Encyclopedia
of Business
Information Sources

ISSN 0071-0210

Encyclopedia of Business Information Sources

A Bibliographic Guide to More Than 35,000 Citations Covering
Over 1,100 subjects of Interest to Business Personnel

Includes: Abstracts and Indexes, Almanacs and Yearbooks,
Bibliographies, Biographical Sources, CD-ROM Databases, Directories,
Encyclopedias and Dictionaries, Financial Ratios, Handbooks and Manuals,
Internet Databases, Online Databases, Periodicals and Newsletters, Price
Sources, Research Centers and Institutes, Statistics Sources, Trade and
Professional Societies, and Other Sources of Information on Each Topic

24th EDITION

Linda D.Hall

GALE
CENGAGE Learning

Detroit • New York • San Francisco • New Haven, Conn • Waterville, Maine • London

GALE
CENGAGE Learning

Encyclopedia of Business Information Sources 24th Edition

Project Editor: Linda Hall

Editorial: Linda Hall

Composition and Electronic Prepress: Gary Leach

Manufacturing: Rita Wimberley

Gale
27500 Drake Rd.
Farmington Hills, MI, 48331-3535

ISBN-13: 978-1-4144-2022-6
ISBN-10: 1-4144-2022-6

ISSN 0071-0210

Printed in the United States of America
1 2 3 4 5 6 7 12 11 10 09 08

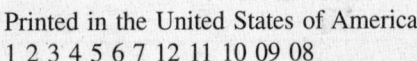

Contents

As the information needs of business managers and information professionals continue to increase, timely and convenient access becomes more valuable. The *Encyclopedia of Business Information Sources (EBIS)* is designed to assist these individuals in locating material relevant to today's rapidly-changing business environment.

EBIS now includes more than 35,000 citations, dealing with more than 1,100 business, financial, and industrial topics. The subjects cover a variety of business-related concerns. These include, for example:

- Business functions—Accounting; Administration; Personnel Management
- Computer-related subjects—Computer Graphics; Computer Software Industry; Local Area Networks
- Foreign trade—International Marketing; Latin American Markets; North American Free Trade Agreement (NAFTA)
- Information industry topics—Electronic Publishing; Internet; Multimedia

Easy to Use

A convenient and accessible grouping of information sources is provided for each business topic. Within these topics, there is the additional convenience of type-of-material categories: directories, periodicals, handbooks, and so forth. An extensive *Outline of Contents* (see p. xiii) makes the exact heading for any subject easy to locate. Many cross-references provide additional assistance in finding needed information.

EBIS thus serves two kinds of information needs: for a quick survey of publications and organizations relating to a particular topic, and for reference to a specific source that will provide a single fact or statistic.

"Sources Cited" Section

For users with a specific title, organization, or service in mind, an alphabetic list of sources follows the main text. This *Sources Cited* section repeats all entries from the main text, sorting them alphabetically by publication title or organization name. The *Sources Cited* section also includes complete contact information.

Extensive Updating

Thousands of changes and additions were required to update this edition of *EBIS*. Information was verified through reliable sources and independent research of the editorial staff. Current editions of *Gale's Encyclopedia of Associationsand Research Centers Directory* were used to update nonprint sources in the categories of "Trade Associations and Professional Societies" and "Research Centers and Institutes."

Standard business or economic compilations, such as the annual *Economic Report of the President* and *Risk Management Association's Annual Statement Studies,* have been carefully examined and entered under topics for which these publications contain significant data. Many out-of-print and discontinued items have been deleted from this edition of *EBIS*, although a few titles considered to be unique or of particular interest have been retained. Should it be desirable to consult these works, they may be available at local libraries.

New material for this edition has been collected in various ways. These include examining publishers' catalogs or brochures, reviewing material in business libraries, scanning lists of recommended titles, and discussing publications with business librarians. Publishers' Internet Web pages have also been useful.

Suggestions Are Welcome

If you have suggestions, concerns, or comments about the

Encyclopedia of Business Information Sources, please contact:

Encyclopedia of Business Information Sources

Gale, Cengage Learning

27500 Drake Road

Farmington Hills, MI 48331-3535

Phone: 248-699-4253

Toll-free: 800-877-GALE

Fax: 248-699-8070

Primary Listings

In the main section of the *Encyclopedia of Business Information Sources (EBIS)*, entries are arranged alphabetically by ▌1▌ topic, and further subdivided by ▌2▌ type of source and ▌3▌ publication title or organization name. For example:

▌1▌ CORPORATE FINANCE

▌2▌ DIRECTORIES

▌3▌ *America's Corporate Finance Directory*. National Register Publishing Co., Reed Elsevier Inc. Annual. $730.00. Adirectory of financial information, covering 5,000 major U. S. corporations.

▌3▌ *Corporate Finance Sourcebook*. National Register Publishing Co., Reed Elsevier Inc. Annual. $650.00. Lists more than 3,700 organizations providing corporate capital.

▌2▌ ONLINE DATABASES

▌3▌ *ABI/INFORM*. Proquest Co. Provides online indexing to business-related material occurring in more than 1,000 periodicals from 1971 to the present. Inquire as to online cost and availability.

▌2▌ RESEARCH CENTERS AND INSTITUTES

▌3▌ Bendheim Center for Finance. Princeton University, Dept. of Economics, Princeton, NJ 08544. Phone: (609)258-4023. Fax: (609)258-6419.

Locate Topics in the Outline of Contents Section

The *Encyclopedia of Business Information Sources* covers more than 1,100 topics. The efficient way to locate a particular topic is to scan the *Outline of Contents* section, which follows this *User's Guide*. The *Outline of Contents* lists topics alphabetically.

Users can determine at a glance the specific form of the subject term that has been employed. Numerous cross-references provide assistance where necessary. For instance, if the term being sought is Cellular Telephones, the *Outline of Contents* provides a cross-reference directing users to the heading "Mobile Telephone Industry," where information on cell phones may be found.

18 Kinds of Sources

Material under each topic is grouped according to the type of source or form in which the information is provided. Auser

can look under the topic of interest (Corporate Finance, for example) to find key information sources arranged as follows:

- General Works
- Abstracts and Indexing Services
- Almanacs and Yearbooks
- Bibliographies
- Biographical Sources
- CD-ROM Databases
- Directories
- Encyclopedias and Dictionaries
- Financial Ratios
- Handbooks and Manuals
- Internet Databases
- Online Databases
- Periodicals and Newsletters
- Price Sources
- Research Centers and Institutes
- Statistics Sources
- Trade/Professional Associations
- Other Sources

Content of the Entries

The content of the entries is described here and illustrated in the sample that appears on the previous page.

Entries for publications and online databases list the title of the work, the name of the author (where applicable), the name of the publisher or provider, frequency or year of publi- cation, and price. Brief descriptive notes are often added to clarify listings. Entries included in the "Internet Databases" category provide the name of the Web site, the name of the provider or host, telephone/fax numbers, E-mail address, the URLaddress, and information on content and cost (most are free).

Entries for trade associations and research centers provide the organization name, address, telephone/fax numbers, and Internet information where available. Many of these entries include a brief description of the organization.

Sources Cited Section

Arrangement—In the Sources Cited section, all entries from the primary listings in *EBIS* are arranged alphabetically by publication title, database title, or organization name.

Contact Information—The Sources Cited section provides contact information—including URL addresses and e-mail in most instances—for print publishers and for publishers or providers of online databases.

Many of the online databases referenced in EBIS are available through the widely used service providers listed below.

ONLINE DATABASE VENDORS

DIALOG

Dialog/Thomson Corp.
11000 Regency Parkway, Suite 10
Cary, NC 27518
(800)334-2564 or (919)462-8600
Fax: (919)468-9890
http://www.dialog.com

DIALOG DataStar

Dialog/Thomson Corp.
11000 Regency Parkway, Suite 10
Cary, NC 27518
(800)334-2564 or (919)462-8600
Fax: (919)468-9890
http://www.dialog.com/products/
datastar

InfoTrac OneFile

Gale, Cengage Learning
27500 Drake Road
Farmington Hills, MI 48331-3535
(800)877-4253 or (248) 699-4253
Fax: (800) 414-5043 or (248)699-8096
gale.cengage.com

LEXIS-NEXIS

Reed-Elsevier Inc.
P. O. Box 933
Dayton, OH 45401-0933
(800)227-4908 or (937)865-6800
Fax: (937)865-6909
http://www.lexisnexis.com

OCLC FirstSearch

OCLC Online Computer Library Center, Inc.
6565 Kilgour Place
Dublin, OH 43017-3395
(800)848-5878 or (614)764-6000
Fax: (614)764-6096
http://www.oclc.org/firstsearch

Ovid Technologies,Inc.

333 Seventh Ave., 20th Floor
New York, NY10001
(800)950-2035 or (646)674-6300
Fax: (646)674-6301
http://www.ovid.com

Questel-Orbit,Inc.

1725 Duke Street, Suite 625
Alexandria, VA22314
(800)456-7248 or (703)519-1820
Fax: (703)519-1821
http://www.questel.orbit.com

WESTLAW

West Group
610 Opperman Drive
Saint Paul, MN 55123
(800)328-4880 or (651)687-7000
Fax: (651)687-7849
http://www.westlaw.com

Outline of Contents

OUTLINE OF CONTENTS

A

ABBREVIATIONS

ENCYCLOPEDIAS AND DICTIONARIES

Abbreviations Dictionary. Dean A. Stahl and Karen Kerchelich. CRC Press, LLC. • 2001. $79.95. 10th edition. Contains about 270,000 abbreviations, acronyms, initialisms, and nicknames. Covers most areas of knowledge, including business, science, and technology.

Acronyms, Initialisms, and Abbreviations Dictionary. Gale Cengage Learning. • Annual. $865.00. Four parts. Provides more than 780,000 definitions in all subject areas.

Acronyms of Computer Science and Communications: A Comprehensive Acronym Dictionary and Illustrated Encyclopedia. Enjob Kajan and Ejub Kajan. Springer Verlag. • 2002. $49.95. Explains more than 4,000 "broadly used" computer, telecommunications, and information technology acronyms. Includes illustrations and Web addresses, where applicable.

Dictionary of Financial Abbreviations. John Paxton. Routledge. • 2002. $50.00. Provides more than 4,000 abbreviations and acronyms relating to finance, currencies, and financial organizations.

International Acronyms, Initialisms, and Abbreviations Dictionary. Gale Cengage Learning. • 2001. $250.00. Fifth edition. Contains over 210,000 English and non-English entries used internationally and in specific countries.

Periodical Title Abbreviations. Gale Cengage Learning. • 2002. $520.00. 14th edition. Two volumes. $260.00 per volume Vol. 1 *By Abbreviation*; vol. 2 *By Title*. Lists more than 145,000 different abbreviations.

Reverse Acronyms, Initialisms, and Abbreviations Dictionary. Gale Cengage Learning. • 2001. $235.00.

Scientific and Technical Acronyms, Symbols, and Abbreviations. Uwe Erb and Harald Keller. John Wiley and Sons, Inc. • 2001. $250.00. Contains more than 200,000 entries covering a wide variety of scientific and technical fields.

INTERNET DATABASES

Acronym Finder: The Web's Most Comprehensive Database of Acronyms, Abbreviations, and Initialisms. Mountain Data Systems. Phone: (970)586-5556 E-mail: acronyms@mtnds.com • URL: http://www.acronymfinder.com • Web site provides more than 345,000 definitions. Searching offers a choice of "exact acronym," "acronym begins with," "acronym (wildcard)," or "reverse lookup (keywords)." Fees: Free.

ABRASIVES INDUSTRY

ABSTRACTS AND INDEXES

Alloys Index. CSA. • Monthly. $775.00 per year. Includes print and online editions.

Chemical Abstracts. Chemical Abstracts Service. • Weekly. $26,000.00 per year. Includes *CA Index Guide*.

Metals Abstracts. CSA. • Monthly. $3,575.00 per year. Includes print and online editions.

FINANCIAL RATIOS

Annual Statement Studies. The Risk Management Association. • Annual. Median and quartile financial ratios are given for over 400 kinds of manufacturing, wholesale, retail, construction, and consumer finance establishments. Data is sorted by both asset size and sales volume. Includes a clearly written "Definition of Ratios" and an alphabetical industry index.

Annual Statement Studies: Industry Default Probabilities and Cash Flow Measures. The Risk Management Association. • Annual. $145.00. Serves as a companion volume to the original *Annual Statement Studies*. Gives probability of default estimates on a percentage scale for more than 450 industries. Includes changes in position year-by-year for eight financial statement line items and provides percentage measures of cash flow.

ONLINE DATABASES

F & S Index. Gale Cengage Learning. • Contains about four million citations to worldwide business, financial, and industrial or consumer product literature appearing from 1972 to date. Weekly updates. Inquire as to online cost and availability.

METADEX. Cambridge Scientific Abstracts. • Covers the worldwide literature of metals, metallurgy, and materials science, 1966 to date. Includes detailed alloys indexing from 1974. Biweekly updating. Inquire as to online cost and availability. (Formerly produced by ASM International.).

PERIODICALS AND NEWSLETTERS

Grinding and Abrasive Magazine. Abrasive Magazine, Inc. • Eight times a year. $27.00 per year. Formerly *Abrasive Magazine*.

Grits and Grinds. Norton Co. • Quarterly. Free.

Visons. Unified Abrasives Manufacturers Association. • Irregular. Newsletter. Price on application.

PRICE SOURCES

Chemical and Engineering News: The Newsmagazine of the Chemical World. American Chemical Society. • Weekly. Institutions, $210.00 per year.

STATISTICS SOURCES

Mineral Commodity Summaries. Available from U. S. Government Printing Office. • Annual. $26.00. Published by the U. S. Geological Survey, Department of the Interior (http://www.usgs.gov). Contains detailed, five-year data for about 90 nonfuel minerals. Covers a wide range of statistics, including production, imports, exports, consumption, reserves, prices, tariff information, and industry employment. (Two pages are devoted to each mineral.).

Minerals Yearbook. Available from U.S. Government Printing Office. • Annual. Three volumes.

United States Census of Mineral Industries. Bureau of the Census, U.S. Department of Commerce. Available from U.S. Government Printing Office. • Quinquennial.

TRADE/PROFESSIONAL ASSOCIATIONS

Abrasive Engineering Society. 144 Moore Rd., Butler, PA 16001. Phone: (724)282-6210 Fax: (724)234-2376 E-mail: aes@abrasiveengineering.com • URL: http://www.abrasiveengineering.com • Promotes knowledge and understanding of abrasives (abrasive wheels, coated abrasives, media, diamonds and diamond products, dressers, dressing devices and abrasive grains) and their application in metalworking. Sponsors courses.

Unified Abrasives Manufacturers Association - Bonded Division. c/o Wherry Associates, 30200 Detroit Ave., Cleveland, OH 44145-1967. Phone: (440)899-0010 Fax: (440)892-1404 E-mail: contact@uama.org • URL: http://www.uama.org • Formerly Grinding Wheel Institute.

Unified Abrasives Manufacturers Association - Coated Division. c/o Wherry Associates, 30200 Detroit Rd., Cleveland, OH 44145-1967. Phone: (440)899-0010 Fax: (440)892-1404 E-mail: contact@uama.org • URL: http://www.uama.org • Formerly Coated Abrasives Manufacturers Institute.

OTHER SOURCES

Abrasive Engineering Society Conference Proceedings. Abrasive Engineering Society. • Irregular. Price on application.

ABSENTEEISM

ABSTRACTS AND INDEXES

Business Periodicals Index. H. W. Wilson Co. • 11 times a year. Quarterly and annual cumulations. Price varies.

Personnel Management Abstracts. • Quarterly.

$190.00 per year. Includes annual cumulation.

DIRECTORIES

Business Organizations, Agencies, and Publications Directory. Gale Cengage Learning. • 2003. $480.00. 15th edition. Over 40,000 entries describing 39 types of business information sources. Classified by type of organization, publication, or serviceIncludes state, national, and international agencies and organizations. Master index to names and keywords. Also includes e-mail addresses and web site URL's.

ONLINE DATABASES

Wilson Business Abstracts Online. H. W. Wilson Co. • Indexes and abstracts 600 major business periodicals, plus the *Wall Street Journal* and the business section of the *New York Times*. Indexing is from 1982, abstracting from 1990, with the two newspapers included from 1993. Updated weekly. Inquire as to online cost and availability. (*Business Periodicals Index* without abstracts is also available online.).

PERIODICALS AND NEWSLETTERS

HR Magazine (Human Resources): Strategies and Solutions for Human Resource Professionals. Society for Human Resource Management. • Monthly. Free to members; non-members, $70.00 per year. Formerly *Personnel Administrator.*

TRADE/PROFESSIONAL ASSOCIATIONS

American Management Association. 1601 Broadway, New York, NY 10019-7420. Phone: 800-262-9699 or (212)586-8100 Fax: (212)903-8168 E-mail: membershjp@amanet.org • URL: http://www.amanet.org • Provides educational forums worldwide where members and their colleagues learn superior, practical business skills and explore best practices of world-class organizations through interaction with each other and expert faculty practitioners. Maintains a publishing program providing tools individuals use to extend learning beyond the classroom in a process of life-long professional growth and development through education.

Society for Human Resource Management. 1800 Duke St., Alexandria, VA 22314. Phone: 800-283-7476 or (703)548-3440 Fax: (703)535-6490 • URL: http://www.shrm.org • Affiliated with Human Resource Certification Institute; Media Human Resources Association and SHRM Global Forum. Formerly American Society for Personnel Administration.

ACADEMIC DEGREES

See also: COLLEGES AND UNIVERSITIES

ABSTRACTS AND INDEXES

Current Index to Journals in Education (CIJE). Oryx Press. • Monthly. $245.00 per year. Semiannual cumulations, $475.00.

Education Index. H. W. Wilson Co. • 10 times a year. Quarterly and annual cumulations. Price varies.

ONLINE DATABASES

Education Index Online. H. W. Wilson Co. • Indexes a wide variety of periodicals related to schools, colleges, and education, 1984 to date. Monthly updates. Inquire as to online cost and availability.

PERIODICALS AND NEWSLETTERS

Resources in Education. Educational Resources Information Center. Available from U.S. Government Printing Office. • Monthly. Reports on educational research.

STATISTICS SOURCES

Digest of Education Statistics. Available from U. S. Government Printing Office. • Annual. $51.00. Covers all areas of education from kindergarten through

graduate school. Includes data from both government and private sources. Compiled by National Center for Education Statistics, U. S. Department of Education.

Occupational Projections and Training Data. Available from U. S. Government Printing Office. • Biennial. $21.00. Issued by Bureau of Labor Statistics, U. S. Department of Labor. Contains projections of employment change and job openings over the next 15 years for about 500 specific occupations. Also includes the number of associate, bachelor's, master's, doctoral, and professional degrees awarded in a recent year for about 900 specific fields of study.

ACADEMIC DISSERTATIONS

See: DISSERTATIONS

ACCIDENT INSURANCE

See also: AUTOMOBILE INSURANCE; CASUALTY INSURANCE; INSURANCE

GENERAL WORKS

Modern Accident Investigation and Analysis: An Executive Guide to Accident Investigation. Theodore S. Ferry. John Wiley and Sons, Inc. • 1988. $160.00. Second edition.

Property and Liability Insurance. Solomon S. Huebner and Kenneth Black. Prentice Hall PTR. • 2000. $72.00. Fourth edition.

ALMANACS AND YEARBOOKS

Insurance Almanac: Who, What, When and Where in Insurance. Underwriter Printing and Publishing Co. • Annual. $175.00. Lists insurance agencies and brokerage firms; U.S. and Canadian insurance companies, adjusters, appraisers, auditors, investigators, insurance officials and insurance organizations.

BIBLIOGRAPHIES

Insurance and Employee Benefits Literature. Special Libraries Association, Insurance and Employee Benefits Div. • Bimonthly. $15.00 per year. Lists a wide variety of literature in all branches of the insurance industry. Includes annotations.

CD-ROM DATABASES

U. S. Insurance: Life, Accident, and Health. Sheshunoff Information Services, Inc. • Monthly. Price on application. CD-ROM provides detailed, current information on the financial characteristics of more than 2,300 life, accident, and health insurance companies.

DIRECTORIES

Best's Directory of Recommended Insurance Attorneys and Adjusters. A.M. Best Co. • Annual. $1,175.00. More than 5,000 American, Canadian, and foreign insurance defense law firms; lists 1,200 national and international insurance adjusting firms. Formerly *Best's Recommended Insurance Adjusters.*

ENCYCLOPEDIAS AND DICTIONARIES

Dictionary of Insurance Terms. Harvey W. Rubin. Barron's Educational Series, Inc. • 2000. $14.95. Fourth edition. Defines terms in a wide variety of insurance fields. (Business Dictionaries Series).

Glossary of Insurance Policy Terms. Organization for Economic Cooperation and Development. • 1999. $30.00. "The selected topics range from insurance policy regulation/supervision to general trade issues and include technical terms related to issues such as claims, premiums, and provisions." Edited for government, academic, business, and insurance organizations.

Insurance Words and Their Meanings: A Glossary of Insurance Terms. The Rough Notes Co., Inc. •

2001. 17th edition. Price on application.

Rupp's Insurance and Risk Management Glossary. Richard V. Rupp. NILS Publishing Co. • 2001. $35.00. Second edition. Provides definitions of 6,400 insurance words and phrases. Includes a guide to acronyms and abbreviations.

FINANCIAL RATIOS

Best's Key Rating Guide. A.M. Best Co. • Annual. $225.00. Financial information and ratings on over 3,300 major property/casualty insurers.

HANDBOOKS AND MANUALS

Life and Health Insurance Law. Muirel L. Crawford. McGraw Hill. • 1997. $118.88. Eighth edition. Covers the legal aspects of life, health, and accident insurance.

ONLINE DATABASES

I.I.I. Data Base Search. Insurance Information Institute. • Provides online citations and abstracts of insurance-related literature in magazines, newspapers, trade journals, and books. Emphasis is on property and casualty insurance issues, including highway safety, product safety, and environmental liability. Inquire as to online cost and availability.

PERIODICALS AND NEWSLETTERS

Journal of Risk and Insurance. American Risk and Insurance Association. Blackwell Publishing, Inc. • Quarterly. Institutions, $243.00 per year. Includes online edition.

PRICE SOURCES

Policy Statistics Service. The National Underwriter Co.

STATISTICS SOURCES

Accident Facts. National Safety Council. • Annual. $37.95.

TRADE/PROFESSIONAL ASSOCIATIONS

American Insurance Association. 1130 Connecticut Ave. NW, Ste. 1000, Washington, DC 20036. Phone: 800-242-2302 or (202)828-7100 or (202)828-7183 Fax: (202)293-1219 E-mail: info@aiadc.org • URL: http://www.aiadc.org/aiadotnet • Represents companies providing property and casualty insurance and suretyship. Monitors and reports on economic, political, and social trends; serves as a clearinghouse for ideas, advice, and technical information. Represents members' interests before state and federal legislative and regulatory bodies; coordinates members' litigation.

Council of Insurance Agents and Brokers. 701 Pennsylvania Ave. NW, Ste. 750, Washington, DC 20004-2608. Phone: (202)783-4400 Fax: (202)783-4410 E-mail: ciab@ciab.com • URL: http://www.ciab.com.

Insurance Information Institute. 110 William St., New York, NY 10038. Phone: 800-331-9146 or (212)346-5500 Fax: (212)791-1807 E-mail: members@iii.org • URL: http://www.iii.org • Property and casualty insurance companies. Provides information and educational services to mass media, educational institutions, trade associations, businesses, government agencies, and the public.

OTHER SOURCES

Life, Health, and Accident Insurance Law Reports. CCH, Inc. • $835.00 per year. Looseleaf service. Monthly updates.

ACCIDENTS

See also: ACCIDENT INSURANCE; SAFETY; TRAFFIC ACCIDENTS AND TRAFFIC SAFETY

GENERAL WORKS

Safety. Alton, L. ThyGerson. Jones and Bartlett Publishers. • 1992. $37.75. Second edition.

ABSTRACTS AND INDEXES

Health and Safety Science Abstracts. Institute of Safety and Systems Management. Cambridge Information Group. • Monthly. Online edition, $850.00 year. Formerly *Safety Science Abstracts Journal.*

Safety and Health at Work. International Labour Office. • Bimonthly. $240.00 per year. Formerly *Occupational Safety and Health Abstracts.*

CD-ROM DATABASES

OSH-ROM: Occupational Safety and Health Information on CD-ROM. Available from Silver-Platter Information, Inc. • Price and frequency on application. Produced in Geneva by the International Occupational Safety and Health Information Centre, International Labour Organization (http://www.ilo. org). Provides about two million citations and abstracts to the worldwide literature of industrial safety, industrial hygiene, hazardous materials, and accident prevention. Material is included from journals, technical reports, books, government publications, and other sources. Time span varies.

ENCYCLOPEDIAS AND DICTIONARIES

Encyclopedia of Occupational Health and Safety. International Labour Organization. • 1998. $990.00. Fourth edition. Four volumes. Includes CD-ROM. Covers safety engineering, industrial medicine, ergonomics, hygiene, epidemiology, toxicology, industrial psychology, and related topics. Includes material related to specific chemical, textile, transport, construction, manufacturing, and other industries. Indexed by subject, chemical name, and author, with a "Directory of Experts.".

Encyclopedia of Occupational Health and Safety. Jeanne M. Stellman. International Labour Office. • 1998. $990.00. Fourth edition. Four volumes. Includes CD-Rom.

HANDBOOKS AND MANUALS

Office Building Safety and Health. Charles D. Reese. CRC Press. • 2004. $89.95. Covers a wide variety of topics relating to office building safety, including management of emergencies, common hazards, accident prevention, environmental health issues, and security.

INTERNET DATABASES

National Center for Health Statistics: Monitoring the Nation's Health. National Center for Health Statistics, Centers for Disease Control and Preventio. Phone: (301)458-4000 E-mail: nchsquery@cdc.gov • URL: http://www.cdc.gov/ nchswww • Web site provides detailed data on diseases, vital statistics, and health care in the U. S. Includes a search facility and links to many other health-related Web sites. "Fastats A to Z" offers quick data on hundreds of topics from Accidents to Work-Loss Days, with links to Comprehensive Data and related sources. Frequent updates. Fees: Free.

ONLINE DATABASES

Embase. Elsevier Science, Inc. • Worldwide medical literature, 1974 to present. Weekly updates. Inquire as to online cost and availability.

Information Bank Abstracts. New York Times Index Dept. • Provides indexing and abstracting of current affairs, primarily from the final late edition of *The New York Times* and the Eastern edition of *The Wall Street Journal.* Time period is 1969 to present, with

daily updates. Inquire as to online cost and availability.

Labordoc. International Labour Organization. • Indexing of labor literature and the publications of the International Labour Organization, 1965 to present. Monthly updates. Inquire as to online cost and availability.

PERIODICALS AND NEWSLETTERS

Accident Analysis and Prevention. Elsevier. • Bimonthly. Qualified personnel, $339.00 per year; institutions, $1,370.00 per year.

Accident Prevention. Flight Safety Foundation Inc. • Description: Carries items of particular value to professional pilots: general air safety material and reports of dangerous situations, incidents, near misses by professional pilots, ground crew, or other persons involved.

BNA's SafetyNet. Bureau of National Affairs Inc. • Description: Designed to help employers deal with occupational safety and health regulations, policies, standards, and practices, and to understand the effects of compliance on employee relations. Covers the establishment, management, evaluation, maintenance, and administration of health and safety programs. Carries information on recordkeeping, inspections, enforcement, employer defenses, and training.

Human Factors and Aviation Medicine. Flight Safety Foundation, Inc. • Bimonthly. Members, $120.00 per year; non-members, $240.00 per year.

Journal of System Safety. System Safety Society, Inc. • Quarterly. Free to members; non-members, $55.00 per year. Formerly *Hazard Prevention.*

Occupational Hazards: Magazine of Health and Environment. Penton Media, Inc. • Monthly. $55.00 per year. Industrial safety and security management.

Safety and Health: The International Safety, Health and Environment Magazine. National Safety Council,. • Monthly. Members, $45.00 per year; non-members, $58.50 per year. Formerly *National Safety and Health News.*

Traffic Safety: The Magazine for Traffic Safety Professionals. National Safety Council, Periodicals Dept. • Bimonthly. Members, $24.00 per year; non-members, $31.20 per year.

STATISTICS SOURCES

Accident Facts. National Safety Council. • Annual. $37.95.

Health and Environment in America's Top-Rated Cities: A Statistical Profile. Grey House Publishing. • Biennial. $125.00. Covers 75 U. S. cities. Includes statistical and other data on a wide variety of topics, such as air quality, water quality, recycling, hospitals, physicians, health care costs, death rates, infant mortality, accidents, and suicides.

Metropolitan Life Insurance Co. Statistical Bulletin SB. Metropolitan Life Insurance Co. • Quarterly. Individuals, $50.00 per year. Covers a wide range of social, economic and demographic health concerns.

Occupational Injuries and Illnesses by Industry. Bureau of Labor Statistics, U.S. Department of Labor. Available from U.S. Government Printing Office. • Annual.

Report on the American Workforce. Available from U. S. Government Printing Office. • Annual. Issued by the U. S. Department of Labor (http://www.dol. gov). Appendix contains tabular statistics, including employment, unemployment, price indexes, consumer expenditures, employee benefits (retirement, insurance, vacation, etc.), wages, productivity, hours of work, and occupational injuries. Annual figures are shown for up to 50 years.

Vital Statistics of the United States. Public Health Service, U.S. Dept. of Health and Human Services.

Available from U.S. Government Printing Office. • Annual.

TRADE/PROFESSIONAL ASSOCIATIONS

International Association of Industrial Accident Boards and Commissions. 5610 Medical Ctr, Ste. 24, Madison, WI 53719. Phone: (608)663-6355 Fax: (608)663-1546 E-mail: fhowe@iaiabc.org • URL: http://www.iaiabc.org • Members are government agencies, insurance companies, lawyers, unions, self-insurers, and others with an interest in industrial safety and the administration of workers' compensation laws.

National Safety Council. 1121 Spring Lake Dr., Itasca, IL 60143-3201. Phone: 800-621-7619 or (630)285-1121 Fax: (630)285-1613 E-mail: nrhc@ nrhcweb.org • URL: http://www.nsc.org • Individuals whose professional activities are related to the safety of employees and college or university students.

OTHER SOURCES

Employment Safety and Health Guide. CCH, Inc. • Weekly. $1,139.00 per year. Four looseleaf volumes.

Worker's Compensation: The Survival Guide for Business. LexisNexis Matthew Bender. • Looseleaf. $100.00. Periodic supplementation available. Edited for business managers and executives. Covers the basics of worker's compensation, including accident prevention, post-accident activities, accident investigation, medical management, insurance issues, and recent legislation. Includes a glossary, checklists, sample letters, a sample employers liability insurance policy, and statistics.

ACCOUNTABILITY, SOCIAL

See: SOCIAL RESPONSIBILITY

ACCOUNTANTS

See: CERTIFIED PUBLIC ACCOUNTANTS

ACCOUNTING

See also: AUDITING; CERTIFIED PUBLIC ACCOUNTANTS; COMPUTERS IN ACCOUNTING; COST ACCOUNTING; GOVERNMENT ACCOUNTING; WOMEN ACCOUNTANTS

GENERAL WORKS

Accounting and Finance for Non-Specialists. Peter Atrill and Eddie McLaney. Pearson Education. • 2003. $77.00. Fourth edition. Includes the measurement and reporting of financial performance and cash flow.

Accounting: The Basis for Business Decisions. Robert Meigs and others. McGraw-Hill. • 2000. $95.63. 11th edition.

Accounting Theory. Ahmed Riahi-Belkaoui. The Thomson Corporation. • 2000. $77.99. Fourth edition. (ITBP Textbook Series.).

Advanced Accounting. Joe B. Hoyle and others. McGraw-Hill. • 2003. $112.50. Seventh edition.

Basic Accounting for the Small Business: Simple, Foolproof Techniques for Keeping Your Books Straight and Staying Out of Trouble. Bobbie Kuhlmann. Pearson Custom Publishing. • 1990. $120.00.

The Financial Numbers Game: Detecting Creative Accounting Practices. Charles W. Mulford and Eugene E. Comiskey. John Wiley and Sons, Inc. • 2002. $39.95. Serves as a guide to financial statement analysis for investors. Explains the "creative" schemes used by corporations to boost earnings-per-share data.

Fundamental Accounting Principles. Kermit D. Larson and others. McGraw-Hill. • 2001. $36.88. 16th edition. (Ready Notes Series).

Fundamentals of Financial and Managerial Accounting. Kermit D. Larson and others. McGraw-Hill. • 1993. $72.00.

Management Accounting. W. Steve Albrecht. South-Western. • 2001. $96.95. Eighth edition.

Managerial Accounting. Paul E. Dascher and others. South-Western. • 2001. $84.95. Second edition.

Movie Money: Understanding Hollywood's (Creative) Accounting Practices. Bill Daniels. Silman-James Press. • 1998. $29.95. Explains the numerous amd mysterious accounting methods used by the film industry to arrive at gross and net profit figures. The authors also discuss profit participation, audits, claims, and negotiating.

ABSTRACTS AND INDEXES

Accounting and Tax Index. UMI. • Quarterly. Price on application. Annual cumulation. Indexes accounting, auditing, and taxation literature appearing in journals, books, pamphlets, conference proceedings, and newsletters.

Accounting Articles. CCH, Inc. • Monthly. $624.00 per year. Looseleaf service.

Business Periodicals Index. H. W. Wilson Co. • 11 times a year. Quarterly and annual cumulations. Price varies.

ALMANACS AND YEARBOOKS

Yearbook. Association of Government Accountants. • Annual.

CD-ROM DATABASES

WILSONDISC: Wilson Business Abstracts. H. W. Wilson Co. • Monthly. Includes unlimited online access to *Wilson Business Abstracts* through WILSONLINE. Provides CD-ROM "cover-to-cover" abstracting and indexing of over 600 prominent business periodicals. Indexing is from 1982, abstracting from 1990. (*Business Periodicals Index* without abstracts is available on CD-ROM at $1,495 per year.).

DIRECTORIES

Emerson's Directory of Leading U.S. Accounting Firms. Emerson Co. • Biennial. $195.00. Provides information on 500 major CPA firms.

National Society of Public Accountants - Yearbook. National Society of Accountants. • Annual. Free to members, government agencies and libraries; not available to others.

Who Audits America: A Directory of Publicly Held Corporations and the Accounting Firms Who Audit Them. Data Financial Press. • 1994. $155.00. 12,000 publicly held corporations that report to the Securities and Exchange Commission, and their accounting firms.

ENCYCLOPEDIAS AND DICTIONARIES

Blackwell Encyclopedic Dictionary of Accounting. Rashad Abdel-khalik. Blackwell Publishing. • 1997. $38.95. The editor is associated with the University of Florida. Contains definitions of key terms combined with longer articles written by various U. S. and foreign business educators. Includes bibliographies and index. (Blackwell Encyclopedia of Management Series).

Dictionary of Accounting. Adrian Joliffe and P.H. Collin. Independent Publishers Group. • 2002. $15. 95. Second edition.

Dictionary of Accounting Terms. Joel G. Siegel. Barron's Educational Series, Inc. • 2000. $13.95. Third edition. (Business Dictionaries Series).

Encyclopedia of Accounting Systems. Tom M. Plank and Lois R. Plank. Prentice Hall Books. • 1994. $132.00. Three volumes.

Encyclopedia of Business. Gale Cengage Learning.

• 2000. $425.00. Second edition. Two volumes. Contains more than 700 signed articles covering major business disciplines and concepts. International in scope. (Encyclopedia of Business Series).

Encyclopedia of Business and Finance. Burton Kaliski, editor. Available from Gale Cengage Learning. • 2001. $275.00. Two volumes. Published by Macmillan Reference USA. Contains articles by various contributors on accounting, business administration, banking, finance, management information systems, and marketing.

The History of Accounting: An Encyclopedia. Michael Chatfield and Richard Vangermeersch. Garland Publishing, Inc. • 1996. $100.00. Contains more than 400 alphabetical entries by various contributors, covering the history of accounting from 750 B.C. to the modern era. Includes a bibliography for each entry and an index. (Reference Library of the Humanities Series: Vol. 1573).

International Dictionary of Accounting Acronyms. Thomas W. Morris, editor. Fitzroy Dearborn Publishers, Inc. • 1999. $45.00. Defines 2,000 acronyms used in worldwide accounting and finance.

FINANCIAL RATIOS

Income and Fees of Accountants in Public Practice. National Society of Accountants. • Triennial. Members, $35.00; non-members, $50.00.

HANDBOOKS AND MANUALS

Accountant's Business Manual. American Institute of Certified Public Accountants. • $189.75. Looseleaf. Two volumes. Semiannual updates. Covers a wide variety of topics relating to financial and accounting management, including types of ownership, business planning, financing, cash management, valuation, retirement plans, estate planning, workers' compensation, unemployment insurance, social security, and employee benefits management.

Accountants' Handbook. Douglas R. Carmichael and Paul Rosenfeld. John Wiley and Sons, Inc. • 2003. $160.00. 10th edition. Two volumes. Vol. one, $95.00; vol. two, $95.00. Chapters are written by various accounting and auditing specialists.

Accountant's Handbook of Fraud and Commercial Crime. G. Jack Bologna and others. John Wiley and Sons, Inc. • 1992. $225.00.

Accounting and Budgeting in Public and Non-profit Organizations: A Manager's Guide. C. William Garner. John Wiley and Sons, Inc. • 1991. $49.00. An accounting primer for non-profit executives with no formal training in accounting. Includes an explanation of Generally Accepted Accounting Principles (GAAP) as applied to non-profit organizations. (Public Administration-Non Profit Sector Series).

Accounting and Recordkeeping for the Self-Employed. Jack Fox. John Wiley and Sons, Inc. • 1994. $19.95.

Accounting Desk Book: The Accountant's Everyday Instant Answer Book. Tom M. Plank and Lois R. Plank. Prentice Hall PTR. • 2000. $100.00. 11th edition. Covers more than 230 accounting topics with examples, checklists, worksheets and tables. (Accounting Desk Book Series).

Accounting for Libraries and Other Not-for-Profit Organizations. G. Stevenson Smith. American Library Association. • 1999. $82.00. Second edition. Covers accounting fundamentals for nonprofit organizations. Includes a glossary.

Accounting Trends and Techniques in Published Corporate Annual Reports. American Institute of Certified Public Accountants. • Annual. Price on application.

AICPA Audit and Accounting Manual. American Institute of Certified Public Accountants. • 1999.

$90.50. Covers working papers, internal control, audit approach, etc.

AICPA Codification of Statements on Auditing Standards. American Institute of Certified Public Accountants. • 1999. $81.25. Includes *Auditing Interpretations* and *International Auditing Guidelines.*

AICPA Professional Standards, U. S. Auditing Standards, Accounting and Review Services, Ethics, Bylaws, International Accounting, International Auditing, Management Advisory Services, Quality Control, and Tax Practice. American Institute of Certified Public Accountants. • 1999. $123.50. Two volumes.

AICPA Technical Practice Aids. American Institute of Certified Public Accountants. • 1998. $119.00 per year. Two volumes. Advisory opinions, statements of position, and other material.

Applying GAAP and GAAS. LexisNexis Matthew Bender. • Biennial. $358.00 per year. Two looseleaf volumes. In-depth explanations of generally accepted accounting principles (GAAP) and generally accepted auditing standards (GAAS).

Bookkeeping Service. Entrepreneur Media, Inc. • Looseleaf. $59.50. A practical guide to starting a computer-oriented bookkeeping business. Covers profit potential, start-up costs, market size evaluation, pricing, accounting, advertising, promotion, etc. (Start-Up Business Guide No. E2335.).

FASB Accounting Standards. Financial Accounting Standards Board. • Annual. Price on application.

Financial Accounting Standards: Explanation and Analysis. CCH, Inc. • 1996. $56.00. 18th edition.

Financial Shenanigans: How to Detect Accounting Gimmicks and Fraud in Financial Reports. Howard M. Schilit. McGraw-Hill. • 2002. $27.95. Second edition. Tells how to interpret the footnotes and fine print in corporate annual and other reports.

GAAP for Governments: Interpretation and Application of Generally Accepted Accounting Principles for State and Local Governments. John Wiley and Sons, Inc. • Annual. $134.00. (Includes CD-ROM.).

Guide to Financial Reporting and Analysis. Eugene E. Comiskey and Charles W. Mulford. John Wiley and Sons, Inc. • 2000. $75.00. Provides financial statement examples to illustrate the application of generally accepted accounting principles.

IAS: Interpretation and Application of International Accounting Standards. John Wiley and Sons, Inc. • Annual. $71.00. (Also available on CD-ROM.).

Managerial Accounting for Libraries and Other Not-for-Profit Organizations. G. Stevenson Smith. American Library Association. • 2002. $55.00. Coverage includes responsibility accounting, life cycle costing, and activity-based accounting, as opposed to traditional cost accounting for profit-based organizations.

Marketing for CPAs, Accountants, and Tax Professionals. William J. Winston. Haworth Press, Inc. • 1995. $49.95. (Marketing Resources Series).

Miller European Accounting Guide. Aspen Publishers. • Annual. $159.00. Presents analysis of accounting standards in 25 European and Eastern European countries.

Miller GAAP Financial Statement Disclosures Manual. Aspen Publishers. • Annual. $105.00. Provides a detailed summary of financial report disclosure requirements, with examples. Includes a CD-ROM.

Miller GAAP Guide: A Comprehensive Restatement of All Current Promulgated Generally Accepted Accounting Principles. Aspen Publishers, Inc. • Annual. $149.00. Includes monthly *Update* service. Includes all current Financial Accounting Standards Board (FASB) statements, interpretations, and technical bulletins.

Miller International Accounting Standards Guide. Aspen Publishers. • Annual. $139.00. Covers all current International Financial Reporting Standards (IFRS), International Accounting Standards (IAS), and related interpretations issued by the International Accounting Standards Board (IASB).

Not-for-Profit GAAP 2001: Interpretation and Application of Generally Accepted Ating Principles for Not-for-Profit Organizations. Richard F. Larkin and Marie DiTommaso. John Wiley and Sons, Inc. • 2001. $65.00.

Practitioner's Guide to GAAS. John Wiley and Sons, Inc. • Annual. $184.95. Covers GAAS: Generally Accepted Auditing Standards, promulgated by the American Institute of Certified Public Accountants. (Includes CD-ROM.).

SEC Accounting Rules. CCH, Inc. • $448.00. Loose-leaf service.

Small Business Accounting Simplefied. Daniel Sitarz. Nova Publishing Co. • 2002. $22.95. Third edition. Includes basic forms and instructions for small business accounting and bookkeeping. (Small Business Library Series).

Transnational Accounting. Dieter Ordelheide and others, editors. Groves Dictionaries, Inc. • 2001. $685.00. Second edition. Three volumes. Published by Macmillan (UK). Provides detailed descriptions of financial accounting principles and practices in 14 major countries (10 European, plus the U. S., Canada, Australia, and Japan). Includes tables, exhibits, index, and a glossary of 244 accounting terms in eight languages.

U. S. Master Accounting Guide. John C. Wisdom. CCH, Inc. • 1999. $52.95. Summarizes key accounting, business, and financial information from various sources. Includes digests, tables, charts, formulas, ratios, examples, and explanatory text. (Master Guide Series).

U. S. Master GAAP Guide. Bill D. Jarnagin. CCH, Inc. • 2000. $62.95. Covers the generally accepted accounting principles (GAAP) contained in the professional pronouncements of the Accounting Principles Board (APB) or the Financial Accounting Standards Board (FASB). Includes general discussions, flow charts, and detailed examples. Arranged by topic.

INTERNET DATABASES

Rutgers Accounting Web (RAW). Rutgers University Accounting Research Center. Phone: (973)353-5172 Fax: (973)353-1283 • URL: http://www.rutgers.edu/accounting • RAW Web site provides extensive links to sources of national and international accounting information, such as the Big Six accounting firms, the Financial Accounting Standards Board (FASB), SEC filings (EDGAR), journals, publishers, software, the International Accounting Network, and "Internet's largest list of accounting firms in USA." Searching is offered. Fees: Free.

ONLINE DATABASES

Accounting and Tax Database. PROQUEST. • Provides indexing and abstracting of the literature of accounting, taxation, and financial management, 1971 to date. Updating is weekly. Especially covers accounting, auditing, banking, bankruptcy, employee compensation and benefits, cash management, financial planning, and credit. Inquire as to online cost and availability.

Management Contents. Gale Cengage Learning. • Covers a wide range of management, financial, marketing, personnel, and administrative topics. About 150 leading business journals are indexed and abstracted from 1974 to date, with monthly updating. Inquire as to online cost and availability.

Wilson Business Abstracts Online. H. W. Wilson Co. • Indexes and abstracts 600 major business periodicals, plus the *Wall Street Journal* and the business section of the *New York Times*. Indexing is

from 1982, abstracting from 1990, with the two newspapers included from 1993. Updated weekly. Inquire as to online cost and availability. (*Business Periodicals Index* without abstracts is also available online.).

PERIODICALS AND NEWSLETTERS

Accounting and Financial Planning for Law Firms. American Lawyer Media, Inc. • Monthly. $225.00 per year. Newsletter. Covers budgeting, liability issues, billing systems, benefits management, and other topics relating to law firm administration. (A Law Journal Newsletter, formerly published by Leader Publications).

Accounting Review. University of Georgia, J.M. Tull School of Accounting. American Accounting Association. • Quarterly. Members, $85.00 per year; non-members, $110.00 per year.

Accounting Today: The Business Newspaper for the Tax & Accounting Community. Thomson Media. • Biweekly. $99.00 per year. Covers news affecting tax and accounting professionals.

Inside Public Accounting. Hudson Sawyer Professional Services Marketing Inc. • Description: Contains articles on CPAs and CPA firms, provides news and analysis of management strategies, politics, marketing, computers, and personnel. Email alert delivers hot and topical news to subscribers' desktops. Recurring features include interviews, commentary, reports of meetings, book reviews, and the columns titled Mergers, New Shareholders, Newsmakers, and Lawsuits.

Journal of Accountancy. American Institute of Certified Public Accountants. • Monthly. Free to members; non-members, $61.00 per year.

Journal of Accounting Research. University of Chicago, Graduate School of Business Institute of Professional Accounting. Blackwell Publishing. • Five times a year. Institutions, $425.00 per year. Includes online edition. Annual *Supplement* available. Accepts for review unpublished research in the fields of empirical and experimental accounting.

Journal of Corporate Accounting and Finance. John Wiley and Sons, Inc., Journals. • Bimonthly. $495.00 per year; with online edition, $520.00 per year. Topics include government regulation, corporate taxation, financial risk, business valuation, and strategic planning.

The Journal of Government Financial Management. Association of Government Accountants. • Quarterly. $90.00 per year. Formerly *Government Accountants Journal.*

National Public Accountant. National Society of Accountants. • 10 times a year. Free to members; non-members, $20.00 per year. For accounting and tax practitioners.

NSPA Washington Reporter. National Society of Accountants. • Monthly. Membership.

The Practical Accountant: Providing the Competitive Edge. Thomson Media. • Monthly. $65.00 per year. Covers tax planning, financial planning, practice management, client relationships, and related topics.

Public Accounting Report: Competitive Intelligence for Accounting Firms. Strafford Publications, Inc. • 23 times a year. $360.00 per year. Newsletter. Presents news and trends affecting the accounting profession.

RESEARCH CENTERS AND INSTITUTES

Accounting Research Program. University of California, The Anderson School, Los Angeles, CA 90095-1481. Phone: (310)206-6462 Fax: (310)267-2163 E-mail: carla.hayn@anderson.ucla.edu.

Center for International Education and Research in Accounting. University of Illinois at Urbana-Champaign. 1206 S. Sixth St., 320 Wohlers Hall, Champaign, IL 61820. Phone: (217)333-4545 Fax:

(217)244-6565 E-mail: ciera@uiuc.edu • URL: http://www.cba.uiuc.edu/.

TRADE/PROFESSIONAL ASSOCIATIONS

American Accounting Association. 5717 Bessie Dr., Sarasota, FL 34233-2330. Phone: (941)921-7747 Fax: (941)923-4093 E-mail: office@aaahq.org • URL: http://aaahq.org • Professors and practitioners of accounting. Promotes worldwide excellence in accounting education, research and practice.

American Institute of Certified Public Accountants. 1211 Ave. of the Americas, New York, NY 10036-8775. Phone: 888-777-7077 or (212)596-6200 Fax: (212)596-6213 • URL: http://www.aicpa.org.

Association for Accounting Administration. 136 S. Keowee St., Dayton, OH 45402. Phone: (937)222-0030 Fax: (937)222-5794 E-mail: aaainfo@cpaadmin.org • URL: http://www.cpaadmin.org • Members are accounting and office systems executives.

Association of Government Accountants. 2208 Mount Vernon Ave., Alexandria, VA 22301-1314. Phone: 800-242-7211 or (703)684-6931 Fax: (703)548-9367 E-mail: agamembers@agacgfm.org • URL: http://www.agacgfm.org • Members are employed by federal, state, county, and city government agencies. Includes accountants, auditors, budget officers, and other government finance administrators and officials.

Financial Executives International. 200 Campus Dr., PO Box 674, Florham Park, NJ 07932-0674. Phone: (973)765-1000 Fax: (973)765-1018 E-mail: mcangemi@financialexecutives.org • URL: http://www.financialexecutives.org • Professional organization of corporate financial executives performing duties of chief financial officer, controller, treasurer, or vice-president-finance. Sponsors research activities through its affiliated Financial Executives Research Foundation. Maintains offices in Toronto, Canada, and Washington, DC.

Governmental Accounting Standards Board. 401 Merritt 7, PO Box 5116, Norwalk, CT 06856-5116. Phone: (203)847-0700 Fax: (203)849-9714 E-mail: webmaster@gasb.org • URL: http://www.gasb.org • Has established and maintains the Financial +Accounting Standards Board and the Financial +Accounting Standards Advisory Council. In 1984, organized the Governmental Accounting Standards Board and the Governmental Accounting Standards Advisory Council (see separate entries). FASB creates and improves standards of financial accounting and reporting by defining, and issuing, such standards; conducts and commissions research, statistical compilations, and other studies and surveys; holds meetings, conferences, and hearings with respect to financial accounting and reporting. FASB consults with FASB about major technical issues, agenda of projects, assignment of priorities, and selection and organization of FASB task forces. GASB establishes accounting standards for state and local governmental entities. GASB consults with GASAC in a fashion similar to the FASB and FASAC. **Convention/Meeting:** none.

Institute of Internal Auditors. 247 Maitland Ave., Altamonte Springs, FL 32701-4201. Phone: (407)937-1100 Fax: (407)937-1101 E-mail: iia@theiia.org • URL: http://www.theiia.org.

Institute of Management Accountants. 10 Paragon Dr., Montvale, NJ 07645-1718. Phone: 800-638-4427 or (201)573-9000 Fax: (201)474-1600 E-mail: ima@imanet.org • URL: http://www.imanet.org • Formerly National Association of Accountants.

National Society of Accountants. 1010 N Fairfax St., Alexandria, VA 22314-1574. Phone: 800-966-6679 or (703)549-6400 Fax: (703)549-2984 E-mail: members@nsacct.org • URL: http://www.nsacct.org

• Formerly National Society of Public Accountants.

OTHER SOURCES

Accounting Research Studies. American Institute of Certified Public Accountants. • Irregular.

FASB Accounting Standards Current Text. Financial Accounting Standards Board. • $395.00. Three looseleaf volumes. Periodic supplementation.

FASB Accounting Standards Current Text: General Standards. Financial Accounting Standards Board. • Irregular. Price on application.

FASB Accounting Standards Current Text: Industries Standards. Financial Accounting Standards Board. • Irregular. Price on application.

FASB Accounting Standards Current Text: Professional Standards. Financial Accounting Standards Board. • Irregular. Price on application.

FASB Accounting Standards Current Text: Technical Practice Aids. Financial Accounting Standards Board. • Irregular. Price on application.

FASB Original Pronouncements. Financial Accounting Standards Board. • $595.00. Seven looseleaf volumes.

FASB Original Pronouncements. John Wiley and Sons, Inc. • 2001. $108.95. Three volumes include all the original pronouncements put forth by the Financial Accounting Standards Board since inception in 1973 and the American Institute of Certified Public Accountants.

FASB Statements of Financial Accounting Concepts. John Wiley and Sons, Inc. • 2001. $35.95. Contains statements of concepts issued by the Financial Accounting Standards Board.

Finance and Accounting for Nonfinancial Managers. American Management Association Extension Institute. • Looseleaf. $159.00. Self-study course. Emphasis is on practical explanations, examples, and problem solving. Quizzes and a case study are included.

Financial Accounting Series. Financial Accounting Standards Board. • Price on application.

Forensic Accounting and Financial Fraud. American Management Association Extension Institute. • Looseleaf. $159.00. Self-study course. Emphasis is on practical explanations, examples, and problem solving. Quizzes and a case study are included.

Keeping the Books: Basic Recordkeeping and Accounting for the Successful Small Business. Linda Pinson. Dearborn Trade Publishing, A Kaplan Professional Co. • 2001. $22.95. Fifth edition. Covers bookkeeping systems, financial statements, and IRS tax record requirements. Includes illustrations, worksheets, and forms.

Management Advisory Services Guideline Series. American Institute of Certified Public Accountants. • Irregular. Price varies.

ACCOUNTING, BANK

See: BANK ACCOUNTING

ACCOUNTING, COMPUTERS IN

See: COMPUTERS IN ACCOUNTING

ACCOUNTING, COST

See: COST ACCOUNTING

ACCOUNTING, GOVERNMENT

See: GOVERNMENT ACCOUNTING

ACCOUNTING RESEARCH

ABSTRACTS AND INDEXES

Business Periodicals Index. H. W. Wilson Co. • 11 times a year. Quarterly and annual cumulations. Price varies.

ALMANACS AND YEARBOOKS

Research in Accounting Regulation. Elsevier. • Dates vary. Price varies. 16 volumes.

BIBLIOGRAPHIES

Accounting Research Directory: Database of Accounting Literature. Lawrence D. Brown and others. Markus Wiener Publishing, Inc. • 1994. $69.95. Third edition. Contains lists and evaluations of all publications in seven leading accounting, journals.

DIRECTORIES

Business Organizations, Agencies, and Publications Directory. Gale Cengage Learning. • 2003. $480.00. 15th edition. Over 40,000 entries describing 39 types of business information sources. Classified by type of organization, publication, or serviceIncludes state, national, and international agencies and organizations. Master index to names and keywords. Also includes e-mail addresses and web site URL's.

ENCYCLOPEDIAS AND DICTIONARIES

Blackwell Encyclopedic Dictionary of Accounting. Rashad Abdel-khalik. Blackwell Publishing. • 1997. $38.95. The editor is associated with the University of Florida. Contains definitions of key terms combined with longer articles written by various U. S. and foreign business educators. Includes bibliographies and index. (Blackwell Encyclopedia of Management Series).

INTERNET DATABASES

Rutgers Accounting Web (RAW). Rutgers University Accounting Research Center. Phone: (973)353-5172 Fax: (973)353-1283 • URL: http://www.rutgers.edu/accounting • RAW Web site provides extensive links to sources of national and international accounting information, such as the Big Six accounting firms, the Financial Accounting Standards Board (FASB), SEC filings (EDGAR), journals, publishers, software, the International Accounting Network, and "Internet's largest list of accounting firms in USA." Searching is offered. Fees: Free.

ONLINE DATABASES

EconLit. American Economic Association. • Covers the worldwide literature of economics as contained in selected monographs and about 550 journals. Subjects include microeconomics, macroeconomics, economic history, inflation, money, credit, finance, accounting theory, trade, natural resource economics, and regional economics. Time period is 1969 to present, with monthly updates. Inquire as to online cost and availability.

Wilson Business Abstracts Online. H. W. Wilson Co. • Indexes and abstracts 600 major business periodicals, plus the *Wall Street Journal* and the business section of the *New York Times.* Indexing is from 1982, abstracting from 1990, with the two newspapers included from 1993. Updated weekly. Inquire as to online cost and availability. (*Business Periodicals Index* without abstracts is also available online.).

PERIODICALS AND NEWSLETTERS

CPA Technology and Internet Tax Advisor (Certified Public Accountant). Aspen Publishers. • Monthly. $261.00 per year. Newsletter. Describes hardware and software products and makes recommendations. Formerly *C P A Technology and Internet Advisor.*

Journal of Accounting Research. University of Chicago, Graduate School of Business Institute of Professional Accounting. Blackwell Publishing. • Five times a year. Institutions, $425.00 per year. Includes online edition. Annual *Supplement*

available. Accepts for review unpublished research in the fields of empirical and experimental accounting.

RESEARCH CENTERS AND INSTITUTES

Accounting Research Program. University of California, The Anderson School, Los Angeles, CA 90095-1481. Phone: (310)206-6462 Fax: (310)267-2163 E-mail: carla.hayn@anderson.ucla.edu.

Bureau of Economic and Business Research. University of Illinois at Urbana-Champaign, 1206 S. Sixth St., 403 Wohlers Hall, Champaign, IL 61820. Phone: (217)333-2330 Fax: (217)244-7410 E-mail: g-oldman@uiuc.edu • URL: http://www.business.uiuc.edu/research.

McGladrey Institute of Accounting Education and Research. University of Iowa, Henry B. Tippie College of Business, 108 John Pappajohn Business Bldg., 21 E. Market St., Iowa City, IA 52242-1000. Phone: (319)335-0862 Fax: (319)335-1956 E-mail: mcg-inst@iuowa.edu • URL: http://www.biz.uiowa.edu/acct.

TRADE/PROFESSIONAL ASSOCIATIONS

American Accounting Association. 5717 Bessie Dr., Sarasota, FL 34233-2330. Phone: (941)921-7747 Fax: (941)923-4093 E-mail: office@aaahq.org • URL: http://aaahq.org • Professors and practitioners of accounting. Promotes worldwide excellence in accounting education, research and practice.

American Woman's Society of Certified Public Accountants. 136 S Keowee St., Dayton, OH 45402. Phone: 800-297-2721 or (973)222-1872 Fax: (973)222-5794 E-mail: info@awscpa.org • URL: http://www.awscpa.org.

Governmental Accounting Standards Board. 401 Merritt 7, PO Box 5116, Norwalk, CT 06856-5116. Phone: (203)847-0700 Fax: (203)849-9714 E-mail: webmaster@gasb.org • URL: http://www.gasb.org • Has established and maintains the Financial +Accounting Standards Board and the Financial +Accounting Standards Advisory Council. In 1984, organized the Governmental Accounting Standards Board and the Governmental Accounting Standards Advisory Council (see separate entries). FASB creates and improves standards of financial accounting and reporting by defining, and issuing, such standards; conducts and commissions research, statistical compilations, and other studies and surveys; holds meetings, conferences, and hearings with respect to financial accounting and reporting. FASAC consults with FASB about major technical issues, agenda of projects, assignment of priorities, and selection and organization of FASB task forces. GASB establishes accounting standards for state and local governmental entities. GASB consults with GASAC in a fashion similar to the FASB and FASAC. **Convention/Meeting:** none.

ACID RAIN

See also: ENVIRONMENT

ABSTRACTS AND INDEXES

Environment Abstracts. Congressional Information Service, Inc. • Monthly. Price varies. Provides multidisciplinary coverage of the world's environmental literature. Incorporates *Acid Rain Abstracts.*

Environment Abstracts Annual: A Guide to the Key Environmental Literature of the Year. Congressional Information Service, Inc. • Annual. $495.00. A yearly cumulation of *Environment Abstracts.*

Environmental Knowledge Base: An Electronic Bibliography Featuring Citations and Abstracts of Scientific and Popular Articles on Environmental Issues, Including Social Policy, Economics, Regulatory, and Legal Topics. Environmental Studies Institute. • Monthly. Price varies. An index to current environmental literature. Formerly

6

For publishers addresses, refer to SOURCES CITED section at the back of the book.

Environmental Periodicals Bibliography.

Pollution Abstracts. Cambridge Information Group. • Monthly. $1,390.00 per year. Includes print and online editions; with index, $1,515.00 per year.

CD-ROM DATABASES

Environment Abstracts on €D-ROM. LEXIS-NEXIS. • Quarterly. $1,295.00 per year. Contains the following CD-ROM databases: *Environment Abstracts, Energy Abstracts,* and *Acid Rain Abstracts.* Length of coverage varies.

DIRECTORIES

Gale Environmental Sourcebook: A Guide to Organizations, Agencies, and Publications. Gale Cengage Learning. • 1993. $115.00. Second edition. A directory of print and non-print information sources on a wide variety of environmental topics.

ENCYCLOPEDIAS AND DICTIONARIES

Encyclopedia of Global Change: Environmental Change and Human Society. Andrew S. Goudie, editor. Oxford University Press. • 2001. $275.00. Two volumes. Contains 300 signed articles on a wide variety of topics relating to changes in the environment and the atmosphere. Includes bibliographies and illustrations.

Wiley Encyclopedia of Energy and the Environment. Attilio Bisio and Sharon Boots. John Wiley and Sons, Inc. • 1996. $285.00. Abriged edition. Two volumes. Covers a wide variety of energy and environmental topics, including legal and policy issues. (Encyclopedia of Energy and the Environment Series: Vol. 2).

ONLINE DATABASES

PAIS International. Public Affairs Information Service, Inc. • Corresponds to the former printed publications, *PAIS Bulletin* (1976-90) and *PAIS Foreign Language Index* (1972-90), and to the current *PAIS International in Print* (1991 to date). Covers economic, political, and sociological material appearing in periodicals, books, government documents, and other publications. Updating is monthly. Inquire as to online cost and availability.

Pollution Abstracts [online]. Cambridge Scientific Abstracts. • Provides indexing and abstracting of international, environmentally related literature, 1970 to date. Monthly updates. Inquire as to online cost and availability.

STATISTICS SOURCES

Statistical Record of the Environment. Gale Cengage Learning. • 1996. $130.00. Third edition. Provides over 875 charts, tables, and graphs of major environmental statistics, arranged by subject. Covers population growth, hazardous waste, nuclear energy, acid rain, pesticides, and other subjects related to the environment. A keyword index is included. (Gale Environmental Library Series).

TRADE/PROFESSIONAL ASSOCIATIONS

Izaak Walton League of America. 707 Conservation Lane, Gaithersburg, MD 20878. Phone: 800-453-5463 or (301)548-0150 Fax: (301)548-0146 E-mail: general@iwla.org • URL: http://www.iwla.org • Sponsors the Acid Rain Project, an environmental protection program. Absorbed Friends of the Land.

OTHER SOURCES

Environment Reporter. BNA, Inc. • Weekly. $3,166.00 per year. 18 looseleaf volumes. Covers legal aspects of wide variety of environmental concerns.

ACOUSTICAL ENGINEERING

See: NOISE CONTROL

ACQUISITIONS AND MERGERS

See: MERGERS AND ACQUISITIONS

ACTUARIAL SCIENCE

ALMANACS AND YEARBOOKS

American Academy of Actuaries Yearbook. American Academy of Actuaries. • Annual. $25.00.

Casualty Actuarial Society Yearbook. Casualty Actuarial Society. • Annual. $40.00. Approximately 2,500 actuaries working in insurance other than life insurance.

Society of Actuaries Yearbook. Society of Actuaries. • Annual. Price on application. Includes alphabetical list of actuaries.

HANDBOOKS AND MANUALS

Actuaries' Survival Guide: How to Succeed in One of the Most Desirable Professions. Fred Szabo. Elsevier Butterworth Heinemann. • 2004. $39.95. Serves as a guide for students and graduates of "number-based disciplines" who are considering a career in actuarial science. Covers careers, education, and jobs. (Imprint: Academic Press.).

PERIODICALS AND NEWSLETTERS

The Actuary. Society of Actuaries. • Description: Features information about actuaries practicing in life and health insurance, pensions, and investments in the U.S. and Canada. Recurring features include letters to the editor, news of research and education, a calendar of events, reports of meetings, notices of publications available, and puzzles.

Contingencies: The Magazine of the Actuarial Profession. American Academy of Actuaries. • Bimonthly. $30.00 per year. Provides non-technical articles on the actuarial aspects of insurance, employee benefits, and pensions.

STATISTICS SOURCES

Vital Statistics of the United States: Life Tables. Available from U. S. Government Printing Office. • Annual. $64.00. Produced by the National Center for Health Statistics, Public Health Service, U. S. Department of Health and Human Services. Provides detailed data on expectation of life by age, race, and sex. Historical data is shown annually from the year 1900. (Vital Statistics, volume 2.).

TRADE/PROFESSIONAL ASSOCIATIONS

American Academy of Actuaries. 1100 17th St., N.W., 7th Fl., Washington, DC 20036. Phone: (202)223-8196 Fax: (202)872-1948 E-mail: lawson@actuary.org • URL: http://www.actuary.org.

Casualty Actuarial Society. 4350 N Fairfax Dr., Ste. 250, Arlington, VA 22203. Phone: (703)276-3100 Fax: (703)276-3108 E-mail: office@casact.org • URL: http://www.casact.org • Professional society of property/casualty actuaries. Seeks to advance the body of knowledge of actuarial science applied to property, casualty and similar risk exposures, to maintain qualification standards, promote high standards of conduct and competence, and increase awareness of actuarial science. Examinations required for membership.

Conference of Consulting Actuaries. 1110 W. Lake Cook Rd., Suite 235, Buffalo Grove, IL 60089-1968. Phone: (847)419-9090 Fax: (847)419-9091 E-mail: cca@ccactuaries.org • URL: http://www.ccactuaries.org • Formerly Conference of Actuaries of Public Practice.

Society of Actuaries. 475 N. Martingale Rd., Suite 800, Schaumburg, IL 60173-2226. Phone: (847)706-3500 Fax: (847)706-3599 E-mail: aabel@soa.org • URL: http://www.soa.org.

ADDITIVES AND FLAVORINGS

ABSTRACTS AND INDEXES

Applied Science and Technology Index. H. W. Wilson Co. • 11 times a year. Quarterly and annual cumulations. Price varies. Indexes a wide variety of English language technical, industrial, and engineering periodicals.

Current Contents: Engineering, Computing and Technology. Thomson/ISI. • Weekly. $730.00 per year. Reproductions of contents pages of technical journals. Includes *Author Index, Address Directory, Current Book Contents* and *Title Word Index.* Formerly *Current Contents: Engineering, Technology and Applied Sciences.*

Food Science and Technology Abstracts. International Food Information Service Publishing. • Monthly. $1,780.00 per year. Provides worldwide coverage of the literature of food technology and food production.

Foods Adlibra: Key to the World's Food Literature. General Mills, Inc. Foods Adlibra Publications. • Semimonthly. $240.00 per year. Provides journal citations and abstracts to the literature of food technology and packaging.

ALMANACS AND YEARBOOKS

Feed Additive Compendium. Miller Publishing Co. • Annual. $265.00. Monthly updates. Covers the use of drugs as additives to livestock and poultry feed.

CD-ROM DATABASES

Food Science and Technology Abstracts [CD-ROM]. Available from SilverPlatter Information, Inc. • Quarterly. Produced by International Food Information Service (home page is http://www.ifis.org). Provides worldwide coverage on CD-ROM of the literature of food technology and production. Various types of publications are indexed, with abstracts, including about 1,800 periodicals. Time period is 1969 to date.

DIRECTORIES

Food Processing Guide and Directory. Putman Media Inc. • Annual. $90.00. Lists over 5,390 food ingredient and equipment manufacturers.

Major Food and Drink Companies of the World. Available from Gale Cengage Learning. • Annual. $880.00. Two volumes. Published by Graham & Whiteside. Contains profiles and trade names for more than 9,800 important food and beverage companies in various countries. In addition to foods, includes both alcoholic and nonalcoholic drink products.

Prepared Foods Sourcebook. Reed Business Information. • Annual. $75.00. Lists approximately 600 food and veverage companies.

Specialty Food Industry Directory. Phoenix Media Network, Inc. • Annual. Included in subscription to Food Distribution Magazine. Lists manufacturers and suppliers of specialty foods, and services and equipment for the specialty food industry. Featured food products include legumes, sauces, spices, upscale cheese, specialty beverages, snack foods, baked goods, ethnic foods, and specialty meats.

Thomas Food and Beverage Market Place. Grey House Publishing. • 2004. $495.00. Three volumes. Contains more than 40,000 entries covering food companies, beverages, food equipment, warehouse companies, food brokers, wholesalers, importers, and exporters. Formerly *Thomas Food Industry Register.*

ENCYCLOPEDIAS AND DICTIONARIES

Dictionary of Food Ingredients. Robert S. Igoe and Y.H. Hui. Aspen Publishers, Inc. • 2001. $44.00. Fourth edition.

Foods and Nutrition Encyclopedia. Audrey H. Ensminger and others. CRC Press, Inc. • 1993. $309.95. Second edition. Two volumes.

Wiley Encyclopedia of Food Science and Technology. Frederick J. Francis, editor. John Wiley and Sons, Inc. • 2000. $1,650.00. Second edition. Four volumes. Contains about 400 entries. Coverage includes biotechnology, genetic engineering, nutrition, regulatory matters, food safety, labeling, food substitutes (sugar, fat, dairy), and many other topics.

ONLINE DATABASES

Applied Science and Technology Index Online. H. W. Wilson Co. • Provides online indexing of 500 major scientific, technical, industrial, and engineering periodicals. Time period is 1983 to date. Monthly updates. Inquire as to online cost and availability.

Food Science and Technology Abstracts [online]. IFIS North American Desk. • Produced by International Food Information Service. Provides about 500,000 online citations, with abstracts, to the international literature of food science, technology, commodities, engineering, and processing. Approximately 2,000 periodicals are covered. Time period is 1969 to date, with monthly updates. Inquire as to online cost and availability.

FOODS ADLIBRA. General Mills, Inc. • Contains online citations, with abstracts, to the technical and business literature of food processing and packaging. New products and new ingredients are featured. Covers about 250 trade journals and 500 research journals from 1974 to date, with monthly updates. Inquire as to online cost and availability.

PROMT: Predicasts Overview of Markets and Technology. Gale Cengage Learning. • Companies, products, applied technologies and markets. U.S. and international literature coverage, 1972 to date. Inquire as to online cost and availability. Provides abstracts from more than 1,600 publications. Weekly updates.

PERIODICALS AND NEWSLETTERS

Flavour and Fragrance Journal. John Wiley and Sons, Inc., Journals. • Bimonthly. Individuals, $890.00 per year; institutions, $1,185.00 per year.

Food Additives and Contaminants: Analysis, Surveillance, Evaluation, Control. Taylor and Francis Group. • Monthly. Institutions $2,038.00 per year.

Food Chemical News. CRC Press L.L.C. • Description: Provides in-depth, timely coverage of the laws affecting food regulation, including additives, colors, pesticides, and allied products. Recurring features include news of research.

Food Distribution Magazine. Phoenix Media Network, Inc. • Monthly. $49.00 per year. Edited for marketers and buyers of domestic and imported, specialty or gourmet food products, including ethnic foods, seasonings, and bakery items.

Food Processing. Putman Media. • Monthly. Free to qualified personnel; others, $89.00 per year. Edited for executive and operating personnel in the food processing industry.

The Monell Connection: From the Monell Chemical Senses Center, a Nonprofit Scientific Institute Devoted to Research on Taste and Smell. Monell Chemical Senses Center. • Three times a year. Free. Newsletter. Includes brief summaries of selected papers describing ongoing work of Monell scientists.

Perfumer and Flavorist. Allured Publishing. • Bimonthly. $135.00 per year. Provides information on the art and technology of flavors and fragrances, including essential oils, aroma chemicals, and spices.

RESEARCH CENTERS AND INSTITUTES

Food Research Institute. University of Wisconsin at Madison, Dept. of Food Microbiology and Toxicology, 1925 Willow Dr., Madison, WI 53706. Phone: (608)263-7777 Fax: (608)263-1114 E-mail: mwpariza@facstaff.wisc.edu • URL: http://www.wisc.edu/fri/.

Institute of Food Science. Cornell University, 114 Stocking Hall, Ithaca, NY 14853-7201. Phone:

(607)255-7900 E-mail: cifs@cornell.edu • URL: http://www.nysaes.cornell.edu/cifs/ • Research areas include the chemistry and processing of food commodities, food processing engineering, food packaging, and nutrition.

Monell Chemical Senses Center. Monell Chemical Senses Center. 3500 Market St., Philadelphia, PA 19104-3308. Phone: (267)519-4700 Fax: (267)898-2084 E-mail: beauchamp@monell.org • URL: http://www.monell.org • Mechanisms and functions of the chemical senses (taste, smell, and chemical irritation), including studies in the areas of biochemistry, biophysics, endocrinology, physiology, ethology, neurology, behavior, genetics, psychophysics, nutrition, organic chemistry, chemical ecology, and zoology. Basic research relates to solutions of problems in health and nutrition, aging and neurodegenerative disease, environmental odors, reproduction, disease diagnosis, expansion of world food supply, and alternative means of vertebrate pest control. Projects focus on biochemistry of receptor mechanisms, sensory qualities of food, role of early diet in shaping food preferences, relationship between chemosensory function and nutritional and disease states, role of body volatiles in disease diagnosis, methods of altering salt preference, role of taste and smell in food utilization, effect of aging on taste and smell, information processing in taste and smell, role of genes in determining sensory perception and hedonic responses, and diagnosis and treatment of taste and smell disorders.

STATISTICS SOURCES

World Food Data and Statistics. Euromonitor International. • 2004. $650.00. Provides five-year data for a wide variety of food products in 52 countries. Includes market size, consumer expenditures, price indicators, and retail distribution data for many kinds of meat, fish, fruits, vegetables, dairy products, baked goods, condiments, canned food, and frozen food.

TRADE/PROFESSIONAL ASSOCIATIONS

Chemical Sources Association. 3301 Rte. 66, Ste. 205, Bldg. C, PO Box 790, Neptune, NJ 07753. Phone: (732)922-3008 Fax: (732)922-3590 E-mail: diane@afius.org • URL: http://www.chemicalsources.org • Representatives of flavor and fragrance manufacturers. Purpose is to find suppliers and manufacturers for rare or hard-to-obtain chemicals and essential oils used in the flavor and fragrance industry. Compiles statistics.

Flavor and Extract Manufacturers Association of the United States. 1620 Eye St., N.W. Suite 925, Washington, DC 20006. Phone: (202)293-5800 Fax: (202)463-8998 E-mail: kearle@thereobertsgroup.net • URL: http://www.femaflavor.org.

International Flavors and Fragrances. 521 W 57th St., New York, NY 10019. Phone: (212)765-5500 Fax: (212)708-7132 E-mail: iffusaflavors@iff.com • URL: http://www.iff.com.

International Food Additives Council. 5775 Peachtree-Dunwoody Rd., Ste. 500G, Atlanta, GA 30342. Phone: (404)252-3663 Fax: (404)252-0774 E-mail: ifac@kellencompany.com • Consists of manufacturers of food additives and businesses using food additives. Aims to: gather and disseminate information on food additives; represent members' interests; provide technical and scientific assistance. Sponsors research; compiles statistics.

National Association of Flavors and Food Ingredient Systems. 3301 Rte. 66, Ste. 205, Bldg. C, Neptune, NJ 07753. Phone: (732)922-3218 Fax: (732)922-3590 E-mail: info@naffs.org • URL: http://www.naffs.org • Manufacturers of fruit and syrup toppings, flavors and stabilizers for the food

industry. Formerly National Association of Fruits, Flavors and Syrups.

OTHER SOURCES

Food Additives. Available from MarketResearch.com. • 2002. $3,700.00. Published by the Freedonia Group. Market data with forecasts to 2006 on coloring agents, flavors, preservatives, stabilizers, etc.

ADHESIVES

GENERAL WORKS

Adhesion Science. J. Comyn. Springer-Verlag. • 1997. $52.95. Published by The Royal Society of Chemistry. Provides basic scientific and technical information on "common adhesives." (RSC Paperback Series).

ABSTRACTS AND INDEXES

Applied Science and Technology Index. H. W. Wilson Co. • 11 times a year. Quarterly and annual cumulations. Price varies. Indexes a wide variety of English language technical, industrial, and engineering periodicals.

Chemical Abstracts. Chemical Abstracts Service. • Weekly. $26,000.00 per year. Includes *CA Index Guide.*

CPI Digest: Key to World Literature Serving the Coatings, Plastics, Fibers, Adhesives, and Related Industries (Chemical Process Industries). CPI Information Services. • Monthly. $397.00 per year. Abstracts of business and technical articles for polymer-based, chemical process industries. Includes a monthly list of relevant U. S. patents. International coverage.

NTIS Alerts: Materials Sciences. National Technical Information Service. • Semimonthly. $220.00 per year. Provides descriptions of government-sponsored research reports and software, with ordering information. Covers ceramics, glass, coatings, composite materials, alloys, plastics, wood, paper, adhesives, fibers, lubricants, and related subjects. Formerly *Abstract Newsletter.*

DIRECTORIES

Adhesives Age Buyers Guide. Chemical Week Associates. • Annual. $60.00. Lists manufacturers and suppliers of raw materials, chemicals, equipment, and machinery for the adhesives industry.

Adhesives Technology Handbook. Arthur H. Landrock. Noyes Data Corp. • 1986. $64.00.

Assembly Buyers Guide. Reed Business Information. • Annual. $68.00. Lists manufacturers and suppliers of equipment relating to assembly automation, fasteners, adhesives, robotics, and power tools.

U. S. Glass, Metal, and Glazing: Buyers Guide. Key Communications, Inc. • Annual. $25.00. A directory of about 3,000 supplies and equipment for the glass fabrication and installation industry.

ENCYCLOPEDIAS AND DICTIONARIES

ASM Materials Engineering Dictionary. Joseph R. Davis, editor. ASM International. • 1992. $166.00. Contains 10,000 entries, 700 illustrations, and 150 tables relating to metals, plastics, ceramics, composites, and adhesives. Includes "Technical Briefs" on 64 key material groups.

FINANCIAL RATIOS

Annual Statement Studies. The Risk Management Association. • Annual. Median and quartile financial ratios are given for over 400 kinds of manufacturing, wholesale, retail, construction, and consumer finance establishments. Data is sorted by both asset size and sales volume. Includes a clearly written "Definition of Ratios" and an alphabetical industry index.

Annual Statement Studies: Industry Default Probabilities and Cash Flow Measures. The Risk

Management Association. • Annual. $145.00. Serves as a companion volume to the original *Annual Statement Studies*. Gives probability of default estimates on a percentage scale for more than 450 industries. Includes changes in position year-by-year for eight financial statement line items and provides percentage measures of cash flow.

HANDBOOKS AND MANUALS

Construction Sealants and Adhesives. Julian R. Panek and John P. Cook. John Wiley and Sons, Inc. • 1991. $150.00. Third edition. (Practical Construction Guides Series).

Handbook of Adhesives and Sealants. Edward M. Petrie. McGraw-Hill. • 1999. $99.95. (Handbook Series).

Handbook of Pressure Sensitive Adhesive Technology. Donatas Satas. Satas and Associates. • 1999. $150.00. Third revised edition.

ONLINE DATABASES

CA Search. Chemical Abstracts Service. • Guide to chemical literature, 1967 to present. Inquire as to online cost and availability.

PaperChem Database. Information Services Div. • Worldwide coverage of the scientific and technical paper industry chemical literature, including patents, 1967 to present. Weekly updates. Inquire as to online cost and availability.

World Surface Coatings Abstracts [Online]. Paint Research Association of Great Britain. • Indexing and abstracting of the literature of paint and surface coatings, 1976 to present. Monthly updates. Inquire as to online cost and availability.

PERIODICALS AND NEWSLETTERS

Adhesives Age. Chemical Week Associates. • Monthly. $60.00 per year. Includes annual *Directory.*

Assembly: Design and Manufacturing Technology for Better Assembled Products. Business News Publishing Co. • Monthly. $68.00 per year. Covers assembly, fastening, and joining systems. Includes information on automation and robotics.

The Composites and Adhesives Newsletter. T-C Press. • Quarterly. $190.00. Presents news of the composite materials and adhesives industries, with particular coverage of new products and applications.

International Journal of Adhesion and Adhesives. Elsevier. • Six times a year. $972.00 per year. Published in England.

Journal of Adhesion. Taylor & Francis Group. • Monthly. Three volumes. Individuals, $1,575.00 per year; institutions, $3,056.00 per year; corporations, $6,760.00 per year.

U. S. Glass, Metal, and Glazing. Key Communications, Inc. • Monthly. $35.00 per year. Edited for glass fabricators, glaziers, distributors, and retailers. Special feature issues are devoted to architectural glass, mirror glass, windows, storefronts, hardware, machinery, sealants, and adhesives. Regular topics include automobile glass and fenestration (window design and placement).

STATISTICS SOURCES

Annual Survey of Manufactures. Available from U. S. Government Printing Office. • Annual. Prices vary. Issued by the U. S. Census Bureau as an interim update to the *Census of Manufactures*. Includes data on number of manufacturing establishments in various industries, employment, labor costs, value of shipments, capital expenditures, inventories, energy costs, and assets. (See also Census Bureau home page, http://www.census. gov/.).

U. S. Industry and Trade Outlook. Available from National Technical Information Service. • Annual. $69.95. Produced by the International Trade Administration, U. S. Department of Commerce, in a "public-private" partnership with DRI/McGraw-Hill and Standard & Poor's. Provides basic data, outlook for the current year, and "Long-Term Prospects" (five-year projections) for a wide variety of products and services. Includes high technology industries. Formerly *U. S. Industrial Outlook.*

TRADE/PROFESSIONAL ASSOCIATIONS

Adhesive and Sealant Council. 7979 Old Georgetown Rd., No. 500, Bethesda, MD 20814. Phone: (301)986-9700 Fax: (301)986-9795 E-mail: info@ascouncil.org • URL: http://www.ascouncil.org.

OTHER SOURCES

Adhesives and Sealants. ASM International. • 1990. $198.00. Volume three. (Engineered Materials Handbook Series).

ADMINISTRATION

See also: BUSINESS; EXECUTIVES; INDUSTRIAL MANAGEMENT; PUBLIC ADMINISTRATION

GENERAL WORKS

Business and Administrative Communication. Kitty O. Locker. McGraw-Hill. • 2003. Sixth edition. Price on application.

Creative Management. Jane Henry. Sage Publications, Inc. • 2001. $101.00. Second edition.

Designing Organizations to Create Value: From Strategy to Structure. Jerry Zimmerman and others. McGraw-Hill. • 2002. $29.95. Describes a process for "identifying the critical aspects of an organization's internal structure" and making administrative enhancements.

Dynamic E-Business Implementation Management: How to Effectively Manage E-Business Implementation. Bennet P. Lientz and Kathryn P. Rea. Elsevier. • 2000. $47.95. (E-Business Solutions Series).

Fundamentals of Management. James H. Donnelly and others. McGraw-Hill. • 1997. $60.50. 10th edition.

The Human Side of Enterprise. Douglas McGregor. McGraw-Hill. • 1985. $53.13.

The Leader of the Future: New Essays by World-Class Leaders and Thinkers. Frances Hesselbein. John Wiley and Sons, Inc. • 2000. $16.50. Contains articles on leadership by "executives, consultants, and commentators." (Management Series).

Management. Luis R. Gomez-Mejia and David B. Balkin. McGraw-Hill. • 2002. Price on application.

Management: Concepts, Practice, and Skills. R. Wayne Mondy and Shane R. Premeaux. Cengage Learning. • 2000. $61.95.

Management: Skills and Application. Lloyd L. Byars. McGraw-Hill. • 2002. 10th edition. Price on application. An introductory text covering the principles of successful management. Arranged according to the following "Skills:" Planning, Organizing, Staffing, Directing, and Controlling. Includes a glossary of key terms and three indexes. (Irwin Professional Publishing.).

Reengineering Management: The Mandate for New Leadership. James Champy. DIANE Publishing Co. • 1998. $25.00.

Reengineering the Corporation: A Manifesto for Business Revolution. Michael Hammer and James Champy. HarperInformation. • 2001. $16.00. Revised edition.

ABSTRACTS AND INDEXES

Business Periodicals Index. H. W. Wilson Co. • 11 times a year. Quarterly and annual cumulations. Price varies.

CD-ROM DATABASES

Profiles in Business and Management: An International Directory of Scholars and Their Research [CD-ROM]. Harvard Business School Publishing. • Annual. $595.00. Fully searchable CD-ROM version of two-volume printed directory. Contains bibliographic and biographical information for over 5600 business and management experts active in 21 subject areas. Formerly *International Directory of Business and Management Scholars.*

WILSONDISC: Wilson Business Abstracts. H. W. Wilson Co. • Monthly. Includes unlimited online access to *Wilson Business Abstracts* through WILSONLINE. Provides CD-ROM "cover-to-cover" abstracting and indexing of over 600 prominent business periodicals. Indexing is from 1982, abstracting from 1990. (*Business Periodicals Index* without abstracts is available on CD-ROM at $1,495 per year.).

DIRECTORIES

Reference Book of Corporate Managements. • Annual. Libraries, $650.00 per year; others, $795.00 per year. Lease basis. Management executives at over 12,000 leading United States companies.

Standard and Poor's Register of Corporations, Directors and Executives. Standard and Poor's. • Annual. $675.00. Looseleaf service. Lease basis. Periodic supplementation. Over 55,000 public and privately held corporations in the U.S.

ENCYCLOPEDIAS AND DICTIONARIES

Blackwell Encyclopedic Dictionary of Strategic Management. Derek F. Channon, editor. Blackwell Publishing. • 1997. $128.95. The editor is associated with Imperial College, London. Contains definitions of key terms combined with longer articles written by various U. S. and foreign business educators. Includes bibliographies and index. (Blackwell Encyclopedia of Management Series.).

Every Manager's Guide to Information Technology: A Glossary of Key Terms and Concepts for Today's Business Leader. Peter G. W. Keen. Harvard Business School Publishing. • 1994. $18.95. Second edition. Provides definitions of terms related to computers, data-communications, and information network systems. (Harvard Business Reference Series).

International Encyclopedia of Business and Management. Malcolm Warner, editor. Cengage Learning. • 2001. $1,899.00.Second edition. Eight volumes. Contains more than 500 articles on global management issues. Includes extensive bibliographies, cross references, and an index of key words and phrases.

International Encyclopedia of Public Policy and Administration. Jay M. Shafritz, editor. Westview Press. • 1997. $550.00. Four volumes. Covers 20 major areas, such as public administration, government budgeting, industrial policy, nonprofit management, organizational theory, public finance, labor relations, and taxation. Includes a brief bibliography for each major entry and a comprehensive index.

HANDBOOKS AND MANUALS

AMA Management Handbook. John J. Hampton, editor. AMACOM. • 1994. $110.00. Third edition. Provides 200 chapters in 16 major subject areas. Covers a wide variety of business and industrial management topics.

Developing E-Business Systems and Architectures: A Manager's Guide. Paul Harmon and others. Elsevier. • 2000. $34.95.

Management: Skills and Application With Powerweb. Leslie W. Rue and Lloyd L. Byars. McGraw-Hill. • 2002. 10th edition. Price on application.

Organization Charts: Structures of More Than 200 Businesses and Non-Profit Organizations. Gale Cengage Learning. • 1999. $180.00. Third edition. Includes an introductory discussion of the history and use of such charts.

Professional's Guide to Successful Management:

The Eight Essentials for Running Your Firm, Practice, or Partnership. Carol A. O'Connor. McGraw-Hill. • 1994. Price on application.

Reengineering Revolution: A Handbook. Michael Hammer and Steven Stanton. HarperInformation. • 1995. $17.95.

INTERNET DATABASES

EBSCO Information Services. Ebsco Publishing. Phone: 800-653-2726 or (978)356-6500 Fax: (978)356-6565 E-mail: ep@epnet.com • URL: http://www.epnet.com • Fee-based Web site providing Internet access to a wide variety of databases, including business-related material. Full text is available for many periodical titles, with daily updates. Fees: Apply.

InSite 2. Intelligence Data/Thomson Financial. Phone: 800-654-0393 or (617)856-1890 Fax: (617)737-3182 E-mail: intelligence.data@tfn.com • URL: http://www.insite2.gale.com/ • Fee-based Web site consolidates information in a "Base Pack" consisting of Business InSite, Market InSite, and Company InSite. Optional databases are Consumer InSite, Health and Wellness InSite, Newsletter InSite, and Computer InSite. Includes fulltext content from more than 2,500 trade publications, journals, newsletters, newspapers, analyst reports, and other sources. Continuous updating. Formerly produced by The Gale Group.

ProQuest Direct. ProQuest Inc. Phone: 800-889-3358 or (734)761-4700 Fax: (734)662-4554 • URL: http://proquest.com • Fee-based Web site providing Internet access to more than 3,000 periodicals, newspapers, and other publications. Many items are available full-text, with daily updates. Includes extensive corporate and financial information. Fees: Apply.

ONLINE DATABASES

Business and Management Practices. Gale Cengage Learning. • Provides fulltext of management articles appearing in more than 350 relevant publications. Emphasis is on "the processes, methods, and strategies of managing a business." Time span is 1995 to date. Inquire as to online cost and availability. (Also available in a CD-ROM version.).

Management Contents. Gale Cengage Learning. • Covers a wide range of management, financial, marketing, personnel, and administrative topics. About 150 leading business journals are indexed and abstracted from 1974 to date, with monthly updating. Inquire as to online cost and availability.

Wilson Business Abstracts Online. H. W. Wilson Co. • Indexes and abstracts 600 major business periodicals, plus the *Wall Street Journal* and the business section of the *New York Times.* Indexing is from 1982, abstracting from 1990, with the two newspapers included from 1993. Updated weekly. Inquire as to online cost and availability. (*Business Periodicals Index* without abstracts is also available online.).

PERIODICALS AND NEWSLETTERS

Academy of Management Executive. Academy of Management. • Bimonthly. $125.00 per year. Contains articles relating to the practical application of management principles and theory.

Academy of Management Journal. Academy of Management. • Bimonthly. $125.00 per year. Presents research papers on management-related topics.

Administrative Science Quarterly. Cornell University, Johnson Graduate School of Management. • Individuals: $65.00 per year; institutions, $130.00 per year.

California Management Review. University of California at Berkeley. • Quarterly. Individuals, $50.00 per year; institutions, $65.00.

Forbes. Forbes, Inc. • Biweekly. $59.95 per year.

Includes supplements: *Forbes ASAP* and *Forbes FYI.*

Fortune Magazine. Time Inc., Business Information Group. • Biweekly. $59.95 per year. Edited for top executives and upper-level managers.

Harvard Management Update. Harvard Business School Publishing. • Description: Provides information on current management techniques and trends.

Leader to Leader. Peter F. Drucker Foundation for Nonprofit Management. Jossey-Bass. • Quarterly. Institutions, $199.00 per year. Contains articles on "management, leadership, and strategy" written by "leading executives, thinkers, and consultants." Covers both business and nonprofit issues.

Management Review. American Management Association. • Membership.

Management Science. INFORMS. • Monthly. Individuals, $185.00 per year; institutions, $488.00 per year. Includes print and online editions. Provides an interchange of information between management and management scientists in industry, academia, the military and go vernment.

MIR: Management International Review: Journal of International Business. Bertelsmann Springer. • Quarterly. $150.00 per year.

SAM Advanced Management Journal. Society for Advancement of Management. Texas A & M University - Corpus Christi, College of Business. • Quarterly. $49.00. Provides information on leading business topics for practicing managers.

Women as Managers: Strategies for Success. Economics Press, Inc. • Biweekly. $69.00 per year. Newsletter. Covers management skills and techniques leading to higher career levels. Discusses problems women face on the job.

RESEARCH CENTERS AND INSTITUTES

Board of Research. Babson College, 204 Babson, Babson Park, MA 02457-0310. Phone: (718)239-5339 Fax: (718)239-6416 E-mail: chern@babson.edu • URL: http://www.babson.edu/bor • Research areas include management, entrepreneurial characteristics, and multi-product inventory analysis.

Conference Board, Inc. The Conference Board, Inc. 845 3rd Ave., New York, NY 10022. Phone: (212)339-0345 Fax: (212)980-7014 E-mail: info@conference-board.org • URL: http://www.conference-board.org • Business management practices worldwide, especially economic, and demographic in nature. Specific concerns include: corporate citizenship, including corporate contributions, diversity, environmental policy and issues, and government relations; corporate governance, including boards of directors, role of chief executives, relations with institutional investors, and shareholder input and influence; economics, including economic and financial forecasts, consumer confidence, leading economic indicators, North American outlook and trends, and global economic environment; human resources and organizational effectiveness, including organization structure and design, compensation and benefits, training and development, and communications; and performance excellence.

Financial Executives Research Foundation. 10 Madison Ave., Morristown, NJ 07962. Phone: (973)898-4600 Fax: (973)898-6636 E-mail: mbace@fei.org • URL: http://www.fei.org/rf.

TRADE/PROFESSIONAL ASSOCIATIONS

Academy of Management. P.O. Box 3020, Briarcliff Manor, NY 10510-3020. Phone: (914)923-2607 Fax: (914)923-2615 E-mail: academy@pace.edu • URL: http://www.aomonline.edu • Members are university professors of management and selected business executives.

American Management Association. 1601 Broadway, New York, NY 10019-7420. Phone: 800-

262-9699 or (212)586-8100 Fax: (212)903-8168 E-mail: membership@amanet.org • URL: http://www.amanet.org • Provides educational forums worldwide where members and their colleagues learn superior, practical business skills and explore best practices of world-class organizations through interaction with each other and expert faculty practitioners. Maintains a publishing program providing tools individuals use to extend learning beyond the classroom in a process of life-long professional growth and development through education.

National Association of Professional Organizers. 4700 W Lake Ave., Glenview, IL 60025. Phone: (847)375-4746 Fax: (847)734-9236 E-mail: hq@napo.net • URL: http://www.napo.net • Members are concerned with time management, productivity, and the efficient organization of documents and activities. Formerly Association of Professional Organizers.

Society for Advancement of Management. Texas A&M University-Corpus Christi, College of Business, 6300 Ocean Dr., Corpus Christi, TX 78412. Phone: 888-827-6077 or (361)825-6045 or (361)825-5574 Fax: (361)825-2725 E-mail: moustafa@falcon.tamucc.edu • URL: http://www.enterprise.tamucc.edu/sam/ • Professional organization of management executives in industry, commerce, government and education. Absorbed Industrial Methods Society.

OTHER SOURCES

How to Manage Conflict in the Organization. American Management Association Extension Institute. • Looseleaf. $139.00. Self-study course. Emphasis is on practical explanations, examples, and problem solving. Quizzes and a case study are included.

ADMINISTRATIVE DECISION MAKING

See: DECISION-MAKING

ADMINISTRATIVE LAW AND REGULATION

See also: BUSINESS LAW; CORPORATION LAW AND REGULATION; LABOR LAW AND REGULATION; LAW; LAWS; LAWYERS

GENERAL WORKS

Administrative Law. Steven J. Cann. Sage Publications, Inc. • 2001. $89.95. Third edition.

From Red Tape to Smart Tape: Administrative Simplification in OECD Countries. Organization for Economic Cooperation and Development. • 2003. $58.00. "This report looks at a set of tools and practices commonly used by governments to make administrative regulations simpler and less burdensome to comply with." Includes information on one-stop facilitation, license/permit simplification, decision-making time limits, small business assistance, and the use of information technology (IT) for administrative simplification.

ABSTRACTS AND INDEXES

Current Law Index: Multiple Access to Legal Periodicals. Gale Cengage Learning. • Monthly. $725.00 per year. Produced in cooperation with the American Association of Law Libraries. Indexes more than 900 law journals, legal newspapers, and specialty publications from the U.S., Canada, U.K., Ireland, Australia, and New Zealand.

Index to Legal Periodicals and Books. H. W. Wilson Co. • Monthly. $490.00 per year. Quarterly and annual cumulations.

BIBLIOGRAPHIES

Current Publications in Legal and Related Fields. American Association of Law Libraries. Fred B.

Rothman and Co. • Nine times a year. $198.00 per year. Looseleaf service. Annual cumulation.

Law Books Published. Glanville Publishers, Inc. • Semiannual. $160.00 per year. Supplement to *Law Books in Print.*

CD-ROM DATABASES

Authority on Administrative Law. LexisNexis/ Matthew Bender. • Periodic updates. Price on request. Full text CD-ROM provides detailed information on Federal administrative procedural law. Contains a large number of judicial, regulatory, and statutory references.

WILSONDISC: Index to Legal Periodicals and Books. H. W. Wilson Co. • Monthly. Includes unlimited online access to *Index to Legal Periodicals* through WILSONLINE. Contains CD-ROM indexing of more than 1,400 English language legal periodicals from 1981 to date and 2,500 books.

ENCYCLOPEDIAS AND DICTIONARIES

Communicating with Legal Databases: Terms and Abbreviations for the Legal Researcher. Anne L. McDonald. Neal-Schuman Publishers, Inc. • 1987. $82.50.

HANDBOOKS AND MANUALS

Administrative Law Desk Manual for Lawyers. John H. Reese. LexisNexis Matthew Bender. • 2003. $90. 00. Provides detailed coverage of the federal Administrative Procedure Act and summarizes relevant state law in 17 of the largest states.

Code of Federal Regulations. Office of the Federal Register, U.S. General Services Administration. Available from U.S. Government Printing Office. • $1,094.00 per year. Complete service.

INTERNET DATABASES

Lexis.com Research System. Lexis-Nexis Group. Phone: 800-227-4908 or (937)865-6800 Fax: (937)865-6909 E-mail: webmaster@prod.lexis-nexis.com • URL: http://www.lexis.com • Fee-based Web site offers extensive searching of a wide variety of legal sources. Additional features include Daily Opinion Service, lexis.com Bookstore, Career Center, CLE Center, Law Schools, and Practice Pages ("Pages specific to areas of specialty").

ONLINE DATABASES

Index to Legal Periodicals and Books (Online). H. W. Wilson Co. • Broad coverage of law journals and books 1981 to date. Monthly updates. Inquire as to online cost and availability.

LEXIS. LEXIS-NEXIS. • The various LEXIS databases provide full text and indexing for a wide variety of legal cases, statutes, orders, and opinions.

PERIODICALS AND NEWSLETTERS

Administrative Law Review. American University, Washington College of Law. • Quarterly. Members; $35.00 per year; non-members, $40.00 per year. Scholarly legal journal on developments in the field of administrative law.

Federal Register. Office of the Federal Register. Available from U.S. Government Printing Office. • Daily except Saturday and Sunday. $764.00 per year. Publishes regulations and legal notices issued by federal agencies, including executive orders and presidential proclamations. Issued by the National Archives and Records Administration (http://www. nara.gov).

TRADE/PROFESSIONAL ASSOCIATIONS

American Bar Association. 321 N Clark St., Chicago, IL 60610. Phone: 800-285-2221 or (312)988-5000 Fax: (312)988-5522 E-mail: askaba@abanet.org • URL: http://www.abanet.org • Attorneys in good standing of the bar of any state. Conducts research and educational projects and activities to: encourage professional improvement; provide public services; improve the administration of civil and criminal justice; increase the availability

of legal services to the public. Sponsors Law Day USA. Administers numerous standing and special committees such as Committee on +Soviet and +East +European +Law, providing seminars and newsletters. Operates 25 sections, including Criminal Justice, Economics of Law Practice, and Family Law. Sponsors essay competitions. Maintains library.

Federal Administrative Law Judges Conference. 2020 Pennsylvania Ave. NW, PMB 260, Washington, DC 20006. Phone: (202)675-3065 Fax: (202)720-8424 E-mail: steven.glazer@ferc.gov • URL: http://www.faljc.org • Administrative law judges employed by federal agencies and departments who perform judicial functions in the federal service, presiding at administrative hearings, ruling on admissibility of evidence, making findings of fact and conclusions of law, and issuing decisions.

OTHER SOURCES

Administrative Law. LexisNexis Matthew Bender. • Three times a year. $1,416.00. Six looseleaf volumes. Covers investigations, adjudications, hearings, licenses, judicial review, and so forth.

ADULT EDUCATION

See also: CORRESPONDENCE SCHOOLS AND COURSES; GRADUATE WORK IN UNIVERSITIES; TRAINING OF EMPLOYEES; VOCATIONAL EDUCATION

GENERAL WORKS

Administering Successful Programs for Adults: Promoting Excellence in Adult, Community, and Continuing Education. Michael W. Galbraith and others. Krieger Publishing Co. • 1996. $24.50. Provides practical advice on the "day-to-day duties and responsibilities of organizing and administering successful programs in adult, community, and continuing education settings." (Professional Practices in Adult Education and Human Resource Development Series).

Adults as Learners: Increasing Participation and Facilities Learning. Kathryn P. Cross. John Wiley and Sons, Inc. • 1981. $35.00. (Classic Series).

ABSTRACTS AND INDEXES

Current Index to Journals in Education (CIJE). Oryx Press. • Monthly. $245.00 per year. Semiannual cumulations, $475.00.

Education Index. H. W. Wilson Co. • 10 times a year. Quarterly and annual cumulations. Price varies.

ALMANACS AND YEARBOOKS

Research and Investigation in Adult Education: Annual Register. American Association for Adult and Continuing Education. • Annual.

BIBLIOGRAPHIES

Education for Older Adult Learning: A Selected, Annotated Bibliography. Reva M. Greenberg. Greenwood Publishing Group, Inc. • 1993. $82.95. Describes more than 700 books, articles, and other items relating to formal and informal education for older adults. (Bibliographies and Indexes in Gerontology Series, No. 20).

CD-ROM DATABASES

ERIC on SilverPlatter. Available from SilverPlatter Information, Inc. • Quarterly. $700.00 per year. Produced by the Office of Educational Research and Improvement, U. S. Dept. of Education. Provides CD-ROM indexing and abstracting of a wide variety of literature relating to education. Archival discs are available from 1966.

DIRECTORIES

American Association for Adult and Continuing Education: Membership Directory. American As-

sociation for Adult and Continuing Education. • Annual. Price on application.

Peterson's Guide to Distance Learning Programs. Peterson's. • 2002. $26.95. Second revised edition. Provides detailed information on accredited college and university programs available through television, radio, computer, videocassette, and audiocassette resources. Covers U. S. and Canadian institutions.

ENCYCLOPEDIAS AND DICTIONARIES

Encyclopedia of Distributed Learning. Anna DiStefano and others, editors. Sage Publications, Inc. • 2004. $125.00. Contains 275 entries on contemporary continuing education and distance learning for adults in corporate, academic, and other settings.

ONLINE DATABASES

Education Index Online. H. W. Wilson Co. • Indexes a wide variety of periodicals related to schools, colleges, and education, 1984 to date. Monthly updates. Inquire as to online cost and availability.

ERIC. Educational Resources Information Center. • Funded by the U. S. Department of Education, Institute of Education Sciences (formerly Office of Educational Research and Improvement). Provides access to more than one million online records covering education-related journal and report literature, 1966 to date. Updating is monthly. Inquire as to online cost and availability.

Information Bank Abstracts. New York Times Index Dept. • Provides indexing and abstracting of current affairs, primarily from the final late edition of *The New York Times* and the Eastern edition of *The Wall Street Journal.* Time period is 1969 to present, with daily updates. Inquire as to online cost and availability.

PERIODICALS AND NEWSLETTERS

Adult and Continuing Education Today. Learning Resources Network. • BiWeekly. $95.00 per year. Newsletter.

Adult Education Quarterly: A Journal of Research and Theory. American Association for Adult and Continuing Education. Sage Publications. • Quarterly. Institutions, $206.00 per year.

Adult Learning. American Association for Adult and Continuing Education. • Quarterly. $45.00 per year.

Journal of Library and Information Services in Distance Learning. Haworth Press, Inc. • Quarterly. $150.00 per year to libraries; $48.00 per year to individuals.

Resources in Education. Educational Resources Information Center. Available from U.S. Government Printing Office. • Monthly. Reports on educational research.

RESEARCH CENTERS AND INSTITUTES

Center for Adult Education. Columbia University. Teachers College, 525 W 120th St., New York, NY 10027. Phone: (212)678-3760 Fax: (212)678-3937 E-mail: vjm5@columbia.edu.

ERIC Clearinghouse on Adult, Career and Vocational Education. Ohio State University. Center on Education and Training for Employment, 1900 Kenny Rd., Columbus, OH 43210-1090. Phone: 800-848-4815 or (614)292-7069 Fax: (614)292-1260 E-mail: ericacve@postbox.acs.ohio-state.edu • URL: http://www.ericacve.org/.

National Institute for Work and Learning. Academy for Educational Development, 1875 Connecticut Ave., N.W., Washington, DC 20009-5721. Phone: (202)884-8186 Fax: (202)884-8422 E-mail: niwl@ aed.org • URL: http://www.niwl.org • Research areas include adult education, training, unemployment insurance, and career development.

STATISTICS SOURCES

Digest of Education Statistics. Available from U. S. Government Printing Office. • Annual. $51.00. Covers all areas of education from kindergarten through graduate school. Includes data from both government and private sources. Compiled by National Center for Education Statistics, U. S. Department of Education.

TRADE/PROFESSIONAL ASSOCIATIONS

American Association for Adult and Continuing Education. 4380 Forbes Blvd., Lanham, MD 20036. Phone: (301)918-1913 Fax: (301)918-1846 E-mail: info@aaace.org • URL: http://www.aaace.org.

Association for Continuing Higher Education. Trident Technical College, P.O. Box 118067 CE-M, Charleston, SC 29423-8067. Phone: 800-807-2243 or (843)574-6658 Fax: (843)574-6470 E-mail: webmaster@acheinc.org • URL: http://www.acheinc.org.

University Continuing Education Association. 1 Dupont Cir., Ste. 615, Washington, DC 20036. Phone: (202)659-3130 Fax: (202)785-0374 E-mail: kjkohl@ucea.edu • URL: http://www.ucea.edu • Institutions of higher education, both public and private, that offer professional and continuing education programs, both degree and non-degree, to nontraditional students at the pre and post baccalaureate levels. Offers accelerated learning opportunities to practitioners through professional development seminars, modules and conferences. Collects and disseminates data on continuing education programs and trends. Compiles statistics on the field. Only those individuals who work for a member institution are eligible to become professional members.

ADVERTISING

See also: ADVERTISING AGENCIES; ADVERTISING MEDIA; ADVERTISING SPECIALTIES; DIRECT MAIL ADVERTISING; INDUSTRIAL ADVERTISING; MARKETING; OUTDOOR ADVERTISING; PUBLIC RELATIONS AND PUBLICITY; RADIO AND TELEVISION ADVERTISING

GENERAL WORKS

Advertising. Ray Wright. Trans-Atlantic Publications, Inc. • 2000. $49.50.

The Advertising Business: Operations, Creativity, Media Planning, Integrated Communications. John P. Jones, editor. Sage Publications, Inc. • 1999. $91.95. Contains articles by professionals in various fields of advertising.

Advertising: Principles and Practice. William Wells and others. Prentice Hall PTR. • 2000. $120.00. Sixth edition.

Breaking Up America: Advertisers and the New Media World. Joseph Turow. The University of Chicago Press. • 1997. $22.50. A social criticism of target marketing, market segmentation, and customized media.

Contemporary Advertising. William F. Arens. McGraw-Hill. • 2001. $71.00. Eighth edition. Includes CD-ROM. (Marketing Series).

Creative Strategy in Advertising; What the Copywriter Should Know About the Creative Side of the Business. A. Jerome Jewler and Bonnie Drewniany. Wadsworth Publishing Co. • 2000. $85.95. Seventh edition. (Mass Communication Series).

How to Promote, Publicize, and Advertise Your Growing Business: Getting the Word Out Without Spending a Fortune. Kim Baker and Sunny Baker. John Wiley and Sons, Inc. • 1992. $12.95.

International Advertising: Realities and Myths. John P. Jones, editor. Sage Publications, Inc. • 1999. $95.95. Includes articles by advertising professionals in 10 different countries. (Advertising Series).

Introduction to Advertising and Promotion: An Integrated Marketing Communications Perspective.

George E. Belch and Michael A. Belch. McGraw-Hill. • 1994. $69.95. Third edition.

Kleppner's Advertising Procedure. Thomas Russell and others. Prentice Hall PTR. • 2001. $115.00. 15th edition.

What's in a Name? Advertising and the Concept of Brands. John P. Jones and Jan S. Slater. M. E. Sharpe, Inc. • 2003. $79.95. Second edition. Covers brand identity and loyalty from the viewpoint of modern marketing theory.

ABSTRACTS AND INDEXES

Business Periodicals Index. H. W. Wilson Co. • 11 times a year. Quarterly and annual cumulations. Price varies.

Communication Abstracts: An International Information Service. Sage Publications, Inc. • Bimonthly. Institutions, $1,150.00 per year. Provides broad coverage of the literature of communications, including broadcasting and advertising.

What's New in Advertising and Marketing. Special Libraries Association, Advertising and Marketing Div. • Quarterly. Non-profit organizations, $20.00 per year; corporations, $30.00 per year. Lists and briefly describes a wide variety of free or inexpensive material relating to advertising, marketing, and media.

ALMANACS AND YEARBOOKS

Advertisers Annual. Hollis Directories Ltd. • Annual. $325.00. About 2,000 advertising and media agencies in the United Kingdom, Ireland and abroad, relevant to all forms of advertising.

BIBLIOGRAPHIES

Topicator: Classified Guide to Articles in the Advertising/Communications/Marketing Periodical Press. • Bimonthly. $110.00 per year. An index of major articles appearing in 20 leading magazines in the advertising, communications, and marketing fields.

BIOGRAPHICAL SOURCES

The Ad Men and Women: A Biographical Dictionary of Advertising. Edd Applegate, editor. Greenwood Publishing Group, Inc. • 1994. $94.95. Provides extended biographical profiles of "54 men and women who have shaped advertising from the nineteenth century to the present." Includes bibliographies.

CD-ROM DATABASES

Advertiser and Agency Red Books Plus. National Register Publishing. • Quarterly. $1,295.00 per year. The CD-ROM version of *Standard Directory of Advertisers,* *Standard Directory of Advertising Agencies,* and *Standard Directory of International Advertisers and Agencies.*

OECD Statistical Compendium. Organization for Economic Cooperation and Development. • Semiannual. $1,905.00 per year for 1 to 10 users. CD-ROM contains more than 730,000 monthly, quarterly, and annual time series for OECD countries, 1960 to date. Includes fully searchable data on agriculture, food, economic indicators, national accounts, employment, energy, finance, industry, technology, and foreign trade. Results can be displayed in various forms.

WILSONDISC: Wilson Business Abstracts. H. W. Wilson Co. • Monthly. Includes unlimited online access to *Wilson Business Abstracts* through WILSONLINE. Provides CD-ROM "cover-to-cover" abstracting and indexing of over 600 prominent business periodicals. Indexing is from 1982, abstracting from 1990. (*Business Periodicals Index* without abstracts is available on CD-ROM at $1,495 per year.).

DIRECTORIES

Advertising Age-Leading National Advertisers. Crain Communications, Inc. • Annual. $5.00. List of

the 100 leading advertisers in terms of the amount spent in national advertising and below-the-line forms of spending.

Advertising Organizations and Publications: A Resource Guide. John P. Jones. Sage Publications, Inc. • 2000. $86.95. Describes advertising associations, books, periodicals, etc.

International Advertising Association Membership Directory. International Advertising Association. • Annual. Membership. Available only online. Over 3,600 advertisers, advertising agencies, media, and other firms involved in advertising.

Plunkett's Advertising and Branding Industry Almanac. Plunkett Research, Ltd. • 2004. $249.99. Provides profiles of 300 leading firms in the areas of advertising, brand promotion, and corporate image, including marketing media, online advertising, and direct mail. Also covers industry trends and statistical data.

Standard Directory of Advertisers: Business Classifications Edition. National Register Publishing. • Annual $799.00; with supplements, $899.00. Arranged by product or service. Provides information on the advertising programs of over 14,000 companies, including advertising/marketing personnel and the names of advertising agencies used.

Standard Directory of Advertisers: Geographic Edition. National Register Publishing. • Annual $659.00; with supplements, $759.00. Arranged geographically by state. Provides information on the advertising programs of over 20,000 companies, including advertising/marketing personnel and the names of advertising agencies used. Includes *Advertiser/Agency* supplement.

ENCYCLOPEDIAS AND DICTIONARIES

Advertising Age Encyclopedia of Advertising. John McDonough and others, editors. Fitzroy Dearborn Publishers. • 2002. $385.00. Three volumes. Contains 600 entries in alphabetical order covering a wide variety of advertising and market research topics. Includes bibliographies.

Blackwell Encyclopedic Dictionary of Marketing. Dale Littler and Barbara R. Lewis, editors. Blackwell Publishers. • 1997. $38.95. The editors are associated with the Manchester School of Management. Contains definitions of key terms combined with longer articles written by various U. S. and foreign business educators. Includes bibliographies and index. (Blackwell Encyclopedia of Management Series.).

Dictionary of Marketing and Advertising. Jerry M. Rosenberg. John Wiley and Sons, Inc. • 1995. $145.00. (Business Dictionary Series).

Dictionary of Marketing Communications. Norman A. P. Govoni. Sage Publications, Inc. • 2003. $69.95. Contains more than 4,000 concise definitions of terms relating to advertising, sales promotion, public relations, direct marketing, and selling.

HANDBOOKS AND MANUALS

Advertising Manager's Handbook. Robert W. Bly. Prentice Hall PTR. • 1998. $79.95. Second edition.

Advertising: What It Is and How to Do It. Roderick White. McGraw-Hill. • 1993. $16.95. Third edition.

Dartnell's Advertising Manager's Handbook. David Bushko, editor. Dartnell Corp. • 1997. $89.95. Fourth revised edition.

Do-It-Yourself Advertising and Promotion: How to Produce Great Ads, Brochures, Catalogs, Direct Mail, Web Sites and more. Fred E. Hahn. John Wiley and Sons, Inc. • 2003. $19.95. Third edition. Covers magazines, newspapers, flyers, brochures, catalogs, direct mail, telemarketing, trade shows, and radio/TV promotions. Includes checklists. (Small Business Series).

Logo Power: Creating World-Class Logos and Effective Business Identities. David E. Carter. DIANE Publishing Co. • 2001. $40.00. Explains how to plan, develop, evaluate, and implement a company logo system.

Marketing Without Advertising. Michael Phillips and Salli Rasberry. Nolo. • 2001. $24.00. Fourth edition. How to market a small business economically.

INTERNET DATABASES

Business 2.0 Web Guide to the Best Business Links. Business 2.0 Media Inc. Phone: (415)293-4800 E-mail: support@business2.com • URL: http://www.business2.com/webguide • Web site presents an extensive, searchable directory of links to "the best, most informative, and authoritative web pages." Twenty main categories cover business, finance, career, company information, people, and technology topics, with thousands of subtopics, all linking to Web sites recommended by experienced business researchers. Fees: Free.

ONLINE DATABASES

Management Contents. Gale Cengage Learning. • Covers a wide range of management, financial, marketing, personnel, and administrative topics. About 150 leading business journals are indexed and abstracted from 1974 to date, with monthly updating. Inquire as to online cost and availability.

Marketing and Advertising Reference Service (MARS). Gale Cengage Learning. • Provides abstracts of literature relating to consumer marketing and advertising, including all forms of advertising media. Time period is 1984 to date. Daily updates. Inquire as to online cost and availability.

National Consumer Survey. Simmons Market Research Bureau. • Market and media survey data relating to the American consumer. Inquire as to online cost and availability.

Wilson Business Abstracts Online. H. W. Wilson Co. • Indexes and abstracts 600 major business periodicals, plus the *Wall Street Journal* and the business section of the *New York Times.* Indexing is from 1982, abstracting from 1990, with the two newspapers included from 1993. Updated weekly. Inquire as to online cost and availability. (*Business Periodicals Index* without abstracts is also available online.).

PERIODICALS AND NEWSLETTERS

Advertising Age: The International Newspaper of Marketing. Crain Communications, Inc. • Weekly. $178.50 per year. Includes supplement *Creativity.*

Advertising Age's Euromarketing. Crain Communications, Inc. • Weekly. $295.00 per year. Newsletter on European advertising and marketing.

ADWEEK. VNU Business Media. • Weekly. $149.00 per year. Covers local, national, and international advertising news and trends. Includes critiques of advertising campaigns.

IAA National & World News. International Advertising Association. • Description: Supplies information on Association policies and activities. Includes reviews of publications and reports from the 62 chapters worldwide.

International Journal of Advertising: The Quarterly Review of Marketing Communications. Advertising Association. NTC Publications Ltd. • Quarterly. Price on application.

Journal of Advertising. M. E. Sharpe, Inc. • Quarterly. $90.00 per year. An academic journal devoted to advertising theory and research.

Journal of Advertising Research. Advertising Research Foundation. • Quarterly. Individuals, $155.00 per year; institutions, $275.00 per year.

Journal of Promotion Management: Innovations in Planning and Applied Research. Haworth Press, Inc. • Semiannual. Institutions, $200.00 per year.

The Licensing Letter. EPM Communications Inc. • Description: Concerned with all aspects of licensed merchandising, "the business of associating

someone's name, likeness or creation with someone else's product or service, for a consideration." Recurring features include statistics, research, events, mechanics, available properties, and identification of licensors, licensing agents, and licensees.

Med Ad News. Engel Publishing Partners. • Monthly. $225.00 per year. Covers the field of pharmaceutical advertising and marketing.

Media Industry Newsletter. Access Intelligence L.L.C. • Description: Covers the media industry, including advertising, marketing, publishing, radio, and television. Recurring features include weekly box scores of advertising pages in major magazines, salaries of top executives, earnings reports, and news of people in the industry.

STATISTICS SOURCES

Advertising Age: National Expenditures in Newspapers. Crain Communications, Inc. • Annual.

U. S. Industry and Trade Outlook. Available from National Technical Information Service. • Annual. $69.95. Produced by the International Trade Administration, U. S. Department of Commerce, in a "public-private" partnership with DRI/McGraw-Hill and Standard & Poor's. Provides basic data, outlook for the current year, and "Long-Term Prospects" (five-year projections) for a wide variety of products and services. Includes high technology industries. Formerly *U. S. Industrial Outlook.*

TRADE/PROFESSIONAL ASSOCIATIONS

Advertising and Marketing International Network. c/o B. Vaughn Sink, 12323 Nantucket, Wichita, KS 67235. Phone: (316)722-2535 Fax: (316)722-8353 E-mail: vaughn.sink@shs.com • URL: http://www.aminworldwide.com.

Advertising Council. 815 2nd Ave., 9th Fl., New York, NY 10017. Phone: 800-933-7727 or (212)922-1500 Fax: (212)922-1676 E-mail: info@adcouncil.org • URL: http://www.adcouncil.org • Founded and supported by American business, media, and advertising sectors to conduct public service advertising campaigns. Encourages advertising media to contribute time and space and advertising agencies to supply creative talent and facilities to further timely national causes. Specific campaigns include: Drug Abuse Prevention; AIDS Prevention; Teen-Alcoholism; Child Abuse; Crime Prevention; Forest Fire Prevention.

American Advertising Federation. 1101 Vermont Ave. NW, Ste. 500, Washington, DC 20005-6306. Phone: 800-999-2231 or (202)898-0089 Fax: (202)898-0159 E-mail: aaf@aaf.org • URL: http://www.aaf.org • Works to advance the business of advertising as a vital and essential part of the American economy and culture through government and public relations; professional development and recognition; community service, social responsibility and high standards; and benefits and services to members. Operates Advertising Hall of Fame, Hall of Achievement, and National Student Advertising Competition. Maintains speakers' bureau.

ARF - Advertising Research Foundation. 432 Park Ave. S, New York, NY 10016. Phone: (212)751-5656 Fax: (212)319-5265 E-mail: info@thearf.org • URL: http://www.thearf.org • Advertisers, advertising agencies, research organizations, associations, and the media are regular members of the foundation; colleges and universities are associate members. Objectives are to: further scientific practices and promote greater effectiveness of advertising and marketing by means of objective and impartial research; develop new research methods and techniques; analyze and evaluate existing methods and techniques, and define proper applications; establish research standards, criteria, and reporting methods. Compiles statistics and conducts research programs.

Association of National Advertisers. 708 3rd Ave.,

New York, NY 10017-4270. Phone: (212)697-5950 Fax: (212)661-8057 • URL: http://www.ana.net.

Direct Marketing Association. 1120 Ave. of the Americas, New York, NY 10036-6700. Phone: (212)768-7277 Fax: (212)302-6714 E-mail: presiden@the-dma.org • URL: http://www.the-dma.org • Manufacturers, wholesalers, public utilities, retailers, mail order firms, publishers, schools, clubs, insurance companies, financial organizations, business equipment manufacturers, paper and envelope manufacturers, list brokers, compilers, managers, owners, computer service bureaus, advertising agencies, letter shops, research organizations, printers, lithographers, creators, and producers of direct mail and direct response advertising. Studies consumer and business attitudes toward direct mail and related direct marketing statistics. Offers Mail Preference Service for consumers who wish to receive less mail advertising, Mail Order Action Line to help resolve difficulties with mail order purchases, and Telephone Preference Service for people who wish to receive fewer telephone sales calls. Maintains hall of fame; offers placement service; compiles statistics. Sponsors several three-day Basic Direct Marketing Institutes, Advanced Direct Marketing Institutes, and special interest seminars and workshops. Maintains Government Affairs office in Washington, DC. Operates Direct Marketing Educational Foundation.

International Advertising Association. 275 Madison Ave., Ste. 2102, New York, NY 10016. Phone: (212)557-1133 Fax: (212)983-0455 E-mail: membership@iaaglobal.org • URL: http://www.iaaglobal.org • Global network of advertisers, advertising agencies, the media and related services, spanning 99 countries. Demonstrates to governments and consumers the benefits of advertising as the foundation of diverse, independent media. Protects and advances freedom of commercial speech and consumer choice, encourages greater practice and acceptance of advertising self-regulation, provides a forum to debate emerging professional marketing communications issues and their consequences in the fast-changing world environment, and takes the lead in state-of-the-art professional development through education and training for the marketing communications industry of tomorrow. Conducts research on such topics as restrictions and taxes on advertising, advertising trade practices and related information, and advertising expenditures around the world. Sponsors IAA Education Program. Has compiled recommendations for international advertising standards and practices.

National Advertising Review Board. 70 W 36th St., 13th Fl., New York, NY 10018. Phone: (866)334-6272 or (212)705-0114 E-mail: bhopewell@narc.bbb.org • URL: http://www.narbreview.org • Individuals from industry and the public. Sponsored by the National +Advertising +Review Council for the purpose of sustaining high standards of truth and accuracy in national advertising. Aims to maintain a self-regulatory mechanism that responds constructively to public complaints about national advertising and which significantly improves advertising performance and credibility.

ADVERTISING AGENCIES

See also: ADVERTISING

GENERAL WORKS

Where the Suckers Moon: The Life and Death of an Advertising Campaign. Randall Rothenberg. Random House, Inc. • 1995. $16.00. Presents the story of an advertising agency's failed automobile campaign.

CD-ROM DATABASES

Advertiser and Agency Red Books Plus. National Register Publishing. • Quarterly. $1,295.00 per year.

The CD-ROM version of *Standard Directory of Advertisers*, *Standard Directory of Advertising Agencies*, and *Standard Directory of International Advertisers and Agencies*.

DIRECTORIES

Standard Directory of Advertising Agencies: The Agency Red Book. National Register Publishing. • Semiannual $969.00. Information on nearly 10,800 Provides advertising agencies and branch offices. Includes annual billings by media and names of clients. Includes *Advertiser/Agency* supplement.

Standard Directory of International Advertisers and Agencies: The International Red Book. National Register Publishing. • Annual. $629.00. Includes more than 5,000 foreign companies and their advertising agencies. Geographic, company name, personal name, and trade name indexes are provided.

FINANCIAL RATIOS

Almanac of Business and Industrial Financial Ratios. Leo Troy. Aspen Publishers, Inc. • 2003. $125.95. Includes CD-Rom. Contains financial ratios derived from federal tax returns. Ratios for each of about 200 industries are arranged according to company asset size. (Almanac of Business and Industrial Financial Ratios Series).

Annual Statement Studies. The Risk Management Association. • Annual. Median and quartile financial ratios are given for over 400 kinds of manufacturing, wholesale, retail, construction, and consumer finance establishments. Data is sorted by both asset size and sales volume. Includes a clearly written "Definition of Ratios" and an alphabetical industry index.

Annual Statement Studies: Industry Default Probabilities and Cash Flow Measures. The Risk Management Association. • Annual. $145.00. Serves as a companion volume to the original *Annual Statement Studies*. Gives probability of default estimates on a percentage scale for more than 450 industries. Includes changes in position year-by-year for eight financial statement line items and provides percentage measures of cash flow.

HANDBOOKS AND MANUALS

Advertising Agency. Entrepreneur Media, Inc. • Looseleaf. $59.50. A practical guide to starting a small advertising agency. Covers profit potential, start-up costs, market size evaluation, pricing, accounting, advertising, promotion, etc. (Start-Up Business Guide No. E1223.).

ONLINE DATABASES

Information Bank Abstracts. New York Times Index Dept. • Provides indexing and abstracting of current affairs, primarily from the final late edition of *The New York Times* and the Eastern edition of *The Wall Street Journal*. Time period is 1969 to present, with daily updates. Inquire as to online cost and availability.

Management Contents. Gale Cengage Learning. • Covers a wide range of management, financial, marketing, personnel, and administrative topics. About 150 leading business journals are indexed and abstracted from 1974 to date, with monthly updating. Inquire as to online cost and availability.

PERIODICALS AND NEWSLETTERS

American Advertising. American Advertising Federation. • Quarterly. Membership.

TRADE/PROFESSIONAL ASSOCIATIONS

American Association of Advertising Agencies. 405 Lexington Ave., 18th Fl., New York, NY 10174-1801. Phone: (212)682-2500 Fax: (212)953-5665 E-mail: obd@aaaa.org • URL: http://www.aaaa.org.

International Advertising Association. 275 Madison Ave., Ste. 2102, New York, NY 10016. Phone: (212)557-1133 Fax: (212)983-0455 E-mail:

membership@iaaglobal.org • URL: http://www. iaaglobal.org • Global network of advertisers, advertising agencies, the media and related services, spanning 99 countries. Demonstrates to governments and consumers the benefits of advertising as the foundation of diverse, independent media. Protects and advances freedom of commercial speech and consumer choice, encourages greater practice and acceptance of advertising self-regulation, provides a forum to debate emerging professional marketing communications issues and their consequences in the fast-changing world environment, and takes the lead in state-of-the-art professional development through education and training for the marketing communications industry of tomorrow. Conducts research on such topics as restrictions and taxes on advertising, advertising trade practices and related information, and advertising expenditures around the world. Sponsors IAA Education Program. Has compiled recommendations for international advertising standards and practices.

International Communications Agency Network. PO Box 490, 1649 Lump Gulch Rd., Rollinsville, CO 80474-0490. Phone: (303)258-9511 Fax: (303)484-4087 E-mail: info@icomagencies.com • URL: http://www.icomagencies.com • Network of non-competing advertising agencies. Provides an interchange of management information, international facilities, and branch office service for partner agencies. Provides discounts on syndicated services and access to 1000 computer databases.

League of Advertising Agencies. 17 Little W 12th St., Ste. 304, New York, NY 10014-1309. Phone: 877-969-2927 or (212)528-0364 Fax: (212)766-1181.

National Meat Association. 1970 Broadway, Ste. 825, 1970 Broadway, No. 825, Oakland, CA 94612. Phone: (510)763-1533 Fax: (510)763-6186 E-mail: staff@nmaonline.org • URL: http://www. nmaonline.org • Meat packers, processors, slaughterers, and jobbers. Promotes interests of independent meat packers in all states. Conducts group purchasing activities and administers group insurance program. Provides legal, freight rate, and contract advisory services. Offers research programs; compiles statistics.

ADVERTISING ART

See: COMMERCIAL ART

ADVERTISING, COOPERATIVE

See: COOPERATIVE ADVERTISING

ADVERTISING COPY

GENERAL WORKS

Advertising Copywriting. Philip W. Burton. McGraw Hill. • 1996. $44.95. Seventh edition. (NTC Business Book Series).

Teach Yourself Copywriting. J. Jonathan Gabay. McGraw-Hill. • 2001. $14.95. Second edition. Includes material on copywriting for e-commerce websites.

ABSTRACTS AND INDEXES

Business Periodicals Index. H. W. Wilson Co. • 11 times a year. Quarterly and annual cumulations. Price varies.

DIRECTORIES

The ADWEEK Directory. ADWEEK Magazines. • Covers: over 6,400 U.S. Advertising agencies, public relations firms, media buying services, direct

marketing and related organizations. Entries include: Agency name, address, phone, fax/e-mail, URL; names and titles of key personnel; major accounts; Ultimate parent company; headquarters location; major subsidiaries and other operating units; year founded; number of employees; fee income; billings; percentage of billings by medium. Individual listings for each agency branch.

HANDBOOKS AND MANUALS

Copywriter's Handbook. Robert W. Bly. Henry Holt & Co., Inc. • 1990. $16.00.

Copywriting Secrets and Tactics: How to Put More Sell into All Your Copy. Herschell G. Lewis. Dartnell Corp. • $91.50. Looseleaf service.

How to Produce Creative Advertising: Traditional Techniques and Computer Applications. Thomas Bivins and Ann Keding. McGraw Hill. • 1993. $37.95. Covers copywriting, advertising design, and the use of desktop publishing techniques in advertising. (NTC Business Books Series).

ONLINE DATABASES

Wilson Business Abstracts Online. H. W. Wilson Co. • Indexes and abstracts 600 major business periodicals, plus the *Wall Street Journal* and the business section of the *New York Times*. Indexing is from 1982, abstracting from 1990, with the two newspapers included from 1993. Updated weekly. Inquire as to online cost and availability. (*Business Periodicals Index* without abstracts is also available online.).

PERIODICALS AND NEWSLETTERS

Print: America's Graphic Design Magazine. Krause Publications, Inc. • Bimonthly. $57.00 per year. Emphasizes creative trends.

TRADE/PROFESSIONAL ASSOCIATIONS

ARF - Advertising Research Foundation. 432 Park Ave. S, New York, NY 10016. Phone: (212)751-5656 Fax: (212)319-5265 E-mail: info@thearf.org • URL: http://www.thearf.org • Advertisers, advertising agencies, research organizations, associations, and the media are regular members of the foundation; colleges and universities are associate members. Objectives are to: further scientific practices and promote greater effectiveness of advertising and marketing by means of objective and impartial research; develop new research methods and techniques; analyze and evaluate existing methods and techniques, and define proper applications; establish research standards, criteria, and reporting methods. Compiles statistics and conducts research programs.

ADVERTISING, INDUSTRIAL

See: INDUSTRIAL ADVERTISING

ADVERTISING LAW AND REGULATION

See also: BUSINESS LAW

GENERAL WORKS

Impact of Advertising Law on Business and Public Policy. Ross D. Petty. Greenwood Publishing Group, Inc. • 1992. $64.95. Analyzes cases under the Federal Trade Commission and Lanham Acts.

ABSTRACTS AND INDEXES

Business Periodicals Index. H. W. Wilson Co. • 11 times a year. Quarterly and annual cumulations. Price varies.

Current Law Index: Multiple Access to Legal Periodicals. Gale Cengage Learning. • Monthly. $725.00 per year. Produced in cooperation with the American Association of Law Libraries. Indexes more than 900 law journals, legal newspapers, and specialty publications from the U.S., Canada, U.K., Ireland, Australia, and New Zealand.

Index to Legal Periodicals and Books. H. W. Wilson Co. • Monthly. $490.00 per year. Quarterly and annual cumulations.

ALMANACS AND YEARBOOKS

Advertising Law: Year in Review. CCH, Inc. • Annual. $85.00. Summarizes the year's significant legal and regulatory developments.

BIBLIOGRAPHIES

Law Books in Print: Law Books in English Published Throughout the World. Glanville Publishers, Inc. • Triennial. $750.00.

Legal Looseleafs in Print. Arlene L. Eis, editor. Infosources Publishing. • 2001. $106.00. Lists over 3,600 titles by more than 250 publishers.

DIRECTORIES

Lawyer's Register International by Specialties and Fields of Law Including a Directory of Corporate Counsel. Lawyer's Register Publishing Co. • Annual. $359.00. Three volumes. Referral source for law firms.

INTERNET DATABASES

Lexis.com Research System. Lexis-Nexis Group. Phone: 800-227-4908 or (937)865-6800 Fax: (937)865-6909 E-mail: webmaster@prod.lexis-nexis.com • URL: http://www.lexis.com • Fee-based Web site offers extensive searching of a wide variety of legal sources. Additional features include Daily Opinion Service, lexis.com Bookstore, Career Center, CLE Center, Law Schools, and Practice Pages ("Pages specific to areas of specialty").

ONLINE DATABASES

Legal Resource Index. Gale Cengage Learning. • Broad coverage of law literature appearing in legal, business, and other periodicals, 1980 to date. Daily updates. Inquire as to online cost and availability.

LEXIS. LEXIS-NEXIS. • The various LEXIS databases provide full text and indexing for a wide variety of legal cases, statutes, orders, and opinions.

Management Contents. Gale Cengage Learning. • Covers a wide range of management, financial, marketing, personnel, and administrative topics. About 150 leading business journals are indexed and abstracted from 1974 to date, with monthly updating. Inquire as to online cost and availability.

PAIS International. Public Affairs Information Service, Inc. • Corresponds to the former printed publications, *PAIS Bulletin* (1976-90) and *PAIS Foreign Language Index* (1972-90), and to the current *PAIS International in Print* (1991 to date). Covers economic, political, and sociological material appearing in periodicals, books, government documents, and other publications. Updating is monthly. Inquire as to online cost and availability.

Trade & Industry Database. Gale Cengage Learning. • Provides indexing of business periodicals, January 1981 to date. Daily updates. (Full text articles from some periodicals are available online, 1983 to date. Inquire as to online cost and availability).

PERIODICALS AND NEWSLETTERS

Media and the Law. SIMBA Information. • Semimonthly. $327.00 per year. Newsletter.

RESEARCH CENTERS AND INSTITUTES

Center for Study of Responsive Law. P.O. Box 19367, Washington, DC 20036. Phone: (202)387-8030 Fax: (202)234-5176 E-mail: csrl@csrl.org • URL: http://www.csrl.org • A consumer-oriented research group.

TRADE/PROFESSIONAL ASSOCIATIONS

National Advertising Review Board. 70 W 36th St., 13th Fl., New York, NY 10018. Phone: (866)334-

6272 or (212)705-0114 E-mail: bhopewell@narc.bbb.org • URL: http://www.narbreview.org • Individuals from industry and the public. Sponsored by the National +Advertising +Review Council for the purpose of sustaining high standards of truth and accuracy in national advertising. Aims to maintain a self-regulatory mechanism that responds constructively to public complaints about national advertising and which significantly improves advertising performance and credibility.

National Consumer Law Center. 77 Summer St., 10th Fl., Boston, MA 02110. Phone: (617)542-8010 or (617)542-9500 Fax: (617)542-8028 E-mail: consumerlaw@nclc.org • URL: http://www.consumerlaw.org • Serves as a specialized resource in consumer and energy law funded by federal, state, and foundation grants and donations. Lawyers provide research, technical consulting, and in-depth assistance to legal services, private lawyers, and state agencies throughout the nation. Defines recurring patterns in the problems of low-income consumers and develops a series of alternative solutions utilizing litigation, legislation, lawyer training, and development of new service delivery systems. Seeks consultants for an interdisciplinary approach to problems. Conducts analyses of weatherization and energy assistance programs for low-income homeowners, renters, and state and federal agencies.

OTHER SOURCES

Advertising Compliance Service Newsletter. John Lichtenberger. • Bimonthly. $495.00 per year.

Lindey on Entertainment, Publishing and the Arts: Agreements and the Law. Alexander Lindey, editor. West Group. • $935.00 per year. Six looseleaf volumes. Periodic supplementation. Provides basic forms, applicable law, and guidance.

ADVERTISING MEDIA

See also: ADVERTISING; MASS MEDIA; RADIO AND TELEVISION ADVERTISING

GENERAL WORKS

Advertising Media Planning. Roger B. Baron and Jack Z. Sissors. McGraw-Hill. • 2002. $64.95. Sixth edition. Introduction to media planning.

Advertising Media Planning: A Brand Management Approach. Larry D. Kelley and Donald W. Jugenheimer. M. E. Sharpe, Inc. • 2003. $69.95. Emphasizes the importance of brand recognition in media planning.

Breaking Up America: Advertisers and the New Media World. Joseph Turow. The University of Chicago Press. • 1997. $22.50. A social criticism of target marketing, market segmentation, and customized media.

Electronic Media Ratings. Karen Buzzard. Elsevier. • 1992. $22.95. Provides basic information about TV and radio audience-rating techniques. Includes glossary and bibliography. (Electronic Media Guide Series).

Essentials of Media Planning: A Marketing Viewpoint. Arnold M. Barban and others. McGraw-Hill. • 1993. $29.95. Third edition. Practical guide to media analysis. (NTC Business Book Series).

Gonzo Marketing: Winning Through Worst Practices. Christopher Locke. John Wiley and Sons, Inc. • 2001. $29.95. An iconoclastic, entertaining view of e-commerce advertising and marketing (banners, pop-ups, spam, etc.). States the obvious: most Web advertising is more annoying than effective.

BIBLIOGRAPHIES

Topicator: Classified Guide to Articles in the Advertising/Communications/Marketing Periodical Press. • Bimonthly. $110.00 per year. An index of major articles appearing in 20 leading magazines in

the advertising, communications, and marketing fields.

DIRECTORIES

CARD The Media Information Network. Rogers Media Publishing. • Covers: Radio and television stations and networks; daily and weekend newspapers; consumer, farm, and business publications; advertising agencies and international media representatives; advertising, marketing, and media associations; and transportation and out-of-home advertising. Entries include: For publications--Title, company name, address, phone, frequency, names and titles of key personnel, advertising rates, discounts, mechanical requirements, copy regulations, circulation, closing and publication dates. For broadcasting stations--Call letters, name of owning company, address, phone, name of firm or individual representing station for advertising, special features, format, facilities, affiliations, rates, participation programs. For agencies and associations--Name, address, phone, personnel.

Hispanic Media and Market Source. SRDS. • Quarterly. $295.00 per year. Provides detailed information on the following Hispanic advertising media in the U. S.: TV, radio, newspapers, magazines, direct mail, outdoor, and special events.

International Media Guide: Business-Professional: Asia/Pacific, Middle East, Africa. SRDS. • Annual. $300.00. Provides information on 14,000 trade journals "from Africa to the Pacific Rim," including advertising rates and circulation data.

International Media Guide Business-Professional Publications: Europe. SRDS. • Annual. $300.00. Describes 6,000 trade journals from Eastern and Western Europe, with advertising rates and circulation data.

International Media Guide: Business/Professional Publications: The Americas. SRDS. • Annual. $300.00. Describes trade journals from North, South, and Central America, with advertising rates and circulation data.

International Media Guide: Newspapers Worldwide. SRDS. • Annual. $350.00. Provides advertising rates, circulation, and other details relating to newspapers in major cities of the world (covers 200 countries, including U. S.).

The SHOOT Directory for Commercial Production and Postproduction. SHOOT. • Annual. $79.00. Lists production companies, advertising agencies, and sources of professional television, motion picture, and audio equipment.

SRDS Business Publication Advertising Source. SRDS. • Monthly. $714.00 per year. Issued in three parts: (1) U. S. Business Publications, (2) U. S. Healthcare Publications, and (3) International Publications. Provides detailed advertising rates, profiles of editorial content, management names, "Multiple Publications Publishers," circulation data, and other trade journal information. Formerly *Business Publication Advertising Source.*

SRDS Community Publication Advertising Source. SRDS. • Semiannual. $186.00 per year. Provides advertising rates for weekly community newspapers, shopping guides, and religious newspapers, with circulation data and other information.

SRDS Consumer Magazine Advertising Source. SRDS. • Annual. $699.00 per year. Contains advertising rates and other data for U. S. consumer magazines and agricultural publications. Also provides consumer market data for population, households, income, and retail sales. Formerly *Consumer Magazine and Advertising Source.*

SRDS Direct Marketing List Source. SRDS. • Bimonthly. $561.00 per year. Provides detailed information and rates for business, farm, and consumer mailing lists (U. S., Canadian, and international). Includes current postal information and directories of list brokers, compilers, and managers. Formerly *Direct Mail List Source*.

SRDS Interactive Advertising Source. SRDS. • Quarterly. $569.00 per year. Provides descriptive profiles, rates, audience, personnel, etc., for producers of various forms of interactive or multimedia advertising: online/Internet, CD-ROM, interactive TV, interactive cable, interactive telephone, interactive kiosk, and others.

SRDS International Media Guides. SRDS. • Covers: In five volumes (Newspapers worldwide, Consumer magazines worldwide, Business Publications: Asia-Pacific/Middle East/Africa, Business Publications: Europe, Business Publications: The Americas), advertising rates and data for 20,000 newspapers, consumer magazines and business publications worldwide. Entries include: contact names, addresses, phone and fax numbers, and e-mail.

SRDS Newspaper Advertising Source. SRDS. • Monthly. $700.00 per year. Lists newspapers geographically, with detailed information on advertising rates, special features, personnel, circulation, etc. Includes a section on college newspapers. Also provides consumer market data for population, households, income, and retail sales. Formerly *Newspaper Advertising Source*.

SRDS Out-of-Home Advertising Source. SRDS. • Annual. $341.00. Provides detailed information on non-traditional or "out-of-home" advertising media: outdoor, aerial, airport, mass transit, bus benches, school, hotel, in-flight, in-store, theater, stadium, taxi, truckstop, kiosk, shopping malls, and others. Formerly*Advertising Options Plus*.

SRDS Print Media Production Source. SRDS. • Quarterly. $808.00 per year. Contains details of printing and mechanical production requirements for advertising in specific trade journals, consumer magazines, and newspapers. Formerly *Print Media Production Source*.

SRDS Radio Advertising Source. SRDS. • Quarterly. $535.00 per year. Contains detailed information on U. S. radio stations, networks, and corporate owners, with maps of market areas. Includes key personnel. Formerly*Radio Advertising Rates and Data*.

SRDS Technology Media Source. SRDS. • Annual. $312.00. Contains detailed information on business publications, consumer magazines, and direct mail lists that may be of interest to "technology marketers." Emphasis is on aviation and telecommunications. Formerly*Technology Media Source*.

SRDS TV and Cable Source. SRDS. • Quarterly. $525.00 per year. Provides detailed information on U. S. television stations, cable systems, networks, and group owners, with maps and market data. Includes key personnel.

VNU Business Media. ADWEEK Directories. • Annual. $100.00. Presents cost, circulation, and audience statistics for various mass media segments, including television, radio, magazines, newspapers, telephone yellow pages, and cinema.

ENCYCLOPEDIAS AND DICTIONARIES

Broadcast Communications Dictionary. Lincoln Diamant, editor. Greenwood Publishing Group Inc. • 1989. $57.95. Third revised edition.

HANDBOOKS AND MANUALS

Click Here! Internet Advertising: How the Pros Attract, Design, Price, Place, and Measure Ads Online. Eugene Marlow. John Wiley and Sons, Inc. • 1997. $29.95. Covers pricing, effectiveness, Web site selection, content, and other aspects of Internet advertising. (Business Technology Series).

Media Math: Basic Techniques for Media Evaluation. Robert W. Hall. McGraw-Hill. • 1988. $14.95. Second edition. (NTC Business Books Series).

Online Marketing Handbook: How to Promote, Advertise and Sell, Your Products and Services on the Internet. Daniel S. Janal. John Wiley and Sons, Inc. • 1999. $29.95. Revised edition. Provides step-by-step instructions for utilizing online publicity, advertising, and sales promotion. Contains chapters on interactive marketing, online crisis communication, and Web home page promotion, with numerous examples and checklists. (Business Technology Series).

ONLINE DATABASES

Arbitron Radio County Coverage. Arbitron Co. • Ratings of radio and TV stations plus audience measurement data, updated frequently. Inquire as to online cost and availability.

Management Contents. Gale Cengage Learning. • Covers a wide range of management, financial, marketing, personnel, and administrative topics. About 150 leading business journals are indexed and abstracted from 1974 to date, with monthly updating. Inquire as to online cost and availability.

Nielsen Station Index. Nielsen Media Research. • Measures local television station audiences in about 220 U. S. geographic areas. Includes current and some historical data. Inquire as to online cost and availability.

Nielsen Television Index. Nielsen Media Research. • Measures national television program audiences by sampling approximately 4,000 U. S. households. Time period is 1970 to date, with weekly updates.

PERIODICALS AND NEWSLETTERS

Advertising Age: The International Newspaper of Marketing. Crain Communications, Inc. • Weekly. $178.50 per year. Includes supplement *Creativity*.

B to B: The Magazine for Marketing and E-Commerce Strategists. Crain Communications, Inc. • 26 times a year. $59.00 per year. Formerly *Advertising Age's Business Marketing*.

Broadcasting and Cable. Reed Business Information. • 51 times a year. $179.00 per year; includes print and online editions. Formerly *Broadcasting*.

Interactive Marketing and P R News: News and Practical Advice on Using Interactive Advertising and Marketing to Sell Your Products. PBI Media, LLC. • Biweekly. $495.00 per year. Newsletter. Provides information and guidance on merchandising via CD-ROM ("multimedia catalogs"), the Internet, and interactive TV. Topics include "cybermoney", addresses for e-mail marketing, "virtual malls," and other interactive subjects. Formerly *Interactive Marketing News*.

Internet Business Report: Software, Tools and Platforms. Jupitermedia. • Semimonthly. $695.00 per year; with electronic software, $795.00 per year. Newsletter. Covers Internet advertising, fee collection, and attempts in general to make the Internet/World Wide Web profitable. Includes news of how businesses are using the Internet for sales promotion and public relations.

The Marketing Pulse: The Exclusive Insight Provider to the Entertainment, Marketing, Advertising and Media Industries. Unlimited Positive Communications, Inc. • Bimonthly. $300.00 per year. Newsletter concerned with advertising media forecasts and analyses. Emphasis is on TV and radio.

Medical Marketing and Media. Haymarket Media, Inc. • Monthly. Individuals, $96.00 per year; institutions, $108.00 per person. Contains articles on marketing, direct marketing, advertising media, and sales personnel for the healthcare and pharmaceutical industries.

SHOOT: The Leading Newsweekly for Commercial Production and Postproduction. VNU Business Media. • Weekly. $125.00 per year. Covers animation, music, sound design, computer graphics, visual effects, cinematography, and other aspects of television and motion picture production, with emphasis on TV commercials.

STATISTICS SOURCES

DMA Statistical Fact Book. Direct Marketing Association. Library and Resource Center. • Annual. Members, $79.95; non-members, $104.95. Provides data in five sections covering direct response advertising, media, mailing lists, market applications, and "Practical Management Information." Includes material on interactive/online marketing. (Cover title: *Direct Marketing Association's Statistical Fact Book*.).

SRDS Circulation [year]. SRDS. • Annual. $297.00. Contains detailed statistical analysis of newspaper circulation by metropolitan area or county and data on television viewing by area. Includes maps. Formerly*Circulation Year*.

TRADE/PROFESSIONAL ASSOCIATIONS

Association of Free Community Papers. 1634 Miner St., Idaho Springs, CO 80452. Phone: 877-203-2327 Fax: (781)459-7770 E-mail: afcp@aspobox.com • URL: http://www.afcp.org.

Magazine Publishers of America. 919 Third Ave., 22nd Fl., New York, NY 10022. Phone: (212)872-3700 Fax: (212)888-4217 E-mail: infocenter@ magazine.org • URL: http://www.magazine.org • Members are publishers of consumer and other periodicals. Affiliated with American Society of Magazine Editors; Media Credit Association; Publishers Information Bureau. Formerly Magazine Publishers Association.

Newsletter and Electronic Publishers Association. 1501 Wilson Blvd., Suite 509, Arlington, VA 22209-2403. Phone: 800-356-9302 or (703)527-2333 Fax: (703)841-0629 E-mail: nepa@newsletter.org • URL: http://www.newsletter.org • Formerly Newsletter Publishers Association.

Radio Advertising Bureau. 1320 Greenway Dr., Ste. 500, 261 Madison Ave., 23rd Fl., Irving, TX 75038-2587. Phone: 800-232-3131 or (212)681-7214 Fax: (212)681-7217 E-mail: jhaley@rab.com • URL: http://www.rab.com • Includes radio stations, radio networks, station sales representatives, and allied industry services, such as producers, research firms, schools, and consultants. Calls on advertisers and agencies to promote the sale of radio time as an advertising medium. Sponsors program to increase professionalism of radio salespeople, awarding Certified Radio Marketing Consultant designation to those who pass examination. Sponsors regional marketing conferences. Conducts extensive research program into all phases of radio sales. Issues reports on use of radio by national, regional, and local advertisers. Speaks before conventions and groups to explain benefits of radio advertising. Sponsors Radio Creative Fund. Compiles statistics.

Television Bureau of Advertising. Three E. 54th St., New York, NY 10022. Phone: (212)486-1111 Fax: (212)935-5631 E-mail: info@tvb.org • URL: http://www.tvb.org.

OTHER SOURCES

eAdvertising Report. Available from MarketResearch.com. • 2001. $495.00. Market research data published by eMarketer. Covers the growth of the Internet online advertising market. Includes future trends and Internet users' attitudes.

ADVERTISING, POINT-OF-SALE

See: POINT-OF-PURCHASE ADVERTISING

ADVERTISING RESEARCH

See also: MARKET RESEARCH; MEDIA RESEARCH

GENERAL WORKS

Super Searchers on Madison Avenue: Top Advertising and Marketing Professionals Share Their Online Research Strategies. Grace A. Villamora. Information Today, Inc. • 2003. $24.95. Provides research "tips, techniques, and resources" from 13 information professionals working in advertising and marketing. (Super Searchers Series).

ABSTRACTS AND INDEXES

Business Periodicals Index. H. W. Wilson Co. • 11 times a year. Quarterly and annual cumulations. Price varies.

HANDBOOKS AND MANUALS

How Advertising Works: The Role of Research. John P. Jones, editor. Sage Publications, Inc. • 1998. $111.00. Includes sections entitled "Research Before the Advertising Runs" and "Research After the Advertising Has Run.".

Successful Advertising Research Methods. Jack B. Haskins and Alice Gagnard-Kendrick. McGraw-Hill. • 1994. $49.95. (NTC Business Books Series).

ONLINE DATABASES

Management Contents. Gale Cengage Learning. • Covers a wide range of management, financial, marketing, personnel, and administrative topics. About 150 leading business journals are indexed and abstracted from 1974 to date, with monthly updating. Inquire as to online cost and availability.

Trade & Industry Database. Gale Cengage Learning. • Provides indexing of business periodicals, January 1981 to date. Daily updates. (Full text articles from some periodicals are available online, 1983 to date. Inquire as to online cost and availability).

PERIODICALS AND NEWSLETTERS

Journal of Advertising. M. E. Sharpe, Inc. • Quarterly. $90.00 per year. An academic journal devoted to advertising theory and research.

Journal of Advertising Research. Advertising Research Foundation. • Quarterly. Individuals, $155.00 per year; institutions, $275.00 per year.

Journal of Website Promotion: Innovations in Internet Business Research, Theory, and Practice. Haworth Press, Inc. • Semiannual. $250.00 per year to libraries; $45.00 per year to individuals. Presents a scholarly view of such items as spam, banner ads, pop-ups, click rates, and the use of search engines for advertising.

Mediaweek: The News Magazine of the Media. VNU Business Media. • 47 times a year. Weekly. $149.00 per year. Published for advertising media buyers and managers.

TRADE/PROFESSIONAL ASSOCIATIONS

American Academy of Advertising. c/o Dennis Martin, Brigham Young University, Dept. of Communications, Provo, UT 84604-6403. Phone: (801)378-6845 Fax: (801)378-6016 E-mail: dmartin@cougar.netutah.net • URL: http://www.americanacademyofadvertising.net

ARF - Advertising Research Foundation. 432 Park Ave. S, New York, NY 10016. Phone: (212)751-5656 Fax: (212)319-5265 E-mail: info@thearf.org • URL: http://www.thearf.org • Advertisers, advertising agencies, research organizations, associations, and the media are regular members of the foundation; colleges and universities are associate members. Objectives are to: further scientific practices and promote greater effectiveness of advertising and marketing by means of objective and impartial research; develop new research methods and techniques; analyze and evaluate existing

methods and techniques, and define proper applications; establish research standards, criteria, and reporting methods. Compiles statistics and conducts research programs.

ADVERTISING SPECIALTIES

See also: ADVERTISING

DIRECTORIES

Creative's Illustrated Guide to P-O-P Exhibits and Promotion. Magazines Creative, Inc. • Annual. $25.00. Lists sources of point-of-purchase displays, signs, and exhibits and sources of other promotional materials and equipment. Available online.

Incentive's Buyer's Guide. VNU Business Media. • Publication includes: List of 1,500 merchandise suppliers, hotels, cruise lines, airlines, and other companies that provide services to companies offering incentive travel and merchandise programs. Entries include: Company name, address, phone, name of sales contact, description of facilities (for hotels).

PROMO Annual SourceBook: The Only Guide to the $70 Billion Promotion Industry. Primedia Business Magazines and Media. • Annual. $49.95. Lists service and supply companies for the promotion industry. Includes annual salary survey and award winning campaigns.

FINANCIAL RATIOS

Annual Statement Studies. The Risk Management Association. • Annual. Median and quartile financial ratios are given for over 400 kinds of manufacturing, wholesale, retail, construction, and consumer finance establishments. Data is sorted by both asset size and sales volume. Includes a clearly written "Definition of Ratios" and an alphabetical industry index.

Annual Statement Studies: Industry Default Probabilities and Cash Flow Measures. The Risk Management Association. • Annual. $145.00. Serves as a companion volume to the original *Annual Statement Studies.* Gives probability of default estimates on a percentage scale for more than 450 industries. Includes changes in position year-by-year for eight financial statement line items and provides percentage measures of cash flow.

HANDBOOKS AND MANUALS

Specialty Advertising. Entrepreneur Media, Inc. • Looseleaf. $59.50. A practical guide to starting a business dealing in advertising specialties. Covers profit potential, market size evaluation, start-up costs, pricing, accounting, advertising, promotion, etc. (Start-Up Business Guide No. E1292.).

ONLINE DATABASES

Management Contents. Gale Cengage Learning. • Covers a wide range of management, financial, marketing, personnel, and administrative topics. About 150 leading business journals are indexed and abstracted from 1974 to date, with monthly updating. Inquire as to online cost and availability.

PERIODICALS AND NEWSLETTERS

Incentive: Managing and Marketing Through Motivation. VNU Business Media. • Monthly. $59.00 per year.

Retail Ad World. Visual Reference Publications, Inc. • Monthly. $299.00 per year. Weekly report on outstanding advertising by department stores, specialty stores and shopping centers with reprints of current advertising. Formerly *Retail Rd Week.*

STATISTICS SOURCES

Incentive-State of the Industry and Annual Facts Review. VNU Business Media. • Annual. $5.00. A special issue of *Incentive* magazine.

TRADE/PROFESSIONAL ASSOCIATIONS

Promotional Products Association International. 3125 Skyway Cir. N, Irving, TX 75038-3526.

Phone: 888-IAM-PPAI or (972)252-0404 Fax: (972)258-3007 E-mail: membership@ppa.org • URL: http://www.ppa.org • Suppliers and distributors of promotional products including incentives, imprinted ad specialties, premiums, and executive gifts. Promotes industry contacts in 60 countries. Holds executive development and sales training seminars. Conducts research and compiles statistics. Administers industry advertising and public relations program. Maintains speakers' bureau. Conducts trade shows, regional training, publishes educational resources.

ADVISORY SERVICES

See: INVESTMENT ADVISORY SERVICES

AEROSOL INDUSTRY

See: PRESSURE PACKAGING

AEROSPACE INDUSTRY

See also: AIRPLANE INDUSTRY; AVIATION INDUSTRY; DEFENSE INDUSTRIES; ROCKET INDUSTRY

GENERAL WORKS

Space Sciences. Patricia Dasch, editor. Gale Cengage Learning. • 2002. $395.00. Four volumes. Includes business and economic aspects of aerospace technology. (Macmillan Reference USA imprint, Macmillan Science Library,).

ABSTRACTS AND INDEXES

Air University Library Index to Military Periodicals. U.S. Air Force. • Quarterly. Free to qualified personnel. Annual cumulation.

Applied Science and Technology Index. H. W. Wilson Co. • 11 times a year. Quarterly and annual cumulations. Price varies. Indexes a wide variety of English language technical, industrial, and engineering periodicals.

Engineering Index Monthly: Abstracting and Indexing Services Covering Sources of the World's Engineering Literature. Engineering Information Inc. • Monthly. Institutions, $5,279.00 per year. Provides indexing and abstracting of the world's engineering and technical literature.

International Aerospace Abstracts. American Institute of Aeronautics and Astronautics, Inc. CSA. • 11 times a year. $2,260.00 per year. Includes print and online editions.

ALMANACS AND YEARBOOKS

Progress in Aerospace Sciences: An International Journal. Elsevier. • Eight times a year. Institutions, $1,533.00 per year. Text in English, French and German.

CD-ROM DATABASES

OECD Statistical Compendium. Organization for Economic Cooperation and Development. • Semiannual. $1,905.00 per year for 1 to 10 users. CD-ROM contains more than 730,000 monthly, quarterly, and annual time series for OECD countries, 1960 to date. Includes fully searchable data on agriculture, food, economic indicators, national accounts, employment, energy, finance, industry, technology, and foreign trade. Results can be displayed in various forms.

DIRECTORIES

International ABC Aerospace Directory. Jane's Information Group Ltd. • Covers: Approximately 28,000 companies and organizations involved in the aerospace industry, including civil and military organizations, aircraft manufacturers, Civil Aviation

Authorities, air force bases, leasing companies, airport authorities, engine manufacturers, distributors of components, and maintenance contractors; international coverage. Entries include: Name, address, phone, fax, names and titles of key personnel, description of products/services.

ENCYCLOPEDIAS AND DICTIONARIES

Encyclopedia of Space Science and Technology. Hans Mark, editor. John Wiley and Sons, Inc. • 2003. $475.00. Two volumes. Covers astronomical background, physical principles, launch technology, control systems, rockets, space vehicles, space stations, satellites, space environment, and related topics.

Macmillan Encyclopedia of Transportation. Available from Gale Cengage Learning. • 1999. $450.00. Six volumes. Published by Macmillan Reference USA. Covers the business, technology, and history of transportation on land, on water, in the air, and in space. Includes definitions, cross-references, and 200 color illustrations.

INTERNET DATABASES

Business 2.0 Web Guide to the Best Business Links. Business 2.0 Media Inc. Phone: (415)293-4800 E-mail: support@business2.com • URL: http://www.business2.com/webguide • Web site presents an extensive, searchable directory of links to "the best, most informative, and authoritative web pages." Twenty main categories cover business, finance, career, company information, people, and technology topics, with thousands of subtopics, all linking to Web sites recommended by experienced business researchers. Fees: Free.

Fedstats. Federal Interagency Council on Statistical Policy. Phone: (202)395-7254 • URL: http://www.fedstats.gov • Web site features an efficient search facility for full-text statistics produced by more than 100 federal agencies, including the Census Bureau, the Bureau of Economic Analysis, and the Bureau of Labor Statistics. Boolean searches can be made within one agency or for all agencies combined. Links are offered to international statistical bureaus, including the UN, IMF, OECD, UNESCO, Eurostat, and 20 individual countries. Fees: Free.

FreeLunch.com. Economy.com, Inc. Phone: (610)696-8700 Fax: (610)696-1678 • URL: http://www.freelunch.com • Web site provides free access to more than 1.5 million economic and financial data series, covering industry, demographics, labor markets, prices, retail sales, government spending, trade, interest rates, housing starts, the stock market, and many other topics. Data is available for various time periods in either chart or table form. Searching is offered. Fees: Free, but registration required. Economy.com, Inc. also offers fee-based economic analysis at *The Dismal Scientist* site (http://www.dismal.com).

Manufacturing Profiles. U. S. Bureau of the Census. Phone: (301)763-4636 E-mail: webmaster@census.gov • URL: http://www.census.gov/prod/www/abs/mfg-prof.html • The Census Bureau makes available free on PDF (Portable Document Format) an annual consolidation of the entire Current Industrial Report series, presenting "all the data compiled." Contains statistics on production, shipments, inventories, consumption, exports, imports, and orders for a wide variety of manufactured products.

ONLINE DATABASES

Aerospace America [online]. American Institute of Aeronautics and Astronautics. • Provides complete text of the periodical, *Aerospace America*, 1984 to date, with monthly updates. Also includes news from the *AIAA Bulletin.* Inquire as to online cost and availability.

Aerospace Database. American Institute of Aeronautics and Astronautics. • Contains abstracts of literature covering all aspects of the aerospace and aircraft industry 1983 to date. Monthly updates.

Inquire as to online cost and availability.

Aerospace/Defense Markets and Technology. Gale Cengage Learning. • Abstracts of commerical aerospace/defense related literature, 1982 to date. Also includes information about major defense contracts awarded by the U. S. Department of Defense. International coverage. Inquire as to online cost and availability.

F & S Index. Gale Cengage Learning. • Contains about four million citations to worldwide business, financial, and industrial or consumer product literature appearing from 1972 to date. Weekly updates. Inquire as to online cost and availability.

PERIODICALS AND NEWSLETTERS

Advanced Composites Monthly. Composite Market Reports Inc. • Description: Covers advanced composite materials processes and markets in the aerospace industry worldwide. "Prepared for engineering, program, and manufacturing management at primes and their subcontractors where aerospace components made of high-performance composite materials are designed, fabricated, or assembled." Discusses subcontract opportunities of interest to U.S., Canadian, and overseas aerospace companies. Recurring features include a calendar of events, reports of meetings, interviews, news of research, and application case histories.

Aerospace Daily. The McGraw-Hill Cos. • Description: Reports on developments in the aerospace industry in the U.S. and overseas. Covers related political decisions. **Remarks:** Available in print, e-mail, and URL format.

Air Force Journal of Logistics. Available from U. S. Government Printing Office. • Quarterly. $15.00 per year. Issued by the Air Force Logistics Management Center, Air Force Department, Defense Department. Presents research and information of interest to professional Air Force logisticians.

Aviation Week and Space Technology. McGraw-Hill Aviation Week Group. • Monthly. $92.00 per year.

Defense Daily: The Daily of Aerospace and Defense. PBI Media, LLC. • Daily (five times a week). $1,897.00 per year. Newsletter.

Flying Safety. U.S. Air Force. Available from U.S. Government Printing Office. • Monthly. $50.00 per year. Published in the interest of safer-flying. Articles cover many fields of flight, aircraft engineering, training and safety measures in the air and on the ground.

Satellite News: The Monthly Newsletter Covering Management, Marketing Technology and Regulation. PBI Media, Inc. • 50 times a year. $1,097.00 per year. Newsletter. Covers business applications in space, including remote sensing and satellites. Incorporates (Space Business News).

Space Times. American Astronautical Society. • Description: Discusses current topics in astronautics, Society events, national and international space programs, and related items of interest to those in the field. Recurring features include a calendar of events, book reviews, editorials, and feature articles on space exploration: past, present, and future.

RESEARCH CENTERS AND INSTITUTES

California Institute of Technology. Jet Propulsion Laboratory, 4800 Oak Grove Dr., Bldg. 180, Rm. 904, Pasadena, CA 91109. Phone: (818)354-4321 Fax: (818)393-4218 E-mail: feefback@jpl.nasa.gov • URL: http://www.jpl.nasa.gov.

Center for Space Research. Massachusetts Institute of Technology. 77 Massachusetts Ave., Room 37-241, Cambridge, MA 02139-4307. Phone: (617)253-7501 Fax: (617)253-8111 E-mail: csr@space.mit.edu • URL: http://www.space.mit.edu.

Earth Data Analysis Center. University of New Mexico. Bandelier West, Albuquerque, NM 87131-6031. Phone: (505)277-3622 Fax: (505)277-3614

E-mail: smorain@spock.unm.edu • URL: http://www.edac.unm.edu.

Graduate Aeronautical Laboratories. California Institute of Technology, Div. of Engineering and Applied Science. 1200 E. California Blvd., MS150-50, Pasadena, CA 91125. Phone: (626)395-4750 Fax: (626)449-2677 E-mail: aero@galcit.caltech.edu • URL: http://www.galcit.caltech.edu/.

Joint Institute for Advancement of Flight Sciences. NASA Langley Research Center, MS 335, 227 Hunting Ave., Hampton, VA 23681-2199. Phone: (757)864-1982 Fax: (757)864-5894 E-mail: jiafs@seas.gwu.edu • URL: http://www.seas.gwu.edu/ • Conducts research in aeronautics, astronautics, and acoustics (flight-produced noise).

OAI. 22800 Cedar Point Rd., Cleveland, OH 44142. Phone: (440)962-3000 Fax: (440)962-3120 E-mail: michaelsalkind@oai.org • URL: http://www.oai.org • Aerospace-related research, education, and technology transfers. Formerly Ohio Aerospace Institute.

Physical Science Laboratory. New Mexico State University. P.O. Box 30002, Las Cruces, NM 88003-0002. Phone: (505)522-9100 Fax: (505)522-9434 E-mail: dbirx@psl.nmsu.edu • URL: http://www.psl.nmsu.edu.

Space Institute. University of Tennessee. B.H. Goethert Parkway, Tullahoma, TN 37388-9700. Phone: (931)393-7213 Fax: (931)393-7211 E-mail: tmccay@utsi.edu • URL: http://www.utsi.edu.

STATISTICS SOURCES

Aerospace Facts and Figures. Aerospace Industries Association of America. • Annual. $35.00. Includes financial data for the aerospace industries.

Annual Survey of Manufactures. Available from U. S. Government Printing Office. • Annual. Prices vary. Issued by the U. S. Census Bureau as an interim update to the *Census of Manufactures.* Includes data on number of manufacturing establishments in various industries, employment, labor costs, value of shipments, capital expenditures, inventories, energy costs, and assets. (See also Census Bureau home page, http://www.census.gov/.).

Business Statistics of the United States. Linz Audain and Cornelia J. Strawser. Bernan Associates. • Annual. $147.00. Based on *Business Statistics,* formerly issue by the Bureau of Economic Analysis, U. S. Department of Commerce. Provides basic data for a wide variety of U. S. industries, services, and economic indicators. Most statistics are shown annually for 30 years and monthly for the most recent four years.

Standard & Poor's Industry Surveys. Standard & Poor's. • Semiannual. $1,800.00. Two looseleaf volumes. Includes monthly *Supplements.* Provides detailed, individual surveys of 52 major industry groups. Each survey is revised on a semiannual basis. Also includes "Monthly Investment Review" (industry group investment analysis) and monthly "Trends & Projections" (economic analysis).

Statistical Handbook on Technology. Paula Bernstein. Greenwood Publishing Group, Inc. • 1999. $69.95. Provides statistical data on such items as the Internet, online services, computer technology, recycling, patents, prescription drug sales, telecommunications, and aerospace. Includes charts, tables, and graphs. Edited for the general reader. (Statistical Handbook Series).

Survey of Current Business. Available from U. S. Government Printing Office. • Monthly. $63.00 per year. Issued by Bureau of Economic Analysis, U. S. Department of Commerce. Presents a wide variety of business and economic data.

TRADE/PROFESSIONAL ASSOCIATIONS

Aerospace Education Foundation. 1501 Lee Hwy., Arlington, VA 22209-1198. Phone: 800-291-8480 or

For publishers addresses, refer to SOURCES CITED section at the back of the book.

(703)247-5839 Fax: (703)247-5853 E-mail: aefstaff@aef.org • URL: http://www.aef.org • Provides America's youth with the tools needed to educate the public and the youth in math and the sciences to help keep America's edge in aerospace technology.

Aerospace Electrical Society. 18231 Fernando Cir., Villa Park, CA 92861. Phone: (714)538-1002 Fax: (714)538-1002 E-mail: aefstaff@aef.org • Technicians, engineers, and management personnel engaged in the development and use of electrical and electronic equipment and systems for air and space craft.

Aerospace Industries Association of America. 1250 Eye St., N.W., Ste. 1200, Washington, DC 20005-3924. Phone: (202)371-8400 Fax: (202)371-8470 E-mail: neale@aia-aerospace.org • URL: http://www.aia-aerospace.org.

ASM International. 9639 Kinsman Rd., Novelty, OH 44073-0002. Phone: 800-336-5152 or (440)338-5151 Fax: (440)338-4634 E-mail: customerservice@asminternational.org • URL: http://asmcommunity.asminternational.org/portal/site/asm • Metallurgists, materials engineers, executives in materials producing and consuming industries; teachers and students. Disseminates technical information about the manufacture, use, and treatment of engineered materials. Offers in-plant, home study, and intensive courses through Materials +Engineering Institute. Conducts career development program. Established ASM Foundation for +Education and Research.

Society for the Advancement of Material and Process Engineering. 1161 Parkview Dr., Covina, CA 91722-3748. Phone: 800-562-7360 or (626)331-0616 Fax: (626)332-8929 E-mail: sampeibo@sampe.org • URL: http://www.sampe.org • Formerly Society of Aerospace Material and Process Engineers.

AFFIRMATIVE ACTION PROGRAMS

See also: EQUAL EMPLOYMENT OPPORTUNITY

GENERAL WORKS

Affirmative Action. Lynne Eisaguirre. ABC-CLIO, Inc. • 1999. $45.00. Provides an impartial survey and analysis of affirmative action controversies, including historical background and statistical data. (Contemporary World Issues.).

Affirmative Action Revisited. Charles V. Dale. Nova Science Publishers, Inc. • 2001. $59.00. Provides an assessment of the history, current status, and future of affirmative action.

Employment Equity and Affirmative Action: An International Comparison. Harish C. Jain and others. M. E. Sharpe, Inc. • 2003. $66.95. Describes and compares the affirmative action and employment equity policies of six countries: the U. S., Canada, Great Britain, India, South Africa, and Malaysia.

BIBLIOGRAPHIES

Affirmative Action: An Annotated Bibliography. A. M. Babkina, editor. Nova Science Publishers, Inc. • 2003. $49.00. Second edition. Covers books, reports, and articles on all aspects of affirmative action. Includes author, title, and subject indexes.

HANDBOOKS AND MANUALS

Employer's Guide to Discrimination Laws. Maureen F. Moore. LexisNexis Matthew Bender. • 2003. $28.00, including CD-ROM. Edited for business owners and managers. Provides a concise guide to federal discrimination laws relating to race, sex, age, disability, pregnancy, religion, and national origin.

Equal Employment Opportunity Compliance Guide. John F. Buckley. Aspen Publishers, Inc. • 2002. $175.00.

Equality in the Workplace: An Equal Opportunities Handbook for Trainers. Helen Collins. Blackwell Publishing. • 1995. $55.95. (Human Resource Management in Action Series).

ONLINE DATABASES

Information Bank Abstracts. New York Times Index Dept. • Provides indexing and abstracting of current affairs, primarily from the final late edition of *The New York Times* and the Eastern edition of *The Wall Street Journal.* Time period is 1969 to present, with daily updates. Inquire as to online cost and availability.

Management Contents. Gale Cengage Learning. • Covers a wide range of management, financial, marketing, personnel, and administrative topics. About 150 leading business journals are indexed and abstracted from 1974 to date, with monthly updating. Inquire as to online cost and availability.

PERIODICALS AND NEWSLETTERS

Affirmative Action Register: The E E O Recruitment Publication. Affirmative Action, Inc. • Monthly. Free to qualified personnel; others, $15.00 per year. "The *Affirmative Action Register* is the only nationwide publication that provides for systematic distribution to mandated minorities, females, handicapped, veterans, and Native Americans." Each issue consists of recruitment advertisements placed by equal opportunity employers (institutions and companies).

Civil Rights: State Capitals. Wakeman-Walworth, Inc. • 50 times a year. $245.00 per year; print and online editions, $350.00 per year. Newsletter. Includes coverage of state affirmative action programs. Formerly *From the State Capitals: Civil Rights.*

MBI: The National Report on Minority, Women-Owned and Disadvantaged Business. Community Development Services, Inc. CD Publications. • Semimonthly. $379.00 per year. Newsletter. Provides news of affirmative action, government contracts, minority business employment, and education/training for minorities in business. Formerly *Minorities in Business.*

School Law News: The Independent Bi-Weekly News Service on Legal Developments inEducation. Aspen Publishers, Inc. • Biweekly. $383.00 per year.

RESEARCH CENTERS AND INSTITUTES

Industrial Relations Section. Massachusetts Institute of Technology. Sloan School of Management, 50 Memorial Dr., E 52-586, Cambridge, MA 02142. Phone: (617)253-2667 Fax: (617)253-7696 E-mail: osterman@mit.edu.

TRADE/PROFESSIONAL ASSOCIATIONS

American Association for Affirmative Action. 11250 Roger Bacon Dr., No. 8, Reston, WA 20190. Phone: 800-252-8952 Fax: (703)435-4390 E-mail: execdir@affirmativeaction.org • URL: http://www.affirmativeaction.org.

National Association for Equal Opportunity in Higher Education. 8701 Georgia Ave., Suite 200, Silver Spring, MD 20910. Phone: (301)650-2440 Fax: (301)495-3306 E-mail: hponder@nafeo.org • URL: http://www.nafeo.org.

OTHER SOURCES

Affirmative Action Compliance Manual for Federal Contractors. BNA, Inc. • Monthly. $410.00 per year. Two looseleaf volumes.

BNA Fair Employment Practices. BNA, Inc. • Biweekly. $938.00 per year. Looseleaf service.

Larson's Employment Discrimination. LexisNexis Matthew Bender. • $1,487.00. 10 looseleaf volumes. Treatise on both substantive and procedural law

governing employment discrimination based on sex, age, race, religion, national origin, etc.

Practical Guide to Equal Employment Opportunity. American Lawyer Media, Inc. • Looseleaf. $199.00. Two volumes. Updated as needed. Serves as a legal manual for EEO compliance. "Volume one analyzes discrimination on the basis of race, religion, sex, age, and physical handicaps including AIDS." Provides information relating to an employer's liability in cases of sexual harassment of employees, including same-sex harassment. Covers affirmative action and reverse discrimination issues. Volume two contains model affirmative action plans, a sample EEO compliance manual, checklists, and other documents. (Law Journal Press).

AFFLUENT MARKET

GENERAL WORKS

Marketing to the Affluent. Thomas J. Stanley. McGraw-Hill. • 1988. $19.95. Discusses demographics, psychographics, and buying habits.

ABSTRACTS AND INDEXES

Business Periodicals Index. H. W. Wilson Co. • 11 times a year. Quarterly and annual cumulations. Price varies.

DIRECTORIES

Business Organizations, Agencies, and Publications Directory. Gale Cengage Learning. • 2003. $480.00. 15th edition. Over 40,000 entries describing 39 types of business information sources. Classified by type of organization, publication, or serviceIncludes state, national, and international agencies and organizations. Master index to names and keywords. Also includes e-mail addresses and web site URL's.

Wealth Ranking Annual. Mark W. Scott. The Taft Group. • Contains reprints of wealth rankings and compensation lists appearing in periodicals and newspapers. Includes about 600 lists naming more than 6,000 individuals.

HANDBOOKS AND MANUALS

Networking with the Affluent. Thomas J. Stanley. McGraw-Hill. • 1993. $17.95. Discusses specific methods of prospecting for wealthy clients, with examples.

Selling to the Affluent: The Professional's Guide to Closing the Sales That Count. Thomas Stanley. McGraw-Hill. • 1990. $19.95.

ONLINE DATABASES

Marketing and Advertising Reference Service (MARS). Gale Cengage Learning. • Provides abstracts of literature relating to consumer marketing and advertising, including all forms of advertising media. Time period is 1984 to date. Daily updates. Inquire as to online cost and availability.

PROMT: Predicasts Overview of Markets and Technology. Gale Cengage Learning. • Companies, products, applied technologies and markets. U.S. and international literature coverage, 1972 to date. Inquire as to online cost and availability. Provides abstracts from more than 1,600 publications. Weekly updates.

Wilson Business Abstracts Online. H. W. Wilson Co. • Indexes and abstracts 600 major business periodicals, plus the *Wall Street Journal* and the business section of the *New York Times.* Indexing is from 1982, abstracting from 1990, with the two newspapers included from 1993. Updated weekly. Inquire as to online cost and availability. (*Business Periodicals Index* without abstracts is also available online.).

PERIODICALS AND NEWSLETTERS

City & Country Club Life: The Social Magazine for South Florida. Club Publications, Inc. • Five times a year. Controlled circulation.

Custom Home. Hanley-Wood, LLC. • Seven times a year. $36.00 per year. Edited for "top of the market" custom builders, designers, and architects.

Fortune Magazine. Time Inc., Business Information Group. • Biweekly. $59.95 per year. Edited for top executives and upper-level managers.

Journal of Wealth Management. Institutional Investor, Inc., Journals Group. • Quarterly. $410.00 per year. Includes print and online editions. Edited for managers of wealthy individuals' investment portfolios. Formerly *Journal of Private Portfolio Management.*

Money. • 13 times a year. $19.95 per year. Covers all aspects of family finance; investments, careers, shopping, taxes, insurance, consumerism, etc.

Palm Beach Illustrated: The Best of Boca Raton to Vero Beach. Palm Beach Media Group. • 10 times a year. $24.95 per year. Includes *Palm Beach Social Observer.* Formerly *Illustrated.*

Private Asset Management. Institutional Investor, Inc., Journals Group. • Biweekly. $2,335.00 per year. Newsletter. Includes print and online editions. Edited for managers investing the private assets of wealthy ("high-net-worth") individuals. Includes marketing, taxation, regulation, and fee topics.

Profit Investor Portfolio: The International Magazine of Money and Style. Profit Publications, Inc. • Bimonthly. $29.95 per year. A glossy consumer magazine featuring specific investment recommendations and articles on upscale travel and shopping.

Robb Report Home Entertaining & Design. CurtCo Robb Media. • Nine times a year. $21.95 per year. Covers "high end" home theaters, audio, video, wireless home networks, and custom installations.

Robb Report Motorcycling. CurtCo Robb Media. • Semiannual. Price on application. Contains reviews of the "newest high-quality motorcycles.".

Robb Report: The Magazine for the Luxury Lifestyle. CurtCo Robb Media. • Monthly. $65.00 per year. Consumer magazine featuring advertisements for expensive items-antique automobiles, boats, airplanes, large houses, etc.

Robb Report Worth: Wealth in Perspective. CurtCo Robb Media. • Monthly. $54.95 per year. Glossy magazine featuring articles for the affluent on personal financial management, investments, estate planning, trusts, private bankers, taxes, travel, yachts, and lifestyle. Formerly *Worth: Financial Intelligence.*

Town and Country. Hearst Corp. • Monthly. $24.00 per year.

Travel and Leisure. American Express Publishing Corp. • Monthly. $39.00 per year. In three regional editions and one demographic edition.

Vanity Fair. Conde Nast Publications, Inc. • Monthly. $18.00 per year.

STATISTICS SOURCES

Social Statistics of the United States. Mark S. Littman, editor. Bernan Press. • 2000. $65.00. Includes statistical data on population growth, labor force, occupations, environmental trends, leisure time use, income, poverty, taxes, and other economic or demographic topics.

SRDS Lifestyle Market Analyst. SRDS. • Annual. $440.00. Published in conjunction with EQUIFAX. Provides extensive lifestyle data on interests, activities, and hobbies within specific geographic and demographic markets. Formerly*Lifestyle Market Analyst.*

Statistical Handbook on Consumption and Wealth in the United States. Greenwood Publishing Group, Inc. • 1999. $69.95. Provides more than 400 graphs, tables, and charts dealing with basic income levels, income inequalities, spending patterns, taxation, subsidies, etc. (Statistical Handbook Series).

A Statistical Portrait of the United States: Social Conditions and Trends. Mark S. Littman, editor. Bernan Press. • 1998. $89.00. Covers "social, economic, and environmental trends in the United States over the past 25 years." Includes statistical tables, graphs, and analysis relating to such topics as population, income, poverty, wealth, labor, housing, education, healthcare, air/water quality, and government. (Statistical Portrait of the United States: Social Conditions and Trends Series).

OTHER SOURCES

The Affluent Market. MarketResearch.com. • 2002. $2,750.00 Consumer market data. Includes demographics of affluent house holds and the expenditures of the affluent on 250 types of products.

AFTER-DINNER SPEAKING

See: PUBLIC SPEAKING

AGE AND EMPLOYMENT

See: EMPLOYMENT OF OLDER WORKERS

AGING

See: RETIREMENT

AGREEMENTS

See: CONTRACTS

AGRIBUSINESS

GENERAL WORKS

Agricultural Biotechnology: An Economic Perspective. Margriet F. Caswell and others. Nova Science Publishers, Inc. • 2003. $30.00. Considers such factors as consumer demand, producer demand, public policies, regulation, food safety, and research funding.

Cases in Agribusiness Management. George J. Seperich and others. Holcomb Hathaway, Inc. • 1995. $28.95. Second edition.

ABSTRACTS AND INDEXES

World Agricultural Economics and Rural Sociology Abstracts: Abstracts of World Literature. Available from CABI Publishing, North America. • Monthly. Institutions, $1,425.00 per year. Print and online edition, $1,460.00 per year. Published in England by CABI Publishing. Provides worldwide coverage of the literature.

ALMANACS AND YEARBOOKS

Research in Domestic and International Agribusiness Management. Elsevier. • Dates vary. $73.25. 12 volumes.

CD-ROM DATABASES

OECD Statistical Compendium. Organization for Economic Cooperation and Development. • Semiannual. $1,905.00 per year for 1 to 10 users. CD-ROM contains more than 730,000 monthly, quarterly, and annual time series for OECD countries, 1960 to date. Includes fully searchable data on agriculture, food, economic indicators, national accounts, employment, energy, finance, industry, technology, and foreign trade. Results can be displayed in various forms.

DIRECTORIES

Agri Marketing: Marketing Services Guide. Doane Agricultural Services. • Annual. $30.00. Wide range of listings related to agricultural marketing.

Agricultural Guide to Washington: Whom to Contact and Where. Dow Elunco. • Biennial. Free. Heads of congressional committees and subcommittees in Washington, D.C. that deal with agricultural matters, and members of federal agencies and trade associations concerned with agribusiness.

Agriculture: Websites and Glossary. Carol Canada. Nova Science Publishers, Inc. • 2003. $29.50. Lists agricultural Web sites according to 24 main categories and 16 subcategories. Includes a glossary and an index.

BioScan: The Worldwide Biotech Industry Reporting Service. Greenwood Publishing Group, Inc. • Annual. $975.00 per year. Bimonthly updates. Provides detailed information on over 1,000 U.S. and foreign companies broadly classified as biotechnological. In addition to medical technology and advanced pharmaceutical firms, includes firms doing research in food processing, waste management, agriculture, and veterinary science.

FINANCIAL RATIOS

IRS Corporate Financial Ratios. Available from MarketResearch.com. • 2002. $225.00. Published by Schonfeld & Associates, Inc. Presents 70 key financial ratios for 260 industries. Ratios are calculated from income statement and balance sheet data available from the Internal Revenue Service. Includes four asset size classes.

HANDBOOKS AND MANUALS

Agricultural Finance. Warren F. Lee and others. Blackwell Publishing. • 1988. $44.95. Eighth revised edition.

INTERNET DATABASES

Business 2.0 Web Guide to the Best Business Links. Business 2.0 Media Inc. Phone: (415)293-4800 E-mail: support@business2.com • URL: http://www.business2.com/webguide • Web site presents an extensive, searchable directory of links to "the best, most informative, and authoritative web pages." Twenty main categories cover business, finance, career, company information, people, and technology topics, with thousands of subtopics, all linking to Web sites recommended by experienced business researchers. Fees: Free.

Fedstats. Federal Interagency Council on Statistical Policy. Phone: (202)395-7254 • URL: http://www.fedstats.gov • Web site features an efficient search facility for full-text statistics produced by more than 100 federal agencies, including the Census Bureau, the Bureau of Economic Analysis, and the Bureau of Labor Statistics. Boolean searches can be made within one agency or for all agencies combined. Links are offered to international statistical bureaus, including the UN, IMF, OECD, UNESCO, Eurostat, and 20 individual countries. Fees: Free.

FreeLunch.com. Economy.com, Inc. Phone: (610)696-8700 Fax: (610)696-1678 • URL: http://www.freelunch.com • Web site provides free access to more than 1.5 million economic and financial data series, covering industry, demographics, labor markets, prices, retail sales, government spending, trade, interest rates, housing starts, the stock market, and many other topics. Data is available for various time periods in either chart or table form. Searching is offered. Fees: Free, but registration required. Economy.com, Inc. also offers fee-based economic analysis at *The Dismal Scientist* site (http://www.dismal.com).

ONLINE DATABASES

Business and Industry. Gale Cengage Learning. • Contains online citations, abstracts, and selected fulltext from more than 1,000 trade journals, newspapers, and other publications. Provides general coverage of both manufacturing and service industries, including marketing, production, industry trends, key events, and information on specific companies. Time span is 1994 to date. Daily updates. Inquire as to online cost and availability. (Also available in a CD-ROM version.).

PROMT: Predicasts Overview of Markets and Technology. Gale Cengage Learning. • Companies, products, applied technologies and markets. U.S. and international literature coverage, 1972 to date. Inquire as to online cost and availability. Provides abstracts from more than 1,600 publications. Weekly updates.

Tablebase. Gale Cengage Learning. • Provides online numerical tabular data from a wide variety of business, organization, and government sources, including about 1,000 trade journals. Includes industry and individual company statistics relating to products, market share, sales forecasts, production, exports, market trends, etc. Time span is 1997 to date. Weekly updates. Inquire as to online cost and availability. (Also available in a CD-ROM version.).

PERIODICALS AND NEWSLETTERS

Ag Executive. Ag Executive Inc. • Description: Focuses on financial, personnel, and risk management issues for commercial agriculture. Covers business analysis and practical management ideas for improving profitability. Includes such topics as accounting, farm business organization, financing, economic forecasting, resource/risk control, and taxes.

Ag Lender. Doane Agricultural Services Co. • Monthly. $139.00 per year. Formerly *Agri Finance.*

AgExporter. Available from U. S. Government Printing Office. • Monthly. $44.00 per year. Issued by the Foreign Agricultural Service, U. S. Department of Agriculture. Edited for U. S. exporters of farm products. Provides practical information on exporting, including overseas trade opportunities.

Agri Marketing: The Magazine for Professionals Selling to the Farm Market. Doane Agricultural Services. • Monthly. $30.00 per year.

Agribusiness Fieldman. Western Agricultural Publishing Co., Inc. • Monthly. $19.95 per year.

Amber Waves. Available from U. S. Government Printing Office. • Quarterly. $38.00 per year. Replaces *Agricultural Outlook; Food Review*; and *Rural America.* Provides research and analysis from the U.S. Department of Agriculture's Economic Research Service. Includes economic data on agriculture, food, trade, and environmental factors.

Doane's Agricultural Report. Doane Agricultural Services. • Description: Covers the marketing of commodities (such as cattle, hogs, corn, wheat, and soybeans), as well as providing agricultural, economic, management, and production information. Discusses such topics as profit management, prices, outlook, machinery, buildings, equipment, taxes, social security, law, and government.

Farm Industry News. Primedia Business Magazines and Media. • Monthly. $25.00 per year. Includes new products for farm use.

Journal of International Food and Agribusiness Marketing. Haworth Press, Inc. • Semiannual. Institutions, $320.00 per year.

The Kiplinger Agriculture Letter. Kiplinger Washington Editors Inc. • Description: Publishes information on actions and proposals by the administration, U.S. Department of Agriculture, and Congress affecting all aspects of agriculture. Includes analysis and forecasts on a broad range of issues affecting the farm/food industry, government production and price support programs, commodity production and consumption data, food marketing and processing, consumer trends, taxes, farm credit, and financial matters.

Outlook for United States Agricultural Trade. Available from U. S. Government Printing Office. • Quarterly. $15.00 per year. Issued by the Economic Research Service, U. S. Department of Agriculture.

(Situation and Outlook Reports.).

The Washington Agricultural Record. Washington Agricultural Record. • Description: Focuses on Washington farm issues and developments, reporting international congressional and United States Department of Agriculture (U.S.D.A.) news and international agricultural developments.

RESEARCH CENTERS AND INSTITUTES

Giannini Foundation of Agricultural Economics. University of California at Berkeley. 248 Giannini Hall, Berkeley, CA 94720-3310. Phone: (510)642-7121 Fax: (510)643-8911 E-mail: dote@are. berkeley.edu • URL: http://www.are.berkeley.edu/library.

STATISTICS SOURCES

Business Statistics of the United States. Linz Audain and Cornelia J. Strawser. Bernan Associates. • Annual. $147.00. Based on *Business Statistics*, formerly issue by the Bureau of Economic Analysis, U. S. Department of Commerce. Provides basic data for a wide variety of U. S. industries, services, and economic indicators. Most statistics are shown annually for 30 years and monthly for the most recent four years.

Encyclopedia of American Industries. Gale Cengage Learning. • 2000. $560.00. Third edition. Two volumes. $280.00 per volume. Volume one is *Manufacturing Industries* and volume two is *Service and Non-Manufacturing Industries.* Provides the history, development, and recent status of approximately 1,000 industries. Includes statistical graphs, with industry and general indexes.

Infrastructure Industries USA. Gale Cengage Learning. • 2001. $260.00. Presents statistics and projections relating to economic activity in a wide variety of natural resource and construction industries.

OECD Agricultural Outlook. Organization for Economic Cooperation and Development. • Annual. $34.00. Provides a five-year outlook for agricultural markets in various countries of the world, including the U. S., other OECD countries, and selected non-OECD nations.

Standard & Poor's Industry Surveys. Standard & Poor's. • Semiannual. $1,800.00. Two looseleaf volumes. Includes monthly *Supplements.* Provides detailed, individual surveys of 52 major industry groups. Each survey is revised on a semiannual basis. Also includes "Monthly Investment Review" (industry group investment analysis) and monthly "Trends & Projections" (economic analysis).

Survey of Current Business. Available from U. S. Government Printing Office. • Monthly. $63.00 per year. Issued by Bureau of Economic Analysis, U. S. Department of Commerce. Presents a wide variety of business and economic data.

TRADE/PROFESSIONAL ASSOCIATIONS

Agribusiness Council. 1312 18th St. NW, Ste. 300, Washington, DC 20036. Phone: (202)296-4563 or (202)887-0238 Fax: (202)887-9178 E-mail: info@agribusinesscouncil.org • URL: http://www.agribusinesscouncil.org • Business organizations, universities and foundations, and individuals interested in stimulating and encouraging agribusiness in cooperation with the public sector, both domestic and international. Seeks to aid in relieving the problems of world food supply. Supports coordinated agribusiness in the developing nations by identifying opportunities for investment of U.S. private-sector technology management and financial resources. Advises agribusiness leaders about selected developing countries with good investment climates; brings potential investment opportunities to the attention of U.S. agribusiness firms; coordinates informal network of state agribusiness councils and grassroots organization; encourages companies to make investment feasibility studies in

agribusiness; provides liaison and information exchange between agribusiness firms, governments, international organizations, universities, foundations, and other groups with the objective of identifying areas of cooperation and mutual interest; encourages projects geared to the conversion of subsistence farming to intensive, higher income agriculture in order to bring the world's rural populations, wherever feasible, into the market economy.

American Society of Agricultural Consultants. 950 S. Cherry St., Suite 508, Denver, CO 80222-2664. Phone: (303)759-5091 Fax: (303)758-0190 E-mail: suggestions@agconsultants.org • URL: http://www.agconsultants.org.

International Trade Council. 3114 Circle Hill Rd., Alexandria, VA 22305-1606. Phone: (703)548-1234 Fax: (703)548-6216 E-mail: ita@titanium.org • Companies and organizations that import and export products, commodities, and services in 300 major industries including agricultural commodities, livestock, food, farm implements, and food machinery; agencies dealing with health and medicine, housing, energy, communications, transportation, forestry, water, and sanitation. Promotes free trade and the elimination of trade barriers and facilitates logistics, research, and marketing for members. Maintains legislative and educational services to develop world trade. Conducts management, technical, and educational programs; conducts financial studies of export banking, insurance, performance bonds, and transportation costs to enable exporters to be more competitive; offers speakers' bureau. Sponsors International Development Institute; offers Opportunity/Risk Analysis Service to help members find new or expandable overseas markets for their commodities, products, services, and investments.

National Agri-Marketing Association. 11020 King St., Ste. 205, Overland Park, KS 66210. Phone: (913)491-6500 Fax: (913)491-6502 E-mail: agrimktg@nama.org • URL: http://www.nama.org • Persons engaged in agricultural marketing for manufacturers, advertising agencies, and the media. Promotes the highest standards of agricultural marketing; provides for the exchange of ideas; encourages the study and better understanding of agricultural advertising, selling, and marketing; works to broaden understanding of the economic importance of agriculture; encourages careers in agricultural marketing. Provides agri-marketing short courses.

National Council of Agricultural Employers. 1112 16th St., N.W. Suite 920, Washington, DC 20036. Phone: (202)728-0300 Fax: (202)728-0303 E-mail: membership@nceaonline.org • URL: http://www.ncaeonline.org.

AGRICULTURAL CHEMICALS

See also: CHEMICAL INDUSTRIES; FERTILIZER INDUSTRY; POTASH INDUSTRY

ABSTRACTS AND INDEXES

Biological and Agricultural Index. H. W. Wilson Co. • 11 times a year. Annual and quarterly cumulations. Price varies.

DIRECTORIES

The Agrochemical Companies Fact File. PJB Publications Ltd. • Covers: 300 agrochemical manufacturers; formulators; biopesticide manufacturers, and agrochemical trading companies worldwide. Entries include: Details on key executives, financial data, operating locations, main markets, products, subsidiaries, joint ventures, and portfolios.

Major Chemical and Petrochemical Companies of

the World. Available from Gale Cengage Learning. • 2002. $880.00. Sixth edition. Published by Graham & Whiteside. Contains profiles of more than 7,000 important chemical and petrochemical companies in various countries. Subject areas include general chemicals, specialty chemicals, agricultural chemicals, petrochemicals, industrial gases, and fertilizers.

ENCYCLOPEDIAS AND DICTIONARIES

Encyclopedia of Agrochemicals. Jack R. Plimmer. John Wiley and Sons, Inc. • 2003. $945.00. Three volumes. Includes pesticides, animal food additives, veterinary drugs, and other compounds.

Kirk-Othmer Encyclopedia of Chemical Technology. Raymond E. Kirk and Donald F. Othmer. John Wiley and Sons, Inc. • 1991-97. $9,895.00, prepaid. 27 volumes. Fourth edition. Four volumes are scheduled to be published each year, with individual volumes available at $415.00. (Kirk-Othmer Encyclopedia of Chemical Technology Series).

FINANCIAL RATIOS

Industry Norms and Key Business Ratios. Desk Top Edition. Dun and Bradstreet Corp. • Annual. Five volumes. $475.00 per volume. $1,890.00 per set. Covers over 800 kinds of businesses, arranged by Standard Industrial Classification number. More detailed editions covering longer periods of time are also available.

HANDBOOKS AND MANUALS

Agrochemicals: Composition, Production, Toxicology, Applications. Franz Muller, editor. John Wiley and Sons, Inc. • 2000. $375.00. Coverage includes fertilizers, herbicides, fungicides, insecticides, and biological control agents. Content is both theoretical and practical.

Crop Protection Chemicals Reference. Chemical and Pharmaceutical Press, Inc. • 1994. $130.00. 10th edition. Contains the complete text of product labels. Indexed by manufacturer, product category, pest use, crop use, chemical name, and brand name.

Farm Chemicals International. Meister Media. • Annual. $99.00. Manufacturers and suppliers of fertilizers, pesticides, and related equipment used in agribusiness.

ONLINE DATABASES

Agricola. U.S. National Agricultural Library. • Covers worldwide agricultural literature. Over 3.3 million citations, 1970 to present, with monthly updates. Inquire as to online cost and availability.

CA Search. Chemical Abstracts Service. • Guide to chemical literature, 1967 to present. Inquire as to online cost and availability.

Derwent Crop Protection File. Derwent, Inc. • Provides citations to the international journal literature of agricultural chemicals and pesticides from 1968 to date, with updating eight times per year. Formerly *PESTDOC.* Inquire as to online cost and availability.

PERIODICALS AND NEWSLETTERS

AOAC International Journal. AOAC International. • Bimonthly. Members $176.00 per year; nonmembers, $242.00 per year; institutions, $262.00 per year. Formerly *Association of Official Analytical Chemist Journal.*

Croplife. Meister Media. • Monthly. $36.00 per year. Formerly *Farm Chemicals.*

Dealer Progress: How Smart Agribusiness is Growing. Fertilizer Institute. • Bimonthly. Free to qualified personnel; others, $40.00 per year. Published in association with the Fertilizer Institute. Includes information on fertilizers and agricultural chemicals, including farm pesticides. Formerly *Progress.*

Soil Science: An Interdisciplinary Approach to Soils Research. Lippincott Williams and Wilkins. •

Monthly. Individuals, $182.00 per year; institutions, $336.00 per year.

PRICE SOURCES

Chemical Market Reporter. Schnell Publishing Co., Inc. • Weekly. $169.00 per year. Quotes current prices for a wide range of chemicals. Formerly *Chemical Marketing Reporter.*

RESEARCH CENTERS AND INSTITUTES

Laboratory for Pest Control Application Technology. Ohio State University, Ohio Agricultural Research and Development Center, 1680 Madison Ave., Wooster, OH 44691-4096. Phone: (330)263-3931 Fax: (330)263-3686 E-mail: downer.2@osu.edu • URL: http://www.oardc.ohio-state.edu/lpcat • Conducts pest control research in cooperation with the U. S. Department of Agriculture.

Mount Vernon Research and Extension Unit. Washington State University. 16650 Memorial Highway, Mount Vernon, WA 98273. Phone: (360)848-6120 Fax: (360)848-6159.

Office of the Texas State Chemist. Texas A & M University. P.O. Box 3160, College Station, TX 77841-3160. Phone: (979)845-1121 Fax: (979)845-1389 E-mail: g-latimer@tamu.edu • URL: http://www.otscweb.tamu.edu.

Soil and Plant Tissue Testing Laboratory. University of Massachusetts at Amherst. West Experimental Station, Amherst, MA 01003-8020. Phone: (413)545-2311 Fax: (413)545-1931 E-mail: bodine@pssci.umass.edu • URL: http://www.umass.edu/plsoils.

Tennessee Agricultural Experiment Station. University of Tennessee, Knoxville. 103 Morgan Hall, Knoxville, TN 37901. Phone: (865)974-6756 Fax: (865)974-6479 E-mail: caspeer@utk.edu • URL: http://www.web.utk.edu/~taescomm/.

STATISTICS SOURCES

U. S. Industry and Trade Outlook. Available from National Technical Information Service. • Annual. $69.95. Produced by the International Trade Administration, U. S. Department of Commerce, in a "public-private" partnership with DRI/McGraw-Hill and Standard & Poor's. Provides basic data, outlook for the current year, and "Long-Term Prospects" (five-year projections) for a wide variety of products and services. Includes high technology industries. Formerly *U. S. Industrial Outlook.*

WEFA Industrial Monitor. John Wiley and Sons, Inc. • Annual. $65.00. Prepared by industry analysts at WEFA, an economic forecasting and consulting firm (originally Wharton Econometric Forecasting Associates). Contains discussions of the outlook for major U. S. industries, with many 10-year forecasts (WEFA Web site is http://www.wefa.com).

TRADE/PROFESSIONAL ASSOCIATIONS

AOAC International. 481 N Frederick Ave., Ste. 500, Gaithersburg, MD 20877-2417. Phone: 800-379-2622 or (301)924-7077 Fax: (301)924-7089 E-mail: aoac@aoac.org • URL: http://www.aoac.org • Government, academic, and industry analytical scientists who develop, test, and collaboratively study methods for analyzing fertilizers, foods, feeds, pesticides, drugs, cosmetics, and other products related to agriculture and public health. Offers short courses for analytical laboratory personnel in chemical and microbiological quality assurance, lab waste management, statistics, giving expert testimony, and technical writing.

CropLife America. 1156 15th St. NW, Washington, DC 20005. Phone: (202)296-1585 Fax: (202)463-0474 E-mail: rrunyon@croplifeamerica.org • URL: http://www.croplifeamerica.org • Fosters the interests of the general public and member companies by promoting innovative and environmentally sound manufacture, distribution

and use of crop protection and production technologies for safe, high quality, affordable, abundant food, fiber and other crops.

The Fertilizer Institute. Union Center Plz., 820 1st St. NE, Ste. 430, Washington, DC 20002. Phone: (202)962-0490 Fax: (202)962-0577 E-mail: informationtfi@tfi.org • URL: http://www.tfi.org • Producers, manufacturers, retailers, trading firms, and equipment manufacturers. Represents members in various legislative, educational, and technical areas. Provides information and public relations programs.

OTHER SOURCES

World Agrochemical Markets. Theta Reports. • 2000. $1,040.00. Market research data. Covers the demand for crop protection products in 11 countries having major markets and 20 countries having minor markets. (Theta Report No. DS196E.).

AGRICULTURAL CREDIT

See also: AGRICULTURAL ECONOMICS; CREDIT

GENERAL WORKS

Financial Management in Agriculture. Peter Barry and others. Prentice Hall PTR. • 2000. $62.00. Sixth edition. Includes *Casebook.*

ABSTRACTS AND INDEXES

Biological and Agricultural Index. H. W. Wilson Co. • 11 times a year. Annual and quarterly cumulations. Price varies.

ALMANACS AND YEARBOOKS

Agricultural Credit and Related Data. American Bankers Association. • Annual.

Farm Mortgage Debt. U.S. Department of Agriculture, Economic Research Service. • Annual.

HANDBOOKS AND MANUALS

Agricultural Finance. Warren F. Lee and others. Blackwell Publishing. • 1988. $44.95. Eighth revised edition.

INTERNET DATABASES

USDA. United States Department of Agriculture. Phone: (202)720-2791 E-mail: agsec@usda.gov • URL: http://www.usda.gov • The USDA home page has six sections: News and Information; What's New; About USDA; Agencies; Opportunities; Search and Help. Keyword searching is offered from the USDA home page and from various individual agency home pages. Agencies are the Economic Research Service, Agricultural Marketing Service, National Agricultural Statistics Service, National Agricultural Library, and about 12 others. Updating varies. Fees: Free.

ONLINE DATABASES

Agricola. U.S. National Agricultural Library. • Covers worldwide agricultural literature. Over 3.3 million citations, 1970 to present, with monthly updates. Inquire as to online cost and availability.

EconLit. American Economic Association. • Covers the worldwide literature of economics as contained in selected monographs and about 550 journals. Subjects include microeconomics, macroeconomics, economic history, inflation, money, credit, finance, accounting theory, trade, natural resource economics, and regional economics. Time period is 1969 to present, with monthly updates. Inquire as to online cost and availability.

PERIODICALS AND NEWSLETTERS

ABA Bankers News. American Bankers Association. • Biweekly. Members, $48.00 per year; nonmembers, $96.00 per year. Formerly *Banker News.*

Ag Lender. Doane Agricultural Services Co. •

Monthly. $139.00 per year. Formerly *Agri Finance.*

RESEARCH CENTERS AND INSTITUTES

Giannini Foundation of Agricultural Economics. University of California at Berkeley. 248 Giannini Hall, Berkeley, CA 94720-3310. Phone: (510)642-7121 Fax: (510)643-8911 E-mail: dote@are. berkeley.edu • URL: http://www.are.berkeley.edu/library.

STATISTICS SOURCES

Agricultural Finance Databook. U. S. Federal Reserve System. • Quarterly. $5.00 per year. (Federal Reserve Statistical Release, E.15.).

Agricultural Statistics. Available from U. S. Government Printing Office. • Annual. $38.00. Produced by the National Agricultural Statistics Service, U. S. Department of Agriculture. Provides a wide variety of statistical data relating to agricultural production, supplies, consumption, prices/price-supports, foreign trade, costs, and returns, as well as farm labor, loans, income, and population. In many cases, historical data is shown annually for 10 years. In addition to farm data, includes detailed fishery statistics.

FAO Production Yearbook. Available from Bernan Associates. • Annual. $45.00. Published by the Food and Agriculture Organization (http://www.fao.org). Contains worldwide data on agriculture, land use, farm crops, livestock, and agricultural prices.

FAO Trade Yearbook. Available from Bernan Associates. • Annual. $45.00. Published by the Food and Agriculture Organization (http://www.fao.org). Provides extensive worldwide data on exports and imports of agricultural commodities, fertilizers, tractors, and pesticides. Includes more than 130 tables of detailed statistics.

TRADE/PROFESSIONAL ASSOCIATIONS

Agribusiness Council. 1312 18th St. NW, Ste. 300, Washington, DC 20036. Phone: (202)296-4563 or (202)887-0238 Fax: (202)887-9178 E-mail: info@agribusinesscouncil.org • URL: http://www.agribusinesscouncil.org • Business organizations, universities and foundations, and individuals interested in stimulating and encouraging agribusiness in cooperation with the public sector, both domestic and international. Seeks to aid in relieving the problems of world food supply. Supports coordinated agribusiness in the developing nations by identifying opportunities for investment of U.S. private-sector technology management and financial resources. Advises agribusiness leaders about selected developing countries with good investment climates; brings potential investment opportunities to the attention of U.S. agribusiness firms; coordinates informal network of state agribusiness councils and grassroots organization; encourages companies to make investment feasibility studies in agribusiness; provides liaison and information exchange between agribusiness firms, governments, international organizations, universities, foundations, and other groups with the objective of identifying areas of cooperation and mutual interest; encourages projects geared to the conversion of subsistence farming to intensive, higher income agriculture in order to bring the world's rural populations, wherever feasible, into the market economy.

AGRICULTURAL ECONOMICS

GENERAL WORKS

Agricultural Economics and Agribusiness. Gail L. Cramer and others. John Wiley and Sons, Inc. • 2000. $104.95. Eighth edition.

ABSTRACTS AND INDEXES

NTIS Alerts: Agriculture & Food. National Technical Information Service. • Semimonthly. $195.00 per year. Provides descriptions of government-sponsored research reports and software, with ordering information. Covers agricultural economics, horticulture, fisheries, veterinary medicine, food technology, and related subjects. Formerly *Abstract Newsletter.*

World Agricultural Economics and Rural Sociology Abstracts: Abstracts of World Literature. Available from CABI Publishing, North America. • Monthly. Institutions, $1,425.00 per year. Print and online edition, $1,460.00 per year. Published in England by CABI Publishing. Provides worldwide coverage of the literature.

ALMANACS AND YEARBOOKS

Agricultural Policies, Markets, and Trade: Monitoring and Evaluation. Organization for Economic Cooperation and Development. Available from OECD Publications and Information Center. • Annual. $62.00. A yearly report on agricultural and trade policy developments in OECD member countries.

CD-ROM DATABASES

AGRICOLA on SilverPlatter. Available from Silver-Platter Information, Inc. • Quarterly. $825.00 per year. Produced by the National Agricultural Library. Provides about three million citations on CD-ROM to the literature of agriculture, agricultural economics, animal sciences, entomology, fertilizer, food, forestry, nutrition, pesticides, plant science, water resources, and other topics. Each quarterly disc covers the past ten years, with archival discs available from 1970.

EconLit. Available from SilverPlatter Information, Inc. • Monthly. Single-user, $1,600.00 per year. Provides CD-ROM citations, with abstracts, to articles from more than 500 economics journals. Time period is 1969 to date. Produced by the American Economic Association.

ENCYCLOPEDIAS AND DICTIONARIES

Dictionary of Agriculture: From Abaca to Zoonosis. Kathryn L. Lipton. Lynne Rienner Publishers, Inc. • 1995. $75.00. Emphasis is on agricultural economics.

Encyclopedia of Agriculture Science. Charles J. Arntzen and Ellen M. Ritter, editors. Elsevier • 1994. $900.00. Four volumes.

Encyclopedia of Food and Culture. Gale Cengage Learning. • 2002. $395.00. Three volumes. Contains 600 articles covering various aspects of food and its place in society, from agronomy to zucchini. Includes illustrations and a detailed index.

INTERNET DATABASES

USDA. United States Department of Agriculture. Phone: (202)720-2791 E-mail: agsec@usda.gov • URL: http://www.usda.gov • The USDA home page has six sections: News and Information; What's New; About USDA; Agencies; Opportunities; Search and Help. Keyword searching is offered from the USDA home page and from various individual agency home pages. Agencies are the Economic Research Service, Agricultural Marketing Service, National Agricultural Statistics Service, National Agricultural Library, and about 12 others. Updating varies. Fees: Free.

ONLINE DATABASES

CAB Abstracts. CAB Publishing North America. • Contains 46 specialized abstract collections covering over 10,000 journals and monographs in the areas of agriculture, horticulture, forest products, farm products, nutrition, dairy science, poultry, grains, animal health, entomology, etc. Time period is 1972 to date, with monthly updates. Inquire as to online cost and availability. *CAB Abstracts on CD-ROM* also available, with annual updating.

EconLit. American Economic Association. • Covers the worldwide literature of economics as contained in selected monographs and about 550 journals. Subjects include microeconomics, macroeconomics, economic history, inflation, money, credit, finance, accounting theory, trade, natural resource economics, and regional economics. Time period is 1969 to present, with monthly updates. Inquire as to online cost and availability.

PERIODICALS AND NEWSLETTERS

Amber Waves. Available from U. S. Government Printing Office. • Quarterly. $38.00 per year. Replaces *Agricultural Outlook; Food Review*; and *Rural America.* Provides research and analysis from the U.S. Department of Agriculture's Economic Research Service. Includes economic data on agriculture, food, trade, and environmental factors.

American Journal of Agricultural Economics. American Agricultural Economics Association Blackwell Publishing, Inc. • Five times a year. $183.00 per year. Includes online edition. Provides a forum for creative and scholarly work in agriculture economics.

Doane's Agricultural Report. Doane Agricultural Services. • Description: Covers the marketing of commodities (such as cattle, hogs, corn, wheat, and soybeans), as well as providing agricultural, economic, management, and production information. Discusses such topics as profit management, prices, outlook, machinery, buildings, equipment, taxes, social security, law, and government.

Land Economics: A Quarterly Journal Devoted to the Study of Economic and Social Institutions. University of Wisconsin at Madison. University of Wisconsin Press, Journals Div. • Quarterly. Individuals, $59.00 per year; institutions, $166.00 per year.

STATISTICS SOURCES

Agricultural Statistics. Available from U. S. Government Printing Office. • Annual. $38.00. Produced by the National Agricultural Statistics Service, U. S. Department of Agriculture. Provides a wide variety of statistical data relating to agricultural production, supplies, consumption, prices/price-supports, foreign trade, costs, and returns, as well as farm labor, loans, income, and population. In many cases, historical data is shown annually for 10 years. In addition to farm data, includes detailed fishery statistics.

Agriculture Fact Book. Available from U. S. Government Printing Office. • Annual. $26.00. Issued by the Office of Communications, U. S. Department of Agriculture. Includes data on U. S. agriculture, farmers, food, nutrition, and rural America. Programs of the Department of Agriculture in six areas are described: rural economic development, foreign trade, nutrition, the environment, inspection, and education.

Economic Accounts for Agriculture. Organization for Economic Cooperation and Development. Available from OECD Publications and Information Center. • Annual. $59.00. Provides data for 14 years on agricultural output and its components, intermediate consumption, and gross value added to net income and capital formation. Relates to various commodities produced by OECD member countries.

FAO Production Yearbook. Available from Bernan Associates. • Annual. $45.00. Published by the Food and Agriculture Organization (http://www.fao.org). Contains worldwide data on agriculture, land use, farm crops, livestock, and agricultural prices.

FAO Trade Yearbook. Available from Bernan Associates. • Annual. $45.00. Published by the Food and Agriculture Organization (http://www.fao.org). Provides extensive worldwide data on exports and imports of agricultural commodities, fertilizers, tractors, and pesticides. Includes more than 130 tables of detailed statistics.

TRADE/PROFESSIONAL ASSOCIATIONS

American Agricultural Economics Association. 555 E Wells, Ste. 1100, Milwaukee, WI 53202. Phone: (414)918-3190 Fax: (414)276-3349 E-mail: info@ aaea.org • URL: http://www.aaea.org • Professional society of agricultural economists. Serves to enhance the skills, knowledge and professional contribution of those economists who serve society by solving problems related to agriculture, food, resources and economic development. Offers placement service.

International Association of Agricultural Economists. c/o Walter Armbruster, 1211 W 22nd St., Ste. 216, Oak Brook, IL 60523-2197. Phone: (603)571-9393 Fax: (603)571-9580 E-mail: iaae@ farmfoundation.org • URL: http://www.iaae-agecon. org/ • Formerly International Conference of Agricultural Economists.

OTHER SOURCES

Agricultural Law. LexisNexis Matthew Bender. • Semiannual. $2,501.00. 15 looseleaf volumes. Covers all aspects of state and federal law relating to farms, ranches and other agricultural interests. Includes five volumes dealing with agricultural estate, tax and business planning.

AGRICULTURAL EXTENSION WORK

DIRECTORIES

County Agents Directory: The Reference Book for Agricultural Extension Workers. Doane Agricultural Services. • Semiannual. $26.95. About 17,000 county agents and university agricultural extension workers.

ONLINE DATABASES

Agricola. U.S. National Agricultural Library. • Covers worldwide agricultural literature. Over 3.3 million citations, 1970 to present, with monthly updates. Inquire as to online cost and availability.

AGRICULTURAL FOREIGN TRADE

See: FOREIGN AGRICULTURE

AGRICULTURAL LABOR

See: FARMERS; LABOR

AGRICULTURAL MACHINERY

GENERAL WORKS

Farm Power and Machinery Management. Donnell Hunt. Blackwell Publishing. • 2001. $59.95. 10th edition.

ABSTRACTS AND INDEXES

Agricultural Engineering Abstracts. Available from CABI Publishing North America. • Bimonthly. Institutions, $1,030.00 per year. Online edition available, $1,050.00 per year. Published in England by CABI Publishing.

DIRECTORIES

FEWA--Membership Directory. Farm Equipment Wholesalers Association. • Covers: Members of the Association, including 64 wholesalers, 28 branches, and 100 associate members. Entries include: Company name, address, phone, fax, web, email, names of executives, territory served illustrated in a

map, branch offices, product code, brief company profile paragraph.

NAEDA Equipment Dealer Buyer's Guide. North American Equipment Dealers Association. • Annual. $28.00. List of manufacturers and suppliers of agricultural, lawn and garden, and light industrial machinery.

Thomas Register of American Manufacturers. Thomas Publishing Co., Inc. • Annual. $149.00. 34 volumes. A three-part system offering information on a wide variety of industrial equipment and supplies. Lists more than 151,000 industrial product and services companies.

FINANCIAL RATIOS

Almanac of Business and Industrial Financial Ratios. Leo Troy. Aspen Publishers, Inc. • 2003. $125.95. Includes CD-Rom. Contains financial ratios derived from federal tax returns. Ratios for each of about 200 industries are arranged according to company asset size. (Almanac of Business and Industrial Financial Ratios Series).

Annual Statement Studies. The Risk Management Association. • Annual. Median and quartile financial ratios are given for over 400 kinds of manufacturing, wholesale, retail, construction, and consumer finance establishments. Data is sorted by both asset size and sales volume. Includes a clearly written "Definition of Ratios" and an alphabetical industry index.

Annual Statement Studies: Industry Default Probabilities and Cash Flow Measures. The Risk Management Association. • Annual. $145.00. Serves as a companion volume to the original *Annual Statement Studies.* Gives probability of default estimates on a percentage scale for more than 450 industries. Includes changes in position year-by-year for eight financial statement line items and provides percentage measures of cash flow.

Industry Norms and Key Business Ratios. Desk Top Edition. Dun and Bradstreet Corp. • Annual. Five volumes. $475.00 per volume. $1,890.00 per set. Covers over 800 kinds of businesses, arranged by Standard Industrial Classification number. More detailed editions covering longer periods of time are also available.

HANDBOOKS AND MANUALS

Regional Official Guides: Tractors and Farm Equipment. Iron Solutions, LLC. • Quarterly. Membership.

INTERNET DATABASES

Manufacturing Profiles. U. S. Bureau of the Census. Phone: (301)763-4636 E-mail: webmaster@census. gov • URL: http://www.census.gov/prod/www/abs/ mfg-prof.html • The Census Bureau makes available free on PDF (Portable Document Format) an annual consolidation of the entire Current Industrial Report series, presenting "all the data compiled." Contains statistics on production, shipments, inventories, consumption, exports, imports, and orders for a wide variety of manufactured products.

ONLINE DATABASES

Agricola. U.S. National Agricultural Library. • Covers worldwide agricultural literature. Over 3.3 million citations, 1970 to present, with monthly updates. Inquire as to online cost and availability.

F & S Index. Gale Cengage Learning. • Contains about four million citations to worldwide business, financial, and industrial or consumer product literature appearing from 1972 to date. Weekly updates. Inquire as to online cost and availability.

Thomas Register Online. Thomas Publishing Co., Inc. • Provides concise information on approximately 194,000 U. S. companies, mainly manufacturers, with over 50,000 product classifications. Indexes over 115,000 trade names. Information is updated semiannually. Inquire as to

online cost and availability.

PERIODICALS AND NEWSLETTERS

Farm Equipment. Cygnus Business Media. • Seven times a year. $48.00 per year. Includes annual *Product* issue.

Implement and Tractor: The Business Magazine of the Farm and Industrial Equipment Industry. Agra USA. • Bimonthly. $35.00 per year. Includes annuals *Product File* and *Red Book.*

NAEDA Equipment Dealer. North American Equipment Dealers Association. • Monthly. $40.00 per year. Covers power equipment for farm, outdoor, and industrial use. Formerly *Farm and Power Equipment Dealer.*

PRICE SOURCES

PPI Detailed Report. Bureau of Labor Statistics, U.S. Department of Labor. Available from U.S. Government Printing Office. • Monthly. $55.00 per year. Formerly *Producer Price Indexes.*

RESEARCH CENTERS AND INSTITUTES

Biological and Agricultural Engineering. Texas A & M University, 201 Scoats Hall, 2117 TAMU, College Station, TX 77843-2117. Phone: (979)845-3931 Fax: (979)862-3932 E-mail: info@baen. tamu.ed • URL: http://www.baen.tamu.edu/.

Idaho Agricultural Experiment Station. University of Idaho. P.O. Box 442337, Moscow, ID 83844-2337. Phone: (208)885-7173 Fax: (208)885-6654 E-mail: agres@uidaho.edu • URL: http://www. uidaho.edu/ag/iaes/.

Milan Experiment Station. University of Tennessee, Knoxville. 6205 Ellington Dr., Milan, TN 38358. Phone: (901)686-7362 Fax: (901)686-3558 E-mail: utmilan@usit.net • URL: http://www.web.utk.edu.

National Soil Dynamics Laboratory-U.S. Dept. of Agriculture Agricultural Research Service. 411 S Donahue Dr., Auburn, AL 36832. Phone: (334)884-4741 Fax: (334)887-8597 E-mail: hrogers@ars. udsa.gov • URL: http://www.msa.ars.usda.gov/area/ mis-bio.

Tennessee Agricultural Experiment Station. University of Tennessee, Knoxville. 103 Morgan Hall, Knoxville, TN 37901. Phone: (865)974-6756 Fax: (865)974-6479 E-mail: caspeer@utk.edu • URL: http://www.web.utk.edu/~taescomm/.

STATISTICS SOURCES

Annual Survey of Manufactures. Available from U. S. Government Printing Office. • Annual. Prices vary. Issued by the U. S. Census Bureau as an interim update to the *Census of Manufactures.* Includes data on number of manufacturing establishments in various industries, employment, labor costs, value of shipments, capital expenditures, inventories, energy costs, and assets. (See also Census Bureau home page, http://www.census. gov/.).

FAO Production Yearbook. Available from Bernan Associates. • Annual. $45.00. Published by the Food and Agriculture Organization (http://www.fao.org). Contains worldwide data on agriculture, land use, farm crops, livestock, and agricultural prices.

FAO Trade Yearbook. Available from Bernan Associates. • Annual. $45.00. Published by the Food and Agriculture Organization (http://www.fao.org). Provides extensive worldwide data on exports and imports of agricultural commodities, fertilizers, tractors, and pesticides. Includes more than 130 tables of detailed statistics.

U. S. Industry and Trade Outlook. Available from National Technical Information Service. • Annual. $69.95. Produced by the International Trade Administration, U. S. Department of Commerce, in a "public-private" partnership with DRI/McGraw-Hill and Standard & Poor's. Provides basic data, outlook for the current year, and "Long-Term Prospects" (five-year projections) for a wide variety of products and services. Includes high technology industries. Formerly *U. S. Industrial Outlook.*

United States Census of Manufactures. U.S. Bureau of the Census. • Quinquennial. Results presented in reports, tape, CD-ROM, and Diskette files.

TRADE/PROFESSIONAL ASSOCIATIONS

Farm Equipment Manufacturers Association. 1000 Executive Pkwy., Ste. 100, St. Louis, MO 63141-6369. Phone: (314)878-2304 Fax: (314)878-1742 E-mail: fema@farmequip.org • URL: http://www.farmequip.org • Manufacturers of "shortlines" (specialized farm equipment).

Farm Equipment Wholesalers Association. PO Box 1347, Box 1347, Iowa City, IA 52244. Phone: (319)354-5156 Fax: (319)354-5157 E-mail: info@fewa.org • URL: http://www.fewa.org • Independent wholesaler-distributors of shortline and specialty farm equipment, light industrial tractors, lawn and garden tractors, turf care equipment, estate and park maintenance equipment, power vehicles for outdoor recreation and sports, and related supply items.

North American Equipment Dealers Association. 1195 Smizer Mill Rd., Fenton, MO 63026-3480. Phone: (636)349-5000 Fax: (636)349-5443 E-mail: kindingerp@naeda.com • URL: http://www.naeda.com • Retailers of farm equipment, implements, light industrial equipment, outdoor power equipment, and related supplies. Conducts programs on management training, and governmental and trade relations.

AGRICULTURAL MARKET

See: FARM MARKETS

AGRICULTURAL PRODUCTS

See: FARM PRODUCE

AGRICULTURAL STATISTICS

See also: BUSINESS STATISTICS

CD-ROM DATABASES

OECD Statistical Compendium. Organization for Economic Cooperation and Development. • Semiannual. $1,905.00 per year for 1 to 10 users. CD-ROM contains more than 730,000 monthly, quarterly, and annual time series for OECD countries, 1960 to date. Includes fully searchable data on agriculture, food, economic indicators, national accounts, employment, energy, finance, industry, technology, and foreign trade. Results can be displayed in various forms.

INTERNET DATABASES

USDA. United States Department of Agriculture. Phone: (202)720-2791 E-mail: agsec@usda.gov • URL: http://www.usda.gov • The USDA home page has six sections: News and Information; What's New; About USDA; Agencies; Opportunities; Search and Help. Keyword searching is offered from the USDA home page and from various individual agency home pages. Agencies are the Economic Research Service, Agricultural Marketing Service, National Agricultural Statistics Service, National Agricultural Library, and about 12 others. Updating varies. Fees: Free.

STATISTICS SOURCES

Agricultural Statistics. Available from U. S. Government Printing Office. • Annual. $38.00. Produced by the National Agricultural Statistics Service, U. S. Department of Agriculture. Provides a wide variety of statistical data relating to agricultural production, supplies, consumption, prices/price-supports,

foreign trade, costs, and returns, as well as farm labor, loans, income, and population. In many cases, historical data is shown annually for 10 years. In addition to farm data, includes detailed fishery statistics.

Agriculture Fact Book. Available from U. S. Government Printing Office. • Annual. $26.00. Issued by the Office of Communications, U. S. Department of Agriculture. Includes data on U. S. agriculture, farmers, food, nutrition, and rural America. Programs of the Department of Agriculture in six areas are described: rural economic development, foreign trade, nutrition, the environment, inspection, and education.

Datapedia of the United States: American History in Numbers. George T. Kurian, editor. Bernan Press. • 2004. $125.00. Third edition. Based on the Census Bureau publication, *Historical Statistics of the United States.* Provides data from Colonial times to the present on agriculture, business, consumer income, energy, finance, labor, national income, population, and many other subjects. Includes "narrative highlights," maps, charts, and statistical projections.

FAO Production Yearbook. Available from Bernan Associates. • Annual. $45.00. Published by the Food and Agriculture Organization (http://www.fao.org). Contains worldwide data on agriculture, land use, farm crops, livestock, and agricultural prices.

FAO Quarterly Bulletin of Statistics. Food and Agriculture Organization of the United Nations. Available from UNIPUB. • Quarterly. $20.00 per year. Provides international data on agricultural production, trade, and prices, covering the major commodities of many countries. Text in English, French, and Spanish. Formerly *FAO Monthly Bulletin of Statistics.*

FAO Trade Yearbook. Available from Bernan Associates. • Annual. $45.00. Published by the Food and Agriculture Organization (http://www.fao.org). Provides extensive worldwide data on exports and imports of agricultural commodities, fertilizers, tractors, and pesticides. Includes more than 130 tables of detailed statistics.

United States Census of Agriculture. U.S. Bureau of the Census. • Quinquennial. Results presented in reports, tape, CD-ROM, and Diskette files.

World Agricultural Supply and Demand Estimates. Available from U. S. Government Printing Office. • Monthly. $52.00 per year. Issued by the Economics and Statistics Service and the Foreign Agricultural Service of the U. S. Department of Agriculture. Consists mainly of statistical data and tables.

AGRICULTURAL SURPLUSES

See: FARM PRODUCE

AGRICULTURE

See also: COOPERATIVES; FOREIGN AGRICULTURE

GENERAL WORKS

Agribusiness Management. Steven P. Erickson and others. McGraw-Hill. • 2001. $111.56. Third edition.

United States Agricultural Trade: Trends, Policy, and Direction. Larry V. Fedorov, editor. Nova Science Publishers, Inc. • 2003. $59.00. Includes data on the impact of NAFTA on the import and export of farm products.

ABSTRACTS AND INDEXES

Agrindex: International Information System for the Agricultural Sciences and Technology. Food and Agriculture Organization of the United Nations.

Bernan Press. • Monthly. $500.00 per year. Text in English, French, and Spanish.

Biological and Agricultural Index. H. W. Wilson Co. • 11 times a year. Annual and quarterly cumulations. Price varies.

ALMANACS AND YEARBOOKS

Advances in Agronomy. American Society for Agronomy, Inc. Elsevier. • Annual. Prices vary.

Agricultural and Mineral Commodities Year Book. Available from Taylor & Francis Group. • Annual. $225.00. Published by Europa Publications. Contains descriptive product profiles, price data, export-import data, and production statistics for major commodities of the world. Includes commodity histories, uses, markets, demand trends, and information about trade agreements and key commodity organizations.

The State of Food and Agriculture. Available from Bernan Associates. • Annual. $55.00. Published by the Food and Agriculture Organization of the United Nations (FAO). A yearly review of world and regional agricultural and food activities. Includes tables and graphs. Text in English.

Yearbook of Agriculture. U.S. Department of Agriculture. Available from U.S. Government Printing Office. • Annual.

BIBLIOGRAPHIES

Using the Agricultural, Environmental, and Food Literature. Barbara S. Hutchinson and Antoinette P. Greider, editors. Marcel Dekker, Inc. • 2002. $125.00. Serves as a guide to both print and electronic sources of information.

CD-ROM DATABASES

AGRICOLA on SilverPlatter. Available from Silver-Platter Information, Inc. • Quarterly. $825.00 per year. Produced by the National Agricultural Library. Provides about three million citations on CD-ROM to the literature of agriculture, agricultural economics, animal sciences, entomology, fertilizer, food, forestry, nutrition, pesticides, plant science, water resources, and other topics. Each quarterly disc covers the past ten years, with archival discs available from 1970.

WILSONDISC: Biological and Agricultural Index. H. W. Wilson Co. • Monthly. Includes unlimited on-line access to *Biological and Agricultural Index* through WILSONLINE. Provides CD-ROM indexing of over 250 periodicals covering agriculture, agricultural chemicals, biochemistry, biotechnology, entomology, horticulture, and related topics.

DIRECTORIES

Agriculture: Websites and Glossary. Carol Canada. Nova Science Publishers, Inc. • 2003. $29.50. Lists agricultural Web sites according to 24 main categories and 16 subcategories. Includes a glossary and an index.

Internet Tools of the Profession: A Guide for Information Professionals. Hope N. Tillman, editor. Special Libraries Association. • 1997. $49.00. Second edition. Consists of 14 sections by various authors or compilers. After two introductory articles on searching the Internet, there are 12 annotated lists of useful Web sites, covering the SLA, business and finance, chemistry, education, food and agriculture, information technology, insurance and employee benefits, law, library management, metals and materials, pharmaceuticals, and telecommunications. An index is provided.

ENCYCLOPEDIAS AND DICTIONARIES

Dictionary of Agriculture: From Abaca to Zoonosis. Kathryn L. Lipton. Lynne Rienner Publishers, Inc. • 1995. $75.00. Emphasis is on agricultural economics.

Encyclopedia of Agriculture Science. Charles J. Arntzen and Ellen M. Ritter, editors. Elsevier. • 1994. $900.00. Four volumes.

FINANCIAL RATIOS

Almanac of Business and Industrial Financial Ratios. Leo Troy. Aspen Publishers, Inc. • 2003. $125.95. Includes CD-Rom. Contains financial ratios derived from federal tax returns. Ratios for each of about 200 industries are arranged according to company asset size. (Almanac of Business and Industrial Financial Ratios Series).

HANDBOOKS AND MANUALS

Dun & Bradstreet/Gale Group Industry Handbooks. Gale Cengage Learning. • 2000. $650.00. Five volumes. $130.00 per volume. Each volume covers two or more major industries: 1. *Entertainment and Hospitality*; 2. *Construction and Agriculture*; 3. *Chemicals and Pharmaceuticals*; 4. *Computers & Software and Broadcasting & Telecommunications*; 5. *Insurance and Health & Medical Services*. The following are included for each industry: overview, statistics, financial ratios, rankings, merger information, company directory, directory of associations, and consultants directory. (Dun and Bradstreet/Gale Industry Reference Handbook Series).

INTERNET DATABASES

FedWorld: A Program of the United States Department of Commerce. National Technical Information Service. Phone: (703)605-6000 Fax: (703)605-6900 E-mail: webmaster@fedworld.gov • URL: http://www.fedworld.gov • Web site offers "a comprehensive central access point for searching, locating, ordering, and acquiring government and business information." Emphasis is on searching the Web pages, databases, and government reports of a wide variety of federal agencies. Fees: Free.

FirstGov: Your First Click to the U. S. Government. General Services Administration. Phone: 800-333-4636 or (202)501-0705 E-mail: public.affairs@gsa.gov • URL: http://www.firstgov.gov • Free Web site provides extensive links to federal agencies covering a wide variety of topics, such as agriculture, business, consumer safety, education, the environment, government jobs, grants, health, social security, statistics sources, taxes, technology, travel, and world affairs. Also provides links to federal forms, including IRS tax forms. Searching is offered, both keyword and advanced.

USDA. United States Department of Agriculture. Phone: (202)720-2791 E-mail: agsec@usda.gov • URL: http://www.usda.gov • The USDA home page has six sections: News and Information; What's New; About USDA; Agencies; Opportunities; Search and Help. Keyword searching is offered from the USDA home page and from various individual agency home pages. Agencies are the Economic Research Service, Agricultural Marketing Service, National Agricultural Statistics Service, National Agricultural Library, and about 12 others. Updating varies. Fees: Free.

WilsonWeb Periodicals Databases. H. W. Wilson. Phone: 800-367-6770 or (718)588-8400 Fax: 800-590-1617 or (718)992-8003 E-mail: custserv@hwwilson.com • URL: http://www.hwwilson.com/ • Web sites provide fee-based access to *Wilson Business Full Text, Applied Science & Technology Full Text, Biological & Agricultural Index, Library Literature & Information Science Full Text,* and *Readers' Guide Full Text, Mega Edition.* Daily updates.

ONLINE DATABASES

Agricola. U.S. National Agricultural Library. • Covers worldwide agricultural literature. Over 3.3 million citations, 1970 to present, with monthly updates. Inquire as to online cost and availability.

CAB Abstracts. CAB Publishing North America. • Contains 46 specialized abstract collections covering over 10,000 journals and monographs in the areas of agriculture, horticulture, forest products, farm products, nutrition, dairy science, poultry, grains, animal health, entomology, etc. Time period is 1972 to date, with monthly updates. Inquire as to online cost and availability. *CAB Abstracts on CD-ROM* also available, with annual updating.

Information Bank Abstracts. New York Times Index Dept. • Provides indexing and abstracting of current affairs, primarily from the final late edition of *The New York Times* and the Eastern edition of *The Wall Street Journal.* Time period is 1969 to present, with daily updates. Inquire as to online cost and availability.

PERIODICALS AND NEWSLETTERS

Agricultural Research. Available from U. S. Government Printing Office. • Monthly. $50.00 per year. Issued by the Agricultural Research Service of the U. S. Department of Agriculture. Presents results of research projects related to a wide variety of farm crops and products.

Agronomy Journal: An International Journal. American Society of Agronomy, Inc. • Bimonthly. Free to members; non-members, $216.00 per year.

Amber Waves. Available from U. S. Government Printing Office. • Quarterly. $38.00 per year. Replaces *Agricultural Outlook; Food Review;* and *Rural America.* Provides research and analysis from the U.S. Department of Agriculture's Economic Research Service. Includes economic data on agriculture, food, trade, and environmental factors.

CSANews. American Society of Agronomy. • Description: Publishes information on agronomy, crop science, soil science, and related topics. Provides news of the societies and members; reports of annual meetings; listings of publications; announcements of awards, retirements, and deaths; job listings; and a calendar of events.

Journal of Agricultural and Food Information. Haworth Press, Inc. • Quarterly. Institutions, $95.00 per year. A journal for librarians and others concerned with the acquisition of information on food and agriculture.

Journal of Sustainable Agriculture: Innovations for the Long-Term and Lasting Maintenance and Enhancement of Agricultural Resources, Production and Environmental Quality. Haworth Press, Inc. • Quarterly. Institutions, $285.00 per year. Two volumes. An academic and practical journal concerned with resource depletion and environmental misuse.

The Kiplinger Agriculture Letter. Kiplinger Washington Editors Inc. • Description: Publishes information on actions and proposals by the administration, U.S. Department of Agriculture, and Congress affecting all aspects of agriculture. Includes analysis and forecasts on a broad range of issues affecting the farm/food industry, government production and price support programs, commodity production and consumption data, food marketing and processing, consumer trends, taxes, farm credit, and financial matters.

National Farmers Union News. National Farmers Union. • Description: Provides news, legislation, and tax information in relation to the farming industry.

The Washington Agricultural Record. Washington Agricultural Record. • Description: Focuses on Washington farm issues and developments, reporting international congressional and United States Department of Agriculture (U.S.D.A.) news and international agricultural developments.

RESEARCH CENTERS AND INSTITUTES

Agricultural Experiment Station. Cornell University. 245 Roberts Hall, Ithaca, NY 14853-5905. Phone: (607)255-2552 Fax: (607)255-9499 E-mail: cuaes@cornell.edu • URL: http://www.cuaes.cornell.edu/cuaes.

California Agricultural Experiment Station. University of California. 1111 Franklin St., 6th Fl., Oakland, CA 94607-5200. Phone: (510)987-0060 Fax: (510)451-2317 E-mail: wr.gomes@ucop.edu • URL: http://www.ucanr.org/aes.

Florida Agricultural Experiment Station. University of Florida. Institute of Food and Agricultural Science, 1022 McCarty Hall, Gainesville, FL 32611. Phone: (352)392-1784 Fax: (352)392-4965 E-mail: rljones@mail.fas.ufl.edu • URL: http://www.research.ifas.ufl.edu.

Michigan Agricultural Experiment Station. Michigan State University. 109 Argricultural Hall, East Lansing, MI 48224-1039. Phone: (517)355-0123 Fax: (517)355-5406 E-mail: maesdir@msu.edu • URL: http://www.maes.msu.edu.

Ohio Agricultural Research and Development Center. Ohio State University. 1680 Madison Ave., 209 Research Services, Wooster, OH 44691-4096. Phone: (330)263-3701 Fax: (330)263-3688 E-mail: oardc@osu.edu • URL: http://www.oardc.ohio-state.edu.

Tennessee Agricultural Experiment Station. University of Tennessee, Knoxville. 103 Morgan Hall, Knoxville, TN 37901. Phone: (865)974-6756 Fax: (865)974-6479 E-mail: caspeer@utk.edu • URL: http://www.web.utk.edu/~taescomm/.

Wisconsin Agricultural Experiment Station. University of Wisconsin - Madison. College of Agricultural and Life Sciences, 140 Agricultural Hall, Madison, WI 53706. Phone: (608)262-4930 Fax: (608)262-4556 E-mail: info@cals.wisc.edu • URL: http://www.cals.wisc.edu/.

STATISTICS SOURCES

Agricultural Statistics. Available from U. S. Government Printing Office. • Annual. $38.00. Produced by the National Agricultural Statistics Service, U. S. Department of Agriculture. Provides a wide variety of statistical data relating to agricultural production, supplies, consumption, prices/price-supports, foreign trade, costs, and returns, as well as farm labor, loans, income, and population. In many cases, historical data is shown annually for 10 years. In addition to farm data, includes detailed fishery statistics.

Agriculture Fact Book. Available from U. S. Government Printing Office. • Annual. $26.00. Issued by the Office of Communications, U. S. Department of Agriculture. Includes data on U. S. agriculture, farmers, food, nutrition, and rural America. Programs of the Department of Agriculture in six areas are described: rural economic development, foreign trade, nutrition, the environment, inspection, and education.

FAO Production Yearbook. Available from Bernan Associates. • Annual. $45.00. Published by the Food and Agriculture Organization (http://www.fao.org). Contains worldwide data on agriculture, land use, farm crops, livestock, and agricultural prices.

FAO Quarterly Bulletin of Statistics. Food and Agriculture Organization of the United Nations. Available from UNIPUB. • Quarterly. $20.00 per year. Provides international data on agricultural production, trade, and prices, covering the major commodities of many countries. Text in English, French, and Spanish. Formerly *FAO Monthly Bulletin of Statistics.*

FAO Trade Yearbook. Available from Bernan Associates. • Annual. $45.00. Published by the Food and Agriculture Organization (http://www.fao.org). Provides extensive worldwide data on exports and imports of agricultural commodities, fertilizers, tractors, and pesticides. Includes more than 130 tables of detailed statistics.

Infrastructure Industries USA. Gale Cengage Learning. • 2001. $260.00. Presents statistics and projections relating to economic activity in a wide variety of natural resource and construction industries.

Monthly Bulletin of Statistics. United Nations Publications. • Monthly. $295.00 per year. Provides current data for about 200 countries on a wide variety of economic, industrial, and demographic subjects. Compiled by United Nations Statistical Office.

OECD Agricultural Outlook. Organization for Economic Cooperation and Development. • Annual. $34.00. Provides a five-year outlook for agricultural markets in various countries of the world, including the U. S., other OECD countries, and selected non-OECD nations.

Statistical Yearbook. United Nations Publications. • Annual. $125.00. Contains statistics for about 200 countries on a wide variety of economic, industrial, and demographic topics. Compiled by United Nations Statistical Office.

United States Census of Agriculture. U.S. Bureau of the Census. • Quinquennial. Results presented in reports, tape, CD-ROM, and Diskette files.

TRADE/PROFESSIONAL ASSOCIATIONS

Agricultural Research Institute. 9650 Rockville Pike, Bethesda, MD 20814-3998. Phone: (301)530-7122 Fax: (301)530-7007 E-mail: info@agribusinesscouncil.org • Originally an integral part of the National Academy of Sciences (see separate entry), incorporated separately in 1973. Analyzes agricultural problems and promotes research by its members to solve them. (ARI does not engage in research activities itself.).

American Farm Bureau Federation. 600 Maryland Ave. SW, Ste. 1000W, Washington, DC 20024. Phone: 800-572-1090 or (202)406-3600 Fax: (202)406-3602 E-mail: bstallman@fb.org • URL: http://www.fb.org • Federation of 50 state farm bureaus and Puerto Rico, with membership on a family basis. Analyzes problems of members and formulates action to achieve educational improvement, economic opportunity, and social advancement. Maintains speakers' bureau; sponsors specialized education program.

American Society of Agricultural Engineers. 2950 Niles Rd., St. Joseph, MI 49085. Phone: (269)429-0300 Fax: (269)429-3852 E-mail: hq@asae.org • URL: http://www.asae.org.

American Society of Agronomy. 677 S. Segoe Rd., Madison, WI 53711. Phone: (608)273-8080 Fax: (608)273-2021 E-mail: headquarters@agronomy.org • URL: http://www.agronomy.org.

National Association of State Departments of Agriculture. 1156 15th St., N.W., Suite 1020, Washington, DC 20005. Phone: (202)296-9680 Fax: (202)296-9686 E-mail: nasda@nasda.org • URL: http://www.nasda.org.

National Grange. 1616 H St. NW, Washington, DC 20006. Phone: 888-4-GRANGE or (202)628-3507 Fax: (202)347-1091 E-mail: info@nationalgrange.org • URL: http://www.nationalgrange.org • Rural family service organization with a special interest in agriculture. Promotes mission and goals through legislative, social, educational, community service, youth and member services programs. Sponsors needlework and stuffed toy contests.

OTHER SOURCES

Agricultural Law. LexisNexis Matthew Bender. • Semiannual. $2,501.00. 15 looseleaf volumes. Covers all aspects of state and federal law relating to farms, ranches and other agricultural interests. Includes five volumes dealing with agricultural estate, tax and business planning.

AGRONOMY

See: AGRICULTURE

AIDS POLICY

GENERAL WORKS

HIV/AIDS and the World of Work: An ILO Code of Practice. International Labour Organization. • 2002. $12.95. Emphasis is on protection from discrimination. Discusses the formation of appropriate policy by governments and organizations.

Women, Men, the Family and HIV/AIDS: A Sociological Perspective on the Epidemic in America. Carole A. Campbell. Cambridge University Press. • 1999. $21.00.

ABSTRACTS AND INDEXES

AIDS: Abstracts of the Psychological and Behavioral Literature, 1983-1991. John Anderson and others, editors. American Psychological Association. • 1991. $19.95. Third edition. (Bibliographies in Psychology Series: No.1).

Business Periodicals Index. H. W. Wilson Co. • 11 times a year. Quarterly and annual cumulations. Price varies.

Current Law Index: Multiple Access to Legal Periodicals. Gale Cengage Learning. • Monthly. $725.00 per year. Produced in cooperation with the American Association of Law Libraries. Indexes more than 900 law journals, legal newspapers, and specialty publications from the U.S., Canada, U.K., Ireland, Australia, and New Zealand.

Readers' Guide to Periodical Literature. H. W. Wilson Co. • Monthly. $345.00 per year. Includes annual *Cumulation*. Indexes about 250 peridicals of general interest.

Social Sciences Index. H. W. Wilson Co. • Quarterly, with annual cumulation. Price varies. Indexes more than 400 periodicals covering economics, environmental policy, government, insurance, labor, health care policy, plannning, public administration, public welfare, urban studies, women's issues, criminology, and related topics.

BIBLIOGRAPHIES

AIDS Literature and Law Review. University Publishing Group, Inc. • Monthly. $225.00 per year. Contains abstracts of journal and newspaper articles. Formerly *AIDS Literature and News Review.*

How to Find Information About AIDS. Jeffrey T. Huber, editor. Haworth Press, Inc. • 1992. $49.95. Second edition. Includes print, electronic, and organizational sources of information. Local and national hotlines are listed.

CD-ROM DATABASES

AGRICOLA on SilverPlatter. Available from Silver-Platter Information, Inc. • Quarterly. $825.00 per year. Produced by the National Agricultural Library. Provides about three million citations on CD-ROM to the literature of agriculture, agricultural economics, animal sciences, entomology, fertilizer, food, forestry, nutrition, pesticides, plant science, water resources, and other topics. Each quarterly disc covers the past ten years, with archival discs available from 1970.

Social Sciences Citation Index. ISI. • Monthly. Price on request. Provides CD-ROM indexing of articles appearing in 1700 leading social science journals worldwide, with additional selections from more than 5700 other journals. Time span is 1992 to date. Coverage includes economics, business, finance, management, communications, demographics, library and information science, political science, sociology, and many other subjects.

Social Sciences Citation Index: Compact Disc Edition with Abstracts. Institute for Scientific Information. • Monthly. Provides CD-ROM indexing and abstracting of "significant articles" from 1,700 social science journals worldwide, with additional selections from 3,200 other journals, 1986 to date. Includes economics, business, finance, management, communications, demographics,

information and library science, political science, sociology, and many other subjects.

WILSONDISC: Wilson Social Sciences Abstracts. H. W. Wilson Co. • Monthly. Includes unlimited online access to *Social Sciences Index* through WILSONLINE. Provides CD-ROM indexing from 1983 and abstracting from 1994 of more than 500 periodicals covering economics, area studies, community health, public administration, public welfare, urban studies, and many other topics related to the social sciences.

ENCYCLOPEDIAS AND DICTIONARIES

Encyclopedia of AIDS: A Social, Political, Cultural, and Scientific Record of the HIV Epidemic. Raymond A. Smith, editor. Fitzroy Dearborn Publishers, Inc. • 1998. $135.00. Emphasis is historical, covering the years 1981 to 1996. Includes information on AIDS law, policy, and activism.

HANDBOOKS AND MANUALS

AIDS and the Law. Margaret C. Jasper. Oceana Publications. • 2000. $27.50. Second edition. (Legal Almanac Series).

AIDS Benefits Handbook: Everything You Need to Know to Get Social Security, Welfare, Medicaid, Medicare, Food Stamps, Housing, Drugs, and Other Benefits. Thomas P. McCormack. Yale University Press. • 1990. $37.50.

AIDS Issues in the Workplace: A Response Model for Human Resource Management. Dale A. Masi. Greenwood Publishing Group, Inc. • 1990. $64.95.

AIDS Law Today: A New Guide for the Public. Yale AIDS Law Project Staff and others. Yale University Press. • 1993. $20.00. Second edition.

AIDS Reference Guide: A Sourcebook for Planners and Decision Makers. Frances Fernald, editor. Atlantic Information Services, Inc. • $448.00 Looseleaf Service. Two volumes. Includes twelve updates and twelve newsletters. Covers a wide range of AIDS topics, including "Employment Policies and Issues," "Legal Issues," "Financing Issues," "Impact on Healthcare Providers," "Global Issues," and "Legislative, Regulatory, and Governance Issues.".

Legal Aspects of AIDS. West Group. • Annual. $254.50 per year. Looseleaf service. Includes issue employment discrimination, housing discrimination, and insurance. This work also "traces the historical progression of the disease and its spread.".

INTERNET DATABASES

Lexis.com Research System. Lexis-Nexis Group. Phone: 800-227-4908 or (937)865-6800 Fax: (937)865-6909 E-mail: webmaster@prod.lexis-nexis.com • URL: http://www.lexis.com • Fee-based Web site offers extensive searching of a wide variety of legal sources. Additional features include Daily Opinion Service, lexis.com Bookstore, Career Center, CLE Center, Law Schools, and Practice Pages ("Pages specific to areas of specialty").

ONLINE DATABASES

Index to Legal Periodicals and Books (Online). H. W. Wilson Co. • Broad coverage of law journals and books 1981 to date. Monthly updates. Inquire as to online cost and availability.

Newspaper Abstracts Daily. ProQuest Inc. • Provides online coverage (citations and abstracts) of 25 major newspapers. Covers business, economics, current affairs, health, fitness, sports, education, technology, government, consumer affairs, psychology, the arts, and the social sciences. Time period is 1986 to date, with daily updates. Inquire as to online cost and availability.

Readers' Guide Abstracts Online. H. W. Wilson Co. • Indexes and abstracts general interest periodicals, 1983 to date. Weekly updates. Inquire as to online cost and availability.

Wilson Business Abstracts Online. H. W. Wilson Co. • Indexes and abstracts 600 major business periodicals, plus the *Wall Street Journal* and the business section of the *New York Times*. Indexing is from 1982, abstracting from 1990, with the two newspapers included from 1993. Updated weekly. Inquire as to online cost and availability. (*Business Periodicals Index* without abstracts is also available online.).

Wilson Social Sciences Abstracts Online. H. W. Wilson Co. • Provides online abstracting and indexing of more than 500 periodicals covering area studies, community health, public administration, public welfare, urban studies, and many other social science topics. Time period is 1994 to date for abstracts and 1983 to date for indexing, with updates weekly. Inquire as to online cost and availability.

PERIODICALS AND NEWSLETTERS

AIDS and Public Policy Journal. University Publishing Group, Inc. • Quarterly. Individuals, $59.00 per year; institutions, $115.00 per year.

AIDS Policy and Law: The Biweekly Newsletter on Legislation, Regulation, and Litigation Concerning AIDS. LRP Publications. • 22 times a year. $514.00 per year. Newsletter for personnel managers, lawyers, and others.

RESEARCH CENTERS AND INSTITUTES

Center for Women Policy Studies. 1211 Connecticut Ave., N.W. Suite 312, Washington, DC 20036. Phone: (202)872-1770 Fax: (202)296-8962 E-mail: cwps@centerwomenpolicy.org • URL: http://www.centerwomenpolicy.org • Conducts research on the policy issues that affect the legal, economic, educational, and social status of women, including sexual harassment in the workplace, and women and AIDS.

TRADE/PROFESSIONAL ASSOCIATIONS

AIDS Action Council. 1730 M St. NW, Ste. 611, Washington, DC 20036. Phone: (202)530-8030 Fax: (202)530-8031 E-mail: members@aidsaction.org • URL: http://www.aidsaction.org • Serves as a representative in Washington, DC, of community-based AIDS service organizations. Advocates, at the federal level, for more effective AIDS policy, legislation, and funding. Works collaboratively with AIDS Action Foundation, a national public policy research organization.

American Foundation for AIDS Research. 120 Wall St., 13th Fl., New York, NY 10005-3902. Phone: 800-392-6327 or (212)806-1600 Fax: (212)806-1601 E-mail: donors@amfar.org; teresa.coffey@amfar.org • URL: http://www.amfar.org • Purpose is to raise funds to support AIDS research.

OTHER SOURCES

AIDS Litigation Reporter (Acquired Immune Deficiency Syndrome): The National Journal of Record of AIDS-Related Litigation. Andrews Publications. • Semimonthly. $951.00 per year. Newsletter. Provides reports on a wide variety of legal cases in which AIDS is a factor.

AIR BASES

See: AIR FORCE

AIR CARGO

See: AIR FREIGHT

AIR CONDITIONING INDUSTRY

See also: HEATING AND VENTILATION; REFRIGERATION INDUSTRY

GENERAL WORKS

Modern Refrigeration and Air Conditioning. Andrew D. Althouse and others. Goodheart-Willcox

Publishers. • 2003. Price on application.

Refrigeration and Air Conditioning. A.R. Trott and T. Welch. Elsevier. • 2000. $64.99. Third edition.

ABSTRACTS AND INDEXES

Applied Science and Technology Index. H. W. Wilson Co. • 11 times a year. Quarterly and annual cumulations. Price varies. Indexes a wide variety of English language technical, industrial, and engineering periodicals.

NTIS Alerts: Energy. National Technical Information Service. • Semimonthly. $245.00 per year. Provides descriptions of government-sponsored research reports and software, with ordering information. Covers electric power, batteries, fuels, geothermal energy, heating/cooling systems, nuclear technology, solar energy, energy policy, and related subjects. Formerly *Abstract Newsletter.*

DIRECTORIES

Air Conditioning, Heating, and Refrigeration News-Directory. Business News Publishing Co. • Annual. $35.00.

AMCA Directory of Licensed Products. Air Movement and Control Association. • Annual. Free. Lists member manufacturers of equipment and supplies for the air and movement control industry.

The Wholesaler "The Wholesaling 100". TMB Publishing, Inc. • Annual. $25.00. Provides information on the 100 leading wholesalers of plumbing, piping, heating, and air conditioning equipment.

ENCYCLOPEDIAS AND DICTIONARIES

Macmillan Encyclopedia of Energy. Available from Gale Cengage Learning. • 2001. $395.00. Three volumes. Published by Macmillan Reference USA. Covers the business, technology, and history of a wide variety of energy sources.

FINANCIAL RATIOS

American Supply Association Operating Performance Report. American Supply Association. • Annual. Members, $45.00; non-members, $150.00.

Annual Statement Studies. The Risk Management Association. • Annual. Median and quartile financial ratios are given for over 400 kinds of manufacturing, wholesale, retail, construction, and consumer finance establishments. Data is sorted by both asset size and sales volume. Includes a clearly written "Definition of Ratios" and an alphabetical industry index.

Annual Statement Studies: Industry Default Probabilities and Cash Flow Measures. The Risk Management Association. • Annual. $145.00. Serves as a companion volume to the original *Annual Statement Studies.* Gives probability of default estimates on a percentage scale for more than 450 industries. Includes changes in position year-by-year for eight financial statement line items and provides percentage measures of cash flow.

Industry Norms and Key Business Ratios. Desk Top Edition. Dun and Bradstreet Corp. • Annual. Five volumes. $475.00 per volume. $1,890.00 per set. Covers over 800 kinds of businesses, arranged by Standard Industrial Classification number. More detailed editions covering longer periods of time are also available.

HANDBOOKS AND MANUALS

Air Conditioning Testing-Adjusting-Balancing: A Field Practice Manual. John Gladstone. Engineers Press. • 1991. $44.95. Second edition.

Guide to Energy Efficient Commercial Equipment. Margaret Suozzo and others. American Council for an Energy Efficient Economy. • 1997. $25.00. Provides information on specifying and purchasing energy-saving systems for buildings (heating, air conditioning, lighting, and motors).

No-Regrets Remodeling: Creating a Comfortable,

Healthy Home That Saves Energy. Home Energy. • 1997. $19.95. Edited by *Home Energy* magazine. Serves as a home remodeling guide to efficient heating, cooling, ventilation, water heating, insulation, lighting, and windows.

INTERNET DATABASES

Manufacturing Profiles. U. S. Bureau of the Census. Phone: (301)763-4636 E-mail: webmaster@census.gov • URL: http://www.census.gov/prod/www/abs/mfg-prof.html • The Census Bureau makes available free on PDF (Portable Document Format) an annual consolidation of the entire Current Industrial Report series, presenting "all the data compiled." Contains statistics on production, shipments, inventories, consumption, exports, imports, and orders for a wide variety of manufactured products.

ONLINE DATABASES

F & S Index. Gale Cengage Learning. • Contains about four million citations to worldwide business, financial, and industrial or consumer product literature appearing from 1972 to date. Weekly updates. Inquire as to online cost and availability.

Management Contents. Gale Cengage Learning. • Covers a wide range of management, financial, marketing, personnel, and miscellaneous topics. About 150 leading business journals are indexed and abstracted from 1974 to date, with monthly updating. Inquire as to online cost and availability.

PERIODICALS AND NEWSLETTERS

Air Conditioning, Heating, and Refrigeration News: The HVACR Contractor's Weekly Newsmagazine. Business News Publishing Co. • Weekly. $87.00 per year. Includes *Supplement.*

ASHRAE Journal: The Magazine of the American Society of Heating, Refrigeration, Air-Conditioning, Ventilation. American Society of Heating, Refrigerating and Air Conditioning Engineers, Inc. • Monthly. Free to members; non-members, $59.00 per year.

Dealerscope: Product and Strategy for Consumer Technology Retailing. North American Publishing Co. • Monthly. Free to qualified personnel; others, $79.00 per year. Formerly *Dealerscope Consumer Electronices Marketplace.*

Heating/Piping/Air Conditioning Engineering: The Magazine of Mechanical Systems Engineering. Penton Media, Inc. • Monthly. $65.00 per year. Covers design, specification, installation, operation, and maintenance for systems in industrial, commercial, and institutional buildings. Formerly (Heating, Piping and Air Conditioning).

Koldfax. Air-Conditioning and Refrigeration Institute. • Monthly. Membership. Newsletter.

Shop Talk. Mobile Air Conditioning Society. • Description: Carries news briefs on happenings in the motor vehicle air conditioning and installed accessories industry. Publishes technical as well as management-oriented articles and listings of manuals, technical services, and training opportunities available. Recurring features include reports of meetings, company and personnel news, reports on the Association's activities and professional interest groups, and monthly supplements on specific topics.

The Wholesaler. TMB Publishing, Inc. • Monthly. $75.00 per year. Edited for wholesalers and distributors of plumbing, piping, heating, and air conditioning equipment.

RESEARCH CENTERS AND INSTITUTES

Energy Systems Laboratory. Texas A & M University. College Station, TX 77843. Phone: (979)845-6402 Fax: (979)845-6334 E-mail: doneal@mengr.tamu.edu • URL: http://www.esl.tamu.edu.

Institute for Environmental Research. Kansas State University. Seaton Hall, Manhattan, KS 66506. Phone: (785)532-5620 Fax: (785)532-6642 E-mail:

hosni@ksu.edu • URL: http://www.engg.ksu.edu/ier.

Mechanical and Nuclear Engineering Research Laboratories. Kansas State University. Rathbone Hall, Room 302, Manhattan, KS 66506. Phone: (785)532-5610 Fax: (785)532-7057 E-mail: hosni@ksu.edu • URL: http://www.mne.ksu.edu/.

Ray W. Herrick Laboratories. Purdue University, 1077 Ray W. Herrick Laboratories, West Lafayette, IN 47907-1077. Phone: (765)494-2132 Fax: (765)494-0787 E-mail: rhlab@ecn.purdue.edu • URL: http://www.herrick.ecn.purdue.edu.

STATISTICS SOURCES

AHAM Major Home Appliance Industry Fact Book: A Comprehensive Reference on the U States Major Home Appliance Industry. Association of Home Appliance Manufacturers. • Biennial. $75.00. Includes statistical data on manufacturing, industry shipments, distribution, and ownership.

Annual Survey of Manufactures. Available from U. S. Government Printing Office. • Annual. Prices vary. Issued by the U. S. Census Bureau as an interim update to the *Census of Manufactures.* Includes data on number of manufacturing establishments in various industries, employment, labor costs, value of shipments, capital expenditures, inventories, energy costs, and assets. (See also Census Bureau home page, http://www.census.gov/.).

Refrigeration, Air Conditioning, and Warm Air Heating Equipment. U. S. Bureau of the Census. • Annual. Provides data on quantity and value of shipments by manufacturers. Formerly *Air Conditioning and Refrigeration Equipment.* (Current Industrial Reports, MA-35M.).

U. S. Industry and Trade Outlook. Available from National Technical Information Service. • Annual. $69.95. Produced by the International Trade Administration, U. S. Department of Commerce, in a "public-private" partnership with DRI/McGraw-Hill and Standard & Poor's. Provides basic data, outlook for the current year, and "Long-Term Prospects" (five-year projections) for a wide variety of products and services. Includes high technology industries. Formerly *U. S. Industrial Outlook.*

TRADE/PROFESSIONAL ASSOCIATIONS

Air-Conditioning and Refrigeration Institute. 4301 N. Fairfax Dr., Suite 425, Arlington, VA 22203. Phone: (703)524-8800 Fax: (703)528-3816 E-mail: ari@ari.org • URL: http://www.ari.org.

Air Conditioning Contractors of America. 2800 Shirlington Rd., Ste. 330, Arlington, VA 22206. Phone: (703)575-4477 Fax: (703)575-4449 E-mail: info@ms.acca.org • URL: http://www.acca.org.

American Society of Heating, Refrigerating and Air Conditioning Engineers. c/o Frank Coda, 1791 Tullie Circle, N.E., Atlanta, GA 30329. Phone: 800-527-4723 or (404)636-8400 Fax: (404)321-5478 E-mail: ashrae@ashrae.org • URL: http://www.ashrae.org.

International Mobile Air Conditioning Association Education Foundation. 6410 Southwest Blvd., Ste. 212, Fort Worth, TX 76109-3920. Phone: (817)732-4600 Fax: (817)732-9610 E-mail: info@imaca.org • URL: http://www.imaca.org • Serves the automotive, boat, and aircraft air conditioning industries. Formerly Automotive Air Conditioning Association.

Sheet Metal and Air Conditioning Contractors' National Association. 4201 Lafayette Center Dr., Chantilly, VA 20151-1209. Phone: (703)803-2980 Fax: (703)803-3732 E-mail: info@smacna.org • URL: http://www.smacna.org • Formerly Sheet Metal Contractors National Association.

OTHER SOURCES

ASHRAE Transactions. American Society of Heating, Refrigerating, and Air Conditioning Engineers, Inc. • Semiannual. Members, $169.00 per year; non-

members, $211.00 per year.

Major Energy Companies of the World. Available from Gale Cengage Learning. • Annual. $880.00. Published by Graham & Whiteside. Contains detailed information on more than 3,300 important energy companies in various countries. Industries include electricity generation, coal, natural gas, nuclear energy, petroleum, fuel distribution, and equipment for energy production.

AIR FORCE

ABSTRACTS AND INDEXES

Air University Library Index to Military Periodicals. U.S. Air Force. • Quarterly. Free to qualified personnel. Annual cumulation.

DIRECTORIES

Directory of U.S. Military Bases Worldwide. William R. Evinger, editor. Greenwood Publishing Group, Inc. • 1998. $125.00. Third edition.

ONLINE DATABASES

Information Bank Abstracts. New York Times Index Dept. • Provides indexing and abstracting of current affairs, primarily from the final late edition of *The New York Times* and the Eastern edition of *The Wall Street Journal.* Time period is 1969 to present, with daily updates. Inquire as to online cost and availability.

PERIODICALS AND NEWSLETTERS

Air Force Magazine: The Force Behind the Force. Air Force Association. • Monthly. $30.00 per year.

Air Force Times. Army Times Publishing Co. • Weekly. $52.00 per year. In two editions: Domestic and International. *Supplement* available.

Airman: Official Magazine of the U.S. Air Force. Available from U.S. Government Printing Office. • Monthly. $41.00 per year.

STATISTICS SOURCES

Annual Report of the Secretary of Defense. U.S. Department of Defense, Office of the Secretary. • Annual.

Budget of the United States Government. U.S. Office of Management and Budget. Available from U.S. Government Printing Office. • Annual. $52.00.

Military Prime Contract Awards and Subcontract Payments. U.S. Department of Defense, Office of the Secretary. • Annual.

TRADE/PROFESSIONAL ASSOCIATIONS

Air Force Aid Society. 241 18th St. S, Ste. 202, Langley Air Force Base, Arlington, VA 22202. Phone: 800-769-8951 or (703)607-3034 Fax: (703)607-3022 E-mail: dvosburg@afas.org • URL: http://www.afas.org • Collects and holds funds to relieve the distress of active, retired, and selected Reserve Air Force personnel and their dependents, including those of deceased personnel. Operates through local units on all major U.S. Air Force installations worldwide. Education Loan programs are offered to members, to assist in financing postsecondary education; education grants are also offered to dependent children of active duty, retired, and deceased Air Force members.

Air Force Association. 1501 Lee Hwy., Arlington, VA 22209-1198. Phone: 800-727-3337 or (703)247-5800 Fax: (703)247-5853 E-mail: polcom@afa.org • URL: http://www.afa.org • Promotes public understanding of aerospace power and the pivotal role it plays in the security of the nation.

Air Force Historical Foundation. 1535 Command Dr., Ste. A-122, 1535 Command Dr., Suite A-122, Andrews AFB, MD 20762-7002. Phone: (301)736-1959 Fax: (301)981-3574 E-mail: afhf@earthlink.net • URL: http://www.afhistoricalfoundation.com • Preserves the history of American air power and the annals of the U.S. Air Force, its components,

subsidiaries, and affiliates. Collects and disseminates historical information on air subjects.

Air Force Sergeants Association. 5211 Auth Rd., Suitland, MD 20746. Phone: 800-638-0594 or (301)899-3500 Fax: (301)899-8136 E-mail: staff@hqafsa.org • URL: http://www.hqafsa.org • Any enlisted man or woman, active or retired, in the Air Force, Air National Guard, Air Force Reserve, Army Air Corps, or Army Air Forces; women auxiliaries. Works to: promote, preserve, and uphold fair and equitable legislation as it pertains to the welfare of the airmen who served and are serving in the U.S.A. F.; maintain the highest professional standards and integrity among members; promote the interests of members, the U.S., and the rest of the "free world"; promote religious, educational, and recreational activities among members, in order to develop a better understanding and mutual respect. Sponsors educational seminars, Air Force training, JOBCAP - a job placement service, and programs for retired members. Provides congressional representation, insurance, and other services.

OTHER SOURCES

Carroll's Defense Organization Charts. Carroll Publishing. • Every six weeks. $1,500.00 per year. Provides more than 200 large, fold-out paper charts showing personnel relationships in 2,400 U. S. military offices. Charts are also available online and on CD-ROM.

AIR FREIGHT

See also: FREIGHT TRANSPORT

ABSTRACTS AND INDEXES

Business Periodicals Index. H. W. Wilson Co. • 11 times a year. Quarterly and annual cumulations. Price varies.

DIRECTORIES

Air Freight Directory. Air Cargo Inc. • Publication includes: Directory of more than 500 motor carriers contracting with Air Cargo, Inc. for delivery and pick up of freight. Air Cargo is a ground service specialist organization jointly owned by 18 major air carriers. Entries include: Airport city and code, firm name, address, phone, and services offered. Principal content of publication is chart of service points and rates.

National Customs Brokers and Forwarders Association of America Membership Direc tory. National Customs Brokers and Forwarders Association of America. • Annual. $25.00. Lists about 600 customs brokers, international air cargo agents, and freight forwarders in the U.S.

OAG Air Cargo Guide. OAG Worldwide. • Monthly. $239.00 per year. Shows current domestic and international air freight schedules. Diskette edition, $449.00 per year.

Quick Caller Area Air Cargo Directory. Fourth Seacoast Publishing Co., Inc. • Annual. $19.95 for each regional edition. Six regionals. Reference source for the air cargo industry.

ENCYCLOPEDIAS AND DICTIONARIES

Macmillan Encyclopedia of Transportation. Available from Gale Cengage Learning. • 1999. $450.00. Six volumes. Published by Macmillan Reference USA. Covers the business, technology, and history of transportation on land, on water, in the air, and in space. Includes definitions, cross-references, and 200 color illustrations.

ONLINE DATABASES

Management Contents. Gale Cengage Learning. • Covers a wide range of management, financial, marketing, personnel, and administrative topics. About 150 leading business journals are indexed and abstracted from 1974 to date, with monthly updating. Inquire as to online cost and availability.

PROMT: Predicasts Overview of Markets and Technology. Gale Cengage Learning. • Companies, products, applied technologies and markets. U.S. and international literature coverage, 1972 to date. Inquire as to online cost and availability. Provides abstracts from more than 1,600 publications. Weekly updates.

Trade & Industry Database. Gale Cengage Learning. • Provides indexing of business periodicals, January 1981 to date. Daily updates. (Full text articles from some periodicals are available online, 1983 to date. Inquire as to online cost and availability).

TRIS: Transportation Research Information Service. National Research Council. • Contains abstracts and citations to a wide range of transportation literature, 1968 to present, with monthly updates. Includes references to the literature of air transportation, highways, ships and shipping, railroads, trucking, and urban mass transportation. Formerly *TRIS-ONLINE.* Inquire as to online cost and availability.

PERIODICALS AND NEWSLETTERS

Air Cargo News. Air Cargo News, Inc. • Monthly. $39.95 per year.

Air Cargo World: International Trends and Analysis. • Monthly. $58.00 per year. Provides news and information concerning air freight carriers, freight forwarding, and cargo operations at airports.

Air Transport World. Penton Media Inc. • Monthly. Free to qualified personnel, others, $55.00 per year. Includes supplement *World Airline Reports.*

Aviation Week and Space Technology. McGraw-Hill Aviation Week Group. • Monthly. $92.00 per year.

Cargo Facts: The Airfreight and Express Industry Newsletter of Record. Air Cargo Management Group. • Monthly. $345.00 per year. Newsletter. Provides analysis of developments in the air freight and express industry.

The Journal of Commerce. Commonwealth Business Media. • Weekly. $146.00 per year. Topics include transatlantic shipping, domestic shipping, customs brokers, freight forwarders, ports, air freight, containerization, and other aspects of transportation and shipping logistics. Formerly *Journal of Commerce.*

RESEARCH CENTERS AND INSTITUTES

Transportation Center. Northwestern University, 600 Foster St., Evanston, IL 60208-4055. Phone: (847)491-7287 Fax: (847)491-3090 E-mail: tc-info@northwestern.edu • URL: http://www.nutc.northwestern.edu/public.

STATISTICS SOURCES

Air Transport. Air Transport Association of America. • Annual. $20.00.

FAA Aviation Forecasts. Federal Aviation Administration. Available from U. S. Government Printing Office. • Annual. $44.00.

TRADE/PROFESSIONAL ASSOCIATIONS

Air and Expedited Motor Carriers Association. 1600 Duke St., Ste. 400, Alexandria, VA 22314. Phone: (703)519-0335 Fax: (703)519-1716 E-mail: info@aemca.org • URL: http://www.aemca.org.

Air Transport Association of America. 1301 Pennsylvania Ave., Suite 1100, Washington, DC 20004-7017. Phone: (202)626-4000 Fax: (202)626-4166 E-mail: ata@air-lines.org • URL: http://www.air-lines.org.

Cargo Airline Association. 1220 19th St. NW, Ste. 400, Washington, DC 20036. Phone: (202)293-1030 Fax: (202)293-4377 E-mail: info@cargoair.org • URL: http://www.cargoair.org • Represents the interests of all-cargo air carriers.

International Federation of Freight Forwarders Associations. Schaffhauserstrasse 104, PO Box 364,

CH-8152 Glattbrugg, Switzerland. Phone: 41 43 2116500 Fax: 41 43 2116565 E-mail: info@fita.com • URL: http://www.fiata.com/.

Regional Airline Association. 2025 M St. NW, Ste. 800, Washington, DC 20036-3309. Phone: (202)367-1170 Fax: (202)367-2170 E-mail: raa@raa.org • URL: http://www.raa.org • Regional air carriers engaged in the transportation of passengers, cargo, or mail on a scheduled basis; persons, companies, and organizations engaged in pursuits related to commercial aviation; colleges and universities, state and local governments, and state aviation associations. Responds to community, consumer, and public needs for air transportation and aviation facilities and to help establish a healthy business, regulatory, and legislative climate that enables members to profit through service to the nation and the flying public. Supports programs for improving safety and reliability of air transportation and air commerce; provides a forum for exchange of ideas and information.

OTHER SOURCES

Aviation Law Reports. CCH, Inc. • Semimonthly. $2,155.00 per year. Four looseleaf volumes.

AIR PILOTS

BIBLIOGRAPHIES

Aviation. Available from U. S. Government Printing Office. • Annual. Free. Lists government publications. (GPO Subject Bibliography Number 18).

DIRECTORIES

Airport/Facility Directory. U.S. National Ocean Service. • Covers: Non-military airports in the continental United States; separate volumes cover the southeast, northeast, northwest, east central, north central, southwest, and south central states (including Puerto Rico and the Virgin Islands). Entries include: Airport name, location, weather service phone number, control center frequencies, and information concerning navigational and other aids and systems.

AOPA Aviation U.S.A. Aircraft Owners and Pilots Association. • Semiannual. Free to members. Price on Application. Primarily for pilots.

Jet and Propjet: Corporate Directory. AvCom International Inc. • Annual. $21.95. Owners of business jet and turboprop aircraft. Worldwide coverage. Formerly *Propjet.*

List of Certificated Pilot Schools. Federal Aviation Administration. Available from U. S. Government Printing Office. • Annual $4.50.

Professional Pilot-FBO Directory. Queensmith Communications Corp. • Annual. $8.00. Includes information for about 1,600 airports and fixed-base operators.

HANDBOOKS AND MANUALS

An Invitation to Fly: Basics for the Private Pilot. Dennis Glaeser and others. Brooks/Cole. • 2003. $77.95. Seventh edition. Prepares beginning pilots for FAA written test. (Aviation Series).

PERIODICALS AND NEWSLETTERS

Air Line Pilot; The Magazine of Professional Flight Deck Crews. Air Line Pilots Association. • 10 times a year. $30.00 per year.

AOPA Pilot. Aircraft Owners and Pilots Association. • Monthly. Members, $39.00 per year; qualified organizations, $21.00 per year.

FAA Aviation News. Federal Aviation Administration. Available from U. S. Government Printing Office. • Bimonthly. $28.00. per year. Designed to help airmen become safer pilots. Includes updates on major rule changes and proposals.

Flight International. Reed Business Information. • Weekly. $140.00 per year. Technical aerospace coverage.

Flying. Hachette Filipacchi Media U.S., Inc. • Monthly. Includes three *Special Issues.* Price on application.

Plane and Pilot. Werner Publishing Corp. • Monthly. $9.97 per year.

Professional Pilot Magazine. Queensmith Communications Corp. • Monthly. $36.00 per year. Edited for career pilots in all areas of aviation: airline, corporate, charter, and military. Includes flying technique, avionics, navigation, accident analysis, career planning, corporate profiles, and business aviation news.

RESEARCH CENTERS AND INSTITUTES

Institute of Aviation. University of Illinois. One Airport Rd., Savoy, IL 61874. Phone: (217)244-8601 E-mail: s-allen2@uiuc.edu • URL: http://www.aviation.uiuc.edu.

TRADE/PROFESSIONAL ASSOCIATIONS

Air Line Pilots Association, International. 1625 Massachusetts Ave. NW, Washington, DC 20036. Phone: (703)689-2270 Fax: (703)689-4370 E-mail: communications@alpa.org • URL: http://www.alpa.org • Conducts collective bargaining activities of airline pilots. Promotes all aspects of aviation safety and security.

Aircraft Owners and Pilots Association. 421 Aviation Way, Frederick, MD 21701. Phone: 800-872-2672 or (301)695-2000 Fax: (301)695-2375 E-mail: aopahq@aopa.org • URL: http://www.aopa.org.

Allied Pilots Association. 14600 Trinity Blvd., Ste. 500, O'Connell Bldg., Fort Worth, TX 76155-2512. Phone: 800-323-1470 or (817)302-2272 Fax: (817)302-2152 E-mail: public-comment@alliedpilots.org • URL: http://www.alliedpilots.org • Independent group originating from the Air Line Pilots Association. Collective bargaining agent for the pilots of American Airlines.

International Council of Aircraft Owner and Pilot Associations. 421 Aviation Way, Frederick, MD 21701. Phone: (301)695-2220 Fax: (301)695-2375 E-mail: airmail@iaopa.org • URL: http://www.iaopa.org.

Lawyer-Pilots Bar Association. PO Box 1510, Edgewater, MD 21037. Phone: (410)571-1750 Fax: (410)571-1780 E-mail: lpba@lan2wan.com • URL: http://www.lpba.org • Lawyers who are licensed pilots and engaged in the practice of aviation law or interested in aviation. Is concerned with law, safety, and general aviation.

National Association of Flight Instructors. EAA Aviation Center. P.O. Box 3086, Oshkosh, WI 54903-3086. Phone: 800-843-3612 or (920)426-6801 Fax: (920)426-4881 E-mail: nafi@eaa.org • URL: http://www.nafinet.org.

Ninety-Nines, International Organization of Women Pilots. Will Rogers World Airport, 7100 Terminal Dr., Oklahoma City, OK 73159. Phone: 800-994-1929 or (405)685-7969 Fax: (405)685-7985 E-mail: ihq99@cs.com • URL: http://www.ninety-nines.org • Licensed women pilots. Formerly Ninety-Nines International Women Pilots.

Society of Experimental Test Pilots. P.O. Box 986, Lancaster, CA 93584-0986. Phone: (661)942-9574 Fax: (661)940-0398 E-mail: setp@setp.org • URL: http://www.setp.org.

Whirly-Girls - International Women Helicopter Pilots. PO Box 265, Pinehurst, TX 77362. Phone: (650)462-1441 Fax: (650)323-3840 E-mail: tcoreywg@aol.com • URL: http://www.whirlygirls.org • Women helicopter pilots. Stimulates interest among women in rotary-wing aircraft.

AIR POLLUTION

See also: ENVIRONMENT

GENERAL WORKS

Pollution: Causes, Effects, and Control. R. M. Harrison. Springer-Verlag. • 2001. $62.00. Fourth edition. Published by The Royal Society of Chemistry. A basic introduction to pollution of air, water, and land. Includes discussions of pollution control technologies.

ABSTRACTS AND INDEXES

Environment Abstracts. Congressional Information Service, Inc. • Monthly. Price varies. Provides multidisciplinary coverage of the world's environmental literature. Incorporates *Acid Rain Abstracts.*

Environment Abstracts Annual: A Guide to the Key Environmental Literature of the Year. Congressional Information Service, Inc. • Annual. $495.00. A yearly cumulation of *Environment Abstracts.*

Environmental Knowledge Base: An Electronic Bibliography Featuring Citations and Abstracts of Scientific and Popular Articles on Environmental Issues, Including Social Policy, Economics, Regulatory, and Legal Topics. Environmental Studies Institute. • Monthly. Price varies. An index to current environmental literature. Formerly *Environmental Periodicals Bibliography.*

Excerpta Medica: Environmental Health and Pollution Control. Elsevier. • 16 times a year. Institutions, $3,246.00 per year. Section 46 of *Excerpta Medica.* Covers air, water, and land pollution and noise control.

NTIS Alerts: Environmental Pollution & Control. National Technical Information Service. • Semimonthly. $245.00 per year. Provides descriptions of government-sponsored research reports and software, with ordering information. Covers the following categories of environmental pollution: air, water, solid wastes, radiation, pesticides, and noise. Formerly *Abstract Newsletter.*

Pollution Abstracts. Cambridge Information Group. • Monthly. $1,390.00 per year. Includes print and online editions; with index, $1,515.00 per year.

ALMANACS AND YEARBOOKS

Environmental Viewpoints. Gale Cengage Learning. • 1993. $195.00. Three volumes. $65.00 per volume. A compendium of excerpts of about 200 articles on a wide variety of environmental topics, selected from both popular and professional periodicals. Arranged alphabetically by topic, with a subject/keyword index.

Gale Environmental Almanac. Gale Cengage Learning. • 1993. $115.00. Contains 15 chapters, each on a broad topic related to the environment, such as "Waste and Recycling." Each chapter has a topical overview, charts, statistics, and illustrations. Includes a glossary of environmental terms and a bibliography.

CD-ROM DATABASES

Environment Abstracts on CD-ROM. LEXIS-NEXIS. • Quarterly. $1,295.00 per year. Contains the following CD-ROM databases: *Environment Abstracts, Energy Abstracts,* and *Acid Rain Abstracts.* Length of coverage varies.

DIRECTORIES

Gale Environmental Sourcebook: A Guide to Organizations, Agencies, and Publications. Gale Cengage Learning. • 1993. $115.00. Second edition. A directory of print and non-print information sources on a wide variety of environmental topics.

Pollution Engineering Buyer's Guide. BNP Media. • Publication includes: Lists of about 32,000 suppliers of equipment and services for the environmental control field, and about 2,500 companies providing independent services as consultants, contractors, or managers for the pollution control industry and other industries concerned with the environment. Entries include: Company name, address, phone.

Pollution Equipment News Buyer's Guide. Rimbach Publishing, Inc. • Annual. $100.00. Over 3,000 manufacturers of pollution control equipment and products.

ENCYCLOPEDIAS AND DICTIONARIES

Encyclopedia of Energy. Cutler J. Cleveland, editor. Elsevier, Inc. • 2004. $1,560.00. Six volumes. Covers all aspects of energy sources and energy-related environmental issues.

Encyclopedia of Environmental Science. John Mongillo and Linda Zierdt-Warshaw, editors. Greenwood Publishing Group, Inc. • 2000. $99.95. Provides information on more than 1,000 topics relating to the environment. Includes graphs, tables, maps, illustrations, and 400 Web site addresses.

Encyclopedia of Global Change: Environmental Change and Human Society. Andrew S. Goudie, editor. Oxford University Press. • 2001. $275.00. Two volumes. Contains 300 signed articles on a wide variety of topics relating to changes in the environment and the atmosphere. Includes bibliographies and illustrations.

Environmental Encyclopedia. Gale Cengage Learning. • 2003. $275.00. Third edition. Provides over 1,300 articles on all aspects of the environment. Written in non-technical style.

Pollution A to Z. Gale Cengage Learning. • 2003. $195.00. Two volumes. Provides encyclopedic coverage of many aspects of environmental pollution, including air, water, noise, and soil. (Macmillan Reference USA imprint.).

Wiley Encyclopedia of Energy and the Environment. Attilio Bisio and Sharon Boots. John Wiley and Sons, Inc. • 1996. $285.00. Abriged edition. Two volumes. Covers a wide variety of energy and environmental topics, including legal and policy issues. (Encyclopedia of Energy and the Environment Series: Vol. 2).

Wiley Encyclopedia of Environmental Pollution and Cleanup. Robert A. Meyers, editor. John Wiley and Sons, Inc. • 1999. $350.00. Two volumes. Presents generally nontechnical, basic coverage of environmental hazards and methods of detection and cleanup, with consideration of risk assessment, regulatory policy, and economic factors.

HANDBOOKS AND MANUALS

Industrial Pollution Prevention Handbook. Harry M. Freeman. McGraw-Hill. • 1994. $115.00.

Statistics for the Environment: Statistical Aspects of Health and the Environment. Vic Barnett and others. John Wiley and Sons, Inc. • 1999. $180.00. Two volumes. Vol. 3, $205.00; vol. 4, $225.00. Contains articles on the statistical analysis and interpretation of environmental monitoring and sampling data. Areas covered include meteorology, pollution of the environment, and forest resources. (Statistics for the Environment Series).

INTERNET DATABASES

Manufacturing Profiles. U. S. Bureau of the Census. Phone: (301)763-4636 E-mail: webmaster@census.gov • URL: http://www.census.gov/prod/www/abs/mfg-prof.html • The Census Bureau makes available free on PDF (Portable Document Format) an annual consolidation of the entire Current Industrial Report series, presenting "all the data compiled." Contains statistics on production, shipments, inventories, consumption, exports, imports, and orders for a wide variety of manufactured products.

ONLINE DATABASES

Pollution Abstracts [online]. Cambridge Scientific Abstracts. • Provides indexing and abstracting of international, environmentally related literature, 1970 to date. Monthly updates. Inquire as to online cost and availability.

PERIODICALS AND NEWSLETTERS

Air and Waste Management Association Journal. • Monthly. Individuals, $150.00 per year; institutions, $329.00 per year: nonprofit institutions, $229.00 per year. Includes annual *Directory of Governmental Air Pollution Agencies.*

Air Pollution Control. BNA, Inc. • Biweekly. $798.00 per year. Newsletter.

Atmospheric Environment. Elsevier Science. • 36 times a year. Qualified personnel, $431.00 per year; institutions, $5,368.00 per year. Text in English, French and German.

Environmental Business Journal: Strategic Information for a Changing Industry. Environmental Business International, Inc. • Monthly. $495.00 per year. Newsletter. Includes both industrial and financial information relating to individual companies and to the environmental industry in general. Covers air pollution, wat es, U. S. Department of Health and Human Services. Provides conference, workshop, and symposium proceedings, as well as extensive reviews of environmental prospects.

Environmental Regulation: State Capitals. Wakeman-Walworth, Inc. • 50 times a year. $245.00 per year; print and online editions, $350.00 per year. Newsletter. Formerly *From the State Capitals: Environmental Regulation.*

RESEARCH CENTERS AND INSTITUTES

Air Pollution Research Center. University of California, Riverside. 205 Fawcett Laboratory, Riverside, CA 92521. Phone: (909)787-5124 Fax: (909)787-5004 E-mail: ratkins@mail.ucr.edu • URL: http://www.cnas.ucr.edu/.

Air Pollution Research Laboratory. University of Rhode Island. 121 Wales Hall, Kingston, RI 02881. Phone: (401)874-2535 Fax: (401)874-2355.

Center for Energy and Environmental Studies. Carnegie Mellon University Department of Engineering and Public Policy. Baker Hall 128-A, Pittsburgh, PA 15213. Phone: (412)268-5897 Fax: (412)268-1089 E-mail: rubin@cmu.edu.

Environmental Health Sciences Research Laboratory. Tulane University. 1440 Canal St., Ste. 2100, New Orleans, LA 70112. Phone: (504)588-5374 Fax: (504)584-1726 E-mail: assafa@tulane.edu • URL: http://www.sph.tulane.edu.

Environmental Resources Research Institute. Pennsylvania State University. 100 Land and Water Resource Bldg., University Park, PA 16802. Phone: (814)863-0291 Fax: (814)865-3378 E-mail: ajm2@psu.edu • URL: http://www.environment.erri.psu.edu.

STATISTICS SOURCES

Air Quality Data. U.S. Environmental Protection Agency. • Annual.

Annual Survey of Manufactures. Available from U. S. Government Printing Office. • Annual. Prices vary. Issued by the U. S. Census Bureau as an interim update to the *Census of Manufactures.* Includes data on number of manufacturing establishments in various industries, employment, labor costs, value of shipments, capital expenditures, inventories, energy costs, and assets. (See also Census Bureau home page, http://www.census.gov/.).

Health and Environment in America's Top-Rated Cities: A Statistical Profile. Grey House Publishing. • Biennial. $125.00. Covers 75 U. S. cities. Includes statistical and other data on a wide variety of topics, such as air quality, water quality, recycling, hospitals, physicians, health care costs, death rates, infant mortality, accidents, and suicides.

OECD Environmental Indicators. Organization for Economic Cooperation and Development. • Annual.

$27.00. Provides statistical information relating to climate change, air pollution, biodiversity, waste management, water resources, and other environmental topics.

Standard & Poor's Industry Surveys. Standard & Poor's. • Semiannual. $1,800.00. Two looseleaf volumes. Includes monthly *Supplements*. Provides detailed, individual surveys of 52 major industry groups. Each survey is revised on a semiannual basis. Also includes "Monthly Investment Review" (industry group investment analysis) and monthly "Trends & Projections" (economic analysis).

Statistical Record of the Environment. Gale Cengage Learning. • 1996. $130.00. Third edition. Provides over 875 charts, tables, and graphs of major environmental statistics, arranged by subject. Covers population growth, hazardous waste, nuclear energy, acid rain, pesticides, and other subjects related to the environment. A keyword index is included. (Gale Environmental Library Series).

U. S. Industry and Trade Outlook. Available from National Technical Information Service. • Annual. $69.95. Produced by the International Trade Administration, U. S. Department of Commerce, in a "public-private" partnership with DRI/McGraw-Hill and Standard & Poor's. Provides basic data, outlook for the current year, and "Long-Term Prospects" (five-year projections) for a wide variety of products and services. Includes high technology industries. Formerly *U. S. Industrial Outlook*.

TRADE/PROFESSIONAL ASSOCIATIONS

Air and Waste Management Association. One Gateway Center, 3rd Fl., 420 Duquesne Blvd., Pittsburgh, PA 15222. Phone: 800-270-3444 or (412)232-3444 Fax: (412)232-3450 E-mail: info@awma.org • URL: http://www.awma.org.

Association of Local Air Pollution Control Officials. 444 N Capitol St., NW, Ste. 307, Washington, DC 20001. Phone: (202)624-7864 Fax: (202)624-7863 E-mail: 4clnair@4cleanair.org • URL: http://www.4cleanairworld.org.

OTHER SOURCES

Environment Reporter. BNA, Inc. • Weekly. $3,166.00 per year. 18 looseleaf volumes. Covers legal aspects of wide variety of environmental concerns.

AIR TRAFFIC

See: AIR TRAVEL

AIR TRANSPORTATION

See: AIR FREIGHT; AIR TRAVEL; AIRLINE INDUSTRY

AIR TRAVEL

See also: AIRLINE INDUSTRY

GENERAL WORKS

Safe Trip Abroad. Available from U. S. Government Printing Office. • 2002. $2.50. Issued by the Bureau of Consular Affairs, U. S. State Department (http://www.state.gov). Provides practical advice for international travel.

ABSTRACTS AND INDEXES

Business Periodicals Index. H. W. Wilson Co. • 11 times a year. Quarterly and annual cumulations. Price varies.

BIBLIOGRAPHIES

Travel and Tourism. Available from U. S. Government Printing Office. • Annual. Free. Issued by the Superintendent of Documents. A list of government publications on the travel industry and tourism. Formerly *Mass Transit, Travel and Tourism.* (Subject Bibliography No. 302.).

DIRECTORIES

ASU Travel Guide. Christopher Gil, editor. Airline Services Unlimited. • Covers: over 3,700 listing for airlines, lodgings, tours, car rental companies, and cruise lines, which allow travel discounts to airline employees worldwide. Entries include: Name, address, and phone of facility or service; description; regular price and type and amount of discount; credit cards accepted; validity dates; booking procedures; whether parents and retired airline employees are eligible.

OAG Desktop Flight Guide, North American Edition. OAG Worldwide. • Biweekly. $285.00 per year. Provides detailed airline travel schedules for the U. S., Canada, Mexico, and the Caribbean. Includes aircraft seat charts and airport diagrams. Formerly *Official Airline Guide, North American Edition*.

OAG Flight Guide: Worldwide. OAG Worldwide. • Monthly. $469.00 per year. Provides detailed airline schedules for international travel. Travel within North America not included.

HANDBOOKS AND MANUALS

Fly-Rights: A Consumer Guide to Air Travel. Available from U. S. Government Printing Office. • 1999. $4.00. 11th edition. Issued by the U. S. Department of Transportation. Explains the rights and responsibilities of air travelers.

Health Information for International Travel. Available from U. S. Government Printing Office. • Annual. Issued by Centers for Disease Control, U. S. Department of Health and Human Services. Discusses potential health risks of international travel and specifies vaccinations required by different countries.

Health Information for International Travel. U.S. Dept. of Health and Human Services, Centers for Disease Control and Prefabricated. • Annual. $20.00. Produced by the Centers for Disease Control and Prevention (CDC). Primarily edited for "healthcare providers who administer pre- and post-travel counseling and care." Also serves as a reference for airlines, cruise lines, and the travel industry in general. Covers such items as injuries during travel, motion sickness, disabilities, vaccines, insect repellents, and travel with children. Sometimes known as "The Yellow Book.".

ONLINE DATABASES

Management Contents. Gale Cengage Learning. • Covers a wide range of management, financial, marketing, personnel, and administrative topics. About 150 leading business journals are indexed and abstracted from 1974 to date, with monthly updating. Inquire as to online cost and availability.

Newspaper Abstracts Daily. ProQuest Inc. • Provides online coverage (citations and abstracts) of 25 major newspapers. Covers business, economics, current affairs, health, fitness, sports, education, technology, government, consumer affairs, psychology, the arts, and the social sciences. Time period is 1986 to date, with daily updates. Inquire as to online cost and availability.

Trade & Industry Database. Gale Cengage Learning. • Provides indexing of business periodicals, January 1981 to date. Daily updates. (Full text articles from some periodicals are available online, 1983 to date. Inquire as to online cost and availability).

United States International Air Travel Statistics. U. S. Department of Transportation, Center for Transportation Information. • Provides detailed statistics on air passenger travel between the U. S. and foreign countries for both scheduled and charter flights. Time period is 1975 to date, with monthly updates. Inquire as to online cost and availability.

PERIODICALS AND NEWSLETTERS

Aviation Week and Space Technology. McGraw-Hill Aviation Week Group. • Monthly. $92.00 per year.

Consumer Reports Travel Letter. Consumers Union of U.S. Inc. • Description: Provides travelers with information and advice on travel goods and services. Discusses such topics as air and rail passes, air fare, hotel rates, car rental fees, and techniques for optimizing foreign exchange rates.

Frequent Flyer: For Business People Who Must Travel. OAG Worldwide. • Monthly. $89.00 per year to individuals. Also known as *OAG Frequent Flyer*. Edited for business travelers. Contains news of frequent flyer programs, airport developments, airline services, and business travel trends. Available only with *OAG Flight Guide*.

Front Row Advisor: Business and First Class Air Travel and the Alluring World of Free Upgrades. Diversified Specialties, Inc. • Bimonthly. $145.00 per year. Newsletter. Contains information on opportunities provided by airlines to upgrade coach seats to business class, including frequent flyer upgrades.

Inside Flyer. • Monthly. $36.00 per year. Newsletter. Provides information relating to frequent flyer awards and air travel.

Jax Fax Travel Marketing Magazine: The Official Leisure Travel Booking Magazine. Jet Airtransport Exchange, Inc. • Monthly. $15.00 per year. Trade magazine for travel agents.

Newsline: Research News from the U. S. Travel Data Center. U.S. National Research Council. • Monthly. $55.00 per year. Newsletter. Covers trends in the U. S. travel industry.

Summary of Health Information for International Travel. U. S. Department of Health and Human Services. • Biweekly. Formerly *Weekly Summary of Health Information for International Travel*.

Travel Smart: Pay Less, Enjoy More. Dunan Communications, Inc. • Monthly. $39.00 per year. Newsletter. Provides information and recommendations for travelers. Emphasis is on travel value and opportunities for bargains. Incorporates *Joy of Travel*.

RESEARCH CENTERS AND INSTITUTES

Travel Industry Association of America-Research Dept. 1100 New York Ave., N.W., No. 450, Washington, DC 20005-3934. Phone: (202)408-8422 Fax: (202)408-1255 E-mail: feedback@tia.org • URL: http://www.tia.org • Conducts economic, statistical, and market research relating to the U. S. travel industry. Affiliated with the Travel Industry Association of America.

STATISTICS SOURCES

Air Carrier Traffic Statistics Monthly. U. S. Department of Transportation. • Monthly. Provides passenger traffic data for large airlines.

Air Transport. Air Transport Association of America. • Annual. $20.00.

Economic Review of Travel in America. Travel Industry Association of America. • Annual. Members, $75.00; non-members, $125.00. Presents a statistical summary of travel in the U.S., including travel expenditures, travel industry employment, tax data, international visitors, etc.

FAA Aviation Forecasts. Federal Aviation Administration. Available from U. S. Government Printing Office. • Annual. $44.00.

Outlook for Travel and Tourism. Travel Industry Association of America. • Annual. Members, $100.00; non-members, $175.00. Contains forecasts of the performance of the U. S. travel industry, including air travel, business travel, recreation (attractions), and accomodations.

Summary of International Travel to the United

States. International Trade Administration, Tourism Industries. U.S. Dept. of Commerce. • Monthly. Quarterly and annual versions available. Provides statistics on air travel to the U.S. from each of 90 countries. Formerly *Summary and Analysis of International Travel to the United States.*

World Air Transport Statistics. International Air Transport Association. • Annual. $225.00.

TRADE/PROFESSIONAL ASSOCIATIONS

Air Traffic Control Association. 1101 King St., Ste. 300, Alexandria, VA 22314. Phone: (703)299-2430 Fax: (703)299-2437 E-mail: info@atca.org • URL: http://www.atca.org • Air traffic controllers; private, commercial, and military pilots; private and business aircraft owners and operators; aircraft and electronics engineers; airlines, aircraft manufacturers, and electronic and human engineering firms. Promotes the establishment and maintenance of a safe and efficient air traffic control system. Conducts special surveys and studies on air traffic control problems. Participates in aviation community conferences.

Air Transport Association of America. 1301 Pennsylvania Ave., Suite 1100, Washington, DC 20004-7017. Phone: (202)626-4000 Fax: (202)626-4166 E-mail: ata@air-lines.org • URL: http://www.air-lines.org.

Aviation Consumer Action Project. 529 14th St. NW, No. 923, Washington, DC 20045. Phone: 800-588-ACAP or (202)638-4000 Fax: (202)638-0746 E-mail: info@awda.org • URL: http://www.acap1971.org • Promotes the interests of consumers in improved ground and air safety, environmental protection, affordable air fares, and expanded passenger rights. Activities include distributing passenger information leaflets and advocating passenger interests before federal regulatory agencies and the courts. Seeks: lower fares and increased competition in domestic and international air transportation; improved airline crash survivability; enhanced standards and equipment for crash prevention; elimination of unfair consumer practices; increased government accessibility.

Aviation Safety Institute. PO Box 690, 6797 N High St., Worthington, OH 43085. Phone: (614)885-4242 Fax: (614)793-1708 E-mail: 110364.3550@compuserve.com • URL: http://www.aviationsafetyinstitute.com • Acts as an independent party not aligned with industry or government to promote and improve aviation safety. Activities include: operating an anonymous hazard reporting system; conducting safety education programs and seminars; maintaining a computerized safety information system; performing safety audits and consulting services; conducting aircraft accident investigations and research projects on topics such as pilot and crew fatigue. Conducts research.

Flight Safety Foundation. 601 Madison St., Ste. 300, Alexandria, VA 22314-1756. Phone: (703)739-6700 Fax: (703)739-6708 E-mail: wahdan@flightsafety.org • URL: http://www.flightsafety.org • Aerospace manufacturers, domestic and foreign airlines, insurance companies, fuel and oil companies, schools, and miscellaneous organizations having an interest in the promotion of safety in flight. Sponsors safety audits. Compiles statistics.

International Air Transport Association. 703 Waterford Way, NW 62nd Ave., Ste. 600, Miami, FL 33126. Phone: (305)264-7772 Fax: (305)264-8088 E-mail: membership@iaaglobal.org • URL: http://www1.iata.org/ • Represents the airline industries; promotes safe, reliable, secure and economical air services worldwide.

International Airline Passengers Association. PO Box 700188, Dallas, TX 75370-0188. Phone: 800-821-4272 or (972)404-9980 Fax: (972)233-5348 E-mail: info.dallas@iapa.com • URL: http://www.iapa.com • Persons who are frequent users of airlines. Represents frequent flyers in matters of safety, comfort, convenience, and economy. Conducts semiannual survey regarding travel preferences and opinions in order to present consumers' viewpoints to airlines and government agencies. Provides discounts on hotels and car rentals. Disseminates travel information through magazines and literature. Compiles statistics. **Convention/Meeting:** none.

National Air Carrier Association. 1000 Wilson Blvd., Ste. 1700, Arlington, VA 22209. Phone: (703)358-8060 Fax: (703)358-8070 E-mail: tzoeller@naca.cc • URL: http://www.naca.cc • Represents U.S. certificated airlines specializing in low-cost scheduled and air charter operations. Assists members in the promotion of air transportation and serves as a liaison between members and U.S. government bodies that regulate air transportation.

OTHER SOURCES

Travel Law. American Lawyer Media, Inc. • Looseleaf. $149.00. Updated as needed. Emphasis is on the legal rights of travelers, including a consideration of class action suits. Includes such matters as tour operator liability, hotel responsibilities, overbooking by airlines, and frequent-flyer issues. (Law Journal Press).

AIRCRAFT INDUSTRY

See: AIRPLANE INDUSTRY

AIRCRAFT OWNERS AND PILOTS

See: AIR PILOTS; BUSINESS AVIATION

AIRLINE INDUSTRY

See also: AIR TRAVEL

GENERAL WORKS

Air Transportation: A Management Perspective. Alexander Wells. Brooks/Cole Publishing Co. • 1998. $81.95. Fourth edition.

Airlines. Alexander T. Wells and Franklin D. Richey. Krieger Publishing Co. • 1996. $275.00. Provides an overview of the commuter airline industry, including operating and management functions.

FAA Historical Chronology: Civil Aviation and the Federal Government, 1926-1996. Edmund Preston, editor. Available from U. S. Government Printing Office. • 1998. $33.50. Third edition. Issued by the Federal Aviation Administration, U. S. Department of Transportation (http://www.dot.gov). Provides a compilation of historical information about the FAA and the earlier Civil Aeronautics Board (CAB). Chronological arrangement.

Pricing and Capacity Determination in International Air Transport. Peter P. C. Haanappel. Kluwer Law International. • 1984. $66.00.

ABSTRACTS AND INDEXES

Business Periodicals Index. H. W. Wilson Co. • 11 times a year. Quarterly and annual cumulations. Price varies.

NTIS Alerts: Transportation. National Technical Information Service. • Semimonthly. $210.00 per year. Provides descriptions of government-sponsored research reports and software, with ordering information. Covers air, marine, highway, inland waterway, pipeline, and railroad transportation. Formerly *Abstract Newsletter.*

BIBLIOGRAPHIES

Federal Aviation Regulations. Available from U. S. Government Printing Office. • Annual. Free. Lists government publications. GPO Subject Bibliography Number 12.

CD-ROM DATABASES

OECD Statistical Compendium. Organization for Economic Cooperation and Development. • Semiannual. $1,905.00 per year for 1 to 10 users. CD-ROM contains more than 730,000 monthly, quarterly, and annual time series for OECD countries, 1960 to date. Includes fully searchable data on agriculture, food, economic indicators, national accounts, employment, energy, finance, industry, technology, and foreign trade. Results can be displayed in various forms.

DIRECTORIES

Airline Handbook. Aerotravel Research. • Covers: 2,000 commercial airlines (scheduled and chartered) serving over 200 nations and territories worldwide. Entries include: Airline name, address of main office, phone, telex, financial keys, number of employees, routes and destinations, aircraft fleets, passenger traffic totals, company history.

Annual Report of the Commuter Regional Airline Industry. Regional Airline Association. • Annual. $75.00. Lists commuter and regional airlines and gives statistical information.

ASU Travel Guide. Christopher Gil, editor. Airline Services Unlimited. • Covers: over 3,700 listing for airlines, lodgings, tours, car rental companies, and cruise lines, which allow travel discounts to airline employees worldwide. Entries include: Name, address, and phone of facility or service; description; regular price and type and amount of discount; credit cards accepted; validity dates; booking procedures; whether parents and retired airline employees are eligible.

International ABC Aerospace Directory. Jane's Information Group Ltd. • Covers: Approximately 28,000 companies and organizations involved in the aerospace industry, including civil and military organizations, aircraft manufacturers, Civil Aviation Authorities, air force bases, leasing companies, airport authorities, engine manufacturers, distributors of components, and maintenance contractors; international coverage. Entries include: Name, address, phone, fax, names and titles of key personnel, description of products/services.

Jane's World Airlines. Jane's Information Group Ltd. • Covers: Approximately 500 scheduled, non-scheduled, cargo, and passenger airlines; international coverage. Entries include: Airline name, address, phone, fax, fleet structure, routes operated, traffic statistics, financial data, cargo capacity, corporate structure and major subsidiaries, names and titles of executives.

National Air Transportation Association Official Membership Directory. National Air Transportation Association. • Annual. $95.00. List more than 1,000 regular, associate, and affiliate members; regular members include airport service organizations, air taxi operators, and commuter airlines.

OAG Desktop Flight Guide, North American Edition. OAG Worldwide. • Biweekly. $285.00 per year. Provides detailed airline travel schedules for the U. S., Canada, Mexico, and the Caribbean. Includes aircraft seat charts and airport diagrams. Formerly *Official Airline Guide, North American Edition.*

OAG Flight Guide: Worldwide. OAG Worldwide. • Monthly. $469.00 per year. Provides detailed airline schedules for international travel. Travel within North America not included.

Plunkett's Airline, Hotel, and Travel Industry Almanac. Plunkett Research, Ltd. • Annual. $249.95. Contains profiles of 300 leading companies, including airlines, hotels, travel agencies, theme parks, cruise lines, casinos, and car rental companies.

Regional Aviation Handbook. Shephard Press Ltd. • Annual. $90.00. Edited for regional, short-haul, and commuter airlines. Includes airline operators worldwide, manufacturers of equipment and supplies, aircraft companies, leasing companies, trade associations, and other listings.

ENCYCLOPEDIAS AND DICTIONARIES

Macmillan Encyclopedia of Transportation. Available from Gale Cengage Learning. • 1999. $450.00. Six volumes. Published by Macmillan Reference USA. Covers the business, technology, and history of transportation on land, on water, in the air, and in space. Includes definitions, cross-references, and 200 color illustrations.

FINANCIAL RATIOS

Almanac of Business and Industrial Financial Ratios. Leo Troy. Aspen Publishers, Inc. • 2003. $125.95. Includes CD-Rom. Contains financial ratios derived from federal tax returns. Ratios for each of about 200 industries are arranged according to company asset size. (Almanac of Business and Industrial Financial Ratios Series).

Annual Statement Studies. The Risk Management Association. • Annual. Median and quartile financial ratios are given for over 400 kinds of manufacturing, wholesale, retail, construction, and consumer finance establishments. Data is sorted by both asset size and sales volume. Includes a clearly written "Definition of Ratios" and an alphabetical industry index.

Annual Statement Studies: Industry Default Probabilities and Cash Flow Measures. The Risk Management Association. • Annual. $145.00. Serves as a companion volume to the original *Annual Statement Studies.* Gives probability of default estimates on a percentage scale for more than 450 industries. Includes changes in position year-by-year for eight financial statement line items and provides percentage measures of cash flow.

Industry Norms and Key Business Ratios. Desk Top Edition. Dun and Bradstreet Corp. • Annual. Five volumes. $475.00 per volume. $1,890.00 per set. Covers over 800 kinds of businesses, arranged by Standard Industrial Classification number. More detailed editions covering longer periods of time are also available.

INTERNET DATABASES

Business 2.0 Web Guide to the Best Business Links. Business 2.0 Media Inc. Phone: (415)293-4800 E-mail: support@business2.com • URL: http://www.business2.com/webguide • Web site presents an extensive, searchable directory of links to "the best, most informative, and authoritative web pages." Twenty main categories cover business, finance, career, company information, people, and technology topics, with thousands of subtopics, all linking to Web sites recommended by experienced business researchers. Fees: Free.

Fedstats. Federal Interagency Council on Statistical Policy. Phone: (202)395-7254 • URL: http://www.fedstats.gov • Web site features an efficient search facility for full-text statistics produced by more than 100 federal agencies, including the Census Bureau, the Bureau of Economic Analysis, and the Bureau of Labor Statistics. Boolean searches can be made within one agency or for all agencies combined. Links are offered to international statistical bureaus, including the UN, IMF, OECD, UNESCO, Eurostat, and 20 individual countries. Fees: Free.

FreeLunch.com. Economy.com, Inc. Phone: (610)696-8700 Fax: (610)696-1678 • URL: http://www.freelunch.com • Web site provides free access to more than 1.5 million economic and financial data series, covering industry, demographics, labor markets, prices, retail sales, government spending, trade, interest rates, housing starts, the stock market, and many other topics. Data is available for various time periods in either chart or table form. Searching

is offered. Fees: Free, but registration required. Economy.com, Inc. also offers fee-based economic analysis at *The Dismal Scientist* site (http://www.dismal.com).

ONLINE DATABASES

Globalbase. Gale Cengage Learning. • Provides more than one million online summaries of business, industrial, and economic news reports from more than 1,000 publications worldwide. Covers a wide range of material appearing in international trade journals, professional magazines, and newspapers. Time period is 1984 to date, with weekly updates. Inquire as to online cost and availability.

Management Contents. Gale Cengage Learning. • Covers a wide range of management, financial, marketing, personnel, and administrative topics. About 150 leading business journals are indexed and abstracted from 1974 to date, with monthly updating. Inquire as to online cost and availability.

PAIS International. Public Affairs Information Service, Inc. • Corresponds to the former printed publications, *PAIS Bulletin* (1976-90) and *PAIS Foreign Language Index* (1972-90), and to the current *PAIS International in Print* (1991 to date). Covers economic, political, and sociological material appearing in periodicals, books, government documents, and other publications. Updating is monthly. Inquire as to online cost and availability.

PROMT: Predicasts Overview of Markets and Technology. Gale Cengage Learning. • Companies, products, applied technologies and markets. U.S. and international literature coverage, 1972 to date. Inquire as to online cost and availability. Provides abstracts from more than 1,600 publications. Weekly updates.

Trade & Industry Database. Gale Cengage Learning. • Provides indexing of business periodicals, January 1981 to date. Daily updates. (Full text articles from some periodicals are available online, 1983 to date. Inquire as to online cost and availability).

TRIS: Transportation Research Information Service. National Research Council. • Contains abstracts and citations to a wide range of transportation literature, 1968 to present, with monthly updates. Includes references to the literature of air transportation, highways, ships and shipping, railroads, trucking, and urban mass transportation. Formerly *TRIS-ONLINE.* Inquire as to online cost and availability.

PERIODICALS AND NEWSLETTERS

Air Transport World. Penton Media Inc. • Monthly. Free to qualified personnel, others, $55.00 per year. Includes supplement *World Airline Reports.*

Airline Business Report. Access Intelligence L.L.C. • Description: Reports on financial aspects of the world airline industry. **Remarks:** Also available online and via e-mail.

Airline Business: The Voice of Airline Managements. Available from Reed Aerospace. • Monthly. $130.00 per year. Published in England by Reed Business Information. Covers management and financial topics for international airline executives.

Aviation Daily. Aviation Week Newsletter. The McGraw-Hill Cos. • Description: Concerned with air transportation and the aviation manufacturing field. Focuses on management developments and trends with specific detail on economic, financial, and operating aspects of domestic and foreign airlines, aircraft manufacturers, and allied associations. Reports on federal legislation affecting the field, and lists relevant statistics.

Aviation Week and Space Technology. McGraw-Hill Aviation Week Group. • Monthly. $92.00 per year.

Frequent Flyer: For Business People Who Must Travel. OAG Worldwide. • Monthly. $89.00 per

year to individuals. Also known as *OAG Frequent Flyer.* Edited for business travelers. Contains news of frequent flyer programs, airport developments, airline services, and business travel trends. Available only with *OAG Flight Guide.*

Professional Pilot Magazine. Queensmith Communications Corp. • Monthly. $36.00 per year. Edited for career pilots in all areas of aviation: airline, corporate, charter, and military. Includes flying technique, avionics, navigation, accident analysis, career planning, corporate profiles, and business aviation news.

Regional Airline World. Shephard Press Ltd. • 10 times a year. $130.00 per year. Covers the business, financial, and technical aspects of regional, short-haul, and commuter airline operations.

RESEARCH CENTERS AND INSTITUTES

Center for Transportation Studies. Massachusetts Institute of Technology. 77 Massachusetts Ave. Room 1-235, Cambridge, MA 02139. Phone: (617)253-5320 Fax: (617)253-4560 E-mail: sheffi@mit.edu • URL: http://www.web.mit.edu/cts/www/.

Transportation Center. Northwestern University, 600 Foster St., Evanston, IL 60208-4055. Phone: (847)491-7287 Fax: (847)491-3090 E-mail: tc-info@northwestern.edu • URL: http://www.nutc.northwestern.edu/public.

STATISTICS SOURCES

Air Carrier Financial Statistics. U. S. Department of Transportation. • Quarterly. Contains profit and loss and asset information for specific airlines.

Air Carrier Industry Scheduled Service Traffic Statistics. U. S. Department of Transportation. • Quarterly. Includes data for commuter airlines.

Air Carrier Traffic Statistics Monthly. U. S. Department of Transportation. • Monthly. Provides passenger traffic data for large airlines.

Air Transport. Air Transport Association of America. • Annual. $20.00.

Airport Activity Statistics of Certificated Route Air Carriers. U. S. Department of Transportation. Available from U. S. Government Printing Office. • Annual. $58.00.

Business Statistics of the United States. Linz Audain and Cornelia J. Strawser. Bernan Associates. • Annual. $147.00. Based on *Business Statistics,* formerly issue by the Bureau of Economic Analysis, U. S. Department of Commerce. Provides basic data for a wide variety of U. S. industries, services, and economic indicators. Most statistics are shown annually for 30 years and monthly for the most recent four years.

FAA Aviation Forecasts. Federal Aviation Administration. Available from U. S. Government Printing Office. • Annual. $44.00.

Standard & Poor's Industry Surveys. Standard & Poor's. • Semiannual. $1,800.00. Two looseleaf volumes. Includes monthly *Supplements.* Provides detailed, individual surveys of 52 major industry groups. Each survey is revised on a semiannual basis. Also includes "Monthly Investment Review" (industry group investment analysis) and monthly "Trends & Projections" (economic analysis).

Standard & Poor's Statistical Service. Current Statistics. Standard & Poor's. • Monthly. $688.00 per year. Includes 10 *Basic Statistics* sections, *Current Statistics Supplements* and *Annual Security Price Index Record.*

Survey of Current Business. Available from U. S. Government Printing Office. • Monthly. $63.00 per year. Issued by Bureau of Economic Analysis, U. S. Department of Commerce. Presents a wide variety of business and economic data.

Transportation Statistics Annual Report. Available from U. S. Government Printing Office. • Annual. $43.00. Issued by the U. S. Bureau of Transportation Statistics, Transportation Department (http://

www.bts.gov). Summarizes national data for various forms of transportation, including airlines, railroads, and motor vehicles. Information on the use of roads and highways is included.

WEFA Industrial Monitor. John Wiley and Sons, Inc. • Annual. $65.00. Prepared by industry analysts at WEFA, an economic forecasting and consulting firm (originally Wharton Econometric Forecasting Associates). Contains discussions of the outlook for major U. S. industries, with many 10-year forecasts (WEFA Web site is http://www.wefa.com).

World Air Transport Statistics. International Air Transport Association. • Annual. $225.00.

TRADE/PROFESSIONAL ASSOCIATIONS

Aeronautical Repair Station Association. 121 N Henry St., Alexandria, VA 22314-2903. Phone: (703)739-9543 Fax: (703)739-9488 E-mail: arsa@arsa.org • URL: http://www.arsa.org • Represents FAA-certified repair stations, suppliers and distributors. Assists members on regulatory and legislative issues before the FAA and other governmental agencies.

Air Line Pilots Association, International. 1625 Massachusetts Ave. NW, Washington, DC 20036. Phone: (703)689-2270 Fax: (703)689-4370 E-mail: communications@alpa.org • URL: http://www.alpa.org • Conducts collective bargaining activities for airline pilots. Promotes all aspects of aviation safety and security.

Air Transport Association of America. 1301 Pennsylvania Ave., Suite 1100, Washington, DC 20004-7017. Phone: (202)626-4000 Fax: (202)626-4166 E-mail: ata@air-lines.org • URL: http://www.air-lines.org.

International Air Transport Association. 703 Waterford Way, NW 62nd Ave., Ste. 600, Miami, FL 33126. Phone: (305)264-7772 Fax: (305)264-8088 E-mail: membership@iaaglobal.org • URL: http://www1.iata.org/ • Represents the airline industries; promotes safe, reliable, secure and economical air services worldwide.

International Airline Passengers Association. PO Box 700188, Dallas, TX 75370-0188. Phone: 800-821-4272 or (972)404-9980 Fax: (972)233-5348 E-mail: info.dallas@iapa.com • URL: http://www.iapa.com • Persons who are frequent users of airlines. Represents frequent flyers in matters of safety, comfort, convenience, and economy. Conducts semiannual survey regarding travel preferences and opinions in order to present consumers' viewpoints to airlines and government agencies. Provides discounts on hotels and car rentals. Disseminates travel information through magazines and literature. Compiles statistics. **Convention/Meeting:** none.

National Air Carrier Association. 1000 Wilson Blvd., Ste. 1700, Arlington, VA 22209. Phone: (703)358-8060 Fax: (703)358-8070 E-mail: tzoeller@naca.cc • URL: http://www.naca.cc • Represents U.S. certificated airlines specializing in low-cost scheduled and air charter operations. Assists members in the promotion of air transportation and serves as a liaison between members and U.S. government bodies that regulate air transportation.

National Air Transportation Association. 4226 King St., Alexandria, VA 22302. Phone: 800-808-6282 or (703)845-9000 Fax: (703)845-8176 E-mail: enews@nata.aero • URL: http://www.nata.aero • Represents the interests of aviation businesses nationwide. Provides vital aviation services to the airlines, the military, and business/corporate/individual aircraft owners and operators; services includes fueling, maintenance, and flight instruction.

Regional Airline Association. 2025 M St. NW, Ste. 800, Washington, DC 20036-3309. Phone: (202)367-1170 Fax: (202)367-2170 E-mail: raa@raa.org • URL: http://www.raa.org • Regional air carriers engaged in the transportation of passengers,

cargo, or mail on a scheduled basis; persons, companies, and organizations engaged in pursuits related to commercial aviation; colleges and universities, state and local governments, and state aviation associations. Responds to community, consumer, and public needs for air transportation and aviation facilities and to help establish a healthy business, regulatory, and legislative climate that enables members to profit through service to the nation and the flying public. Supports programs for improving safety and reliability of air transportation and air commerce; provides a forum for exchange of ideas and information.

OTHER SOURCES

Aviation Law Reports. CCH, Inc. • Semimonthly. $2,155.00 per year. Four looseleaf volumes.

AIRLINES TIME TABLES

See: TIMETABLES

AIRPLANE ELECTRONICS

See: AVIONICS

AIRPLANE INDUSTRY

See also: AEROSPACE INDUSTRY; AVIATION INDUSTRY

ABSTRACTS AND INDEXES

Applied Science and Technology Index. H. W. Wilson Co. • 11 times a year. Quarterly and annual cumulations. Price varies. Indexes a wide variety of English language technical, industrial, and engineering periodicals.

Business Periodicals Index. H. W. Wilson Co. • 11 times a year. Quarterly and annual cumulations. Price varies.

Science Citation Index. Thomson/ISI. • Bimonthly. $15,020.00 per year. Annual cumulation. Includes *Source Index*, *Citation Index*, *Permuterm Subject Index*, and *Corporate Index*.

CD-ROM DATABASES

OECD Statistical Compendium. Organization for Economic Cooperation and Development. • Semiannual. $1,905.00 per year for 1 to 10 users. CD-ROM contains more than 730,000 monthly, quarterly, and annual time series for OECD countries, 1960 to date. Includes fully searchable data on agriculture, food, economic indicators, national accounts, employment, energy, finance, industry, technology, and foreign trade. Results can be displayed in various forms.

DIRECTORIES

ABD--Aviation Buyer's Directory. Air Service Directory Inc. • Covers: aircraft, parts, and equipment manufacturers and dealers, and service firms in the aviation industry. Entries include: Company name, address, phone.

International ABC Aerospace Directory. Jane's Information Group Ltd. • Covers: Approximately 28,000 companies and organizations involved in the aerospace industry, including civil and military organizations, aircraft manufacturers, Civil Aviation Authorities, air force bases, leasing companies, airport authorities, engine manufacturers, distributors of components, and maintenance contractors; international coverage. Entries include: Name, address, phone, fax, names and titles of key personnel, description of products/services.

FINANCIAL RATIOS

Almanac of Business and Industrial Financial Ratios. Leo Troy. Aspen Publishers, Inc. • 2003.

$125.95. Includes CD-Rom. Contains financial ratios derived from federal tax returns. Ratios for each of about 200 industries are arranged according to company asset size. (Almanac of Business and Industrial Financial Ratios Series).

Annual Statement Studies. The Risk Management Association. • Annual. Median and quartile financial ratios are given for over 400 kinds of manufacturing, wholesale, retail, construction, and consumer finance establishments. Data is sorted by both asset size and sales volume. Includes a clearly written "Definition of Ratios" and an alphabetical industry index.

Annual Statement Studies: Industry Default Probabilities and Cash Flow Measures. The Risk Management Association. • Annual. $145.00. Serves as a companion volume to the original *Annual Statement Studies*. Gives probability of default estimates on a percentage scale for more than 450 industries. Includes changes in position year-by-year for eight financial statement line items and provides percentage measures of cash flow.

Industry Norms and Key Business Ratios. Desk Top Edition. Dun and Bradstreet Corp. • Annual. Five volumes. $475.00 per volume. $1,890.00 per set. Covers over 800 kinds of businesses, arranged by Standard Industrial Classification number. More detailed editions covering longer periods of time are also available.

HANDBOOKS AND MANUALS

A Field Guide to Airplanes of North America. M. R. Montgomery and Gerald L. Foster. Houghton Mifflin Co. • 1992. $18.00. Second revised edition.

INTERNET DATABASES

Business 2.0 Web Guide to the Best Business Links. Business 2.0 Media Inc. Phone: (415)293-4800 E-mail: support@business2.com • URL: http://www.business2.com/webguide • Web site presents an extensive, searchable directory of links to "the best, most informative, and authoritative web pages." Twenty main categories cover business, finance, career, company information, people, and technology topics, with thousands of subtopics, all linking to Web sites recommended by experienced business researchers. Fees: Free.

Fedstats. Federal Interagency Council on Statistical Policy. Phone: (202)395-7254 • URL: http://www.fedstats.gov • Web site features an efficient search facility for full-text statistics produced by more than 100 federal agencies, including the Census Bureau, the Bureau of Economic Analysis, and the Bureau of Labor Statistics. Boolean searches can be made within one agency or for all agencies combined. Links are offered to international statistical bureaus, including the UN, IMF, OECD, UNESCO, Eurostat, and 20 individual countries. Fees: Free.

FreeLunch.com. Economy.com, Inc. Phone: (610)696-8700 Fax: (610)696-1678 • URL: http://www.freelunch.com • Web site provides free access to more than 1.5 million economic and financial data series, covering industry, demographics, labor markets, prices, retail sales, government spending, trade, interest rates, housing starts, the stock market, and many other topics. Data is available for various time periods in either chart or table form. Searching is offered. Fees: Free, but registration required. Economy.com, Inc. also offers fee-based economic analysis at *The Dismal Scientist* site (http://www.dismal.com).

Manufacturing Profiles. U. S. Bureau of the Census. Phone: (301)763-4636 E-mail: webmaster@census.gov • URL: http://www.census.gov/prod/www/abs/mfg-prof.html • The Census Bureau makes available free on PDF (Portable Document Format) an annual consolidation of the entire Current Industrial Report series, presenting "all the data compiled." Contains statistics on production, shipments, inventories, consumption, exports, imports, and orders for a wide variety of manufactured products.

ONLINE DATABASES

Aerospace America [online]. American Institute of Aeronautics and Astronautics. • Provides complete text of the periodical, *Aerospace America*, 1984 to date, with monthly updates. Also includes news from the *AIAA Bulletin.* Inquire as to online cost and availability.

Aerospace Database. American Institute of Aeronautics and Astronautics. • Contains abstracts of literature covering all aspects of the aerospace and aircraft industry 1983 to date. Monthly updates. Inquire as to online cost and availability.

Aerospace/Defense Markets and Technology. Gale Cengage Learning. • Abstracts of commerical aerospace/defense related literature, 1982 to date. Also includes information about major defense contracts awarded by the U. S. Department of Defense. International coverage. Inquire as to online cost and availability.

Globalbase. Gale Cengage Learning. • Provides more than one million online summaries of business, industrial, and economic news reports from more than 1,000 publications worldwide. Covers a wide range of material appearing in international trade journals, professional magazines, and newspapers. Time period is 1984 to date, with weekly updates. Inquire as to online cost and availability.

Management Contents. Gale Cengage Learning. • Covers a wide range of management, financial, marketing, personnel, and administrative topics. About 150 leading business journals are indexed and abstracted from 1974 to date, with monthly updating. Inquire as to online cost and availability.

PROMT: Predicasts Overview of Markets and Technology. Gale Cengage Learning. • Companies, products, applied technologies and markets. U.S. and international literature coverage, 1972 to date. Inquire as to online cost and availability. Provides abstracts from more than 1,600 publications. Weekly updates.

Scisearch. Institute for Scientific Information. • Broad, multidisciplinary index to the literature of science and technology, 1974 to present. Inquire as to online cost and availability. Coverage of literature is worldwide, with weekly updates.

Trade & Industry Database. Gale Cengage Learning. • Provides indexing of business periodicals, January 1981 to date. Daily updates. (Full text articles from some periodicals are available online, 1983 to date. Inquire as to online cost and availability).

PERIODICALS AND NEWSLETTERS

A/C Flyer: Best Read Resale Magazine Worldwide (Aircraft). McGraw-Hill. • Monthly. Individuals $49.00 per year; students, $28.00 per year. Lists used airplanes for sale by dealers, brokers, and private owners. Provides news and trends relating to the aircraft resale industry. Special issues include "Product & Service Buyer's Guide" and "Dealer/Broker Directory.".

Aerospace America. American Institute of Aeronautics and Astronautics, Inc. • Monthly. Free to members; non-members, $140.00 per year. Provides coverage of key issues affecting the aerospace field.

Aerospace Engineering Magazine. Society of Automotive Engineers. • Monthly. $66.00 per year. Provides technical information that can be used in the design of new and improved aerospace systems.

Air Market News. General Publications Co. • Bimonthly. Free to qualified personnel. Subject matter is news of aircraft products and services.

Aviation Maintenance. PBI Media, LLC. • Monthly. Free to qualified personnel; others, $189.00 per year. Formerly *Aviation Equipment Maintenance.*

Aviation Week and Space Technology. McGraw-Hill Aviation Week Group. • Monthly. $92.00 per year.

Flight International. Reed Business Information. • Weekly. $140.00 per year. Technical aerospace coverage.

Flying. Hachette Filipacchi Media U.S., Inc. • Monthly. Includes three *Special Issues.* Price on application.

Journal of Aircraft: Devoted to Aeronautical Science and Technology. American Institute of Aeronautics and Astronautics, Inc. • Bimonthly. Members, $55.00 per year; institutions, $520.00 per year. Online edition available.

Trade-a-Plane. • 36 times a year. $42.00 per year. Subject matter is aircraft for sale or trade.

RESEARCH CENTERS AND INSTITUTES

Center for Aeromechanics Research. University of Texas at Austin. Aerospace Engineering & Engineering Mechanics, WRW Room 220, Austin, TX 78712-1085. Phone: (512)471-5962 Fax: (512)471-3788 E-mail: varghese@mail.utexas.edu • URL: http://www.ae.utexas.edu/research/car.

OAI. 22800 Cedar Point Rd., Cleveland, OH 44142. Phone: (440)962-3000 Fax: (440)962-3120 E-mail: michaelsalkind@oai.org • URL: http://www.oai.org • Aerospace-related research, education, and technology transfers. Formerly Ohio Aerospace Institute.

STATISTICS SOURCES

Aerospace Facts and Figures. Aerospace Industries Association of America. • Annual. $35.00. Includes financial data for the aerospace industries.

Annual Survey of Manufactures. Available from U. S. Government Printing Office. • Annual. Prices vary. Issued by the U. S. Census Bureau as an interim update to the *Census of Manufactures.* Includes data on number of manufacturing establishments in various industries, employment, labor costs, value of shipments, capital expenditures, inventories, energy costs, and assets. (See also Census Bureau home page, http://www.census.gov/.).

Business Statistics of the United States. Linz Audain and Cornelia J. Strawser. Bernan Associates. • Annual. $147.00. Based on *Business Statistics,* formerly issue by the Bureau of Economic Analysis, U. S. Department of Commerce. Provides basic data for a wide variety of U. S. industries, services, and economic indicators. Most statistics are shown annually for 30 years and monthly for the most recent four years.

Standard & Poor's Statistical Service. Current Statistics. Standard & Poor's. • Monthly. $688.00 per year. Includes 10 *Basic Statistics* sections, *Current Statistics Supplements* and *Annual Security Price Index Record.*

Survey of Current Business. Available from U. S. Government Printing Office. • Monthly. $63.00 per year. Issued by Bureau of Economic Analysis, U. S. Department of Commerce. Presents a wide variety of business and economic data.

WEFA Industrial Monitor. John Wiley and Sons, Inc. • Annual. $65.00. Prepared by industry analysts at WEFA, an economic forecasting and consulting firm (originally Wharton Econometric Forecasting Associates). Contains discussions of the outlook for major U. S. industries, with many 10-year forecasts (WEFA Web site is http://www.wefa.com).

TRADE/PROFESSIONAL ASSOCIATIONS

Aeronautical Repair Station Association. 121 N Henry St., Alexandria, VA 22314-2903. Phone: (703)739-9543 Fax: (703)739-9488 E-mail: arsa@arsa.org • URL: http://www.arsa.org • Represents FAA-certified repair stations, suppliers and distributors. Assists members on regulatory and legislative issues before the FAA and other governmental agencies.

Aerospace Industries Association of America. 1250 Eye St., N.W., Ste. 1200, Washington, DC 20005-3924. Phone: (202)371-8400 Fax: (202)371-8470 E-mail: neale@aia-aerospace.org • URL: http://www.aia-aerospace.org.

American Institute of Aeronautics and Astronautics. 1801 Alexander Bell Dr., Suite 500, c/o Michael Lewis, Reston, VA 20191-4344. Phone: 800-639-2422 or (703)264-7500 Fax: (703)264-7551 E-mail: custserv@aiaa.org • URL: http://www.aiaa.org.

Flight Safety Foundation. 601 Madison St., Ste. 300, Alexandria, VA 22314-1756. Phone: (703)739-6700 Fax: (703)739-6708 E-mail: wahdan@flightsafety.org • URL: http://www.flightsafety.org • Aerospace manufacturers, domestic and foreign airlines, insurance companies, fuel and oil companies, schools, and miscellaneous organizations having an interest in the promotion of safety in flight. Sponsors safety audits. Compiles statistics.

General Aviation Manufacturers Association. 1400 K St. NW, Ste. 801, Washington, DC 20005. Phone: (202)393-1500 Fax: (202)842-4063 E-mail: webmaster@gama.aero • URL: http://www.gama.aero • Manufacturers of aviation airframes, engines, avionics, and components. Seeks to create a better climate for the growth of general aviation.

National Business Aviation Association. 1200 18th St. NW, Ste. 400, Washington, DC 20036-2527. Phone: (202)783-9000 Fax: (202)331-8364 E-mail: info@nbaa.org • URL: http://www.nbaa.org • Companies owning and operating aircraft for business use, suppliers, and maintenance and air fleet service companies. Compiles statistics; provides literature for researchers and students.

OTHER SOURCES

Aircraft, Engines, Parts, and Equipment Industry. Available from MarketResearch.com. • 2002. $4,450.00. Published by Global Industry Analysts. Provides worldwide market research data, including profiles of major aircraft and equipment companies.

Aviation Law Reports. CCH, Inc. • Semimonthly. $2,155.00 per year. Four looseleaf volumes.

Jane's All the World's Aircraft. Jane's Information Group, Inc. • Annual. $630.00; CD-ROM edition, $1,455.00; online edition, $1,566.00; microfiche edition, $3,075.00. Lists civil and military aircraft, helicopters, airships, and aero engines.

AIRPLANES, BUSINESS

See: BUSINESS AVIATION

AIRPORTS

ABSTRACTS AND INDEXES

Business Periodicals Index. H. W. Wilson Co. • 11 times a year. Quarterly and annual cumulations. Price varies.

DIRECTORIES

Airport/Facility Directory. U.S. National Ocean Service. • Covers: Non-military airports in the continental United States; separate volumes cover the southeast, northeast, northwest, east central, north central, southwest, and south central states (including Puerto Rico and the Virgin Islands). Entries include: Airport name, location, weather service phone number, control center frequencies, and information concerning navigational and other aids and systems.

AOPA Aviation U.S.A. Aircraft Owners and Pilots Association. • Semiannual. Free to members. Price on Application. Primarily for pilots.

Jane's Air Traffic Control. Jane's Information Group, Inc. • Annual. $495.00. International coverage of equipment and supplies for both civil and military airports. Formerly *Jane's Airport and ATC Equipment*.

OAG Business Travel Planner: North America. OAG. • Quarterly. $142.00 per year. $55.00 per issue. Arranged according to more than 14,500 destinations in the U. S., Canada, Mexico, and the Caribbean. Lists more than 31,500 hotels, with AAA ratings where available. Provides information on airports, ground transportation, coming events, and climate. Includes maps.

OAG Travel Planner: Europe Worldwide. OAG. • Quarterly. $149.00 per year. Arranged according to more than 13,850 destinations in Europe. Lists more than 14,700 hotels, with information on airports, ground transportation, coming events, and climate.

OAG Travel Planner Hotel and Motel Redbook: Asia Pacific. OAG. • Quarterly. $130.00 per year. Arranged according to more than 5,000 destinations throughout Asia and the Pacific. Lists about 3,000 hotels, with information on airports, ground transportation, coming events, and climate.

Professional Pilot-FBO Directory. Queensmith Communications Corp. • Annual. $8.00. Includes information for about 1,600 airports and fixed-base operators.

FINANCIAL RATIOS

Annual Statement Studies. The Risk Management Association. • Annual. Median and quartile financial ratios are given for over 400 kinds of manufacturing, wholesale, retail, construction, and consumer finance establishments. Data is sorted by both asset size and sales volume. Includes a clearly written "Definition of Ratios" and an alphabetical industry index.

Annual Statement Studies: Industry Default Probabilities and Cash Flow Measures. The Risk Management Association. • Annual. $145.00. Serves as a companion volume to the original *Annual Statement Studies*. Gives probability of default estimates on a percentage scale for more than 450 industries. Includes changes in position year-by-year for eight financial statement line items and provides percentage measures of cash flow.

ONLINE DATABASES

Management Contents. Gale Cengage Learning. • Covers a wide range of management, financial, marketing, personnel, and administrative topics. About 150 leading business journals are indexed and abstracted from 1974 to date, with monthly updating. Inquire as to online cost and availability.

PAIS International. Public Affairs Information Service, Inc. • Corresponds to the former printed publications, *PAIS Bulletin* (1976-90) and *PAIS Foreign Language Index* (1972-90), and to the current *PAIS International in Print* (1991 to date). Covers economic, political, and sociological material appearing in periodicals, books, government documents, and other publications. Updating is monthly. Inquire as to online cost and availability.

Trade & Industry Database. Gale Cengage Learning. • Provides indexing of business periodicals, January 1981 to date. Daily updates. (Full text articles from some periodicals are available online, 1983 to date. Inquire as to online cost and availability).

PERIODICALS AND NEWSLETTERS

Airport Business. Cygnus Business Media. • 10 times a year. $55.00 per year.

Airports: The Weekly for Airport Users, Managers, and Suppliers. Aviation Week Business Intelligence Services. • Weekly. $649.00 per year. Newsletter. Covers news of worldwide airport development, financing, operations, marketing, bidding, improvements, and personnel.

Aviation Week and Space Technology. McGraw-Hill Aviation Week Group. • Monthly. $92.00 per year.

Homeland Security and Defense: Weekly Intelligence for the Global Homeland Security and Defense Community. Aviation Week Business Intelligence Services. • Weekly. $595.00 per year. Newsletter. Emphasis is on airline and airport programs (federal, state, and local). Also covers counterterrorism, protection of military units, Department of Homeland Security activities, industrial security, communications equipment, and other topics related to homeland security.

Jane's Airport Review: The Global Airport Business Magazine. Jane's Information Group, Inc. • 10 times a year. $190.00 per year. CD-Rom edition, $775.00 per year. Edited for airport managers. Covers all aspects of airport operations.

STATISTICS SOURCES

Airport Activity Statistics of Certificated Route Air Carriers. U. S. Department of Transportation. Available from U. S. Government Printing Office. • Annual. $58.00.

FAA Aviation Forecasts. Federal Aviation Administration. Available from U. S. Government Printing Office. • Annual. $44.00.

TRADE/PROFESSIONAL ASSOCIATIONS

Air Transport Association of America. 1301 Pennsylvania Ave., Suite 1100, Washington, DC 20004-7017. Phone: (202)626-4000 Fax: (202)626-4166 E-mail: ata@air-lines.org • URL: http://www.air-lines.org.

Airports Council International - North America. 1775 K St. NW, Ste. 500, Washington, DC 20006. Phone: 888-424-7767 or (202)293-8500 Fax: (202)331-1362 E-mail: memberservices@aci-na.org • URL: http://www.aci-na.org • Represents local, regional, and state governing organizations that own and operate commercial airports in the U.S., Canada, and Bermuda. Represents a variety of industries that provide products and services to the air transportation industry.

American Association of Airport Executives. 601 Madison St., Ste. 400, Alexandria, VA 22314. Phone: (703)824-0500 Fax: (703)820-1395 E-mail: member.services@airportnet.org • URL: http://www.airportnet.org.

International Air Transport Association. 703 Waterford Way, NW 62nd Ave., Ste. 600, Miami, FL 33126. Phone: (305)264-7772 Fax: (305)264-8088 E-mail: membership@iaaglobal.org • URL: http://www1.iata.org/ • Represents the airline industries; promotes safe, reliable, secure and economical air services worldwide.

National Air Transportation Association. 4226 King St., Alexandria, VA 22302. Phone: 800-808-6282 or (703)845-9000 Fax: (703)845-8176 E-mail: enews@nata.aero • URL: http://www.nata.aero • Represents the interests of aviation businesses nationwide. Provides vital aviation services to the airlines, the military, and business/corporate/ individual aircraft owners and operators; services includes fueling, maintenance, and flight instruction.

ALARMS

See: ELECTRONIC SECURITY SYSTEMS

ALCOHOL AS FUEL

See: FUEL

ALCOHOLIC BEVERAGES

See: DISTILLING INDUSTRY

ALCOHOLISM

See also: DRUG ABUSE AND TRAFFIC

GENERAL WORKS

Alcohol and Drug Problems at Work: The Shift to Prevention. International Labour Organization. • 2003. $9.95. Discusses workplace substance abuse initiatives for both large and small businesses.

Drugs, Alcohol, and Tobacco: Learning About Addictive Behavior. Gale Cengage Learning. • 2002. $295.00. Three volumes. Contains 200 articles on various aspects of addiction. Includes color illustrations, a glossary, and comprehensive indexing. (Macmillan Reference USA imprint.).

The Facts About Drug Use: Coping with Drugs and Alcohol in Your Family, at Work, in Your Community. The Haworth Press, Inc. • 1992. $14.95. A comprehensive overview of drug dependence, including alcoholism.

Sober for Good: New Solutions for Drinking Problems - Advice from Those Who Have Succeeded. Anne M. Fletcher. Houghton Mifflin Co. • 2001. $25.00. Describes the various methods that problem drinkers have used to attain sobriety.

ABSTRACTS AND INDEXES

Alcoholism Digest Annual. Information Planning Associates, Inc. • Annual. Price on application.

Excerpta Medica: Drug Dependence, Alcohol Abuse, and Alcoholism. Elsevier. • Bimonthly. Institutions, $1,398.00 per year. Section 40 of *Excerpta Medica*.

Psychological Abstracts. American Psychological Association. • Monthly. Members, $815.00 per year; individuals and institutions, $1,207.00 per year. Covers the international literature of psychology and the behavioral sciences. Includes journals, technical reports, dissertations, and other sources.

BIBLIOGRAPHIES

Alcoholism: The Health and Social Consequences of Alcohol Use: An Annotated Bibliography with Analytical Introduction. Cecilia M. Schmitz and Richard A. Gray. Pierian Press. • 1998. $40.00. Provides detailed summaries of more than 100 significant books and major articles on the subject of alcoholism. (Science and Social Responsibility Series, No. 3.).

International Bibliography of Studies on Alcohol. Sarah S. Jordy, compiler. Rutgers Center of Alcohol Studies Publications. • $200.00. Three volumes. Volume one, *References*, 1901-1950; volume two, *Indexes*, 1901-1980; volume three, *References* and *Indexes*, 1951-1960.

CD-ROM DATABASES

Magazine Index Plus. Gale Cengage Learning. • Monthly. $4,000.00 per year (includes InfoTrac workstation). Provides full text on CD-ROM for about 100 popular, general interest magazines and indexing for 300 others. Includes special indexing of reviews and product evaluations. Time period is 1980 to date.

DIRECTORIES

National Directory of Drug and Alcohol Abuse Treatment Programs. Substance Abuse and Mental Health Services Administration. • Annual. Free. Lists 11,000 federal, state, local, and privately funded agencies administering or providing drug abuse and alcoholism treatment services. Formerly *National Directory of Drug Abuse and Alcoholism Treatment and Prevention Programs*.

ENCYCLOPEDIAS AND DICTIONARIES

Encyclopedia of Drugs, Alcohol, and Addictive Behavior. Available from Gale Cengage Learning. • 2001. $425.00. Second edition. Four volumes. Published by Macmillan Reference USA. Covers the social, economic, political, and medical aspects of addiction.

HANDBOOKS AND MANUALS

Drug Abuse Handbook. Steven B. Karch, editor. CRC Press LLC. • 1997. $129.95. Provides comprehensive coverage of drug abuse issues and trends. Edited for healthcare professionals.

Substance Abuse: A Comprehensive Textbook. Joyce Lowinson and others. Lippincott Williams and Wilkins. • 1997. $179.00. Third edition. Covers the medical, psychological, socioeconomic, and public health aspects of drug and alcohol abuse.

ONLINE DATABASES

Embase. Elsevier Science, Inc. • Worldwide medical literature, 1974 to present. Weekly updates. Inquire as to online cost and availability.

Information Bank Abstracts. New York Times Index Dept. • Provides indexing and abstracting of current affairs, primarily from the final late edition of *The New York Times* and the Eastern edition of *The Wall Street Journal.* Time period is 1969 to present, with daily updates. Inquire as to online cost and availability.

Mental Health Abstracts. IFI/Plenum Data Corp. • Provides indexing and abstracting of mental health and mental illness literature appearing in more than 1,200 journals and other sources from 1969 to date. Monthly updates. Inquire as to online cost and availability.

PsycINFO. American Psychological Association. • Provides indexing and abstracting of the worldwide literature of psychology and the behavioral sciences. Time period is 1967 to date, with monthly updates. Inquire as to online cost and availability.

PERIODICALS AND NEWSLETTERS

Addiction Research Foundation Journal: Addiction News for Professionals. Addiction Research Foundation of Ontario, Subscription-Marketing Dept. • Six times a year. $19.00 per year. News and opinions from the drug and alcohol field around the world. Formerly *Alcoholism and Drug Addiction Research Foundation Journal.*

Alcohol Research and Health. Available from U. S. Government Printing Office. • Quarterly. $25.00 per year. Issued by the National Institute on Alcohol Abuse and Alcoholism. Presents alcohol-related research findings and descriptions of alcoholism prevention and treatment programs.

Alcoholism: Clinical and Experimental Research. Research Society on Alcoholism. Lippincott Williams and Wilkins. • Monthly. Individuals, $331.00 per year; institutions, $639.00 per year.

Alcoholism Treatment Quarterly: The Practitioner's Quarterly for Individual, Group, and Family Therapy. Haworth Press, Inc. • Quarterly. $535.00 per year. Edited for professionals working with alcoholics and their families. Formerly *Alcoholism Counseling and Treatment.*

American Journal of Drug and Alcohol Abuse. Marcel Dekker, Inc. • Quarterly. Institutions, $995.00 per year; with online edition, $1,124.00 per year.

Counselor: The Magazine for Addiction Professionals. Health Communications, Inc. • Bimonthly. $26.00 per year. Covers both clinical and societal aspects of substance abuse.

Drug and Alcohol Abuse Education. Editorial Resources, Inc. • Monthly. $84.00 per year. Newsletter covering education, prevention, and treatment relating to abuse of drugs and alcohol.

Employee Assistance Quarterly. Haworth Press, Inc. • Quarterly. $535.00 per year. An academic and practical journal focusing on employee alcoholism and mental health problems. Formerly *Labor-Management Alcoholism Journal.*

A Journal of Ethnicity in Substance Abuse. Haworth Press, Inc. • Quarterly. $380.00 per year. Includes print and online editions. Edited for researchers and practitioners. Covers various areas of susbstance abuse, including alcoholism. Formerly *Drugs and Society.*

Journal of Studies on Alcohol. Rutgers Center of Alcohol Studies. Alcohol Research Documentation, Inc. • Bimonthly. Individuals, $140.00 per year; institutions, $175.00 per year.

Workplace Substance Abuse Advisor. LRP Publications. • Description: Reviews federal, state, and local laws and regulations concerning alcohol and drug use, testing, and policies. Discusses significant court decisions. Contains information on the drug enforcement budgets at all levels of government. Examines employee assistance plans and other educational programs designed to help substance abusers.

RESEARCH CENTERS AND INSTITUTES

Mental Sciences Institute. University of Texas Houston Health Science Center. 1300 Moursund Ave., Houston, TX 77030. Phone: (713)500-2500 Fax: (713)500-2553 E-mail: robert.w.guynn@uth.tmc.edu • URL: http://www.msi.uth.tmc.edu.

Research Institute on Addictions. State University of New York at Buffalo, 1021 Main St., Buffalo, NY 14203-1016. Phone: (716)887-2566 Fax: (716)887-2252 E-mail: connors@ria.org • URL: http://www.ria.org/.

STATISTICS SOURCES

Statistics on Alcohol, Drug, and Tobacco Use: A Selection of Statistical Charts, Graphs and Tables about Alcohol, Drug and Tobacco Use from a Variety of Published Sources with Explanatory Comments. Gale Cengage Learning. • 1995. $85.00. Includes graphs, charts, and tables arranged within subject chapters. Citations to data sources are provided. (Statistics on...Series: vol. 1).

TRADE/PROFESSIONAL ASSOCIATIONS

Al-Anon Family Group Headquarters, World Service Office. 1600 Corporate Landing Pkwy., Virginia Beach, VA 23454-5617. Phone: 888-4AL-ANON or (757)563-1600 or (757)563-1600 Fax: (757)563-1655 E-mail: wso@al-anon.org • URL: http://www.al-anon.alateen.org • Offers a twelve-step program for the relatives and friends of individuals with an alcohol problem. Operates Alateen for members 12-18 years of age whose lives have been adversely affected by someone else's drinking problem, usually by parents.

Alcoholics Anonymous World Services. PO Box 459, Grand Central Sta., 475 Riverside Dr., 11th Fl., New York, NY 10163. Phone: (212)870-3400 Fax: (212)870-3003 E-mail: wso@al-anon.org • URL: http://www.aa.org • Individuals recovering from alcoholism. Maintains that members can solve their common problem and help others achieve sobriety through a twelve step program that includes sharing their experience, strength, and hope with each other. Self-supported through members' contributions, not an allied with any sect, denomination, political organization, or institution and does not endorse nor oppose any cause.

American Council on Alcoholism. P.O. Box 25126, Arlington, VA 22202. Phone: 800-527-5344 or (703)248-9005 Fax: (703)248-9007 E-mail: aca2@earthlink.net • URL: http://aca.usa.org/.

International Health and Temperance Association. 12501 Old Columbia Pike, Silver Spring, MD 20904. Phone: (301)680-6719 Fax: (301)680-6707 E-mail: 74617.1663@compuserve.com • URL: http://www.health20-20.org • Seeks to "enlighten the public concerning the harmful effects of alcohol, tobacco and narcotics and to mount an educational campaign to solve these problems". Formerly International Temperance Association.

National Council on Alcoholism and Drug Dependence. 20 Exchange Place, Suite 2902, New York, NY 10005-3201. Phone: 800-622-2255 or (212)269-7797 Fax: (212)269-7510 E-mail: national@ncadd.org • URL: http://www.ncadd.org • Works for the prevention and treatment of alcoholism and other drug dependence through programs of public education, information and public policy advocacy.

ALKALI INDUSTRY

See also: POTASH INDUSTRY

DIRECTORIES

OPD Chemical Buyers Directory. Schnell Publishing Company Inc. • Covers: about 1,500 suppliers of chemical process materials and more than 300 companies that transport and store chemicals in the United States. Entries include: Company name, address, phone, list of products or services, telex, fax, e-mail address, internet address, branch offices.

ONLINE DATABASES

CA Search. Chemical Abstracts Service. • Guide to chemical literature, 1967 to present. Inquire as to online cost and availability.

F & S Index. Gale Cengage Learning. • Contains about four million citations to worldwide business, financial, and industrial or consumer product literature appearing from 1972 to date. Weekly updates. Inquire as to online cost and availability.

PERIODICALS AND NEWSLETTERS

Better Crops With Plant Food. Potash and Phosphate Institute. • Quarterly. $8.00.

PRICE SOURCES

Chemical Market Reporter. Schnell Publishing Co., Inc. • Weekly. $169.00 per year. Quotes current prices for a wide range of chemicals. Formerly *Chemical Marketing Reporter.*

STATISTICS SOURCES

Minerals Yearbook. Available from U.S. Government Printing Office. • Annual. Three volumes.

TRADE/PROFESSIONAL ASSOCIATIONS

Potash and Phosphate Institute. 655 Engineering Dr., No. 110, Norcross, GA 30092-2837. Phone: (770)447-0335 Fax: (770)448-0439 E-mail: ppi@ppi-ppic.org • URL: http://www.ppi-ppic.org • Formerly Potash Institute.

ALLOYS

See: METAL INDUSTRY

ALUMINUM FOIL

See: ALUMINUM INDUSTRY

ALUMINUM INDUSTRY

ABSTRACTS AND INDEXES

Aluminum Industry Abstracts: A Monthly Review of the World's Technical Literature on Aluminum. Aluminum Association. • Monthly. $975.00 per year. Includes print and online editions. Formerly-*World Aluminum Abstracts.*

ALMANACS AND YEARBOOKS

Agricultural and Mineral Commodities Year Book. Available from Taylor & Francis Group. • Annual. $225.00. Published by Europa Publications. Contains descriptive product profiles, price data, export-import data, and production statistics for major commodities of the world. Includes commodity histories, uses, markets, demand trends, and information about trade agreements and key commodity organizations.

CRB Commodity Yearbook. Commodity Research Bureau. CRB. • Annual. $99.95.

CD-ROM DATABASES

METADEX Materials Collection: Metals-Polymers-Ceramics. Cambridge Scientific Abstracts. • Quarterly. Provides CD-ROM citations to the worldwide literature of materials science and metallurgy. Corresponds to *Metals Abstracts, Alloys*

Index, Steels Alert, Nonferrous Alert, Polymers/ Ceramics/Composites Alert, and *Engineered Materials Abstracts.* (Formerly produced by ASM International.).

DIRECTORIES

Dun's Industrial Guide: The Metalworking Directory. Dun and Bradstreet Corp. • Annual. Libraries, $485; commercial institutions, $795.00. Lease basis. Three volumes. Lists about 65,000 U. S. manufacturing plants using metal and suppliers of metalworking equipment and materials. Includes names and titles of key personnel. Products, purchases, and processes are indicated.

INTERNET DATABASES

Manufacturing Profiles. U. S. Bureau of the Census. Phone: (301)763-4636 E-mail: webmaster@census. gov • URL: http://www.census.gov/prod/www/abs/ mfg-prof.html • The Census Bureau makes available free on PDF (Portable Document Format) an annual consolidation of the entire Current Industrial Report series, presenting "all the data compiled." Contains statistics on production, shipments, inventories, consumption, exports, imports, and orders for a wide variety of manufactured products.

ONLINE DATABASES

F & S Index. Gale Cengage Learning. • Contains about four million citations to worldwide business, financial, and industrial or consumer product literature appearing from 1972 to date. Weekly updates. Inquire as to online cost and availability.

Materials Business File. Cambridge Scientific Abstracts. • Provides online abstracts and citations to worldwide materials literature, covering the business and industrial aspects of metals, plastics, ceramics, and composites. Corresponds to *Steels Alert, Nonferrous Metals Alert,* and *Polymers/ Ceramics/Composites Alert.* Time period is 1985 to date, with monthly updates. (Formerly produced by ASM International.) Inquire as to online cost and availability.

METADEX. Cambridge Scientific Abstracts. • Covers the worldwide literature of metals, metallurgy, and materials science, 1966 to date. Includes detailed alloys indexing from 1974. Biweekly updating. Inquire as to online cost and availability. (Formerly produced by ASM International.).

PERIODICALS AND NEWSLETTERS

Light Metal Age. Fellom Publishing Co. • Bimonthly. $40.00 per year. Edited for production and engineering executives of the aluminum industry and other nonferrous light metal industries.

Metal Center News. Sackett Business Media Inc. • Quadriennial 13 times a year. $99.00 per year.

33 Metalproducing: For Primary Producers of Steel, Aluminum, and Copper-Base Alloys. Penton Media, Inc. • Monthly. $65.00 per year. Covers metal production technology and methods and industry news. Includes a bimonthly *Nonferrous Supplement.*

PRICE SOURCES

Chemical and Engineering News: The Newsmagazine of the Chemical World. American Chemical Society. • Weekly. Institutions, $210.00 per year.

Chemical Market Reporter. Schnell Publishing Co., Inc. • Weekly. $169.00 per year. Quotes current prices for a wide range of chemicals. Formerly *Chemical Marketing Reporter.*

Platt's Metals Week. Platt's. • Weekly. $770.00 per year.

STATISTICS SOURCES

Aluminum Standards and Data. Aluminum Association. • Biennial. $25.00.

Aluminum Statistical Review. Aluminum Association. • Annual. $50.00.

Annual Survey of Manufactures. Available from U.

S. Government Printing Office. • Annual. Prices vary. Issued by the U. S. Census Bureau as an interim update to the *Census of Manufactures.* Includes data on number of manufacturing establishments in various industries, employment, labor costs, value of shipments, capital expenditures, inventories, energy costs, and assets. (See also Census Bureau home page, http://www.census. gov/.).

Metal Statistics. Reed Business Information. • Annual. $250.00. Provides statistical data on a wide variety of metals, metal products, ores, alloys, and scrap metal. Includes data on prices, production, consumption, shipments, imports, and exports.

Mineral Commodity Summaries. Available from U. S. Government Printing Office. • Annual. $26.00. Published by the U. S. Geological Survey, Department of the Interior (http://www.usgs.gov). Contains detailed, five-year data for about 90 nonfuel minerals. Covers a wide range of statistics, including production, imports, exports, consumption, reserves, prices, tariff information, and industry employment. (Two pages are devoted to each mineral.).

Minerals Yearbook. Available from U.S. Government Printing Office. • Annual. Three volumes.

Standard & Poor's Industry Surveys. Standard & Poor's. • Semiannual. $1,800.00. Two looseleaf volumes. Includes monthly *Supplements.* Provides detailed, individual surveys of 52 major industry groups. Each survey is revised on a semiannual basis. Also includes "Monthly Investment Review" (industry group investment analysis) and monthly "Trends & Projections" (economic analysis).

U. S. Industry and Trade Outlook. Available from National Technical Information Service. • Annual. $69.95. Produced by the International Trade Administration, U. S. Department of Commerce, in a "public-private" partnership with DRI/McGraw-Hill and Standard & Poor's. Provides basic data, outlook for the current year, and "Long-Term Prospects" (five-year projections) for a wide variety of products and services. Includes high technology industries. Formerly *U. S. Industrial Outlook.*

United States Census of Mineral Industries. Bureau of the Census, U.S. Department of Commerce. Available from U.S. Government Printing Office. • Quinquennial.

WEFA Industrial Monitor. John Wiley and Sons, Inc. • Annual. $65.00. Prepared by industry analysts at WEFA, an economic forecasting and consulting firm (originally Wharton Econometric Forecasting Associates). Contains discussions of the outlook for major U. S. industries, with many 10-year forecasts (WEFA Web site is http://www.wefa.com).

TRADE/PROFESSIONAL ASSOCIATIONS

Aluminum Association. 1525 Wilson Blvd., Ste. 600, Arlington, VA 22209. Phone: (703)358-2960 Fax: (703)358-2961 E-mail: slarkin@aluminum.org • URL: http://www.aluminum.org • Producers of aluminum and manufacturers of semi-fabricated aluminum products. Represents members' interests in legislative activity. Conducts seminars and workshops. Provides publications on aluminum technology and the aluminum industry. Sponsors competition; compiles statistics.

Aluminum Extruders Council. 1000 N Rand Rd., Ste. 214, Wauconda, IL 60084. Phone: (847)526-2010 Fax: (847)526-3993 E-mail: mail@aec.org • URL: http://www.aec.org • Manufacturers of extruded aluminum shapes and their suppliers. Compiles statistics; provides technical assistance and develops markets. Conducts workshops for management, sales, and plant personnel.

American Architectural Manufacturers Association. 1827 Walden Office Sq., Ste. 550, Schaumburg, IL 60173-4287. Phone: (847)303-5664 Fax: (847)303-5774 E-mail: rwalker@aamanet.org • URL: http://

www.aamanet.org • Provides performance standards, product certification and educational programs for the fenestration industry, including product testing and market research.

National Association of Aluminum Distributors. 1900 Arch St., Philadelphia, PA 19103-1498. Phone: (215)564-3484 Fax: (215)963-9784 E-mail: naad@ fernley.com • URL: http://www.naad.org.

AMERICAN STOCK EXCHANGE

See: STOCK EXCHANGES

AMUSEMENT INDUSTRY

See also: CONCESSIONS; FAIRS; MOTION PICTURE INDUSTRY; RADIO BROADCASTING INDUSTRY; RECREATION INDUSTRY; SHOW BUSINESS; TELEVISION BROADCASTING INDUSTRY

ABSTRACTS AND INDEXES

IMM Abstracts and Index: A Survey of World Literature on the Economic Geology and Mining of All Minerals (Except Coal), Mineral Processing, and Nonferrous Extraction Metallurgy. Institution of Mining and Metallurgy. • Bimonthly. $500.00 per year. Provides international coverage of the literature of mining and nonferrous metallurgy. Includes mineral economics, tunnelling, and rock mechanics.

BIBLIOGRAPHIES

The Influence of Disney Entertainment Parks on Architecture and Development. Stephen J. Rebori. Sage Publications, Inc. • 1995. $10.00. (CPL Bibliographies Series: Vol. 321).

DIRECTORIES

Cavalcade of Acts and Attractions. Amusement Business. • Annual. $85.00. Directory of personal appearance artists, touring shows and other specialized entertainment. Lists promoters, producers, managers and booking agents.

Directory of Funparks and Attractions: International Guide to Amusement Parks, Family Entertainment Centers, Waterparks, and Attractions. Amusement Business. • Annual. $69. 00. Over 2,800, amusement parks, theme parks, family entertainment centers, water parks, zoos, kiddielands and other tourist attractions in U.S., Canada and overseas. Formerly *Amusement Business Directory of Funparks and Attractions.*

Directory of North American Fairs, Festivals and Expositions. Amusement Business. • Annual. $79. 00. Lists over 5,000 fairs, festivals and expositions in the U.S. and Canada which run three days or more.

Entertainment Sourcebook: An Insider's Guide on Where to Find Everything. Applause Theatre & Cinema Books. • Annual. $45.00. Compiled by the Association of Theatrical Artists and Craftspeople (http://www.entertainmentsourcebook.com/ATAC. htm). Lists more than 5,000 sources of theatrical and entertainment supplies and services, such as props, costumes, publicity agencies, scenic shops, amusement park equipment, audio/video products, balloons, wigs, make-up, magic supplies, etc.

The Grey House Performing Arts Directory. Grey House Publishing. • Covers: More than 9,000 dance companies, instrumental music programs, opera companies, choral groups, theatre companies, performing arts series, and performing arts facilities. Entries include: Mailing address, telephone and fax numbers, e-mail addresses, Web sites, mission statement, key management contacts, and facility

For publishers addresses, refer to SOURCES CITED section at the back of the book.

39

information such as capacity, season, and attendance.

International Amusement Industry Buyers Guide. Amusement Business. • Covers: manufacturers, importers, and suppliers of amusement rides, games, and merchandise as well as food and drink equipment and supplies. Entries include: Company name, address, phone, fax, name of principal executive, list of products or services.

International Association of Amusement Parks and Attractions International Directory and Buyers' Guide. International Association of Amusement Parks and Attractions. • Annual. $83.00. Over 1,800 member amusement parks, attractions and industry suppliers.

Plunkett's Airline, Hotel, and Travel Industry Almanac. Plunkett Research, Ltd. • Annual. $249.95. Contains profiles of 300 leading companies, including airlines, hotels, travel agencies, theme parks, cruise lines, casinos, and car rental companies.

Resorts and Parks Purchasing Guide. Klevens Publications, Inc. • Annual. $85.00. Lists suppliers of products and services for resorts and parks, including national parks, amusement parks, dude ranches, golf resorts, ski areas, and national monument areas.

FINANCIAL RATIOS

Almanac of Business and Industrial Financial Ratios. Leo Troy. Aspen Publishers, Inc. • 2003. $125.95. Includes CD-Rom. Contains financial ratios derived from federal tax returns. Ratios for each of about 200 industries are arranged according to company asset size. (Almanac of Business and Industrial Financial Ratios Series).

Annual Statement Studies. The Risk Management Association. • Annual. Median and quartile financial ratios are given for over 400 kinds of manufacturing, wholesale, retail, construction, and consumer finance establishments. Data is sorted by both asset size and sales volume. Includes a clearly written "Definition of Ratios" and an alphabetical industry index.

Annual Statement Studies: Industry Default Probabilities and Cash Flow Measures. The Risk Management Association. • Annual. $145.00. Serves as a companion volume to the original *Annual Statement Studies*. Gives probability of default estimates on a percentage scale for more than 450 industries. Includes changes in position year-by-year for eight financial statement line items and provides percentage measures of cash flow.

HANDBOOKS AND MANUALS

Complete Guide to Special Event Management: Business Insights, Financial Advice and Successful Strategies from Ernst and Young, Consultants to the Olympics. John Wiley and Sons, Inc. • 1992. $39.95. Covers the marketing, financing, and general management of special events in the fields of art, entertainment, and sports.

Dun & Bradstreet/Gale Group Industry Handbooks. Gale Cengage Learning. • 2000. $650.00. Five volumes. $130.00 per volume. Each volume covers two or more major industries: 1. *Entertainment and Hospitality*; 2. *Construction and Agriculture*; 3. *Chemicals and Pharmaceuticals*; 4. *Computers & Software and Broadcasting & Telecommunications*; 5. *Insurance and Health & Medical Services.* The following are included for each industry: overview, statistics, financial ratios, rankings, merger information, company directory, directory of associations, and consultants directory. (Dun and Bradstreet/Gale Industry Reference Handbook Series).

Entertainment Law: Legal Concepts and Business

Practices. West Group. • Annual. $560.00. Five looseleaf volumes.

ONLINE DATABASES

F & S Index. Gale Cengage Learning. • Contains about four million citations to worldwide business, financial, and industrial or consumer product literature appearing from 1972 to date. Weekly updates. Inquire as to online cost and availability.

Information Bank Abstracts. New York Times Index Dept. • Provides indexing and abstracting of current affairs, primarily from the final late edition of *The New York Times* and the Eastern edition of *The Wall Street Journal.* Time period is 1969 to present, with daily updates. Inquire as to online cost and availability.

Management Contents. Gale Cengage Learning. • Covers a wide range of management, financial, marketing, personnel, and administrative topics. About 150 leading business journals are indexed and abstracted from 1974 to date, with monthly updating. Inquire as to online cost and availability.

PERIODICALS AND NEWSLETTERS

Amusement Business: International Live Entertainment and Amusement Industry Newsletter. VNU Business Media. • Weekly. $129.00 per year.

Funworld. International Association of Amusement Parks and Attractions. • 11 times a year. Members, $22.00 per year; non-members, $40.00 per year. Analysis and statistics of the international amusement park industry. Text in English; sections in French, German, Japanese and Spanish.

IEG's Sponsorship Report: The International Newsletter of Event Sponsorship and Lifestyle Marketing. International Events Group, Inc. • Biweekly. $445.00 per year. Includes print and online editions. Newsletter reporting on corporate sponsorship of special events: sports, music, festivals, and the arts. Edited for event producers, directors, and marketing personnel.

TRADE/PROFESSIONAL ASSOCIATIONS

Amusement Industry Manufacturers and Suppliers International. 1250 S.E. Port St., Lucie Blvd., Suite C, Port Lucie, FL 34952. Phone: (772)398-6701 Fax: (772)398-6702 E-mail: info@aimsintl.org • URL: http://www.aimsintl.org.

Association of Theatrical Artists and Craftspeople (ATAC). 604 Riverside Dr., New York, NY 10031. Phone: (212)234-9001 • Members are artists and craftspeople working in theatre, film, TV, and advertising. Areas of expertise include props, costumes, millinery, puppetry, display, and special effects.

International Association of Amusement Parks and Attractions. 1448 Duke St., Alexandria, VA 22314. Phone: (703)836-4800 Fax: (703)836-9678 E-mail: iaapa@iaapa.org • URL: http://www.iaapa.org • Formerly International Association of Amusement Parks.

Outdoor Amusement Business Association. 1035 S Semoran Blvd., Ste. 1045A, Winter Park, FL 32792. Phone: 800-517-OABA or (407)681-9444 Fax: (407)681-9445 E-mail: oaba@aol.com • URL: http://www.oaba.org • Represents executives and employees of carnivals and fairs; ride owners; independent food and games concessionaires; manufacturers and suppliers of equipment. Promotes and lobbies on behalf of the interests of the outdoor amusement industry; provides a center for dissemination of information.

OTHER SOURCES

Lindey on Entertainment, Publishing and the Arts: Agreements and the Law. Alexander Lindey, editor. West Group. • $935.00 per year. Six looseleaf volumes. Periodic supplementation. Provides basic forms, applicable law, and guidance.

Sports and Entertainment Litigation Reporter. An-

drews Publications. • Monthly. $899.00 per year. Newsletter. Provides reports on lawsuits involving films, TV, cable broadcasting, stage productions, radio, and other areas of the entertainment business. Formerly *Sports and Entertainment Litigation Reporter.*

AMUSEMENT PARKS

See: AMUSEMENT INDUSTRY

ANIMAL INDUSTRY

See: LIVESTOCK INDUSTRY

ANIMATION, COMPUTER

See: COMPUTER ANIMATION

ANNIVERSARIES AND HOLIDAYS

See also: CHRONOLOGY; SPECIAL EVENT PLANNING

GENERAL WORKS

The Folklore of American Holidays. Gale Cengage Learning. • 1999. $140.00. Third edition. Festivals, rituals, beliefs, superstitions, etc., arranged according to holiday.

The Folklore of World Holidays. Gale Cengage Learning. • 1999. $140.00. Third edition. Contains descriptions of the important holidays in more than 150 countries.

DIRECTORIES

Chase's Calendar of Events: The Day-by-Day Directory. McGraw-Hill. • Annual. $52.95. Provides information for over 12,000 special days and special events throughout the world. Chronological arrangement with an alphabetical index. Formerly *Chase's Annual Events.*

ENCYCLOPEDIAS AND DICTIONARIES

Holidays, Festivals, and Celebrations of the World Dictionary: Detailing More Than 2,500 Observances from All 50 States and More Than 100 Nations. Helen Henderson and Sue Ellen Thompson, editors. Omnigraphics, Inc. • 2001. $98.00. Third edition.

HANDBOOKS AND MANUALS

Anniversaries and Holidays. Bernard Trawicky. American Library Association. • 2000. $68.00. Fifth edition. Provides information on 3,500 holidays and anniversaries.

Holidays and Anniversaries of the World. Gale Cengage Learning. • 1998. $125.00. Third edition. Lists 23,000 regional, national and international holidays and anniversaries. Includes birthdays of famous people, days of the saints and other days of religious significance.

TRADE/PROFESSIONAL ASSOCIATIONS

Holiday Institute of Yonkers. c/o William Bickel, P.O. Box 2, Kenvil, NJ 07847-0002. E-mail: bbickel@cris.com • Seeks to research, study, celebrate and promote interest in holidays in general.

ANNUAL REPORTS OF CORPORATIONS

See: CORPORATION REPORTS

ANNUAL WAGE PLANS

See: WAGES AND SALARIES

ANNUITIES

ALMANACS AND YEARBOOKS

Investment Company Yearbook. Thomson Financial. • Annual. $310.00. Provides an "entire history of recent events in the mutual funds industry," with emphasis on changes during the past year. About 100 pages are devoted to general information and advice for fund investors. Includes 600 full-page profiles of popular mutual funds, with brief descriptions of 10,000 others, plus 7,000 variable annuities and 500 closed-end funds. Contains a glossary of technical terms, a Web site index, and an overall book index. Also known as *Wiesenberger Investment Companies Yearbook.*

DIRECTORIES

S & P's Insurance Book. Standard & Poor's Ratings Group, Insurance Rating Services. • Quarterly. Price on application. Contains detailed financial analyses and ratings of various kinds of insurance companies.

S & P's Insurance Digest: Life Insurance Edition. Standard & Poor's Ratings Group, Insurance Rating Services. • Quarterly. Contains concise financial analyses and ratings of life insurance companies.

ENCYCLOPEDIAS AND DICTIONARIES

Dictionary of Finance and Investment Terms. John Downes. Barron's Educational Series, Inc. • 2002. $14.95. Sixth edition. Provides clear explanations of more than 5,000 business, banking, financial, investment, and tax terms. Includes a separate list of financial abbreviations and acronyms. (Business Dictionaries Series).

Rupp's Insurance and Risk Management Glossary. Richard V. Rupp. NILS Publishing Co. • 2001. $35.00. Second edition. Provides definitions of 6,400 insurance words and phrases. Includes a guide to acronyms and abbreviations.

HANDBOOKS AND MANUALS

Charitable Planning Primer. Ralph G. Miller and Adam Smalley. CCH, Inc. • 1999. $99.00. Covers the legal and tax aspects of charitable giving and planned gifts. Includes annuity documents, tax forms, tables, and examples.

The Complete Book of Insurance: Protecting Your Life, Health Property, and Income. Ben G. Baldwin. McGraw-Hill. • 1991. $24.95. Provides basic information and advice on various kinds of insurance: life, health, property (fire), disability, long-term care, automobile, liability, and annuities.

Federal Tax Course. Aspen Publishers, Inc. • Annual. $210.00. Provides basic reference and training for various forms of federal taxation: individual, business, corporate, partnership, estate, gift, etc.

Federal Tax Manual. CCH, Inc. • Monthly. $342.00 per year. Looseleaf service. Covers "basic federal tax rules and forms affecting individuals and businesses." Includes a copy of *Annuity, Depreciation, and Withholding Tables.*

Financial Planning Applications. Thomas P. Langdon and William J. Ruckstuhl. The American College. • 2003. $70.00. 19th edition. Emphasis on annuities and life insurance.

How to Build Wealth with Tax-Sheltered Investments. Kerry Anne Lynch. American Institute for Economic Research. • 2000. $6.00. Provides practical information on conservative tax shelters, including defined-contribution pension plans, individual retirement accounts, Keogh plans, U. S. savings bonds, municipal bonds, and various kinds of annuities: deferred, variable-rate, immediate, and foreign-currency. (Economic Education Bulletin.).

McGill's Life Insurance. Edward E. Graves, editor. The American College. • 2002. $80.00. Fourth edition. Contains chapters by various authors on diverse kinds of life insurance, as well as annuities, disability insurance, long-term care insurance, risk management, reinsurance, and other insurance topics. (Huebner School Series).

Working with Tax-Sheltered Annuities: 403(b) Plans Explained. Steven Leventhal. CCH, Inc. • 2001. $75.95. Fourth edition. Emphasis is on legal aspects of tax-deferred annuities.

INTERNET DATABASES

ACGA: Partners in Philanthropy. American Council on Gift Annuities. Phone: (317)269-6271 Fax: (317)269-6276 E-mail: acga@acga-web.org • URL: http://www.acga-web.org • Web site provides detailed information on gift annuities, including suggested charitable gift annuity rates for use by charities and their donors. Rates for immediate and deferred annuities are presented in the form of tables for ages 20 to 90 (and over), for both "Single Life" and "Two Lives - Joint and Survivor." Other items covered include the philosophy of gift annuities, state regulations, "What's New," and a search site. Fees: Free.

InsWeb. InsWeb Corp. Phone: (916)853-3300 E-mail: info@insweb.com • URL: http://www.insweb.com • Web site offers a wide variety of advice and information on automobile, life, health, and "other" insurance. Includes glossaries of insurance terms, Standard & Poor's ratings of individual insurance companies, and "Financial Needs Estimators." Searching is available. Fees: Free.

PERIODICALS AND NEWSLETTERS

Annuity and Life Insurance Shopper. United States Annuities. • Semiannual. $25.00 per year. Provides information on rates and performance for fixed annuities, variable annuities, and term life policies issued by more than 250 insurance companies.

Annuity Market News. Thomson Media. • Monthly. $625.00 per year. Newsletter. Edited for investment and insurance professionals. Covers the marketing, management, and servicing of variable and fixed annuity products.

Best's Review: Inurance Issues and Analysis. A.M. Best Co. • Monthly. $25.00 per year. Editorial coverage of significant industry trends, developments, and important events. Formerly Best's Review: Property-Casualty Insurance.

Broker World. Insurance Publications, Inc. • Bimonthly. $6.00 per year. Edited for independent insurance agents and brokers. Special feature issue topics include annuities, disability insurance, estate planning, and life insurance.

Financial Planning: The Magazine for Financial Service Professionals. Thomson Media. • Monthly. $79.00 per year. Edited for independent financial planners and insurance agents. Covers retirement planning, estate planning, tax planning, and insurance, including long-term healthcare considerations. Special features include a Retirement Planning Issue, Mutual Fund Performance Survey, and Variable Life and Annuity Survey.

Guide to Life, Health, and Annuity Insurers: A Quarterly Compilation of Insurance Company Ratings and Analysis. Weiss Ratings, Inc. • Quarterly. $438.00 per year. Emphasis is on rating of financial safety and relative risk. Includes annual summary.

National Underwriter. The National Underwriter Co. • Weekly. Two editions: *Life* or *Health.* $86.00 per year, each edition.

On Wall Street. Thomson Media. • Monthly. $96.00 per year. Edited for securities dealers. Includes articles on financial planning, retirement planning, variable annuities, and money management, with special coverage of 401(k) plans and IRAs.

TRADE/PROFESSIONAL ASSOCIATIONS

Association for Advanced Life Underwriting. 2901 Telestar Court, Falls Church, VA 22042. Phone: 888-275-0092 or (703)641-9400 Fax: (703)641-9885 E-mail: info@aalu.org • URL: http://www.aalu.org.

ANNUITY TABLES

See: INTEREST

ANSWERING SERVICE

See: TELEPHONE ANSWERING SERVICE

ANTHRACITE COAL

See: COAL INDUSTRY

ANTIMONY INDUSTRY

See: METAL INDUSTRY

ANTIQUES AS AN INVESTMENT

See also: ART AS AN INVESTMENT

DIRECTORIES

Antique Shop Guide--Central Edition. Mayhill Publications. • Covers: antique shops in Illinois, Indiana, Iowa, Kentucky, Michigan, Minnesota, Missouri, Ohio, Tennessee, Wisconsin, western Pennsylvania, and West Virginia. Entries include: For antique shops--Shop name, address, map reference, specialty, whether reproductions are stocked, hours and seasons open, phone. Listings for other categories have similar detail.

National Antique and Art Dealers Association of America Membership Directory. National Antique and Art Dealers Association of America. • Annual. Price on application. Provides a list of 46 members and their areas of specialization in the decorative arts.

HANDBOOKS AND MANUALS

Collectibles Broker. Entrepreneur Media, Inc. • Looseleaf. $59.50. A practical guide to starting a brokerage service for collectibles. Covers profit potential, start-up costs, market size evaluation, owner's time required, pricing, accounting, advertising, promotion, etc. (Start-Up Business Guide No. E1360.).

PERIODICALS AND NEWSLETTERS

Antique Dealer and Collector's Guide: The International Magazine for Dealers and Collectors. Statuscourt Ltd. • Monthly. $44.00 per year. Incorporates *Art and Antiques.*

Art and Antiques. Trans World Publishing Co. • 11 times a year. $24.95 per year. Incorporates *Antique Monthly.*

The Magazine Antiques. Brant Publications, Inc. • Monthly. Individuals. $39.95 per year; libraries, $34.95 per year. Emphasizes antique furniture, but also covers paintings, architecture, glass and textiles. Formerly *Antiques.*

PRICE SOURCES

Kovels' on Antiques and Collectibles: The Newsletter for Dealers, Collectors, and Investors. Antiques Inc. • Monthly. $46.00 per year.

Miller's Antiques Shops, Fairs and Auctions. Antique Collectors' Club. • Annual. $35.00.

Pictorial Price Guide to American Antiques: 2002-2003. Dorothy Hammond. Antique Collectors Club. • 2002 $19.95 (Pictorial Price Guide to American Antiques Series).

Warman's Antiques and Collectibles Price Guide. Krause Publications, Inc. • Annual. $19.99. Manufacturer profiles, key events, current status, collector's clubs, museums, resources available for Americana and collectibles.

TRADE/PROFESSIONAL ASSOCIATIONS

Antique Appraisal Association of America. 386 Park Ave. S, Ste. 2000, New York, NY 10016. Phone: (212)889-5404 Fax: (212)889-5503 E-mail: aaa1@rcn.com • URL: http://www.appraisersassoc.org

Art and Antique Dealers League of America. 1040 Madison Ave., New York, NY 10021-0111. Phone: (212)879-7558 Fax: (212)772-7197 • URL: http://www.artantiquedealersleague.com • Members are retailers and wholesalers of antiques and art objects.

Mid-Am Antique Appraisers Association. PO Box 123, Springfield, MO 65801-0123. Phone: (417)865-7269 Fax: (417)865-7269 E-mail: info@mpif.org • Antique, art, and collectible dealers. To maintain a high standard of ethics for appraising by exhibiting honesty, integrity, and professional conduct while evaluating merchandise at the current fair market value.

The Questers. 210 S Quince St., Philadelphia, PA 19107-5534. Phone: (215)923-5183 Fax: (212)251-0890 E-mail: wjones@pinechemicals.org • URL: http://www.questers1944.org • Promotes the study and appreciation of antiques and objects of art and their historical backgrounds; aids in the restoration and preservation of historical places. Has donated several antique pieces to the White House and has contributed financially to historic houses, villages, and foundations. Sponsors annual scholarship at Columbia University for graduate studies in the field of architectural restoration. Maintains library of 1000 volumes on history, people, and artifacts.

World Antique Dealers Association. 818 Marion Ave., 818 Marion Ave., Mansfield, OH 44906. Phone: (419)756-4374 Fax: (419)756-4979 E-mail: drjm@richnet.net • Antique dealers, educators, authors, auctioneers, show managers, and museum professionals dedicated to the promotion and preservation of the antiques profession and fair and honest representation of antiques. Seeks to build a more professional and reliable approach to the purchase and sale of antiques. Establishes standards to clearly price merchandise, refund purchase money if merchandise is found to be other than represented. Receives and transmits pertinent information, actively engages in curbing unethical practices, and promotes the dignity of the antiques profession. Conducts seminars and study groups.

ANTITRUST ACTIONS

GENERAL WORKS

American Industry: Structure, Conduct, Performance. Richard E. Caves. Prentice Hall PTR. • 1992. $60.00. Seventh edition.

Monopolies in America: Empire Builders and Their Enemies from Jay Gould to Bill Gates. Charles R. Geisst. DIANE Publishing Co. • 2000. $30.00. Provides a panoramic, historical view of U. S. trusts, monopolies, and antitrust activities.

ABSTRACTS AND INDEXES

Current Law Index: Multiple Access to Legal Periodicals. Gale Cengage Learning. • Monthly. $725.00 per year. Produced in cooperation with the American Association of Law Libraries. Indexes more than 900 law journals, legal newspapers, and specialty publications from the U.S., Canada, U.K.,

Ireland, Australia, and New Zealand.

HANDBOOKS AND MANUALS

Antitrust Division Manual. Available from U. S. Government Printing Office. • Looseleaf. $60.00. Includes basic manual, with supplementary material for an indeterminate period. Serves as a guide to the operating policies and procedures of the Antitrust Division of the U. S. Department of Justice (http://www.usdoj.gov). Covers suggested methods of conducting investigations and litigation.

Antitrust-Intellectual Property Handbook. Alan J. Weinschel. Glasser Legalworks. • Looseleaf. $175.00. Periodic supplementation. Covers patent licensing, patent antitrust issues, innovation markets, intervention by government agencies, standard-setting activities, royalty arrangements, and related intellectual property/antitrust topics. Provides explanations, legal guidance, and historical background.

Antitrust Law and Practice. West Publishing Co. • Periodic supplementation. Price on application.

Antitrust Law Handbook. William C. Holmes. West Group. • 2004. $286.50. Overview of antitrust law from procedural to substantive issues.

Antitrust Laws and Trade Regulation: Desk Edition. LexisNexis Matthew Bender. • $709.00. Two looseleaf volumes. Periodic supplementation. The history and organization of the antitrust laws.

INTERNET DATABASES

Lexis.com Research System. Lexis-Nexis Group. Phone: 800-227-4908 or (937)865-6800 Fax: (937)865-6909 E-mail: webmaster@prod.lexisnexis.com • URL: http://www.lexis.com • Fee-based Web site offers extensive searching of a wide variety of legal sources. Additional features include Daily Opinion Service, lexis.com Bookstore, Career Center, CLE Center, Law Schools, and Practice Pages ("Pages specific to areas of specialty").

PERIODICALS AND NEWSLETTERS

The Antitrust Bulletin. Federal Legal Publications, Inc. • Quarterly. Institutions, $85.00 per year.

Antitrust Law and Economics Review. Charles E. Mueller, editor. Antitrust Law and Economics Review, Inc. • Quarterly. $144.50 per year.

Antitrust Law Journal. American Bar Association, Antitrust Law Section. • Three times a year. Free to members; non-members, $40.00 per year.

OTHER SOURCES

Antitrust and Trade Regulation Report. BNA, Inc. • Weekly. $1,479.00 per year. Looseleaf service.

Antitrust Basics. American Lawyer Media, Inc. • Looseleaf. $179.00. Updated as needed. Discusses "business practices consistently upheld, as well as those consistently condemned." Covers a wide variety of antitrust legal topics. (Law Journal Press).

Antitrust Counseling and Litigation Techniques. LexisNexis Matthew Bender. • Annual. $938.00 per year. Five looseleaf volumes.

Antitrust Laws and Trade Regulation. LexisNexis Matthew Bender. • $1,990.00. 11 looseleaf volumes. Periodic supplementation. Covers provisions and applications of the Sherman, Clayton, Robinson-Patman, and Federal Trade Commission Acts. Also covers state antitrust laws.

Antitrust Litigation Reporter: The National Journal of Record on Antitrust Litigation. Andrews Publications. • Monthly. $775.00 per year. Newsletter. Provides reports on federal and state antitrust statutes.

Callmann on Unfair Competition, Trademarks and Monopolies. Louis Altman and Rudolf Callmann. West Group. • Semiannual. $1,270.00 per year. 10 looseleaf volumes. Covers various aspects of anti-competitive behavior.

Intellectual Property and Antitrust Law. William C.

Holmes. West Group. • Semiannual. $389.00 per year. Two looseleaf volumes. Includes patent, trademark, and copyright practices.

White Collar Crime: Business and Regulatory Offenses. American Lawyer Media, Inc. • Looseleaf. $249.00. Updated as needed. Covers such legal matters as criminal tax cases, securities fraud, computer crime, mail fraud, bank embezzlement, criminal antitrust activities, extortion, perjury, the criminal liability of corporations, and RICO (Racketeer Influenced and Corrupt Organization Act). (Law Journal Press).

ANXIETY

See: STRESS (ANXIETY)

APARTMENT HOUSES

See also: BUILDING INDUSTRY; CONDOMINIUMS; REAL ESTATE BUSINESS

GENERAL WORKS

Real Estate Finance and Investments. William B. Brueggeman and Jeffrey Fisher. McGraw-Hill. • 2001. 11th edition. Price on application. Covers mortgage loans, financing, risk analysis, income properties, land development, real estate investment trusts, and related topics. (Finance, Insurance and Real Estate Series).

Rethinking Rental Housing. John I. Gilderbloom and Richard P. Applebaum. Temple University Press. • 1987. $44.95. Emphasis on social and political factors.

CD-ROM DATABASES

Sourcebooks America CD-ROM. CACI Marketing Systems. • Annual. $1,250.00. Provides the CD-ROM version of *The Sourcebook of ZIP Code Demographics: Census Edition* and *The Sourcebook of County Demographics: Census Edition.*

HANDBOOKS AND MANUALS

Every Landlord's Legal Guide. Marcia Stewart and others. Nolo. • 2003. $44.99. Sixth edition.

Every Tenant's Legal Guide. Janet Portman and Marcia Stewart. Nolo. • 2002. $29.99. Third edition.

The Landlord's Handbook: A Complete Guide to Managing Small Residential and Commercial Properties. Daniel Goodwin and Richard Rusdorf. Dearborn Trade Publishing, A Kaplan Professional Co. • 2003. $29.95. Third edition. Covers such topics as finding good tenants, rent collection, insurance, taxes, environmental issues, leases, security deposits, and evictions.

Real Estate Finance and Investment Manual: A Guide to Money Making Strategies. Jack Cummings. Prentice Hall PTR. • 1997. $34.95. Second edition.

ONLINE DATABASES

Information Bank Abstracts. New York Times Index Dept. • Provides indexing and abstracting of current affairs, primarily from the final late edition of *The New York Times* and the Eastern edition of *The Wall Street Journal.* Time period is 1969 to present, with daily updates. Inquire as to online cost and availability.

PERIODICALS AND NEWSLETTERS

Affordable Housing Finance. Alexander & Edwards Publishing. • Ten times a year. $119.00 per year. Provides advice and information on obtaining financing for lower-cost housing. Covers both government and private sources.

Apartment Finance Today. Alexander & Edwards Publishing. • Bimonthly. $29.00 per year. Covers mortgages and financial services for apartment developers, builders, and owners.

Apartment Management Magazine. Apartment News Publications, Inc. • Monthly. $24.00 per year. In four Los Angeles area editions, one Orange County edition.

Apartment Management Newsletter: Wealth Building Techniques for Apartment Owners and Their Managers. Apartment Management Publishing Co., Inc. • Monthly. $95.00 per year.

Buildings: The Source for Facilities Decision-Makers. Stamats Communications, Inc. • Monthly. $70.00 per year. Serves professional building ownership/management organizations.

Housing the Elderly Report. Community Development Services, Inc. CD Publications. • Monthly. $249.00 per year. Newsletter. Edited for retirement communities, apartment projects, and nursing homes. Covers news relative to business and property management issues.

Ledger Quarterly: A Financial Review for Community Association Practitioners. Community Associations Institute. • Quarterly. $67.00 per year. Newsletter. Provides current information on issues affecting the finances of condominium, cooperative, homeowner, apartment, and other community housing associations.

Managing Housing Letter. Community Development Services, Inc. CD Publications. • Description: Provides news and advice for owners and managers of rental housing--public, private, and subsidized--including news from Washington and practical management tips. Recurring features include news of research.

Marketscore. CB Richard Ellis. • Quarterly. Price on application. Newsletter. Provides proprietary forecasts of commercial real estate performance in metropolitan areas.

Metropolitan Home: Style for Our Generation. Hachette Filipacchi Media U.S., Inc. • Bimonthly. $17.94 per year.

Multi-Housing News (MHN). VNU Business Media. • Monthly. $80.00 per year. Individuals and firms primarily engaged in the development, construction, planning and management of multi-housing.

Quarterly Market Report. Property and Portfolio Research. • Quarterly. $1,000.00 per year for one property type; 2,000 per year for six property types. Newsletter. Reviews current prices, rents, capitalization rates, and occupancy trends for commercial real estate.

PRICE SOURCES

National Real Estate Index. CB Richard Ellis. • Price and frequency on application. Provides reports on commercial real estate prices, rents, capitalization rates, and trends in more than 65 metropolitan areas. Time span is 12 years. Includes urban office buildings, suburban offices, warehouses, retail properties, and apartments.

STATISTICS SOURCES

American Housing Survey for the United States in [year]. Available from U. S. Government Printing Office. • Biennial. $51.00. Issued by the U. S. Census Bureau (http://www.census.gov). Covers both owner-occupied and renter-occupied housing. Includes data on such factors as condition of building, type of mortgage, utility costs, and housing occupied by minorities. (Current Housing Reports, H150.).

Characteristics of Apartments Completed. U.S. Bureau of the Census. Available from U.S. Government Printing Office. • Annual.

Characteristics of Apartments Completed: [year]. U.S. Census Bureau. • Annual. Free. Covers privately financed, nonsubsidized apartments in buildings with five units or more.

Housing Starts. U.S. Bureau of the Census. Available from U.S. Government Printing Office. •

Monthly. Construction Reports: C-20.

Housing Statistics of the United States. Patrick A. Simmons. Bernan Press. • 2000. $89.00. Third edition. (Housing Statistics of the United States Series).

Market Absorption of Apartments. U.S. Bureau of the Census. Available from U.S. Government Printing Office. • Quarterly and annual. $16.00 per year. Current Housing Report H-130.

U. S. Housing Markets. Hanley-Wood, LLC. • Monthly. $345.00 per year. Includes eight interim reports. Provides data on residential building permits, apartment building completions, rental vacancy rates, sales of existing homes, average home prices, housing affordability, etc. All major U. S. cities and areas are covered.

Value of New Construction Put in Place. U.S. Bureau of the Census. Available from U.S. Government Printing Office. • Monthly. $42.00 per year.

TRADE/PROFESSIONAL ASSOCIATIONS

Community Associations Institute. 225 Reinekers Ln., Ste. 300, Alexandria, VA 22314. Phone: 888-CAI-4321 or (703)548-8600 Fax: (703)684-1581 E-mail: caidirect@caionline.org • URL: http://www.caionline.org • Condominium and homeowner associations, cooperatives, and association-governed planned communities of all sizes and architectural types; community or property managers and management firms; individual homeowners; community association managers and management firms; public officials; and lawyers, accountants, engineers, reserve specialists, builder/developers and other providers of professional services and products for CAs. Seeks to educate and represent America's 250,000 residential condominium, cooperative and homeowner associations and related professionals and service providers. Aims to foster vibrant, responsive, competent community associations that promote harmony, community and responsible leadership.

OTHER SOURCES

Apartment Building Income-Expense Analysis. Institute of Real Estate Management. • Annual.

APPARATUS, SCIENTIFIC

See: SCIENTIFIC APPARATUS AND INSTRUMENT INDUSTRIES

APPAREL, CHILDREN'S

See: CHILDREN'S APPAREL INDUSTRY

APPAREL INDUSTRY

See: CLOTHING INDUSTRY

APPAREL, MEN'S

See: MEN'S CLOTHING INDUSTRY

APPAREL, WOMEN'S

See: WOMEN'S APPAREL

APPLE INDUSTRY

See also: FRUIT INDUSTRY

ALMANACS AND YEARBOOKS

CRB Commodity Yearbook. Commodity Research Bureau. CRB. • Annual. $99.95.

CD-ROM DATABASES

Food Science and Technology Abstracts [CD-ROM]. Available from SilverPlatter Information,

Inc. • Quarterly. Produced by International Food Information Service (home page is http://www.ifis.org). Provides worldwide coverage on CD-ROM of the literature of food technology and production. Various types of publications are indexed, with abstracts, including about 1,800 periodicals. Time period is 1969 to date.

DIRECTORIES

Major Food and Drink Companies of the World. Available from Gale Cengage Learning. • Annual. $880.00. Two volumes. Published by Graham & Whiteside. Contains profiles and trade names for more than 9,800 important food and beverage companies in various countries. In addition to foods, includes both alcoholic and nonalcoholic drink products.

Thomas Food and Beverage Market Place. Grey House Publishing. • 2004. $495.00. Three volumes. Contains more than 40,000 entries covering food companies, beverages, food equipment, warehouse companies, food brokers, wholesalers, importers, and exporters. Formerly *Thomas Food Industry Register.*

FINANCIAL RATIOS

Industry Norms and Key Business Ratios. Desk Top Edition. Dun and Bradstreet Corp. • Annual. Five volumes. $475.00 per volume. $1,890.00 per set. Covers over 800 kinds of businesses, arranged by Standard Industrial Classification number. More detailed editions covering longer periods of time are also available.

INTERNET DATABASES

USDA. United States Department of Agriculture. Phone: (202)720-2791 E-mail: agsec@usda.gov • URL: http://www.usda.gov • The USDA home page has six sections: News and Information; What's New; About USDA; Agencies; Opportunities; Search and Help. Keyword searching is offered from the USDA home page and from various individual agency home pages. Agencies are the Economic Research Service, Agricultural Marketing Service, National Agricultural Statistics Service, National Agricultural Library, and about 12 others. Updating varies. Fees: Free.

ONLINE DATABASES

Agricola. U.S. National Agricultural Library. • Covers worldwide agricultural literature. Over 3.3 million citations, 1970 to present, with monthly updates. Inquire as to online cost and availability.

CAB Abstracts. CAB Publishing North America. • Contains 46 specialized abstract collections covering over 10,000 journals and monographs in the areas of agriculture, horticulture, forest products, farm products, nutrition, dairy science, poultry, grains, animal health, entomology, etc. Time period is 1972 to date, with monthly updates. Inquire as to online cost and availability. *CAB Abstracts on CD-ROM* also available, with annual updating.

Food Science and Technology Abstracts [online]. IFIS North American Desk. • Produced by International Food Information Service. Provides about 500,000 online citations, with abstracts, to the international literature of food science, technology, commodities, engineering, and processing. Approximately 2,000 periodicals are covered. Time period is 1969 to date, with monthly updates. Inquire as to online cost and availability.

PERIODICALS AND NEWSLETTERS

American Fruit Grower. Meister Media. • Monthly. $27.47 per year.

Apple News. U.S. Apple Association. • Description: Reports national and international events in the apple industry; includes statistics and article title index in each issue.

Good Fruit Grower. Fruit Commission. • Semimonthly. $30.00 per year.

Journal of Tree Fruit Production. Haworth Press, Inc. • Semiannual. Institutions, $95.00 per year. A research journal for tree fruit growers.

PRICE SOURCES

PPI Detailed Report. Bureau of Labor Statistics, U.S. Department of Labor. Available from U.S. Government Printing Office. • Monthly. $55.00 per year. Formerly *Producer Price Indexes*.

RESEARCH CENTERS AND INSTITUTES

Fruit Research and Extension Center. Pennsylvania State University. 239 University Dr., Biglerville, PA 17307. Phone: (717)677-6116 Fax: (717)677-4112 E-mail: lah4@psu.edu • URL: http://www.frec.cas. psu.edu/.

Kearneysville Tree Fruit Research and Education Center. West Virginia University. P.O. Box 609, Kearneysville, WV 25430-0609. Phone: (304)876-6353 Fax: (304)876-6034 E-mail: dleach@wvu.edu • URL: http://www.caf.wvu.edu/kearneysville.

Peninsular Agricultural Research Station. University of Wisconsin - Madison. 4312 Highway 42, Sturgeon Bay, WI 54235. Phone: (414)743-5406 Fax: (414)743-1080 E-mail: rweidman@facstaff. wisc.edu • URL: http://www.wisc.edu/.

Rutgers Agricultural Research and Extension Center. Rutgers University. 121 Northville Rd., Bridgeton, NJ 08302-5919. Phone: (856)455-3100 Fax: (856)455-3133 E-mail: nicholson@aesop. rutgers.edu.

Sandhills Research Station. North Carolina Dept. of Agriculture and Consumer Services. 2664 Windblow Rd., Jackson Springs, NC 27281. Phone: (910)974-4673 Fax: (910)974-4462.

STATISTICS SOURCES

Agricultural Statistics. Available from U. S. Government Printing Office. • Annual. $38.00. Produced by the National Agricultural Statistics Service, U. S. Department of Agriculture. Provides a wide variety of statistical data relating to agricultural production, supplies, consumption, prices/price-supports, foreign trade, costs, and returns, as well as farm labor, loans, income, and population. In many cases, historical data is shown annually for 10 years. In addition to farm data, includes detailed fishery statistics.

FAO Production Yearbook. Available from Bernan Associates. • Annual. $45.00. Published by the Food and Agriculture Organization (http://www.fao.org). Contains worldwide data on agriculture, land use, farm crops, livestock, and agricultural prices.

FAO Trade Yearbook. Available from Bernan Associates. • Annual. $45.00. Published by the Food and Agriculture Organization (http://www.fao.org). Provides extensive worldwide data on exports and imports of agricultural commodities, fertilizers, tractors, and pesticides. Includes more than 130 tables of detailed statistics.

United States Census of Agriculture. U.S. Bureau of the Census. • Quinquennial. Results presented in reports, tape, CD-ROM, and Diskette files.

World Food Data and Statistics. Euromonitor International. • 2004. $650.00. Provides five-year data for a wide variety of food products in 52 countries. Includes market size, consumer expenditures, price indicators, and retail distribution data for many kinds of meat, fish, fruits, vegetables, dairy products, baked goods, condiments, canned food, and frozen food.

TRADE/PROFESSIONAL ASSOCIATIONS

Apple Products Research and Education Council. 5775 Peachtree-Dunwoody Rd., Bldg. G, Ste. 500, Atlanta, GA 30342. Phone: (404)252-3663 Fax: (404)252-0774 E-mail: info@appleproducts.org • URL: http://www.appleproducts.org • Represents processors of apple products and suppliers to the industry. Conducts program to improve business

conditions in the apple products industry and to enable the industry to serve the interests of consumers. Conducts research programs on the health benefits of apple products.

US Apple Association. 8233 Old Courthouse Rd., Ste. 200, Vienna, VA 22182. Phone: 800-781-4443 or (703)442-8850 Fax: (703)790-0845 E-mail: jdaly@usapple.org • URL: http://www.usapple.org • Formerly International Apple Institute.

APPLIANCES

See: ELECTRIC APPLIANCE INDUSTRY

APPLICATIONS FOR POSITIONS

See: JOB RESUMES

APPRAISAL (ALL PROPERTY)

See: VALUATION

APPRAISAL OF REAL ESTATE

See: REAL PROPERTY VALUATION

AQUACULTURE

ABSTRACTS AND INDEXES

Aquatic Sciences and Fisheries Abstracts: Aquatic Pollution and Environmental Quality. Food and Agriculture Organization of the United Nations. CSA. • Bimonthly. $520.00 per year. Part three. Includes print and online editions.

ENCYCLOPEDIAS AND DICTIONARIES

Encyclopedia of Aquaculture. Robert R. Stickney. John Wiley and Sons, Inc. • 2000. $415.00. Includes both economic and biological aspects of aquaculture and fish farming.

ONLINE DATABASES

ASFA Aquaculture Abstracts [Online]. Cambridge Scientific Abstracts. • Indexing and abstracting of the literature of marine life, 1984 to present. Inquire as to online cost and availability.

PERIODICALS AND NEWSLETTERS

Aquaculture Magazine. Achill River Corp. • Bimonthly. $24.00 per year.

Aquaculture Magazine. Aquill River Corp. • Bimonthly. $24.00 per year.

Journal of Aquatic Food Product Technology: An International Journal Devoted to Foods from Marine and Inland Waters of the World. Haworth Press, Inc. • Quarterly. $375.00 per year.

North American Journal of Aquaculture. American Fisheries Society. • Quarterly. $195.00 per year. Covers research and new developments relating to aquaculture.

RESEARCH CENTERS AND INSTITUTES

Aquacultural Research and Teaching Facility. Texas A & M University, Wildlife and Fisheries Sciences, College Station, TX 77843. Phone: (979)272-3422 Fax: (979)845-3786 E-mail: d-gatlin@tamu.edu.

Department of Fisheries and Allied Aquacultures. Auburn University - Alabama Agricultural Experiment Station, Auburn, AL 36849-5419. Phone: (334)844-4786 Fax: (334)844-9208 E-mail:

jjensen@acesag.auburn.edu • URL: http://www.ag. auburn.edu/dept/faa/.

TRADE/PROFESSIONAL ASSOCIATIONS

American Fisheries Society. 5410 Grosvenor Ln., Ste. 110, Bethesda, MD 20814-2199. Phone: (301)897-8616 Fax: (301)897-8096 E-mail: main@ fisheries.org • URL: http://www.fisheries.org • International scientific organization of fisheries and aquatic science professionals, including fish culturists, fish biologists, water quality scientists, fish health professionals, fish technologists, educators, limnologists, and oceanographers. Promotes the development of all branches of fishery science and practice, and the conservation, development, and wise utilization of fisheries, both recreational and commercial. Strengthens professional standards by certifying fisheries scientists, stressing professional ethics, and providing forums for the exchange of scientific and management information. Represents members through written and verbal testimony before legislative and administrative bodies concerning aquatic environmental issues. Maintains over 30 committees.

Aquatic Research Interactive. 1100 W Columbus Dr., East Chicago, IL 46312. Phone: (219)391-4138 Fax: (219)391-4168 E-mail: fishmail@arii.org • URL: http://www.arii.org.

ARBITRATION

GENERAL WORKS

Arbitration: Essential Concepts. Steven C. Bennett. American Lawyer Media, Inc. • 2002. $32.95. Provides basic explanations of arbitration law, history, and relevant case law. Describes practical procedures for arbitration in various fields (labor, employment, securities, international). (ALM Publishing).

Labor Relations. Arthur A. Sloan and Fred Witney. Prentice Hall PTR. • 2000. $115.00. 10th edition. Emphasizes collective bargaining and arbitration.

When Talk Works: Profiles of Mediators. Deborah M. Kolb. John Wiley and Sons, Inc. • 1997. $38.00. Provides interview-based profiles of expert mediators in labor, business, education, family matters, community relations, foreign affairs, and other fields. (Business Management Series).

BIBLIOGRAPHIES

Labor Arbitration: An Annotated Bibliography, 1991-1996. Charles J. Coleman and others, editors. Cornell Universtiy Press. • 1997. $27.50. (ILR Bibliography Series, No. 18).

DIRECTORIES

Martindale-Hubbell International Dispute Resolution Directory. Martindale-Hubbell. • Irregular. $195.00. Produced in cooperation with the American Arbitration Association. Over 45,000 judges, attorneys, law firms, and other neutral experts that specialize in dispute resolution and arbitration.

ONLINE DATABASES

Instant Computer Arbitration Search. LRP Publications. • Provides citations to U. S. labor arbitration cases and a detailed directory of about 2,500 public and private labor arbitrators. Weekly updates. Cases date from 1970. Inquire as to online cost and availability.

PERIODICALS AND NEWSLETTERS

Dispute Resolution Journal. American Arbitration Association. • Quarterly. $125.00 per year. Formerly *Arbitration Journal*.

Labor Relations Bulletin. Aspen Publishers Inc. • Description: Provides information and insight to management and labor officials to help them avoid or resolve conflicts. Recurring features include reports on current developments in labor law and relations, discipline and grievance cases based on actual arbitration, a question and answer column on labor and employment relations, and a column titled Reflections of an Arbitrator, offering the insight and experience of prominent national arbitrators.

Securities Arbitration Commentator: Covering Significant Issues and Events in Securities-Commodities Arbitration. Richard P. Ryder. • Monthly. $348.00 per year. Newsletter. Edited for attorneys and other professionals concerned with securities arbitration.

Summary of Labor Arbitration Awards. American Arbitration Association, Inc. • Monthly. $120.00 per year.

Weekly Summary of the National Labor Relations Board Cases. Available from U. S. Government Printing Office. • Weekly. $237.00 per year. Issued by the Division of Information, National Labor Relations Board.

TRADE/PROFESSIONAL ASSOCIATIONS

American Arbitration Association. 1633 Broadway, 10th Fl., New York, NY 10019. Phone: 800-778-7879 or (212)716-5800 Fax: (212)716-5905 E-mail: websitemail@adr.org • URL: http://www.adr.org • Works to achieve the resolution of disputes through the use of mediation, arbitration, democratic elections, and other voluntary methods. Provides administrative services for arbitrating, mediating, or negotiating disputes and impartial administration of elections. Maintains National Roster of Arbitrators and Mediators for referrals to parties involved in disputes. Conducts skill-building sessions to promote a more complete understanding of conflict resolution processes.

National Academy of Arbitrators. One N Main St., Ste. 412, Cortland, NY 13045. Phone: 800-872-5617 or (607)756-8363 Fax: (607)756-8365 E-mail: naa@igc.org • URL: http://www.naarb.org.

OTHER SOURCES

Labor Arbitration Awards. CCH, Inc. • Weekly. $1,239.00 per year. Looseleaf service.

ARCHITECTURE

See also: BUILDING INDUSTRY

ABSTRACTS AND INDEXES

Architectural Publications Index. British Architectural Library. RIBA Publications Ltd. • Quarterly. Individuals, $450.00 per year. Formerly *Architectural Periodicals Index.*

Art Index. H. W. Wilson Co. • Quarterly. Annual cumulations. Price varies. Subject and author index to periodicals in art, architecture, industrial design, city planning, photography, and various related topics.

Avery Index to Architectural Periodicals. Columbia University, Avery Architectural Library. Available from G.K. Hall Co. • Annual. $995.00.

NTIS Alerts: Building Industry Technology. National Technical Information Service. • Semimonthly. $210.00 per year. Provides descriptions of government-sponsored research reports and software, with ordering information. Covers architecture, construction management, building materials, maintenance, furnishings, and related subjects. Formerly *Abstract Newsletter.*

BIOGRAPHICAL SOURCES

Contemporary Architects. Available from Gale Cengage Learning. • 1994. $190.00. Third edition. Published by St. James Press. Living architects of the world and influential architects of earlier times.

DIRECTORIES

Accredited Programs in Architecture. National Architectural Accrediting Board. • Annual. Free.

Guide to Architecture Schools: Comprehensive Guide to Accredited Schools of Architecture in the United States and Canada. Association of Collegiate Schools of Architecture. • 1994. $19.95. Fifth edition. Descriptions of 120 accredited degree programs and related organizations in architecture. Formerly *Guide to Architecture Schools in North America.*

Plunkett's Real Estate and Construction Industry Almanac. Plunkett Research, Ltd. • 2004. $249.99. Contains profiles of 300 leading firms concerned with real estate or construction. Specialties include architecture, development, mortgages, building engineering, real estate sales, etc. Also covers industry trends and statistical data.

ENCYCLOPEDIAS AND DICTIONARIES

Classical Architecture: An Introduction to Its Vocabulary and Essentials, with a Select Glossary of Terms. James S. Curl. W. W. Norton & Co., Inc. • 2003. $29.95. Second edition. Covers the architectural terminology of the Renaissance, the baroque period, rococo, neoclassicism, and the modern era.

Dictionary of Architecture. James S. Curl. Oxford University Press. • 1999. $55.00. (Reference Series).

Dictionary of Architecture and Construction. Cyril M. Harris. McGraw-Hill. • 2000. $69.95. Third edition.

Illustrated Dictionary of Historic Architecture. Cyril M. Harris, editor. Dover Publications, Inc. • 1983. $16.95.

International Dictionary of Architects and Architecture. Saint James Press. • 1993. $295.00. Two volumes. Volume one: *Architects.* Volume two: *Architecture.*

Penguin Dictionary of Architecture and Landscape Architecture. Nikolas Pevsner and others. Penguin Group. • 2000. $16.95. Fifth edition. (Penguin Reference Series).

FINANCIAL RATIOS

Almanac of Business and Industrial Financial Ratios. Leo Troy. Aspen Publishers, Inc. • 2003. $125.95. Includes CD-Rom. Contains financial ratios derived from federal tax returns. Ratios for each of about 200 industries are arranged according to company asset size. (Almanac of Business and Industrial Financial Ratios Series).

Annual Statement Studies. The Risk Management Association. • Annual. Median and quartile financial ratios are given for over 400 kinds of manufacturing, wholesale, retail, construction, and consumer finance establishments. Data is sorted by both asset size and sales volume. Includes a clearly written "Definition of Ratios" and an alphabetical industry index.

Annual Statement Studies: Industry Default Probabilities and Cash Flow Measures. The Risk Management Association. • Annual. $145.00. Serves as a companion volume to the original *Annual Statement Studies.* Gives probability of default estimates on a percentage scale for more than 450 industries. Includes changes in position year-by-year for eight financial statement line items and provides percentage measures of cash flow.

HANDBOOKS AND MANUALS

Architects Handbook of Professional Practice. David Haviland. American Institute of Architects Press. • 2000. $225.00. 12th edition.

Architectural Graphic Standards. Charles G. Ramsey and others. John Wiley and Sons, Inc. • 2000. $675.00. 10th edition.

Interior Graphic Standards. Maryrose T. McGowan. John Wiley and Sons, Inc. • 2003. $175.00. Provides guidelines for the planning and detailing of commercial and residential interiors. Includes more than

3,000 architectural drawings.

New Uses for Obsolete Buildings. Urban Land Institute. • 1996. $65.95. Covers various aspects of redevelopment: zoning, building codes, environment, economics, financing, and marketing. Includes eight case studies and 75 descriptions of completed "adaptive use projects.".

ONLINE DATABASES

Art Index Online. H. W. Wilson Co. • Indexes a wide variety of art-related periodicals, 1984 to date. Monthly updates. Inquire as to online cost and availability.

Avery Architectural Periodicals Index. Avery Architectural and Fine Arts Library. • Indexes a wide range of periodicals related to architecture and design. Subjects include building design, building materials, interior design, housing, land use, and city planning. Time span: 1977 to date. *bul* URL: http://www-rlg.stanford.edu/cit-ave.html.

PERIODICALS AND NEWSLETTERS

Architectural Record. American Institute of Architects. McGraw-Hill. • Monthly $59.00 per year. Includes supplements *Record Interiors.* and *Record Houses.*

Architectural Review. Fenner, Reed and Jackson. • Monthly. Individuals, $64.00 per year; students, $40.50 per year. Visits innovative buildings around the world.

Architecture. VNU Business Media. • Monthly. $49.00 per year. Incorporates *Building Renovation.*

Custom Home. Hanley-Wood, LLC. • Seven times a year. $36.00 per year. Edited for "top of the market" custom builders, designers, and architects.

Design Cost Data: The Cost Estimating Magazine for Architects, Builders and Specifiers. L. M. Rector Corp. • Bimonthly. $64.80 per year. Provides a preliminary cost estimating system for architects, contractors, builders, and developers, utilizing historical data. Includes case studies of actual costs. Formerly *Design Cost and Data.*

Journal of Architectural Education. Association of Collegiate Schools of Architecture. MIT Press. • Quarterly. Free to members; non-members, $50.00. Articles on architectural education, theory and practice.

Masonry Construction. Hanley-Wood, LLC. • 10 times a year. $30.00 per year. Covers masonry design, materials, equipment, and techniques.

Residential Architect: Exclusively Housing. Hanley-Wood, LLC. • Monthly. $39.95 per year. Edited for architects specializing in home design.

PRICE SOURCES

Building Construction Cost Data. RSMeans. • Annual. $108.95. Lists over 20,000 entries for estimating.

RESEARCH CENTERS AND INSTITUTES

Center for Environmental Design Research. University of California at Berkeley. 390 Wurster Hall, MC 1839, Berkeley, CA 94720-1839. Phone: (510)642-2896 Fax: (510)643-5571 E-mail: cedr@ced.berkley.edu • URL: http://www.ced.berkley.edu/cedr.

TRADE/PROFESSIONAL ASSOCIATIONS

American Institute of Architects. 1735 New York Ave., N.W., Washington, DC 20006. Phone: 800-242-3837 or (202)626-7300 Fax: (202)626-7547 E-mail: infocentral@aia.org • URL: http://www.aia.org.

National Architectural Accrediting Board. 1735 New York Ave. NW, Washington, DC 20006. Phone: (202)783-2007 Fax: (202)783-2822 E-mail: info@naab.org • URL: http://www.naab.org • Formed by the American Institute of Architects, Association of Collegiate Schools of Architecture, and National Council of Architectural Registration Boards (see separate entries) to stimulate the improvement of architectural education. Conducts continuing program of accreditation of programs of architecture. Compiles statistics; maintains library of 100 volumes of descriptions and self-evaluations of architecture schools.

Society of American Registered Architects. 305 E 46th St., New York, NY 10017. Phone: 888-385-7272 or (914)631-3600 Fax: 888-385-7272 E-mail: rick@hjarchitects.com • URL: http://www.sara-national.org.

OTHER SOURCES

Forms and Agreements for Architects, Engineers and Contractors. Albert Dib. West Group. • Three times a year. $900.00. Five looseleaf volume. Covers evaluation of construction documents and alternative clauses. Includes pleadings for litigation and resolving of claims. (Real Property Law Series).

ARCHIVES MANAGEMENT

See: RECORDS MANAGEMENT

AREA DEVELOPMENT

See: INDUSTRIAL DEVELOPMENT

ARMAMENT AND DEFENSE

See: DEFENSE INDUSTRIES

ARMAMENTS MARKET

See: MILITARY MARKET

ARMY

CD-ROM DATABASES

Leadership Library on CD-ROM: Who's Who in the Leadership of the United States. Leadership Directories, Inc. • Quarterly. Including access to Internet version (weekly updates). Contains all 14 *Yellow Book* personnel directories on CD-ROM, providing contact and brief biographical information for about 400,000 individuals. Covers business, government, financial institutions, news media, law firms, associations, foreign representatives, and nonprofit organizations. Includes photographs.

DIRECTORIES

Carroll's Federal & Federal Regional Directory. Carroll Publishing. • Semiannual. $325.00 per year; with online edition, $1,200 per year. Lists more than 23,000 U. S. government officials throughout the country, including military installations.

Carroll's Federal Regional Directory. Carroll Publishing. • Covers: Over 32,000 officials in federal congressional, judicial, and executive branch departments and agencies outside the District of Columbia. Entries include: Organization or agency name; names, addresses, and phone numbers of key personnel.

Directory of U.S. Military Bases Worldwide. William R. Evinger, editor. Greenwood Publishing Group, Inc. • 1998. $125.00. Third edition.

Federal Regional Yellow Book: Who's Who in the Federal Government's Departments, Agencies, Military Installations, and Service Academies Outside of Washington, DC. Leadership Directories, Inc. • Semiannual. $265.00 per year. Lists over 35,000 federal officials and support staff at 8,000 regional offices.

HANDBOOKS AND MANUALS

The Army Officer's Guide. Keith E. Bonn. Stackpole Books. • 1999. $22.95. 48th edition. (Army Officer's Guide Series).

NCO Guide. Robert L. Rush. Stackpole Books, Inc. • 2003. $18.95. 7th edition.

PERIODICALS AND NEWSLETTERS

Armed Forces Comptroller. American Society of Military Comptrollers. • Quarterly. $18.00 per year.

Armed Forces Journal International. Armed Forces Journal International, Inc. • Monthly. $45.00 per year. A defense magazine for career military officers and industry executives. Covers defense events, plans, policies, budgets, and innovations.

Army Logistician: The Professional Bulletin of United States Army Logistics. United States Army Logistics Management College. Available from U.S. Government Printing Office. • Bimonthly. $21.00 per year.

Army Reserve Magazine. Available from U. S. Government Printing Office. • Quarterly. $14.00 per year. Issued by the Army Reserve, U. S. Department of Defense.

Army Times. Army Times Publishing Co. • Weekly. $52.00 per year. In two editions: Domestic and International.

Soldiers. Available from U. S. Government Printing Office. • Monthly. $38.00 per year. Provides information on the policies, plans, operations, and technical developments of the U.S. Department of the Army (http://www.army.mil).

STATISTICS SOURCES

Annual Report of the Secretary of Defense. U.S. Department of Defense, Office of the Secretary. • Annual.

Budget of the United States Government. U.S. Office of Management and Budget. Available from U.S. Government Printing Office. • Annual. $52.00.

Labour Force Statistics. Organization for Economic Cooperation and Development. Available from OECD Publications and Information Center. • Annual. $98.00. Provides 21 years of data for OECD member countries on population, employment, unemployment, civilian labor force, armed forces, and other labor factors.

Military Prime Contract Awards and Subcontract Payments. U.S. Department of Defense, Office of the Secretary. • Annual.

Quarterly Labour Force Statistics. Organization for Economic Cooperation and Development. Available from OECD Publications and Information Center. • Quarterly. $90.00 per year. Provides current data for OECD member countries on population, employment, unemployment, civilian labor force, armed forces, and other labor factors.

TRADE/PROFESSIONAL ASSOCIATIONS

Army and Air Force Mutual Aid Association. 102 Sheridan Ave., Bldg. 468, Fort Myer, VA 22211-1110. Phone: 800-336-4538 or (703)522-3060 Fax: (703)522-1336 E-mail: info@aafmaa.com • URL: http://www.aafmaa.com • A mutual aid organization providing aid to families of deceased career Army and Airforce officers and noncommissioned officers.

Army Aviation Association of America. 755 Main St., Suite 4D, Monroe, CT 06468-2830. Phone: (203)268-2450 Fax: (203)268-5870 E-mail: aaaa@quad-a.org • URL: http://www.quad-a.org.

Army Emergency Relief. 200 Stovall St., Alexandria, VA 22332-0001. Phone: (866)878-6378 or (703)428-0000 Fax: (703)325-7183 E-mail: aer@aerhq.org • URL: http://www.aerhq.org • A private organization whose primary purpose is to relieve distress of members of the Army (active and retired) and their dependents, and to provide assistance to needy spouses and orphans of deceased Army members; a secondary purpose is to make available educational assistance (scholarships) to unmarried dependent children of soldiers (active, retired, or deceased) who need such assistance to pursue undergraduate studies.

Association of the United States Army. 2425 Wilson Blvd., Arlington, VA 22201-3385. Phone: 800-336-4570 or (703)841-4300 Fax: (703)525-9039 E-mail: ausa-info@ausa.org • URL: http://www.ausa.org.

OTHER SOURCES

Army AL&T: Acquisitions, Logistics, and Technology Bulletin. Available from U. S. Government Printing Office. • Bimonthly. $20.00 per year. Produced by the U. S. Army Materiel Command (http://www.amc.army.mil). Reports on Army research, development, and acquisition. Formerly *Army RD&A.*

Carroll's Defense Organization Charts. Carroll Publishing. • Every six weeks. $1,500.00 per year. Provides more than 200 large, fold-out paper charts showing personnel relationships in 2,400 U. S. military offices. Charts are also available online and on CD-ROM.

ART AS AN INVESTMENT

See also: ANTIQUES AS AN INVESTMENT

ABSTRACTS AND INDEXES

Art Index. H. W. Wilson Co. • Quarterly. Annual cumulations. Price varies. Subject and author index to periodicals in art, architecture, industrial design, city planning, photography, and various related topics.

BIOGRAPHICAL SOURCES

Contemporary Artists. Available from Gale Cengage Learning. • 2002. $265.00. Fifth edition. Published by St. James Press. International coverage.

Who's Who in American Art. Available from Reed Elsevier. • Biennial. $229.00. Lists about 11,800 people active in visual arts. Published by Marquis Who's Who.

Who's Who in Art. Available from Gale Cengage Learning. • Biennial. $140.00 per year. Contains about 3,000 brief biographies of artists, designers, curators, critics, and other art-related individuals. International coverage, with British emphasis. Published by Art Trade Press.

DIRECTORIES

American Art Directory. LexisNexis Group. • Covers: over 7,000 museums, art libraries, and art organizations, and 1,700 art schools; also includes lists of state directors and supervisors of art education in schools, traveling exhibition booking agencies, corporations having art holdings for public viewing, newspapers that carry art notes, art scholarships and fellowships; and 190 national, regional, and state open art exhibitions. Entries include: For museums--Name, address, phone, fax, electronic mail address, name of curator; days and hours of operation, collection, budget, publications. For exhibits--Name, address, phone, fax, electronic mail address, name of contact; date, deadline. For schools--Name, address, phone, name of director, names of faculty members, majors or degrees offered, tuition fees; summer school or adult hobby class information. For newspapers--Name, address, phone, name of art editor.

Art Now Gallery Guides. Art Now Inc. • Covers: in '[M Art Now Gallery Guide--International Edition]' current exhibitions in over 1,800 museums and galleries. Separate regional editions cover metropolitan New York, Boston and New England, the Philadelphia area, the southeast, Chicago and the midwest, the southwest, California and the northwest, Latin America, and Europe. Listings are paid. Entries include: Gallery or museum name, address, phone, days and hours of operation, artist's name or name of the exhibit, medium, and dates of showing.

International Directory of Arts. Available from Gale Cengage Learning. • Annual. $305.00. Three volumes. A guide to more than 126,000 art sources and markets in 175 countries. Includes artists, collectors, dealers, galleries, museums, art schools, auctioneers, restorers, publishers, libraries, and associations. Published by K. G. Saur.

National Antique and Art Dealers Association of America Membership Directory. National Antique and Art Dealers Association of America. • Annual. Price on application. Provides a list of 46 members and their areas of specialization in the decorative arts.

HANDBOOKS AND MANUALS

How to Invest in Your First Works of Art: A Guide for the New Collector. John Carlin. Yarrow Press. • 1990. $11.95.

ONLINE DATABASES

Art Index Online. H. W. Wilson Co. • Indexes a wide variety of art-related periodicals, 1984 to date. Monthly updates. Inquire as to online cost and availability.

PERIODICALS AND NEWSLETTERS

Antique Dealer and Collector's Guide: The International Magazine for Dealers and Collectors. Statuscourt Ltd. • Monthly. $44.00 per year. Incorporates *Art and Antiques.*

Art and Auction. Auction Guild. • 11 times a year. $89.00 per year.

Art in America. Brant Publications, Inc. • Monthly. $39.95 per year; libraries, $34.95. Comprehensive reviews of U.S. and worldwide exhibits.

ARTnews. Artnews LLC. • 11 times a year. $39.95 per year.

PRICE SOURCES

International Auction Records: Engravings, Drawings, Watercolors, Paintings, Sculpture. Archer Fields, Inc. • 1993. $179.00. Back volumes available for most years.

Leonard's Annual Price Index of Art Auctions. Auction Index, Inc. • Annual. $245.00. List major auction houses.

TRADE/PROFESSIONAL ASSOCIATIONS

Allied Artists of America. 15 Gramercy Park, S., New York, NY 10003. Phone: (212)582-6411.

American Artists Professional League. 47 5th Ave., New York, NY 10003. Phone: (212)645-1345 Fax: (212)645-1345 E-mail: aaplinc@gmail.com • URL: http://www.americanartistsprofessionalleague.org • Advances the cause of fine arts in America through the promotion of high standards of beauty, integrity and craftsmanship in painting, sculpture and the graphic arts.

Art and Antique Dealers League of America. 1040 Madison Ave., New York, NY 10021-0111. Phone: (212)879-7558 Fax: (212)772-7197 • URL: http://www.artantiquedealersleague.com • Members are retailers and wholesalers of antiques and art objects.

Art Dealers Association of America. 575 Madison Ave., New York, NY 10022. Phone: (212)940-8590 Fax: (212)940-6484 E-mail: adaa@artdealers.org • URL: http://www.artdealers.org.

Art Information Center. 55 Mercer St., 3rd Fl., New York, NY 10013. Phone: (212)966-3443 E-mail: info@adcglobal.org • Serves as a clearinghouse of information on contemporary fine arts. Assists artists in finding outlets for their work; assists art dealers in finding new talent; aids curators, and collectors. Data collected is donated to the Archives of American Art. **Convention/Meeting:** none.

International Confederation of Art Dealers. 32 rue Ernest Allard, B-1000 Brussels, Belgium. Phone: 32 2 5116777 E-mail: secretry@cinoa.org • URL: http://www.cinoa.org.

National Association of Women Artists, Inc. NAWA Fifth Avenue Gallery, 80 5th Ave., Ste. 1405, New York, NY 10011. Phone: (212)675-1616 Fax:

(212)675-8257 E-mail: nawomena@msn.com • URL: http://www.nawanet.org • Formerly Women's Art Club of the City of New York.

ART BUSINESS

See also: ARTS MANAGEMENT

GENERAL WORKS

Opportunities in Visual Arts Careers. Mark Salmon. McGraw-Hill. • 2001. $15.95. Edited for students and job seekers. Includes education requirements and salary data. (Opportunities in...Series).

ABSTRACTS AND INDEXES

Art Index. H. W. Wilson Co. • Quarterly. Annual cumulations. Price varies. Subject and author index to periodicals in art, architecture, industrial design, city planning, photography, and various related topics.

BIBLIOGRAPHIES

Subject Bibliography: Art and Artists. Available from U. S. Government Printing Office. • Annual. Free. Lists books, pamphlets, periodicals, and other government publications on art-related topics. (Subject Bibliography No. SB-107.).

BIOGRAPHICAL SOURCES

Who's Who in American Art. Available from Reed Elsevier. • Biennial. $229.00. Lists about 11,800 people active in visual arts. Published by Marquis Who's Who.

Who's Who in Art. Available from Gale Cengage Learning. • Biennial. $140.00 per year. Contains about 3,000 brief biographies of artists, designers, curators, critics, and other art-related individuals. International coverage, with British emphasis. Published by Art Trade Press.

CD-ROM DATABASES

WILSONDISC: Art Index. H. W. Wilson Co. • Monthly. Provides CD-ROM indexing of art-related literature from 1982 to date. Price includes online service.

DIRECTORIES

American Art Directory. LexisNexis Group. • Covers: over 7,000 museums, art libraries, and art organizations, and 1,700 art schools; also includes lists of state directors and supervisors of art education in schools, traveling exhibition booking agencies, corporations having art holdings for public viewing, newspapers that carry art notes, art scholarships and fellowships; and 190 national, regional, and state open art exhibitions. Entries include: For museums--Name, address, phone, fax, electronic mail address, name of curator; days and hours of operation, collection, budget, publications. For exhibits--Name, address, phone, fax, electronic mail address, name of contact; date, deadline. For schools--Name, address, phone, name of director, names of faculty members, majors or degrees offered, tuition fees; summer school or adult hobby class information. For newspapers--Name, address, phone, name of art editor.

Art Business News Buyer's Guide. Advanstar Communications. • Annual. $25.00. Lists companies furnishing supplies and services to art dealers and framers. Includes art by subject and media.

Art Marketing Sourcebook. ArtNetwork. • Covers: over 2,000 representatives, consultants, galleries, architects, interior designers, museums. and specialty markets. Entries include: Company name, address, phone, description of services, style represented, mediums, years in business, types of companies dealt with, geographical limitations, number of clients, requirements for viewing slides.

Art Now Gallery Guides. Art Now Inc. • Covers: in '[M Art Now Gallery Guide--International Edition]'

current exhibitions in over 1,800 museums and galleries. Separate regional editions cover metropolitan New York, Boston and New England, the Philadelphia area, the southeast, Chicago and the midwest, the southwest, California and the northwest, Latin America, and Europe. Listings are paid. Entries include: Gallery or museum name, address, phone, days and hours of operation, artist's name or name of the exhibit, medium, and dates of showing.

Artist's and Graphic Designer's Market. F&W Publications, Inc. • Annual. $24.99. Lists art galleries, advertising agencies, TV producers, publishers, and other buyers of free-lance art work. Formerly *Artist's Market.*

International Directory of Arts. Available from Gale Cengage Learning. • Annual. $305.00. Three volumes. A guide to more than 126,000 art sources and markets in 175 countries. Includes artists, collectors, dealers, galleries, museums, art schools, auctioneers, restorers, publishers, libraries, and associations. Published by K. G. Saur.

Who's Who in Art Materials/NAMTA Membership. National Art Materials Trade Association. • Annual. Free to members; non-members, $110.00 per year. Lists retailers and manufacturers of artists' supplies.

ENCYCLOPEDIAS AND DICTIONARIES

Art Business Encyclopedia. Leonard DuBoff. Allworth Press. • 1994. $18.95. Defines words, phrases, and concepts relating to the business of art, with emphasis on legal matters. Includes relevant statutes, arranged by state. Published in cooperation with the American Council for the Arts.

HANDBOOKS AND MANUALS

Art Law: The Guide for Collectors, Investors, Dealers, and Artists. Ralph E. Lerner and Judith Bresler. Practising Law Institute. • 1989. $170.00. Two volumes. Second edition. Covers artist/dealer relationships, artists' rights, appraisals, museum law, tax aspects, estate planning issues, and other legal topics relating to visual art. There are six main headings: Dealers, Artwork Transactions, Artists' Rights, Collectors, Taxes and Estate Planning, and Museums and Multimedia.

ONLINE DATABASES

Art Index Online. H. W. Wilson Co. • Indexes a wide variety of art-related periodicals, 1984 to date. Monthly updates. Inquire as to online cost and availability.

Newspaper Abstracts Daily. ProQuest Inc. • Provides online coverage (citations and abstracts) of 25 major newspapers. Covers business, economics, current affairs, health, fitness, sports, education, technology, government, consumer affairs, psychology, the arts, and the social sciences. Time period is 1986 to date, with daily updates. Inquire as to online cost and availability.

PERIODICALS AND NEWSLETTERS

Art Business News. Advanstar Communications. • Monthly. $43.00 per year.

The ARTnewsletter: The International Bi-Weekly Business Report on the Art Market. ARTnews LLC. • Biweekly. $249.00 per year. Newsletter on forthcoming auctions, price trends, ownership squabbles, criminal cases, etc.

Picture Framing Magazine. Hobby Publications, Inc. • Monthly. $20.00 per year. Published for retailers, wholesalers, and manufacturers of picture frames.

RESEARCH CENTERS AND INSTITUTES

International Foundation for Art Research, Inc. 500 Fifth Ave., Suite 1234, New York, NY 10110. Phone: (212)391-6234 Fax: (212)391-8794 E-mail: kferg@ifar.org • URL: http://www.ifar.org • Research fields are art theft and the authenticity of art objects. Maintains an information archive on stolen art and operates an authentication service.

STATISTICS SOURCES

United States Census of Service Industries. U.S. Bureau of the Census. • Quinquennial. Various reports available.

TRADE/PROFESSIONAL ASSOCIATIONS

Americans for the Arts. 1000 Vermont Ave., N.W., 12th Fl., Washington, DC 20005. Phone: 800-321-4510 or (202)371-2830 Fax: (202)371-0424 E-mail: info@artusa.org • URL: http://www.artsusa.org • Members are arts organizations and interested individuals. Conducts research and provides information and clearinghouse services relating to the visual arts.

Art and Antique Dealers League of America. 1040 Madison Ave., New York, NY 10021-0111. Phone: (212)879-7558 Fax: (212)772-7197 • URL: http://www.artantiquedealersleague.com • Members are retailers and wholesalers of antiques and art objects.

Art and Creative Materials Institute. PO Box 479, Hanson, MA 02341-0479. Phone: (781)293-4100 Fax: (781)293-0808 E-mail: debbief@acminet.com • URL: http://www.acminet.org • Members are manufacturers of school and professional art and craft materials.

Art Dealers Association of America. 575 Madison Ave., New York, NY 10022. Phone: (212)940-8590 Fax: (212)940-6484 E-mail: adaa@artdealers.org • URL: http://www.artdealers.org

Art Information Center. 55 Mercer St., 3rd Fl., New York, NY 10013. Phone: (212)966-3443 E-mail: info@adcglobal.org • Serves as a clearinghouse of information on contemporary fine arts. Assists artists in finding outlets for their work; assists art dealers in finding new talent; aids curators, and collectors. Data collected is donated to the Archives of American Art. **Convention/Meeting:** none.

National Antique and Art Dealers Association of America. 220 E. 57th St., New York, NY 10022. Phone: (212)826-9707 Fax: (212)832-9493 E-mail: inquiries@naadaa.org • URL: http://www.naadaa.org.

ART, COMMERCIAL

See: COMMERCIAL ART

ART DEALERS

See: ART BUSINESS

ART IN INDUSTRY

See also: ARCHITECTURE; COMMERCIAL ART; DESIGN IN INDUSTRY; GRAPHIC ARTS INDUSTRY

ABSTRACTS AND INDEXES

Art Index. H. W. Wilson Co. • Quarterly. Annual cumulations. Price varies. Subject and author index to periodicals in art, architecture, industrial design, city planning, photography, and various related topics.

CD-ROM DATABASES

WILSONDISC: Art Index. H. W. Wilson Co. • Monthly. Provides CD-ROM indexing of art-related literature from 1982 to date. Price includes online service.

DIRECTORIES

International Directory of Corporate Art Collections. ARTnews. • Biennial. $109.95. Contains information on about 1,300 corporate art collections maintained or sponsored in the U. S.,

Canada, Europe, and Japan.

ONLINE DATABASES

Art Index Online. H. W. Wilson Co. • Indexes a wide variety of art-related periodicals, 1984 to date. Monthly updates. Inquire as to online cost and availability.

TRADE/PROFESSIONAL ASSOCIATIONS

American Institute of Graphic Arts. 164 Fifth Ave., New York, NY 10010. Phone: 800-548-1634 or (212)807-1990 Fax: (212)807-1799 E-mail: comments@aiga.org • URL: http://www.aiga.org.

Society of Illustrators. 128 E 63rd St., New York, NY 10021-7303. Phone: (212)838-2560 Fax: (212)838-2561 E-mail: sil901@aol.com • URL: http://www.societyillustrators.org • Professional society of illustrators and art directors.

OTHER SOURCES

Arts Management. Radius Group Inc. • Five times a year. $22.00 per year. National news service for those who finance, manage and communicate the arts.

ARTIFICIAL INTELLIGENCE

See also: MICROCOMPUTERS AND MINICOMPUTERS; ROBOTS

GENERAL WORKS

The Age of Spiritual Machines: When Computers Exceed Human Intelligence. Ray Kurzweil. Penguin Group. • 1998. $25.95. Provides speculation on the future of artificial intelligence and "computer consciousness.".

Artificial Intelligence. Winston P. Henry. Addison-Wesley. • 2001. Fourth edition. Price on application.

Artificial Intelligence: A Guide to Intelligent Systems. Michael Negnevitsky. Addison-Wesley. • 2001. $62.00.

Artificial Intelligence in Perspective. Daniel G. Bobrow, editor. MIT Press. • 1994. $45.00. (Special Issues of Artificial Intelligence, an International Journal Series).

ABSTRACTS AND INDEXES

Applied Science and Technology Index. H. W. Wilson Co. • 11 times a year. Quarterly and annual cumulations. Price varies. Indexes a wide variety of English language technical, industrial, and engineering periodicals.

Business Periodicals Index. H. W. Wilson Co. • 11 times a year. Quarterly and annual cumulations. Price varies.

Computer and Control Abstracts. Available from INSPEC, Inc. • Monthly. $2,400.00 per year. Section C of *Science Abstracts*.

Computer and Information Systems Abstracts Journal: An Abstract Journal Pertaining to the Theory, Design, Fabrication and Application of Computer and Information Systems. CSA. • 11 times a year. $1,750 per year.

Computer Literature Index: A Subject/Author Index to Computer and Data Processing Literature. EBSCO Publishing. • Quarterly, with annual cumulation. $245.00 per year. Contains brief abstracts of book and periodical literature covering all phases of computing, including approximately 70 specific application areas.

Current Contents: Engineering, Computing and Technology. Thomson/ISI. • Weekly. $730.00 per year. Reproductions of contents pages of technical journals. Includes *Author Index, Address Directory, Current Book Contents* and *Title Word Index.* Formerly *Current Contents: Engineering, Technology and Applied Sciences.*

Key Abstracts: Artificial Intelligence. Available from INSPEC, Inc. • Monthly. $250.00 per year. Provides

international coverage of journal and proceedings literature, including material on expert systems and knowledge engineering. Published in England by the Institution of Electrical Engineers (IEE).

NTIS Alerts: Biomedical Technology & Human Factors Engineering. National Technical Information Service. • Semimonthly. $210.00 per year. Provides descriptions of government-sponsored research reports and software, with ordering information. Covers biotechnology, ergonomics, bionics, artificial intelligence, prosthetics, and related subjects. Formerly *Abstract Newsletter.*

Science Citation Index. Thomson/ISI. • Bimonthly. $15,020.00 per year. Annual cumulation. Includes *Source Index, Citation Index, Permuterm Subject Index,* and *Corporate Index.*

BIBLIOGRAPHIES

Computer Book Review. • Quarterly. $30.00 per year. Includes annual index. Reviews new computer books. Back issues available.

CD-ROM DATABASES

Science Citation Index: Compact Disc Edition. Institute for Scientific Information. • Monthly. Provides CD-ROM indexing of the world's scientific and technical literature. Corresponds to online *Scisearch* and printed *Science Citation Index.*

DIRECTORIES

Business Organizations, Agencies, and Publications Directory. Gale Cengage Learning. • 2003. $480.00. 15th edition. Over 40,000 entries describing 39 types of business information sources. Classified by type of organization, publication, or serviceIncludes state, national, and international agencies and organizations. Master index to names and keywords. Also includes e-mail addresses and web site URL's.

Information Sources: The Annual Directory of the Information Industry Association. Software and Information Industry Association. • Annual. Members, $75.00; non-members, $125.00.

MicroLeads Vendor Directory on Disk (Personal Computer Industry). Chromatic Communications Enterprises, Inc. • Annual. $495.00. Includes computer hardware manufacturers, software producers, book-periodical publishers, and franchised or company-owned chains of personal computer equipment retailers, support services and accessory manufacturers. Formerly *MicroLeads U.S. Vender Directory.*

The Software Encyclopedia: A Guide for Personal, Professional, and Business Users. Gale. • Annual. $335.00. Two volumes. Volume one lists software programs by title and producer. Volume two provides information on programs according to application and operating system. Includes prices and requirements for hardware and memory.

ENCYCLOPEDIAS AND DICTIONARIES

Artificial Intelligence Dictionary: A Dictionary Specifically for Artificial Intelligence Users and Specialists. Ellen Thro. Slawson Communications, Inc. • 1991. $24.95. Includes common lay words that lead to correct medical terms. (Lance A. Levanthal Microtrend Series).

Dictionary of Computing. Valerie Illingworth, editor. Oxford University Press. • 1997. $18.00. Fourth edition.

Dictionary of Information Technology and Computer Science. Tony Gunton. Blackwell Publishing. • 1994. $62.95. Second edition. Covers key words, phrases, abbreviations, and acronyms used in computing and data communications.

World of Computer Science. Gale Cengage Learning. • 2002. $160.00. Alphabetical arrangement. Contains 650 entries covering discoveries, theories, concepts, issues, ethics, and people in the broad area of computer science and technology.

HANDBOOKS AND MANUALS

Artificial Intelligence and Software Engineering: Understanding the Promise of the future. Darek Partridge. Fitzroy Dearborn Publishers, Inc. • 1999. $55.00. Includes applications of artificial intelligence software to banking and financial services.

Expert Systems for Business: Concepts and Applications. D. V. Pigford and Gregory R. Baur. Course Technology. • 1995. $35.00. Second edition. (Introduction to Computing Series).

Managing Expert Systems. Efraim Tuban and Jay Liebowitz. Idea Group Publishing. • 1992. $53.50.

ONLINE DATABASES

Applied Science and Technology Index Online. H. W. Wilson Co. • Provides online indexing of 500 major scientific, technical, industrial, and engineering periodicals. Time period is 1983 to date. Monthly updates. Inquire as to online cost and availability.

Globalbase. Gale Cengage Learning. • Provides more than one million online summaries of business, industrial, and economic news reports from more than 1,000 publications worldwide. Covers a wide range of material appearing in international trade journals, professional magazines, and newspapers. Time period is 1984 to date, with weekly updates. Inquire as to online cost and availability.

Internet and Personal Computing Abstracts. Information Today, Inc. • Contains abstracts covering a wide variety of personal and business microcomputer literature appearing in more than 100 journals and popular magazines. Time period is 1981 to date, with monthly updates. Formerly *Microcomputer Index.* Inquire as to online cost and availability.

PROMT: Predicasts Overview of Markets and Technology. Gale Cengage Learning. • Companies, products, applied technologies and markets. U.S. and international literature coverage, 1972 to date. Inquire as to online cost and availability. Provides abstracts from more than 1,600 publications. Weekly updates.

Scisearch. Institute for Scientific Information. • Broad, multidisciplinary index to the literature of science and technology, 1974 to present. Inquire as to online cost and availability. Coverage of literature is worldwide, with weekly updates.

Wilson Business Abstracts Online. H. W. Wilson Co. • Indexes and abstracts 600 major business periodicals, plus the *Wall Street Journal* and the business section of the *New York Times.* Indexing is from 1982, abstracting from 1990, with the two newspapers included from 1993. Updated weekly. Inquire as to online cost and availability. (*Business Periodicals Index* without abstracts is also available online.).

PERIODICALS AND NEWSLETTERS

AI Magazine (Artificial Intelligence). American Association for Artificial Intelligence. AAAI Press. • Quarterly. Individuals, $95.00 per year; institutions, $190.00 per year. Information on artificial intelligence research and innovative applications of the science.

Computer Languages, Systems and Structures. Elsevier. • Quarterly. Individuals, $208.00 per year; institutions, $951.00 per year.

Computers in Human Behavior. Elsevier. • Bimonthly. Qualified personnel, $242.00 per year; institutions, $1,100.00 per year.

EDP Weekly: The Leading Weekly Computer News Summary. Computer Age and EDP News Services. • Weekly. $495.00 per year. Newsletter. Summarizes news from all areas of the computer and microcomputer industries.

The Gray Sheet. F-D-C Reports Inc. • Description: Monitors the complex regulatory environment for devices, instrumentation, and diagnostics. Topics include device-related Congressional activity, Medicare reimbursement policies, international regulatory intiatives, enforcement and premarket approval programs at FDA's Center for Devices and Radiological Health. Recurring features include device approvals, 510(k) clearances, FDA recalls and seizures, mergers and acquisitions, and sales and earnings.

Industrial Computing. Industrial Computing Society. ISA Services, Inc. • Monthly. Members $100.00 per year; non-members, $80.00 per year. Published by the Instrument Society of America. Edited for engineering managers and systems integrators. Subject matter includes industrial software, programmable controllers, artificial intelligence systems, and industrial computer networking systems.

Intelligent Systems Report (ISR). Lionheart Publishing, Inc. • Monthly. $299.00 per year. Newsletter. Formed by merger of *Neural Network News* and *AI Week.*

International Journal of Intelligent Systems. John Wiley and Sons, Inc., Journals. • Monthly. $1,925.00 per year; with online edition, $2,022.00 per year.

Release 1.0 Esther Dysons Monthly Report. EDventure Holdings Inc. • Description: Reports on technology, communications, and the Internet. Reviews and analyzes the technology business. Recurring features include a calendar of events.

Report. Robinson and Associates. • Monthly. $295.00 per year. Newsletter. Articles cover the artificial intelligence field. Formerly *Artificial Intelligence Report.*

Telematics and Informatics: An International Journal on Telecommunications and Internet Technology. Elsevier. • Four times a year. Institutions, $938.00 per year.

RESEARCH CENTERS AND INSTITUTES

Artificial Intelligence Laboratory. University of Texas at Austin, Taylor Hall 2.124, Austin, TX 78712-1188. Phone: (512)471-9565 Fax: (512)471-8885 E-mail: porter@cs.utexas.edu • URL: http://www.cs.utexas.edu/users.

Carnegie Mellon Research Institute-Computer Automation and Robotics. Carnegie Mellon University, 700 Technology Dr., Pittsburgh, PA 15219. Phone: (412)268-3363 Fax: (412)368-7759 • URL: http://www.cmu.edu/cmri • Multidisciplinary research activities include expert systems applications, minicomputer and microcomputer systems design, genetic engineering, and transportation systems analysis.

Center for Artificial Intelligence. University of Pennsylvania, Computer and Information Science Dept., Moore School of Electrical Engineering, 200 S. 33rd St., Philadelphia, PA 19104-6389. Phone: (215)898-3191 Fax: (215)898-0587.

Center for Intelligent Machines and Robotics. University of Florida, Dept. of Mechanical Engineering, P.O. Box 116300, Gainesville, FL 32611. Phone: (352)392-9461 Fax: (352)392-1071 E-mail: cimar@cimar.me.ufl.edu • URL: http://www.me.ufl.edu/cimar/.

Collaboratory for Research on Electronic Work. University of Michigan, 1075 Beal Ave., Ann Arbor, MI 48109-2112. Phone: (734)647-4948 Fax: (734)647-8044 E-mail: finholt@umich.edu • URL: http://www.crew.umich.edu/ • Concerned with the design and use of computer-based tools for thinking and planning in the professional office.

Digital Image Analysis Laboratory. University of Arizona, Dept. of Electrical and Computer Engineering, Tucson, AZ 85721. Phone: (520)621-2706 Fax: (520)621-8076 E-mail: schowengerdt@ece.arizona.edu • URL: http://www.ece.arizona.edu/ • Research fields include image processing, computer vision, and artificial intelligence.

Imaging and Computer Vision Center. Drexel University, 32nd and Market Sts., Room 110-7, Philadelphia, PA 19104. Phone: (215)895-2279 Fax: (215)895-4987 E-mail: icvc-support@cbis.ece.drexel.edu • URL: http://www.cbis.ece.drexel.edu/icvc • Fields of research include computer vision, robot vision, and expert systems.

Institute for Systems Research. University of Maryland at College Park, A. V. Williams Bldg., 2nd Fl., No. 115, College Park, MD 20742-3311. Phone: (301)405-6615 Fax: (301)314-9220 E-mail: isr@isr.umd.edu • URL: http://www.isr.umd.edu/ • A National Science Foundation Engineering Research Center. Areas of research include communication systems, manufacturing systems, chemical process systems, artificial intelligence, and systems integration.

Institute of Advanced Manufacturing Sciences. 1111 Edison Dr., Cincinnati, OH 45230. Phone: (513)948-2000 Fax: 800-345-4482 • Fields of research include quality improvement, computer-aided design, artificial intelligence, and employee training.

Laboratory for Computer Science. Massachusetts Institute of Technology, 200 Technology Square, Bldg. NE43, Cambridge, MA 02139. Phone: (617)253-5851 Fax: (617)258-8682 E-mail: zue@mit.edu • URL: http://www.lcs.mit.edu/ • Research is in four areas: Intelligent Systems; Parallel Systems; Systems, Languages, and Networks; and Theory. Emphasis is on the application of online computing.

McGill Centre for Intelligent Machines. McGill University, 3480 University St., Room 410, Montreal, QC, Canada H3A 2A7. Phone: (514)398-6319 Fax: (514)398-7348 E-mail: cim@cim.mcgill.ca • URL: http://www.cim.mcgill.ca.

Robot Vision Laboratory. Purdue University, School of Electrical and Computer Engineering, 1285 EE Bldg., West Lafayette, IN 47907-1285. Phone: (765)494-3456 Fax: (765)494-6440 E-mail: kak@ecn.purdue.edu • URL: http://www.ecn.purdue.edu.

Studio for Creative Inquiry. Carnegie Mellon University, College of Fine Arts, Pittsburgh, PA 15213-3890. Phone: (412)268-3454 Fax: (412)268-2829 E-mail: mmbm@andrew.cmu.edu/ • URL: http://www.cmu.edu/studio/ • Research areas include artificial intelligence, virtual reality, hypermedia, multimedia, and telecommunications, in relation to the arts.

STATISTICS SOURCES

U. S. Industry and Trade Outlook. Available from National Technical Information Service. • Annual. $69.95. Produced by the International Trade Administration, U. S. Department of Commerce, in a "public-private" partnership with DRI/McGraw-Hill and Standard & Poor's. Provides basic data, outlook for the current year, and "Long-Term Prospects" (five-year projections) for a wide variety of products and services. Includes high technology industries. Formerly *U. S. Industrial Outlook.*

TRADE/PROFESSIONAL ASSOCIATIONS

American Association for Artificial Intelligence. 445 Burgess Dr., Menlo Park, CA 94025-3442. Phone: (650)328-3123 Fax: (650)321-4457 E-mail: info@aaai.org • URL: http://www.aaai.org.

Cognitive Science Society, Inc. c/o Thomas B. Ward, Center for Creative Media, Univ. of Alabama, Tuscaloosa, IL 35487-0172. Phone: (205)348-3178 E-mail: cogsci@psy.utexas.edu • URL: http://www.cognitivesciencesociety.org.

Instrumentation Systems and Automation Society.

67 Alexander Dr., Research Triangle Park, NC 27709. Phone: (919)549-8411 Fax: (919)549-8288 E-mail: info@isa.org • URL: http://www.isa.org • Members are engineers and others concerned with industrial instrumentation, systems, computers, and automation. Formerly Instrument Society of America.

Society for Computer Simulation International. PO Box 17900, San Diego, CA 92177-1810. Phone: (858)277-3888 Fax: (858)277-3930 E-mail: info@scs.org • URL: http://www.scs.org • Formerly Society for Computer Simulation.

Special Interest Group on Artificial Intelligence. c/o Association for Computing Machinery, 1515 Broadway, New York, NY 10036. Phone: 800-342-6626 or (212)869-7440 Fax: (212)944-1318 E-mail: acmhelp@acm.org • URL: http://www.acm.org/sigart/.

OTHER SOURCES

Artificial Intelligence: Reality or Fantasy?. Leslie Chase and Robert Landers, editors. Software and Information Industry Association. • 1984. $59.95. General information and market considerations.

ARTIFICIAL LIMBS

See: PROSTHETICS INDUSTRY

ARTS MANAGEMENT

See also: ART BUSINESS; FOUNDATIONS; FUND-RAISING; GRANTS-IN-AID

GENERAL WORKS

Management Control in Nonprofit Organizations. Robert N. Anthony and David W. Young. McGraw-Hill. • 2002. $115.31. Seventh edition.

Marketing for Non-Profit Organizations. David L. Rados. Greenwood Publishing Group, Inc. • 1996. $64.95. Second edition.

ABSTRACTS AND INDEXES

Art Index. H. W. Wilson Co. • Quarterly. Annual cumulations. Price varies. Subject and author index to periodicals in art, architecture, industrial design, city planning, photography, and various related topics.

DIRECTORIES

Gale's Guide to the Arts: A Gale Ready Reference Handbook. Gale Cengage Learning. • 2000. $125.00. Contains descriptions of information sources of interest to nonprofit art groups, including publications, online databases, museums, government agencies, and associations. Three indexes and a glossary are provided.

Guide to Arts Administration Training and Research. Americans for the Arts. • Triennial. $12.95. Lists 33 institutions.

HANDBOOKS AND MANUALS

Art Law: The Guide for Collectors, Investors, Dealers, and Artists. Ralph E. Lerner and Judith Bresler. Practising Law Institute. • 1989. $170.00. Two volumes. Second edition. Covers artist/dealer relationships, artists' rights, appraisals, museum law, tax aspects, estate planning issues, and other legal topics relating to visual art. There are six main headings: Dealers, Artwork Transactions, Artists' Rights, Collectors, Taxes and Estate Planning, and Museums and Multimedia.

Art Marketing Handbook: Marketing Art in the 21st Century. Calvin J. Goodman. Gee Tee Bee. • 2003. $65.00. Seventh enlarged revised edition. A complete guide to all aspects of the art market.

Arts Management: A Guide to Finding Funds and Winning Audiences. Alvin H. Reiss. Fund Raising Institute. • 1992. $45.00.

Complete Guide to Special Event Management: Business Insights, Financial Advice and Successful Strategies from Ernst and Young, Consultants to the Olympics. John Wiley and Sons, Inc. • 1992. $39.95. Covers the marketing, financing, and general management of special events in the fields of art, entertainment, and sports.

Presenting Performances: A Basic Handbook for the Twenty-First Century. Thomas Wolf. Association of Performing Arts Presenters, Inc. • 2001. $21.95. Revised edition.

ONLINE DATABASES

Art Index Online. H. W. Wilson Co. • Indexes a wide variety of art-related periodicals, 1984 to date. Monthly updates. Inquire as to online cost and availability.

PERIODICALS AND NEWSLETTERS

Art Business News. Advanstar Communications. • Monthly. $43.00 per year.

Art Reference Services Quarterly. Haworth Press, Inc. • Quarterly. Institutions, $110.00 per year. A journal for art librarians.

Journal of Arts Management, Law, and Society. Helen Dwight Reid Educational Foundation. Publications. • Quarterly. Individuals, $73.00 per year; institutions, $136.00 per year. Addresses current and ongoing issues in arts policy, management, low and governance from a range of philosophical and national perspectives encompassing diverse disciplinary viewpoints. Formerly *Journal of Arts Management and Law.*

Variety: The International Entertainment Weekly. Reed Business Information. • 50 times a year. $259.00 per year. Contains national and international news of show business, with emphasis on motion pictures and television. Includes *Market* and *Special Focus* issues.

Washington International Arts Letter. Allied Business Consultants Inc. • Description: Publishes information about cultural developments; personalities in the arts; and the workings and actions of the National Endowments of the Arts and Humanities, Congress, and federal offices as they affect this field. Recurring features include announcements of jobs, scholarships, grants, and other forms of assistance available in the arts and humanities; bibliographies; publications reviews; and listings of names and addresses of businesses and organizations that contribute to the arts.

RESEARCH CENTERS AND INSTITUTES

Center for Arts Administration Program. Florida State University. 123 Carothers Hall, Tallahassee, FL 32306-4408. Phone: (850)644-2158 Fax: (850)644-5067 E-mail: cdorn@mailer.fsu.edu • URL: http://www.fsu.edu.

Foundation Center. Foundation Center. 79 5th Ave./16th St., New York, NY 10003-3076. Phone: 800-424-9836 or (212)620-4230 Fax: (212)807-3677 E-mail: communications@foundationcenter.org • URL: http://foundationcenter.org • Strengthens the nonprofit sector by advancing knowledge about U.S. philanthropy, maintains a comprehensive database on U.S. grantmakers and their grants, and operates research, education and training programs designed to advance philanthropy.

TRADE/PROFESSIONAL ASSOCIATIONS

Americans for the Arts. 1000 Vermont Ave., N.W., 12th Fl., Washington, DC 20005. Phone: 800-321-4510 or (202)371-2830 Fax: (202)371-0424 E-mail: info@artusa.org • URL: http://www.artsusa.org • Members are arts organizations and interested individuals. Conducts research and provides information and clearinghouse services relating to the visual arts.

Association of Performing Arts Presenters. 1112 16th St., N.W., Ste. 400, Washington, DC 20036.

Phone: (202)833-2787 Fax: (202)833-1543 E-mail: artspres@artspresenters.org • URL: http://www.artspresenter.org.

Business Committee for the Arts. 27 Queens Plz., N, 4th Fl., Long Island City, NY 11101. Phone: (718)482-9900 Fax: (718)-482-9911 E-mail: info@bcainc.org • URL: http://www.bcainc.org.

International Society for the Performing Arts. 17 Prudy Ave., Rye, NY 10580. Phone: (914)921-1550 Fax: (914)921-1593 E-mail: info@ispa.org • URL: http://www.ispa.org • Formerly International Society of Performing Arts Administrators.

Professional Arts Management Institute. 110 Riverside Dr., No. 4E, New York, NY 10024. Phone: (212)579-2039 or (212)787-1194 Fax: (212)579-2049 E-mail: skipreiss@aol.com • URL: http://www.artsmanagementnews.com • Intensive training program designed to supplement the knowledge and skills of both professionals and students interested in or involved in managing cultural institutions and performing arts programs. Conducts one three-day seminar per year; compiles statistics.

OTHER SOURCES

Arts Management. Radius Group Inc. • Five times a year. $22.00 per year. National news service for those who finance, manage and communicate the arts.

Financial Management Strategies for Arts Organization. Frederick J. Turk and Robert P. Gallo. Americans for the Arts. • 1984. $16.95.

Lindey on Entertainment, Publishing and the Arts: Agreements and the Law. Alexander Lindey, editor. West Group. • $935.00 per year. Six looseleaf volumes. Periodic supplementation. Provides basic forms, applicable law, and guidance.

ASBESTOS INDUSTRY

ABSTRACTS AND INDEXES

Environment Abstracts. Congressional Information Service, Inc. • Monthly. Price varies. Provides multidisciplinary coverage of the world's environmental literature. Incorporates *Acid Rain Abstracts.*

Environment Abstracts Annual: A Guide to the Key Environmental Literature of the Year. Congressional Information Service, Inc. • Annual. $495.00. A yearly cumulation of *Environment Abstracts.*

Pollution Abstracts. Cambridge Information Group. • Monthly. $1,390.00 per year. Includes print and online editions; with index, $1,515.00 per year.

CD-ROM DATABASES

Environment Abstracts on CD-ROM. LEXIS-NEXIS. • Quarterly. $1,295.00 per year. Contains the following CD-ROM databases: *Environment Abstracts*, *Energy Abstracts*, and *Acid Rain Abstracts*. Length of coverage varies.

DIRECTORIES

OPD Chemical Buyers Directory. Schnell Publishing Company Inc. • Covers: about 1,500 suppliers of chemical process materials and more than 300 companies that transport and store chemicals in the United States. Entries include: Company name, address, phone, list of products or services, telex, fax, e-mail address, internet address, branch offices.

ONLINE DATABASES

CA Search. Chemical Abstracts Service. • Guide to chemical literature, 1967 to present. Inquire as to online cost and availability.

F & S Index. Gale Cengage Learning. • Contains about four million citations to worldwide business, financial, and industrial or consumer product literature appearing from 1972 to date. Weekly updates. Inquire as to online cost and availability.

Toxline. National Library of Medicine. • Abstracting service covering human and animal toxicity studies,

1965 to present (older studies available in *Toxback* file). Monthly updates. Inquire as to online cost and availability.

PRICE SOURCES

Chemical and Engineering News: The Newsmagazine of the Chemical World. American Chemical Society. • Weekly. Institutions, $210.00 per year.

Chemical Market Reporter. Schnell Publishing Co., Inc. • Weekly. $169.00 per year. Quotes current prices for a wide range of chemicals. Formerly *Chemical Marketing Reporter.*

RESEARCH CENTERS AND INSTITUTES

Asbestos Institute. Asbestos Institute. 1200 McGill College, Ste. 1640, Montreal, QC, Canada H3B 4G7. Phone: (514)877-9797 Fax: (514)877-9717 E-mail: info@chrysotile.com • URL: http://www. chrysotile.com • Safe of asbestos.

STATISTICS SOURCES

Mineral Commodity Summaries. Available from U. S. Government Printing Office. • Annual. $26.00. Published by the U. S. Geological Survey, Department of the Interior (http://www.usgs.gov). Contains detailed, five-year data for about 90 nonfuel minerals. Covers a wide range of statistics, including production, imports, exports, consumption, reserves, prices, tariff information, and industry employment. (Two pages are devoted to each mineral.).

Minerals Yearbook. Available from U.S. Government Printing Office. • Annual. Three volumes.

TRADE/PROFESSIONAL ASSOCIATIONS

Asbestos Information Association/North America. PMB 114, 1235 Jefferson Davis Hwy., Arlington, VA 22202-3283. Phone: (703)560-2980 Fax: (703)560-2981 E-mail: aiabjpigg@aol.com • Manufacturers, processors, and miners/millers of asbestos or products containing asbestos. Purposes are: to provide industry wide information on asbestos and health and on industry efforts to eliminate existing hazards; to cooperate with government agencies in developing and implementing industry wide standards for exposure to asbestos dust and for the control of asbestos dust emissions into community air and water; to exchange information on methods and techniques of asbestos dust control; to assist in the solution of problems arising from the health effects of asbestos; to increase public knowledge of the unique benefits and importance of asbestos products. Acts as central agency for the collection and dissemination of medical and technical information on asbestos-related disease, asbestos dust control, and other asbestos-related ecological considerations.

OTHER SOURCES

Asbestos Litigation Reporter: The National Journal of Record of Asbestos Litigation. Andrews Publications. • Semimonthly. $995.00 per year. Provides reports on legal cases involving asbestos as a health hazard.

ASIAN MARKETS

GENERAL WORKS

China in the World Economy: The Domestic Challenges. Organization for Economic Cooperation and Development. • 2002. $120.00. Analyzes the domestic and international effects of China's entry into the World Trade Organization. (China in the Global Economy Series).

Doing Business in China: The Last Great Market. Geoffrey Murray. Saint Martin's Press. • 1994. $80.00.

Economic and Social Survey of Asia and the Pacific. United Nations Publications. • Annual. $65.00. Emphasis is on trends in economic policy and economic development strategies.

Trade Policy Review - Japan. Bernan Press. • 1999. $60.00. Available in English, French, or Spanish versions. Provides WTO analysis of Japan's overall economic environment, trade policy objectives, and "policy developments affecting trade and investment.".

World Trade Issues. Lambert S. Martin, editor. Nova Science Publishers, Inc. • 2002. $69.00. Provides articles by various authors on foreign trade and the influence of globalization, including discussion of the World Trade Organization. Emphasis is on Asian countries and Latin America.

ABSTRACTS AND INDEXES

F & S Index: International. Gale Cengage Learning. • Monthly. $1,450.00 per year, including quarterly and annual cumulations. Provides annotated citations to marketing, business, financial, and industrial literature. Coverage of international business activity includes trade journals, financial magazines, business newspapers, and special reports. Areas included are Asia, Latin America, Africa, the Middle East, Oceania, and Canada.

PAIS International in Print. Public Affairs Information Service, Inc. • Monthly. $850.00 per year; cumulations three times a year. Provides topical citations to the worldwide literature of public affairs, economics, demographics, sociology, and trade. Text in English; indexed materials in English, French, German, Italian, Portuguese and Spanish.

ALMANACS AND YEARBOOKS

Emerging Markets Analyst. • Monthly. $895.00 per year. Provides an annual overview of the emerging financial markets in 24 countries of Latin America, Asia, and Europe. Includes data on international mutual funds and closed-end funds.

Japan Economic Almanac. • Annual. $59.50. Lists of Japanese government agencies, and professional and trade organizations. Text in English.

People's Republic of China Year Book. Current Publications Ltd. • Annual. $98.00. Serves as the official yearbook of the People's Republic of China. Covers developments in various aspects of life in China, including the economy, industry, transportation, telecommunications, agriculture, technology, demographics, the legal system, health, and foreign relations. Includes many statistical tables and photographs. Text in Chinese.

BIBLIOGRAPHIES

Japanese Automobile Industry: An Annotated Bibliography. Sheau-Yueh J. Chao, compiler. Greenwood Publishing Group, Inc. • 1994. $82.95. Describes about 600 books, articles, papers, and documents written in English. Emphasis is on material published since 1980. (Bibliographies and Indexes in Economics and Economic History Series: No. 15).

CD-ROM DATABASES

Asia Pacific Kompass on Disc. Available from Kompass USA, Inc. • Annual. CD-ROM provides information on more than 200,000 companies in Australia, China, Hong Kong, India, Korea, Malaysia, New Zealand, Philippines, Singapore, Thailand, and Taiwan. Classification system covers approximately 50,000 products and services.

Hoover's Company Capsules on CD-ROM. Hoover's, Inc. • Quarterly. $399.95 per year (single-user). Provides the CD-ROM version of *Hoover's Handbook of American Business, Hoover's Handbook of Emerging Companies, Hoover's Handbook of World Business, Hoover's Guide to Computer Companies, Hoover's Guide to Media Companies, Hoover's Handbook of Private Companies,* and various regional guides. Includes more than 11,000 profiles of companies.

Kompass CD-ROM Editions. Available from Kompass USA, Inc. • Semiannual or annual. Prices

vary. CD-ROM versions of Kompass international trade directories are available for each of 36 major countries and nine world regions. Searching is provided for 50,000 product/service items and for many company details.

PAIS on CD-ROM. Public Affairs Information Service, Inc. • Quarterly. $1,995.00 per year. Provides a CD-ROM version of the online service, *PAIS International.* Contains over 500,000 citations to the literature of contemporary social, political, and economic issues.

World Consumer Markets. Gale Cengage Learning. • Annual. $2,500.00. Pblished by Euromonitor. Provides five- year historical data, current data, and forecasts, on CD-ROM for 330 consumer products in 55 countries. Market data is presented in a standardized format for each country.

World Database of Consumer Brands and Their Owners on CD-ROM. Gale Cengage Learning. • Annual. $3,190.00. Produced by Euromonitor. Provides detailed information on CD-ROM for about 10,000 companies and 80,000 brands around the world. Covers 1,000 product sectors.

World Marketing Forecasts on CD-ROM. Gale Cengage Learning. • Annual. $2,500.00. Produced by Euromonitor. Provides detailed forecast data for the years to 2012 on CD-ROM for 54 countries in all parts of the world. Covers a wide range of social, demographic, economic, and market factors. Includes specific forecasts for many kinds of consumer products.

DIRECTORIES

Asia Pacific Securities Handbook. Hoover's Inc. • Covers: stock exchanges and brokers in Australia, Bangladesh, China, Hong Kong, India, Indonesia, Japan, Malaysia, Nepal, New Zealand, Pakistan, Philippines, Singapore, South Korea, Sri Lanka, Taiwan, and Thailand. Entries include: Name, address, phone, fax; exchanges also list market practices, most active and highest capitalized stocks.

Asian Marketing Information Sourcebook. Euromonitor International. • 2003. $475.00. Lists trade associations, statistical offices, government agencies, special libraries, trade journals, websites, and other sources of business information for the countries of Asia.

Asian Pacific Markets: A Guide to Company and Industry Information Sources. Washington Researchers Ltd. • Irregular. $335.00. A directory of government offices, "experts," publications, and databases related to Asian markets and companies. Includes individual chapters on "the 11 most important nations in Asia." Formerly *Asian Markets.*

Asia's 7,500 Largest Companies. ELC International. • Covers: top 7,500 companies of Hong Kong, Indonesia, Japan, Korea, Malaysia, the Philippines, Singapore, Taiwan, Thailand, and China. Entries include: Company name, address, line of business, International SIC numbers, financial data including assets, turnover, and capital.

Business Directory of Hong Kong. Estrin & Diamond Publications. • Annual. $180.00. Published in Hong Kong by Current Publications Ltd. Provides information on more than 12,300 Hong Kong businesses in various fields, including manufacturing, finance, services, construction, transportation, and foreign trade.

China: A Directory and Sourcebook. Euromonitor International, Business Referene Div. • 1998. $590.00. Second edition. Describes about 500 companies in both China and Hong Kong. Sourcebook section provides 1,000 information sources.

Directory of Consumer Brands and Their Owners: Asia Pacific. Euromonitor International, Business Reference Div. • 1998. $990.00. Provides information about brands available from major Asia Pacific companies. Descriptions of companies are also included.

Dun's Asia Pacific Key Business Enterprises. Dun & Bradstreet Corp. • Covers: 30,000 leading companies in 14 Pacific Rim countries whose annual sales are $10 million and who have 500 or more employees. Entries include: Company name, address, phone, fax, telex, number of employees, import/export designation, primary and secondary Standard Industrial Classification (SIC) codes, sales volume.

Dun's Key Decision-Makers in Hong Kong Business. • Annual. $380.00. Provides information on over 8,000 major Hong Kong companies.

Global Market Share Planner. Euromonitor International. • 2003. $5,900.00. Six volumes. Second edition. Provides detailed profiles and market share rankings of major consumer product companies in North America, Latin America, Europe, South Africa, and the Asia-Pacific region. Covers firms operating in key consumer markets: beverages, food products, household products, and personal care items. (Volumes are available individually.).

Hoover's Handbook of World Business: Profiles of Major European, Asian, Latin American, and Canadian Companies. Hoover's, Inc. • Annual. $165.00. Contains detailed profiles for approximately 300 large foreign companies. Includes indexes by industry, location, executive name, company name, and brand name.

International Media Guide: Business-Professional: Asia/Pacific, Middle East, Africa. SRDS. • Annual. $300.00. Provides information on 14,000 trade journals "from Africa to the Pacific Rim," including advertising rates and circulation data.

Japan Company Handbook. Toyo Keizai Inc. • Covers: in two sections: over 3,939 Japanese corporations listed on the 'First Section' of Tokyo, Osaka, and Nagoya stock exchanges, listed in one volume; about 900 firms, smaller in capital but 'considered promising' and listed on the 'Second Section,' are given in a separate volume titled 'Japan Company Handbook--Second Section'; 800 over-the counter companies; and nearly 80 local market companies. Entries include: Company name, address, phone, fax, telex, description, outlook, year established, fiscal year, overseas offices, president, references, capital, other financial data, stock exchanges on which listed, underwriters, number of employees, names of major stockholders and percentage of Japanese and foreign ownership, principal products, export ratio.

Japan Trade Directory. Japan External Trade Organization. • Covers: nearly 2,000 Japanese firms; trade and industrial associations. Entries include: For companies--Name, address, cable address, fax, e-mail, URL, name of chief executive officer, year established, line of business, amount of capital, annual sales, number of employees, bank references, office hours, trade names, whether catalog is available, languages spoken, countries with which business relationship is desired, products desired and those available for export, contact name and phone.

Kompass International Trade Directories. Kompass International/Kompass USA, Inc. • Annual. Prices and volumes vary. Kompass directories are published internationally for each of more than 70 countries, from Algeria to Uzbekistan. The Kompass classification system covers more than 50,000 individual product and service categories, with most directories containing a tradename index and company profiles. Total number of companies in Kompass volumes is about two million.

Major Companies of South West Asia. Available from Gale Cengage Learning. • 2001. $570.00. Fifth edition. Published by Graham and Whiteside. Provides information on 6,000 leading businesses in India, Turkey, Pakistan, Iran and other countries of the region.

Major Companies of the Far East and Australasia. Gale Cengage Learning. • Annual. $1,595.00. Three volumes. Published by Graham & Whiteside. Volume one: *South East Asia,* volume two: *East Asia,* volume three: *Australia, New Zealand, and Papua New Guinea.* Includes a total of 13,000 leading companies, with the names of 81,000 senior executives. (Volumes are available individually.).

Major Market Share Companies: Asia Pacific. Available from Gale Cengage Learning. • 2003. $990.00. Second edition. Published by Euromonitor. Provides consumer market share data and rankings for multinational and regional companies. Covers leading firms in Japan, China, Australia, South Korea, Indonesia, Malaysia, Philippines, and Thailand.

Who Owns Whom: Australasia, Asia, Middle East and Africa. Dun & Bradstreet Corp. • Annual. $550.00. Two volumes. Published in England by Dun & Bradstreet Ltd. Provides information on 32,000 parent companies and their foreign and domestic subsidiaries. Parent companies are located in Singapore, Hong Kong, Japan, the Philippines, South Korea, Taiwan, Thailand, Papua New Guinea, Malaysia, Indonesia, New Zealand, and Australia. Formerly *Who Owns Whom: Australasia and Far East.*

ENCYCLOPEDIAS AND DICTIONARIES

Encyclopedia of Business. Gale Cengage Learning. • 2000. $425.00. Second edition. Two volumes. Contains more than 700 signed articles covering major business disciplines and concepts. International in scope. (Encyclopedia of Business Series).

HANDBOOKS AND MANUALS

Business Guide to Modern China. Jon P. Alston and Yongxin He. Michigan State University Press. • 1997. $29.95. (International Business Series).

China Business: The Portable Encyclopedia for Doing Business with China. Christine Genzberger and others. World Trade Press. • 1994. $24.95. Covers economic data, import/export possibilities, basic tax and trade laws, travel information, and other useful facts for doing business with the People's Republic of China. (Country Business Guides Series).

Guidebook on Trading with China. United Nations Publications. • 1999. $75.00. Fifth edition. Serves to provide "a better understanding of China's economic policies, rules, and regulations." Includes information on China's trade and development planning.

Hong Kong Business: The Portable Encyclopedia for Doing Business with Hong Kong. Christine Genzberger and others. World Trade Press. • 1994. $24.95. Covers economic data, import/export possibilities, basic tax and trade laws, travel information, and other useful facts for doing business with Hong Kong. (Country Business Guides Series).

Japan Business: The Portable Encyclopedia for Doing Business with Japan. Christine Genzberger and others. World Trade Press. • 1994. $24.95. (Country Business Guide Series).

Singapore Business: The Portable Encyclopedia for Doing Business with Singapore. Christine Genzberger and others. World Trade Press. • 1994. $24.95. Covers economic data, import/export possibilities, basic tax and trade laws, travel information, and other useful facts for doing business with Singapore. (Country Business Guides Series).

Taiwan Business: The Portable Encyclopedia for Doing Business with Taiwan. Christine Genzberger and others. World Trade Press. • 1994. $24.95. Covers economic data, import/export possibilities, basic tax and trade laws, travel information, and other use-ful facts for doing business with Taiwan. (Country Business Guide Series).

INTERNET DATABASES

Trade Show Center. Global Sources/Trade Media Holdings Ltd. [Singapore]. Phone: (656)574-2800 E-mail: service@globalsources.com • URL: http://www.globalsources.com/TRADESHW/TRDSHFRM.HTM • Free Web site provides current, detailed information on more than 1,000 major trade shows worldwide, including events in the U.S., but with an emphasis on "Asia and Greater China." Searching is offered by product, supplier, country, and month of year. Includes links to "Trade Information.".

ONLINE DATABASES

F & S Index. Gale Cengage Learning. • Contains about four million citations to worldwide business, financial, and industrial or consumer product literature appearing from 1972 to date. Weekly updates. Inquire as to online cost and availability.

Globalbase. Gale Cengage Learning. • Provides more than one million online summaries of business, industrial, and economic news reports from more than 1,000 publications worldwide. Covers a wide range of material appearing in international trade journals, professional magazines, and newspapers. Time period is 1984 to date, with weekly updates. Inquire as to online cost and availability.

Japan Economic Newswire Plus. Kyodo News International, Inc. • Provides full text in English of news items relating to business, economics, industry, trade, and finance in Japan and the Pacific Rim countries. Time period is 1982 to date, with daily updates. Inquire as to online cost and availability.

PAIS International. Public Affairs Information Service, Inc. • Corresponds to the former printed publications, *PAIS Bulletin* (1976-90) and *PAIS Foreign Language Index* (1972-90), and to the current *PAIS International in Print* (1991 to date). Covers economic, political, and sociological material appearing in periodicals, books, government documents, and other publications. Updating is monthly. Inquire as to online cost and availability.

PROMT: Predicasts Overview of Markets and Technology. Gale Cengage Learning. • Companies, products, applied technologies and markets. U.S. and international literature coverage, 1972 to date. Inquire as to online cost and availability. Provides abstracts from more than 1,600 publications. Weekly updates.

PERIODICALS AND NEWSLETTERS

Asia Inc.: The Region's Business Magazine. Asia, Inc., Ltd. • Monthly. $79.00 per year. Contains business, financial, and other news and commentary from various countries in Asia. Main sections are "At Work," "Asia Abroad: A World of Business," and "After Hours: Travel and Leisure." Text in English.

Asia Pacific Economic Review: Bridging Pacific Rim Business and Society. Zencore, Inc. • Monthly. $35.00 per year. Includes special issues on individual countries: Taiwan, Malaysia, China/Hong Kong, Japan, and Korea.

Asia Times Online.

The Asian Wall Street Journal. Dow Jones & Co., Inc. • Daily. $970.00 per year (air mail). Published in Hong Kong. Also available in a weekly edition at $259.00 per year: *Asian Wall Street Journal Weekly.*

Business Week China. Ministry of Foreign Economic Relations and Trade, Institute of International Tra. McGraw-Hill. • Bimonthly. Price on application. Edited for business and government officials in the People's Republic of China. Selected Chinese translation of *Business Week.*

Business Week International: The World's Only International Newsweekly of Business. McGraw-

Hill. • Weekly. $95.00 per year.

China Business Review. United States-China Business Council. • Bimonthly. $99.00 per year. Covers trends and issues affecting U. S. investment and trade with China and Hong Kong.

East Asian Executive Reports. International Executive Reports. • Description: Features legal, financial, and practical aspects of doing business in East Asia. Features articles on local requirements for agents and sponsors, branch offices, joint ventures, importing, government tendering, licensing, and sourcing. Reports on technology transfer, labor, product liability, taxes, investment, repatriation of profits, marketing, and financing.

Emerging Markets Quarterly. Institutional Investor, Inc., Journals Group. • Quarterly. Price on application. Newsletter on financial markets in developing areas, such as Africa, Latin America, Southeast Asia, and Eastern Europe. Topics include institutional investment opportunities and regulatory matters. Formerly *Emerging Markets Weekly*.

Far Eastern Economic Review. Dow Jones International Marketing Service. • Weekly. $205.00 per year (air mail). Published in Hong Kong by Review Publishing Co., a Dow Jones subsidiary (GPO Box 160, Hong Kong). Covers Asian business, economics, politics, and international relations. Includes reports on individual countries and companies, business trends, and stock price quotations.

Hong Kong Week. Dow Jones & Co. • Weekly. $260.00 per year (air mail). A guide to investing in Hong Kong and China. Provides stock prices, market analysis, and commentary. Edited and published in Hong Kong by the *Asian Wall Street Journal*.

Institutional Investor International Edition: The Magazine for International Finance and Investment. Institutional Investor, Inc., Journals Group. • Monthly. $475.00 per year. Covers the international aspects of professional investing and finance. Emphasis is on Europe, the Far East, and Latin America.

International Economic Scoreboard. The Conference Board Inc. • Description: Provides current data on the business outlook in 11 major industrial countries: Australia, Canada, France, West Germany, Italy, Japan, Korea, New Zealand, Taiwan, the United Kingdom, and the U.S. **Remarks:** A source for additional information on this indicator system and its uses is available at the Center for International Business Cycle Research, Columbia University Business School.

The Japan Times. • Weekly. $120.00 per year. Provides news and commentary on Japan's economy, trade policies, and Japanese life in general. Regular features include "Business Briefs," "Market Reports," "Lifestyle," and "Issue Analysis." Supplement available *The Japan Times Weekly*. Text in English.

Journal of Asia-Pacific Business. Haworth Press, Inc. • Quarterly. $225.00 per year. Includes print and online editions. An academic and practical journal concerned with marketing, finance, and other aspects of doing business in Asia.

Journal of Asian Business. Southeast Asia Business Program. University of Michigan. • Quarterly. Individuals, $25.00 per year; institutions, $40.00 per year. An international academic journal covering business in all parts of Asia.

Journal of East-West Business. Haworth Press, Inc. • Quarterly. $300.00 per year; Includes print and on-line editions. An academic and practical journal focusing on business in the developing regions of Asia and Eastern Europe.

Journal of the Asia Pacific Economy. Taylor and Francis Group. • Three times a year. Individuals, $76.00 per year; institutions, $347.00 per year. Cov-

ers economic, political, social, cultural, and historical factors affecting Asian commerce and trade.

Market: Asia Pacific. Edimax. • Description: Concerned with demographics, lifestyles, and business opportunities in the Asia Pacific region. Profiles a particular city or country in each issue, providing consumer market trends, surveys results, and articles on direct marketing and marketing management.

The Nikkei Weekly: Japan's Leading Business Newspaper. Nikkei America, Inc. • Weekly. $129.00 per year. A newspaper in English "dedicated to all aspects of Japanese business and its influence on people, markets and political trends around the world." Includes English versions of articles appearing in leading Japanese business newspapers, such as *Nihon Keizai Shimbun, Nikkei Marketing Journal*, and *Nikkei Financial Daily*.

RESEARCH CENTERS AND INSTITUTES

Center on Japanese Economy and Business. Columbia University, Graduate School of Business, 322 Uris Hall, 3022 Broadway, New York, NY 10027-6902. Phone: (212)854-3976 Fax: (212)678-6958 E-mail: htp1@colombia.edu • URL: http://www.gsb.columbia.edu/japan/ • Research areas include Pacific Basin trade policy.

Industrial Research Institute for Pacific Nations. California State Polytechnic University, Pomona, School of Business Administration, 3801 W. Temple Ave., Bldg. 66, Room 217, Pomona, CA 91768. Phone: (909)869-2399 Fax: (909)869-6799 E-mail: hkj@csupomona.edu • URL: http://www.hkjinacsu.edu • Conducts research on the Pacific nations marketplace.

STATISTICS SOURCES

China Marketing Data and Statistics. Available from Gale Cengage Learning. • 2000. $445.00. Second edition. Two volumes. Published by Euromonitor. In addition to national statistics, includes data for 30 cities and 400 administrative areas. Major source is the Chinese State Statistical Bureau.

Consumer Asia. Available from Gale Cengage Learning. • Annual. $1,090.00. Published by Euromonitor. Provides statistical andanalytical surveys of factors affecting Asian consumer markets: energy, labor, population, finance, debt, tourism, consumer expenditures, household characteristics, etc. Emphasis is on Hong Kong, Singapore, Taiwan, South Korea, Indonesia, and Malaysia.

Consumer China. 2001. Available from Gale Cengage Learning. • Annual. $1,090.00. Published by Euromonitor. Provides demographic and consumer market data for China.

Consumer International. Available from Gale Cengage Learning. • Annual. $1,290.00. Published by Euromonitor. Contains extensive consumer market, economic, and demographic data for 25 major, non-European countries, including the U. S. and Canada. Includes consumer market size (volume and value) for 150 product types in 14 categories (food, clothing, automobiles, cosmetics, appliances, etc.).

Emerging Stock Markets Factbook 1999. International Finance Corp. • 1998. $150.00. Provides statistical profiles for emerging stock markets in various countries of the world. Includes regional, composite, and industry indexes.

The Far East and Australasia 2000. Taylor and Francis Group. • Annual. $480.00. Published by Europa. Includes country statistical surveys of demographics, finance, trade, and agriculture. (Regional Surveys of the World.).

Gale Country and World Rankings Reporter. Gale Cengage Learning. • 1997. $160.00. Second edition. Provides about 3,000 statistical ranking tables and charts covering more than 235 nations. Sources

include the United Nations and various government publications.

International Marketing Forecasts. Available from Gale Cengage Learning. • Annual. $1,250.00. Published by Euromonitor. Contains demographic, economic, and market forecasts to the year 2013 for major, non-European countries, including the U. S. and Canada. Forecasts include market-size data for 15 consumer product sectors, such as food, clothing, and automobiles.

Retail Trade International. Gale Cengage Learning. • 2002. $1,990.00. 11th edition. Eight volumes. Published by Euromonitor. Presents comprehensive data on retail trends in 52 countries. Includes textual analysis and profiles of major retailers. Covers Europe, Asia, the Middle East, Africa and the Americas.

Statistical Indicators for Asia and the Pacific. United Nations Publications. • Quarterly. $80.00 per year. Provides data on economic and demographic trends in the region. Text in English.

Statistical Yearbook for Asia and the Pacific. United Nations Publications. • Annual. $90.00. Includes 56 countries of the region. Contains data on national accounts, trade, industry, banking, wages, consumption, population, and other economic and demographic subjects. Text in English and French.

TRADE/PROFESSIONAL ASSOCIATIONS

American Indonesian Chamber of Commerce. 317 Madison Ave., Room 520, New York, NY 10017-5201. Phone: (212)687-4505 Fax: (212)687-5844 E-mail: aiccny@bigplanet.com • URL: http://www.aiccusa.org • Holds briefings on new trade policies in Indonesia and offers orientation workshops to company personnel traveling in Indonesia.

Chinese American Association of Commerce. 778 Clay St., Suite C, San Francisco, CA 94108. Phone: (415)362-4306 Fax: (415)362-1478 • Members are individuals interested in improving trade between the U. S. and the People's Republic of China.

Japan External Trade Organization. 1221 Ave. of the Americas, McGraw Hill Bldg., 42nd Fl., New York, NY 10020. Phone: (212)997-0400 Fax: (212)997-0464 E-mail: epj_la@jetro.go.jp • URL: http://www.jetro.org • Supports foreign companies in export and/or investment to Japan-related business ventures. Disseminates comprehensive information on the Japanese economy and market through surveys, reports, publications, and newsletters. Conducts trade and investment promotion seminars and symposia. Sponsors trade shows and exhibitions. Provides professional business consultation services and handles trade-related inquiries and provides opportunities for international exchange.

Korea Trade Promotion Center. 460 Park Ave., Ste. 402, New York, NY 10022. Phone: (212)826-0900 Fax: (212)888-4930 E-mail: kotrany@ix.netcom.com • URL: http://nyc.kotra.or.kr • Works as an agency of the Korean government. Provides information about Korean export commodities and exporters, and import commodities and importers. Sponsors visits of foreign businesspersons to the Republic of Korea; arranges introductions of potential traders to Korean manufacturers and sales and buying missions of traders with the Republic of Korea. Compiles statistics; conducts economic and marketing research for distribution to Korean industry, business, and government; participates in U.S. trade shows. Maintains 35,000 volume international trade library.

OTHER SOURCES

Japanese Company Factfinder: Teikoku Databank. Teikoku Databank America, Inc. • Quarterly. $1,920.00 per year to academic and public libraries. $3,200 per year to businesses. CD-ROM provides detailed financial and descriptive information on more than 186,000 Japanese companies doing business overseas.

The Market for Consumer Products in Southeast Asia. MarketResearch.com. • 1997. $3,250.00. Market research report. Covers Asian consumer markets for food, cosmetics, pharmaceuticals, medical devices, and building materials. Market projections are provided to the year 2001.

ASPHALT INDUSTRY

BIBLIOGRAPHIES

Catalog of Asphalt Institute Publications. Asphalt Institute. • Annual. Free.

DIRECTORIES

OPD Chemical Buyers Directory. Schnell Publishing Company Inc. • Covers: about 1,500 suppliers of chemical process materials and more than 300 companies that transport and store chemicals in the United States. Entries include: Company name, address, phone, list of products or services, telex, fax, e-mail address, internet address, branch offices.

ONLINE DATABASES

F & S Index. Gale Cengage Learning. • Contains about four million citations to worldwide business, financial, and industrial or consumer product literature appearing from 1972 to date. Weekly updates. Inquire as to online cost and availability.

PERIODICALS AND NEWSLETTERS

Asphalt. Asphalt Institute. • Three times a year. Free.

HMAT (Hot Mix Asphalt Technology). National Asphalt Pavement Association. • Bimonthly. Free.

Oil Daily: Daily Newspaper of the Petroleum Industry. Energy Intelligence Group, Inc. • Daily. Email, $1,595.00 per year; fax, $2,395.00 per year, online, $1,495.00 per year. Newspaper for the petroleum industry.

PRICE SOURCES

Chemical Market Reporter. Schnell Publishing Co., Inc. • Weekly. $169.00 per year. Quotes current prices for a wide range of chemicals. Formerly *Chemical Marketing Reporter.*

PPI Detailed Report. Bureau of Labor Statistics, U.S. Department of Labor. Available from U.S. Government Printing Office. • Monthly. $55.00 per year. Formerly *Producer Price Indexes.*

RESEARCH CENTERS AND INSTITUTES

Engineering Experiment Station. Ohio State University. 2070 Neil Ave., Columbus, OH 43210-1275. Phone: (614)292-3149 Fax: (614)292-9615 E-mail: fortner.1@osu.edu • URL: http://www.osu.edu.

Texas Transportation Institute, Systems Planning. Texas A & M University. 3135 TAMU, College Station, TX 77843-3135. Phone: (979)845-6002 Fax: (979)945-6008 E-mail: k-turnbull@tamu.edu • URL: http://www.tti.tamu.edu.

STATISTICS SOURCES

Minerals Yearbook. Available from U.S. Government Printing Office. • Annual. Three volumes.

TRADE/PROFESSIONAL ASSOCIATIONS

Asphalt Emulsion Manufacturers Association. 3 Church Cir., PMB 250, Annapolis, MD 21401. Phone: (410)267-0023 Fax: (410)267-7546 E-mail: krissoff@aema.org • URL: http://www.aema.org • Seeks to foster: advancement and improvement of the asphalt emulsion industry; expanded and more efficient use of emulsion as a result of an improved state of the art; provision of information to users through guide specifications and answers to specific questions.

Asphalt Institute. 2696 Research Park Dr., PO Box 14052, Lexington, KY 40511-8480. Phone: (859)288-4960 Fax: (859)288-4999 E-mail: info@asphaltinstitute.org • URL: http://www.asphaltinstitute.org • Composed of petroleum asphalt/bitumen producers, manufacturers and affiliated businesses. Promotes the use, benefits, and quality performance of petroleum asphalt through environmental marketing, research, engineering, and technical development, and through the resolution of issues affecting the industry.

Association of Asphalt Paving Technologists. 4711 Clark Ave., Ste. G, White Bear Lake, MN 55110. Phone: (651)293-9188 Fax: (651)293-9193 E-mail: aapt@qwest.net • URL: http://www.asphalttechnology.org.

National Asphalt Pavement Association. 5100 Forbes Blvd., 5100 Forbes Blvd., Lanham, MD 20706. Phone: 888-468-6499 or (301)731-4748 or (301)731-4748 Fax: (301)731-4621 E-mail: mcervarich@hotmix.org • URL: http://www.hotmix.org • Manufacturers and producers of scientifically proportioned Hot Mix Asphalt for use in all paving, including highways, airfields, and environmental usages. Membership includes hot mix producers, paving contractors, equipment manufacturers, engineering consultants, and others. Supports research and publishes information on: producing, stockpiling, and feeding of the aggregate to the manufacturing facility; drying; methods of screening, storing, and proportioning in the manufacturing facility; production of the hot mix asphalt; transporting mix to paver; lay down procedure and rolling; general workmanship; and related construction practices and materials. Commits to product quality, environmental control, safety and health, and energy conservation. Conducts training programs on a variety of technical and managerial topics for industry personnel. Maintains speakers' bureau and Hot Mix Asphalt Hall of Fame.

OTHER SOURCES

Asphalt Products and Markets. Available from MarketResearch.com. • 2001. $3,200.00. Published by the Freedonia Group. Market data with forecasts to 2007. Includes information on paving, coating, and roofing asphalt products.

ASSOCIATIONS

See also: CLUBS; WOMEN'S CLUBS

ALMANACS AND YEARBOOKS

Association Meeting Trends. American Society of Association Executives. • 1999. $90.00. (Management Research Series).

BIOGRAPHICAL SOURCES

Who's Who in Association Management. American Society of Association Executives. • Annual. $160.00. Lists paid executives who are members of the association and suppliers of products and services to the association.

CD-ROM DATABASES

Associations Unlimited. Gale Cengage Learning. • Semiannual. Includes all information on CD-ROM from all of the Gale *Encyclopedia of Associations* directories, plus association materials from about 2,500 of the associations-full-text documents and membership applications.

Encyclopedia of Associations CD-ROM. Gale Cengage Learning. • Semiannual. $1,095.00 per year, single user; $1,895.00 per year, network. Available for IBM or MAC. Provides detailed CD-ROM information on over 170,000 international, national, regional, state, and local organizations. Corresponds to the various volumes and supplements that make up the Gale *Encyclopedia of Associations* series.

World Database of Business Information Sources on CD-ROM. Gale Cengage Learning. • Annual. Produced by Euromonitor. Presents Euromonitor's entire information source database on CD-ROM. Contains a worldwide total of about 35,000 publications, organizations, libraries, trade fairs, and online databases.

Yearbook of International Organizations PLUS. R. R. Bowker. • Annual. Compiled by the Union of International Organizations, Brussels. Includes the *Yearbook of International Organizations* and *Who's Who in International Organizations.*

DIRECTORIES

Association Meeting and Event Planners Directory. Douglas Publications, Inc. • Annual. $650.00. Lists planners of meetings for over 8,000 national associations. Provides past and future convention locations, dates held, number of attendees, exhibit space required, and other convention information. Formerly *Association Meeting Planners.*

Associations Canada: The Directory of Associations in Canada. Micromedia. • Annual. $299.00. Provides detailed information in English and French on 20,000 active Canadian associations. Includes subject, keyword, personal name, and other indexes. Formerly *Directory of Associations in Canada.*

Associations Yellow Book: Who's Who at the Leading U. S. Trade and Professional Associations. Leadership Directories, Inc. • Semiannual. $265.00 per year. Gives the names and titles of over 44,000 staff members in about 1,100 major associations. Six indexes are included: association name, individual name, industry, budget, acronym, and political action committee (PAC).

Directory of British Associations and Associations in Ireland. CBD Research Research Ltd. • Biennial. $350.00. Lists about 7,000 national organizations of England, Wales, Scotland, Northern Ireland and the Irish Republic. Published by CBD Research.

The Directory of Business Information Resources: Associations, Newsletters, Magazine Trade Shows. Grey House Publishing, Inc. • Annual. $250.00. Provides concise information on associations, newsletters, magazines, and trade shows for each of 90 major industry groups. An "Entry & Company Index" serves as a guide to titles, publishers, and organizations.

Directory of Trade and Professional Associations in the European Union - The Blue Book. Euroconfidentiel S. A. • Annual. $160.00. Includes more than 9,000 EU-related associations.

Encyclopedia of Associations. Gale Cengage Learning. • Annual. $1,530.00. Three volumes. Volume 1, National Organizations, $585.00; Volume 2, Geographic and Executive Indexes, $460.00; Volume 3, supplement, $485.00.

Encyclopedia of Associations: International Organizations. Gale Cengage Learning. • Annual. $695.00. Two volumes. Includes detailed information on approximately 24,000 international nonprofit membership organizations.

Encyclopedia of Associations: Regional, State, and Local Organizations. Gale Cengage Learning. • Annual. $660.00. Five volumes. $170.00 per volume. Each volume covers a particular region of the U. S.

Europa Directory of International Organizations. Available from Taylor & Francis Group. • 2001. $250.00. Published by Europa Publications (http://www.europapublications.com). Describes about 1,700 associations and other organizations around the world.

National Directory of Nonprofit Organizations. Available from Gale Cengage Learning. • 2003. $590.00. 16th edition. Three volumes. Published by the TAFT Group. Contains over 250,000 listings of nonprofit organizations, indexed by 260 areas of activity. Indicates income range and IRS tax filing status for each organization.

National Trade and Professional Associations of the

United States. Columbia Books, Inc. • Annual. $149.00. Provides key facts on approximately 7,500 trade associations, labor and professional organizations.

Public Interest Profiles, 2001-2002. CQ Press. • 2002. $215.00. Provides detailed information on more than 250 influential public interest and public policy organizations (lobbyists) in the U.S. Includes e-mail addresses and Web sites where available. (Public Interest Profile Series).

State and Regional Associations of the United States. Columbia Books, Inc. • Annual. $149.00. Provides information on over 7,400 state and regional business associations, professional societies, and labor unions.

Trade Associations amd Professional Bodies of Continental Europe. Available from Gale Cengage Learning. • 2003. $290.00. Second edition. Published by Graham & Whiteside. Provides detailed information on more than 3,600 business and professional organizations in Europe.

Washington: A Comprehensive Directory of the Key Institutions and Leaders in th e National Capitol Area. Columbia Books, Inc. • Annual. $149.00. Provides information on about 5,000 Washington, DC key businesses, government offices, non-profit organizations, and cultural institutions, with the names of about 25,000 principal executives. Includes Washington media, law offices, foundations, labor unions, international organizations, clubs, etc.

Washington Information Directory. CQ Press. • Covers: 5,000 governmental agencies, congressional committees, and non-governmental associations considered competent sources of specialized information. Entries include: Name of agency, committee, or association; address, phone, fax, and Internet; annotation concerning function or activities of the office; and name of contact.

World Directory of Marketing Information Sources. Available from Gale Cengage Learning. • 2003. $650.00. Fourth edition. Published by Euromonitor. Provides details on approximately 6,000 sources of marketing information, including publications, libraries, associations, market research companies, online databases, and governmental organizations. Coverage is worldwide.

World Directory of Trade and Business Associations. Available from Gale Cengage Learning. • 2003. $650.00. Fourth edition. Published by Euromonitor. Provides detailed information on approximately 3,000 trade associations in various countries of the world. Includes subject and geographic indexes.

Yearbook of International Organizations. Available from Gale Cengage Learning. • Annual. $1,460,00. Five volumes. Vol. 1 *Organization Descriptions and Cross-References*; Vol. 2 *Geographic*; Vol. 4 *Bibliographic*; Vol. 5 *Statistics, Visualizations and Patterns.* Published by K. G. Saur.

FINANCIAL RATIOS

Association Operating Ratio Report. American Society of Association Executives The ASAE Bldg. • 1997. $165.00. 10th edition. Contains comparison data from associations.

HANDBOOKS AND MANUALS

The Law of Associations: An Operating Legal Manual for Executives and Counsel. George D. Webster, editor. LexisNexis Matthew Bender. • Annual. $301.00. Looseleaf service. Coverage of all legal and tax aspects of non-profit associations.

Principles of Association Management. Henry Ernstthal and Bob Jones. American Society of Association Executives. • 2001. Fourth edition. Price on application.

Professional Corporations and Associations. Berrien C. Eaton. LexisNexis Matthew Bender. •

Semiannual. $1,432.00 per year. Six looseleaf volumes. Detailed information on forming, operating and changing a professional corporation or association.

ONLINE DATABASES

Encyclopedia of Associations [Online]. Gale Cengage Learning. • Provides detailed information on about 170,000 U. S. and International non-profit organizations. Semiannual updates. Inquire as to online cost and availability.

Industry Insider. Thomson Financial. • Contains full-text online industry research reports from more than 200 leading trade associations, covering 50 specific industries. Reports include extensive statistics and market research data. Inquire as to online cost and availability.

PERIODICALS AND NEWSLETTERS

Association Management. American Society of Association Executives. • Monthly. $50.00.

Association Trends. Martineau Corporation. • Weekly. $129.00 per year. For staff executives of national, local, regional trade and professional associations. Contains news and information on association management and related issues.

Nonprofit Issues. Donald W. Kramer. • Description: Presents legal information for nonprofit executives and their professional advisors.

STATISTICS SOURCES

Association Executive Compensation and Benefits Study. American Society of Association Executives. • 1999. $195.00. 11th edition. A salary survey.

TRADE/PROFESSIONAL ASSOCIATIONS

American Society of Association Executives. 1575 Eye St., N.W., Washington, DC 20005-1103. Phone: 888-950-2723 or (202)626-2723 or (202)626-2803 Fax: (202)371-8825 E-mail: pr@asaenet.org • URL: http://www.asaenet.org.

International Association of Association Management Companies. 414 Plaza Dr., Suite 209, Westmont, IL 60559. Phone: (630)655-1669 Fax: (630)655-0391 E-mail: info@iaamc.org • URL: http://www.iaamc.org • Formerly Institute of Association Management Companies.

OTHER SOURCES

Company of Military Historians. • Represents professional society of military historians, museologists, artists, writers, journalists, military personnel, teachers, researchers, and other individuals interested in the history of American military units, organization, tactics, uniforms, arms, and equipment. Maintains museum.

Orders and Medals Society of America. • Persons, including 300 members outside the U.S., interested in collecting and studying insignias of the orders of knighthood and merit, the decorations of valor and honor, the medals of distinction and service, and allied material and historical data.

ASSOCIATIONS, INTERNATIONAL

See: INTERNATIONAL AGENCIES

ASTRONAUTICS

See: ROCKET INDUSTRY

ATHLETIC GOODS

See: SPORTING GOODS INDUSTRY

ATLASES

See: MAPS

ATOMIC POWER

See: NUCLEAR ENERGY

ATTORNEYS

See: LAWYERS

AUCTIONS

GENERAL WORKS

Deal Engines: The Science of Auctions, Stock markets, and e-Markets. Robert E. Hall. W. W. Norton & Co., Inc. • 2003. $14.95. A practical, economic analysis of how auction markets work, whether simple (eBay) or complex (stock exchanges). Covers both theory and application. (Originally published as *Digital Dealing.*).

PERIODICALS AND NEWSLETTERS

The Auctioneer. National Auctioneers Association. • Monthly. Membership. News of interest to auctioneers.

PRICE SOURCES

Book Auction Records. RoweCom UK Ltd. • Annual. $150.00.

TRADE/PROFESSIONAL ASSOCIATIONS

Burley Auction Warehouse Association. 620 S. Broadway St., Lexington, KY 40508-3126. Phone: (859)255-4504 Fax: (859)255-4534 E-mail: bawa@gte.net.

Livestock Marketing Association. 10510 NW Ambassador Dr., Kansas City, MO 64153. Phone: 800-821-2048 or (816)891-0502 Fax: (816)891-7926 E-mail: lmainfo@lmaweb.com • URL: http://www.lmaweb.com • Livestock marketing businesses and livestock dealers. Sponsors annual World Livestock Auctioneer Championships. Offers management and promotional services.

National Auctioneers Association. 8880 Ballentine, Overland Park, KS 66214. Phone: (913)541-8084 Fax: (913)894-5281 E-mail: info@auctioneers.org • URL: http://www.auctioneers.org • Professional auctioneers. Provides continuing education classes for auctioneers, promotes use of the auction method of marketing in both the private and public sectors. Encourages the highest ethical standards for the profession.

National Auto Auction Association. 5320 Spectrum Dr., Ste. D, Frederick, MD 21703. Phone: (301)696-0400 Fax: (301)631-1359 E-mail: naaa@naaa.com • URL: http://www.naaa.com • Owners/operators of wholesale automobile and truck auctions; associate members are car and truck manufacturers, insurers of checks and titles, car and truck rental companies, publishers of auto price guide books, and others connected with the industry. Maintains hall of fame.

AUDIENCE RESEARCH

See: ADVERTISING MEDIA; MARKET RESEARCH

AUDIO EQUIPMENT INDUSTRY

See: HIGH FIDELITY/STEREO

AUDIOVISUAL AIDS IN EDUCATION

See also: AUDIOVISUAL AIDS IN INDUSTRY

ALMANACS AND YEARBOOKS

Educational Media and Technology Yearbook. Libraries Unlimited, Inc. • Annual. $75.00.

BIBLIOGRAPHIES

Films and Audiovisual Information. Available from U. S. Government Printing Office. • Annual. Free.

Issued by the Superintendent of Documents. A list of government publications on motion picture and audiovisual topics. Formerly *Motion Pictures, Films and Audiovisual Information*. (Subject Bibliography No. 73.).

CD-ROM DATABASES

A-V Online (CD-ROM). Access Innovations, Inc. • Annual. $795.00 per year. Provides CD-ROM descriptions of all types of non-print educational materials, covering all learning levels.

ERIC on SilverPlatter. Available from SilverPlatter Information, Inc. • Quarterly. $700.00 per year. Produced by the Office of Educational Research and Improvement, U. S. Dept. of Education. Provides CD-ROM indexing and abstracting of a wide variety of literature relating to education. Archival discs are available from 1966.

DIRECTORIES

AV Market Place: The Complete Business Directory of Audio, Audio Visual, Computer Systems, Film, Video, and Programming, with Industry Yellow Pages. Information Today, Inc. • Annual. $195.00. Provides information on "more than 7,500 companies that create, apply, or distribute AV equipment and services for business, education, science, and government." Multimedia, virtual reality, presentation software, and interactive video are among the categories. Formerly published by R. R. Bowker.

Film and Video Finder. National Information Center for Educational Media. c/o Plexus Publishing, Inc. • Biennial. $295.00. Contains 92,000 listings of film and video educational, technical and vocational children's programs and literary materials.

Filmstrip and Slide Set Finder, 1990: A Comprehensive Index to 35mm Educational Filmstrips and Slide Sets. c/o Plexus Publishing, Inc. • 1990. $225.00. Three volumes. (NICEM Series).

Index to AV Producers and Distributors (Educational Audiovisual Materials). National Information Center for Educational Media. c/o Plexus Publishing, Inc. • Biennial. $89.00. A directory listing about 23,300 producers and distributors of all types of audiovisual educational materials.

Peterson's Guide to Distance Learning Programs. Peterson's. • 2002. $26.95. Second revised edition. Provides detailed information on accredited college and university programs available through television, radio, computer, videocassette, and audiocassette resources. Covers U. S. and Canadian institutions.

Video Source Book. Gale. • Covers: Approximately 160,000 videos covering more than 120,000 complete programs available from more than 2,100 distributors. Entries include: Video title, release year, description, run time, format, audience, MPAA rating, credits, producer, awards, distributor, price. Distributor's address and phone are given in a separate list.

HANDBOOKS AND MANUALS

Educators Guide to Free Films, Filmstrips and Slides. Educators Progress Service, Inc. • Annual. $36.95. Lists educational and recreational films in all subject areas for free use by teachers and other educators. Formerly *Educators Guide to Free Filmstrips and Slides*.

Educators Guide to Free Videotapes - Secondary Education. James Berger, editor. Educators Progress Service, Inc. • Annual. $34.95. Lists free-loan audiotapes, videotapes and records. Formerly *Educators Guide to Free Audio and Video Materials*.

ONLINE DATABASES

A-V Online. Access Innovations, Inc. • Provides online descriptions of non-print educational materials for all levels, kindergarten to graduate school. Includes all types of audio, film, and video media.

Updated quarterly. Inquire as to online cost and availability.

ERIC. Educational Resources Information Center. • Funded by the U. S. Department of Education, Institute of Education Sciences (formerly Office of Educational Research and Improvement). Provides access to more than one million online records covering education-related journal and report literature, 1966 to date. Updating is monthly. Inquire as to online cost and availability.

PERIODICALS AND NEWSLETTERS

Educational Marketer: The Educational Publishing Industry's Voice of Authority Since 1968. SIMBA Information. • Three times a month. $599.00 per year. Newsletter. Edited for suppliers of educational materials to schools and colleges at all levels. Covers print and electronic publishing, software, audiovisual items, and multimedia. Includes corporate news and educational statistics.

Educational Technology Research and Development. Association for Educational Communications and Technology. • Quarterly. $75.00 per year.

Multimedia Schools: A Practical Journal of Technology for Education including Multimedia, CD-ROM, Online and Internet and Hardware in K-12. Information Today, Inc. • Six times a year. $39.95 per year. Edited for school librarians, media center directors, computer coordinators, and others concerned with educational multimedia. Coverage includes the use of CD-ROM sources, the Internet, online services, and library technology.

Pro AV: Real-World Solutions for AV Professionals. • Monthly. Free. Formerly *Presenting Communications*.

Syllabus: New Directions in Educational Technology. Syllabus Press. • 10 times a year. $24.00 per year. Covers the use of advanced technology in higher education systems, including video, multimedia, the Internet, distance learning systems, and electronic publishing.

TechTrends: For Leaders in Education and Training. Association for Educational Communications and Technology. • Bimonthly. $65.00 per year.

RESEARCH CENTERS AND INSTITUTES

Division of Educational Research and Service. Louisiana Tech University. Tech Station, P.O. Box 3163, Ruston, LA 71272. Phone: (318)257-3036.

Instructional Media Development Center. University of Wisconsin at Madison. 142 Education Sciences Bldg., 1025 W. Johnson, Madison, WI 53706. Phone: (608)262-3330 Fax: (608)262-6447 E-mail: imdcinfo@education.wisc.edu • URL: http://www.imdc.education.wisc.edu.

TRADE/PROFESSIONAL ASSOCIATIONS

Association for Educational Communications and Technology. 1800 N. Stonelake Dr., Suite 2, Bloomington, IN 47404. Phone: 877-677-2328 or (812)335-7675 Fax: (812)335-7678 E-mail: aect@aect.org • URL: http://www.aect.org.

InfoComm International. 11242 Waples Mill Rd., Ste. 200, Fairfax, VA 22030-6079. Phone: 800-659-7469 or (703)273-7200 Fax: (703)278-8082 E-mail: customerservice@infocomm.org • URL: http://www.infocomm.org • Represents for-profit individuals and organizations that derive revenue from the commercialization or utilization of communications technology. Ensures the credibility and desirability of its members' products and services by representing the communications industry to the public, business, education, and governments.

AUDIOVISUAL AIDS IN INDUSTRY

See also: AUDIOVISUAL AIDS IN EDUCATION

BIBLIOGRAPHIES

Films and Audiovisual Information. Available from U. S. Government Printing Office. • Annual. Free. Issued by the Superintendent of Documents. A list of government publications on motion picture and audiovisual topics. Formerly *Motion Pictures, Films and Audiovisual Information*. (Subject Bibliography No. 73.).

DIRECTORIES

AV Market Place: The Complete Business Directory of Audio, Audio Visual, Computer Systems, Film, Video, and Programming, with Industry Yellow Pages. Information Today, Inc. • Annual. $195.00. Provides information on "more than 7,500 companies that create, apply, or distribute AV equipment and services for business, education, science, and government." Multimedia, virtual reality, presentation software, and interactive video are among the categories. Formerly published by R. R. Bowker.

Video Source Book. Gale. • Covers: Approximately 160,000 videos covering more than 120,000 complete programs available from more than 2,100 distributors. Entries include: Video title, release year, description, run time, format, audience, MPAA rating, credits, producer, awards, distributor, price. Distributor's address and phone are given in a separate list.

ONLINE DATABASES

ERIC. Educational Resources Information Center. • Funded by the U. S. Department of Education, Institute of Education Sciences (formerly Office of Educational Research and Improvement). Provides access to more than one million online records covering education-related journal and report literature, 1966 to date. Updating is monthly. Inquire as to online cost and availability.

PERIODICALS AND NEWSLETTERS

Harvard Management Communication Letter. Harvard Business School Publishing. • Description: Provides information and techniques for managers on effective communication.

Presentations: Technology and Techniques for Effective Communication. VNU Business Media. • Monthly. Free to qualified personnel; others, $69.00 per year. Covers the use of presentation hardware and software, including audiovisual equipment and computerized display systems. Includes an annual "Buyers Guide to Presentation Products.".

Video Librarian: The Video Review Magazine. Video Librarian. • Bimonthly. $64.00 per year. $99.00 per year with online access to archives (15,000 reviews). Edited for public and school libraries. Each issue includes reviews of hundreds of video DVDs or cassettes, in various subject areas.

TRADE/PROFESSIONAL ASSOCIATIONS

Communications Media Management Association. 20423 State Rd. 7, Ste. F6-491, Boca Raton, FL 33498. Phone: (561)477-8100 Fax: (973)543-0166 E-mail: cmma@cmma.org • URL: http://www.cmma.net • Professional association of managers of communications media departments of business, education, or government. Aims to provide networking and educational opportunities for communications media managers that build peer professional relationships, facilitate leadership development, deepen managerial skills, expand technical knowledge, and develop skills in business strategy.

AUDIOVISUAL EQUIPMENT INDUSTRY

BIBLIOGRAPHIES

Films and Audiovisual Information. Available from U. S. Government Printing Office. • Annual. Free. Issued by the Superintendent of Documents. A list of government publications on motion picture and audiovisual topics. Formerly *Motion Pictures, Films and Audiovisual Information.* (Subject Bibliography No. 73.).

DIRECTORIES

AV Market Place: The Complete Business Directory of Audio, Audio Visual, Computer Systems, Film, Video, and Programming, with Industry Yellow Pages. Information Today, Inc. • Annual. $195.00. Provides information on "more than 7,500 companies that create, apply, or distribute AV equipment and services for business, education, science, and government." Multimedia, virtual reality, presentation software, and interactive video are among the categories. Formerly published by R. R. Bowker.

AV Presentation--Buyer's Guide. Cygnus Business Media Inc. • Covers: lists of film and slide laboratory services and manufacturers of media production and presentation equipment and audiovisual supplies. Entries include: Company name, address, product or service.

Entertainment Sourcebook: An Insider's Guide on Where to Find Everything. Applause Theatre & Cinema Books. • Annual. $45.00. Compiled by the Association of Theatrical Artists and Craftspeople (http://www.entertainmentsourcebook.com/ATAC.htm). Lists more than 5,000 sources of theatrical and entertainment supplies and services, such as props, costumes, publicity agencies, scenic shops, amusement park equipment, audio/video products, balloons, wigs, make-up, magic supplies, etc.

Library Journal Sourcebook. Reed Business Information. • Publication includes: List of over 600 suppliers of products and services used by libraries from abstracting to word processing equipment. Entries include: Company name, address, phone, list of products or services. Complete listings for more than 100 architectural firms; Disaster planning for librarians.

ENCYCLOPEDIAS AND DICTIONARIES

Multimedia and the Web from A to Z. David C. Leonard and Patrick M. Dillon. Greenwood Publishing Group, Inc. • 1998. $42.95. Second enlarged revised edition. Defines more than 1,500 terms relating to software and hardware in the areas of computing, online technology, telecommunications, audio, video, motion pictures, CD-ROM, and the Internet. Includes acronyms and an annotated bibliography. Formerly *Multimedia Technology from A to Z* (1994).

PERIODICALS AND NEWSLETTERS

AV Guide: The Learning Media Newsletter. Educational Screen, Inc. • Monthly. $15.00 per year. Provides information on audiovisual aids. Formerly *AV Guide Newsletter.*

Media and Methods: Educational Products, Technologies and Programs for Schools and Universities. American Society of Educators. • Five times a year. $33.50 per year.

Presentations: Technology and Techniques for Effective Communication. VNU Business Media. • Monthly. Free to qualified personnel; others, $69.00 per year. Covers the use of presentation hardware and software, including audiovisual equipment and computerized display systems. Includes an annual "Buyers Guide to Presentation Products.".

TRADE/PROFESSIONAL ASSOCIATIONS

Association of Theatrical Artists and Craftspeople (ATAC). 604 Riverside Dr., New York, NY 10031.

Phone: (212)234-9001 • Members are artists and craftspeople working in theatre, film, TV, and advertising. Areas of expertise include props, costumes, millinery, puppetry, display, and special effects.

Content Delivery and Storage Association. 182 Nassau St., Ste. 204, Princeton, NJ 08542-7005. Phone: (609)279-1700 Fax: (609)279-1999 E-mail: info@ contentdeliveryandstorage.org • URL: http://www.recordingmedia.org • Serves as the advocate for the growth and development of all recording media and as a forum for the exchange of information regarding global trends and innovations. Provides members an opportunity to join forces and be a strong industry voice allowing them to grow and expand their business. Encompasses all facets of the recording media.

InfoComm International. 11242 Waples Mill Rd., Ste. 200, Fairfax, VA 22030-6079. Phone: 800-659-7469 or (703)273-7200 Fax: (703)278-8082 E-mail: customerservice@infocomm.org • URL: http://www.infocomm.org • Represents for-profit individuals and organizations that derive revenue from the commercialization or utilization of communications technology. Ensures the credibility and desirability of its members' products and services by representing the communications industry to the public, business, education, and governments.

AUDITING

See also: ACCOUNTING; CERTIFIED PUBLIC ACCOUNTANTS; COST ACCOUNTING; INTERNAL AUDITING

GENERAL WORKS

Auditing. Jack C. Robertson and Timothy J. Louwers. McGraw-Hill. • 2001. $41.88. 10th edition.

Auditing: Integrated Approach. Alvin A. Arens. Prentice Hall PTR. • 2000. $105.00. Eighth edition.

The Financial Numbers Game: Detecting Creative Accounting Practices. Charles W. Mulford and Eugene E. Comiskey. John Wiley and Sons, Inc. • 2002. $39.95. Serves as a guide to financial statement analysis for investors. Explains the "creative" schemes used by corporations to boost earnings-per-share data.

Principles of Auditing. O. Ray Whittington and Kurt Pany. McGraw-Hill. • 2000. $90.31. 13th edition.

ABSTRACTS AND INDEXES

Accounting and Tax Index. UMI. • Quarterly. Price on application. Annual cumulation. Indexes accounting, auditing, and taxation literature appearing in journals, books, pamphlets, conference proceedings, and newsletters.

Accounting Articles. CCH, Inc. • Monthly. $624.00 per year. Looseleaf service.

DIRECTORIES

America's Corporate Finance Directory. LexisNexis Group. • Covers: Financial personnel and outside financial services relationships of 5,000 leading United States corporations and their wholly-owned United States subsidiaries. Entries include: Company name, address, phone, fax, telex, e-mail addresses, stock exchange information, earnings, total assets, size of pension/profit-sharing fund portfolio, number of employees, description of business, wholly-owned U.S. Subsidiaries of parent company; name and title of key executives; outside suppliers of financial services.

Who Audits America: A Directory of Publicly Held Corporations and the Accounting Firms Who Audit Them. Data Financial Press. • 1994. $155.00. 12,000 publicly held corporations that report to the Securi-

ties and Exchange Commission, and their accounting firms.

ENCYCLOPEDIAS AND DICTIONARIES

Blackwell Encyclopedic Dictionary of Accounting. Rashad Abdel-khalik. Blackwell Publishing. • 1997. $38.95. The editor is associated with the University of Florida. Contains definitions of key terms combined with longer articles written by various U. S. and foreign business educators. Includes bibliographies and index. (Blackwell Encyclopedia of Management Series).

Dictionary of Accounting Terms. Joel G. Siegel. Barron's Educational Series, Inc. • 2000. $13.95. Third edition. (Business Dictionaries Series).

International Dictionary of Accounting Acronyms. Thomas W. Morris, editor. Fitzroy Dearborn Publishers, Inc. • 1999. $45.00. Defines 2,000 acronyms used in worldwide accounting and finance.

HANDBOOKS AND MANUALS

Accountants' Handbook. Douglas R. Carmichael and Paul Rosenfeld. John Wiley and Sons, Inc. • 2003. $160.00. 10th edition. Two volumes. Vol. one, $95.00; vol. two, $95.00. Chapters are written by various accounting and auditing specialists.

Accountant's Handbook of Fraud and Commercial Crime. G. Jack Bologna and others. John Wiley and Sons, Inc. • 1992. $225.00.

AICPA Audit and Accounting Manual. American Institute of Certified Public Accountants. • 1999. $90.50. Covers working papers, internal control, audit approach, etc.

AICPA Codification of Statements on Auditing Standards. American Institute of Certified Public Accountants. • 1999. $81.25. Includes *Auditing Interpretations* and *International Auditing Guidelines.*

AICPA Professional Standards. U. S. Auditing Standards, Accounting and Review Services, Ethics, Bylaws, International Accounting, International Auditing, Management Advisory Services, Quality Control, and Tax Practice. American Institute of Certified Public Accountants. • 1999. $123.50. Two volumes.

AICPA Technical Practice Aids. American Institute of Certified Public Accountants. • 1998. $119.00 per year. Two volumes. Advisory opinions, statements of position, and other material.

Applying GAAP and GAAS. LexisNexis Matthew Bender. • Biennial. $358.00 per year. Two looseleaf volumes. In-depth explanations of generally accepted accounting principles (GAAP) and generally accepted auditing standards (GAAS).

Financial Accounting Standards: Explanation and Analysis. CCH, Inc. • 1996. $56.00. 18th edition.

Financial Investigations: A Forensic Accounting Approach to Detecting and Resolving Crimes. Available from U. S. Government Printing Office. • 2002. $54.00. Two volumes: textbook and workbook. Issued by the Internal Revenue Service (http://www.irs.ustreas.gov). Serves as a text "for courses on conducting financial investigations." (IRS Publications 1714 and 1816.).

Government Auditing Standards. Available from U. S. Government Printing Office. • 1994. $6.50. Revised edition. Issued by the U. S. General Accounting Office (http://www.gao.gov). Contains standards for CPA firms to follow in financial and performance audits of federal government agencies and programs. Also known as the "Yellow Book.".

Handbook of Accounting and Auditing. John C. Burton and others. RIA. • Annual. $310.00. Looseleaf service.

Miller GAAS Guide: A Comprehensive Restatement of Generally Accepted Auditing Standards for Auditing, Attestation, Compilation and Review and the Code of Professional Conduct. Larry P. Bailey.

Aspen Publishers. • Annual. $139.00. Includes monthly update. Includes industry audit guides and a model audit program.

Modern Auditing. William C. Boynton. John Wiley and Sons, Inc. • 2001. $111.95. Seventh edition.

Montgomery's Auditing. Vincent M. O'Reilly and others. John Wiley and Sons, Inc. • 1999. $225.00. 12th edition. 2001 *Supplement*, $72.00. Provides comprehensive coverage of auditing strategies and methods, including detailed guidelines.

Practitioner's Guide to GAAS. John Wiley and Sons, Inc. • Annual. $184.95. Covers GAAS: Generally Accepted Auditing Standards, promulgated by the American Institute of Certified Public Accountants. (Includes CD-ROM.).

SEC Accounting Rules. CCH, Inc. • $448.00. Loose-leaf service.

U. S. Master Auditing Guide. CCH, Inc. • 2002. $65.00. Covers such topics as auditing standards, audit management, compliance, consulting, governmental audits, forensic auditing, and fraud. Includes checklists, charts, graphs, and sample reports.

U. S. Master GAAP Guide. Bill D. Jarnagin. CCH, Inc. • 2000. $62.95. Covers the generally accepted accounting principles (GAAP) contained in the professional pronouncements of the Accounting Principles Board (APB) or the Financial Accounting Standards Board (FASB). Includes general discussions, flow charts, and detailed examples. Arranged by topic.

ONLINE DATABASES

Accounting and Tax Database. PROQUEST. • Provides indexing and abstracting of the literature of accounting, taxation, and financial management, 1971 to date. Updating is weekly. Especially covers accounting, auditing, banking, bankruptcy, employee compensation and benefits, cash management, financial planning, and credit. Inquire as to online cost and availability.

PERIODICALS AND NEWSLETTERS

Internal Auditor. Institute of Internal Auditors, Inc. • Bimonthly. $60.00 per year.

Journal of Accounting, Auditing and Finance. New York University Vincent C. Ross Institute of Accounting Research. Greenwood Publishing Group Inc. • Quarterly. Individuals, $70.00 per year; institutions, $165.00 per year.

TRADE/PROFESSIONAL ASSOCIATIONS

American Institute of Certified Public Accountants. 1211 Ave. of the Americas, New York, NY 10036-8775. Phone: 888-777-7077 or (212)596-6200 Fax: (212)596-6213 • URL: http://www.aicpa.org.

Information Systems Audit and Control Association and Foundation. 3701 Algonquin Rd., Suite 1010, Rolling Meadows, IL 60008. Phone: (847)253-1545 Fax: (847)253-1443 E-mail: membership@isaca.org • URL: http://www.isaca.org • Formerly EDP Auditors Association.

Institute of Internal Auditors. 247 Maitland Ave., Altamonte Springs, FL 32701-4201. Phone: (407)937-1100 Fax: (407)937-1101 E-mail: iia@theiia.org • URL: http://www.theiia.org.

OTHER SOURCES

Auditing Research Monographs. American Institute of Certified Public Accountants. • Irregular. Price varies.

FASB Accounting Standards Current Text. Financial Accounting Standards Board. • $395.00. Three looseleaf volumes. Periodic supplementation.

FASB Accounting Standards Current Text: General Standards. Financial Accounting Standards Board. • Irregular. Price on application.

FASB Accounting Standards Current Text: Industries Standards. Financial Accounting Standards Board. • Irregular. Price on application.

FASB Accounting Standards Current Text: Professional Standards. Financial Accounting Standards Board. • Irregular. Price on application.

FASB Accounting Standards Current Text: Technical Practice Aids. Financial Accounting Standards Board. • Irregular. Price on application.

FASB Original Pronouncements. Financial Accounting Standards Board. • $595.00. Seven looseleaf volumes.

FASB Original Pronouncements. John Wiley and Sons, Inc. • 2001. $108.95. Three volumes include all the original pronouncements put forth by the Financial Accounting Standards Board since inception in 1973 and the American Institute of Certified Public Accountants.

FASB Statements of Financial Accounting Concepts. John Wiley and Sons, Inc. • 2001. $35.95. Contains statements of concepts issued by the Financial Accounting Standards Board.

Financial Accounting Series. Financial Accounting Standards Board. • Price on application.

AUDITING, INTERNAL

See: INTERNAL AUDITING

AUTHORITIES

See: CONSULTANTS

AUTHORS

See: WRITERS AND WRITING

AUTOMATED TELLER MACHINES (ATM)

See: BANK AUTOMATION

AUTOMATIC CONTROL EQUIPMENT

See: SCIENTIFIC APPARATUS AND INSTRUMENT INDUSTRIES

AUTOMATIC DATA SYSTEMS

See: AUTOMATION; COMPUTERS; SYSTEMS IN MANAGEMENT

AUTOMATIC IDENTIFICATION SYSTEMS

See also: POINT-OF-SALE SYSTEMS (POS)

ABSTRACTS AND INDEXES

Applied Science and Technology Index. H. W. Wilson Co. • 11 times a year. Quarterly and annual cumulations. Price varies. Indexes a wide variety of English language technical, industrial, and engineering periodicals.

CompuMath Citation Index. Institute for Scientific Information. • Three times a year. $1,090.00 per year. Provides citations to the worldwide literature of computer science and mathematics.

Computer and Information Systems Abstracts Journal: An Abstract Journal Pertaining to the Theory, Design, Fabrication and Application of Computer and Information Systems. CSA. • 11 times a year. $1,750.00 per year.

Computer Literature Index: A Subject/Author Index to Computer and Data Processing Literature. EBSCO Publishing. • Quarterly, with annual cumulation. $245.00 per year. Contains brief abstracts of book and periodical literature covering all phases of computing, including approximately 70 specific application areas.

NTIS Alerts: Computers, Control & Information Theory. National Technical Information Service. • Semimonthly. $235.00 per year. Provides descriptions of government-sponsored research reports and software, with ordering information. Covers computer hardware, software, control systems, pattern recognition, image processing, and related subjects. Formerly *Abstract Newsletter.*

CD-ROM DATABASES

WILSONDISC: Applied Science and Technology Abstracts. H. W. Wilson Co. • Monthly. Includes unlimited access to the online version of *Applied Science and Technology Abstracts* through WILSONLINE. Provides CD-ROM indexing and abstracting of 500 prominent scientific, technical, engineering, and industrial periodicals. Indexing coverage is provided from 1983 to date and abstracting from 1993 to date.

DIRECTORIES

Frontline Solutions Buyer's Guide. Advanstar Communications. • Publication includes: List of manufacturers, suppliers, consultants, value added resellers, and dealers/distributors of automatic identification and data capture software, technology, equipment, and products for bar code, biometric identification, electronic data interchange, machine vision, magnetic stripe, optical character recognition, radio frequency data communications, radio frequency identification, smart cards, and voice data entry; also includes related organizations, and sources for industry standards. Entries include: Company name, address, phone, e-mail, web address, products or services.

Manufacturing Systems: Buyers Guide. Reed Business Information. • Annual. Price on application. Contains information on companies manufacturing or supplying materials handling systems, CAD/CAM systems, specialized software for manufacturing, programmable controllers, machine vision systems, and automatic identification systems.

Sensors Buyers Guide. Advanstar Communications. • Covers: Lists manufacturers and vendors of sensors and transducers for use in high-technology applications engineering. Also covers related products and services. Entries include: Company name, address, phone, fax, e-mail, URL, contact person, type of sensors manufactured and/or physical, chemical, or biological characteristics utilized in sensing.

ONLINE DATABASES

Applied Science and Technology Index Online. H. W. Wilson Co. • Provides online indexing of 500 major scientific, technical, industrial, and engineering periodicals. Time period is 1983 to date. Monthly updates. Inquire as to online cost and availability.

PROMT: Predicasts Overview of Markets and Technology. Gale Cengage Learning. • Companies, products, applied technologies and markets. U.S. and international literature coverage, 1972 to date. Inquire as to online cost and availability. Provides abstracts from more than 1,600 publications. Weekly updates.

PERIODICALS AND NEWSLETTERS

Card Technology. Thomson Media. • Monthly. $79.00 per year. Covers advanced technology for credit, debit, and other cards. Topics include smart cards, optical recognition, and card design.

Frontline Solutions. Advanstar Communications. • Thirteen times per year. $41.00 per year. Provides news and information about the applications and technology of automated data capture systems. Formerly (Automatic I.D. News).

Item Processing Report. Access Intelligence L.L.C. • Description: Monitors developments in the processing of remittances and checks, including image processing, optical character recognition, check truncation, hardware, and software. **Remarks:** Absorbed The Powell Report, 1992.

Manufacturing Computer Solutions. • Monthly. $88.00 per year. Edited for managers of factory automation, emphasizing the integration of systems in manufacturing. Subjects include materials handling, CAD/CAM, specialized software for manufacturing, programmable controllers, machine vision, and automatic identification systems. Formerly *Manufacturing Systems.*

Sensors: Your Resource for Sensing, Communications, and Control. Advantar Communications. • Monthly. $70.00 per year. Edited for design, production, and manufacturing engineers involved with sensing systems. Emphasis is on emerging technology.

Supply Chain Systems: The Resource for Supply Chain Automation. Helmers Publishing, Inc. • Monthly. Free to qualified personnel; others, $55.00 per year. Covers trends in automatic identification technology and management. Formerly *ID Systems7.*.

TRADE/PROFESSIONAL ASSOCIATIONS

AIM Global. 125 Warrendale-Bayne Rd., Ste. 100, Warrendale, PA 15086. Phone: (724)934-4470 Fax: (724)934-4495 E-mail: dan@aimglobal.org • URL: http://www.aimglobal.org • Serves as a trade association for the automatic identification data captures technology industry.

AIM, Inc. 125 Warrendale Bayne Rd., Warrendale, PA 15086. Phone: 800-338-0206 or (724)934-4470 Fax: (724)934-4495 E-mail: info@aimglobal.org • URL: http://www.aimglobal.org • Members are companies concerned with automatic identification and data capture, including bar code systems, magnetic stripes, machine vision, voice technology, optical character recognition, and systems integration technology.

GS1 US. Princeton Pike Corporate Center, 1009 Lenox Dr., Ste. 202, Lawrenceville, NJ 08648. Phone: (609)620-0200 Fax: (609)620-1200 E-mail: info@gs1us.org • URL: http://www.uc-council.org • Develops and implements standard-based, global supply chain solutions. Operates two wholly owned subsidiaries, UCCnet and RosettaNet, and co-manages the global EAN.UCC System with EAN International. Manages the United Nations Standard Products and Services Code (UNSPSC) for the United Nations Development Programme (UNDP). Evaluates the effects of brand and size demand, competitor actions, pricing policy, and shelf location of merchandise. Administers Universal Product Code and Symbol (UPC), Uniform Communications Standard (UCS), Warehouse Information Network Standard (WINS), and Voluntary Inter-Industry Communications Standard (VICSEDI).

AUTOMATIC TRANSLATING

See: MACHINE TRANSLATING

AUTOMATION

See also: COMPUTERS; CONTROL EQUIPMENT INDUSTRY; LINEAR PROGRAMMING; MACHINE VISION; ONLINE INFORMATION SYSTEMS; OPERATIONS RESEARCH; ROBOTS

GENERAL WORKS

Automatic Control Systems. Benjamin C. Kuo and Farid Golnaraghi. John Wiley and Sons, Inc. • 2002. $119.95. Eighth edition.

ABSTRACTS AND INDEXES

Applied Science and Technology Index. H. W. Wilson Co. • 11 times a year. Quarterly and annual cumulations. Price varies. Indexes a wide variety of English language technical, industrial, and engineering periodicals.

Internet and Personal Computing Abstracts [print edition]. EBSCO Publishing. • Quarterly. $269.00 per year, including cumulative index. Provides more than 10,000 abstracts annually from both trade and academic publications. Covers computer hardware, software, product reviews, Web sites, e-commerce, networks, corporate news, security, and related topics. Formerly *Microcomputer Abstracts.*

Key Abstracts: Factory Automation. Available from INSPEC, Inc. • Monthly. $250.00 per year. Provides international coverage of journal and proceedings literature, including publications on CAD/CAM, materials handling, robotics, and factory management. Published in England by the Institution of Electrical Engineers (IEE).

NTIS Alerts: Manufacturing Technology. National Technical Information Service. • Semimonthly. $265.00 per year. Provides descriptions of government-sponsored research reports and software, with ordering information. Covers computer-aided design and manufacturing (CAD/CAM), engineering materials, quality control, machine tools, robots, lasers, productivity, and related subjects. Formerly *Abstract Newsletter.*

BIBLIOGRAPHIES

Automation. Available from U. S. Government Printing Office. • Annual. Free. Issued by the Superintendent of Documents. A list of government publications on automation, computers, and related topics. Formerly *Computers and Data Processing.* (Subject Bibliography No. 51.).

CD-ROM DATABASES

Computer Database. Gale Cengage Learning. • Provides one year of full-text on CD-ROM for 150 leading computer-related publications. Also includes 70,000 product specifications and brief profiles of 13,000 computer product vendors and manufacturers.

DIRECTORIES

Assembly Buyers Guide. Reed Business Information. • Annual. $68.00. Lists manufacturers and suppliers of equipment relating to assembly automation, fasteners, adhesives, robotics, and power tools.

Control Engineering Buyers Guide. Reed Business Information. • Annual. Price on application. Contains specifications, prices, and manufacturers' listings for computer software, as related to control engineering.

Data Sources: The Comprehensive Guide to the Data Processing Industry: Hardware, Data Communications Products, Software, Company Profiles. Gale Cengage Learning. • Semiannual. $455.00 per year. Two volumes. Describes hardware and software for all computer operating sysems, including prices and technical details. Lists about 75,000 products from 14,000 suppliers. Industry-specific software applications are described.

Sensors Buyers Guide. Advantar Communications. • Covers: Lists manufacturers and vendors of sensors and transducers for use in high-technology applications engineering. Also covers related products and services. Entries include: Company name, address, phone, fax, e-mail, URL, contact person, type of sensors manufactured and/or physical, chemical, or biological characteristics utilized in sensing.

ENCYCLOPEDIAS AND DICTIONARIES

Acronyms of Computer Science and Communications: A Comprehensive Acronym Dictionary and Illustrated Encyclopedia. Enjob Kajan and Ejub Kajan. Springer Verlag. • 2002. $49.95. Explains more than 4,000 "broadly used" computer, telecommunications, and information technology acronyms. Includes illustrations and Web addresses, where applicable.

Encyclopedia of Information Systems. Hossein Bidgoli, editor. Elsevier. • 2002. $1,200.00. Four volumes. Contains a wide range of articles relating to computers, databases, communication, and information technology. The 200 topics include coverage of hardware, software, artificial intelligence, the Internet, networks, knowledge management, electronic commerce, search engines, and systems design.

ONLINE DATABASES

INSPEC. Institution of Electrical Engineers (IEE). • Provides online citations, with abstracts, to the world literature of electrical engineering, electronics, optoelectronics, telecommunications, industrial controls, instrumentation, computer technology, information technology, and physics. Coverage includes more than 4,000 technical and scientific journals from 1969 to date, with weekly updating. (INSPEC is Information Services in Physics, Electronics, and Computing.) Inquire as to online cost and availability.

PERIODICALS AND NEWSLETTERS

Advanced Manufacturing Technology: Monthly Report. Technical Insights. • Monthly. Institutions, $695.00 per year. Newsletter. Covers technological developments relating to robotics, computer graphics, automation, computer-integrated manufacturing, and machining.

Assembly: Design and Manufacturing Technology for Better Assembled Products. Business News Publishing Co. • Monthly. $68.00 per year. Covers assembly, fastening, and joining systems. Includes information on automation and robotics.

Automatica. Elsevier. • Monthly. Qualifed personnel, $74.00 per year; institutions, $2,332.00 per year. Text in English, French, German and Russian.

Industrial Computing. Industrial Computing Society. ISA Services, Inc. • Monthly. Members $100.00 per year; non-members, $80.00 per year. Published by the Instrument Society of America. Edited for engineering managers and systems integrators. Subject matter includes industrial software, programmable controllers, artificial intelligence systems, and industrial computer networking systems.

Information Week: Business Innovation Powered by Technology. CMP Publications, Inc. • Weekly. $199.00 per year. The magazine for information systems management.

Managing Automation. Thomas Publishing Co., LLC. • Monthly. Free to qualified personnel; others, $60.00 per year. Coverage includes software for manufacturing, systems planning, integration in process industry automation, computer integrated manufacturing (CIM), computer networks for manufacturing, management problems, industry news, and new products.

Sensors: Your Resource for Sensing, Communications, and Control. Advantar Communications. • Monthly. $70.00 per year. Edited for design, production, and manufacturing engineers involved with sensing systems. Emphasis is on emerging technology.

RESEARCH CENTERS AND INSTITUTES

Alliance for Innovative Manufacturing. Stanford University, Bldg.02-530, Rm. 225, Stanford, CA 94305-3036. Phone: (650)723-9038 Fax: (650)723-5034 E-mail: cborn@stanford.edu • URL: http://www.stanford.edu/group/aim • Development of new products and processing. Formerly Stanford Integrated Manufacturing Association.

Coordinated Science Laboratory. University of Illinois at Urbana-Champaign. 1308 W. Main St,. Room 202, Urbana, IL 61801-2307. Phone: (217)333-2511 Fax: (217)244-1764 E-mail: iyer@uiuc.edu • URL: http://www.csl.uiuc.edu.

Division of Engineering Research. Michigan State University. B-100 Engineering Research Complex, East Lansing, MI 48824. Phone: (517)355-5104 Fax: (517)353-5547 E-mail: wadem@egr.msu.edu • URL: http://www.egr.msu.edu/der.

Industrial Relations Research Institute. University of Wisconsin-Madison, 4226 Social Science Bldg., Madison, WI 53706-1393. Phone: (608)262-1882 Fax: (608)265-4591 E-mail: irri@mhub.facstaff.wisc.edu • URL: http://www.wisc.edu/irr.

TRADE/PROFESSIONAL ASSOCIATIONS

Computer and Automated Systems Techincal Group of Society of Manufacturing Engin. Technical Activities Dept. 1 SME Dr., Dearborn, MI 48121. Phone: 800-733-4763 or (313)271-1500 Fax: (313)425-3400 E-mail: service@sme.org • URL: http://www.sme.org/casa • Sponsored by the Society of Manufacturing Engineers. Formerly Computer and Automated Systems Association.

Instrumentation Systems and Automation Society. 67 Alexander Dr., Research Triangle Park, NC 27709. Phone: (919)549-8411 Fax: (919)549-8288 E-mail: info@isa.org • URL: http://www.isa.org • Members are engineers and others concerned with industrial instrumentation, systems, computers, and automation, Formerly Instrument Society of America.

Special Interest Group for Design Automation. c/o Association for Computing Machinery, 1515 Broadway, New York, NY 10036. Phone: 800-342-6626 or (212)626-0500 Fax: (212)302-5826 E-mail: sigs@acm.org • URL: http://www.acm.org/sigda.

OTHER SOURCES

Annual Reviews in Control. Elsevier. • Annual. $471.00 per year. Formerly*Annual Review in Automatic Programming.*

Factory Automation-Related Equipment and Accessories. Available from MarketResearch.com. • 2002. $3,850.00. Published by Global Industry Analysts. Provides worldwide market research data, including profiles of major automation equipment and software companies.

AUTOMATION, BANK

See: BANK AUTOMATION

AUTOMATION, LIBRARY

See: LIBRARY AUTOMATION

AUTOMATION, OFFICE

See: OFFICE AUTOMATION

AUTOMATION, RETAIL

See: POINT-OF-SALE SYSTEMS (POS)

AUTOMATONS

See: ROBOTS

AUTOMOBILE ACCESSORIES INDUSTRY

See: AUTOMOBILE EQUIPMENT INDUSTRY

AUTOMOBILE ACCIDENTS

See: TRAFFIC ACCIDENTS AND TRAFFIC SAFETY

AUTOMOBILE BATTERIES

See: BATTERY INDUSTRY

AUTOMOBILE DEALERS

See also: AUTOMOTIVE INDUSTRY; USED CAR INDUSTRY

GENERAL WORKS

Car Ownership Forecasting. E.W. Allanson, editor. Gordon and Breach Publishing Group. • 1982. $211.00. Volume one. (Transporation Studies Series).

What Your Car Really Costs: How to Keep a Financially Safe Driving Record. American Institute for Economic Research. • 2002. $6.00. Contains "Should You Buy or Lease?," "Should You Buy New or Used?," "Dealer Trade-in or Private Sale?," "Lemon Laws," and other car buying information. Includes rankings of specific models for resale value, 1995 to 2001. (Economic Education Bulletin.).

DIRECTORIES

NAFA Annual Reference Book. National Association of Fleet Administrators. • Annual. $45.00. Automobile manufacturers' sales and leasing representatives throughout the country.

FINANCIAL RATIOS

Almanac of Business and Industrial Financial Ratios. Leo Troy. Aspen Publishers, Inc. • 2003. $125.95. Includes CD-Rom. Contains financial ratios derived from federal tax returns. Ratios for each of about 200 industries are arranged according to company asset size. (Almanac of Business and Industrial Financial Ratios Series).

Annual Statement Studies. The Risk Management Association. • Annual. Median and quartile financial ratios are given for over 400 kinds of manufacturing, wholesale, retail, construction, and consumer finance establishments. Data is sorted by both asset size and sales volume. Includes a clearly written "Definition of Ratios" and an alphabetical industry index.

Annual Statement Studies: Industry Default Probabilities and Cash Flow Measures. The Risk Management Association. • Annual. $145.00. Serves as a companion volume to the original *Annual Statement Studies.* Gives probability of default estimates on a percentage scale for more than 450 industries. Includes changes in position year-by-year for eight financial statement line items and provides percentage measures of cash flow.

Industry Norms and Key Business Ratios. Desk Top Edition. Dun and Bradstreet Corp. • Annual. Five volumes. $475.00 per volume. $1,890.00 per set. Covers over 800 kinds of businesses, arranged by Standard Industrial Classification number. More

detailed editions covering longer periods of time are also available.

HANDBOOKS AND MANUALS

Used Car Sales. Entrepreneur Media, Inc. • Looseleaf. $59.50. A practical guide to getting started in the business of selling used cars. Covers profit potential, start-up costs, market size evaluation, owner's time required, site selection, lease negotiation, pricing, accounting, advertising, etc. (Start-Up Business Guide No. E2330.).

INTERNET DATABASES

Advance Monthly Sales for Retail Trade and Food Services. U. S. Census Bureau. Phone: 800-541-8345 or (301)763-4636 Fax: (301)457-3842 E-mail: rcb@census.gov • URL: http://www.census.gov/svsd/www/fullpub.html • Web pages provide monthly sales figures for a wide range of retail businesses. Advance, preliminary, and final statistics are provided for the latest month available in each case, with a previous-year comparison. Updates are monthly.

PERIODICALS AND NEWSLETTERS

Automotive News: Engineering, Financial, Manufacturing, Sales, Marketing, Servicing. Crain Communications, Inc. • Weekly. $129.00 per year. Business news coverage of the automobile industry at the retail, wholesale, and manufacturing levels. Includes statistics.

Car Dealer Insider: Profit Making Secrets for the Competitive Dealer. United Communications Group. • Weekly. $275.00 per year. Newsletter. Provides automotive industry news, with ideas and advice for car dealers on advertising, marketing, and management. Formerly *Car and Truck Dealer Insider Newsletter.*

Chilton's Automotive Marketing: A Monthly Publication for the Retail Jobber and Distributor of Automotive Aftermarket. Reed Business Information. • Monthly. Free to qualified personnel; others, $48.00 per year. Includes marketing of automobile batteries. Formerly *Automotive Aftermarket News.*

NADA'S Automotive Executive. National Automobile Dealers Association. • Monthly. $24.00 per year.

Used Car Dealer. National Independent Automobile Dealers Association. • Monthly. Free to members; non-members, $60.00 per year.

STATISTICS SOURCES

Annual Benchmark Report for Retail Trade and Food Services...A Detailed Summary of Retail Sales, Purchases, Accounts Receivable, Inventories, and Food Service Sales. Available from U. S. Government Printing Office. • Annual. $13.00. Issued by the U.S. Census Bureau. Provides detailed annual and monthly retail statistics for the most recent 10 years. Includes data for various kinds of retail outlets, including automobiles, furniture, appliances, building supplies, grocery stores, drug stores, gasoline stations, clothing, sporting goods, department stores, and restaurants.

U. S. Industry and Trade Outlook. Available from National Technical Information Service. • Annual. $69.95. Produced by the International Trade Administration, U. S. Department of Commerce, in a "public-private" partnership with DRI/McGraw-Hill and Standard & Poor's. Provides basic data, outlook for the current year, and "Long-Term Prospects" (five-year projections) for a wide variety of products and services. Includes high technology industries. Formerly *U. S. Industrial Outlook.*

TRADE/PROFESSIONAL ASSOCIATIONS

National Automobile Dealers Association. 8400 Westpark Dr., McLean, VA 22102. Phone: 800-252-6232 or (703)821-7000 Fax: (703)821-7075 E-mail: nadainfo@nada.org • URL: http://www.nada.org •

Franchised new car and truck dealers. Provides representation for franchised new car and truck dealers in the areas of government, industry, and public affairs. Offers management services and retirement and insurance programs to member dealers. Maintains National +Automobile +Dealers Charitable Foundation.

National Independent Automobile Dealers Association. 2521 Brown Blvd., Arlington, TX 76006. Phone: 800-682-3837 or (817)640-3838 Fax: (817)649-5866 E-mail: mike@niada.com • URL: http://www.niada.com • Individuals, companies, or corporations licensed by their states as dealers to buy and sell used motor vehicles; associate members are businesses related to or associated with the buying or selling of motor vehicles. Gathers and disseminates information relative to the used car industry; represents used car dealers before regulatory and legislative bodies; provides educational and other programs to help used car dealers understand their responsibilities; works for the betterment of the automobile industry. Works closely with local and state independent automobile dealers' associations and others concerning dealers and the public. Maintains code of fair dealing for members. Conducts seminars, meetings, and professional training programs. Maintains speakers' bureau, services for children, and charitable programs. Sponsors competitions; compiles statistics.

AUTOMOBILE EQUIPMENT INDUSTRY

See also: AUTOMOBILE DEALERS; AUTOMOTIVE INDUSTRY

DIRECTORIES

Directory of Automotive Aftermarket Suppliers. Chain Store Guide. • Annual. $327.00. Covers auto supply store chains. Includes distributors.

Plunkett's Automobile Industry Almanac. Plunkett Research Ltd. • Covers: 300 leading companies in the automotive industry. Entries include: Name, address, phone, fax, and key executives. Also includes analysis and information on trends, technology, and statistics in the field.

FINANCIAL RATIOS

Industry Norms and Key Business Ratios. Desk Top Edition. Dun and Bradstreet Corp. • Annual. Five volumes. $475.00 per volume. $1,890.00 per set. Covers over 800 kinds of businesses, arranged by Standard Industrial Classification number. More detailed editions covering longer periods of time are also available.

ONLINE DATABASES

Ward's AutoInfoBank. Ward's Communications, Inc. • Provides weekly, monthly, quarterly, and annual statistical data from 1980 to date for U. S. and imported cars and trucks. Covers production, shipments, sales, inventories, optional equipment, etc. Updating varies by series. Inquire as to online cost and availability.

PERIODICALS AND NEWSLETTERS

Automotive Recycling. Automotive Recyclers Association. • Bimonthly. Free to members; nonmembers, $40.00 per year. Formerly *Dismantlers Digest.*

Brake and Frontend: The Complete Undercar Service Magazine. Babcox. • Monthly. $64.00 per year.

Chilton's Automotive Marketing; A Monthly Publication for the Retail Jobber and Distributor of Automotive Aftermarket. Reed Business Information. • Monthly. Free to qualified personnel; others, $48.00 per year. Includes marketing of automobile batteries. Formerly *Automotive Aftermarket News.*

SEMA News. Specialty Equipment Market Association. • Description: Covers the automotive specialty, performance equipment, and accessory sectors. Recurring features include news of government and legislative actions, new products, international markets, and member and Association activities.

PRICE SOURCES

Car Stereo. Orion Research Corp. • Annual. $144.00. Quotes retail and wholesale prices of used stereo sound equipment for automobiles. Original list prices and years of manufacture are also shown.

STATISTICS SOURCES

Annual Survey of Manufactures. Available from U. S. Government Printing Office. • Annual. Prices vary. Issued by the U. S. Census Bureau as an interim update to the *Census of Manufactures.* Includes data on number of manufacturing establishments in various industries, employment, labor costs, value of shipments, capital expenditures, inventories, energy costs, and assets. (See also Census Bureau home page, http://www.census.gov/.).

Standard & Poor's Industry Surveys. Standard & Poor's. • Semiannual. $1,800.00. Two looseleaf volumes. Includes monthly *Supplements.* Provides detailed, individual surveys of 52 major industry groups. Each survey is revised on a semiannual basis. Also includes "Monthly Investment Review" (industry group investment analysis) and monthly "Trends & Projections" (economic analysis).

U. S. Industry and Trade Outlook. Available from National Technical Information Service. • Annual. $69.95. Produced by the International Trade Administration, U. S. Department of Commerce, in a "public-private" partnership with DRI/McGraw-Hill and Standard & Poor's. Provides basic data, outlook for the current year, and "Long-Term Prospects" (five-year projections) for a wide variety of products and services. Includes high technology industries. Formerly *U. S. Industrial Outlook.*

TRADE/PROFESSIONAL ASSOCIATIONS

Automotive Aftermarket Industry Association. 7101 Wisconsin Ave., Ste. 1300, Bethesda, MD 20814-3415. Phone: (301)654-6664 Fax: (301)654-3299 E-mail: aaia@aftermarket.org • URL: http://www.aftermarket.org • Automotive parts and accessories retailers, distributors, manufacturers, and manufacturers' representatives. Conducts research and compiles statistics. Conducts seminars and provides specialized education program.

International Mobile Air Conditioning Association Education Foundation. 6410 Southwest Blvd., Ste. 212, Fort Worth, TX 76109-3920. Phone: (817)732-4600 Fax: (817)732-9610 E-mail: info@imaca.org • URL: http://www.imaca.org • Serves the automotive, boat, and aircraft air conditioning industries. Formerly Automotive Air Conditioning Association.

Motor and Equipment Manufacturers Association. 10 Laboratory Dr., Research Triangle Park, NC 27709-3966. Phone: (919)549-4800 Fax: (919)549-4824 E-mail: info@amema.org • URL: http://www.mema.org.

OTHER SOURCES

Automotive Air Bags. Available from MarketResearch.com. • 2002. $4,450.00. Published by Global Industry Analysts. Provides worldwide market research data, including profiles of major air bag manufacturers.

AUTOMOBILE INDUSTRY

See: AUTOMOTIVE INDUSTRY

AUTOMOBILE INSURANCE

See also: ACCIDENT INSURANCE; CASUALTY INSURANCE; INSURANCE

GENERAL WORKS

Smarter Insurance Solutions. Janet Bamford. Bloomberg. • 1996. $19.95. Provides practical advice to consumers, with separate chapters on the following kinds of insurance: automobile, homeowners, health, disability, and life. (Bloomberg Personal Bookshelf Series).

ABSTRACTS AND INDEXES

Insurance Periodicals Index. Specials Libraries Association, Insurance and Employees Benefits Div. NILS Publishing Co. • Annual. $250.00. Compiled by the Insurance and Employee Benefits Div., Special Libraries Association. A yearly index of over 15,000 articles from about 35 insurance periodicals. Arrangement is by subject, with an index to authors.

BIBLIOGRAPHIES

Insurance and Employee Benefits Literature. Special Libraries Association, Insurance and Employee Benefits Div. • Bimonthly. $15.00 per year. Lists a wide variety of literature in all branches of the insurance industry. Includes annotations.

CD-ROM DATABASES

U. S. Insurance: Property and Casualty. Sheshunoff Information Services, Inc. • Monthly. Price on application. CD-ROM provides detailed, current financial information on more than 3,200 property and casualty insurance companies.

ENCYCLOPEDIAS AND DICTIONARIES

Dictionary of Insurance Terms. Harvey W. Rubin. Barron's Educational Series, Inc. • 2000. $14.95. Fourth edition. Defines terms in a wide variety of insurance fields. (Business Dictionaries Series).

Glossary of Insurance Policy Terms. Organization for Economic Cooperation and Development. • 1999. $30.00. "The selected topics range from insurance policy regulation/supervision to general trade issues and include technical terms related to issues such as claims, premiums, and provisions." Edited for government, academic, business, and insurance organizations.

Insurance Words and Their Meanings: A Glossary of Insurance Terms. The Rough Notes Co., Inc. • 2001. 17th edition. Price on application.

Rupp's Insurance and Risk Management Glossary. Richard V. Rupp. NILS Publishing Co. • 2001. $35.00. Second edition. Provides definitions of 6,400 insurance words and phrases. Includes a guide to acronyms and abbreviations.

HANDBOOKS AND MANUALS

The Complete Book of Insurance: Protecting Your Life, Health Property, and Income. Ben G. Baldwin. McGraw-Hill. • 1991. $24.95. Provides basic information and advice on various kinds of insurance: life, health, property (fire), disability, long-term care, automobile, liability, and annuities.

INTERNET DATABASES

InsWeb. InsWeb Corp. Phone: (916)853-3300 E-mail: info@insweb.com • URL: http://www.insweb.com • Web site offers a wide variety of advice and information on automobile, life, health, and "other" insurance. Includes glossaries of insurance terms, Standard & Poor's ratings of individual insurance companies, and "Financial Needs Estimators." Searching is available. Fees: Free.

ONLINE DATABASES

I.I.I. Data Base Search. Insurance Information Institute. • Provides online citations and abstracts of insurance-related literature in magazines, newspapers, trade journals, and books. Emphasis is on property and casualty insurance issues, including highway safety, product safety, and environmental liability. Inquire as to online cost and availability.

PERIODICALS AND NEWSLETTERS

Automobile Insurance Losses, Collision Coverages, Variations by Make and Series. Highway Loss Data Institute. • Semiannual. Membership.

New York No-Fault Arbitration Reports. American Arbitration Association. • Description: Addresses developing laws under the no-fault law in the state of New York. Summarizes awards rendered under state-sponsored arbitration.

STATISTICS SOURCES

Property-Casualty Insurance Facts. Insurance Information Institute. • Annual. $22.50. Formerly *Insurance Facts.*

TRADE/PROFESSIONAL ASSOCIATIONS

Alliance of American Insurers. 3025 Highland Pky., Ste. 800, Downers Grove, IL 60515. Phone: (630)724-2100 Fax: (630)724-2190 E-mail: cstonehill@allianceai.org • URL: http://www.allianceai.org.

Insurance Services Office (ISO). 545 Washington Blvd., Jersey City, NJ 07310-1686. Phone: 800-888-4476 or (201)469-2000 Fax: (201)748-1472 E-mail: info@iso.com • URL: http://www.iso.com • Provides statistical, actuarial, underwriting, and claims information to property and casualty insurance companies.

OTHER SOURCES

Automobile Liability Insurance. 3d. Irvin E. Schermer and William J. Schermer. West Group. • Seminannual. $501.00. Four looseleaf volumes.

The Law of Liability Insurance. LexisNexis Matthew Bender. • $1,451.00. Five looseleaf volumes. Periodic supplementation. Explains the terms and phases essential for a general understanding of liability insurance, and discusses injuries to both persons and property.

AUTOMOBILE LAWS

See: MOTOR VEHICLE LAW AND REGULATION

AUTOMOBILE LEASE AND RENTAL SERVICES

GENERAL WORKS

What Your Car Really Costs: How to Keep a Financially Safe Driving Record. American Institute for Economic Research. • 2002. $6.00. Contains "Should You Buy or Lease?," "Should You Buy New or Used?," "Dealer Trade-in or Private Sale?," "Lemon Laws," and other car buying information. Includes rankings of specific models for resale value, 1995 to 2001. (Economic Education Bulletin.).

DIRECTORIES

Avis Licensee Directory. Avis Licensee Association. • Covers: about 125 owners of licensed Avis Rent-a-Car franchises; coverage includes Canada. Entries include: Company name, address, phone, names and titles of key officials; branch office or subsidiary names, locations, and phone numbers; name of owner, home address, phone, name of spouse (if any).

Plunkett's Airline, Hotel, and Travel Industry Almanac. Plunkett Research, Ltd. • Annual. $249.95. Contains profiles of 300 leading companies, including airlines, hotels, travel agencies, theme parks, cruise lines, casinos, and car rental companies.

FINANCIAL RATIOS

Annual Statement Studies. The Risk Management Association. • Annual. Median and quartile financial

ratios are given for over 400 kinds of manufacturing, wholesale, retail, construction, and consumer finance establishments. Data is sorted by both asset size and sales volume. Includes a clearly written "Definition of Ratios" and an alphabetical industry index.

Annual Statement Studies: Industry Default Probabilities and Cash Flow Measures. The Risk Management Association. • Annual. $145.00. Serves as a companion volume to the original *Annual Statement Studies.* Gives probability of default estimates on a percentage scale for more than 450 industries. Includes changes in position year-by-year for eight financial statement line items and provides percentage measures of cash flow.

HANDBOOKS AND MANUALS

CCH Guide to Car, Travel, Entertainment, and Home Office Deductions. CCH, Inc. • Annual. $45.00. Explains how to claim maximum tax deductions for common business expenses. Includes automobile depreciation tables, lease value tables, worksheets, and examples of filled-in tax forms.

Limousine Service. Entrepreneur Media, Inc. • Looseleaf. $59.50. A practical guide to starting a limousine service. Covers profit potential, start-up costs, market size evaluation, owner's time required, site selection, lease negotiation, pricing, accounting, advertising, promotion, etc. (Start-Up Business Guide No. E1224.).

Used-Car Rental Agency. Entrepreneur Media, Inc. • Looseleaf. $59.50. A practical guide to starting a used-car rental business. Covers profit potential, start-up costs, market size evaluation, owner's time required, site selection, lease negotiation pricing, accounting, advertising, promotion, etc. (Start-Up Business Guide No. E1108.).

Vehicle Leasing. Entrepreneur Media, Inc. • Looseleaf. $59.50. A practical guide to starting an automobile leasing business. Covers profit potential, start-up costs, market size evaluation, owner's time required, site selection, lease negotiation, pricing, accounting, advertising, promotion, etc. (Start-Up Business Guide No. E2329.).

TRADE/PROFESSIONAL ASSOCIATIONS

American Automotive Leasing Association. 675 N Washington St., Ste. 410, Alexandria, VA 22314. Phone: (703)548-0777 Fax: (703)548-1925 E-mail: peters@aalafleet.com • URL: http://www.aalafleet.com • Represents the commercial automotive fleet leasing and management industry.

AUTOMOBILE LICENSES

See: MOTOR VEHICLE LAW AND REGULATION

AUTOMOBILE PARTS INDUSTRY

See: AUTOMOBILE EQUIPMENT INDUSTRY

AUTOMOBILE RENTAL SERVICES

See: AUTOMOBILE LEASE AND RENTAL SERVICES

AUTOMOBILE REPAIR INDUSTRY

ABSTRACTS AND INDEXES

Business Periodicals Index. H. W. Wilson Co. • 11 times a year. Quarterly and annual cumulations. Price varies.

CD-ROM DATABASES

ABI/INFORM. PROQUEST. • Monthly. Provides CD-ROM indexing and abstracting of worldwide

business literature. Archival discs are available from 1971. Formerly *ABI/INFORM OnDisc.*

WILSONDISC: Wilson Business Abstracts. H. W. Wilson Co. • Monthly. Includes unlimited online access to *Wilson Business Abstracts* through WILSONLINE. Provides CD-ROM "cover-to-cover" abstracting and indexing of over 600 prominent business periodicals. Indexing is from 1982, abstracting from 1990. (*Business Periodicals Index* without abstracts is available on CD-ROM at $1,495 per year.).

DIRECTORIES

Fleet Owner Specs and Buyers' Directory. Primedia Business Magazines and Media. • Annual. $5.00. Lists of manufacturers of equipment and materials used in the operation, management, and maintenance of truck and bus fleets.

FINANCIAL RATIOS

Almanac of Business and Industrial Financial Ratios. Leo Troy. Aspen Publishers, Inc. • 2003. $125.95. Includes CD-Rom. Contains financial ratios derived from federal tax returns. Ratios for each of about 200 industries are arranged according to company asset size. (Almanac of Business and Industrial Financial Ratios Series).

ONLINE DATABASES

F & S Index. Gale Cengage Learning. • Contains about four million citations to worldwide business, financial, and industrial or consumer product literature appearing from 1972 to date. Weekly updates. Inquire as to online cost and availability.

PROMT: Predicasts Overview of Markets and Technology. Gale Cengage Learning. • Companies, products, applied technologies and markets. U.S. and international literature coverage, 1972 to date. Inquire as to online cost and availability. Provides abstracts from more than 1,600 publications. Weekly updates.

Trade & Industry Database. Gale Cengage Learning. • Provides indexing of business periodicals, January 1981 to date. Daily updates. (Full text articles from some periodicals are available online, 1983 to date. Inquire as to online cost and availability).

Wilson Business Abstracts Online. H. W. Wilson Co. • Indexes and abstracts 600 major business periodicals, plus the *Wall Street Journal* and the business section of the *New York Times.* Indexing is from 1982, abstracting from 1990, with the two newspapers included from 1993. Updated weekly. Inquire as to online cost and availability. (*Business Periodicals Index* without abstracts is also available online.).

PERIODICALS AND NEWSLETTERS

Fleet Owner. Primedia Business Magazines and Media. • Monthly. $45.00 per year.

Motor Age: For the Professional Automotive Import and Domestic Service Industry. Reed Business Information. • Monthly. $49.00 per year. Published for independent automotive repair shops and gasoline service stations.

MOTOR: Covering the World of Automotive Service. Hearst Business Publishing. • Monthly. $48.00 per year. Edited for professional automobile and light-truck mechanics. Includes industry news and market trends.

TRADE/PROFESSIONAL ASSOCIATIONS

Automotive Aftermarket Industry Association. 7101 Wisconsin Ave., Ste. 1300, Bethesda, MD 20814-3415. Phone: (301)654-6664 Fax: (301)654-3299 E-mail: aaia@aftermarket.org • URL: http://www.aftermarket.org • Automotive parts and accessories retailers, distributors, manufacturers, and manufacturers' representatives. Conducts research and compiles statistics. Conducts seminars and provides specialized education program.

Automotive Service Association. PO Box 929, PO Box 929, Bedford, TX 76095-0929. Phone: 800-272-7467 or (817)283-6205 Fax: (817)685-0225 E-mail: asainfo@asashop.org • URL: http://www.asashop.org • Automotive service businesses including body, paint, and trim shops, engine rebuilders, radiator shops, brake and wheel alignment services, transmission shops, tune-up services, and air conditioning services; associate members are manufacturers and wholesalers of automotive parts, and the trade press. Represents independent business owners and managers before private agencies and national and state legislative bodies. Promotes confidence between consumer and the automotive service industry, safety inspection of motor vehicles, and better highways.

Gasoline and Automotive Service Dealers Association. 9520 Seaview Ave., Brooklyn, NY 11236. Phone: (718)241-1111 Fax: (718)763-6589 E-mail: gasdal@cs.com • Members are owners and operators of automobile service stations and repair shops. Formerly Gasoline Merchants.

National Institute for Automotive Service Excellence. 101 Blue Seal Dr. SE, Leesburg, VA 20175. Phone: 877-273-8324 or (703)669-6600 Fax: (703)713-0727 E-mail: webmaster@asecert.org • URL: http://www.asecert.org • A public interest organization which promotes high standards in automotive service and repair. Encourages effective training programs for automobile mechanics/technicians. Affiliated with National Automotive Technicians Education Foundation.

AUTOMOBILE ROAD GUIDES

See: MAPS

AUTOMOBILE SERVICE STATIONS

See: GASOLINE SERVICE STATIONS

AUTOMOBILE TELEPHONES

See: MOBILE TELEPHONE INDUSTRY

AUTOMOBILES

See also: AUTOMOTIVE INDUSTRY; FOREIGN AUTOMOBILES; USED CAR INDUSTRY

GENERAL WORKS

What Your Car Really Costs: How to Keep a Financially Safe Driving Record. American Institute for Economic Research. • 2002. $6.00. Contains "Should You Buy or Lease?," "Should You Buy New or Used?," "Dealer Trade-in or Private Sale?," "Lemon Laws," and other car buying information. Includes rankings of specific models for resale value, 1995 to 2001. (Economic Education Bulletin.).

CD-ROM DATABASES

Magazine Index Plus. Gale Cengage Learning. • Monthly. $4,000.00 per year (includes InfoTrac workstation). Provides full text on CD-ROM for about 100 popular, general interest magazines and indexing for 300 others. Includes special indexing of reviews and product evaluations. Time period is 1980 to date.

OECD Statistical Compendium. Organization for Economic Cooperation and Development. • Semiannual. $1,905.00 per year for 1 to 10 users.

CD-ROM contains more than 730,000 monthly, quarterly, and annual time series for OECD countries, 1960 to date. Includes fully searchable data on agriculture, food, economic indicators, national accounts, employment, energy, finance, industry, technology, and foreign trade. Results can be displayed in various forms.

Sourcebooks America CD-ROM. CACI Marketing Systems. • Annual. $1,250.00. Provides the CD-ROM version of *The Sourcebook of ZIP Code Demographics: Census Edition* and *The Sourcebook of County Demographics: Census Edition.*

ENCYCLOPEDIAS AND DICTIONARIES

Elsevier's Dictionary of Automotive Engineering. A. Schellings. Elsevier. • 1998. $149.50.

Macmillan Encyclopedia of Transportation. Available from Gale Cengage Learning. • 1999. $450.00. Six volumes. Published by Macmillan Reference USA. Covers the business, technology, and history of transportation on land, on water, in the air, and in space. Includes definitions, cross-references, and 200 color illustrations.

HANDBOOKS AND MANUALS

CCH Guide to Car, Travel, Entertainment, and Home Office Deductions. CCH, Inc. • Annual. $45.00. Explains how to claim maximum tax deductions for common business expenses. Includes automobile depreciation tables, lease value tables, worksheets, and examples of filled-in tax forms.

INTERNET DATABASES

Business 2.0 Web Guide to the Best Business Links. Business 2.0 Media Inc. Phone: (415)293-4800 E-mail: support@business2.com • URL: http://www.business2.com/webguide • Web site presents an extensive, searchable directory of links to "the best, most informative, and authoritative web pages." Twenty main categories cover business, finance, career, company information, people, and technology topics, with thousands of subtopics, all linking to Web sites recommended by experienced business researchers. Fees: Free.

Fedstats. Federal Interagency Council on Statistical Policy. Phone: (202)395-7254 • URL: http://www.fedstats.gov • Web site features an efficient search facility for full-text statistics produced by more than 100 federal agencies, including the Census Bureau, the Bureau of Economic Analysis, and the Bureau of Labor Statistics. Boolean searches can be made within one agency or for all agencies combined. Links are offered to international statistical bureaus, including the UN, IMF, OECD, UNESCO, Eurostat, and 20 individual countries. Fees: Free.

FreeLunch.com. Economy.com, Inc. Phone: (610)696-8700 Fax: (610)696-1678 • URL: http://www.freelunch.com • Web site provides free access to more than 1.5 million economic and financial data series, covering industry, demographics, labor markets, prices, retail sales, government spending, trade, interest rates, housing starts, the stock market, and many other topics. Data is available for various time periods in either chart or table form. Searching is offered. Fees: Free, but registration required. Economy.com, Inc. also offers fee-based economic analysis at *The Dismal Scientist* site (http://www.dismal.com).

ONLINE DATABASES

Ward's AutoInfoBank. Ward's Communications, Inc. • Provides weekly, monthly, quarterly, and annual statistical data from 1980 to date for U. S. and imported cars and trucks. Covers production, shipments, sales, inventories, optional equipment, etc. Updating varies by series. Inquire as to online cost and availability.

PERIODICALS AND NEWSLETTERS

Antique Automobile. Antique Automobile Club of America. • Membership.

Automobile Quarterly: The Connoisseur's Magazine of Motoring Today, Yesterday and Tomorrow. Automobile Quarterly, Inc. • Five times a year. $89.95 per year.

Car and Driver. Hachette Filipacchi Media U.S., Inc. • Monthly. $11.97 per year.

Motor Trend. PRIMEDIA Inc. • Monthly. $10.00. per year.

Special Interest Autos. Watering Inc., Special Interest Publications. • Bimonthly. $19.95 per year.

PRICE SOURCES

Edmund's New Cars. Edmund Publications Corp. • Four times a year. Individuals, $39.96 per year; libraries, $26.80 per year. Wholesale and retail prices for all American and import models and accessories. Includes federal crash reports, leasing facts, and accident report forms. Formerly *Edmund's New Car Prices.*

NADA Appraisal Guides. National Automobile Dealers Association. • Prices and frequencies vary. Guides to prices of used cars, old used cars, motorcycles, mobile homes, recreational vehicles, and mopeds.

RESEARCH CENTERS AND INSTITUTES

Engineering Experiment Station. Ohio State University. 2070 Neil Ave., Columbus, OH 43210-1275. Phone: (614)292-3149 Fax: (614)292-9615 E-mail: fortner.1@osu.edu • URL: http://www.osu.edu.

Southwest Research Institute. Southwest Research Institute. PO Box 28510, 6220 Culebra Rd., San Antonio, TX 78228-0510. Phone: (210)684-5111 Fax: (210)522-3547 E-mail: bd@swri.org • URL: http://www.swri.org • Automation, robotics, intelligent systems, space sciences, environmental sciences and engineering, bioengineering, micro encapsulation, chemistry, plant machinery and piping dynamics, radiolocation sciences and development, communications, electromagnetic compatibility, electronic systems, geophysical instrumentation, nondestructive evaluation research, nuclear waste regulatory analysis, fluid dynamics and hydraulics, offshore systems, structural analysis and testing, terminal ballistics and blast effects, materials development, solid mechanics, nonmetallic materials, engine systems engineering, engine emissions analysis and control, fuels and lubricants evaluation, fluids and lubrication technology, alternate energy systems, alternate fuels, mining systems engineering, vehicle and highway safety, and fire research.

STATISTICS SOURCES

Business Statistics of the United States. Linz Audain and Cornelia J. Strawser. Bernan Associates. • Annual. $147.00. Based on *Business Statistics,* formerly issue by the Bureau of Economic Analysis, U. S. Department of Commerce. Provides basic data for a wide variety of U. S. industries, services, and economic indicators. Most statistics are shown annually for 30 years and monthly for the most recent four years.

Highway Statistics. Federal Highway Administration, U.S. Department of Transportation. Available from U.S. Government Printing Office. • Annual. $26.00.

Survey of Current Business. Available from U. S. Government Printing Office. • Monthly. $63.00 per year. Issued by Bureau of Economic Analysis, U. S. Department of Commerce. Presents a wide variety of business and economic data.

Transportation Statistics Annual Report. Available from U. S. Government Printing Office. • Annual. $43.00. Issued by the U. S. Bureau of Transportation Statistics, Transportation Department (http://www.bts.gov). Summarizes national data for various forms of transportation, including airlines, railroads, and motor vehicles. Information on the use of roads and highways is included.

TRADE/PROFESSIONAL ASSOCIATIONS

American Automobile Association. One River Pl., Wilmington, DE 19801. Phone: 800-763-9900 or (302)299-4700 Fax: (407)444-8030 E-mail: ahaddad@eec.nwv.edu • URL: http://www.aaa.com • Federation of automobile clubs (1,000 offices) providing domestic and foreign travel services, emergency road services, and insurance. Sponsors public services for traffic safety, better highways, more efficient and safer cars, energy conservation, and improvement of motoring and travel conditions.

AUTOMOBILES, USED

See: USED CAR INDUSTRY

AUTOMOTIVE INDUSTRY

See also: AUTOMOBILES; FOREIGN AUTOMOBILES; USED CAR INDUSTRY

ABSTRACTS AND INDEXES

Engineering Index Monthly: Abstracting and Indexing Services Covering Sources of the World's Engineering Literature. Engineering Information Inc. • Monthly. Institutions, $5,279.00 per year. Provides indexing and abstracting of the world's engineering and technical literature.

ALMANACS AND YEARBOOKS

Automotive News Market Data Book. Crain Communications, Inc. • Annual. $19.95. Directory of automotive vendors and worldwide vehicle manufacturing. Formerly *Automotive News Almanac.*

Ward's Automotive Yearbook. Ward's Communications. • Annual. $425.00. Comprehensive statistical information on automotive production, sales, truck data and suppliers. Included with subscription to *Ward's Automotive Reports.*

BIBLIOGRAPHIES

Japanese Automobile Industry: An Annotated Bibliography. Sheau-Yueh J. Chao, compiler. Greenwood Publishing Group, Inc. • 1994. $82.95. Describes about 600 books, articles, papers, and documents written in English. Emphasis is on material published since 1980. (Bibliographies and Indexes in Economics and Economic History Series: No. 15).

CD-ROM DATABASES

OECD Statistical Compendium. Organization for Economic Cooperation and Development. • Semiannual. $1,905.00 per year for 1 to 10 users. CD-ROM contains more than 730,000 monthly, quarterly, and annual time series for OECD countries, 1960 to date. Includes fully searchable data on agriculture, food, economic indicators, national accounts, employment, energy, finance, industry, technology, and foreign trade. Results can be displayed in various forms.

World Marketing Forecasts on CD-ROM. Gale Cengage Learning. • Annual. $2,500.00. Produced by Euromonitor. Provides detailed forecast data for the years to 2012 on CD-ROM for 54 countries in all parts of the world. Covers a wide range of social, demographic, economic, and market factors. Includes specific forecasts for many kinds of consumer products.

DIRECTORIES

Automotive Warehouse Distributors Association-Membership Directory. Automotive Warehouse Distributors Association. • Annual. $200.00. Over 175 automotive parts distributors, 150 manufacturers of automotive parts, and marketing associations,

manufacturer representatives, and affiliate members. *Plunkett's Automobile Industry Almanac.* Plunkett Research Ltd. • Covers: 300 leading companies in the automotive industry. Entries include: Name, address, phone, fax, and key executives. Also includes analysis and information on trends, technology, and statistics in the field.

ENCYCLOPEDIAS AND DICTIONARIES

Macmillan Encyclopedia of Transportation. Available from Gale Cengage Learning. • 1999. $450.00. Six volumes. Published by Macmillan Reference USA. Covers the business, technology, and history of transportation on land, on water, in the air, and in space. Includes definitions, cross-references, and 200 color illustrations.

FINANCIAL RATIOS

Almanac of Business and Industrial Financial Ratios. Leo Troy. Aspen Publishers, Inc. • 2003. $125.95. Includes CD-Rom. Contains financial ratios derived from federal tax returns. Ratios for each of about 200 industries are arranged according to company asset size. (Almanac of Business and Industrial Financial Ratios Series).

Annual Statement Studies. The Risk Management Association. • Annual. Median and quartile financial ratios are given for over 400 kinds of manufacturing, wholesale, retail, construction, and consumer finance establishments. Data is sorted by both asset size and sales volume. Includes a clearly written "Definition of Ratios" and an alphabetical industry index.

Annual Statement Studies: Industry Default Probabilities and Cash Flow Measures. The Risk Management Association. • Annual. $145.00. Serves as a companion volume to the original *Annual Statement Studies.* Gives probability of default estimates on a percentage scale for more than 450 industries. Includes changes in position year-by-year for eight financial statement line items and provides percentage measures of cash flow.

Industry Norms and Key Business Ratios. Desk Top Edition. Dun and Bradstreet Corp. • Annual. Five volumes. $475.00 per volume. $1,890.00 per set. Covers over 800 kinds of businesses, arranged by Standard Industrial Classification number. More detailed editions covering longer periods of time are also available.

IRS Corporate Financial Ratios. Available from MarketResearch.com. • 2002. $225.00. Published by Schonfeld & Associates, Inc. Presents 70 key financial ratios for 260 industries. Ratios are calculated from income statement and balance sheet data available from the Internal Revenue Service. Includes four asset size classes.

HANDBOOKS AND MANUALS

SAE Handbook. Society of Automotive Engineers. • Annual. $425.00. Three volumes. Contains standards, recommended practices and information reports on ground vehicle design, manufacturing, testing and performance.

INTERNET DATABASES

Business 2.0 Web Guide to the Best Business Links. Business 2.0 Media Inc. Phone: (415)293-4800 E-mail: support@business2.com • URL: http://www.business2.com/webguide • Web site presents an extensive, searchable directory of links to "the best, most informative, and authoritative web pages." Twenty main categories cover business, finance, career, company information, people, and technology topics, with thousands of subtopics, all linking to Web sites recommended by experienced business researchers. Fees: Free.

Fedstats. Federal Interagency Council on Statistical Policy. Phone: (202)395-7254 • URL: http://www.fedstats.gov • Web site features an efficient search facility for full-text statistics produced by more than

100 federal agencies, including the Census Bureau, the Bureau of Economic Analysis, and the Bureau of Labor Statistics. Boolean searches can be made within one agency or for all agencies combined. Links are offered to international statistical bureaus, including the UN, IMF, OECD, UNESCO, Eurostat, and 20 individual countries. Fees: Free.

FreeLunch.com. Economy.com, Inc. Phone: (610)696-8700 Fax: (610)696-1678 • URL: http://www.freelunch.com • Web site provides free access to more than 1.5 million economic and financial data series, covering industry, demographics, labor markets, prices, retail sales, government spending, trade, interest rates, housing starts, the stock market, and many other topics. Data is available for various time periods in either chart or table form. Searching is offered. Fees: Free, but registration required. Economy.com, Inc. also offers fee-based economic analysis at *The Dismal Scientist* site (http://www.dismal.com).

ONLINE DATABASES

Business and Industry. Gale Cengage Learning. • Contains online citations, abstracts, and selected fulltext from more than 1,000 trade journals, newspapers, and other publications. Provides general coverage of both manufacturing and service industries, including marketing, production, industry trends, key events, and information on specific companies. Time span is 1994 to date. Daily updates. Inquire as to online cost and availability. (Also available in a CD-ROM version.).

F & S Index. Gale Cengage Learning. • Contains about four million citations to worldwide business, financial, and industrial or consumer product literature appearing from 1972 to date. Weekly updates. Inquire as to online cost and availability.

Tablebase. Gale Cengage Learning. • Provides online numerical tabular data from a wide variety of business, organization, and government sources, including about 1,000 trade journals. Includes industry and individual company statistics relating to products, market share, sales forecasts, production, exports, market trends, etc. Time span is 1997 to date. Weekly updates. Inquire as to online cost and availability. (Also available in a CD-ROM version.).

Ward's AutoInfoBank. Ward's Communications, Inc. • Provides weekly, monthly, quarterly, and annual statistical data from 1980 to date for U. S. and imported cars and trucks. Covers production, shipments, sales, inventories, optional equipment, etc. Updating varies by series. Inquire as to online cost and availability.

PERIODICALS AND NEWSLETTERS

Autocar. Haymarket Publishing, Ltd. • Monthly. $172.00 per year. Formerly *Autocar and Motor.*

Automotive Engineering International. Society of Automotive Engineers. • Monthly. $96.00 per year. Provides 86,000 automotive product planners and engineers with state-of-the-art technology that can be applied to the development of new and improved vehicles. Supplement available *Off-Highway Engineering.* Formerly *Automotive Engineering.*

Automotive Industries. Randall Publishing Co. • Monthly. $74.00 per year.

Automotive News: Engineering, Financial, Manufacturing, Sales, Marketing, Servicing. Crain Communications, Inc. • Weekly. $129.00 per year. Business news coverage of the automobile industry at the retail, wholesale, and manufacturing levels. Includes statistics.

Car Dealer Insider: Profit Making Secrets for the Competitive Dealer. United Communications Group. • Weekly. $275.00 per year. Newsletter. Provides automotive industry news, with ideas and advice for car dealers on advertising, marketing, and management. Formerly *Car and Truck Dealer Insider Newsletter.*

NADA'S Automotive Executive. National Automobile Dealers Association. • Monthly. $24.00 per year.

Road and Track. Hachette Filipacchi Media U.S., Inc. • Monthly. $11.97 per year.

Ward's Auto World. Primedia Business Magazines and Media. • Monthly. Free to members; non-members, $55.00 per year. In-depth news and analysis of the automotive industry.

Ward's Automotive Reports. Ward's Communications. • Description: Reports "vital statistical information and exclusive news of critical interest" to the automotive industry. **Remarks:** Subscription includes Ward's Automotive Yearbook. Ward's Communications, Inc. is a subsidiary of Intertec Publishing Corp..

PRICE SOURCES

Automotive Market Report. Automotive Auction Publishing, Inc. • Biweekly. $130.00 Per Year. Current wholesale values of used vehicles.

STATISTICS SOURCES

American Trucking Trends. American Trucking Associations. Trucking Information Services, Inc. • Annual. $45.00.

Annual Survey of Manufactures. Available from U. S. Government Printing Office. • Annual. Prices vary. Issued by the U. S. Census Bureau as an interim update to the *Census of Manufactures.* Includes data on number of manufacturing establishments in various industries, employment, labor costs, value of shipments, capital expenditures, inventories, energy costs, and assets. (See also Census Bureau home page, http://www.census.gov/.).

Business Statistics of the United States. Linz Audain and Cornelia J. Strawser. Bernan Associates. • Annual. $147.00. Based on *Business Statistics,* formerly issue by the Bureau of Economic Analysis, U. S. Department of Commerce. Provides basic data for a wide variety of U. S. industries, services, and economic indicators. Most statistics are shown annually for 30 years and monthly for the most recent four years.

Consumer International. Available from Gale Cengage Learning. • Annual. $1,290.00. Published by Euromonitor. Contains extensive consumer market, economic, and demographic data for 25 major, non-European countries, including the U. S. and Canada. Includes consumer market size (volume and value) for 150 product types in 14 categories (food, clothing, automobiles, cosmetics, appliances, etc.).

Encyclopedia of American Industries. Gale Cengage Learning. • 2000. $560.00. Third edition. Two volumes. $280.00 per volume. Volume one is *Manufacturing Industries* and volume two is *Service and Non-Manufacturing Industries.* Provides the history, development, and recent status of approximately 1,000 industries. Includes statistical graphs, with industry and general indexes.

European Marketing Forecasts. Available from Gale Cengage Learning. • Annual. $1,250.00. Published by Euromonitor. Contains demographic, economic, and market forecasts for the countries of Europe to the year 2010. Forecasts include market-size data for 15 consumer product sectors (food, clothing, automobiles, consumer electronics, etc.).

International Marketing Forecasts. Available from Gale Cengage Learning. • Annual. $1,250.00. Published by Euromonitor. Contains demographic, economic, and market forecasts to the year 2013 for major, non-European countries, including the U. S. and Canada. Forecasts include market-size data for 15 consumer product sectors, such as food, clothing, and automobiles.

Standard & Poor's Industry Surveys. Standard & Poor's. • Semiannual. $1,800.00. Two looseleaf volumes. Includes monthly *Supplements.* Provides detailed, individual surveys of 52 major industry groups. Each survey is revised on a semiannual basis. Also includes "Monthly Investment Review" (industry group investment analysis) and monthly "Trends & Projections" (economic analysis).

Statistics of Income: Corporation Income Tax Returns. U.S. Internal Revenue Service. Available from U.S. Government Printing Office. • Annual. $26.00.

Survey of Current Business. Available from U. S. Government Printing Office. • Monthly. $63.00 per year. Issued by Bureau of Economic Analysis, U. S. Department of Commerce. Presents a wide variety of business and economic data.

United States Census of Manufactures. U.S. Bureau of the Census. • Quinquennial. Results presented in reports, tape, CD-ROM, and Diskette files.

TRADE/PROFESSIONAL ASSOCIATIONS

ASM International. 9639 Kinsman Rd., Novelty, OH 44073-0002. Phone: 800-336-5152 or (440)338-5151 Fax: (440)338-4634 E-mail: customerservice@asminternational.org • URL: http://asmcommunity.asminternational.org/portal/site/asm • Metallurgists, materials engineers, executives in materials producing and consuming industries; teachers and students. Disseminates technical information about the manufacture, use, and treatment of engineered materials. Offers in-plant, home study, and intensive courses through Materials +Engineering Institute. Conducts career development program. Established ASM Foundation for +Education and Research.

Automotive Aftermarket Industry Association. 7101 Wisconsin Ave., Ste. 1300, Bethesda, MD 20814-3415. Phone: (301)654-6664 Fax: (301)654-3299 E-mail: aaia@aftermarket.org • URL: http://www.aftermarket.org • Automotive parts and accessories retailers, distributors, manufacturers, and manufacturers' representatives. Conducts research and compiles statistics. Conducts seminars and provides specialized education program.

Automotive Engine Rebuilders Association. 500 Coventry Ln., Crystal Lake, IL 60014-7592. Phone: 888-326-2372 or (847)541-6550 Fax: (847)541-5808 E-mail: john@aera.org • URL: http://www.aera.org • Wholesalers of automotive replacement parts and equipment with machine shop operations; associate members are suppliers of parts, equipment, tools, and services to the rebuilder members. Acts as clearinghouse for automotive jobber machine shop information.

Automotive Market Research Council. PO Box 5887, PO Box 13966, Denver, CO 80202. Phone: (303)744-4884 Fax: (919)549-4824 E-mail: info@amrc.org • URL: http://www.amrc.org • Represents manufacturers of automotive service equipment, automotive parts, components, subassemblies, accessories as original or replacement equipment, and employees whose principal responsibility is market research analysis and business planning. Promotes more complete, prompt, and accurate gathering and dissemination of marketing data; seeks to increase the reliability of forecasts of demand in the industry; works to improve the professional abilities of market analysis. Works with government agencies to improve collection of statistics.

Automotive Trade Association Executives. 8400 Westpark Dr., McLean, VA 22102. Phone: (703)821-7072 Fax: (703)556-8581 E-mail: aaia@aftermarket.org • URL: http://www.atae.info • Executives of state and local automotive dealer associations.

Automotive Warehouse Distributors Association. 7101 Wisconsin Ave., Ste. 1300, Bethesda, MD 20814. Phone: (301)654-6664 Fax: (301)654-3299 E-mail: info@awda.org • URL: http://www.awda.org • Warehouse distributors of automotive parts and supplies; manufacturers of automotive parts and suppliers; publishers. Compiles statistics.

SAE International. 400 Commonwealth Dr., Warrendale, PA 15096-0001. Phone: 877-606-7323 or (724)776-4841 Fax: (724)776-5760 E-mail: custsvc@sae.org • URL: http://www.sae.org • Affiliated with Service Technicians Society. Formerly Society of Automobile Engineers.

AV EQUIPMENT INDUSTRY

See: AUDIOVISUAL EQUIPMENT INDUSTRY

AVIATION, BUSINESS

See: BUSINESS AVIATION

AVIATION ELECTRONICS

See: AVIONICS

AVIATION INDUSTRY

See also: AEROSPACE INDUSTRY; AIRLINE INDUSTRY; AIRPLANE INDUSTRY; BUSINESS AVIATION

GENERAL WORKS

ATP-FAR 135, Airline Transport Pilot: A Comprehensive Text and Workbook for the en Exam. K.T. Boyd. Iowa State University Press. • 1994. $29.95. Third edition.

FAA Historical Chronology: Civil Aviation and the Federal Government, 1926-1996. Edmund Preston, editor. Available from U. S. Government Printing Office. • 1998. $33.50. Third edition. Issued by the Federal Aviation Administration, U. S. Department of Transportation (http://www.dot.gov). Provides a compilation of historical information about the FAA and the earlier Civil Aeronautics Board (CAB). Chronological arrangement.

BIBLIOGRAPHIES

Aviation. Available from U. S. Government Printing Office. • Annual. Free. Lists government publications. (GPO Subject Bibliography Number 18).

DIRECTORIES

Air Freight Directory. Air Cargo Inc. • Publication includes: Directory of more than 500 motor carriers contracting with Air Cargo, Inc. for delivery and pick up of freight. Air Cargo is a ground service specialist organization jointly owned by 18 major air carriers. Entries include: Airport city and code, firm name, address, phone, and services offered. Principal content of publication is chart of service points and rates.

Regional Aviation Handbook. Shephard Press Ltd. • Annual. $90.00. Edited for regional, short-haul, and commuter airlines. Includes airline operators worldwide, manufacturers of equipment and supplies, aircraft companies, leasing companies, trade associations, and other listings.

ENCYCLOPEDIAS AND DICTIONARIES

Macmillan Encyclopedia of Transportation. Available from Gale Cengage Learning. • 1999. $450.00. Six volumes. Published by Macmillan Reference USA. Covers the business, technology, and history of transportation on land, on water, in the air, and in space. Includes definitions, cross-references, and 200 color illustrations.

FINANCIAL RATIOS

Industry Norms and Key Business Ratios. Desk Top Edition. Dun and Bradstreet Corp. • Annual. Five volumes. $475.00 per volume. $1,890.00 per set. Covers over 800 kinds of businesses, arranged by Standard Industrial Classification number. More detailed editions covering longer periods of time are also available.

ONLINE DATABASES

F & S Index. Gale Cengage Learning. • Contains about four million citations to worldwide business, financial, and industrial or consumer product literature appearing from 1972 to date. Weekly updates. Inquire as to online cost and availability.

PERIODICALS AND NEWSLETTERS

AIAA Journal: Devoted to Aerospace Research and Development. American Institute of Aeronautics and Astronautics, Inc. • Monthly. Members, $68.00 per year. Includes print and online editions. Non-members, $890.00 per year; with online edition, $1,025.00 per year.

Air Transport World. Penton Media Inc. • Monthly. Free to qualified personnel, others, $55.00 per year. Includes supplement *World Airline Reports.*

Aviation Daily. Aviation Week Newsletter. The McGraw-Hill Cos. • Description: Concerned with air transportation and the aviation manufacturing field. Focuses on management developments and trends with specific detail on economic, financial, and operating aspects of domestic and foreign airlines, aircraft manufacturers, and allied associations. Reports on federal legislation affecting the field, and lists relevant statistics.

Aviation Week and Space Technology. McGraw-Hill Aviation Week Group. • Monthly. $92.00 per year.

Human Factors and Aviation Medicine. Flight Safety Foundation, Inc. • Bimonthly. Members, $120.00 per year; non-members, $240.00 per year.

The ICAO Journal. International Civil Aviation Organization c/o Document Sales Unit. • Ten times a year. $25.00 per year. Editions in English, French and Spanish.

The Weekly of Business Aviation. Aviation Week Newsletter. McGraw-Hill. • Weekly. $595.00 per year.

RESEARCH CENTERS AND INSTITUTES

Avionics Engineering Center. Ohio University. 239 Stocker Center, Athens, OH 45701. Phone: (740)593-1534 Fax: (740)593-1604 E-mail: rankinj@ohiou.edu • URL: http://www.ent.ohiou.edu/avn/.

Flight Mechanics Laboratory. Texas A & M University, College Station, TX 77843-3141. Phone: (979)845-1685 Fax: (979)845-6051 E-mail: valasek@aero.tamu.edu • URL: http://www.flutie.tamu.edu.

Flight Research Laboratory. Kansas University Center for Research. Dept. of Aerospace Engineering, 2004 Learned Hall, 1530 W 15th St., Lawrence, KS 66045-7609. Phone: (785)864-4267 Fax: (785)864-3597 E-mail: mewing@ku.edu • URL: http://www.engr.ku.edu/ae.

Institute of Aviation. University of Illinois. One Airport Rd., Savoy, IL 61874. Phone: (217)244-8601 E-mail: s-allen2@uiuc.edu • URL: http://www.aviation.uiuc.edu.

Joint Institute for Advancement of Flight Sciences. NASA Langley Research Center, MS 335, 227 Hunting Ave., Hampton, VA 23681-2199. Phone: (757)864-1982 Fax: (757)864-5894 E-mail: jiafs@seas.gwu.edu • URL: http://www.seas.gwu.edu/ • Conducts research in aeronautics, astronautics, and acoustics (flight-produced noise).

STATISTICS SOURCES

Aerospace Facts and Figures. Aerospace Industries Association of America. • Annual. $35.00. Includes financial data for the aerospace industries.

Air Transport. Air Transport Association of America. • Annual. $20.00.

Handbook of Airline Statistics. National Aeronautics and Space Administration. • Biennial.

International Civil Aviation Organization Digests of Statistics. International Civil Aviation Organization c/o Document Sales Unit. • Irregular. $54.00. Contains financial data and traffic data for international airports. Text in English, French, Russian and Spanish.

TRADE/PROFESSIONAL ASSOCIATIONS

Air Transport Association of America. 1301 Pennsylvania Ave., Suite 1100, Washington, DC 20004-7017. Phone: (202)626-4000 Fax: (202)626-4166 E-mail: ata@air-lines.org • URL: http://www.air-lines.org.

Aviation Development Council. 141-07 20th Ave., Ste. 404, Whitestone, NY 11357. Phone: (718)746-0212 Fax: (718)746-1006 E-mail: root@aviationdevelopmentcouncil.org • URL: http://www.aviationdevelopmentcouncil.org • U.S. and foreign scheduled air carriers serving the New York-New Jersey metropolitan area; Port Authority of New York and New Jersey; Allied Pilots Association; and Air Line Pilots Association, International. Aims to explore, evaluate, and recommend to the proper authorities measures in various fields that will afford possible relief to people affected by noise of aircraft. Initiates public information on significant developments in the metropolitan area. Compiles runway analysis data on New York City area airports. Administers industry funded outreach programs designed to encourage local purchasing; administers "crime and security watch" programs for JFK, LGA & EWR.

Aviation Distributors and Manufacturers Association. 1900 Arch St., Philadelphia, PA 19103-1498. Phone: (215)564-3484 Fax: (215)963-9784 E-mail: adma@fernley.com • URL: http://www.adma.org.

General Aviation Manufacturers Association. 1400 K St. NW, Ste. 801, Washington, DC 20005. Phone: (202)393-1500 Fax: (202)842-4063 E-mail: webmaster@gama.aero • URL: http://www.gama.aero • Manufacturers of aviation airframes, engines, avionics, and components. Seeks to create a better climate for the growth of general aviation.

International Air Transport Association. 703 Waterford Way, NW 62nd Ave., Ste. 600, Miami, FL 33126. Phone: (305)264-7772 Fax: (305)264-8088 E-mail: membership@iaaglobal.org • URL: http://www1.iata.org/ • Represents the airline industries; promotes safe, reliable, secure and economical air services worldwide.

National Aeronautic Association of the U.S.A. 1815 N. Fort Myer Dr., Suite 700, Arlington, VA 22209-1805. Phone: 800-644-9777 or (703)527-0226 Fax: (703)527-0229 E-mail: naa@naa-usa.org • URL: http://www.naa.usa.org.

National Air Transportation Association. 4226 King St., Alexandria, VA 22302. Phone: 800-808-6282 or (703)845-9000 Fax: (703)845-8176 E-mail: enews@nata.aero • URL: http://www.nata.aero • Represents the interests of aviation businesses nationwide. Provides vital aviation services to the airlines, the military, and business/corporate/individual aircraft owners and operators; services includes fueling, maintenance, and flight instruction.

National Association of State Aviation Officials. 8401 Colesville Rd., Suite 505, Silver Spring, MD 20910. Phone: (301)588-0587 Fax: (301)588-1803 E-mail: henryo@nasa.org • URL: http://www.nasao.org.

University Aviation Association. 3410 Skyway Dr., Auburn, AL 36830. Phone: (334)844-2434 Fax: (334)844-2432 E-mail: uaamail@uaa.aero • URL: http://www.uaa.aero • Professional organization of educators, industry representatives, institutions and corporations interested in promoting aviation educa-

tion at the higher education level. Fosters exchange and dissemination of information among colleges and governmental and industrial organizations in the aerospace field. Supports aerospace-oriented teacher education. Sponsors research programs and compiles statistics.

OTHER SOURCES

Aviation Law Reports. CCH, Inc. • Semimonthly. $2,155.00 per year. Four looseleaf volumes.

Jane's All the World's Aircraft. Jane's Information Group, Inc. • Annual. $630.00; CD-ROM edition, $1,455.00; online edition, $1,566.00; microfiche edition, $3,075.00. Lists civil and military aircraft, helicopters, airships, and aero engines.

AVIONICS

See also: ELECTRONICS INDUSTRY

ABSTRACTS AND INDEXES

Applied Science and Technology Index. H. W. Wilson Co. • 11 times a year. Quarterly and annual cumulations. Price varies. Indexes a wide variety of English language technical, industrial, and engineering periodicals.

Science Citation Index. Thomson/ISI. • Bimonthly. $15,020.00 per year. Annual cumulation. Includes *Source Index, Citation Index, Permuterm Subject Index,* and *Corporate Index.*

CD-ROM DATABASES

Science Citation Index: Compact Disc Edition. Institute for Scientific Information. • Monthly. Provides CD-ROM indexing of the world's scientific and technical literature. Corresponds to online *Scisearch* and printed *Science Citation Index.*

DIRECTORIES

ECN's Electronic Industry Telephone Directory. Reed Business Information. • Covers: 30,000 electronics manufacturers, distributors, and representatives. Entries include: Company name, address, phone, fax, and type of establishment.

International ABC Aerospace Directory. Jane's Information Group Ltd. • Covers: Approximately 28,000 companies and organizations involved in the aerospace industry, including civil and military organizations, aircraft manufacturers, Civil Aviation Authorities, air force bases, leasing companies, airport authorities, engine manufacturers, distributors of components, and maintenance contractors; international coverage. Entries include: Name, address, phone, fax, names and titles of key personnel, description of products/services.

Jane's Avionics. Jane's Information Group Ltd. • Covers: Civil/military airborne equipment, including radio, radar, electro-optic, and electronic warfare data processors; worldwide coverage. Entries include: Technical information on equipment, including specifications, uses. Manufacturer information contained in separate index.

ENCYCLOPEDIAS AND DICTIONARIES

Wiley Encyclopedia of Electrical and Electronics Engineering. John G. Webster, editor. John Wiley and Sons, Inc. • 1999. $9,630.00. 25 volumes. Includes *Supplement I* and *Supplement II.* Contains about 1,400 articles, each with bibliography. Arrangement is according to 64 categories.

ONLINE DATABASES

Aerospace America [online]. American Institute of Aeronautics and Astronautics. • Provides complete text of the periodical, *Aerospace America,* 1984 to date, with monthly updates. Also includes news from the *AIAA Bulletin.* Inquire as to online cost and availability.

Aerospace Database. American Institute of Aeronautics and Astronautics. • Contains abstracts of literature covering all aspects of the aerospace and aircraft industry 1983 to date. Monthly updates. Inquire as to online cost and availability.

Aerospace/Defense Markets and Technology. Gale Cengage Learning. • Abstracts of commerical aerospace/defense related literature, 1982 to date. Also includes information about major defense contracts awarded by the U. S. Department of Defense. International coverage. Inquire as to online cost and availability.

Globalbase. Gale Cengage Learning. • Provides more than one million online summaries of business, industrial, and economic news reports from more than 1,000 publications worldwide. Covers a wide range of material appearing in international trade journals, professional magazines, and newspapers. Time period is 1984 to date, with weekly updates. Inquire as to online cost and availability.

INSPEC. Institution of Electrical Engineers (IEE). • Provides online citations, with abstracts, to the world literature of electrical engineering, electronics, optoelectronics, telecommunications, industrial controls, instrumentation, computer technology, information technology, and physics. Coverage includes more than 4,000 technical and scientific journals from 1969 to date, with weekly updating. (INSPEC is Information Services in Physics, Electronics, and Computing.) Inquire as to online cost and availability.

Scisearch. Institute for Scientific Information. • Broad, multidisciplinary index to the literature of science and technology, 1974 to present. Inquire as to online cost and availability. Coverage of literature is worldwide, with weekly updates.

PERIODICALS AND NEWSLETTERS

Aerospace America. American Institute of Aeronautics and Astronautics, Inc. • Monthly. Free to members; non-members, $140.00 per year. Provides coverage of key issues affecting the aerospace field.

Aerospace Engineering Magazine. Society of Automotive Engineers. • Monthly. $66.00 per year. Provides technical information that can be used in the design of new and improved aerospace systems.

Aviation Week and Space Technology. McGraw-Hill Aviation Week Group. • Monthly. $92.00 per year.

Avionics Magazine The Monthly Magazine of the Global Avionics Industry. PBI Media LLC. • Monthly. Free to qualified personnel.

Defense Electronics. Primedia Business Magazines and Media. • Monthly. $52.00 per year.

Flight International. Reed Business Information. • Weekly. $140.00 per year. Technical aerospace coverage.

Journal of Electronic Defense. Association of Old Crows. Horizon House Publications. • Monthly. Free to members; non-members, $115.00 per year.

Professional Pilot Magazine. Queensmith Communications Corp. • Monthly. $36.00 per year. Edited for career pilots in all areas of aviation: airline, corporate, charter, and military. Includes flying technique, avionics, navigation, accident analysis, career planning, corporate profiles, and business aviation news.

RESEARCH CENTERS AND INSTITUTES

Avionics Engineering Center. Ohio University. 239 Stocker Center, Athens, OH 45701. Phone: (740)593-1534 Fax: (740)593-1604 E-mail: rankinj@ohiou.edu • URL: http://www.ent.ohiou.edu/avn/.

TRADE/PROFESSIONAL ASSOCIATIONS

Aeronautical Repair Station Association. 121 N Henry St., Alexandria, VA 22314-2903. Phone: (703)739-9543 Fax: (703)739-9488 E-mail: arsa@arsa.org • URL: http://www.arsa.org • Represents FAA-certified repair stations, suppliers and distributors. Assists members on regulatory and legislative issues before the FAA and other governmental agencies.

Aerospace Electrical Society. 18231 Fernando Cir., Villa Park, CA 92861. Phone: (714)538-1002 Fax: (714)538-1002 E-mail: aefstaff@aef.org • Technicians, engineers, and management personnel engaged in the development and use of electrical and electronic equipment and systems for air and space craft.

Aircraft Electronics Association. 4217 S Hocker, Independence, MO 64055-0963. Phone: (816)373-6565 Fax: (816)478-3100 E-mail: info@aea.net • URL: http://www.aea.net • Companies engaged in the sales, engineering, installation, and service of electronic aviation equipment and systems. Seeks to: advance the science of aircraft electronics; promote uniform and stable regulations and uniform standards of performance; establish and maintain a code of ethics; gather and disseminate technical data; advance the education of members and the public in the science of aircraft electronics. Offers supplement type certificates, test equipment licensing, temporary FCC licensing for new installations, spare parts availability and pricing, audiovisual technician training, equipment and spare parts loan, profitable installation, and service facility operation. Provides employment information, equipment exchange information and service assistance on member installations anywhere in the world.

American Institute of Aeronautics and Astronautics. 1801 Alexander Bell Dr., Suite 500, c/o Michael Lewis, Reston, VA 20191-4344. Phone: 800-639-2422 or (703)264-7500 Fax: (703)264-7551 E-mail: custserv@aiaa.org • URL: http://www.aiaa.org.

Aviation Distributors and Manufacturers Association. 1900 Arch St., Philadelphia, PA 19103-1498. Phone: (215)564-3484 Fax: (215)963-9784 E-mail: adma@fernley.com • URL: http://www.adma.org.

Avionics Maintenance Conference. 2551 Riva Rd., 2551 Riva Rd., Annapolis, MD 21401. Phone: 800-633-6882 or (410)266-2008 Fax: (410)266-2047 E-mail: sbuckwal@arinc.com • URL: http://www.arinc.com/amc • Avionics maintenance professionals from commercial airlines, airframe manufacturers, avionics suppliers, and government organizations. Seeks to improve safety and reliability and reduce the costs of operating and supporting avionics equipment. Contributes to reduce the growth of avionics maintenance costs per flight hour despite growth in avionics capital costs. Conducts projects such as: the establishment of a standard language source document for writing automatic test programs; definition of an economic alternative to costly dedicated automatic test systems provided by manufacturers; development of an industry standard for automated preparation of test software; specification of documentation standards for software-based avionics; coordination of technical training needs for maintenance; and development of voluntary standards for the avionics industry.

IEEE Aerospace and Electronic Systems Society. c/o IEEE Corporate Office, 3 Park Ave., 17th Fl., New York, NY 10016-5997. Phone: 800-678-4333 or (212)419-7900 Fax: (212)752-4929 E-mail: ieeeusa@ieee.org • URL: http://www.ieee.org.

ISA-Instrumentation, Systems, and Automation Society. 67 Alexander Dr., Research Triangle Park, NC 27709. Phone: (919)549-8411 Fax: (919)549-8288 E-mail: info@isa.org • URL: http://www.isa.org.

RTCA. 1828 L St. NW, Ste. 805, Washington, DC 20036. Phone: (202)833-9339 Fax: (202)833-9434 E-mail: info@rtca.org • URL: http://www.rtca.org • Addresses requirements, operational concepts, and industry standards for aviation. Advances the art and science of aviation and aviation electronic systems for the benefit of the public. Products are developed by volunteers from the entire aviation community and include consensus-based recommendations addressing the implementation of new operational capabilities, performance standards, transition and implementation strategies, as well as technical guidance documents and special topic reports. Recommendations are often used as the foundation for government policy and industry business decisions. Most activities function as Federal Advisory Committees.

AWARDS

See: CONTESTS, PRIZES, AND AWARDS

B

BABY CLOTHES

See: CHILDREN'S APPAREL INDUSTRY

BABY SITTING

See also: DAY CARE CENTERS

HANDBOOKS AND MANUALS

Babysitter's Survival Kit: A Guide for Parents and Sitters. Time-Life, Inc. • 2001. $14.95.

ONLINE DATABASES

ERIC. Educational Resources Information Center. • Funded by the U. S. Department of Education, Institute of Education Sciences (formerly Office of Educational Research and Improvement). Provides access to more than one million online records covering education-related journal and report literature, 1966 to date. Updating is monthly. Inquire as to online cost and availability.

BAG INDUSTRY

See: PAPER BAG INDUSTRY

BAKING INDUSTRY

See also: FOOD INDUSTRY; SNACK FOOD INDUSTRY

ABSTRACTS AND INDEXES

Flour Milling and Baking Abstracts. CCFAA Technology Ltd. • Bimonthly. Members, $275.00 per year; non-members, $325.00 per year. Includes print and online editions.

Food Science and Technology Abstracts. International Food Information Service Publishing. • Monthly. $1,780.00 per year. Provides worldwide coverage of the literature of food technology and food production.

Foods Adlibra: Key to the World's Food Literature. General Mills, Inc. Foods Adlibra Publications. • Semimonthly. $240.00 per year. Provides journal citations and abstracts to the literature of food technology and packaging.

CD-ROM DATABASES

Food Science and Technology Abstracts [CD-ROM]. Available from SilverPlatter Information, Inc. • Quarterly. Produced by International Food Information Service (home page is http://www.ifis.org). Provides worldwide coverage on CD-ROM of the literature of food technology and production.

Various types of publications are indexed, with abstracts, including about 1,800 periodicals. Time period is 1969 to date.

DIRECTORIES

Directory of Delicatessen Products. Pacific Rim Publishing Co. • Annual. Included with February issue of *Deli News.* Lists suppliers of cheeses, lunch meats, packaged fresh meats, kosher foods, gourmet-specialty items, and bakery products.

Major Food and Drink Companies of the World. Available from Gale Cengage Learning. • Annual. $880.00. Two volumes. Published by Graham & Whiteside. Contains profiles and trade names for more than 9,800 important food and beverage companies in various countries. In addition to foods, includes both alcoholic and nonalcoholic drink products.

Plunkett's Food Industry Almanac. Plunkett Research Ltd. • Covers: 340 leading companies in the global food industry. Entries include: Name, address, phone, fax, and key executives. Also includes analysis and information on trends, technology, and statistics in the field.

Specialty Food Industry Directory. Phoenix Media Network, Inc. • Annual. Included in subscription to Food Distribution Magazine. Lists manufacturers and suppliers of specialty foods, and services and equipment for the specialty food industry. Featured food products include legumes, sauces, spices, upscale cheese, specialty beverages, snack foods, baked goods, ethnic foods, and specialty meats.

Thomas Food and Beverage Market Place. Grey House Publishing. • 2004. $495.00. Three volumes. Contains more than 40,000 entries covering food companies, beverages, food equipment, warehouse companies, food brokers, wholesalers, importers, and exporters. Formerly *Thomas Food Industry Register.*

World Food Marketing Directory. Euromonitor International. • Covers: Over 2,000 retailers and wholesalers, 1,600 manufacturers, over 2,000 international and European organizations, statistical agencies, trade journals and associations, databases, and trade fairs in the grocery and food industries worldwide. Entries include: Company name, address, phone, telex, names of parent company and subsidiaries, number of employees, financial data, products and brand names handled; retailers and wholesalers include type of outlet, names and titles of key personnel.

FINANCIAL RATIOS

Almanac of Business and Industrial Financial Ratios. Leo Troy. Aspen Publishers, Inc. • 2003. $125.95. Includes CD-Rom. Contains financial ratios derived from federal tax returns. Ratios for

each of about 200 industries are arranged according to company asset size. (Almanac of Business and Industrial Financial Ratios Series).

Annual Statement Studies. The Risk Management Association. • Annual. Median and quartile financial ratios are given for over 400 kinds of manufacturing, wholesale, retail, construction, and consumer finance establishments. Data is sorted by both asset size and sales volume. Includes a clearly written "Definition of Ratios" and an alphabetical industry index.

Annual Statement Studies: Industry Default Probabilities and Cash Flow Measures. The Risk Management Association. • Annual. $145.00. Serves as a companion volume to the original *Annual Statement Studies.* Gives probability of default estimates on a percentage scale for more than 450 industries. Includes changes in position year-by-year for eight financial statement line items and provides percentage measures of cash flow.

Industry Norms and Key Business Ratios. Desk Top Edition. Dun and Bradstreet Corp. • Annual. Five volumes. $475.00 per volume. $1,890.00 per set. Covers over 800 kinds of businesses, arranged by Standard Industrial Classification number. More detailed editions covering longer periods of time are also available.

HANDBOOKS AND MANUALS

Baker's Manual. Joseph Amendola. John Wiley and Sons, Inc. • 2002. $29.95. Fifth edition.

Bakery. Entrepreneur Media, Inc. • Looseleaf. $59.50. A practical guide to starting a retail bakery. Covers profit potential, start-up costs, market size evaluation, owner's time required, site selection, lease negotiation, pricing, accounting, advertising, promotion, etc. (Start-Up Business Guide No. E1158.).

Donut Shop. Entrepreneur Media, Inc. • Looseleaf. $59.50. A practical guide to starting a doughnut shop. Covers profit potential, start-up costs, market size evaluation, owner's time required, site selection, lease negotiation, pricing, accounting, advertising, promotion, etc. (Start-Up Business Guide No. E1126.).

Pizzeria. Entrepreneur Media, Inc. • Looseleaf. $59.50. A practical guide to starting a pizza shop. Covers profit potential, start-up costs, market size evaluation, owner's time required, site selection, lease negotiation, pricing, accounting, advertising, promotion, etc. (Start-Up Business Guide No. E1006.).

Practical Baking. William J. Sultan. John Wiley and

Sons, Inc. • 1990. $55.95. Fifth edition.

ONLINE DATABASES

F & S Index. Gale Cengage Learning. • Contains about four million citations to worldwide business, financial, and industrial or consumer product literature appearing from 1972 to date. Weekly updates. Inquire as to online cost and availability.

Food Science and Technology Abstracts [online]. IFIS North American Desk. • Produced by International Food Information Service. Provides about 500,000 online citations, with abstracts, to the international literature of food science, technology, commodities, engineering, and processing. Approximately 2,000 periodicals are covered. Time period is 1969 to date, with monthly updates. Inquire as to online cost and availability.

FOODS ADLIBRA. General Mills, Inc. • Contains online citations, with abstracts, to the technical and business literature of food processing and packaging. New products and new ingredients are featured. Covers about 250 trade journals and 500 research journals from 1974 to date, with monthly updates. Inquire as to online cost and availability.

PERIODICALS AND NEWSLETTERS

Baking and Snack. Sosland Publishing Co. • Monthly. Free to qualified personnel; others, $30.00 per year. Covers manufacturing systems and ingredients for baked goods and snack foods.

Deli News. Delicatessen Council of Southern California, Inc. Pacific Rim Publishing Co. • Monthly. $25.00 per year. Includes product news and comment related to cheeses, lunch meats, packaged fresh meats, kosher foods, gourmet-specialty items, and bakery products.

Fancy Food and Culinary Products. Talcott Communications Corp. • Monthly. $34.00 per year. Emphasizes new specialty food products and the business management aspects of the specialty food and confection industries. Includes special issues on wine, cheese, candy, "upscale" cookware, and gifts. Formerly (Fancy Foods).

Food Distribution Magazine. Phoenix Media Network, Inc. • Monthly. $49.00 per year. Edited for marketers and buyers of domestic and imported, specialty or gourmet food products, including ethnic foods, seasonings, and bakery items.

Gourmet Retailer. VNU Business Media. • Monthly. Free to qualified personnel; others, $75.00 per year. Covers upscale food and housewares, including confectionery items, bakery operations, and coffee.

Reference Source. Sosland Publishing Co. • Annual. $45.00 per year. A statistical reference manual and specification guide for wholesale baking.

Snack Food and Wholesale Bakery: The Magazine That Defines the Snack Food Industry. Stagnito Publishing Co. • Monthly. Free to qualified personnel; others, $85.06 per year. Provides news and information for producers of pretzels, potato chips, cookies, crackers, nuts, and other snack foods. Includes *Annual Buyers Guide* and *State of Industry Report.*

Specialty Baker's Voice. Specialty Bakery Owners of America. • Monthly. $25.00 per year.

PRICE SOURCES

PPI Detailed Report. Bureau of Labor Statistics, U.S. Department of Labor. Available from U.S. Government Printing Office. • Monthly. $55.00 per year. Formerly *Producer Price Indexes.*

RESEARCH CENTERS AND INSTITUTES

Food and Feed Grains Institute. Kansas State University. 105 Waters Hall, Manhattan, KS 66506-4030. Phone: (785)532-4056 Fax: (785)532-5861 E-mail: ffgi@ksu.edu • URL: http://www.ksu.edu/ffgi.

Quality Bakers of America Cooperative Laboratory.

70 Riverdale Ave., Greenwich, CT 06831. Phone: (203)531-7100 Fax: (203)531-1406 E-mail: info@qba.com • URL: http://www.qba.com/service.

STATISTICS SOURCES

Annual Survey of Manufactures. Available from U. S. Government Printing Office. • Annual. Prices vary. Issued by the U. S. Census Bureau as an interim update to the *Census of Manufactures.* Includes data on number of manufacturing establishments in various industries, employment, labor costs, value of shipments, capital expenditures, inventories, energy costs, and assets. (See also Census Bureau home page, http://www.census.gov/.).

U. S. Industry and Trade Outlook. Available from National Technical Information Service. • Annual. $69.95. Produced by the International Trade Administration, U. S. Department of Commerce, in a "public-private" partnership with DRI/McGraw-Hill and Standard & Poor's. Provides basic data, outlook for the current year, and "Long-Term Prospects" (five-year projections) for a wide variety of products and services. Includes high technology industries. Formerly *U. S. Industrial Outlook.*

United States Census of Manufactures. U.S. Bureau of the Census. • Quinquennial. Results presented in reports, tape, CD-ROM, and Diskette files.

World Food Data and Statistics. Euromonitor International. • 2004. $650.00. Provides five-year data for a wide variety of food products in 52 countries. Includes market size, consumer expenditures, price indicators, and retail distribution data for many kinds of meat, fish, fruits, vegetables, dairy products, baked goods, condiments, canned food, and frozen food.

TRADE/PROFESSIONAL ASSOCIATIONS

Allied Trades of the Baking Industry. 1200 Central Ave., Ste. 360, Whilmette, IL 60091. Phone: (847)920-9885 Fax: (847)920-9886 E-mail: atb1@atbi.org • URL: http://www.atbi.org.

American Bakers Association. 1300 I St. NW, Ste. 700 W, Washington, DC 20005. Phone: (202)789-0300 Fax: (202)898-1164 E-mail: info@americanbakers.org • URL: http://www.americanbakers.org • Manufacturers and wholesale distributors of bread, rolls, and pastry products; suppliers of goods and services to bakers. Conducts seminars and expositions.

American Institute of Baking. 1213 Bakers Way, Manhattan, KS 66505. Phone: 800-633-5137 or (785)537-4750 Fax: (785)537-1493 E-mail: info@aibonline.org • URL: http://www.aibonline.org.

American Society of Baking. 1200 Central Ave., Suite 360, Wilmette, IL 60091. Phone: (866)920-9885 or (847)920-9885 Fax: (847)920-9886 E-mail: asbe@asbe.org • URL: http://www.asbe.org.

Baking Industry Sanitation Standards Committee. PO Box 3999, 1400 W. Devon Ave., Ste. 422, Manhattan, KS 66505-3999. Phone: (866)342-4772 or (785)537-4750 Fax: (785)565-6060 E-mail: bissc@bissc.org • URL: http://www.bissc.org • Industry association representing 120 bakery equipment manufacturers. Seeks to establish standards of sanitation in bakery food processing equipment. Receives advisory assistance from national and international public health and food sanitation groups. Develops and publishes sanitation standards for the baking industry. Offers an equipment certification program for bakery equipment conforming to standards (annual).

BEMA, The Bakery Industry Suppliers Association. 825 Green Bay Rd., Ste. 120, Wilmette, IL 60091. Phone: (847)920-1230 Fax: (847)920-1253 E-mail: office@bema.org • URL: http://www.bema.org.

Retail Bakers of America. 8201 Greensboro Dr., Ste. 300, 14239 Park Ctr. Dr., McLean, VA 22102. Phone: 800-638-0924 or (703)610-9035 Fax:

(703)610-9005 E-mail: info@rbanet.com • URL: http://www.rbanet.com • Independent and in-store bakeries, food service, specialty bakeries, suppliers of ingredients, tools and equipment; other. Provides information, management, production, merchandising, and small business services.

OTHER SOURCES

American Society of Baking Proceedings. American Society of Bakery Engineers. • Annual. Membership.

Bakery Products. Available from MarketResearch.com. • 2002. $3,850.00. Published by Global Industry Analysts. Provides worldwide market research data, including profiles of major baked food companies.

The Bread Market. Available from MarketResearch.com. • 2000. $1,800.00. Published by Packaged Facts. Provides market data on a wide variety of packaged, frozen, and fresh- baked bread products.

The Market for Sweet Baked Goods. MarketResearch.com. • 2000. $2,750.00. Market research data. Covers both fresh and frozen, bakery products.

BALANCE OF PAYMENTS

See also: FOREIGN TRADE

CD-ROM DATABASES

EconLit. Available from SilverPlatter Information, Inc. • Monthly. Single-user, $1,600.00 per year. Provides CD-ROM citations, with abstracts, to articles from more than 500 economics journals. Time period is 1969 to date. Produced by the American Economic Association.

OECD Statistical Compendium. Organization for Economic Cooperation and Development. • Semiannual. $1,905.00 per year for 1 to 10 users. CD-ROM contains more than 730,000 monthly, quarterly, and annual time series for OECD countries, 1960 to date. Includes fully searchable data on agriculture, food, economic indicators, national accounts, employment, energy, finance, industry, technology, and foreign trade. Results can be displayed in various forms.

World Trade Atlas CD-ROM. Global Trade Information Services, Inc. • Monthly. $4,920.00 per year. ($3,650.00 per year with quarterly updates.) Provides government statistics on trade between the U. S. and each of more than 200 countries. Includes import-export data, trade balances, product information, market share, price data, etc. Time period is the most recent three years.

INTERNET DATABASES

Business 2.0 Web Guide to the Best Business Links. Business 2.0 Media Inc. Phone: (415)293-4800 E-mail: support@business2.com • URL: http://www.business2.com/webguide • Web site presents an extensive, searchable directory of links to "the best, most informative, and authoritative web pages." Twenty main categories cover business, finance, career, company information, people, and technology topics, with thousands of subtopics, all linking to Web sites recommended by experienced business researchers. Fees: Free.

Fedstats. Federal Interagency Council on Statistical Policy. Phone: (202)395-7254 • URL: http://www.fedstats.gov • Web site features an efficient search facility for full-text statistics produced by more than 100 federal agencies, including the Census Bureau, the Bureau of Economic Analysis, and the Bureau of Labor Statistics. Boolean searches can be made within one agency or for all agencies combined. Links are offered to international statistical bureaus, including the UN, IMF, OECD, UNESCO, Eurostat, and 20 individual countries. Fees: Free.

FreeLunch.com. Economy.com, Inc. Phone:

(610)696-8700 Fax: (610)696-1678 • URL: http://www.freelunch.com • Web site provides free access to more than 1.5 million economic and financial data series, covering industry, demographics, labor markets, prices, retail sales, government spending, trade, interest rates, housing starts, the stock market, and many other topics. Data is available for various time periods in either chart or table form. Searching is offered. Fees: Free, but registration required. Economy.com, Inc. also offers fee-based economic analysis at *The Dismal Scientist* site (http://www.dismal.com).

ONLINE DATABASES

Balance of Payments Statistics. International Monetary Fund. • Time series compiled by IMF, mid-1960's to present. Inquire as to online cost and availability.

EconLit. American Economic Association. • Covers the worldwide literature of economics as contained in selected monographs and about 550 journals. Subjects include microeconomics, macroeconomics, economic history, inflation, money, credit, finance, accounting theory, trade, natural resource economics, and regional economics. Time period is 1969 to present, with monthly updates. Inquire as to online cost and availability.

OECD Main Economic Indicators. Organization for Economic Cooperation and Development. • International statistics provided by OECD, 1960 to date. Monthly updates. Inquire as to online cost and availability.

PERIODICALS AND NEWSLETTERS

IMF Survey. International Monetary Fund. • Description: Timely news on topics of general interest in the fields of international finance, country economics, trade, and commodities. Contains information on the IMF's activities, including press releases, major management speeches, and lending activity data rates.

International Monetary Fund Staff Papers. International Monetary Fund, Publication Services. • Quarterly. Individuals, $56.00 per year; students, $28.00 per year. Contains studies by IMF staff members on balance of payments, foreign exchange, fiscal policy, and related topics. Formerly *International Monetary Fund Staff Papers.*

STATISTICS SOURCES

Business Statistics of the United States. Linz Audain and Cornelia J. Strawser. Bernan Associates. • Annual. $147.00. Based on *Business Statistics*, formerly issue by the Bureau of Economic Analysis, U. S. Department of Commerce. Provides basic data for a wide variety of U. S. industries, services, and economic indicators. Most statistics are shown annually for 30 years and monthly for the most recent four years.

International Financial Statistics. International Monetary Fund, Publications Services. • Monthly. Individuals, $495.00 per year; students, $247.00 per year. Includes a wide variety of current data for individual countries in Europe and elsewhere. Includes *Annual* issue.

Monthly Bulletin of Statistics. United Nations Publications. • Monthly. $295.00 per year. Provides current data for about 200 countries on a wide variety of economic, industrial, and demographic subjects. Compiled by United Nations Statistical Office.

Statistical Yearbook. United Nations Publications. • Annual. $125.00. Contains statistics for about 200 countries on a wide variety of economic, industrial, and demographic topics. Compiled by United Nations Statistical Office.

Survey of Current Business. Available from U. S. Government Printing Office. • Monthly. $63.00 per year. Issued by Bureau of Economic Analysis, U. S. Department of Commerce. Presents a wide variety

of business and economic data.

BALANCE OF TRADE

See: BALANCE OF PAYMENTS; FOREIGN TRADE

BALL BEARINGS

See: BEARINGS AND BALL BEARINGS

BALL POINT PENS

See: WRITING INSTRUMENTS

BANANA INDUSTRY

See also: FRUIT INDUSTRY

ALMANACS AND YEARBOOKS

Agricultural and Mineral Commodities Year Book. Available from Taylor & Francis Group. • Annual. $225.00. Published by Europa Publications. Contains descriptive product profiles, price data, export-import data, and production statistics for major commodities of the world. Includes commodity histories, uses, markets, demand trends, and information about trade agreements and key commodity organizations.

CD-ROM DATABASES

Food Science and Technology Abstracts [CD-ROM]. Available from SilverPlatter Information, Inc. • Quarterly. Produced by International Food Information Service (home page is http://www.ifis.org). Provides worldwide coverage on CD-ROM of the literature of food technology and production. Various types of publications are indexed, with abstracts, including about 1,800 periodicals. Time period is 1969 to date.

DIRECTORIES

Major Food and Drink Companies of the World. Available from Gale Cengage Learning. • Annual. $880.00. Two volumes. Published by Graham & Whiteside. Contains profiles and trade names for more than 9,800 important food and beverage companies in various countries. In addition to foods, includes both alcoholic and nonalcoholic drink products.

Thomas Food and Beverage Market Place. Grey House Publishing. • 2004. $495.00. Three volumes. Contains more than 40,000 entries covering food companies, beverages, food equipment, warehouse companies, food brokers, wholesalers, importers, and exporters. Formerly *Thomas Food Industry Register.*

INTERNET DATABASES

USDA. United States Department of Agriculture. Phone: (202)720-2791 E-mail: agsec@usda.gov • URL: http://www.usda.gov • The USDA home page has six sections: News and Information; What's New; About USDA; Agencies; Opportunities; Search and Help. Keyword searching is offered from the USDA home page and from various individual agency home pages. Agencies are the Economic Research Service, Agricultural Marketing Service, National Agricultural Statistics Service, National Agricultural Library, and about 12 others. Updating varies. Fees: Free.

ONLINE DATABASES

Agricola. U.S. National Agricultural Library. • Covers worldwide agricultural literature. Over 3.3 million citations, 1970 to present, with monthly updates. Inquire as to online cost and availability.

Food Science and Technology Abstracts [online].

IFIS North American Desk. • Produced by International Food Information Service. Provides about 500,000 online citations, with abstracts, to the international literature of food science, technology, commodities, engineering, and processing. Approximately 2,000 periodicals are covered. Time period is 1969 to date, with monthly updates. Inquire as to online cost and availability.

PERIODICALS AND NEWSLETTERS

BGF Bulletin. Banana Growers Federation Co-Operative Ltd. • Monthly. $35.00 per year. Formerly *Banana Bulletin.*

PRICE SOURCES

PPI Detailed Report. Bureau of Labor Statistics, U.S. Department of Labor. Available from U.S. Government Printing Office. • Monthly. $55.00 per year. Formerly *Producer Price Indexes.*

RESEARCH CENTERS AND INSTITUTES

College of Tropical Agriculture and Human Resources. University of Hawaii at Manoa, 2515 Campus Rd., Miller Hall 110, Honolulu, HI 96822. Phone: (808)956-8105 Fax: (808)956-8105 E-mail: fcs@ctahr.hawaii.edu • URL: http://www.ctahr.hawaii.edu/ • Concerned with the production and marketing of tropical food and ornamental plant products, including pineapples, bananas, coffee, and macadamia nuts.

Kauai Agricultural Station. University of Hawaii at Manoa. 7370 Kuamoo Rd., Kapaa, HI 96746. Phone: (808)822-4984 Fax: (808)822-2190.

STATISTICS SOURCES

Agricultural Statistics. Available from U. S. Government Printing Office. • Annual. $38.00. Produced by the National Agricultural Statistics Service, U. S. Department of Agriculture. Provides a wide variety of statistical data relating to agricultural production, supplies, consumption, prices/price-supports, foreign trade, costs, and returns, as well as farm labor, loans, income, and population. In many cases, historical data is shown annually for 10 years. In addition to farm data, includes detailed fishery statistics.

FAO Production Yearbook. Available from Bernan Associates. • Annual. $45.00. Published by the Food and Agriculture Organization (http://www.fao.org). Contains worldwide data on agriculture, land use, farm crops, livestock, and agricultural prices.

FAO Trade Yearbook. Available from Bernan Associates. • Annual. $45.00. Published by the Food and Agriculture Organization (http://www.fao.org). Provides extensive worldwide data on exports and imports of agricultural commodities, fertilizers, tractors, and pesticides. Includes more than 130 tables of detailed statistics.

World Food Data and Statistics. Euromonitor International. • 2004. $650.00. Provides five-year data for a wide variety of food products in 52 countries. Includes market size, consumer expenditures, price indicators, and retail distribution data for many kinds of meat, fish, fruits, vegetables, dairy products, baked goods, condiments, canned food, and frozen food.

BANK ACCOUNTING

HANDBOOKS AND MANUALS

Handbook of Bank Accounting: Understanding and Applying Standards and Regulations. Charles J. Woelfel. McGraw-Hill. • 1992. $65.00. "Written to meet the practical needs of senior- and middle-level bank accountants." Covers managerial accounting, the theory and practice of bank accounting, financial statement analysis, bank examinations, audits, and related topics.

INTERNET DATABASES

Rutgers Accounting Web (RAW). Rutgers University Accounting Research Center. Phone: (973)353-5172

Fax: (973)353-1283 • URL: http://www.rutgers.edu/ accounting • RAW Web site provides extensive links to sources of national and international accounting information, such as the Big Six accounting firms, the Financial Accounting Standards Board (FASB), SEC filings (EDGAR), journals, publishers, software, the International Accounting Network, and "Internet's largest list of accounting firms in USA." Searching is offered. Fees: Free.

PERIODICALS AND NEWSLETTERS

Bank Accounting and Finance. Aspen Publishers, Inc. • Quarterly. $345.00 per year. Emphasis is on the practical aspects of bank accounting and bank financial management.

Bank Auditing and Accounting Report. RIA Group. • Monthly. $199.00 per year. Newsletter covering bank regulations, accounting techniques, and audit controls.

Journal of Bank Cost and Management Accounting. Association for Management Information in Financial Services. • Three times a year. $100.00 per year.

TRADE/PROFESSIONAL ASSOCIATIONS

Association for Management Information in Financial Services. 3895 Fairfax Court, Atlanta, GA 30339. Phone: (770)444-3557 Fax: (770)444-9084 E-mail: ami@amifs.org • URL: http://www.amifs. org • Members are financial institution employees interested in management accounting and cost analysis.

Bank Administration Institute. 1 N Franklin St., Ste. 1000, Chicago, IL 60606-3421. Phone: 888-284-4078 or (312)683-2464 Fax: (312)683-2373 E-mail: info@bai.org • URL: http://www.bai.org • Works to improve the competitive position of banking companies through strategic research and educational offerings.

BANK AUTOMATION

ABSTRACTS AND INDEXES

Business Periodicals Index. H. W. Wilson Co. • 11 times a year. Quarterly and annual cumulations. Price varies.

DIRECTORIES

Bank Systems and Technology-Directory and Buyer's Guide. CMP Media LLC. • Annual. $25.00. List of more than 1,800 manufacturers, distributors, and other suppliers of equipment and materials to the banking industry.

HANDBOOKS AND MANUALS

Bank Systems Management: The Project Management Guide to Planning and Implementing Systems. Kent S. Belasco. McGraw-Hill. • 1993. $62.50.

Bank Technology Review: A Bank Manager's Guide to New Technology Products, Systems, and Applications. Tom Groenfeldt. McGraw-Hill. • 1995. $37.50.

ONLINE DATABASES

Management Contents. Gale Cengage Learning. • Covers a wide range of management, financial, marketing, personnel, and administrative topics. About 150 leading business journals are indexed and abstracted from 1974 to date, with monthly updating. Inquire as to online cost and availability.

Trade & Industry Database. Gale Cengage Learning. • Provides indexing of business periodicals, January 1981 to date. Daily updates. (Full text articles from some periodicals are available online, 1983 to date. Inquire as to online cost and availability).

PERIODICALS AND NEWSLETTERS

Bank Automation News. PBI Media LCC. • Biweekly. $651.65 per year. Newsletter.

Bank Systems and Technology: For Senior-Level

Executives in Operations and Technology Management. CMP Media LLC. • 13 times a year. $65.00 per year. Focuses on strategic planning for banking executives. Formerly *Bank Systems and Equipment.*

Card Technology. Thomson Media. • Monthly. $79.00 per year. Covers advanced technology for credit, debit, and other cards. Topics include smart cards, optical recognition, and card design.

Corporate EFT Report (Electronic Funds Tranfer). Phillips International, Inc. • Biweekly. $695.00 per year. Newsletter on subject of electronic funds transfer.

Electronic Banking Law and Commerce Report. Glasser Legalworks. • 10 times a year. $300.00 per year. Newsletter. Provides coverage of the legal aspects of online banking services, bank cards, and "smart phones.".

End Point Express: Exclusive Report for Bank Operations Professionals. United Communications Group. • Biweekly. $247.00 per year. Newsletter. Covers bank payment systems, including checks, electronic funds transfer (EFT), point-of-sale (POS), and automated teller machine (ATM) operations. Formerly *Bank Office Bulletin.*

Item Processing Report. Access Intelligence L.L.C. • Description: Monitors developments in the processing of remittances and checks, including image processing, optical character recognition, check truncation, hardware, and software. **Remarks:** Absorbed The Powell Report, 1992.

Loan Market Week: The Newsweekly of the Loan Syndication, Trading and Investment Markets. Institutional Investor, Inc., Journals Group. • Weekly. $2,370.00 per year. Newsletter. Includes print and online editions. Covers retail banking, commercial lending, foreign loans, bank technology, government regulations, and other topics related to banking. Formerly *Bank Letter.*

U.S. Banker. IMG Media. • Monthly. $79.00 per year. Covers technology innovation for the banking industry, including online banking. Incorporates *Future Banker.*

WebFinance. Thomson Media. • Semimonthly. $995.00 per year. Newsletter (also available online at www.webfinance.net). Covers the Internet-based provision of online financial services by banks, online brokers, mutual funds, and insurance companies. Provides news stories, analysis, and descriptions of useful resources.

STATISTICS SOURCES

Statistical Information on the Financial Services Industry. American Bankers Association. • Annual. Members, $150.00; non-members, $275.00. Presents a wide variety of data relating to banking and financial services, including consumer economics, personal finance, credit, government loans, capital markets, and international banking.

TRADE/PROFESSIONAL ASSOCIATIONS

Association for Financial Technology. Blendonview Office Park, 5008-2 Pine Creek Dr., Westerville, OH 43081-4899. Phone: (614)895-1208 Fax: (614)895-3466 E-mail: aft@fitech.org • URL: http://www. fitech.org • Concerned with bank computer technology.

Bank Administration Institute; Operations and Technology Commission. One N. Franklin St., Suite 1000, Chicago, IL 60606. Phone: 800-224-9889 or (312)653-2464 Fax: (312)683-2373 E-mail: info@ bai.org • URL: http://www.bai.org.

Electronic Funds Transfer Association. 11350 Random Hills Rd., Ste. 800, Fairfax, VA 22030. Phone: (703)934-6052 Fax: (703)934-6058 E-mail: melanierenner@efta.org • URL: http://www.efta. org • Financial institutions, credit card companies, ATM owners, networks and processors, hardware and software manufacturers and e-commerce

companies dedicated to the advancement of electronic payment systems and commerce.

NACHA: The Electronic Payments Association. 13450 Sunrise Valley Dr., Ste. 100, Herndon, VA 20171. Phone: 800-487-9180 or (703)561-1100 Fax: (703)787-0996 E-mail: info@nacha.org • URL: http://www.nacha.org • Automated Clearing House (ACH) association. Provides an interregional exchange for electronic debits and credits among ACHs and to establish and administer nationwide standards and operating rules for ACHs. Conducts national seminars and conferences on ACH operations and products; sponsors annual Payments and Electronic Commerce Institute; sponsors Accredited ACH Professional (AAP) program. Sponsors national marketing campaign; compiles statistics.

National Independent Bank Equipment and Systems Association. 5300 Sequoia NW, Ste. 205, Albuquerque, NM 87120. Phone: 800-843-6082 or (505)839-7958 Fax: (505)839-0017 E-mail: nibesa@nibesa.com • URL: http://www.nibesa.com • Formerly National Independent Bank Equipment Suppliers Association.

OTHER SOURCES

Online Banking. MarketResearch.com. • 2000. $3,000.00. Market research report. Includes demographics relating to the users and nonusers of online banking services. Provides market forecasts.

The U. S. Market for Plastic Payment Cards. Available from MarketResearch.com. • 1998. $1,375.00. Market research report published by Packaged Facts. Covers credit cards, charge cards, debit cards, and smart cards. Provides profiles of Visa, Mastercard, American Express, Discover, Diners Club, and others.

BANK CREDIT

See: BANK LOANS

BANK DEPOSITS

See also: BANKS AND BANKING; ELECTRONIC FUNDS TRANSFER SYSTEMS (EFTS)

GENERAL WORKS

Consumer Reports Money Book: How to Get It, Save It, and Spend It Wisely. Janet Bamford and others. Consumers Union of the United States, Inc. • 2000. $19.95. Third edition. Covers budgeting, retirement planning, bank accounts, insurance, and other personal finance topics.

ABSTRACTS AND INDEXES

Accounting and Tax Index. UMI. • Quarterly. Price on application. Annual cumulation. Indexes accounting, auditing, and taxation literature appearing in journals, books, pamphlets, conference proceedings, and newsletters.

HANDBOOKS AND MANUALS

Deposit Account Operations and Services. The Institute of Financial Education. • 1997. $49.95.

Deposit Operations. David H. Friedman. American Bankers Association. • 1992. Price on application.

Insurance of Accounts Handbook: A Practical Guide to the FDIC Regulations. The Institute of Financial Education. • 1993. $39.95. Second edition. A guide for bankers to the regulations of the Federal Deposit Insurance Corporation.

ONLINE DATABASES

EconLit. American Economic Association. • Covers the worldwide literature of economics as contained in selected monographs and about 550 journals. Subjects include microeconomics, macroeconomics, economic history, inflation, money, credit, finance, accounting theory, trade, natural resource economics, and regional economics. Time period is 1969 to present, with monthly updates. Inquire as to online cost and availability.

PERIODICALS AND NEWSLETTERS

Jumbo Rate News. BauerFinancial, Inc. • Description: Reports on high-yielding, insured Jumbo CD (Certificate of Deposit) rates nationwide. Analyzes each institution by current credit-worthiness, and lists current assets and capital ratios. Provides phone numbers, contacts, methods of computation, and information on how interest is paid. Also contains financial news, insights, and commentary of interest to Jumbo CD investors. Recurring features include editorials and news of interest.

STATISTICS SOURCES

Aggregate Reserves of Depository Institutions and the Monetary Base. U.S. Federal Reserve System. • Weekly. $20.00 per year.

Assets and Liabilities of Commercial Banks in the United States. U. S. Federal Reserve System. • Weekly. $30.00 per year. (Federal Reserve Statistical Release, H.8.).

Debits and Deposit Turnover at Commercial Banks. Board of Governors. • Monthly. $5.00 per year.

Economic Indicators. Council of Economic Advisors, Executive Office of the President. Available from U.S. Government Printing Office. • Monthly. $55.00 per year.

Federal Reserve Bulletin. U.S. Federal Reserve System. • Monthly. $25.00 per year. Provides statistics on banking and the economy, including interest rates, money supply, and the Federal Reserve Board indexes of industrial production.

Statistical Information on the Financial Services Industry. American Bankers Association. • Annual. Members, $150.00; non-members, $275.00. Presents a wide variety of data relating to banking and financial services, including consumer economics, personal finance, credit, government loans, capital markets, and international banking.

BANK FAILURES

GENERAL WORKS

Does Financial Deregulation Work? A Critique of Free Market Approaches. Bruce Coggins. Edward Elgar Publishing, Inc. • 1998. $95.00. Provides a critique of bank deregulation in the United States. Includes suggestions for more effective financial regulation. (New Directions in Modern Economics Series).

Financial Institutions and Markets. Meir J. Kohn. Oxford University Press, Inc. • 2003. $115.00. Second edition.

Preventing Bank Crises: Lessons from Recent Global Bank Failures. Gerand Caprio. The World Bank Group. • 1998. $40.00. Examines worldwide problems with bank regulation, bank infrastructure, public accountability, and political influence.(EDI Development Studies).

Transnational Bank Behavior and the International Debt Crisis. United Nations Publications. • 1990.

ABSTRACTS AND INDEXES

Business Periodicals Index. H. W. Wilson Co. • 11 times a year. Quarterly and annual cumulations. Price varies.

BIBLIOGRAPHIES

The Savings and Loan Crisis: An Annotated Bibliography. Pat L. Talley, compiler. Greenwood Publishing Group, Inc. • 1993. $65.00. Includes 360 scholarly and popular titles (books and research papers). (Bibliographies and Indexes in Economic History, No. 14).

CD-ROM DATABASES

ABI/INFORM. PROQUEST. • Monthly. Provides CD-ROM indexing and abstracting of worldwide business literature. Archival discs are available from 1971. Formerly *ABI/INFORM OnDisc*.

PAIS on CD-ROM. Public Affairs Information Service, Inc. • Quarterly. $1,995.00 per year. Provides a CD-ROM version of the online service, *PAIS International*. Contains over 500,000 citations to the literature of contemporary social, political, and economic issues.

WILSONDISC: Business Periodicals Index. H. W. Wilson Co. • Monthly. Provides CD-ROM indexing of business periodicals from 1982 to date. Price includes online service.

HANDBOOKS AND MANUALS

Analyzing and Managing Banking Risk: A Framework for Assessing Corporate Governacial Risk Management. Hennie van Greuning and Sonja Brajovic Bratanovic. The World Bank Group. • 2003. $100.00. Provides a guide to the analysis of banking risk for bank executives, bank supervisors, and risk analysts. Includes a CD-ROM with spreadsheet-based tables to assist in the interpretation and analysis of a bank's financial risk.

ONLINE DATABASES

American Banker Full Text. American Banker-Bond Buyer, Database Services. • Provides complete text online of the daily *American Banker*. Inquire as to online cost and availability.

Banking Information Source. PROQUEST. • Provides indexing and abstracting of periodical and other literature from 1982 to date, with weekly updates. Covers the financial services industry: banks, savings institutions, investment houses, credit unions, insurance companies, and real estate organizations. Emphasis is on marketing and management. Inquire as to online cost and availability. (Formerly *FINIS: Financial Industry Information Service*.).

F & S Index. Gale Cengage Learning. • Contains about four million citations to worldwide business, financial, and industrial or consumer product literature appearing from 1972 to date. Weekly updates. Inquire as to online cost and availability.

PAIS International. Public Affairs Information Service, Inc. • Corresponds to the former printed publications, *PAIS Bulletin* (1976-90) and *PAIS Foreign Language Index* (1972-90), and to the current *PAIS International in Print* (1991 to date). Covers economic, political, and sociological material appearing in periodicals, books, government documents, and other publications. Updating is monthly. Inquire as to online cost and availability.

Trade & Industry Database. Gale Cengage Learning. • Provides indexing of business periodicals, January 1981 to date. Daily updates. (Full text articles from some periodicals are available online, 1983 to date. Inquire as to online cost and availability).

Wilson Business Abstracts Online. H. W. Wilson Co. • Indexes and abstracts 600 major business periodicals, plus the *Wall Street Journal* and the business section of the *New York Times*. Indexing is from 1982, abstracting from 1990, with the two newspapers included from 1993. Updated weekly. Inquire as to online cost and availability. (*Business Periodicals Index* without abstracts is also available online.).

PERIODICALS AND NEWSLETTERS

American Banker: The Financial Services Daily. Thomson Media. • Daily. $895.00 per year. Provides news of banking, investment products, mortgages, credit unions, finance, bank technology, and legal developments.

Bank Mergers & Acquisitions: The Authoritative Newsletter Providing In-Depth Analysis of the Restructuring of American Banking. SNL Financial LLC. • Monthly. $795.00 per year. Newsletter. Includes information on transactions assisted by the Federal Deposit Insurance Corporation (FDIC) for commercial banks or by the Resolution Trust Corporation (RTC) for savings and loan institutions.

Troubled and Problematic Bank and Thrift Report. BauerFinancial, Inc. • Quarterly. $225.00 per year. Newsletter provides information on seriously undercapitalized ("Troubled") banks and savings institutions, as defined by a federal Prompt Corrective Action Rule. "Problematic" banks and thrifts are those meeting regulatory capital levels, but showing negative trends.

U. S. Banker. Thomson Media. • Monthly. $65.00 per year. Edited for bank executives and managers. Covers a wide variety of banking and financial topics.

RESEARCH CENTERS AND INSTITUTES

Banking Research Center. Northwestern University, 401 Anderson Hall, 2001 Sheridan Rd., Evanston, IL 60208. Phone: (847)491-3562 Fax: (847)491-5719 E-mail: k-hagerty@northwestern.edu • Does research in the management and public regulation of financial institutions. A unit of the J. L. Kellogg Graduate School of Management.

Morin Center for Banking and Financial Law. Boston University, School of Law, 765 Commonwealth Ave., Boston, MA 02215. Phone: (617)353-3023 Fax: (617)353-2444 E-mail: banklaw@bu.edu • URL: http://www.web.bu.edu/law • Research fields include banking law, regulation of depository institutions, and deposit insurance.

Salomon Center. New York University. Stern School of Business, 44 W. Fourth St., Ste. 9-60, New York, NY 10012-1126. Phone: (212)998-0707 Fax: (212)995-4220 E-mail: iwalter@stern.nyu.edu • URL: http://www.stern.nyu.edu/salmon/.

TRADE/PROFESSIONAL ASSOCIATIONS

American Council of State Savings Supervisors. P.O. Box 1904, Leesburg, VA 20177. Phone: (703)669-5440 Fax: (703)699-5441 E-mail: amfalz@csss.org • URL: http://www.acsss.org • Members are state savings and loan supervisors. Includes a Joint Committee on Examinations and Education.

Conference of State Bank Supervisors. 1155 Connecticut Ave., NW, 5th Fl., Washington, DC 20036. Phone: 800-886-2727 or (202)728-5702 Fax: (202)296-1928 E-mail: nmilner@csbs.org • URL: http://www.csbs.org • Members are state officials responsible for supervision of state-chartered banking institutions.

OTHER SOURCES

Bank and Lender Litigation Reporter: The Nationwide Litigation Report of Failed National and State Banks and Savings and Loan Associations, including FDIC and FSLIC Complaints and Related Actions Among Shareholders, Officers, Directors, Ins. Andrews Publications. • Semimonthly. $875.00 per year. Newsletter. Provides summaries of significant litigation and regulatory agency complaints. Formerly *Lender Liability Litigation Reporter*.

BANK FINANCE

See: BANK LOANS

BANK LAW

See: BANKING LAW AND REGULATION

BANK LOANS

See also: COMMERCIAL LENDING; CONSUMER CREDIT; CREDIT

GENERAL WORKS

Spilled Milk: A Special Collection from The Journal of Commercial Bank Lending on Loans that Went

---

Sour. The Risk Management Association. • 1987. $16.75. Two volumes.

ABSTRACTS AND INDEXES

Business Periodicals Index. H. W. Wilson Co. • 11 times a year. Quarterly and annual cumulations. Price varies.

CD-ROM DATABASES

OECD Statistical Compendium. Organization for Economic Cooperation and Development. • Semiannual. $1,905.00 per year for 1 to 10 users. CD-ROM contains more than 730,000 monthly, quarterly, and annual time series for OECD countries, 1960 to date. Includes fully searchable data on agriculture, food, economic indicators, national accounts, employment, energy, finance, industry, technology, and foreign trade. Results can be displayed in various forms.

DIRECTORIES

Business Capital Sources. Tyler G. Hicks. IWS Inc. • Covers: about 1,500 banks, insurance and mortgage companies, commercial finance, leasing, and venture capital firms that lend money for business investment. Entries include: Company or institution name, address, phone.

ENCYCLOPEDIAS AND DICTIONARIES

Credit and Lending Dictionary. Shelley W. Geehr and Daphne Smith, editors. The Risk Management Association. • 1994. $25.00.

HANDBOOKS AND MANUALS

Financing Your Small Business. Robert Walter. Barron's Educational Series, Inc. • 2004. $18.95. Explains various sources of capital for small businesses, including bank loans, venture capital, and initial public offerings of stock.

Problem Loan Strategies; A Decision Process for Commercial Bankers. John E. McKinley and others. The Risk Management Association. • 1998. $53.00. Revised edition.

SBA Loan Guide. Entrepreneur Meida, Inc. • Looseleaf. $59.50. A practical guide to obtaining loans through the Small Business Administration. (Start-Up Business Guide No. E1315.).

Where to Go When the Bank Says No: Alternatives to Financing Your Business. David R. Evanson. Bloomberg. • 1998. $24.95. Emphasis is on obtaining business financing in the $250,000 to $15,000,000 range. Business plans are discussed. (Bloomberg Small Business Series).

INTERNET DATABASES

BanxQuote Banking, Mortgage, and Finance Center. BanxQuote, Inc. Phone: (914)722-1600 Fax: (914)722-6630 E-mail: info@banx.com • URL: http://www.banx.com • Web site quotes interest rates paid by banks around the country on various savings products, as well as rates paid by consumers for automobile loans, mortgages, credit cards, home equity loans, and personal loans. Also provided: stock quotes, indexes, stock options, futures trading data, economic indicators, and links to many other financial sites. Daily updates. Fees: Free.

Business 2.0 Web Guide to the Best Business Links. Business 2.0 Media Inc. Phone: (415)293-4800 E-mail: support@business2.com • URL: http://www.business2.com/webguide • Web site presents an extensive, searchable directory of links to "best, most informative, and authoritative web pages." Twenty main categories cover business, finance, career, company information, people, and technology topics, with thousands of subtopics, all linking to Web sites recommended by experienced business researchers. Fees: Free.

Fedstats. Federal Interagency Council on Statistical Policy. Phone: (202)395-7254 • URL: http://www.fedstats.gov • Web site features an efficient search facility for full-text statistics produced by more than 100 federal agencies, including the Census Bureau, the Bureau of Economic Analysis, and the Bureau of Labor Statistics. Boolean searches can be made within one agency or for all agencies combined. Links are offered to international statistical bureaus, including the UN, IMF, OECD, UNESCO, Eurostat, and 20 individual countries. Fees: Free.

FreeLunch.com. Economy.com, Inc. Phone: (610)696-8700 Fax: (610)696-1678 • URL: http://www.freelunch.com • Web site provides free access to more than 1.5 million economic and financial data series, covering industry, demographics, labor markets, prices, retail sales, government spending, trade, interest rates, housing starts, the stock market, and many other topics. Data is available for various time periods in either chart or table form. Searching is offered. Fees: Free, but registration required. Economy.com, Inc. also offers fee-based economic analysis at *The Dismal Scientist* site (http://www.dismal.com).

ONLINE DATABASES

Management Contents. Gale Cengage Learning. • Covers a wide range of management, financial, marketing, personnel, and administrative topics. About 150 leading business journals are indexed and abstracted from 1974 to date, with monthly updating. Inquire as to online cost and availability.

Trade & Industry Database. Gale Cengage Learning. • Provides indexing of business periodicals, January 1981 to date. Daily updates. (Full text articles from some periodicals are available online, 1983 to date. Inquire as to online cost and availability).

PERIODICALS AND NEWSLETTERS

Bank Credit Analyst. BCA Publications Ltd. • Monthly. $695.00 per year. "The independent monthly forecast and analysis of trends in business conditions and major investment markets based on a continuous appraisal of money and credit flows." Includes many charts and graphs relating to money, credit, and securities in the U. S.

Bank Loan Report. IDD Enterprises L.P. • Description: Discusses banking loans and transactions made by large corporations. Recurring features include a column titled Term Sheets.

Commercial Lending Litigation News. LRP Publications. • Description: Covers liability claims and their policies and procedures, case strategies, court decisions, and jury verdicts.

Consumer Credit and Truth-in-Lending Compliance Report. RIA. • Monthly. $183.75 per year. Newsletter. Focuses on the latest regulatory rulings and findings involving consumer lending and credit activity. Incorporates (Consumer Lending Report).

Consumer Finance Newsletter. Financial Publishing Co. • Description: Provides information on effective and pending credit insurance and installment loan regulations on the state and federal levels. Supplies news of potential state changes in regulations.

Grant's Interest Rate Observer. James Grant, editor. Grant's Financial Publishing Inc. • Biweekly. $725.00 per year. Newsletter containing detailed analysis of money-related topics, including interest rate trends, global credit markets, fixed-income investments, bank loan policies, and international money markets.

International Bank Credit Analyst. BCA Publications Ltd. • Monthly. $795.00 per year. "A monthly forecast and analysis of currency movements, interest rates, and stock market developments in the principal countries, based on a continuous appraisal of money and credit trends worldwide." Includes many charts and graphs providing international coverage of money, credit, and securities.

Lender Liability Law Report. RIA. • Description: Discusses the impact of relevant cases and legislation on lenders and spotlights legal landmines which lenders may encounter. Recurring features include summaries of recent cases and avoidance techniques.

The RMA Journal. The Risk Management Association. • 10 times a year. Members, $40.00 per year; non-members, $95.00 per year. *The Journal of Lending and Credit Risk Management.*

RESEARCH CENTERS AND INSTITUTES

Credit Research Center. Georgetown University. 3240 Prospect St. NW, Ste. 300, Washington, DC 20007. Phone: (202)625-0103 Fax: (202)625-0104 E-mail: statenm@msb.edu • URL: http://www.msb.edu/prog/crc • Economic trends and public policy issues in consumer and mortgage credit, with emphasis on regulatory policy (including rate ceilings, restrictions on creditor remedies, and consumer bankruptcies), consumer behavior, medical debt, and managerial decision systems.

STATISTICS SOURCES

Business Statistics of the United States. Linz Audain and Cornelia J. Strawser. Bernan Associates. • Annual. $147.00. Based on *Business Statistics,* formerly issue by the Bureau of Economic Analysis, U. S. Department of Commerce. Provides basic data for a wide variety of U. S. industries, services, and economic indicators. Most statistics are shown annually for 30 years and monthly for the most recent four years.

Statistical Information on the Financial Services Industry. American Bankers Association. • Annual. Members, $150.00; non-members, $275.00. Presents a wide variety of data relating to banking and financial services, including consumer economics, personal finance, credit, government loans, capital markets, and international banking.

Survey of Current Business. Available from U. S. Government Printing Office. • Monthly. $63.00 per year. Issued by Bureau of Economic Analysis, U. S. Department of Commerce. Presents a wide variety of business and economic data.

TRADE/PROFESSIONAL ASSOCIATIONS

Credit Research Foundation. 8840 Columbia 100 Pkwy., 100 Pky., Columbia, MD 21045. Phone: (410)740-5499 Fax: (410)740-4620 E-mail: crf_info@crfonline.org • URL: http://www.crfonline.org • Represents credit, financial, and working capital executives of manufacturing and banking concerns. Aims to create a better understanding of the impact of credit on the economy. Plans, supervises, and administers research and educational programs. Conducts surveys on economic conditions, trends, policies, practices, theory, systems, and methodology. Sponsors formal educational programs in credit and financial management. Maintains library on credit, collections, and management.

Risk Management Association. 1801 Market St., Ste. 300, 1650 Market St., Ste. 2300, Philadelphia, PA 19103-1628. Phone: 800-677-7621 or (215)446-4000 Fax: (215)446-4101 E-mail: member@rmahq.org • URL: http://www.rmahq.org/RMA • Commercial and savings banks, and savings and loan, and other financial services companies. Conducts research and professional development activities in areas of loan administration, asset management, and commercial lending and credit to increase professionalism.

OTHER SOURCES

Bank and Lender Litigation Reporter: The Nationwide Litigation Report of Failed National and State Banks and Savings and Loan Associations, including FDIC and FSLIC Complaints and Related Actions Among Shareholders, Officers, Directors, Ins. Andrews Publications. • Semimonthly. $875.00 per year. Newsletter. Provides summaries of significant litigation and regulatory agency complaints. Formerly *Lender Li-*

ability Litigation Reporter.

Consumer and Commercial Credit: Installment Sales. Prentice Hall PTR. • Three looseleaf volumes. Periodic supplementation. Price on application. Covers secured transactions under the Uniform Commercial Code and the Uniform Consumer Credit Code. Includes retail installment sales, home improvement loans, higher education loans, and other kinds of installment loans.

Country Finance. Economist Intelligence Unit. • Annual $425.00 per year. Discusses banking and financial conditions in each of 47 countries. Includes foreign exchange regulations, the currency outlook, sources of capital, financing techniques, and tax considerations.

BANK MANAGEMENT

See also: BANKS AND BANKING

GENERAL WORKS

Bank Management. Timothy W. Koch and Steven S. MacDonald. Dryden Press. • 2002. Fifth edition. Price on application.

Reengineering the Bank: A Blueprint for Survival and Success. Paul H. Allen. McGraw-Hill. • 1994. $40.00.

ABSTRACTS AND INDEXES

Business Periodicals Index. H. W. Wilson Co. • 11 times a year. Quarterly and annual cumulations. Price varies.

BIBLIOGRAPHIES

Financial Institutions. Available from U. S. Government Printing Office. • Annual. Free. Lists government publications. Formerly *Banks and Banking.* GPO Subject Bibliography No. 128.

BIOGRAPHICAL SOURCES

Who's Who in Finance and Industry. Marquis Who's Who. • Biennial. $259.95. Provides over 21,000 concise biographies of business leaders in all fields.

Who's Who in International Banking. Bowker-Saur. • Irregular. $400.00. Contains biographical sketches of about 4,000 bankers. Worldwide coverage.

HANDBOOKS AND MANUALS

Bank CEO's Operating and Management Desk Reference. Thomson Media. • $395.00. Two looseleaf volumes. Periodic updates available. Provides up-to-date information and advice on all areas of bank management. (A Sheshunoff publication.)

Bank Investments and Funds Management. Gerald O. Hatler. American Bankers Association. • 1991. $49.00. Second edition. Focuses on portfolio management, risk analysis, and investment strategy.

Bank Systems Management: The Project Management Guide to Planning and Implementing Systems. Kent S. Belasco. McGraw-Hill. • 1993. $62.50.

Banking Crimes: Fraud, Money Laundering and Embezzlement. John K. Villa. West Group. • Annual. $280.00. Looseleaf service. Covers fraud and embezzlement.

Commercial Bank Management: Producing and Selling Financial Services. Peter S. Rose. McGraw-Hill. • 2001. $110.94. Fifth edition. (Finance Series).

Handbook of Bank Accounting: Understanding and Applying Standards and Regulations. Charles J. Woelfel. McGraw-Hill. • 1992. $65.00. "Written to meet the practical needs of senior- and middle-level bank accountants." Covers managerial accounting, the theory and practice of bank accounting, financial statement analysis, bank examinations, audits, and related topics.

Trust Department Administration and Operations. LexisNexis Matthew Bender. • Biennial. $360.00

per year. Two looseleaf volumes. A procedural manual, training guide and idea source.

ONLINE DATABASES

American Banker Full Text. American Banker-Bond Buyer, Database Services. • Provides complete text online of the daily *American Banker.* Inquire as to online cost and availability.

Banking Information Source. PROQUEST. • Provides indexing and abstracting of periodical and other literature from 1982 to date, with weekly updates. Covers the financial services industry: banks, savings institutions, investment houses, credit unions, insurance companies, and real estate organizations. Emphasis is on marketing and management. Inquire as to online cost and availability. (Formerly *FINIS: Financial Industry Information Service.*).

Management Contents. Gale Cengage Learning. • Covers a wide range of management, financial, marketing, personnel, and administrative topics. About 150 leading business journals are indexed and abstracted from 1974 to date, with monthly updating. Inquire as to online cost and availability.

Trade & Industry Database. Gale Cengage Learning. • Provides indexing of business periodicals, January 1981 to date. Daily updates. (Full text articles from some periodicals are available online, 1983 to date. Inquire as to online cost and availability).

PERIODICALS AND NEWSLETTERS

ABA Banking Journal. American Bankers Association, Member Communications. Simmons-Boardman Books. • Monthly. Free to qualified personnel; others, $25.00 per year.

American Banker: The Financial Services Daily. Thomson Media. • Daily. $895.00 per year. Provides news of banking, investment products, mortgages, credit unions, finance, bank technology, and legal developments.

Bank Systems and Technology: For Senior-Level Executives in Operations and Technology Management. CMP Media LLC. • 13 times a year. $65.00 per year. Focuses on strategic planning for banking executives. Formerly *Bank Systems and Equipment.*

Banking Strategies. Bank Administration Institute. • Monthly. Free to qualified personnel; others, $64.50 per year. For senior bankers and financial services executives.

The Community Bank President. Siefer Consultants, Inc. • Monthly. $329.00 per year.

Fee Income Growth Strategies. Siefer Consultants Inc. • Description: Discusses the role of fees and service charges for money orders, cashier's checks, nonsufficient funds, loans, automatic teller machine cards, and other ancillary services in the profitability of financial institutions.

Operations Alert. America's Community Bankers. • Description: Reviews recent regulatory and product developments that affect community bank operations.

U. S. Banker. Thomson Media. • Monthly. $65.00 per year. Edited for bank executives and managers. Covers a wide variety of banking and financial topics.

U.S. Banker. IMG Media. • Monthly. $79.00 per year. Covers technology innovation for the banking industry, including online banking. Incorporates *Future Banker.*

RESEARCH CENTERS AND INSTITUTES

Banking Research Center. Northwestern University, 401 Anderson Hall, 2001 Sheridan Rd., Evanston, IL 60208. Phone: (847)491-3562 Fax: (847)491-5719 E-mail: k-hagerty@northwestern.edu • Does research in the management and public regulation of financial institutions. A unit of the J. L. Kellogg

Graduate School of Management.

STATISTICS SOURCES

Bank Operating Statistics. Federal Deposit Insurance Corp. • Annual. Price on application. Based on Reports of Condition and Reports of Income.

TRADE/PROFESSIONAL ASSOCIATIONS

American Bankers Association. 1120 Connecticut Ave. NW, Washington, DC 20036. Phone: 800-BAN-KERS or (202)663-5000 Fax: (202)663-7543 E-mail: custserv@aba.com • URL: http://www.aba.com • Members are principally commercial banks and trust companies; combined assets of members represent approximately 90% of the U.S. banking industry; approximately 94% of members are community banks with less than $500 million in assets. Seeks to enhance the role of commercial bankers as preeminent providers of financial services through communications, research, legal action, lobbying of federal legislative and regulatory bodies, and education and training programs. Serves as spokesperson for the banking industry; facilitates exchange of information among members. Maintains the American Institute of +Banking, an industry-sponsored adult education program. Conducts educational and training programs for bank employees and officers through a wide range of banking schools and national conferences. Maintains liaison with federal bank regulators; lobbies Congress on issues affecting commercial banks; testifies before congressional committees; represents members in U.S. postal rate proceedings. Serves as secretariat of the International Monetary Conference and the Financial Institutions Committee for the American National Standards Institute. Files briefs and lawsuits in major court cases affecting the industry. Conducts teleconferences with state banking associations on such issues as regulatory compliance; works to build consensus and coordinate activities of leading bank and financial service trade groups. Provides services to members including: public advocacy; news media contact; insurance program providing directors and officers with liability coverage, financial institution bond, and trust errors and omissions coverage; research service operated through ABA Center for Banking Information; fingerprint set processing in conjunction with the Federal Bureau of Investigation; discounts on operational and income-producing projects through the Corporation for American Banking. Conducts conferences, forums, and workshops covering subjects such as small business, consumer credit, agricultural and community banking, trust management, bank operations, and automation. Sponsors ABA Educational Foundation and the Personal +Economics Program, which educates schoolchildren and the community on banking, economics, and personal finance.

Bank Administration Institute. 1 N Franklin St., Ste. 1000, Chicago, IL 60606-3421. Phone: 888-284-4078 or (312)683-2464 Fax: (312)683-2373 E-mail: info@bai.org • URL: http://www.bai.org • Works to improve the competitive position of banking companies through strategic research and educational offerings.

Financial Women International. 1027 W Roselawn Ave., Roseville, MN 55113. Phone: (866)236-2007 or (651)487-7632 Fax: (651)489-1322 E-mail: info@fwi.org • URL: http://www.fwi.org • Individuals working in or with the financial services industry. Maintains FWI Educational Foundation.

Independent Community Bankers of America. One Thomas Circle, N.W., Suite 400, Washington, DC 20005. Phone: 800-422-8439 or (202)659-8111 Fax: (202)659-9216 E-mail: info@icba.org • URL: http://www.icba.org • Formerly Independent Bankers Association of America.

National Bankers Association. 1513 P St. NW, Washington, DC 20005. Phone: (202)588-5432 Fax: (202)588-5443 E-mail: nahart@nationalbankers.org

• URL: http://www.nationalbankers.org • Minority banking institutions owned by minority individuals and institutions. Serves as an advocate for the minority banking industry. Organizes banking services, government relations, marketing, scholarship, and technical assistance programs. Offers placement services; compiles statistics.

OTHER SOURCES

Control of Banking. Prentice Hall PTR. • Two loose-leaf volumes. $465.00 per year. Periodic supplementation. Banking rules and regulations affecting day-to-day operations and financial practices of banks.

BANK MARKETING

GENERAL WORKS

Bank Marketing for the Nineties: New Ideas from 55 of the Best Marketers in Banking. Don Wright. John Wiley and Sons, Inc. • 1991. $175.00.

Bankers in the Selling Role: A Consultative Guide to Cross Selling Financial Services. Linda Richardson. John Wiley and Sons, Inc. • 1992. $29.95. Second edition.

ABSTRACTS AND INDEXES

Business Periodicals Index. H. W. Wilson Co. • 11 times a year. Quarterly and annual cumulations. Price varies.

ONLINE DATABASES

Banking Information Source. PROQUEST. • Provides indexing and abstracting of periodical and other literature from 1982 to date, with weekly updates. Covers the financial services industry: banks, savings institutions, investment houses, credit unions, insurance companies, and real estate organizations. Emphasis is on marketing and management. Inquire as to online cost and availability. (Formerly *FINIS: Financial Industry Information Service.*).

Management Contents. Gale Cengage Learning. • Covers a wide range of management, financial, marketing, personnel, and administrative topics. About 150 leading business journals are indexed and abstracted from 1974 to date, with monthly updating. Inquire as to online cost and availability.

Trade & Industry Database. Gale Cengage Learning. • Provides indexing of business periodicals, January 1981 to date. Daily updates. (Full text articles from some periodicals are available online, 1983 to date. Inquire as to online cost and availability).

PERIODICALS AND NEWSLETTERS

ABA Bank Marketing. Bank Marketing Association. • 10 times a year. Members, $80.00 per year; non-members, $120.00 per year. Includes a *Buyer's Guide.* Formerly *Bank Marketing.*

American Banker: The Financial Services Daily. Thomson Media. • Daily. $895.00 per year. Provides news of banking, investment products, mortgages, credit unions, finance, bank technology, and legal developments.

Bank Investment Consultant: Sales Strategies for the Financial Adviser. Thomson Media. • Monthly. Controlled circulation. Covers sales and marketing techniques for bank investment and asset management divisions. Formerly *Bank Investment Marketing.*

Bank Investment Product News. Institutional Investor, Inc., Journals Group. • Weekly. $1,195.00 per year. Newsletter. Edited for bank executives. Covers the marketing and regulation of financial products sold through banks, such as mutual funds, stock brokerage services, and insurance.

International Journal of Bank Marketing. Emerald (North America). • Seven times a year. $12,519.00 per year.

U. S. Banker. Thomson Media. • Monthly. $65.00 per year. Edited for bank executives and managers. Covers a wide variety of banking and financial topics.

TRADE/PROFESSIONAL ASSOCIATIONS

ABA Marketing Network. 1120 Connecticut Ave. NW, Washington, DC 20036. Phone: 800-BAN-KERS or (202)663-5360 Fax: (202)828-4540 E-mail: webmaster@aba.com • URL: http://www.aba.com/MarketingNetwork/default.htm • Marketing and public relations executives for commercial and savings banks, credit unions, and savings and loans associations, and related groups such as advertising agencies and research firms. Provides marketing education, information, and services to the financial services industry. Conducts research; cosponsors summer sessions of fundamentals and advanced courses in marketing at the University of Colorado at Boulder; compiles statistics.

American Bankers Association. 1120 Connecticut Ave. NW, Washington, DC 20036. Phone: 800-BAN-KERS or (202)663-5000 Fax: (202)663-7543 E-mail: custserv@aba.com • URL: http://www.aba.com • Members are principally commercial banks and trust companies; combined assets of members represent approximately 90% of the U.S. banking industry; approximately 94% of members are community banks with less than $500 million in assets. Seeks to enhance the role of commercial bankers as preeminent providers of financial services through communications, research, legal action, lobbying of federal legislative and regulatory bodies, and education and training programs. Serves as spokesperson for the banking industry; facilitates exchange of information among members. Maintains the American Institute of +Banking, an industry-sponsored adult education program. Conducts educational and training programs for bank employees and officers through a wide range of banking schools and national conferences. Maintains liaison with federal bank regulators; lobbies Congress on issues affecting commercial banks; testifies before congressional committees; represents members in U.S. postal rate proceedings. Serves as secretariat of the International Monetary Conference and the Financial Institutions Committee for the American National Standards Institute. Files briefs and lawsuits in major court cases affecting the industry. Conducts teleconferences with state banking associations on such issues as regulatory compliance; works to build consensus and coordinate activities of leading bank and financial service trade groups. Provides services to members including: public advocacy; news media contact; insurance program providing directors and officers with liability coverage, financial institution bond, and trust errors and omissions coverage; research service operated through ABA Center for Banking Information; fingerprint set processing in conjunction with the Federal Bureau of Investigation; discounts on operational and income-producing projects through the Corporation for American Banking. Conducts conferences, forums, and workshops covering subjects such as small business, consumer credit, agricultural and community banking, trust management, bank operations, and automation. Sponsors ABA Educational Foundation and the Personal +Economics Program, which educates schoolchildren and the community on banking, economics, and personal finance.

OTHER SOURCES

Home Banking Report. JupiterMedia. • Annual. $695.00. Market research report. Covers banking from home by phone or online, with projections of growth in future years.

BANK RESERVES

See also: BANKS AND BANKING

CD-ROM DATABASES

CreditDisk 2.0. Fitch, Inc. • Price and frequency on application. CD-ROM provides credit research and ratings on individual banks throughout the world, with Internet updating. Includes graphic displays of rating histories and financial ratios.

INTERNET DATABASES

Federal Reserve Board Publications and Education Resources. Board of Governors of the Federal Reserve System. Phone: (202)452-3000 Fax: (202)452-3819 • URL: http://www.federalreserve.gov/publications.htm • Web site provides convenient access to statistics, surveys, and research from the Federal Reserve Board. *Federal Reserve Bulletin* articles are available as abstracts or full text (PDF) currently or from six-year archives. The link "Statistics: Releases and Historical Data" offers daily, weekly, monthly, quarterly, and annual data in great detail for interest rates, foreign exchange, consumer credit, money stock measures, industrial production indexes, bank reserves, and other items. Historical tabulations are available for various time periods. Fees: Free.

STATISTICS SOURCES

Assets and Liabilities of Commercial Banks in the United States. U. S. Federal Reserve System. • Weekly. $30.00 per year. (Federal Reserve Statistical Release, H.8.).

Federal Reserve Bulletin. U.S. Federal Reserve System. • Monthly. $25.00 per year. Provides statistics on banking and the economy, including interest rates, money supply, and the Federal Reserve Board indexes of industrial production.

Statistical Information on the Financial Services Industry. American Bankers Association. • Annual. Members, $150.00; non-members, $275.00. Presents a wide variety of data relating to banking and financial services, including consumer economics, personal finance, credit, government loans, capital markets, and international banking.

BANK TECHNOLOGY

See: BANK AUTOMATION

BANK TELLER MACHINES

See: BANK AUTOMATION

BANKING LAW AND REGULATION

GENERAL WORKS

Does Financial Deregulation Work? A Critique of Free Market Approaches. Bruce Coggins. Edward Elgar Publishing, Inc. • 1998. $95.00. Provides a critique of bank deregulation in the United States. Includes suggestions for more effective financial regulation. (New Directions in Modern Economics Series).

Improving Access to Bank Information for Tax Purposes. Organization for Economic Cooperation and Development. • 2000. $66.00. Discusses ways to improve the international exchange of bank account information for tax determinations.

Law and Banking: Principles. Kathleen L. Farrell and James C. Conboy. American Bankers Association. • 2000. Fourth edition. Price on application. Discusses legal issues facing the banking industry.

Preventing Bank Crises: Lessons from Recent

Global Bank Failures. Gerand Caprio. The World Bank Group. • 1998. $40.00. Examines worldwide problems with bank regulation, bank infrastructure, public accountability, and political influence.(EDI Development Studies).

Reforming the Bank Regulatory Structure. Andrew S. Carron. Brookings Institution Press. • 1985. $8.95. (Studies in the Regulation of Economic Activity).

ABSTRACTS AND INDEXES
Business Periodicals Index. H. W. Wilson Co. • 11 times a year. Quarterly and annual cumulations. Price varies.

Index to Legal Periodicals and Books. H. W. Wilson Co. • Monthly. $490.00 per year. Quarterly and annual cumulations.

ALMANACS AND YEARBOOKS
Securities, Commodities, and Federal Banking: 1999 in Review. CCH, Inc. • Irregular. $57.00. Summarizes the year's significant legal and regulatory developments.

BIBLIOGRAPHIES
Financial Institutions. Available from U. S. Government Printing Office. • Annual. Free. Lists government publications. Formerly *Banks and Banking.* GPO Subject Bibliography No. 128.

Law Books in Print: Law Books in English Published Throughout the World. Glanville Publishers, Inc. • Triennial. $750.00.

Legal Looseleafs in Print. Arlene L. Eis, editor. Infosources Publishing. • 2001. $106.00. Lists over 3,600 titles by more than 250 publishers.

DIRECTORIES
Lawyer's Register International by Specialties and Fields of Law Including a Directory of Corporate Counsel. Lawyer's Register Publishing Co. • Annual. $359.00. Three volumes. Referral source for law firms.

HANDBOOKS AND MANUALS
Bank Tax Guide. CCH, Inc. • Annual. $199.00. Summarizes and explains federal tax rules affecting financial institutions.

Banking Law. LexisNexis Matthew Bender. • $2,325.00. 20 looseleaf volumes. Periodic supplementation. Operational guidance for bank officers, with analysis of statutory law and agency regulations. Includes *Checks, Drafts* and *Notes* as volumes 7, 7a, 8, 8a.

Banking Law Manual: Federal Regulation of Financial Holding Companies, Banks and Thrifts. LexisNexis Matthew Bender. • $254.00. Second edition. Desk reference, procedural guide, or training and management tool for the banking professional.

Law and Banking: Applications. Craig W. Smith. American Bankers Association. • 1990. $57.00. Third edition. Covers laws pertaining to collections, secured transactions, letters of credit, check processing, collateral, fraud, and default.

INTERNET DATABASES
Lexis.com Research System. Lexis-Nexis Group. Phone: 800-227-4908 or (937)865-6800 Fax: (937)865-6909 E-mail: webmaster@prod.lexisnexis.com • URL: http://www.lexis.com • Fee-based Web site offers extensive searching of a wide variety of legal sources. Additional features include Daily Opinion Service, lexis.com Bookstore, Career Center, CLE Center, Law Schools, and Practice Pages ("Pages specific to areas of specialty").

ONLINE DATABASES
Legal Resource Index. Gale Cengage Learning. • Broad coverage of law literature appearing in legal, business, and other periodicals, 1980 to date. Daily updates. Inquire as to online cost and availability.

LEXIS. LEXIS-NEXIS. • The various LEXIS databases provide full text and indexing for a wide variety of legal cases, statutes, orders, and opinions.

Management Contents. Gale Cengage Learning. • Covers a wide range of management, financial, marketing, personnel, and administrative topics. About 150 leading business journals are indexed and abstracted from 1974 to date, with monthly updating. Inquire as to online cost and availability.

PAIS International. Public Affairs Information Service, Inc. • Corresponds to the former printed publications, *PAIS Bulletin* (1976-90) and *PAIS Foreign Language Index* (1972-90), and to the current *PAIS International in Print* (1991 to date). Covers economic, political, and sociological material appearing in periodicals, books, government documents, and other publications. Updating is monthly. Inquire as to online cost and availability.

Trade & Industry Database. Gale Cengage Learning. • Provides indexing of business periodicals, January 1981 to date. Daily updates. (Full text articles from some periodicals are available online, 1983 to date. Inquire as to online cost and availability).

PERIODICALS AND NEWSLETTERS
Electronic Banking Law and Commerce Report. Glasser Legalworks. • 10 times a year. $300.00 per year. Newsletter. Provides coverage of the legal aspects of online banking services, bank cards, and "smart phones.".

International Financial Law Review. American Educational Systems. • Monthly. $750.00 per year. Includes print and online editions.

RESEARCH CENTERS AND INSTITUTES
Banking Research Center. Northwestern University, 401 Anderson Hall, 2001 Sheridan Rd., Evanston, IL 60208. Phone: (847)491-3562 Fax: (847)491-5719 E-mail: k-hagerty@northwestern.edu • Does research in the management and public regulation of financial institutions. A unit of the J. L. Kellogg Graduate School of Management.

Center for Study of Responsive Law. P.O. Box 19367, Washington, DC 20036. Phone: (202)387-8030 Fax: (202)234-5176 E-mail: csrl@csrl.org • URL: http://www.csrl.org • A consumer-oriented research group.

Morin Center for Banking and Financial Law. Boston University, School of Law, 765 Commonwealth Ave., Boston, MA 02215. Phone: (617)353-3023 Fax: (617)353-2444 E-mail: banklaw@bu.edu • URL: http://www.web.bu.edu/law • Research fields include banking law, regulation of depository institutions, and deposit insurance.

Rodney L. White Center for Financial Research. University of Pennsylvania, 3254 Steinberg Hall-Dietrich Hall, Philadelphia, PA 19104. Phone: (215)898-7616 Fax: (215)573-8084 E-mail: rlwtcr@finance.wharton.upenn.edu • URL: http://www.finance.wharton.upenn.edu • Research areas include financial management, money markets, real estate finance, and international finance.

TRADE/PROFESSIONAL ASSOCIATIONS
BANKPAC. 1120 Connecticut Ave. NW, 1120 Connecticut Ave. NW, 1120 Connecticut Ave., N.W., Washington, DC 20036. Phone: 800-BAN-KERS or (202)663-5121 Fax: (202)828-6071 E-mail: scrochet@aba.com • URL: http://www.aba.com • Members of the banking community united to help elect to the U.S. Congress, without regard to party affiliation, those who have shown an interest, understanding, and a concern for banking business and a free economic system in which it can function properly. Acts as the political action committee of the American Bankers Association (see separate entry); makes contributions for campaign expenditures in political contests for seats in the

House of Representatives and the Senate; does not make contributions in presidential contests or in contests for state and local offices.

Conference of State Bank Supervisors. 1155 Connecticut Ave., NW, 5th Fl., Washington, DC 20036. Phone: 800-886-2727 or (202)728-5702 Fax: (202)296-1928 E-mail: nmilner@csbs.org • URL: http://www.csbs.org • Members are state officials responsible for supervision of state-chartered banking institutions.

Independent Community Bankers of America. One Thomas Circle, N.W., Suite 400, Washington, DC 20005. Phone: 800-422-8439 or (202)659-8111 Fax: (202)659-9216 E-mail: info@icba.org • URL: http://www.icba.org • Formerly Independent Bankers Association of America.

OTHER SOURCES
Control of Banking. Prentice Hall PTR. • Two looseleaf volumes. $465.00 per year. Periodic supplementation. Banking rules and regulations affecting day-to-day operations and financial practices of banks.

Federal Banking Law Reports. CCH, Inc. • Weekly. $1,533.00 per year. Looseleaf service.

BANKRUPTCY

See also: BUSINESS FAILURES; BUSINESS LAW; LAW

GENERAL WORKS
Bankruptcy: A Primer. D. Ellsworth Blanc. Nova Science Publishers, Inc. • 2002. $27.50. Serves as a basic guide to liquidation, reorganization, the U. S. Bankruptcy Code, and economic issues.

Bankruptcy Law Fundamentals. West Group. • Annual. $180.00. Looseleaf service.

The Fragile Middle Class: Americans in Debt. Teresa A. Sullivan and others. Yale University Press. • 2000. $40.00. Provides an analysis of a 1991 survey of personal bankruptcies in five states of the U. S. Serves as a sequel to the authors' *As We Forgive Our Debtors* (1989), an analysis of 1981 bankruptcies.

Mergers, Acquisitions, and Corporate Restructurings. Patrick A. Gaughan. John Wiley and Sons, Inc. • 2001. $75.00. Third edition. Covers mergers, acquisitions, divestitures, internal reorganizations, joint ventures, leveraged buyouts, bankruptcy workouts, and recapitalizations.

ABSTRACTS AND INDEXES
Accounting and Tax Index. UMI. • Quarterly. Price on application. Annual cumulation. Indexes accounting, auditing, and taxation literature appearing in journals, books, pamphlets, conference proceedings, and newsletters.

Current Law Index: Multiple Access to Legal Periodicals. Gale Cengage Learning. • Monthly. $725.00 per year. Produced in cooperation with the American Association of Law Libraries. Indexes more than 900 law journals, legal newspapers, and specialty publications from the U.S., Canada, U.K., Ireland, Australia, and New Zealand.

Index to Legal Periodicals and Books. H. W. Wilson Co. • Monthly. $490.00 per year. Quarterly and annual cumulations.

ALMANACS AND YEARBOOKS
American Law Yearbook. Gale Cengage Learning. • Annual. $165.00. Serves as a yearly supplement to *West's Encyclopedia of American Law.* Describes new legal developments in many subject areas.

Bankruptcy Yearbook and Almanac. New Generation Research, Inc. • Annual. Price on application.

CD-ROM DATABASES
Authority Collier Bankruptcy Library. LexisNexis/Matthew Bender. • Periodic revisions. Price on

request. CD-ROM contains updated full text of *Collier on Bankruptcy* and 13 other Collier publications. Various aspects of bankruptcy are covered, including attorney compensation, proceedings, farm insolvencies, real estate failures, family law, taxation, and business workouts.

WILSONDISC: Index to Legal Periodicals and Books. H. W. Wilson Co. • Monthly. Includes unlimited online access to *Index to Legal Periodicals* through WILSONLINE. Contains CD-ROM indexing of more than 1,400 English language legal periodicals from 1981 to date and 2,500 books.

ENCYCLOPEDIAS AND DICTIONARIES

West's Encyclopedia of American Law. Available from Gale Cengage Learning. • 2003. $1,195.00. Second edition. 12 volumes. Published by West Group. Covers a wide variety of legal topics for the general reader.

HANDBOOKS AND MANUALS

Bankruptcy and Insolvency Accounting. Grant Newton. John Wiley and Sons, Inc. • 2000. $380.00. 6th edition. Two volumes. $190.00 per volume. *2001 Supplement, $65.00*.

Bankruptcy and Insolvency Taxation. Grant W. Newton and Gilbert D. Bloom. John Wiley and Sons, Inc. • 1993. $235.00. Second edition. 2002 cumulative supplement, $95.00.

Bankruptcy Basics. Available from U. S. Government Printing Office. • 1998. $4.25. Second edition. Issued by the Bankruptcy Judges Division, Administrative Office of the United States Courts. Provides concise explanation of five Chapters of the U.S. Bankruptcy Code: Chapter 7 (Liquidation), Chapter 9 (Municipal), Chapter 11 (Reorganization), Chapter 12 (Family Farmer), and Chapter 13 (Debt Adjustment). Includes a seven-page glossary, "Bankruptcy Terminology." (Public Information Series.).

Bankruptcy Concepts: A Desk Reference for Lenders. Bonnie K. Donahue. The Risk Management Association. • 1994. $55.00. Designed to help loan officers deal with the intricacies of bankruptcy law. Chapters include a brief history of bankruptcy law, basic bankruptcy principles, and "Adjustments of Debts.".

Bankruptcy Law Manual. West Group. • Annual. $298.00. Looseleaf service. Complete, practical to modern bankruptcy practice and procedure.

Bankruptcy Practice Handbook, 2d. West Group. • Annual. $290.00. Two looseleaf volumes.

Business Taxpayer Information Publications. Available from U. S. Government Printing Office. • Annual. $63.00. Two volumes, consisting of *Circular E, Employer's Tax Guide* and *Employer's Supplemental Tax Guide*. Issued by the Internal Revenue Service (http://www.irs.ustreas.gov). Includes a wide variety of business-related tax information, including withholding tables, tax calendars, self-employment issues, partnership matters, corporation topics, depreciation, and bankruptcy.

Chapter 13: Practice and Procedure. West Group. • Annual. $160.00. Looseleaf service.

Collier Bankruptcy Practice Guide. LexisNexis Matthew Bender. • $1,393.00. Six looseleaf volumes. Periodic supplementation. Strategic and procedural guide for all cases instituted under the code.

Consumer Bankruptcy Law and Practice. The National Consumer Law Center. • 2000. $140.00. Sixth edition. (Consumer Credit and Sales Legal Practice Series).

Corporate Financial Distress and Bankruptcy: A Complete Guide to Predicting and Avoiding Distress and Profiting from Bankruptcy. Edward I. Altman. John Wiley and Sons, Inc. • 1993. $110.00. Second edition. Provides practical advice on analyzing the financial position of a corporation, with case studies. Includes a discussion of the junk bond market. (Finance Series).

Debt Free: The National Bankruptcy Kit. Daniel Sitarz. Nova Publishing Co. • 1999. $19.95. Second edition. Includes basic forms and instructions for use in uncomplicated personal bankruptcy situations. (Legal Self-Help Series).

INTERNET DATABASES

Lexis.com Research System. Lexis-Nexis Group. Phone: 800-227-4908 or (937)865-6800 Fax: (937)865-6909 E-mail: webmaster@prod.lexisnexis.com • URL: http://www.lexis.com • Fee-based Web site offers extensive searching of a wide variety of legal sources. Additional features include Daily Opinion Service, lexis.com Bookstore, Career Center, CLE Center, Law Schools, and Practice Pages ("Pages specific to areas of specialty").

ONLINE DATABASES

Accounting and Tax Database. PROQUEST. • Provides indexing and abstracting of the literature of accounting, taxation, and financial management, 1971 to date. Updating is weekly. Especially covers accounting, auditing, banking, bankruptcy, employee compensation and benefits, cash management, financial planning, and credit. Inquire as to online cost and availability.

Index to Legal Periodicals and Books (Online). H. W. Wilson Co. • Broad coverage of law journals and books 1981 to date. Monthly updates. Inquire as to online cost and availability.

LEXIS. LEXIS-NEXIS. • The various LEXIS databases provide full text and indexing for a wide variety of legal cases, statutes, orders, and opinions.

PERIODICALS AND NEWSLETTERS

American Bankruptcy Law Journal. National Conference of Bankruptcy Judges. • Quarterly. $65.00.

The Bankruptcy Strategist. Law Journal Newsletter. • Description: Reports on substantive legal developments and successful strategy decisions by bankruptcy attorneys. Recurring features include a calendar of upcoming seminars.

Chapter 11 Update: Monitors All Major Developments in Today's Corporate Bankruptcies and Examines Pertinent Court Decisions Related to Chapter 11 Filings. Andrews Publications. • Semimonthly. $500.00 per year. Newsletter on corporate Chapter 11 bankruptcy filings.

Collections and Credit Risk: The Authority for Commercial and Consumer Credit Professionals. Thomson Media. • Monthly. $95.00 per year. Contains articles on the technology and business management of credit and collection functions. Includes coverage of bad debts, bankruptcy, and credit risk management.

Credit Risk Management. Phillips International, Inc. • Biweekly. $695.00 per year. Newsletter on consumer credit, including delinquency aspects.

Insolvency Law & Practice. LexisNexis Butterworths Tolley. • Bimonthly. $181.00 per year. United Kingdom emphasis.

Norton Bankruptcy Law Adviser. William L. Norton, Jr. West Group. • Monthly. $598.00 per year. Newsletter.

STATISTICS SOURCES

Weekly Business Failures. Dun & Bradstreet Corp. • Weekly. $445.00 per year.

TRADE/PROFESSIONAL ASSOCIATIONS

American Bankruptcy Institute. 44 Canal Center Plz., Ste. 400, Alexandria, VA 22314. Phone: (703)739-0800 Fax: (703)739-1060 E-mail: sgerdano@abiworld.org • URL: http://www.abiworld.org • Attorneys, accountants, and other providers of financial services, lending institutions, credit organizations, consumer groups, federal and state governments, and other interested individuals. Provides a multidisciplinary forum for the exchange of information on bankruptcy and insolvency issues. Fosters dialogue among lawyers, businesspersons, and legislators on current and potential bankruptcy problems. Reviews existing and proposed legislation as it affects bankruptcy and insolvency. Conducts nationally televised panel discussions and research projects; provides information to the public and legislators. Maintains speakers bureau; compiles statistics. Conducts research and educational programs.

Association of Insolvency and Restructuring Advisors. 132 W. Main, Suite 200, Medford, OR 97501. Phone: (541)858-1665 or (541)848-9362 Fax: (541)858-9187 E-mail: info@airacira.org • URL: http://www.airacira.org.

National Conference of Bankruptcy Judges. c/o Christine J. Molick, 235 Secret Cove Dr., Lexington, SC 29072. Phone: (803)957-6225 • URL: http://www.ncbj.org.

OTHER SOURCES

Bankruptcy Law Reports. CCH, Inc. • Biweekly. $1,150.00 per year. Three looseleaf volumes.

Collier on Bankruptcy. LexisNexis Matthew Bender. • $2,880.00. 23 looseleaf volumes. Periodic supplementation. Detailed discussion, by the leading bankruptcy authorities, of the Bankruptcy Code as amended.

BANKS AND BANKING

See also: ELECTRONIC FUNDS TRANSFER SYSTEMS (EFTS)

GENERAL WORKS

Bankers in the Selling Role: A Consultative Guide to Cross Selling Financial Services. Linda Richardson. John Wiley and Sons, Inc. • 1992. $29.95. Second edition.

The Bankers: The Next Generation: The New Worlds of Money, Credit, and Banking in an Electronic Age. Martin Mayer. Dutton/Plume. • 1998. $16.95. A popularly written discussion of the future of banks, bankers, and banking.

The Business of Banking for Bank Directors. George K. Darling and James F. Chaston. The Risk Management Association. • 1995. $33.00. Presents basic banking concepts and issues for new directors of financial institutions. Emphasis is on the specific duties of directors.

The Economics of Money, Banking and Financial Markets. Frederic S. Mishkin. Addison Wesley. • 2003. $110.00. Seventh edition. (Economics Series).

A Guide to the World Bank. The World Bank. • 2003. $15.00. Covers history of the World Bank, with its organization, mission, and purpose.

Michie on Banks on Banking, 1999. Mary J. Divine and Paul Ernest. LEXIS Publishing. • 1999. $440.00. Revised edition.

Money, Banking, and Financial Markets. Roger L. Miller and David D. VanHoose. South-Western. • 2003. $102.95. Second edition.

Money, Banking, and the Economy. Thomas Mayer and others. W. W. Norton & Co., Inc. • 1996. $92.45. Sixth edition.

Money: Its Origins, Development, Debasement, and Prospects. John H. Wood. American Institute for Economic Research. • 1999. $10.00. A politically conservative view of monetary history, the gold standard, banking systems, and inflation. Includes a list of references. (Economic Education Bulletin.).

Principles of Banking. Eric N. Compton. American Bankers Association. • 2001. $65.00. Seventh edition.

Principles of Money, Banking and Financial Markets. Addison-Wesley. • 2000. $67.00. 10th edition.

Resumes for Banking and Financial Careers. McGraw-Hill. • 2001. $10.95. Second edition. Contains 100 sample resumes and 20 cover letters. (VGM Professional Resumes Series.).

ABSTRACTS AND INDEXES

Business Periodicals Index. H. W. Wilson Co. • 11 times a year. Quarterly and annual cumulations. Price varies.

NTIS Alerts: Business & Economics. National Technical Information Service. • Text: Semimonthly. $210.00 per year.

World Banking Abstracts: The International Journal of the Financial Services Industry. Institution of European Finance. Blackwell Publishing Ltd. • Bimonthly. Institutions, $1,393.00 per year. Includes print and online editions. Provides worldwide coverage of articles appearing in over 400 financial publications.

ALMANACS AND YEARBOOKS

Bankers' Almanac. Reed Business Information. • Semiannual. $1,170.00. Six volumes. Lists more than 27,000 financial institutions; international coverage. Formerly *Bankers' Almanac and Yearbook.*

BIBLIOGRAPHIES

Banking in the U. S.: An Annotated Bibliography. Jean Deuss. Scarecrow Press, Inc. • 1990. $35.00.

FED in Print: Economics and Banking Topics. Federal Reserve Bank of Philadelphia. • Semiannual. Free. Business and banking topics.

BIOGRAPHICAL SOURCES

Who's Who in Finance and Industry. Marquis Who's Who. • Biennial. $259.95. Provides over 21,000 concise biographies of business leaders in all fields.

Who's Who in International Banking. Bowker-Saur. • Irregular. $400.00. Contains biographical sketches of about 4,000 bankers. Worldwide coverage.

CD-ROM DATABASES

CreditDisk 2.0. Fitch, Inc. • Price and frequency on application. CD-ROM provides credit research and ratings on individual banks throughout the world, with Internet updating. Includes graphic displays of rating histories and financial ratios.

OECD Statistical Compendium. Organization for Economic Cooperation and Development. • Semiannual. $1,905.00 per year for 1 to 10 users. CD-ROM contains more than 730,000 monthly, quarterly, and annual time series for OECD countries, 1960 to date. Includes fully searchable data on agriculture, food, economic indicators, national accounts, employment, energy, finance, industry, technology, and foreign trade. Results can be displayed in various forms.

WILSONDISC: Wilson Business Abstracts. H. W. Wilson Co. • Monthly. Includes unlimited online access to *Wilson Business Abstracts* through WILSONLINE. Provides CD-ROM "cover-to-cover" abstracting and indexing of over 600 prominent business periodicals. Indexing is from 1982, abstracting from 1990. (*Business Periodicals Index* without abstracts is available on CD-ROM at $1,495 per year.).

DIRECTORIES

American Bankers Association Key to Routing Numbers. American Bankers Association. Thomas Financial Publishing. • Annual. $169.00. per year. Lists over 30,000 finanical institutions in the U.S. and their routing members.

American Financial Directory. Accuity. • Covers: Approximately 23,000 banks, bank holding companies, credit unions, savings and loans, and other financial institutions and their approximately 56,000 branch offices. Entries include: Institution name, address, phone, fax, holding company affiliation, names and titles of key personnel, correspondent banks, FEDWIRE data and ABA number, balance sheet highlights, branches.

America's Corporate Finance Directory. LexisNexis Group. • Covers: Financial personnel and outside financial services relationships of 5,000 leading United States corporations and their wholly-owned United States subsidiaries. Entries include: Company name, address, phone, fax, telex, e-mail addresses, stock exchange information, earnings, total assets, size of pension/profit-sharing fund portfolio, number of employees, description of business, wholly-owned U.S. Subsidiaries of parent company; name and title of key executives; outside suppliers of financial services.

Directory of Trust Banking. Thomson Financial Publishing. • Annual. $344.00. Contains profiles of bank affiliated trust companies, independent trust companies, trust investment advisors, and trust fund managers. Provides contact information for professional personnel at more than 3,000 banking and other financial institutions.

Financial Yellow Book: Who's Who at the Leading U. S. Financial Institutions. Leadership Directories, Inc. • Semiannual. $265.00. Gives the names and titles of over 28,000 key executives in financial institutions. Includes the areas of banking, investment, money management, and insurance. Five indexes are provided: institution, executive name, geographic by state, financial service segment, and parent company.

Institutional Buyers of Bank and Thrift Stocks: A Targeted Directory. Investment Data Corp. • Annual. $645.00. Provides detailed profiles of about 600 institutional buyers of bank and savings and loan stocks. Includes names of financial analysts and portfolio managers.

Major Financial Institutions of Europe. Available from Gale Cengage Learning. • Annual. $510.00. Contains profiles of over 2,000 financial institutions in Europe such as banks, investment companies, and insurance companies. Formerly *Major Financial Institutions of Continental Europe.*

Major Financial Institutions of the World 2001. Available from Gale Cengage Learning. • 2003. $880.00. Sixth edition. Two volumes. Published by Graham & Whiteside. Contains detailed information on more than 7,500 important financial institutions in various countries. Includes banks, investment companies, and insurance companies.

Morgan Stanley Central Bank Directory. Central Banking Publications Ltd. • 2003. $160.00. Provides detailed information on over 160 central banks around the world. A full page is devoted to each country included. Included in subscription to *Central Banking.*

Plunkett's Financial Services Industry Almanac: The Only Comprehensive Overview of the Banking, Insurance, Credit and Investment Sectors. Plunkett Research, Ltd. • Annual. $229.99. Includes CD-ROM. Discusses important trends in various sectors of the financial industry. Five hundred major banking, credit card, investment, and financial services companies are profiled. (Business, Careers and Internet Reference Tools Series).

Thomson Bank Directory. Accuity. • Covers: in five volumes, about 11,000 banks and 50,000 branches of United States banks, and 60,000 foreign banks and branches engaged in foreign banking; Federal Reserve system and other United States government and state government banking agencies; 500 largest North American and International commercial banks; paper and automated clearinghouses. Volumes 1 and 2 contain North American listings; volumes 3 and 4, international listings (also cited as 'Thomson International Bank Directory'); volume 5, Worldwide Correspondents Guide containing key correspondent data to facilitate funds transfer. Entries include: For domestic banks--Bank name, address, phone, telex, cable, date established, routing number, charter type, bank holding company affiliation, memberships in Federal Reserve System and other banking organizations, principal officers by function performed, principal correspondent banks, and key financial data (deposits, etc.). For international banks--Bank name, address, phone, fax, telex, cable, SWIFT address, transit or sort codes within home country, ownership, financial data, names and titles of key personnel, branch locations. For branches--Bank name, address, phone, charter type, ownership and other details comparable to domestic bank listings.

Thomson World Bank Directory. Accuity. • Covers: Over 10,000 international banks and their branches in around 200 countries around the globe, including the top 1,000 U.S. Banks. Entries include: Institution name, address, phone, fax, key banking officers by functional title, directors, data established, expanded statement of condition, including a profit and loss account and historic performance ratios.

The Top 5,000 European Companies 2002. Available from Gale Cengage Learning. • 2002. $645.00. Third edition. Published by Graham & Whiteside. In addition to about 5,000 manufacturing and service companies, includes the 500 largest banks in Europe and the 100 largest insurance companies.

The Top 5,000 Global Companies 2002. Available from Gale Cengage Learning. • 2002. $730.00. Third edition. Published by Graham & Whiteside. Includes about 5,000 manufacturing and service companies worldwide, plus the world's 500 largest banks and 100 largest insurance companies.

Vickers Directory of Institutional Investors. Vickers Stock Research Corp. • Semiannual. $195.00 per year. Detailed alphabetical listing of more than 4,000 U. S., Canadian, and foreign institutional investors. Includes insurance companies, banks, endowment funds, and investment companies. Formerly *Directory of Institutional Investors.*

ENCYCLOPEDIAS AND DICTIONARIES

The A-Z Vocabulary for Investors. American Institute for Economic Research. • 1997. $7.00. Second half of book is a "General Glossary" of about 400 financial terms "most-commonly used" in investing. First half contains lengthier descriptions of types of banking institutions (commercial banks, thrift institutions, credit unions), followed by succinct explanations of various forms of investment: stocks, bonds, options, futures, commodities, and "Other Investments" (collectibles, currencies, mortgages, precious metals, real estate, charitable trusts). (Economic Education Bulletin.).

Blackwell Encyclopedic Dictionary of Finance. Dean Paxson and Douglas Wood, editors. Blackwell Publishing. • 1997. $110.00. The editors are associated with the University of Manchester. Contains definitions of key terms combined with longer articles written by various U. S. and foreign business educators. Includes bibliographies and index. (Blackwell Encyclopedia of Management Series).

Dictionary of Banking and Finance Terms: 'AAA to Zloty'. John Clark. State Mutual Book and Periodical Services Ltd. • 1998. $60.00.

Dictionary of Banking: Over 4,000 Terms Defined and Explained. Charles J. Woelfel. McGraw-Hill. • 1994. $24.95. Contains brief definitions of more than 4,000 banking terms.

Dictionary of Banking Terms. Jack P. Friedman and Thomas Fitch. Barron's Educational Series, Inc. • 2000. $13.95. Fifth edition. (Business Dictionaries Series).

Dictionary of Finance and Investment Terms. John Downes. Barron's Educational Series, Inc. • 2002.

$14.95. Sixth edition. Provides clear explanations of more than 5,000 business, banking, financial, investment, and tax terms. Includes a separate list of financial abbreviations and acronyms. (Business Dictionaries Series).

Encyclopedia of Banking and Finance. Charles J. Woelfel. McGraw-Hill. • 1996. $150.00. 10th revised edition. Includes CD-ROM.

Encyclopedia of Business. Gale Cengage Learning. • 2000. $425.00. Second edition. Two volumes. Contains more than 700 signed articles covering major business disciplines and concepts. International in scope. (Encyclopedia of Business Series).

Encyclopedia of Business and Finance. Burton Kaliski, editor. Available from Gale Cengage Learning. • 2001. $275.00. Two volumes. Published by Macmillan Reference USA. Contains articles by various contributors on accounting, business administration, banking, finance, management information systems, and marketing.

Encyclopedic Dictionary of International Finance and Banking. Jae K. Shim and Michael Constas. CRC Press. • 2001. $64.95. Contains 550 detailed entries covering multinational business, international finance, money, investments, financial planning, financial economics, and banking. Includes statistics, charts, exhibits, diagrams, rules-of-thumb and checklists.

The Language of Banking: Terms and Phrases Used in the Financial Industry. Michael G. Hales. McFarland & Co., Inc., Publishers. • 1994. $35.00. Provides detailed explanations of about 1,200 banking and finance terms.

The New Palgrave Dictionary of Money and Finance. Peter Newman and others, editors. Palgrave Macmillan. • 1992. $595.00. Two volumes. Consists of signed essays on over 1,000 financial topics, each with a bibliography. Covers a wide variety of financial, monetary, and investment areas. A detailed subject index is provided.

FINANCIAL RATIOS

Almanac of Business and Industrial Financial Ratios. Leo Troy. Aspen Publishers, Inc. • 2003. $125.95. Includes CD-Rom. Contains financial ratios derived from federal tax returns. Ratios for each of about 200 industries are arranged according to company asset size. (Almanac of Business and Industrial Financial Ratios Series).

HANDBOOKS AND MANUALS

The Bank Director's Handbook. Edwin B Cox and others. Greenwood Publishing Group, Inc. • 1986. $79.95. Second edition.

Banking and Finance on the Internet. Mary J. Cronin, editor. John Wiley and Sons, Inc. • 1997. $45.00. Contains articles on Internet services, written by bankers, money mangers, investment analysts, and stockbrokers. Emphasis is on operations management. (Communications Series).

How to Charter a Commercial Bank. Douglas V. Austin. CCH, Inc. • 1999. $350.00. Provides detailed information on how to start a commercial bank, including both technical and practical requirements.

International Banking. Peter K. Oppenheim. American Bankers Association. • 1991. $51.00. Sixth edition. Covers letters of credit, money transfers, collections, and other aspects of global banking.

Moody's Bank and Finance Manual. Mergent. • Annual. $1,750.00 per year. Four volumes. Includes biweekly supplements in *Moody's Bank and Finance News Report.*

INTERNET DATABASES

The Bauer Group: Reporting On and Analyzing the Performance of U. S. Banks, Thrifts, and Credit Unions. Bauer Financial Reports, Inc. Phone: 800-388-6686 or (305)445-9500 Fax: 800-230-9569 or (305)445-6775 • URL: http://www.bauerfinancial.com • Web site provides ratings (0 to 5 stars) of individual banks and credit unions, based on capital ratios and other financial criteria. Online searching for bank or credit union names is offered. Fees: Free.

Business 2.0 Web Guide to the Best Business Links. Business 2.0 Media Inc. Phone: (415)293-4800 E-mail: support@business2.com • URL: http://www.business2.com/webguide • Web site presents an extensive, searchable directory of links to "the best, most informative, and authoritative web pages." Twenty main categories cover business, finance, career, company information, people, and technology topics, with thousands of subtopics, all linking to Web sites recommended by experienced business researchers. Fees: Free.

Factiva. Dow Jones Reuters Business Interactive, LLC. Phone: 800-369-7466 or (609)452-1511 Fax: (609)520-5770 E-mail: solutions@factiva.com • URL: http://www.factiva.com • Fee-based Web site provides "global news and business information through Web sites and content integration solutions." Includes Dow Jones and Reuters newswires, The Wall Street Journal, and more than 7,000 other sources of current news, historical articles, market research reports, and investment analysis. Content includes 96 major U. S. newspapers, 900 non-English sources, trade publications, media transcripts, country profiles, news photos, etc.

Federal Reserve Board Publications and Education Resources. Board of Governors of the Federal Reserve System. Phone: (202)452-3000 Fax: (202)452-3819 • URL: http://www.federalreserve.gov/publications.htm • Web site provides convenient access to statistics, surveys, and research from the Federal Reserve Board. *Federal Reserve Bulletin* articles are available as abstracts or full text (PDF) currently or from six-year archives. The link "Statistics: Releases and Historical Data" offers daily, weekly, monthly, quarterly, and annual data in great detail for interest rates, foreign exchange, consumer credit, money stock measures, industrial production indexes, bank reserves, and other items. Historical tabulations are available for various time periods. Fees: Free.

Fedstats. Federal Interagency Council on Statistical Policy. Phone: (202)395-7254 • URL: http://www.fedstats.gov • Web site features an efficient search facility for full-text statistics produced by more than 100 federal agencies, including the Census Bureau, the Bureau of Economic Analysis, and the Bureau of Labor Statistics. Boolean searches can be made within one agency or for all agencies combined. Links are offered to international statistical bureaus, including the UN, IMF, OECD, UNESCO, Eurostat, and 20 individual countries. Fees: Free.

FreeLunch.com. Economy.com, Inc. Phone: (610)696-8700 Fax: (610)696-1678 • URL: http://www.freelunch.com • Web site provides free access to more than 1.5 million economic and financial data series, covering industry, demographics, labor markets, prices, retail sales, government spending, trade, interest rates, housing starts, the stock market, and many other topics. Data is available for various time periods in either chart or table form. Searching is offered. Fees: Free, but registration required. Economy.com, Inc. also offers fee-based economic analysis at *The Dismal Scientist* site (http://www.dismal.com).

Gateway to the European Union. European Union. E-mail: pressoffice@eurostat.cec.be • URL: http://www.europa.eu.int • Web site provides access to a wide variety of EU information, including statistics (Eurostat), news, policies, publications, key issues, and official exchange rates for the euro. Includes links to the European Central Bank, the European Investment Bank, and other institutions. Fees: Free.

Nexis.com. Lexis-Nexis Group. Phone: 800-227-4908 or (937)865-6800 Fax: (937)865-6909 E-mail: webmaster@prod.lexis-nexis.com • URL: http://www.nexis.com • Fee-based Web site offers searching of about 2.8 billion documents in some 30,000 news, business, and legal information sources. Features include a subject directory covering 1,200 topics in 34 categories and a Company Dossier containing information on more than 500,000 public and private companies. Boolean searching is offered.

ONLINE DATABASES

American Banker Full Text. American Banker-Bond Buyer, Database Services. • Provides complete text online of the daily *American Banker.* Inquire as to online cost and availability.

Banking Information Source. PROQUEST. • Provides indexing and abstracting of periodical and other literature from 1982 to date, with weekly updates. Covers the financial services industry: banks, savings institutions, investment houses, credit unions, insurance companies, and real estate organizations. Emphasis is on marketing and management. Inquire as to online cost and availability. (Formerly *FINIS: Financial Industry Information Service.*).

Wilson Business Abstracts Online. H. W. Wilson Co. • Indexes and abstracts 600 major business periodicals, plus the *Wall Street Journal* and the business section of the *New York Times.* Indexing is from 1982, abstracting from 1990, with the two newspapers included from 1993. Updated weekly. Inquire as to online cost and availability. (*Business Periodicals Index* without abstracts is also available online.).

PERIODICALS AND NEWSLETTERS

ABA Bank Marketing. Bank Marketing Association. • 10 times a year. Members, $80.00 per year; nonmembers, $120.00 per year. Includes a *Buyer's Guide.* Formerly *Bank Marketing.*

ABA Bankers News. American Bankers Association. • Biweekly. Members, $48.00 per year; nonmembers, $96.00 per year. Formerly *Banker News.*

ABA Banking Journal. American Bankers Association, Member Communications. Simmons-Boardman Books. • Monthly. Free to qualified personnel; others, $25.00 per year.

American Banker: The Financial Services Daily. Thomson Media. • Daily. $895.00 per year. Provides news of banking, investment products, mortgages, credit unions, finance, bank technology, and legal developments.

Applied Financial Economics. Taylor and Francis Group. • Monthly. Institutions, $1,277.00 per year. Covers practical aspects of financial economics, banking, and monetary economics. Supplement to *Applied Economics.*

Bank Rate Monitor: The Weekly Financial Rate Reporter. Advertising News Service, Inc. • Weekly. $895.00 per year. Newsletter. Includes online addition and monthly supplement. Provides detailed information on interest rates currently paid by U. S. banks and savings institutions.

The Banker. • Monthly. $283.00 per year. Includes supplement. Published in England.

Banking Strategies. Bank Administration Institute. • Monthly. Free to qualified personnel; others, $64.50 per year. For senior bankers and financial services executives.

Central Banking: Policy, Markets, Supervision. Available from European Business Publications, Inc. • Quarterly. $260.00 per year, including annual *Central Banking Directory.* Published in England by Central Banking Publications. Reports and comments on the activities of central banks around the world. Also provides discussions of the International Monetary Fund (IMF), the Organization for Economic Cooperation and Development (OECD), the Bank for International Settlements (BIS), and the World Bank.

Financial Markets, Institutions, and Instruments. New York University, Salomon Center. Blackwell Publishing. • Five times a year. Institutions, $338.00 per year. Includes online edition. Edited to "bridge the gap between the academic and professional finance communities." Special fifth issue each year provides surveys of developments in four areas: money and banking, derivative securities, corporate finance, and fixed-income securities.

Guide to Banks and Thrifts: A Quarterly Compilation of Financial Institutions Ratings and Analysis. Weiss Ratings, Inc. • Quarterly. $438.00 per year. Emphasis is on rating of financial safety and relative risk. Includes annual summary.

Journal of Money, Credit and Banking. Ohio State University Press. • Quarterly. $210.00 per year, with online edition, $294.00 per year. Reports major findings in the study of financial markets, monetary and fiscal policy credit markets, money and banking, portfolio management and related subjects.

Jumbo Rate News. BauerFinancial, Inc. • Description: Reports on high-yielding, insured Jumbo CD (Certificate of Deposit) rates nationwide. Analyzes each institution by current credit-worthiness, and lists current assets and capital ratios. Provides phone numbers, contacts, methods of computation, and information on how interest is paid. Also contains financial news, insights, and commentary of interest to Jumbo CD investors. Recurring features include editorials and news of interest.

Loan Market Week: The Newsweekly of the Loan Syndication, Trading and Investment Markets. Institutional Investor, Inc., Journals Group. • Weekly. $2,370.00 per year. Newsletter. Includes print and online editions. Covers retail banking, commercial lending, foreign loans, bank technology, government regulations, and other topics related to banking. Formerly *Bank Letter.*

Martin Weiss' Safe Money Report. Weiss Ratings, Inc. • Monthly. $189.00 per year. Newsletter. Provides financial advice and current safety ratings of various banks, savings and loan companies, insurance companies, and securities dealers. Formerly (The Safe Money Report).

One Hundred Highest Yields. Advertising News Service, Inc. • Weekly. $124.00 per year. Newsletter. List CD's and money markets offered by federally insured banks. National coverage.

Recommended Bank and Thrift Report. BauerFinancial, Inc. • Quarterly. $585.00 per year. Newsletter provides information on "safe, financially sound" commercial banks, savings banks, and savings and loan institutions. Various factors are considered, including tangible capital ratios and total risk-based capital ratios. (Six regional editions are also available at $150.00 per edition per year.).

The RMA Journal. The Risk Management Association. • 10 times a year. Members, $40.00 per year; non-members, $95.00 per year. *The Journal of Lending and Credit Risk Management.*

Treasury Manager's Report: Strategic Information for the Financial Executive. PBI Media, LLC. • Biweekly. $630.00. Newsletter reporting on legal developments affecting the operations of banks, savings institutions, and other financial service organizations. Formerly *Financial Services Law Report.*

Troubled and Problematic Bank and Thrift Report. BauerFinancial, Inc. • Quarterly. $225.00 per year. Newsletter provides information on seriously undercapitalized ("Troubled") banks and savings institutions, as defined by a federal Prompt Corrective Action Rule. "Problematic" banks and thrifts are those meeting regulatory capital levels, but showing negative trends.

U. S. Banker. Thomson Media. • Monthly. $65.00

per year. Edited for bank executives and managers. Covers a wide variety of banking and financial topics.

RESEARCH CENTERS AND INSTITUTES

American Institute for Economic Research. P.O. Box 1000, Great Barrington, MA 01230. Phone: (413)528-1216 Fax: (413)528-0103 E-mail: info@aier.org • URL: http://www.aier.org.

National Opinion Research Center. National Opinion Research Center. 1155 E 60th St., Chicago, IL 60637. Phone: (773)256-6000 Fax: (773)753-7886 E-mail: norcinfo@norcmail.uchicago.edu • URL: http://www.norc.uchicago.edu • Sociology, social psychology, education, demography, child studies, and policy studies, including studies of political behavior, religious attitudes, economic behavior, career development, family behavior, and survey research methodology. Research group consists of the Center on Aging, Sloan Center on Families and Work, the Data and Research and Development Center, and the Population Research Center. Conducts the General Social Survey (GSS). Maintains a national sample frame that allows national representative samples for complex, multi-year surveys.

STATISTICS SOURCES

Assets and Liabilities of Commercial Banks in the United States. U. S. Federal Reserve System. • Weekly. $30.00 per year. (Federal Reserve Statistical Release, H.8.).

Bank Operating Statistics. Federal Deposit Insurance Corp. • Annual. Price on application. Based on Reports of Condition and Reports of Income.

Bank Profitability: Financial Statements of Banks. Organization for Economic Cooperation and Development. Available from OECD Publications and Information Center. • Annual. $85.00. Presents data for 10 years on bank profitability in OECD member countries.

Business Statistics of the United States. Linz Audain and Cornelia J. Strawser. Bernan Associates. • Annual. $147.00. Based on *Business Statistics,* formerly issue by the Bureau of Economic Analysis, U. S. Department of Commerce. Provides basic data for a wide variety of U. S. industries, services, and economic indicators. Most statistics are shown annually for 30 years and monthly for the most recent four years.

Economic Indicators. Council of Economic Advisors, Executive Office of the President. Available from U.S. Government Printing Office. • Monthly. $55.00 per year.

Federal Reserve Bulletin. U.S. Federal Reserve System. • Monthly. $25.00 per year. Provides statistics on banking and the economy, including interest rates, money supply, and the Federal Reserve Board indexes of industrial production.

Financial Market Trends. Organization for Economic Cooperation and Development. • Quarterly. $80.00 per year. Provides analysis of developments and trends in international and national capital markets. Includes charts and graphs on interest rates, exchange rates, stock market indexes, bank stock indexes, trading volumes, and loans outstanding. Data from OECD countries includes international direct investment, bank profitability, institutional investment, and privatization.

Information, Finance, and Services USA. Gale Cengage Learning. • 2001. $240.00. Replaces *Service Industries USA* and *Finance, Insurance, and Real Estate USA.* Presents statistics and projections relating to economic activity in a wide variety of non-manufacturing areas.

Ranking the Banks. American Banker. • Annual. Price on application. Ranks domestic and foreign banks by 75 financial parameters.

Standard & Poor's Industry Surveys. Standard &

Poor's. • Semiannual. $1,800.00. Two looseleaf volumes. Includes monthly *Supplements.* Provides detailed, individual surveys of 52 major industry groups. Each survey is revised on a semiannual basis. Also includes "Monthly Investment Review" (industry group investment analysis) and monthly "Trends & Projections" (economic analysis).

Statistical Information on the Financial Services Industry. American Bankers Association. • Annual. Members, $150.00; non-members, $275.00. Presents a wide variety of data relating to banking and financial services, including consumer economics, personal finance, credit, government loans, capital markets, and international banking.

Survey of Current Business. Available from U. S. Government Printing Office. • Monthly. $63.00 per year. Issued by Bureau of Economic Analysis, U. S. Department of Commerce. Presents a wide variety of business and economic data.

TRADE/PROFESSIONAL ASSOCIATIONS

American Bankers Association. 1120 Connecticut Ave. NW, Washington, DC 20036. Phone: 800-BAN-KERS or (202)663-5000 Fax: (202)663-7543 E-mail: custserv@aba.com • URL: http://www.aba.com • Members are principally commercial banks and trust companies; combined assets of members represent approximately 90% of the U.S. banking industry; approximately 94% of members are community banks with less than $500 million in assets. Seeks to enhance the role of commercial bankers as preeminent providers of financial services through communications, research, legal action, lobbying of federal legislative and regulatory bodies, and education and training programs. Serves as spokesperson for the banking industry; facilitates exchange of information among members. Maintains the American Institute of +Banking, an industry-sponsored adult education program. Conducts educational and training programs for bank employees and officers through a wide range of banking schools and national conferences. Maintains liaison with federal bank regulators; lobbies Congress on issues affecting commercial banks; testifies before congressional committees; represents members in U.S. postal rate proceedings. Serves as secretariat of the International Monetary Conference and the Financial Institutions Committee for the American National Standards Institute. Files briefs and lawsuits in major court cases affecting the industry. Conducts teleconferences with state banking associations on such issues as regulatory compliance; works to build consensus and coordinate activities of leading bank and financial service trade groups. Provides services to members including: public advocacy; news media contact; insurance program providing directors and officers with liability coverage, financial institution bond, and trust errors and omissions coverage; research service operated through ABA Center for Banking Information; fingerprint set processing in conjunction with the Federal Bureau of Investigation; discounts on operational and income-producing projects through the Corporation for American Banking. Conducts conferences, forums, and workshops covering subjects such as small business, consumer credit, agricultural and community banking, trust management, bank operations, and automation. Sponsors ABA Educational Foundation and the Personal +Economics Program, which educates schoolchildren and the community on banking, economics, and personal finance.

Bankers' Association for Finance and Trade. 1717 Pennsylvania Ave., N.W., Ste. 450, Washington, DC 20006. Phone: (202)452-0952 Fax: (202)452-0959 E-mail: baft@baft.org • URL: http://www.baft.org • Formerly Bankers' Association for Foreign Trade.

Bretton Woods Committee. 1726 M St. NW, Ste. 200, Washington, DC 20036. Phone: (202)331-1616 Fax: (202)785-9423 E-mail: info@brettonwoods.

org • URL: http://www.brettonwoods.org • Corporate CEOs, university administrators, former government officials, state governors, association and trade union executives, and bankers. Seeks to inform and educate the public regarding the activities of the World Bank, International Monetary Fund, and other Multinational Development Banks (MDB). Promotes U.S. participation in MDBs.

Consumer Bankers Association. 1000 Wilson Blvd., Ste. 2500, Arlington, VA 22209-3912. Phone: (703)276-1750 Fax: (703)528-1290 E-mail: membership@cbanet.org • URL: http://www.cbanet.org • Federally insured deposit-taking institutions. Sponsors Graduate School of Retail Bank Management at the university of Virginia.

Financial Services Round Table. 1001 Pennsylvania Ave. NW, Ste. 500 S, Washington, DC 20004. Phone: (202)289-4322 Fax: (202)628-2507 E-mail: info@fsround.org • URL: http://www.fsround.org • Companies registered with the Federal Reserve Board under the Bank Holding Company Act of 1956.

Independent Community Bankers of America. One Thomas Circle, N.W., Suite 400, Washington, DC 20005. Phone: 800-422-8439 or (202)659-8111 Fax: (202)659-9216 E-mail: info@icba.org • URL: http://www.icba.org • Formerly Independent Bankers Association of America.

Mortgage Bankers Association of America. 1919 Pennsylvania Ave., NW, Washington, DC 20006. Phone: (202)557-2700 E-mail: membership@mbaa.org • URL: http://www.mbaa.org.

World Bank Group. 1818 H St. NW, Washington, DC 20433. Phone: (202)473-1000 or (202)473-1000 Fax: (202)477-6391 E-mail: wbannualreport@worldbank.org • URL: http://www.worldbank.org • Comprises of the International Bank for Reconstruction and Development, the International Development Association, International Finance Corporation and the Multilateral Investment Guarantee Agency. Established by the United Nations to assist in raising the standards of living in developing countries by channeling financial resources from developed countries. Emphasis is placed on investments which foster active participation in the development process. Programs concentrate on rural and urban development, agriculture, and education. Activities include improving water and sewage facilities, building low-cost housing, and increasing the productivity of small industries. Assists organizations with identifying, designing, and executing development projects; offers financial aid to national development institutions. Encourages discussion on common development problems such as income distribution, rural poverty, unemployment, excessive population growth, and rapid urbanization. Conducts research programs on topics including economic planning and public utilities. Works in association with the United Nations Development Program and executes many UNDP projects.

OTHER SOURCES

BANKPAC. • Members of the banking community united to help elect to the U.S. Congress, without regard to party affiliation, those who have shown an interest, understanding, and a concern for banking business and a free economic system in which it can function properly. Acts as the political action committee of the American Bankers Association (see separate entry); makes contributions for campaign expenditures in political contests for seats in the House of Representatives and the Senate; does not make contributions in presidential contests or in contests for state and local offices.

BNA's Banking Report: Legal and Regulatory Developments in the Financial Services Industry. BNA, Inc. • Weekly. $1,221.00 per year. Two looseleaf volumes. Emphasis on federal regulations.

Federal Banking Law Reports. CCH, Inc. • Weekly. $1,533.00 per year. Looseleaf service.

Online Banking. MarketResearch.com. • 2000. $3,000.00. Market research report. Includes demographics relating to the users and nonusers of online banking services. Provides market forecasts.

BAR CODES

See: AUTOMATIC IDENTIFICATION SYSTEMS; POINT-OF-SALE SYSTEMS (POS)

BARBER AND BEAUTY SHOPS

See also: COSMETICS INDUSTRY

GENERAL WORKS

Cosmetology. Jack Rudman. National Learning Corp. • 2002. $49.95. (Occupational Competency Examination Series: OCE-13).

The Professional Cosmetologist. John Dalton. West Group. • 1992. $42.50. Fourth edition.

FINANCIAL RATIOS

Annual Statement Studies. The Risk Management Association. • Annual. Median and quartile financial ratios are given for over 400 kinds of manufacturing, wholesale, retail, construction, and consumer finance establishments. Data is sorted by both asset size and sales volume. Includes a clearly written "Definition of Ratios" and an alphabetical industry index.

Annual Statement Studies: Industry Default Probabilities and Cash Flow Measures. The Risk Management Association. • Annual. $145.00. Serves as a companion volume to the original *Annual Statement Studies.* Gives probability of default estimates on a percentage scale for more than 450 industries. Includes changes in position year-by-year for eight financial statement line items and provides percentage measures of cash flow.

Dealer Operating Analysis. Beauty and Barber Supply Institute. • Annual.

HANDBOOKS AND MANUALS

Beauty Supply Store. Entrepreneur Media, Inc. • Looseleaf. $59.50. A practical guide to starting a store for professional beauty supplies. Covers profit potential, start-up costs, market size evaluation, owner's time required, site selection, lease negotiation, pricing, accounting, advertising, promotion, etc. (Start-Up Business Guide No. E1277.).

Van Dean Manual. Delmar Learning. • 1990. $36.95. (Cosmetology Series).

ONLINE DATABASES

F & S Index. Gale Cengage Learning. • Contains about four million citations to worldwide business, financial, and industrial or consumer product literature appearing from 1972 to date. Weekly updates. Inquire as to online cost and availability.

PERIODICALS AND NEWSLETTERS

American Salon. National Hairdressers and Cosmetologists Association. Advanstar Communications. • Monthly. $26.50 per year. Supplement available *American Salon Distributor-Manufacturer News.*

Hairdressers' Journal International. Reed Business Information. • Weekly. $112.00 per year.

Modern Salon Magazine. Vance Publishing Corp. • Monthly. $20.00 per year.

STATISTICS SOURCES

United States Census of Service Industries. U.S. Bureau of the Census. • Quinquennial. Various reports available.

TRADE/PROFESSIONAL ASSOCIATIONS

Beauty and Barber Supply Institute. 15825 N 71st St., Ste. 100, Scottsdale, AZ 85254. Phone: 800-468-

2274 or (480)281-0424 Fax: (480)905-0708 E-mail: info@bbsi.org • URL: http://www.bbsi.org.

Hair International/Associated Masters Barbers and Beauticians of America. 2017 Church St., Lebanon, PA 17046-2733. Phone: (717)838-0795 Fax: (717)838-0796 E-mail: hairint@nbn.net.

National Cosmetology Association. 401 N Michigan Ave., 22nd Fl., Chicago, IL 60611. Phone: (866)871-0656 or (312)527-6765 Fax: (312)464-6118 E-mail: nca1@ncacares.com • URL: http://www.ncacares.org • Owners of cosmetology salons; cosmetologists. Sponsors: National Cosmetology Month; National Beauty Show. Provides special sections for estheticians, school owners, salon owners, and nail technicians. Maintains hall of fame. Conducts educational and charitable programs.

Textile Processors, Service Trades, Health Care, Professional and Technical Employees International Union. 2210 Midwest Rd., No. 310, Oak Brook, IL 60523. Phone: (630)574-0422.

OTHER SOURCES

Beauty Salons. Available from MarketResearch.com. • 1997. $995.00. Market research report published by Specialists in Business Information. Covers beauty salon revenues, as well as sales of supplies and equipment for beauty salons and barber shops.

BARLEY INDUSTRY

See: AGRICULTURE

BARRELS

See: COOPERAGE INDUSTRY

BARTER AND COUNTERTRADE

HANDBOOKS AND MANUALS

Personal and Business Bartering. James Stout. McGraw-Hill. • 1985. $14.95.

PERIODICALS AND NEWSLETTERS

Barter Update. Update Publicare Co. • Description: Presents examples of ways to use bartering. Updates information and ideas associated with bartering. Recurring features include news of research and ideas on barter.

BarterNews. BarterNews Publications. • Quarterly. $40.00 per year. How to barter information, contacts, and other unique trades.

Countertrade and Offset: Weekly Intelligence on Unconventional and Reciprocal International Trade. CTO Data Services. • 24 times a year. $688.00 per year. Newsletter. Intelligence on reciprocal international trade and unconventional trade finance. Covers developments and trends in the directory publishing industry, including publisher profiles, start-ups, corporate acquisitions, and business opportunities. Includes *Directory of Countertrade Services.* Formerly *Countertrade Outlook.*

Trade Channel. Trade Channel Europe. • Monthly. $88.00 per year. Features export "offers" and import "wants." Worldwide coverage. Technical products and consumer products. Each edition $88.00 per year. Formerly *Export Channel.*

TRADE/PROFESSIONAL ASSOCIATIONS

International Reciprocal Trade Association. 140 Metro Park, Rochester, NY 14623-2641. Phone: (585)424-2940 Fax: (585)424-2964 E-mail: ron@irta.com • URL: http://www.irta.com • Individuals, partnerships, corporations, and firms that engage in the commercial barter industry worldwide, including local trade exchanges which act as clearinghouses, and corporate trade companies which arrange domestic and international barter transactions. Works to foster and promote the interests of the commercial barter industry through the establishment of ethical standards and self-regulation; to represent members before government agencies in matters affecting the industry; to introduce firms engaged in bartering activities; to resolve disputes between members; influence public laws and regulations affecting the industry; disseminate information and conduct public relations programs. Serves as a clearinghouse for industry and public inquiries. Compiles statistics on the segment of commercial barter accounted for by organized trade exchanges and corporate trade companies. Conducts consumer protection, educational, and training programs. Operates Corporate Barter Council as a self-governing body for the corporate trade sector. Awards professional accreditation; operates referral and placement services; maintains speakers' bureau; supports charitable programs.

OTHER SOURCES

International Counterpurchase Contracts. United Nations Publications. • 1990. Trade agreements.

BATTERY INDUSTRY

ABSTRACTS AND INDEXES

Applied Science and Technology Index. H. W. Wilson Co. • 11 times a year. Quarterly and annual cumulations. Price varies. Indexes a wide variety of English language technical, industrial, and engineering periodicals.

Current Contents: Engineering, Computing and Technology. Thomson/ISI. • Weekly. $730.00 per year. Reproductions of contents pages of technical journals. Includes *Author Index, Address Directory, Current Book Contents* and *Title Word Index.* Formerly *Current Contents: Engineering, Technology and Applied Sciences.*

NTIS Alerts: Energy. National Technical Information Service. • Semimonthly. $245.00 per year. Provides descriptions of government-sponsored research reports and software, with ordering information. Covers electric power, batteries, fuels, geothermal energy, heating/cooling systems, nuclear technology, solar energy, energy policy, and related subjects. Formerly *Abstract Newsletter.*

DIRECTORIES

SLIG Buyers' Guide: Starting, Lighting, Ignition, Generating Systems. Independent Battery Manufacturers Association. • Biennial. $25.00 per year. Over 1,900 manufacturers and rebuilders of heavy-duty storage batteries.

Thomas Register of American Manufacturers. Thomas Publishing Co., Inc. • Annual. $149.00. 34 volumes. A three-part system offering information on a wide variety of industrial equipment and supplies. Lists more than 151,000 industrial product and services companies.

ENCYCLOPEDIAS AND DICTIONARIES

Encyclopedia of Energy. Cutler J. Cleveland, editor. Elsevier, Inc. • 2004. $1,560.00. Six volumes. Covers all aspects of energy sources and energy-related environmental issues.

Macmillan Encyclopedia of Energy. Available from Gale Cengage Learning. • 2001. $395.00. Three volumes. Published by Macmillan Reference USA. Covers the business, technology, and history of a wide variety of energy sources.

HANDBOOKS AND MANUALS

Handbook of Batteries. David Linden and Thomas Reddy. McGraw-Hill. • 2001. $125.00. Third edition. (Electronics Book Series).

Handbook of Fuel Cells: Fundamentals, Technology, and Applications. Wolf Vielstich, editor. John

Wiley and Sons, Inc. • 2003. $1,225.00. Four volumes. Volume one: *Fundamentals and Survey of Systems.* Volume two: *Fuel Cell Electrocatalysis.* Volumes three and four: *Fuel Cell Technology and Applications.*

ONLINE DATABASES

Applied Science and Technology Index Online. H. W. Wilson Co. • Provides online indexing of 500 major scientific, technical, industrial, and engineering periodicals. Time period is 1983 to date. Monthly updates. Inquire as to online cost and availability.

PROMT: Predicasts Overview of Markets and Technology. Gale Cengage Learning. • Companies, products, applied technologies and markets. U.S. and international literature coverage, 1972 to date. Inquire as to online cost and availability. Provides abstracts from more than 1,600 publications. Weekly updates.

Thomas Register Online. Thomas Publishing Co., Inc. • Provides concise information on approximately 194,000 U. S. companies, mainly manufacturers, with over 50,000 product classifications. Indexes over 115,000 trade names. Information is updated semiannually. Inquire as to online cost and availability.

PERIODICALS AND NEWSLETTERS

Advanced Battery Technology. Seven Mountains Scientific, Inc. • Monthly. $165.00 per year. Newsletter. Provides technical and marketing information for the international battery industry.

Aftermarket Business. Advanstar Communications. • Monthly. $48.00 per year. Automobile aftermarket, including batteries.

Battery and EV Technology News. Business Communications Co., Inc. • Monthly. $450.00 per year. Newsletter. Technical and economic studies of electric vehicles and battery technology.

The Battery Man: International Journal for Starting, Lighting, Ignition and Generating Systems. Independent Battery Manufacturers Association, Inc. • Monthly. $20.00 per year.

Chilton's Automotive Marketing: A Monthly Publication for the Retail Jobber and Distributor of Automotive Aftermarket. Reed Business Information. • Monthly. Free to qualified personnel; others, $48.00 per year. Includes marketing of automobile batteries. Formerly *Automotive Aftermarket News.*

Industrial Equipment News. Thomas Publishing Co., LLC. • Monthly. $65.00 per year. What's new in equipment, parts and materials.

New Equipment Digest. Penton Media, Inc. • Monthly. Free to qualified personnel; others, $60.00 per year. Formerly *Material Handling Engineering.*

New Equipment Reporter: New Products Industrial News. De Roche Publications. • Monthly. Controlled circulation.

RESEARCH CENTERS AND INSTITUTES

Electrochemical Analysis and Diagnostic Laboratory. Argonne National Laboratory, Chemical Technology Div., Bldg. 205, 9700 S. Cass Ave., Argonne, IL 60439. Phone: (630)252-4516 Fax: (630)252-4176 E-mail: bloom@cmt.anl.gov.

STATISTICS SOURCES

Annual Survey of Manufactures. Available from U. S. Government Printing Office. • Annual. Prices vary. Issued by the U. S. Census Bureau as an interim update to the *Census of Manufactures.* Includes data on number of manufacturing establishments in various industries, employment, labor costs, value of shipments, capital expenditures, inventories, energy costs, and assets. (See also

Census Bureau home page, http://www.census.gov/.).

TRADE/PROFESSIONAL ASSOCIATIONS

Automotive Aftermarket Industry Association. 7101 Wisconsin Ave., Ste. 1300, Bethesda, MD 20814-3415. Phone: (301)654-6664 Fax: (301)654-3299 E-mail: aaia@aftermarket.org • URL: http://www.aftermarket.org • Automotive parts and accessories retailers, distributors, manufacturers, and manufacturers' representatives. Conducts research and compiles statistics. Conducts seminars and provides specialized education program.

Battery Council International. 401 N Michigan Ave., 24th Fl., Chicago, IL 60611-4267. Phone: (312)644-6610 Fax: (312)527-6640 E-mail: info@batterycouncil.org • URL: http://www.batterycouncil.org • Manufacturers, suppliers of materials, and national distributors of lead-acid storage batteries. Recommends industry standards; compiles statistics.

Independent Battery Manufacturers Association. 401 N Michigan Ave., 24th Fl., Chicago, IL 60611. Phone: (312)245-1074 Fax: (312)527-6640 E-mail: info@thebatteryman.com • URL: http://www.thebatteryman.com • Domestic and foreign manufacturers of lead-acid storage batteries; associate members are suppliers of battery parts and battery manufacturing equipment. Purpose is to advance the manufacture of batteries and to promote and develop standards of quality.

OTHER SOURCES

Consumer Batteries. Available from MarketResearch.com. • 2002. $4,450.00. Published by Global Industry Analysts. Provides worldwide market research data, including profiles of major battery companies. Includes the market for cellular phone and laptop computer batteries.

Major Energy Companies of the World. Available from Gale Cengage Learning. • Annual. $880.00. Published by Graham & Whiteside. Contains detailed information on more than 3,300 important energy companies in various countries. Industries include electricity generation, coal, natural gas, nuclear energy, petroleum, fuel distribution, and equipment for energy production.

BAUXITE

See: MINES AND MINERAL RESOURCES

BAZAARS

See: FAIRS

BEAN INDUSTRY

See: AGRICULTURE; CANNED FOOD INDUSTRY

BEARINGS AND BALL BEARINGS

See also: ENGINES

ABSTRACTS AND INDEXES

Applied Science and Technology Index. H. W. Wilson Co. • 11 times a year. Quarterly and annual cumulations. Price varies. Indexes a wide variety of English language technical, industrial, and engineering periodicals.

DIRECTORIES

Dun's Industrial Guide: The Metalworking Directory. Dun and Bradstreet Corp. • Annual. Libraries, $485; commercial institutions, $795.00.

Lease basis. Three volumes. Lists about 65,000 U. S. manufacturing plants using metal and suppliers of metalworking equipment and materials. Includes names and titles of key personnel. Products, purchases, and processes are indicated.

HANDBOOKS AND MANUALS

International Bearing Interchange (IBI Guide). Interchange, Inc. • Biennial. $195.00. Two volumes. Cross-references for ball bearing, straight and curved roller bearings, tappered cones and cups, pillow blocks and flange units; from the latest back to 1918.

INTERNET DATABASES

Manufacturing Profiles. U. S. Bureau of the Census. Phone: (301)763-4636 E-mail: webmaster@census. gov • URL: http://www.census.gov/prod/www/abs/ mfg-prof.html • The Census Bureau makes available free on PDF (Portable Document Format) an annual consolidation of the entire Current Industrial Report series, presenting "all the data compiled." Contains statistics on production, shipments, inventories, consumption, exports, imports, and orders for a wide variety of manufactured products.

ONLINE DATABASES

Applied Science and Technology Index Online. H. W. Wilson Co. • Provides online indexing of 500 major scientific, technical, industrial, and engineering periodicals. Time period is 1983 to date. Monthly updates. Inquire as to online cost and availability.

METADEX. Cambridge Scientific Abstracts. • Covers the worldwide literature of metals, metallurgy, and materials science, 1966 to date. Includes detailed alloys indexing from 1974. Biweekly updating. Inquire as to online cost and availability. (Formerly produced by ASM International.).

STATISTICS SOURCES

Annual Survey of Manufactures. Available from U. S. Government Printing Office. • Annual. Prices vary. Issued by the U. S. Census Bureau as an interim update to the *Census of Manufactures.* Includes data on number of manufacturing establishments in various industries, employment, labor costs, value of shipments, capital expenditures, inventories, energy costs, and assets. (See also Census Bureau home page, http://www.census. gov/.).

Anti-Friction Bearings. U.S. Bureau of the Census. • Annual.

U. S. Industry and Trade Outlook. Available from National Technical Information Service. • Annual. $69.95. Produced by the International Trade Administration, U. S. Department of Commerce, in a "public-private" partnership with DRI/McGraw-Hill and Standard & Poor's. Provides basic data, outlook for the current year, and "Long-Term Prospects" (five-year projections) for a wide variety of products and services. Includes high technology industries. Formerly *U. S. Industrial Outlook.*

TRADE/PROFESSIONAL ASSOCIATIONS

American Bearing Manufacturers Association. 2025 M St. NW, Ste. 800, Washington, DC 20036-2422. Phone: (202)367-1155 Fax: (202)367-2155 E-mail: info@americanbearings.org • URL: http://www. abma-dc.org • Represents manufacturers of anti-friction bearings, balls, and rollers and major components used in anti-friction bearings. Promotes bearing standardization.

Bearing Specialists Association. 800 Roosevelt Rd., Bldg. C, Ste. 312, Bldg. C, Ste. 312, Glen Ellyn, IL 60137. Phone: (630)858-3838 Fax: (630)790-3095 E-mail: info@bsahome.org • URL: http://www. bsahome.org • Distributors of anti-friction bearings. Promotes networking and knowledge sharing and promotes the sale of bearings through authorized distributors.

BEAUTY INDUSTRY

See: BARBER AND BEAUTY SHOPS; COSMETICS INDUSTRY

BEAUTY SHOPS AND BARBER SHOPS

See: BARBER AND BEAUTY SHOPS

BEDDING INDUSTRY

See: FURNITURE INDUSTRY

BEE INDUSTRY

See: HONEY INDUSTRY

BEEF INDUSTRY

See: CATTLE INDUSTRY

BEER INDUSTRY

See: BREWING INDUSTRY

BEETS AND BEET SUGAR INDUSTRY

See: SUGAR INDUSTRY

BEHAVIORAL SCIENCES

See: HUMAN RELATIONS; INDUSTRIAL PSYCHOLOGY

BENEFITS, EMPLOYEE

See: EMPLOYEE BENEFIT PLANS

BEQUESTS

See: WILLS

BERYLLIUM INDUSTRY

See: METAL INDUSTRY

BETTER BUSINESS BUREAUS

See also: CONSUMER EDUCATION

DIRECTORIES

Directory of Better Business Bureaus. Council of Better Business Bureaus, Inc. • Annual. Free. Send stamped, self-addressed envelope. Lists about 185 Better Business Bureaus in the United States and Canada.

TRADE/PROFESSIONAL ASSOCIATIONS

BBB Wise Giving Alliance. 4200 Wilson Blvd., Ste. 800, Arlington, VA 22203-1838. Phone: (703)276-0100 Fax: (703)525-8277 E-mail: kbrannigan@ cottoninc.com • URL: http://www.give.org • Supported by companies and local Better Business Bureaus operated autonomously in the United States and Puerto Rico, which are in turn supported by

270,000 local business members. Seeks to promote and foster the highest ethical relationship between businesses and the public through voluntary self-regulation, consumer and business education, and service excellence. Provides support to local Better Business Bureaus. Administers the advertising industry's self-regulatory program that monitors and investigates the truth and accuracy of national advertising claims; monitors and pre-screens advertising directed towards children. Develops information on national charitable organizations and whether they meet voluntary ethical standards for soliciting organizations. Provides information to help consumers and businesses make informed purchasing decisions and avoid costly scams and frauds; and settles consumer complaints through arbitration and other means. Operates BBB AUTO LINE, a national mediation and arbitration service providing an independent forum to resolve consumer complaints involving 32 participating auto manufacturers; Local Better Business Bureaus respond to more than 23 million requests for service annually, fielding 20 million pre-purchase inquiries and 3 million complaints.

BEVERAGE INDUSTRY

See also: BREWING INDUSTRY; DISTILLING INDUSTRY; SOFT DRINK INDUSTRY

ABSTRACTS AND INDEXES

Food Science and Technology Abstracts. International Food Information Service Publishing. • Monthly. $1,780.00 per year. Provides worldwide coverage of the literature of food technology and food production. .

Foods Adlibra: Key to the World's Food Literature. General Mills, Inc. Foods Adlibra Publications. • Semimonthly. $240.00 per year. Provides journal citations and abstracts to the literature of food technology and packaging.

CD-ROM DATABASES

Food Science and Technology Abstracts [CD-ROM]. Available from SilverPlatter Information, Inc. • Quarterly. Produced by International Food Information Service (home page is http://www.ifis. org). Provides worldwide coverage on CD-ROM of the literature of food technology and production. Various types of publications are indexed, with abstracts, including about 1,800 periodicals. Time period is 1969 to date.

World Marketing Forecasts on CD-ROM. Gale Cengage Learning. • Annual. $2,500.00. Produced by Euromonitor. Provides detailed forecast data for the years to 2012 on CD-ROM for 54 countries in all parts of the world. Covers a wide range of social, demographic, economic, and market factors. Includes specific forecasts for many kinds of consumer products.

DIRECTORIES

Beverage Industry - Annual Manual. Stagnito Communications, Inc. • Annual. $55.00. Provides statistical information on multiple beverage markets. Includes an industry directory. Supplement to *Beverage Industry.*

Beverage Marketing Directory. Beverage Marketing Corp. • Covers: About 11,000 beer wholesalers, wine and spirits wholesalers, soft drink bottlers and franchisors, breweries, wineries, distilleries, alcoholic beverage importers, bottled water companies; and trade associations, government agencies, micro breweries, juice, coffee, tea, milk companies, and others concerned with the beverage and bottling industries; coverage includes Canada. Entries include: Beverage and bottling company listings contain company name, address, phone, names of key executives, number of employees, brand names, and other information, including number of franchisees, number of delivery trucks, sales volume. Suppliers and related companies and organizations listings include similar but less detailed information.

Food Chemicals News Directory. Food Chemical News. CRC Press LLC. • Semiannual. $497.00. Over 2,000 subsidiaries belonging to nearly 250 corporate parents plus an additional 3,000 independent processors. Formerly *Hereld's 1,500.*

Global Market Share Planner. Euromonitor International. • 2003. $5,900.00. Six volumes. Second edition. Provides detailed profiles and market share rankings of major consumer product companies in North America, Latin America, Europe, South Africa, and the Asia-Pacific region. Covers firms operating in key consumer markets: beverages, food products, household products, and personal care items. (Volumes are available individually.).

Major Food and Drink Companies of the World. Available from Gale Cengage Learning. • Annual. $880.00. Two volumes. Published by Graham & Whiteside. Contains profiles and trade names for more than 9,800 important food and beverage companies in various countries. In addition to foods, includes both alcoholic and nonalcoholic drink products.

Specialty Food Industry Directory. Phoenix Media Network, Inc. • Annual. Included in subscription to Food Distribution Magazine. Lists manufacturers and suppliers of specialty foods, and services and equipment for the specialty food industry. Featured food products include legumes, sauces, spices, upscale cheese, specialty beverages, snack foods, baked goods, ethnic foods, and specialty meats.

Thomas Food and Beverage Market Place. Grey House Publishing. • 2004. $495.00. Three volumes. Contains more than 40,000 entries covering food companies, beverages, food equipment, warehouse companies, food brokers, wholesalers, importers, and exporters. Formerly *Thomas Food Industry Register.*

World Drinks Marketing Directory. Euromonitor International. • Covers: 500 retailers and wholesalers, 1,000 manufacturers, over 2,000 international and European organizations, statistical agencies, market research companies, trade journals and associations, databases, and trade fairs in the beverage industry worldwide. Entries include: Company name, address, phone, telex, number of employees, parent company and subsidiary names, financial data, products and brand names handled; retailers and wholesalers include type of outlets, names and titles of key personnel.

World Leading Global Brand Owners. Euromonitor International. • 2003. $1,190.00. Second edition. Contains detailed profiles of multinational consumer product companies. Includes sales, market share, brand names, and financial information. (*Global Market Share Planner,* vol. 3.).

ENCYCLOPEDIAS AND DICTIONARIES

Oxford Encyclopedia of Food and Drink in America. Andrew F. Smith, editor. Oxford University Press. • 2004. $250.00. Two volumes. Emphasis is on historical and cultural aspects of food and beverages in the U. S.

Wiley Encyclopedia of Food Science and Technology. Frederick J. Francis, editor. John Wiley and Sons, Inc. • 2000. $1,650.00. Second edition. Four volumes. Contains about 400 entries. Coverage includes biotechnology, genetic engineering, nutrition, regulatory matters, food safety, labeling, food substitutes (sugar, fat, dairy), and many other topics.

FINANCIAL RATIOS

Industry Norms and Key Business Ratios. Desk Top Edition. Dun and Bradstreet Corp. • Annual. Five volumes. $475.00 per volume. $1,890.00 per set.

Covers over 800 kinds of businesses, arranged by Standard Industrial Classification number. More detailed editions covering longer periods of time are also available.

ONLINE DATABASES

Food Science and Technology Abstracts [online]. IFIS North American Desk. • Produced by International Food Information Service. Provides about 500,000 online citations, with abstracts, to the international literature of food science, technology, commodities, engineering, and processing. Approximately 2,000 periodicals are covered. Time period is 1969 to date, with monthly updates. Inquire as to online cost and availability.

FOODS ADLIBRA. General Mills, Inc. • Contains online citations, with abstracts, to the technical and business literature of food processing and packaging. New products and new ingredients are featured. Covers about 250 trade journals and 500 research journals from 1974 to date, with monthly updates. Inquire as to online cost and availability.

PERIODICALS AND NEWSLETTERS

Advertising Age: The International Newspaper of Marketing. Crain Communications, Inc. • Weekly. $178.50 per year. Includes supplement *Creativity.*

Beverage World: Magazine of the Beverage Industry. VNU Business Media. • Monthly. $79.00 per year.

Food Distribution Magazine. Phoenix Media Network, Inc. • Monthly. $49.00 per year. Edited for marketers and buyers of domestic and imported, specialty or gourmet food products, including ethnic foods, seasonings, and bakery items.

Soft Drink Letter. Whitaker Newsletters Inc. • Description: Covers news pertaining to the beverage industry with emphasis on soft drinks, mixers, and bottled water. Includes reports on new products and federal/state regulations, interviews with leading industry executives, marketing trends, and advertising and marketing research.

PRICE SOURCES

Beverage Industry News. BIN Publications. • Monthly. $49.00 per year. Incorporates *Beverage Industry News Merchandiser.*

Beverage Media. Beverage Network. Beverage Media, Ltd. • Monthly. $78.00 per year. Wholesale prices.

PPI Detailed Report. Bureau of Labor Statistics, U.S. Department of Labor. Available from U.S. Government Printing Office. • Monthly. $55.00 per year. Formerly *Producer Price Indexes.*

STATISTICS SOURCES

Consumer International. Available from Gale Cengage Learning. • Annual. $1,290.00. Published by Euromonitor. Contains extensive consumer market, economic, and demographic data for 25 major, non-European countries, including the U. S. and Canada. Includes consumer market size (volume and value) for 150 product types in 14 categories (food, clothing, automobiles, cosmetics, appliances, etc.).

European Marketing Forecasts. Available from Gale Cengage Learning. • Annual. $1,250.00. Published by Euromonitor. Contains demographic, economic, and market forecasts for the countries of Europe to the year 2010. Forecasts include market-size data for 15 consumer product sectors (food, clothing, automobiles, consumer electronics, etc.).

The Global Drinks Market Impact Databank. M. Shanken Communications, Inc. • Annual. $2,975.00. Detailed compilations of data for various segments of the liquor, beer, and soft drink industries.

International Marketing Forecasts. Available from Gale Cengage Learning. • Annual. $1,250.00. Published by Euromonitor. Contains demographic, economic, and market forecasts to the year 2013 for major, non-European countries, including the U. S.

and Canada. Forecasts include market-size data for 15 consumer product sectors, such as food, clothing, and automobiles.

Standard & Poor's Industry Surveys. Standard & Poor's. • Semiannual. $1,800.00. Two looseleaf volumes. Includes monthly *Supplements.* Provides detailed, individual surveys of 52 major industry groups. Each survey is revised on a semiannual basis. Also includes "Monthly Investment Review" (industry group investment analysis) and monthly "Trends & Projections" (economic analysis).

U. S. Industry and Trade Outlook. Available from National Technical Information Service. • Annual. $69.95. Produced by the International Trade Administration, U. S. Department of Commerce, in a "public-private" partnership with DRI/McGraw-Hill and Standard & Poor's. Provides basic data, outlook for the current year, and "Long-Term Prospects" (five-year projections) for a wide variety of products and services. Includes high technology industries. Formerly *U. S. Industrial Outlook.*

United States Census of Manufactures. U.S. Bureau of the Census. • Quinquennial. Results presented in reports, tape, CD-ROM, and Diskette files.

World Drinks Data and Statistics. Euromonitor International. • 2004. $650.00. Provides five-year data for both alcoholic and non-alcoholic beverages in 52 countries. Includes market size, consumer expenditures, price indicators, and retail distribution data for beer, wine, spirits, tea, coffee, soft drinks, fruit juices, bottled water, and other drinks.

TRADE/PROFESSIONAL ASSOCIATIONS

American Beverage Association. 1101 16th St. NW, Washington, DC 20036-4803. Phone: (202)463-6732 Fax: (202)659-5349 E-mail: info@ameribev.org • URL: http://www.ameribev.org • Active members are bottlers and distributors of soft drinks and franchise companies; associate members are suppliers of materials and services. Conducts government affairs activities on the national and state levels, discussion of industry problems, and general improvement of operating procedures. Conducts research on beverage laws.

International Beverage Packaging Association. Anheuser-Busch, Inc., One Ocean Spray Dr., Fort Collins, CO 80524. Phone: 888-662-3263 or (508)946-1000 Fax: (702)566-7166 E-mail: info@ibpa.org • URL: http://www.ibpa.org • Beverage industry personnel interested in the concerns of the beverage packaging industry, including soft drink, beer, bottled water, juice manufacturers and packagers, allied suppliers.

International Bottled Water Association. 1700 Diagonal Rd., Ste. 650, Alexandria, VA 22314. Phone: 800-WAT-ER11 or (703)683-5213 Fax: (703)683-4074 E-mail: ibwainfo@bottledwater.org • URL: http://www.bottledwater.org • Bottled water plants; distributors; manufacturers of bottled water supplies; international bottlers, distributors and suppliers. Conducts seminars and technical research.

OTHER SOURCES

Fruit Juices. Available from MarketResearch.com. • 2001. $4,500.00. Published by Euromonitor Publications Ltd. Provides consumer market data and forecasts to 2004 for the United States, the United Kingdom, Germany, France, and Italy. Includes fresh, frozen, bottled, and canned fruit and vegetable juices.

Market Share Tracker. Euromonitor International. • 2003. $1,190.00. Second edition. Contains market share rankings of more than 1,800 consumer product companies in 30 countries. Covers 16 kinds of products within "Drinks," "Household and Personal Care," and "Foods." Includes brand shares for leading brands. (*Global Market Share Planner,* vol. 1.).

BIBLIOGRAPHY

See also: BOOK CATALOGS; BUSINESS LITERATURE

GENERAL WORKS

Elements of Bibliography: A Guide to Information Sources and Practical Applications. Robert B. Harmon. Scarecrow Press, Inc. • 1998. $55.00. Third edition.

Elements of Bibliography: A Simplified Approach. Robert B. Harmon. Scarecrow Press, Inc. • 1989. $37.00. Revised edition.

New Introduction to Bibliography. Philip Gaskell. Oak Knoll Press. • 2000. $39.95.

ABSTRACTS AND INDEXES

Bibliographic Index: A Subject List of Bibliographies in English and Foreign Languages. H. W. Wilson Co. • Three times a year. Third issues cumulates all three issues. Price varies.

CD-ROM DATABASES

Books in Print On Disc: The Complete Books in Print System on Compact Laser Disc. Bowker Electronic Publishing. • Monthly. $550.00 per year. The CD-ROM version of *Books in Print, Forthcoming Books,* and other Bowker bibliographic publications: lists the books of over 50,000 U.S. publishers. Includes books recently declared out-of-print. Also available with full text book reviews.

LISA Plus. Available from Cambridge Scientific Abstracts (CSA). • Quarterly. $2,000.00 per year. CD-ROM version of Library Information and Science Abstracts, providing abstracting and indexing of the world's library and information science literature, 1969 to date. Contains more than 180,000 citations.

World Database of Business Information Sources on CD-ROM. Gale Cengage Learning. • Annual. Produced by Euromonitor. Presents Euromonitor's entire information source database on CD-ROM. Contains a worldwide total of about 35,000 publications, organizations, libraries, trade fairs, and online databases.

ENCYCLOPEDIAS AND DICTIONARIES

Dictionary of Bibliometrics. Virgil Diodato. Haworth Press, Inc. • 1994. $39.95. Contains detailed explanations of 225 terms, with references. (Bibliometrics is "the application of mathematical and statistical techniques to the study of publishing and professional communication.").

HANDBOOKS AND MANUALS

The Chicago Manual of Style: The Essential Guide for Authors, Editors, and Publishers. The University of Chicago Press. • 1993. $40.00. 14th edition.

Columbia Guide to Online Style. Janice R. Walker and Todd W. Taylor. Columbia University Press. • 1998. $40.50. Includes rules for bibliographic citation of online sources, formatting guidelines for online documents, and information on the electronic preparation of texts for print publication.

ONLINE DATABASES

Books in Print Online. Bowker Electronic Publishing. • The online version of *Books in Print, Forthcoming Books, Paperbound Books in Print,* and other Bowker bibliographic publications: lists the books of over 50,000 U. S. publishers. Includes books recently declared out-of-print. Updated monthly. Inquire as to online cost and availability.

LC MARC: Books. U. S. Library of Congress. • Contains online bibliographic records for over five million books cataloged by the Library of Congress since 1968. Updating is weekly or monthly. Inquire as to online cost and availability. (MARC is machine readable cataloging.).

LISA: Library and Information Science Abstracts.

Available from Cambridge Scientific Abstracts (CSA). • Provides abstracting and indexing of the world's library and information science literature, 1969 to date. Covers more than 440 periodicals from 68 countries. Updating is biweekly. Inquire as to online cost and availability.

PERIODICALS AND NEWSLETTERS

Bulletin of Bibliography. Greenwood Publishing Group, Inc. • Quarterly. $125.00 per year.

Research Strategies: A Journal of Library Concepts and Instruction. Elsevier. • Quarterly. Individuals, $76.00 per year; institutions, $152.00 per year. Edited for librarians involved in bibliographic or library instruction.

TRADE/PROFESSIONAL ASSOCIATIONS

Bibliographical Society of America. Lenox Hill Station, PO Box 1537, New York, NY 10021. Phone: (212)452-2710 Fax: (212)452-2710 E-mail: tavisgordon@mindspring.com • URL: http://www.bibsocamer.org.

Bibliographical Society of the University of Virginia. c/o Kathy Morgon, University of Virginia, Alderman Library, Charlottesville, VA 22903. Phone: (434)924-7013 or (434)924-7951 Fax: (434)924-1431 E-mail: bibsoc@virginia.edu • URL: http://www.etext.lib.virginia.edu/bsuva.

BICYCLE INDUSTRY

DIRECTORIES

Bicycle Dealer Showcase Buyers Guide. Skies America Publishing Co. • Annual. Free to qualified personnel.

Industry Directory. CMP Media LLC. • Covers: Approximately 1,800 manufacturers and distributors of bicycle products and related organizations and events; international coverage. Entries include: Company or organization name, address, phone, fax, E-mail, URL, toll-free number, name of contact, distributors list, lines distributed, and representatives.

PERIODICALS AND NEWSLETTERS

American Bicyclist. Willow Publishing Co. • Monthly. Free to qualified personnel; others, $35.00 per year. Trade journal edited for bicycle retailers and wholesalers. Includes product reviews.

Bicycling. Rodale. • 11 times a year. $14.94 per year. Information on buying and repairing bicycles.

Outspokin'. National Bicycle Dealers Association. • Description: Offers bicycle retailing and management tips, and provides consumer survey results. Recurring features include Association and industry news.

RESEARCH CENTERS AND INSTITUTES

Human Power, Biochemechanics, and Robotics Laboratory. Cornell University, Dept. of Theoretical and Applied Mechanics, 306 Kimball Hall, Ithaca, NY 14853-1503. Phone: (607)255-7108 Fax: (607)255-2011 E-mail: ruina@cornell.edu • URL: http://www.tam.cornell.edu/~ruina • Conducts research relating to human muscle-powered machines, such as bicycles and rowers.

STATISTICS SOURCES

U. S. Industry and Trade Outlook. Available from National Technical Information Service. • Annual. $69.95. Produced by the International Trade Administration, U. S. Department of Commerce, in a "public-private" partnership with DRI/McGraw-Hill and Standard & Poor's. Provides basic data, outlook for the current year, and "Long-Term Prospects" (five-year projections) for a wide variety of products and services. Includes high technology industries. Formerly *U. S. Industrial Outlook.*

United States Census of Manufactures. U.S. Bureau of the Census. • Quinquennial. Results presented in

reports, tape, CD-ROM, and Diskette files.

TRADE/PROFESSIONAL ASSOCIATIONS

Bicycle Product Suppliers Association. PO Box 187, Montgomeryville, PA 18936. Phone: (215)393-3144 Fax: (215)893-4872 E-mail: bpsa@bpsa.org • URL: http://www.bpsa.org • Wholesalers of bicycles, bicycle parts, and accessories; vendor members are manufacturers and suppliers. Affiliate members supply services and products to bicycle retailers. Offers educational programs; compiles statistics and safety information.

National Bicycle Dealers Association. 777 W 19th St., Ste. O, Costa Mesa, CA 92627. Phone: (949)722-6909 Fax: (949)722-1747 E-mail: info@nbda.com • URL: http://www.nbda.com • Represents independent retail dealers who sell and service bicycles. Sponsors workshops and provides programs.

OTHER SOURCES

Bicycles. Available from MarketResearch.com. • 2002. $3,950.00 Published by Global Industry Analysts. ProvidesU.S. and international market data for bicycles and bicycle parts. Gives profiles of major manufacturers.

BILLBOARDS

See: OUTDOOR ADVERTISING

BINDING OF BOOKS

See: BOOKBINDING

BIOENGINEERING

See: BIOTECHNOLOGY

BIOGRAPHY

ABSTRACTS AND INDEXES

Abridged Biography and Genealogy Master Index. Gale Cengage Learning. • 1994. $475.00. Second edition. Three volumes. Indexes 266 widely held biographical reference sources, with approximately 2.2 million citations. Based on the larger *Biography and Genealogy Master Index.*

Author Biographies Master Index. Gale Cengage Learning. • 1997. $299.00. Fifth edition. Two volumes. Contains over 1,140,000 references to biographies of 550,000 different authors.

Bio-Base: A Master Index on Microfiche to Biographical Sketches Found in Current and Retrospective Biographical Dictionaries. Gale Cengage Learning. • $1,095.00; update, $295.00. Indexes more than 12.7 million biographical sketches.

Biography and Genealogy Master Index. Gale Cengage Learning. • Annual. $1,095.00. Four volumes. $295.00 per volume. Previous editions available.

Biography Index. H. W. Wilson Co. • Quarterly. $280.00 per year. Annual and biennial cumulations.

Index to Marquis Who's Who Publications. Marquis Who's Who. • Annual. $115.00. A combined index to current editions of most Marquis Who's Who publications. Contains over 320,000 entries.

BIOGRAPHICAL SOURCES

Almanac of Famous People. Gale Cengage Learning. • 2000. $145.00. Two volumes. Seventh edition. Contains about 30,000 short biographies, with bibliographic citations. Chronological, geographic, and occupational indexes. Formerly *Biography Almanac.*

American Business Leaders: From Colonial Times

to the Present. Neil A. Hamilton. ABC-CLIO, Inc. • 1999. $175.00. Two volumes. Contains biographies of 413 notable business figures. Historical coverage is from the 17th century to the 1990s.

American Men and Women of Science A Biographical Directory of Today's Leaders in Physical, Biological and Related Sciences. Gale. • 2002. $950.00. 21st edition. Eight volumes. Over 119,600 United States and Canadian scientists active in the physical, biological, mathematical, computer science and engineering fields.

American National Biography. John A. Garraty and Mark C. Carnes, editors. Oxford University Press. • 1999. $795.00. 24 volumes. Contains about 17,500 entries, including business leaders who were important to the American economy. Includes an index by occupation. *Supplement* available, 2002, $150.00.

Canadian Who's Who. University of Toronto Press. • Annual. $185.00. Provides concise biographical information in English and French on 15,000 prominent Canadians.

Celebrity Register. Gale Cengage Learning. • 1990. $115.00. 90th edition. Compiled by Celebrity Services International (Earl Blackwell). Contains profiles of 1,300 famous individuals in the performing arts, sports, politics, business, and other fields.

Current Biography. H. W. Wilson Co. • 11 times a year. $130.00 per year. Includes profiles of business people and economists who have been prominent in the news.

Current Biography Yearbook. H. W. Wilson Co. • Annual. $115.00. The yearly cumulation of *Current Biography.*

Directory of American Scholars. Gale Cengage Learning. • 2001. $595.00. 10th edition. Six volumes. Volumes one to volume five, $145.00; volume six, $50.00. Provides biographical information and publication history for more than 24,000 scholars in the humanities.

Directory of Directors (Canada). Financial Post Datagroup. • Annual. $175.00. Provides brief biographical information on 16,000 directors and key officers of Canadian companies who are also Canadian residents.

Encyclopedia of World Biography. Gale Cengage Learning. • 1998. $1,095.00. Second edition. 17 volumes. Provides biographies of about 7,000 "internationally renowned" individuals from all eras and subject fields. Includes illustrations, bibliographies, and index. *Supplement* available, $125.00.

International Who's Who. Available from Taylor & Francis Group. • Annual. $440.00. Includes print and online editions. Published by Europa Publications (http://www.europapublications.com). Contains brief biographical information on important people in many different countries.

International Who's Who of Women. Available from Taylor and Francis, Inc. • 2002. $395.00. Published by Europa. Contains biographical profiles of more than 5,000 eminent women from all countries.

International Who's Who, 2002. Taylor & Francis. • 2001. $395.00. Includes CD-ROM. Provides up-to-date biographical information on important individuals in international affairs, government, diplomacy, the liberal professions, and all branches of the arts and sports. Published by Europa.

Leaders of American Business and Industry. Gale Cengage Learning. • 2002. $145.00. Three volumes. Provides popularly written biographies of influential American entrepreneurs and business leaders, past and present. Includes detailed profiles of major companies. (UXL imprint).

Net.people: The Personalities and Passions Behind the Web Sites. Thomas E. Bleier and Eric C. Steinert. Information Today, Inc. • 2000. $19.95. Presents the personal stories of 36 Web "entrepreneurs and visionaries." (CyberAge Books.).

Newsmakers. Gale Cengage Learning. • Annual. $155.00. Three softbound issues and one hardbound annual. Biographical information on individuals currently in the news. Includes photographs. Formerly *Contemporary Newsmakers.*

Who Knows Who: Networking Through Corporate Boards. Jeannette E. Glynn. Who Knows Who Publishing. • 1998. $165.00. Fifth edition. Shows the connections between the board members of major U. S. corporations and major foundations and nonprofit organizations.

Who's Who Among African Americans. Gale Cengage Learning. • 2002. $195.00. 15th edition. Includes many business leaders.

Who's Who: An Annual Biographical Dictionary. Saint Martin's Press. • Annual. $275.00. Over 29,000 prominent individuals worldwide, but with emphasis on the United Kingdom.

Who's Who in America. Marquis Who's Who. • Annual. $575.00. Three volumes. Contains over 90,000 concise biographies, with a Geographic/Professional Index.

Who's Who in Canadian Business. University of Toronto Press. • Annual. $179.95. Contains brief biographies of 5,200 individuals prominent in Canadian business.

Who's Who in Finance and Industry. Marquis Who's Who. • Biennial. $259.95. Provides over 21,000 concise biographies of business leaders in all fields.

Who's Who in Science and Engineering. Marquis Who's Who. • Biennial. $269.00. Provides concise biographical information on 35,000 prominent engineers and scientists. International coverage, with geographical and professional indexes.

Who's Who in the World. Marquis Who's Who. • Annual. $329.95. Provides biographical profiles of about 35,000 prominent individuals. International coverage.

Who's Who of American Women. Marquis Who's Who. • Biennial. $275.00. Provides over 25,000 biographical profiles of important women, including individuals prominent in business, finance, and industry.

CD-ROM DATABASES

Complete Marquis Who's Who. Marquis Who's Who, Reed Reference Publishing. • Frequency and price on application. Contains CD-ROM biographical profiles of over 800,000 notable individuals. Includes *Who's Who in America, Who Was Who in America,* and 14 regional and professonal directories.

Current Biography on WILSONDISC. H. W. Wilson Co. • Annual. Provides *Current Biography* on CD-ROM.

OECD Statistical Compendium. Organization for Economic Cooperation and Development. • Semiannual. $1,905.00 per year for 1 to 10 users. CD-ROM contains more than 730,000 monthly, quarterly, and annual time series for OECD countries, 1960 to date. Includes fully searchable data on agriculture, food, economic indicators, national accounts, employment, energy, finance, industry, technology, and foreign trade. Results can be displayed in various forms.

WILSONDISC: Biography Index. H. W. Wilson Co. • Quarterly. Includes unlimited online access to *Biography Index* through WILSONLINE. Provides CD-ROM indexing of biographical information appearing in books, critical studies, fiction, periodicals, obituaries, and other printed sources. Time period is 1984 to date. Corresponds to the printed and online *Biography Index.*

DIRECTORIES

Cyberhound's Guide to People on the Internet. Gale Cengage Learning. • 1996. $79.00. Second edition. Provides descriptions of about 5,500 Internet databases maintained by or for prominent individuals in business, the professions, entertainment, and sports. Indexed by name, subject, and keyword (master index). (Cyberhound's Series).

ENCYCLOPEDIAS AND DICTIONARIES

Dictionary of International Biography. Taylor & Francis Group. • 2001. $245.00. 29th edition. Published in England by Melrose.

Knowledge Exchange Business Encyclopedia: Your Complete Business Advisor. Lorraine Spurge. Knowledge Exchange LLC. • 1998. $45.00. Provides definitions of business terms and financial expressions, profiles of leading industries, tables of economic statistics, biographies of business leaders, and other business information. Includes "A Chronology of Business from 3000 B.C. Through 1995." Contains illustrations and three indexes.

INTERNET DATABASES

Business 2.0 Web Guide to the Best Business Links. Business 2.0 Media Inc. Phone: (415)293-4800 E-mail: support@business2.com • URL: http://www.business2.com/webguide • Web site presents an extensive, searchable directory of links to "the best, most informative, and authoritative web pages." Twenty main categories cover business, finance, career, company information, people, and technology topics, with thousands of subtopics, all linking to Web sites recommended by experienced business researchers. Fees: Free.

ONLINE DATABASES

Biography Index Online. H. W. Wilson Co. • An index to biographies appearing in periodicals, newspapers, current books, and other sources. Covers 1984 to date. Inquire as to online cost and availability.

Biography Master Index [Online]. Gale Cengage Learning. • An index to biographies appearing in biographical reference volumes, both historical and current. Inquire as to online cost and availability.

Complete Marquis Who's Who. Marquis Who's Who. • Contains information on over 825,000 prominent individuals, present and past. Semiannual updates. Inquire as to online cost and availability.

Gale Biographies. Gale Cengage Learning. • Provides online biographical profiles (text) of more than 140,000 prominent individuals, past and present, from all fields of activity. Corresponds to various Gale print sources. Quarterly updates. Inquire as to online cost and availability.

The New York Times Biographical File. New York Times Online Services. • Makes available online the full text of more than 15,000 biographies that have appeared in *The New York Times* from 1980 to the present. Updating is weekly. Inquire as to online cost and availability.

Standard & Poor's Register: Biographical. Standard & Poor's Corp. • Contains brief biographies of approximately 70,000 business executives and directors. Corresponds to the biographical volume of *Standard & Poor's Register of Corporations, Directors, and Executives.* Updated twice a year. Inquire as to online cost and availability.

PERIODICALS AND NEWSLETTERS

Biography: An Interdisciplinary Quarterly. Biographical Research Center. University of Hawaii Press, Journals Dept. • Quarterly. Individuals, $30.00 per year; institutions, $50.00 per year.

The New York Times Biographical Service. UMI. •

Monthly. Price on application. Looseleaf service.

TRADE/PROFESSIONAL ASSOCIATIONS

New York Genealogical and Biographical Society. 122 E. 58th St., New York, NY 10022-1939. Phone: (212)755-8532 Fax: (212)754-4218 E-mail: nygbs@nygbs.org • URL: http://www.nygbs.org.

BIOTECHNOLOGY

See also: GENETIC ENGINEERING

GENERAL WORKS

Agricultural Biotechnology: An Economic Perspective. Margriet F. Caswell and others. Nova Science Publishers, Inc. • 2003. $30.00. Considers such factors as consumer demand, producer demand, public policies, regulation, food safety, and research funding.

Biotechnology. John E. Smith. Cambridge University Press. • 1996. $59.95. Third edition. Provides discussions of biotechnology in relation to medicine, agriculture, food, the environment, biological fuel generation, genetics, ethics, safety, etc. Includes a glossary and bibliography. (Studies in Biology Series).

Introduction to Biotechnology. William Thieman and Michael A. Palladino. Benjamin Cummings Publishing Co. • 2003. $70.00.

ABSTRACTS AND INDEXES

Agricultural and Environmental Biotechnology Abstracts. CSA. • Online edition, $390.00 per year. Formerly *Biotechnology Research Abstracts.*

Applied Science and Technology Index. H. W. Wilson Co. • 11 times a year. Quarterly and annual cumulations. Price varies. Indexes a wide variety of English language technical, industrial, and engineering periodicals.

BioCommerce Abstracts. Available from Pharmabooks Ltd. • Semimonthly. $996.00 per year. Quarterly cumulation. Includes CD-Rom. Emphasis is on commercial biotechnology.

Current Biotechnology Abstracts. DECHEMA. • Monthly. $1,229.00 per year. Reports on the latest scientific, technical and commercial advances in the field of technology.

Current Contents: Engineering, Computing and Technology. Thomson/ISI. • Weekly. $730.00 per year. Reproductions of contents pages of technical journals. Includes *Author Index, Address Directory, Current Book Contents* and *Title Word Index.* Formerly *Current Contents: Engineering, Technology and Applied Sciences.*

Excerpta Medica: Biophysics, Bioengineering, and Medical Instrumentation. Elsevier. • 16 times a year. Institutions, $2,859 per year. Section 27 of *Excerpta Medica.*

Index Medicus. National Library of Medicine. Available from U. S. Government Printing Office. • Monthly. $620.00 per year. Bibliographic listing of references to current articles from approximately 3,000 of the world's biomedical journals.

NTIS Alerts: Biomedical Technology & Human Factors Engineering. National Technical Information Service. • Semimonthly. $210.00 per year. Provides descriptions of government-sponsored research reports and software, with ordering information. Covers biotechnology, ergonomics, bionics, artificial intelligence, prosthetics, and related subjects. Formerly *Abstract Newsletter.*

Science Citation Index. Thomson/ISI. • Bimonthly. $15,020.00 per year. Annual cumulation. Includes *Source Index, Citation Index, Permuterm Subject Index,* and *Corporate Index.*

ALMANACS AND YEARBOOKS

Annual Review of Biophysics and Biomolecular Structure. Annual Reviews. • Annual. Individuals, $80.00. Includes print and online editions. Institutions, $180.00; with online edition, $216.00.

BIBLIOGRAPHIES

Reference Reviews. Available from Information Today, Inc. • Eight times a year. Price on application. Published in London by Aslib: The Association for Information Management. Incorporates*Aslib Book Guide.*

BIOGRAPHICAL SOURCES

Dictionary of American Medical Biography. Joseph Carvalho and others. Greenwood Publishing Group Inc. • 1984. $210.00. Two volumes. Vol. one, $110.00; vol. two, $110.00.

Who's Who in Science and Engineering. Marquis Who's Who. • Biennial. $269.00. Provides concise biographical information on 35,000 prominent engineers and scientists. International coverage, with geographical and professional indexes.

CD-ROM DATABASES

Biotechnology Abstracts on CD-ROM. Thomson Derwent, Inc. • Quarterly. Price on application. Provides CD-ROM indexing and abstracting of the world's biotechnology journal literature since 1982, including genetic engineering topics.

Science Citation Index: Compact Disc Edition. Institute for Scientific Information. • Monthly. Provides CD-ROM indexing of the world's scientific and technical literature. Corresponds to online *Scisearch* and printed *Science Citation Index.*

WILSONDISC: Biological and Agricultural Index. H. W. Wilson Co. • Monthly. Includes unlimited online access to *Biological and Agricultural Index* through WILSONLINE. Provides CD-ROM indexing of over 250 periodicals covering agriculture, agricultural chemicals, biochemistry, biotechnology, entomology, horticulture, and related topics.

DIRECTORIES

BioScan: The Worldwide Biotech Industry Reporting Service. Greenwood Publishing Group, Inc. • Annual. $975.00 per year. Bimonthly updates. Provides detailed information on over 1,000 U.S. and foreign companies broadly classified as biotechnological. In addition to medical technology and advanced pharmaceutical firms, includes firms doing research in food processing, waste management, agriculture, and veterinary science.

Biotechnology Directory. Nature Publishing Group. • Covers: more than 11,000 companies, universities, research centers, and government agencies, and suppliers of products and services to the field. Entries include: Organization name, address, phone, telex, fax, contact; description of products, services, or research.

Genetic Engineering and Biotechnology Firms Worldwide Directory. Mega-Type Publishing. • Annual. $299.00. About 6,000 firms, including major firms with biotechnology divisions as well as small independent firms.

International Instrumentation and Controls Buyers Guide. Keller International Publishing, LLC. • Annual. Included in subscription to *International Instrumentation and Controls.* Lists over 310 suppliers of precision instrument products and services.

Medical and Health Information Directory. Gale Cengage Learning. • 2002. $675.00. Three volumes. 14th edition. Three volumes. $285.00 per volume. Vol. one covers medical organizations, agencies, and institutions; vol. two includes bibliographic, library, and database information; vol. three is a guide to services available for various medical and health problems.

Medical Research Centres: A World Directory of Organizations and Programmes. FT Healthcare. • Biennial. $470.00. Two volumes. Contains profiles of more than 7,000 medical research facilities around the world. Includes medical, dental, nursing, pharmaceutical, psychiatric, and surgical research centers.

Plunkett's Biotech and Genetics Industry Almanac. Plunkett Research, Ltd. • Annual. $249.99. Provides detailed profiles of 400 leading biotech corporations. Includes information on current trends and research in the field of biotechnology/genetics.

ENCYCLOPEDIAS AND DICTIONARIES

Biotechnology from A to Z. William Bains. Oxford University Press. • 2004. $47.50. Third edition. Covers the terminology of biotechnology for non-specialists.

Wiley Encyclopedia of Food Science and Technology. Frederick J. Francis, editor. John Wiley and Sons, Inc. • 2000. $1,650.00. Second edition. Four volumes. Contains about 400 entries. Coverage includes biotechnology, genetic engineering, nutrition, regulatory matters, food safety, labeling, food substitutes (sugar, fat, dairy), and many other topics.

INTERNET DATABASES

National Library of Medicine (NLM). National Institutes of Health (NIH). Phone: 888-346-3656 or (301)496-1131 Fax: (301)480-3537 E-mail: access@nlm.nih.gov • URL: http://www.nlm.nih.gov • NLM Web site offers free access through MEDLINE ("PubMed") to about nine million references to articles appearing in some 4,000 biomedical journals, with abstracts. Search interfaces range from "simple keywords to advanced Boolean expressions." The NLM site offers many links to other sources of biomedical and technical information (the National Center for Biotechnology Information, for example). Fees: Free.

ONLINE DATABASES

Applied Science and Technology Index Online. H. W. Wilson Co. • Provides online indexing of 500 major scientific, technical, industrial, and engineering periodicals. Time period is 1983 to date. Monthly updates. Inquire as to online cost and availability.

CSA Life Sciences Collection. Cambridge Scientific Abstracts. • Includes online versions of *Biotechnology Research Abstracts, Entomology Abstracts, Genetics Abstracts,* and about 20 other abstract collections. Time period is 1978 to date, with monthly updates. Inquire as to online cost and availability.

Derwent Biotechnology Abstracts. Derwent, Inc. • Provides indexing and abstracting of the world's biotechnology journal literature since 1982, including genetic engineering topics. Monthly updates. Inquire as to online cost and availability.

F-D-C Reports. FDC Reports, Inc. • An online version of "The Gray Sheet" (medical devices), "The Pink Sheet" (pharmaceuticals), "The Rose Sheet" (cosmetics), "The Blue Sheet" (biomedical), and "The Tan Sheet" (nonprescription). Contains full-text information on legal, technical, corporate, financial, and marketing developments from 1987 to date, with weekly updates. Inquire as to online cost and availability.

Globalbase. Gale Cengage Learning. • Provides more than one million online summaries of business, industrial, and economic news reports from more than 1,000 publications worldwide. Covers a wide range of material appearing in international trade journals, professional magazines, and newspapers. Time period is 1984 to date, with weekly updates. Inquire as to online cost and availability.

PROMT: Predicasts Overview of Markets and Technology. Gale Cengage Learning. • Companies, products, applied technologies and markets. U.S. and international literature coverage, 1972 to date. Inquire as to online cost and availability. Provides abstracts from more than 1,600 publications. Weekly updates.

Scisearch. Institute for Scientific Information. • Broad, multidisciplinary index to the literature of science and technology, 1974 to present. Inquire as to online cost and availability. Coverage of literature is worldwide, with weekly updates.

PERIODICALS AND NEWSLETTERS

Applied Genetics News. BCC Research. • Description: Concerned primarily with the application of genetic research to industry and technology. Evaluates ongoing research in the areas of aging, cancer, disease, and cell differentiation. Discusses research funding and finances. Analyzes new developments in venture capital and stock price movement.

Biomedical Products. Reed Business Information. • Monthly. $55.90 per year. Features new products and services. Formerly *Biomedical Products.*

Bioscience. American Institute of Biological Sciences. • Monthly. $267.00 per year. Includes print and online editions.

BioTechniques: The Journal of Laboratory Technology for Bioresearch. Eaton Publishing Co. • 12 times a year. $110.00 per year.

BioWorld Today: The Daily Biotechnology Newspaper. American Health Consultants, Inc., Bio-World Publishing Group. • Daily. $1,897.00 per year; with online edition, $1,927.00 per year. Covers news of the biotechnology and genetic engineering industries, with emphasis on finance, investments, and marketing.

BioWorld Week: The Weekly Biotechnology Report. American Health Consultants, Inc., BioWorld Publishing Group. • Weekly. $789.00 per year. Newsletter. Provides a weekly summary of business and financial news relating to the biotechnology and genetic engineering industries.

Genetic Engineering News: The Information Source of the Biotechnology Industry. Mary Ann Liebert, Inc. • 21 times a year. Institutions, $666.00 per year. Newsletter. Business and financial coverage.

Genetic Technology News. Technical Insights/John Wiley & Sons Inc. • Description: Informs corporate development and research managers of advances in genetic engineering with applications in medical, agricultural, chemical, food, and other businesses. Covers areas such as recombinant DNA, monoclonal antibodies, and interferon. Recurring features include news of research, company reports, a calendar of events, and supplements titled Market Forecasts, Patent Update, and Strategic Partners. **Remarks:** Also available as part of Biotechnology Information Package, which includes Industrial Bioprocessing (see separate listings).

Health News Daily. F-D-C Reports Inc. • Description: Tracks developments in health care policy, legislation and regulation, insurance, pharmaceuticals, delivery, manufacturing, technology and treatment, funding, and research.

Health Policy and Biomedical Research: The Blue Sheet. F-D-C Reports, Inc. • 51 times a year. $716.00 per year. Newsletter. Emphasis is on news of medical research agencies and institutions, especially the National Institutes of Health (NIH).

IEEE Engineering in Medicine and Biology Magazine. Institute of Electrical and Electronics Engineers, Inc. • Six times a year, $250.00 per year. Published for biomedical engineers.

Journal of Biotechnology. Elsevier. • Semimonthly. Institutions, $3,338.00 per year. Text and summaries in English.

Journal of Chemical Technology and Biotechnology. John Wiley and Sons, Inc., Journals. • Monthly. Individuals, $1,120.00 per year; institutions, $1,495.00 per year.

Journal of Crop Improvement. Haworth Press, Inc. • Semiannual. $300.00 per year to libraries; $80.00 per year to individuals. Topics include plant biotechnology, plant genetics, crop productivity, quality,

safety, pest control, and environmental concerns. Formerly *Journal of Crop Production.*

McGraw-Hill's Biotechnology Newswatch. McGraw-Hill. • Semimonthly. Price on application. Newsletter.

The Pink Sheet: Prescription Pharmaceuticals and Biotechnology. F-D-C Reports, Inc. • 51 times a year. Institutions, $1,431.00 per year. Newsletter covering business and regulatory developments affecting the pharmaceutical and biotechnology industries. Provides information on generic drug approvals and includes a drug sector stock index.

RESEARCH CENTERS AND INSTITUTES

Biotechnology Process Engineering Center. Massachusetts Institute of Technology, 77 Massachusetts Ave., Bldg. 16, Rm. 429, Cambridge, MA 02139-4480. Phone: (617)253-0805 Fax: (617)253-2400 E-mail: lauffen@mit.edu • URL: http://www.web.mit.edu/bpec/ • Includes an Industrial Advisory Board and a Biotechnology Industrial Consortium.

Laboratory of Electronics. Rockefeller University, 1230 York Ave., New York, NY 10021. Phone: (212)327-8613 Fax: (212)327-7613 E-mail: ros@rockvax.rockefeller.edu • Studies the application of computer engineering and electronics to biomedicine.

Laser Biomedical Research Center. Massachusetts Institute of Technology, 77 Massachusetts Ave., Cambridge, MA 02139. Phone: (617)253-7700 Fax: (617)253-4513 E-mail: msfeld@mit.edu • Concerned with the medical use of lasers.

Mayo Biomedical Imaging Resource. Mayo Clinic, 200 First St., S. W., Rochester, MN 55902. Phone: (507)284-4937 Fax: (507)284-1632 E-mail: rar@mayo.edu • URL: http://www.mayo.edu/bir • Develops three-dimensional medical imaging systems and software.

Molecular Biology Institute. University of California, Los Angeles, P.O. Box 951570, Los Angeles, CA 90095-1570. Phone: (310)825-1018 Fax: (310)206-7286 E-mail: clarke@mbi.ucla.edu • URL: http://www.mbi.ucla.edu.

Salk Institute for Biological Studies. P.O. Box 85800, San Diego, CA 92186-5800. Phone: (858)453-4100 Fax: (858)552-8285 E-mail: murphy@salk.edu • URL: http://www.salk.edu.

STATISTICS SOURCES

Standard & Poor's Industry Surveys. Standard & Poor's. • Semiannual. $1,800.00. Two looseleaf volumes. Includes monthly *Supplements.* Provides detailed, individual surveys of 52 major industry groups. Each survey is revised on a semiannual basis. Also includes "Monthly Investment Review" (industry group investment analysis) and monthly "Trends & Projections" (economic analysis).

TRADE/PROFESSIONAL ASSOCIATIONS

American Institute for Medical and Biological Engineering. 1901 Pennsylvania Ave., N.W., Suite 401, Washington, DC 20006. Phone: (202)496-9660 Fax: (202)466-8489 E-mail: info@aimbe.org • URL: http://www.aimbe.org.

American Institute of Biological Sciences. 1444 Eye St., N.W., Suite 200, Washington, DC 20005-2210. Phone: 800-992-2427 or (202)628-1500 Fax: (202)628-1509 E-mail: rogrady@aibs.org • URL: http://www.aibs.org.

Biomedical Engineering Society. 8401 Corporate Dr., Ste. 140, Landover, MD 20785-2224. Phone: (301)459-1999 Fax: (301)459-2444 E-mail: info@bmes.org • URL: http://www.bmes.org • Biomedical, chemical, electrical, civil, agricultural and mechanical engineers, physicians, managers, and university professors representing all fields of biomedical engineering; students and corporations. Encourages the development, dissemination, integration, and utilization of knowledge in biomedical engineering.

Biotechnology Industry Organization. 1201 Maryland Ave. SW, Ste. 900, Washington, DC 20024. Phone: 800-255-3304 or (202)962-9200 Fax: (202)962-9201 E-mail: info@bio.org • URL: http://www.bio.org • Represents biotechnology companies, academic institutions, state biotechnology centers and related organizations in all 50 U.S. states and 33 other nations. Members are involved in the research and development of healthcare, agricultural, industrial and environmental biotechnology products.

IEEE Engineering in Medicine and B iology Society. c/o IEEE Corporate Office, 3 Park Ave., 17th Fl., New York, NY 10016-5997. Phone: 800-678-4333 or (212)419-7900 Fax: (212)752-4929 E-mail: ieeeusa@ieee.org • URL: http://www.ieee.org • Members are engineers,technicians, physicians, manufacturers and others with an interest in medical instrumentation.

OTHER SOURCES

Biotechnology and the Law. Iver P. Cooper. West Group. • Annual. $424.50. Three looseleaf volumes.

Biotechnology Instrumentation. Available from MarketResearch.com. • 2002. $3,950.00. Published by Global Industry Analysts. Provides worldwide market research data, including profiles of major biotech instrument companies.

Global Seed Markets. Theta Reports. • 2000. $1,040.00. Market research data. Covers the major seed sectors, including cereal crops, legumes, oilseed crops, fibre crops, and beet crops. Provides analysis of biotechnology developments. (Theta Report No. DS208E.).

New and Breaking Technologies in the Pharmaceutical and Medical Device Industries. Theta Reports. • 1999. $1,695.00. Contains market research predictions of medical technology trends over the next 5 to 10 years (2004-2009), including developments in biotechnology, genetic engineering, medical device technology, therapeutic vaccines, non-invasive diagnostics, and minimally-invasive surgery. (Theta Report No. 931.).

BIRTH CERTIFICATES

See: VITAL STATISTICS

BIRTHS AND DEATHS

See: VITAL STATISTICS

BITUMINOUS COAL

See: COAL INDUSTRY

BLACK BUSINESS

See: MINORITY BUSINESS

BLACK CONSUMERS

See: MINORITY MARKETS

BLACK NEWSPAPERS

See: MINORITY NEWSPAPERS

BLOOD PRESSURE

See: HYPERTENSION

BLUE COLLAR THEFT

See: CRIME AND CRIMINALS; FRAUD AND EMBEZZLEMENT

BLUE COLLAR WORKERS

See: LABOR

BLUE SKY LAW

See: SECURITIES LAW AND REGULATION

BOARDING SCHOOLS

See: PRIVATE SCHOOLS

BOARDS OF DIRECTORS

See: CORPORATE DIRECTORS AND OFFICERS

BOARDS OF TRADE

See: CHAMBERS OF COMMERCE

BOAT INDUSTRY

See also: MARINAS; SHIPS, SHIPPING AND SHIPBUILDING

ALMANACS AND YEARBOOKS

Pacific Boating Almanac. ProStar Publications, Inc. • Annual. $24.95 per volume. Three volumes. Volume one, *Pacific Northwest*; volume two, *Northern California and the Delta*; volume three *Southern California and Mexico.* Lists over 3,000 marine facilities serving recreational boating.

DIRECTORIES

National Marine Representatives Association-- Directory. National Marine Representatives Association. • Covers: Approximately 400 independent representatives selling pleasure craft and other small boats, motors, and marine accessories. Entries include: Name, address, phone, fax, e-mail, manufacturers represented, territories covered, customer classifications.

Sailboat Buyers Guide. Primedia Inc. (New York, New York). • Covers: over 2,000 sailboat and equipment manufacturers. Entries include: Firm name, address, phone; many entries have description or photo.

FINANCIAL RATIOS

Almanac of Business and Industrial Financial Ratios. Leo Troy. Aspen Publishers, Inc. • 2003. $125.95. Includes CD-Rom. Contains financial ratios derived from federal tax returns. Ratios for each of about 200 industries are arranged according to company asset size. (*Almanac of Business and Industrial Financial Ratios* Series).

Annual Statement Studies. The Risk Management Association. • Annual. Median and quartile financial ratios are given for over 400 kinds of manufacturing, wholesale, retail, construction, and consumer finance establishments. Data is sorted by both asset size and sales volume. Includes a clearly written "Definition of Ratios" and an alphabetical industry index.

Annual Statement Studies: Industry Default Probabilities and Cash Flow Measures. The Risk Management Association. • Annual. $145.00. Serves as a companion volume to the original *An-*

nual Statement Studies. Gives probability of default estimates on a percentage scale for more than 450 industries. Includes changes in position year-by-year for eight financial statement line items and provides percentage measures of cash flow.

ONLINE DATABASES

Magazine Index. Gale Cengage Learning. • General magazine indexing (popular literature), 1973 to present. Daily updates. Inquire as to online cost and availability.

PERIODICALS AND NEWSLETTERS

Boat and Motor Dealer. Preston Publications, Inc. • 11 times a year. $48.00. Boat retailing.

Boating. Hachette Filipacchi Media U.S., Inc. • Monthly. $28.00 per year.

Boating Industry Buyers Guide and Directory. Ehlert Publishing Group. • Monthly. $38.00 per year.

Commercial Fisheries News. Compass Publications, Fisheries Division. • Monthly. $21.95 per year. Covers the commercial fishing industry in New England. Includes news of marine technology, boatbuilding, fish and lobster prices, business trends, government regulation, and other topics.

The Lookout. National Boating Federation. • Bimonthly. Newsletter. Membership.

Vapor Trail's Boating News and International Yachting and Cruiser and Manufacturers Report. Gemini Productions, Ltd. • Monthly. $24.00 per year.

Workboat. Diversified Business Communications. • Monthly. $49.00 per year. Covers equipment, products, and services for commercial boats such as tugboats, ferries, fireboats, fishing boats, and excursion boats.

PRICE SOURCES

BUC Used Boat Price Guide. BUC International Corp. • Semiannual. $183.00 per year. Formerly *Older Boat Price Guide.*

NADA Marine Appraisal Guide. National Automobile Dealers Association. N.A.D.A. Appraisal Guides. • Three times a year. $100.00 per year. Formerly *NADA Small Boat Appraisal Guide.*

STATISTICS SOURCES

Annual Survey of Manufactures. Available from U. S. Government Printing Office. • Annual. Prices vary. Issued by the U. S. Census Bureau as an interim update to the *Census of Manufactures.* Includes data on number of manufacturing establishments in various industries, employment, labor costs, value of shipments, capital expenditures, inventories, energy costs, and assets. (See also Census Bureau home page, http://www.census. gov/.).

U. S. Industry and Trade Outlook. Available from National Technical Information Service. • Annual. $69.95. Produced by the International Trade Administration, U. S. Department of Commerce, in a "public-private" partnership with DRI/McGraw-Hill and Standard & Poor's. Provides basic data, outlook for the current year, and "Long-Term Prospects" (five-year projections) for a wide variety of products and services. Includes high technology industries. Formerly *U. S. Industrial Outlook.*

TRADE/PROFESSIONAL ASSOCIATIONS

American Boat and Yacht Council. 3069 Solomons Island Rd., Edgewater, MD 21037-1416. Phone: (410)956-1050 Fax: (410)956-2737 E-mail: info@ abycinc.org • URL: http://www.abycinc.org.

American Boat Builders and Repairers Association. 50 Water St., Warren, RI 02885. Phone: (401)247-0318 Fax: (401)247-0074 • URL: http://www.abbra. org.

Boat Owners Association of the United States. 880 S. Pickett St., Alexandria, VA 22304. Phone: 800-990-9825 or (703)823-9550 Fax: (703)461-2847

E-mail: mail@boatus.com • URL: http://www. boatus.com • Absorbed American Yachtmen's Association.

National Marine Manufacturers Association. 1819 L St. NW, Ste. 700, Washington, DC 20036-3830. Phone: (202)861-1180 Fax: (202)861-1181 E-mail: webmaster@nmma.org • URL: http://www.nmma. org • Manufacturers of marine propulsion engines. Staff services and publications provided by National Marine Manufacturers Association (see separate entry).

National Marine Representatives Association. PO Box 360, Gurnee, IL 60031. Phone: (847)662-3167 Fax: (847)336-7126 E-mail: info@nmraonline.org • URL: http://www.nmraonline.org • Works to serve the marine industry independent sales representatives and the manufacturers selling through representatives. Serves as industry voice, networking tool and information source promoting benefits of utilizing independent marine representatives for sales. Aims to assist manufacturers find the right marine sales reps for product lines.

OTHER SOURCES

Pleasure Boats. Available from MarketResearch. com. • 1997. $1,495.00. Market research report published by Specialists in Business Information. Covers inboard, outboard, sterndrive, sail, inflatable, personal watercraft, and canoes.

BOILERS

See: HEATING AND VENTILATION

BONDS

See also: GOVERNMENT BONDS; MUNICIPAL BONDS

GENERAL WORKS

Getting Started in Bonds. Sharon S. Wright. John Wiley and Sons, Inc. • 2003. $19.95. Second edition. Serves as a primer on bonds for the individual investor. Covers government, municipal, corporate, mortgage-backed, international, and convertible bonds. Four parts: "Types of Bonds," "Fixed Income Fundamentals," "Factors Affecting Bonds," and "Fixed Income Investment Strategies." (Getting Started in...Series).

Investing in the Over-the-Counter Markets: Stocks, Bonds, IPOs. Alvin D. Hall. John Wiley and Sons, Inc. • 1995. $29.95. Provides advice and information on investing in "unlisted" or NASDAQ (National Association of Securities Dealers Automated Quotation System) stocks, bonds, and initial public offerings (IPOs).

The Strategic Bond Investor: Strategies and Tools to Unlock the Power of the Bond Market. Anthony Crescenzi. McGraw-Hill. • 2002. $29.95. Covers management strategies for fixed-income investment portfolios. (Teach Yourself Series).

Understanding Corporate Bonds. Harold Kerzner. McGraw-Hill. • 1991. $24.95. A general introduction to investing in corporate bonds. Includes a discussion of high-risk (junk) bonds.

ABSTRACTS AND INDEXES

Investment Statistics Locator. Linda H. Bentley and Jennifer J. Kiesl, editors. Greenwood Publishing Group, Inc. • 1994. $69.95. Expanded revised edition. Provides detailed subject indexing of more than 50 of the most-used sources of financial and investment data. Includes an annotated bibliography.

ALMANACS AND YEARBOOKS

Fixed Income Almanac: The Bond Investor's Compendium of Key Market, Product, and Performance Data. Livingston G. Douglas. McGraw-Hill. • 1993. $75.00. Presents 20 years of data in 350 graphs and charts. Covers bond market volatility, yield spreads, high-yield (junk) corporate bonds, default rates, and other items, such as Federal Reserve policy.

CD-ROM DATABASES

OECD Statistical Compendium. Organization for Economic Cooperation and Development. • Semiannual. $1,905.00 per year for 1 to 10 users. CD-ROM contains more than 730,000 monthly, quarterly, and annual time series for OECD countries, 1960 to date. Includes fully searchable data on agriculture, food, economic indicators, national accounts, employment, energy, finance, industry, technology, and foreign trade. Results can be displayed in various forms.

DIRECTORIES

Corporate Bond Desk Reference: U. S. Buyside and Sellside Profiles. Capital Access International. • Annual. $395.00. Provides "detailed buyside and sellside profiles and contacts" for the the corporate bond market. (Desk Reference Series, volume one.).

Mergent Municipal and Government Manual. Mergent, Inc. • Annual. $3,250.00 per year. Updated weekly online.

Mortgage & Asset-Based Desk Reference: U. S. Buyside and Sellside Profiles. Capital Access International. • Annual. $395.00. Provides "detailed buyside and sellside profiles and contacts" for the mortgage and asset-based securities market.

Standard and Poor's Corporate Registered Bond Interest Record. Standard and Poor's. • Annual. $2,600.00 per year. Weekly updates.

Standard and Poor's Directory of Bond Agents. Standard and Poor's. • Bimonthly. $1,250.00 per year. *Supplement available.*

Value Line Options: the All-in-One Service for Listed Options. Value Line Publishing, Inc. • Weekly. $445.00 per year. Formerly *Value Line Option and Convertible Survey.*

ENCYCLOPEDIAS AND DICTIONARIES

The A-Z Vocabulary for Investors. American Institute for Economic Research. • 1997. $7.00. Second half of book is a "General Glossary" of about 400 financial terms "most-commonly used" in investing. First half contains lengthier descriptions of types of banking institutions (commercial banks, thrift institutions, credit unions), followed by succinct explanations of various forms of investment: stocks, bonds, options, futures, commodities, and "Other Investments" (collectibles, currencies, mortgages, precious metals, real estate, charitable trusts). (Economic Education Bulletin.).

Blackwell Encyclopedic Dictionary of Finance. Dean Paxson and Douglas Wood, editors. Blackwell Publishing. • 1997. $110.00. The editors are associated with the University of Manchester. Contains definitions of key terms combined with longer articles written by various U. S. and foreign business educators. Includes bibliographies and index. (Blackwell Encyclopedia of Management Series).

Dictionary of Finance and Investment Terms. John Downes. Barron's Educational Series, Inc. • 2002. $14.95. Sixth edition. Provides clear explanations of more than 5,000 business, banking, financial, investment, and tax terms. Includes a separate list of financial abbreviations and acronyms. (Business Dictionaries Series).

HANDBOOKS AND MANUALS

Advanced Fixed Income Analysis. Moorad Choudhry. Elsevier Butterworth Heinemann. • 2004. $60.00. Edited for "experienced practitioners in the corporate bond markets." Covers trading, hedging, interest rate models, corporate bond default risk, the yield curve, long bond yields, and other topics.

The Bond and Money Markets: Strategy, Trading, Analysis. Moorad Choudhry. Elsevier Butterworth Heinemann. • 2003. $115.00. Serves as a reference work on corporate bonds, government bonds, currency markets, interest-rate futures, convertible securities, various kinds of derivatives, and technical analysis of financial securities.

Convertible Securities: The Latest Instruments, Portfolio Strategies, and Valuation Analysis. John P. Calamos. McGraw-Hill. • 1998. $65.00. Second revised edition. (Irwin Library of Investment and Finance Series).

Fixed Income Analytics: State-of-the-Art Analysis and Valuation Modeling. Ravi E. Dattatreya, editor. McGraw-Hill. • 1991. $69.95. Discusses the yield curve, structure and value in corporate bonds, mortgage-backed securities, and other topics. (Institutional Investor Publications).

Fixed Income Mathematics: Analytical and Statistical Techniques. Frank J. Fabozzi. McGraw-Hill. • 1996. $65.00. Third edition. Covers the basics of fixed income analysis, as well as more advanced techniques used for complex securities.

Handbook of Fixed Income Securities. Frank J. Fabozzi. McGraw-Hill. • 2000. $99.95. Sixth edition. Topics include risk measurement, valuation techniques, and portfolio strategy.

Introduction to Option-Adjusted Spread Analysis. Tom Windas. Bloomberg. • 1996. $40.00. Revised edition. Discusses the limitations of traditional, yield-based, risk and return analysis of bonds. (Bloomberg Professional Library.).

Municipal Bonds: The Comprehensive Review of Municipal Securities and Public Finance. Robert Lamb and Stephen Rappaport. McGraw-Hill. • 1987. $34.95. Second edition.

INTERNET DATABASES

Bondtalk.com: Live Talk & Analysis on the Bond Market & the Economy. Miller Tabak & Co., LLC. Phone: (212)370-0040 E-mail: acrescenzi@bondtalk.com • URL: http://www.bondtalk.com • Web site provides extensive, free data on the fixed income securities market, including individual bond prices, yields, interest rates, Federal Reserve information, charts, bond market news, and economic analysis. Also offered on a fee basis is "Bondtalkpro.com: The New and Enhanced Service for Market Professionals.".

Business 2.0 Web Guide to the Best Business Links. Business 2.0 Media Inc. Phone: (415)293-4800 E-mail: support@business2.com • URL: http://www.business2.com/webguide • Web site presents an extensive, searchable directory of links to "the best, most informative, and authoritative web pages." Twenty main categories cover business, finance, career, company information, people, and technology topics, with thousands of subtopics, all linking to Web sites recommended by experienced business researchers. Fees: Free.

Factiva. Dow Jones Reuters Business Interactive, LLC. Phone: 800-369-7466 or (609)452-1511 Fax: (609)520-5770 E-mail: solutions@factiva.com • URL: http://www.factiva.com • Fee-based Web site provides "global news and business information through Web sites and content integration solutions." Includes Dow Jones and Reuters newswires, The Wall Street Journal, and more than 7,000 other sources of current news, historical articles, market research reports, and investment analysis. Content includes 96 major U. S. newspapers, 900 non-English sources, trade publications, media transcripts, country profiles, news photos, etc.

Federal Reserve Board Publications and Education Resources. Board of Governors of the Federal Reserve System. Phone: (202)452-3000 Fax: (202)452-3819 • URL: http://www.federalreserve.gov/publications.htm • Web site provides convenient access to statistics, surveys, and research from the Federal Reserve Board. *Federal Reserve Bulletin* articles are available as abstracts or full text

(PDF) currently or from six-year archives. The link "Statistics: Releases and Historical Data" offers daily, weekly, monthly, quarterly, and annual data in great detail for interest rates, foreign exchange, consumer credit, money stock measures, industrial production indexes, bank reserves, and other items. Historical tabulations are available for various time periods. Fees: Free.

Fedstats. Federal Interagency Council on Statistical Policy. Phone: (202)395-7254 • URL: http://www.fedstats.gov • Web site features an efficient search facility for full-text statistics produced by more than 100 federal agencies, including the Census Bureau, the Bureau of Economic Analysis, and the Bureau of Labor Statistics. Boolean searches can be made within one agency or for all agencies combined. Links are offered to international statistical bureaus, including the UN, IMF, OECD, UNESCO, Eurostat, and 20 individual countries. Fees: Free.

FreeLunch.com. Economy.com, Inc. Phone: (610)696-8700 Fax: (610)696-1678 • URL: http://www.freelunch.com • Web site provides free access to more than 1.5 million economic and financial data series, covering industry, demographics, labor markets, prices, retail sales, government spending, trade, interest rates, housing starts, the stock market, and many other topics. Data is available for various time periods in either chart or table form. Searching is offered. Fees: Free, but registration required. Economy.com, Inc. also offers fee-based economic analysis at *The Dismal Scientist* site (http://www.dismal.com).

Nexis.com. Lexis-Nexis Group. Phone: 800-227-4908 or (937)865-6800 Fax: (937)865-6909 E-mail: webmaster@prod.lexis-nexis.com • URL: http://www.nexis.com • Fee-based Web site offers searching of about 2.8 billion documents in some 30,000 news, business, and legal information sources. Features include a subject directory covering 1,200 topics in 34 categories and a Company Dossier containing information on more than 500,000 public and private companies. Boolean searching is offered.

U. S. Securities and Exchange Commission. Phone: 800-732-0330 or (202)942-7040 Fax: (202)942-9634 E-mail: webmaster@sec.gov • URL: http://www.sec.gov • SEC Web site offers free access through EDGAR to text of official corporate filings, such as annual reports (10-K), quarterly reports (10-Q), and proxies. (EDGAR is "Electronic Data Gathering, Analysis, and Retrieval System.") An example is given of how to obtain executive compensation data from proxies. Text of the daily *SEC News Digest* is offered, as are links to other government sites, non-government market regulators, and U. S. stock exchanges. Search facilities are extensive. Fees: Free.

Wall Street Journal Interactive Edition. Dow Jones & Co., Inc. Phone: 800-369-2834 or (212)416-2000 Fax: (212)416-2658 E-mail: inquiries@interactive.wsj.com • URL: http://www.wsj.com • Fee-based Web site providing online searching of worldwide information from the *The Wall Street Journal.* Includes "Company Snapshots," "The Journal's Greatest Hits," "Index to Market Data," "Journal Links," etc. Financial price quotes are available. Fees: $49.00 per year; $29.00 per year to print subscribers.

ONLINE DATABASES

Disclosure SEC Database. Thomson Financial. • Provides online information from records filed with the Securities and Exchange Commission by more than 12,000 publicly-owned companies in the U.S. Includes about 200 financial data items and information relating to executives. Time span is 1977 to date, with weekly updates. Inquire as to online cost and availability.

EdgarPlus: SEC Basic Filings. Thomson Financial. • Online service provides full text of about 60,000 documents that have been filed with the U.S. Securities and Exchange Commission, 1987 to date, with daily updates. Filings include 6-K, 8-K, 10-K, 10-C, 10-Q, 20-F, and proxy statements. Inquire as to online cost and availability.

Fitch Ratings Delivery Service. Fitch Inc. • Provides online delivery of Fitch financial ratings in three sectors: "Corporate Finance" (corporate bonds, insurance companies), "Structured Finance" (asset-backed securities), and "U.S. Public Finance" (municipal bonds). Daily updates. Inquire as to online cost and availability.

Value Line Convertible Data Base. Value Line Publishing, Inc. • Provides online data for about 600 convertible bonds and other convertible securities: price, yield, premium, issue size, liquidity, and maturity. Information is current, with weekly updates. Inquire as to online cost and availability.

PERIODICALS AND NEWSLETTERS

Barron's: The Dow Jones Business and Financial Weekly. • Weekly. $145.00 per year.

The Bond Buyer. Veronis, Suhler and Associates Inc. • Daily edition, $1,897 per year. Weekly edition, $525.00 per year. Reports on new municipal bond issues.

Bondweek: The Newsweekly of Fixed Income and Credit Markets. Institutional Investor, Inc., Journals Group. • Weekly. $2,425.00 per year. Newsletter. Includes print and online editions. Covers taxable, fixed-income securities for professional investors, including corporate, government, foreign, mortgage, and high-yield.

CreditWeek. Standard & Poor's. • Description: Standard & Poor's flagship print information and news publication that covers the global credit markets. Includes insightful feature articles on market events and trends, plus columns titled Rating News and Credit Watch.

Emerging Markets Debt Report. Thomson Media. • Weekly. $895.00 per year. Newsletter. Provides information on new and prospective sovereign and corporate bond issues from developing countries. Includes an emerging market bond index and pricing data.

Financial Markets, Institutions, and Instruments. New York University, Salomon Center. Blackwell Publishing. • Five times a year. Institutions, $338.00 per year. Includes online edition. Edited to "bridge the gap between the academic and professional finance communities." Special fifth issue each year provides surveys of developments in four areas: money and banking, derivative securities, corporate finance, and fixed-income securities.

The Financial Post: Canadian's Business Voice. Financial Post Datagroup. • Daily. $200.00 per year. Provides Canadian business, economic, financial, and investment news. Features extensive price quotes from all major Canadian markets: stocks, bonds, mutual funds, commodities, and currencies. Supplement available: *Financial Post 500.* Includes annual supplement.

Financial Times [London]. The Financial Times, Inc. • Daily, except Sunday. $572.88 per year. An international business and financial newspaper, featuring news from London, Paris, Frankfurt, New York, and Tokyo. Includes worldwide stock and bond market data, commodity market data, and monetary/currency exchange information.

Grant's Interest Rate Observer. James Grant, editor. Grant's Financial Publishing Inc. • Biweekly. $725.00 per year. Newsletter containing detailed analysis of money-related topics, including interest rate trends, global credit markets, fixed-income investments, bank loan policies, and international money markets.

Investor's Business Daily. Investor's Business Daily, Inc. • Daily. $295.00 per year. Newspaper.

Journal of Fixed Income. Institutional Investor, Inc.,

Journals Group. • Quarterly. $360.00 per year. Includes print and online editions. Covers a wide range of fixed-income investments for institutions, including bonds, interest-rate options, high-yield securities, and mortgages.

Journal of Investing. Institutional Investor, Inc., Journals Group. • Quarterly. $350.00 per year. Includes print and online editions. Edited for professional investors. Topics include equities, fixed-income securities, derivatives, asset allocation, and other institutional investment subjects.

Mergent Bond Record and Annual Bond Record. Mergent, Inc. • Monthly. Price on application. Formerly *Moody's Bond Record and Annual Bond Record.*

Moody's Bond Survey. Moody's Investors Service Inc. • Description: Presents statistical information and analysis of corporate, municipal, government, federal agency, and international bonds, preferred stock, and commercial paper. Includes ratings changes and withdrawals, calendars of recent and prospective bond offerings, and Moody's bond and preferred stock yield averages.

Private Placement Letter: The Weekly for Privately Placed Fixed-Income Securities. Thomson Media. • Weekly. $895.00 per year. Newsletter. Provides information on private financing of debt and convertible securities.

Richard C. Young's Intelligence Report. Access Intelligence L.L.C. • Description: Provides information for "serious, conservative investors (buy and hold as opposed to active traders)." Features investing advice and recommendations for best funds, stocks, and bonds for current or retirement income.

Standard and Poor's Bond Guide. Standard and Poor's. • Monthly. $239.00 per year.

Standard and Poor's Ratings Handbook. Standard & Poor's. • Monthly. $275.00 per year. Newsletter. Provides news and analysis of international credit markets, including information on new bond issues. Formerly *Credit Week International Ratings.*

Standard and Poor's Semi-Weekly Called Bond Record. Standard & Poor's. • Semiweekly. $1,175.00 per year.

The Wall Street Journal. Dow Jones & Co., Inc. • Daily. $189.00 per year. Covers news and trends relating to business, industry, finance, the economy, and international commerce. Provides extensive price and other data for the securities, commodity, options, futures, foreign exchange, and money markets.

PRICE SOURCES

National Bond Summary. Pink Sheets LLC. • Monthly, with semiannual cumulations. $504.00 per year. Includes price quotes for both active and inactive issues, with transfer agents, market makers (brokers), capital changes, name changes, and other corporate information. Formerly published by the National Quotation Bureau.

STATISTICS SOURCES

Business Statistics of the United States. Linz Audain and Cornelia J. Strawser. Bernan Associates. • Annual. $147.00. Based on *Business Statistics,* formerly issue by the Bureau of Economic Analysis, U. S. Department of Commerce. Provides basic data for a wide variety of U. S. industries, services, and economic indicators. Most statistics are shown annually for 30 years and monthly for the most recent four years.

International Guide to Securities Market Indices. Henry Shilling, editor. Fitzroy Dearborn Publishers, Inc. • 1996. $150.00. Describes 400 stock market, bond market, and other financial price indexes maintained in various countries of the world (300 of the indexes are described in detail, including graphs and 10-year data).

Standard & Poor's Stock and Bond Guide.

McGraw-Hill. • Annual. $24.95. Contains concise data on 6,000 stocks, 7,000 bonds, and 700 mutual funds. Includes year-end prices, earnings estimates for stocks, and debt ratings for bonds.

Stocks, Bonds, Bills, and Inflation Yearbook. Ibbotson Associates. • Annual. $92.00. Provides detailed data from 1926 to the present on inflation and the returns from various kinds of financial investments, such as small-cap stocks and long-term government bonds.

Survey of Current Business. Available from U. S. Government Printing Office. • Monthly. $63.00 per year. Issued by Bureau of Economic Analysis, U. S. Department of Commerce. Presents a wide variety of business and economic data.

TRADE/PROFESSIONAL ASSOCIATIONS

Security Traders Association. 420 Lexington Ave., Ste. 2334, New York, NY 10170. Phone: (212)867-7002 Fax: (212)867-7030 E-mail: traders@securitytraders.org • URL: http://www.securitytraders.org • Brokers and dealers handling listed and OTC securities, stocks, and bonds, and all securities. Conducts educational programs. Promotes the interests of members throughout the global financial markets. Provides representation of these interests in the legislative, regulatory and technological processes. Fosters goodwill and high standards of integrity in accord with the Association's founding principle.

OTHER SOURCES

Fitch Insights. Fitch Investors Service, Inc. • Biweekly. $1,040.00 per year. Includes bond rating actions and explanation of actions. Provides commentary and Fitch's view of the financial markets.

BONDS, GOVERNMENT

See: GOVERNMENT BONDS

BONDS, JUNK

See: JUNK BOND FINANCING

BONDS, MUNICIPAL

See: MUNICIPAL BONDS

BOOK CATALOGS

See also: BIBLIOGRAPHY; BUSINESS LITERATURE

BIBLIOGRAPHIES

American Book Publishing Record: Arranged by Dewey Decimal Classification and Indexed by Author, Title, and Subject. R. R. Bowker. • Monthly. $395.00 per year. Includes annual cumulation.

American Reference Books Annual. Bohdan S. Wynar, editor. Libraries Unlimited, Inc. • Annual. $125.00.

Books in Print. R. R. Bowker. • Annual. $769.00. Eight volumes.

Forthcoming Books. R. R. Bowker. • Bimonthly. $299.95 per year. Supplement to *Books in Print.*

Subject Guide to Books in Print. R. R. Bowker. • Annual. $525.00. Six volumes.

CD-ROM DATABASES

Bowker/Whitaker Global Books in Print On Disc. R. R. Bowker. • Monthly. $2,055.00 per year. Provides CD-ROM listing of English language books published throughout the world, including U. S., U. K., Canada, and Australia. Combines data from R. R. Bowker's *Books in Print Plus* and J. Whitaker &

Sons Ltd.'s *Bookbank*. Includes more than two million titles.

LISA Plus. Available from Cambridge Scientific Abstracts (CSA). • Quarterly. $2,000.00 per year. CD-ROM version of Library Information and Science Abstracts, providing abstracting and indexing of the world's library and information science literature, 1969 to date. Contains more than 180,000 citations.

INTERNET DATABASES

Publishers' Catalogues Home Page. EBSCO Publishing. Phone: (306)931-0020 Fax: (306)931-7667 E-mail: info@lights.com • URL: http://www.lights.com/publisher • Provides links to the Web home pages of about 1,700 U. S. publishers (including about 80 University presses) and publishers in 48 foreign countries. "International/Multinational Publishers" are included, such as the International Monetary Fund, the World Bank, and the World Trade Organization. Publishers are arranged in convenient alphabetical lists. Searching is offered. Fees: Free.

ONLINE DATABASES

Book Review Index [Online]. Gale Cengage Learning. • Cites reviews of books and periodicals in journals, 1969 to present. Inquire as to online cost and availability.

LC MARC: Books. U. S. Library of Congress. • Contains online bibliographic records for over five million books cataloged by the Library of Congress since 1968. Updating is weekly or monthly. Inquire as to online cost and availability. (MARC is machine readable cataloging.).

LISA: Library and Information Science Abstracts. Available from Cambridge Scientific Abstracts (CSA). • Provides abstracting and indexing of the world's library and information science literature, 1969 to date. Covers more than 440 periodicals from 68 countries. Updating is biweekly. Inquire as to online cost and availability,

PERIODICALS AND NEWSLETTERS

Publishers Weekly: The International News Magazine of Book Publishing. Reed Business Information. • 51 times a year. $214.00 per year. The international news magazine of book publishing.

BOOK COLLECTING

See also: BIBLIOGRAPHY

DIRECTORIES

International Directory of Book Collectors. Oak Knoll Press. • 1992. $50.00. Over 1,500 listings. Published in England by Trigon Press.

Sheppard's Bookdealers in Europe: A Directory of Dealers in Secondhand and Antiquarian Books on the Continent of Europe. Richard Joseph Publishers, Ltd. • Biennial. $54.00. 1,746 dealers in antiquarian and secondhand books in 24 European countries.

HANDBOOKS AND MANUALS

Book Collecting: A Comprehensive Guide. Allen Ahearn and Patricia Ahearn. Penguin Group. • 2000. $45.00. Revised edition.

PERIODICALS AND NEWSLETTERS

Collector. Nicolas J. Barker. Collector Ltd. • Quarterly. $68.00 per year.

PRICE SOURCES

American Book Prices Current. Bancroft-Parkman, Inc. • Annual. $119.95.

Bookman's Price Index. Gale Cengage Learning. • Annual. 71 volumes in print. $375.00 per volume. Price guide to out more than 17,000 out-of-print and rare books.

TRADE/PROFESSIONAL ASSOCIATIONS

Antiquarian Booksellers Association of America. 20 W. 44th St., 4th Fl., New York, NY 10036-6604.

Phone: (212)944-8291 Fax: (212)944-8293 E-mail: inquiries@abaa.org • URL: http://www.abaa.org.

Bibliographical Society of America. Lenox Hill Station, PO Box 1537, New York, NY 10021. Phone: (212)452-2710 Fax: (212)452-2710 E-mail: tavisgordon@mindspring.com • URL: http://www.bibsocamer.org.

Grolier Club. 47 E 60th St., New York, NY 10022. Phone: (212)838-6690 Fax: (212)838-2445 E-mail: ejh@grolierclub.org • URL: http://www.grolierclub.org • Persons concerned with the book arts. Named after Jean Grolier (1489-1565), French bibliophile. Conducts free public exhibitions per year.

BOOK INDUSTRY

See also: BIBLIOGRAPHY; BOOK COLLECTING; BOOKSELLING; PAPERBOUND BOOK INDUSTRY; PUBLISHING INDUSTRY

ALMANACS AND YEARBOOKS

The Bowker Annual: Library and Book Trade Almanac. Information Today, Inc. • Annual. $199.00. Reviews key trends and events and provides basic statistical information. Includes financial averages: library expenditures, salaries, and book prices. Contains lists of "best books, literary prizes, winners, and bestsellers." Formerly published by R. R. Bowker.

Trade Book Publishing: Analysis by Category. Kathleen Martucci and others. SIMBA Information, Inc. • 1998. $1,495.00. 6th revised edition. Reviews current conditions in the book publishing industry, including analysis of market segments, retailing aspects, and profiles of major publishers.

BIBLIOGRAPHIES

American Book Publishing Record: Arranged by Dewey Decimal Classification and Indexed by Author, Title, and Subject. R. R. Bowker. • Monthly. $395.00 per year. Includes annual cumulation.

Managing the Publishing Process: An Annotated Bibliography. Bruce W. Speck. Greenwood Publishing Group, Inc. • 1995. $82.95. (Bibliographies and Indexes in Mass Media and Communications Series: No. 9).

CD-ROM DATABASES

LISA Plus. Available from Cambridge Scientific Abstracts (CSA). • Quarterly. $2,000.00 per year. CD-ROM version of Library Information and Science Abstracts, providing abstracting and indexing of the world's library and information science literature, 1969 to date. Contains more than 180,000 citations.

DIRECTORIES

American Book Trade Directory. Information Today Inc. • Covers: Nearly 25,500 retail and antiquarian book dealers, plus 1,200 book and magazine wholesalers, distributors, and jobbers-in all 50 states and U.S. territories. Also included are sections of auctioneers of literary property, exporters/importers, booktrade associations, foreign language book dealers, book and literary appraisers, and rental library chains. Entries include: Bookstore name, address, phone, owner or manager, types and subjects of books stocked, specialty, sidelines, year established, SAN (Standard Address Number), number of volumes stocked, square footage.

International Literary Market Place: The Directory of the International Book Publishing Industry. Information Today, Inc. • Annual. $219.00. Covers more than 180 countries. Listings include publishers, literary agents, major booksellers, book clubs, literary prizes, trade associations, etc. Formerly published by R. R. Bowker.

Literary Market Place: The Directory of the American Book Publishing Industry. Information

Today, Inc. • Annual. $299.00. Two volumes. Listings include publishers, agents, ad agencies, associations, distributors, events, key executives, services, and suppliers (50 directory sections in all). Formerly published by R. R. Bowker.

Publishers Directory: A Guide to New and Established Private and Special-Interest, Avant-Garde and Alternative, Organizational Association, Government and Institution Presses. Gale Cengage Learning. • 2003. $450.00. 26th edition. Contains detailed information on more than 20,000 U.S. and Canadian publishers as well as small, independent presses.

Publishers, Distributors, and Wholesalers of the United States: A Directory of Publishers, Distributors, Associations, Wholesalers, Software Producers and Manufactureres Listing Editorial and Ordering Addresses, and and ISBN Publisher Prefi. Gale. • Annual. $349.00. Two volumes. Lists more than 101,000 publishers, book distributors, and wholesalers. Includes museum and association imprints, inactive publishers, and publishers' fields of activity.

Publishers' International ISBN Directory. International ISBN Agency. • Covers: About 620,000 publishers in the United States and 218 other countries, of which about 555,000 have been assigned International Standard Book Numbers (ISBNs) by one of 140 ISBN Group Agencies. Entries include: For publishers--Name, address, phone, fax, telex, e-mail, ISBN, group, and prefix numbers. For agencies--Name, address, phone, fax, e-mail, group number, names and titles of key personnel in charge of ISBN matters. Publication is a merger of "International ISBN Publishers' Directory" and "Publishers' International Directory.".

Sheppard's Bookdealers in North America. Richard Joseph Publishers, Ltd. • Biennial. $60.00. Over 3,364 dealers in antiquarian and secondhand books in the U.S. and Canada.

Writer's Guide to Book Editors, Publishers, and Literary Agents, Who They Are, What They Want, and How to Win Them Over. Prima Publishing. • Annual. $27.95; with CD-ROM, $49.95. Directory for authors includes information on publishers' response times and pay rates.

FINANCIAL RATIOS

Annual Statement Studies. The Risk Management Association. • Annual. Median and quartile financial ratios are given for over 400 kinds of manufacturing, wholesale, retail, construction, and consumer finance establishments. Data is sorted by both asset size 'and sales volume. Includes a clearly written "Definition of Ratios" and an alphabetical industry index.

Annual Statement Studies: Industry Default Probabilities and Cash Flow Measures. The Risk Management Association. • Annual. $145.00. Serves as a companion volume to the original *Annual Statement Studies*. Gives probability of default estimates on a percentage scale for more than 450 industries. Includes changes in position year-by-year for eight financial statement line items and provides percentage measures of cash flow.

HANDBOOKS AND MANUALS

ABA Book Buyer's Handbook. American Booksellers Association. • Annual. Membership. Trade policies. Formerly *Book Buyer's Handbook*.

Buying Books: A How-To-Do-It Manual for Librarians. Audrey Eaglen. Neal-Schuman Publishers, Inc. • 2000. $45.00. Second edition. Discusses vendor selection and book ordering in the age of electronic commerce. Covers both print and electronic bibliographic sources. (How-to-Do-It Manuals Series).

Getting Your Book Published. Christine S. Smedley and Mitchell Allen. Sage Publications, Inc. • 1993. $59.95. A practical guide for academic and professional authors. Covers the initial book prospectus, contract negotiation, production procedures, and marketing. (Survival Skills for Scholars, vol. 10).

INTERNET DATABASES

Publishers' Catalogues Home Page. EBSCO Publishing. Phone: (306)931-0020 Fax: (306)931-7667 E-mail: info@lights.com • URL: http://www.lights.com/publisher • Provides links to the Web home pages of about 1,700 U. S. publishers (including about 80 University presses) and publishers in 48 foreign countries. "International/Multinational Publishers" are included, such as the International Monetary Fund, the World Bank, and the World Trade Organization. Publishers are arranged in convenient alphabetical lists. Searching is offered. Fees: Free.

ONLINE DATABASES

LISA: Library and Information Science Abstracts. Available from Cambridge Scientific Abstracts (CSA). • Provides abstracting and indexing of the world's library and information science literature, 1969 to date. Covers more than 440 periodicals from 68 countries. Updating is biweekly. Inquire as to online cost and availability.

PERIODICALS AND NEWSLETTERS

Advertising Age: The International Newspaper of Marketing. Crain Communications, Inc. • Weekly. $178.50 per year. Includes supplement *Creativity*.

Book Marketing Update. Open Horizons. • Description: Surveys resources for publishers interested in marketing their books to bookstores, libraries, wholesalers, catalogs, book clubs, and other special markets.

Book Publishing Report: Weekly News and Analysis of Events Shaping the Book Industry. SIMBA Information. • 50 times a year. $549.00 per year. Newsletter. Covers book publishing mergers, marketing, finance, personnel, and trends in general. Formerly *BP Report on the Business of Book Publishing*.

Publishers Weekly: The International News Magazine of Book Publishing. Reed Business Information. • 51 times a year. $214.00 per year. The international news magazine of book publishing.

PRICE SOURCES

American Book Prices Current. Bancroft-Parkman, Inc. • Annual. $119.95.

STATISTICS SOURCES

Annual Survey of Manufactures. Available from U. S. Government Printing Office. • Annual. Prices vary. Issued by the U. S. Census Bureau as an interim update to the *Census of Manufactures*. Includes data on number of manufacturing establishments in various industries, employment, labor costs, value of shipments, capital expenditures, inventories, energy costs, and assets. (See also Census Bureau home page, http://www.census.gov/.).

Book Industry Trends. Book Industry Study Group, Inc. • Annual. $750.00.

U. S. Industry and Trade Outlook. Available from National Technical Information Service. • Annual. $69.95. Produced by the International Trade Administration, U. S. Department of Commerce, in a "public-private" partnership with DRI/McGraw-Hill and Standard & Poor's. Provides basic data, outlook for the current year, and "Long-Term Prospects" (five-year projections) for a wide variety of products and services. Includes high technology industries. Formerly *U. S. Industrial Outlook*.

TRADE/PROFESSIONAL ASSOCIATIONS

Association of American Publishers. 71 Fifth Ave., New York, NY 10003-3004. Phone: (212)255-0200 Fax: (212)255-7007 E-mail: amyg@publishers.org • URL: http://www.publishers.org.

Book Industry Study Group. 370 Lexington Ave., Ste. 900, New York, NY 10017. Phone: (646)336-7141 Fax: (646)336-6214 E-mail: info@bisg.org • URL: http://www.bisg.org • Represents publishers, manufacturers, suppliers, wholesalers, retailers, librarians, and other engaged in the business of print and electronic media.

Book Manufacturers' Institute. Two Armand Beach Dr., Ste. 1B, Palm Coast, FL 32137-2612. Phone: (386)986-4552 Fax: (386)986-4553 E-mail: info@bmibook.com • URL: http://www.bmibook.com • Represents the trade association for manufacturers of books.

Women's National Book Association. PO Box 237, 26 W 17th St., No. 504, New York, NY 10150. Phone: (212)208-4629 Fax: (212)208-4629 E-mail: publicity@bookbuzz.com • URL: http://www.wnba-books.org • Women and men who work with and value books. Exists to promote reading and to support the role of women in the book community.

BOOK REVIEWS

ABSTRACTS AND INDEXES

Book Review Digest: An Index to Reviews of Current Books. H. W. Wilson Co. • 10 times a year. Quarterly and annual cumulation. Price varies.

Book Review Index. Gale Cengage Learning. • Annual. $310.00. Three yearly issues. An index to reviews appearing in hundreds of periodicals. Back volumes available.

Children's Book Review Index. Gale Cengage Learning. • Annual. $165.00. Back volumes available. Contains more than 25,000 review citations.

BIBLIOGRAPHIES

American Reference Books Annual. Bohdan S. Wynar, editor. Libraries Unlimited, Inc. • Annual. $125.00.

Booklist. American Library Association. • 22 times a year. $79.95. Reviews library materials for school and public libraries. Incorporates *Reference Books Bulletin*.

Reference Books Bulletin: A Compilation of Evaluations. Mary Ellen Quinn, editor. American Library Association. • Annual. $79.95. Contains reference book reviews that appeared during the year in *Booklist*.

CD-ROM DATABASES

Books in Print with Book Reviews On Disc. Bowker Electronic Publishing. • Monthly. $2,075 per year. The CD-ROM version of *Books in Print, Forthcoming Books*, and other Bowker bibliographic publications, with the addition of full text book reviews from *Publishers Weekly, Library Journal, Booklist, Choice*, and other periodicals.

ONLINE DATABASES

Book Review Index [Online]. Gale Cengage Learning. • Cites reviews of books and periodicals in journals, 1969 to present. Inquire as to online cost and availability.

PERIODICALS AND NEWSLETTERS

Choice Magazine: Current Reviews for Academic Libraries. Association of College Research Libraries. American Library Association. • 11 times a year. $237.00 per year. A publication of the Association of College and Research Libraries. Contains book reviews, primarily for college and university libraries.

Library Journal. Reed Business Information. • 20 times a year. $134.00 per year. Includes *Buyer's Guide*, six *Supplements* and weekly *Newswire*.

New York Times Book Review. New York Times Co. • Weekly. $54.60 per year. Supplement to *New York Times*.

Reference and User Services Quarterly. American Library Association, Reference and Adult Services Div. • Quarterly. $50.00 per year. In addition to articles, includes reviews of databases, reference books, and library professional material. Formerly *RQ*.

BOOK STORES

See: BOOKSELLING

BOOKBINDING

CD-ROM DATABASES

LISA Plus. Available from Cambridge Scientific Abstracts (CSA). • Quarterly. $2,000.00 per year. CD-ROM version of Library Information and Science Abstracts, providing abstracting and indexing of the world's library and information science literature, 1969 to date. Contains more than 180,000 citations.

DIRECTORIES

Guild of Book Workers-Membership List. Guild of Book Workers. • Annual. $60.00. About 900 amateur and professional workers in the handbook crafts of bookbinding, calligraphy, illuminating, and decorative papermaking.

Opportunities for Study in Hand Bookbinding and Calligraphy. Guild of Book Workers, Inc. • Free. About 150 teachers, schools, and centers offering hand bookbinding and calligraphic services; international coverage.

FINANCIAL RATIOS

Annual Statement Studies. The Risk Management Association. • Annual. Median and quartile financial ratios are given for over 400 kinds of manufacturing, wholesale, retail, construction, and consumer finance establishments. Data is sorted by both asset size and sales volume. Includes a clearly written "Definition of Ratios" and an alphabetical industry index.

Annual Statement Studies: Industry Default Probabilities and Cash Flow Measures. The Risk Management Association. • Annual. $145.00. Serves as a companion volume to the original *Annual Statement Studies*. Gives probability of default estimates on a percentage scale for more than 450 industries. Includes changes in position year-by-year for eight financial statement line items and provides percentage measures of cash flow.

HANDBOOKS AND MANUALS

Book Repair: A How-To-Do-It Manual for Librarians. Kenneth Lavender. Neal-Schuman Publishers, Inc. • 2001. $49.95. Second edition. Covers basic book repair and conservation techniques. (How-to-Do-It Manuals Series).

ONLINE DATABASES

LISA: Library and Information Science Abstracts. Available from Cambridge Scientific Abstracts (CSA). • Provides abstracting and indexing of the world's library and information science literature, 1969 to date. Covers more than 440 periodicals from 68 countries. Updating is biweekly. Inquire as to online cost and availability.

PIRA. PIRA International Information Centre. • Citations and abstracts pertaining to bookbinding and other pulp, paper, and packaging industries, 1975 to present. Weekly updates. Inquire as to online cost and availability.

PERIODICALS AND NEWSLETTERS

The New Library Scene. Library Binding Institute. • Quarterly. $24.00 per year.

TRADE/PROFESSIONAL ASSOCIATIONS

Binding Industries Association of America. 70 E Lake St., No. 300, Chicago, IL 60601. Phone:

(312)372-7606 or (312)704-5000 Fax: (312)709-5025 E-mail: info@bindingindustries.org • URL: http://www.bindingindustries.org • Formerly Binding Industries of America.

Guild of Book Workers. 521 Fifth Ave., 17th Fl., New York, NY 10175. Phone: (212)363-7946.

Library Binding Institute. 4300 S U.S. Hwy. One, No. 203-296, Jupiter, FL 33477. Phone: (561)745-6821 Fax: (561)472-8401 E-mail: dnolan@lbibinders.org • URL: http://www.lbibinders.org • Firms and certified library binders doing library binding in accordance with LBI Standard for Library Binding, including rebinding of worn volumes, prebinding of new volumes, initial hardcover binding of periodicals, and other binding principally for libraries and schools; associate members are suppliers and manufacturers of library binding materials and equipment. Certifies qualified binding companies after examination of work and investigation of experience, insurance for protection of customers' property, and examination of bank and library references. Conducts research on materials used in library binding. Conducts statistical surveys of unit production, operating statement data, and wage data.

OTHER SOURCES
Early American Bookbindings from the Collection of Michael Papantonio. Michael Papantonio. Oak Knoll Press. • 1985. $27.50. Second edition.

BOOKKEEPING

See: ACCOUNTING

BOOKSELLER'S CATALOGS

See: BOOK CATALOGS

BOOKSELLING

See also: BIBLIOGRAPHY; BOOK COLLECTING; BOOK INDUSTRY

GENERAL WORKS
The Business of Publishing: How to Survive and Prosper in the Publishing and Bookselling Industry. Leonard Shatzkin. McGraw-Hill. • 1995. $24.95.

BIBLIOGRAPHIES
American Book Publishing Record: Arranged by Dewey Decimal Classification and Indexed by Author, Title, and Subject. R. R. Bowker. • Monthly. $395.00 per year. Includes annual cumulation.

DIRECTORIES
American Book Trade Directory. Information Today Inc. • Covers: Nearly 25,500 retail and antiquarian book dealers, plus 1,200 book and magazine wholesalers, distributors, and jobbers-in all 50 states and U.S. territories. Also included are sections of auctioneers of literary property, exporters/importers, booktrade associations, foreign language book dealers, book and literary appraisers, and rental library chains. Entries include: Bookstore name, address, phone, owner or manager, types and subjects of books stocked, specialty, sidelines, year established, SAN (Standard Address Number), number of volumes stocked, square footage.

Antiquarian Booksellers' Association of America-Membership List. Antiquarian Booksellers' Association of America. • Annual. Free. Lists about 470 rare book dealers. Send self-addressed business-size envelope with $1.43 postage.

Sheppard's Bookdealers in Europe: A Directory of Dealers in Secondhand and Antiquarian Books on the Continent of Europe. Richard Joseph Publishers, Ltd. • Biennial. $54.00. 1,746 dealers in antiquarian and secondhand books in 24 European countries.

Sheppard's Bookdealers in North America. Richard Joseph Publishers, Ltd. • Biennial. $60.00. Over 3,364 dealers in antiquarian and secondhand books in the U.S. and Canada.

FINANCIAL RATIOS
Annual Statement Studies. The Risk Management Association. • Annual. Median and quartile financial ratios are given for over 400 kinds of manufacturing, wholesale, retail, construction, and consumer finance establishments. Data is sorted by both asset size and sales volume. Includes a clearly written "Definition of Ratios" and an alphabetical industry index.

Annual Statement Studies: Industry Default Probabilities and Cash Flow Measures. The Risk Management Association. • Annual. $145.00. Serves as a companion volume to the original *Annual Statement Studies.* Gives probability of default estimates on a percentage scale for more than 450 industries. Includes changes in position year-by-year for eight financial statement line items and provides percentage measures of cash flow.

HANDBOOKS AND MANUALS
ABA Book Buyer's Handbook. American Booksellers Association. • Annual. Membership. Trade policies. Formerly *Book Buyer's Handbook.*

Children's Bookstore. Entrepreneur Media, Inc. • Looseleaf. $59.50. A practical guide to starting a children's bookstore. Covers profit potential, start-up costs, market size evaluation, owner's time required, site selection, lease negotiation, pricing, accounting, advertising, promotion, etc. (Start-Up Business Guide No. E1293.).

Used Book Store. Entrepreneur Media, Inc. • Looseleaf. $59.50. A practical guide to starting a used book store. Covers profit potential, start-up costs, market size evaluation, owner's time required, site selection, lease negotiation, pricing, accounting, advertising, promotion, etc. (Start-Up Business Guide No. E1117.).

INTERNET DATABASES
Advance Monthly Sales for Retail Trade and Food Services. U. S. Census Bureau. Phone: 800-541-8345 or (301)763-4636 Fax: (301)457-3842 E-mail: rcb@census.gov • URL: http://www.census.gov/svsd/www/fullpub.html • Web pages provide monthly sales figures for a wide range of retail businesses. Advance, preliminary, and final statistics are provided for the latest month available in each case, with a previous-year comparison. Updates are monthly.

BookWeb. American Booksellers Association. Phone: 800-637-0037 or (914)591-2665 Fax: (914)591-2720 E-mail: info@bookweb.org • URL: http://www.bookweb.org/bookstores • Web site provides descriptions of more than 4,500 independent bookstores, searchable by name, specialty, or zip code. Fees: Free.

PERIODICALS AND NEWSLETTERS
The Bookseller: The Organ of the Book Trade. J. Whitaker and Sons, Ltd. • Weekly. $160.00 per year. Provides international book trade news.

Bookselling This Week. American Booksellers Association. • Description: Contains information on book selling.

CBA Marketplace. Christian Booksellers Association. CBA Service Corp. • Monthly. $49.95 per year. Edited for religious book stores. Formerly *Bookstore Journal.*

The Library Bookseller; Books Wanted by College and University Libraries. Danna D'Esopo Jackson, editor. • Monthly. $50.00 per year.

Publishers Weekly: The International News Magazine of Book Publishing. Reed Business Information. • 51 times a year. $214.00 per year. The international news magazine of book publishing.

PRICE SOURCES
American Book Prices Current. Bancroft-Parkman, Inc. • Annual. $119.95.

Bookman's Price Index. Gale Cengage Learning. • Annual. 71 volumes in print. $375.00 per volume. Price guide to out more than 17,000 out-of-print and rare books.

STATISTICS SOURCES
Annual Benchmark Report for Retail Trade and Food Services...A Detailed Summary of Retail Sales, Purchases, Accounts Receivable, Inventories, and Food Service Sales. Available from U. S. Government Printing Office. • Annual. $13.00. Issued by the U.S. Census Bureau. Provides detailed annual and monthly retail statistics for the most recent 10 years. Includes data for various kinds of retail outlets, including automobiles, furniture, appliances, building supplies, grocery stores, drug stores, gasoline stations, clothing, sporting goods, department stores, and restaurants.

United States Census of Retail Trade. U.S. Bureau of the Census. • Quinquennial.

TRADE/PROFESSIONAL ASSOCIATIONS
American Booksellers Association. 200 White Plains Rd., Ste. 600, Tarrytown, NY 10591. Phone: 800-637-0037 or (914)591-2665 Fax: (914)591-2720 E-mail: info@bookweb.org • URL: http://www.bookweb.org • Seeks to meet the needs of members, independently owned bookstores with storefront locations, through education, information dissemination, and advocacy. Supports free speech, literacy, and programs that encourage reading.

Antiquarian Booksellers Association of America. 20 W. 44th St., 4th Fl., New York, NY 10036-6604. Phone: (212)944-8291 Fax: (212)944-8293 E-mail: inquiries@abaa.org • URL: http://www.abaa.org.

CBA. PO Box 62000, Colorado Springs, CO 80962-2000. Phone: 800-252-1950 or (719)265-9895 Fax: (719)272-3510 E-mail: info@cbaonline.org • URL: http://www.cbaonline.org • Serves as trade association for retail stores selling Christian books, Bibles, gifts, and Sunday school and church supplies. Compiles statistics; conducts specialized education programs.

International Booksellers Federation. rue de la Science 10, B-1000 Brussels, Belgium. Phone: 32 2 2234940 Fax: 32 2 2234938 E-mail: ibf.booksellers@skynet.be • URL: http://www.ibf-booksellers.org • Booksellers' associations (20) are members and booksellers (200) are associate members. Promotes international cooperation among booksellers and associations of booksellers. Encourages exchange of ideas and experiences and discussion of common problems.

BOOTS AND SHOES

See: SHOE INDUSTRY

BORING MACHINERY

See: MACHINERY

BOTANY, ECONOMIC

See: ECONOMIC BOTANY

BOTTLE INDUSTRY

See: CONTAINER INDUSTRY; GLASS CONTAINER INDUSTRY

BOTTLED WATER INDUSTRY

See: WATER SUPPLY

BOX INDUSTRY

See also: PAPER BOX AND PAPER CONTAINER INDUSTRIES

DIRECTORIES
National Paperbox Association Membership Directory. National Paperbox Association. • Annual. $150.00.

FINANCIAL RATIOS
Annual Statement Studies. The Risk Management Association. • Annual. Median and quartile financial ratios are given for over 400 kinds of manufacturing, wholesale, retail, construction, and consumer finance establishments. Data is sorted by both asset size and sales volume. Includes a clearly written "Definition of Ratios" and an alphabetical industry index.

Annual Statement Studies: Industry Default Probabilities and Cash Flow Measures. The Risk Management Association. • Annual. $145.00. Serves as a companion volume to the original *Annual Statement Studies.* Gives probability of default estimates on a percentage scale for more than 450 industries. Includes changes in position year-by-year for eight financial statement line items and provides percentage measures of cash flow.

ONLINE DATABASES
PIRA. PIRA International Information Centre. • Citations and abstracts pertaining to bookbinding and other pulp, paper, and packaging industries, 1975 to present. Weekly updates. Inquire as to on-line cost and availability.

PERIODICALS AND NEWSLETTERS
Paperboard Packaging Worldwide. Advanstar Communications. • Monthly. $39.00 per year.

PRICE SOURCES
PPI Detailed Report. Bureau of Labor Statistics, U.S. Department of Labor. Available from U.S. Government Printing Office. • Monthly. $55.00 per year. Formerly *Producer Price Indexes.*

STATISTICS SOURCES
Fibre Box Industry Annual Report. Fibre Box Association. • Annual. Free to members; non-members, $250.00.

United States Census of Manufactures. U.S. Bureau of the Census. • Quinquennial. Results presented in reports, tape, CD-ROM, and Diskette files.

TRADE/PROFESSIONAL ASSOCIATIONS
Fibre Box Association. 25 NW Point Blvd., Ste. 510, Elk Grove Village, IL 60007. Phone: (847)364-9600 Fax: (847)364-9639 E-mail: fba@fibrebox.org • URL: http://www.fibrebox.org • Works to bring together North American manufacturers of corrugated paperboard products to provide comprehensive services for the industry. Compiles statistical reports and industry forecasts; disseminates information on labor negotiations and settlements; presents industry positions to government agencies; develops performance test methods, standards and requirements; monitors environmental issues and/or regulations.

North American Packaging Association. 113 S West St., 3rd Fl., Alexandria, VA 22314. Phone: (703)684-2212 Fax: (703)683-6920 E-mail: info@paperbox.org • URL: http://www.paperbox.org • Independent package converters, including manufacturers of rigid (set-up) and folding paper boxes; suppliers to the industry. Aims to further the development, use, and sale of members' products; to deal with common industry problems; to foster greater operating

economies and efficiencies. Represents the industry before legislative and regulatory bodies. Conducts technical workshops and seminars on sales, marketing, costing, computers, and management methods. Compiles statistics.

Pacific Coast Paper Box Manufacturers' Association. 1350 Main St., Ste. 1508, Springfield, MA 01103-1628. Phone: (413)686-9191 Fax: (413)747-7777 E-mail: paperboardpackaging@ppcnet.org • URL: http://www.ppcnet.org • Represents folding carton and rigid carton manufacturers. Furthers the success and development of paperboard packaging in the territory west of the Rocky Mountains. Offers statistical, and labor data summary programs for members. Conducts technical and production seminars and employee training in plant and equipment operations. Sponsors student design-school competition.

Wirebound Box Manufacturers Association. PO Box 531335, Mountain Brook, AL 35253-1335. Phone: (205)823-3448 Fax: (205)823-3449 E-mail: hrushing@usit.net • Manufacturers of wirebound boxes and crates.

BOXES, PAPER

See: PAPER BOX AND PAPER CONTAINER INDUSTRIES

BOY'S CLOTHING

See: CHILDREN'S APPAREL INDUSTRY; MEN'S CLOTHING INDUSTRY

BRAINSTORMING

See: CREATIVITY

BRANCH STORES

See: CHAIN STORES

BRAND AWARENESS STUDIES

See: MARKET RESEARCH

BRAND NAMES

See: TRADEMARKS AND TRADE NAMES

BREAD INDUSTRY

See: BAKING INDUSTRY

BREWING INDUSTRY

See also: BEVERAGE INDUSTRY; DISTILLING INDUSTRY

ALMANACS AND YEARBOOKS
Brewers Almanac. Beer Institute. • Annual. $170.00.

The U.S. Beer Market: Impact Databank Review and Forecast. M. Shanken Communications, Inc. • Annual. $845.00. Includes industry commentary and statistics.

CD-ROM DATABASES
OECD Statistical Compendium. Organization for Economic Cooperation and Development. • Semiannual. $1,905.00 per year for 1 to 10 users.

CD-ROM contains more than 730,000 monthly, quarterly, and annual time series for OECD countries, 1960 to date. Includes fully searchable data on agriculture, food, economic indicators, national accounts, employment, energy, finance, industry, technology, and foreign trade. Results can be displayed in various forms.

DIRECTORIES
Brewers Digest Annual Buyers Guide and Brewery Directory. Siebel Publishing Company, Inc. • Annual. $50.00. Lists all breweries throughout the western hemisphere.

Major Food and Drink Companies of the World. Available from Gale Cengage Learning. • Annual. $880.00. Two volumes. Published by Graham & Whiteside. Contains profiles and trade names for more than 9,800 important food and beverage companies in various countries. In addition to foods, includes both alcoholic and nonalcoholic drink products.

Modern Brewery Age Blue Book. Business Journals Inc. • Covers: Over 3,000 breweries, beer wholesalers, importers, trade associations, regulatory agencies, and suppliers to the malt beverage industry; international coverage. Entries include: For breweries, distribution plants, wholesalers, importers and suppliers--Company name, address, names of key personnel, phone, products. For government officials--Name, address. For trade associations--Association name, address, phone.

Thomas Food and Beverage Market Place. Grey House Publishing. • 2004. $495.00. Three volumes. Contains more than 40,000 entries covering food companies, beverages, food equipment, warehouse companies, food brokers, wholesalers, importers, and exporters. Formerly *Thomas Food Industry Register.*

INTERNET DATABASES
Business 2.0 Web Guide to the Best Business Links. Business 2.0 Media Inc. Phone: (415)293-4800 E-mail: support@business2.com • URL: http://www.business2.com/webguide • Web site presents an extensive, searchable directory of links to "the best, most informative, and authoritative web pages." Twenty main categories cover business, finance, career, company information, people, and technology topics, with thousands of subtopics, all linking to Web sites recommended by experienced business researchers. Fees: Free.

Fedstats. Federal Interagency Council on Statistical Policy. Phone: (202)395-7254 • URL: http://www.fedstats.gov • Web site features an efficient search facility for full-text statistics produced by more than 100 federal agencies, including the Census Bureau, the Bureau of Economic Analysis, and the Bureau of Labor Statistics. Boolean searches can be made within one agency or for all agencies combined. Links are offered to international statistical bureaus, including the UN, IMF, OECD, UNESCO, Eurostat, and 20 individual countries. Fees: Free.

FreeLunch.com. Economy.com, Inc. Phone: (610)696-8700 Fax: (610)696-1678 • URL: http://www.freelunch.com • Web site provides free access to more than 1.5 million economic and financial data series, covering industry, demographics, labor markets, prices, retail sales, government spending, trade, interest rates, housing starts, the stock market, and many other topics. Data is available for various time periods in either chart or table form. Searching is offered. Fees: Free, but registration required. Economy.com, Inc. also offers fee-based economic analysis at *The Dismal Scientist* site (http://www.dismal.com).

PERIODICALS AND NEWSLETTERS
American Society of Brewing Chemists Journal. American Society of Brewing Chemists. • Quarterly. Free to members; non-members, $164.00 per year; corporate members, $195.00 per year;

student members, $25.00 per year.

ASBC Newsletter. American Society of Brewing Chemists. • Description: Provides news items and technical reports on brewing and related matters. Recurring features include news items, abstracts of technical papers, convention news, book reviews, and membership listings and changes.

Beer Marketer's Insights. Beer Marketer's Insights, Inc. • Semimonthly. $485.00 per year. Newsletter for brewers and wholesalers.

Brewers Digest. Siebel Publishing Co., Inc. • Monthly. $25.00 per year. Covers all aspects of brewing. Annual *Buyers' Guide* and *Directory* available.

Brewing and Distilling International. Brewery Traders Publications, Ltd. • Monthly. $82.00 per year.

Impact: U.S. News and Research for the Wine, Spirits, and Beer Industries. M. Shanken Communications, Inc. • Semimonthly. $375.00 per year. Newsletter covering the marketing, economic, and financial aspects of alcoholic beverages.

Kane's Beverage Week: The Newsletter of Beverage Marketing. Whitaker Newsletters, Inc. • Weekly. $469.00 per year. Newsletter. Covers news relating to the alcoholic beverage industries, including social, health, and legal issues.

Malt Advocate: Beer and Whiskey Magazine. Malt Advocate, Inc. • Quarterly. $16.00 per year. Provides information for consumers of upscale whiskey and beer.

MBAA Technical Quarterly. Master Brewers Association of the Americas. • Quarterly. $100.00 per year. Includes membership.

Modern Brewery Age. Business Journals, Inc. • Bimonthly. $85.00 per year. Annual supplement available *Blue Book.*

PRICE SOURCES

Beverage Media. Beverage Network. Beverage Media, Ltd. • Monthly. $78.00 per year. Wholesale prices.

Feedstuffs: The Weekly Newspaper for Agribusiness. Farm Progress Companies. • Weekly. $135.00 per year. Newsletter.

RESEARCH CENTERS AND INSTITUTES

Cereal Crops Research Unit U.S. Department of Agricultural Research Service. 501 N. Walnut St., Madison, WI 53705. Phone: (608)262-3355 Fax: (608)264-5528 E-mail: dmpeter4@facstaff.wisc.edu • URL: http://www.dfrc.ars.usda.gov/ccru

STATISTICS SOURCES

Annual Survey of Manufactures. Available from U. S. Government Printing Office. • Annual. Prices vary. Issued by the U. S. Census Bureau as an interim update to the *Census of Manufactures.* Includes data on number of manufacturing establishments in various industries, employment, labor costs, value of shipments, capital expenditures, inventories, energy costs, and assets. (See also Census Bureau home page, http://www.census. gov/.).

Beer Statistics News. Beer Marketer's Insights, Inc. • Semimonthly. $485.00 per year. Market share and shipments by region and brewer.

Business Statistics of the United States. Linz Audain and Cornelia J. Strawser. Bernan Associates. • Annual. $147.00. Based on *Business Statistics,* formerly issue by the Bureau of Economic Analysis, U. S. Department of Commerce. Provides basic data for a wide variety of U. S. industries, services, and economic indicators. Most statistics are shown annually for 30 years and monthly for the most recent four years.

The Global Drinks Market Impact Databank. M. Shanken Communications, Inc. • Annual. $2,975. 00. Detailed compilations of data for various segments of the liquor, beer, and soft drink industries.

Monthly Statistical Release: Beer. U. S. Bureau of Alcohol, Tobacco, and Firearms. • Monthly.

Standard & Poor's Industry Surveys. Standard & Poor's. • Semiannual. $1,800.00. Two looseleaf volumes. Includes monthly *Supplements.* Provides detailed, individual surveys of 52 major industry groups. Each survey is revised on a semiannual basis. Also includes "Monthly Investment Review" (industry group investment analysis) and monthly "Trends & Projections" (economic analysis).

Survey of Current Business. Available from U. S. Government Printing Office. • Monthly. $63.00 per year. Issued by Bureau of Economic Analysis, U. S. Department of Commerce. Presents a wide variety of business and economic data.

World Drinks Data and Statistics. Euromonitor International. • 2004. $650.00. Provides five-year data for both alcoholic and non-alcoholic beverages in 52 countries. Includes market size, consumer expenditures, price indicators, and retail distribution data for beer, wine, spirits, tea, coffee, soft drinks, fruit juices, bottled water, and other drinks.

TRADE/PROFESSIONAL ASSOCIATIONS

American Society of Brewing Chemists. 3340 Pilot Knob Rd., Saint Paul, MN 55121-2097. Phone: (612)454-7250 Fax: (612)454-0766 E-mail: asbc@ scisoc.org • URL: http://www.asbcnet.org.

Beer Institute. 122 C St. NW, Ste. 350, Washington, DC 20001. Phone: 800-379-BREW or (202)737-2337 Fax: (202)737-7004 E-mail: info@ beerinstitute.org • URL: http://www.beerinstitute. org • Brewers, importers, and suppliers to the industry. Committed to the development of public policy and to the values of civic duty and personal responsibility.

Brewers' Association of America. 501 Washington St., Ste. H, Durham, NC 27701. Phone: (919)530-8140 Fax: (919)530-8160 E-mail: www.65.23.136. 214/ • URL: http://www207.8.155.214/.

Brewery and Soft Drink Workers Conference-U. S.A. and Canada. 25 Louisiana Ave., NW, Washington, DC 20001. Phone: (202)624-6921 Fax: (202)624-8137 E-mail: brewery@teamster.org • URL: http://www.teamster.org • Promotes the interests of brewery and soft drink workers in the United States and Canada.

Master Brewers Association of the Americas. 3340 Pilot Knot Rd., Saint Paul, MN 55121-2097. Phone: (651)454-7250 Fax: (651)454-0766 E-mail: mbaa@ mbaa.com • URL: http://www.mbaa.com • Formerly Master Brewers Association of America.

National Beer Wholesalers Association. 1101 King St., Ste. 600, Alexandria, VA 22314-2944. Phone: 800-300-6417 or (703)683-4300 Fax: (703)683-8965 E-mail: info@nbwa.org • URL: http://www. nbwa.org • Independent wholesalers of malt beverages and affiliates of the malt beverage industry. Conducts specialized education programs.

World Association of Alcohol Beverage Industries. P.O. Box 45-1057, Garland, TX 75045. Phone: 800-466-6920 or (972)675-3246 Fax: (972)675-3673 E-mail: woodgateh@aol.com • URL: http://www. waabi.org • Volunteer men and women working together for personal growth and for the benefit of the legal alcohol beverage industry. Formerly National Women's Association of Allied Beverage Industries.

OTHER SOURCES

Liquor Control Law Reporter: Federal and All States. CCH, Inc. • Biweekly. $3,649.00 per year. Nine looseleaf volumes. Federal and state regulation and taxation of alcoholic beverages.

The Market for Craft and Specialty Beer. MarketResearch.com. • 1997. $1,625.00. Market research report with projections. Includes brewing company profiles.

BRIBES AND PAYOFFS

See: BUSINESS ETHICS

BRICK INDUSTRY

See: CLAY INDUSTRY; REFRACTORIES

BROADCASTING

See: RADIO BROADCASTING INDUSTRY; TELEVISION BROADCASTING INDUSTRY

BROKERS, STOCK

See: STOCK BROKERS

BUDGET, FEDERAL

See: FEDERAL BUDGET

BUDGETING, BUSINESS

GENERAL WORKS

Basics of Budgeting. Robert G. Finney. AMACOM. • 1993. $19.95.

Internet Prophets: Enlightened E-Business Strategies for Every Budget. Mary Diffley. Information Today, Inc. • 2002. $29.95. Emphasizes the specific dollar costs of having a successful online business. The "Internet Prophets" are four individual guides for developing business on the Web, arranged according to size of budget. (CyberAge Books.).

ABSTRACTS AND INDEXES

Accounting and Tax Index. UMI. • Quarterly. Price on application. Annual cumulation. Indexes accounting, auditing, and taxation literature appearing in journals, books, pamphlets, conference proceedings, and newsletters.

HANDBOOKS AND MANUALS

Budgeting: A How-to-Do-it Manual for Librarians. Alice S. Warner. Neal-Schuman Publishers, Inc. • 1998. $49.95. Explains six forms of budgeting suitable for various kinds of libraries. Includes a bibliography. (How-to-Do-It Manuals Series).

Film and Video Budgets. Deke Simon and Michael Wiese. Michael Wiese Productions. • 2001. $26.95. Third edition. Contains detailed, sample budgets for a wide variety of productions from shoestring documentaries to expensive feature films. Includes practical explanations and information.

Handbook of Budgeting. William R. Lalli. John Wiley and Sons, Inc. • 2003. $145.00. Fifth edition.

Little Black Book of Budgets and Forecasts. Michael C. Thomsett. AMACOM. • 1988. $14.95. A concise guide to business budgeting and forecasting. (Little Black Book Series).

Total Business Budgeting: A Step-by-Step Guide with Forms. Robert Rachlin. John Wiley and Sons, Inc. • 1999. $90.00. Second edition.

PERIODICALS AND NEWSLETTERS

Journal of Cost Management. RIA. • Bimonthly. $230.00 per year. Includes articles on business budgeting.

Strategic Finance. Institute of Management Accountants. • Monthly. Institutions, $140.00 per year; non-profit libraries, $70,00 per year. Provides articles on corporate finance, cost control, cash flow, budgeting, corporate taxes, and other financial management topics.

Successful Cost Control Strategies for CEOs, Managers, and Administrators. Siefer Consultants,

Inc. • Monthly. $279.00 per year. Newsletter. Provides a variety of ideas on business budgeting and controlling company expenses. Formerly *Employee Cost Conrol Strategies for CEOs, Managers, and Administrators.*

TRADE/PROFESSIONAL ASSOCIATIONS

National Association of State Budget Officers. Hall of States, 444 N Capitol St. NW, Ste. 642, Washington, DC 20001-1511. Phone: (202)624-5382 Fax: (202)624-7745 E-mail: nasbo-direct@nasbo.org • URL: http://www.nasbo.org.

BUDGETING, PERSONAL

See: PERSONAL FINANCE

BUILDING AND LOAN ASSOCIATIONS

See: SAVINGS AND LOAN ASSOCIATIONS

BUILDING CONTRACTS

See also: BUILDING INDUSTRY; CONTRACTS

GENERAL WORKS

Construction Contracting. Richard H. Clough and Glenn A. Sears. John Wiley and Sons, Inc. • 1994. $110.00. Sixth edition.

ABSTRACTS AND INDEXES

Current Law Index: Multiple Access to Legal Periodicals. Gale Cengage Learning. • Monthly. $725.00 per year. Produced in cooperation with the American Association of Law Libraries. Indexes more than 900 law journals, legal newspapers, and specialty publications from the U.S., Canada, U.K., Ireland, Australia, and New Zealand.

DIRECTORIES

ABC Today-Associated Builders and Contractors National Membership Directory. Associated Builders and Contractors, Inc. • Annual. $150.00. List of approximately 19,000 member construction contractors and suppliers. Formerly *Builder and Contractor-Associated Builders and Contractors Membership Directory.*

Blue Book of Building and Construction. Contractors Register, Inc. • Annual. Controlled circulation. 15 regional editions. Lists architects, contractors, subcontractors, manufacturers and suppliers of constructions materials and equipment.

ENR Top 400 Construction Contractors (Engineering News-Record). McGraw-Hill. • Annual. $10.00. Lists 400 United States contractors receiving largest dollar volume of contracts in preceding calendar year.

INTERNET DATABASES

Lexis.com Research System. Lexis-Nexis Group. Phone: 800-227-4908 or (937)865-6800 Fax: (937)865-6909 E-mail: webmaster@prod.lexisnexis.com • URL: http://www.lexis.com • Fee-based Web site offers extensive searching of a wide variety of legal sources. Additional features include Daily Opinion Service, lexis.com Bookstore, Career Center, CLE Center, Law Schools, and Practice Pages ("Pages specific to areas of specialty").

PERIODICALS AND NEWSLETTERS

ASA Today. American Subcontractors Association. • Weekly. $40.00 per year.

Constructor: The Management Magazine of the Construction Industry. Associated General Contractors of America. AGC Information, Inc. • Monthly. Members, $15.00 per year; non-members, $250.00

per year. Includes *Directory.*

Government Contractor. West DC Editorial. • Weekly. $1,700.00 per year.

TRADE/PROFESSIONAL ASSOCIATIONS

American Institute of Constructors. 466 94th Ave., N., Saint Petersburg, FL 33702. Phone: (727)578-0317 Fax: (727)578-9982 E-mail: admin@aicnet.org • URL: http://www.aicnet.org.

American Subcontractors Association. 1004 Duke St., Alexandria, VA 22314-3588. Phone: 888-374-3133 or (703)684-3450 Fax: (703)836-3482 E-mail: asaoffice@asa-hq.com • URL: http://www.asaonline.com • Construction subcontractors of trades and specialties such as foundations, concrete, masonry, steel, mechanical, drywall, electrical, painting, plastering, roofing, and acoustical. Formed to deal with issues common to subcontractors. Works with other segments of the construction industry in promoting ethical practices, beneficial legislation, and education of construction subcontractors and suppliers. Manages the Foundation of the American +Subcontractors Association (FASA).

Associated Builders and Contractors. 1300 N. 17th St., Suite 800, Arlington, VA 22209. Phone: (703)812-2000 Fax: (703)812-8200 E-mail: info@abc.org • URL: http://www.abc.org.

Associated General Contractors of America. 333 John Carlyle St., Suite 200, Alexandria, VA 22314. Phone: (703)548-3118 Fax: (703)548-3119 E-mail: info@agc.org • URL: http://www.agc.org.

Associated Specialty Contractors. 3 Bethesda Metro Ctr., Ste. 1100, Bethesda, MD 20814. Phone: (703)548-3118 Fax: (301)215-4500 E-mail: dgw@necanet.org • URL: http://www.assoc-spec-con.org • Works to promote efficient management and productivity. Coordinates the work of specialized branches of the industry in management information, research, public information, government relations and construction relations. Serves as a liaison among specialty trade associations in the areas of public relations, government relations, and with other organizations. Seeks to avoid unnecessary duplication of effort and expense or conflicting programs among affiliates. Identifies areas of interest and problems shared by members, and develops positions and approaches on such problems.

OTHER SOURCES

Forms and Agreements for Architects, Engineers and Contractors. Albert Dib. West Group. • Three times a year. $900.00. Five looseleaf volume. Covers evaluation of construction documents and alternative clauses. Includes pleadings for litigation and resolving of claims. (Real Property Law Series).

Government Contracts Reports. CCH, Inc. • Weekly. $2,600.00 per year. 10 looseleaf volumes. Laws and regulations affecting government contracts.

BUILDING EQUIPMENT

See: CONSTRUCTION EQUIPMENT

BUILDING ESTIMATING

See: ESTIMATING

BUILDING INDUSTRY

See also: APARTMENT HOUSES; ARCHITECTURE; BUILDING MATERIALS INDUSTRY; CONSTRUCTION EQUIPMENT; DOOR INDUSTRY; ELECTRICAL CONSTRUCTION INDUSTRY; ESTIMATING; HOME IMPROVEMENT INDUSTRY; OFFICE BUILDINGS; PREFABRICATED HOUSE INDUSTRY

GENERAL WORKS

Fundamentals of Construction Estimating and Cost Accounting. Keith Collier. Prentice Hall PTR. • 2000. Third edition. Price on application.

ABSTRACTS AND INDEXES

Applied Science and Technology Index. H. W. Wilson Co. • 11 times a year. Quarterly and annual cumulations. Price varies. Indexes a wide variety of English language technical, industrial, and engineering periodicals.

NTIS Alerts: Building Industry Technology. National Technical Information Service. • Semimonthly. $210.00 per year. Provides descriptions of government-sponsored research reports and software, with ordering information. Covers architecture, construction management, building materials, maintenance, furnishings, and related subjects. Formerly *Abstract Newsletter.*

CD-ROM DATABASES

OECD Statistical Compendium. Organization for Economic Cooperation and Development. • Semiannual. $1,905.00 per year for 1 to 10 users. CD-ROM contains more than 730,000 monthly, quarterly, and annual time series for OECD countries, 1960 to date. Includes fully searchable data on agriculture, food, economic indicators, national accounts, employment, energy, finance, industry, technology, and foreign trade. Results can be displayed in various forms.

DIRECTORIES

ABC Today-Associated Builders and Contractors National Membership Directory. Associated Builders and Contractors, Inc. • Annual. $150.00. List of approximately 19,000 member construction contractors and suppliers. Formerly *Builder and Contractor-Associated Builders and Contractors Membership Directory.*

Builder: Buyer's Guide. Hanley-Wood, LLC. • Annual. $10.00. A directory of products and services for the home building and remodeling industry.

Building Officials and Code Administrators International-Membership Directory. • Annual. $16.00. Approximately 14,000 construction code officials, architects, engineers, trade associations, and manufacturers.

Concrete Construction Buyers' Guide. Hanley-Wood, LLC. • Annual. $5.00. Lists sources of products and services related to building with concrete.

Construction Specifier Member Directory. Construction Specifications Institute. • Annual. $30.00. Roster of construction specifers by the institute, and 17,200 members.

Masonry Construction Buyers' Guide. Mason Contractors Association of America. • Annual. $3.00. Lists manufacturers or suppliers of products and services related to masonry construction.

Plunkett's Real Estate and Construction Industry Almanac. Plunkett Research, Ltd. • 2004. $249.99. Contains profiles of 300 leading firms concerned with real estate or construction. Specialties include architecture, development, mortgages, building engineering, real estate sales, etc. Also covers industry trends and statistical data.

ProSales Buyer's Guide. Hanley-Wood, LLC. • Annual. Price on application. A directory of equipment for professional builders.

Tools of the Trade Annual Buyers Guide. Hanley-Wood, LLC. • Annual. Price on application. A directory of tools for the construction industry.

ENCYCLOPEDIAS AND DICTIONARIES

Dictionary of Architecture and Construction. Cyril M. Harris. McGraw-Hill. • 2000. $69.95. Third edition.

Dictionary of Building. Randall McMullan. GP. • 1991. $59.50.

Wiley Dictionary of Civil Engineering and Construction. Len F. Webster, editor. John Wiley and Sons, Inc. • 1997. $85.00. Provides more than 30,000 definitions in the fields of civil engineering, construction, architecture, forestry, mining, and public works. (Professional Series)

FINANCIAL RATIOS

Almanac of Business and Industrial Financial Ratios. Leo Troy. Aspen Publishers, Inc. • 2003. $125.95. Includes CD-Rom. Contains financial ratios derived from federal tax returns. Ratios for each of about 200 industries are arranged according to company asset size. (Almanac of Business and Industrial Financial Ratios Series).

Construction Industry Annual Financial Survey. Construction Financial Management Association. • Annual. $149.00. Contains key financial ratios for various kinds and sizes of construction contractors.

IRS Corporate Financial Ratios. Available from MarketResearch.com. • 2002. $225.00. Published by Schonfeld & Associates, Inc. Presents 70 key financial ratios for 260 industries. Ratios are calculated from income statement and balance sheet data available from the Internal Revenue Service. Includes four asset size classes.

HANDBOOKS AND MANUALS

Building Construction Handbook. Ray Chudley. Elsevier. • 2001. $34.95. Fourth edition.

Dun & Bradstreet/Gale Group Industry Handbooks. Gale Cengage Learning. • 2000. $650.00. Five volumes. $130.00 per volume. Each volume covers two or more major industries: 1. *Entertainment and Hospitality*; 2. *Construction and Agriculture*; 3. *Chemicals and Pharmaceuticals*; 4. *Computers & Software and Broadcasting & Telecommunications*; 5. *Insurance and Health & Medical Services.* The following are included for each industry: overview, statistics, financial ratios, rankings, merger information, company directory, directory of associations, and consultants directory. (Dun and Bradstreet/Gale Industry Reference Handbook Series).

Guide to Energy Efficient Commercial Equipment. Margaret Suozzo and others. American Council for an Energy Efficient Economy. • 1997. $25.00. Provides information on specifying and purchasing energy-saving systems for buildings (heating, air conditioning, lighting, and motors).

New Uses for Obsolete Buildings. Urban Land Institute. • 1996. $65.95. Covers various aspects of redevelopment: zoning, building codes, environment, economics, financing, and marketing. Includes eight case studies and 75 descriptions of completed "adaptive use projects.".

Standard Handbook of Structural Details for Building Construction. Morton Newman. McGraw-Hill. • 1993. $99.95. Second edition.

INTERNET DATABASES

Business 2.0 Web Guide to the Best Business Links. Business 2.0 Media Inc. Phone: (415)293-4800 E-mail: support@business2.com • URL: http://www.business2.com/webguide • Web site presents an extensive, searchable directory of links to "the best, most informative, and authoritative web pages." Twenty main categories cover business, finance, career, company information, people, and technology topics, with thousands of subtopics, all

linking to Web sites recommended by experienced business researchers. Fees: Free.

Fedstats. Federal Interagency Council on Statistical Policy. Phone: (202)395-7254 • URL: http://www.fedstats.gov • Web site features an efficient search facility for full-text statistics produced by more than 100 federal agencies, including the Census Bureau, the Bureau of Economic Analysis, and the Bureau of Labor Statistics. Boolean searches can be made within one agency or for all agencies combined. Links are offered to international statistical bureaus, including the UN, IMF, OECD, UNESCO, Eurostat, and 20 individual countries. Fees: Free.

FreeLunch.com. Economy.com, Inc. Phone: (610)696-8700 Fax: (610)696-1678 • URL: http://www.freelunch.com • Web site provides free access to more than 1.5 million economic and financial data series, covering industry, demographics, labor markets, prices, retail sales, government spending, trade, interest rates, housing starts, the stock market, and many other topics. Data is available for various time periods in either chart or table form. Searching is offered. Fees: Free, but registration required. Economy.com, Inc. also offers fee-based economic analysis at *The Dismal Scientist* site (http://www.dismal.com).

ONLINE DATABASES

Business and Industry. Gale Cengage Learning. • Contains online citations, abstracts, and selected fulltext from more than 1,000 trade journals, newspapers, and other publications. Provides general coverage of both manufacturing and service industries, including marketing, production, industry trends, key events, and information on specific companies. Time span is 1994 to date. Daily updates. Inquire as to online cost and availability. (Also available in a CD-ROM version.).

Tablebase. Gale Cengage Learning. • Provides online numerical tabular data from a wide variety of business, organization, and government sources, including about 1,000 trade journals. Includes industry and individual company statistics relating to products, market share, sales forecasts, production, exports, market trends, etc. Time span is 1997 to date. Weekly updates. Inquire as to online cost and availability. (Also available in a CD-ROM version.).

PERIODICALS AND NEWSLETTERS

Builder: The Voice of America's Housing Industry. National Association of Home Builders of the United States, Economics, Mortgage Finance and Housing Policy Div. Hanley-Wood, LLC. • Monthly. $29.95 per year. Covers the home building and remodeling industry in general, including design, construction, and marketing.

Building Design and Construction: The Magazine for the Building Team. Reed Business Information. • Monthly. $119.00 per year. For non-residential building owners, contractors, engineers and architects.

Building Products. Hanley-Wood, LLC. • Quarterly. $36.00 per year. Covers building products and materials for the construction industry, including new products.

Buildings: The Source for Facilities Decision-Makers. Stamats Communications, Inc. • Monthly. $70.00 per year. Serves professional building ownership/management organizations.

CFMA Building Profits. Construction Financial Management Association. • Bimonthly. Controlled circulation. Covers the financial side of the construction industry.

Commercial Building: Tranforming Plans into Buildings. Stamats Communications. • Bimonthly. $48.00 per year. Edited for building contractors, engineers, and architects. Includes special features on new products, climate control, plumbing, and vertical transportation.

Construction Law Digest. LexisNexis Matthew Bender. • Monthly. $425.00 per year. Newsletter. Provides practical information on emerging legal trends, issues, and court decisions relevant to the construction industry.

Construction Specifier: For Commercial and Industrial Construction. Construction Specifications Institute. • Monthly. Free to members; non-members, $36.00 per year; libraries, $30.00 per year. Technical aspects of the construction industry.

Custom Home. Hanley-Wood, LLC. • Seven times a year. $36.00 per year. Edited for "top of the market" custom builders, designers, and architects.

Design Cost Data: The Cost Estimating Magazine for Architects, Builders and Specifiers. L. M. Rector Corp. • Bimonthly. $64.80 per year. Provides a preliminary cost estimating system for architects, contractors, builders, and developers, utilizing historical data. Includes case studies of actual costs. Formerly *Design Cost and Data.*

ENR: Connecting the Industry Worldwide (Engineering News-Record). McGraw-Hill. • Weekly. $74.00 per year.

Journal of Light Construction. Hanley-Wood, LLC. • Monthly. $35.95 per year. Provides jobsite tips, techniques, and product advice for builders and contractors.

Masonry Construction. Hanley-Wood, LLC. • 10 times a year. $30.00 per year. Covers masonry design, materials, equipment, and techniques.

Professional Builder: Small Builders and Contractors Business Magazine. Reed Business Information. • 11 times a year. $39.00 per year. Provides price and market forecasts on industrial products, components and materials. Office products, business systems and transportation. Includes supplement *Luxury Homes.* Formerly *Professional Builder and Remodeler.*

ProSales: For Dealers and Distributors Serving the Professional Contractor. Hanley-Wood LLC. • Monthly. $36.00 per year. Includes special feature issues on selling, credit, financing, and the marketing of power tools.

Tools of the Trade. Hanley-Wood, LLC. • Five times a year. $19.80 per year. Provides advice and information on tools for the construction industry. Includes product tests and evaluations.

PRICE SOURCES

Building Construction Cost Data. RSMeans. • Annual. $108.95. Lists over 20,000 entries for estimating.

Means Construction Cost Indexes. RSMeans. • Quarterly. $237.95 per year.

Means Labor Rates for the Construction Industry. RSMeans. • Annual. $239.95. Formerly *Labor Rates for the Construction Industry.*

RESEARCH CENTERS AND INSTITUTES

Construction Industry Institute. Construction Industry Institute. 3925 W Braker Ln., No. R4500, Austin, TX 78759-5316. Phone: (512)232-3000 Fax: (512)499-8101 E-mail: wcrew@mail.utexas.edu • URL: http://construction-institute.org • Management, planning, design, and technology aspects of construction project execution, as well as methods and materials of construction and craft labor techniques. Links owners, contractors, and others directly active in the construction industry with academic resources to develop techniques and databases to improve the cost, schedule, quality and safety of the constructed project, the capital investment process, and total quality of the construction industry. Identifies immediate, long-range, and breakthrough research needs; directs appropriate research and studies; collects information from engineering and construction projects; and provides implementation guides on how to get research into actual engineering and construction projects. Also

---

addresses education needs of the industry and conducts benchmarking studies for "best practices" comparisons.

Construction Research Center. University of Texas at Arlington, P.O. Box 19347, Arlington, TX 76019. Phone: (817)272-3701 Fax: (817)272-7575 E-mail: matthys@uta.edu • Addresses the needs of the construction industry through construction research and educational programs.

STATISTICS SOURCES

Annual Bulletin of Housing and Building Statistics for Europe and North America. United Nations Publications. • Annual. $25.00. Provides basic data on housing and construction in European countries, Canada, and the U. S., including non-residential buildings, value of construction, building materials, prices, costs, and rents. Includes base years of 1990 and 1995 and recent calendar years.

Business Statistics of the United States. Linz Audain and Cornelia J. Strawser. Bernan Associates. • Annual. $147.00. Based on *Business Statistics*, formerly issue by the Bureau of Economic Analysis, U. S. Department of Commerce. Provides basic data for a wide variety of U. S. industries, services, and economic indicators. Most statistics are shown annually for 30 years and monthly for the most recent four years.

Encyclopedia of American Industries. Gale Cengage Learning. • 2000. $560.00. Third edition. Two volumes. $280.00 per volume. Volume one is *Manufacturing Industries* and volume two is *Service and Non-Manufacturing Industries.* Provides the history, development, and recent status of approximately 1,000 industries. Includes statistical graphs, with industry and general indexes.

Expenditures for Residential Improvements and Repairs. Available from U. S. Government Printing Office. • Quarterly. $16.00 per year. Bureau of the Census Construction Report, C50. Provides estimates of spending for housing maintenance, repairs, additions, alterations, and major replacements.

Infrastructure Industries USA. Gale Cengage Learning. • 2001. $260.00. Presents statistics and projections relating to economic activity in a wide variety of natural resource and construction industries.

Standard & Poor's Industry Surveys. Standard & Poor's. • Semiannual. $1,800.00. Two looseleaf volumes. Includes monthly *Supplements.* Provides detailed, individual surveys of 52 major industry groups. Each survey is revised on a semiannual basis. Also includes "Monthly Investment Review" (industry group investment analysis) and monthly "Trends & Projections" (economic analysis).

Survey of Current Business. Available from U. S. Government Printing Office. • Monthly. $63.00 per year. Issued by Bureau of Economic Analysis, U. S. Department of Commerce. Presents a wide variety of business and economic data.

U. S. Industry Profiles: The Leading 100. Gale Cengage Learning. • 1998. $130.00. Second edition. Contains detailed profiles, with statistics, of 100 industries in the areas of manufacturing, construction, transportation, wholesale trade, retail trade, and entertainment.

United States Census of Construction Industries. U.S. Bureau of the Census. • Quinquennial. Results presented in reports, tape, and CD-ROM files.

Value of New Construction Put in Place. U.S. Bureau of the Census. Available from U.S. Government Printing Office. • Monthly. $42.00 per year.

WEFA Industrial Monitor. John Wiley and Sons, Inc. • Annual. $65.00. Prepared by industry analysts at WEFA, an economic forecasting and consulting firm (originally Wharton Econometric Forecasting Associates). Contains discussions of the outlook for major U. S. industries, with many 10-year forecasts (WEFA Web site is http://www.wefa.com).

TRADE/PROFESSIONAL ASSOCIATIONS

Building and Construction Trades Department - AFL-CIO. 815 16th, Ste. 600, Washington, DC 20006. Phone: (202)347-1461 Fax: (202)628-0724 E-mail: severn@bctd.org • URL: http://www. buildingtrades.org.

Building Officials and Code Administrators International. 4051 W Flossmoor Rd., Country Club Hills, IL 60478-5795. Phone: 800-214-4321 or (708)799-2300 Fax: 800-214-7167 E-mail: webmaster@bocai.org • URL: http://www.bocai.org • Formerly Building Officials Conference of America.

Construction Financial Management Association. 29 Emmons Dr., Ste. F-50, Princeton, NJ 08540. Phone: (609)452-8000 Fax: (609)452-0474 E-mail: info@ cfma.org • URL: http://www.cfma.org • Contractors, subcontractors, architects, real estate developers, and engineers; associate members are equipment and material suppliers, accountants, lawyers, bankers, and others involved with the financial management of the construction industry. Provides a forum for the exchange of ideas; coordinates educational programs dedicated to improving the professional standards of financial management in the construction industry. Offers expanded national programs, technical assistance, and industry representation. Conducts research programs; maintains speakers' bureau and placement service; compiles statistics.

Construction Industry Manufacturers Association. 111 E. Wisconsin Ave., Ste. 1000, Milwaukee, WI 53202. Phone: (414)272-0943 Fax: (414)272-1170 E-mail: info@cfma.org • URL: http://www.cimanet. com • Manufacturers of off-highway earthmoving and construction machinery and allied equipment and components. Compiles statistics.

National Association of Home Builders. 1201 15th St., N.W., Washington, DC 20005. Phone: 800-368-5242 or (202)266-8200 • URL: http://www.nahb. com • Members are single and multifamily home builders, commercial builders and others associated with the building industry.

National Association of the Remodeling Industry. 780 Lee St., Suite 200, Des Plaines, IL 60016. Phone: 800-611-6274 or (847)298-9200 Fax: (847)298-9225 E-mail: info@nari.org • URL: http:// www.nari.org.

National Association of Women In Construction. 327 S. Adams St., Fort Worth, TX 76104. Phone: 800-552-3506 or (817)877-5551 Fax: (817)877-0324 E-mail: nawic@nawic.org • URL: http://www. nawic.org.

National Constructors Association. 1730 M St. NW, Ste. 503, Washington, DC 20036. Phone: (703)560-2391 Fax: (703)560-2392 E-mail: nfpa@nfpa.com • URL: http://www.nccc.org • Engineering and construction contractors specializing in design and installation of chemical plants, steel mills, power plants, oil refineries, and atomic energy facilities. Serves as a clearinghouse for collecting, analyzing, and exchanging information about field labor and working conditions on industrial construction projects, wages, and safety. Negotiates union labor agreements with members of Building Constitution Trades Department. Sponsors Work +Environment +Safety Training Program.

OTHER SOURCES

Construction Labor Report. BNA, Inc. • Weekly. $1,189.00 per year. Two looseleaf volumes.

Construction Law. LexisNexis Matthew Bender. • Looseleaf. $935.00. Six volumes. Periodic supplementation available. Edited for lawyers who prepare construction contracts or engage in construction dispute litigation.

Dodge Reports. F. W. Dodge Group. • Daily. Price on application. Individual reports on new construction jobs.

Dodge/SCAN. F. W. Dodge Group. • Price on application. Provides plans and specifications of new construction jobs.

Door Hardware. Available from MarketResearch. com. • 1997. $495.00. Market research report published by Specialists in Business Information. Covers locks, closers, doorknobs, security devices, and other door hardware. Presents market data relative to demographics, sales growth, shipments, exports, imports, price trends, and end-use. Includes company profiles.

Doors. Available from MarketResearch.com. • 1999. $2,250.00. Market research report published by Specialists in Business Information. Covers residential doors, including garage doors. Presents market data relative to demographics, sales growth, shipments, exports, imports, price trends, and end-use. Includes company profiles.

Forms and Agreements for Architects, Engineers and Contractors. Albert Dib. West Group. • Three times a year. $900.00. Five looseleaf volume. Covers evaluation of construction documents and alternative clauses. Includes pleadings for litigation and resolving of claims. (Real Property Law Series).

International Code Council, Uniform Building Code. International Conference of Building Officials. • Triennial. Two volumes. Members, $144. 55; non-members, $180.70. (International Conference of Building Officials. Uniform Building Code).

Windows. Available from MarketResearch.com. • 2001. $2,250.00. Market research report published by Specialists in Business Information. Covers metal, wood, and vinyl windows. Presents market data relative to demographics, sales growth, shipments, exports, imports, price trends, and end-use. Includes company profiles.

BUILDING LOANS

See: MORTGAGES

BUILDING MAINTENANCE

See: MAINTENANCE OF BUILDINGS

BUILDING MANAGEMENT

See: PROPERTY MANAGEMENT

BUILDING MATERIALS INDUSTRY

GENERAL WORKS

Basic Construction Materials. Theodore Marotta. Prentice-Hall PTR. • 2001. $88.00. Sixth edition.

Construction Materials and Processes. Donald A. Watson. McGraw-Hill. • 1986. $83.34. Third edition.

Materials of Construction. James Lai. Kendall/Hunt Publishing Co. • 1999. $65.95. Second edition.

CD-ROM DATABASES

OECD Statistical Compendium. Organization for Economic Cooperation and Development. • Semiannual. $1,905.00 per year for 1 to 10 users. CD-ROM contains more than 730,000 monthly, quarterly, and annual time series for OECD countries, 1960 to date. Includes fully searchable data on agriculture, food, economic indicators, national accounts, employment, energy, finance, industry, technology, and foreign trade. Results can

be displayed in various forms.

DIRECTORIES

Builder: Buyer's Guide. Hanley-Wood, LLC. • Annual. $10.00. A directory of products and services for the home building and remodeling industry.

Construction Equipment Buyers Guide. Reed Business Information. • Annual. $49.95.

Directory of Home Center Operators and Hardware Chains. Chain Store Guide. • Annual. $327.00. On-line edition, $747.00. Nearly 4,700 home center operators, paint and home decorating chains, and lumber and building materials companies. Covers United States and Canada.

International Conference of Building Officials - Membership Directory. International Conference of Building Officials. • Annual. Price on application.

North American Building Material Distribution Association-Membership. North American Building Material Distribution Association. • Annual. Free to members; non-members, $795.00. About 200 wholesale distributors of building products who are members, and 150 manufacturers in that field who are associate members and over 600 of their locations. Formerly *National Building Material Distributors Association Membership and Product Directory.*

North American Wholesale Lumber Association - Distribution Directory. North American Wholesale Lumber Association. • Annual. $50.00. Over 600 wholesalers and manufacturers of lumber and related forest products.

Remodeling--Product Guide. Hanley-Wood L.L.C. • Publication includes: List of more than 2,000 manufacturers and suppliers serving the remodeling contracting industry; list of industry-related associations. Entries include: For manufacturers and suppliers--Company name, address, phone, name and title of contact, product line, geographical area served. For associations--Association name, address, phone, director.

U. S. Glass, Metal, and Glazing: Buyers Guide. Key Communications, Inc. • Annual. $25.00. A directory of about 3,000 supplies and equipment for the glass fabrication and installation industry.

ENCYCLOPEDIAS AND DICTIONARIES

Dictionary of Architecture, Building Construction and Materials. Herbert Bucksch. French and European Publications, Inc. • 1983. $295.00. Second edition. Volume two. Text in English and German.

Encyclopedia of Materials: Science and Technology. K.H.J. Buschow and others, editors. Elsevier. • 2001. $4,985.00. Eleven volumes. Provides extensive technical information on a wide variety of materials, including metals, ceramics, plastics, optical materials, and building materials. Includes more than 2,000 articles and 5,000 illustrations.

Illustrated Dictionary of Building Materials and Techniques: An Invaluable Sourcebook to the Tools, Terms, Materials, and Techniques Used by Building Professionals. Paul Bianchina. John Wiley and Sons, Inc. • 1993. $19.95. Contains 4,000 definitions of building and building materials terms, with 500 illustrations. Includes materials grades, measurements, and specifications.

FINANCIAL RATIOS

Almanac of Business and Industrial Financial Ratios. Leo Troy. Aspen Publishers, Inc. • 2003. $125.95. Includes CD-Rom. Contains financial ratios derived from federal tax returns. Ratios for each of about 200 industries are arranged according to company asset size. (Almanac of Business and Industrial Financial Ratios Series).

Annual Statement Studies. The Risk Management Association. • Annual. Median and quartile financial ratios are given for over 400 kinds of manufactur-

ing, wholesale, retail, construction, and consumer finance establishments. Data is sorted by both asset size and sales volume. Includes a clearly written "Definition of Ratios" and an alphabetical industry index.

Annual Statement Studies: Industry Default Probabilities and Cash Flow Measures. The Risk Management Association. • Annual. $145.00. Serves as a companion volume to the original *Annual Statement Studies.* Gives probability of default estimates on a percentage scale for more than 450 industries. Includes changes in position year-by-year for eight financial statement line items and provides percentage measures of cash flow.

Annual Statement Studies: Industry Default Probabilities and Cash Flow Measures. The Risk Management Association. • Annual. $145.00. Serves as a companion volume to the original *Annual Statement Studies.* Gives probability of default estimates on a percentage scale for more than 450 industries. Includes changes in position year-by-year for eight financial statement line items and provides percentage measures of cash flow.

HANDBOOKS AND MANUALS

Construction Materials: Types, Uses, and Applications. Caleb Hornbostel. John Wiley and Sons, Inc. • 1991. $250.00. Second edition. (Practical Construction Guides Series).

Materials Handbook. John A. Vaccari and others. McGraw-Hill. • 2002. $99.95. 15th edition. (Handbook Series).

INTERNET DATABASES

Advance Monthly Sales for Retail Trade and Food Services. U. S. Census Bureau. Phone: 800-541-8345 or (301)763-4636 Fax: (301)457-3842 E-mail: rcb@census.gov • URL: http://www.census.gov/svsd/www/fullpub.html • Web pages provide monthly sales figures for a wide range of retail businesses. Advance, preliminary, and final statistics are provided for the latest month available in each case, with a previous-year comparison. Updates are monthly.

Business 2.0 Web Guide to the Best Business Links. Business 2.0 Media Inc. Phone: (415)293-4800 E-mail: support@business2.com • URL: http://www.business2.com/webguide • Web site presents an extensive, searchable directory of links to "the best, most informative, and authoritative web pages." Twenty main categories cover business, finance, career, company information, people, and technology topics, with thousands of subtopics, all linking to Web sites recommended by experienced business researchers. Fees: Free.

Fedstats. Federal Interagency Council on Statistical Policy. Phone: (202)395-7254 • URL: http://www.fedstats.gov • Web site features an efficient search facility for full-text statistics produced by more than 100 federal agencies, including the Census Bureau, the Bureau of Economic Analysis, and the Bureau of Labor Statistics. Boolean searches can be made within one agency or for all agencies combined. Links are offered to international statistical bureaus, including the UN, IMF, OECD, UNESCO, Eurostat, and 20 individual countries. Fees: Free.

FreeLunch.com. Economy.com, Inc. Phone: (610)696-8700 Fax: (610)696-1678 • URL: http://www.freelunch.com • Web site provides free access to more than 1.5 million economic and financial data series, covering industry, demographics, labor markets, prices, retail sales, government spending, trade, interest rates, housing starts, the stock market, and many other topics. Data is available for various time periods in either chart or table form. Searching is offered. Fees: Free, but registration required. Economy.com, Inc. also offers fee-based economic

analysis at *The Dismal Scientist* site (http://www.dismal.com).

PERIODICALS AND NEWSLETTERS

Building Material Dealer. National Lumber and Building Material Dealers Association. • Monthly. $48.00 per year. Includes special feature issues on hand and power tools, lumber, roofing, kitchens, flooring, windows and doors, and insulation. Formerly *Builder Material Retailer.*

National Home Center News: News and Analysis for the Home Improvement, Building Material Industry. Lebhar-Friedman, Inc. • 22 times a year. $99.00 per year. Includes special feature issues on hardware and tools, building materials, millwork, electrical supplies, lighting, and kitchens.

U. S. Glass, Metal, and Glazing. Key Communications, Inc. • Monthly. $35.00 per year. Edited for glass fabricators, glaziers, distributors, and retailers. Special feature issues are devoted to architectural glass, mirror glass, windows, storefronts, hardware, machinery, sealants, and adhesives. Regular topics include automobile glass and fenestration (window design and placement).

PRICE SOURCES

PPI Detailed Report. Bureau of Labor Statistics, U.S. Department of Labor. Available from U.S. Government Printing Office. • Monthly. $55.00 per year. Formerly *Producer Price Indexes.*

RESEARCH CENTERS AND INSTITUTES

Building Research Council. University of Illinois at Urbana-Champaign. One E. Saint Mary's Rd., Champaign, IL 61820. Phone: 800-336-0616 or (217)333-1801 Fax: (217)244-2204 • Integral unit of School of Architecture.

National Association of Home Builders Research Center. 400 Prince George's Blvd., Upper Marlboro, MD 20774. Phone: 800-638-8556 or (301)249-4000 Fax: (301)430-6180 • URL: http://www.nahbrc.org.

STATISTICS SOURCES

Annual Benchmark Report for Retail Trade and Food Services...A Detailed Summary of Retail Sales, Purchases, Accounts Receivable, Inventories, and Food Service Sales. Available from U. S. Government Printing Office. • Annual. $13.00. Issued by the U.S. Census Bureau. Provides detailed annual and monthly retail statistics for the most recent 10 years. Includes data for various kinds of retail outlets, including automobiles, furniture, appliances, building supplies, grocery stores, drug stores, gasoline stations, clothing, sporting goods, department stores, and restaurants.

Business Statistics of the United States. Linz Audain and Cornelia J. Strawser. Bernan Associates. • Annual. $147.00. Based on *Business Statistics,* formerly issue by the Bureau of Economic Analysis, U. S. Department of Commerce. Provides basic data for a wide variety of U. S. industries, services, and economic indicators. Most statistics are shown annually for 30 years and monthly for the most recent four years.

Survey of Current Business. Available from U. S. Government Printing Office. • Monthly. $63.00 per year. Issued by Bureau of Economic Analysis, U. S. Department of Commerce. Presents a wide variety of business and economic data.

TRADE/PROFESSIONAL ASSOCIATIONS

International Conference of Building Officials. 5360 Workman Mill Rd., Whittier, CA 90601-2298. Phone: 800-423-6587 or (562)699-0541 or (562)699-0543 Fax: (562)695-4694 • URL: http://www.icbo.org • Formerly Pacific Coast Building Officials Conference.

National Lumber and Building Materials Dealers Association. 40 Ivy St., S.E., Washington, DC 20003. Phone: 800-634-8645 or (202)547-2230 Fax: (202)547-7640 E-mail: nikki@dealer.org • URL:

http://www.dealer.org • Formerly National Retail Lumber Dealers Association.

North American Building Material Distribution Association. 401 N. Michigan Ave., Chicago, IL 60611. Phone: 888-747-7862 Fax: (312)644-0310 E-mail: nbmda@sba.com • URL: http://www.nbmda.org • Formerly National Building Material Distributors Association.

OTHER SOURCES

The Home Improvement Market. Available from MarketResearch.com. • 1999. $2,750.00. Market research report published by Packaged Facts. Covers the market for lumber, finishing materials, tools, hardware, etc.

BUILDING REPAIR AND RECONSTRUCTION

See: HOME IMPROVEMENT INDUSTRY

BUILDING RESEARCH

See also: ARCHITECTURE; BUILDING INDUSTRY; BUSINESS RESEARCH

RESEARCH CENTERS AND INSTITUTES

Building Research Council. University of Illinois at Urbana-Champaign. One E. Saint Mary's Rd., Champaign, IL 61820. Phone: 800-336-0616 or (217)333-1801 Fax: (217)244-2204 • Integral unit of School of Architecture.

Centre for Building Science. University of Toronto Department of Civil Engineering. 35 Saint George St., Toronto, ON, Canada M5S 1A4. Phone: (416)978-6813 Fax: (416)978-6813 E-mail: pressna@civ.utoronto.ca • URL: http://www.civ.utoronto.ca.

National Association of Home Builders Research Center. 400 Prince George's Blvd., Upper Marlboro, MD 20774. Phone: 800-638-8556 or (301)249-4000 Fax: (301)430-6180 • URL: http://www.nahbrc.org.

TRADE/PROFESSIONAL ASSOCIATIONS

Building Officials and Code Administrators International. 4051 W Flossmoor Rd., Country Club Hills, IL 60478-5795. Phone: 800-214-4321 or (708)799-2300 Fax: 800-214-7167 E-mail: webmaster@bocai.org • URL: http://www.bocai.org • Formerly Building Officials Conference of America.

BUILDING STONE

See: QUARRYING

BUILDING SUPPLY INDUSTRY

See: BUILDING MATERIALS INDUSTRY

BUILDINGS, PREFABRICATED

See: PREFABRICATED HOUSE INDUSTRY

BUILDINGS, RESIDENTIAL

See: HOUSING

BULLION

See: MONEY

BUREAUCRACY

See also: GOVERNMENT EMPLOYEES

GENERAL WORKS

Bureaucracy: What Government Agencies Do and Why They Do It. James Q. Wilson. Basic Books. • 2000. $24.00. Second edition.

Businesses' Views on Red Tape: Administrative and Regulatory Burdens on Small and Medium-Sized Enterprises. Organization for Economic Cooperation and Development. • 2001. $22.00. Based on a survey of about 8,000 firms in 11 OECD countries. Provides opinions on the costs of complying with governmental rules, regulations, and formalities.

From Red Tape to Smart Tape: Administrative Simplification in OECD Countries. Organization for Economic Cooperation and Development. • 2003. $58.00. "This report looks at a set of tools and practices commonly used by governments to make administrative regulations simpler and less burdensome to comply with." Includes information on one-stop facilitation, license/permit simplification, decision-making time limits, small business assistance, and the use of information technology (IT) for administrative simplification.

The Logic of Organizations. Bengt Abrahamsson. Sage Publications, Inc. • 1992. $39.95. Consists of two major sections: "The Emergence of Bureaucracy.." and "Administration Theory..".

Unmasking Administrative Evil. Guy B. Adams and Danny L. Balfour. M. E. Sharpe, Inc. • 2004. $59.95. Revised edition. Discusses bureaucratic mismanagement and the resulting evil or even tragedy.

ABSTRACTS AND INDEXES

Business Periodicals Index. H. W. Wilson Co. • 11 times a year. Quarterly and annual cumulations. Price varies.

BIBLIOGRAPHIES

Census of Governments: Subject Bibliography No. 156. Available from U. S. Government Printing Office. • Annual. Free. Lists government publications.

Intergovernmental Relations. Available from U. S. Government Printing Office. • Annual. Free. Lists government publications. (Subject Bibliography 211.).

CD-ROM DATABASES

Leadership Library on CD-ROM: Who's Who in the Leadership of the United States. Leadership Directories, Inc. • Quarterly. Including access to Internet version (weekly updates). Contains all 14 *Yellow Book* personnel directories on CD-ROM, providing contact and brief biographical information for about 400,000 individuals. Covers business, government, financial institutions, news media, law firms, associations, foreign representatives, and nonprofit organizations. Includes photographs.

Newspaper Abstracts Ondisc. PROQUEST. • Monthly. $2,950.00 per year (covers 1989 to date; archival discs are available for 1985-88). Provides cover-to-cover CD-ROM indexing and abstracting of 19 major newspapers, including the *New York Times, Wall Street Journal, Washington Post, Chicago Tribune,* and *Los Angeles Times.*

DIRECTORIES

The Almanac of the Executive Branch. Maximov Publications. • Annual. $149.00. Provides detailed information on more than 830 key staff memebers of the executive branch of the federal government. Includes educational background, previous employment, job responsibilities, etc.

Almanac of the Unelected: Staff of the U. S. Congress. Bernan Associates. • Annual. $275.00. Provides detailed information on key staff members

of the legislative branch of the federal government. Includes educational background, previous employment, job responsibilities, etc.

Carroll's Federal & Federal Regional Directory. Carroll Publishing. • Semiannual. $325.00 per year; with online edition, $1,200 per year. Lists more than 23,000 U. S. government officials throughout the country, including military installations.

Carroll's Federal Directory. Carroll Publishing. • Covers: About 38,000 executive managers in federal government offices in Washington, DC, including executive, congressional and judicial branches; members of Congress and Congressional committees and staff. Entries include: Agency names, titles, office address (including room numbers), e-mail addresses, and telephone and fax numbers. Also available as part of a "library edition" titled "Federal Directory Annual".

Carroll's Federal Regional Directory. Carroll Publishing. • Covers: Over 32,000 officials in federal congressional, judicial, and executive branch departments and agencies outside the District of Columbia. Entries include: Organization or agency name; names, addresses, and phone numbers of key personnel.

Congressional Yellow Book: Who's Who in Congress, Including Committees and Key Staff. Leadership Directories, Inc. • Quarterly. $360.00 per year. Looseleaf. A directory of members of congress, including their committees and their key aides.

Federal Regional Yellow Book: Who's Who in the Federal Government's Departments, Agencies, Military Installations, and Service Academies Outside of Washington, DC. Leadership Directories, Inc. • Semiannual. $265.00 per year. Lists over 35,000 federal officials and support staff at 8,000 regional offices.

Federal Staff Directory: With Biographical Information on Executive Staff Personnel. CQ Press. • Three times a year. $259.00 per year. Single copies, $149.00. Lists 35,000 staff members of federal departments and agencies, with biographies of 3,200 key executives. Includes keyword and name indexes.

Government Phone Book USA: Your Comprehensive Guide to Federal, State, County, and Local Government Offices in the United States. Omnigraphics, Inc. • Annual. $265.00. Contains more than 270,000 listings of federal, state, county, and local government offices and personnel, including legislatures. Formerly *Government Directory of Addresses and Phone Numbers.*

United States Government Manual. National Archives and Records Administration. Office of the Federal Register. • Description: Provides information on the agencies of the executive, judicial, and legislative branches of the Federal government. Contains a section on terminated or transferred agencies.

ENCYCLOPEDIAS AND DICTIONARIES

International Encyclopedia of Public Policy and Administration. Jay M. Shafritz, editor. Westview Press. • 1997. $550.00. Four volumes. Covers 20 major areas, such as public administration, government budgeting, industrial policy, nonprofit management, organizational theory, public finance, labor relations, and taxation. Includes a brief bibliography for each major entry and a comprehensive index.

HANDBOOKS AND MANUALS

Banishing Bureaucratese: Using Plain English in Government Writing. Judith G. Myers. Management Concepts, Inc. • 2001. $39.00. Covers plain writing style for government memos, letters, e-mail, agency communications, budget justification statements, and other bureaucratic documents.

ONLINE DATABASES

Information Bank Abstracts. New York Times Index Dept. • Provides indexing and abstracting of current affairs, primarily from the final late edition of *The New York Times* and the Eastern edition of *The Wall Street Journal.* Time period is 1969 to present, with daily updates. Inquire as to online cost and availability.

Management Contents. Gale Cengage Learning. • Covers a wide range of management, financial, marketing, personnel, and administrative topics. About 150 leading business journals are indexed and abstracted from 1974 to date, with monthly updating. Inquire as to online cost and availability.

PAIS International. Public Affairs Information Service, Inc. • Corresponds to the former printed publications, *PAIS Bulletin* (1976-90) and *PAIS Foreign Language Index* (1972-90), and to the current *PAIS International in Print* (1991 to date). Covers economic, political, and sociological material appearing in periodicals, books, government documents, and other publications. Updating is monthly. Inquire as to online cost and availability.

Trade & Industry Database. Gale Cengage Learning. • Provides indexing of business periodicals, January 1981 to date. Daily updates. (Full text articles from some periodicals are available online, 1983 to date. Inquire as to online cost and availability).

PERIODICALS AND NEWSLETTERS

Administration and Society. Sage Publications, Inc. • Bimonthly. Institutions, $612.00 per year. Scholarly journal concerned with public administration and the effects of bureaucracy.

Federal Manager. Federal Managers' Association. • Quarterly. $24.00 per year. Formerly *Federal Managers Quarterly.*

Government Computer News: The Newspaper Serving Computer Users Throughout the Federal Government. Business Information, Inc. • 32 times a year. Free to qualified personnel.

Government Executive: Federal Government's Business Magazine. National Journal Group, Inc. • Monthly. $48.00 per year. Includes management of computerized information systems in the federal government.

Legal Times: Law and Lobbying in the Nation's Capital. American Lawyer Media, Inc. • Weekly. $318.00 per year. Published in Washington, DC. Provides news relating to lawyers and the federal government. Special features cover a variety of topics relating to law firm administration.

Public Administration Review. American Society for Public Administration. • Bimonthly. Institutions, $209.00 per year. Includes online edition.

The Public Manager: The Journal for Practitioners. Bureaucrat, Inc. • Quarterly. Individuals, $35.00 per year; institutions, $65.00 per year. Formerly *Bureaucrat.*

TRADE/PROFESSIONAL ASSOCIATIONS

American Society for Public Administration. 1120 G St., N.W., Suite 700, Washington, DC 20005-3885. Phone: (202)393-7878 Fax: (202)638-4952 E-mail: mhamilton@aspanet.org • URL: http://www.aspanet.org.

Federal Managers Association. 1641 Prince St., Alexandria, VA 22314-2818. Phone: (703)683-8700 Fax: (703)683-8707 E-mail: info@fedmanagers.org • URL: http://www.fedmanagers.org • Represents managers and supervisors in all federal agencies. Promotes excellence in public service through effective management. Promotes and supports legislation beneficial to members, including workforce reshaping through mission analysis; compensation reform; and health and retirement benefits. Sponsors profes-

sional development program for managers as well as training seminars.

Fund for Constitutional Government. 122 Maryland Ave., N.E., 3rd Fl., Washington, DC 20002. Phone: (202)546-3799 Fax: (202)543-3156 E-mail: funcongov@aol.com • URL: http://www.epic.org/fcg • Provides legal and strategic counsel to government "whistleblowers.".

International Association of Professional Bureaucrats. c/o Dr. James H. Boren, 2400 Jolinda, Whitesboro, TX 76273. Phone: (903)564-9290 Fax: (903)564-9430 E-mail: jimboren@cox-intenet.com • URL: http://www.jimboren.com/inataprobu • Motto of Association: "When in doubt, mumble.".

Public Citizen/Freedom of Information Clearinghouse. 1600 20th St. NW, Washington, DC 20036. Phone: (202)588-1000 Fax: (202)588-7795 E-mail: member@citizen.org • URL: http://www.citizen.org/litigation/ • Promotes citizen access to government-held information.

OTHER SOURCES

Government Employee Relations Report. BNA, Inc. • Weekly. $1,144.00 per year. Three looseleaf volumes. Concerned with labor relations in the public sector.

BUREAUS OF BUSINESS RESEARCH

See also: BUSINESS RESEARCH; ECONOMIC RESEARCH

CD-ROM DATABASES

Profiles in Business and Management: An International Directory of Scholars and Their Research [CD-ROM]. Harvard Business School Publishing. • Annual. $595.00. Fully searchable CD-ROM version of two-volume printed directory. Contains bibliographic and biographical information for over 5600 business and management experts active in 21 subject areas. Formerly *International Directory of Business and Management Scholars.*

ONLINE DATABASES

EconLit. American Economic Association. • Covers the worldwide literature of economics as contained in selected monographs and about 550 journals. Subjects include microeconomics, macroeconomics, economic history, inflation, money, credit, finance, accounting theory, trade, natural resource economics, and regional economics. Time period is 1969 to present, with monthly updates. Inquire as to online cost and availability.

RESEARCH CENTERS AND INSTITUTES

Bureau of Economic and Business Research. University of Florida. 221 Matherly Hall, Gainesville, FL 32611-7145. Phone: (352)392-0171 Fax: (352)392-4739 E-mail: info@bebr.ufl.edu • URL: http://www.bebr.ufl.edu.

BURGLAR ALARMS

See: ELECTRONIC SECURITY SYSTEMS

BURLAP INDUSTRY

See also: JUTE INDUSTRY

ABSTRACTS AND INDEXES

Textile Technology Digest. Institute of Textile Technology. • Annual. $535.00. Provides indexing and abstracting of a wide variety of textile technology literature.

ALMANACS AND YEARBOOKS

CRB Commodity Yearbook. Commodity Research Bureau. CRB. • Annual. $99.95.

CD-ROM DATABASES

Textile Technology Digest [CD-ROM]. Textile Information Center, Institute of Textile Technology.

• Quarterly. Provides CD-ROM indexing and abstracting of worldwide journals and monographs in various areas of textile technology, production, and management. Covers 1978 to date.

ENCYCLOPEDIAS AND DICTIONARIES

Textile Terms and Definitions. J.E. McIntyre and Paul N. Daniels, editors. Available from State Mutual Book and Periodical Service Ltd. • 1996. $180.00. 10th edition. Published by the Textile Institute (UK). Includes more than 1,000 definitions of textile processes, fiber types, and end products. Illustrated.

ONLINE DATABASES

Agricola. U.S. National Agricultural Library. • Covers worldwide agricultural literature. Over 3.3 million citations, 1970 to present, with monthly updates. Inquire as to online cost and availability.

Textile Technology Digest [online]. Institute of Textile Technology. • Contains indexing and abstracting of more than 300 worldwide journals and monographs in various areas of textile technology, production, and management. Time period is 1978 to date, with monthly updating. Inquire as to online cost and availability.

World Textiles. Elsevier Science, Inc. • Provides abstracting and indexing from 1970 of worldwide textile literature (periodicals, books, pamphlets, and reports). Includes U. S., European, and British patent information. Updating is monthly. Inquire as to online cost and availability.

PRICE SOURCES

PPI Detailed Report. Bureau of Labor Statistics, U.S. Department of Labor. Available from U.S. Government Printing Office. • Monthly. $55.00 per year. Formerly *Producer Price Indexes.*

STATISTICS SOURCES

FAO Quarterly Bulletin of Statistics. Food and Agriculture Organization of the United Nations. Available from UNIPUB. • Quarterly. $20.00 per year. Provides international data on agricultural production, trade, and prices, covering the major commodities of many countries. Text in English, French, and Spanish. Formerly *FAO Monthly Bulletin of Statistics.*

TRADE/PROFESSIONAL ASSOCIATIONS

Burlap and Jute Association. c/o Susan Spiegel, Drawer 8, Dayton, OH 45401. Phone: 800-543-3400 or (937)476-8272 Fax: (937)258-0029 E-mail: tbpa@aol.com.

Textile Bag and Packaging Association. Drawer 8, Dayton, OH 45401. Phone: 800-543-3400 or (937)476-8272 Fax: (937)258-0029 E-mail: tbpa@aol.com • Formerly Textile Bag Packaging Association.

Textile Institute. St. James's Buildings, 1st Fl., 79 Oxford St., Manchester M1 6FQ, United Kingdom. Phone: 44 161 2371188 Fax: 44 161 2361991 E-mail: tiihq@textileinst.org.uk • URL: http://www.texi.org • Companies and individuals in 100 countries involved in management, science, technology, design, information transfer, and marketing of textiles including clothing and footwear. Promotes interests of the textile industry worldwide; serves professional interests of members; confers qualifications and recognizes achievements in research, application of ideas, education, business, and public affairs. Maintains Information Service to collect information relating to textile industrial and economic conditions in different countries and economic sectors.

BUS LINE TIME TABLES

See: TIMETABLES

BUSES

See: MOTOR BUSES

BUSINESS

See also: ADMINISTRATION; CORPORA-
TIONS; ECONOMICS; EXECUTIVES;
INDUSTRY; INTERNATIONAL BUSINESS

GENERAL WORKS

Business Essentials. Robert J. Ebert and Ricky W.
Griffin. Prentice Hall PTR. • 2002. $73.33. Fourth
edition.

*Reengineering Management: The Mandate for New
Leadership.* James Champy. DIANE Publishing Co.
• 1998. $25.00.

*Reengineering the Corporation: A Manifesto for
Business Revolution.* Michael Hammer and James
Champy. HarperInformation. • 2001. $16.00.
Revised edition.

Understanding Business. William G. Nickels.
McGraw-Hill. • 2001. $56.25. Sixth edition.

ABSTRACTS AND INDEXES

Business Periodicals Index. H. W. Wilson Co. • 11
times a year. Quarterly and annual cumulations.
Price varies.

NTIS Alerts: Business & Economics. National
Technical Information Service. • Text:
Semimonthly. $210.00 per year.

Social Sciences Citation Index. Thomson/ISI. •
Three times a year. $6,900 per year. Annual
cumulation. Includes *Source Index, Citation Index,
Permuterm Subject Index,* and *Corporate Index.*

ALMANACS AND YEARBOOKS

*Information Please Business Almanac and Desk
Reference.* Information Please LLC. • Annual. $21.
95.

*Irwin Business and Investment Almanac, 1994: Dow
Jones and Company Edition.* Summer N. Levine and
Caroline Levine. McGraw-Hill. • 1994. $75.00. 18th
edition. A review of last year's business activity.
Covers a wide variety of business and economic
data: stock market statistics, industrial information,
commodity futures information, art market trends,
comparative living costs for U. S. metropolitan
areas, foreign stock market data, etc. Formerly *Business One Irwin Business and Investment Almanac.*

BIBLIOGRAPHIES

The Basic Business Library: Core Resources.
Rashells S. Karp and Bernard S. Schlessinger.
Greenwood Publishing Group, Inc. • 2002. $64.95.
Fourth edition. Consists of three parts: (1) "Core List
of Printed Business Reference Sources," (2) "The
Literature of Business Reference and Business
Libraries: 1976-1994," and (3) "Business Reference
Sources and Services: Essays." Part one lists 200
basic titles, with annotations and evaluations.

Bibliographic Guide to Business and Economics.
Available from Gale Cengage Learning. • Annual.
$835.00. Three volumes. Published by G. K. Hall &
Co. Lists current business and economics publications cataloged by the New York Public Library and
the Library of Congress.

Bibliographic Guide to Conference Publications.
Available from Gale Cengage Learning. • Annual.
$600.00. Two volumes. Published by G. K. Hall &
Co., Lists a wide range of conference publications
cataloged by the New York Public Library and the
Library of Congress.

BIOGRAPHICAL SOURCES

Who's Who in Finance and Industry. Marquis
Who's Who. • Biennial. $259.95. Provides over
21,000 concise biographies of business leaders in all
fields.

CD-ROM DATABASES

ABI/INFORM. PROQUEST. • Monthly. Provides
CD-ROM indexing and abstracting of worldwide
business literature. Archival discs are available from
1971. Formerly *ABI/INFORM OnDisc.*

D & B Business Locator. Dun & Bradstreet, Inc. •
Quarterly. $2,495.00 per year. CD-ROM provides
concise information on more than 10 million U. S.
companies or businesses. Includes data on number
of employees.

Hoover's Company Capsules on CD-ROM.
Hoover's, Inc. • Quarterly. $399.95 per year (single-
user). Provides the CD-ROM version of *Hoover's
Handbook of American Business, Hoover's
Handbook of Emerging Companies, Hoover's
Handbook of World Business, Hoover's Guide to
Computer Companies, Hoover's Guide to Media
Companies, Hoover's Handbook of Private
Companies,* and various regional guides. Includes
more than 11,000 profiles of companies.

OECD Statistical Compendium. Organization for
Economic Cooperation and Development. •
Semiannual. $1,905.00 per year for 1 to 10 users.
CD-ROM contains more than 730,000 monthly,
quarterly, and annual time series for OECD
countries, 1960 to date. Includes fully searchable
data on agriculture, food, economic indicators,
national accounts, employment, energy, finance,
industry, technology, and foreign trade. Results can
be displayed in various forms.

16 Million Businesses Phone Directory. Info USA. •
Annual. $29.95. Provides more than 16 million yel-
low pages telephone directory listings on CD-ROM
for all ZIP Code areas of the U. S.

Social Sciences Citation Index. ISI. • Monthly. Price
on request. Provides CD-ROM indexing of articles
appearing in 1700 leading social science journals
worldwide, with additional selections from more
than 5700 other journals. Time span is 1992 to date.
Coverage includes economics, business, finance,
management, communications, demographics,
library and information science, political science,
sociology, and many other subjects.

*Social Sciences Citation Index: Compact Disc Edi-
tion with Abstracts.* Institute for Scientific
Information. • Monthly. Provides CD-ROM indexing and abstracting of "significant articles" from
1,700 social science journals worldwide, with additional selections from 3,200 other journals, 1986
to date. Includes economics, business, finance,
management, communications, demographics,
information and library science, political science,
sociology, and many other subjects.

WILSONDISC: Wilson Business Abstracts. H. W.
Wilson Co. • Monthly. Includes unlimited online access to *Wilson Business Abstracts* through
WILSONLINE. Provides CD-ROM "cover-to-
cover" abstracting and indexing of over 600
prominent business periodicals. Indexing is from
1982, abstracting from 1990. (*Business Periodicals
Index* without abstracts is available on CD-ROM at
$1,495 per year.).

DIRECTORIES

American Big Businesses Directory. infoUSA Inc. •
Covers: 218,000 U.S. businesses with more than 100
employees, and 500,000 key executives and
directors. CD-ROM version contains 160,000 top
firms and 431,000 key executives. Entries include:
Name, address, phone, names and titles of key
personnel, number of employees, sales volume,
Standard Industrial Classification (SIC) codes,
subsidiaries and parent company names, stock
exchanges on which traded.

American Manufacturers Directory. infoUSA Inc. •
Covers: more than 150,000 manufacturing
companies with 20 or more employees. CD-ROM
version lists all 531,000 U.S. manufacturers, in all
employee size ranges. Entries include: Company
name, address, phone, contact name, Standard
Industrial Classification (SIC) codes, number of
employees, sales volume code, credit rating scores.

America's Corporate Families. Dun & Bradstreet
Corp. • Covers: Approximately 12,700 U.S.
corporations. Ultimate companies must meet all of
the following criteria for inclusion: two or more
business locations, 250 or more employees at that
location or in excess of $25 million in sales volume
or a tangible net worth greater than $500,000, and
controlling interest in one or more subsidiary
company. Entries include: D&B D-U-N-S number,
company name, address, phone, state of incorporation, line of business, primary/secondary SIC codes,
sales volume, net worth, number of employees, current ownership date, year started, number of sites,
key executives' names/titles, directors and than officers, primary bank and accounting firm, import/
export designation, stock exchange symbol and
indicator for publicly owned companies, parent
company and location.

*Business Organizations, Agencies, and Publications
Directory.* Gale Cengage Learning. • 2003. $480.00.
15th edition. Over 40,000 entries describing 39
types of business information sources. Classified by
type of organization, publication, or serviceIncludes
state, national, and international agencies and
organizations. Master index to names and keywords.
Also includes e-mail addresses and web site URL's.

The Corporate Directory of U.S. Public Companies.
Walker's Research, LLC. • Annual. $360.00. Two
volumes. Contains information on more than 10,000
publicly-traded companies, including names of
executives and major subsidiaries. Includes financial
and stock data.

Cyberhound's Guide to Companies on the Internet.
Gale Cengage Learning. • 1996. $79.00. Presents
critical descriptions and ratings of more than 2,000
company or corporate Internet databases. Includes a
glossary of Internet terms, a bibliography, and
indexes. (Cyberhound's Series).

D and B Million Dollar Directory. • Annual. Commercial institutions, $1,395.00; libraries, $1,275.00.
Lease basis.

*Directory of Companies Required to File Annual
Reports with the Securities and Exchange
Commission.* Securities and Exchange Commission.
Available from U.S. Government Printing Office. •
Annual. $46.00.

Guide to American Directories. Todd Publications. •
Biennial. $125.00. Provides more than 11,000 list-
ings with descriptions, prices, etc.

*Headquarters USA: A Directory of Contact Informa-
tion for Headquarters and Other Central Offices of
Major Businesses and Organizations Nationwide.*
Omnigraphics, Inc. • Annual. $185.00. Two
volumes. Volume one is alphabetical by name of
business or organization. Volume two is classified by
subject. Includes more than 112,000 businesses,
organizations, agencies, institutions, and "high-
profile" individuals. Listings include addresses,
telephone numbers, fax numbers, and toll-free
numbers and Web addresses where available.
Formerly *Business Phone Book USA.*

Hoover's Masterlist of Major U. S. Companies.
Hoover's, Inc. • 2003. $275.00. Provides brief
information, including annual sales, number of
employees, and chief executive, for about 5,000 U.
S. companies, both public and private.

*Internet Tools of the Profession: A Guide for
Information Professionals.* Hope N. Tillman, editor.
Special Libraries Association. • 1997. $49.00.
Second edition. Consists of 14 sections by various
authors or compilers. After two introductory articles
on searching the Internet, there are 12 annotated lists
of useful Web sites, covering the SLA, business and
finance, chemistry, education, food and agriculture,
information technology, insurance and employee
benefits, law, library management, metals and
materials, pharmaceuticals, and
telecommunications. An index is provided.

Kompass USA. Kompass International/Kompass USA, Inc. • Annual. Price on application. Two volumes. Includes information on about 125,000 U.S. companies. Classification system covers approximately 50,000 products and services. Product and tradename indexes are provided.

Peterson's Job Opportunities for Business Majors. Peterson's. • 1999. $18.95. Provides career information for the 2,000 largest U. S. employers in various industries.

Principal International Businesses: The World Marketing Directory. • Annual. $5,000. Provides information about 50,000 major businesses located in over 145 countries. Geographic arrangement with company name and product indexes.

Standard and Poor's Register of Corporations, Directors and Executives. Standard and Poor's. • Annual. $675.00. Looseleaf service. Lease basis. Periodic supplementation. Over 55,000 public and privately held corporations in the U.S.

Thomas Register of American Manufacturers. Thomas Publishing Co., Inc. • Annual. $149.00. 34 volumes. A three-part system offering information on a wide variety of industrial equipment and supplies. Lists more than 151,000 industrial product and services companies.

Ward's Business Directory of U. S. Private and Public Companies. Gale Cengage Learning. • 2002. $2,765.00. 45th edition. Eight volumes. *Ward's* contains basic information on about 120,000 business firms, of which 90 percent are private companies. Includes mid-year *Supplement.* Volumes available individually. Prices vary.

ENCYCLOPEDIAS AND DICTIONARIES

Encyclopedia of Business. Gale Cengage Learning. • 2000. $425.00. Second edition. Two volumes. Contains more than 700 signed articles covering major business disciplines and concepts. International in scope. (Encyclopedia of Business Series).

Encyclopedia of Business and Finance. Burton Kaliski, editor. Available from Gale Cengage Learning. • 2001. $275.00. Two volumes. Published by Macmillan Reference USA. Contains articles by various contributors on accounting, business administration, banking, finance, management information systems, and marketing.

Every Manager's Guide to Information Technology: A Glossary of Key Terms and Concepts for Today's Business Leader. Peter G. W. Keen. Harvard Business School Publishing. • 1994. $18.95. Second edition. Provides definitions of terms related to computers, data communications, and information network systems. (Harvard Business Reference Series).

International Encyclopedia of Business and Management. Malcolm Warner, editor. Cengage Learning. • 2001. $1,899.00.Second edition. Eight volumes. Contains more than 500 articles on global management issues. Includes extensive bibliographies, cross references, and an index of key words and phrases.

Knowledge Exchange Business Encyclopedia: Your Complete Business Advisor. Lorraine Spurge. Knowledge Exchange LLC. • 1998. $45.00. Provides definitions of business terms and financial expressions, profiles of leading industries, tables of economic statistics, biographies of business leaders, and other business information. Includes "A Chronology of Business from 3000 B.C. Through 1995." Contains illustrations and three indexes.

HANDBOOKS AND MANUALS

Doing Business in the United States: Legal Opportunities and Pitfalls. Lawrence B. Landman. John Wiley and Sons, Inc. • 1997. $55.00. (Essential Facts Series).

Industry and Product Classification Manual (SIC Basis). Available from National Technical Information Service. • 1992. Issued by U. S. Bureau of the Census. Contains extended Standard Industrial Classification (SIC) numbers used by the Census Bureau to allow a more detailed classification of industry, services, and agriculture.

North American Industry Classification System (NAICS). Available from Bernan Press. • 2002. $45.00. Issued by the Executive Office of the President, Office of Management and Budget (OMB).

Organization Charts: Structures of More Than 200 Businesses and Non-Profit Organizations. Gale Cengage Learning. • 1999. $180.00. Third edition. Includes an introductory discussion of the history and use of such charts.

Reengineering Revolution: A Handbook. Michael Hammer and Steven Stanton. HarperInformation. • 1995. $17.95.

Standard Industrial Classification Manual. U.S. Department of Commerce, Bureau of the Census. Available from U.S. Government Printing Office. • 1987. $36.00.

INTERNET DATABASES

Bureau of Economic Analysis (BEA). U. S. Department of Commerce, Bureau of Economic Analysis. Phone: (202)606-9900 Fax: (202)606-5310 E-mail: webmaster@bea.doc.gov • URL: http://www.bea.doc.gov • Web site includes "News Release Information" covering national, regional, and international economic estimates from the BEA. Highlights of releases appear online the same day, complete text and tables appear the next day. "Recent News Releases" section provides titles for past nine months, with links. "BEA Data and Methodology" includes "Frequently Requested NIPA Data" (national income and product accounts, such as gross domestic product and personal income). Other statistics are available. Fees: Free.

Business 2.0 Web Guide to the Best Business Links. Business 2.0 Media Inc. Phone: (415)293-4800 E-mail: support@business2.com • URL: http://www.business2.com/webguide • Web site presents an extensive, searchable directory of links to "the best, most informative, and authoritative web pages." Twenty main categories cover business, finance, career, company information, people, and technology topics, with thousands of subtopics, all linking to Web sites recommended by experienced business researchers. Fees: Free.

Business Week Online. McGraw-Hill. Phone: (212)512-2511 Fax: (684)842-6101 • URL: http://www.businessweek.com • Web site provides complete contents of current issue of *Business Week* plus "BW Daily" with additonal business news, financial market quotes, and corporate information from Standard & Poor's. Includes various features, such as "Banking Center" with mortgage and interest data, and "Interactive Computer Buying Guide." The "Business Week Archive" is fully searchable back to 1996.

Factiva. Dow Jones Reuters Business Interactive, LLC. Phone: 800-369-7466 or (609)452-1511 Fax: (609)520-5770 E-mail: solutions@factiva.com • URL: http://www.factiva.com • Fee-based Web site provides "global news and business information through Web sites and content integration solutions." Includes Dow Jones and Reuters newswires, The Wall Street Journal, and more than 7,000 other sources of current news, historical articles, market research reports, and investment analysis. Content includes 96 major U. S. newspapers, 900 non-English sources, trade publications, media transcripts, country profiles, news photos, etc.

Fedstats. Federal Interagency Council on Statistical Policy. Phone: (202)395-7254 • URL: http://www.fedstats.gov • Web site features an efficient search facility for full-text statistics produced by more than 100 federal agencies, including the Census Bureau, the Bureau of Economic Analysis, and the Bureau of Labor Statistics. Boolean searches can be made within one agency or for all agencies combined. Links are offered to international statistical bureaus, including the UN, IMF, OECD, UNESCO, Eurostat, and 20 individual countries. Fees: Free.

FreeLunch.com. Economy.com, Inc. Phone: (610)696-8700 Fax: (610)696-1678 • URL: http://www.freelunch.com • Web site provides free access to more than 1.5 million economic and financial data series, covering industry, demographics, labor markets, prices, retail sales, government spending, trade, interest rates, housing starts, the stock market, and many other topics. Data is available for various time periods in either chart or table form. Searching is offered. Fees: Free, but registration required. Economy.com, Inc. also offers fee-based economic analysis at *The Dismal Scientist* site (http://www.dismal.com).

InSite 2. Intelligence Data/Thomson Financial. Phone: 800-654-0393 or (617)856-1890 Fax: (617)737-3182 E-mail: intelligence.data@tfn.com • URL: http://www.insite2.gale.com/ • Fee-based Web site consolidates information in a "Base Pack" consisting of Business InSite, Market InSite, and Company InSite. Optional databases are Consumer InSite, Health and Wellness InSite, Newsletter InSite, and Computer InSite. Includes fulltext content from more than 2,500 trade publications, journals, newsletters, newspapers, analyst reports, and other sources. Continuous updating. Formerly produced by The Gale Group.

Nexis.com. Lexis-Nexis Group. Phone: 800-227-4908 or (937)865-6800 Fax: (937)865-6909 E-mail: webmaster@prod.lexis-nexis.com • URL: http://www.nexis.com • Fee-based Web site offers searching of about 2.8 billion documents in some 30,000 news, business, and legal information sources. Features include a subject directory covering 1,200 topics in 34 categories and a Company Dossier containing information on more than 500,000 public and private companies. Boolean searching is offered.

1997 NAICS and 1987 SIC Correspondence Tables. U. S. Census Bureau. Phone: (301)457-4100 Fax: (301)457-1296 E-mail: naics@census.gov • URL: http://www.census.gov/epcd/www/naicstab.htm • Web site provides detailed tables for converting four-digit Standard Industrial Classification (SIC) numbers to the six-digit North American Industrial Classification System (NAICS) or vice versa: "1987 SIC Matched to 1997 NAICS" or "1997 NAICS Matched to 1987 SIC." Fees: Free.

Switchboard. Switchboard, Inc. Phone: (508)898-8000 Fax: (508)898-1755 E-mail: webmaster@switchboard.com • URL: http://www.switchboard.com • Web site provides telephone numbers and street addresses for more than 100 million business locations and residences in the U. S. Broad industry categories are available. Fees: Free.

U. S. Business Advisor. Small Business Administration. Phone: (202)205-6600 Fax: (202)205-7064 • URL: http://www.business.gov • Web site provides "a one-stop electronic link to all the information and services government provides for the business community." Covers about 60 federal agencies that exist to assist or regulate business. Detailed information is provided on financial assistance, workplace issues, taxes, regulations, international trade, and other business topics. Searching is offered. Fees: Free.

Wall Street Journal Interactive Edition. Dow Jones & Co., Inc. Phone: 800-369-2834 or (212)416-2000 Fax: (212)416-2658 E-mail: inquiries@interactive.wsj.com • URL: http://www.wsj.com • Fee-based Web site providing online searching of worldwide information from the *The Wall Street Journal.* Includes "Company Snapshots," "The Journal's Greatest Hits," "Index to Market Data," "Journal Links," etc. Financial price quotes are available.

Fees: $49.00 per year; $29.00 per year to print subscribers.

WilsonWeb Periodicals Databases. H. W. Wilson. Phone: 800-367-6770 or (718)588-8400 Fax: 800-590-1617 or (718)992-8003 E-mail: custserv@hwwilson.com • URL: http://www.hwwilson.com/ • Web sites provide fee-based access to *Wilson Business Full Text, Applied Science & Technology Full Text, Biological & Agricultural Index, Library Literature & Information Science Full Text,* and *Readers' Guide Full Text, Mega Edition.* Daily updates.

ONLINE DATABASES

Business and Industry. Gale Cengage Learning. • Contains online citations, abstracts, and selected fulltext from more than 1,000 trade journals, newspapers, and other publications. Provides general coverage of both manufacturing and service industries, including marketing, production, industry trends, key events, and information on specific companies. Time span is 1994 to date. Daily updates. Inquire as to online cost and availability. (Also available in a CD-ROM version.).

Dow Jones News Service. Dow Jones and Co., Inc. • Full text and edited news stories and articles on business affairs. Inquire as to online cost and availability.

F & S Index. Gale Cengage Learning. • Contains about four million citations to worldwide business, financial, and industrial or consumer product literature appearing from 1972 to date. Weekly updates. Inquire as to online cost and availability.

PROMT: Predicasts Overview of Markets and Technology. Gale Cengage Learning. • Companies, products, applied technologies and markets. U.S. and international literature coverage, 1972 to date. Inquire as to online cost and availability. Provides abstracts from more than 1,600 publications. Weekly updates.

Social Scisearch. Institute for Scientific Information. • Broad, multidisciplinary index to the literature of the social sciences, 1972 to present. Weekly updates. Worldwide coverage. Inquire as to online cost and availability.

Thomas Register Online. Thomas Publishing Co., Inc. • Provides concise information on approximately 194,000 U. S. companies, mainly manufacturers, with over 50,000 product classifications. Indexes over 115,000 trade names. Information is updated semiannually. Inquire as to online cost and availability.

Trade & Industry Database. Gale Cengage Learning. • Provides indexing of business periodicals, January 1981 to date. Daily updates. (Full text articles from some periodicals are available online, 1983 to date. Inquire as to online cost and availability).

Wilson Business Abstracts Online. H. W. Wilson Co. • Indexes and abstracts 600 major business periodicals, plus the *Wall Street Journal* and the business section of the *New York Times.* Indexing is from 1982, abstracting from 1990, with the two newspapers included from 1993. Updated weekly. Inquire as to online cost and availability. (*Business Periodicals Index* without abstracts is also available online.).

PERIODICALS AND NEWSLETTERS

Barron's: The Dow Jones Business and Financial Weekly. • Weekly. $145.00 per year.

Business Strategies Bulletin. CCH Inc. • Description: Reports tax and business planning information for all sizes of business, with emphasis on small to mid-sized business advisors.

Business 2.0. Time Inc. • Monthly. $30.00 per year. General business magazine emphasizing ideas, insight, and innovation.

Business Week. McGraw-Hill. • Weekly. $45.97 per year. Last volume is a double issue.

Canadian Business. Canadian Business Media. • Biweekly. $64.95 per year. Edited for corporate managers and executives, this is a major periodical in Canada covering a variety of business, economic, and financial topics. Emphasis is on the top 500 Canadian corporations.

Commerce Business Daily. Industry and Trade Administration, U.S. Department of Commerce. U.S. Department of Commerce. • Description: Lists notices of proposed government procurement actions, contract awards, sales of government property, and other procurement information. Includes 500-1,000 notices in each edition; notices appear in the publication only once.

Commercial and Financial Chronicle. William B. Dana Co. • Weekly. $140.00. per year.

Daily Report for Executives. BNA, Inc. • Daily. $7,698.00 per year. Newsletter. Covers legal, regulatory, economic, and tax developments affecting corporations.

Fast Company: How Smart Business Works. Fast Company, Inc. • Monthly. $12.00 per year. Covers business management, with emphasis on creativity, leadership, innovation, career advancement, teamwork, the global economy, and the "new workplace.".

Forbes. Forbes, Inc. • Biweekly. $59.95 per year. Includes supplements: *Forbes ASAP* and *Forbes FYI.*

Fortune Magazine. Time Inc., Business Information Group. • Biweekly. $59.95 per year. Edited for top executives and upper-level managers.

Harvard Business Review. Harvard University, Graduate School of Business Administration. Harvard Business School Publishing. • Monthly. $118.00 per year.

IndustryWeek: The Management Resource. Penton Media, Inc. • 22 times a year. Free to qualified personnel; others, $65.00 per year. Edited for industrial and business managers. Covers organizational and technological developments affecting industrial management.

The Journal of Business. The University of Chicago Press, Journals Div. • Quarterly. Individuals, $31.00 per year; institutions, $125.00 per year; students, $25.00 per year.

Journal of World Business. Columbia University, Trustees of Columbia University. Elsevier. • Quarterly. Individuals, $131.00 per year; institutions, $315.00 per year.

The Kiplinger Letter. Kiplinger Washington Editors Inc. • Description: Provides information on current events and future outlook in business, economics, legislation, politics, finance, labor, and other topics of interest to business professionals.

Smart Business for the New Economy. Element K Journals. • Monthly. $12.00 per year. Provides practical advice for doing business in an economy dominated by technology and electronic commerce.

The Wall Street Journal. Dow Jones & Co., Inc. • Daily. $189.00 per year. Covers news and trends relating to business, industry, finance, the economy, and international commerce. Provides extensive price and other data for the securities, commodity, options, futures, foreign exchange, and money markets.

RESEARCH CENTERS AND INSTITUTES

Board of Research. Babson College, 204 Babson, Babson Park, MA 02457-0310. Phone: (718)239-5339 Fax: (718)239-6416 E-mail: chern@babson.edu • URL: http://www.babson.edu/bor • Research areas include management, entrepreneurial characteristics, and multi-product inventory analysis.

Conference Board, Inc. The Conference Board, Inc. 845 3rd Ave., New York, NY 10022. Phone: (212)339-0345 Fax: (212)980-7014 E-mail: info@conference-board.org • URL: http://www.conference-board.org • Business management practices worldwide, especially economic, and demographic in nature. Specific concerns include: corporate citizenship, including corporate contributions, diversity, environmental policy and issues, and government relations; corporate governance, including boards of directors, role of chief executives, relations with institutional investors, and shareholder input and influence; economics, including economic and financial forecasts, consumer confidence, leading economic indicators, North American outlook and trends, and global economic environment; human resources and organizational effectiveness, including organization structure and design, compensation and benefits, training and development, and communications; and performance excellence.

STATISTICS SOURCES

American Business Climate and Economic Profiles. Priscilla C. Geahigan. Gale Cengage Learning. • 1993. $170.00. Provides business, industrial, demographic, and economic figures for all states and 300 metropolitan areas. Includes production, taxation, population, growth rates, labor force data, incomes, total sales, etc.

Business Statistics of the United States. Linz Audain and Cornelia J. Strawser. Bernan Associates. • Annual. $147.00. Based on *Business Statistics,* formerly issue by the Bureau of Economic Analysis, U. S. Department of Commerce. Provides basic data for a wide variety of U. S. industries, services, and economic indicators. Most statistics are shown annually for 30 years and monthly for the most recent four years.

County Business Patterns. Available from U. S. Government Printing Office. • Irregular. 52 issues containing annual data for each state, the District of Columbia, and a U. S. Summary. Produced by U.S. Bureau of the Census (http://www.census.gov). Provides local establishment and employment statistics by industry.

Economic Indicators. Council of Economic Advisors, Executive Office of the President. Available from U.S. Government Printing Office. • Monthly. $55.00 per year.

Gale Book of Averages. Gale Cengage Learning. • 1994. $75.00. Contains 1,100-1,200 statistical averages on a variety of topics, with references to published sources. Subjects include business, labor, consumption, crime, and other areas of contemporary society.

Manufacturing and Distribution USA. Gale Cengage Learning. • 2002. $395.00. Second edition. Three volumes. Presents statistics and projections relating to economic activity in more than 500 business classifications.

Statistical Abstract of the United States. Available from U. S. Government Printing Office. • Annual. $51.00. Issued by the U. S. Bureau of the Census.

Survey of Current Business. Available from U. S. Government Printing Office. • Monthly. $63.00 per year. Issued by Bureau of Economic Analysis, U. S. Department of Commerce. Presents a wide variety of business and economic data.

TRADE/PROFESSIONAL ASSOCIATIONS

American Management Association. 1601 Broadway, New York, NY 10019-7420. Phone: 800-262-9699 or (212)586-8100 Fax: (212)903-8168 E-mail: membership@amanet.org • URL: http://www.amanet.org • Provides educational forums worldwide where members and their colleagues learn superior, practical business skills and explore best practices of world-class organizations through interaction with each other and expert faculty practitioners. Maintains a publishing program providing tools individuals use to extend learning beyond the classroom in a process of life-long professional growth and development through education.

Business Council. PO Box 20147, Washington, DC 20041. Phone: (202)298-7650 Fax: (202)785-0296 E-mail: margie@buildingstoneinstitute.org • URL: http://www.businesscouncil.com • Represents business executives. Aims to serve the national interest, with the primary objectives of developing a constructive point of view on matters of public policy affecting the business interests of the country and by providing a medium for a better understanding of government problems by business. Members are former and present chief executive officers of corporations.

OTHER SOURCES

Business Organizations with Tax Planning. Zolman Cavitch, editor. LexisNexis Matthew Bender. • Quarterly. $2,750. 16 looseleaf volumes. Periodic supplementation. In-depth analytical coverage of corporation law and all relevant aspects of federal corporation taxation.

Business Rankings Annual. Gale Cengage Learning. • Annual. $325.00. Two volumes. Compiled by the Business Library Staff of the Brooklyn Public Library. This is a guide to lists and rankings appearing in major business publications. The top ten names are listed in each case.

Business Strategies. CCH, Inc. • Semimonthly. $795.00 per year. Four looseleaf volumes. Semimonthly updates. Legal, tax, and accounting aspects of business planning and decision-making. Provides information on start-ups, forms of ownership (partnerships, corporations), failing businesses, reorganizations, acquisitions, and so forth. Includes *Business Strategies Bulletin,* a monthly newsletter.

World Business Rankings Annual. Gale Cengage Learning. • 1998. $189.00. Provides 2,500 ranked lists of international companies, compiled from a variety of published sources. Each list shows the "top ten" in a particular category. Keyword indexing, a country index, and citations are provided.

BUSINESS ADMINISTRATION

See: ADMINISTRATION

BUSINESS AIRPLANES

See: BUSINESS AVIATION

BUSINESS AND GOVERNMENT

See: REGULATION OF INDUSTRY

BUSINESS AND PROFESSIONAL WOMEN

See: EMPLOYMENT OF WOMEN

BUSINESS AND SOCIETY

See: SOCIAL RESPONSIBILITY

BUSINESS APPRAISAL

See: VALUATION

BUSINESS ARCHIVES

See: RECORDS MANAGEMENT

BUSINESS AVIATION

See also: AVIATION INDUSTRY

ABSTRACTS AND INDEXES

Business Periodicals Index. H. W. Wilson Co. • 11 times a year. Quarterly and annual cumulations. Price varies.

BIBLIOGRAPHIES

Aviation. Available from U. S. Government Printing Office. • Annual. Free. Lists government publications. (GPO Subject Bibliography Number 18).

DIRECTORIES

ABD--Aviation Buyer's Directory. Air Service Directory Inc. • Covers: aircraft, parts, and equipment manufacturers and dealers, and service firms in the aviation industry. Entries include: Company name, address, phone.

Airport/Facility Directory. U.S. National Ocean Service. • Covers: Non-military airports in the continental United States; separate volumes cover the southeast, northwest, northwest, east central, north central, southwest, and south central states (including Puerto Rico and the Virgin Islands). Entries include: Airport name, location, weather service phone number, control center frequencies, and information concerning navigational and other aids and systems.

Jet and Propjet: Corporate Directory. AvCom International Inc. • Annual. $21.95. Owners of business jet and turboprop aircraft. Worldwide coverage. Formerly *Propjet.*

Professional Pilot-FBO Directory. Queensmith Communications Corp. • Annual. $8.00. Includes information for about 1,600 airports and fixed-base operators.

ONLINE DATABASES

Management Contents. Gale Cengage Learning. • Covers a wide range of management, financial, marketing, personnel, and administrative topics. About 150 leading business journals are indexed and abstracted from 1974 to date, with monthly updating. Inquire as to online cost and availability.

PROMT: Predicasts Overview of Markets and Technology. Gale Cengage Learning. • Companies, products, applied technologies and markets. U.S. and international literature coverage, 1972 to date. Inquire as to online cost and availability. Provides abstracts from more than 1,600 publications. Weekly updates.

Trade & Industry Database. Gale Cengage Learning. • Provides indexing of business periodicals, January 1981 to date. Daily updates. (Full text articles from some periodicals are available online, 1983 to date. Inquire as to online cost and availability).

PERIODICALS AND NEWSLETTERS

A/C Flyer: Best Read Resale Magazine Worldwide (Aircraft). McGraw-Hill. • Monthly. Individuals $49.00 per year; students, $28.00 per year. Lists used airplanes for sale by dealers, brokers, and private owners. Provides news and trends relating to the aircraft resale industry. Special issues include "Product & Service Buyer's Guide" and "Dealer/ Broker Directory.".

AOPA Pilot. Aircraft Owners and Pilots Association. • Monthly. Members, $39.00 per year; qualified organizations, $21.00 per year.

Aviation Week and Space Technology. McGraw-Hill Aviation Week Group. • Monthly. $92.00 per year.

Business and Commercial Aviation. McGraw-Hill Aviation Week Group. • Monthly. $52.00 per year. Supplement available: *Annual Planning Purchasing Handbook.*

FAA Aviation News. Federal Aviation

Administration. Available from U. S. Government Printing Office. • Bimonthly. $28.00. per year. Designed to help airmen become safer pilots. Includes updates on major rule changes and proposals.

Flying. Hachette Filipacchi Media U.S., Inc. • Monthly. Includes three *Special Issues.* Price on application.

General Aviation News. • Biweekly. $29.50 per year. Formerly *Flyer.*

Professional Pilot Magazine. Queensmith Communications Corp. • Monthly. $36.00 per year. Edited for career pilots in all areas of aviation: airline, corporate, charter, and military. Includes flying technique, avionics, navigation, accident analysis, career planning, corporate profiles, and business aviation news.

Trade-a-Plane. • 36 times a year. $42.00 per year. Subject matter is aircraft for sale or trade.

The Weekly of Business Aviation. Aviation Week Newsletter. McGraw-Hill. • Weekly. $595.00 per year.

RESEARCH CENTERS AND INSTITUTES

OAI. 22800 Cedar Point Rd., Cleveland, OH 44142. Phone: (440)962-3000 Fax: (440)962-3120 E-mail: michaelsalkind@oai.org • URL: http://www.oai.org • Aerospace-related research, education, and technology transfers. Formerly Ohio Aerospace Institute.

STATISTICS SOURCES

Air Transport. Air Transport Association of America. • Annual. $20.00.

TRADE/PROFESSIONAL ASSOCIATIONS

Aircraft Owners and Pilots Association. 421 Aviation Way, Frederick, MD 21701. Phone: 800-872-2672 or (301)695-2000 Fax: (301)695-2375 E-mail: aopahq@aopa.org • URL: http://www.aopa.org.

General Aviation Manufacturers Association. 1400 K St. NW, Ste. 801, Washington, DC 20005. Phone: (202)393-1500 Fax: (202)842-4063 E-mail: webmaster@gama.aero • URL: http://www.gama. aero • Manufacturers of aviation airframes, engines, avionics, and components. Seeks to create a better climate for the growth of general aviation.

International Council of Aircraft Owner and Pilot Associations. 421 Aviation Way, Frederick, MD 21701. Phone: (301)695-2220 Fax: (301)695-2375 E-mail: airmail@iaopa.org • URL: http://www. iaopa.org.

National Business Aviation Association. 1200 18th St. NW, Ste. 400, Washington, DC 20036-2527. Phone: (202)783-9000 Fax: (202)331-8364 E-mail: info@nbaa.org • URL: http://www.nbaa.org • Companies owning and operating aircraft for business use, suppliers, and maintenance and air fleet service companies. Compiles statistics; provides literature for researchers and students.

OTHER SOURCES

Aviation Law Reports. CCH, Inc. • Semimonthly. $2,155.00 per year. Four looseleaf volumes.

BUSINESS BROKERS

See: BUSINESS ENTERPRISES, SALE OF

BUSINESS BUDGETING

See: BUDGETING, BUSINESS

BUSINESS CHOICE

See: OCCUPATIONS

BUSINESS COLLEGES

See: BUSINESS EDUCATION; COLLEGES AND UNIVERSITIES

BUSINESS COMMUNICATION

See: BUSINESS CORRESPONDENCE; COMMUNICATION

BUSINESS CONDITIONS

See also: BANKRUPTCY; BUSINESS CYCLES; BUSINESS FORECASTING

GENERAL WORKS

Dow 40,000: Strategies for Profiting from the Greatest Bull Market in History. David Elias. Soaring Eagle Communications. • 1999. $15.95. Predicts continuing strong growth in the U. S. economy, low interest rates, and low inflation, resulting in a level of 40,000 for the Dow Jones Industrial Average in the year 2016.

Recreation Trends and Markets: Info the 21st Century. John R. Kelly and Rodney Warnick. Sagamore Publishing, Inc. • 1999. $25.00. Second edition.

ALMANACS AND YEARBOOKS

Political Risk Yearbook. The PRS Group, Inc. • Annual. $2,415.00. Seven regional volumes; $345.00 per volume. Each volume covers a separate region of the world and assesses economic and political conditions as they relate to the risk of doing business.

CD-ROM DATABASES

Magazine Index Plus. Gale Cengage Learning. • Monthly. $4,000.00 per year (includes InfoTrac workstation). Provides full text on CD-ROM for about 100 popular, general interest magazines and indexing for 300 others. Includes special indexing of reviews and product evaluations. Time period is 1980 to date.

Newspaper Abstracts Ondisc. PROQUEST. • Monthly. $2,950.00 per year (covers 1989 to date; archival discs are available for 1985-88). Provides cover-to-cover CD-ROM indexing and abstracting of 19 major newspapers, including the *New York Times, Wall Street Journal, Washington Post, Chicago Tribune,* and *Los Angeles Times.*

OECD Statistical Compendium. Organization for Economic Cooperation and Development. • Semiannual. $1,905.00 per year for 1 to 10 users. CD-ROM contains more than 730,000 monthly, quarterly, and annual time series for OECD countries, 1960 to date. Includes fully searchable data on agriculture, food, economic indicators, national accounts, employment, energy, finance, industry, technology, and foreign trade. Results can be displayed in various forms.

INTERNET DATABASES

Business 2.0 Web Guide to the Best Business Links. Business 2.0 Media Inc. Phone: (415)293-4800 E-mail: support@business2.com • URL: http://www.business2.com/webguide • Web site presents an extensive, searchable directory of links to "best, most informative, and authoritative web pages." Twenty main categories cover business, finance, career, company information, people, and technology topics, with thousands of subtopics, all linking to Web sites recommended by experienced business researchers. Fees: Free.

Factiva. Dow Jones Reuters Business Interactive, LLC. Phone: 800-369-7466 or (609)452-1511 Fax: (609)520-5770 E-mail: solutions@factiva.com •

URL: http://www.factiva.com • Fee-based Web site provides "global news and business information through Web sites and content integration solutions." Includes Dow Jones and Reuters newswires, The Wall Street Journal, and more than 7,000 other sources of current news, historical articles, market research reports, and investment analysis. Content includes 96 major U. S. newspapers, 900 non-English sources, trade publications, media transcripts, country profiles, news photos, etc.

Fedstats. Federal Interagency Council on Statistical Policy. Phone: (202)395-7254 • URL: http://www.fedstats.gov • Web site features an efficient search facility for full-text statistics produced by more than 100 federal agencies, including the Census Bureau, the Bureau of Economic Analysis, and the Bureau of Labor Statistics. Boolean searches can be made within one agency or for all agencies combined. Links are offered to international statistical bureaus, including the UN, IMF, OECD, UNESCO, Eurostat, and 20 individual countries. Fees: Free.

FreeLunch.com. Economy.com, Inc. Phone: (610)696-8700 Fax: (610)696-1678 • URL: http://www.freelunch.com • Web site provides free access to more than 1.5 million economic and financial data series, covering industry, demographics, labor markets, prices, retail sales, government spending, trade, interest rates, housing starts, the stock market, and many other topics. Data is available for various time periods in either chart or table form. Searching is offered. Fees: Free, but registration required. Economy.com, Inc. also offers fee-based economic analysis at *The Dismal Scientist* site (http://www.dismal.com).

Nexis.com. Lexis-Nexis Group. Phone: 800-227-4908 or (937)865-6800 Fax: (937)865-6909 E-mail: webmaster@prod.lexis-nexis.com • URL: http://www.nexis.com • Fee-based Web site offers searching of about 2.8 billion documents in some 30,000 news, business, and legal information sources. Features include a subject directory covering 1,200 topics in 34 categories and a Company Dossier containing information on more than 500,000 public and private companies. Boolean searching is offered.

Summary of Commentary on Current Economic Conditions by Federal Reserve District [the Beige Book]. Board of Governors of the Federal Reserve System. Phone: (202)452-3000 Fax: (202)452-3819 • URL: http://www.federalreserve.gov/fomc/beigebook/2004/ • Free Web site provides current "anecdotal information" eight times a year on economic conditions within each of the 12 Federal Reserve Districts, plus an extensive national *Summary.* Text is based on the opinions of bank officials, business executives, economists, financial market experts, and others. Typically contains views of consumer spending, manufacturing, services, credit, employment, prices, wages, and the economy in general. Usually referred to as the Beige Book.

ONLINE DATABASES

Country Report Services. The PRS Group. • Provides full text of reports describing the business risks and opportunities currently existing in more than 150 countries of the world. Contains a wide variety of statistics and forecasts relating to economics political and social conditions. Also includes demographics, tax, and currency information. Updated monthly. Inquire as to online cost and availability.

Information Bank Abstracts. New York Times Index Dept. • Provides indexing and abstracting of current affairs, primarily from the final late edition of *The New York Times* and the Eastern edition of *The Wall Street Journal.* Time period is 1969 to present, with daily updates. Inquire as to online cost and availability.

Newspaper Abstracts Daily. ProQuest Inc. • Provides online coverage (citations and abstracts) of 25 major newspapers. Covers business, economics,

current affairs, health, fitness, sports, education, technology, government, consumer affairs, psychology, the arts, and the social sciences. Time period is 1986 to date, with daily updates. Inquire as to online cost and availability.

OECD Main Economic Indicators. Organization for Economic Cooperation and Development. • International statistics provided by OECD, 1960 to date. Monthly updates. Inquire as to online cost and availability.

PERIODICALS AND NEWSLETTERS

Economic Perspectives (Chicago). Federal Reserve Bank of Chicago. • Quarterly. Free.

Federal Reserve Bank of Atlanta: Economic Review. Federal Reserve Bank of Atlanta. • Quarterly. Free.

Federal Reserve Bank of Dallas: Southwest Ecomomy Economic Review. Federal Reserve Bank of Dallas. • Quarterly. Free.

Federal Reserve Bank of Kansas City. Federal Reserve Bank of Kansas City. • Quarterly. Free.

Federal Reserve Bank of Minneapolis: Quarterly Review. Federal Reserve Bank of Minneapolis, Research Dept. • Quarterly. Free.

Federal Reserve Bank of New York: Economic Policy Review. Federal Reserve Bank of New York, Public Information Office. • Quarterly. Free.

Federal Reserve Bank of Philadelphia: Business Review. Federal Reserve Bank of Philadelphia, Research Dept. • Quarterly. Free. Contains articles on current topics in economics, finance, and banking.

Federal Reserve Bank of Richmond: Economic Quarterly. Federal Reserve Bank of Richmond, Research Dept. • Quarterly. Free. Formerly *Federal Reserve Bank of Richmond: Economic Review.*

Federal Reserve Bank of Saint Louis: Review. Federal Reserve Bank of Saint Louis. • Bimonthly. Free.

Federal Reserve Bank of San Francisco Economic Letter. Federal Reserve Bank of San Francisco. Economic Letter. • 38 times a year. Free. Formerly *Federal Reserve Bank of San Francisco: Weekly Letter.*

Federal Reserve Bank of San Francisco: Economic Review. Federal Reserve Bank of San Francisco. • Annual. Free.

The Levy Institute Forecast. Forecasting Center. • Description: Provides analyses and forecasts of U.S. business conditions. Reports on production, sales, inflation, corporate profits, and interest rates.

Ragan's Annual Report Review. Lawrence Ragan Communications Inc. • Description: Provides business trends, tips, and tactics.

Regional Economics and Markets: A Quarterly Analysis from the Conference Board. The Conference Board. • Quarterly. Members, $145.00 per year; non-members, $295.00 per year. Summarizes economic trends and prospects for nine geographic regions of the U. S. Provides data on key predictive indexes, including employment, housing permits, retail sales, consumer confidence, and help-wanted advertising. Charts and graphs are included.

Research Reports. American Institute for Economic Research. • Semimonthly. $59.00 per year. Newsletter. Alternate issues include charts of "Primary Leading Indicators," "Primary Roughly Coincident Indicators," and "Primary Lagging Indicators," as issued by The Conference Board (formerly provided by the U. S. Department of Commerce).

StraightTalk. The Conference Board. • 10 times a year. Members, $195.00 per year; non-members, $395.00 per year. Newsletter. Provides analysis of domestic and international economic issues.

Includes coverage of interest rate trends and the currency exchange outlook.

STATISTICS SOURCES

Business Statistics of the United States. Linz Audain and Cornelia J. Strawser. Bernan Associates. • Annual. $147.00. Based on *Business Statistics,* formerly issue by the Bureau of Economic Analysis, U. S. Department of Commerce. Provides basic data for a wide variety of U. S. industries, services, and economic indicators. Most statistics are shown annually for 30 years and monthly for the most recent four years.

Economic Indicators. Council of Economic Advisors, Executive Office of the President. Available from U.S. Government Printing Office. • Monthly. $55.00 per year.

Economic Indicators Handbook: Time Series, Conversions, Documentation. Gale Cengage Learning. • 2002. $205.00. Sixth edition. Provides data for about 175 U. S. economic indicators, such as the consumer price index (CPI), gross national product (GNP), and the rate of inflation. Values for series are given since inception, in both original form and adjusted for inflation. A bibliography of sources is included.

Main Economic Indicators. OECD Publication and Information Center. • Monthly. $450.00 per year. "The essential source of timely statistics for OECD member countries." Includes a wide variety of business, economic, and industrial data for the 29 OECD nations.

Main Economic Indicators: Historical Statistics. OECD Publications and Information Center. • Annual. $475.00. Includes online edition.

Nations of the World: A Political, Economic, and Business Handbook. Grey House Publishing. • 2002. $135.00. Third edition. Includes descriptive data on economic characteristics, population, gross domestic product (GDP), banking, inflation, agriculture, tourism, and other factors. Covers "all the nations of the world.".

OECD Economic Outlook. OECD Publications and Information Center. • Semiannual. Price on application. $95.00 per year. Contains a wide range of economic and monetary data relating to the member countries of the Organization for Economic Cooperation and Development. Includes about 100 statistical tables and graphs, with 24-month forecasts for each of the OECD countries. Provides extensive review and analysis of recent economic trends.

OECD Economic Survey of the United States. OECD Publications and Information Center. • Annual. $26.00.

OECD Economic Surveys. OECD Publications and Information Center. • Annual. $26.00 each. These are separate, yearly reviews for each of the economies of the industrialized nations that comprise the OECD. Each edition includes forecasts, analyses, and detailed statistical tables for the country being surveyed. (The combined series, one annual volume for each nation, is available at $485.00.).

Standard & Poor's Industry Surveys. Standard & Poor's. • Semiannual. $1,800.00. Two looseleaf volumes. Includes monthly *Supplements.* Provides detailed, individual surveys of 52 major industry groups. Each survey is revised on a semiannual basis. Also includes "Monthly Investment Review" (industry group investment analysis) and monthly "Trends & Projections" (economic analysis).

Survey of Current Business. Available from U. S. Government Printing Office. • Monthly. $63.00 per year. Issued by Bureau of Economic Analysis, U. S. Department of Commerce. Presents a wide variety of business and economic data.

Working Americans, 1880-1999, Volume One: The

Working Class. Scott Derks, editor. Grey House Publishing. • 2000. $375.00. Provides detailed information on the lifestyles and economic life of working class families in the 12 decades from 1880 to 1999. Includes such items as selected consumer prices, income, family finances, budgets, life at home, jobs, and working conditions. (Universal Reference Publications.).

Working Americans, 1880-1999, Volume Two: The Middle Class. Scott Derks, editor. Grey House Publishing. • 2000. $135.00. Three volumes. Furnishes details of the social and economic lives of middle class Americans during the years 1880 to 1999. Describes such items as selected consumer prices, income, family finances, budgets, life at home, jobs, and working conditions. (Universal Reference Publications.).

The World Economic Factbook. Available from Gale Cengage Learning. • Annual. $530.00. Published by Euromonitor. Presents key economic facts and figures for each of 200 countries, including details of chief industries, export-import trade, currency, political risk, household expenditures, and the economic situation in general.

World Economic Outlook: A Survey by the Staff of the International Monetary Fund. International Monetary Fund, Publications Services. • Semiannual. $78.00 per year. Presents international statistics combined with forecasts and analyses of the world economy.

World Economic Prospects: A Planner's Guide to International Market Conditions. Available from Gale Cengage Learning. • 2002. $490.00. Second edition. Published by Euromonitor. Ranks countries by specific economic characteristics, such as gross domestic product (GDP) per capita and short term growth prospects. Discusses the economic situation, prospects, and market potential of each of the countries.

OTHER SOURCES

Consensus Forecasts: A Worldwide Survey. Consensus Economics Inc. • Monthly. $565.00 per year. Provides a survey of more than 200 "prominent" financial and economic forecasters, covering 20 major countries. Two-year forecasts for each country include future growth, inflation, interest rates, and exchange rates. Each issue contains analysis of business conditions in various countries.

World Economic and Social Survey: Trends and Policies in the World Economy. United Nations Publications. • Annual. $55.00. Includes discussion and "an extensive statistical annex of economic, trade, and financial indicators, incorporating current data and forecasts.".

World Economic Situation and Prospects. United Nations Publications. • Annual. $15.00. Serves as a supplement and update to the UN *World Economic and Social Survey.*

BUSINESS CONSOLIDATION

See: MERGERS AND ACQUISITIONS

BUSINESS CONSULTANTS

See: CONSULTANTS; MANAGEMENT CONSULTANTS

BUSINESS CORRESPONDENCE

See also: COMMUNICATION; REPORT WRITING

GENERAL WORKS

Business English. Mary E. Guffey. South-Western. • 2001. $78.95. Seventh edition. (South-Western Col-

lege Busines Communications Series).

Writing Business Letters for Dummies. Sheryl Lindsell-Roberts. John Wiley. • 1999. $21.99. (For Dummies Series).

Writing That Works: How to Write Effective E-Mails, Letters, Resumes, Presentations, Plans, Reports and Other Business Communications. Kenneth Roman. HarperInformation. • 2000. $13.00. Third edition.

ENCYCLOPEDIAS AND DICTIONARIES

Lifetime Encyclopedia of Letters. Harold E. Meyer. Prentice Hall PTR. • 2001. $50.00. Third edition. Includes CD-ROM. Contains about 800 model letters and 400 alternative opening and closing sentences. Model letters are for sales, collection, complaints, apology, congratulations, fund raising, resignation, termination, etc.

HANDBOOKS AND MANUALS

AMA Handbook of Business Letters. Jeffrey L. Seglin and Edward Coleman. AMACOM. • 2002. $69.95. Third edition. Includes audio compact disk. Contains 300 sample letters, with advice on business correspondence.

Business English: A Complete Guide to Developing an Effective Business Writing Style. Andrea B. Geffner. Barron's Educational Series, Inc. • 2004. $16.95. Fourth edition. Covers both traditional and electronic business communication.

Business Letters for Busy People: Time-Saving Ready-to-Use Business Letters for Any Occasion. Jim Dugger. Career Press, Inc. • 2002. $19.99. Fourth edition.

Business Letters Ready to Go. Ann Basye. McGraw-Hill. • 1998. $12.95. Includes CD-Rom. (Contemporary Books Series).

Complete Book of Model Business Letters. Jack Griffin. Prentice Hall PTR. • 1997. $34.95.

Handbook for Business Writing. L. Sue Baug and others. McGraw-Hill. • 1993. $24.95. Second edition. Covers reports, letters, memos, and proposals. (Handbook for... Series).

Handbook for Memo Writing. L. Sue Baugh. McGraw-Hill. • 1995. $32.95. (NTC Business Book Series).

Handbook for Practical Letter Writing. L. Sue Baugh. McGraw-Hill. • 1993. $12.95.

Little Black Book of Business Letters. Michael C. Thomsett. AMACOM. • 1988. $14.95. Includes examples of various kinds of business correspondence. (Little Black Book Series).

Logo Power: Creating World-Class Logos and Effective Business Identities. David E. Carter. DIANE Publishing Co. • 2001. $40.00. Explains how to plan, develop, evaluate, and implement a company logo system.

McGraw-Hill Handbook of Business Letters. Roy W. Poe. McGraw-Hill. • 1993. $59.50. Third edition. Contains about 200 model business letters in 13 categories. Writing style, organization, objective, and underlying psychology are discussed for each example.

175 High-Impact Cover Letters. Richard H. Beatty. John Wiley and Sons, Inc. • 2002. $14.95. Third edition. Provides samples of cover letters for resumes.

Wall Street Journal Guide to Business Style and Usage. Paul R. Martin, editor. The Free Press. • 2002. $30.00. Contains definitions and explanations relating to grammar, spelling, punctuation, and the use of specialized business terms. (Wall Street Journal Book Series).

PERIODICALS AND NEWSLETTERS

Harvard Management Communication Letter. Harvard Business School Publishing. • Description: Provides information and techniques for managers on effective communication.

BUSINESS CYCLES

See also: BUSINESS CONDITIONS; BUSINESS FORECASTING; BUSINESS RESEARCH

GENERAL WORKS

Business Cycles: A Theoretical, Historical and Statistical Analysis of the Capitalist Process. Joseph A. Schumpeter. Porcupine Press, Inc. • 1989. $24.95. Abridged edition.

Business Cycles: Theory, History, Indications, and Forecasting. Victor Zarnowitz. The University of Chicago Press. • 1992. $77.00. (National Bureau of Economic Research Monograph Series: Vol. 27).

Forecasting Business Trends. American Institute for Economic Research. • 2000. $6.00. Summarizes methods of economic forecasting, statistical indicators, methods of analyzing business cycles, and use of leading, coincident, and lagging indicators. Includes charts, tables, and a glossary of terms. (Economic Education Bulletin.).

The Great Depression and New Deal Reference Library. Gale Cengage Learning. • 2002. $145.00. Three volumes. Individual volumes are available at $55.00. Includes *Great Depression and New Deal: Almanac; Great Depression and New Deal: Biographies* and *Great Depression and New Deal: Primary Sources*. (UXL imprint).

Great Inflations of the 20th Century: Theories, Policies, and Evidence. Pierre L. Siklos, editor. Edward Elgar Publishing, Inc. • 1995. $100.00. Contains reprints of papers on the history and economic analysis of major inflations.

It Was a Very Good Year: Extraordinary Moments in Stock Market History. Martin S. Fridson. John Wiley and Sons, Inc. • 1997. $29.95. Provides details on what happened during each of the ten best years for the stock market since 1900. (Investment Series).

Manias, Panics, and Crashes: A History of Financial Crises. Charles P. Kindleberger. John Wiley and Sons, Inc. • 2000. $19.95. Fourth edition. Provides a history of financial troubles from 1618 to modern times, with greed as a central theme. (Investment Classic Series).

A Short History of Financial Euphoria. John Kenneth Galbraith. Penguin Group. • 1994. $13.00. An analysis of speculative euphoria and subsequent crashes, from the Holland tulip mania in 1637 to the 1987 unpleasantness in the U. S. stock market. (Whittle Series).

Stock Market Crashes and Speculative Manias. Eugene N. White, editor. Edward Elgar Publishing, Inc. • 1996. $255.00. Contains reprints of 23 articles dating from 1905 to 1994. (International Library of Macroeconomic and Financial History Series: No. 13).

What Will Recession Mean to You?. C. Edgar Murray, editor. American Institute for Economic Research. • 2001. $6.00. A revision of *What Will the Next Recession Mean to You?* (1998). Covers the history of U. S. recessions, future recessions, forecasting, and "Coping with a Recession." (Economic Education Bulletin.).

CD-ROM DATABASES

OECD Statistical Compendium. Organization for Economic Cooperation and Development. • Semiannual. $1,905.00 per year for 1 to 10 users. CD-ROM contains more than 730,000 monthly, quarterly, and annual time series for OECD countries, 1960 to date. Includes fully searchable data on agriculture, food, economic indicators, national accounts, employment, energy, finance, industry, technology, and foreign trade. Results can be displayed in various forms.

ENCYCLOPEDIAS AND DICTIONARIES

Business Cycles and Depressions: An Encyclopedia. David Glasner. Garland Publishing, Inc. • 1997.

$155.00. Contains 327 alphabetical entries by various contributors. Defines and reviews all significant depressions, recessions, and financial crises in the U. S. and Europe since 1790. Includes chronologies, bibliographies, and indexes.

Encyclopedia of the Great Depression. Gale Cengage Learning. • 2003. $265.00. Two volumes. Covers about two decades of U. S. economic history, from "the farm crisis of the mid-1920s," through the gradual recovery of the 1930s, to the beginning of World War II. (Macmillan Reference USA imprint.).

Encyclopedia of the Great Depression and the New Deal. James Ciment, editor. M. E. Sharpe, Inc. • 2001. $199.00. Two volumes. Covers the major movements, events, and people of the 1930's depression. Includes many illustrations, a bibliography, and an index.

HANDBOOKS AND MANUALS

BCI Handbook. The Conference Board, Inc. • 2001. $20.00. Provides detailed descriptions of the economic series - Business Cycle Indicators - used by The Conference Board to determine current business conditions and predict the future direction of the U. S. economy. Data sources are indicated. (A previous version was published in 1982.).

Fibonacci Applications and Strategies for Traders. Robert Fischer. John Wiley and Sons, Inc. • 1993. $60.00. Provides a new look at the Elliott Wave Theory and Fibonacci numbers as applied to commodity prices, business cycles, and interest rate movements. (Traders Advantage Series).

Investor's Guide to Economic Indicators. Charles R. Nelson. John Wiley and Sons, Inc. • 1989. $17.95.

INTERNET DATABASES

Business 2.0 Web Guide to the Best Business Links. Business 2.0 Media Inc. Phone: (415)293-4800 E-mail: support@business2.com • URL: http://www.business2.com/webguide • Web site presents an extensive, searchable directory of links to "the best, most informative, and authoritative web pages." Twenty main categories cover business, finance, career, company information, people, and technology topics, with thousands of subtopics, all linking to Web sites recommended by experienced business researchers. Fees: Free.

Fedstats. Federal Interagency Council on Statistical Policy. Phone: (202)395-7254 • URL: http://www.fedstats.gov • Web site features an efficient search facility for full-text statistics produced by more than 100 federal agencies, including the Census Bureau, the Bureau of Economic Analysis, and the Bureau of Labor Statistics. Boolean searches can be made within one agency or for all agencies combined. Links are offered to international statistical bureaus, including the UN, IMF, OECD, UNESCO, Eurostat, and 20 individual countries. Fees: Free.

FreeLunch.com. Economy.com, Inc. Phone: (610)696-8700 Fax: (610)696-1678 • URL: http://www.freelunch.com • Web site provides free access to more than 1.5 million economic and financial data series, covering industry, demographics, labor markets, prices, retail sales, government spending, trade, interest rates, housing starts, the stock market, and many other topics. Data is available for various time periods in either chart or table form. Searching is offered. Fees: Free, but registration required. Economy.com, Inc. also offers fee-based economic analysis at *The Dismal Scientist* site (http://www.dismal.com).

ONLINE DATABASES

EconLit. American Economic Association. • Covers the worldwide literature of economics as contained in selected monographs and about 550 journals. Subjects include microeconomics, macroeconomics, economic history, inflation, money, credit, finance, accounting theory, trade, natural resource economics, and regional economics. Time period is 1969 to

present, with monthly updates. Inquire as to online cost and availability.

PERIODICALS AND NEWSLETTERS

Crawford Perspectives. Arch Crawford. • Description: Publishes information on the stock market based on a "unique cycle approach using elipses instead of pure cycles to gain higher resolution in determining turning points." Employs technical analyses to back up astronomic cycles. "Ranked 1 market timer 5 year period by independent rating service".

Cycle Projections. Foundation for the Study of Cycles. • Monthly. $125.00 per year. Newsletter includes trend projections for stocks, commodities, real estate, and the economy. Short, intermediate, and long-term cycles are covered.

Cycles. Service Directions Inc. • Description: Describes new laundry equipment, advances in laundryroom management, and analyzes problems in residential laundryrooms. Recurring features include interviews.

Trading Cycles. R.E. Andrews, editor. Andrews Publications, Inc. • Monthly. $97.99 per year. Newsletter. Technical investment newsletter. Formerly *Andrews Trading Cycles*.

RESEARCH CENTERS AND INSTITUTES

Bureau of Economic and Business Research. University of Florida. 221 Matherly Hall, Gainesville, FL 32611-7145. Phone: (352)392-0171 Fax: (352)392-4739 E-mail: info@bebr.ufl.edu • URL: http://www.bebr.ufl.edu.

Conference Board, Inc. The Conference Board, Inc. 845 3rd Ave., New York, NY 10022. Phone: (212)339-0345 Fax: (212)980-7014 E-mail: info@conference-board.org • URL: http://www.conference-board.org • Business management practices worldwide, especially economic, and demographic in nature. Specific concerns include: corporate citizenship, including corporate contributions, diversity, environmental policy and issues, and government relations; corporate governance, including boards of directors, role of chief executives, relations with institutional investors, and shareholder input and influence; economics, including economic and financial forecasts, consumer confidence, leading economic indicators, North American outlook and trends, and global economic environment; human resources and organizational effectiveness, including organization structure and design, compensation and benefits, training and development, and communications; and performance excellence.

STATISTICS SOURCES

The AIER Chart Book. AIER Research Staff. American Institute for Economic Research. • Annual. $4.00. A compact compilation of long-range charts ("Purchasing Power of the Dollar," for example, goes back to 1780) covering various aspects of the U. S. economy. Includes inflation, interest rates, debt, gold, taxation, stock prices, etc. (Economic Education Bulletin.).

Business Cycle Indicators: A Monthly Report from the Conference Board. Conference Board. • Monthly. $130.00 per year. Contains detailed business and economic statistics in tables that were formerly published by the U. S. Department of Commerce in *Survey of Current Business*, and before that, in the discontinued *Business Conditions Digest.* Includes composite indexes of leading economic indicators, coincident indicators, and lagging indicators.

Business Statistics of the United States. Linz Audain and Cornelia J. Strawser. Bernan Associates. • Annual. $147.00. Based on *Business Statistics,* formerly issue by the Bureau of Economic Analysis, U. S. Department of Commerce. Provides basic data for a wide variety of U. S. industries, services, and economic indicators. Most statistics are shown annually for 30 years and monthly for the most recent four years.

Leading Economic Indicators and Related Composite Indexes. The Conference Board. • Monthly. $24.00 per year. Shows monthly changes in the composite indexes of leading, coincident, and lagging economic indicators, formerly computed by the U. S. Department of Commerce. Tables present monthly data for up to 10 years, with a one-page line chart covering 18 years. (The Conference Board News.).

Survey of Current Business. Available from U. S. Government Printing Office. • Monthly. $63.00 per year. Issued by Bureau of Economic Analysis, U. S. Department of Commerce. Presents a wide variety of business and economic data.

BUSINESS DEPRESSIONS

See: BUSINESS CYCLES

BUSINESS DIRECTORIES

See: CATALOGS AND DIRECTORIES

BUSINESS ECONOMICS

GENERAL WORKS

Managerial Economics. Mark Hirschey. South-Western. • 2002. Ninth edition. Price on application.

Managerial Economics: Analysis, Problems, Cases. Lila Truett and Dale B. Turett. John Wiley and Sons, Inc. • 2000. $101.95. Seventh edition.

ABSTRACTS AND INDEXES

Business Periodicals Index. H. W. Wilson Co. • 11 times a year. Quarterly and annual cumulations. Price varies.

CD-ROM DATABASES

EconLit. Available from SilverPlatter Information, Inc. • Monthly. Single-user, $1,600.00 per year. Provides CD-ROM citations, with abstracts, to articles from more than 500 economics journals. Time period is 1969 to date. Produced by the American Economic Association.

DIRECTORIES

Business Organizations, Agencies, and Publications Directory. Gale Cengage Learning. • 2003. $480.00. 15th edition. Over 40,000 entries describing 39 types of business information sources. Classified by type of organization, publication, or serviceIncludes state, national, and international agencies and organizations. Master index to names and keywords. Also includes e-mail addresses and web site URL's.

National Association for Business Economics Membership Directory. National Association for Business Economics. • Annual. Membership.

ENCYCLOPEDIAS AND DICTIONARIES

Blackwell Encyclopedic Dictionary of Managerial Economics. Robert McAuliffe, editor. Blackwell Publishers. • 1999. $138.95. The editor is associated with Boston College. Contains definitions of key terms combined with longer articles written by various U. S. and foreign business educators. Includes bibliographies and index. *Blackwell Encyclopedia of Management Series.*

Dictionary of Economics. Donald Rutherford. Routledge. • 2002. $90.00. Second edition.

HANDBOOKS AND MANUALS

Tracking America's Economy. Norman Frumkin. M. E. Sharpe, Inc. • 2004. $72.95. Fourth edition. Provides detailed explanations of the meaning and methodology of the leading U. S. economic

indicators. Covers such topics as employment data, financial indicators, productivity, housing, government spending, balance of payments, and taxation.

ONLINE DATABASES

Wilson Business Abstracts Online. H. W. Wilson Co. • Indexes and abstracts 600 major business periodicals, plus the *Wall Street Journal* and the business section of the *New York Times.* Indexing is from 1982, abstracting from 1990, with the two newspapers included from 1993. Updated weekly. Inquire as to online cost and availability. (*Business Periodicals Index* without abstracts is also available online.).

PERIODICALS AND NEWSLETTERS

Applied Economics Letters. Taylor and Francis Group. • 15 times a year. Individuals, $115.00 per year; institutions, $809.00 per year. Provides short accounts of new, original research in practical economics. Supplement to *Applied Economics.*

Applied Financial Economics. Taylor and Francis Group. • Monthly. Institutions, $1,277.00 per year. Covers practical aspects of financial economics, banking, and monetary economics. Supplement to *Applied Economics.*

Business Economics: Designed to Serve the Needs of People Who Use Economics in Their Work. National Association for Business Economics. • Quarterly. $85.00 per year. Features articles on applied economics.

Challenge: The Magazine of Economic Affairs. M. E. Sharpe, Inc. • Bimonthly. Individuals, $52.00 per year; institutions, $220.00 per year. Includes print and online editions. A nontechnical journal on current economic policy and economic trends.

The Economist. Economist Intelligence Unit. • 51 times a year. $125.00 per year.

Fortune Magazine. Time Inc., Business Information Group. • Biweekly. $59.95 per year. Edited for top executives and upper-level managers.

Harvard Business Review. Harvard University, Graduate School of Business Administration. Harvard Business School Publishing. • Monthly. $118.00 per year.

The Journal of Business. The University of Chicago Press, Journals Div. • Quarterly. Individuals, $31.00 per year; institutions, $125.00 per year; students, $25.00 per year.

Managerial and Decision Economics: The International Journal of Research and Progress in Management Economics. John Wiley and Sons, Inc., Journals. • Eight times a year. Individuals, $340.00 per year; institutions, $1,180.00 per year. Deals with economic problems in the field of managerial and decision economics. International coverage. Published in England by John Wiley and Sons Ltd.

MIT Sloan Management Review. Sloan Management Review Association. Massachusetts Institute of Technology. • Quarterly. Individuals, $89.00 per year; institutions, $148.00 per year. Formerly *Sloan Management Review..*

NABE News. National Association for Business Economics. • Description: Concerned with business economics. Serves this professional Association of persons employed by private, institutional, or government concerns in the area of business-related economic analysis. Recurring features include results of the NABE quarterly outlook survey, featured articles of timely interest, reviews of seminars and annual meetings, news from local chapters and roundtables, and personal notes.

Quarterly Journal of Business and Economics. University of Nebraska at Lincoln, College of Business Administration. • Quarterly. Individuals, $24.00 per year; institutions, $45.00 per year.

The Quarterly Review of Economics and Finance. University of Illinois at Urbana-Champaign, Bureau of Economics and Business Research. Available

from JAI Press, Inc. • Five times a year. Individuals, $95.00 per year; institutions, $426.00 per year. Includes annual *Supplement.* Formerly *Quarterly Review of Economics and Business.*

StraightTalk. The Conference Board. • 10 times a year. Members, $195.00 per year; non-members, $395.00 per year. Newsletter. Provides analysis of domestic and international economic issues. Includes coverage of interest rate trends and the currency exchange outlook.

TRADE/PROFESSIONAL ASSOCIATIONS

National Association for Business Economics. 1233 20th St., N.W., Suite 505, Washington, DC 20036. Phone: (202)463-6223 Fax: (202)463-6239 E-mail: nabe@nabe.com • URL: http://www.nabe.com • Formerly National Association of Business Economists.

Society of American Business Editors and Writers, Inc. c/o University of Missouri,, School of Journalism, 134 Neff Annex, Columbia, MO 65211-1200. Phone: (573)882-7862 or (573)882-8985 Fax: (573)884-1372 E-mail: sabew@missouri.edu • URL: http://www.sabew.org • Affiliated with Association for Education in Journalism and Mass Communication. Formerly Society of American Business and Economic Writers.

BUSINESS EDUCATION

See also: ADULT EDUCATION; COLLEGES AND UNIVERSITIES; GRADUATE WORK IN UNIVERSITIES; VOCATIONAL EDUCATION

GENERAL WORKS

Can Ethics Be Taught? Perspectives, Challenges, and Approaches at the Harvard Business School. Thomas R. Piper and others. Harvard Business School Publishing. • 1993. $24.95.

Gravy Training: Inside the Real World of Business Schools. Stuart Crainer and Des Dearlove. Jossey-Bass. • 1999. $25.00. Provides a critical look at major American business schools. (Business and Management Series).

Mastering Management Education: Innovations in Teaching Effectiveness. Charles M. Vance, editor. Sage Publications, Inc. • 1993. $80.95. A collection of articles from the *Journal of Management Education.* Chapters cover lecture and discussion methods, case-study teaching, group-learning skills, and other business education topics.

Teaching Business Studies. David Needham and others. McGraw-Hill. • 1992. $15.99.

Trends and Developments in Business Administration Programs. Donald L. Joyal. Greenwood Publishing Group, Inc. • 1982. $52.50.

ABSTRACTS AND INDEXES

Current Index to Journals in Education (CIJE). Oryx Press. • Monthly. $245.00 per year. Semiannual cumulations, $475.00.

Education Index. H. W. Wilson Co. • 10 times a year. Quarterly and annual cumulations. Price varies.

Educational Administration Abstracts. Sage Publication, Inc. • Quarterly. Institutions, $722.00 per year.

ALMANACS AND YEARBOOKS

National Business Education Yearbook. National Business Education Association. • Annual. $40.00.

BIOGRAPHICAL SOURCES

Who's Who in American Education. Marquis Who's Who. • Biennial. $159.95. Contains over 27,000 concise biographies of teachers, administrators, and other individuals involved in all levels of American education.

CD-ROM DATABASES

College Blue Book CD-ROM. Available from Gale Cengage Learning. • Annual. $250.00. Produced by

Macmillan Reference USA. Serves as electronic version of printed *College Blue Book*. Provides detailed information on programs, degrees, and financial aid sources in the U.S. and Canada.

ERIC on SilverPlatter. Available from SilverPlatter Information, Inc. • Quarterly. $700.00 per year. Produced by the Office of Educational Research and Improvement, U. S. Dept. of Education. Provides CD-ROM indexing and abstracting of a wide variety of literature relating to education. Archival discs are available from 1966.

OECD Statistical Compendium. Organization for Economic Cooperation and Development. • Semiannual. $1,905.00 per year for 1 to 10 users. CD-ROM contains more than 730,000 monthly, quarterly, and annual time series for OECD countries, 1960 to date. Includes fully searchable data on agriculture, food, economic indicators, national accounts, employment, energy, finance, industry, technology, and foreign trade. Results can be displayed in various forms.

WILSONDISC: Education Index. H. W. Wilson Co. • Monthly. Provides CD-ROM indexing of education-related literature from 1983 to date. Price includes online service.

DIRECTORIES

American Universities and Colleges. American Council on Education USA. Walter de Gruyter, Inc. • Quadrennial. $249.50. Two volumes. Produced in collaboration with the American Council on Education. Provides full descriptions of more than 1,900 institutions of higher learning, including details of graduate and professional programs.

Barron's Guide to Graduate Business Schools. Barron's Educational Series. • Biennial. Contains profiles of more than 600 business schools offering graduate business degrees in the U. S. and Canada. Includes advice on choosing a school.

Business Week's Guide to the Best Business Schools. John A. Byrne. McGraw-Hill. • 2002. $16.95. Seventh edition. Includes the best regional business schools. (Business Week Guide to the Best Business Schools Series).

Faculty White Pages. Gale Cengage Learning. • 1991. $135.00. 91st edition. "Telephone book" classified arrangement of over 537,000 U. S. college faculty members in 41 subject sections. A roster of institutions is included.

Peterson's Graduate and Professional Programs: Business, Education, Health, Information Studies, Law, and Social Work. Peterson's. • 2002. $49.95. Provides details of graduate and professional programs in business, law, information, and other fields at colleges and universities. (Peterson's Graduate and Professional Program Series). Formerly *Peterson's Guide to Graduate Programs in Business, Education, Health, Information Studies, Law and Social Work.*

Peterson's Guide to MBA Programs: The Most Comprehensive Guide to U. S., Canadian, and International Business Schools. Peterson's. • 2002. $29.95. Provides detailed information on about 850 graduate programs in business at 700 colleges and universities in the U. S., Canada, and other countries.

Wall Street Journal Guide to the Top Business Schools. Simon & Schuster, Inc. • Annual. $17.00. Rankings are based on surveys of recruiters of MBA graduates. Includes detailed descriptions of the leading U.S. business schools and information for applicants.

ENCYCLOPEDIAS AND DICTIONARIES

Encyclopedia of Distributed Learning. Anna DiStefano and others, editors. Sage Publications, Inc. • 2004. $125.00. Contains 275 entries on contemporary continuing education and distance

learning for adults in corporate, academic, and other settings.

HANDBOOKS AND MANUALS

Financing Graduate School: How to Get Money for Your Master's or Ph.D. Patricia McWade. Peterson's. • 1996. $16.95. Second revised edition. Discusses the practical aspects of various types of financial aid for graduate students. Includes bibliographic and directory information.

Official Guide for GMAT Review (Graduate Management Admission Test). Graduate Management Admissions Council. Educational Testing Service. • 2003. 10th edition. Price on application. Provides sample tests, answers, and explanations for the Graduate Management Admission Test (GMAT).

INTERNET DATABASES

Business 2.0 Web Guide to the Best Business Links. Business 2.0 Media Inc. Phone: (415)293-4800 E-mail: support@business2.com • URL: http://www.business2.com/webguide • Web site presents an extensive, searchable directory of links to "the best, most informative, and authoritative web pages." Twenty main categories cover business, finance, career, company information, people, and technology topics, with thousands of subtopics, all linking to Web sites recommended by experienced business researchers. Fees: Free.

ONLINE DATABASES

ERIC. Educational Resources Information Center. • Funded by the U. S. Department of Education, Institute of Education Sciences (formerly Office of Educational Research and Improvement). Provides access to more than one million online records covering education-related journal and report literature, 1966 to date. Updating is monthly. Inquire as to online cost and availability.

PERIODICALS AND NEWSLETTERS

Business Education Forum. National Business Education Association. • Four times a year. Libraries, $70.00 per year. Includes *Yearbook* and *Keying In*, a newsletter.

International Review for Business Education. SIEC-ISBE. • Semiannual. $36.00 per year. Text in English, French, German, Italian, and Spanish.

Journal of Education for Business. Helen Dwight Reid Educational Foundation. Heldref Publications. • Bimonthly. Individuals, $51.00 per year; institutions, $87.00 per year. Features basic and applied research-based articles on business fundamentals, career education, consumer economics, distributive education, management, and trends in communications, information systems, and knowledge systems in business.

Journal of Management Education. Organizational Behavior Teaching Society. Sage Publications, Inc. • Bimonthly. Institutions, $397.00 per year; includes print and online editions. A scholarly journal dealing with the teaching and training of business students and managers.

Journal of Teaching in International Business. Haworth Press, Inc. • Quarterly. Institutions, $315.00 per year.

Resources in Education. Educational Resources Information Center. Available from U.S. Government Printing Office. • Monthly. Reports on educational research.

RESEARCH CENTERS AND INSTITUTES

Center for Financial Responsibility. College of Human Sciences, Box 41162, Texas Tech University, Lubbock, TX 79409-1162. Phone: (806)742-9781 Fax: (806)742-9784 E-mail: bill.gustafson@ttu.edu • URL: http://www.hs.ttu.edu/cfr/ • Research areas include financial preparation for retirement, financial education, determinants of financial satisfaction, risk tolerance, and the career prepara-

tion of retirement industry professionals.

STATISTICS SOURCES

Degrees and Other Awards Conferred by Institutions of Higher Education. Available from U. S. Government Printing Office. • Annual. Issued by the National Center for Education Statistics, U. S. Department of Education. Provides data on the number of degrees awarded at the associate's, bachelor's, master's, and doctor's levels. Includes fields of study and racial-ethnic-sex data by major field or discipline.

Occupational Projections and Training Data. Available from U. S. Government Printing Office. • Biennial. $21.00. Issued by Bureau of Labor Statistics, U. S. Department of Labor. Contains projections of employment change and job openings over the next 15 years for about 500 specific occupations. Also includes the number of associate, bachelor's, master's, doctoral, and professional degrees awarded in a recent year for about 900 specific fields of study.

TRADE/PROFESSIONAL ASSOCIATIONS

Delta Pi Epsilon. PO Box 4340, Little Rock, AR 72214. Phone: (501)219-1866 Fax: (501)219-1876 E-mail: dpe@ipa.net • URL: http://www.dpe.org • Professional society - men and women, business education.

Delta Sigma Pi. 330 S Campus Ave., Oxford, OH 45056-2405. Phone: (513)523-1907 Fax: (513)523-7292 E-mail: centraloffice@dspnet.org • URL: http://www.dspnet.org • Professional fraternity - commerce and business administration. Operates Delta Sigma Pi Leadership Foundation. Maintains museum; sponsors competitions; offers computerized services; compiles statistics. Provides educational and career assistance.

Graduate Management Admission Council. 1600 Tysons Blvd., Ste. 1400, McLean, VA 22102. Phone: (866)505-6559 or (703)749-0131 Fax: (703)749-0169 E-mail: webmaster1@gmac.com • URL: http://www.gmac.com • Graduate schools of management and business administration. Works to establish criteria for use in admission to graduate management programs. Provides professional development for academic administrators and seminars for admissions officers. Maintains Graduate +Management Admission Search Service, a program that provides institutions with the names of qualified students with desirable characteristics. Employs Educational Testing Service to develop and administer the Graduate Management Admission Test. Conducts research on student selection issues and political and social issues related to graduate management education.

National Business Education Association. 1914 Association Dr., Reston, VA 20191-1596. Phone: (703)860-8300 Fax: (703)620-4483 E-mail: nbea@nbea.org • URL: http://www.nbea.org • Teachers of business subjects in secondary and postsecondary schools and colleges; administrators and research workers in business education; businesspersons interested in business education; teachers in educational institutions training business teachers; high school and college students preparing for careers in business.

OTHER SOURCES

Educational Rankings Annual: A Compilation of Approximately 3,500 Published Rankings and Lists on Every Aspect of Education. Gale Cengage Learning. • Annual. $265.00. Provides national, regional, local, and international rankings of a wide variety of educational institutions, including business and professional schools.

BUSINESS ENTERPRISES, SALE OF

See also: SMALL BUSINESS

GENERAL WORKS

Buying and Selling a Small Business: A Complete Guide to a Successful Deal. Ernest J. Honigmann. CCH, Inc. • 1999. $91.95.

How to Sell Your Business for More Money. Gary Schine. The Consultants Press, Ltd. • 1991. $29.95.

ABSTRACTS AND INDEXES

Business Periodicals Index. H. W. Wilson Co. • 11 times a year. Quarterly and annual cumulations. Price varies.

Index to Legal Periodicals and Books. H. W. Wilson Co. • Monthly. $490.00 per year. Quarterly and annual cumulations.

CD-ROM DATABASES

ABI/INFORM. PROQUEST. • Monthly. Provides CD-ROM indexing and abstracting of worldwide business literature. Archival discs are available from 1971. Formerly *ABI/INFORM OnDisc.*

WILSONDISC: Index to Legal Periodicals and Books. H. W. Wilson Co. • Monthly. Includes unlimited online access to *Index to Legal Periodicals* through WILSONLINE. Contains CD-ROM indexing of more than 1,400 English language legal periodicals from 1981 to date and 2,500 books.

WILSONDISC: Wilson Business Abstracts. H. W. Wilson Co. • Monthly. Includes unlimited online access to *Wilson Business Abstracts* through WILSONLINE. Provides CD-ROM "cover-to-cover" abstracting and indexing of over 600 prominent business periodicals. Indexing is from 1982, abstracting from 1990. (*Business Periodicals Index* without abstracts is available on CD-ROM at $1,495 per year.).

DIRECTORIES

Business Brokers Directory. infoUSA Inc. • Number of listings: 3,487 Entries include: Name, address, phone (including area code), size of advertisement, year first in "Yellow Pages," name of owner or manager, number of employees. Compiled from telephone company "Yellow Pages," nationwide.

HANDBOOKS AND MANUALS

Business Brokerage. Entrepreneur Media, Inc. • Looseleaf. $59.50. A practical guide to starting a brokerage service for the sale and purchase of small businesses. Covers profit potential, start-up costs, market size evaluation, owner's time required, pricing, accounting, advertising, promotion, etc. (Start-Up Business Guide No. E1317.).

CCH Guide to Business Valuation. CCH, Inc. • Looseleaf. $295.00 per year, including quarterly newsletter. Covers latest developments and trends in the evaluation of businesses.

Corporate Valuation: Tools for Effective Appraisal and Decision Making. Stephen A. Ross and others. McGraw-Hill. • 1994. $76.95. Discusses the four most widely-used corporate appraisal methods.

ONLINE DATABASES

Index to Legal Periodicals and Books (Online). H. W. Wilson Co. • Broad coverage of law journals and books 1981 to date. Monthly updates. Inquire as to online cost and availability.

Management Contents. Gale Cengage Learning. • Covers a wide range of management, financial, marketing, personnel, and administrative topics. About 150 leading business journals are indexed and abstracted from 1974 to date, with monthly updating. Inquire as to online cost and availability.

Trade & Industry Database. Gale Cengage Learning. • Provides indexing of business periodicals, January 1981 to date. Daily updates.

(Full text articles from some periodicals are available online, 1983 to date. Inquire as to online cost and availability).

Wilson Business Abstracts Online. H. W. Wilson Co. • Indexes and abstracts 600 major business periodicals, plus the *Wall Street Journal* and the business section of the *New York Times.* Indexing is from 1982, abstracting from 1990, with the two newspapers included from 1993. Updated weekly. Inquire as to online cost and availability. (*Business Periodicals Index* without abstracts is also available online.).

BUSINESS ETHICS

See also: SOCIAL RESPONSIBILITY

GENERAL WORKS

American Business Values: With International Perspectives. Gerald F. Cavanaugh. Prentice Hall PTR. • 1997. $48.00. Fourth edition.

Business Ethics. J. Michael Hoffman and others. McGraw-Hill. • 2000. $39.25. Fourth edition.

Business Ethics: Roles and Responsibilities. Joseph Badaracco. McGraw-Hill. • 1994. $63.50.

Business, Government, and Society: A Managerial Perspective: Text and Cases. George A. Steiner and John F. Steiner. McGraw-Hill. • 1999. $88.75. Ninth edition. (Management Series).

Can Ethics Be Taught? Perspectives, Challenges, and Approaches at the Harvard Business School. Thomas R. Piper and others. Harvard Business School Publishing. • 1993. $24.95.

Case Studies in Business Ethics. Thomas Donaldson and Al Gini, editors. Prentice Hall PTR. • 1995. $49.00. Fourth edition.

Case Studies in Business, Society, and Ethics. Thomas L. Beauchamp, editor. Prentice Hall PTR. • 1997. $42.00. Fourth edition.

Corporate Social Challenge: Cases and Commentaries. James E. Stacey and Frederick D. Sturdivant, editors. McGraw-Hill. • 1994. $41.95. Fifth edition.

The Ethics of Management. LaRue T. Hosmer. McGraw-Hill. • 2002. $50.00. Fourth edition.

BIBLIOGRAPHIES

A Bibliography of Business Ethics, 1981-1985: University of Virginia. Donald G. Jones and Patricia Bennett, editors. The Edwin Mellen Press. • 1986. $99.95. (Mellen Studies in Business Series: Vol. 2).

ENCYCLOPEDIAS AND DICTIONARIES

Blackwell Encyclopedic Dictionary of Business Ethics. Patricia H. Werhane and R. Edward Freeman. Blackwell Publishing. • 1997. $38.95. The editors are associated with the University of Virginia. Contains definitions of key terms combined with longer articles written by various U. S. and foreign business educators. Includes bibliographies and index. (Blackwell Encyclopedia of Management Series).

HANDBOOKS AND MANUALS

ABA/BNA Lawyer's Manual on Professional Conduct. American Bar Association. BNA, Inc. • Bimonthly. $595.00 per year. Looseleaf service. Covers American Bar Association's model rules governing ethical practice of law.

Codes of Professional Responsibility: Ethic Standards in Business, Health and Law. Rena Gorlin, editor. BNA, Inc. • 1999. $95.00. Fourth edition. Contains full text or substantial excerpts of the official codes of ethics of major professional groups in the fields of law, business, and health care.

Legal Ethics in the Practice of Law. Richard A. Zitrin and Carol M. Langford. LexisNexis Matthew Bender. • 2002. $57.00. Provides "real-life examples

of ethical dilemmas" occurring in the law profession.

Managing Business Ethics: Straight Talk About How to Do It Right. Linda K. Trevino and others. John Wiley and Sons, Inc. • 2002. Third edition. Price on application. Includes "Ethics and the Individual," "Ethics and the Manager," and "Ethics and the Organization.".

Managing Finance: A Socially Responsible Approach. David Crowther. Elsevier Butterworth Heinemann. • 2004. $37.50. Explains how to manage an ethical approach to such items as accounting, company reports, profit analysis, costing, budgeting, performance data, and investment appraisal.

PERIODICALS AND NEWSLETTERS

Business and Society: A Journal of Interdisciplinary Exploration. International Association for Business and Society Research Committee. Sage Publications, Inc. • Quarterly. $402.00 per year.

Journal of Business Ethics. Kluwer Academic Publishers. • 28 times a year. Institutions, $1,743.00 per year. Includes print and online editions.

Positive Leadership: Improving Performance Through Value-Centered Management. Lawrence Ragan Communications, Inc. • Monthly. $99.00 per year. Newsletter. Emphasis is on employee motivation, family issues, ethics, and community relations.

RESEARCH CENTERS AND INSTITUTES

Business, Government, and Society Research Institute. University of Pittsburgh. School of Business, Mervis Hall, Pittsburgh, PA 15260. Phone: (412)648-1555 Fax: (412)648-1693 E-mail: mitnick@pitt.edu.

Olsson Center for Applied Ethics. University of Virginia. The Darden School, P.O. Box 6550, Charlottesville, VA 22906. Phone: (434)924-0935 Fax: (434)924-6378 E-mail: ref8d@virginia.edu • URL: http://www.darden.virginia.edu.

STATISTICS SOURCES

Business Ethics Survey. Available from Paul & Co. • Annual. $99.95. Published by the Society for Human Resource Management (http://www.shrm.org). Provides benchmarks, with trends in business ethics data since 1997.

BUSINESS ETIQUETTE

See: ETIQUETTE

BUSINESS FAILURES

See also: BANK FAILURES; BANKRUPTCY

GENERAL WORKS

Why Entreprenuers Fail: Avoid the 20 Fatal Pitfalls of Running Your Own Business. James W. Halloran. Waterview Press, Inc. • 1999. $17.00. Second revised edition.

ABSTRACTS AND INDEXES

Business Periodicals Index. H. W. Wilson Co. • 11 times a year. Quarterly and annual cumulations. Price varies.

CD-ROM DATABASES

Authority Collier Bankruptcy Library. LexisNexis/ Matthew Bender. • Periodic revisions. Price on request. CD-ROM contains updated full text of *Collier on Bankruptcy* and 13 other Collier publications. Various aspects of bankruptcy are covered, including attorney compensation, proceedings, farm insolvencies, real estate failures, family law, taxation, and business workouts.

OECD Statistical Compendium. Organization for Economic Cooperation and Development. • Semiannual. $1,905.00 per year for 1 to 10 users. CD-ROM contains more than 730,000 monthly, quarterly, and annual time series for OECD countries, 1960 to date. Includes fully searchable data on agriculture, food, economic indicators, national accounts, employment, energy, finance, industry, technology, and foreign trade. Results can be displayed in various forms.

INTERNET DATABASES

Business 2.0 Web Guide to the Best Business Links. Business 2.0 Media Inc. Phone: (415)293-4800 E-mail: support@business2.com • URL: http://www.business2.com/webguide • Web site presents an extensive, searchable directory of links to "the best, most informative, and authoritative web pages." Twenty main categories cover business, finance, career, company information, people, and technology topics, with thousands of subtopics, all linking to Web sites recommended by experienced business researchers. Fees: Free.

Fedstats. Federal Interagency Council on Statistical Policy. Phone: (202)395-7254 • URL: http://www.fedstats.gov • Web site features an efficient search facility for full-text statistics produced by more than 100 federal agencies, including the Census Bureau, the Bureau of Economic Analysis, and the Bureau of Labor Statistics. Boolean searches can be made within one agency or for all agencies combined. Links are offered to international statistical bureaus, including the UN, IMF, OECD, UNESCO, Eurostat, and 20 individual countries. Fees: Free.

FreeLunch.com. Economy.com, Inc. Phone: (610)696-8700 Fax: (610)696-1678 • URL: http://www.freelunch.com • Web site provides free access to more than 1.5 million economic and financial data series, covering industry, demographics, labor markets, prices, retail sales, government spending, trade, interest rates, housing starts, the stock market, and many other topics. Data is available for various time periods in either chart or table form. Searching is offered. Fees: Free, but registration required. Economy.com, Inc. also offers fee-based economic analysis at *The Dismal Scientist* site (http://www.dismal.com).

ONLINE DATABASES

Trade & Industry Database. Gale Cengage Learning. • Provides indexing of business periodicals, January 1981 to date. Daily updates. (Full text articles from some periodicals are available online, 1983 to date. Inquire as to online cost and availability).

PERIODICALS AND NEWSLETTERS

Business Strategies Bulletin. CCH Inc. • Description: Reports tax and business planning information for all sizes of business, with emphasis on small to mid-sized business advisors.

Insolvency Law & Practice. LexisNexis Butterworths Tolley. • Bimonthly. $181.00 per year. United Kingdom emphasis.

STATISTICS SOURCES

Business Failure Record. Dun Bradstreet Corp. • Annual. Free upon request. Provides historical business failure data.

Business Statistics of the United States. Linz Audain and Cornelia J. Strawser. Bernan Associates. • Annual. $147.00. Based on *Business Statistics,* formerly issue by the Bureau of Economic Analysis, U. S. Department of Commerce. Provides basic data for a wide variety of U. S. industries, services, and economic indicators. Most statistics are shown annually for 30 years and monthly for the most recent four years.

Monthly Business Failures. Dun & Bradstreet Corp. • Monthly. $30.00 per year. Provides number of failures and liabilities in over 100 lines of business.

Quarterly Analysis of Failures. Dun & Bradstreet Corp. • Quarterly. $20.00.

Standard & Poor's Statistical Service. Current *Statistics.* Standard & Poor's. • Monthly. $688.00 per year. Includes 10 *Basic Statistics* sections, *Current Statistics Supplements* and *Annual Security Price Index Record.*

Survey of Current Business. Available from U. S. Government Printing Office. • Monthly. $63.00 per year. Issued by Bureau of Economic Analysis, U. S. Department of Commerce. Presents a wide variety of business and economic data.

Weekly Business Failures. Dun & Bradstreet Corp. • Weekly. $445.00 per year.

OTHER SOURCES

Business Strategies. CCH, Inc. • Semimonthly. $795.00 per year. Four looseleaf volumes. Semimonthly updates. Legal, tax, and accounting aspects of business planning and decision-making. Provides information on start-ups, forms of ownership (partnerships, corporations), failing businesses, reorganizations, acquisitions, and so forth. Includes *Business Strategies Bulletin,* a monthly newsletter.

BUSINESS FICTION

See: BUSINESS IN FICTION

BUSINESS FILMS

See: AUDIOVISUAL AIDS IN INDUSTRY

BUSINESS FINANCE

See: FINANCE; FINANCIAL ANALYSIS

BUSINESS FLYING

See: AIR TRAVEL; AIRLINE INDUSTRY; BUSINESS AVIATION

BUSINESS FORECASTING

See also: BUSINESS CYCLES; BUSINESS STATISTICS; ECONOMIC POLICY

GENERAL WORKS

The Art of the Long View: Planning for the Future in an Uncertain World. Peter Schwartz. Doubleday. • 1996. $30.95. Covers strategic planning for corporations and smaller firms. Includes "The World in 2005: Three Scenarios.".

Business Cycles: Theory, History, Indications, and Forecasting. Victor Zarnowitz. The University of Chicago Press. • 1992. $77.00. (National Bureau of Economic Research Monograph Series: Vol. 27).

Business Forecasting. J. Holton Wilson and Barry Keating. McGraw-Hill. • 2001. $67.50. Fourth edition.

Business Forecasting. John E. Hanke and others. Prentice Hall PTR. • 2001. $117.33. Seventh edition.

Business Forecasting for Management. Branko Pecar. McGraw-Hill. • 1994. $14.95.

Econometric Models and Economic Forecasts. Robert S. Pindyck and Daniel L. Rubinfield. McGraw-Hill. • 1997. $110.00. Fourth edition. Includes CD-ROM.

The 500 Year Delta: What Happens After What Comes Next. Jim Taylor and others. HarperInformation. • 1998. $14.00. Provides analysis of major corporate and political trends.

Forecasting Business Trends. American Institute for Economic Research. • 2000. $6.00. Summarizes methods of economic forecasting, statistical indicators, methods of analyzing business cycles, and use of leading, coincident, and lagging indicators. Includes charts, tables, and a glossary of terms. (Economic Education Bulletin.).

The Fortune Sellers: The Big Business of Buying and Selling Predictions. William A. Sherden. John Wiley and Sons, Inc. • 1997. $29.95. The author states that predictions are notoriously unreliable in any field, including the stock market, the economy, and the weather. (Forecasters in all areas don't have to be right; they just have to be interesting.).

BIBLIOGRAPHIES

Future Survey Annual: A Guide to the Recent Literature of Trends, Forecasts, and Policy Proposals. World Future Society. • Annual. $35.00.

CD-ROM DATABASES

World Marketing Forecasts on CD-ROM. Gale Cengage Learning. • Annual. $2,500.00. Produced by Euromonitor. Provides detailed forecast data for the years to 2012 on CD-ROM for 54 countries in all parts of the world. Covers a wide range of social, demographic, economic, and market factors. Includes specific forecasts for many kinds of consumer products.

HANDBOOKS AND MANUALS

Guide to Everyday Economic Statistics. Gary E. Clayton and Martin G. Giesbrecht. McGraw-Hill. • 2001. $19.90. Fifth edition. Contains clear explanations of the commonly used economic indicators.

Using Econometrics: A Practical Guide. Addison-Wesley. • 2000. $114.00. Fourth edition. (Economics Series).

ONLINE DATABASES

EconLit. American Economic Association. • Covers the worldwide literature of economics as contained in selected monographs and about 550 journals. Subjects include microeconomics, macroeconomics, economic history, inflation, money, credit, finance, accounting theory, trade, natural resource economics, and regional economics. Time period is 1969 to present, with monthly updates. Inquire as to online cost and availability.

Globalbase. Gale Cengage Learning. • Provides more than one million online summaries of business, industrial, and economic news reports from more than 1,000 publications worldwide. Covers a wide range of material appearing in international trade journals, professional magazines, and newspapers. Time period is 1984 to date, with weekly updates. Inquire as to online cost and availability.

MarkIntel. Thomson Financial. • Provides the current full text online of more than 50,000 market research reports covering 54 industries, from 85 leading research firms worldwide. Reports include extensive forecasts and market analysis. Inquire as to online cost and availability.

PERIODICALS AND NEWSLETTERS

Barometer of Business. Harris Trust and Savings Bank. • Bimonthly. Free.

Blue Chip Economic Indicators: What Top Economists Are Saying About the U.S. Outlook for the Year Ahead. Aspen Publishers, Inc. • Monthly. $665.00 per year. Newsletter containing U. S. economic consensus forecasts.

Blue Chip Financial Forecasts: What Top Analysts are Saying About U. S. and Foreign Interest Rates, Monetary Policy, Inflation, and Economic Growth. Aspen Publishers, Inc. • Monthly. $665.00 per year. Newsletter. Gives forecasts about a year in advance for interest rates, inflation, currency exchange rates, monetary policy, and economic growth rates.

International Economic Scoreboard. The Conference Board Inc. • Description: Provides current data on the business outlook in 11 major industrial countries: Australia, Canada, France, West Germany, Italy, Japan, Korea, New Zealand,

Taiwan, the United Kingdom, and the U.S. **Remarks:** A source for additional information on this indicator system and its uses is available at the Center for International Business Cycle Research, Columbia University Business School.

Journal of Business Forecasting Methods and Systems. Graceway Publishing Co. • Quarterly. $85.00 per year. Includes articles on forecasting methods and provides actual business and economic forecasts.

Journal of Forecasting. John Wiley and Sons, Inc., Journals Div. • Seven times a year. Individuals, $200.00 per year; institutions, $1,025.00 per year. A centralized focus on recent development in the art and science of forecasting International coverage. Published in England by John Wiley and Sons Ltd.

Long Range Planning. Strategic Planning Society. Elsevier. • Bimonthly. Qualified personnel, $197.00 per year; institutions, $1,346.00 per year.

Technological Forecasting and Social Change: An International Journal of the Dragon Project. Elsevier. • Nine times a year. Individuals, $131.00 per year; institutions, $839.00 per year.

The Trends Journal: The Authority on Trends Management. Gerald Celente, editor. Trends Research Institute. • Quarterly. $185.00 per year. Newsletter. Provides forecasts on a wide variety of economic, social, and political topics. Includes "Hot Trends to Watch.".

RESEARCH CENTERS AND INSTITUTES

Bureau of Economic and Business Research. University of Florida. 221 Matherly Hall, Gainesville, FL 32611-7145. Phone: (352)392-0171 Fax: (352)392-4739 E-mail: info@bebr.ufl.edu • URL: http://www.bebr.ufl.edu.

Business Forecasting Project. University of California, Los Angeles. 110 Westwood Plaza, Gold Hall B302, Los Angeles, CA 90095. Phone: (310)825-1623 Fax: (310)206-9440 E-mail: forecast@anderson.ucla.edu • URL: http://www.anderson.ucla.edu/research.

Economic Forecasting Center. Georgia State University, College of Business Administration, University Plaza, 35 Broad St., Atlanta, GA 30303-3083. Phone: (404)651-3298 Fax: (404)651-3299 E-mail: rdhawan@gsu.edu • URL: http://www.robinson.gsu.edu/efc/~egcenter • Concerned with national and regional economic analysis and forecasting.

STATISTICS SOURCES

Consumer International. Available from Gale Cengage Learning. • Annual. $1,290.00. Published by Euromonitor. Contains extensive consumer market, economic, and demographic data for 25 major, non-European countries, including the U. S. and Canada. Includes consumer market size (volume and value) for 150 product types in 14 categories (food, clothing, automobiles, cosmetics, appliances, etc.).

Country Data Forecasts. Bank of America, World Information Services, Dept. 3015. • Looseleaf, with semiannual updates. $495.00 per year. Provides detailed statistical tables for 80 countries, showing historical data and five-year forecasts of 23 key economic series. Includes population, inflation figures, debt, per capita income, foreign trade, exchange rates, and other data.

Economic Indicators. Council of Economic Advisors, Executive Office of the President. Available from U.S. Government Printing Office. • Monthly. $55.00 per year.

European Marketing Forecasts. Available from Gale Cengage Learning. • Annual. $1,250.00. Published by Euromonitor. Contains demographic, economic, and market forecasts for the countries of Europe to the year 2010. Forecasts include market-size data for 15 consumer product sectors (food, clothing, automobiles, consumer electronics, etc.).

International Marketing Forecasts. Available from Gale Cengage Learning. • Annual. $1,250.00. Published by Euromonitor. Contains demographic, economic, and market forecasts to the year 2013 for major, non-European countries, including the U. S. and Canada. Forecasts include market-size data for 15 consumer product sectors, such as food, clothing, and automobiles.

International Survey of Business Expectations. Dun & Bradstreet Corp., Economic Analysis Dept. • Quarterly. $40.00 per year. A survey of international business executives regarding their quarterly expectations for sales, profits, prices, inventories, employment, and new orders. Results are given for each of 14 major foreign countries and the U. S.

Source OECD. Economic Outlook Statistics. • 2000. $325.00. Includes country and global forecasts of over 170 economic and business variables. Actual data is shown for two years, with forecasts up to ten years.

Statistical Forecasts of the United States. Gale Cengage Learning. • 1995. $115.00. Second edition. Provides both long-term and short-term statistical forecasts relating to basic items in the U. S.: population, employment, labor, crime, education, and health care. Data in the form of charts, graphs, and tables has been taken from a wide variety of government and private sources. Includes a subject index and an "Index of Forecast by Year.".

U. S. Market Trends and Forecasts. Gale Cengage Learning. • 2002. $325.00. Third edition. Provides graphic representation of market statistics by means of pie charts and tables for each of 30 major industries and 400 market segments. Includes market forecasts and historical overviews.

U. S. Survey of Business Expectations. Dun & Bradstreet Corp. • Quarterly. 40.00 per year. A survey of 3,000 U. S. business executives as to their expectations for next quarter's sales, profits, prices, inventories, employment, exports, and new orders.

TRADE/PROFESSIONAL ASSOCIATIONS

Hudson Institute. 1015 15th St. NW, 6th Fl., 1015 18th St., NW, Ste. 300, Washington, DC 20005. Phone: 800-HUDSON-0 or (202)974-2400 Fax: (202)974-2410 E-mail: info@hudson.org • URL: http://www.hudson.org • Members of this research center are elected from academic, governmental, and business/industrial sectors. Studies public policy issues in areas of national security, international and domestic economics, education and employment, energy and technology, agriculture and environment, and future studies. Studies are funded through contract or grant from government agencies, private businesses, foundations, associations, and individuals. Sometimes referred to as a "think tank", the institute focuses on "providing policymakers with a broad, workable, conceptual framework within which intelligent and successful policy decisions can be developed"; seeks to determine what issues will have the greatest long-term impact and to identify issues that may become urgent though they are not yet recognized as such. Conducts briefings on policy issues to corporate and other audiences. Distributes research reports to depository libraries.

Institute for the Future. 2744 Sand Hill Rd., Menlo Park, CA 94025-7020. Phone: (650)854-6322 Fax: (650)854-7850 E-mail: info@iftf.org • URL: http://www.iftf.org • Assists organizations, businesses, industry and the government in conducting long-term futures research.

National Policy Association. 3424 Porter St. NW, Washington, DC 20016-3126. Phone: (202)265-7685 Fax: (202)797-5516 E-mail: npa@npa1.org • URL: http://www.npa1.org • Research institution that helps private and public sector leaders from agriculture, business, labor, and academia to better understand national economic and social issues. Conducts research and analysis on national and

international economic and social issues.

Renewable Natural Resources Foundation. 5430 Grosvenor Ln., Bethesda, MD 20814-2142. Phone: (301)493-9101 Fax: (301)493-6148 E-mail: info@rnrf.org • URL: http://www.rnrf.org • Members are American Fisheries Society, American Geophysical Union, American Meteorological Society, American Society of Agronomy, American Society of Civil Engineers, Society of Landscape Architects, American Society for Photogrammetry and Remote Sensing, American Water Resources Association, Association of American Geographers, Humane Society of the United States, Society for Range Management, Society of Wood Science and Technology, Society of Environmental Toxicology and Chemistry, Soil and Water Conservation Society, Universities Council on Water Resources, and Wildlife Society. Concerned with renewable natural resources subjects and public policy alternatives. Develops 35-acre, forested Renewable Natural Resources Center, an office-park complex for natural resources and other nonprofit organizations.

World Future Society. 7910 Woodmont Ave., Ste. 450, Bethesda, MD 20814. Phone: 800-989-8274 or (301)656-8274 Fax: (301)951-0394 E-mail: info@wfs.org • URL: http://www.wfs.org • Helps individuals, organizations, and communities see, understand, and respond appropriately and effectively to change. Raises awareness of change and encourages development of creative solutions through media, meetings, and dialogue among its members. Serves as a neutral forum for exploring possible, probable, and preferable futures.

OTHER SOURCES

Consensus Forecasts: A Worldwide Survey. Consensus Economics Inc. • Monthly. $565.00 per year. Provides a survey of more than 200 "prominent" financial and economic forecasters, covering 20 major countries. Two-year forecasts for each country include future growth, inflation, interest rates, and exchange rates. Each issue contains analysis of business conditions in various countries.

BUSINESS FORMS

See: FORMS AND BLANKS

BUSINESS GIFTS

See: GIFT BUSINESS

BUSINESS HISTORY

GENERAL WORKS

Age of Giant Corporations: A Microeconomic History of American Business, 1914-1992. Robert Sobel. Greenwood Publishing Group Inc. • 1993. $57.95. Third edition. (Contributions in Economics and Economic History Series, No. 146).

American Decades. Gale Cengage Learning. • 1994-2001. $990.00. 10 volumes. $99.00 per volume. Each volume covers a decade during the period 1900-1989. "Each volume begins with an overview and chronology covering the entire decade. Subject chapters follow, each including an overview, subject-specific timeline and alphabetically arranged entries..".

Business History of the World: A Chronology. Richard B. Robinson. Greenwood Publishing Group, Inc. • 1993. $85.00. Provides "a basic chronology of the business world outside the United States from prehistory through the 1980s.".

Computer Sciences. Roger Flynn, editor. Gale Cengage Learning. • 2002. $395.00. Four volumes. Presents a general and historical review of the impact of computers on modern society. Includes biographical information and multidisciplinary examples. (Macmillan Reference USA imprint, Macmillan Science Library.).

Crystal Fire: The Birth of the Information Age. Michael Riordan and Lillian Hoddeson. W. W. Norton & Co., Inc. • 1997. $27.50. A history of the transistor, from early electronic experiments to practical development at the former Bell Telephone Laboratories. (Sloan Technology Series).

Devil Take the Hindmost: A History of Financial Speculation. Edward Chancellor. Dutton/Plume. • 2000. $15.00. Covers such events as the Dutch tulip mania of 1637, the South Sea bubble of 1720, and the Japanese real estate and stock market boom of the 1980's.

FAA Historical Chronology: Civil Aviation and the Federal Government, 1926-1996. Edmund Preston, editor. Available from U. S. Government Printing Office. • 1998. $33.50. Third edition. Issued by the Federal Aviation Administration, U. S. Department of Transportation (http://www.dot.gov). Provides a compilation of historical information about the FAA and the earlier Civil Aeronautics Board (CAB). Chronological arrangement.

Financial History of the United States. Jerry W. Markham. M. E. Sharpe, Inc. • 2002. $349.00. Three volumes. Vol. 1: *From Christopher Columbus to the Robber Barons (1492-1900).* Vol. 2: *From J. P. Morgan to the Institutional Investor (1900-1970).* Vol. 3: *From the Age of Derivatives to the Internet (1970-2000).* Each volume contains name and subject indexes, with cumulative indexes in volume three.

The Great Depression and New Deal Reference Library. Gale Cengage Learning. • 2002. $145.00. Three volumes. Individual volumes are available at $55.00. Includes *Great Depression and New Deal: Almanac; Great Depression and New Deal: Biographies* and *Great Depression and New Deal: Primary Sources.* (UXL imprint).

The Great Game: The Emergence of Wall Street as a World Power, 1653-2000. John S. Gordon. Gale Cengage Learning. • 1999. $25.00. Provides a history of U. S. financial markets, featuring such key figures as Alexander Hamilton, Commodore Vanderbilt, J. P. Morgan, Charles Merrill, and Michael Milken.

Great Inflations of the 20th Century: Theories, Policies, and Evidence. Pierre L. Siklos, editor. Edward Elgar Publishing, Inc. • 1995. $100.00. Contains reprints of papers on the history and economic analysis of major inflations.

The History of Black Business in America: Capitalism, Race, Entrepreneurship. Juliet E. Walker. Available from Gale Cengage Learning. • 1998. $50.00. Published by Twayne Publishers. Includes profiles of African American business pioneers. (Evolution of Modern Business Series.).

History of the Internet: A Chronology, 1843 to the Present. Christos J. P. Moschovitis and others. ABC-CLIO, Inc. • 1999. $65.00. Early entries cover the history of the computer. Includes biographical information, bibliography, and glossary.

In the Black: A History of African Americans on Wall Street. Gregory S. Bell. John Wiley and Sons, Inc. • 2001. $24.95. Written by the son of Travers Bell, co-founder of Daniels Bell stockbrokers, the first black-owned New York Stock Exchange member firm.

Industrial Revolution Reference Library. Gale Cengage Learning. • 2003. $165.00. Three volumes. Individual volumes are available at $55.00. Includes *Industrial Revolution: Almanac; Industrial Revolution: Biographies* and *Industrial Revolution: Primary Sources.* (UXL imprint).

It Was a Very Good Year: Extraordinary Moments in Stock Market History. Martin S. Fridson. John Wiley

and Sons, Inc. • 1997. $29.95. Provides details on what happened during each of the ten best years for the stock market since 1900. (Investment Series).

Manias, Panics, and Crashes: A History of Financial Crises. Charles P. Kindleberger. John Wiley and Sons, Inc. • 2000. $19.95. Fourth edition. Provides a history of financial troubles from 1618 to modern times, with greed as a central theme. (Investment Classic Series).

100 Years of Wall Street. Charles R. Geisst. McGraw-Hill. • 1999. $29.95. A popularly written, illustrated history of the American stock market. About 200 photographs, charts, cartoons, and reproductions of stock certificates are included.

The Power of Gold: The History of an Obsession. Peter L. Bernstein. John Wiley and Sons, Inc. • 2000. $27.95. Covers the economic and financial history of gold from ancient times to the present.

Reinventing the Bazaar: A Natural History of Markets. John McMillan. W. W. Norton & Co., Inc. • 2002. $25.05. Covers marketing from early times to modern times. Takes the viewpoint that markets are desirable, occur naturally, and require intelligent regulation.

Stock Market Crashes and Speculative Manias. Eugene N. White, editor. Edward Elgar Publishing, Inc. • 1996. $255.00. Contains reprints of 23 articles dating from 1905 to 1994. (International Library of Macroeconomic and Financial History Series: No. 13).

U. S. Trade Policy: History, Theory, and the WTO. William A. Lovett and others. M. E. Sharpe, Inc. • 2004. $66.95. Second edition. Discusses the consequences of free trade and the activities of the World Trade Organization. Covers U. S. trade history from colonial times to recent years.

United States Business History, 1602-1988: A Chronology. Richard B. Robinson. Greenwood Publishing Group, Inc. • 1990. $99.95.

Wall Street: A History. Charles R. Geisst. Oxford University Press. • 1997. $18.95. Presents the history of the U. S. stock market according to four distinct eras: 1790 to the Civil War, the Civil War to 1929, 1929 to 1954, and from 1954 to recent years.

Wheels of Fortune: The History of Speculation from Scandal to Respectability. Charles R. Geisst. John Wiley and Sons, Inc. • 2002. $29.95. Provides a colorful history of speculation in the U. S. commodity futures markets from 1850 to about 2000.

Worldwide History of Telecommunications. Anton Huurdeman. John Wiley and Sons, Inc. • 2003. $125.00. Covers the evolution and history of telecommunications from before 1800 to 2000. Topics include telegraph, telephone, radio, satellite transmission, optical fiber transmission, electronic switching, telefax, multimedia, and many other subjects. Includes a two-century chronology, worldwide statistics, a glossary, and an index.

BIOGRAPHICAL SOURCES

American Business Leaders: From Colonial Times to the Present. Neil A. Hamilton. ABC-CLIO, Inc. • 1999. $175.00. Two volumes. Contains biographies of 413 notable business figures. Historical coverage is from the 17th century to the 1990s.

American National Biography. John A. Garraty and Mark C. Carnes, editors. Oxford University Press. • 1999. $795.00. 24 volumes. Contains about 17,500 entries, including business leaders who were important to the American economy. Includes an index by occupation. *Supplement* available, 2002, $150.00.

DIRECTORIES

International Directory of Company Histories. Saint James Press. • 53 volumes. $199.00 per volume. Provides detailed histories of about 4,550 major corporations. Cumulative indexing is provided for company names, personal names, and industries.

Notable Corporate Chronologies. Gale. • Covers: Company name, address, phone, fax, URL, e-mail address, and cable and telex number.

ENCYCLOPEDIAS AND DICTIONARIES

Business Cycles and Depressions: An Encyclopedia. David Glasner. Garland Publishing, Inc. • 1997. $155.00. Contains 327 alphabetical entries by various contributors. Defines and reviews all significant depressions, recessions, and financial crises in the U. S. and Europe since 1790. Includes chronologies, bibliographies, and indexes.

Encyclopedia of the Great Depression. Gale Cengage Learning. • 2003. $265.00. Two volumes. Covers about two decades of U. S. economic history, from "the farm crisis of the mid-1920s," through the gradual recovery of the 1930s, to the beginning of World War II. (Macmillan Reference USA imprint.).

Gale Encyclopedia of U.S. Economic History. Gale Cengage Learning. • 2000. $225.00. Two volumes. Contains about 1,000 alphabetically arranged entries. Includes industry profiles, biographies, social issue profiles, geographic profiles, and chronological tables.

The History of Accounting: An Encyclopedia. Michael Chatfield and Richard Vangermeersch. Garland Publishing, Inc. • 1996. $100.00. Contains more than 400 alphabetical entries by various contributors, covering the history of accounting from 750 B.C. to the modern era. Includes a bibliography for each entry and an index. (Reference Library of the Humanities Series: Vol. 1573).

Oxford Encyclopedia of Economic History. Joel Mokyr, editor. Oxford University Press. • 2003. $695.00. Five volumes. Provides extensive coverage of a wide variety of topics relating to business, industrial, and economic history.

Work in America: An Encyclopedia of History, Policy, and Society. Carl E. Van Horn and Herbert A. Schaffner. ABC-CLIO, Inc. • 2003. $185.00. Two volumes. Contains 265 A-Z entries covering work in the U. S. from the Industrial Revolution to modern times. Covers labor-related topics in economics, history, law, welfare, employment policy, and other areas.

FINANCIAL RATIOS

IRS Corporate Financial Ratios. Available from MarketResearch.com. • 2002. $225.00. Published by Schonfeld & Associates, Inc. Presents 70 key financial ratios for 260 industries. Ratios are calculated from income statement and balance sheet data available from the Internal Revenue Service. Includes four asset size classes.

PERIODICALS AND NEWSLETTERS

Business History. Frank Cass Publishers. • Quarterly. Institutions, $382.00 per year. Includes print and online editions.

Business History Review. Harvard Business School Publishing. • Quarterly. Individuals, $50.00 per year; institutions, $100.00 per year; students, $35.00 per year.

Explorations in Economic History. Elsevier. • Quarterly. Individuals, $214.00 per year; institutions, $439.00 per year.

Financial History: Chronicling the History of America's Capital Markets. Museum of American Financial History. • Quarterly. Membership. Contains articles on early stock and bond markets and trading in the U. S., with photographs and other illustrations. Current trading in rare and unusual, obsolete stock and bond certificates is featured. Formerly *Friends or Financial History.*

Journal of Economic History. Economic History Association. Cambridge University Press, Journals Dept. • Quarterly. Institutions, $144.00 per year.

RESEARCH CENTERS AND INSTITUTES

John W. Hartman Center for Sales, Advertising, and Marketing History. Special Collections Library,

Duke University, P.O. Box 90185, Durham, NC 27708-0185. Phone: (919)660-5827 Fax: (919)660-5934 E-mail: hartman-center@duke.edu • URL: http://www.scriptorium.lib.duke.edu/hartman/ • Concerned with the study of the roles of sales, advertising, and marketing in society.

STATISTICS SOURCES

Datapedia of the United States: American History in Numbers. George T. Kurian, editor. Bernan Press. • 2004. $125.00. Third edition. Based on the Census Bureau publication, *Historical Statistics of the United States.* Provides data from Colonial times to the present on agriculture, business, consumer income, energy, finance, labor, national income, population, and many other subjects. Includes "narrative highlights," maps, charts, and statistical projections.

Encyclopedia of American Industries. Gale Cengage Learning. • 2000. $560.00. Third edition. Two volumes. $280.00 per volume. Volume one is *Manufacturing Industries* and volume two is *Service and Non-Manufacturing Industries.* Provides the history, development, and recent status of approximately 1,000 industries. Includes statistical graphs, with industry and general indexes.

The World Economy: A Millennial Perspective. Angus Maddison. Organization for Economic Cooperation and Development. • 2001. $63.00. "...covers the development of the entire world economy over the past 2000 years," including data on world population and gross domestic product (GDP) since the year 1000, and exports since 1820. Focuses primarily on the disparity in economic performance among nations over the very long term. More than 200 statistical tables and figures are provided.

TRADE/PROFESSIONAL ASSOCIATIONS

Business History Conference. Hagley Museum and Library, PO Box 3630, PO Box 3630, Wilmington, DE 19807-0630. Phone: (302)658-2400 Fax: (302)655-3188 E-mail: rh@udel.edu • URL: http://www.thebhc.org • Business historians and economic historians (most are from the academic community but a number of business firms are represented through their corporate historians). Brings together persons who are active historians of American and international business, with interests ranging from writing biographies of businessmen and histories of firms to the application of economic theory to analysis of the evolution of American business.

Economic History Association. Santa Clara University, Department of Economics, 500 El Camino Real, Santa Clara, CA 95053-0385. Phone: (408)554-4348 or (785)864-2847 Fax: (408)554-2331 E-mail: afield@scu.edu • URL: http://eh.net/eha • Represents scholars, teachers and students of economic history.

The Newcomen Society of the United States. 211 Welsh Pool Rd., Ste. 240, Exton, PA 19341. Phone: 800-466-7604 or (610)363-6600 Fax: (610)363-0612 E-mail: info@newcomen.org • URL: http://www.newcomen.org • Formerly Newcomen Society in North America.

OTHER SOURCES

Goldsmiths' Kress Library of Economic Literature: A Consolidated Guide to the Microfilm Collection, 1976-1983. Primary Source Microfilm. • $1,200.00. Four volumes. Individual volumes, $300.00. An estimated 60,000 titles on 1,500 reels of microfilm (or fiche).

BUSINESS IN FICTION

ONLINE DATABASES

Magazine Index. Gale Cengage Learning. • General magazine indexing (popular literature), 1973 to present. Daily updates. Inquire as to online cost and availability.

BUSINESS INDICATORS

See: ECONOMIC INDICATORS

BUSINESS INFORMATION SOURCES

See: INFORMATION SOURCES

BUSINESS INNOVATION

See also: BUSINESS START-UP PLANS AND PROPOSALS; NEW PRODUCTS; RESEARCH AND DEVELOPMENT

GENERAL WORKS

Cases in Corporate Innovation. Gale Cengage Learning. • 2002. $310.00. Reviews and analyzes about 300 cases to illustrate both successful and failed management of innovation.

Innovation: Leadership Strategies for the Competitive Edge. Thomas D. Kuczmarski. McGraw-Hill. • 1995. $37.95. (NTC Business Books Series).

The Innovator's Dilemma: When New Technologies Cause Great Firms to Fail. Clayton M. Christensen. Harvard Business School Publishing. • 1997. $27.50. Discusses management myths relating to innovation, change, and research and development. (Mangement of Innovation and Change Series).

ABSTRACTS AND INDEXES

Business Periodicals Index. H. W. Wilson Co. • 11 times a year. Quarterly and annual cumulations. Price varies.

ONLINE DATABASES

Wilson Business Abstracts Online. H. W. Wilson Co. • Indexes and abstracts 600 major business periodicals, plus the *Wall Street Journal* and the business section of the *New York Times.* Indexing is from 1982, abstracting from 1990, with the two newspapers included from 1993. Updated weekly. Inquire as to online cost and availability. (*Business Periodicals Index* without abstracts is also available online.).

PERIODICALS AND NEWSLETTERS

Business 2.0. Time Inc. • Monthly. $30.00 per year. General business magazine emphasizing ideas, insight, and innovation.

Fast Company: How Smart Business Works. Fast Company, Inc. • Monthly. $12.00 per year. Covers business management, with emphasis on creativity, leadership, innovation, career advancement, teamwork, the global economy, and the "new workplace.".

Journal of Product Innovation Management: An International Publication of the Product Development and Management Association. Product Development and Management Association. Elsevier. • Bimonthly. Institutions, $535.00 per year. Includes print and online editions. Covers new product planning and development.

RESEARCH CENTERS AND INSTITUTES

Mack Center on Managing Technological Innovation. University of Pennsylvania, 3620 Locust Walk, Suite 1400, Philadelphia, PA 19104. Phone: (215)898-2104 Fax: (215)573-2129 E-mail: dayg@wharton.upenn.edu • URL: http://www.emertech.wharton.upenn.edu • Conducts research related to international business. Formerly Huntsman Center for Global Competition and Innovation.

OTHER SOURCES

Joint Ventures. Glasser Legalworks. • Looseleaf. $225.00, including CD-ROM version. Periodic Supplementation. Includes explanations of legal procedures for joint ventures, with annotated forms.

(Emerging Growth Companies Series.).

BUSINESS INTELLIGENCE

See: COMPETITIVE INTELLIGENCE

BUSINESS, INTERNATIONAL

See: INTERNATIONAL BUSINESS

BUSINESS INTERRUPTION INSURANCE

See also: INSURANCE

HANDBOOKS AND MANUALS

Business Interruption Coverage. American Bar Association. • 1987. $29.95. Produced by ABA Tort and Insurance Practice Section. Covers legal aspects of business interruption insurance.

Insuring Your Business: What You Need to Know to Get the Best Insurance Coverage for Your Business. Sean Mooney. Insurance Information Institute. • 1992. $22.50.

PERIODICALS AND NEWSLETTERS

Business Insurance: News Magazine for Corporate Risk, Employee Benefit and Financial Executives. Crain Communications, Inc. • Weekly. $95.00 per year. Covers a wide variety of business insurance topics, including risk management, employee benefits, workers compensation, marine insurance, and casualty insurance.

Jounal of Finacial Services Professionals. Society of Financial Services Professional. • Bimonthly. $95.00 per year. Provides information on life insurance and financial planning, including estate planning, retirement, tax planning, trusts, business insurance, long-term care insurance, disability insurance, and employee benefits. Formerly (American Society of CLU and Ch F C Journal).

BUSINESS JOURNALISM

See also: FARM JOURNALS; HOUSE ORGANS; TRADE JOURNALS

GENERAL WORKS

The Art of Editing. Brian S. Brooks and others. Allyn and Bacon, Inc. • 2000. $82.00. 7th edition.

Super Searcher, Author, Scribe: Successful Writers Share Their Internet Research Secrets. Loraine Page. Information Today, Inc. • 2002. $24.95. Presents the results of interviews with 14 leading journalists, book authors, writing teachers, and professional literary researchers. Tips, techniques, and sources for searching the Web are featured. (Super Searchers Series).

Super Searchers in the News: The Online Secrets of Journalists and News Researchers. Paula J. Hane. Information Today, Inc. • 2000. $24.95. Contains online searching advice from 10 professional news researchers and fact checkers. (Super Searchers Series).

DIRECTORIES

Cabell's Directory of Publishing Opportunities in Management. Cabell Publishing Co. • 1997. $149.95. Seventh edition. Four volumes. Over 540 scholarly periodicals in management.

Editor and Publisher Market Guide. Editor and Publisher Co., Inc. • Annual. $150.00. More than 1,700 newspaper markets in the United States and Canada.

Magazines Career Directory: A Practical One-Stop Guide to Getting a Job in Publc Relations. Visible

---

Ink Press. • 1993. $39.00. Fifth edition. Includes information on magazine publishing careers in art, editing, sales, and business management. Provides advice from "insiders," resume suggestions, a directory of companies that may offer entry-level positions, and a directory of career information sources. (Career Advisor Series).

Professional Freelance Writers Directory. The National Writers Association. • Database covers: about 200 professional members selected from the club's membership on the basis of significant articles or books, or production of plays or movies. Entries include: Name, address, phone (home and business numbers), special fields of writing competence, titles of books published by royalty firms, mention of contributions to specific magazines, journals, newspapers or anthologies, recent awards received, relevant activities and skills (photography, etc.).

Writer's Market. Writer's Digest Books. • Covers: Over 8,000 buyers of books, articles, short stories, plays, gags, verse, fillers, and other original written material. Includes book and periodical publishers, greeting card publishers, play producers and publishers, audiovisual material producers, syndicates, and contests and awards. Entries include: Name and address of buyer, phone, payment rates, editorial requirements, reporting time, how to break in.

PERIODICALS AND NEWSLETTERS

ASBPE Editor's Notes. American Society of Business Press Editors. • Bimonthly. Membership. Newsletter.

Freelance Writer's Report. Dana K. Cassell, editor. CNW Publishing, Editing & Promotion Inc. • Description: Offers up-to-date news and information concerning effective marketing/production techniques, writing tips, self-promotion, and other topics of interest "to freelance writers who intend to earn a good income from their work and improve the quality of their work." Recurring features include interviews, book reviews, news of writing seminars, conferences, and market news. **Remarks:** Members of the Florida Freelance Writers Association receive an extra association section (4 pages).

Journal of Technical Writing and Communication. Baywood Publishing Co., Inc. • Quarterly. Individuals, $60.00 per year; institutions, $237.00 per year.

RESEARCH CENTERS AND INSTITUTES

Knight Center for Specialized Journalism. University of Maryland, 1117 Cole Field House, College Park, MD 20742-1024. Phone: (301)405-4817 E-mail: knight@umail.umd.edu • URL: http://www.knightcenter.umd.edu/ • Research area is media coverage of complex subjects, such as economics, law, science, and medicine.

TRADE/PROFESSIONAL ASSOCIATIONS

American Society of Business Publications Editors. 710 E Ogden Ave., Ste. 600, Naperville, IL 60563-8603. Phone: (603)579-3288 Fax: (603)369-2488 E-mail: info@asbpe.org • URL: http://www.asbpe.com.

International Association of Business Communicators. One Hallidie Plaza, Suite 600, San Francisco, CA 94102-2818. Phone: (415)544-4700 Fax: (415)544-4747 E-mail: service_centre@iabc.com • URL: http://www.iabc.com.

Society of Publication Designers. 60 E. 42nd St., Suite 721, New York, NY 10165. Phone: (212)983-8585 Fax: (212)983-6043 E-mail: spdnyc@aol.com • URL: http://www.spd.org • Supersedes Society of Publication Designers.

BUSINESS LAW

GENERAL WORKS

Business Law. Kevin Wardman and others. Continnum International Publishing Group, Inc. • 2002.

$99.95. Seventh edition. (Letts Higher Education List Series).

Business Law and Regulatory Environment: Concepts and Cases. Jane Mallor Frona Powell. McGraw-Hill Higher Education. • 1997. $38.75. 10th edition. (Legal Studies in Business Series).

Business Law: Ethical, International and E-Commerce Environment. Henry R. Cheesman. Prentice Hall PTR. • 2000. $140.00. Fourth edition.

Business Law: Principles and Practices. Arnold J. Goldman and William D. Sigismond. Houghton Mifflin Co. • 2001. $64.36. Fifth edition.

Contemporary Business: Alternate Study Guide. Louis E. Boone. Harcourt College Publishers. • 2002. 10th edition. Price on application. (Management Series).

Contemporary Business Law and the Legal Environment: Principles, Cases and Regulation. James Highsmith. McGraw-Hill. • 1994. $32.81. Fifth edition.

Law for Business. John Ashcroft and Janet Ashcroft. South-Western. • 2001. $82.95. 14th edition. (Business Law Series).

Law of the Super Searchers: The Online Secrets of Top Legal Researchers. T. R. Halvorson. Information Today, Inc. • 1999. $24.95. Eight law researchers explain how to find useful legal information online. (Super Searchers Series).

Modern Business Law: The Regulatory Environment. Thomas W. Dunfee and others. McGraw-Hill. • 1995. $132.50. Third edition.

West's Business Law: Text and Cases, Legal, Ethical, Regulatory and International Environment. Kenneth Clarkson. South-Western. • 2000. $125.95. Eighth edition.

ABSTRACTS AND INDEXES

Current Law Index: Multiple Access to Legal Periodicals. Gale Cengage Learning. • Monthly. $725.00 per year. Produced in cooperation with the American Association of Law Libraries. Indexes more than 900 law journals, legal newspapers, and specialty publications from the U.S., Canada, U.K., Ireland, Australia, and New Zealand.

Index to Legal Periodicals and Books. H. W. Wilson Co. • Monthly. $490.00 per year. Quarterly and annual cumulations.

ALMANACS AND YEARBOOKS

American Law Yearbook. Gale Cengage Learning. • Annual. $165.00. Serves as a yearly supplement to *West's Encyclopedia of American Law.* Describes new legal developments in many subject areas.

BIBLIOGRAPHIES

Encyclopedia of Legal Information Sources. Gale Cengage Learning. • 1992. $180.00. Second edition. Lists more than 23,000 law-related information sources, including print, nonprint, and organizational.

Legal Information: How to Find It, How to Use It. Kent Olson. Greenwood Publishing Group, Inc. • 1998. $64.95. Includes CD-ROM. Recommends sources for various kinds of legal information.

CD-ROM DATABASES

Authority Computer and Telecommunications Law Library. LexisNexis/Matthew Bender. • Quarterly. Price on request. Full text CD-ROM provides cases, analysis, sample agreements, and other information relating to computer law, telecommunications regulation (cable, broadcasting, satellite, Internet), international computer law, and computer contracts.

WILSONDISC: Index to Legal Periodicals and Books. H. W. Wilson Co. • Monthly. Includes unlimited online access to *Index to Legal Periodicals* through WILSONLINE. Contains CD-ROM indexing of more than 1,400 English language

legal periodicals from 1981 to date and 2,500 books.

DIRECTORIES

Law and Legal Information Directory. Gale Cengage Learning. • Annual. $440.00. Contains a wide range of sources of legal information, such as associations, law schools, courts, federal agencies, referral services, libraries, publishers, and research centers. There is a separate chapter for each of 23 types of information source or service.

ENCYCLOPEDIAS AND DICTIONARIES

Communicating with Legal Databases: Terms and Abbreviations for the Legal Researcher. Anne L. McDonald. Neal-Schuman Publishers, Inc. • 1987. $82.50.

Dictionary of Commercial, Financial and Legal Terms in Two Languages. R. Herbst. Adler's Foreign Books, Inc. • Two volumes. Vol. A, $179.50; vol. B $179.50. Text in English and German.

HANDBOOKS AND MANUALS

Anderson on Uniform Commercial Code. Lary Lawrence. West Group. • $1,050.00. Annual updates.

Digest of Commercial Laws of the World. N. Stephan Kinsella and Paul E. Comeaux. Oceana Publications, Inc. • $495.00. Five volumes. Losseleaf service. Periodic supplementation.

The Law in (Plain English) for Small Businesses. Leonard D. DuBoff. Allworth Press. • 1998. $19.95. Third revised edition. Discusses and explains legal issues relating to the organization, financing, and operation of a small business.

Manual of Credit and Commercial Laws. National Association of Credit Management. • Annual. Free to members; non-members, $125.00. Formerly *Credit Manual of Commercial Laws.*

Manual of Credit and Commercial Laws. National Association of Credit Management. • Annual. Free to members; non-members, $100.00. Formerly *Credit Manual of Commercial Laws.*

Small Business Legal Smarts. Deborah L. Jacobs. Bloomberg. • 1998. $16.95. Discusses common legal problems encountered by small business owners. (Small Business Series).

Warren's Forms of Agreements. LexisNexis Matthew Bender. • Biennial. $1,110.00. Eight looseleaf volumes. A compact source of forms that business transaction lawyers are most frequently asked to document.

INTERNET DATABASES

Factiva. Dow Jones Reuters Business Interactive, LLC. Phone: 800-369-7466 or (609)452-1511 Fax: (609)520-5770 E-mail: solutions@factiva.com • URL: http://www.factiva.com • Fee-based Web site provides "global news and business information through Web sites and content integration solutions." Includes Dow Jones and Reuters newswires, The Wall Street Journal, and more than 7,000 other sources of current news, historical articles, market research reports, and investment analysis. Content includes 96 major U. S. newspapers, 900 non-English sources, trade publications, media transcripts, country profiles, news photos, etc.

Lexis.com Research System. Lexis-Nexis Group. Phone: 800-227-4908 or (937)865-6800 Fax: (937)865-6909 E-mail: webmaster@prod.lexis-nexis.com • URL: http://www.lexis.com • Fee-based Web site offers extensive searching of a wide variety of legal sources. Additional features include Daily Opinion Service, lexis.com Bookstore, Career Center, CLE Center, Law Schools, and Practice Pages ("Pages specific to areas of specialty").

Nexis.com. Lexis-Nexis Group. Phone: 800-227-4908 or (937)865-6800 Fax: (937)865-6909 E-mail: webmaster@prod.lexis-nexis.com • URL: http://www.nexis.com • Fee-based Web site offers searching of about 2.8 billion documents in some 30,000 news, business, and legal information sources. Features include a subject directory covering 1,200 topics in 34 categories and a Company Dossier containing information on more than 500,000 public and private companies. Boolean searching is offered.

ONLINE DATABASES

Index to Legal Periodicals and Books (Online). H. W. Wilson Co. • Broad coverage of law journals and books 1981 to date. Monthly updates. Inquire as to online cost and availability.

Legal Resource Index. Gale Cengage Learning. • Broad coverage of law literature appearing in legal, business, and other periodicals, 1980 to date. Daily updates. Inquire as to online cost and availability.

LEXIS. LEXIS-NEXIS. • The various LEXIS databases provide full text and indexing for a wide variety of legal cases, statutes, orders, and opinions.

PERIODICALS AND NEWSLETTERS

Business Lawyer. American Bar Association, Business Law Section. • Quarterly. Members $99.00 per year; non-members, $149.00 per year.

Commercial Law Journal. Legalease Ltd. • 10 times a year. $99.00 per year.

E-Commerce Law Report: Buying and Selling on the Internet. Glasser Legalworks. • Monthly. $300.00 per year. Newsletter. Provides coverage of the legal and regulatory aspects of doing business online.

Federal Register. Office of the Federal Register. Available from U.S. Government Printing Office. • Daily except Saturday and Sunday. $764.00 per year. Publishes regulations and legal notices issued by federal agencies, including executive orders and presidential proclamations. Issued by the National Archives and Records Administration (http://www.nara.gov).

Privacy and Information Law Report. Glasser Legalworks. • 10 times a year. $375.00 per year. Newsletter. Coverage includes the legal aspects of health record privacy, employee records, anti-spam, and privacy-enhancing technology. Provides reports on relevant court cases and consumer advocacy.

UCC Bulletin. West Group. • Monthly. $560.00 per year. Newsletter. Includes case summaries of recent UCC decisions.

RESEARCH CENTERS AND INSTITUTES

Alabama Law Institute. University of Alabama. P.O. Box 861425, Tuscaloosa, AL 35486-0013. Phone: (205)348-7411 Fax: (205)348-8411 E-mail: mccurle@law.ua.edu • URL: http://www.law.ua.edu/ali.

TRADE/PROFESSIONAL ASSOCIATIONS

Commercial Law League of America. 150 N. Michigan Ave., No. 600, Chicago, IL 60601. Phone: 800-978-2552 or (312)781-2000 Fax: (312)781-2010 E-mail: clla@clla.org • URL: http://www.clla.org.

OTHER SOURCES

Business Law Monographs. LexisNexis Matthew Bender. • Quarterly. $1,599.00. 38 volumes. Intended for in-house and outside corporate counsel. Each monograph concentrates on a particular subject.

Computer Law: Evidence and Procedures. David Bender. LexisNexis Matthew Bender. • $686.00. Three looseleaf volumes. Periodic supplementation. Covers the concepts and techniques of evidence and discovery procedures as they apply to computer-based information, and to the protection of computer software under intellectual property.

Current Legal Forms with Tax Analysis. LexisNexis Matthew Bender. • Quarterly. $2,183.00 per year. 34 looseleaf volumes.

Documents of Title Under the Uniform Commercial Code. American Law Institute-American Bar Association Committee on Continuing Professional

Education. • 1990. $90.00. Second edition.

Forms of Business Agreements and Resolutions-Annotated, Tax Tested. Prentice Hall PTR. • Three looseleaf volumes. Periodic supplementation. Price on application.

Joint Ventures. Glasser Legalworks. • Looseleaf. $225.00, including CD-ROM version. Periodic Supplementation. Includes explanations of legal procedures for joint ventures, with annotated forms. (Emerging Growth Companies Series.).

BUSINESS LETTERS

See: BUSINESS CORRESPONDENCE

BUSINESS LIBRARIES

See: SPECIAL LIBRARIES

BUSINESS LITERATURE

See also: BUSINESS; BUSINESS HISTORY; BUSINESS RESEARCH; ECONOMIC RESEARCH; GOVERNMENT PUBLICATIONS

GENERAL WORKS

The Web Library: Building a World Class Personal Library with Free Web Resources. Nicholas G. Tomaiuolo. Information Today, Inc. • 2003. $24.95. Provides advice on obtaining free, useful information and literature by way of the Internet. (Cyber-Age Books).

ABSTRACTS AND INDEXES

Business Periodicals Index. H. W. Wilson Co. • 11 times a year. Quarterly and annual cumulations. Price varies.

Index of Economic Articles in Journals and Collective Volumes. American Economic Association. • Irregular. $160.00.

BIBLIOGRAPHIES

The Basic Business Library: Core Resources. Rashells S. Karp and Bernard S. Schlessinger. Greenwood Publishing Group, Inc. • 2002. $64.95. Fourth edition. Consists of three parts: (1) "Core List of Printed Business Reference Sources," (2) "The Literature of Business Reference and Business Libraries: 1976-1994," and (3) "Business Reference Sources and Services: Essays." Part one lists 200 basic titles, with annotations and evaluations.

Bibliographic Guide to Business and Economics. Available from Gale Cengage Learning. • Annual. $835.00. Three volumes. Published by G. K. Hall & Co. Lists current business and economics publications cataloged by the New York Public Library and the Library of Congress.

Bibliographic Guide to Conference Publications. Available from Gale Cengage Learning. • Annual. $600.00. Two volumes. Published by G. K. Hall & Co., Lists a wide range of conference publications cataloged by the New York Public Library and the Library of Congress.

Guide to Special Issues and Indexes of Periodicals. Miriam Uhlan and Doris B. Katz, editors. Special Libraries Association. • 1994. $59.00. Fourth edition. A listing, with prices, of the special issues of over 1700 U. S. and Canadian periodicals in business, industry, technology, science, and the arts. Includes a comprehensive subject index.

U. S. Government Information for Business. U. S. Government Printing Office. • Annual. Free. A selected list of currently available publications, periodicals, and electronic products on business, trade, labor, federal regulations, economics, and other topics. Also known as *Business Catalog.*

Using the Financial and Business Literature. Thomas P. Slavens. Marcel Dekker, Inc. • 2004. $165.00. Provides detailed descriptions of both print and electronic information sources. (Books in Library and Information Science Series/64.).

DIRECTORIES

Cabell's Directory of Publishing Opportunities in Management. Cabell Publishing Co. • 1997. $149.95. Seventh edition. Four volumes. Over 540 scholarly periodicals in management.

INTERNET DATABASES

EBSCO Information Services. Ebsco Publishing. Phone: 800-653-2726 or (978)356-6500 Fax: (978)356-6565 E-mail: ep@epnet.com • URL: http://www.epnet.com • Fee-based Web site providing Internet access to a wide variety of databases, including business-related material. Full text is available for many periodical titles, with daily updates. Fees: Apply.

InSite 2. Intelligence Data/Thomson Financial. Phone: 800-654-0393 or (617)856-1890 Fax: (617)737-3182 E-mail: intelligence.data@tfn.com • URL: http://www.insite2.gale.com/ • Fee-based Web site consolidates information in a "Base Pack" consisting of Business InSite, Market InSite, and Company InSite. Optional databases are Consumer InSite, Health and Wellness InSite, Newsletter InSite, and Computer InSite. Includes fulltext content from more than 2,500 trade publications, journals, newsletters, newspapers, analyst reports, and other sources. Continuous updating. Formerly produced by The Gale Group.

ProQuest Direct. ProQuest Inc. Phone: 800-889-3358 or (734)761-4700 Fax: (734)662-4554 • URL: http://proquest.com • Fee-based Web site providing Internet access to more than 3,000 periodicals, newspapers, and other publications. Many items are available full-text, with daily updates. Includes extensive corporate and financial information. Fees: Apply.

ONLINE DATABASES

EconLit. American Economic Association. • Covers the worldwide literature of economics as contained in selected monographs and about 550 journals. Subjects include microeconomics, macroeconomics, economic history, inflation, money, credit, finance, accounting theory, trade, natural resource economics, and regional economics. Time period is 1969 to present, with monthly updates. Inquire as to online cost and availability.

Newsletter Database. Gale Cengage Learning. • Contains the full text of about 600 U. S. and international newsletters covering a wide range of business and industrial topics. Time period is 1988 to date, with daily updates. Inquire as to online cost and availability.

Trade & Industry Database. Gale Cengage Learning. • Provides indexing of business periodicals, January 1981 to date. Daily updates. (Full text articles from some periodicals are available online, 1983 to date. Inquire as to online cost and availability).

PERIODICALS AND NEWSLETTERS

Business and Finance Division Bulletin. Special Libraries Association, Business and Finance Div. • Quarterly. $12.00 per year.

Business Information Alert: Sources, Strategies and Signposts for Information Professionals. Alert Publications, Inc. • 10 times per year. Libraries, $162.00 per year. Newsletter for business librarians and information specialists.

The Information Report. Washington Researchers. • Description: Contains 40-140 items in each issue identifying little-known sources of information. Lists and describes directories, special libraries, booklets, seminars, studies, and other research sources available on markets, competition, federal regulation, and economic conditions. Covers government as well as corporate sources, trade, and professional organizations.

Journal of Economic Literature. American Economic Association. • Quarterly. $135.00 per year. Includes *American Economic Review* and *Journal of Economic Perspectives*.

SI: Special Issues. Trip Wyckoff, editor. Hoover's, Inc. • Bimonthly. $149.95 per year. Newsletter. Serves as a supplement to *Directory of Business Periodical Special Issues*. Provides current information on trade journal special issues and editorial calendars.

BUSINESS LOANS

See: BANK LOANS

BUSINESS MACHINES

See: OFFICE EQUIPMENT AND SUPPLIES

BUSINESS MANAGEMENT

See: ADMINISTRATION; INDUSTRIAL MANAGEMENT

BUSINESS MARKETING

See: INDUSTRIAL MARKETING

BUSINESS MATHEMATICS

See also: STATISTICAL METHODS

GENERAL WORKS
Applied Calculus with Linear Programming for Business, Economics, Life Sciences, and Social Science. Michael R. Ziegler and Raymond A. Barnett. Pearson Custom Publishing. • 1999. $80.00. Fifth edition.

Business Math: Practical Applications. Cheryl Cleaves and Margie J. Hobbs. Prentice Hall PTR. • 2001. $79.93. Sixth edition.

Business Mathematics. William L. Kindsfather and W. Alton Parish. Prentice Hall PTR. • 2003. Price on application.

Business Mathematics. Charles D. Miller and others. Addison-Wesley. • 2002. $97.00. Ninth edition.

Business Mathematics for College. Jeffrey Slater and Rick Ponticelli. McGraw-Hill. • 1996. $81.56.

Contemporary Business Mathematics. Southam Dietz. McGraw-Hill. • 2001. $91.95. 13th edition. (General Business and Business Education Series).

Mathematics with Applications in Management and Economics. Gordon D. Prichett and John C. Saber. McGraw-Hill. • 1993. $72.75. Seventh revised edition.

ABSTRACTS AND INDEXES
CompuMath Citation Index. Institute for Scientific Information. • Three times a year. $1,090.00 per year. Provides citations to the worldwide literature of computer science and mathematics.

CD-ROM DATABASES
MathSci Disc. American Mathematical Society. • Semiannual. Price on application. Provides CD-ROM citations, with abstracts, to the literature of mathematics, statistics, and computer science, 1940 to date.

HANDBOOKS AND MANUALS
Computational Finance: Numerical Methods for Pricing Financial Instruments. George Levy.

Elsevier Butterworth Heinemann. • 2003. $89.95. Explains advanced financial modeling techniques using Windows software.

Fixed Income Mathematics: Analytical and Statistical Techniques. Frank J. Fabozzi. McGraw-Hill. • 1996. $65.00. Third edition. Covers the basics of fixed income analysis, as well as more advanced techniques used for complex securities.

An Introduction to the Mathematics of Financial Derivatives. Salih N. Neftci. Elsevier. • 2000. $64.95. Second edition. Covers the mathematical models underlying the pricing of derivatives. Includes explanations of basic financial calculus for students, derivatives traders, risk managers, and others concerned with derivatives.

ONLINE DATABASES
MathSci. American Mathematical Society. • Provides online citations, with abstracts, to the literature of mathematics, statistics, and computer science. Time period is 1940 to date, with monthly updates. Inquire as to online cost and availability.

PERIODICALS AND NEWSLETTERS
Mathematical Finance: An International Journal of Mathematics, Statistics, and Financial Economics. Blackwell Publishing. • Quarterly. Institutions, $683.00 per year. Includes online edition. Covers the use of sophisticated mathematical tools in financial research and practice.

RESEARCH CENTERS AND INSTITUTES
Center for Mathematical Studies in Economics and Management Sciences. Northwestern University, Weinberg College of Arts and Sciences, Dept. of Economics, 2001 Sheridan Rd., 302 Arthur Andersen Hall, Evanston, IL 60208-2600. Phone: (847)491-5140 Fax: (847)491-7001 • URL: http://www.kellogg.nwu.edu/research/math.

Institute for Mathematics and Its Applications. University of Minnesota, 400 Lind, 206 Church St., S. E., Minneapolis, MN 55455-0436. Phone: (612)624-6066 Fax: (612)626-7370 E-mail: staff@ima.umn.edu • URL: http://www.ima.umn.edu • Research areas include various topics connected with industrial and applied mathematics.

TRADE/PROFESSIONAL ASSOCIATIONS
Industrial Mathematics Society. PO Box 159, Roseville, MI 48066. E-mail: ihea@ihea.org • Mathematicians, scientists, engineers, and economists. To extend the understanding and application of mathematics in industry. Supports study group on mathematics of gear design. Areas of interest include applied mathematics, engineering mechanics, computers, statistics, automatic control, operations analysis, and biomechanics.

Society for Industrial and Applied Mathematics. 3600 University City Science Center, Philadelphia, PA 19104-2688. Phone: 800-447-7426 or (215)382-9800 Fax: (215)386-7999 E-mail: siam@siam.org • URL: http://www.siam.org.

BUSINESS MERGERS

See: MERGERS AND ACQUISITIONS

BUSINESS MORALE

See: HUMAN RELATIONS

BUSINESS ORGANIZATION AND ADMINISTRATION

See: INDUSTRIAL MANAGEMENT

BUSINESS PERIODICALS

See: TRADE JOURNALS

BUSINESS PLANNING

See: BUSINESS START-UP PLANS AND PROPOSALS; PLANNING

BUSINESS PROPOSALS

See: BUSINESS START-UP PLANS AND PROPOSALS

BUSINESS PSYCHOLOGY

See: INDUSTRIAL PSYCHOLOGY

BUSINESS RATIOS

See: FINANCIAL RATIOS

BUSINESS RECORDS MANAGEMENT

See: RECORDS MANAGEMENT

BUSINESS REPORTS

See: CORPORATION REPORTS; REPORT WRITING

BUSINESS RESEARCH

See also: BUSINESS LITERATURE; BUREAUS OF BUSINESS RESEARCH; COMPETITIVE INTELLIGENCE; ECONOMIC RESEARCH

GENERAL WORKS
Business Research for Decision Making. Duane Davis. Wadsworth Publishing Co. • 1999. $62.00. Fifth edition. (Business Statistics Series).

Super Searchers Cover the World: The Online Secrets of International Business Researchers. Mary E. Bates. Information Today, Inc. • 2001. $24.95. Presents interviews with 15 experts in the area of online searching for international business information. (Super Searchers Series).

Super Searchers Do Business: The Online Secrets of Top Business Researchers. Mary E.Bates. Information Today, Inc. • 1999. $24.95. Presents the results of interviews with "11 leading researchers who use the Internet and online services to find critical business information." (Super Searchers Series.).

Super Searchers on Competitive Intelligence: The Online and Offline Secrets of Top CI Researchers. Margaret M. Carr. Information Today, Inc. • 2003. $24.95. Presents the views of business intelligence experts from 15 major corporations and organizations. Contains information on sources for "monitoring competitive forces." (Super Searchers Series).

Super Searchers on Madison Avenue: Top Advertising and Marketing Professionals Share Their Online Research Strategies. Grace A. Villamora. Information Today, Inc. • 2003. $24.95. Provides research "tips, techniques, and resources" from 13 information professionals working in advertising and marketing. (Super Searchers Series).

Super Searchers on Mergers & Acquisitions: The Online Secrets of Top Corporate Researchers and M & A Professionals. Jan Tudor. Information Today, Inc. • 2001. $24.95. Presents the results of interviews with 13 "top M & A information pros." Covers the finding, evaluating, and delivering of relevant data on companies and industries. (Super Searchers Series).

Super Searchers on Wall Street: Top Investment Professionals Share Their Online Research Secrets. Amelia Kassel. Information Today, Inc. • 2000. $24.95. Gives the results of interviews with "10 leading financial industry research experts." Explains how online information is used by stock brokers, investment bankers, and individual investors. Includes relevant Web sites and other sources. (Super Searchers Series).

BIBLIOGRAPHIES

Analyzing Your Competition: Simple, Low-Cost Techniques for Intelligence Gathering. Michael Strenges. MarketResearch.com. • 1997. $95.00. Third edition. Mainly an annotated listing of specific, business information sources, but also contains concise discussions of information-gathering techniques. Indexed by publisher and title.

Bibliographic Guide to Business and Economics. Available from Gale Cengage Learning. • Annual. $835.00. Three volumes. Published by G. K. Hall & Co. Lists current business and economics publications cataloged by the New York Public Library and the Library of Congress.

Bibliographic Guide to Conference Publications. Available from Gale Cengage Learning. • Annual. $600.00. Two volumes. Published by G. K. Hall & Co., Lists a wide range of conference publications cataloged by the New York Public Library and the Library of Congress.

Business Information: How to Find It, How to Use It. Michael R. Lavin. Greenwood Publishing Group, Inc. • 2001. $61.00. Third edition. Combines discussions of business research techniques with detailed descriptions of major business publications and databases. Includes title and subject indexes.

Business Research Handbook: Methods and Sources for Lawyers and Business Professionals. Kathy E. Shimpock. Aspen Publishers, Inc. • $155.00. Loose-leaf service. Periodic supplementation. Provides detailed advice on how to find business information. Describes a wide variety of data sources, both private and government.

International Business Information: How to Find It, How to Use It. Ruth A. Pagell and Michael Halperin. Glenlake Publishing Co., Ltd. • 2000. $65.00.

CD-ROM DATABASES

OECD Statistical Compendium. Organization for Economic Cooperation and Development. • Semiannual. $1,905.00 per year for 1 to 10 users. CD-ROM contains more than 730,000 monthly, quarterly, and annual time series for OECD countries, 1960 to date. Includes fully searchable data on agriculture, food, economic indicators, national accounts, employment, energy, finance, industry, technology, and foreign trade. Results can be displayed in various forms.

Profiles in Business and Management: An International Directory of Scholars and Their Research [CD-ROM]. Harvard Business School Publishing. • Annual. $595.00. Fully searchable CD-ROM version of two-volume printed directory. Contains bibliographic and biographical information for over 5600 business and management experts active in 21 subject areas. Formerly *International Directory of Business and Management Scholars.*

World Database of Business Information Sources on CD-ROM. Gale Cengage Learning. • Annual. Produced by Euromonitor. Presents Euromonitor's entire information source database on CD-ROM. Contains a worldwide total of about 35,000 publications, organizations, libraries, trade fairs, and online databases.

DIRECTORIES

Association for University Business and Economic Research Membership Directory. Association for University Business and Economic Research. • Annual. $10.00. Member institutions in the United States and abroad with centers, bureaus, departments, etc., concerned with business and economic research.

Business Organizations, Agencies, and Publications Directory. Gale Cengage Learning. • 2003. $480.00. 15th edition. Over 40,000 entries describing 39 types of business information sources. Classified by type of organization, publication, or serviceIncludes state, national, and international agencies and organizations. Master index to names and keywords. Also includes e-mail addresses and web site URL's.

The Core Business Web: A Guide to Key Information Sources. Gary W. White, editor. Haworth Press, Inc. • 2003. $49.95. Business librarians select Web sites in 25 areas of business, such as banking, e-commerce, investments, tourism, and small business.

Directory of Special Libraries and Information Centers. Gale Cengage Learning. • 2003. $975.00. 28th edition. Three volumes. Two available separately: volume one,*Directory of Special Libraries and Information Centers*, $740.00; volume two *Geographic and Personnel Indexes*, $560.00. Contains 34,000 entries from the U.S., Canada, and 80 other countries. A detailed subject index is included in volume one.

Research Centers Directory. Gale. • Covers: About 13,600 university, government, and other nonprofit research organizations established on a permanent basis to carry on continuing research programs in all areas of study; includes research institutes, laboratories, experiment stations, research parks, technology transfer centers, and other facilities and activities; coverage includes Canada. Entries include: Unit name, name of parent institution, address, phone, fax, name of director, e-mail addresses, URLs, year founded, governance, staff, educational activities, public services, sources of support, annual volume of research, principal fields of research, publications, special library facilities, special research facilities.

Subject Directory of Special Libraries and Information Centers. Gale Cengage Learning. • Annual. $960.00. Three volumes, available separately: volume one, *Business, Government, and Law Libraries*, $375.00; volume two, *Computer, Engineering, and Law Libraries*, $375.00; volume three, *Health Sciences Libraries*, $375.00. Altogether, 14,000 entries from the *Directory of Special Libraries and Information Centers* are arranged in 14 subject chapters.

World Directory of Business Information Web Sites. Available from Gale Cengage Learning. • 2003. $690.00. Sixth edition. Published by Euromonitor. Provides detailed descriptions of a wide variety of business-related Web sites. More than 1,500 sites are included from around the world. Covers statistics sources, market research, company information, rankings, surveys, economic data, etc.

HANDBOOKS AND MANUALS

The Business Library and How to Use It: A Guide to Sources and Research Strategies for Information on Business and Management. Elizabeth Wood and others, editors. Omnigraphics, Inc. • 1996. $28.00. Sixth edition. Explains library research methods and describes specific sources of business information. A revision of *How to Use the Business Library*, by H. Webster Johnson and others.

Find It Online: The Complete Guide to Online Research. Alan M. Schlein. Facts on Demand Press. • 2002. $19.95. Third edition. Presents the general principles of online searching for information about people, phone numbers, public records, news, business, investments, etc. Covers both free and fee-based sources. (On Line Ease Series).

Finding Market Research on the Web: Best

Practices of Professional Researchers. Robert I. Berkman. MarketResearch.com. • 2003. $279.00. Provides tips and techniques for locating useful market research data through the Internet.

Handbook of Entrepreneurial Dynamics. William B. Gartner and others, editors. Sage Publications, Inc. • 2004. $115.00. Covers current academic research in entrepreneurship.

International Business Information on the Web: Searcher Magazine's Guide to Sites and Strategies for Global Business Research. Sheri R. Lanza. Information Today, Inc. • 2001. $29.95. (CyberAge Books.).

Internet Business Intelligence: How to Build a Big Company System on a Small Company Budget. David Vine. Information Today, Inc. • 2000. $29.95. Covers the obtaining of valuable business intelligence data through use of the Internet.

Mining for Gold on the Internet: How to Find Investment and Financial Information on the Internet. Mary Ellen Bates. McGraw-Hill. • 2000. $24.95. Tells how to effectively search the Internet for financial advice and information. Specific websites are discussed.

A New Archetype for Competitive Intelligence. John J. McGonagle and Carolyn M. Vella. Greenwood Publishing Group, Inc. • 1996. $64.95. Covers competitive intelligence, strategic intelligence, market intelligence, defensive intelligence, and cyber-intelligence. Includes an overview of sources and techniques for data gathering. A bibliography, glossary, and index are provided.

Recruiter's Research Blue Book: A How-To Guide for Researchers, Consultants, Corporate Recruiters, Small Business Owners, Venture Capitalists, and Line Executives. Andrea A. Jupina. Kennedy Information, Inc. • 2000. $179.00. Second edition. Provides detailed coverage of the role that research plays in executive recruiting. Includes such practical items as "Telephone Interview Guide," "Legal Issues in Executive Search," and "How to Create an Executive Search Library." Covers both person-to-person research and research using printed and online business information sources. Includes an extensive directory of recommended sources. Formerly *Handbook of Executive Search Research.*

Researching Company Financial Information. Washington Researchers, Ltd. • 2002. $59.00.

The Skeptical Business Searcher: The Information Advisor's Guide to Evaluating Web Data, Sites, and Sources. Robert Berkman. Information Today, Inc. • 2003. $29.95. Covers free Internet sources of company backgrounds, sales data, earnings, SEC documents, competitive intelligence information, poll data, business news, economic statistics, etc. The author is editor of *The Information Advisor* newsletter. (CyberAge Books).

INTERNET DATABASES

Business 2.0 Web Guide to the Best Business Links. Business 2.0 Media Inc. Phone: (415)293-4800 E-mail: support@business2.com • URL: http://www.business2.com/webguide • Web site presents an extensive, searchable directory of links to "the best, most informative, and authoritative web pages." Twenty main categories cover business, finance, career, company information, people, and technology topics, with thousands of subtopics, all linking to Web sites recommended by experienced business researchers. Fees: Free.

FedWorld: A Program of the United States Department of Commerce. National Technical Information Service. Phone: (703)605-6000 Fax: (703)605-6900 E-mail: webmaster@fedworld.gov • URL: http://www.fedworld.gov • Web site offers "a comprehensive central access point for searching, locating, ordering, and acquiring government and business information." Emphasis is on searching the Web pages, databases, and government reports of a wide variety of federal agencies. Fees: Free.

FirstGov: Your First Click to the U. S. Government. General Services Administration. Phone: 800-333-4636 or (202)501-0705 E-mail: public.affairs@gsa.gov • URL: http://www.firstgov.gov • Free Web site provides extensive links to federal agencies covering a wide variety of topics, such as agriculture, business, consumer safety, education, the environment, government jobs, grants, health, social security, statistics sources, taxes, technology, travel, and world affairs. Also provides links to federal forms, including IRS tax forms. Searching is offered, both keyword and advanced.

ONLINE DATABASES

EconLit. American Economic Association. • Covers the worldwide literature of economics as contained in selected monographs and about 550 journals. Subjects include microeconomics, macroeconomics, economic history, inflation, money, credit, finance, accounting theory, trade, natural resource economics, and regional economics. Time period is 1969 to present, with monthly updates. Inquire as to online cost and availability.

NTIS Database. National Technical Information Service. • Contains citations and abstracts to unrestricted reports of government-sponsored research, 1964 to date. Covers a wide range of technical, engineering, business, and social science topics. Monthly updates. Inquire as to online cost and availability.

PERIODICALS AND NEWSLETTERS

The CyberSkeptic's Guide to Internet Research. Information Today, Inc. • 10 times a year. Individuals, $159.00 per year; nonprofit organizations, $134.00 per year. Newsletter. Presents critical reviews of World Wide Web sites and databases, written by information professionals. Includes "Late Breaking News" of Web sites.

The Information Advisor: Tips and Techniques for Smart Information Users. MarketResearch.com. • Monthly. $159.00 per year. Newsletter. Evaluates and discusses online, CD-ROM, and published sources of business, financial, and market research information.

Journal of Business and Finance Librarianship. Haworth Press, Inc. • Quarterly. $165.00 per year.

The Journal of Business Research. Elsevier.. • Monthly. Qualified personnel, $181.00 per year; institutions, $1,471.00 per year. Covers theoretical and empirical advances in marketing, finance, international business, risk management, and other business topics.

The Journal of Research Administration. Society of Research Administrators. • Quarterly. Members, $35.00 per year; non-members, $45.00 per year. Formerly *SRA Journal.*

RESEARCH CENTERS AND INSTITUTES

Bureau of Economic and Business Research. University of Illinois at Urbana-Champaign, 1206 S. Sixth St., 403 Wohlers Hall, Champaign, IL 61820. Phone: (217)333-2330 Fax: (217)244-7410 E-mail: g-oldman@uiuc.edu • URL: http://www.business.uiuc.edu/research.

Bureau of Economic and Business Research. University of Florida. 221 Matherly Hall, Gainesville, FL 32611-7145. Phone: (352)392-0171 Fax: (352)392-4739 E-mail: info@bebr.ufl.edu • URL: http://www.bebr.ufl.edu.

Conference Board, Inc. The Conference Board, Inc. 845 3rd Ave., New York, NY 10022. Phone: (212)339-0345 Fax: (212)980-7014 E-mail: info@conference-board.org • URL: http://www.conference-board.org • Business management practices worldwide, especially economic, and demographic in nature. Specific concerns include: corporate citizenship, including corporate contributions, diversity, environmental policy and issues,

and government relations; corporate governance, including boards of directors, role of chief executives, relations with institutional investors, and shareholder input and influence; economics, including economic and financial forecasts, consumer confidence, leading economic indicators, North American outlook and trends, and global economic environment; human resources and organizational effectiveness, including organization structure and design, compensation and benefits, training and development, and communications; and performance excellence.

Institute of Business and Economic Research. University of California at Berkeley, Hass School of Business, Berkeley, CA 94720-1900. Phone: (510)642-5905 Fax: (510)642-1420 E-mail: shapiro@haas.berkeley.edu • URL: http://www.haas.berkeley.edu/groups/iber • Research fields are business administration, economics, finance, real estate, and international development.

TRADE/PROFESSIONAL ASSOCIATIONS

Industrial Research Institute. 2200 Clarendon Blvd., Ste. 1102, Arlington, VA 22201. Phone: (703)647-2580 Fax: (703)647-2581 E-mail: bernstein@iriinc.org • URL: http://www.iriinc.org • Manufacturers and industrial firms maintaining industrial research laboratories. Identifies and promotes effective techniques for the organization and management of research, development, and engineering in support of technological innovation.

National Association for Business Economics. 1233 20th St., N.W., Suite 505, Washington, DC 20036. Phone: (202)463-6223 Fax: (202)463-6239 E-mail: nabe@nabe.com • URL: http://www.nabe.com • Formerly National Association of Business Economists.

Society of Research Administrators International. 1901 N Moore St., Ste. 1004, Arlington, VA 22209. Phone: (703)741-0140 Fax: (703)741-0142 E-mail: info@srainternational.org • URL: http://www.srainternational.org • Dedicated to advancing the profession and improving the efficiency and effectiveness of research administration.

OTHER SOURCES

Business Information Desk Reference: Where to Find Answers to Your Business Questions. Melvyn N. Freed and Virgil P. Diodato. Prentice Hall PTR. • 1992. $20.00. Offers a unique, question and answer approach to business information sources. Covers print sources, online databases, trade associations, and government agencies.

The Information Catalog. MarketResearch.com. • Bimonthly. Free. Mainly a catalog of market research reports from various publishers, but also includes business and marketing reference sources. Includes keyword title index. Formerly *The Information Catalog: Marketing Intelligence Studies, Competitor Reports, Business and Marketing Sources.*

On-the-Job Research: How Usable are Corporate Research Intranets?. Alison J. Head and Shannon Staley. Special Libraries Association. • 2002. Members, $100.00; non-members, $135.00. Presents the results of a survey of how employees at seven major corporations make use of company intranets for news and information research. Searching by individual employees generally had a success rate of less than 50 percent.

BUSINESS RESPONSIBILITY

See: SOCIAL RESPONSIBILITY

BUSINESS SCHOOLS

See: BUSINESS EDUCATION

BUSINESS, SMALL

See: SMALL BUSINESS

BUSINESS START-UP PLANS AND PROPOSALS

See also: BUSINESS INNOVATION; VENTURE CAPITAL

GENERAL WORKS

Business Plan: Planning for the Small Business. Alan West. Nichols Publishing Co. • 1988. $21.95.

Entrepreneurship.com. Tim Burns. Dearborn Trade Publishing, A Kaplan Professional Co. • 2000. $19.95. Provides basic advice and information on the topic of dot.com startups, including business plan creation and financing.

ABSTRACTS AND INDEXES

Business Periodicals Index. H. W. Wilson Co. • 11 times a year. Quarterly and annual cumulations. Price varies.

ENCYCLOPEDIAS AND DICTIONARIES

Encyclopedia of Small Business. Gale Cengage Learning. • 2002. $450.00. Second edition. Two volumes. Contains about 600 informative entries on a wide variety of topics affecting small business. Arrangement is alphabetical.

HANDBOOKS AND MANUALS

Anatomy of a Business Plan: A Step-by-Step Guide to Starting Smart, Building thesiness and Securing Your Company's Future. Linda J. Pinson. Dearborn Trade Publishing, A Kaplan Professional Co. • 2001. $21.95. Fifth edition.

Business Plans Handbook. Gale Cengage Learning. • 2003. $150.00. Contains examples of detailed plans for starting or developing various kinds of businesses. Categories within plans include statement of purpose, market description, personnel requirements, financial needs, etc.

Business Plans that Work for Your Small Business. Alice H. Magos and Steve Crow, editors. CCH, Inc. • 2003. $19.95. Second edition. Part one is "Creating a Business Plan that Works" and part two is "Five Sample Business Plans.".

Cyberfinance: Raising Capital for the E-Business. Martin B. Robins. CCH, Inc. • 2001. $79.00. Covers the taxation, financial, and legal aspects of raising money for new Internet-based ("dot.com") companies, including the three stages of startup, growth, and initial public offering. (Solutions for Professional Advisers Series).

Entrepreneur's Guide to Finance and Business: Wealth Creation Techniques for Growing a Business. Steven Rogers. McGraw-Hill. • 2003. $49.95. Coverage includes entrepreneurial financing, business plan development, and structuring a deal.

How to Write Proposals that Produce. Joel P. Bowman and Bernadine P. Branchaw. Greenwood Publishing Group, Inc. • 1992. $23.50. An extensive guide to effective proposal writing for both nonprofit organizations and businesses. Covers writing style, intended audience, format, use of graphs, charts, and tables, documentation, evaluation, oral presentation, and related topics.

New Venture Creation: Entrepreneurship for the 21st Century. Jeffrey A. Timmons and Stephen Spinelli. McGraw-Hill. • 2003. Sixth edition. Price on application.

Preparing a Successful Business Plan: How to Plan to Succeed and Secure Financial Banking. Rodger D. Touchie. Self-Counsel Press Inc. • 2001. $16.95. Fourth edition.

Proposal Development: How to Respond and Win

the Bid. Bud Porter-Roth. PSI Research. • 1998. $21.95. Third revised edition. A step-by-step guide to the practical details of preparing, printing, and submitting business proposals of various kinds. (Successful Business Library Series).

Proposal Planning and Writing. Lynn E. Miner and Jeremy T. Miner. Greenwood Publishing Group, Inc. • 2003. $39.95. Third edition. Discusses the steps necessary to locate and obtain funding from the federal government, foundations, and corporations.

Proposal Preparation. Rodney D. Stewart and Ann L. Stewart. John Wiley and Sons, Inc. • 1992. $150.00. Second edition. Covers proposals of various kinds. (New Dimensions in Engineering Series, vol. 6).

Restaurant Start-Up Guide: A 12-Month Plan for Successfully Starting a Restaurant. Peter Rainsford and David H. Bangs. Dearborn Trade Publishing, A Kaplan Professional Co. • 2000. $22.95. Second edition. Emphasizes the importance of advance planning for restaurant startups.

Start Right in E-Business: A Step-by-Step Guide to Successful E-Business Implementation. Bennet P. Lientz and Kathryn P. Rea. Elsevier. • 2000. $47.95. (E-Business Solutions Series).

Start-Up Business Guides. Entrepreneur Media, Inc. • Looseleaf. $59.50 each. Practical guides to starting a wide variety of small businesses.

Starting on a Shoestring: Building a Business Without a Bankroll. Arnold S. Goldstein. John Wiley and Sons, Inc. • 2002. $19.95. Fourth edition. Includes chapters on venture capital and Small Business Administration (SBA) loans.

Startup: An Entrepreneur's Guide to Launching and Managing a New Venture. William J. Stolze. Rock Beach Press. • 1989. $24.95.

Steps to Small Business Start-Up: Everything You Need to Know to Turn Your Idea into a Successful Business. Linda Pinson and Jerry Jinnett. Dearborn Trade Publishing, A Kaplan Professional Co. • 2003. $22.95. Fifth edition. Covers such topics as location, legal structure, cash flow, financing, appropriateness, taxes, and insurance. Includes charts, sample calculations, spreadsheets, and forms.

Successful Business Plan: Secrets and Strategies. Rhonda M. Abrams. Rhonda, Inc. • 1999. $27.95. Third edition. (Successful Business Library Series).

Ultimate Guide to Raising Money for Growing Companies. Michael C. Thomsett. McGraw-Hill. • 1990. $45.00. Discusses the preparation of a practical business plan, how to manage cash flow, and debt vs. equity decisions.

Where to Go When the Bank Says No: Alternatives to Financing Your Business. David R. Evanson. Bloomberg. • 1998. $24.95. Emphasis is on obtaining business financing in the $250,000 to $15,000,000 range. Business plans are discussed. (Bloomberg Small Business Series).

Writing Effective Business Plans. Entrepreneur Media, Inc. • Looseleaf. $49.50. A step-by-step guide. Includes a sample business plan.

INTERNET DATABASES

U. S. Business Advisor. Small Business Administration. Phone: (202)205-6600 Fax: (202)205-7064 • URL: http://www.business.gov • Web site provides "a one-stop electronic link to all the information and services government provides for the business community." Covers about 60 federal agencies that exist to assist or regulate business. Detailed information is provided on financial assistance, workplace issues, taxes, regulations, international trade, and other business topics. Searching is offered. Fees: Free.

ONLINE DATABASES

Wilson Business Abstracts Online. H. W. Wilson Co. • Indexes and abstracts 600 major business periodicals, plus the *Wall Street Journal* and the

business section of the *New York Times.* Indexing is from 1982, abstracting from 1990, with the two newspapers included from 1993. Updated weekly. Inquire as to online cost and availability. (*Business Periodicals Index* without abstracts is also available online.).

PERIODICALS AND NEWSLETTERS

Business Start-Ups: Smart Ideas for Your Small Business. Entrepreneur Media, Inc. • Monthly. $14.97 per year. Provides advice for starting a small business. Includes business trends, new technology, E-commerce, and case histories ("real-life stories").

Small Business Opportunities. Harris Publications, Inc. • Bimonthly. $11.97.

RESEARCH CENTERS AND INSTITUTES

Berkley Center for Entrepreneurial Studies. New York University, Kaufman Management Center, Stern School of Business, 44 W. Fourth St., Ste. 8-180, New York, NY 10012. Phone: (212)998-0070 Fax: (212)995-4211 E-mail: aginsber@stern.nyu.edu • URL: http://www.stern.nyu.edu/bces.

TRADE/PROFESSIONAL ASSOCIATIONS

National Business Incubation Association. 20 E Circle Dr., No. 37198, Athens, OH 45701-3571. Phone: (740)593-4331 Fax: (740)593-1996 E-mail: info@nbia.org • URL: http://www.NBIA.org • Incubator developers and managers; corporate joint venture partners, venture capital investors; economic development professionals. (Incubators are business assistance programs providing business consulting services and financing assistance to start-up and fledgling companies.) Helps newly formed businesses to succeed. Educates businesses and investors on incubator benefits; offers specialized training in incubator formation and management. Conducts research and referral services; compiles statistics; maintains speakers' bureau; publishes information relevant to business incubation and growing companies.

OTHER SOURCES

Formation and Financing of Emerging Companies. Daniel E. O'Connor and others. Glasser Legalworks. • Looseleaf. $225.00, including CD-ROM version. Periodic Supplementation. Covers incorporation, bylaws, indemnification, intellectual property, financing sources, venture capital, due diligence, bridge loans, investor rights, compliance, and other legal issues associated with company formation. (Emerging Growth Companies Series.).

How to Write a Business Plan. American Management Association Extension Institute. • Looseleaf. $159.00. Self-study course. Emphasis is on practical explanations, examples, and problem solving. Quizzes and a case study are included.

Start-Up and Emerging Companies: Planning, Financing, and Operating the Successful Business, with Forms on Disk. American Lawyer Media, Inc. • Looseleaf. $289.00. Two volumes. Updated as needed. Covers a wide variety of business and legal topics relating to new enterprises. Provides information on venture financing, formation of corporations, tax laws, limited liability companies, employee benefits, contracts, and accounting. Includes a CD-ROM containing more than 75 sample legal forms, clauses, agreements, organizational resolutions, and checklists. (Law Journal Press).

BUSINESS STATISTICS

See also: ECONOMIC STATISTICS; MARKET STATISTICS; STATISTICAL METHODS

GENERAL WORKS

Business Statistics: A Decision-Making Approach. David F. Groebner and others. Prentice Hall PTR. •

2001. $115.00 Fifth edition.

Business Statistics: Contemporary Decision Making. Ken Black. South-Western. • 2000. $107.95. Third edition.

Business Statistics for Management and Economics. Wayne W. Daniel and James C. Terrell. Houghton Mifflin Co. • 1995. $23.96. Seventh edition.

Business Statistics for Quality and Productivity. John M. Levine. Prentice Hall PTR. • 1994. $94.07. (Prentice Hall College Title Series).

Business Statistics Practice. Bruce L. Bowerman and others. McGraw-Hill. • 2001. $68.00. Second edition.

Complete Business Statistics. Amir D. Aczel and Jayavel Sounderpandian. McGraw-Hill. • 2001. $104.38. Fifth edition. Includes CD-ROM.

Statistics for Management. Richard I. Levin and David S. Rubin. Prentice Hall PTR. • 1997. $93.33. Seventh edition.

Understanding Business Statistics. John E. Hanke and Arthur G. Reitsch. McGraw-Hill. • 1993. $71.25. Second edition.

ABSTRACTS AND INDEXES

Current Index to Statistics: Applications, Methods, and Theory. American Statistical Association. • Annual. Price on application. An index to journal articles on statistical applications and methodology.

Statistical Reference Index: A Selective Guide to American Statistical Publications from Sources Other than the United States Government. Congressional Information Service, Inc. • Monthly. Price varies. Quarterly and annual cumulations. Service basis.

ALMANACS AND YEARBOOKS

National Accounts Statistics: Main Aggregates and Detailed Tables. United Nations Publications. • Annual. $160.00.

BIBLIOGRAPHIES

Statistics Sources: A Subject Guide to Data on Industrial, Business, Social, Educational, Financial and Other Topics for the U. S. and Selected Foreign Countries. Gale Cengage Learning. • 2003. $515.00. 27th edition. Two volumes. Lists sources of statistical information for more than 20,000 topics.

World Directory of Non-Official Statistical Sources. Gale Group, Inc. • 2002. $650.00. Fourth edition. Provides detailed descriptions of more than 4,000 regularly published, non-governmental statistics sources. Includes surveys, studies, market research reports, trade journals, databank compilations, and other print sources. Coverage is international, with four indexes.

CD-ROM DATABASES

OECD Statistical Compendium. Organization for Economic Cooperation and Development. • Semiannual. $1,905.00 per year for 1 to 10 users. CD-ROM contains more than 730,000 monthly, quarterly, and annual time series for OECD countries, 1960 to date. Includes fully searchable data on agriculture, food, economic indicators, national accounts, employment, energy, finance, industry, technology, and foreign trade. Results can be displayed in various forms.

Statistical Abstract of the United States on CD-ROM. Hoover's, Inc. • Annual. $49.95. Provides all statistics from official print version, plus expanded historical data, greater detail, and keyword searching features.

DIRECTORIES

Directory of Statisticians. American Statistical Association. • Triennial. Free to members; non-members, $125.00. List more than 25,000 members.

Major Performance Rankings. Available from Gale Cengage Learning. • 2003. $1,190.00. Second edition. Published by Euromonitor. Ranks 2,500

leading consumer product companies worldwide by various kinds of business and financial data, such as sales, profit, and market share. Includes international, regional, and country rankings.

ENCYCLOPEDIAS AND DICTIONARIES

A Dictionary of Statistical Terms. F.H. Marriott. Addison-Wesley. • 1996. $76.67. Fifth edition.

HANDBOOKS AND MANUALS

Business Statistics by Example. Simon Sincich. Pearson Custom Publishing. • 2001. $45.00.

Business Statistics on the Web: Find Them Fast, at Little or No Cost. Paula Berinstein. Information Today, Inc. • 2003. $29.95. Serves as a practical guide to finding and evaluating business data through the Internet. Includes advice on the organization and presentation of business statistics. (CyberAge Books).

Dun & Bradstreet/Gale Group Industry Handbooks. Gale Cengage Learning. • 2000. $650.00. Five volumes. $130.00 per volume. Each volume covers two or more major industries: 1. *Entertainment and Hospitality*; 2. *Construction and Agriculture*; 3. *Chemicals and Pharmaceuticals*; 4. *Computers & Software and Broadcasting & Telecommunications*; 5. *Insurance and Health & Medical Services.* The following are included for each industry: overview, statistics, financial ratios, rankings, merger information, company directory, directory of associations, and consultants directory. (Dun and Bradstreet/Gale Industry Reference Handbook Series).

Finding Statistics Online: How to Locate the Elusive Numbers You Need. Paula Berinstein. Information Today, Inc. • 1998. $29.95. Provides advice on efficient searching when looking for statistical data on the World Wide Web or from commercial online services and database producers. (CyberAge Books.).

Little Black Book of Business Statistics. Michael C. Thomsett. AMACOM. • 1990. $14.95. A practical guide to the effective use and interpretation of statistics by business managers. (Little Black Book Series).

INTERNET DATABASES

Business 2.0 Web Guide to the Best Business Links. Business 2.0 Media Inc. Phone: (415)293-4800 E-mail: support@business2.com • URL: http://www.business2.com/webguide • Web site presents an extensive, searchable directory of links to "the best, most informative, and authoritative web pages." Twenty main categories cover business, finance, career, company information, people, and technology topics, with thousands of subtopics, all linking to Web sites recommended by experienced business researchers. Fees: Free.

Federal Reserve Board Publications and Education Resources. Board of Governors of the Federal Reserve System. Phone: (202)452-3000 Fax: (202)452-3819 • URL: http://www.federalreserve.gov/publications.htm • Web site provides convenient access to statistics, surveys, and research from the Federal Reserve Board. *Federal Reserve Bulletin* articles are available as abstracts or full text (PDF) currently or from six-year archives. The link "Statistics: Releases and Historical Data" offers daily, weekly, monthly, quarterly, and annual data in great detail for interest rates, foreign exchange, consumer credit, money stock measures, industrial production indexes, bank reserves, and other items. Historical tabulations are available for various time periods. Fees: Free.

Fedstats. Federal Interagency Council on Statistical Policy. Phone: (202)395-7254 • URL: http://www.fedstats.gov • Web site features an efficient search facility for full-text statistics produced by more than 100 federal agencies, including the Census Bureau, the Bureau of Economic Analysis, and the Bureau of Labor Statistics. Boolean searches can be made

within one agency or for all agencies combined. Links are offered to international statistical bureaus, including the UN, IMF, OECD, UNESCO, Eurostat, and 20 individual countries. Fees: Free.

FedWorld: A Program of the United States Department of Commerce. National Technical Information Service. Phone: (703)605-6000 Fax: (703)605-6900 E-mail: webmaster@fedworld.gov • URL: http://www.fedworld.gov • Web site offers "a comprehensive central access point for searching, locating, ordering, and acquiring government and business information." Emphasis is on searching the Web pages, databases, and government reports of a wide variety of federal agencies. Fees: Free.

FirstGov: Your First Click to the U. S. Government. General Services Administration. Phone: 800-333-4636 or (202)501-0705 E-mail: public.affairs@gsa.gov • URL: http://www.firstgov.gov • Free Web site provides extensive links to federal agencies covering a wide variety of topics, such as agriculture, business, consumer safety, education, the environment, government jobs, grants, health, social security, statistics sources, taxes, technology, travel, and world affairs. Also provides links to federal forms, including IRS tax forms. Searching is offered, both keyword and advanced.

FreeLunch.com. Economy.com, Inc. Phone: (610)696-8700 Fax: (610)696-1678 • URL: http://www.freelunch.com • Web site provides free access to more than 1.5 million economic and financial data series, covering industry, demographics, labor markets, prices, retail sales, government spending, trade, interest rates, housing starts, the stock market, and many other topics. Data is available for various time periods in either chart or table form. Searching is offered. Fees: Free, but registration required. Economy.com, Inc. also offers fee-based economic analysis at *The Dismal Scientist* site (http://www.dismal.com).

InSite 2. Intelligence Data/Thomson Financial. Phone: 800-654-0393 or (617)856-1890 Fax: (617)737-3182 E-mail: intelligence.data@tfn.com • URL: http://www.insite2.gale.com/ • Fee-based Web site consolidates information in a "Base Pack" consisting of Business InSite, Market InSite, and Company InSite. Optional databases are Consumer InSite, Health and Wellness InSite, Newsletter InSite, and Computer InSite. Includes fulltext content from more than 2,500 trade publications, journals, newsletters, newspapers, analyst reports, and other sources. Continuous updating. Formerly produced by The Gale Group.

U. S. Census Bureau: The Official Statistics. U. S. Bureau of the Census. Phone: (301)763-4100 Fax: (301)763-4794 • URL: http://www.census.gov • Web site is "Your Source for Social, Demographic, and Economic Information." Contains "Current U. S. Population Count," "Current Economic Indicators," and a wide variety of data under "Other Official Statistics." Keyword searching is provided. Fees: Free.

ONLINE DATABASES

Industry Insider. Thomson Financial. • Contains full-text online industry research reports from more than 200 leading trade associations, covering 50 specific industries. Reports include extensive statistics and market research data. Inquire as to online cost and availability.

OECD Main Economic Indicators. Organization for Economic Cooperation and Development. • International statistics provided by OECD, 1960 to date. Monthly updates. Inquire as to online cost and availability.

Tablebase. Gale Cengage Learning. • Provides online numerical tabular data from a wide variety of business, organization, and government sources, including about 1,000 trade journals. Includes industry and individual company statistics relating

to products, market share, sales forecasts, production, exports, market trends, etc. Time span is 1997 to date. Weekly updates. Inquire as to online cost and availability. (Also available in a CD-ROM version.).

PERIODICALS AND NEWSLETTERS

American Statistician. American Statistical Association. • Quarterly. Individuals, $15.00 per year; libraries, $75.00 per year; students, $15.00 per year.

JASA (Journal of the American Statistical Association). American Statistical Association. • Quarterly. Members, $39.00 per year; non-members, $310.00 per year; students, $10.00 per year.

Journal of Business and Economic Statistics. American Statistical Association. • Quarterly. Libraries, $90.00 per year. Emphasis is on statistical measurement and applications for business and economics.

STATISTICS SOURCES

Business Statistics of the United States. Linz Audain and Cornelia J. Strawser. Bernan Associates. • Annual. $147.00. Based on *Business Statistics*, formerly issue by the Bureau of Economic Analysis, U. S. Department of Commerce. Provides basic data for a wide variety of U. S. industries, services, and economic indicators. Most statistics are shown annually for 30 years and monthly for the most recent four years.

County Business Patterns. Available from U. S. Government Printing Office. • Irregular. 52 issues containing annual data for each state, the District of Columbia, and a U. S. Summary. Produced by U.S. Bureau of the Census (http://www.census.gov). Provides local establishment and employment statistics by industry.

Datapedia of the United States: American History in Numbers. George T. Kurian, editor. Bernan Press. • 2004. $125.00. Third edition. Based on the Census Bureau publication, *Historical Statistics of the United States.* Provides data from Colonial times to the present on agriculture, business, consumer income, energy, finance, labor, national income, population, and many other subjects. Includes "narrative highlights," maps, charts, and statistical projections.

Economic Indicators. Council of Economic Advisors, Executive Office of the President. Available from U.S. Government Printing Office. • Monthly. $55.00 per year.

Economic Report of the President: Together with the Annual Report of the Council of Economic Advisors. Available from U. S. Government Printing Office. • Annual. $32.00. Includes about 130 pages of "Statistical Tables Relating to Income, Employment, and Production." Tables cover national income, employment, wages, productivity, manufacturing, prices, credit, money (public and private), corporate profits, and foreign trade.

Industrial Commodity Statistics Yearbook. United Nations Dept. of Economic and Social Affairs. United Nations Publications. • Annual.

International Trade Statistics Yearbook. United Nations Statistical Office. United Nations Publications. • Annual. $135.00. Two volumes.

Main Economic Indicators. OECD Publication and Information Center. • Monthly. $450.00 per year. "The essential source of timely statistics for OECD member countries." Includes a wide variety of business, economic, and industrial data for the 29 OECD nations.

Manufacturers' Shipments, Inventories, and Orders. Available from U. S. Government Printing Office. • Monthly. $79.00 per year. Issued by Bureau of the Census, U. S. Department of Commerce. Includes monthly *Advance Report on Durable Goods.*

Provides data on production, value, shipments, and consumption for a wide variety of manufactured products. (Current Industrial Reports, M3-1.).

Metropolitan Life Insurance Co. Statistical Bulletin SB. Metropolitan Life Insurance Co. • Quarterly. Individuals, $50.00 per year. Covers a wide range of social, economic and demographic health concerns.

Statistical Abstract of the United States. Available from U. S. Government Printing Office. • Annual. $51.00. Issued by the U. S. Bureau of the Census.

Survey of Current Business. Available from U. S. Government Printing Office. • Monthly. $63.00 per year. Issued by Bureau of Economic Analysis, U. S. Department of Commerce. Presents a wide variety of business and economic data.

World Consumer Income and Expenditure Patterns. Available from Gale Cengage Learning. • Annual. $1,090.00. Two volumes. Published by Euromonitor. Provides data for countries worldwide on consumer income, earning power, spending patterns, and savings. Expenditures are detailed for product or service categories.

TRADE/PROFESSIONAL ASSOCIATIONS

American Statistical Association. 732 N Washington St., Alexandria, VA 22314-1943. Phone: 888-231-3473 or (703)684-1221 Fax: (703)684-2037 E-mail: asainfo@amstat.org • URL: http://www.amstat.org • Professional society of persons interested in the theory, methodology, and application of statistics to all fields of human endeavor.

Econometric Society. New York University, Department of Economics, 19 W 4th St., 6th Fl., New York, NY 10012. Phone: (212)998-3820 Fax: (212)995-4487 E-mail: sashi@econometricsociety.org • URL: http://www.econometricsociety.org • Economists, statisticians, and mathematicians. Promotes studies that are directed towards unification of the theoretical and empirical approaches to economic problems and advancement of economic theory in its relation to statistics and mathematics.

International Statistical Institute. Prinses Beatrixlaan 428, PO Box 950, NL-2270 AZ Voorburg, Netherlands. Phone: 31 70 3860025 or 31 70 3375737 Fax: 31 70 3860025 E-mail: isi@cbs.nl • URL: http://isi.cbs.nl • Persons from more than 130 countries who have contributed to the development or application of statistical methods or to the administration of statistical services. Works toward the development and improvement of statistical methods and their application worldwide. Sponsors statistics course at the ISEC in Calcutta, India. Compiles and publishes information pertaining to international statistics; has established an abstracting service of statistical publications.

OTHER SOURCES

Business Rankings Annual. Gale Cengage Learning. • Annual. $325.00. Two volumes. Compiled by the Business Library Staff of the Brooklyn Public Library. This is a guide to lists and rankings appearing in major business publications. The top ten names are listed in each case.

BUSINESS STRATEGY

See also: PLANNING

GENERAL WORKS

The Art of the Long View: Planning for the Future in an Uncertain World. Peter Schwartz. Doubleday. • 1996. $30.95. Covers strategic planning for corporations and smaller firms. Includes "The World in 2005: Three Scenarios.".

Business Strategy and Policy. McGraw-Hill. • 1999. $45.00.

Cases in Strategic Management. Thomas J. Wheelen and J. David Hunger. Addison-Wesley. • 1996. Fifth edition. Price on application.

Cases in Strategic Marketing: An Integrated Approach. Strickland. McGraw-Hill. • 2000. $41. 25. 12th edition.

Designing Organizations to Create Value: From Strategy to Structure. Jerry Zimmerman and others. McGraw-Hill. • 2002. $29.95. Describes a process for "identifying the critical aspects of an organization's internal structure" and making administrative enhancements.

Developing Business Strategies. David A. Aaker. John Wiley and Sons, Inc. • 2001. $39.95. Sixth edition.

The Leader of the Future: New Essays by World-Class Leaders and Thinkers. Frances Hesselbein. John Wiley and Sons, Inc. • 2000. $16.50. Contains articles on leadership by "executives, consultants, and commentators." (Management Series).

Marketing Strategy. Orville C. Walker and others. McGraw Hill. • 1998. $73.13. Third edition.

Strategic Management. Fred R. David. Prentice Hall PTR. • 2002. $80.00. Ninth edition.

Strategic Management: Formulation, Implementation, and Control. John A. Pearce and Richard B. Robinson. McGraw-Hill. • 2002. Eighth edition. Price on application.

Strategic Marketing. David W. Cravens and Nigel Percy. McGraw-Hill. • 2002. $110.00. Seventh edition. (Marketing Series).

Strategic Planning Plus: An Organizational Guide. Roger Kaufman. Sage Publications, Inc. • 1992. $80.95.

Strategy-Specific Decision Making: A Guide for Executing Competitive Strategy. William G. Forgang. M. E. Sharpe, Inc. • 2004. $72.95. Includes a bibliography and case studies in the area of competitive strategy.

ABSTRACTS AND INDEXES

Business Periodicals Index. H. W. Wilson Co. • 11 times a year. Quarterly and annual cumulations. Price varies.

DIRECTORIES

Business Organizations, Agencies, and Publications Directory. Gale Cengage Learning. • 2003. $480.00. 15th edition. Over 40,000 entries describing 39 types of business information sources. Classified by type of organization, publication, or serviceIncludes state, national, and international agencies and organizations. Master index to names and keywords. Also includes e-mail addresses and web site URL's.

ENCYCLOPEDIAS AND DICTIONARIES

Blackwell Encyclopedic Dictionary of Strategic Management. Derek F. Channon, editor. Blackwell Publishing. • 1997. $128.95. The editor is associated with Imperial College, London. Contains definitions of key terms combined with longer articles written by various U. S. and foreign business educators. Includes bibliographies and index. (Blackwell Encyclopedia of Management Series.).

Dictionary of Strategy: Strategic Management A-Z. Louise Kelly. Sage Publications, Inc. • 2004. $69. 95. Defines more than 550 terms relating to strategy in management.

Field Guide to Strategy: A Glossary to Essential Tools and Concepts for Today's Manager. McGraw-Hill. • 1993. $29.95. Defines fundamental terms.

HANDBOOKS AND MANUALS

Manager's Guide to Financial Statement Analysis. Stephen F. Jablonsky and Noah P. Barsky. John Wiley and Sons, Inc. • 2001. $49.95. Second edition. The two main sections are "Financial Statements and Business Strategy" and "Market Valuation and Business Strategy.".

Strategic Planning: A Practical Guide. Peter J. Rea and Harold Kerzner. John Wiley and Sons, Inc. • 1997. $90.00. Covers strategic planning for

manufacturing firms, small businesses, and large corporations. (Industrial Engineering Series).

INTERNET DATABASES

Intelligence Data. Thomson Financial. Phone: 800-654-0393 Fax: (617)824-2477 • URL: http://www.intelligencedata.com • Fee-based Web site provides a wide variety of information relating to competitive intelligence, strategic planning, business development, mergers, acquisitions, sales, and marketing. "Intelliscope" feature offers searching of other Thomson units, such as Investext, MarkIntel, InSite 2, and Industry Insider. Weekly updating.

ONLINE DATABASES

Business and Management Practices. Gale Cengage Learning. • Provides fulltext of management articles appearing in more than 350 relevant publications. Emphasis is on "the processes, methods, and strategies of managing a business." Time span is 1995 to date. Inquire as to online cost and availability. (Also available in a CD-ROM version.).

Wilson Business Abstracts Online. H. W. Wilson Co. • Indexes and abstracts 600 major business periodicals, plus the *Wall Street Journal* and the business section of the *New York Times.* Indexing is from 1982, abstracting from 1990, with the two newspapers included from 1993. Updated weekly. Inquire as to online cost and availability. (*Business Periodicals Index* without abstracts is also available online.).

PERIODICALS AND NEWSLETTERS

Daily Report for Executives. BNA, Inc. • Daily. $7,698.00 per year. Newsletter. Covers legal, regulatory, economic, and tax developments affecting corporations.

Journal of Business Strategy. Thomson Media. • Bimonthly. $98.00 per year. Covers managememt planning techniques and corporate strategy for senior executives.

Journal of Economics and Management Strategy. MIT Press. • Quarterly. Institutions, $195.00 per year. Includes print and online editions. Covers "theoretical and empirical industrial organization, applied game theory, and management strategy.".

Leader to Leader. Peter F. Drucker Foundation for Nonprofit Management. Jossey-Bass. • Quarterly. Institutions, $199.00 per year. Contains articles on "management, leadership, and strategy" written by "leading executives, thinkers, and consultants." Covers both business and nonprofit issues.

The Manager's Intelligence Report: An Insider's Fast Track to Better Management. Lawrence Ragan Communications, Inc. • Monthly. $129.00 per year. Newsletter on various aspects of management, including strategy, employee morale, and time management.

Strategic Management Journal. John Wiley and Sons, Inc., Journals. • Monthly. Individuals, $315.00 per year; institutions, $1,325.00 per year. Original refereed material concerned with all aspects of strategic management. Devoted to the development and improvement of both theory and practice. Provides international coverage.

Strategy and Business. • Quarterly. $38.00 per year.

RESEARCH CENTERS AND INSTITUTES

Hubert H. Humphrey Institute of Public Affairs. University of Minnesota, 300 HHH Center, 301 19th Ave., S., Minneapolis, MN 55455. Phone: (612)625-0669 Fax: (612)626-6351 E-mail: jbrandl@hhh.umn.edu • URL: http://www.hhh.umn.edu/centers • Studies strategic management in both the private and the public sectors.

Strategic Planning Institute. 1030 Massachusetts Ave., Newton Center, MA 01238-5388. Phone: (617)491-9200 Fax: (617)491-1634 • Conducts research in business information and strategy.

BUSINESS TO BUSINESS MARKETING

See: INDUSTRIAL MARKETING

BUSINESS TRAVEL

See also: AIR TRAVEL; TRAVEL INDUSTRY

GENERAL WORKS

Safe Trip Abroad. Available from U. S. Government Printing Office. • 2002. $2.50. Issued by the Bureau of Consular Affairs, U. S. State Department (http://www.state.gov). Provides practical advice for international travel.

Unofficial Business Traveler's Pocket Guide: 249 Tips Even the Best Business Travelers May Not Know. Christopher J. McGinnis. McGraw-Hill. • 1998. $10.95. Arranged by subject categories, such as airports, frequent traveler programs, eating, and staying well.

ABSTRACTS AND INDEXES

Business Periodicals Index. H. W. Wilson Co. • 11 times a year. Quarterly and annual cumulations. Price varies.

Leisure, Recreation, and Tourism Abstracts. Available from CABI Publishing North America. • Quarterly. Members, $280.00 per year; Institutions, $610.00 per year. Includes single site internet access. Published in England by CABI Publishing. Provides coverage of the worldwide literature of travel, recreation, sports, and the hospitality industry. Emphasis is on research.

Readers' Guide to Periodical Literature. H. W. Wilson Co. • Monthly. $345.00 per year. Includes annual *Cumulation.* Indexes about 250 periodicals of general interest.

BIBLIOGRAPHIES

Travel and Tourism. Available from U. S. Government Printing Office. • Annual. Free. Issued by the Superintendent of Documents. A list of government publications on the travel industry and tourism. Formerly *Mass Transit, Travel and Tourism.* (Subject Bibliography No. 302.).

DIRECTORIES

City Profiles USA: A Traveler's Guide to Major U. S. and Canadian Cities. Darren L. Smith, editor. Omnigraphics, Inc. • 2003. $130.00. A directory of information useful to business and other travelers in major cities. Includes services, facilities, attractions, and events. Arranged by city.

Corporate Travel's Blackbook. CMP Books. • Annual. $15.00. Included with subscription to *Corporate Travel.* Gives sources of corporate travel packages. Formerly *Corporate Travel-Directory.*

Internet Resources and Services for International Business: A Global Guide. Lewis-Guodo Liu. Greenwood Publishing Group, Inc. • 1998. $62.95. Describes more than 2,500 business-related Web sites from 176 countries. Includes five major categories: general information, economics, business and trade, business travel, and contacts. Indexed by Web site name, country, and subject.

OAG Business Travel Planner: North America. OAG. • Quarterly. $142.00 per year. $55.00 per issue. Arranged according to more than 14,500 destinations in the U. S., Canada, Mexico, and the Caribbean. Lists more than 31,500 hotels, with AAA ratings where available. Provides information on airports, ground transportation, coming events, and climate. Includes maps.

OAG Travel Planner: Europe Worldwide. OAG. • Quarterly. $149.00 per year. Arranged according to more than 13,850 destinations in Europe. Lists more than 14,700 hotels, with information on airports,

ground transportation, coming events, and climate.

OAG Travel Planner Hotel and Motel Redbook: Asia Pacific. OAG. • Quarterly. $130.00 per year. Arranged according to more than 5,000 destinations throughout Asia and the Pacific. Lists about 3,000 hotels, with information on airports, ground transportation, coming events, and climate.

HANDBOOKS AND MANUALS

CCH Guide to Car, Travel, Entertainment, and Home Office Deductions. CCH, Inc. • Annual. $45.00. Explains how to claim maximum tax deductions for common business expenses. Includes automobile depreciation tables, lease value tables, worksheets, and examples of filled-in tax forms.

Health Information for International Travel. U.S. Dept. of Health and Human Services, Centers for Disease Control and Prefabricated. • Annual. $20.00. Produced by the Centers for Disease Control and Prevention (CDC). Primarily edited for "healthcare providers who administer pre- and post-travel counseling and care." Also serves as a reference for airlines, cruise lines, and the travel industry in general. Covers such items as injuries during travel, motion sickness, disabilities, vaccines, insect repellents, and travel with children. Sometimes known as "The Yellow Book.".

Health Information for International Travel. Available from U. S. Government Printing Office. • Annual. Issued by Centers for Disease Control, U. S. Department of Health and Human Services. Discusses potential health risks of international travel and specifies vaccinations required by different countries.

ONLINE DATABASES

Readers' Guide Abstracts Online. H. W. Wilson Co. • Indexes and abstracts general interest periodicals, 1983 to date. Weekly updates. Inquire as to online cost and availability.

Wilson Business Abstracts Online. H. W. Wilson Co. • Indexes and abstracts 600 major business periodicals, plus the *Wall Street Journal* and the business section of the *New York Times.* Indexing is from 1982, abstracting from 1990, with the two newspapers included from 1993. Updated weekly. Inquire as to online cost and availability. (*Business Periodicals Index* without abstracts is also available online.).

PERIODICALS AND NEWSLETTERS

Business Travel News: News and Ideas for Business Travel Management. VNU Business Media. • 29 times a year. $119.00 per year. Includes annual directory of travel sources. Formerly *Corporate Travel.*

Frequent Flyer: For Business People Who Must Travel. OAG Worldwide. • Monthly. $89.00 per year to individuals. Also known as *OAG Frequent Flyer.* Edited for business travelers. Contains news of frequent flyer programs, airport developments, airline services, and business travel trends. Available only with *OAG Flight Guide.*

Front Row Advisor: Business and First Class Air Travel and the Alluring World of Free Upgrades. Diversified Specialties, Inc. • Bimonthly. $145.00 per year. Newsletter. Contains information on opportunities provided by airlines to upgrade coach seats to business class, including frequent flyer upgrades.

Inside Flyer. • Monthly. $36.00 per year. Newsletter. Provides information relating to frequent flyer awards and air travel.

Newsline: Research News from the U. S. Travel Data Center. U.S. National Research Council. • Monthly. $55.00 per year. Newsletter. Covers trends in the U. S. travel industry.

Runzheimer Reports on Travel Management. Runzheimer International. • Monthly. $295.00 per year. Newsletter on the control of business travel costs.

Summary of Health Information for International Travel. U. S. Department of Health and Human Services. • Biweekly. Formerly *Weekly Summary of Health Information for International Travel.*

Travel Manager's Executive Briefing. American Business Publishing. • Description: Follows developments in the field of travel and expense cost control. Recurring features include news of discounted air fares, car rentals, and hotel bills; case histories of other companies cutting costs; travel alternatives, phone savings, planning for meetings; and trends in government legislation affecting business travel costs.

Travel Weekly. Northstar Travel Media, LLC. • Weekly. $266.00 per year. Includes cruise guides, a weekly "Business Travel Update," and special issues devoted to particular destinations and areas. Edited mainly for travel agents and tour operators.

STATISTICS SOURCES

Economic Review of Travel in America. Travel Industry Association of America. • Annual. Members, $75.00; non-members, $125.00. Presents a statistical summary of travel in the U.S., including travel expenditures, travel industry employment, tax data, international visitors, etc.

Outlook for Travel and Tourism. Travel Industry Association of America. • Annual. Members, $100.00; non-members, $175.00. Contains forecasts of the performance of the U. S. travel industry, including air travel, business travel, recreation (attractions), and accomodations.

Summary of International Travel to the United States. International Trade Administration, Tourism Industries. U.S. Dept. of Commerce. • Monthly. Quarterly and annual versions available. Provides statistics on air travel to the U.S. from each of 90 countries. Formerly *Summary and Analysis of International Travel to the United States.*

Survey of Business Travelers. Travel Industry Association of America. • Biennial. Members, $100.00 per year; non-members, $175.00 per year.

TRADE/PROFESSIONAL ASSOCIATIONS

American Hotel and Lodging Association. 1201 New York Ave., N.W., No. 600, Washington, DC 20005-3931. Phone: (202)289-3180 Fax: (202)289-3199 E-mail: info@ahla.com • URL: http://www.ahla.com • Formerly American Hotel and Motel Association.

International Airline Passengers Association. PO Box 700188, Dallas, TX 75370-0188. Phone: 800-821-4272 or (972)404-9980 Fax: (972)233-5348 E-mail: info.dallas@iapa.com • URL: http://www.iapa.com • Persons who are frequent users of airlines. Represents frequent flyers in matters of safety, comfort, convenience, and economy. Conducts semiannual survey regarding travel preferences and opinions in order to present consumers' viewpoints to airlines and government agencies. Provides discounts on hotels and car rentals. Disseminates travel information through magazines and literature. Compiles statistics. **Convention/Meeting:** none.

National Association of Business Travel Agents. 3699 Wilshire Blvd., Ste. 700, Los Angeles, CA 90010. Phone: (213)382-3335 Fax: (213)480-7712 E-mail: sjfaber@earthlink.net • Members specialize in corporate and business travel services.

Society of Incentive and Travel Executives. 401 N Michigan Ave., Chicago, IL 60611. Phone: (312)321-5148 Fax: (312)527-6783 • URL: http://www.site-intl.org • Members include both users and suppliers of incentive travel. Formerly Society of Incentive Travel Executives.

BUSINESS TRENDS

See: BUSINESS CYCLES; BUSINESS FORECASTING

BUSINESS VALUATION

See: VALUATION

BUSINESS WRITING

See: BUSINESS CORRESPONDENCE; REPORT WRITING; WRITERS AND WRITING

BUSINESSMEN IN FICTION

See: BUSINESS IN FICTION

BUTANE

See: PROPANE AND BUTANE GAS INDUSTRY

BUTCHER SHOPS

See: MEAT INDUSTRY

BUTTER INDUSTRY

See: DAIRY INDUSTRY

BUYING

See: PURCHASING

BUYING A BUSINESS

See: BUSINESS ENTERPRISES, SALE OF

BUYING POWER

See: PURCHASING POWER

BUYOUTS, LEVERAGED

See: LEVERAGED BUYOUTS

BY-PRODUCTS

See: WASTE PRODUCTS

C

CABLE ADDRESSES

DIRECTORIES
Thomas Register of American Manufacturers. Thomas Publishing Co., Inc. • Annual. $149.00. 34 volumes. A three-part system offering information on a wide variety of industrial equipment and supplies. Lists more than 151,000 industrial product and services companies.

CABLE TELEVISION INDUSTRY

See also: TELEVISION BROADCASTING INDUSTRY

ABSTRACTS AND INDEXES
Business Periodicals Index. H. W. Wilson Co. • 11 times a year. Quarterly and annual cumulations. Price varies.

BIOGRAPHICAL SOURCES
The Highwaymen: Warriors on the Information Superhighway. Ken Auletta. Harcourt Trade Publications. • 1998. $13.00. Revised expanded edition. Contains critical articles about Ted Turner, Rupert Murdoch, Barry Diller, Michael Eisner, and other key figures in electronic communications, entertainment, and information. (Harvest Book Series).

CD-ROM DATABASES
Hoover's Company Capsules on CD-ROM. Hoover's, Inc. • Quarterly. $399.95 per year (single-user). Provides the CD-ROM version of *Hoover's Handbook of American Business, Hoover's Handbook of Emerging Companies, Hoover's Handbook of World Business, Hoover's Guide to Computer Companies, Hoover's Guide to Media Companies, Hoover's Handbook of Private Companies,* and various regional guides. Includes more than 11,000 profiles of companies.

DIRECTORIES
Bacon's Radio/TV/Cable Directory. Bacon's Information, Inc. • Annual. $325.00. Includes educational and public broadcasters. Covers all United States broadcast media.

Broadcasting and Cable Yearbook. Gale. • Annual. $179.95. Provides information on U. S. and Canadian TV stations, radio stations, cable TV companies, and radio-TV services of various kinds.

Burrelle's Media Directory: Broadcast Media. Burrelle's Information Services. • Annual. $550.00. Approximately 48,000 print and electronic media in North America. Provides detailed descriptions, including programming and key personnel.

Gale Directory of Publications and Broadcast Media. Gale Cengage Learning. • Annual. $770.00. Five volumes. *Interedition Supplement,* Free. A guide to publications and broadcasting stations in the U. S. and Canada, including newspapers, magazines, journals, radio stations, television stations, and cable systems. Geographic arrangement. Volume three consists of statistical tables, maps, subject indexes, and title index.

International Television and Video Almanac: Reference Tool of the Television and Home Video Industries. Quigley Publishing Co., Inc. • Annual. $130.00.

SRDS Interactive Advertising Source. SRDS. • Quarterly. $569.00 per year. Provides descriptive profiles, rates, audience, personnel, etc., for producers of various forms of interactive or multimedia advertising: online/Internet, CD-ROM, interactive TV, interactive cable, interactive telephone, interactive kiosk, and others.

SRDS TV and Cable Source. SRDS. • Quarterly. $525.00 per year. Provides detailed information on U. S. television stations, cable systems, networks, and group owners, with maps and market data. Includes key personnel.

ENCYCLOPEDIAS AND DICTIONARIES
Jones Dictionary of Cable Television Terminology, Including Related Computer andSatellite Definitions. Glenn R. Jones. Jones Twenty-First Century Ltd. • 1988. $14.95. Third edition.

HANDBOOKS AND MANUALS
Cable and Station Coverage Atlas. Warren Publishing Inc. • 1997. $410.00.

ONLINE DATABASES
ERIC. Educational Resources Information Center. • Funded by the U. S. Department of Education, Institute of Education Sciences (formerly Office of Educational Research and Improvement). Provides access to more than one million online records covering education-related journal and report literature, 1966 to date. Updating is monthly. Inquire as to online cost and availability.

Gale Database of Publications and Broadcast Media. Gale Cengage Learning. • An online directory containing detailed information on over 67,000 periodicals, newspapers, broadcast stations, cable systems, directories, and newsletters. Corresponds to the following print sources: *Gale Directory of Publications and Broadcast Media; Directories in Print; City and State Directories in Print; Newsletters in Print.* Semiannual updates. Inquire as to online cost and availability.

Magazine Index. Gale Cengage Learning. • General magazine indexing (popular literature), 1973 to present. Daily updates. Inquire as to online cost and availability.

Management Contents. Gale Cengage Learning. • Covers a wide range of management, financial, marketing, personnel, and administrative topics. About 150 leading business journals are indexed and abstracted from 1974 to date, with monthly updating. Inquire as to online cost and availability.

PROMT: Predicasts Overview of Markets and Technology. Gale Cengage Learning. • Companies, products, applied technologies and markets. U.S. and international literature coverage, 1972 to date. Inquire as to online cost and availability. Provides abstracts from more than 1,600 publications. Weekly updates.

Trade & Industry Database. Gale Cengage Learning. • Provides indexing of business periodicals, January 1981 to date. Daily updates. (Full text articles from some periodicals are available online, 1983 to date. Inquire as to online cost and availability).

PERIODICALS AND NEWSLETTERS
Broadband Technology: Newsletter on Technical Advances, Construction of New Systms and Rebuild of Existing Systems. Paul Kagan Associates, Inc. • Monthly. $895.00 per year. Newsletter. Contains news of cable TV technical advances. Formerly (Cable TV Technology).

Broadcasting and Cable. Reed Business Information. • 51 times a year. $179.00 per year; includes print and online editions. Formerly *Broadcasting.*

Cable TV Investor: Newsletter on Investments in Cable TV Systems and Publicly Held Cable TV Stocks. Paul Kagan Associates, Inc. • Monthly. $995.00 per year.

Cable TV Programming: Newsletter on Programs for Pay Cable TV and Analysis of Basic Cable Networks. Paul Kagan Associates, Inc. • Monthly. $895.00 per year.

Communications Daily: The Authoritative News Service of Electronic Communications. Warren Publishing, Inc. • Daily. $3,006.00 per year. Newsletter. Covers telecommunications, including the telephone industry, broadcasting, cable TV, satellites, data communications, and electronic publishing. Features corporate and industry news.

The Hollywood Reporter. • Daily. $219.00 per year. Covers the latest news in film, TV, cable, multimedia, music, and theatre. Includes box office grosses and entertainment industry financial data.

Multichannel News. Reed Business Information. • 51 times a year. $139.00 per year. Covers the business, programming, market and technology concerns of cable television operators and their suppliers.

Television Digest with Consumer Electronics. Warren Publishing, Inc. • Weekly. $944.00 per year. Newsletter featuring new consumer entertainment products utilizing electronics. Also covers the television broadcasting and cable TV industries, with corporate and industry news.

Television Week. Crain Communications, Inc. • Weekly. $119.00 per year. Formerly *Electronic Media.*

Warren's Cable Regulation Monitor: The Authoritative Weekly News Service Covering Federal, State, and Local Cable Activities and Trends. Warren Publishing, Inc. • Weekly. $594.00 per year. Newsletter. Emphasis is on Federal Communications Commission regulations affecting cable television systems. Covers rate increases made by local systems and cable subscriber complaints filed with the FCC.

STATISTICS SOURCES

Cable Television Revenues. U.S. Federal Communications Commission. • Annual.

Cable TV Facts. Cabletelevision Advertising Bureau. • Annual. $12.00. Provides statistics on cable TV and cable TV advertising in the U. S.

Infrastructure Industries USA. Gale Cengage Learning. • 2001. $260.00. Presents statistics and projections relating to economic activity in a wide variety of natural resource and construction industries.

Standard & Poor's Industry Surveys. Standard & Poor's. • Semiannual. $1,800.00. Two looseleaf volumes. Includes monthly *Supplements.* Provides detailed, individual surveys of 52 major industry groups. Each survey is revised on a semiannual basis. Also includes "Monthly Investment Review" (industry group investment analysis) and monthly "Trends & Projections" (economic analysis).

Television and Cable Factbook. Warren Publishing, Inc. • Annual. $595.00. Three volumes. Weekly updates. Commercial and noncommercial television stations and networks.

U. S. Industry and Trade Outlook. Available from National Technical Information Service. • Annual. $69.95. Produced by the International Trade Administration, U. S. Department of Commerce, in a "public-private" partnership with DRI/McGraw-Hill and Standard & Poor's. Provides basic data, outlook for the current year, and "Long-Term Prospects" (five-year projections) for a wide variety of products and services. Includes high technology industries. Formerly *U. S. Industrial Outlook.*

TRADE/PROFESSIONAL ASSOCIATIONS

Alliance for Community Media. 666 11th St., N.W., Suite 740, Washington, DC 20001. Phone: (202)393-2650 Fax: (202)393-2653 E-mail: acm@alliancecm.org • URL: http://www.alliancecm.org • Formerly National Federation of Local Cable Programmers.

Cabletelevision Advertising Bureau. 830 Third Ave., 2nd Fl., New York, NY 10022. Phone: (212)508-1200 Fax: (212)832-3268 E-mail: info@bta.org • URL: http://www.onetvworld.org • Ad-supported cable networks. Provides marketing and advertising support to members and promotes the use of cable by advertisers and ad agencies locally, regionally, and nationally.

CTAM-Cable and Telecommunications Association for Marketing. 201 N. Union, Suite 440, Alexandria, VA 23314. Phone: (703)549-4200 Fax: (703)684-1167 E-mail: ctam@ctam.com • URL: http://www.ctam.com • Formerly CTAM, The Marketing Society for Cable and Telecommunications Industry.

National Cable and Telecommunications Association. 1724 Massachusetts Ave., N.W., Washington, DC 20036. Phone: (202)775-3550 Fax:

(202)775-3675 E-mail: webmaster@ncta.com • URL: http://www.ncta.com • Affiliated with Motion Picture Association of America. Formerly National Cable Television Association.

National Cable Television Institute. 9697 E Mineral Ave., Centennial, CO 80112. Phone: (866)575-7206 or (303)797-9393 Fax: (303)797-9394 E-mail: info@jonesncti.com • URL: http://www.ncti.com • Provides comprehensive broadband training for the cable television industry. Offers career training resources and courses in areas ranging from customer service procedures to optical fiber system design, installation, and maintenance.

Society of Cable Telecommunications Engineers. 140 Philips Rd., Exton, PA 19341-1318. Phone: 800-542-5040 or (610)363-6888 Fax: (610)363-5898 E-mail: info@scte.org • URL: http://www.scte.org • Formerly Society of Cable Television Engineers.

Women in Cable and Telecommunications. 230 W. Monroe St., Suite 2630, Chicago, IL 60606-4702. Phone: (312)634-2330 Fax: (312)634-2345 E-mail: information@wict.org • URL: http://www.wict.org • Formerly Women in Cable.

OTHER SOURCES

Telecommunications Regulation: Cable, Broadcasting, Satellite, and the Internet. LexisNexis Matthew Bender. • Semiannual. $826.00. Four looseleaf volumes. Covers local, state, and federal regulation, with emphasis on the Telecommunications Act of 1996. Includes regulation of television, telephone, cable, satellite, computer communication, and online services. Formerly *Cable Television Law.*

CAD/CAM

See: COMPUTER-AIDED DESIGN AND MANUFACTURING (CAD/CAM)

CAFETERIAS

See: RESTAURANTS, LUNCHROOMS, ETC.

CAFETERIAS, EMPLOYEE

See: EMPLOYEE LUNCHROOMS AND CAFETERIAS

CALENDAR

See: CHRONOLOGY

CAMCORDERS

See: VIDEO RECORDING INDUSTRY

CAMERA INDUSTRY

See also: PHOTOGRAPHIC INDUSTRY

GENERAL WORKS

A Century of Cameras. Eaton S. Lothrop. Morgan and Morgan, Inc. • 1982. $24.00. Revised edition.

Photography in Focus. Mark Jacobs and Ken Kokrda. McGraw-Hill. • 2001. $48.64. Fifth edition.

DIRECTORIES

Photographer's Market: 2000 Places to Sell Your Photographs. F&W Publications, Inc. • Annual. $24.99. Lists 2,000 companies and publications that purchase original photographs.

Who's Who in Professional Imaging. Professional Photographers of America, Inc. • Annual. $110.00. Lists over 18,000 members. Formerly *Buyers Guide*

to Qualified Photographers.

ENCYCLOPEDIAS AND DICTIONARIES

Focal Encyclopedia of Photography. Leslie Stroebel and Richard D. Zakia, editors. Elsevier. • 1996. $69.95. Third edition.

FINANCIAL RATIOS

Almanac of Business and Industrial Financial Ratios. Leo Troy. Aspen Publishers, Inc. • 2003. $125.95. Includes CD-Rom. Contains financial ratios derived from federal tax returns. Ratios for each of about 200 industries are arranged according to company asset size. (Almanac of Business and Industrial Financial Ratios Series).

Annual Statement Studies. The Risk Management Association. • Annual. Median and quartile financial ratios are given for over 400 kinds of manufacturing, wholesale, retail, construction, and consumer finance establishments. Data is sorted by both asset size and sales volume. Includes a clearly written "Definition of Ratios" and an alphabetical industry index.

Annual Statement Studies: Industry Default Probabilities and Cash Flow Measures. The Risk Management Association. • Annual. $145.00. Serves as a companion volume to the original *Annual Statement Studies.* Gives probability of default estimates on a percentage scale for more than 450 industries. Includes changes in position year-by-year for eight financial statement line items and provides percentage measures of cash flow.

Cost of Doing Business Survey. Photo Marketing Association International. • Biennial. $225.00. Emphasis is on photographic retailing.

HANDBOOKS AND MANUALS

Black and White Photography: A Basic Manual. Henry Horenstein. Little, Brown and Co. • 1983. $24.95. Second revised edition.

PERIODICALS AND NEWSLETTERS

Japan Camera Trade News: Monthly Information on Photographic Products, Optical Instruments and Accessories. K. Eda, editor. Genyosha Publications, Inc. • Monthly. $130.00 per year. Information on the photographic industry worldwide. Text in English.

PRICE SOURCES

Camera. Orion Research Corp. • Annual. $144.00. Quotes retail and wholesale prices of used cameras and equipment. Original list prices and years of manufacture are also shown.

STATISTICS SOURCES

U. S. Industry and Trade Outlook. Available from National Technical Information Service. • Annual. $69.95. Produced by the International Trade Administration, U. S. Department of Commerce, in a "public-private" partnership with DRI/McGraw-Hill and Standard & Poor's. Provides basic data, outlook for the current year, and "Long-Term Prospects" (five-year projections) for a wide variety of products and services. Includes high technology industries. Formerly *U. S. Industrial Outlook.*

United States Census of Manufactures. U.S. Bureau of the Census. • Quinquennial. Results presented in reports, tape, CD-ROM, and Diskette files.

TRADE/PROFESSIONAL ASSOCIATIONS

International Imaging Industry Association. 701 Westchester Ave., Ste. 317W, White Plains, NY 10604-3018. Phone: (914)285-4933 Fax: (914)285-4937 E-mail: i3ainfo@i3a.org • URL: http://www.i3a.org • Develops and promotes the adoption of open industry standards, addressing environmental issues and providing a voice for the industry that will benefit all users. Promotes environment, health and safety concerns; works with various government agencies including the EPA, TSA, and WTO to ensure the best interests of the imaging industry are represented.

National Association of Photo Equipment Technicians. 3000 Picture Place, Jackson, MI 49201. Phone: (517)788-8100 Fax: (517)788-8371 • URL: http://www.pmai.org • Affiliated with Photo Marketing Association International.

Photoimaging Manufacturers and Distributors Association. 109 White Oak Lane, Suite 72F, Old Bridge, NJ 08857. Phone: (732)679-3460 Fax: (732)679-2294 E-mail: bclarkpmda@aol.com • Formerly Photographic Manufacturers and Distributors Association.

OTHER SOURCES

Cameras. Available from MarketResearch.com. • 2002. $3,950.00. Published by Global Industry Analysts. Provides worldwide market research data, including profiles of major camera companies.

CAMPER INDUSTRY

See: RECREATIONAL VEHICLE INDUSTRY

CAMPING INDUSTRY

See: RECREATION INDUSTRY

CANADIAN MARKETS

ABSTRACTS AND INDEXES

Canadian Periodical Index. Gale Cengage Learning. • Monthly. $595.00 per year. Annual cumulation. Indexes more than 400 English and French language periodicals.

F & S Index: International. Gale Cengage Learning. • Monthly. $1,450.00 per year, including quarterly and annual cumulations. Provides annotated citations to marketing, business, financial, and industrial literature. Coverage of international business activity includes trade journals, financial magazines, business newspapers, and special reports. Areas included are Asia, Latin America, Africa, the Middle East, Oceania, and Canada.

ALMANACS AND YEARBOOKS

Canadian Almanac and Directory. Micromedia Proquest. • Annual. $269.00. Contains general information and statistical data relating to Canada and provides information on about 60,000 Canadian agencies, associations, institutions, museums, libraries, etc.

BIOGRAPHICAL SOURCES

Canadian Who's Who. University of Toronto Press. • Annual. $185.00. Provides concise biographical information in English and French on 15,000 prominent Canadians.

Directory of Directors (Canada). Financial Post Datagroup. • Annual. $175.00. Provides brief biographical information on 16,000 directors and key officers of Canadian companies who are also Canadian residents.

Who's Who in Canadian Business. University of Toronto Press. • Annual. $179.95. Contains brief biographies of 5,200 individuals prominent in Canadian business.

CD-ROM DATABASES

Canada Year Book on CD-ROM. Statistics Canada, Publications Division. • Annual. $90.00. CD-ROM in English and French provides basic statistical and other information on Canada. Contains multimedia features and search capabilities.

CanCorp Plus Canadian Financial Database. Micromedia Ltd. • Monthly. $3,600.00 per year. Also available quarterly at $2,975.00 per year. Provides comprehensive information on CD-ROM for more than 11,000 public and private Canadian corporations. Emphasis is on detailed financial data for up to seven years.

CPI.Q: The Canadian Periodical Index Full-Text on CD-ROM. Gale Cengage Learning. • Bimonthly. Provides CD-ROM citations from 1988 to date for more than 400 English and French language periodicals. Contains full-text coverage from 1995 to date for 150 periodicals.

Hoover's Company Capsules on CD-ROM. Hoover's, Inc. • Quarterly. $399.95 per year (single-user). Provides the CD-ROM version of *Hoover's Handbook of American Business, Hoover's Handbook of Emerging Companies, Hoover's Handbook of World Business, Hoover's Guide to Computer Companies, Hoover's Guide to Media Companies, Hoover's Handbook of Private Companies,* and various regional guides. Includes more than 11,000 profiles of companies.

World Database of Consumer Brands and Their Owners on CD-ROM. Gale Cengage Learning. • Annual. $3,190.00. Produced by Euromonitor. Provides detailed information on CD-ROM for about 10,000 companies and 80,000 brands around the world. Covers 1,000 product sectors.

World Marketing Forecasts on CD-ROM. Gale Cengage Learning. • Annual. $2,500.00. Produced by Euromonitor. Provides detailed forecast data for the years to 2012 on CD-ROM for 54 countries in all parts of the world. Covers a wide range of social, demographic, economic, and market factors. Includes specific forecasts for many kinds of consumer products.

DIRECTORIES

Associations Canada: The Directory of Associations in Canada. Micromedia. • Annual. $299.00. Provides detailed information in English and French on 20,000 active Canadian associations. Includes subject, keyword, personal name, and other indexes. Formerly *Directory of Associations in Canada.*

Canadian Directory of Shopping Centres. Rogers Media Publishing. • Annual. $400.00. Two volumes (Eastern Canada and Western Canada). Describes about 2,200 shopping centers and malls, including those under development.

Canadian Trade Index. MacRae's Blue Book. • Covers: in one volumes, over 30,000 manufacturers in Canada. Also includes distributors, service companies, and exporters. Entries include: Company name, address, names and titles of key personnel, products, trademarks, number of employees, annual sales, non-manufacturing locations, subsidiaries and associates, foreign representatives, headquarters phone, ISO information, export regions.

CARD The Media Information Network. Rogers Media Publishing. • Covers: Radio and television stations and networks; daily and weekend newspapers; consumer, farm, and business publications; advertising agencies and international media representatives; advertising, marketing, and media associations; and transportation and out-of-home advertising. Entries include: For publications--Title, company name, address, phone, frequency, names and titles of key personnel, advertising rates, discounts, mechanical requirements, copy regulations, circulation, closing and publication dates. For broadcasting stations--Call letters, name of owning company, address, phone, name of firm or individual representing station for advertising, special features, format, facilities, affiliations, rates, participation programs. For agencies and associations--Name, address, phone, personnel.

Directory of Canadian Trademarks. Thomson & Thomson. • Annual. Price on application. Provides owner, registration, and classification information for Canadian trademarks registered with the Canadian Intellectual Property Office (CIPO).

Directory of Retail Chains in Canada. Rogers Media Publishing. • Annual. $340.00. Provides detailed information on approximately 1,600 retail chains of all sizes in Canada.

Dun and Bradstreet Canadian Key Business Directory. Dun and Bradstreet Corp. • Annual. Corporations, $495.00; libraries, $435.00. Published by Dun & Bradstreet Canada Ltd. Provides information in English and French on 20,000 leading Canadian business firms.

FP Survey Industrials (Canada). Globe Information Services. • Annual. $49.95. Provides information on more than 3,000 Canadian manufacturing and service companies.

FP Survey of Industrials (Canadian Firms). Financial Post Datagroup. • Annual. $124.95. Contains detailed information on more than 2,700 publicly owned Canadian manufacturing, retailing, and service corporations. Includes the "Financial Post 500," a ranking of the largest Canadian companies.

Frasers Canadian Trade Directory. Rogers Media Publishing. • Covers: over 42,000 manufacturers and distributors and over 14,000 foreign companies with Canadian representatives. Entries include: Company name, address. Products are included for manufacturers; name and address of Canadian representative is included for foreign firms.

Global Market Share Planner. Euromonitor International. • 2003. $5,900.00. Six volumes. Second edition. Provides detailed profiles and market share rankings of major consumer product companies in North America, Latin America, Europe, South Africa, and the Asia-Pacific region. Covers firms operating in key consumer markets: beverages, food products, household products, and personal care items. (Volumes are available individually.).

Hoover's Handbook of World Business: Profiles of Major European, Asian, Latin American, and Canadian Companies. Hoover's, Inc. • Annual. $165.00. Contains detailed profiles for approximately 300 large foreign companies. Includes indexes by industry, location, executive name, company name, and brand name.

International Media Guide: Business/Professional Publications: The Americas. SRDS. • Annual. $300.00. Describes trade journals from North, South, and Central America, with advertising rates and circulation data.

Major Market Share Companies: The Americas. Available from Gale Cengage Learning. • 2003. $990.00. Second edition. Published by Euromonitor. Provides consumer market share data and rankings for multinational and regional companies. Covers leading firms in the U.S., Canada, Mexico, Brazil, Argentina, Venezuela, and Chile.

INTERNET DATABASES

CANOE: Canadian Online Explorer. Canoe Limited Partnership. Phone: (416)947-2154 Fax: (416)947-2209 • URL: http://www.canoe.ca • Web site provides a wide variety of Canadian news and information, including business and financial data. Includes "Money," "Your Investment," "Technology," and "Stock Quotes." Allows keyword searching, with links to many other sites. Daily updating. Fees: Free.

The Financial Post (Web site). National Post Online. Phone: 800-805-1184 or (244)383-2300 Fax: (416)383-2443 • URL: http://www.nationalpost.com/financialpost/ • Provides a broad range of Canadian business news online, with daily updates. Includes news, opinion, and special reports, as well as "Investing," "Money Rates," "Market Watch," and "Daily Mutual Funds." Allows advanced searching (Boolean operators), with links to various other sites. Fees: Free.

Globeandmail.com: Canada's Best Source for News. Bell Globemedia Publishing, Inc. Phone: 800-

268-9128 or (416)585-5000 Fax: (416)585-5249 • URL: http://www.globeandmail.ca • Web site provides access to selected sections of *The Globe and Mail: Canada's National Newspaper*. Includes current news, national issues, career information, "Report on Business," and other topics. Keyword searching is offered for "a seven-day archive of the portion of the *Globe and Mail* that we publish online" (refers to the Web site). Daily updates. Fees: free.

Statistics Canada!. Statistics Canada. Phone: 800-263-1136 or (613)951-8116 Fax: 877-287-4369 • URL: http://www.statcan.ca • Web site in English and French provides basic statistical information relating to economic and social conditions in Canada: "The Land," "The People," "The Economy," "The State." Includes daily news, latest indicators, products and services, and links to other sites. Keyword searching is provided. Fees: Free.

TAXNET.PRO. Carswell. Phone: 800-387-5164 or (416)609-3800 Fax: (416)298-5082 E-mail: orders@carswell.com • URL: http://www.carswell.com/taxnetpro.asp • Fee-based Web site provides complete coverage of Canadian tax law and regulation, including income tax, provincial taxes, accounting, and payrolls. Daily updates. Base price varies according to product.

ONLINE DATABASES

Canada NewsWire. Canada NewsWire Ltd. • Provides the complete online text of currrent press releases from more than 5,000 Canadian companies, institutions, and government agencies, including stock exchanges and the Ontario Securities Commission. Emphasis is on mining, petroleum, technology, and pharmaceuticals. Time span is 1996 to date, with daily updates. Inquire as to online cost and availability.

Canadian Business and Current Affairs Fulltext. Micromedia Ltd. • Provides full-text of eight Canadian daily newspapers and more than 330 Canadian business magazines and trade journals. Indexing is 1982 to date, with selected full text from 1993. Updates are twice a month. Inquire as to online cost and availability.

CANSIM Time Series Database. Statistics Canada, Statistical Reference Center. • CANSIM is the Canadian Socio-Economic Information Management System. Contains more than 700,000 statistical time series relating to Canadian business, industry, trade, economics, finance, labor, health, welfare, and demographics. Time period is mainly 1946 to date, with daily updating. Inquire as to online cost and availability.

The Globe and Mail Online. The Globe and Mail Co. • Contains full text of more than 1.1 million news stories and articles that have appeared daily in *The Globe and Mail: Canada's National Newspaper*, including "Report on Business." Time span is 1977 to date. Daily updates of the complete newspaper are provided. Inquire as to online cost and availability.

PERIODICALS AND NEWSLETTERS

Canadian Business. Canadian Business Media. • Biweekly. $64.95 per year. Edited for corporate managers and executives, this is a major periodical in Canada covering a variety of business, economic, and financial topics. Emphasis is on the top 500 Canadian corporations.

The Canadian Employer. MPL Communications Inc. • Description: Provides information regarding Canadian employment laws.

The Canadian Taxpayer. Thomson Carswell • Description: Provides "analyses of Canadian tax trends, political appointments, tax policies and landmark cases.".

The Financial Post: Canadian's Business Voice. Financial Post Datagroup. • Daily. $200.00 per year. Provides Canadian business, economic, financial,

and investment news. Features extensive price quotes from all major Canadian markets: stocks, bonds, mutual funds, commodities, and currencies. Supplement available: *Financial Post 500*. Includes annual supplement.

Globe and Mail Report on Business. Globe and Mail Publishing. • Daily. Controlled circulation. Provides general coverage of business activity in Canada, with emphasis on the economy, foreign trade, technology, and personal finance.

Marketing Magazine: Canada's Weekly Newspaper for Marketing, Advertising and Sales Executives. Rogers Media Publishing. • Weekly. $95.00 per year. "Canada's national weekly publication dedicated to the businesses of marketing, advertising, and media." Includes annual Marketing Awards, quarterly Digital Marketing (emerging technology), Promo Marketing, and PR Quarterly (special issues on public relations).

RESEARCH CENTERS AND INSTITUTES

Canadian-American Center. University of Maine - Canada House, 154 College Ave., Orono, ME 04473. Phone: (207)581-4220 Fax: (207)581-4223 E-mail: hornsby@maine.edu • URL: http://www.umaine.edu/canam/ • Research areas include Canadian-American business, economics, and trade.

Canadian Studies Program. University of Vermont, 589 Main St., Burlington, VT 05401. Phone: (802)656-3541 Fax: (802)656-8518 E-mail: canada@zoo.uvm.edu • URL: http://www.uvm.edu/~canada • Research areas include Canadian corporate strategies, telecommunications, and natural resources.

Center for Canadian-American Studies. Western Washington University, Canada House High St., Ste. 516, Bellingham, WA 98225-9110. Phone: (360)650-3728 Fax: (360)650-3995 E-mail: canam@cc.wwu.edu • URL: http://www.wwu.edu/~ • Research areas include Canadian business and economics.

Conference Board of Canada. 255 Smyth Rd., Ottawa, ON, Canada K1H 8M7. Phone: (613)526-3280 Fax: (613)526-4857 E-mail: contactcboc@conferenceboard.ca • URL: http://www.conferenceboard.ca • Research areas include economics, finance, international business, and consumer buying intentions.

Statistical Reference Centre. Holland Ave., Room 1500, Ottawa, ON, Canada K1A OT6. Phone: 800-263-1136 or (613)951-8116 Fax: 877-287-4369 E-mail: infostats@statcan.ca • URL: http://www.statcan.ca • Issues compilations of census data and other facts relating to Canadian business, finance, industry, economics, and society in general. Statistics Canada is the country's national statistical agency, required to collect data according to the Statistics Act.

STATISTICS SOURCES

Canada Year Book. Statistics Canada, Operations and Integration Div., Circulation Management. • 2001. $75.00. Contains "fifteen chapters on the social, economic, demographic and cultural life of Canada," with more than 260 tables, charts and graphs.

Consumer International. Available from Gale Cengage Learning. • Annual. $1,290.00. Published by Euromonitor. Contains extensive consumer market, economic, and demographic data for 25 major, non-European countries, including the U. S. and Canada. Includes consumer market size (volume and value) for 150 product types in 14 categories (food, clothing, automobiles, cosmetics, appliances, etc.).

Financial Post Markets Canadian Demographics: Complete Demographics for Canadian Urban Markets. Financial Post Datagroup. • Annual. $135.00 Provides demographic and economic profiles of Canadian urban consumer regions with populations of 10,000 or more. Includes current data

and projections for population, retail sales, personal income, and other market characteristics. CD-ROM available. Formerly *Canadian Markets*.

Handbook of North American Industry: NAFTA and the Economies of its Member Nations. John E. Cremeans. Bernan Press. • 1999. $115.00. Second revised edition. Provides detailed industry statistics for the U.S., Canada, and Mexico.

International Marketing Forecasts. Available from Gale Cengage Learning. • Annual. $1,250.00. Published by Euromonitor. Contains demographic, economic, and market forecasts to the year 2013 for major, non-European countries, including the U. S. and Canada. Forecasts include market-size data for 15 consumer product sectors, such as food, clothing, and automobiles.

Market Research Handbook. Statistics Reference Centre (National Capital Region). • Annual. $125.00. Contains a wide variety of demographic and other data relevant to Canadian markets.

Provincial Outlook. Conference Board of Canada. • Quarterly. Free to members; non-members, $2,500.00 per year. Contains detailed forecasts of economic conditions in each of the Canadian provinces.

TRADE/PROFESSIONAL ASSOCIATIONS

Canada-United States Business Association. 600 Renaissance Ctr., Ste. 1100, Ste. 1100, Detroit, MI 48243. Phone: (313)446-7013 Fax: (313)567-2164 E-mail: cheryl.clark@international.gc.ca • URL: http://www.dfait-maeci.gc.ca/can-am/detroit/home_page/cusba-en.asp • Consists of supporters of business such as labor, banking, consulting, government, and academia. Promotes stronger business and trading lineages between the U.S. and Canada by providing a forum to exchange information and ideas and to build relationships. Conducts educational programs; maintains speakers' bureau, panels, and special events.

Canadian-American Business Council. 1900 K St. NW, Washington, DC 20006. Phone: (202)496-7430 Fax: (202)496-7756 E-mail: sgreenwood@mckennalong.com • URL: http://www.canambusco.org • Individuals, corporations, institutions, and organizations with an interest in trade between the United States and Canada. Promotes free trade. Gathers and disseminates information; maintains speakers' bureau.

Canadian Manufacturers and Exporters. 1 Nicholas St., Ste. 1500, Ottawa, ON, Canada K1N 7B7. Phone: (613)238-8888 Fax: (613)563-9218 E-mail: pbeatty@cme-mec.ca • URL: http://www.the-alliance.com • Formerly Alliance of Manufacturers and Exporters of Canada.

CANDY INDUSTRY

See also: CHOCOLATE INDUSTRY; COCOA INDUSTRY

ABSTRACTS AND INDEXES

Food Science and Technology Abstracts. International Food Information Service Publishing. • Monthly. $1,780.00 per year. Provides worldwide coverage of the literature of food technology and food production.

Foods Adlibra: Key to the World's Food Literature. General Mills, Inc. Foods Adlibra Publications. • Semimonthly. $240.00 per year. Provides journal citations and abstracts to the literature of food technology and packaging.

CD-ROM DATABASES

Food Science and Technology Abstracts [CD-ROM]. Available from SilverPlatter Information, Inc. • Quarterly. Produced by International Food Information Service (home page is http://www.ifis.org). Provides worldwide coverage on CD-ROM of the literature of food technology and production. Various types of publications are indexed, with abstracts, including about 1,800 periodicals. Time period is 1969 to date.

DIRECTORIES

Candy Buyers' Directory. Manufacturing Confectioner Publishing Co. • Covers: Wholesale confectionery manufacturers and candy importers. Entries include: Company name, address, phone, name of sales manager (for manufacturers and importers), and products and brand names manufactured or distributed. Broker and importer listings also show territory covered and countries from which imported.

Candy Industry Buyer's Guide. Stagnito Communications Inc. • Publication includes: List of approximately 682 suppliers of ingredients, equipment, and services to the candy industry. Entries include: Company name, address, phone.

Food Chemicals News Directory. Food Chemical News. CRC Press LLC. • Semiannual. $497.00. Over 2,000 subsidiaries belonging to nearly 250 corporate parents plus an additional 3,000 independent processors. Formerly *Hereld's 1,500.*

Major Food and Drink Companies of the World. Available from Gale Cengage Learning. • Annual. $880.00. Two volumes. Published by Graham & Whiteside. Contains profiles and trade names for more than 9,800 important food and beverage companies in various countries. In addition to foods, includes both alcoholic and nonalcoholic drink products.

Thomas Food and Beverage Market Place. Grey House Publishing. • 2004. $495.00. Three volumes. Contains more than 40,000 entries covering food companies, beverages, food equipment, warehouse companies, food brokers, wholesalers, importers, and exporters. Formerly *Thomas Food Industry Register.*

FINANCIAL RATIOS

Annual Statement Studies. The Risk Management Association. • Annual. Median and quartile financial ratios are given for over 400 kinds of manufacturing, wholesale, retail, construction, and consumer finance establishments. Data is sorted by both asset size and sales volume. Includes a clearly written "Definition of Ratios" and an alphabetical industry index.

Annual Statement Studies: Industry Default Probabilities and Cash Flow Measures. The Risk Management Association. • Annual. $145.00. Serves as a companion volume to the original *Annual Statement Studies.* Gives probability of default estimates on a percentage scale for more than 450 industries. Includes changes in position year-by-year for eight financial statement line items and provides percentage measures of cash flow.

INTERNET DATABASES

Manufacturing Profiles. U. S. Bureau of the Census. Phone: (301)763-4636 E-mail: webmaster@census. gov • URL: http://www.census.gov/prod/www/abs/mfg-prof.html • The Census Bureau makes available free on PDF (Portable Document Format) an annual consolidation of the entire Current Industrial Report series, presenting "all the data compiled." Contains statistics on production, shipments, inventories, consumption, exports, imports, and orders for a wide variety of manufactured products.

ONLINE DATABASES

F & S Index. Gale Cengage Learning. • Contains about four million citations to worldwide business, financial, and industrial or consumer product literature appearing from 1972 to date. Weekly updates. Inquire as to online cost and availability.

Food Science and Technology Abstracts [online]. IFIS North American Desk. • Produced by

International Food Information Service. Provides about 500,000 online citations, with abstracts, to the international literature of food science, technology, commodities, engineering, and processing. Approximately 2,000 periodicals are covered. Time period is 1969 to date, with monthly updates. Inquire as to online cost and availability.

FOODS ADLIBRA. General Mills, Inc. • Contains online citations, with abstracts, to the technical and business literature of food processing and packaging. New products and new ingredients are featured. Covers about 250 trade journals and 500 research journals from 1974 to date, with monthly updates. Inquire as to online cost and availability.

PERIODICALS AND NEWSLETTERS

Candy Industry: The Global Magazine of Chocolate and Confectionery. Stagnito Publishing Co. • Monthly. Free to qualified personnel; othres, $70.10 per year.

Confectioner: The Magazine. Stagnito Communcations, Inc. • Bimonthly. $70.17 per year. Covers a wide variety of topics relating to the distribution and retailing of candy and snacks.

Distribution Channels: The Magazine for Candy, Tobacco, Grocery and General Merchandise Distributors. American Wholesalers Marketers Association. • 10 times a year. $36.00 per year. Formerly *Candy Wholesaler.*

Fancy Food and Culinary Products. Talcott Communications Corp. • Monthly. $34.00 per year. Emphasizes new specialty food products and the business management aspects of the specialty food and confection industries. Includes special issues on wine, cheese, candy, "upscale" cookware, and gifts. Formerly (*Fancy Foods*).

Gourmet Retailer. VNU Business Media. • Monthly. Free to qualified personnel; others, $75.00 per year. Covers upscale food and housewares, including confectionery items, bakery operations, and coffee.

Manufacturing Confectioner. Manufacturing Confectioner Publishing Co. • Monthly. $35.00 per year. Buying guide available *Purchasing Executives' Number.*

Spotlight. World Affairs Council of Northern California. • Description: Includes one major and 30-40 brief annotated reviews of books on international relations, world politics, and economics. Includes transcripts of council programs.

PRICE SOURCES

PPI Detailed Report. Bureau of Labor Statistics, U.S. Department of Labor. Available from U.S. Government Printing Office. • Monthly. $55.00 per year. Formerly *Producer Price Indexes.*

STATISTICS SOURCES

Annual Survey of Manufactures. Available from U. S. Government Printing Office. • Annual. Prices vary. Issued by the U. S. Census Bureau as an interim update to the *Census of Manufactures.* Includes data on number of manufacturing establishments in various industries, employment, labor costs, value of shipments, capital expenditures, inventories, energy costs, and assets. (See also Census Bureau home page, http://www.census. gov/.)

U. S. Industry and Trade Outlook. Available from National Technical Information Service. • Annual. $69.95. Produced by the International Trade Administration, U. S. Department of Commerce, in a "public-private" partnership with DRI/McGraw-Hill and Standard & Poor's. Provides basic data, outlook for the current year, and "Long-Term Prospects" (five-year projections) for a wide variety of products and services. Includes high technology industries. Formerly *U. S. Industrial Outlook.*

United States Census of Manufactures. U.S. Bureau of the Census. • Quinquennial. Results presented in

reports, tape, CD-ROM, and Diskette files.

TRADE/PROFESSIONAL ASSOCIATIONS

American Wholesale Marketers Association. 2750 Prosperity Ave., Ste. 530, Fairfax, VA 22031. Phone: 800-482-2962 or (703)208-3358 Fax: (703)573-5738 E-mail: info@awmanet.org • URL: http://www.awmanet.org • Represents the interests of distributors of convenience products. Its members include wholesalers, retailers, manufacturers, brokers and allied organizations from across the U.S. and abroad. Programs include strong legislative representation in Washington and a broad spectrum of targeted education, business and information services. Sponsors the country's largest show for candy and convenience related products in conjunction with its semi-annual convention.

Bakery, Confectionery, Tobacco Workers and Grain Millers International Union. 10401 Connecticut Ave., Room 400, Kensington, MD 20895. Phone: (301)933-8600 Fax: (301)946-8452 • URL: http://www.bctgm.org • Formerly Bakery, Confectionery and Tobacco Workers International Union.

National Confectioners Association of the U.S. 8320 Old Courthouse Rd., Ste. 300, McLean, VA 22182-3811. Phone: 800-433-1200 or (703)790-5750 Fax: (703)790-5752 E-mail: info@candyusa.org • URL: http://www.candyusa.org • Affiliated with American Cocoa Research Institute and the Chocolate Manufacturers Associations of the U.S.A.

National Confectionery Sales Association. 10225 Berea Rd., Ste. B, Cleveland, OH 44102. Phone: (216)631-8200 Fax: (216)631-8210 E-mail: ttarantino@propressinc.com • URL: http://www.candyhalloffame.org • Salespersons, brokers, sales managers, wholesalers, and manufacturers in the candy industry. Maintains Candy Hall of Fame.

Retail Confectioners International. 1807 Glenview Rd., Glenview, IL 60025. Phone: 800-545-5381 or (847)724-6120 Fax: (847)724-2719 E-mail: van@retailconfectioners.org • URL: http://www.retailconfectioners.org • Manufacturing retail confectioners who make and sell their own candies through directly owned retail candy shops; associates are suppliers to the industry. Provides education, promotion, and legislative and information service. Monitors legislative activities that affect the industry at state and national levels. Holds comprehensive two-week course and one-week specialized course on retail candy making biennially.

OTHER SOURCES

The Candy Dish. National Candy Brokers and Salesmen's Association. • Monthly. Price on application. Provides industry news and event information for candy brokers and distributors.

The Candy Market. Available from MarketResearch. com. • 1998. $2,500.00. Published by Packaged Facts. Provides market data on chocolate and non-chocolate candy.

Confectioneries. Available from MarketResearch. com. • 2002. $3,950.00. Published by Global Industry Analysts. Provides worldwide market research data, including profiles of companies producing candy and other confectionery products.

NCBA Membership Roster. National Candy Brokers Association. • Annual. $25.00. Lists broker, manufacturer, and distributor members of the National Candy Brokers Association.

CANNED BEVERAGES

See: BEVERAGE INDUSTRY

CANNED FOOD INDUSTRY

See also: FISH INDUSTRY; FOOD
INDUSTRY; FROZEN FOOD INDUSTRY

ABSTRACTS AND INDEXES

Food Science and Technology Abstracts.
International Food Information Service Publishing.
• Monthly. $1,780.00 per year. Provides worldwide
coverage of the literature of food technology and
food production.

Foods Adlibra: Key to the World's Food Literature.
General Mills, Inc. Foods Adlibra Publications. •
Semimonthly. $240.00 per year. Provides journal
citations and abstracts to the literature of food
technology and packaging.

ALMANACS AND YEARBOOKS

*Almanac of the Canning, Freezing, Preserving
Industries, Vol. Two.* Edward E. Judge and Sons, Inc.
• Annual. $73.00. Contains U. S. food laws and
regulations and detailed production statistics.

CD-ROM DATABASES

*Food Science and Technology Abstracts [CD-
ROM].* Available from SilverPlatter Information,
Inc. • Quarterly. Produced by International Food
Information Service (home page is http://www.ifis.
org). Provides worldwide coverage on CD-ROM of
the literature of food technology and production.
Various types of publications are indexed, with
abstracts, including about 1,800 periodicals. Time
period is 1969 to date.

DIRECTORIES

Judge's Peerless Food Processors. Edward E. Judge
& Sons Inc. • Covers: over 4,000 North American
plants producing frozen, refrigerated, and shelf-
stable foods, fruits, vegetables, juices, preserves,
jams and jellies (SIC 2033); canned specialties (SIC
2032); frozen fruits and vegetables (SIC 2037);
frozen specialties (SIC 2038); pickles, sauces and
salad dressings (SIC 2035); canned and cured
seafood (SIC 2091); fresh or frozen packaged fish
(SIC 2092); refrigerated canned and frozen meat and
poultry (SIC's 2013 and 2015); meat slaughtering
(SIC 2011); butter (SIC 2021); cheese (SIC 2022);
ice cream (SIC 2024); fluid milk and dry milk (SIC
2026, 2023). Entries include: Company name, address, phone, divisions, subsidiaries, factories, pack
volume, names and titles of key personnel, container
sizes, association affiliation, brands, products by factory and process. Plant SIC codes, number of
employees for each plant.

Major Food and Drink Companies of the World.
Available from Gale Cengage Learning. • Annual.
$880.00. Two volumes. Published by Graham &
Whiteside. Contains profiles and trade names for
more than 9,800 important food and beverage
companies in various countries. In addition to foods,
includes both alcoholic and nonalcoholic drink
products.

Plunkett's Food Industry Almanac. Plunkett
Research Ltd. • Covers: 340 leading companies in
the global food industry. Entries include: Name, address, phone, fax, and key executives. Also includes
analysis and information on trends, technology, and
statistics in the field.

Prepared Foods Sourcebook. Reed Business
Information. • Annual. $75.00. Lists approximately
600 food and veverage companies.

Thomas Food and Beverage Market Place. Grey
House Publishing. • 2004. $495.00. Three volumes.
Contains more than 40,000 entries covering food
companies, beverages, food equipment, warehouse
companies, food brokers, wholesalers, importers,
and exporters. Formerly *Thomas Food Industry
Register.*

World Food Marketing Directory. Euromonitor
International. • Covers: Over 2,000 retailers and
wholesalers, 1,600 manufacturers, over 2,000
international and European organizations, statistical
agencies, trade journals and associations, databases,
and trade fairs in the grocery and food industries
worldwide. Entries include: Company name, address, phone, telex, names of parent company and
subsidiaries, number of employees, financial data,
products and brand names handled; retailers and
wholesalers include type of outlet, names and titles
of key personnel.

ENCYCLOPEDIAS AND DICTIONARIES

*Encyclopedia of Food Science, Food Technology,
and Nutrition.* Robert Macrae and others, editors.
Elsevier. • 1993. Eight volumes. $3,056.00. $382.00
per volume.

*Wiley Encyclopedia of Food Science and
Technology.* Frederick J. Francis, editor. John Wiley
and Sons, Inc. • 2000. $1,650.00. Second edition.
Four volumes. Contains about 400 entries. Coverage includes biotechnology, genetic engineering,
nutrition, regulatory matters, food safety, labeling,
food substitutes (sugar, fat, dairy), and many other
topics.

INTERNET DATABASES

USDA. United States Department of Agriculture.
Phone: (202)720-2791 E-mail: agsec@usda.gov •
URL: http://www.usda.gov • The USDA home page
has six sections: News and Information; What's
New; About USDA; Agencies; Opportunities;
Search and Help. Keyword searching is offered from
the USDA home page and from various individual
agency home pages. Agencies are the Economic
Research Service, Agricultural Marketing Service,
National Agricultural Statistics Service, National
Agricultural Library, and about 12 others. Updating
varies. Fees: Free.

ONLINE DATABASES

F & S Index. Gale Cengage Learning. • Contains
about four million citations to worldwide business,
financial, and industrial or consumer product
literature appearing from 1972 to date. Weekly
updates. Inquire as to online cost and availability.

Food Science and Technology Abstracts [online].
IFIS North American Desk. • Produced by
International Food Information Service. Provides
about 500,000 online citations, with abstracts, to the
international literature of food science, technology,
commodities, engineering, and processing. Approximately 2,000 periodicals are covered. Time
period is 1969 to date, with monthly updates. Inquire
as to online cost and availability.

FOODS ADLIBRA. General Mills, Inc. • Contains
online citations, with abstracts, to the technical and
business literature of food processing and
packaging. New products and new ingredients are
featured. Covers about 250 trade journals and 500
research journals from 1974 to date, with monthly
updates. Inquire as to online cost and availability.

PERIODICALS AND NEWSLETTERS

*Food Production-Management: Monthly Publica-
tion of the Canning, Glass-Packing, As eptic, and
Frozen Food Industry.* CTI Publications, Inc. •
Monthly. $35.00 per year.

Prepared Foods. Business News Publishing Co. •
Monthly. $99.90 per year. Edited for food
manufacturing management, marketing, and operations personnel.

PRICE SOURCES

*Supermarket News: The Industry's Weekly
Newspaper.* Fairchild Publications. • Weekly.
Individuals, $196.00 per year; retailers, $45.00 per
year; manufacturers, $89.00 per year.

STATISTICS SOURCES

Agricultural Statistics. Available from U. S. Government Printing Office. • Annual. $38.00. Produced by
the National Agricultural Statistics Service, U. S.
Department of Agriculture. Provides a wide variety
of statistical data relating to agricultural production,
supplies, consumption, prices/price-supports,
foreign trade, costs, and returns, as well as farm
labor, loans, income, and population. In many cases,
historical data is shown annually for 10 years. In addition to farm data, includes detailed fishery
statistics.

Annual Survey of Manufactures. Available from U.
S. Government Printing Office. • Annual. Prices
vary. Issued by the U. S. Census Bureau as an
interim update to the *Census of Manufactures.*
Includes data on number of manufacturing establishments in various industries, employment, labor
costs, value of shipments, capital expenditures,
inventories, energy costs, and assets. (See also
Census Bureau home page, http://www.census.
gov/.).

FAO Production Yearbook. Available from Bernan
Associates. • Annual. $45.00. Published by the Food
and Agriculture Organization (http://www.fao.org).
Contains worldwide data on agriculture, land use,
farm crops, livestock, and agricultural prices.

FAO Trade Yearbook. Available from Bernan
Associates. • Annual. $45.00. Published by the Food
and Agriculture Organization (http://www.fao.org).
Provides extensive worldwide data on exports and
imports of agricultural commodities, fertilizers, tractors, and pesticides. Includes more than 130 tables
of detailed statistics.

United States Census of Manufactures. U.S. Bureau
of the Census. • Quinquennial. Results presented in
reports, tape, CD-ROM, and Diskette files.

World Food Data and Statistics. Euromonitor
International. • 2004. $650.00. Provides five-year
data for a wide variety of food products in 52
countries. Includes market size, consumer
expenditures, price indicators, and retail distribution
data for many kinds of meat, fish, fruits, vegetables,
dairy products, baked goods, condiments, canned
food, and frozen food.

TRADE/PROFESSIONAL ASSOCIATIONS

Food Processing Machinery Association. 200
Daingerfield Rd., Alexandria, VA 22314-2800.
Phone: 800-331-8816 or (703)684-1080 Fax:
(703)548-6563 E-mail: info@fpmamail.com • URL:
http://www.foodprocessingmachinery.com •
Represents firms manufacturing machinery and
providing services and supplies for the canning,
freezing, food, beverage, and pharmaceutical
processing industries. Produces annual exposition of
food processing equipment, supplies, and services,
the International Exposition for Food Processors
(IEFP); offers export and marketing services for
members.

Food Products Association. 1350 I St. NW, Ste. 300,
Washington, DC 20005. Phone: 800-355-0983 or
(202)639-5900 Fax: (202)639-5932 E-mail:
membership@fpa-food.org • URL: http://www.fpa-
food.org • Leading authority on food science and
food safety for the food industry. Members produce
processed and packaged fruits and vegetables, meat
and poultry, seafood, cereals, dairy products, drinks,
juices, and other specialty items or provides supplies and services to food manufacturers.

Shelf-Stable Food Processors Association. 1150
Connecticut Ave. NW, 12th Fl., Washington, DC
20036. Phone: (202)587-4273 Fax: (202)587-4303
E-mail: sfpa@meatami.com • URL: http://www.
meatami.com/content/AboutAMI/canners.htm •
Serves the shelf-stable prepared food industry.
Represents the interests of shelf-stable food processors and their suppliers on issues affecting the
industry. Members include companies of all sizes,
from regional processors to large multi-plant
operations.

For publishers addresses, refer to SOURCES CITED section at the back of the book.

CANVASSING

See: DIRECT MARKETING

CAPITAL EQUIPMENT

See: INDUSTRIAL EQUIPMENT INDUSTRY

CAPITAL GAINS TAX

See also: TAXATION

ABSTRACTS AND INDEXES

Accounting and Tax Index. UMI. • Quarterly. Price on application. Annual cumulation. Indexes accounting, auditing, and taxation literature appearing in journals, books, pamphlets, conference proceedings, and newsletters.

INTERNET DATABASES

Internal Revenue Service IRS.gov. Internal Revenue Service. Phone: 800-829-1040 or (202)622-5000 Fax: (202)622-5844 • URL: http://www.irs.gov • Web site provides a wide variety of tax information, including IRS forms and publications. Searching is available. Fees: Free.

ONLINE DATABASES

Accounting and Tax Database. PROQUEST. • Provides indexing and abstracting of the literature of accounting, taxation, and financial management, 1971 to date. Updating is weekly. Especially covers accounting, auditing, banking, bankruptcy, employee compensation and benefits, cash management, financial planning, and credit. Inquire as to online cost and availability.

EconLit. American Economic Association. • Covers the worldwide literature of economics as contained in selected monographs and about 550 journals. Subjects include microeconomics, macroeconomics, economic history, inflation, money, credit, finance, accounting theory, trade, natural resource economics, and regional economics. Time period is 1969 to present, with monthly updates. Inquire as to online cost and availability.

PERIODICALS AND NEWSLETTERS

National Tax Journal. National Tax Association - Tax Institute of America. • Quarterly. Membership. Topics of current interest in the field of taxation and public finance in the U.S. and foreign countries.

RESEARCH CENTERS AND INSTITUTES

Institute for Tax Administration. 900 Wilshire Blvd., Suite 624, Los Angeles, CA 90017-4707. Phone: (213)623-1103 Fax: (818)842-3930.

International Tax Program. Harvard University, 1563 Massachusetts Ave., Pound Hall, Room 400, Cambridge, MA 02138. Phone: (617)495-4406 Fax: (617)495-0423 E-mail: itp@law.harvard.edu • URL: http://www.law.harvard.edu/programs/itp • Studies the worldwide problems of taxation, including tax law and tax administration.

STATISTICS SOURCES

Statistics of Income Bulletin. Available from U.S. Government Printing Office. • Quarterly. $44.00 per year. Current data compiled from tax returns relating to income, assets, and expenses of individuals and businesses. (U. S. Internal Revenue Service.).

TRADE/PROFESSIONAL ASSOCIATIONS

Citizens for a Sound Economy. 1250 H St., NW, Ste. 700, Washington, DC 20005-3908. Phone: 888-564-6273 or (202)783-3870 Fax: (202)783-4687 E-mail: cse@cse.org • URL: http://www.cse.org • Absorbed Council for a Competitive Economy and Tax Foundation.

Federation of Tax Administrators. 444 N. Capitol St., Suite 348, Washington, DC 20001. Phone:

(202)624-5890 Fax: (202)624-7888 E-mail: fta@taxadmin.org • URL: http://www.taxadmin.org.

Tax Executives Institute. 1200 G St. NW, Ste. 300, Washington, DC 20005-3814. Phone: (202)638-5601 Fax: (202)638-5607 E-mail: administration@tei.org • URL: http://www.tei.org • Professional society of executives administering and directing tax affairs for corporations and businesses. Maintains TEI +Education Fund.

OTHER SOURCES

Taxation of Securities Transactions. LexisNexis Matthew Bender. • Semiannual. $307.00. Looseleaf service. Covers taxation of a wide variety of securities transactions, including those involving stocks, bonds, options, short sales, new issues, mutual funds, dividend distributions, foreign securities, and annuities.

CAPITAL, VENTURE

See: VENTURE CAPITAL

CAR PHONES

See: MOBILE TELEPHONE INDUSTRY

CARBONATED BEVERAGES

See: BEVERAGE INDUSTRY

CARDS, GREETING

See: GREETING CARD INDUSTRY

CAREER PLANNING

See: VOCATIONAL GUIDANCE

CAREERS

See: JOB HUNTING; OCCUPATIONS

CARIBBEAN AREA

See: LATIN AMERICAN MARKETS

CARPENTRY

See also: HOME IMPROVEMENT INDUSTRY; WOODWORKING INDUSTRIES

GENERAL WORKS

Carpentry and Building Construction. John Feirer and others. Glencoe/McGraw-Hill. • 1999. $53.25. Fifth edition.

Modern Carpentry: Building Construction Details in Easy-To-Understand Form. Willis H. Wagner and Howard S. Smith. Goodheart-Willcox Publishers. • 2003. Price on application.

DIRECTORIES

Wood Digest-Showcase. Cygnus Business Media. • Publication includes: List of suppliers of materials, machinery, tools, and services for woodworking, cabinetry, casegoods, and furniture manufacturing processes (SIC 24, 25, 37, and 39). Entries include: Company name, phone number, photograph of product, services.

ENCYCLOPEDIAS AND DICTIONARIES

Illustrated Dictionary of Building Materials and Techniques: An Invaluable Sourcebook to the Tools,

Terms, Materials, and Techniques Used by Building Professionals. Paul Bianchina. John Wiley and Sons, Inc. • 1993. $19.95. Contains 4,000 definitions of building and building materials terms, with 500 illustrations. Includes materials grades, measurements, and specifications.

FINANCIAL RATIOS

Annual Statement Studies. The Risk Management Association. • Annual. Median and quartile financial ratios are given for over 400 kinds of manufacturing, wholesale, retail, construction, and consumer finance establishments. Data is sorted by both asset size and sales volume. Includes a clearly written "Definition of Ratios" and an alphabetical industry index.

Annual Statement Studies: Industry Default Probabilities and Cash Flow Measures. The Risk Management Association. • Annual. $145.00. Serves as a companion volume to the original *Annual Statement Studies.* Gives probability of default estimates on a percentage scale for more than 450 industries. Includes changes in position year-by-year for eight financial statement line items and provides percentage measures of cash flow.

ONLINE DATABASES

Magazine Index. Gale Cengage Learning. • General magazine indexing (popular literature), 1973 to present. Daily updates. Inquire as to online cost and availability.

PERIODICALS AND NEWSLETTERS

The Carpenter. United Brotherhood of Carpenters and Joiners of America. • Bimonthly. Free to members; non-members, $10.00 per year.

TRADE/PROFESSIONAL ASSOCIATIONS

International Association of Machinists and Aerospace Workers. 9000 Machinists Place, Upper Marlboro, MD 20772-2687. Phone: (301)967-4500 Fax: (301)967-4595 E-mail: websteward@goiam.org • URL: http://www.iamaw.org/ • Formerly International Association of Machinists.

United Brotherhood of Carpenters and Joiners of America. 1221 Massachusetts Ave. NW, Washington, DC 20005. Phone: (202)546-0580 Fax: (202)543-0580 • URL: http://www.carpenters.org/home.

CARPET CLEANING INDUSTRY

See: CLEANING INDUSTRY

CARPET INDUSTRY

See: FLOOR COVERINGS; ORIENTAL RUG INDUSTRY

CARRIERS

See: AUTOMOBILES; FREIGHT TRANSPORT

CARTOGRAPHY

See: MAPS

CARWASH INDUSTRY

ONLINE DATABASES

Trade & Industry Database. Gale Cengage Learning. • Provides indexing of business periodicals, January 1981 to date. Daily updates. (Full text articles from some periodicals are available online, 1983 to date. Inquire as to online cost and availability).

PERIODICALS AND NEWSLETTERS

American Clean Car. Crain Communications, Inc. • Bimonthly. $135.00 per year. Provides articles on new products and management for the carwash industry.

Auto Laundry News: The Voice of the Car Care Industry. EW Williams Publications Co. • Monthly. $56.00 per year. Covers management, technical information, trends, and marketing for the vehicle cleaning industry. Edited for owners, operators, managers, and investors.

Professional Carwashing and Detailing. National Trade Publications, Inc. • Monthly. Free to qualified personnel. Edited for owners, operators, and managers of automatic carwashes, custom hand carwash facilities, detail shops, and coin-operated, self-service carwashes.

TRADE/PROFESSIONAL ASSOCIATIONS

Car Wash Owners and Suppliers Association. 1822 South St., Racine, WI 53404. Phone: (262)639-2289 Fax: (262)639-4393 • Formerly Car Wash Manufacturers and Suppliers Association.

CASE STUDIES

GENERAL WORKS

Case Studies in Business Ethics. Thomas Donaldson and Al Gini, editors. Prentice Hall PTR. • 1995. $49.00. Fourth edition.

Case Studies in Business, Society, and Ethics. Thomas L. Beauchamp, editor. Prentice Hall PTR. • 1997. $42.00. Fourth edition.

Case Studies in Finance: Managing for Corporate Value Creation. Robert Bruner. McGraw-Hill. • 2002. $109.69. Fourth edition. (Finance, Insurance and Real Estate Series).

Cases in Corporate Acquisitions, Buyouts, Mergers, and Takeovers. Gale Cengage Learning. • 1999. $350.00. Reviews and analyzes about 300 cases of both success and failure in corporate acquisitiveness.

Cases in Corporate Innovation. Gale Cengage Learning. • 2002. $310.00. Reviews and analyzes about 300 cases to illustrate both successful and failed management of innovation.

Cases in Financial Mangement: Directed Versions. Eugene Brigham and Louis Gapenski. Dryden Press. • 1993. $32.00.

Cases in International Finance. Gunter Duffey. Addison-Wesley. • 2001. 3rd edition. Price on application.

Cases in Marketing Management. Kenneth L. Bernhardt and Thomas C. Kinnear. McGraw-Hill. • 1997. Ninth edition. Price on application.

Cases in Portfolio Management. John W. Peavy and Katrina F. Sherrerd. Association of Investment Management and Research. • 1991. $30.00.

Cases in Strategic Management. Thomas J. Wheelen and J. David Hunger. Addison-Wesley. • 1996. Fifth edition. Price on application.

Cases in Strategic Marketing: An Integrated Approach. Strickland. McGraw-Hill. • 2000. $41.25. 12th edition.

Cases in Total Quality Management: Manufacturing and Services. Jay H. Heizer. Course Technology, Inc. • 1997. $48.95. (GC Principles in Management Series.).

Corporate Social Challenge: Cases and Commentaries. James E. Stacey and Frederick D. Sturdivant, editors. McGraw-Hill. • 1994. $41.95. Fifth edition.

Creating Web-Accessible Databases: Case Studies for Libraries, Museums, and Other Non-Profits.

Julie M. Still, editor. Information Today, Inc. • 2001. $39.50. Presents case studies of successful Web projects in libraries and other institutions.

Dirty Business: Exploring Corporate Misconduct: Analysis and Cases. Maurice Punch. Sage Publications, Inc. • 1996. $113.00. Covers organizational misbehavior and white-collar crime. Includes "Ten Cases of Corporate Deviance.".

Managing Quality in America's Most Admired Companies. Jay W. Spechler. Engineering and Management Press. • 1993. $49.95. Part one provides "Guidelines for Implementing Quality Management," including detailed information on the Malcolm Baldrige National Quality Award. Part two contains 30 "Case Studies of Quality Management in Leading Companies.".

Marketing Management: Text and Cases. Robert Dolan. McGraw Hill. • 2001. $108.75. (Marketing Series).

Operating an E-Business. Andrew McAfee. McGraw-Hill. • 2002. $61.25. Provides case studies covering B-to-B (business-to-business) Internet endeavors, B-to-C (business-to-consumer), and the electronic business activities of traditional "bricks-and-mortar" companies. Illustrates what went right and what went wrong. The author is a professor at Harvard Business School.

PR News Casebook. Gale Cengage Learning. • 1993. $110.00. A collection of about 1,000 case studies covering major public relations campaigns and events, taken from the pages of *PR News.* Covers such issues as boycotts, new products, anniversaries, plant closings, downsizing, and stockholder relations.

Project Management Casebook. David I. Cleland and others, editors. Project Management Institute. • 1998. $69.95. Provides 50 case studies in various areas of project management.

Public Relations Practices: Managerial Case Studies and Problems. Allen H. Center. Prentice Hall PTR. • 2002. $84.00. Sixth edition.

Strategic Marketing Problems: Cases and Comments. Roger A. Kerin and Robert A. Peterson. Prentice Hall PTR. • 2003. $113.33. 10th edition.

CASH FLOW AND CASH MANAGEMENT

GENERAL WORKS

Accounting and Finance for Non-Specialists. Peter Atrill and Eddie McLaney. Pearson Education. • 2003. $77.00. Fourth edition. Includes the measurement and reporting of financial performance and cash flow.

Operational Cash Flow Management and Control. Morris A. Nunes. Prentice Hall PTR. • 1982. $34.95.

ABSTRACTS AND INDEXES

Accounting and Tax Index. UMI. • Quarterly. Price on application. Annual cumulation. Indexes accounting, auditing, and taxation literature appearing in journals, books, pamphlets, conference proceedings, and newsletters.

ENCYCLOPEDIAS AND DICTIONARIES

Blackwell Encyclopedic Dictionary of Accounting. Rashad Abdel-khalik. Blackwell Publishing. • 1997. $38.95. The editor is associated with the University of Florida. Contains definitions of key terms combined with longer articles written by various U.S. and foreign business educators. Includes bibliographies and index. (Blackwell Encyclopedia of Management Series).

HANDBOOKS AND MANUALS

Analysis and Use of Financial Statements. Gerald I. White. John Wiley and Sons, Inc. • 2002. $123.95.

Third edition. Includes analysis of financial ratios, cash flow, inventories, assets, debt, etc. Also covered are employee benefits, corporate investments, multinational operations, financial derivatives, and hedging activities.

Corporate Liquidity: Management and Measurement. Jarl G. Kallberg and Kenneth L. Parkinson. McGraw-Hill. • 1992. $67.95. Topics include cash management and risk.

Cost Management Handbook. Barry J. Brinker. John Wiley and Sons, Inc. • 2000. $140.00.

Essentials of Cash Management. Peter S. Adams and William Harrison, editors. The Association for Financial Professionals. • 1998. $95.50. Sixth edition.

How to Manage Corporate Cash Effectively. Joseph E. Finnerty. AMACOM. • 1991. $59.95. A practical approach to cash flow problems.

Small Business Survival Guide: How to Manage Your Cash, Profits and Taxes. Robert E. Fleury. Sourcebooks, Inc. • 1995. $17.95. Third revised edition. (Small Business Series).

Ultimate Guide to Raising Money for Growing Companies. Michael C. Thomsett. McGraw-Hill. • 1990. $45.00. Discusses the preparation of a practical business plan, how to manage cash flow, and debt vs. equity decisions.

ONLINE DATABASES

Accounting and Tax Database. PROQUEST. • Provides indexing and abstracting of the literature of accounting, taxation, and financial management, 1971 to date. Updating is weekly. Especially covers accounting, auditing, banking, bankruptcy, employee compensation and benefits, cash management, financial planning, and credit. Inquire as to online cost and availability.

PERIODICALS AND NEWSLETTERS

AFP Exchange. Association for Financial Professionals. • Monthly. Membership. Newsletter.

Strategic Finance. Institute of Management Accountants. • Monthly. Institutions, $140.00 per year; non-profit libraries, $70,00 per year. Provides articles on corporate finance, cost control, cash flow, budgeting, corporate taxes, and other financial management topics.

Successful Cost Control Strategies for CEOs, Managers, and Administrators. Siefer Consultants, Inc. • Monthly. $279.00 per year. Newsletter. Provides a variety of ideas on business budgeting and controlling company expenses. Formerly *Employee Cost Conrol Strategies for CEOs, Managers, and Administrators.*

TRADE/PROFESSIONAL ASSOCIATIONS

Association for Financial Professionals. 7315 Wisconsin Ave., Suite 600 W, Bethesda, MD 20814-3211. Phone: (301)907-2862 Fax: (301)907-2864 E-mail: afp@afponline.org • URL: http://www.afponline.org • Goal is to raise the stature and visibility of the finance profession. Formerly Treasury Management Association.

IRCDA/SDA. 1900 Cross Beam Dr., Charlotte, NC 28217. Phone: (704)357-3124 Fax: (704)357-3127 E-mail: info@icrda.org • URL: http://www.icrda.org • Formerly Independent Cash Register Dealers Association.

OTHER SOURCES

Planning Cash Flow. American Management Association Extension Institute. • Looseleaf. $139.00. Self-study course. Emphasis is on practical explanations, examples, and problem solving. Quizzes and a case study are included.

CASINOS

See: GAMBLING INDUSTRY

CASKS

See: COOPERAGE INDUSTRY

CASSETTE RECORDING

See: SOUND RECORDERS AND RECORD-ING; VIDEO RECORDING INDUSTRY

CASTING

See: FOUNDRIES

CASTOR BEAN INDUSTRY

See: OIL AND FATS INDUSTRY

CASUALTY INSURANCE

See also: ACCIDENT INSURANCE; INSUR-ANCE

ABSTRACTS AND INDEXES

Insurance Periodicals Index. Specials Libraries Association, Insurance and Employees Benefits Div. NILS Publishing Co. • Annual. $250.00. Compiled by the Insurance and Employee Benefits Div., Special Libraries Association. A yearly index of over 15,000 articles from about 35 insurance periodicals. Arrangement is by subject, with an index to authors.

ALMANACS AND YEARBOOKS

Casualty Actuarial Society Yearbook. Casualty Actuarial Society. • Annual. $40.00. Approximately 2,500 actuaries working in insurance other than life insurance.

BIBLIOGRAPHIES

Insurance and Employee Benefits Literature. Special Libraries Association, Insurance and Employee Benefits Div. • Bimonthly. $15.00 per year. Lists a wide variety of literature in all branches of the insurance industry. Includes annotations.

CD-ROM DATABASES

U. S. Insurance: Property and Casualty. Sheshunoff Information Services, Inc. • Monthly. Price on application. CD-ROM provides detailed, current financial information on more than 3,200 property and casualty insurance companies.

DIRECTORIES

S & P's Insurance Book. Standard & Poor's Ratings Group, Insurance Rating Services. • Quarterly. Price on application. Contains detailed financial analyses and ratings of various kinds of insurance companies.

S & P's Insurance Digest: Property-Casualty and Reinsurance Edition. Standard & Poor's Ratings Group, Insurance Rating Services. • Quarterly. Contains concise financial analyses and ratings of property-casualty insurance companies.

ENCYCLOPEDIAS AND DICTIONARIES

Dictionary of Insurance Terms. Harvey W. Rubin. Barron's Educational Series, Inc. • 2000. $14.95. Fourth edition. Defines terms in a wide variety of insurance fields. (Business Dictionaries Series).

Glossary of Insurance Policy Terms. Organization for Economic Cooperation and Development. • 1999. $30.00. "The selected topics range from insurance policy regulation/supervision to general trade issues and include technical terms related to issues such as claims, premiums, and provisions." Edited for government, academic, business, and insurance organizations.

Insurance Words and Their Meanings: A Glossary of Insurance Terms. The Rough Notes Co., Inc. •

2001. 17th edition. Price on application.

Rupp's Insurance and Risk Management Glossary. Richard V. Rupp. NILS Publishing Co. • 2001. $35.00. Second edition. Provides definitions of 6,400 insurance words and phrases. Includes a guide to acronyms and abbreviations.

ONLINE DATABASES

I.I.I. Data Base Search. Insurance Information Institute. • Provides online citations and abstracts of insurance-related literature in magazines, newspapers, trade journals, and books. Emphasis is on property and casualty insurance issues, including highway safety, product safety, and environmental liability. Inquire as to online cost and availability.

PERIODICALS AND NEWSLETTERS

Best's Review: Inurance Issues and Analysis. A.M. Best Co. • Monthly. $25.00 per year. Editorial coverage of significant industry trends, developments, and important events. Formerly Best's Review: Property-Casualty Insurance.

Business Insurance: News Magazine for Corporate Risk, Employee Benefit and Financial Executives. Crain Communications, Inc. • Weekly. $95.00 per year. Covers a wide variety of business insurance topics, including risk management, employee benefits, workers compensation, marine insurance, and casualty insurance.

Chartered Property and Casualty Underwriters Society Journal. Chartered Property and Casualty Underwriters Society. • Quarterly. $30.00 per year. Published by the Chartered Property and Casualty Underwriters Society (CPCU). Edited for professional insurance underwriters and agents.

Fire, Casualty and Surety Bulletin. The National Underwriter Co. • Monthly. $420.00 per year. Five looseleaf volumes.

Guide to Property and Casualty Insurers: A Quarterly Compilation of Insurance Company Ratings and Analysis. Weiss Ratings, Inc. • Quarterly. $438.00 per year. Emphasis is on rating of financial safety and relative risk. Includes annual summary.

Insurance and Technology. CMP Media LLC. • Monthly. $65.00 per year. Covers information technology and systems management as applied to the operation of life, health, casualty, and property insurance companies.

Insurance Day. Available from Informa Publishing Group Ltd. • Three times a week. $440.00 per year. Published in the UK by Lloyd's List (http://www.lloydslist.com). A newspaper providing international coverage of property/casualty/liability insurance, reinsurance, and risk, with an emphasis on marine insurance.

Journal of Risk and Insurance. American Risk and Insurance Association. Blackwell Publishing, Inc. • Quarterly. Institutions, $243.00 per year. Includes online edition.

National Underwriter, Property and Casualty Edition. The National Underwriter Co. • Weekly. $92.00 per year.

Risk Management. Risk and Insurance Management Society. Risk Management Society Publishing, Inc. • Monthly. $59.00 per year.

RESEARCH CENTERS AND INSTITUTES

S. S. Huebner Foundation. University of Pennsylvania, 3733 Spruce St., Vance Hall, Suite 430, Philadelphia, PA 19104-6301. Phone: (215)898-9631 Fax: (215)573-2218 E-mail: cummins@wharton.upenn.edu • URL: http://www.rider.wharton.upenn.edu/ • Awards grants for research in various areas of insurance.

STATISTICS SOURCES

Best's Aggregates and Averages: Property-Casualty. A.M. Best Co., Inc. • Annual. $335.00. Statistical summary of composite property casualty

business. 400 pages of historical data, underwriting expenses and underwriting experience by line.

Property-Casualty Insurance Facts. Insurance Information Institute. • Annual. $22.50. Formerly *Insurance Facts.*

Standard & Poor's Industry Surveys. Standard & Poor's. • Semiannual. $1,800.00. Two looseleaf volumes. Includes monthly *Supplements.* Provides detailed, individual surveys of 52 major industry groups. Each survey is revised on a semiannual basis. Also includes "Monthly Investment Review" (industry group investment analysis) and monthly "Trends & Projections" (economic analysis).

TRADE/PROFESSIONAL ASSOCIATIONS

American Insurance Association. 1130 Connecticut Ave. NW, Ste. 1000, Washington, DC 20036. Phone: 800-242-2302 or (202)828-7100 or (202)828-7183 Fax: (202)293-1219 E-mail: info@aiadc.org • URL: http://www.aiadc.org/aiadotnet • Represents companies providing property and casualty insurance and suretyship. Monitors and reports on economic, political, and social trends; serves as a clearinghouse for ideas, advice, and technical information. Represents members' interests before state and federal legislative and regulatory bodies; coordinates members' litigation.

Casualty Actuarial Society. 4350 N Fairfax Dr., Ste. 250, Arlington, VA 22203. Phone: (703)276-3100 Fax: (703)276-3108 E-mail: office@casact.org • URL: http://www.casact.org • Professional society of property/casualty actuaries. Seeks to advance the body of knowledge of actuarial science applied to property, casualty and similar risk exposures, to maintain qualification standards, promote high standards of conduct and competence, and increase awareness of actuarial science. Examinations required for membership.

CPCU Society. 720 Providence Rd., 720 Providence Rd., PO Box 3009, Malvern, PA 19355-3402. Phone: 800-932-2728 or (610)251-2727 Fax: (610)251-2780 E-mail: membercenter@cpcusociety.org • URL: http://www.cpcusociety.org • Serves as a professional society of individuals who have passed national examinations of the American Institute for Chartered Property Casualty Underwriters (see separate entry), have 3 years of work experience, have agreed to be bound by a code of ethics, and have been awarded CPCU designation. Promotes education, research, social responsibility, and professionalism in the field. Holds seminars, symposia, and workshops.

Insurance Services Office (ISO). 545 Washington Blvd., Jersey City, NJ 07310-1686. Phone: 800-888-4476 or (201)469-2000 Fax: (201)748-1472 E-mail: info@iso.com • URL: http://www.iso.com • Provides statistical, actuarial, underwriting, and claims information to property and casualty insurance companies.

National Association of Professional Insurance Agents. 400 N. Washington St., Alexandria, VA 22314. Phone: (703)836-9340 Fax: (703)836-1279 E-mail: piaweb@pianet.org • URL: http://www.pianet.com • Members are independent agents in various fields of insurance. Formerly National Association of Mutual Insurance Agents.

OTHER SOURCES

Best's Insurance Reports: Property-Casualty. A.M. Best Co. • Annual. $750.00. Guide to over 3,200 major property/casualty companies.

BestWeek: Insurance News and Analysis. A.M. Best Co. • Weekly. $495.00 per year. Newsletter. Focuses on key areas of the insurance industry.

Casualty Insurance Claims: Coverage-Investigation-Law. Pat Magarick and Ken Brownlee. West Group. • Semiannual. $400.00 per year. Three looseleaf volumes.

Fire and Casualty Insurance Law Reports. CCH,

Inc. • $870.00 per year. Looseleaf service. Semimonthly updates.

CATALOGS AND DIRECTORIES

See also: ASSOCIATIONS; BOOK CATALOGS

BIBLIOGRAPHIES

Books in Print. R. R. Bowker. • Annual. $769.00. Eight volumes.

Guide to Special Issues and Indexes of Periodicals. Miriam Uhlan and Doris B. Katz, editors. Special Libraries Association. • 1994. $59.00. Fourth edition. A listing, with prices, of the special issues of over 1700 U. S. and Canadian periodicals in business, industry, technology, science, and the arts. Includes a comprehensive subject index.

CD-ROM DATABASES

MediaFinder CD-ROM: Oxbridge Directories of Print Media and Catalogs. Oxbridge Communications, Inc. • Quarterly. $1,995.00 per year. CD-ROM includes about 100,000 listings from *Standard Periodical Directory, National Directory of Catalogs, National Directory of British Mail Order Catalogs, National Directory of German Mail Order Catalogs, Oxbridge Directory of Newsletters, National Directory of Mailing Lists, College Media Directory,* and *National Directory of Magazines.*

DIRECTORIES

Catalog Age--Direct Sourcebook. Primedia Business. • Publication includes: List of approximately 300 suppliers of equipment, products, and services to the direct marketing industry; related trade associations. Entries include: Name, address, phone, key personnel, geographical area covered, description of products or services, branch offices or subsidiary names and locations.

Directories in Print. Gale Cengage Learning. • Annual. $565.00. Two volumes. *Midyear Supplement,* $440.00. Two volumes. An annotated guide to approximately 15,500 business, industrial, professional, and scientific directories. Formerly *Directory of Directories.*

Grey House Directory of Special Issues: A Guide to Business Magazines' Buyer's Guides & Directory Issues. Grey House Publishing. • 2001. $175.00. Second edition. Provides information on more than 2,500 specialized directories issued by business and trade journals, arranged according to 90 industry groups.

Guide to American Directories. Todd Publications. • Biennial. $125.00. Provides more than 11,000 listings with descriptions, prices, etc.

Library Journal: Reference [year]: Print, CD-ROM, Online. Reed Business Information. • Annual. Issued in November as a supplement to *Library Journal.* Lists new and updated reference material, including general and trade print titles, directories, annuals, CD-ROM titles, and online sources. Includes material from more than 200 publishers, arranged by company name, with an index by subject. Addresses include e-mail and Web information.

Library Journal Sourcebook. Reed Business Information. • Publication includes: List of over 600 suppliers of products and services used by libraries from abstracting to word processing equipment. Entries include: Company name, address, phone, list of products or services. Complete listings for more than 100 architectural firms; Disaster planning for librarians.

The National Directory of Catalogs. Oxbridge Communications. • Annual. $645.00. Describes over 9,000 United States and Canadian catalogs within 78 subject areas.

Trade Directories of the World. Croner Publications, Inc. • Annual. 100.00. Looseleaf service. Monthly supplements. Lists over 3,300 publications.

HANDBOOKS AND MANUALS

Do-It-Yourself Advertising and Promotion: How to Produce Great Ads, Brochures, Catalogs, Direct Mail, Web Sites and more. Fred E. Hahn. John Wiley and Sons, Inc. • 2003. $19.95. Third edition. Covers magazines, newspapers, flyers, brochures, catalogs, direct mail, telemarketing, trade shows, and radio/TV promotions. Includes checklists. (Small Business Series).

The Perfect Sales Piece: A Complete Do-It-Yourself Guide to Creating Brochures, Catalogs, Fliers, and Pamphlets. Robert W. Bly. John Wiley and Sons, Inc. • 1994. $50.00. A guide to the use of various forms of printed literature for direct selling, sales promotion, and marketing. (Small Business Series).

ONLINE DATABASES

Books in Print Online. Bowker Electronic Publishing. • The online version of *Books in Print, Forthcoming Books, Paperbound Books in Print,* and other Bowker bibliographic publications: lists the books of over 50,000 U. S. publishers. Includes books recently declared out-of-print. Updated monthly. Inquire as to online cost and availability.

Gale Database of Publications and Broadcast Media. Gale Cengage Learning. • An online directory containing detailed information on over 67,000 periodicals, newspapers, broadcast stations, cable systems, directories, and newsletters. Corresponds to the following print sources: *Gale Directory of Publications and Broadcast Media; Directories in Print; City and State Directories in Print; Newsletters in Print.* Semiannual updates. Inquire as to online cost and availability.

PERIODICALS AND NEWSLETTERS

Catalog Age. PRIMEDIA Business Magazine and Media. • 13 times a year. Free to qualified personnel; others, $85.00 per year. Edited for catalog marketing and management personnel.

CSM. CSM Marketing, Inc. • Monthly. $30.00 per year. Formerly *Catalog Showroom Merchandiser.*

DM News: The Newspaper of Direct Marketing. Courtenay Communications Corp. • 48 times a year. $49.00 per year. Includes special feature issues on catalog marketing, telephone marketing, database marketing, and fundraising. Includes monthly supplements, *DM News International, DRTV News,* and *TeleServices.*

The SIMBA Report on Directory Publishing. SIMBA Information. • Monthly. $359.00 per year. Newsletter.

Yellow Pages and Directory Report: The Newsletter for the Yellow Page and Directory Publishing Industry. SIMBA Information. • 22 times a year. $689.00 per year. Newsletter. Covers the yellow pages publishing industry, including electronic directory publishing, directory advertising, and special interest directories.

STATISTICS SOURCES

DMA State of the Catalog Industry Report. Direct Marketing Association, Inc. • Annual. $495.00. Provides merchandising, operating, and financial statistics on consumer and business-to-business marketing through both print and electronic (interactive) catalogs. (Produced in association with W. A. Dean & Associates.).

TRADE/PROFESSIONAL ASSOCIATIONS

Association of Directory Publishers. 116 Cass St., Traverse City, MI 49685-1929. Phone: 800-267-9002 Fax: (231)486-2182 E-mail: hg@adp.org • URL: http://www.adp.org.

National Catalog Managers Association. 7101 Wisconsin Ave., Ste. 1300, Bethesda, MD 20814-3415. Phone: (301)654-6664 Fax: (301)654-3299

E-mail: ncma@aftermarket.org • URL: http://www.ncmacat.org • Individuals actively engaged in the management, preparation, production, and distribution of automotive product catalogs. Purposes are to: exchange practical and useful ideas in the creation, compilation, production, and distribution of catalogs; raise standards of catalogs in automotive and related industries; create a better understanding of the current developments in the field of graphics; establish a professional and fraternal relationship with colleagues; improve professional recognition of the catalog specialist; promote high standards of ethics in the cataloging industry. Operates placement service.

OTHER SOURCES

DMA Direct and Interactive Marketing Buying Practices Study. Direct Marketing Association, Inc. • 2000. $1,295.00. Provides marketing research data relating to consumer purchasing from catalogs. "Incidence and profile of Internet buying" is also included. (Research conducted by Elrick & Lavidge.).

The U. S. Market for Catalog Shopping. Available from MarketResearch.com. • 1997. $1,375.00. Market research report published by Packaged Facts. Includes analysis of catalog shopping market by age, ethnic groups, and income.

CATERERS AND CATERING

See also: HOTEL AND MOTEL INDUSTRY; RESTAURANTS, LUNCHROOMS, ETC.

GENERAL WORKS

Fundamentals of Professional Food Preparation: A Laboratory Text-Workbook. Donald V. Laconi. John Wiley and Sons, Inc. • 1995. $60.00.

Successful Catering. Bernard Splaver. John Wiley and Sons, Inc. • 1991. $70.00. Third edition.

HANDBOOKS AND MANUALS

Catering Handbook. Edith Weiss and Hal Weiss. John Wiley and Sons, Inc. • 1990. $60.00.

Catering Service. Entrepreneur Media, Inc. • Looseleaf. $59.50. A practical guide to starting a food and beverage catering business. Covers profit potential, start-up costs, market size evaluation, owner's time required, site selection, pricing, accounting, advertising, promotion, etc. (Start-Up Business Guide No. E1215.).

Club Manager's Guide to Private Parties and Club Functions. Joe Perdue and others. John Wiley and Sons, Inc. • 1998. $65.00. Covers on-premises catering at clubs, including member relations, meal functions, beverage functions, room setup, staffing, etc.

How to Manage a Successful Catering Business. Manfred Ketterer. John Wiley and Sons, Inc. • 1990. $65.00. Second edition.

PERIODICALS AND NEWSLETTERS

Catering Industry Employee. Hotel Employees and Restaurant Employees International Union, AFL0-CIO. • Quarterly. $5.00.

Catering Magazine: The Magazine for Off-Premise Caterers. GP Publishing, Inc. • Bimonthly. $35.00 per year. Covers the marketing and management aspects of the catering business.

Chef. Talcott Communications Corp. • Monthly. $24.00 per year. Edited for executive chefs, food and beverage directors, caterers, banquet and club managers, and others responsible for food buying and food service. Special coverage of regional foods is provided.

TRADE/PROFESSIONAL ASSOCIATIONS

Convenience Caterers and Food Manufacturers Association. 1205 Spartan Dr., Madison Heights, MI 48071. Phone: 800-620-6422 or (248)982-5379 Fax: (248)582-3268 E-mail: ccfma@sbcglobal.net •

URL: http://www.mobilecaterers.com • Firms and corporations engaged in the mobile catering business and in any other business catering to industrial feeding by mobile equipment; associate members are suppliers and manufacturers. Deals with common intra-industry problems through exchange of ideas, advice on legal problems, and safety standards and licensing regulations.

International Food Service Executives Association. 8155 Briar Cliff Dr., Castle Rock, CO 80108-8215. Phone: 800-893-5499 or (720)733-8001 Fax: (720)733-8999 E-mail: hq@ifsea.com • URL: http://www.ifsea.com • Owners, managers, stewards, caterers, proprietors, purchasing agents, dietitians, and other management-level personnel of hotels, clubs, restaurants, cafeterias, schools, hospitals, institutions, and airlines. Associate members are providers of goods and services to the food service industry. Seeks to raise standards in the food service industry by educating members. Underwrites scholarships; provides assistance to universities and other educational institutions establishing programs for professional food service training. Maintains Certified Food Executive Program, through which individuals in the food service industry who have demonstrated outstanding leadership capabilities receive certification training.

CATTLE INDUSTRY

See also: DAIRY INDUSTRY; LIVESTOCK INDUSTRY

CD-ROM DATABASES

OECD Statistical Compendium. Organization for Economic Cooperation and Development. • Semiannual. $1,905.00 per year for 1 to 10 users. CD-ROM contains more than 730,000 monthly, quarterly, and annual time series for OECD countries, 1960 to date. Includes fully searchable data on agriculture, food, economic indicators, national accounts, employment, energy, finance, industry, technology, and foreign trade. Results can be displayed in various forms.

FINANCIAL RATIOS

Annual Statement Studies. The Risk Management Association. • Annual. Median and quartile financial ratios are given for over 400 kinds of manufacturing, wholesale, retail, construction, and consumer finance establishments. Data is sorted by both asset size and sales volume. Includes a clearly written "Definition of Ratios" and an alphabetical industry index.

Annual Statement Studies: Industry Default Probabilities and Cash Flow Measures. The Risk Management Association. • Annual. $145.00. Serves as a companion volume to the original *Annual Statement Studies.* Gives probability of default estimates on a percentage scale for more than 450 industries. Includes changes in position year-by-year for eight financial statement line items and provides percentage measures of cash flow.

INTERNET DATABASES

BEEF. National Cattlemen's Beef Association. Phone: (303)694-0305 Fax: (303)694-2851 E-mail: cows@beef.org • URL: http://www.beef.org • Web site provides detailed information from the "Cattle and Beef Handbook," including "Beef Economics" (production, sales, consumption, retail value, foreign competition, etc.). Text of monthly newsletter is also available: "The Beef Brief-Issues & Trends in the Cattle Industry." Keyword searching is offered. Fees: Free.

Business 2.0 Web Guide to the Best Business Links. Business 2.0 Media Inc. Phone: (415)293-4800 E-mail: support@business2.com • URL: http://www.business2.com/webguide • Web site presents

an extensive, searchable directory of links to "the best, most informative, and authoritative web pages." Twenty main categories cover business, finance, career, company information, people, and technology topics, with thousands of subtopics, all linking to Web sites recommended by experienced business researchers. Fees: Free.

Fedstats. Federal Interagency Council on Statistical Policy. Phone: (202)395-7254 • URL: http://www.fedstats.gov • Web site features an efficient search facility for full-text statistics produced by more than 100 federal agencies, including the Census Bureau, the Bureau of Economic Analysis, and the Bureau of Labor Statistics. Boolean searches can be made within one agency or for all agencies combined. Links are offered to international statistical bureaus, including the UN, IMF, OECD, UNESCO, Eurostat, and 20 individual countries. Fees: Free.

FreeLunch.com. Economy.com, Inc. Phone: (610)696-8700 Fax: (610)696-1678 • URL: http://www.freelunch.com • Web site provides free access to more than 1.5 million economic and financial data series, covering industry, demographics, labor markets, prices, retail sales, government spending, trade, interest rates, housing starts, the stock market, and many other topics. Data is available for various time periods in either chart or table form. Searching is offered. Fees: Free, but registration required. Economy.com, Inc. also offers fee-based economic analysis at *The Dismal Scientist* site (http://www.dismal.com).

USDA. United States Department of Agriculture. Phone: (202)720-2791 E-mail: agsec@usda.gov • URL: http://www.usda.gov • The USDA home page has six sections: News and Information; What's New; About USDA; Agencies; Opportunities; Search and Help. Keyword searching is offered from the USDA home page and from various individual agency home pages. Agencies are the Economic Research Service, Agricultural Marketing Service, National Agricultural Statistics Service, National Agricultural Library, and about 12 others. Updating varies. Fees: Free.

PERIODICALS AND NEWSLETTERS

Beef. Primedia Business Magazines and Media. • 13 times a year. $35.00 per year.

Cattleman. Texas and Southwestern Cattle Raisers Association, Inc. • Monthly. $25.00 per year.

Livestock Market Digest. Livestock Market Digest, Inc. • Weekly. $20.00 per year.

Livestock Weekly. Southwest Publishing, Inc. • Weekly. $25.00 per year.

PRICE SOURCES

The National Provisioner: Serving Meat, Poultry, and Seafood Processors. Stagnito Communications, Inc. • Monthly. Free to qualified personnel; others, $85.04 per year. Annual *Buyer's Guide* available. Meat, poultry and seafood newsletter.

RESEARCH CENTERS AND INSTITUTES

Beef Cattle and Sheep Research Center. Pennsylvania State University. 324 Henning Bldg., University Park, PA 16802. Phone: (814)865-5893 Fax: (814)863-6042 E-mail: rswope@das.psu.edu • URL: http://www.das.cas.psu.edu/.

Cottonwood Range and Livestock Research Station. South Dakota State University. HCR 1, P.O. Box 66, Philip, SD 57567. Phone: (605)386-4445 Fax: (605)386-4505 E-mail: sdsuctwd@gwtc.net • URL: http://www.abs.sdstate.edu/ars/cotton.

Iberia Research Station. Louisiana State University. P.O. Box 466, Jeanerette, LA 70544-0466. Phone: (318)276-5527 Fax: (318)276-9088 E-mail: sviator@agctr.lsu.edu.

Montana State University-Bozeman. Montana Agricultural Experiment Station. 202 Linfied Hall, Bozeman, MT 59717. Phone: (406)994-3681 Fax: (406)994-6579 E-mail: agdean@montana.edu •

URL: http://www.montana.edu.

STATISTICS SOURCES

Agricultural Statistics. Available from U. S. Government Printing Office. • Annual. $38.00. Produced by the National Agricultural Statistics Service, U. S. Department of Agriculture. Provides a wide variety of statistical data relating to agricultural production, supplies, consumption, prices/price-supports, foreign trade, costs, and returns, as well as farm labor, loans, income, and population. In many cases, historical data is shown annually for 10 years. In addition to farm data, includes detailed fishery statistics.

Business Statistics of the United States. Linz Audain and Cornelia J. Strawser. Bernan Associates. • Annual. $147.00. Based on *Business Statistics*, formerly issue by the Bureau of Economic Analysis, U. S. Department of Commerce. Provides basic data for a wide variety of U. S. industries, services, and economic indicators. Most statistics are shown annually for 30 years and monthly for the most recent four years.

FAO Production Yearbook. Available from Bernan Associates. • Annual. $45.00. Published by the Food and Agriculture Organization (http://www.fao.org). Contains worldwide data on agriculture, land use, farm crops, livestock, and agricultural prices.

FAO Trade Yearbook. Available from Bernan Associates. • Annual. $45.00. Published by the Food and Agriculture Organization (http://www.fao.org). Provides extensive worldwide data on exports and imports of agricultural commodities, fertilizers, tractors, and pesticides. Includes more than 130 tables of detailed statistics.

Survey of Current Business. Available from U. S. Government Printing Office. • Monthly. $63.00 per year. Issued by Bureau of Economic Analysis, U. S. Department of Commerce. Presents a wide variety of business and economic data.

TRADE/PROFESSIONAL ASSOCIATIONS

Livestock Marketing Association. 10510 NW Ambassador Dr., Kansas City, MO 64153. Phone: 800-821-2048 or (816)891-0502 Fax: (816)891-7926 E-mail: lmainfo@lmaweb.com • URL: http://www.lmaweb.com • Livestock marketing businesses and livestock dealers. Sponsors annual World Livestock Auctioneer Championships. Offers management and promotional services.

National Cattlemen's Beef Association. 9110 E Nichols Ave., Ste. 300, Centennial, CO 80112. Phone: (866)233-3872 or (303)694-0305 Fax: (303)694-2851 E-mail: membership@beef.org • URL: http://www.beefusa.org • Represents 149 organizations of livestock marketers, growers, meat packers, food retailers, and food service firms. Conducts extensive program of promotion, education and information about beef, veal, and associated meat products. Conducts projects such as recipe testing and development, food demonstrations, food photography, educational service to colleges, experimental meat cutting methods, merchandising programs, and preparation of materials for newspapers, magazines, radio, and television.

Society for Range Management. 445 Union Blvd., Ste. 230, Lakewood, CO 80228-1259. Phone: (303)986-3309 Fax: (303)986-3892 E-mail: srmweb@rangelands.org • URL: http://www.rangelands.org • Formerly American Society of Range Management.

Texas Longhorn Breeders Association of America. 2315 N Main St., Ste. 402, Fort Worth, TX 76164. Phone: (817)625-6241 Fax: (817)625-1388 E-mail: tlbaa@tlbaa.org • URL: http://www.tlbaa.org • Individuals, firms and organizations interested in the Texas Longhorn breed of cattle.

United Producers. PO Box 29800, PO Box 29800, Columbus, OH 43229. Phone: 800-456-3276 or (614)890-6666 Fax: (614)839-8659 E-mail:

erayburn@uproducers.com • URL: http://www.
uproducers.com • Cooperative marketing organization for livestock producers in the Midwest.
Conducts livestock marketing program. Owns Illinois Livestock Marketing Company. Works with
Illinois, Iowa, and Missouri farm bureaus.

United States Hide, Skin and Leather Association.
1700 N. Moore St., Suite 1600, Arlington, VA
22209. Phone: (703)841-5485 Fax: (703)841-9656
E-mail: lcondon@ushsla.org • URL: http://www.
meatami.org • Affiliated with American Meat
Institute.

CATV

See: CABLE TELEVISION INDUSTRY

CD-ROM DEVICES

See: MULTIMEDIA; OPTICAL DISK STOR-
AGE DEVICES

CELLULAR TELEPHONES

See: MOBILE TELEPHONE INDUSTRY

CEMENT INDUSTRY

See also: CONCRETE INDUSTRY

CD-ROM DATABASES

OECD Statistical Compendium. Organization for
Economic Cooperation and Development. •
Semiannual. $1,905.00 per year for 1 to 10 users.
CD-ROM contains more than 730,000 monthly,
quarterly, and annual time series for OECD
countries, 1960 to date. Includes fully searchable
data on agriculture, food, economic indicators,
national accounts, employment, energy, finance,
industry, technology, and foreign trade. Results can
be displayed in various forms.

DIRECTORIES

American Cement Directory. Bradley Pulverizer Co.
• Covers: Approximately 100 cement manufacturing companies in the United States, Canada,
Mexico, Central and South America. Entries
include: Company Name, address, phone, fax,
names of principal executives, capacity, capitalization, brand names and process, plant locations.

*Pit and Quarry Reference Manual and Buyers'
Guide.* Advanstar Communications. • Annual. $25.
00. Lists approximately 1,000 manufacturers and
other suppliers of equipment products and services
to the nonmetallic mining and quarrying industry.
Absorbed: *Ready-Mix-Reference Manual.*

FINANCIAL RATIOS

*Almanac of Business and Industrial Financial
Ratios.* Leo Troy. Aspen Publishers, Inc. • 2003.
$125.95. Includes CD-Rom. Contains financial
ratios derived from federal tax returns. Ratios for
each of about 200 industries are arranged according
to company asset size. (Almanac of Business and
Industrial Financial Ratios Series).

HANDBOOKS AND MANUALS

*Cement Data Book: International Process Engineer-
ing in the Cement Industry.* Walter H. Duda. French
and European Publications, Inc. • Dates vary. $950.
00. Three volumes. Vol.1, $375.00; vol.2, $325.00;
vol.3, $250.00. Text in English and German.

INTERNET DATABASES

Business 2.0 Web Guide to the Best Business Links.
Business 2.0 Media Inc. Phone: (415)293-4800
E-mail: support@business2.com • URL: http://
www.business2.com/webguide • Web site presents

an extensive, searchable directory of links to "the
best, most informative, and authoritative web
pages." Twenty main categories cover business,
finance, career, company information, people, and
technology topics, with thousands of subtopics, all
linking to Web sites recommended by experienced
business researchers. Fees: Free.

Fedstats. Federal Interagency Council on Statistical
Policy. Phone: (202)395-7254 • URL: http://www.
fedstats.gov • Web site features an efficient search
facility for full-text statistics produced by more than
100 federal agencies, including the Census Bureau,
the Bureau of Economic Analysis, and the Bureau of
Labor Statistics. Boolean searches can be made
within one agency or for all agencies combined.
Links are offered to international statistical bureaus,
including the UN, IMF, OECD, UNESCO, Eurostat,
and 20 individual countries. Fees: Free.

FreeLunch.com. Economy.com, Inc. Phone:
(610)696-8700 Fax: (610)696-1678 • URL: http://
www.freelunch.com • Web site provides free access
to more than 1.5 million economic and financial data
series, covering industry, demographics, labor
markets, prices, retail sales, government spending,
trade, interest rates, housing starts, the stock market,
and many other topics. Data is available for various
time periods in either chart or table form. Searching
is offered. Fees: Free, but registration required.
Economy.com, Inc. also offers fee-based economic
analysis at *The Dismal Scientist* site (http://www.
dismal.com).

ONLINE DATABASES

F & S Index. Gale Cengage Learning. • Contains
about four million citations to worldwide business,
financial, and industrial or consumer product
literature appearing from 1972 to date. Weekly
updates. Inquire as to online cost and availability.

PERIODICALS AND NEWSLETTERS

Cement and Concrete Research. Elsevier. •
Monthly. Qualified personnel, $347.00 per year;
institutions, $2,147.00 per year. Text in English,
French, German and Russian.

Pit and Quarry. Advanstar Communications. •
Monthly. $45.00 per year. Covers crushed stone,
sand and gravel, etc.

*Quarry Management: The Monthly Journal for the
Quarrying, Asphalt, Concrete and Recycling
Industries.* QMJ Publishing Ltd. • Monthly. $100.00
per year.

*Rock Products: The Aggregate Industry's Journal of
Applied Technology.* Primedia Business Magazines
and Media. • Monthly. $56.00 per year.

RESEARCH CENTERS AND INSTITUTES

Center for Cement Composite Materials. University
of Illinois at Urbana-Champaign. 2129 Newmark
Civil Engineering Laboratory, 205 Mathews Ave.,
Urbana, IL 61801. Phone: (217)333-6900 Fax:
(217)265-8040 E-mail: lstruble@uiuc.edu.

STATISTICS SOURCES

Annual Survey of Manufactures. Available from U.
S. Government Printing Office. • Annual. Prices
vary. Issued by the U. S. Census Bureau as an
interim update to the *Census of Manufactures.*
Includes data on number of manufacturing establishments in various industries, employment, labor
costs, value of shipments, capital expenditures,
inventories, energy costs, and assets. (See also
Census Bureau home page, http://www.census.
gov/.).

Business Statistics of the United States. Linz Audain
and Cornelia J. Strawser. Bernan Associates. •
Annual. $147.00. Based on *Business Statistics,*
formerly issue by the Bureau of Economic Analysis,
U. S. Department of Commerce. Provides basic data
for a wide variety of U. S. industries, services, and
economic indicators. Most statistics are shown an-

nually for 30 years and monthly for the most recent
four years.

Mineral Commodity Summaries. Available from U.
S. Government Printing Office. • Annual. $26.00.
Published by the U. S. Geological Survey, Department of the Interior (http://www.usgs.gov). Contains
detailed, five-year data for about 90 nonfuel
minerals. Covers a wide range of statistics, including production, imports, exports, consumption,
reserves, prices, tariff information, and industry
employment. (Two pages are devoted to each
mineral.).

Minerals Yearbook. Available from U.S. Government Printing Office. • Annual. Three volumes.

Survey of Current Business. Available from U. S.
Government Printing Office. • Monthly. $63.00 per
year. Issued by Bureau of Economic Analysis, U. S.
Department of Commerce. Presents a wide variety
of business and economic data.

United States Census of Manufactures. U.S. Bureau
of the Census. • Quinquennial. Results presented in
reports, tape, CD-ROM, and Diskette files.

WEFA Industrial Monitor. John Wiley and Sons, Inc.
• Annual. $65.00. Prepared by industry analysts at
WEFA, an economic forecasting and consulting firm
(originally Wharton Econometric Forecasting
Associates). Contains discussions of the outlook for
major U. S. industries, with many 10-year forecasts
(WEFA Web site is http://www.wefa.com).

TRADE/PROFESSIONAL ASSOCIATIONS

Cement Employers Association. 122 E Broad St.,
2nd Fl., Bethlehem, PA 18018. Phone: (610)868-
8060 Fax: (610)861-2884 E-mail: emcgehee@
cementemployers.com • Cement companies. Aims
to improve labor and employee relations.

Cement, Lime, Gypsum, and Allied Workers
Division. c/o James Hickenbotham, 3112 Peters
Creek Rd., North Roanoke Plaza, Roanoke, VA
24019. Phone: (540)362-7110 Fax: (540)362-7116
E-mail: union2@rbnet.com • URL: http://www.
boilermakers.org • Affiliated with International
Brotherhood of Boilermakers, Iron Ship Builders,
Blacksmiths, Forgers and Helpers.

Operative Plasterers and Cement Masons
International Association of U.S. and Canada. 14405
Laurel Place, Suite 300, Laurel, MD 20707. Phone:
(301)470-4200 Fax: (301)470-2502 E-mail:
opcmiaintl@opcmia.org • URL: http://www.
opcmia.org.

Portland Cement Association. 5420 Old Orchard
Rd., Skokie, IL 60077-1053. Phone: (847)966-6200
Fax: (847)966-8389 E-mail: info@cement.org •
URL: http://www.cement.org • Companies in the
U.S. and Canada. Seeks to improve and extend the
uses of Portland cement and concrete through
market promotion, research and development,
educational programs, and representation with
governmental entities. Conducts research on
concrete technology and durability; concrete pavement design; load-bearing capacities, field
performance, and fire resistance of concrete;
transportation, building, and structural uses of
concrete. Operates Construction +Technology
+Laboratories, which conducts research and technical services in construction materials, products, and
applications. Sponsors a public affairs program in
Washington, DC.

CEMETERIES

See: FUNERAL HOMES AND DIRECTORS

CENSUS REPORTS

See also: GOVERNMENT PUBLICATIONS; POPULATION

GENERAL WORKS

Moving Power and Money: The Politics of Census Taking. Barbara E. Bryant and William Dunn. New Strategist Publications, Inc. • 1995. $24.95. Barbara Everitt Bryant was Director of the U. S. Census Bureau from 1989 to 1993. She provides a plan for reducing the costs of census taking, improving accuracy, and overcoming public resistance to the census.

BIBLIOGRAPHIES

Census Catalog and Guide. U. S. Government Printing Office. • Annual. Lists publications and electronic media products currently available from the U. S. Bureau of the Census, along with some out of print items. Includes comprehensive title and subject indexes. Formerly *Bureau of the Census Catalog.*

Monthly Product Announcement. U. S. Bureau of the Census. • Monthly. Lists Census Bureau publications and products that became available during the previous month.

CD-ROM DATABASES

OECD Statistical Compendium. Organization for Economic Cooperation and Development. • Semiannual. $1,905.00 per year for 1 to 10 users. CD-ROM contains more than 730,000 monthly, quarterly, and annual time series for OECD countries, 1960 to date. Includes fully searchable data on agriculture, food, economic indicators, national accounts, employment, energy, finance, industry, technology, and foreign trade. Results can be displayed in various forms.

Sourcebooks America CD-ROM. CACI Marketing Systems. • Annual. $1,250.00. Provides the CD-ROM version of *The Sourcebook of ZIP Code Demographics: Census Edition* and *The Sourcebook of County Demographics: Census Edition.*

HANDBOOKS AND MANUALS

Industry and Product Classification Manual (SIC Basis). Available from National Technical Information Service. • 1992. Issued by U. S. Bureau of the Census. Contains extended Standard Industrial Classification (SIC) numbers used by the Census Bureau to allow a more detailed classification of industry, services, and agriculture.

North American Industry Classification System (NAICS). Available from Bernan Press. • 2002. $45.00. Issued by the Executive Office of the President, Office of Management and Budget (OMB).

Understanding the Census: A Guide for Marketers, Planners, Grant Writers, and Other Data Users. Michael R. Lavin. Epoch Books, Inc. • 1996. $49.95. Contains basic explanations of U. S. Census "concepts, methods, terminology, and data sources." Includes practical advice for locating and using Census data.

INTERNET DATABASES

Business 2.0 Web Guide to the Best Business Links. Business 2.0 Media Inc. Phone: (415)293-4800 E-mail: support@business2.com • URL: http://www.business2.com/webguide • Web site presents an extensive, searchable directory of links to "the best, most informative, and authoritative web pages." Twenty main categories cover business, finance, career, company information, people, and technology topics, with thousands of subtopics, all linking to Web sites recommended by experienced business researchers. Fees: Free.

Fedstats. Federal Interagency Council on Statistical Policy. Phone: (202)395-7254 • URL: http://www.fedstats.gov • Web site features an efficient search facility for full-text statistics produced by more than 100 federal agencies, including the Census Bureau, the Bureau of Economic Analysis, and the Bureau of Labor Statistics. Boolean searches can be made within one agency or for all agencies combined. Links are offered to international statistical bureaus, including the UN, IMF, OECD, UNESCO, Eurostat, and 20 individual countries. Fees: Free.

FreeLunch.com. Economy.com, Inc. Phone: (610)696-8700 Fax: (610)696-1678 • URL: http://www.freelunch.com • Web site provides free access to more than 1.5 million economic and financial data series, covering industry, demographics, labor markets, prices, retail sales, government spending, trade, interest rates, housing starts, the stock market, and many other topics. Data is available for various time periods in either chart or table form. Searching is offered. Fees: Free, but registration required. Economy.com, Inc. also offers fee-based economic analysis at *The Dismal Scientist* site (http://www.dismal.com).

1997 NAICS and 1987 SIC Correspondence Tables. U. S. Census Bureau. Phone: (301)457-4100 Fax: (301)457-1296 E-mail: naics@census.gov • URL: http://www.census.gov/epcd/www/naicstab.htm • Web site provides detailed tables for converting four-digit Standard Industrial Classification (SIC) numbers to the six-digit North American Industrial Classification System (NAICS) or vice versa: "1987 SIC Matched to 1997 NAICS" or "1997 NAICS Matched to 1987 SIC." Fees: Free.

PERIODICALS AND NEWSLETTERS

Population and Development Review. Blackwell Publishing. • Quarterly. Institutions, $105.00 per year. Includes print and online editions. *Supplement* available. Text in English; summaries in English, French and Spanish.

Population Bulletin. Population Reference Bureau, Inc. • Quarterly. $49.00 per year.

RESEARCH CENTERS AND INSTITUTES

Alabama State Data Center. University of Alabama. P.O. Box 870221, Tuscaloosa, AL 35487. Phone: (205)348-6191 Fax: (205)348-2951 E-mail: awatters@cba.ua.edu • URL: http://www.cber.cba.ua.edu.

Policy Research Institute. University of Kansas. 607 Blake Hall, 1541 Lilac Ln., Lawrence, KS 66044-3177. Phone: (785)864-9105 Fax: (785)864-3683 E-mail: thelyar@ukans.edu • URL: http://www.ukans.edu/pri • Formerly Institute for Public Policy and Business Research.

STATISTICS SOURCES

County and City Data Book 2000: A Statistical Abstract Supplement. Available from U. S. Government Printing Office. • 2002. $68.00. 13th edition. Issued by the U. S. Bureau of the Census (http://www.census.gov). Contains a wide variety of data on 3,141 U.S. counties, 1,078 cities, and 11,097 places of 2,500 or more inhabitants. Includes statistical information on retailing, manufacturing, banking, service industries, income, employment, housing, education, crime, and population. Updated metropolitan areas are included.

County and City Extra: Annual Metro, City and County Data Book. Deirdre A. Gaquin and Mark S. Littman. Bernan Press. • 2001. $120.00. Updates and augments data published irregularly in print form by the U. S. Census Bureau in *County and City Data Book.* Covers "every state, county, metropolitan area, and congressional district in the United States, as well as all U. S. cities with a 1990 population of 25,000 or more." Contains a wide range tic maps.

County and City Extra: Special Decennial Census Edition. Deirdre A. Gaquin and Katherine A. De-Brandt, editors. Bernan Press. • 2002. $95.00. Presents conveniently arranged population, housing, and other data from the 2000 census, with many 1980 and 1990 comparisons. Includes maps and tables with rankings of about 20 items for various geographic locations. Complements the annual *County and City Extra.*

County Business Patterns. Available from U. S. Government Printing Office. • Irregular. 52 issues containing annual data for each state, the District of Columbia, and a U. S. Summary. Produced by U.S. Bureau of the Census (http://www.census.gov). Provides local establishment and employment statistics by industry.

Current Population Reports: Household Economic Studies, Series P-70. Available from U. S. Government Printing Office. • Irregular. $21.00 per year. Issued by the U.S. Bureau of the Census (http://www.census.gov). Each issue covers a special topic relating to household socioeconomic characteristics.

Current Population Reports: Population Characteristics, Special Studies, and Consumer Income, Series P-20, P-23, and P-60. Available from U. S. Government Printing Office. • Irregular. $80.00 per year. Issued by the U.S. Bureau of the Census (http://www.census.gov). Each issue covers a special topic relating to population or income. Series P-20, *Population Characteristics*, provides statistical studies on such items as mobility, fertility, education, and marital status. Series P-23, *Special Studies*, consists of occasional reports on methodology. Series P-60, *Consumer Income*, publishes reports on income in relation to age, sex, education, occupation, family size, etc.

Historical Statistics of the United States, Colonial Times to 1970: A Statistical Abstract Supplement. U.S. Bureau of the Census. Available from U.S. Government Printing Office. • 1975. $109.00. Two volumes.

Places, Towns, and Townships, 1998. Deirdre A. Gaquin and Richard W. Dodge, editors. Bernan Press. • 1997. $89.00. Second edition. Presents demographic and economic statistics from the U. S. Census Bureau and other government sources for places, cities, towns, villages, census designated places, and minor civil divisions. Contains more than 60 data categories. (Places, Towns and Townships Series).

Population Abstract of the U. S. Gale Cengage Learning. • 1999. $190.00. Historical emphasis. Includes a "breakdown of urban and rural population from the earliest census to the present.".

Population of States and Counties of the United States: 1790-1990. Available from National Technical Information Service. • 1996. $35.00. Issued by the U. S. Census Bureau (http://www.census.gov). Provides data on the number of inhabitants of the U. S., states, territories, and counties according to 21 decennial censuses from 1790 to 1990. Includes descriptions of county origins and lists prior county names, where applicable.

The Sourcebook of ZIP Code Demographics. Available from Gale Cengage Learning. • Annual. $495.00. Published by ESRI Business Information Systems. Presents detailed statistical profiles of every ZIP code in America. Each profile contains data on more than 70 variables with 2003 updates and 2008 forecasts.

State and Metropolitan Area Data Book. Available from U. S. Government Printing Office. • 1998. Issued by the U. S. Bureau of the Census. Presents a wide variety of statistical data for U. S. regions, states, counties, metropolitan areas, and central cities, with ranking tables. Time period is 1970 to 1990.

Statistical Abstract of the United States. Available from U. S. Government Printing Office. • Annual. $51.00. Issued by the U. S. Bureau of the Census.

United States Census of Agriculture. U.S. Bureau of the Census. • Quinquennial. Results presented in reports, tape, CD-ROM, and Diskette files.

United States Census of Construction Industries. U.S. Bureau of the Census. • Quinquennial. Results presented in reports, tape, and CD-ROM files.

United States Census of Governments. Bureau of the Census, U.S. Department of Commerce. Available from U.S. Government Printing Office. • Quinquennial.

United States Census of Manufactures. U.S. Bureau of the Census. • Quinquennial. Results presented in reports, tape, CD-ROM, and Diskette files.

United States Census of Mineral Industries. Bureau of the Census, U.S. Department of Commerce. Available from U.S. Government Printing Office. • Quinquennial.

United States Census of Population. Bureau of the Census, U.S. Department of Commerce. Available from U.S. Government Printing Office. • Quinquennial.

United States Census of Retail Trade. U.S. Bureau of the Census. • Quinquennial.

United States Census of Service Industries. U.S. Bureau of the Census. • Quinquennial. Various reports available.

United States Census of Transportation. Bureau of the Census, U.S. Department of Commerce. Available from U.S. Government Printing Office. • Quinquennial.

United States Census of Wholesale Trade. Bureau of the Census, U.S. Department of Commerce. Available from U.S. Government Printing Office. • Quinquennial.

TRADE/PROFESSIONAL ASSOCIATIONS

Population Association of America. 8630 Fenton St., Ste. 722, Silver Spring, MD 20910. Phone: (301)565-6710 Fax: (301)565-7850 E-mail: info@popassoc.org • URL: http://www.popassoc.org • Individuals interested in demography and its scientific aspects.

Population Council. 1 Dag Hammarskjold Plz., New York, NY 10017. Phone: (212)339-0500 Fax: (212)755-6052 E-mail: pubinfo@popcouncil.org • URL: http://www.popcouncil.org • Seeks to improve the well-being and reproductive health of current and future generations around the world. Helps achieve a humane, equitable, and sustainable balance between people and resources.

Population Reference Bureau. 1875 Connecticut Ave. NW, Ste. 520, Washington, DC 20009-5728. Phone: 800-877-9881 or (202)483-1100 Fax: (202)328-3937 E-mail: popref@prb.org • URL: http://www.prb.org • Gathers, interprets, and disseminates information on the facts and implications of national and world population trends.

CENTRAL AMERICA

See: LATIN AMERICAN MARKETS

CERAMIC TILE INDUSTRY

See: TILE INDUSTRY

CERAMICS INDUSTRY

See also: CLAY INDUSTRY; POTTERY INDUSTRY

ABSTRACTS AND INDEXES

Applied Science and Technology Index. H. W. Wilson Co. • 11 times a year. Quarterly and annual cumulations. Price varies. Indexes a wide variety of English language technical, industrial, and engineering periodicals.

Ceramics Abstracts/ World Ceramics Abstracts.

American Ceramic Society. Cambridge Scientific Abstracts. • Five times a year. $225.00 per year. Online edition available.

Engineered Materials Abstracts. Cambridge Information Group. • Monthly. $995.00 per year. Provides citations to the technical and engineering literature of plastic, ceramic, and composite materials.

NTIS Alerts: Materials Sciences. National Technical Information Service. • Semimonthly. $220.00 per year. Provides descriptions of government-sponsored research reports and software, with ordering information. Covers ceramics, glass, coatings, composite materials, alloys, plastics, wood, paper, adhesives, fibers, lubricants, and related subjects. Formerly *Abstract Newsletter*.

CD-ROM DATABASES

METADEX Materials Collection: Metals-Polymers-Ceramics. Cambridge Scientific Abstracts. • Quarterly. Provides CD-ROM citations to the worldwide literature of materials science and metallurgy. Corresponds to *Metals Abstracts, Alloys Index, Steels Alert, Nonferrous Alert, Polymers/Ceramics/Composites Alert*, and *Engineered Materials Abstracts*. (Formerly produced by ASM International.).

ENCYCLOPEDIAS AND DICTIONARIES

ASM Materials Engineering Dictionary. Joseph R. Davis, editor. ASM International. • 1992. $166.00. Contains 10,000 entries, 700 illustrations, and 150 tables relating to metals, plastics, ceramics, composites, and adhesives. Includes "Technical Briefs" on 64 key material groups.

Encyclopedia of Advanced Materials. David Bloor and others. Elsevier. • 1994. $1,534.00. Four volumes.

Encyclopedia of Materials: Science and Technology. K.H.J. Buschow and others, editors. Elsevier. • 2001. $4,985.00. Eleven volumes. Provides extensive technical information on a wide variety of materials, including metals, ceramics, plastics, optical materials, and building materials. Includes more than 2,000 articles and 5,000 illustrations.

HANDBOOKS AND MANUALS

ASM Engineered Materials Reference Book. Michael L. Bauccio, editor. ASM International. • 1994. $155.00. Third edition. Provides information on a wide range of materials, with special sections on ceramics, industrial glass products, and plastics.

Ceramics: A Potter's Handbook. Glenn C. Nelson. Wadsworth Publishing Co. • 2001. $63.95. Sixth edition.

Handbook of Materials Selection. Myer Kutz. John Wiley and Sons, Inc. • 2002. $225.00. First section of handbook covers materials relative to the type of engineering application. Second section deals with the specific properties of materials. Covers both traditional materials and high-tech composites.

ONLINE DATABASES

Applied Science and Technology Index Online. H. W. Wilson Co. • Provides online indexing of 500 major scientific, technical, industrial, and engineering periodicals. Time period is 1983 to date. Monthly updates. Inquire as to online cost and availability.

Engineered Materials Abstracts [online]. Cambridge Scientific Abstracts. • Provides online citations to the technical and engineering literature of plastic, ceramic, and composite materials. Time period is 1986 to date, with monthly updates. (Formerly produced by ASM International.) Inquire as to online cost and availability.

F & S Index. Gale Cengage Learning. • Contains about four million citations to worldwide business, financial, and industrial or consumer product literature appearing from 1972 to date. Weekly

updates. Inquire as to online cost and availability.

Materials Business File. Cambridge Scientific Abstracts. • Provides online abstracts and citations to worldwide materials literature, covering the business and industrial aspects of metals, plastics, ceramics, and composites. Corresponds to *Steels Alert, Nonferrous Metals Alert*, and *Polymers/Ceramics/Composites Alert*. Time period is 1985 to date, with monthly updates. (Formerly produced by ASM International.) Inquire as to online cost and availability.

METADEX. Cambridge Scientific Abstracts. • Covers the worldwide literature of metals, metallurgy, and materials science, 1966 to date. Includes detailed alloys indexing from 1974. Biweekly updating. Inquire as to online cost and availability. (Formerly produced by ASM International.).

PERIODICALS AND NEWSLETTERS

American Ceramic Society Bulletin. American Ceramic Society. • Monthly. Members, $50.00 per year; non-members, $100.00 per year.

American Ceramic Society Journal. American Ceramic Society. • Monthly. Members, $150.00 per year; non-members, $750.00 per year. Includes subscription to *Ceramic Bulletin and Abstracts*.

Ceramic Industries International. Turret RAI plc. • Bimonthly. $94.00. per year.

Ceramic Industry: The Magazine for Refractories, Traditional and Advanced Ceramic Manufacturers. Business News Publishing Co. • 13 times a year. $65.00 per year. Includes *Data Buyers Guide, Materials Handbook, Economic Forecast*, and *Giants in Ceramic*.

Ceramics Monthly. American Ceramic Society. • 10 times a year. Member, $30.00 per year; non-members, $48.00 per year.

High-Tech Materials Alert: Advanced Materials: Their Uses and Manufacture. Technical Insights. • Monthly. Institutions, $695.00 per year. Newsletter on technical developments relating to high-performance materials, including metals and ceramics. Includes market forecasts.

RESEARCH CENTERS AND INSTITUTES

Alliance for Innovative Manufacturing. Stanford University, Bldg.02-530, Rm. 225, Stanford, CA 94305-3036. Phone: (650)723-9038 Fax: (650)723-5034 E-mail: cborn@stanford.edu • URL: http://www.stanford.edu/group/aim • Development of new products and processing. Formerly Stanford Integrated Manufacturing Association.

Materials Processing Center. Massachusetts Institute of Technology, 77 Massachusetts Ave., Room 12-007, Cambridge, MA 02139-4307. Phone: (617)253-5179 Fax: (617)258-6900 E-mail: fmpage@.mit.edu • URL: http://www.web.mit.edu/mpc • Conducts processing, engineering, and economic research in ferrous and nonferrous metals, ceramics, polymers, photonic materials, superconductors, welding, composite materials, and other materials.

STATISTICS SOURCES

Ceramic Industry Data Book Buyers' Guide. Business News Publishing Co. • Annual. $25.00. Included with subscription to *Ceramic Industry*. Formerly *Ceramic Data Book*.

Refractories. U. S. Bureau of the Census. • Annual. Provides data on value of manufacturers' shipments, quantity, exports, imports, etc. (Current Industrial Reports, MA-32C.).

TRADE/PROFESSIONAL ASSOCIATIONS

American Ceramic Society. 600 N Cleveland Ave., Ste. 210, Westerville, OH 43082. Phone: (866)721-3322 or (240)646-7054 Fax: (301)206-9789 E-mail: customerservice@ceramics.org • URL: http://www.ceramics.org • Professional society of scientists, engineers, educators, plant operators, and others interested in the glass, cements, refractories, nuclear ceramics, whitewares, electronics, engineering, and structural clay products industries. Disseminates scientific and technical information through its publications and technical meetings. Conducts continuing education courses and training such as the Precollege Education Program. Sponsors over 10 meetings yearly; encourages high school and college students' interest in ceramics. Maintains Ross C. Purdy Museum of Ceramics; offers placement service and speakers' bureau.

Associated Glass and Pottery Manufacturers. 912 Country Club Dr., Greensburg, PA 15601. Phone: (724)837-9451 Fax: (724)523-2022 E-mail: robrupp@helicon.net.

Glass Molders, Pottery, Plastics, and Allied Workers International Union. 608 E. Baltimore Pike, Media, PA 19063. Phone: (610)565-5051 Fax: (610)565-0983 E-mail: gmpiu@ix.netcom.com • URL: http://www.gmpiu.org.

Hobby Industry Association. 319 E. 54th St., Elmwood Park, NJ 07407. Phone: (201)794-1133 Fax: (201)797-0657 E-mail: hia@hobby.org • URL: http://www.hobby.org • Formerly Hobby Industry Association of America.

International Ceramic Association. 17098 Pheasant Meadow Ln. SW, Prior Lake, MN 55372. Phone: (952)447-6421 E-mail: ceramicteacher@msn.com • URL: http://www.ceramic-ica.com • Manufacturers, distributors, dealers, teachers, and finished ceramists in 7 countries. Conducts promotional activities; seeks to improve relations between the industry and raw material suppliers, transportation companies, and governments. Recommends standards for sales policy and buying, pricing, and inventory; promotes standardization of entries and judging at shows. Encourages improved teaching methods; conducts pilot programs for the handicapped; organizes teachers' meetings, business seminars, and competitions. Maintains International Ceramic Association Educational Foundation. Operates hall of fame.

National Institute of Ceramic Engineers. c/o Diane C. Folz, Virginia Polytechnic Institute and State University, Dept. of Materials Science and Engineering, 213 Holden Hall, Blacksburg, VA 24061. Phone: (540)231-3897 Fax: (540)231-8919 E-mail: dfolz@vt.edu • URL: http://www.acers.org • Affiliated with Ceramic Education Council and Keramos.

United Steelworkers of America. Aluminum, Brick and Glassworkers Division. c/o Unitrd Steelworkers of America, Five Gateway Center, Pittsburgh, PA 15222. Phone: (412)562-2400 E-mail: webmaster@uswa.org • URL: http://www.uswa.org.

CEREAL INDUSTRY

See: GRAIN INDUSTRY

CERTIFIED PUBLIC ACCOUNTANTS

See also: ACCOUNTING; WOMEN ACCOUNTANTS

ABSTRACTS AND INDEXES
Accounting and Tax Index. UMI. • Quarterly. Price on application. Annual cumulation. Indexes accounting, auditing, and taxation literature appearing in journals, books, pamphlets, conference proceedings, and newsletters.

Accounting Articles. CCH, Inc. • Monthly. $624.00 per year. Looseleaf service.

CD-ROM DATABASES
The Tax Directory [CD-ROM]. Tax Analysts. • Quarterly. Provides *The Tax Directory* listings on CD-ROM, covering federal, state, and international

tax officials, tax practitioners, and corporate tax executives.

DIRECTORIES
Emerson's Directory of Leading U.S. Accounting Firms. Emerson Co. • Biennial. $195.00. Provides information on 500 major CPA firms.

The Tax Directory. Tax Analysts. • Covers: Volume One--Approximately 15,000 federal and state government tax legislators, policymakers, administrators, and employees; tax regulation attorneys; over 500 international tax officials with central banks, ministries of finance, foreign embassies and consulate, and chambers of commerce; over 300 tax and business journalists and editors working for magazines, journals, newspapers, television, and radio; tax sections of over 100 trade and professional associations; state CPA, bar, and enrolled agent associations. Volume Two--Over 5,000 corporate tax managers of large U.S. and international firms. Entries include: For government and international officials--Name, title, address, phone, fax, email and website. For corporate tax managers--Name, address, phone, fax, email, website, and company name. For journalists--Name, address, phone, fax, email, website, and name of publication/network. For organizations and associations--Name, address, phone, fax, email, website, budget, membership, background information, and description of purpose.

ENCYCLOPEDIAS AND DICTIONARIES
Encyclopedia of Accounting Systems. Tom M. Plank and Lois R. Plank. Prentice Hall Books. • 1994. $132.00. Three volumes.

HANDBOOKS AND MANUALS
Accountant's Business Manual. American Institute of Certified Public Accountants. • $189.75. Looseleaf. Two volumes. Semiannual updates. Covers a wide variety of topics relating to financial and accounting management, including types of ownership, business planning, financing, cash management, valuation, retirement plans, estate planning, workers' compensation, unemployment insurance, social security, and employee benefits management.

Accountants' Liability. Practising Law Institute. • $160.00. Covers all aspects of accountants' professional liability issues, including depositions and court cases.

AICPA Audit and Accounting Manual. American Institute of Certified Public Accountants. • 1999. $90.50. Covers working papers, internal control, audit approach, etc.

AICPA Technical Practice Aids. American Institute of Certified Public Accountants. • 1998. $119.00 per year. Two volumes. Advisory opinions, statements of position, and other material.

Best Practices for Financial Advisors. Mary Rowland. Bloomberg. • 1997. $40.00. Provides advice for professional financial advisors on practice management, ethics, marketing, and legal concerns. (Bloomberg Professional Library.).

CPA Examination Review Business Law and Professional Responsibilities. Patrick R. Delaney and Debra R. Hopkins. John Wiley and Sons, Inc. • 2001. $41.00.

Getting Started in Investment Planning Services. James E. Grant. CCH, Inc. • 1999. $85.00. Second edition. Provides advice and information for lawyers and accountants who are planning to initiate fee-based investment services.

Marketing for CPAs, Accountants, and Tax Professionals. William J. Winston. Haworth Press, Inc. • 1995. $49.95. (Marketing Resources Series).

Mastering the Art of Marketing Professional Services: A Step-by-Step Best Practices Guide. Allan S. Boress and Michael G. Cummings. American Institute of Certified Public Accountants. • 2002. $74.00. Discusses recommended marketing

practices for accounting firms, including networking, advertising, press release writing, public speaking, seminar planning, and use of trade shows.

Professional Resumes for Accounting, Tax, Finance and Law: A Special Gallery of Best Resumes by Professional Resume Writers. David H. Noble. JIST Publishing. • 1999. $19.95. Written for accounting, tax, law, and finance professionals. In addition to advice, provides 335 sample resumes and 22 cover letters.

Valuing Professional Practices: A Practitioner's Guide. Robert Reilly and Robert Schweihs. CCH, Inc. • 1997. $99.00. Provides a basic introduction to estimating the dollar value of practices in various professional fields.

INTERNET DATABASES
Rutgers Accounting Web (RAW). Rutgers University Accounting Research Center. Phone: (973)353-5172 Fax: (973)353-1283 • URL: http://www.rutgers.edu/accounting • RAW Web site provides extensive links to sources of national and international accounting information, such as the Big Six accounting firms, the Financial Accounting Standards Board (FASB), SEC filings (EDGAR), journals, publishers, software, the International Accounting Network, and "Internet's largest list of accounting firms in USA." Searching is offered. Fees: Free.

PERIODICALS AND NEWSLETTERS
The CPA Journal (Certified Public Accountants). New York State Society of Certified Public Accountants. • Monthly. Individuals, $42.00 per year; students, $18.00 per year.

The CPA Letter: A News Report to Members. Public Relations-Communications. American Institute of Certified Public Accountants. • 10 times a year. Free to members; non-members, $40.00 per year.

CPA Managing Partner Report: Management News for Accounting Executives. Strafford Publications, Inc. • Monthly. $396.00 per year. Newsletter. Covers practice management and professional relationships.

CPA Marketing Report. CCH Inc. • Description: Helps public accounting firms design, implement, and evaluate effective programs to attract new clients, enhance the firm's image, improve client relations, and build sound practices.

CPA Personnel Report. Aspen Publishers Inc. • Description: Helps CPA firms excel in recruiting and retaining professional and non-professional staff, in competing with other firms to attract the best talent, in making informed hiring and firing decisions, and in staying abreast of evaluation, compensation, and benefits strategies and management and motivational techniques.

Inside Public Accounting. Hudson Sawyer Professional Services Marketing Inc. • Description: Contains articles on CPAs and CPA firms, provides news and analysis of management strategies, politics, marketing, computers, and personnel. Email alert delivers hot and topical news to subscribers' desktops. Recurring features include interviews, commentary, reports of meetings, book reviews, and the columns titled Mergers, New Shareholders, Newsmakers, and Lawsuits.

Journal of Accountancy. American Institute of Certified Public Accountants. • Monthly. Free to members; non-members, $61.00 per year.

National Public Accountant. National Society of Accountants. • 10 times a year. Free to members; non-members, $20.00 per year. For accounting and tax practitioners.

The Practical Accountant: Providing the Competitive Edge. Thomson Media. • Monthly. $65.00 per year. Covers tax planning, financial planning, practice management, client relationships, and related topics.

Practical Tax Strategies. RIA. • Monthly. $275.00.

per year. Emphasis is on current tax developments as they affect accountants and their clients. Includes advice on tax software and computers. Formerly *Taxation for Accountants.*

Public Accounting Report: Competitive Intelligence for Accounting Firms. Strafford Publications, Inc. • 23 times a year. $360.00 per year. Newsletter. Presents news and trends affecting the accounting profession.

Tax Practice. Tax Analysts. • Weekly. $199.00 per year. Newsletter. Covers news affecting tax practitioners and litigators, with emphasis on federal court decisions, rules and regulations, and tax petitions. Provides a guide to Internal Revenue Service audit issues.

RESEARCH CENTERS AND INSTITUTES

Accounting Research Program. University of California, The Anderson School, Los Angeles, CA 90095-1481. Phone: (310)206-6462 Fax: (310)267-2163 E-mail: carla.hayn@anderson.ucla.edu.

STATISTICS SOURCES

U. S. Industry and Trade Outlook. Available from National Technical Information Service. • Annual. $69.95. Produced by the International Trade Administration, U. S. Department of Commerce, in a "public-private" partnership with DRI/McGraw-Hill and Standard & Poor's. Provides basic data, outlook for the current year, and "Long-Term Prospects" (five-year projections) for a wide variety of products and services. Includes high technology industries. Formerly *U. S. Industrial Outlook.*

TRADE/PROFESSIONAL ASSOCIATIONS

American Institute of Certified Public Accountants. 1211 Ave. of the Americas, New York, NY 10036-8775. Phone: 888-777-7077 or (212)596-6200 Fax: (212)596-6213 • URL: http://www.aicpa.org.

American Woman's Society of Certified Public Accountants. 136 S Keowee St., Dayton, OH 45402. Phone: 800-297-2721 or (973)222-1872 Fax: (973)222-5794 E-mail: info@awscpa.org • URL: http://www.awscpa.org.

National Association of State Boards of Accountancy. 150 Fourth Ave., N., Suite. 00, Nashville, TN 37219. Phone: (615)880-4200 Fax: (615)880-4290 E-mail: communications@nasba.org • URL: http://www.nasba.org • Formerly Association of Certified Public Accountants.

National Society of Accountants. 1010 N Fairfax St., Alexandria, VA 22314-1574. Phone: 800-966-6679 or (703)549-6400 Fax: (703)549-2984 E-mail: members@nsacct.org • URL: http://www.nsacct.org • Formerly National Society of Public Accountants.

Tax Analysts. 400 S Maple Ave., Ste. 400, Falls Church, VA 22046. Phone: 800-955-2444 or (703)533-4400 Fax: (703)533-4444 E-mail: cservice@tax.org • URL: http://www.tax.org • Reviews all tax law developments, federal, state, international comprehensively; compiles statistics. **Convention/Meeting:** none.

OTHER SOURCES

Andrews' Professional Liability Litigation Reporter. Andrews Publications. • Monthly. $550.00 per year. Provides reports on lawsuits against attorneys, accountants, and investment professionals.

Avoiding Tax Malpractice. CCH, Inc. • 2000. $75.00. Covers malpractice considerations for professional tax practitioners.

CHAIN STORES

See also: DISCOUNT HOUSES; DRUG STORES; FRANCHISES; RETAIL TRADE

CD-ROM DATABASES

OECD Statistical Compendium. Organization for Economic Cooperation and Development. •

Semiannual. $1,905.00 per year for 1 to 10 users. CD-ROM contains more than 730,000 monthly, quarterly, and annual time series for OECD countries, 1960 to date. Includes fully searchable data on agriculture, food, economic indicators, national accounts, employment, energy, finance, industry, technology, and foreign trade. Results can be displayed in various forms.

DIRECTORIES

Directory of Automotive Aftermarket Suppliers. Chain Store Guide. • Annual. $327.00. Covers auto supply store chains. Includes distributors.

Directory of Chain Restaurant Operators. Chain Store Guide. • Annual. $335.00. Includes fast food establishments, and leading chain hotel copanies operating foodservice unit.

Directory of Discount and General Merchandise Stores. Chain Store Guide. • Annual. $327.00. On-line edition, $747.00. Includes retailers and wholesalers of housewares, giftwares, novelties, toys, hobby materials, crafts, and stationery.

Directory of Home Center Operators and Hardware Chains. Chain Store Guide. • Annual. $327.00. On-line edition, $747.00. Nearly 4,700 home center operators, paint and home decorating chains, and lumber and building materials companies. Covers United States and Canada.

Directory of Retail Chains in Canada. Rogers Media Publishing. • Annual. $340.00. Provides detailed information on approximately 1,600 retail chains of all sizes in Canada.

Directory of Supermarket, Grocery, and Convenience Store Chains. Chain Store Guide. • Annual. $327.00. Online edition, $747.00. Provides information on about 3,300 food store chains operating 120,000 individual stores. Store locations are given.

Discount Store News - Top Chains. Lebhar-Friedman, Inc. • Annual. $79.00.

National Association of Chain Drug Stores - Communications Directory. National Association of Chain Drug Stores. • Annual. Membership. About 150 chain drug retailers and their 31,000 individual pharmacies; 900 supplier companies; state boards of pharmacy, pharmaceutical and retail associations, colleges of pharmacy; drug trade associations.

Plunkett's Retail Industry Almanac: Complete Profiles on the Retail 500-The Leading Firms in Retail Stores, Services, Catalogs, and On-Line Sales. Plunkett Research, Ltd. • 2001. $229.99. Includes CD-ROM. Provides detailed profiles of 500 major U. S. retailers. Industry trends are discussed.

INTERNET DATABASES

Business 2.0 Web Guide to the Best Business Links. Business 2.0 Media Inc. Phone: (415)293-4800 E-mail: support@business2.com • URL: http://www.business2.com/webguide • Web site presents an extensive, searchable directory of links to "the best, most informative, and authoritative web pages." Twenty main categories cover business, finance, career, company information, people, and technology topics, with thousands of subtopics, all linking to Web sites recommended by experienced business researchers. Fees: Free.

Fedstats. Federal Interagency Council on Statistical Policy. Phone: (202)395-7254 • URL: http://www.fedstats.gov • Web site features an efficient search facility for full-text statistics produced by more than 100 federal agencies, including the Census Bureau, the Bureau of Economic Analysis, and the Bureau of Labor Statistics. Boolean searches can be made within one agency or for all agencies combined. Links are offered to international statistical bureaus, including the UN, IMF, OECD, UNESCO, Eurostat, and 20 individual countries. Fees: Free.

FreeLunch.com. Economy.com, Inc. Phone: (610)696-8700 Fax: (610)696-1678 • URL: http://

www.freelunch.com • Web site provides free access to more than 1.5 million economic and financial data series, covering industry, demographics, labor markets, prices, retail sales, government spending, trade, interest rates, housing starts, the stock market, and many other topics. Data is available for various time periods in either chart or table form. Searching is offered. Fees: Free, but registration required. Economy.com, Inc. also offers fee-based economic analysis at *The Dismal Scientist* site (http://www.dismal.com).

ONLINE DATABASES

F & S Index. Gale Cengage Learning. • Contains about four million citations to worldwide business, financial, and industrial or consumer product literature appearing from 1972 to date. Weekly updates. Inquire as to online cost and availability.

PERIODICALS AND NEWSLETTERS

Chain Drug Review: The Reporter for the Chain Drug Store Industry. Racher Press, Inc. • 21 times a year. $136.00 per year. Covers news and trends of concern to the chain drug store industry. Includes special articles on OTC (over-the-counter) drugs.

Chain Store Age: The NewsMagazine for Retail Executives. Lebhar-Friedman, Inc. • Monthly. $105.00 per year. Formerly *Chain Store Age Executive with Shopping Center Age.*

Drug Topics. Thomson Medical Economics. • 23 times a year. $61.00 per year. Edited for retail pharmacists, hospital pharmacists, pharmacy chain store executives, wholesalers, buyers, and others concerned with drug dispensing and drug store management. Provides information on new products, including personal care items and cosmetics.

DSN Retailing Today (Discount Store News). Lebhar-Friedman, Inc. • 23 times a year. $119.00 per year. Includes supplement *Apparel Merchandising.* Formerly (Discount Store News).

Franchising World. International Franchise Association. • Eight times a year. $18.00 per year. Formerly *Franchising Opportunities.*

Retail Pharmacy Management. McMahon Group. • Monthly. $60.00 per year. Featues include product news for pharmacists and financial news for chain store executives. Formerly *Retail Pharmacy Management News.*

Stores. National Retail Federation. NRF Enterprises, Inc. • Monthly. Individuals $49.00 per year; institutions, $120.00 per year.

Value Retail News: The Journal of Outlet and Off-Price Retail and Development. Off-Price Specialists, Inc. Value Retail News. • Monthly. Members, $144.00 per year; non-members, $175.00 per year. Provides news of the off-price and outlet store industry. Emphasis is on real estate for outlet store centers.

RESEARCH CENTERS AND INSTITUTES

Center for Retail Management. Kellogg School of Management, Northwestern University, 2001 Sheridan Rd., Evanston, IL 60208. Phone: (847)467-3600 Fax: (847)467-3620 E-mail: r-blattberg@kellogg.northwestern.edu • URL: http://www.kellogg.northwestern.edu • Conducts research related to retail marketing and management.

Center for Retailing Studies. Texas A & M University, Department of Marketing, 4112 TAMU, College Station, TX 77843-4112. Phone: (979)845-0325 Fax: (979)845-5230 E-mail: d-szymanski@tamu.edu • URL: http://www.crstamu.org • Research areas include retailing issues and consumer economics.

STATISTICS SOURCES

Business Statistics of the United States. Linz Audain and Cornelia J. Strawser. Bernan Associates. • Annual. $147.00. Based on *Business Statistics,* formerly issue by the Bureau of Economic Analysis, U. S. Department of Commerce. Provides basic data for a wide variety of U. S. industries, services, and economic indicators. Most statistics are shown annually for 30 years and monthly for the most recent four years.

Survey of Current Business. Available from U. S. Government Printing Office. • Monthly. $63.00 per year. Issued by Bureau of Economic Analysis, U. S. Department of Commerce. Presents a wide variety of business and economic data.

TRADE/PROFESSIONAL ASSOCIATIONS

CIES, Food Business Forum. 8455 Colesville Rd., Ste. 705, Silver Spring, MD 20910. Phone: (301)563-3383 Fax: (301)563-3386 E-mail: us.office@ciesnet.com • URL: http://www.ciesnet.com • Membership in 44 countries includes: food industry chain store firms with combined outlets of over 100,000; associations; firms supplying articles and services to chain food stores. Fosters cooperation between chain store organizations and their suppliers. Serves as a liaison between members. Assists in the exchange of trainees among member firms. Conducts studies on methods, technical progress, and the growth rate of chain store organizations throughout the world.

International Mass Retail Association. 1700 N. Moore St., Suite 2250, Arlington, VA 22209. Phone: (703)841-2300 Fax: (703)841-1184 E-mail: klasu@imra.org • URL: http://www.imra.org • Formerly National Mass Retailing Institute.

National Association of Chain Drug Stores. 413 N Lee St., Alexandria, VA 22313. Phone: (703)549-3001 Fax: (703)836-4869 • URL: http://www.nacds.org.

CHAMBERS OF COMMERCE

DIRECTORIES

World Chamber of Commerce Directory. • Annual. $50.00.

PERIODICALS AND NEWSLETTERS

Chamber Executive. American Chamber of Commerce Executives. • Description: Covers Chamber management issues, including economic development, international trade, membership development and retention, government relations, small business, and tourism development.

TRADE/PROFESSIONAL ASSOCIATIONS

American Chamber of Commerce Executives. 4232 King St., Alexandria, VA 22302. Phone: (703)998-0072 Fax: (703)931-5624 E-mail: mfleming@acce.org • URL: http://www.acce.org.

United States Council for International Business. 1212 Ave. of the Americas, 21st Fl., New York, NY 10036. Phone: (212)354-4480 Fax: (212)575-0327 E-mail: info@uscib.org • URL: http://www.uscib.org • Formerly United States Council of the International Chamber of Commerce.

CHARITABLE TRUSTS

See: FOUNDATIONS

CHARITY

See: PHILANTHROPY

CHARTS

See: GRAPHS AND CHARTS

CHARTS, STOCK MARKET

See: TECHNICAL ANALYSIS (FINANCE)

CHECKLESS BANKING

See: ELECTRONIC FUNDS TRANSFER SYSTEMS (EFTS)

CHEESE INDUSTRY

See also: DAIRY INDUSTRY

ABSTRACTS AND INDEXES

Food Science and Technology Abstracts. International Food Information Service Publishing. • Monthly. $1,780.00 per year. Provides worldwide coverage of the literature of food technology and food production.

Foods Adlibra: Key to the World's Food Literature. General Mills, Inc. Foods Adlibra Publications. • Semimonthly. $240.00 per year. Provides journal citations and abstracts to the literature of food technology and packaging.

ALMANACS AND YEARBOOKS

CRB Commodity Yearbook. Commodity Research Bureau. CRB. • Annual. $99.95.

CD-ROM DATABASES

Food Science and Technology Abstracts [CD-ROM]. Available from SilverPlatter Information, Inc. • Quarterly. Produced by International Food Information Service (home page is http://www.ifis.org). Provides worldwide coverage on CD-ROM of the literature of food technology and production. Various types of publications are indexed, with abstracts, including about 1,800 periodicals. Time period is 1969 to date.

DIRECTORIES

Cheese Market News--Market Directory. Quarne Publishing L.L.C. • Publication includes: List of suppliers of equipment, ingredients and services/supplies to the cheese industry and cheese manufacturers/marketers-including variety and style of cheese. Entries include: Company name, address, phone, fax, telex, and name and title of contact.

Dairy Foods Market Directory. Gorman Publishing Co. • Covers: Manufacturers of equipment, supplies and ingredients in the dairy foods industry. Entries include: Contact information.

Directory of Delicatessen Products. Pacific Rim Publishing Co. • Annual. Included with February issue of *Deli News.* Lists suppliers of cheeses, lunch meats, packaged fresh meats, kosher foods, gourmet-specialty items, and bakery products.

Major Food and Drink Companies of the World. Available from Gale Cengage Learning. • Annual. $880.00. Two volumes. Published by Graham & Whiteside. Contains profiles and trade names for more than 9,800 important food and beverage companies in various countries. In addition to foods, includes both alcoholic and nonalcoholic drink products.

Specialty Food Industry Directory. Phoenix Media Network, Inc. • Annual. Included in subscription to Food Distribution Magazine. Lists manufacturers and suppliers of specialty foods, and services and equipment for the specialty food industry. Featured food products include legumes, sauces, spices, upscale cheese, specialty beverages, snack foods, baked goods, ethnic foods, and specialty meats.

Thomas Food and Beverage Market Place. Grey House Publishing. • 2004. $495.00. Three volumes. Contains more than 40,000 entries covering food companies, beverages, food equipment, warehouse companies, food brokers, wholesalers, importers,

and exporters. Formerly *Thomas Food Industry Register.*

HANDBOOKS AND MANUALS

The Cheese Handbook. Bob Farand. Sterling Publishing Co., Inc. • 2001. $24.95.

INTERNET DATABASES

USDA. United States Department of Agriculture. Phone: (202)720-2791 E-mail: agsec@usda.gov • URL: http://www.usda.gov • The USDA home page has six sections: News and Information; What's New; About USDA; Agencies; Opportunities; Search and Help. Keyword searching is offered from the USDA home page and from various individual agency home pages. Agencies are the Economic Research Service, Agricultural Marketing Service, National Agricultural Statistics Service, National Agricultural Library, and about 12 others. Updating varies. Fees: Free.

ONLINE DATABASES

F & S Index. Gale Cengage Learning. • Contains about four million citations to worldwide business, financial, and industrial or consumer product literature appearing from 1972 to date. Weekly updates. Inquire as to online cost and availability.

Food Science and Technology Abstracts [online]. IFIS North American Desk. • Produced by International Food Information Service. Provides about 500,000 online citations, with abstracts, to the international literature of food science, technology, commodities, engineering, and processing. Approximately 2,000 periodicals are covered. Time period is 1969 to date, with monthly updates. Inquire as to online cost and availability.

FOODS ADLIBRA. General Mills, Inc. • Contains online citations, with abstracts, to the technical and business literature of food processing and packaging. New products and new ingredients are featured. Covers about 250 trade journals and 500 research journals from 1974 to date, with monthly updates. Inquire as to online cost and availability.

PERIODICALS AND NEWSLETTERS

Cheese Importers Association of America Bulletin. Cheese Importer Association of America. • Irregular. Membership.

Cheese Market News. Quarne Publishing LLC. • Weekly. $85.00 per year. Covers market trends, legislation, and new products.

Cheese Reporter. Richard Groves, editor. Cheese Reporter Publishing Co., Inc. • Weekly. $80.00 per year. Reports technology, production, sales, merchandising, promotion, research and general industry news of and pertaining to the manufacture and marketing of cheese.

Dairy Foods: Innovative Ideas and Technologies for Dairy Processors. Business News Publishing Co. • Monthly. $99.90 per year. Provides broad coverage of new developments in the dairy industry, including cheese and ice cream products. Includes an annual *Supplement.*

Deli News. Delicatessen Council of Southern California, Inc. Pacific Rim Publishing Co. • Monthly. $25.00 per year. Includes product news and comment related to cheeses, lunch meats, packaged fresh meats, kosher foods, gourmet-specialty items, and bakery products.

Fancy Food and Culinary Products. Talcott Communications Corp. • Monthly. $34.00 per year. Emphasizes new specialty food products and the business management aspects of the specialty food and confection industries. Includes special issues on wine, cheese, candy, "upscale" cookware, and gifts. Formerly (Fancy Foods).

Food Distribution Magazine. Phoenix Media Network, Inc. • Monthly. $49.00 per year. Edited for marketers and buyers of domestic and imported, specialty or gourmet food products, including ethnic foods, seasonings, and bakery items.

PRICE SOURCES

Dairy Market Statistics. U.S. Department of Agriculture, Agricultural Marketing Service. • Annual.

STATISTICS SOURCES

Agricultural Statistics. Available from U. S. Government Printing Office. • Annual. $38.00. Produced by the National Agricultural Statistics Service, U. S. Department of Agriculture. Provides a wide variety of statistical data relating to agricultural production, supplies, consumption, prices/price-supports, foreign trade, costs, and returns, as well as farm labor, loans, income, and population. In many cases, historical data is shown annually for 10 years. In addition to farm data, includes detailed fishery statistics.

Annual Survey of Manufactures. Available from U. S. Government Printing Office. • Annual. Prices vary. Issued by the U. S. Census Bureau as an interim update to the *Census of Manufactures.* Includes data on number of manufacturing establishments in various industries, employment, labor costs, value of shipments, capital expenditures, inventories, energy costs, and assets. (See also Census Bureau home page, http://www.census. gov/.).

FAO Production Yearbook. Available from Bernan Associates. • Annual. $45.00. Published by the Food and Agriculture Organization (http://www.fao.org). Contains worldwide data on agriculture, land use, farm crops, livestock, and agricultural prices.

FAO Trade Yearbook. Available from Bernan Associates. • Annual. $45.00. Published by the Food and Agriculture Organization (http://www.fao.org). Provides extensive worldwide data on exports and imports of agricultural commodities, fertilizers, tractors, and pesticides. Includes more than 130 tables of detailed statistics.

World Food Data and Statistics. Euromonitor International. • 2004. $650.00. Provides five-year data for a wide variety of food products in 52 countries. Includes market size, consumer expenditures, price indicators, and retail distribution data for many kinds of meat, fish, fruits, vegetables, dairy products, baked goods, condiments, canned food, and frozen food.

TRADE/PROFESSIONAL ASSOCIATIONS

Cheese Importers Association of America. 460 Park Ave., 11th Fl., New York, NY 10022. Phone: (212)753-7500 Fax: (212)688-2870 • URL: http:// www.cheesemarketnews.com.

National Cheese Institute. 1250 H St. NW, Ste. 900, Washington, DC 20005-3952. Phone: (202)737-4332 Fax: (202)331-7820 E-mail: membership@ idfa.org • URL: http://www.idfa.org • Represents manufacturers, processors, marketers, assemblers, and distributors of cheese and cheese products; advocates before government and regulatory bodies on behalf of members.

Wisconsin Cheese Makers' Association. 8030 Excelsior Dr., Ste. 305, Madison, WI 53717-1950. Phone: (608)828-4550 Fax: (608)828-4551 E-mail: office@wischeesemakersassn.org • URL: http:// www.wischeesemakersassn.org • Active licensed cheese plants; active licensed cheese making employees; suppliers of goods and services to the industry. Seeks to educate members for better work in the art of making cheese, the care and management of factories, and the sale of the product. Works to curb competency in the business and enforce laws that will protect the manufacturer against deceitful imitations.

OTHER SOURCES

U. S. Cheese Market. Available from MarketResearch.com. • 2002. $2,950.00. Market

research data published by Packaged Facts. Includes projections to 2006.

CHEMICAL ENGINEERING

See also: CHEMICAL INDUSTRIES

GENERAL WORKS

Chemical Engineering for Chemists. Richard G. Griskey. American Chemical Society. • 1997. $140. 00. Provides basic knowledge of chemical engineering and engineering economics.

ABSTRACTS AND INDEXES

Applied Science and Technology Index. H. W. Wilson Co. • 11 times a year. Quarterly and annual cumulations. Price varies. Indexes a wide variety of English language technical, industrial, and engineering periodicals.

Chemical Abstracts. Chemical Abstracts Service. • Weekly. $26,000.00 per year. Includes *CA Index Guide.*

Engineering Index Monthly: Abstracting and Indexing Services Covering Sources ofthe World's Engineering Literature. Engineering Information Inc. • Monthly. Institutions, $5,279.00 per year. Provides indexing and abstracting of the world's engineering and technical literature.

ALMANACS AND YEARBOOKS

Advances in Chemical Engineering. Elsevier. • Irregular. Prices vary.

BIBLIOGRAPHIES

Encyclopedia of Physical Science and Engineering Information. Gale Cengage Learning. • 1996. $160. 00. Second edition. Includes print, electronic, and other information sources for a wide range of scientific, technical, and engineering topics.

BIOGRAPHICAL SOURCES

Who's Who in Science and Engineering. Marquis Who's Who. • Biennial. $269.00. Provides concise biographical information on 35,000 prominent engineers and scientists. International coverage, with geographical and professional indexes.

DIRECTORIES

Chemical and Engineering News-Career and Employment. American Chemical Society. • Annual. $9.00.

Chemical Engineering Buyers Guide. McGraw-Hill Inc. • Publication includes: List of over 4,000 firms supplying equipment, materials, and services to the chemical process industries. Entries include: Company name, address, phone, fax, toll-free phone, all sales office locations and phones.

Consulting Services. Association of Consulting Chemists and Chemical Engineers Inc. • Covers: about 160 member consultants in chemistry, chemical engineering, metallurgy, etc. Entries include: Individual name, address, certificate number, qualifications, affiliation, experience, facilities, staff.

Peterson's Graduate and Professional Programs in Engineering and Applied Sciences. Peterson's. • Annual. $49.95. Provides details of more than 3,400 graduate and professional programs in engineering and related fields at colleges and universities. (Peterson's Graduate in Professional Programs Series). Formerly *Peterson's Guide to Graduate Programs in Engineering and Professional Sciences.*

Plunkett's Engineering and Research Industry Almanac. Plunkett Research, Ltd. • Annual. $179. 99. Contains detailed profiles of major engineering and technology corporations. Includes CD-ROM.

ENCYCLOPEDIAS AND DICTIONARIES

Kirk-Othmer Concise Encyclopedia of Chemical Technology. John Wiley and Sons, Inc. • 2001. $295. 00. Fourth edition. Contains abstracts of articles

from the multivolume *Kirk-Othmer Encyclopedia of Chemical Technology.*

HANDBOOKS AND MANUALS

Handbook of Chemical Engineering Calculations. Nicolas P. Chopey. McGraw-Hill Professional. • 2003. $125.00. Third edition.

ONLINE DATABASES

Applied Science and Technology Index Online. H. W. Wilson Co. • Provides online indexing of 500 major scientific, technical, industrial, and engineering periodicals. Time period is 1983 to date. Monthly updates. Inquire as to online cost and availability.

CA Search. Chemical Abstracts Service. • Guide to chemical literature, 1967 to present. Inquire as to online cost and availability.

Current Contents Connect. Institute for Scientific Information. • Provides online abstracts of articles listed in the tables of contents of about 7,500 journals. Coverage is very broad, including science, social science, life science, technology, engineering, industry, agriculture, the environment, economics, and arts and humanities. Time period is two years, with weekly updates. Inquire as to online cost and availability.

NTIS Database. National Technical Information Service. • Contains citations and abstracts to unrestricted reports of government-sponsored research, 1964 to date. Covers a wide range of technical, engineering, business, and social science topics. Monthly updates. Inquire as to online cost and availability.

Who's Who in Technology [Online]. Gale Cengage Learning. • Provides online biographical profiles of over 25,000 American scientists, engineers, and others in technology-related occupations. Inquire as to online cost and availability.

PERIODICALS AND NEWSLETTERS

AIChe Journal. American Institute of Chemical Engineers. • Monthly. Members, $105.00 per year; non-members, $950.00 per year. Devoted to research and technological developments in chemical engineering and allied fields. Available online.

CEC Communications (Chemical Engineering Communications). Taylor and Francis Group. • Bimonthly. Institutions, $87.00 per year; corporations, $135.00 per year. Formerly *Chemical Engineering Communications.*

Chemical Engineering. Chemical Week Associates. • Monthly. $39.50 per year. Includes annual *Chemical Engineering Buyers Guide.*

Chemical Engineering Progress. American Institute of Chemical Engineers. • Monthly. Individuals, $100.00 per year. Covers current advances and trends in the chemical process and related industries. Supplement available *AICh Extra.*

Chemical Equipment. Reed Business Information. • Monthly. Free to qualified personnel. Covers the design, building, and operation of chemical process plants. Includes end-of-year *Chemical Equipment Literature Review.*

Industrial and Engineering Chemistry Research. American Chemical Society. • Monthly. Members, $169.00 per year; institutions, $1,445.00 per year; students, $127.00 per year. Available on line . Formerly *Industrial and Engineering Chemistry Product Research and Development.*

Journal of Chemical and Engineering Data. American Chemical Society. • Bimonthly. Members, $81.00 per year; institutions, $770.00 per year; students, $61.00 per year.

PRICE SOURCES

Chemical and Engineering News: The Newsmagazine of the Chemical World. American Chemical

Society. • Weekly. Institutions, $210.00 per year.

RESEARCH CENTERS AND INSTITUTES

Alberta Research Council, Inc. 250 Karl Clark Rd., Edmonton, AB, Canada T6N 1E4. Phone: (780)450-5111 Fax: (780)450-5333 E-mail: solutions@arc.ab.ca • URL: http://www.arc.ab.ca.

Division of Engineering Research. Michigan State University. B-100 Engineering Research Complex, East Lansing, MI 48824. Phone: (517)355-5104 Fax: (517)353-5547 E-mail: wadem@egr.msu.edu • URL: http://www.egr.msu.edu/der.

Institute for Systems Research. University of Maryland at College Park, A. V. Williams Bldg., 2nd Fl., No. 115, College Park, MD 20742-3311. Phone: (301)405-6615 Fax: (301)314-9220 E-mail: isr@isr.umd.edu • URL: http://www.isr.umd.edu/ • A National Science Foundation Engineering Research Center. Areas of research include communication systems, manufacturing systems, chemical process systems, artificial intelligence, and systems integration.

STATISTICS SOURCES

Chemical and Engineering News: Facts and Figures. American Chemical Society. • Annual. $20.00. List of 100 largest chemical producers by total chemical sales.

TRADE/PROFESSIONAL ASSOCIATIONS

American Chemical Society. 1155 16th St. NW, Washington, DC 20036. Phone: 800-227-5558 or (202)872-4600 Fax: (202)872-4615 E-mail: help@acs.org • URL: http://portal.chemistry.org/portal/acs/corg/memberapp • Scientific and educational society of chemists and chemical engineers. Conducts: studies and surveys; special programs for disadvantaged persons; legislation monitoring, analysis, and reporting; courses for graduate chemists and chemical engineers; radio and television programming. Offers career guidance counseling; administers the Petroleum Research Fund and other grants and fellowship programs. Operates Employment Clearing Houses. Compiles statistics. Maintains Speaker's Bureau and 33 divisions.

American Institute of Chemical Engineers. Three Park Ave., New York, NY 10016-5991. Phone: 800-242-4363 or (212)591-7338 Fax: (212)591-8897 E-mail: xpress@aiche.org • URL: http://www.aiche.org.

Association of Consulting Chemists and Chemical Engineers. P.O. Box 297, Sparta, NJ 07871. Phone: (973)729-6671 Fax: (973)729-7088 E-mail: info@chemconsult.org • URL: http://www.chemconsult.org.

CHEMICAL INDUSTRIES

See also: AGRICULTURAL CHEMICALS; FERTILIZER INDUSTRY; PLASTICS INDUSTRY

GENERAL WORKS

Chemistry Today and Tomorrow: The Central, Useful, and Creative Science. Ronald Breslow. Jones and Bartlett Publishers, Inc. • 1996. $37.95. Written in nontechnical language for the general reader. Discusses the various disciplines of chemistry, such as medicinal, environmental, and industrial. (Chemistry Series).

Understanding Toxicology: Chemicals, Their Benefits and Uses. Bruno H. Schiefer and others. CRC Press LLC. • 1997. $39.95. Provides a basic introduction to chemical interactions and toxicology for the general reader.

ABSTRACTS AND INDEXES

Applied Science and Technology Index. H. W. Wilson Co. • 11 times a year. Quarterly and annual cumulations. Price varies. Indexes a wide variety of English language technical, industrial, and engineering periodicals.

Chemical Abstracts. Chemical Abstracts Service. • Weekly. $26,000.00 per year. Includes *CA Index Guide.*

BIBLIOGRAPHIES

How to Find Chemical Information: A Guide for Practicing Chemists, Educators, and Students. Robert E. Maizell. John Wiley and Sons, Inc. • 1998. $89.95. Third edition.

Information Sources in Chemistry. Peter Rhodes and Fy Hon Rowland. K.G. Saur Publishing. • 2003. Price on application. Evaluates information sources on a wide range of chemical topics. (Guides to Information Sources Series).

CD-ROM DATABASES

Hazardous Substances Data Bank. SilverPlatter Information, Inc. • Provides CD-ROM information on hazardous substances, including 140,000 chemicals in the *Registry of Toxic Effects of Chemical Substances* and 60,000 materials covered by the *Toxic Substances Control Act Initial Inventory.*

OECD Statistical Compendium. Organization for Economic Cooperation and Development. • Semiannual. $1,905.00 per year for 1 to 10 users. CD-ROM contains more than 730,000 monthly, quarterly, and annual time series for OECD countries, 1960 to date. Includes fully searchable data on agriculture, food, economic indicators, national accounts, employment, energy, finance, industry, technology, and foreign trade. Results can be displayed in various forms.

DIRECTORIES

Chem Sources--International. Chem Sources International Inc. • Publication includes: List of 8,000 chemical producers and distributors in 135 countries; 275,000 chemicals; and 25,000 chemical trade names. Entries include: For producers and distributors--Company name, address, phone, locations of manufacturing plants, shipping points, sales offices, telex, TWX, cable address. For agents and representatives--Name, company name and address. Principal content of publication is alphabetical listing of 200,000 organic and inorganic chemical compounds by chemical nomenclature; includes classified list of trade names for 7,000 products.

Chem Sources--USA. Chem Sources International Inc. • Publication includes: List of 800 United States and Canadian chemical producers and distributors; 160,000 chemicals. Entries include: company name, address, phone, locations of manufacturing plants, shipping points, e-mail addresses, sales offices, telex, fax, cable address. Principal content of directory is alphabetical listing of 160,000 chemical products by chemical nomenclature.

Chemcyclopedia. American Chemical Society. • Publication includes: List of over 900 chemical manufacturers and suppliers in the United States and Canada. Entries include: Company name, address, phone, fax, telex, trade name; chemical available grades, packaging, special shipping requirements, and potential applications. Principal content of publication is technical and commercial information on about 10,000 chemicals produced and sold arranged by product group.

Chemical Week-Buyers Guide. Chemical Week Associates. • Annual. $115.00. About 4,200 manufacturers and suppliers of chemical raw materials to the chemical process industries. Included in subscription to *Chemical Week.*

Directory of Chemical Producers - United States. SRI Consulting. • Annual. $2,070.00. Information on over 1,200 United States basic chemical producers, manufacturing nearly 7,900 chemicals in commercial quantities at 3,500 plant locations.

Internet Tools of the Profession: A Guide for Information Professionals. Hope N. Tillman, editor.

Special Libraries Association. • 1997. $49.00. Second edition. Consists of 14 sections by various authors or compilers. After two introductory articles on searching the Internet, there are 12 annotated lists of useful Web sites, covering the SLA, business and finance, chemistry, education, food and agriculture, information technology, insurance and employee benefits, law, library management, metals and materials, pharmaceuticals, and telecommunications. An index is provided.

Major Chemical and Petrochemical Companies of Europe. Available from Gale Cengage Learning. • 2003. $880.00. Fifth edition. Two volumes. Published by Graham & Whiteside Ltd., London. Includes financial, personnel, and product information for chemical companies in Western Europe.

Major Chemical and Petrochemical Companies of the World. Available from Gale Cengage Learning. • 2002. $880.00. Sixth edition. Published by Graham & Whiteside. Contains profiles of more than 7,000 important chemical and petrochemical companies in various countries. Subject areas include general chemicals, specialty chemicals, agricultural chemicals, petrochemicals, industrial gases, and fertilizers.

McCutcheon's Functional Materials Volumes 2. MC Publishing Co. • Annual. $170.00. Edited for product development, quality control and research and development chemists.

McCutcheon's Volume 1: Emulsifiers and Detergents. MC Publishing Co. • Annual. $190.00. Two volumes. International coverage.

OPD Chemical Buyers Directory. Schnell Publishing Company Inc. • Covers: about 1,500 suppliers of chemical process materials and more than 300 companies that transport and store chemicals in the United States. Entries include: Company name, address, phone, list of products or services, telex, fax, e-mail address, internet address, branch offices.

Purchasing/CPI Chemicals Yellow Pages. Reed Business Information. • Annual. $85.00. Manufacturers and distributors of 10,000 chemicals and raw materials, containers and packaging, transportation services and storage facilities; includes environmental servicer companies. Formerly *CPI Purchasing-Chemicals Directory.*

ENCYCLOPEDIAS AND DICTIONARIES

Encyclopedia of Polymer Science and Technology. Corinna Czekaj. John Wiley and Sons, Inc. • 2004. $3,600. Third edition. 12 volumes. Covers new techniques and methods, as well as "traditional topics of continuing interest.".

Hawley's Condensed Chemical Dictionary. Richard J. Lewis. John Wiley and Sons, Inc. • 2002. $155.00. 14th edition. Contains information about thousands of chemicals. Entries cover properties, occurence, shipping regulations, hazards, synonyms, applications, and other characteristics. (CD-ROM edition also available.).

Kirk-Othmer Concise Encyclopedia of Chemical Technology. John Wiley and Sons, Inc. • 2001. $295.00. Fourth edition. Contains abstracts of articles from the multivolume *Kirk-Othmer Encyclopedia of Chemical Technology.*

Kirk-Othmer Encyclopedia of Chemical Technology. Raymond E. Kirk and Donald F. Othmer. John Wiley and Sons, Inc. • 1991-97. $9,895.00, prepaid. 27 volumes. Fourth edition. Four volumes are scheduled to be published each year, with individual volumes available at $415.00. (Kirk-Othmer Encyclopedia of Chemical Technology Series).

McGraw-Hill Encyclopedia of Science & Technology. McGraw-Hill. • 2002. $2,495.00. Ninth edition. 20 volumes.

Ullmann's Encyclopedia of Industrial Chemistry. Matthias Bonet and others, editors. John Wiley and

Sons, Inc. • 2003. $4,500.00. Sixth edition. 40 volumes.

FINANCIAL RATIOS

Almanac of Business and Industrial Financial Ratios. Leo Troy. Aspen Publishers, Inc. • 2003. $125.95. Includes CD-Rom. Contains financial ratios derived from federal tax returns. Ratios for each of about 200 industries are arranged according to company asset size. (Almanac of Business and Industrial Financial Ratios Series).

Annual Statement Studies. The Risk Management Association. • Annual. Median and quartile financial ratios are given for over 400 kinds of manufacturing, wholesale, retail, construction, and consumer finance establishments. Data is sorted by both asset size and sales volume. Includes a clearly written "Definition of Ratios" and an alphabetical industry index.

Annual Statement Studies: Industry Default Probabilities and Cash Flow Measures. The Risk Management Association. • Annual. $145.00. Serves as a companion volume to the original *Annual Statement Studies.* Gives probability of default estimates on a percentage scale for more than 450 industries. Includes changes in position year-by-year for eight financial statement line items and provides percentage measures of cash flow.

IRS Corporate Financial Ratios. Available from MarketResearch.com. • 2002. $225.00. Published by Schonfeld & Associates, Inc. Presents 70 key financial ratios for 260 industries. Ratios are calculated from income statement and balance sheet data available from the Internal Revenue Service. Includes four asset size classes.

Quarterly Financial Report for Manufacturing, Mining, and Trade Corporations. U.S. Federal Trade Commission and U.S. Securities and Exchange Commission. Available from U.S. Government Printing Office. • Quarterly. $49.00 per year.

HANDBOOKS AND MANUALS

Comprehensive Guide to the Hazardous Properties of Chemical Substances. Pradyot Patnaik. John Wiley and Sons, Inc. • 1999. $210.00. Second edition.

Dun & Bradstreet/Gale Group Industry Handbooks. Gale Cengage Learning. • 2000. $650.00. Five volumes. $130.00 per volume. Each volume covers two or more major industries: 1. *Entertainment and Hospitality*; 2. *Construction and Agriculture*; 3. *Chemicals and Pharmaceuticals*; 4. *Computers & Software and Broadcasting & Telecommunications*; 5. *Insurance and Health & Medical Services.* The following are included for each industry: overview, statistics, financial ratios, rankings, merger information, company directory, directory of associations, and consultants directory. (Dun and Bradstreet/Gale Industry Reference Handbook Series).

Hazardous Chemicals Desk Reference. Richard J. Lewis. John Wiley and Sons, Inc. • 2002. $185.00. Fifth edition. Summarizes the hazardous properties of about 5,000 chemical substances.

INTERNET DATABASES

Business 2.0 Web Guide to the Best Business Links. Business 2.0 Media Inc. Phone: (415)293-4800 E-mail: support@business2.com • URL: http://www.business2.com/webguide • Web site presents an extensive, searchable directory of links to "the best, most informative, and authoritative web pages." Twenty main categories cover business, finance, career, company information, people, and technology topics, with thousands of subtopics, all linking to Web sites recommended by experienced business researchers. Fees: Free.

Fedstats. Federal Interagency Council on Statistical Policy. Phone: (202)395-7254 • URL: http://www.fedstats.gov • Web site features an efficient search facility for full-text statistics produced by more than 100 federal agencies, including the Census Bureau, the Bureau of Economic Analysis, and the Bureau of Labor Statistics. Boolean searches can be made within one agency or for all agencies combined. Links are offered to international statistical bureaus, including the UN, IMF, OECD, UNESCO, Eurostat, and 20 individual countries. Fees: Free.

FreeLunch.com. Economy.com, Inc. Phone: (610)696-8700 Fax: (610)696-1678 • URL: http://www.freelunch.com • Web site provides free access to more than 1.5 million economic and financial data series, covering industry, demographics, labor markets, prices, retail sales, government spending, trade, interest rates, housing starts, the stock market, and many other topics. Data is available for various time periods in either chart or table form. Searching is offered. Fees: Free, but registration required. Economy.com, Inc. also offers fee-based economic analysis at *The Dismal Scientist* site (http://www.dismal.com).

Manufacturing Profiles. U. S. Bureau of the Census. Phone: (301)763-4636 E-mail: webmaster@census.gov • URL: http://www.census.gov/prod/www/abs/mfg-prof.html • The Census Bureau makes available free on PDF (Portable Document Format) an annual consolidation of the entire Current Industrial Report series, presenting "all the data compiled." Contains statistics on production, shipments, inventories, consumption, exports, imports, and orders for a wide variety of manufactured products.

ONLINE DATABASES

Business and Industry. Gale Cengage Learning. • Contains online citations, abstracts, and selected fulltext from more than 1,000 trade journals, newspapers, and other publications. Provides general coverage of both manufacturing and service industries, including marketing, production, industry trends, key events, and information on specific companies. Time span is 1994 to date. Daily updates. Inquire as to online cost and availability. (Also available in a CD-ROM version.).

CA Search. Chemical Abstracts Service. • Guide to chemical literature, 1967 to present. Inquire as to online cost and availability.

F & S Index. Gale Cengage Learning. • Contains about four million citations to worldwide business, financial, and industrial or consumer product literature appearing from 1972 to date. Weekly updates. Inquire as to online cost and availability.

Tablebase. Gale Cengage Learning. • Provides online numerical tabular data from a wide variety of business, organization, and government sources, including about 1,000 trade journals. Includes industry and individual company statistics relating to products, market share, sales forecasts, production, exports, market trends, etc. Time span is 1997 to date. Weekly updates. Inquire as to online cost and availability. (Also available in a CD-ROM version.).

PERIODICALS AND NEWSLETTERS

Chemical Equipment. Reed Business Information. • Monthly. Free to qualified personnel. Covers the design, building, and operation of chemical process plants. Includes end-of-year *Chemical Equipment Literature Review.*

Chemical Processing. Putman Media. • Monthly. Free to qualified personnel; others, $67.00 per year.

Chemical Week. Chemical Week Associates. • 49 times a year. $139.00 per year. Includes annual *Buyers' Guide.*

JOACS (Journal of the American Oil Chemists' Society). American Oil Chemists' Society. AOCS Press. • Monthly. Individuals, $120.00 per year; institutions, $278.00 per year. Includes *INFORM: International News on Fats, Oils and Related Materials.*

Journal of Chemical Information and Computer Sciences. American Chemical Society. • Bimonthly. Members, $75.00; institutions, $531.00 per year; students, $56.00 per year. others, price on application.

PetroChemical News: A Weekly News Service in English Devoted to the Worldwide Petrochemical Industry. William F. Bland Co. • Weekly. $807.00 per year. Report of current and significant news about the petrochemical business worldwide.

Today's Chemist at Work. American Chemical Society. • Monthly. Institutions, $200.00 per year; others, price on application. Provide practrical information for chemists on day-to-day operations. Product coverage includes chemicals, equipment, apparatus, instruments, and supplies.

PRICE SOURCES

Chemical and Engineering News: The Newsmagazine of the Chemical World. American Chemical Society. • Weekly. Institutions, $210.00 per year.

Chemical Market Reporter. Schnell Publishing Co., Inc. • Weekly. $169.00 per year. Quotes current prices for a wide range of chemicals. Formerly *Chemical Marketing Reporter.*

STATISTICS SOURCES

Annual Review of the Chemical Industry. United Nations Publications. • Annual. $100.00.

Annual Survey of Manufactures. Available from U. S. Government Printing Office. • Annual. Prices vary. Issued by the U. S. Census Bureau as an interim update to the *Census of Manufactures.* Includes data on number of manufacturing establishments in various industries, employment, labor costs, value of shipments, capital expenditures, inventories, energy costs, and assets. (See also Census Bureau home page, http://www.census.gov/.).

Business Statistics of the United States. Linz Audain and Cornelia J. Strawser. Bernan Associates. • Annual. $147.00. Based on *Business Statistics,* formerly issue by the Bureau of Economic Analysis, U. S. Department of Commerce. Provides basic data for a wide variety of U. S. industries, services, and economic indicators. Most statistics are shown annually for 30 years and monthly for the most recent four years.

Encyclopedia of American Industries. Gale Cengage Learning. • 2000. $560.00. Third edition. Two volumes. $280.00 per volume. Volume one is *Manufacturing Industries* and volume two is *Service and Non-Manufacturing Industries.* Provides the history, development, and recent status of approximately 1,000 industries. Includes statistical graphs, with industry and general indexes.

Standard & Poor's Industry Surveys. Standard & Poor's. • Semiannual. $1,800.00. Two looseleaf volumes. Includes monthly *Supplements.* Provides detailed, individual surveys of 52 major industry groups. Each survey is revised on a semiannual basis. Also includes "Monthly Investment Review" (industry group investment analysis) and monthly "Trends & Projections" (economic analysis).

Survey of Current Business. Available from U. S. Government Printing Office. • Monthly. $63.00 per year. Issued by Bureau of Economic Analysis, U. S. Department of Commerce. Presents a wide variety of business and economic data.

Synthetic Organic Chemicals: United States Production and Sales. International Trade Commission. Available from U.S. Government Printing Office. • Annual.

United States Census of Manufactures. U.S. Bureau of the Census. • Quinquennial. Results presented in reports, tape, CD-ROM, and Diskette files.

WEFA Industrial Monitor. John Wiley and Sons, Inc. • Annual. $65.00. Prepared by industry analysts at WEFA, an economic forecasting and consulting firm (originally Wharton Econometric Forecasting Associates). Contains discussions of the outlook for major U. S. industries, with many 10-year forecasts (WEFA Web site is http://www.wefa.com).

TRADE/PROFESSIONAL ASSOCIATIONS

American Chemical Society. 1155 16th St. NW, Washington, DC 20036. Phone: 800-227-5558 or (202)872-4600 Fax: (202)872-4615 E-mail: help@acs.org • URL: http://portal.chemistry.org/portal/acs/corg/memberapp • Scientific and educational society of chemists and chemical engineers. Conducts: studies and surveys; special programs for disadvantaged persons; legislation monitoring, analysis, and reporting; courses for graduate chemists and chemical engineers; radio and television programming. Offers career guidance counseling; administers the Petroleum Research Fund and other grants and fellowship programs. Operates Employment Clearing Houses. Compiles statistics. Maintains Speaker's Bureau and 33 divisions.

American Chemistry Council. 1300 Wilson Blvd., Arlington, VA 22209. Phone: (703)741-5000 Fax: (703)741-6050 E-mail: aygoyer@one.net • URL: http://www.americanchemistry.com • Represents the leading companies engaged in the business of chemistry. Members apply the science of chemistry to make innovative products and services that make people's lives "better, healthier and safer." Improves environmental, health and safety performance through "Responsible Care"(R), common sense advocacy designed to address major public policy issues, and health and environmental research and product testing.

Association of Consulting Chemists and Chemical Engineers. P.O. Box 297, Sparta, NJ 07871. Phone: (973)729-6671 Fax: (973)729-7088 E-mail: info@chemconsult.org • URL: http://www.chemconsult.org.

Chemical Specialties Manufacturers Association. 1913 Eye St., N.W., Washington, DC 20006. (202)872-8110 Fax: (202)872-8114 E-mail: csma@juno.com • Formerly National Association Insecticide and Disinfectant Manufacturers.

Commercial Development and Marketing Association. 1900 Arch St., Philadelphia, PA 19103. Phone: (215)564-3484 Fax: (215)963-9784 E-mail: info@cdmaonline.org • URL: http://www.cdmaonline.com • Formerly Commercial Chemical Development Association.

National Association of Chemical Distributors. 1560 Wilson Blvd., Suite 1250, Arlington, VA 22209. Phone: (703)527-6223 Fax: (703)527-7747 E-mail: publicaffairs@nacd.com • URL: http://www.nacd.com.

Sales Association of the Chemical Industry. 66 Morris Ave., Ste. 2A, Springfield, NJ 07081. Phone: (973)379-1100 Fax: (973)379-6507 E-mail: veronicagaamc@earthlink.net • Members are chemical sales personnel, including sales managers and executives. Formerly Salesmen's Association of the American Chemical Industry.

United Food and Commercial Workers Union International. 1775 K St., N.W., Washington, DC 20006. Phone: (202)223-3111 Fax: (202)466-1562 • URL: http://www.ufcw.org.

OTHER SOURCES

Chemical Regulation Reporter: A Weekly Review of Activity Affecting Chemical Users and Manufacturers. BNA, Inc. • Weekly. $2,226 per year. Looseleaf service.

CHEMICAL LABORATORIES

See: LABORATORIES

CHEMICAL MARKETING

ABSTRACTS AND INDEXES

Business Periodicals Index. H. W. Wilson Co. • 11 times a year. Quarterly and annual cumulations. Price varies.

DIRECTORIES

Chem Sources--International. Chem Sources International Inc. • Publication includes: List of 8,000 chemical producers and distributors in 135 countries; 275,000 chemicals; and 25,000 chemical trade names. Entries include: For producers and distributors--Company name, address, phone, locations of manufacturing plants, shipping points, sales offices, telex, TWX, cable address. For agents and representatives--Name, company name and address. Principal content of publication is alphabetical listing of 200,000 organic and inorganic chemical compounds by chemical nomenclature; includes classified list of trade names for 7,000 products.

Chem Sources--USA. Chem Sources International Inc. • Publication includes: List of 800 United States and Canadian chemical producers and distributors; 160,000 chemicals. Entries include: company name, address, phone, locations of manufacturing plants, shipping points, e-mail addresses, sales offices, telex, fax, cable address. Principal content of directory is alphabetical listing of 160,000 chemical products by chemical nomenclature.

Chemical Wholesalers Directory. infoUSA. • Annual. Price on application. Lists 8,082 United States wholesalers and 1,199 Canadian wholesalers. Compiled from telephone company yellow pages.

OPD Chemical Buyers Directory. Schnell Publishing Company Inc. • Covers: about 1,500 suppliers of chemical process materials and more than 300 companies that transport and store chemicals in the United States. Entries include: Company name, address, phone, list of products or services, telex, fax, e-mail address, internet address, branch offices.

ONLINE DATABASES

PROMT: Predicasts Overview of Markets and Technology. Gale Cengage Learning. • Companies, products, applied technologies and markets. U.S. and international literature coverage, 1972 to date. Inquire as to online cost and availability. Provides abstracts from more than 1,600 publications. Weekly updates.

Wilson Business Abstracts Online. H. W. Wilson Co. • Indexes and abstracts 600 major business periodicals, plus the *Wall Street Journal* and the business section of the *New York Times*. Indexing is from 1982, abstracting from 1990, with the two newspapers included from 1993. Updated weekly. Inquire as to online cost and availability. (*Business Periodicals Index* without abstracts is also available online.).

PERIODICALS AND NEWSLETTERS

Chemical Week. Chemical Week Associates. • 49 times a year. $139.00 per year. Includes annual *Buyers' Guide*.

PRICE SOURCES

Chemical Market Reporter. Schnell Publishing Co., Inc. • Weekly. $169.00 per year. Quotes current prices for a wide range of chemicals. Formerly *Chemical Marketing Reporter*.

STATISTICS SOURCES

Annual Bulletin of Trade in Chemical Products. Economic Commission for Europe. United Nations Publications. • Annual. $47.00.

Chemical and Engineering News: Facts and Figures. American Chemical Society. • Annual. $20.00. List of 100 largest chemical producers by total chemical sales.

Chemical Week: Financial Survey of the 300 Largest Companies in the U. S. Chemical Process Industries. Chemical Week Associates. • Annual. $8.00. Supersedes *Chemical Week-Chemical Week 300*.

Synthetic Organic Chemicals: United States Production and Sales. International Trade Commission. Available from U.S. Government Printing Office. • Annual.

TRADE/PROFESSIONAL ASSOCIATIONS

American Chemical Society. 1155 16th St. NW, Washington, DC 20036. Phone: 800-227-5558 or (202)872-4600 Fax: (202)872-4615 E-mail: help@acs.org • URL: http://portal.chemistry.org/portal/acs/corg/memberapp • Scientific and educational society of chemists and chemical engineers. Conducts: studies and surveys; special programs for disadvantaged persons; legislation monitoring, analysis, and reporting; courses for graduate chemists and chemical engineers; radio and television programming. Offers career guidance counseling; administers the Petroleum Research Fund and other grants and fellowship programs. Operates Employment Clearing Houses. Compiles statistics. Maintains Speaker's Bureau and 33 divisions.

American Chemistry Council. 1300 Wilson Blvd., Arlington, VA 22209. Phone: (703)741-5000 Fax: (703)741-6050 E-mail: aygoyer@one.net • URL: http://www.americanchemistry.com • Represents the leading companies engaged in the business of chemistry. Members apply the science of chemistry to make innovative products and services that make people's lives "better, healthier and safer." Improves environmental, health and safety performance through "Responsible Care"(R), common sense advocacy designed to address major public policy issues, and health and environmental research and product testing.

National Association of Chemical Distributors. 1560 Wilson Blvd., Suite 1250, Arlington, VA 22209. Phone: (703)527-6223 Fax: (703)527-7747 E-mail: publicaffairs@nacd.com • URL: http://www.nacd.com.

Sales Association of the Chemical Industry. 66 Morris Ave., Ste. 2A, Springfield, NJ 07081. Phone: (973)379-1100 Fax: (973)379-6507 E-mail: veronicagaamc@earthlink.net • Members are chemical sales personnel, including sales managers and executives. Formerly Salesmen's Association of the American Chemical Industry.

CHILD CARE

See: DAY CARE CENTERS

CHILD LABOR

See also: LABOR; LABOR LAW AND REGULATION

GENERAL WORKS

Child Labor: An American History. Hugh D. Hindman. M. E. Sharpe, Inc. • 2002. $88.95.

ONLINE DATABASES

Labordoc. International Labour Organization. • Indexing of labor literature and the publications of the International Labour Organization, 1965 to present. Monthly updates. Inquire as to online cost and availability.

LEXIS. LEXIS-NEXIS. • The various LEXIS databases provide full text and indexing for a wide variety of legal cases, statutes, orders, and opinions.

TRADE/PROFESSIONAL ASSOCIATIONS

National Child Labor Committee. 1501 Broadway, Ste. 1908, New York, NY 10036. Phone: (212)840-1801 Fax: (212)768-0963 E-mail: info@nationalchildlabor.org • URL: http://www.nationalchildlabor.org • Parent organization of National Committee on Employment of Youth and

National Committee on the Education of Migrant Children. Provides direct and technical assistance to programs on youth-related issues, particularly education, job training, and employment.

National Youth Employment Coalition. 1836 Jefferson Pl. NW, Washington, DC 20036. Phone: (202)659-1064 Fax: (202)659-0399 E-mail: nyec@nyec.org • URL: http://www.nyec.org • A network of over 180 community-based organizations, research organizations, public interest groups, policy analysis organizations, and others dedicated to promoting improved policies and practices related to youth employment/development, to help youth succeed in becoming lifelong learners, productive workers and self-sufficient citizens.

CHILD MARKET

See: YOUTH MARKET

CHILDREN'S APPAREL INDUSTRY

See also: CLOTHING INDUSTRY

DIRECTORIES

Buyer's Guide to the New York Market. Earnshaw Publications, Inc. • Annual. Included with *Earnshaw's Magazine.*

Directory of Apparel Specialty Stores. Chain Store Guide. • Annual. $335.00. 4,700 apparel and sporting goods specialty stores in the United States and Canada, operating more than 80,000 stores. Include company name, phone and fax numbers, company e-mail and web addresses and other information.

Garment Manufacturers Index. Klevens Publications Inc. • Covers: about 8,000 manufacturers and suppliers of products and services such as fabrics, trimmings, factory equipment, and sewing contractors used in the manufacture of apparel. Publication includes: fabrics, trimmings, supplies, services, equipment, and contractors. Entries include: Company name, address, phone, fax, list of products or services, brief description of product.

Women's and Children's Wear Buyers Directory. Douglas Publications, Inc. • Annual. $329.00. About 10,500 retail stores selling women's dresses, coats, sportswear, intimate apparel, and women's accessories, infants' to teens wear, and accessories; coverage does not include New York metropolitan area. *Salesman's Guide Directories.*

FINANCIAL RATIOS

Annual Statement Studies. The Risk Management Association. • Annual. Median and quartile financial ratios are given for over 400 kinds of manufacturing, wholesale, retail, construction, and consumer finance establishments. Data is sorted by both asset size and sales volume. Includes a clearly written "Definition of Ratios" and an alphabetical industry index.

Annual Statement Studies: Industry Default Probabilities and Cash Flow Measures. The Risk Management Association. • Annual. $145.00. Serves as a companion volume to the original *Annual Statement Studies.* Gives probability of default estimates on a percentage scale for more than 450 industries. Includes changes in position year-by-year for eight financial statement line items and provides percentage measures of cash flow.

HANDBOOKS AND MANUALS

Children's Clothing Store. Entrepreneur Media, Inc. • Looseleaf. $59.50. A practical guide to starting a children's clothing shop. Covers profit potential, start-up costs, market size evaluation, owner's time required, site selection, lease negotiation, pricing, accounting, advertising, promotion, etc. (Start-Up

Business Guide No. E1161.).

INTERNET DATABASES

Manufacturing Profiles. U. S. Bureau of the Census. Phone: (301)763-4636 E-mail: webmaster@census.gov • URL: http://www.census.gov/prod/www/abs/mfg-prof.html • The Census Bureau makes available free on PDF (Portable Document Format) an annual consolidation of the entire Current Industrial Report series, presenting "all the data compiled." Contains statistics on production, shipments, inventories, consumption, exports, imports, and orders for a wide variety of manufactured products.

ONLINE DATABASES

F & S Index. Gale Cengage Learning. • Contains about four million citations to worldwide business, financial, and industrial or consumer product literature appearing from 1972 to date. Weekly updates. Inquire as to online cost and availability.

PERIODICALS AND NEWSLETTERS

Apparel Merchandising. Lebhar-Friedman, Inc. • Eight times a year. $24.00 per year. Reports on fashion trends in women's, men's, and children's clothing. Supplement to (DSN Retailing Today).

Baby and Junior: International Trade Magazine for Children's and Youth Fashions and Supplies. Verbond der Korbwaren-, Korbmoebel-und Kinderwagen-Industrie. Meisenbach GmbH. • 10 times a year. 131.00 per year. Text in German.

Earnshaw's Infants, Girls and Boys Wear Review - Children's Wear Directory. Earnshaw Publications, Inc. • Annual. Controlled circulation.

Tobe Report. Tobe. • 38 times a year. Price on application. Edited for fashion retailers. Provides detailed information and analysis relating to current trends in the women's, children's, and men's apparel and accessories markets.

STATISTICS SOURCES

Annual Survey of Manufactures. Available from U. S. Government Printing Office. • Annual. Prices vary. Issued by the U. S. Census Bureau as an interim update to the *Census of Manufactures.* Includes data on number of manufacturing establishments in various industries, employment, labor costs, value of shipments, capital expenditures, inventories, energy costs, and assets. (See also Census Bureau home page, http://www.census.gov/.).

TRADE/PROFESSIONAL ASSOCIATIONS

Bureau of Wholesale Sales Representatives. 1100 Spring St. N.W., Suite 700, Atlanta, GA 30309. Phone: 800-877-1808 or (404)870-7600 Fax: (404)870-7601 E-mail: info@bwsr.com • URL: http://www.bwsr.com • Formerly Bureau of Salesmen's National Association.

Infant and Juvenile Manufacturers Association. 125 Ramona Ct., New Rochelle, NY 10804. Phone: (914)235-9258 Fax: (914)235-9258 E-mail: inj@ferster.com.

CHINA

See: ASIAN MARKETS

CHINAWARE

See: TABLEWARE

CHLORINE INDUSTRY

See: CHEMICAL INDUSTRIES

CHOCOLATE INDUSTRY

See also: CANDY INDUSTRY; COCOA INDUSTRY

GENERAL WORKS

Chocolate Fads, Folklore, and Fantasies: 1,000 Chunks of Chocolate Information. Linda K. Fuller.

The Haworth Press, Inc. • 1994. $49.95. Includes "Choco-Marketing-Mania Survey," "Media Citations: Chocolate 1979-1992," "Choco-References," and addresses of chocolate companies. (Original Book Series).

ABSTRACTS AND INDEXES

Food Science and Technology Abstracts. International Food Information Service Publishing. • Monthly. $1,780.00 per year. Provides worldwide coverage of the literature of food technology and food production.

Foods Adlibra: Key to the World's Food Literature. General Mills, Inc. Foods Adlibra Publications. • Semimonthly. $240.00 per year. Provides journal citations and abstracts to the literature of food technology and packaging.

CD-ROM DATABASES

Food Science and Technology Abstracts [CD-ROM]. Available from SilverPlatter Information, Inc. • Quarterly. Produced by International Food Information Service (home page is http://www.ifis.org). Provides worldwide coverage on CD-ROM of the literature of food technology and production. Various types of publications are indexed, with abstracts, including about 1,800 periodicals. Time period is 1969 to date.

DIRECTORIES

Major Food and Drink Companies of the World. Available from Gale Cengage Learning. • Annual. $880.00. Two volumes. Published by Graham & Whiteside. Contains profiles and trade names for more than 9,800 important food and beverage companies in various countries. In addition to foods, includes both alcoholic and nonalcoholic drink products.

Thomas Food and Beverage Market Place. Grey House Publishing. • 2004. $495.00. Three volumes. Contains more than 40,000 entries covering food companies, beverages, food equipment, warehouse companies, food brokers, wholesalers, importers, and exporters. Formerly *Thomas Food Industry Register.*

ONLINE DATABASES

Food Science and Technology Abstracts [online]. IFIS North American Desk. • Produced by International Food Information Service. Provides about 500,000 online citations, with abstracts, to the international literature of food science, technology, commodities, engineering, and processing. Approximately 2,000 periodicals are covered. Time period is 1969 to date, with monthly updates. Inquire as to online cost and availability.

FOODS ADLIBRA. General Mills, Inc. • Contains online citations, with abstracts, to the technical and business literature of food processing and packaging. New products and new ingredients are featured. Covers about 250 trade journals and 500 research journals from 1974 to date, with monthly updates. Inquire as to online cost and availability.

STATISTICS SOURCES

Statistical Bulletin of the International Office of Cocoa, Chocolate and Sugar Confectionary. International Office of Cocoa, Chocolate and Sugar Confectionary. • Annual.

World Food Data and Statistics. Euromonitor International. • 2004. $650.00. Provides five-year data for a wide variety of food products in 52 countries. Includes market size, consumer expenditures, price indicators, and retail distribution data for many kinds of meat, fish, fruits, vegetables, dairy products, baked goods, condiments, canned food, and frozen food.

TRADE/PROFESSIONAL ASSOCIATIONS

American Cocoa Research Institute. 8320 Old Courthouse Rd., Ste. 300, Vienna, VA 22182. Phone: (703)790-5011 Fax: (703)790-5752 E-mail: larry.

graham@candyusa.org • URL: http://www.chocolateandcocoa.org/acri.

Chocolate Manufacturers Association of the U.S.A. 8320 Old Courthouse Rd., Ste. 300, Vienna, VA 22182-3811. Phone: (703)790-5750 Fax: (703)790-5752 E-mail: info@candyusa.org • URL: http://www.candyusa.org • Formerly Association of Cocoa and Chocolate Manufacturers of the U.S.

The Cocoa Merchants' Association of America, Inc. 39 Broadway, 3rd Fl., New York, NY 10006. Phone: (212)201-8819 Fax: (212)785-5475 E-mail: cmaa@cocoamerchants.com • URL: http://www.cocoamerchants.com.

OTHER SOURCES
The Candy Market. Available from MarketResearch.com. • 1998. $2,500.00. Published by Packaged Facts. Provides market data on chocolate and non-chocolate candy.

CHRISTMAS CARDS

See: GREETING CARD INDUSTRY

CHROMIUM INDUSTRY

See: METAL INDUSTRY

CHRONOLOGY

See also: ANNIVERSARIES AND HOLIDAYS
GENERAL WORKS
American Decades. Gale Cengage Learning. • 1994-2001. $990.00. 10 volumes. $99.00 per volume. Each volume covers a decade during the period 1900-1989. "Each volume begins with an overview and chronology covering the entire decade. Subject chapters follow, each including an overview, subject-specific timeline and alphabetically arranged entries..".

Business History of the World: A Chronology. Richard B. Robinson. Greenwood Publishing Group, Inc. • 1993. $85.00. Provides "a basic chronology of the business world outside the United States from prehistory through the 1980s.".

FAA Historical Chronology: Civil Aviation and the Federal Government, 1926-1996. Edmund Preston, editor. Available from U. S. Government Printing Office. • 1998. $33.50. Third edition. Issued by the Federal Aviation Administration, U. S. Department of Transportation (http://www.dot.gov). Provides a compilation of historical information about the FAA and the earlier Civil Aeronautics Board (CAB). Chronological arrangement.

It Was a Very Good Year: Extraordinary Moments in Stock Market History. Martin S. Fridson. John Wiley and Sons, Inc. • 1997. $29.95. Provides details on what happened during each of the ten best years for the stock market since 1900. (Investment Series).

United States Business History, 1602-1988: A Chronology. Richard B. Robinson. Greenwood Publishing Group, Inc. • 1990. $99.95.

ALMANACS AND YEARBOOKS
The Annual Register: A Record of World Events. Keesing's Worldwide, LLC. • Annual. $185.00. Published by Keesings Worldwide. Lists major economic, social, and cultural events of the past year. International coverage.

DIRECTORIES
Chase's Calendar of Events: The Day-by-Day Directory. McGraw-Hill. • Annual. $52.95. Provides information for over 12,000 special days and special events throughout the world. Chronological arrange-

ment with an alphabetical index. Formerly *Chase's Annual Events.*

ENCYCLOPEDIAS AND DICTIONARIES
Encyclopedia of American Facts and Dates. Gorton Carruth. HarperInformation. • 1997. $50.00. 10th edition. (Encyclopedia of American Facts and Dates Series).

Gale Encyclopedia of U.S. Economic History. Gale Cengage Learning. • 2000. $225.00. Two volumes. Contains about 1,000 alphabetically arranged entries. Includes industry profiles, biographies, social issue profiles, geographic profiles, and chronological tables.

Knowledge Exchange Business Encyclopedia: Your Complete Business Advisor. Lorraine Spurge. Knowledge Exchange LLC. • 1998. $45.00. Provides definitions of business terms and financial expressions, profiles of leading industries, tables of economic statistics, biographies of business leaders, and other business information. Includes "A Chronology of Business from 3000 B.C. Through 1995." Contains illustrations and three indexes.

CIGAR AND CIGARETTE INDUSTRY

See also: SMOKING POLICY; TOBACCO AND TOBACCO INDUSTRY

GENERAL WORKS
Cigarettes: Anatomy of an Industry from Seed to Smoke. Tara Parker-Pope. The New Press. • 2001. $24.95. Covers the history, economic ramifications, marketing strategies, and legal problems of the cigarette industry. Popularly written.

Rise and Fall of the Cigarette: A Social and Cultural History of Smoking in the U. S. Allan Brandt. Basic Books. • 2000. $25.00. Second edition.

Smoking and Politics: Policy Making and the Federal Bureaucracy. A. Lee Fritschler and James M. Hoepler. Prentice Hall PTR. • 1995. $44.00. Fifth edition.

ALMANACS AND YEARBOOKS
Tobacco Retailers Almanac. Retail Tobacco Dealers of America Inc. • Annual. Price on application. Lists virtually every tobacco related product available (including cigars, cigarettes, pipes, tobacco, lighters and gift items).

CD-ROM DATABASES
OECD Statistical Compendium. Organization for Economic Cooperation and Development. • Semiannual. $1,905.00 per year for 1 to 10 users. CD-ROM contains more than 730,000 monthly, quarterly, and annual time series for OECD countries, 1960 to date. Includes fully searchable data on agriculture, food, economic indicators, national accounts, employment, energy, finance, industry, technology, and foreign trade. Results can be displayed in various forms.

DIRECTORIES
Perelman's Pocket Cyclopedia of Cigars. Perelman, Pioneer and Co. • Annual. $12.95. Contains profiles of more than 1,000 brands of cigars marketed in the U. S.

Tobacco International Buyers' Guide and Directory. Lockwood Publications, Inc. • Annual. $40.00. Formerly *Tobacco Internatonal Directory and Buyers' Guide.*

INTERNET DATABASES
Business 2.0 Web Guide to the Best Business Links. Business 2.0 Media Inc. Phone: (415)293-4800 E-mail: support@business2.com • URL: http://www.business2.com/webguide • Web site presents an extensive, searchable directory of links to "the best, most informative, and authoritative web

pages." Twenty main categories cover business, finance, career, company information, people, and technology topics, with thousands of subtopics, all linking to Web sites recommended by experienced business researchers. Fees: Free.

Fedstats. Federal Interagency Council on Statistical Policy. Phone: (202)395-7254 • URL: http://www.fedstats.gov • Web site features an efficient search facility for full-text statistics produced by more than 100 federal agencies, including the Census Bureau, the Bureau of Economic Analysis, and the Bureau of Labor Statistics. Boolean searches can be made within one agency or for all agencies combined. Links are offered to international statistical bureaus, including the UN, IMF, OECD, UNESCO, Eurostat, and 20 individual countries. Fees: Free.

FreeLunch.com. Economy.com, Inc. Phone: (610)696-8700 Fax: (610)696-1678 • URL: http://www.freelunch.com • Web site provides free access to more than 1.5 million economic and financial data series, covering industry, demographics, labor markets, prices, retail sales, government spending, trade, interest rates, housing starts, the stock market, and many other topics. Data is available for various time periods in either chart or table form. Searching is offered. Fees: Free, but registration required. Economy.com, Inc. also offers fee-based economic analysis at *The Dismal Scientist* site (http://www.dismal.com).

ONLINE DATABASES
Agricola. U.S. National Agricultural Library. • Covers worldwide agricultural literature. Over 3.3 million citations, 1970 to present, with monthly updates. Inquire as to online cost and availability.

PERIODICALS AND NEWSLETTERS
Smokeshop. • Bimonthly. $32.00 per year.

TMA Tobacco Tax Guide: Summaries of Key Provisions of Tobacco Tax Laws, All Tobacco Products, All States. Tobacco Merchant's Association of the United States, Inc. • Looseleaf service. Members, $750.00 per year; non-members, $2,250.00 per year. Quarterly updates.

Tobacco-Cigarette News. International Press Cutting Service. • Weekly. $85.00 per year. Text in English. Formerly *Tobacco News.*

PRICE SOURCES
Tobacco Market Review. U.S. Department of Agriculture, Agricultural Marketing Service. • Annual.

RESEARCH CENTERS AND INSTITUTES
Border Belt Tobacco Research Station. North Carolina Dept. of Agriculture and Consumer Services, 86 Border Belt Dr., Whiteville, NC 28472-6828. Phone: (910)648-4703 Fax: (910)648-4858 E-mail: borderbelt.resst@ncmail.net • URL: http://www.ncagr.com/research.

Lower Coastal Plain Research Station/Cunningham Research Station. North Carolina Dept. of Agricultural and Consumer Services, 200 Cunningham Rd., Kinston, NC 28501-1700. Phone: (252)527-3579 Fax: (252)527-2036 E-mail: lowercoastal.resst@ncmail.net • URL: http://www.ncagr.com/research.

Oxford Tobacco Research Station. North Carolina Department of Agriculture and Consumer Services. 300 Providence Rd., Oxford, NC 27565. Phone: (919)693-2483 Fax: (919)693-6747 E-mail: oxford.resst@ncmail.net • URL: http://www.agr.state.nc.us/research/otrs.

Tobacco and Health Research Institute. University of Kentucky. Cooper and University Drives, Lexington, KY 40546-0236. Phone: (859)257-5798 Fax: (859)323-1077 E-mail: mdavies@pop.uky.edu • URL: http://www.uky.edu/~rgs/thri.

STATISTICS SOURCES
Annual Survey of Manufactures. Available from U. S. Government Printing Office. • Annual. Prices

vary. Issued by the U. S. Census Bureau as an interim update to the *Census of Manufactures.* Includes data on number of manufacturing establishments in various industries, employment, labor costs, value of shipments, capital expenditures, inventories, energy costs, and assets. (See also Census Bureau home page, http://www.census.gov/.).

Business Statistics of the United States. Linz Audain and Cornelia J. Strawser. Bernan Associates. • Annual. $147.00. Based on *Business Statistics,* formerly issue by the Bureau of Economic Analysis, U. S. Department of Commerce. Provides basic data for a wide variety of U. S. industries, services, and economic indicators. Most statistics are shown annually for 30 years and monthly for the most recent four years.

Monthly Statistical Bulletin. Cigar Association of America. • Monthly. Membership.

Standard & Poor's Industry Surveys. Standard & Poor's. • Semiannual. $1,800.00. Two looseleaf volumes. Includes monthly *Supplements.* Provides detailed, individual surveys of 52 major industry groups. Each survey is revised on a semiannual basis. Also includes "Monthly Investment Review" (industry group investment analysis) and monthly "Trends & Projections" (economic analysis).

Survey of Current Business. Available from U. S. Government Printing Office. • Monthly. $63.00 per year. Issued by Bureau of Economic Analysis, U. S. Department of Commerce. Presents a wide variety of business and economic data.

TRADE/PROFESSIONAL ASSOCIATIONS

American Wholesale Marketers Association. 2750 Prosperity Ave., Ste. 530, Fairfax, VA 22031. Phone: 800-482-2962 or (703)208-3358 Fax: (703)573-5738 E-mail: info@awmanet.org • URL: http://www.awmanet.org • Represents the interests of distributors of convenience products. Its members include wholesalers, retailers, manufacturers, brokers and allied organizations from across the U.S. and abroad. Programs include strong legislative representation in Washington and a broad spectrum of targeted education, business and information services. Sponsors the country's largest show for candy and convenience related products in conjunction with its semi-annual convention.

Cigar Association of America. 1707 H St., N.W., Ste. 800, Washington, DC 20006. Phone: (202)223-8204 Fax: (202)833-0379.

Retail Tobacco Dealers of America. 12 Galloway Ave., Suite 1B, Cockeysville, MD 21030. Phone: (410)628-1674 Fax: (410)628-1679 E-mail: info@rtda.org • URL: http://www.rtda.org.

Retail, Wholesale and Department Store Union. 30 E. 29th St., New York, NY 10016. Phone: (212)684-5300 Fax: (212)779-2809 E-mail: rwdsu@aol.com • URL: http://www.rwdsu.org.

Tobacconists' Association of America. 1211 Tutor Ln., Evansville, IN 47715-4001. Phone: (812)479-8070 Fax: (812)479-5939 E-mail: t_a_a_@hotmail.com • URL: http://www.t-a-a.org • Retail tobacco merchants.

OTHER SOURCES

The Cigar Market. Available from MarketResearch.com. • 1997. $1,230.00. Market research report published by Packaged Facts. Who smokes cigars? Why are they smoking? Are they likely to continue? Sales projections are provided.

Tobacco Industry Litigation Reporter: The National Journal of Record of Litigation Affecting the Tobacco Industry. Andrews Publications. • Monthly. $725.00 per year. Newsletter. Reports on major lawsuits brought against tobacco companies.

CIGARETTE INDUSTRY

See: CIGAR AND CIGARETTE INDUSTRY

CINEMA

See: MOTION PICTURE THEATERS

CINEMATOGRAPHY

See: MOTION PICTURE PHOTOGRAPHY

CIRCULATION MANAGEMENT (PUBLISHING)

See also: PERIODICALS

HANDBOOKS AND MANUALS

Grossman on Circulation. Gordon W. Grossman. Primedia Business Magazines and Media. • Annual. $99.95. Covers magazine circulation management and marketing, with emphasis on circulaton incentives, such as free-issue offers, sweepstakes, premiums, "freemiums," and professional courtesy offers. Includes examples of promotions used by consumer and trade publications.

ONLINE DATABASES

Management Contents. Gale Cengage Learning. • Covers a wide range of management, financial, marketing, personnel, and administrative topics. About 150 leading business journals are indexed and abstracted from 1974 to date, with monthly updating. Inquire as to online cost and availability.

Trade & Industry Database. Gale Cengage Learning. • Provides indexing of business periodicals, January 1981 to date. Daily updates. (Full text articles from some periodicals are available online, 1983 to date. Inquire as to online cost and availability).

PERIODICALS AND NEWSLETTERS

Circulation Management. Media Central. • Monthly. $39.00 per year. Edited for circulation professionals in the magazine and newsletter publishing industry. Covers marketing, planning, promotion, management, budgeting, and related topics.

STATISTICS SOURCES

SRDS Circulation [year]. SRDS. • Annual. $297.00. Contains detailed statistical analysis of newspaper circulation by metropolitan area or county and data on television viewing by area. Includes maps. Formerly*Circulation Year.*

TRADE/PROFESSIONAL ASSOCIATIONS

American Business Press. 675 Third Ave., Suite 415, New York, NY 10017. Phone: (212)661-6360 Fax: (212)370-0736 E-mail: info@abumail.com • URL: http://www.americanbusinesspress.com • Members are publishers of business and technical periodicals with audited circulation. Includes a Publishing Management Committee.

Audit Bureau of Circulations. 900 N. Meacham Rd., Schaumburg, IL 60173-4968. Phone: (847)605-0909 Fax: (847)605-0483 E-mail: corpcomdebt@accessabc.com • URL: http://www.accessabc.com • Verifies newspaper and periodical circulation statements. Includes a Business Publications Industry Committee and a Magazine Directors Advisory Committee.

BPA International. 2 Corporate Dr., Ste. 900, Shelton, CT 06484. Phone: (203)447-2800 Fax: (203)447-2900 E-mail: info@bpai.com • URL: http://www.bpai.com • Verifies business and consumer periodical circulation statements. Includes a Circulation Managers Committee. Formerly Business Publications Audit of Circulation.

Circulation Council of DMA. 1120 Ave. of the Americas, New York, NY 10036. Phone: (212)768-7277 Fax: (212)302-6714 E-mail: councils@the-dma.org • URL: http://www.the-dma.org • A division of the Direct Marketing Association. Members include publishers and circulation directors.

Fulfillment Management Association (FMA). 60 E 42nd St., Ste. 1166, New York, NY 10165. Phone: (815)734-5821 Fax: (815)734-5824 • URL: http://www.fmanational.org • Members includes publishing circulation executives. Includes a Training and Education Committee and a Career Guidance Committee. Formerly Subscription Fulfillment Managers Association.

Magazine Publishers of America. 919 Third Ave., 22nd Fl., New York, NY 10022. Phone: (212)872-3700 Fax: (212)888-4217 E-mail: infocenter@magazine.org • URL: http://www.magazine.org • Members are publishers of consumer and other periodicals. Affiliated with American Society of Magazine Editors; Media Credit Association; Publishers Information Bureau. Formerly Magazine Publishers Association.

CITIES AND TOWNS

See also: MUNICIPAL GOVERNMENT; URBAN DEVELOPMENT

GENERAL WORKS

Cities for the 21st Century. OECD Publications and Information Center. • 1994. $39.00. Contains discussions of the economic, social, and environmental problems of today's cities.

Urban Economics and Land Use in America: The Transformation of Cities in the Twentieth Century. Alan Rabinowitz. M. E. Sharpe, Inc. • 2004. $72.95. Covers suburbanization and its problems from 1900 to modern times.

ABSTRACTS AND INDEXES

PAIS International in Print. Public Affairs Information Service, Inc. • Monthly. $850.00 per year; cumulations three times a year. Provides topical citations to the worldwide literature of public affairs, economics, demographics, sociology, and trade. Text in English; indexed materials in English, French, German, Italian, Portuguese and Spanish.

Readers' Guide to Periodical Literature. H. W. Wilson Co. • Monthly. $345.00 per year. Includes annual *Cumulation.* Indexes about 250 peridicals of general interest.

Sage Public Administration Abstracts. Sage Publications, Inc. • Quarterly. Institutions, $785.00 per year.

Sage Urban Studies Abstracts. Sage Publications, Inc. • Quarterly. Institutions, $797.00 per year.

Social Sciences Index. H. W. Wilson Co. • Quarterly, with annual cumulation. Price varies. Indexes more than 400 periodicals covering economics, environmental policy, government, insurance, labor, health care policy, plannning, public administration, public welfare, urban studies, women's issues, criminology, and related topics.

ALMANACS AND YEARBOOKS

Municipal Year Book. International City-County Management Association. • Annual. $84.95. An authoritative resume of activities and statistical data of American cities.

CD-ROM DATABASES

Newspaper Abstracts Ondisc. PROQUEST. • Monthly. $2,950.00 per year (covers 1989 to date; archival discs are available for 1985-88). Provides cover-to-cover CD-ROM indexing and abstracting of 19 major newspapers, including the *New York Times, Wall Street Journal, Washington Post, Chicago Tribune,* and *Los Angeles Times.*

PAIS on CD-ROM. Public Affairs Information Service, Inc. • Quarterly. $1,995.00 per year. Provides a CD-ROM version of the online service,

PAIS International. Contains over 500,000 citations to the literature of contemporary social, political, and economic issues.

Social Sciences Citation Index. ISI. • Monthly. Price on request. Provides CD-ROM indexing of articles appearing in 1700 leading social science journals worldwide, with additional selections from more than 5700 other journals. Time span is 1992 to date. Coverage includes economics, business, finance, management, communications, demographics, library and information science, political science, sociology, and many other subjects.

Social Sciences Citation Index: Compact Disc Edition with Abstracts. Institute for Scientific Information. • Monthly. Provides CD-ROM indexing and abstracting of "significant articles" from 1,700 social science journals worldwide, with additional selections from 3,200 other journals, 1986 to date. Includes economics, business, finance, management, communications, demographics, information and library science, political science, sociology, and many other subjects.

Sourcebooks America CD-ROM. CACI Marketing Systems. • Annual. $1,250.00. Provides the CD-ROM version of *The Sourcebook of ZIP Code Demographics: Census Edition* and *The Sourcebook of County Demographics: Census Edition.*

WILSONDISC: Readers' Guide to Periodical Literature. H. W. Wilson Co. • Monthly. $1,095.00 per year, including unlimited online access to *Readers' Guide to Periodical Literature* through WILSONLINE. Provides CD-ROM indexing of about 270 general interest periodicals. Covers 1983 to date. (*Readers' Guide Abstracts* also available on CD-ROM at $1,995 per year.).

WILSONDISC: Wilson Social Sciences Abstracts. H. W. Wilson Co. • Monthly. Includes unlimited online access to *Social Sciences Index* through WILSONLINE. Provides CD-ROM indexing from 1983 and abstracting from 1994 of more than 500 periodicals covering economics, area studies, community health, public administration, public welfare, urban studies, and many other topics related to the social sciences.

DIRECTORIES

American City and County Municipal Index: Purchasing Guide for City, Township, County Officials and Consulting Engineers. Primedia Business Magazines and Media. • Annual. $61.95. Includes a directory of city and county governments with populations of 10,000 or more. Names and telephone numbers of municipal purchasing officials are listed. Also includes a directory of manufacturers and suppliers of materials, equipment, and services for municipalities.

Carroll's Municipal/County Directory. Carroll Publishing. • Annual. $250.00 per year. Provides listings of about 90,000 city, town, and county officials in the U. S.

Carroll's Municipal Directory. Carroll Publishing. • Covers: about 50,000 officials in more than 7,900 cities towns and villages: includes top elected council or elected board members. Entries include: Name, county name, locator phone, address, population; officials' names, titles, addresses, and phone numbers.

City Profiles USA: A Traveler's Guide to Major U. S. and Canadian Cities. Darren L. Smith, editor. Omnigraphics, Inc. • 2003. $130.00. A directory of information useful to business and other travelers in major cities. Includes services, facilities, attractions, and events. Arranged by city.

Encyclopedia of Associations: Regional, State, and Local Organizations. Gale Cengage Learning. • Annual. $660.00. Five volumes. $170.00 per volume. Each volume covers a particular region of the U. S.

Municipal Yellow Book: Who's Who in the Leading

City and County Governments and Local Authorities. Leadership Directories, Inc. • Annual. $265.00 per year. Lists approximately 30,000 key personnel in city and county departments, agencies, subdivisions, and branches.

INTERNET DATABASES

U. S. Census Bureau: The Official Statistics. U. S. Bureau of the Census. Phone: (301)763-4100 Fax: (301)763-4794 • URL: http://www.census.gov • Web site is "Your Source for Social, Demographic, and Economic Information." Contains "Current U. S. Population Count," "Current Economic Indicators," and a wide variety of data under "Other Official Statistics." Keyword searching is provided. Fees: Free.

ONLINE DATABASES

Newspaper Abstracts Daily. ProQuest Inc. • Provides online coverage (citations and abstracts) of 25 major newspapers. Covers business, economics, current affairs, health, fitness, sports, education, technology, government, consumer affairs, psychology, the arts, and the social sciences. Time period is 1986 to date, with daily updates. Inquire as to online cost and availability.

PAIS International. Public Affairs Information Service, Inc. • Corresponds to the former printed publications, *PAIS Bulletin* (1976-90) and *PAIS Foreign Language Index* (1972-90), and to the current *PAIS International in Print* (1991 to date). Covers economic, political, and sociological material appearing in periodicals, books, government documents, and other publications. Updating is monthly. Inquire as to online cost and availability.

Readers' Guide Abstracts Online. H. W. Wilson Co. • Indexes and abstracts general interest periodicals, 1983 to date. Weekly updates. Inquire as to online cost and availability.

Wilson Social Sciences Abstracts Online. H. W. Wilson Co. • Provides online abstracting and indexing of more than 500 periodicals covering area studies, community health, public administration, public welfare, urban studies, and many other social science topics. Time period is 1994 to date for abstracts and 1983 to date for indexing, with updates weekly. Inquire as to online cost and availability.

PERIODICALS AND NEWSLETTERS

American City and County: Administration, Engineering and Operations in Relation to Local Government. Primedia Business Magazines and Media. • Monthly. Free to qualified personnel. Edited for mayors, city managers, and other local officials. Emphasis is on equipment and basic services.

Downtown Idea Exchange: Essential Information for Downtown Research and Development Center. Downtown Research and Development Center. Alexander Communications Group, Inc. • Semimonthly. $187.00 per year. Newsletter for those concerned with central business districts. Provides news and other information on planning, development, parking, mass transit, traffic, funding, and other topics.

Downtown Promotion Reporter. Downtown Research and Development Center. Alexander Communications Group Inc. • Description: Focuses primarily on helping downtown areas be as competitive and successful as possible on a day-to-day basis. Reports on market research, retailing, advertising approaches, public relations techniques, budgeting, and organization. Provides news of promotional strategies used in cities throughout the nation. Recurring features include case studies.

ICMA Newsletter. International City/County Management Association. • Description: Discusses local government, professional management, and federal regulation. Publishes news of Association activities. Recurring features include news of

members; reports of publications, educational workshops, positions open in public management; and two main supplements titled Nuts & Bolts and ICMA University.

Nation's Cities Weekly. National League of Cities. • Description: Presents news on the latest developments in Congress, the White House, federal agencies, and other public interest groups which may affect the nation's cities.

RESEARCH CENTERS AND INSTITUTES

Institute of Urban and Regional Development. University of California at Berkeley, 316 Wurster Hall, Berkeley, CA 94720-1870. Phone: (510)642-4874 Fax: (510)643-9576 E-mail: iurd@uclink. berkeley.edu • URL: http://www.ced.berkeley.edu/ iurd • Research topics include the effects of changing economic trends in urban areas.

Urban Institute. Urban Institute. 2100 M St. NW, Washington, DC 20037. Phone: (202)833-7200 Fax: (202)728-0232 E-mail: paffairs@ui.urban.org • URL: http://www.urban.org • Domestic, social, and economic affairs, including multidisciplinary studies and government program evaluations in the areas of tax and budget reform, education policy, health policy, crime and justice, housing and community development, labor and human services, income security and retirement, welfare reform, international activities, nonprofit sector and philanthropy, public finance, productivity and economic development, social services, and immigration. Also conducts research programs on employment and training, children's issues and family policy, minorities and social policy, poverty, state and local governments, and community impact and demography.

Urban Land Institute. Urban Land Institute. 1025 Thomas Jefferson St. NW, Ste. 500 W, Washington, DC 20007. Phone: (202)624-7000 Fax: (202)624-7140 E-mail: customerservice@uli.org • URL: http://www.uli.org • Urban land use policy, planning, and development issues, including studies on central city problems, industrial development, new community development, residential developments of all types, taxation, smart growth, shopping center development and economics, metropolitan and urbanized area growth and development, mixed use development, and environmental factors affecting development.

STATISTICS SOURCES

American Business Climate and Economic Profiles. Priscilla C. Geahigan. Gale Cengage Learning. • 1993. $170.00. Provides business, industrial, demographic, and economic figures for all states and 300 metropolitan areas. Includes production, taxation, population, growth rates, labor force data, incomes, total sales, etc.

American Cost of Living Survey. Gale Cengage Learning. • 2001. $245.00. Third edition. Cost of living data is provided for 455 U.S. cities and metropolitan areas.

American Places Dictionary: A Guide to Populated Places, Natural Features , and Other United States Places. Frank R. Abate, editor. Omnigraphics, Inc. • 1994. $350.00. Four regional volumes: Northeast, South, Midwest, and West. Provides statistical data and other information on 45,000 U. S. cities, towns, townships, boroughs, and villages. Includes detailed state profiles, county profiles, and more than 10,000 name origins. Arranged by state, then by county. (Individual regional volumes are available at $100. 00.).

America's Top Rated Cities: A Statistical Handbook. Grey House Publishing. • Annual. $195. 00. Four volumes. $59.95 per volume. Each volume covers major cities in a region of the U. S.: Eastern, Southern, Central, and Western. City statistics cover the "Business Environment" (finances, employment, taxes, utilities, etc.) and the "Living Environment"

(cost of living, housing, education, health care, climate, etc.).

America's Top-Rated Smaller Cities: A Statistical Handbook. Grey House Publishing. • Biennial. $160.00. Provides detailed profiles of 60 smaller U. S. cities ranging in population from 25,000 to 100,000. Includes data on cost of living, employment, income, taxes, climate, media, and many other factors.

Cities of the United States. Gale Cengage Learning. • 2001. $445.00. Fourth edition. Four regional volumes. $125.00 per volume. Detailed information is provided on 164 U. S. cities. Includes economic data, climate, geography, government, and history, with maps and photographs.

Cities of the World. Gale Cengage Learning. • 1998. $370.00. Fifth edition. Four regional volumes. $95.00 per volume. Detailed information is provided for more than 3,407 cities in 177 countries (excluding U.S.) Includes maps and photographs. Based in U.S. State Department reports.

Comparative Guide to American Suburbs, 2003/ 2004. Grey House Publishing. • 2003. $130.00. Third edition. Contains detailed profiles of 1,800 suburban communities having a population of 10,000 or more and located within the 50 largest metropolitan areas. Includes ranking tables for income, unemployment, new housing permits, home prices, and crime, as well as information on school districts. (Universal Reference Publications.).

County and City Data Book, a Statistical Abstract Supplement. U.S. Bureau of the Census. Available from U.S. Government Printing Office. • 1994. $60. 00.

County and City Data Book 2000: A Statistical Abstract Supplement. Available from U. S. Government Printing Office. • 2002. $68.00. 13th edition. Issued by the U. S. Bureau of the Census (http:// www.census.gov). Contains a wide variety of data on 3,141 U.S. counties, 1,078 cities, and 11,097 places of 2,500 or more inhabitants. Includes statistical information on retailing, manufacturing, banking, service industries, income, employment, housing, education, crime, and population. Updated metropolitan areas are included.

County and City Extra: Annual Metro, City and County Data Book. Deirdre A. Gaquin and Mark S. Littman. Bernan Press. • 2001. $120.00. Updates and augments data published irregularly in print form by the U. S. Census Bureau in *County and City Data Book.* Covers "every state, county, metropolitan area, and congressional district in the United States, as well as all U. S. cities with a 1990 population of 25,000 or more." Contains a wide range tic maps.

County and City Extra: Special Decennial Census Edition. Deidre A. Gaquin and Katherine A. De- Brandt, editors. Bernan Press. • 2002. $95.00. Presents conveniently arranged population, housing, and other data from the 2000 census, with many 1980 and 1990 comparisons. Includes maps and tables with rankings of about 20 items for various geographic locations. Complements the annual *County and City Extra.*

Crime in America's Top-Rated Cities: A Statistical Profile. Grey House Publishing. • 2000. $155.00. Third edition. Contains 20-year data for major crime categories in 76 cities, suburbs, metropolitan areas, and the U. S. Also includes statistics on correctional facilities, inmates, hate crimes, illegal drugs, and other crime-related matters.

Datapedia of the United States: American History in Numbers. George T. Kurian, editor. Bernan Press. • 2004. $125.00. Third edition. Based on the Census Bureau publication, *Historical Statistics of the United States.* Provides data from Colonial times to the present on agriculture, business, consumer income, energy, finance, labor, national income,

population, and many other subjects. Includes "narrative highlights," maps, charts, and statistical projections.

Ernst & Young Almanac and Guide to U. S. Business Cities: 65 Leading Places to Do Business. John Wiley and Sons, Inc. • 1994. $16.95. Provides demographic, business, economic, and site selection data for 65 major U. S. cities.

Facts About the Cities. Allan Carpenter and Carl Provorse. H. W. Wilson Co. • 1996. $100.00. Second edition. Contains a wide variety of information on 300 American cities, including cities in Puerto Rico, Guam, and the U. S. Virgin Islands. Data is provided on the workplace, taxes, revenues, cost of living, population, climate, housing, transportation, etc.

Geographic Reference Report: Annual Report of Costs, Wages, Salaries, and Human Resource Statistics for the United States and Canada. ERI (Economic Research Institute). • Annual. $389.00. Provides demographic and other data for each of 298 North American metropolitan areas, including local salaries, wage differentials, cost-of-living, housing costs, income taxation, employment, unemployment, population, major employers, crime rates, weather, etc.

Health and Environment in America's Top-Rated Cities: A Statistical Profile. Grey House Publishing. • Biennial. $125.00. Covers 75 U. S. cities. Includes statistical and other data on a wide variety of topics, such as air quality, water quality, recycling, hospitals, physicians, health care costs, death rates, infant mortality, accidents, and suicides.

Moving and Relocation Sourcebook and Directory: Reference Guide to the 120 Largest Metropolitan Areas in the United States. Omnigraphics, Inc. • Annual. $225.00 Provides extensive statistical and other descriptive data for the 120 largest metropolitan areas in the U. S. Includes maps and a discussion of factors to be considered when relocating.

Places, Towns, and Townships, 1998. Deirdre A. Gaquin and Richard W. Dodge, editors. Bernan Press. • 1997. $89.00. Second edition. Presents demographic and economic statistics from the U. S. Census Bureau and other government sources for places, cities, towns, villages, census designated places, and minor civil divisions. Contains more than 60 data categories. (Places, Towns and Townships Series).

Population Abstract of the U. S. Gale Cengage Learning. • 1999. $190.00. Historical emphasis. Includes a "breakdown of urban and rural population from the earliest census to the present.".

Social Statistics of the United States. Mark S. Littman, editor. Bernan Press. • 2000. $65.00. Includes statistical data on population growth, labor force, occupations, environmental trends, leisure time use, income, poverty, taxes, and other economic or demographic topics.

State and Metropolitan Area Data Book. Available from U. S. Government Printing Office. • 1998. Issued by the U. S. Bureau of the Census. Presents a wide variety of statistical data for U. S. regions, states, counties, metropolitan areas, and central cities, with ranking tables. Time period is 1970 to 1990.

Statistical Abstract of the United States. Available from U. S. Government Printing Office. • Annual. $51.00. Issued by the U. S. Bureau of the Census.

A Statistical Portrait of the United States: Social Conditions and Trends. Mark S. Littman, editor. Bernan Press. • 1998. $89.00. Covers "social, economic, and environmental trends in the United States over the past 25 years." Includes statistical tables, graphs, and analysis relating to such topics as population, income, poverty, wealth, labor, housing, education, healthcare, air/water quality, and

government. (Statistical Portrait of the United States: Social Conditions and Trends Series).

ULI Market Profiles: North America. Urban Land Institute. • Annual. Members, $249.95; nonmembers, $299.95. Provides real estate marketing data for residential, retail, office, and industrial sectors. Covers 76 U. S. metropolitan areas and 13 major foreign metropolitan areas.

TRADE/PROFESSIONAL ASSOCIATIONS

International City/County Management Association. 777 N Capitol St. NE, Ste. 500, Washington, DC 20002-4201. Phone: 800-745-8780 or (202)289-4262 or (202)962-3680 Fax: (202)962-3500 E-mail: roneill@icma.org • URL: http://icma.org • International professional and educational organization for appointed administrators and assistant administrators serving cities, counties, districts, and regions. Provides publications, training, and management assistance to help local government professionals improve their skills and increase their knowledge. Collects data on local governments.

National Association of Towns and Townships. 444 N Capitol St. NW, Ste. 397, Washington, DC 20001-1202. Phone: (202)624-3550 Fax: (202)625-3554 E-mail: natat@sos.org • URL: http://www.natat.org • Provides technical and other assistance to officials of small communities. Absorbed National Association of Smaller Communities.

National League of Cities. 1301 Pennsylvania Ave. NW, Washington, DC 20004-1763. Phone: (202)626-3000 Fax: (202)626-3043 E-mail: inet@ nlc.org • URL: http://www.nlc.org • Formerly American Municipal Association.

United States Conference of Mayors. 1620 Eye St., N. W., Washington, DC 20006. Phone: (202)293-7330 Fax: (202)293-2352 E-mail: info@usmayors. org • URL: http://www.usmayors.org • Promotes improved municipal government, with emphasis on federal cooperation.

OTHER SOURCES

Commercial Atlas and Marketing Guide. Rand McNally. • Annual. $395.00. Includes maps and marketing data: population, transportation, communication, and local area business statistics. Provides information on more than 128,000 U.S. locations. (Commercial Atlas and Marketing Guide series).

Omni Gazetteer of the United States of America: A Guide to 1,500,000 Place Names in the United States and Territories. Frank R. Abate, editor. Omnigraphics, Inc. • 1991. $700.00. 11 volumes. Comprehensive listing of cities, towns, suburbs, villages, boroughs, structures, facilities, locales, historic places, and named geographic features. Population is shown where applicable. Individual regional volumes are available at $150.00.

Township Atlas of the United States. Gale Cengage Learning. • 2000. $85.00. Fourth edition. Covers the 48 contiguous states. Includes state maps, county maps, townships, subdivisions, and indexes.

Zip Code Mapbook of Metropolitan Areas. ESRI Business Information Solutions. • 1992. $195.00. Second edition. Contains Zip Code two-color maps of 326 metropolitan areas. Includes summary statistical profiles of each area: population characteristics, employment, housing, and income.

CITIZENSHIP

See also: CIVIL RIGHTS

HANDBOOKS AND MANUALS

Complete Guide to Becoming a U. S. Citizen. Eve P. Steinberg. Peterson's. • 1994. $11.95.

ONLINE DATABASES

Magazine Index. Gale Cengage Learning. • General magazine indexing (popular literature), 1973 to present. Daily updates. Inquire as to online cost and availability.

PERIODICALS AND NEWSLETTERS
Presidential Studies Quarterly. Center for the Study of the Presidency. Sage Publications, Inc. • Quarterly. Institutions, $255.00 per year. Includes print and online editions.

STATISTICS SOURCES
Statistical Yearbook of the Immigration and Naturalization Service. Available from U. S. Government Printing Office. • Annual. $40.00. Provides data on legal immigrants, deportable aliens, refugees, persons naturalized, political asylum cases, foreign tourists, and foreign students.

TRADE/PROFESSIONAL ASSOCIATIONS
Center for the Study of the Presidency. 1020 19th St., NW, Ste. 250, Washington, DC 20036. Phone: (202)872-9800 Fax: (202)872-9811 E-mail: center@thepresidency.org • URL: http://www.thepresidency.org • Counsels the White House and Executive Branch on policy issues critical to strengthening presidential leadership and improving executive-congressional relations. Formerly Library of Presidential Papers.

Ethics Resource Center. 2345 Crystal Dr., Ste. 201, Arlington, VA 22202. Phone: 800-777-1285 or (703)647-2185 Fax: (703)647-2180 E-mail: ethics@ethics.org • URL: http://www.ethics.org • Seeks to serve as a catalyst to improve the ethical practices of individuals and organizations from the classroom to the boardroom. Fulfills its mission through three distinct areas of expertise: as a leader in the fields of organizational/business ethics consulting; as a provider and facilitator of character education programs; and as an ethics information clearinghouse.

National Conference on Citizenship. 200 Park Ave., Ste. 106, Falls Church, VA 22046. Phone: (703)237-1500 Fax: (703)237-4500 E-mail: phil.duncan@ncoc.net • URL: http://www.ncoc.net.

National Immigration Forum. 50 F St. NW, Ste. 300, Washington, DC 20001. Phone: (202)347-0040 Fax: (202)347-0058 E-mail: info@nicyra.org • URL: http://www.immigrationforum.org • Dedicated to extending and defending America's tradition as a nation of immigrants. Supports the reunification of families, the rescue and resettlement of refugees fleeing persecution, and the equitable treatment of immigrants under the law. Encourages immigrants to become U.S. citizens and promote cooperation and understanding between immigrants and other Americans.

CITRUS FRUIT INDUSTRY

ABSTRACTS AND INDEXES
Food Science and Technology Abstracts. International Food Information Service Publishing. • Monthly. $1,780.00 per year. Provides worldwide coverage of the literature of food technology and food production.

Foods Adlibra: Key to the World's Food Literature. General Mills, Inc. Foods Adlibra Publications. • Semimonthly. $240.00 per year. Provides journal citations and abstracts to the literature of food technology and packaging.

ALMANACS AND YEARBOOKS
Agricultural and Mineral Commodities Year Book. Available from Taylor & Francis Group. • Annual. $225.00. Published by Europa Publications. Contains descriptive product profiles, price data, export-import data, and production statistics for major commodities of the world. Includes commodity histories, uses, markets, demand trends, and

information about trade agreements and key commodity organizations.

CD-ROM DATABASES
Food Science and Technology Abstracts [CD-ROM]. Available from SilverPlatter Information, Inc. • Quarterly. Produced by International Food Information Service (home page is http://www.ifis.org). Provides worldwide coverage on CD-ROM of the literature of food technology and production. Various types of publications are indexed, with abstracts, including about 1,800 periodicals. Time period is 1969 to date.

DIRECTORIES
American Fruit Grower Source Book. Meister Publishing Co. • Annual. $5.00. Manufacturers and distributors of equipment and supplies for the commericial fruit growing industry.

Major Food and Drink Companies of the World. Available from Gale Cengage Learning. • Annual. $880.00. Two volumes. Published by Graham & Whiteside. Contains profiles and trade names for more than 9,800 important food and beverage companies in various countries. In addition to foods, includes both alcoholic and nonalcoholic drink products.

Thomas Food and Beverage Market Place. Grey House Publishing. • 2004. $495.00. Three volumes. Contains more than 40,000 entries covering food companies, beverages, food equipment, warehouse companies, food brokers, wholesalers, importers, and exporters. Formerly *Thomas Food Industry Register.*

FINANCIAL RATIOS
Annual Statement Studies. The Risk Management Association. • Annual. Median and quartile financial ratios are given for over 400 kinds of manufacturing, wholesale, retail, construction, and consumer finance establishments. Data is sorted by both asset size and sales volume. Includes a clearly written "Definition of Ratios" and an alphabetical industry index.

Annual Statement Studies: Industry Default Probabilities and Cash Flow Measures. The Risk Management Association. • Annual. $145.00. Serves as a companion volume to the original *Annual Statement Studies.* Gives probability of default estimates on a percentage scale for more than 450 industries. Includes changes in position year-by-year for eight financial statement line items and provides percentage measures of cash flow.

INTERNET DATABASES
USDA. United States Department of Agriculture. Phone: (202)720-2791 E-mail: agsec@usda.gov • URL: http://www.usda.gov • The USDA home page has six sections: News and Information; What's New; About USDA; Agencies; Opportunities; Search and Help. Keyword searching is offered from the USDA home page and from various individual agency home pages. Agencies are the Economic Research Service, Agricultural Marketing Service, National Agricultural Statistics Service, National Agricultural Library, and about 12 others. Updating varies. Fees: Free.

ONLINE DATABASES
Agricola. U.S. National Agricultural Library. • Covers worldwide agricultural literature. Over 3.3 million citations, 1970 to present, with monthly updates. Inquire as to online cost and availability.

Food Science and Technology Abstracts [online]. IFIS North American Desk. • Produced by International Food Information Service. Provides about 500,000 online citations, with abstracts, to the international literature of food science, technology, commodities, engineering, and processing. Approximately 2,000 periodicals are covered. Time period is 1969 to date, with monthly updates. Inquire

as to online cost and availability.

FOODS ADLIBRA. General Mills, Inc. • Contains online citations, with abstracts, to the technical and business literature of food processing and packaging. New products and new ingredients are featured. Covers about 250 trade journals and 500 research journals from 1974 to date, with monthly updates. Inquire as to online cost and availability.

PERIODICALS AND NEWSLETTERS
Agricultural Research and Extension Center at Uvalde. Overeas Development Institute. • Semiannual. Price on application. Newsletter.

Citrograph: Magazine of the Citrus Industry. Western Agricultural Publishing Co., Inc. • Monthly. $19.95 per year. Gives produce growing tips.

Citrus Industry Magazine. Associated Publications Corp. • Monthly. $20.00 per year. Gives food growing tips.

Triangle. Florida Citrus Mutual. • Description: Contains items of interest to citrus growers, including statistical data, market information, ongoing scientific research, and action by various government agencies. Recurring features include weather forecasts, market information, production statistics, news of research, a calendar of events, and reports of meetings.

PRICE SOURCES
California Farmer: The Business Magazine for Commercial Agriculture. Farm Progress Companies. • 15 times a year. $23.95 per year. Three editions: Northern, Southern and Central Valley.

Supermarket News: The Industry's Weekly Newspaper. Fairchild Publications. • Weekly. Individuals, $196.00 per year; retailers, $45.00 per year; manufacturers, $89.00 per year.

RESEARCH CENTERS AND INSTITUTES
Citrus Center. Texas A & M University at Kingsville. 312 N. International Blvd., Weslaco, TX 78596. Phone: (956)968-2132 Fax: (956)969-0649 E-mail: j-dagraca@tamu.edu • URL: http://www.primera.tamu.edu/kcchome.

Citrus Research and Education Center, Lake Alfred. University of Florida. 700 Experiment Station Rd., Lake Alfred, FL 33850-2299. Phone: (863)956-1151 Fax: (863)956-4631 E-mail: jill@lal.ufl.edu • URL: http://www.lal.ufl.edu.

Citrus Research Center and Agricultural Experiment Station. University of California at Riverside. 202 College Bldg., North, Riverside, CA 92521. Phone: (909)787-7291 Fax: (909)787-4190 E-mail: donald.cooksey@ucr.edu • URL: http://www.cnas.ucr.edu.

Lindcove Research and Extension Center. University of California. 22963 Carson Ave., Exeter, CA 93221. Phone: (559)592-2408 Fax: (559)592-5947 E-mail: llwhitendale@ucdavis.edu • URL: http://www.danrrec.ucdavis.edu/lindcove.

STATISTICS SOURCES
Agricultural Statistics. Available from U. S. Government Printing Office. • Annual. $38.00. Produced by the National Agricultural Statistics Service, U. S. Department of Agriculture. Provides a wide variety of statistical data relating to agricultural production, supplies, consumption, prices/price-supports, foreign trade, costs, and returns, as well as farm labor, loans, income, and population. In many cases, historical data is shown annually for 10 years. In addition to farm data, includes detailed fishery statistics.

FAO Production Yearbook. Available from Bernan Associates. • Annual. $45.00. Published by the Food and Agriculture Organization (http://www.fao.org). Contains worldwide data on agriculture, land use, farm crops, livestock, and agricultural prices.

FAO Trade Yearbook. Available from Bernan Associates. • Annual. $45.00. Published by the Food and Agriculture Organization (http://www.fao.org). Provides extensive worldwide data on exports and imports of agricultural commodities, fertilizers, tractors, and pesticides. Includes more than 130 tables of detailed statistics.

United States Census of Agriculture. U.S. Bureau of the Census. • Quinquennial. Results presented in reports, tape, CD-ROM, and Diskette files.

World Food Data and Statistics. Euromonitor International. • 2004. $650.00. Provides five-year data for a wide variety of food products in 52 countries. Includes market size, consumer expenditures, price indicators, and retail distribution data for many kinds of meat, fish, fruits, vegetables, dairy products, baked goods, condiments, canned food, and frozen food.

TRADE/PROFESSIONAL ASSOCIATIONS

Florida Citrus Mutual. PO Box 89, 302 S Massachusetts Ave., Lakeland, FL 33802. Phone: (863)682-1111 Fax: (863)682-1074 E-mail: info@ flcitrusmutual.com • URL: http://www. flcitrusmutual.com/content • Supplies market and price information to members; marketing of fruit is handled by affiliated shippers and processors.

Florida Department of Citrus. P.O. Box 148, Lakeland, FL 33802-0148. Phone: (863)499-2500 Fax: (863)499-4300 E-mail: vmsodek@mail.ifas.ufl.edu • URL: http://www.floridajuice.com.

Florida Gift Fruit Shippers Association. 5500 W Concord Ave., Orlando, FL 32808. Phone: 800-741-1491 or (407)295-1491 Fax: (407)290-0918 E-mail: donnag@fgfsa.com • URL: http://www.fgfsa.com • Firms packing and shipping gift fruit packages.

Sunkist Growers. PO Box 7888, Van Nuys, CA 91409-7888. Phone: (818)986-4800 Fax: (818)379-7511 E-mail: info@sunkistgrowers.com • URL: http://www.sunkist.com • Serves as a citrus fruit marketing cooperative.

CITY ATTORNEYS

See: MUNICIPAL GOVERNMENT

CITY CLERKS

See: MUNICIPAL GOVERNMENT

CITY FINANCE

See: MUNICIPAL FINANCE

CITY GOVERNMENT

See: MUNICIPAL GOVERNMENT

CITY PLANNING

See also: REGIONAL PLANNING; URBAN DEVELOPMENT; ZONING

GENERAL WORKS

City Planning in America: Between Promise and Despair. Mary E. Hommann. Greenwood Publishing Group, Inc. • 1993. $57.95.

The Practice of Local Government Planning. Charles Hoch and others. International City/County Management Association. • 2000. $42.95. Third edition. (Municipal Management Series).

ABSTRACTS AND INDEXES

Art Index. H. W. Wilson Co. • Quarterly. Annual cumulations. Price varies. Subject and author index to periodicals in art, architecture, industrial design,

city planning, photography, and various related topics.

Journal of Planning Literature. Ohio State University, Dept. of City and Regional Planning. Sage Publications, Inc. • Quarterly. Institutions, $682.00 per year; includes print and online editions. Provides reviews and abstracts of city and regional planning lierature.

Social Sciences Index. H. W. Wilson Co. • Quarterly, with annual cumulation. Price varies. Indexes more than 400 periodicals covering economics, environmental policy, government, insurance, labor, health care policy, plannning, public administration, public welfare, urban studies, women's issues, criminology, and related topics.

ALMANACS AND YEARBOOKS

Institute on Planning, Zoning and Eminent Domain. LexisNexis. • 1971. $199.00.

CD-ROM DATABASES

Social Sciences Citation Index. ISI. • Monthly. Price on request. Provides CD-ROM indexing of articles appearing in 1700 leading social science journals worldwide, with additional selections from more than 5700 other journals. Time span is 1992 to date. Coverage includes economics, business, finance, management, communications, demographics, library and information science, political science, sociology, and many other subjects.

Social Sciences Citation Index: Compact Disc Edition with Abstracts. Institute for Scientific Information. • Monthly. Provides CD-ROM indexing and abstracting of "significant articles" from 1,700 social science journals worldwide, with additional selections from 3,200 other journals, 1986 to date. Includes economics, business, finance, management, communications, demographics, information and library science, political science, sociology, and many other subjects.

WILSONDISC: Wilson Social Sciences Abstracts. H. W. Wilson Co. • Monthly. Includes unlimited online access to *Social Sciences Index* through WILSONLINE. Provides CD-ROM indexing from 1983 and abstracting from 1994 of more than 500 periodicals covering economics, area studies, community health, public administration, public welfare, urban studies, and many other topics related to the social sciences.

HANDBOOKS AND MANUALS

Progress in Planning. Elsevier. • Eight times a year. $755.00 per year.

Urban Parks and Open Space. Gayle L. Berens and others. Urban Land Institute. • 1997. $40.95. Covers financing, design, management, and public-private partnerships relative to the development of open space for new urban parks. Includes color illustrations and the history of urban parks.

Zoning and Planning Deskbook, 2d. Douglas W. Kmiec. West Group. • $220.00. Two looseleaf volumes. Annual supplementation. Emphasis is on legal issues.

Zoning and Planning Law Handbook. West Group. • $264.50.

ONLINE DATABASES

Art Index Online. H. W. Wilson Co. • Indexes a wide variety of art-related periodicals, 1984 to date. Monthly updates. Inquire as to online cost and availability.

Wilson Social Sciences Abstracts Online. H. W. Wilson Co. • Provides online abstracting and indexing of more than 500 periodicals covering area studies, community health, public administration, public welfare, urban studies, and many other social science topics. Time period is 1994 to date for abstracts and 1983 to date for indexing, with updates weekly.

Inquire as to online cost and availability.

PERIODICALS AND NEWSLETTERS

American Planning Association Journal. American Planning Association. • Quarterly. Members, $33.00 per year; non-members $75.00 per year.

Journal of Housing and Community Development. National Association of Housing and Redevelopment Officials (NAHRO). • Bimonthly. $33.00 per year. Formerly *Journal of Housing.*

Land Use Law and Zoning Digest. American Planning Association. • Monthly. $275.00 per year. Covers judicial decisions and state laws affecting zoning and land use. Edited for city planners and lawyers. Monthly supplement available *Zoning News.*

Planning. American Planning Association. • Monthly. Free to members; non-members, $65.00 per year.

Planning and Zoning News. Planning and Zoning Center, Inc. • Monthly. $175.00 per year. Newsletter on planning and zoning issues in the United States.

Urban Land: News and Trends in Land Development. Urban Land Institute. • Monthly. Membership.

Zoning and Planning Law Report. West Group. • Monthly. $483.00 per year. Newsletter.

RESEARCH CENTERS AND INSTITUTES

Center for Urban and Regional Studies. University of North Carolina at Chapel Hill. 108 Battle Ln., Chapel Hill, NC 27599. Phone: (919)962-3074 Fax: (919)962-2518 E-mail: brohe.@unc.edu • URL: http://www.unc.edu/depts/curs.

Program in International Studies in Planning. Cornell University, Dept. of City Regional Planning. 106 W. Sibley Hall, Ithaca, NY 14853-3901. Phone: (607)255-4331 Fax: (607)255-1971 E-mail: bdl5@ cornell.edu • URL: http://www.inet.crp.cornell.edu/ organizations/isp • Research activities are related to international urban and regional planning, with emphasis on developing areas.

STATISTICS SOURCES

Facts About the Cities. Allan Carpenter and Carl Provorse. H. W. Wilson Co. • 1996. $100.00. Second edition. Contains a wide variety of information on 300 American cities, including cities in Puerto Rico, Guam, and the U. S. Virgin Islands. Data is provided on the workplace, taxes, revenues, cost of living, population, climate, housing, transportation, etc.

TRADE/PROFESSIONAL ASSOCIATIONS

American Planning Association. 122 S Michigan Ave., Ste. 1600, Chicago, IL 60603-6107. Phone: (312)431-9100 Fax: (312)431-9985 E-mail: customerservice@planning.org • URL: http://www. planning.org • Public and private planning agency officials, professional planners, planning educators, elected and appointed officials, and other persons involved in urban and rural development. Works to foster the best techniques and decisions for the planned development of communities and regions. Provides extensive professional services and publications to professionals and laypeople in planning and related fields; serves as a clearinghouse for information. Through Planning Advisory Service, a research and inquiry-answering service, provides, on an annual subscription basis, advice on specific inquiries and a series of research reports on planning, zoning, and environmental regulations. Supplies information on job openings and makes definitive studies on salaries and recruitment of professional planners. Conducts research; collaborates in joint projects with local, national, and international organizations.

National Association of Housing and Redevelopment Officials. 630 Eye St., N.W., Washington, DC 20001. Phone: 877-866-2476 or (202)289-3500 Fax: (202)289-8181 E-mail: nahro@nahro.org • URL:

http://www.nahro.org • Formerly National Association of Housing Officials.

National Community Development Association. 522 21st St. NW, No. 120, Washington, DC 20006-5059. Phone: (202)293-7587 Fax: (202)887-5546 E-mail: ncda@ncdaonline.org • URL: http://www.ncdaonline.org • Represents community development program directors. Supports the interests of Community Development Block Grant Programs as well as other community and economic development issues; disseminates information; operates workshops on various aspects of housing, economic, and community development.

OTHER SOURCES

American Land Planning Law. John Taylor and Norma Williams. West Group. • $780.00. Eight volumes. Annual cumulative updates. (Real Property and Zoning Series).

CIVIL ENGINEERING

ABSTRACTS AND INDEXES

Applied Science and Technology Index. H. W. Wilson Co. • 11 times a year. Quarterly and annual cumulations. Price varies. Indexes a wide variety of English language technical, industrial, and engineering periodicals.

Engineering Index Monthly: Abstracting and Indexing Services Covering Sources of the World's Engineering Literature. Engineering Information Inc. • Monthly. Institutions, $5,279.00 per year. Provides indexing and abstracting of the world's engineering and technical literature.

Fluid Abstracts: Civil Engineering. Elsevier. • Monthly. Institutions, $1,709.00 per year. Includes annual cumulation. Includes the literature of coastal structures.Published in England by Elsevier Science Publishing Ltd. Formerly *Civil Engineering Hydraulics Abstracts.*

BIBLIOGRAPHIES

Encyclopedia of Physical Science and Engineering Information. Gale Cengage Learning. • 1996. $160.00. Second edition. Includes print, electronic, and other information sources for a wide range of scientific, technical, and engineering topics.

BIOGRAPHICAL SOURCES

Who's Who in Engineering. American Association of Engineering Societies. • 1995. $250.00. Lists about 15,000 engineers who have received professional recognition for outstanding achievement.

DIRECTORIES

American Society of Civil Engineers-Official Register. American Society of Civil Engineers. • Annual. Free.

Peterson's Graduate and Professional Programs in Engineering and Applied Sciences. Peterson's. • Annual. $49.95. Provides details of more than 3,400 graduate and professional programs in engineering and related fields at colleges and universities. (Peterson's Graduate in Professional Programs Series). Formerly *Peterson's Guide to Graduate Programs in Engineering and Professional Sciences.*

ENCYCLOPEDIAS AND DICTIONARIES

Wiley Dictionary of Civil Engineering and Construction. Len F. Webster, editor. John Wiley and Sons, Inc. • 1997. $85.00. Provides more than 30,000 definitions in the fields of civil engineering, construction, architecture, forestry, mining, and public works. (Professional Series).

HANDBOOKS AND MANUALS

Civil Engineering Practice: Engineering Success By Analysis of Failure. David D. Piesold. McGraw-Hill. • 1991. $52.00.

Environmental Engineering. Joseph A. Salvato and others. John Wiley and Sons, Inc. • 2003. $240.00.

Fifth edition. Written for environmental engineers, civil engineers, environmental scientists, public health professionals, and others concerned with the technical aspects of protecting the environment. Covers a wide range of topics, including sanitation management, groundwater contamination, incineration, wastewater treatment, communicable diseases, and noise control.

Standard Handbook for Civil Engineers. Frederick S. Merritt and others. McGraw-Hill. • 2003. $150.00. Fifth edition. (Scientic, Technical and Medical Series).

ONLINE DATABASES

Applied Science and Technology Index Online. H. W. Wilson Co. • Provides online indexing of 500 major scientific, technical, industrial, and engineering periodicals. Time period is 1983 to date. Monthly updates. Inquire as to online cost and availability.

Civil Engineering Database (CEDB). American Society of Civil Engineers. • Provides abstracts of the U. S. and international literature of civil engineering, 1975 to date. Inquire as to online cost and availability.

NTIS Database. National Technical Information Service. • Contains citations and abstracts to unrestricted reports of government-sponsored research, 1964 to date. Covers a wide range of technical, engineering, business, and social science topics. Monthly updates. Inquire as to online cost and availability.

TRIS: Transportation Research Information Service. National Research Council. • Contains abstracts and citations to a wide range of transportation literature, 1968 to present, with monthly updates. Includes references to the literature of air transportation, highways, ships and shipping, railroads, trucking, and urban mass transportation. Formerly *TRIS-ONLINE.* Inquire as to online cost and availability.

PERIODICALS AND NEWSLETTERS

American Society of Civil Engineers. Proceedings. American Society of Civil Engineers. • Monthly. $2,289.00 per year. Consists of the Journals of the various Divisions of the Society.

ASCE News. American Society of Civil Engineers. • Description: Reports on activities of the society and news of the civil engineering profession.

Civil Engineering: Engineered Design and Construction. American Society of Civil Engineers. • Monthly. $160.00 per year.

ENR: Connecting the Industry Worldwide (Engineering News-Record). McGraw-Hill. • Weekly. $74.00 per year.

RESEARCH CENTERS AND INSTITUTES

Engineering Dean's Office. University of California at Berkeley, 308 Mclaughin Hall, MC. 1702, Berkeley, CA 94720-1706. Phone: (510)642-7594 Fax: (510)643-8653 E-mail: dma@coe.berkeley.edu • Research fields include civil, electrical, industrial, mechanical, and other types of engineering.

New Mexico Engineering Research Institute. University of New Mexico. 901 University Blvd., S.E., Albuquerque, NM 87106-4339. Phone: (505)272-7200 Fax: (505)272-7203 E-mail: oneil@nmeri.umm.edu • URL: http://www.nmeri.umn.edu.

TRADE/PROFESSIONAL ASSOCIATIONS

American Society of Civil Engineers. 1801 Alexander Bell Dr., Reston, VA 20191-4400. Phone: 800-548-2723 or (703)295-6300 Fax: (703)295-6222 E-mail: jdavis@asce.org • URL: http://www.asce.org.

OTHER SOURCES

American Society of Civil Engineers: Transactions. American Society of Civil Engineers. • Annual. $254.00.

Forms and Agreements for Architects, Engineers and Contractors. Albert Dib. West Group. • Three times a year. $900.00. Five looseleaf volume. Covers evaluation of construction documents and alternative clauses. Includes pleadings for litigation and resolving of claims. (Real Property Law Series).

CIVIL RIGHTS

See also: CITIZENSHIP; HUMAN RELATIONS

GENERAL WORKS

Civil Liberties Under the Constitution. M. Glenn Abernathy and others. University of South Carolina Press. • 1993. $34.95. Sixth edition.

The Limits of Liberty: Between Anarchy and Leviathan. James M. Buchanan. Liberty Fund, Inc. • 2000. $20.00. (Collected Works of James M. Buchanan: Vol. 7).

ABSTRACTS AND INDEXES

Current Law Index: Multiple Access to Legal Periodicals. Gale Cengage Learning. • Monthly. $725.00 per year. Produced in cooperation with the American Association of Law Libraries. Indexes more than 900 law journals, legal newspapers, and specialty publications from the U.S., Canada, U.K., Ireland, Australia, and New Zealand.

Social Sciences Index. H. W. Wilson Co. • Quarterly, with annual cumulation. Price varies. Indexes more than 400 periodicals covering economics, environmental policy, government, insurance, labor, health care policy, plannning, public administration, public welfare, urban studies, women's issues, criminology, and related topics.

ALMANACS AND YEARBOOKS

World Labour Report. International Labour Office. • Irregular. Price varies. Volume eight. International coverage. Reviews significant recent events and labor policy developments in the following areas: employment, human rights, labor relations, and working conditions.

CD-ROM DATABASES

Social Sciences Citation Index. ISI. • Monthly. Price on request. Provides CD-ROM indexing of articles appearing in 1700 leading social science journals worldwide, with additional selections from more than 5700 other journals. Time span is 1992 to date. Coverage includes economics, business, finance, management, communications, demographics, library and information science, political science, sociology, and many other subjects.

Social Sciences Citation Index: Compact Disc Edition with Abstracts. Institute for Scientific Information. • Monthly. Provides CD-ROM indexing and abstracting of "significant articles" from 1,700 social science journals worldwide, with additional selections from 3,200 other journals, 1986 to date. Includes economics, business, finance, management, communications, demographics, information and library science, political science, sociology, and many other subjects.

WILSONDISC: Wilson Social Sciences Abstracts. H. W. Wilson Co. • Monthly. Includes unlimited online access to *Social Sciences Index* through WILSONLINE. Provides CD-ROM indexing from 1983 and abstracting from 1994 of more than 500 periodicals covering economics, area studies, community health, public administration, public welfare, urban studies, and many other topics related to the social sciences.

DIRECTORIES

Human Rights Organizations and Periodicals Directory. Meiklejohn Civil Liberties Institute. • Biennial. Individuals, $75.00 per year; libraries and institutions, $125.00 per year. Over 1,200 United

States organiations and periodicals dedicated to improving human rights.

ENCYCLOPEDIAS AND DICTIONARIES

Encyclopedia of Crime and Justice. Available from Gale Cengage Learning. • 2001. $475.00. Second edition. Four volumes. Published by Macmillan Reference USA. Contains extensive information on a wide variety of topics pertaining to crime, criminology, social issues, and the courts. (A complete revision of 1982 edition.).

Encyclopedia of Crime and Punishment. David Levinson, editor. Sage Publications, Inc. • 2002. $600.00. Four volumes. Contains 425 signed entries dealing with civil, criminal, media, corporate, and international issues. Includes material on fraud, police science, correctional institutions, social matters, methodology, national surveys, and crime statistics.

World of Criminal Justice. Gale Cengage Learning. • 2002. $160.00. Two volumes. Contains both topical and biographical entries relating to the criminal justice system and criminology.

HANDBOOKS AND MANUALS

Federal Civil Rights Acts. West Group. • Semiannual. $410.00 per year. Two looseleaf volumes. Covers current legislation relating to a wide range of civil rights issues, including discrimination in employment, housing, property rights, and voting.

Legal Aspects of AIDS. West Group. • Annual. $254.50 per year. Looseleaf service. Includes issue employment discrimination, housing discrimination, and insurance. This work also "traces the historical progression of the disease and its spread.".

Manual on Employment Discrimination Law and Civil Rights Action in the Federal Courts. West Group. • Biennial. $236.00. Two looseleaf volumes.

Women and the Law. Carol H. Lefcourt, editor. West Group. • Annual. $302.00. Looseleaf service. Covers such topics as employment discrimination, pay equity (comparable worth), sexual harassment in the workplace, property rights, and child custody issues.

INTERNET DATABASES

Lexis.com Research System. Lexis-Nexis Group. Phone: 800-227-4908 or (937)865-6800 Fax: (937)865-6909 E-mail: webmaster@prod.lexis-nexis.com • URL: http://www.lexis.com • Fee-based Web site offers extensive searching of a wide variety of legal sources. Additional features include Daily Opinion Service, lexis.com Bookstore, Career Center, CLE Center, Law Schools, and Practice Pages ("Pages specific to areas of specialty").

ONLINE DATABASES

Legal Resource Index. Gale Cengage Learning. • Broad coverage of law literature appearing in legal, business, and other periodicals, 1980 to date. Daily updates. Inquire as to online cost and availability.

Wilson Social Sciences Abstracts Online. H. W. Wilson Co. • Provides online abstracting and indexing of more than 500 periodicals covering area studies, community health, public administration, public welfare, urban studies, and many other social science topics. Time period is 1994 to date for abstracts and 1983 to date for indexing, with updates weekly. Inquire as to online cost and availability.

PERIODICALS AND NEWSLETTERS

Civil Liberties. American Civil Liberties Union. • Description: Supplies news of the legal defense, research, and public education projects of the ACLU, conducted to enable citizens to know and assert their rights. Focuses on civil liberties issues relating to freedom of expression, due process of law, equality, and privacy. Recurring features include news of significant legislation.

Civil Rights: State Capitals. Wakeman-Walworth, Inc. • 50 times a year. $245.00 per year; print and

online editions, $350.00 per year. Newsletter. Includes coverage of state affirmative action programs. Formerly *From the State Capitals: Civil Rights.*

CORE Magazine. Congress of Racial Equality. CORE Publications. • Quarterly. $10.00 per year.

Police Misconduct and Civil Rights Law Report. National Lawyers Guild. West Group. • $297.00. Newsletter. Periodic supplementation.

RESEARCH CENTERS AND INSTITUTES

Center for National Policy. One Massachusetts Ave., N.W., Suite 333, Washington, DC 20001-1401. Phone: (202)682-1800 Fax: (202)682-1818 E-mail: mostein@cnponline.org • URL: http://www.cnponline.org.

Earl Warren Legal Institute. University of California at Berkeley. Boalt Hall, Berkeley, CA 94720. Phone: (510)642-5125 Fax: (510)643-2698 E-mail: zimring@mail.law.berkeley.edu.

TRADE/PROFESSIONAL ASSOCIATIONS

American Civil Liberties Union. 125 Broad St., 18th Fl., New York, NY 10004. Phone: 888-567-ACLU or (212)549-2500 Fax: (212)549-2646 E-mail: membership@aclu.org • URL: http://www.aclu.org • Champions the rights set forth in the Bill of Rights of the U.S. Constitution: freedom of speech, press, assembly, and religion; due process of law and fair trial; equality before the law regardless of race, color, sexual orientation, national origin, political opinion, or religious belief. Conducts activities including litigation, advocacy, and public education. Sponsors litigation projects on topics such as women's rights, gay and lesbian rights, and children's rights.

Leadership Conference on Civil Rights. 1629 K St., N.W., Suite 1010, Washington, DC 20006. Phone: (202)466-3311 Fax: (202)466-3435 E-mail: webmaster@civilrights.org • URL: http://www.civilrights.org • Formerly Civil Rights Mobilization.

National Association for the Advancement of Colored People. 4805 Mount Hope Dr., Baltimore, MD 21215. Phone: 877-622-2798 or (410)521-4939 Fax: (410)358-3818 • URL: http://www.naacp.org/.

National Urban League. 120 Wall St., 8th Fl., New York, NY 10005. Phone: (212)558-5300 Fax: (212)344-5332 E-mail: info@nul.org • URL: http://www.nul.org • Voluntary nonpartisan community service agency of civic, professional, business, labor, and religious leaders with a staff of trained social workers and other professionals. Aims to eliminate racial segregation and discrimination in the United States and to achieve parity for blacks and other minorities in every phase of American life. Works to eliminate institutional racism and to provide direct service to minorities in the areas of employment, housing, education, social welfare, health, family planning, mental retardation, law and consumer affairs, youth and student affairs, labor affairs, veterans' affairs, and community and minority business development. Maintains research department in Washington, DC.

Southern Christian Leadership Conference. PO Box 89128, PO Box 89128, Atlanta, GA 30312. Phone: (404)522-1420 Fax: (404)527-4333 E-mail: president@sclcnational.org • URL: http://www.sclcnational.org • Nonsectarian coordinating and service agency for local organizations seeking full citizenship rights, equality, and the integration of African-Americans in all aspects of life in the U.S. and subscribing to the Ghandian philosophy of nonviolence. Works primarily in 16 southern and border states to improve civic, religious, economic, and cultural conditions. Fosters nonviolent resistance to all forms of racial injustice, including state and local laws and practices. Conducts leadership training program embracing such subjects as registration and voting, social protest, use of the boycott, picketing, nature of prejudice, and

understanding politics. Sponsors citizenship education schools to teach reading and writing, help persons pass literacy tests for voting, and provide information about income tax forms, tax-supported resources, aid to handicapped children, public health facilities, how government is run, and social security. Conducts Crusade for the Ballot, which aims to double the black vote in the South through increased voter registrations. Sponsors lectures; disseminates literature.

OTHER SOURCES

Civil Rights Actions. LexisNexis Matthew Bender. • $1,157.00. Seven looseleaf volumes. Periodic supplementation. Contains legal analysis of civil rights activities.

Employment Discrimination: Law and Litigation. Lexis Law Publishing. • $185.00 per year. Two looseleaf volumes. Periodic supplementation. Covers employment provisions of the Civil Rights Act, the Equal Pay Act, and related topics.

Government Discrimination: Equal Protection Law and Litigation. James A. Kushner. West Group. • Semiannual. $244.00 per year. Looseleaf service. Covers discrimination in employment, housing, and other areas by local, state, and federal offices or agencies. (Civil Rights Series).

Housing Discrimination: Law and Litigation. Robert G. Schwemm. West Group. • Annual. $256.00. Looseleaf service. Covers provisions of the Fair Housing Act and related topics.

Larson's Employment Discrimination. LexisNexis Matthew Bender. • $1,487.00. 10 looseleaf volumes. Treatise on both substantive and procedural law governing employment discrimination based on sex, age, race, religion, national origin, etc.

CIVIL SERVICE

See also: GOVERNMENT EMPLOYEES

GENERAL WORKS

Opportunities in Government Careers. Neale J. Baxter. McGraw-Hill. • 2001. $15.95. Edited for students and job seekers. Includes education requirements and salary data. (VGM Career Books.).

Public Personnel Administration: Problems and Prospects. Steven W. Hays and Richard C. Kearney, editors. Prentice Hall PTR. • 2002. $44.00.

ABSTRACTS AND INDEXES

Social Sciences Index. H. W. Wilson Co. • Quarterly, with annual cumulation. Price varies. Indexes more than 400 periodicals covering economics, environmental policy, government, insurance, labor, health care policy, plannning, public administration, public welfare, urban studies, women's issues, criminology, and related topics.

ALMANACS AND YEARBOOKS

Federal Employees Almanac. Federal Employees New Digest, Inc. • Annual. $11.95. Comprehensive guide for federal employees.

CD-ROM DATABASES

Social Sciences Citation Index. ISI. • Monthly. Price on request. Provides CD-ROM indexing of articles appearing in 1700 leading social science journals worldwide, with additional selections from more than 5700 other journals. Time span is 1992 to date. Coverage includes economics, business, finance, management, communications, demographics, library and information science, political science, sociology, and many other subjects.

Social Sciences Citation Index: Compact Disc Edition with Abstracts. Institute for Scientific Information. • Monthly. Provides CD-ROM indexing and abstracting of "significant articles" from 1,700 social science journals worldwide, with additional selections from 3,200 other journals, 1986 to date. Includes economics, business, finance, management, communications, demographics, information and library science, political science, sociology, and many other subjects.

WILSONDISC: Wilson Social Sciences Abstracts. H. W. Wilson Co. • Monthly. Includes unlimited online access to *Social Sciences Index* through WILSONLINE. Provides CD-ROM indexing from 1983 and abstracting from 1994 of more than 500 periodicals covering economics, area studies, community health, public administration, public welfare, urban studies, and many other topics related to the social sciences.

ENCYCLOPEDIAS AND DICTIONARIES

International Encyclopedia of Public Policy and Administration. Jay M. Shafritz, editor. Westview Press. • 1997. $550.00. Four volumes. Covers 20 major areas, such as public administration, government budgeting, industrial policy, nonprofit management, organizational theory, public finance, labor relations, and taxation. Includes a brief bibliography for each major entry and a comprehensive index.

HANDBOOKS AND MANUALS

Civil Service Handbook: How to Get a Civil Service Job. Peterson's. • 1999. $12.95. 14th edition. (Arco Civil Service Series).

The Federal Manager's Handbook: A Guide to Rehabilitating or Removing the Problem Employee. G. Jerry Shaw and William L. Bransford. FPMI Communications, Inc. • 1997. $29.95. Third revised edition.

Federal Personnel Manual. U.S. Office of Personnel Management. Available from U.S. Government Printing Office. • Looseleaf service. Periodic supplementation. Available in parts.

ONLINE DATABASES

Magazine Index. Gale Cengage Learning. • General magazine indexing (popular literature), 1973 to present. Daily updates. Inquire as to online cost and availability.

Wilson Social Sciences Abstracts Online. H. W. Wilson Co. • Provides online abstracting and indexing of more than 500 periodicals covering area studies, community health, public administration, public welfare, urban studies, and many other social science topics. Time period is 1994 to date for abstracts and 1983 to date for indexing, with updates weekly. Inquire as to online cost and availability.

PERIODICALS AND NEWSLETTERS

The Federal Employee. National Federation of Federal Employees. • Description: Provides news and information on issues (legislative and regulatory) affecting federal employees.

Federal Human Resources Week: News, Strategies and Best Practices for the HR Professional. LRP Publications. • 48 times a year. $350.00 per year. Newsletter. Covers federal personnel issues, including legislation, benefits, budgets, and downsizing.

Federal Jobs Digest. • Biweekly. Individuals, $125.00 per year; libraries, $112.50 per year. Lists 15,000 immediate job openings within the federal government in each issue.

Federal Times. Army Times Publishing Co. • Weekly. $52.00 per year.

Public Personnel Management. International Personnel Management Association. • Quarterly. $50.00 per year.

TRADE/PROFESSIONAL ASSOCIATIONS

Federation of International Civil Servants' Associations. 304 E 45th St., New York, NY 10017. Phone: (212)906-6549 E-mail: 76521.335@compuserve.com • URL: http://www.ficsa.org.

International Personnel Management Association. 1617 Duke St., Alexandria, VA 22314. Phone: (703)549-7100 Fax: (703)684-0948 E-mail: ipma@

impa-hr.org • URL: http://www.ipma-hr.org.

OTHER SOURCES

Carroll's Federal Organization Charts. Carroll Publishing. • Every six weeks. $1,000.00 per year. Provides 200 large, fold-out paper charts showing personnel relationships in 2,100 federal departments and agencies. Charts are also available online and on CD-ROM.

CLAY INDUSTRY

See also: CERAMICS INDUSTRY; POTTERY INDUSTRY

GENERAL WORKS

An Introduction to Clay Colloid Chemistry: For Clay Technologists, Geologists and Soil Scientists. H. Van Olphen. Krieger Publishing Co. • 1991. $69.50. Second edition.

CD-ROM DATABASES

OECD Statistical Compendium. Organization for Economic Cooperation and Development. • Semiannual. $1,905.00 per year for 1 to 10 users. CD-ROM contains more than 730,000 monthly, quarterly, and annual time series for OECD countries, 1960 to date. Includes fully searchable data on agriculture, food, economic indicators, national accounts, employment, energy, finance, industry, technology, and foreign trade. Results can be displayed in various forms.

HANDBOOKS AND MANUALS

Clay Mineralogy. M. J. Wilson. John Wiley and Sons, Inc. • 1992. $105.00.

INTERNET DATABASES

Business 2.0 Web Guide to the Best Business Links. Business 2.0 Media Inc. Phone: (415)293-4800 E-mail: support@business2.com • URL: http://www.business2.com/webguide • Web site presents an extensive, searchable directory of links to "the best, most informative, and authoritative web pages." Twenty main categories cover business, finance, career, company information, people, and technology topics, with thousands of subtopics, all linking to Web sites recommended by experienced business researchers. Fees: Free.

Fedstats. Federal Interagency Council on Statistical Policy. Phone: (202)395-7254 • URL: http://www.fedstats.gov • Web site features an efficient search facility for full-text statistics produced by more than 100 federal agencies, including the Census Bureau, the Bureau of Economic Analysis, and the Bureau of Labor Statistics. Boolean searches can be made within one agency or for all agencies combined. Links are offered to international statistical bureaus, including the UN, IMF, OECD, UNESCO, Eurostat, and 20 individual countries. Fees: Free.

FreeLunch.com. Economy.com, Inc. Phone: (610)696-8700 Fax: (610)696-1678 • URL: http://www.freelunch.com • Web site provides free access to more than 1.5 million economic and financial data series, covering industry, demographics, labor markets, prices, retail sales, government spending, trade, interest rates, housing starts, the stock market, and many other topics. Data is available for various time periods in either chart or table form. Searching is offered. Fees: Free, but registration required. Economy.com, Inc. also offers fee-based economic analysis at *The Dismal Scientist* site (http://www.dismal.com).

Manufacturing Profiles. U. S. Bureau of the Census. Phone: (301)763-4636 E-mail: webmaster@census.gov • URL: http://www.census.gov/prod/www/abs/mfg-prof.html • The Census Bureau makes available free on PDF (Portable Document Format) an annual consolidation of the entire Current Industrial Report series, presenting "all the data compiled."

Contains statistics on production, shipments, inventories, consumption, exports, imports, and orders for a wide variety of manufactured products.

PERIODICALS AND NEWSLETTERS

Clays and Clay Minerals. The Clay Minerals Society. • Bimonthly. $235.00 per year. Includes online edition.

PRICE SOURCES

Chemical Market Reporter. Schnell Publishing Co., Inc. • Weekly. $169.00 per year. Quotes current prices for a wide range of chemicals. Formerly *Chemical Marketing Reporter.*

RESEARCH CENTERS AND INSTITUTES

Geotechnical Materials Research Laboratories. Iowa State University of Science and Technology. Dept. of Civil and Construction Engineering, College of Engineering, 486 Town Engineering, Ames, IA 50011. Phone: (515)294-3925 Fax: (515)294-8216 E-mail: bkjartan@iastate.edu.

STATISTICS SOURCES

Annual Survey of Manufactures. Available from U. S. Government Printing Office. • Annual. Prices vary. Issued by the U. S. Census Bureau as an interim update to the *Census of Manufactures.* Includes data on number of manufacturing establishments in various industries, employment, labor costs, value of shipments, capital expenditures, inventories, energy costs, and assets. (See also Census Bureau home page, http://www.census.gov/.).

Business Statistics of the United States. Linz Audain and Cornelia J. Strawser. Bernan Associates. • Annual. $147.00. Based on *Business Statistics,* formerly issue by the Bureau of Economic Analysis, U. S. Department of Commerce. Provides basic data for a wide variety of U. S. industries, services, and economic indicators. Most statistics are shown annually for 30 years and monthly for the most recent four years.

Mineral Commodity Summaries. Available from U. S. Government Printing Office. • Annual. $26.00. Published by the U. S. Geological Survey, Department of the Interior (http://www.usgs.gov). Contains detailed, five-year data for about 90 nonfuel minerals. Covers a wide range of statistics, including production, imports, exports, consumption, reserves, prices, tariff information, and industry employment. (Two pages are devoted to each mineral.).

Minerals Yearbook. Available from U.S. Government Printing Office. • Annual. Three volumes.

Survey of Current Business. Available from U. S. Government Printing Office. • Monthly. $63.00 per year. Issued by Bureau of Economic Analysis, U. S. Department of Commerce. Presents a wide variety of business and economic data.

United States Census of Mineral Industries. Bureau of the Census, U.S. Department of Commerce. Available from U.S. Government Printing Office. • Quinquennial.

TRADE/PROFESSIONAL ASSOCIATIONS

Brick Industry Association. 1850 Centennial Park Dr., Ste. 301, Reston, VA 20191. Phone: (703)620-0010 Fax: (703)620-3928 E-mail: brickinfo@bia.org • URL: http://www.bia.org • Manufacturers and distributors of clay brick. Promotes clay brick with the goal of increasing its market share.

Clay Minerals Society. 3635 Concorde Pkwy., Ste. 500, Chantilly, VA 20151-1125. Phone: (703)652-9960 Fax: (703)652-9951 E-mail: cms@clays.org • URL: http://www.clays.org • Professionals concerned with clay mineralogy and technology in industry, university research, and government. Includes students of mineralogy, geology, soil science, astronomy, physics, geochemistry, and engineering, and representatives of such firms as oil companies, instrument makers, and clay mining companies. Seeks to stimulate research and disseminate information relating to all aspects of clay science and technology. Provides a forum for exchange of information and ideas. Maintains quantities of Source and Special Clays at the Source Clays Repository.

Expanded Shale Clay and Slate Institute. 2225 E. Murray Holladay Rd., Suite 102, Salt Lake City, UT 84117. Phone: (801)272-7070 Fax: (801)272-3377 E-mail: info@escsi.org • URL: http://www.escsi.org • Formerly Expanded Shale Institute.

United Steelworkers of America. Aluminum, Brick and Glassworkers Division. c/o Unitrd Steelworkers of America, Five Gateway Center, Pittsburgh, PA 15222. Phone: (412)562-2400 E-mail: webmaster@uswa.org • URL: http://www.uswa.org.

CLEANING COMPOSITIONS

See: CLEANING PRODUCTS INDUSTRY

CLEANING INDUSTRY

See also: LAUNDRY INDUSTRY

ABSTRACTS AND INDEXES

Textile Technology Digest. Institute of Textile Technology. • Annual. $535.00. Provides indexing and abstracting of a wide variety of textile technology literature.

CD-ROM DATABASES

Textile Technology Digest [CD-ROM]. Textile Information Center, Institute of Textile Technology. • Quarterly. Provides CD-ROM indexing and abstracting of worldwide journals and monographs in various areas of textile technology, production, and management. Covers 1978 to date.

DIRECTORIES

National Association of Institutional Linen Management Membership Directory. National Association of Institutional Linen Management. • Annual. $100.00. Lists managers of in-house laundries for institutions, hotels, schools, etc.

ENCYCLOPEDIAS AND DICTIONARIES

Textile Terms and Definitions. J.E. McIntyre and Paul N. Daniels, editors. Available from State Mutual Book and Periodical Service Ltd. • 1996. $180.00. 10th edition. Published by the Textile Insitute (UK). Includes more than 1,000 definitions of textile processes, fiber types, and end products. Illustrated.

FINANCIAL RATIOS

Annual Statement Studies. The Risk Management Association. • Annual. Median and quartile financial ratios are given for over 400 kinds of manufacturing, wholesale, retail, construction, and consumer finance establishments. Data is sorted by both asset size and sales volume. Includes a clearly written "Definition of Ratios" and an alphabetical industry index.

Annual Statement Studies: Industry Default Probabilities and Cash Flow Measures. The Risk Management Association. • Annual. $145.00. Serves as a companion volume to the original *Annual Statement Studies.* Gives probability of default estimates on a percentage scale for more than 450 industries. Includes changes in position year-by-year for eight financial statement line items and provides percentage measures of cash flow.

HANDBOOKS AND MANUALS

Carpet Cleaning Service. Entrepreneur Media, Inc. • Looseleaf. $59.50. A practical guide to starting a carpet cleaning business. Covers profit potential, start-up costs, market size evaluation, owner's time required, pricing, accounting, advertising, promotion, etc. (Start-Up Business Guide No. E1053.).

Dry Cleaning Shop. Entrepreneur Media, Inc. • Looseleaf. $59.50. A practical guide to starting a dry cleaning business. Covers profit potential, start-up costs, market size evaluation, owner's time required, site selection, lease negotiation, pricing, accounting, advertising, promotion, etc. (Start-Up Business Guide No. E1037.).

Everything You Need to Know to Start a House Cleaning Service. Mary P. Johnson. Cleaning Consultant Services, Inc. • 1999. $38.00. Revised edition.

ONLINE DATABASES

Textile Technology Digest [online]. Institute of Textile Technology. • Contains indexing and abstracting of more than 300 worldwide journals and monographs in various areas of textile technology, production, and management. Time period is 1978 to date, with monthly updating. Inquire as to online cost and availability.

PERIODICALS AND NEWSLETTERS

American Coin-Op: The Magazine for Coin-Operated Laundry and Drycleaning Businessmen. Crain Communications, Inc. • Monthly. Free.

American Drycleaner. Crain Communications, Inc. • Monthly. Free.

Cleaning Business: Published Monthly for the Self-Employed Cleaning and Maintenance Professionals. William R. Griffin, Publisher. • Monthly. $20.00 per year. Formerly *Service Business.*

Drycleaners News. Zackin Publications, Inc. • Monthly. $36.00.

Industrial Launderer. Institute of Industrial Launderers. • Monthly. $100.00 per year.

STATISTICS SOURCES

Annual Survey of Manufactures. Available from U. S. Government Printing Office. • Annual. Prices vary. Issued by the U. S. Census Bureau as an interim update to the *Census of Manufactures.* Includes data on number of manufacturing establishments in various industries, employment, labor costs, value of shipments, capital expenditures, inventories, energy costs, and assets. (See also Census Bureau home page, http://www.census.gov/.).

United States Census of Service Industries. U.S. Bureau of the Census. • Quinquennial. Various reports available.

TRADE/PROFESSIONAL ASSOCIATIONS

Coin Laundry Association. 1315 Butterfield Rd., Ste. 212, Downers Grove, IL 60515. Phone: 877-CLA-IDEA or (630)963-5547 Fax: (630)963-5864 E-mail: info@coinlaundry.org • URL: http://www.coinlaundry.org • Manufacturers of equipment or supplies used in self-service (coin-operated) laundry or dry cleaning establishments; distributors of equipment services and supplies; owners and operators of self-service laundry and/or dry cleaning stores. Compiles statistics.

International Fabricare Institute. 14700 Sweitzer Ln., Laurel, MD 20707. Phone: 800-638-2627 or (301)622-1900 Fax: (240)295-0685 E-mail: techline@ifi.org • URL: http://www.ifi.org • Retail and industrial drycleaners, hospital laundries, linen supply and drapery services, distributors and manufacturers of supplies and machinery, dry-cleaning and laundry associations, and individual launders in 43 countries. Provides washability and dry-cleanability testing for manufacturers of fabrics and related products; offers quality testing and consulting services; conducts research for members. Organizes courses in dry-cleaning, laundering, management, and maintenance. Maintains consulting service, speakers' bureau, research facilities, and library.

Multi-Housing Laundry Association. 1500 Sunday Dr., Ste. 102, Raleigh, NC 27607. Phone: 800-380-3652 or (919)861-5579 Fax: (919)787-4916 E-mail: nshore@mla-online.com • URL: http://www.mla-online.com • Operating and supplier companies. Strives to provide tenants with professionally operated laundry facilities. Sponsors annual convention and trade show.

National Association of Institutional Linen Management. 2130 Lexington Rd., Suite H, Richmond, KY 40475. Phone: 800-669-0863 or (859)624-0177 Fax: (859)624-3580 E-mail: linda@nlmnet.org • URL: http://www.nlmnet.org • Formerly National Assoiciation of Institutional Laundry Managers.

National Cleaners Association. 252 W 29th St., New York, NY 10001. Phone: (212)967-3002 Fax: (212)967-2240 E-mail: info@nca-i.com • URL: http://www.nca-i.com • Members are dry cleaning establishments.

Textile Care Allied Trades Association. 271 Rte. 46 W, No. D203, Fairfield, NJ 07004. Phone: (973)244-1790 Fax: (973)244-4455 E-mail: info@tcata.org • URL: http://www.tcata.org • Represents Manufacturers and distributors of laundry and dry-cleaning machinery, and supplies.

Textile Institute. St. James's Buildings, 1st Fl., 79 Oxford St., Manchester M1 6FQ, United Kingdom. Phone: 44 161 2371188 Fax: 44 161 2361991 E-mail: tiihq@textileinst.org.uk • URL: http://www.texi.org • Companies and individuals in 100 countries involved in management, science, technology, design, information transfer, and marketing of textiles including clothing and footwear. Promotes interests of the textile industry worldwide; serves professional interests of members; confers qualifications and recognizes achievements in research, application of ideas, education, business, and public affairs. Maintains Information Service to collect information relating to textile industrial and economic conditions in different countries and economic sectors.

Textile Processors, Service Trades, Health Care, Professional and Technical Employees International Union. 2210 Midwest Rd., No. 310, Oak Brook, IL 60523. Phone: (630)574-0422.

CLEANING PRODUCTS INDUSTRY

ABSTRACTS AND INDEXES

Applied Science and Technology Index. H. W. Wilson Co. • 11 times a year. Quarterly and annual cumulations. Price varies. Indexes a wide variety of English language technical, industrial, and engineering periodicals.

CD-ROM DATABASES

World Marketing Forecasts on CD-ROM. Gale Cengage Learning. • Annual. $2,500.00. Produced by Euromonitor. Provides detailed forecast data for the years to 2012 on CD-ROM for 54 countries in all parts of the world. Covers a wide range of social, demographic, economic, and market factors. Includes specific forecasts for many kinds of consumer products.

DIRECTORIES

Global Market Share Planner. Euromonitor International. • 2003. $5,900.00. Six volumes. Second edition. Provides detailed profiles and market share rankings of major consumer product companies in North America, Latin America, Europe, South Africa, and the Asia-Pacific region. Covers firms operating in key consumer markets: beverages, food products, household products, and personal care items. (Volumes are available individually.).

Household and Personal Products Industry - Buyers

Guide. Rodman Publications. • Annual. $12.00. Lists of suppliers to manufacturers of cosmetics, toiletries, soaps, detergents, and related household and personal products.

Household and Personal Products Industry Contract Packaging and Private Label Directory. Rodman Publications. • Annual. $12.00. Provides information for about 450 companies offering private label or contract packaged household and personal care products, such as detergents, cosmetics, polishes, insecticides, and various aerosol items.

McCutcheon's Functional Materials Volumes 2. MC Publishing Co. • Annual. $170.00. Edited for product development, quality control and research and development chemists.

McCutcheon's Volume 1: Emulsifiers and Detergents. MC Publishing Co. • Annual. $190.00. Two volumes. International coverage.

OPD Chemical Buyers Directory. Schnell Publishing Company Inc. • Covers: about 1,500 suppliers of chemical process materials and more than 300 companies that transport and store chemicals in the United States. Entries include: Company name, address, phone, list of products or services, telex, fax, e-mail address, internet address, branch offices.

Soap/Cosmetics/Blue Book. Cygnus Business Media, Inc. • Annual. $15.00. Sources of raw materials, equipment and services for the soap, cosmetic and chemical specialities. Formerly *Blue Book of the Soap, Detergent, Cosmetic, and Chemical Specialty Industries.*

World Leading Global Brand Owners. Euromonitor International. • 2003. $1,190.00. Second edition. Contains detailed profiles of multinational consumer product companies. Includes sales, market share, brand names, and financial information. (*Global Market Share Planner*, vol. 3.).

FINANCIAL RATIOS

Annual Statement Studies. The Risk Management Association. • Annual. Median and quartile financial ratios are given for over 400 kinds of manufacturing, wholesale, retail, construction, and consumer finance establishments. Data is sorted by both asset size and sales volume. Includes a clearly written "Definition of Ratios" and an alphabetical industry index.

Annual Statement Studies: Industry Default Probabilities and Cash Flow Measures. The Risk Management Association. • Annual. $145.00. Serves as a companion volume to the original *Annual Statement Studies.* Gives probability of default estimates on a percentage scale for more than 450 industries. Includes changes in position year-by-year for eight financial statement line items and provides percentage measures of cash flow.

ONLINE DATABASES

CA Search. Chemical Abstracts Service. • Guide to chemical literature, 1967 to present. Inquire as to online cost and availability.

PROMT: Predicasts Overview of Markets and Technology. Gale Cengage Learning. • Companies, products, applied technologies and markets. U.S. and international literature coverage, 1972 to date. Inquire as to online cost and availability. Provides abstracts from more than 1,600 publications. Weekly updates.

PERIODICALS AND NEWSLETTERS

Household and Personal Products Industry: The Magazine for the Detergent, Soap, Cosmetic and Toiletry, Wax, Polish and Aerosol Industries. Rodman Publications. • Monthly. $48.00 per year. Covers marketing, packaging, production, technical innovations, private label developments, and aerosol packaging for soap, detergents, cosmetics, insecticides, and a variety of other household products.

ISSA Today. International Sanitary Supply Association. • 10 times a year. $75.00 per year.

Soap and Cosmetics. Cygnus Business Media. • Monthly. $60.00 per year. Formerly *Soap, Cosmetics, Chemical Specialities.*

PRICE SOURCES

Chemical and Engineering News: The Newsmagazine of the Chemical World. American Chemical Society. • Weekly. Institutions, $210.00 per year.

Chemical Market Reporter. Schnell Publishing Co., Inc. • Weekly. $169.00 per year. Quotes current prices for a wide range of chemicals. Formerly *Chemical Marketing Reporter.*

STATISTICS SOURCES

Consumer International. Available from Gale Cengage Learning. • Annual. $1,290.00. Published by Euromonitor. Contains extensive consumer market, economic, and demographic data for 25 major, non-European countries, including the U. S. and Canada. Includes consumer market size (volume and value) for 150 product types in 14 categories (food, clothing, automobiles, cosmetics, appliances, etc.).

European Marketing Forecasts. Available from Gale Cengage Learning. • Annual. $1,250.00. Published by Euromonitor. Contains demographic, economic, and market forecasts for the countries of Europe to the year 2010. Forecasts include market-size data for 15 consumer product sectors (food, clothing, automobiles, consumer electronics, etc.).

International Marketing Forecasts. Available from Gale Cengage Learning. • Annual. $1,250.00. Published by Euromonitor. Contains demographic, economic, and market forecasts to the year 2013 for major, non-European countries, including the U. S. and Canada. Forecasts include market-size data for 15 consumer product sectors, such as food, clothing, and automobiles.

U. S. Industry and Trade Outlook. Available from National Technical Information Service. • Annual. $69.95. Produced by the International Trade Administration, U. S. Department of Commerce, in a "public-private" partnership with DRI/McGraw-Hill and Standard & Poor's. Provides basic data, outlook for the current year, and "Long-Term Prospects" (five-year projections) for a wide variety of products and services. Includes high technology industries. Formerly *U. S. Industrial Outlook.*

TRADE/PROFESSIONAL ASSOCIATIONS

International Housewares Association. 6400 Shafer Ct., Ste. 650, Rosemont, IL 60018. Phone: 800-843-6462 or (847)292-4200 Fax: (847)292-4211 E-mail: pbrandl@housewares.org • URL: http://www. housewares.org • Manufacturers and distributors of housewares and small appliances. Conducts annual market research survey of the housewares industry. Manages the international housewares show.

The Soap and Detergent Association. 1500 K St., NW, Ste. 300, Washington, DC 20005. Phone: (202)347-2900 Fax: (202)347-4110 E-mail: info@cleaning101.com • URL: http://www.cleaning101.com • Represents over 100 North American manufacturers of household, industrial and institutional cleaning projucts, their ingredients and finished packaging. Formerly Glycerine and Oleochemicals Association.

OTHER SOURCES

Household Cleaning Agents. Available from MarketResearch.com. • 2001. $5,900.00. Published by Euromonitor Publications Ltd. Provides consumer market data and forecasts to 2005 for the United States, the United Kingdom, Germany, France, and Italy. Covers dishwashing detergents, floor cleaning products, scourers, polishes, bleaching products, etc.

Market Share Tracker. Euromonitor International. • 2003. $1,190.00. Second edition. Contains market share rankings of more than 1,800 consumer product companies in 30 countries. Covers 16 kinds of products within "Drinks," "Household and Personal Care," and "Foods." Includes brand shares for leading brands. (*Global Market Share Planner*, vol. 1.).

CLIMATE

See also: TRAVEL INDUSTRY; WEATHER AND WEATHER FORECASTING

ABSTRACTS AND INDEXES

Meteorological and Geoastrophysical Abstracts. American Meteorological Society. • Bimonthly. $1,685.00 per year.

ALMANACS AND YEARBOOKS

The Weather Almanac: A Reference Guide to Weather, Climate, and Air Quality in the United States and Its Key Cities, Comprising Statistics, Principles, and Terminology. Gale Cengage Learning. • 2001. $165.00. 10th edition. Weather reports for 108 major U.S. cities and a climatic overview of the country.

DIRECTORIES

Curricula in the Atmospheric Oceanic, Hydrologic and Related Sciences - Colleges and Universities in the United States and Canada. American Meteorological Society. • Free. Available online only. Includes approximately 100 schools. Formerly *Curricula in the Atmospheric and Oceanographic Sciences-Colleges and Universities in the U.S. and Canada.*

ENCYCLOPEDIAS AND DICTIONARIES

Encyclopedia of Climate and Weather. Stephen H. Schneider, editor. Oxford University Press. • 1996. $275.00. Two volumes. Contains more than 300 multidisciplinary entries, with photographs, line drawings, and charts.

Encyclopedia of Global Change: Environmental Change and Human Society. Andrew S. Goudie, editor. Oxford University Press. • 2001. $275.00. Two volumes. Contains 300 signed articles on a wide variety of topics relating to changes in the environment and the atmosphere. Includes bibliographies and illustrations.

HANDBOOKS AND MANUALS

Climates of the States. Gale Cengage Learning. • 2002. $275.00. Fourth edition. Two volumes. State-by-state summaries of climatebased on first order weather reporting stations.

Handbook of Weather, Climate, and Water: Atmospheric Chemistry, Hydrology, and Societal Impacts. Thomas D. Potter and Bradley R. Coleman. John Wiley and Sons, Inc. • 2003. $275.00. Two volumes. $150.00 per volume. Provides a detailed weather and climate reference for "both professionals and laypersons.".

Statistics for the Environment: Statistical Aspects of Health and the Environment. Vic Barnett and others. John Wiley and Sons, Inc. • 1999. $180.00. Two volumes. Vol. 3, $205.00; vol. 4, $225.00. Contains articles on the statistical analysis and interpretation of environmental monitoring and sampling data. Areas covered include meteorology, pollution of the environment, and forest resources. (Statistics for the Environment Series).

USA Today Weather Book. Jack Williams. Random House, Inc. • 1997. $20.00. Contains a state-by-state guide to U. S. climate, with color illustrations. Author (weather editor of *USA Today*) includes discussions of weather patterns and computerized forecasting.

Weather of U.S. Cities. Gale Cengage Learning. • 1996. $235.00. Fifth edition.

PERIODICALS AND NEWSLETTERS

International Journal of Climatology. Royal Meteorological Society. John Wiley and Sons, Inc.,

Journals. • 15 times a year. $1,065.00 per year; institutions, $2,135.00 per year. Published in England by John Wiley and Sons Ltd.

Journal of the Atmospheric Sciences. American Meteorological Society. • Semimonthly. Members, $80.00 per year; institutions, $545.00 per year.

Weather and Climate Report. Nautilus Press, Inc. • Monthly. $95.00 per year. Newsletter.

Weatherwise: The Magazine About the Weather. Helen Dwight Reid Educational Foundation. Heldref Publications. • Bimonthly. Individuals, $38.00 per year; institutions, $80.00 per year. Popular magazine devoted to weather.

RESEARCH CENTERS AND INSTITUTES

Atmospheric Sciences Research Center. University of Albany, State University of New York. 251 Fuller Rd., Albany, NY 12203. Phone: (518)437-8700 Fax: (518)437-8758 E-mail: info@asrc.cestm.albany.edu • URL: http://www.asrc.cestm.albany.edu.

Center for Climatic Research. University of Wisconsin - Madison. 1225 W. Dayton St., Madison, WI 53706-1695. Phone: (608)262-2839 Fax: (608)263-4190 E-mail: jek@facstaff.wisc.edu • URL: http://www.aos.905.wisc/edu.

Institute of Atmospheric Physics. University of Arizona. Dept. of Atmospheric Sciences, P.O. Box 210081, Tucson, AZ 85721-0081. Phone: (520)621-6831 Fax: (520)621-6833 E-mail: atmosci@atmo.arizona.edu • URL: http://www.atmo.arizona.edu.

Office of Climatology. Arizona State University. Tempe, AZ 85287-1508. Phone: (480)965-6265 Fax: (480)965-1473 E-mail: robert.balling@asu.edu.

STATISTICS SOURCES

Local Climatological Data. U.S. National Climatic Data Center. • Monthly.

OECD Environmental Indicators. Organization for Economic Cooperation and Development. • Annual. $27.00. Provides statistical information relating to climate change, air pollution, biodiversity, waste management, water resources, and other environmental topics.

TRADE/PROFESSIONAL ASSOCIATIONS

American Institute of Biomedical Climatology. 1050 Eagle Rd., Newtown, PA 18940. Phone: (215)968-4483 • URL: http://www.aibc.cc • Formerly American Institute of Medical Climatology.

American Meteorological Society. 45 Beacon St., Boston, MA 02108-3693. Phone: (617)227-2425 Fax: (617)742-8718 E-mail: amsinfo@ametsoc.org • URL: http://www.ametsoc.org • Professional meteorologists, oceanographers, and hydrologists; interested students and nonprofessionals. Develops and disseminates information on the atmospheric and related oceanic and hydrospheric sciences; seeks to advance professional applications. Activities include guidance service, scholarship programs, career information, certification of consulting meteorologists, and a seal of approval program to recognize competence in radio and television weathercasting. Issues statements of policy to assist public understanding on subjects such as weather modification, forecasting, tornadoes, hurricanes, flash floods, and meteorological satellites. Provides abstracting services. Prepares educational films, filmstrips, and slides for a new curriculum in meteorology at the ninth grade level. Issues monthly announcements of job openings for meteorologists.

International Association of Meteorology and Atmospheric Sciences. c/o Professor R. List, Dept. of Physics, University of Toronto, Toronto, ON, Canada M5S 1A7. Phone: (416)978-2982 Fax: (416)978-8905 E-mail: list@atmosp.physics.utoronto.ca • URL: http://www.iamas.org.

World Meteorological Organization. 7bis, ave. de la Paix, CH-1211 Geneva, Switzerland. Phone: 41 22 7308111 Fax: 41 22 7308181 E-mail: wmo@wmo.int • URL: http://www.wmo.ch • States, territories, and groups of territories. Supports international cooperation in establishing networks for meteorological observations and hydrological and geophysical observations related to meteorology. Promotes the creation of centers offering meteorological services and systems to facilitate exchange of information. Encourages uniform publication of observations and statistics and the application of meteorology as it involves aviation, shipping, water problems, and agriculture. Fosters activities in operational hydrology and cooperation between meteorological and hydrological services. Organizes courses in meteorology and operational hydrology.

CLINICAL LABORATORY INDUSTRY

BIBLIOGRAPHIES

Encyclopedia of Health Information Sources. Gale Cengage Learning. • 1993. $180.00. Second edition. Both print and nonprint sources of information are listed for 450 health-related topics.

DIRECTORIES

AHA Integrated Delivery Network Directory: U.S. Health Care Systems, Networks, and Alliances. American Hospital Association. • Annual. $250.00. Provides information about a wide variety of U.S. health care groups and affiliations, including hospitals, nursing homes, rehabilitation centers, psychiatric facilities, home health care agencies, clinical laboratories, outpatient facilities, and diagnostic imaging centers. Includes names of more than 8,000 key executives.

CLR (Clinical Laboratory Reference). Medical Economics Co. • Annual. $32.00. Describes diagnostic reagents, test systems, instruments, equipment, and services for medical laboratories. Includes "Directory of Diagnostic Marketers" and "Index of Tests, Equipment, and Services.".

Encyclopedia of Medical Organizations and Agencies. Gale Cengage Learning. • 2001. $295.00. 11th edition. Information on over 18,000 public and private organizations in medicine and related fields.

Health Devices Sourcebook. ECRI. • Covers: Over 6,800 suppliers of patient care equipment, medical and surgical instruments, implants, clinical laboratory equipment and supplies, medical and hospital disposable supplies, and testing instruments; also lists companies that service, recondition, lease, or buy and sell used equipment; coverage includes U.S. and Canada. Entries include: Company name, address, phone, toll-free phone, fax, toll-free fax, URL, e-mail, total sales, names of key executives and contacts, product categories handled, trade names, methods of distribution, typical pricing, annual volume. Price of directory includes custom updates upon request.

Health Industry Buyers Guide. Lippincott Williams & Wilkins. • Covers: 4,000 manufacturers of hospital and physician's supplies and equipment, including medical laboratory, oxygen therapy, and X-ray supplies, home health care products, and orthopedic appliances. Entries include: Manufacturer name, address, phone, fax, full product line.

Laboratories Medical Directory. infoUSA Inc. • Number of listings: 9,073. Entries include: Name, address, phone (including area code), size of advertisement, year first in "Yellow Pages," name of owner or manager, number of employees. Compiled from telephone company "Yellow Pages," nationwide.

FINANCIAL RATIOS

Almanac of Business and Industrial Financial Ratios. Leo Troy. Aspen Publishers, Inc. • 2003. $125.95. Includes CD-Rom. Contains financial ratios derived from federal tax returns. Ratios for each of about 200 industries are arranged according to company asset size. (Almanac of Business and Industrial Financial Ratios Series).

Annual Statement Studies. The Risk Management Association. • Annual. Median and quartile financial ratios are given for over 400 kinds of manufacturing, wholesale, retail, construction, and consumer finance establishments. Data is sorted by both asset size and sales volume. Includes a clearly written "Definition of Ratios" and an alphabetical industry index.

Annual Statement Studies: Industry Default Probabilities and Cash Flow Measures. The Risk Management Association. • Annual. $145.00. Serves as a companion volume to the original *Annual Statement Studies.* Gives probability of default estimates on a percentage scale for more than 450 industries. Includes changes in position year-by-year for eight financial statement line items and provides percentage measures of cash flow.

Industry Norms and Key Business Ratios. Desk Top Edition. Dun and Bradstreet Corp. • Annual. Five volumes. $475.00 per volume. $1,890.00 per set. Covers over 800 kinds of businesses, arranged by Standard Industrial Classification number. More detailed editions covering longer periods of time are also available.

PERIODICALS AND NEWSLETTERS

Clinical Leadership and Management Review. Clinical Laboratory Management Association. Lippincott Williams and Wilkins. • Bimonthly. Individuals, $132.00 per year; institutions, $181.00 per year. Formerly *Cinical Laboratory Management Review.*

Journal of Clinical Laboratory Analysis. John Wiley and Sons, Inc., Journals. • Bimonthly. $1,225.00 per year; with online edition, $1,287.00 per year. Original articles on newly developing assays.

MLO (Medical Laboratory Observer). Thomson Medical Economics. • Monthly. $70.00 per year. Covers management, regulatory, and technical topics for clinical laboratory administrators.

TRADE/PROFESSIONAL ASSOCIATIONS

American Association of Bioanalysts. 917 Locust St., Suite 1100, St. Louis, MO 63101-1419. Phone: (314)241-1445 Fax: (314)241-1449 E-mail: aab@aab.org • URL: http://www.aab.org • Members are owners and managers of bioanalytical clinical laboratories. Affiliated with American Board of Bioanalysis.

American Clinical Laboratory Association. 1250 H St. NW, Ste. 880, Washington, DC 20005-5943. Phone: (202)637-9466 Fax: (202)637-2050 E-mail: info@clinical-labs.org • URL: http://www.clinical-labs.org • Corporations, partnerships, or individuals owning or controlling one or more independent clinical laboratory facilities operating for a profit and licensed under the Clinical Laboratories Improvement Act of 1967 or the Clinical Laboratories Improvement Amendment of 1988, or accredited by the Medicare program. Promotes the development of uniformly high quality laboratory testing; eliminates the present inequalities in the standards applied to different segments of the clinical laboratory market; discourages the enactment of restrictive legislative or regulatory policies that may impede the free flow of commerce or operate to the detriment of the public. Examines federal and state health care and laboratory regulatory and legislative proposals and submits comments and opinions to the appropriate agencies or legislative bodies.

American Medical Technologists. 710 Higgins Rd., Park Ridge, IL 60068-5765. Phone: 800-275-1268 or (847)823-5169 Fax: (847)823-0458 E-mail: dfisher@amga.org • URL: http://www.amt1.com • A program of the American Medical Technologists (see separate entry). Certified assistants to physicians in office practice, clinics, hospitals, and private health care facilities. Works to establish standards of training; provides continuing education and home study programs; promotes quality care in allied health. Works with the Accrediting Bureau of Health Education Schools (see separate entry) in regard to certification examinations and student societies. Offers group insurance programs.

American Society for Clinical Laboratory Science. 6701 Democracy Blvd., Ste. 300, Bethesda, MD 20817. Phone: (301)657-2768 Fax: (301)657-2909 E-mail: ascls@ascls.org • URL: http://www.ascls. org • Seeks to promote high standards in clincal laboratory methods. Formerly American Society for Medical Technology.

Clinical and Laboratory Standards Institute. 940 W Valley Rd., Ste. 1400, Wayne, PA 19087-1898. Phone: 877-447-1888 or (610)688-0100 Fax: (610)688-0700 E-mail: customerservice@clsi.org • URL: http://www.clsi.org • Government agencies, professional societies, clinical laboratories, and industrial firms with interests in medical testing. Purposes are to promote the development of national and international standards for medical testing and to provide a consensus mechanism for defining and resolving problems that influence the quality and cost of healthcare work performed.

Clinical Laboratory Management Association. 989 Old Eagle School Rd., Ste. 815, Wayne, PA 19087. Phone: (610)995-9580 Fax: (610)995-9568 E-mail: website@clma.org • URL: http://www.clma.org • Individuals holding managerial or supervisory positions with clinical laboratories; persons engaged in education of such individuals; manufacturers or distributors of equipment or services to clinical laboratories. Objectives are: to enhance management skills and promote more efficient and productive department operations; to further exchange of professional knowledge, new technology, and colleague experience; to encourage cooperation among those engaged in management or supervisory functions. Activities include: workshops, seminars, and expositions; dissemination of information about legislation and other topics.

CLIPPING SERVICES

See also: NEWSPAPERS; PERIODICALS

ABSTRACTS AND INDEXES

Vertical File Index: Guide to Pamphlets and References to Current Topics. H. W. Wilson Co. • 11 times a year. $115.00 per year. A subject and title index to selected pamphlet material.

ALMANACS AND YEARBOOKS

Editor and Publisher International Yearbook: Encyclopedia of the Newspaper Industry. Editor and Publisher Co., Inc. • Annual. $150.00. Daily and Sunday newspapers in the United States and Canada.

ONLINE DATABASES

National Newspaper Index. Gale Cengage Learning. • Citations to news items in five major newspapers, 1970 to present. Weekly updates. Inquire as to online cost and availability.

TRADE/PROFESSIONAL ASSOCIATIONS

International Federation of Press Cutting Agencies. Streulistrasse 19, CH-8030 Zurich, Switzerland. Phone: 41 1 3888200 Fax: 41 1 3888201.

OTHER SOURCES

Bacon's Newspaper and Magazine Directories. Bacon's Information Inc. • Annual. $325.00 per year. Two volumes: Magazines and Newspapers. Covers print media in the United States and Canada. Formerly *Bacon's Publicity Checker.*

CLOCK AND WATCH INDUSTRY

See also: JEWELRY BUSINESS

GENERAL WORKS

From Sundials to Atomic Clocks: Understanding Time and Frequency. James Jespersen. Dover Publications, Inc. • 1999. $12.95. Second revised edition.

HANDBOOKS AND MANUALS

The Watch Repairer's Manual. Henry B. Fried. American Watchmakers Institute. • $35.00. 1986. Fourth revised edition.

PERIODICALS AND NEWSLETTERS

Journal Suisse d'Horlogerie et de Bijouterie Internationale. Editions Scriptar S.A. • Six times a year. $95.00. Text in English, French and German. Formery J S H- Journal Suisse d'Horlogerie e+ de Bijouterie Internationale.

Modern Jeweler. Cygnus Business Media. • Monthly. $60.00 per year. Edited for retail jewelers. Covers the merchandising of jewelry, gems, and watches. Supersedes in part *Modern Jeweler.*

National Jeweler. VNU Business Media. • Bimonthly. $65.00 per year. For jewelry retailers.

Watch and Clock Review. Golden Bell Press Inc. • 10 times a year. $19.50 per year. Formerly *American Horologist and Jeweler.*

STATISTICS SOURCES

Annual Survey of Manufactures. Available from U. S. Government Printing Office. • Annual. Prices vary. Issued by the U. S. Census Bureau as an interim update to the *Census of Manufactures.* Includes data on number of manufacturing establishments in various industries, employment, labor costs, value of shipments, capital expenditures, inventories, energy costs, and assets. (See also Census Bureau home page, http://www.census. gov/.).

TRADE/PROFESSIONAL ASSOCIATIONS

American Watch Association. PO Box 464, 1201 Pennsylvania Ave. NW, Washington, DC 20044. Phone: (703)759-3377 Fax: (703)759-1639 E-mail: avmainfo@avma.org • Importers of watch movements, watches, and clocks; assemblers of watches, using imported or domestic movements and cases; domestic manufacturers of watch products; suppliers of goods and services.

American Watchmakers and Clockmakers Institute. 701 Enterprise Dr., Harrison, OH 45030. Phone: (866)367-2924 or (513)367-2924 Fax: (513)367-1414 E-mail: jlubic@awi-net.org • URL: http://www.awi-net.org • Formerly American Watchmakers Institute.

CLOSED-END FUNDS

See also: INVESTMENT COMPANIES

ALMANACS AND YEARBOOKS

Emerging Markets Analyst. • Monthly. $895.00 per year. Provides an annual overview of the emerging financial markets in 24 countries of Latin America, Asia, and Europe. Includes data on international mutual funds and closed-end funds.

Investment Company Yearbook. Thomson Financial. • Annual. $310.00. Provides an "entire history of recent events in the mutual funds industry," with emphasis on changes during the past year. About 100 pages are devoted to general information and advice for fund investors. Includes 600 full-page profiles of popular mutual funds, with brief descriptions of 10,000 others, plus 7,000 variable annuities and 500 closed-end funds. Contains a glossary of

technical terms, a Web site index, and an overall book index. Also known as *Wiesenberger Investment Companies Yearbook.*

DIRECTORIES

Morningstar Closed-End Fund 250. McGraw-Hill. • 1996. $35.00. Second edition. Provides detailed information on 50 actively traded closed-end investment companies. Past data is included for up to 12 years, depending on life of the fund.

INTERNET DATABASES

ETF Connect. Nuveen Investments. Phone: 800-257-8787 • URL: http://www.etfconnect.com • Free Web site makes available extensive, searchable information on individual closed-end investment funds, preferred share funds, and exchange-traded index funds. Information on a particular fund is available by name or as part of a classification (high yield, investment grade, municipal, emerging markets, global equity, etc.). Fund charts are available for various time periods, as is data concerning premiums or discounts, dividends, annualized total return, credit quality, "Top 10 Holdings," and so forth.

Factiva. Dow Jones Reuters Business Interactive, LLC. Phone: 800-369-7466 or (609)452-1511 Fax: (609)520-5770 E-mail: solutions@factiva.com • URL: http://www.factiva.com • Fee-based Web site provides "global news and business information through Web sites and content integration solutions." Includes Dow Jones and Reuters newswires, The Wall Street Journal, and more than 7,000 other sources of current news, historical articles, market research reports, and investment analysis. Content includes 96 major U. S. newspapers, 900 non-English sources, trade publications, media transcripts, country profiles, news photos, etc.

Nexis.com. Lexis-Nexis Group. Phone: 800-227-4908 or (937)865-6800 Fax: (937)865-6909 E-mail: webmaster@prod.lexis-nexis.com • URL: http://www.nexis.com • Fee-based Web site offers searching of about 2.8 billion documents in some 30,000 news, business, and legal information sources. Features include a subject directory covering 1,200 topics in 34 categories and a Company Dossier containing information on more than 500,000 public and private companies. Boolean searching is offered.

U. S. Securities and Exchange Commission. Phone: 800-732-0330 or (202)942-7040 Fax: (202)942-9634 E-mail: webmaster@sec.gov • URL: http:// www.sec.gov • SEC Web site offers free access through EDGAR to text of official corporate filings, such as annual reports (10-K), quarterly reports (10-Q), and proxies. (EDGAR is "Electronic Data Gathering, Analysis, and Retrieval System.") An example is given of how to obtain executive compensation data from proxies. Text of the daily *SEC News Digest* is offered, as are links to other government sites, non-government market regulators, and U. S. stock exchanges. Search facilities are extensive. Fees: Free.

Wall Street Journal Interactive Edition. Dow Jones & Co., Inc. Phone: 800-369-2834 or (212)416-2000 Fax: (212)416-2658 E-mail: inquiries@interactive. wsj.com • URL: http://www.wsj.com • Fee-based Web site providing online searching of worldwide information from the *The Wall Street Journal.* Includes "Company Snapshots," "The Journal's Greatest Hits," "Index to Market Data," "Journal Links," etc. Financial price quotes are available. Fees: $49.00 per year; $29.00 per year to print subscribers.

PERIODICALS AND NEWSLETTERS

The Investor's Guide to Closed-End Funds. Thomas J. Herzfeld Advisors, Inc. • Monthly. $475.00 per year. Looseleaf service. Provides detailed information on closed-end investment funds, including charts and recommendations.

Mutual Funds Update. Thomson Financial. •

Monthly. $325.00 per year. Provides recent performance information and statistics for approximately 10,000 mutual funds and closed-end funds as compiled from the CDA/Wiesenberger database. Includes commentary and analysis relating to the mutual fund industry. Information is provided on new funds, name changes, mergers, and liquidations.

The Wall Street Journal. Dow Jones & Co., Inc. • Daily. $189.00 per year. Covers news and trends relating to business, industry, finance, the economy, and international commerce. Provides extensive price and other data for the securities, commodity, options, futures, foreign exchange, and money markets.

TRADE/PROFESSIONAL ASSOCIATIONS

Investment Company Institute. 1401 H St. NW, 12th Fl., Washington, DC 20005. Phone: (202)326-5800 Fax: (202)326-8309 E-mail: memberservices@ici. org • URL: http://www.ici.org • Represents open-end and closed-end investment companies registered under Investment Company Act of 1940; investment advisers to, and underwriters of, such companies; unit investment trust sponsors; interested others. Represents members in matters of legislation, taxation, regulation, economic research marketing, and public information. Provides a clearinghouse for information on the mutual fund industry. Compiles statistics.

OTHER SOURCES

Fund Governance: Legal Duties of Investment Company Directors. American Lawyer Media, Inc. • Looseleaf. $159.00. Updated as needed. Covers the legal obligations of directors of mutual funds and closed-end funds. (Law Journal Press).

CLOSELY HELD CORPORATIONS

See also: PRIVATE COMPANIES

ABSTRACTS AND INDEXES

Business Periodicals Index. H. W. Wilson Co. • 11 times a year. Quarterly and annual cumulations. Price varies.

DIRECTORIES

Business Organizations, Agencies, and Publications Directory. Gale Cengage Learning. • 2003. $480.00. 15th edition. Over 40,000 entries describing 39 types of business information sources. Classified by type of organization, publication, or serviceIncludes state, national, and international agencies and organizations. Master index to names and keywords. Also includes e-mail addresses and web site URL's.

HANDBOOKS AND MANUALS

Managing and Operating a Closely-Held Corporation. Michael Diamond. John Wiley and Sons, Inc. • 1991. $225.00.

Valuing a Business: Analysis and Appraisal of Closely Held Companies. Shannon P. Pratt and others. McGraw-Hill. • 2000. $95.00. Fourth edition. Includes information on how to appraise partial interests and how to write a valuation report.

INTERNET DATABASES

Lexis.com Research System. Lexis-Nexis Group. Phone: 800-227-4908 or (937)865-6800 Fax: (937)865-6909 E-mail: webmaster@prod.lexis-nexis.com • URL: http://www.lexis.com • Fee-based Web site offers extensive searching of a wide variety of legal sources. Additional features include Daily Opinion Service, lexis.com Bookstore, Career Center, CLE Center, Law Schools, and Practice Pages ("Pages specific to areas of specialty").

ONLINE DATABASES

Wilson Business Abstracts Online. H. W. Wilson Co. • Indexes and abstracts 600 major business

periodicals, plus the *Wall Street Journal* and the business section of the *New York Times.* Indexing is from 1982, abstracting from 1990, with the two newspapers included from 1993. Updated weekly. Inquire as to online cost and availability. (*Business Periodicals Index* without abstracts is also available online.).

PERIODICALS AND NEWSLETTERS

Inc.: The Magazine for Growing Companies. INC. • 18 times a year. $14.00 per year. Edited for small office and office-in-the-home businesses with from one to 25 employees. Covers management, office technology, and lifestyle. Incorporates *Self-Employed Professional.*

CLOTHING, CHILDREN'S

See: CHILDREN'S APPAREL INDUSTRY

CLOTHING INDUSTRY

See also: CHILDREN'S APPAREL INDUSTRY; FASHION INDUSTRY; MEN'S CLOTHING INDUSTRY; TAILORING; WOMEN'S APPAREL

GENERAL WORKS

Fashion Merchandising: An Introduction. Elaine Stone. McGraw-Hill. • 1989. $45.72. Fifth edition. (Marketing Series).

ABSTRACTS AND INDEXES

Textile Technology Digest. Institute of Textile Technology. • Annual. $535.00. Provides indexing and abstracting of a wide variety of textile technology literature.

ALMANACS AND YEARBOOKS

International Association of Clothing Designers Convention Yearbook. International Association of Clothing Designers. • Annual. Price on application. For designers of men's and boy's clothing.

CD-ROM DATABASES

OECD Statistical Compendium. Organization for Economic Cooperation and Development. • Semiannual. $1,905.00 per year for 1 to 10 users. CD-ROM contains more than 730,000 monthly, quarterly, and annual time series for OECD countries, 1960 to date. Includes fully searchable data on agriculture, food, economic indicators, national accounts, employment, energy, finance, industry, technology, and foreign trade. Results can be displayed in various forms.

Textile Technology Digest [CD-ROM]. Textile Information Center, Institute of Textile Technology. • Quarterly. Provides CD-ROM indexing and abstracting of worldwide journals and monographs in various areas of textile technology, production, and management. Covers 1978 to date.

World Marketing Forecasts on CD-ROM. Gale Cengage Learning. • Annual. $2,500.00. Produced by Euromonitor. Provides detailed forecast data for the years to 2012 on CD-ROM for 54 countries in all parts of the world. Covers a wide range of social, demographic, economic, and market factors. Includes specific forecasts for many kinds of consumer products.

DIRECTORIES

American Apparel Manufacturers Association Directory of Members and Associate Members. American Apparel Manufacturers Association. • Annual. $100.00. Lists 900 clothing manufacturers and suppliers of goods and services to apparel manufacturers.

Garment Manufacturers Index. Klevens Publications Inc. • Covers: about 8,000 manufacturers and suppliers of products and services such as fabrics,

trimmings, factory equipment, and sewing contractors used in the manufacture of apparel. Publication includes: fabrics, trimmings, supplies, services, equipment, and contractors. Entries include: Company name, address, phone, fax, list of products or services, brief description of product.

Mass Merchandisers and Off-Price Apparel Buyers Directory. Douglas Publications, Inc. • Annual. $229.00. Lists buyers of clothing for major retailers. (Does not include the metropolitan New York City area.) *Salesman's Guide Directories.*

Plunkett's Apparel and Textiles Industry Almanac. Plunkett Research, Ltd. • 2004. $249.99. Includes detailed profiles of 300 leading companies in such industries as clothing, footware, textile design, textile manufacturing, and apparel retailing. Also covers industry trends and statistical data.

ENCYCLOPEDIAS AND DICTIONARIES

Fashion, Fad, and Style. Gale Cengage Learning. • 2003. $250.00. Five volumes. Contains 500 entries covering "human decoration and adornment throughout history." Includes information on clothing, hairstyles, jewelry, and related items. (U-X-L imprint.).

Textile Terms and Definitions. J.E. McIntyre and Paul N. Daniels, editors. Available from State Mutual Book and Periodical Service Ltd. • 1996. $180.00. 10th edition. Published by the Textile Insitute (UK). Includes more than 1,000 definitions of textile processes, fiber types, and end products. Illustrated.

FINANCIAL RATIOS

Almanac of Business and Industrial Financial Ratios. Leo Troy. Aspen Publishers, Inc. • 2003. $125.95. Includes CD-Rom. Contains financial ratios derived from federal tax returns. Ratios for each of about 200 industries are arranged according to company asset size. (Almanac of Business and Industrial Financial Ratios Series).

INTERNET DATABASES

Advance Monthly Sales for Retail Trade and Food Services. U. S. Census Bureau. Phone: 800-541-8345 or (301)763-4636 Fax: (301)457-3842 E-mail: rcb@census.gov • URL: http://www.census.gov/svsd/www/fullpub.html • Web pages provide monthly sales figures for a wide range of retail businesses. Advance, preliminary, and final statistics are provided for the latest month available in each case, with a previous-year comparison. Updates are monthly.

Business 2.0 Web Guide to the Best Business Links. Business 2.0 Media Inc. Phone: (415)293-4800 E-mail: support@business2.com • URL: http://www.business2.com/webguide • Web site presents an extensive, searchable directory of links to "the best, most informative, and authoritative web pages." Twenty main categories cover business, finance, career, company information, people, and technology topics, with thousands of subtopics, all linking to Web sites recommended by experienced business researchers. Fees: Free.

Fedstats. Federal Interagency Council on Statistical Policy. Phone: (202)395-7254 • URL: http://www.fedstats.gov • Web site features an efficient search facility for full-text statistics produced by more than 100 federal agencies, including the Census Bureau, the Bureau of Economic Analysis, and the Bureau of Labor Statistics. Boolean searches can be made within one agency or for all agencies combined. Links are offered to international statistical bureaus, including the UN, IMF, OECD, UNESCO, Eurostat, and 20 individual countries. Fees: Free.

FreeLunch.com. Economy.com, Inc. Phone: (610)696-8700 Fax: (610)696-1678 • URL: http://www.freelunch.com • Web site provides free access to more than 1.5 million economic and financial data series, covering industry, demographics, labor markets, prices, retail sales, government spending, trade, interest rates, housing starts, the stock market, and many other topics. Data is available for various time periods in either chart or table form. Searching is offered. Fees: Free, but registration required. Economy.com, Inc. also offers fee-based economic analysis at *The Dismal Scientist* site (http://www.dismal.com).

Manufacturing Profiles. U. S. Bureau of the Census. Phone: (301)763-4636 E-mail: webmaster@census.gov • URL: http://www.census.gov/prod/www/abs/mfg-prof.html • The Census Bureau makes available free on PDF (Portable Document Format) an annual consolidation of the entire Current Industrial Report series, presenting "all the data compiled." Contains statistics on production, shipments, inventories, consumption, exports, imports, and orders for a wide variety of manufactured products.

ONLINE DATABASES

Textile Technology Digest [online]. Institute of Textile Technology. • Contains indexing and abstracting of more than 300 worldwide journals and monographs in various areas of textile technology, production, and management. Time period is 1978 to date, with monthly updating. Inquire as to online cost and availability.

World Textiles. Elsevier Science, Inc. • Provides abstracting and indexing from 1970 of worldwide textile literature (periodicals, books, pamphlets, and reports). Includes U. S., European, and British patent information. Updating is monthly. Inquire as to online cost and availability.

PERIODICALS AND NEWSLETTERS

Apparel Merchandising. Lebhar-Friedman, Inc. • Eight times a year. $24.00 per year. Reports on fashion trends in women's, men's, and children's clothing. Supplement to (DSN Retailing Today).

Textile Hi-Lights. American Textile Manufacturers Institute, Inc. • Quarterly. $125.00 per year. Monthly *Supplements.*

Textile World. Biilian Publishing Inc. • Monthly. Free to qualified personnel.

WWD: The Retailer's Daily Newspaper (Women's Wear Daily). Fairchild Publications. • Daily. Individuals, $195.00 per year; retailers, $99.00 per year; manufacturers, $135.00 per year.

RESEARCH CENTERS AND INSTITUTES

International Textile Center. Texas Tech University. P.O. Box 45019, Lubbock, TX 79409-5019. Phone: (806)747-3790 Fax: (806)747-3796 E-mail: itc@ttu.edu • URL: http://www.depts.ttu.edu/itc.

Textiles and Materials. Philadelphia University, Schoolhouse Lane and Henry Ave., Philadelphia, PA 19144-5497. Phone: (215)951-2751 Fax: (215)951-2651 E-mail: brooksteind@philau.edu • URL: http://www.philaau.edu/schools • Many research areas, including industrial and nonwoven textiles.

STATISTICS SOURCES

Annual Benchmark Report for Retail Trade and Food Services...A Detailed Summary of Retail Sales, Purchases, Accounts Receivable, Inventories, and Food Service Sales. Available from U. S. Government Printing Office. • Annual. $13.00. Issued by the U.S. Census Bureau. Provides detailed annual and monthly retail statistics for the most recent 10 years. Includes data for various kinds of retail outlets, including automobiles, furniture, appliances, building supplies, grocery stores, drug stores, gasoline stations, clothing, sporting goods, department stores, and restaurants.

Annual Survey of Manufactures. Available from U. S. Government Printing Office. • Annual. Prices vary. Issued by the U. S. Census Bureau as an interim update to the *Census of Manufactures.* Includes data on number of manufacturing establishments in various industries, employment, labor

costs, value of shipments, capital expenditures, inventories, energy costs, and assets. (See also Census Bureau home page, http://www.census.gov/.).

Business Statistics of the United States. Linz Audain and Cornelia J. Strawser. Bernan Associates. • Annual. $147.00. Based on *Business Statistics,* formerly issue by the Bureau of Economic Analysis, U. S. Department of Commerce. Provides basic data for a wide variety of U. S. industries, services, and economic indicators. Most statistics are shown annually for 30 years and monthly for the most recent four years.

Consumer International. Available from Gale Cengage Learning. • Annual. $1,290.00. Published by Euromonitor. Contains extensive consumer market, economic, and demographic data for 25 major, non-European countries, including the U. S. and Canada. Includes consumer market size (volume and value) for 150 product types in 14 categories (food, clothing, automobiles, cosmetics, appliances, etc.).

European Marketing Forecasts. Available from Gale Cengage Learning. • Annual. $1,250.00. Published by Euromonitor. Contains demographic, economic, and market forecasts for the countries of Europe to the year 2010. Forecasts include market-size data for 15 consumer product sectors (food, clothing, automobiles, consumer electronics, etc.).

International Marketing Forecasts. Available from Gale Cengage Learning. • Annual. $1,250.00. Published by Euromonitor. Contains demographic, economic, and market forecasts to the year 2013 for major, non-European countries, including the U. S. and Canada. Forecasts include market-size data for 15 consumer product sectors, such as food, clothing, and automobiles.

Standard & Poor's Industry Surveys. Standard & Poor's. • Semiannual. $1,800.00. Two looseleaf volumes. Includes monthly *Supplements.* Provides detailed, individual surveys of 52 major industry groups. Each survey is revised on a semiannual basis. Also includes "Monthly Investment Review" (industry group investment analysis) and monthly "Trends & Projections" (economic analysis).

Survey of Current Business. Available from U. S. Government Printing Office. • Monthly. $63.00 per year. Issued by Bureau of Economic Analysis, U. S. Department of Commerce. Presents a wide variety of business and economic data.

WEFA Industrial Monitor. John Wiley and Sons, Inc. • Annual. $65.00. Prepared by industry analysts at WEFA, an economic forecasting and consulting firm (originally Wharton Econometric Forecasting Associates). Contains discussions of the outlook for major U. S. industries, with many 10-year forecasts (WEFA Web site is http://www.wefa.com).

TRADE/PROFESSIONAL ASSOCIATIONS

American Apparel and Footwear Association. 1601 N. Kent St., Suite 1200, Arlington, VA 22209. Phone: 800-520-2262 or (703)524-1864 Fax: (703)522-6741 E-mail: mrhowell@apparelandfootwear.org • URL: http://www.americanapparel.org • Formerly American Apparel Manufacturers Associations.

Chamber of Commerce of the Apparel Industry. 118 River Rd., Ste. 18, Harriman, NY 10926-3022. Phone: (845)781-7337 Fax: (845)781-7340 • A worker's compensation group authorized by the New York State Insurance Funds.

Clothing Manufacturers Association of the U.S.A. 730 Broadway, 10th Fl., New York, NY 10003. Phone: (212)529-0823 Fax: (212)529-1443.

International Association of Clothing Designers and Executives. 475 Park Ave. S, 9th Fl., New York, NY 10016. Fax: (212)545-1709 E-mail: dmschmida@aol.com • Formerly International Associatin of Clothing Designers.

Textile Institute. St. James's Buildings, 1st Fl., 79 Oxford St., Manchester M1 6FQ, United Kingdom. Phone: 44 161 2371188 Fax: 44 161 2361991 E-mail: tiihq@textileinst.org.uk • URL: http://www.texi.org • Companies and individuals in 100 countries involved in management, science, technology, design, information transfer, and marketing of textiles including clothing and footwear. Promotes interests of the textile industry worldwide; serves professional interests of members; confers qualifications and recognizes achievements in research, application of ideas, education, business, and public affairs. Maintains Information Service to collect information relating to textile industrial and economic conditions in different countries and economic sectors.

Unite!-The Union of Needletrades, Industrial and Textile Employees. 1710 Broadway, New York, NY 10019. Phone: (212)265-7000 Fax: (212)315-3803 E-mail: kkirsch@uniteunion.org • URL: http://www.uniteunion.org.

UNITE!-Union of Needletrades, Industrial and Textile Employees. 275 Seventh Ave., New York, NY 10001-6708. Phone: (212)265-7000 Fax: (212)315-3803 E-mail: kkirsch@uniteunion.org • URL: http://www.uniteunion.org.

United Food and Commercial Workers International Union. 1775 K. St., N.W., Washington, DC 20006. Phone: (202)223-3111 Fax: (202)466-1562 • URL: http://www.ufcw.org.

CLOTHING, MEN'S

See: MEN'S CLOTHING INDUSTRY

CLOTHING, WOMEN'S

See: WOMEN'S APPAREL

CLUBS

See also: ASSOCIATIONS; WOMEN'S CLUBS

GENERAL WORKS

The American Country Club: Its Origins and Development. James M. Mayo. Rutgers University Press. • 1998. $25.00.

ALMANACS AND YEARBOOKS

CMAA Yearbook. Club Managers Association of America. • Annual. Membership directory.

DIRECTORIES

Club Industry: Buyers Guide. Primedia Business Magazines and Media. • Annual. $25.00. A directory of over 1,000 companies furnishing equipment, supplies, and services to health and fitness clubs.

Washington: A Comprehensive Directory of the Key Institutions and Leaders in th e National Capitol Area. Columbia Books, Inc. • Annual. $149.00. Provides information on about 5,000 Washington, DC key businesses, government offices, non-profit organizations, and cultural institutions, with the names of about 25,000 principal executives. Includes Washington media, law offices, foundations, labor unions, international organizations, clubs, etc.

FINANCIAL RATIOS

Annual Statement Studies. The Risk Management Association. • Annual. Median and quartile financial ratios are given for over 400 kinds of manufacturing, wholesale, retail, construction, and consumer finance establishments. Data is sorted by both asset size and sales volume. Includes a clearly written "Definition of Ratios" and an alphabetical industry index.

Annual Statement Studies: Industry Default Probabilities and Cash Flow Measures. The Risk Management Association. • Annual. $145.00. Serves as a companion volume to the original *Annual Statement Studies.* Gives probability of default estimates on a percentage scale for more than 450 industries. Includes changes in position year-by-year for eight financial statement line items and provides percentage measures of cash flow.

HANDBOOKS AND MANUALS

Club Manager's Guide to Private Parties and Club Functions. Joe Perdue and others. John Wiley and Sons, Inc. • 1998. $65.00. Covers on-premises catering at clubs, including member relations, meal functions, beverage functions, room setup, staffing, etc.

Federal Taxes and the Private Club. PKF - Pannell Kerr Forster. • Annual. $25.00. Provides a summary of tax issues affecting private clubs.

Robert's Rules of Order. Henry M. Roberts, editors. Perseus Books Group. • 2000. $35.00. 10th revised edition.

ONLINE DATABASES

Magazine Index. Gale Cengage Learning. • General magazine indexing (popular literature), 1973 to present. Daily updates. Inquire as to online cost and availability.

PERIODICALS AND NEWSLETTERS

Bottomline. Hospitality Financial and Technology Professionals. • Bimonthly. Free to members, educational institutions and libraries; non-members, $50.00 per year. Contains articles on accounting, finance, information technology, and management for hotels, resorts, casinos, clubs, and other hospitality businesses.

Club Director. National Club Association. • Bimonthly. $18.00 per year. Magazine for directors, owners and managers of private clubs.

Club Management: The Resource for Successful Club Operations. Club Managers Association of America. Finan Publishing Co. • Bimonthly. $21.95 per year.

GFWC Clubwoman: Magazine of the General Federation of Women's Club. General Federation of Women's Clubs. • Bimonthly. $6.00 per year.

Hospitality Technology: Guiding High-Growth Businesses to Best-Choice IT Solutions. Edgell Communications, Inc. • 10 times a year. Price on application. Covers information technology, computer communications, and software for food-service and lodging enterprises.

STATISTICS SOURCES

Profiles of Success. International Health, Racquet, and Sportsclub Association. • Annual. Members, $125.00; non-members, $500.00. Provides detailed financial statistics for commercial health clubs, sports clubs, and gyms.

TRADE/PROFESSIONAL ASSOCIATIONS

Club Managers Association of America. 1733 King St., Alexandria, VA 22314-2720. Phone: (703)739-9500 Fax: (703)739-0124 E-mail: cmaa@cmaa.org • URL: http://www.cmaa.org.

Hospitality Financial and Technology Professionals. 11709 Boulder Lane, Suite 110, Austin, TX 78726. Phone: 800-646-4387 or (512)249-5333 Fax: (512)249-1533 E-mail: frank.wolfe@hftp.org • URL: http://www.hftp.org • Members are accounting and finance officers in the hotel, motel, casino, club, and other areas of the hospitality industry. Formerly International Association of Hospitality Accountants.

International Health, Racquet and Sportsclub Association. 263 Summer St., Boston, MA 02210. Phone: 800-228-4772 or (617)951-0055 Fax: (617)951-0056 E-mail: info@ihrsa.org • URL: http://www.ihrsa.org • Members are for-profit health

clubs, sports clubs, and gyms. Formerly IRSA, The Association of Quality Clubs.

International Military Community Executives Association. 2100 E Stan Schlueter Loop, Ste. G, Killeen, TX 76542. Phone: (254)554-6619 Fax: (254)554-6629 E-mail: mhanson@imcea.com • URL: http://www.imcea.com.

National Club Association. 1201 15th St., Ste. 450, 1120 20th St., N.W., Suite 725, Washington, DC 20005. Phone: 800-625-6221 or (202)822-9822 Fax: (202)822-9808 E-mail: info@nationalclub.org • URL: http://www.natlclub.org • Represents the business and legal interests of private clubs. Analyzes proposed laws and regulations affecting clubs; compiles statistics and economic data; drafts model legislation; and acts as a general center of information about club matters.

CLUBS, WOMEN'S

See: WOMEN'S CLUBS

COAL GASIFICATION

See: ENERGY SOURCES

COAL INDUSTRY

See also: COKE INDUSTRY; ENERGY SOURCES

ALMANACS AND YEARBOOKS

Agricultural and Mineral Commodities Year Book. Available from Taylor & Francis Group. • Annual. $225.00. Published by Europa Publications. Contains descriptive product profiles, price data, export-import data, and production statistics for major commodities of the world. Includes commodity histories, uses, markets, demand trends, and information about trade agreements and key commodity organizations.

CRB Commodity Yearbook. Commodity Research Bureau. CRB. • Annual. $99.95.

UK Coal. OECD Publications and Information Center. • Annual. $200.00. A yearly report on world coal market trends and prospects.

BIBLIOGRAPHIES

Coal Industry. Charles Kernot. American Educational Systems. • $710.00. Looseleaf service. Periodic supplementation.

CD-ROM DATABASES

OECD Statistical Compendium. Organization for Economic Cooperation and Development. • Semiannual. $1,905.00 per year for 1 to 10 users. CD-ROM contains more than 730,000 monthly, quarterly, and annual time series for OECD countries, 1960 to date. Includes fully searchable data on agriculture, food, economic indicators, national accounts, employment, energy, finance, industry, technology, and foreign trade. Results can be displayed in various forms.

DIRECTORIES

Financial Times Business Global Mining Directory. Available from Gale Cengage Learning. • Annual. $355.00. Published by Financial Times Business. Provides detailed information on 1,000 leading mining companies worldwide. Includes financial data for three years. Formerly *Financial Times Energy Yearbook: Mining.*

Keystone Coal Industry Manual. Primedia Business. • Covers: coal companies and mines, coke plants, coal preparation plants, domestic and export coal sales companies; industry organizations, steam power plants, portland cement plants, industrial coal-burning plants, consultants, mining contrac-

tors; river docks, tidewater piers, river transportation companies, railroads; financial institutions; includes list of leading coal mining companies and mines. Entries include: Company or organization name, address, names of executives; coal mine directory includes analysis, tonnage, capacity, seam mined and facilities; consultants directory includes services offered.

ENCYCLOPEDIAS AND DICTIONARIES

Wiley Encyclopedia of Energy and the Environment. Attilio Bisio and Sharon Boots. John Wiley and Sons, Inc. • 1996. $285.00. Abriged edition. Two volumes. Covers a wide variety of energy and environmental topics, including legal and policy issues. (Encyclopedia of Energy and the Environment Series: Vol. 2).

FINANCIAL RATIOS

Almanac of Business and Industrial Financial Ratios. Leo Troy. Aspen Publishers, Inc. • 2003. $125.95. Includes CD-Rom. Contains financial ratios derived from federal tax returns. Ratios for each of about 200 industries are arranged according to company asset size. (Almanac of Business and Industrial Financial Ratios Series).

Annual Statement Studies. The Risk Management Association. • Annual. Median and quartile financial ratios are given for over 400 kinds of manufacturing, wholesale, retail, construction, and consumer finance establishments. Data is sorted by both asset size and sales volume. Includes a clearly written "Definition of Ratios" and an alphabetical industry index.

Annual Statement Studies: Industry Default Probabilities and Cash Flow Measures. The Risk Management Association. • Annual. $145.00. Serves as a companion volume to the original *Annual Statement Studies.* Gives probability of default estimates on a percentage scale for more than 450 industries. Includes changes in position year-by-year for eight financial statement line items and provides percentage measures of cash flow.

HANDBOOKS AND MANUALS

Coal Data. National Mining Association. • Annual. Free to members; non-members, $75.00.

INTERNET DATABASES

Business 2.0 Web Guide to the Best Business Links. Business 2.0 Media Inc. Phone: (415)293-4800 E-mail: support@business2.com • URL: http://www.business2.com/webguide • Web site presents an extensive, searchable directory of links to "the best, most informative, and authoritative web pages." Twenty main categories cover business, finance, career, company information, people, and technology topics, with thousands of subtopics, all linking to Web sites recommended by experienced business researchers. Fees: Free.

Fedstats. Federal Interagency Council on Statistical Policy. Phone: (202)395-7254 • URL: http://www.fedstats.gov • Web site features an efficient search facility for full-text statistics produced by more than 100 federal agencies, including the Census Bureau, the Bureau of Economic Analysis, and the Bureau of Labor Statistics. Boolean searches can be made within one agency or for all agencies combined. Links are offered to international statistical bureaus, including the UN, IMF, OECD, UNESCO, Eurostat, and 20 individual countries. Fees: Free.

FreeLunch.com. Economy.com, Inc. Phone: (610)696-8700 Fax: (610)696-1678 • URL: http://www.freelunch.com • Web site provides free access to more than 1.5 million economic and financial data series, covering industry, demographics, labor markets, prices, retail sales, government spending, trade, interest rates, housing starts, the stock market, and many other topics. Data is available for various time periods in either chart or table form. Searching is offered. Fees: Free, but registration required.

Economy.com, Inc. also offers fee-based economic analysis at *The Dismal Scientist* site (http://www.dismal.com).

NMA. National Mining Association. Phone: (202)463-2600 Fax: (202)463-2666 • URL: http://www.nma.org • Web site provides information on the U. S. coal and mineral industries. Includes "Salient Statistics of the Mining Industry," showing a wide variety of annual data (six years) for coal and non-fuel minerals. Publications of the National Mining Association are described and links are provided to other sites. (National Mining Association formerly known as National Coal Association.) Fees: Free.

PERIODICALS AND NEWSLETTERS

Coal Leader: Coal's National Newspaper. Coal, Inc. • Monthly. $18.00 per year. Formerly *National Coal Leader.*

Coal Outlook. FT Energy. • Description: Reports on government action affecting the coal industry. Analyzes court cases and legislation, plus market, transportation, and regulatory trends. Also provides information on production and productivity, utility coal specifications and delivered prices, overseas coal markets, union organizing activities and contract negotiations, and company news. Recurring features include statistics, coal price and consumption data, and the column titled Marketscoop. **Remarks:** Includes supplements containing price charts for steam, metallurgical, industrial, or anthracite coal. Also available via daily e-mail service.

Energy and Fuels. American Chemical Society. • Bimonthly. Institutions, $852.00 per year; others, price on application. An interdisciplinary technical journal covering non-nuclear energy sources: petroleum, gas, synthetic fuels, etc.

Mining Week. National Mining Association. Weekly. Free to members; non-members, $100.00 per year. Newsletter. Covers legislative, business, research, and other developments of interest to the mining industry.

Power Generation Technology and Markets. Pasha Publishing Inc. • Weekly. $790.00 per year. Newsletter. Formerly *Coal and Synfuels Technology.*

PRICE SOURCES

Energy Prices and Taxes. International Energy Agency. OECD Publications and Information Center. • Quarterly. $385.00 per year. Includes print and online edition. Compiled by the International Energy Agency. Provides data on prices and taxation of petroleum products, natural gas, coal, and electricity. Diskette edition, $800.00. (Published in Paris).

Energy Prices and Taxes. Organization for Economic Cooperation and Development. • Quarterly. $355.00 per year. Includes both industrial and consumer prices for oil products, natural gas, coal, and electricity in various countries. (Also available on CD-ROM.).

RESEARCH CENTERS AND INSTITUTES

Canadian Energy Research Institute. Canadian Energy Research Institute. 3512 33rd St. NW, No. 150, Calgary, AB, Canada T2L 2A6. Phone: (403)282-1231 Fax: (403)284-4181 E-mail: mmasri@ceri.ca • URL: http://www.ceri.ca • Economic issues relating to all forms of energy, including oil, natural gas, coal, nuclear and hydroelectric power, and alternative energy sources. Develops software such as the World Oil Market Model.

Center for Applied Energy Research. University of Kentucky, 2540 Research Dr., Lexington, KY 40511-8410. Phone: (859)257-0305 Fax: (859)257-0302 E-mail: mcalister@caer.uky.edu • URL: http://www.caer.uky.edu.

Coal Research Center. Southern Illinois University at Carbondale. Mail Code 4623, Carbondale, IL 62901-4623. Phone: (618)536-5521 Fax: (618)453-7346 E-mail: jmead@siu.edu • URL: http://www.siu.edu.

Energy and Environmental Research Center. University of North Dakota. P.O. Box 9018, Grand Forks, ND 58202-9018. Phone: (701)777-5000 Fax: (701)777-5181 E-mail: ggroenewold@undeerc.org • URL: http://www.undeerc.org.

Energy Institute. Pennsylvania State University. 120 Hosler Bldg., C211 Coal Utilization Laboratory, University Park, PA 16802-5000. Phone: (814)863-1337 Fax: (814)863-7432 E-mail: schobert@ems.psu.edu • URL: http://www.energyinstitute.psu.edu/.

STATISTICS SOURCES

Annual Energy Outlook [year], with Projections to [year]. Available from U. S. Government Printing Office. • Annual. $42.00. Issued by the Energy Information Administration, U. S. Department of Energy (http://www.eia.doe.gov). Contains detailed statistics and 20-year projections for electricity, oil, natural gas, coal, and renewable energy. Text provides extensive discussion of energy issues and "Market Trends.".

Annual Energy Review. Available from U. S. Government Printing Office. • Annual. $51.00. Issued by the Energy Information Administration, Office of Energy Markets and End Use, U. S. Department of Energy. Presents long-term historical as well as recent data on production, consumption, stocks, imports, exports, and prices of the principal energy commodities in the U. S.

Business Statistics of the United States. Linz Audain and Cornelia J. Strawser. Bernan Associates. • Annual. $147.00. Based on *Business Statistics,* formerly issue by the Bureau of Economic Analysis, U. S. Department of Commerce. Provides basic data for a wide variety of U. S. industries, services, and economic indicators. Most statistics are shown annually for 30 years and monthly for the most recent four years.

Coal Information. Organization for Economic Cooperation and Development. • Annual. $200.00. Presents comprehensive data from the International Energy Agency (IEA) on the world coal market, including supply, demand, production, trade, and prices. In addition to coal itself, provides country-specific data on coal-fired power stations and coal-related environmental issues.

Coal Transportation Statistics. National Mining Association. • Annual. Non-profit organizations, $25.00; others, $35.00. Formerly *Coal Traffic Annual.*

Energy Balances of OECD Countries. Organization for Economic Cooperation and Development. Available from OECD Publications and Information Center. • Annual. $115.00. Presents two-year data on the supply and consumption of solid fuels, oil, gas, and electricity, expressed in oil equivalency terms. Historical tables are also provided. Relates to OECD member countries.

Minerals Yearbook. Available from U.S. Government Printing Office. • Annual. Three volumes.

Monthly Energy Review. Available from U. S. Government Printing Office. • Monthly. $126.00 per year. Issued by the Energy Information Administration, Office of Energy Markets and End Use, U. S. Department of Energy. Contains current and historical statistics on U. S. production, storage, imports, and consumption of petroleum, natural gas, and coal.

Oil, Gas, Coal, and Electricity: Quarterly Statistics. Organization for Economic Cooperation and Development. • Quarterly. $355.00 per year. Provides detailed data for OECD countries. Covers crude oil, nine oil product groups, hard coal, brown

coal (lignite), natural gas, and electric power.

Quarterly Coal Report. Energy Information Administration, U.S. Department of Energy. Available from U.S. Government Printing Office. • Quarterly. $30.00 per year. Annual summary.

Quarterly Mining Review. National Mining Association. • Quarterly. $300.00 per year. Contains detailed data on production, shipments, consumption, stockpiles, and trade for coal and various minerals. (Publisher formerly National Coal Association.).

Steam Electric Market Analysis. National Mining Association. • Monthly. Free to members; non-members, $300.00 per year. Covers 400 major electric power plants, with detailed data on coal consumption and stockpiles. Shows percent of power generated by fuel type. (Publisher formerly National Coal Association.).

Survey of Current Business. Available from U. S. Government Printing Office. • Monthly. $63.00 per year. Issued by Bureau of Economic Analysis, U. S. Department of Commerce. Presents a wide variety of business and economic data.

United States Census of Mineral Industries. Bureau of the Census, U.S. Department of Commerce. Available from U.S. Government Printing Office. • Quinquennial.

Weekly Statistical Summary. National Mining Association. • Weekly. Newsletter. Free to members; non-members, $100.00 per year. A detailed report on coal production and consumption.

WEFA Industrial Monitor. John Wiley and Sons, Inc. • Annual. $65.00. Prepared by industry analysts at WEFA, an economic forecasting and consulting firm (originally Wharton Econometric Forecasting Associates). Contains discussions of the outlook for major U. S. industries, with many 10-year forecasts (WEFA Web site is http://www.wefa.com).

TRADE/PROFESSIONAL ASSOCIATIONS

National Mining Association. 101 Constitution Ave. NW, Ste. 500 E, Washington, DC 20001-2133. Phone: (202)463-2600 Fax: (202)463-2666 E-mail: craulston@nma.org • URL: http://www.nma.org • Producers and sellers of coal and hardrock minerals, equipment manufacturers, distributors, equipment suppliers, other energy suppliers, consultants, utility companies, and coal transporters. Serves as liaison between the industry and federal government agencies. Keeps members informed of legislative and regulatory actions. Works with industry, consumers, and government agencies on mining industry issues. Seeks improved conditions for export of steam and metallurgical coal. Collects, analyzes, and distributes industry statistics; makes special studies of competitive fuels, coal and metal markets, production and consumption forecasts, and industry planning.

Rocky Mountain Coal Mining Institute. 8057 S Yukon Way, Littleton, CO 80128-5510. Phone: (303)948-3300 Fax: (303)948-1132 E-mail: mail@rmcmi.org • URL: http://www.rmcmi.org • Coal industry persons, including producers, users, equipment manufacturers, suppliers, coal transporters, lawyers, bankers, and others. Promotes the use of western coal through education.

United Mine Workers of America. 8315 Lee Highway, Fairfax, VA 22031. Phone: (703)208-7200 • URL: http://www.umwa.org • Formerly International Union United Mine Workers in America.

COAL MINING INDUSTRY

See: COAL INDUSTRY

COAL TAR PRODUCTS

See: CHEMICAL INDUSTRIES

COAST GUARD

DIRECTORIES
Register of Officers [United States Coast Guard].
U.S. Coast Guard. • Annual.

HANDBOOKS AND MANUALS
Coast Guardsman's Manual. George E. Krietmeyer.
Naval Institute Press. • 2000. $21.95. Ninth edition.

PERIODICALS AND NEWSLETTERS
The Coast Guard Reservist. Commandant, U.S.
Coast Guard. • Monthly. Free.

Ocean Navigator: Marine Navigation and Ocean Voyaging. Navigator Publishing LLC. • Bimonthly.
$26.00 per year.

TRADE/PROFESSIONAL ASSOCIATIONS
United States Coast Guard Auxiliary. Commandant,
U.S. Coast Guard HQ (G-OCX), 2100 Second St.
SW, Washington, DC 20593. Phone: 800-368-5647
or (202)267-0780 or (202)267-1001 Fax: (202)267-
4460 E-mail: info@cgaux.org • URL: http://www.
cgaux.org.

United States Coast Guard Chief Petty Officer
Association. 5520G Hempstead Way, Springfield,
VA 22151. Phone: (703)941-0395 Fax: (703)941-
0397 E-mail: cgcpoa@aol.com • URL: http://www.
uscgcpoa.org.

COATINGS, INDUSTRIAL

See: INDUSTRIAL COATINGS

COBALT INDUSTRY

See: METAL INDUSTRY

COCOA INDUSTRY

See also: CHOCOLATE INDUSTRY

ALMANACS AND YEARBOOKS
Agricultural and Mineral Commodities Year Book.
Available from Taylor & Francis Group. • Annual.
$225.00. Published by Europa Publications.
Contains descriptive product profiles, price data,
export-import data, and production statistics for
major commodities of the world. Includes commodity histories, uses, markets, demand trends, and
information about trade agreements and key commodity organizations.

CRB Commodity Yearbook. Commodity Research
Bureau. CRB. • Annual. $99.95.

CD-ROM DATABASES
*Food Science and Technology Abstracts [CD-
ROM].* Available from SilverPlatter Information,
Inc. • Quarterly. Produced by International Food
Information Service (home page is http://www.ifis.
org). Provides worldwide coverage on CD-ROM of
the literature of food technology and production.
Various types of publications are indexed, with
abstracts, including about 1,800 periodicals. Time
period is 1969 to date.

DIRECTORIES
Major Food and Drink Companies of the World.
Available from Gale Cengage Learning. • Annual.
$880.00. Two volumes. Published by Graham &
Whiteside. Contains profiles and trade names for
more than 9,800 important food and beverage
companies in various countries. In addition to foods,
includes both alcoholic and nonalcoholic drink
products.

OPD Chemical Buyers Directory. Schnell Publishing Company Inc. • Covers: about 1,500 suppliers
of chemical process materials and more than 300

companies that transport and store chemicals in the
United States. Entries include: Company name, address, phone, list of products or services, telex, fax,
e-mail address, internet address, branch offices.

Thomas Food and Beverage Market Place. Grey
House Publishing. • 2004. $495.00. Three volumes.
Contains more than 40,000 entries covering food
companies, beverages, food equipment, warehouse
companies, food brokers, wholesalers, importers,
and exporters. Formerly *Thomas Food Industry
Register.*

ONLINE DATABASES
Food Science and Technology Abstracts [online].
IFIS North American Desk. • Produced by
International Food Information Service. Provides
about 500,000 online citations, with abstracts, to the
international literature of food science, technology,
commodities, engineering, and processing. Approximately 2,000 periodicals are covered. Time
period is 1969 to date, with monthly updates. Inquire
as to online cost and availability.

PERIODICALS AND NEWSLETTERS
*Barron's: The Dow Jones Business and Financial
Weekly.* • Weekly. $145.00 per year.

Coffee and Cocoa International. DMG World Media
Ltd. • Seven times a year. $124.00 per year.

PRICE SOURCES
The New York Times. New York Times Co. • Daily.
$374.40 per year. Supplements available: *New York
Times Book Review, New York Times Magazine,
Sophisticated Traveler* and *Fashions of the Times.*

STATISTICS SOURCES
FAO Production Yearbook. Available from Bernan
Associates. • Annual. $45.00. Published by the Food
and Agriculture Organization (http://www.fao.org).
Contains worldwide data on agriculture, land use,
farm crops, livestock, and agricultural prices.

FAO Quarterly Bulletin of Statistics. Food and
Agriculture Organization of the United Nations.
Available from UNIPUB. • Quarterly. $20.00 per
year. Provides international data on agricultural
production, trade, and prices, covering the major
commodities of many countries. Text in English,
French, and Spanish. Formerly *FAO Monthly Bulletin of Statistics.*

FAO Trade Yearbook. Available from Bernan
Associates. • Annual. $45.00. Published by the Food
and Agriculture Organization (http://www.fao.org).
Provides extensive worldwide data on exports and
imports of agricultural commodities, fertilizers, tractors, and pesticides. Includes more than 130 tables
of detailed statistics.

World Food Data and Statistics. Euromonitor
International. • 2004. $650.00. Provides five-year
data for a wide variety of food products in 52
countries. Includes market size, consumer
expenditures, price indicators, and retail distribution
data for many kinds of meat, fish, fruits, vegetables,
dairy products, baked goods, condiments, canned
food, and frozen food.

TRADE/PROFESSIONAL ASSOCIATIONS
American Cocoa Research Institute. 8320 Old
Courthouse Rd., Ste. 300, Vienna, VA 22182. Phone:
(703)790-5011 Fax: (703)790-5752 E-mail: larry.
graham@candyusa.org • URL: http://www.
chocolateandcocoa.org/acri.

The Cocoa Merchants' Association of America, Inc.
39 Broadway, 3rd Fl., New York, NY 10006. Phone:
(212)201-8819 Fax: (212)785-5475 E-mail: cmaa@
cocoamerchants.com • URL: http://www.
cocoamerchants.com.

Coffee, Sugar and Cocoa Exchange. 1 N End Ave.,
New York, NY 10282-1101. Phone: (212)748-4000
E-mail: webmaster@nybot.com • URL: http://www.
csce.com • Members are commodity traders.

COCONUT OIL INDUSTRY

See: OIL AND FATS INDUSTRY

CODING, PRODUCT

See: POINT-OF-SALE SYSTEMS (POS)

COFFEE INDUSTRY

See also: TEA INDUSTRY

GENERAL WORKS
*The Book of Coffee and Tea: A Guide to the Appreciation of Fine Coffees, Teas and Herbal
Beverages.* Joel Schapira and others. Saint Martin's
Press. • 1996. $14.95. Second revised edition.

ALMANACS AND YEARBOOKS
Agricultural and Mineral Commodities Year Book.
Available from Taylor & Francis Group. • Annual.
$225.00. Published by Europa Publications.
Contains descriptive product profiles, price data,
export-import data, and production statistics for
major commodities of the world. Includes commodity histories, uses, markets, demand trends, and
information about trade agreements and key commodity organizations.

CRB Commodity Yearbook. Commodity Research
Bureau. CRB. • Annual. $99.95.

HANDBOOKS AND MANUALS
Coffee and Tea Store. Entrepreneur Media, Inc. •
Looseleaf. $59.50. A practical guide to starting a
coffee and tea store. Covers profit potential, start-up
costs, market size evaluation, owner's time required,
site selection, lease negotiation, pricing, accounting,
advertising, promotion, etc. (Start-Up Business
Guide No. E1202.).

INTERNET DATABASES
USDA. United States Department of Agriculture.
Phone: (202)720-2791 E-mail: agsec@usda.gov •
URL: http://www.usda.gov • The USDA home page
has six sections: News and Information; What's
New; About USDA; Agencies; Opportunities;
Search and Help. Keyword searching is offered from
the USDA home page and from various individual
agency home pages. Agencies are the Economic
Research Service, Agricultural Marketing Service,
National Agricultural Statistics Service, National
Agricultural Library, and about 12 others. Updating
varies. Fees: Free.

PERIODICALS AND NEWSLETTERS
*Barron's: The Dow Jones Business and Financial
Weekly.* • Weekly. $145.00 per year.

Coffee and Cocoa International. DMG World Media
Ltd. • Seven times a year. $124.00 per year.

Coffee Intelligence. Coffee Publications. • Monthly.
$95.00 per year. Provides trade information for the
coffee industry.

The Coffee Reporter. National Coffee Association of
U.S.A Inc. • Weekly. Free to members; nonmembers, $65.00 per year. Newsletter.

Fancy Food and Culinary Products. Talcott Communications Corp. • Monthly. $34.00 per year.
Emphasizes new specialty food products and the
business management aspects of the specialty food
and confection industries. Includes special issues on
wine, cheese, candy, "upscale" cookware, and gifts.
Formerly (Fancy Foods).

Gourmet Retailer. VNU Business Media. • Monthly.
Free to qualified personnel; others, $75.00 per year.
Covers upscale food and housewares, including
confectionery items, bakery operations, and coffee.

Tea and Coffee Trade Journal. Lockwood
Publications. • Monthly. $30.00 per year. Current

trends in coffee roasting and tea packing industry.

PRICE SOURCES

Supermarket News: The Industry's Weekly Newspaper. Fairchild Publications. • Weekly. Individuals, $196.00 per year; retailers, $45.00 per year; manufacturers, $89.00 per year.

RESEARCH CENTERS AND INSTITUTES

College of Tropical Agriculture and Human Resources. University of Hawaii at Manoa, 2515 Campus Rd., Miller Hall 110, Honolulu, HI 96822. Phone: (808)956-8105 Fax: (808)956-8105 E-mail: fcs@ctahr.hawaii.edu • URL: http://www.ctahr.hawaii.edu/ • Concerned with the production and marketing of tropical food and ornamental plant products, including pineapples, bananas, coffee, and macadamia nuts.

STATISTICS SOURCES

Agricultural Statistics. Available from U. S. Government Printing Office. • Annual. $38.00. Produced by the National Agricultural Statistics Service, U. S. Department of Agriculture. Provides a wide variety of statistical data relating to agricultural production, supplies, consumption, prices/price-supports, foreign trade, costs, and returns, as well as farm labor, loans, income, and population. In many cases, historical data is shown annually for 10 years. In addition to farm data, includes detailed fishery statistics.

Annual Survey of Manufactures. Available from U. S. Government Printing Office. • Annual. Prices vary. Issued by the U. S. Census Bureau as an interim update to the *Census of Manufactures.* Includes data on number of manufacturing establishments in various industries, employment, labor costs, value of shipments, capital expenditures, inventories, energy costs, and assets. (See also Census Bureau home page, http://www.census.gov/.).

FAO Production Yearbook. Available from Bernan Associates. • Annual. $45.00. Published by the Food and Agriculture Organization (http://www.fao.org). Contains worldwide data on agriculture, land use, farm crops, livestock, and agricultural prices.

FAO Quarterly Bulletin of Statistics. Food and Agriculture Organization of the United Nations. Available from UNIPUB. • Quarterly. $20.00 per year. Provides international data on agricultural production, trade, and prices, covering the major commodities of many countries. Text in English, French, and Spanish. Formerly *FAO Monthly Bulletin of Statistics.*

FAO Trade Yearbook. Available from Bernan Associates. • Annual. $45.00. Published by the Food and Agriculture Organization (http://www.fao.org). Provides extensive worldwide data on exports and imports of agricultural commodities, fertilizers, tractors, and pesticides. Includes more than 130 tables of detailed statistics.

World Drinks Data and Statistics. Euromonitor International. • 2004. $650.00. Provides five-year data for both alcoholic and non-alcoholic beverages in 52 countries. Includes market size, consumer expenditures, price indicators, and retail distribution data for beer, wine, spirits, tea, coffee, soft drinks, fruit juices, bottled water, and other drinks.

TRADE/PROFESSIONAL ASSOCIATIONS

Coffee, Sugar and Cocoa Exchange. 1 N End Ave., New York, NY 10282-1101. Phone: (212)748-4000 E-mail: webmaster@nybot.com • URL: http://www.csce.com • Members are commodity traders.

National Coffee Association of U.S.A. 15 Maiden Lane, Ste. 1405, New York, NY 10038-4003. Phone: (212)766-4007 Fax: (212)766-5815 E-mail: info@ncausa.org • URL: http://www.ncausa.org •

Formerly Associated Coffee Industries of America.

OTHER SOURCES

Coffee and Tea Market. MarketResearch.com. • 1999. $2,750.00. Market data with forecasts to 2004. Covers many types of coffee and tea.

International Coffee Organization.

COGENERATION OF ENERGY

GENERAL WORKS

Renewables for Power Generation: Status and Prospect. Organization for Economic Cooperation and Development. • 2003. $75.00. Presents the global outlook for electrical power generation from renewable sources, including water power, wind power, solar power, and geothermal power.

BIOGRAPHICAL SOURCES

Energy and Nuclear Sciences International Who's Who. Addison Wesley/Benjamin Cummings. • 1990. $310.00. Third edition.

CD-ROM DATABASES

Environment Abstracts on CD-ROM. LEXIS-NEXIS. • Quarterly. $1,295.00 per year. Contains the following CD-ROM databases: *Environment Abstracts, Energy Abstracts,* and *Acid Rain Abstracts.* Length of coverage varies.

DIRECTORIES

Energy User News: Energy Technology Buyers Guide. Business News Publishing Co. • Annual. $10.00. List of about 400 manufacturers, manufacturers' representatives, dealers, and distributors of energy management equipment. *Annual Review* and *Forecast* issue.

The International Competitive Power Industry Directory. PennWell Corp. • Publication includes: List of 1,400 companies active in the global power industry, providing information on developers, financial firms, law firms, engineering and construction firms, fuel suppliers, consultants, manufacturers and other suppliers of products, equipment ot the hydro, geothermal, solar and wind industries. Entries include: Company name, address, phone, fax; contact name; business area or tyope; technology used; region covered; products.

Plunkett's Energy Industry Almanac: Complete Profiles on the Energy Industry 500 Companies. Plunkett Research Ltd. • Annual. $199.99. Includes major oil companies, utilities, pipelines, alternative energy companies, etc. Provides information on industry trends.

SYNERJY: A Directory of Renewable Energy. Synerjy. • Semiannual. Individuals, $30.00 per year; others, $62.00 per year. Includes organizations, publishers, and other resources. Lists articles, patents, government publications, research groups and facilities.

ENCYCLOPEDIAS AND DICTIONARIES

Wiley Encyclopedia of Energy and the Environment. Attilio Bisio and Sharon Boots. John Wiley and Sons, Inc. • 1996. $285.00. Abriged edition. Two volumes. Covers a wide variety of energy and environmental topics, including legal and policy issues. (Encyclopedia of Energy and the Environment Series: Vol. 2).

ONLINE DATABASES

PROMT: Predicasts Overview of Markets and Technology. Gale Cengage Learning. • Companies, products, applied technologies and markets. U.S. and international literature coverage, 1972 to date. Inquire as to online cost and availability. Provides abstracts from more than 1,600 publications. Weekly updates.

PERIODICALS AND NEWSLETTERS

Alternative Energy Retailer. Zackin Publications, Inc. • Monthly. $32.00 per year.

Energy Conversion and Management. Elsevier. • 20 times a year. Institutions, $3,457.00 per year. Presents a scholarly approach to alternative or renewable energy sources. Text in English, French and German.

Energy Today. Trends Publishing Inc. • Description: Examines energy programs, policy, regulation, and conservation. Discusses fossil, solar, and nuclear energy and other power sources. Includes a section titled Energy Trends, which reports in brief on upcoming conferences, papers and studies, energy education, new multimedia items, and international energy news.

Global Power Report: An Exclusive Biweekly Covering the Cogeneration and Small Power Market. Platts. • Biweekly. $1,165.00 per year. Newsletter. Covers industry trends, new projects, new contracts, rate changes, and regulations, with emphasis on the Federal Energy Regulatory Commission (FERC). Formerly *Cogeneration Report.*

Independent Energy: The Power Industry's Business Magazine. PennWell Corp., Industrial Div. • 10 times a year. $127.00 per year. Covers non-utility electric power plants (cogeneration) and other alternative sources of electric energy.

Journal of Energy Engineering: The International Journal. American Society of Civil Engineers. • Three times a year. Members, $40.00 per year; with online edition, $46.00 per year; non-members, $60.00 per year; with online edition, $69.00 per year.

Power. McGraw-Hill Inc. • Description: Covers design, operation, construction, and maintenance of power plants for utilities, process industries, and manufacturers.

Private Power Executive. Pequot Publishing, Inc. • Bimonthly. $90.00 per year. Covers private power (non-utility) enterprises, including cogeneration projects and industrial self-generation.

World Cogeneration: A Power Source for Partnering in the 90's. Dick Flanagan. • Five times a year. $36.00 per year. Edited for managers and executives of independent and cogeneration electric power plants. Provides analysis of industry trends.

RESEARCH CENTERS AND INSTITUTES

Hawaii Natural Energy Institute. University of Hawaii at Manoa, 2540 Dole St., Holmes Hall 246, Honolulu, HI 96822. Phone: (808)956-8890 Fax: (808)956-2336 E-mail: hnei@hawaii.edu • URL: http://www.soest.hawaii.edu • Research areas include geothermal, wind, solar, hydroelectric, and other energy sources.

Laboratory for Energy and the Environment. Massachusetts Institute of Technology. 77 Massachusetts Ave., Bldg. E40-455, Cambridge, MA 02139-4307. Phone: (617)258-8891 Fax: (617)253-8013 E-mail: jwilmson@mit.edu • URL: http://www.lfee.mit.edu • Formerly Energy Laboratory.

STATISTICS SOURCES

Annual Energy Outlook [year], with Projections to [year]. Available from U. S. Government Printing Office. • Annual. $42.00. Issued by the Energy Information Administration, U. S. Department of Energy (http://www.eia.doe.gov). Contains detailed statistics and 20-year projections for electricity, oil, natural gas, coal, and renewable energy. Text provides extensive discussion of energy issues and "Market Trends.".

International Energy Annual. Available from U. S. Government Printing Office. • Annual. $34.00. Issued by the Energy Information Administration, U. S. Department of Energy. Provides production, consumption, import, and export data for primary energy commodities in more than 200 countries and areas. In addition to petroleum products and alcohol, renewable energy sources are covered (hydroelectric, geothermal, solar, and wind).

TRADE/PROFESSIONAL ASSOCIATIONS

American Wind Energy Association. 1101 14th St. NW, 12th Fl., Washington, DC 20005. Phone: (202)383-2500 Fax: (202)383-2505 E-mail: windmail@awea.org • URL: http://www.awea.org • Wind energy equipment manufacturers; project developers and dealers; individuals from industry, government, and academia; interested others. Works to: advance the art and science of using energy from the wind for human purposes; encourage the use of wind turbines and wind power plants as alternatives to current energy systems that depend on depletable fuels; facilitate the widespread use of wind as a renewable, non-polluting energy source by fostering communication within the field of wind energy and between the technical community and the public. Provides federal and state legislators with information on wind as an energy source; offers consultation to federal, state, and local government and private industry. Promotes exportation of U.S. manufactured wind energy equipment.

Association of Energy Engineers. 4025 Pleasantdale Rd., Ste. 420, Atlanta, GA 30340-4264. Phone: (770)447-5083 Fax: (770)446-3969 E-mail: info@ aeecenter.org • URL: http://www.aeecenter.org • Members are engineers and other professionals concerned with energy management and cogeneration.

Electric Power Supply Association. 1401 New York Ave. NW, 11th Fl., Washington, DC 20005-2110. Phone: (202)628-8200 Fax: (202)628-8260 E-mail: etsinfo@ets.org • URL: http://www.epsa.org • Represents competitive power suppliers, including generators and power marketers. Provides reliable, competitively priced electricity from environmentally responsible facilities serving global power markets. Seeks to bring the benefits of competition to all power customers.

COIN MACHINES

See: VENDING MACHINES

COINS AS AN INVESTMENT

ALMANACS AND YEARBOOKS

Coin Yearbook. British Royal Mint. • Annual. $15.95.

DIRECTORIES

Stamp Exchangers Directory. Levine Publications. • Covers: over 1000 people who are interested in exchanging stamps, coins, and other collectibles with Americans; international coverage. Entries include: Name, address, item collected.

PERIODICALS AND NEWSLETTERS

The Coin Dealer Newsletter. CDN Publications. • Description: Provides information on U.S. coinage, 1793 to present. Gives current prices and market commentary and analysis. Issues "The Monthly Supplement and Complete Series Pricing Guide" as an adjunct to the newsletter. Recurring features include columns titled The Market in Depth and This Week's Market.

Coinage. Miller Magazines, Inc. • Monthly. $24.00 per year.

Coins. Krause Publications, Inc. • Monthly. $25.98 per year.

Numismatic News: The Complete Information Source for Coin Collectors. Krause Publications, Inc. • Weekly. $32.00 per year.

Coin World: World's #1 Publication for Coin Collectors. Amos Press, Inc. • Weekly. $36.95 per year.

PRICE SOURCES

Coin Prices: Complete Guide to U.S. Coin Values. Krause Publications, Inc. • Bimonthly. $18.98 per

year. Gives current values of U. S. coins.

TRADE/PROFESSIONAL ASSOCIATIONS

American Numismatic Association. 818 N Cascade Ave., Colorado Springs, CO 80903-3279. Phone: 800-367-9723 or (719)632-2646 Fax: (719)634-4085 E-mail: ana@money.org • URL: http://www. money.org • Collectors of coins, medals, tokens, and paper money. Promotes the study, research, and publication of articles on coins, coinage, and history of money. Sponsors correspondence courses; conducts research. Maintains museum, archive, authentication service for coins, and hall of fame. Sponsors National Coin Week; operates speakers' bureau.

American Numismatic Society. 96 Fulton St., New York, NY 10038. Phone: (212)571-4470 Fax: (212)571-4479 E-mail: wartenberg@numismatics. org • URL: http://www.numismatics.org • Collectors and others interested in coins, medals, and related materials. Advances numismatic knowledge as it relates to history, art, archaeology, and economics by collecting coins, medals, tokens, decorations, and paper money. Maintains only museum devoted entirely to numismatics. Presents annual Graduate Fellowship in Numismatics. Sponsors Graduate Seminar in Numismatics, a nine-week individual study program for ten students.

International Numismatic Society Authentication Bureau. 3386 Rasmont Rd., Apt. F, Roanoke, VA 24018-6326. Fax: (610)494-2270 E-mail: broke. bode@inma.org • Numismatic organizations, coin dealers, and private coin collectors from 8 countries. Offers an authentication bureau for coins from all countries and eras; holds seminars on authentication, coin grading, coin photography, and related subjects. Conducts research into microscopic characteristics of genuine coin dies.

Numismatics International. PO Box 570842, Dallas, TX 75357-0842. Phone: (940)440-2213 Fax: (940)365-2072 E-mail: johnvan@grandecom.net • URL: http://www.numis.org • Numismatists, coin dealers, students, and numismatic authors in 35 countries. Works to: encourage and promote the science of numismatics; cultivate fraternal relations among collectors and numismatic students; encourage new collectors and foster the interest of youth in numismatics; stimulate and advance affiliations among collectors and kindred organizations; acquire, share, and disseminate numismatic knowledge including cultural and historical information on coins. Sponsors periodic lectures. Maintains coin collection. **Convention/Meeting:** none.

Professional Numismatists Guild. 3950 Concordia Ln., 3950 Concordia Lane, Fallbrook, CA 92028. Phone: (760)728-1300 Fax: (760)728-8507 E-mail: info@pngdealers.com • URL: http://www. pngdealers.com • Represents coin dealers who have been involved full-time in the profession for at least five years. Establishes, promotes, and defends ethics in the hobby of numismatics.

Society for International Numismatics. c/o The American Numismatic Society, Broadway at 155th St., New York, NY 10032. Phone: (212)234-3130 Fax: (212)234-3381 E-mail: metcalf@amnumsoc. org • URL: http://www.amnumsoc.org.

COKE INDUSTRY

See also: COAL INDUSTRY

ALMANACS AND YEARBOOKS

CRB Commodity Yearbook. Commodity Research Bureau. CRB. • Annual. $99.95.

RESEARCH CENTERS AND INSTITUTES

Energy and Environmental Research Center. University of North Dakota. P.O. Box 9018, Grand

Forks, ND 58202-9018. Phone: (701)777-5000 Fax: (701)777-5181 E-mail: ggroenewold@undeerc.org • URL: http://www.undeerc.org.

Energy Institute. Pennsylvania State University. 120 Hosler Bldg., C211 Coal Utilization Laboratory, University Park, PA 16802-5000. Phone: (814)863-1337 Fax: (814)863-7432 E-mail: schobert@ems. psu.edu • URL: http://www.energyinstitute.psu. edu/.

Engineering Experiment Station. Ohio State University. 2070 Neil Ave., Columbus, OH 43210-1275. Phone: (614)292-3149 Fax: (614)292-9615 E-mail: fortner.1@osu.edu • URL: http://www.osu. edu.

STATISTICS SOURCES

American Iron and Steel Annual Statistical Report. American Iron and Steel Institute. • Annual. $100.00 per year.

Minerals Yearbook. Available from U.S. Government Printing Office. • Annual. Three volumes.

Quarterly Coal Report. Energy Information Administration, U.S. Department of Energy. Available from U.S. Government Printing Office. • Quarterly. $30.00 per year. Annual summary.

TRADE/PROFESSIONAL ASSOCIATIONS

American Coke and Coal Chemicals Institute. 1255 23rd St., N.W., Washington, DC 20037. Phone: (202)452-1140 Fax: (202)833-3636 E-mail: information@accci.org • URL: http://www.accci. org.

COLD STORAGE WAREHOUSES

See: REFRIGERATION INDUSTRY; WAREHOUSES

COLLECTIBLES

See: ANTIQUES AS AN INVESTMENT; ART AS AN INVESTMENT; COINS AS AN INVESTMENT; HOBBY INDUSTRY

COLLECTING OF ACCOUNTS

See also: CREDIT

DIRECTORIES

Blue Book of Commercial Collection. International Association of Commercial Collectors. • Annual. Membership.

Membership Roster. ACA International. • Annual. Membership.

Regency International Directory of Private Investigators, Private Detectives, Security Guards, and Security Equipment Suppliers. Regency International Directory. • Annual. $60.00. Over 5,000 detective agencies, firms specializing in security. bailiffs, and trade protection societies; worldwide coverage.

FINANCIAL RATIOS

Annual Statement Studies. The Risk Management Association. • Annual. Median and quartile financial ratios are given for over 400 kinds of manufacturing, wholesale, retail, construction, and consumer finance establishments. Data is sorted by both asset size and sales volume. Includes a clearly written "Definition of Ratios" and an alphabetical industry index.

Annual Statement Studies: Industry Default Probabilities and Cash Flow Measures. The Risk Management Association. • Annual. $145.00.

Serves as a companion volume to the original *Annual Statement Studies*. Gives probability of default estimates on a percentage scale for more than 450 industries. Includes changes in position year-by-year for eight financial statement line items and provides percentage measures of cash flow.

HANDBOOKS AND MANUALS

The Check is Not in the Mail: How to Get Paid More, in Full, on Time, at Less Cost, and Without Losing Valued Customers. Leonard Sklar. Baroque Publishing. • 1990. $19.95. Explains how to establish the right collection cycle, what is harassment, choosing a collection agency, and collection procedures in general.

Collection Agency. Entrepreneur Media, Inc. • Looseleaf. $59.50. A practical guide to starting a collection agency. Covers profit potential, start-up costs, market size evaluation, owner's time required, pricing, accounting, advertising, promotion, etc. (Start-Up Business Guide No. E1207.).

IRS Tax Collection Procedures. CCH, Inc. • $195.00. Looseleaf service. Periodic supplementation. Covers IRS collection personnel, payment arrangements, penalties, abatements, summons, liens, etc.

Practical Guide to Credit and Collection. George O. Bancroft. AMACOM. • 1989. $29.95.

PERIODICALS AND NEWSLETTERS

Collections and Credit Risk: The Authority for Commercial and Consumer Credit Professionals. Thomson Media. • Monthly. $95.00 per year. Contains articles on the technology and business management of credit and collection functions. Includes coverage of bad debts, bankruptcy, and credit risk management.

Collector. American Collectors Association, Inc. • Monthly. Members, $30.00 per year; non-members, $60.00 per year. Provides news and education in the field of credit and collections.

TRADE/PROFESSIONAL ASSOCIATIONS

ACA-The International Association of Credit and Collections Professionals. ACA International, PO Box 390106, Minneapolis, MN 55439. Phone: (959)926-6547 Fax: (959)926-1624 • URL: http://www.acainternational.org • Formerly American Collectors Association.

International Association of Commercial Collectors. 4040 W. 70th St., Minneapolis, MN 55435. Phone: (952)925-0760 Fax: (952)926-1624 E-mail: iacc@collector.com • URL: http://www.commercialcollector.com • Collection agencies specializing in the recovery of commercial accounts receivable. Formerly American Commercial Collectors Association.

OTHER SOURCES

Consumer and Commercial Credit: Installment Sales. Prentice Hall PTR. • Three looseleaf volumes. Periodic supplementation. Price on application. Covers secured transactions under the Uniform Commercial Code and the Uniform Consumer Credit Code. Includes retail installment sales, home improvement loans, higher education loans, and other kinds of installment loans.

Debtor-Creditor Law. LexisNexis Matthew Bender. • $2,078.00. 13 looseleaf volumes. Periodic supplementation. Covers all aspects of the creation and enforcement of the debtor-creditor relationship.

U. S. Credit Bureaus and Collection Agencies: An Industry Analysis. Available from MarketResearch.com. • 2003. $1,435.00. Market research report published by Marketdata Enterprises. Includes forecasts of industry growth to the year 2006 and provides profiles of Dun & Bradstreet, Equifax, Experion, and TransUnion.

COLLECTIVE BARGAINING

See also: ARBITRATION; LABOR UNIONS

GENERAL WORKS

Labor Relations. Arthur A. Sloan and Fred Witney. Prentice Hall PTR. • 2000. $115.00. 10th edition. Emphasizes collective bargaining and arbitration.

Labor Relations: Development, Structure, Process. John A. Fossum. McGraw-Hill. • 2001. $112.50. Eighth edition.

ALMANACS AND YEARBOOKS

OECD Employment Outlook. OECD Publications and Information Center. • 2000. $48.00. Outlines the employment prospects for the coming year in OECD countries. Also discusses labor force growth, job creation, labor standards, and collective bargaining.

DIRECTORIES

International Centre for Settlement of Investment Disputes - Annual Report. International Centre for Settlement of Investment Disputes. • Annual. Free. Editions available in French and Spanish.

IRRA-Membership Directory. Industrial Relations Research Association. • Quadrennial. $25.00. About 3,200 business people, union leaders, government officials, lawyers, arbitrators, academics, consultants, and others interested in labor relations.

Profiles of American Labor Unions. Gale Cengage Learning. • 1998. $315.00. Second edition. Provides detailed information on more than 280 national labor unions. Includes descriptions of about 800 bargaining agreements and biographies of more than 170 union officials. Local unions are also listed. Four indexes. Formerly *American Directory of Organized Labor* (1992).

ONLINE DATABASES

Labordoc. International Labour Organization. • Indexing of labor literature and the publications of the International Labour Organization, 1965 to present. Monthly updates. Inquire as to online cost and availability.

LEXIS. LEXIS-NEXIS. • The various LEXIS databases provide full text and indexing for a wide variety of legal cases, statutes, orders, and opinions.

PERIODICALS AND NEWSLETTERS

Dispute Resolution Journal. American Arbitration Association. • Quarterly. $125.00 per year. Formerly *Arbitration Journal.*

Labor Relations Bulletin. Aspen Publishers Inc. • Description: Provides information and insight to management and labor officials to help them avoid or resolve conflicts. Recurring features include reports on current developments in labor law and relations, discipline and grievance cases based on actual arbitration, a question and answer column on labor and employment relations, and a column titled Reflections of an Arbitrator, offering the insight and experience of prominent national arbitrators.

Summary of Labor Arbitration Awards. American Arbitration Association, Inc. • Monthly. $120.00 per year.

Union Labor Report. Bureau of National Affairs Inc. • Description: Covers legal, legislative, and regulatory developments and trends affecting management and labor in the workplace.

RESEARCH CENTERS AND INSTITUTES

Center for Labor Education and Research. University of Alabama at Birmingham. 1044 11th St., S., Birmingham, AL 35294-4500. Phone: (205)934-2101 Fax: (205)975-5087 E-mail: judiking@uab.edu • URL: http://www.main.uab.edu/.

Institute of Industrial Relations. University of California, Los Angeles. UCLA Box 951478, Los Angeles, CA 90095-1478. Phone: (310)794-5957 Fax: (310)794-6410 E-mail: milkman@soc.ucla.edu • URL: http://www.iir.ucla.edu/.

TRADE/PROFESSIONAL ASSOCIATIONS

American Arbitration Association. 1633 Broadway, 10th Fl., New York, NY 10019. Phone: 800-778-7879 or (212)716-5800 Fax: (212)716-5905 E-mail: websitemail@adr.org • URL: http://www.adr.org • Works to achieve the resolution of disputes through the use of mediation, arbitration, democratic elections, and other voluntary methods. Provides administrative services for arbitrating, mediating, or negotiating disputes and impartial administration of elections. Maintains National Roster of Arbitrators and Mediators for referrals to parties involved in disputes. Conducts skill-building sessions to promote a more complete understanding of conflict resolution processes.

National Academy of Arbitrators. One N Main St., Ste. 412, Cortland, NY 13045. Phone: 800-872-5617 or (607)756-8363 Fax: (607)756-8365 E-mail: naa@igc.org • URL: http://www.naarb.org.

OTHER SOURCES

Collective Bargaining Negotiations and Contracts. BNA, Inc. • Biweekly. $1,187.00. Two looseleaf volumes.

COLLEGE AND SCHOOL NEWSPAPERS

See also: NEWSPAPERS

GENERAL WORKS

The Mass Media and the School Newspaper. De Witt C. Reddick. West Group. • 1986. $24.75. Second edition. (Mass Communication Series).

Scholastic Journalism. Tom Rolnicki and others. Blackwell Publishing. • 2001 $44.95. 10th edition.

CD-ROM DATABASES

MediaFinder CD-ROM: Oxbridge Directories of Print Media and Catalogs. Oxbridge Communications, Inc. • Quarterly. $1,995.00 per year. CD-ROM includes about 100,000 listings from *Standard Periodical Directory, National Directory of Catalogs, National Directory of British Mail Order Catalogs, National Directory of German Mail Order Catalogs, Oxbridge Directory of Newsletters, National Directory of Mailing Lists, College Media Directory,* and *National Directory of Magazines.*

DIRECTORIES

Burrelle's Media Directory: Newspapers and Related Media. Burrelle's Information Services. • Annual. $550.00. *Daily Newspapers* volume lists more than 2,200 daily publications in the U. S., Canada, and Mexico. *Non-Daily Newspapers* volume lists more than 10,400 items published no more than three times a week. Provides detailed descriptions, including key personnel.

SRDS Newspaper Advertising Source. SRDS. • Monthly. $700.00 per year. Lists newspapers geographically, with detailed information on advertising rates, special features, personnel, circulation, etc. Includes a section on college newspapers. Also provides consumer market data for population, households, income, and retail sales. Formerly *Newspaper Advertising Source.*

ONLINE DATABASES

Magazine Index. Gale Cengage Learning. • General magazine indexing (popular literature), 1973 to present. Daily updates. Inquire as to online cost and availability.

PERIODICALS AND NEWSLETTERS

College Media Review. College Media Advisors. University of Memphis. • Quarterly. Free to members; non-members, $15.00 per year.

Columbia Journalism Review. Columbia University, Graduate School of Journalism. • Bimonthly. $19.95 per year. Critical review of news media.

Quill and Scroll. International Honorary Society for High School Journalists. Quill and Scroll Society. • Quarterly. $13.00 per year. Devoted exclusively to the field of high school publications.

TRADE/PROFESSIONAL ASSOCIATIONS

Associated Collegiate Press. University of Minnesota. University of Minnesota, 2221 University Ave. SE, Ste. 121, Minneapolis, MN 55414. Phone: (612)625-8335 Fax: (612)626-0720 E-mail: info@studentpress.org • URL: http://www. studentpress.org/acp • Conducts annual critique of newspapers and annual critique of magazines and yearbooks. Sponsors competitions.

College Media Advisers, Inc. University of Memphis. c/o Dept. of Journalism, MJ-300, Memphis, TN 38152-6661. Phone: (901)678-2403 Fax: (901)678-4798 E-mail: vsplbrgr@cc.memphis. edu • URL: http://www.collegemedia.org • Formerly National Council of College Publications Advisers.

College Press Service. 435 N Michigan Ave., Ste. 1500, Chicago, IL 60611. Phone: 800-245-6536 or (312)222-4444 Fax: (312)222-3459.

Columbia Scholastic Press Association. Columbia University. Columbia University, Mail Code 5711, New York, NY 10027-6902. Phone: (212)854-9400 Fax: (212)854-9401 E-mail: cspa@columbia.edu • URL: http://www.columbia.edu/cu/cspa • Newspapers, magazines, and yearbooks issued by schools from junior high school level through college and university, with the majority being from secondary schools. Works to promote student writing through the medium of the school publication. Improves publications in all phases. Offers critiques for each regular member. Compiles statistics. Provides consultation and referral services to student publications.

National Scholastic Press Association. University of Minnesota. University of Minnesota, 2221 University Ave. SE, Ste. 121, Minneapolis, MN 55414-3074. Phone: (612)625-8335 Fax: (612)626-0720 E-mail: info@studentpress.org • URL: http:// www.studentpress.org/nspa • Represents publishers of high school newspapers, yearbooks, and magazines. Offers critical services for newspapers, yearbooks, and magazines.

Quill and Scroll Society. School of Journalism. University of Iowa. Iowa City, IA 52242. Phone: (319)335-5210 or (319)335-5795 E-mail: quill-scroll@uiowa.edu • URL: http://www.uiowa.edu.

COLLEGE AND UNIVERSITY LIBRARIES

GENERAL WORKS

The Academic Library in Transition: Planning for the 1990s. Beverly P. Lynch, editor. Neal-Schuman Publishers, Inc. • 1989. $49.95.

ABSTRACTS AND INDEXES

Library Literature and Information Science Index. H. W. Wilson Co. • Quarterly. Annual cumulation. Price varies.

ALMANACS AND YEARBOOKS

The Bowker Annual: Library and Book Trade Almanac. Information Today, Inc. • Annual. $199.00. Reviews key trends and events and provides basic statistical information. Includes financial averages: library expenditures, salaries, and book prices. Contains lists of "best books, literary prizes, winners, and bestsellers." Formerly published by R. R. Bowker.

CD-ROM DATABASES

ERIC on SilverPlatter. Available from SilverPlatter Information, Inc. • Quarterly. $700.00 per year.

Produced by the Office of Educational Research and Improvement, U. S. Dept. of Education. Provides CD-ROM indexing and abstracting of a wide variety of literature relating to education. Archival discs are available from 1966.

LISA Plus. Available from Cambridge Scientific Abstracts (CSA). • Quarterly. $2,000.00 per year. CD-ROM version of Library Information and Science Abstracts, providing abstracting and indexing of the world's library and information science literature, 1969 to date. Contains more than 180,000 citations.

WILSONDISC: Library Literature and Information Science Index. H. W. Wilson Co. • Quarterly. Includes unlimited access to the online version of *Library Literature.* Provides CD-ROM indexing of about 300 periodicals, covering a wide range of topics having to do with libraries, library management, and the information industry.

DIRECTORIES

American Library Directory. Information Today Inc. • Covers: Over 37,000 U.S. and Canadian academic, public, county, provincial, and regional libraries; library systems; medical, law, and other special libraries; and libraries for the blind and physically handicapped. Separate section lists over 350 library networks and consortia and 220 accredited and un-accredited library school programs. Entries include: For libraries--Name, supporting or affiliated institution or firm name, address, phone, fax, electronic mail address, Standard Address Number (SANs), names of librarian and department heads, income, collection size, special collections, computer hardware, automated functions, and type of catalog. For library systems--Name, location. For library schools--Name, address, phone, fax, electronic mail address, director, type of training and degrees, admission requirements, tuition, faculty size. For networks and consortia--Name, address, phone, names of affiliates, name of director, function.

Cyberhound's Guide to Internet Libraries. Gale Cengage Learning. • 1996. 79.00. Presents critical descriptions and ratings of more than 2,000 library Internet databases. Includes a glossary of Internet terms, a bibliography, and indexes. (Cyberhound's Series).

Gale Directory of Learning Worldwide: A Guide to Faculty and Institutions of Higher Education, Research, and Culture. Gale Cengage Learning. • 2001. $425.00. Three volumes. Describes about 26,000 colleges, universities, research institutes, libraries, museums, scholarly associations, academies, and archives around the world. Arranged by country.

World Guide to Libraries. Available from Gale Cengage Learning. • 2003. $465.00. 17th edition. Two volumes. Provides information on more than 43,000 academic, government, and public libraries in 200 countries. Published by K. G. Saur.

ENCYCLOPEDIAS AND DICTIONARIES

World Encyclopedia of Library and Information Services. Robert Wedgeworth, editor. American Library Association. • 1993. $200.00. Third edition. Contains about 340 articles from various contributors.

HANDBOOKS AND MANUALS

Raising Money for Academic and Research Libraries: A How-To- Do-It Manual for Librarians. Barbara I. Dewey, editor. Neal-Schuman Publishers, Inc. • 1991. $45.00. (How-to-Do-It Manuals Series).

Strategic Management for Academic Libraries: A Handbook. Robert M. Hayes. Greenwood Publishing Group, Inc. • 1993. $69.95. (Library Management Collection).

Teaching Information Literacy: 35 Practical, Standards-based Exercises for College Students. Joanna M. Burkhardt and others. American Library

Association. • 2003. $35.00. Provides a step-by-step guide for teaching students the intricacies of library and online research.

Working with Faculty to Design Undergraduate Information Literacy Programs: A How-To-Do-It Manual for Librarians. Rosemary M. Young and Stephana Harmony. Neal-Schuman Publishers, Inc. • 1999. $45.00. Includes sample forms, surveys, evaluations, and assignments for credit courses or single sessions. (How-to-Do-It Manuals Series).

ONLINE DATABASES

American Library Directory Online. Information Today, Inc. • Provides information on more than 30,000 public, college, and special libraries in the U.S. and Canada, with annual updates. Includes library networks, consortia, organizations, and schools. Inquire as to online cost and availability.

ERIC. Educational Resources Information Center. • Funded by the U. S. Department of Education, Institute of Education Sciences (formerly Office of Educational Research and Improvement). Provides access to more than one million online records covering education-related journal and report literature, 1966 to date. Updating is monthly. Inquire as to online cost and availability.

LISA: Library and Information Science Abstracts. Available from Cambridge Scientific Abstracts (CSA). • Provides abstracting and indexing of the world's library and information science literature, 1969 to date. Covers more than 440 periodicals from 68 countries. Updating is biweekly. Inquire as to online cost and availability.

PERIODICALS AND NEWSLETTERS

American Libraries. American Library Association. • 11 times a year. Institutions, $60.00 per year. Current news and information concerning the library industry.

ARL: A Bimonthly Report on Research Library Issues and Actions. Association of Research Libraries. • Bimonthly. Members, $25.00; non-members, $50.00 per year. Formerly ARL: A Bimonthly Newsletter of Research Library Issues and Actions.

Choice Magazine: Current Reviews for Academic Libraries. Association of College Research Libraries. American Library Association. • 11 times a year. $237.00 per year. A publication of the Association of College and Research Libraries. Contains book reviews, primarily for college and university libraries.

College and Research Libraries (CRL). Association of College and Research Libraries. American Library Association. • Bimonthly. $60.00 per year. Supplement available *C and R L News.*

College and Research Libraries News. Association of College and Research Libraries. American Library Association. • 11 times per year. Free to members; non-members, $40.00 per year. Supplement to *College and Research Libraries.*

College and Undergraduate Libraries. Haworth Press, Inc. • Semiannual. $105.00 per year. A practical journal dealing with everyday library problems.

Community and Junior College Libraries: The Journal for Learning Resources Centers. Haworth Press, Inc. • Quarterly. $85.00 per year.

Focus: On the Center for Research Libraries. Center for Research Libraries. • Bimonthly. Free. Newsletter. Provides news of Center activites.

The Journal of Academic Librarianship: Articles, Features, and Book Reviews for the Academic Library Professional. Elsevier. • Bimonthly. Qualified personnel, $101.00 per year; institutions, $253.00 per year.

STATISTICS SOURCES

ALA Survey of Librarian Salaries. American Library Association. • Annual. $55.00. Provides data on salaries paid to librarians in academic and public libraries. Position categories range from beginning librarian to director.

ARL Annual Salary Survey. Association of Research Libraries. • Annual. Members, $44.00; non-members, $100.00. Statistics on salaries by institution, region, position, sex/race and other data for the 119 research libraries in ARL.

ARL Statistics. Association of Research Libraries. • Annual. Members, $44.00; non-members, $100.00. Presents a variety of statistics for about 120 university and other major research libraries.

TRADE/PROFESSIONAL ASSOCIATIONS

Association of College and Research Libraries. 50 E. Huron St., Chicago, IL 60611-2795. Phone: 800-545-2433 or (312)280-2523 Fax: (312)280-2520 E-mail: acrl@ala.org • URL: http://www.ala.org/acrl.

Association of Research Libraries. 21 Dupont Circle N.W., Washington, DC 20036. Phone: (202)296-2296 Fax: (202)872-0884 E-mail: duane@arl.org • URL: http://www.arl.org.

International Association of Technological University Libraries. c/o Dr. Judith Palmer, Univeristy of Oxford, Radcliffe Science Library, Park Rd., Oxford OX1 30P, United Kingdom. Phone: 44 1865 27282 Fax: 44 1865 27283 E-mail: iatul@qut.edu.au • URL: http://www.iatul.org.

Research Libraries Group. 2029 Stierlin Ct., Ste. 100, Mountain View, CA 94043-4684. Phone: 800-537-7546 or (650)691-2333 or (650)691-2333 Fax: (650)964-0943 E-mail: ric@rlg.org • URL: http://www.rlg.org • Universities, archives, historical societies, museums, and related institutions devoted to improving access to information that supports research and learning. Maintains the Research Libraries Information Network (RLIN), an online bibliographic database of more than 22 million items, including books, serials, archival materials, maps, music scores, sound recordings, films, photographs, and computer-readable files. RLIN contains the Library of Congress Name Authority and Subject Authority Files, the Art and Architecture thesaurus, and special databases for 18th-century printed material, art auction catalogs, and library collection management. CitaDel, a citation and document-delivery service, is available through RLIN.

COLLEGE DEGREES

See: ACADEMIC DEGREES

COLLEGE ENROLLMENT

See also: COLLEGE ENTRANCE REQUIRE-MENTS; COLLEGES AND UNIVERSITIES

DIRECTORIES

American Universities and Colleges. American Council on Education USA. Walter de Gruyter, Inc. • Quadrennial. $249.50. Two volumes. Produced in collaboration with the American Council on Education. Provides full descriptions of more than 1,900 institutions of higher learning, including details of graduate and professional programs.

College Blue Book. Macmillan Reference USA. • Covers: Listings and detailed descriptions of thousands of two and four year schools, their programs, degrees, financial aid sources, and scholarships.

ONLINE DATABASES

ERIC. Educational Resources Information Center. • Funded by the U. S. Department of Education, Institute of Education Sciences (formerly Office of Educational Research and Improvement). Provides access to more than one million online records

covering education-related journal and report literature, 1966 to date. Updating is monthly. Inquire as to online cost and availability.

RESEARCH CENTERS AND INSTITUTES

ERIC Clearinghouse on Adult, Career and Vocational Education. Ohio State University. Center on Education and Training for Employment, 1900 Kenny Rd., Columbus, OH 43210-1090. Phone: 800-848-4815 or (614)292-7069 Fax: (614)292-1260 E-mail: ericacve@postbox.acs.ohio-state.edu • URL: http://www.ericacve.org/.

Records and Research Office. University of the Pacific. 3601 Pacific Ave., Stockton, CA 95211. Phone: (209)946-2569 Fax: (209)946-2596 E-mail: rbrodnick@upo.edu • URL: http://www.1.uop.edu/iro • Formerly Institutional Research Office.

STATISTICS SOURCES

College Facts Chart. National Beta Club. • Annual. $7.00. Reference guide to 3,500 institutions of higher education in the United States, Puerto Rico, Guam, and the Virgin Islands. Charts locate tuition and fee costs, telephone numbers and school size.

Digest of Education Statistics. Available from U. S. Government Printing Office. • Annual. $51.00. Covers all areas of education from kindergarten through graduate school. Includes data from both government and private sources. Compiled by National Center for Education Statistics, U. S. Department of Education.

Ethnic Enrollment Data From Institutions of Higher Education. U.S. Dept. of Health and Human Services, Office for Civil Rights. • Annual.

Occupational Projections and Training Data. Available from U. S. Government Printing Office. • Biennial. $21.00. Issued by Bureau of Labor Statistics, U. S. Department of Labor. Contains projections of employment change and job openings over the next 15 years for about 500 specific occupations. Also includes the number of associate, bachelor's, master's, doctoral, and professional degrees awarded in a recent year for about 900 specific fields of study.

Projections of Education Statistics. Available from U. S. Government Printing Office. • Annual. $26.00. Issued by the U. S. Department of Education, National Center for Education Statistics (http://www.ed.gov). Provides 10-year projections of data relating to elementary schools, secondary schools, and institutions of higher learning. Includes projections of enrollment, graduates, classroom teachers, and expenditures.

COLLEGE ENTRANCE REQUIREMENTS

See also: COLLEGE ENROLLMENT; COL-LEGES AND UNIVERSITIES; GRADUATE WORK IN UNIVERSITIES

BIBLIOGRAPHIES

College Admissions: A Selected Annotated Bibliography. Linda Sparks, compiler. Greenwood Publishing Group, Inc. • 1993. $60.00. Describes about 1,000 professional or academic items relating to undergraduate college admissions in the United States. Topics include marketing and recruitment. (Popular guides are not included.) (Bibliographies and Indexes in Education Series, No.11).

DIRECTORIES

College Admissions Data Handbook. Riverside Publishing/Wintergreen Orchard House. • Covers: about 1,700 accredited four-year undergraduate and upper division institutions offering bachelor's degrees; published in a national edition and four regional editions (Northeast, Southeast, Midwest, and West). Entries include: Institution name, phone,

location, names of president and admissions officer, accreditation, number of students, admission policies, Scholastic Aptitude Test and American College Test (SAT-ACT) board score distribution, costs, financial aid availability, advance placement policy, subject majors offered, degrees offered, extracurricular activities, academic calendar, religious requirements, and policies on housing, cars, alcohol, attendance, and marriage. Index volume titled 'College Admissions Index of Majors & Sports' (see separate entry).

College Blue Book. Macmillan Reference USA. • Covers: Listings and detailed descriptions of thousands of two and four year schools, their programs, degrees, financial aid sources, and scholarships.

Lovejoy's College Guide. IDG Books Worldwide Inc. • Covers: 2,500 American colleges, universities, and technical institutes, and selected foreign colleges accredited by United States regional accrediting associations. Entries include: School name, location, date founded, name changes, enrollment figures, SAT/ACT figures, library size, faculty-student ratio, religious affiliation, admission information, tuition, room and board costs, scholarships and loans, athletic programs, curricula and degrees offered, special programs, summer sessions.

ONLINE DATABASES

ERIC. Educational Resources Information Center. • Funded by the U. S. Department of Education, Institute of Education Sciences (formerly Office of Educational Research and Improvement). Provides access to more than one million online records covering education-related journal and report literature, 1966 to date. Updating is monthly. Inquire as to online cost and availability.

PERIODICALS AND NEWSLETTERS

College Board Review. College Board Publications. • Quarterly. $25.00 per year.

NACAC Bulletin. National Association for College Admission Counseling. • Description: Discusses college admissions counseling, financial aid, and legislation affecting these areas. Recurring features include statistics, book reviews, news of research, a calendar of events, news of members, and columns titled Perspective, NACACTION, Capitol Outlook, News Briefs, F.Y.I., and On the Move.

TRADE/PROFESSIONAL ASSOCIATIONS

ACT. PO Box 168, PO Box 168, Iowa City, IA 52244-0168. Phone: (319)337-1000 Fax: (319)339-3020 E-mail: mediarelations@act.org • URL: http://www.act.org • Provides guidance-oriented assessment and research programs for students, schools, colleges, universities, vocational-technical institutes, and scholarship agencies. ACT Assessment Program, which consists of a profile questionnaire, interest inventory, and four 35-60 minute tests in English, mathematics, reading, and scientific reasoning, is completed by more than 1,700,000 students annually. Provides colleges and universities with information used in admission, placement, and advising. ASSET and COMPASS, placement programs for two-year colleges, are completed by more than 1,600,000 students annually. Also offers eighth grade and tenth grade assessments; Work Keys, the nation's leading work skills testing system; and DISCOVER, an interactive educational and career planning program. Conducts more than 90 other assessment programs on behalf of organizations, and agencies. Conducts research, compiles statistics, and processes federal financial aid applications.

American Association of Collegiate Registrars and Admissions Officers. One Dupont Circle, N.W., Suite 520, Washington, DC 20036. Phone: (202)293-9161 Fax: (202)872-8857 E-mail: info@aacrao.edu • URL: http://www.aacrao.org.

The College Board. 45 Columbus Ave., 45

Columbus Ave., New York, NY 10023-6992. Phone: (866)392-3017 or (212)713-8000 Fax: (212)649-8442 E-mail: publicaffairs@collegeboard.org • URL: http://www.collegeboard.com • Represents the schools, colleges, universities, and other educational organizations that seeks to connect members to success and opportunity. Serves students, parents, high schools, and colleges through major programs and services in college admission, guidance, assessment, financial aid, enrollment, and teaching and learning.

Educational Testing Service. Rosedale Rd., Princeton, NJ 08541. Phone: (609)921-9000 Fax: (609)734-5410 E-mail: etsinfo@ets.org • URL: http://www.ets.org • Educational measurement and research organization, founded by merger of the testing activities of American Council on Education, Carnegie Foundation for the Advancement of Teaching, and The College Board. Provides tests and related services for schools, colleges, governmental agencies, and the professions; offers advisory services in the sound application of measurement techniques and materials; conducts educational, psychological, and measurement research. Offers a summer program in educational testing for scholars and educators from other countries, continuing education programs, and measurement, evaluation, and other instructional activities.

Graduate Management Admission Council. 1600 Tysons Blvd., Ste. 1400, McLean, VA 22102. Phone: (866)505-6559 or (703)749-0131 Fax: (703)749-0169 E-mail: webmaster1@gmac.com • URL: http://www.gmac.com • Graduate schools of management and business administration. Works to establish criteria for use in admission to graduate management programs. Provides professional development for academic administrators and seminars for admissions officers. Maintains Graduate +Management Admission Search Service, a program that provides institutions with the names of qualified students with desirable characteristics. Employs Educational Testing Service to develop and administer the Graduate Management Admission Test. Conducts research on student selection issues and political and social issues related to graduate management education.

National Association for College Admission Counseling. 1631 Prince St., Alexandria, VA 22314-2818. Phone: 800-822-6285 or (703)836-2222 Fax: (703)836-8015 E-mail: info@nacac.com • URL: http://www.nacac.com • Formerly National Association of College Admissions Counselors.

COLLEGE FACULTIES

GENERAL WORKS

Rhythms of Academic Life: Personal Accounts of Careers in Academia. M. Susan Taylor. Sage Publications, Inc. • 1996. $97.95. Contains articles by various authors on college teaching, research, publishing, tenure, and related topics. Contributions are described as "sometimes poignant and often humorous." (Foundations for Organizational Science Series).

Technology and Teaching. Les Lloyd, editor. Information Today, Inc. • 1997. $42.50. Contains multimedia computer application case studies relating to college level curricula and teaching.

BIOGRAPHICAL SOURCES

Directory of American Scholars. Gale Cengage Learning. • 2001. $595.00. 10th edition. Six volumes. Volumes one to volume five, $145.00; volume six, $50.00. Provides biographical information and publication history for more than 24,000 scholars in the humanities.

Who's Who in American Education. Marquis Who's Who. • Biennial. $159.95. Contains over 27,000 concise biographies of teachers, administrators, and

other individuals involved in all levels of American education.

CD-ROM DATABASES

Profiles in Business and Management: An International Directory of Scholars and Their Research [CD-ROM]. Harvard Business School Publishing. • Annual. $595.00. Fully searchable CD-ROM version of two-volume printed directory. Contains bibliographic and biographical information for over 5600 business and management experts active in 21 subject areas. Formerly *International Directory of Business and Management Scholars.*

DIRECTORIES

Faculty White Pages. Gale Cengage Learning. • 1991. $135.00. 91st edition. "Telephone book" classified arrangement of over 537,000 U. S. college faculty members in 41 subject sections. A roster of institutions is included.

Fulbright Scholar Program Grants for U.S. Faculty and Professionals. Council for International Exchange of Scholars. • Annual. Free. Lists about 800 grants.

Gale Directory of Learning Worldwide: A Guide to Faculty and Institutions of Higher Education, Research, and Culture. Gale Cengage Learning. • 2001. $425.00. Three volumes. Describes about 26,000 colleges, universities, research institutes, libraries, museums, scholarly associations, academies, and archives around the world. Arranged by country.

National Faculty Directory. Gale. • Covers: More than 740,000 (90,000 more in supplement) teaching faculty members at over 3,600 junior colleges, colleges, and universities in the United States and those in Canada that give instruction in English. Entries include: Name, department name, institution, address, and phone and fax numbers. Directory combines main edition and supplement.

HANDBOOKS AND MANUALS

Getting Your Book Published. Christine S. Smedley and Mitchell Allen. Sage Publications, Inc. • 1993. $59.95. A practical guide for academic and professional authors. Covers the initial book prospectus, contract negotiation, production procedures, and marketing. (Survival Skills for Scholars, vol. 10).

ONLINE DATABASES

ERIC. Educational Resources Information Center. • Funded by the U. S. Department of Education, Institute of Education Sciences (formerly Office of Educational Research and Improvement). Provides access to more than one million online records covering education-related journal and report literature, 1966 to date. Updating is monthly. Inquire as to online cost and availability.

PERIODICALS AND NEWSLETTERS

ACADEME. American Association of University Professors. • Bimonthly. $64.00 per year.

College Teaching: International Quarterly Journal. Helen Dwight Reid Educational Foundation. Heldref Publications. • Quarterly. Individuals, $47.00 per year; institutions, $93.00 per year. Practical ideas, successful methods, and new programs for faculty development.

Journal of Higher Education. Ohio State University Press. • Bimonthly. Individuals, $50.00 per year; institutions, $110.00 per year. Issues important to faculty administrators and program managers in higher education.

RESEARCH CENTERS AND INSTITUTES

ERIC Clearinghouse for Community Colleges. University of California, Los Angeles. 3051 Moore Hall, Los Angeles, CA 90095. Phone: 800-832-8256 or (310)825-3931 Fax: (310)206-8095 E-mail: ericc@ucla.edu • URL: http://www.gseis.ucla.edu/eric.

ERIC Clearinghouse on Higher Education. George Washington University. Graduate School of Education and Human Development, One Dupont Circle, Suite 630, Washington, DC 20036. Phone: 800-773-3742 or (202)296-2597 Fax: (202)452-1844 E-mail: wcummings@eric-he.edu • URL: http://www.eriche.org.

STATISTICS SOURCES

The Annual Report on the Economic Status of the Profession. American Association of University Professors. • Special annual issue of *ACADEME.*

Biennial Survey of Education in the United States. U.S. Department of Education. • Biennial.

Digest of Education Statistics. Available from U. S. Government Printing Office. • Annual. $51.00. Covers all areas of education from kindergarten through graduate school. Includes data from both government and private sources. Compiled by National Center for Education Statistics, U. S. Department of Education.

TRADE/PROFESSIONAL ASSOCIATIONS

American Association of University Professors. 1012 14th St., N.W., 5th Fl., Washington, DC 20005. Phone: 800-424-2973 or (202)737-5900 Fax: (202)737-5526 E-mail: aaup@aaup.org • URL: http://www.aaup.org.

University Professors for Academic Order. 724 Walnut Ave., Redlands, CA 92373. Phone: (909)792-1264.

COLLEGE INSTRUCTORS AND PROFESSORS

See: COLLEGE FACULTIES

COLLEGE LIBRARIES

See: COLLEGE AND UNIVERSITY LIBRARIES

COLLEGE NEWSPAPERS

See: COLLEGE AND SCHOOL NEWSPAPERS

COLLEGE PLACEMENT BUREAUS

DIRECTORIES

NACE Directory: Who's Who in Career Services and HR/Staffing t. National Association of Colleges and Employers. • Annual. Free to members; nonmembers, $47.95. Lists over 2,200 college placement offices and about 2,000 companies interested in recruiting college graduates. Gives names of placement and recruitment personnel. Formerly *CPC National Dierctory.*

PERIODICALS AND NEWSLETTERS

Journal of Career Planning and Employment: The International Magazine of Placement and Recruitment. National Association of Colleges and Employers. • Quarterly. Free to members; nonmembers, $72.00 per year. Includes *Spotlight* newsletter. Formerly *Journal of College Placement.*

STATISTICS SOURCES

NACE Salary Survey: A Study of Beginning Salary Offers. National Association of Colleges and Employers. • Quarterly. Free to members; nonmembers, $220.00 per year. Formerly *PC Salary Survey.* Formerly College Placement Council, Inc.

TRADE/PROFESSIONAL ASSOCIATIONS

Association of Master of Business Administration Executives. c/o AMBA Center, 388 E Main St., Ste.

A, Branford, CT 06405. Phone: (203)315-5221 Fax: (203)483-6186.

National Student Employment Association. PO Box 23606, Career Services/JLD/CWE, Collin Community College, 2200 W University, Eugene, OR 97402. Phone: (541)484-6935 Fax: (541)484-6935 E-mail: claire.adams@comcast.net • URL: http://www.nsea.info • Directors, coordinators, and senior staff personnel of postsecondary educational institutions, including proprietary schools and corporate human resource directors, who are involved in student employment, internships, cooperative and experiential education, federal work-study, job location and development, and student placement. Answers problems associated with the management of student employment programs. Provides financial support for students in higher education. Creates and conducts training and professional development programs for higher education student employment professionals. Sponsors State Work Study Clearinghouse on state sponsored student employment programs. Compiles statistics. Conducts research programs. Provides legislative updates on current issues.

COLLEGE PRESIDENTS

See also: COLLEGES AND UNIVERSITIES

BIOGRAPHICAL SOURCES

Who's Who in American Education. Marquis Who's Who. • Biennial. $159.95. Contains over 27,000 concise biographies of teachers, administrators, and other individuals involved in all levels of American education.

PERIODICALS AND NEWSLETTERS

For Your Information. Western New York Library Resources Council. • Bimonthly. Free.

STATISTICS SOURCES

Digest of Education Statistics. Available from U. S. Government Printing Office. • Annual. $51.00. Covers all areas of education from kindergarten through graduate school. Includes data from both government and private sources. Compiled by National Center for Education Statistics, U. S. Department of Education.

TRADE/PROFESSIONAL ASSOCIATIONS

American Association of University Administrators. Rhode Island College, Robert Halls 407, Providence, RI 02908-1991. Phone: (401)456-2808 Fax: (401)456-8287 E-mail: allanw@allianceedu.org • URL: http://www.aaua.org.

Association of American Universities. 1200 New York Ave., Suite 550, Washington, DC 20005. Phone: (202)408-7500 Fax: (202)408-8184 E-mail: nils_hasselmo@aau.edu • URL: http://www.aau.edu.

Center for Institutional and Intern. c/o American Council on Education. 1 Dupont Cir., NW, 8th Fl., Washington, DC 20036. Phone: (202)939-9300 E-mail: membership@ace.nche.edu • URL: http://www.acenet.edu.

COLLEGE PUBLISHERS

See: UNIVERSITY PRESSES

COLLEGE STORES

See also: BOOKSELLING; DEPARTMENT STORES; RETAIL TRADE

DIRECTORIES

Directory of College Stores. B. Klein Publications, Inc. • 1999. $95.00. Covers about 4,400 stores selling books, stationery, personal care items, gifts, etc., which serve primarily a college student population.

PERIODICALS AND NEWSLETTERS

The College Store. National Association of College Stores. • Six times a year. Members, $54.00 per year; non-members, $64.00 per year. Formerly *College Store Journal.*

College Store Executive. Executive Business Media, Inc. • 10 times a year. $40.00 per year.

TRADE/PROFESSIONAL ASSOCIATIONS

National Association of College Auxiliary Services. Seven Boar's Head Lane, Charlottesville, VA 22903-4610. Phone: (434)245-8425 Fax: (434)245-8453 E-mail: info@nacas.org • URL: http://www.nacas.org • Formerly Association of College Auxiliary Services.

National Association of College Stores. 500 E Lorain St., Oberlin, OH 44074. Phone: 800-622-7498 or (440)775-7777 Fax: (440)775-4769 E-mail: info@nacs.org • URL: http://www.nacs.org • Formerly College Bookstore Association.

COLLEGE TEACHERS

See: COLLEGE FACULTIES

COLLEGES AND UNIVERSITIES

See also: COLLEGE ENROLLMENT; COLLEGE ENTRANCE REQUIREMENTS; COLLEGE FACULTIES; COLLEGE PRESIDENTS; GRADUATE WORK IN UNIVERSITIES; SCHOLARSHIPS AND STUDENT AID

ABSTRACTS AND INDEXES

Current Index to Journals in Education (CIJE). Oryx Press. • Monthly. $245.00 per year. Semiannual cumulations, $475.00.

Education Index. H. W. Wilson Co. • 10 times a year. Quarterly and annual cumulations. Price varies.

Educational Administration Abstracts. Sage Publication, Inc. • Quarterly. Institutions, $722.00 per year.

Index of Majors. College Board Publications. • Annual. $22.95.

CD-ROM DATABASES

College Blue Book CD-ROM. Available from Gale Cengage Learning. • Annual. $250.00. Produced by Macmillan Reference USA. Serves as electronic version of printed *College Blue Book.* Provides detailed information on programs, degrees, and financial aid sources in the U.S. and Canada.

ERIC on SilverPlatter. Available from SilverPlatter Information, Inc. • Quarterly. $700.00 per year. Produced by the Office of Educational Research and Improvement, U. S. Dept. of Education. Provides CD-ROM indexing and abstracting of a wide variety of literature relating to education. Archival discs are available from 1966.

Leadership Library on CD-ROM: Who's Who in the Leadership of the United States. Leadership Directories, Inc. • Quarterly. Including access to Internet version (weekly updates). Contains all 14 *Yellow Book* personnel directories on CD-ROM, providing contact and brief biographical information for about 400,000 individuals. Covers business, government, financial institutions, news media, law firms, associations, foreign representatives, and nonprofit organizations. Includes photographs.

WILSONDISC: Education Index. H. W. Wilson Co. • Monthly. Provides CD-ROM indexing of education-related literature from 1983 to date. Price includes online service.

DIRECTORIES

Accredited Institutions of Postsecondary Education, Programs, Candidates. Greenwood Publishing Group, Inc. • Annual. $80.00. Lists more than 6,600 public and private accredited institutions and programs.

American Universities and Colleges. American Council on Education USA. Walter de Gruyter, Inc. • Quadrennial. $249.50. Two volumes. Produced in collaboration with the American Council on Education. Provides full descriptions of more than 1,900 institutions of higher learning, including details of graduate and professional programs.

Chronicle Four-Year College Databook. Chronicle Guidance Publications Inc. • Covers: More than 825 baccalaureate, master's, doctoral, and first professional programs offered by more than 2,450 colleges and universities in the United States. Entries include: College charts section gives college name, address, phone; accreditation, enrollment, admissions, costs, financial aid; accreditation associations' names, addresses, and phone numbers. Appendices gives details on admissions and other information special to each college.

College Blue Book. Macmillan Reference USA. • Covers: Listings and detailed descriptions of thousands of two and four year schools, their programs, degrees, financial aid sources, and scholarships.

Faculty White Pages. Gale Cengage Learning. • 1991. $135.00. 91st edition. "Telephone book" classified arrangement of over 537,000 U. S. college faculty members in 41 subject sections. A roster of institutions is included.

Gale Directory of Learning Worldwide: A Guide to Faculty and Institutions of Higher Education, Research, and Culture. Gale Cengage Learning. • 2001. $425.00. Three volumes. Describes about 26,000 colleges, universities, research institutes, libraries, museums, scholarly associations, academies, and archives around the world. Arranged by country.

Lovejoy's College Guide. IDG Books Worldwide Inc. • Covers: 2,500 American colleges, universities, and technical institutes, and selected foreign colleges accredited by United States regional accrediting associations. Entries include: School name, location, date founded, name changes, enrollment figures, SAT/ACT figures, library size, faculty-student ratio, religious affiliation, admission information, tuition, room and board costs, scholarships and loans, athletic programs, curricula and degrees offered, special programs, summer sessions.

National Faculty Directory. Gale. • Covers: More than 740,000 (90,000 more in supplement) teaching faculty members at over 3,600 junior colleges, colleges, and universities in the United States and those in Canada that give instruction in English. Entries include: Name, department name, institution, address, and phone and fax numbers. Directory combines main edition and supplement.

New Riders' Official World Wide Web Yellow Pages. New Riders Publishing. • 1998. $34.99. Sixth edition. A broadly classified listing of Web sites, with brief descriptions of sites and a subject index to narrower topics. Includes a guide to using the Internet and a separate, alphabetical listing of more than 1,500 college and university Web sites, both U. S. and foreign. Includes CD-ROM.

Nonprofit Sector Yellow Book: Who's Who in the Management of the Leading Foundations, Universities, Museums, and Other Nonprofit Organizations. Leadership Directories, Inc. • Semiannual. $265.00 per year. Covers management personnel and board members of about 1,300 prominent, nonprofit organizations: foundations, colleges, museums, performing arts groups, medical institutions, libraries, private preparatory schools, and charitable service organizations.

Patterson's Schools Classified. Educational Directories Inc. • Covers: Over 7,000 accredited colleges, universities, community colleges, junior colleges, career schools and teaching hospitals. Entries include: School name, address, phone, URL, e-mail, name of administrator or admissions officer, description, professional accreditation (where applicable). Updated from previous year's edition of 'Patterson's American Education' (see separate entry).

Peterson's Guide to Distance Learning Programs. Peterson's. • 2002. $26.95. Second revised edition. Provides detailed information on accredited college and university programs available through television, radio, computer, videocassette, and audiocassette resources. Covers U. S. and Canadian institutions.

Peterson's Guide to Four-Year Colleges. Peterson's. • Annual. $29.95. Provides information on more than 2,000 accredited degree-granting colleges and universities in the U. S. and Canada.

Peterson's Guide to Graduate and Professional Programs: An Overview. Peterson's. • Annual. $49.95. Provide details for more than 31,000 graduate programs at 1,700 colleges and universities. (Peterson's Graduate and Professional Program Series).

Peterson's Register of Higher Education. Peterson's. • Annual. $49.95. Provides concise information on 3,700 colleges and other postsecondary educational institutions in the U. S.

The World of Learning. Available from Taylor and Francis, Inc. • Annual. $525.00. Covers about 30,000 colleges, libraries, museums, learned societies, academies, and research institutions throughout the world. Published by Europa Publications.

HANDBOOKS AND MANUALS

The College Handbook. The College Board. • 2003. $27.95. Includes CD-Rom. Over 3,200 undergraduate schools. (College Handbook Series).

Office Procedures and Technology for Colleges. Patsy J. Fulton. South-Western. • 1998. $39.95. 11th edition. (KF-Office Education Series).

INTERNET DATABASES

U. S. Census Bureau: The Official Statistics. U. S. Bureau of the Census. Phone: (301)763-4100 Fax: (301)763-4794 • URL: http://www.census.gov • Web site is "Your Source for Social, Demographic, and Economic Information." Contains "Current U. S. Population Count," "Current Economic Indicators," and a wide variety of data under "Other Official Statistics." Keyword searching is provided. Fees: Free.

ONLINE DATABASES

Education Index Online. H. W. Wilson Co. • Indexes a wide variety of periodicals related to schools, colleges, and education, 1984 to date. Monthly updates. Inquire as to online cost and availability.

ERIC. Educational Resources Information Center. • Funded by the U. S. Department of Education, Institute of Education Sciences (formerly Office of Educational Research and Improvement). Provides access to more than one million online records covering education-related journal and report literature, 1966 to date. Updating is monthly. Inquire as to online cost and availability.

PERIODICALS AND NEWSLETTERS

American School and University: Facilities, Purchasing, and Business Administration. Primedia Business Magazines and Media. • Monthly. Free to qualified personnel; others, $50.00 per year.

Athletic Management. MomentumMedia. • Bimonthly. $24.00 per year. Formerly *College Athletic Management.*

Change: The Magazine of Higher Learning. American Association of Higher Education. Heldref Publications. • Bimonthly. Individuals, $55.00 per year; institutions, $112.00 per year.

The Chronicle of Higher Education. Chronicle of

Higher Education, Inc. • 49 times a year. $82.50 per year. Includes *Almanac.* Provides news, book reviews and job listings for college professors and administrators.

College and University. American Association of Collegiate Registrars and Admissions Officers. • Quarterly. Free to members; non-members, $50.00 per year. Addresses issues in higher education; looks at new procedures, policies, technology; reviews new publications.

Community College Journal. American Association of Community Colleges. • Bimonthly. $28.00 per year. Formerly *Community, Technical and Junior College Journal.*

Community College Week: The Independent Voice Serving Community, Technical and Junior Colleges. Cox, Matthews & Associates, Inc. • Biweekly. $40.00 per year. Covers a wide variety of current topics relating to the administration and operation of community colleges.

Higher Education and National Affairs. American Council on Education, Office of Research. • Biweekly. $60.00 per year. Newsletter.

Journal of Higher Education. Ohio State University Press. • Bimonthly. Individuals, $50.00 per year; institutions, $110.00 per year. Issues important to faculty administrators and program managers in higher education.

Journal of Marketing for Higher Education. Haworth Press, Inc. • Semiannual. $365.00 per year.

New Directions for Higher Education. Jossey-Bass. • Quarterly. Institutions, $145.00 per year; with on-line edition, $153.00 per year. Sample issue free to librarians.

The Presidency: The Magazine for Higher Education Leaders. American Council on Education, Office of Research. • Three times a year. Members, $27.00 per year; non-members, $30.00 per year. Formerly *Educational Record.*

Resources in Education. Educational Resources Information Center. Available from U.S. Government Printing Office. • Monthly. Reports on educational research.

University Business: Solutions for Today's Higher Education. Educational Media Inc. • 10 times a year. $60.00 per year. Edited for college administrators, including managers of business services, finance, computing, and telecommunications. Includes information on relevant technological advances.

RESEARCH CENTERS AND INSTITUTES

Center for the Study of Higher Education. Pennsylvania State University. 400 Rackley Bldg., University Park, PA 16802. Phone: (814)865-6346 Fax: (814)865-3638 E-mail: cshe@psu.edu • URL: http://www.ed.psu.edu/cshe.

ERIC Clearinghouse for Community Colleges. University of California, Los Angeles. 3051 Moore Hall, Los Angeles, CA 90095. Phone: 800-832-8256 or (310)825-3931 Fax: (310)206-8095 E-mail: ericc@ucla.edu • URL: http://www.gseis.ucla.edu/eric.

ERIC Clearinghouse on Adult, Career and Vocational Education. Ohio State University. Center on Education and Training for Employment, 1900 Kenny Rd., Columbus, OH 43210-1090. Phone: 800-848-4815 or (614)292-7069 Fax: (614)292-1260 E-mail: ericacve@postbox.acs.ohio-state.edu • URL: http://www.ericacve.org/.

STATISTICS SOURCES

Datapedia of the United States: American History in Numbers. George T. Kurian, editor. Bernan Press. • 2004. $125.00. Third edition. Based on the Census Bureau publication, *Historical Statistics of the United States.* Provides data from Colonial times to the present on agriculture, business, consumer income, energy, finance, labor, national income, population, and many other subjects. Includes "nar-

rative highlights," maps, charts, and statistical projections.

Degrees and Other Awards Conferred by Institutions of Higher Education. Available from U. S. Government Printing Office. • Annual. Issued by the National Center for Education Statistics, U. S. Department of Education. Provides data on the number of degrees awarded at the associate's, bachelor's, master's, and doctor's levels. Includes fields of study and racial-ethnic-sex data by major field or discipline.

Digest of Education Statistics. Available from U. S. Government Printing Office. • Annual. $51.00. Covers all areas of education from kindergarten through graduate school. Includes data from both government and private sources. Compiled by National Center for Education Statistics, U. S. Department of Education.

Projections of Education Statistics. Available from U. S. Government Printing Office. • Annual. $26.00. Issued by the U. S. Department of Education, National Center for Education Statistics (http://www.ed.gov). Provides 10-year projections of data relating to elementary schools, secondary schools, and institutions of higher learning. Includes projections of enrollment, graduates, classroom teachers, and expenditures.

School Enrollment, Social and Economic Characteristics of Students. Available from U. S. Government Printing Office. • Annual. $2.25. Issued by the U. S. Bureau of the Census. Presents detailed tabulations of data on school enrollment of the civilian noninstitutional population three years old and over. Covers nursery school, kindergarten, elementary school, high school, college, and graduate school. Information is provided on age, race, sex, family income, marital status, employment, and other characteristics.

Social Statistics of the United States. Mark S. Littman, editor. Bernan Press. • 2000. $65.00. Includes statistical data on population growth, labor force, occupations, environmental trends, leisure time use, income, poverty, taxes, and other economic or demographic topics.

Statistical Abstract of the United States. Available from U. S. Government Printing Office. • Annual. $51.00. Issued by the U. S. Bureau of the Census.

A Statistical Portrait of the United States: Social Conditions and Trends. Mark S. Littman, editor. Bernan Press. • 1998. $89.00. Covers "social, economic, and environmental trends in the United States over the past 25 years." Includes statistical tables, graphs, and analysis relating to such topics as population, income, poverty, wealth, labor, housing, education, healthcare, air/water quality, and government. (Statistical Portrait of the United States: Social Conditions and Trends Series).

UNESCO Statistical Yearbook. Bernan Press. • 1998. $95.00. Co-published by Bernan Press and the United Nations Educational, Scientific, and Cultural Organization (http://www.unesco.org). Presents statistical data from more than 200 countries on education, technology, research, broadcasting, cinema, book publishing, newspapers, libraries, museums, and population. Includes charts, maps, and graphs.

TRADE/PROFESSIONAL ASSOCIATIONS

Academy for Educational Development. c/o Eileen D'Andrea, 1825 Connecticut Ave. NW, Washington, DC 20009-5721. Phone: (202)884-8000 Fax: (202)884-8400 E-mail: adminc@aed.org • URL: http://www.aed.org.

American Council on Education. One Dupont Circle, N.W., Suite 800, Washington, DC 20036. Phone: (202)939-9300 Fax: (202)833-4760 E-mail: web@ace.nche.edu • URL: http://www.acenet.edu.

Association of American Colleges and Universities. 1818 R St., N.W., Washington, DC 20009. Phone:

800-297-3775 or (202)387-3760 Fax: (202)265-9532 E-mail: info@aacu.org • URL: http://www.aacu-edu.org.

Association of American Universities. 1200 New York Ave., Suite 550, Washington, DC 20005. Phone: (202)408-7500 Fax: (202)408-8184 E-mail: nils_hasselmo@aau.edu • URL: http://www.aau.edu.

Association of American University Presses. 71 W. 23rd St., Suite 901, New York, NY 10010-4102. Phone: (212)989-1010 Fax: (212)989-0275 E-mail: info@aaupnet.org • URL: http://www.aaupnet.org.

Association of Governing Boards of Universities and Colleges. One Dupont Circle, N.W., Suite 400, Washington, DC 20036. Phone: 800-356-6317 or (202)296-8400 Fax: (202)223-7053 E-mail: tomi@agb.org • URL: http://www.agb.org.

Association of Graduate Schools in Association of American Universities. 1200 New York Ave., Suite 550, Washington, DC 20005. Phone: (202)408-7500 Fax: (202)408-8184 E-mail: matt_owens@aau.edu.

The College Board. 45 Columbus Ave., 45 Columbus Ave., New York, NY 10023-6992. Phone: (866)392-3017 or (212)713-8000 Fax: (212)649-8442 E-mail: publicaffairs@collegeboard.org • URL: http://www.collegeboard.com • Represents the schools, colleges, universities, and other educational organizations that seeks to connect members to success and opportunity. Serves students, parents, high schools, and colleges through major programs and services in college admission, guidance, assessment, financial aid, enrollment, and teaching and learning.

Council for Advancement and Support of Education. 1307 New York Ave. N.W., Suite 1000, Washington, DC 20005-4701. Phone: (202)328-2273 Fax: (202)387-4973 E-mail: membersservicecenter@case.org • URL: http://www.case.org • Formerly American College Public Relations Association.

Council of Graduate Schools. One Dupont Circle, N.W., Suite 430, Washington, DC 20036-1173. Phone: (202)223-3791 Fax: (202)331-7157 E-mail: cflagg@cgs.nche.edu • URL: http://www.cgsnet.org • Formerly Council of Graduate Schools in the United States.

OTHER SOURCES

Educational Rankings Annual: A Compilation of Approximately 3,500 Published Rankings and Lists on Every Aspect of Education. Gale Cengage Learning. • Annual. $265.00. Provides national, regional, local, and international rankings of a wide variety of educational institutions, including business and professional schools.

COLOR IN INDUSTRY

See also: ART IN INDUSTRY

GENERAL WORKS

Color: A Multidisciplinary Approach. Heinrich Zollinger. John Wiley and Sons, Inc. • 1999. $125.00. Written for a wide audience, including "interested laymen." Among the chapter headings are "Physics of Light and Color," "Chemistry of Color," "How Do We See Colors?" and "How Do We Name Colors?".

Color in the Office: Design Trends from 1950 to 1990 and Beyond. Sara O. Marberry. John Wiley and Sons, Inc. • 1993. $90.00. Presents past, present, and future color trends in corporate office design. Features color photographs of traditional, postmodern, and neoclassical office designs. (Architecture Series).

HANDBOOKS AND MANUALS

Color Chemistry. Heinrich Zollinger. John Wiley and Sons, Inc. • 2003. $150.00. Third edition. Includes technical information for industrial chemists and others on dyes and pigments.

Color Science: Concepts and Methods, Quantitative Data and Formulae. Gunter Wyszecki and W. S. Stiles. John Wiley and Sons, Inc. • 1982. $66.50. Second edition. (Pure and Applied Optics Series).

Dimensional Color. Lois Swirnoff. W. W. Norton & Co., Inc. • 2003. $39.95. Second edition. Explores the three-dimensional interaction between light, color, and surface, with 230 color illustrations. Written chiefly for architects and designers. (Previous edition was published by Van Nostrand Reinhold.).

Industrial Color Testing: Fundamentals and Techniques. Hans G. Volz. John Wiley and Sons, Inc. • 2001. $140.00. Second edition.

Industrial Dyes: Chemistry, Properties, Applications. Klaus Hunger, editor. John Wiley and Sons, Inc. • 2003. $185.00. Covers textile dyeing, nontextile dyeing, functional dyes, and optical brighteners. Includes health and safety aspects and examples of commercially available dyes.

The Physics and Chemistry of Color: The Fifteen Causes of Color. Kurt Nassau. John Wiley and Sons, Inc. • 2001. $115.00. Second edition. (Pure and Applied Optics Series).

ONLINE DATABASES

CA Search. Chemical Abstracts Service. • Guide to chemical literature, 1967 to present. Inquire as to online cost and availability.

PERIODICALS AND NEWSLETTERS

Chromatographia: An International Journal for Rapid Communication in Chromatography and Associated Techniques. Elsevier. • 24 times a year. $1,299.00 per year. Text in English; summaries in English, French and German.

Color Publishing. PennWell Corp., Advanced Technology Div. • Bimonthly. $29.70 per year.

Color Research and Application. John Wiley and Sons, Inc. • Bimonthly. Institutions, $840 per year; with online edition, $882.00 per year. International coverage.

PRICE SOURCES

Chemical Market Reporter. Schnell Publishing Co., Inc. • Weekly. $169.00 per year. Quotes current prices for a wide range of chemicals. Formerly *Chemical Marketing Reporter.*

RESEARCH CENTERS AND INSTITUTES

Center for Imaging Science. Rochester Institute of Technology, 54 Lomb Memorial Dr., Rochester, NY 14623. Phone: (716)475-5994 Fax: (716)475-5988 E-mail: gatley@cis.rit.edu • URL: http://www.cis.rit.edu • Activities include research in color science and digital image processing.

Chemistry Laboratories. Rensselaer Polytechnic Institute. Cogswell Laboratory, Troy, NY 12180-3590. Phone: (518)276-6344 Fax: (518)276-4887 E-mail: bailer@rpi.edu.

TRADE/PROFESSIONAL ASSOCIATIONS

American Association of Textile Chemists and Colorists. P.O. Box 12215, Research Triangle Park, NC 27709-2215. Phone: (919)549-8141 Fax: (919)549-8933 E-mail: hammona@aatcc.org • URL: http://www.aatcc.org.

Color Association of the United States. 315 W 39th St., Studio 507, New York, NY 10018. Phone: (212)947-7774 Fax: (212)594-6987 E-mail: caus@colorassociation.com • URL: http://www.colorassociation.com • Formerly The Textile Color Card Association of America.

Color Marketing Group. 5845 Richmond Hwy., No. 410, Alexandria, VA 22303. Phone: (703)329-8500 Fax: (703)329-0155 E-mail: cmg@colormarketing.org • URL: http://www.colormarketing.org • International group of professionals who forecast colors for consumer and contract markets. Examines color as it applies to the profitable marketing of products and services. Provides a forum for the exchange of ideas for all phases of color marketing, including styling, design, trends, merchandising, sales, education, and research.

Color Pigments Manufacturers Association. 300 N Washington St., Ste. 102, Alexandria, VA 22314. Phone: (703)684-4044 Fax: (703)684-1795 E-mail: cpma@cpma.com • URL: http://www.pigments.org • Manufacturers of inorganic and organic color pigments. Disseminates technical, regulatory, and legislative information on laboratory testing, toxicity, and subjects of general interest to manufacturers of pigments.

Optical Society of America. 2010 Massachusetts Ave., N.W., Washington, DC 20036-1023. Phone: (202)223-8130 Fax: (202)223-1096 E-mail: info@osa.org • URL: http://www.osa.org.

COLOR PHOTOGRAPHY

See: PHOTOGRAPHIC INDUSTRY

COLOR TELEVISION

See: TELEVISION APPARATUS INDUSTRY

COLUMNISTS

See: WRITERS AND WRITING

COMMERCIAL ART

See also: ART IN INDUSTRY; CREATIVITY; DESIGN IN INDUSTRY; GRAPHIC ARTS INDUSTRY

GENERAL WORKS

Opportunities in Visual Arts Careers. Mark Salmon. McGraw-Hill. • 2001. $15.95. Edited for students and job seekers. Includes education requirements and salary data. (Opportunities in...Series).

ABSTRACTS AND INDEXES

Art Index. H. W. Wilson Co. • Quarterly. Annual cumulations. Price varies. Subject and author index to periodicals in art, architecture, industrial design, city planning, photography, and various related topics.

ALMANACS AND YEARBOOKS

Art Directors Annual. Art Directors Club Inc. • Annual. $70.00. Formerly *Annual of Advertising, Editorial and Television Art and Design with the Annual Copy Awards.*

Graphis Design: International Annual of Design and Illustration. Watson-Guptill Publications. • Annual. $69.00. Text in English, French, and German. Formerly *Graphis Annual.*

CD-ROM DATABASES

WILSONDISC: Art Index. H. W. Wilson Co. • Monthly. Provides CD-ROM indexing of art-related literature from 1982 to date. Price includes online service.

DIRECTORIES

Graphic Arts Blue Book. Reed Business Information. • Covers: printing plants, bookbinders, imagesetters, platemakers, paper merchants, paper manufacturers, printing machinery manufacturers and dealers, and others serving the graphic arts industry (Standard Industrial Classification (SIC) code 2600, 2700). Eight editions: New York edition (7,000 establishments) covers metropolitan New York and the state of New Jersey; Southeastern edition (10,500 establishments) covers Kentucky, Tennessee, Alabama, Mississippi, Virginia (except

Washington suburbs), North Carolina, South Carolina, Georgia, and Florida; Northeastern edition (6,000 establishments) covers Connecticut, Maine, Massachusetts, New Hampshire, New York (upstate only), Rhode Island, and Vermont and the eastern Canadian provinces; Delaware Valley-Ohio edition (8,500 establishments) covers Pennsylvania, Maryland, Delaware, District of Columbia and its Virginia suburbs, and Ohio; Midwestern edition (13,000 establishments) covers Illinois, Indiana, Iowa, Michigan, Minnesota, Wisconsin, North and South Dakota; Southwestern edition (5,500 establishments) covers Arizona, southern California, Hawaii, southern Nevada; Pacific Northwestern edition (5,500 establishments), covers northern California, northern Nevada, Oregon, Washington, Montana, Idaho, Wyoming, Utah, Alaska, and the western provinces of Canada. Texas central edition (8000 establishments) covering Texas, Colorado, New Mexico, Oklahoma, Louisiana, Kansas, Missouri, and Nebraska. Entries include: Company name, address, phone, names and titles of executives, name of buyer, list of products or services, year established.

Magazines Career Directory: A Practical One-Stop Guide to Getting a Job in Publ c Relations. Visible Ink Press. • 1993. $39.00. Fifth edition. Includes information on magazine publishing careers in art, editing, sales, and business management. Provides advice from "insiders," resume suggestions, a directory of companies that may offer entry-level positions, and a directory of career information sources. (Career Advisor Series).

Peterson's Professional Degree Programs in the Visual and Performing Arts. Peterson's. • Annual. $21.95. A directory of more than 900 degree programs in art, music, theater, and dance at 600 colleges and professional schools.

ONLINE DATABASES

Art Index Online. H. W. Wilson Co. • Indexes a wide variety of art-related periodicals, 1984 to date. Monthly updates. Inquire as to online cost and availability.

PERIODICALS AND NEWSLETTERS

Graphic Design: U.S.A. Kaye Publishing Corp. • Monthly. $60.00.

Graphis: International Journal of Visual Communication. Graphis Inc. • Bimonthly. $90.00 per year. Text in English, French and German.

RESEARCH CENTERS AND INSTITUTES

Chester F. Carlson Center for Imaging Science. Rochester Institute of Technology, 54 Lomb Memorial Dr., Rochester, NY 14623. Phone: 800-724-2536 or (716)475-5944 Fax: (716)475-5988 E-mail: garley@cis.rit.edu • URL: http://www.cis.rit.edu/.

TRADE/PROFESSIONAL ASSOCIATIONS

Art Directors Club. 106 W 29th St., New York, NY 10001. Phone: (212)643-1440 Fax: (212)643-4266 E-mail: info@adcglobal.org • URL: http://www.adcglobal.org • Art directors of advertising magazines and agencies, visual information specialists, and graphic designers; associate members are artists, cinematographers, photographers, copywriters, educators, journalists, and critics. Promotes and stimulates interest in the practice of art direction. Sponsors Annual Exhibition of Advertising, Editorial and Television Art and Design; International Traveling Exhibition. Provides educational, professional, and entertainment programs; on-premise art exhibitions; portfolio review program. Conducts panels for students and faculty.

Graphic Artists Guild. 32 Broadway, Ste. 1114, New York, NY 10004-1612. Phone: (212)791-3400 Fax: (212)791-0333 E-mail: admin@gag.org • URL: http://gag.org • Professional graphic artists who work in the disciplines of illustration, graphic design, surface design, computer graphics, and

cartoons, and create work for national magazines, newspaper syndicates, books, television, advertising, corporate and promotional materials. Aims to: raise the business and ethical standards in the industry; provide legal and educational services to members; increase public appreciation of graphic artists as professionals. Maintains professional discipline meetings and provides professional education services for each chapter.

Society of American Graphic Artists. 32 Union Square, Room 1214, New York, NY 10003. Phone: (212)260-5706 • URL: http://www.clt.astate.edu • Formerly Society of American Erchers, Engravers, Lithographers and Woodcutters.

COMMERCIAL AVIATION

See: BUSINESS AVIATION

COMMERCIAL CODE

See: BUSINESS LAW

COMMERCIAL CORRESPONDENCE

See: BUSINESS CORRESPONDENCE

COMMERCIAL CREDIT

See: COMMERCIAL LENDING

COMMERCIAL EDUCATION

See: BUSINESS EDUCATION

COMMERCIAL FINANCE COMPANIES

See: FINANCE COMPANIES

COMMERCIAL LAW AND REGULATION

See: BUSINESS LAW

COMMERCIAL LENDING

See also: BANK LOANS

GENERAL WORKS

The Art of Commercial Lending. Edgar M. Morsman. Robert Morris Associates. • 1997. $64.00. Describes the diverse skills required for success as a commercial lender. Covers both personal and institutional aspects.

ABSTRACTS AND INDEXES

Business Periodicals Index. H. W. Wilson Co. • 11 times a year. Quarterly and annual cumulations. Price varies.

DIRECTORIES

Business Organizations, Agencies, and Publications Directory. Gale Cengage Learning. • 2003. $480.00. 15th edition. Over 40,000 entries describing 39 types of business information sources. Classified by type of organization, publication, or serviceIncludes state, national, and international agencies and organizations. Master index to names and keywords.

Also includes e-mail addresses and web site URL's.

ENCYCLOPEDIAS AND DICTIONARIES

Credit and Lending Dictionary. Shelley W. Geehr and Daphne Smith, editors. The Risk Management Association. • 1994. $25.00.

HANDBOOKS AND MANUALS

Commercial Lending. George E. Ruth. American Bankers Association. • 1990. $57.00. Second edition. Discusses the practical aspects of commercial lending.

How to Charter a Commercial Bank. Douglas V. Austin. CCH, Inc. • 1999. $350.00. Provides detailed information on how to start a commercial bank, including both technical and practical requirements.

Manual of Credit and Commercial Laws. National Association of Credit Management. • Annual. Free to members; non-members, $100.00. Formerly *Credit Manual of Commercial Laws.*

ONLINE DATABASES

TRW Business Credit Profiles. Experian. • Provides credit history (trade payments, payment trends, payment totals, payment history, etc.) for public and private U. S. companies. Key facts and banking information are also given. Updates are weekly. Inquire as to online cost and availability.

Wilson Business Abstracts Online. H. W. Wilson Co. • Indexes and abstracts 600 major business periodicals, plus the *Wall Street Journal* and the business section of the *New York Times.* Indexing is from 1982, abstracting from 1990, with the two newspapers included from 1993. Updated weekly. Inquire as to online cost and availability. (*Business Periodicals Index* without abstracts is also available online.).

PERIODICALS AND NEWSLETTERS

Commercial Lending Litigation News. LRP Publications. • Description: Covers liability claims and their policies and procedures, case strategies, court decisions, and jury verdicts.

Commercial Lending Review. American Bankers Association. Aspen Publishers, Inc. • Quarterly. $315.00 per year. Edited for senior-level lending officers. Includes specialized lending techniques, management issues, legal developments, and reviews of specific industries.

Lender Liability Law Report. RIA. • Description: Discusses the impact of relevant cases and legislation on lenders and spotlights legal landmines which lenders may encounter. Recurring features include summaries of recent cases and avoidance techniques.

Loan Market Week: The Newsweekly of the Loan Syndication, Trading and Investment Markets. Institutional Investor, Inc., Journals Group. • Weekly. $2,370.00 per year. Newsletter. Includes print and online editions. Covers retail banking, commercial lending, foreign loans, bank technology, government regulations, and other topics related to banking. Formerly *Bank Letter.*

The RMA Journal. The Risk Management Association. • 10 times a year. Members, $40.00 per year; non-members, $95.00 per year. *The Journal of Lending and Credit Risk Management.*

TRADE/PROFESSIONAL ASSOCIATIONS

International Association of Commercial Collectors. 4040 W. 70th St., Minneapolis, MN 55435. Phone: (952)925-0760 Fax: (952)926-1624 E-mail: iacc@collector.com • URL: http://www.commercialcollector.com • Collection agencies specializing in the recovery of commercial accounts receivable. Formerly American Commercial Collectors Association.

Risk Management Association. 1801 Market St., Ste. 300, 1650 Market St., Ste. 2300, Philadelphia,

PA 19103-1628. Phone: 800-677-7621 or (215)446-4000 Fax: (215)446-4101 E-mail: member@rmahq.org • URL: http://www.rmahq.org/RMA • Commercial and savings banks, and savings and loan, and other financial services companies. Conducts research and professional development activities in areas of loan administration, asset management, and commercial lending and credit to increase professionalism.

OTHER SOURCES

Bank and Lender Litigation Reporter: The Nationwide Litigation Report of Failed National and State Banks and Savings and Loan Associations, including FDIC and FSLIC Complaints and Related Actions Among Shareholders, Officers, Directors, Ins. Andrews Publications. • Semimonthly. $875.00 per year. Newsletter. Provides summaries of significant litigation and regulatory agency complaints. Formerly *Lender Liability Litigation Reporter.*

COMMERCIAL PHOTOGRAPHY

See also: PHOTOGRAPHIC INDUSTRY

ABSTRACTS AND INDEXES

Art Index. H. W. Wilson Co. • Quarterly. Annual cumulations. Price varies. Subject and author index to periodicals in art, architecture, industrial design, city planning, photography, and various related topics.

BIOGRAPHICAL SOURCES

Contemporary Photographers. Available from Gale Cengage Learning. • 1995. $190.00. Third edition. Provides biographical and critical information on more than 850 international photographers.

DIRECTORIES

American Society of Photographers - Membership Directory. American Society of Photographers, Inc. • Annual. Membership.

Photographer's Market: 2000 Places to Sell Your Photographs. F&W Publications, Inc. • Annual. $24.99. Lists 2,000 companies and publications that purchase original photographs.

Who's Who in Professional Imaging. Professional Photographers of America, Inc. • Annual. $110.00. Lists over 18,000 members. Formerly *Buyers Guide to Qualified Photographers.*

ENCYCLOPEDIAS AND DICTIONARIES

Focal Encyclopedia of Photography. Leslie Stroebel and Richard D. Zakia, editors. Elsevier. • 1996. $69.95. Third edition.

FINANCIAL RATIOS

Annual Statement Studies. The Risk Management Association. • Annual. Median and quartile financial ratios are given for over 400 kinds of manufacturing, wholesale, retail, construction, and consumer finance establishments. Data is sorted by both asset size and sales volume. Includes a clearly written "Definition of Ratios" and an alphabetical industry index.

Annual Statement Studies: Industry Default Probabilities and Cash Flow Measures. The Risk Management Association. • Annual. $145.00. Serves as a companion volume to the original *Annual Statement Studies.* Gives probability of default estimates on a percentage scale for more than 450 industries. Includes changes in position year-by-year for eight financial statement line items and provides percentage measures of cash flow.

ONLINE DATABASES

Art Index Online. H. W. Wilson Co. • Indexes a wide variety of art-related periodicals, 1984 to date.

Monthly updates. Inquire as to online cost and availability.

Magazine Index. Gale Cengage Learning. • General magazine indexing (popular literature), 1973 to present. Daily updates. Inquire as to online cost and availability.

PERIODICALS AND NEWSLETTERS

News Photographer: Dedicated to the Service and Advancement of News Photography. National Press Photographers Association, Inc. • Monthly. $38.00 per year.

Professional Photographer. Professional Photographers of America. • Monthly. $27.00 per year.

Studio Photography and Design. Cygnus Business Media, Inc. • Monthly. Free to qualified personnel; others, $60.00 per year. Incorporates *Comercial Image.*

TRADE/PROFESSIONAL ASSOCIATIONS

American Society of Media Photographers. 150 N. Second St., Philadelphia, PA 19106. Phone: (215)451-2767 Fax: (215)451-0880 E-mail: info@asmp.org • URL: http://www.asmp.org.

National Press Photographers Association. 3200 Croasdaile Dr., Ste. 306, Durham, NC 27705-2588. Phone: (919)383-7246 Fax: (919)383-7261 E-mail: info@nppa.org • URL: http://www.nppa.org • Professional news photographers and others whose occupation has a direct professional relationship with photojournalism, the art of news communication by photographic image through publication, television film, or theater screen. Sponsors annual television-news film workshop and annual cross-country (five locations) short course. Conducts annual competition for news photos and for television-news film, and monthly contest for still clipping and television-news film.

Professional Photographers of America. 229 Peachtree St., N.E., Suite 2200, Atlanta, GA 30303. Phone: 800-786-6277 or (404)522-8600 Fax: (404)614-6404 E-mail: csc@ppa.com • URL: http://www.ppa.com • Formerly Photographer's Association of America.

COMMERCIAL REAL ESTATE

See: INDUSTRIAL REAL ESTATE

COMMERCIAL STATISTICS

See: BUSINESS STATISTICS

COMMODITIES

See also: COMMODITY FUTURES TRADING

ALMANACS AND YEARBOOKS

Agricultural and Mineral Commodities Year Book. Available from Taylor & Francis Group. • Annual. $225.00. Published by Europa Publications. Contains descriptive product profiles, price data, export-import data, and production statistics for major commodities of the world. Includes commodity histories, uses, markets, demand trends, and information about trade agreements and key commodity organizations.

Commodity Market Review. Available from Bernan Associates. • Annual. $18.00 Published by the Food and Agriculture Organization of the United Nations (FAO). Reviews the global outlook for over 20 specific commodities.

CRB Commodity Yearbook. Commodity Research Bureau. CRB. • Annual. $99.95.

Securities, Commodities, and Federal Banking: 1999 in Review. CCH, Inc. • Irregular. $57.00. Summarizes the year's significant legal and regulatory developments.

UNCTAD Commodity Yearbook. United Nations Conference on Trade and Development. United Nations Publications. • Annual.

CD-ROM DATABASES

World Trade Analyzer. Statistics Canada, International Trade Division. • Annual. CD-ROM provides 20 years of export-import data for 800 commodities traded by the 180 member countries of the United Nations.

ENCYCLOPEDIAS AND DICTIONARIES

Dictionary of Agriculture: From Abaca to Zoonosis. Kathryn L. Lipton. Lynne Rienner Publishers, Inc. • 1995. $75.00. Emphasis is on agricultural economics.

INTERNET DATABASES

USDA. United States Department of Agriculture. Phone: (202)720-2791 E-mail: agsec@usda.gov • URL: http://www.usda.gov • The USDA home page has six sections: News and Information; What's New; About USDA; Agencies; Opportunities; Search and Help. Keyword searching is offered from the USDA home page and from various individual agency home pages. Agencies are the Economic Research Service, Agricultural Marketing Service, National Agricultural Statistics Service, National Agricultural Library, and about 12 others. Updating varies. Fees: Free.

ONLINE DATABASES

CAB Abstracts. CAB Publishing North America. • Contains 46 specialized abstract collections covering over 10,000 journals and monographs in the areas of agriculture, horticulture, forest products, farm products, nutrition, dairy science, poultry, grains, animal health, entomology, etc. Time period is 1972 to date, with monthly updates. Inquire as to online cost and availability. *CAB Abstracts on CD-ROM* also available, with annual updating.

EconLit. American Economic Association. • Covers the worldwide literature of economics as contained in selected monographs and about 550 journals. Subjects include microeconomics, macroeconomics, economic history, inflation, money, credit, finance, accounting theory, trade, natural resource economics, and regional economics. Time period is 1969 to present, with monthly updates. Inquire as to online cost and availability.

PERIODICALS AND NEWSLETTERS

CRB Futures Market Service. Commodity Research Bureau Inc. • Description: "Discusses developments that will affect the future status of supply, demand, and price movements for the different commodities traded on the futures markets.".

Financial Times [London]. The Financial Times, Inc. • Daily, except Sunday. $572.88 per year. An international business and financial newspaper, featuring news from London, Paris, Frankfurt, New York, and Tokyo. Includes worldwide stock and bond market data, commodity market data, and monetary/currency exchange information.

The Journal of Futures Markets. John Wiley and Sons, Inc., Journals. • Monthly. Institutions, $1,460.00 per year; with online edition, $1,533.00 per year.

PRICE SOURCES

CRB Commodity Index Report. Commodity Research Bureau. • Weekly. $295.00 per year. Quotes the CRB Futures Price Index and the CRB Spot Market Index for the last five business days, plus the previous week, month, and year. Includes tables and graphs.

Monthly Commodity Price Bulletin. United Nations

Publications. • Monthly. $125.00 per year. Provides monthly average prices for the previous 12 months for a wide variety of commodities traded internationally.

PPI Detailed Report. Bureau of Labor Statistics, U.S. Department of Labor. Available from U.S. Government Printing Office. • Monthly. $55.00 per year. Formerly *Producer Price Indexes.*

Wholesale Commodity Report. Financial Times. • Weekly. $144.00 to $165.00 per year depending on postal rates.

STATISTICS SOURCES

Agricultural Statistics. Available from U. S. Government Printing Office. • Annual. $38.00. Produced by the National Agricultural Statistics Service, U. S. Department of Agriculture. Provides a wide variety of statistical data relating to agricultural production, supplies, consumption, prices/price-supports, foreign trade, costs, and returns, as well as farm labor, loans, income, and population. In many cases, historical data is shown annually for 10 years. In addition to farm data, includes detailed fishery statistics.

Economic Accounts for Agriculture. Organization for Economic Cooperation and Development. Available from OECD Publications and Information Center. • Annual. $59.00. Provides data for 14 years on agricultural output and its components, intermediate consumption, and gross value added to net income and capital formation. Relates to various commodities produced by OECD member countries.

FAO Production Yearbook. Available from Bernan Associates. • Annual. $45.00. Published by the Food and Agriculture Organization (http://www.fao.org). Contains worldwide data on agriculture, land use, farm crops, livestock, and agricultural prices.

FAO Quarterly Bulletin of Statistics. Food and Agriculture Organization of the United Nations. Available from UNIPUB. • Quarterly. $20.00 per year. Provides international data on agricultural production, trade, and prices, covering the major commodities of many countries. Text in English, French, and Spanish. Formerly *FAO Monthly Bulletin of Statistics.*

FAO Trade Yearbook. Available from Bernan Associates. • Annual. $45.00. Published by the Food and Agriculture Organization (http://www.fao.org). Provides extensive worldwide data on exports and imports of agricultural commodities, fertilizers, tractors, and pesticides. Includes more than 130 tables of detailed statistics.

Foreign Trade by Commodities (Series C). OECD Publications and Information Center. • Annual. $625.00. Five volumes. Presents detailed five-year export-import data for specific commodities in OECD member countries.

Industrial Commodity Statistics Yearbook. United Nations Dept. of Economic and Social Affairs. United Nations Publications. • Annual.

International Trade by Commodities Statistics. Organization for Economic Cooperation and Development. • Five times a year. $605.00 per year. Presents extensive, detailed statistical tables of OECD countries' imports and exports. Products are grouped by Standard International Trade Classification and by country.

Monthly Bulletin of Statistics. United Nations Publications. • Monthly. $295.00 per year. Provides current data for about 200 countries on a wide variety of economic, industrial, and demographic subjects. Compiled by United Nations Statistical Office.

Statistical Yearbook. United Nations Publications. • Annual. $125.00. Contains statistics for about 200 countries on a wide variety of economic, industrial,

and demographic topics. Compiled by United Nations Statistical Office.

TRADE/PROFESSIONAL ASSOCIATIONS

Futures Industry Association. 2001 Pennsylvania Ave. NW, Ste. 600, Washington, DC 20006. Phone: (202)466-5460 Fax: (202)296-3184 E-mail: info@futuresindustry.org • URL: http://www.futuresindustry.org • Acts as a principal spokesman for the futures and options industry. Represents all facets of the futures industry, including many international exchanges. Works to preserve the system of free and competitive markets by representing the interests of the industry in connection with legislative and regulatory issues.

New York Mercantile Exchange. World Financial Ctr., 1 N End Ave., New York, NY 10282-1101. Phone: 800-438-8616 or (212)299-2000 or (212)748-5265 Fax: (212)301-4700 E-mail: exchangeinfo@nymex.com • URL: http://www.nymex.com • Brokerage houses, businesses with commercial interests in commodities, and professional traders. Provides a mechanism for trading futures and options. Compiles trading statistics for public distribution. Operates library of government and trade publications related to commodity futures contracts currently traded. Maintains numerous committees.

COMMODITY EXCHANGES

See: COMMODITY FUTURES TRADING

COMMODITY FUTURES TRADING

GENERAL WORKS

Education of a Speculator. Victor Niederhoffer. John Wiley and Sons, Inc. • 1998. $18.95. An autobiography providing basic advice on speculation, investment, and the commodity futures market.

Futures Markets. A. G. Malliaris, editor. Edward Elgar Publishing, Inc. • 1997. $550.00. Three volumes. Consists of reprints of 70 articles dating from 1959 to 1993, on futures market volatility, speculation, hedging, stock indexes, portfolio insurance, interest rates, and foreign currencies. (International Library of Critical Writings in Financial Economics Series: No. 2).

Getting Started in Futures. Todd Lofton. John Wiley and Sons, Inc. • 2001. $19.95. Fourth edition. A general introduction to commodity and financial futures trading. Includes case studies and a glossary. (Getting Started in.... Series).

Inside the Financial Futures Markets. Mark Powers and Mark Castelino. John Wiley and Sons, Inc. • 1991. $55.00. Third edition. (Finance Series).

Trading to Win: The Psychology of Mastering the Markets. Ari Kiev. John Wiley and Sons, Inc. • 1998. $39.95. A mental health guide for stock, bond, and commodity traders. Tells how to keep speculative emotions in check, overcome self-doubt, and focus on a winning strategy. (Trading Series).

Wheels of Fortune: The History of Speculation from Scandal to Respectability. Charles R. Geisst. John Wiley and Sons, Inc. • 2002. $29.95. Provides a colorful history of speculation in the U. S. commodity futures markets from 1850 to about 2000.

ALMANACS AND YEARBOOKS

Commodity Trading Guide. Commodity Research Bureau. • Annual. $22.50. Serves as a concise "Almanac, Encyclopedia, Yearbook, and Calendar for the Futures Market." Includes many price charts, tables, government report dates, contract specifications, and price outlooks.

CRB Commodity Yearbook. Commodity Research

Bureau. CRB. • Annual. $99.95.

Irwin Business and Investment Almanac, 1994: Dow Jones and Company Edition. Summer N. Levine and Caroline Levine. McGraw-Hill. • 1994. $75.00. 18th edition. A review of last year's business activity. Covers a wide variety of business and economic data: stock market statistics, industrial information, commodity futures information, art market trends, comparative living costs for U. S. metropolitan areas, foreign stock market data, etc. Formerly *Business One Irwin Business and Investment Almanac.*

Supertrader's Almanac-Reference Manual: Reference Guide and Analytical Techniques for Investors. Frank A. Taucher. • 1991. $55.00. Explains technical methods for the trading of commodity futures, and includes data on seasonality, cycles, trends, contract characteristics, highs and lows, etc.

DIRECTORIES

Futures Magazine SourceBook: The Most Complete List of Exchanges, Companies, Regulators, Organizations, etc., Offering Products and Services to the Futures and Options Industry. Futures Magazine, Inc. • Annual. $19.50. Provides information on commodity futures brokers, trading method services, publications, and other items of interest to futures traders and money managers.

Handbook of World Stock and Commodity Exchanges. Blackwell Publishing. • Annual. $265.00. Provides detailed information on over 200 stock and commodity exchanges in more than 50 countries.

ENCYCLOPEDIAS AND DICTIONARIES

Encyclopedia of Chart Patterns. Thomas N. Bulkowski. John Wiley and Sons, Inc. • 2000. $79.95. Provides explanations of the predictive value of various chart patterns formed by stock and commodity price movements. (Trading Series).

International Encyclopedia of Futures and Options. Fitzroy Dearborn Publishers, Inc. • 2000. $285.00. Two volumes. Covers terminology, concepts, events, individuals, and markets.

HANDBOOKS AND MANUALS

Agricultural Options: Trading, Risk Management, and Hedging. Christopher A. Bobin. John Wiley and Sons, Inc. • 1990. $49.95. Practical advice on trading commodity futures options (puts and calls).

Commodity Trading Manual. Frank S. Rose, editor. AMACOM. • 1999. $55.00. Textbook and reference manual.

Derivatives: A Comprehensive Resource for Options, Futures, Interest Rate Swaps, and Mortgage Securities. Fred D. Arditti. Harvard Business School Publishing. • 1996. $60.00. Published by Harvard Business School Press. Provides detailed explanations of various kinds of financial derivatives (options, futures, swaps, etc.) and their trading tactics, uses, and risks. (Financial Management Association Survey and Synthesis Series).

Fibonacci Applications and Strategies for Traders. Robert Fischer. John Wiley and Sons, Inc. • 1993. $60.00. Provides a new look at the Elliott Wave Theory and Fibonacci numbers as applied to commodity prices, business cycles, and interest rate movements. (Traders Advantage Series).

Money Management Strategies for Futures Traders. Nauzer J. Balsara. John Wiley and Sons, Inc. • 1992. $75.00. How to limit risk and avoid catastrophic losses. (Finance Series).

Money Manager's Compliance Guide. Thompson Publishing Group, Inc. • $649.00 per year. Two looseleaf volumes. Monthly updates and newletters. Edited for investment advisers and investment companies to help them be in compliance with governmental regulations, including SEC rules, restrictions based on the Employee Retirement Income Security Act (ERISA), and regulations issued by the Commodity Futures Trading Commission (CFTC).

National Futures Association Manual. National Futures Association. • Quarterly. Price on application. Looseleaf service. Rules and regulations concerning commodity futures trading.

101 Rules of Trading Discipline. Pejman Hamidi. McGraw-Hill. • 2002. $39.95. Trading rules for investors or speculators are presented in three categories: "Trading Disciplines," "Market Disciplines," and "Personal Disciplines." (Teach Yourself Series).

Options: The International Guide to Valuation and Trading Strategies. Gordon Gemmill. McGraw-Hill. • 1992. $37.95. Covers valuation techniques for American, European, and Asian options. Trading strategies are discussed for options on currencies, stock indexes, interest rates, and commodities.

Trading for a Living: Psychology, Trading Tactics, Money Management. Alexander Elder. John Wiley and Sons, Inc. • 1993. $70.00. Covers technical and chart methods of trading in commodity and financial futures, options, and stocks. Includes Elliott Wave Theory, oscillators, moving averages, point-and-figure, and other technical approaches. (Finance Series).

INTERNET DATABASES

BanxQuote Banking, Mortgage, and Finance Center. BanxQuote, Inc. Phone: (914)722-1600 Fax: (914)722-6630 E-mail: info@banx.com • URL: http://www.banx.com • Web site quotes interest rates paid by banks around the country on various savings products, as well as rates paid by consumers for automobile loans, mortgages, credit cards, home equity loans, and personal loans. Also provided: stock quotes, indexes, stock options, futures trading data, economic indicators, and links to many other financial sites. Daily updates. Fees: Free.

Chicago Board of Trade: The World's Leading Futures Exchange. Chicago Board of Trade. Phone: (312)535-3500 Fax: (312)341-3392 E-mail: comments@cbot.com • URL: http://www.cbot.com • Web site provides a wide variety of statistics, commentary, charts, and news relating to both agricultural and financial futures trading. For example, Web page "MarketPlex: Information MarketPlace to the World" offers prices & volume, contract specifications & margins, government reports, etc. Searching is available, with daily updates for current data. Fees: Mostly free (some specialized services are fee-based).

CRB Markets Overview. Commodity Research Bureau. Phone: 800-621-5271 or (312)554-8456 Fax: (312)939-4135 E-mail: info@crbtrader.com • URL: http://www.crbtrader.com/data/ • Web site provides free, detailed, current price quotes for about 100 futures contracts, covering Currencies, Energies, Financials, Grains, Meats, Metals, "Softs" (orange juice, coffee, etc.) and stock price indexes. Includes contract specifications and detailed prices of options on futures.

Factiva. Dow Jones Reuters Business Interactive, LLC. Phone: 800-369-7466 or (609)452-1511 Fax: (609)520-5770 E-mail: solutions@factiva.com • URL: http://www.factiva.com • Fee-based Web site provides "global news and business information through Web sites and content integration solutions." Includes Dow Jones and Reuters newswires, The Wall Street Journal, and more than 7,000 other sources of current news, historical articles, market research reports, and investment analysis. Content includes 96 major U. S. newspapers, 900 non-English sources, trade publications, media transcripts, country profiles, news photos, etc.

Futures Online. Futures Magazine Inc. Phone: (312)846-4600 Fax: (312)846-4638 • URL: http://www.futuresmag.com • Web site presents updates of

Futures magazine and links to other futures-related sites.

Nexis.com. Lexis-Nexis Group. Phone: 800-227-4908 or (937)865-6800 Fax: (937)865-6909 E-mail: webmaster@prod.lexis-nexis.com • URL: http://www.nexis.com • Fee-based Web site offers searching of about 2.8 billion documents in some 30,000 news, business, and legal information sources. Features include a subject directory covering 1,200 topics in 34 categories and a Company Dossier containing information on more than 500,000 public and private companies. Boolean searching is offered.

Wall Street Journal Interactive Edition. Dow Jones & Co., Inc. Phone: 800-369-2834 or (212)416-2000 Fax: (212)416-2658 E-mail: inquiries@interactive.wsj.com • URL: http://www.wsj.com • Fee-based Web site providing online searching of worldwide information from the *The Wall Street Journal.* Includes "Company Snapshots," "The Journal's Greatest Hits," "Index to Market Data," "Journal Links," etc. Financial price quotes are available. Fees: $49.00 per year; $29.00 per year to print subscribers.

PERIODICALS AND NEWSLETTERS

Consensus: National Futures and Financial Weekly. Consensus, Inc. • Weekly. $365.00 per year. Newspaper. Contains news, statistics, and special reports relating to agricultural, industrial, and financial futures markets. Features daily basis price charts, reprints of market advice, and "The Consensus Index of Bullish Market Opinion" (charts show percent bullish of advisors for various futures).

CRB Futures Market Service. Commodity Research Bureau Inc. • Description: "Discusses developments that will affect the future status of supply, demand, and price movements for the different commodities traded on the futures markets.".

The Financial Post: Canadian's Business Voice. Financial Post Datagroup. • Daily. $200.00 per year. Provides Canadian business, economic, financial, and investment news. Features extensive price quotes from all major Canadian markets: stocks, bonds, mutual funds, commodities, and currencies. Supplement available: *Financial Post 500.* Includes annual supplement.

Futures and Derivatives Law Report: The Journal on the Law of Investment and Risk Management Products. Glasser Legalworks. • Monthly. $305.00 per year. Newsletter. Covers developments in regulation, legislation, and litigation concerning financial derivatives, futures trading, and options trading.

Futures Market Service. Commodity Research Bureau. • Weekly. $155.00 per year.

Futures: News, Analysis, and Strategies for Futures, Options, and Derivatives Traders. Futures Magazine. • Monthly. $39.00 per year. Edited for institutional money managers and traders, brokers, risk managers, and individual investors or speculators. Includes special feature issues on interest rates, technical indicators, currencies, charts, precious metals, hedge funds, and derivatives. Supplements available.

The Journal of Futures Markets. John Wiley and Sons, Inc., Journals. • Monthly. Institutions, $1,460.00 per year; with online edition, $1,533.00 per year.

Managed Account Reports: The Clearing House for Commodity Money Management. Managed Account Reports, Inc. • Monthly. $425.00 per year. Newsletter. Reviews the performance and other characteristics of commodity trading advisors and their commodity futures funds or managed accounts. Includes tables and graphs.

SFO: Stocks, Futures & Options. Wasendorf & Associates, Inc. • Monthly. $49.95 per year. Subtitle: *Official Journal for Personal Investing in Stocks, Futures, and Options.* Covers mainly speculative

techniques for stocks, commodity futures, financial futures, stock index futures, foreign exchange, short selling, and various kinds of options.

The Wall Street Journal. Dow Jones & Co., Inc. • Daily. $189.00 per year. Covers news and trends relating to business, industry, finance, the economy, and international commerce. Provides extensive price and other data for the securities, commodity, options, futures, foreign exchange, and money markets.

PRICE SOURCES

CRB Commodity Index Report. Commodity Research Bureau. • Weekly. $295.00 per year. Quotes the CRB Futures Price Index and the CRB Spot Market Index for the last five business days, plus the previous week, month, and year. Includes tables and graphs.

CRB Futures Perspective: Agricultural Edition. Commodity Research Bureau. • Weekly. $230.00 per year. Service provides comprehensive price charts for more than 20 agricultural commodity futures, from cocoa to wheat (includes lumber). Also provides technical analysis of price movements and market commentary. Formerly part of *CRB Futures Chart Service.*

STATISTICS SOURCES

Information, Finance, and Services USA. Gale Cengage Learning. • 2001. $240.00. Replaces *Service Industries USA* and *Finance, Insurance, and Real Estate USA.* Presents statistics and projections relating to economic activity in a wide variety of non-manufacturing areas.

Statistical Annual: Grains, Options on Agricultural Futures. Chicago Board of Trade. • Annual. Includes historical data on Wheat Futures, Options on Wheat Futures, Corn Futures, Options on Corn Futures, Oats Futures, Soybean Futures, Options on Soybean Futures, Soybean Oil Futures, Soybean Meal Futures.

Statistical Annual: Interest Rates, Metals, Stock Indices, Options on Financial Futures, Options on Metals Futures. Chicago Board of Trade. • Annual. Includes historical data on GNMA CDR Futures, Cash-Settled GNMA Futures, U. S. Treasury Bond Futures, U. S. Treasury Note Futures, Options on Treasury Note Futures, NASDAQ-100 Futures, Major Market Index Futures, Major Market Index MAXI Futures, Municipal Bond Index Futures, 1,000-Ounce Silver Futures, Options on Silver Futures, and Kilo Gold Futures.

TRADE/PROFESSIONAL ASSOCIATIONS

Coffee, Sugar and Cocoa Exchange. 1 N End Ave., New York, NY 10282-1101. Phone: (212)748-4000 E-mail: webmaster@nybot.com • URL: http://www.csce.com • Members are commodity traders.

National Futures Association. 300 S Riverside Plaza, No. 1800, Chicago, IL 60606-6615. Phone: 800-621-3570 or (312)781-1300 Fax: (312)781-1467 E-mail: information@nfa.futures.org • URL: http://www.nfa.futures.org • Futures commission merchants; commodity trading advisors; commodity pool operators; brokers and their associated persons. Works to: strengthen and expand industry self-regulation to include all segments of the futures industry; provide uniform standards to eliminate duplication of effort and conflict; remove unnecessary regulatory constraints to aid effective regulation. Conducts member qualification screening, financial surveillance, and registration. Monitors and enforces customer protection rules and uniform business standards. Maintains information center. Arbitrates customer disputes; audits non-exchange member FCM's.

New York Cotton Exchange. 1 N End Ave., 23-10 43rd Ave., New York, NY 10282-1101. Phone: 800-HED-GEIT or (212)748-4094 E-mail: webmaster@nybot.com • URL: http://www.nybot.com • Commodity exchange - cotton and frozen concentrated orange juice. Develops new products; provides market information; compiles statistics. Collaborates with the Citrus Associates of the +New York +Cotton Exchange; operates Financial Instruments Exchange, in conjunction with the New York Stock Exchange.

New York Mercantile Exchange. World Financial Ctr., 1 N End Ave., New York, NY 10282-1101. Phone: 800-438-8616 or (212)299-2000 or (212)748-5265 Fax: (212)301-4700 E-mail: exchangeinfo@nymex.com • URL: http://www.nymex.com • Brokerage houses, businesses with commercial interests in commodities, and professional traders. Provides a mechanism for trading futures and options. Compiles trading statistics for public distribution. Operates library of government and trade publications related to commodity futures contracts currently traded. Maintains numerous committees.

OTHER SOURCES

Commodity Futures Law Reports. CCH, Inc. • Semimonthly. $948.00 per year. Looseleaf service. Periodic supplementation. Includes legal aspects of financial futures and stock options trading.

Securities Litigation and Regulation Reporter: The National Journal of Record ofCommodities Litigation. Andrews Publications. • Semimonthly. $1,250.00 per year. Newsletter. Provides reports on litigation involving the rules and decisions of the Commodity Futures Trading Commission. Formerly *Securities and Commodities Litigation Reporter.*

COMMON MARKET

See: EUROPEAN MARKETS

COMMUNICATION

See also: BUSINESS CORRESPONDENCE; BUSINESS JOURNALISM; COMMUNICATION SYSTEMS; COMMUNICATIONS SATELLITES; COMPUTER COMMUNICATIONS; CORPORATION REPORTS; TELECOMMUNICATIONS

GENERAL WORKS

Business and Administrative Communication. Kitty O. Locker. McGraw-Hill. • 2003. Sixth edition. Price on application.

Business Communication. Betty S. Johnson and Marsha L. Bayless. Cengage Learning Custom Publishing. • 2001. $72.95. Third edition.

Business Communications. Sherron Bienvenu and Paul R. Timm. Prentice Hall PTR. • 2002. $90.00. Includes CD-ROM.

Business Communications Made Simple. Butterworth-Heinemann. • Date not set. Price on application.

Business English. Mary E. Guffey. South-Western. • 2001. $78.95. Seventh edition. (South-Western College Busines Communications Series).

Contemporary Business Communication. Scot Ober. Houghton Mifflin Co. • 2003. $106.36. Fifth edition.

Crisis Response: Inside Stories on Managing Image Under Siege. Gale Cengage Learning. • 1993. $80.00. Presents first-hand accounts by media relations professionals of major business crises and how they were handled. Topics include the following kinds of crises: environmental, governmental, corporate image, communications, and product.

Interface Culture: How New Technology Transforms the Way We Create and Communicate. Steven Johnson. HarperSanFrancisco. • 1997. $24.00. A discussion of how computer interfaces and online technology ("cyberspace") affect society in general.

Introduction to Mass Communication. Phillip H. Agee. Addison-Wesley. • 2000. 13th edition. Price on application.

ABSTRACTS AND INDEXES

Communication Abstracts: An International Information Service. Sage Publications, Inc. • Bimonthly. Institutions, $1,150.00 per year. Provides broad coverage of the literature of communications, including broadcasting and advertising.

Psychological Abstracts. American Psychological Association. • Monthly. Members, $815.00 per year; individuals and institutions, $1,207.00 per year. Covers the international literature of psychology and the behavioral sciences. Includes journals, technical reports, dissertations, and other sources.

Social Sciences Citation Index. Thomson/ISI. • Three times a year. $6,900 per year. Annual cumulation. Includes *Source Index, Citation Index, Permuterm Subject Index,* and *Corporate Index.*

Social Sciences Index. H. W. Wilson Co. • Quarterly, with annual cumulation. Price varies. Indexes more than 400 periodicals covering economics, environmental policy, government, insurance, labor, health care policy, plannning, public administration, public welfare, urban studies, women's issues, criminology, and related topics.

ALMANACS AND YEARBOOKS

Communication Yearbook. International Communication Association. • Annual. Membership.

CD-ROM DATABASES

Social Sciences Citation Index. ISI. • Monthly. Price on request. Provides CD-ROM indexing of articles appearing in 1700 leading social science journals worldwide, with additional selections from more than 5700 other journals. Time span is 1992 to date. Coverage includes economics, business, finance, management, communications, demographics, library and information science, political science, sociology, and many other subjects.

Social Sciences Citation Index. ISI. • Monthly. Price on request. Provides CD-ROM indexing of articles appearing in 1700 leading social science journals worldwide, with additional selections from more than 5700 other journals. Time span is 1992 to date. Coverage includes economics, business, finance, management, communications, demographics, library and information science, political science, sociology, and many other subjects.

Social Sciences Citation Index: Compact Disc Edition with Abstracts. Institute for Scientific Information. • Monthly. Provides CD-ROM indexing and abstracting of "significant articles" from 1,700 social science journals worldwide, with additional selections from 3,200 other journals, 1986 to date. Includes economics, business, finance, management, communications, demographics, information and library science, political science, sociology, and many other subjects.

WILSONDISC: Wilson Business Abstracts. H. W. Wilson Co. • Monthly. Includes unlimited online access to *Wilson Business Abstracts* through WILSONLINE. Provides CD-ROM "cover-to-cover" abstracting and indexing of over 600 prominent business periodicals. Indexing is from 1982, abstracting from 1990. (*Business Periodicals Index* without abstracts is available on CD-ROM at $1,495 per year.).

WILSONDISC: Wilson Social Sciences Abstracts. H. W. Wilson Co. • Monthly. Includes unlimited online access to *Social Sciences Index* through WILSONLINE. Provides CD-ROM indexing from 1983 and abstracting from 1994 of more than 500 periodicals covering economics, area studies, community health, public administration, public welfare,

urban studies, and many other topics related to the social sciences.

ENCYCLOPEDIAS AND DICTIONARIES

Blackwell Encyclopedic Dictionary of Organizational Behavior. Nigel Nicholson, editor. Blackwell Publishing. • 1997. $130.95. The editor is associated with the London Business School. Contains definitions of key terms combined with longer articles written by various U. S. and foreign business educators. Includes bibliographies and index. *Blackwell Encyclopedia of Management Series.*

Dictionary of Bibliometrics. Virgil Diodato. Haworth Press, Inc. • 1994. $39.95. Contains detailed explanations of 225 terms, with references. (Bibliometrics is "the application of mathematical and statistical techniques to the study of publishing and professional communication.").

Encyclopedia of Communication and Information. Available from Gale Cengage Learning. • 2001. $395.00. Three volumes. Published by Macmillan Reference USA.

Hargrave's Communications Dictionary. Frank Hargrave. Available from John Wiley and Sons, Inc. • 2001. $140.00. Published by IEEE. Contains more than 10,000 definitions relating to voice and data communications, plus definitions in the areas of computer science, optics, networks, and the Internet. Includes acronyms, charts, equations, and drawings.

HANDBOOKS AND MANUALS

Business English: A Complete Guide to Developing an Effective Business Writing Style. Andrea B. Geffner. Barron's Educational Series, Inc. • 2004. $16.95. Fourth edition. Covers both traditional and electronic business communication.

Gower Handbook of Internal Communications. Eileen Scholes, editor. Ashgate Publishing Co. • 1997. $124.95. Consists of 38 chapters written by various authors, with case studies. Covers more than 45 communication techniques, "from team meetings to web sites." Published by Gower in England.

Handbook of Interpersonal Communication. Mark L. Knapp and John A. Daly. Sage Publications, Inc. • 2003. $115.00. Third edition. Includes "Computer Mediated Communications and Relationships.".

Lesly's Handbook of Public Relations and Communications. Philip Lesly. McGraw-Hill. • 1997. $100.00. Fifth edition.

Personnel Management: Communications. Prentice Hall PTR. • Looseleaf. Periodic supplementation. Price on application. Includes how to write effectively and how to prepare employee publications.

ONLINE DATABASES

PsycINFO. American Psychological Association. • Provides indexing and abstracting of the worldwide literature of psychology and the behavioral sciences. Time period is 1967 to date, with monthly updates. Inquire as to online cost and availability.

Social Scisearch. Institute for Scientific Information. • Broad, multidisciplinary index to the literature of the social sciences, 1972 to present. Weekly updates. Worldwide coverage. Inquire as to online cost and availability.

Wilson Business Abstracts Online. H. W. Wilson Co. • Indexes and abstracts 600 major business periodicals, plus the *Wall Street Journal* and the business section of the *New York Times.* Indexing is from 1982, abstracting from 1990, with the two newspapers included from 1993. Updated weekly. Inquire as to online cost and availability. (*Business Periodicals Index* without abstracts is also available online.).

Wilson Social Sciences Abstracts Online. H. W. Wilson Co. • Provides online abstracting and indexing of more than 500 periodicals covering area studies, community health, public administration, public welfare, urban studies, and many other social science topics. Time period is 1994 to date for abstracts and 1983 to date for indexing, with updates weekly. Inquire as to online cost and availability.

PERIODICALS AND NEWSLETTERS

Business Communication Quarterly. Association for Business Communication. • Quarterly. Members, $65.00 per year; institutions, $160.00 per year. Features articles about teaching and writing course outlines. Description of training programs, problems, soutions, etc. Includes *Journal of Business Communcation.*

Business Communications Review. Key3Media Group, Inc. • Monthly. $45.00 per year. Edited for communications managers in large end-user companies and institutions. Includes special feature issues on intranets and network management.

Communication Briefings: A Monthly Idea Source for Decision Makers. Briefings Publishing Group. • Monthly. $139.00 per year. Newsletter. Presents useful ideas for communication, public relations, customer service, human resources, and employee training.

Communication Research. Sage Publications, Inc. • Bimonthly. Institutions, $599.00 per year.

Communication World: The Magazine for Communication Professionals. International Association of Business Communicators. • Seven times a year. Free to members; libraries, $95.00 per year. Emphasis is on public relations, media relations, corporate communication, and writing.

Communications News. Nelson Publishing Co. • Monthly. Free to qualified personnel; others, $84.00 per year.

Communications News: Solutions for Today's Networking Decision Managers. Nelson Publishing, Inc. • Monthly. Free to qualified personnel; others, $84.00 per year. Includes coverage of "Internetworking" and "Intranetworking." Emphasis is on emerging telecommunications technologies.

The Customer Communicator. The Customer Service Group. • Description: Serves as a guideline for customer relations skills while it "boosts morale." Covers customer representative skills and provides tips on customer contact, handling complaints, checklists, and promotional contests. **Remarks:** a monthly training module.

Harvard Management Communication Letter. Harvard Business School Publishing. • Description: Provides information and techniques for managers on effective communication.

Homeland Security and Defense: Weekly Intelligence for the Global Homeland Security and Defense Community. Aviation Week Business Intelligence Services. • Weekly. $595.00 per year. Newsletter. Emphasis is on airline and airport programs (federal, state, and local). Also covers counterterrorism, protection of military units, Department of Homeland Security activities, industrial security, communications equipment, and other topics related to homeland security.

Human Communication Research. International Communication Association. Oxford University Press, Journals. • Quarterly. Institutions, $294.00 per year; with online edition, $309.00 per year. A scholarly journal of interpersonal communication.

Journal of Business and Technical Communication. Sage Publications, Inc. • Institutions, $445.00 per year; includes print and online editions.

Journal of Business Communication. Association for Business Communication. • Quarterly. Individuals, $65.00 per year; insititutions, $160.00 per year. Includes *Association for Business Communiation Bulletin.*

Management Communication Quarterly: An International Journal. Sage Publications, Inc. • Quarterly. Institutions, $515.00 per year; includes

print and online editions. A scholarly journal on managerial and organizational communication effectiveness.

9-1-1 Magazine: Public Safety Communications and Response. Official Publications, Inc. • Bimonthly. $29.95 per year. Covers technical information and applications for public safety communications personnel.

PR Reporter: The Newsletter of Behavioral Public Relations, Public Affairs, and Communication Strategies. Lawrence Ragan Communications, Inc. • Weekly. $250.00 per year. Newsletter. Presents a "digest of theories, research, public opinion, case studies, and successful public relations techniques.".

Presentations: Technology and Techniques for Effective Communication. VNU Business Media. • Monthly. Free to qualified personnel; others, $69.00 per year. Covers the use of presentation hardware and software, including audiovisual equipment and computerized display systems. Includes an annual "Buyers Guide to Presentation Products.".

The Successful Benefits Communicator. Lawrence Ragan Communications Inc. • Description: Offers ideas, techniques, and tips for those who communicate benefits information.

Written Communication: A Quarterly Journal of Research, Theory, and Application. Sage Publications, Inc. • Quarterly. Institutions, $499.00 per year; includes print and online editions.

RESEARCH CENTERS AND INSTITUTES

East-West Center. 1601 East-West Rd., Honolulu, HI 96848-1601. Phone: (808)944-7111 Fax: (808)944-7376 E-mail: ewcinfo@eastwestcenter.org • URL: http://www.eastwestcenter.org.

STATISTICS SOURCES

AM/FM Broadcast Financial Data/TV Broadcast Financial Data. U.S. Federal Communications Commission. • Annual. Free.

World Factbook. U.S. National Technical Information Service. • Annual. $83.00. Prepared by the Central Intelligence Agency. For all countries of the world, provides current economic, demographic, geographic, communications, government, defense force, and illicit drug trade information (where applicable).

TRADE/PROFESSIONAL ASSOCIATIONS

Association for Business Communication. Baruch College, Communications Studies, One Bernard Baruch Way, New York, NY 10010. Phone: (646)312-3726 Fax: (646)349-5297 E-mail: abcrjm@cs.com • URL: http://www.theabc.org.

International Association of Business Communicators. One Hallidie Plaza, Suite 600, San Francisco, CA 94102-2818. Phone: (415)544-4700 Fax: (415)544-4747 E-mail: service_centre@iabc.com • URL: http://www.iabc.com.

International Institute of Communications. 24-25 Nutford Pl., London WH1 5YN, England. Phone: 44 207 3239622 Fax: 44 207 3239623 E-mail: enquiries@iicom.org • URL: http://www. iicom.org.

Society for Technical Communication. 901 N. Stuart St., Suite 904, Arlington, VA 22203-1822. Phone: (703)522-4114 Fax: (703)522-2075 E-mail: stc@stc.org • URL: http://www.stc.org • Formerly Society of Technical Writers and Publishers.

OTHER SOURCES

Commodities Regulation: Fraud, Manipulation, and Other Claims. Jerry W. Markham. West Group. • Semiannual. $567.00 per year. Two looseleaf volumes. $250.00. Covers the commodity futures trading prohibitions of the Commodity Exchange Act. (Securities Law Series).

COMMUNICATION, COMPUTER

See: COMPUTER COMMUNICATIONS

COMMUNICATION EQUIPMENT INDUSTRY

See: TELECOMMUNICATIONS; TELEPHONE INDUSTRY

COMMUNICATION, MASS

See: MASS MEDIA

COMMUNICATION SYSTEMS

See also: COMPUTERS; TELECOMMUNICATIONS

GENERAL WORKS

Analog and Digital Communications. Hwei P. Hsu. McGraw-Hill. • 2003. $16.95. Second edition. (Schaum's Outlines Series).

ABSTRACTS AND INDEXES

Electronics and Communications Abstracts Journal: Comprehensive Coverage of Essential Scientific Literature. CSA. • Monthly. $1,665.00 per year. Includes print and online editions.

ALMANACS AND YEARBOOKS

OECD Communications Outlook. OECD Publications and Information Center. • Annual. $104.00. Provides international coverage of yearly telecommunications activity. Includes charts, graphs, and maps.

CD-ROM DATABASES

Datapro on CD-ROM: Communications Analyst. Gartner Group, Inc. • Monthly. Price on application. Provides detailed information on products and services for communications systems, including local area networks and voice systems.

DIRECTORIES

Major Information Technology Companies of the World 2001. Available from Gale Cengage Learning. • Annual. $880.00. Published by Graham & Whiteside. Contains profiles of more than 3,100 leading information technology companies in various countries.

Plunkett's E-Commerce and Internet Business Almanac. Plunkett Research, Ltd. • Annual. $249.99. Contains detailed profiles of 250 large companies engaged in various areas of Internet commerce, including e-business Web sites, communications equipment manufacturers, and Internet service providers. Includes CD-ROM.

Telecommunications Directory. Gale. • Covers: Two volumes-North America and International, Cover approximately 6,000 national and international voice and data communications networks, electronic mail services, teleconferencing facilities and services, facsimile services, Internet access providers, videotex and teletext operations, transactional services, local area networks, audiotex services, microwave systems/networkers, satellite facilities, and others involved in telecommunications, including related consultants, advertisers/marketers; associations, regulatory bodies, and publishers. Entries include: Company or organization name, address, phone, fax, year established, name and title of contact, executive officers and board of directors, function or type of service; geographical area served; NAICS and SIC codes; number of employees; general description, including telecommunications-related activities; product/service; specific applications; means of access and equipment required; publications; intended market and availability; pricing; stock exchanges traded and ticker symbols; financial figures.

Telehealth Buyer's Guide. Miller Freeman. • Annual. $10.00. Lists sources of telecommunications and information technology products and services for the health care industry.

ENCYCLOPEDIAS AND DICTIONARIES

Acronyms of Computer Science and Communications: A Comprehensive Acronym Dictionary and Illustrated Encyclopedia. Enjob Kajan and Ejub Kajan. Springer Verlag. • 2002. $49.95. Explains more than 4,000 "broadly used" computer, telecommunications, and information technology acronyms. Includes illustrations and Web addresses, where applicable.

Encyclopedia of New Media: An Essential Reference to Communication and Technology. Steve Jones, editor. Sage Publications, Inc. • 2003. $125.00. Contains more than 250 entries dealing with such areas as multimedia, broadband access, information communication technology (ICT), content filtering, wireless networks, and cyberethics.

HANDBOOKS AND MANUALS

Business Multimedia Explained: A Manager's Guide to Key Terms and Concepts. Peter G. W. Keen. Harvard Business School Publishing. • 1997. $39.95.

Reference Manual for Telecommunications Engineering. Roger L. Freeman. John Wiley and Sons, Inc. • 2001. $695.00. Third edition. Two volumes. Presents detailed information and specific data on the most commonly used telecommunications standards.

ONLINE DATABASES

INSPEC. Institution of Electrical Engineers (IEE). • Provides online citations, with abstracts, to the world literature of electrical engineering, electronics, optoelectronics, telecommunications, industrial controls, instrumentation, computer technology, information technology, and physics. Coverage includes more than 4,000 technical and scientific journals from 1969 to date, with weekly updating. (INSPEC is Information Services in Physics, Electronics, and Computing.) Inquire as to online cost and availability.

PERIODICALS AND NEWSLETTERS

C E D: The Premier Magazine of Technology. Reed Business Information. • Monthly. $54.00 per year. Formerly *Communications Engineering and Design.*

Call Center. CMP Media LLC. • Monthly. Free to qualified personnel. Emphasis is on telemarketing, selling, and customer service. Includes articles on communication technology. Formerly *Call Center Solutions.*

CC News: The Business Newspaper for Call Center and Customer Care Professionals. United Publications, Inc. • Monthly. Free to qualified personnel; others, $60.00 per year. Includes news of call center technical developments.

IEEE Transactions on Communications. Institute of Electrical and Electronics Engineers, Inc. • Monthly. $600.00 per year.

Poptronics. Gernsback Publications, Inc. • Monthly. $19.99 per year. Incorporates *Electronics Now.*

RCR Wireless News: The Newspaper for the Wireless Communications Industry. Crain Communications. • Weekly. $64.00 per year. Covers news of the wireless communications industry, including business and financial developments. Formerly *RCR.*

Telecommunications Reports. • Weekly. Institutions, $1,695.00 per year. Includes *TR Daily.* Regulatory newsletter.

Telecons. Applied Business Telecommunications. • Bimonthly. $30.00 per year. Topics include teleconferencing, videoconferencing, distance learning, telemedicine, and telecommuting.

Wireless Review: Intelligence for Competitive Providers. Primedia Business Magazines and Media. • Semimonthly. $48.00 per year. Covers business and technology developments for wireless service providers. Includes special issues on a wide variety of wireless topics. Formed by merger of *Cellular Business* and *Wireless World.*

RESEARCH CENTERS AND INSTITUTES

Communications and Signal Processing Laboratory. University of Michigan. 4110 EECS Bldg., 1301 Beal Ave., Ann Arbor, MI 48109-2122. Phone: (734)763-0390 Fax: (734)763-8041 E-mail: stark@eecs.umich.edu • URL: http://www.eecs.umich.edu/systems.

Institute for Systems Research. University of Maryland at College Park, A. V. Williams Bldg., 2nd Fl., No. 115, College Park, MD 20742-3311. Phone: (301)405-6615 Fax: (301)314-9220 E-mail: isr@isr.umd.edu • URL: http://www.isr.umd.edu/ • A National Science Foundation Engineering Research Center. Areas of research include communication systems, manufacturing systems, chemical process systems, artificial intelligence, and systems integration.

Laboratory for Information and Decision Systems. Massachusetts Institute of Technology, 127 Massachusetts Ave., Bldg. 35, Room 308, Cambridge, MA 02139-4307. Phone: (617)258-8222 Fax: (617)253-3578 E-mail: chan@mit.edu • URL: http://www.justice.mit.edu • Research areas include data communication networks and fiber optic networks.

Space, Telecommunications and Radioscience Laboratory. Stanford University. David Packard Electrical and Engineering Bldg., Room 355, Stanford, CA 94305-9515. Phone: (650)723-4994 Fax: (650)723-9251 E-mail: inan@nova.stanford.edu • URL: http://www.nova.stanford.edu.

STATISTICS SOURCES

Communication Equipment, and Other Electronic Systems and Equipment. U. S. Bureau of the Census. • Annual. Provides data on shipments: value, quantity, imports, and exports. (Current Industrial Reports, MA-36P.).

Electronic Market Data Book. Consumer Electronics Association. • Annual. Price on application.

OECD Information Technology Outlook 2000: ICTs, E-Commerce and the Information Economy. Organization for Economic Cooperation and Development. • 2000. $72.00. Provides data on information and communications technology (ICT) and electronic commerce in 11 OECD nations (includes U. S.). Coverage includes network infrastructure, electronic payment systems, financial transaction technologies, intelligent agents, global navigation systems, and portable flat panel display technologies.

TRADE/PROFESSIONAL ASSOCIATIONS

Armed Forces Communications and Electronics Association. 4400 Fair Lakes Court, Fairfax, VA 22033. Phone: 800-336-4583 or (703)631-6100 Fax: (703)631-4693 E-mail: promo@afcea.org • URL: http://www.afcea.org.

Interactive Multimedia and Collaborative Communications Alliance. PO Box 756, Syosset, NY 11791-0756. Phone: (516)818-8184 Fax: (516)922-2170 E-mail: staff@imcca.org • URL: http://www.imcca.org • Members are vendors and users of teleconferencing equipment. Formerly International Teleconferencing Association.

TCA - The Information Technology and Telecommunications Association-Sacramento Valley. PO Box 278076, Sacramento, CA 95827-8076. Phone:
(916)845-3140 Fax: (916)845-3140 E-mail: shirley.helfand@ftb.ca.gov • URL: http://www.tca.org.

COMMUNICATIONS SATELLITES

See also: TELECOMMUNICATIONS

GENERAL WORKS

Principles of Communications Satellites. Gary D. Gordon and Walter L. Morgan. John Wiley and Sons, Inc. • 1993. $130.00.

Satellite Communications: The First Quarter Century of Service. David W. Rees. John Wiley and Sons, Inc. • 1990. $130.00. A survey of the history of communications satellites, emphasizing business applications. (Telecommunications and Signal Processing Series).

ABSTRACTS AND INDEXES

NTIS Alerts: Communication. National Technical Information Service. • Semimonthly. $210.00 per year. . Provides descriptions of government-sponsored research reports and software, with ordering information. Covers common carriers, satellites, radio/TV equipment, telecommunication regulations, and related subjects.

DIRECTORIES

International Satellite Directory: A Complete Guide to the Satellite Communications Industry. Satnews Publishers. • Annual. $395.00. Lists over 25,000 satellite operators, common carriers, earth stations, manufacturers, associations, etc.

Major Telecommunications Companies of the World. Available from Gale Cengage Learning. • 2003. $885.00. Sixth edition. Published by Graham & Whiteside. Contains detailed information and trade names for more than 3,500 important telecommunications companies in various countries.

Phillips Satellite Industry Directory. PBI Media LLC. • Annual. $267.00. Provides information for more than 5,800 contacts and 2,000 providers of equipment and services for the satellite communications industry.

Phillips World Satellite Almanac. Access Intelligence L.L.C. • Covers: all commercial satellite systems and operators (operational and planned), booking contacts, PTT decision makers, and transponder brokers. Entries include: Owner/operator/system name, corporate contact, booking contact, public relations contact, tariff information or lease price, remarks, TT&C stations, satellites, transponder details.

ENCYCLOPEDIAS AND DICTIONARIES

Jones Dictionary of Cable Television Terminology, Including Related Computer and Satellite Definitions. Glenn R. Jones. Jones Twenty-First Century Ltd. • 1988. $14.95. Third edition.

HANDBOOKS AND MANUALS

Satellite Broadcasting: The Politics and Implications of the New Media. Ralph M. Negrine, editor. Taylor & Francis. • 1988. $65.00. Second edition.

Video Engineering. Arch Luther and Andrew Inglis. McGraw-Hill. • 2000. $65.00. Third edition. Covers such topics as digital postproduction technology, streaming video on the Internet, digital HDTV, digital cameras, and satellite TV systems.

PERIODICALS AND NEWSLETTERS

Communications Daily: The Authoritative News Service of Electronic Communications. Warren Publishing, Inc. • Daily. $3,006.00 per year. Newsletter. Covers telecommunications, including the telephone industry, broadcasting, cable TV, satellites, data communications, and electronic publishing. Features corporate and industry news.

Satellite News: The Monthly Newsletter Covering

Management, Marketing Technology and Regulation. PBI Media, Inc. • 50 times a year. $1,097.00 per year. Newsletter. Covers business applications in space, including remote sensing and satellites. Incorporates (Space Business News).

Satellite Week: The Authoritative News Service for Satellite Communications and Allied Fields. Warren Publishing, Inc. • Weekly. $495.00 per year. Newsletter. Covers satellite broadcasting, telecommunications, and the industrialization of space.

Via Satellite. PBI Media, LLC. • Monthly. $49.00 per year. Covers the communications satellite industry.

Wireless Week. Reed Business Information. • 50 times a year. $99.00 per year. Covers news of cellular telephones, mobile radios, communications satellites, microwave transmission, and the wireless industry in general. Includes annual *Directory*.

RESEARCH CENTERS AND INSTITUTES

Applied Research Laboratories. University of Texas at Austin. University Station, P.O. Box 8029, Austin, TX 78713-8029. Phone: (512)835-3200 Fax: (512)835-3529 E-mail: penrod@arlut.utexas.edu • URL: http://www.arlut.utexas.edu.

Center for Space Research. Massachusetts Institute of Technology. 77 Massachusetts Ave., Room 37-241, Cambridge, MA 02139-4307. Phone: (617)253-7501 Fax: (617)253-8111 E-mail: csr@space.mit.edu • URL: http://www.space.mit.edu.

Engineering Experiment Station. Ohio State University. 2070 Neil Ave., Columbus, OH 43210-1275. Phone: (614)292-3149 Fax: (614)292-9615 E-mail: fortner.1@osu.edu • URL: http://www.osu.edu.

Space Institute. University of Tennessee. B.H. Goethert Parkway, Tullahoma, TN 37388-9700. Phone: (931)393-7213 Fax: (931)393-7211 E-mail: tmccay@utsi.edu • URL: http://www.utsi.edu.

Space, Telecommunications and Radioscience Laboratory. Stanford University. David Packard Electrical and Engineering Bldg., Room 355, Stanford, CA 94305-9515. Phone: (650)723-4994 Fax: (650)723-9251 E-mail: inan@nova.stanford.edu • URL: http://www.nova.stanford.edu.

STATISTICS SOURCES

U. S. Industry and Trade Outlook. Available from National Technical Information Service. • Annual. $69.95. Produced by the International Trade Administration, U. S. Department of Commerce, in a "public-private" partnership with DRI/McGraw-Hill and Standard & Poor's. Provides basic data, outlook for the current year, and "Long-Term Prospects" (five-year projections) for a wide variety of products and services. Includes high technology industries. Formerly *U. S. Industrial Outlook*.

TRADE/PROFESSIONAL ASSOCIATIONS

International Telecommunications Satellite Organization. 3400 International Dr., N.W., Washington, DC 20008. Phone: (202)243-5096 Fax: (202)243-5018 • URL: http://www.itso.int.

OTHER SOURCES

Telecommunications Regulation: Cable, Broadcasting, Satellite, and the Internet. LexisNexis Matthew Bender. • Semiannual. $826.00. Four looseleaf volumes. Covers local, state, and federal regulation, with emphasis on the Telecommunications Act of 1996. Includes regulation of television, telephone, cable, satellite, computer communication, and on-line services. Formerly *Cable Television Law*.

Wireless Data Networks. Gupta. Prentice Hall PTR. • 2000. Price on application. Presents market research information relating to cellular data networks, paging networks, packet radio networks, satellite systems, and other areas of wireless communication. Contains "summaries of recent developments and trends in wireless markets.".

COMMUNITY ANTENNA TELEVISION

See: CABLE TELEVISION INDUSTRY

COMMUNITY CHESTS

See: COMMUNITY FUNDS

COMMUNITY COLLEGES

See: JUNIOR COLLEGES

COMMUNITY DEVELOPMENT

See also: PLANNING; URBAN DEVELOPMENT

GENERAL WORKS

Housing the Poor: An Overview. Morton J. Schussheim. Nova Science Publishers, Inc. • 2003. $29.50. Discusses currrent and emerging housing problems affecting the poor. Covers housing rehabilitation programs, community development block grants, and other programs for low-income households.

Placemaking: The Art and Practice of Building Communities. Lynda H. Schneekloth and Robert G. Shibley. John Wiley and Sons, Inc. • 1995. $70.00.

ABSTRACTS AND INDEXES

Social Sciences Index. H. W. Wilson Co. • Quarterly, with annual cumulation. Price varies. Indexes more than 400 periodicals covering economics, environmental policy, government, insurance, labor, health care policy, plannning, public administration, public welfare, urban studies, women's issues, criminology, and related topics.

CD-ROM DATABASES

Social Sciences Citation Index. ISI. • Monthly. Price on request. Provides CD-ROM indexing of articles appearing in 1700 leading social science journals worldwide, with additional selections from more than 5700 other journals. Time span is 1992 to date. Coverage includes economics, business, finance, management, communications, demographics, library and information science, political science, sociology, and many other subjects.

Social Sciences Citation Index: Compact Disc Edition with Abstracts. Institute for Scientific Information. • Monthly. Provides CD-ROM indexing and abstracting of "significant articles" from 1,700 social science journals worldwide, with additional selections from 3,200 other journals, 1986 to date. Includes economics, business, finance, management, communications, demographics, information and library science, political science, sociology, and many other subjects.

WILSONDISC: Wilson Social Sciences Abstracts. H. W. Wilson Co. • Monthly. Includes unlimited online access to *Social Sciences Index* through WILSONLINE. Provides CD-ROM indexing from 1983 and abstracting from 1994 of more than 500 periodicals covering economics, area studies, community health, public administration, public welfare, urban studies, and many other topics related to the social sciences.

DIRECTORIES

Funding Sources for Community and Economic Development 2003-2004: A Guide to Current Sources for Local Programs and Projects. Greenwood Publishing Group, Inc. • 2003. $64.95. Sixth edition. Provides information on 2,600 funding sources. Includes "A Guide to Proposal

Planning." (Funding Sources for Community and Economic Development Series).

HANDBOOKS AND MANUALS

New Uses for Obsolete Buildings. Urban Land Institute. • 1996. $65.95. Covers various aspects of redevelopment: zoning, building codes, environment, economics, financing, and marketing. Includes eight case studies and 75 descriptions of completed "adaptive use projects.".

Zoning and Planning Law Handbook. West Group. • $264.50.

ONLINE DATABASES

Magazine Index. Gale Cengage Learning. • General magazine indexing (popular literature), 1973 to present. Daily updates. Inquire as to online cost and availability.

Wilson Social Sciences Abstracts Online. H. W. Wilson Co. • Provides online abstracting and indexing of more than 500 periodicals covering area studies, community health, public administration, public welfare, urban studies, and many other social science topics. Time period is 1994 to date for abstracts and 1983 to date for indexing, with updates weekly. Inquire as to online cost and availability.

PERIODICALS AND NEWSLETTERS

Community Development Digest: Semi-Monthly Report on Development, Planning, Inf structure Financing. Community Services Development, Inc. CD Publications. • Semimonthly. $483.00 per year. Newsletter.

Community Journal. Community Service Inc. • Description: Aims to promote the small community as a basic social institution. Publishes articles pertaining to community life with an emphasis on small towns, neighborhoods, rural life, and intentional communities. Discusses economics, education, land trusts, and other related issues. Recurring features include announcements of conferences, resources, an other events, letters to the editor, and news of the activities of the Service.

International Society for Community Development Newsletter. • Semiannual. Membership.

Ledger Quarterly: A Financial Review for Community Association Practitioners. Community Associations Institute. • Quarterly. $67.00 per year. Newsletter. Provides current information on issues affecting the finances of condominium, cooperative, homeowner, apartment, and other community housing associations.

Zoning and Planning Law Report. West Group. • Monthly. $483.00 per year. Newsletter.

RESEARCH CENTERS AND INSTITUTES

Institute of Cultural Affairs. c/o ICA Counterpoints, 4750 N. Sheridan Rd., Chicago, IL 60640. Phone: (773)769-6363 Fax: (773)769-1144 E-mail: dmcicac@igc.apc.org • URL: http://www.ica-usa.org.

Midwest Research Institute. Midwest Research Institute. 425 Volker Blvd., Kansas City, MO 64110-2241. Phone: (816)753-7600 Fax: (816)753-8420 E-mail: info@mriresearch.org • URL: http://www.mriresearch.org • Conducts research, development, and engineering activities in the major areas of health, chemistry, the environment, national security and defense, agriculture and food safety, and technology. Specific interests in the health area are pharmaceutical development and regulatory support, vaccine development, preclinical toxicology, metabolism studies, integrated clinical and preclinical drug development support, phytochemicals and designer foods, pesticide product registration support, chemistry support for toxicology, biotechnology, immunoassay development, DNA assay development, proteomics, high through-put automated assay systems, nanotechnology, food safety, seed technology, antibody production, biosensor development, electromagnetic field effects, neurobehavioral toxicology, reversal theory, and health risk behavior. In the field of chemistry, MRI focuses on analytical chemistry methods, including method development, improvement, validation, and application for programs involving immunoanalytical chemistry, exposure assessment, biological monitoring, industrial hygiene, environmental monitoring, chemical surety, site remediation, demilitarization, atmospheric chemistry, and product analysis of foods, consumer and commercial products, drinking water, and other materials. Environmental programs address environmental measurements, emission inventory development, emission factor development, modeling, water quality, waste minimization, pollution prevention, environmental control strategy development, process analysis and industry profiling, nonpoint source pollution, ambient air toxics, indoor air quality, industrial hygiene, multimedia environmental sampling and analysis, environmental impact assessment, facility assessment, environmental audits, waste processing and characterization, waste combustion, solar soil detoxification, risk analysis, regulatory support, policy analysis, cooling tower performance testing, permitting assistance, and tank and pipeline management. Technology areas include thermo electrics, microclimate conditioning systems, industrial systems evaluation, safety engineering, engineering design, prototype development, bench-scale testing, technology testing, dental biomaterial formulation, dental polymer development, pipeline coating technology, deicing chemical evaluation, traffic engineering, economic impact assessment, financial and business analysis, economic development, strategic planning, international programs, instructional material development, training program design and presentation, technology transfer, etc.

Regional Developement Services. East Carolina University. Willis Bldg., 300 E. First St., Greenville, NC 27858-4353. Phone: (252)328-6650 Fax: (252)328-4356 E-mail: deliaa@mail.ecu.edu • URL: http://www.ecu.edu/rds.

Urban Land Institute. Urban Land Institute. 1025 Thomas Jefferson St. NW, Ste. 500 W, Washington, DC 20007. Phone: (202)624-7000 Fax: (202)624-7140 E-mail: customerservice@uli.org • URL: http://www.uli.org • Urban land use policy, planning, and development issues, including studies on central city problems, industrial development, new community development, residential developments of all types, taxation, smart growth, shopping center development and economics, metropolitan and urbanized area growth and development, mixed use development, and environmental factors affecting development.

STATISTICS SOURCES

Agriculture Fact Book. Available from U. S. Government Printing Office. • Annual. $26.00. Issued by the Office of Communications, U. S. Department of Agriculture. Includes data on U. S. agriculture, farmers, food, nutrition, and rural America. Programs of the Department of Agriculture in six areas are described: rural economic development, foreign trade, nutrition, the environment, inspection, and education.

Budget of the United States Government. U.S. Office of Management and Budget. Available from U.S. Government Printing Office. • Annual. $52.00.

TRADE/PROFESSIONAL ASSOCIATIONS

Community Associations Institute. 225 Reinekers Ln., Ste. 300, Alexandria, VA 22314. Phone: 888-CAI-4321 or (703)548-8600 Fax: (703)684-1581 E-mail: caidirect@caionline.org • URL: http://www.caionline.org • Condominium and homeowner associations, cooperatives, and association-governed planned communities of all sizes and architectural

types; community or property managers and management firms; individual homeowners; community association managers and management firms; public officials; and lawyers, accountants, engineers, reserve specialists, builder/developers and other providers of professional services and products for CAs. Seeks to educate and represent America's 250,000 residential condominium, cooperative and homeowner associations and related professionals and service providers. Aims to foster vibrant, responsive, competent community associations that promote harmony, community and responsible leadership.

Community Development Society. 17 S High St., Ste. 200, Columbus, OH 43215. Phone: (614)221-1900 Fax: (614)221-1989 E-mail: cds@assnoffices.com • URL: http://www.comm-dev.org • Professionals and practitioners in community development; international, national, state, and local groups interested in community development efforts. Provides a forum for exchange of ideas and experiences; disseminates information to the public; advocates excellence in community programs, scholarship, and research; promotes citizen participation as essential to effective community development. Sponsors educational programs.

Small Towns Institute. PO Box 13530, PO Box 517, Burton, WA 98013-3530. Phone: (509)925-1830 Fax: (509)963-1753 E-mail: pmiller@mwcapitol.com • Individuals and institutions interested in small town problems and potentials. Collects, assembles, and disseminates information on small town living, especially in regard to planning, revitalization, and environmental programs. Provides research data on topics such as historic preservation and arts development for small towns, innovative job resources, and improving the quality of life in community development projects.

OTHER SOURCES

American Land Planning Law. John Taylor and Norma Williams. West Group. • $780.00. Eight volumes. Annual cumulative updates. (Real Property and Zoning Series).

COMMUNITY FUNDS

See also: FUND-RAISING

DIRECTORIES

Funding Sources for Community and Economic Development 2003-2004: A Guide to Current Sources for Local Programs and Projects. Greenwood Publishing Group, Inc. • 2003. $64.95. Sixth edition. Provides information on 2,600 funding sources. Includes "A Guide to Proposal Planning." (Funding Sources for Community and Economic Development Series).

STATISTICS SOURCES

Giving U.S.A: The Annual Report on Philanthropy. American Association of Fund-Raising Counsel. AAFRC Trust for Philanthropy. • Annual. $65.00.

United Way Annual Report. United Way of America. • Annual. Price on application.

TRADE/PROFESSIONAL ASSOCIATIONS

Association of Fundraising Professionals. 1101 King St., Ste. 700, Alexandria, VA 22314-2967. Phone: 800-666-3863 or (703)684-0410 Fax: (703)684-0540 • URL: http://www.afpnet.org • Formerly National Society of Fundraising Executives.

United Way of America. 701 N. Fairfax St., Alexandria, VA 22314. Phone: (703)836-7112 Fax: (703)683-7840 • URL: http://www.national.unitedway.org • Formerly United Community Funds and Councils of America.

COMMUNITY PLANNING

See: CITY PLANNING

COMMUNITY RELATIONS

See also: SOCIAL RESPONSIBILITY

ABSTRACTS AND INDEXES

Business Periodicals Index. H. W. Wilson Co. • 11 times a year. Quarterly and annual cumulations. Price varies.

Readers' Guide to Periodical Literature. H. W. Wilson Co. • Monthly. $345.00 per year. Includes annual *Cumulation.* Indexes about 250 peridicals of general interest.

Social Sciences Index. H. W. Wilson Co. • Quarterly, with annual cumulation. Price varies. Indexes more than 400 periodicals covering economics, environmental policy, government, insurance, labor, health care policy, plannning, public administration, public welfare, urban studies, women's issues, criminology, and related topics.

CD-ROM DATABASES

Newspaper Abstracts Ondisc. PROQUEST. • Monthly. $2,950.00 per year (covers 1989 to date; archival discs are available for 1985-88). Provides cover-to-cover CD-ROM indexing and abstracting of 19 major newspapers, including the *New York Times, Wall Street Journal, Washington Post, Chicago Tribune,* and *Los Angeles Times.*

Social Sciences Citation Index. ISI. • Monthly. Price on request. Provides CD-ROM indexing of articles appearing in 1700 leading social science journals worldwide, with additional selections from more than 5700 other journals. Time span is 1992 to date. Coverage includes economics, business, finance, management, communications, demographics, library and information science, political science, sociology, and many other subjects.

Social Sciences Citation Index: Compact Disc Edition with Abstracts. Institute for Scientific Information. • Monthly. Provides CD-ROM indexing and abstracting of "significant articles" from 1,700 social science journals worldwide, with additional selections from 3,200 other journals, 1986 to date. Includes economics, business, finance, management, communications, demographics, information and library science, political science, sociology, and many other subjects.

WILSONDISC: Wilson Social Sciences Abstracts. H. W. Wilson Co. • Monthly. Includes unlimited online access to *Social Sciences Index* through WILSONLINE. Provides CD-ROM indexing from 1983 and abstracting from 1994 of more than 500 periodicals covering economics, area studies, community health, public administration, public welfare, urban studies, and many other topics related to the social sciences.

DIRECTORIES

Business Organizations, Agencies, and Publications Directory. Gale Cengage Learning. • 2003. $480.00. 15th edition. Over 40,000 entries describing 39 types of business information sources. Classified by type of organization, publication, or serviceIncludes state, national, and international agencies and organizations. Master index to names and keywords. Also includes e-mail addresses and web site URL's.

National Directory of Corporate Public Affairs. Columbia Books, Inc. • Annual. $109.00. Lists about 1,900 corporations that have foundations or other public affairs activities.

Shopping for a Better World: A Quick and Easy Guide to Socially Responsible Supermarket Shopping. Council on Economic Priorities. • Annual. $14.00. Rates 186 major corporations according to 10 social criteria: advancement of minorities, advancement of women, environmental concerns, South African investments, charity, community outreach, nuclear power, animal testing, military contracts, and social disclosure. Includes

American, Japanese and British firms.

ENCYCLOPEDIAS AND DICTIONARIES

Blackwell Encyclopedic Dictionary of Business Ethics. Patricia H. Werhane and R. Edward Freeman. Blackwell Publishing. • 1997. $38.95. The editors are associated with the University of Virginia. Contains definitions of key terms combined with longer articles written by various U. S. and foreign business educators. Includes bibliographies and index. (Blackwell Encyclopedia of Management Series).

ONLINE DATABASES

Information Bank Abstracts. New York Times Index Dept. • Provides indexing and abstracting of current affairs, primarily from the final late edition of *The New York Times* and the Eastern edition of *The Wall Street Journal.* Time period is 1969 to present, with daily updates. Inquire as to online cost and availability.

Readers' Guide Abstracts Online. H. W. Wilson Co. • Indexes and abstracts general interest periodicals, 1983 to date. Weekly updates. Inquire as to online cost and availability.

Wilson Business Abstracts Online. H. W. Wilson Co. • Indexes and abstracts 600 major business periodicals, plus the *Wall Street Journal* and the business section of the *New York Times.* Indexing is from 1982, abstracting from 1990, with the two newspapers included from 1993. Updated weekly. Inquire as to online cost and availability. (*Business Periodicals Index* without abstracts is also available online.).

Wilson Social Sciences Abstracts Online. H. W. Wilson Co. • Provides online abstracting and indexing of more than 500 periodicals covering area studies, community health, public administration, public welfare, urban studies, and many other social science topics. Time period is 1994 to date for abstracts and 1983 to date for indexing, with updates weekly. Inquire as to online cost and availability.

PERIODICALS AND NEWSLETTERS

The Community Relations Report. Joe Williams Communications. • Description: Reports on innovative and creative corporate community relations activities throughout the country. Covers different techniques of improving community relations such as programs, activities, cultural events, and philanthropy grants. Recurring features include profiles of community relations practitioners and announcements of useful programs and books.

Corporate Public Issues and Their Management: The Executive Systems Approach to Public Policy Formation. Issue Action Publications, Inc. • Monthly. $235.00 per year. Newsletter.

Positive Leadership: Improving Performance Through Value-Centered Management. Lawrence Ragan Communications, Inc. • Monthly. $99.00 per year. Newsletter. Emphasis is on employee motivation, family issues, ethics, and community relations.

RESEARCH CENTERS AND INSTITUTES

Center for Corporate Citizenship. Boston College, 55 Lee Rd., Chestnut Hill, MA 02467. Phone: (617)552-4545 Fax: (617)552-8499 E-mail: cccr@bc.edu • URL: http://www.bc.edu/cccbc • Areas of study include corporate images within local communities, corporate community relations, social vision, and philanthropy. Formerly Center for Corporate Community Relations.

Center for Public-Private Sector Cooperation. The Centers, University of Colorado-Denver, Campus Box 133, P.O.Box 173364, Denver, CO 80202-3364. Phone: (303)352-3800 Fax: (303)352-3810 E-mail: centers@cudenver.edu • URL: http://www.centers.cudenver.edu.

TRADE/PROFESSIONAL ASSOCIATIONS

Community Leadership Association. Fanning Institute, 1240 S Lumpkin St., University of

Georgia, Athens, GA 30602. Phone: (706)542-0301 Fax: (706)542-7007 E-mail: info@communityleadership.org • URL: http://www.communityleadership.org • Local, regional, and state community leadership organizations. Provides for exchange of creative ideas concerning community leadership; promotes existing community leadership programs and their alumni organizations; helps establish new programs worldwide. Offers training, publications, and volunteer experts to community leadership organizations. Sponsors educational programs; compiles statistics.

COMMUNITY SHOPPING CENTERS

See: SHOPPING CENTERS

COMMUTER AIRLINES

See: AIRLINE INDUSTRY

COMPACT DISCS

See: OPTICAL DISK STORAGE DEVICES

COMPANIES

See: CORPORATIONS; INDUSTRY; PRIVATE COMPANIES

COMPANY ANNIVERSARIES

See: ANNIVERSARIES AND HOLIDAYS

COMPANY HISTORIES

See: BUSINESS HISTORY

COMPENSATION OF EMPLOYEES

See: WAGES AND SALARIES

COMPENSATION OF EXECUTIVES

See: EXECUTIVE COMPENSATION

COMPETITIVE INTELLIGENCE

See also: BUSINESS RESEARCH

GENERAL WORKS

Competitive Intelligence. Jim Underwood. John Wiley and Sons, Inc. • 2001. $16.50. Describes the basic elements of competitive intelligence. Chapter headings include "What is Competitive Intelligence?", "Key Concepts and Thinkers," and "Ten Steps to Making It Work.".

Essentials of Knowledge Management. Bryan Bergeron. John Wiley and Sons, Inc. • 2003. $29.95. Covers current strategies, trends, and technologies in knowledge management. Includes examples of best practices. (Essentials Series).

Information Management for the Intelligent Organization: The Art of Scanning the Environment. Chun Wei Choo. Information Today, Inc. • 2001.

$39.50. Third edition. Published on behalf of the American Society for Information Science (ASIS). Covers the general principles of acquiring, creating, organizing, and using information within organizations.

Knowledge Management for the Information Professional. T. Kanti Srikantaiah and Michael Koenig. Information Today, Inc. • 2000. $44.50. Contains articles by 26 contributors on the concept of "knowledge management." (ASIS Mongraph Series).

Knowledge Management Lessons Learned: What Works and What Doesn't. Michael Koenig and T. Kanti Srikantaiah, editors. Information Today, Inc. • 2003. $44.50. Contains more than 30 articles by KM experts, covering recent applications, innovations, strategy, implementation, cost analysis, training, content management, and other topics related to knowledge management. (ASIS Management Series).

Millennium Intelligence: Understanding and Conducting Competitive Intelligence in the Digital Age. Jerry Miller, editor. Information Today, Inc. • 1999. $29.95. Contains essays by various authors on competitive intelligence information sources, legal aspects, intelligence skills, corporate security, and other topics. (CyberAge Books.).

Online Competitive Intelligence: Move Your Business to the Top Using Cyber-Intelligence. Helen P. Burwell. Facts on Demand Press. • 1999. $25.95. Covers the selection and use of online sources for competitive intelligence. Includes descriptions of many Internet Web sites, classified by subject. (Online Ease Series).

Smart Services: Competitive Information Strategies, Solutions, and Success Stories for Service Businesses. Deborah C. Sawyer. Information Today, Inc. • 2002. $29.95. Covers the use of competitive information by service-oriented firms. (CyberAge Books.).

Strategy-Specific Decision Making: A Guide for Executing Competitive Strategy. William G. Forgang. M. E. Sharpe, Inc. • 2004. $72.95. Includes a bibliography and case studies in the area of competitive strategy.

Super Searchers Go to the Source: The Interviewing and Hands-On Information Strategies of Top Primary Researchers - Online, On the Phone, and In Person. Risa Sacks. Information Today, Inc. • 2001. $24.95. Explains how information-search experts use various print, electronic, and live sources for competitive intelligence and other purposes. (Super Searchers Series).

Super Searchers on Competitive Intelligence: The Online and Offline Secrets of Top CI Researchers. Margaret M. Carr. Information Today, Inc. • 2003. $24.95. Presents the views of business intelligence experts from 15 major corporations and organizations. Contains information on sources for "monitoring competitive forces." (Super Searchers Series).

Super Searchers on Mergers & Acquisitions: The Online Secrets of Top Corporate Researchers and M & A Professionals. Jan Tudor. Information Today, Inc. • 2001. $24.95. Presents the results of interviews with 13 "top M & A information pros." Covers the finding, evaluating, and delivering of relevant data on companies and industries. (Super Searchers Series).

BIBLIOGRAPHIES

Analyzing Your Competition: Simple, Low-Cost Techniques for Intelligence Gathering. Michael Strenges. MarketResearch.com. • 1997. $95.00. Third edition. Mainly an annotated listing of specific, business information sources, but also contains concise discussions of information-gathering techniques. Indexed by publisher and title.

Knowledge Management: The Bibliography. Paul

Burden and others. Information Today, Inc. • 2000. $22.50. Provides citations to more than 1,500 articles, 150 Web sites, and 400 books. Arranged according to specific KM topics, such as "KM and E-Commerce." Published in conjunction with the American Society for Information Science and Technology (ASIST).

DIRECTORIES

KMWorld Buyer's Guide. Knowledge Asset Media. • Semiannual. Controlled circulation as part of *KMWorld.* Contains corporate and product profiles related to various aspects of knowledge management and information systems. (Knowledge Asset Media is a an affiliate of Information Today, Inc.).

HANDBOOKS AND MANUALS

Assessing Competitive Intelligence Software: A Guide to Evaluating CI Technology. France Bouthillier and Kathleen Shearer. Information Today, Inc. • 2003. $39.50. Provides a 32-step methodology for making an evaluation of competitive intelligence software. (An ASIST publication: American Society for Information Science and Technology).

Competitive Intelligence From Black Ops to Boardrooms: How Businesses Gather, Analyze, and Use Information to Succeed in the Global Marketplace. Larry Kahaner. Simon & Schuster Trade. • 1996. $24.00. Emphasizes corporate espionage as opposed to more traditional information gathering (the author is a former licensed private investigator). Includes a "Glossary of Competitive Intelligence.".

Intelligence Essentials for Everyone. Available from U. S. Government Printing Office. • 1999. $6.50. Issued by the Joint Military Intelligence College, Defense Intelligence Agency, U. S. Department of Defense (http://www.dia.mil/). Written for "businesses worldwide." Explains how to collect, process, analyze, and manage business intelligence information.

Internet Business Intelligence: How to Build a Big Company System on a Small Company Budget. David Vine. Information Today, Inc. • 2000. $29.95. Covers the obtaining of valuable business intelligence data through use of the Internet.

Naked in Cyberspace: How to Find Personal Information Online. Carole A. Lane. Information Today, Inc. • 2002. $29.95. Second edition. Covers the availability of personal records on the Internet, including competitive intelligence data, customer characteristics, employee information, backgrounds of experts, public records, criminal records, and genealogical data. From an opposite viewpoint, advice is offered relative to the maintenance of privacy. Includes a Web directory with about 1,000 sources of information. (CyberAge Books.).

A New Archetype for Competitive Intelligence. John J. McGonagle and Carolyn M. Vella. Greenwood Publishing Group, Inc. • 1996. $64.95. Covers competitive intelligence, strategic intelligence, market intelligence, defensive intelligence, and cyber-intelligence. Includes an overview of sources and techniques for data gathering. A bibliography, glossary, and index are provided.

New Competitor Intelligence: The Complete Resource for Finding, Analyzing, and Using Information About Your Competitors. Leonard M. Fuld. John Wiley and Sons, Inc. • 1994. $145.00. Second edition. Topics include data sources, strategy, analysis of competition, and how to establish a competitive intelligence system.

The Skeptical Business Searcher: The Information Advisor's Guide to Evaluating Web Data, Sites, and Sources. Robert Berkman. Information Today, Inc. • 2003. $29.95. Covers free Internet sources of company backgrounds, sales data, earnings, SEC documents, competitive intelligence information, poll data, business news, economic statistics, etc.

The author is editor of *The Information Advisor* newsletter. (CyberAge Books).

INTERNET DATABASES

Competitive Intelligence Guide. Fuld & Co. Phone: (617)492-5900 Fax: (617)492-7108 E-mail: info@fuld.com • URL: http://www.fuld.com • Web site includes "Intelligence Index" (links to Internet sites), "Strategic Intelligence Organizer" (game-board format), "Intelligence Pyramid" (graphics), "Thoughtleaders" (expert commentary), "Intelligence System Evaluator" (interactive questionnaire), and "Reference Resource" (book excerpts from *New Competitor Intelligence*). Fees: information provided by Web site is free, but Fuld & Co. offers fee-based research and consulting services.

EBSCO Information Services. Ebsco Publishing. Phone: 800-653-2726 or (978)356-6500 Fax: (978)356-6565 E-mail: ep@epnet.com • URL: http://www.epnet.com • Fee-based Web site providing Internet access to a wide variety of databases, including business-related material. Full text is available for many periodical titles, with daily updates. Fees: Apply.

Ebusiness Forum: Global Business Intelligence for the Digital Age. Economist Intelligence Unit (EIU), Economist Group. Phone: 800-938-4685 or (212)554-0600 Fax: (212)586-0248 E-mail: newyork@eiu.com • URL: http://www.ebusinessforum.com • Web site provides information relating to multinational business, with an emphasis on activities in specific countries. Includes rankings of countries for "e-business readiness," additional data on the political, economic, and business environment in 180 nations ("Doing Business in.."), and "Today's News Analysis." Fees: Free, but registration is required for access to all content. Daily updates.

Factiva. Dow Jones Reuters Business Interactive, LLC. Phone: 800-369-7466 or (609)452-1511 Fax: (609)520-5770 E-mail: solutions@factiva.com • URL: http://www.factiva.com • Fee-based Web site provides "global news and business information through Web sites and content integration solutions." Includes Dow Jones and Reuters newswires, The Wall Street Journal, and more than 7,000 other sources of current news, historical articles, market research reports, and investment analysis. Content includes 96 major U. S. newspapers, 900 non-English sources, trade publications, media transcripts, country profiles, news photos, etc.

InSite 2. Intelligence Data/Thomson Financial. Phone: 800-654-0393 or (617)856-1890 Fax: (617)737-3182 E-mail: intelligence.data@tfn.com • URL: http://www.insite2.gale.com/ • Fee-based Web site consolidates information in a "Base Pack" consisting of Business InSite, Market InSite, and Company InSite. Optional databases are Consumer InSite, Health and Wellness InSite, Newsletter InSite, and Computer InSite. Includes fulltext content from more than 2,500 trade publications, journals, newsletters, newspapers, analyst reports, and other sources. Continuous updating. Formerly produced by The Gale Group.

Intelligence Data. Thomson Financial. Phone: 800-654-0393 Fax: (617)824-2477 • URL: http://www.intelligencedata.com • Fee-based Web site provides a wide variety of information relating to competitive intelligence, strategic planning, business development, mergers, acquisitions, sales, and marketing. "Intelliscope" feature offers searching of other Thomson units, such as Investext, MarkIntel, InSite 2, and Industry Insider. Weekly updating.

Nexis.com. Lexis-Nexis Group. Phone: 800-227-4908 or (937)865-6800 Fax: (937)865-6909 E-mail: webmaster@prod.lexis-nexis.com • URL: http://www.nexis.com • Fee-based Web site offers searching of about 2.8 billion documents in some 30,000 news, business, and legal information sources. Features include a subject directory covering 1,200

topics in 34 categories and a Company Dossier containing information on more than 500,000 public and private companies. Boolean searching is offered.

ProQuest Direct. ProQuest Inc. Phone: 800-889-3358 or (734)761-4700 Fax: (734)662-4554 • URL: http://proquest.com • Fee-based Web site providing Internet access to more than 3,000 periodicals, newspapers, and other publications. Many items are available full-text, with daily updates. Includes extensive corporate and financial information. Fees: Apply.

PERIODICALS AND NEWSLETTERS

Competitive Intelligence Magazine. Society of Competitive Intelligence Professionals. • Quarterly. $49.00 per year. Covers the "legal and ethical collection and analysis of information" relating to business competition.

DM Review: The Premier Publication for Business Intelligence and Analytics. Thomson Media. • Monthly. $49.00 per year. Edited for corporate executives and information technology personnel. Covers data management, business intelligence, data warehousing, systems management, data integration, knowledge management, data mining, and related topics.

KM World: Creating and Managing the Knowledge-Based Enterprise (Knowledge Management). Asset Media. • 10 times a year. Free to qualified personnel; others, $63.95 per year. Provides articles on knowledge management, including business intelligence, multimedia content management, document management, e-business, and intellectual property. Emphasis is on business-to-business information technology. (Knowledge Asset Media is a an affiliate of Information Today, Inc.).

Ragan's Journal of Business Intelligence. Lawence Ragan Communications, Inc. • Bimonthly. $199.00 per year. Includes articles on competitive intelligence, knowledge management, legalities, ethics, and counterintelligence.

Strategy and Business. • Quarterly. $38.00 per year.

TRADE/PROFESSIONAL ASSOCIATIONS

Society of Competitive Intelligence Professionals. 1700 Diagonal Rd., Suite 600, Alexandria, VA 22314. Phone: (703)739-0696 Fax: (703)739-2524 E-mail: info@scip.org • URL: http://www.scip.org • Members are professionals involved in competitor intelligence and analysis. Formerly Society of Competitor Intelligence Professionals.

COMPOSITE MATERIALS

See also: MATERIALS

ABSTRACTS AND INDEXES

Applied Science and Technology Index. H. W. Wilson Co. • 11 times a year. Quarterly and annual cumulations. Price varies. Indexes a wide variety of English language technical, industrial, and engineering periodicals.

Engineered Materials Abstracts. Cambridge Information Group. • Monthly. $995.00 per year. Provides citations to the technical and engineering literature of plastic, ceramic, and composite materials.

Engineering Index Monthly: Abstracting and Indexing Services Covering Sources of the World's Engineering Literature. Engineering Information Inc. • Monthly. Institutions, $5,279.00 per year. Provides indexing and abstracting of the world's engineering and technical literature.

Key Abstracts: Advanced Materials. Available from INSPEC, Inc. • Monthly. $250.00 per year. Provides international coverage of journal and proceedings literature, including publications on ceramics and composite materials. Published in England by the Institution of Electrical Engineers (IEE).

NTIS Alerts: Manufacturing Technology. National Technical Information Service. • Semimonthly. $265.00 per year. Provides descriptions of government-sponsored research reports and software, with ordering information. Covers computer-aided design and manufacturing (CAD/CAM), engineering materials, quality control, machine tools, robots, lasers, productivity, and related subjects. Formerly *Abstract Newsletter.*

NTIS Alerts: Materials Sciences. National Technical Information Service. • Semimonthly. $220.00 per year. Provides descriptions of government-sponsored research reports and software, with ordering information. Covers ceramics, glass, coatings, composite materials, alloys, plastics, wood, paper, adhesives, fibers, lubricants, and related subjects. Formerly *Abstract Newsletter.*

CD-ROM DATABASES

Materials Science Citation Index. Institute for Scientific Information. • Bimonthly. Contains current, CD-ROM citations and abstracts, providing international coverage of materials science journals.

METADEX Materials Collection: Metals-Polymers-Ceramics. Cambridge Scientific Abstracts. • Quarterly. Provides CD-ROM citations to the worldwide literature of materials science and metallurgy. Corresponds to *Metals Abstracts, Alloys Index, Steels Alert, Nonferrous Alert, Polymers/Ceramics/Composites Alert,* and *Engineered Materials Abstracts.* (Formerly produced by ASM International.).

WILSONDISC: Applied Science and Technology Abstracts. H. W. Wilson Co. • Monthly. Includes unlimited access to the online version of *Applied Science and Technology Abstracts* through WILSONLINE. Provides CD-ROM indexing and abstracting of 500 prominent scientific, technical, engineering, and industrial periodicals. Indexing coverage is provided from 1983 to date and abstracting from 1993 to date.

DIRECTORIES

Engineering Plastics and Composites. William A. Woishnis and others, editors. ASM International. • 1993. $149.00. Second edition. In four sections: (1) Trade names of plastics, reinforced plastics, and resin composites; (2) Index to materials, with suppliers and other information; (3) Suppliers alphabetically, with trade names; (4) Supplier contact information. (Materials Data Series).

ENCYCLOPEDIAS AND DICTIONARIES

ASM Materials Engineering Dictionary. Joseph R. Davis, editor. ASM International. • 1992. $166.00. Contains 10,000 entries, 700 illustrations, and 150 tables relating to metals, plastics, ceramics, composites, and adhesives. Includes "Technical Briefs" on 64 key material groups.

Comprehensive Composite Materials. Anthony Kelly and Carl Zweben. Elsevier. • 2000. $2,905.50. Six volumes. Provides detailed information on a wide variety of materials used in composites, including metals, polymers, cements, concrete, carbon, ceramics, and fibers. (Pergamon Press.).

Encyclopedia of Advanced Materials. David Bloor and others. Elsevier. • 1994. $1,534.00. Four volumes.

Encyclopedia of Materials: Science and Technology. K.H.J. Buschow and others, editors. Elsevier. • 2001. $4,985.00. Eleven volumes. Provides extensive technical information on a wide variety of materials, including metals, ceramics, plastics, optical materials, and building materials. Includes more than 2,000 articles and 5,000 illustrations.

Encyclopedia of Smart Materials. Mel Schwartz, editor. John Wiley and Sons, Inc. • 2002. $725.00. Three volumes. Covers materials "that combine two or more functions in a single material or element.".

Materials Science and Technology: A

Comprehensive Treatment. R. W. Cahn and others, editors. John Wiley and Sons, Inc. • 1997. $4,250.00. 18 volumes. Each volume covers a particular area of high-performance materials technology.

HANDBOOKS AND MANUALS

Handbook of Materials Selection. Myer Kutz. John Wiley and Sons, Inc. • 2002. $225.00. First section of handbook covers materials relative to the type of engineering application. Second section deals with the specific properties of materials. Covers both traditional materials and high-tech composites.

Joining of Composite Matrix Materials. Mel M. Schwartz. ASM International. • 1994. $59.00.

ONLINE DATABASES

Applied Science and Technology Index Online. H. W. Wilson Co. • Provides online indexing of 500 major scientific, technical, industrial, and engineering periodicals. Time period is 1983 to date. Monthly updates. Inquire as to online cost and availability.

Current Contents Connect. Institute for Scientific Information. • Provides online abstracts of articles listed in the tables of contents of about 7,500 journals. Coverage is very broad, including science, social science, life science, technology, engineering, industry, agriculture, the environment, economics, and arts and humanities. Time period is two years, with weekly updates. Inquire as to online cost and availability.

Engineered Materials Abstracts [online]. Cambridge Scientific Abstracts. • Provides online citations to the technical and engineering literature of plastic, ceramic, and composite materials. Time period is 1986 to date, with monthly updates. (Formerly produced by ASM International.) Inquire as to online cost and availability.

Materials Business File. Cambridge Scientific Abstracts. • Provides online abstracts and citations to worldwide materials literature, covering the business and industrial aspects of metals, plastics, ceramics, and composites. Corresponds to *Steels Alert, Nonferrous Metals Alert,* and *Polymers/Ceramics/Composites Alert.* Time period is 1985 to date, with monthly updates. (Formerly produced by ASM International.) Inquire as to online cost and availability.

METADEX. Cambridge Scientific Abstracts. • Covers the worldwide literature of metals, metallurgy, and materials science, 1966 to date. Includes detailed alloys indexing from 1974. Biweekly updating. Inquire as to online cost and availability. (Formerly produced by ASM International.).

PROMT: Predicasts Overview of Markets and Technology. Gale Cengage Learning. • Companies, products, applied technologies and markets. U.S. and international literature coverage, 1972 to date. Inquire as to online cost and availability. Provides abstracts from more than 1,600 publications. Weekly updates.

PERIODICALS AND NEWSLETTERS

Advanced Composites Monthly. Composite Market Reports Inc. • Description: Covers advanced composite materials processes and markets in the aerospace industry worldwide. "Prepared for engineering, program, and manufacturing management at primes and their subcontractors where aerospace components made of high-performance composite materials are designed, fabricated, or assembled." Discusses subcontract opportunities of interest to U.S., Canadian, and overseas aerospace companies. Recurring features include a calendar of events, reports of meetings, interviews, news of research, and application case histories.

The Composites and Adhesives Newsletter. T-C Press. • Quarterly. $190.00. Presents news of the composite materials and adhesives industries, with particular coverage of new products and applications.

Composites Industry Monthly. Composite Market Reports Inc. • Description: Directed toward companies seeking to diversify their line of non-aerospace applications of advanced composites. Discusses composite materials, processes, and markets worldwide with a focus on fabricators and users. Recurring features include interviews, news of research, a calendar of events, reports of meetings, and application case histories.

High-Tech Materials Alert: Advanced Materials: Their Uses and Manufacture. Technical Insights. • Monthly. Institutions, $695.00 per year. Newsletter on technical developments relating to high-performance materials, including metals and ceramics. Includes market forecasts.

International Materials Review. ASM International. • Bimonthly. $865.00 per year. Provides technical and research coverage of metals, alloys, and advanced materials. Formerly *International Metals Review.*

Journal of Advanced Materials. Society for the Advancement of Material and Process Engineering. • Quarterly. Individuals, $60.00 per year; institutions, $150.00 per year. Contains technical and research articles. Formerly *SAMPE Quarterly.*

Journal of Materials Research. Materials Research Society. • Monthly. $785.00 per year. Includes print and online editions. Covers the preparation, properties, and processing of advanced materials.

SAMPE Journal. Society for the Advancement of Material and Process Engineering. • Bimonthly. Members, $78.00 per year; non-members, $80.00 per year. Provides technical information.

RESEARCH CENTERS AND INSTITUTES

Alliance for Innovative Manufacturing. Stanford University, Bldg.02-530, Rm. 225, Stanford, CA 94305-3036. Phone: (650)723-9038 Fax: (650)723-5034 E-mail: cborn@stanford.edu • URL: http://www.stanford.edu/group/aim • Development of new products and processing. Formerly Stanford Integrated Manufacturing Association.

Center for Composite Materials. University of Delaware, Newark, DE 19716-3144. Phone: (302)831-8149 Fax: (302)831-8525 E-mail: info@ccm.udel.edu • URL: http://www.ccm.udel.edu

Composite Materials and Structures Center. Michigan State University, College of Engineering, 2100 Engineering Bldg., East Lansing, MI 48824-1226. Phone: (517)353-5466 Fax: (517)432-1634 E-mail: drzal@msu.edu • URL: http://www.egr.msu.edu/cmsc • Studies polymer, metal, and ceramic based composites.

Composite Materials Research Group. University of Wyoming, Department of Mechanical Engineering, P.O. Box 3295, Laramie, WY 82071. Phone: (307)766-2371 Fax: (307)766-4444 E-mail: dadams@uwyo.edu • URL: http://www.eng.uwyo.edu/cmrg.

Materials Processing Center. Massachusetts Institute of Technology, 77 Massachusetts Ave., Room 12-007, Cambridge, MA 02139-4307. Phone: (617)253-5179 Fax: (617)258-6900 E-mail: fmpage@.mit.edu • URL: http://www.web.mit.edu/mpc • Conducts processing, engineering, and economic research in ferrous and nonferrous metals, ceramics, polymers, photonic materials, superconductors, welding, composite materials, and other materials.

TRADE/PROFESSIONAL ASSOCIATIONS

American Composites Manufacturers Association. 1010 N Glebe Rd., Ste. 450, Arlington, VA 22201. Phone: (703)525-0511 Fax: (703)525-0743 E-mail: info@acmanet.org • URL: http://www.acmanet.org • Companies engaged in the hand lay up or spray up of fiberglass in open molds or engaged in filament winding or resin transfer molding. Products requiring this process include boats, swimming pools, and bathroom fixtures. Conducts educational and

---

research programs; compiles statistics. Sponsors product specialty seminars.

ASM International. 9639 Kinsman Rd., Novelty, OH 44073-0002. Phone: 800-336-5152 or (440)338-5151 Fax: (440)338-4634 E-mail: customerservice@asminternational.org • URL: http://asmcommunity.asminternational.org/portal/site/asm • Metallurgists, materials engineers, executives in materials producing and consuming industries; teachers and students. Disseminates technical information about the manufacture, use, and treatment of engineered materials. Offers inplant, home study, and intensive courses through Materials +Engineering Institute. Conducts career development program. Established ASM Foundation for +Education and Research.

Composites Manufacturing Association of the Society of Manufacturing Engineers. 1 SME Dr., Dearborn, MI 48121. Phone: 800-733-4763 or (313)271-1500 Fax: (313)271-2861 E-mail: service@sme.org • URL: http://www.sme.org/cma • Members are composites manufacturing professionals and students.

Materials Research Society. 506 Keystone Dr., Warrendale, PA 15086-7573. Phone: (724)779-3003 Fax: (724)779-8313 E-mail: info@mrs.org • URL: http://www.mrs.org • Represents the interests of materials researchers from academia, industry, and government that promotes communication for the advancement of interdisciplinary materials research to improve the quality of life. Fosters interaction among researchers working on different classes of inorganic and organic materials and to promote interdisciplinary basic research on materials. Provides forum for industry, government, and university cooperation; conducts technical conferences, tutorial lectures. Maintains speakers' bureau.

COMPRESSORS

See: PUMPS AND COMPRESSORS

COMPTROLLERS

See: CORPORATE DIRECTORS AND OFFICERS

COMPUTER ACCESSORIES

See: COMPUTER PERIPHERALS AND ACCESSORIES

COMPUTER-AIDED DESIGN AND MANUFACTURING (CAD/CAM)

See also: COMPUTER GRAPHICS

GENERAL WORKS

Computer Aided Design. Robert Becker and Carmo J. Pereira, editors. Marcel Dekker, Inc. • 1993. $250.00. (Chemical Industries Series: Vol. 51).

Systems Approach to Computer-Integrated Design and Manufacturing. Nanua Singh. John Wiley and Sons, Inc. • 1995. $105.95.

ABSTRACTS AND INDEXES

Applied Science and Technology Index. H. W. Wilson Co. • 11 times a year. Quarterly and annual cumulations. Price varies. Indexes a wide variety of English language technical, industrial, and engineering periodicals.

Key Abstracts: Factory Automation. Available from INSPEC, Inc. • Monthly. $250.00 per year. Provides international coverage of journal and proceedings literature, including publications on CAD/CAM, materials handling, robotics, and factory management. Published in England by the Institution of Electrical Engineers (IEE).

NTIS Alerts: Manufacturing Technology. National Technical Information Service. • Semimonthly. $265.00 per year. Provides descriptions of government-sponsored research reports and software, with ordering information. Covers computer-aided design and manufacturing (CAD/CAM), engineering materials, quality control, machine tools, robots, lasers, productivity, and related subjects. Formerly *Abstract Newsletter.*

Science Citation Index. Thomson/ISI. • Bimonthly. $15,020.00 per year. Annual cumulation. Includes *Source Index, Citation Index, Permuterm Subject Index,* and *Corporate Index.*

DIRECTORIES

CAD/CAM,CAE: Survey, Review and Buyers' Guide. Daratech, Inc. • $2,998.00 per year. Looseleaf service. Three editions. Mechanical edition, $972.00 per year; AEC and Plant design editon, $1,498.00 per year. Includes computer-aided engineering (CAE).

Manufacturing Systems: Buyers Guide. Reed Business Information. • Annual. Price on application. Contains information on companies manufacturing or supplying materials handling systems, CAD/CAM systems, specialized software for manufacturing, programmable controllers, machine vision systems, and automatic identification systems.

Modern Machine Shop Material Working Technology Guide. Gardner Publications, Inc. • Annual. $15.00. Lists products and services for the metalworking industry. Formerly *Modern Machine Shop CNC and Software Guide.*

HANDBOOKS AND MANUALS

Mechanical Engineer's Reference Book. E. H. Smith, editor. Society of Automotive Engineers. • 1994. $135.00. 12th edition. Covers mechanical engineering principles, computer integrated engineering systems, design standards, materials, power transmission, and many other engineering topics. (Authored Series).

ONLINE DATABASES

Globalbase. Gale Cengage Learning. • Provides more than one million online summaries of business, industrial, and economic news reports from more than 1,000 publications worldwide. Covers a wide range of material appearing in international trade journals, professional magazines, and newspapers. Time period is 1984 to date, with weekly updates. Inquire as to online cost and availability.

Scisearch. Institute for Scientific Information. • Broad, multidisciplinary index to the literature of science and technology, 1974 to present. Inquire as to online cost and availability. Coverage of literature is worldwide, with weekly updates.

PERIODICALS AND NEWSLETTERS

ACM Transactions on Graphics. Association for Computing Machinery. • Quarterly. Members, $41.00 per year; non-members, $170.00 per year; students, $36.00 per year.

Commline. Numeridex, Inc. • Bimonthly. Free to qualified personnel; others, $20.00 per year. Emphasizes NC/CNC (numerically controlled and computer numerically controlled machinery).

Computer-Aided Engineering: Data Base Applications in Design and Manufacturing. Penton Media, Inc. • Quarterly. $55.00 per year.

IEEE Computer Graphics and Applications. Insitute of Electrical and Electronics Engineers, Inc. • Bimonthly. $695.00 per year.

IEEE Transactions on Visualization and Computer Graphics. Institute of Electrical and Electronics Engineers, Inc. • Quarterly. $676.00 per year. Topics include computer vision, computer graphics, image processing, signal processing, computer-aided design, animation, and virtual reality.

Manufacturing Computer Solutions. • Monthly. $88.00 per year. Edited for managers of factory automation, emphasizing the integration of systems in manufacturing. Subjects include materials handling, CAD/CAM, specialized software for manufacturing, programmable controllers, machine vision, and automatic identification systems. Formerly *Manufacturing Systems.*

Robotics and Computer-Integrated Manufacturing: An International Journal. Elsevier. • Bimonthly. Institutions, $1,098.00 per year.

RESEARCH CENTERS AND INSTITUTES

Advanced Manufacturing Engineering Institute. University of Hartford, United Technologies Hall, Room 215, West Hartford, CT 06117. Phone: 800-678-4844 or (860)768-4615 Fax: (860)768-5073 E-mail: shetty@mail.hartford.edu.

Computer Network Center. Purdue University at Indianapolis, 799 W. Michigan St., ET 141-148, Indianapolis, IN 46202-5160. Phone: (317)274-0814 Fax: (317)274-8470 E-mail: cnhelp@engr.iupui.edu • URL: http://www.engr.iupui.edu.

Institute of Advanced Manufacturing Sciences. 1111 Edison Dr., Cincinnati, OH 45230. Phone: (513)948-2000 Fax: 800-345-4482 • Fields of research include quality improvement, computer-aided design, artificial intelligence, and employee training.

Laboratory for Manufacturing and Productivity. Massachusetts Institute of Technology, 77 Massachusetts Ave., Room 35-234, Cambridge, MA 02139. Phone: (617)253-2113 Fax: (617)253-1556 E-mail: gutowski@mit.edu • URL: http://www.web.mit.edu/lmp/.

STATISTICS SOURCES

U. S. Industry and Trade Outlook. Available from National Technical Information Service. • Annual. $69.95. Produced by the International Trade Administration, U. S. Department of Commerce, in a "public-private" partnership with DRI/McGraw-Hill and Standard & Poor's. Provides basic data, outlook for the current year, and "Long-Term Prospects" (five-year projections) for a wide variety of products and services. Includes high technology industries. Formerly *U. S. Industrial Outlook.*

TRADE/PROFESSIONAL ASSOCIATIONS

American Automatic Control Council. Northwestern University, 2145 Sheridan Rd., 3640 Col Glenn Highway, Evanston, IL 60208-3118. Phone: (937)775-5062 Fax: (937)775-3936 E-mail: ahaddad@eec.nwv.edu • URL: http://www.a2c2.org • Control engineering divisions of: American Institute of Aeronautics and Astronautics, American Institute of Chemical Engineers, American Society of Mechanical Engineers, Association of Iron and Steel Engineers, Institute of Electrical and Electronics Engineers, Instrument Society of America, and Society for Computer Simulation International (see separate entries). Covers the field of automatic control including control of manufacturing processes, computer control, process control, navigation, and guidance.

Computer Aided Manufacturing International. 7850 N Belt Line Rd., No. 631, Irving, TX 75063-6064. Phone: (817)860-1654 Fax: (817)275-6450 E-mail: eredd@phila.k12.pa.us • Companies, organizations, corporations, and individuals who are interested or engaged in computer-aided manufacturing. Seeks to develop and execute a long-range plan for the advancement of the use of computers in manufacturing. Engages in research and development activities, educational seminars, and forums for the generation and dissemination of information.

Maintains library of over 1000 public-domain holdings (publications and software, including video- and magnetic tapes) relating to computer-aided design and manufacturing, cost management, and activity based costing. Compiles statistics.

Computer and Automated Systems Techical Group of Society of Manufacturing Engin. Technical Activities Dept. 1 SME Dr., Dearborn, MI 48121. Phone: 800-733-4763 or (313)271-1500 Fax: (313)425-3400 E-mail: service@sme.org • URL: http://www.sme.org/casa • Sponsored by the Society of Manufacturing Engineers. Formerly Computer and Automated Systems Association.

IEEE Computer Society. 1828 L St. NW, Ste. 1202, Washington, DC 20036. Phone: (202)371-0101 Fax: (202)728-9614 E-mail: help@computer.org • URL: http://www.computer.org • Computer professionals. Promotes the development of computer and information sciences and fosters communication within the information processing community. Sponsors conferences, symposia, workshops, tutorials, technical meetings, and seminars. Operates Computer Society Press. Presents scholarships; bestows technical achievement and service awards and certificates.

Special Interest Group on Design Automation. c/o Association for Computing Machinery, 1515 Broadway, New York, NY 10036. Phone: 800-342-6626 or (212)869-7440 Fax: (212)944-1318 E-mail: acmhelp@acm.org • URL: http://www.acm.org/sigda • Concerned with computer-aided design systems and software. Publishes the semiannual *SIGDA Newsletter*.

COMPUTER ANIMATION

See also: VIRTUAL REALITY

GENERAL WORKS

Animation 101. Ernest Pintoff. Michael Wiese Productions. • 1999. $16.95. Presents the history of animation from "Disney to Bakski, traditional to computer-generated." Includes comments from Stan Lee, Bill Hanna, Nick Park, and John Lasseter.

Multimedia: Concepts and Practice. Stephen McGloughlin. Prentice Hall Books. • 2000. $73.33. Includes audio compact disk. Provides basic information and instruction on multimedia graphic design, animation, video editing, sound editing, authoring, product creation, and other multimedia topics.

ABSTRACTS AND INDEXES

Internet and Personal Computing Abstracts [print edition]. EBSCO Publishing. • Quarterly. $269.00 per year, including cumulative index. Provides more than 10,000 abstracts annually from both trade and academic publications. Covers computer hardware, software, product reviews, Web topics, e-commerce, networks, corporate news, security, and related topics. Formerly *Microcomputer Abstracts.*

ALMANACS AND YEARBOOKS

Computer Animation Proceedings. Institute of Electrical and Electronic Engineers. • Annual. $110.00.

CD-ROM DATABASES

Computer Database. Gale Cengage Learning. • Provides one year of full-text on CD-ROM for 150 leading computer-related publications. Also includes 70,000 product specifications and brief profiles of 13,000 computer product vendors and manufacturers.

DIRECTORIES

Data Sources: The Comprehensive Guide to the Data Processing Industry: Hardware, Data Communications Products, Software, Company Profiles. Gale Cengage Learning. • Semiannual. $455.00 per year. Two volumes. Describes hardware and software for all computer operating sysems, including prices and technical details. Lists about 75,000 products from 14,000 suppliers. Industry-specific software applications are described.

The SHOOT Directory for Commercial Production and Postproduction. SHOOT. • Annual. $79.00. Lists production companies, advertising agencies, and sources of professional television, motion picture, and audio equipment.

ENCYCLOPEDIAS AND DICTIONARIES

Acronyms of Computer Science and Communications: A Comprehensive Acronym Dictionary and Illustrated Encyclopedia. Enjob Kajan and Ejub Kajan. Springer Verlag. • 2002. $49.95. Explains more than 4,000 "broadly used" computer, telecommunications, and information technology acronyms. Includes illustrations and Web addresses, where applicable.

Encyclopedia of Information Systems. Hossein Bidgoli, editor. Elsevier. • 2002. $1,200.00. Four volumes. Contains a wide range of articles relating to computers, databases, communication, and information technology. The 200 topics include coverage of hardware, software, artificial intelligence, the Internet, networks, knowledge management, electronic commerce, search engines, and systems design.

New Hacker's Dictionary. Eric S. Raymond. MIT Press. • 1996. $65.00. Third edition. Includes three classifications of hacker communication: slang, jargon, and "techspeak.".

HANDBOOKS AND MANUALS

The Art of 3-D Computer Animation and Imaging. Isaac V. Kerlow. John Wiley and Sons, Inc. • 2000. $59.95. Second edition. Covers special effects, hypermedia formats, video output, the post-production process, etc. Includes full-color illustrations and step-by-step examples. (Design and Graphic Design Series).

Guide to Computer Animation: For TV, Games, Multimedia and Web. Marcia Kuperberg and others. Elsevier. • 2002. $34.00. Covers the principles and techniques of digital animation, with advice on both software and hardware. (Visual Effects and Animation Series).

PC Graphics Handbook. Julio Sanchez and Maria P. Canton. CRC Press. • 2003. $129.95. Covers both the hardware and software specifics of PC graphics programming. Includes such practical and theoretical topics as graphics algorithms, relevant mathematics, artificial life, virtual reality, device drivers, antimation techniques, and video games.

INTERNET DATABASES

Wired News. Lycos, Inc. Phone: (415)276-8400 Fax: (415)276-8500 E-mail: newsfeedback@wired.com • URL: http://www.wired.com • Provides summaries and full-text of "Top Stories" relating to the Internet, computers, multimedia, telecommunications, and the electronic information industry in general. These news stories are placed in the broad categories of Politics, Business, Culture, and Technology. Affiliated with *Wired* magazine. Fees: Free.

PERIODICALS AND NEWSLETTERS

Digital Video Magazine. CMP Media LLC. • Monthly. $29.97 per year. Edited for producers and creators of digital media. Includes topics relating to video, audio, animation, multimedia, interactive design, and special effects. Covers both hardware and software, with product reviews. Formerly *Digital Video Magazine.*

SHOOT: The Leading Newsweekly for Commercial Production and Postproduction. VNU Business Media. • Weekly. $125.00 per year. Covers animation, music, sound design, computer graphics, visual effects, cinematography, and other aspects of television and motion picture production, with emphasis on TV commercials.

RESEARCH CENTERS AND INSTITUTES

Computer Graphics Laboratory. New York Institute of Technology, Fine Arts, Old Westbury, NY 11568. Phone: (516)686-7542 Fax: (516)686-7428 E-mail: pvoci@nyit.edu • Research areas include computer graphics, computer animation, and digital sound.

Graphics, Visualization, and Usability Center. Georgia Institute of Technology. GVU Center, 801 Atlantic Dr., Atlanta, GA 30332-0280. Phone: (404)894-4488 Fax: (404)894-0673 E-mail: afb@cc.gatech.edu • URL: http://www.cc.gatech.edu/gvu/ • Research areas include computer graphics, multimedia, image recognition, interactive graphics systems, animation, and virtual realities.

Inter-Arts Center. San Francisco State University, School of Creative Arts, 1600 Holloway Ave., San Francisco, CA 94132. Phone: (415)338-1478 Fax: (415)338-6159 E-mail: jimdavis@sfsu.edu • URL: http://www.sfsu.edu/~iac • Research areas include multimedia, computerized experimental arts processes, and digital sound.

UCLA Film and Television Archive-Research and Study Center. University of California, Los Angeles, 405 Hilgard Ave., 46 Powell Library, Los Angeles, CA 90095-1517. Phone: (310)206-5388 Fax: (310)206-5392 E-mail: arsc@ucla.edu • URL: http://www.cinema.ucla.edu/ • Research areas include animation.

TRADE/PROFESSIONAL ASSOCIATIONS

International Animated Film Society, ASIFA - Hollywood. 2114 W Burbank Blvd., Burbank, CA 91506. Phone: (818)842-8330 Fax: (818)842-5645 E-mail: info@asifa-hollywood.org • URL: http://www.asifa-hollywood.org • Represents professional animation artists, fans, and students of animation. Works to promote and advance the art of animation.

COMPUTER BULLETIN BOARDS

See: COMPUTER COMMUNICATIONS

COMPUTER COMMUNICATIONS

See also: INTERNET; LOCAL AREA NETWORKS; MICROCOMPUTERS AND MINICOMPUTERS; ONLINE INFORMATION SYSTEMS; TELECOMMUNICATIONS; TELECOMMUTING

GENERAL WORKS

Analog and Digital Communications. Hwei P. Hsu. McGraw-Hill. • 2003. $16.95. Second edition. (Schaum's Outlines Series).

Computer Networks. Andrew S. Tanenbaum. Prentice Hall PTR. • 2002. $89.00. Fourth edition.

Data Smog: Surviving the Information Glut. David Shenk. HarperSanFrancisco. • 1997. $14.00. A critical view of both the electronic and print information industries. Emphasis is on information overload.

Digital Literacy: Personal Preparation for the Internet Age. Paul Gilster. John Wiley and Sons, Inc. • 1997. $22.95. Provides practical advice for the on-line consumer on how to evaluate various aspects of the Internet ("digital literacy" is required, as well as "print literacy").

Interface Culture: How New Technology Transforms the Way We Create and Communicate. Steven Johnson. HarperSanFrancisco. • 1997. $24.00. A discussion of how computer interfaces and online technology ("cyberspace") affect society in general.

What Will Be: How the New World of Information Will Change Our Lives. Michael L. Dertouzos. DIANE Publishing Co. • 1997. $25.00. A discussion of the "information market place" of the future, including telecommuting, virtual reality, and computer recognition of speech. The author is director of the MIT Laboratory for Computer Science.

Wired Neighborhood. Stephen Doheny-Farina. Yale University Press. • 1996. $40.00. The author examines both the hazards and the advantages of "making the computer the center of our public and private lives," as exemplified by the Internet and telecommuting.

ABSTRACTS AND INDEXES

Applied Science and Technology Index. H. W. Wilson Co. • 11 times a year. Quarterly and annual cumulations. Price varies. Indexes a wide variety of English language technical, industrial, and engineering periodicals.

Business Periodicals Index. H. W. Wilson Co. • 11 times a year. Quarterly and annual cumulations. Price varies.

Communication Abstracts: An International Information Service. Sage Publications, Inc. • Bimonthly. Institutions, $1,150.00 per year. Provides broad coverage of the literature of communications, including broadcasting and advertising.

Computer and Control Abstracts. Available from INSPEC, Inc. • Monthly. $2,400.00 per year. Section C of *Science Abstracts.*

Computer and Information Systems Abstracts Journal: An Abstract Journal Pertaining to the Theory, Design, Fabrication and Application of Computer and Information Systems. CSA. • 11 times a year. $1,750 per year.

Computer Literature Index: A Subject/Author Index to Computer and Data Processing Literature. EBSCO Publishing. • Quarterly, with annual cumulation. $245.00 per year. Contains brief abstracts of book and periodical literature covering all phases of computing, including approximately 70 specific application areas.

Current Contents: Engineering, Computing and Technology. Thomson/ISI. • Weekly. $730.00 per year. Reproductions of contents pages of technical journals. Includes *Author Index, Address Directory, Current Book Contents* and *Title Word Index.* Formerly *Current Contents: Engineering, Technology and Applied Sciences.*

Electronics and Communications Abstracts Journal: Comprehensive Coverage of Essential Scientific Literature. CSA. • Monthly. $1,665.00 per year. Includes print and online editions.

Key Abstracts: Computer Communications and Storage. Available from INSPEC, Inc. • Monthly. $250.00 per year. Provides international coverage of journal and proceedings literature, including material on optical disks and networks. Published in England by the Institution of Electrical Engineers (IEE).

LAMP (Literature Analysis of Microcomputer Publications). Soft Images. • Bimonthly. $89.95 per year. Annual cumulation.

Science Citation Index. Thomson/ISI. • Bimonthly. $15,020.00 per year. Annual cumulation. Includes *Source Index, Citation Index, Permuterm Subject Index,* and *Corporate Index.*

ALMANACS AND YEARBOOKS

Communication Technology Update. Elsevier. • 2000. $36.95. 7th edition. A yearly review of developments in electronic media, telecommunications, and the Internet.

BIBLIOGRAPHIES

Computer Book Review. • Quarterly. $30.00 per year. Includes annual index. Reviews new computer

books. Back issues available.

CD-ROM DATABASES

Authority Computer and Telecommunications Law Library. LexisNexis/Matthew Bender. • Quarterly. Price on request. Full text CD-ROM provides cases, analysis, sample agreements, and other information relating to computer law, telecommunications regulation (cable, broadcasting, satellite, Internet), international computer law, and computer contracts.

DIRECTORIES

Business Organizations, Agencies, and Publications Directory. Gale Cengage Learning. • 2003. $480.00. 15th edition. Over 40,000 entries describing 39 types of business information sources. Classified by type of organization, publication, or serviceIncludes state, national, and international agencies and organizations. Master index to names and keywords. Also includes e-mail addresses and web site URL's.

Computer Review. Computer Review. • Covers: Technology solution providers. Entries include: Company name, address, phone, fax, e-mail, product/service. Three sections--"Solution Providers", including computer hardware and software companies, telecom infrastructure and services, and Internet applications and new media; "Trends and Profiles", including products, services, and business affiliations; and the "Market Directory".

Information Sources: The Annual Directory of the Information Industry Association. Software and Information Industry Association. • Annual. Members, $75.00; non-members, $125.00.

Major Information Technology Companies of the World 2001. Available from Gale Cengage Learning. • Annual. $880.00. Published by Graham & Whiteside. Contains profiles of more than 3,100 leading information technology companies in various countries.

Major Telecommunications Companies of the World. Available from Gale Cengage Learning. • 2003. $885.00. Sixth edition. Published by Graham & Whiteside. Contains detailed information and trade names for more than 3,500 important telecommunications companies in various countries.

MicroLeads Vendor Directory on Disk (Personal Computer Industry). Chromatic Communications Enterprises, Inc. • Annual. $495.00. Includes computer hardware manufacturers, software producers, book-periodical publishers, and franchised or company-owned chains of personal computer equipment retailers, support services and accessory manufacturers. Formerly *MicroLeads U.S. Vender Directory.*

Network Buyers Guide. CMP Media LLC. • Annual. $5.00. Lists suppliers of products for local and wide area computer networks. Formerly *LAN Buyers Guide Issue.*

Plunkett's E-Commerce and Internet Business Almanac. Plunkett Research, Ltd. • Annual. $249.99. Contains detailed profiles of 250 large companies engaged in various areas of Internet commerce, including e-business Web sites, communications equipment manufacturers, and Internet service providers. Includes CD-ROM.

Plunkett's InfoTech Industry Almanac: Complete Profiles on the InfoTech 500-the Leading Firms in the Movement and Management of Voice, Data, and Video. Plunkett Research, Ltd. • Biennial. $229.99. Includes CD-ROM. Five hundred major information companies are profiled, with corporate culture aspects. Discusses major trends in various sectors of the computer and information industry, including data on careers and job growth. Includes several indexes.

Telecommunications Directory. Gale. • Covers: Two volumes-North America and International, Cover approximately 6,000 national and international voice and data communications networks, electronic

mail services, teleconferencing facilities and services, facsimile services, Internet access providers, videotex and teletext operations, transactional services, local area networks, audiotex services, microwave systems/networkers, satellite facilities, and others involved in telecommunications, including related consultants, advertisers/marketers; associations, regulatory bodies, and publishers. Entries include: Company or organization name, address, phone, fax, year established, name and title of contact, executive officers and board of directors, function or type of service; geographical area served; NAICS and SIC codes; number of employees; general description, including telecommunications-related activities; product/service; specific applications; means of access and equipment required; publications; intended market and availability; pricing; stock exchanges traded and ticker symbols; financial figures.

ENCYCLOPEDIAS AND DICTIONARIES

Acronyms of Computer Science and Communications: A Comprehensive Acronym Dictionary and Illustrated Encyclopedia. Enjob Kajan and Ejub Kajan. Springer Verlag. • 2002. $49.95. Explains more than 4,000 "broadly used" computer, telecommunications, and information technology acronyms. Includes illustrations and Web addresses, where applicable.

CyberDictionary: Your Guide to the Wired World. Spurge ink!. • 1996. $17.95. Includes many illustrations.

Dictionary of Computing. Valerie Illingworth, editor. Oxford University Press. • 1997. $18.00. Fourth edition.

Dictionary of Information Technology and Computer Science. Tony Gunton. Blackwell Publishing. • 1994. $62.95. Second edition. Covers key words, phrases, abbreviations, and acronyms used in computing and data communications.

Encyclopedia of Communication and Information. Available from Gale Cengage Learning. • 2001. $395.00. Three volumes. Published by Macmillan Reference USA.

Every Manager's Guide to Information Technology: A Glossary of Key Terms and Concepts for Today's Business Leader. Peter G. W. Keen. Harvard Business School Publishing. • 1994. $18.95. Second edition. Provides definitions of terms related to computers, data communications, and information network systems. (Harvard Business Reference Series).

Hargrave's Communications Dictionary. Frank Hargrave. Available from John Wiley and Sons, Inc. • 2001. $140.00. Published by IEEE. Contains more than 10,000 definitions relating to voice and data communications, plus definitions in the areas of computer science, optics, networks, and the Internet. Includes acronyms, charts, equations, and drawings.

Wiley Encyclopedia of Telecommunications and Signal Processing. John G. Proakis, editor. John Wiley and Sons, Inc. • 2002. $1,250.00. Five volumes. Contains about 300 articles covering both fundamentals and recent advances in telecommunications and signal processing. Emphasis is on material for electrical engineers.

HANDBOOKS AND MANUALS

The Cybrarian's Manual. Pat Ensor, editor. American Library Association. • 2000. $45.00. Second edition. Provides information for librarians concerning the Internet, expert systems, computer networks, client/server architecture, Web pages, multimedia, information industry careers, and other "cyberspace" topics.

The Essential Guide to Bulletin Board Systems. Patrick R. Dewey. Information Today, Inc. • 1998. $39.50. Provides details on the setup and operation of online bulletin board systems. Covers both hardware and software.

For publishers addresses, refer to SOURCES CITED section at the back of the book.

The Modem Reference: The Complete Guide to PC Communications. Michael A. Banks. Information Today, Inc. • 2000. $29.95. Fourth edition. Covers personal computer data communications technology, including fax transmissions, computer networks, modems, and the Internet. Popularly written.

The Official America Online Tour Guide. Jennifer Watson and Dave Marx. John Wiley and Sons, Inc. • 2000. $24.99.Fifth edition. Provides a detailed explanation of the various features of versio of America Online, including electronic mail procedures and "Using the Internet.".

Reference Manual for Telecommunications Engineering. Roger L. Freeman. John Wiley and Sons, Inc. • 2001. $695.00. Third edition. Two volumes. Presents detailed information and specific data on the most commonly used telecommunications standards.

INTERNET DATABASES

InfoTech Trends. Data Analysis Group. Phone: (925)462-1202 Fax: (925)462-1225 E-mail: support@infotechtrends.com • URL: http://www. infotechtrends.com • Web site provides both free and fee-based market research data on the information technology industry, including computers, peripherals, telecommunications, the Internet, software, CD-ROM/DVD, e-commerce, and workstations. Fees: Free for current (most recent year) data; more extensive information has various fee structures. Formerly *Computer Industry Forecasts.*

ONLINE DATABASES

Applied Science and Technology Index Online. H. W. Wilson Co. • Provides online indexing of 500 major scientific, technical, industrial, and engineering periodicals. Time period is 1983 to date. Monthly updates. Inquire as to online cost and availability.

Globalbase. Gale Cengage Learning. • Provides more than one million online summaries of business, industrial, and economic news reports from more than 1,000 publications worldwide. Covers a wide range of material appearing in international trade journals, professional magazines, and newspapers. Time period is 1984 to date, with weekly updates. Inquire as to online cost and availability.

INSPEC. Institution of Electrical Engineers (IEE). • Provides online citations, with abstracts, to the world literature of electrical engineering, electronics, optoelectronics, telecommunications, industrial controls, instrumentation, computer technology, information technology, and physics. Coverage includes more than 4,000 technical and scientific journals from 1969 to date, with weekly updating. (INSPEC is Information Services in Physics, Electronics, and Computing.) Inquire as to online cost and availability.

Internet and Personal Computing Abstracts. Information Today, Inc. • Contains abstracts covering a wide variety of personal and business microcomputer literature appearing in more than 100 journals and popular magazines. Time period is 1981 to date, with monthly updates. Formerly *Microcomputer Index.* Inquire as to online cost and availability.

Management Contents. Gale Cengage Learning. • Covers a wide range of management, financial, marketing, personnel, and administrative topics. About 150 leading business journals are indexed and abstracted from 1974 to date, with monthly updating. Inquire as to online cost and availability.

PROMT: Predicasts Overview of Markets and Technology. Gale Cengage Learning. • Companies, products, applied technologies and markets. U.S. and international literature coverage, 1972 to date. Inquire as to online cost and availability. Provides

abstracts from more than 1,600 publications. Weekly updates.

Scisearch. Institute for Scientific Information. • Broad, multidisciplinary index to the literature of science and technology, 1974 to present. Inquire as to online cost and availability. Coverage of literature is worldwide, with weekly updates.

Trade & Industry Database. Gale Cengage Learning. • Provides indexing of business periodicals, January 1981 to date. Daily updates. (Full text articles from some periodicals are available online, 1983 to date. Inquire as to online cost and availability).

Wilson Business Abstracts Online. H. W. Wilson Co. • Indexes and abstracts 600 major business periodicals, plus the *Wall Street Journal* and the business section of the *New York Times.* Indexing is from 1982, abstracting from 1990, with the two newspapers included from 1993. Updated weekly. Inquire as to online cost and availability. (*Business Periodicals Index* without abstracts is also available online.).

PERIODICALS AND NEWSLETTERS

Boardwatch: Analysis of Telecom Software, Services and Strategy. Light Reading, Inc. • Monthly. $72.00 per year. Covers World Wide Web publishing, internet technology, educational aspects of online communication, internet legalities, and other computer communication topics.

Business Communications Review. Key3Media Group, Inc. • Monthly. $45.00 per year. Edited for communications managers in large end-user companies and institutions. Includes special feature issues on intranets and network management.

CIO: The Magazine for Chief Information Officers. CXO Media, Inc. • 23 times a year. $150.00 per year. Edited for chief information officers. Includes a monthly "Web Business" section (incorporates the former *WebMaster* periodical) and a monthly "Enterprise" section for company executives other than CIOs.

Communications News. Nelson Publishing Co. • Monthly. Free to qualified personnel; others, $84.00 per year.

Communications News: Solutions for Today's Networking Decision Managers. Nelson Publishing, Inc. • Monthly. Free to qualified personnel; others, $84.00 per year. Includes coverage of "Internetworking" and "Intranetworking." Emphasis is on emerging telecommunications technologies.

Computer Communications Review. Association for Computing Machinery, Special Interest Group on Data Communicatio. • Quarterly. Membership.

Computerworld: Newsweekly for Information Technology Leaders. Computerworld, Inc. • Weekly. $190.00 per year.

Electronic Messaging News: Strategies, Applications, and Standards. PBI Media, LLC. • Biweekly. $597.00 per year. Newsletter.

The Gray Sheet. F-D-C Reports Inc. • Description: Monitors the complex regulatory environment for devices, instrumentation, and diagnostics. Topics include device-related Congressional activity, Medicare reimbursement policies, international regulatory intiatives, enforcement and premarket approval programs at FDA's Center for Devices and Radiological Health. Recurring features include device approvals, 510(k) clearances, FDA recalls and seizures, mergers and acquisitions, and sales and earnings.

Handheld Computing: The Number One Guide to Handheld Devices. Mobile Media Group. • Nine times a year. $18.95 per year. Covers handheld devices for consumers, including PDAs, cell phones, digital cameras, MP3 players, tablet PCs, accessories, and software. Includes product reviews.

IEEE Communications Magazine. Institute of

Electrical and Electronics Engineers, Inc. • Monthly. $270.00 per year.

Information Processing and Management: An International Journal. Elsevier Science. • Bimonthly. Qualified personnel, $301.00 per year; institutions, $1,196.00 per year. Text in English, French, German and Italian.

Information Today: The Newspaper for Users and Producers of Electronic Information Services. Information Today, Inc. • 11 times a year. $68.95 per year.

Insurance Networking: Strategies and Solutions for Electronic Commerce. Thomson Media. • 10 times a year. Price on application. Covers information technology for the insurance industry, with emphasis on computer communications and the Internet.

Interactive Marketing and P R News: News and Practical Advice on Using Interactive Advertising and Marketing to Sell Your Products. PBI Media, LLC. • Biweekly. $495.00 per year. Newsletter. Provides information and guidance on merchandising via CD-ROM ("multimedia catalogs"), the Internet, and interactive TV. Topics include "cybermoney", addresses for e-mail marketing, "virtual malls," and other interactive subjects. Formerly *Interactive Marketing News.*

International Journal of Communication Systems. John Wiley and Sons, Inc., Journals. • Bimonthly. Individuals, $1,055.00 per year; institutions, $1,405.00 per year. Published in England by John Wiley and Sons Ltd. Formerly *International Journal of Digital and Analog Communication Systems.*

Laptop: Mobile Solutions for Business and Life. Bedford Communications. • Monthly. $18.00 per year. Consumer magazine containing articles and product reviews for notebook/laptop computers, handheld computers, tablet devices, cell phones, digital cameras, and other consumer electronic products.

Mobile PC. Future Network USA. • Monthly. $20.00 per year. Provides information and detailed product reviews for consumers. Covers notebook/ laptop computers, personal digital assistants (PDAs), wireless network equipment, cell phones, digital cameras, and other electronic products.

Mobility: Handheld and Wireless Solutions for Today's Business. Mobile Media Group. • Quarterly. $14.95 per year. Edited for business users of wireless handheld devices and notebook computers.

NetMag: Strategies and Solutions for the Network Professional. CMP Media LLC. • 13 times a year. Free to qualified personnel. Incorporates *Data Communications.*

Network Computing: Computing in a Network Environment. CMP Publications, Inc. • Semimonthly. Free to qualified personnel.

Network: Strategies and Solutions for the Network Professional. CMP Media LLC. • 13 times a year. Free to qualified personnel. Covers network products and peripherals for computer professionals. Includes annual network managers salary survey and annual directory issue. Formerly *LAN: The Network Solutions Magazine.*

Network World: The Newsweekly of Enterprise Network Computing. Network World Inc. • Weekly. $129.00 per year. Includes special feature issues on enterprise Internets, network operating systems, network management, high-speed modems, LAN management systems, and Internet access providers.

Telematics and Informatics: An International Journal on Telecommunications and Internet Technology. Elsevier. • Four times a year. Institutions, $938.00 per year.

Wired. Wired Ventures Ltd. • Monthly. $10.00 per year. Edited for creators and managers in various areas of electronic information and entertainment, including multimedia, the Internet, and video. Often

---

considered to be the primary publication of the "digital generation.".

Wireless Data News. Access Intelligence L.L.C. • Description: Provides analysis of technology, applications, marketing, and competition in the mobile communications industry. Scope is international. Recurring features include news of research.

Wireless Review: Intelligence for Competitive Providers. Primedia Business Magazines and Media. • Semimonthly. $48.00 per year. Covers business and technology developments for wireless service providers. Includes special issues on a wide variety of wireless topics. Formed by merger of *Cellular Business* and *Wireless World*.

RESEARCH CENTERS AND INSTITUTES

Concord Consortium, Inc. Concord Consortium. 25 Love Ln., Concord, MA 01742. Phone: (978)405-3200 Fax: (978)405-2076 E-mail: info@concord.org • URL: http://www.concord.org • Global technology-based Science and Math education, including educational applications of networking, computers and electronics.

Information Sciences Institute. University of Southern California, 4676 Admiralty Way, Suite 1001, Marina del Rey, CA 90292-6695. Phone: (310)822-1511 Fax: (310)823-6714 E-mail: schorr@isis.edu • URL: http://www.isi.edu • Research fields include online information and computer science, with emphasis on the World Wide Web.

Laboratory for Information and Decision Systems. Massachusetts Institute of Technology, 127 Massachusetts Ave., Bldg. 35, Room 308, Cambridge, MA 02139-4307. Phone: (617)258-8222 Fax: (617)253-3578 E-mail: chan@mit.edu • URL: http://www.justice.mit.edu • Research areas include data communication networks and fiber optic networks.

STATISTICS SOURCES

Communication Equipment, and Other Electronic Systems and Equipment. U. S. Bureau of the Census. • Annual. Provides data on shipments: value, quantity, imports, and exports. (Current Industrial Reports, MA-36P.).

OECD Information Technology Outlook 2000: ICTs, E-Commerce and the Information Economy. Organization for Economic Cooperation and Development. • 2000. $72.00. Provides data on information and communications technology (ICT) and electronic commerce in 11 OECD nations (includes U. S.). Coverage includes network infrastructure, electronic payment systems, financial transaction technologies, intelligent agents, global navigation systems, and portable flat panel display technologies.

Standard & Poor's Industry Surveys. Standard & Poor's. • Semiannual. $1,800.00. Two looseleaf volumes. Includes monthly *Supplements*. Provides detailed, individual surveys of 52 major industry groups. Each survey is revised on a semiannual basis. Also includes "Monthly Investment Review" (industry group investment analysis) and monthly "Trends & Projections" (economic analysis).

TRADE/PROFESSIONAL ASSOCIATIONS

Association for Interactive Marketing. 1430 Broadway, 8th Fl., New York, NY 10018. Phone: 888-337-0008 or (212)790-1408 Fax: (212)391-9233 • URL: http://www.interactivehq.com • Members are companies engaged in various interactive enterprises, utilizing the internet, interactive television, computer communications and multimedia. Formerly Association for Interactive Media.

Association of Internet Professionals. 2929 Main St., No. 136, Santa Monica, CA 90405. Phone: (866)247-9700 or (501)423-2248 Fax: (501)423-2248 E-mail: info@association.org • URL: http://

www.iproa.org • Members are interactive media professionals concerned with intetractive arts and technologies. Formerly International Interactive Communications Society.

Computer and Communications Industry Association. 666 11th St., N.W., Suite 600, Washington, DC 20001. Phone: (202)783-0070 Fax: (202)783-0534 E-mail: asteinem@ccianet.org • URL: http://www.ccianet.org • Formerly Computer Industry Association.

Electronic Frontier Foundation. 454 Shotwell St., San Francisco, CA 94110-1914. Phone: (415)436-9333 Fax: (415)436-9993 E-mail: information@eff.org • URL: http://www.eff.org • Promotes the creation of legal and structural approaches to help ease the assimilation of new technologies by society. Seeks to: help policymakers develop a better understanding of issues underlying telecommunications; increase public understanding of the opportunities and challenges posed by computing and telecommunications fields. Fosters awareness of civil liberties issues arising from the advancements in new computer-based communications media and supports litigation to preserve, protect, and extend First Amendment rights in computing and telecommunications technology. Maintains speakers' bureau; conducts educational programs. Encourages and supports the development of tools to endow non-technical users with access to computer-based telecommunications.

IEEE Computer Society. 1828 L St. NW, Ste. 1202, Washington, DC 20036. Phone: (202)371-0101 Fax: (202)728-9614 E-mail: help@computer.org • URL: http://www.computer.org • Computer professionals. Promotes the development of computer and information sciences and fosters communication within the information processing community. Sponsors conferences, symposia, workshops, tutorials, technical meetings, and seminars. Operates Computer Society Press. Presents scholarships; bestows technical achievement and service awards and certificates.

International Council for Computer Communication. P.O. Box 9745, Washington, DC 20016-9745. Phone: (703)836-7787 Fax: (703)836-7787 E-mail: office@icccgovernors.org • URL: http://www.icccgovernors.org • Affiliated with International Federation for Information Processing.

Special Interest Group on Management of Data. c/o Association for Computing Machinery, 1515 Broadway, New York, NY 10036. Phone: 800-342-6626 or (212)869-7440 Fax: (212)944-1318 E-mail: acmhelp@acm.org • URL: http://www.acm.org/sigmod • Focuses on network architecture, protocols, and distributed systems. Publishes a quarterly newsletter *Computer Communication Review*. Formerly Special Interest Group on Data Communication.

OTHER SOURCES

Wireless Data Networks. Gupta. Prentice Hall PTR. • 2000. Price on application. Presents market research information relating to cellular data networks, paging networks, packet radio networks, satellite systems, and other areas of wireless communication. Contains "summaries of recent developments and trends in wireless markets.".

COMPUTER CRIME AND SECURITY

GENERAL WORKS

Computer Fraud and Abuse Laws: An Overview of Federal Criminal Laws. Charles Doyle. Nova Science Publishers, Inc. • 2002. $27.50. The author is concerned mainly with the federal computer fraud and abuse statute, 18 U.S.C. 1030.

Computer Virus Crisis. Philip E. Fites and others. DIANE Publishing Co. • 1999. $15.00. Second edition.

Cybercrime and Cyberterrorism: Current Issues. John V. Blane. Nova Science Publishers, Inc. • 2003. $29.50. Emphasizes the legal fight against cybercrime that is taking place in various countries of the world.

Information Security Fundamentals. Thomas R. Peltier and others. CRC Press. • 2004. $59.95. Provides basic information on computer security, employee responsibilities, and "common threats." (Imprint: Auerbach Publications.).

ABSTRACTS AND INDEXES

Applied Science and Technology Index. H. W. Wilson Co. • 11 times a year. Quarterly and annual cumulations. Price varies. Indexes a wide variety of English language technical, industrial, and engineering periodicals.

Business Periodicals Index. H. W. Wilson Co. • 11 times a year. Quarterly and annual cumulations. Price varies.

Computer and Control Abstracts. Available from INSPEC, Inc. • Monthly. $2,400.00 per year. Section C of *Science Abstracts*.

Computer and Information Systems Abstracts Journal: An Abstract Journal Pertaining to the Theory, Design, Fabrication and Application of Computer and Information Systems. CSA. • 11 times a year. $1,750 per year.

Computer Literature Index: A Subject/Author Index to Computer and Data Processing Literature. EBSCO Publishing. • Quarterly, with annual cumulation. $245.00 per year. Contains brief abstracts of book and periodical literature covering all phases of computing, including approximately 70 specific application areas.

Current Contents: Engineering, Computing and Technology. Thomson/ISI. • Weekly. $730.00 per year. Reproductions of contents pages of technical journals. Includes *Author Index, Address Directory, Current Book Contents* and *Title Word Index*. Formerly *Current Contents: Engineering, Technology and Applied Sciences*.

BIBLIOGRAPHIES

Computer Security: A Bibliography with Indexes. John S. Potts, editor. Nova Science Publishers, Inc. • 2002. $59.00. Covers literature on computer hackers, viruses, identity theft, electronic spying, and other security issues. Includes author, title, and subject indexes.

CD-ROM DATABASES

Authority Computer and Telecommunications Law Library. LexisNexis/Matthew Bender. • Quarterly. Price on request. Full text CD-ROM provides cases, analysis, sample agreements, and other information relating to computer law, telecommunications regulation (cable, broadcasting, satellite, Internet), international computer law, and computer contracts.

OECD Statistical Compendium. Organization for Economic Cooperation and Development. • Semiannual. $1,905.00 per year for 1 to 10 users. CD-ROM contains more than 730,000 monthly, quarterly, and annual time series for OECD countries, 1960 to date. Includes fully searchable data on agriculture, food, economic indicators, national accounts, employment, energy, finance, industry, technology, and foreign trade. Results can be displayed in various forms.

DIRECTORIES

Business Organizations, Agencies, and Publications Directory. Gale Cengage Learning. • 2003. $480.00. 15th edition. Over 40,000 entries describing 39 types of business information sources. Classified by type of organization, publication, or serviceIncludes state, national, and international agencies and organizations. Master index to names and keywords. Also includes e-mail addresses and web site URL's.

Computer Security Buyers Guide. Computer

Security Institute. • Covers: about 650 suppliers and consultants of computer security products, including communications and network security, disaster recovery, media security, personnel security, and security training. Entries include: Firm name, address, phone, name and title of contact, product or service provided.

Security: Product Service Suppliers Guide. Reed Business Information. • Annual. $50.00 Includes computer and information protection products. Formerly *Security World Product Directory.*

ENCYCLOPEDIAS AND DICTIONARIES

Dictionary of Computing. Valerie Illingworth, editor. Oxford University Press. • 1997. $18.00. Fourth edition.

HANDBOOKS AND MANUALS

Computer Security Basics. Deborah F. Russell and G. T. Gangemi. O'Reilly and Associates, Inc. • 1991. $29.95. (Computer Science Series).

Corporate Fraud. Michael J. Comer. Ashgate Publishing Co. • 1997. Third edition. $139.95. Examines new risks of corporate fraud related to "electronic commerce, derivatives, computerization, empowerment, downsizing, and other recent developments." Covers fraud detection, prevention, and internal control systems. Published by Gower in England.

Cyber Crime Investigator's Field Guide. Bruce Middleton. CRC Press. • 2004. $69.95. Second edition. Provides a step-by-step routine for investigating cybercrime, including the use of key forensic software, sample questions for clients, evidence collection, and examples from case studies. (Imprint: Auerbach Publications.).

The Ethical Hack: A Framework for Business Value Penetration Testing. James S. Tiller. CRC Press. • 2004. $69.95. Provides practical information relating to the deliberate, "ethical hacking" of a computer system to uncover security flaws. Includes hacker technology, interpretation of results, protection of security professionals, staff politics, and details of various testing procedures. (Imprint: Auerbach Publications.).

Guidelines for Consumer Protection in the Context of Electronic Commerce. Organization for Economic Cooperation and Development. • 2000. $20.00. Provides a guide to effective consumer protection in online business-to-consumer transactions. Text in English and French.

Hacker's Handbook: The Strategy Behind Breaking Into and Defending Networks. Susan Young and Dave Aitel. CRC Press. • 2003. $79.95. Reveals "the technical aspects of hacking that are least understood by network administrators." Practical defenses are outlined. (Imprint: Auerbach Publications.).

Halting the Hacker: A Practical Guide to Computer Security. Donald L. Pipkin. Prentice Hall PTR. • 2002. $44.99. Second edition. (Hewlett-Packard Professional Book Series).

Net Crimes and Misdemeanors: Outmaneuvering the Spammers, Swindlers, and Stalkers Who Are Targeting You Online. Jayne Hitchcock. Information Today, Inc. • 2002. $24.95. Provides specific strategies and techniques for dealing with a wide range of online abusive practices. (CyberAge Books.).

Short Course on Computer Viruses. Frederick B. Cohen. John Wiley and Sons, Inc. • 1994. $44.95. Second edition. Includes CD-Rom. (Professional Computing Series).

Trade Secret Protection in an Information Age. Gale R. Peterson. Glasser LegalWorks. • Looseleaf. $149. 00, including sample forms on disk. Periodic supplementation available. Covers trade secret law relating to computer software, online databases, and multimedia products. Explanations are based on more than 1,000 legal cases. Sample forms on disk include work-for-hire examples and covenants not to compete.

INTERNET DATABASES

Business 2.0 Web Guide to the Best Business Links. Business 2.0 Media Inc. Phone: (415)293-4800 E-mail: support@business2.com • URL: http://www.business2.com/webguide • Web site presents an extensive, searchable directory of links to "the best, most informative, and authoritative web pages." Twenty main categories cover business, finance, career, company information, people, and technology topics, with thousands of subtopics, all linking to Web sites recommended by experienced business researchers. Fees: Free.

ONLINE DATABASES

Applied Science and Technology Index Online. H. W. Wilson Co. • Provides online indexing of 500 major scientific, technical, industrial, and engineering periodicals. Time period is 1983 to date. Monthly updates. Inquire as to online cost and availability.

Internet and Personal Computing Abstracts. Information Today, Inc. • Contains abstracts covering a wide variety of personal and business microcomputer literature appearing in more than 100 journals and popular magazines. Time period is 1981 to date, with monthly updates. Formerly *Microcomputer Index.* Inquire as to online cost and availability.

PROMT: Predicasts Overview of Markets and Technology. Gale Cengage Learning. • Companies, products, applied technologies and markets. U.S. and international literature coverage, 1972 to date. Inquire as to online cost and availability. Provides abstracts from more than 1,600 publications. Weekly updates.

Wilson Business Abstracts Online. H. W. Wilson Co. • Indexes and abstracts 600 major business periodicals, plus the *Wall Street Journal* and the business section of the *New York Times.* Indexing is from 1982, abstracting from 1990, with the two newspapers included from 1993. Updated weekly. Inquire as to online cost and availability. (*Business Periodicals Index* without abstracts is also available online.).

PERIODICALS AND NEWSLETTERS

Computer Fraud and Security. Elsevier. • Monthly. $833.00 per year. Newsletter. Formerly *Computer Fraud and Security Bulletin.*

Computer Security Digest. Jack Bologna. Computer Protection Systems Inc. • Description: Provides information on computer security; company lawsuits; software viruses, failures, and piracy; and international privacy protection.

Computers and Security: The International Journal Devoted to the Study of the Technical and Financial Aspects of Computer Security. International Federation for Information Processing AUT Technical Committee on Computer Security. Elsevier. • Eight times a year. Institutions, $760.00 per year.

CSO: The Resource for Security Executives. CXO Media, Inc. • Monthly. $64.95 per year. Edited for corporate chief security officers (CSOs). Covers a wide variety of business security issues, including computer security, identity theft, spam, physical security, loss prevention, risk management, privacy, and investigations.

EDP Weekly: The Leading Weekly Computer News Summary. Computer Age and EDP News Services. • Weekly. $495.00 per year. Newsletter. Summarizes news from all areas of the computer and microcomputer industries.

FBI Law Enforcement Bulletin. Available from U. S. Government Printing Office. • Monthly. $36.00 per year. Issued by Federal Bureau of Investigation, U. S. Department of Justice. Contains articles on a wide variety of law enforcement and crime topics, including computer-related crime.

The Gray Sheet. F-D-C Reports Inc. • Description: Monitors the complex regulatory environment for devices, instrumentation, and diagnostics. Topics include device-related Congressional activity, Medicare reimbursement policies, international regulatory intiatives, enforcement and premarket approval programs at FDA's Center for Devices and Radiological Health. Recurring features include device approvals, 510(k) clearances, FDA recalls and seizures, mergers and acquisitions, and sales and earnings.

IEEE Security & Privacy: Building Confidence in a Networked World. IEEE Computer Society. • Bimonthly. $72.00 per year to individuals; $525.00 to institutions. Emphasis is on computer and netwoek security for large systems.

Information Systems Security. Auerbach Publications. • Bimonthly. $175.00 per year. Formerly *Journal of Information Systems Security.*

Journal of Computer Security. Sushil Jajodia and Jonathan K. Millen, editors. IOS Press, Inc. • Six times a year. Institutions, $542.00 per year.

Security Management. American Society for Industrial Security. • Monthly. Members, $38.00 per year; non-members, $48.00 per year. Articles cover the protection of corporate assets, including personnel property and information security.

Security: The Magazine for Buyers of Security Products, Systems and Service. Business News Publishing Co. • Monthly. $82.90 per year.

White-Collar Crime Reporter: Information and Analyses Concerning White-Collar Practice. Andrews Publications. • 10 times a year. $550.00 per year. Newsletter. Provides information on trends in white collar crime.

TRADE/PROFESSIONAL ASSOCIATIONS

American Society for Industrial Security. 1625 Prince St., Alexandria, VA 22314-2818. Phone: (703)519-6200 Fax: (703)519-6299 E-mail: asis@asisonline • URL: http://www.asisonline.org.

Computer Security Institute. 600 Harrison St., San Francisco, CA 94107. Phone: 800-250-2429 or (415)947-6320 Fax: (415)947-6023 E-mail: csi@techweb.com • URL: http://www.gocsi.com • Serves the information security professional.

IEEE Computer Society. 1828 L St. NW, Ste. 1202, Washington, DC 20036. Phone: (202)371-0101 Fax: (202)728-9614 E-mail: help@computer.org • URL: http://www.computer.org • Computer professionals. Promotes the development of computer and information sciences and fosters communication within the information processing community. Sponsors conferences, symposia, workshops, tutorials, technical meetings, and seminars. Operates Computer Society Press. Presents scholarships; bestows technical achievement and service awards and certificates.

National Center for Computer Crime Data. 1714 Brommer St., Santa Cruz, CA 95062. Phone: (831)475-4457 Fax: (831)475-5336 E-mail: anudnic@aol.com • Conducts research, compiles statistics, provides case studies and other information.

Special Interest Group on Security, Audit, and Control. c/o Association for Computing Machinery, 1515 Broadway, New York, NY 10036. Phone: 800-342-6626 or (212)869-7440 Fax: (212)944-1318 E-mail: acmhelp@acm.org • URL: http://www.acm.org/sigsac.

OTHER SOURCES

White Collar Crime: Business and Regulatory Offenses. American Lawyer Media, Inc. • Looseleaf. $249.00. Updated as needed. Covers such legal matters as criminal tax cases, securities fraud, computer crime, mail fraud, bank embezzlement, criminal antitrust activities, extortion, perjury, the criminal liability of corporations, and RICO (Racketeer Influenced and Corrupt Organization Act). (Law Journal Press).

COMPUTER DEALERS

See: COMPUTER RETAILING

COMPUTER GRAPHICS

See also: COMPUTER-AIDED DESIGN AND MANUFACTURING (CAD/CAM); COMPUTER ANIMATION

GENERAL WORKS

Computer Graphics. Prentice Hall PTR. • 2000. $72.00.

Multimedia: Concepts and Practice. Stephen McGloughlin. Prentice Hall Books. • 2000. $73.33. Includes audio compact disk. Provides basic information and instruction on multimedia graphic design, animation, video editing, sound editing, authoring, product creation, and other multimedia topics.

ABSTRACTS AND INDEXES

Computer Literature Index: A Subject/Author Index to Computer and Data Processing Literature. EBSCO Publishing. • Quarterly, with annual cumulation. $245.00 per year. Contains brief abstracts of book and periodical literature covering all phases of computing, including approximately 70 specific application areas.

LAMP (Literature Analysis of Microcomputer Publications). Soft Images. • Bimonthly. $89.95 per year. Annual cumulation.

BIBLIOGRAPHIES

Computer Book Review. • Quarterly. $30.00 per year. Includes annual index. Reviews new computer books. Back issues available.

DIRECTORIES

The SHOOT Directory for Commercial Production and Postproduction. SHOOT. • Annual. $79.00. Lists production companies, advertising agencies, and sources of professional television, motion picture, and audio equipment.

ENCYCLOPEDIAS AND DICTIONARIES

Graphically Speaking: An Illustrated Guide to the Working Language of Design and Publishing. Mark Beach. Coast to Coast Books. • 1992. $29.50. Provides practical definitions of 2,800 terms used in printing, graphic design, publishing, and desktop publishing. Over 300 illustrations are included, about 40 in color.

HANDBOOKS AND MANUALS

Columbia Guide to Digital Publishing: In Print and On the Web. William E. Kasdorf, editor. Columbia University Press. • 2002. $65.00. Covers the practical production of both written and graphic material in digital format, including archives, new technology, "information architecture," and copyright.

Handbook of Digital Publishing. Michael L. Kleper. Prentice Hall PTR. • 2001. $129.99. Two volumes. Edited for the digital publishing industry. Covers print publishing, electronic documents, and Internet (Web) publishing, including basic desktop procedures. Provides information on typography, design, layout, image creation, and page creation.

Learning Web Design: A Beginner's Guide to HTML, Graphics, and Beyond. Jennifer Niederst. O'Reilly & Associates, Inc. • 2001. $34.95. Written for beginners who have no previous knowledge of how Web design works.

PC Graphics Handbook. Julio Sanchez and Maria P. Canton. CRC Press. • 2003. $129.95. Covers both the hardware and software specifics of PC graphics programming. Includes such practical and theoretical topics as graphics algorithms, relevant mathematics, artificial life, virtual reality, device drivers, antimation techniques, and video games.

Web Style Guide: Basic Design Principles for Creating Web Sites. Patrick J. Lynch and Sarah Horton. Yale University Press. • 2002. $35.00. Second edition. Covers design of content, interface, page layout, graphics, and multimedia aspects.

ONLINE DATABASES

Internet and Personal Computing Abstracts. Information Today, Inc. • Contains abstracts covering a wide variety of personal and business microcomputer literature appearing in more than 100 journals and popular magazines. Time period is 1981 to date, with monthly updates. Formerly *Microcomputer Index.* Inquire as to online cost and availability.

PROMT: Predicasts Overview of Markets and Technology. Gale Cengage Learning. • Companies, products, applied technologies and markets. U.S. and international literature coverage, 1972 to date. Inquire as to online cost and availability. Provides abstracts from more than 1,600 publications. Weekly updates.

PERIODICALS AND NEWSLETTERS

ACM Transactions on Graphics. Association for Computing Machinery. • Quarterly. Members, $41.00 per year; non-members, $170.00 per year; students, $36.00 per year.

Advanced Manufacturing Technology: Monthly Report. Technical Insights. • Monthly. Institutions, $695.00 per year. Newsletter. Covers technological developments relating to robotics, computer graphics, automation, computer-integrated manufacturing, and machining.

Computer Graphics. Special Interest Group on Computer Graphics. Association for Computing Machinery. • Quarterly. Members, $59.00 per year; non-members, $95.00 per year; students, $50.00 per year.

Computer Graphics World. PennWell Publishing Co., Advanced Technology Div. • Monthly. $55.00 per year.

Computers and Graphics: International Journal of Systems Applications in Computer Graphics. Elsevier. • Bimonthly. Qualified personnel, $180.00 per year; institutions, $1,760.00 per year.

Engineering Design Graphics Journal. American Society for Engineering Education. • Three times a year. Free to members; Non-members, $24.00 per year. Concerned with engineering graphics, computer graphics, geometric modeling, computer-aided drafting, etc.

IEEE Computer Graphics and Applications. Insitute of Electrical and Electronics Engineers, Inc. • Bimonthly. $695.00 per year.

IEEE Transactions on Visualization and Computer Graphics. Institute of Electrical and Electronics Engineers, Inc. • Quarterly. $676.00 per year. Topics include computer vision, computer graphics, image processing, signal processing, computer-aided design, animation, and virtual reality.

IMAGES. IMAGE Society. • Semiannual. $25.00 per year. Newsletter Provides news of virtual reality developments and the IMAGE Society.

The Journal of Visualization and Computer Animation. John Wiley and Sons, Inc., Journals. • Quarterly. Individuals, $743.00 per year; institutions, $955.00 per year. Research papers on the technological developments (both hardware and software) that will make animation tools more accessible to end-users. International coverage. Published in England by John Wiley and Sons Ltd.

The Magazine for Electronic Publishing Professionals. Publish Media. • Monthly. $39.90 per year. Edited for professional publishers, graphic designers, and industry service providers. Covers new products and emerging technologies for the electronic publishing industry.

SHOOT: The Leading Newsweekly for Commercial Production and Postproduction. VNU Business Media. • Weekly. $125.00 per year. Covers animation, music, sound design, computer graphics, visual effects, cinematography, and other aspects of television and motion picture production, with emphasis on TV commercials.

Step-By-Step Electronic Design: The How-To Newsletter for Electronic Designers. Dynamic Graphics, Inc. • Monthly. $48.00 per year.

Step Inside Design: The World of Design from Inside Out. Dynamic Graphics, Inc. • Bimonthly. $42.00 per year. Formerly*Step-by-Step Graphics.*

RESEARCH CENTERS AND INSTITUTES

Computer Graphics Laboratory. New York Institute of Technology, Fine Arts, Old Westbury, NY 11568. Phone: (516)686-7542 Fax: (516)686-7428 E-mail: pvoci@nyit.edu • Research areas include computer graphics, computer animation, and digital sound.

Electronic Visualization Laboratory. University of Illinois at Chicago, Engineering Research Facility, 842 W. Taylor St., Room 2032, Chicago, IL 60607-7053. Phone: (312)996-3002 Fax: (312)413-7585 E-mail: tom@uic.edu • URL: http://www.evl.uic.edu • Research areas include computer graphics, virtual reality, multimedia, and interactive techniques.

Graphics, Visualization, and Usability Center. Georgia Institute of Technology. GVU Center, 801 Atlantic Dr., Atlanta, GA 30332-0280. Phone: (404)894-4488 Fax: (404)894-0673 E-mail: afb@cc.gatech.edu • URL: http://www.cc.gatech.edu/gvu/ • Research areas include computer graphics, multimedia, image recognition, interactive graphics systems, animation, and virtual realities.

Image Science Research Group. Worcester Polytechnic Institute, Computer Science Dept., 100 Institute Rd., Worcester, MA 01609-2208. Phone: (508)831-5357 Fax: (508)831-5776 E-mail: matt@wpi.edu • URL: http://www.cs.wpi.edu/research/isrg • Areas of research include image processing, computer graphics, and computational vision.

Institute for Information Science and Technology. George Washington University, 801 22nd St., N. W., 6th Fl., Washington, DC 20052. Phone: (202)994-6208 Fax: (202)994-0227 E-mail: helgert@seas.gwu.edu • Research areas include computer graphics and image processing.

TRADE/PROFESSIONAL ASSOCIATIONS

IEEE Computer Society. 1828 L St. NW, Ste. 1202, Washington, DC 20036. Phone: (202)371-0101 Fax: (202)728-9614 E-mail: help@computer.org • URL: http://www.computer.org • Computer professionals. Promotes the development of computer and information sciences and fosters communication within the information processing community. Sponsors conferences, symposia, workshops, tutorials, technical meetings, and seminars. Operates Computer Society Press. Presents scholarships; bestows technical achievement and service awards and certificates.

IMAGE Society. PO Box 6221, Chandler, AZ 85246-6221. Phone: (602)839-8709 E-mail: image@asu.edu • URL: http://image-society.org • Individuals and organizations interested in the technological advancement and application of real-time visual simulation (medical, virtual reality, telepresence, aeronautical, and automotive) and other related virtual reality technologies.

InfoComm International. 11242 Waples Mill Rd., Ste. 200, Fairfax, VA 22030-6079. Phone: 800-659-7469 or (703)273-7200 Fax: (703)278-8082 E-mail: customerservice@infocomm.org • URL: http://

www.infocomm.org • Represents for-profit individuals and organizations that derive revenue from the commercialization or utilization of communications technology. Ensures the credibility and desirability of its members' products and services by representing the communications industry to the public, business, education, and governments.

Special Interest Group on Design Automation. c/o Association for Computing Machinery, 1515 Broadway, New York, NY 10036. Phone: 800-342-6626 or (212)869-7440 Fax: (212)944-1318 E-mail: acmhelp@acm.org • URL: http://www.acm.org/sigda • Concerned with computer-aided design systems and software. Publishes the semiannual *SIGDA Newsletter*.

COMPUTER IMAGING

See: DOCUMENT IMAGING

COMPUTER INDUSTRY

See: COMPUTERS; MICROCOMPUTERS AND MINICOMPUTERS

COMPUTER INTEGRATED MANUFACTURING (CIM)

See: COMPUTER-AIDED DESIGN AND MANUFACTURING (CAD/CAM); SYSTEMS INTEGRATION

COMPUTER LAW

GENERAL WORKS

Law of the Super Searchers: The Online Secrets of Top Legal Researchers. T. R. Halvorson. Information Today, Inc. • 1999. $24.95. Eight law researchers explain how to find useful legal information online. (Super Searchers Series).

ABSTRACTS AND INDEXES

Computer Literature Index: A Subject/Author Index to Computer and Data Processing Literature. EBSCO Publishing. • Quarterly, with annual cumulation. $245.00 per year. Contains brief abstracts of book and periodical literature covering all phases of computing, including approximately 70 specific application areas.

Current Law Index: Multiple Access to Legal Periodicals. Gale Cengage Learning. • Monthly. $725.00 per year. Produced in cooperation with the American Association of Law Libraries. Indexes more than 900 law journals, legal newspapers, and specialty publications from the U.S., Canada, U.K., Ireland, Australia, and New Zealand.

Index to Legal Periodicals and Books. H. W. Wilson Co. • Monthly. $490.00 per year. Quarterly and annual cumulations.

BIBLIOGRAPHIES

Encyclopedia of Legal Information Sources. Gale Cengage Learning. • 1992. $180.00. Second edition. Lists more than 23,000 law-related information sources, including print, nonprint, and organizational.

CD-ROM DATABASES

Authority Computer and Telecommunications Law Library. LexisNexis/Matthew Bender. • Quarterly. Price on request. Full text CD-ROM provides cases, analysis, sample agreements, and other information relating to computer law, telecommunications regulation (cable, broadcasting, satellite, Internet), international computer law, and computer contracts.

Authority Intellectual Property Library. LexisNexis/Matthew Bender. • Quarterly. Price on request. CD-ROM contains updated full text of *Intellectual Property Counseling and Litigation, Computer Law, International Computer Law, Nimmer on Copyright, Milgrim on Trade Secrets, Patent Litigation, Patent Licensing Transactions, Trademark Protection and Practice,* and other Matthew Bender publications relating to the law of intellectual property.

LegalTrac. Gale Cengage Learning. • Monthly. $5,000.00 per year. Price includes workstation. Provides CD-ROM indexing of periodical literature relating to legal matters from 1980 to date. Corresponds to online *Legal Resource Index.*

WILSONDISC: Index to Legal Periodicals and Books. H. W. Wilson Co. • Monthly. Includes unlimited online access to *Index to Legal Periodicals* through WILSONLINE. Contains CD-ROM indexing of more than 1,400 English language legal periodicals from 1981 to date and 2,500 books.

DIRECTORIES

Law and Legal Information Directory. Gale Cengage Learning. • Annual. $440.00. Contains a wide range of sources of legal information, such as associations, law schools, courts, federal agencies, referral services, libraries, publishers, and research centers. There is a separate chapter for each of 23 types of information source or service.

Lawyer's Register International by Specialties and Fields of Law Including a Directory of Corporate Counsel. Lawyer's Register Publishing Co. • Annual. $359.00. Three volumes. Referral source for law firms.

HANDBOOKS AND MANUALS

Computer Law: Cases, Comments, Questions. Peter B. Maggs and others. West Publishing Co. • 1991. $62.50. (Amrican Casebook Series).

Fundamentals of Computer-High Technology Law. James V. Vergari and Virginia V. Shue. American Law Institute-American Bar Association Committee on Continuing Professional Education. • 1991. $29.00.

INTERNET DATABASES

Lexis.com Research System. Lexis-Nexis Group. Phone: 800-227-4908 or (937)865-6800 Fax: (937)865-6909 E-mail: webmaster@prod.lexisnexis.com • URL: http://www.lexis.com • Fee-based Web site offers extensive searching of a wide variety of legal sources. Additional features include Daily Opinion Service, lexis.com Bookstore, Career Center, CLE Center, Law Schools, and Practice Pages ("Pages specific to areas of specialty").

ONLINE DATABASES

Index to Legal Periodicals and Books (Online). H. W. Wilson Co. • Broad coverage of law journals and books 1981 to date. Monthly updates. Inquire as to online cost and availability.

Legal Resource Index. Gale Cengage Learning. • Broad coverage of law literature appearing in legal, business, and other periodicals, 1980 to date. Daily updates. Inquire as to online cost and availability.

PERIODICALS AND NEWSLETTERS

Computer Law Reporter: A Monthly Journal of Computer Law and Practice, Intellectual Property, Copyright and Trademark Law. Computer Law Reporter, Inc. • Monthly. $1,650.00 per year. Newsletter.

Computer Law Strategist. American Lawyer Media Inc. • Monthly. $265.00 per year. Newsletter.

Cyberspace Lawyer. Glasser Legalworks. • 11 times a year. $300.00 per year. Newsletter. Covers various legal topics pertaining to use of the Internet. Includes advice on legal research via the Web.

Internet Law Researcher. Glasser Legalworks. • 11 times a year. $200.00 per year. Newsletter for legal professionals on how to search the Web efficiently. Provides detailed information on individual Web sites.

Privacy and Information Law Report. Glasser Legalworks. • 10 times a year. $375.00 per year. Newsletter. Coverage includes the legal aspects of health record privacy, employee records, anti-spam, and privacy-enhancing technology. Provides reports on relevant court cases and consumer advocacy.

Technology Law Alert: Monthly Newsletter Covering Computer-Related Law and Tax Issues. Roditti Reports Corp. • Monthly. $297.00 per year. Newsletter. Formerly *Computer Law and Tax Report.*

RESEARCH CENTERS AND INSTITUTES

Center for the Study of Law, Science, and Technology. Arizona State University, College of Law, P.O. Box 877906, Tempe, AZ 85287-7906. Phone: (480)965-2554 Fax: (480)965-2427 E-mail: gary.marchant@asu.edu • URL: http://www.law.asu.edu • Studies the legal problems created by technological advances.

TRADE/PROFESSIONAL ASSOCIATIONS

International Technology Law Association. 401 Edgewater Pl., Ste. 600, Wakefield, MA 01880. Phone: (781)876-8877 Fax: (781)224-1239 E-mail: office@itechlaw.org • URL: http://www.itechlaw.org • Lawyers, law students, and others interested in legal problems related to computer-communications technology. Aids in: contracting for computer-communications goods and services; perfecting and protecting proprietary rights chiefly in software; and taxing computer-communications goods, services, and transactions, and liability for acquisition and use of computer-communications goods and services. Provides specialized educational programs; and offers limited placement service. Holds Annual Computer Law Update.

OTHER SOURCES

Computer and Online Industry Litigation Reporter: The National Journal of Record of Computer Online Industry. Andrews Publications, Inc. • Semimonthly. $875.00 per year. Newsletter. Provides complete text of key decisions relating to copyright, patents, trademarks, breach of contract, etc. Formerly *Computer Industry Litigation Reporter.*

Computer Software: Protection, Liability, Forms. L. J. Kutten. West Group. • Semiannual. $576.00 per year. Four looseleaf volumes. Covers copyright law, patents, trade secrets, licensing, publishing contracts, and other legal topics related to computer software.

E-Commerce and Internet Law: Treatise with Forms. Ian C. Ballon. Glasser Legalworks. • Three looseleaf volumes. $595.00. Periodic supplementation. Analyzes Internet legalities. including litigious matters relating to downloading, streaming, music, video, content aggregation, domain names, chatrooms, and search engines. Includes forms, contracts, checklists, sample pleadings, and an extensive glossary.

Guide to Computer Law. CCH, Inc. • Semimonthly. $602.00 per year. Two looseleaf volumes.

COMPUTER NETWORKS

See: COMPUTER COMMUNICATIONS; LOCAL AREA NETWORKS

COMPUTER OUTPUT MICROFILM (COM)

See: MICROFORMS

COMPUTER PERIPHERALS AND ACCESSORIES

See also: MICROCOMPUTERS AND MINICOMPUTERS

ABSTRACTS AND INDEXES

Applied Science and Technology Index. H. W. Wilson Co. • 11 times a year. Quarterly and annual cumulations. Price varies. Indexes a wide variety of English language technical, industrial, and engineering periodicals.

Business Periodicals Index. H. W. Wilson Co. • 11 times a year. Quarterly and annual cumulations. Price varies.

Computer and Control Abstracts. Available from INSPEC, Inc. • Monthly. $2,400.00 per year. Section C of *Science Abstracts.*

Computer and Information Systems Abstracts Journal: An Abstract Journal Pertaining to the Theory, Design, Fabrication and Application of Computer and Information Systems. CSA. • 11 times a year. $1,750 per year.

Computer Literature Index: A Subject/Author Index to Computer and Data Processing Literature. EBSCO Publishing. • Quarterly, with annual cumulation. $245.00 per year. Contains brief abstracts of book and periodical literature covering all phases of computing, including approximately 70 specific application areas.

CD-ROM DATABASES

Datapro on CD-ROM: Computer Systems Hardware and Software. Gartner Group, Inc. • Monthly. Price on application. CD-ROM provides product specifications, product reports, user surveys, and market forecasts for a wide range of computer hardware and software.

DIRECTORIES

Better Buys for Business: The Independent Consumer Guide to Office Equipment. What to Buy for Business, Inc. • 10 times a year. $134.00 per year. Each issue is on a particular office product, with detailed evaluation of specific models: 1. Low-Volume Copier Guide, 2. Mid-Volume Copier Guide, 3. High-Volume Copier Guide, 4. Plain Paper Fax and Low-Volume Multifunctional Guide, 5. Mid/High-Volume Multifunctional Guide, 6. Laser Printer Guide, 7. Color Printer and Color Copier Guide, 8. Scan-to-File Guide, 9. Business Phone Systems Guide, 10. Postage Meter Guide, with a Short Guide to Shredders.

Computer Parts and Supplies Directory. infoUSA. • Annual. Price on application. Lists 7,020 companies. Compiled from telephone company yellow pages.

Control Engineering Buyers Guide. Reed Business Information. • Annual. Price on application. Contains specifications, prices, and manufacturers' listings for computer software, as related to control engineering.

Directory of Computer VAR's and Systems Integrators. Chain Store Guide. • Annual. $327.00. Provides information on computer companies that modify, enhance, or customize hardware or software. Includes systems houses, systems integrators, turnkey systems specialists, original equipment manufacturers, and value added retailers. Formerly *Directory of Value Added Resellers.*

Laptop: Mobile Solutions for Business and Life. Bedford Communications, Inc. • Monthly. $12.00 per year. Contains informative articles and critical reviews of laptop, notebook, subnotebook, and handheld computers. Includes portable peripheral equipment, such as printers and scanners. Directory information includes company profiles (major manufacturers), product comparison charts, street price guide, list of manufacturers, and list of dealers.

Formerly *Laptop Buyer's Guide and Handbook.*

Network Buyers Guide. CMP Media LLC. • Annual. $5.00. Lists suppliers of products for local and wide area computer networks. Formerly *LAN Buyers Guide Issue.*

FINANCIAL RATIOS

Industry Norms and Key Business Ratios. Desk Top Edition. Dun and Bradstreet Corp. • Annual. Five volumes. $475.00 per volume. $1,890.00 per set. Covers over 800 kinds of businesses, arranged by Standard Industrial Classification number. More detailed editions covering longer periods of time are also available.

HANDBOOKS AND MANUALS

Guide to Energy Efficient Office Equipment. Loretta A. Smith and others. American Council for an Energy Efficient Economy. • 1996. $12.00. Second edition. Provides information on selecting, purchasing, and using energy-saving computers, monitors, printers, copiers, and other office devices.

The Modem Reference: The Complete Guide to PC Communications. Michael A. Banks. Information Today, Inc. • 2000. $29.95. Fourth edition. Covers personal computer data communications technology, including fax transmissions, computer networks, modems, and the Internet. Popularly written.

INTERNET DATABASES

InfoTech Trends. Data Analysis Group. Phone: (925)462-1202 Fax: (925)462-1225 E-mail: support@infotechtrends.com • URL: http://www.infotechtrends.com • Web site provides both free and fee-based market research data on the information technology industry, including computers, peripherals, telecommunications, the Internet, software, CD-ROM/DVD, e-commerce, and workstations. Fees: Free for current (most recent year) data; more extensive information has various fee structures. Formerly *Computer Industry Forecasts.*

ONLINE DATABASES

Applied Science and Technology Index Online. H. W. Wilson Co. • Provides online indexing of 500 major scientific, technical, industrial, and engineering periodicals. Time period is 1983 to date. Monthly updates. Inquire as to online cost and availability.

Internet and Personal Computing Abstracts. Information Today, Inc. • Contains abstracts covering a wide variety of personal and business microcomputer literature appearing in more than 100 journals and popular magazines. Time period is 1981 to date, with monthly updates. Formerly *Microcomputer Index.* Inquire as to online cost and availability.

PROMT: Predicasts Overview of Markets and Technology. Gale Cengage Learning. • Companies, products, applied technologies and markets. U.S. and international literature coverage, 1972 to date. Inquire as to online cost and availability. Provides abstracts from more than 1,600 publications. Weekly updates.

Wilson Business Abstracts Online. H. W. Wilson Co. • Indexes and abstracts 600 major business periodicals, plus the *Wall Street Journal* and the business section of the *New York Times.* Indexing is from 1982, abstracting from 1990, with the two newspapers included from 1993. Updated weekly. Inquire as to online cost and availability. (*Business Periodicals Index* without abstracts is also available online.).

PERIODICALS AND NEWSLETTERS

EDP Weekly: The Leading Weekly Computer News Summary. Computer Age and EDP News Services. • Weekly. $495.00 per year. Newsletter. Summarizes news from all areas of the computer and

microcomputer industries.

Interactive Home: Consumer Technology Monthly. Jupiter Communications. • Monthly. $625.00 per year; with online edition, $725.00 per year. Newsletter on devices to bring the Internet into the average American home. Covers TV set-top boxes, game devices, telephones with display screens, handheld computer communication devices, the usual PCs, etc.

Network: Strategies and Solutions for the Network Professional. CMP Media LLC. • 13 times a year. Free to qualified personnel. Covers network products and peripherals for computer professionals. Includes annual network managers salary survey and annual directory issue. Formerly *LAN: The Network Solutions Magazine.*

Presentations: Technology and Techniques for Effective Communication. VNU Business Media. • Monthly. Free to qualified personnel; others, $69.00 per year. Covers the use of presentation hardware and software, including audiovisual equipment and computerized display systems. Includes an annual "*Buyers Guide to Presentation Products.*".

PRICE SOURCES

Computer. Orion Research Corp. • Quarterly. $516.00 per year. $129.00 per issue. Quotes retail and wholesale prices of used computers and equipment. Original list prices and years of manufacture are also shown.

RESEARCH CENTERS AND INSTITUTES

Battelle Memorial Institute. Battelle Memorial Institute. 505 King Ave., Columbus, OH 43201. Phone: 800-201-2011 or (614)424-5853 Fax: (614)424-5263 E-mail: solutions@battelle.org • URL: http://www.battelle.org/ • Environment and energy; national security; transportation; health and life sciences; medical, pharmaceutical, agrochemical, and consumer product development. Conducts marine research at three coastal locations: Florida Marine Research Facility (Daytona Beach), Northwest Marine Research Laboratory (Sequim, Washington), and the Ocean Sciences Laboratory (Duxbury, Massachusetts). Specialized facilities and units include: Aviation Safety Reporting System Office; the Breakthrough Center for Strategic Product Development; the Human Engineering, Ergonomics, and Organizational Research Center; and the William R. Wiley Environmental Molecular Sciences Laboratory.

Carnegie Mellon Research Institute-Computer Automation and Robotics. Carnegie Mellon University, 700 Technology Dr., Pittsburgh, PA 15219. Phone: (412)268-3363 Fax: (412)368-7759 • URL: http://www.cmu.edu/cmri • Multidisciplinary research activities include expert systems applications, minicomputer and microcomputer systems design, genetic engineering, and transportation systems analysis.

Center for Advanced Technology in Information Management. Columbia University, Vanderbilt Clinic, 622 W 168th St., 5th Fl., New York, NY 10032. Phone: (212)305-2944 Fax: (212)305-0196 E-mail: shortliffe@dmi.columbia.edu • URL: http://www.dmi.columbia.edu/cat.

STATISTICS SOURCES

Computers and Office and Accounting Machines. U. S. Bureau of the Census. • Annual. Provides data on shipments: value, quantity, imports, and exports. (Current Industrial Reports, MA-35R.).

Standard & Poor's Industry Surveys. Standard & Poor's. • Semiannual. $1,800.00. Two looseleaf volumes. Includes monthly *Supplements.* Provides detailed, individual surveys of 52 major industry groups. Each survey is revised on a semiannual basis. Also includes "Monthly Investment Review" (industry group investment analysis) and monthly

"Trends & Projections" (economic analysis).

TRADE/PROFESSIONAL ASSOCIATIONS

Computing Technology Industry Association. 1815 S Meyers Rd., Ste. 300, Oakbrook Terrace, IL 60181-5228. Phone: (630)678-8300 Fax: (630)678-8384 E-mail: information@comptia.org • URL: http://www.comptia.org • Trade association of more than 19,000 companies and professional IT members in the rapidly converging computing and communications market. Has members in more than 89 countries and provides a unified voice for the industry in the areas of e-commerce standards, vendor-neutral certification, service metrics, public policy and workforce development. Serves as information clearinghouse and resource for the industry; sponsors educational programs.

Information Technology Resellers Association. 11921 Freedom Dr., Ste. 550, Reston, VA 20190-5608. Phone: (703)904-4337 Fax: (703)736-8062 E-mail: info@itra.net • URL: http://www.itra.net • Companies that buy, sell, and lease new and used computer equipment, including central processing units and peripheral devices; associate members are companies that are actively engaged in business related to the computer industry. Promotes enhanced status of computer lessors and dealers; assures ethical business dealings for the benefit of members and their customers.

COMPUTER PROGRAMMING

See: COMPUTER SOFTWARE INDUSTRY

COMPUTER RESELLERS

See: COMPUTER RETAILING

COMPUTER RETAILING

DIRECTORIES

Computer Dealers Directory. infoUSA. • Annual. Price on application. Lists over 30,847 computer dealers. Brand names are indicated. Compiled from telephone company yellow pages. Regional editions and franchise editions available.

Directory of Computer VAR's and Systems Integrators. Chain Store Guide. • Annual. $327.00. Provides information on computer companies that modify, enhance, or customize hardware or software. Includes systems houses, systems integrators, turnkey systems specialists, original equipment manufacturers, and value added retailers. Formerly *Directory of Value Added Resellers.*

MicroLeads Vendor Directory on Disk (Personal Computer Industry). Chromatic Communications Enterprises, Inc. • Annual. $495.00. Includes computer hardware manufacturers, software producers, book-periodical publishers, and franchised or company-owned chains of personal computer equipment retailers, support services and accessory manufacturers. Formerly *MicroLeads U.S. Vender Directory.*

FINANCIAL RATIOS

Annual Statement Studies. The Risk Management Association. • Annual. Median and quartile financial ratios are given for over 400 kinds of manufacturing, wholesale, retail, construction, and consumer finance establishments. Data is sorted by both asset size and sales volume. Includes a clearly written "Definition of Ratios" and an alphabetical industry index.

Annual Statement Studies: Industry Default Probabilities and Cash Flow Measures. The Risk Management Association. • Annual. $145.00.

Serves as a companion volume to the original *Annual Statement Studies.* Gives probability of default estimates on a percentage scale for more than 450 industries. Includes changes in position year-by-year for eight financial statement line items and provides percentage measures of cash flow.

HANDBOOKS AND MANUALS

Software Store. Entrepreneur Media, Inc. • Looseleaf. $59.50. A practical guide to opening a computer software retail establishment. Covers profit potential, start-up costs, market size evaluation, owner's time required, site selection, lease negotiation, pricing, accounting, advertising, promotion, etc. (Start-Up Business Guide No. E1261.).

INTERNET DATABASES

Advance Monthly Sales for Retail Trade and Food Services. U. S. Census Bureau. Phone: 800-541-8345 or (301)763-4636 Fax: (301)457-3842 E-mail: rcb@census.gov • URL: http://www.census.gov/svsd/www/fullpub.html • Web pages provide monthly sales figures for a wide range of retail businesses. Advance, preliminary, and final statistics are provided for the latest month available in each case, with a previous-year comparison. Updates are monthly.

PERIODICALS AND NEWSLETTERS

Computer Reseller News: The Newsweekly for Builders of Technology Solutions. CMP Worldwide Media Networks. • Weekly. $199.00 per year. Includes bimonthly supplement. Incorporates *Computer Reseller Sources and Macintosh News.* Formerly *Computer Retailer News.*

Computer Shopper: The Computer Magazine for Direct Buyers. Media Inc. • Monthly. $14.99 per year. Nationwide marketplace for computer equipment.

STATISTICS SOURCES

Annual Benchmark Report for Retail Trade and Food Services...A Detailed Summary of Retail Sales, Purchases, Accounts Receivable, Inventories, and Food Service Sales. Available from U. S. Government Printing Office. • Annual. $13.00. Issued by the U.S. Census Bureau. Provides detailed annual and monthly retail statistics for the most recent 10 years. Includes data for various kinds of retail outlets, including automobiles, furniture, appliances, building supplies, grocery stores, drug stores, gasoline stations, clothing, sporting goods, department stores, and restaurants.

TRADE/PROFESSIONAL ASSOCIATIONS

Computing Technology Industry Association. 1815 S Meyers Rd., Ste. 300, Oakbrook Terrace, IL 60181-5228. Phone: (630)678-8300 Fax: (630)678-8384 E-mail: information@comptia.org • URL: http://www.comptia.org • Trade association of more than 19,000 companies and professional IT members in the rapidly converging computing and communications market. Has members in more than 89 countries and provides a unified voice for the industry in the areas of e-commerce standards, vendor-neutral certification, service metrics, public policy and workforce development. Serves as information clearinghouse and resource for the industry; sponsors educational programs.

Information Technology Resellers Association. 11921 Freedom Dr., Ste. 550, Reston, VA 20190-5608. Phone: (703)904-4337 Fax: (703)736-8062 E-mail: info@itra.net • URL: http://www.itra.net • Companies that buy, sell, and lease new and used computer equipment, including central processing units and peripheral devices; associate members are companies that are actively engaged in business related to the computer industry. Promotes enhanced status of computer lessors and dealers; assures ethical business dealings for the benefit of members and their customers.

COMPUTER SECURITY

See: COMPUTER CRIME AND SECURITY

COMPUTER SOFTWARE INDUSTRY

See also: COMPUTERS; MICROCOMPUTERS AND MINICOMPUTERS; UNIX; WINDOWS (SOFTWARE)

GENERAL WORKS

Managing Software Development Projects: Formula for Success. Neal Whitten. John Wiley and Sons, Inc. • 1995. $70.00. Second edition.

Microsoft Secrets: How the World's Most Powerful Software Company Creates Technology, Shapes Markets, and Manages People. Michael A. Cusumano and Richard W. Selby. The Free Press. • 1995. $30.00. Describes the internal workings of the Microsoft Corporation, including marketing, technical innovation, and human relations. Includes CD-ROM.

ABSTRACTS AND INDEXES

Computer Literature Index: A Subject/Author Index to Computer and Data Processing Literature. EBSCO Publishing. • Quarterly, with annual cumulation. $245.00 per year. Contains brief abstracts of book and periodical literature covering all phases of computing, including approximately 70 specific application areas.

Internet and Personal Computing Abstracts [print edition]. EBSCO Publishing. • Quarterly. $269.00 per year, including cumulative index. Provides more than 10,000 abstracts annually from both trade and academic publications. Covers computer hardware, software, product reviews, Web topics, e-commerce, networks, corporate news, security, and related topics. Formerly *Microcomputer Abstracts.*

Key Abstracts: Software Engineering. Available from INSPEC, Inc. • Monthly. $250.00 per year. Provides international coverage of journal and proceedings literature. Published in England by the Institution of Electrical Engineers (IEE).

LAMP (Literature Analysis of Microcomputer Publications). Soft Images. • Bimonthly. $89.95 per year. Annual cumulation.

ALMANACS AND YEARBOOKS

Computer Industry Almanac. Egil Juliussen and Karen Petska, editors. Computer Industry Almanac, Inc. • Annual. $53.00. Analyzes recent trends in various segments of the computer industry, with forecasts, employment data and industry salary information. Includes directories of computer companies, industry organizations, and publications.

BIBLIOGRAPHIES

Computer Book Review. • Quarterly. $30.00 per year. Includes annual index. Reviews new computer books. Back issues available.

BIOGRAPHICAL SOURCES

Gates: How Microsoft's Mogul Reinvented an Industry and Made Himself the Richest Man in America. Stephen Manes and Paul Andrews. Simon & Schuster Trade. • 1994. $15.00.

Hard Drive: Bill Gates and the Making of the Microsoft Empire. James Wallace and Jim Erickson. HarperInformation. • 1992. $16.00. A biography of William H. Gates, chief executive of the Microsoft Corporation.

CD-ROM DATABASES

Computer Database. Gale Cengage Learning. • Provides one year of full-text on CD-ROM for 150 leading computer-related publications. Also includes 70,000 product specifications and brief profiles of

13,000 computer product vendors and manufacturers.

Datapro on CD-ROM: Computer Systems Hardware and Software. Gartner Group, Inc. • Monthly. Price on application. CD-ROM provides product specifications, product reports, user surveys, and market forecasts for a wide range of computer hardware and software.

Datapro Software Finder. Gartner Group, Inc. • Quarterly. $1,770.00 per year. CD-ROM provides detailed information on more than 18,000 software products for a wide variety of computers, personal to mainframe. Covers software for 130 types of business, finance, and industry. (Editions limited to either microcomputer or mainframe software are available at $995.00 per year.).

Hoover's Company Capsules on CD-ROM. Hoover's, Inc. • Quarterly. $399.95 per year (single-user). Provides the CD-ROM version of *Hoover's Handbook of American Business, Hoover's Handbook of Emerging Companies, Hoover's Handbook of World Business, Hoover's Guide to Computer Companies, Hoover's Guide to Media Companies, Hoover's Handbook of Private Companies,* and various regional guides. Includes more than 11,000 profiles of companies.

OECD Statistical Compendium. Organization for Economic Cooperation and Development. • Semiannual. $1,905.00 per year for 1 to 10 users. CD-ROM contains more than 730,000 monthly, quarterly, and annual time series for OECD countries, 1960 to date. Includes fully searchable data on agriculture, food, economic indicators, national accounts, employment, energy, finance, industry, technology, and foreign trade. Results can be displayed in various forms.

DIRECTORIES

Computing and Software Career Directory. Gale Cengage Learning. • 1993. $39.00. Includes career information relating to programmers, software engineers, technical writers, systems experts, and other computer specialists. Provides advice from "insiders," resume suggestions, a directory of companies that may offer entry-level positions, and a directory of career information sources. (Career Advisor Series.).

Data Sources: The Comprehensive Guide to the Data Processing Industry: Hardware, Data Communications Products, Software, Company Profiles. Gale Cengage Learning. • Semiannual. $455.00 per year. Two volumes. Describes hardware and software for all computer operating sysems, including prices and technical details. Lists about 75,000 products from 14,000 suppliers. Industry-specific software applications are described.

MicroLeads Vendor Directory on Disk (Personal Computer Industry). Chromatic Communications Enterprises, Inc. • Annual. $495.00. Includes computer hardware manufacturers, software producers, book-periodical publishers, and franchised or company-owned chains of personal computer equipment retailers, support services and accessory manufacturers. Formerly *MicroLeads U.S. Vender Directory.*

Music Technology Buyer's Guide. United Entertainment Media. • $6.95. Annual. Lists more than 4,000 hardware and software music production products from 350 manufacturers. Includes synthesizers, MIDI hardware and software, mixers, microphones, music notation software, etc. Produced by the editorial staffs of *Keyboard* and *EQ* magazines.

The Software Encyclopedia: A Guide for Personal, Professional, and Business Users. Gale. • Annual. $335.00. Two volumes. Volume one lists software programs by title and producer. Volume two provides information on programs according to application and operating system. Includes prices and requirements for hardware and memory.

303 Software Programs to Use in Your Library: Descriptions, Evaluations, and Practical Advice. Patrick R. Dewey. American Library Association. • 1997. $36.00. Contains profiles of a wide variety of software (21 categories) that may be useful in libraries. Includes prices, company addresses, glossary, bibliography, and an index.(101 Micro Series).

ENCYCLOPEDIAS AND DICTIONARIES

Acronyms of Computer Science and Communications: A Comprehensive Acronym Dictionary and Illustrated Encyclopedia. Enjob Kajan and Ejub Kajan. Springer Verlag. • 2002. $49.95. Explains more than 4,000 "broadly used" computer, telecommunications, and information technology acronyms. Includes illustrations and Web addresses, where applicable.

Dictionary of Information Technology and Computer Science. Tony Gunton. Blackwell Publishing. • 1994. $62.95. Second edition. Covers key words, phrases, abbreviations, and acronyms used in computing and data communications.

Encyclopedia of Information Systems. Hossein Bidgoli, editor. Elsevier. • 2002. $1,200.00. Four volumes. Contains a wide range of articles relating to computers, databases, communication, and information technology. The 200 topics include coverage of hardware, software, artificial intelligence, the Internet, networks, knowledge management, electronic commerce, search engines, and systems design.

Encyclopedia of Software Engineering. John J. Marciniak, editor. John Wiley and Sons, Inc. • 2002. $695.00. Second edition. Two volumes. Contains more than 500 entries covering 35 software classifications.

New Hacker's Dictionary. Eric S. Raymond. MIT Press. • 1996. $65.00. Third edition. Includes three classifications of hacker communication: slang, jargon, and "techspeak.".

World of Computer Science. Gale Cengage Learning. • 2002. $160.00. Alphabetical arrangement. Contains 650 entries covering discoveries, theories, concepts, issues, ethics, and people in the broad area of computer science and technology.

HANDBOOKS AND MANUALS

Artificial Intelligence and Software Engineering: Understanding the Promise of the future. Darek Partridge. Fitzroy Dearborn Publishers, Inc. • 1999. $55.00. Includes applications of artificial intelligence software to banking and financial services.

Assessing Competitive Intelligence Software: A Guide to Evaluating CI Technology. France Bouthillier and Kathleen Shearer. Information Today, Inc. • 2003. $39.50. Provides a 32-step methodology for making an evaluation of competitive intelligence software. (An ASIST publication: American Society for Information Science and Technology).

Dun & Bradstreet/Gale Group Industry Handbooks. Gale Cengage Learning. • 2000. $650.00. Five volumes. $130.00 per volume. Each volume covers two or more major industries: 1. *Entertainment and Hospitality*; 2. *Construction and Agriculture*; 3. *Chemicals and Pharmaceuticals*; 4. *Computers & Software and Broadcasting & Telecommunications*; 5. *Insurance and Health & Medical Services.* The following are included for each industry: overview, statistics, financial ratios, rankings, merger information, company directory, directory of associations, and consultants directory. (Dun and Bradstreet/Gale Industry Reference Handbook Series).

Software Engineering. Ian Sommerville. Addison-Wesley. • 2000. $98.00. Sixth edition. (International Computer Science Series).

Software for Indexing. Sandi Schroeder, editor. Information Today, Inc. • 2003. $35.00. Published

in conjunction with the American Society of Indexers (ASI). Material by professional indexers covers dedicated indexing programs, embedded software, online indexing, Web indexing, database software, customized software, automatic indexing, and other indexing software topics.

INTERNET DATABASES

Business 2.0 Web Guide to the Best Business Links. Business 2.0 Media Inc. Phone: (415)293-4800 E-mail: support@business2.com • URL: http://www.business2.com/webguide • Web site presents an extensive, searchable directory of links to "the best, most informative, and authoritative web pages." Twenty main categories cover business, finance, career, company information, people, and technology topics, with thousands of subtopics, all linking to Web sites recommended by experienced business researchers. Fees: Free.

InfoTech Trends. Data Analysis Group. Phone: (925)462-1202 Fax: (925)462-1225 E-mail: support@infotechtrends.com • URL: http://www.infotechtrends.com • Web site provides both free and fee-based market research data on the information technology industry, including computers, peripherals, telecommunications, the Internet, software, CD-ROM/DVD, e-commerce, and workstations. Fees: Free for current (most recent year) data; more extensive information has various fee structures. Formerly *Computer Industry Forecasts.*

Wired News. Lycos, Inc. Phone: (415)276-8400 Fax: (415)276-8500 E-mail: newsfeedback@wired.com • URL: http://www.wired.com • Provides summaries and full-text of "Top Stories" relating to the Internet, computers, multimedia, telecommunications, and the electronic information industry in general. These news stories are placed in the broad categories of Politics, Business, Culture, and Technology. Affiliated with *Wired* magazine. Fees: Free.

ONLINE DATABASES

Internet and Personal Computing Abstracts. Information Today, Inc. • Contains abstracts covering a wide variety of personal and business microcomputer literature appearing in more than 100 journals and popular magazines. Time period is 1981 to date, with monthly updates. Formerly *Microcomputer Index.* Inquire as to online cost and availability.

PROMT: Predicasts Overview of Markets and Technology. Gale Cengage Learning. • Companies, products, applied technologies and markets. U.S. and international literature coverage, 1972 to date. Inquire as to online cost and availability. Provides abstracts from more than 1,600 publications. Weekly updates.

SoftBase: Reviews, Companies, and Products. Information Sources, Inc. • Describes and reviews business software packages. Inquire as to online cost and availability.

PERIODICALS AND NEWSLETTERS

Computer Languages, Systems and Structures. Elsevier. • Quarterly. Individuals, $208.00 per year; institutions, $951.00 per year.

Computerworld: Newsweekly for Information Technology Leaders. Computerworld, Inc. • Weekly. $190.00 per year.

Dr. Dobb's Journal: Software Tools for the Professional Programmer. CMP Media LLC. • Monthly. $34.95 per year. A technical publication covering software development, languages, operating systems, and applications.

EQ: The Project Recording and Sound Magazine. United Entertainment Media, Inc. • Monthly. $24.95 per year. Provides advice on professional music recording equipment and technique.

IEEE Software. Institute of Electrical and Electronic

Engineers, Inc. • Bimonthly. $695.00 per year. Covers software engineering, technology, and development. Affiliated with the Institute of Electrical and Electronics Engineers.

Industrial Computing. Industrial Computing Society. ISA Services, Inc. • Monthly. Members $100.00 per year; non-members, $80.00 per year. Published by the Instrument Society of America. Edited for engineering managers and systems integrators. Subject matter includes industrial software, programmable controllers, artificial intelligence systems, and industrial computer networking systems.

InfoWorld: Defining Technology for Business. InfoWorld Publishing. • Weekly. $195.00 per year. For personal computing professionals.

Insurance and Technology. CMP Media LLC. • Monthly. $65.00 per year. Covers information technology and systems management as applied to the operation of life, health, casualty, and property insurance companies.

Journal of Software Maintenance and Evolution: Research and Practice. John Wiley and Sons, Inc., Journals. • Bimonthly. Individuals, $1,125.00 per year; institutions, $1,500.00 per year. Published in England by John Wiley and Sons Ltd. Provides international coverage of subject matter.

Managing Automation. Thomas Publishing Co., LLC. • Monthly. Free to qualified personnel; others, $60.00 per year. Coverage includes software for manufacturing, systems planning, integration in process industry automation, computer integrated manufacturing (CIM), computer networks for manufacturing, management problems, industry news, and new products.

MSDN Magazine (Microsoft Systems for Developers). CMP Media LLC. • Monthly. $84.95 per year. Produced for professional software developers using Windows, MS-DOS, Visual Basic, and other Microsoft Corporation products. Incorporates *Microsoft Internet Developer*.

Network Computing: Computing in a Network Environment. CMP Publications, Inc. • Semimonthly. Free to qualified personnel.

Soft-Letter: Trends and Strategies in Software Publishing. UCG Technologies. • Semimonthly. $395.00 per year. Newsletter on the software industry, including new technology and financial aspects.

Software Development. CMP Media LLC. • Monthly. $39.00 per year. Edited for professional software developers and managers.

Software Digest: The Independent Comparative Ratings Report for PC and LAN Software. NSTL. • 12 times a year. $450.00 per year. Critical evaluations of personal computer software.

Software Economics Letter: Maximizing Your Return on Corporate Software. Computer Economics, Inc. • Monthly. $395.00 per year. Newsletter for information systems managers. Contains data on business software trends, vendor licensing policies, and other corporate software management issues.

Software Magazine. Wiesner Publishing, Inc. • Monthly. Free to qualified personnel; others, $42.00 per year.

Telematics and Informatics: An International Journal on Telecommunications and Internet Technology. Elsevier. • Four times a year. Institutions, $938.00 per year.

Upgrade. Software and Information Industry Association. • Monthly. $79.00 per year. Covers news and trends relating to the software, information, and Internet industries. Formerly *SPA News* from Software Publisers Association.

STATISTICS SOURCES
Standard & Poor's Industry Surveys. Standard & Poor's. • Semiannual. $1,800.00. Two looseleaf

volumes. Includes monthly *Supplements*. Provides detailed, individual surveys of 52 major industry groups. Each survey is revised on a semiannual basis. Also includes "Monthly Investment Review" (industry group investment analysis) and monthly "Trends & Projections" (economic analysis).

U. S. Industry and Trade Outlook. Available from National Technical Information Service. • Annual. $69.95. Produced by the International Trade Administration, U. S. Department of Commerce, in a "public-private" partnership with DRI/McGraw-Hill and Standard & Poor's. Provides basic data, outlook for the current year, and "Long-Term Prospects" (five-year projections) for a wide variety of products and services. Includes high technology industries. Formerly *U. S. Industrial Outlook.*

TRADE/PROFESSIONAL ASSOCIATIONS
Entertainment Software Association. 575 7th St. NW, Ste. 300, Washington, DC 20004. Phone: (202)223-2400 E-mail: esa@theesa.com • URL: http://www.theesa.com • Represents the interactive entertainment software publishing industry. Established an autonomous rating board to rate interactive entertainment software. Established a program to combat piracy in the United States and around the world. Represents members on industry issues at the federal and state level. Provides market research and information. **Publications:** none.

IEEE Computer Society. 1828 L St. NW, Ste. 1202, Washington, DC 20036. Phone: (202)371-0101 Fax: (202)728-9614 E-mail: help@computer.org • URL: http://www.computer.org • Computer professionals. Promotes the development of computer and information sciences and fosters communication within the information processing community. Sponsors conferences, symposia, workshops, tutorials, technical meetings, and seminars. Operates Computer Society Press. Presents scholarships; bestows technical achievement and service awards and certificates.

Information Technology Association of America. 1401 Wilson Blvd., Suite 1100, Arlington, VA 22209. Phone: (703)522-5055 Fax: (703)525-2279 E-mail: hmiller@itaa.org • URL: http://www.itaa.org • Members are computer software and services companies. Maintains an Information Systems Integration Services Section. Formerly Software Industry Division of ADAPSO.

Instrumentation Systems and Automation Society. 67 Alexander Dr., Research Triangle Park, NC 27709. Phone: (919)549-8411 Fax: (919)549-8288 E-mail: info@isa.org • URL: http://www.isa.org • Members are engineers and others concerned with industrial instrumentation, systems, computers, and automation. Formerly Instrument Society of America.

Software and Information Industry Association. 1090 Vermont Ave. NW, 6th Fl., Washington, DC 20005. Phone: (202)289-7442 Fax: (202)289-7097 • URL: http://www.siia.net • A trade association for the software and digital content industry. Affiliated with Massachusetts Software and Internet Council.

Special Interest Group on Programming Languages. c/o Association for Computing Machinery, 1515 Broadway, New York, NY 10036. Phone: 800-342-6626 or (212)869-7440 Fax: (212)944-1318 E-mail: acmhelp@acm.org • URL: http://www.acm.org/sigplan/.

Special Interest Group on Software Engineering. c/o Association for Computing Machinery, 1515 Broadway, New York, NY 10036. Phone: 800-342-6626 or (212)869-7440 Fax: (212)944-1318 E-mail: acmhelp@acm.org • URL: http://www.acm.org/sigsoft • Concerned with all aspects of software development and maintenance. Publishes *Software*

Engineering Notes, a bimonthly newsletter.

OTHER SOURCES
Computer Software: Protection, Liability, Forms. L. J. Kutten. West Group. • Semiannual. $576.00 per year. Four looseleaf volumes. Covers copyright law, patents, trade secrets, licensing, publishing contracts, and other legal topics related to computer software.

Keyboard: The World's Leading Music Technology Magazine. United Entertainment Media, Inc. • Monthly. $25.95 per year. Emphasis is on recording systems, keyboard technique, and computer-assisted music (MIDI) systems.

COMPUTER STORES

See: COMPUTER RETAILING

COMPUTER VIRUSES

See: COMPUTER CRIME AND SECURITY

COMPUTER VISION

See: MACHINE VISION

COMPUTERIZED TRANSLATION

See: MACHINE TRANSLATING

COMPUTERS

See also: AUTOMATION; COMMUNICATION SYSTEMS; COMPUTER SOFTWARE INDUSTRY; LINEAR PROGRAMMING; MICROCOMPUTERS AND MINICOMPUTERS; OPERATIONS RESEARCH; PORTABLE COMPUTERS

GENERAL WORKS
The Age of Spiritual Machines: When Computers Exceed Human Intelligence. Ray Kurzweil. Penguin Group. • 1998. $25.95. Provides speculation on the future of artificial intelligence and "computer consciousness.".

Being Digital. Nicholas Negroponte. Knopf Publishing Group. • 1995. $30.00. A kind of history of multimedia, with visions of future technology and public participation. Predicts how computers will affect society in years to come.

Computer Sciences. Roger Flynn, editor. Gale Cengage Learning. • 2002. $395.00. Four volumes. Presents a general and historical review of the impact of computers on modern society. Includes biographical information and multidisciplinary examples. (Macmillan Reference USA imprint, Macmillan Science Library.).

Computers. Larry Long and Nancy Long. Prentice Hall PTR. • 2003. $46.67. Eighth edition.

Computers: The User Perspective. Sarah E. Hutchinson and Stacey C. Sawyer. McGraw-Hill. • 1991. $41.95. Third edition.

Designing the User Interface: Strategies for Effective Human-Computer Interaction. Ben Shneiderman. Addison-Wesley. • 2002. $70.00. Third edition. Provides an introduction to computer user-interface design. Covers usability testing, dialog boxes, menus, command languages, interaction devices, tutorials, printed user manuals, and related subjects.

History of the Internet: A Chronology, 1843 to the Present. Christos J. P. Moschovitis and others. ABC-

CLIO, Inc. • 1999. $65.00. Early entries cover the history of the computer. Includes biographical information, bibliography, and glossary.

Introducing Computers: Concepts, Systems, and Applications. Robert H. Blissmer. John Wiley and Sons, Inc. • 1995. $38.95.

Introduction to Computer Theory. Daniel I. Cohen. John Wiley and Sons, Inc. • 1996. $98.95. Second edition.

Probable Tomorrows: How Science and Technology Will Transform Our Lives in the Next Twenty Years. Marvin J. Cetron and Owen L. Davies. Saint Martin's Press. • 1997. $24.95. Predicts the developments in technological products, services, and "everyday conveniences" by the year 2017. Covers such items as personal computers, artificial intelligence, telecommunications, highspeed railroads, and healthcare.

Recent Advances and Issues in Computers. Martin K. Gay. Greenwood Publishing Group, Inc. • 2000. $49.95. Includes recent developments in computer science, computer engineering, and commercial software applications. (Oryx Frontiers of Science Series.).

The Trouble with Computers: Usefulness, Useability, and Productivity. Thomas K. Landauer. MIT Press. • 1995. $30.00. A critical view of computers and how they are being used.

ABSTRACTS AND INDEXES

Applied Science and Technology Index. H. W. Wilson Co. • 11 times a year. Quarterly and annual cumulations. Price varies. Indexes a wide variety of English language technical, industrial, and engineering periodicals.

CompuMath Citation Index. Institute for Scientific Information. • Three times a year. $1,090.00 per year. Provides citations to the worldwide literature of computer science and mathematics.

Computer Abstracts. Emerald. • Bimonthly. $4,739.00 per year.

Computer and Information Systems Abstracts Journal: An Abstract Journal Pertaining to the Theory, Design, Fabrication and Application of Computer and Information Systems. CSA. • 11 times a year. $1,750 per year.

Computer Literature Index: A Subject/Author Index to Computer and Data Processing Literature. EBSCO Publishing. • Quarterly, with annual cumulation. $245.00 per year. Contains brief abstracts of book and periodical literature covering all phases of computing, including approximately 70 specific application areas.

Computing Reviews. Association for Computing Machinery. • Monthly. Members, $45.00 per year; non-members, $190.00 per year; students, $40.00 per year.

Internet and Personal Computing Abstracts [print edition]. EBSCO Publishing. • Quarterly. $269.00 per year, including cumulative index. Provides more than 10,000 abstracts annually from both trade and academic publications. Covers computer hardware, software, product reviews, Web topics, e-commerce, networks, corporate news, security, and related topics. Formerly *Microcomputer Abstracts*.

NTIS Alerts: Computers, Control & Information Theory. National Technical Information Service. • Semimonthly. $235.00 per year. Provides descriptions of government-sponsored research reports and software, with ordering information. Covers computer hardware, software, control systems, pattern recognition, image processing, and related subjects. Formerly *Abstract Newsletter*.

ALMANACS AND YEARBOOKS

Advances in Computers. Elsevier. • Irregular. Price on application.

Computer Industry Almanac. Egil Juliussen and Karen Petska, editors. Computer Industry Almanac,

Inc. • Annual. $53.00. Analyzes recent trends in various segments of the computer industry, with forecasts, employment data and industry salary information. Includes directories of computer companies, industry organizations, and publications.

Information Technology Outlook. OECD Publications and Information Center. • Biennial. $57.00. A review of recent developments in international markets for computer hardware, software, and services. Also examines current legal provisions for information systems security and privacy in OECD countries.

BIBLIOGRAPHIES

Automation. Available from U. S. Government Printing Office. • Annual. Free. Issued by the Superintendent of Documents. A list of government publications on automation, computers, and related topics. Formerly *Computers and Data Processing*. (Subject Bibliography No. 51.).

A C M Electronic Guide to Computing Literature: Bibliographic Listing, Author Index, Keyword Index, Category Index, Proper Noun Subject Index, Reviewer Index, Source Index. Association for Computing Machinery. • Quarterly. Members, $175.00; non-members, $499.00 per year. A comprehensive guide to each year's computer literature (books, proceedings, journals, etc.), with an emphasis on technical material. Indexed by author, keyword, category, proper noun, reviewer, and source. Formerly *A C M Guide to Computing Literature*.

IEEE Products and Publications Bulletin. Institute of Electrical and Electronics Engineers, Inc. • Quarterly. Free. Provides information on all IEEE journals, proceedings, and other publications. Formerly *IEEE Publications Bulletin*.

Reference Reviews. Available from Information Today, Inc. • Eight times a year. Price on application. Published in London by Aslib: The Association for Information Management. Incorporates *Aslib Book Guide*.

BIOGRAPHICAL SOURCES

Who's Who in Science and Engineering. Marquis Who's Who. • Biennial. $269.00. Provides concise biographical information on 35,000 prominent engineers and scientists. International coverage, with geographical and professional indexes.

CD-ROM DATABASES

Computer Database. Gale Cengage Learning. • Provides one year of full-text on CD-ROM for 150 leading computer-related publications. Also includes 70,000 product specifications and brief profiles of 13,000 computer product vendors and manufacturers.

Datapro on CD-ROM: Computer Systems Hardware and Software. Gartner Group, Inc. • Monthly. Price on application. CD-ROM provides product specifications, product reports, user surveys, and market forecasts for a wide range of computer hardware and software.

Hoover's Company Capsules on CD-ROM. Hoover's, Inc. • Quarterly. $399.95 per year (single-user). Provides the CD-ROM version of *Hoover's Handbook of American Business, Hoover's Handbook of Emerging Companies, Hoover's Handbook of World Business, Hoover's Guide to Computer Companies, Hoover's Guide to Media Companies, Hoover's Handbook of Private Companies,* and various regional guides. Includes more than 11,000 profiles of companies.

MathSci Disc. American Mathematical Society. • Semiannual. Price on application. Provides CD-ROM citations, with abstracts, to the literature of mathematics, statistics, and computer science, 1940 to date.

WILSONDISC: Wilson Business Abstracts. H. W. Wilson Co. • Monthly. Includes unlimited online ac-

cess to *Wilson Business Abstracts* through WILSONLINE. Provides CD-ROM "cover-to-cover" abstracting and indexing of over 600 prominent business periodicals. Indexing is from 1982, abstracting from 1990. (*Business Periodicals Index* without abstracts is available on CD-ROM at $1,495 per year.).

DIRECTORIES

Data Sources: The Comprehensive Guide to the Data Processing Industry: Hardware, Data Communications Products, Software, Company Profiles. Gale Cengage Learning. • Semiannual. $455.00 per year. Two volumes. Describes hardware and software for all computer operating systems, including prices and technical details. Lists about 75,000 products from 14,000 suppliers. Industry-specific software applications are described.

Directory of Computer VAR's and Systems Integrators. Chain Store Guide. • Annual. $327.00. Provides information on computer companies that modify, enhance, or customize hardware or software. Includes systems houses, systems integrators, turnkey systems specialists, original equipment manufacturers, and value added retailers. Formerly *Directory of Value Added Resellers*.

Peterson's Computer Science and Electrical Engineering Programs. Peterson's. • 1996. $24.95. A guide to 900 accredited graduate degree programs related to computers or electrical engineering at colleges and universities in the U. S. and Canada.

Plunkett's InfoTech Industry Almanac: Complete Profiles on the InfoTech 500-the Leading Firms in the Movement and Management of Voice, Data, and Video. Plunkett Research, Ltd. • Biennial. $229.99. Includes CD-ROM. Five hundred major information companies are profiled, with corporate culture aspects. Discusses major trends in various sectors of the computer and information industry, including data on careers and job growth. Includes several indexes.

ENCYCLOPEDIAS AND DICTIONARIES

Acronyms of Computer Science and Communications: A Comprehensive Acronym Dictionary and Illustrated Encyclopedia. Enjob Kajan and Ejub Kajan. Springer Verlag. • 2002. $49.95. Explains more than 4,000 "broadly used" computer, telecommunications, and information technology acronyms. Includes illustrations and Web addresses, where applicable.

Computer Glossary: The Complete Illustrated Dictionary. Alan Freedman. AMACOM. • 2000. $29.95. Ninth edition. Includes CD-Rom.

Dictionary of Information Technology and Computer Science. Tony Gunton. Blackwell Publishing. • 1994. $62.95. Second edition. Covers key words, phrases, abbreviations, and acronyms used in computing and data communications.

Encyclopedia of Computer Science and Technology. Marcel Dekker, Inc. • Dates vary. 45 volumes. $8,775.00. $195.00 per volume. Contains scholarly articles written by computer experts. Includes bibliographies.

Encyclopedia of Information Systems. Hossein Bidgoli, editor. Elsevier. • 2002. $1,200.00. Four volumes. Contains a wide range of articles relating to computers, databases, communication, and information technology. The 200 topics include coverage of hardware, software, artificial intelligence, the Internet, networks, knowledge management, electronic commerce, search engines, and systems design.

New Hacker's Dictionary. Eric S. Raymond. MIT Press. • 1996. $65.00. Third edition. Includes three classifications of hacker communication: slang, jargon, and "techspeak.".

1001 Computer Words You Need to Know. Jerry Pournelle. Oxford University Press. • 2004. $17.95.

World of Computer Science. Gale Cengage Learning. • 2002. $160.00. Alphabetical arrangement. Contains 650 entries covering discoveries, theories, concepts, issues, ethics, and people in the broad area of computer science and technology.

HANDBOOKS AND MANUALS

Computer Repair Service. Entrepreneur Media, Inc. • Looseleaf. $59.50. A practical guide to starting a computer repair service. Covers profit potential, start-up costs, market size evaluation, owner's time required, site selection, lease negotiation, pricing, accounting, advertising, promotion, etc. (Start-Up Business Guide No. E1256.).

Computer Science Handbook. Allen B. Tucker. CRC Press. • 2004. $139.95. Second edition. Provides 70 chapters on 11 computer subject areas. Includes material from 150 contributing authors.

Dun & Bradstreet/Gale Group Industry Handbooks. Gale Cengage Learning. • 2000. $650.00. Five volumes. $130.00 per volume. Each volume covers two or more major industries: 1. *Entertainment and Hospitality;* 2. *Construction and Agriculture;* 3. *Chemicals and Pharmaceuticals;* 4. *Computers & Software and Broadcasting & Telecommunications;* 5. *Insurance and Health & Medical Services.* The following are included for each industry: overview, statistics, financial ratios, rankings, merger information, company directory, directory of associations, and consultants directory. (Dun and Bradstreet/Gale Industry Reference Handbook Series).

Guide to Energy Efficient Office Equipment. Loretta A. Smith and others. American Council for an Energy Efficient Economy. • 1996. $12.00. Second edition. Provides information on selecting, purchasing, and using energy-saving computers, monitors, printers, copiers, and other office devices.

INTERNET DATABASES

InfoTech Trends. Data Analysis Group. Phone: (925)462-1202 Fax: (925)462-1225 E-mail: support@infotechtrends.com • URL: http://www. infotechtrends.com • Web site provides both free and fee-based market research data on the information technology industry, including computers, peripherals, telecommunications, the Internet, software, CD-ROM/DVD, e-commerce, and workstations. Fees: Free for current (most recent year) data; more extensive information has various fee structures. Formerly *Computer Industry Forecasts.*

Manufacturing Profiles. U. S. Bureau of the Census. Phone: (301)763-4636 E-mail: webmaster@census. gov • URL: http://www.census.gov/prod/www/abs/ mfg-prof.html • The Census Bureau makes available free on PDF (Portable Document Format) an annual consolidation of the entire Current Industrial Report series, presenting "all the data compiled." Contains statistics on production, shipments, inventories, consumption, exports, imports, and orders for a wide variety of manufactured products.

Wired News. Lycos, Inc. Phone: (415)276-8400 Fax: (415)276-8500 E-mail: newsfeedback@wired.com • URL: http://www.wired.com • Provides summaries and full-text of "Top Stories" relating to the Internet, computers, multimedia, telecommunications, and the electronic information industry in general. These news stories are placed in the broad categories of Politics, Business, Culture, and Technology. Affiliated with *Wired* magazine. Fees: Free.

ONLINE DATABASES

Applied Science and Technology Index Online. H. W. Wilson Co. • Provides online indexing of 500 major scientific, technical, industrial, and engineering periodicals. Time period is 1983 to date. Monthly updates. Inquire as to online cost and availability.

INSPEC. Institution of Electrical Engineers (IEE). •

Provides online citations, with abstracts, to the world literature of electrical engineering, electronics, optoelectronics, telecommunications, industrial controls, instrumentation, computer technology, information technology, and physics. Coverage includes more than 4,000 technical and scientific journals from 1969 to date, with weekly updating. (INSPEC is Information Services in Physics, Electronics, and Computing.) Inquire as to online cost and availability.

MathSci. American Mathematical Society. • Provides online citations, with abstracts, to the literature of mathematics, statistics, and computer science. Time period is 1940 to date, with monthly updates. Inquire as to online cost and availability.

Wilson Business Abstracts Online. H. W. Wilson Co. • Indexes and abstracts 600 major business periodicals, plus the *Wall Street Journal* and the business section of the *New York Times.* Indexing is from 1982, abstracting from 1990, with the two newspapers included from 1993. Updated weekly. Inquire as to online cost and availability. (*Business Periodicals Index* without abstracts is also available online.).

PERIODICALS AND NEWSLETTERS

ACM Computing Surveys: The Survey and Tutorial Journal of the ACM. Association for Computing Machinery. • Quarterly. Members, $26.00 per year; non-members, $160.00 per year; students, $21.00 per year.

Association for Computing Machinery Communications. Association for Computing Machinery. • Monthly. Members, $36.00 per year; non-members, $174.00 per year; students, $41.00 per year.

Association for Computing Machinery Journal. Association for Computing Machinery. • Bimonthly. Members, $45.00 per year; non-members, $220.00 per year; students, $40.00 per year.

CIO: The Magazine for Chief Information Officers. CXO Media, Inc. • 23 times a year. $150.00 per year. Edited for chief information officers. Includes a monthly "Web Business" section (incorporates the former *WebMaster* periodical) and a monthly "Enterprise" section for company executives other than CIOs.

Computer. Institute of Electrical and Electronic Engineers, Inc. • Monthly. $1,060.00 per year. Edited for computer technology professionals.

Computer Economics Networking Strategies Report: Advising IT Decision Maker ractices and Current Trends. Computer Economics, Inc. • Monthly. $395.00 per year. Newsletter. Edited for information technology managers. Covers news and trends relating to a variety of corporate computer network and management information systems topics. Emphasis is on costs. Formerly *Intranet and Networking Strategies Report.*

Computer Economics Report: The Financial Advisor of Data Processing Users. Computer Economics, Inc. • Monthly. $595.00 per year. Newsletter on lease/purchase decisions, prices, discounts, residual value forecasts, personnel allocation, cost control, and other corporate computer topics. Edited for information technology (IT) executives.

Computer Letter: Business Issues in Technology. Technologic Partners, Inc. • 40 times a year. $695.00 per year. Newsletter. Computer industry newsletter with emphasis on information for investors.

Computer Reseller News: The Newsweekly for Builders of Technology Solutions. CMP Worldwide Media Networks. • Weekly. $199.00 per year. Includes bimonthly supplement. Incorporates *Computer Reseller Sources and Macintosh News.* Formerly *Computer Retailer News.*

Computer Shopper: The Computer Magazine for Direct Buyers. Media Inc. • Monthly. $14.99 per

year. Nationwide marketplace for computer equipment.

Computerworld: Newsweekly for Information Technology Leaders. Computerworld, Inc. • Weekly. $190.00 per year.

The Electronic Library: The International Journal for the Application of Technology in Information Environments. Sage Publications, Inc. • Bimonthly. $469.00 per year. Incorporated*Library Computing.*

IBM Journal of Research and Development. International Business Machines Corp. • Bimonthly. $220.00 per year.

Industrial Computing. Industrial Computing Society. ISA Services, Inc. • Monthly. Members $100.00 per year; non-members, $80.00 per year. Published by the Instrument Society of America. Edited for engineering managers and systems integrators. Subject matter includes industrial software, programmable controllers, artificial intelligence systems, and industrial computer networking systems.

Information Processing and Management: An International Journal. Elsevier Science. • Bimonthly. Qualified personnel, $301.00 per year; institutions, $1,196.00 per year. Text in English, French, German and Italian.

Information Retrieval and Library Automation. Lomond Publications, Inc. • Monthly. $75.00 per year. Summarizes research events and literature worldwide.

IT Cost Management Strategies: The Planning Assistant for IT Directors. Computer Economics, Inc. • Monthly. $495.00 per year. Newsletter for information technology professionals. Covers data processing costs, budgeting, financial management, and related topics.

Network Computing: Computing in a Network Environment. CMP Publications, Inc. • Semimonthly. Free to qualified personnel.

Smart Computing. Sandhills Publishing Co. • Monthly. $29.00 per year. Provides basic computer advice "in plain English." Includes reviews of hardware and software.

PRICE SOURCES

Computer Price Guide: The Blue Book of Used IBM Computer Prices. Computer Economics, Inc. • Quarterly. $140.00 per year. Provides average prices of used IBM computer equipment, including "complete lists of obsolete IBM equipment." Includes a newsletter on trends in the used computer market. Edited for dealers, leasing firms, and business computer buyers.

RESEARCH CENTERS AND INSTITUTES

Center for Integrated Systems. Stanford University, 420 Via Palou Mall, Stanford, CA 94305-4070. Phone: (650)725-3621 Fax: (650)725-0991 E-mail: rdasher@stanford.edu • URL: http://www.cis. stanford.edu • Research programs include manufacturing science, design science, computer architecture, semiconductor technology, and telecommunications.

Engineering Systems Research Center. University of California at Berkeley. 3115 Etcheverry Hall, MC 1750, Berkeley, CA 94720-1750. Phone: (510)643-9150 Fax: (510)643-0966 E-mail: esrc@esrc. berkeley.edu • URL: http://www.esrc.berkeley.edu/.

International Data Corp. (IDC). Five Speen St., Framingham, MA 01701. Phone: (508)872-8200 Fax: (508)935-4015 E-mail: leads@idc.com • URL: http://www.idc.com • Private research firm specializing in market research related to computers, multimedia, and telecommunications.

Laboratory for Computer Science. Massachusetts Institute of Technology, 200 Technology Square, Bldg. NE43, Cambridge, MA 02139. Phone: (617)253-5851 Fax: (617)258-8682 E-mail: zue@ mit.edu • URL: http://www.lcs.mit.edu/ • Research is in four areas: Intelligent Systems; Parallel Systems; Systems, Languages, and Networks; and Theory. Emphasis is on the application of online computing.

RAND. RAND. 1776 Main St., PO Box 2138, Santa Monica, CA 90407-2138. Phone: (310)393-0411 Fax: (310)393-4818 E-mail: correspondence@rand. org • URL: http://www.rand.org/ • Analysis and effective solutions that address the challenges facing the nation and the world, including critical issues surrounding education, homeland security, social security, health care and international development, as well as a range of national security issues.

SRI International. SRI International. 333 Ravenswood Ave., Menlo Park, CA 94025-3493. Phone: (650)859-2000 Fax: (650)859-4111 E-mail: inquiry. line@sri.com • URL: http://www.sri.com • Physical and life sciences, engineering, industrial management, business, social sciences, and public policy. Areas of research include biosciences, economics, energy, engineering systems and development, environment, health, industry consulting, information and communications, public policy, national security, and physical, life, and social sciences.

STATISTICS SOURCES

Annual Survey of Manufactures. Available from U. S. Government Printing Office. • Annual. Prices vary. Issued by the U. S. Census Bureau as an interim update to the *Census of Manufactures.* Includes data on number of manufacturing establishments in various industries, employment, labor costs, value of shipments, capital expenditures, inventories, energy costs, and assets. (See also Census Bureau home page, http://www.census. gov/.).

Computer Publishing Market Forecast. SIMBA Information. • Biennial. $1,895.00. Provides market data on computer-related books, magazines, newsletters, and other publications. Includes profiles of major publishers of computer-related material.

Computers and Office and Accounting Machines. U. S. Bureau of the Census. • Annual. Provides data on shipments: value, quantity, imports, and exports. (Current Industrial Reports, MA-35R.).

Information Systems Spending: An Analysis of Trends and Strategies. Computer Economics, Inc. • Annual. $1,595.00. Three volumes. Based on "in-depth surveys of public and private companies amd government organizations." Provides detailed data on management information systems spending, budgeting, and benchmarks. Includes charts, graphs, and analysis.

Standard & Poor's Industry Surveys. Standard & Poor's. • Semiannual. $1,800.00. Two looseleaf volumes. Includes monthly *Supplements.* Provides detailed, individual surveys of 52 major industry groups. Each survey is revised on a semiannual basis. Also includes "Monthly Investment Review" (industry group investment analysis) and monthly "Trends & Projections" (economic analysis).

Statistical Handbook on Technology. Paula Bernstein. Greenwood Publishing Group, Inc. • 1999. $69.95. Provides statistical data on such items as the Internet, online services, computer technology, recycling, patents, prescription drug sales, telecommunications, and aerospace. Includes charts, tables, and graphs. Edited for the general reader. (Statistical Handbook Series).

U. S. Industry and Trade Outlook. Available from National Technical Information Service. • Annual. $69.95. Produced by the International Trade Administration, U. S. Department of Commerce, in a "public-private" partnership with DRI/McGraw-Hill and Standard & Poor's. Provides basic data, outlook for the current year, and "Long-Term Prospects" (five-year projections) for a wide variety of products and services. Includes high technology industries. Formerly *U. S. Industrial Outlook.*

WEFA Industrial Monitor. John Wiley and Sons, Inc. • Annual. $65.00. Prepared by industry analysts at WEFA, an economic forecasting and consulting firm (originally Wharton Econometric Forecasting Associates). Contains discussions of the outlook for major U. S. industries, with many 10-year forecasts (WEFA Web site is http://www.wefa.com).

TRADE/PROFESSIONAL ASSOCIATIONS

AFCOM. 742 E Chapman Ave., Orange, CA 92866. Phone: (714)997-7966 Fax: (714)997-9743 E-mail: afcom@afcom.com • URL: http://www.afcom.com • Data center, networking and enterprise systems management professionals from medium and large scale mainframe, midrange and client/server data centers worldwide. Works to meet the professional needs of the enterprise system management community. Provides information and support through educational events, research and assistance hotlines, and surveys.

Association for Computing Machinery. 1515 Broadway, 17th Fl., New York, NY 10036-5701. Phone: 800-342-6626 or (212)626-0500 Fax: (212)944-1318 E-mail: acmhelp@acm.org • URL: http://www.acm.org • Includes many Special Interest Groups.

Association of Information Technology Professionals. 401 N Michigan Ave., Ste. 2200, Chicago, IL 60611-4267. Phone: 800-224-9371 or (312)245-1070 Fax: (312)527-6636 • URL: http://www.aitp.org.

Computer and Automated Systems Techincal Group of Society of Manufacturing Engin. Technical Activities Dept. 1 SME Dr., Dearborn, MI 48121. Phone: 800-733-4763 or (313)271-1500 Fax: (313)425-3400 E-mail: service@sme.org • URL: http://www.sme.org/casa • Sponsored by the Society of Manufacturing Engineers. Formerly Computer and Automated Systems Association.

Information Technology Association of America. 1401 Wilson Blvd., Suite 1100, Arlington, VA 22209. Phone: (703)522-5055 Fax: (703)525-2279 E-mail: hmiller@itaa.org • URL: http://www.itaa. org • Members are computer software and services companies. Maintains an Information Systems Integration Services Section. Formerly Software Industry Division of ADAPSO.

Institute of Electrical and Electronics Engineers. c/o IEEE Corporate Office, 3 Park Ave., 17th Fl., New York, NY 10016-5997. Phone: 800-678-4333 or (212)419-7900 Fax: (212)752-4929 E-mail: ieeeusa@ieee.org • URL: http://www.ieee.org.

Instrumentation Systems and Automation Society. 67 Alexander Dr., Research Triangle Park, NC 27709. Phone: (919)549-8411 Fax: (919)549-8288 E-mail: info@isa.org • URL: http://www.isa.org • Members are engineers and others concerned with industrial instrumentation, systems, computers, and automation. Formerly Instrument Society of America.

Special Interest Group on Applied Computing. c/o Association for Computing Machinery, 1515 Broadway, New York, NY 10036. Phone: 800-342-6626 or (212)626-0500 Fax: (212)302-5826 E-mail: sigs@acm.org • URL: http://www.acm.org/sigapp • Concerned with "innovative applications, technology transfer, experimental computing, strategic research, and the management of computing." Publishes a semiannual newsletter, *Applied Computing Review.*

OTHER SOURCES

Survey of Advanced Technology: A Strategic Analysis of Today's Leading-edge Information Technologies. I.T. Works, Innovation Center. • Annual. $795.00. Surveys the corporate use (or neglect) of advanced computer technology. Topics include major technology trends and emerging technologies.

COMPUTERS, HOME

See: MICROCOMPUTERS AND MINICOMPUTERS

COMPUTERS IN ACCOUNTING

ABSTRACTS AND INDEXES

Accounting and Tax Index. UMI. • Quarterly. Price on application. Annual cumulation. Indexes accounting, auditing, and taxation literature appearing in journals, books, pamphlets, conference proceedings, and newsletters.

Accounting Articles. CCH, Inc. • Monthly. $624.00 per year. Looseleaf service.

Business Periodicals Index. H. W. Wilson Co. • 11 times a year. Quarterly and annual cumulations. Price varies.

Computer Literature Index: A Subject/Author Index to Computer and Data Processing Literature. EB-SCO Publishing. • Quarterly, with annual cumulation. $245.00 per year. Contains brief abstracts of book and periodical literature covering all phases of computing, including approximately 70 specific application areas.

Key Abstracts: Business Automation. Available from INSPEC, Inc. • Monthly. $250.00 per year. Provides international coverage of journal and proceedings literature. Published in England by the Institution of Electrical Engineers (IEE).

CD-ROM DATABASES

ABI/INFORM. PROQUEST. • Monthly. Provides CD-ROM indexing and abstracting of worldwide business literature. Archival discs are available from 1971. Formerly *ABI/INFORM OnDisc.*

WILSONDISC: Business Periodicals Index. H. W. Wilson Co. • Monthly. Provides CD-ROM indexing of business periodicals from 1982 to date. Price includes online service.

ENCYCLOPEDIAS AND DICTIONARIES

Blackwell Encyclopedic Dictionary of Accounting. Rashad Abdel-khalik. Blackwell Publishing. • 1997. $38.95. The editor is associated with the University of Florida. Contains definitions of key terms combined with longer articles written by various U. S. and foreign business educators. Includes bibliographies and index. (Blackwell Encyclopedia of Management Series).

INTERNET DATABASES

Rutgers Accounting Web (RAW). Rutgers University Accounting Research Center. Phone: (973)353-5172 Fax: (973)353-1283 • URL: http://www.rutgers.edu/accounting • RAW Web site provides extensive links to sources of national and international accounting information, such as the Big Six accounting firms, the Financial Accounting Standards Board (FASB), SEC filings (EDGAR), journals, publishers, software, the International Accounting Network, and "Internet's largest list of accounting firms in USA." Searching is offered. Fees: Free.

ONLINE DATABASES

Wilson Business Abstracts Online. H. W. Wilson Co. • Indexes and abstracts 600 major business periodicals, plus the *Wall Street Journal* and the business section of the *New York Times.* Indexing is from 1982, abstracting from 1990, with the two newspapers included from 1993. Updated weekly. Inquire as to online cost and availability. (*Business Periodicals Index* without abstracts is also available online.).

PERIODICALS AND NEWSLETTERS

Accounting Technology: Turning Technology into Business Know How. Thomson Media. • 11 times a year. $61.00 per year. Provides advice and information on computers and software for the accounting profession. Formerly *Computers in Accounting*.

The CPA Software News (Certified Public Accountant). Cygnus Business Media. • Eight times a year. $39.95 per year. Provides articles and reviews relating to computer technology and software for accountants.

CPA Technology and Internet Tax Advisor (Certified Public Accountant). Aspen Publishers. • Monthly. $261.00 per year. Newsletter. Describes hardware and software products and makes recommendations. Formerly *C P A Technology and Internet Advisor*.

Quantum PC Report for CPAs. QNet. • Monthly. $235.00 per year. Newsletter on personal computer software and hardware for the accounting profession.

RESEARCH CENTERS AND INSTITUTES

Accounting Research Program. University of California, The Anderson School, Los Angeles, CA 90095-1481. Phone: (310)206-6462 Fax: (310)267-2163 E-mail: carla.hayn@anderson.ucla.edu.

TRADE/PROFESSIONAL ASSOCIATIONS

American Institute of Certified Public Accountants. 1211 Ave. of the Americas, New York, NY 10036-8775. Phone: 888-777-7077 or (212)596-6200 Fax: (212)596-6213 • URL: http://www.aicpa.org.

Association for Accounting Administration. 136 S. Keowee St., Dayton, OH 45402. Phone: (937)222-0030 Fax: (937)222-5794 E-mail: aaainfo@cpaadmin.org • URL: http://www.cpaadmin.org • Members are accounting and office systems executives.

Institute of Internal Auditors. 247 Maitland Ave., Altamonte Springs, FL 32701-4201. Phone: (407)937-1100 Fax: (407)937-1101 E-mail: iia@theiia.org • URL: http://www.theiia.org.

COMPUTERS IN BANKING

See: BANK AUTOMATION; COMPUTERS IN FINANCE

COMPUTERS IN EDUCATION

See also: MICROCOMPUTERS AND MINICOMPUTERS

GENERAL WORKS

Computer Studies: Computers in Education. John Hirschbuhl and Dwight Bishop. McGraw-Hill. • 1999. $18.44. Ninth edition. (Annual Editions Series).

Computers in Education Today. Steven L. Mandell. West Publishing Co. • $52.00. Date not set.

The Evolving Virtual Library: Practical and Philosophical Perspectives. Laverna M. Saunders, editor. Information Today, Inc. • 1999. $39.50. Various authors cover trends in library and school use of the Internet, intranets, extranets, and electronic databases.

Net Curriculum: An Educator's Guide to Using the Internet. Linda Joseph. Information Today, Inc. • 1999. $29.95. Covers various educational aspects of the Internet. Written for K-12 teachers, librarians, and media specialists by a columnist for *Multimedia Schools*. (CyberAge Books.).

NetSavvy: Building Information Literacy in the Classroom. Ian Jukes and others. Corwin Press, Inc. • 2000. $69.95. Second edition. Provides practical advice on the teaching of computer, Internet, and technological literacy. Includes sample lesson plans and grade-level objectives. (One-Off Series).

Technology and Teaching. Les Lloyd, editor. Information Today, Inc. • 1997. $42.50. Contains multimedia computer application case studies relat-

ing to college level curricula and teaching.

Using Technology to Increase Student Learning. Linda E. Reksten. Corwin Press, Inc. • 2000. $74.95. Emphasis is on the use of computer technology in schools. (Technology Series).

ABSTRACTS AND INDEXES

Computer Literature Index: A Subject/Author Index to Computer and Data Processing Literature. EBSCO Publishing. • Quarterly, with annual cumulation. $245.00 per year. Contains brief abstracts of book and periodical literature covering all phases of computing, including approximately 70 specific application areas.

ALMANACS AND YEARBOOKS

Educational Media and Technology Yearbook. Libraries Unlimited, Inc. • Annual. $75.00.

DIRECTORIES

TESS: (The Educational Software Selector). EPIE Institute. • Semiannual. $82.50 per year. Lists over 900 suppliers of educational software for Mackintosh, Apple II, MS-DOS and Windows compatible computers and videodisc players. Formerly *The Latest and Best of TESS: The Educational Software Selector*.

ENCYCLOPEDIAS AND DICTIONARIES

Dictionary of Computing. Valerie Illingworth, editor. Oxford University Press. • 1997. $18.00. Fourth edition.

ONLINE DATABASES

Education Index Online. H. W. Wilson Co. • Indexes a wide variety of periodicals related to schools, colleges, and education, 1984 to date. Monthly updates. Inquire as to online cost and availability.

PERIODICALS AND NEWSLETTERS

Boardwatch: Analysis of Telecom Software, Services and Strategy. Light Reading, Inc. • Monthly. $72.00 per year. Covers World Wide Web publishing, internet technology, educational aspects of online communication, internet legalities, and other computer communication topics.

Computers in the Schools: The Interdisciplinary Journal of Practice, Theory, and Applied Research. Haworth Press, Inc. • Quarterly. $450.00 per year. Includes print and online editions.

Education Technology News: Insiders Guide to Multimedia in the K-12 Classroom. Business Publishers, Inc. • Biweekly. $357.00 per year. Looseleaf service. Formerly *Education Computer News*.

Electronic Learning. Scholastic, Inc. • Eight times a year. $19.95 per year. Includes classroom applications for computers. For teachers of grades K-12.

The Gray Sheet. F-D-C Reports Inc. • Description: Monitors the complex regulatory environment for devices, instrumentation, and diagnostics. Topics include device-related Congressional activity, Medicare reimbursement policies, international regulatory intiatives, enforcement and premarket approval programs at FDA's Center for Devices and Radiological Health. Recurring features include device approvals, 510(k) clearances, FDA recalls and seizures, mergers and acquisitions, and sales and earnings.

Mathematics and Computer Education. George M. Miller, editor. MATYC Journal, Inc. • Quarterly. Individuals, $18.00 per year; institutions, $30.00 per year. Articles for high school and college teachers.

Multimedia Schools: A Practical Journal of Technology for Education including Multimedia, CD-ROM, Online and Internet and Hardware in K-12. Information Today, Inc. • Six times a year. $39.95 per year. Edited for school librarians, media center directors, computer coordinators, and others concerned with educational multimedia. Coverage includes the use of CD-ROM sources, the Internet,

online services, and library technology.

Syllabus: New Directions in Educational Technology. Syllabus Press. • 10 times a year. $24.00 per year. Covers the use of advanced technology in higher education systems, including video, multimedia, the Internet, distance learning systems, and electronic publishing.

T H E Journal (Technological Horizons in Education). Ed Warnshuis Ltd. • 11 times a year. $29.00 per year. For educators of all levels.

Technology and Learning: The Leading Magazine of Electronic Education. CMP Media LLC. • Eight times a year. $29.95 per year. Covers all levels of computer/electronic education-elementary to college. Formerly *Classroom Computer Learning*.

University Business: Solutions for Today's Higher Education. Educational Media Inc. • 10 times a year. $60.00 per year. Edited for college administrators, including managers of business services, finance, computing, and telecommunications. Includes information on relevant technological advances.

RESEARCH CENTERS AND INSTITUTES

Computer-Based Education and Instructional Design Project. Temple University. Broad and Montgomery, Ritter Annex, Room 217, Philadelphia, PA 19122. Phone: (215)204-6109 Fax: (215)204-6103 E-mail: snelbeck@astro.temple.edu.

Concord Consortium, Inc. Concord Consortium. 25 Love Ln., Concord, MA 01742. Phone: (978)405-3200 Fax: (978)405-2076 E-mail: info@concord.org • URL: http://www.concord.org • Global technology-based Science and Math education, including educational applications of networking, computers and electronics.

Instructional Technology Center. University of Delaware, College of Education, 305 Willard Hall, Wilmington, DE 19716. Phone: (302)831-8164 Fax: (302)831-4110 E-mail: fth@udel.edu • URL: http://www.udel.edu.

TRADE/PROFESSIONAL ASSOCIATIONS

IEEE Computer Society. 1828 L St. NW, Ste. 1202, Washington, DC 20036. Phone: (202)371-0101 Fax: (202)728-9614 E-mail: help@computer.org • URL: http://www.computer.org • Computer professionals. Promotes the development of computer and information sciences and fosters communication within the information processing community. Sponsors conferences, symposia, workshops, tutorials, technical meetings, and seminars. Operates Computer Society Press. Presents scholarships; bestows technical achievement and service awards and certificates.

International Society for Technology in Education. 480 Chamelton St., Eugene, OR 97401-2626. Phone: 800-336-5191 or (541)302-3777 Fax: (541)302-3778 E-mail: iste@iste.org • URL: http://www.iste.org.

Special Interest Group for Computer Science Education. c/o Association for Computing Machinery, 1515 Broadway, New York, NY 10036-5701. Phone: 800-342-6626 or (212)626-0500 E-mail: acmhelp@acm.org • URL: http://www.acm.org • Concerned with education relating to computer science and technology on various levels, ranging from secondary school to graduate degree programs.

COMPUTERS IN FINANCE

GENERAL WORKS

Mastering Online Investing: How to Use the Internet to Become a More Successful Investor. Michael C. Thomsett. Dearborn Trading Publishing, A Kaplan Professional Co. • 2001. $19.95. Emphasis is on the Internet as an information source for intelligent investing, avoiding "speculation and fads.".

Super Searchers on Wall Street: Top Investment

Professionals Share Their Online Research Secrets. Amelia Kassel. Information Today, Inc. • 2000. $24.95. Gives the results of interviews with "10 leading financial industry research experts." Explains how online information is used by stock brokers, investment bankers, and individual investors. Includes relevant Web sites and other sources. (Super Searchers Series).

ABSTRACTS AND INDEXES

Business Periodicals Index. H. W. Wilson Co. • 11 times a year. Quarterly and annual cumulations. Price varies.

Computer Literature Index: A Subject/Author Index to Computer and Data Processing Literature. EBSCO Publishing. • Quarterly, with annual cumulation. $245.00 per year. Contains brief abstracts of book and periodical literature covering all phases of computing, including approximately 70 specific application areas.

CD-ROM DATABASES

ABI/INFORM. PROQUEST. • Monthly. Provides CD-ROM indexing and abstracting of worldwide business literature. Archival discs are available from 1971. Formerly *ABI/INFORM OnDisc.*

WILSONDISC: Business Periodicals Index. H. W. Wilson Co. • Monthly. Provides CD-ROM indexing of business periodicals from 1982 to date. Price includes online service.

DIRECTORIES

Futures Magazine SourceBook: The Most Complete List of Exchanges, Companies, Regulators, Organizations, etc., Offering Products and Services to the Futures and Options Industry. Futures Magazine, Inc. • Annual. $19.50. Provides information on commodity futures brokers, trading method services, publications, and other items of interest to futures traders and money managers.

Microbanker Software Buyer's Guide. Microbanker Inc. • Covers: 600 suppliers of approximately 1,550 financial application programs for microcomputers. Entries include: Name, address, and phone of supplier; description of program, including application, hardware requirements, price, and type of documentation or software support provided.

HANDBOOKS AND MANUALS

Artificial Intelligence and Software Engineering: Understanding the Promise of the future. Darek Partridge. Fitzroy Dearborn Publishers, Inc. • 1999. $55.00. Includes applications of artificial intelligence software to banking and financial services.

INTERNET DATABASES

Futures Online. Futures Magazine Inc. Phone: (312)846-4600 Fax: (312)846-4638 • URL: http://www.futuresmag.com • Web site presents updates of *Futures* magazine and links to other futures-related sites.

ONLINE DATABASES

Banking Information Source. PROQUEST. • Provides indexing and abstracting of periodical and other literature from 1982 to date, with weekly updates. Covers the financial services industry: banks, savings institutions, investment houses, credit unions, insurance companies, and real estate organizations. Emphasis is on marketing and management. Inquire as to online cost and availability. (Formerly *FINIS: Financial Industry Information Service.*).

Wilson Business Abstracts Online. H. W. Wilson Co. • Indexes and abstracts 600 major business periodicals, plus the *Wall Street Journal* and the business section of the *New York Times.* Indexing is from 1982, abstracting from 1990, with the two newspapers included from 1993. Updated weekly. Inquire as to online cost and availability. (*Business*

Periodicals Index without abstracts is also available online.).

PERIODICALS AND NEWSLETTERS

American Banker: The Financial Services Daily. Thomson Media. • Daily. $895.00 per year. Provides news of banking, investment products, mortgages, credit unions, finance, bank technology, and legal developments.

Computerized Investing. American Association of Individual Investors. • Description: Furnishes articles on computer-aided investment analysis and investment-related software programs and database. Contains information on hardware and software, new product announcements, and editorial commentary. Recurring features include columns titled Product Reviews, New Products, Product Comparisons, BBS Update, Bookshelf, and Member Software Services.

Online Investor: Personal Investing for the Digital Age. Stock Trends, Inc. • Monthly. $14.95 per year. Provides advice and Web site reviews for online traders.

Securities Industry News. Thomson Financial Corporate Communications. • Weekly. $275.00 per year. Newsletter covers securities dealing and processing, including regulatory compliance, shareholder services, human resources, transaction clearing, and technology.

U. S. Banker. Thomson Media. • Monthly. $65.00 per year. Edited for bank executives and managers. Covers a wide variety of banking and financial topics.

U.S. Banker. IMG Media. • Monthly. $79.00 per year. Covers technology innovation for the banking industry, including online banking. Incorporates *Future Banker.*

Wall Street and Technology: For Senior-Level Executives in Technology and Information Management in Securities and Invesment Firms. CMP Media LLC. • Monthly. $85.00 per year. Includes material on the use of computers in technical investment strategies. Formerly *Wall Computer Review.*

WebFinance. Thomson Media. • Semimonthly. $995.00 per year. Newsletter (also available online at www.webfinance.net). Covers the Internet-based provision of online financial services by banks, online brokers, mutual funds, and insurance companies. Provides news stories, analysis, and descriptions of useful resources.

Windows in Financial Services. • Quarterly. $39.00 per year. Covers information technology applications and products for Microsoft Windows users in the financial sector.

RESEARCH CENTERS AND INSTITUTES

Institute for Quantitative Research in Finance. Church Street Station, P.O. Box 6194, New York, NY 10249-6194. Phone: (212)744-6825 Fax: (212)517-2259 E-mail: daleberman@compuserve • Financial research areas include quantitative methods, securities analysis, and the financial structure of industries. Also known as the "Q Group.".

OTHER SOURCES

The Options Workbook: Proven Strategies from a Market Wizard. Anthony J. Saliba. Dearborn Trade Publishing, A Kaplan Professional Co. • 2001. $40.00. Emphasis is on computerized trading on the Chicago Board Options Exchange. Includes information on specific trading strategies.

COMPUTERS IN GOVERNMENT

ABSTRACTS AND INDEXES

Computer Literature Index: A Subject/Author Index to Computer and Data Processing Literature. EB-

SCO Publishing. • Quarterly, with annual cumulation. $245.00 per year. Contains brief abstracts of book and periodical literature covering all phases of computing, including approximately 70 specific application areas.

Sage Public Administration Abstracts. Sage Publications, Inc. • Quarterly. Institutions, $785.00 per year.

CD-ROM DATABASES

NTIS on SilverPlatter. Available from SilverPlatter Information, Inc. • Quarterly. $2,850.00 per year. Produced by the National Technical Information Service. Provides a CD-ROM guide to over 500,000 government reports on a wide variety of technical, industrial, and business topics.

PAIS on CD-ROM. Public Affairs Information Service, Inc. • Quarterly. $1,995.00 per year. Provides a CD-ROM version of the online service, *PAIS International.* Contains over 500,000 citations to the literature of contemporary social, political, and economic issues.

ONLINE DATABASES

NTIS Database. National Technical Information Service. • Contains citations and abstracts to unrestricted reports of government-sponsored research, 1964 to date. Covers a wide range of technical, engineering, business, and social science topics. Monthly updates. Inquire as to online cost and availability.

PAIS International. Public Affairs Information Service, Inc. • Corresponds to the former printed publications, *PAIS Bulletin* (1976-90) and *PAIS Foreign Language Index* (1972-90), and to the current *PAIS International in Print* (1991 to date). Covers economic, political, and sociological material appearing in periodicals, books, government documents, and other publications. Updating is monthly. Inquire as to online cost and availability.

PERIODICALS AND NEWSLETTERS

Federal Computer Week: The Newspaper for the Government Systems Community. FCW Government Technology Group. • 41 times a year. $95.00 per year.

Governing: The States and Localities. • Monthly. $39.95 per year. Edited for state and local government officials. Covers finance, office management, computers, telecommunications, environmental concerns, etc.

Government Computer News: The Newspaper Serving Computer Users Throughout the Federal Government. Business Information, Inc. • 32 times a year. Free to qualified personnel.

Government Executive: Federal Government's Business Magazine. National Journal Group, Inc. • Monthly. $48.00 per year. Includes management of computerized information systems in the federal government.

Government Technology: Solutions for State and Local Government in the Information Age. E. Republic Inc. • Monthly. Free to qualified personnel.

Journal of E-Government. Haworth Press, Inc. • Quarterly. $300.00 per year to libraries; $45.00 per year to individuals. Contains material on "government usage of information technology to enhance the delivery of public services and information.".

RESEARCH CENTERS AND INSTITUTES

Government Finance Officers Association. Government Finance Officers Association. 203 N LaSalle St., Ste. 2700, Chicago, IL 60601-1210. Phone: (312)977-9700 Fax: (312)977-4806 E-mail: communications@foundationcenter.org • URL: http://www.gfoa.org • Provides consulting and research services in state and local government finance and management. Areas of expertise include: accounting, budgeting, cash management, debt management, pension/benefits, revenue and expenditure forecasting, technology procurement, reengineering/privatization, and state/local fiscal relations.

COMPUTERS IN INVESTING

See: COMPUTERS IN FINANCE

COMPUTERS IN LIBRARIES

See: LIBRARY AUTOMATION; ONLINE INFORMATION SYSTEMS

COMPUTERS, PERSONAL

See: MICROCOMPUTERS AND MINICOMPUTERS

COMPUTERS, PORTABLE

See: PORTABLE COMPUTERS

CONCESSIONS

See also: FAIRS; FRANCHISES

DIRECTORIES
Concession Profession. National Association of Concessionaires. • Covers: about 900 member equipment manufacturers, suppliers, jobber/distributors, popcorn processors, theaters, amusement parks, stadiums, rinks, and other concession operators in the United States and Canada. Entries include: For operators--Company name, address, phone, name of contact. For manufacturers and suppliers--Company name, address, phone, names and titles of up to four executives, brief description of service or products.

TRADE/PROFESSIONAL ASSOCIATIONS
National Association of Concessionaires. 35 E. Wacker Dr., Suite 1816, Chicago, IL 60601. Phone: (312)236-3858 Fax: (312)236-7809 E-mail: info@naconline.org • URL: http://www.naconline.org • Formerly Popcorn and Concessions Association.

National Park Hospitality Association. 1225 New York Ave. NW, Ste. 450, Washington, DC 20005. Phone: (202)682-9530 Fax: (202)682-9529 E-mail: info@nphassn.org • URL: http://parkpartners.org • Represents private concessionaires operating in the U.S. national parks. Acts as liaison between members and the National Park Service and Congress.

CONCILIATION, INDUSTRIAL

See: ARBITRATION

CONCRETE INDUSTRY

See also: BUILDING INDUSTRY; CEMENT INDUSTRY

GENERAL WORKS
Design of Concrete Structures. Arthur H. Nilson and others. McGraw-Hill. • 2003. $134.90. 13th edition. (Construction Engineering and Project Management Series).

Reinforced Concrete Fundamentals. Phil M. Ferguson and others. John Wiley and Sons, Inc. • 1988. $116.95. Fifth edition.

ALMANACS AND YEARBOOKS
The Concrete Yearbook. EMAP Construction Ltd. • Annual. $100.00.

DIRECTORIES
Concrete Construction. Hanley-Wood, LLC. • Monthly. $30.00 per year. Lists manufacturers or suppliers of concrete-related products and services.
Concrete Construction Buyers' Guide. Hanley-Wood, LLC. • Annual. $5.00. Lists sources of products and services related to building with concrete.
Masonry Construction Buyers' Guide. Mason Contractors Association of America. • Annual. $3.00. Lists manufacturers or suppliers of products and services related to masonry construction.

FINANCIAL RATIOS
Annual Statement Studies. The Risk Management Association. • Annual. Median and quartile financial ratios are given for over 400 kinds of manufacturing, wholesale, retail, construction, and consumer finance establishments. Data is sorted by both asset size and sales volume. Includes a clearly written "Definition of Ratios" and an alphabetical industry index.

Annual Statement Studies: Industry Default Probabilities and Cash Flow Measures. The Risk Management Association. • Annual. $145.00. Serves as a companion volume to the original *Annual Statement Studies.* Gives probability of default estimates on a percentage scale for more than 450 industries. Includes changes in position year-by-year for eight financial statement line items and provides percentage measures of cash flow.

HANDBOOKS AND MANUALS
ACI Manual of Concrete Practice. American Concrete Institute. • Annual. Free to members; nonmembers, $595.00. Five volumes.

PERIODICALS AND NEWSLETTERS
Concrete International. American Concrete Institute. • Monthly. $126.00 per year. Covers practical technology, industry news, and business management relating to the concrete construction industry.
The Concrete Producer. Hanley-Wood, LLC. • Monthly. $27.00 per year. Covers the production and marketing of various concrete products, including precast and prestressed concrete. Formerly *Aberdeen's Concrete Trader.*
Concrete Products. Primedia Business Magazines and Media. • Monthly. $61.00 per year. Free to qualified personnel; others, $61.00 per year.

RESEARCH CENTERS AND INSTITUTES
Center for Cement Composite Materials. University of Illinois at Urbana-Champaign. 2129 Newmark Civil Engineering Laboratory, 205 Mathews Ave., Urbana, IL 61801. Phone: (217)333-6900 Fax: (217)265-8040 E-mail: lstruble@uiuc.edu.

STATISTICS SOURCES
Annual Survey of Manufactures. Available from U. S. Government Printing Office. • Annual. Prices vary. Issued by the U. S. Census Bureau as an interim update to the *Census of Manufactures.* Includes data on number of manufacturing establishments in various industries, employment, labor costs, value of shipments, capital expenditures, inventories, energy costs, and assets. (See also Census Bureau home page, http://www.census.gov/.).

TRADE/PROFESSIONAL ASSOCIATIONS
American Concrete Institute. PO Box 9094, Farmington Hills, MI 48333-9094. Phone: (248)848-3700 Fax: (248)848-3701 E-mail: bill.tolley@concrete.org • URL: http://www.aci-int.org • Technical and educational society of engineers, architects, contractors, educators, and others interested in improving techniques of design construction and maintenance of concrete products and structures. Offers certification program.

National Concrete Masonry Association. 13750 Sunrise Valley Dr., Herndon, VA 20171-4662. Phone: (703)713-1900 Fax: (703)713-1910 E-mail:

ncma@ncma.org • URL: http://www.ncma.org • Manufacturers of concrete masonry units (concrete blocks), segmental retaining wall units and paving block; associate members are machinery, cement, and aggregate manufacturers. Conducts testing and research on masonry units and masonry assemblies. Compiles statistics.

National Ready Mixed Concrete Association. 900 Spring St., Silver Spring, MD 20910. Phone: 888-846-7622 or (301)587-1400 or (301)587-1400 Fax: (301)585-4219 E-mail: info@nrmca.org • URL: http://www.nrmca.org • Concrete plant manufacturers. Develops engineering standards with a view toward simplification and standardization of sizes, capacities, and other criteria associated with the manufacture of concrete plants. Performs services leading to higher quality concrete plant equipment.

CONDIMENTS INDUSTRY

See: SPICE INDUSTRY

CONDOMINIUMS

See also: APARTMENT HOUSES; HOUSING; REAL ESTATE BUSINESS

CD-ROM DATABASES
Sourcebooks America CD-ROM. CACI Marketing Systems. • Annual. $1,250.00. Provides the CD-ROM version of *The Sourcebook of ZIP Code Demographics: Census Edition* and *The Sourcebook of County Demographics: Census Edition.*

FINANCIAL RATIOS
Almanac of Business and Industrial Financial Ratios. Leo Troy. Aspen Publishers, Inc. • 2003. $125.95. Includes CD-Rom. Contains financial ratios derived from federal tax returns. Ratios for each of about 200 industries are arranged according to company asset size. (Almanac of Business and Industrial Financial Ratios Series).

HANDBOOKS AND MANUALS
Condos, Co-ops, and Townhomes: A Complete Guide to Finding, Buying, Maintaining, and Enjoying Your New Home. Mark B. Weiss. Dearborn Trade Publishing, A Kaplan Professional Co. • 2003. $18.95. Covers financing, assessments, investment for rental, common areas, homeowners associations, and other topics relating to "association-managed communities.".

How to Buy a House, Condo, or Co-op. Jean C. Thomsett. Consumers Union of the United States, Inc. • 1996. $84.75. Fifth edition.

Your Dream Home: A Comprehensive Guide to Buying a House, Condo, or Co-op. Marguerite Smith. Warner Books, Inc. • 1997. $10.99. (Money, America's Financial Advisor Series).

PERIODICALS AND NEWSLETTERS
CondoBusiness. Shelter Publications. • Monthly. $55.00 per year. Covers condominum development and administration industries.

Ledger Quarterly: A Financial Review for Community Association Practitioners. Community Associations Institute. • Quarterly. $67.00 per year. Newsletter. Provides current information on issues affecting the finances of condominium, cooperative, homeowner, apartment, and other community housing associations.

Mortgage and Real Estate Executives Report. West Group. • Biweekly. $368.00 per year. Newsletter. Source of ideas and new updates. Covers the latest opportunities and developments.

STATISTICS SOURCES
American Housing Survey for the United States in [year]. Available from U. S. Government Printing

Office. • Biennial. $51.00. Issued by the U. S. Census Bureau (http://www.census.gov). Covers both owner-occupied and renter-occupied housing. Includes data on such factors as condition of building, type of mortgage, utility costs, and housing occupied by minorities. (Current Housing Reports, H150.).

Housing Statistics of the United States. Patrick A. Simmons. Bernan Press. • 2000. $89.00. Third edition. (Housing Statistics of the United States Series).

TRADE/PROFESSIONAL ASSOCIATIONS

Community Associations Institute. 225 Reinekers Ln., Ste. 300, Alexandria, VA 22314. Phone: 888-CAI-4321 or (703)548-8600 Fax: (703)684-1581 E-mail: caidirect@caionline.org • URL: http://www.caionline.org • Condominium and homeowner associations, cooperatives, and association-governed planned communities of all sizes and architectural types; community or property managers and management firms; individual homeowners; community association managers and management firms; public officials; and lawyers, accountants, engineers, reserve specialists, builder/developers and other providers of professional services and products for CAs. Seeks to educate and represent America's 250,000 residential condominium, cooperative and homeowner associations and related professionals and service providers. Aims to foster vibrant, responsive, competent community associations that promote harmony, community and responsible leadership.

Institute of Real Estate Management. 430 N. Michigan Ave., Chicago, IL 60611-4090. Phone: 800-837-0706 or (312)329-6000 Fax: 800-837-4736 E-mail: custserv@irem.org • URL: http://www.irem.org.

National Association of Realtors. 430 N. Michigan Ave., Chicago, IL 60611. Phone: 800-874-6500 or (312)329-8313 Fax: (312)329-5962 E-mail: infocentral@realtors.org • URL: http://www.realtor.org.

OTHER SOURCES

Real Estate Transactions: Condominium Law and Practice Forms. Patrick J. Rohan and Melvin A. Reskin. LexisNexis Matthew Bender. • Three times a year. $1,649.00. Eight looseleaf volumes. Guide for handling condominium transactions.

CONFECTIONERY INDUSTRY

See: CANDY INDUSTRY

CONFERENCE MANAGEMENT

See: MEETING MANAGEMENT

CONFERENCES, WORKSHOPS, AND SEMINARS

See also: CONVENTIONS; SALES CONVENTIONS

BIBLIOGRAPHIES

Bibliographic Guide to Conference Publications. Available from Gale Cengage Learning. • Annual. $600.00. Two volumes. Published by G. K. Hall & Co., Lists a wide range of conference publications cataloged by the New York Public Library and the Library of Congress.

DIRECTORIES

Corporate Meeting and Event Planners. Douglas Publications L.L.C. • Covers: Approximately 11,200

corporations that hold regular, off-site meetings arranged by nearly 14,300 corporate meeting planners. Includes companies in the United States, Puerto Rico, the Virgin Islands, and Canada. Entries include: Company name, address, phone, fax; e-mail; URL; names and titles of key personnel; geographical area served; branch/subsidiary office name and address; products and/or services provided; type of business; number of meetings; months when meetings are held; number of attendees; type of facility used; whether company utilizes services of professional speakers or entertainers.

International Congress Calendar. Union of International Associations. • Covers: over 12,000 scheduled international meetings; mostly covers meetings within the next two years, but extends through the next 10 years. Entries include: Name and address of sponsoring body, theme, meeting dates, meeting place, estimated number of participants, concurrent exhibition, reference to organization listing in "Yearbook of International Organizations.".

Trade Shows Worldwide: An International Directory of Events, Facilities and Suppliers. Gale Cengage Learning. • 2003. $355.00. 19th edition. Provides detailed information from over 75 countries on more than 10,800 trade shows and exhibitions. Separate sections are provided for trade shows/exhibitions, for sponsors/organizers, and for services, facilities, and information sources. Indexing is by date, location, subject, name, and keyword.

HANDBOOKS AND MANUALS

How to Develop and Promote Successful Seminars and Workshops: A Definitive Guide to Creating and Marketing Seminars, Workshops, Classes, and Conferences. Howard L. Shenson. John Wiley and Sons, Inc. • 1990. $34.95.

How to Make it Big in the Seminar Business. Paul Karasik. McGraw-Hill. • 1995. $15.95. Covers the organizing and marketing of seminars or workshops, including fee determination, promotion, scheduling, and evaluation.

Seminar Promoting. Entrepreneur Media, Inc. • Looseleaf. $59.50. A practical guide to starting a seminar promotion business. Covers profit potential, start-up costs, market size evaluation, owner's time required, site selection, pricing, accounting, advertising, promotion, etc. (Start-Up Business Guide No. E1071.).

Workshops: Designing and Facilitating Experiential Learning. Jeff E. Brooks-Harris and Susan R. Stock-Ward. Sage Publications, Inc. • 1999. $80.95. Presents a practical approach to designing, running, and evaluating workshops in business, adult education, and other areas. Includes references.

INTERNET DATABASES

Trade Show Center. Global Sources/Trade Media Holdings Ltd. [Singapore]. Phone: (656)574-2800 E-mail: service@globalsources.com • URL: http://www.globalsources.com/TRADESHW/TRDSHFRM.HTM • Free Web site provides current, detailed information on more than 1,000 major trade shows worldwide, including events in the U. S., but with an emphasis on "Asia and Greater China." Searching is offered by product, supplier, country, and month of year. Includes links to "Trade Information.".

PERIODICALS AND NEWSLETTERS

The Meeting Professional. Meeting Professionals International. • Monthly. $50.00 per year. Published for professionals in the meeting and convention industry. Contains news, features, and how-to's for domestic and international meetings management. Formerly *Meeting Manager.*

Scientific Meetings. Scientific Meetings Publications. • Quarterly. $85.00 per year. Provides

information on forthcoming scientific, technical, medical, health, engineering and management meetings held throughout the world.

World Meetings: Outside United States and Canada. Gale Group. • Three times a year. $195.00 per year.

World Meetings: United States and Canada. Gale Cengage Learning. • Three times a year. $195.00 per year.

TRADE/PROFESSIONAL ASSOCIATIONS

International Association of Conference Translators. 15, route des Morillons, CH-1218 Grand-Saconnex, Geneva, Switzerland. Phone: 41 22 7910666 Fax: 41 22 7885644 E-mail: webmaster@aitc.ch • URL: http://www.aitc.ch.

CONFLICT MANAGEMENT

See: ARBITRATION; NEGOTIATION

CONGLOMERATES

See: CORPORATIONS

CONGRESS

See: UNITED STATES CONGRESS

CONSERVATION

See: NATURAL RESOURCES

CONSTRUCTION CONTRACTS

See: BUILDING CONTRACTS

CONSTRUCTION, ELECTRICAL

See: ELECTRICAL CONSTRUCTION INDUSTRY

CONSTRUCTION EQUIPMENT

See also: BUILDING INDUSTRY; CIVIL ENGINEERING; HOUSING

GENERAL WORKS

Construction Contracting. Richard H. Clough and Glenn A. Sears. John Wiley and Sons, Inc. • 1994. $110.00. Sixth edition.

DIRECTORIES

Builder: Buyer's Guide. Hanley-Wood, LLC. • Annual. $10.00. A directory of products and services for the home building and remodeling industry.

Construction Equipment Buyers Guide. Reed Business Information. • Annual. $49.95.

Construction Equipment Distribution-Directory. Associated Equipment Distributors. • Annual. $100.00 per year. Lists about 1,300 members of the association.

ProSales Buyer's Guide. Hanley-Wood, LLC. • Annual. Price on application. A directory of equipment for professional builders.

Tools of the Trade Annual Buyers Guide. Hanley-Wood, LLC. • Annual. Price on application. A directory of tools for the construction industry.

FINANCIAL RATIOS

Almanac of Business and Industrial Financial Ratios. Leo Troy. Aspen Publishers, Inc. • 2003. $125.95. Includes CD-Rom. Contains financial ratios derived from federal tax returns. Ratios for each of about 200 industries are arranged according to company asset size. (Almanac of Business and Industrial Financial Ratios Series).

Annual Statement Studies. The Risk Management Association. • Annual. Median and quartile financial ratios are given for over 400 kinds of manufacturing, wholesale, retail, construction, and consumer finance establishments. Data is sorted by both asset size and sales volume. Includes a clearly written "Definition of Ratios" and an alphabetical industry index.

Annual Statement Studies: Industry Default Probabilities and Cash Flow Measures. The Risk Management Association. • Annual. $145.00. Serves as a companion volume to the original *Annual Statement Studies*. Gives probability of default estimates on a percentage scale for more than 450 industries. Includes changes in position year-by-year for eight financial statement line items and provides percentage measures of cash flow.

HANDBOOKS AND MANUALS

Complete Building Equipment Maintenance Desk Book. Sheldon J. Fuchs, editor. Prentice Hall PTR. • 1992. $69.95. Second edition. *Supplement* available, $39.95.

INTERNET DATABASES

Manufacturing Profiles. U. S. Bureau of the Census. Phone: (301)763-4636 E-mail: webmaster@census. gov • URL: http://www.census.gov/prod/www/abs/ mfg-prof.html • The Census Bureau makes available free on PDF (Portable Document Format) an annual consolidation of the entire Current Industrial Report series, presenting "all the data compiled." Contains statistics on production, shipments, inventories, consumption, exports, imports, and orders for a wide variety of manufactured products.

PERIODICALS AND NEWSLETTERS

Building Products. Hanley-Wood, LLC. • Quarterly. $36.00 per year. Covers building products and materials for the construction industry, including new products.

Construction Equipment Distribution. Associated Equipment Distributors. • Monthly. Members, $20.00 per year; non-members, $40.00 per year.

Construction Equipment Operation and Maintenance. Construction Publications Inc. • Bimonthly. $12.00 per year. Information for users of construction equipment and industry news.

Equipment Today. Cygnus Business Media. • Monthly. $65.00 per year. Includes annual *Product* issue Formerly *Equipment Guide News.*

Journal of Light Construction. Hanley-Wood, LLC. • Monthly. $35.95 per year. Provides jobsite tips, techniques, and product advice for builders and contractors.

Tools of the Trade. Hanley-Wood, LLC. • Five times a year. $19.80 per year. Provides advice and information on tools for the construction industry. Includes product tests and evaluations.

STATISTICS SOURCES

Annual Survey of Manufactures. Available from U. S. Government Printing Office. • Annual. Prices vary. Issued by the U. S. Census Bureau as an interim update to the *Census of Manufactures*. Includes data on number of manufacturing establishments in various industries, employment, labor costs, value of shipments, capital expenditures, inventories, energy costs, and assets. (See also Census Bureau home page, http://www.census. gov/.).

U. S. Industry and Trade Outlook. Available from National Technical Information Service. • Annual. $69.95. Produced by the International Trade Administration, U. S. Department of Commerce, in a "public-private" partnership with DRI/McGraw-Hill and Standard & Poor's. Provides basic data, outlook for the current year, and "Long-Term Prospects" (five-year projections) for a wide variety of products and services. Includes high technology industries. Formerly *U. S. Industrial Outlook*.

TRADE/PROFESSIONAL ASSOCIATIONS

AEM Marketing Council. 6737 W Washington St., Ste. 2400, Milwaukee, WI 53214-5647. Phone: (866)AEM-0442 or (414)272-0943 Fax: (414)272-1170 E-mail: us.office@ciesnet.com • URL: http:// www.aem.org • Advertising and marketing executives of equipment manufacturers and their advertising agencies directly interested in the marketing, advertising and sales promotion of construction equipment.

Associated Equipment Distributors. 615 W 22nd St., Oak Brook, IL 60523. Phone: 800-388-0650 or (630)574-0650 Fax: (630)574-0132 E-mail: info@ aednet.org • URL: http://www.aednet.org • Represents distributors and manufacturers of agriculture, and construction, mining, logging, forestry, public works and road maintenance equipment in the U.S., Canada, and overseas. Includes activities such as industry information and statistics, educational programs on customer service, financial management, rental management, sales management, and service and parts management program for younger executives. Maintains Washington, DC office. Oversees AED Foundation which offers industry educational programs and career/vocational services. Offers group and business insurance to members; conducts ongoing industry relations program with construction equipment manufacturers and users. Operates Market Trends Index Program, covering monthly distributor sales and inventories.

Construction Industry Manufacturers Association. 111 E. Wisconsin Ave., Ste. 1000, Milwaukee, WI 53202. Phone: (414)272-0943 Fax: (414)272-1170 E-mail: info@cfma.org • URL: http://www.cimanet. com • Manufacturers of off-highway earthmoving and construction machinery and allied equipment and components. Compiles statistics.

CONSTRUCTION ESTIMATING

See: ESTIMATING

CONSTRUCTION INDUSTRIES, ELECTRICAL

See: ELECTRICAL CONSTRUCTION INDUSTRY

CONSTRUCTION INDUSTRY

See: BUILDING INDUSTRY

CONSULAR SERVICE

See: DIPLOMATIC AND CONSULAR SERVICE

CONSULTANTS

See also: ENGINEERING CONSULTANTS; MANAGEMENT CONSULTANTS

GENERAL WORKS

Is It Too Late to Run Away and Join the Circus? Finding the Life You Really Want. Marti Smye. John Wiley. • 1998. $14.95. Provides philosophical and inspirational advice on leaving corporate life and becoming self-employed as a consultant or whatever. Central theme is dealing with major changes in life style and career objectives.

DIRECTORIES

AMA International Member and Marketing Services Guide. American Marketing Association. • Annual. $150.00. Lists professional members of the American Marketing Association. Also contains information on providers of marketing support services and products, including software, communications, direct marketing, promotion, research, and consulting companies. Includes geographical and alphabetical indexes. Formerly *Marketing Yellow Pages and AMA International Membership Directory*.

Consultants and Consulting Organizations Directory. Gale Cengage Learning. • 2003. $840.00. 25th edition. Three volumes. Includes mid-year *Supplement*. Lists more than 27,000 firms and individuals covering 14 general fields of consulting activity.

Directory of Management Consultants. Kennedy Information, Inc. • Biennial. $295.00. Contains profiles of more than 2,100 general and specialty management consulting firms in the U. S., Canada, and Mexico.

Emerson's Directory of Leading U.S. Technology Consulting Firms. Emerson Co. • 2000. $195.00. Provides information on major consulting firms specializing in technology.

Nelson Information's Directory of Pension Fund Consultants. Nelson Information. • Annual. $610. 00. Covers the pension plan sponsor industry. More than 325 worldwide consulting firms are described. Formerly *Nelson's Guide to Pension Fund Consultants*.

HANDBOOKS AND MANUALS

The Consultant's Proposal, Fee, and Contract Problem-Solver. Ronald Tepper. John Wiley and Sons, Inc. • 1993. $29.95. Provides advice for consultants on fees, contracts, proposals, and client communications. Includes case histories in 10 specific fields, such as finance, marketing, engineering, and management.

Consulting Business. Entrepreneur Media, Inc. • Looseleaf. $59.50. A practical guide to becoming a business consultant. Covers profit potential, start-up costs, market size evaluation, pricing, accounting, advertising, promotion, etc. (Start-Up Business Guide No. E1151.).

The Contract and Fee-Setting Guide for Consultants and Professionals. Howard L. Shenson. John Wiley and Sons, Inc. • 1990. $175.00.

Flawless Consulting: A Guide to Getting Your Expertise Used. Peter Block. John Wiley and Sons, Inc. • 1999. $45.00. Second edition.

How to Become a Successful Consultant in Your Own Field. Hubert Bermont. Prima Publishing. • 2000. $14.00. Third editon.

How to Make It Big as a Consultant. William A. Cohen. AMACOM • 2001. $17.95. Third edition. Step-by-step instructions for finding clients, writing proposals, pricing services, etc.

How to Succeed as an Independent Consultant. Herman Holtz. John Wiley and Sons, Inc. • 1993. $34. 95. Third edition. Covers a wide variety of marketing, financial, professional, and ethical issues for consultants. Includes bibliographic and organizational information.

Million Dollar Consulting: The Professional's Guide to Growing a Practice. Alan Weiss. McGraw-Hill. • 2002. $15.95. Third edition. Provides step-by-step advice on raising capital, finding new clients, and setting fees.

INTERNET DATABASES

FindLaw: Internet Legal Resources. FindLaw, Inc. Phone: (650)940-4300 E-mail: info@findlaw.com • URL: http://www.findlaw.com • Web site provides a wide variety of information and links relating to laws, law schools, professional development, lawyers, the U. S. Supreme Court, consultants (experts), law reviews, legal news, etc. Online searching is provided. Fees: Free.

PERIODICALS AND NEWSLETTERS

Consultants News: Independent Commentary on Management Consulting Since 1970. Kennedy Information, Inc. • Monthly. $295.00 per year. Newsletter. News and ideas for management consultants.

TRADE/PROFESSIONAL ASSOCIATIONS

American Consultants League. 245 NE 4th Ave., Ste. 102, Delray Beach, FL 33483. Phone: (866)344-7200 or (410)651-4869 Fax: (561)265-3542 E-mail: support@earlytorise.com • URL: http://www. americanconsultantsleague.com • Full-time and part-time consultants in varied fields of expertise. Provides assistance to consultants in establishing and managing the business component of their consultancies; offers marketing and legal advice. Maintains the Consultants Institute, which offers a home study program and bestows Certified Professional Consultants designation upon completion of program. Conducts research programs; compiles statistics. **Convention/Meeting:** none.

Society for Advancement of Management. Texas A&M University-Corpus Christi, College of Business, 6300 Ocean Dr., Corpus Christi, TX 78412. Phone: 888-827-6077 or (361)825-6045 or (361)825-5574 Fax: (361)825-2725 E-mail: moustafa@falcon.tamucc.edu • URL: http://www. enterprise.tamucc.edu/sam/ • Professional organization of management executives in industry, commerce, government and education. Absorbed Industrial Methods Society.

CONSULTANTS, ENGINEERING

See: ENGINEERING CONSULTANTS

CONSULTANTS, MANAGEMENT

See: MANAGEMENT CONSULTANTS

CONSUMER AFFAIRS

ABSTRACTS AND INDEXES

Business Periodicals Index. H. W. Wilson Co. • 11 times a year. Quarterly and annual cumulations. Price varies.

NTIS Alerts: Business & Economics. National Technical Information Service. • Text: Semimonthly. $210.00 per year.

Readers' Guide to Periodical Literature. H. W. Wilson Co. • Monthly. $345.00 per year. Includes annual *Cumulation.* Indexes about 250 peridicals of general interest.

CD-ROM DATABASES

Magazine Index Plus. Gale Cengage Learning. • Monthly. $4,000.00 per year (includes InfoTrac workstation). Provides full text on CD-ROM for about 100 popular, general interest magazines and indexing for 300 others. Includes special indexing of reviews and product evaluations. Time period is 1980 to date.

Newspaper Abstracts Ondisc. PROQUEST. • Monthly. $2,950.00 per year (covers 1989 to date; archival discs are available for 1985-88). Provides cover-to-cover CD-ROM indexing and abstracting of 19 major newspapers, including the *New York Times, Wall Street Journal, Washington Post, Chicago Tribune,* and *Los Angeles Times.*

WILSONDISC: Readers' Guide to Periodical Literature. H. W. Wilson Co. • Monthly. $1,095.00 per year, including unlimited online access to *Readers' Guide to Periodical Literature* through WILSONLINE. Provides CD-ROM indexing of about 270 general interest periodicals. Covers 1983 to date. (*Readers' Guide Abstracts* also available on CD-ROM at $1,995 per year.).

DIRECTORIES

Business Organizations, Agencies, and Publications Directory. Gale Cengage Learning. • 2003. $480.00. 15th edition. Over 40,000 entries describing 39 types of business information sources. Classified by type of organization, publication, or serviceIncludes state, national, and international agencies and organizations. Master index to names and keywords. Also includes e-mail addresses and web site URL's.

Consumer Sourcebook: A Directory and Guide. Gale Cengage Learning. • 2003. $305.00. 16th edition. Consumer-oriented agencies, associations, institutes, centers, etc.

ONLINE DATABASES

Information Bank Abstracts. New York Times Index Dept. • Provides indexing and abstracting of current affairs, primarily from the final late edition of *The New York Times* and the Eastern edition of *The Wall Street Journal.* Time period is 1969 to present, with daily updates. Inquire as to online cost and availability.

Newspaper Abstracts Daily. ProQuest Inc. • Provides online coverage (citations and abstracts) of 25 major newspapers. Covers business, economics, current affairs, health, fitness, sports, education, technology, government, consumer affairs, psychology, the arts, and the social sciences. Time period is 1986 to date, with daily updates. Inquire as to online cost and availability.

Readers' Guide Abstracts Online. H. W. Wilson Co. • Indexes and abstracts general interest periodicals, 1983 to date. Weekly updates. Inquire as to online cost and availability.

Wilson Business Abstracts Online. H. W. Wilson Co. • Indexes and abstracts 600 major business periodicals, plus the *Wall Street Journal* and the business section of the *New York Times.* Indexing is from 1982, abstracting from 1990, with the two newspapers included from 1993. Updated weekly. Inquire as to online cost and availability. (*Business Periodicals Index* without abstracts is also available online.).

PERIODICALS AND NEWSLETTERS

Journal of Consumer Affairs. The American Council on Consumer Interests. • Semiannual. Membership. $100.00 per year; institutions, $240.00 per year. Includes *Consumer News and Reviews, Advancing the Consumer Interest* and *Consumer Interest Annual.*

Privacy and Information Law Report. Glasser Legalworks. • 10 times a year. $375.00 per year. Newsletter. Coverage includes the legal aspects of health record privacy, employee records, anti-spam, and privacy-enhancing technology. Provides reports on relevant court cases and consumer advocacy.

RESEARCH CENTERS AND INSTITUTES

American Council on Consumer Awareness, Inc. 125 Kent St., N., St. Paul, MN 55117-4263. Phone: (651)489-2835 Fax: (651)489-5650 E-mail: bennerassociates@aol.com.

Center for Consumer Research. University of

Florida, P.O. Box 117160, Gainesville, FL 32611-7160. Phone: (352)392-0161 Fax: (352)846-0457 E-mail: joel.cohen@cba.ufl.edu • URL: http://www. cba.ufl.edu/.

Consumer Education Research Center. 439 Clark St., South Orange, NJ 07079. Phone: (973)374-0263.

Consumer Research Center. Conference Board, Inc., 845 Third Ave., New York, NY 10022. Phone: (212)339-0304 Fax: (212)836-9714 E-mail: crc@ conference-board.org • URL: http://www.crc-conquest.org • Conducts research on the consumer market, including elderly and working women segments.

TRADE/PROFESSIONAL ASSOCIATIONS

American Consumers Association. 2633 Flossmoor Rd., Flossmoor, IL 60422. Phone: (708)957-2900 Fax: (708)957-4155 E-mail: amerconassn@ ameritech.net • Provides information on consumer goods and services, including product quality, cost, safety, and effectiveness. Promotes exchange of information beneficial to the health and welfare of the American consumer. Cooperates with individual or group efforts with the same goals. Offers a group insurance program and referrals on questions related to health and welfare. Issues public service announcements; conducts radio and direct mail advertising; endorses products. Compiles statistics; plans to establish a library.

American Council on Consumer Interests. 415 S Duff Ave., Ste. C, Ames, IA 50010-6600. Phone: (515)956-4666 Fax: (515)233-3101 E-mail: info@ consumerinterests.org • URL: http://www. consumerinterests.org • Formerly Council on Consumer Information.

Consumer Federation of America. 1424 16th St., N. W., Suite 604, Washington, DC 20036. Phone: (202)387-6121 Fax: (202)265-7989 E-mail: cfa@ essential.org • URL: http://www.consumerfed.org • Members are national, regional, state, and local consumer groups. Absorbed Electric Consumers Information Committee.

Federal Consumer Information Center. General Services Administration, 1800 F St., NW, Rm. G-142, Pueblo, CO 81009. Phone: 888-8-PUEBLO Fax: (202)501-4281 E-mail: catalog.pueblo@gsa. gov • URL: http://www.pueblo.gsa.gov • A department of the General Services Administration. Established by Presidential Order in 1970 to assist federal agencies to develop, promote, and distribute information of interest to consumers and to increase public awareness of this information.

National Consumers League. 1701 K St. NW, Ste. 1200, Washington, DC 20006. Phone: (202)835-3323 Fax: (202)835-0747 E-mail: info@nclnet.org • URL: http://www.nclnet.org • Identifies, protects, represents, and advances the economic and social interests of consumers and workers. Addresses issues including healthcare, food and drug safety, and consumer fraud. Promotes fairness and safety at the marketplace and in the workplace. Coordinates the Alliance Against Fraud in Telemarketing and the Child +Labor Coalition. Administers the National Fraud Information Center and Internet Fraud Watch.

People's Medical Society. PO Box 868, Allentown, PA 18105-0868. Phone: 800-624-8773 or (610)770-1670 Fax: (610)770-0607 E-mail: cbi@peoplesmed. org • URL: http://www.peoplesmed.org • Promotes citizen involvement in the cost, quality, and management of the American health care system. Seeks to: train and encourage individuals to study local health care systems, practitioners, and institutions and promote preventive health care and medical cost control by these groups; address major policy issues and control health costs; encourage more preventive practice and research; promote self-care and alternative health care procedures; launch an information campaign to assist individuals in maintaining personal health and to prepare them for appointments with medical professionals. **Convention/ Meeting:** none.

Public Citizen. 1600 20th St. NW, Washington, DC 20009. Phone: (202)588-1000 Fax: (202)588-7798 E-mail: member@citizen.org • URL: http://www. citizen.org • Formed by Ralph Nader to support the work of citizen advocates. Areas of focus include: consumer rights in the marketplace, safe products, a healthful environment and workplace, clean and safe energy sources, corporate and government accountability, and citizen empowerment. Methods for change include lobbying, litigation, monitoring government agencies, research, and public education including special reports, periodicals, expert testimony, and news media coverage. Acquires funding primarily through direct mail and also through payment for publications and court awards.

Society of Consumer Affairs Professionals in Business. 675 Washington St., Ste. 200, Alexandria, VA 22314. Phone: (703)519-3700 Fax: (703)549-4886 E-mail: socap@socap.org • URL: http://www. socap.org • Members are managers of consumer affairs departments of business firms.

OTHER SOURCES

Consumer Protection and the Law. Mary D. Pridgen. West Group. • Annual. $269.00. Looseleaf service. Covers advertising, sales practices, unfair trade practices, consumer fraud, and product warranties.

CONSUMER CREDIT

See also: CREDIT; INSTALLMENT PLAN PURCHASING

GENERAL WORKS

The Fragile Middle Class: Americans in Debt. Teresa A. Sullivan and others. Yale University Press. • 2000. $40.00. Provides an analysis of a 1991 survey of personal bankruptcies in five states of the U. S. Serves as a sequel to the authors' *As We Forgive Our Debtors* (1989), an analysis of 1981 bankruptcies.

CD-ROM DATABASES

OECD Statistical Compendium. Organization for Economic Cooperation and Development. • Semiannual. $1,905.00 per year for 1 to 10 users. CD-ROM contains more than 730,000 monthly, quarterly, and annual time series for OECD countries, 1960 to date. Includes fully searchable data on agriculture, food, economic indicators, national accounts, employment, energy, finance, industry, technology, and foreign trade. Results can be displayed in various forms.

FINANCIAL RATIOS

Annual Statement Studies. The Risk Management Association. • Annual. Median and quartile financial ratios are given for over 400 kinds of manufacturing, wholesale, retail, construction, and consumer finance establishments. Data is sorted by both asset size and sales volume. Includes a clearly written "Definition of Ratios" and an alphabetical industry index.

Annual Statement Studies: Industry Default Probabilities and Cash Flow Measures. The Risk Management Association. • Annual. $145.00. Serves as a companion volume to the original *Annual Statement Studies.* Gives probability of default estimates on a percentage scale for more than 450 industries. Includes changes in position year-by-year for eight financial statement line items and provides percentage measures of cash flow.

HANDBOOKS AND MANUALS

Cost of Personal Borrowing in the United States. Financial Publishing Co. • Annual. $175.00.

Credit Consulting. Entrepreneur Media, Inc. • Looseleaf. $59.50. A practical guide to starting a

consumer credit and debt counseling and consulting service. Covers profit potential, start-up costs, market size evaluation, owner's time required, pricing, accounting, advertising, promotion, etc. (Start-Up Business Guide No. E1321.).

INTERNET DATABASES

BanxQuote Banking, Mortgage, and Finance Center. BanxQuote, Inc. Phone: (914)722-1600 Fax: (914)722-6630 E-mail: info@banx.com • URL: http://www.banx.com • Web site quotes interest rates paid by banks around the country on various savings products, as well as rates paid by consumers for automobile loans, mortgages, credit cards, home equity loans, and personal loans. Also provided: stock quotes, indexes, stock options, futures trading data, economic indicators, and links to many other financial sites. Daily updates. Fees: Free.

Business 2.0 Web Guide to the Best Business Links. Business 2.0 Media Inc. Phone: (415)293-4800 E-mail: support@business2.com • URL: http:// www.business2.com/webguide • Web site presents an extensive, searchable directory of links to "the best, most informative, and authoritative web pages." Twenty main categories cover business, finance, career, company information, people, and technology topics, with thousands of subtopics, all linking to Web sites recommended by experienced business researchers. Fees: Free.

Federal Reserve Board Publications and Education Resources. Board of Governors of the Federal Reserve System. Phone: (202)452-3000 Fax: (202)452-3819 • URL: http://www.federalreserve. gov/publications.htm • Web site provides convenient access to statistics, surveys, and research from the Federal Reserve Board. *Federal Reserve Bulletin* articles are available as abstracts or full text (PDF) currently or from six-year archives. The link "Statistics: Releases and Historical Data" offers daily, weekly, monthly, quarterly, and annual data in great detail for interest rates, foreign exchange, consumer credit, money stock measures, industrial production indexes, bank reserves, and other items. Historical tabulations are available for various time periods. Fees: Free.

Fedstats. Federal Interagency Council on Statistical Policy. Phone: (202)395-7254 • URL: http://www. fedstats.gov • Web site features an efficient search facility for full-text statistics produced by more than 100 federal agencies, including the Census Bureau, the Bureau of Economic Analysis, and the Bureau of Labor Statistics. Boolean searches can be made within one agency or for all agencies combined. Links are offered to international statistical bureaus, including the UN, IMF, OECD, UNESCO, Eurostat, and 20 individual countries. Fees: Free.

FreeLunch.com. Economy.com, Inc. Phone: (610)696-8700 Fax: (610)696-1678 • URL: http:// www.freelunch.com • Web site provides free access to more than 1.5 million economic and financial data series, covering industry, demographics, labor markets, prices, retail sales, government spending, trade, interest rates, housing starts, the stock market, and many other topics. Data is available for various time periods in either chart or table form. Searching is offered. Fees: Free, but registration required. Economy.com, Inc. also offers fee-based economic analysis at *The Dismal Scientist* site (http://www. dismal.com).

ONLINE DATABASES

Banking Information Source. PROQUEST. • Provides indexing and abstracting of periodical and other literature from 1982 to date, with weekly updates. Covers the financial services industry: banks, savings institutions, investment houses, credit unions, insurance companies, and real estate organizations. Emphasis is on marketing and management. Inquire as to online cost and

availability. (Formerly *FINIS: Financial Industry Information Service.*).

PERIODICALS AND NEWSLETTERS

American Banker: The Financial Services Daily. Thomson Media. • Daily. $895.00 per year. Provides news of banking, investment products, mortgages, credit unions, finance, bank technology, and legal developments.

Business Credit. National Association of Credit Management. • 10 tims a year. $48.00 per year. Formerly *Credit and Financial Management.*

Consumer Credit and Truth-in-Lending Compliance Report. RIA. • Monthly. $183.75 per year. Newsletter. Focuses on the latest regulatory rulings and findings involving consumer lending and credit activity. Incorporates (Consumer Lending Report).

Consumer Finance Law Bulletin. American Financial Services Association. • Description: Provides a digest of recent cases in consumer finance law, covering Truth In Lending Act, Equal Credit Opportunity Act, Fair Credit Reporting Act, Fair Debt Collection Practices Act, consumer bankruptcy, state usury and consumer protection laws, and practice notes on recent regulatory activity. **Remarks:** Subscription includes membership in AFSA's Law Forum.

Consumer Finance Newsletter. Financial Publishing Co. • Description: Provides information on effective and pending credit insurance and installment loan regulations on the state and federal levels. Supplies news of potential state changes in regulations.

Credit Risk Management. Phillips International, Inc. • Biweekly. $695.00 per year. Newsletter on consumer credit, including delinquency aspects.

Loan Market Week: The Newsweekly of the Loan Syndication, Trading and Investment Markets. Institutional Investor, Inc., Journals Group. • Weekly. $2,370.00 per year. Newsletter. Includes print and online editions. Covers retail banking, commercial lending, foreign loans, bank technology, government regulations, and other topics related to banking. Formerly *Bank Letter.*

U. S. Banker. Thomson Media. • Monthly. $65.00 per year. Edited for bank executives and managers. Covers a wide variety of banking and financial topics.

STATISTICS SOURCES

Business Statistics of the United States. Linz Audain and Cornelia J. Strawser. Bernan Associates. • Annual. $147.00. Based on *Business Statistics,* formerly issue by the Bureau of Economic Analysis, U. S. Department of Commerce. Provides basic data for a wide variety of U. S. industries, services, and economic indicators. Most statistics are shown annually for 30 years and monthly for the most recent four years.

Consumer Credit. U. S. Federal Reserve System. • Monthly. $5.00 per year. (Federal Reserve Statistical Release, G.19.).

Statistical Information on the Financial Services Industry. American Bankers Association. • Annual. Members, $150.00; non-members, $275.00. Presents a wide variety of data relating to banking and financial services, including consumer economics, personal finance, credit, government loans, capital markets, and international banking.

Survey of Current Business. Available from U. S. Government Printing Office. • Monthly. $63.00 per year. Issued by Bureau of Economic Analysis, U. S. Department of Commerce. Presents a wide variety of business and economic data.

TRADE/PROFESSIONAL ASSOCIATIONS

American Financial Services Association. 919 18th St. NW, Ste. 300, Washington, DC 20006-5517. Phone: (202)296-5544 Fax: (202)223-0321 E-mail: cstinebert@afsamail.org • URL: http://www.

afsaonline.org • Represents companies whose business is primarily direct credit lending to consumers and/or the purchase of sales finance paper on consumer goods. Has members that have insurance and retail subsidiaries; some are themselves subsidiaries of highly diversified parent corporations. Encourages the business of financing individuals and families for necessary and useful purposes at reasonable charges, including interest; promotes consumer understanding of basic money management principles as well as constructive uses of consumer credit. Includes educational services such as films, textbooks, and study units for the classroom and budgeting guides for individuals and families. Compiles statistical reports; offers seminars.

Consumer Credit Industry Association. 2911 S Shore Blvd., Ste. 130, League City, TX 77573. Phone: (281)535-7446 Fax: (281)535-7435 E-mail: jim.pangburn@anico.com • URL: http://www.cciaonline.com • Insurance companies underwriting consumer credit insurance in areas of life insurance, accident and health insurance, and property insurance.

National Association of Consumer Credit Administrators. PO Box 20871, Columbus, OH 43220-0871. Phone: (614)326-1165 Fax: (614)326-1162 • URL: http://www.naccaonline.org • State government officials who administer consumer finance laws in the United States, Guam, Puerto Rico and Canada.

National Foundation for Credit Counseling. 801 Roeder Rd., Ste. 900, Silver Spring, MD 20910. Phone: 800-388-2227 or (301)589-5600 Fax: (301)495-5623 • URL: http://www.nfcc.org • Supersedes Retail Credit Institute of America.

OTHER SOURCES

Consumer and Commercial Credit: Installment Sales. Prentice Hall PTR. • Three looseleaf volumes. Periodic supplementation. Price on application. Covers secured transactions under the Uniform Commercial Code and the Uniform Consumer Credit Code. Includes retail installment sales, home improvement loans, higher education loans, and other kinds of installment loans.

Consumer Credit and the Law. Mary D. Pridgen. West Group. • Annual. $280.00. Looseleaf service.

Consumer Credit Guide. CCH, Inc. • Biweekly. $1,255.00 per year. Looseleaf service.

Consumer Credit: Law Transactions and Forms. LexisNexis Matthew Bender. • $849.00. Six looseleaf volumes. Periodic supplementation. Detailed treatment of the law with practical step-by-step guidance for every stage of a consumer credit transaction.

U. S. Credit Bureaus and Collection Agencies: An Industry Analysis. Available from MarketResearch.com. • 2003. $1,435.00. Market research report published by Marketdata Enterprises. Includes forecasts of industry growth to the year 2006 and provides profiles of Dun & Bradstreet, Equifax, Experion, and TransUnion.

CONSUMER ECONOMICS

See also: CONSUMER EDUCATION; ECONOMIC RESEARCH; MARKET RESEARCH

GENERAL WORKS

Consumer Behavior. Leon Schiffman and Leslie Kanut. Harcourt College Publishers. • 2003. $120.00. Eighth edition.

Money: Who Has How Much and Why. Andrew Hacker. Simon & Schuster Trade. • 1997. $24.50. A discourse on the distribution of wealth in America,

with emphasis on the gap between rich and poor.

CD-ROM DATABASES

EconLit. Available from SilverPlatter Information, Inc. • Monthly. Single-user, $1,600.00 per year. Provides CD-ROM citations, with abstracts, to articles from more than 500 economics journals. Time period is 1969 to date. Produced by the American Economic Association.

OECD Statistical Compendium. Organization for Economic Cooperation and Development. • Semiannual. $1,905.00 per year for 1 to 10 users. CD-ROM contains more than 730,000 monthly, quarterly, and annual time series for OECD countries, 1960 to date. Includes fully searchable data on agriculture, food, economic indicators, national accounts, employment, energy, finance, industry, technology, and foreign trade. Results can be displayed in various forms.

Sourcebook America. Gale Cengage Learning. • Annual. $995.00. Produced by CACI Marketing Systems. A combination on CD-ROM of *The Sourcebook of ZIP Code Demographics* and *The Sourcebook of County Demographics*. Provides detailed population and socio-economic data (about 75 items) for each of 3,141 U. S. counties and approximately 30,000 ZIP codes, plus states, metropolitan areas, and media market areas. Includes forecasts to the year 2004.

World Marketing Forecasts on CD-ROM. Gale Cengage Learning. • Annual. $2,500.00. Produced by Euromonitor. Provides detailed forecast data for the years to 2012 on CD-ROM for 54 countries in all parts of the world. Covers a wide range of social, demographic, economic, and market factors. Includes specific forecasts for many kinds of consumer products.

HANDBOOKS AND MANUALS

Hispanic Market Handbook. Gale Cengage Learning. • 1995. $95.00. Provides advice on marketing consumer items to Hispanic Americans. Includes case studies and demographic profiles. (Professional Library).

INTERNET DATABASES

Bureau of Economic Analysis (BEA). U. S. Department of Commerce, Bureau of Economic Analysis. Phone: (202)606-9900 Fax: (202)606-5310 E-mail: webmaster@bea.doc.gov • URL: http://www.bea.doc.gov • Web site includes "News Release Information" covering national, regional, and international economic estimates from the BEA. Highlights of releases appear online the same day, complete text and tables appear the next day. "Recent News Releases" section provides titles for past nine months, with links. "BEA Data and Methodology" includes "Frequently Requested NIPA Data" (national income and product accounts, such as gross domestic product and personal income). Other statistics are available. Fees: Free.

Business 2.0 Web Guide to the Best Business Links. Business 2.0 Media Inc. Phone: (415)293-4800 E-mail: support@business2.com • URL: http://www.business2.com/webguide • Web site presents an extensive, searchable directory of links to "the best, most informative, and authoritative web pages." Twenty main categories cover business, finance, career, company information, people, and technology topics, with thousands of subtopics, all linking to Web sites recommended by experienced business researchers. Fees: Free.

Fedstats. Federal Interagency Council on Statistical Policy. Phone: (202)395-7254 • URL: http://www.fedstats.gov • Web site features an efficient search facility for full-text statistics produced by more than 100 federal agencies, including the Census Bureau, the Bureau of Economic Analysis, and the Bureau of Labor Statistics. Boolean searches can be made within one agency or for all agencies combined. Links are offered to international statistical bureaus,

including the UN, IMF, OECD, UNESCO, Eurostat, and 20 individual countries. Fees: Free.

FreeLunch.com. Economy.com, Inc. Phone: (610)696-8700 Fax: (610)696-1678 • URL: http://www.freelunch.com • Web site provides free access to more than 1.5 million economic and financial data series, covering industry, demographics, labor markets, prices, retail sales, government spending, trade, interest rates, housing starts, the stock market, and many other topics. Data is available for various time periods in either chart or table form. Searching is offered. Fees: Free, but registration required. Economy.com, Inc. also offers fee-based economic analysis at *The Dismal Scientist* site (http://www.dismal.com).

ONLINE DATABASES

EconLit. American Economic Association. • Covers the worldwide literature of economics as contained in selected monographs and about 550 journals. Subjects include microeconomics, macroeconomics, economic history, inflation, money, credit, finance, accounting theory, trade, natural resource economics, and regional economics. Time period is 1969 to present, with monthly updates. Inquire as to online cost and availability.

PERIODICALS AND NEWSLETTERS

American Demographics: Consumer Trends for Business Leaders. Media Central. • Monthly. $58.00 per year.

Family Economics and Nutrition Review. Available from U. S. Government Printing Office. • Semiannual. $13.00 per year. Issued by the Consumer and Food Economics Institute, U. S. Department of Agriculture. Provides articles on consumer expenditures and budgeting for food, clothing, housing, energy, education, etc.

Journal of Consumer Research; An Interdisciplinary Quarterly. The University of Chicago Press, Journals Div. • Quarterly. Members, $62.00 per year; non-members, $145.00 per year; institutions, $152.00 per year; students, $25.00. Covers various aspects of consumer behavior.

Regional Economics and Markets: A Quarterly Analysis from the Conference Board. The Conference Board. • Quarterly. Members, $145.00 per year; non-members, $295.00 per year. Summarizes economic trends and prospects for nine geographic regions of the U. S. Provides data on key predictive indexes, including employment, housing permits, retail sales, consumer confidence, and help-wanted advertising. Charts and graphs are included.

PRICE SOURCES

The Value of a Dollar: Millennium Edition, 1860-1999. Grey House Publishing. • 1999. $135.00. Second edition. Shows the actual prices of thousands of items available to consumers from the Civil War era to recent years. Includes selected data on consumer expenditures, investments, income, and jobs. (Universal Reference Publications.).

STATISTICS SOURCES

Business Statistics of the United States. Linz Audain and Cornelia J. Strawser. Bernan Associates. • Annual. $147.00. Based on *Business Statistics*, formerly issue by the Bureau of Economic Analysis, U. S. Department of Commerce. Provides basic data for a wide variety of U. S. industries, services, and economic indicators. Most statistics are shown annually for 30 years and monthly for the most recent four years.

Consumer Expenditure Survey. Available from U. S. Government Printing Office. • Biennial. Issued by the Bureau of Labor Statistics, U. S. Department of Labor (http://www.bls.gov). Contains data on various kinds of consumer spending, according to household income, education, etc. (Bureau of Labor Statistics Bulletin.).

Consumer International. Available from Gale-Cengage Learning. • Annual. $1,290.00. Published by Euromonitor. Contains extensive consumer market, economic, and demographic data for 25 major, non-European countries, including the U. S. and Canada. Includes consumer market size (volume and value) for 150 product types in 14 categories (food, clothing, automobiles, cosmetics, appliances, etc.).

Consumer Power: How Americans Spend. Margaret Ambry. McGraw-Hill. • 1992. $27.50. Contains detailed statistics on consumer income and spending. Nine major categories of products and services are covered, with spending data and dollar size of market for each item.

Consumer USA. Available from Gale Cengage Learning. • Annual. $1,090.00. Fifth edition. Published by Euromonitor. Provides demographic and consumer market data for the United States. Forecasts to the year 2005.

Current Population Reports: Household Economic Studies, Series P-70. Available from U. S. Government Printing Office. • Irregular. $21.00 per year. Issued by the U.S. Bureau of the Census (http://www.census.gov). Each issue covers a special topic relating to household socioeconomic characteristics.

Current Population Reports: Population Characteristics, Special Studies, and Consumer Income, Series P-20, P-23, and P-60. Available from U. S. Government Printing Office. • Irregular. $80.00 per year. Issued by the U.S. Bureau of the Census (http://www.census.gov). Each issue covers a special topic relating to population or income. Series P-20, *Population Characteristics,* provides statistical studies on such items as mobility, fertility, education, and marital status. Series P-23, *Special Studies,* consists of occasional reports on methodology. Series P-60, *Consumer Income,* publishes reports on income in relation to age, sex, education, occupation, family size, etc.

Demographics USA: County Edition. Trade Dimensions. • Annual. $435.00. Contains 200 statistical series for each of 3,000 counties. Includes population, household income, employment, retail sales, and consumer expenditures. Also provides Effective Buying Income, Buying Power Index, and data summaries by Metro Market, Media Market, and State. (CD-ROM version is available.).

Demographics USA: ZIP Edition. Trade Dimensions. • Annual. $435.00. Contains 50 statistical series for each of 40,000 ZIP codes. Includes population, household income, employment, retail sales, and consumer expenditures. Also provides Effective Buying Income, Business Characteristics, and data summaries by state, region, and the first three digits of ZIP codes. (CD-ROM version is available.).

European Marketing Forecasts. Available from Gale Cengage Learning. • Annual. $1,250.00. Published by Euromonitor. Contains demographic, economic, and market forecasts for the countries of Europe to the year 2010. Forecasts include market-size data for 15 consumer product sectors (food, clothing, automobiles, consumer electronics, etc.).

Gale Book of Averages. Gale Cengage Learning. • 1994. $75.00. Contains 1,100-1,200 statistical averages on a variety of topics, with references to published sources. Subjects include business, labor, consumption, crime, and other areas of contemporary society.

Handbook of U. S. Labor Statistics: Employment, Earnings, Prices, Productivity, and Other Labor Data. Eva E. Jacobs, editor. Bernan Associates. • 1999. $74.00. Based on *Handbook of Labor Statistics,* formerly issued by the Bureau of Labor Statistics, U. S. Department of Labor. Includes the Bureau's projections of employment in the U. S. by industry and occupation. Provides a wide variety of data on the work force, prices, fringe benefits, and consumer expenditures.

Household Spending: Who Spends How Much On What. New Strategist Publications, Inc. • 1999. $94.95. Fifth edition. Gives facts about the buying habits of U. S. consumers according to income, age, household type, and household size. Includes spending data for about 1,000 products and services.

International Marketing Forecasts. Available from Gale Cengage Learning. • Annual. $1,250.00. Published by Euromonitor. Contains demographic, economic, and market forecasts to the year 2013 for major, non-European countries, including the U. S. and Canada. Forecasts include market-size data for 15 consumer product sectors, such as food, clothing, and automobiles.

Key Indicators of the Labour Market. Available from Routledge. • Biennial. $125.00. Published by the International Labour Office (http://www.ilo.org). Provides data on 20 key indicators in 220 countries. Includes labor force statistics, employment, unemployment, part-time workers, wages, productivity, poverty indicators, and related topics.

Money Income in the United States. Available from U. S. Government Printing Office. • Annual. $5.50. Issued by the U. S. Bureau of the Census. Presents data on consumer income in current and constant dollars, both totals and averages (means, medians, distributions). Includes figures for a wide variety of demographic and occupational characteristics. (Current Population Reports.).

Sourcebook of Zip Code Demographics. ESRI Business Information Solutions. • 2002. $495.00. 16th edition. Provides data on 75 demographic and socioeconomic characteristics for each ZIP code in the U. S.

Statistical Handbook on Consumption and Wealth in the United States. Greenwood Publishing Group, Inc. • 1999. $69.95. Provides more than 400 graphs, tables, and charts dealing with basic income levels, income inequalities, spending patterns, taxation, subsidies, etc. (Statistical Handbook Series).

Statistical Handbook on the American Family. Bruce A. Chadwick and Tim B. Heaton. Greenwood Publishing Group, Inc. • 1998. $69.95. Second edition. Includes data on education, health, politics, employment, expenditures, social characteristics, the elderly, and women in the labor force. Historical statistics on marriage, birth, and divorce are shown from 1900 on. A list of sources and a subject index are provided. (Statistical Handbooks Series).

Statistical Information on the Financial Services Industry. American Bankers Association. • Annual. Members, $150.00; non-members, $275.00. Presents a wide variety of data relating to banking and financial services, including consumer economics, personal finance, credit, government loans, capital markets, and international banking.

Working Americans, 1880-1999, Volume One: The Working Class. Scott Derks, editor. Grey House Publishing. • 2000. $375.00. Provides detailed information on the lifestyles and economic life of working class families in the 12 decades from 1880 to 1999. Includes such items as selected consumer prices, income, family finances, budgets, life at home, jobs, and working conditions. (Universal Reference Publications.).

Working Americans, 1880-1999, Volume Two: The Middle Class. Scott Derks, editor. Grey House Publishing. • 2000. $135.00. Three volumes. Furnishes details of the social and economic lives of middle class Americans during the years 1880 to 1999. Describes such items as selected consumer prices, income, family finances, budgets, life at home, jobs, and working conditions. (Universal Reference Publications.).

World Consumer Expenditure Patterns. Euromonitor International. • 2003. $1,190.00. Contains detailed consumer expenditure data for 71 countries. Covers 70 specific categories within the areas of food, beverages, tobacco, clothing, housing, appliances, health, transportation, leisure, etc. Provides 10 years of data and includes consumer price indexes.

World Consumer Income and Expenditure Patterns. Available from Gale Cengage Learning. • Annual. $1,090.00. Two volumes. Published by Euromonitor. Provides data for countries worldwide on consumer income, earning power, spending patterns, and savings. Expenditures are detailed for product or service categories.

World Consumer Income Patterns. Euromonitor International. • 2003. $1,190.00. Provides detailed data on household income in 71 countries (10-year statistics). Covers income by age, sex, and level of education, with further data on savings, earnings, and average taxes.

World Consumer Lifestyles Databook: Key Trends. Euromonitor International. • 2003. $1,190.00. Second edition. Covers 71 countries. Presents statistical data relating to such consumer lifestyle characteristics as family size, household income, family expenditures, home ownership, shopping habits, eating habits, drinking habits, savings, transportation, travel, health characteristics, and education.

CONSUMER EDUCATION

See also: BETTER BUSINESS BUREAUS; CONSUMER ECONOMICS

CD-ROM DATABASES

Consumers Reference Disc. National Information Services Corp. • Quarterly. Provides the CD-ROM version of *Consumer Health and Nutrition Index* from Oryx Press and *Consumers Index to Product Evaluations and Information Sources* from Pierian Press. Contains citations to consumer health articles and consumer product evaluations, tests, warnings, and recalls.

DIRECTORIES

Consumer Sourcebook: A Directory and Guide. Gale Cengage Learning. • 2003. $305.00. 16th edition. Consumer-oriented agencies, associations, institutes, centers, etc.

HANDBOOKS AND MANUALS

The Consumer Health Information Source Book. Alan Rees, editor. Greenwood Publishing Group, Inc. • 2003. $65.00. Seventh edition. Bibliography of current literature and guide to organizations.

PERIODICALS AND NEWSLETTERS

Bottom Line/Personal. Boardroom Inc. • Description: Publishes "expert advice on how to live longer, better, richer, and wiser." Covers topical issues with a personal slant aimed at helping those involved with careers handle their personal lives more successfully. Features articles on tax issues, money information, traveling, family, friends, and general health and happiness. Contains informational items throughout on various aspects of business/personal life.

Consumer Reports. Consumers Union of the United States, Inc. • Monthly. $26.00 per year. Includes *Annual Buying Guide.*

Consumer's Research Magazine: Analyzing Consumer Issues. Consumers' Research Inc. • Monthly. $24.00 per year.

eShopper: Where Style Meets the Net. Element K Journals. • Bimonthly. $9.97 per year. A consumer magazine providing advice and information for "shopping on the Web.".

FDA Consumer. Available from U. S. Government Printing Office. • Bimonthly. $14.00 per year. Issued by the U. S. Food and Drug Administration. Provides consumer information about FDA regulations and product safety.

Journal of Consumer Affairs. The American Council on Consumer Interests. • Semiannual. Membership, $100.00 per year; institutions, $240.00 per year. Includes *Consumer News and Reviews, Advancing the Consumer Interest* and *Consumer Interest Annual.*

RESEARCH CENTERS AND INSTITUTES

Consumer Education Research Center. 439 Clark St., South Orange, NJ 07079. Phone: (973)374-0263.

Consumers' Research. 800 Maryland Ave., N.E., Washington, DC 20002. Phone: (202)546-1713 Fax: (202)546-1638 E-mail: crmag@aol.com.

TRADE/PROFESSIONAL ASSOCIATIONS

American Council on Consumer Interests. 415 S Duff Ave., Ste. C, Ames, IA 50010-6600. Phone: (515)956-4666 Fax: (515)233-3101 E-mail: info@consumerinterests.org • URL: http://www.consumerinterests.org • Formerly Council on Consumer Information.

Consumer Federation of America. 1424 16th St., N. W., Suite 604, Washington, DC 20036. Phone: (202)387-6121 Fax: (202)265-7989 E-mail: cfa@essential.org • URL: http://www.consumerfed.org • Members are national, regional, state, and local consumer groups. Absorbed Electric Consumers Information Committee.

Consumers Education and Protective Association International. 6048 Ogontz Ave., Philadelphia, PA 19141-1347. Phone: (215)424-1441 Fax: (215)424-8045.

National Consumers League. 1701 K St. NW, Ste. 1200, Washington, DC 20006. Phone: (202)835-3323 Fax: (202)835-0747 E-mail: info@nclnet.org • URL: http://www.nclnet.org • Identifies, protects, represents, and advances the economic and social interests of consumers and workers. Addresses issues including healthcare, food and drug safety, and consumer fraud. Promotes fairness and safety at the marketplace and in the workplace. Coordinates the Alliance Against Fraud in Telemarketing and the Child +Labor Coalition. Administers the National Fraud Information Center and Internet Fraud Watch.

CONSUMER ELECTRONICS

See also: ELECTRIC APPLIANCE INDUSTRY

GENERAL WORKS

The Consumer Electronics Industry and the Future of American Manufacturing: How the U. S. Lost the Lead and Why We Must Get Back in the Game. Susan W. Sanderson. Economic Policy Institute. • 1990. $12.00.

ABSTRACTS AND INDEXES

Readers' Guide to Periodical Literature. H. W. Wilson Co. • Monthly. $345.00 per year. Includes annual *Cumulation.* Indexes about 250 periodicals of general interest.

CD-ROM DATABASES

World Marketing Forecasts on CD-ROM. Gale Cengage Learning. • Annual. $2,500.00. Produced by Euromonitor. Provides detailed forecast data for the years to 2012 on CD-ROM for 54 countries in all parts of the world. Covers a wide range of social, demographic, economic, and market factors. Includes specific forecasts for many kinds of consumer products.

DIRECTORIES

Directory of Computer and Consumer Electronics Retailers. Chain Store Guide. • Annual. $335.00. Online edition, $775.00. Lists 4,500 United States and Canada companies operating almost 59,000 stores with at least $1,000,000 in sales.

FINANCIAL RATIOS

Industry Norms and Key Business Ratios. Desk Top Edition. Dun and Bradstreet Corp. • Annual. Five volumes. $475.00 per volume. $1,890.00 per set. Covers over 800 kinds of businesses, arranged by Standard Industrial Classification number. More detailed editions covering longer periods of time are also available.

INTERNET DATABASES

Advance Monthly Sales for Retail Trade and Food Services. U. S. Census Bureau. Phone: 800-541-8345 or (301)763-4636 Fax: (301)457-3842 E-mail: rcb@census.gov • URL: http://www.census.gov/svsd/www/fullpub.html • Web pages provide monthly sales figures for a wide range of retail businesses. Advance, preliminary, and final statistics are provided for the latest month available in each case, with a previous-year comparison. Updates are monthly.

Manufacturing Profiles. U. S. Bureau of the Census. Phone: (301)763-4636 E-mail: webmaster@census. gov • URL: http://www.census.gov/prod/www/abs/mfg-prof.html • The Census Bureau makes available free on PDF (Portable Document Format) an annual consolidation of the entire Current Industrial Report series, presenting "all the data compiled." Contains statistics on production, shipments, inventories, consumption, exports, imports, and orders for a wide variety of manufactured products.

ONLINE DATABASES

Readers' Guide Abstracts Online. H. W. Wilson Co. • Indexes and abstracts general interest periodicals, 1983 to date. Weekly updates. Inquire as to online cost and availability.

PERIODICALS AND NEWSLETTERS

Audio Week: The Authoritative News Service of the Audio Consumer Electronics Industry. Warren Publishing, Inc. • Weekly. $663.00. Newsletter. Provdies audio industry news, company news, and new product information.

Dealerscope: Product and Strategy for Consumer Technology Retailing. North American Publishing Co. • Monthly. Free to qualified personnel; others, $79.00 per year. Formerly *Dealerscope Consumer Electronics Marketplace.*

Handheld Computing: The Number One Guide to Handheld Devices. Mobile Media Group. • Nine times a year. $18.95 per year. Covers handheld devices for consumers, including PDAs, cell phones, digital cameras, MP3 players, tablet PCs, accessories, and software. Includes product reviews.

Laptop: Mobile Solutions for Business and Life. Bedford Communications. • Monthly. $18.00 per year. Consumer magazine containing articles and product reviews for notebook/laptop computers, handheld computers, tablet devices, cell phones, digital cameras, and other consumer electronic products.

Mobile PC. Future Network USA. • Monthly. $20.00 per year. Provides information and detailed product reviews for consumers. Covers notebook/laptop computers, personal digital assistants (PDAs), wireless network equipment, cell phones, digital cameras, and other electronic products.

Mobility: Handheld and Wireless Solutions for Today's Business. Mobile Media Group. • Quarterly. $14.95 per year. Edited for business users of wireless handheld devices and notebook computers.

T W I C E: This Week in Consumer Electronics. Reed Business Information. • 29 times a year. $129.90 per year. Contains marketing and manufacturing news relating to a wide variety of consumer electronic products, including video, audio, telephone, and home office equipment.

Television Digest with Consumer Electronics. Warren Publishing, Inc. • Weekly. $944.00 per year. Newsletter featuring new consumer entertainment products utilizing electronics. Also covers the television broadcasting and cable TV industries, with corporate and industry news.

PRICE SOURCES

Audio. Orion Research Corp. • Annual. $179.00. Quotes retail and wholesale prices of used audio equipment. Original list prices and years of manufacture are also shown.

Video and Television. Orion Research Corp. • Annual. $144.00. Quotes retail and wholesale prices of used video and TV equipment. Original list prices and years of manufacture are also shown.

STATISTICS SOURCES

Annual Benchmark Report for Retail Trade and Food Services...A Detailed Summary of Retail Sales, Purchases, Accounts Receivable, Inventories, and Food Service Sales. Available from U. S. Government Printing Office. • Annual. $13.00. Issued by the U.S. Census Bureau. Provides detailed annual and monthly retail statistics for the most recent 10 years. Includes data for various kinds of retail outlets, including automobiles, furniture, appliances, building supplies, grocery stores, drug stores, gasoline stations, clothing, sporting goods, department stores, and restaurants.

Annual Survey of Manufactures. Available from U. S. Government Printing Office. • Annual. Prices vary. Issued by the U. S. Census Bureau as an interim update to the *Census of Manufactures.* Includes data on number of manufacturing establishments in various industries, employment, labor costs, value of shipments, capital expenditures, inventories, energy costs, and assets. (See also Census Bureau home page, http://www.census. gov/.).

Consumer International. Available from Gale Cengage Learning. • Annual. $1,290.00. Published by Euromonitor. Contains extensive consumer market, economic, and demographic data for 25 major, non-European countries, including the U. S. and Canada. Includes consumer market size (volume and value) for 150 product types in 14 categories (food, clothing, automobiles, cosmetics, appliances, etc.).

European Marketing Forecasts. Available from Gale Cengage Learning. • Annual. $1,250.00. Published by Euromonitor. Contains demographic, economic, and market forecasts for the countries of Europe to the year 2010. Forecasts include market-size data for 15 consumer product sectors (food, clothing, automobiles, consumer electronics, etc.).

International Marketing Forecasts. Available from Gale Cengage Learning. • Annual. $1,250.00. Published by Euromonitor. Contains demographic, economic, and market forecasts to the year 2013 for major, non-European countries, including the U. S. and Canada. Forecasts include market-size data for 15 consumer product sectors, such as food, clothing, and automobiles.

Standard & Poor's Industry Surveys. Standard & Poor's. • Semiannual. $1,800.00. Two looseleaf volumes. Includes monthly *Supplements.* Provides detailed, individual surveys of 52 major industry groups. Each survey is revised on a semiannual basis. Also includes "Monthly Investment Review" (industry group investment analysis) and monthly "Trends & Projections" (economic analysis).

U. S. Industry and Trade Outlook. Available from National Technical Information Service. • Annual. $69.95. Produced by the International Trade Administration, U. S. Department of Commerce, in a "public-private" partnership with DRI/McGraw-Hill and Standard & Poor's. Provides basic data, outlook for the current year, and "Long-Term Prospects" (five-year projections) for a wide variety of products and services. Includes high technology industries. Formerly *U. S. Industrial Outlook.*

TRADE/PROFESSIONAL ASSOCIATIONS

Electronic Industries Alliance. 2500 Wilson Blvd., Arlington, VA 22201. Phone: (703)907-7500 Fax:

(703)907-7501 E-mail: mflanigan@eia.org • URL: http://www.eia.org • Seeks for the competitiveness of the American producer, represents all companies involved in the design and manufacture of electronic components, parts, systems and equipment for communications, industrial, government and consumer uses.

Electronics Representatives Association. 300 W Adams St., Ste. 617, Chicago, IL 60606. Phone: 800-776-7377 or (312)527-3050 Fax: (312)527-3783 E-mail: info@era.org • URL: http://www.era.org • Professional field sales organizations selling components and materials; computer, instrumentation, and data communications products; audiovisual, security, land/mobile communications and commercial sound components, and consumer products to the electronics industry. Sponsors insurance programs and educational conference for members.

IEEE Consumer Electronics Society. 4115 Clendenning Rd., 445 Hoes Ln., Gibsonia, PA 15044. Phone: 800-678-4333 or (732)981-0025 Fax: (732)981-0225 E-mail: ckobert@zbzoom.net • URL: http://www.ewh.ieee.org/soc/ces • A society of the Institute of Electrical and Electronics Engineers. Gathers and disseminates information regarding the design and manufacture of consumer electronics components and products, particularly those with recreational or educational applications.

Professional Audiovideo Retailers Association. 2500 Wilson Blvd., Arlington, VA 22201-3834. Phone: (630)268-1500 Fax: (630)953-8957 E-mail: para@ce.org • URL: http://www.paralink.org • Retailers of specialty high end audio/video equipment. To educate the public on the value, desirability, and quality of audio equipment; to unite manufacturers for the exchange of information on the latest equipment and technological advancements in the industry. Provides computer seminar, service managers seminar, sales training course, and retail financial management course. Offers correspondence course leading to certification as professional audio specialist.

OTHER SOURCES

U. S. Home Theater Market. Available from MarketResearch.com. • 1997. $1,3750.00. Market research report published by Packaged Facts. Covers big-screen TV, high definition TV, audio equipment, and video sources. Market projections are provided.

CONSUMER FINANCE COMPANIES

See: FINANCE COMPANIES

CONSUMER LOANS

See: CONSUMER CREDIT

CONSUMER PRICE INDEXES

CD-ROM DATABASES

OECD Statistical Compendium. Organization for Economic Cooperation and Development. • Semiannual. $1,905.00 per year for 1 to 10 users. CD-ROM contains more than 730,000 monthly, quarterly, and annual time series for OECD countries, 1960 to date. Includes fully searchable data on agriculture, food, economic indicators, national accounts, employment, energy, finance, industry, technology, and foreign trade. Results can be displayed in various forms.

INTERNET DATABASES

Business 2.0 Web Guide to the Best Business Links. Business 2.0 Media Inc. Phone: (415)293-4800 E-mail: support@business2.com • URL: http://www.business2.com/webguide • Web site presents an extensive, searchable directory of links to "the best, most informative, and authoritative web pages." Twenty main categories cover business, finance, career, company information, people, and technology topics, with thousands of subtopics, all linking to Web sites recommended by experienced business researchers. Fees: Free.

Fedstats. Federal Interagency Council on Statistical Policy. Phone: (202)395-7254 • URL: http://www.fedstats.gov • Web site features an efficient search facility for full-text statistics produced by more than 100 federal agencies, including the Census Bureau, the Bureau of Economic Analysis, and the Bureau of Labor Statistics. Boolean searches can be made within one agency or for all agencies combined. Links are offered to international statistical bureaus, including the UN, IMF, OECD, UNESCO, Eurostat, and 20 individual countries. Fees: Free.

FreeLunch.com. Economy.com, Inc. Phone: (610)696-8700 Fax: (610)696-1678 • URL: http://www.freelunch.com • Web site provides free access to more than 1.5 million economic and financial data series, covering industry, demographics, labor markets, prices, retail sales, government spending, trade, interest rates, housing starts, the stock market, and many other topics. Data is available for various time periods in either chart or table form. Searching is offered. Fees: Free, but registration required. Economy.com, Inc. also offers fee-based economic analysis at *The Dismal Scientist* site (http://www.dismal.com).

PRICE SOURCES

CPI Detailed Report: Consumer Price Index. Available from U.S. Government Printing Office. • Monthly. $45.00 per year. Cost of living data.

The Value of a Dollar: Millennium Edition, 1860-1999. Grey House Publishing. • 1999. $135.00. Second edition. Shows the actual prices of thousands of items available to consumers from the Civil War era to recent years. Includes selected data on consumer expenditures, investments, income, and jobs. (Universal Reference Publications.).

STATISTICS SOURCES

ACCRA Cost of Living Index (Association for Applied Community Reseach). ACCRA. • Quarterly. $130.00 per year. Compares price levels for 280-310 U.S. cities.

American Cost of Living Survey. Gale Cengage Learning. • 2001. $245.00. Third edition. Cost of living data is provided for 455 U.S. cities and metroploitan areas.

Bulletin of Labour Statistics: Supplementing the Annual Data Presented in the Year Book of Labour Statistics. International Labour Ofice. • Quarterly. $84.00 per year. Includes five *Supplements*. A supplement to *Yearbook of Labour Statistics*. Provides current labor and price index statistics for over 130 countries. Generally includes data for the most recent four years. Text in English, French and Spanish.

Business Statistics of the United States. Linz Audain and Cornelia J. Strawser. Bernan Associates. • Annual. $147.00. Based on *Business Statistics*, formerly issue by the Bureau of Economic Analysis, U. S. Department of Commerce. Provides basic data for a wide variety of U. S. industries, services, and economic indicators. Most statistics are shown annually for 30 years and monthly for the most recent four years.

Economic Indicators. Council of Economic Advisors, Executive Office of the President. Available from U.S. Government Printing Office. • Monthly. $55.00 per year.

Economic Indicators Handbook: Time Series, Conversions, Documentation. Gale Cengage Learning. • 2002. $205.00. Sixth edition. Provides data for about 175 U. S. economic indicators, such as the consumer price index (CPI), gross national product (GNP), and the rate of inflation. Values for series are given since inception, in both original form and adjusted for inflation. A bibliography of sources is included.

Geographic Reference Report: Annual Report of Costs, Wages, Salaries, and Human Resource Statistics for the United States and Canada. ERI (Economic Research Institute). • Annual. $389.00. Provides demographic and other data for each of 298 North American metropolian areas, including local salaries, wage differentials, cost-of-living, housing costs, income taxation, employment, unemployment, population, major employers, crime rates, weather, etc.

Monthly Labor Review. Available from U. S. Government Printing Office. • Monthly. $49.00 per year. Issued by the Bureau of Labor Statistics, U. S. Department of Labor. Contains data on the labor force, wages, work stoppages, price indexes, productivity, economic growth, and occupational injuries and illnesses.

Prices and Earnings Around the Globe. Union Bank of Switzerland. • Triennial. Free. Published in Zurich. Compares prices and purchasing power in 48 major cities of the world. Wages and hours are also compared.

Report on the American Workforce. Available from U. S. Government Printing Office. • Annual. Issued by the U. S. Department of Labor (http://www.dol.gov). Appendix contains tabular statistics, including employment, unemployment, price indexes, consumer expenditures, employee benefits (retirement, insurance, vacation, etc.), wages, productivity, hours of work, and occupational injuries. Annual figures are shown for up to 50 years.

Survey of Current Business. Available from U. S. Government Printing Office. • Monthly. $63.00 per year. Issued by Bureau of Economic Analysis, U. S. Department of Commerce. Presents a wide variety of business and economic data.

United States Department of State Indexes of Living Costs Abroad, Quarters Allowances, and Hardship Differentials. Available from U. S. Government Printing Office. • Quarterly. $15.00 per year. Provides data on the difference in living costs between Washington, DC and each of 160 foreign cities.

The Value of a Dollar: Millenium Edition. Scott Derks, editor. Grey House Publishing, Inc. • 1999. $135.00. Second edition.

Working Americans, 1880-1999, Volume One: The Working Class. Scott Derks, editor. Grey House Publishing. • 2000. $375.00. Provides detailed information on the lifestyles and economic life of working class families in the 12 decades from 1880 to 1999. Includes such items as selected consumer prices, income, family finances, budgets, life at home, jobs, and working conditions. (Universal Reference Publications.).

Working Americans, 1880-1999, Volume Two: The Middle Class. Scott Derks, editor. Grey House Publishing. • 2000. $135.00. Three volumes. Furnishes details of the social and economic lives of middle class Americans during the years 1880 to 1999. Describes such items as selected consumer prices, income, family finances, budgets, life at home, jobs, and working conditions. (Universal Reference Publications.).

World Consumer Expenditure Patterns. Euromonitor International. • 2003. $1,190.00. Contains detailed consumer expenditure data for 71 countries. Covers 70 specific categories within the areas of food, beverages, tobacco, clothing, housing, appliances, health, transportation, leisure, etc. Provides 10 years of data and includes consumer price indexes.

World Cost of Living Survey. Gale Cengage Learning. • 1999. $275.00. Second edition. Arranged by country and then by city within each country. Provides cost of living data for many products and services. Includes indexes and an annotated bibliography.

Yearbook of Labour Statistics. Available from Bernan Associates. • Annual. $168.00. Published by the International Labour Organizaton (http://www.ilo.org). Provides data for more than 180 countries on employment, unemployment, wages, hours of work, cost of labor, strikes, industrial accidents, and consumer prices.

CONSUMER RESEARCH

See: CONSUMER ECONOMICS

CONSUMER SURVEYS

See also: MARKET RESEARCH

GENERAL WORKS

Consumer Behavior. Leon Schiffman and Leslie Kanut. Harcourt College Publishers. • 2003. $120.00. Eighth edition.

ALMANACS AND YEARBOOKS

Research Alert Yearbook: Vital Facts on Consumer Behavior and Attitudes. EPM Communications, Inc. • Annual. $295.00. Provides summaries of consumer market research from the newsletters *Research Alert, Youth Markets Alert, and Minority Markets Alert.* Includes tables, charts, graphs, and textual summaries for 41 subject categories. Sources include reports, studies, polls, and focus groups.

DIRECTORIES

Bradford's International Directory of Marketing Research Agencies. Business Research Services, Inc. • Annual. $95.00. Over 1,700 marketing research agencies and management consultants in market research. Formerly *Bradford's Directory of Marketing Research of the United States and the World.*

Findex: The Worldwide Directory of Market Research Reports, Studies, and Surveys. MarketResearch.com. • Annual. $425.00. Provides brief annotations of market research reports and related publications from about 1,000 publishers, arranged by topic. Back of book includes Report Titles by Publisher, Publishers/Distributors Directory, Subject Index, Geography Index, and Company Index. (Formerly published by Cambridge Information Group.).

GreenBook. New York AMA. • Annual. $100.00. Contains information on companies offering focus group facilities, including recruiting, moderating, and transcription services.

GreenBook Worldwide Directory of Marketing Research Companies and Services. New York AMA-Green Book. • Annual. $250.00. Contains information in 300 categories on more than 2,500 market research companies, consultants, field services, computer services, survey research companies, etc. Indexed by specialty, industry, company, computer program, and personnel. Available online. Formerly *Greenbook Worldwide International Directory of Marketing Research Companies and Services.*

Marketing Know-How: Your Guide to the Best Marketing Tools and Sources. Primedia Business Magazines and Media. • 1996. $49.95. Describes more than 700 public and private sources of consumer marketing data. Also discusses market trends and provides information on such marketing techniques as cluster analysis, focus groups, and geodemographic analysis.

MRA Blue Book Research Services Directory. Marketing Research Association. • Covers: over 1,200 marketing research companies and field interviewing services. Entries include: Company name, address, phone, names of executives, services, facilities, special interviewing capabilities.

ENCYCLOPEDIAS AND DICTIONARIES

The Sage Encyclopedia of Social Science Research Methods. Michael S. Lewis-Beck and others, editors. Sage Publications, Inc. • 2004. $550.00. Three volumes. Includes more than 800 signed entries on such topics as basic statistics, econometrics, evaluation, linear models, data analysis, sampling, and survey design.

HANDBOOKS AND MANUALS

An American Profile: Attitudes and Behaviors of the American People, 1972-1989. Gale Cengage Learning. • 1990. $89.50. A summary of responses to about 300 questions in the General Social Survey conducted annually by the National Opinion Research Center, covering family characteristics, social behavior, religion, political opinions, etc. Includes a chronology of significant world events from 1972 to 1989 and a subject-keyword index.

Constructing Effective Questionnaires. Robert A. Peterson. Sage Publications, Inc. • 1999. $86.95. Covers the construction and wording of questionnaires for survey research.

Focus Group Kit. David L. Morgan and Richard A. Krueger. Sage Publications, Inc. • 1997. $150.00. Six volumes. Various authors cover the basics of focus group research, including planning, developing questions, moderating, and analyzing results. (Focus Group Kit Series).

Handbook for Focus Group Research. Thomas L. Greenbaum. Sage Publications, Inc. • 1998. $97.95. Second edition. Includes glossary and index.

The Survey Kit. Arlene Fink, editor. Sage Publications, Inc. • 2003. $130.00. Second edition. Ten volumes. Covers various survey research topics, such as in-person interviews, telephone interviewing, focus groups, content analysis, sampling, database management, and Internet surveys. Each volume contains a glossary.

INTERNET DATABASES

Summary of Commentary on Current Economic Conditions by Federal Reserve District [the Beige Book]. Board of Governors of the Federal Reserve System. Phone: (202)452-3000 Fax: (202)452-3819 • URL: http://www.federalreserve.gov/fomc/beigebook/2004/ • Free Web site provides current "anecdotal information" eight times a year on economic conditions within each of the 12 Federal Reserve Districts, plus an extensive national *Summary.* Text is based on the opinions of bank officials, business executives, economists, financial market experts, and others. Typically contains views of consumer spending, manufacturing, services, credit, employment, prices, wages, and the economy in general. Usually referred to as the Beige Book.

ONLINE DATABASES

National Consumer Survey. Simmons Market Research Bureau. • Market and media survey data relating to the American consumer. Inquire as to online cost and availability.

PERIODICALS AND NEWSLETTERS

Consumer Confidence Survey. The Conference Board Inc. • Description: Publishes results of a special ongoing consumer attitude survey. Carries information on appraisal of business conditions and employment; plans to buy major durable goods such as homes, cars, and appliances; and intended vacations and chosen means of travel.

Public Pulse: Roper's Authoritative Report on What Americans are Thinking, Doing, and Buying. Roper Starch Worldwide. • Monthly. $297.00. Newsletter.

Contains news of surveys of American attitudes, values, and behavior. Each issue includes a research supplement giving "complete facts and figures behind each survey question.".

Research Alert: A Bi-Weekly Report of Consumer Marketing Studies. EPM Communications, Inc. • Biweekly. $369.00 per year. Newsletter. Provides descriptions (abstracts) of new, consumer market research reports from private, government, and academic sources. Includes sample charts and tables.

RESEARCH CENTERS AND INSTITUTES

Conference Board, Inc. The Conference Board, Inc. 845 3rd Ave., New York, NY 10022. Phone: (212)339-0345 Fax: (212)980-7014 E-mail: info@conference-board.org • URL: http://www.conference-board.org • Business management practices worldwide, especially economic, and demographic in nature. Specific concerns include: corporate citizenship, including corporate contributions, diversity, environmental policy and issues, and government relations; corporate governance, including boards of directors, role of chief executives, relations with institutional investors, and shareholder input and influence; economics, including economic and financial forecasts, consumer confidence, leading economic indicators, North American outlook and trends, and global economic environment; human resources and organizational effectiveness, including organization structure and design, compensation and benefits, training and development, and communications; and performance excellence.

STATISTICS SOURCES

Consumer Expenditure Survey. Available from U. S. Government Printing Office. • Biennial. Issued by the Bureau of Labor Statistics, U. S. Department of Labor (http://www.bls.gov). Contains data on various kinds of consumer spending, according to household income, education, etc. (Bureau of Labor Statistics Bulletin.).

SRDS Lifestyle Market Analyst. SRDS. • Annual. $440.00. Published in conjunction with EQUIFAX. Provides extensive lifestyle data on interests, activities, and hobbies within specific geographic and demographic markets. Formerly *Lifestyle Market Analyst.*

TRADE/PROFESSIONAL ASSOCIATIONS

National Council on Public Polls. c/o Edward J. Efchak, 150 River St., Hackensack, NJ 07601. Phone: (201)646-4379 E-mail: info@ncpp.org • URL: http://www.ncpp.org • Members are public opinion polling organizations.

CONSUMERS' COOPERATIVE SOCIETIES

See: COOPERATIVES

CONSUMERS' LEAGUES

See: COOPERATIVES

CONSUMERS, MATURE

See: MATURE CONSUMER MARKET

CONSUMERS' PRODUCTS RESEARCH

See: QUALITY OF PRODUCTS

CONTACT LENS AND INTRAOCULAR LENS INDUSTRIES

See also: OPHTHALMIC INDUSTRY

ABSTRACTS AND INDEXES

Index Medicus. National Library of Medicine. Available from U. S. Government Printing Office. • Monthly. $620.00 per year. Bibliographic listing of references to current articles from approximately 3,000 of the world's biomedical journals.

BIBLIOGRAPHIES

Medical and Health Care Books and Serials in Print: An Index to Literature in Health Sciences. R. R. Bowker. • Annual. $359.00. Two volumes.

DIRECTORIES

Contact Lens Manufacturers Association: Directory of Members. Contact Lens Manufacturers Association. • Annual. Membership.

Medical and Health Information Directory. Gale Cengage Learning. • 2002. $675.00. Three volumes. 14th edition. Three volumes. $285.00 per volume. Vol. one covers medical organizations, agencies, and institutions; vol. two includes bibliographic, library, and database information; vol. three is a guide to services available for various medical and health problems.

HANDBOOKS AND MANUALS

Physicians' Desk Reference for Ophthalmology. Medical Economics Co. • Annual. $49.95. Provides detailed descriptions of ophthalmological instrumentation, equipment, supplies, lenses, and prescription drugs. Indexed by manufacturer, product name, product category, active drug ingredient, and instrumentation. Editorial discussion is included.

ONLINE DATABASES

Embase. Elsevier Science, Inc. • Worldwide medical literature, 1974 to present. Weekly updates. Inquire as to online cost and availability.

Medline. Medlars Management Section. • Provides indexing and abstracting of worldwide medical literature, 1966 to date. Weekly updates. Inquire as to online cost and availability.

PERIODICALS AND NEWSLETTERS

Contact Lens Spectrum. Boucher Communications, Inc. • 20 times a year. $43.00 per year. Provides news and information on clinical issues and the contact lens industry. Incorporates *Contact Lens Forum.*

Eye and Contact Lens: Science and Clinical Practices. University of Texas, Dept. of Ophthalmology. Lippincott Williams and Wilkins. • Quarterly. Individuals, $88.00 per year; institutions, $108.00 per year. Formerly *The CLAO Journal.*

International Contact Lens Clinic. Elsevier. • Bimonthly. Individuals, $139.00 per year; institutions, $272.00 per year.

Ocular Surgery News. SLACK, Inc. • Biweekly. Individuals, $399.00 per year; institutions, $384.00 per year. Formerly *IOL & Ocular Surgery News.*

TRADE/PROFESSIONAL ASSOCIATIONS

American Optometric Association; Contact Lens Section. 243 N. Lindbergh Blvd., St. Louis, MO 63141. Phone: (314)991-4100 Fax: (314)991-4101 • URL: http://www.aoanet.org • Members are optometrists, students of optometry and paraoptometric assistants and technicians. Formerly American Optical Association.

American Society of Cataract and Refractive Surgery. 4000 Legato Rd., No. 850, Fairfax, VA 22033. Phone: 800-451-1339 or (703)591-2220 Fax: (703)591-0614 E-mail: ascrs@ascrs.org • URL:

http://www.ascrs.org • Affiliated with American Medical Association and American Society Ophthalmic Administrators.

Contact Lens Association of Ophthalmologists. c/o John S. Massare, 721 Papworth Ave., Ste. 206, Metairie, LA 70005. Phone: (504)835-3937 Fax: (504)833-5884 E-mail: eyes@clao.org • URL: http://www.clao.org • Affiliated with American Academy of Ophthalmology, American Medical Association and American National Standards Institute.

Contact Lens Manufacturers Association. PO Box 29398, Lincoln, NE 68529. Phone: 800-344-9060 or (402)465-4122 Fax: (402)465-4187 E-mail: clmassociation@aol.com • URL: http://www.clma.net • Represents contact lens laboratories, material, solution and equipment manufacturers in the United States and abroad. Aims to increase awareness and utilization of custom manufactured contact lenses.

Contact Lens Society of America. 441 Carlisle Dr., Herndon, VA 20170-4837. Phone: 800-296-9776 or (703)437-5100 Fax: (703)437-0727 E-mail: info@theclsa.com • URL: http://www.clsa.info.

OTHER SOURCES

New Ophthalmology: Treatments and Technologies. Theta Reports. • 2000. $1,695. Provides market research data relating to eye surgery, including LASIK, cataract surgery, and associated technology. (Theta Report No. 911.).

CONTAINER INDUSTRY

See also: COOPERAGE INDUSTRY; GLASS CONTAINER INDUSTRY; PAPER BAG INDUSTRY; PAPER BOX AND PAPER CONTAINER INDUSTRIES

CD-ROM DATABASES

OECD Statistical Compendium. Organization for Economic Cooperation and Development. • Semiannual. $1,905.00 per year for 1 to 10 users. CD-ROM contains more than 730,000 monthly, quarterly, and annual time series for OECD countries, 1960 to date. Includes fully searchable data on agriculture, food, economic indicators, national accounts, employment, energy, finance, industry, technology, and foreign trade. Results can be displayed in various forms.

DIRECTORIES

Packaging Digest Machinery/Materials Guide. Reed Business Information. • Annual. $46.00. List of more than 3,100 manufacturers of machinery and materials for the packaging industry, and about 260 contract packagers.

Paperboard Packaging Resource Directory. Advanstar Communications. • Covers: about 3,000 manufacturers of corrugated and solid fiber containers, folding cartons, rigid boxes, fiber cans and tubes, and fiber drums. Entries include: For manufacturers--Company name, address, phone, equipment, names of executives, plants, and type of containers manufactured.

ENCYCLOPEDIAS AND DICTIONARIES

Wiley Encyclopedia of Packaging Technology. Aaron Brody and Kenneth Marsh, editors. John Wiley and Sons, Inc. • 1997. $330.00. Second edition.

FINANCIAL RATIOS

Annual Statement Studies. The Risk Management Association. • Annual. Median and quartile financial ratios are given for over 400 kinds of manufacturing, wholesale, retail, construction, and consumer finance establishments. Data is sorted by both asset size and sales volume. Includes a clearly written "Definition of Ratios" and an alphabetical industry index.

Annual Statement Studies: Industry Default Prob-

abilities and Cash Flow Measures. The Risk Management Association. • Annual. $145.00. Serves as a companion volume to the original *Annual Statement Studies.* Gives probability of default estimates on a percentage scale for more than 450 industries. Includes changes in position year-by-year for eight financial statement line items and provides percentage measures of cash flow.

INTERNET DATABASES

Business 2.0 Web Guide to the Best Business Links. Business 2.0 Media Inc. Phone: (415)293-4800 E-mail: support@business2.com • URL: http://www.business2.com/webguide • Web site presents an extensive, searchable directory of links to "the best, most informative, and authoritative web pages." Twenty main categories cover business, finance, career, company information, people, and technology topics, with thousands of subtopics, all linking to Web sites recommended by experienced business researchers. Fees: Free.

Fedstats. Federal Interagency Council on Statistical Policy. Phone: (202)395-7254 • URL: http://www.fedstats.gov • Web site features an efficient search facility for full-text statistics produced by more than 100 federal agencies, including the Census Bureau, the Bureau of Economic Analysis, and the Bureau of Labor Statistics. Boolean searches can be made within one agency or for all agencies combined. Links are offered to international statistical bureaus, including the UN, IMF, OECD, UNESCO, Eurostat, and 20 individual countries. Fees: Free.

FreeLunch.com. Economy.com, Inc. Phone: (610)696-8700 Fax: (610)696-1678 • URL: http://www.freelunch.com • Web site provides free access to more than 1.5 million economic and financial data series, covering industry, demographics, labor markets, prices, retail sales, government spending, trade, interest rates, housing starts, the stock market, and many other topics. Data is available for various time periods in either chart or table form. Searching is offered. Fees: Free, but registration required. Economy.com, Inc. also offers fee-based economic analysis at *The Dismal Scientist* site (http://www.dismal.com).

Manufacturing Profiles. U. S. Bureau of the Census. Phone: (301)763-4636 E-mail: webmaster@census.gov • URL: http://www.census.gov/prod/www/abs/mfg-prof.html • The Census Bureau makes available free on PDF (Portable Document Format) an annual consolidation of the entire Current Industrial Report series, presenting "all the data compiled." Contains statistics on production, shipments, inventories, consumption, exports, imports, and orders for a wide variety of manufactured products.

PERIODICALS AND NEWSLETTERS

Packaging Digest. Reed Business Information. • 13 times a year. $119.90 per year.

PRICE SOURCES

Official Board Markets: "The Yellow Sheet". Mark Arzoumanian. Advantstar Communications. • Weekly. $160.00 per year. Covers the corrugated container, folding carton, rigid box and waste paper industries.

STATISTICS SOURCES

American Iron and Steel Annual Statistical Report. American Iron and Steel Institute. • Annual. $100.00 per year.

Annual Survey of Manufactures. Available from U. S. Government Printing Office. • Annual. Prices vary. Issued by the U. S. Census Bureau as an interim update to the *Census of Manufactures.* Includes data on number of manufacturing establishments in various industries, employment, labor costs, value of shipments, capital expenditures, inventories, energy costs, and assets. (See also Census Bureau home page, http://www.census.gov/.).

Business Statistics of the United States. Linz Audain and Cornelia J. Strawser. Bernan Associates. • Annual. $147.00. Based on *Business Statistics*, formerly issue by the Bureau of Economic Analysis, U. S. Department of Commerce. Provides basic data for a wide variety of U. S. industries, services, and economic indicators. Most statistics are shown annually for 30 years and monthly for the most recent four years.

Survey of Current Business. Available from U. S. Government Printing Office. • Monthly. $63.00 per year. Issued by Bureau of Economic Analysis, U. S. Department of Commerce. Presents a wide variety of business and economic data.

TRADE/PROFESSIONAL ASSOCIATIONS

Associated Cooperage Industries of America. 2100 Gardiner Lane, Suite 100-E, Louisville, KY 40205-2947. Phone: (502)459-6113 Fax: (502)459-6114 E-mail: aciainc@acia.net • URL: http://www.acia. net.

Can Manufacturers Institute. 1730 Rhode Island Ave. NW, Ste. 1000, Washington, DC 20036. Phone: (202)232-4677 Fax: (202)232-5756 E-mail: clee@ cancentral.com • URL: http://www.cancentral.com • Represents can makers and can industry suppliers. Aims to foster the prosperity of the industry and bring value to its members in a cost effective way.

Containerization and Intermodal Institute. 195 Fairfield Ave., Suite 4D, West Caldwell, NJ 07006. Phone: (973)226-0160 Fax: (973)364-1212 E-mail: cii@bsya.com • Formerly Containerization Institute.

International Beverage Packaging Association. Anheuser-Busch, Inc., One Ocean Spray Dr., Fort Collins, CO 80524. Phone: 888-662-3263 or (508)946-1000 Fax: (702)566-7166 E-mail: info@ ibpa.org • URL: http://www.ibpa.org • Beverage industry personnel interested in the concerns of the beverage packaging industry, including soft drink, beer, bottled water, juice manufacturers and packagers, allied suppliers.

Steel Shipping Container Institute. S-1101 14th St. NW, Washington, DC 20005. Phone: (202)408-1900 Fax: (202)408-1972 E-mail: ssci_office@ steelcontainers.com • URL: http://www. steelcontainers.com • Manufacturers of steel drums, barrels, pails, accessories, fittings, equipment, and materials used by the industry. Underwrites U.S. Bureau of Census monthly report on steel pail and drum production. Sponsors development programs on container design, safety features, testing, quality control, and product protection systems.

CONTESTS, PRIZES, AND AWARDS

DIRECTORIES

Awards, Honors, and Prizes. Gale Cengage Learning. • 2003. $525.00. Two volumes. 21th edition. Domestic volume, $275.00. International volume, $305.00.

Contests for Students: All You Need to Know to Enter and Win 600 Contests. Gale Cengage Learning. • 1999. $65.00. Second edition. details 600 regional, national, and international contests for elementary, junior high, and high school students.

Peterson's Scholarships, Grants, and Prizes: Your Complete Guide to College Aid from Private Sources. Peterson's. • 1998. $26.95. Third edition.

The PROMO 100 Promotion Agency Ranking. PROMO Magazine. • Covers: Ranking of the top 100 U.S. Promotion agencies. Entries include: Name, address, phone, financial data, client lists, rate of growth, name of CEO, and description of product/service.

R and I Blue Book (Recognition and Identification). The Engravers Journal, Inc. • Annual. Price on application. Over 200 manufacturers and suppliers of trophies, plaques, engraving and marking equipment and supplies to the recognition and identification (R&I) industry. Formerly *Awards Specialist Directory.*

World of Winners: A Current and Historical Perspective on Awards and Their Winners. Gale Cengage Learning. • 1991. $99.00. Second edition. Lists 100,000 recipients of 2,500 awards, honors, and prizes in 12 subject categories. Indexed by organization, recipient, and award. Covers all years for each award.

ONLINE DATABASES

Marketing and Advertising Reference Service (MARS). Gale Cengage Learning. • Provides abstracts of literature relating to consumer marketing and advertising, including all forms of advertising media. Time period is 1984 to date. Daily updates. Inquire as to online cost and availability.

PERIODICALS AND NEWSLETTERS

Potentials: Ideas and Products that Motivate. VNU Business Media. • Monthly. $59.00 per year. Covers incentives, premiums, awards, and gifts as related to promotional activities. Formerly *Potentials in Marketing.*

PROMO: Promotion Marketing Worldwide. Primedia Business Magazines and Media. • Monthly. $65.00 per year. Edited for companies and agencies that utilize couponing, point-of-purchase advertising, special events, games, contests, premiums, product samples, and other unique promotional items.

TRADE/PROFESSIONAL ASSOCIATIONS

Awards and Recognition Association. 4700 W Lake Ave., Glenview, IL 60025. Phone: 800-344-2148 or (847)375-4800 Fax: (847)375-6309 E-mail: info@ ara.org • URL: http://www.ara.org.

CONTRACTIONS

See: ABBREVIATIONS

CONTRACTORS

See: BUILDING CONTRACTS; BUILDING INDUSTRY

CONTRACTORS, ELECTRICAL

See: ELECTRICAL CONSTRUCTION INDUSTRY

CONTRACTS

See also: BUILDING CONTRACTS; GOVERNMENT CONTRACTS

GENERAL WORKS

An Introduction to the Law of Contract. Patrick S. Atiyah. Oxford University Press. • 2005. $35.00. Sixth edition. (Claredon Law Series).

ABSTRACTS AND INDEXES

Current Law Index: Multiple Access to Legal Periodicals. Gale Cengage Learning. • Monthly. $725.00 per year. Produced in cooperation with the American Association of Law Libraries. Indexes more than 900 law journals, legal newspapers, and specialty publications from the U.S., Canada, U.K., Ireland, Australia, and New Zealand.

Index to Legal Periodicals and Books. H. W. Wilson Co. • Monthly. $490.00 per year. Quarterly and annual cumulations.

ALMANACS AND YEARBOOKS

American Law Yearbook. Gale Cengage Learning. • Annual. $165.00. Serves as a yearly supplement to *West's Encyclopedia of American Law.* Describes new legal developments in many subject areas.

CD-ROM DATABASES

WILSONDISC: Index to Legal Periodicals and Books. H. W. Wilson Co. • Monthly. Includes unlimited online access to *Index to Legal Periodicals* through WILSONLINE. Contains CD-ROM indexing of more than 1,400 English language legal periodicals from 1981 to date and 2,500 books.

ENCYCLOPEDIAS AND DICTIONARIES

West's Encyclopedia of American Law. Available from Gale Cengage Learning. • 2003. $1,195.00. Second edition. 12 volumes. Published by West Group. Covers a wide variety of legal topics for the general reader.

HANDBOOKS AND MANUALS

Contracts for the Film and Television Industry. Mark Litwak. Silman-James Press. • 1999. $35.95. Second expanded edition. Contains a wide variety of sample entertainment contracts. Includes material on rights, employment, joint ventures, music, financing, production, distribution, merchandising, and the retaining of attorneys.

Corbin on Contracts. LexisNexis. • $999.00. 14 volumes. Includes looseleaf volume and cumulative *Supplement.*

Legal Guide to Independent Contractor Status. Robert W. Wood. Aspen Publishers, Inc. • 2003. Price on application. A guide to the legal and tax-related differences between employers and independent contractors. Includes examples of both "safe" and "troublesome" independent contractor designations. Penalties and fines are discussed.

Williston on Contracts. Richard A. Lord. West Group. • $1,963.00. 23 volumes. Periodic supplementation. Encyclopedic coverage of contract law.

INTERNET DATABASES

Lexis.com Research System. Lexis-Nexis Group. Phone: 800-227-4908 or (937)865-6800 Fax: (937)865-6909 E-mail: webmaster@prod.lexis-nexis.com • URL: http://www.lexis.com • Fee-based Web site offers extensive searching of a wide variety of legal sources. Additional features include Daily Opinion Service, lexis.com Bookstore, Career Center, CLE Center, Law Schools, and Practice Pages ("Pages specific to areas of specialty").

ONLINE DATABASES

Index to Legal Periodicals and Books (Online). H. W. Wilson Co. • Broad coverage of law journals and books 1981 to date. Monthly updates. Inquire as to online cost and availability.

LEXIS. LEXIS-NEXIS. • The various LEXIS databases provide full text and indexing for a wide variety of legal cases, statutes, orders, and opinions.

PERIODICALS AND NEWSLETTERS

Contract Management. National Contract Management Association. • Monthly. $72.00 per year.

TRADE/PROFESSIONAL ASSOCIATIONS

National Contract Management Association. 21740 Beaumeade Cir., Ste. 125, Ashburn, VA 20147. Phone: 800-344-8096 or (571)382-0082 Fax: (703)448-0939 E-mail: couture@ncmahq.org • URL: http://www.ncmahq.org • Professional individuals concerned with administration, procurement, acquisition, negotiation and management of contracts and subcontracts. Works for the education, improvement and professional development of members and nonmembers through national and chapter programs, symposia and educational materials. Offers certification in Contract Management (CPCM, CFCM, and CCCM) designations as well as a credential program. Operates speakers' bureau.

OTHER SOURCES

Government Contracts Reports. CCH, Inc. • Weekly. $2,600.00 per year. 10 looseleaf volumes. Laws and regulations affecting government contracts.

CONTRACTS, GOVERNMENT

See: GOVERNMENT CONTRACTS

CONTROL EQUIPMENT INDUSTRY

See also: AUTOMATION; FLUIDICS INDUSTRY

ABSTRACTS AND INDEXES

Applied Science and Technology Index. H. W. Wilson Co. • 11 times a year. Quarterly and annual cumulations. Price varies. Indexes a wide variety of English language technical, industrial, and engineering periodicals.

Engineering Index Monthly: Abstracting and Indexing Services Covering Sources of the World's Engineering Literature. Engineering Information Inc. • Monthly. Institutions, $5,279.00 per year. Provides indexing and abstracting of the world's engineering and technical literature.

Key Abstracts: Machine Vision. Available from INSPEC, Inc. • Monthly. $250.00 per year. Provides international coverage of journal and proceedings literature on optical noncontact sensing. Published in England by the Institution of Electrical Engineers (IEE).

Key Abstracts: Robotics and Control. Available from INSPEC, Inc. • Monthly. $250.00 per year. Provides international coverage of journal and proceedings literature. Published in England by the Institution of Electrical Engineers (IEE).

NTIS Alerts: Computers, Control & Information Theory. National Technical Information Service. • Semimonthly. $235.00 per year. Provides descriptions of government-sponsored research reports and software, with ordering information. Covers computer hardware, software, control systems, pattern recognition, image processing, and related subjects. Formerly *Abstract Newsletter.*

Science Citation Index. Thomson/ISI. • Bimonthly. $15,020.00 per year. Annual cumulation. Includes *Source Index, Citation Index, Permuterm Subject Index,* and *Corporate Index.*

DIRECTORIES

Control Engineering Buyers Guide. Reed Business Information. • Annual. Price on application. Contains specifications, prices, and manufacturers' listings for computer software, as related to control engineering.

Frontline Solutions Buyer's Guide. Advanstar Communications. • Publication includes: List of manufacturers, suppliers, consultants, value added resellers, and dealers/distributors of automatic identification and data capture software, technology, equipment, and products for bar code, biometric identification, electronic data interchange, machine vision, magnetic stripe, optical character recognition, radio frequency data communications, radio frequency identification, smart cards, and voice data entry; also includes related organizations, and sources for industry standards. Entries include: Company name, address, phone, e-mail, web address, products or services.

International Instrumentation and Controls Buyers Guide. Keller International Publishing, LLC. • Annual. Included in subscription to *International Instrumentation and Controls.* Lists over 310 suppliers of precision instrument products and services.

ISA Directory of Instrumentation. ISA - The Instrumentation Systems and Automation Society. • Annual. $100.00. Over 2,400 manufacturers of control and instrumentation equipment, over 1,000 manufacturers' representatives, and several hundred service companies; coverage includes Canada.

Manufacturing Systems: Buyers Guide. Reed Business Information. • Annual. Price on application. Contains information on companies manufacturing or supplying materials handling systems, CAD/CAM systems, specialized software for manufacturing, programmable controllers, machine vision systems, and automatic identification systems.

Sensors Buyers Guide. Advanstar Communications. • Covers: Lists manufacturers and vendors of sensors and transducers for use in high-technology applications engineering. Also covers related products and services. Entries include: Company name, address, phone, fax, e-mail, URL, contact person, type of sensors manufactured and/or physical, chemical, or biological characteristics utilized in sensing.

Test and Measurement World Annual Buyer's Guide. Reed Business Information. • Annual. $29.95. List of suppliers of test, measurement, inspection, and monitoring products and services.

Thomas Register of American Manufacturers. Thomas Publishing Co., Inc. • Annual. $149.00. 34 volumes. A three-part system offering information on a wide variety of industrial equipment and supplies. Lists more than 151,000 industrial product and services companies.

FINANCIAL RATIOS

Industry Norms and Key Business Ratios. Desk Top Edition. Dun and Bradstreet Corp. • Annual. Five volumes. $475.00 per volume. $1,890.00 per set. Covers over 800 kinds of businesses, arranged by Standard Industrial Classification number. More detailed editions covering longer periods of time are also available.

HANDBOOKS AND MANUALS

Control Handbook. William S. Levine, editor. CRC Press LLC. • 1996. $179.95. Contains about 140 articles by various authors on automatic control, control theory, and control engineering. (Electrical Engineering Handbook Series).

INTERNET DATABASES

Manufacturing Profiles. U. S. Bureau of the Census. Phone: (301)763-4636 E-mail: webmaster@census.gov • URL: http://www.census.gov/prod/www/abs/mfg-prof.html • The Census Bureau makes available free on PDF (Portable Document Format) an annual consolidation of the entire Current Industrial Report series, presenting "all the data compiled." Contains statistics on production, shipments, inventories, consumption, exports, imports, and orders for a wide variety of manufactured products.

ONLINE DATABASES

FLUIDEX. Elsevier Science, Inc. • Produced in the Netherlands by Elsevier Science B.V. Provides indexing and abstracting of the international literature of fluid engineering and technology, 1973 to date, with monthly updates. Also known as *Fluid Engineering Abstracts.* Inquire as to online cost and availability.

Globalbase. Gale Cengage Learning. • Provides more than one million online summaries of business, industrial, and economic news reports from more than 1,000 publications worldwide. Covers a wide range of material appearing in international trade journals, professional magazines, and newspapers. Time period is 1984 to date, with

weekly updates. Inquire as to online cost and availability.

INSPEC. Institution of Electrical Engineers (IEE). • Provides online citations, with abstracts, to the world literature of electrical engineering, electronics, optoelectronics, telecommunications, industrial controls, instrumentation, computer technology, information technology, and physics. Coverage includes more than 4,000 technical and scientific journals from 1969 to date, with weekly updating. (INSPEC is Information Services in Physics, Electronics, and Computing.) Inquire as to online cost and availability.

Scisearch. Institute for Scientific Information. • Broad, multidisciplinary index to the literature of science and technology, 1974 to present. Inquire as to online cost and availability. Coverage of literature is worldwide, with weekly updates.

Thomas Register Online. Thomas Publishing Co., Inc. • Provides concise information on approximately 194,000 U. S. companies, mainly manufacturers, with over 50,000 product classifications. Indexes over 115,000 trade names. Information is updated semiannually. Inquire as to online cost and availability.

PERIODICALS AND NEWSLETTERS

Control Engineering: Covering Control, Instrumentation and Automation Systems Worldwide. Reed Business Information. • Monthly. $109.90 per year.

IEEE Industry Applications Magazine. Institute of Electrical and Electronics Engineers. • Bimonthly. $190.00 per year. Covers new industrial applications of power conversion, drives, lighting, and control. Emphasis is on the petroleum, chemical, rubber, plastics, textile, and mining industries.

Industrial Computing. Industrial Computing Society. ISA Services, Inc. • Monthly. Members $100.00 per year; non-members, $80.00 per year. Published by the Instrument Society of America. Edited for engineering managers and systems integrators. Subject matter includes industrial software, programmable controllers, artificial intelligence systems, and industrial computer networking systems.

Instrumentation and Automation News: Instruments, Controls, Manufacturing Software, Electronic and Mechanical Components. Reed Business Information. • Monthly. $61.90 per year.

INTECH: The International Journal of Instrumentation and Control. ISA Services, Inc. • Monthly. $72.00 per year.

Manufacturing Computer Solutions. • Monthly. $88.00 per year. Edited for managers of factory automation, emphasizing the integration of systems in manufacturing. Subjects include materials handling, CAD/CAM, specialized software for manufacturing, programmable controllers, machine vision, and automatic identification systems. Formerly *Manufacturing Systems.*

Measurements and Control. Measurements and Data Corp. • Bimonthly. $24.00 per year. Supplement available: *M & C: Measurement and Control News.*

Processing. Putman Media. • 14 times a year. $54.00 per year. Emphasis is on descriptions of new products for all areas of industrial processing, including valves, controls, filters, pumps, compressors, fluidics, and instrumentation.

Sensor Technology: A Monthly Intgelligence Service. Technical Insights. • Monthly. Institutions, $685.00 per year. Newsletter on technological developments relating to industrial sensors and process control.

Sensors: Your Resource for Sensing, Communications, and Control. Advanstar Communications. • Monthly. $70.00 per year. Edited for design, production, and manufacturing engineers involved with sensing systems. Emphasis is on emerging technology.

Test and Measurement World: The Magazine for Quality in Electronics. Reed Electronics Group. • 15 times a year. $93.99 per year.

RESEARCH CENTERS AND INSTITUTES

Instrumentation and Control Laboratory. Princeton University. Dept. of Mechanical and Aerospace Engineering, Engineering Quadrangle, Princeton, NJ 08544. Phone: (609)452-5154 Fax: (609)452-6109 E-mail: enoch@princeton.edu.

STATISTICS SOURCES

Annual Survey of Manufactures. Available from U. S. Government Printing Office. • Annual. Prices vary. Issued by the U. S. Census Bureau as an interim update to the *Census of Manufactures.* Includes data on number of manufacturing establishments in various industries, employment, labor costs, value of shipments, capital expenditures, inventories, energy costs, and assets. (See also Census Bureau home page, http://www.census.gov/.).

U. S. Industry and Trade Outlook. Available from National Technical Information Service. • Annual. $69.95. Produced by the International Trade Administration, U. S. Department of Commerce, in a "public-private" partnership with DRI/McGraw-Hill and Standard & Poor's. Provides basic data, outlook for the current year, and "Long-Term Prospects" (five-year projections) for a wide variety of products and services. Formerly *U. S. Industrial Outlook.*

TRADE/PROFESSIONAL ASSOCIATIONS

American Automatic Control Council. Northwestern University, 2145 Sheridan Rd., 3640 Col Glenn Highway, Evanston, IL 60208-3118. Phone: (937)775-5062 Fax: (937)775-3936 E-mail: ahaddad@eec.nwv.edu • URL: http://www.a2c2.org • Control engineering divisions of: American Institute of Aeronautics and Astronautics, American Institute of Chemical Engineers, American Society of Mechanical Engineers, Association of Iron and Steel Engineers, Institute of Electrical and Electronics Engineers, Instrument Society of America, and Society for Computer Simulation International (see separate entries). Covers the field of automatic control including control of manufacturing processes, computer control, process control, navigation, and guidance.

Fluid Controls Institute. 1300 Sumner Ave., Cleveland, OH 44115. Phone: (216)241-7333 Fax: (216)241-0105 E-mail: fci@fluidcontrolsinstitute. org • URL: http://www.fluidcontrolsinstitute.org • Works for technical advancement, promotion and understanding of a broad range of fluid control and fluid conditioning devices. Concentrates its efforts on the manufacturing and engineering aspects of control valves, solenoid valves, regulators, steam traps, pipeline strainers, secondary pressure drainers and gauges. Maintains the flexibility to adapt to changing technology by including a general products section, out of which new sections can be formed to better serve the industry and the general public.

IEEE Control Systsems Society. c/o IEEE Corporate Office, 3 Park Ave., 17th Fl., New York, NY 10016-5997. Phone: 800-678-4333 or (212)419-7900 Fax: (212)752-4929 E-mail: ieeeusa@ieee.org • URL: http://www.ieee.org.

Instrumentation Systems and Automation Society. 67 Alexander Dr., Research Triangle Park, NC 27709. Phone: (919)549-8411 Fax: (919)549-8288 E-mail: info@isa.org • URL: http://www.isa.org • Members are engineers and others concerned with industrial instrumentation, systems, computers, and automation. Formerly Instrument Society of America.

ISA-Instrumentation, Systems, and Automation

Society. 67 Alexander Dr., Research Triangle Park, NC 27709. Phone: (919)549-8411 Fax: (919)549-8288 E-mail: info@isa.org • URL: http://www.isa.org.

ISA-The Instrumentation, Systems, and Automation Society:. 67 Alexander Dr., Research Triangle Park, NC 27709. Phone: (919)549-8411 Fax: (919)549-8288 E-mail: info@isa.org • URL: http://www.isa.org.

Process Equipment Manufacturers Association. 201 Park Washington Ct., Falls Church, VA 22046-4527. Phone: (703)538-1796 Fax: (703)241-5603 E-mail: info@pemanet.org • URL: http://www.pemanet.org • Represents North American process equipment companies. Maintains an organization of capital equipment manufacturers. Provides a social/business base where members can meet to share and exchange views on common interests.

SAMA Group of Associations. 225 Reinekers Lane, Ste. 625, Alexandria, VA 23314. Phone: (703)836-1360 Fax: (703)836-6644 • Formerly Apparatus Makers Association of America.

OTHER SOURCES

Industrial Controls. Available from MarketResearch.com. • 2001. $4,100.00. Published by the Freedonia Group. Market data with forecasts to 2005 and 2009. Includes computerized controls and conventional controls.

CONTROLLERS

See: CORPORATE DIRECTORS AND OFFICERS

CONVENIENCE STORES

ABSTRACTS AND INDEXES

Business Periodicals Index. H. W. Wilson Co. • 11 times a year. Quarterly and annual cumulations. Price varies.

CD-ROM DATABASES

ABI/INFORM. PROQUEST. • Monthly. Provides CD-ROM indexing and abstracting of worldwide business literature. Archival discs are available from 1971. Formerly *ABI/INFORM OnDisc.*

WILSONDISC: Wilson Business Abstracts. H. W. Wilson Co. • Monthly. Includes unlimited online access to *Wilson Business Abstracts* through WILSONLINE. Provides CD-ROM "cover-to-cover" abstracting and indexing of over 600 prominent business periodicals. Indexing is from 1982, abstracting from 1990. (*Business Periodicals Index* without abstracts is available on CD-ROM at $1,495 per year.).

DIRECTORIES

Convenience Store News Buyers Guide. Bill Communications. • Annual. $200.00. Provides information on convenience store chains, including service station stores, and suppliers of products, equipment, and services to convenience stores.

Directory of Convenience Stores. Trade Dimensions. • Annual. $260.00. Provides information on over 1,400 convenience store chains having four or more convenience stores.

Directory of Supermarket, Grocery, and Convenience Store Chains. Chain Store Guide. • Annual. $327.00. Online edition, $747.00. Provides information on about 3,300 food store chains operating 120,000 individual stores. Store locations are given.

HANDBOOKS AND MANUALS

Convenience Food Store. Entrepreneur Media, Inc. • Looseleaf. $59.50. A practical guide to starting a convenience food store. Covers profit potential, start-up costs, market size evaluation, owner's time

required, site selection, lease negotiation, pricing, accounting, advertising, promotion, etc. (Start-Up Business Guide No. E1173.).

ONLINE DATABASES

F & S Index. Gale Cengage Learning. • Contains about four million citations to worldwide business, financial, and industrial or consumer product literature appearing from 1972 to date. Weekly updates. Inquire as to online cost and availability.

PROMT: Predicasts Overview of Markets and Technology. Gale Cengage Learning. • Companies, products, applied technologies and markets. U.S. and international literature coverage, 1972 to date. Inquire as to online cost and availability. Provides abstracts from more than 1,600 publications. Weekly updates.

Trade & Industry Database. Gale Cengage Learning. • Provides indexing of business periodicals, January 1981 to date. Daily updates. (Full text articles from some periodicals are available online, 1983 to date. Inquire as to online cost and availability).

Wilson Business Abstracts Online. H. W. Wilson Co. • Indexes and abstracts 600 major business periodicals, plus the *Wall Street Journal* and the business section of the *New York Times.* Indexing is from 1982, abstracting from 1990, with the two newspapers included from 1993. Updated weekly. Inquire as to online cost and availability. (*Business Periodicals Index* without abstracts is also available online.).

PERIODICALS AND NEWSLETTERS

Convenience Store Decisions. Donohue-Meehan Publishing Co. • Monthly. $60.00 per year. Edited for headquarters and regional management personnel of convenience store chains.

Convenience Store News: The Information Source for the Industry. VNU Business Media. • 15 times a year. Free to qualified personnel; others, $89.00 per year. Contains news of industry trends and merchandising techniques.

CSP: The Magazine for C-Store People. CSP Information Group. • 14 times a year. $48.00 per year. Emphasizes the influence of people (both store personnel and consumers) on the C-store industry.

Oil Express: Inside Report on Trends in Petroleum Marketing Without the Influ nce of Advertising. United Communications Group. • 50 times a year. $337.00 per year. Newsletter. Provides news of trends in petroleum marketing and convenience store operations. Includes *U. S. Oil Week's Price Monitor* (petroleum product prices) and *C-Store Digest* (news concerning convenience stores operated by the major oil companies) and *Fuel Oil Update.* Formerly *U.S. Oil Week.*

RESEARCH CENTERS AND INSTITUTES

Center for Retail Management. Kellogg School of Management, Northwestern University, 2001 Sheridan Rd., Evanston, IL 60208. Phone: (847)467-3600 Fax: (847)467-3620 E-mail: r-blattberg@kellogg. northwestern.edu • URL: http://www.kellogg. northwestern.edu • Conducts research related to retail marketing and management.

Center for Retailing Studies. Texas A & M University, Department of Marketing, 4112 TAMU, College Station, TX 77843-4112. Phone: (979)845-0325 Fax: (979)845-5230 E-mail: d-szymanski@tamu.edu • URL: http://www.crstamu.org • Research areas include retailing issues and consumer economics.

TRADE/PROFESSIONAL ASSOCIATIONS

National Association of Convenience Stores. 1605 King St., Alexandria, VA 22314-2792. Phone: 800-966-6227 or (703)684-3600 Fax: (703)836-4564 E-mail: bremoyer@nacsonline.com • URL: http://www.nacsonline.com • Members are small retail stores that sell a variety of food and nonfood items and that usually have extended hours of opening.

CONVENTION MANAGEMENT

See: MEETING MANAGEMENT

CONVENTIONS

See also: CONFERENCES, WORKSHOPS, AND SEMINARS; SALES CONVENTIONS; TRADE SHOWS

DIRECTORIES

Association Meeting and Event Planners Directory. Douglas Publications, Inc. • Annual. $650.00. Lists planners of meetings for over 8,000 national associations. Provides past and future convention locations, dates held, number of attendees, exhibit space required, and other convention information. Formerly *Association Meeting Planners.*

AudArena Stadium International Guide and Facility Buyers Guide. San Diego Technical Books, Inc. • 2002. $99.00. More than 4,500 arenas, auditoriums, stadiums, exhibit halls, and coliseums in U.S., Canada and in less depth, Europe and South America. Formerly *Audarena Stadium International Guide.*

Directory of Conventions Regional Editions. VNU Business Media. • Annual. $155.00 per volume. Four volumes. Set, $285.00. Over 14,000 meetings of North American national, regional, and state and local organizations.

The HCEA Directory of Healthcare Meetings and Conventions. Healthcare Convention Exhibitors Association. • Semiannual. Free to members; nonmembers, $245.00 per year. Lists more than 6,000 health care meetings, most of which have an exhibit program. Formerly *Handbook-A Directory of Health Care Meetings and Conventions.*

Trade Shows Worldwide: An International Directory of Events, Facilities and Suppliers. Gale Cengage Learning. • 2003. $355.00. 19th edition. Provides detailed information from over 75 countries on more than 10,800 trade shows and exhibitions. Separate sections are provided for trade shows/exhibitions, for sponsors/organizers, and for services, facilities, and information sources. Indexing is by date, location, subject, name, and keyword.

HANDBOOKS AND MANUALS

Sports, Convention, and Entertainment Facilities. David C. Petersen. Urban Land Institute. • 1996. $61.95. Provides advice and information on developing, financing, and operating amphitheaters, arenas, convention centers, and stadiums. Includes case studies of 70 projects.

INTERNET DATABASES

Trade Show Center. Global Sources/Trade Media Holdings Ltd. [Singapore]. Phone: (656)574-2800 E-mail: service@globalsources.com • URL: http://www.globalsources.com/TRADESHW/TRDSHFRM.HTM • Free Web site provides current, detailed information on more than 1,000 major trade shows worldwide, including events in the U.S., but with an emphasis on "Asia and Greater China." Searching is offered by product, supplier, country, and month of year. Includes links to "Trade Information.".

ONLINE DATABASES

Conference Papers Index. Cambridge Scientific Abstracts. • Citations to scientific and technical papers presented at meetings, 1973 to present. Inquire as to online cost and availability.

PERIODICALS AND NEWSLETTERS

Journal of Convention and Event Tourism. Haworth Press, Inc. • Quarterly. $165.00 per year. Formerly

Journal of Convention and Exhibition Management.

Scientific Meetings. Scientific Meetings Publications. • Quarterly. $85.00 per year. Provides information on forthcoming scientific, technical, medical, health, engineering and management meetings held throughout the world.

Successful Meetings: The Authority on Meetings and Incentive Travel Management. VNU Business Media. • Monthly. $79.00 per year.

World Meetings: United States and Canada. Gale Cengage Learning. • Three times a year. $195.00 per year.

TRADE/PROFESSIONAL ASSOCIATIONS

International Association for Exhibition Management. 8111 LBJ Fwy., Ste. 750, Dallas, TX 75251-1313. Phone: (972)458-8002 Fax: (972)458-8119 E-mail: iaem@iaem.org • URL: http://www.iaem.org • Formerly International Association of Exposition Management.

International Association of Convention and Visitor Bureaus. 2025 M St., N.W., Suite 500, Washington, DC 20036. Phone: (202)296-7888 Fax: (202)296-7889 E-mail: info@iacvb.org • URL: http://www.iacvb.org.

Meeting Professionals International. 3030 Lyndon B. Johnson Fwy., Ste. 1700, Dallas, TX 75234-2759. Phone: (972)702-3000 Fax: (972)702-3070 E-mail: feedback@mpiweb.org • URL: http://www.mpiweb.org • Meeting planners, full meeting consultants, and suppliers of goods and services. Works to: improve meeting method education; create an "open platform" for research and experimentation. Provides survey results, statistics, supply sources, and technical information; offers members assistance with specific problems; encourages information and idea exchange. Maintains professional code; standardizes terminology; monitors legislation affecting the industry. Maintains resource center. Conducts educational, charitable, and research programs.

Professional Convention Management Association. 2301 S Lake Shore Dr., Ste. 1001, Chicago, IL 60616-1419. Phone: 877-827-7262 or (312)423-7262 Fax: (312)423-7222 E-mail: president@pcma.org • URL: http://www.pcma.org • Represents the interests of meeting management executives from associations, non-profit organizations, corporations, independent meeting planning companies, and multi-management firms who recognize the importance of meetings to their organization. Provides education, research and advocacy to advance the meetings and hospitality industry. Empowers members with the tools they need to succeed as meeting professionals and to promote the value of the industry to their organizations and the general public.

Religious Conference Management Association. 7702 Woodland Dr., Ste. 120, Indianapolis, IN 46278. Phone: (317)632-1888 Fax: (317)632-7909 E-mail: rcma@rcmaweb.org • URL: http://www.rcmaweb.org • Represents persons responsible for planning and/or managing religious conventions, meetings, and assemblies; associate members are individuals who directly support the logistics of religious meetings. Promotes professional excellence through exchange of ideas, techniques, and methods of management.

CONVERTIBILITY OF CURRENCY

See: FOREIGN EXCHANGE

CONVERTIBLE SECURITIES

See also: SECURITIES

HANDBOOKS AND MANUALS

Convertible Securities: The Latest Instruments, Portfolio Strategies, and Valuation Analysis. John P. Calamos. McGraw-Hill. • 1998. $65.00. Second revised edition. (Irwin Library of Investment and Finance Series).

Handbook of Derivative Instruments: Investment Research, Analysis, and Portfolio Applications. Arsuo Konishi and Ravi Dattatreya, editors. McGraw-Hill. • 1996. $80.00. Second revised edition. Contains 41 chapters by various authors on all aspects of derivative securities, including such esoterica as "Inverse Floaters," "Positive Convexity," "Exotic Options," and "How to Use the Holes in Black-Scholes.".

Handbook of Equity Derivatives. Jack C. Francis and others, editors. John Wiley and Sons, Inc. • 1999. $105.00. Revised edition. Contains 27 chapters by various authors. Covers options (puts and calls), stock index futures, warrants, convertibles, over-the-counter options, swaps, legal issues, taxation, etc. (Financial Engineering Series).

International Handbook of Convertible Securities: A Global Guide to the Convertible Market. Thomas C. Noddings and others. Fitzroy Dearborn Publishers, Inc. • 2001. $75.00. Second edition. Includes new structures for convertible securities and advanced hedging strategies.

INTERNET DATABASES

Factiva. Dow Jones Reuters Business Interactive, LLC. Phone: 800-369-7466 or (609)452-1511 Fax: (609)520-5770 E-mail: solutions@factiva.com • URL: http://www.factiva.com • Fee-based Web site provides "global news and business information through Web sites and content integration solutions." Includes Dow Jones and Reuters newswires, The Wall Street Journal, and more than 7,000 other sources of current news, historical articles, market research reports, and investment analysis. Content includes 96 major U. S. newspapers, 900 non-English sources, trade publications, media transcripts, country profiles, news photos, etc.

Nexis.com. Lexis-Nexis Group. Phone: 800-227-4908 or (937)865-6800 Fax: (937)865-6909 E-mail: webmaster@prod.lexis-nexis.com • URL: http://www.nexis.com • Fee-based Web site offers searching of about 2.8 billion documents in some 30,000 news, business, and legal information sources. Features include a subject directory covering 1,200 topics in 34 categories and a Company Dossier containing information on more than 500,000 public and private companies. Boolean searching is offered.

U. S. Securities and Exchange Commission. Phone: 800-732-0330 or (202)942-7040 Fax: (202)942-9634 E-mail: webmaster@sec.gov • URL: http://www.sec.gov • SEC Web site offers free access through EDGAR to text of official corporate filings, such as annual reports (10-K), quarterly reports (10-Q), and proxies. (EDGAR is "Electronic Data Gathering, Analysis, and Retrieval System.") An example is given of how to obtain executive compensation data from proxies. Text of the daily *SEC News Digest* is offered, as are links to other government sites, non-government market regulators, and U. S. stock exchanges. Search facilities are extensive. Fees: Free.

Wall Street Journal Interactive Edition. Dow Jones & Co., Inc. Phone: 800-369-2834 or (212)416-2000 Fax: (212)416-2658 E-mail: inquiries@interactive.wsj.com • URL: http://www.wsj.com • Fee-based Web site providing online searching of worldwide information from the *The Wall Street Journal.* Includes "Company Snapshots," "The Journal's Greatest Hits," "Index to Market Data," "Journal

Links," etc. Financial price quotes are available. Fees: $49.00 per year; $29.00 per year to print subscribers.

ONLINE DATABASES

Disclosure SEC Database. Thomson Financial. • Provides online information from records filed with the Securities and Exchange Commission by more than 12,000 publicly-owned companies in the U.S. Includes about 200 financial data items and information relating to executives. Time span is 1977 to date, with weekly updates. Inquire as to online cost and availability.

EdgarPlus: SEC Basic Filings. Thomson Financial. • Online service provides full text of about 60,000 documents that have been filed with the U.S. Securities and Exchange Commission, 1987 to date, with daily updates. Filings include 6-K, 8-K, 10-K, 10-C, 10-Q, 20-F, and proxy statements. Inquire as to online cost and availability.

Value Line Convertible Data Base. Value Line Publishing, Inc. • Provides online data for about 600 convertible bonds and other convertible securities: price, yield, premium, issue size, liquidity, and maturity. Information is current, with weekly updates. Inquire as to online cost and availability.

PERIODICALS AND NEWSLETTERS

Bondweek: The Newsweekly of Fixed Income and Credit Markets. Institutional Investor, Inc., Journals Group. • Weekly. $2,425.00 per year. Newsletter. Includes print and online editions. Covers taxable, fixed-income securities for professional investors, including corporate, government, foreign, mortgage, and high-yield.

Private Placement Letter: The Weekly for Privately Placed Fixed-Income Securities. Thomson Media. • Weekly. $895.00 per year. Newsletter. Provides information on private financing of debt and convertible securities.

The Wall Street Journal. Dow Jones & Co., Inc. • Daily. $189.00 per year. Covers news and trends relating to business, industry, finance, the economy, and international commerce. Provides extensive price and other data for the securities, commodity, options, futures, foreign exchange, and money markets.

CONVEYING MACHINERY

See also: MACHINERY; MATERIALS HANDLING

DIRECTORIES

Modern Materials Handling Casebook Directory. Reed Business Information. • Annual. $25.00. Lists about 2,300 manufacturers of equipment and supplies in the materials handling industry. Supplement to *Modern Materials Handling.*

PERIODICALS AND NEWSLETTERS

CEMA Bulletin. Conveyor Equipment Manufacturers Association. • Description: Covers information about the conveyor equipment industry. Recurring features include reports of meetings and news of members.

Material Handling Management: Educating Industry on Product Handling, Flow Strategies, and Automation Technology. Penton Media, Inc. • 13 times a year. Free to qualified personnel; others, $50.00 per year. Formerly *Material Handling Engineering.*

Modern Materials Handling. Reed Business Information. • 14 times a year. $99.90 per year. For managers and engineers who buy or specify equipment used to move, store, control and protect products throughout the manufacturing and warehousing cycles. Includes *Casebook Directory* and *Planning Guide.* Also includes *ADC News and Solutions.*

On the Mhove. Material Handling Industry of America. • Quarterly. Free. Formerly *MHI News.*

PHL Bulletin (Packaging, Handling, Logistics). National Institute of Packaging, Handling, and Logistics Engineers. • Monthly. $50.00 per year.

TRADE/PROFESSIONAL ASSOCIATIONS

Association of Professional Material Handling Consultants. 8720 Red Oak Blvd., Suite 201, Charlotte, NC 28217-3992. Phone: (704)676-1184 or (704)676-1190 Fax: (704)676-1199 E-mail: bcurtis@mhia.org • URL: http://www.mhia.org/apmhc.

Conveyor Equipment Manufacturers Association. 6724 Lone Oak Blvd., Naples, FL 34109. Phone: (239)514-3441 Fax: (239)514-3470 E-mail: cema@cemanet.org • URL: http://www.cemanet.org • Manufacturers and engineers of conveyors and conveying systems, and portable and stationary machinery used in the transportation of raw materials and finished products in warehouses and on assembly line operations. Aims to standardize design, manufacture, and application of conveying machinery and component parts.

Material Handling Equipment Distributors Association. 201 U.S. Hwy. 45, Vernon Hills, IL 60061-2398. Phone: (847)680-3500 Fax: (847)362-6989 E-mail: connect@mheda.org • URL: http://www.mheda.org • Distributors and manufacturers of material handling equipment. Aims to improve the proficiency of independent material handling distributors.

Material Handling Industry of America. 8720 Red Oak Blvd., Suite 201, Charlotte, NC 28217. Phone: 800-345-1815 or (704)676-1190 Fax: (704)676-1199 E-mail: jnofsinger@mhia.org • URL: http://www.mhia.org • Formerly Material Handling Industry.

COOKIE INDUSTRY

See: BAKING INDUSTRY; SNACK FOOD INDUSTRY

COOKING UTENSILS

See: HOUSEWARES INDUSTRY

COOKWARE

See: HOUSEWARES INDUSTRY

COOPERAGE INDUSTRY

See also: CONTAINER INDUSTRY

DIRECTORIES

Association of Container Reconditioners-Membership and Industrial Supply Directory. Association of Container Reconditioners. • Annual. $30.00. Lists approximately 215 container reconditioners and dealers, worldwide. Also lists suppliers of machinery and accessories.

TRADE/PROFESSIONAL ASSOCIATIONS

Associated Cooperage Industries of America. 2100 Gardiner Lane, Suite 100-E, Louisville, KY 40205-2947. Phone: (502)459-6113 Fax: (502)459-6114 E-mail: aciainc@acia.net • URL: http://www.acia.net.

COOPERATIVE ADVERTISING

ABSTRACTS AND INDEXES

Business Periodicals Index. H. W. Wilson Co. • 11 times a year. Quarterly and annual cumulations. Price varies.

DIRECTORIES

Business Organizations, Agencies, and Publications Directory. Gale Cengage Learning. • 2003. $480.00.

15th edition. Over 40,000 entries describing 39 types of business information sources. Classified by type of organization, publication, or serviceIncludes state, national, and international agencies and organizations. Master index to names and keywords. Also includes e-mail addresses and web site URL's.

Co-op Advertising Programs Sourcebook. National Register Publishing Co. • Covers: More than 4,000 cooperative advertising programs offered by manufacturers. Entries include: Manufacturer name, address, phone; name, phone, fax of contact; products, trade names, regional variations, international availability, mechanical requirements, participation percentage, eligible media, ad specifications, reimbursement method, claim documentation, claim address.

Radio Co-op Directory. Radio Advertising Bureau. • Database covers: Over 5,000 manufacturers that provide cooperative allowances for radio advertising. Database includes: Company name, address, name of contact, phone, fax, allowance, accrual rate, whether plan is administered by distributor, expiration dates.

ONLINE DATABASES

Marketing and Advertising Reference Service (MARS). Gale Cengage Learning. • Provides abstracts of literature relating to consumer marketing and advertising, including all forms of advertising media. Time period is 1984 to date. Daily updates. Inquire as to online cost and availability.

Wilson Business Abstracts Online. H. W. Wilson Co. • Indexes and abstracts 600 major business periodicals, plus the *Wall Street Journal* and the business section of the *New York Times.* Indexing is from 1982, abstracting from 1990, with the two newspapers included from 1993. Updated weekly. Inquire as to online cost and availability. (*Business Periodicals Index* without abstracts is also available online.).

STATISTICS SOURCES

Radio Facts: The Voice of Urban Culture. RadioMan Publishing Inc. • Annual. $50.00.

TRADE/PROFESSIONAL ASSOCIATIONS

Newsletter and Electronic Publishers Association. 1501 Wilson Blvd., Suite 509, Arlington, VA 22209-2403. Phone: 800-356-9302 or (703)527-2333 Fax: (703)841-0629 E-mail: nepa@newsletter.org • URL: http://www.newsletter.org • Formerly Newsletter Publishers Association.

Radio Advertising Bureau. 1320 Greenway Dr., Ste. 500, 261 Madison Ave., 23rd Fl., Irving, TX 75038-2587. Phone: 800-232-3131 or (212)681-7214 Fax: (212)681-7217 E-mail: jhaley@rab.com • URL: http://www.rab.com • Includes radio stations, radio networks, station sales representatives, and allied industry services, such as producers, research firms, schools, and consultants. Calls on advertisers and agencies to promote the sale of radio time as an advertising medium. Sponsors program to increase professionalism of radio salespeople, awarding Certified Radio Marketing Consultant designation to those who pass examination. Sponsors regional marketing conferences. Conducts extensive research program into all phases of radio sales. Issues reports on use of radio by national, regional, and local advertisers. Speaks before conventions and groups to explain benefits of radio advertising. Sponsors Radio Creative Fund. Compiles statistics.

COOPERATIVE AGRICULTURE

See: COOPERATIVES

COOPERATIVE HOUSING

See: CONDOMINIUMS; COOPERATIVES

COOPERATIVE MOVEMENT

See: COOPERATIVES

COOPERATIVES

DIRECTORIES
Directory of Wholesale Grocers. Chain Store Guide. • Annual. $327.00. Online edition, $747.00. Profiles over 1,100 cooperatives, voluntaries, non-sponsoring wholesalers, cash and carry warehouses, and nearly 220 service merchandisers. Covers United States and Canada.

HANDBOOKS AND MANUALS
How to Buy a House, Condo, or Co-op. Jean C. Thomsett. Consumers Union of the United States, Inc. • 1996. $84.75. Fifth edition.

Your Dream Home: A Comprehensive Guide to Buying a House, Condo, or Co-op. Marguerite Smith. Warner Books, Inc. • 1997. $10.99. (Money, America's Financial Advisor Series).

PERIODICALS AND NEWSLETTERS
CHF Newsbriefs. Cooperative Housing Foundation. • Description: Seeks to "help families throughout the world by focusing on the development of communities, habitat, and finance.".

Communities: Journal of Cooperative Living. Fellowship for Intentional Communities. • Monthly. $20.00 per year.

Cooperative Housing Bulletin. National Association of Housing Cooperatives. • Bimonthly. $75.00 per year. Includes *Cooperative Housing Journal.*

Rural Cooperatives. Available from U. S. Government Printing Office. • Bimonthly. $21.00 per year. Issued by the U. S. Department of Agriculture. Contains articles on cooperatives in rural America. Formerly *Farmer Cooperatives.*

TRADE/PROFESSIONAL ASSOCIATIONS
International Co-operative Alliance-Switzerland. 15, route des Morillons, CH-1218 Grand-Saconnex, Switzerland. Phone: 41 22 9298888 Fax: 41 22 7984122 E-mail: ica@coop.org • URL: http://www.ica.coop/ica.

National Cooperative Business Association. 1401 New York Ave. NW, Ste. 1100, Washington, DC 20005. Phone: (202)638-6222 Fax: (202)638-1374 E-mail: ncba@ncba.coop • URL: http://www.ncba.coop • Local, state, regional, and national cooperative business organizations including farm supply, agricultural marketing, insurance, banking, housing, health care, consumer goods and services, student, worker, fishery, and other cooperatives. Represents, strengthens, and expands cooperative businesses. Programs include: supporting the development of cooperative businesses in the U.S.; developing and providing technical assistance to cooperatives in developing nations; representing American cooperatives in Washington, DC and abroad; promoting and developing commercial relations among the world's cooperatives. Operates Cooperative Action for +Congressional Trust. Supports the Cooperative +Hall of Fame, and the Cooperative Development Foundation. Maintains hall of fame.

Universal Cooperatives. 1300 Corporate Center Curve, Eagan, MN 55121. Phone: (651)239-1000 Fax: (651)239-1080 E-mail: info@ucoop.com • URL: http://www.ucoop.com • Works as a federation of regional agricultural cooperative associations. Engages in buying, manufacturing, importing and distributing activities. Focuses on tires, batteries, and accessories; twine; farm supplies; lubricants; animal health products; agricultural chemicals.

OTHER SOURCES
Real Estate Transactions: Cooperative Housing Law and Practice-Forms. Patrick J. Rohan and Melvin A. Reskin. LexisNexis Matthew Bender. • Semiannual. $999.00 per year. Six looseleaf volumes. Covers every aspect of the creation, financing, operation, sale and tax consequences of cooperatives. (Real Estate Transaction Series).

COPIERS

See: COPYING MACHINE INDUSTRY

COPPER INDUSTRY

See also: METAL INDUSTRY; MINES AND MINERAL RESOURCES

ABSTRACTS AND INDEXES
IMM Abstracts and Index: A Survey of World Literature on the Economic Geology and Mining of All Minerals (Except Coal), Mineral Processing, and Nonferrous Extraction Metallurgy. Institution of Mining and Metallurgy. • Bimonthly. $500.00 per year. Provides international coverage of the literature of mining and nonferrous metallurgy. Includes mineral economics, tunnelling, and rock mechanics.

ALMANACS AND YEARBOOKS
CRB Commodity Yearbook. Commodity Research Bureau. CRB. • Annual. $99.95.

CD-ROM DATABASES
METADEX Materials Collection: Metals-Polymers-Ceramics. Cambridge Scientific Abstracts. • Quarterly. Provides CD-ROM citations to the worldwide literature of materials science and metallurgy. Corresponds to *Metals Abstracts, Alloys Index, Steels Alert, Nonferrous Alert, Polymers/Ceramics/Composites Alert,* and *Engineered Materials Abstracts.* (Formerly produced by ASM International.).

ONLINE DATABASES
Materials Business File. Cambridge Scientific Abstracts. • Provides online abstracts and citations to worldwide materials literature, covering the business and industrial aspects of metals, plastics, ceramics, and composites. Corresponds to *Steels Alert, Nonferrous Metals Alert,* and *Polymers/Ceramics/Composites Alert.* Time period is 1985 to date, with monthly updates. (Formerly produced by ASM International.) Inquire as to online cost and availability.

METADEX. Cambridge Scientific Abstracts. • Covers the worldwide literature of metals, metallurgy, and materials science, 1966 to date. Includes detailed alloys indexing from 1974. Biweekly updating. Inquire as to online cost and availability. (Formerly produced by ASM International.).

PERIODICALS AND NEWSLETTERS
Barron's: The Dow Jones Business and Financial Weekly. • Weekly. $145.00 per year.

Oil Daily: Daily Newspaper of the Petroleum Industry. Energy Intelligence Group, Inc. • Daily. Email, $1,595.00 per year; fax, $2,395.00 per year, online, $1,495.00 per year. Newspaper for the petroleum industry.

33 Metalproducing: For Primary Producers of Steel, Aluminum, and Copper-Base Alloys. Penton Media, Inc. • Monthly. $65.00 per year. Covers metal production technology and methods and industry news. Includes a bimonthly *Nonferrous Supplement.*

PRICE SOURCES
Chemical and Engineering News: The Newsmagazine of the Chemical World. American Chemical Society. • Weekly. Institutions, $210.00 per year.

The New York Times. New York Times Co. • Daily. $374.40 per year. Supplements available: *New York* *Times Book Review, New York Times Magazine, Sophisticated Traveler* and *Fashions of the Times.*

Platt's Metals Week. Platt's. • Weekly. $770.00 per year.

STATISTICS SOURCES
Annual Survey of Manufactures. Available from U. S. Government Printing Office. • Annual. Prices vary. Issued by the U. S. Census Bureau as an interim update to the *Census of Manufactures.* Includes data on number of manufacturing establishments in various industries, employment, labor costs, value of shipments, capital expenditures, inventories, energy costs, and assets. (See also Census Bureau home page, http://www.census.gov/.).

Mineral Commodity Summaries. Available from U. S. Government Printing Office. • Annual. $26.00. Published by the U. S. Geological Survey, Department of the Interior (http://www.usgs.gov). Contains detailed, five-year data for about 90 nonfuel minerals. Covers a wide range of statistics, including production, imports, exports, consumption, reserves, prices, tariff information, and industry employment. (Two pages are devoted to each mineral.).

Minerals Yearbook. Available from U.S. Government Printing Office. • Annual. Three volumes.

Non-Ferrous Metal Data Yearbook. American Bureau of Metal Statistics. • Annual. $405.00. Provides worldwide data on approximately about 200 statistical tables covering many nonferrous metals. Includes production, consumption, inventories, exports, imports, and other data.

Standard & Poor's Industry Surveys. Standard & Poor's. • Semiannual. $1,800.00. Two looseleaf volumes. Includes monthly *Supplements.* Provides detailed, individual surveys of 52 major industry groups. Each survey is revised on a semiannual basis. Also includes "Monthly Investment Review" (industry group investment analysis) and monthly "Trends & Projections" (economic analysis).

U. S. Industry and Trade Outlook. Available from National Technical Information Service. • Annual. $69.95. Produced by the International Trade Administration, U. S. Department of Commerce, in a "public-private" partnership with DRI/McGraw-Hill and Standard & Poor's. Provides basic data, outlook for the current year, and "Long-Term Prospects" (five-year projections) for a wide variety of products and services. Includes high technology industries. Formerly *U. S. Industrial Outlook.*

United States Census of Mineral Industries. Bureau of the Census, U.S. Department of Commerce. Available from U.S. Government Printing Office. • Quinquennial.

WEFA Industrial Monitor. John Wiley and Sons, Inc. • Annual. $65.00. Prepared by industry analysts at WEFA, an economic forecasting and consulting firm (originally Wharton Econometric Forecasting Associates). Contains discussions of the outlook for major U. S. industries, with many 10-year forecasts (WEFA Web site is http://www.wefa.com).

TRADE/PROFESSIONAL ASSOCIATIONS
American Bureau of Metal Statistics. P.O. Box 805, Chatham, NJ 07928. Phone: (973)701-2299 Fax: (973)701-2152 E-mail: info@abms.com • URL: http://www.abms.com • Members are metal companies. Compiles and publishes detailed statistical data on a wide variety of nonferrous metals: aluminum, copper, gold, lead, nickel, platinum, silver, tin, titanium, uranium, zinc, and others.

Copper and Brass Fabricators Council. 1050 17th St., N.W., Suite 440, Washington, DC 20036. Phone: (202)833-8575 Fax: (202)331-8267 E-mail: copbrass@aol.com • Formerly Copper and Brass Fabricators Foreign Trade Association.

Copper and Brass Servicenter Association. 994 Old

Eagle School Rd., Suite 1019, Wayne, PA 19087-1802. Phone: (610)971-4850 Fax: (610)971-4859 E-mail: ifo@cbsa.copper-brass.org • URL: http://www.cbsa.copper-brass.org.

Copper Development Association. 260 Madison Ave., New York, NY 10016. Phone: 800-CDA-DATA or (212)251-7200 Fax: (212)251-7234 E-mail: questions@cda.copper.org • URL: http://www.copper.org • Represents U.S. and foreign copper mining, smelting and refining companies, U.S. fabricating companies such as brass and wire mills, foundries, and ingot makers. Seeks to expand the uses and applications and to broaden the markets of copper and copper products. Functions in groups or divisions corresponding to principal market areas such as transportation, building construction, electrical and electronic products, industrial machinery and equipment, and consumer and general products. Provides technical service to users of copper and copper alloy products. Has industrywide responsibility for market statistics and research. Maintains 10 field offices in the U.S.

International Copper Association. 260 Madison Ave., 16th Fl., New York, NY 10016-2401. Phone: (212)251-7240 Fax: (212)251-7245 E-mail: info@copperinfo.com • URL: http://www.copperinfo.com • Copper producing and fabricating companies. Conducts market development and research on uses for copper through contracts with commercial, institutional, and university organizations.

Non-Ferrous Metals Producers Committee. 2030 M St. NW, Ste. 800, 2030 M St. NW, Ste. 800, 2030 M. St., N.W., Suite 800, Washington, DC 20036. Phone: (202)466-7720 Fax: (202)466-2710 E-mail: nffstaff@nffs.org • URL: http://www.arcat.com/arcatcos/cos37/arc37679.cfm • Represents domestic copper, lead, and zinc producers. Promotes the interests of copper, lead, and zinc mining and metal industries in the U.S. with emphasis on tariffs, laws, regulations, and government policies affecting international trade and foreign imports.

COPYING MACHINE INDUSTRY

DIRECTORIES

Better Buys for Business: The Independent Consumer Guide to Office Equipment. What to Buy for Business, Inc. • 10 times a year. $134.00 per year. Each issue is on a particular office product, with detailed evaluation of specific models: 1. Low-Volume Copier Guide, 2. Mid-Volume Copier Guide, 3. High-Volume Copier Guide, 4. Plain Paper Fax and Low-Volume Multifunctional Guide, 5. Mid/High-Volume Multifunctional Guide, 6. Laser Printer Guide, 7. Color Printer and Color Copier Guide, 8. Scan-to-File Guide, 9. Business Phone Systems Guide, 10. Postage Meter Guide, with a Short Guide to Shredders.

HANDBOOKS AND MANUALS

Guide to Energy Efficient Office Equipment. Loretta A. Smith and others. American Council for an Energy Efficient Economy. • 1996. $12.00. Second edition. Provides information on selecting, purchasing, and using energy-saving computers, monitors, printers, copiers, and other office devices.

PERIODICALS AND NEWSLETTERS

Digital Information Network. Buyers Laboratory, Inc. • Monthly. $725.00 per year. Newsletter. Information on the copier industry, including test reports on individual machines. Formerly *Digital Information Network.*

TRADE/PROFESSIONAL ASSOCIATIONS

International Reprographic Association. 401 N Michigan Ave., Chicago, IL 60611-4255. Phone: 800-833-4742 or (312)245-1026 Fax: (312)527-6724 E-mail: sbova@irga.com • URL: http://www.irga.com • Commercial blue print and photocopy firms, engineering supply stores, and materials and equipment suppliers. Conducts annual photo-tech, marketing, management, and business planning seminars.

COPYRIGHT

GENERAL WORKS

Copyright: Current Issues and Laws. John V. Martin, editor. Nova Science Publishers, Inc. • 2002. $59.00. Contains articles by various authors on many aspects of copyright, such as copyright term extension, public domain, fair use, infringement, Internet issues, and online music delivery.

Copyright, Patent, Trademark and Related State Doctrines; Cases and Materials on the Law of Intellectual Property. Paul Goldstein. Foundation Press, Inc. • 2002. $80.50. Fifth edition. (University Casebook Series).

ABSTRACTS AND INDEXES

Current Law Index: Multiple Access to Legal Periodicals. Gale Cengage Learning. • Monthly. $725.00 per year. Produced in cooperation with the American Association of Law Libraries. Indexes more than 900 law journals, legal newspapers, and specialty publications from the U.S., Canada, U.K., Ireland, Australia, and New Zealand.

Library Literature and Information Science Index. H. W. Wilson Co. • Quarterly. Annual cumulation. Price varies.

ALMANACS AND YEARBOOKS

Intellectual Property Law Review. West Group. • 1999. $299.00. Patent, trademark, and copyright practices.

CD-ROM DATABASES

Authority Intellectual Property Library. LexisNexis/Matthew Bender. • Quarterly. Price on request. CD-ROM contains updated full text of *Intellectual Property Counseling and Litigation, Computer Law, International Computer Law, Nimmer on Copyright, Milgrim on Trade Secrets, Patent Litigation, Patent Licensing Transactions, Trademark Protection and Practice*, and other Matthew Bender publications relating to the law of intellectual property.

WILSONDISC: Library Literature and Information Science Index. H. W. Wilson Co. • Quarterly. Includes unlimited access to the online version of *Library Literature.* Provides CD-ROM indexing of about 300 periodicals, covering a wide range of topics having to do with libraries, library management, and the information industry.

DIRECTORIES

Directory of Intellectual Property Attorneys, 1995. Aspen Publishers, Inc. • 1994. $195.00.

ENCYCLOPEDIAS AND DICTIONARIES

McCarthy's Desk Encyclopedia of Intellectual Property. J. Thomas McCarthy. BNA, Inc. • 1995. $75.00.Second edition. Defines legal terms relating to patents, trademarks, copyrights, trade secrets, entertainment, and the computer industry.

HANDBOOKS AND MANUALS

Clearance and Copyright: Everything the Independent Filmmaker Needs to Know. Michael C. Donaldson. Silman-James Press. • 1996. $26.95. Covers film rights problems in pre-production, production, post-production, and final release. Includes sample contracts and forms.

Columbia Guide to Digital Publishing: In Print and On the Web. William E. Kasdorf, editor. Columbia University Press. • 2002. $65.00. Covers the practical production of both written and graphic material in digital format, including archives, new technology, "information architecture," and copyright.

Complete Copyright: An Everyday Guide for Librarians. Carrie Russell. American Library Association. • 2004. $50.00. Covers the fundamentals of U. S. copyright law, including the Digital Millennium Copyright Act (DMCA, 1998) and the Technology, Education, and Copyright Harmonization Act (the TEACH Act, 2002). The author is copyright specialist for the ALA Office for Information Technology Policy.

The Copyright Book: A Practical Guide. William S. Strong. MIT Press. • 1999. $34.95. Fifth edition.

Copyright Essentials for Librarians and Educators. Kenneth D. Crews. American Library Association. • 2000. $45.00. Explains the basics of modern copyright law. Includes checklists and summaries of legislation.

Copyright Handbook: How to Protect and Use Written Works. Stephen Fishman. Nolo Press-Occidental. • 2002. Sixth edition. Price on application. Includes sample forms and copyright agreements.

Copyright Law '99 and Beyond Handbook. Glasser LegalWorks. • 1999. $95.00. Examines current trends in copyright litigation. Based on a 1999 seminar held in cooperation with the U. S. Copyright Office.

Copyright Law of the United States of America. Available from U. S. Government Printing Office. • Annual. Issued by U. S. Copyright Office, Library of Congress. Provides the text of copyright law contained in Title 17 of the U. S. Code.

Copyright Primer for Librarians and Educators. Janis H. Bruwelheide. American Library Association. • 1995. $25.00. Second edition.

Copyright Principles, Law, and Practice. Paul Goldstein. Aspen Publishers, Inc. • 1989. $375.00. Three volumes.

Copyrights, Patents, and Trademarks: Protect Your Rights Worldwide. Hoyt L. Barber. McGraw-Hill. • 1996. $32.95. Second edition.

Coyle's Information Highway Handbook: A Practical File on the New Information Order. Karen Coyle. American Library Association. • 1997. $30.00. Provides useful "essays on copyright, access, privacy, censorship, and the information marketplace.".

The Fair Use Privilege in Copyright Law. William F. Patry. BNA, Inc. • 1995. $115.00. Second edition. A comprehensive analysis of fair use.

Handbook of Digital Publishing. Michael L. Kleper. Prentice Hall PTR. • 2001. $129.99. Two volumes. Edited for the digital publishing industry. Covers print publishing, electronic documents, and Internet (Web) publishing, including basic desktop procedures. Provides information on typography, design, layout, image creation, and page creation.

Intellectual Property Infringement Damages: A Litigation Support Handbook 2003 Cumulative Supplement. Russell L. Parr. John Wiley and Sons, Inc. • 2003. $78.00. Second edition. Describes how to calculate damages for patent, trademark, and copyright infringement. (Intellectual Property-General, Law, Accounting and Finance, Management, Licensing and Special Topics Series).

Intellectual Property Primary Law Soucebook. LexisNexis Matthew Bender. • Annual. $88.00. Provides federal copyright, patent, and trademark statutes and regulations.

Librarian's Guide to Intellectual Property in the Digital Age: Copyrights, Patents, and Trademarks. Timothy L. Wherry. American Library Association. • 2002. $38.00. Includes lists of patent and trademark depositories, relevant Web sites, and questions & answers.

Libraries and Copyright: A Guide to Copyright Law in the Nineties. Laura N. Gasaway and Sarah K. Wiant. Special Libraries Association. • 1994. $59.00. Provides practical explanations of copyright law.

Includes an extensive bibliography.

Nimmer on Copyright. David Nimmer. LexisNexis Matthew Bender. • $1,369.00. 10 looseleaf volumes. Periodic supplementation. Analytical and practical guide on the law of literary, musical, and artistic proprerty.

Patent, Copyright, and Trademark: An Intellectual Property Desk Reference. Stephen Elias. Nolo. • 2003. $39.99. Sixth revised edition. Contains practical explanations of the legalities of patents, copyrights, trademarks, and trade secrets. Includes examples of relevant legal forms. A 1985 version was called *Nolo's Intellectual Property Law Dictionary.* (Nolo Press Self-Help Law Series).

Patent, Trademark, and Copyright Laws, 2003. Jeffrey Samuels, editor. BNA, Inc. • 2003. $115.00. Contains text of "all pertinent intellectual property legislation to date.".

Protecting Trade Secrets, Patents, Copyrights, and Trademarks. Robert C. Dorr and Christopher H. Munch. Aspen Publishers, Inc. • $165.00. Looseleaf service.

INTERNET DATABASES

Lexis.com Research System. Lexis-Nexis Group. Phone: 800-227-4908 or (937)865-6800 Fax: (937)865-6909 E-mail: webmaster@prod.lexis-nexis.com • URL: http://www.lexis.com • Fee-based Web site offers extensive searching of a wide variety of legal sources. Additional features include Daily Opinion Service, lexis.com Bookstore, Career Center, CLE Center, Law Schools, and Practice Pages ("Pages specific to areas of specialty").

ONLINE DATABASES

LEXIS. LEXIS-NEXIS. • The various LEXIS databases provide full text and indexing for a wide variety of legal cases, statutes, orders, and opinions.

U. S. Copyrights. Available from DIALOG. • Provides access to registration details for all active copyright registrations on file at the U. S. Copyright Office since 1978. Contains information on initial registration, renewal, assignments, and ownership status. Weekly updates. Inquire as to online cost and availability.

PERIODICALS AND NEWSLETTERS

BNA's Patent, Trademark and Copyright Journal. BNA, Inc. • Weekly. $1,495.00 per year. Looseleaf service.

Copyright Bulletin: Quarterly Review. Available from Bernan Associates. • Quarterly. Available online only.

Copyright Society of the United States of America Journal. The Copyright Society of the United States of America. • Quarterly. Individuals, $125.00 per year; nonprofit organizations, $50.00 per year; corporations, $500.00 per year.

Information Outlook: The Monthly Magazine of the Special Libraries Association. Special Libraries Association. • Monthly. $65.00 per year. Topics include information technology, the Internet, copyright, research techniques, library management, and professional development. Replaces *Special Libraries* and *SpeciaList.*

Intellectual Property Today. • Monthly. $96.00 per year. Covers legal developments in copyright, patents, trademarks, and licensing. Emphasizes the effect of new technology on intellectual property. Formerly *Law Works.*

RESEARCH CENTERS AND INSTITUTES

PTC Research Foundation. 24 Warren St., Concord, NH 03301. Phone: (603)228-4530 Fax: (603)228-4730 E-mail: anharr@cybertours.com • URL: http://www.ptcforum.org.

TRADE/PROFESSIONAL ASSOCIATIONS

Copyright Clearance Center. 222 Rosewood Dr., Danvers, MA 01923. Phone: (978)750-8400 Fax:

(978)646-8600 E-mail: info@copyright.com • URL: http://www.copyright.com • Facilitates compliance with U.S. copyright law. Provides licensing systems for the reproduction and distribution of copyrighted materials in print and electronic formats throughout the world. Manages rights relating to over 1.75 million works and represents more than 9600 publishers and hundreds of thousands of authors and other creators, directly or through their representatives.

The Copyright Society of the U.S.A. 352 Seventh Ave., Ste. 307, New York, NY 10001. Phone: (212)354-6401 E-mail: bpannone@csusa.org • URL: http://www.csusa.org.

OTHER SOURCES

Catalog of Copyright Entries. U.S. Library of Congress, Copyright Office. Available from U.S. Government Printing Office. • Frequency and prices vary.

Copyright Law in Business and Practice. John W. Hazard. West Group. • Semiannual. $274.00 per year. Two looseleaf volumes.

Copyright Law Reports. CCH, Inc. • Monthly. $768.00 per year. Two looseleaf volumes.

Cyberlaw: Intellectual Property in the Digital Millennium. American Lawyer Media, Inc. • Looseleaf. $159.00. Updated as needed. A basic guide to copyright as applied to the Internet and other electronic sources. (Law Journal Press).

Intellectual Property and Antitrust Law. William C. Holmes. West Group. • Semiannual. $389.00 per year. Two looseleaf volumes. Includes patent, trademark, and copyright practices.

Lindey on Entertainment, Publishing and the Arts: Agreements and the Law. Alexander Lindey, editor. West Group. • $935.00 per year. Six looseleaf volumes. Periodic supplementation. Provides basic forms, applicable law, and guidance.

COPYWRITING

See: ADVERTISING COPY

CORDAGE INDUSTRY

See: ROPE AND TWINE INDUSTRY

CORN INDUSTRY

See also: FEED AND FEEDSTUFFS INDUSTRY

GENERAL WORKS

Corn: Origin, History, Technology, and Production. C. Wayne Smith and others, editors. John Wiley and Sons, Inc. • 2002. $250.00. (Crop Science Series.).

ABSTRACTS AND INDEXES

Field Crop Abstracts: Monthly Abstract Journal on World Annual Cereal, Legume, Root, Oilseed and Fibre Crops. Available from CABI Publishing North America. • Monthly. Institutions, $1,775.00 per year. Online edition available, $1,820.00 per year. Published in England by CABI Publishing, formerly Commonwealth Agricultural Bureaux. Provides worldwide coverage of the literature.

Maize Abstracts. Available from CABI Publishing, North America. • Bimonthly. $840.00 per year. Published in England by CABI Publishing. Provides worldwide coverage of the literature.

ALMANACS AND YEARBOOKS

Agricultural and Mineral Commodities Year Book. Available from Taylor & Francis Group. • Annual. $225.00. Published by Europa Publications. Contains descriptive product profiles, price data, export-import data, and production statistics for

major commodities of the world. Includes commodity histories, uses, markets, demand trends, and information about trade agreements and key commodity organizations.

Corn Annual. Corn Refiners Association, Inc. • Annual. Single copies free.

CRB Commodity Yearbook. Commodity Research Bureau. CRB. • Annual. $99.95.

CD-ROM DATABASES

Food Science and Technology Abstracts [CD-ROM]. Available from SilverPlatter Information, Inc. • Quarterly. Produced by International Food Information Service (home page is http://www.ifis.org). Provides worldwide coverage on CD-ROM of the literature of food technology and production. Various types of publications are indexed, with abstracts, including about 1,800 periodicals. Time period is 1969 to date.

OECD Statistical Compendium. Organization for Economic Cooperation and Development. • Semiannual. $1,905.00 per year for 1 to 10 users. CD-ROM contains more than 730,000 monthly, quarterly, and annual time series for OECD countries, 1960 to date. Includes fully searchable data on agriculture, food, economic indicators, national accounts, employment, energy, finance, industry, technology, and foreign trade. Results can be displayed in various forms.

DIRECTORIES

American Vegetable Grower--Source Book. Meister Media Worldwide. • Publication includes: Lists of suppliers of agricultural chemicals and manufacturers and suppliers of other agricultural products, equipment, and services including packaging equipment, transportation services, direct marketing suppliers, plants and seeds, etc. Entries include: Company name, address, phone, fax, e-mail.

Major Food and Drink Companies of the World. Available from Gale Cengage Learning. • Annual. $880.00. Two volumes. Published by Graham & Whiteside. Contains profiles and trade names for more than 9,800 important food and beverage companies in various countries. In addition to foods, includes both alcoholic and nonalcoholic drink products.

Thomas Food and Beverage Market Place. Grey House Publishing. • 2004. $495.00. Three volumes. Contains more than 40,000 entries covering food companies, beverages, food equipment, warehouse companies, food brokers, wholesalers, importers, and exporters. Formerly *Thomas Food Industry Register.*

INTERNET DATABASES

Business 2.0 Web Guide to the Best Business Links. Business 2.0 Media Inc. Phone: (415)293-4800 E-mail: support@business2.com • URL: http://www.business2.com/webguide • Web site presents an extensive, searchable directory of links to "the best, most informative, and authoritative web pages." Twenty main categories cover business, finance, career, company information, people, and technology topics, with thousands of subtopics, all linking to Web sites recommended by experienced business researchers. Fees: Free.

Fedstats. Federal Interagency Council on Statistical Policy. Phone: (202)395-7254 • URL: http://www.fedstats.gov • Web site features an efficient search facility for full-text statistics produced by more than 100 federal agencies, including the Census Bureau, the Bureau of Economic Analysis, and the Bureau of Labor Statistics. Boolean searches can be made within one agency or for all agencies combined. Links are offered to international statistical bureaus, including the UN, IMF, OECD, UNESCO, Eurostat, and 20 individual countries. Fees: Free.

FreeLunch.com. Economy.com, Inc. Phone: (610)696-8700 Fax: (610)696-1678 • URL: http://

www.freelunch.com • Web site provides free access to more than 1.5 million economic and financial data series, covering industry, demographics, labor markets, prices, retail sales, government spending, trade, interest rates, housing starts, the stock market, and many other topics. Data is available for various time periods in either chart or table form. Searching is offered. Fees: Free, but registration required. Economy.com, Inc. also offers fee-based economic analysis at *The Dismal Scientist* site (http://www.dismal.com).

USDA. United States Department of Agriculture. Phone: (202)720-2791 E-mail: agsec@usda.gov • URL: http://www.usda.gov • The USDA home page has six sections: News and Information; What's New; About USDA; Agencies; Opportunities; Search and Help. Keyword searching is offered from the USDA home page and from various individual agency home pages. Agencies are the Economic Research Service, Agricultural Marketing Service, National Agricultural Statistics Service, National Agricultural Library, and about 12 others. Updating varies. Fees: Free.

ONLINE DATABASES

CAB Abstracts. CAB Publishing North America. • Contains 46 specialized abstract collections covering over 10,000 journals and monographs in the areas of agriculture, horticulture, forest products, farm products, nutrition, dairy science, poultry, grains, animal health, entomology, etc. Time period is 1972 to date, with monthly updates. Inquire as to online cost and availability. *CAB Abstracts on CD-ROM* also available, with annual updating.

Food Science and Technology Abstracts [online]. IFIS North American Desk. • Produced by International Food Information Service. Provides about 500,000 online citations, with abstracts, to the international literature of food science, technology, commodities, engineering, and processing. Approximately 2,000 periodicals are covered. Time period is 1969 to date, with monthly updates. Inquire as to online cost and availability.

PERIODICALS AND NEWSLETTERS

Barron's: The Dow Jones Business and Financial Weekly. • Weekly. $145.00 per year.

PRICE SOURCES

Agricultural Letter. Federal Reserve Bank of Chicago. • Quarterly. Free. Looseleaf service.

The New York Times. New York Times Co. • Daily. $374.40 per year. Supplements available: *New York Times Book Review, New York Times Magazine, Sophisticated Traveler* and *Fashions of the Times.*

RESEARCH CENTERS AND INSTITUTES

Agricultural Experiment Station. New Mexico State University. P.O. Box 30003, MSC 3BF, Las Cruces, NM 88003-8003. Phone: (505)646-3125 Fax: (505)646-2816 E-mail: milgonza@nmsu.edu • URL: http://www.cahe.nmsu.edu/aes.

Agricultural Research Division. University of Nebraska - Lincoln. 207 Agricultural Hall, Lincoln, NE 68583-0704. Phone: (402)472-2045 Fax: (402)472-9071 E-mail: dnelson1@unl.edu.

California Agricultural Experiment Station. University of California. 1111 Franklin St., 6th Fl., Oakland, CA 94607-5200. Phone: (510)987-0060 Fax: (510)451-2317 E-mail: wr.gomes@ucop.edu • URL: http://www.ucanr.org/aes.

New York State Agricultural Experiment Station. Cornell University. 630 W. North St., Geneva, NY 14456. Phone: (315)787-2211 Fax: (315)787-2276 E-mail: jeh3@cornell.edu • URL: http://www.nysaes.cornell.edu/.

STATISTICS SOURCES

Agricultural Statistics. Available from U. S. Government Printing Office. • Annual. $38.00. Produced by the National Agricultural Statistics Service, U. S.

Department of Agriculture. Provides a wide variety of statistical data relating to agricultural production, supplies, consumption, prices/price-supports, foreign trade, costs, and returns, as well as farm labor, loans, income, and population. In many cases, historical data is shown annually for 10 years. In addition to farm data, includes detailed fishery statistics.

Business Statistics of the United States. Linz Audain and Cornelia J. Strawser. Bernan Associates. • Annual. $147.00. Based on *Business Statistics,* formerly issue by the Bureau of Economic Analysis, U. S. Department of Commerce. Provides basic data for a wide variety of U. S. industries, services, and economic indicators. Most statistics are shown annually for 30 years and monthly for the most recent four years.

FAO Production Yearbook. Available from Bernan Associates. • Annual. $45.00. Published by the Food and Agriculture Organization (http://www.fao.org). Contains worldwide data on agriculture, land use, farm crops, livestock, and agricultural prices.

FAO Trade Yearbook. Available from Bernan Associates. • Annual. $45.00. Published by the Food and Agriculture Organization (http://www.fao.org). Provides extensive worldwide data on exports and imports of agricultural commodities, fertilizers, tractors, and pesticides. Includes more than 130 tables of detailed statistics.

Statistical Annual: Grains, Options on Agricultural Futures. Chicago Board of Trade. • Annual. Includes historical data on Wheat Futures, Options on Wheat Futures, Corn Futures, Options on Corn Futures, Oats Futures, Soybean Futures, Options on Soybean Futures, Soybean Oil Futures, Soybean Meal Futures.

Survey of Current Business. Available from U. S. Government Printing Office. • Monthly. $63.00 per year. Issued by Bureau of Economic Analysis, U. S. Department of Commerce. Presents a wide variety of business and economic data.

United States Census of Agriculture. U.S. Bureau of the Census. • Quinquennial. Results presented in reports, tape, CD-ROM, and Diskette files.

WEFA Industrial Monitor. John Wiley and Sons, Inc. • Annual. $65.00. Prepared by industry analysts at WEFA, an economic forecasting and consulting firm (originally Wharton Econometric Forecasting Associates). Contains discussions of the outlook for major U. S. industries, with many 10-year forecasts (WEFA Web site is http://www.wefa.com).

World Food Data and Statistics. Euromonitor International. • 2004. $650.00. Provides five-year data for a wide variety of food products in 52 countries. Includes market size, consumer expenditures, price indicators, and retail distribution data for many kinds of meat, fish, fruits, vegetables, dairy products, baked goods, condiments, canned food, and frozen food.

TRADE/PROFESSIONAL ASSOCIATIONS

Corn Refiners Association. 1701 Pennsylvania Ave., Ste. 950, Washington, DC 20006. Phone: (202)331-1634 Fax: (202)331-2054 E-mail: info@ropecord.com • URL: http://www.corn.org • Corn refining firms that manufacture corn starches, sugars, syrups, oils, feed and alcohol by wet process.

National Corn Growers Association. 632 Cepi Dr., Chesterfield, MO 63005-1221. Phone: (636)733-9004 Fax: (636)733-9005 E-mail: corninfo@ncga.com • URL: http://www.ncga.com • Growers of corn. Furthers the use, proper marketing, legislative position, and efficient production of corn. Conducts research and educational programs. Sponsors National Yield Contest; compiles statistics.

CORPORATE ACQUISITIONS AND MERGERS

See: MERGERS AND ACQUISITIONS

CORPORATE CULTURE

GENERAL WORKS

Corporate Culture and Organizational Effectiveness. Daniel R. Denison. Aviat, Inc. • 1997. Second edition. Price on application.

Corporate Cultures: The Rites and Rituals of Corporate Life. Terrance E. Deal and Allan Kennedy. Perseus Books Group. • 1982. $15.00.

Creating a Culture of Competence. Michael Zwell. John Wiley and Sons, Inc. • 2000. $35.95. Emphasizes employee participation to arrive at a desired change in organizational culture.

The Web of Inclusion: Building an Organization for Everyone. Sally Helgesen. Doubleday Publishing. • 1995. $24.95.

ABSTRACTS AND INDEXES

Business Periodicals Index. H. W. Wilson Co. • 11 times a year. Quarterly and annual cumulations. Price varies.

DIRECTORIES

Business Organizations, Agencies, and Publications Directory. Gale Cengage Learning. • 2003. $480.00. 15th edition. Over 40,000 entries describing 39 types of business information sources. Classified by type of organization, publication, or serviceIncludes state, national, and international agencies and organizations. Master index to names and keywords. Also includes e-mail addresses and web site URL's.

ENCYCLOPEDIAS AND DICTIONARIES

International Encyclopedia of Business and Management. Malcolm Warner, editor. Cengage Learning. • 2001. $1,899.00.Second edition. Eight volumes. Contains more than 500 articles on global management issues. Includes extensive bibliographies, cross references, and an index of key words and phrases.

HANDBOOKS AND MANUALS

Gaining Control of the Corporate Culture. Ralph H. Kilmann and others. John Wiley and Sons, Inc. • 1985. $48.00. (Management Series).

ONLINE DATABASES

Wilson Business Abstracts Online. H. W. Wilson Co. • Indexes and abstracts 600 major business periodicals, plus the *Wall Street Journal* and the business section of the *New York Times.* Indexing is from 1982, abstracting from 1990, with the two newspapers included from 1993. Updated weekly. Inquire as to online cost and availability. (*Business Periodicals Index* without abstracts is also available online.).

PERIODICALS AND NEWSLETTERS

Chief Executive Magazine. Chief Executive Group, Inc. • Monthly. $95.00 per year.

Corporate Public Issues and Their Management: The Executive Systems Approach to Public Policy Formation. Issue Action Publications, Inc. • Monthly. $235.00 per year. Newsletter.

Fortune Magazine. Time Inc., Business Information Group. • Biweekly. $59.95 per year. Edited for top executives and upper-level managers.

Harvard Business Review. Harvard University, Graduate School of Business Administration. Harvard Business School Publishing. • Monthly. $118.00 per year.

RESEARCH CENTERS AND INSTITUTES

Business, Government, and Society Research Institute. University of Pittsburgh. School of Business, Mervis Hall, Pittsburgh, PA 15260. Phone: (412)648-1555 Fax: (412)648-1693 E-mail: mitnick@pitt.edu.

CORPORATE DIRECTORS AND OFFICERS

See also: EXECUTIVES

GENERAL WORKS

The Business of Banking for Bank Directors. George K. Darling and James F. Chaston. The Risk Management Association. • 1995. $33.00. Presents basic banking concepts and issues for new directors of financial institutions. Emphasis is on the specific duties of directors.

BIOGRAPHICAL SOURCES

Newsmakers. Gale Cengage Learning. • Annual. $155.00. Three softbound issues and one hardbound annual. Biographical information on individuals currently in the news. Includes photographs. Formerly *Contemporary Newsmakers.*

Who Knows Who: Networking Through Corporate Boards. Jeannette E. Glynn. Who Knows Who Publishing. • 1998. $165.00. Fifth edition. Shows the connections between the board members of major U. S. corporations and major foundations and nonprofit organizations.

Who's Who in Finance and Industry. Marquis Who's Who. • Biennial. $259.95. Provides over 21,000 concise biographies of business leaders in all fields.

CD-ROM DATABASES

Standard & Poor's Corporations. Available from Dialog OnDisc. • Monthly. Price on application. Produced by Standard & Poor's. Contains three CD-ROM files: Executives, Private Companies, and Public Companies, providing detailed information on more than 70,000 business executives, 55,000 private companies, and 12,000 publicly-traded corporations.

DIRECTORIES

Reference Book of Corporate Managements. • Annual. Libraries, $650.00 per year; others, $795.00 per year. Lease basis. Management executives at over 12,000 leading United States companies.

Standard and Poor's Register of Corporations, Directors and Executives. Standard and Poor's. • Annual. $675.00. Looseleaf service. Lease basis. Periodic supplementation. Over 55,000 public and privately held corporations in the U.S.

ENCYCLOPEDIAS AND DICTIONARIES

Encyclopedia of Corporate Meetings, Minutes and Resolutions. William Sardell, editor. Prentice Hall PTR. • 1985. $125.00. Third edition. Two volumes.

HANDBOOKS AND MANUALS

Organization Charts: Structures of More Than 200 Businesses and Non-Profit Organizations. Gale Cengage Learning. • 1999. $180.00. Third edition. Includes an introductory discussion of the history and use of such charts.

Principles of Corporate Governance: Analysis and Recommendations. Mike Greenwald, editor. American Law Institute-American Bar Association Committee on Continuing Professional Education. • 1994. $135.00. Two volumes. An examination of the duties and responsibilities of directors and officers of business corporations. Seven parts cover (1) definitions, (2) objectives and conduct, (3) corporate structure and oversight committees, (4) business judgment, (5) fair dealing, (6) tender offers, and (7) legal remedies.

Responsibilities of Corporate Officers and Directors Under Federal Securities Law. CCH, Inc. • Annual. $79.00. Includes discussions of indemnification, "D

& O" insurance, corporate governance, and insider liability.

ONLINE DATABASES

Standard & Poor's Register: Biographical. Standard & Poor's Corp. • Contains brief biographies of approximately 70,000 business executives and directors. Corresponds to the biographical volume of *Standard & Poor's Register of Corporations, Directors, and Executives.* Updated twice a year. Inquire as to online cost and availability.

PERIODICALS AND NEWSLETTERS

Corporate Board Member: The Magazine for Directors of Public Companies. Board Member Inc. • Bimonthly. $155.00 per year. Edited for board members of publicly traded corporations. Includes such topics as liability, executive compensation, mergers, corporate administration, and management succession.

Corporate Controller. RIA. • Bimonthly. $130.00 per year.

D & O Advisor: Risk Management for Directors and Officers. American Lawyer Media, Inc. • Quarterly. $125.00 per year. Covers a wide range of legal topics of concern to corporate boards and key executives.

Director's Monthly. National Association of Corporate Directors. • Description: Reports current issues and events of interest to corporate directors. Covers such topics as director independence, ethics, directors, audit, compensation, nominating committees, and changing regulatory requirements. Recurring features include roundtable discussions and interviews.

Forbes. Forbes, Inc. • Biweekly. $59.95 per year. Includes supplements: *Forbes ASAP* and *Forbes FYI.*

Fortune Magazine. Time Inc., Business Information Group. • Biweekly. $59.95 per year. Edited for top executives and upper-level managers.

RESEARCH CENTERS AND INSTITUTES

Financial Executives Research Foundation. 10 Madison Ave., Morristown, NJ 07962. Phone: (973)898-4600 Fax: (973)898-6636 E-mail: mbace@fei.org • URL: http://www.fei.org/rf.

TRADE/PROFESSIONAL ASSOCIATIONS

American Management Association. 1601 Broadway, New York, NY 10019-7420. Phone: 800-262-9699 or (212)586-8100 Fax: (212)903-8168 E-mail: membership@amanet.org • URL: http://www.amanet.org • Provides educational forums worldwide where members and their colleagues learn superior, practical business skills and explore best practices of world-class organizations through interaction with each other and expert faculty practitioners. Maintains a publishing program providing tools individuals use to extend learning beyond the classroom in a process of life-long professional growth and development through education.

American Society of Corporate Secretaries. 521 Fifth Ave., New York, NY 10175-0003. Phone: (212)681-2000 Fax: (212)681-2005 E-mail: dsmith@ascs.org • URL: http://www.ascs.org.

International Management Council of the YMCA. 7502 Maple St., Omaha, NE 68134-6602. Phone: 800-688-9622 or (402)330-6310 Fax: (402)330-7424 E-mail: imcoffice@msn.com • URL: http://www.imc-ymca.org • Formerly International Management Council.

National Association of Corporate Directors. 1828 L St., N.W., Ste. 801, Washington, DC 20036. Phone: (202)775-0509 Fax: (202)775-4857 E-mail: info@nacdonline.org • URL: http://www.nacdonline.org.

Professional Services Management Association. 44 Canal Center Plz., Ste. 44, Alexandria, VA 22314.

Phone: (866)739-0277 or (703)739-0277 Fax: (703)549-2498 E-mail: info@psmanet.org • URL: http://www.psmanet.org • Individuals responsible for any or all aspects of business management in a professional design firm. Aims to improve the effectiveness of professional design firms through the growth and development of business management skills. Seeks to: provide a forum for the exchange of ideas and information and discussion and resolution of common problems and issues; establish guidelines for approaches to common management concerns; initiate and maintain professional relationships among members; improve recognition and practice of management as a science in professional design firms; advance and improve reputable service to clients; offer a variety of comprehensive educational programs and opportunities. Maintains speakers' bureau and placement service. Holds seminars. Conducts surveys and research programs. Compiles statistics.

OTHER SOURCES

Corporate Directors' Compensation. The Conference Board. • Irregular.

Corporate Officers and Directors Liability Litigation Reporter: The Twice Monthly National Journal of Record of Litigation Based on Fiduciary Responsibility. Andrews Publications. • Semimonthly. $890.00 per year. Newsletter. Provides reports on lawsuits in the area of corporate officers' fiduciary responsibility.

Corporate Secretary's Guide. CCH, Inc. • Monthly. $645.00 per year. Looseleaf service. Includes newsletter and semimonthly updates. Published in consultation with the American Society of Corporate Secretaries. Covers the duties of corporate secretaries, especially as related to taxation and securities.

Corporation Forms. Prentice Hall PTR. • Looseleaf. Periodic supplementation. Price on application.

Directors and Officers Liability: Prevention, Insurance, and Indemnification. American Lawyer Media, Inc. • Looseleaf. $179.00. Updated as needed. Covers the legal risks faced by corporate directors and officers. (Law Journal Press).

Fund Governance: Legal Duties of Investment Company Directors. American Lawyer Media, Inc. • Looseleaf. $159.00. Updated as needed. Covers the legal obligations of directors of mutual funds and closed-end funds. (Law Journal Press).

CORPORATE FINANCE

See also: FINANCE; FINANCIAL MANAGEMENT

GENERAL WORKS

Accounting and Finance for Non-Specialists. Peter Atrill and Eddie McLaney. Pearson Education. • 2003. $77.00. Fourth edition. Includes the measurement and reporting of financial performance and cash flow.

Case Studies in Finance: Managing for Corporate Value Creation. Robert Bruner. McGraw-Hill. • 2002. $109.69. Fourth edition. (Finance, Insurance and Real Estate Series).

Corporate Finance. Stephen A. Ross and others. McGraw-Hill. • 2001. $76.25. Sixth edition. (Finance, Insurance, and Real Estate Series).

Corporate Finance and the Securities Laws. Charles J. Johnson and Joseph McLaughlin. Aspen Publishers, Inc. • 1997. $175.00. Second edition.

Corporate Financial Reporting: Text and Cases. David B. Hawkins. McGraw-Hill. • 1997. $118.13. Fourth edition.

The Financial Numbers Game: Detecting Creative Accounting Practices. Charles W. Mulford and Eugene E. Comiskey. John Wiley and Sons, Inc. • 2002. $39.95. Serves as a guide to financial statement analysis for investors. Explains the "creative" schemes used by corporations to boost earnings-per-share data.

Mergers, Acquisitions, and Corporate Restructurings. Patrick A. Gaughan. John Wiley and Sons, Inc. • 2001. $75.00. Third edition. Covers mergers, acquisitions, divestitures, internal reorganizations, joint ventures, leveraged buyouts, bankruptcy workouts, and recapitalizations.

Theory of Corporate Finance. Michael J. Brennan, editor. Edward Elgar Publishing, Inc. • 1996. $760.00. Two volumes. Consists of reprints of 46 articles dating from 1976 to 1994. (International Library of Critical Writings in Financial Economics Series: Vol. 1).

ABSTRACTS AND INDEXES

Business Periodicals Index. H. W. Wilson Co. • 11 times a year. Quarterly and annual cumulations. Price varies.

CD-ROM DATABASES

ABI/INFORM. PROQUEST. • Monthly. Provides CD-ROM indexing and abstracting of worldwide business literature. Archival discs are available from 1971. Formerly *ABI/INFORM OnDisc.*

Buyout Financing Sources/M & A Intermediaries. Thomson Media. • Annual. $895.00. Provides the CD-ROM combination of *Directory of Buyout Financing Sources* and *Directory of M & A Intermediaries.* Contains information on more than 1,000 financing sources (banks, insurance companies, venture capital firms, etc.) and 850 intermediaries (corporate acquirers, valuation firms, lawyers, accountants, etc.). Also includes back issues of *Buyouts Newsletter* and *Mergers & Acquisitions Report.* Fully searchable.

Compact D/SEC. Thomson Financial. • Monthly. Provides 200 financial data items for 12,000 U. S. publicly-held corporations filing reports with the Securities and Exchange Commission. Includes company profiles.

Corporate Affiliations Plus. National Register Publishing, Reed Reference Publishing. • Quarterly. $1,995.00 per year. Provides CD-ROM discs corresponding to *Directory of Corporate Affiliations* and *Corporate Finance Bluebook.* Contains corporate financial services information and worldwide data on subsidiaries and affiliates.

WILSONDISC: Business Periodicals Index. H. W. Wilson Co. • Monthly. Provides CD-ROM indexing of business periodicals from 1982 to date. Price includes online service.

DIRECTORIES

America's Corporate Finance Directory. LexisNexis Group. • Covers: Financial personnel and outside financial services relationships of 5,000 leading United States corporations and their wholly-owned United States subsidiaries. Entries include: Company name, address, phone, fax, telex, e-mail addresses, stock exchange information, earnings, total assets, size of pension/profit-sharing fund portfolio, number of employees, description of business, wholly-owned U.S. Subsidiaries of parent company; name and title of key executives; outside suppliers of financial services.

Corporate Bond Desk Reference: U. S. Buyside and Sellside Profiles. Capital Access International. • Annual. $395.00. Provides "detailed buyside and sellside profiles and contacts" for the the corporate bond market. (Desk Reference Series, volume one.).

Directory of Buyout Financing Sources. Thomson Financial. • Annual. $445.00. Describes more than 1,000 U. S. and foreign sources of financing for buyout deals. Indexed by personnel, company, industry, and location.

Major Financial Institutions of the World 2001. Available from Gale Cengage Learning. • 2003. $880.00. Sixth edition. Two volumes. Published by

Graham & Whiteside. Contains detailed information on more than 7,500 important financial institutions in various countries. Includes banks, investment companies, and insurance companies.

Mergent's Handbook of Common Stocks. Mergent, Inc. • Quarterly. $350.00 per year ($100.00 per copy). Contains one-page profiles of about 1,000 major corporations listed on the New York Stock Exchange. Includes analysis, comment, stock price performance data, and 10-year financial statistics. Formerly *Moody's Handbook of Common Stocks.*

Mergent's Handbook of NASDAQ Stocks. Mergent, Inc. • Quarterly. $350.00 per year ($100.00 per copy). Contains one-page profiles of more than 600 major companies traded on the NASDAQ National Exchange or the American Stock Exchange. Includes price performance scores, analysis, comment, and seven-year financial statistics. Formerly *Moody's Handbook of NASDAQ Stocks.*

Zacks Analyst Directory: Listed by Broker. Zacks Investment Research. • Quarterly. $395.00 per year. Lists stockbroker investment analysts and gives the names of major U. S. corporations covered by those analysts.

Zacks Analyst Directory: Listed by Company. Zacks Investment Research. • Quarterly. $395.00 per year. Lists major U. S. corporations and gives the names of stockbroker investment analysts covering those companies.

Zacks EPS Calendar. Zacks Investment Research. • Biweekly. $1,250.00 per year. (Also available monthly at $895.00 per year.) Lists anticipated reporting dates of earnings per share for major U. S. corporations.

ENCYCLOPEDIAS AND DICTIONARIES

Blackwell Encyclopedic Dictionary of Finance. Dean Paxson and Douglas Wood, editors. Blackwell Publishing. • 1997. $110.00. The editors are associated with the University of Manchester. Contains definitions of key terms combined with longer articles written by various U. S. and foreign business educators. Includes bibliographies and index. (Blackwell Encyclopedia of Management Series).

Dictionary of Finance and Investment Terms. John Downes. Barron's Educational Series, Inc. • 2002. $14.95. Sixth edition. Provides clear explanations of more than 5,000 business, banking, financial, investment, and tax terms. Includes a separate list of financial abbreviations and acronyms. (Business Dictionaries Series).

The New Palgrave Dictionary of Money and Finance. Peter Newman and others, editors. Palgrave Macmillan. • 1992. $595.00. Two volumes. Consists of signed essays on over 1,000 financial topics, each with a bibliography. Covers a wide variety of financial, monetary, and investment areas. A detailed subject index is provided.

FINANCIAL RATIOS

IRS Corporate Financial Ratios. Available from MarketResearch.com. • 2002. $225.00. Published by Schonfeld & Associates, Inc. Presents 70 key financial ratios for 260 industries. Ratios are calculated from income statement and balance sheet data available from the Internal Revenue Service. Includes four asset size classes.

HANDBOOKS AND MANUALS

Analysis and Use of Financial Statements. Gerald I. White. John Wiley and Sons, Inc. • 2002. $123.95. Third edition. Includes analysis of financial ratios, cash flow, inventories, assets, debt, etc. Also covered are employee benefits, corporate investments, multinational operations, financial derivatives, and hedging activities.

Corporate Financial Analysis: Decisions in a Global Environment. Diana R. Harrington and Brent D. Wilson. McGraw-Hill. • 1993. $50.00. Fourth edition.

Corporate Financial Distress and Bankruptcy: A Complete Guide to Predicting and Avoiding Distress and Profiting from Bankruptcy. Edward I. Altman. John Wiley and Sons, Inc. • 1993. $110.00. Second edition. Provides practical advice on analyzing the financial position of a corporation, with case studies. Includes a discussion of the junk bond market. (Finance Series).

Corporate Liquidity: Management and Measurement. Jarl G. Kallberg and Kenneth L. Parkinson. McGraw-Hill. • 1992. $67.95. Topics include cash management and risk.

Cyberfinance: Raising Capital for the E-Business. Martin B. Robins. CCH, Inc. • 2001. $79.00. Covers the taxation, financial, and legal aspects of raising money for new Internet-based ("dot.com") companies, including the three stages of startup, growth, and initial public offering. (Solutions for Professional Advisers Series).

Dividend Policy: Theory and Practice. George W. Frankfurter and Bob G. Wood. Elsevier Butterworth Heinemann. • 2003. $59.95. Covers the history of dividends, preferred stock dividends, dividend reinvestment plans, extensive academic research, and "New Ways of Thinking About Dividends and Dividend Policy.".

Financial Investigations: A Forensic Accounting Approach to Detecting and Resolving Crimes. Available from U. S. Government Printing Office. • 2002. $54.00. Two volumes: textbook and workbook. Issued by the Internal Revenue Service (http://www.irs.ustreas.gov). Serves as a text "for courses on conducting financial investigations." (IRS Publications 1714 and 1816.).

Financing the Corporation. Richard A. Booth. West Group. • Annual. $160.00. Looseleaf service. Covers a wide variety of corporate finance legal topics, from initial capital structure to public sale of securities.

Fundamentals of Corporate Finance. Richard A. Brealey and others. McGraw-Hill. • 2003. Third edition. Price on application. (Finance, Insurance, and Real Estate Series).

Managing Finance: A Socially Responsible Approach. David Crowther. Elsevier Butterworth Heinemann. • 2004. $37.50. Explains how to manage an ethical approach to such items as accounting, company reports, profit analysis, costing, budgeting, performance data, and investment appraisal.

Miller GAAP Financial Statement Disclosures Manual. Aspen Publishers. • Annual. $105.00. Provides a detailed summary of financial report disclosure requirements, with examples. Includes a CD-ROM.

Principles of Corporate Finance. Richard A. Brealey and Stewart C. Myers. McGraw-Hill. • 2002. $79.50. Seventh edition. (Finance, Insurance and Real Estate Series).

SEC Handbook: Rules and Forms for Financial Statements and Related Disclosures. CCH, Inc. • Annual. $59.00. Contains full text of rules and requirements set by the Securities and Exchange Commisssion for preparation of corporate financial statements.

Swap Literacy. Elizabeth Ungar. Bloomberg. • 1996. $40.00. Written for corporate finance officers. Provides basic information on arbitrage, hedging, and speculation, involving interest rate, currency, and other types of financial swaps. (Bloomberg Professional Library.).

INTERNET DATABASES

Mergent Online. Mergent, Inc. Phone: 800-342-5647 or (704)559-7601 Fax: (704)559-6945 E-mail: customerservice@mergent.com • URL: http://www.mergentonline.com • Fee-based Web site provides detailed information on 20,000 publicly-owned companies in 100 foreign countries, as well as more than 10,000 corporations listed on the New York Stock Exchange, American Stock Exchange, NASDAQ, and U. S. regional exchanges. Searching is offered on many financial variables and text fields. Weekly updating. Formerly *FIS Online*.

U. S. Securities and Exchange Commission. Phone: 800-732-0330 or (202)942-7040 Fax: (202)942-9634 E-mail: webmaster@sec.gov • URL: http://www.sec.gov • SEC Web site offers free access through EDGAR to text of official corporate filings, such as annual reports (10-K), quarterly reports (10-Q), and proxies. (EDGAR is "Electronic Data Gathering, Analysis, and Retrieval System.") An example is given of how to obtain executive compensation data from proxies. Text of the daily *SEC News Digest* is offered, as are links to other government sites, non-government market regulators, and U. S. stock exchanges. Search facilities are extensive. Fees: Free.

ONLINE DATABASES

Banking Information Source. PROQUEST. • Provides indexing and abstracting of periodical and other literature from 1982 to date, with weekly updates. Covers the financial services industry: banks, savings institutions, investment houses, credit unions, insurance companies, and real estate organizations. Emphasis is on marketing and management. Inquire as to online cost and availability. (Formerly *FINIS: Financial Industry Information Service.*).

First Call Consensus Earnings Estimates. Thomson Financial. • Online service provides corporate earnings estimates for more than 2,500 U. S. companies, based on data from leading brokerage firms. Weekly updates. Inquire as to online cost and availability.

Fitch Ratings Delivery Service. Fitch Inc. • Provides online delivery of Fitch financial ratings in three sectors: "Corporate Finance" (corporate bonds, insurance companies), "Structured Finance" (asset-backed securities), and "U.S. Public Finance" (municipal bonds). Daily updates. Inquire as to online cost and availability.

Management Contents. Gale Cengage Learning. • Covers a wide range of management, financial, marketing, personnel, and administrative topics. About 150 leading business journals are indexed and abstracted from 1974 to date, with monthly updating. Inquire as to online cost and availability.

Trade & Industry Database. Gale Cengage Learning. • Provides indexing of business periodicals, January 1981 to date. Daily updates. (Full text articles from some periodicals are available online, 1983 to date. Inquire as to online cost and availability).

Wilson Business Abstracts Online. H. W. Wilson Co. • Indexes and abstracts 600 major business periodicals, plus the *Wall Street Journal* and the business section of the *New York Times*. Indexing is from 1982, abstracting from 1990, with the two newspapers included from 1993. Updated weekly. Inquire as to online cost and availability. (*Business Periodicals Index* without abstracts is also available online.).

Zacks Earnings Estimates. Zacks Investment Research. • Provides online earnings projections for about 6,000 U. S. corporations, based on investment analysts' reports. Data is mainly from 200 major brokerage firms. Time span varies according to online provider, with daily or weekly updates. Inquire as to online cost and availability.

PERIODICALS AND NEWSLETTERS

American Banker: The Financial Services Daily. Thomson Media. • Daily. $895.00 per year. Provides news of banking, investment products, mortgages, credit unions, finance, bank technology, and legal developments.

Bank Loan Report. IDD Enterprises L.P. • Description: Discusses banking loans and transactions made by large corporations. Recurring features include a column titled Term Sheets.

Business Finance. Penton Technology and Lifestyle Media. • Monthly. $59.00 per year. Covers trends in finance, technology, and economics for corporate financial executives.

CFO: The Magazine for Senior Financial Executives. CFO Publishing Corp. • Monthly. $65.00 per year.

Corporate Financing Week: The Newsweekly of Corporate Finance, Investment Banking and M and A. Institutional Investor, Inc., Journals Group. • Weekly. $2,550.00 per year. Includes print and online editions. Newsletter for corporate finance officers. Emphasis is on debt and equity financing, mergers, leveraged buyouts, investment banking, and venture capital.

Financial Markets, Institutions, and Instruments. New York University, Salomon Center. Blackwell Publishing. • Five times a year. Institutions, $338.00 per year. Includes online edition. Edited to "bridge the gap between the academic and professional finance communities." Special fifth issue each year provides surveys of developments in four areas: money and banking, derivative securities, corporate finance, and fixed-income securities.

Global Finance. Global Finance Media, Inc. • Monthly. $350.00 per year. Edited for corporate financial executives and money managers responsible for "cross-border" financial transactions.

Journal of Corporate Accounting and Finance. John Wiley and Sons, Inc., Journals. • Bimonthly. $495.00 per year; with online edition, $520.00 per year. Topics include government regulation, corporate taxation, financial risk, business valuation, and strategic planning.

Private Placement Letter: The Weekly for Privately Placed Fixed-Income Securities. Thomson Media. • Weekly. $895.00 per year. Newsletter. Provides information on private financing of debt and convertible securities.

Strategic Finance. Institute of Management Accountants. • Monthly. Institutions, $140.00 per year; non-profit libraries, $70,00 per year. Provides articles on corporate finance, cost control, cash flow, budgeting, corporate taxes, and other financial management topics.

U. S. Banker. Thomson Media. • Monthly. $65.00 per year. Edited for bank executives and managers. Covers a wide variety of banking and financial topics.

Wallstreetlawyer.com: Securities in the Electronic Age. Glasser Legalworks. • Monthly. $345.00 per year. Newsletter. Covers the latest regulatory developments in capital raising, disclosure, and enforcement.

Zacks Analyst Watch. Zacks Investment Research. • Biweekly. $250.00 per year. Provides the results of research by stockbroker investment analysts on major U. S. corporations.

Zacks Earnings Forecaster. Zacks Investment Research. • Biweekly. $495.00 per year. (Also available monthly at $375.00 per year.) Provides estimates by stockbroker investment analysts of earnings per share of individual U. S. companies.

Zacks Profit Guide. Zacks Investment Research. • Quarterly. $375.00 per year. Provides analysis of total return and stock price performance of major U. S. companies.

RESEARCH CENTERS AND INSTITUTES

Bendheim Center for Finance. Princeton University, 26 Prospect Ave., Princeton, NJ 08540-5296. Phone: (609)258-0770 Fax: (609)258-0771 E-mail: yacine@princeton.edu • URL: http://www.princeton.edu/~bcf/ • Research areas include securities markets, portfolio analysis, credit markets, and corporate finance. Emphasis is on quantitative and mathematical perspectives.

Center for Finance and Real Estate. University of California, Los Angeles, John E. Anderson Graduate School of Management, 110 Westwood Plaza, Los Angeles, CA 90095-1481. Phone: (310)206-5455 Fax: (310)206-5455 E-mail: wtorous@anderson.ucla.edu • URL: http://www.agsm.ucla.edu.

STATISTICS SOURCES

Economic Report of the President: Together with the Annual Report of the Council of Economic Advisors. Available from U. S. Government Printing Office. • Annual. $32.00. Includes about 130 pages of "Statistical Tables Relating to Income, Employment, and Production." Tables cover national income, employment, wages, productivity, manufacturing, prices, credit, finance (public and private), corporate profits, and foreign trade.

Standard & Poor's Stock Reports: NASDAQ and Regional Exchanges. Standard & Poor's. • Irregular. $1,100.00 per year. Looseleaf service. Provides two pages of financial details and other information for each corporation included.

Standard & Poor's Stock Reports: New York Stock Exchange. Standard & Poor's. • Irregular. $1,295.00 per year. Looseleaf service. Provides two pages of financial details and other information for each corporation with stock listed on the N. Y. Stock Exchange.

TRADE/PROFESSIONAL ASSOCIATIONS

Association for Financial Professionals. 7315 Wisconsin Ave., Suite 600 W, Bethesda, MD 20814-3211. Phone: (301)907-2862 Fax: (301)907-2864 E-mail: afp@afponline.org • URL: http://www.afponline.org • Goal is to raise the stature and visibility of the finance profession. Formerly Treasury Management Association.

Financial Executives International. 200 Campus Dr., PO Box 674, Florham Park, NJ 07932-0674. Phone: (973)765-1000 Fax: (973)765-1018 E-mail: mcangemi@financialexecutives.org • URL: http://www.financialexecutives.org • Professional organization of corporate financial executives performing duties of chief financial officer, controller, treasurer, or vice-president-finance. Sponsors research activities through its affiliated Financial Executives Research Foundation. Maintains offices in Toronto, Canada, and Washington, DC.

Financial Management Association International. University of South Florida, College of Business Administration, 4202 E Fowler Ave., BSN 3331, Tampa, FL 33620-5500. Phone: (813)974-2084 Fax: (813)974-3318 E-mail: fma@coba.usf.edu • URL: http://www.fma.org • Professors of financial management; corporate financial officers. Facilitates exchange of ideas among persons involved in financial management or the study thereof. Conducts workshops for comparison of current research projects and development of cooperative ventures in writing and research. Sponsors honorary society for superior students at 300 colleges and universities. Offers placement services.

National Association of Corporate Treasurers. 11250 Roger Bacon Dr., Ste. 8, Reston, VA 20190-5202. Phone: (703)318-4227 Fax: (703)435-4390 E-mail: nact@nact.org • URL: http://www.nact.org • Members are corporate financial executives.

OTHER SOURCES

Corporate Dividends and Stock Repurchases. Barbara Black. West Group. • Annual. $173.00. Looseleaf service. Covers the law relating to dividends in general, illegal dividends, stock splits, stock dividends, corporate repurchases, and other dividend topics.

FASB Accounting Standards Current Text. Financial Accounting Standards Board. • $395.00. Three looseleaf volumes. Periodic supplementation.

FASB Accounting Standards Current Text: General

Standards. Financial Accounting Standards Board. • Irregular. Price on application.

FASB Accounting Standards Current Text: Industries Standards. Financial Accounting Standards Board. • Irregular. Price on application.

FASB Accounting Standards Current Text: Professional Standards. Financial Accounting Standards Board. • Irregular. Price on application.

FASB Accounting Standards Current Text: Technical Practice Aids. Financial Accounting Standards Board. • Irregular. Price on application.

FASB Original Pronouncements. Financial Accounting Standards Board. • $595.00. Seven looseleaf volumes.

Finance and Accounting for Nonfinancial Managers. American Management Association Extension Institute. • Looseleaf. $159.00. Self-study course. Emphasis is on practical explanations, examples, and problem solving. Quizzes and a case study are included.

Financial Accounting Series. Financial Accounting Standards Board. • Price on application.

Formation and Financing of Emerging Companies. Daniel E. O'Connor and others. Glasser Legalworks. • Looseleaf. $225.00, including CD-ROM version. Periodic Supplementation. Covers incorporation, bylaws, indemnification, intellectual property, financing sources, venture capital, due diligence, bridge loans, investor rights, compliance, and other legal issues associated with company formation. (Emerging Growth Companies Series.).

Managing Financial Risk with Forwards, Futures, Options, and Swaps. American Management Association Extension Institute. • Looseleaf. $159.00. Self-study course. Emphasis is on practical explanations, examples, and problem solving. Quizzes and a case study are included.

CORPORATE FORMATION

See: INCORPORATION

CORPORATE GIVING

See: PHILANTHROPY

CORPORATE HISTORIES

See: BUSINESS HISTORY

CORPORATE IMAGE

GENERAL WORKS

Crisis Response: Inside Stories on Managing Image Under Siege. Gale Cengage Learning. • 1993. $80.00. Presents first-hand accounts by media relations professionals of major business crises and how they were handled. Topics include the following kinds of crises: environmental, governmental, corporate image, communications, and product.

Living Logos: How U. S. Corporations Revitalize Their Trademarks. David E. Carter, editor. Art Direction Book Co., Inc. • 1993. $22.95. Traces the history and evolution of 70 famous U. S. company logos.

Shaping the Corporate Image: An Analytical Guide for Executive Decision Makers. Marion G. Sobol and others. Greenwood Publishing Group, Inc. • 1992. $59.95.

The 22 Immutable Laws of Branding: How to Build a Product or Service Into a World-Class Brand. Al Ries and Laura Ries. HarperInformation. • 1998. $25.00. Provides advice on attaining positive brand recognition.

ABSTRACTS AND INDEXES

Business Periodicals Index. H. W. Wilson Co. • 11 times a year. Quarterly and annual cumulations. Price varies.

PAIS International in Print. Public Affairs Information Service, Inc. • Monthly. $850.00 per year; cumulations three times a year. Provides topical citations to the worldwide literature of public affairs, economics, demographics, sociology, and trade. Text in English; indexed materials in English, French, German, Italian, Portuguese and Spanish.

CD-ROM DATABASES

ABI/INFORM. PROQUEST. • Monthly. Provides CD-ROM indexing and abstracting of worldwide business literature. Archival discs are available from 1971. Formerly *ABI/INFORM OnDisc.*

PAIS on CD-ROM. Public Affairs Information Service, Inc. • Quarterly. $1,995.00 per year. Provides a CD-ROM version of the online service, *PAIS International.* Contains over 500,000 citations to the literature of contemporary social, political, and economic issues.

WILSONDISC: Wilson Business Abstracts. H. W. Wilson Co. • Monthly. Includes unlimited online access to *Wilson Business Abstracts* through WILSONLINE. Provides CD-ROM "cover-to-cover" abstracting and indexing of over 600 prominent business periodicals. Indexing is from 1982, abstracting from 1990. (*Business Periodicals Index* without abstracts is available on CD-ROM at $1,495 per year.).

DIRECTORIES

Plunkett's Advertising and Branding Industry Almanac. Plunkett Research, Ltd. • 2004. $249.99. Provides profiles of 300 leading firms in the areas of advertising, brand promotion, and corporate image, including marketing media, online advertising, and direct mail. Also covers industry trends and statistical data.

HANDBOOKS AND MANUALS

Corporate Image: A Practical Guide to the Implementation of a Corporate Identity Program. Nicholas Ind. Beekman Publishers, Inc. • 1992. $44.95. Revised edition.

Corporate Image: Communicating Visions and Values. Allyson LaBorde, editor. The Conference Board. • 1993. $100.00. (Report No. 1038).

Logo Power: Creating World-Class Logos and Effective Business Identities. David E. Carter. DIANE Publishing Co. • 2001. $40.00. Explains how to plan, develop, evaluate, and implement a company logo system.

ONLINE DATABASES

Management Contents. Gale Cengage Learning. • Covers a wide range of management, financial, marketing, personnel, and administrative topics. About 150 leading business journals are indexed and abstracted from 1974 to date, with monthly updating. Inquire as to online cost and availability.

PAIS International. Public Affairs Information Service, Inc. • Corresponds to the former printed publications, *PAIS Bulletin* (1976-90) and *PAIS Foreign Language Index* (1972-90), and to the current *PAIS International in Print* (1991 to date). Covers economic, political, and sociological material appearing in periodicals, books, government documents, and other publications. Updating is monthly. Inquire as to online cost and availability.

Trade & Industry Database. Gale Cengage Learning. • Provides indexing of business periodicals, January 1981 to date. Daily updates. (Full text articles from some periodicals are available online, 1983 to date. Inquire as to online cost and availability).

Wilson Business Abstracts Online. H. W. Wilson Co. • Indexes and abstracts 600 major business periodicals, plus the *Wall Street Journal* and the business section of the *New York Times.* Indexing is from 1982, abstracting from 1990, with the two newspapers included from 1993. Updated weekly.

Inquire as to online cost and availability. (*Business Periodicals Index* without abstracts is also available online.).

PERIODICALS AND NEWSLETTERS

Directors & Boards. • Quarterly. $295.00 per year. Edited for corporate board members and senior executive officers.

RESEARCH CENTERS AND INSTITUTES

Center for Corporate Citizenship. Boston College, 55 Lee Rd., Chestnut Hill, MA 02467. Phone: (617)552-4545 Fax: (617)552-8499 E-mail: cccr@bc.edu • URL: http://www.bc.edu/cccbc • Areas of study include corporate images within local communities, corporate community relations, social vision, and philanthropy. Formerly Center for Corporate Community Relations.

TRADE/PROFESSIONAL ASSOCIATIONS

Public Relations Society of America. 33 Irving Pl., 3rd Fl., New York, NY 10003-2376. Phone: (212)995-2230 Fax: (212)995-0757 E-mail: hq@prsa.org • URL: http://www.prsa.org • Absorbed American Public Relations Association and National Communication Council for Human Services.

CORPORATE INCOME TAX

See also: TAXATION

ABSTRACTS AND INDEXES

Accounting and Tax Index. UMI. • Quarterly. Price on application. Annual cumulation. Indexes accounting, auditing, and taxation literature appearing in journals, books, pamphlets, conference proceedings, and newsletters.

CD-ROM DATABASES

Authority Tax and Estate Planning Library. LexisNexis/Matthew Bender. • Periodic revisions. Price on request. CD-ROM contains updated full text of *Bender's Payroll Tax Guide, Depreciation Handbook, Federal Income Taxation of Corporations, Tax Planning for Corporations, Modern Estate Planning, Planning for Large Estates, Murphy's Will Clauses, Tax & Estate Planning for the Elderly,* and 12 other Matthew Bender publications. The Internal Revenue Code is also included.

Federal Tax Products. Available from U. S. Government Printing Office. • Annual. $27.00. CD-ROM issued by the Internal Revenue Service (http://www.irs.treas.gov/forms_pubs/). Provides current tax forms, instructions, and publications. Also includes older tax forms beginning with 1991.

OECD Statistical Compendium. Organization for Economic Cooperation and Development. • Semiannual. $1,905.00 per year for 1 to 10 users. CD-ROM contains more than 730,000 monthly, quarterly, and annual time series for OECD countries, 1960 to date. Includes fully searchable data on agriculture, food, economic indicators, national accounts, employment, energy, finance, industry, technology, and foreign trade. Results can be displayed in various forms.

The Tax Directory [CD-ROM]. Tax Analysts. • Quarterly. Provides *The Tax Directory* listings on CD-ROM, covering federal, state, and international tax officials, tax practitioners, and corporate tax executives.

DIRECTORIES

The Tax Directory. Tax Analysts. • Covers: Volume One--Approximately 15,000 federal and state government tax legislators, policymakers, administrators, and employees; tax regulation attorneys; over 500 international tax officials with central banks, ministries of finance, foreign embassies and consulate, and chambers of commerce; over 300 tax and business journalists and editors working for magazines, journals, newspapers, television, and radio; tax sections of over 100 trade and professional associations; state CPA, bar, and enrolled agent associations. Volume Two--Over 5,000 corporate tax managers of large U.S. and international firms. Entries include: For government and international officials--Name, title, address, phone, fax, email and website. For corporate tax managers--Name, address, phone, fax, email, website, and company name. For journalists--Name, address, phone, fax, email, website, and name of publication/network. For organizations and associations--Name, address, phone, fax, email, website, budget, membership, background information, and description of purpose.

HANDBOOKS AND MANUALS

Business Taxpayer Information Publications. Available from U. S. Government Printing Office. • Annual. $63.00. Two volumes, consisting of *Circular E, Employer's Tax Guide* and *Employer's Supplemental Tax Guide.* Issued by the Internal Revenue Service (http://www.irs.ustreas.gov). Includes a wide variety of business-related tax information, including withholding tables, tax calendars, self-employment issues, partnership matters, corporation topics, depreciation, and bankruptcy.

Corporate, Partnership, Estate, and Gift Taxation 1997. James W. Pratt and William Kulsrud, editors. McGraw-Hill. • 1996. $71.25. 10th edition.

Corporate Taxes: Worldwide Summaries. John Wiley and Sons, Inc. • 2003. $105.00. Summarizes the corporate tax regulations of more than 125 countries. Provides information useful for international tax planning and foreign investments.

Corporation and Partnership Tax Return Guide (1999 Taxes). Bill Massey and others. RIA. • 2000. $16.50. Revised edition.

Corporation-Partnership-Fiduciary Filled-in Tax Return Forms, 2002. CCH, Inc. • 2002. $34.00.

Federal Tax Course. Aspen Publishers, Inc. • Annual. $210.00. Provides basic reference and training for various forms of federal taxation: individual, business, corporate, partnership, estate, gift, etc.

Federal Tax Manual. CCH, Inc. • Monthly. $342.00 per year. Looseleaf service. Covers "basic federal tax rules and forms affecting individuals and businesses." Includes a copy of *Annuity, Depreciation, and Withholding Tables.*

Tax Planning for Corporations and Shareholders: Forms. LexisNexis Matthew Bender. • Annual. $236.00. Looseleaf service.

U. S. Master Multistate Corporate Tax Guide. CCH, Inc. • Annual. $72.00. Provides corporate income tax information for 47 states, New York City, and the District of Columbia.

INTERNET DATABASES

Business 2.0 Web Guide to the Best Business Links. Business 2.0 Media Inc. Phone: (415)293-4800 E-mail: support@business2.com • URL: http://www.business2.com/webguide • Web site presents an extensive, searchable directory of links to "the best, most informative, and authoritative web pages." Twenty main categories cover business, finance, career, company information, people, and technology topics, with thousands of subtopics, all linking to Web sites recommended by experienced business researchers. Fees: Free.

CCH Essentials: An Internet Tax Research and Primary Source Library. CCH, Inc. Phone: 800-248-3248 or (773)866-6000 Fax: 800-224-8299 or (773)866-3608 E-mail: cust_serv@cch.com • URL: http://tax.cch.com/essentials • Fee-based Web site provides full-text coverage of federal tax law and regulations, including rulings, procedures, tax court decisions, and IRS publications, announcements, notices, and penalties. Includes explanation, analysis, tax planning guides, and a daily tax news

service. Searching is offered, including citation search.

Factiva. Dow Jones Reuters Business Interactive, LLC. Phone: 800-369-7466 or (609)452-1511 Fax: (609)520-5770 E-mail: solutions@factiva.com • URL: http://www.factiva.com • Fee-based Web site provides "global news and business information through Web sites and content integration solutions." Includes Dow Jones and Reuters newswires, The Wall Street Journal, and more than 7,000 other sources of current news, historical articles, market research reports, and investment analysis. Content includes 96 major U. S. newspapers, 900 non-English sources, trade publications, media transcripts, country profiles, news photos, etc.

Fedstats. Federal Interagency Council on Statistical Policy. Phone: (202)395-7254 • URL: http://www.fedstats.gov • Web site features an efficient search facility for full-text statistics produced by more than 100 federal agencies, including the Census Bureau, the Bureau of Economic Analysis, and the Bureau of Labor Statistics. Boolean searches can be made within one agency or for all agencies combined. Links are offered to international statistical bureaus, including the UN, IMF, OECD, UNESCO, Eurostat, and 20 individual countries. Fees: Free.

FreeLunch.com. Economy.com, Inc. Phone: (610)696-8700 Fax: (610)696-1678 • URL: http://www.freelunch.com • Web site provides free access to more than 1.5 million economic and financial data series, covering industry, demographics, labor markets, prices, retail sales, government spending, trade, interest rates, housing starts, the stock market, and many other topics. Data is available for various time periods in either chart or table form. Searching is offered. Fees: Free, but registration required. Economy.com, Inc. also offers fee-based economic analysis at *The Dismal Scientist* site (http://www.dismal.com).

Internal Revenue Service IRS.gov. Internal Revenue Service. Phone: 800-829-1040 or (202)622-5000 Fax: (202)622-5844 • URL: http://www.irs.gov • Web site provides a wide variety of tax information, including IRS forms and publications. Searching is available. Fees: Free.

Nexis.com. Lexis-Nexis Group. Phone: 800-227-4908 or (937)865-6800 Fax: (937)865-6909 E-mail: webmaster@prod.lexis-nexis.com • URL: http://www.nexis.com • Fee-based Web site offers searching of about 2.8 billion documents in some 30,000 news, business, and legal information sources. Features include a subject directory covering 1,200 topics in 34 categories and a Company Dossier containing information on more than 500,000 public and private companies. Boolean searching is offered.

Rutgers Accounting Web (RAW). Rutgers University Accounting Research Center. Phone: (973)353-5172 Fax: (973)353-1283 • URL: http://www.rutgers.edu/accounting • RAW Web site provides extensive links to sources of national and international accounting information, such as the Big Six accounting firms, the Financial Accounting Standards Board (FASB), SEC filings (EDGAR), journals, publishers, software, the International Accounting Network, and "Internet's largest list of accounting firms in USA." Searching is offered. Fees: Free.

Tax Analysts [Web site]. Tax Analysts. Phone: 800-955-3444 or (703)533-4400 Fax: (703)533-4444 • URL: http://www.tax.org • The three main sections of Tax Analysts home page are "Tax News" (Today's Tax News, Feature of the Week, Tax Snapshots, Tax Calendar); "Products & Services" (Product Catalog, Press Releases); and "Public Interest" (Discussion Groups, Tax Clinic, Tax History Project). Fees: Free for coverage of current tax events; fee-based for

comprehensive information. Daily updating.

ONLINE DATABASES

Accounting and Tax Database. PROQUEST. • Provides indexing and abstracting of the literature of accounting, taxation, and financial management, 1971 to date. Updating is weekly. Especially covers accounting, auditing, banking, bankruptcy, employee compensation and benefits, cash management, financial planning, and credit. Inquire as to online cost and availability.

PERIODICALS AND NEWSLETTERS

Corporate Taxation. RIA. • Bimonthly. $400.00 per year. Analysis and guidance for practitioners. Provides ongoing coverage of currently proposed tax reform bills. Formerly (Journal of Corporate Taxation).

Highlights and Documents. Tax Analysts. • Daily. $2,249.00 per year, including monthly indexes. Newsletter. Provides daily coverage of IRS, congressional, judicial, state, and international tax developments. Includes abstracts and citations for "all tax documents released within the previous 24 to 48 hours." Annual compilation available *Highlights and Documents on Microfiche.*

Journal of Taxation of Corporate Transactions. CCH, Inc. • Bimonthly. $225.00 per year. Covers the planning and compliance issues faced by corporate taxpayers.

Strategic Finance. Institute of Management Accountants. • Monthly. Institutions, $140.00 per year; non-profit libraries, $70,00 per year. Provides articles on corporate finance, cost control, cash flow, budgeting, corporate taxes, and other financial management topics.

Tax Notes: The Weekly Tax Service. Tax Analysts. • Weekly. $1,699.00 per year. Includes an *Annual* and 1985-1996 compliations on CD-ROM. Newsletter. Covers "tax news from all federal sources," including congressional committees, tax courts, and the Internal Revenue Service. Each issue contains "summaries of every document that pertains to federal tax law," with citations. Commentary is provided.

Tax Practice. Tax Analysts. • Weekly. $199.00 per year. Newsletter. Covers news affecting tax practitioners and litigators, with emphasis on federal court decisions, rules and regulations, and tax petitions. Provides a guide to Internal Revenue Service audit issues.

STATISTICS SOURCES

Business Statistics of the United States. Linz Audain and Cornelia J. Strawser. Bernan Associates. • Annual. $147.00. Based on *Business Statistics,* formerly issue by the Bureau of Economic Analysis, U. S. Department of Commerce. Provides basic data for a wide variety of U. S. industries, services, and economic indicators. Most statistics are shown annually for 30 years and monthly for the most recent four years.

Statistics of Income Bulletin. Available from U.S. Government Printing Office. • Quarterly. $44.00 per year. Current data compiled from tax returns relating to income, assets, and expenses of individuals and businesses. (U. S. Internal Revenue Service.).

Statistics of Income: Corporation Income Tax Returns. U.S. Internal Revenue Service. Available from U.S. Government Printing Office. • Annual. $26.00.

Survey of Current Business. Available from U. S. Government Printing Office. • Monthly. $63.00 per year. Issued by Bureau of Economic Analysis, U. S. Department of Commerce. Presents a wide variety of business and economic data.

TRADE/PROFESSIONAL ASSOCIATIONS

Tax Analysts. 400 S Maple Ave., Ste. 400, Falls Church, VA 22046. Phone: 800-955-2444 or (703)533-4400 Fax: (703)533-4444 E-mail:

cservice@tax.org • URL: http://www.tax.org • Reviews all tax law developments, federal, state, international comprehensively; compiles statistics. **Convention/Meeting:** none.

Tax Executives Institute. 1200 G St. NW, Ste. 300, Washington, DC 20005-3814. Phone: (202)638-5601 Fax: (202)638-5607 E-mail: administration@tei.org • URL: http://www.tei.org • Professional society of executives administering and directing tax affairs for corporations and businesses. Maintains TEI +Education Fund.

OTHER SOURCES

Capital Changes Reports. CCH, Inc. • Weekly. $1,395.00. Six looseleaf volumes. Arranged alphabetically by company. This service presents a chronological capital history that includes reorganizations, mergers and consolidations. Recent actions are found in Volume One - "New Matters.".

Corporation Forms. Prentice Hall PTR. • Looseleaf. Periodic supplementation. Price on application.

Federal Income Taxation of Corporations Filing Consolidated Returns. LexisNexis Matthew Bender. • Semiannual. $768.00. Four looseleaf volumes.

Manufacturers' Tax Alert. CCH, Inc. • Monthly $297.00 per year. Newsletter. Covers the major tax issues affecting manufacturing companies. Includes current developments in various kind of federal, state, and international taxes: sales, use, franchise, property, and corporate income.

Reproducible Copies of Federal Tax Forms and Instructions. Available from U. S. Government Printing Office. • Annual. $54.00. Two looseleaf volumes issued by the Internal Revenue Service (http://www.irs.gov). "Contains the most frequently requested tax forms and instructions," prepared especially for libraries.

CORPORATE PLANNING

See: PLANNING

CORPORATE REAL ESTATE

See: INDUSTRIAL REAL ESTATE

CORPORATE RESPONSIBILITY

See: SOCIAL RESPONSIBILITY

CORPORATION LAW AND REGULATION

See also: ADMINISTRATIVE LAW AND REGULATION; BUSINESS LAW; INCORPORATION; LAW

GENERAL WORKS

Economics of Corporation Law and Securities Regulation. Richard A. Posner and Kenneth E. Scott. Aspen Publishers, Inc. • 1981. $32.95.

ABSTRACTS AND INDEXES

Current Law Index: Multiple Access to Legal Periodicals. Gale Cengage Learning. • Monthly. $725.00 per year. Produced in cooperation with the American Association of Law Libraries. Indexes more than 900 law journals, legal newspapers, and specialty publications from the U.S., Canada, U.K., Ireland, Australia, and New Zealand.

Index to Legal Periodicals and Books. H. W. Wilson Co. • Monthly. $490.00 per year. Quarterly and annual cumulations.

ALMANACS AND YEARBOOKS

American Law Yearbook. Gale Cengage Learning. • Annual. $165.00. Serves as a yearly supplement to

West's Encyclopedia of American Law. Describes new legal developments in many subject areas.

BIBLIOGRAPHIES

Encyclopedia of Legal Information Sources. Gale Cengage Learning. • 1992. $180.00. Second edition. Lists more than 23,000 law-related information sources, including print, nonprint, and organizational.

Legal Information: How to Find It, How to Use It. Kent Olson. Greenwood Publishing Group, Inc. • 1998. $64.95. Includes CD-ROM. Recommends sources for various kinds of legal information.

CD-ROM DATABASES

WILSONDISC: Index to Legal Periodicals and Books. H. W. Wilson Co. • Monthly. Includes unlimited online access to *Index to Legal Periodicals* through WILSONLINE. Contains CD-ROM indexing of more than 1,400 English language legal periodicals from 1981 to date and 2,500 books.

DIRECTORIES

Law and Legal Information Directory. Gale Cengage Learning. • Annual. $440.00. Contains a wide range of sources of legal information, such as associations, law schools, courts, federal agencies, referral services, libraries, publishers, and research centers. There is a separate chapter for each of 23 types of information source or service.

ENCYCLOPEDIAS AND DICTIONARIES

Communicating with Legal Databases: Terms and Abbreviations for the Legal Researcher. Anne L. McDonald. Neal-Schuman Publishers, Inc. • 1987. $82.50.

West's Encyclopedia of American Law. Available from Gale Cengage Learning. • 2003. $1,195.00. Second edition. 12 volumes. Published by West Group. Covers a wide variety of legal topics for the general reader.

HANDBOOKS AND MANUALS

Model Business Corporation Act Annotated. American Bar Association. • 1998. $600.00. Four volumes. $150.00 per volume.

INTERNET DATABASES

Lexis.com Research System. Lexis-Nexis Group. Phone: 800-227-4908 or (937)865-6800 Fax: (937)865-6909 E-mail: webmaster@prod.lexis-nexis.com • URL: http://www.lexis.com • Fee-based Web site offers extensive searching of a wide variety of legal sources. Additional features include Daily Opinion Service, lexis.com Bookstore, Career Center, CLE Center, Law Schools, and Practice Pages ("Pages specific to areas of specialty").

ONLINE DATABASES

Index to Legal Periodicals and Books (Online). H. W. Wilson Co. • Broad coverage of law journals and books 1981 to date. Monthly updates. Inquire as to online cost and availability.

Legal Resource Index. Gale Cengage Learning. • Broad coverage of law literature appearing in legal, business, and other periodicals, 1980 to date. Daily updates. Inquire as to online cost and availability.

LEXIS. LEXIS-NEXIS. • The various LEXIS databases provide full text and indexing for a wide variety of legal cases, statutes, orders, and opinions.

PERIODICALS AND NEWSLETTERS

Corporate Counselor. American Lawyer Media, Inc. • Monthly. $229.00 per year. Newsletter. Covers issues involved with managing the legal department of a corporation, including relations with outside counsel. (A Law Journal Newsletter, formerly published by Leader Publications).

D & O Advisor: Risk Management for Directors and Officers. American Lawyer Media, Inc. • Quarterly. $125.00 per year. Covers a wide range of legal top-

ics of concern to corporate boards and key executives.

Daily Report for Executives. BNA, Inc. • Daily. $7,698.00 per year. Newsletter. Covers legal, regulatory, economic, and tax developments affecting corporations.

Federal Register. Office of the Federal Register. Available from U.S. Government Printing Office. • Daily except Saturday and Sunday. $764.00 per year. Publishes regulations and legal notices issued by federal agencies, including executive orders and presidential proclamations. Issued by the National Archives and Records Administration (http://www.nara.gov).

Fletcher Corporation Law Adviser. West Group. • Description: Comments on recent developments in corporation law. Discusses age discrimination, bankruptcy, civil rights, arbitration, appraisals, bylaws, derivative suits, fraud, hazardous waste, liability, mergers liens, pensions, insurance, proxies, profits, stocks, and taxation.

Securities and Federal Corporate Law Report. West Group. • $526.00 per year. Newsletter. Periodic supplementation.

Securities Regulation and Law Report. BNA, Inc. • Weekly. $1,479.00 per year. Looseleaf service.

TRADE/PROFESSIONAL ASSOCIATIONS

Academy of Legal Studies in Business. Dept. of Finance, 120 Upham Hall, Miami University, Oxford, OH 45056. Phone: 800-831-2903 or (513)529-2945 Fax: (513)523-8180 • URL: http://www.alsb.org.

OTHER SOURCES

Business Law Monographs. LéxisNexis Matthew Bender. • Quarterly. $1,599.00. 38 volumes. Intended for in-house and outside corporate counsel. Each monograph concentrates on a particular subject.

Corporate Compliance Series. Joseph E. Murphy and Paul H. Dawes. West Group. • $1,210.00. 12 looseleaf volumes. Covers criminal and civil liability problems for corporations. Includes employee safety, product liability, pension requirements, securities violations, equal employment opportunity issues, intellectual property, employee hiring and firing, and other corporate compliance topics.

Corporate Criminal Liability. Kathleen F. Brickley. West Group. • Annual. $365.00 per year. Three looseleaf volumes. Discusses how the general principles of criminal law apply to the corporate world. Provides a detailed analysis of liability under major federal crime statutes.

Corporate Practice Series. BNA, Inc. • Weekly. $1,937.00 per year. Looseleaf service. Series of about 30 "portfolios" on various aspects of corporate law.

Corporation Forms. Prentice Hall PTR. • Looseleaf. Periodic supplementation. Price on application.

Fletcher Corporation Forms Annotated. West Group. • Annual. $1,263.00. 26 volumes.

Going Private. American Lawyer Media, Inc. • Looseleaf. $169.00. Updated as needed. Discusses the legal ramifications of a publicly-owned company "going private" by way of a sale, leveraged buyout, reverse stock split, or merger. (Law Journal Press).

How to Form Your Own Corporation Without a Lawyer for Under $75.00. Ted Nicholas and Sean P. Melvin. Dearborn Trade Publishing, A Kaplan Professional Co. • 1999. $19.95. 26th edition.

CORPORATION REPORTS

See also: BUSINESS JOURNALISM; COM-
MUNICATION

GENERAL WORKS

Corporate Financial Reporting: Text and Cases.
David B. Hawkins. McGraw-Hill. • 1997. $118.13.
Fourth edition.

*The Financial Numbers Game: Detecting Creative
Accounting Practices.* Charles W. Mulford and
Eugene E. Comiskey. John Wiley and Sons, Inc. •
2002. $39.95. Serves as a guide to financial state-
ment analysis for investors. Explains the "creative"
schemes used by corporations to boost earnings-per-
share data.

*Financial Statement Analysis: Theory, Application
and Interpretation.* Leopold A. Bernstein and John J
Wild. McGraw-Hill. • 1997. $95.31. Sixth edition.

Understanding Financial Statements. Lyn M. Fraser
and Aileen Orminston. Prentice Hall PTR. • 2003.
$42.67. Seventh edition. Emphasis is on the evalua-
tion and interpretation of financial statements.

CD-ROM DATABASES

Compact D/SEC. Thomson Financial. • Monthly.
Provides 200 financial data items for 12,000 U. S.
publicly-held corporations filing reports with the
Securities and Exchange Commission. Includes
company profiles.

DIRECTORIES

Mergent's Handbook of Common Stocks. Mergent,
Inc. • Quarterly. $350.00 per year ($100.00 per
copy). Contains one-page profiles of about 1,000
major corporations listed on the New York Stock
Exchange. Includes analysis, comment, stock price
performance data, and 10-year financial statistics.
Formerly *Moody's Handbook of Common Stocks.*

Mergent's Handbook of NASDAQ Stocks. Mergent,
Inc. • Quarterly. $350.00 per year ($100.00 per
copy). Contains one-page profiles of more than 600
major companies traded on the NASDAQ National
Exchange or the American Stock Exchange.
Includes price performance scores, analysis, com-
ment, and seven-year financial statistics. Formerly
Moody's Handbook of NASDAQ Stocks.

HANDBOOKS AND MANUALS

*Accounting Trends and Techniques in Published
Corporate Annual Reports.* American Institute of
Certified Public Accountants. • Annual. Price on
application.

Analysis and Use of Financial Statements. Gerald I.
White. John Wiley and Sons, Inc. • 2002. $123.95.
Third edition. Includes analysis of financial ratios,
cash flow, inventories, assets, debt, etc. Also covered
are employee benefits, corporate investments,
multinational operations, financial derivatives, and
hedging activities.

*Environmental Accounting: Current Issues,
Abstracts, and Bibliography.* United Nations
Publications. • 1992. Provides guidelines for
environmental disclosure in corporate annual
reports.

*Financial Shenanigans: How to Detect Accounting
Gimmicks and Fraud in Financial Reports.* Howard
M. Schilit. McGraw-Hill. • 2002. $27.95. Second
edition. Tells how to interpret the footnotes and fine
print in corporate annual and other reports.

*Financial Statement Analysis: A Practitioner's
Guide.* Martin Fridson and Fernando Alvarez. John
Wiley and Sons, Inc. • 2002. $69.95. Third edition.
(Finance Series).

*Financial Statement Analysis: The Investor's Self
Study Guide to Interpreting and Analyzing.* Charles
J. Woelfel. McGraw-Hill. • 1993. $24.95. Revised
edition.

Guide to Financial Reporting and Analysis. Eugene

E. Comiskey and Charles W. Mulford. John Wiley
and Sons, Inc. • 2000. $75.00. Provides financial
statement examples to illustrate the application of
generally accepted accounting principles.

Guide to Preparing Financial Statements. John R.
Clay and others. Practitioners Publishing Co. •
1998. Three looseleaf volumes. Price on application.

*How to Produce Creative Advertising: Traditional
Techniques and Computer Applications.* Thomas
Bivins and Ann Keding. McGraw Hill. • 1993. $37.
95. Covers copywriting, advertising design, and the
use of desktop publishing techniques in advertising.
(NTC Business Books Series).

*How to Produce Creative Publications: Traditional
Techniques and Computer Applications.* Thomas
Bivins and Ann Keding. McGraw-Hill. • 1993. $37.
95. A practical guide to the writing, designing, and
production of magazines, annual reports, brochures,
and newsletters by traditional methods and by
desktop publishing. (NTC Business Books Series).

*How to Read a Financial Report: Wringing Vital
Signs Out of the Numbers.* John A. Tracy. John
Wiley and Sons, Inc. • 1999. $29.95. Fifth edition.

Manager's Guide to Financial Statement Analysis.
Stephen F. Jablonsky and Noah P. Barsky. John
Wiley and Sons, Inc. • 2001. $49.95. Second
edition. The two main sections are "Financial Statements and Business Strategy" and "Market Valuation
and Business Strategy.".

*Miller GAAP Financial Statement Disclosures
Manual.* Aspen Publishers. • Annual. $105.00.
Provides a detailed summary of financial report
disclosure requirements, with examples. Includes a
CD-ROM.

*Reliable Financial Reporting and Internal Control:
A Global Implementation Guide.* Dmitris N.
Chorafas. John Wiley and Sons, Inc. • 2000. $75.00.
Discusses financial reporting and control as related
to doing business internationally.

*SEC Financial Reporting: Annual Reports to
Shareholders, Form 10-K, and Quarterly Financial
Reporting.* LexisNexis Matthew Bender. • Annual.
$254.00. Looseleaf service. Coverage of aspects of
financial reporting with GAAP disclosure and
Regulation S-X preparation Step-by-step procedures
for preparing information for Form 10-K and annual
shareholders reports.

*SEC Handbook: Rules and Forms for Financial
Statements and Related Disclosures.* CCH, Inc. •
Annual. $59.00. Contains full text of rules and
requirements set by the Securities and Exchange
Commisssion for preparation of corporate financial
statements.

INTERNET DATABASES

Factiva. Dow Jones Reuters Business Interactive,
LLC. Phone: 800-369-7466 or (609)452-1511 Fax:
(609)520-5770 E-mail: solutions@factiva.com •
URL: http://www.factiva.com • Fee-based Web site
provides "global news and business information
through Web sites and content integration solutions."
Includes Dow Jones and Reuters newswires, The
Wall Street Journal, and more than 7,000 other
sources of current news, historical articles, market
research reports, and investment analysis. Content
includes 96 major U. S. newspapers, 900 non-
English sources, trade publications, media
transcripts, country profiles, news photos, etc.

Nexis.com. Lexis-Nexis Group. Phone: 800-227-
4908 or (937)865-6800 Fax: (937)865-6909 E-mail:
webmaster@prod.lexis-nexis.com • URL: http://
www.nexis.com • Fee-based Web site offers searching of about 2.8 billion documents in some 30,000
news, business, and legal information sources.
Features include a subject directory covering 1,200
topics in 34 categories and a Company Dossier
containing information on more than 500,000 public
and private companies. Boolean searching is offered.

Wall Street Journal Interactive Edition. Dow Jones
& Co., Inc. Phone: 800-369-2834 or (212)416-2000
Fax: (212)416-2658 E-mail: inquiries@interactive.
wsj.com • URL: http://www.wsj.com • Fee-based
Web site providing online searching of worldwide
information from the *The Wall Street Journal.*
Includes "Company Snapshots," "The Journal's
Greatest Hits," "Index to Market Data," "Journal
Links," etc. Financial price quotes are available.
Fees: $49.00 per year; $29.00 per year to print
subscribers.

ONLINE DATABASES

Compustat. Standard and Poor's. • Financial data on
publicly held U.S. and some foreign corporations;
data held for 20 years. Inquire as to online cost and
availability.

Disclosure SEC Database. Thomson Financial. •
Provides online information from records filed with
the Securities and Exchange Commission by more
than 12,000 publicly-owned companies in the U.S.
Includes about 200 financial data items and information relating to executives. Time span is 1977 to
date, with weekly updates. Inquire as to online cost
and availability.

EdgarPlus: SEC Basic Filings. Thomson Financial.
• Online service provides full text of about 60,000
documents that have been filed with the U.S. Securities and Exchange Commission, 1987 to date, with
daily updates. Filings include 6-K, 8-K, 10-K, 10-C,
10-Q, 20-F, and proxy statements. Inquire as to online cost and availability.

F & S Index. Gale Cengage Learning. • Contains
about four million citations to worldwide business,
financial, and industrial or consumer product
literature appearing from 1972 to date. Weekly
updates. Inquire as to online cost and availability.

First Call Consensus Earnings Estimates. Thomson
Financial. • Online service provides corporate earnings estimates for more than 2,500 U. S. companies,
based on data from leading brokerage firms. Weekly
updates. Inquire as to online cost and availability.

PERIODICALS AND NEWSLETTERS

Ragan's Annual Report Review. Lawrence Ragan
Communications Inc. • Description: Provides business trends, tips, and tactics.

The Wall Street Journal. Dow Jones & Co., Inc. •
Daily. $189.00 per year. Covers news and trends
relating to business, industry, finance, the economy,
and international commerce. Provides extensive
price and other data for the securities, commodity,
options, futures, foreign exchange, and money
markets.

RESEARCH CENTERS AND INSTITUTES

Design Research Unit. Massachusetts College of
Art, 621 Huntington Ave., Boston, MA 02115.
Phone: (617)879-7733 Fax: (617)566-4034 E-mail:
rstreit@massart.edu • URL: http://www.babel.
massart.edu/dru • Conducts research related to the
design of printed matter, including annual reports,
letterheads, posters, and brochures.

STATISTICS SOURCES

*Standard & Poor's Stock Reports: NASDAQ and
Regional Exchanges.* Standard & Poor's. • Irregular.
$1,100.00 per year. Looseleaf service. Provides two
pages of financial details and other information for
each corporation included.

*Standard & Poor's Stock Reports: New York Stock
Exchange.* Standard & Poor's. • Irregular. $1,295.00
per year. Looseleaf service. Provides two pages of
financial details and other information for each
corporation with stock listed on the N. Y. Stock
Exchange.

TRADE/PROFESSIONAL ASSOCIATIONS

Financial Executives International. 200 Campus Dr.,
PO Box 674, Florham Park, NJ 07932-0674. Phone:
(973)765-1000 Fax: (973)765-1018 E-mail:

mcangemi@financialexecutives.org • URL: http://www.financialexecutives.org • Professional organization of corporate financial executives performing duties of chief financial officer, controller, treasurer, or vice-president-finance. Sponsors research activities through its affiliated Financial Executives Research Foundation. Maintains offices in Toronto, Canada, and Washington, DC.

Financial Management Association International. University of South Florida, College of Business Administration, 4202 E Fowler Ave., BSN 3331, Tampa, FL 33620-5500. Phone: (813)974-2084 Fax: (813)974-3318 E-mail: fma@coba.usf.edu • URL: http://www.fma.org • Professors of financial management; corporate financial officers. Facilitates exchange of ideas among persons involved in financial management or the study thereof. Conducts workshops for comparison of current research projects and development of cooperative ventures in writing and research. Sponsors honorary society for superior students at 300 colleges and universities. Offers placement services.

Governmental Accounting Standards Board. 401 Merritt 7, PO Box 5116, Norwalk, CT 06856-5116. Phone: (203)847-0700 Fax: (203)849-9714 E-mail: webmaster@gasb.org • URL: http://www.gasb.org • Has established and maintains the Financial +Accounting Standards Board and the Financial +Accounting Standards Advisory Council. In 1984, organized the Governmental Accounting Standards Board and the Governmental Accounting Standards Advisory Council (see separate entries). FASB creates and improves standards of financial accounting and reporting by defining, and issuing, such standards; conducts and commissions research, statistical compilations, and other studies and surveys; holds meetings, conferences, and hearings with respect to financial accounting and reporting. FASAC consults with FASB about major technical issues, agenda of projects, assignment of priorities, and selection and organization of FASB task forces. GASB establishes accounting standards for state and local governmental entities. GASB consults with GASAC in a fashion similar to the FASB and FASAC. **Convention/Meeting:** none.

OTHER SOURCES

Corporation Forms. Prentice Hall PTR. • Looseleaf. Periodic supplementation. Price on application.

CORPORATIONS

See also: MULTINATIONAL CORPORATIONS
GENERAL WORKS
Cases and Materials on Corporations-Including Partnerships and Limited Partnerships. Robert W. Hamilton. West Publishing Co. • 2001. $83.00. Seventh edition. American Case book Series.

Cases in Corporate Acquisitions, Buyouts, Mergers, and Takeovers. Gale Cengage Learning. • 1999. $350.00. Reviews and analyzes about 300 cases of both success and failure in corporate acquisitiveness.

Cases in Corporate Innovation. Gale Cengage Learning. • 2002. $310.00. Reviews and analyzes about 300 cases to illustrate both successful and failed management of innovation.

Corporate Cultures: The Rites and Rituals of Corporate Life. Terrance E. Deal and Allan Kennedy. Perseus Books Group. • 1982. $15.00.

Dirty Business: Exploring Corporate Misconduct: Analysis and Cases. Maurice Punch. Sage Publications, Inc. • 1996. $113.00. Covers organizational misbehavior and white-collar crime. Includes "Ten Cases of Corporate Deviance.".

The ERC Closely-Held Corporation Guide. Prentice Hall PTR. • 1983. $59.95. Second edition.

Reengineering Management: The Mandate for New Leadership. James Champy. DIANE Publishing Co. • 1998. $25.00.

Reengineering the Corporation: A Manifesto for Business Revolution. Michael Hammer and James Champy. HarperInformation. • 2001. $16.00. Revised edition.

CD-ROM DATABASES
CanCorp Plus Canadian Financial Database. Micromedia Ltd. • Monthly. $3,600.00 per year. Also available quarterly at $2,975.00 per year. Provides comprehensive information on CD-ROM for more than 11,000 public and private Canadian corporations. Emphasis is on detailed financial data for up to seven years.

Corporate Affiliations Plus. National Register Publishing, Reed Reference Publishing. • Quarterly. $1,995.00 per year. Provides CD-ROM discs corresponding to *Directory of Corporate Affiliations* and *Corporate Finance Bluebook.* Contains corporate financial services information and worldwide data on subsidiaries and affiliates.

Hoover's Company Capsules on CD-ROM. Hoover's, Inc. • Quarterly. $399.95 per year (single-user). Provides the CD-ROM version of *Hoover's Handbook of American Business, Hoover's Handbook of Emerging Companies, Hoover's Handbook of World Business, Hoover's Guide to Computer Companies, Hoover's Guide to Media Companies, Hoover's Handbook of Private Companies,* and various regional guides. Includes more than 11,000 profiles of companies.

InvesText [CD-ROM]. Thomson Financial. • Monthly. Contains full text on CD-ROM of investment research reports from about 630 sources, including leading brokers and investment bankers. Reports are available on both U. S. and international publicly traded corporations. Separate industry reports cover more than 50 industries. Time span is 1982 to date.

OECD Statistical Compendium. Organization for Economic Cooperation and Development. • Semiannual. $1,905.00 per year for 1 to 10 users. CD-ROM contains more than 730,000 monthly, quarterly, and annual time series for OECD countries, 1960 to date. Includes fully searchable data on agriculture, food, economic indicators, national accounts, employment, energy, finance, industry, technology, and foreign trade. Results can be displayed in various forms.

Standard & Poor's Corporations. Available from Dialog OnDisc. • Monthly. Price on application. Produced by Standard & Poor's. Contains three CD-ROM files: Executives, Private Companies, and Public Companies, providing detailed information on more than 70,000 business executives, 55,000 private companies, and 12,000 publicly-traded corporations.

WILSONDISC: Wilson Business Abstracts. H. W. Wilson Co. • Monthly. Includes unlimited online access to *Wilson Business Abstracts* through WILSONLINE. Provides CD-ROM "cover-to-cover" abstracting and indexing of over 600 prominent business periodicals. Indexing is from 1982, abstracting from 1990. (*Business Periodicals Index* without abstracts is available on CD-ROM at $1,495 per year.).

DIRECTORIES
American Big Businesses Directory. infoUSA Inc. • Covers: 218,000 U.S. businesses with more than 100 employees, and 500,000 key executives and directors. CD-ROM version contains 160,000 top firms and 431,000 key executives. Entries include: Name, address, phone, names and titles of key personnel, number of employees, sales volume, Standard Industrial Classification (SIC) codes, subsidiaries and parent company names, stock exchanges on which traded.

American Manufacturers Directory. infoUSA Inc. • Covers: more than 150,000 manufacturing companies with 20 or more employees. CD-ROM version lists all 531,000 U.S. manufacturers, in all employee size ranges. Entries include: Company name, address, phone, contact name, Standard Industrial Classification (SIC) codes, number of employees, sales volume code, credit rating scores.

The Corporate Directory of U.S. Public Companies. Walker's Research, LLC. • Annual. $360.00. Two volumes. Contains information on more than 10,000 publicly-traded companies, including names of executives and major subsidiaries. Includes financial and stock data.

Corporate Yellow Book: Who's Who at the Leading U.S. Companies. Leadership Directions, Inc. • Quarterly. $360.00 per year. Lists names and titles of over 42,000 key executives in major U. S. corporations. Includes four indexes: industry, personnel, geographic by state, and company/subsidiary. Companion volume to *Financial Yellow Book.*

Cyberhound's Guide to Companies on the Internet. Gale Cengage Learning. • 1996. $79.00. Presents critical descriptions and ratings of more than 2,000 company or corporate Internet databases. Includes a glossary of Internet terms, a bibliography, and indexes. (Cyberhound's Series).

D and B Million Dollar Directory. • Annual. Commercial institutions, $1,395.00; libraries, $1,275.00. Lease basis.

Directory of Companies Required to File Annual Reports with the Securities and Exchange Commission. Securities and Exchange Commission. Available from U.S. Government Printing Office. • Annual. $46.00.

FP Survey of Industrials (Canadian Firms). Financial Post Datagroup. • Annual. $124.95 Contains detailed information on more than 2,700 publicly owned Canadian manufacturing, retailing, and service corporations. Includes the "Financial Post 500," a ranking of the largest Canadian companies.

Headquarters USA: A Directory of Contact Information for Headquarters and Other Central Offices of Major Businesses and Organizations Nationwide. Omnigraphics, Inc. • Annual. $185.00. Two volumes. Volume one is alphabetical by name of business or organization. Volume two is classified by subject. Includes more than 112,000 businesses, organizations, agencies, institutions, and "high-profile" individuals. Listings include addresses, telephone numbers, fax numbers, and toll-free numbers and Web addresses where available. Formerly *Business Phone Book USA.*

Hoover's Handbook of American Business: Profiles of Major U. S. Companies. Hoover's, Inc. • Annual. $195.95. Two volumes. Provides detailed profiles of more than 750 large public and private companies, including history, executives, brand names, key competitors, and up to 10 years of financial data. Includes indexes by industry, location, executive name, company name, and brand name.

Hoover's Handbook of Emerging Companies: Profiles of America's Most Exciting Growth Enterprises. Hoover's, Inc. • Annual. $125.00. Contains detailed profiles of 600 rapidly growing corporations. Includes indexes by industry, location, executive name, company name, and brand name.

Hoover's Masterlist of Major U. S. Companies. Hoover's, Inc. • 2003. $275.00. Provides brief information, including annual sales, number of employees, and chief executive, for about 5,000 U. S. companies, both public and private.

International Directory of Company Histories. Saint James Press. • 53 volumes. $199.00 per volume. Provides detailed histories of about 4,550 major corporations. Cumulative indexing is provided for company names, personal names, and industries.

Job Seeker's Guide to Private and Public Companies. Gale Cengage Learning. • 1993. $390.00. Second edition. $99.00 per volume. Four regional volumes: *The West, The Midwest, The Northeast,* and *The South.* Covers about 15,000 companies, providing information on personnel department contacts, corporate officials, company benefits, application procedures, etc.

Kompass USA. Kompass International/Kompass USA, Inc. • Annual. Price on application. Two volumes. Includes information on about 125,000 U.S. companies. Classification system covers approximately 50,000 products and services. Product and tradename indexes are provided.

Major Performance Rankings. Available from Gale Cengage Learning. • 2003. $1,190.00. Second edition. Published by Euromonitor. Ranks 2,500 leading consumer product companies worldwide by various kinds of business and financial data, such as sales, profit, and market share. Includes international, regional, and country rankings.

Peterson's Job Opportunities for Business Majors. Peterson's. • 1999. $18.95. Provides career information for the 2,000 largest U. S. employers in various industries.

Reference Book of Corporate Managements. • Annual. Libraries, $650.00 per year; others, $795.00 per year. Lease basis. Management executives at over 12,000 leading United States companies.

S & P MidCap 400 Directory. Standard and Poors Corp. • Annual. $66.00. Contains detailed profiles of the companies included in Standard & Poor's MidCap 400 Index of stock prices. Includes income and balance sheet data for up to 10 years, with growth and stability rankings for 400 midsized corporations.

Standard & Poor's 500 Guide. McGraw-Hill. • Annual. $27.95. Contains detailed profiles of the companies included in Standard & Poor's 500 Index of stock prices. Includes income and balance sheet data for up to 10 years, with growth and stability rankings for 500 major corporations.

Standard and Poor's Register of Corporations, Directors and Executives. Standard and Poor's. • Annual. $675.00. Looseleaf service. Lease basis. Periodic supplementation. Over 55,000 public and privately held corporations in the U.S.

Ward's Business Directory of U. S. Private and Public Companies. Gale Cengage Learning. • 2002. $2,765.00. 45th edition. Eight volumes. *Ward's* contains basic information on about 120,000 business firms, of which 90 percent are private companies. Includes mid-year *Supplement.* Volumes available individually. Prices vary.

FINANCIAL RATIOS

Quarterly Financial Report for Manufacturing, Mining, and Trade Corporations. U.S. Federal Trade Commission and U.S. Securities and Exchange Commission. Available from U.S. Government Printing Office. • Quarterly. $49.00 per year.

HANDBOOKS AND MANUALS

Analysis of Financial Statements. Leopold A. Bernstein and John J. Wild. McGraw-Hill. • 1999. $65.00. Fifth edition. Includes practical examples of analysis.

Corporate Valuation: Tools for Effective Appraisal and Decision Making. Stephen A. Ross and others. McGraw-Hill. • 1994. $76.95. Discusses the four most widely-used corporate appraisal methods.

Dun & Bradstreet/Gale Group Industry Handbooks. Gale Cengage Learning. • 2000. $650.00. Five volumes. $130.00 per volume. Each volume covers two or more major industries: 1. *Entertainment and Hospitality*; 2. *Construction and Agriculture*; 3. *Chemicals and Pharmaceuticals*; 4. *Computers &*

Software and Broadcasting & Telecommunications; 5. *Insurance and Health & Medical Services.* The following are included for each industry: overview, statistics, financial ratios, rankings, merger information, company directory, directory of associations, and consultants directory. (Dun and Bradstreet/Gale Industry Reference Handbook Series).

Incorporating Your Business: The Complete Guide That Tells All You Should Know About Establishing and Operating a Small Corporation. McGraw-Hill. • 1986. $14.95.

Incorporation Kit. Entrepreneur Media, Inc. • Looseleaf. $59.50. A practical guide to incorporating a small business. Includes sample forms and information on how to construct bylaws and articles of incorporation. (Start-Up Business Guide No. E7100.).

Reengineering Revolution: A Handbook. Michael Hammer and Steven Stanton. HarperInformation. • 1995. $17.95.

INTERNET DATABASES

Business 2.0 Web Guide to the Best Business Links. Business 2.0 Media Inc. Phone: (415)293-4800 E-mail: support@business2.com • URL: http://www.business2.com/webguide • Web site presents an extensive, searchable directory of links to "the best, most informative, and authoritative web pages." Twenty main categories cover business, finance, career, company information, people, and technology topics, with thousands of subtopics, all linking to Web sites recommended by experienced business researchers. Fees: Free.

Business Week Online. McGraw-Hill. Phone: (212)512-2511 Fax: (684)842-6101 • URL: http://www.businessweek.com • Web site provides complete contents of current issue of *Business Week* plus "BW Daily" with additonal business news, financial market quotes, and corporate information from Standard & Poor's. Includes various features, such as "Banking Center" with mortgage and interest data, and "Interactive Computer Buying Guide." The "Business Week Archive" is fully searchable back to 1996.

EBSCO Information Services. Ebsco Publishing. Phone: 800-653-2726 or (978)356-6500 Fax: (978)356-6565 E-mail: ep@epnet.com • URL: http://www.epnet.com • Fee-based Web site providing Internet access to a wide variety of databases, including business-related material. Full text is available for many periodical titles, with daily updates. Fees: Apply.

Factiva. Dow Jones Reuters Business Interactive, LLC. Phone: 800-369-7466 or (609)452-1511 Fax: (609)520-5770 E-mail: solutions@factiva.com • URL: http://www.factiva.com • Fee-based Web site provides "global news and business information through Web sites and content integration solutions." Includes Dow Jones and Reuters newswires, The Wall Street Journal, and more than 7,000 other sources of current news, historical articles, market research reports, and investment analysis. Content includes 96 major U. S. newspapers, 900 non-English sources, trade publications, media transcripts, country profiles, news photos, etc.

Hoover's Online. Hoover's, Inc. Phone: 800-486-8666 or (512)374-4500 Fax: (512)374-4501 • URL: http://www.hoovers.com • Web site provides stock quotes, lists of companies, and a variety of business information at no charge. In-depth company profiles are available.

InSite 2. Intelligence Data/Thomson Financial. Phone: 800-654-0393 or (617)856-1890 Fax: (617)737-3182 E-mail: intelligence.data@tfn.com • URL: http://www.insite2.gale.com/ • Fee-based Web site consolidates information in a "Base Pack" consisting of Business InSite, Market InSite, and Company InSite. Optional databases are Consumer InSite, Health and Wellness InSite, Newsletter In-

Site, and Computer InSite. Includes fulltext content from more than 2,500 trade publications, journals, newsletters, newspapers, analyst reports, and other sources. Continuous updating. Formerly produced by The Gale Group.

Mergent Online. Mergent, Inc. Phone: 800-342-5647 or (704)559-7601 Fax: (704)559-6945 E-mail: customerservice@mergent.com • URL: http://www.mergentonline.com • Fee-based Web site provides detailed information on 20,000 publicly-owned companies in 100 foreign countries, as well as more than 10,000 corporations listed on the New York Stock Exchange, American Stock Exchange, NASDAQ, and U. S. regional exchanges. Searching is offered on many financial variables and text fields. Weekly updating. Formerly *FIS Online.*

Nexis.com. Lexis-Nexis Group. Phone: 800-227-4908 or (937)865-6800 Fax: (937)865-6909 E-mail: webmaster@prod.lexis-nexis.com • URL: http://www.nexis.com • Fee-based Web site offers searching of about 2.8 billion documents in some 30,000 news, business, and legal information sources. Features include a subject directory covering 1,200 topics in 34 categories and a Company Dossier containing information on more than 500,000 public and private companies. Boolean searching is offered.

ProQuest Direct. ProQuest Inc. Phone: 800-889-3358 or (734)761-4700 Fax: (734)662-4554 • URL: http://proquest.com • Fee-based Web site providing Internet access to more than 3,000 periodicals, newspapers, and other publications. Many items are available full-text, with daily updates. Includes extensive corporate and financial information. Fees: Apply.

Switchboard. Switchboard, Inc. Phone: (508)898-8000 Fax: (508)898-1755 E-mail: webmaster@switchboard.com • URL: http://www.switchboard.com • Web site provides telephone numbers and street addresses for more than 100 million business locations and residences in the U. S. Broad industry categories are available. Fees: Free.

ONLINE DATABASES

Business and Industry. Gale Cengage Learning. • Contains online citations, abstracts, and selected fulltext from more than 1,000 trade journals, newspapers, and other publications. Provides general coverage of both manufacturing and service industries, including marketing, production, industry trends, key events, and information on specific companies. Time span is 1994 to date. Daily updates. Inquire as to online cost and availability. (Also available in a CD-ROM version.).

Dow Jones News Service. Dow Jones and Co., Inc. • Full text and edited news stories and articles on business affairs. Inquire as to online cost and availability.

InvesText. Thomson Financial. • Provides full text online of investment research reports from more than 600 sources, including leading brokers and investment bankers. Reports are available on approximately 60,000 U. S. and international corporations. Separate industry reports cover 54 industries. Time span is 1982 to date, with daily updates. Inquire as to online cost and availability.

Moody's Corporate News: International. Moody's Investors Service, Inc. • Provides financial and other business news relating to over 5,000 corporations in 100 countries, excluding the U. S. Time period is 1983 to date, with weekly updates. Inquire as to online cost and availability.

Standard & Poor's Corporate Descriptions. Standard & Poor's Corp. • Provides current, detailed financial and other information on approximately 12,000 publicly held U. S. and foreign corporations. Corresponds to the printed *Standard & Poor's Corporation Records.* Updating is twice a month. Inquire as to online cost and availability.

Standard and Poor's Daily News Online. Standard and Poor's Corp. • Full text of business news and

other information, 1984 to present. Inquire as to online cost and availability.

Standard & Poor's Register: Corporate. Standard & Poor's Corp. ⚫ Contains brief descriptions, with names of key executives, of about 55,000 public and private U. S. companies. Corresponds to the corporate volume of *Standard & Poor's Register of Corporations, Directors, and Executives.* Updated quarterly. Inquire as to online cost and availability.

Tablebase. Gale Cengage Learning. ⚫ Provides online numerical tabular data from a wide variety of business, organization, and government sources, including about 1,000 trade journals. Includes industry and individual company statistics relating to products, market share, sales forecasts, production, exports, market trends, etc. Time span is 1997 to date. Weekly updates. Inquire as to online cost and availability. (Also available in a CD-ROM version.).

Wilson Business Abstracts Online. H. W. Wilson Co. ⚫ Indexes and abstracts 600 major business periodicals, plus the *Wall Street Journal* and the business section of the *New York Times.* Indexing is from 1982, abstracting from 1990, with the two newspapers included from 1993. Updated weekly. Inquire as to online cost and availability. (*Business Periodicals Index* without abstracts is also available online.).

Worldscope. Thomson Financial. ⚫ Online service provides detailed financial and other information on more than 32,000 publicly-owned companies in 50 countries. Includes business description, balance sheets, earnings statements, senior officers, major shareholders, financial ratios, and 20-year historical data. Monthly updates. Inquire as to online cost and availability.

PERIODICALS AND NEWSLETTERS

Business Strategies Bulletin. CCH Inc. ⚫ Description: Reports tax and business planning information for all sizes of business, with emphasis on small to mid-sized business advisors.

Corporate Jobs Outlook!. Plunkett Research Ltd. ⚫ Description: Provides information about corporate employment opportunities. Includes salaries, benefits, and hiring policies.

The Corporate Secretary & Governance Professional. American Society of Corporate Secretaries Inc. ⚫ Description: News items of interest to the corporate secretary. Occasional articles covering SEC briefings, ASCS events, Chapter news, etc.

Forbes. Forbes, Inc. ⚫ Biweekly. $59.95 per year. Includes supplements: *Forbes ASAP* and *Forbes FYI.*

Fortune Magazine. Time Inc., Business Information Group. ⚫ Biweekly. $59.95 per year. Edited for top executives and upper-level managers.

Standard & Poor's SmallCap 600 Guide. McGraw-Hill. ⚫ Monthly. $24.95. Contains detailed profiles of the companies included in Standard & Poor's SmallCap 600 Index of stock prices. Includes income and balance sheet data for up to 10 years, with growth and stability rankings for 600 small capitalization corporations.

RESEARCH CENTERS AND INSTITUTES

Business, Government, and Society Research Institute. University of Pittsburgh. School of Business, Mervis Hall, Pittsburgh, PA 15260. Phone: (412)648-1555 Fax: (412)648-1693 E-mail: mitnick@pitt.edu.

Olsson Center for Applied Ethics. University of Virginia. The Darden School, P.O. Box 6550, Charlottesville, VA 22906. Phone: (434)924-0935 Fax: (434)924-6378 E-mail: ref8d@virginia.edu ⚫ URL: http://www.darden.virginia.edu.

STATISTICS SOURCES

New Business Incorporations. Dun & Bradstreet Corp. ⚫ Monthly. $25.00 per year. Gives the number of new business incorporations in each of the 50 states. Includes commentary.

Statistics of Income: Corporation Income Tax Returns. U.S. Internal Revenue Service. Available from U.S. Government Printing Office. ⚫ Annual. $26.00.

TRADE/PROFESSIONAL ASSOCIATIONS

American Society of Corporate Secretaries. 521 Fifth Ave., New York, NY 10175-0003. Phone: (212)681-2000 Fax: (212)681-2005 E-mail: dsmith@ascs.org ⚫ URL: http://www.ascs.org.

Association for Corporate Growth. 1926 Waukegan Rd., Suite 1, Glenview, IL 60025-1770. Phone: 800-699-1331 or (847)657-6730 Fax: (847)657-6819 E-mail: acghq@tcag.com ⚫ URL: http://www.acg.org.

Strategic Leadership Forum. 230 E Ohio St., No. 400, PO Box 5329, Chicago, IL 60611-3265. Phone: (403)240-1245 Fax: (403)240-0776 E-mail: ssci_office@steelcontainers.com ⚫ URL: http://www.strategicleadershipforum.org ⚫ Professional society primarily comprised of executives involved in international strategic management and planning. Conducts education programs. Maintains numerous committees.

OTHER SOURCES

Business Organizations with Tax Planning. Zolman Cavitch, editor. LexisNexis Matthew Bender. ⚫ Quarterly. $2,750. 16 looseleaf volumes. Periodic supplementation. In-depth analytical coverage of corporation law and all relevant aspects of federal corporation taxation.

Business Rankings Annual. Gale Cengage Learning. ⚫ Annual. $325.00. Two volumes. Compiled by the Business Library Staff of the Brooklyn Public Library. This is a guide to lists and rankings appearing in major business publications. The top ten names are listed in each case.

Business Strategies. CCH, Inc. ⚫ Semimonthly. $795.00 per year. Four looseleaf volumes. Semimonthly updates. Legal, tax, and accounting aspects of business planning and decision-making. Provides information on start-ups, forms of ownership (partnerships, corporations), failing businesses, reorganizations, acquisitions, and so forth. Includes *Business Strategies Bulletin,* a monthly newsletter.

Corporation Forms. Prentice Hall PTR. ⚫ Looseleaf. Periodic supplementation. Price on application.

World Business Rankings Annual. Gale Cengage Learning. ⚫ 1998. $189.00. Provides 2,500 ranked lists of international companies, compiled from a variety of published sources. Each list shows the "top ten" in a particular category. Keyword indexing, a country index, and citations are provided.

CORPORATIONS, CLOSELY HELD

See: CLOSELY HELD CORPORATIONS; PRIVATE COMPANIES

CORPORATIONS, MULTINATIONAL

See: MULTINATIONAL CORPORATIONS

CORPORATIONS, PROFESSIONAL

See: PROFESSIONAL CORPORATIONS

CORRECTIONAL INSTITUTIONS

See: LAW ENFORCEMENT INDUSTRIES

CORRESPONDENCE

See: BUSINESS CORRESPONDENCE

CORRESPONDENCE SCHOOLS AND COURSES

See also: ADULT EDUCATION

DIRECTORIES

Directory of Accredited Home Study Schools. Distance Education and Training Council. ⚫ Annual. Free. Lists accredited home study schools and the subjects they offer.

ENCYCLOPEDIAS AND DICTIONARIES

Encyclopedia of Distributed Learning. Anna DiStefano and others, editors. Sage Publications, Inc. ⚫ 2004. $125.00. Contains 275 entries on contemporary continuing education and distance learning for adults in corporate, academic, and other settings.

PERIODICALS AND NEWSLETTERS

DETC News. Distance Education & Training Council. ⚫ Description: Discusses issues pertaining to distance study education and reports activities of the Council. Recurring features include news of research, book reviews, news of members, and a calendar of events.

RESEARCH CENTERS AND INSTITUTES

ERIC Clearinghouse on Adult, Career and Vocational Education. Ohio State University. Center on Education and Training for Employment, 1900 Kenny Rd., Columbus, OH 43210-1090. Phone: 800-848-4815 or (614)292-7069 Fax: (614)292-1260 E-mail: ericacve@postbox.acs.ohio-state.edu ⚫ URL: http://www.ericacve.org/.

TRADE/PROFESSIONAL ASSOCIATIONS

Distance Education and Training Council. 1601 18th St., N.W., Washington, DC 20009. Phone: (202)234-5100 Fax: (202)332-1386 E-mail: detc@detc.org ⚫ URL: http://www.detc.org ⚫ Formerly National Home Study Council.

University Continuing Education Association. 1 Dupont Cir., Ste. 615, Washington, DC 20036. Phone: (202)659-3130 Fax: (202)785-0374 E-mail: kjkohl@ucea.edu ⚫ URL: http://www.ucea.edu ⚫ Institutions of higher education, both public and private, that offer professional and continuing education programs, both degree and non-degree, to nontraditional students at the pre and post baccalaureate levels. Offers accelerated learning opportunities to practitioners through professional development seminars, modules and conferences. Collects and disseminates data on continuing education programs and trends. Compiles statistics on the field. Only those individuals who work for a member institution are eligible to become professional members.

CORROSION CONTROL INDUSTRY

See also: INDUSTRIAL COATINGS

ABSTRACTS AND INDEXES

Corrosion Abstracts: Abstracts of the World's Literature on Corrosion and Corrosion Mitigation. National Association of Corrosion Engineers. CSA.

• Bimonthly. Individuals, $240.00 per year; institutions, $340.00 per year. Includes print and online editions. Provides abstracts of the worldwide literature of corrosion and corrosion control. Also available on CD-ROM.

DIRECTORIES

Coatings-Protective (Manufacturers) Directory. infoUSA Inc. • Number of listings: 3,246. Entries include: Name, address, phone (including area code), size of advertisement, year first in "Yellow Pages," name of owner or manager, number of employees. Compiled from telephone company "Yellow Pages," nationwide.

HANDBOOKS AND MANUALS

Corrosion of Stainless Steels. A. John Sedriks. John Wiley and Sons, Inc. • 1996. $105.00. Second edition. Covers the corrosion and corrosion control of stainless steels used in a variety of applications. (Corrosion Monograph Series).

Maintenance Engineering Handbook. Lindley R. Higgins and R. Keith Mobley. McGraw-Hill. • 2001. $150.00. Sixth edition. Contains about 60 chapters by various authors in 12 major sections covering all elements of industrial and plant maintenance.

Uhlig's Corrosion Handbook. R. Winston Revie and Herbert H. Uhlig, editors. John Wiley and Sons, Inc. • 2000. $248.00. Second edition. Covers the basics of corrosion science and the use of modern materials for corrosion control. (Electrochemical Society Series, vol. 39).

PERIODICALS AND NEWSLETTERS

Corrosion: Journal of Science and Engineering. National Association of Corrosion Engineers. NACE International. • Monthly. Individuals, $160.00 per year; institutions, $290.00 per year. Covers corrosion control science, theory, engineering, and practice.

Materials Performance: Articles on Corrosion Science and Engineering Solutions for Corrosion Problems. National Association of Corrosion Engineers. NACE International. • Monthly. Individuals, $115.00 per year; institutions, $205.00 per year. Covers the protection and performance of materials in corrosive environments. Includes information on new materials and industrial coatings.

RESEARCH CENTERS AND INSTITUTES

Center for Applied Thermodynamics Studies. University of Idaho, College of Engineering, Moscow, ID 83843. Phone: (208)885-6107 Fax: (208)885-6007 E-mail: steve@uidaho.edu • URL: http://www.uidaho.edu/cats.

Corrosion Research Center. University of Minnesota, 221 Church St., S. E., Minneapolis, MN 55455. Phone: (612)625-4048 Fax: (612)626-7246 E-mail: dshores@maroon.tc.umn.edu • URL: http://www.cems.umn.edu/crc • Research areas include the effect of corrosion on high technology materials and devices.

Fontana Corrosion Center. Ohio State University, 477 Watts Halls, 2041 College Rd., Columbus, OH 43210. Phone: (614)292-9857 Fax: (614)292-9857 E-mail: fcc@osu.edu/ • URL: http://www.mse.eng.ohio-state.edu • Research areas include metal coatings and corrosion of alloys.

TRADE/PROFESSIONAL ASSOCIATIONS

NACE International: The Corrosion Society. 1440 S Creek Dr., Houston, TX 77084-4906. Phone: 800-797-6223 or (281)228-6200 Fax: (281)228-6300 E-mail: firstservice@nace.org • URL: http://www.nace.org • Serves as professional technical society dedicated to reducing the economic impact of corrosion, promoting public safety, and protecting the environment by advancing the knowledge of corrosion engineering and science. Conducts programs

for technical training, sponsors technical conferences, and produces standards, publications, and software. Maintains certification program for engineers, technicians, and coating inspectors.

National Association of Metal Finishers. 21165 Whitfield Pl., Ste. 105, Potomac Falls, VA 20165. Phone: (703)433-2522 Fax: (703)433-0369 E-mail: namf@erols.com • URL: http://www.namf.org • Members are management personnel of metal and plastic finishing companies. Finishing includes plating, coating, polishing, rustproofing, and other processes.

CORRUGATED PAPERBOARD

See: PAPERBOARD AND PAPERBOARD PACKAGING INDUSTRIES

COSMETICS INDUSTRY

See also: BARBER AND BEAUTY SHOPS; PERFUME INDUSTRY

GENERAL WORKS

Cosmetics: Science and Technology. M.S. Balsam and Edward Sagarin. Krieger Publishing Co. • 1992. $375.00. Second edition. Three volumes. Vol. one, $135.00; vol. two, $143.50; vol. three, $163.50.

CD-ROM DATABASES

World Marketing Forecasts on CD-ROM. Gale Cengage Learning. • Annual. $2,500.00. Produced by Euromonitor. Provides detailed forecast data for the years to 2012 on CD-ROM for 54 countries in all parts of the world. Covers a wide range of social, demographic, economic, and market factors. Includes specific forecasts for many kinds of consumer products.

DIRECTORIES

Global Market Share Planner. Euromonitor International. • 2003. $5,900.00. Six volumes. Second edition. Provides detailed profiles and market share rankings of major consumer product companies in North America, Latin America, Europe, South Africa, and the Asia-Pacific region. Covers firms operating in key consumer markets: beverages, food products, household products, and personal care items. (Volumes are available individually.).

Household and Personal Products Industry - Buyers Guide. Rodman Publications. • Annual. $12.00. Lists of suppliers to manufacturers of cosmetics, toiletries, soaps, detergents, and related household and personal products.

Household and Personal Products Industry Contract Packaging and Private Label Directory. Rodman Publications. • Annual. $12.00. Provides information for about 450 companies offering private label or contract packaged household and personal care products, such as detergents, cosmetics, polishes, insecticides, and various aerosol items.

Who's Who: The CTFA Membership Directory (Cosmetics Industry). Cosmetic, Toiletry, and Fragrance Association. • Annual. Free to members; non-members, $100.00. Lists 600 member companies, with key personnel, products, and services.

World Cosmetics and Toiletries Marketing Directory. Available from Gale Cengage Learning. • 2002. $1,190.00. Third edition. Three volumes. Published by Euromonitor. Provides detailed descriptions of the world's cosmetics and toiletries companies. Includes consumers market research data.

World Leading Global Brand Owners. Euromonitor International. • 2003. $1,190.00. Second edition.

Contains detailed profiles of multinational consumer product companies. Includes sales, market share, brand names, and financial information. (*Global Market Share Planner,* vol. 3.).

ENCYCLOPEDIAS AND DICTIONARIES

The Consumer's Dictionary of Cosmetic Ingredients. Ruth Winter. Crown Publishing Group, Inc. • 1999. $16.00. Fifth edition. (Consumer's Dictionaries Series).

FINANCIAL RATIOS

Annual Statement Studies. The Risk Management Association. • Annual. Median and quartile financial ratios are given for over 400 kinds of manufacturing, wholesale, retail, construction, and consumer finance establishments. Data is sorted by both asset size and sales volume. Includes a clearly written "Definition of Ratios" and an alphabetical industry index.

Annual Statement Studies: Industry Default Probabilities and Cash Flow Measures. The Risk Management Association. • Annual. $145.00. Serves as a companion volume to the original *Annual Statement Studies.* Gives probability of default estimates on a percentage scale for more than 450 industries. Includes changes in position year-by-year for eight financial statement line items and provides percentage measures of cash flow.

HANDBOOKS AND MANUALS

Beauty Supply Store. Entrepreneur Media, Inc. • Looseleaf. $59.50. A practical guide to starting a store for professional beauty supplies. Covers profit potential, start-up costs, market size evaluation, owner's time required, site selection, lease negotiation, pricing, accounting, advertising, promotion, etc. (Start-Up Business Guide No. E1277.).

Formulary of Cosmetic Preparations. Anthony L. Hunting, editor. Micelle Press, Inc. • 1991. $135.00. Two volumes. Volume one, *Decorative Cosmetics* $60.00; volume two *Creams, Lotions and Milks* $105.00.

Standard Textbook of Cosmetology 2000: A Practical Course on the Scientific Fundals of Beauty Culture for Students and Practicing Cosmetologists. Constance V. Kibbe. Delmar Learning. • 1999. $57.95. Ninth deluxe edition. (Standard Texts of Cosmetology).

ONLINE DATABASES

F & S Index. Gale Cengage Learning. • Contains about four million citations to worldwide business, financial, and industrial or consumer product literature appearing from 1972 to date. Weekly updates. Inquire as to online cost and availability.

PERIODICALS AND NEWSLETTERS

Cosmetic World News: The International News Magazine of the Perfumery, Cosmetic s and Toiletries Industry. World News Publications. • Bimonthly. $192.00 per year.

Cosmetics and Toiletries: The International Journal of Cosmetic Technology. Allured Publishing. • Monthly. $98.00 per year.

CTFA News. Cosmetic, Toiletry, and Fragrance Association. • Bimonthly. Newsletter.

Drug Topics. Thomson Medical Economics. • 23 times a year. $61.00 per year. Edited for retail pharmacists, hospital pharmacists, pharmacy chain store executives, wholesalers, buyers, and others concerned with drug dispensing and drug store management. Provides information on new products, including personal care items and cosmetics.

Household and Personal Products Industry: The Magazine for the Detergent, Soap, Cosmetic and Toiletry, Wax, Polish and Aerosol Industries. Rodman Publications. • Monthly. $48.00 per year. Covers marketing, packaging, production, technical innovations, private label developments, and aerosol packaging for soap, detergents, cosmetics, insecticides, and a variety of other household products.

The Rose Sheet: Toiletries, Fragrances and Skin Care. F-D-C Reports, Inc. • 51 times a year. $916.00 per year. Newsletter. Provides industry news, regulatory news, market data, and a "Weekly Trademark Review" for the cosmetics industry.

Soap and Cosmetics. Cygnus Business Media. • Monthly. $60.00 per year. Formerly *Soap, Cosmetics, Chemical Specialities.*

STATISTICS SOURCES

Consumer International. Available from Gale Cengage Learning. • Annual. $1,290.00. Published by Euromonitor. Contains extensive consumer market, economic, and demographic data for 25 major, non-European countries, including the U. S. and Canada. Includes consumer market size (volume and value) for 150 product types in 14 categories (food, clothing, automobiles, cosmetics, appliances, etc.).

European Marketing Forecasts. Available from Gale Cengage Learning. • Annual. $1,250.00. Published by Euromonitor. Contains demographic, economic, and market forecasts for the countries of Europe to the year 2010. Forecasts include market-size data for 15 consumer product sectors (food, clothing, automobiles, consumer electronics, etc.).

International Marketing Forecasts. Available from Gale Cengage Learning. • Annual. $1,250.00. Published by Euromonitor. Contains demographic, economic, and market forecasts to the year 2013 for major, non-European countries, including the U. S. and Canada. Forecasts include market-size data for 15 consumer product sectors, such as food, clothing, and automobiles.

U. S. Industry and Trade Outlook. Available from National Technical Information Service. • Annual. $69.95. Produced by the International Trade Administration, U. S. Department of Commerce, in a "public-private" partnership with DRI/McGraw-Hill and Standard & Poor's. Provides basic data, outlook for the current year, and "Long-Term Prospects" (five-year projections) for a wide variety of products and services. Includes high technology industries. Formerly *U. S. Industrial Outlook.*

WEFA Industrial Monitor. John Wiley and Sons, Inc. • Annual. $65.00. Prepared by industry analysts at WEFA, an economic forecasting and consulting firm (originally Wharton Econometric Forecasting Associates). Contains discussions of the outlook for major U. S. industries, with many 10-year forecasts (WEFA Web site is http://www.wefa.com).

World Cosmetics and Toiletries Data and Statistics. Euromonitor International. • 2004. $650.00. Provides five-year data for a wide variety of cosmetics and toiletries in 52 countries. Includes market size, consumer expenditures, price indicators, and retail distribution data for such items as perfume, shampoo, sun products, soap, deodorants, toothpaste, hair care products, and skin care products.

TRADE/PROFESSIONAL ASSOCIATIONS

American Association of Cosmetology Schools/ Cosmetology Educators of America. 15825 N. 71st St., Suite 100, Scottsdale, AZ 85254-1521. Phone: 800-831-1086 or (480)281-0431 Fax: (480)905-0993 E-mail: jim@beautyschools.org • URL: http://www.beautyschools.org.

Cosmetic, Toiletry and Fragrance Association. 1101 17th St., N.W., Suite 300, Washington, DC 20036. Phone: (202)331-1770 Fax: (202)331-1969 E-mail: membership@ctfa.org • URL: http://www.ctfa.org/ • Formerly Associated Manufacturers of Toilet Articles.

National Beauty Culturists' League. 25 Logan Cir. NW, Washington, DC 20005-3725. Phone: (202)332-2695 Fax: (202)332-0940 E-mail: nbcl@

bellsouth.net • URL: http://www.nbcl.org • Beauticians, cosmetologists, and beauty products manufacturers. Encourages standardized, scientific, and approved methods of hair, scalp, and skin treatments. Offers scholarships and plans to establish a research center. Sponsors: National Institute of +Cosmetology, a training course in operating and designing and business techniques. Maintains hall of fame; conducts research program.

National Cosmetology Association. 401 N Michigan Ave., 22nd Fl., Chicago, IL 60611. Phone: (866)871-0656 or (312)527-6765 Fax: (312)464-6118 E-mail: nca1@ncacares.org • URL: http://www.ncacares.org • Owners of cosmetology salons; cosmetologists. Sponsors: National Cosmetology Month; National Beauty Show. Provides special sections for estheticians, school owners, salon owners, and nail technicians. Maintains hall of fame. Conducts educational and charitable programs.

National Interstate Council of State Boards of Cosmetology. 3949 Nighthawk Dr., Weston, FL 33331. Phone: (954)389-5302 Fax: (954)389-2837 E-mail: jwilson@nictesting.org • URL: http://www.nictesting.org.

Society of Cosmetic Chemists. 120 Wall St., Suite 2400, New York, NY 10005. Phone: (212)668-1500 Fax: (212)668-1504 E-mail: scc@scconline.org • URL: http://www.scconline.org • Affiliated with International Federation of Societies o Cosmetic Chemists.

OTHER SOURCES

Food Law Reports. CCH, Inc. • Weekly. $1,459.00 per year. Six looseleaf volumes. Covers regulation of adulteration, packaging, labeling, and additives. Formerly *Food Drug Cosmetic Law Reports.*

Hair Care Products. Available from MarketResearch.com. • 2002. $3,950.00. Published by Global Industry Analysts. Provides worldwide market research data, including profiles of major hair care product companies.

Market Share Tracker. Euromonitor International. • 2003. $1,190.00. Second edition. Contains market share rankings of more than 1,800 consumer product companies in 30 countries. Covers 16 kinds of products within "Drinks," "Household and Personal Care," and "Foods." Includes brand shares for leading brands. (*Global Market Share Planner*, vol. 1.).

The Suncare Products Market. Available from MarketResearch.com. • 2001. $2,100.00. Published by Packaged Facts. Provides market data on sun screen lotions, after-sun products, and sunless tanning cosmetics, with sales projections.

The U.S. Skincare Market. Available from MarketResearch.com. • 2001. $2,750.00. Published by Packaged Facts. Provides market data on skincare products such as moisturizers, cleansers, and toners, with sales projections to 2005.

COST ACCOUNTING

See also: ACCOUNTING; COST CONTROL

GENERAL WORKS

Cost Accounting. William K. Carter and Milton Usry. South-Western. • 2002. $83.95. 13th edition. (Prentice Hall Accounting Series).

Cost Accounting: A Managerial Emphasis. Charles T. Horngren. Prentice Hall PTR. • 2002. $132.00. 11th edition. (Charles T. Horngren Accounting Series).

ABSTRACTS AND INDEXES

Accounting Articles. CCH, Inc. • Monthly. $624.00 per year. Looseleaf service.

Business Periodicals Index. H. W. Wilson Co. • 11

times a year. Quarterly and annual cumulations. Price varies.

ENCYCLOPEDIAS AND DICTIONARIES

Blackwell Encyclopedic Dictionary of Accounting. Rashad Abdel-khalik. Blackwell Publishing. • 1997. $38.95. The editor is associated with the University of Florida. Contains definitions of key terms combined with longer articles written by various U. S. and foreign business educators. Includes bibliographies and index. (Blackwell Encyclopedia of Management Series).

Dictionary of Accounting Terms. Joel G. Siegel. Barron's Educational Series, Inc. • 2000. $13.95. Third edition. (Business Dictionaries Series).

International Dictionary of Accounting Acronyms. Thomas W. Morris, editor. Fitzroy Dearborn Publishers, Inc. • 1999. $45.00. Defines 2,000 acronyms used in worldwide accounting and finance.

FINANCIAL RATIOS

Income and Fees of Accountants in Public Practice. National Society of Accountants. • Triennial. Members, $35.00; non-members, $50.00.

HANDBOOKS AND MANUALS

Accountants' Handbook. Douglas R. Carmichael and Paul Rosenfeld. John Wiley and Sons, Inc. • 2003. $160.00. 10th edition. Two volumes. Vol. one, $95.00; vol. two, $95.00. Chapters are written by various accounting and auditing specialists.

Cost Accounting Standards Board Regulations. CCH, Inc. • 2002. $27.00. Covers Federal Acquisition Regulation (FAR) cost accounting standards for both defense and civilian government contracts. Provides the rules for estimating and reporting costs for contracts of more than $500,000.

Handbook of Cost Accounting. Sidney Davidson and Roman L. Weil. Prentice Hall PTR. • 1989. $79.95.

Handbook of Cost Accounting Theory and Techniques. Ahmed Righi-Belkaoui. Greenwood Publishing Group, Inc. • 1991. $94.95.

INTERNET DATABASES

Rutgers Accounting Web (RAW). Rutgers University Accounting Research Center. Phone: (973)353-5172 Fax: (973)353-1283 • URL: http://www.rutgers.edu/ accounting • RAW Web site provides extensive links to sources of national and international accounting information, such as the Big Six accounting firms, the Financial Accounting Standards Board (FASB), SEC filings (EDGAR), journals, publishers, software, the International Accounting Network, and "Internet's largest list of accounting firms in USA." Searching is offered. Fees: Free.

ONLINE DATABASES

Wilson Business Abstracts Online. H. W. Wilson Co. • Indexes and abstracts 600 major business periodicals, plus the *Wall Street Journal* and the business section of the *New York Times*. Indexing is from 1982, abstracting from 1990, with the two newspapers included from 1993. Updated weekly. Inquire as to online cost and availability. (*Business Periodicals Index* without abstracts is also available online.).

PERIODICALS AND NEWSLETTERS

Journal of Bank Cost and Management Accounting. Association for Management Information in Financial Services. • Three times a year. $100.00 per year.

Management for Strategic Business Ideas. Society of Management Accountants of Canada. • 10 times a year. $60.00 per year. Text in English and French.

TRADE/PROFESSIONAL ASSOCIATIONS

American Institute of Certified Public Accountants. 1211 Ave. of the Americas, New York, NY 10036-8775. Phone: 888-777-7077 or (212)596-6200 Fax:

(212)596-6213 • URL: http://www.aicpa.org.
Association for Management Information in Financial Services. 3895 Fairfax Court, Atlanta, GA 30339. Phone: (770)444-3557 Fax: (770)444-9084 E-mail: ami@amifs.org • URL: http://www.amifs. org • Members are financial institution employees interested in management accounting and cost analysis.

Institute of Internal Auditors. 247 Maitland Ave., Altamonte Springs, FL 32701-4201. Phone: (407)937-1100 Fax: (407)937-1101 E-mail: iia@theiia.org • URL: http://www.theiia.org.

Institute of Management Accountants. 10 Paragon Dr., Montvale, NJ 07645-1718. Phone: 800-638-4427 or (201)573-9000 Fax: (201)474-1600 E-mail: ima@imanet.org • URL: http://www.imanet.org • Formerly National Association of Accountants.

OTHER SOURCES
Cost Accounting Standards Guide. CCH, Inc. • $385.00 per year. Looseleaf serivce. Monthly updates.

COST CONTROL

See also: COST ACCOUNTING

GENERAL WORKS
Controllership: The Work of the Managerial Accountant. James D. Willson and others. John Wiley and Sons, Inc. • 1999. $220.00. Sixth edition. *2002 Cumulative Supplement,* $70.00.

Cost Estimating. Rodney D. Stewart. John Wiley and Sons, Inc. • 1991. $150.00. Second edition. Discusses high technology engineering cost forecasting, including the estimation of software costs. (New Dimensions in Engineering Series).

Internet Prophets: Enlightened E-Business Strategies for Every Budget. Mary Diffley. Information Today, Inc. • 2002. $29.95. Emphasizes the specific dollar costs of having a successful online business. The "Internet Prophets" are four individual guides for developing business on the Web, arranged according to size of budget. (CyberAge Books.).

A Manager's Guide to Creative Cost Cutting: 101 Ways to Build the Bottom Line. David W. Young. McGraw-Hill. • 2002. $16.95. Mainly concerned with reducing expenses without reducing staff. (Teach Yourself Series).

CD-ROM DATABASES
Authority Health Care Law Library. LexisNexis/ Matthew Bender. • Periodic updates. Price on request. Full text CD-ROM provides legal information, case law, and analysis relating to health care facilities, health insurance, longterm care, Medigap, and Medicare.

DIRECTORIES
AACE International-Directory of Members. AACE International. • Annual. $20.00 per year. 6,000 cost engineers, estimators, and cost management professionals worldwide.

ENCYCLOPEDIAS AND DICTIONARIES
Blackwell Encyclopedic Dictionary of Operations Management. Nigel Slack, editor. Blackwell Publishing. • 1997. $130.95. The editor is associated with the University of Warwick, England. Contains definitions of key terms combined with longer articles written by various U. S. and foreign business educators. Includes bibliographies and index. (Blackwell Encyclopedia of Management Series.).

HANDBOOKS AND MANUALS
Cost Control Handbook. R. M. Wilson. Ashgate Publishing Co. • 1983. $102.95. Second edition. Published by Gower in England.
Cost Management Handbook. Barry J. Brinker. John

Wiley and Sons, Inc. • 2000. $140.00.

PERIODICALS AND NEWSLETTERS
Cost Engineering: The Journal of Cost Estimating, Cost Control, and Project Management. • Monthly. $60.00 per year. Subjects include cost estimation and cost control.

IT Cost Management Strategies: The Planning Assistant for IT Directors. Computer Economics, Inc. • Monthly. $495.00 per year. Newsletter for information technology professionals. Covers data processing costs, budgeting, financial management, and related topics.

Journal of Cost Management. RIA. • Bimonthly. $230.00 per year. Includes articles on business budgeting.

Strategic Finance. Institute of Management Accountants. • Monthly. Institutions, $140.00 per year; non-profit libraries, $70.00 per year. Provides articles on corporate finance, cost control, cash flow, budgeting, corporate taxes, and other financial management topics.

Successful Cost Control Strategies for CEOs, Managers, and Administrators. Siefer Consultants, Inc. • Monthly. $279.00 per year. Newsletter. Provides a variety of ideas on business budgeting and controlling company expenses. Formerly *Employee Cost Conrol Strategies for CEOs, Managers, and Administrators.*

OTHER SOURCES
AACE International. Transactions of the Annual Meetings. American Assoiciation of Cost Engineers. AACE International. • Annual. Price varies. Contains texts of papers presented at AACE meetings.

COST OF LIVING INDEXES

See: CONSUMER PRICE INDEXES

COSTUME JEWELRY

See: JEWELRY BUSINESS

COTTON INDUSTRY

See also: TEXTILE INDUSTRY

GENERAL WORKS
Cotton: Origin, History, Technology, and Production. Joe T. Cothren and C. Wayne Smith, editors. John Wiley and Sons, Inc. • 1999. $299.00. (Crop Science Series: Vol. 4).

ABSTRACTS AND INDEXES
Textile Technology Digest. Institute of Textile Technology. • Annual. $535.00. Provides indexing and abstracting of a wide variety of textile technology literature.

ALMANACS AND YEARBOOKS
Agricultural and Mineral Commodities Year Book. Available from Taylor & Francis Group. • Annual. $225.00. Published by Europa Publications. Contains descriptive product profiles, price data, export-import data, and production statistics for major commodities of the world. Includes commodity histories, uses, markets, demand trends, and information about trade agreements and key commodity organizations.

CD-ROM DATABASES
OECD Statistical Compendium. Organization for Economic Cooperation and Development. • Semiannual. $1,905.00 per year for 1 to 10 users. CD-ROM contains more than 730,000 monthly, quarterly, and annual time series for OECD

countries, 1960 to date. Includes fully searchable data on agriculture, food, economic indicators, national accounts, employment, energy, finance, industry, technology, and foreign trade. Results can be displayed in various forms.

Textile Technology Digest [CD-ROM]. Textile Information Center, Institute of Textile Technology. • Quarterly. Provides CD-ROM indexing and abstracting of worldwide journals and monographs in various areas of textile technology, production, and management. Covers 1978 to date.

DIRECTORIES
Cotton International. Meister Publishing Co. • Annual. $30.00.

Davison's Textile Blue Book. Davison Publishing Company L.L.C. • Covers: Over 8,400 companies in the textile industry in the United States, Canada, and Mexico including about 4,400 textile plants. Covers mills, manufacturers, dyers, bleachers, finishers, dealers, importers, exporters, brokers, shippers, and agents for various textiles, fibers, yarns, and cordage. Also includes supplies of equipment, materials and services. Entries include: Company name, address, phone, fax, e-mail, website addresses, names of executives, description of product/service, and trade names. Mill and other production facility listings include data on equipment and capacity.

ENCYCLOPEDIAS AND DICTIONARIES
Textile Terms and Definitions. J.E. McIntyre and Paul N. Daniels, editors. Available from State Mutual Book and Periodical Service Ltd. • 1996. $180.00. 10th edition. Published by the Textile Insitute (UK). Includes more than 1,000 definitions of textile processes, fiber types, and end products. Illustrated.

INTERNET DATABASES
Business 2.0 Web Guide to the Best Business Links. Business 2.0 Media Inc. Phone: (415)293-4800 E-mail: support@business2.com • URL: http:// www.business2.com/webguide • Web site presents an extensive, searchable directory of links to "the best, most informative, and authoritative web pages." Twenty main categories cover business, finance, career, company information, people, and technology topics, with thousands of subtopics, all linking to Web sites recommended by experienced business researchers. Fees: Free.

Fedstats. Federal Interagency Council on Statistical Policy. Phone: (202)395-7254 • URL: http://www. fedstats.gov • Web site features an efficient search facility for full-text statistics produced by more than 100 federal agencies, including the Census Bureau, the Bureau of Economic Analysis, and the Bureau of Labor Statistics. Boolean searches can be made within one agency or for all agencies combined. Links are offered to international statistical bureaus, including the UN, IMF, OECD, UNESCO, Eurostat, and 20 individual countries. Fees: Free.

FreeLunch.com. Economy.com, Inc. Phone: (610)696-8700 Fax: (610)696-1678 • URL: http:// www.freelunch.com • Web site provides free access to more than 1.5 million economic and financial data series, covering industry, demographics, labor markets, prices, retail sales, government spending, trade, interest rates, housing starts, the stock market, and many other topics. Data is available for various time periods in either chart or table form. Searching is offered. Fees: Free, but registration required. Economy.com, Inc. also offers fee-based economic analysis at *The Dismal Scientist* site (http://www. dismal.com).

Manufacturing Profiles. U. S. Bureau of the Census. Phone: (301)763-4636 E-mail: webmaster@census. gov • URL: http://www.census.gov/prod/www/abs/ mfg-prof.html • The Census Bureau makes available free on PDF (Portable Document Format) an annual consolidation of the entire Current Industrial

Report series, presenting "all the data compiled." Contains statistics on production, shipments, inventories, consumption, exports, imports, and orders for a wide variety of manufactured products.

USDA. United States Department of Agriculture. Phone: (202)720-2791 E-mail: agsec@usda.gov • URL: http://www.usda.gov • The USDA home page has six sections: News and Information; What's New; About USDA; Agencies; Opportunities; Search and Help. Keyword searching is offered from the USDA home page and from various individual agency home pages. Agencies are the Economic Research Service, Agricultural Marketing Service, National Agricultural Statistics Service, National Agricultural Library, and about 12 others. Updating varies. Fees: Free.

ONLINE DATABASES

Textile Technology Digest [online]. Institute of Textile Technology. • Contains indexing and abstracting of more than 300 worldwide journals and monographs in various areas of textile technology, production, and management. Time period is 1978 to date, with monthly updating. Inquire as to online cost and availability.

World Textiles. Elsevier Science, Inc. • Provides abstracting and indexing from 1970 of worldwide textile literature (periodicals, books, pamphlets, and reports). Includes U. S., European, and British patent information. Updating is monthly. Inquire as to online cost and availability.

PERIODICALS AND NEWSLETTERS

Barron's: The Dow Jones Business and Financial Weekly. • Weekly. $145.00 per year.

Cotton Digest International. Cotton Digest Co., Inc. • Monthly. $40.00 per year. Formerly *Cotton Digest*.

Cotton Farming. Vance Publishing Corp. • Nine times a year. $35.00 per year.

Cotton Grower. Meister Media. • 10 times a year. $32.10 per year.

Cotton's Week. National Cotton Council of America. • Description: Reports legislative, administrative, and economic actions and issues affecting the cotton industry from the field to the fabric. Recurring features include news of research and reports of meetings.

Journal of Natural Fibers. Haworth Press, Inc. • Quarterly. $400.00 per year to libraries; $45.00 per year to individuals. Covers applications, technology, research, and world markets relating to fibers from silk, wool, cotton, flax, hemp, jute, etc. Previously *Natural Fibres*, published annually.

PRICE SOURCES

Cotton Price Statistics. U.S. Department of Agriculture. • Monthly.

The New York Times. New York Times Co. • Daily. $374.40 per year. Supplements available: *New York Times Book Review, New York Times Magazine, Sophisticated Traveler* and *Fashions of the Times*.

Weekly Board of Trade, Cotton Exchange. New York Cotton Exchange. • Weekly. $100.00 per year.

RESEARCH CENTERS AND INSTITUTES

Institute of Textile Technology. 2551 Ivy Rd., Charlottesville, VA 22903-4614. Phone: (434)296-5511 Fax: (434)296-2957 E-mail: library@itt.edu • URL: http://www.itt.edu.

Tropical Research and Education Center. University of Florida, 18905 S.W. 280th St., Homestead, FL 33031. Phone: (305)246-7001 Fax: (305)246-7003 E-mail: hom@gnv.ifas.ufl.edu • URL: http://www.ifas.ufl.edu/~trecweb.

STATISTICS SOURCES

Agricultural Statistics. Available from U. S. Government Printing Office. • Annual. $38.00. Produced by the National Agricultural Statistics Service, U. S.

Department of Agriculture. Provides a wide variety of statistical data relating to agricultural production, supplies, consumption, prices/price-supports, foreign trade, costs, and returns, as well as farm labor, loans, income, and population. In many cases, historical data is shown annually for 10 years. In addition to farm data, includes detailed fishery statistics.

Annual Survey of Manufactures. Available from U. S. Government Printing Office. • Annual. Prices vary. Issued by the U. S. Census Bureau as an interim update to the *Census of Manufactures*. Includes data on number of manufacturing establishments in various industries, employment, labor costs, value of shipments, capital expenditures, inventories, energy costs, and assets. (See also Census Bureau home page, http://www.census.gov/.).

Business Statistics of the United States. Linz Audain and Cornelia J. Strawser. Bernan Associates. • Annual. $147.00. Based on *Business Statistics*, formerly issue by the Bureau of Economic Analysis, U. S. Department of Commerce. Provides basic data for a wide variety of U. S. industries, services, and economic indicators. Most statistics are shown annually for 30 years and monthly for the most recent four years.

FAO Production Yearbook. Available from Bernan Associates. • Annual. $45.00. Published by the Food and Agriculture Organization (http://www.fao.org). Contains worldwide data on agriculture, land use, farm crops, livestock, and agricultural prices.

FAO Trade Yearbook. Available from Bernan Associates. • Annual. $45.00. Published by the Food and Agriculture Organization (http://www.fao.org). Provides extensive worldwide data on exports and imports of agricultural commodities, fertilizers, tractors, and pesticides. Includes more than 130 tables of detailed statistics.

International Textile Machinery Shipment Statistics. International Textile Manufacturers Federation. • Annual. 250 Swiss francs. Formerly *International Cotton Industry Statistics*.

Quality of Cotton Report. Agricultural Marketing Service. U.S. Department of Agriculture. • Weekly.

Survey of Current Business. Available from U. S. Government Printing Office. • Monthly. $63.00 per year. Issued by Bureau of Economic Analysis, U. S. Department of Commerce. Presents a wide variety of business and economic data.

United States Census of Agriculture. U.S. Bureau of the Census. • Quinquennial. Results presented in reports, tape, CD-ROM, and Diskette files.

WEFA Industrial Monitor. John Wiley and Sons, Inc. • Annual. $65.00. Prepared by industry analysts at WEFA, an economic forecasting and consulting firm (originally Wharton Econometric Forecasting Associates). Contains discussions of the outlook for major U. S. industries, with many 10-year forecasts (WEFA Web site is http://www.wefa.com).

TRADE/PROFESSIONAL ASSOCIATIONS

American Cotton Shipper's Association. PO Box 3366, Memphis, TN 38173. Phone: (901)525-2272 Fax: (901)527-8303 E-mail: jonnichols@acfsa.org • URL: http://www.acsa-cotton.org • Purposes are to protect the financial well-being of exporters of U.S. grown cotton, to foster and improve international trade, and to preserve the principal of the sanctity of contracts.

American Textile Manufacturers Institute. 1130 Connecticut Ave. NW, Washington, DC 20036-3954. Phone: (202)862-0500 Fax: (202)862-0570 E-mail: info@atmanet.org • URL: http://www.textileweb.com/storefronts/amertextile.html • Textile mill firms operating machinery for manufacturing and processing cotton, man-made, wool, and silk textile products; includes spinning, weaving, bleaching, finishing, knitting, and allied

plants; does not include manufacturers of hosiery or firms that produce man-made fibers and yarn by a chemical process. Operates public relations program for the industry, government relations program, textile market program, and statistical and economic information service. Holds seminars and meetings. Sponsors safety contest among textile mills.

Cotton Council International. 1521 New Hampshire Ave. NW, Washington, DC 20036. Phone: (202)745-7805 Fax: (202)483-4040 E-mail: cottonusa@cotton.org • URL: http://www.cottonusa.org • Representatives of all segments of the U.S. cotton industry. Works as an international cotton sales promotion organization cooperating with cotton interests in foreign countries.

Cotton Incorporated. 6399 Weston Pkwy., Cary, NC 27513. Phone: (919)678-2220 Fax: (919)678-2230 E-mail: kbrannigan@cottoninc.com • URL: http://www.cottoninc.com • Represents 45,000 cotton producers for research and promotion.

National Cotton Council of America. 1918 N Parkway, Memphis, TN 38112-0285. Phone: (901)274-9030 Fax: (901)725-0510 E-mail: info@cotton.org • URL: http://www.cotton.org/ncc • Delegates are from 19 cotton producing states.

New York Cotton Exchange. 1 N End Ave., 23-10 43rd Ave., New York, NY 10282-1101. Phone: 800-HED-GEIT or (212)748-4094 E-mail: webmaster@nybot.com • URL: http://www.nybot.com • Commodity exchange - cotton and frozen concentrated orange juice. Develops new products; provides market information; compiles statistics. Collaborates with the Citrus Associates of the +New York +Cotton Exchange; operates Financial Instruments Exchange, in conjunction with the New York Stock Exchange.

Textile Institute. St. James's Buildings, 1st Fl., 79 Oxford St., Manchester M1 6FQ, United Kingdom. Phone: 44 161 2371188 Fax: 44 161 2361991 E-mail: tiihq@textileinst.org.uk • URL: http://www.texi.org • Companies and individuals in 100 countries involved in management, science, technology, design, information transfer, and marketing of textiles including clothing and footwear. Promotes interests of the textile industry worldwide; serves professional interests of members; confers qualifications and recognizes achievements in research, application of ideas, education, business, and public affairs. Maintains Information Service to collect information relating to textile industrial and economic conditions in different countries and economic sectors.

COTTON TEXTILE INDUSTRY

See: TEXTILE INDUSTRY

COTTONSEED OIL INDUSTRY

See: OIL AND FATS INDUSTRY

COUNCIL MANAGER PLAN

See: MUNICIPAL GOVERNMENT

COUNSELING

See also: PERSONNEL MANAGEMENT; VOCATIONAL GUIDANCE

GENERAL WORKS

The Helping Relationship: Process and Skills. Lawrence M. Brammer and Ginger A. MacDonald.

Allyn and Bacon, Inc. • 2002. $53.00. Eighth edition.

Is It Too Late to Run Away and Join the Circus? Finding the Life You Really Want. Marti Smye. John Wiley. • 1998. $14.95. Provides philosophical and inspirational advice on leaving corporate life and becoming self-employed as a consultant or whatever. Central theme is dealing with major changes in life style and career objectives.

ABSTRACTS AND INDEXES

Psychological Abstracts. American Psychological Association. • Monthly. Members, $815.00 per year; individuals and institutions, $1,207.00 per year. Covers the international literature of psychology and the behavioral sciences. Includes journals, technical reports, dissertations, and other sources.

DIRECTORIES

Directory of Counseling Services. International Association of Counseling Services. • Annual. $50.00. About 200 accredited services in the United States and Canada concerned with psychological educational, and vocational counseling, including those at colleges and universities and public and private agencies.

HANDBOOKS AND MANUALS

Handbook of Counseling Psychology. Steven D. Brown and Robert W. Lent, editors. John Wiley and Sons, Inc. • 2000. $110.00. Third edition. Includes material on counseling policy, research methods, and preventive interventions, as well as group, educational, career and family counseling.

Handbook of Group Counseling and Psychotherapy. Janice L. DeLucia-Waack and others, editors. Sage Publications, Inc. • 2004. $99.95. Contains 48 chapters by various "experts in group work.".

Introduction to the Counseling Profession. Dave Capuzzi and Douglas Gross. Allyn and Bacon, Inc. • 2000. $97.00. Third edition.

On Becoming a Counselor: A Basic Guide for Nonprofessional Counselors and the Helping Professionals. Eugene Kennedy and Sara Charles. Crossroad Publishing Co. • 2001. $24.95. Third expanded revised edition.

Sexual Orientation in the Workplace: Gays, Lesbians, Bisexuals and Heterosexuals Working Together. Amy J. Zuckerman and George F. Simons. Sage Publications, Inc. • 1994. $34.95. A workbook containing "a variety of simple tools and exercises" to provide skills for "working realistically and effectively with diverse colleagues.".

ONLINE DATABASES

PsycINFO. American Psychological Association. • Provides indexing and abstracting of the worldwide literature of psychology and the behavioral sciences. Time period is 1967 to date, with monthly updates. Inquire as to online cost and availability.

PERIODICALS AND NEWSLETTERS

Counseling and Values. Association for Spiritual, Ethical and Religious Values in Counseling. American Counseling Association. • Three times a year. Institutions, $35.00 per year.

The Counseling Psychologist. American Psychological Association. Sage Publications, Inc. • Bimonthly. Institutions, $495.00 per year.

Counseling Services: IACS Newsletter. International Association of Counseling Services. • Three times a year. Membership.

Counselor: The Magazine for Addiction Professionals. Health Communications, Inc. • Bimonthly. $26.00 per year. Covers both clinical and societal aspects of substance abuse.

Employee Assistance Quarterly. Haworth Press, Inc. • Quarterly. $535.00 per year. An academic and practical journal focusing on employee alcoholism and mental health problems. Formerly *Labor-*

Management Alcoholism Journal.

Journal of Counseling Psychology. American Psychological Association. • Quarterly. Members, $39.00 per year; non-members, $78.00 per year; institutions, $182.00 per year.

Journal of Mental Health Counseling. American Counseling Association. • Quarterly. $175.00 per year. The official journal of the American Mental Health Counselors Association.

RESEARCH CENTERS AND INSTITUTES

Bureau of Educational Research and Evaluation. Mississippi State University. P.O. Box 9710, Mississippi State, MS 39762. Phone: (662)325-3717 Fax: (662)325-8784 E-mail: rhr2@colled.msstate.edu • URL: http://www.msstate.edu.

TRADE/PROFESSIONAL ASSOCIATIONS

American Counseling Association. 5999 Stevenson Ave., Alexandria, VA 22304. Phone: 800-347-6647 or (703)823-9800 Fax: (703)823-0252 E-mail: ryep@counseling.org • URL: http://www.counseling.org • Counseling professionals in elementary and secondary schools, higher education, community agencies and organizations, rehabilitation programs, government, industry, business, private practice, career counseling, and mental health counseling. Conducts professional development institutes and provides liability insurance. Maintains Counseling and Human Development Foundation to fund counseling projects.

American Mental Health Counselors Association. 801 N Fairfax St., Ste. 304, Alexandria, VA 22314. Phone: 800-326-2642 or (703)548-6002 Fax: (703)548-4775 E-mail: mhamilton@amhca.org • URL: http://www.amhca.org • Professional counselors employed in mental health services; students. Aims to: deliver quality mental health services to children, youth, adults, families, and organizations; improve the availability and quality of counseling services through licensure and certification, training standards, and consumer advocacy. Supports specialty and special interest networks. Fosters communication among members. A division of the American Counseling Association (see separate entry).

American Rehabilitation Counseling Association. PO Box 6500, Pan American Department of Rehabilitation, College of Health Sciences and Human Services, 1201 W University Dr., Brea, CA 92822. Phone: 800-347-6647 or (714)674-5728 Fax: (956)380-6499 E-mail: patricia.nunez@cna.com • URL: http://www.arcaweb.org • A division of the American Counseling Association (see separate entry). Rehabilitation counselors and interested professionals and students. Aims to improve the rehabilitation counseling profession and its services to individuals with disabilities. Promotes high standards in rehabilitation counseling, practice, research, and education. Encourages the exchange of information between rehabilitation professionals and consumer groups. Serves as liaison among members and public and private rehabilitation counselors across the country. Sponsors educational and training programs.

Association of Career Management Consulting Firms International. 204 E St., NE, Washington, DC 20002. Phone: (202)547-6344 Fax: (202)547-6348 E-mail: aocfi@aocfi.org • URL: http://www.aocfi.org • Firms providing displaced employees who are sponsored by their organization, with counsel and assistance in job searching and the techniques and practices of choosing a career.

International Association of Counseling Services. 101 S Whiting St., Ste. 211, Alexandria, VA 22304. Phone: (703)823-9840 Fax: (703)823-9843 E-mail: iacsinc@earthlink.net • URL: http://www.iacsinc.org • Formerly American Board on Professional Standards in Vocational Counseling.

National Institute of Management Counsellors. P.O.

Box 193, Great Neck, NY 11022. Phone: (516)482-5683 Fax: (516)482-5683.

COUNTERFEITING

See also: CRIME AND CRIMINALS; FORGERIES

GENERAL WORKS

Becker the Counterfeiter. G. F. Hill. Sanford J. Durst. • 1979. $20.00.

ENCYCLOPEDIAS AND DICTIONARIES

Encyclopedia of White-Collar and Corporate Crime. Lawrence M. Salinger, editor. Sage Publications, Inc. • 2004. $295.00. Two volumes. Covers such items as fraud, kickbacks, price fixing, tax evasion, bribery, forgery, counterfeiting, embezzlement, extortion, graft, bid rigging, and assorted scams and swindles.

COUNTERTRADE

See: BARTER AND COUNTERTRADE

COUNTRY CLUBS

See: CLUBS

COUNTY FINANCE

See also: PUBLIC FINANCE

DIRECTORIES

Mergent Municipal and Government Manual. Mergent, Inc. • Annual. $3,250.00 per year. Updated weekly online.

RESEARCH CENTERS AND INSTITUTES

Institute for Tax Administration. 900 Wilshire Blvd., Suite 624, Los Angeles, CA 90017-4707. Phone: (213)623-1103 Fax: (818)842-3930.

STATISTICS SOURCES

Facts and Figures on Government Finance. Tax Foundation. • Annual. $45.00.

United States Census of Governments. Bureau of the Census, U.S. Department of Commerce. Available from U.S. Government Printing Office. • Quinquennial.

TRADE/PROFESSIONAL ASSOCIATIONS

Association of Government Accountants. 2208 Mount Vernon Ave., Alexandria, VA 22301-1314. Phone: 800-242-7211 or (703)684-6931 Fax: (703)548-9367 E-mail: agamembers@agacgfm.org • URL: http://www.agacgfm.org • Members are employed by federal, state, county, and city government agencies. Includes accountants, auditors, budget officers, and other government finance administrators and officials.

National Association of County Treasurers and Finance Officers. c/o National Association of Counties, 440 First St., N.W., 8th Fl., Washington, DC 20001. Phone: (202)393-6226 Fax: (202)393-2630 E-mail: rvaldes@seminoletax.org • URL: http://www.nactfo.org.

COUNTY GOVERNMENT

See also: MUNICIPAL GOVERNMENT

BIOGRAPHICAL SOURCES

Who's Who in American Politics. Marquis Who's Who. • Biennial. $275.00. Two volumes. Contains about 27,000 biographical sketches of local, state, and national elected or appointed individuals.

DIRECTORIES

Carroll's County Directory. Carroll Publishing. • Covers: Over 57,000 officials in more than 3,000 counties; includes elected, appointed, and career office holders. Entries include: County seat, locator phone, address, population, officials' names, titles, addresses, and phone numbers. Available as part of a "library volume" titled "Municipal/County Directory Annual Edition" (see separate entry).

Carroll's Municipal/County Directory. Carroll Publishing. • Annual. $250.00 per year. Provides listings of about 90,000 city, town, and county officials in the U. S.

Directory of Regional Councils. National Association of Regional Councils. • Annual. $100.00. Lists about 526 regional councils within U.S., including contacts and counties they serve. Formerly *National Association of Regional Councils-Directory of Regional Councils.*

Government Phone Book USA: Your Comprehensive Guide to Federal, State, County, and Local Government Offices in the United States. Omnigraphics, Inc. • Annual. $265.00. Contains more than 270,000 listings of federal, state, county, and local government offices and personnel, including legislatures. Formerly *Government Directory of Addresses and Phone Numbers.*

Municipal Yellow Book: Who's Who in the Leading City and County Governments and Local Authorities. Leadership Directories, Inc. • Annual. $265.00 per year. Lists approximately 30,000 key personnel in city and county departments, agencies, subdivisions, and branches.

PERIODICALS AND NEWSLETTERS

County News. National Association of Counties. • Biweekly. $82.50 per year.

Governing: The States and Localities. • Monthly. $39.95 per year. Edited for state and local government officials. Covers finance, office management, computers, telecommunications, environmental concerns, etc.

Public Risk. Public Risk Management Association. • 10 times a year. $125.00 per year. Covers risk management for state and local governments, including various kinds of liabilities.

RESEARCH CENTERS AND INSTITUTES

Citizens League Research Institute. Citizens League Research Institute. 1331 Euclid Ave., Cleveland, OH 44113. Phone: (216)241-5340 Fax: (216)736-7626 E-mail: staff@citizensleague.org • URL: http://www.citizensleague.org • Local government structure, performance, and financing focusing on the Greater Cleveland (7-county) region. Cooperates with public officials and civic organizations on improvement of local governmental procedures in order to obtain greater economy and efficiency in administration of public affairs.

Urban Institute. Urban Institute. 2100 M St. NW, Washington, DC 20037. Phone: (202)833-7200 Fax: (202)728-0232 E-mail: paffairs@ui.urban.org • URL: http://www.urban.org • Domestic, social, and economic affairs, including multidisciplinary studies and government program evaluations in the areas of tax and budget reform, education policy, health policy, crime and justice, housing and community development, labor and human services, income security and retirement, welfare reform, international activities, nonprofit sector and philanthropy, public finance, productivity and economic development, social services, and immigration. Also conducts research programs on employment and training, children's issues and family policy, minorities and social policy, poverty, state

and local governments, and community impact and demography.

STATISTICS SOURCES

County and City Data Book, a Statistical Abstract Supplement. U.S. Bureau of the Census. Available from U.S. Government Printing Office. • 1994. $60.00.

United States Census of Governments. Bureau of the Census, U.S. Department of Commerce. Available from U.S. Government Printing Office. • Quinquennial.

TRADE/PROFESSIONAL ASSOCIATIONS

National Association of Counties. 440 First St., N.W., Ste. 800, Washington, DC 20001. Phone: (202)393-6226 or (202)942-4287 Fax: (202)393-2630 E-mail: tgoodman@naco.org • URL: http://www.naco.org • Formerly National Association of County Human Services Administrators.

National Association of County Planners. c/o National Association of Counties, 440 First St., N.W., 8th Fl., Washington, DC 20001. Phone: (202)661-8807 or (202)942-4276 Fax: (202)737-0480 E-mail: jdavenpo@naco.org • URL: http://www.naco.org • Formerly National Association of County Planning Directors.

Public Risk Management Association. 500 Montgomery St., Ste. 750, Alexandria, VA 22314. Phone: (703)528-7701 Fax: (703)739-0200 E-mail: info@primacentral.org • URL: http://www.primacentral.org • Public agency risk, insurance, human resources, attorneys, and/or safety managers from cities, counties, villages, towns, school boards, and other related areas. Provides an information clearinghouse and communications network for public risk managers to share resources, ideas, and experiences. Offers information on risk, insurance, and safety management. Monitors state and federal legislative actions and court decisions that deal with immunity, tort liability, and intergovernmental risk pools. Maintains library containing current reports from governmental units on their insurance procedures, self-insurance plans, and loss control and safety programs; and copies of policy statements, job descriptions, contractual arrangements, and indemnification clauses.

OTHER SOURCES

Local Government Law. Chester J. Antieau. LexisNexis Matthew Bender. • $1,113.00. Six looseleaf volumes. Periodic supplementation. States the principle of law for all types of local governments, and backs those principles with case citations from all jurisdictions. Examines the laws and their impact in three primary cases.

COUNTY OFFICIALS

See: COUNTY GOVERNMENT

COUNTY PLANNING

See: REGIONAL PLANNING

COUPONS AND REFUNDS

ABSTRACTS AND INDEXES

Business Periodicals Index. H. W. Wilson Co. • 11 times a year. Quarterly and annual cumulations. Price varies.

CD-ROM DATABASES

WILSONDISC: Wilson Business Abstracts. H. W. Wilson Co. • Monthly. Includes unlimited online access to *Wilson Business Abstracts* through WILSONLINE. Provides CD-ROM "cover-to-cover" abstracting and indexing of over 600

prominent business periodicals. Indexing is from 1982, abstracting from 1990. (*Business Periodicals Index* without abstracts is available on CD-ROM at $1,495 per year.).

DIRECTORIES

The PROMO 100 Promotion Agency Ranking. PROMO Magazine. • Covers: Ranking of the top 100 U.S. Promotion agencies. Entries include: Name, address, phone, financial data, client lists, rate of growth, name of CEO, and description of product/service.

HANDBOOKS AND MANUALS

Coupon Mailer Service. Entrepreneur Media, Inc. • Looseleaf. $59.50. A practical guide to starting a service for mailing business promotion discount coupons to consumers. Covers profit potential, start-up costs, market size evaluation, owner's time required, pricing, accounting, advertising, promotion, etc. (Start-Up Business Guide No. E1232.).

ONLINE DATABASES

Wilson Business Abstracts Online. H. W. Wilson Co. • Indexes and abstracts 600 major business periodicals, plus the *Wall Street Journal* and the business section of the *New York Times.* Indexing is from 1982, abstracting from 1990, with the two newspapers included from 1993. Updated weekly. Inquire as to online cost and availability. (*Business Periodicals Index* without abstracts is also available online.).

PERIODICALS AND NEWSLETTERS

Moneytalk. Jean Kwiatowski. • Description: Provides suggestions for saving money through the use of coupons and refund offers. Recurring features include letters to the editor and news of research.

PROMO: Promotion Marketing Worldwide. Primedia Business Magazines and Media. • Monthly. $65.00 per year. Edited for companies and agencies that utilize couponing, point-of-purchase advertising, special events, games, contests, premiums, product samples, and other unique promotional items.

Refundable Bundle. • Bimonthly. $10.00 per year. Newsletter for grocery shoppers. Each issue provides details of new coupon and refund offers.

COURTS

See also: LAW; LAWS; LAWYERS

GENERAL WORKS

Courts, Judges and Politics: An Introduction to the Judicial Process. Walter Murphy and others, editors. McGraw-Hill. • 2001. $56.25. Fifth edition. (Humanities, Social Sciences and World Languages Series).

Government by Judiciary: The Transformation of the Fourteenth Amendment. Raoul Berger. Liberty Fund, Inc. • 1997. $22.00. Second revised edition.

ABSTRACTS AND INDEXES

Current Law Index: Multiple Access to Legal Periodicals. Gale Cengage Learning. • Monthly. $725.00 per year. Produced in cooperation with the American Association of Law Libraries. Indexes more than 900 law journals, legal newspapers, and specialty publications from the U.S., Canada, U.K., Ireland, Australia, and New Zealand.

Index to Legal Periodicals and Books. H. W. Wilson Co. • Monthly. $490.00 per year. Quarterly and annual cumulations.

ALMANACS AND YEARBOOKS

American Law Yearbook. Gale Cengage Learning. • Annual. $165.00. Serves as a yearly supplement to *West's Encyclopedia of American Law.* Describes new legal developments in many subject areas.

BIBLIOGRAPHIES

Court System of the United States: A Bibliography. D. Ellsworth Blanc, editor. Nova Science Publishers, Inc. • 2002. $69.00. Covers literature dealing with district, circuit, and appeals courts. Includes author, title, and subject indexes.

Criminal Justice Information: How to Find It, How to Use It. Dennis C. Benamati and others. Greenwood Publishing Group, Inc. • 1997. $64.95. A guide to print, electronic, and online criminal justice information resources. Includes statistical reports, directories, periodicals, monographs, databases, and other sources.

BIOGRAPHICAL SOURCES

Who's Who in American Law. Marquis Who's Who. • Biennial. $295.00. Contains over 23,000 concise biographies of American lawyers, judges, and others in the legal field.

CD-ROM DATABASES

Leadership Library on CD-ROM: Who's Who in the Leadership of the United States. Leadership Directories, Inc. • Quarterly. Including access to Internet version (weekly updates). Contains all 14 *Yellow Book* personnel directories on CD-ROM, providing contact and brief biographical information for about 400,000 individuals. Covers business, government, financial institutions, news media, law firms, associations, foreign representatives, and nonprofit organizations. Includes photographs.

WILSONDISC: Index to Legal Periodicals and Books. H. W. Wilson Co. • Monthly. Includes unlimited online access to *Index to Legal Periodicals* through WILSONLINE. Contains CD-ROM indexing of more than 1,400 English language legal periodicals from 1981 to date and 2,500 books.

DIRECTORIES

Almanac of the Federal Judiciary. Aspen Publishers, Inc. • Annual. $295.00 per set. Two volumes. Volume one provides information on federal district judges; volume two relates to federal circuit judges.

American Bench: Judges of the Nation. Forster Long, Inc. • Annual. $395.00. Features biographies of 18,000 members of the U.S. Judiciary at federal, state and local levels.

Carroll's Federal & Federal Regional Directory. Carroll Publishing. • Semiannual. $325.00 per year; with online edition, $1,200 per year. Lists more than 23,000 U. S. government officials throughout the country, including military installations.

Carroll's Federal Directory. Carroll Publishing. • Covers: About 38,000 executive managers in federal government offices in Washington, DC, including executive, congressional and judicial branches; members of Congress and Congressional committees and staff. Entries include: Agency names, titles, office address (including room numbers), e-mail addresses, and telephone and fax numbers. Also available as part of a "library edition" titled "Federal Directory Annual".

Judicial Staff Directory: With Biographical Information on Judges and Key Court Staff. CQ Press. • Semiannual. $450.00. $225.00 per volume. Lists 33,500 federal court personnel, including 1,900 federal judges and their staffs, including biographies of judges and key executives. Includes maps of court jurisdictions.

Judicial Yellow Book: Who's Who in Federal and State Courts. Leadership Directories, Inc. • Semiannual. $245.00 per year. Lists more than 3,200 judges and staffs in various federal courts and 1,200 judges and staffs in state courts. Includes biographical profiles of judges.

Want's Federal-State Court Directory. Want Publishing Co. • Covers: All federal court judges and clerks of court, and United States attorneys and magistrates, judges; state supreme court chief justices and state court administrators; Supreme Court Chief Justices of Canada and other nations. Entries include: Judge, clerk, probation office, or magistrate's name, address, phone.

ENCYCLOPEDIAS AND DICTIONARIES

Concise Dictionary of Crime and Justice. Mark S. Davis. Sage Publications, Inc. • 2002. $64.95. Contains more than 2,000 definitions of terms relating to the criminal justice system and criminology.

Encyclopedia of Crime and Justice. Available from Gale Cengage Learning. • 2001. $475.00. Second edition. Four volumes. Published by Macmillan Reference USA. Contains extensive information on a wide variety of topics pertaining to crime, criminology, social issues, and the courts. (A complete revision of 1982 edition.).

Encyclopedia of Crime and Punishment. David Levinson, editor. Sage Publications, Inc. • 2002. $600.00. Four volumes. Contains 425 signed entries dealing with civil, criminal, media, corporate, and international issues. Includes material on fraud, police science, correctional institutions, social matters, methodology, national surveys, and crime statistics.

Encyclopedia of White-Collar and Corporate Crime. Lawrence M. Salinger, editor. Sage Publications, Inc. • 2004. $295.00. Two volumes. Covers such items as fraud, kickbacks, price fixing, tax evasion, bribery, forgery, counterfeiting, embezzlement, extortion, graft, bid rigging, and assorted scams and swindles.

Legal Systems of the World: A Political, Social, and Cultural Encyclopedia. Herbert M. Kritzer, editor. ABC-CLIO, Inc. • 2002. $385.00. Four volumes. Describes how the courts and legal systems operate in many different countries.

West's Encyclopedia of American Law. Available from Gale Cengage Learning. • 2003. $1,195.00. Second edition. 12 volumes. Published by West Group. Covers a wide variety of legal topics for the general reader.

World of Criminal Justice. Gale Cengage Learning. • 2002. $160.00. Two volumes. Contains both topical and biographical entries relating to the criminal justice system and criminology.

INTERNET DATABASES

Lexis.com Research System. Lexis-Nexis Group. Phone: 800-227-4908 or (937)865-6800 Fax: (937)865-6909 E-mail: webmaster@prod.lexis-nexis.com • URL: http://www.lexis.com • Fee-based Web site offers extensive searching of a wide variety of legal sources. Additional features include Daily Opinion Service, lexis.com Bookstore, Career Center, CLE Center, Law Schools, and Practice Pages ("Pages specific to areas of specialty").

ONLINE DATABASES

Index to Legal Periodicals and Books (Online). H. W. Wilson Co. • Broad coverage of law journals and books 1981 to date. Monthly updates. Inquire as to online cost and availability.

LEXIS. LEXIS-NEXIS. • The various LEXIS databases provide full text and indexing for a wide variety of legal cases, statutes, orders, and opinions.

PERIODICALS AND NEWSLETTERS

Court Review. American Judges Association. National Center for State Courts. • Quarterly. Free to members; non-members, $25.00 per year.

Family Court Review: An Interdisciplinary Journal. Association of Family and Conciliation Courts. Sage Publications, Inc. • Quarterly. Institutions, $456.00 per year.

Judges' Journal. American Bar Association, Judicial Administration Div., Section of Environment, Energy and Resources. • Quarterly. Free to members; non-members, $25.00 per year. Focuses on the court.

U. S. Supreme Court Bulletin. CCH, Inc. • Monthly and on each decision day while the Court is in session.

United States Law Week: A National Survey of Current Law. BNA, Inc. • Weekly. $1,152.00 per year. Covers U.S. Supreme Court proceedings and gives full text of decisions. Also provides detailed reports on important legislative and regulatory actions.

STATISTICS SOURCES

Annual Report of the Director. Administrative Office of the United States Courts. • Annual.

Statistics on Crime, Justice, and Punishment. Gale Cengage Learning. • 1996. $850.00. Volume three. Includes graphs, charts, and tables arranged within subject chapters. Citations to data sources are provided. (Statistics on...Series: vol. 3).

TRADE/PROFESSIONAL ASSOCIATIONS

Fund for Modern Courts. 351 W. 54th St., New York, NY 10019. Phone: (212)541-6741 Fax: (212)541-7301 E-mail: justice@moderncourts.org • URL: http://www.moderncourts.org • Members seek public support for the improvement of the judicial system.

National Association for Court Management. c/o Association Management National Center for State Courts, 300 Newport Ave., Williamsburg, VA 23185-4147. Phone: 800-616-6165 or (757)259-1841 Fax: (757)259-1520 E-mail: nacm@ncsc.dni.us • URL: http://www.nacmnet.org.

National Center for State Courts. 300 Newport Ave., Williamsburg, VA 23185. Phone: 800-616-6164 or (757)253-2000 Fax: (757)220-0449 E-mail: webmaster@ncsc.dni.us • URL: http://www.ncsconline.org.

National Council of Juvenile and Family Court Judges. P.O. Box 8907, Reno, NV 89507. Phone: (775)784-6012 Fax: (775)784-6628 E-mail: admin@ncjfcj.org • URL: http://www.ncjfcj.org/.

CRACKER INDUSTRY

See: BAKING INDUSTRY; SNACK FOOD INDUSTRY

CRAFTS

See: GIFT BUSINESS; HOBBY INDUSTRY

CREATIVITY

GENERAL WORKS

Corporate Creativity: How Innovation and Improvement Actually Happen. Alan G. Robinson and Sam Stern. Berrett-Koehler Pulishers, Inc. • 1997. $29.95. Describes the six "essential elements" of business creativity.

Creative Management. Jane Henry. Sage Publications, Inc. • 2001. $101.00. Second edition.

Interface Culture: How New Technology Transforms the Way We Create and Communicate. Steven Johnson. HarperSanFrancisco. • 1997. $24.00. A discussion of how computer interfaces and online technology ("cyberspace") affect society in general.

Lateral Thinking: Creativity Step by Step. Edward de Bono. HarperTrade. • 1990. $15.00.

ABSTRACTS AND INDEXES

Psychological Abstracts. American Psychological Association. • Monthly. Members, $815.00 per year; individuals and institutions, $1,207.00 per year. Covers the international literature of psychology and the behavioral sciences. Includes journals, technical reports, dissertations, and other sources.

ALMANACS AND YEARBOOKS

Creativity. Art Direction Magazine. Art Directon Book Co., Inc. • Annual. $62.95.

ONLINE DATABASES

PsycINFO. American Psychological Association. • Provides indexing and abstracting of the worldwide literature of psychology and the behavioral sciences. Time period is 1967 to date, with monthly updates. Inquire as to online cost and availability.

PERIODICALS AND NEWSLETTERS

Business 2.0. Time Inc. • Monthly. $30.00 per year. General business magazine emphasizing ideas, insight, and innovation.

Fast Company: How Smart Business Works. Fast Company, Inc. • Monthly. $12.00 per year. Covers business management, with emphasis on creativity, leadership, innovation, career advancement, teamwork, the global economy, and the "new workplace.".

Journal of Creative Behavior. Creative Education Foundation, Inc. • Quarterly. Individuals, $75.00 per year; institutions, $95.00 per year.

RESEARCH CENTERS AND INSTITUTES

Center for Studies in Creativity. State University of New York College at Buffalo. 244 Chase Hall, 1300 Elmwood Ave., Buffalo, NY 14222-1095. Phone: (716)878-6223 Fax: (716)878-4040 E-mail: creatcps@buffalostate.edu • URL: http://www.buffalostate.edu/creativity.

Institute of Personality and Social Research. University of California at Berkeley. 4143 Tolman Hall, Berkeley, CA 94720. Phone: (510)642-5050 Fax: (510)643-9334 • URL: http://www.ls.berkeley.edu/dept/ipsr.

TRADE/PROFESSIONAL ASSOCIATIONS

Supporting Emotional Needs of the Gifted. P.O. Box 6047, Scottsdale, AZ 85261. Phone: (773)857-6250 E-mail: office@sengifted.org • URL: http://www.sengifted.org.

CREDIT

See also: AGRICULTURAL CREDIT; CONSUMER CREDIT; CREDIT INSUR-ANCE; CREDIT MANAGEMENT; FOREIGN CREDIT

CD-ROM DATABASES

CreditDisk 2.0. Fitch, Inc. • Price and frequency on application. CD-ROM provides credit research and ratings on individual banks throughout the world, with Internet updating. Includes graphic displays of rating histories and financial ratios.

EconLit. Available from SilverPlatter Information, Inc. • Monthly. Single-user, $1,600.00 per year. Provides CD-ROM citations, with abstracts, to articles from more than 500 economics journals. Time period is 1969 to date. Produced by the American Economic Association.

OECD Statistical Compendium. Organization for Economic Cooperation and Development. • Semiannual. $1,905.00 per year for 1 to 10 users. CD-ROM contains more than 730,000 monthly, quarterly, and annual time series for OECD countries, 1960 to date. Includes fully searchable data on agriculture, food, economic indicators, national accounts, employment, energy, finance, industry, technology, and foreign trade. Results can be displayed in various forms.

WILSONDISC: Wilson Business Abstracts. H. W. Wilson Co. • Monthly. Includes unlimited online access to *Wilson Business Abstracts* through WILSONLINE. Provides CD-ROM "cover-to-cover" abstracting and indexing of over 600 prominent business periodicals. Indexing is from 1982, abstracting from 1990. (*Business Periodicals Index* without abstracts is available on CD-ROM at $1,495 per year.).

ENCYCLOPEDIAS AND DICTIONARIES

Blackwell Encyclopedic Dictionary of Finance. Dean Paxson and Douglas Wood, editors. Blackwell Publishing. • 1997. $110.00. The editors are associ-

ated with the University of Manchester. Contains definitions of key terms combined with longer articles written by various U. S. and foreign business educators. Includes bibliographies and index. (Blackwell Encyclopedia of Management Series).

Credit and Lending Dictionary. Shelley W. Geehr and Daphne Smith, editors. The Risk Management Association. • 1994. $25.00.

Encyclopedia of Banking and Finance. Charles J. Woelfel. McGraw-Hill. • 1996. $150.00. 10th revised edition. Includes CD-ROM.

HANDBOOKS AND MANUALS

Manual of Credit and Commercial Laws. National Association of Credit Management. • Annual. Free to members; non-members, $125.00. Formerly *Credit Manual of Commercial Laws.*

Manual of Credit and Commercial Laws. National Association of Credit Management. • Annual. Free to members; non-members, $100.00. Formerly *Credit Manual of Commercial Laws.*

Practical Guide to Credit and Collection. George O. Bancroft. AMACOM. • 1989. $29.95.

INTERNET DATABASES

Business 2.0 Web Guide to the Best Business Links. Business 2.0 Media Inc. Phone: (415)293-4800 E-mail: support@business2.com • URL: http://www.business2.com/webguide • Web site presents an extensive, searchable directory of links to "the best, most informative, and authoritative web pages." Twenty main categories cover business, finance, career, company information, people, and technology topics, with thousands of subtopics, all linking to Web sites recommended by experienced business researchers. Fees: Free.

EBSCO Information Services. Ebsco Publishing. Phone: 800-653-2726 or (978)356-6500 Fax: (978)356-6565 E-mail: ep@epnet.com • URL: http://www.epnet.com • Fee-based Web site providing Internet access to a wide variety of databases, including business-related material. Full text is available for many periodical titles, with daily updates. Fees: Apply.

Fedstats. Federal Interagency Council on Statistical Policy. Phone: (202)395-7254 • URL: http://www.fedstats.gov • Web site features an efficient search facility for full-text statistics produced by more than 100 federal agencies, including the Census Bureau, the Bureau of Economic Analysis, and the Bureau of Labor Statistics. Boolean searches can be made within one agency or for all agencies combined. Links are offered to international statistical bureaus, including the UN, IMF, OECD, UNESCO, Eurostat, and 20 individual countries. Fees: Free.

FreeLunch.com. Economy.com, Inc. Phone: (610)696-8700 Fax: (610)696-1678 • URL: http://www.freelunch.com • Web site provides free access to more than 1.5 million economic and financial data series, covering industry, demographics, labor markets, prices, retail sales, government spending, trade, interest rates, housing starts, the stock market, and many other topics. Data is available for various time periods in either chart or table form. Searching is offered. Fees: Free, but registration required. Economy.com, Inc. also offers fee-based economic analysis at *The Dismal Scientist* site (http://www.dismal.com).

InSite 2. Intelligence Data/Thomson Financial. Phone: 800-654-0393 or (617)856-1890 Fax: (617)737-3182 E-mail: intelligence.data@tfn.com • URL: http://www.insite2.gale.com/ • Fee-based Web site consolidates information in a "Base Pack" consisting of Business InSite, Market InSite, and Company InSite. Optional databases are Consumer InSite, Health and Wellness InSite, Newsletter In-Site, and Computer InSite. Includes fulltext content from more than 2,500 trade publications, journals, newsletters, newspapers, analyst reports, and other

sources. Continuous updating. Formerly produced by The Gale Group.

ProQuest Direct. ProQuest Inc. Phone: 800-889-3358 or (734)761-4700 Fax: (734)662-4554 • URL: http://proquest.com • Fee-based Web site providing Internet access to more than 3,000 periodicals, newspapers, and other publications. Many items are available full-text, with daily updates. Includes extensive corporate and financial information. Fees: Apply.

Summary of Commentary on Current Economic Conditions by Federal Reserve District [the Beige Book]. Board of Governors of the Federal Reserve System. Phone: (202)452-3000 Fax: (202)452-3819 • URL: http://www.federalreserve.gov/fomc/beigebook/2004/ • Free Web site provides current "anecdotal information" eight times a year on economic conditions within each of the 12 Federal Reserve Districts, plus an extensive national *Summary.* Text is based on the opinions of bank officials, business executives, economists, financial market experts, and others. Typically contains views of consumer spending, manufacturing, services, credit, employment, prices, wages, and the economy in general. Usually referred to as the Beige Book.

ONLINE DATABASES

Accounting and Tax Database. PROQUEST. • Provides indexing and abstracting of the literature of accounting, taxation, and financial management, 1971 to date. Updating is weekly. Especially covers accounting, auditing, banking, bankruptcy, employee compensation and benefits, cash management, financial planning, and credit. Inquire as to online cost and availability.

Banking Information Source. PROQUEST. • Provides indexing and abstracting of periodical and other literature from 1982 to date, with weekly updates. Covers the financial services industry: banks, savings institutions, investment houses, credit unions, insurance companies, and real estate organizations. Emphasis is on marketing and management. Inquire as to online cost and availability. (Formerly *FINIS: Financial Industry Information Service.*).

EconLit. American Economic Association. • Covers the worldwide literature of economics as contained in selected monographs and about 550 journals. Subjects include microeconomics, macroeconomics, economic history, inflation, money, credit, finance, accounting theory, trade, natural resource economics, and regional economics. Time period is 1969 to present, with monthly updates. Inquire as to online cost and availability.

TRW Business Credit Profiles. Experian. • Provides credit history (trade payments, payment trends, payment totals, payment history, etc.) for public and private U. S. companies. Key facts and banking information are also given. Updates are weekly. Inquire as to online cost and availability.

Wilson Business Abstracts Online. H. W. Wilson Co. • Indexes and abstracts 600 major business periodicals, plus the *Wall Street Journal* and the business section of the *New York Times.* Indexing is from 1982, abstracting from 1990, with the two newspapers included from 1993. Updated weekly. Inquire as to online cost and availability. (*Business Periodicals Index* without abstracts is also available online.).

PERIODICALS AND NEWSLETTERS

American Banker: The Financial Services Daily. Thomson Media. • Daily. $895.00 per year. Provides news of banking, investment products, mortgages, credit unions, finance, bank technology, and legal developments.

Bank Credit Analyst. BCA Publications Ltd. • Monthly. $695.00 per year. "The independent monthly forecast and analysis of trends in business conditions and major investment markets based on a continuous appraisal of money and credit flows." Includes many charts and graphs relating to money, credit, and securities in the U. S.

Bondweek: The Newsweekly of Fixed Income and Credit Markets. Institutional Investor, Inc., Journals Group. • Weekly. $2,425.00 per year. Newsletter. Includes print and online editions. Covers taxable, fixed-income securities for professional investors, including corporate, government, foreign, mortgage, and high-yield.

Credit Executive Letter. American Financial Services Association. • Monthly. Members, $12.00 per year; non-members, $22.00 per year.

Grant's Interest Rate Observer. James Grant, editor. Grant's Financial Publishing Inc. • Biweekly. $725.00 per year. Newsletter containing detailed analysis of money-related topics, including interest rate trends, global credit markets, fixed-income investments, bank loan policies, and international money markets.

International Bank Credit Analyst. BCA Publications Ltd. • Monthly. $795.00 per year. "A monthly forecast and analysis of currency movements, interest rates, and stock market developments in the principal countries, based on a continuous appraisal of money and credit trends worldwide." Includes many charts and graphs providing international coverage of money, credit, and securities.

U. S. Banker. Thomson Media. • Monthly. $65.00 per year. Edited for bank executives and managers. Covers a wide variety of banking and financial topics.

RESEARCH CENTERS AND INSTITUTES

Bendheim Center for Finance. Princeton University, 26 Prospect Ave., Princeton, NJ 08540-5296. Phone: (609)258-0770 Fax: (609)258-0771 E-mail: yacine@princeton.edu • URL: http://www.princeton.edu/~bcf/ • Research areas include securities markets, portfolio analysis, credit markets, and corporate finance. Emphasis is on quantitative and mathematical perspectives.

STATISTICS SOURCES

Business Statistics of the United States. Linz Audain and Cornelia J. Strawser. Bernan Associates. • Annual. $147.00. Based on *Business Statistics*, formerly issue by the Bureau of Economic Analysis, U. S. Department of Commerce. Provides basic data for a wide variety of U. S. industries, services, and economic indicators. Most statistics are shown annually for 30 years and monthly for the most recent four years.

Economic Report of the President: Together with the Annual Report of the Council of Economic Advisors. Available from U. S. Government Printing Office. • Annual. $32.00. Includes about 130 pages of "Statistical Tables Relating to Income, Employment, and Production." Tables cover national income, employment, wages, productivity, manufacturing, prices, credit, finance (public and private), corporate profits, and foreign trade.

Statistical Information on the Financial Services Industry. American Bankers Association. • Annual. Members, $150.00; non-members, $275.00. Presents a wide variety of data relating to banking and financial services, including consumer economics, personal finance, credit, government loans, capital markets, and international banking.

Survey of Current Business. Available from U. S. Government Printing Office. • Monthly. $63.00 per year. Issued by Bureau of Economic Analysis, U. S. Department of Commerce. Presents a wide variety of business and economic data.

TRADE/PROFESSIONAL ASSOCIATIONS

National Association of Credit Management. 8815 Columbia, 100 Pky., Columbia, MD 21045-2158. Phone: 800-955-8815 or (410)740-5560 Fax: (410)740-5574 E-mail: nacm_info@nacm.org •

URL: http://www.nacm.org • Formerly National Institute of Credit.

OTHER SOURCES

Consumer and Commercial Credit: Installment Sales. Prentice Hall PTR. • Three looseleaf volumes. Periodic supplementation. Price on application. Covers secured transactions under the Uniform Commercial Code and the Uniform Consumer Credit Code. Includes retail installment sales, home improvement loans, higher education loans, and other kinds of installment loans.

Debtor-Creditor Law. LexisNexis Matthew Bender. • $2,078.00. 13 looseleaf volumes. Periodic supplementation. Covers all aspects of the creation and enforcement of the debtor-creditor relationship.

CREDIT, BANK

See: BANK LOANS

CREDIT CARD INDUSTRY

ABSTRACTS AND INDEXES

Business Periodicals Index. H. W. Wilson Co. • 11 times a year. Quarterly and annual cumulations. Price varies.

DIRECTORIES

BIN Number Directory of all Visa and Mastercard Issuing Banks. Fraud and Theft Information Bureau. • Annual. $1,175.00. Base edition. Semiannual updates, $360.00 per year. Numerical arrangement of about 30,000 banks worldwide. BIN numbers (also called ISO or prefix numbers) identify a credit card holder's issuing bank.

Business Organizations, Agencies, and Publications Directory. Gale Cengage Learning. • 2003. $480.00. 15th edition. Over 40,000 entries describing 39 types of business information sources. Classified by type of organization, publication, or serviceIncludes state, national, and international agencies and organizations. Master index to names and keywords. Also includes e-mail addresses and web site URL's.

Card Industry Directory and Debit Card Directory. Thomson Media. • Annual. Price on application.

Credit Card Management Buyers Guide. Thomson Financial (New York, New York). • Database covers: Credit and debit card contacts, products and services. Entries include: Company name, address, phone.

International Association of Financial Crimes Investigators: Membership Directory. International Association of Financial Crimes Investigators. • Annual. Membership. About 3,500 firms and individuals engaged in investigation of fraudulent use of credit cards. Formerly *International Association of Credit Card Investigators-Membership Directory.* Formerly International Association of Credit Card Investigators.

Low Rate and No Fee Credit Card List. Bankcard Holders of America. • Quarterly. $4.00 per copy. Lists about 50 banks offering relatively low interest rates and/or no annual fee for credit card accounts. Formerly *Low Interest Rate.*

Plunkett's Financial Services Industry Almanac: The Only Comprehensive Overview of the Banking, Insurance, Credit and Investment Sectors. Plunkett Research, Ltd. • Annual. $229.99. Includes CD-ROM. Discusses important trends in various sectors of the financial industry. Five hundred major banking, credit card, investment, and financial services companies are profiled. (Business, Careers and Internet Reference Tools Series).

INTERNET DATABASES

BanxQuote Banking, Mortgage, and Finance Center. BanxQuote, Inc. Phone: (914)722-1600 Fax:

(914)722-6630 E-mail: info@banx.com • URL: http://www.banx.com • Web site quotes interest rates paid by banks around the country on various savings products, as well as rates paid by consumers for automobile loans, mortgages, credit cards, home equity loans, and personal loans. Also provided: stock quotes, indexes, stock options, futures trading data, economic indicators, and links to many other financial sites. Daily updates. Fees: Free.

ONLINE DATABASES

Marketing and Advertising Reference Service (MARS). Gale Cengage Learning. • Provides abstracts of literature relating to consumer marketing and advertising, including all forms of advertising media. Time period is 1984 to date. Daily updates. Inquire as to online cost and availability.

Wilson Business Abstracts Online. H. W. Wilson Co. • Indexes and abstracts 600 major business periodicals, plus the *Wall Street Journal* and the business section of the *New York Times.* Indexing is from 1982, abstracting from 1990, with the two newspapers included from 1993. Updated weekly. Inquire as to online cost and availability. (*Business Periodicals Index* without abstracts is also available online.).

PERIODICALS AND NEWSLETTERS

Bankcard Consumer News. Bankcard Holders of America. • Bimonthly. $24.00 per year. Newsletter for consumers.

Card News: The Executive Report on the Transaction Card Marketplace. PBI Media, LLC. • 25 times per year. $997.00 per year. Newsletter on transaction cards, debit and credit cards, automatic teller machines, etc.

Card Technology. Thomson Media. • Monthly. $79.00 per year. Covers advanced technology for credit, debit, and other cards. Topics include smart cards, optical recognition, and card design.

Credit Card Management: The Magazine of Electronic Payments. Thomson Media. • Monthly. $98.00 per year. Edited for bankers and other managers of electronic payment systems.

Credit Executive Letter. American Financial Services Association. • Monthly. Members, $12.00 per year; non-members, $22.00 per year.

Credit Risk Management. Phillips International, Inc. • Biweekly. $695.00 per year. Newsletter on consumer credit, including delinquency aspects.

The Nilson Report. HSN Consultants Inc. • Description: Provides information about the credit card industry.

Online Marketplace. Jupiter Communications. • Description: Keeps abreast of the fast-emerging developments in the digital marketplace and emerging interactive technologies. Reports on players and devices to provide the "inside scoop" on this marketplace. Topics include screen phones, interactive television, and smart cards, to name a few. Recurring features include interviews, and columns titled Tool Watch, Site Watch, and News Digest.

RESEARCH CENTERS AND INSTITUTES

Credit Research Center. Georgetown University. 3240 Prospect St. NW, Ste. 300, Washington, DC 20007. Phone: (202)625-0103 Fax: (202)625-0104 E-mail: statenm@msb.edu • URL: http://www.msb.edu/prog/crc • Economic trends and public policy issues in consumer and mortgage credit, with emphasis on regulatory policy (including rate ceilings, restrictions on creditor remedies, and consumer bankruptcies), consumer behavior, medical debt, and managerial decision systems.

STATISTICS SOURCES

Statistical Information on the Financial Services Industry. American Bankers Association. • Annual. Members, $150.00; non-members, $275.00. Presents a wide variety of data relating to banking and financial services, including consumer economics, personal finance, credit, government loans, capital markets, and international banking.

TRADE/PROFESSIONAL ASSOCIATIONS

American Financial Services Association. 919 18th St. NW, Ste. 300, Washington, DC 20006-5517. Phone: (202)296-5544 Fax: (202)223-0321 E-mail: cstinebert@afsamail.org • URL: http://www.afsaonline.org • Represents companies whose business is primarily direct credit lending to consumers and/or the purchase of sales finance paper on consumer goods. Has members that have insurance and retail subsidiaries; some are themselves subsidiaries of highly diversified parent corporations. Encourages the business of financing individuals and families for necessary and useful purposes at reasonable charges, including interest; promotes consumer understanding of basic money management principles as well as constructive uses of consumer credit. Includes educational services such as films, textbooks, and study units for the classroom and budgeting guides for individuals and families. Compiles statistical reports; offers seminars.

CardTrak. PO Box 1700, Frederick, MD 21702. Phone: (301)631-9100 Fax: (301)631-9112 E-mail: cardstaff@cardweb.com • URL: http://www.cardweb.com/cardtrak • Promotes the "wise and careful" use of credit cards. A consumer organization.

Credit Card Users of America. P.O. Box 7100, Beverly Hills, CA 90212. Phone: (818)343-4434 • Supports the rights of credit card users.

International Association of Financial Crimes Investigators. 837 Embarcadero Ave., Suite 5, El Dorado Hills, CA 95762. Phone: (919)939-5000 Fax: (919)939-0395 E-mail: admin@iafci.org • URL: http://www.iafci.org • Members are officials who investigate criminal violations of credit card laws. Formerly International Association of Financial Crimes.

MasterCard International. 2000 Purchase St., Purchase, NY 10577. Phone: 800-622-7747 or (914)249-2000 Fax: (914)249-5510 E-mail: customerservicecenter@mastercard.com • URL: http://www.mastercard.com • Represents banks and financial institutions. Serves as a licensor of the MasterCard credit card, the MasterCard business card, the Gold MasterCard credit card, and the MasterCard Travelers Cheque.

National Foundation for Credit Counseling. 801 Roeder Rd., Ste. 900, Silver Spring, MD 20910. Phone: 800-388-2227 or (301)589-5600 Fax: (301)495-5623 • URL: http://www.nfcc.org • Supersedes Retail Credit Institute of America.

OTHER SOURCES

Internet Payments Report. JupiterMedia. • Annual. $1,095.00. Market research report. Provides data, comment, and forecasts on the collection of electronic payments ("e-money") for goods and services offered through the Internet.

The U. S. Market for Plastic Payment Cards. Available from MarketResearch.com. • 1998. $1,375.00. Market research report published by Packaged Facts. Covers credit cards, charge cards, debit cards, and smart cards. Provides profiles of Visa, Mastercard, American Express, Discover, Diners Club, and others.

CREDIT, CONSUMER

See: CONSUMER CREDIT

CREDIT INSURANCE

See also: INSURANCE

BIOGRAPHICAL SOURCES

Who's Who in Insurance. Underwriter Printing and Publishing Co. • Annual. $150.00. Contains over 5,000 biographies of insurance officials, leading agents and brokers, and high-ranking company officials.

PERIODICALS AND NEWSLETTERS

CCIA Newsletter. Consumer Credit Insurance Association. • Description: Focuses on consumer credit insurance in the areas of life insurance, accident and health insurance, and property insurance. Includes news of the Association.

TRADE/PROFESSIONAL ASSOCIATIONS

Consumer Credit Industry Association. 2911 S Shore Blvd., Ste. 130, League City, TX 77573. Phone: (281)535-7446 Fax: (281)535-7435 E-mail: jim.pangburn@anico.com • URL: http://www.cciaonline.com • Insurance companies underwriting consumer credit insurance in areas of life insurance, accident and health insurance, and property insurance.

Foreign Credit Insurance Association. 125 Park Ave., 14th Fl., New York, NY 10017. Phone: (212)885-1500 Fax: (212)885-1535 E-mail: service@fcia.org • URL: http://www.fcia.org • Represents marine, property, and casualty insurance companies. Insures companies against the risks of nonpayment by buyers for commercial and/or political reasons. Facilitates the financing of term credit sales, thus providing companies with support to meet competitive terms of payment offered by others.

CREDIT MANAGEMENT

See also: CREDIT

HANDBOOKS AND MANUALS

Credit Department Management. D. Laurence Blackstone. The Risk Management Association. • 1992. $65.00. Second edition.

Credit Management Handbook. Burt Edwards and others. Ashgate Publishing Co. • 1997. $119.95. Fourth edition. Published by Gower in England.

Credit Risk Management: A Guide to Sound Business Decisions. H. A. Schaeffer. John Wiley and Sons, Inc. • 2000. $95.00. Covers corporate credit policies, credit authorization procedures, and analysis of business credit applications. Includes 12 "real-life" case studies.

PERIODICALS AND NEWSLETTERS

Business Credit. National Association of Credit Management. • 10 tims a year. $48.00 per year. Formerly *Credit and Financial Management.*

Collections and Credit Risk: The Authority for Commercial and Consumer Credit Professionals. Thomson Media. • Monthly. $95.00 per year. Contains articles on the technology and business management of credit and collection functions. Includes coverage of bad debts, bankruptcy, and credit risk management.

TRADE/PROFESSIONAL ASSOCIATIONS

Credit Research Foundation. 8840 Columbia 100 Pkwy., 100 Pky., Columbia, MD 21045. Phone: (410)740-5499 Fax: (410)740-4620 E-mail: crf_info@crfonline.org • URL: http://www.crfonline.org • Represents credit, financial, and working capital executives of manufacturing and banking concerns. Aims to create a better understanding of the impact of credit on the economy. Plans, supervises, and administers research and educational programs. Conducts surveys on economic conditions, trends, policies, practices, theory, systems, and methodology. Sponsors formal educational programs in credit and financial management. Maintains library on credit, collections, and management.

National Association of Consumer Credit Administrators. PO Box 20871, Columbus, OH 43220-0871. Phone: (614)326-1165 Fax: (614)326-1162 • URL: http://www.naccaonline.org • State government officials who administer consumer finance laws in the United States, Guam, Puerto Rico and Canada.

Society of Certified Credit Executives. c/o Association of Credit and Collection Professionals, PO Box 390106, Minneapolis, MN 55439. Phone: (952)926-6547 E-mail: scce@collector.com • URL: http://www.acainternational.org.

OTHER SOURCES

Consumer and Commercial Credit: Installment Sales. Prentice Hall PTR. • Three looseleaf volumes. Periodic supplementation. Price on application. Covers secured transactions under the Uniform Commercial Code and the Uniform Consumer Credit Code. Includes retail installment sales, home improvement loans, higher education loans, and other kinds of installment loans.

CREDIT UNIONS

See also: SAVINGS AND LOAN ASSOCIATIONS

ALMANACS AND YEARBOOKS

Credit Union Report. Credit Union National Association. • Annual. $15.00. Credit union leagues, associations, for each of the 50 states and the District of Columbia.

DIRECTORIES

American Financial Directory. Accuity. • Covers: Approximately 23,000 banks, bank holding companies, credit unions, savings and loans, and other financial institutions and their approximately 56,000 branch offices. Entries include: Institution name, address, phone, fax, holding company affiliation, names and titles of key personnel, correspondent banks, FEDWIRE data and ABA number, balance sheet highlights, branches.

Callahan's Credit Union Directory. Callahan & Associates Inc. • Covers: 11,843 state, federal, and U.S. credit unions; regulators, organizations, and leagues. Entries include: For credit unions--Name, address, phone, fax, chief executive officer, charter number; financial data, including total assets, loans, capital, and investments; number of members, rate of deposit growth, and routing and transit numbers. For regulators, associations and leagues--Organization or agency name, address, phone, contact.

Thomson Credit Union Directory. Credit Union National Association, Inc. Accuity. • Covers: Approximately 12,000 credit unions and head offices and over 6,000 branches. Entries include: Institution name, address, phone, fax, routing and transit number, managing officer, financial data, charter number, year established, number of members, number of employees.

HANDBOOKS AND MANUALS

National Credit Union Administration Rules and Regulations. Available from U. S. Government Printing Office. • Looseleaf. $130.00 for basic manual, including updates for an indeterminate period. Incorporates all amendments and revisions.

INTERNET DATABASES

The Bauer Group: Reporting On and Analyzing the Performance of U. S. Banks, Thrifts, and Credit Unions. Bauer Financial Reports, Inc. Phone: 800-

388-6686 or (305)445-9500 Fax: 800-230-9569 or (305)445-6775 • URL: http://www.bauerfinancial. com • Web site provides ratings (0 to 5 stars) of individual banks and credit unions, based on capital ratios and other financial criteria. Online searching for bank or credit union names is offered. Fees: Free.

ONLINE DATABASES

Banking Information Source. PROQUEST. • Provides indexing and abstracting of periodical and other literature from 1982 to date, with weekly updates. Covers the financial services industry: banks, savings institutions, investment houses, credit unions, insurance companies, and real estate organizations. Emphasis is on marketing and management. Inquire as to online cost and availability. (Formerly *FINIS: Financial Industry Information Service.*).

PERIODICALS AND NEWSLETTERS

American Banker: The Financial Services Daily. Thomson Media. • Daily. $895.00 per year. Provides news of banking, investment products, mortgages, credit unions, finance, bank technology, and legal developments.

The CEO Report. United Communications Group. • Description: Contains information for managers of credit unions.

Credit Union Executive Journal: For Active Leaders and Managers of Credit Unions. Credit Union National Association, Inc., Communications Div. CUNA Publications. • Bimonthly. $110.00 per year. A management journal for credit union CEOs and senior executives.

Credit Union Journal: The Nation's Leading Independent Credit Union Newsweekly. Thomson Media. • Weekly. $109.00 per year. Edited for credit union executives. Covers trends and developments in lending, insurance, investments, mortgages, check processing, relevant technology, and other topics.

Credit Union Magazine: For Credit Union Elected Officials, Managers and Employees. Credit Union National Association, Inc. CUNA Publications. • Monthly. $45.00 per year. News analysis and operational information for credit union management, staff, directors, and committee executives.

CUIS (Credit Union Information Service). United Communications Group. • Biweekly. $277.00 per year. Newsletter. Supplement available *CUIS Special Reoprt.*

U. S. Banker. Thomson Media. • Monthly. $65.00 per year. Edited for bank executives and managers. Covers a wide variety of banking and financial topics.

United States National Credit Union Administration NCUA Quarterly. National Credit Union Administration.

STATISTICS SOURCES

Statistical Information on the Financial Services Industry. American Bankers Association. • Annual. Members, $150.00; non-members, $275.00. Presents a wide variety of data relating to banking and financial services, including consumer economics, personal finance, credit, government loans, capital markets, and international banking.

U. S. Industry and Trade Outlook. Available from National Technical Information Service. • Annual. $69.95. Produced by the International Trade Administration, U. S. Department of Commerce, in a "public-private" partnership with DRI/McGraw-Hill and Standard & Poor's. Provides basic data, outlook for the current year, and "Long-Term Prospects" (five-year projections) for a wide variety of products and services. Includes high technology industries. Formerly *U. S. Industrial Outlook.*

TRADE/PROFESSIONAL ASSOCIATIONS

Credit Union Executives Society. PO Box 14167, Madison, WI 53708-0167. Phone: 800-252-2664 or

(608)271-2664 Fax: (608)271-2303 E-mail: cues@cues.org • URL: http://www.cues.org • Advances the professional development of credit union CEOs, senior management and directors. Serves as an international membership association dedicated to the professional development of credit union CEOs, senior management and directors.

Credit Union National Association. PO Box 431, PO Box 431, Madison, WI 53701-0431. Phone: 800-356-9655 or (608)231-4000 Fax: (608)231-4263 E-mail: dorothy@cuna.org • URL: http://www.cuna.org • Serves as trade association serving more than 90% of credit unions in the U.S. through their respective state leagues with a total membership of more than 77 million persons. (A credit union is a member-owned, nonprofit institution formed to encourage saving and to offer low interest loans to members, usually people working for the same employer, belonging to the same association, or living in the same community.) Promotes credit union membership, use of services, and organization of new credit unions. Seeks to perfect credit union laws; aids in the development of new credit union services, including new payment systems techniques; assists in the training of credit union officials and employees; compiles statistics, annually, by state. Offers charitable program.

Defense Credit Union Council. South Bldg., Ste. 600, 601 Pennsylvania Ave. NW, Washington, DC 20004-2601. Phone: 800-356-9655 or (202)638-3950 Fax: (202)638-3410 E-mail: dcuc1@cuna.com • URL: http://www.dcuc.org • Credit unions serving Department of Defense military and civilian personnel. Aims to assist credit unions serving DOD personnel with problems peculiar to military installations and personnel, and to maintain close liaison with DOD.

National Association of Federal Credit Unions. 3138 N 10th St., Arlington, VA 22201-2149. Phone: 800-336-4644 or (703)522-4770 Fax: (703)524-1082 E-mail: webmaster@nafcunet.org • URL: http://www.nafcunet.org.

World Council of Credit Unions, Inc. 5710 Mineral Point Rd., Madison, WI 53705. Phone: (608)231-7130 Fax: (608)238-8020 E-mail: mail@woccu.org • URL: http://www.woccu.org • A worldwide representative organization of credit unions. Supersedes World Division CUNA International.

OTHER SOURCES

Credit Union Guide. Credit Union National Association. Prentice Hall PTR. • Four looseleaf volumes. Periodic supplementation. Price on application. Laws, regulations, and developments affecting credit unions.

CRIME AND CRIMINALS

See also: COMPUTER CRIME AND SECURITY; COUNTERFEITING; FORGERIES; FRAUD AND EMBEZZLEMENT

GENERAL WORKS

Dirty Business: Exploring Corporate Misconduct: Analysis and Cases. Maurice Punch. Sage Publications, Inc. • 1996. $113.00. Covers organizational misbehavior and white-collar crime. Includes "Ten Cases of Corporate Deviance.".

Introduction to Security. Robert J. Fishcher and Gion Green. Elsevier. • 2003. Seventh edition. Price on application.

ABSTRACTS AND INDEXES

Current Law Index: Multiple Access to Legal Periodicals. Gale Cengage Learning. • Monthly. $725.00 per year. Produced in cooperation with the American Association of Law Libraries. Indexes more than 900 law journals, legal newspapers, and specialty publications from the U.S., Canada, U.K.,

Ireland, Australia, and New Zealand.

Index to Legal Periodicals and Books. H. W. Wilson Co. • Monthly. $490.00 per year. Quarterly and annual cumulations.

Social Sciences Index. H. W. Wilson Co. • Quarterly, with annual cumulation. Price varies. Indexes more than 400 periodicals covering economics, environmental policy, government, insurance, labor, health care policy, plannning, public administration, public welfare, urban studies, women's issues, criminology, and related topics.

ALMANACS AND YEARBOOKS

American Law Yearbook. Gale Cengage Learning. • Annual. $165.00. Serves as a yearly supplement to *West's Encyclopedia of American Law.* Describes new legal developments in many subject areas.

BIBLIOGRAPHIES

Criminal Justice Information: How to Find It, How to Use It. Dennis C. Benamati and others. Greenwood Publishing Group, Inc. • 1997. $64.95. A guide to print, electronic, and online criminal justice information resources. Includes statistical reports, directories, periodicals, monographs, databases, and other sources.

CD-ROM DATABASES

Newspaper Abstracts Ondisc. PROQUEST. • Monthly. $2,950.00 per year (covers 1989 to date; archival discs are available for 1985-88). Provides cover-to-cover CD-ROM indexing and abstracting of 19 major newspapers, including the *New York Times, Wall Street Journal, Washington Post, Chicago Tribune,* and *Los Angeles Times.*

Social Sciences Citation Index. ISI. • Monthly. Price on request. Provides CD-ROM indexing of articles appearing in 1700 leading social science journals worldwide, with additional selections from more than 5700 other journals. Time span is 1992 to date. Coverage includes economics, business, finance, management, communications, demographics, library and information science, political science, sociology, and many other subjects.

Social Sciences Citation Index: Compact Disc Edition with Abstracts. Institute for Scientific Information. • Monthly. Provides CD-ROM indexing and abstracting of "significant articles" from 1,700 social science journals worldwide, with additional selections from 3,200 other journals, 1986 to date. Includes economics, business, finance, management, communications, demographics, information and library science, political science, sociology, and many other subjects.

WILSONDISC: Index to Legal Periodicals and Books. H. W. Wilson Co. • Monthly. Includes unlimited online access to *Index to Legal Periodicals* through WILSONLINE. Contains CD-ROM indexing of more than 1,400 English language legal periodicals from 1981 to date and 2,500 books.

WILSONDISC: Wilson Social Sciences Abstracts. H. W. Wilson Co. • Monthly. Includes unlimited online access to *Social Sciences Index* through WILSONLINE. Provides CD-ROM indexing from 1983 and abstracting from 1994 of more than 500 periodicals covering economics, area studies, community health, public administration, public welfare, urban studies, and many other topics related to the social sciences.

ENCYCLOPEDIAS AND DICTIONARIES

Concise Dictionary of Crime and Justice. Mark S. Davis. Sage Publications, Inc. • 2002. $64.95. Contains more than 2,000 definitions of terms relating to the criminal justice system and criminology.

Encyclopedia of Crime and Justice. Available from Gale Cengage Learning. • 2001. $475.00. Second edition. Four volumes. Published by Macmillan Reference USA. Contains extensive information on a wide variety of topics pertaining to crime,

---

criminology, social issues, and the courts. (A complete revision of 1982 edition.).

Encyclopedia of Crime and Punishment. David Levinson, editor. Sage Publications, Inc. • 2002. $600.00. Four volumes. Contains 425 signed entries dealing with civil, criminal, media, corporate, and international issues. Includes material on fraud, police science, correctional institutions, social matters, methodology, national surveys, and crime statistics.

Encyclopedia of White-Collar and Corporate Crime. Lawrence M. Salinger, editor. Sage Publications, Inc. • 2004. $295.00. Two volumes. Covers such items as fraud, kickbacks, price fixing, tax evasion, bribery, forgery, counterfeiting, embezzlement, extortion, graft, bid rigging, and assorted scams and swindles.

West's Encyclopedia of American Law. Available from Gale Cengage Learning. • 2003. $1,195.00. Second edition. 12 volumes. Published by West Group. Covers a wide variety of legal topics for the general reader.

World of Criminal Justice. Gale Cengage Learning. • 2002. $160.00. Two volumes. Contains both topical and biographical entries relating to the criminal justice system and criminology.

HANDBOOKS AND MANUALS

Accountant's Handbook of Fraud and Commercial Crime. G. Jack Bologna and others. John Wiley and Sons, Inc. • 1992. $225.00.

Banking Crimes: Fraud, Money Laundering and Embezzlement. John K. Villa. West Group. • Annual. $280.00. Looseleaf service. Covers fraud and embezzlement.

Burglar Alarm Sales and Installation. Entrepreneur Media, Inc. • Looseleaf. $59.50. A practical guide to starting a burglar alarm service. Covers profit potential, start-up costs, market size evaluation, owner's time required, pricing, accounting, advertising, promotion, etc. (Start-Up Business Guide No. E1091.).

Criminal Law Deskbook. Patrick McCloskey and Ronald Schoenberg. LexisNexis Matthew Bender. • $276.00. Looseleaf service. Periodic supplementation. Discussions of the basic principles of criminal procedure, substantive law, and criminal trial strategy and tactics.

Criminal Procedure Handbook. J.J. Joubert, editor. Available from Gaunt, Inc. • 1999. $42.50. Fourth edition.

Financial Investigations: A Forensic Accounting Approach to Detecting and Resolving Crimes. Available from U. S. Government Printing Office. • 2002. $54.00. Two volumes: textbook and workbook. Issued by the Internal Revenue Service (http://www.irs.ustreas.gov). Serves as a text "for courses on conducting financial investigations." (IRS Publications 1714 and 1816.).

Private Investigator. Entrepreneur Media, Inc. • Looseleaf. $59.50. A practical guide to starting a private investigation agency. Covers profit potential, start-up costs, market size evaluation, pricing, accounting, advertising, promotion, etc. (Start-Up Business Guide No. E1320.).

Securities Crimes. West Group. • Annual. $225.00. Two looseleaf volumes. Analyzes the enfo of federal securities laws from the viewpoint of the defendant. Discusses Securities and Exchange Commission (SEC) investigations and federal sentencing guidelines. (Securities Law Series).

INTERNET DATABASES

Lexis.com Research System. Lexis-Nexis Group. Phone: 800-227-4908 or (937)865-6800 Fax: (937)865-6909 E-mail: webmaster@prod.lexisnexis.com • URL: http://www.lexis.com • Fee-based Web site offers extensive searching of a wide variety of legal sources. Additional features include

Daily Opinion Service, lexis.com Bookstore, Career Center, CLE Center, Law Schools, and Practice Pages ("Pages specific to areas of specialty").

U. S. Census Bureau: The Official Statistics. U. S. Bureau of the Census. Phone: (301)763-4100 Fax: (301)763-4794 • URL: http://www.census.gov • Web site is "Your Source for Social, Demographic, and Economic Information." Contains "Current U. S. Population Count," "Current Economic Indicators," and a wide variety of data under "Other Official Statistics." Keyword searching is provided. Fees: Free.

ONLINE DATABASES

Index to Legal Periodicals and Books (Online). H. W. Wilson Co. • Broad coverage of law journals and books 1981 to date. Monthly updates. Inquire as to online cost and availability.

Information Bank Abstracts. New York Times Index Dept. • Provides indexing and abstracting of current affairs, primarily from the final late edition of *The New York Times* and the Eastern edition of *The Wall Street Journal.* Time period is 1969 to present, with daily updates. Inquire as to online cost and availability.

LEXIS. LEXIS-NEXIS. • The various LEXIS databases provide full text and indexing for a wide variety of legal cases, statutes, orders, and opinions.

NCJRS: National Criminal Justice Reference Service. U.S. Department of Justice. • References print and non-print information on law enforcement and criminal justice, 1972 to present. Monthly updates. Inquire as to online cost and availability.

Newspaper Abstracts Daily. ProQuest Inc. • Provides online coverage (citations and abstracts) of 25 major newspapers. Covers business, economics, current affairs, health, fitness, sports, education, technology, government, consumer affairs, psychology, the arts, and the social sciences. Time period is 1986 to date, with daily updates. Inquire as to online cost and availability.

Wilson Social Sciences Abstracts Online. H. W. Wilson Co. • Provides online abstracting and indexing of more than 500 periodicals covering area studies, community health, public administration, public welfare, urban studies, and many other social science topics. Time period is 1994 to date for abstracts and 1983 to date for indexing, with updates weekly. Inquire as to online cost and availability.

PERIODICALS AND NEWSLETTERS

Business Crimes Bulletin. American Lawyer Media, Inc. • Monthly. $229.00 per year. Newsletter. Provides news of the "multifaceted world of financial and white collar crime." Covers such items as foreign corrupt practices, mail fraud, money laundering, tax fraud, securities law violations, environmental crime, and antitrust violations. Includes developments in sentencing guidelines for white collar perpetrators. (A Law Journal Newsletter, formerly published by Leader Publications).

Criminal Law Advocacy Reporter. LexisNexis Matthew Bender. • Monthly. $447.00 per year. Newsletter. Analysis of the latest cases and trends in criminal law and procedure.

Criminology; An Interdisciplinary Journal. American Society of Criminology. • Quarterly. Individuals, $120.00 per year; institutions, $140.00 per year.

FBI Law Enforcement Bulletin. Available from U. S. Government Printing Office. • Monthly. $36.00 per year. Issued by Federal Bureau of Investigation, U. S. Department of Justice. Contains articles on a wide variety of law enforcement and crime topics, including computer-related crime.

Security: The Magazine for Buyers of Security Products, Systems and Service. Business News Publishing Co. • Monthly. $82.90 per year.

White-Collar Crime Reporter: Information and

Analyses Concerning White-Collar Practice. Andrews Publications. • 10 times a year. $550.00 per year. Newsletter. Provides information on trends in white collar crime.

RESEARCH CENTERS AND INSTITUTES

Academy for State and Local Government. 444 N. Capitol St., N.W., Suite 345, Washington, DC 20001. Phone: (202)434-4850 Fax: (202)434-4851 E-mail: aelsbree@sso.org.

National Council on Crime and Delinquency. 1970 Broadway, Suite 500, Oakland, CA 94612. Phone: (510)208-0500 Fax: (510)208-0511 E-mail: kxfisher@chorus.net • URL: http://www.nccd-crc.org.

STATISTICS SOURCES

Crime in America's Top-Rated Cities: A Statistical Profile. Grey House Publishing. • 2000. $155.00. Third edition. Contains 20-year data for major crime categories in 76 cities, suburbs, metropolitan areas, and the U. S. Also includes statistics on correctional facilities, inmates, hate crimes, illegal drugs, and other crime-related matters.

Datapedia of the United States: American History in Numbers. George T. Kurian, editor. Bernan Press. • 2004. $125.00. Third edition. Based on the Census Bureau publication, *Historical Statistics of the United States.* Provides data from Colonial times to the present on agriculture, business, consumer income, energy, finance, labor, national income, population, and many other subjects. Includes "narrative highlights," maps, charts, and statistical projections.

Gale Book of Averages. Gale Cengage Learning. • 1994. $75.00. Contains 1,100-1,200 statistical averages on a variety of topics, with references to published sources. Subjects include business, labor, consumption, crime, and other areas of contemporary society.

Gale Country and World Rankings Reporter. Gale Cengage Learning. • 1997. $160.00. Second edition. Provides about 3,000 statistical ranking tables and charts covering more than 235 nations. Sources include the United Nations and various government publications.

Gale State Rankings Reporter. Gale Cengage Learning. • 1996. $130.00. Second edition Provides 3,000 ranked lists of states under 35 subject headings. Sources are newspapers, periodicals, books, research institute publications, and government publications.

Prisoners in State and Federal Institutions. Bureau of Justice Statistics, U.S. Department of Justice. Available from U.S. Government Printing Office. • Annual.

Social Statistics of the United States. Mark S. Littman, editor. Bernan Press. • 2000. $65.00. Includes statistical data on population growth, labor force, occupations, environmental trends, leisure time use, income, poverty, taxes, and other economic or demographic topics.

Social Trends and Indicators USA. Monique D. Magee, editor. Gale Cengage Learning. • 2003. $450.00. Four volumes. Includes data on labor, economics, the health care industry, crime, leisure, population, education, social security, and many other topics. Sources include various government agencies and major publications.

Sourcebook of Criminal Justice Statistics. Available from U. S. Government Printing Office. • Annual. $56.00. Issued by the Bureau of Justice Statistics, U. S. Department of Justice (http://www.usdoj.gov/bjs). Contains both crime data and corrections statistics.

Statistical Abstract of the United States. Available from U. S. Government Printing Office. • Annual. $51.00. Issued by the U. S. Bureau of the Census.

Statistical Abstract of the World. Gale Cengage

Learning. • 1997. $85.00. Third edition. Provides data on a wide variety of economic, social, and political topics for about 200 countries. Arranged by country.

Statistical Forecasts of the United States. Gale Cengage Learning. • 1995. $115.00. Second edition. Provides both long-term and short-term statistical forecasts relating to basic items in the U. S.: population, employment, labor, crime, education, and health care. Data in the form of charts, graphs, and tables has been taken from a wide variety of government and private sources. Includes a subject index and an "Index of Forecast by Year.".

A Statistical Portrait of the United States: Social Conditions and Trends. Mark S. Littman, editor. Bernan Press. • 1998. $89.00. Covers "social, economic, and environmental trends in the United States over the past 25 years." Includes statistical tables, graphs, and analysis relating to such topics as population, income, poverty, wealth, labor, housing, education, healthcare, air/water quality, and government. (Statistical Portrait of the United States: Social Conditions and Trends Series).

Statistics on Crime, Justice, and Punishment. Gale Cengage Learning. • 1996. $850.00. Volume three. Includes graphs, charts, and tables arranged within subject chapters. Citations to data sources are provided. (Statistics on...Series: vol. 3).

Statistics on Weapons and Violence: A Selection of Statistical Charts, Graphs and Tables about Weapons and Violence from a Variety of Published Sources with Explanatory Comments. Gale Cengage Learning. • 1995. $85.00. Includes graphs, charts, and tables arranged within subject chapters. Citations to data sources are provided. (Statistics for Students Series).

Uniform Crime Reports for the United States. Federal Bureau of Investigation, U.S. Department of Justice. Available from U.S. Government Printing Office. • Annual. $45.00.

Vital Statistics of the United States. Public Health Service, U.S. Dept. of Health and Human Services. Available from U.S. Government Printing Office. • Annual.

TRADE/PROFESSIONAL ASSOCIATIONS

American Society of Criminology. 1314 Kinnear Rd., Suite 212, Columbus, OH 43212-1156. Phone: (614)292-9207 Fax: (614)292-6767 E-mail: asc41@infinet.com • URL: http://www.asc41.com • Formerly Society for the Advancement of Criminology.

OTHER SOURCES

Corporate Criminal Liability. Kathleen F. Brickley. West Group. • Annual. $365.00 per year. Three looseleaf volumes. Discusses how the general principles of criminal law apply to the corporate world. Provides a detailed analysis of liability under major federal crime statutes.

Criminal Law Reporter. BNA, Inc. • Weekly. $896.00 per year. Includes full text of U. S. Supreme Court criminal law decisions.

White Collar Crime: Business and Regulatory Offenses. American Lawyer Media, Inc. • Looseleaf. $249.00. Updated as needed. Covers such legal matters as criminal tax cases, securities fraud, computer crime, mail fraud, bank embezzlement, criminal antitrust activities, extortion, perjury, the criminal liability of corporations, and RICO (Racketeer Influenced and Corrupt Organization Act). (Law Journal Press).

CRIME, COMPUTER

See: COMPUTER CRIME AND SECURITY

CRITICAL PATH METHOD/PERT (PROGRAM EVALUATION AND REVIEW TECHNIQUE)

GENERAL WORKS

Critical Path Analysis and Linear Programming. Mik Wisniewski and Jonathan Klein. Palgrave Macmillan Ltd. • 2001. f29.99. Contains "Book 1: Linear Programming" and "Book 2: Critical Path Analysis." Chapters include "Linear Programming in the Real World" and "Critical Path Analysis Techniques." Emphasis is on software applications, with a non-mathematical orientation.

Project Management with CPM, Pert and Precedence Diagramming. Joseph J. Moder and others. Blitz Publishing Co. • 1995. $40.00. Third edition.

HANDBOOKS AND MANUALS

Project Manager's Desk Reference: A Comprehensive Guide to Project Planning, Evaluation and Control. James P. Lewis. McGraw-Hill. • 1999. $70.00. Second edition. Includes scheduling with PERT (Program Evaluation and Review Technique), CPM (Critical Path Method), and Gantt schedules. Covers the steps for "planning, monitoring, and controlling any project.".

PERIODICALS AND NEWSLETTERS

Project Management Journal. Project Management Institute. • Four times a year. Membership. Contains technical articles dealing with the interests of the field of project management.

TRADE/PROFESSIONAL ASSOCIATIONS

Project Management Institute. 14 Campus Blvd., Newtown Square, PA 19073-3299. Phone: (610)356-4600 Fax: (610)356-4647 E-mail: customercare@pmi.org • URL: http://www.pmi.org • Corporations and individuals engaged in the practice of project management; project management students and educators. Seeks to advance the study, teaching, and practice of project management. Establishes project management standards; conducts educational and professional certification courses; bestows Project Management Professional credential upon qualified individuals. Offers educational seminars and global congresses.

CROPS

See: FARM PRODUCE

CRUISE LINES

See: STEAMSHIP LINES

CRYOGENICS

GENERAL WORKS

Progress in Low Temperature Physics. W. P. Halperin, editor. Elsevier. • 1996. $228.00. Volume 14.

Recent Advances in Cryogenic Engineering. J. P. Kelley and J. Goodman, editors. American Society of Mechanical Engineers International. • 1993. $30.00.

ABSTRACTS AND INDEXES

Applied Science and Technology Index. H. W. Wilson Co. • 11 times a year. Quarterly and annual cumulations. Price varies. Indexes a wide variety of English language technical, industrial, and engineering periodicals.

Current Contents: Engineering, Computing and Technology. Thomson/ISI. • Weekly. $730.00 per year. Reproductions of contents pages of technical journals. Includes *Author Index, Address Directory, Current Book Contents* and *Title Word Index.* Formerly *Current Contents: Engineering, Technology and Applied Sciences.*

ALMANACS AND YEARBOOKS

Advances in Cryogenic Engineering. Perseus Publishing. • Irregular. Price varies. Represents *Cryogenic Engineering Conference Proceedings.*

BIBLIOGRAPHIES

Encyclopedia of Physical Science and Engineering Information. Gale Cengage Learning. • 1996. $160.00. Second edition. Includes print, electronic, and other information sources for a wide range of scientific, technical, and engineering topics.

CD-ROM DATABASES

Science Citation Index: Compact Disc Edition. Institute for Scientific Information. • Monthly. Provides CD-ROM indexing of the world's scientific and technical literature. Corresponds to online *Scisearch* and printed *Science Citation Index.*

WILSONDISC: Applied Science and Technology Abstracts. H. W. Wilson Co. • Monthly. Includes unlimited access to the online version of *Applied Science and Technology Abstracts* through WILSONLINE. Provides CD-ROM indexing and abstracting of 500 prominent scientific, technical, engineering, and industrial periodicals. Indexing coverage is provided from 1983 to date and abstracting from 1993 to date.

ONLINE DATABASES

Applied Science and Technology Index Online. H. W. Wilson Co. • Provides online indexing of 500 major scientific, technical, industrial, and engineering periodicals. Time period is 1983 to date. Monthly updates. Inquire as to online cost and availability.

F & S Index. Gale Cengage Learning. • Contains about four million citations to worldwide business, financial, and industrial or consumer product literature appearing from 1972 to date. Weekly updates. Inquire as to online cost and availability.

Globalbase. Gale Cengage Learning. • Provides more than one million online summaries of business, industrial, and economic news reports from more than 1,000 publications worldwide. Covers a wide range of material appearing in international trade journals, professional magazines, and newspapers. Time period is 1984 to date, with weekly updates. Inquire as to online cost and availability.

PROMT: Predicasts Overview of Markets and Technology. Gale Cengage Learning. • Companies, products, applied technologies and markets. U.S. and international literature coverage, 1972 to date. Inquire as to online cost and availability. Provides abstracts from more than 1,600 publications. Weekly updates.

Scisearch. Institute for Scientific Information. • Broad, multidisciplinary index to the literature of science and technology, 1974 to present. Inquire as to online cost and availability. Coverage of literature is worldwide, with weekly updates.

PERIODICALS AND NEWSLETTERS

Cold Facts. Cryogenic Society of America. • Description: Technical newsletter serving individuals interested in cryogenics and cryobiology.

CryoGas International: The Source of Timely and Relevant Information for the Industrial Gas and Cyrogenics Industries. J. R. Campbell & Associates, Inc. • 11 times a year. $150.00 per year. Reports developments in technology market development and new products for the industrial gases and cryogenic equipment industries. Formerly *Cryogenic Information Report.*

Cryogenics: The International Journal of Low Temperature Engineering and Research. Elsevier. •

Monthly. Institutions, $2,169.00 per year.

Journal of Low Temperature Physics. Kluwer Academic Publishers. • Semimonthly. Institutions, $1,941.00 per year; with online edition, $2,329.20 per year. Covers the science of cryogenics.

RESEARCH CENTERS AND INSTITUTES

Edward L. Ginzton Laboratory. Stanford University, 450 Via Palou, Stanford, CA 94305-4085. Phone: (650)723-0111 Fax: (650)725-9355 E-mail: dabm@ee.stanford.edu • URL: http://www.stanford.edu/group/ginzton • Research fields include low-temperature physics and superconducting electronics.

Kurata Thermodynamics Laboratory. University of Kansas, Dept. of Chemical and Petroleum Engineering, Lawrence, KS 66045. Phone: (785)864-3860 Fax: (785)864-7399 E-mail: cshowat@ukans.edu • URL: http://www.engr.ukans.edu/~ktl • Investigates the behavior of various materials over a wide range of temperatures.

Laboratory for Electromagnetic and Electronic Systems. Massachusetts Institute of Technology, 77 Massachusetts Ave., Room 10-172, Cambridge, MA 02139. Phone: (617)253-4631 Fax: (617)258-6774 E-mail: jgk@mit.edu • URL: http://www.power.mit.edu/index • Research areas include heat transfer and cryogenics.

Microkelvin Laboratory. University of Florida, Dept. of Physics, 2348 New Physics Bldg., Gainsville, FL 32611-5803. Phone: (352)392-5803 E-mail: adams@phys.ufl.edu • URL: http://www.phys.ufl.edu/~mkelvin • Focuses on electronic behavior changes in metals, insulators, and semiconductors at ultra-low temperatures.

Thermophysical Properties Research Laboratory. 3080 Kent Ave., West Lafayette, IN 47906. Phone: (765)463-1581 Fax: (765)463-5235 E-mail: rtaylor@tprl.com • URL: http://www.tprl.com • Studies the thermophysical properties of materials from cryogenic to very high temperatures.

W. W. Hansen Experimental Physics Laboratory. Stanford University, 445 Via Palou St., Stanford, CA 94305-4085. Phone: (650)723-0280 Fax: (650)725-8311 • URL: http://www.hepl.stanford.edu • Conducts large-scale cryogenic research.

TRADE/PROFESSIONAL ASSOCIATIONS

Cryogenic Engineering Conference. PO Box 500, Fermi National Lab, Kirk & Wilson Rds., PO Box 500, Batavia, IL 60510-0500. Phone: (630)840-3238 Fax: (630)840-4989 E-mail: tnicol@fnal.gov • URL: http://tdserver1.fnal.gov/nicol/cec • Represents academic, industrial and governmental researchers, and managers involved in basic and applied work in cryogenics (the branch of physics and engineering dealing with the phenomena of extreme cold). Provides a forum for a four-day presentation of papers and seminars concerning advances in the science and technology of cryogenics in areas such as superconductivity, heat transfer, insulation, instrumentation, aerospace, liquefied gases, cryo-health services, cryobiology, LNG and power generation.

Cryogenic Society of America. c/o Laurie Huget, Huget Advertising, 1033 South Blvd., Oak Park, IL 60302-2881. Phone: (708)383-6220 Fax: (708)383-9337 E-mail: csa@huget.com • URL: http://www.cryogenicsociety.gov/ • Seeks to encourage the dissemination of information on low temperature industrial technology. Formerly Helium Society.

OTHER SOURCES

Superconductor Week: The Newsletter of Record in the Field of Superconductivity. WestTech. • 30 times a year. $437.00 per year. Newsletter. Covers applications of superconductivity and cryogenics, including new markets and products.

CULINARY

TRADE/PROFESSIONAL ASSOCIATIONS

Chefs de Cuisine Association of America. 155 E 55th St., Ste. 302B, New York, NY 10022. Phone: (212)832-4939 Fax: (212)599-2717 E-mail: info@chefsdecuisineofamerica.com • URL: http://www.chefsdecuisineofamerica.com • Professional executive chefs; chefs who own restaurants; pastry chefs for hotels, clubs, and restaurants. Maintains 350 volume library and placement service for members.

International Chefs' Association. GPO Box 1889, New York, NY 10116-1889. Phone: (201)825-8455 E-mail: info@chefsdecuisineofamerica.com • Professional chefs and cooks for restaurants, hotels, and clubs. Aims to improve the cooking profession and to guide young culinarians. Promotes international exchange. Conducts seminars, competitions, and culinary art exhibitions. Maintains placement service; bestows scholarships and Chef of the Year Award. Maintains library of 350 cookbooks.

United States Personal Chef Association. 610 Quantum Rd. NE, Rio Rancho, NM 87124. Phone: 800-995-2138 or (505)994-6372 E-mail: customerservice@uspca.com • URL: http://www.uspca.com • Promotes the personal chef; committed in advancing the profession of personal chef as a legitimate career choice in the culinary arts field; ensures the credibility of the personal chef with the industry-wide implementation of Educational Standards of Knowledge.

OTHER SOURCES

American Culinary Federation. • Aims to promote the culinary profession and provide on-going educational training and networking for members. Provides opportunities for competition, professional recognition, and access to educational forums with other culinary experts at local, regional, national, and international events. Operates the National +Apprenticeship Program for +Cooks and pastry cooks. Offers programs that address certification of the individual chef's skills, accreditation of culinary programs, apprenticeship of cooks and pastry cooks, professional development, and the fight against childhood hunger.

Commanderie des Cordons Bleus de France. • Chefs, cooks, and other culinary professionals. Encourages appreciation of good food and the establishment of high standards among culinary professionals. Promotes accuracy in the naming of dishes.

U.S. Pastry Alliance. • Pastry chefs. Dedicated to the advancement of professional pastry making through education, networking, and communication.

Vatel Club. • Social club for chefs, cooks, and other members of the culinary profession.

Women Chefs and Restaurateurs. • Seeks to educate and advance women in the restaurant industry.

CULTURE, CORPORATE

See: CORPORATE CULTURE

CURRENCY

See: MONEY

CURRENCY CONVERTIBILITY

See: FOREIGN EXCHANGE

CURRENCY EXCHANGE RATES

See also: FOREIGN EXCHANGE

ALMANACS AND YEARBOOKS

World Currrency Yearbook. International Currency Analysis, Inc. • Annual. $250.00. Directory of more than 110 central banks worldwide.

HANDBOOKS AND MANUALS

International Guide to Foreign Currency Management. Gary Shoup, editor. Glenlake Publishing Co., Ltd. • 1999. $65.00. Written for corporate financial managers. Covers the market for currencies, price forecasting, exposure of various kinds, and risk management.

Strategic Trading in the Foreign Exchange Markets. Gary Klopfenstein. Fitzroy Dearborn Publishers, Inc. • 2000. $65.00. Describes the tactics of successful foreign exchange traders.

INTERNET DATABASES

The Financial Post (Web site). National Post Online. Phone: 800-805-1184 or (244)383-2300 Fax: (416)383-2443 • URL: http://www.nationalpost.com/financialpost/ • Provides a broad range of Canadian business news online, with daily updates. Includes news, opinion, and special reports, as well as "Investing," "Money Rates," "Market Watch," and "Daily Mutual Funds." Allows advanced searching (Boolean operators), with links to various other sites. Fees: Free.

Financial Times: Where Information Becomes Intelligence. FT Group. Phone: 800-628-8088 • URL: http://www.ft.com • Web site provides extensive data and information relating to international business and finance, with daily updates. Includes Markets Today, Company News, Economic Indicators, Equities, Currencies, Capital Markets, Euro Prices, etc. Fees: Free (registration required).

Gateway to the European Union. European Union. E-mail: pressoffice@eurostat.cec.be • URL: http://www.europa.eu.int • Web site provides access to a wide variety of EU information, including statistics (Eurostat), news, policies, publications, key issues, and official exchange rates for the euro. Includes links to the European Central Bank, the European Investment Bank, and other institutions. Fees: Free.

PERIODICALS AND NEWSLETTERS

Blue Chip Financial Forecasts: What Top Analysts are Saying About U. S. and Foreign Interest Rates, Monetary Policy, Inflation, and Economic Growth. Aspen Publishers, Inc. • Monthly. $665.00 per year. Newsletter. Gives forecasts about a year in advance for interest rates, inflation, currency exchange rates, monetary policy, and economic growth rates.

The Financial Post: Canadian's Business Voice. Financial Post Datagroup. • Daily. $200.00 per year. Provides Canadian business, economic, financial, and investment news. Features extensive price quotes from all major Canadian markets: stocks, bonds, mutual funds, commodities, and currencies. Supplement available: *Financial Post 500.* Includes annual supplement.

Financial Times Currency Forecaster: Consensus Forecasts of the Worldwide Currency and Economic Outlook. Briefings Publishing Group. • Monthly. $695.00 per year. Newsletter. Provides forecasts of foreign currency exchange rates and economic conditions. Supplement available: *Mid-Month Global Financial Report.*

Financial Times [London]. The Financial Times, Inc. • Daily, except Sunday. $572.88 per year. An international business and financial newspaper, featuring news from London, Paris, Frankfurt, New York, and Tokyo. Includes worldwide stock and

250

For publishers addresses, refer to SOURCES CITED section at the back of the book.

bond market data, commodity market data, and monetary/currency exchange information.

International Market Alert. United Communications Group. • Description: Provides a fax service covering financial markets, world economy developments, foreign exchange, and U.S. interest rates.

Rundt's World Business Intelligence. S. J. Rundt and Associates, Inc. • Weekly. $695.00 per year. Formerly *Rundt's Weekly Intelligence.*

StraightTalk. The Conference Board. • 10 times a year. Members, $195.00 per year; non-members, $395.00 per year. Newsletter. Provides analysis of domestic and international economic issues. Includes coverage of interest rate trends and the currency exchange outlook.

RESEARCH CENTERS AND INSTITUTES

Institute for International Economics. 1750 Massachusetts Ave., N.W., Washington, DC 20036. Phone: (202)328-9000 Fax: (202)328-5432 E-mail: alreeves@iie.com • URL: http://www.iie.com • Research fields include a wide range of international economic issues, including foreign exchange rates.

STATISTICS SOURCES

International Financial Statistics. International Monetary Fund, Publications Services. • Monthly. Individuals, $495.00 per year; students, $247.00 per year. Includes a wide variety of current data for individual countries in Europe and elsewhere. Includes *Annual* issue.

CURRENT EVENTS

See also: CLIPPING SERVICES; NEWSPAPERS; PERIODICALS

GENERAL WORKS

Super Searchers in the News: The Online Secrets of Journalists and News Researchers. Paula J. Hane. Information Today, Inc. • 2000. $24.95. Contains online searching advice from 10 professional news researchers and fact checkers. (Super Searchers Series).

ALMANACS AND YEARBOOKS

The Annual Register: A Record of World Events. Keesing's Worldwide, LLC. • Annual. $185.00. Published by Keesings Worldwide. Lists major economic, social, and cultural events of the past year. International coverage.

Facts-on-File Yearbook. Facts on File, Inc. • Annual. $100.00.

The World Almanac and Book of Facts. World Almanac Books. • Annual. $11.95.

Worldmark Yearbook. Gale Cengage Learning. • 2001. $295.00. Three volumes. Covers economic, social, and political events in about 230 countries. Includes statistical data, directories, and a bibliography.

BIOGRAPHICAL SOURCES

Newsmakers. Gale Cengage Learning. • Annual. $155.00. Three softbound issues and one hardbound annual. Biographical information on individuals currently in the news. Includes photographs. Formerly *Contemporary Newsmakers.*

CD-ROM DATABASES

Newspaper Abstracts Ondisc. PROQUEST. • Monthly. $2,950.00 per year (covers 1989 to date; archival discs are available for 1985-88). Provides cover-to-cover CD-ROM indexing and abstracting of 19 major newspapers, including the *New York Times, Wall Street Journal, Washington Post, Chicago Tribune,* and *Los Angeles Times.*

DIRECTORIES

Cyberhound's Guide to People on the Internet. Gale Cengage Learning. • 1996. $79.00. Second edition.

Provides descriptions of about 5,500 Internet databases maintained by or for prominent individuals in business, the professions, entertainment, and sports. Indexed by name, subject, and keyword (master index). (Cyberhound's Series).

ENCYCLOPEDIAS AND DICTIONARIES

Americana Annual. Grolier Inc. • Annual. $29.95.

BBC World Glossary of Current Affairs. Available from the Gale Group. • 1991. $85.00. Published by Longman Group Ltd. Provides definitions of 7,000 terms used in world affairs. Arranged by country, with an alphabetical index.

INTERNET DATABASES

Globeandmail.com: Canada's Best Source for News. Bell Globemedia Publishing, Inc. Phone: 800-268-9128 or (416)585-5000 Fax: (416)585-5249 • URL: http://www.globeandmail.ca • Web site provides access to selected sections of *The Globe and Mail: Canada's National Newspaper.* Includes current news, national issues, career information, "Report on Business," and other topics. Keyword searching is offered for "a seven-day archive of the portion of the *Globe and Mail* that we publish online" (refers to the Web site). Daily updates. Fees: free.

Law.com: First in Legal News and Information. American Lawyer Media, Inc. Phone: 800-888-8300 or (212)779-9200 Fax: (212)481-8110 • URL: http://www.law.com • Web site provides free, law-related, current news (National News Sites and Regional News Sites). Free searching of martindale.com lawyer locator is offered, including lawyer ratings. Fee-based premium services for the legal profession are also available.

ONLINE DATABASES

The Globe and Mail Online. The Globe and Mail Co. • Contains full text of more than 1.1 million news stories and articles that have appeared daily in *The Globe and Mail: Canada's National Newspaper,* including "Report on Business." Time span is 1977 to date. Daily updates of the complete newspaper are provided. Inquire as to online cost and availability.

Information Bank Abstracts. New York Times Index Dept. • Provides indexing and abstracting of current affairs, primarily from the final late edition of *The New York Times* and the Eastern edition of *The Wall Street Journal.* Time period is 1969 to present, with daily updates. Inquire as to online cost and availability.

Newspaper Abstracts Daily. ProQuest Inc. • Provides online coverage (citations and abstracts) of 25 major newspapers. Covers business, economics, current affairs, health, fitness, sports, education, technology, government, consumer affairs, psychology, the arts, and the social sciences. Time period is 1986 to date, with daily updates. Inquire as to online cost and availability.

PERIODICALS AND NEWSLETTERS

Canadian News Facts: The Indexed Digest of Canadian Current Events. MPL Communications Inc. • Bimonthly. $280.00 per year. Monthly and quarterly indexes. A summary of current events in Canada.

Facts-on-File World News Digest With Index. Facts on File. • Weekly. $725.00 per year. Looseleaf service.

Intelligence Digest: A Review of World Affairs; International Political, Economic and Strategic Intelligence. Janes Information Group. • Weekly. $240.00 per year. Provides political, strategic and economic information. Gives warnings on political trends and current affairs. Published in England.

Keesing's Record of World Events. Keesing's Worldwide, LLC. • Monthly. $365.00 per year.

CURTAIN INDUSTRY

See: WINDOW COVERING INDUSTRY

CUSTOMER SERVICE

GENERAL WORKS

Keeping Customers for Life. Joan K. Cannie and Donald Caplin. National Institute of Business Management. • 1996. $14.95.

Keeping Customers Happy: Strategies for Success. Jacqueline Dunckel. Self-Counsel Press. • 1994. $9.95. Third edition. (Business Series).

Total Customer Service: The Ultimate Weapon. William H. Davidow and Bro Uttal. HarperTrade. • 1990. $13.00.

ABSTRACTS AND INDEXES

Business Periodicals Index. H. W. Wilson Co. • 11 times a year. Quarterly and annual cumulations. Price varies.

Readers' Guide to Periodical Literature. H. W. Wilson Co. • Monthly. $345.00 per year. Includes annual *Cumulation.* Indexes about 250 peridicals of general interest.

HANDBOOKS AND MANUALS

Assessing Service Quality: Satisfying the Expectations of Library Customers. Peter Hernon and Ellen Altman. American Library Association. • 1998. $40.00. Discusses surveys, focus groups, and other data collection methods for measuring the quality of library service. Includes sample forms and an annotated bibliography.

Customer Service: A Practical Approach. Elaine K. Harris. Prentice Hall PTR. • 2002. $43.00. Third edition. Covers various topics in relation to providing good customer service: problem solving; strategy; planning; communication; coping with difficult customers; motivation; leadership. Glossary, information sources, and index are included.

Customer Service Excellence: A Concise Guide for Librarians. Darlene E. Weingand. American Library Association. • 1997. $30.00. Includes information on quality of service benchmarks, teamwork, patron-librarian conflict management, "customer service language," and other library service topics. (ALA Editions Series).

Gower Handbook of Customer Service. Peter Murley, editor. Ashgate Publishing Co. • 1996. $129.95. Consists of 40 articles (chapters) written by various authors. Among the topics covered are benchmarking, customer surveys, focus groups, control groups, employee selection, incentives, training, teamwork, and telephone techniques. Published by Gower in England.

Marketing Manager's Handbook. Sidney J. Levy and others. Prentice Hall PTR. • 2000. Price on application. Contains 71 chapters by various authors on a wide variety of marketing topics, including market segmentation, market research, international marketing, industrial marketing, survey methods, customer service, advertising, pricing, planning, strategy, and ethics.

Service Quality Handbook. Eberhard E. Scheuing and William F. Christopher, editors. AMACOM. • 1993. $75.00. Contains articles by various authors on the management of service to customers.

ONLINE DATABASES

Readers' Guide Abstracts Online. H. W. Wilson Co. • Indexes and abstracts general interest periodicals, 1983 to date. Weekly updates. Inquire as to online cost and availability.

Wilson Business Abstracts Online. H. W. Wilson Co. • Indexes and abstracts 600 major business periodicals, plus the *Wall Street Journal* and the business section of the *New York Times.* Indexing is from 1982, abstracting from 1990, with the two newspapers included from 1993. Updated weekly. Inquire as to online cost and availability. (*Business Periodicals Index* without abstracts is also available online.).

PERIODICALS AND NEWSLETTERS

Call Center. CMP Media LLC. • Monthly. Free to qualified personnel. Emphasis is on telemarketing, selling, and customer service. Includes articles on communication technology. Formerly *Call Center Solutions.*

CC News: The Business Newspaper for Call Center and Customer Care Professionals. United Publications, Inc. • Monthly. Free to qualified personnel; others, $60.00 per year. Includes news of call center technical developments.

Communication Briefings: A Monthly Idea Source for Decision Makers. Briefings Publishing Group. • Monthly. $139.00 per year. Newsletter. Presents useful ideas for communication, public relations, customer service, human resources, and employee training.

The Customer Communicator. The Customer Service Group. • Description: Serves as a guideline for customer relations skills while it "boosts morale." Covers customer representative skills and provides tips on customer contact, handling complaints, checklists, and promotional contests. **Remarks:** a monthly training module.

Customer Service Newsletter. The Customer Service Group. • Description: Reports on practical, action-oriented techniques and tactics for improving your customer service operations.

Journal of Relationship Marketing: Innovations and Enhancement for Customer Service. Haworth Press, Inc. • Quarterly. $325.00 per year.

RESEARCH CENTERS AND INSTITUTES

Center for the Study of Services. 733 15th St., N.W., Suite 820, Washington, DC 20005. Phone: 800-475-7283 or (202)347-9612 Fax: (202)347-4000 E-mail: editors@checkbook.org • URL: http://www. checkbook.org • Evaluates local consumer services and retailers in Washington, D.C. and San Francisco metropolitan areas.

Marketing Science Institute. Marketing Science Institute. 1000 Massachusetts Ave., Cambridge, MA 02138-5396. Phone: (617)491-2060 Fax: (617)491-2065 E-mail: mclippinger@msi.org • URL: http:// www.msi.org • Marketing, including studies on marketing management and strategy, international/ global marketing, impact of information technology on marketing, marketing models and methods, advertising, sales promotion, sales force, channels of distribution, consumer services marketing, business-to-business marketing, and marketing of consumer durables and packaged goods.

TRADE/PROFESSIONAL ASSOCIATIONS

International Customer Service Association. 24 Wernik Pl., Metuchen, NJ 08840. Phone: 800-360-4272 or (732)767-0330 Fax: (732)767-1423 E-mail: info@icsatoday.org • URL: http://www.icsa.com • Customer service professionals in public and private sectors united to develop the theory and understanding of customer service and management. Goals are to: promote professional development; standardize terminology and phrases; provide career counseling and placement services; establish hiring guidelines, performance standards, and job descriptions. Provides a forum for shared problems and solutions. Compiles statistics.

National Retail Federation. 325 7th St. NW, Ste. 1100, Washington, DC 20004. Phone: 800-673-4692 or (202)783-7971 Fax: (202)737-2849 E-mail: mullint@nrf.com • URL: http://www.nrf.com •

Represents state retail associations, several dozen national retail associations, as well as large and small corporate members representing the breadth and diversity of the retail industry's establishment and employees. Conducts informational and educational conferences related to all phases of retailing including financial planning and cash management, taxation, economic forecasting, expense planning, shortage control, credit, electronic data processing, telecommunications, merchandise management, buying, traffic, security, supply, materials handling, store planning and construction, personnel administration, recruitment and training, and advertising and display.

CUSTOMS BROKERS

See also: CUSTOMS HOUSE, U.S. CUSTOMS SERVICE; EXPORT-IMPORT TRADE; FOREIGN TRADE

DIRECTORIES

American Export Register. Thomas Publishing Co. • Covers: over 45,000 companies in the United States exporting products and services, United States and foreign government services to exporters and importers, chambers of commerce abroad, embassies and consulates in the U.S., and financial and transportation services such as airlines, steamship lines, freight forwarders, customs brokers, and banks, international cargo carriers and carriers, world trade centers. Entries include: Company name, address, phone, URL address, fax, markets served, contact name, product or service, company description.

National Customs Brokers and Forwarders Association of America Membership Direc tory. National Customs Brokers and Forwarders Association of America. • Annual. $25.00. Lists about 600 customs brokers, international air cargo agents, and freight forwarders in the U.S.

PERIODICALS AND NEWSLETTERS

International Trade Reporter Export Reference Manual. BNA, Inc. • Biweekly. $874.00 per year. Looseleaf service.

TRADE/PROFESSIONAL ASSOCIATIONS

National Customs Brokers and Forwarders Association of America. 1200 18th St., N.W., Suite 901, Washington, DC 20036. Phone: (202)466-0222 Fax: (202)466-0226 E-mail: staff@ncbfaa.org • URL: http://www.ncbfaa.org • Formerly Customs Brokers and Forwarders Association of America.

CUSTOMS HOUSE, U.S. CUSTOMS SERVICE

CD-ROM DATABASES

U. S. Exports of Merchandise on CD-ROM. U. S. Bureau of the Census, Foreign Trade Div.,. • Monthly. $1,200 per year. Provides export data in the most extensive detail available, including product, quantity, value, shipping weight, country of destination, customs district of exportation, etc.

U. S. Imports of Merchandise (CD-ROM). U. S. Bureau of the Census, Foreign Trade Division. • Monthly. $1,200 per year. Provides import data in the most extensive detail available, including product, quantity, value, shipping weight, country of origin, customs district of entry, rate provision, etc.

DIRECTORIES

U.S. Custom House Guide. Commonwealth Business Media Inc. • Publication includes: List of ports having customs facilities, customs officials, port

authorities, chambers of commerce, embassies and consulates, foreign trade zones, and other organizations; related trade services. Entries include: For each principal port--Name of organization or agency, address, phone, fax, names and titles of key personnel; description and limitations of port facilities. For service firms--Company name, address, phone, fax. Principal content is U.S. tariff schedules and customs regulations, and a "How to Import" manual.

HANDBOOKS AND MANUALS

Importers Manual U. S. A.: The Single Source Reference Encyclopedia for Importined States. Edward G. Hinkelman. World Trade Press. • 1998. $87.00. Third edition. Published by World Trade Press. Covers U. S. customs regulations, letters of credit, contracts, shipping, insurance, and other items relating to importing. Includes 60 essays on practical aspects of importing.

INTERNET DATABASES

FedWorld: A Program of the United States Department of Commerce. National Technical Information Service. Phone: (703)605-6000 Fax: (703)605-6900 E-mail: webmaster@fedworld.gov • URL: http:// www.fedworld.gov • Web site offers "a comprehensive central access point for searching, locating, ordering, and acquiring government and business information." Emphasis is on searching the Web pages, databases, and government reports of a wide variety of federal agencies. Fees: Free.

PERIODICALS AND NEWSLETTERS

Customs Bulletin and Decisions. Available from U. S. Government Printing Office. • Weekly. $247.00 per year. Issued by U. S. Customs Service, Department of the Treasury. Contains regulations, rulings, decisions, and notices relating to customs laws.

The Journal of Commerce. Commonwealth Business Media. • Weekly. $146.00 per year. Topics include transatlantic shipping, domestic shipping, customs brokers, freight forwarders, ports, air freight, containerization, and other aspects of transportation and shipping logistics. Formerly *Journal of Commerce.*

TRADE/PROFESSIONAL ASSOCIATIONS

National Treasury Employees Union. 1750 H St. NW, Ste. 600, Washington, DC 20006. Phone: (202)572-5500 Fax: (202)572-5641 E-mail: nteu-pr@nteu.org • URL: http://www.nteu.org • Employees of the federal government. Conducts research and educational training programs. Sponsors Federal Employees Education and Assistance Fund.

OTHER SOURCES

Customs Law and Administration: Statutes and Treaties. Oceana Publications, Inc. • $475.00. Five volumes. Looseleaf service. Periodic supplementation.

Customs Regulations of the United States. Available from U. S. Government Printing Office. • Looseleaf. $175.00. Issued by U. S. Customs Service, Department of the Treasury. Reprint of regulations published to carry out customs laws of the U. S. Includes supplementary material for an indeterminate period.

CUSTOMS TAX

See: TARIFF

CYCLES, BUSINESS

See: BUSINESS CYCLES

D

DAIRY INDUSTRY

See also: CHEESE INDUSTRY; DAIRY
PRODUCTS

ABSTRACTS AND INDEXES
Biological and Agricultural Index. H. W. Wilson Co. • 11 times a year. Annual and quarterly cumulations. Price varies.

Dairy Science Abstracts. Available from CABI Publishing North America. • Monthly. Institutions, $1,305.00 per year. Online edition available. Published in England by CABI Publishing. Provides worldwide coverage of the literature.

DIRECTORIES
Dairy Foods Market Directory. Gorman Publishing Co. • Covers: Manufacturers of equipment, supplies and ingredients in the dairy foods industry. Entries include: Contact information.

ONLINE DATABASES
CAB Abstracts. CAB Publishing North America. • Contains 46 specialized abstract collections covering over 10,000 journals and monographs in the areas of agriculture, horticulture, forest products, farm products, nutrition, dairy science, poultry, grains, animal health, entomology, etc. Time period is 1972 to date, with monthly updates. Inquire as to online cost and availability. *CAB Abstracts on CD-ROM* also available, with annual updating.

PERIODICALS AND NEWSLETTERS
Dairy Foods: Innovative Ideas and Technologies for Dairy Processors. Business News Publishing Co. • Monthly. $99.90 per year. Provides broad coverage of new developments in the dairy industry, including cheese and ice cream products. Includes an annual *Supplement.*

DFISA Reporter. Dairy and Food Industries Supply Association, Inc. • Monthly. Free. Provides industry and association news to manufacturers of equipment products and services to the dairy and food industry.

International Association of Food Industry Suppliers Reporter. International Association on Food Industry Suppliers. • Monthly. Free.

Journal of Dairy Research. Institute of Food Research. Cambridge University Press, Journals Dept. • Quarterly. Institutions, $446.00 per year.

RESEARCH CENTERS AND INSTITUTES
Caine Dairy Center. Utah State University. 4300 S. Highway 89-91, Wellsville, UT 84339. Phone: (435)245-6067 Fax: (435)245-7680.

Quebec Dairy Herd Analyses Service. 555 Blvd. des Anciens Combattants, Saint-Anne de Bellevue, QC, Canada H9X 3R4. Phone: (514)398-7880 Fax:

(514)398-7963 E-mail: bfarmer@patlq.com • URL: http://www.patlq.com.

STATISTICS SOURCES
United States Census of Agriculture. U.S. Bureau of the Census. • Quinquennial. Results presented in reports, tape, CD-ROM, and Diskette files.

TRADE/PROFESSIONAL ASSOCIATIONS
Dairy Industry Committee. 1451 Dolley Madison Blvd., 1451 Dolley Madison Blvd., Mc Lean, VA 22101-3850. Phone: (703)761-2600 Fax: (703)761-4334 E-mail: tnicol@fnal.gov • URL: http://www.iafis.org • Federation of associations in the dairy industry. Deals with national matters common to all segments of dairy processing and distributing industry.

Dairy Management, Inc. 10255 W Higgins Rd., Ste. 900, Rosemont, IL 60018-5616. Phone: 800-853-2479 or (847)627-3252 Fax: (847)803-2077 E-mail: marykateg@rosedmi.com • URL: http://www.dairyinfo.com • Operates under the auspices of the United Dairy Industry Association. Milk producers, milk dealers, and manufacturers of butter, cheese, ice cream, dairy equipment, and supplies. Conducts programs of nutrition research and nutrition education in the use of milk and its products.

International Association of Food Industry Suppliers. 1451 Dolley Madison Blvd., McLean, VA 22101-3850. Phone: (703)761-2600 Fax: (703)761-4334 E-mail: info@iafis.org • URL: http://www.iafis.org • Formerly Dairy and Food Industries Supply Association.

United Dairy Industry Association. O'Hare International Center, 10255 W Higgins Rd., Ste. 900, Rosemont, IL 60018. Phone: (847)803-2000 Fax: (847)803-2077 E-mail: info@gs1us.org • Aims to promote the sale and consumption of U.S.-produced milk and milk products. Sponsors the advertising and sales promotion campaigns of the American Dairy Association and the nutrition research and education programs of the National Dairy Council. Maintains reference library. **Publications:** none.

DAIRY PRODUCTS

See also: DAIRY INDUSTRY

ABSTRACTS AND INDEXES
Food Science and Technology Abstracts. International Food Information Service Publishing. • Monthly. $1,780.00 per year. Provides worldwide coverage of the literature of food technology and food production.

Foods Adlibra: Key to the World's Food Literature.

General Mills, Inc. Foods Adlibra Publications. • Semimonthly. $240.00 per year. Provides journal citations and abstracts to the literature of food technology and packaging.

CD-ROM DATABASES
Food Science and Technology Abstracts [CD-ROM]. Available from SilverPlatter Information, Inc. • Quarterly. Produced by International Food Information Service (home page is http://www.ifis.org). Provides worldwide coverage on CD-ROM of the literature of food technology and production. Various types of publications are indexed, with abstracts, including about 1,800 periodicals. Time period is 1969 to date.

OECD Statistical Compendium. Organization for Economic Cooperation and Development. • Semiannual. $1,905.00 per year for 1 to 10 users. CD-ROM contains more than 730,000 monthly, quarterly, and annual time series for OECD countries, 1960 to date. Includes fully searchable data on agriculture, food, economic indicators, national accounts, employment, energy, finance, industry, technology, and foreign trade. Results can be displayed in various forms.

DIRECTORIES
Dairy Field--Buyer's Guide. Stagnito Communications Inc. • Publication includes: List of over 500 suppliers of equipment and services and distributors for the dairy processing industry. Entries include: Company or organization name, address, phone.

Major Food and Drink Companies of the World. Available from Gale Cengage Learning. • Annual. $880.00. Two volumes. Published by Graham & Whiteside. Contains profiles and trade names for more than 9,800 important food and beverage companies in various countries. In addition to foods, includes both alcoholic and nonalcoholic drink products.

Thomas Food and Beverage Market Place. Grey House Publishing. • 2004. $495.00. Three volumes. Contains more than 40,000 entries covering food companies, beverages, food equipment, warehouse companies, food brokers, wholesalers, importers, and exporters. Formerly *Thomas Food Industry Register.*

ENCYCLOPEDIAS AND DICTIONARIES
Foods and Nutrition Encyclopedia. Audrey H. Ensminger and others. CRC Press, Inc. • 1993. $309.95. Second edition. Two volumes.

FINANCIAL RATIOS
Almanac of Business and Industrial Financial Ratios. Leo Troy. Aspen Publishers, Inc. • 2003. $125.95. Includes CD-Rom. Contains financial ratios derived from federal tax returns. Ratios for

Encyclopedia of Business Information Sources • 24th Edition

each of about 200 industries are arranged according to company asset size. (Almanac of Business and Industrial Financial Ratios Series).

Annual Statement Studies. The Risk Management Association. • Annual. Median and quartile financial ratios are given for over 400 kinds of manufacturing, wholesale, retail, construction, and consumer finance establishments. Data is sorted by both asset size and sales volume. Includes a clearly written "Definition of Ratios" and an alphabetical industry index.

Annual Statement Studies: Industry Default Probabilities and Cash Flow Measures. The Risk Management Association. • Annual. $145.00. Serves as a companion volume to the original *Annual Statement Studies.* Gives probability of default estimates on a percentage scale for more than 450 industries. Includes changes in position year-by-year for eight financial statement line items and provides percentage measures of cash flow.

INTERNET DATABASES

Business 2.0 Web Guide to the Best Business Links. Business 2.0 Media Inc. Phone: (415)293-4800 E-mail: support@business2.com • URL: http://www.business2.com/webguide • Web site presents an extensive, searchable directory of links to "the best, most informative, and authoritative web pages." Twenty main categories cover business, finance, career, company information, people, and technology topics, with thousands of subtopics, all linking to Web sites recommended by experienced business researchers. Fees: Free.

Fedstats. Federal Interagency Council on Statistical Policy. Phone: (202)395-7254 • URL: http://www.fedstats.gov • Web site features an efficient search facility for full-text statistics produced by more than 100 federal agencies, including the Census Bureau, the Bureau of Economic Analysis, and the Bureau of Labor Statistics. Boolean searches can be made within one agency or for all agencies combined. Links are offered to international statistical bureaus, including the UN, IMF, OECD, UNESCO, Eurostat, and 20 individual countries. Fees: Free.

FreeLunch.com. Economy.com, Inc. Phone: (610)696-8700 Fax: (610)696-1678 • URL: http://www.freelunch.com • Web site provides free access to more than 1.5 million economic and financial data series, covering industry, demographics, labor markets, prices, retail sales, government spending, trade, interest rates, housing starts, the stock market, and many other topics. Data is available for various time periods in either chart or table form. Searching is offered. Fees: Free, but registration required. Economy.com, Inc. also offers fee-based economic analysis at *The Dismal Scientist* site (http://www.dismal.com).

USDA. United States Department of Agriculture. Phone: (202)720-2791 E-mail: agsec@usda.gov • URL: http://www.usda.gov • The USDA home page has six sections: News and Information; What's New; About USDA; Agencies; Opportunities; Search and Help. Keyword searching is offered from the USDA home page and from various individual agency home pages. Agencies are the Economic Research Service, Agricultural Marketing Service, National Agricultural Statistics Service, National Agricultural Library, and about 12 others. Updating varies. Fees: Free.

ONLINE DATABASES

Food Science and Technology Abstracts [online]. IFIS North American Desk. • Produced by International Food Information Service. Provides about 500,000 online citations, with abstracts, to the international literature of food science, technology, commodities, engineering, and processing. Approximately 2,000 periodicals are covered. Time period is 1969 to date, with monthly updates. Inquire as to online cost and availability.

FOODS ADLIBRA. General Mills, Inc. • Contains online citations, with abstracts, to the technical and business literature of food processing and packaging. New products and new ingredients are featured. Covers about 250 trade journals and 500 research journals from 1974 to date, with monthly updates. Inquire as to online cost and availability.

PERIODICALS AND NEWSLETTERS

Journal of Dairy Science. American Dairy Science Association. • Monthly. $400.00 per year. Provides primary scientific research on all aspects of dairy foods and dairy cattle production and management.

Monthly Price Review. Urner Barry Publications Inc. • Description: Provides daily price information and monthly averages on dairy, egg, and poultry products. **Remarks:** Subscription includes a supplement titled Annual Price Review.

Weekly Insiders Dairy and Egg Letter. Urner Barry Publications, Inc. • Weekly. $173.00 per year.

PRICE SOURCES

Supermarket News: The Industry's Weekly Newspaper. Fairchild Publications. • Weekly. Individuals, $196.00 per year; retailers, $45.00 per year; manufacturers, $89.00 per year.

RESEARCH CENTERS AND INSTITUTES

Dairy Research and Education Center. Pennsylvania State University. 320 Hening Bldg., University Park, PA 16802. Phone: (814)863-3666 Fax: (814)863-6042 E-mail: cjohansen@psu.edu • URL: http://www.das.psu.edu.

STATISTICS SOURCES

Agricultural Statistics. Available from U. S. Government Printing Office. • Annual. $38.00. Produced by the National Agricultural Statistics Service, U. S. Department of Agriculture. Provides a wide variety of statistical data relating to agricultural production, supplies, consumption, prices/price-supports, foreign trade, costs, and returns, as well as farm labor, loans, income, and population. In many cases, historical data is shown annually for 10 years. In addition to farm data, includes detailed fishery statistics.

Annual Survey of Manufactures. Available from U. S. Government Printing Office. • Annual. Prices vary. Issued by the U. S. Census Bureau as an interim update to the *Census of Manufactures.* Includes data on number of manufacturing establishments in various industries, employment, labor costs, value of shipments, capital expenditures, inventories, energy costs, and assets. (See also Census Bureau home page, http://www.census.gov/.)

Business Statistics of the United States. Linz Audain and Cornelia J. Strawser. Bernan Associates. • Annual. $147.00. Based on *Business Statistics,* formerly issue by the Bureau of Economic Analysis, U. S. Department of Commerce. Provides basic data for a wide variety of U. S. industries, services, and economic indicators. Most statistics are shown annually for 30 years and monthly for the most recent four years.

FAO Production Yearbook. Available from Bernan Associates. • Annual. $45.00. Published by the Food and Agriculture Organization (http://www.fao.org). Contains worldwide data on agriculture, land use, farm crops, livestock, and agricultural prices.

FAO Trade Yearbook. Available from Bernan Associates. • Annual. $45.00. Published by the Food and Agriculture Organization (http://www.fao.org). Provides extensive worldwide data on exports and imports of agricultural commodities, fertilizers, tractors, and pesticides. Includes more than 130 tables of detailed statistics.

Survey of Current Business. Available from U. S. Government Printing Office. • Monthly. $63.00 per year. Issued by Bureau of Economic Analysis, U. S.

Department of Commerce. Presents a wide variety of business and economic data.

World Food Data and Statistics. Euromonitor International. • 2004. $650.00. Provides five-year data for a wide variety of food products in 52 countries. Includes market size, consumer expenditures, price indicators, and retail distribution data for many kinds of meat, fish, fruits, vegetables, dairy products, baked goods, condiments, canned food, and frozen food.

TRADE/PROFESSIONAL ASSOCIATIONS

American Butter Institute. 2101 Wilson Blvd., Ste. 400, Arlington, VA 22201. Phone: (703)243-5630 Fax: (703)841-9328 E-mail: aminer@nmpf.org • URL: http://www.butterinstitute.org • Represents butter manufacturers, processors, packagers, and distributors based on volume. Aims to promote and protect the interests and welfare of the butter industry.

Certified Milk Producers Association of America. 8300 Pine Ave., Chino, CA 91710. Phone: (909)399-3560 Fax: (909)399-3627.

Dairy Management, Inc. 10255 W Higgins Rd., Ste. 900, Rosemont, IL 60018-5616. Phone: 800-853-2479 or (847)627-3252 Fax: (847)803-2077 E-mail: marykateg@rosedmi.com • URL: http://www.dairyinfo.com • Operates under the auspices of the United Dairy Industry Association. Milk producers, milk dealers, and manufacturers of butter, cheese, ice cream, dairy equipment, and supplies. Conducts programs of nutrition research and nutrition education in the use of milk and its products.

Milk Industry Foundation. 1250 H St. NW, Ste. 900, Washington, DC 20005-3952. Phone: (202)737-4332 Fax: (202)331-7820 E-mail: membership@idfa.org • URL: http://www.idfa.org • Represents processors of fluid milk and milk products. Advocates before government and regulatory bodies on behalf of members.

National Cheese Institute. 1250 H St. NW, Ste. 900, Washington, DC 20005-3952. Phone: (202)737-4332 Fax: (202)331-7820 E-mail: membership@idfa.org • URL: http://www.idfa.org • Represents manufacturers, processors, marketers, assemblers, and distributors of cheese and cheese products; advocates before government and regulatory bodies on behalf of members.

DANGEROUS MATERIALS

See: HAZARDOUS MATERIALS

DATA BASES, ONLINE

See: ONLINE INFORMATION SYSTEMS

DATA COMMUNICATIONS

See: COMPUTER COMMUNICATIONS

DATA IDENTIFICATION SYSTEMS, AUTOMATIC

See: AUTOMATIC IDENTIFICATION SYSTEMS

DATA SYSTEMS

See: SYSTEMS IN MANAGEMENT

DATES (CHRONOLOGY)

See: CHRONOLOGY

For publishers addresses, refer to SOURCES CITED section at the back of the book.

DAY CARE CENTERS

See also: BABY SITTING

FINANCIAL RATIOS

Annual Statement Studies. The Risk Management Association. • Annual. Median and quartile financial ratios are given for over 400 kinds of manufacturing, wholesale, retail, construction, and consumer finance establishments. Data is sorted by both asset size and sales volume. Includes a clearly written "Definition of Ratios" and an alphabetical industry index.

Annual Statement Studies: Industry Default Probabilities and Cash Flow Measures. The Risk Management Association. • Annual. $145.00. Serves as a companion volume to the original *Annual Statement Studies.* Gives probability of default estimates on a percentage scale for more than 450 industries. Includes changes in position year-by-year for eight financial statement line items and provides percentage measures of cash flow.

HANDBOOKS AND MANUALS

Child Care Service. Entrepreneur Media, Inc. • Looseleaf. $59.50. A practical guide to starting a day care center for children. Covers profit potential, start-up costs, market size evaluation, owner's time required, site selection, pricing, accounting, advertising, promotion, etc. (Start-Up Business Guide No. E1058.).

Senior Day Care Center. Entrepreneur Media, Inc. • Looseleaf. $59.50. A practical guide to starting a day care center for older adults (supervised environment for frail individuals). Covers profit potential, start-up costs, market size evaluation, owner's time required, site selection, lease negotiation, pricing, accounting, advertising, promotion, etc. (Start-Up Business Guide No. E1335.).

PERIODICALS AND NEWSLETTERS

Day Care USA: The Independent Biweekly for Day Care Professionals. United Communications Group. • Biweekly. $239.00 per year. Newsletter. Provides current information on child day care center funding, legislation, and regulation.

TRADE/PROFESSIONAL ASSOCIATIONS

Comprehensive Day Care Programs. Stevens Administrative Center. Stevens Adm. Center, 1301 Spring Garden at 13th St., Rm. 203, Philadelphia, PA 19123. Phone: (215)351-7200 Fax: (215)351-7165 E-mail: eredd@phila.k12.pa.us • Day care centers serving 3900 children of low-income families. Aims to help each child fulfill his or her own potential in intellectual, social, emotional, and physical development. Provides opportunities in self-development to parents; seeks to emphasize the parental role and responsibility in the development of the child. Services provided comprise six components: Curriculum; Food Services; Health Services; Parent Involvement; Social Services; Volunteer Services. Is funded by the School District of Philadelphia and the Pennsylvania Department of Public Welfare, under Title XX of the Federal Social Security Act.

DDT

See: PESTICIDE INDUSTRY

DEATH TAX

See: INHERITANCE TAX

DEATHS AND BIRTHS

See: VITAL STATISTICS

DEBATES AND DEBATING

See also: PUBLIC SPEAKING

GENERAL WORKS

How to Win Arguments; More Often Than Not. William A. Rusher. University Press of America. • 1985. $25.00.

Mastering Competitive Debate. Dana Hensley and Diana Carlin. Clark Publishing, Inc. • 1999. $38.00. Fifth edition.

DIRECTORIES

American Forensic Association Newsletter - Directory. American Forensic Association. • Annual. Free with subscription; non-subscription, $15.00. List of 500 member teachers of argumentation and debate.

PERIODICALS AND NEWSLETTERS

Argumentation and Advocacy: Journal of the American Forensic Association. American Forensic Association. • Quarterly. Members, $60.00 per year; institutions, $70.00 per year; students, $20.00 per year. Formerly *American Forensic Association Journal.*

TRADE/PROFESSIONAL ASSOCIATIONS

American Forensic Association. Box 256, River Falls, WI 54022. Phone: 800-228-5424 or (715)425-3198 Fax: (715)425-9533 E-mail: amforensicassoc@aol.com • URL: http://www.americanforensics.org • High school and college directors of forensics and debate coaches. Promotes debate and other speech activities. Sponsors annual collegiate National Individual Events Tournament and National Debate Tournament; sells debate ballots; makes studies of professional standards and debate budgets. Supports research grants.

National Forensic League. PO Box 38, PO Box 38, Ripon, WI 54971. Phone: (920)748-6206 Fax: (920)748-9478 E-mail: nfl@nflonline.org • URL: http://nflonline.org • High school honor society. Promotes the art of debate, oratory, interpretation, and extemporaneous speaking. Conducts educational and outreach programs; maintains speakers' bureau; maintains hall of fame; compiles statistics.

DEBENTURES

See: BONDS

DEBT COLLECTION

See: COLLECTING OF ACCOUNTS

DEBT, NATIONAL

See: NATIONAL DEBT

DECEPTIVE ADVERTISING

See: ADVERTISING LAW AND REGULATION

DECISION-MAKING

See also: OPERATIONS RESEARCH

GENERAL WORKS

Business Statistics: Contemporary Decision Making. Ken Black. South-Western. • 2000. $107.95. Third edition.

The Dynamic Decision Maker: Five Decision Styles for Executive and Business Success. Michael J.

Driver and others. HarperInformation. • 1990. $24.95. The five styles are decisive, flexible, hierarchial, integrative, and systemic.

The Psychology of Decision Making: People in Organizations. Lee R. Beach. Sage Publications, Inc. • 1997. $97.95. Includes references and index. (Foundations for Organizational Science Series: Vol. 6).

Smart Choices: A Practical Guide to Making Better Decisions. John S. Hammond and others. Harvard Business School Publishing. • 1998. $22.50. Provides a systematic approach to effective decision-making. Eight fundamentals of decision-analysis are described, involving problems, objectives, alternatives, consequences, tradeoffs, uncertainty, risks, and choices.

ABSTRACTS AND INDEXES

Psychological Abstracts. American Psychological Association. • Monthly. Members, $815.00 per year; individuals and institutions, $1,207.00 per year. Covers the international literature of psychology and the behavioral sciences. Includes journals, technical reports, dissertations, and other sources.

ENCYCLOPEDIAS AND DICTIONARIES

Blackwell Encyclopedic Dictionary of Strategic Management. Derek F. Channon, editor. Blackwell Publishing. • 1997. $128.95. The editor is associated with Imperial College, London. Contains definitions of key terms combined with longer articles written by various U. S. and foreign business educators. Includes bibliographies and index. (Blackwell Encyclopedia of Management Series.).

HANDBOOKS AND MANUALS

AMA Management Handbook. John J. Hampton, editor. AMACOM. • 1994. $110.00. Third edition. Provides 200 chapters in 16 major subject areas. Covers a wide variety of business and industrial management topics.

ONLINE DATABASES

PsycINFO. American Psychological Association. • Provides indexing and abstracting of the worldwide literature of psychology and the behavioral sciences. Time period is 1967 to date, with monthly updates. Inquire as to online cost and availability.

PERIODICALS AND NEWSLETTERS

Communication Briefings: A Monthly Idea Source for Decision Makers. Briefings Publishing Group. • Monthly. $139.00 per year. Newsletter. Presents useful ideas for communication, public relations, customer service, human resources, and employee training.

Decision Line. Decision Sciences Institute. • Description: Informs business executives and faculty of research and developments in the area of decision sciences. Promotes further education in the processes of decision-making for business students. Recurring features include reports on Institute activities and programs.

Decision Sciences. Decision Sciences Institute. Decision Sciences Institute. • Description: Discusses the topic of decision sciences.

RESEARCH CENTERS AND INSTITUTES

Center for Decision Research. University of Chicago Graduate School of Business. 1101 E. 58th St., Chicago, IL 60637. Phone: (773)702-4877 Fax: (773)702-0458 E-mail: richardthaler@gsb.uchicago.edu.

Center for Research in Regulated Industries. Rutgers University. Graduate School of Management, 180 University Ave., Newark, NJ 07102-1897. Phone: (973)353-5049 Fax: (973)353-1348 E-mail: crri@andromeda.rutgers.edu • URL: http://www.crri.rutgers.edu/.

TRADE/PROFESSIONAL ASSOCIATIONS

Decision Sciences Institute. Georgia State University, J. Mack Robinson College of Business,

---

University Plz., Atlanta, GA 30303. Phone: (404)413-7710 Fax: (404)413-7714 E-mail: clatta@gsu.edu • URL: http://www.decisionsciences.org • Businesspersons and members of business school faculties. Maintains placement service.

North American Simulation and Gaming Association. P.O. Box 78636, Indianapolis, IN 46278. Phone: 888-432-4263 or (317)387-1424 Fax: (317)387-1921 E-mail: info@nasaga.org • URL: http://www.nasaga.org • Members are professionals interested in the use of games and simulations for problem solving and decision-making in all types of organizations. Formerly National Gaming Council.

DECORATION, INTERIOR

See: INTERIOR DECORATION

DEDUCTIONS (INCOME TAX)

See: INCOME TAX

DEFENSE CONTRACTS

See: GOVERNMENT CONTRACTS

DEFENSE INDUSTRIES

See also: AEROSPACE INDUSTRY; AVIATION INDUSTRY; GOVERNMENT CONTRACTS; MILITARY MARKET

ABSTRACTS AND INDEXES
Air University Library Index to Military Periodicals. U.S. Air Force. • Quarterly. Free to qualified personnel. Annual cumulation.

ALMANACS AND YEARBOOKS
Brassey's Defence Yearbook. Brassey's Inc. • 1998. $55.00.

United Nations Disarmament Yearbook. United Nations Publications. • Annual. $55.00.

BIBLIOGRAPHIES
Defense and Security. Available from U. S. Government Printing Office. • Annual. Free. Issued by the Superintendent of Documents. A list of government publications on defense and related topics. Formerly *Defense Supply and Logistics.* (Subject Bibliography No. 153.).

CD-ROM DATABASES
OECD Statistical Compendium. Organization for Economic Cooperation and Development. • Semiannual. $1,905.00 per year for 1 to 10 users. CD-ROM contains more than 730,000 monthly, quarterly, and annual time series for OECD countries, 1960 to date. Includes fully searchable data on agriculture, food, economic indicators, national accounts, employment, energy, finance, industry, technology, and foreign trade. Results can be displayed in various forms.

DIRECTORIES
Military Helicopter Handbook. The Shephard Press Ltd. • Annual. $110.00. Data includes specifications of fighter helicopters, inventory of world helicopter forces, government contacts, directory of services & products, and listing of exhibits & conferences. Coverage is international.

INTERNET DATABASES
Business 2.0 Web Guide to the Best Business Links. Business 2.0 Media Inc. Phone: (415)293-4800 E-mail: support@business2.com • URL: http://www.business2.com/webguide • Web site presents an extensive, searchable directory of links to "the best, most informative, and authoritative web pages." Twenty main categories cover business, finance, career, company information, people, and technology topics, with thousands of subtopics, all linking to Web sites recommended by experienced business researchers. Fees: Free.

Fedstats. Federal Interagency Council on Statistical Policy. Phone: (202)395-7254 • URL: http://www.fedstats.gov • Web site features an efficient search facility for full-text statistics produced by more than 100 federal agencies, including the Census Bureau, the Bureau of Economic Analysis, and the Bureau of Labor Statistics. Boolean searches can be made within one agency or for all agencies combined. Links are offered to international statistical bureaus, including the UN, IMF, OECD, UNESCO, Eurostat, and 20 individual countries. Fees: Free.

FreeLunch.com. Economy.com, Inc. Phone: (610)696-8700 Fax: (610)696-1678 • URL: http://www.freelunch.com • Web site provides free access to more than 1.5 million economic and financial data series, covering industry, demographics, labor markets, prices, retail sales, government spending, trade, interest rates, housing starts, the stock market, and many other topics. Data is available for various time periods in either chart or table form. Searching is offered. Fees: Free, but registration required. Economy.com, Inc. also offers fee-based economic analysis at *The Dismal Scientist* site (http://www.dismal.com).

ONLINE DATABASES
Aerospace America [online]. American Institute of Aeronautics and Astronautics. • Provides complete text of the periodical, *Aerospace America,* 1984 to date, with monthly updates. Also includes news from the *AIAA Bulletin.* Inquire as to online cost and availability.

Aerospace Database. American Institute of Aeronautics and Astronautics. • Contains abstracts of literature covering all aspects of the aerospace and aircraft industry 1983 to date. Monthly updates. Inquire as to online cost and availability.

Aerospace/Defense Markets and Technology. Gale Cengage Learning. • Abstracts of commerical aerospace/defense related literature, 1982 to date. Also includes information about major defense contracts awarded by the U. S. Department of Defense. International coverage. Inquire as to online cost and availability.

PERIODICALS AND NEWSLETTERS
Air Force Journal of Logistics. Available from U. S. Government Printing Office. • Quarterly. $15.00 per year. Issued by the Air Force Logistics Management Center, Air Force Department, Defense Department. Presents research and information of interest to professional Air Force logisticians.

Armed Forces Journal International. Armed Forces Journal International, Inc. • Monthly. $45.00 per year. A defense magazine for career military officers and industry executives. Covers defense events, plans, policies, budgets, and innovations.

Defence & Public Service Helicopter. Shephard Press Ltd. • Monthly. $130.00 per year. Provides international coverage of both the public service (police, emergency, etc.) and military helicopter industries and markets. Includes technical, piloting, and safety topics. Formerly *Defence Helicopter.*

Defense Daily: The Daily of Aerospace and Defense. PBI Media, LLC. • Daily (five times a week). $1,897.00 per year. Newsletter.

The Defense Monitor. Center for Defense Information. • Description: Concerned with U.S. military issues such as nuclear and conventional weapons; research, development, and procurement; armed force levels; foreign commitments; arms control; annual military budget; and economic, environmental, and political implications. Provides analysis and conclusions for a single military subject in each issue, and recommends changes and areas for further study.

Homeland Security and Defense: Weekly Intelligence for the Global Homeland Security and Defense Community. Aviation Week Business Intelligence Services. • Weekly. $595.00 per year. Newsletter. Emphasis is on airline and airport programs (federal, state, and local). Also covers counterterrorism, protection of military units, Department of Homeland Security activities, industrial security, communications equipment, and other topics related to homeland security.

Inside R and D: A Weekly Report on Technical Innovation. Technical Insights. • Weekly. Institutions, $840.00 per year. Concentrates on new and significant developments. Formerly *Technolog Transfer Week.*

National Defense: NDIA's Business and Technology Journal. National Defense Industrial Association. • 10 times a year. $35.00 per year.

Soldiers. Available from U. S. Government Printing Office. • Monthly. $38.00 per year. Provides information on the policies, plans, operations, and technical developments of the U.S. Department of the Army (http://www.army.mil).

RESEARCH CENTERS AND INSTITUTES
Applied Research Laboratory. Pennsylvania State University. P.O. Box 30, State College, PA 16804. Phone: (814)865-6343 Fax: (814)865-3105 E-mail: lrh3@psu.edu • URL: http://www.arl.psu.edu.

Center for Defense Information. 1779 Massachusetts Ave., N.W., Washington, DC 20036. Phone: (202)332-0600 Fax: (202)462-4559 E-mail: info@cdi.org • URL: http://www.cdi.org.

Institute for Defense Analyses. 4850 Mark Center Dr., Alexandria, VA 22311-1882. Phone: (703)845-2000 • URL: http://www.ida.org.

Structures and Composites Laboratory. Stanford University. Dept. of Aeronautics and Astronautics, 496 Lomita Mall, Stanford, CA 94305. Phone: (650)723-3524 Fax: (650)723-0062 E-mail: gspringer@stanford.edu • URL: http://www.structure.stanford.edu/.

STATISTICS SOURCES
Business Statistics of the United States. Linz Audain and Cornelia J. Strawser. Bernan Associates. • Annual. $147.00. Based on *Business Statistics,* formerly issue by the Bureau of Economic Analysis, U. S. Department of Commerce. Provides basic data for a wide variety of U. S. industries, services, and economic indicators. Most statistics are shown annually for 30 years and monthly for the most recent four years.

Standard & Poor's Industry Surveys. Standard & Poor's. • Semiannual. $1,800.00. Two looseleaf volumes. Includes monthly *Supplements.* Provides detailed, individual surveys of 52 major industry groups. Each survey is revised on a semiannual basis. Also includes "Monthly Investment Review" (industry group investment analysis) and monthly "Trends & Projections" (economic analysis).

Survey of Current Business. Available from U. S. Government Printing Office. • Monthly. $63.00 per year. Issued by Bureau of Economic Analysis, U. S. Department of Commerce. Presents a wide variety of business and economic data.

World Factbook. U.S. National Technical Information Service. • Annual. $83.00. Prepared by the Central Intelligence Agency. For all countries of the world, provides current economic, demographic, geographic, communications, government, defense force, and illicit drug trade information (where applicable).

TRADE/PROFESSIONAL ASSOCIATIONS
National Defense Industrial Association. 2111 Wilson Blvd., Ste. 400, Arlington, VA 22201-3061.

Phone: (703)522-1820 or (703)247-2589 Fax: (703)522-1885 E-mail: info@ndia.org • URL: http://www.adpa.org • Concerned citizens, military and government personnel, and defense-related industry workers interested in industrial preparedness for the national defense of the United States. Operates Technology Services that provides a forum for discussion of defense industry programs and issues. Conducts 55 technical meetings per year.

National Defense Transportation Association. 50 S Pickett St., Ste. 220, Alexandria, VA 22304-7296. Phone: (703)751-5011 Fax: (703)823-8761 E-mail: info@ndtahq.com • URL: http://www.ndtahq.com • Men and women in the field of transportation, travel logistics and related areas in the Armed Forces, federal government, private industry and the academic sector. Strives to foster a strong and efficient transportation system in support of national defense. Serves as link between government and industry on transportation matters. Operates a job placement service for members.

OTHER SOURCES

Army AL&T: Acquisitions, Logistics, and Technology Bulletin. Available from U. S. Government Printing Office. • Bimonthly. $20.00 per year. Produced by the U. S. Army Materiel Command (http://www.amc.army.mil). Reports on Army research, development, and acquisition. Formerly *Army RD&A.*

Carroll's Defense Industry Charts. Carroll Publishing. • Quarterly. $1,500.00 per year. Provides 180 large, fold-out paper charts showing personnel relationships at more than 100 major U. S. defense contractors. Charts are also available online and on CD-ROM.

Government Contract Litigation Reporter: Covers Defense Procurement Fraud Litigation As Well as False Claims Acts (Qui Tam) Litigation. Andrews Publications. • Semimonthly. $875.00 per year. Newsletter. Provides reports on defense procurement fraud lawsuits.

DEFENSE MARKET

See: MILITARY MARKET

DEFICIT, FEDERAL

See: NATIONAL DEBT

DEHYDRATED FOODS

See: FOOD INDUSTRY

DEMOGRAPHY

See: MARKET STATISTICS; POPULATION; VITAL STATISTICS

DENTAL SUPPLY INDUSTRY

DIRECTORIES

Dentistry Today: Equipment Buyers' Guide. Dentistry Today, Inc. • Annual. Price on application. Provides purchasing information for more than 500 dental products.

Proofs' Buyers' Guide and United States Manufacturers' Directory. PennWell Publishing, Dental Economics Div. • Annual. $30.00. List of over 600 manufacturers of dental products and equipment; coverage includes foreign listings.

PERIODICALS AND NEWSLETTERS

Dental Lab Products. MEDEC Dental Communications. • Bimonthly. $35.00 per year.

Edited for dental laboratory managers. Covers new products and technical developments.

Dental Products Report Europe. MEDEC Dental Communications. • Seven times a year. $40.00 per year. Covers new dental products for the Europea market.

Dental Products Report: Trends in Dentistry. MEDEC Dental Communications. • 11 times a year. $120.00 per year. Provides information on new dental products, technology, and trends in dentistry.

Dental Trade Newsletter. American Dental Trade Association. • Bimonthly. Price on application.

Proofs: The Magazine of Dental Sales. PennWell Corp., Industrial Div. • Five times a year. $35.00 per year.

STATISTICS SOURCES

U. S. Industry and Trade Outlook. Available from National Technical Information Service. • Annual. $69.95. Produced by the International Trade Administration, U. S. Department of Commerce, in a "public-private" partnership with DRI/McGraw-Hill and Standard & Poor's. Provides basic data, outlook for the current year, and "Long-Term Prospects" (five-year projections) for a wide variety of products and services. Includes high technology industries. Formerly *U. S. Industrial Outlook.*

TRADE/PROFESSIONAL ASSOCIATIONS

Advanced Medical Technology Association. 701 Pennsylvania Ave. NW, Ste. 800, Washington, DC 20004-2654. Phone: (202)783-8700 Fax: (202)783-8750 E-mail: info@advamed.org • URL: http://www.advamed.org • Represents domestic (including U.S. territories and possessions) manufacturers of medical devices, diagnostic products, and healthcare information systems. Develops programs and activities on economic, technical, medical, and scientific matters affecting the industry. Gathers and disseminates information concerning the United States and international developments in legislative, regulatory, scientific or standards-making areas. Conducts scientific and educational seminars and programs.

American Dental Association. 211 E Chicago Ave., Chicago, IL 60611-2678. Phone: (312)440-2500 Fax: (312)440-2800 E-mail: publicinfo@ada.org • URL: http://www.ada.org • Professional society of dentists. Encourages the improvement of the health of the public and promotes the art and science of dentistry in matters of legislation and regulations. Inspects and accredits dental schools and schools for dental hygienists, assistants, and laboratory technicians. Conducts research programs at ADA Foundation +Research Institute. Produces dental health education material used in the U.S. Sponsors National Children's Dental Health Month and Give Kids a Smile Day. Compiles statistics on personnel, practice, and dental care needs and attitudes of patients with regard to dental health. Sponsors 13 councils.

American Dental Trade Association. 4222 King St., W., Alexandria, VA 22302-1597. Phone: (703)379-7755 Fax: (703)931-9429 E-mail: adta@adta.com • URL: http://www.adata.com.

Dental Dealers of America. 123 S. Broad St., Ste. 1960, Philadelphia, PA 19109-1025. Phone: (215)731-9982 Fax: (215)731-9983 E-mail: staff@dmanews.org.

Dental Manufacturers of America. 123 S. Broad St., Suite 2030, Philadelphia, PA 19109-1020. Phone: (215)731-9975 or (215)731-9982 Fax: (215)731-9984 E-mail: staff@dmanews.org • URL: http://www.dmanews.org.

OTHER SOURCES

Dental Supplies. Available from MarketResearch.com. • 2002. $3,450.00. Published by Global Industry Analysts. Provides worldwide market

research data, including profiles of major dental supply companies.

DEPARTMENT STORES

See also: CHAIN STORES; MARKETING; RETAIL TRADE

CD-ROM DATABASES

OECD Statistical Compendium. Organization for Economic Cooperation and Development. • Semiannual. $1,905.00 per year for 1 to 10 users. CD-ROM contains more than 730,000 monthly, quarterly, and annual time series for OECD countries, 1960 to date. Includes fully searchable data on agriculture, food, economic indicators, national accounts, employment, energy, finance, industry, technology, and foreign trade. Results can be displayed in various forms.

DIRECTORIES

Directory of Department Stores. Chain Store Guide. • Annual. $327.00. Available online. Lists 214 department stores, 1,500 shoe stores, 200 jewelry stores, 95 optical stores, and 70 leather and luggage stores in the United States and Canada, with annual sales of at least $250.00.

Directory of Discount and General Merchandise Stores. Chain Store Guide. • Annual. $327.00. Online edition, $747.00. Includes retailers and wholesalers of housewares, giftwares, novelties, toys, hobby materials, crafts, and stationery.

Plunkett's Retail Industry Almanac: Complete Profiles on the Retail 500-The Leading Firms in Retail Stores, Services, Catalogs, and On-Line Sales. Plunkett Research, Ltd. • 2001. $229.99. Includes CD-ROM. Provides detailed profiles of 500 major U. S. retailers. Industry trends are discussed.

Sheldon's Major Stores and Chains. Phelon Sheldon and Marsar, Inc. • Annual. $200.00. Lists department stores and chains in, women's specialty and chains, home furnishing chains and resident buying offices in the U.S. and Canada. Formerly *Sheldon's Retail Stores.*

FINANCIAL RATIOS

Annual Statement Studies. The Risk Management Association. • Annual. Median and quartile financial ratios are given for over 400 kinds of manufacturing, wholesale, retail, construction, and consumer finance establishments. Data is sorted by both asset size and sales volume. Includes a clearly written "Definition of Ratios" and an alphabetical industry index.

Annual Statement Studies: Industry Default Probabilities and Cash Flow Measures. The Risk Management Association. • Annual. $145.00. Serves as a companion volume to the original *Annual Statement Studies.* Gives probability of default estimates on a percentage scale for more than 450 industries. Includes changes in position year-by-year for eight financial statement line items and provides percentage measures of cash flow.

Financial and Operating Results of Department and Specialty Stores. National Retail Federation. John Wiley and Sons, Inc. • Annual. Members, $80.00; non-members, $100.00.

INTERNET DATABASES

Advance Monthly Sales for Retail Trade and Food Services. U. S. Census Bureau. Phone: 800-541-8345 or (301)763-4636 Fax: (301)457-3842 E-mail: rcb@census.gov • URL: http://www.census.gov/svsd/www/fullpub.html • Web pages provide monthly sales figures for a wide range of retail businesses. Advance, preliminary, and final statistics are provided for the latest month available in each case, with a previous-year comparison. Updates are monthly.

Business 2.0 Web Guide to the Best Business Links. Business 2.0 Media Inc. Phone: (415)293-4800 E-mail: support@business2.com • URL: http://www.business2.com/webguide • Web site presents an extensive, searchable directory of links to "the best, most informative, and authoritative web pages." Twenty main categories cover business, finance, career, company information, people, and technology topics, with thousands of subtopics, all linking to Web sites recommended by experienced business researchers. Fees: Free.

Fedstats. Federal Interagency Council on Statistical Policy. Phone: (202)395-7254 • URL: http://www.fedstats.gov • Web site features an efficient search facility for full-text statistics produced by more than 100 federal agencies, including the Census Bureau, the Bureau of Economic Analysis, and the Bureau of Labor Statistics. Boolean searches can be made within one agency or for all agencies combined. Links are offered to international statistical bureaus, including the UN, IMF, OECD, UNESCO, Eurostat, and 20 individual countries. Fees: Free.

FreeLunch.com. Economy.com, Inc. Phone: (610)696-8700 Fax: (610)696-1678 • URL: http://www.freelunch.com • Web site provides free access to more than 1.5 million economic and financial data series, covering industry, demographics, labor markets, prices, retail sales, government spending, trade, interest rates, housing starts, the stock market, and many other topics. Data is available for various time periods in either chart or table form. Searching is offered. Fees: Free, but registration required. Economy.com, Inc. also offers fee-based economic analysis at *The Dismal Scientist* site (http://www.dismal.com).

PERIODICALS AND NEWSLETTERS

Chain Store Age: The NewsMagazine for Retail Executives. Lebhar-Friedman, Inc. • Monthly. $105.00 per year. Formerly *Chain Store Age Executive with Shopping Center Age.*

Retailing Today. Robert Kahn and Associates. • Description: Focuses on general merchandise, apparel, furniture, hardware, automotive, and food retailing. Offers "original research, comments on current trends and conditions, recommendations for company policy, and emphasis on ethical conduct in business.".

Stores. National Retail Federation. NRF Enterprises, Inc. • Monthly. Individuals $49.00 per year; institutions, $120.00 per year.

RESEARCH CENTERS AND INSTITUTES

Center for Retail Management. Kellogg School of Management, Northwestern University, 2001 Sheridan Rd., Evanston, IL 60208. Phone: (847)467-3600 Fax: (847)467-3620 E-mail: r-blattberg@kellogg.northwestern.edu • URL: http://www.kellogg.northwestern.edu • Conducts research related to retail marketing and management.

Center for Retailing Studies. Texas A & M University, Department of Marketing, 4112 TAMU, College Station, TX 77843-4112. Phone: (979)845-0325 Fax: (979)845-5230 E-mail: d-szymanski@tamu.edu • URL: http://www.crstamu.org • Research areas include retailing issues and consumer economics.

STATISTICS SOURCES

Annual Benchmark Report for Retail Trade and Food Services...A Detailed Summary of Retail Sales, Purchases, Accounts Receivable, Inventories, and Food Service Sales. Available from U. S. Government Printing Office. • Annual. $13.00. Issued by the U.S. Census Bureau. Provides detailed annual and monthly retail statistics for the most recent 10 years. Includes data for various kinds of retail outlets, including automobiles, furniture, appliances, building supplies, grocery stores, drug stores, gasoline stations, clothing, sporting goods, department stores, and restaurants.

Business Statistics of the United States. Linz Audain and Cornelia J. Strawser. Bernan Associates. • Annual. $147.00. Based on *Business Statistics,* formerly issue by the Bureau of Economic Analysis, U. S. Department of Commerce. Provides basic data for a wide variety of U. S. industries, services, and economic indicators. Most statistics are shown annually for 30 years and monthly for the most recent four years.

Merchandise and Operating Results of Department and Specialty Stores. National Retail Federation, Financial Executive Div. John Wiley and Sons, Inc. • Annual. Members, $80.00; non-members, $100.00.

Survey of Current Business. Available from U. S. Government Printing Office. • Monthly. $63.00 per year. Issued by Bureau of Economic Analysis, U. S. Department of Commerce. Presents a wide variety of business and economic data.

WEFA Industrial Monitor. John Wiley and Sons, Inc. • Annual. $65.00. Prepared by industry analysts at WEFA, an economic forecasting and consulting firm (originally Wharton Econometric Forecasting Associates). Contains discussions of the outlook for major U. S. industries, with many 10-year forecasts (WEFA Web site is http://www.wefa.com).

TRADE/PROFESSIONAL ASSOCIATIONS

International Mass Retail Association. 1700 N. Moore St., Suite 2250, Arlington, VA 22209. Phone: (703)841-2300 Fax: (703)841-1184 E-mail: klasu@imra.org • URL: http://www.imra.org • Formerly National Mass Retailing Institute.

National Retail Federation. 325 7th St. NW, Ste. 1100, Washington, DC 20004. Phone: 800-673-4692 or (202)783-7971 Fax: (202)737-2849 E-mail: mullint@nrf.com • URL: http://www.nrf.com • Represents state retail associations, several dozen national retail associations, as well as large and small corporate members representing the breadth and diversity of the retail industry's establishment and employees. Conducts informational and educational conferences related to all phases of retailing including financial planning and cash management, taxation, economic forecasting, expense planning, shortage control, credit, electronic data processing, telecommunications, merchandise management, buying, traffic, security, supply, materials handling, store planning and construction, personnel administration, recruitment and training, and advertising and display.

North American Retail Dealers Association. 4700 W Lake Ave., Glenview, IL 60025. Phone: 800-621-0298 or (847)375-4713 Fax: (866)879-7505 E-mail: nardasvc@narda.com • URL: http://www.narda.com • Firms engaged in the retailing of electronic and electrical devices and components. Promotes and represents members' interests. Makes available services to members including: legal and technical consulting; employee screening; bank card processing; long-distance phone discounts; financial statements analysis; in-store promotion kits; customer check authorization. Advocates for members' interests before federal regulatory bodies; disseminates information on new regulations affecting members. Conducts educational programs.

Retail, Wholesale and Department Store Union. 30 E. 29th St., New York, NY 10016. Phone: (212)684-5300 Fax: (212)779-2809 E-mail: rwdsu@aol.com • URL: http://www.rwdsu.org.

DEPRECIATION

See also: ACCOUNTING

CD-ROM DATABASES

Authority Tax and Estate Planning Library. LexisNexis/Matthew Bender. • Periodic revisions. Price on request. CD-ROM contains updated full

text of *Bender's Payroll Tax Guide, Depreciation Handbook, Federal Income Taxation of Corporations, Tax Planning for Corporations, Modern Estate Planning, Planning for Large Estates, Murphy's Will Clauses, Tax & Estate Planning for the Elderly,* and 12 other Matthew Bender publications. The Internal Revenue Code is also included.

HANDBOOKS AND MANUALS

Business Taxpayer Information Publications. Available from U. S. Government Printing Office. • Annual. $63.00. Two volumes, consisting of *Circular E, Employer's Tax Guide* and *Employer's Supplemental Tax Guide.* Issued by the Internal Revenue Service (http://www.irs.ustreas.gov). Includes a wide variety of business-related tax information, including withholding tables, tax calendars, self-employment issues, partnership matters, corporation topics, depreciation, and bankruptcy.

CCH Guide to Car, Travel, Entertainment, and Home Office Deductions. CCH, Inc. • Annual. $45.00. Explains how to claim maximum tax deductions for common business expenses. Includes automobile depreciation tables, lease value tables, worksheets, and examples of filled-in tax forms.

Depreciation Handbook. LexisNexis Matthew Bender. • Annual. $213.00. Looseleaf service. Treatment of depreciation in one volume.

Federal Tax Course. Aspen Publishers, Inc. • Annual. $210.00. Provides basic reference and training for various forms of federal taxation: individual, business, corporate, partnership, estate, gift, etc.

Federal Tax Manual. CCH, Inc. • Monthly. $342.00 per year. Looseleaf service. Covers "basic federal tax rules and forms affecting individuals and businesses." Includes a copy of *Annuity, Depreciation, and Withholding Tables.*

U. S. Master Depreciation Guide. CCH, Inc. • Annual. $52.00. Contains explanations of ADR (asset depreciation range), ACRS (accelerated cost recovery system), and MACRS (modified accelerated cost recovery system). Includes the historical background of depreciation.

RESEARCH CENTERS AND INSTITUTES

Center for International Education and Research in Accounting. University of Illinois at Urbana-Champaign. 1206 S. Sixth St., 320 Wohlers Hall, Champaign, IL 61820. Phone: (217)333-4545 Fax: (217)244-6565 E-mail: ciera@uiuc.edu • URL: http://www.cba.uiuc.edu/.

STATISTICS SOURCES

Statistics of Income: Corporation Income Tax Returns. U.S. Internal Revenue Service. Available from U.S. Government Printing Office. • Annual. $26.00.

DEPRESSION

See: MENTAL HEALTH

DEPRESSIONS, BUSINESS

See: BUSINESS CYCLES

DERIVATIVE SECURITIES

GENERAL WORKS

Financial Institutions and Markets. Meir J. Kohn. Oxford University Press, Inc. • 2003. $115.00. Second edition.

DIRECTORIES

Derivatives Desk Reference: Buyside and Sellside Profiles. Capital Access International. • Annual. $295.00. A directory of about 900 firms active in the use of such derivatives as options, futures, currency swaps, interest rate swaps, and structured notes. Includes names of derivatives specialists in each firm.

Futures Magazine SourceBook: The Most Complete List of Exchanges, Companies, Regulators, Organizations, etc., Offering Products and Services to the Futures and Options Industry. Futures Magazine, Inc. • Annual. $19.50. Provides information on commodity futures brokers, trading method services, publications, and other items of interest to futures traders and money managers.

HedgeWorld Annual Compendium: The Hedge Fund Industry's Definitive Reference Guide. HedgeWorld USA. • Annual. $499.00. Contains profiles of 500 domestic and offshore hedge funds with more than $50 million in assets under management. Includes articles on "The Basics of Investing in Hedge Funds," "Beyond the Basics," and other information.

HedgeWorld Service Provider League Tables & Analyses. HedgeWorld USA. • Annual. $595.00. Provides quantitative and qualitative information on firms providing services to hedge funds: accountants/auditors, administrators, custodians, legal counsel, and prime brokers. Detailed categories cover banks, clearing services, consultants, derivatives business, investment companies, wealth management services, etc.

Thomson Derivatives and Risk Management Directory. Cengage Learning. • 1998. $247.00. Lists "over 9,000 contacts at more than 4,000 institutions." (Thomson Derivatives and Risk Management Directory 1999 Series: Vol. 1).

ENCYCLOPEDIAS AND DICTIONARIES

Dictionary of Finance and Investment Terms. John Downes. Barron's Educational Series, Inc. • 2002. $14.95. Sixth edition. Provides clear explanations of more than 5,000 business, banking, financial, investment, and tax terms. Includes a separate list of financial abbreviations and acronyms. (Business Dictionaries Series).

HANDBOOKS AND MANUALS

Advanced Fixed Income Analysis. Moorad Choudhry. Elsevier Butterworth Heinemann. • 2004. $60.00. Edited for "experienced practitioners in the corporate bond markets." Covers trading, hedging, interest rate models, corporate bond default risk, the yield curve, long bond yields, and other topics.

Analysis and Use of Financial Statements. Gerald I. White. John Wiley and Sons, Inc. • 2002. $123.95. Third edition. Includes analysis of financial ratios, cash flow, inventories, assets, debt, etc. Also covered are employee benefits, corporate investments, multinational operations, financial derivatives, and hedging activities.

The Bond and Money Markets: Strategy, Trading, Analysis. Moorad Choudhry. Elsevier Butterworth Heinemann. • 2003. $115.00. Serves as a reference work on corporate bonds, government bonds, currency markets, interest-rate futures, convertible securities, various kinds of derivatives, and technical analysis of financial securities.

Computational Finance: Numerical Methods for Pricing Financial Instruments. George Levy. Elsevier Butterworth Heinemann. • 2003. $89.95. Explains advanced financial modeling techniques using Windows software.

Corporate Fraud. Michael J. Comer. Ashgate Publishing Co. • 1997. Third edition. $139.95. Examines new risks of corporate fraud related to "electronic commerce, derivatives, computerization, empowerment, downsizing, and other recent developments." Covers fraud detection, prevention, and internal control systems. Published by Gower in England.

Derivative Instruments: A Guide to Theory and Practice. Brian A. Eales. Elsevier Butterworth

Heinemann. • 2003. $94.95. Includes examples and spreadsheet models.

Derivatives: A Comprehensive Resource for Options, Futures, Interest Rate Swaps, and Mortgage Securities. Fred D. Arditti. Harvard Business School Publishing. • 1996. $60.00. Published by Harvard Business School Press. Provides detailed explanations of various kinds of financial derivatives (options, futures, swaps, etc.) and their trading tactics, uses, and risks. (Financial Management Association Survey and Synthesis Series).

Derivatives Handbook: Risk Management and Control. Robert J. Schwartz and Clifford W. Smith. John Wiley and Sons, Inc. • 1997. $90.00. Some chapter topics are legal risk, risk measurement, and risk oversight. Includes "Derivatives Debacles: Case Studies of Losses in DerivativesMarkets." A glossary of derivatives terminology is provided. (Financial Engineering Series, vol. 6).

Econometrics of Financial Markets. John Y. Campbell and others. Princeton University Press. • 1996. $70.00. Written for advanced students and industry professionals. Includes chapters on "The Predictability of Asset Returns," "Derivative Pricing Models," and "Fixed-Income Securities." Provides a discussion of the random walk theory of investing and tests of the theory.

Guide to Federal Regulation of Derivatives. James Hamilton and others. CCH, Inc. • 1998. $85.00. Explains the complex derivatives regulations of the Securities and Exchange Commission. Covers swap agreements, third-party derivatives, credit derivatives, mutual fund liquidity, and other topics.

Handbook of Alternative Investment Strategies. Thomas Schneeweis and Joseph F. Pescatore, editors. Institutional Investor, Inc., Journals Group. • 1999. $95.00. Covers various forms of alternative investment, including hedge funds, managed futures, derivatives, venture capital, and natural resource financing.

Handbook of Derivative Instruments: Investment Research, Analysis, and Portfolio Applications. Arsuo Konishi and Ravi Dattatreya, editors. McGraw-Hill. • 1996. $80.00. Second revised edition. Contains 41 chapters by various authors on all aspects of derivative securities, including such esoterica as "Inverse Floaters," "Positive Convexity," "Exotic Options," and "How to Use the Holes in Black-Scholes.".

Handbook of Equity Derivatives. Jack C. Francis and others, editors. John Wiley and Sons, Inc. • 1999. $105.00. Revised edition. Contains 27 chapters by various authors. Covers options (puts and calls), stock index futures, warrants, convertibles, over-the-counter options, swaps, legal issues, taxation, etc. (Financial Engineering Series).

Interest Rate Risk Measurement and Management. Sanjay K. Nawalkha and Donald R. Chambers, editors. Institutional Investor, Inc. • 1999. $95.00. Provides interest rate risk models for fixed-income derivatives and for investments by various kinds of financial institutions.

An Introduction to the Mathematics of Financial Derivatives. Salih N. Neftci. Elsevier. • 2000. $64.95. Second edition. Covers the mathematical models underlying the pricing of derivatives. Includes explanations of basic financial calculus for students, derivatives traders, risk managers, and others concerned with derivatives.

Risk Management, Speculation, and Derivative Securities. Geoffrey Poitras. Elsevier Butterworth Heinemann. • 2002. $99.95. In addition to "Risk Management Concepts" and "Speculative Concepts," topics include financial futures, forward contracts, arbitrage, spread trading, hedging, and diversification. Three appendices are devoted to mathematical concepts and calculations.

Swap Literacy. Elizabeth Ungar. Bloomberg. • 1996.

$40.00. Written for corporate finance officers. Provides basic information on arbitrage, hedging, and speculation, involving interest rate, currency, and other types of financial swaps. (Bloomberg Professional Library.).

Understanding Financial Derivatives: How to Protect Your Investments. Donald Strassheim. McGraw-Hill. • 1996. $40.00. Covers three basic risk management instruments: options, futures, and swaps. Includes advice on equity index options, financial futures contracts, and over-the-counter derivatives markets.

INTERNET DATABASES

Derivatives. Imagine Software Inc. Phone: (212)317-7600 Fax: (212)317-7601 • URL: http://www.derivatives.com • Web site mainly promotes proprietary software for the use of derivatives in risk management, but also provides free access to articles on a variety of derivatives-related topics.

Factiva. Dow Jones Reuters Business Interactive, LLC. Phone: 800-369-7466 or (609)452-1511 Fax: (609)520-5770 E-mail: solutions@factiva.com • URL: http://www.factiva.com • Fee-based Web site provides "global news and business information through Web sites and content integration solutions." Includes Dow Jones and Reuters newswires, The Wall Street Journal, and more than 7,000 other sources of current news, historical articles, market research reports, and investment analysis. Content includes 96 major U. S. newspapers, 900 non-English sources, trade publications, media transcripts, country profiles, news photos, etc.

Futures Online. Futures Magazine Inc. Phone: (312)846-4600 Fax: (312)846-4638 • URL: http://www.futuresmag.com • Web site presents updates of *Futures* magazine and links to other futures-related sites.

Nexis.com. Lexis-Nexis Group. Phone: 800-227-4908 or (937)865-6800 Fax: (937)865-6909 E-mail: webmaster@prod.lexis-nexis.com • URL: http://www.nexis.com • Fee-based Web site offers searching of about 2.8 billion documents in some 30,000 news, business, and legal information sources. Features include a subject directory covering 1,200 topics in 34 categories and a Company Dossier containing information on more than 500,000 public and private companies. Boolean searching is offered.

U. S. Securities and Exchange Commission. Phone: 800-732-0330 or (202)942-7040 Fax: (202)942-9634 E-mail: webmaster@sec.gov • URL: http://www.sec.gov • SEC Web site offers free access through EDGAR to text of official corporate filings, such as annual reports (10-K), quarterly reports (10-Q), and proxies. (EDGAR is "Electronic Data Gathering, Analysis, and Retrieval System.") An example is given of how to obtain executive compensation data from proxies. Text of the daily *SEC News Digest* is offered, as are links to other government sites, non-government market regulators, and U. S. stock exchanges. Search facilities are extensive. Fees: Free.

Wall Street Journal Interactive Edition. Dow Jones & Co., Inc. Phone: 800-369-2834 or (212)416-2000 Fax: (212)416-2658 E-mail: inquiries@interactive.wsj.com • URL: http://www.wsj.com • Fee-based Web site providing online searching of worldwide information from the *The Wall Street Journal.* Includes "Company Snapshots," "The Journal's Greatest Hits," "Index to Market Data," "Journal Links," etc. Financial price quotes are available. Fees: $49.00 per year; $29.00 per year to print subscribers.

ONLINE DATABASES

Disclosure SEC Database. Thomson Financial. • Provides online information from records filed with the Securities and Exchange Commission by more than 12,000 publicly-owned companies in the U.S. Includes about 200 financial data items and information relating to executives. Time span is 1977 to date, with weekly updates. Inquire as to online cost and availability.

EdgarPlus: SEC Basic Filings. Thomson Financial. • Online service provides full text of about 60,000 documents that have been filed with the U.S. Securities and Exchange Commission, 1987 to date, with daily updates. Filings include 6-K, 8-K, 10-K, 10-C, 10-Q, 20-F, and proxy statements. Inquire as to online cost and availability.

PERIODICALS AND NEWSLETTERS

Derivatives Quarterly. Institutional Investor, Inc., Journals Group. • Quarterly. Price on application. Emphasis is on the practical use of derivatives. Includes case studies to demonstrate "real-life" risks and benefits.

Derivatives Week: The Newsweekly on Derivatives Worldwide. Institutional Investor, Inc., Journals Group. • Weekly. $2,475.00 per year. Includes print and online editions. Newsletter on financial derivatives linked to equities, interest rates, commodities, and currencies. Covers new products, investment opportunities, legalities, etc.

Financial Markets, Institutions, and Instruments. New York University, Salomon Center. Blackwell Publishing. • Five times a year. Institutions, $338.00 per year. Includes online edition. Edited to "bridge the gap between the academic and professional finance communities." Special fifth issue each year provides surveys of developments in four areas: money and banking, derivative securities, corporate finance, and fixed-income securities.

Futures and Derivatives Law Report: The Journal on the Law of Investment and Risk Management Products. Glasser Legalworks. • Monthly. $305.00 per year. Newsletter. Covers developments in regulation, legislation, and litigation concerning financial derivatives, futures trading, and options trading.

Futures: News, Analysis, and Strategies for Futures, Options, and Derivatives Traders. Futures Magazine. • Monthly. $39.00 per year. Edited for institutional money managers and traders, brokers, risk managers, and individual investors or speculators. Includes special feature issues on interest rates, technical indicators, currencies, charts, precious metals, hedge funds, and derivatives. Supplements available.

Journal of Derivatives. Institutional Investor, Inc., Journals Group. • Quarterly. $365.00 per year. Includes print and online editions. Covers the structure and management of financial derivatives. Includes graphs, equations, and detailed analyses.

Journal of Investing. Institutional Investor, Inc., Journals Group. • Quarterly. $350.00 per year. Includes print and online editions. Edited for professional investors. Topics include equities, fixed-income securities, derivatives, asset allocation, and other institutional investment subjects.

Journal of Risk Finance: The Convergence of Financial Products and Insurance. Institutional Investor, Inc., Journals Group. • Quarterly. $500.00 per year. Includes print and online editions. Covers the field of customized risk management, including securitization, insurance, hedging, derivatives, and credit arbitrage.

Journal of Taxation of Financial Products. CCH, Inc. • Bimonthly. $249.00 per year.

Quantitative Finance. Available from American Institute of Physics. • Bimonthly. $340.00 per year. Print and online edition, $765.00 per year. Published in the UK by the Institute of Physics. A technical journal on the use of quantitative tools and applications in financial analysis and financial engineering. Covers such topics as portfolio theory, derivatives, asset allocation, return on assets, risk management, price volatility, financial econometrics, market anomalies, and trading systems.

SFO: Stocks, Futures & Options. Wasendorf & Associates, Inc. • Monthly. $49.95 per year. Subtitle: *Official Journal for Personal Investing in Stocks, Futures, and Options.* Covers mainly speculative techniques for stocks, commodity futures, financial futures, stock index futures, foreign exchange, short selling, and various kinds of options.

The Wall Street Journal. Dow Jones & Co., Inc. • Daily. $189.00 per year. Covers news and trends relating to business, industry, finance, the economy, and international commerce. Provides extensive price and other data for the securities, commodity, options, futures, foreign exchange, and money markets.

STATISTICS SOURCES

Statistical Information on the Financial Services Industry. American Bankers Association. • Annual. Members, $150.00; non-members, $275.00. Presents a wide variety of data relating to banking and financial services, including consumer economics, personal finance, credit, government loans, capital markets, and international banking.

TRADE/PROFESSIONAL ASSOCIATIONS

EMTA-Trade Association for the Emerging Markets. 360 Madison Ave., 18th Fl., New York, NY 10017. Phone: (646)637-9100 Fax: (646)637-9128 • URL: http://www.emta.org • Promotes orderly trading markets for emerging market instruments. Formerly Emerging Markets Traders Association.

DESALINATION INDUSTRY

ABSTRACTS AND INDEXES

Applied Science and Technology Index. H. W. Wilson Co. • 11 times a year. Quarterly and annual cumulations. Price varies. Indexes a wide variety of English language technical, industrial, and engineering periodicals.

Current Contents: Engineering, Computing and Technology. Thomson/ISI. • Weekly. $730.00 per year. Reproductions of contents pages of technical journals. Includes *Author Index, Address Directory, Current Book Contents* and *Title Word Index.* Formerly *Current Contents: Engineering, Technology and Applied Sciences.*

Environment Abstracts. Congressional Information Service, Inc. • Monthly. Price varies. Provides multidisciplinary coverage of the world's environmental literature. Incorporates *Acid Rain Abstracts.*

Environment Abstracts Annual: A Guide to the Key Environmental Literature of the Year. Congressional Information Service, Inc. • Annual. $495.00. A yearly cumulation of *Environment Abstracts.*

Oceanic Abstracts. CSA. • 11 times a year. $1,645.00 per year. Includes print and online editions. Covers oceanography, marine biology, ocean shipping, and a wide range of other marine-related subject areas.

BIBLIOGRAPHIES

Encyclopedia of Physical Science and Engineering Information. Gale Cengage Learning. • 1996. $160.00. Second edition. Includes print, electronic, and other information sources for a wide range of scientific, technical, and engineering topics.

CD-ROM DATABASES

Environment Abstracts on CD-ROM. LEXIS-NEXIS. • Quarterly. $1,295.00 per year. Contains the following CD-ROM databases: *Environment Abstracts, Energy Abstracts,* and *Acid Rain Abstracts.* Length of coverage varies.

NTIS on SilverPlatter. Available from SilverPlatter Information, Inc. • Quarterly. $2,850.00 per year. Produced by the National Technical Information Service. Provides a CD-ROM guide to over 500,000 government reports on a wide variety of technical, industrial, and business topics.

Science Citation Index: Compact Disc Edition. Institute for Scientific Information. • Monthly. Provides CD-ROM indexing of the world's scientific and technical literature. Corresponds to online *Scisearch* and printed *Science Citation Index.*

WILSONDISC: Applied Science and Technology Abstracts. H. W. Wilson Co. • Monthly. Includes unlimited access to the online version of *Applied Science and Technology Abstracts* through WILSONLINE. Provides CD-ROM indexing and abstracting of 500 prominent scientific, technical, engineering, and industrial periodicals. Indexing coverage is provided from 1983 to date and abstracting from 1993 to date.

ENCYCLOPEDIAS AND DICTIONARIES

Encyclopedia of Global Change: Environmental Change and Human Society. Andrew S. Goudie, editor. Oxford University Press. • 2001. $275.00. Two volumes. Contains 300 signed articles on a wide variety of topics relating to changes in the environment and the atmosphere. Includes bibliographies and illustrations.

ONLINE DATABASES

Applied Science and Technology Index Online. H. W. Wilson Co. • Provides online indexing of 500 major scientific, technical, industrial, and engineering periodicals. Time period is 1983 to date. Monthly updates. Inquire as to online cost and availability.

Aqualine. Cambridge Scientific Abstracts. • Provides online citations and abstracts to a wide variety of literature relating to the aquatic environment, including 400 journals, from 1960 to date. Updating is monthly. Inquire as to online cost and availability.

F & S Index. Gale Cengage Learning. • Contains about four million citations to worldwide business, financial, and industrial or consumer product literature appearing from 1972 to date. Weekly updates. Inquire as to online cost and availability.

Globalbase. Gale Cengage Learning. • Provides more than one million online summaries of business, industrial, and economic news reports from more than 1,000 publications worldwide. Covers a wide range of material appearing in international trade journals, professional magazines, and newspapers. Time period is 1984 to date, with weekly updates. Inquire as to online cost and availability.

NTIS Database. National Technical Information Service. • Contains citations and abstracts to unrestricted reports of government-sponsored research, 1964 to date. Covers a wide range of technical, engineering, business, and social science topics. Monthly updates. Inquire as to online cost and availability.

Oceanic Abstracts (Online). Cambridge Scientific Abstracts. • Oceanographic and other marine-related technical literature, 1981 to present. Monthly updates. Inquire as to online cost and availability.

PROMT: Predicasts Overview of Markets and Technology. Gale Cengage Learning. • Companies, products, applied technologies and markets. U.S. and international literature coverage, 1972 to date. Inquire as to online cost and availability. Provides abstracts from more than 1,600 publications. Weekly updates.

Scisearch. Institute for Scientific Information. • Broad, multidisciplinary index to the literature of science and technology, 1974 to present. Inquire as to online cost and availability. Coverage of literature is worldwide, with weekly updates.

PERIODICALS AND NEWSLETTERS

Water Desalination Report. Maria C. Smith. • Description: Concentrates on the activities of government and industry worldwide concerning the desalination of seawater and brackish water.

      For publishers addresses, refer to SOURCES CITED section at the back of the book.

Discusses such topics as problems with water supply and reuse, resource planning, and pollution control. Reports on federal budgets, regulation, new and future programs, opportunities in business, and research. Recurring features include book reviews and a schedule of activities.

RESEARCH CENTERS AND INSTITUTES

Pacific International Center for High Technology Research. 1020 Auahi St., Bldg. 5, Bay 14, Honolulu, HI 96814. Phone: (808)591-6490 Fax: (808)591-6491 E-mail: harold.masumoto@.pichtr. org • URL: http://www.pichtr.org • Desalination is included as a field of research.

TRADE/PROFESSIONAL ASSOCIATIONS

International Desalination Association. PO Box 387, Topsfield, MA 01983. Phone: (978)887-0410 Fax: (978)887-0411 E-mail: info@idadesal.org • URL: http://www.idadesal.org • Users and suppliers of desalination equipment; water reuse and reclamation consultants. Seeks to develop and promote worldwide application of desalination and desalination technology in maintaining water supplies, controlling water pollution, and purifying, treating, and reusing water. Disseminates information on desalination-related subjects and water reuse. Encourages the establishment of standards, specifications, procedures, and the efficient use of water for energy. Conducts seminars and workshops.

DESIGN AND MANUFACTURING, COMPUTER-AIDED

See: COMPUTER-AIDED DESIGN AND MANUFACTURING (CAD/CAM)

DESIGN IN INDUSTRY

See also: ART IN INDUSTRY; ARTS MANAGEMENT; COMMERCIAL ART; GRAPHIC ARTS INDUSTRY; OFFICE DESIGN

ABSTRACTS AND INDEXES

Art Index. H. W. Wilson Co. • Quarterly. Annual cumulations. Price varies. Subject and author index to periodicals in art, architecture, industrial design, city planning, photography, and various related topics.

BIOGRAPHICAL SOURCES

Contemporary Designers. Gale Cengage Learning. • 1997. $190.00. Third edition. Profiles the careers and accomplishments of 685 designers from throughout the world.

DIRECTORIES

Design News OEM Directory. Reed Business Information. • Covers: about 5,000 manufacturers and suppliers of power transmission products, fluid power products, and electrical/electronic components to the OEM (original equipment manufacturer) market in SIC groups 34-39. Entries include: Company name, address, phone, fax, url, e-mail.

Directory of Minority-Owned Professional and Personnel Services Consultants. San Francisco Redevelopment Agency. • Annual. Free. About 650 minority firms in Northern California.

ENR-Top International Design Firms (Engineering News Record). McGraw-Hill. • Annual. $10.00. Lists 200 firms. Includes U. S. firms. Formerly *Engineering News Record-Top International Design Firms.*

The Top 500 Design Firms Sourcebook. McGraw-Hill. • Annual. $25.00. Lists 500 leading architectural, engineering and speciality design firms selected on basis of annual billings. Formerly *ENR Directory of Design Firms.*

ENCYCLOPEDIAS AND DICTIONARIES

Design Encyclopedia. Mel Byars. John Wiley and Sons, Inc. • 1994. $60.00. Contains more than 3,000 entries covering various aspects of design and decoration since the 19th century.

HANDBOOKS AND MANUALS

Dimensional Color. Lois Swirnoff. W. W. Norton & Co., Inc. • 2003. $39.95. Second edition. Explores the three-dimensional interaction between light, color, and surface, with 230 color illustrations. Written chiefly for architects and designers. (Previous edition was published by Van Nostrand Reinhold.).

Logo Power: Creating World-Class Logos and Effective Business Identities. David E. Carter. DIANE Publishing Co. • 2001. $40.00. Explains how to plan, develop, evaluate, and implement a company logo system.

Office Interior Design Guide: An Introduction for Facility and Design. Julie K. Rayfield. John Wiley and Sons, Inc. • 1997. $70.00. (Professional Series).

ONLINE DATABASES

Art Index Online. H. W. Wilson Co. • Indexes a wide variety of art-related periodicals, 1984 to date. Monthly updates. Inquire as to online cost and availability.

PERIODICALS AND NEWSLETTERS

Design Drafting News. American Design Drafting Association. • Description: Monitors new developments, techniques, and products related to design and drafting. Carries information about metrication and standards. Recurring features include news of the Association and its members, book reviews, and a calendar of events.

Design Management Journal. Design Management Institute. • Quarterly. $96.00 per year. Covers the management of product-related design.

Design Perspectives. Industrial Designers Society of America. • Description: The largest newsletter examining the news and trends of industrial design. Recurring features include: new and cutting-edge products, news of people and events in industrial design, resource section, reports of chapter and national activities of IDSA, and a calendar of events. The classified ad section is the largest of its kind and, for advertisers, the newsletter is the best way to reach new product decision-making VPs of industrial design.

Engineering Design Graphics Journal. American Society for Engineering Education. • Three times a year. Free to members; Non-members; $24.00 per year. Concerned with engineering graphics, computer graphics, geometric modeling, computer-aided drafting, etc.

Machine Design: Magazine of Applied Technology for Design Engineering. Penton Media, Inc. • 21 times a year. $110.00 per year. Includes *Machine Design Reference Issues* and *Penton Executive Network.*

TRADE/PROFESSIONAL ASSOCIATIONS

American Design Drafting Association. 105 E Main St., Newbern, TN 38059. Phone: (731)627-0802 Fax: (731)627-9321 E-mail: cadboss@gmail.com • URL: http://www.adda.org • Designers, drafters, drafting managers, chief drafters, supervisors, administrators, instructors, and students of design and drafting. Encourages a continued program of education for self-improvement and professionalism in design and drafting and computer-aided design/drafting. Informs members of effective techniques and materials used in drawings and other graphic presentations. Evaluates curriculum of educational institutions through certification program; sponsors drafter certification program.

American Institute of Building Design. 2505 Main St., Suite 209B, Stratford, CT 06615. Phone: 800-366-2423 or (203)227-3640 Fax: (203)378-3568 E-mail: aibdnat@aol.com • URL: http://www.aibd. org.

Design Management Institute. 101 Tremont St., Ste. 300, Boston, MA 02108. Phone: (617)338-6380 Fax: (617)338-6570 E-mail: dmistaff@dmi.org • URL: http://www.dmi.org • In-house design groups and consultant design firms; individuals involved in the management of designers with in-house corporate design groups or consultant design firms. Aims to share management techniques as applied to design groups, and to facilitate better understanding by business management of the role design can play in achieving business goals. Design disciplines included are: architecture, advertising, communications, exhibit design, graphics, interior design, packaging and product design. Develops and distributes design management education materials. Sponsors seminars for design professionals. Identifies critical areas of design management study; conducts surveys and research on corporate design management. Maintains design management archive. Operates Center for Research, Center for Education, and Center for +Design and Management Resources.

Industrial Designers Society of America. 45195 Business Court, No. 250, Dulles, VA 20166. Phone: (703)707-6000 Fax: (703)787-8501 E-mail: idsa@idsa.org • URL: http://www.idsa.org • A professional society of industrial designers.

International Council of Societies of Industrial Design. PO Box 100820, FIN-D45008 Essen, Finland. Phone: 49 201 3010420 or 49 201 3010440 E-mail: office@icsid.org • URL: http://www.icsid. org.

DESKTOP PUBLISHING

See also: MICROCOMPUTERS AND MINICOMPUTERS; WORD PROCESSING

GENERAL WORKS

Teach Yourself Desktop Publishing. Christopher Lumgair. McGraw-Hill. • 2001. $10.95. Describes current desktop publishing software and techniques.

ABSTRACTS AND INDEXES

Applied Science and Technology Index. H. W. Wilson Co. • 11 times a year. Quarterly and annual cumulations. Price varies. Indexes a wide variety of English language technical, industrial, and engineering periodicals.

Business Periodicals Index. H. W. Wilson Co. • 11 times a year. Quarterly and annual cumulations. Price varies.

Computer and Control Abstracts. Available from INSPEC, Inc. • Monthly. $2,400.00 per year. Section C of *Science Abstracts.*

Computer and Information Systems Abstracts Journal: An Abstract Journal Pertaining to the Theory, Design, Fabrication and Application of Computer and Information Systems. CSA. • 11 times a year. $1,750 per year.

Computer Literature Index: A Subject/Author Index to Computer and Data Processing Literature. EBSCO Publishing. • Quarterly, with annual cumulation. $245.00 per year. Contains brief abstracts of book and periodical literature covering all phases of computing, including approximately 70 specific application areas.

Current Contents: Engineering, Computing and Technology. Thomson/ISI. • Weekly. $730.00 per year. Reproductions of contents pages of technical journals. Includes *Author Index, Address Directory, Current Book Contents* and *Title Word Index.* Formerly *Current Contents: Engineering, Technology and Applied Sciences.*

Internet and Personal Computing Abstracts [print edition]. EBSCO Publishing. • Quarterly. $269.00 per year, including cumulative index. Provides more than 10,000 abstracts annually from both trade and academic publications. Covers computer hardware, software, product reviews, Web topics, e-commerce, networks, corporate news, security, and related topics. Formerly *Microcomputer Abstracts.*

CD-ROM DATABASES

Computer Database. Gale Cengage Learning. • Provides one year of full-text on CD-ROM for 150 leading computer-related publications. Also includes 70,000 product specifications and brief profiles of 13,000 computer product vendors and manufacturers.

DIRECTORIES

Business Organizations, Agencies, and Publications Directory. Gale Cengage Learning. • 2003. $480.00. 15th edition. Over 40,000 entries describing 39 types of business information sources. Classified by type of organization, publication, or serviceIncludes state, national, and international agencies and organizations. Master index to names and keywords. Also includes e-mail addresses and web site URL's.

Data Sources: The Comprehensive Guide to the Data Processing Industry: Hardware, Data Communications Products, Software, Company Profiles. Gale Cengage Learning. • Semiannual. $455.00 per year. Two volumes. Describes hardware and software for all computer operating sysems, including prices and technical details. Lists about 75,000 products from 14,000 suppliers. Industry-specific software applications are described.

MicroLeads Vendor Directory on Disk (Personal Computer Industry). Chromatic Communications Enterprises, Inc. • Annual. $495.00. Includes computer hardware manufacturers, software producers, book-periodical publishers, and franchised or company-owned chains of personal computer equipment retailers, support services and accessory manufacturers. Formerly *MicroLeads U.S. Vender Directory.*

The Software Encyclopedia: A Guide for Personal, Professional, and Business Users. Gale. • Annual. $335.00. Two volumes. Volume one lists software programs by title and producer. Volume two provides information on programs according to application and operating system. Includes prices and requirements for hardware and memory.

ENCYCLOPEDIAS AND DICTIONARIES

Acronyms of Computer Science and Communications: A Comprehensive Acronym Dictionary and Illustrated Encyclopedia. Enjob Kajan and Ejub Kajan. Springer Verlag. • 2002. $49.95. Explains more than 4,000 "broadly used" computer, telecommunications, and information technology acronyms. Includes illustrations and Web addresses, where applicable.

Dictionary of Computing. Valerie Illingworth, editor. Oxford University Press. • 1997. $18.00. Fourth edition.

Dictionary of Information Technology and Computer Science. Tony Gunton. Blackwell Publishing. • 1994. $62.95. Second edition. Covers key words, phrases, abbreviations, and acronyms used in computing and data communications.

Encyclopedia of Information Systems. Hossein Bidgoli, editor. Elsevier. • 2002. $1,200.00. Four volumes. Contains a wide range of articles relating to computers, databases, communication, and information technology. The 200 topics include coverage of hardware, software, artificial intelligence, the Internet, networks, knowledge management, electronic commerce, search engines, and systems design.

Graphically Speaking: An Illustrated Guide to the Working Language of Design and Publishing. Mark Beach. Coast to Coast Books. • 1992. $29.50. Provides practical definitions of 2,800 terms used in printing, graphic design, publishing, and desktop publishing. Over 300 illustrations are included, about 40 in color.

HANDBOOKS AND MANUALS

Columbia Guide to Digital Publishing: In Print and On the Web. William E. Kasdorf, editor. Columbia University Press. • 2002. $65.00. Covers the practical production of both written and graphic material in digital format, including archives, new technology, "information architecture," and copyright.

The Desktop Designer's Illustration Handbook. Marcelle L. Toor. John Wiley and Sons, Inc. • 1996. $29.95. Serves as a guide to locating, selecting, and using illustrations for desktop publications. (ITCP Computer Science Series).

Desktop Publishing. Entrepreneur Media, Inc. • Looseleaf. $59.50. A practical guide to starting a desktop publishing service. Covers profit potential, start-up costs, market size evaluation, pricing, accounting, advertising, promotion, etc. (Start-Up Business Guide No. E1288.).

Handbook of Digital Publishing. Michael L. Kleper. Prentice Hall PTR. • 2001. $129.99. Two volumes. Edited for the digital publishing industry. Covers print publishing, electronic documents, and Internet (Web) publishing, including basic desktop procedures. Provides information on typography, design, layout, image creation, and page creation.

How to Produce Creative Advertising: Traditional Techniques and Computer Applications. Thomas Bivins and Ann Keding. McGraw Hill. • 1993. $37.95. Covers copywriting, advertising design, and the use of desktop publishing techniques in advertising. (NTC Business Books Series).

How to Produce Creative Publications: Traditional Techniques and Computer Applications. Thomas Bivins and Ann Keding. McGraw-Hill. • 1993. $37.95. A practical guide to the writing, designing, and production of magazines, annual reports, brochures, and newsletters by traditional methods and by desktop publishing. (NTC Business Books Series).

Looking Good in Print: A Guide to Basic Design for Desktop Publishing. Roger C. Parker. Paraglyph, Inc. • 2003. $29.99. Fifth edition. Includes CD-ROM. Covers newsletters, advertisements, brochures, manuals, and correspondence.

Using Desktop Publishing to Create Newsletters, Library Guides, and Web Pages: A How-To-Do-It Manual for Librarians. John Maxymuk. Neal-Schuman Publishers, Inc. • 1997. $55.00. Includes more than 90 illustrations. (How-to-Do-It Manuals Series).

INTERNET DATABASES

InfoTech Trends. Data Analysis Group. Phone: (925)462-1202 Fax: (925)462-1225 E-mail: support@infotechtrends.com • URL: http://www.infotechtrends.com • Web site provides both free and fee-based market research data on the information technology industry, including computers, peripherals, telecommunications, the Internet, software, CD-ROM/DVD, e-commerce, and workstations. Fees: Free for current (most recent year) data; more extensive information has various fee structures. Formerly *Computer Industry Forecasts.*

Wired News. Lycos, Inc. Phone: (415)276-8400 Fax: (415)276-8500 E-mail: newsfeedback@wired.com • URL: http://www.wired.com • Provides summaries and full-text of "Top Stories" relating to the Internet, computers, multimedia, telecommunications, and the electronic information industry in general. These news stories are placed in the broad categories of Politics, Business, Culture, and Technology. Affiliated with *Wired* magazine. Fees: Free.

ONLINE DATABASES

Applied Science and Technology Index Online. H. W. Wilson Co. • Provides online indexing of 500 major scientific, technical, industrial, and engineering periodicals. Time period is 1983 to date. Monthly updates. Inquire as to online cost and availability.

Internet and Personal Computing Abstracts. Information Today, Inc. • Contains abstracts covering a wide variety of personal and business microcomputer literature appearing in more than 100 journals and popular magazines. Time period is 1981 to date, with monthly updates. Formerly *Microcomputer Index.* Inquire as to online cost and availability.

PROMT: Predicasts Overview of Markets and Technology. Gale Cengage Learning. • Companies, products, applied technologies and markets. U.S. and international literature coverage, 1972 to date. Inquire as to online cost and availability. Provides abstracts from more than 1,600 publications. Weekly updates.

Wilson Business Abstracts Online. H. W. Wilson Co. • Indexes and abstracts 600 major business periodicals, plus the *Wall Street Journal* and the business section of the *New York Times.* Indexing is from 1982, abstracting from 1990, with the two newspapers included from 1993. Updated weekly. Inquire as to online cost and availability. (*Business Periodicals Index* without abstracts is also available online.).

PERIODICALS AND NEWSLETTERS

Digital Imaging: The Magazine for the Imaging Professional. Cygnus Business Media, Inc. • Bimonthly. $24.95 per year. Edited for business and professional users of electronic publishing products and services. Topics covered include document imaging, CD-ROM publishing, digital video, and multimedia services. Formerly *Micro Publishing News.*

EDP Weekly: The Leading Weekly Computer News Summary. Computer Age and EDP News Services. • Weekly. $495.00 per year. Newsletter. Summarizes news from all areas of the computer and microcomputer industries.

The Gray Sheet. F-D-C Reports Inc. • Description: Monitors the complex regulatory environment for devices, instrumentation, and diagnostics. Topics include device-related Congressional activity, Medicare reimbursement policies, international regulatory intiatives, enforcement and premarket approval programs at FDA's Center for Devices and Radiological Health. Recurring features include device approvals, 510(k) clearances, FDA recalls and seizures, mergers and acquisitions, and sales and earnings.

Innovative Publisher: Publishing Strategies for New Markets. Emmelle Publishing Co., Inc. • Biweekly. $69.00 per year. Provides articles and news on electronic publishing (CD-ROM or online) and desktop publishing.

The Magazine for Electronic Publishing Professionals. Publish Media. • Monthly. $39.90 per year. Edited for professional publishers, graphic designers, and industry service providers. Covers new products and emerging technologies for the electronic publishing industry.

The Page. The Cobb Group. • Description: Acts as a visual guide to McIntosh computer desktop publishing.

The Seybold Report (Analyzing Publishing Technologies). Seybold Publications. • Semimonthly. $595.00 per year. Newsletter. Formerly *Seybold Report on Publishing Systems.*

Step-By-Step Electronic Design: The How-To

Newsletter for Electronic Designers. Dynamic Graphics, Inc. • Monthly. $48.00 per year.

RESEARCH CENTERS AND INSTITUTES
Chester F. Carlson Center for Imaging Science. Rochester Institute of Technology, 54 Lomb Memorial Dr., Rochester, NY 14623. Phone: 800-724-2536 or (716)475-5944 Fax: (716)475-5988 E-mail: garley@cis.rit.edu • URL: http://www.cis.rit.edu/.

DETERGENTS

See: CLEANING PRODUCTS INDUSTRY

DEVELOPING AREAS

See also: FOREIGN INVESTMENTS

GENERAL WORKS
Developing Countries: Definitions, Concepts, and Comparisons. Jonathan E. Sanford. Nova Science Publishers, Inc. • 2003. $29.50. Describes four basic measures of levels of national development: per capita income, economic structure, social conditions (quality of life), and political freedom.

Economic Development. Michael P. Todaro and Stephen C. Smith. Addison-Wesley. • 2002. Eight edition. Price on application. (Addison-Wesley Economic Series).

Global Economic Prospects 2004. The World Bank Group. • 2003. $38.00. "..offers an in-depth analysis of the economic prospects of developing countries.." Emphasis is on the impact of recessions and financial crises. Regional statistical data is included.

Marketing in the Third World. Denise M. Johnson and Erdener Kaynak, editors. Haworth Press, Inc. • 1996. $29.95. Various authors discuss marketing, advertising, government regulations, and other topics relating to business promotion in developing countries. (Also published in the *Journal of Global Marketing*, vol. 9, no. 4).

Trade and Employment in Developing Countries. Anne O. Krueger, editor. The University of Chicago Press. • Two volumes. Vol. 2, 1982, $35.00; Vol. 3, 1983, $16.00. (National Bureau of Economic Research Project Report Series).

ABSTRACTS AND INDEXES
World Agricultural Economics and Rural Sociology Abstracts: Abstracts of World Literature. Available from CABI Publishing, North America. • Monthly. Institutions, $1,425.00 per year. Print and online edition, $1,460.00 per year. Published in England by CABI Publishing. Provides worldwide coverage of the literature.

ALMANACS AND YEARBOOKS
Emerging Markets Analyst. • Monthly. $895.00 per year. Provides an annual overview of the emerging financial markets in 24 countries of Latin America, Asia, and Europe. Includes data on international mutual funds and closed-end funds.

World Development Report 2004. The World Bank Group. • Annual. $26.00. Covers history, conditions, and trends relating to economic globalization and localization. Includes selected data from *World Development Indicators* for 132 countries or economies. Key indicators are provided for 78 additional countries or economies.

Worldmark Yearbook. Gale Cengage Learning. • 2001. $295.00. Three volumes. Covers economic, social, and political events in about 230 countries. Includes statistical data, directories, and a bibliography.

BIBLIOGRAPHIES
Catalogue of Statistical Materials of Developing Countries. Institute of Developing Economies/Ajia

Keizai Kenkyusho. • Semiannual. Price varies. Text in English and Japanese.

Regional Economic Development: Theories amd Strategies for Developing Countries. Marguerite N. Abd El-Shahid. Sage Publications, Inc. • 1994. $10.00.

CD-ROM DATABASES
International Development Statistics. Organization for Economic Cooperation and Development. • Annual. $71.00. Issued by the OECD Development Assistance Committee. CD-ROM contains data on aid to more than 180 recipient countries, including amount, origin, type, and recipients' external debt.

Kompass Concord CD-ROM. Available from Kompass USA, Inc. • Semiannual. CD-ROM provides information on more than 280,000 companies in 17 rapidly developing East European countries: Armenia, Azerbaijan, Belarus, Bulgaria, Czech Republic, Estonia, Hungary, Kazakhstan, Kyrgyzstan, Latvia, Lithuania, Moldova, Poland, Romania, Russia, Ukraine, and Uzbekistan. Classification system covers approximately 50,000 products and services.

World Development Report [CD-ROM]. The World Bank, Office of the Publisher. • Annual. CD-ROM includes the current edition of *World Development Report* and 21 previous editions.

ENCYCLOPEDIAS AND DICTIONARIES
Worldmark Encyclopedia of National Economies. Gale Cengage Learning. • 2002. $325.00. Four volumes. Covers both the current and historical development of the economies of 200 foreign nations. Includes analysis and statistics.

HANDBOOKS AND MANUALS
Third World Handbook. Guy Arnold. Fitzroy Dearborn Publishers, Inc. • 1994. $45.00. Second revised edition. Published by Cassell Publications. Discusses background, organizations, and movements within each country and region. Includes maps and photographs.

INTERNET DATABASES
ETF Connect. Nuveen Investments. Phone: 800-257-8787 • URL: http://www.etfconnect.com • Free Web site makes available extensive, searchable information on individual closed-end investment funds, preferred share funds, and exchange-traded index funds. Information on a particular fund is available by name or as part of a classification (high yield, investment grade, municipal, emerging markets, global equity, etc.). Fund charts are available for various time periods, as is data concerning premiums or discounts, dividends, annualized total return, credit quality, "Top 10 Holdings," and so forth.

ONLINE DATABASES
EconLit. American Economic Association. • Covers the worldwide literature of economics as contained in selected monographs and about 550 journals. Subjects include microeconomics, macroeconomics, economic history, inflation, money, credit, finance, accounting theory, trade, natural resource economics, and regional economics. Time period is 1969 to present, with monthly updates. Inquire as to online cost and availability.

PERIODICALS AND NEWSLETTERS
Development Business. United Nations Publications. • Semimonthly. $495.00 per year. Provides leads on contract opportunities worldwide for engineering firms and multinational corporations. Text in English, French, Portuguese, and Spanish.

Emerging Markets Debt Report. Thomson Media. • Weekly. $895.00 per year. Newsletter. Provides information on new and prospective sovereign and corporate bond issues from developing countries. Includes an emerging market bond index and pricing data.

Emerging Markets Finance & Trade. M. E. Sharpe, Inc. • Bimonthly. $1,150.00 per year to institutions; $140.00 to individuals. Provides research papers on developing markets in Europe, Asia, Latin America, the Middle East, and Africa.

Emerging Markets Quarterly. Institutional Investor, Inc., Journals Group. • Quarterly. Price on application. Newsletter on financial markets in developing areas, such as Africa, Latin America, Southeast Asia, and Eastern Europe. Topics include institutional investment opportunities and regulatory matters. Formerly *Emerging Markets Weekly*.

Journal of Developing Areas. Tennessee State University. • Semiannual. Individuals, $30.00 per year; institutions, $36.50 per year.

The Journal of Development Studies. Frank Cass Publishers. • Bimonthly. Institutions, $490.00 per year. Includes print and online editions.

Journal of East-West Business. Haworth Press, Inc. • Quarterly. $300.00 per year; Includes print and online editions. An academic and practical journal focusing on business in the developing regions of Asia and Eastern Europe.

The Journal of International Trade and Economic Development. Taylor and Francis Group. • Quarterly. Individuals, $81.00 per year; institutions, $529.00 per year. Emphasizes the effect of trade on the economies of developing nations.

World Development. Elsevier. • Monthly. Qualified personnel, $286.00 per year; institutions, $1,887.00 per year; students, $84.00 per year.

RESEARCH CENTERS AND INSTITUTES
Center for International Policy. 1755 Massachusetts Ave., N. W., Ste. 550, Washington, DC 20036. Phone: (202)232-3317 Fax: (202)232-3440 E-mail: cip@ciponline.org • URL: http://www.ciponline.org • Research subjects include the International Monetary Fund, the World Bank, and other international financial institutions. Analyzes the impact of policies on social and economic conditions in developing countries.

Program in International Studies in Planning. Cornell University, Dept. of City Regional Planning, 106 W. Sibley Hall, Ithaca, NY 14853-3901. Phone: (607)255-4331 Fax: (607)255-1971 E-mail: bdl5@cornell.edu • URL: http://www.inet.crp.cornell.edu/organizations/isp • Research activities are related to international urban and regional planning, with emphasis on developing areas.

STATISTICS SOURCES
Emerging Stock Markets Factbook 1999. International Finance Corp. • 1998. $150.00. Provides statistical profiles for emerging stock markets in various countries of the world. Includes regional, composite, and industry indexes.

Global Development Finance. The World Bank Group. • Annual. $400.00.

Handbook of International Economic Statistics. Available from National Technical Information Service. • Annual. $40.00. Prepared by U. S. Central Intelligence Agency. Provides basic statistics for comparing worldwide economic performance, with an emphasis on Europe, including Eastern Europe.

Handbook of International Trade and Development Statistics. United Nations Publications. • Annual. $80.00. Text in English and French.

Least Developed Countries. United Nations Publications. • Annual. $45.00 Report on least developed countries compiled by the United Nations Conference on Trade and Development (UNCTAD). Contains basic data.

The Little Data Book. The World Bank. • 2003. $15.00. Contains "key development data for 208 countries," including country profiles and 54 statistical indicators relating to such factors as population, economics, trade, technology, finance, and environment.

MiniAtlas of Global Development. The World Bank. • 2003. $7.00. Presents concise data for 208 countries, based on the *World Bank Atlas* and other World Bank publications. Includes maps, tables, and graphs summarizing social, economic, and environmental statistics.

Monthly Bulletin of Statistics. United Nations Publications. • Monthly. $295.00 per year. Provides current data for about 200 countries on a wide variety of economic, industrial, and demographic subjects. Compiled by United Nations Statistical Office.

Nations of the World: A Political, Economic, and Business Handbook. Grey House Publishing. • 2002. $135.00. Third edition. Includes descriptive data on economic characteristics, population, gross domestic product (GDP), banking, inflation, agriculture, tourism, and other factors. Covers "all the nations of the world.".

Statistical Abstract of the World. Gale Cengage Learning. • 1997. $85.00. Third edition. Provides data on a wide variety of economic, social, and political topics for about 200 countries. Arranged by country.

Statistical Handbook on Poverty in the Developing World. Chandrika Kaul. Greenwood Publishing Group, Inc. • 1999. $69.95. Provides international coverage, including special sections on women and children, and on selected cities. (Statistical Handbooks Series).

Statistical Yearbook. United Nations Publications. • Annual. $125.00. Contains statistics for about 200 countries on a wide variety of economic, industrial, and demographic topics. Compiled by United Nations Statistical Office.

UNESCO Statistical Yearbook. Bernan Press. • 1998. $95.00. Co-published by Bernan Press and the United Nations Educational, Scientific, and Cultural Organization (http://www.unesco.org). Presents statistical data from more than 200 countries on education, technology, research, broadcasting, cinema, book publishing, newspapers, libraries, museums, and population. Includes charts, maps, and graphs.

The World Bank Atlas. World Bank Group. • Annual. $10.00. Contains "color maps, charts, and graphs representing the main social, economic, and environmental indicators for 209 countries and territories" (publisher).

World Development Indicators. The World Bank Group. • Annual. $60.00. Provides data and information on the people, economy, environment, and markets of 148 countries. Emphasis is on statistics relating to major development issues.

TRADE/PROFESSIONAL ASSOCIATIONS

International Development Association. The World Bank, 1818 H St. NW, Washington, DC 20433. Phone: (202)477-6391 or (202)473-1000 Fax: (202)477-6391 E-mail: info@idadesal.org • URL: http://www.worldbank.org • Functional member of the World Bank (see separate entry); membership is open to countries of the World Bank. Promotes the economic development of the World Bank's poorer member countries by extending credits on easier terms than are normally available. Makes loans for projects aimed at strengthening the economies of developing countries in Asia, the Middle East, Africa, and the Western Hemisphere. Provides economic advice.

National Democratic Institute for International Affairs. 2030 M St., NW, 5th Fl., Washington, DC 20036-3306. Phone: (202)728-5500 Fax: (202)728-5520 E-mail: contactndi@ndi.org • URL: http://www.ndi.org.

OXFAM America. 226 Causeway St., 5th Fl., Boston, MA 02114. Phone: 800-77-OXFAM or (617)482-1211 Fax: (617)728-2594 E-mail: info@oxfamamerica.org • URL: http://www.

oxfamamerica.org • Autonomous development and disaster assistance organization cooperating in a worldwide network known as Oxfam, a name derived from the Oxford Committee for Famine Relief, which began in England in 1942. Provides funds for self-help projects in the poorer countries of Asia, Africa, and the Americas. Emphasizes on promoting economic and food self-reliance. Responds to emergency needs of political and natural disaster refugees by funding food, water resources, and medical aid programs. Supports development programs that address underlying causes of such disasters. Educates U.S. public about root causes of hunger; advocates for policy changes.

Peaceworkers Nonviolent Peaceforce. 425 Oak Grove St., Minneapolis, MN 55403. Phone: (612)871-0005 Fax: (612)871-0006 E-mail: information@nonviolentpeaceforce.org • URL: http://www.nonviolentpeaceforce.org • Promotes the widespread implementation of effective nonviolent peacemaking in conflict areas around the world. Currently working to create the Nonviolent Peaceforce, an international organization to send hundreds and eventually thousands of trained peacemakers to work in areas of conflict at the invitation of local peacemakers or human rights workers. The Peace Force will be sent to conflict areas to prevent death and destruction, and protect human rights, thus creating the space for local groups to struggle nonviolently, enter into dialogue, and seek peaceful resolution.

Society for International Development USA. 1875 Connecticut Ave. NW, Washington, DC 20009. Phone: (202)884-8590 Fax: (202)884-8499 E-mail: sid@aed.org • URL: http://www.sidint.org.

OTHER SOURCES

World Migration Report. United Nations Publications. • Annual. $39.00. Analyzes major trends in world migration, including individual country profiles.

DEVELOPMENT, COMMUNITY

See: COMMUNITY DEVELOPMENT

DEVELOPMENT CREDIT CORPORATIONS

See: CREDIT

DEVELOPMENT, INDUSTRIAL

See: INDUSTRIAL DEVELOPMENT

DEVELOPMENT, URBAN

See: URBAN DEVELOPMENT

DIAMOND INDUSTRY

See also: GEMS AND GEMSTONES; INDUSTRIAL DIAMONDS

GENERAL WORKS

Diamonds. Irene Franck and David Brownstone. Scholastic Library Publishing. • 2003. $38.99. Price on application.

Diamonds and Conflict: Problems and Solutions. Arthur V. Levy. Nova Science Publishers, Inc. • 2003. $29.50. Describes reforms and legislative initiatives that have been undertaken in efforts to

stop illicit trade in diamonds ("conflict diamonds").

Diamonds and Precious Stones. Patrick Voillot. Abrams, Harry N., Inc. • 1998. $12.95. (Discoveries Series).

ALMANACS AND YEARBOOKS

Diamond Manufacturers and Importers Association of America Yearbook. • Annual.

DIRECTORIES

Jewelers' Circular/Keystone-Jewelers' Directory. Reed Business Information. • Annual. $33.95. About 8,500 manufacturers, importers and wholesale jewelers providing merchandise and supplies to the jewelry retailing industry; and related trade organizations. Included with subscription to *Jewelers' Circular Keystone.*

HANDBOOKS AND MANUALS

Diamond Ring Buying Guide: How to Evaluate, Identify, and Select Diamonds and Diamond Jewelry. Renee Newman. International Jewelry Publications. • 2003. $17.95. Sixth edition. A well known gemologist explains diamond "cut, color, clarity, and carat." Color photographs are included, as well as information on diamond settings.

PERIODICALS AND NEWSLETTERS

Diamond World Review. World Federation of Diamond Bourses. International Diamond Publications, Ltd. • Bimonthly. $78.00 per year. Text in English.

Israel Diamond and Precious Stones. International Diamond Publications, Ltd. • Bimonthly. $78.00 per year. Text in English. Formerly *Israel Diamonds.*

STATISTICS SOURCES

Mineral Commodity Summaries. Available from U. S. Government Printing Office. • Annual. $26.00. Published by the U. S. Geological Survey, Department of the Interior (http://www.usgs.gov). Contains detailed, five-year data for about 90 nonfuel minerals. Covers a wide range of statistics, including production, imports, exports, consumption, reserves, prices, tariff information, and industry employment. (Two pages are devoted to each mineral.).

TRADE/PROFESSIONAL ASSOCIATIONS

Diamond Council of America. c/o Jerry Fogel, 3212 W End Ave., Ste. 202, Nashville, TN 37203-5835. Phone: (615)385-5301 Fax: (615)385-4955 • URL: http://www.diamondcouncil.org.

Diamond Dealers Club. 580 5th Ave. at 11 W 47th St., New York, NY 10036. Phone: (212)869-9777 Fax: (212)869-5164 E-mail: mhochbaum@ddcny.com • URL: http://www.nyddc.com • Seeks to foster the interests of the diamond industry, promote equitable trade principles, eliminate abuses and unfair trade practices, disseminate accurate and reliable information concerning the industry, establish uniform business ethics, and cooperate with other persons and organizations for the advancement of the trade. Maintains active trading floor for all categories of wholesale diamonds and offers all members arbitration tribunals for dispute settlement. Operates charitable program.

Industrial Diamond Association. PO Box 29460, Columbus, OH 43229. Phone: (614)797-2265 Fax: (614)797-2264 E-mail: tkane-ida@insight.rr.com • URL: http://www.superabrasives.org • Represents industrial diamond, CBN, CVD diamond and polycrystalline and other superabrasive manufacturers, toolmakers, end users, contractors, machine tool builders and related suppliers.

DIAMONDS, INDUSTRIAL

See: INDUSTRIAL DIAMONDS

DICTATING MACHINES

See: OFFICE EQUIPMENT AND SUPPLIES

DIE CASTING

See: TOOL INDUSTRY

DIESEL ENGINES

See: ENGINES

DIET

See also: HEALTH FOOD INDUSTRY;
HERBS; VITAMINS

GENERAL WORKS

Fast Food Nation: The Dark Side of the All-American Meal. Eric Schlosser. Gale Cengage Learning. • 2001. $30.95. Explains how the fast food industry is contributing to obesity, disease, urban sprawl, and other bad things. Special attention is given to the meatpacking industry, *E.coli*, worker injuries, fast food franchise problems, detrimental labor practices, and the effect of fast food diets on children. Companies prominently mentioned are McDonald's, Burger King, Wendy's, Taco Bell, Pizza Hut, Jack in the Box, ConAgra, and Iowa Beef Packers. Includes many research notes, a bibliography, and a detailed index.

ABSTRACTS AND INDEXES

Nutrition Abstracts and Reviews, Series A: Human and Experimental. Available from CABI Publishing, North America. • Monthly. Institutions, $1,835.00 per year. Includes single site internet access. Published in England by CABI Publishing. Provides worldwide coverage of the literature.

CD-ROM DATABASES

Consumers Reference Disc. National Information Services Corp. • Quarterly. Provides the CD-ROM version of *Consumer Health and Nutrition Index* from Oryx Press and *Consumers Index to Product Evaluations and Information Sources* from Pierian Press. Contains citations to consumer health articles and consumer product evaluations, tests, warnings, and recalls.

Magazine Index Plus. Gale Cengage Learning. • Monthly. $4,000.00 per year (includes InfoTrac workstation). Provides full text on CD-ROM for about 100 popular, general interest magazines and indexing for 300 others. Includes special indexing of reviews and product evaluations. Time period is 1980 to date.

DIRECTORIES

American Society of Bariatric Physicians - Directory. American Society of Bariatric Physicians. • Annual. $50.00. Lists 1,300 physicians concerned with obesity.

ENCYCLOPEDIAS AND DICTIONARIES

CRC Desk Reference for Nutrition. Carolyn D. Berdanier. CRC Press LLC. • 1997. $79.95. Encyclopedic, alphabetical arrangement of topics. (Desk Reference Series).

Encyclopedia of Food and Culture. Gale Cengage Learning. • 2002. $395.00. Three volumes. Contains 600 articles covering various aspects of food and its place in society, from agronomy to zucchini. Includes illustrations and a detailed index.

Encyclopedia of Food Science, Food Technology, and Nutrition. Robert Macrae and others, editors. Elsevier. • 1993. Eight volumes. $3,056.00. $382.00 per volume.

Foods and Nutrition Encyclopedia. Audrey H. Ensminger and others. CRC Press, Inc. • 1993. $309.95. Second edition. Two volumes.

HANDBOOKS AND MANUALS

Advanced Nutrition: Micronutrients. Carolyn D. Berdanier. CRC Press LLC. • 2000. $119.95.

Provides detailed coverage of essential vitamins and minerals. Written for professional dietitions and nutritionists. (Modern Nutrition Series).

Calories and Carbohydrates: A Dictionary Listing of over 8500 Brand Names and Basic Foods with their Calorie and Carbohydrate Count. Barbara Kraus. NAL. • 2001. $6.99. 14th revised edition.

Diet and Meal Planning. Entrepreneur Media, Inc. • Looseleaf. $59.50. A practical guide to starting a diet and meal planning service. Covers profit potential, start-up costs, market size evaluation, pricing, accounting, advertising, promotion, etc. (Start-Up Business Guide No. E2333.).

Mayo Clinic Diet Manual: A Handbook of Nutrition Practices. Jennifer K. Nelson and others. Mosby Inc. • 1994. $79.00. Seventh edition.

Personal Health Reporter. Gale Cengage Learning. • 1992. $150.00. Two volumes. Volume one, $115.00; volume two, $115.00. Presents a collection of professional and popular articles on 150 topics relating to physical and mental health conditions and treatments.

INTERNET DATABASES

National Library of Medicine (NLM). National Institutes of Health (NIH). Phone: 888-346-3656 or (301)496-1131 Fax: (301)480-3537 E-mail: access@nlm.nih.gov • URL: http://www.nlm.nih.gov • NLM Web site offers free access through MEDLINE ("PubMed") to about nine million references to articles appearing in some 4,000 biomedical journals, with abstracts. Search interfaces range from "simple keywords to advanced Boolean expressions." The NLM site offers many links to other sources of biomedical and technical information (the National Center for Biotechnology Information, for example). Fees: Free.

ONLINE DATABASES

CAB Abstracts. CAB Publishing North America. • Contains 46 specialized abstract collections covering over 10,000 journals and monographs in the areas of agriculture, horticulture, forest products, farm products, nutrition, dairy science, poultry, grains, animal health, entomology, etc. Time period is 1972 to date, with monthly updates. Inquire as to online cost and availability. *CAB Abstracts on CD-ROM* also available, with annual updating.

PERIODICALS AND NEWSLETTERS

American Dietetic Association Journal. American Dietetic Association. Elsevier. • Monthly. Individuals, $208.00 per year; institutions, $288.00 per year.

American Journal of Clinical Nutrition: A Journal Reporting the Practical Application of Our World-Wide Knowledge of Nutrition. American Society for Clinical Nutrition, Inc. • Monthly, Individuals, $155.00 per year; Institutions, $245.00 per year; Students, $100.00 per year. Includes online edition.

Family Economics and Nutrition Review. Available from U. S. Government Printing Office. • Semi-annual. $13.00 per year. Issued by the Consumer and Food Economics Institute, U. S. Department of Agriculture. Provides articles on consumer expenditures and budgeting for food, clothing, housing, energy, education, etc.

International Journal for Vitamin and Nutrition Research. Hogrefe & Huber Publishers. • Quarterly. $202.00 per year.

Journal of Nutrition. American Society for Nutritional Science. • Bimonthly. Individuals, $175.00 per year; institutions, $550.00 per year.

Journal of Nutrition Education and Behavior. Society for Nutrition Education. B. C. Decker, Inc. • Bimonthly. Individuals, $159.00 per year; institutions, $234.00 per year.

Nutrition Reviews. International Life Science Institute. • Monthly. Individuals, $122.50 per year; institutions, $195.00 per year.

Nutrition Today. Lippincott Williams and Wilkins. • Bimonthly. Individuals, $69.00 per year; institutions, $169.00 per year.

RESEARCH CENTERS AND INSTITUTES

Institute of Human Nutrition. Columbia University. College of Physicians and Surgeons, 630 W. 168th St., PH 15E, Room 1512, New York, NY 10032. Phone: (212)305-4808 Fax: (212)305-3079 E-mail: rjd20@columbia.edu • URL: http://www.cpmcnet.columbia.edu/dept/ihn/.

STATISTICS SOURCES

Agriculture Fact Book. Available from U. S. Government Printing Office. • Annual. $26.00. Issued by the Office of Communications, U. S. Department of Agriculture. Includes data on U. S. agriculture, farmers, food, nutrition, and rural America. Programs of the Department of Agriculture in six areas are described: rural economic development, foreign trade, nutrition, the environment, inspection, and education.

TRADE/PROFESSIONAL ASSOCIATIONS

American Dietetic Association. 120 S Riverside Plz., Ste. 2000, Chicago, IL 60606-6995. Phone: 800-877-1600 or (312)899-0040 Fax: (312)899-1979 E-mail: rmoen@eatright.org • URL: http://www.eatright.org • Represents food and nutrition professionals. Promotes nutrition, health and well-being.

American Society for Nutritional Sciences. 9650 Rockville Pike, Bethesda, MD 20814-3990. Phone: (301)634-7050 Fax: (301)634-7892 E-mail: sec@asns.org • URL: http://www.asns.org • Affiliated with American Society for Clinical Nutrition. Formerly American Institute of Nutrition.

Natural Products Association. 2112 E 4th St., Ste. 200, Santa Ana, CA 92705. Phone: 800-966-6632 or (714)460-7732 Fax: (714)460-7444 E-mail: natural@naturalproductsassoc.org • URL: http://www.naturalproductsassoc.org • Represents retailers, wholesalers, brokers, distributors and manufacturers of natural, nutritional, dietetic foods, supplements, and natural body care products.

OTHER SOURCES

Weight Loss and Diet Control Market. Available from MarketResearch.com. • 2002. $795.00. Market research report published by Marketdata Enterprises. Covers commercial diet programs, medical plans, nonprescription appetite suppressants low-calorie foods, artifical sweeteners, health clubs, and diet books. Includes forecasts to the year 2006.

DIGITAL COMPUTERS

See: COMPUTERS

DIGITAL MEDIA

See: ELECTRONIC PUBLISHING;
MULTIMEDIA; ONLINE INFORMATION
SYSTEMS; OPTICAL DISK STORAGE
DEVICES

DINERS

See: RESTAURANTS, LUNCHROOMS, ETC.

DINNERWARE

See: TABLEWARE

DIPLOMATIC AND CONSULAR SERVICE

GENERAL WORKS

Safe Trip Abroad. Available from U. S. Government Printing Office. • 2002. $2.50. Issued by the Bureau of Consular Affairs, U. S. State Department (http://www.state.gov). Provides practical advice for international travel.

ABSTRACTS AND INDEXES

PAIS International in Print. Public Affairs Information Service, Inc. • Monthly. $850.00 per year; cumulations three times a year. Provides topical citations to the worldwide literature of public affairs, economics, demographics, sociology, and trade. Text in English; indexed materials in English, French, German, Italian, Portuguese and Spanish.

ALMANACS AND YEARBOOKS

The Statesman's Yearbook: Statistical and Historical Annual of the States of the World. Saint Martin's Press. • Annual. $120.00.

BIBLIOGRAPHIES

Diplomatic Bookshelf and Review. Arthur H. Thrower, Ltd. • Monthly. $4.00 per year.

CD-ROM DATABASES

Leadership Library on CD-ROM: Who's Who in the Leadership of the United States. Leadership Directories, Inc. • Quarterly. Including access to Internet version (weekly updates). Contains all 14 *Yellow Book* personnel directories on CD-ROM, providing contact and brief biographical information for about 400,000 individuals. Covers business, government, financial institutions, news media, law firms, associations, foreign representatives, and nonprofit organizations. Includes photographs.

PAIS on CD-ROM. Public Affairs Information Service, Inc. • Quarterly. $1,995.00 per year. Provides a CD-ROM version of the online service, *PAIS International.* Contains over 500,000 citations to the literature of contemporary social, political, and economic issues.

DIRECTORIES

Diplomatic List. U.S. Department of State. Department of Foreign Affairs and Trade. • Covers: offices of diplomatic representatives to Australia. Entries include: Diplomat name, delegation, office address, names of personnel with diplomatic status.

Foreign Consular Offices in the United States. U.S. Department of State. Available from U.S. Government Printing Office. • Semiannual. $17.00 per copy.

Foreign Representatives in the U. S. Yellow Book: Who's Who in the U. S. Offices of Foreign Corporations, Foreign Nations, the Foreign Press, and Intergovernmental Organizations. Leadership Directories, Inc. • Annual. $265.00 per year. Lists executives located in the U. S. for 1,200 foreign companies, 300 foreign banks and other financial institutions, 175 embassies and consulates, and 375 foreign press outlets. Includes five indexes.

United States Government Manual. National Archives and Records Administration. Office of the Federal Register. • Description: Provides information on the agencies of the executive, judicial, and legislative branches of the Federal government. Contains a section on terminated or transferred agencies.

ONLINE DATABASES

PAIS International. Public Affairs Information Service, Inc. • Corresponds to the former printed publications, *PAIS Bulletin* (1976-90) and *PAIS Foreign Language Index* (1972-90), and to the current *PAIS International in Print* (1991 to date). Covers economic, political, and sociological material appearing in periodicals, books, government documents, and other publications. Updating is monthly. Inquire as to online cost and availability.

PERIODICALS AND NEWSLETTERS

Diplomatic History. Society for Historians of American Foreign Relations. Blackwell Publishing.

• Quarterly. Institutions, $208.00 per year. Includes print and online edition.

Diplomatic Observer. Institute for International Sociological Research. • Monthly. $16.50 per year.

Diplomatic World Bulletin and Delegates World Bulletin: Dedicated to Serving the United Nations and the International Community. Diplomatic World Bulletin Publications, Inc. • Biweekly. $45.00 per year.

Foreign Service Journal. American Foreign Service Association. • Monthly. Individuals, $40.00 per year; students, $20.00 per year. Written for United States foreign service members.

Society for Historians of American Foreign Relations Newsletter. Society for Historians of American Foreign Relations. • Quarterly. $15.00 per year.

RESEARCH CENTERS AND INSTITUTES

Center of International Studies. Princeton University. Bendheim Hall, Princeton, NJ 08544. Phone: (609)258-4851 Fax: (609)258-3988 • URL: http://www.princeton.edu/cis.

TRADE/PROFESSIONAL ASSOCIATIONS

American Foreign Service Association. 2101 E St. NW, Washington, DC 20037. Phone: 800-704-AFSA or (202)338-4045 Fax: (202)338-6820 E-mail: member@afsa.org • URL: http://www.afsa.org • Associate membership is open to individuals and international organizations and corporations interested in foreign affairs, international trade, and economic policy. Conducts international conferences and symposia; holds monthly speaker programs. Operates the Foreign Service Club; sponsors member insurance programs. Maintains Speakers' Bureau.

Diplomatic and Consular Officers, Retired. 1801 F St., N.W., Washington, DC 20006. Phone: 800-344-9127 or (202)682-0500 Fax: (202)842-3295 E-mail: dacor@dacorbacon.org • URL: http://www.dacorbacon.org • Formerly Retired Foreign Service Officers Association.

DIRECT COSTING

See: COST ACCOUNTING

DIRECT DEBIT SYSTEMS

See: POINT-OF-SALE SYSTEMS (POS)

DIRECT MAIL ADVERTISING

See also: ADVERTISING; MAIL ORDER BUSINESS; MAILING LISTS

DIRECTORIES

Directory of Mail Order Catalogs. Grey House Publishing. • Annual. $165.00. Contains 12,000 entries for mail order companies selling consumer products throughout the U.S.

Directory of Mailing List Companies. Todd Publications. • Biennial. $75.00. Lists and describes approximately 1,000 of the most active list brokers, owners, managers and compilers.

Mail Order Business Directory. B. Klein Publications. • Covers: 5,000 firms in the United States and doing business by mail order and catalogs. Entries include: Name, address, phone, name of owner or contact, and products or services.

Plunkett's Advertising and Branding Industry Almanac. Plunkett Research, Ltd. • 2004. $249.99. Provides profiles of 300 leading firms in the areas of advertising, brand promotion, and corporate image, including marketing media, online advertising, and

direct mail. Also covers industry trends and statistical data.

Who's Who-Masa's Buyers' Guide to Blue Ribbon Mailing Service. Mailing and Fulfillment Service Association. • Annual. Free. Member firms that provide printing, addressing, inserting, sorting, and other mailing services, and mailing list brokers.

FINANCIAL RATIOS

Annual Statement Studies. The Risk Management Association. • Annual. Median and quartile financial ratios are given for over 400 kinds of manufacturing, wholesale, retail, construction, and consumer finance establishments. Data is sorted by both asset size and sales volume. Includes a clearly written "Definition of Ratios" and an alphabetical industry index.

Annual Statement Studies: Industry Default Probabilities and Cash Flow Measures. The Risk Management Association. • Annual. $145.00. Serves as a companion volume to the original *Annual Statement Studies.* Gives probability of default estimates on a percentage scale for more than 450 industries. Includes changes in position year-by-year for eight financial statement line items and provides percentage measures of cash flow.

HANDBOOKS AND MANUALS

Do-It-Yourself Advertising and Promotion: How to Produce Great Ads, Brochures, Catalogs, Direct Mail, Web Sites and more. Fred E. Hahn. John Wiley and Sons, Inc. • 2003. $19.95. Third edition. Covers magazines, newspapers, flyers, brochures, catalogs, direct mail, telemarketing, trade shows, and radio/TV promotions. Includes checklists. (Small Business Series).

The Greatest Direct Mail Sales Letters of All Time: Why They Succeed, How They Are Created, How You Can Create Great Sales Letters, Too. Richard S. Hodgson. Dartnell Corp. • 1995. $69.95. Second revised edition. About 100 direct mail sales lettes on a variety of products are reprinted and analyzed.

The Perfect Sales Piece: A Complete Do-It-Yourself Guide to Creating Brochures, Catalogs, Fliers, and Pamphlets. Robert W. Bly. John Wiley and Sons, Inc. • 1994. $50.00. A guide to the use of various forms of printed literature for direct selling, sales promotion, and marketing. (Small Business Series).

PERIODICALS AND NEWSLETTERS

Advertising Age: The International Newspaper of Marketing. Crain Communications, Inc. • Weekly. $178.50 per year. Includes supplement *Creativity.*

Database Marketer. SIMBA Information. • Monthly. $329.00 per year.

Direct Marketing: Using Direct Response Advertising to Enhance Marketing Database. Hoke Communications, Inc. • Monthly. $65.00 per year. Direct marketing to consumers and business.

DMA Washington Report: Federal and State Regulatory Issues of Concern. Direct Marketing Association. • Monthly. Membership.

Inside Direct Mail: The Monthly Newsletter Analysis and Record of the Direct Ma reting Archive. North American Publishing Co. • Monthly. $295.00 per year. Newsletter and listing of promotional mailings. Photocopies of mailings are available to subscribers. Formerly *Who's Mailing What!.*

Public Affairs Report. Institute of Governmental Studies. • Description: Publishes essays on emerging governmental and public policy issues of significance to public officials and citizens in both California and the nation. Covers such subjects as pollution, politics, finance, transportation, health and housing policy, and California-Mexico trade relations. Recurring features include bibliographies.

Target Marketing: The Leading Magazine for Integrated Database Marketing. North American

Publishing Co. • Monthly. $65.00 per year. Dedicated to direct marketing excellence. Formerly *Zip Target Marketing*.

STATISTICS SOURCES

DMA Statistical Fact Book. Direct Marketing Association. Library and Resource Center. • Annual. Members, $79.95; non-members, $104.95. Provides data in five sections covering direct response advertising, media, mailing lists, market applications, and "Practical Management Information." Includes material on interactive/online marketing. (Cover title: *Direct Marketing Association's Statistical Fact Book.*).

TRADE/PROFESSIONAL ASSOCIATIONS

Alliance of Nonprofit Mailers. 1211 Connecticut Ave., No. 620, Washington, DC 20036. Phone: (202)462-5132 Fax: (202)462-0423 E-mail: alliance@nonprofitmailers.org • URL: http://www.nonprofitmailers.org.

Direct Marketing Association. 1120 Ave. of the Americas, New York, NY 10036-6700. Phone: (212)768-7277 Fax: (212)302-6714 E-mail: presiden@the-dma.org • URL: http://www.the-dma.org • Manufacturers, wholesalers, public utilities, retailers, mail order firms, publishers, schools, clubs, insurance companies, financial organizations, business equipment manufacturers, paper and envelope manufacturers, list brokers, compilers, managers, owners, computer service bureaus, advertising agencies, letter shops, research organizations, printers, lithographers, creators, and producers of direct mail and direct response advertising. Studies consumer and business attitudes toward direct mail and related direct marketing statistics. Offers Mail Preference Service for consumers who wish to receive less mail advertising, Mail Order Action Line to help resolve difficulties with mail order purchases, and Telephone Preference Service for people who wish to receive fewer telephone sales calls. Maintains hall of fame; offers placement service; compiles statistics. Sponsors several three-day Basic Direct Marketing Institutes, Advanced Direct Marketing Institutes, and special interest seminars and workshops. Maintains Government Affairs office in Washington, DC. Operates Direct Marketing Educational Foundation.

Direct Marketing Educational Foundation. 1120 Ave. of the Americas, New York, NY 10036-6700. Phone: (212)768-7277 Fax: (212)790-1561 E-mail: dmef@the-dma.org • URL: http://www.the-dma.org/dmef • Represents individuals, firms, and organizations interested in furthering college-level education in direct marketing. Functions as the collegiate arm of the direct marketing profession. Sponsors a summer internship, programs for students and professors, and campaign competition for students. Provides educational materials and course outlines to faculty members; arranges for speakers for college classes and clubs. Co-sponsors academic research competitions. Maintains hall of fame.

DMA Nonprofit Federation. 1615 L St. NW, Ste. 1100, Washington, DC 20036. Phone: (202)628-4380 Fax: (202)628-4383 E-mail: nonprofitfederation@the-dma.org • URL: http://www.the-dma.org/nonprofitfederation • Trade and lobbying group for non-profit organizations that use direct and online marketing to raise funds and communicate with members. Sponsors professional development conferences and seminars, lobbies on state and federal legislation, regulation, and standards related to direct marketing and related issues. Provides information about and participants in litigation affecting non-profits. Promotes the overall welfare of non-profits. Represents health care charities, social service agencies, religious groups, colleges and universities and fraternal organizations.

Mailing and Fulfillment Service Association. 1421 Prince St., Alexandria, VA 22314-2806. Phone: 800-

333-6272 or (703)836-9200 Fax: (703)548-8204 E-mail: masa-mail@mfsanet.org • URL: http://www.mfsanet.org • Formerly Mail Advertising Service Association International.

DIRECT MARKETING

GENERAL WORKS

Creative Strategy in Direct Marketing. Susan K. Jones. McGraw-Hill. • 1993. $39.95. Second edition. (NTC Business Books Series).

Direct Marketing, Direct Selling, and the Mature Consumer: A Research Study. James R. Lumpkin and others. Greenwood Publishing Group, Inc. • 1989. $64.95. A study of older consumers and their use of mail order, telephone shopping, party-plans, etc.

Do-It-Yourself Direct Marketing: Secrets for Small Business. Mark S. Bacon. John Wiley and Sons, Inc. • 1997. $19.95. Second edition.

ABSTRACTS AND INDEXES

Business Periodicals Index. H. W. Wilson Co. • 11 times a year. Quarterly and annual cumulations. Price varies.

DIRECTORIES

AMA International Member and Marketing Services Guide. American Marketing Association. • Annual. $150.00. Lists professional members of the American Marketing Association. Also contains information on providers of marketing support services and products, including software, communications, direct marketing, promotion, research, and consulting companies. Includes geographical and alphabetical indexes. Formerly *Marketing Yellow Pages and AMA International Membership Directory.*

Catalog Age--Direct Sourcebook. Primedia Business. • Publication includes: List of approximately 300 suppliers of equipment, products, and services to the direct marketing industry; related trade associations. Entries include: Name, address, phone, key personnel, geographical area covered, description of products or services, branch offices or subsidiary names and locations.

Direct Marketing Market Place: The Networking Source of the Direct Marketing Industry. LexisNexis. • Annual. $324.99. Lists direct marketers, service companies, creative sources, professional groups, photographers, paper suppliers, etc.

SRDS Direct Marketing List Source. SRDS. • Bimonthly. $561.00 per year. Provides detailed information and rates for business, farm, and consumer mailing lists (U. S., Canadian, and international). Includes current postal information and directories of list brokers, compilers, and managers. Formerly *Direct Mail List Source.*

WFDSA Directory of Members (World Federation of Direct Selling Association). World Federation of Direct Selling Associations. • Annual. Price on application.

ENCYCLOPEDIAS AND DICTIONARIES

Dictionary of Marketing Communications. Norman A. P. Govoni. Sage Publications, Inc. • 2003. $69.95. Contains more than 4,000 concise definitions of terms relating to advertising, sales promotion, public relations, direct marketing, and selling.

HANDBOOKS AND MANUALS

Direct Marketing Success: What Works and Why. Freeman F. Gosden. John Wiley and Sons, Inc. • 1989. $24.95.

The New Direct Marketing: How to Implement a Profit-Driven Database Marketing Strategy. McGraw-Hill. • 1999. $79.95. Third edition. Discusses the construction, analysis, practical use, and evaluation of direct marketing databases containing primary and/or secondary data.

Sales Manager's Handbook. John P. Steinbrink. Dartnell Corp. • 1989. $93.50. 14th edition.

ONLINE DATABASES

Wilson Business Abstracts Online. H. W. Wilson Co. • Indexes and abstracts 600 major business periodicals, plus the *Wall Street Journal* and the business section of the *New York Times*. Indexing is from 1982, abstracting from 1990, with the two newspapers included from 1993. Updated weekly. Inquire as to online cost and availability. (*Business Periodicals Index* without abstracts is also available online.).

PERIODICALS AND NEWSLETTERS

Catalog Age. PRIMEDIA Business Magazine and Media. • 13 times a year. Free to qualified personnel; others, $85.00 per year. Edited for catalog marketing and management personnel.

Direct: Magazine for Direct Marketing Management. Primedia Business Magazines and Media. • 16 times a year. Free to qualified personnel; others, $85.00 per year.

Direct Marketing: Using Direct Response Advertising to Enhance Marketing Database. Hoke Communications, Inc. • Monthly. $65.00 per year. Direct marketing to consumers and business.

Direct Selling Association World Federation News. Direct Selling Association. World Federation of Direct Selling Associations. • Six times a year. Membership.

DM News: The Newspaper of Direct Marketing. Courtenay Communications Corp. • 48 times a year. $49.00 per year. Includes special feature issues on catalog marketing, telephone marketing, database marketing, and fundraising. Includes monthly supplements, *DM News International*, *DRTV News*, and *TeleServices*.

Fred Goss' What's Working in Direct Marketing. United Communications Group (UCG). • Biweekly. $242.00 per year. Newsletter. Provides ideas for direct marketing promotions.

Inside Direct Mail: The Monthly Newsletter Analysis and Record of the Direct Ma reting Archive. North American Publishing Co. • Monthly. $295.00 per year. Newsletter and listing of promotional mailings. Photocopies of mailings are available to subscribers. Formerly *Who's Mailing What!.*

Journal of Interactive Marketing. Direct Marketing Educational Foundation. John Wiley and Sons, Inc., Journals. • Quarterly. Institutions, $699.00 per year; with online edition, $734.00 per year. Exchange of ideas in the field of direct marketing. Formerly *Journal of Direct Marketing.*

STATISTICS SOURCES

DMA Statistical Fact Book. Direct Marketing Association. Library and Resource Center. • Annual. Members, $79.95; non-members, $104.95. Provides data in five sections covering direct response advertising, media, mailing lists, market applications, and "Practical Management Information." Includes material on interactive/online marketing. (Cover title: *Direct Marketing Association's Statistical Fact Book.*).

TRADE/PROFESSIONAL ASSOCIATIONS

Direct Marketing Educational Foundation. 1120 Ave. of the Americas, New York, NY 10036-6700. Phone: (212)768-7277 Fax: (212)790-1561 E-mail: dmef@the-dma.org • URL: http://www.the-dma.org/dmef • Represents individuals, firms, and organizations interested in furthering college-level education in direct marketing. Functions as the collegiate arm of the direct marketing profession. Sponsors a summer internship, programs for students and professors, and campaign competition for students. Provides educational materials and course outlines to faculty members; arranges for speakers for college classes and clubs. Co-sponsors academic research competitions. Maintains hall of fame.

Direct Selling Association. 1667 K St. NW, Ste. 1100, Washington, DC 20006. Phone: (202)452-8866 Fax: (202)452-9010 E-mail: info@dsa.org • URL: http://www.dsa.org • Manufacturers and distributors selling consumer products through person-to-person sales, by appointment, and through home-party plans. Products include food, gifts, house wares, dietary supplements, cosmetics, apparel, jewelry, decorative accessories, reference books, and telecommunications products and services. Offers specialized education; conducts research programs; compiles statistics. Maintains hall of fame. Sponsors Direct Selling Education Foundation (see separate entry).

DIRECT SELLING

See: DIRECT MARKETING

DIRECTORIES

See: CATALOGS AND DIRECTORIES

DIRECTORS

See: CORPORATE DIRECTORS AND OFFICERS

DISABILITY INSURANCE

See also: EMPLOYEE BENEFIT PLANS

GENERAL WORKS

Smarter Insurance Solutions. Janet Bamford. Bloomberg. • 1996. $19.95. Provides practical advice to consumers, with separate chapters on the following kinds of insurance: automobile, homeowners, health, disability, and life. (Bloomberg Personal Bookshelf Series).

Social Security, Medicare, and Government Pensions: Get the Most Out of Your Retirement and Medical Benefits. Joseph Matthews and Dorothy M. Berman. Nolo. • 2002. $29.99. Eighth edition. In addition to the basic topics, includes practical information on Supplemental Security Income (SSI), disability benefits, veterans benefits, 401(k) plans, Medicare HMOs, medigap insurance, Medicaid, and how to appeal decisions. (Social Security, Medicare and Pensions Series).

ABSTRACTS AND INDEXES

Business Periodicals Index. H. W. Wilson Co. • 11 times a year. Quarterly and annual cumulations. Price varies.

Current Law Index: Multiple Access to Legal Periodicals. Gale Cengage Learning. • Monthly. $725.00 per year. Produced in cooperation with the American Association of Law Libraries. Indexes more than 900 law journals, legal newspapers, and specialty publications from the U.S., Canada, U.K., Ireland, Australia, and New Zealand.

Index to Legal Periodicals and Books. H. W. Wilson Co. • Monthly. $490.00 per year. Quarterly and annual cumulations.

Insurance Periodicals Index. Specials Libraries Association, Insurance and Employees Benefits Div. NILS Publishing Co. • Annual. $250.00. Compiled by the Insurance and Employee Benefits Div., Special Libraries Association. A yearly index of over 15,000 articles from about 35 insurance periodicals. Arrangement is by subject, with an index to authors.

ALMANACS AND YEARBOOKS

American Law Yearbook. Gale Cengage Learning. • Annual. $165.00. Serves as a yearly supplement to

West's Encyclopedia of American Law. Describes new legal developments in many subject areas.

BIBLIOGRAPHIES

Insurance and Employee Benefits Literature. Special Libraries Association, Insurance and Employee Benefits Div. • Bimonthly. $15.00 per year. Lists a wide variety of literature in all branches of the insurance industry. Includes annotations.

CD-ROM DATABASES

U. S. Insurance: Life, Accident, and Health. Sheshunoff Information Services, Inc. • Monthly. Price on application. CD-ROM provides detailed, current information on the financial characteristics of more than 2,300 life, accident, and health insurance companies.

WILSONDISC: Index to Legal Periodicals and Books. H. W. Wilson Co. • Monthly. Includes unlimited online access to *Index to Legal Periodicals* through WILSONLINE. Contains CD-ROM indexing of more than 1,400 English language legal periodicals from 1981 to date and 2,500 books.

WILSONDISC: Wilson Business Abstracts. H. W. Wilson Co. • Monthly. Includes unlimited online access to *Wilson Business Abstracts* through WILSONLINE. Provides CD-ROM "cover-to-cover" abstracting and indexing of over 600 prominent business periodicals. Indexing is from 1982, abstracting from 1990. (*Business Periodicals Index* without abstracts is available on CD-ROM at $1,495 per year.).

ENCYCLOPEDIAS AND DICTIONARIES

Glossary of Insurance Policy Terms. Organization for Economic Cooperation and Development. • 1999. $30.00. "The selected topics range from insurance policy regulation/supervision to general trade issues and include technical terms related to issues such as claims, premiums, and provisions." Edited for government, academic, business, and insurance organizations.

West's Encyclopedia of American Law. Available from Gale Cengage Learning. • 2003. $1,195.00. Second edition. 12 volumes. Published by West Group. Covers a wide variety of legal topics for the general reader.

HANDBOOKS AND MANUALS

The Complete Book of Insurance: Protecting Your Life, Health Property, and Income. Ben G. Baldwin. McGraw-Hill. • 1991. $24.95. Provides basic information and advice on various kinds of insurance: life, health, property (fire), disability, long-term care, automobile, liability, and annuities.

U. S. Master Employee Benefits Guide. CCH, Inc. • $56.95. Seventh edition. Explains federal tax and labor laws relating to health care benefits, disability benefits, workers' compensation, employee assistance plans, etc.

INTERNET DATABASES

Lexis.com Research System. Lexis-Nexis Group. Phone: 800-227-4908 or (937)865-6800 Fax: (937)865-6909 E-mail: webmaster@prod.lexis-nexis.com • URL: http://www.lexis.com • Fee-based Web site offers extensive searching of a wide variety of legal sources. Additional features include Daily Opinion Service, lexis.com Bookstore, Career Center, CLE Center, Law Schools, and Practice Pages ("Pages specific to areas of specialty").

Social Security Online: The Official Web Site of the Social Security Administration. U. S. Social Security Administration. Phone: 800-772-1213 or (410)965-7700 • URL: http://www.ssa.gov • Web site provides a wide variety of online information relating to social security and Medicare. Topics include benefits, disability, employer wage reporting, personal earnings statements, statistics, government

financing, social security law, and public welfare reform legislation.

ONLINE DATABASES

I.I.I. Data Base Search. Insurance Information Institute. • Provides online citations and abstracts of insurance-related literature in magazines, newspapers, trade journals, and books. Emphasis is on property and casualty insurance issues, including highway safety, product safety, and environmental liability. Inquire as to online cost and availability.

Index to Legal Periodicals and Books (Online). H. W. Wilson Co. • Broad coverage of law journals and books 1981 to date. Monthly updates. Inquire as to online cost and availability.

Management Contents. Gale Cengage Learning. • Covers a wide range of management, financial, marketing, personnel, and administrative topics. About 150 leading business journals are indexed and abstracted from 1974 to date, with monthly updating. Inquire as to online cost and availability.

Wilson Business Abstracts Online. H. W. Wilson Co. • Indexes and abstracts 600 major business periodicals, plus the *Wall Street Journal* and the business section of the *New York Times.* Indexing is from 1982, abstracting from 1990, with the two newspapers included from 1993. Updated weekly. Inquire as to online cost and availability. (*Business Periodicals Index* without abstracts is also available online.).

PERIODICALS AND NEWSLETTERS

Advisor Today. National Association of Insurance and Finacial Advisors. • Monthly. Free to members; non-members, $7.00 per year. Edited for individual life and health insurance agents. Among the topics included are disability insurance and long-term care insurance. Formerly Life Association News.

Broker World. Insurance Publications, Inc. • Bimonthly. $6.00 per year. Edited for independent insurance agents and brokers. Special feature issue topics include annuities, disability insurance, estate planning, and life insurance.

Health Insurance Underwriter. National Association of Health Underwriters. • Monthly. $25.00 per year. Includes special feature issues on long-term care insurance, disability insurance, managed health care, and insurance office management.

Jounal of Finacial Services Professionals. Society of Financial Services Professional. • Bimonthly. $95.00 per year. Provides information on life insurance and financial planning, including estate planning, retirement, tax planning, trusts, business insurance, long-term care insurance, disability insurance, and employee benefits. Formerly (American Society of CLU and Ch F C Journal).

TRADE/PROFESSIONAL ASSOCIATIONS

Health Insurance Association of America. 1201 F St., N.W., No. 500, Washington, DC 20004. Phone: (202)824-1600 Fax: (202)824-1722 E-mail: jbalda@hiaa.org • URL: http://www.hiaa.org • Members are commercial health insurers. Includes a Disability Insurance Committee, a Medicare Administration Committee, and a Long-Term Care Committee.

National Association of Health Underwriters. 200 N. 14th St., Suite. 450, Arlington, VA 22201. Phone: (703)276-0220 Fax: (703)841-7797 E-mail: info@nahu.org • URL: http://www.nahu.org • Members are engaged in the sale of health and disability insurance. Formerly International Association of Health Underwriters.

National Association of Insurance and Financial Advisors. 2901 Telestar Court, Falls Church, VA 22042-1205. Phone: 877-866-2432 or (703)770-8100 Fax: (703)770-8142 E-mail: membersupport@naifa.org • URL: http://www.naifa.org • Affiliated with Association for Advanced Life Underwriting. Formerly National Association of Life Underwriters.

DISABLED

See: HANDICAPPED WORKERS

DISCHARGED SERVICEMEN

See: VETERANS

DISCIPLINE OF EMPLOYEES

See: EMPLOYEE DISCIPLINE

DISCOUNT HOUSES

See also: CHAIN STORES; DEPARTMENT STORES; MARKETING; RETAIL TRADE

DIRECTORIES

Discount Store News - Top Chains. Lebhar-Friedman, Inc. • Annual. $79.00.

Phelon's Discount/Jobbing Trade. Phelon, Sheldon & Marsar Inc. • Covers: Approximately 2,050 mass merchandisers, including discount stores and discount chains, TV shopping clubs, wholesalers clubs, drug store chains, auto chains, toy store chains, audio and TV chains, leased department operators, catalog showrooms; also includes 5,000 jobbers, wholesalers, and distributors of all types of merchandise. Entries include: Company name, address, phone, names and titles of key executives, sales volume, number of stores, resident buying offices, merchandise lines with buyers' names, trade and brand names.

Plunkett's Retail Industry Almanac: Complete Profiles on the Retail 500-The Leading Firms in Retail Stores, Services, Catalogs, and On-Line Sales. Plunkett Research, Ltd. • 2001. $229.99. Includes CD-ROM. Provides detailed profiles of 500 major U. S. retailers. Industry trends are discussed.

INTERNET DATABASES

Advance Monthly Sales for Retail Trade and Food Services. U. S. Census Bureau. Phone: 800-541-8345 or (301)763-4636 Fax: (301)457-3842 E-mail: rcb@census.gov • URL: http://www.census.gov/svsd/www/fullpub.html • Web pages provide monthly sales figures for a wide range of retail businesses. Advance, preliminary, and final statistics are provided for the latest month available in each case, with a previous-year comparison. Updates are monthly.

PERIODICALS AND NEWSLETTERS

Chain Store Age: The NewsMagazine for Retail Executives. Lebhar-Friedman, Inc. • Monthly. $105.00 per year. Formerly *Chain Store Age Executive with Shopping Center Age.*

DSN Retailing Today (Discount Store News). Lebhar-Friedman, Inc. • 23 times a year. $119.00 per year. Includes supplement *Apparel Merchandising.* Formerly (Discount Store News).

Retail Merchandiser. • Monthly. $55.00 per year. Mass merchandising retail industry. Formerly *Discount Merchandiser.*

Value Retail News: The Journal of Outlet and Off-Price Retail and Development. Off-Price Specialists, Inc. Value Retail News. • Monthly. Members, $144.00 per year; non-members, $175.00 per year. Provides news of the off-price and outlet store industry. Emphasis is on real estate for outlet store centers.

RESEARCH CENTERS AND INSTITUTES

Center for Retail Management. Kellogg School of Management, Northwestern University, 2001 Sheridan Rd., Evanston, IL 60208. Phone: (847)467-3600 Fax: (847)467-3620 E-mail: r-blattberg@kellogg.

northwestern.edu • URL: http://www.kellogg.northwestern.edu • Conducts research related to retail marketing and management.

Center for Retailing Studies. Texas A & M University, Department of Marketing, 4112 TAMU, College Station, TX 77843-4112. Phone: (979)845-0325 Fax: (979)845-5230 E-mail: d-szymanski@tamu.edu • URL: http://www.crstamu.org • Research areas include retailing issues and consumer economics.

STATISTICS SOURCES

Annual Benchmark Report for Retail Trade and Food Services...A Detailed Summary of Retail Sales, Purchases, Accounts Receivable, Inventories, and Food Service Sales. Available from U. S. Government Printing Office. • Annual. $13.00. Issued by the U.S. Census Bureau. Provides detailed annual and monthly retail statistics for the most recent 10 years. Includes data for various kinds of retail outlets, including automobiles, furniture, appliances, building supplies, grocery stores, drug stores, gasoline stations, clothing, sporting goods, department stores, and restaurants.

TRADE/PROFESSIONAL ASSOCIATIONS

International Mass Retail Association. 1700 N. Moore St., Suite 2250, Arlington, VA 22209. Phone: (703)841-2300 Fax: (703)841-1184 E-mail: klasu@imra.org • URL: http://www.imra.org • Formerly National Mass Retailing Institute.

National Association of Wholesaler-Distributors. 1725 K St., N.W., Ste. 00, Washington, DC 20006. Phone: (202)872-0885 Fax: (202)785-0586 E-mail: naw@nawd.org • URL: http://www.naw.org • Formerly National Association of Wholesalers.

DISCOVERIES, SCIENTIFIC AND TECHNOLOGICAL

See: INVENTIONS; PATENTS

DISCRIMINATION IN EMPLOYMENT

See: AFFIRMATIVE ACTION PROGRAMS

DISHWARE

See: TABLEWARE

DISINFECTION AND DISINFECTANT

See: SANITATION INDUSTRY

DISK STORAGE DEVICES, OPTICAL

See: OPTICAL DISK STORAGE DEVICES

DISMISSAL OF EMPLOYEES

See also: JOB HUNTING; UNEMPLOYMENT

GENERAL WORKS

Healing the Wounds: Overcoming the Trauma of Layoffs, and Revitalizing Downsized Organizations. David M. Noer. John Wiley and Sons, Inc. • 1993. $34.00. (Management Series).

PR News Casebook. Gale Cengage Learning. • 1993. $110.00. A collection of about 1,000 case studies covering major public relations campaigns

and events, taken from the pages of *PR News.* Covers such issues as boycotts, new products, anniversaries, plant closings, downsizing, and stockholder relations.

When You Lose Your Job: Laid Off, Fired, Early Retired, Relocated, Demoted. Cliff Hakim. Berrett-Koehler Publishers, Inc. • 1993. $14.95. A guide to overcoming job loss. Covers emotional responses, as well as practical matters such as networking, resumes, and preparing for interviews.

ABSTRACTS AND INDEXES

Business Periodicals Index. H. W. Wilson Co. • 11 times a year. Quarterly and annual cumulations. Price varies.

Current Law Index: Multiple Access to Legal Periodicals. Gale Cengage Learning. • Monthly. $725.00 per year. Produced in cooperation with the American Association of Law Libraries. Indexes more than 900 law journals, legal newspapers, and specialty publications from the U.S., Canada, U.K., Ireland, Australia, and New Zealand.

Human Resources Abstracts: An International Information Service. Sage Publications, Inc. • Quarterly. Institutions, $968.00 per year; includes print and online editions.

Index to Legal Periodicals and Books. H. W. Wilson Co. • Monthly. $490.00 per year. Quarterly and annual cumulations.

Personnel Management Abstracts. • Quarterly. $190.00 per year. Includes annual cumulation.

ALMANACS AND YEARBOOKS

American Law Yearbook. Gale Cengage Learning. • Annual. $165.00. Serves as a yearly supplement to *West's Encyclopedia of American Law.* Describes new legal developments in many subject areas.

CD-ROM DATABASES

WILSONDISC: Index to Legal Periodicals and Books. H. W. Wilson Co. • Monthly. Includes unlimited online access to *Index to Legal Periodicals* through WILSONLINE. Contains CD-ROM indexing of more than 1,400 English language legal periodicals from 1981 to date and 2,500 books.

DIRECTORIES

Business Organizations, Agencies, and Publications Directory. Gale Cengage Learning. • 2003. $480.00. 15th edition. Over 40,000 entries describing 39 types of business information sources. Classified by type of organization, publication, or serviceIncludes state, national, and international agencies and organizations. Master index to names and keywords. Also includes e-mail addresses and web site URL's.

Directory of Outplacement and Career Management Firms. Kennedy Information, Inc. • Annual. $149.95. Contains profiles of more than 390 firms specialize in helping "downsized" executives find new employment. Formerly *Directory of Outplacement Firms.*

ENCYCLOPEDIAS AND DICTIONARIES

West's Encyclopedia of American Law. Available from Gale Cengage Learning. • 2003. $1,195.00. Second edition. 12 volumes. Published by West Group. Covers a wide variety of legal topics for the general reader.

HANDBOOKS AND MANUALS

Employment Termination: Rights and Remedies. William J. Holloway and Michael J. Leech. BNA, Inc. • 1993. $145.00. Second edition. Discusses employment contracts and wrongful-discharge claims.

Fair, Square, and Legal: Safe Hiring, Managing, and Firing Practices to Keep You and Your Company Out of Court. Donald Weiss. AMACOM. • 1999. $29.95. Third edition. Covers recruiting, interviewing, sexual discrimination, evaluation of

---

employees, disipline, defamation charges, and wrongful discharge.

The Federal Manager's Handbook: A Guide to Rehabilitating or Removing the Problem Employee. G. Jerry Shaw and William L. Bransford. FPMI Communications, Inc. • 1997. $29.95. Third revised edition.

The Hiring and Firing Book: A Complete Legal Guide for Employers. Steven M. Sack. Legal Strategies, Inc. • 1996. $149.95. Revised edition. Covers a wide range of legal considerations relative to employment and dismissal. Includes checklists, a glossary, and samples of applications, agreements, contracts, and other documents.

WARN Act: A Manager's Compliance Guide to Workforce Reductions. Joseph A. Brislin. BNA, Inc. • 1990. $195.00.

INTERNET DATABASES

EBSCO Information Services. Ebsco Publishing. Phone: 800-653-2726 or (978)356-6500 Fax: (978)356-6565 E-mail: ep@epnet.com • URL: http://www.epnet.com • Fee-based Web site providing Internet access to a wide variety of databases, including business-related material. Full text is available for many periodical titles, with daily updates. Fees: Apply.

InSite 2. Intelligence Data/Thomson Financial. Phone: 800-654-0393 or (617)856-1890 Fax: (617)737-3182 E-mail: intelligence.data@tfn.com • URL: http://www.insite2.gale.com/ • Fee-based Web site consolidates information in a "Base Pack" consisting of Business InSite, Market InSite, and Company InSite. Optional databases are Consumer InSite, Health and Wellness InSite, Newsletter InSite, and Computer InSite. Includes fulltext content from more than 2,500 trade publications, journals, newsletters, newspapers, analyst reports, and other sources. Continuous updating. Formerly produced by The Gale Group.

Lexis.com Research System. Lexis-Nexis Group. Phone: 800-227-4908 or (937)865-6800 Fax: (937)865-6909 E-mail: webmaster@prod.lexis-nexis.com • URL: http://www.lexis.com • Fee-based Web site offers extensive searching of a wide variety of legal sources. Additional features include Daily Opinion Service, lexis.com Bookstore, Career Center, CLE Center, Law Schools, and Practice Pages ("Pages specific to areas of specialty").

ProQuest Direct. ProQuest Inc. Phone: 800-889-3358 or (734)761-4700 Fax: (734)662-4554 • URL: http://proquest.com • Fee-based Web site providing Internet access to more than 3,000 periodicals, newspapers, and other publications. Many items are available full-text, with daily updates. Includes extensive corporate and financial information. Fees: Apply.

ONLINE DATABASES

Index to Legal Periodicals and Books (Online). H. W. Wilson Co. • Broad coverage of law journals and books 1981 to date. Monthly updates. Inquire as to online cost and availability.

Wilson Business Abstracts Online. H. W. Wilson Co. • Indexes and abstracts 600 major business periodicals, plus the *Wall Street Journal* and the business section of the *New York Times*. Indexing is from 1982, abstracting from 1990, with the two newspapers included from 1993. Updated weekly. Inquire as to online cost and availability. (*Business Periodicals Index* without abstracts is also available online.).

PERIODICALS AND NEWSLETTERS

Employee Terminations Law Bulletin. Quinlan Publishing Co. • Description: Advises employers on preventable errors and lawful procedure regarding employee dismissal. Reports on court decisions involving employee terminations.

HR Briefing (Human Resources). Aspen Publishers.

• Monthly. $249.00 per year. Newsletter. Provides HR professionals and other business people with concise, up-to-date information on employment practices and trends, with an emphasis on compliance with federal employment laws.

ReCareering Newsletter: An Idea and Resource Guide to Second Career and Relocation Planning. Publications Plus, Inc. • Monthly. $59.00 per year. Edited for "downsized managers, early retirees, and others in career transition after leaving traditional employment." Offers advice on second careers, franchises, starting a business, finances, education, training, skills assessment, and other matters of interest to the newly unemployed.

TRADE/PROFESSIONAL ASSOCIATIONS

Association of Career Management Consulting Firms International. 204 E St., NE, Washington, DC 20002. Phone: (202)547-6344 Fax: (202)547-6348 E-mail: aocfi@aocfi.org • URL: http://www.aocfi.org • Firms providing displaced employees who are sponsored by their organization, with counsel and assistance in job searching and the techniques and practices of choosing a career.

OTHER SOURCES

Corporate Compliance Series. Joseph E. Murphy and Paul H. Dawes. West Group. • $1,210.00. 12 looseleaf volumes. Covers criminal and civil liability problems for corporations. Includes employee safety, product liability, pension requirements, securities violations, equal employment opportunity issues, intellectual property, employee hiring and firing, and other corporate compliance topics.

Employment Litigation Reporter: The National Journal of Record for Termination Lawsuits Alleging Tort and Contract Claims Against Employers. Andrews Publications. • Semimonthly. $825.00 per year. Newsletter. Provides reports on wrongful dismissal lawsuits.

Employment Practice Guide. CCH, Inc. • Weekly. $1,129.00 per year. Four looseleaf volumes.

DISPLAY OF MERCHANDISE

See also: POINT-OF-PURCHASE ADVERTISING; TRADE SHOWS

DIRECTORIES

Creative's Illustrated Guide to P-O-P Exhibits and Promotion. Magazines Creative, Inc. • Annual. $25.00. Lists sources of point-of-purchase displays, signs, and exhibits and sources of other promotional materials and equipment. Available online.

HANDBOOKS AND MANUALS

Library Displays Handbook. Mark Schaeffer. H. W. Wilson Co. • 1991. $65.00. Provides detailed instructions for signs, posters, wall displays, bulletin boards, and exhibits.

PERIODICALS AND NEWSLETTERS

Journal of Convention and Event Tourism. Haworth Press, Inc. • Quarterly. $165.00 per year. Formerly *Journal of Convention and Exhibition Management.*

Signs of the Times: The Industry Journal Since 1906. ST Media Group International. • 13 times a year. $36.00 per year. For designers and manufacturers of all types of signs. Features how-to-tips. Includes *Sign Erection, Maintenance Directory* and annual *Buyer's Guide.*

VM & SD (Visual Merchandising and Store Design). International Authority on Visual Merchandising and Store Design. S T Publications, Inc. • Monthly. $39.00 per year. Ideas for retailers on store design and display. Includes *Buyers' Guide.* Formerly *Visual Merchandising and Store Design.*

TRADE/PROFESSIONAL ASSOCIATIONS

National Association of Display Industries. 3595 Sheridan St., Ste. 200, Hollywood, FL 33021.

Phone: (954)893-7225 Fax: (954)893-8375 E-mail: nadi@nadi-global.com • URL: http://www.nadi-global.com.

Point-of-Purchase Advertising International. 1600 Duke St., Ste. 400, Alexandria, VA 22314. Phone: (703)373-8800 Fax: (703)373-8801 E-mail: info@popai.com • URL: http://www.popai.com • Producers and suppliers of point-of-purchase advertising signs and displays and national and regional advertisers and retailers interested in use and effectiveness of signs, displays, and other point-of-purchase media. Conducts student education programs; maintains speakers' bureau.

DISPOSABLE FABRICS

See: NONWOVEN FABRICS INDUSTRY

DISPUTES, LABOR

See: ARBITRATION; STRIKES AND LOCKOUTS

DISSERTATIONS

GENERAL WORKS

Doing Exemplary Research. Ralph E. Stablein. Sage Publications, Inc. • 1992. $43.95. Contains discussions of research methodologies.

Surviving Your Dissertation: A Comprehensive Guide to Content and Process. Kjell E. Rudestam and Rae R. Newton. Sage Publications, Inc. • 2000. $72.95. Second edition. Provides general advice on how to successfully complete a dissertation or thesis.

ABSTRACTS AND INDEXES

Dissertation Abstracts International. UMI. • Monthly. Price on application. Section A: Humanities and Social Sciences. Author-written summaries of current doctoral dissertations from over 500 educational institutions.

HANDBOOKS AND MANUALS

The Chicago Manual of Style: The Essential Guide for Authors, Editors, and Publishers. The University of Chicago Press. • 1993. $40.00. 14th edition.

Columbia Guide to Online Style. Janice R. Walker and Todd W. Taylor. Columbia University Press. • 1998. $40.50. Includes rules for bibliographic citation of online sources, formatting guidelines for online documents, and information on the electronic preparation of texts for print publication.

Manual for Writers of Term Papers, Theses, and Dissertations. Kate L. Turabian. The University of Chicago Press. • 1996. $27.50. Sixth revised edition.

MLA Handbook for Writers of Research Papers. Joseph Gibaldi. Modern Language Association of America. • 2003. $25.00. Fifth edition. Includes style guidelines for both print and online citations. (MLA Handbook for Writers of Research Papers).

MLA Style Manual and Guide to Scholarly Publishing. Joseph Gibaldi. Modern Language Association of America. • 1998. $25.00. Second edition. Covers preparation of manuscripts for publication, legal issues, basic writing principles, documentation, and use of abbreviations.

ONLINE DATABASES

Dissertation Abstracts Online. PROQUEST. • Citations to all dissertations accepted for doctoral degrees by accredited U.S. educational institutions, 1861 to date. Includes British theses, 1988 to date. Inquire as to online cost and availability.

PERIODICALS AND NEWSLETTERS

American Doctoral Dissertations. Association of Research Libraries. UMI. • Annual. Price on application.

Resources in Education. Educational Resources Information Center. Available from U.S. Government Printing Office. • Monthly. Reports on educational research.

DISTILLING INDUSTRY

See also: BEVERAGE INDUSTRY; BREWING INDUSTRY; WINE INDUSTRY

ALMANACS AND YEARBOOKS

The U.S. Distilled Spirits Market: Impact Databank Market Review and Forecast. M. Shanken Communications, Inc. • Annual. $865.00. Includes industry commentary and statistics.

CD-ROM DATABASES

OECD Statistical Compendium. Organization for Economic Cooperation and Development. • Semiannual. $1,905.00 per year for 1 to 10 users. CD-ROM contains more than 730,000 monthly, quarterly, and annual time series for OECD countries, 1960 to date. Includes fully searchable data on agriculture, food, economic indicators, national accounts, employment, energy, finance, industry, technology, and foreign trade. Results can be displayed in various forms.

DIRECTORIES

Beverage Industry - Annual Manual. Stagnito Communications, Inc. • Annual. $55.00. Provides statistical information on multiple beverage markets. Includes an industry directory. Supplement to *Beverage Industry*.

Beverage Marketing Directory. Beverage Marketing Corp. • Covers: About 11,000 beer wholesalers, wine and spirits wholesalers, soft drink bottlers and franchisors, breweries, wineries, distilleries, alcoholic beverage importers, bottled water companies; and trade associations, government agencies, micro breweries, juice, coffee, tea, milk companies, and others concerned with the beverage and bottling industries; coverage includes Canada. Entries include: Beverage and bottling company listings contain company name, address, phone, names of key executives, number of employees, brand names, and other information, including number of franchisees, number of delivery trucks, sales volume. Suppliers and related companies and organizations listings include similar but less detailed information.

Brewers Digest Annual Buyers Guide and Brewery Directory. Siebel Publishing Company, Inc. • Annual. $50.00. Lists all breweries throughout the western hemisphere.

Major Food and Drink Companies of the World. Available from Gale Cengage Learning. • Annual. $880.00. Two volumes. Published by Graham & Whiteside. Contains profiles and trade names for more than 9,800 important food and beverage companies in various countries. In addition to foods, includes both alcoholic and nonalcoholic drink products.

Thomas Food and Beverage Market Place. Grey House Publishing. • 2004. $495.00. Three volumes. Contains more than 40,000 entries covering food companies, beverages, food equipment, warehouse companies, food brokers, wholesalers, importers, and exporters. Formerly *Thomas Food Industry Register*.

FINANCIAL RATIOS

Almanac of Business and Industrial Financial Ratios. Leo Troy. Aspen Publishers, Inc. • 2003. $125.95. Includes CD-Rom. Contains financial ratios derived from federal tax returns. Ratios for each of about 200 industries are arranged according to company asset size. (Almanac of Business and Industrial Financial Ratios Series).

Annual Statement Studies. The Risk Management Association. • Annual. Median and quartile financial ratios are given for over 400 kinds of manufacturing, wholesale, retail, construction, and consumer finance establishments. Data is sorted by both asset size and sales volume. Includes a clearly written "Definition of Ratios" and an alphabetical industry index.

Annual Statement Studies: Industry Default Probabilities and Cash Flow Measures. The Risk Management Association. • Annual. $145.00. Serves as a companion volume to the original *Annual Statement Studies*. Gives probability of default estimates on a percentage scale for more than 450 industries. Includes changes in position year-by-year for eight financial statement line items and provides percentage measures of cash flow.

HANDBOOKS AND MANUALS

Liquor Store. Entrepreneur Media, Inc. • Looseleaf. $59.50. A practical guide to starting a liquor store. Covers profit potential, start-up costs, market size evaluation, owner's time required, site selection, lease negotiation, pricing, accounting, advertising, promotion, etc. (Start-Up Business Guide No. E1024.).

INTERNET DATABASES

Business 2.0 Web Guide to the Best Business Links. Business 2.0 Media Inc. Phone: (415)293-4800 E-mail: support@business2.com • URL: http://www.business2.com/webguide • Web site presents an extensive, searchable directory of links to "the best, most informative, and authoritative web pages." Twenty main categories cover business, finance, career, company information, people, and technology topics, with thousands of subtopics, all linking to Web sites recommended by experienced business researchers. Fees: Free.

Fedstats. Federal Interagency Council on Statistical Policy. Phone: (202)395-7254 • URL: http://www.fedstats.gov • Web site features an efficient search facility for full-text statistics produced by more than 100 federal agencies, including the Census Bureau, the Bureau of Economic Analysis, and the Bureau of Labor Statistics. Boolean searches can be made within one agency or for all agencies combined. Links are offered to international statistical bureaus, including the UN, IMF, OECD, UNESCO, Eurostat, and 20 individual countries. Fees: Free.

FreeLunch.com. Economy.com, Inc. Phone: (610)696-8700 Fax: (610)696-1678 • URL: http://www.freelunch.com • Web site provides free access to more than 1.5 million economic and financial data series, covering industry, demographics, labor markets, prices, retail sales, government spending, trade, interest rates, housing starts, the stock market, and many other topics. Data is available for various time periods in either chart or table form. Searching is offered. Fees: Free, but registration required. Economy.com, Inc. also offers fee-based economic analysis at *The Dismal Scientist* site (http://www.dismal.com).

PERIODICALS AND NEWSLETTERS

American Society of Brewing Chemists Journal. American Society of Brewing Chemists. • Quarterly. Free to members; non-members, $164.00 per year; corporate members, $195.00 per year; student members, $25.00 per year.

ASBC Newsletter. American Society of Brewing Chemists. • Description: Provides news items and technical reports on brewing and related matters. Recurring features include news items, abstracts of technical papers, convention news, book reviews, and membership listings and changes.

Brewing and Distilling International. Brewery Traders Publications, Ltd. • Monthly. $82.00 per year.

Bureau of Alcohol, Tobacco, and Firearms Quarterly Bulletin. Bureau of Alcohol, Tobacco, and Firearms, U.S. Department of the Treasury. Available from U.S. Government Printing Office. • Quarterly. $25.00 per year. Laws and regulations.

Communications. Master Brewer's Association of America. • Bimonthly. Membership.

Impact: U.S. News and Research for the Wine, Spirits, and Beer Industries. M. Shanken Communications, Inc. • Semimonthly. $375.00 per year. Newsletter covering the marketing, economic, and financial aspects of alcoholic beverages.

Kane's Beverage Week: The Newsletter of Beverage Marketing. Whitaker Newsletters, Inc. • Weekly. $469.00 per year. Newsletter. Covers news relating to the alcoholic beverage industries, including social, health, and legal issues.

Malt Advocate: Beer and Whiskey Magazine. Malt Advocate, Inc. • Quarterly. $16.00 per year. Provides information for consumers of upscale whiskey and beer.

STATISTICS SOURCES

Annual Survey of Manufactures. Available from U. S. Government Printing Office. • Annual. Prices vary. Issued by the U. S. Census Bureau as an interim update to the *Census of Manufactures*. Includes data on number of manufacturing establishments in various industries, employment, labor costs, value of shipments, capital expenditures, inventories, energy costs, and assets. (See also Census Bureau home page, http://www.census.gov/.).

Business Statistics of the United States. Linz Audain and Cornelia J. Strawser. Bernan Associates. • Annual. $147.00. Based on *Business Statistics*, formerly issue by the Bureau of Economic Analysis, U. S. Department of Commerce. Provides basic data for a wide variety of U. S. industries, services, and economic indicators. Most statistics are shown annually for 30 years and monthly for the most recent four years.

The Global Drinks Market Impact Databank. M. Shanken Communications, Inc. • Annual. $2,975.00. Detailed compilations of data for various segments of the liquor, beer, and soft drink industries.

Monthly Statistical Release: Distilled Spirits. U. S. Bureau of Alcohol, Tobacco, and Firearms. • 1995.

Standard & Poor's Industry Surveys. Standard & Poor's. • Semiannual. $1,800.00. Two looseleaf volumes. Includes monthly *Supplements*. Provides detailed, individual surveys of 52 major industry groups. Each survey is revised on a semiannual basis. Also includes "Monthly Investment Review" (industry group investment analysis) and monthly "Trends & Projections" (economic analysis).

Survey of Current Business. Available from U. S. Government Printing Office. • Monthly. $63.00 per year. Issued by Bureau of Economic Analysis, U. S. Department of Commerce. Presents a wide variety of business and economic data.

World Drinks Data and Statistics. Euromonitor International. • 2004. $650.00. Provides five-year data for both alcoholic and non-alcoholic beverages in 52 countries. Includes market size, consumer expenditures, price indicators, and retail distribution data for beer, wine, spirits, tea, coffee, soft drinks, fruit juices, bottled water, and other drinks.

TRADE/PROFESSIONAL ASSOCIATIONS

Distilled Spirits Council of the United States. 1250 Eye St., N.W., Suite 400, Washington, DC 20005. Phone: (202)628-3544 Fax: (202)682-8888 • URL: http://www.discus.org.

United Food and Commercial Workers International Union. 1775 K. St., N.W., Washington, DC 20006. Phone: (202)223-3111 Fax: (202)466-1562 • URL: http://www.ufcw.org.

OTHER SOURCES

Liquor Control Law Reporter: Federal and All States. CCH, Inc. • Biweekly. $3,649.00 per year.

Nine looseleaf volumes. Federal and state regulation and taxation of alcoholic beverages.

DISTRIBUTION

See also: MARKETING; RACK JOBBERS; TRANSPORTATION INDUSTRY; TRUCKING INDUSTRY; WHOLESALE TRADE

ABSTRACTS AND INDEXES

Business Periodicals Index. H. W. Wilson Co. • 11 times a year. Quarterly and annual cumulations. Price varies.

BIBLIOGRAPHIES

Marketing Information Revolution. Robert C. Blattberg, editor. McGraw-Hill. • 1993. $39.95. Third edition. Includes a wide variety of sources for specific kinds of marketing.

DIRECTORIES

American Wholesalers and Distributors Directory. Gale Cengage Learning. • 2003. $250.00. 12th edition. Lists more than 30,000 national, regional, state, and local wholesalesrs.

Grocery Headquarters: The Newspaper for the Food Industry. Trend Publishing. • Monthly. $80.00 per year. Covers the sale and distribution of food products and other items sold in supermarkets and grocery stores. Edited mainly for retailers and wholesalers. Incorporates (Grocery Distribution).

Plunkett's Transportation and Logistics Industry Almanac. Plunkett Research, Ltd. • 2004. $249.99. Contains profiles of 300 leading companies in the fields of transportation, logistics, supply chain management, warehousing, distribution, and intermodal shipment systems. Includes industry trends and statistics.

Warehouse Management's Guide to Public Warehousing. Reed Business Information. • Annual. $55.00. List of general merchandise,contract and refrigerated warehouses.

Warehousing Distribution Directory. Commonwealth Business Media Inc. • Publication includes: List of about 800 warehousing and consolidation companies and firms offering trucking, trailer on flatcar, container on flatcar, and piggyback carrier services. Entries include: Name of firm, address, phone, name and title of contact, services, insurance provided, bank references, territory covered, restrictions, number of staff, and branches or subsidiaries with their locations.

ENCYCLOPEDIAS AND DICTIONARIES

Blackwell Encyclopedic Dictionary of Marketing. Dale Littler and Barbara R. Lewis, editors. Blackwell Publishers. • 1997. $38.95. The editors are associated with the Manchester School of Management. Contains definitions of key terms combined with longer articles written by various U. S. and foreign business educators. Includes bibliographies and index. (Blackwell Encyclopedia of Management Series.).

ONLINE DATABASES

Wilson Business Abstracts Online. H. W. Wilson Co. • Indexes and abstracts 600 major business periodicals, plus the *Wall Street Journal* and the business section of the *New York Times.* Indexing is from 1982, abstracting from 1990, with the two newspapers included from 1993. Updated weekly. Inquire as to online cost and availability. (*Business Periodicals Index* without abstracts is also available online.).

PERIODICALS AND NEWSLETTERS

B to B: The Magazine for Marketing and E-Commerce Strategists. Crain Communications, Inc. • 26 times a year. $59.00 per year. Formerly *Advertising Age's Business Marketing.*

Chilton's Distribution: The Transportation and Business Logistics Magazine. Reed Business Information. • Monthly. $65.00 per year.

Distribution Center Management. Alexander Research & Communications Inc. • Description: The monthly newsletter for distribution centers and warehouse managers with ideas and information on how to run their facilities more productively.

Industrial Distribution: For Industrial Distributors and Their Sales Personnel. Reed Business Information. • Monthly. $109.90 per year.

Journal of Marketing Channels: Distribution Systems, Strategy, and Management. Haworth Press, Inc. • Quarterly. $315.00 per year. Subject matter has to do with the management of product distribution systems.

Marketing Management: Shaping the Profession of Marketing. American Marketing Association. • Quarterly. Members, $45.00 per year; nonmembers, $70.00 per year; institutions, $90.00 per year. Covers trends in the management of marketing, sales, and distribution.

Transportation and Distribution: Integrating Logistics in Supply Chain Management. Penton Media, Inc. • Monthly. Free to qualified personnel; others, $50.00 per year. Essential information on transportation and distribution practices in domestic and international trade.

RESEARCH CENTERS AND INSTITUTES

Center for Research and Management Services. Indiana State University. School of Business, Terre Haute, IN 47809. Phone: (812)237-6311 Fax: (812)237-8720.

Marketing Science Institute. Marketing Science Institute. 1000 Massachusetts Ave., Cambridge, MA 02138-5396. Phone: (617)491-2060 Fax: (617)491-2065 E-mail: mclippinger@msi.org • URL: http://www.msi.org • Marketing, including studies on marketing management and strategy, international/global marketing, impact of information technology on marketing, marketing models and methods, advertising, sales promotion, sales force, channels of distribution, consumer services marketing, business-to-business marketing, and marketing of consumer durables and packaged goods.

STATISTICS SOURCES

Industry Profile and Healthcare Factbook. Healthcare Distribution Management Association. • Annual. $349.00. Provides 266 statistical tables in three sections: "Industry Profile" (financial ratios related to drug distribution), "Pharmaceutical and Healthcare Distribution Trends and Facts," and "Healthcare Factbook" (expenditures, insurance utilization, company/product rankings, drug price inflation, generics, OTC, drug store data, hospital statistics, healthcare consumer summaries, etc.). Also known as *HDMA Factbook.* The Healthcare Distribution Management Association was formerly the National Wholesale Druggists' Association.

Manufacturing and Distribution USA. Gale Cengage Learning. • 2002. $395.00. Second edition. Three volumes. Presents statistics and projections relating to economic activity in more than 500 business classifications.

TRADE/PROFESSIONAL ASSOCIATIONS

Council of Logistics Management. 2803 Butterfield Rd., Ste. 200, Oak Brook, IL 60523-1170. Phone: (630)574-0985 Fax: (630)574-0989 E-mail: clmadmin@clm1.org • URL: http://www.clm1.org.

National Association of Wholesaler-Distributors. 1725 K St., N.W., Ste. 00, Washington, DC 20006. Phone: (202)872-0885 Fax: (202)785-0586 E-mail: naw@nawd.org • URL: http://www.naw.org • Formerly National Association of Wholesalers.

OTHER SOURCES

Product Distribution Law Guide. CCH, Inc. • $199. 00. Looseleaf service. Annual updates available.

Covers the legal aspects of various methods of product distribution, including franchising.

DIVIDENDS

See also: INVESTMENTS; STOCKS

GENERAL WORKS

How to Invest Wisely. Lawrence S. Pratt. American Institute for Economic Research. • 2002. $12.00. Presents a conservative policy of investing, with emphasis on dividend-paying common stocks. Gold and other inflation hedges are compared. Includes a reprint of *Toward an Optimal Stock Selection Strategy* (1997). (Economic Education Bulletin.).

What Works on Wall Street: A Guide to the Best Performing Investment Strategies of All Time. James P. O'Shaughnessy. McGraw-Hill. • 1998. $49.95. Second revised edition. Examines investment strategies over a 43-year period and concludes that large capitalization, high-dividend-yield stocks produce the best results. Includes digital audio.

CD-ROM DATABASES

OECD Statistical Compendium. Organization for Economic Cooperation and Development. • Semiannual. $1,905.00 per year for 1 to 10 users. CD-ROM contains more than 730,000 monthly, quarterly, and annual time series for OECD countries, 1960 to date. Includes fully searchable data on agriculture, food, economic indicators, national accounts, employment, energy, finance, industry, technology, and foreign trade. Results can be displayed in various forms.

DIRECTORIES

American Stock Exchange Directory. CCH, Inc. • 2000. $30.00.

Mergent's Handbook of Dividend Achievers. Mergent, Inc. • Quarterly. $160.00 per year ($45.00 per copy). Provides information on about 300 companies that have increased cash dividends for the past 10 or more consecutive years. Formerly *Moody's Handbook of Dividend Achievers.*

Standard and Poor's Security Dealers of North America. Standard & Poor's. • Semiannual. $480.00 per year; with *Supplements* every six weeks. Geographical listing of over 12,000 stock, bond, and commodity dealers.

FINANCIAL RATIOS

Quarterly Financial Report for Manufacturing, Mining, and Trade Corporations. U.S. Federal Trade Commission and U.S. Securities and Exchange Commission. Available from U.S. Government Printing Office. • Quarterly. $49.00 per year.

HANDBOOKS AND MANUALS

Dividend Policy: Theory and Practice. George W. Frankfurter and Bob G. Wood. Elsevier Butterworth Heinemann. • 2003. $59.95. Covers the history of dividends, preferred stock dividends, dividend reinvestment plans, extensive academic research, and "New Ways of Thinking About Dividends and Dividend Policy.".

Moody's Dividend Record and Annual Dividend Record. • Semiweekly. $775.00 per year. Includes annual and cumulative supplement. Formerly *Moody's Dividend Record.*

Standard and Poor's Dividend Record. Standard and Poor's. • Daily. $825.00 per year.

INTERNET DATABASES

Business 2.0 Web Guide to the Best Business Links. Business 2.0 Media Inc. Phone: (415)293-4800 E-mail: support@business2.com • URL: http://www.business2.com/webguide • Web site presents an extensive, searchable directory of links to "the best, most informative, and authoritative web pages." Twenty main categories cover business, finance, career, company information, people, and technology topics, with thousands of subtopics, all linking to Web sites recommended by experienced business researchers. Fees: Free.

ETF Connect. Nuveen Investments. Phone: 800-257-8787 • URL: http://www.etfconnect.com • Free Web site makes available extensive, searchable information on individual closed-end investment funds, preferred share funds, and exchange-traded index funds. Information on a particular fund is available by name or as part of a classification (high yield, investment grade, municipal, emerging markets, global equity, etc.). Fund charts are available for various time periods, as is data concerning premiums or discounts, dividends, annualized total return, credit quality, "Top 10 Holdings," and so forth.

Fedstats. Federal Interagency Council on Statistical Policy. Phone: (202)395-7254 • URL: http://www.fedstats.gov • Web site features an efficient search facility for full-text statistics produced by more than 100 federal agencies, including the Census Bureau, the Bureau of Economic Analysis, and the Bureau of Labor Statistics. Boolean searches can be made within one agency or for all agencies combined. Links are offered to international statistical bureaus, including the UN, IMF, OECD, UNESCO, Eurostat, and 20 individual countries. Fees: Free.

FreeLunch.com. Economy.com, Inc. Phone: (610)696-8700 Fax: (610)696-1678 • URL: http://www.freelunch.com • Web site provides free access to more than 1.5 million economic and financial data series, covering industry, demographics, labor markets, prices, retail sales, government spending, trade, interest rates, housing starts, the stock market, and many other topics. Data is available for various time periods in either chart or table form. Searching is offered. Fees: Free, but registration required. Economy.com, Inc. also offers fee-based economic analysis at *The Dismal Scientist* site (http://www.dismal.com).

ONLINE DATABASES

Disclosure SEC Database. Thomson Financial. • Provides online information from records filed with the Securities and Exchange Commission by more than 12,000 publicly-owned companies in the U.S. Includes about 200 financial data items and information relating to executives. Time span is 1977 to date, with weekly updates. Inquire as to online cost and availability.

Dow Jones News Service. Dow Jones and Co., Inc. • Full text and edited news stories and articles on business affairs. Inquire as to online cost and availability.

EdgarPlus: SEC Basic Filings. Thomson Financial. • Online service provides full text of about 60,000 documents that have been filed with the U.S. Securities and Exchange Commission, 1987 to date, with daily updates. Filings include 6-K, 8-K, 10-K, 10-C, 10-Q, 20-F, and proxy statements. Inquire as to online cost and availability.

PERIODICALS AND NEWSLETTERS

Barron's: The Dow Jones Business and Financial Weekly. • Weekly. $145.00 per year.

Commercial and Financial Chronicle. William B. Dana Co. • Weekly. $140.00. per year.

DRIP Investor: Your Guide to Buying Stocks Without a Broker. Horizon Publishing, Co., LLC. • Monthly. $89.00 per year. Newsletter covering the dividend reinvestment plans (DRIPs) of various publicly-owned corporations. Includes model portfolios and *Directory of Dividend Reinvestment Plans.*

Investment Guide. American Investment Services Inc. • Description: Contains analyses of stock market activity and strategies for investment. Recurring features include market statistics, Dow high-yield stock investing.

The Moneypaper. Temper of the Times Communications, Inc. Temper of the Times Communications Inc. • Description: Contains strategies to minimize stock sales costs and articles on investing and market trends. Includes a summary of monthly financial news drawn from over 70 financial publications and advisory services. Recurring features include columns titled Summing Up, Market Outlook, and Stocktrack.

Wall Street Transcript: A Professional Publication for the Business and Financial Community. Wall Street Transcript Corp. • Weekly. $1,890.00. per year. Provides reprints of investment research reports.

PRICE SOURCES

Stock Market Values and Yields 2000. RIA. • 2000. $22.00. Revised edition. Gives year-end prices and dividends for tax purposes.

RESEARCH CENTERS AND INSTITUTES

Center for Research in Security Prices. University of Chicago, 725 S. Wells St., Suite 800, Chicago, IL 60607. Phone: (773)834-4610 Fax: (773)702-3036 E-mail: custom@crsp.uchicago.edu • URL: http://gsbwww.uchicago.edu/research/crsp.

Rodney L. White Center for Financial Research. University of Pennsylvania, 3254 Steinberg Hall-Dietrich Hall, Philadelphia, PA 19104. Phone: (215)898-7616 Fax: (215)573-8084 E-mail: rlwtcr@finance.wharton.upenn.edu • URL: http://www.finance.wharton.upenn.edu • Research areas include financial management, money markets, real estate finance, and international finance.

STATISTICS SOURCES

Business Statistics of the United States. Linz Audain and Cornelia J. Strawser. Bernan Associates. • Annual. $147.00. Based on *Business Statistics,* formerly issue by the Bureau of Economic Analysis, U. S. Department of Commerce. Provides basic data for a wide variety of U. S. industries, services, and economic indicators. Most statistics are shown annually for 30 years and monthly for the most recent four years.

Survey of Current Business. Available from U. S. Government Printing Office. • Monthly. $63.00 per year. Issued by Bureau of Economic Analysis, U. S. Department of Commerce. Presents a wide variety of business and economic data.

OTHER SOURCES

Corporate Dividends and Stock Repurchases. Barbara Black. West Group. • Annual. $173.00. Looseleaf service. Covers the law relating to dividends in general, illegal dividends, stock splits, stock dividends, corporate repurchases, and other dividend topics.

Mergent's Annual Dividend Record. Mergent, Inc. • Annual. $49.00. Provides detailed dividend data, including tax information, for 12,000 stocks and 18,000 mutual funds. Covers the most recent year. Formerly *Moody's Annual Dividend Record.*

DIVORCE

See also: FAMILY LAW

GENERAL WORKS

Economics of Divorce: The Effect on Parents and Children. Craig A. Everett. Haworth Press, Inc. • 1994. $39.95. (Journal of Divorce and Remarriage Series).

Smart Questions to Ask Your Financial Advisers. Lynn Brenner. Bloomberg. • 1997. $19.95. Provides practical advice on how to deal with financial planners, stockbrokers, insurance agents, and lawyers. Some of the areas covered are investments, estate planning, tax planning, house buying, prenuptial agreements, divorce arrangements, loss of a job, and

retirement. (Bloomberg Personal Bookshelf Series).

ABSTRACTS AND INDEXES

Current Law Index: Multiple Access to Legal Periodicals. Gale Cengage Learning. • Monthly. $725.00 per year. Produced in cooperation with the American Association of Law Libraries. Indexes more than 900 law journals, legal newspapers, and specialty publications from the U.S., Canada, U.K., Ireland, Australia, and New Zealand.

Index to Legal Periodicals and Books. H. W. Wilson Co. • Monthly. $490.00 per year. Quarterly and annual cumulations.

Psychological Abstracts. American Psychological Association. • Monthly. Members, $815.00 per year; individuals and institutions, $1,207.00 per year. Covers the international literature of psychology and the behavioral sciences. Includes journals, technical reports, dissertations, and other sources.

Sage Family Studies Abstracts. Sage Publications, Inc. • Quarterly. Institutions, $847.00 per year.

Women Studies Abstracts. Transaction Publishers. • Quarterly. Individuals, $102.00 per year; institutions, $240.00 per year.

CD-ROM DATABASES

Magazine Index Plus. Gale Cengage Learning. • Monthly. $4,000.00 per year (includes InfoTrac workstation). Provides full text on CD-ROM for about 100 popular, general interest magazines and indexing for 300 others. Includes special indexing of reviews and product evaluations. Time period is 1980 to date.

DIRECTORIES

American Academy of Matrimonial Lawyers: List of Certified Fellows. American Academy of Matrimonial Lawyers. • Annual. Membership.

Where to Write for Vital Records: Births, Deaths, Marriages, and Divorces. Available from U. S. Government Printing Office. • 2002. $3.00. Issued by the National Center for Health Statistics, U. S. Department of Health and Human Services. Arranged by state. Provides addresses, telephone numbers, and cost of copies for various kinds of vital records or certificates. (DHHS Publication No. PHS 93-1142.).

HANDBOOKS AND MANUALS

Divorce Decisions Workbook: A Planning and Action Guide. Marjorie L. Engel. McGraw-Hill. • 1992. $27.95. Covers the business, financial, legal, and tax aspects of divorce.

Divorce Yourself: The National No-Fault Divorce Kit. Daniel Sitarz. Nova Publishing Co. • 2002. $34.95. Fifth edition. Provides instructions, checklists, questionnaires, worksheets, and forms for use in uncomplicated divorce proceedings. Forms are also available on IBM or MAC diskettes.

Negotiating to Settlement in Divorce. Sanford N. Katz, editor. Aspen Publishers, Inc. • $75.00. Looseleaf service. Periodic supplementation.

Valuation Strategies in Divorce: Cumulative Supplement. Robert D. Feder. Aspen Publishers, Inc. • 2002. Fourth edition. Explains the basic principles of asset valuation in divorce cases. Discusses financial statements, tax returns, retirement benefits, real estate, and personal property.

INTERNET DATABASES

Lexis.com Research System. Lexis-Nexis Group. Phone: 800-227-4908 or (937)865-6800 Fax: (937)865-6909 E-mail: webmaster@prod.lexis-nexis.com • URL: http://www.lexis.com • Fee-based Web site offers extensive searching of a wide variety of legal sources. Additional features include Daily Opinion Service, lexis.com Bookstore, Career Center, CLE Center, Law Schools, and Practice

Pages ("Pages specific to areas of specialty").

ONLINE DATABASES

Contemporary Women's Issues. Gale Cengage Learning. • Provides fulltext articles online from 150 periodicals and a wide variety of additional sources relating to economic, legal, social, political, education, health, and other women's issues. Time span is 1992 to date. Weekly updates. Inquire as to online cost and availability. (Also available in a CD-ROM version.).

Index to Legal Periodicals and Books (Online). H. W. Wilson Co. • Broad coverage of law journals and books 1981 to date. Monthly updates. Inquire as to online cost and availability.

Legal Resource Index. Gale Cengage Learning. • Broad coverage of law literature appearing in legal, business, and other periodicals, 1980 to date. Daily updates. Inquire as to online cost and availability.

LEXIS. LEXIS-NEXIS. • The various LEXIS databases provide full text and indexing for a wide variety of legal cases, statutes, orders, and opinions.

PsycINFO. American Psychological Association. • Provides indexing and abstracting of the worldwide literature of psychology and the behavioral sciences. Time period is 1967 to date, with monthly updates. Inquire as to online cost and availability.

PERIODICALS AND NEWSLETTERS

Family Advocate. American Bar Association, Family Law Section. • Quarterly. Members $39.50; non-members, $44.50 per year. Practical advice for attorneys practicing family law.

Journal of Divorce and Remarriage: Research and Clinical Studies in Family Theory, Family Law, Family Meditation and Family Therapy. Haworth Press, Inc. • Quarterly. $520.00 per year. Two volumes.

STATISTICS SOURCES

Current Population Reports: Population Characteristics, Special Studies, and Consumer Income, Series P-20, P-23, and P-60. Available from U. S. Government Printing Office. • Irregular. $80.00 per year. Issued by the U.S. Bureau of the Census (http://www.census.gov). Each issue covers a special topic relating to population or income. Series P-20, *Population Characteristics*, provides statistical studies on such items as mobility, fertility, education, and marital status. Series P-23, *Special Studies*, consists of occasional reports on methodology. Series P-60, *Consumer Income*, publishes reports on income in relation to age, sex, education, occupation, family size, etc.

Monthly Vital Statistics Report. U. S. Department of Health and Human Services. • Monthly. Provides data on births, deaths, cause of death, marriage, and divorce.

Statistical Handbook on the American Family. Bruce A. Chadwick and Tim B. Heaton. Greenwood Publishing Group, Inc. • 1998. $69.95. Second edition. Includes data on education, health, politics, employment, expenditures, social characteristics, the elderly, and women in the labor force. Historical statistics on marriage, birth, and divorce are shown from 1900 on. A list of sources and a subject index are provided. (Statistical Handbooks Series).

TRADE/PROFESSIONAL ASSOCIATIONS

American Academy of Matrimonial Lawyers. 150 N. Michigan Ave., Suite 2040, Chicago, IL 60601. Phone: (312)263-6477 Fax: (312)263-7682 E-mail: aaml@aaml.org • URL: http://www.aaml.org • Members are attorneys specializing in family law.

The National Organization for Men. 11 Park Pl., Ste. 1100, New York, NY 10007. Phone: (212)686-6253 or (212)766-4030 Fax: (212)791-3056 E-mail: info@tnom.com • URL: http://www.tnom.com • Encourages rational and objective state and national divorce laws. Absorbed National Committee for Fair

Divorce and Alimony Laws.

OTHER SOURCES

Divorce and Taxes. CCH, Inc. • 2000. $25.00. Second edition. In addition to tax problems, topics include alimony, division of property, and divorce decrees.

Divorce, Separation, and the Distribution of Property. American Lawyer Media, Inc. • Looseleaf. $169.00. Updated as needed. Covers such thorny divorce settlement issues as earning power, stock options, pensions, repayment of student loans, tort claims, closely held businesses, premarital agreement enforcement, and alimony awards. (Law Journal Press).

DO-IT-YOURSELF

See: HOME IMPROVEMENT INDUSTRY

DOCKS

See: PORTS

DOCTORS' DEGREES

See: ACADEMIC DEGREES

DOCUMENT IMAGING

See also: MICROFORMS

GENERAL WORKS

Essentials of Knowledge Management. Bryan Bergeron. John Wiley and Sons, Inc. • 2003. $29.95. Covers current strategies, trends, and technologies in knowledge management. Includes examples of best practices. (Essentials Series).

Knowledge Management Lessons Learned: What Works and What Doesn't. Michael Koenig and T. Kanti Srikantaiah, editors. Information Today, Inc. • 2003. $44.50. Contains more than 30 articles by KM experts, covering recent applications, innovations, strategy, implementation, cost analysis, training, content management, and other topics related to knowledge management. (ASIS Management Series).

ABSTRACTS AND INDEXES

Applied Science and Technology Index. H. W. Wilson Co. • 11 times a year. Quarterly and annual cumulations. Price varies. Indexes a wide variety of English language technical, industrial, and engineering periodicals.

Computer Literature Index: A Subject/Author Index to Computer and Data Processing Literature. EBSCO Publishing. • Quarterly, with annual cumulation. $245.00 per year. Contains brief abstracts of book and periodical literature covering all phases of computing, including approximately 70 specific application areas.

F & S Index: United States. Gale Cengage Learning. • Monthly. $1,450.00 per year, including quarterly and annual cumulations. Provides annotated citations to marketing, business, financial, and industrial literature. Coverage of U. S. business activity includes trade journals, financial magazines, business newspapers, and special reports.

Imaging Abstracts. Royal Photographic Society of Great Britain, Imaging Science and Technology Grou. Elsevier. • Bimonthly. $860.00 per year. Formerly *Photographic Abstracts*.

Key Abstracts: Business Automation. Available from INSPEC, Inc. • Monthly. $250.00 per year. Provides international coverage of journal and proceedings literature. Published in England by the Institution of

Electrical Engineers (IEE).

NTIS Alerts: Computers, Control & Information Theory. National Technical Information Service. • Semimonthly. $235.00 per year. Provides descriptions of government-sponsored research reports and software, with ordering information. Covers computer hardware, software, control systems, pattern recognition, image processing, and related subjects. Formerly *Abstract Newsletter*.

BIBLIOGRAPHIES

Knowledge Management: The Bibliography. Paul Burden and others. Information Today, Inc. • 2000. $22.50. Provides citations to more than 1,500 articles, 150 Web sites, and 400 books. Arranged according to specific KM topics, such as "KM and E-Commerce." Published in conjunction with the American Society for Information Science and Technology (ASIST).

CD-ROM DATABASES

Datapro on CD-ROM: Computer Systems Analyst. Gartner Group, Inc. • Monthly. Price on application. Includes detailed information on specific computer hardware and software products, such as peripherals, security systems, document imaging systems, and UNIX-related products.

WILSONDISC: Applied Science and Technology Abstracts. H. W. Wilson Co. • Monthly. Includes unlimited access to the online version of *Applied Science and Technology Abstracts* through WILSONLINE. Provides CD-ROM indexing and abstracting of 500 prominent scientific, technical, engineering, and industrial periodicals. Indexing coverage is provided from 1983 to date and abstracting from 1993 to date.

DIRECTORIES

Advanced Imaging Buyers Guide: The Most Comprehensive Worldwide Directory of Imaging Product and Equipment Vendors. Cygnus Business Media. • Annual. $19.95. Lists 800 electronic imaging companies and their products.

Better Buys for Business: The Independent Consumer Guide to Office Equipment. What to Buy for Business, Inc. • 10 times a year. $134.00 per year. Each issue is on a particular office product, with detailed evaluation of specific models: 1. Low-Volume Copier Guide, 2. Mid-Volume Copier Guide, 3. High-Volume Copier Guide, 4. Plain Paper Fax and Low-Volume Multifunctional Guide, 5. Mid/High-Volume Multifunctional Guide, 6. Laser Printer Guide, 7. Color Printer and Color Copier Guide, 8. Scan-to-File Guide, 9. Business Phone Systems Guide, 10. Postage Meter Guide, with a Short Guide to Shredders.

KMWorld Buyer's Guide. Knowledge Asset Media. • Semiannual. Controlled circulation as part of *KMWorld*. Contains corporate and product profiles related to various aspects of knowledge management and information systems. (Knowledge Asset Media is a an affiliate of Information Today, Inc.).

The Software Encyclopedia: A Guide for Personal, Professional, and Business Users. Gale. • Annual. $335.00. Two volumes. Volume one lists software programs by title and producer. Volume two provides information on programs according to application and operating system. Includes prices and requirements for hardware and memory.

ENCYCLOPEDIAS AND DICTIONARIES

Every Manager's Guide to Information Technology: A Glossary of Key Terms and Concepts for Today's Business Leader. Peter G. W. Keen. Harvard Business School Publishing. • 1994. $18.95. Second edition. Provides definitions of terms related to computers, data communications, and information network systems. (Harvard Business Reference Series).

HANDBOOKS AND MANUALS

Electronic Document Management Systems: A Practical Guide for Evaluators and Users. Thomas M. Koulopoulos. McGraw-Hill. • 1995. $45.00.

ONLINE DATABASES

Applied Science and Technology Index Online. H. W. Wilson Co. • Provides online indexing of 500 major scientific, technical, industrial, and engineering periodicals. Time period is 1983 to date. Monthly updates. Inquire as to online cost and availability.

F & S Index. Gale Cengage Learning. • Contains about four million citations to worldwide business, financial, and industrial or consumer product literature appearing from 1972 to date. Weekly updates. Inquire as to online cost and availability.

Internet and Personal Computing Abstracts. Information Today, Inc. • Contains abstracts covering a wide variety of personal and business microcomputer literature appearing in more than 100 journals and popular magazines. Time period is 1981 to date, with monthly updates. Formerly *Microcomputer Index.* Inquire as to online cost and availability.

PROMT: Predicasts Overview of Markets and Technology. Gale Cengage Learning. • Companies, products, applied technologies and markets. U.S. and international literature coverage, 1972 to date. Inquire as to online cost and availability. Provides abstracts from more than 1,600 publications. Weekly updates.

PERIODICALS AND NEWSLETTERS

Advanced Imaging: Solutions for the Electronic Imaging Professional. Cygnus Business Media. • Monthly. $60.00 per year Covers document-based imaging technologies, products, systems, and services. Coverage is also devoted to multimedia and electronic printing and publishing.

Digital Imaging: The Magazine for the Imaging Professional. Cygnus Business Media, Inc. • Bimonthly. $24.95 per year. Edited for business and professional users of electronic publishing products and services. Topics covered include document imaging, CD-ROM publishing, digital video, and multimedia services. Formerly *Micro Publishing News.*

Document Imaging Report. Access Intelligence L.L.C. • Description: Aims to keep readers current with all developments in the optical media field. Reports on new products, applications, and licensing programs. Also provides coverage of the Association for Information and Image Management (AIIM), Optical Storage, and Rothchild conferences.

Document Processing Technology. RB Publishing Co. • Seven times a year. Controlled circulation. Edited for "high volume document printing" professionals. Covers imaging, printing, and mailing.

IEEE Transactions on Visualization and Computer Graphics. Institute of Electrical and Electronics Engineers, Inc. • Quarterly. $676.00 per year. Topics include computer vision, computer graphics, image processing, signal processing, computer-aided design, animation, and virtual reality.

Imaging Business: The Voice of the Document Imaging Channel. PBI Media, LLC. • Monthly. Free to qualified personnel. Edited for resellers of document imaging equipment.

Imaging KM: Creating and Managing the Knowledge-Based Enterprise. Knowledge Management World. • 10 times a year. Free to qualified personnel; others, $48.00 per year. Covers automated and networked document image handling.

Item Processing Report. Access Intelligence L.L.C.

• Description: Monitors developments in the processing of remittances and checks, including image processing, optical character recognition, check truncation, hardware, and software. **Remarks:** Absorbed The Powell Report, 1992.

KM World: Creating and Managing the Knowledge-Based Enterprise (Knowledge Management). Asset Media. • 10 times a year. Free to qualified personnel; others, $63.95 per year. Provides articles on knowledge management, including business intelligence, multimedia content management, document management, e-business, and intellectual property. Emphasis is on business-to-business information technology. (Knowledge Asset Media is a an affiliate of Information Today, Inc.).

Transform: Reinventing Business with Content and Collaboration Technologies. CMP Media LLC. • Monthly. $25.00 per year. Emphasis is on descriptions of new imaging products, including CD-ROM items. Formerly *Imaging and Document Solutions.*

RESEARCH CENTERS AND INSTITUTES

Bibliographical Center for Research, Inc., Rocky Mountain Region. 14394 E. Evans Ave., Aurora, CO 80014-1478. Phone: 800-397-1552 or (303)751-6277 Fax: (303)751-9787 E-mail: dbrunell@bcr.org • URL: http://www.bcr.org • Fields of research include information retrieval systems, Internet technology, CD-ROM technology, document delivery, and library automation.

Center for Imaging Science. Rochester Institute of Technology, 54 Lomb Memorial Dr., Rochester, NY 14623. Phone: (716)475-5994 Fax: (716)475-5988 E-mail: gatley@cis.rit.edu • URL: http://www.cis.rit.edu • Activities include research in color science and digital image processing.

Center for Integrated Manufacturing Studies. Rochester Institute of Technology, 111 Lomb Memorial Dr., Rochester, NY 14623-5608. Phone: (716)475-5101 Fax: (716)475-5250 E-mail: wjasp@rit.edu • URL: http://www.cims.rit.edu • Research areas include electronics, imaging, printing, and publishing.

Digital Image Analysis Laboratory. University of Arizona, Dept. of Electrical and Computer Engineering, Tucson, AZ 85721. Phone: (520)621-2706 Fax: (520)621-8076 E-mail: schowengerdt@ece.arizona.edu • URL: http://www.ece.arizona.edu/ • Research fields include image processing, computer vision, and artificial intelligence.

Graphics, Visualization, and Usability Center. Georgia Institute of Technology. GVU Center, 801 Atlantic Dr., Atlanta, GA 30332-0280. Phone: (404)894-4488 Fax: (404)894-0673 E-mail: afb@cc.gatech.edu • URL: http://www.cc.gatech.edu/gvu/ • Research areas include computer graphics, multimedia, image recognition, interactive graphics systems, animation, and virtual realities.

Image Science Research Group. Worcester Polytechnic Institute, Computer Science Dept., 100 Institute Rd., Worcester, MA 01609-2208. Phone: (508)831-5357 Fax: (508)831-5776 E-mail: matt@wpi.edu • URL: http://www.cs.wpi.edu/research/isrg • Areas of research include image processing, computer graphics, and computational vision.

Imaging Systems Laboratory. Carnegie Mellon University, Robotics Institute, 5000 Forbes Ave., Pittsburgh, PA 15213. Phone: (412)268-3824 Fax: (412)683-3763 E-mail: rht@cs.cmu.edu • Fields of research include computer vision and document interpretation.

Institute for Information Science and Technology. George Washington University, 801 22nd St., N. W., 6th Fl., Washington, DC 20052. Phone: (202)994-6208 Fax: (202)994-0227 E-mail: helgert@seas.

gwu.edu • Research areas include computer graphics and image processing.

TRADE/PROFESSIONAL ASSOCIATIONS

AIIM - The Enterprise Content Management Association. 1100 Wayne Ave., Ste. 1100, Silver Spring, MD 20910. Phone: 800-477-2446 or (301)587-8202 Fax: (301)587-2711 E-mail: aiim@aiim.org • URL: http://www.aiim.org • Manufacturers, vendors, and individual users of information and image management equipment, products, and services. Holds special meetings for trade members and companies. Maintains speakers' bureau. Operates resource center. Compiles statistics.

DOCUMENTATION (INFORMATION RETRIEVAL)

See: ONLINE INFORMATION SYSTEMS

DOCUMENTS

See: GOVERNMENT PUBLICATIONS

DOG FOOD

See: PET INDUSTRY

DOMESTIC APPLIANCES

See: ELECTRIC APPLIANCE INDUSTRY

DONATIONS, CHARITABLE

See: PHILANTHROPY

DOOR INDUSTRY

See also: BUILDING INDUSTRY

ABSTRACTS AND INDEXES

NTIS Alerts: Building Industry Technology. National Technical Information Service. • Semimonthly. $210.00 per year. Provides descriptions of government-sponsored research reports and software, with ordering information. Covers architecture, construction management, building materials, maintenance, furnishings, and related subjects. Formerly *Abstract Newsletter.*

ONLINE DATABASES

Trade & Industry Database. Gale Cengage Learning. • Provides indexing of business periodicals, January 1981 to date. Daily updates. (Full text articles from some periodicals are available online, 1983 to date. Inquire as to online cost and availability).

PERIODICALS AND NEWSLETTERS

Door and Operator Industry. International Door Association. • Bimonthly. Free. Edited for garage door and opener dealers.

Door and Window Retailing. Jervis and Associates. • Bimonthly. $15.00 per year. Edited for door and window retailers. Formerly *Door and Window Business.*

Doors and Hardware. Door and Hardware Institute. • Monthly. $49.00 per year.

TRADE/PROFESSIONAL ASSOCIATIONS

American Architectural Manufacturers Association. 1827 Walden Office Sq., Ste. 550, Schaumburg, IL 60173-4287. Phone: (847)303-5664 Fax: (847)303-5774 E-mail: rwalker@aamanet.org • URL: http://www.aamanet.org • Provides performance

---

standards, product certification and educational programs for the fenestration industry, including product testing and market research.

Door and Access Systems Manufacturers Association International. 1300 Sumner Ave., Cleveland, OH 44115-2851. Phone: (216)241-7333 Fax: (216)241-0105 E-mail: dasma@dasma.com • URL: http://www.dasma.com • Members are manufacturers of "upward-acting" garage doors and related products, both residential and commercial.

Door and Hardware Institute. 14150 Newbrook Dr., Suite 200, Chantilly, VA 20151-2232. Phone: (703)222-2010 Fax: (703)222-2410 E-mail: info@dhi.org • URL: http://www.dhi.org.

International Door Association. PO Box 246, 28 Lowry Dr., West Milton, OH 45383-0246. Phone: 800-355-4432 or (937)698-8042 Fax: (937)698-6153 E-mail: info@longmgt.com • URL: http://www.doors.org • Individuals and companies who manufacture, sell, or install overhead garage doors and openers. Aims to promote the industry and increase training and educational opportunities. Sets a code of business practices; compiles statistics. Conducts seminars.

National Fenestration Rating Council. 6305 Ivy Ln., Ste. 140, Greenbelt, MD 20770. Phone: (301)589-1776 Fax: (301)589-3884 E-mail: info@nfrc.org • URL: http://www.nfrc.org • Individuals, organizations, and corporations interested in production, regulation, promotion, and development of technology related to fenestration products. Develops national voluntary energy performance rating system for fenestration products; coordinates certification and labeling activities to ensure uniform rating application. Promotes consumer awareness of fenestration ratings in an effort to encourage informed purchase of windows, doors, and skylights. Conducts efficiency testing. Maintains speakers' bureau; conducts educational and research programs.

National Sash and Door Jobbers Association. 10047 Robert Trent Jones Parkway, New Port Richey, FL 34655-4649. Phone: 800-786-7274 or (727)372-3665 Fax: (727)372-2879 E-mail: mail@nsdja.com • URL: http://www.nsdja.com • Members are wholesale distributors of door and window products.

Steel Door Institute. 30200 Detroit Rd., Cleveland, OH 44145-1967. Phone: (440)899-0010 Fax: (440)892-1404 E-mail: info@steeldoor.org • URL: http://www.steeldoor.org • Represents manufacturers of standard, all-metal doors and frames used in commercial applications. Aims to promote the use of steel doors and frames in the construction industry.

Window and Door Manufacturers Association. 1400 E Touhy Ave., No. 470, Des Plaines, IL 60018. Phone: 800-223-2301 or (847)299-5200 Fax: (847)299-1286 E-mail: admin@wdma.com • URL: http://www.wdma.com • Members are manufacturers of wooden door and window products. Absorbed Ponderosa Pine Woodwork Association. Formerly National Wood Window and Door Association.

OTHER SOURCES

Door Hardware. Available from MarketResearch.com. • 1997. $495.00. Market research report published by Specialists in Business Information. Covers locks, closers, doorknobs, security devices, and other door hardware. Presents market data relative to demographics, sales growth, shipments, exports, imports, price trends, and end-use. Includes company profiles.

Doors. Available from MarketResearch.com. • 1999. $2,250.00. Market research report published by Specialists in Business Information. Covers residential doors, including garage doors. Presents market data relative to demographics, sales growth, shipments, exports, imports, price trends, and end-use. Includes company profiles.

DOOR-TO-DOOR SELLING

See: DIRECT MARKETING

DOUGLAS FIR

See: LUMBER INDUSTRY

DOW THEORY

See also: INVESTMENTS; STOCKS; TECHNICAL ANALYSIS (FINANCE)

ONLINE DATABASES

Dow Jones News Service. Dow Jones and Co., Inc. • Full text and edited news stories and articles on business affairs. Inquire as to online cost and availability.

PERIODICALS AND NEWSLETTERS

Dow Theory Forecasts: Business and Stock Market. Dow Theory Forecasts, Inc. • Weekly. $233.00 per year. Provides information and advice on blue chip and income stocks.

Dow Theory Letters. Dow Theory Letters, Inc. • 17 times a year. $250.00 per year. Newsletter on stock market trends, investing, and economic conditions.

STATISTICS SOURCES

Advance-Decline Album. Dow Theory Letters, Inc. • Annual. Contains one page for each year since 1931. Includes charts of the New York Stock Exchange advance-decline ratio and the Dow Jones industrial average.

Dow Jones Averages Chart Album. Dow Theory Letters, Inc. • Annual. $140.00. Contains one page for each year since 1885. Includes line charts of the Dow Jones industrial, transportation, utilities, and bond averages. Important historical and economic dates are shown.

DOWNSIZING

See: DISMISSAL OF EMPLOYEES

DRAFTING, MECHANICAL

See: MECHANICAL DRAWING

DRAPERY INDUSTRY

See: WINDOW COVERING INDUSTRY

DRIED FOODS

See: FOOD INDUSTRY

DRILLING AND BORING MACHINERY

See: MACHINERY

DRINKING AND TRAFFIC ACCIDENTS

See: TRAFFIC ACCIDENTS AND TRAFFIC SAFETY

DRIVE-IN AND CURB SERVICES

See also: RESTAURANTS, LUNCHROOMS, ETC.

DIRECTORIES

Directory of Chain Restaurant Operators. Chain Store Guide. • Annual. $335.00. Includes fast food

establishments, and leading chain hotel copanies operating foodservice unit.

HANDBOOKS AND MANUALS

Donut Shop. Entrepreneur Media, Inc. • Looseleaf. $59.50. A practical guide to starting a doughnut shop. Covers profit potential, start-up costs, market size evaluation, owner's time required, site selection, lease negotiation, pricing, accounting, advertising, promotion, etc. (Start-Up Business Guide No. E1126.).

PERIODICALS AND NEWSLETTERS

QSR: The Magazine of Quick Service Restaurant Success. Journalistic, Inc. • Ten times a year. $30.00 per year. Provides news and management advice for quick-service restaurants, including franchisors and franchisees.

TRADE/PROFESSIONAL ASSOCIATIONS

National Frozen Food Dessert and Fast Food Association. P.O. Box 1116, Millbrook, NY 12545. Phone: 800-535-7748 or (845)677-9301 Fax: (845)677-3387 E-mail: director@nfdffa.org • URL: http://www.nfdffa.org • Formerly National Soft Serve and Fast Food Association.

DRUG ABUSE AND TRAFFIC

See also: ALCOHOLISM; NARCOTICS; PHARMACEUTICAL INDUSTRY

GENERAL WORKS

Alcohol and Drug Problems at Work: The Shift to Prevention. International Labour Organization. • 2003. $9.95. Discusses workplace substance abuse initiatives for both large and small businesses.

A Brief History of Cocaine. Steven B. Karch. CRC Press LLC. • 1997. $29.95. Emphasizes the societal effects of cocaine abuse in various regions of the world.

The Chemistry of Mind-Altering Drugs: History, Pharmacology, and Cultural Context. Daniel M. Perrine. American Chemical Society. • 1996. $45.00. Contains detailed descriptions of the pharmacological and psychological effects of a wide variety of drugs, "from alcohol to zopiclone.".

Drugs, Alcohol, and Tobacco: Learning About Addictive Behavior. Gale Cengage Learning. • 2002. $295.00. Three volumes. Contains 200 articles on various aspects of addiction. Includes color illustrations, a glossary, and comprehensive indexing. (Macmillan Reference USA imprint.).

Drugs of Abuse. Available from U. S. Government Printing Office. • 2003. $9.00. Issued by the Drug Enforcement Administration, U. S. Department of Justice (http://www.usdoj.gov). Provides detailed information on various kinds of narcotics, depressants, stimulants, hallucinogens, cannabis, steroids, and inhalants. Contains many color illustrations and a detailed summary of the Controlled Substances Act.

The Facts About Drug Use: Coping with Drugs and Alcohol in Your Family, at Work, in Your Community. The Haworth Press, Inc. • 1992. $14.95. A comprehensive overview of drug dependence, including alcoholism.

The United Nations and Drug Abuse Control. United Nations Publications. • 1992. An overview of international drug control efforts.

ABSTRACTS AND INDEXES

Excerpta Medica: Drug Dependence, Alcohol Abuse, and Alcoholism. Elsevier. • Bimonthly. Institutions, $1,398.00 per year. Section 40 of *Excerpta Medica.*

CD-ROM DATABASES

Magazine Index Plus. Gale Cengage Learning. • Monthly. $4,000.00 per year (includes InfoTrac workstation). Provides full text on CD-ROM for about 100 popular, general interest magazines and indexing for 300 others. Includes special indexing of reviews and product evaluations. Time period is 1980 to date.

ENCYCLOPEDIAS AND DICTIONARIES

American Drug Index. Facts and Comparisons. • Annual. $69.95. Lists over 20,000 drug entries in dictionary style.

Drugs and Controlled Substances: Information for Students. Gale Cengage Learning. • 2002. $115.00. Arranged alphabetically by drug name. Provides detailed information on the psychological and physiological effects of addictive drugs and substances. Includes illegal drugs, addictive prescription drugs, and over-the-counter items.

Encyclopedia of Crime and Justice. Available from Gale Cengage Learning. • 2001. $475.00. Second edition. Four volumes. Published by Macmillan Reference USA. Contains extensive information on a wide variety of topics pertaining to crime, criminology, social issues, and the courts. (A complete revision of 1982 edition.).

Encyclopedia of Crime and Punishment. David Levinson, editor. Sage Publications, Inc. • 2002. $600.00. Four volumes. Contains 425 signed entries dealing with civil, criminal, media, corporate, and international issues. Includes material on fraud, police science, correctional institutions, social matters, methodology, national surveys, and crime statistics.

Encyclopedia of Drugs, Alcohol, and Addictive Behavior. Available from Gale Cengage Learning. • 2001. $425.00. Second edition. Four volumes. Published by Macmillan Reference USA. Covers the social, economic, political, and medical aspects of addiction.

World of Criminal Justice. Gale Cengage Learning. • 2002. $160.00. Two volumes. Contains both topical and biographical entries relating to the criminal justice system and criminology.

HANDBOOKS AND MANUALS

Drug Abuse and the Law Sourcebook. Victor G. Haddox and Gerald G. Haddox. West Group. • Annual. $419.00. Two looseleaf volumes. Covers drugs of abuse, criminal responsibility, possessory offenses, trafficking offenses, and related topics. (Criminal Law Series).

Drug Abuse Handbook. Steven B. Karch, editor. CRC Press LLC. • 1997. $129.95. Provides comprehensive coverage of drug abuse issues and trends. Edited for healthcare professionals.

Drug Abuse in Society: A Reference Handbook. Geraldine Woods. ABC-CLIO, Inc. • 1993. $39.50. (Contemporary World Issues Series).

Drug Testing Legal Manual and Practice Aids. Kevin B. Zeese. West Group. • Semiannual. $394.00 per year. Two looseleaf volumes. Covers methods of testing for illegal drugs, pre-employment drug testing, technological problems, testing of school students, and related topics. (Criminal Law Series).

Narcotics and Drug Abuse A to Z. Croner Publications. • 1990. Three volumes. Price on application. Lists treatment centers.

Substance Abuse: A Comprehensive Textbook. Joyce Lowinson and others. Lippincott Williams and Wilkins. • 1997. $179.00. Third edition. Covers the medical, psychological, socioeconomic, and public health aspects of drug and alcohol abuse.

ONLINE DATABASES

Mental Health Abstracts. IFI/Plenum Data Corp. • Provides indexing and abstracting of mental health and mental illness literature appearing in more than 1,200 journals and other sources from 1969 to date. Monthly updates. Inquire as to online cost and availability.

Pharmaceutical News Index. ProQuest Inc. • Indexes major pharmaceutical industry newsletters, 1974 to present. Weekly updates. Inquire as to online cost and availability.

Toxline. National Library of Medicine. • Abstracting service covering human and animal toxicity studies, 1965 to present (older studies available in *Toxback* file). Monthly updates. Inquire as to online cost and availability.

PERIODICALS AND NEWSLETTERS

American Journal of Drug and Alcohol Abuse. Marcel Dekker, Inc. • Quarterly. Institutions, $995.00 per year; with online edition, $1,124.00 per year.

Contemporary Drug Problems. Federal Legal Publications, Inc. • Quarterly. Individuals, $30.00 per year; institutions, $36.00 per year.

Counselor: The Magazine for Addiction Professionals. Health Communications, Inc. • Bimonthly. $26.00 per year. Covers both clinical and societal aspects of substance abuse.

Drug and Alcohol Abuse Education. Editorial Resources, Inc. • Monthly. $84.00 per year. Newsletter covering education, prevention, and treatment relating to abuse of drugs and alcohol.

International Drug Report. International Narcotic Enforcement Officers Association Inc. • Description: Discusses current trends in narcotic abuse and enforcement, legal decisions concerning drug abuse, and related subjects. Carries news articles, scientific reports, statistics, and agency information. Recurring features include book reviews, notices of meetings, and news from U.S. Customs and the Drug Enforcement Administration.

Journal of Alcohol and Drug Education. American Alcohol and Drug Information Foundation. • Three times a year. $45.00 per year.

Journal of Drug Education. Baywood Publishing Co., Inc. • Quarterly. Individuals, $60.00 per year; institutions, $237.00 per year.

Journal of Drug Issues. Florida State University, School of Criminology and Criminal Justice. • Quarterly. Individuals, $95.00 per year; institutions, $120.00 per year.

A Journal of Ethnicity in Substance Abuse. Haworth Press, Inc. • Quarterly. $380.00 per year. Includes print and online editions. Edited for researchers and practitioners. Covers various areas of susbstance abuse, including alcoholism. Formerly *Drugs and Society.*

Workplace Substance Abuse Advisor. LRP Publications. • Description: Reviews federal, state, and local laws and regulations concerning alcohol and drug use, testing, and policies. Discusses significant court decisions. Contains information on the drug enforcement budgets at all levels of government. Examines employee assistance plans and other educational programs designed to help substance abusers.

STATISTICS SOURCES

Crime in America's Top-Rated Cities: A Statistical Profile. Grey House Publishing. • 2000. $155.00. Third edition. Contains 20-year data for major crime categories in 76 cities, suburbs, metropolitan areas, and the U. S. Also includes statistics on correctional facilities, inmates, hate crimes, illegal drugs, and other crime-related matters.

Statistics on Alcohol, Drug, and Tobacco Use: A Selection of Statistical Charts, Graphs and Tables about Alcohol, Drug and Tobacco Use from a Variety of Published Sources with Explanatory Comments. Gale Cengage Learning. • 1995. $85.00. Includes graphs, charts, and tables arranged within subject chapters. Citations to data sources are provided. (Statistics on...Series: vol. 1).

World Factbook. U.S. National Technical Information Service. • Annual. $83.00. Prepared by the Central Intelligence Agency. For all countries of the world, provides current economic, demographic, geographic, communications, government, defense force, and illicit drug trade information (where applicable).

TRADE/PROFESSIONAL ASSOCIATIONS

American Pharmaceutical Association-Academy of Pharmacy Practice and Management. c/o Anne Burns, 2215 Constitution Ave., N.W., Washington, DC 20037-2895. Phone: 800-237-2742 or (202)628-4410 Fax: (202)783-2351 E-mail: apha-appm@mail.aphanet.org • URL: http://www.aphanet.org • Pharmacists concerned with rendering professional services directly to the public, without regard for status of employment or environment of practice. Formerly Academy of Pharmacy Practice and Management.

Drug, Chemical and Allied Trades Association. 510 Route 130, Suite B1, East Windsor, NJ 08520. Phone: 800-640-3228 or (609)448-1000 Fax: (609)448-1944 E-mail: mtimony@dcat.org • URL: http://www.dcat.org • Formerly Drug, Chemical and Allied Trades Section of the New York Board of Trade.

International Narcotic Enforcement Officers Association. 112 State St., Suite 1200, Albany, NY 12207-2079. Phone: (518)463-6232 Fax: (518)432-3378 E-mail: inepa@iopener.net • URL: http://www.ineoa.org • Formerly National Narcotic Enforcement Officers Association.

Section for Psychiatric and Substance Abuse Services. c/o American Hospital Association, 1 N Franklin St., Chicago, IL 60606-3421. Phone: 800-242-4890 or (312)422-3000 Fax: (312)422-4796 E-mail: hromero@aha.org • URL: http://www.aha.org.

OTHER SOURCES

World Drug Report. United Nations Publications. • Annual. $25.00. Issued by the United Nations Office for Drug Control and Crime Prevention. Includes maps, graphs, charts, and tables.

DRUG INDUSTRY

See: PHARMACEUTICAL INDUSTRY

DRUG STORES

See also: CHAIN STORES; DISCOUNT HOUSES; PHARMACEUTICAL INDUSTRY

GENERAL WORKS

Pharmaceutical Marketing in the 21st Century. Mickey C. Smith, editor. Haworth Press, Inc. • 1996. $49.95. Various authors discuss the marketing, pricing, distribution, and retailing of prescription drugs. (Pharmaceutical Marketing and Management Series, Vol. 10, Nos. 2,3&4).

Pharmacy: What It Is and How It Works. William N. Kelly. CRC Press. • 2002. $39.95. Serves as an introduction to the field of pharmacy, including a history of the profession and information on career opportunities. Chapters are included on drug development, uses of drugs, pricing, information technology for pharmacies, and career planning.

ALMANACS AND YEARBOOKS

Family Almanac. National Asociation of Retail Druggists. Creative Publishing. • Annual. Free at participating pharmacies. Formerly *NARD Almanac and Health Guide.*

CD-ROM DATABASES

OECD Statistical Compendium. Organization for Economic Cooperation and Development. • Semiannual. $1,905.00 per year for 1 to 10 users. CD-ROM contains more than 730,000 monthly, quarterly, and annual time series for OECD countries, 1960 to date. Includes fully searchable data on agriculture, food, economic indicators, national accounts, employment, energy, finance, industry, technology, and foreign trade. Results can be displayed in various forms.

FINANCIAL RATIOS

Almanac of Business and Industrial Financial Ratios. Leo Troy. Aspen Publishers, Inc. • 2003. $125.95. Includes CD-Rom. Contains financial ratios derived from federal tax returns. Ratios for each of about 200 industries are arranged according to company asset size. (Almanac of Business and Industrial Financial Ratios Series).

HANDBOOKS AND MANUALS

Financial Management for Pharmacists: A Decision-Making Approach. Norman V. Carroll. Lippincott Williams and Wilkins. • 1997. $39.00. Second edition.

Managing Pharmacy Practice: Principles, Strategies, and Systems. Andrew M. Peterson. CRC Press. • 2004. $69.95. Covers basic management theory and systems as applied to pharmacies. Includes discussion of current trends in managed care systems, reimbursement, formularies, and drug benefit systems.

INTERNET DATABASES

Advance Monthly Sales for Retail Trade and Food Services. U. S. Census Bureau. Phone: 800-541-8345 or (301)763-4636 Fax: (301)457-3842 E-mail: rcb@census.gov • URL: http://www.census.gov/svsd/www/fullpub.html • Web pages provide monthly sales figures for a wide range of retail businesses. Advance, preliminary, and final statistics are provided for the latest month available in each case, with a previous-year comparison. Updates are monthly.

Business 2.0 Web Guide to the Best Business Links. Business 2.0 Media Inc. Phone: (415)293-4800 E-mail: support@business2.com • URL: http://www.business2.com/webguide • Web site presents an extensive, searchable directory of links to "the best, most informative, and authoritative web pages." Twenty main categories cover business, finance, career, company information, people, and technology topics, with thousands of subtopics, all linking to Web sites recommended by experienced business researchers. Fees: Free.

Fedstats. Federal Interagency Council on Statistical Policy. Phone: (202)395-7254 • URL: http://www.fedstats.gov • Web site features an efficient search facility for full-text statistics produced by more than 100 federal agencies, including the Census Bureau, the Bureau of Economic Analysis, and the Bureau of Labor Statistics. Boolean searches can be made within one agency or for all agencies combined. Links are offered to international statistical bureaus, including the UN, IMF, OECD, UNESCO, Eurostat, and 20 individual countries. Fees: Free.

FreeLunch.com. Economy.com, Inc. Phone: (610)696-8700 Fax: (610)696-1678 • URL: http://www.freelunch.com • Web site provides free access to more than 1.5 million economic and financial data series, covering industry, demographics, labor markets, prices, retail sales, government spending, trade, interest rates, housing starts, the stock market, and many other topics. Data is available for various time periods in either chart or table form. Searching is offered. Fees: Free, but registration required. Economy.com, Inc. also offers fee-based economic analysis at *The Dismal Scientist* site (http://www.dismal.com).

PERIODICALS AND NEWSLETTERS

America's Pharmacist. National Community Pharmacists Association. • Monthly. $50.00 per year. Formerly *N A R D Journal.*

Chain Drug Review: The Reporter for the Chain Drug Store Industry. Racher Press, Inc. • 21 times a year. $136.00 per year. Covers news and trends of concern to the chain drug store industry. Includes special articles on OTC (over-the-counter) drugs.

Community Pharmacist: Meeting the Professional and Educational Needs of Today's Practitioner. ELF Publicatons, Inc. • Bimonthly. $25.00 per year. Edited for retail pharmacists in various settings, whether independent or chain-operated. Covers both pharmaceutical and business topics.

Computertalk: For Contemporary Pharmacy Management. Computertalk Associates, Inc. • Bimonthly. $50.00 per year. Provides detailed advice and information on computer systems for pharmacies, including a buyers' guide issue.

Drug Store News. Lebhar-Friedman Inc. • Biweekly. Free to qualified personnel; others, $99.00 per year.

Drug Topics. Thomson Medical Economics. • 23 times a year. $61.00 per year. Edited for retail pharmacists, hospital pharmacists, pharmacy chain store executives, wholesalers, buyers, and others concerned with drug dispensing and drug store management. Provides information on new products, including personal care items and cosmetics.

The Green Sheet. F-D-C Reports, Inc. • Weekly. $109.00 per year. Newsletter for retailers and wholesalers of pharmaceutical products. Includes pricing developments and new drug announcements.

Pharmacy Times: Practical Information for Today's Pharmacists. Medical World Communications. • Monthly. Individuals, $57.00 per year; institutions, $103.00 per year. Edited for pharmacists. Covers store management, new products, regulations, home health care products, managed care issues, etc.

Retail Pharmacy Management. McMahon Group. • Monthly. $60.00 per year. Features include product news for pharmacists and financial news for chain store executives. Formerly *Retail Pharmacy Management News.*

U. S. Pharmacist. Jobson Publishing LLC. • Monthly. $30.00 per year. Covers a wide variety of topics for independent, chain store, hospital, and other pharmacists.

PRICE SOURCES

First DataBank Blue Book. Hearst Corp. • Annual. $65.00. List of manufacturers of prescription and over-the-counter drugs, sold in retail drug stores. Formerly *American Druggist Blue Book.*

RESEARCH CENTERS AND INSTITUTES

Pharmaceutical Marketing and Management Research Program. University of Mississippi, Waller Lab Complex, Room 101, University, MS 38677. Phone: (662)915-5948 Fax: (662)915-5262 E-mail: mkolassa@olemiss.edu • URL: http://www.olemiss.edu/depts/rips.

STATISTICS SOURCES

Annual Benchmark Report for Retail Trade and Food Services...A Detailed Summary of Retail Sales, Purchases, Accounts Receivable, Inventories, and Food Service Sales. Available from U. S. Government Printing Office. • Annual. $13.00. Issued by the U.S. Census Bureau. Provides detailed annual and monthly retail statistics for the most recent 10 years. Includes data for various kinds of retail outlets, including automobiles, furniture, appliances, building supplies, grocery stores, drug stores, gasoline stations, clothing, sporting goods, department stores, and restaurants.

Business Statistics of the United States. Linz Audain and Cornelia J. Strawser. Bernan Associates. • Annual. $147.00. Based on *Business Statistics,* formerly issue by the Bureau of Economic Analysis, U. S. Department of Commerce. Provides basic data for a wide variety of U. S. industries, services, and economic indicators. Most statistics are shown annually for 30 years and monthly for the most recent four years.

Industry Profile and Healthcare Factbook. Healthcare Distribution Management Association. • Annual. $349.00. Provides 266 statistical tables in three sections: "Industry Profile" (financial ratios related to drug distribution), "Pharmaceutical and Healthcare Distribution Trends and Facts," and "Healthcare Factbook" (expenditures, insurance utilization, company/product rankings, drug price inflation, generics, OTC, drug store data, hospital statistics, healthcare consumer summaries, etc.). Also known as *HDMA Factbook.* The Healthcare Distribution Management Association was formerly the National Wholesale Druggists' Association.

Lilly Digest. Eli Lilly and Co. • Annual. $30.00. Includes drug store financial data.

Lilly Hospital Pharmacy Survey. Eli Lilly and Co. • Annual. $30.00. Includes financial data for drug stores located in hospitals.

Standard & Poor's Industry Surveys. Standard & Poor's. • Semiannual. $1,800.00. Two looseleaf volumes. Includes monthly *Supplements.* Provides detailed, individual surveys of 52 major industry groups. Each survey is revised on a semiannual basis. Also includes "Monthly Investment Review" (industry group investment analysis) and monthly "Trends & Projections" (economic analysis).

Survey of Current Business. Available from U. S. Government Printing Office. • Monthly. $63.00 per year. Issued by Bureau of Economic Analysis, U. S. Department of Commerce. Presents a wide variety of business and economic data.

WEFA Industrial Monitor. John Wiley and Sons, Inc. • Annual. $65.00. Prepared by industry analysts at WEFA, an economic forecasting and consulting firm (originally Wharton Econometric Forecasting Associates). Contains discussions of the outlook for major U. S. industries, with many 10-year forecasts (WEFA Web site is http://www.wefa.com).

TRADE/PROFESSIONAL ASSOCIATIONS

American Pharmaceutical Association-Academy of Pharmacy Practice and Management. c/o Anne Burns, 2215 Constitution Ave., N.W., Washington, DC 20037-2895. Phone: 800-237-2742 or (202)628-4410 Fax: (202)783-2351 E-mail: apha-appm@mail.aphanet.org • URL: http://www.aphanet.org • Pharmacists concerned with rendering professional services directly to the public, without regard for status of employment or environment of practice. Formerly Academy of Pharmacy Practice and Management.

Healthcare Distribution Management Association. 901 N Glebe Rd., Ste. 1000, 1821 Michael Faraday Dr., Ste. 400, Arlington, VA 22203. Phone: (703)787-0000 Fax: (703)935-3200 E-mail: info@hdmanet.org • URL: http://www.healthcaredistribution.org • Wholesalers and manufacturers of drug and health care products and industry service providers. Seeks to secure safe and effective distribution of health care products, create and exchange industry knowledge affecting the future of distribution management, and influence standards and business processes that produce efficient health care commerce. Compiles statistics; sponsors research and specialized education programs.

National Association of Chain Drug Stores. 413 N Lee St., Alexandria, VA 22313. Phone: (703)549-3001 Fax: (703)836-4869 • URL: http://www.nacds.org.

OTHER SOURCES

Mail Service Pharmacy Market. MarketResearch.com. • 1999. $3,250.00. Provides detailed market data, with forecasts to the year 2003.

DRUGS

See: DRUG ABUSE AND TRAFFIC;
NARCOTICS; PHARMACEUTICAL
INDUSTRY

DRUGS, GENERIC

See: GENERIC DRUG INDUSTRY

DRUGS, NONPRESCRIPTION

See: NONPRESCRIPTION DRUG INDUSTRY

DRUNKENNESS

See: ALCOHOLISM

DRY CLEANING INDUSTRY

See: CLEANING INDUSTRY

DUPLICATING MACHINES

See: COPYING MACHINE INDUSTRY

DUTIES

See: TARIFF; TAXATION

DYES AND DYEING

See also: TEXTILE INDUSTRY

ABSTRACTS AND INDEXES

AATC Review. American Association of Textile Chemists and Colorists. • Monthly. Free to members; non-members, $60.00 per year. Annual *Buyer's Guide* available. Formerly *Textile Chemist and Colorist and American Dyestuff Reporter.*

CPI Digest: Key to World Literature Serving the Coatings, Plastics, Fibers, Adhesives, and Related Industries (Chemical Process Industries). CPI Information Services. • Monthly. $397.00 per year. Abstracts of business and technical articles for polymer-based, chemical process industries. Includes a monthly list of relevant U. S. patents. International coverage.

DIRECTORIES

OPD Chemical Buyers Directory. Schnell Publishing Company Inc. • Covers: about 1,500 suppliers of chemical process materials and more than 300 companies that transport and store chemicals in the United States. Entries include: Company name, address, phone, list of products or services, telex, fax, e-mail address, internet address, branch offices.

HANDBOOKS AND MANUALS

Color Chemistry. Heinrich Zollinger. John Wiley and Sons, Inc. • 2003. $150.00. Third edition. Includes technical information for industrial chemists and others on dyes and pigments.

Industrial Dyes: Chemistry, Properties, Applications. Klaus Hunger, editor. John Wiley and Sons, Inc. • 2003. $185.00. Covers textile dyeing, nontextile dyeing, functional dyes, and optical brighteners. Includes health and safety aspects and examples of commercially available dyes.

ONLINE DATABASES

CA Search. Chemical Abstracts Service. • Guide to chemical literature, 1967 to present. Inquire as to on-line cost and availability.

PERIODICALS AND NEWSLETTERS

International Dyer. World Textile Publications Ltd. • Monthly. $90.00 per year.

International Textile Bulletin: Dyeing-Printing-Finishing Edition. ITS Publishing, International Textile Service. • Quarterly. $170.00 per year. Editions in Chinese, English, French, German, Italian and Spanish.

TRADE/PROFESSIONAL ASSOCIATIONS

Textile Processors, Service Trades, Health Care, Professional and Technical Employees International Union. 2210 Midwest Rd., No. 310, Oak Brook, IL 60523. Phone: (630)574-0422.

E

E-COMMERCE

See: ELECTRONIC COMMERCE

EATING FACILITIES, EMPLOYEES

See: EMPLOYEE LUNCHROOMS AND CAFETERIAS

EATING PLACES

See: RESTAURANTS, LUNCHROOMS, ETC.

ECOLOGY

See: ENVIRONMENT

ECONOMETRICS

See also: ECONOMIC RESEARCH; ECONOMIC STATISTICS; ECONOMICS

GENERAL WORKS

Advances in Econometrics and Quantitative Economics. Morris H. DeGroot and others. Blackwell Publishing. • 1995. $122.95.

An Introduction to the Theory and Practice of Econometrics. George G. Judge and others. John Wiley and Sons, Inc. • 1988. $106.95. Second edition.

The Theory and Practice of Econometrics. George G. Judge and others. John Wiley and Sons, Inc. • 1985. $109.95. Second edition. (Probability and Statistics Series).

CD-ROM DATABASES

EconLit. Available from SilverPlatter Information, Inc. • Monthly. Single-user, $1,600.00 per year. Provides CD-ROM citations, with abstracts, to articles from more than 500 economics journals. Time period is 1969 to date. Produced by the American Economic Association.

ENCYCLOPEDIAS AND DICTIONARIES

Dictionary of Econometrics. Adrian C. Darnell. Edward Elgar Publishing, Inc. • 1994. $160.00. Published by Edward Elgar Publishing Co. (UK).

Dictionary of Economics. Donald Rutherford. Routledge. • 2002. $90.00. Second edition.

HANDBOOKS AND MANUALS

Econometric Analysis. William H. Greene. Prentice Hall PTR. • 2000. Fourth edition. Price on application. Includes bibliographical references.

Econometric Methods. John Johnston and John N. DiNardo. McGraw-Hill. • 1996. $109.06. Fourth edition. Covers various models, equations, variables, relationships, and "A Smorgasbord of Computationally Intense Methods.".

Econometrics of Financial Markets. John Y. Campbell and others. Princeton University Press. • 1996. $70.00. Written for advanced students and industry professionals. Includes chapters on "The Predictability of Asset Returns," "Derivative Pricing Models," and "Fixed-Income Securities." Provides a discussion of the random walk theory of investing and tests of the theory.

Using Econometrics: A Practical Guide. Addison-Wesley. • 2000. $114.00. Fourth edition. (Economics Series).

ONLINE DATABASES

EconLit. American Economic Association. • Covers the worldwide literature of economics as contained in selected monographs and about 550 journals. Subjects include microeconomics, macroeconomics, economic history, inflation, money, credit, finance, accounting theory, trade, natural resource economics, and regional economics. Time period is 1969 to present, with monthly updates. Inquire as to online cost and availability.

PERIODICALS AND NEWSLETTERS

Econometric Theory. Cambridge University Press, Journals Dept. • Bimonthly. Individuals, $152.00 per year; institutions, $440.00 per year. Devoted to the advancement of theoretical research in econometrics.

Econometrica. Blackwell Publishing. • Bimonthly. Institutions, $301.00 per year. Includes print and online editions. Published in England by Basil Blackwell Ltd.

Journal of Applied Econometrics. John Wiley and Sons, Inc., Journals. • Bimonthly. Individuals, $85.00 per year; institutions, $1,050.00 per year.

Journal of Econometrics. Elsevier. • Monthly. Individuals, $160.00 per year; institutions, $2,463.00 per year.

Quantitative Finance. Available from American Institute of Physics. • Bimonthly. $340.00 per year. Print and online edition, $765.00 per year. Published in the UK by the Institute of Physics. A technical journal on the use of quantitative tools and applications in financial analysis and financial engineering. Covers such topics as portfolio theory, derivatives, asset allocation, return on assets, risk management, price volatility, financial econometrics, market anomalies, and trading systems.

RESEARCH CENTERS AND INSTITUTES

Center for Mathematical Studies in Economics and Management Sciences. Northwestern University, Weinberg College of Arts and Sciences, Dept. of Economics, 2001 Sheridan Rd., 302 Arthur Andersen Hall, Evanston, IL 60208-2600. Phone: (847)491-5140 Fax: (847)491-7001 • URL: http://www.kellogg.nwu.edu/research/math.

Cowles Foundation for Research in Economics. Yale University. 30 Hillhouse Ave., New Haven, CT 06520-8281. Phone: (203)432-3704 Fax: (203)432-6167 E-mail: john.geanakoplos@yale.edu • URL: http://www.cowles.econ.yale.edu.

Gregory C. Chow Econometric Research Program. Princeton University. Dept. of Economics, Princeton, NJ 08544-1021. Phone: (609)258-4014 Fax: (609)258-5561 E-mail: honore@princeton.edu • URL: http://www.princeton.edu/~erp.

TRADE/PROFESSIONAL ASSOCIATIONS

Econometric Society. New York University, Department of Economics, 19 W 4th St., 6th Fl., New York, NY 10012. Phone: (212)998-3820 Fax: (212)995-4487 E-mail: sashi@econometricsociety.org • URL: http://www.econometricsociety.org • Economists, statisticians, and mathematicians. Promotes studies that are directed towards unification of the theoretical and empirical approaches to economic problems and advancement of economic theory in its relation to statistics and mathematics.

ECONOMIC BOTANY

See also: AGRICULTURE

ABSTRACTS AND INDEXES

Biological and Agricultural Index. H. W. Wilson Co. • 11 times a year. Annual and quarterly cumulations. Price varies.

ENCYCLOPEDIAS AND DICTIONARIES

Dictionary of Economic Plants. J.C. Uphof. Lubrecht and Cramer, Ltd. • 1998. $80.00. Second enlarged revised edition.

PERIODICALS AND NEWSLETTERS

American Journal of Botany: Devoted to All Branches of Plant Sciences. Botanical Society of America. • Monthly. $295.00 per year. Includes *Plant Science Bulletin.*

The Botanical Review: Interpreting Botanical Progress. Society for Economic Botany. The New York Botanical Garden Press. • Quarterly. Individuals, $82.00 per year; institutions, $96.00 per year. Reviews articles in all fields of botany.

Economic Botany: Devoted to Applied Botany and Plant Utilization. Society for Economic Botany. New York Botanical Garden Press. • Quarterly. Individuals, $88.00 per year; institutions, $102.00 per year. Includes *Plants and People.* Newsletter. Original research and review articles on the uses of plants.

Journal of Crop Improvement. Haworth Press, Inc. • Semiannual. $300.00 per year to libraries; $80.00 per year to individuals. Topics include plant biotechnology, plant genetics, crop productivity, quality, safety, pest control, and environmental concerns. Formerly *Journal of Crop Production.*

Plant Science Bulletin. Department of Biology. • Description: Carries news of this Association of plant scientists, with some issues including brief articles of more general interest in the field. Recurring features include notices of awards, meetings, courses, and study and professional opportunities; annotated lists of botanical books; and book reviews.

RESEARCH CENTERS AND INSTITUTES

Morton Collectanea. University of Miami Dept. of Biology. P.O. Box 249118, Coral Gables, FL 33124-0421. Phone: (305)284-3973 Fax: (305)284-3039 E-mail: mgaines@umiami.edu • URL: http://www.fig.cox.miami.edu.

TRADE/PROFESSIONAL ASSOCIATIONS

Botanical Society of America. PO Box 299, Saint Louis, MO 63166-0299. Phone: (314)577-9566 Fax: (314)577-9515 E-mail: bsa-manager@botany.org • URL: http://www.botany.org.

Society for Economic Botany. PO Box 7075, Lawrence, KS 66044. Phone: 800-627-0629 or (785)843-1235 Fax: (785)843-1274 E-mail: info@econbot.org • URL: http://www.econbot.org • Botanists, anthropologist, pharmacologists and others interested in scientific studies of useful plants. Affiliated with American Association for the Advancement of Science and the Botanical Society of America.

OTHER SOURCES

Global Seed Markets. Theta Reports. • 2000. $1,040.00. Market research data. Covers the major seed sectors, including cereal crops, legumes, oilseed crops, fibre crops, and beet crops. Provides analysis of biotechnology developments. (Theta Report No. DS208E.).

ECONOMIC CONDITIONS

See: BUSINESS CONDITIONS

ECONOMIC CYCLES

See: BUSINESS CYCLES

ECONOMIC DEVELOPMENT

See also: DEVELOPING AREAS; INDUSTRIAL DEVELOPMENT; URBAN DEVELOPMENT

GENERAL WORKS

Economic and Social Survey of Asia and the Pacific. United Nations Publications. • Annual. $65.00. Emphasis is on trends in economic policy and economic development strategies.

Economic Development. Michael P. Todaro and Stephen C. Smith. Addison-Wesley. • 2002. Eight edition. Price on application. (Addison-Wesley Economic Series).

Economics of Development. Malcolm Gillis and others. W. W. Norton and Co., Inc. • 2001. $105.10. Fifth edition.

Global Economic Prospects and the Developing Countries, 1999-2000. The World Bank Group. • 2001. $25.00. Examines the economic connections between industrial and developing countries, with a different theme in each edition.

Global Economic Prospects 2004. The World Bank Group. • 2003. $38.00. "..offers an in-depth analysis of the economic prospects of developing countries.." Emphasis is on the impact of recessions and financial crises. Regional statistical data is included.

Towards a Sustainable Energy Future. Organization for Economic Cooperation and Development. • 2001. $100.00. Prepared by the International Energy Agency (IEA). Describes various policies for promoting sustainable energy, especially as related to economic development. Discusses "growing concerns about climate change and energy-supply security.".

ABSTRACTS AND INDEXES

PAIS International in Print. Public Affairs Information Service, Inc. • Monthly. $850.00 per year; cumulations three times a year. Provides topical citations to the worldwide literature of public affairs, economics, demographics, sociology, and trade. Text in English; indexed materials in English, French, German, Italian, Portuguese and Spanish.

Social Sciences Index. H. W. Wilson Co. • Quarterly, with annual cumulation. Price varies. Indexes more than 400 periodicals covering economics, environmental policy, government, insurance, labor, health care policy, plannning, public administration, public welfare, urban studies, women's issues, criminology, and related topics.

ALMANACS AND YEARBOOKS

Trade and Development Report and Overview. Available from United Nations Publications. • Annual. $45.00. Yearly overview of trends in international trade, including an analysis of the economic and trade situation in developing countries. Published by the United Nations Conference on Trade and Development (UNCTAD).

BIBLIOGRAPHIES

Regional Economic Development: Theories amd Strategies for Developing Countries. Marguerite N. Abd El-Shahid. Sage Publications, Inc. • 1994. $10.00.

CD-ROM DATABASES

International Development Statistics. Organization for Economic Cooperation and Development. • Annual. $71.00. Issued by the OECD Development Assistance Committee. CD-ROM contains data on aid to more than 180 recipient countries, including amount, origin, type, and recipients' external debt.

PAIS on CD-ROM. Public Affairs Information Service, Inc. • Quarterly. $1,995.00 per year. Provides a CD-ROM version of the online service, *PAIS International.* Contains over 500,000 citations to the literature of contemporary social, political, and economic issues.

Social Sciences Citation Index. ISI. • Monthly. Price on request. Provides CD-ROM indexing of articles appearing in 1700 leading social science journals worldwide, with additional selections from more than 5700 other journals. Time span is 1992 to date. Coverage includes economics, business, finance, management, communications, demographics, library and information science, political science, sociology, and many other subjects.

Social Sciences Citation Index: Compact Disc Edition with Abstracts. Institute for Scientific Information. • Monthly. Provides CD-ROM indexing and abstracting of "significant articles" from 1,700 social science journals worldwide, with additional selections from 3,200 other journals, 1986 to date. Includes economics, business, finance, management, communications, demographics,

information and library science, political science, sociology, and many other subjects.

WILSONDISC: Wilson Social Sciences Abstracts. H. W. Wilson Co. • Monthly. Includes unlimited online access to *Social Sciences Index* through WILSONLINE. Provides CD-ROM indexing from 1983 and abstracting from 1994 of more than 500 periodicals covering economics, area studies, community health, public administration, public welfare, urban studies, and many other topics related to the social sciences.

DIRECTORIES

Funding Sources for Community and Economic Development 2003-2004: A Guide to Current Sources for Local Programs and Projects. Greenwood Publishing Group, Inc. • 2003. $64.95. Sixth edition. Provides information on 2,600 funding sources. Includes "A Guide to Proposal Planning." (Funding Sources for Community and Economic Development Series).

ENCYCLOPEDIAS AND DICTIONARIES

Worldmark Encyclopedia of National Economies. Gale Cengage Learning. • 2002. $325.00. Four volumes. Covers both the current and historical development of the economies of 200 foreign nations. Includes analysis and statistics.

FINANCIAL RATIOS

IRS Corporate Financial Ratios. Available from MarketResearch.com. • 2002. $225.00. Published by Schonfeld & Associates, Inc. Presents 70 key financial ratios for 260 industries. Ratios are calculated from income statement and balance sheet data available from the Internal Revenue Service. Includes four asset size classes.

ONLINE DATABASES

Business and Industry. Gale Cengage Learning. • Contains online citations, abstracts, and selected fulltext from more than 1,000 trade journals, newspapers, and other publications. Provides general coverage of both manufacturing and service industries, including marketing, production, industry trends, key events, and information on specific companies. Time span is 1994 to date. Daily updates. Inquire as to online cost and availability. (Also available in a CD-ROM version.).

PAIS International. Public Affairs Information Service, Inc. • Corresponds to the former printed publications, *PAIS Bulletin* (1976-90) and *PAIS Foreign Language Index* (1972-90), and to the current *PAIS International in Print* (1991 to date). Covers economic, political, and sociological material appearing in periodicals, books, government documents, and other publications. Updating is monthly. Inquire as to online cost and availability.

Tablebase. Gale Cengage Learning. • Provides online numerical tabular data from a wide variety of business, organization, and government sources, including about 1,000 trade journals. Includes industry and individual company statistics relating to products, market share, sales forecasts, production, exports, market trends, etc. Time span is 1997 to date. Weekly updates. Inquire as to online cost and availability. (Also available in a CD-ROM version.).

Wilson Social Sciences Abstracts Online. H. W. Wilson Co. • Provides online abstracting and indexing of more than 500 periodicals covering area studies, community health, public administration, public welfare, urban studies, and many other social science topics. Time period is 1994 to date for abstracts and 1983 to date for indexing, with updates weekly. Inquire as to online cost and availability.

PERIODICALS AND NEWSLETTERS

Economic Development and Cultural Change. The University of Chicago Press, Journals Div. • Quarterly. Individuals, $50.00 per year; institutions,

$218.00 per year; students, $38.00 per year. Examines the economic and social forces that affect development and the impact of development on culture.

Economic Development Monitor. Whitaker Newsletters, Inc. • Biweekly. $247.00 per year. Newsletter. Covers the news of U. S. economic and industrial development, including legislation, regulation, planning, and financing.

Economic Development Quarterly: The Journal of American Revitalization. Sage Publications, Inc. • Quarterly. Institutions, $486.00 per year; includes print and online editions.

Economic Development Review. American Economic Development Council. • Quarterly. $50.00 per year.

Financial Flows and the Developing Countries. The World Bank Group. • Quarterly. $150.00 per year. Concerned mainly with debt, capital markets, and foreign direct investment. Includes statistical tables.

The Journal of Development Economics. Elsevier. • Bimonthly. Individuals, $135.00 per year; institutions, $1,491.00 per year.

The Journal of International Trade and Economic Development. Taylor and Francis Group. • Quarterly. Individuals, $81.00 per year; institutions, $529.00 per year. Emphasizes the effect of trade on the economies of developing nations.

Plants, Sites, and Parks. Reed Business Information. • Seven times a year. Free to qualified personnel; others, $43.90 per year. Covers economic development, site location, industrial parks, and industrial development programs.

RESEARCH CENTERS AND INSTITUTES

Center for International Policy. 1755 Massachusetts Ave., N. W., Ste. 550, Washington, DC 20036. Phone: (202)232-3317 Fax: (202)232-3440 E-mail: cip@ciponline.org • URL: http://www.ciponline.org • Research subjects include the International Monetary Fund, the World Bank, and other international financial institutions. Analyzes the impact of policies on social and economic conditions in developing countries.

Economic Growth Center. Yale University. 27 Hillhouse Ave., New Haven, CT 06520-8269. Phone: (203)432-3610 Fax: (203)432-3898 E-mail: louise. danishevsky@yale.edu • URL: http://www.econ. yale.edu.

Regional Economic Development Center. University of Memphis. Johnson Hall, Room 226, Memphis, TN 38152. Phone: (901)678-2056 Fax: (901)678-4162 E-mail: lburrell@memphis.edu • URL: http://www.planning.memphis.edu.

W. E. Upjohn Institute for Employment Research. 300 S. Westnedge Ave., Kalamazoo, MI 49007-4686. Phone: (616)343-5541 Fax: (616)343-3308 E-mail: eberts@we.upjohninst.org • URL: http:// www.upjohninst.org • Research fields include unemployment, unemployment insurance, worker's compensation, labor productivity, profit sharing, the labor market, economic development, earnings, training, and other areas related to employment.

STATISTICS SOURCES

Encyclopedia of American Industries. Gale Cengage Learning. • 2000. $560.00. Third edition. Two volumes. $280.00 per volume. Volume one is *Manufacturing Industries* and volume two is *Service and Non-Manufacturing Industries.* Provides the history, development, and recent status of approximately 1,000 industries. Includes statistical graphs, with industry and general indexes.

Global Development Finance. The World Bank Group. • Annual. $400.00.

Handbook of International Economic Statistics. Available from National Technical Information Service. • Annual. $40.00. Prepared by U. S. Central Intelligence Agency. Provides basic statistics for

comparing worldwide economic performance, with an emphasis on Europe, including Eastern Europe.

National Accounts of OECD Countries. OECD Publications and Information Center. • Annual. Two volumes. Price varies.

UNCTAD Handbook of Statistics. United Nations Conference on Trade and Development. United Nations Publications. • Annual. $80.00. Contains a "comprehensive collection of statistical data relevant to the analysis of world trade, investment, and development." Includes rank-orderings, growth rates, and 20-year time series.

The World Economy: A Millennial Perspective. Angus Maddison. Organization for Economic Cooperation and Development. • 2001. $63.00. "...covers the development of the entire world economy over the past 2000 years," including data on world population and gross domestic product (GDP) since the year 1000, and exports since 1820. Focuses primarily on the disparity in economic performance among nations over the very long term. More than 200 statistical tables and figures are provided.

TRADE/PROFESSIONAL ASSOCIATIONS

Bretton Woods Committee. 1726 M St. NW, Ste. 200, Washington, DC 20036. Phone: (202)331-1616 Fax: (202)785-9423 E-mail: info@brettonwoods. org • URL: http://www.brettonwoods.org • Corporate CEOs, university administrators, former government officials, state governors, association and trade union executives, and bankers. Seeks to inform and educate the public regarding the activities of the World Bank, International Monetary Fund, and other Multinational Development Banks (MDB). Promotes U.S. participation in MDBs.

Committee for Economic Development. 2000 L St., N.W., Suite 700, Washington, DC 20036. Phone: (202)296-5860 Fax: (202)223-0776 E-mail: info@ ced.org • URL: http://www.ced.org • Committee conducts research and formulates policy recommendations on national and international economic issues, including education and trade policy.

International Economic Development Council. 734 15th St. NW, Ste. 900, Washington, DC 20005. Phone: (202)223-7800 Fax: (202)223-4745 E-mail: cziegler@iedconline.org • URL: http://www. iedconline.org • Works to help economic development professionals improve the quality of life in their communities. Represents all levels of government, academia, and private industry; provides a broad range of member services including research, advisory services, conferences, professional certification, professional development, publications, legislative tracking and more.

National Association of State Development Agencies. 12884 Harbor Dr., Woodbridge, VA 22192. Phone: (703)490-6777 Fax: (703)492-4404 E-mail: spope@nasda.com • URL: http://www. nasda.com • Formerly Association of State Planning and Development Agencies.

National Policy Association. 3424 Porter St. NW, Washington, DC 20016-3126. Phone: (202)265-7685 Fax: (202)797-5516 E-mail: npa@npa1.org • URL: http://www.npa1.org • Research institution that helps private and public sector leaders from agriculture, business, labor, and academia to better understand national economic and social issues. Conducts research and analysis on national and international economic and social issues.

Organisation for Economic Co-Operation and Development. 2, rue Andre Pascal, F-75775 Paris Cedex 16, France. Phone: 33 1 45248200 E-mail: webmaster@oecd.org • URL: http://www.oecd.org. Society for International Development USA. 1875 Connecticut Ave. NW, Washington, DC 20009. Phone: (202)884-8590 Fax: (202)884-8499 E-mail:

sid@aed.org • URL: http://www.sidint.org.

OTHER SOURCES

World Investment Report. United Nations Publications. • Annual. $49.00. Concerned with foreign direct investment, economic development, regional trends, transnational corporations, and globalization.

ECONOMIC ENTOMOLOGY

See also: PESTICIDE INDUSTRY

ABSTRACTS AND INDEXES

Biological and Agricultural Index. H. W. Wilson Co. • 11 times a year. Annual and quarterly cumulations. Price varies.

Review of Agricultural Entomology: Consisting of Abstracts of Reviews of Current Literature on Applied Entomology Throughout the World. Available from CABI Publishing, North America. • Monthly. Institutions, $1,505.00 per year. Print and online edition, $1,505.00 per year. Published in England by CABI Publishing. Provides worldwide coverage of the literature. (Formerly *Review of Applied Entomology, Series A: Agricultural*.).

Review of Medical and Veterinary Entomology. Available from CABI Publishing, North America. • Monthly. Institutions, $855.00 per year. Print and online edition, $885.00 per year. Provides worldwide coverage of the literature. Formerly *Review of Applied Entomology, Series B: Medical and Veterinary*.

ALMANACS AND YEARBOOKS

Annual Review of Entomology. Annual Reviews. • Annual. Individuals, $70.00. Includes print and online editions. Institutions, $160.00; with online editions, $192.00.

CD-ROM DATABASES

AGRICOLA on SilverPlatter. Available from SilverPlatter Information, Inc. • Quarterly. $825.00 per year. Produced by the National Agricultural Library. Provides about three million citations on CD-ROM to the literature of agriculture, agricultural economics, animal sciences, entomology, fertilizer, food, forestry, nutrition, pesticides, plant science, water resources, and other topics. Each quarterly disc covers the past ten years, with archival discs available from 1970.

ENCYCLOPEDIAS AND DICTIONARIES

Encyclopedia of Agriculture Science. Charles J. Arntzen and Ellen M. Ritter, editors. Elsevier. • 1994. $900.00. Four volumes.

HANDBOOKS AND MANUALS

Introduction to Insect Pest Management. Robert L. Metcalf and William H. Luckmann. John Wiley and Sons, Inc. • 1994. $199.00. Third edition. (Environmental Science and Technology Series).

ONLINE DATABASES

Derwent Crop Protection File. Derwent, Inc. • Provides citations to the international journal literature of agricultural chemicals and pesticides from 1968 to date, with updating eight times per year. Formerly *PESTDOC.* Inquire as to online cost and availability.

PERIODICALS AND NEWSLETTERS

American Entomologist: Entomological Articles of General Interest. Entomological Society of America. • Quarterly. Individuals, $38.00 per year; institutions, $70.00 per year. Formerly *Entomological Society of America Bulletin.*

Entomological Society of America Annals: Devoted to the Interest of Classical Entomology. Entomological Society of America. • Bimonthly. Individuals,

For publishers addresses, refer to SOURCES CITED section at the back of the book.

283

$84.00 per year; institutions, $162.00 per year.

RESEARCH CENTERS AND INSTITUTES

Cattle Fever Tick Research Laboratory. U.S. Department of Agricultural Livestock Insects Laboratory, Rte. 3, PO Box 1010, Edinburg, TX 78539. Phone: (956)580-7268 Fax: (956)580-7261 E-mail: ronald.b.davey@aphis.udsa.gov.

Center for Integrated Plant Systems. Michigan State University. East Lansing, MI 48824-1311. Phone: (517)353-9430 Fax: (517)353-5598 E-mail: cips@msu.edu • URL: http://www.cips.msu.edu.

Food and Environmental Toxicology Laboratory. University of Florida. SW 23rd Dr., Bldg. 685, Gainesville, FL 32611. Phone: (352)392-1978 Fax: (352)392-1988.

Integrated Plant Protection Center. Oregon State University. 2040 Cordley Hall, Corvallis, OR 97331-2915. Phone: (541)737-3541 Fax: (541)737-3080 E-mail: koganm@bcc.orst.edu • URL: http://www.ippc.orst.edu.

Laboratory for Pest Control Application Technology. Ohio State University, Ohio Agricultural Research and Development Center, 1680 Madison Ave., Wooster, OH 44691-4096. Phone: (330)263-3931 Fax: (330)263-3686 E-mail: downer.2@osu.edu • URL: http://www.oardc.ohio-state.edu/lpcat • Conducts pest control research in cooperation with the U. S. Department of Agriculture.

Toxic Chemicals Laboratory. Cornell University. New York State College of Agriculture, Tower Rd., Ithaca, NY 14853-7401. Phone: (607)255-4538 Fax: (607)255-0599 E-mail: djl22@cornell.edu.

TRADE/PROFESSIONAL ASSOCIATIONS

American Entomological Society. 9301 Annapolis Rd., Ste. 300, Lanham, MD 20706. Phone: (301)731-4535 Fax: (301)731-4538 E-mail: esa@entsoc.org • URL: http://www.entsoc.org/ • Professional and amateur entomologists. Promotes the study of insects and publishes the results of research in the systematics and morphology of insects.

OTHER SOURCES

World Non-Agricultural Pesticide Markets. Theta Reports. • 2000. $1,670.00. Market research data. Includes home/garden pesticides, herbicides, professional pest-control products, and turf pesticides. (Theta Report No. DS191E.).

ECONOMIC FORECASTING

See: BUSINESS FORECASTING

ECONOMIC GEOLOGY

See also: MINES AND MINERAL RESOURCES

ENCYCLOPEDIAS AND DICTIONARIES

Glossary of Geology. Robert L. Bates and Julia A. Jackson. American Geological Institute. • 2000. $110.00. Fourth edition.

ONLINE DATABASES

GEOARCHIVE. Geosystems. • Citations to literature on geoscience and water. 1974 to present. Monthly updates. Inquire as to online cost and availability.

GEOREF. American Geological Institute. • Bibliography and index of geology and geosciences literature, 1785 to present. Inquire as to online cost and availability.

PERIODICALS AND NEWSLETTERS

Economic Geology and the Bulletin of the Society of Economic Geologists. Society of Economic Geologist. Economic Geology Publishing Co. •

Irregular. Individuals, $75.00 per year; institutions, $145.00 per year.

RESEARCH CENTERS AND INSTITUTES

Bureau of Economic Geology. University of Texas at Austin. University Station, P.O. Box X, Austin, TX 78713-8924. Phone: 888-839-4365 or (512)471-1534 Fax: (512)471-0140 E-mail: begmain@beg.utexas.edu • URL: http://www.utexas.edu/research/beg/.

Mineral Industry Research Laboratory. University of Alaska Fairbanks. P.O. Box 757240, Fairbanks, AK 99775-7240. Phone: (907)474-6347 Fax: (907)474-1121 E-mail: fysme@uaf.edu • URL: http://www.sme.uaf.edu.

TRADE/PROFESSIONAL ASSOCIATIONS

Society of Economic Geologists. 7811 Shaffer Parkway, Littleton, CO 80127. Phone: (720)981-7882 Fax: (720)981-7874 E-mail: seg@segweb.org • URL: http://www.segweb.org.

ECONOMIC HISTORY

See: BUSINESS HISTORY

ECONOMIC INDICATORS

GENERAL WORKS

Business Cycles: Theory, History, Indications, and Forecasting. Victor Zarnowitz. The University of Chicago Press. • 1992. $77.00. (National Bureau of Economic Research Monograph Series: Vol. 27).

Forecasting Business Trends. American Institute for Economic Research. • 2000. $6.00. Summarizes methods of economic forecasting, statistical indicators, methods of analyzing business cycles, and use of leading, coincident, and lagging indicators. Includes charts, tables, and a glossary of terms. (Economic Education Bulletin.).

Global Economic Prospects 2004. The World Bank Group. • 2003. $38.00. "..offers an in-depth analysis of the economic prospects of developing countries.." Emphasis is on the impact of recessions and financial crises. Regional statistical data is included.

ALMANACS AND YEARBOOKS

State of the World [year]. Worldwatch Institute. • Annual. $16.95. Provides yearly analysis of factors influencing the global environment.

Vital Signs [year]: The Trends That Are Shaping Our Future. Worldwatch Institute. • Annual. $14.95. Provides access to selected indicators showing social, economic, and environmental trends throughout the world. Includes data relating to food, energy, transportation, finance, population, and other topics.

World Development Report 2004. The World Bank Group. • Annual. $26.00. Covers history, conditions, and trends relating to economic globalization and localization. Includes selected data from *World Development Indicators* for 132 countries or economies. Key indicators are provided for 78 additional countries or economies.

CD-ROM DATABASES

OECD Statistical Compendium. Organization for Economic Cooperation and Development. • Semiannual. $1,905.00 per year for 1 to 10 users. CD-ROM contains more than 730,000 monthly, quarterly, and annual time series for OECD countries, 1960 to date. Includes fully searchable data on agriculture, food, economic indicators, national accounts, employment, energy, finance, industry, technology, and foreign trade. Results can be displayed in various forms.

World Development Report [CD-ROM]. The World Bank, Office of the Publisher. • Annual. CD-ROM includes the current edition of *World Development*

Report and 21 previous editions.

HANDBOOKS AND MANUALS

BCI Handbook. The Conference Board, Inc. • 2001. $20.00. Provides detailed descriptions of the economic series - Business Cycle Indicators - used by The Conference Board to determine current business conditions and predict the future direction of the U. S. economy. Data sources are indicated. (A previous version was published in 1982.).

Guide to Economic Indicators. Norman Frumkin. M. E. Sharpe, Inc. • 2000. $24.95. Third expanded revised edition. Provides detailed descriptions and sources of 50 economic indicators.

Guide to Everyday Economic Statistics. Gary E. Clayton and Martin G. Giesbrecht. McGraw-Hill. • 2001. $19.90. Fifth edition. Contains clear explanations of the commonly used economic indicators.

Investor's Guide to Economic Indicators. Charles R. Nelson. John Wiley and Sons, Inc. • 1989. $17.95.

Tracking America's Economy. Norman Frumkin. M. E. Sharpe, Inc. • 2004. $72.95. Fourth edition. Provides detailed explanations of the meaning and methodology of the leading U. S. economic indicators. Covers such topics as employment data, financial indicators, productivity, housing, government spending, balance of payments, and taxation.

INTERNET DATABASES

BanxQuote Banking, Mortgage, and Finance Center. BanxQuote, Inc. Phone: (914)722-1600 Fax: (914)722-6630 E-mail: info@banx.com • URL: http://www.banx.com • Web site quotes interest rates paid by banks around the country on various savings products, as well as rates paid by consumers for automobile loans, mortgages, credit cards, home equity loans, and personal loans. Also provided: stock quotes, indexes, stock options, futures trading data, economic indicators, and links to many other financial sites. Daily updates. Fees: Free.

Bondtalk.com: Live Talk & Analysis on the Bond Market & the Economy. Miller Tabak & Co., LLC. Phone: (212)370-0040 E-mail: acrescenzi@bondtalk.com • URL: http://www.bondtalk.com • Web site provides extensive, free data on the fixed income securities market, including individual bond prices, yields, interest rates, Federal Reserve information, charts, bond market news, and economic analysis. Also offered on a fee basis is "Bondtalkpro.com: The New and Enhanced Service for Market Professionals.".

Bureau of Economic Analysis (BEA). U. S. Department of Commerce, Bureau of Economic Analysis. Phone: (202)606-9900 Fax: (202)606-5310 E-mail: webmaster@bea.doc.gov • URL: http://www.bea.doc.gov • Web site includes "News Release Information" covering national, regional, and international economic estimates from the BEA. Highlights of releases appear online the same day, complete text and tables appear the next day. "Recent News Releases" section provides titles for past nine months, with links. "BEA Data and Methodology" includes "Frequently Requested NIPA Data" (national income and product accounts, such as gross domestic product and personal income). Other statistics are available. Fees: Free.

Business 2.0 Web Guide to the Best Business Links. Business 2.0 Media Inc. Phone: (415)293-4800 E-mail: support@business2.com • URL: http://www.business2.com/webguide • Web site presents an extensive, searchable directory of links to "the best, most informative, and authoritative web pages." Twenty main categories cover business, finance, career, company information, people, and technology topics, with thousands of subtopics, all linking to Web sites recommended by experienced business researchers. Fees: Free.

Business Week Online. McGraw-Hill. Phone: (212)512-2511 Fax: (684)842-6101 • URL: http://www.businessweek.com • Web site provides complete contents of current issue of *Business Week* plus "BW Daily" with additonal business news, financial market quotes, and corporate information from Standard & Poor's. Includes various features, such as "Banking Center" with mortgage and interest data, and "Interactive Computer Buying Guide." The "Business Week Archive" is fully searchable back to 1996.

Fedstats. Federal Interagency Council on Statistical Policy. Phone: (202)395-7254 • URL: http://www.fedstats.gov • Web site features an efficient search facility for full-text statistics produced by more than 100 federal agencies, including the Census Bureau, the Bureau of Economic Analysis, and the Bureau of Labor Statistics. Boolean searches can be made within one agency or for all agencies combined. Links are offered to international statistical bureaus, including the UN, IMF, OECD, UNESCO, Eurostat, and 20 individual countries. Fees: Free.

FreeLunch.com. Economy.com, Inc. Phone: (610)696-8700 Fax: (610)696-1678 • URL: http://www.freelunch.com • Web site provides free access to more than 1.5 million economic and financial data series, covering industry, demographics, labor markets, prices, retail sales, government spending, trade, interest rates, housing starts, the stock market, and many other topics. Data is available for various time periods in either chart or table form. Searching is offered. Fees: Free, but registration required. Economy.com, Inc. also offers fee-based economic analysis at *The Dismal Scientist* site (http://www.dismal.com).

Summary of Commentary on Current Economic Conditions by Federal Reserve District [the Beige Book]. Board of Governors of the Federal Reserve System. Phone: (202)452-3000 Fax: (202)452-3819 • URL: http://www.federalreserve.gov/fomc/beigebook/2004/ • Free Web site provides current "anecdotal information" eight times a year on economic conditions within each of the 12 Federal Reserve Districts, plus an extensive national *Summary*. Text is based on the opinions of bank officials, business executives, economists, financial market experts, and others. Typically contains views of consumer spending, manufacturing, services, credit, employment, prices, wages, and the economy in general. Usually referred to as the Beige Book.

U. S. Census Bureau: The Official Statistics. U. S. Bureau of the Census. Phone: (301)763-4100 Fax: (301)763-4794 • URL: http://www.census.gov • Web site is "Your Source for Social, Demographic, and Economic Information." Contains "Current U. S. Population Count," "Current Economic Indicators," and a wide variety of data under "Other Official Statistics." Keyword searching is provided. Fees: Free.

ONLINE DATABASES

OECD Main Economic Indicators. Organization for Economic Cooperation and Development. • International statistics provided by OECD, 1960 to date. Monthly updates. Inquire as to online cost and availability.

PERIODICALS AND NEWSLETTERS

Financial Times Currency Forecaster: Consensus Forecasts of the Worldwide Currency and Economic Outlook. Briefings Publishing Group. • Monthly. $695.00 per year. Newsletter. Provides forecasts of foreign currency exchange rates and economic conditions. Supplement available: *Mid-Month Global Financial Report.*

Regional Economics and Markets: A Quarterly Analysis from the Conference Board. The Conference Board. • Quarterly. Members, $145.00 per year; non-members, $295.00 per year. Summarizes economic trends and prospects for nine geographic regions of the U. S. Provides data on key predictive indexes, including employment, housing permits, retail sales, consumer confidence, and help-wanted

advertising. Charts and graphs are included.

Research Reports. American Institute for Economic Research. • Semimonthly. $59.00 per year. Newsletter. Alternate issues include charts of "Primary Leading Indicators," "Primary Roughly Coincident Indicators," and "Primary Lagging Indicators," as issued by The Conference Board (formerly provided by the U. S. Department of Commerce).

World Watch: Working for a Sustainable Future. Worldwatch Institute. • Bimonthly. $25.00 per year. Emphasis is on environmental trends, including developments in population growth, climate change, human behavior, the role of government, and other factors.

RESEARCH CENTERS AND INSTITUTES

Conference Board, Inc. The Conference Board, Inc. 845 3rd Ave., New York, NY 10022. Phone: (212)339-0345 Fax: (212)980-7014 E-mail: info@conference-board.org • URL: http://www.conference-board.org • Business management practices worldwide, especially economic, and demographic in nature. Specific concerns include: corporate citizenship, including corporate contributions, diversity, environmental policy and issues, and government relations; corporate governance, including boards of directors, role of chief executives, relations with institutional investors, and shareholder input and influence; economics, including economic and financial forecasts, consumer confidence, leading economic indicators, North American outlook and trends, and global economic environment; human resources and organizational effectiveness, including organization structure and design, compensation and benefits, training and development, and communications; and performance excellence.

Worldwatch Institute. Worldwatch Institute. 1776 Massachusetts Ave. NW, Washington, DC 20036-1904. Phone: (202)452-1999 or (202)452-1999 Fax: (202)296-7365 E-mail: worldwatch@worldwatch.org • URL: http://www.worldwatch.org • Global trends in the availability and management of both human and natural resources, including research in energy, food policy, population, development, technology, the environment, economics, toxics, and recycling.

STATISTICS SOURCES

The AIER Chart Book. AIER Research Staff. American Institute for Economic Research. • Annual. $4.00. A compact compilation of long-range charts ("Purchasing Power of the Dollar," for example, goes back to 1780) covering various aspects of the U. S. economy. Includes inflation, interest rates, debt, gold, taxation, stock prices, etc. (Economic Education Bulletin.).

Business Cycle Indicators: A Monthly Report from the Conference Board. Conference Board. • Monthly. $130.00 per year. Contains detailed business and economic statistics in tables that were formerly published by the U. S. Department of Commerce in *Survey of Current Business*, and before that, in the discontinued *Business Conditions Digest*. Includes composite indexes of leading economic indicators, coincident indicators, and lagging indicators.

Business Statistics of the United States. Linz Audain and Cornelia J. Strawser. Bernan Associates. • Annual. $147.00. Based on *Business Statistics*, formerly issue by the Bureau of Economic Analysis, U. S. Department of Commerce. Provides basic data for a wide variety of U. S. industries, services, and economic indicators. Most statistics are shown annually for 30 years and monthly for the most recent four years.

Country Outlooks. Pyramid Research. • Looseleaf. $495.00 per year. Covers 81 major countries, with each country updated quarterly. Provides detailed

economic data and financial forecasts, including tables of key economic indicators.

Country Profile: Annual Survey of Political and Economic Background. Economist Intelligence Unit. • Annual. $245.00 per country or country group. Contains statistical tables "showing the last 6 year run of macro-economic indicators, and an overview of a country's politics, economy and industry." Covers 180 countries in 115 annual editions.

Economic and Budget Outlook: Fiscal Years 2004-2013. Available from U. S. Government Printing Office. • 2002. $27.00. Issued by the Congressional Budget Office (http://www.cbo.gov). Contains CBO economic projections and federal budget projections annually in billions of dollars. An appendix contains "Historical Budget Data" annually from, including revenues, outlays, deficits, surpluses, and debt held by the public.

Economic Indicators. Council of Economic Advisors, Executive Office of the President. Available from U.S. Government Printing Office. • Monthly. $55.00 per year.

Economic Indicators Handbook: Time Series, Conversions, Documentation. Gale Cengage Learning. • 2002. $205.00. Sixth edition. Provides data for about 175 U. S. economic indicators, such as the consumer price index (CPI), gross national product (GNP), and the rate of inflation. Values for series are given since inception, in both original form and adjusted for inflation. A bibliography of sources is included.

Leading Economic Indicators and Related Composite Indexes. The Conference Board. • Monthly. $24.00 per year. Shows monthly changes in the composite indexes of leading, coincident, and lagging economic indicators, formerly computed by the U. S. Department of Commerce. Tables present monthly data for up to 10 years, with a one-page line chart covering 18 years. (The Conference Board News.).

Main Economic Indicators. OECD Publication and Information Center. • Monthly. $450.00 per year. "The essential source of timely statistics for OECD member countries." Includes a wide variety of business, economic, and industrial data for the 29 OECD nations.

Main Economic Indicators: Historical Statistics. OECD Publications and Information Center. • Annual. $475.00. Includes online edition.

Survey of Current Business. Available from U. S. Government Printing Office. • Monthly. $63.00 per year. Issued by Bureau of Economic Analysis, U. S. Department of Commerce. Presents a wide variety of business and economic data.

The World Bank Atlas. World Bank Group. • Annual. $10.00. Contains "color maps, charts, and graphs representing the main social, economic, and environmental indicators for 209 countries and territories" (publisher).

World Development Indicators. The World Bank Group. • Annual. $60.00. Provides data and information on the people, economy, environment, and markets of 148 countries. Emphasis is on statistics relating to major development issues.

TRADE/PROFESSIONAL ASSOCIATIONS

Institute for Economic Analysis. c/o John S. Atlee, Four High St., No. 3, Brattleboro, VT 05301. Phone: (802)254-0089 Fax: (802)254-0089 E-mail: jatlee@sover.net • URL: http://www.iea-macro-economics.org.

ECONOMIC PLANNING

See: ECONOMIC POLICY

ECONOMIC POLICY

See also: ECONOMIC DEVELOPMENT;
ECONOMICS

GENERAL WORKS

Age of Diminished Expectations: U. S. Economic Policy in the 1990s. Paul Krugman. MIT Press. • 1997. $50.00. Third edition. States that the big problem is slow growth in productivity.

Economic Parables and Policies: An Introduction to Economics. Laurence S. Seidman. M. E. Sharpe, Inc. • 2004. $64.95. Third edition. Emphasis is on current economic policy in such areas as taxation, trade, health care, education, social security, and the environment. Popularly written.

Manias, Panics, and Crashes: A History of Financial Crises. Charles P. Kindleberger. John Wiley and Sons, Inc. • 2000. $19.95. Fourth edition. Provides a history of financial troubles from 1618 to modern times, with greed as a central theme. (Investment Classic Series).

Money, Banking, and the Economy. Thomas Mayer and others. W. W. Norton & Co., Inc. • 1996. $92. 45. Sixth edition.

The New Financial Order: Risk in the 21st Century. Robert J. Shiller. Princeton University Press. • 2003. $29.95. By the author of *Irrational Exuberance* (2000). Recommends that risk management schemes be developed for application to the risks of everyday life, as in such chapters as "Insurance for Livelihoods and Home Values," "Inequality Insurance: Protecting the Distribution of Income," and "Intergenerational Social Security: Sharing Risks Between Young and Old.".

Setting National Priorities: Budget Choices for the Next Century. Robert D. Reischauer, editor. Brookings Institution Press. • 1996. $42.95. Contains discussions of the federal budget, economic policy, and government spending policy.

U. S. Trade Policy: History, Theory, and the WTO. William A. Lovett and others. M. E. Sharpe, Inc. • 2004. $66.95. Second edition. Discusses the consequences of free trade and the activities of the World Trade Organization. Covers U. S. trade history from colonial times to recent years.

Women and the Economy: A Reader. Ellen Mutari and Deborah M. Figart, editors. M. E. Sharpe, Inc. • 2003. $69.95. A collection of essays presenting a feminist approach to economic issues.

ABSTRACTS AND INDEXES

Social Sciences Index. H. W. Wilson Co. • Quarterly, with annual cumulation. Price varies. Indexes more than 400 periodicals covering economics, environmental policy, government, insurance, labor, health care policy, planning, public administration, public welfare, urban studies, women's issues, criminology, and related topics.

CD-ROM DATABASES

Social Sciences Citation Index. ISI. • Monthly. Price on request. Provides CD-ROM indexing of articles appearing in 1700 leading social science journals worldwide, with additional selections from more than 5700 other journals. Time span is 1992 to date. Coverage includes economics, business, finance, management, communications, demographics, library and information science, political science, sociology, and many other subjects.

Social Sciences Citation Index: Compact Disc Edition with Abstracts. Institute for Scientific Information. • Monthly. Provides CD-ROM indexing and abstracting of "significant articles" from 1,700 social science journals worldwide, with additional selections from 3,200 other journals, 1986 to date. Includes economics, business, finance, management, communications, demographics, information and library science, political science,

sociology, and many other subjects.

WILSONDISC: Wilson Social Sciences Abstracts. H. W. Wilson Co. • Monthly. Includes unlimited online access to *Social Sciences Index* through WILSONLINE. Provides CD-ROM indexing from 1983 and abstracting from 1994 of more than 500 periodicals covering economics, area studies, community health, public administration, public welfare, urban studies, and many other topics related to the social sciences.

ENCYCLOPEDIAS AND DICTIONARIES

Blackwell Encyclopedic Dictionary of Managerial Economics. Robert McAuliffe, editor. Blackwell Publishers. • 1999. $138.95. The editor is associated with Boston College. Contains definitions of key terms combined with longer articles written by various U. S. and foreign business educators. Includes bibliographies and index. *Blackwell Encyclopedia of Management Series.*

Dictionary of Economics. Donald Rutherford. Routledge. • 2002. $90.00. Second edition.

Work in America: An Encyclopedia of History, Policy, and Society. Carl E. Van Horn and Herbert A. Schaffner. ABC-CLIO, Inc. • 2003. $185.00. Two volumes. Contains 265 A-Z entries covering work in the U. S. from the Industrial Revolution to modern times. Covers labor-related topics in economics, history, law, welfare, employment policy, and other areas.

INTERNET DATABASES

Factiva. Dow Jones Reuters Business Interactive, LLC. Phone: 800-369-7466 or (609)452-1511 Fax: (609)520-5770 E-mail: solutions@factiva.com • URL: http://www.factiva.com • Fee-based Web site provides "global news and business information through Web sites and content integration solutions." Includes Dow Jones and Reuters newswires, The Wall Street Journal, and more than 7,000 other sources of current news, historical articles, market research reports, and investment analysis. Content includes 96 major U. S. newspapers, 900 non-English sources, trade publications, media transcripts, country profiles, news photos, etc.

Nexis.com. Lexis-Nexis Group. Phone: 800-227-4908 or (937)865-6800 Fax: (937)865-6909 E-mail: webmaster@prod.lexis-nexis.com • URL: http://www.nexis.com • Fee-based Web site offers searching of about 2.8 billion documents in some 30,000 news, business, and legal information sources. Features include a subject directory covering 1,200 topics in 34 categories and a Company Dossier containing information on more than 500,000 public and private companies. Boolean searching is offered.

Wall Street Journal Interactive Edition. Dow Jones & Co., Inc. Phone: 800-369-2834 or (212)416-2000 Fax: (212)416-2658 E-mail: inquiries@interactive. wsj.com • URL: http://www.wsj.com • Fee-based Web site providing online searching of worldwide information from the *The Wall Street Journal*. Includes "Company Snapshots," "The Journal's Greatest Hits," "Index to Market Data," "Journal Links," etc. Financial price quotes are available. Fees: $49.00 per year; $29.00 per year to print subscribers.

ONLINE DATABASES

Wilson Social Sciences Abstracts Online. H. W. Wilson Co. • Provides online abstracting and indexing of more than 500 periodicals covering area studies, community health, public administration, public welfare, urban studies, and many other social science topics. Time period is 1994 to date for abstracts and 1983 to date for indexing, with updates weekly. Inquire as to online cost and availability.

PERIODICALS AND NEWSLETTERS

Blue Chip Financial Forecasts: What Top Analysts are Saying About U. S. and Foreign Interest Rates, Monetary Policy, Inflation, and Economic Growth.

Aspen Publishers, Inc. • Monthly. $665.00 per year. Newsletter. Gives forecasts about a year in advance for interest rates, inflation, currency exchange rates, monetary policy, and economic growth rates.

Challenge: The Magazine of Economic Affairs. M. E. Sharpe, Inc. • Bimonthly. Individuals, $52.00 per year; institutions, $220.00 per year. Includes print and online editions. A nontechnical journal on current economic policy and economic trends.

International Monetary Fund Staff Papers. International Monetary Fund, Publication Services. • Quarterly. Individuals, $56.00 per year; students, $28.00 per year. Contains studies by IMF staff members on balance of payments, foreign exchange, fiscal policy, and related topics. Formerly *International Monetary Fund Staff Papers.*

Journal of Economic Perspectives. American Economic Association. • Quarterly. Membership. Emphasis is on the economic analysis of public policy issues.

The Wall Street Journal. Dow Jones & Co., Inc. • Daily. $189.00 per year. Covers news and trends relating to business, industry, finance, the economy, and international commerce. Provides extensive price and other data for the securities, commodity, options, futures, foreign exchange, and money markets.

RESEARCH CENTERS AND INSTITUTES

Bradley Policy Research Center. University of Rochester, William E. Simon Graduate School of Business Administration, Rochester, NY 14627. Phone: (585)275-2668 Fax: (585)275-0095 E-mail: hansen@simon.rochester.edu • URL: http://www. ssb.rochester.edu • Corporate control and corporate takeovers are among the research areas covered.

Brookings Institution. Brookings Institution. 1775 Massachusetts Ave. NW, Washington, DC 20036. Phone: (202)797-6000 Fax: (202)797-6004 E-mail: communications@brookings.edu • URL: http:// www.brookings.edu/ • Economics, including studies on what economic policies are most conducive to sustained growth of the U.S. economy, how social programs can be made more effective in an era of constrained resources, and how international economic relations can be improved; government, including studies on political institutions, the media, regulation and economic policy, and social policy; and foreign policy, including defense analysis and international economics and trade studies, and U.S. relations with, and regional studies on, the former Soviet Union, East Asia, China, the Middle East, Latin America, and Africa.

STATISTICS SOURCES

Budget and Economic Outlook: Fiscal Years [10-year period]. Available from U. S. Government Printing Office. • Annual. $27.00. Issued by the Congressional Budget Office (CBO). Reports on fiscal policy and provides baseline projections of federal budget for 10 years. Also offers "impartial analysis with no recommendations.".

TRADE/PROFESSIONAL ASSOCIATIONS

Hudson Institute. 1015 15th St. NW, 6th Fl., 1015 18th St., NW, Ste. 300, Washington, DC 20005. Phone: 800-HUDSON-0 or (202)974-2400 Fax: (202)974-2410 E-mail: info@hudson.org • URL: http://www.hudson.org • Members of this research center are elected from academic, governmental, and business/industrial sectors. Studies public policy issues in areas of national security, international and domestic economics, education and employment, energy and technology, agriculture and environment, and future studies. Studies are funded through contract or grant from government agencies, private businesses, foundations, associations, and individuals. Sometimes referred to as a "think tank", the institute focuses on "providing policymakers with a broad, workable, conceptual framework within which intelligent and successful policy decisions can be developed"; seeks to determine what issues will have the greatest long-term impact and to identify issues that may become urgent though they are not yet recognized as such. Conducts briefings on policy issues to corporate and other audiences. Distributes research reports to depository libraries.

ECONOMIC RESEARCH

See also: BUREAUS OF BUSINESS RESEARCH; BUSINESS RESEARCH

ABSTRACTS AND INDEXES

Social Sciences Index. H. W. Wilson Co. • Quarterly, with annual cumulation. Price varies. Indexes more than 400 periodicals covering economics, environmental policy, government, insurance, labor, health care policy, plannning, public administration, public welfare, urban studies, women's issues, criminology, and related topics.

ALMANACS AND YEARBOOKS

Research in Experimental Economics. Elsevier. • Dates vary. $84.00. Nine volumes. Supplement available *An Experiment in Non-Cooperative Oligopoly.*

Research in Law and Economics: A Research Annual. Richard O. Zerbe. Elsevier. • Dates vary. $78.50. 20 volumes. Supplement available:*Economics of Nonproprietary Organizations.*

BIBLIOGRAPHIES

Bibliographic Guide to Business and Economics. Available from Gale Cengage Learning. • Annual. $835.00. Three volumes. Published by G. K. Hall & Co. Lists current business and economics publications cataloged by the New York Public Library and the Library of Congress.

Bibliographic Guide to Conference Publications. Available from Gale Cengage Learning. • Annual. $600.00. Two volumes. Published by G. K. Hall & Co., Lists a wide range of conference publications cataloged by the New York Public Library and the Library of Congress.

CD-ROM DATABASES

Profiles in Business and Management: An International Directory of Scholars and Their Research [CD-ROM]. Harvard Business School Publishing. • Annual. $595.00. Fully searchable CD-ROM version of two-volume printed directory. Contains bibliographic and biographical information for over 5600 business and management experts active in 21 subject areas. Formerly *International Directory of Business and Management Scholars.*

Social Sciences Citation Index. ISI. • Monthly. Price on request. Provides CD-ROM indexing of articles appearing in 1700 leading social science journals worldwide, with additional selections from more than 5700 other journals. Time span is 1992 to date. Coverage includes economics, business, finance, management, communications, demographics, library and information science, political science, sociology, and many other subjects.

Social Sciences Citation Index: Compact Disc Edition with Abstracts. Institute for Scientific Information. • Monthly. Provides CD-ROM indexing and abstracting of "significant articles" from 1,700 social science journals worldwide, with additional selections from 3,200 other journals, 1986 to date. Includes economics, business, finance, management, communications, demographics, information and library science, political science, sociology, and many other subjects.

WILSONDISC: Wilson Social Sciences Abstracts. H. W. Wilson Co. • Monthly. Includes unlimited online access to *Social Sciences Index* through WILSONLINE. Provides CD-ROM indexing from 1983 and abstracting from 1994 of more than 500 periodicals covering economics, area studies, community health, public administration, public welfare, urban studies, and many other topics related to the social sciences.

DIRECTORIES

Association for University Business and Economic Research Membership Directory. Association for University Business and Economic Research. • Annual. $10.00. Member institutions in the United States and abroad with centers, bureaus, departments, etc., concerned with business and economic research.

ENCYCLOPEDIAS AND DICTIONARIES

The Sage Encyclopedia of Social Science Research Methods. Michael S. Lewis-Beck and others, editors. Sage Publications, Inc. • 2004. $550.00. Three volumes. Includes more than 800 signed entries on such topics as basic statistics, econometrics, evaluation, linear models, data analysis, sampling, and survey design.

HANDBOOKS AND MANUALS

Using Government Information Sources, Electronic and Print. Marilyn K. Moody and Jean L. Sears. Greenwood Publishing Group, Inc. • 2001. $125.00. Third edition. Contains detailed information in four sections on subject searches, agency searches, statistical searches, and special techniques for searching. Appendixes give selected agency and publisher addresses, telephone numbers, and computer communications numbers.

ONLINE DATABASES

Current Contents Connect. Institute for Scientific Information. • Provides online abstracts of articles listed in the tables of contents of about 7,500 journals. Coverage is very broad, including science, social science, life science, technology, engineering, industry, agriculture, the environment, economics, and arts and humanities. Time period is two years, with weekly updates. Inquire as to online cost and availability.

Wilson Social Sciences Abstracts Online. H. W. Wilson Co. • Provides online abstracting and indexing of more than 500 periodicals covering area studies, community health, public administration, public welfare, urban studies, and many other social science topics. Time period is 1994 to date for abstracts and 1983 to date for indexing, with updates weekly. Inquire as to online cost and availability.

PERIODICALS AND NEWSLETTERS

Applied Economics Letters. Taylor and Francis Group. • 15 times a year. Individuals, $115.00 per year; institutions, $809.00 per year. Provides short accounts of new, original research in practical economics. Supplement to *Applied Economics.*

Mathematical Finance: An International Journal of Mathematics, Statistics, and Financial Economics. Blackwell Publishing. • Quarterly. Institutions, $683.00 per year. Includes online edition. Covers the use of sophisticated mathematical tools in financial research and practice.

Research Reports. American Institute for Economic Research. • Semimonthly. $59.00 per year. Newsletter. Alternate issues include charts of "Primary Leading Indicators," "Primary Roughly Coincident Indicators," and "Primary Lagging Indicators," as issued by The Conference Board (formerly provided by the U. S. Department of Commerce).

Review of Financial Economics. Elsevier. • Three times a year. Individuals, $95.00 per year; institutions, $350.00 per year. Formerly *Review of Business and Economic Research.*

RESEARCH CENTERS AND INSTITUTES

American Institute for Economic Research. P.O. Box 1000, Great Barrington, MA 01230. Phone: (413)528-1216 Fax: (413)528-0103 E-mail: info@ aier.org • URL: http://www.aier.org.

Brookings Institution. Brookings Institution. 1775 Massachusetts Ave. NW, Washington, DC 20036. Phone: (202)797-6000 Fax: (202)797-6004 E-mail: communications@brookings.edu • URL: http:// www.brookings.edu/ • Economics, including studies on what economic policies are most conducive to sustained growth of the U.S. economy, how social programs can be made more effective in an era of constrained resources, and how international economic relations can be improved; government, including studies on political institutions, the media, regulation and economic policy, and social policy; and foreign policy, including defense analysis and international economics and trade studies, and U.S. relations with, and regional studies on, the former Soviet Union, East Asia, China, the Middle East, Latin America, and Africa.

Bureau of Economic and Business Research. University of Illinois at Urbana-Champaign, 1206 S. Sixth St., 403 Wohlers Hall, Champaign, IL 61820. Phone: (217)333-2330 Fax: (217)244-7410 E-mail: g-oldman@uiuc.edu • URL: http://www.business. uiuc.edu/research.

Cowles Foundation for Research in Economics. Yale University. 30 Hillhouse Ave., New Haven, CT 06520-8281. Phone: (203)432-3704 Fax: (203)432-6167 E-mail: john.geanakoplos@yale.edu • URL: http://www.cowles.econ.yale.edu.

Institute for Economic Research. University of Washington. 302 Savery Hall, Seattle, WA 98195. Phone: (206)543-5955 Fax: (206)685-7477 E-mail: econ.dept@u.washington.edu • URL: http://www. econ.washington.edu/.

Institute of Business and Economic Research. University of California at Berkeley, Hass School of Business, Berkeley, CA 94720-1900. Phone: (510)642-5905 Fax: (510)642-1420 E-mail: shapiro@haas.berkeley.edu • URL: http://www. haas.berkeley.edu/groups/iber • Research fields are business administration, economics, finance, real estate, and international development.

National Bureau of Economic Research, Inc. 1050 Massachusetts Ave., Cambridge, MA 02138.

National Opinion Research Center. National Opinion Research Center. 1155 E 60th St., Chicago, IL 60637. Phone: (773)256-6000 Fax: (773)753-7886 E-mail: norcinfo@norcmail.uchicago.edu • URL: http://www.norc.uchicago.edu • Sociology, social psychology, education, demography, child studies, and policy studies, including studies of political behavior, religious attitudes, economic behavior, career development, family behavior, and survey research methodology. Research group consists of the Center on Aging, Sloan Center on Families and Work, the Data and Research and Development Center, and the Population Research Center. Conducts the General Social Survey (GSS). Maintains a national sample frame that allows national representative samples for complex, multiyear surveys.

TRADE/PROFESSIONAL ASSOCIATIONS

National Association for Business Economics. 1233 20th St., N.W., Suite 505, Washington, DC 20036. Phone: (202)463-6223 Fax: (202)463-6239 E-mail: nabe@nabe.com • URL: http://www.nabe.com • Formerly National Association of Business Economists.

ECONOMIC RESPONSIBILITY

See: SOCIAL RESPONSIBILITY

ECONOMIC STATISTICS

See also: BUSINESS STATISTICS;
ECONOMETRICS; ECONOMICS; MARKET
STATISTICS; STATISTICAL METHODS;
STATISTICS SOURCES

GENERAL WORKS

Business Statistics for Management and Economics.
Wayne W. Daniel and James C. Terrell. Houghton
Mifflin Co. • 1995. $23.96. Seventh edition.

ABSTRACTS AND INDEXES

*Current Index to Statistics: Applications, Methods,
and Theory.* American Statistical Association. •
Annual. Price on application. An index to journal
articles on statistical applications and methodology.

Social Sciences Index. H. W. Wilson Co. • Quarterly,
with annual cumulation. Price varies. Indexes more
than 400 periodicals covering economics,
environmental policy, government, insurance, labor,
health care policy, planning, public administration,
public welfare, urban studies, women's issues,
criminology, and related topics.

ALMANACS AND YEARBOOKS

*Irwin Business and Investment Almanac, 1994: Dow
Jones and Company Edition.* Summer N. Levine and
Caroline Levine. McGraw-Hill. • 1994. $75.00. 18th
edition. A review of last year's business activity.
Covers a wide variety of business and economic
data: stock market statistics, industrial information,
commodity futures information, art market trends,
comparative living costs for U. S. metropolitan
areas, foreign stock market data, etc. Formerly *Business One Irwin Business and Investment Almanac.*

BIBLIOGRAPHIES

Global Data Locator. George T. Kurian. Bernan
Associates. • 1997. $89.00. Provides detailed
descriptions of international statistical sourcebooks
and electronic databases. Covers a wide variety of
trade, economic, and demographic topics.

*Statistics Sources: A Subject Guide to Data on
Industrial, Business, Social, Educational, Financial
and Other Topics for the U. S. and Selected Foreign
Countries.* Gale Cengage Learning. • 2003. $515.
00. 27th edition. Two volumes. Lists sources of
statistical information for more than 20,000 topics.

World Directory of Non-Official Statistical Sources.
Gale Group, Inc. • 2002. $650.00. Fourth edition.
Provides detailed descriptions of more than 4,000
regularly published, non-governmental statistics
sources. Includes surveys, studies, market research
reports, trade journals, databank compilations, and
other print sources. Coverage is international, with
four indexes.

CD-ROM DATABASES

OECD Statistical Compendium. Organization for
Economic Cooperation and Development. •
Semiannual. $1,905.00 per year for 1 to 10 users.
CD-ROM contains more than 730,000 monthly,
quarterly, and annual time series for OECD
countries, 1960 to date. Includes fully searchable
data on agriculture, food, economic indicators,
national accounts, employment, energy, finance,
industry, technology, and foreign trade. Results can
be displayed in various forms.

Social Sciences Citation Index. ISI. • Monthly. Price
on request. Provides CD-ROM indexing of articles
appearing in 1700 leading social science journals
worldwide, with additional selections from more
than 5700 other journals. Time span is 1992 to date.
Coverage includes economics, business, finance,
management, communications, demographics,
library and information science, political science,
sociology, and many other subjects.

Social Sciences Citation Index: Compact Disc Edition with Abstracts. Institute for Scientific
Information. • Monthly. Provides CD-ROM index-

ing and abstracting of "significant articles" from
1,700 social science journals worldwide, with additional selections from 3,200 other journals, 1986
to date. Includes economics, business, finance,
management, communications, demographics,
information and library science, political science,
sociology, and many other subjects.

Statistical Abstract of the United States on CD-ROM. Hoover's, Inc. • Annual. $49.95. Provides all
statistics from official print version, plus expanded
historical data, greater detail, and keyword searching features.

USA Trade. U. S. Department of Commerce. •
Monthly. $650.00 per year. Provides over 150,000
trade-related data series on CD-ROM. Includes full
text of many government publications. Specific data
is included on national income, labor, price indexes,
foreign exchange, technical standards, and
international markets. Website address is http://
www.stat-usa.gov/.

WILSONDISC: Wilson Social Sciences Abstracts. H.
W. Wilson Co. • Monthly. Includes unlimited online
access to *Social Sciences Index* through
WILSONLINE. Provides CD-ROM indexing from
1983 and abstracting from 1994 of more than 500
periodicals covering economics, area studies, community health, public administration, public welfare,
urban studies, and many other topics related to the
social sciences.

World Marketing Forecasts on CD-ROM. Gale Cengage Learning. • Annual. $2,500.00. Produced by
Euromonitor. Provides detailed forecast data for the
years to 2012 on CD-ROM for 54 countries in all
parts of the world. Covers a wide range of social,
demographic, economic, and market factors.
Includes specific forecasts for many kinds of
consumer products.

DIRECTORIES

*The Internet Blue Pages: The Guide to Federal
Government Web Sites.* Information Today, Inc. •
Annual. $34.95. Provides information on more than
1,800 Web sites used by various agencies of the
federal government. Includes indexes to agencies
and topics. Links to all Web sites listed are available
at http://www.fedweb.com. (CyberAge Books.).

ENCYCLOPEDIAS AND DICTIONARIES

*Knowledge Exchange Business Encyclopedia: Your
Complete Business Advisor.* Lorraine Spurge.
Knowledge Exchange LLC. • 1998. $45.00.
Provides definitions of business terms and financial
expressions, profiles of leading industries, tables of
economic statistics, biographies of business leaders,
and other business information. Includes "A
Chronology of Business from 3000 B.C. Through
1995." Contains illustrations and three indexes.

HANDBOOKS AND MANUALS

*Finding Statistics Online: How to Locate the Elusive
Numbers You Need.* Paula Berinstein. Information
Today, Inc. • 1998. $29.95. Provides advice on efficient searching when looking for statistical data on
the World Wide Web or from commercial online
services and database producers. (CyberAge
Books.).

Guide to Everyday Economic Statistics. Gary E.
Clayton and Martin G. Giesbrecht. McGraw-Hill. •
2001. $19.90. Fifth edition. Contains clear explanations of the commonly used economic indicators.

INTERNET DATABASES

Business 2.0 Web Guide to the Best Business Links.
Business 2.0 Media Inc. Phone: (415)293-4800
E-mail: support@business2.com • URL: http://
www.business2.com/webguide • Web site presents
an extensive, searchable directory of links to "the
best, most informative, and authoritative web
pages." Twenty main categories cover business,
finance, career, company information, people, and
technology topics, with thousands of subtopics, all

linking to Web sites recommended by experienced
business researchers. Fees: Free.

Fedstats. Federal Interagency Council on Statistical
Policy. Phone: (202)395-7254 • URL: http://www.
fedstats.gov • Web site features an efficient search
facility for full-text statistics produced by more than
100 federal agencies, including the Census Bureau,
the Bureau of Economic Analysis, and the Bureau of
Labor Statistics. Boolean searches can be made
within one agency or for all agencies combined.
Links are offered to international statistical bureaus,
including the UN, IMF, OECD, UNESCO, Eurostat,
and 20 individual countries. Fees: Free.

FreeLunch.com. Economy.com, Inc. Phone:
(610)696-8700 Fax: (610)696-1678 • URL: http://
www.freelunch.com • Web site provides free access
to more than 1.5 million economic and financial data
series, covering industry, demographics, labor
markets, prices, retail sales, government spending,
trade, interest rates, housing starts, the stock market,
and many other topics. Data is available for various
time periods in either chart or table form. Searching
is offered. Fees: Free, but registration required.
Economy.com, Inc. also offers fee-based economic
analysis at *The Dismal Scientist* site (http://www.
dismal.com).

FreeLunch.com. Economy.com, Inc. Phone:
(610)696-8700 Fax: (610)696-1678 • URL: http://
www.freelunch.com • Web site provides free access
to more than 1.5 million economic and financial data
series, covering industry, demographics, labor
markets, prices, retail sales, government spending,
trade, interest rates, housing starts, the stock market,
and many other topics. Data is available for various
time periods in either chart or table form. Searching
is offered. Fees: Free, but registration required.
Economy.com, Inc. also offers fee-based economic
analysis at *The Dismal Scientist* site (http://www.
dismal.com).

ONLINE DATABASES

OECD Main Economic Indicators. Organization for
Economic Cooperation and Development. •
International statistics provided by OECD, 1960 to
date. Monthly updates. Inquire as to online cost and
availability.

Wilson Social Sciences Abstracts Online. H. W.
Wilson Co. • Provides online abstracting and indexing of more than 500 periodicals covering area studies, community health, public administration, public
welfare, urban studies, and many other social science topics. Time period is 1994 to date for abstracts
and 1983 to date for indexing, with updates weekly.
Inquire as to online cost and availability.

PERIODICALS AND NEWSLETTERS

Journal of Business and Economic Statistics.
American Statistical Association. • Quarterly.
Libraries, $90.00 per year. Emphasis is on statistical
measurement and applications for business and
economics.

STATISTICS SOURCES

American Business Climate and Economic Profiles.
Priscilla C. Geahigan. Gale Cengage Learning. •
1993. $170.00. Provides business, industrial,
demographic, and economic figures for all states and
300 metropolitan areas. Includes production, taxation, population, growth rates, labor force data,
incomes, total sales, etc.

Consumer International. Available from Gale Cengage Learning. • Annual. $1,290.00. Published by
Euromonitor. Contains extensive consumer market,
economic, and demographic data for 25 major, non-European countries, including the U. S. and Canada.
Includes consumer market size (volume and value)
for 150 product types in 14 categories (food, clothing, automobiles, cosmetics, appliances, etc.).

Country Data Forecasts. Bank of America, World
Information Services, Dept. 3015. • Looseleaf, with

semiannual updates. $495.00 per year. Provides detailed statistical tables for 80 countries, showing historical data and five-year forecasts of 23 key economic series. Includes population, inflation figures, debt, per capita income, foreign trade, exchange rates, and other data.

County and City Data Book 2000: A Statistical Abstract Supplement. Available from U. S. Government Printing Office. • 2002. $68.00. 13th edition. Issued by the U. S. Bureau of the Census (http://www.census.gov). Contains a wide variety of data on 3,141 U.S. counties, 1,078 cities, and 11,097 places of 2,500 or more inhabitants. Includes statistical information on retailing, manufacturing, banking, service industries, income, employment, housing, education, crime, and population. Updated metropolitan areas are included.

County and City Extra: Annual Metro, City and County Data Book. Deirdre A. Gaquin and Mark S. Littman. Bernan Press. • 2001. $120.00. Updates and augments data published irregularly in print form by the U. S. Census Bureau in *County and City Data Book.* Covers "every state, county, metropolitan area, and congressional district in the United States, as well as all U. S. cities with a 1990 population of 25,000 or more." Contains a wide range tic maps.

County and City Extra: Special Decennial Census Edition. Deidre A. Gaquin and Katherine A. DeBrandt, editors. Bernan Press. • 2002. $95.00. Presents conveniently arranged population, housing, and other data from the 2000 census, with many 1980 and 1990 comparisons. Includes maps and tables with rankings of about 20 items for various geographic locations. Complements the annual *County and City Extra.*

Current Population Reports: Household Economic Studies, Series P-70. Available from U. S. Government Printing Office. • Irregular. $21.00 per year. Issued by the U.S. Bureau of the Census (http://www.census.gov). Each issue covers a special topic relating to household socioeconomic characteristics.

Datapedia of the United States: American History in Numbers. George T. Kurian, editor. Bernan Press. • 2004. $125.00. Third edition. Based on the Census Bureau publication, *Historical Statistics of the United States.* Provides data from Colonial times to the present on agriculture, business, consumer income, energy, finance, labor, national income, population, and many other subjects. Includes "narrative highlights," maps, charts, and statistical projections.

Economic Indicators. Council of Economic Advisors, Executive Office of the President. Available from U.S. Government Printing Office. • Monthly. $55.00 per year.

Economic Report of the President: Together with the Annual Report of the Council of Economic Advisors. Available from U. S. Government Printing Office. • Annual. $32.00. Includes about 130 pages of "Statistical Tables Relating to Income, Employment, and Production." Tables cover national income, employment, wages, productivity, manufacturing, prices, credit, finance (public and private), corporate profits, and foreign trade.

European Marketing Forecasts. Available from Gale Cengage Learning. • Annual. $1,250.00. Published by Euromonitor. Contains demographic, economic, and market forecasts for the countries of Europe to the year 2010. Forecasts include market-size data for 15 consumer product sectors (food, clothing, automobiles, consumer electronics, etc.).

Handbook of International Economic Statistics. Available from National Technical Information Service. • Annual. $40.00. Prepared by U. S. Central Intelligence Agency. Provides basic statistics for comparing worldwide economic performance, with an emphasis on Europe, including Eastern Europe.

International Marketing Forecasts. Available from Gale Cengage Learning. • Annual. $1,250.00. Published by Euromonitor. Contains demographic, economic, and market forecasts to the year 2013 for major, non-European countries, including the U. S. and Canada. Forecasts include market-size data for 15 consumer product sectors, such as food, clothing, and automobiles.

The Little Data Book. The World Bank. • 2003. $15.00. Contains "key development data for 208 countries," including country profiles and 54 statistical indicators relating to such factors as population, economics, trade, technology, finance, and environment.

Main Economic Indicators. OECD Publication and Information Center. • Monthly. $450.00 per year. "The essential source of timely statistics for OECD member countries." Includes a wide variety of business, economic, and industrial data for the 29 OECD nations.

Main Economic Indicators: Historical Statistics. OECD Publications and Information Center. • Annual. $475.00. Includes online edition.

Metropolitan Life Insurance Co. Statistical Bulletin SB. Metropolitan Life Insurance Co. • Quarterly. Individuals, $50.00 per year. Covers a wide range of social, economic and demographic health concerns.

Monthly Bulletin of Statistics. United Nations Publications. • Monthly. $295.00 per year. Provides current data for about 200 countries on a wide variety of economic, industrial, and demographic subjects. Compiled by United Nations Statistical Office.

OECD Economic Outlook. OECD Publications and Information Center. • Semiannual. Price on application. $95.00 per year. Contains a wide range of economic and monetary data relating to the member countries of the Organization for Economic Cooperation and Development. Includes about 100 statistical tables and graphs, with 24-month forecasts for each of the OECD countries. Provides extensive review and analysis of recent economic trends.

OECD Economic Survey of the United States. OECD Publications and Information Center. • Annual. $26.00.

OECD in Figures. Organization for Economic Cooperation and Development. • Annual. $13.00. A "pocket data book" providing a summary of key statistics for OECD countries, including economic growth, employment, education, the environment, and transportation.

Places, Towns, and Townships, 1998. Deirdre A. Gaquin and Richard W. Dodge, editors. Bernan Press. • 1997. $89.00. Second edition. Presents demographic and economic statistics from the U. S. Census Bureau and other government sources for places, cities, towns, villages, census designated places, and minor civil divisions. Contains more than 60 data categories. (Places, Towns and Townships Series).

Social Statistics of the United States. Mark S. Littman, editor. Bernan Press. • 2000. $65.00. Includes statistical data on population growth, labor force, occupations, environmental trends, leisure time use, income, poverty, taxes, and other economic or demographic topics.

Standard & Poor's Industry Surveys. Standard & Poor's. • Semiannual. $1,800.00. Two looseleaf volumes. Includes monthly *Supplements.* Provides detailed, individual surveys of 52 major industry groups. Each survey is revised on a semiannual basis. Also includes "Monthly Investment Review" (industry group investment analysis) and monthly "Trends & Projections" (economic analysis).

State and Metropolitan Area Data Book. Available from U. S. Government Printing Office. • 1998. Issued by the U. S. Bureau of the Census. Presents a wide variety of statistical data for U. S. regions, states, counties, metropolitan areas, and central cities, with ranking tables. Time period is 1970 to 1990.

Statistical Abstract of the United States. Available from U. S. Government Printing Office. • Annual. $51.00. Issued by the U. S. Bureau of the Census.

Statistical Abstract of the World. Gale Cengage Learning. • 1997. $85.00. Third edition. Provides data on a wide variety of economic, social, and political topics for about 200 countries. Arranged by country.

Statistical Forecasts of the United States. Gale Cengage Learning. • 1995. $115.00. Second edition. Provides both long-term and short-term statistical forecasts relating to basic items in the U. S.: population, employment, labor, crime, education, and health care. Data in the form of charts, graphs, and tables has been taken from a wide variety of government and private sources. Includes a subject index and an "Index of Forecast by Year.".

A Statistical Portrait of the United States: Social Conditions and Trends. Mark S. Littman, editor. Bernan Press. • 1998. $89.00. Covers "social, economic, and environmental trends in the United States over the past 25 years." Includes statistical tables, graphs, and analysis relating to such topics as population, income, poverty, wealth, labor, housing, education, healthcare, air/water quality, and government. (Statistical Portrait of the United States: Social Conditions and Trends Series).

Statistical Yearbook. United Nations Publications. • Annual, $125.00. Contains statistics for about 200 countries on a wide variety of economic, industrial, and demographic topics. Compiled by United Nations Statistical Office.

The World Economic Factbook. Available from Gale Cengage Learning. • Annual. $530.00. Published by Euromonitor. Presents key economic facts and figures for each of 200 countries, including details of chief industries, export-import trade, currency, political risk, household expenditures, and the economic situation in general.

World Economic Outlook: A Survey by the Staff of the International Monetary Fund. International Monetary Fund, Publications Services. • Semiannual. $78.00 per year. Presents international statistics combined with forecasts and analyses of the world economy.

World Economic Prospects: A Planner's Guide to International Market Conditions. Available from Gale Cengage Learning. • 2002. $490.00. Second edition. Published by Euromonitor. Ranks countries by specific economic characteristics, such as gross domestic product (GDP) per capita and short term growth prospects. Discusses the economic situation, prospects, and market potential of each of the countries.

TRADE/PROFESSIONAL ASSOCIATIONS

American Statistical Association. 732 N Washington St., Alexandria, VA 22314-1943. Phone: 888-231-3473 or (703)684-1221 Fax: (703)684-2037 E-mail: asainfo@amstat.org • URL: http://www.amstat.org • Professional society of persons interested in the theory, methodology, and application of statistics to all fields of human endeavor.

Econometric Society. New York University, Department of Economics, 19 W 4th St., 6th Fl., New York, NY 10012. Phone: (212)998-3820 Fax: (212)995-4487 E-mail: sashi@econometricsociety.org • URL: http://www.econometricsociety.org • Economists, statisticians, and mathematicians. Promotes studies that are directed towards unification of the theoretical and empirical approaches to economic problems and advancement of economic theory in its relation to statistics and mathematics.

ECONOMICS

See also: BUSINESS RESEARCH;
ECONOMETRICS

GENERAL WORKS

Economic Parables and Policies: An Introduction to Economics. Laurence S. Seidman. M. E. Sharpe, Inc. • 2004. $64.95. Third edition. Emphasis is on current economic policy in such areas as taxation, trade, health care, education, social security, and the environment. Popularly written.

Economics. William D. Nordhaus and Paul A. Samuelson. McGraw-Hill. • 2000. $92.50. 17th edition.

Economics Explained: Everything You Need to Know About How the Economy Works and Where It's Going. Robert L. Heilbroner and Lester C. Thurow. Peter Smith Publishing, Inc. • 1988. $27.50. Fourth revised edition.

Economics: Principles, Problems, and Policies. Campbell R. McConnell. McGraw-Hill. • 2001. $111.50. 14th edition.

Economics Today. Roger L. Miller. Addison-Wesley. • 2003. $118.00. 11th edition. Includes CD-ROM.

Economists and Their Theories for Students. Gale Cengage Learning. • 2003. $95.00. Provides detailed information on major economic theories and the economists who developed them. Includes a glossary and chronology.

Fundamentals of Managerial Economics. Mark Hirschey. South-Western. • 2002. $107.95. Seventh edition.

Managerial Economics. William Sanuelson and Stephen G. Marks. John Wiley and Sons, Inc. • 2002. $104.95. Fourth edition.

Managerial Economics: Analysis, Problems, Cases. Lila Truett and Dale B. Turett. John Wiley and Sons, Inc. • 2000. $101.95. Seventh edition.

Managerial Economics and Business Strategy. Michael R. Baye. McGraw-Hill. • 2002. $109.38. Seventh edition.

Modern Economics. Jan S. Hogendorn. Prentice Hall PTR. • 1994. $75.00.

Principles of Economics. Fred M. Gottheil. South-Western. • 2001. $88.95. Third edition. (Economics Series).

Principles of Macroeconomics. Joseph E. Stiglitz and John Walsh. Norton, W.W. and Co., Inc. • 2002. $62.00. Third edition.

Understanding Economics Today. Gary M. Walton and Frank C. Wykoff. McGraw-Hill. • 2000. $82.19. Seventh edition.

ABSTRACTS AND INDEXES

Index of Economic Articles in Journals and Collective Volumes. American Economic Association. • Irregular. $160.00.

NTIS Alerts: Business & Economics. National Technical Information Service. • Text: Semimonthly. $210.00 per year.

Social Sciences Citation Index. Thomson/ISI. • Three times a year. $6,900 per year. Annual cumulation. Includes *Source Index, Citation Index, Permuterm Subject Index,* and *Corporate Index.*

Social Sciences Index. H. W. Wilson Co. • Quarterly, with annual cumulation. Price varies. Indexes more than 400 periodicals covering economics, environmental policy, government, insurance, labor, health care policy, plannning, public administration, public welfare, urban studies, women's issues, criminology, and related topics.

BIBLIOGRAPHIES

Bibliographic Guide to Business and Economics. Available from Gale Cengage Learning. • Annual. $835.00. Three volumes. Published by G. K. Hall &

Co. Lists current business and economics publications cataloged by the New York Public Library and the Library of Congress.

Bibliographic Guide to Conference Publications. Available from Gale Cengage Learning. • Annual. $600.00. Two volumes. Published by G. K. Hall & Co., Lists a wide range of conference publications cataloged by the New York Public Library and the Library of Congress.

International Bibliography of the Social Sciences: Economics. British Library of Political and Economic Science. Routledge. • 1995. $250.00. (International Bibliography of the Social Sciences Series).

CD-ROM DATABASES

EconLit. Available from SilverPlatter Information, Inc. • Monthly. Single-user, $1,600.00 per year. Provides CD-ROM citations, with abstracts, to articles from more than 500 economics journals. Time period is 1969 to date. Produced by the American Economic Association.

Social Sciences Citation Index. ISI. • Monthly. Price on request. Provides CD-ROM indexing of articles appearing in 1700 leading social science journals worldwide, with additional selections from more than 5700 other journals. Time span is 1992 to date. Coverage includes economics, business, finance, management, communications, demographics, library and information science, political science, sociology, and many other subjects.

Social Sciences Citation Index: Compact Disc Edition with Abstracts. Institute for Scientific Information. • Monthly. Provides CD-ROM indexing and abstracting of "significant articles" from 1,700 social science journals worldwide, with additional selections from 3,200 other journals, 1986 to date. Includes economics, business, finance, management, communications, demographics, information and library science, political science, sociology, and many other subjects.

WILSONDISC: Wilson Social Sciences Abstracts. H. W. Wilson Co. • Monthly. Includes unlimited online access to *Social Sciences Index* through WILSONLINE. Provides CD-ROM indexing from 1983 and abstracting from 1994 of more than 500 periodicals covering economics, area studies, community health, public administration, public welfare, urban studies, and many other topics related to the social sciences.

ENCYCLOPEDIAS AND DICTIONARIES

Blackwell Encyclopedic Dictionary of Managerial Economics. Robert McAuliffe, editor. Blackwell Publishers. • 1999. $138.95. The editor is associated with Boston College. Contains definitions of key terms combined with longer articles written by various U. S. and foreign business educators. Includes bibliographies and index. *Blackwell Encyclopedia of Management Series.*

Dictionary of Economics. Donald Rutherford. Routledge. • 2002. $90.00. Second edition.

Gale Encyclopedia of U.S. Economic History. Gale Cengage Learning. • 2000. $225.00. Two volumes. Contains about 1,000 alphabetically arranged entries. Includes industry profiles, biographies, social issue profiles, geographic profiles, and chronological tables.

Oxford Encyclopedia of Economic History. Joel Mokyr, editor. Oxford University Press. • 2003. $695.00. Five volumes. Provides extensive coverage of a wide variety of topics relating to business,

industrial, and economic history.

HANDBOOKS AND MANUALS

Handbook of Mathematical Economics. Elsevier. • $625.00. Dates vary. Four volumes. $125.00 per volume.

ONLINE DATABASES

Dow Jones News Service. Dow Jones and Co., Inc. • Full text and edited news stories and articles on business affairs. Inquire as to online cost and availability.

EconLit. American Economic Association. • Covers the worldwide literature of economics as contained in selected monographs and about 550 journals. Subjects include microeconomics, macroeconomics, economic history, inflation, money, credit, finance, accounting theory, trade, natural resource economics, and regional economics. Time period is 1969 to present, with monthly updates. Inquire as to online cost and availability.

Newspaper Abstracts Daily. ProQuest Inc. • Provides online coverage (citations and abstracts) of 25 major newspapers. Covers business, economics, current affairs, health, fitness, sports, education, technology, government, consumer affairs, psychology, the arts, and the social sciences. Time period is 1986 to date, with daily updates. Inquire as to online cost and availability.

Social Scisearch. Institute for Scientific Information. • Broad, multidisciplinary index to the literature of the social sciences, 1972 to present. Weekly updates. Worldwide coverage. Inquire as to online cost and availability.

Wilson Social Sciences Abstracts Online. H. W. Wilson Co. • Provides online abstracting and indexing of more than 500 periodicals covering area studies, community health, public administration, public welfare, urban studies, and many other social science topics. Time period is 1994 to date for abstracts and 1983 to date for indexing, with updates weekly. Inquire as to online cost and availability.

PERIODICALS AND NEWSLETTERS

American Economic Review. American Economic Association. • Five times a year. Institutions, $195.00 per year. Includes *Journal of Economic Literature* and *Journal of Economic Persepective.*

Applied Economics. Taylor and Francis Group. • 18 times a year. Institutions, $3,352.00 per year. Emphasizes quantitative studies having results of practical use. Supplements available, *Applied Financial Economics* and *Applied Economics Letters.*

Applied Economics Letters. Taylor and Francis Group. • 15 times a year. Individuals, $115.00 per year; institutions, $809.00 per year. Provides short accounts of new, original research in practical economics. Supplement to *Applied Economics.*

Applied Financial Economics. Taylor and Francis Group. • Monthly. Institutions, $1,277.00 per year. Covers practical aspects of financial economics, banking, and monetary economics. Supplement to *Applied Economics.*

Blue Chip Economic Indicators: What Top Economists Are Saying About the U.S. Outlook for the Year Ahead. Aspen Publishers, Inc. • Monthly. $665.00 per year. Newsletter containing U. S. economic consensus forecasts.

Econometrica. Blackwell Publishing. • Bimonthly. Institutions, $301.00 per year. Includes print and online editions. Published in England by Basil Blackwell Ltd.

The Economist. Economist Intelligence Unit. • 51 times a year. $125.00 per year.

International Review of Applied Economics. Routledge. • Quarterly. Individuals, $310.00 per year; institutions, $1,007.00 per year.

Journal of Economic Literature. American Economic Association. • Quarterly. $135.00 per year. Includes *American Economic Review* and *Journal of Economic Perspectives.*

Journal of Economics and Business. Temple University, School of Business Administration. Elsevier. • Bimonthly. Individuals, $86.00 per year; institutions, $510.00 per year. Professional and academic research primarily in economics, finance and related business disciplines.

NABE News. National Association for Business Economics. • Description: Concerned with business economics. Serves this professional Association of persons employed by private, institutional, or government concerns in the area of business-related economic analysis. Recurring features include results of the NABE quarterly outlook survey, featured articles of timely interest, reviews of seminars and annual meetings, news from local chapters and roundtables, and personal notes.

Quarterly Journal of Economics. Harvard University, Dept. of Economics. MIT Press. • Quarterly. Individuals, $44.00 per year; instututions, $190.00 per year; students, $28.00 per year. Includes print and online editions.

The Quarterly Review of Economics and Finance. University of Illinois at Urbana-Champaign, Bureau of Economics and Business Research. Available from JAI Press, Inc. • Five times a year. Individuals, $95.00 per year; institutions, $426.00 per year. Includes annual *Supplement.* Formerly *Quarterly Review of Economics and Business.*

Review of Social Economy. Association for Social Economics. Taylor and Francis Group. • Quarterly. Individuals, $78.00 per year; institutions, $211.00 per year. Subject matter is concerned with the relationships between social values and economics. Includes articles on income distribution, poverty, labor, and class.

RESEARCH CENTERS AND INSTITUTES

American Institute for Economic Research. P.O. Box 1000, Great Barrington, MA 01230. Phone: (413)528-1216 Fax: (413)528-0103 E-mail: info@aier.org • URL: http://www.aier.org.

Bureau of Economic and Business Research. University of Florida. 221 Matherly Hall, Gainesville, FL 32611-7145. Phone: (352)392-0171 Fax: (352)392-4739 E-mail: info@bebr.ufl.edu • URL: http://www.bebr.ufl.edu.

Cowles Foundation for Research in Economics. Yale University. 30 Hillhouse Ave., New Haven, CT 06520-8281. Phone: (203)432-3704 Fax: (203)432-6167 E-mail: john.geanakoplos@yale.edu • URL: http://www.cowles.econ.yale.edu.

National Bureau of Economic Research, Inc. 1050 Massachusetts Ave., Cambridge, MA 02138.

National Opinion Research Center. National Opinion Research Center. 1155 E 60th St., Chicago, IL 60637. Phone: (773)256-6000 Fax: (773)753-7886 E-mail: norcinfo@norcmail.uchicago.edu • URL: http://www.norc.uchicago.edu • Sociology, social psychology, education, demography, child studies, and policy studies, including studies of political behavior, religious attitudes, economic behavior, career development, family behavior, and survey research methodology. Research group consists of the Center on Aging, Sloan Center on Families and Work, the Data and Research and Development Center, and the Population Research Center. Conducts the General Social Survey (GSS). Maintains a national sample frame that allows national representative samples for complex, multi-year surveys.

STATISTICS SOURCES

Economic Indicators. Council of Economic Advisors, Executive Office of the President. Available from U.S. Government Printing Office. • Monthly. $55.00 per year.

Social Trends and Indicators USA. Monique D. Ma-

gee, editor. Gale Cengage Learning. • 2003. $450.00. Four volumes. Includes data on labor, economics, the health care industry, crime, leisure, population, education, social security, and many other topics. Sources include various government agencies and major publications.

TRADE/PROFESSIONAL ASSOCIATIONS

American Economic Association. 2014 Broadway, Ste. 305, Nashville, TN 37203. Phone: (615)322-2595 Fax: (615)343-7590 E-mail: aeainfo@vanderbilt.edu • URL: http://www.vanderbilt.edu/AEA • Educators, business executives, government administrators, journalists, lawyers, and others interested in economics and its application to present-day problems. Encourages historical and statistical research into actual conditions of industrial life and provides a nonpartisan forum for economic discussion.

Econometric Society. New York University, Department of Economics, 19 W 4th St., 6th Fl., New York, NY 10012. Phone: (212)998-3820 Fax: (212)995-4487 E-mail: sashi@econometricsociety.org • URL: http://www.econometricsociety.org • Economists, statisticians, and mathematicians. Promotes studies that are directed towards unification of the theoretical and empirical approaches to economic problems and advancement of economic theory in its relation to statistics and mathematics.

Foundation for Economic Education. 30 S. Broadway, Irvington, NY 10533. Phone: 800-960-4333 or (914)591-7230 Fax: (914)591-8910 E-mail: fee@fee.org • URL: http://www.fee.org.

Hudson Institute. 1015 15th St. NW, 6th Fl., 1015 18th St., NW, Ste. 300, Washington, DC 20005. Phone: 800-HUDSON-0 or (202)974-2400 Fax: (202)974-2410 E-mail: info@hudson.org • URL: http://www.hudson.org • Members of this research center are elected from academic, governmental, and business/industrial sectors. Studies public policy issues in areas of national security, international and domestic economics, education and employment, energy and technology, agriculture and environment, and future studies. Studies are funded through contract or grant from government agencies, private businesses, foundations, associations, and individuals. Sometimes referred to as a "think tank", the institute focuses on "providing policymakers with a broad, workable, conceptual framework within which intelligent and successful policy decisions can be developed"; seeks to determine what issues will have the greatest long-term impact and to identify issues that may become urgent though they are not yet recognized as such. Conducts briefings on policy issues to corporate and other audiences. Distributes research reports to depository libraries.

National Association for Business Economics. 1233 20th St., N.W., Suite 505, Washington, DC 20036. Phone: (202)463-6223 Fax: (202)463-6239 E-mail: nabe@nabe.com • URL: http://www.nabe.com • Formerly National Association of Business Economists.

National Council on Economic Education. 1140 Ave. of the Americas, 2nd Fl., New York, NY 10036. Phone: 800-338-1192 or (212)730-7007 Fax: (212)730-1793 E-mail: econed@ncee.net • URL: http://www.nationalcouncil.org • Formerly Joint Council in Economic Education.

ECONOMICS, BUSINESS

See: BUSINESS ECONOMICS

ECONOMICS, MATHEMATICAL

See: ECONOMETRICS

EDITORS AND EDITING

See also: BUSINESS JOURNALISM; HOUSE ORGANS; JOURNALISM; NEWSPAPERS; PERIODICALS; PUBLISHING INDUSTRY

GENERAL WORKS

The Elements of Editing: A Modern Guide for Editors and Journalists. Arthur Plotnik. John Wiley and Sons, Inc. • 1986. $5.95.

Thinking Like Your Editor: How to Write Great Serious Nonfiction and Get It Published. Susan Rabiner and Alfred Fortunato. W. W. Norton & Co., Inc. • 2003. $14.95. Emphasizes the importance of submitting an effective proposal. The authors operate the Susan Rabiner Literary Agency in New York.

ALMANACS AND YEARBOOKS

Editor and Publisher International Yearbook: Encyclopedia of the Newspaper Industry. Editor and Publisher Co., Inc. • Annual. $150.00. Daily and Sunday newspapers in the United States and Canada.

BIBLIOGRAPHIES

Editing: An Annotated Bibliography. Bruce W. Speck. Greenwood Publishing Group, Inc. • 1991. $67.95. (Bibliographies and Indexes in Mass Media and Communications Series, No. 4).

CD-ROM DATABASES

Leadership Library on CD-ROM: Who's Who in the Leadership of the United States. Leadership Directories, Inc. • Quarterly. Including access to Internet version (weekly updates). Contains all 14 *Yellow Book* personnel directories on CD-ROM, providing contact and brief biographical information for about 400,000 individuals. Covers business, government, financial institutions, news media, law firms, associations, foreign representatives, and nonprofit organizations. Includes photographs.

DIRECTORIES

Editor and Publisher Market Guide. Editor and Publisher Co., Inc. • Annual. $150.00. More than 1,700 newspaper markets in the United States and Canada.

Editor and Publisher Syndicate Directory: Annual Directory of Syndicate Services. Editor and Publisher Co., Inc. • Annual. $28.00. Directory of several hundred syndicates serving newspapers in the United States and abroad with news, columns, features, comic strips, editorial cartoons, etc.

Magazines Career Directory: A Practical One-Stop Guide to Getting a Job in Publ c Relations. Visible Ink Press. • 1993. $39.00. Fifth edition. Includes information on magazine publishing careers in art, editing, sales, and business management. Provides advice from "insiders," resume suggestions, a directory of companies that may offer entry-level positions, and a directory of career information sources. (Career Advisor Series).

News Media Yellow Book: Who's Who Among Reporters, Writers, Editors, and Producers in the Leading National News Media. Leadership Directories, Inc. • Quarterly. $360.00 per year. Lists the staffs of major newspapers and news magazines, TV and radio networks, news services and bureaus, and feature syndicates. Includes syndicated columnists and programs. Seven specialized indexes are provided.

Working Press of the Nation. R. R. Bowker. • Annual. $530.00. $295.00 per volume. Three volumes: (1) *Newspaper Directory*; (2) *Magazine and Internal Publications Directory*; (3) *Radio and Television Directory.* Includes names of editors and other personnel.

Writer's Guide to Book Editors, Publishers, and Literary Agents, Who They Are, What They Want, and How to Win Them Over. Prima Publishing. •

Annual. $27.95; with CD-ROM, $49.95. Directory for authors includes information on publishers' response times and pay rates.

HANDBOOKS AND MANUALS

The Chicago Manual of Style: The Essential Guide for Authors, Editors, and Publishers. The University of Chicago Press. • 1993. $40.00. 14th edition.

PERIODICALS AND NEWSLETTERS

American Editor. American Society of Newspaper Editors. • Nine times a year. $29.00 per year. Formerly *American Society of Newspaper Editors Bulletin.*

ASBPE Editor's Notes. American Society of Business Press Editors. • Bimonthly. Membership. Newsletter.

Copy Editor: Language News for the Publishing Profession. McMurry Newsletters. • Bimonthly. $69.00 per year. Newsletter for professional copy editors and proofreaders. Includes such items as "Top Ten Resources for Copy Editors.".

Editor and Publisher - The Newsmagazine of the Fourth Estate Since 1894. Editor and Publisher Co., Inc. • Weekly. $99.00 per year. Includes print and online edition. Trade journal of the newspaper industry.

Folio: The New Dynamics of Magazine Publishing. Primedia Business Magazines and Media. • Monthly. $96.00 per year.

Freelance Writer's Report. Dana K. Cassell, editor. CNW Publishing, Editing & Promotion Inc. • Description: Offers up-to-date news and information concerning effective marketing/production techniques, writing tips, self-promotion, and other topics of interest "to freelance writers who intend to earn a good income from their work and improve the quality of their work." Recurring features include interviews, book reviews, news of writing seminars, conferences, and market news. **Remarks:** Members of the Florida Freelance Writers Association receive an extra association section (4 pages).

Quill: The Magazine for Journalists. Society of Professional Journalists, Eugene S. Pullman Nationalo Journalism Center. • Monthly. $35.00 per year.

Writing That Works: The Business Communications Report. Writing That Works. • Monthly. $119.00 per year.

TRADE/PROFESSIONAL ASSOCIATIONS

American Society of Business Publications Editors. 710 E Ogden Ave., Ste. 600, Naperville, IL 60563-8603. Phone: (603)579-3288 Fax: (603)369-2488 E-mail: info@asbpe.org • URL: http://www.asbpe.com.

American Society of Magazine Editors. c/o Magazine Publishers of America, 810 Seventh Ave., 24th Fl., New York, NY 10019. Phone: (212)872-3737 E-mail: asme@magazine.org • URL: http://www.magazine.org.

American Society of Newspaper Editors. 11690B Sunrise Valley Dr., Reston, VA 20191-1409. Phone: (703)453-1122 Fax: (703)453-1133 E-mail: asne@asne.org • URL: http://www.asne.org.

Associated Press Managing Editors. 450 W 33rd St., New York, NY 10001. Phone: (212)621-1838 Fax: (212)506-6102 E-mail: apme@ap.org • URL: http://www.apme.com • Represents managing editors or executives on the news or editorial staff of The Associated Press newspapers. Aims to: advance the journalism profession; examine the news and other services of the Associated Press in order to provide member newspapers with services that best suit their needs; provide a means of cooperation between the management and the editorial representatives of the members of the Associated Press. Maintains committees dealing with newspapers and news services.

International Association of Business

Communicators. One Hallidie Plaza, Suite 600, San Francisco, CA 94102-2818. Phone: (415)544-4700 Fax: (415)544-4747 E-mail: service_centre@iabc.com • URL: http://www.iabc.com.

EDUCATION

See: SCHOOLS

EDUCATION, BUSINESS

See: BUSINESS EDUCATION

EDUCATION, COMPUTERS IN

See: COMPUTERS IN EDUCATION

EDUCATION, EMPLOYEE

See: TRAINING OF EMPLOYEES

EDUCATION, EXECUTIVE

See: EXECUTIVE TRAINING AND DEVELOPMENT

EDUCATION, FEDERAL AID

See: FEDERAL AID

EDUCATION, HIGHER

See: COLLEGES AND UNIVERSITIES

EDUCATION, TECHNICAL

See: TECHNICAL EDUCATION

EDUCATION, VOCATIONAL

See: VOCATIONAL EDUCATION

EDUCATIONAL FILMS

See: AUDIOVISUAL AIDS IN EDUCATION

EFFICIENCY, INDUSTRIAL

See: TIME AND MOTION STUDY

EFTPOS (ELECTRONIC FUNDS TRANSFER POINT-OF-SALE SYSTEMS)

See: POINT-OF-SALE SYSTEMS (POS)

EFTS

See: ELECTRONIC FUNDS TRANSFER SYSTEMS (EFTS)

EGG INDUSTRY

See: POULTRY INDUSTRY

ELECTRIC APPARATUS

See: ELECTRICAL EQUIPMENT INDUSTRY

ELECTRIC APPLIANCE INDUSTRY

See also: CONSUMER ELECTRONICS

CD-ROM DATABASES

OECD Statistical Compendium. Organization for Economic Cooperation and Development. • Semiannual. $1,905.00 per year for 1 to 10 users. CD-ROM contains more than 730,000 monthly, quarterly, and annual time series for OECD countries, 1960 to date. Includes fully searchable data on agriculture, food, economic indicators, national accounts, employment, energy, finance, industry, technology, and foreign trade. Results can be displayed in various forms.

World Marketing Forecasts on CD-ROM. Gale Cengage Learning. • Annual. $2,500.00. Produced by Euromonitor. Provides detailed forecast data for the years to 2012 on CD-ROM for 54 countries in all parts of the world. Covers a wide range of social, demographic, economic, and market factors. Includes specific forecasts for many kinds of consumer products.

DIRECTORIES

AM-Appliance Manufacturer Directory. Business News Publishing Co. • Annual. $25.00. Formerly *Appliance Manufacturer Directory.*

Appliance - Appliance Industry Purchasing Directory. Dana Chase Publications, Inc. • Annual. $40.00. Suppliers to manufacturers of consumer, commercial, and business appliances.

FINANCIAL RATIOS

Almanac of Business and Industrial Financial Ratios. Leo Troy. Aspen Publishers, Inc. • 2003. $125.95. Includes CD-Rom. Contains financial ratios derived from federal tax returns. Ratios for each of about 200 industries are arranged according to company asset size. (Almanac of Business and Industrial Financial Ratios Series).

Annual Statement Studies. The Risk Management Association. • Annual. Median and quartile financial ratios are given for over 400 kinds of manufacturing, wholesale, retail, construction, and consumer finance establishments. Data is sorted by both asset size and sales volume. Includes a clearly written "Definition of Ratios" and an alphabetical industry index.

Annual Statement Studies: Industry Default Probabilities and Cash Flow Measures. The Risk Management Association. • Annual. $145.00. Serves as a companion volume to the original *Annual Statement Studies.* Gives probability of default estimates on a percentage scale for more than 450 industries. Includes changes in position year-by-year for eight financial statement line items and provides percentage measures of cash flow.

NARDA's Cost of Doing Business Survey. North American Retail Dealers Association. • Annual. $295.00.

INTERNET DATABASES

Advance Monthly Sales for Retail Trade and Food Services. U. S. Census Bureau. Phone: 800-541-8345 or (301)763-4636 Fax: (301)457-3842 E-mail: rcb@census.gov • URL: http://www.census.gov/svsd/www/fullpub.html • Web pages provide monthly sales figures for a wide range of retail businesses. Advance, preliminary, and final statistics are provided for the latest month available in each case, with a previous-year comparison. Updates are monthly.

Business 2.0 Web Guide to the Best Business Links. Business 2.0 Media Inc. Phone: (415)293-4800 E-mail: support@business2.com • URL: http://www.business2.com/webguide • Web site presents an extensive, searchable directory of links to "the best, most informative, and authoritative web pages." Twenty main categories cover business, finance, career, company information, people, and technology topics, with thousands of subtopics, all linking to Web sites recommended by experienced business researchers. Fees: Free.

Fedstats. Federal Interagency Council on Statistical Policy. Phone: (202)395-7254 • URL: http://www.fedstats.gov • Web site features an efficient search facility for full-text statistics produced by more than 100 federal agencies, including the Census Bureau, the Bureau of Economic Analysis, and the Bureau of Labor Statistics. Boolean searches can be made within one agency or for all agencies combined. Links are offered to international statistical bureaus, including the UN, IMF, OECD, UNESCO, Eurostat, and 20 individual countries. Fees: Free.

FreeLunch.com. Economy.com, Inc. Phone: (610)696-8700 Fax: (610)696-1678 • URL: http://www.freelunch.com • Web site provides free access to more than 1.5 million economic and financial data series, covering industry, demographics, labor markets, prices, retail sales, government spending, trade, interest rates, housing starts, the stock market, and many other topics. Data is available for various time periods in either chart or table form. Searching is offered. Fees: Free, but registration required. Economy.com, Inc. also offers fee-based economic analysis at *The Dismal Scientist* site (http://www.dismal.com).

Manufacturing Profiles. U. S. Bureau of the Census. Phone: (301)763-4636 E-mail: webmaster@census.gov • URL: http://www.census.gov/prod/www/abs/mfg-prof.html • The Census Bureau makes available free on PDF (Portable Document Format) an annual consolidation of the entire Current Industrial Report series, presenting "all the data compiled." Contains statistics on production, shipments, inventories, consumption, exports, imports, and orders for a wide variety of manufactured products.

PERIODICALS AND NEWSLETTERS

Appliance. Dana Chase Publications, Inc. • Monthly. $75.00 per year.

Appliance Manufacturer. Business News Publishing Co. • Monthly. $55.00 per year.

Appliance Service News. Gamit Enterprises, Inc. • Monthly. $59.95.

Dealerscope: Product and Strategy for Consumer Technology Retailing. North American Publishing Co. • Monthly. Free to qualified personnel; others, $79.00 per year. Formerly *Dealerscope Consumer Electronices Marketplace.*

NARDA Independent Retailer. North American Retail Dealers Association. • Monthly. $78.00. Formerly *NARDA News.*

Product Design and Development. Reed Business Information. • Monthly. Free to qualified personnel; others, $114.90 per year.

STATISTICS SOURCES

AHAM Major Home Appliance Industry Fact Book: A Comprehensive Reference on the U States Major Home Appliance Industry. Association of Home Appliance Manufacturers. • Biennial. $75.00. Includes statistical data on manufacturing, industry shipments, distribution, and ownership.

Annual Benchmark Report for Retail Trade and Food Services...A Detailed Summary of Retail Sales, Purchases, Accounts Receivable, Inventories, and

Food Service Sales. Available from U. S. Government Printing Office. • Annual. $13.00. Issued by the U.S. Census Bureau. Provides detailed annual and monthly retail statistics for the most recent 10 years. Includes data for various kinds of retail outlets, including automobiles, furniture, appliances, building supplies, grocery stores, drug stores, gasoline stations, clothing, sporting goods, department stores, and restaurants.

Annual Survey of Manufactures. Available from U. S. Government Printing Office. • Annual. Prices vary. Issued by the U. S. Census Bureau as an interim update to the *Census of Manufactures.* Includes data on number of manufacturing establishments in various industries, employment, labor costs, value of shipments, capital expenditures, inventories, energy costs, and assets. (See also Census Bureau home page, http://www.census.gov/.).

Business Statistics of the United States. Linz Audain and Cornelia J. Strawser. Bernan Associates. • Annual. $147.00. Based on *Business Statistics,* formerly issue by the Bureau of Economic Analysis, U. S. Department of Commerce. Provides basic data for a wide variety of U. S. industries, services, and economic indicators. Most statistics are shown annually for 30 years and monthly for the most recent four years.

Consumer International. Available from Gale Cengage Learning. • Annual. $1,290.00. Published by Euromonitor. Contains extensive consumer market, economic, and demographic data for 25 major, non-European countries, including the U. S. and Canada. Includes consumer market size (volume and value) for 150 product types in 14 categories (food, clothing, automobiles, cosmetics, appliances, etc.).

European Marketing Forecasts. Available from Gale Cengage Learning. • Annual. $1,250.00. Published by Euromonitor. Contains demographic, economic, and market forecasts for the countries of Europe to the year 2010. Forecasts include market-size data for 15 consumer product sectors (food, clothing, automobiles, consumer electronics, etc.).

International Marketing Forecasts. Available from Gale Cengage Learning. • Annual. $1,250.00. Published by Euromonitor. Contains demographic, economic, and market forecasts to the year 2013 for major, non-European countries, including the U. S. and Canada. Forecasts include market-size data for 15 consumer product sectors, such as food, clothing, and automobiles.

Major Household Appliances. U.S. Bureau of the Census. • Annual. (Current Industrial Reports MA-36F.).

Standard & Poor's Industry Surveys. Standard & Poor's. • Semiannual. $1,800.00. Two looseleaf volumes. Includes monthly *Supplements.* Provides detailed, individual surveys of 52 major industry groups. Each survey is revised on a semiannual basis. Also includes "Monthly Investment Review" (industry group investment analysis) and monthly "Trends & Projections" (economic analysis).

Survey of Current Business. Available from U. S. Government Printing Office. • Monthly. $63.00 per year. Issued by Bureau of Economic Analysis, U. S. Department of Commerce. Presents a wide variety of business and economic data.

TRADE/PROFESSIONAL ASSOCIATIONS

Appliance Parts Distributors Association. 4700 W Lake Ave., Glenview, IL 60025. Phone: 800-621-0298 or (847)375-4713 Fax: (866)879-7505 E-mail: apda@apda.com • URL: http://www.apda.com • Wholesale distributors of appliance parts, supplies, and accessories. Promotes the sale of appliance parts through independent parts distributors.

Association of Home Appliance Manufacturers. 1111 19th St. NW, Ste. 402, Washington, DC 20036. Phone: (202)872-5955 Fax: (202)872-9354 E-mail:

aham@aham.org • URL: http://www.aham.org.

International Housewares Association. 6400 Shafer Ct., Ste. 650, Rosemont, IL 60018. Phone: 800-843-6462 or (847)292-4200 Fax: (847)292-4211 E-mail: pbrandl@housewares.org • URL: http://www.housewares.org • Manufacturers and distributors of housewares and small appliances. Conducts annual market research survey of the housewares industry. Manages the international housewares show.

National Appliance Service Association. PO Box 2514, Kokomo, IN 46904. Phone: (765)453-1820 Fax: (765)453-1895 E-mail: nasahq@sbcglobal.net • URL: http://www.nasa1.org • Owners of factory-authorized portable appliance repair centers servicing small electrical appliances and commercial food equipment. Promotes the interests and welfare of the commercial-domestic appliance service industry.

North American Retail Dealers Association. 4700 W Lake Ave., Glenview, IL 60025. Phone: 800-621-0298 or (847)375-4713 Fax: (866)879-7505 E-mail: nardasvc@narda.com • URL: http://www.narda.com • Firms engaged in the retailing of electronic and electrical devices and components. Promotes and represents members' interests. Makes available services to members including: legal and technical consulting; employee screening; bank card processing; long-distance phone discounts; financial statements analysis; in-store promotion kits; customer check authorization. Advocates for members' interests before federal regulatory bodies; disseminates information on new regulations affecting members. Conducts educational programs.

ELECTRIC CONTRACTORS

See: ELECTRICAL CONSTRUCTION INDUSTRY

ELECTRIC LAMPS

See: LIGHTING

ELECTRIC LIGHTING

See: LIGHTING

ELECTRIC MOTOR INDUSTRY

See: ELECTRICAL EQUIPMENT INDUSTRY

ELECTRIC POWER

See: ELECTRIC UTILITIES

ELECTRIC POWER COGENERATION

See: COGENERATION OF ENERGY

ELECTRIC POWER PLANTS

See also: ELECTRIC UTILITIES; ELECTRICAL EQUIPMENT INDUSTRY; PUBLIC UTILITIES

GENERAL WORKS

Power System Operation. Robert H. Miller. McGraw-Hill. • 1994. $65.00. Third edition.

Renewables for Power Generation: Status and Prospect. Organization for Economic Cooperation and Development. • 2003. $75.00. Presents the global outlook for electrical power generation from renewable sources, including water power, wind power, solar power, and geothermal power.

ABSTRACTS AND INDEXES

Key Abstracts: Computing in Electronics and Power. Available from INSPEC, Inc. • Monthly. $250.00 per year. Provides international coverage of journal and proceedings literature. Published in England by the Institution of Electrical Engineers (IEE).

Key Abstracts: Power Systems and Applications. Available from INSPEC, Inc. • Monthly. $250.00 per year. Provides international coverage of journal and proceedings literature, including publications on electric power apparatus and machines. Published in England by the Institution of Electrical Engineers (IEE).

DIRECTORIES

Platt's Directory of Electric Power Producers and Distributors. Platts. • Annual. $410.00. Over 3,500 investor-owned, municipal, rural cooperative and government electric utility systems in the U.S. and Canada. Formerly *Directory of Electric Power Producers and Distributors.*

FINANCIAL RATIOS

Annual Statement Studies. The Risk Management Association. • Annual. Median and quartile financial ratios are given for over 400 kinds of manufacturing, wholesale, retail, construction, and consumer finance establishments. Data is sorted by both asset size and sales volume. Includes a clearly written "Definition of Ratios" and an alphabetical industry index.

Annual Statement Studies: Industry Default Probabilities and Cash Flow Measures. The Risk Management Association. • Annual. $145.00. Serves as a companion volume to the original *Annual Statement Studies.* Gives probability of default estimates on a percentage scale for more than 450 industries. Includes changes in position year-by-year for eight financial statement line items and provides percentage measures of cash flow.

HANDBOOKS AND MANUALS

Standard Handbook of Power Plant Engineering. Thomas C. Elliott and others. McGraw-Hill. • 1997. $115.00. Second edition.

PERIODICALS AND NEWSLETTERS

Electrial Construction and Maintenance. Primedia Business Magazines and Media. • Monthly. Free to qualified personnel; individuals, $30.00 per year; libraries, $25.00 per year.

Global Power Report: An Exclusive Biweekly Covering the Cogeneration and Small Power Market. Platts. • Biweekly. $1,165.00 per year. Newsletter. Covers industry trends, new projects, new contracts, rate changes, and regulations, with emphasis on the Federal Energy Regulatory Commission (FERC). Formerly *Cogeneration Report.*

Power Engineering International. PennWell Corp., Industrial Div. • Monthly. $170.00 per year.

Private Power Executive. Pequot Publishing, Inc. • Bimonthly. $90.00 per year. Covers private power (non-utility) enterprises, including cogeneration projects and industrial self-generation.

STATISTICS SOURCES

Coal Information. Organization for Economic Cooperation and Development. • Annual. $200.00. Presents comprehensive data from the International Energy Agency (IEA) on the world coal market, including supply, demand, production, trade, and prices. In addition to coal itself, provides country-specific data on coal-fired power stations and coal-related environmental issues.

Financial Statistics of Major Publicly Owned Electric Utilities in the U.S. U.S. Energy Informa-

tion Administration, U.S. Department of Energy. Available from U.S. Government Printing Office. • Annual.

Inventory of Electrtic Utility Power Plants in the United States. Energy Information Administration, U.S. Department of Energy. Available from U.S. Government Printing Office. • Annual. $33.00.

Statistical YearBook of the Electric Utility Industry. Edison Electric Institute. • Annual. Members, $270.00; non-members, $550.00.

Steam Electric Market Analysis. National Mining Association. • Monthly. Free to members; non-members, $300.00 per year. Covers 400 major electric power plants, with detailed data on coal consumption and stockpiles. Shows percent of power generated by fuel type. (Publisher formerly National Coal Association.).

TRADE/PROFESSIONAL ASSOCIATIONS

Association of Edison Illuminating Companies. 600 N. 18th St., Birmingham, AL 35291-0992. Phone: (205)257-2530 Fax: (205)257-2540 E-mail: diraeic@abinter.net • URL: http://www.aeic.org.

Association of Energy Engineers. 4025 Pleasantdale Rd., Ste. 420, Atlanta, GA 30340-4264. Phone: (770)447-5083 Fax: (770)446-3969 E-mail: info@aeecenter.org • URL: http://www.aeecenter.org • Members are engineers and other professionals concerned with energy management and cogeneration.

Edison Electric Institute. 701 Pennsylvania Ave. NW, Washington, DC 20004-2696. Phone: 800-334-4688 or (202)508-5000 Fax: (202)508-5360 E-mail: bfarrell@eei.org • URL: http://www.eei.org • Shareholder-owned electric utility companies operating in the U.S.; international affiliates and associates worldwide.

Electrical Generating Systems Association. 1650 S Dixie Hwy., Ste. 500, Boca Raton, FL 33432-7462. Phone: (561)750-5575 Fax: (561)395-8557 E-mail: e-mail@egsa.org • URL: http://www.egsa.org • Manufacturers, distributor/dealers, and manufacturers' representatives of devices used to generate electrical power through the use of an internal combustion engine or a gas turbine coupled to a generator. Conducts training programs and publishes material on On-Site Power Generation.

ELECTRIC POWER, RURAL

See: RURAL ELECTRIFICATION

ELECTRIC RATES

See also: PUBLIC UTILITIES

PERIODICALS AND NEWSLETTERS

Electric Utility Week: The Electric Utility Industry Newsletter. Platts. • Weekly. $1,625.00 per year. Newsletter. Formerly *Electric Week.*

STATISTICS SOURCES

EIA Residential Electric Bills in Major Cities. Energy Information Administration. U.S. Department of Energy. • Annual.

ELECTRIC SIGNS

See: SIGNS AND SIGN BOARDS

ELECTRIC UTILITIES

See also: COGENERATION OF ENERGY; ELECTRIC POWER PLANTS; HYDROELECTRIC INDUSTRY; PUBLIC UTILITIES

GENERAL WORKS

Electricity Supply Industry: Structure, Ownership, and Regulation. OECD Publications and Informa-

tion Center. • 1994. $113.00. Discusses the "extensive reform" of the electric utility industry that is underway worldwide. Includes profiles of the electricity supply industry.

ABSTRACTS AND INDEXES

Business Periodicals Index. H. W. Wilson Co. • 11 times a year. Quarterly and annual cumulations. Price varies.

NTIS Alerts: Energy. National Technical Information Service. • Semimonthly. $245.00 per year. Provides descriptions of government-sponsored research reports and software, with ordering information. Covers electric power, batteries, fuels, geothermal energy, heating/cooling systems, nuclear technology, solar energy, energy policy, and related subjects. Formerly *Abstract Newsletter.*

CD-ROM DATABASES

OECD Statistical Compendium. Organization for Economic Cooperation and Development. • Semiannual. $1,905.00 per year for 1 to 10 users. CD-ROM contains more than 730,000 monthly, quarterly, and annual time series for OECD countries, 1960 to date. Includes fully searchable data on agriculture, food, economic indicators, national accounts, employment, energy, finance, industry, technology, and foreign trade. Results can be displayed in various forms.

DIRECTORIES

The International Competitive Power Industry Directory. PennWell Corp. • Publication includes: List of 1,400 companies active in the global power industry, providing information on developers, financial firms, law firms, engineering and construction firms, fuel suppliers, consultants, manufacturers and other suppliers of products, equipment ot the hydro, geothermal, solar and wind industries. Entries include: Company name, address, phone, fax; contact name; business area or tyope; technology used; region covered; products.

Platt's Directory of Electric Power Producers and Distributors. Platts. • Annual. $410.00. Over 3,500 investor-owned, municipal, rural cooperative and government electric utility systems in the U.S. and Canada. Formerly *Directory of Electric Power Producers and Distributors.*

Plunkett's Energy Industry Almanac: Complete Profiles on the Energy Industry 500 Companies. Plunkett Research Ltd. • Annual. $199.99. Includes major oil companies, utilities, pipelines, alternative energy companies, etc. Provides information on industry trends.

Public Power Annual Directory and Statistical Reprot. American Public Power Association. • Annual. $125.00. Lists approximately 2,000 local publicly owned electric utilities in United States and possessions. Formerly *Public Power Directory of Local Publicly Owned Electric Utilities.*

Utility Automation Buying Guide. Pennwell Corp., Industrial Div. • Annual. Price on application. A directory of information technology products and services for electric utility companies.

ENCYCLOPEDIAS AND DICTIONARIES

Encyclopedia of Energy. Cutler J. Cleveland, editor. Elsevier, Inc. • 2004. $1,560.00. Six volumes. Covers all aspects of energy sources and energy-related environmental issues.

Macmillan Encyclopedia of Energy. Available from Gale Cengage Learning. • 2001. $395.00. Three volumes. Published by Macmillan Reference USA. Covers the business, technology, and history of a wide variety of energy sources.

FINANCIAL RATIOS

Almanac of Business and Industrial Financial Ratios. Leo Troy. Aspen Publishers, Inc. • 2003. $125.95. Includes CD-Rom. Contains financial ratios derived from federal tax returns. Ratios for each of about 200 industries are arranged according to company asset size. (Almanac of Business and Industrial Financial Ratios Series).

HANDBOOKS AND MANUALS

Moody's Public Utility Manual. Mergent, Inc. • Annual. $1,995.00. Updated weekly online. Contains financial and other information concerning publicly-held utility companies (electric, gas, telephone, water).

INTERNET DATABASES

Business 2.0 Web Guide to the Best Business Links. Business 2.0 Media Inc. Phone: (415)293-4800 E-mail: support@business2.com • URL: http://www.business2.com/webguide • Web site presents an extensive, searchable directory of links to "the best, most informative, and authoritative web pages." Twenty main categories cover business, finance, career, company information, people, and technology topics, with thousands of subtopics, all linking to Web sites recommended by experienced business researchers. Fees: Free.

Fedstats. Federal Interagency Council on Statistical Policy. Phone: (202)395-7254 • URL: http://www.fedstats.gov • Web site features an efficient search facility for full-text statistics produced by more than 100 federal agencies, including the Census Bureau, the Bureau of Economic Analysis, and the Bureau of Labor Statistics. Boolean searches can be made within one agency or for all agencies combined. Links are offered to international statistical bureaus, including the UN, IMF, OECD, UNESCO, Eurostat, and 20 individual countries. Fees: Free.

FreeLunch.com. Economy.com, Inc. Phone: (610)696-8700 Fax: (610)696-1678 • URL: http://www.freelunch.com • Web site provides free access to more than 1.5 million economic and financial data series, covering industry, demographics, labor markets, prices, retail sales, government spending, trade, interest rates, housing starts, the stock market, and many other topics. Data is available for various time periods in either chart or table form. Searching is offered. Fees: Free, but registration required. Economy.com, Inc. also offers fee-based economic analysis at *The Dismal Scientist* site (http://www.dismal.com).

PERIODICALS AND NEWSLETTERS

Electric Perspectives. Edison Electric Institute. • Bimonthly. $50.00 per year. Covers business, financial, and operational aspects of the investor-owned electric utility industry. Edited for utility executives and managers.

Electric Utility Week: The Electric Utility Industry Newsletter. Platts. • Weekly. $1,625.00 per year. Newsletter. Formerly *Electric Week.*

Electrical Wholesaling. Primedia Business Magazines and Media. • Monthly. $20.00 per year.

Electrical World T and D Magazine. Platts. • Monthly. Free to qualified personnel. Formerly *Electrical World.*

Energy Services Marketing Letter: Covering Electric and Gas Utility Marketing Programs. • Monthly. $295.00 per year. Newsletter. Formerly *DSM Letter.*

EPRI Journal. Electric Power Research Institute. • Bimonthly. Free to members; non-members, $29.00 per year.

Public Power. American Public Power Association. • Bimonthly. $50.00 per year.

Public Power Weekly. American Public Power Association. • Description: Reports on legislative, regulatory, judicial, and technical developments affecting local and state-owned electric utilities. Recurring features include employment notices and news briefs.

Utility Automation. PennWell Corp., Industrial Div. • 10 times a year. $69.00 per year; schools and public libraries, $10.00 per year. Covers new information technologies for electric utilities, including automated meter reading, distribution management systems, and customer information systems.

PRICE SOURCES

Energy Prices and Taxes. International Energy Agency. OECD Publications and Information Center. • Quarterly. $385.00 per year. Includes print and online edition. Compiled by the International Energy Agency. Provides data on prices and taxation of petroleum products, natural gas, coal, and electricity. Diskette edition, $800.00. (Published in Paris).

Energy Prices and Taxes. Organization for Economic Cooperation and Development. • Quarterly. $355.00 per year. Includes both industrial and consumer prices for oil products, natural gas, coal, and electricity in various countries. (Also available on CD-ROM.).

PPI Detailed Report. Bureau of Labor Statistics, U.S. Department of Labor. Available from U.S. Government Printing Office. • Monthly. $55.00 per year. Formerly *Producer Price Indexes.*

RESEARCH CENTERS AND INSTITUTES

Laboratory for Electromagnetic and Electronic Systems. Massachusetts Institute of Technology, 77 Massachusetts Ave., Room 10-172, Cambridge, MA 02139. Phone: (617)253-4631 Fax: (617)258-6774 E-mail: jgk@mit.edu • URL: http://www.power.mit.edu/index • Research areas include heat transfer and cryogenics.

Lamme Power Systems Laboratory. Ohio State University. 2015 Neil Ave., Columbus, OH 43210. Phone: (614)292-7410 Fax: (614)292-7596 E-mail: sebo.1@osu.edu.

STATISTICS SOURCES

Annual Energy Outlook [year], with Projections to [year]. Available from U. S. Government Printing Office. • Annual. $42.00. Issued by the Energy Information Administration, U. S. Department of Energy (http://www.eia.doe.gov). Contains detailed statistics and 20-year projections for electricity, oil, natural gas, coal, and renewable energy. Text provides extensive discussion of energy issues and "Market Trends.".

Annual Energy Review. Available from U. S. Government Printing Office. • Annual. $51.00. Issued by the Energy Information Administration, Office of Energy Markets and End Use, U. S. Department of Energy. Presents long-term historical as well as recent data on production, consumption, stocks, imports, exports, and prices of the principal energy commodities in the U. S.

Business Statistics of the United States. Linz Audain and Cornelia J. Strawser. Bernan Associates. • Annual. $147.00. Based on *Business Statistics,* formerly issue by the Bureau of Economic Analysis, U. S. Department of Commerce. Provides basic data for a wide variety of U. S. industries, services, and economic indicators. Most statistics are shown annually for 30 years and monthly for the most recent four years.

Electric Power Monthly. Available from U. S. Government Printing Office. • Monthly. $137.00 per year. Issued by the Energy Information Administration, U. S. Department of Energy. Contains statistical data relating to electric utility operation, capability, fuel use, and prices.

Electricity Information. OECD Publications and Information Center. • Annual. $130.00. Compiled by the International Energy Agency (IEA). Provides detailed electric power statistics for each OECD country, including data on prices, production, and consumption.

Energy Balances of OECD Countries. Organization for Economic Cooperation and Development. Available from OECD Publications and Information Center. • Annual. $115.00. Presents two-year data on the supply and consumption of solid fuels, oil, gas, and electricity, expressed in oil equivalency terms. Historical tables are also provided. Relates to OECD member countries.

Financial Statistics of Major Publicly Owned Electric Utilities in the U.S. U.S. Energy Information Administration, U.S. Department of Energy. Available from U.S. Government Printing Office. • Annual.

Infrastructure Industries USA. Gale Cengage Learning. • 2001. $260.00. Presents statistics and projections relating to economic activity in a wide variety of natural resource and construction industries.

Inventory of Electrtic Utility Power Plants in the United States. Energy Information Administration, U.S. Department of Energy. Available from U.S. Government Printing Office. • Annual. $33.00.

OECD Nuclear Energy Data. Organization for Economic Cooperation and Development. Available from OECD Publications and Information Center. • Annual. $32.00. Produced by the OECD Nuclear Energy Agency. Provides a yearly compilation of basic statistics on electricity generation and nuclear power in OECD member countries. Text in English and French.

Oil, Gas, Coal, and Electricity: Quarterly Statistics. Organization for Economic Cooperation and Development. • Quarterly. $355.00 per year. Provides detailed data for OECD countries. Covers crude oil, nine oil product groups, hard coal, brown coal (lignite), natural gas, and electric power.

Standard & Poor's Industry Surveys. Standard & Poor's. • Semiannual. $1,800.00. Two looseleaf volumes. Includes monthly *Supplements.* Provides detailed, individual surveys of 52 major industry groups. Each survey is revised on a semiannual basis. Also includes "Monthly Investment Review" (industry group investment analysis) and monthly "Trends & Projections" (economic analysis).

Statistical YearBook of the Electric Utility Industry. Edison Electric Institute. • Annual. Members, $270.00; non-members, $550.00.

Steam Electric Market Analysis. National Mining Association. • Monthly. Free to members; non-members, $300.00 per year. Covers 400 major electric power plants, with detailed data on coal consumption and stockpiles. Shows percent of power generated by fuel type. (Publisher formerly National Coal Association.).

Survey of Current Business. Available from U. S. Government Printing Office. • Monthly. $63.00 per year. Issued by Bureau of Economic Analysis, U. S. Department of Commerce. Presents a wide variety of business and economic data.

World Energy Outlook. OECD Publications and Information Center. • Annual. $150.00. Provides detailed, 15-year projections by the International Energy Agency (IEA) for world energy supply and demand.

TRADE/PROFESSIONAL ASSOCIATIONS

American Public Power Association. 1875 Connecticut Ave. NW, Ste. 200, Washington, DC 20009. Phone: (202)467-2900 Fax: (202)467-2910 E-mail: mrufe@appanet.org • URL: http://www.appanet.org • Municipally owned electric utilities, public utility districts, state and county-owned electric systems, and rural cooperatives. Conducts research programs; compiles statistics; offers utility education courses; sponsors competitions.

Association of Edison Illuminating Companies. 600 N. 18th St., Birmingham, AL 35291-0992. Phone: (205)257-2530 Fax: (205)257-2540 E-mail: diraeic@abinter.net • URL: http://www.aeic.org.

Edison Electric Institute. 701 Pennsylvania Ave.

NW, Washington, DC 20004-2696. Phone: 800-334-4688 or (202)508-5000 Fax: (202)508-5360 E-mail: bfarrell@eei.org • URL: http://www.eei.org • Shareholder-owned electric utility companies operating in the U.S.; international affiliates and associates worldwide.

International League of Electrical Associations. 2901 Metro Dr., Ste. 203, Bloomington, MN 55425. Phone: (952)854-4405 Fax: (952)854-7076 E-mail: sue@ncel.org • URL: http://www.ileaweb.org • Formerly International Association of Electric Leagues.

OTHER SOURCES

Major Energy Companies of the World. Available from Gale Cengage Learning. • Annual. $880.00. Published by Graham & Whiteside. Contains detailed information on more than 3,300 important energy companies in various countries. Industries include electricity generation, coal, natural gas, nuclear energy, petroleum, fuel distribution, and equipment for energy production.

Utilities Industry Litigation Reporter: National Coverage of the Many Types of Litigation Stemming From the Transmission and Distribution of Energy By Publicly and Privately Owned Utilities. Andrews Publications. • Monthly. $775.00 per year. Newsletter. Reports on legal cases involving the generation or distribution of energy.

ELECTRIC WIRE

See: WIRE INDUSTRY

ELECTRICAL CONSTRUCTION INDUSTRY

ALMANACS AND YEARBOOKS

EC&M's Electrical Products Yearbook (Electrical Construction and Maintenance). Primedia Business Magazines and Media. • Annual. $10.00.

BIBLIOGRAPHIES

Census of Construction: Subject Bibliography No. 157. Available from U. S. Government Printing Office. • Annual. Free. Lists government publications.

DIRECTORIES

Electrical Construction Materials Directory. Underwriters Laboratories, Inc. • Annual. $22.00. Lists construction materials manufacturers authorized to use UL label.

Plastics Recognized Component Directory. Underwriters Laboratories Inc. • Covers: Companies that have qualified to use the UL recognized component marking on or in connection with materials that have been found to be in compliance with UL's requirements. Coverage includes foreign companies that manufacture for distribution in the U.S. Entries include: Company name, city, ZIP code, UL file number, type of product.

FINANCIAL RATIOS

Almanac of Business and Industrial Financial Ratios. Leo Troy. Aspen Publishers, Inc. • 2003. $125.95. Includes CD-Rom. Contains financial ratios derived from federal tax returns. Ratios for each of about 200 industries are arranged according to company asset size. (Almanac of Business and Industrial Financial Ratios Series).

Annual Statement Studies. The Risk Management Association. • Annual. Median and quartile financial ratios are given for over 400 kinds of manufacturing, wholesale, retail, construction, and consumer finance establishments. Data is sorted by both asset size and sales volume. Includes a clearly written "Definition of Ratios" and an alphabetical industry index.

Annual Statement Studies: Industry Default Probabilities and Cash Flow Measures. The Risk Management Association. • Annual. $145.00. Serves as a companion volume to the original *Annual Statement Studies.* Gives probability of default estimates on a percentage scale for more than 450 industries. Includes changes in position year-by-year for eight financial statement line items and provides percentage measures of cash flow.

Construction Industry Annual Financial Survey. Construction Financial Management Association. • Annual. $149.00. Contains key financial ratios for various kinds and sizes of construction contractors.

HANDBOOKS AND MANUALS

CEE News Buyers' Guide. Primedia Business Magazines and Media. • Annual. $25.00. List of approximately 1,900 manufacturers of products used in the electrical construction industry; coverage includes Canada.

PERIODICALS AND NEWSLETTERS

Electrial Construction and Maintenance. Primedia Business Magazines and Media. • Monthly. Free to qualified personnel; individuals, $30.00 per year; libraries, $25.00 per year.

Electrical Contractor. National Electrical Contractors Association. • Monthly. Membership.

STATISTICS SOURCES

United States Census of Construction Industries. U.S. Bureau of the Census. • Quinquennial. Results presented in reports, tape, and CD-ROM files.

TRADE/PROFESSIONAL ASSOCIATIONS

Independent Electrical Contractors. 4401 Ford Ave., Ste. 1100, Alexandria, VA 22302-1432. Phone: 800-456-4324 or (703)549-7351 Fax: (703)549-7448 E-mail: info@ieci.org • URL: http://www.ieci.org • Independent electrical contractors, small and large, primarily open shop. Promotes the interests of members; works to eliminate "unwise and unfair business practices" and to protect its members against "unfair or unjust taxes and legislative enactments." Sponsors electrical apprenticeship programs; conducts educational programs on cost control and personnel motivation. Represents independent electrical contractors to the National Electrical Code panel. Conducts surveys on volume of sales and purchases and on type of products used. Has formulated National Pattern Standards for Apprentice Training for Electricians.

International Association of Electrical Inspectors. 901 Waterfall Way, Suite 602, Richardson, TX 75080-0848. Phone: 800-786-4234 or (972)235-1455 Fax: (972)235-3855 E-mail: iaei@iaei.org • URL: http://www.iaei.org.

Joint Industry Board of the Electrical Industry. 158-11 Harry Van Arsdale, Jr. Ave., Flushing, NY 11365. Phone: (718)591-2000 Fax: (718)380-7741 • Concerned with labor-management relations of electrical contractors.

National Electrical Contractors Association. 3 Bethesda Metro Ctr., Ste. 1100, Bethesda, MD 20814. Phone: (301)657-3110 or (301)215-4500 Fax: (301)215-4500 E-mail: webmaster@necanet.org • URL: http://www.necanet.org • Contractors erecting, installing, repairing, servicing, and maintaining electric wiring, equipment, and appliances. Provides management services and labor relations programs for electrical contractors; conducts seminars for contractor sales and training. Conducts research and educational programs; compiles statistics. Sponsors honorary society, the Academy of +Electrical +Contracting.

Power and Communication Contractors Association. 103 Oronoco St., Ste. 200, Alexandria, VA 22314. Phone: 800-542-7222 or (703)212-7734 Fax: (703)548-3733 E-mail: info@pccaweb.org • URL: http://www.pccaweb.org • Contractors engaged in electrical power and communication line construction.

ELECTRICAL ENGINEERING

ABSTRACTS AND INDEXES

Applied Science and Technology Index. H. W. Wilson Co. • 11 times a year. Quarterly and annual cumulations. Price varies. Indexes a wide variety of English language technical, industrial, and engineering periodicals.

Engineering Index Monthly: Abstracting and Indexing Services Covering Sources of the World's Engineering Literature. Engineering Information Inc. • Monthly. Institutions, $5,279.00 per year. Provides indexing and abstracting of the world's engineering and technical literature.

BIBLIOGRAPHIES

Encyclopedia of Physical Science and Engineering Information. Gale Cengage Learning. • 1996. $160.00. Second edition. Includes print, electronic, and other information sources for a wide range of scientific, technical, and engineering topics.

IEEE Products and Publications Bulletin. Institute of Electrical and Electronics Engineers, Inc. • Quarterly. Free. Provides information on all IEEE journals, proceedings, and other publications. Formerly *IEEE Publications Bulletin.*

Reference Reviews. Available from Information Today, Inc. • Eight times a year. Price on application. Published in London by Aslib: The Association for Information Management. Incorporates *Aslib Book Guide.*

BIOGRAPHICAL SOURCES

Who's Who in Science and Engineering. Marquis Who's Who. • Biennial. $269.00. Provides concise biographical information on 35,000 prominent engineers and scientists. International coverage, with geographical and professional indexes.

DIRECTORIES

IEEE Membership Directory. Institute of Electrical and Electronics Engineers. • Annual. $190.00.

Peterson's Computer Science and Electrical Engineering Programs. Peterson's. • 1996. $24.95. A guide to 900 accredited graduate degree programs related to computers or electrical engineering at colleges and universities in the U. S. and Canada.

Peterson's Graduate and Professional Programs in Engineering and Applied Sciences. Peterson's. • Annual. $49.95. Provides details of more than 3,400 graduate and professional programs in engineering and related fields at colleges and universities. (Peterson's Graduate in Professional Programs Series). Formerly *Peterson's Guide to Graduate Programs in Engineering and Professional Sciences.*

Plunkett's Engineering and Research Industry Almanac. Plunkett Research, Ltd. • Annual. $179.99. Contains detailed profiles of major engineering and technology corporations. Includes CD-ROM.

ENCYCLOPEDIAS AND DICTIONARIES

Wiley Encyclopedia of Electrical and Electronics Engineering. John G. Webster, editor. John Wiley and Sons, Inc. • 1999. $9,630.00. 25 volumes. Includes Supplement 1 and *Supplement II.* Contains about 1,400 articles, each with bibliography. Arrangement is according to 64 categories.

Wiley Encyclopedia of Telecommunications and Signal Processing. John G. Proakis, editor. John Wiley and Sons, Inc. • 2002. $1,250.00. Five volumes. Contains about 300 articles covering both fundamentals and recent advances in telecommunications and signal processing. Emphasis is on material for electrical engineers.

HANDBOOKS AND MANUALS

Standard Handbook for Electrical Engineers. Douglas G. Fink. McGraw-Hill. • 1999. $150.00. 14th edtion. (Engineering and Technology Management Series).

ONLINE DATABASES

Current Contents Connect. Institute for Scientific Information. • Provides online abstracts of articles listed in the tables of contents of about 7,500 journals. Coverage is very broad, including science, social science, life science, technology, engineering, industry, agriculture, the environment, economics, and arts and humanities. Time period is two years, with weekly updates. Inquire as to online cost and availability.

INSPEC. Institution of Electrical Engineers (IEE). • Provides online citations, with abstracts, to the world literature of electrical engineering, electronics, optoelectronics, telecommunications, industrial controls, instrumentation, computer technology, information technology, and physics. Coverage includes more than 4,000 technical and scientific journals from 1969 to date, with weekly updating. (INSPEC is Information Services in Physics, Electronics, and Computing.) Inquire as to online cost and availability.

NTIS Database. National Technical Information Service. • Contains citations and abstracts to unrestricted reports of government-sponsored research, 1964 to date. Covers a wide range of technical, engineering, business, and social science topics. Monthly updates. Inquire as to online cost and availability.

Who's Who in Technology [Online]. Gale Cengage Learning. • Provides online biographical profiles of over 25,000 American scientists, engineers, and others in technology-related occupations. Inquire as to online cost and availability.

PERIODICALS AND NEWSLETTERS

Electronic Engineering Times: The Industry Newspaper for Engineers and Technical Management. CMP Publications, Inc. • Weekly. Free to qualified personnel; others, $319.00 per year.

IEEE Industry Applications Magazine. Institute of Electrical and Electronics Engineers. • Bimonthly. $190.00 per year. Covers new industrial applications of power conversion, drives, lighting, and control. Emphasis is on the petroleum, chemical, rubber, plastics, textile, and mining industries.

IEEE Proceedings-Circuits, Devices and Systems. Institute of Electrical and Electronics Engineers, Inc. • Monthly. $720.00 per year.

IEEE Spectrum. Institute of Electrical and Electronics Engineers, Inc. • Monthly. $195.00 per year. Includes print and online editions. Supplement available *The Institute.*

RESEARCH CENTERS AND INSTITUTES

Communications and Signal Processing Laboratory. University of Michigan. 4110 EECS Bldg., 1301 Beal Ave., Ann Arbor, MI 48109-2122. Phone: (734)763-0390 Fax: (734)763-8041 E-mail: stark@ eecs.umich.edu • URL: http://www.eecs.umich.edu/ systems.

Electrical and Computer Engineering. University of Texas at Austin. 143 Engineering Science Bldg., Austin, TX 78712. Phone: (512)471-6179 Fax: (512)471-3652 E-mail: ambler@mail.utexas.edu • URL: http://www.utexas.edu.

Electrical and Computer Engineering Industrial Institute. Purdue University School of Electrical and Computer Engineering. Administration Bldg., Rm. 101, 400 Centennial Mall Dr., West Lafayette, IN 47907-2016. Phone: (765)494-5345 Fax: (765)494-9321 E-mail: dean.of.engineering@purdue.edu • URL: http://www.ecn.purdue.edu.

Laboratory for Electromagnetic and Electronic Systems. Massachusetts Institute of Technology, 77 Massachusetts Ave., Room 10-172, Cambridge, MA 02139. Phone: (617)253-4631 Fax: (617)258-6774 E-mail: jgk@mit.edu • URL: http://www.power.mit.

edu/index • Research areas include heat transfer and cryogenics.

TRADE/PROFESSIONAL ASSOCIATIONS

Institute of Electrical and Electronics Engineers. c/o IEEE Corporate Office, 3 Park Ave., 17th Fl., New York, NY 10016-5997. Phone: 800-678-4333 or (212)419-7900 Fax: (212)752-4929 E-mail: ieeeusa@ieee.org • URL: http://www.ieee.org.

Joint Electron Device Engineering Council (JEDC). 2500 Wilson Blvd., Arlington, VA 22201-3834. Phone: (703)907-7534 Fax: (703)907-7583 E-mail: arlenec@jedec.org • URL: http://www.jedec.org • Affiliated with Electronic Industries Alliance. Formerly Joint Electron Device Engineering Council.

ELECTRICAL EQUIPMENT INDUSTRY

See also: ELECTRIC APPLIANCE INDUSTRY; ELECTRIC POWER PLANTS

ABSTRACTS AND INDEXES

Applied Science and Technology Index. H. W. Wilson Co. • 11 times a year. Quarterly and annual cumulations. Price varies. Indexes a wide variety of English language technical, industrial, and engineering periodicals.

Business Periodicals Index. H. W. Wilson Co. • 11 times a year. Quarterly and annual cumulations. Price varies.

Key Abstracts: Power Systems and Applications. Available from INSPEC, Inc. • Monthly. $250.00 per year. Provides international coverage of journal and proceedings literature, including publications on electric power apparatus and machines. Published in England by the Institution of Electrical Engineers (IEE).

DIRECTORIES

Design News OEM Directory. Reed Business Information. • Covers: about 5,000 manufacturers and suppliers of power transmission products, fluid power products, and electrical/electronic components to the OEM (original equipment manufacturer) market in SIC groups 34-39. Entries include: Company name, address, phone, fax, url, e-mail.

Directory of Electrical Wholesale Distributors. Primedia Business Magazines and Media. • Biennial. $1,390.00. Lists more than 10,000 locations.

Electrical Apparatus: Electromechanical Bench Reference Supplement. Barks Publications, Inc. • Monthly. $24.00. Included in subscription to *Electric Apparatus Magazine.* Lists 3,000 manufacturers and distributors of electrical and electronic products. Formerly *Electrical Apparatus Magazine. Electromechanical Bench Reference Book.*

Thomas Register of American Manufacturers. Thomas Publishing Co., Inc. • Annual. $149.00. 34 volumes. A three-part system offering information on a wide variety of industrial equipment and supplies. Lists more than 151,000 industrial product and services companies.

FINANCIAL RATIOS

Annual Statement Studies. The Risk Management Association. • Annual. Median and quartile financial ratios are given for over 400 kinds of manufacturing, wholesale, retail, construction, and consumer finance establishments. Data is sorted by both asset size and sales volume. Includes a clearly written "Definition of Ratios" and an alphabetical industry index.

Annual Statement Studies: Industry Default Probabilities and Cash Flow Measures. The Risk Management Association. • Annual. $145.00.

Serves as a companion volume to the original *Annual Statement Studies.* Gives probability of default estimates on a percentage scale for more than 450 industries. Includes changes in position year-by-year for eight financial statement line items and provides percentage measures of cash flow.

IRS Corporate Financial Ratios. Available from MarketResearch.com. • 2002. $225.00. Published by Schonfeld & Associates, Inc. Presents 70 key financial ratios for 260 industries. Ratios are calculated from income statement and balance sheet data available from the Internal Revenue Service. Includes four asset size classes.

HANDBOOKS AND MANUALS

CEE News Buyers' Guide. Primedia Business Magazines and Media. • Annual. $25.00. List of approximately 1,900 manufacturers of products used in the electrical construction industry; coverage includes Canada.

Guide to Energy Efficient Commercial Equipment. Margaret Suozzo and others. American Council for an Energy Efficient Economy. • 1997. $25.00. Provides information on specifying and purchasing energy-saving systems for buildings (heating, air conditioning, lighting, and motors).

INTERNET DATABASES

Manufacturing Profiles. U. S. Bureau of the Census. Phone: (301)763-4636 E-mail: webmaster@census. gov • URL: http://www.census.gov/prod/www/abs/ mfg-prof.html • The Census Bureau makes available free on PDF (Portable Document Format) an annual consolidation of the entire Current Industrial Report series, presenting "all the data compiled." Contains statistics on production, shipments, inventories, consumption, exports, imports, and orders for a wide variety of manufactured products.

ONLINE DATABASES

Business and Industry. Gale Cengage Learning. • Contains online citations, abstracts, and selected fulltext from more than 1,000 trade journals, newspapers, and other publications. Provides general coverage of both manufacturing and service industries, including marketing, production, industry trends, key events, and information on specific companies. Time span is 1994 to date. Daily updates. Inquire as to online cost and availability. (Also available in a CD-ROM version.).

Tablebase. Gale Cengage Learning. • Provides online numerical tabular data from a wide variety of business, organization, and government sources, including about 1,000 trade journals. Includes industry and individual company statistics relating to products, market share, sales forecasts, production, exports, market trends, etc. Time span is 1997 to date. Weekly updates. Inquire as to online cost and availability. (Also available in a CD-ROM version.).

Thomas Register Online. Thomas Publishing Co., Inc. • Provides concise information on approximately 194,000 U. S. companies, mainly manufacturers, with over 50,000 product classifications. Indexes over 115,000 trade names. Information is updated semiannually. Inquire as to online cost and availability.

PERIODICALS AND NEWSLETTERS

Appliance Manufacturer. Business News Publishing Co. • Monthly. $55.00 per year.

Canadian Industrial Equipment News: Reader Service On New, Improved and Redesigned Industrial Equipment and Supplies. Business Information Group. • Monthly. $68.95 per year. Supplement available. Formerly *Electrical Equipment News.*

Dealerscope: Product and Strategy for Consumer Technology Retailing. North American Publishing Co. • Monthly. Free to qualified personnel; others,

$79.00 per year. Formerly *Dealerscope Consumer Electronices Marketplace*.

EE Product News (Electronics-Electrical). Penton Media, Inc. • Monthly. Free to qualified personnel; others, $60.00 per year.

National Home Center News: News and Analysis for the Home Improvement, Building Material Industry. Lebhar-Friedman, Inc. • 22 times a year. $99.00 per year. Includes special feature issues on hardware and tools, building materials, millwork, electrical supplies, lighting, and kitchens.

STATISTICS SOURCES

Annual Survey of Manufactures. Available from U. S. Government Printing Office. • Annual. Prices vary. Issued by the U. S. Census Bureau as an interim update to the *Census of Manufactures*. Includes data on number of manufacturing establishments in various industries, employment, labor costs, value of shipments, capital expenditures, inventories, energy costs, and assets. (See also Census Bureau home page, http://www.census. gov/.).

Encyclopedia of American Industries. Gale Cengage Learning. • 2000. $560.00. Third edition. Two volumes. $280.00 per volume. Volume one is *Manufacturing Industries* and volume two is *Service and Non-Manufacturing Industries*. Provides the history, development, and recent status of approximately 1,000 industries. Includes statistical graphs, with industry and general indexes.

Standard & Poor's Industry Surveys. Standard & Poor's. • Semiannual. $1,800.00. Two looseleaf volumes. Includes monthly *Supplements*. Provides detailed, individual surveys of 52 major industry groups. Each survey is revised on a semiannual basis. Also includes "Monthly Investment Review" (industry group investment analysis) and monthly "Trends & Projections" (economic analysis).

U. S. Industry and Trade Outlook. Available from National Technical Information Service. • Annual. $69.95. Produced by the International Trade Administration, U. S. Department of Commerce, in a "public-private" partnership with DRI/McGraw-Hill and Standard & Poor's. Provides basic data, outlook for the current year, and "Long-Term Prospects" (five-year projections) for a wide variety of products and services. Includes high technology industries. Formerly *U. S. Industrial Outlook*.

United States Census of Manufactures. U.S. Bureau of the Census. • Quinquennial. Results presented in reports, tape, CD-ROM, and Diskette files.

TRADE/PROFESSIONAL ASSOCIATIONS

Association of Home Appliance Manufacturers. 1111 19th St. NW, Ste. 402, Washington, DC 20036. Phone: (202)872-5955 Fax: (202)872-9354 E-mail: aham@aham.org • URL: http://www.aham.org.

Electrical Equipment Representatives Association. 638 W 39th St., Kansas City, MO 64111. Phone: (816)561-5323 Fax: (816)561-1249 E-mail: info2005@eera.org • URL: http://www.eera.org • Represents sales agents for manufacturers of electrical equipment used by utilities, industrial firms, and the government.

Electrical Generating Systems Association. 1650 S Dixie Hwy., Ste. 500, Boca Raton, FL 33432-7462. Phone: (561)750-5575 Fax: (561)395-8557 E-mail: e-mail@egsa.org • URL: http://www.egsa.org • Manufacturers, distributor/dealers, and manufacturers' representatives of devices used to generate electrical power through the use of an internal combustion engine or a gas turbine coupled to a generator. Conducts training programs and publishes material on On-Site Power Generation.

National Appliance Parts Suppliers Association. 4015 W Marshall Ave., PO Box 87907, Longview, TX 75604-4916. Phone: 888-309-9676 or (903)759-3983 Fax: (360)834-3507 E-mail: info@napsaweb.

org • URL: http://www.napsaweb.org • Wholesale distributors of replacement parts for major home appliance. Promotes and supports good relations among groups in the supply and distribution of appliance service parts. Sponsors Young +Executives Society of NAPSA to prepare younger generations for leadership in the appliance parts wholesale and distribution industry, and to handle problems characteristic of family businesses.

National Electrical Manufacturers Association. 1300 N 17th St., Ste. 1752, Rosslyn, VA 22209. Phone: (703)841-3200 Fax: (703)841-5900 E-mail: communications@nema.org • URL: http://www. nema.org • Aims to maintain and improve quality and reliability of products; insure safety standards in manufacture and use of products; organize and act upon members' interests in productivity, competition from overseas suppliers, energy conservation and efficiency, marketing opportunities, economic matters, and product liability. Develops product standards covering such matters as nomenclature, ratings, performance, testing, and dimensions; actively participates in regional and international standards process for electrical products; participates in developing National Electrical Code and National Electrical Safety Codes, and advocates their acceptance by state and local authorities; conducts regulatory and legislative analyses on issues of concern to electrical manufacturers; compiles and issues market data of all kinds, and statistical data on such factors as sales, new orders, unfilled orders, cancellations, production, and inventories. Sponsors geographical projects, advisory services, and statistical and management services.

ELECTRONIC COMMERCE

See also: INTERNET

GENERAL WORKS

Deal Engines: The Science of Auctions, Stock markets, and e-Markets. Robert E. Hall. W. W. Norton & Co., Inc. • 2003. $14.95. A practical, economic analysis of how auction markets work, whether simple (eBay) or complex (stock exchanges). Covers both theory and application. (Originally published as *Digital Dealing*.).

Dynamic E-Business Implementation Management: How to Effectively Manage E-Business Implementation. Bennet P. Lientz and Kathryn P. Rea. Elsevier. • 2000. $47.95. (E-Business Solutions Series).

The E-Commerce Book: Building the E-Empire. Steffano Korper and Juanita Ellis. Elsevier. • 2000. $41.95. Second edition. Covers the practical aspects of Internet commerce, including sales, marketing, advertising, payment systems, and security. Written for a general audience. (Communications, Networking and Multimedia Series).

eBrands: Building an Internet Business at Breakneck Speed. Phil Carpenter. Harvard Business School Publishing. • 2000. $25.95. Emphasis is on the marketing aspects of electronic commerce.

Economic Perspectives on the Internet. Alan E. Wiseman. Nova Science Publishers, Inc. • 2003. $59.00. Discusses the pricing of Internet access, pricing of goods and services sold through the Internet, network effects, and Internet taxation.

Entrepreneurship.com. Tim Burns. Dearborn Trade Publishing, A Kaplan Professional Co. • 2000. $19. 95. Provides basic advice and information on the topic of dot.com startups, including business plan creation and financing.

Essentials of Knowledge Management. Bryan Bergeron. John Wiley and Sons, Inc. • 2003. $29. 95. Covers current strategies, trends, and technologies in knowledge management. Includes examples

of best practices. (Essentials Series).

Executive's Guide to E-Business: From Tactics to Strategy. Martin Deise and others. John Wiley and Sons, Inc. • 2000. $39.95. Covers the basic principles of doing business successfully by way of the Internet.

Gonzo Marketing: Winning Through Worst Practices. Christopher Locke. John Wiley and Sons, Inc. • 2001. $29.95. An iconoclastic, entertaining view of e-commerce advertising and marketing (banners, pop-ups, spam, etc.). States the obvious: most Web advertising is more annoying than effective.

The Internet Bubble: Inside the Overvalued World of High-Tech Stocks, and What You Should Know to Avoid the Coming Catastrophe. Anthony Perkins and Michael C. Perkins. HarperInformation. • 2001. $28.00. Revised edition. The authors predict a shakeout in e-commerce stocks and other Internet-related investments. (HarperBusiness.).

Internet Prophets: Enlightened E-Business Strategies for Every Budget. Mary Diffley. Information Today, Inc. • 2002. $29.95. Emphasizes the specific dollar costs of having a successful online business. The "Internet Prophets" are four individual guides for developing business on the Web, arranged according to size of budget. (CyberAge Books).

Internet Taxation. Albert Tokin, editor. Nova Science Publishers, Inc. • 2003. $29.50. Several authors discuss the controversial issue of local taxation of e-commerce transactions.

Knowledge Management Lessons Learned: What Works and What Doesn't. Michael Koenig and T. Kanti Srikantaiah, editors. Information Today, Inc. • 2003. $44.50. Contains more than 30 articles by KM experts, covering recent applications, innovations, strategy, implementation, cost analysis, training, content management, and other topics related to knowledge management. (ASIS Management Series).

The Leap: A Memoir of Love and Madness in the Internet Gold Rush. Tom Ashbrook. Houghton Mifflin Co. • 2000. $25.00. The author relates his personal and family tribulations while attempting to obtain financing for an eventually successful e-business startup, HomePortfolio.com.

Operating an E-Business. Andrew McAfee. McGraw-Hill. • 2002. $61.25. Provides case studies covering B-to-B (business-to-business) Internet endeavors, B-to-C (business-to-consumer) and the electronic business activities of traditional "bricks-and-mortar" companies. Illustrates what went right and what went wrong. The author is a professor at Harvard Business School.

ABSTRACTS AND INDEXES

Internet and Personal Computing Abstracts [print edition]. EBSCO Publishing. • Quarterly. $269.00 per year, including cumulative index. Provides more than 10,000 abstracts annually from both trade and academic publications. Covers computer hardware, software, product reviews, Web topics, e-commerce, networks, corporate news, security, and related topics. Formerly *Microcomputer Abstracts*.

BIBLIOGRAPHIES

Knowledge Management: The Bibliography. Paul Burden and others. Information Today, Inc. • 2000. $22.50. Provides citations to more than 1,500 articles, 150 Web sites, and 400 books. Arranged according to specific KM topics, such as "KM and E-Commerce." Published in conjunction with the American Society for Information Science and Technology (ASIST).

BIOGRAPHICAL SOURCES

Net.people: The Personalities and Passions Behind the Web Sites. Thomas E. Bleier and Eric C. Steinert. Information Today, Inc. • 2000. $19.95. Presents the personal stories of 36 Web "entrepreneurs and visionaries." (CyberAge Books.).

CD-ROM DATABASES

OECD Statistical Compendium. Organization for Economic Cooperation and Development. • Semiannual. $1,905.00 per year for 1 to 10 users. CD-ROM contains more than 730,000 monthly, quarterly, and annual time series for OECD countries, 1960 to date. Includes fully searchable data on agriculture, food, economic indicators, national accounts, employment, energy, finance, industry, technology, and foreign trade. Results can be displayed in various forms.

DIRECTORIES

Gale E-Commerce Sourcebook. Gale. • Covers: Over 4,700 organizations, associations, and agencies related to e-commerce such as Web site designers, government regulatory agencies, publications, and trade shows. Also covers 250 leading e-commerce companies worldwide. Entries include: Name, address, phone, fax, e-mail address, URL, and name and title of contact person. For companies--Same as above along with year of founding, company revenue, and number of employees.

Guide to EU Information Sources on the Internet. Euroconfidentiel S. A. • Annual. $210.00. Contains descriptions of more than 1,700 Web sites providing information relating to the European Union and European commerce and industry. Includes a quarterly e-mail newsletter with new sites and address changes.

Handbook of Internet Stocks. Mergent. • Annual. $19.95. Contains detailed financial information on more than 200 Internet-related corporations, including e-commerce firms and telecommunications hardware manufacturers. Lists and rankings are provided.

KMWorld Buyer's Guide. Knowledge Asset Media. • Semiannual. Controlled circulation as part of *KMWorld.* Contains corporate and product profiles related to various aspects of knowledge management and information systems. (Knowledge Asset Media is a an affiliate of Information Today, Inc.).

Plunkett's E-Commerce and Internet Business Almanac. Plunkett Research, Ltd. • Annual. $249.99. Contains detailed profiles of 250 large companies engaged in various areas of Internet commerce, including e-business Web sites, communications equipment manufacturers, and Internet service providers. Includes CD-ROM.

ENCYCLOPEDIAS AND DICTIONARIES

Acronyms of Computer Science and Communications: A Comprehensive Acronym Dictionary and Illustrated Encylopedia. Enjob Kajan and Ejub Kajan. Springer Verlag. • 2002. $49.95. Explains more than 4,000 "broadly used" computer, telecommunications, and information technology acronyms. Includes illustrations and Web addresses, where applicable.

Encyclopedia of Information Systems. Hossein Bidgoli, editor. Elsevier. • 2002. $1,200.00. Four volumes. Contains a wide range of articles relating to computers, databases, communication, and information technology. The 200 topics include coverage of hardware, software, artificial intelligence, the Internet, networks, knowledge management, electronic commerce, search engines, and systems design.

Gale Encyclopedia of E-Commerce. Gale Cengage Learning. • 2002. $295.00. Two volumes. Contains about 470 entries covering Web site development, e-commerce financing, advertising, marketing, legal issues, and other topics related to doing business through the Internet. Includes a bibliography.

Internet Encyclopedia. Hossein Bidgoli, editor. John Wiley and Sons, Inc. • 2003. $750.00. Four volumes. Covers various aspects of the Internet,

including information technology, electronic business, and telecommunications.

HANDBOOKS AND MANUALS

Complete E-Commerce Book: Design, Build & Maintain a Successful Web-Based Business. Janice Reynolds and Roya Mofazali. CMP Books. • 2000. $29.95. Provides basic information for small firms wishing to do part of their business through a Web site. Covers both hardware and software for various system configurations.

Cyberfinance: Raising Capital for the E-Business. Martin B. Robins. CCH, Inc. • 2001. $79.00. Covers the taxation, financial, and legal aspects of raising money for new Internet-based ("dot.com") companies, including the three stages of startup, growth, and initial public offering. (Solutions for Professional Advisers Series).

Cybertaxation: The Taxation of E-Commerce. Karl A. Frieden. CCH, Inc. • 2000. $75.00. Includes state sales and use tax issues and corporate income tax rules, as related to doing business over the Internet.

Developing E-Business Systems and Architectures: A Manager's Guide. Paul Harmon and others. Elsevier. • 2000. $34.95.

Guidelines for Consumer Protection in the Context of Electronic Commerce. Organization for Economic Cooperation and Development. • 2000. $20.00. Provides a guide to effective consumer protection in online business-to-consumer transactions. Text in English and French.

Hot Text: Web Writing That Works. Jonathan Price and Lisa Price. New Riders Publishing. • 2002. $40.00. Provides practical advice on writing text for Web sites, including such details as headlines and menu design. As the attention span of many Web surfers is limited, clarity and brevity become of great importance.

How to Start a Home-Based Web Design Business. Jim Smith. Globe Pequot Press. • 2004. $17.95. Second edition. Covers planning, marketing, subcontracting, setting fees, customer presentations, and other topics related to starting a freelance, web design business at home. Includes a sample customer contract. (Home-Based Business Series).

Intellectual Property in the International Marketplace. Melvi Simensky and others. John Wiley and Sons, Inc. • 1999. $350.00. Second edition. Two volumes. Volume one: *Valuation, Protection, and Electronic Commerce.* Volume two: *Exploitation and Country-by-Country Profiles.* Includes contributions from lawyers and consultants in various countries. (Intellectual Property-General, Law, Accounting and Finance, Management, Licensing, Special Topics Series).

Learning Web Design: A Beginner's Guide to HTML, Graphics, and Beyond. Jennifer Niederst. O'Reilly & Associates, Inc. • 2001. $34.95. Written for beginners who have no previous knowledge of how Web design works.

Marketer's Guide to E-Commerce: Everything You Need to Know to Successfully Sell, Promote, and Market Your Business, Product, or Service Online. Arthur Bell and Vincent Leger. McGraw-Hill. • 2001. $39.95. Covers website marketing strategies, including guidelines and examples. (NTC Business Books Series).

Sales and Use Taxation of E-Commerce: State Tax Administrators' Current Thinking, with CCH Commentary. CCH, Inc. • 2000. $129.00. Provides advice and information on the impact of state sales taxes on e-commerce activity.

Start Right in E-Business: A Step-by-Step Guide to Successful E-Business Implementation. Bennet P. Lientz and Kathryn P. Rea. Elsevier. • 2000. $47.95. (E-Business Solutions Series).

Web Style Guide: Basic Design Principles for Creating Web Sites. Patrick J. Lynch and Sarah Horton.

Yale University Press. • 2002. $35.00. Second edition. Covers design of content, interface, page layout, graphics, and multimedia aspects.

INTERNET DATABASES

Business 2.0 Web Guide to the Best Business Links. Business 2.0 Media Inc. Phone: (415)293-4800 E-mail: support@business2.com • URL: http://www.business2.com/webguide • Web site presents an extensive, searchable directory of links to "the best, most informative, and authoritative web pages." Twenty main categories cover business, finance, career, company information, people, and technology topics, with thousands of subtopics, all linking to Web sites recommended by experienced business researchers. Fees: Free.

Ebusiness Forum: Global Business Intelligence for the Digital Age. Economist Intelligence Unit (EIU), Economist Group. Phone: 800-938-4685 or (212)554-0600 Fax: (212)586-0248 E-mail: newyork@eiu.com • URL: http://www.ebusinessforum.com • Web site provides information relating to multinational business, with an emphasis on activities in specific countries. Includes rankings of countries for "e-business readiness," additional data on the political, economic, and business environment in 180 nations ("Doing Business in.."), and "Today's News Analysis." Fees: Free, but registration is required for access to all content. Daily updates.

Factiva. Dow Jones Reuters Business Interactive, LLC. Phone: 800-369-7466 or (609)452-1511 Fax: (609)520-5770 E-mail: solutions@factiva.com • URL: http://www.factiva.com • Fee-based Web site provides "global news and business information through Web sites and content integration solutions." Includes Dow Jones and Reuters newswires, The Wall Street Journal, and more than 7,000 other sources of current news, historical articles, market research reports, and investment analysis. Content includes 96 major U. S. newspapers, 900 non-English sources, trade publications, media transcripts, country profiles, news photos, etc.

InfoTech Trends. Data Analysis Group. Phone: (925)462-1202 Fax: (925)462-1225 E-mail: support@infotechtrends.com • URL: http://www.infotechtrends.com • Web site provides both free and fee-based market research data on the information technology industry, including computers, peripherals, telecommunications, the Internet, software, CD-ROM/DVD, e-commerce, and workstations. Fees: Free for current (most recent year) data; more extensive information has various fee structures. Formerly *Computer Industry Forecasts.*

Nexis.com. Lexis-Nexis Group. Phone: 800-227-4908 or (937)865-6800 Fax: (937)865-6909 E-mail: webmaster@prod.lexis-nexis.com • URL: http://www.nexis.com • Fee-based Web site offers searching of about 2.8 billion documents in some 30,000 news, business, and legal information sources. Features include a subject directory covering 1,200 topics in 34 categories and a Company Dossier containing information on more than 500,000 public and private companies. Boolean searching is offered.

PERIODICALS AND NEWSLETTERS

E-Commerce Law and Strategy. American Lawyer Media, Inc. • Monthly. $245.00 per year. Newsletter. Covers electronic commerce contracts, licensing, copyright, fraud, taxation, etc. (A Law Journal Newsletter, formerly published by Leader Publications).

E-Commerce Law Report: Buying and Selling on the Internet. Glasser Legalworks. • Monthly. $300.00 per year. Newsletter. Provides coverage of the legal and regulatory aspects of doing business online.

E-Commerce Tax Alert. CCH Inc. • Description: Print and online newsletter covering e-commerce taxation issues, including compliance and sourcing, e-cash implications, the Internet tax debate, and other topics.

E-Retailing World. VNU Business Media. • Bimonthly. Controlled circulation. Covers various kinds of online retailing, including store-based, catalog-based, pure play, and "click-and-mortar." Includes both technology and management issues.

EC.COM Magazine: The Magazine for Electronic Commerce Management. Electronic Commerce Media, Inc. • Monthly. $48.00 per year. Covers both technical and business issues relating to e-commerce. information.

Electronic Banking Law and Commerce Report. Glasser Legalworks. • 10 times a year. $300.00 per year. Newsletter. Provides coverage of the legal aspects of online banking services, bank cards, and "smart phones.".

Electronic Commerce World. Thomson Media. • Monthly. $45.00 per year. Provides practical information on the application of electronic commerce technology. Also covers such items as taxation of e-business, cash management, copyright, and legal issues.

Electronic Commerce World: Business Solutions Through Technology Integration. EC Media Group. • Monthly. $45.00 per year. Edited for managers and executives of business-to-business Internet commerce firms. Covers the planning, purchasing, and use of e-commerce services or products.

eShopper: Where Style Meets the Net. Element K Journals. • Bimonthly. $9.97 per year. A consumer magazine providing advice and information for "shopping on the Web.".

eWEEK: Building the e-Business Enterprise. Element K Journals. • Weekly. $195.00 per year. Serves as an "information source for companies undertaking e-commerce and Internet-based business initiatives." Formerly *PC Week*.

iMarketing News: The Newspaper of E-Business and Internet Marketing. Courtenay Communications. • Monthly. Controlled circulation.

International Journal of Electronic Commerce. M. E. Sharpe, Inc. • Quarterly. Individuals, $78.00 per year; institutions, $499.00 per year. Inlcudes print and online editions. A scholarly journal published to advance the understanding and practice of electronic commerce.

Internet Retailer: E-Business Strategies. Thomson Financial. • 10 times a year. $98.00 per year. Trade journal on the selling of retail merchandise through the Internet. Provides information on pricing, payment systems, order management, fraud, digital imaging, advertising, Web trends, and other topics.

Journal of Internet Commerce. Haworth Press, Inc. • Quarterly. $285.00 per year to libraries; $48.00 per year to individuals. Presents scholarly articles on marketing and other aspects of electronic commerce.

Journal of Internet Law. Aspen Publishers, Inc. • Monthly. $360.00 per year. Covers such Internet and e-commerce topics as domain name disputes, copyright protection, Uniform Commercial Code issues, international law, privacy regulation, electronic records, digital signatures, liability, and security.

Journal of Website Promotion: Innovations in Internet Business Research, Theory, and Practice. Haworth Press, Inc. • Semiannual. $250.00 per year to libraries; $45.00 per year to individuals. Presents a scholarly view of such items as spam, banner ads, pop-ups, click rates, and the use of search engines for advertising.

KM World: Creating and Managing the Knowledge-Based Enterprise (Knowledge Management). Asset Media. • 10 times a year. Free to qualified personnel; others, $63.95 per year. Provides articles on knowledge management, including business intelligence, multimedia content management, document

management, e-business, and intellectual property. Emphasis is on business-to-business information technology. (Knowledge Asset Media is a an affiliate of Information Today, Inc.).

Mobile Business Advisor: Technology Strategies for Business Innovators. Advisor Media, Inc. • Monthly. $39.00 per year. Covers electronic commerce management and technology, including payment technology, Web development, knowledge management, and e-business market research. Formerly *E-Buisness Advisor*.

Online Investor: Personal Investing for the Digital Age. Stock Trends, Inc. • Monthly. $14.95 per year. Provides advice and Web site reviews for online traders.

Smart Business for the New Economy. Element K Journals. • Monthly. $12.00 per year. Provides practical advice for doing business in an economy dominated by technology and electronic commerce.

WebFinance. Thomson Media. • Semimonthly. $995.00 per year. Newsletter (also available online at www.webfinance.net). Covers the Internet-based provision of online financial services by banks, online brokers, mutual funds, and insurance companies. Provides news stories, analysis, and descriptions of useful resources.

STATISTICS SOURCES

DMA State of the Catalog Industry Report. Direct Marketing Association, Inc. • Annual. $495.00. Provides merchandising, operating, and financial statistics on consumer and business-to-business marketing through both print and electronic (interactive) catalogs. (Produced in association with W. A. Dean & Associates.)

DMA Statistical Fact Book. Direct Marketing Association. Library and Resource Center. • Annual. Members, $79.95; non-members, $104.95. Provides data in five sections covering direct response advertising, media, mailing lists, market applications, and "Practical Management Information." Includes material on interactive/online marketing. (Cover title: *Direct Marketing Association's Statistical Fact Book*.).

OECD Information Technology Outlook 2000: ICTs, E-Commerce and the Information Economy. Organization for Economic Cooperation and Development. • 2000. $72.00. Provides data on information and communications technology (ICT) and electronic commerce in 11 OECD nations (includes U. S.). Coverage includes network infrastructure, electronic payment systems, financial transaction technologies, intelligent agents, global navigation systems, and portable flat panel display technologies.

OTHER SOURCES

DMA Direct and Interactive Marketing Buying Practices Study. Direct Marketing Association, Inc. • 2000. $1,295.00. Provides marketing research data relating to consumer purchasing from catalogs. "Incidence and profile of Internet buying" is also included. (Research conducted by Elrick & Lavidge.).

E-Business, Internet, and Online Transactions. Michael L. Taviss and others. Glasser Legalworks. • Looseleaf. $225.00, including CD-ROM version. Periodic Supplementation. Covers the legal aspects of online content, marketing, advertising, domain names, software licensing, and other Internet issues. Includes many sample forms. (Emerging Growth Companies Series).

E-Commerce and Internet Law: Treatise with Forms. Ian C. Ballon. Glasser Legalworks. • Three looseleaf volumes. $595.00. Periodic supplementation. Analyzes Internet legalities, including litigious matters relating to downloading, streaming, music, video, content aggregation, domain names, chatrooms, and search engines. Includes forms, contracts, checklists, sample plead-

ings, and an extensive glossary.

eAdvertising Report. Available from MarketResearch.com. • 2001. $495.00. Market research data published by eMarketer. Covers the growth of the Internet online advertising market. Includes future trends and Internet users' attitudes.

North American Interactive Television Markets. Available from MarketResearch.com. • 1999. $3,450.00. Published by Frost & Sullivan. Contains market research data on growth, end-user trends, and market strategies. Company profiles are included.

ELECTRONIC COMPONENTS

See: ELECTRONICS INDUSTRY; SEMICONDUCTOR INDUSTRY

ELECTRONIC FUNDS TRANSFER POINT-OF-SALE SYSTEMS (EFTPOS)

See: POINT-OF-SALE SYSTEMS (POS)

ELECTRONIC FUNDS TRANSFER SYSTEMS (EFTS)

See also: BANK AUTOMATION; BANKS AND BANKING

DIRECTORIES

Bank Systems and Technology-Directory and Buyer's Guide. CMP Media LLC. • Annual. $25.00. List of more than 1,800 manufacturers, distributors, and other suppliers of equipment and materials to the banking industry.

PERIODICALS AND NEWSLETTERS

Bank Systems and Technology: For Senior-Level Executives in Operations and Technology Management. CMP Media LLC. • 13 times a year. $65.00 per year. Focuses on strategic planning for banking executives. Formerly *Bank Systems and Equipment*.

End Point Express: Exclusive Report for Bank Operations Professionals. United Communications Group. • Biweekly. $247.00 per year. Newsletter. Covers bank payment systems, including checks, electronic funds transfer (EFT), point-of-sale (POS), and automated teller machine (ATM) operations. Formerly *Bank Office Bulletin*.

Item Processing Report. Access Intelligence L.L.C. • Description: Monitors developments in the processing of remittances and checks, including image processing, optical character recognition, check truncation, hardware, and software. **Remarks:** Absorbed The Powell Report, 1992.

U.S. Banker. IMG Media. • Monthly. $79.00 per year. Covers technology innovation for the banking industry, including online banking. Incorporates *Future Banker*.

OTHER SOURCES

The U. S. Market for Plastic Payment Cards. Available from MarketResearch.com. • 1998. $1,375.00. Market research report published by Packaged Facts. Covers credit cards, charge cards, debit cards, and smart cards. Provides profiles of Visa, Mastercard, American Express, Discover, Diners Club, and others.

ELECTRONIC MAIL

See: COMPUTER COMMUNICATIONS

ELECTRONIC MEDIA

See: INTERACTIVE MEDIA; MULTIMEDIA

ELECTRONIC OPTICS

See: OPTOELECTRONICS

ELECTRONIC PUBLISHING

See also: MULTIMEDIA

GENERAL WORKS

Future Libraries: Dreams, Madness, and Reality. Walt Crawford and Michael Gorman. American Library Association. • 1995. $28.00. Discusses the "over-hyped virtual library" and electronic-publishing "fantasies." Presents the argument for the importance of books, physical libraries, and library personnel.

The Impact of Electronic Publishing: The Future for Libraries and Publishers. David J. Brown. Available from Gale Cengage Learning. • 2003. $80.00. Published by K. G. Saur. Explains how libraries and publishers should prepare for a significant expansion in electronic publishing.

Towards Electronic Journals: Realities for Scientists, Librarians, and Publishers. Carol Tenopir and Donald W. King. Special Libraries Association. • 2000. $59.00. Discusses journals in electronic form vs. traditional (paper) scholarly journals, including the impact of subscription prices.

ABSTRACTS AND INDEXES

Computer Literature Index: A Subject/Author Index to Computer and Data Processing Literature. EBSCO Publishing. • Quarterly, with annual cumulation. $245.00 per year. Contains brief abstracts of book and periodical literature covering all phases of computing, including approximately 70 specific application areas.

F & S Index: United States. Gale Cengage Learning. • Monthly. $1,450.00 per year, including quarterly and annual cumulations. Provides annotated citations to marketing, business, financial, and industrial literature. Coverage of U. S. business activity includes trade journals, financial magazines, business newspapers, and special reports.

Internet and Personal Computing Abstracts [print edition]. EBSCO Publishing. • Quarterly. $269.00 per year, including cumulative index. Provides more than 10,000 abstracts annually from both trade and academic publications. Covers computer hardware, software, product reviews, Web topics, e-commerce, networks, corporate news, security, and related topics. Formerly *Microcomputer Abstracts.*

Key Abstracts: Business Automation. Available from INSPEC, Inc. • Monthly. $250.00 per year. Provides international coverage of journal and proceedings literature. Published in England by the Institution of Electrical Engineers (IEE).

ALMANACS AND YEARBOOKS

Communication Technology Update. Elsevier. • 2000. $36.95. 7th edition. A yearly review of developments in electronic media, telecommunications, and the Internet.

CD-ROM DATABASES

Computer Database. Gale Cengage Learning. • Provides one year of full-text on CD-ROM for 150 leading computer-related publications. Also includes 70,000 product specifications and brief profiles of 13,000 computer product vendors and manufacturers.

Hoover's Company Capsules on CD-ROM. Hoover's, Inc. • Quarterly. $399.95 per year (single-user). Provides the CD-ROM version of *Hoover's*

Handbook of American Business, Hoover's Handbook of Emerging Companies, Hoover's Handbook of World Business, Hoover's Guide to Computer Companies, Hoover's Guide to Media Companies, Hoover's Handbook of Private Companies, and various regional guides. Includes more than 11,000 profiles of companies.

DIRECTORIES

Advanced Imaging Buyers Guide: The Most Comprehensive Worldwide Directory of Imaging Product and Equipment Vendors. Cygnus Business Media. • Annual. $19.95. Lists 800 electronic imaging companies and their products.

CD-ROMS in Print. Gale Cengage Learning. • 2003. $185.00. 17th edition. Describes more than 20,000 currrently available reference and multimedia CD-ROM titles and provides contact information for about 4,000 CD-ROM publishing and distribution companies. Includes several indexes.

Data Sources: The Comprehensive Guide to the Data Processing Industry: Hardware, Data Communications Products, Software, Company Profiles. Gale Cengage Learning. • Semiannual. $455.00 per year. Two volumes. Describes hardware and software for all computer operating sysems, including prices and technical details. Lists about 75,000 products from 14,000 suppliers. Industry-specific software applications are described.

The Software Encyclopedia: A Guide for Personal, Professional, and Business Users. Gale. • Annual. $335.00. Two volumes. Volume one lists software programs by title and producer. Volume two provides information on programs according to application and operating system. Includes prices and requirements for hardware and memory.

ENCYCLOPEDIAS AND DICTIONARIES

Acronyms of Computer Science and Communications: A Comprehensive Acronym Dictionary and Illustrated Encyclopedia. Enjob Kajan and Ejub Kajan. Springer Verlag. • 2002. $49.95. Explains more than 4,000 "broadly used" computer, telecommunications, and information technology acronyms. Includes illustrations and Web addresses, where applicable.

Cyberspace Lexicon: An Illustrated Dictionary of Terms from Multimedia to Virtual Reality. Bob Cotton and Richard Oliver. Phaidon Press. • 1994. $29.95. Defines more than 800 terms, with manyillustrations. Includes a bibliography.

Encyclopedia of Information Systems. Hossein Bidgoli, editor. Elsevier. • 2002. $1,200.00. Four volumes. Contains a wide range of articles relating to computers, databases, communication, and information technology. The 200 topics include coverage of hardware, software, artificial intelligence, the Internet, networks, knowledge management, electronic commerce, search engines, and systems design.

Every Manager's Guide to Information Technology: A Glossary of Key Terms and Concepts for Today's Business Leader. Peter G. W. Keen. Harvard Business School Publishing. • 1994. $18.95. Second edition. Provides definitions of terms related to computers, data communications, and information network systems. (Harvard Business Reference Series).

New Hacker's Dictionary. Eric S. Raymond. MIT Press. • 1996. $65.00. Third edition. Includes three classifications of hacker communication: slang, jargon, and "techspeak.".

HANDBOOKS AND MANUALS

Beyond Book Indexing: How to Get Started in Web Indexing, Embedded Indexing, and Other Computer-Based Media. Information Today, Inc. • 1999. $31.25. Published for the American Society of Indexers. Contains 12 chapters written by professional indexers. Part one discusses making an index by

marking items in an electronic document (embedded indexing); part two is on indexing to make Web pages more accessible; part three covers CD-ROM and multimedia indexing; part four provides career and promotional advice for professionals in the field. Includes an index by Janet Perlman and a glossary.

Columbia Guide to Digital Publishing: In Print and On the Web. William E. Kasdorf, editor. Columbia University Press. • 2002. $65.00. Covers the practical production of both written and graphic material in digital format, including archives, new technology, "information architecture," and copyright.

Columbia Guide to Online Style. Janice R. Walker and Todd W. Taylor. Columbia University Press. • 1998. $40.50. Includes rules for bibliographic citation of online sources, formatting guidelines for online documents, and information on the electronic preparation of texts for print publication.

Developing and Managing Electronic Journal Collections: A How-To-Do It Manual forLibrarians. Donnelyn Curtis and others. Neal-Schuman Publishers, Inc. • 2000. $55.00. Covers the acquisition, management, and integration of journals published in electronic form. (How-To-Do-It Manuals Series).

Electronic Media Management. William E. McCavitt and others. Elsevier. • 1999. $59.95. Fourth edition.

Electronic Publishing: Applications and Implications. Myke Gluck and Elisabeth Logan, editors. Information Today, Inc. • 1997. $34.95. Provides information on copyright, preservation, standards, and other issues relating to the substitution of electronic media for paper-based print.

Handbook of Digital Publishing. Michael L. Kleper. Prentice Hall PTR. • 2001. $129.99. Two volumes. Edited for the digital publishing industry. Covers print publishing, electronic documents, and Internet (Web) publishing, including basic desktop procedures. Provides information on typography, design, layout, image creation, and page creation.

Internet Literacy. Fred Hofstetter. McGraw-Hill. • 2002. $38.75. Third edition. Provides practical information on a wide variety of topics relating to Web creation and electronic publishing.

INTERNET DATABASES

InfoTech Trends. Data Analysis Group. Phone: (925)462-1202 Fax: (925)462-1225 E-mail: support@infotechtrends.com • URL: http://www.infotechtrends.com • Web site provides both free and fee-based market research data on the information technology industry, including computers, peripherals, telecommunications, the Internet, software, CD-ROM/DVD, e-commerce, and workstations. Fees: Free for current (most recent year) data; more extensive information has various fee structures. Formerly *Computer Industry Forecasts.*

Wired News. Lycos, Inc. Phone: (415)276-8400 Fax: (415)276-8500 E-mail: newsfeedback@wired.com • URL: http://www.wired.com • Provides summaries and full-text of "Top Stories" relating to the Internet, computers, multimedia, telecommunications, and the electronic information industry in general. These news stories are placed in the broad categories of Politics, Business, Culture, and Technology. Affiliated with *Wired* magazine. Fees: Free.

ONLINE DATABASES

F & S Index. Gale Cengage Learning. • Contains about four million citations to worldwide business, financial, and industrial or consumer product literature appearing from 1972 to date. Weekly updates. Inquire as to online cost and availability.

Internet and Personal Computing Abstracts. Information Today, Inc. • Contains abstracts covering a wide variety of personal and business microcomputer literature appearing in more than

100 journals and popular magazines. Time period is 1981 to date, with monthly updates. Formerly *Microcomputer Index.* Inquire as to online cost and availability.

PROMT: Predicasts Overview of Markets and Technology. Gale Cengage Learning. • Companies, products, applied technologies and markets. U.S. and international literature coverage, 1972 to date. Inquire as to online cost and availability. Provides abstracts from more than 1,600 publications. Weekly updates.

PERIODICALS AND NEWSLETTERS

Advanced Imaging: Solutions for the Electronic Imaging Professional. Cygnus Business Media. • Monthly. $60.00 per year Covers document-based imaging technologies, products, systems, and services. Coverage is also devoted to multimedia and electronic printing and publishing.

Digital Imaging: The Magazine for the Imaging Professional. Cygnus Business Media, Inc. • Bimonthly. $24.95 per year. Edited for business and professional users of electronic publishing products and services. Topics covered include document imaging, CD-ROM publishing, digital video, and multimedia services. Formerly *Micro Publishing News.*

EContent: Digital Content Strategies and Resources. Online, Inc. • Monthly. $110.00 per year. Emphasis is on the business management and financial aspects of the digital content industry. (Formerly published by Online, Inc.).

Educational Marketer: The Educational Publishing Industry's Voice of Authority Since 1968. SIMBA Information. • Three times a month. $599.00 per year. Newsletter. Edited for suppliers of educational materials to schools and colleges at all levels. Covers print and electronic publishing, software, audiovisual items, and multimedia. Includes corporate news and educational statistics.

Electronic Information Report: Empowering Industry Decision Makers Since 1979. SIMBA Information. • 46 times a year. $649.00 per year. Newsletter. Provides business and financial news and trends for online services, electronic publishing, storage media, multimedia, and voice services. Includes information on relevant IPOs (initial public offerings) and mergers. Formerly *Electronic Information Week.*

Electronic Publishing: For the Business Leaders Who Buy Technology. PennWell Corp., Advanced Technology Div. • Monthly. Free to qualified personnel; others, 55.00 per year. Edited for digital publishing professionals. New products are featured.

eMedia: The Digital Studio Magazine. Online, Inc. • Monthly. $98.00 per year. Covers video production equipment, digital video editing, electronic publishing, digital content streaming, encoding, and other topics related to digital content creation and multimedia. (Formerly published by Online, Inc.).

Interactive Content: Consumer Media Strategies Monthly. Jupitermedia. • Monthly. $675.00 per year; with online edition, $775.00 per year. Newsletter. Covers the broad field of providing content (information, news, entertainment) for the Internet/World Wide Web.

The Magazine for Electronic Publishing Professionals. Publish Media. • Monthly. $39.90 per year. Edited for professional publishers, graphic designers, and industry service providers. Covers new products and emerging technologies for the electronic publishing industry.

Syllabus: New Directions in Educational Technology. Syllabus Press. • 10 times a year. $24.00 per year. Covers the use of advanced technology in higher education systems, including video, multimedia, the Internet, distance learning systems, and electronic publishing.

Wired. Wired Ventures Ltd. • Monthly. $10.00 per year. Edited for creators and managers in various areas of electronic information and entertainment, including multimedia, the Internet, and video. Often considered to be the primary publication of the "digital generation.".

Yellow Pages and Directory Report: The Newsletter for the Yellow Page and Directory Publishing Industry. SIMBA Information. • 22 times a year. $689.00 per year. Newsletter. Covers the yellow pages publishing industry, including electronic directory publishing, directory advertising, and special interest directories.

RESEARCH CENTERS AND INSTITUTES

Center for Integrated Manufacturing Studies. Rochester Institute of Technology, 111 Lomb Memorial Dr., Rochester, NY 14623-5608. Phone: (716)475-5101 Fax: (716)475-5250 E-mail: wjasp@rit.edu • URL: http://www.cims.rit.edu • Research areas include electronics, imaging, printing, and publishing.

International Data Corp. (IDC). Five Speen St., Framingham, MA 01701. Phone: (508)872-8200 Fax: (508)935-4015 E-mail: leads@idc.com • URL: http://www.idc.com • Private research firm specializing in market research related to computers, multimedia, and telecommunications.

Media Laboratory. Massachusetts Institute of Technology, 20 Ames St., Room E-15, Cambridge, MA 02139-4307. Phone: (617)253-0300 Fax: (617)258-6264 E-mail: casr@media.mit.edu • URL: http://www.media.mit.edu • Research areas include electronic publishing, spatial imaging, human-machine interface, computer vision, and advanced television.

STATISTICS SOURCES

By the Numbers: Electronic and Online Publishing. Gale Cengage Learning. • 1997-98. $305.00. Four volumes. $85.00 per volume. Covers "high-interest" industries: 1. *By the Numbers: Electronic and Online Publishing*; 2. *By the Numbers: Emerging Industries*; 3. *By the Numbers: Nonprofits*; 4. *By the Numbers: Publishing.* Each volume provides about 600 tabulations of industry data on revenues, market share, employment, trends, financial ratios, profits, salaries, and so forth. Citations to data sources are included. (By the Numbers Series).

OTHER SOURCES

Consumer Online Services Report. JupiterMedia. • Annual. $1,895.00. Market research report. Provides analysis of trends in the online information industry, with projections of growth in future years (five-year forecasts). Contains profiles of electronic media companies.

Creating the Corporate Digital Library. Primary Research Group, Inc. • 2003. $135.00. Provides a survey of the electronic data policies of specific corporate libraries. Covers electronic journals, e-books, user training, alert services, vendor negotiation, web site development, knowledge management, outsourcing, and other topics.

DVD Assessment, No. 3. Julie B. Schwerin and Theodore A. Pine. InfoTech, Inc. • 1998. $1,295.00. Third edition. Provides detailed market research data on Digital Video Discs (also known as Digital Versatile Discs). Includes history of DVD, technical specifications, DVD publishing outlook, "Industry Overview," "Market Context," "Infrastructure Analysis," "Long-Range Forecast to 2005," and emerging technologies.

Optical Publishing Industry Assessment. Julie B. Schwerin and Theodore A. Pine. InfoTech, Inc. • 1997. $1,295.00. Ninth edition. Provides market research data and forecasts to 2005 for DVD-ROM, "Hybrid ROM/Online Media," and other segments of the interactive entertainment, digital information, and consumer electronics industries. Covers both

software (content) and hardware. Includes Video-CD, DVD- Video, CD-Audio, DVD-Audio, DVD-ROM, PC-Desktop, TV Set-Top, CD-R, CD-RW, DVD-R and DVD-RAM.

ELECTRONIC SECURITY SYSTEMS

See also: INDUSTRIAL SECURITY PROGRAMS

DIRECTORIES

National Burglar and Fire Alarm Association Members Services Directory. National Burglar and Fire Alarm Association. • Annual. Membership. Names and addresses of about 4,000 alarm security companies. Formerly *National Burglar and Fire Alarm Association-Directory of Members.*

Security Distributing and Marketing-Security Products and Services Locater. Reed Business Information. • Annual. $50.00. Formerly *SDM: Security Distributing and Marketing-Security Products and Services Directory.*

Security: Product Service Suppliers Guide. Reed Business Information. • Annual. $50.00 Includes computer and information protection products. Formerly *Security World Product Directory.*

HANDBOOKS AND MANUALS

Burglar Alarm Sales and Installation. Entrepreneur Media, Inc. • Looseleaf. $59.50. A practical guide to starting a burglar alarm service. Covers profit potential, start-up costs, market size evaluation, owner's time required, pricing, accounting, advertising, promotion, etc. (Start-Up Business Guide No. E1091.).

Effective Physical Security: Design, Equipment, and Operations. Lawrence J. Fennelly, editor. Elsevier. • 1996. $44.99. Second edition. Contains chapters written by various U. S. security equipment specialists. Covers architectural considerations, locks, safes, alarms, intrusion detection systems, closed circuit television, identification systems, etc.

PERIODICALS AND NEWSLETTERS

CSO: The Resource for Security Executives. CXO Media, Inc. • Monthly. $64.95 per year. Edited for corporate chief security officers (CSOs). Covers a wide variety of business security issues, including computer security, identity theft, spam, physical security, loss prevention, risk management, privacy, and investigations.

9-1-1 Magazine: Public Safety Communications and Response. Official Publications, Inc. • Bimonthly. $29.95 per year. Covers technical information and applications for public safety communications personnel.

Security Distributing and Marketing. Business News Publishing. • 13 times a year. $82.00 per year. Covers applications, merchandising, new technology and management.

Security Management. American Society for Industrial Security. • Monthly. Members, $38.00 per year; non-members, $48.00 per year. Articles cover the protection of corporate assets, including personnel property and information security.

Security Systems Administration. Cygnus Business Media, Inc. • Monthly. $10.00 per year.

Security: The Magazine for Buyers of Security Products, Systems and Service. Business News Publishing Co. • Monthly. $82.90 per year.

TRADE/PROFESSIONAL ASSOCIATIONS

American Society for Industrial Security. 1625 Prince St., Alexandria, VA 22314-2818. Phone: (703)519-6200 Fax: (703)519-6299 E-mail: asis@asisonline • URL: http://www.asisonline.org.

Automatic Fire Alarm Association. PO Box 1569,

Jasper, GA 30143. Phone: (678)454-3473 Fax: (678)454-3474 E-mail: fire-alarm@afaa.org • URL: http://www.afaa.org • Represents automatic fire detection and fire alarm systems industry. Membership is made up of state and regional member associations, manufacturers, installing distributors, authorities having jurisdiction, and end users. Promotes Life Safety in America through involvement in the codes and standards making process and by providing training seminars on a national basis.

Central Station Alarm Association. 440 Maple Ave., Ste. 201, Vienna, VA 22180-4723. Phone: (703)242-4670 Fax: (703)242-4675 E-mail: communications@csaaul.org • URL: http://www.csaaul.org • Individuals, firms, associations, and burglar and fire alarm corporations engaged primarily in the operation of central station burglar and fire alarm businesses. Aims to foster and improve the relationship between sellers, users, bureaus, and other agencies for the advancement of the central station electrical protection services industry.

National Burglar and Fire Alarm Association. 8300 Colesville Rd., Ste. 750, Silver Spring, MD 20910-6225. Phone: (301)585-1855 Fax: (301)585-1866 E-mail: staff@alarm.org • URL: http://www.alarm.org.

ELECTRONICS, AVIATION

See: AVIONICS

ELECTRONICS, CONSUMER

See: CONSUMER ECONOMICS

ELECTRONICS INDUSTRY

See also: AVIONICS; ELECTRICAL ENGINEERING; MEDICAL ELECTRONICS; OPTOELECTRONICS; RADIO EQUIPMENT INDUSTRY; SEMICONDUCTOR INDUSTRY; TELEVISION APPARATUS INDUSTRY

GENERAL WORKS

Basic Electronics. Bernard Grob. McGraw-Hill. • 1997. $46.43. Eight edition.

Electronics Fundamentals: Circuits, Devices, and Applications. Thomas L. Floyd. Prentice Hall PTR. • 2000. $110.00. Fifth edition.

ABSTRACTS AND INDEXES

Applied Science and Technology Index. H. W. Wilson Co. • 11 times a year. Quarterly and annual cumulations. Price varies. Indexes a wide variety of English language technical, industrial, and engineering periodicals.

Electrical and Electronic Abstracts. INSPEC, Inc. • Monthly. $3,605.00 per year, with annual cumulation. *Science Abstracts. Section B.*

Electronics and Communications Abstracts Journal: Comprehensive Coverage of Essential Scientific Literature. CSA. • Monthly. $1,665.00 per year. Includes print and online editions.

Key Abstracts: Computing in Electronics and Power. Available from INSPEC, Inc. • Monthly. $250.00 per year. Provides international coverage of journal and proceedings literature. Published in England by the Institution of Electrical Engineers (IEE).

Key Abstracts: Electronic Circuits. INSPEC, Inc. • Monthly. $250.00 per year. Provides international coverage of journal and proceedings literature. Published in England by the Institution of Electrical Engineers (IEE).

Key Abstracts: Electronic Instrumentation. Avail-

able from INSPEC, Inc. • Monthly. $250.00 per year. Provides international coverage of journal and proceedings literature. Published in England by the Institution of Electrical Engineers (IEE).

NTIS Alerts: Electrotechnology. National Technical Information Service. • Semimonthly. $210.00 per year. Provides descriptions of government-sponsored research reports and software, with ordering information. Covers electronic components, semiconductors, antennas, circuits, optoelectronic devices, and related subjects. Formerly *Abstract Newsletter.*

Solid State and Superconductivity Abstracts. CSA. • Bimonthly. $1,695.00 per year. Includes print and online editions. Formerly *Solid State Abstracts Journal.*

DIRECTORIES

Directory of Computer and Consumer Electronics Retailers. Chain Store Guide. • Annual. $335.00. Online edition. $775.00. Lists 4,500 United States and Canada companies operating almost 59,000 stores with at least $1,000,000 in sales.

ECN's Electronic Industry Telephone Directory. Reed Business Information. • Covers: 30,000 electronics manufacturers, distributors, and representatives. Entries include: Company name, address, phone, fax, and type of establishment.

ENCYCLOPEDIAS AND DICTIONARIES

Dictionary of Electronics. S.W. Amos and Roger Amos. Elsevier. • 1996. $34.95. Third edition.

McGraw-Hill Encyclopedia of Science & Technology. McGraw-Hill. • 2002. $2,495.00. Ninth edition. 20 volumes.

Modern Dictionary of Electronics. Rudolf F. Graf. Elsevier. • 1999. $69.95. Seventh edition.

Wiley Encyclopedia of Electrical and Electronics Engineering. John G. Webster, editor. John Wiley and Sons, Inc. • 1999. $9,630.00. 25 volumes. Includes *Supplement I* and *Supplement II.* Contains about 1,400 articles, each with bibliography. Arrangement is according to 64 categories.

FINANCIAL RATIOS

Almanac of Business and Industrial Financial Ratios. Leo Troy. Aspen Publishers, Inc. • 2003. $125.95. Includes CD-Rom. Contains financial ratios derived from federal tax returns. Ratios for each of about 200 industries are arranged according to company asset size. (Almanac of Business and Industrial Financial Ratios Series).

Annual Statement Studies. The Risk Management Association. • Annual. Median and quartile financial ratios are given for over 400 kinds of manufacturing, wholesale, retail, construction, and consumer finance establishments. Data is sorted by both asset size and sales volume. Includes a clearly written "Definition of Ratios" and an alphabetical industry index.

Annual Statement Studies: Industry Default Probabilities and Cash Flow Measures. The Risk Management Association. • Annual. $145.00. Serves as a companion volume to the original *Annual Statement Studies.* Gives probability of default estimates on a percentage scale for more than 450 industries. Includes changes in position year-by-year for eight financial statement line items and provides percentage measures of cash flow.

HANDBOOKS AND MANUALS

Electronic Instrument Handbook. Clyde F. Coombs. McGraw-Hill. • 2001. $125.00. Fifth edition. (Engineering Handbook Series).

Solid State Electronic Devices. Prentice Hall PTR. • 1999. $107.00. Fifth edition. (Solid State Physical Electronics Series).

INTERNET DATABASES

Manufacturing Profiles. U. S. Bureau of the Census. Phone: (301)763-4636 E-mail: webmaster@census.

gov • URL: http://www.census.gov/prod/www/abs/mfg-prof.html • The Census Bureau makes available free on PDF (Portable Document Format) an annual consolidation of the entire Current Industrial Report series, presenting "all the data compiled." Contains statistics on production, shipments, inventories, consumption, exports, imports, and orders for a wide variety of manufactured products.

ONLINE DATABASES

INSPEC. Institution of Electrical Engineers (IEE). • Provides online citations, with abstracts, to the world literature of electrical engineering, electronics, optoelectronics, telecommunications, industrial controls, instrumentation, computer technology, information technology, and physics. Coverage includes more than 4,000 technical and scientific journals from 1969 to date, with weekly updating. (INSPEC is Information Services in Physics, Electronics, and Computing.) Inquire as to online cost and availability.

Who's Who in Technology [Online]. Gale Cengage Learning. • Provides online biographical profiles of over 25,000 American scientists, engineers, and others in technology-related occupations. Inquire as to online cost and availability.

PERIODICALS AND NEWSLETTERS

Electronic Business: The Management Magazine for the Electronics Industry. Reed Business Information. • Monthly. $100.99 per year. For the non-technical manager and executive in the electronics industry. Offers news, trends, figures and forecasts. Formerly *Electronic Business Today.*

Electronic Design. Penton Media, Inc. • Biweekly. Free to qualified personnel; others, $100.00 per year. Provides technical information for U.S. design engineers and managers.

Electronic News. Reed Business Information. • 51 times a year. $119.00 per year. Serves the electronic OEM industry.

Electronic Products: The Engineer's Magazine of Product Technology. Hearst Business Communications, UTP Div. • Monthly. $65.00 per year.

Mainly Marketing: The Schoonmaker Report to Technical Managements. Warren K. Schoonmaker, editor. Schoonmaker Associates. • Monthly. $200.00 per year. Report to technical managements focusing on methods of marketing high technology.

MEEN Imaging Technology News. Reilly Publishing Co. • Bimonthly. Free to qualified personnel. Provides medical electronics industry news and new product information. Formerly *Medical Electronics and Equipment News.*

RESEARCH CENTERS AND INSTITUTES

Communications and Signal Processing Laboratory. University of Michigan. 4110 EECS Bldg., 1301 Beal Ave., Ann Arbor, MI 48109-2122. Phone: (734)763-0390 Fax: (734)763-8041 E-mail: stark@eecs.umich.edu • URL: http://www.eecs.umich.edu/systems.

Electronics Research Laboratory. University of California at Berkeley. 253 Cory Hall, Berkeley, CA 94720. Phone: (510)642-2301 Fax: (510)643-8426.

Laboratory for Electromagnetic and Electronic Systems. Massachusetts Institute of Technology, 77 Massachusetts Ave., Room 10-172, Cambridge, MA 02139. Phone: (617)253-4631 Fax: (617)258-6774 E-mail: jgk@mit.edu • URL: http://www.power.mit.edu/index • Research areas include heat transfer and cryogenics.

Laboratory of Electronics. Rockefeller University. 1230 York Ave., New York, NY 10021. Phone: (212)327-8613 Fax: (212)327-7613 E-mail: ros@rockvax.rockefeller.edu.

Research Laboratory of Electronics. Massachusetts Institute of Technology. 77 Massachusetts Ave., Bldg. 46, Room 413, Cambridge, MA 02139-4307.

Phone: (617)253-2519 Fax: (617)258-1301 E-mail: jhs@mit.edu • URL: http://www.rleweb.mit.edu.

SRI International. SRI International. 333 Ravenswood Ave., Menlo Park, CA 94025-3493. Phone: (650)859-2000 Fax: (650)859-4111 E-mail: inquiry. line@sri.com • URL: http://www.sri.com • Physical and life sciences, engineering, industrial management, business, social sciences, and public policy. Areas of research include biosciences, economics, energy, engineering systems and development, environment, health, industry consulting, information and communications, public policy, national security, and physical, life, and social sciences.

Telecommunications and Signal Processing Research Center. University of Texas at Austin. 439 Engineering Science Bldg., Austin, TX 78712-1084. Phone: (512)471-3954 Fax: (512)471-1856 E-mail: ejpowers@mail.utexas.edu • URL: http://www.ece. utexas.edu/projects/telecom/.

STATISTICS SOURCES

Annual Survey of Manufactures. Available from U. S. Government Printing Office. • Annual. Prices vary. Issued by the U. S. Census Bureau as an interim update to the *Census of Manufactures.* Includes data on number of manufacturing establishments in various industries, employment, labor costs, value of shipments, capital expenditures, inventories, energy costs, and assets. (See also Census Bureau home page, http://www.census. gov/.).

Communication Equipment, and Other Electronic Systems and Equipment. U. S. Bureau of the Census. • Annual. Provides data on shipments: value, quantity, imports, and exports. (Current Industrial Reports, MA-36P.).

Electromedical Equipment and Irradiation Equipment, Including X-Ray. U. S. Bureau of the Census. • Annual. Contains shipment quantity, value of shipment, export, and import data. (Current Industrial Report No. MA-38R.).

Electronic Market Data Book. Consumer Electronics Association. • Annual. Price on application.

Semiconductors, Printed Circuit Boards, and Other Electronic Components. U. S. Bureau of the Census. • Annual. Provides data on shipments: value, quantity, imports, and exports. (Current Industrial Reports, MA-36Q.).

Standard & Poor's Industry Surveys. Standard & Poor's. • Semiannual. $1,800.00. Two looseleaf volumes. Includes monthly *Supplements.* Provides detailed, individual surveys of 52 major industry groups. Each survey is revised on a semiannual basis. Also includes "Monthly Investment Review" (industry group investment analysis) and monthly "Trends & Projections" (economic analysis).

U. S. Industry and Trade Outlook. Available from National Technical Information Service. • Annual. $69.95. Produced by the International Trade Administration, U. S. Department of Commerce, in a "public-private" partnership with DRI/McGraw-Hill and Standard & Poor's. Provides basic data, outlook for the current year, and "Long-Term Prospects" (five-year projections) for a wide variety of products and services. Includes high technology industries. Formerly *U. S. Industrial Outlook.*

WEFA Industrial Monitor. John Wiley and Sons, Inc. • Annual. $65.00. Prepared by industry analysts at WEFA, an economic forecasting and consulting firm (originally Wharton Econometric Forecasting Associates). Contains discussions of the outlook for major U. S. industries, with many 10-year forecasts (WEFA Web site is http://www.wefa.com).

TRADE/PROFESSIONAL ASSOCIATIONS

AEA - Advancing the Business of Technology. 601 Pennsylvania Ave., North Bldg., Ste. 1600, Washington, DC 20004. Phone: 800-284-4232 or (202)682-9110 Fax: (202)682-9111 E-mail: rhonda_

starr@aeanet.org • URL: http://www.aeanet.org • Formerly American Electronics Association.

ASM International. 9639 Kinsman Rd., Novelty, OH 44073-0002. Phone: 800-336-5152 or (440)338-5151 Fax: (440)338-4634 E-mail: customerservice@asminternational.org • URL: http://asmcommunity.asminternational.org/portal/ site/asm • Metallurgists, materials engineers, executives in materials producing and consuming industries; teachers and students. Disseminates technical information about the manufacture, use, and treatment of engineered materials. Offers in-plant, home study, and intensive courses through Materials +Engineering Institute. Conducts career development program. Established ASM Foundation for +Education and Research.

Electronic Industries Alliance. 2500 Wilson Blvd., Arlington, VA 22201. Phone: (703)907-7500 Fax: (703)907-7501 E-mail: mflanigan@eia.org • URL: http://www.eia.org • Seeks for the competitiveness of the American producer, represents all companies involved in the design and manufacture of electronic components, parts, systems and equipment for communications, industrial, government and consumer uses.

National Electronic Distributors Association. 1111 Alderman Dr., Ste. 400, Alpharetta, GA 30005. Phone: 800-347-NEDA or (678)393-9900 Fax: (678)393-9998 E-mail: admin@nedassoc.org • URL: http://www.nedassoc.org • Represents authorized distributors and manufacturers of electronic components. Conducts research. Compiles statistical reports and surveys.

OTHER SOURCES

Electronic Market Trends. Consumer Electronics Association, CEA Market Research Dept. • Monthly. Free to members; non-members, $150.00 per year.

ELECTRONICS, MEDICAL

See: MEDICAL ELECTRONICS

ELECTROPLATING

See: METAL FINISHING

ELEVATORS

See also: BUILDING INDUSTRY

DIRECTORIES

Source Directory. Elevator World Inc. • Publication includes: Lists of over 700 elevator manufacturers/ suppliers, contractors and consultants; and 130 elevator/escalator trade associations; international coverage. Entries include: For firms--Company name, address, phone, URL, e-mail, fax, names of marketing and engineering contacts, list of products or services, description or history, market area. For consultants--Name, address, phone, area of specialization. For contractors--Name, address, phone, URL, e-mail, name of key personnel, company statement, area of operation. For trade associations--Name, address, phone, URL, e-mail, names of key personnel, responsibilities, statement of purpose (when available).

PERIODICALS AND NEWSLETTERS

Commercial Building: Tranforming Plans into Buildings. Stamats Communications. • Bimonthly. $48.00 per year. Edited for building contractors, engineers, and architects. Includes special features on new products, climate control, plumbing, and vertical transportation.

Elevator World. Elevator World, Inc. • Monthly. $67.00 per year.

TRADE/PROFESSIONAL ASSOCIATIONS

American Society of Mechanical Engineers. Three Park Ave., New York, NY 10016-5990. Phone: 800-

843-2763 or (212)591-7722 Fax: (212)591-7674 E-mail: infocentral@asme.org • URL: http://www. asme.org.

National Association of Elevator Contractors. 1298 Wellbrook Circle, N.E., Suite A, Conyers, GA 30012. Phone: (770)760-9660 Fax: (770)760-9714 E-mail: info@naec.org • URL: http://www.naec. org.

National Elevator Industry, Inc. 1677 County Rte. 64, PO Box 838, Salem, NY 12865-0838. Phone: (518)854-3100 Fax: (518)854-3257 E-mail: info@ neii.org • URL: http://www.neii.org • Serves as a trade association of the building transportation industry. Promotes safe building transportation for new and existing products and technologies, and adoption of the current codes by local government agencies.

EMBASSIES

See: DIPLOMATIC AND CONSULAR SERVICE

EMBEZZLEMENT

See: FRAUD AND EMBEZZLEMENT

EMERGING MARKETS

See: DEVELOPING AREAS

EMIGRATION

See: IMMIGRATION AND EMIGRATION

EMPLOYEE BENEFIT PLANS

See also: FRINGE BENEFITS; PENSIONS; PROFIT SHARING

GENERAL WORKS

Fundamentals of Employee Benefit Programs. Employee Benefit Research Institute. • 1996. $49. 95. Fifth edition. Provides basic explanation of employee benefit programs in both the private and public sectors, including health insurance, pension plans, retirement planning, social security, and long-term care insurance.

ABSTRACTS AND INDEXES

Business Periodicals Index. H. W. Wilson Co. • 11 times a year. Quarterly and annual cumulations. Price varies.

Insurance Periodicals Index. Specials Libraries Association, Insurance and Employees Benefits Div. NILS Publishing Co. • Annual. $250.00. Compiled by the Insurance and Employee Benefits Div., Special Libraries Association. A yearly index of over 15,000 articles from about 35 insurance periodicals. Arrangement is by subject, with an index to authors.

BIBLIOGRAPHIES

Employee Assistance Programs: An Annotated Bibliography. Donna Kemp. Garland Publishing, Inc. • 1989. $15.00. (Public Affairs and Administration Series).

Insurance and Employee Benefits Literature. Special Libraries Association, Insurance and Employee Benefits Div. • Bimonthly. $15.00 per year. Lists a wide variety of literature in all branches of the insurance industry. Includes annotations.

DIRECTORIES

Business Insurance: Employee Benefit Consultants. Crain Communications, Inc. • Annual. $4.00. List of about 130 firms that offer empolyee benefit counseling services.

EBN Benefits Sourcebook. Thomson Media. • Annual. $36.95. Lists vendors of products and services for the employee benefits industry. Includes industry trends and statistics.

Internet Tools of the Profession: A Guide for Information Professionals. Hope N. Tillman, editor. Special Libraries Association. • 1997. $49.00. Second edition. Consists of 14 sections by various authors or compilers. After two introductory articles on searching the Internet, there are 12 annotated lists of useful Web sites, covering the SLA, business and finance, chemistry, education, food and agriculture, information technology, insurance and employee benefits, law, library management, metals and materials, pharmaceuticals, and telecommunications. An index is provided.

ENCYCLOPEDIAS AND DICTIONARIES

Employee Benefit Plans: A Glossary of Terms. Judith A. Sankey, editor. International Foundation of Employee Benefit Plans. • 2000. $34.00. 10th edition. Contains updated and new definitions derived from all aspects of the employee benefits field in the U.S. and Canada.

Glossary of Insurance Policy Terms. Organization for Economic Cooperation and Development. • 1999. $30.00. "The selected topics range from insurance policy regulation/supervision to general trade issues and include technical terms related to issues such as claims, premiums, and provisions." Edited for government, academic, business, and insurance organizations.

HANDBOOKS AND MANUALS

Accountant's Business Manual. American Institute of Certified Public Accountants. • $189.75. Looseleaf. Two volumes. Semiannual updates. Covers a wide variety of topics relating to financial and accounting management, including types of ownership, business planning, financing, cash management, valuation, retirement plans, estate planning, workers' compensation, unemployment insurance, social security, and employee benefits management.

Handbook of Employee Benefits: Design, Funding, and Administration. Jerry S. Rosenbloom, editor. McGraw-Hill. • 2001. $95.00. Fourth edition.

Medicare: Employer Health Plans. Available from Consumer Information Center. • Free. Published by the U. S. Department of Health and Human Services. Explains the special rules that apply to Medicare beneficiaries who have employer group health plan coverage. (Publication No. 520-Y.).

Money Manager's Compliance Guide. Thompson Publishing Group, Inc. • $649.00 per year. Two looseleaf volumes. Monthly updates and newletters. Edited for investment advisers and investment companies to help them be in compliance with governmental regulations, including SEC rules, restrictions based on the Employee Retirement Income Security Act (ERISA), and regulations issued by the Commodity Futures Trading Commission (CFTC).

U. S. Master Employee Benefits Guide. CCH, Inc. • $56.95. Seventh edition. Explains federal tax and labor laws relating to health care benefits, disability benefits, workers' compensation, employee assistance plans, etc.

ONLINE DATABASES

Accounting and Tax Database. PROQUEST. • Provides indexing and abstracting of the literature of accounting, taxation, and financial management, 1971 to date. Updating is weekly. Especially covers accounting, auditing, banking, bankruptcy, employee compensation and benefits, cash management, financial planning, and credit. Inquire as to online cost and availability.

Employee Benefits Infosource. International Founda-

tion of Employee Benefit Plans. • Provides citations and abstracts to the literature of employee benefits, 1986 to present. Monthly updates. Inquire as to on-line cost and availability.

Labordoc. International Labour Organization. • Indexing of labor literature and the publications of the International Labour Organization, 1965 to present. Monthly updates. Inquire as to online cost and availability.

PAIS International. Public Affairs Information Service, Inc. • Corresponds to the former printed publications, *PAIS Bulletin* (1976-90) and *PAIS Foreign Language Index* (1972-90), and to the current *PAIS International in Print* (1991 to date). Covers economic, political, and sociological material appearing in periodicals, books, government documents, and other publications. Updating is monthly. Inquire as to online cost and availability.

Wilson Business Abstracts Online. H. W. Wilson Co. • Indexes and abstracts 600 major business periodicals, plus the *Wall Street Journal* and the business section of the *New York Times*. Indexing is from 1982, abstracting from 1990, with the two newspapers included from 1993. Updated weekly. Inquire as to online cost and availability. (*Business Periodicals Index* without abstracts is also available online.).

PERIODICALS AND NEWSLETTERS

Benefits News Analysis. Benefits News Analysis, Inc. • Bimonthly. $89.00. Analysis of corporate employee benefit practices. Includes review of benefit program changes at a number of large corporations.

Business Insurance: News Magazine for Corporate Risk, Employee Benefit and Financial Executives. Crain Communications, Inc. • Weekly. $95.00 per year. Covers a wide variety of business insurance topics, including risk management, employee benefits, workers compensation, marine insurance, and casualty insurance.

Compensation and Benefits Update. RIA. • Monthly. $149.00 per year. Provides information on the latest ideas and developments in the field of employee benefits. In-depth exploration of popular benefits programs. Formerly *Benefits and Compensation Update.*

Contingencies: The Magazine of the Actuarial Profession. American Academy of Actuaries. • Bimonthly. $30.00 per year. Provides non-technical articles on the actuarial aspects of insurance, employee benefits, and pensions.

Employee Benefit News: The News Magazine for Employee Benefit Management. Thomson Media. • Monthly. $94.00 per year. Edited for human relations directors and other managers of employee benefits.

Employee Benefit Plan Review. Charles D. Spencer and Associates, Inc. • Monthly. $302.00 per year. Provides a review of recent events affecting the administration of employee benefit programs.

Employee Benefits Digest. International Foundation of Employee Benefit Plans. • Description: Covers the field of employee benefits. Recurring features include notices of publications and educational opportunities, news and announcements for members, and a review of current literature.

Employee Benefits Journal. International Foundation of Employee Benefit Plans. • Quarterly. $80.00 per year. Selected articles on timely and important benefit subjects.

Human Resource Executive. LRP Publications. • 16 times a year. $89.95 per year. Edited for directors of corporate human resource departments. Special issues emphasize training, benefits, retirement planning, recruitment, outplacement, workers' compensation, legal pitfalls, and oes emphasize training, benefits, retirement planning, recruitment,

outplacement, workers' compensation, legal pitfalls, and other personnel topics.

IOMA's Report on Defined Contribution Plan Investing. Institute of Management and Administration, Inc. • Semimonthly. $1,189.90 per year. Newsletter. Edited for 401(k) and other defined contribution retirement plan managers, sponsors, and service providers. Reports on such items as investment manager performance, guaranteed investment contract (GIC) yields, and asset allocation trends.

Jounal of Finacial Services Professionals. Society of Financial Services Professional. • Bimonthly. $95.00 per year. Provides information on life insurance and financial planning, including estate planning, retirement, tax planning, trusts, business insurance, long-term care insurance, disability insurance, and employee benefits. Formerly (American Society of CLU and Ch F C Journal).

Law Firm Partnership and Benefits Report. American Lawyer Media, Inc. • Monthly. $215.00 per year. Newsletter. Covers personnel issues for law firms, including compensation, partnership agreements, malpractice, employment discrimination, training, health insurance, pension plans, and other matters relating to human resources management. (A Law Journal Newsletter, formerly published by Leader Publications).

Legal-Legislative Reporter News Bulletin. International Foundation of Employee Benefit Plans, Inc. • Monthly. $190.00 per year. Review of legislative developments, court cases, arbitration awards and administrative decisions of importance.

Pension Plan Guide. CCH, Inc. • Weekly. $1,279.00 per year. Newsletter. Formerly *Pension Plan Guide Summary.*

Risk and Insurance. LRP Publications. • 15 times a year. Price on application. Topics include risk management, workers' compensation, reinsurance, employee benefits, and managed care.

The Successful Benefits Communicator. Lawrence Ragan Communications Inc. • Description: Offers ideas, techniques, and tips for those who communicate benefits information.

Workforce: H R Trends and Tools for Business Results. Crain Communications, Inc. • Monthly. $59.00 per year. Edited for human resources managers. Covers employee benefits, compensation, relocation, recruitment, training, personnel legalities, and related subjects. Supplements include bimonthly "New Product News" and semiannual "Recruitment/Staffing Sourcebook." Formerly *Personnel Journal.*

RESEARCH CENTERS AND INSTITUTES

Employee Benefit Research Institute. Employee Benefit Research Institute. 1100 13 St. NW, Ste. 878, Washington, DC 20005. Phone: (202)659-0670 Fax: (202)775-6312 E-mail: salisbury@ebri.org • URL: http://www.ebri.org • Employee benefits in the public and private sectors, including studies on individual retirement accounts, retirement income, flexible benefits, financing health care for the elderly, health care costs, long-term care, employee benefits and federal tax policy, social security, changing benefits, and government regulation of employee benefit plans.

STATISTICS SOURCES

Benefits and Wages: OECD Indicators. Organization for Economic Cooperation and Development. • Biennial. $19.00. Provides data for 28 countries on unemployment benefits and related welfare benefits. Includes a cross-country comparison of family incomes, in work and out of work. Formerly *Benefit Systems and Work Incentives.*

Benefits Survey. Available from Paul & Co. • Annual. $99.95. Published by the Society for Human Resource Management (http://www.shrm.org).

Provides five-year data, with discussion, for 200 kinds of employee benefits.

Compensation and Working Conditions. Available from U. S. Government Printing Office. • Quarterly. Issued by the Bureau of Labor Statistics, U. S. Department of Labor. Presents wage and benefit changes that result from collective bargaining settlements and unilateral management decisions. Includes statistical summaries and special reports on wage trends. Formerly *Current Wage Developments.*

EBRI's Databook on Employee Benefits: What is the Promise?. Ken McDonnell and others. Employee Benefit Research Institute. • 1997 $99.00. Fourth edition. Contains more than 350 tables and charts presenting data on employee benefits in the U. S., including pensions, health insurance, social security, and medicare. Includes a glossary of employee benefit terms.

Employee Benefits in Medium and Large Private Establishments. Available from U. S. Government Printing Office. • Biennial. Issued by Bureau of Labor Statistics, U. S. Department of Labor. Provides data on benefits provided by companies with 100 or more employees. Covers benefits for both full-time and part-time workers, including health insurance, pensions, a wide variety of paid time-off policies (holidays, vacations, personal leave, maternity leave, etc.), and other fringe benefits.

Employee Benefits in Small Private Establishments. Available from U. S. Government Printing Office. • Biennial. $12.00. Issued by Bureau of Labor Statistics, U. S. Department of Labor. Supplies data on a wide variety of benefits provided by companies with fewer than 100 employees. Includes statistics for both full-time and part-time workers.

Report on the American Workforce. Available from U. S. Government Printing Office. • Annual. Issued by the U. S. Department of Labor (http://www.dol.gov). Appendix contains tabular statistics, including employment, unemployment, price indexes, consumer expenditures, employee benefits (retirement, insurance, vacation, etc.), wages, productivity, hours of work, and occupational injuries. Annual figures are shown for up to 50 years.

Social Security Bulletin. Social Security Administration. Available from U.S. Government Printing Office. • Quarterly. $27.00 per year. Annual statistical supplement.

TRADE/PROFESSIONAL ASSOCIATIONS

American Benefits Council. 1212 New York Ave. NW, Ste. 1250, Washington, DC 20005-3987. Phone: (202)289-6700 Fax: (202)289-4582 E-mail: info@abcstaff.org • URL: http://www.americanbenefitscouncil.org • Serves as national trade association for companies concerned about federal legislation and regulations affecting all aspects of the employee benefits system. Represents the entire spectrum of the private employee benefits community and sponsors or administers retirement and health plans covering more than one hundred million Americans.

American Society of Pension Actuaries. 4245 N. Fairfax Dr., Suite 750, Arlington, VA 22203. Phone: (703)516-9300 Fax: (703)516-9308 E-mail: aspa@aspa.org • URL: http://www.aspa.org • Members are involved in the pension and insurance aspects of employee benefits. Includes an Insurance and Risk Management Committee, and sponsors an annual 401(k) Workshop.

Council on Employee Benefits. 4910 Moorland Ln., Bethesda, MD 20814. Phone: (301)664-5940 Fax: (301)664-5944 E-mail: vschieber@ceb.org • URL: http://www.ceb.org • Formerly Council on Employee Benefits Plans.

Employers Council on Flexible Compensation. 927 15th St., N.W., Suite 1000, Washington, DC 20005. Phone: (202)659-4300 Fax: (202)371-1467 E-mail: info@ecfc.org • URL: http://www.ecfc.org • Promotes flexible or "cafeteria" plans for employee compensation and benefits.

International Foundation of Employee Benefit Plans. 18700 W. Bluemound Rd., Brookfield, WI 53008. Phone: 888-334-3327 or (262)786-6700 or (262)786-6710 Fax: (262)786-8670 E-mail: pr@ifebp.org • URL: http://www.ifebp.org • Formerly National Foundation of Health, Welfare and Pension Plans.

International Society of Certified Employee Beneift Plan Specialists. 18700 W. Bluemound Rd., Brookfield, WI 53008. Phone: (262)786-8771 Fax: (262)786-8650 E-mail: iscebs@iscebs.org • URL: http://www.iscebs.org • Affiliated with International Foundation of Employee Benefit Plans.

National Employee Benefits Institute. 1350 Connecticut Ave. NW, No. 600, Washington, DC 20036. Phone: 888-822-1344 or (202)822-6432 or (202)833-7366 Fax: (202)466-5109 E-mail: memark@federlaw.com • URL: http://www.nebif.org • Fortune 1000 corporations with an interest in employee benefits legislation and regulation. Works to improve government regulation of employee benefits. Supports and introduces what the institute considers realistic legislation. Invites government spokespersons, legislators, and regulators to speak at special meetings. Conducts educational programs.

Profit Sharing/401(K) Education Foundation. 10 S. Riverside Plaza, Chicago, IL 60606-3802. Phone: (312)441-8550 Fax: (312)441-8559 E-mail: psca@psca.org • URL: http://www.psca.org • Affiliated with Profit Sharing/401(k) Council of America. Formerly Profit Sharing Research Foundation.

OTHER SOURCES

Employee Benefit Cases. BNA, Inc. • 50 times a year. $1,269.00 per year. Looseleaf service.

Employee Benefits Law: ERISA and Beyond. American Lawyer Media, Inc. • Looseleaf. $249.00. Two volumes. Updated as needed. Explains the rules and regulations put forth by the Employee Retirement Income Security Act. Three federal agencies are involved: the Internal Revenue Service, the Labor Department, and the Pension Benefit Guaranty Corporation. (Law Journal Press).

Employee Benefits Management. CCH, Inc. • Semimonthly. $839.00 per year. Looseleaf service. Emphasis on pension plans.

Employment Forms and Policies. LexisNexis Matthew Bender. • Looseleaf. $120.00, including CD-ROM. Periodic supplementation available. Contains more than 300 forms, policies, and checklists for use by small or medium-sized businesses. Covers such topics as employee selection, payroll issues, benefits, performance appraisal, dress codes, and employee termination.

Health Care Benefits Law. American Lawyer Media, Inc. • Looseleaf. $169.00. Updated as needed. Covers the legal compliance aspects of employer health care plans. Includes checklists and sample forms. (Law Journal Press).

EMPLOYEE COUNSELING

See: COUNSELING

EMPLOYEE DISCIPLINE

ABSTRACTS AND INDEXES

Business Periodicals Index. H. W. Wilson Co. • 11 times a year. Quarterly and annual cumulations. Price varies.

Personnel Management Abstracts. • Quarterly. $190.00 per year. Includes annual cumulation.

DIRECTORIES

Business Organizations, Agencies, and Publications Directory. Gale Cengage Learning. • 2003. $480.00.

15th edition. Over 40,000 entries describing 39 types of business information sources. Classified by type of organization, publication, or serviceIncludes state, national, and international agencies and organizations. Master index to names and keywords. Also includes e-mail addresses and web site URL's.

HANDBOOKS AND MANUALS

Fair, Square, and Legal: Safe Hiring, Managing, and Firing Practices to Keep You and Your Company Out of Court. Donald Weiss. AMACOM. • 1999. $29.95. Third edition. Covers recruiting, interviewing, sexual discrimination, evaluation of employees, disipline, defamation charges, and wrongful discharge.

The Federal Manager's Handbook: A Guide to Rehabilitating or Removing the Problem Employee. G. Jerry Shaw and William L. Bransford. FPMI Communications, Inc. • 1997. $29.95. Third revised edition.

Investigations in the Workplace. Eugene F. Ferraro. CRC Press. • 2004. $79.95. Written for security professionals, lawyers, and human resource directors. Explains how to properly conduct internal investigations in the private sector and avoid litigation. Such investigations may relate to loss prevention, asset protection, or employee rights issues. (Imprint: Auerbach Publications.).

ONLINE DATABASES

Wilson Business Abstracts Online. H. W. Wilson Co. • Indexes and abstracts 600 major business periodicals, plus the *Wall Street Journal* and the business section of the *New York Times*. Indexing is from 1982, abstracting from 1990, with the two newspapers included from 1993. Updated weekly. Inquire as to online cost and availability. (*Business Periodicals Index* without abstracts is also available online.).

PERIODICALS AND NEWSLETTERS

HR Briefing (Human Resources). Aspen Publishers. • Monthly.. $249.00 per year. Newsletter. Provides HR professionals and other business people with concise, up-to-date information on employment practices and trends, with an emphasis on compliance with federal employment laws.

Labor Relations Bulletin. Aspen Publishers Inc. • Description: Provides information and insight to management and labor officials to help them avoid or resolve conflicts. Recurring features include reports on current developments in labor law and relations, discipline and grievance cases based on actual arbitration, a question and answer column on labor and employment relations, and a column titled Reflections of an Arbitrator, offering the insight and experience of prominent national arbitrators.

OTHER SOURCES

Employment Practice Guide. CCH, Inc. • Weekly. $1,129.00 per year. Four looseleaf volumes.

EMPLOYEE DISMISSAL

See: DISMISSAL OF EMPLOYEES

EMPLOYEE EDUCATION

See: TRAINING OF EMPLOYEES

EMPLOYEE EFFICIENCY

See: TIME AND MOTION STUDY

EMPLOYEE HEALTH PROGRAMS

See: EMPLOYEE WELLNESS PROGRAMS

EMPLOYEE LUNCHROOMS AND CAFETERIAS

See also: RESTAURANTS, LUNCHROOMS, ETC.

GENERAL WORKS
Fundamentals of Professional Food Preparation: A Laboratory Text-Workbook. Donald V. Laconi. John Wiley and Sons, Inc. • 1995. $60.00.

PERIODICALS AND NEWSLETTERS
Chef. Talcott Communications Corp. • Monthly. $24.00 per year. Edited for executive chefs, food and beverage directors, caterers, banquet and club managers, and others responsible for food buying and food service. Special coverage of regional foods is provided.

TRADE/PROFESSIONAL ASSOCIATIONS
Society for Foodservice Management. 304 W Liberty St., Ste. 201, Louisville, KY 40202. Phone: (502)583-3783 Fax: (502)589-3602 E-mail: sfm@ hqtrs.com • URL: http://www.sfm-online.org.

EMPLOYEE MAGAZINES

See: HOUSE ORGANS

EMPLOYEE MANUALS

See: PROCEDURE MANUALS

EMPLOYEE MOTIVATION

See: MOTIVATION (PSYCHOLOGY)

EMPLOYEE PAMPHLETS

See: PAMPHLETS

EMPLOYEE PARTICIPATION

See: PARTICIPATIVE MANAGEMENT

EMPLOYEE RATING

See: RATING OF EMPLOYEES

EMPLOYEE RELOCATION

See: RELOCATION OF EMPLOYEES

EMPLOYEE REPRESENTATION IN MANAGEMENT

GENERAL WORKS
Employee Representation: Alternatives and Future Directions. Bruce E. Kaufman and Morris Kleiner, editors. Industrial Realtions Research Association. • 1993. $35.00. (Industrial Relations Research Association Series).

DIRECTORIES
Employee Involvement Association--Membership Directory. Employee Involvement Association. • Covers: About 400 companies, associations, and federal, state, county, and municipal government agencies operating or contemplating employee suggestion systems or employee involvement programs. Entries include: Company, association, or agency name; address; employee involvement administrator.

ONLINE DATABASES
Labordoc. International Labour Organization. • Indexing of labor literature and the publications of the International Labour Organization, 1965 to present. Monthly updates. Inquire as to online cost and availability.

Management Contents. Gale Cengage Learning. • Covers a wide range of management, financial, marketing, personnel, and administrative topics. About 150 leading business journals are indexed and abstracted from 1974 to date, with monthly updating. Inquire as to online cost and availability.

PERIODICALS AND NEWSLETTERS
New Horizons. Horticultural Research Institute. • Description: Explores research of the science and art of nursery, retail garden center, and landscape plant production, marketing, and care.

STATISTICS SOURCES
Employee Involvement Association Statistical Report. Employee Involvement Association. • Annual. 150.00.

TRADE/PROFESSIONAL ASSOCIATIONS
Employee Involvement Association. PO Box 2307, Dayton, OH 45401-2307. Phone: (937)586-3724 Fax: (937)586-3699 E-mail: eia@meinet.com • URL: http://www.eianet.org • Represents finance, commerce, industry, and government professionals. Dedicated to the worth, contributions, and benefits of employee suggestion systems and other employee involvement processes. Supports communication between employees and employer for the purpose of exchanging ideas.

EMPLOYEE SELECTION

See: RECRUITMENT OF PERSONNEL

EMPLOYEE STOCK OWNERSHIP PLANS

ABSTRACTS AND INDEXES
Business Periodicals Index. H. W. Wilson Co. • 11 times a year. Quarterly and annual cumulations. Price varies.

DIRECTORIES
Business Organizations, Agencies, and Publications Directory. Gale Cengage Learning. • 2003. $480.00. 15th edition. Over 40,000 entries describing 39 types of business information sources. Classified by type of organization, publication, or serviceIncludes state, national, and international agencies and organizations. Master index to names and keywords. Also includes e-mail addresses and web site URL's.

HANDBOOKS AND MANUALS
The 401(k) Plan Handbook. Julie Jason. Prentice Hall PTR. • 1997. $79.95. Provides technical, legal, administrative, and investment details of 401(k) retirement plans.

U. S. Master Pension Guide. CCH, Inc. • Annual. $56.95. Explains IRS rules and regulations applying to 401(k) plans, 403(k) plans, ESOPs (employee stock ownership plans), IRAs, SEPs (simplified employee pension plans), Keogh plans, and non-qualified plans.

ONLINE DATABASES
Wilson Business Abstracts Online. H. W. Wilson Co. • Indexes and abstracts 600 major business periodicals, plus the *Wall Street Journal* and the business section of the *New York Times.* Indexing is from 1982, abstracting from 1990, with the two newspapers included from 1993. Updated weekly.

Inquire as to online cost and availability. (*Business Periodicals Index* without abstracts is also available online.).

PERIODICALS AND NEWSLETTERS
Employee Ownership Report. National Center for Employee Ownership. • Description: Provides information and news regarding employee ownership, employee stock ownership plans, participation, and communication.

ESOP Report (Employee Stock Ownership Plan). ESOP Association. • Monthly. Membership. Newsletter.

Journal of Compensation and Benefits. West Group. • Bimonthly. $335.00 per year. Working advisor for benefits administrators, company specialists and consultants.

TRADE/PROFESSIONAL ASSOCIATIONS
ESOP Association. 1726 M St. NW, Ste. 501, Washington, DC 20036. Phone: (866)366-3832 or (202)293-2971 Fax: (202)293-7568 E-mail: esop@ esopassociation.org • URL: http://www. esopassociation.org • Companies with employee stock ownership plans; associate members are lawyers, accountants, appraisers, actuaries, brokers, management and benefit consultants, and bankers specializing in working with ESOP. Acts as national information clearinghouse for the press and public interested in the concept of employee ownership; provides forum for the exchange of ideas, experience, and advice among members; lobbies for favorable legislation and regulation on national and state levels; produces and distributes communications material to educate employees on stock ownership. Holds seminars and roundtables. Compiles statistics; maintains speakers' bureau.

National Center for Employee Ownership. 1736 Franklin St., 8th Fl., Oakland, CA 94612. Phone: (510)208-1300 Fax: (510)272-9510 E-mail: nceo@ nceo.org • URL: http://www.nceo.org • Association promotes an increased awareness and understanding of employee ownership of companies.

OTHER SOURCES
Executive Compensation for Emerging Companies. Daniel Niehans and Shawn E. Lampron. Glasser Legalworks. • Looseleaf. $225.00, including CD-ROM version. Periodic Supplementation. Covers various aspects of executive compensation, with emphasis on stock option plans and stock ownership. Includes many annotated legal forms. (Emerging Growth Companies Series.).

Executive Stock Options and Stock Appreciation Rights. American Lawyer Media, Inc. • Looseleaf. $189.00. Updated as needed. Coverage includes non-qualified stock options and incentive stock options. Contains sample forms and documents. (Law Journal Press).

EMPLOYEE SUGGESTIONS

See: SUGGESTION SYSTEMS

EMPLOYEE THEFT

See: CRIME AND CRIMINALS; FRAUD AND EMBEZZLEMENT

EMPLOYEE TRAINING

See: TRAINING OF EMPLOYEES

EMPLOYEE TURNOVER

See: LABOR TURNOVER

For publishers addresses, refer to SOURCES CITED section at the back of the book.

EMPLOYEE WELLNESS PROGRAMS

See also: HEALTH CARE INDUSTRY

GENERAL WORKS

Principles of Health and Hygiene in the Workplace. Timothy J. Key and Michael A. Mueller. Lewis Publishers. • Date not set. $69.95.

Work and Health: Strategies for Maintaining a Vital Workforce. Aspen Publishers, Inc. • 1989. $79.00.

ABSTRACTS AND INDEXES

Excerpta Medica: Occupational Health and Industrial Medicine. Elsevier. • Monthly. Institutions, $2,375.00 per year. Section 35 of *Excerpta Medica.*

Safety and Health at Work. International Labour Office. • Bimonthly. $240.00 per year. Formerly *Occupational Safety and Health Abstracts.*

DIRECTORIES

Fitness Management Products and Services Source Guide. Leisure Publications. • Annual. $24.00. A directory of more than 1,250 fitness equipment manufacturers and suppliers of services. Includes a glossary of terms related to the fitness industry and employee wellness programs.

ENCYCLOPEDIAS AND DICTIONARIES

Encyclopedia of Occupational Health and Safety. International Labour Organization. • 1998. $990.00. Fourth edition. Four volumes. Includes CD-ROM. Covers safety engineering, industrial medicine, ergonomics, hygiene, epidemiology, toxicology, industrial psychology, and related topics. Includes material related to specific chemical, textile, transport, construction, manufacturing, and other industries. Indexed by subject, chemical name, and author, with a "Directory of Experts.".

HANDBOOKS AND MANUALS

How to Cut Your Company's Health Care Costs. George Halvorson. Prentice Hall PTR. • 1987. $27.50.

Stress and Well-Being at Work: Assessments and Interventions for Occupational Mental Health. James C. Quick and others, editors. American Psychological Association. • 1992. $19.95.

PERIODICALS AND NEWSLETTERS

Fitness Management. Leisure Publications, Inc. • Monthly. $24.00 per year. Published for owners and managers of physical fitness centers, both commercial and corporate.

Job Safety and Health Quarterly. Available from U. S. Government Printing Office. • Quarterly. $17.00 per year. Issued by the Occupational Safety and Health Administration (OSHA), U. S. Department of Labor. Contains articles on employee safety and health, with information on current OSHA activities.

RESEARCH CENTERS AND INSTITUTES

Center for Health Promotion and Prevention Research. University of Texas, Houston Health Science Center, School of Public Health, 7000 Fanin St., 25th Fl., Houston, TX 77030. Phone: (713)500-9609 Fax: (713)500-9602 E-mail: chppr@sph.uth.tmc.edu • URL: http://www.sph.uth.tmc.edu/chppr • Fields of study include worksite health promotion. Formerly Center for Health Promotion Research and Development.

Health Policy Institute. University of Texas-Houston Health Science Center, 1200 Herman Pressler Dr., Suite 301, Houston, TX 77030. Phone: (713)500-9485 Fax: (713)500-9493.

National Wellness Institute. College Court, Stevens Point, WI 54481. Phone: 800-243-8694 or (715)342-2969 Fax: (715)342-2979 E-mail: nwi@ nationalwellness.org • URL: http://www. nationalwellness.org.

TRADE/PROFESSIONAL ASSOCIATIONS

Wellness Center. 2315 Stockton Blvd., 2315 Stockton Blvd., Sacramento, CA 95817. Phone: (916)734-9797 Fax: (916)734-2011 E-mail: mprager@forengineers.org • URL: http://www. wellness.ucdavis.edu • Individuals concerned with wellness and preventive health care; firms, institutions, and organizations with wellness centers or employee assistance programs. Educates health practitioners and the public on methods of developing healthier lifestyles through the prevention and treatment of degenerative diseases and other health disorders. Provides professional training workshops in wellness counseling, an approach that integrates many scientific and medical disciplines, to assist members with problems related to weight control, stress, alcoholism, personal relationships, drug addiction, and other physical, mental, or social problems. Conducts individual and group counseling sessions and support groups. Provides speakers on topics such as wellness, lifestyle changes, longevity, diseases and alternative therapies. **Convention/Meeting:** none.

EMPLOYEES, TEMPORARY

See: TEMPORARY EMPLOYEES

EMPLOYMENT

See also: JOB HUNTING; LABOR SUPPLY; OCCUPATIONS; UNEMPLOYMENT

GENERAL WORKS

Global Employment Trends. Claire Harasty and Dorothea Schmidt. International Labour Organization. • 2003. $22.95. Provides an analysis of "current labour market trends around the world." Emphasis is on how the "global economic downturn" has affected various regions and economic groups.

ABSTRACTS AND INDEXES

Human Resources Abstracts: An International Information Service. Sage Publications, Inc. • Quarterly. Institutions, $968.00 per year; includes print and online editions.

ALMANACS AND YEARBOOKS

OECD Employment Outlook. OECD Publications and Information Center. • 2000. $48.00. Outlines the employment prospects for the coming year in OECD countries. Also discusses labor force growth, job creation, labor standards, and collective bargaining.

World Labour Report. International Labour Office. • Irregular. Price varies. Volume eight. International coverage. Reviews significant recent events and labor policy developments in the following areas: employment, human rights, labor relations, and working conditions.

CD-ROM DATABASES

OECD Statistical Compendium. Organization for Economic Cooperation and Development. • Semiannual. $1,905.00 per year for 1 to 10 users. CD-ROM contains more than 730,000 monthly, quarterly, and annual time series for OECD countries, 1960 to date. Includes fully searchable data on agriculture, food, economic indicators, national accounts, employment, energy, finance, industry, technology, and foreign trade. Results can be displayed in various forms.

Sourcebooks America CD-ROM. CACI Marketing Systems. • Annual. $1,250.00. Provides the CD-ROM version of *The Sourcebook of ZIP Code Demographics: Census Edition* and *The Sourcebook of County Demographics: Census Edition.*

WILSONDISC: Wilson Business Abstracts. H. W. Wilson Co. • Monthly. Includes unlimited online access to *Wilson Business Abstracts* through WILSONLINE. Provides CD-ROM "cover-to-cover" abstracting and indexing of over 600 prominent business periodicals. Indexing is from 1982, abstracting from 1990. (*Business Periodicals Index* without abstracts is available on CD-ROM at $1,495 per year.).

DIRECTORIES

Directory of Counseling Services. International Association of Counseling Services. • Annual. $50.00. About 200 accredited services in the United States and Canada concerned with psychological, educational, and vocational counseling, including those at colleges and universities and public and private agencies.

NACE Directory: Who's Who in Career Services and HR/Staffing t. National Association of Colleges and Employers. • Annual. Free to members; nonmembers, $47.95. Lists over 2,200 college placement offices and about 2,000 companies interested in recruiting college graduates. Gives names of placement and recruitment personnel. Formerly *CPC National Dierctory.*

National Directory of Personnel Service Firms. National Association of Personnel Services. • Annual. $15.95. Lists over 1,100 member private (for-profit) employment firms. Formerly *ACCESS.*

ENCYCLOPEDIAS AND DICTIONARIES

Work in America: An Encyclopedia of History, Policy, and Society. Carl E. Van Horn and Herbert A. Schaffner. ABC-CLIO, Inc. • 2003. $185.00. Two volumes. Contains 265 A-Z entries covering work in the U. S. from the Industrial Revolution to modern times. Covers labor-related topics in economics, history, law, welfare, employment policy, and other areas.

HANDBOOKS AND MANUALS

Career Guide to Industries. Available from U. S. Government Printing Office. • 2002. $32.00. Issued by the Bureau of Labor Statistics, U. S. Department of Labor (http://www.bls.gov). Presents background career information (text) and statistics for the 40 industries that account for 70 percent of wage and salary jobs in the U. S. Includes nature of the industry, employment data, working conditions, training, earnings, rate of job growth, outlook, and other career factors. (BLS Bulletin 2541.).

Civil Service Handbook: How to Get a Civil Service Job. Peterson's. • 1999. $12.95. 14th edition. (Arco Civil Service Series).

Law of the Workplace: Rights of Employers and Employees. James Hunt and Patricia Strongin. BNA, Inc. • 1994. $45.00. Third edition. Wages, hours, working conditions, benefits, and so forth.

Legal Guide to Independent Contractor Status. Robert W. Wood. Aspen Publishers, Inc. • 2003. Price on application. A guide to the legal and tax-related differences between employers and independent contractors. Includes examples of both "safe" and "troublesome" independent contractor designations. Penalties and fines are discussed.

Occupational Outlook Handbook. Bureau of Labor Statistics, U.S. Department of Labor. Available from U.S. Government Printing Office. • Biennial. $53.00. Issued as one of the Bureau's *Bulletin* series and kept up to date by *Occupational Outlook Quarterly.*

Practical Guide to Tax Issues in Employment. Julia K. Brazelton. CCH, Inc. • 1999. $95.00. Covers income taxation as related to labor law and tax law, including settlements and awards. Written for tax professionals.

Standard Occupational Classification Manual. Available from Bernan Associates. • 2000. $38.00. Replaces the *Dictionary of Occupational Titles.* Produced by the federal Office of Management and

Budget, Executive Office of the President. "Occupations are classified based on the work performed, and on the required skills, education, training, and credentials for each one." Six-digit codes contain elements for 23 Major Groups, 96 Minor Groups, 451 Broad Occupations, and 820 Detailed Occupations. Designed to reflect the occupational structure currently existing in the U. S.

INTERNET DATABASES

Bureau of Economic Analysis (BEA). U. S. Department of Commerce, Bureau of Economic Analysis. Phone: (202)606-9900 Fax: (202)606-5310 E-mail: webmaster@bea.doc.gov • URL: http://www.bea.doc.gov • Web site includes "News Release Information" covering national, regional, and international economic estimates from the BEA. Highlights of releases appear online the same day, complete text and tables appear the next day. "Recent News Releases" section provides titles for past nine months, with links. "BEA Data and Methodology" includes "Frequently Requested NIPA Data" (national income and product accounts, such as gross domestic product and personal income). Other statistics are available. Fees: Free.

Business 2.0 Web Guide to the Best Business Links. Business 2.0 Media Inc. Phone: (415)293-4800 E-mail: support@business2.com • URL: http://www.business2.com/webguide • Web site presents an extensive, searchable directory of links to "the best, most informative, and authoritative web pages." Twenty main categories cover business, finance, career, company information, people, and technology topics, with thousands of subtopics, all linking to Web sites recommended by experienced business researchers. Fees: Free.

Fedstats. Federal Interagency Council on Statistical Policy. Phone: (202)395-7254 • URL: http://www.fedstats.gov • Web site features an efficient search facility for full-text statistics produced by more than 100 federal agencies, including the Census Bureau, the Bureau of Economic Analysis, and the Bureau of Labor Statistics. Boolean searches can be made within one agency or for all agencies combined. Links are offered to international statistical bureaus, including the UN, IMF, OECD, UNESCO, Eurostat, and 20 individual countries. Fees: Free.

FreeLunch.com. Economy.com, Inc. Phone: (610)696-8700 Fax: (610)696-1678 • URL: http://www.freelunch.com • Web site provides free access to more than 1.5 million economic and financial data series, covering industry, demographics, labor markets, prices, retail sales, government spending, trade, interest rates, housing starts, the stock market, and many other topics. Data is available for various time periods in either chart or table form. Searching is offered. Fees: Free, but registration required. Economy.com, Inc. also offers fee-based economic analysis at *The Dismal Scientist* site (http://www.dismal.com).

Summary of Commentary on Current Economic Conditions by Federal Reserve District [the Beige Book]. Board of Governors of the Federal Reserve System. Phone: (202)452-3000 Fax: (202)452-3819 • URL: http://www.federalreserve.gov/fomc/beigebook/2004/ • Free Web site provides current "anecdotal information" eight times a year on economic conditions within each of the 12 Federal Reserve Districts, plus an extensive national *Summary.* Text is based on the opinions of bank officials, business executives, economists, financial market experts, and others. Typically contains views of consumer spending, manufacturing, services, credit, employment, prices, wages, and the economy in general. Usually referred to as the Beige Book.

ONLINE DATABASES

Labordoc. International Labour Organization. • Indexing of labor literature and the publications of the International Labour Organization, 1965 to present. Monthly updates. Inquire as to online cost and availability.

Wilson Business Abstracts Online. H. W. Wilson Co. • Indexes and abstracts 600 major business periodicals, plus the *Wall Street Journal* and the business section of the *New York Times.* Indexing is from 1982, abstracting from 1990, with the two newspapers included from 1993. Updated weekly. Inquire as to online cost and availability. (*Business Periodicals Index* without abstracts is also available online.).

PERIODICALS AND NEWSLETTERS

Employment Law Strategist. Law Journal Newsletter. • Monthly. 279 individuals for print version per year. Covers employment law topics, including immigration laws, repetitive stress claims, workplace violence, liability of actions of intoxicated employees, record keeping, liability for fetal injury, independent contractor, and employee issues. Monthly. 229 individuals electronic edition. Description: Reports on legal strategy and substantive developments in the area of matrimonial law, including such topics as tax considerations, custody, visitation, division of property, and valuation. Recurring features include litigation roundup and a legislative update.

Occupational Outlook Quarterly. U.S. Department of Labor. Available from U.S. Government Printing Office. • Quarterly. $15.00 per year.

People to People. American Public Power Association. • Description: Reports on public sector labor and personnel issues, especially those concerning the electric utility industry. Summarizes case studies in public labor relations.

Recruiting Trends: The Monthly Newsletter for the Recruiting Executive. Kennedy Information, Inc. • Monthly. $179.00 per year.

Regional Economics and Markets: A Quarterly Analysis from the Conference Board. The Conference Board. • Quarterly. Members, $145.00 per year; non-members, $295.00 per year. Summarizes economic trends and prospects for nine geographic regions of the U. S. Provides data on key predictive indexes, including employment, housing permits, retail sales, consumer confidence, and help-wanted advertising. Charts and graphs are included.

Vocational Training News: The Independent Weekly Report on Employment, Training, and Vocational Education. Aspen Publishers, Inc. • Biweekly. $377.00 per year. Newsletter. Emphasis is on federal job training and vocational education programs. Formerly *Manpower and Vocational Education Weekly.*

Working USA: The Journal of Labor and Society. M. E. Sharpe, Inc. • Quarterly. $160.00 per year to institutions; $45.00 to individuals. Provides a wide range of material on employment, labor markets, societal issues, and present-day labor unions.

RESEARCH CENTERS AND INSTITUTES

W. E. Upjohn Institute for Employment Research. 300 S. Westnedge Ave., Kalamazoo, MI 49007-4686. Phone: (616)343-5541 Fax: (616)343-3308 E-mail: eberts@we.upjohninst.org • URL: http://www.upjohninst.org • Research fields include unemployment, unemployment insurance, worker's compensation, labor productivity, profit sharing, the labor market, economic development, earnings, training, and other areas related to employment.

STATISTICS SOURCES

Bulletin of Labour Statistics: Supplementing the Annual Data Presented in the Year Book of Labour Statistics. International Labour Ofice. • Quarterly. $84.00 per year. Includes five *Supplements.* A supplement to *Yearbook of Labour Statistics.* Provides current labor and price index statistics for over 130 countries. Generally includes data for the most recent four years. Text in English, French and Spanish.

Business Statistics of the United States. Linz Audain and Cornelia J. Strawser. Bernan Associates. • Annual. $147.00. Based on *Business Statistics,* formerly issue by the Bureau of Economic Analysis, U. S. Department of Commerce. Provides basic data for a wide variety of U. S. industries, services, and economic indicators. Most statistics are shown annually for 30 years and monthly for the most recent four years.

County and City Data Book 2000: A Statistical Abstract Supplement. Available from U. S. Government Printing Office. • 2002. $68.00. 13th edition. Issued by the U. S. Bureau of the Census (http://www.census.gov). Contains a wide variety of data on 3,141 U.S. counties, 1,078 cities, and 11,097 places of 2,500 or more inhabitants. Includes statistical information on retailing, manufacturing, banking, service industries, income, employment, housing, education, crime, and population. Updated metropolitan areas are included.

County and City Extra: Annual Metro, City and County Data Book. Deirdre A. Gaquin and Mark S. Littman. Bernan Press. • 2001. $120.00. Updates and augments data published irregularly in print form by the U. S. Census Bureau in *County and City Data Book.* Covers "every state, county, metropolitan area, and congressional district in the United States, as well as all U. S. cities with a 1990 population of 25,000 or more." Contains a wide range tic maps.

County and City Extra: Special Decennial Census Edition. Deidre A. Gaquin and Katherine A. DeBrandt, editors. Bernan Press. • 2002. $95.00. Presents conveniently arranged population, housing, and other data from the 2000 census, with many 1980 and 1990 comparisons. Includes maps and tables with rankings of about 20 items for various geographic locations. Complements the annual *County and City Extra.*

County Business Patterns. Available from U. S. Government Printing Office. • Irregular. 52 issues containing annual data for each state, the District of Columbia, and a U. S. Summary. Produced by U.S. Bureau of the Census (http://www.census.gov). Provides local establishment and employment statistics by industry.

Demographics USA: County Edition. Trade Dimensions. • Annual. $435.00. Contains 200 statistical series for each of 3,000 counties. Includes population, household income, employment, retail sales, and consumer expenditures. Also provides Effective Buying Income, Buying Power Index, and data summaries by Metro Market, Media Market, and State. (CD-ROM version is available.).

Demographics USA: ZIP Edition. Trade Dimensions. • Annual. $435.00. Contains 50 statistical series for each of 40,000 ZIP codes. Includes population, household income, employment, retail sales, and consumer expenditures. Also provides Effective Buying Income, Business Characteristics, and data summaries by state, region, and the first three digits of ZIP codes. (CD-ROM version is available.).

Economic Report of the President: Together with the Annual Report of the Council of Economic Advisors. Available from U. S. Government Printing Office. • Annual. $32.00. Includes about 130 pages of "Statistical Tables Relating to Income, Employment, and Production." Tables cover national income, employment, wages, productivity, manufacturing, prices, credit, finance (public and private), corporate profits, and foreign trade.

Employment and Earnings. Available from U. S. Government Printing Office. • Monthly. $50.00 per year, including annual supplement. Produced by the Bureau of Labor Statistics, U. S. Department of Labor. Provides current data on employment, hours, and earnings for the U. S. as a whole, for states, and for more than 200 local areas.

For publishers addresses, refer to SOURCES CITED section at the back of the book.

Employment and Wages: Annual Averages. Available from U. S. Government Printing Office. • Annual. $53.00. Issued by the Bureau of Labor Statistics, U. S. Department of Labor. Presents a wide variety of data arranged by state and industry.

Employment Outlook, 1998-2008: A Summary of BLS Projections. Available from U. S. Government Printing Office. • 2000. $10.00. Issued by the Bureau of Labor Statistics, U. S. Department of Labor (http://www.bls.gov). Provides 1998 employment data and 2008 projections for a wide variety of managerial, professional, technical, marketing, clerical, service, agricultural, and production occupations. Includes factors affecting the employment growth of various industries. (Bureau of Labor Statistics Bulletin 2522.).

Gale Country and World Rankings Reporter. Gale Cengage Learning. • 1997. $160.00. Second edition. Provides about 3,000 statistical ranking tables and charts covering more than 235 nations. Sources include the United Nations and various government publications.

Gale State Rankings Reporter. Gale Cengage Learning. • 1996. $130.00. Second edition Provides 3,000 ranked lists of states under 35 subject headings. Sources are newspapers, periodicals, books, research institute publications, and government publications.

Geographic Profile of Employment and Unemployment. Available from U. S. Government Printing Office. • Annual. $23.00. Issued by Bureau of Labor Statistics, U. S. Department of Labor. Presents detailed, annual average employment, unemployment, and labor force data for regions, states, and metropolitan areas. Characteristics include sex, age, race, Hispanic origin, marital status, occupation, and type of industry.

Geographic Reference Report: Annual Report of Costs, Wages, Salaries, and Human Resource Statistics for the United States and Canada. ERI (Economic Research Institute). • Annual. $389.00. Provides demographic and other data for each of 298 North American metropolian areas, including local salaries, wage differentials, cost-of-living, housing costs, income taxation, employment, unemployment, population, major employers, crime rates, weather, etc.

Job Patterns for Minorities and Women in Private Industry. Available from U. S. Government Printing Office. • Annual. $61.00. Issued by the Equal Employment Opportunity Commission (http://www.eeoc.gov). "Provides statistical information on the composition of the United States workforce in private industry by sex, race, and ethnic category.".

Labour Force Statistics. Organization for Economic Cooperation and Development. Available from OECD Publications and Information Center. • Annual. $98.00. Provides 21 years of data for OECD member countries on population, employment, unemployment, civilian labor force, armed forces, and other labor factors.

Monthly Labor Review. Available from U. S. Government Printing Office. • Monthly. $49.00 per year. Issued by the Bureau of Labor Statistics, U. S. Department of Labor. Contains data on the labor force, wages, work stoppages, price indexes, productivity, economic growth, and occupational injuries and illnesses.

Occupational Projections and Training Data. Available from U. S. Government Printing Office. • Biennial. $21.00. Issued by Bureau of Labor Statistics, U. S. Department of Labor. Contains projections of employment change and job openings over the next 15 years for about 500 specific occupations. Also includes the number of associate, bachelor's, master's, doctoral, and professional degrees awarded in a recent year for about 900 specific fields of study.

OECD in Figures. Organization for Economic Cooperation and Development. • Annual. $13.00. A "pocket data book" providing a summary of key statistics for OECD countries, including economic growth, employment, education, the environment, and transportation.

Quarterly Labour Force Statistics. Organization for Economic Cooperation and Development. Available from OECD Publications and Information Center. • Quarterly. $90.00 per year. Provides current data for OECD member countries on population, employment, unemployment, civilian labor force, armed forces, and other labor factors.

Report on the American Workforce. Available from U. S. Government Printing Office. • Annual. Issued by the U. S. Department of Labor (http://www.dol.gov). Appendix contains tabular statistics, including employment, unemployment, price indexes, consumer expenditures, employee benefits (retirement, insurance, vacation, etc.), wages, productivity, hours of work, and occupational injuries. Annual figures are shown for up to 50 years.

Services: Statistics on Value Added and Employment. Organization for Economic Cooperation and Development. • 2000. $69.00. Provides 10-year data on service industry employment and output (value added) for all OECD countries. Covers such industries as telecommunications, business services, and information technology services.

Social Trends and Indicators USA. Monique D. Magee, editor. Gale Cengage Learning. • 2003. $450.00. Four volumes. Includes data on labor, economics, the health care industry, crime, leisure, population, education, social security, and many other topics. Sources include various government agencies and major publications.

State Profiles: The Population and Economy of Each U. S. State. Courtenay Slater and Others. Bernan Press. • 1999. $89.00. Presents charts, tables, and text in an eight-page profile for each state. Covers population, labor force, income, poverty, employment, wages, industry, trade, housing, education, health, taxes, and government finances. (The Population and Economy of Each United States Series).

Statistical Abstract of the World. Gale Cengage Learning. • 1997. $85.00. Third edition. Provides data on a wide variety of economic, social, and political topics for about 200 countries. Arranged by country.

Statistical Forecasts of the United States. Gale Cengage Learning. • 1995. $115.00. Second edition. Provides both long-term and short-term statistical forecasts relating to basic items in the U. S.: population, employment, labor, crime, education, and health care. Data in the form of charts, graphs, and tables has been taken from a wide variety of government and private sources. Includes a subject index and an "Index of Forecast by Year.".

Statistical Handbook of Working America. Gale Cengage Learning. • 1997. $130.00. Second edition. Provides statistics, rankings, and forecasts relating to a wide variety of careers, occupations, and working conditions.

Statistical Handbook on the American Family. Bruce A. Chadwick and Tim B. Heaton. Greenwood Publishing Group, Inc. • 1998. $69.95. Second edition. Includes data on education, health, politics, employment, expenditures, social characteristics, the elderly, and women in the labor force. Historical statistics on marriage, birth, and divorce are shown from 1900 on. A list of sources and a subject index are provided. (Statistical Handbooks Series).

Structural Statistics for Industry and Services: Core Data. Organization for Economic Cooperation and Development. • Annual. $63.00. Provides annual data for eight years for both industrial and service sectors. Industries include mining, manufacturing,

utilities, and construction. Statistics for OECD countries cover production, value added, investment, employment, wages, hours worked, and number of establishments.

Survey of Current Business. Available from U. S. Government Printing Office. • Monthly. $63.00 per year. Issued by Bureau of Economic Analysis, U. S. Department of Commerce. Presents a wide variety of business and economic data.

Working Americans, 1880-1999, Volume One: The Working Class. Scott Derks, editor. Grey House Publishing. • 2000. $375.00. Provides detailed information on the lifestyles and economic life of working class families in the 12 decades from 1880 to 1999. Includes such items as selected consumer prices, income, family finances, budgets, life at home, jobs, and working conditions. (Universal Reference Publications.).

Working Americans, 1880-1999, Volume Two: The Middle Class. Scott Derks, editor. Grey House Publishing. • 2000. $135.00. Three volumes. Furnishes details of the social and economic lives of middle class Americans during the years 1880 to 1999. Describes such items as selected consumer prices, income, family finances, budgets, life at home, jobs, and working conditions. (Universal Reference Publications.).

World Employment Report. International Labour Organization. • Annual. $34.95. Contains detailed information on the world employment situation and world employment trends.

Yearbook of Labour Statistics. Available from Bernan Associates. • Annual. $168.00. Published by the International Labour Organizaton (http://www.ilo.org). Provides data for more than 180 countries on employment, unemployment, wages, hours of work, cost of labor, strikes, industrial accidents, and consumer prices.

TRADE/PROFESSIONAL ASSOCIATIONS

Association of Master of Business Administration Executives. c/o AMBA Center, 388 E Main St., Ste. A, Branford, CT 06405. Phone: (203)315-5221 Fax: (203)483-6186.

International Association of Personnel in Employment Security. 1801 Louisville Rd., Frankfort, KY 40601. Phone: 888-898-9960 or (502)223-4459 Fax: (502)233-4127 E-mail: iapes@iapes.org • URL: http://www.iapes.org • Formerly International Association of Public Employment Services.

National Association of Personnel Services. 10905 Fort Washington Rd., Ste. 400, Fort Washington, MD 20744. Phone: (301)203-6700 Fax: (301)203-4346 E-mail: conrad.taylor@recrutinglife.com • URL: http://www.napsweb.org • Members are private employment agencies. Formerly National Association of Personnel Consultants.

OTHER SOURCES

Business Immigration Law: Strategies for Employing Foreign Nationals. American Lawyer Media, Inc. • Looseleaf. $169.00. Updated as needed. Provides step-by-step employment procedures relating to the law and regulations of the State Department, the Immigration and Naturalization Service, specific visa programs, and the Labor Department. Includes guidelines and samples of forms. (Law Journal Press).

Employment and Training Reporter. MII Publications, Inc. • Weekly. $897.00 per year. Looseleaf service. Two volumes. Online edition, $747.00 per year.

Employment Discrimination: Law and Litigation. Lexis Law Publishing. • $185.00 per year. Two looseleaf volumes. Periodic supplementation. Covers employment provisions of the Civil Rights Act, the Equal Pay Act, and related topics.

Employment Forms and Policies. LexisNexis Matthew Bender. • Looseleaf. $120.00, including CD-

ROM. Periodic supplementation available. Contains more than 300 forms, policies, and checklists for use by small or medium-sized businesses. Covers such topics as employee selection, payroll issues, benefits, performance appraisal, dress codes, and employee termination.

Employment Litigation Reporter: The National Journal of Record for Termination Lawsuits Alleging Tort and Contract Claims Against Employers. Andrews Publications. • Semimonthly. $825.00 per year. Newsletter. Provides reports on wrongful dismissal lawsuits.

Labor Relations. CCH, Inc. • $2,589.00 per year. Seven looseleaf volumes. Weekly updates. Covers labor relations, wages and hours, state labor laws, and employment practices. Supplement available, *Labor Law Reports.* Summary Newsletter.

EMPLOYMENT AGENCIES AND SERVICES

See also: CIVIL SERVICE; COLLEGE PLACEMENT BUREAUS

DIRECTORIES

Directory of Executive Recruiters. Kennedy Information, Inc. • Annual. $49.95. Contains profiles of more than 5,500 executive search firms in the U. S., Canada, and Mexico.

Directory of Outplacement and Career Management Firms. Kennedy Information, Inc. • Annual. $149.95. Contains profiles of more than 390 firms specialize in helping "downsized" executives find new employment. Formerly *Directory of Outplacement Firms.*

NACE Directory: Who's Who in Career Services and HR/Staffing t. National Association of Colleges and Employers. • Annual. Free to members; nonmembers, $47.95. Lists over 2,200 college placement offices and about 2,000 companies interested in recruiting college graduates. Gives names of placement and recruitment personnel. Formerly *CPC National Dierctory.*

National Directory of Personnel Service Firms. National Association of Personnel Services. • Annual. $15.95. Lists over 1,100 member private (for-profit) employment firms. Formerly *ACCESS.*

HANDBOOKS AND MANUALS

Employment Agency. Entrepreneur Media, Inc. • Looseleaf. $59.50. A practical guide to starting an employment agency. Covers profit potential, start-up costs, market size evaluation, owner's time required, site selection, lease negotiation, pricing, accounting, advertising, promotion, etc. (Start-Up Business Guide No. E1051.).

Executive Recruiting Service. Entrepreneur Media, Inc. • Looseleaf. $59.50. A practical guide to starting an executive recruitment service. Covers profit potential, start-up costs, market size evaluation, owner's time required, pricing, accounting, advertising, promotion, etc. (Start-Up Business Guide No. E1228.).

Recruiter's Research Blue Book: A How-To Guide for Researchers, Consultants, Corporate Recruiters, Small Business Owners, Venture Capitalists, and Line Executives. Andrea A. Jupina. Kennedy Information, Inc. • 2000. $179.00. Second edition. Provides detailed coverage of the role that research plays in executive recruiting. Includes such practical items as "Telephone Interview Guide," "Legal Issues in Executive Search," and "How to Create an Execuive Search Library." Covers both person-to-person research and research using printed and on-line business information sources. Includes an extensive directory of recommended sources. Formerly *Handbook of Executive Search Research.*

Temporary Help Service. Entrepreneur Media, Inc. •

Looseleaf. $59.50. A practical guide to starting an employment agency for temporary workers. Covers profit potential, start-up costs, market size evaluation, owner's time required, site selection, lease negotiation, pricing, accounting, advertising, promotion, etc. (Start-Up Business Guide No. E1189.).

PERIODICALS AND NEWSLETTERS

Journal of Career Planning and Employment: The International Magazine of Placement and Recruitment. National Association of Colleges and Employers. • Quarterly. Free to members; nonmembers, $72.00 per year. Includes *Spotlight* newsletter. Formerly *Journal of College Placement.*

Recruiting Trends: The Monthly Newsletter for the Recruiting Executive. Kennedy Information, Inc. • Monthly. $179.00 per year.

RESEARCH CENTERS AND INSTITUTES

Women Employed Institute. Women Employed Institute. 111 N Wabash, 13th Fl., Chicago, IL 60602. Phone: (312)782-3902 Fax: (312)782-5249 E-mail: info@womenemployed.org • URL: http://www.womenemployed.org • Economic status of working women, working women and the law, sexual harassment in the workplace, equal employment opportunity, women's access to vocational education and job training, comparable worth, working mothers, and career development.

STATISTICS SOURCES

Handbook of U. S. Labor Statistics: Employment, Earnings, Prices, Productivity, and Other Labor Data. Eva E. Jacobs, editor. Bernan Associates. • 1999. $74.00. Based on *Handbook of Labor Statistics,* formerly issued by the Bureau of Labor Statistics, U. S. Department of Labor. Includes the Bureau's projections of employment in the U. S. by industry and occupation. Provides a wide variety of data on the work force, prices, fringe benefits, and consumer expenditures.

Key Indicators of the Labour Market. Available from Routledge. • Biennial. $125.00. Published by the International Labour Office (http://www.ilo.org). Provides data on 20 key indicators in 220 countries. Includes labor force statistics, employment, unemployment, part-time workers, wages, productivity, poverty indicators, and related topics.

TRADE/PROFESSIONAL ASSOCIATIONS

American Staffing Association. 277 S Washington St., Ste. 200, Alexandria, VA 22314-3675. Phone: (703)253-2020 Fax: (703)253-2053 E-mail: asa@americanstaffing.net • URL: http://www.americanstaffing.net • Promotes and represents the staffing industry through legal and legislative advocacy, public relations, education, and the establishment of high standards of ethical conduct.

Association of Career Management Consulting Firms International. 204 E St., NE, Washington, DC 20002. Phone: (202)547-6344 Fax: (202)547-6348 E-mail: aocfi@aocfi.org • URL: http://www.aocfi.org • Firms providing displaced employees who are sponsored by their organization, with counsel and assistance in job searching and the techniques and practices of choosing a career.

Association of Executive Search Consultants. 500 Fifth Ave., Suite 930, New York, NY 10110-0999. Phone: 877-843-2372 or (212)398-9556 Fax: (212)398-9560 E-mail: aesc@aesc.org • URL: http://www.aesc.org.

National Association of Personnel Services. 10905 Fort Washington Rd., Ste. 400, Fort Washington, MD 20744. Phone: (301)203-6700 Fax: (301)203-4346 E-mail: conrad.taylor@recrutinglife.com • URL: http://www.napsweb.org • Members are private employment agencies. Formerly National Association of Personnel Consultants.

Opportunities Industrialization Centers of America.

1415 N Broad St., Philadelphia, PA 19122-3323. Phone: 800-621-4642 or (215)236-4500 Fax: (215)236-7480 E-mail: gsyounger@oicworld.org • URL: http://www.oicafamerica.org • Network of employment and training programs. Serves disadvantaged and unskilled workers.

EMPLOYMENT IN FOREIGN COUNTRIES

DIRECTORIES

American Jobs Abroad. Gale. • Covers: over 800 U.S. corporations and 100 government agencies, associations, and other organizations that employ Americans overseas, generally on an ongoing or long-term basis at wages or salaries comparable to those in the U.S. Entries include: Company or organization name, address; recruiter's name, address, phone, fax, title; name of CEO; products and services; profile, annual sales, number of employees, number of U.S. employees abroad and countries where employed, application information, salaries, job categories, general requirements, length of assignment, language requirement, training, benefits. Paper back edition published by Visible Ink Press, an imprint of Gale Research.

Directory of American Firms Operating in Foreign Countries. Uniworld Business Publications. • Biennial. $355.00. Three volumes. Lists approximately 3,000 American companies with more than 34,500 subsidiaries and affiliates in 190 foreign countries.

ONLINE DATABASES

Labordoc. International Labour Organization. • Indexing of labor literature and the publications of the International Labour Organization, 1965 to present. Monthly updates. Inquire as to online cost and availability.

PERIODICALS AND NEWSLETTERS

International Employment Hotline. Carlyle Corp. • Description: Covers the latest developments in the international job market. Summarizes hiring cycles of major employers. Lists current overseas job openings by job title, description, employer contact, and address. Recurring features include editorials and news of research.

Transitions Abroad: The Guide to Learning, Living, and Working Overseas. Transitions Abroad Publishing, Inc. • Bimonthly. $28.00 per year, including annual directory of information sources. Provides practical information and advice on foreign education and employment. Supplement available *Overseas Travel Planner.*

OTHER SOURCES

Foreign Labor Trends. Available from U. S. Government Printing Office. • Irregular (50 to 60 issues per year, each on an individual country). $95.00 per year. Prepared by various American Embassies. Issued by the Bureau of International Labor Affairs, U. S. Department of Labor. Covers labor developments in important foreign countries, including trends in wages, working conditions, labor supply, employment, and unemployment.

EMPLOYMENT INTERVIEWING

See: INTERVIEWING; JOB HUNTING

EMPLOYMENT MANAGEMENT

See: PERSONNEL MANAGEMENT

EMPLOYMENT OF OLDER WORKERS

See also: EQUAL EMPLOYMENT OPPORTUNITY; RETIREMENT

ALMANACS AND YEARBOOKS

Older Americans Information Directory. Grey House Publshing, Inc. • 2002. $165.00. Fourth edition. Presents articles (text) and sources of information on a wide variety of aging and retirement topics. Includes an index to personal names, organizations, and subjects.

DIRECTORIES

Older Americans Information Directory. Grey House Publishing. • Covers: Information on national and state organizations, government agencies, health, research centers, libraries and information Centers, print and electronic media, disability aids and assistive devices, assisted living centers and independent living facilities, legal resources, continuing education programs, and travel information; for and about older Americans.

ENCYCLOPEDIAS AND DICTIONARIES

Encyclopedia of Aging. David J. Ekerdt, editor. Available from Gale Cengage Learning. • 2002. $450.00. Four volumes. Published by Macmillan Reference USA. Includes articles relating to the financial aspects of aging, such as housing, long-term care insurance, pensions, social security, individual retirement accounts, savings, and retirement planning.

HANDBOOKS AND MANUALS

Employer's Guide to Discrimination Laws. Maureen F. Moore. LexisNexis Matthew Bender. • 2003. $28.00, including CD-ROM. Edited for business owners and managers. Provides a concise guide to federal discrimination laws relating to race, sex, age, disability, pregnancy, religion, and national origin.

ONLINE DATABASES

Labordoc. International Labour Organization. • Indexing of labor literature and the publications of the International Labour Organization, 1965 to present. Monthly updates. Inquire as to online cost and availability.

STATISTICS SOURCES

Income of the Population 55 and Older. Available from U. S. Government Printing Office. • Biennial. $23.00. Issued by the Social Security Administration (http://www.ssa.gov). Covers major sources and amounts of income for the 55 and older population in the U. S., "with special emphasis on some aspects of the income of the population 65 and older.".

Social Security Bulletin. Social Security Administration. Available from U.S. Government Printing Office. • Quarterly. $27.00 per year. Annual statistical supplement.

Statistical Handbook on Aging Americans. Renee Schick. Greenwood Publishing Group, Inc. • 1994. $69.95. Second edition. Provides data on demographics, social characteristics, health, employment, economic conditions, income, pensions, and social security. Includes bibliographic information and a glossary. (Statistical Handbook Series).

Statistical Record of Older Americans. Gale Cengage Learning. • 1996. $130.00. Second edition. Includes income and pension data.

TRADE/PROFESSIONAL ASSOCIATIONS

Gerontological Society of America. 1030 15th St., N.W., Suite 250, Washington, DC 20005-1503. Phone: (202)842-1275 Fax: (202)842-1150 E-mail: cshutz@geron.org • URL: http://www.geron.org.

National Interfaith Coalition on Aging. c/o National Council on the Aging, 300 D St. SW, Ste. 801,

Washington, DC 20024. Phone: 800-424-9046 or (202)479-1200 Fax: (202)479-0735 E-mail: info@ncoa.org • URL: http://www.ncoa.org • Affiliated with National Council on Aging.

EMPLOYMENT OF THE HANDICAPPED

See: HANDICAPPED WORKERS

EMPLOYMENT OF WOMEN

See also: EQUAL EMPLOYMENT OPPORTUNITY; WOMEN ACCOUNTANTS; WOMEN ENGINEERS; WOMEN IN THE WORK FORCE; WOMEN LAWYERS; WOMEN PHYSICIANS

GENERAL WORKS

Advancing Women in Business-The Catalyst Guide: Best Practices from the Corporate Leaders. Catalyst Staff. John Wiley and Sons, Inc. • 1998. $26.00. Explains the human resources practices of corporations providing a favorable climate for the advancement of female employees. (Jossey-Bass Business and Management Series).

Breaking Out of the Pink-Collar Ghetto: Policy Solutions for Non-College Women. Sharon H. Mastracci. M. E. Sharpe, Inc. • 2004. $65.95. Emphasis is on innovative education and training programs for women in low-paying service jobs.

Breaking Through the Glass Ceiling: Women in Management. Linda Wirth. International Labour Organization. • 2001. $16.95. Portrays "national and international efforts to improve equal opportunities amd promote gender equality in management." Includes statistical information and discussion of earnings gaps, recruitment of women, education, training, and career-building strategies for women.

Women and Careers: Issues and Challenges. Carol W. Konek and Sally L. Kitch. Sage Publications, Inc. • 1993. $77.95. Based on a major survey assessing women's experiences in the workplace.

Women Breaking Through: Overcoming the Final 10 Obstacles at Work. Deborah J. Swiss. Peterson's. • 1996. $24.95. Discusses specific strategies for women to use to advance beyond the middle management level. Based on a survey of 300 women "on the leading edge of change.".

Women, Gender, and Work: What is Equality and How Do We Get There?. Martha F. Loutfi, editor. International Labour Organization. • 2001. $26.95. A collection of articles from the *International Labour Review* covering such topics as equal opportunity for women, family concerns, legal issues, the glass ceiling, wage inequality, and sexual harassment in the workplace. Includes statistical data.

ABSTRACTS AND INDEXES

Women Studies Abstracts. Transaction Publishers. • Quarterly. Individuals, $102.00 per year; institutions, $240.00 per year.

BIOGRAPHICAL SOURCES

Who's Who of American Women. Marquis Who's Who. • Biennial. $275.00. Provides over 25,000 biographical profiles of important women, including individuals prominent in business, finance, and industry.

DIRECTORIES

Women's Information Directory. Gale. • Covers: Nearly 10,800 sources of information for and about women in the U.S., including national, state, and local organizations; publishers and booksellers of women's materials; newspapers, magazines, newsletters, other directories, and videos; museums; awards, honors, and prizes; government agencies

and assistance programs; research centers; women's studies programs at colleges and universities; consultants; scholarships and other financial aids; electronic resources; and library collections. Entries include: Organization or publication name, address, phone, name and title of contact, description of services, activities, etc.

HANDBOOKS AND MANUALS

Employer's Guide to Discrimination Laws. Maureen F. Moore. LexisNexis Matthew Bender. • 2003. $28.00, including CD-ROM. Edited for business owners and managers. Provides a concise guide to federal discrimination laws relating to race, sex, age, disability, pregnancy, religion, and national origin.

Women and the Law. Carol H. Lefcourt, editor. West Group. • Annual. $302.00. Looseleaf service. Covers such topics as employment discrimination, pay equity (comparable worth), sexual harassment in the workplace, property rights, and child custody issues.

ONLINE DATABASES

Contemporary Women's Issues. Gale Cengage Learning. • Provides fulltext articles online from 150 periodicals and a wide variety of additional sources relating to economic, legal, social, political, education, health, and other women's issues. Time span is 1992 to date. Weekly updates. Inquire as to online cost and availability. (Also available in a CD-ROM version.).

Labordoc. International Labour Organization. • Indexing of labor literature and the publications of the International Labour Organization, 1965 to present. Monthly updates. Inquire as to online cost and availability.

PERIODICALS AND NEWSLETTERS

AAUW Outlook. American Association of University Women. • Quarterly. Free to members; non-members, $15.00 per year. Formerly *Graduate Woman*.

Business Woman Magazine. National Federation of Business and Professional Women's Clubs, Inc. • Quarterly. $12.00 per year. Focuses on the activities and interests of working women.

The Equal Employer. Y. S. Publications, Inc. • Biweekly. $245.00 per year. Newsletter on fair employment practices.

Family Relations: State Capitals. Wakeman-Walworth, Inc. • 50 times a year. $245.00 per year.; print and online editions, $350.00 per year. Newsletter. Formerly *From the State Capitals: Family Relations*.

Feminist Economics. International Association for Feminist Economics. Taylor and Francis Group. • Three times a year. Individuals, $68.00 per year; institutions, $184.00 per year. Includes articles on issues relating to the employment and economic opportunities of women.

MS. Liberty Media for Women, L.L.C. • Bimonthly. $45.00 per year.

National Now Times. National Organization for Women. • Bimonthly. Free to members; non-members, $35.00 per year.

New Woman. Endeavour House. • Monthly. $57.00 per year.

Perspective. Magna Publications Inc. • Description: Provides administrators with guidelines for keeping their schools out of court. Examines current trends in law related to higher education, as well as past and future legal issues affecting students, faculty, administrators and the public. Recurring features include columns titled Key Case Review, Follow-Up, Resources, Legislative Note, Outside the Courts, Cross-Examination, and Cases Noted.

Women's Studies International Forum: A Multidisciplinary Journal for the Rapid Publication of Research Communications and Review Articles in Women's Studies. Elsevier. • Bimonthly. Individuals, $122.00 per year; institutions $585.00 per year; students, $38.00 per year.

Women's Studies Quarterly: The First U.S. Journal Devoted to Teaching about Women. Feminist Press. • Four times a year. Individuals, $30.00 per year; institutions, $40.00 per year. Provides coverage of issues and events in women's studies and feminist education, including in-depth articles on research about women and current projects to transform traditional curricula. Includes two double thematic issues.

RESEARCH CENTERS AND INSTITUTES

Business and Professional Women's Foundation. 2012 Massachusetts Ave., N.W., Washington, DC 20036. Phone: (202)293-1200 Fax: (202)861-0298 E-mail: jsmith@bpwusa.org • URL: http://www. bpwusa.org.

Women Employed Institute. Women Employed Institute. 111 N Wabash, 13th Fl., Chicago, IL 60602. Phone: (312)782-3902 Fax: (312)782-5249 E-mail: info@womenemployed.org • URL: http:// www.womenemployed.org • Economic status of working women, working women and the law, sexual harassment in the workplace, equal employment opportunity, women's access to vocational education and job training, comparable worth, working mothers, and career development.

STATISTICS SOURCES

Statistical Handbook on Women in America. Cynthia M. Taeuber, editor. Greenwood Publishing Group, Inc. • 1996. $69.95. Second edition. Includes data on demographics, employment, earnings, economic status, educational status, marriage, divorce, household units, health, and other topics. (Statistical Handbook Series).

Statistical Record of Women Worldwide. Gale Cengage Learning. • 1995. $130.00. Second edition. Includes employment data and other economic statistics relating to women in the U. S. and internationally.

United States Equal Employment Opportunity Commission Annual Report: Job Patterns for Minorities and Women in Private Industry. U.S. Equal Employment Opportunity Commission. • Annual.

Women in the World of Work: Statistical Analysis and Projections to the Year 2000. Shirley Nuss and others. International Labour Office. • 1989. $18.00. (Women, Work, and Development Series, No. 18).

TRADE/PROFESSIONAL ASSOCIATIONS

American Association of University Women. 1111 16th St., N.W., Washington, DC 20036. Phone: 800-326-2289 or (202)785-7700 Fax: (202)872-1425 E-mail: info@aauw.org • URL: http://www.aauw. org.

American Business Women's Association. PO Box 8728, PO Box 8728, Kansas City, MO 64114-0728. Phone: 800-228-0007 or (816)361-6621 Fax: (816)361-4991 E-mail: abwa@abwa.org • URL: http://www.abwa.org • Women in business, including women owning or operating their own businesses, women in professions, and women employed in any level of government, education, or retailing, manufacturing, and service companies. Provides opportunities for businesswomen to help themselves and others grow personally and professionally through leadership, education, networking support, and national recognition. Offers leadership training, business skills training and business education; special membership options for retired businesswomen and the Company Connection for business owners, a resume service, credit card and programs, various travel and insurance benefits. Sponsors American Business Women's Day and National Convention and regional conferences held annually.

Business and Professional Women International. PO Box 568, Horsham RH13 9ZP, United Kingdom.

Phone: 44 1403 739343 Fax: 44 1403 734432 E-mail: members@bpw-international.org • URL: http://www.bpw.international.org.

Business and Professional Women USA. 1900 M St., NW, Ste. 310, Washington, DC 20036. Phone: (202)293-1100 Fax: (202)861-0298 E-mail: memberservices@bpwusa.org • URL: http://www. bpwusa.org • Formerly National Federation of Business and Professional Women's Clubs.

Catalyst. 120 Wall St., 5th Fl., New York, NY 10005-3904. Phone: (212)514-7600 Fax: (212)514-8470 E-mail: info@catalyst.org • URL: http://www. catalystwomen.org • Works to advance women in Business and the professions. Serves as a source of information on women in business for past four decades. Helps companies and women maximize their potential. Holds current statistics, print media, and research materials on issues related to women in business.

Coalition of Labor Union Women. 1925 K St. NW, Ste. 402, Washington, DC 20036. Phone: (202)223-8360 Fax: (202)776-0537 E-mail: info@cluw.org • URL: http://www.cluw.org.

Federally Employed Women. 700 N Fairfax St., Ste. 510, Alexandria, VA 22314. Phone: (202)898-0994 Fax: (202)898-0994 E-mail: few@few.org • URL: http://www.few.org • Represents men and women employed by the federal government. Seeks to end sexual discrimination in government service; to increase job opportunities for women in government service and to further the potential of all women in the government; to improve the merit system in government employment; to assist present and potential government employees who are discriminated against because of sex; to work with other organizations and individuals concerned with equal employment opportunity in the government. Provides speakers and sponsors seminars to publicize the Federal Women's Program; furnishes members with information on pending legislation designed to end discrimination against working women; informs and provides members opportunities for training to improve their job potential; issues fact sheets interpreting civil service rules and regulations and other legislative issues; provides annual training conference for over 3,000 women and men.

Federation of Organizations for Professional Women. P.O. Box 6234, Falls Church, VA 22040. Phone: (202)328-1415 Fax: (703)532-7295 E-mail: fop@hers.com • URL: http://www.fopw.org • Women's groups concerned with economic, educational and professional equality for women.

International Association for Feminist Economics. c/o Barbara Krohn, 100D Roberts Hall, Bucknell University, Lewisburg, PA 17837. Phone: (570)577-3637 Fax: (570)577-3451 E-mail: iaffe@bucknell. edu • URL: http://www.iaffe.org • Members are economists having a feminist viewpoint. Promotes greater economic opportunities for women.

National Association for Female Executives. P.O. Box 156, Congers, NY 10920-0156. Phone: 800-634-6233 Fax: (212)351-6486 E-mail: nafe@nafe. com • URL: http://www.nafe.com.

National Association of Women Business Owners. 8405 Greensboro Dr., Ste. 800, McLean, VA 22102. Phone: 800-556-2926 or (703)506-3268 Fax: (703)506-3266 E-mail: national@nawbo.org • URL: http://www.nawbo.org • Formerly Association of Women Business Owners.

National Organization for Women. 733 15th St., N.W., 2nd Fl., Washington, DC 20005. Phone: (202)628-8669 Fax: (202)785-8576 E-mail: now@ now.org • URL: http://www.now.org • Includes men and women seeking equality for women.

National Partnership for Women and Families. 1875 Connecticut Ave., N. W., Suite 710, Washington, DC 20009. Phone: (202)986-2600 Fax: (202)986-2539 E-mail: info@nationalpartnership.org • URL: http://

www.nationalpartnership.org • Formerly Women's Legal Defense Fund.

National Women's Law Center. 11 Dupont Cir. NW, Ste. 800, Washington, DC 20036. Phone: (202)588-5180 Fax: (202)588-5185 E-mail: info@nwlc.org • URL: http://www.nwlc.org • Has "expanded the possibilities for women and girls in our country". Uses the law in all its forms: getting new laws on the books; litigating ground-breaking lawsuits all the way to the Supreme Court; and educating the public about how to make the law and public policies work for women and their families. "Takes on the issues that cut to the core of women's and girls' lives" in health, education, employment, and family economic security, with special priority given to the needs of low-income women and their families.

OTHER SOURCES

Practical Guide to Equal Employment Opportunity. American Lawyer Media, Inc. • Looseleaf. $199.00. Two volumes. Updated as needed. Serves as a legal manual for EEO compliance. "Volume one analyzes discrimination on the basis of race, religion, sex, age, and physical handicaps including AIDS." Provides information relating to an employer's liability in cases of sexual harassment of employees, including same-sex harassment. Covers affirmative action and reverse discrimination issues. Volume two contains model affirmative action plans, a sample EEO compliance manual, checklists, and other documents. (Law Journal Press).

EMPLOYMENT RESUMES

See: JOB RESUMES

EMPLOYMENT SECURITY

See: UNEMPLOYMENT INSURANCE

EMPLOYMENT TESTS

See: PSYCHOLOGICAL TESTING

ENDOWMENTS

See: FOUNDATIONS

ENERGY COGENERATION

See: COGENERATION OF ENERGY

ENERGY, GEOTHERMAL

See: GEOTHERMAL ENERGY

ENERGY, NUCLEAR

See: NUCLEAR ENERGY

ENERGY, SOLAR

See: SOLAR ENERGY

ENERGY SOURCES

See also: COAL INDUSTRY; ELECTRIC UTILITIES; GEOTHERMAL ENERGY; NATURAL GAS; NUCLEAR ENERGY; PETROLEUM INDUSTRY; SOLAR ENERGY

GENERAL WORKS

Energy and Problems of a Technical Society. Jack J. Kraushaar and Robert A. Ristinen. John Wiley and

Sons, Inc. • 1993. $64.95. Second edition.

Energy Management. Paul Ocallaghan. McGraw-Hill. • 1993. $55.00.

Energy Management and Conservation. Clive Beggs. Elsevier. • 2000. $39.95.

Towards a Sustainable Energy Future. Organization for Economic Cooperation and Development. • 2001. $100.00. Prepared by the International Energy Agency (IEA). Describes various policies for promoting sustainable energy, especially as related to economic development. Discusses "growing concerns about climate change and energy-supply security.".

ABSTRACTS AND INDEXES

Applied Science and Technology Index. H. W. Wilson Co. • 11 times a year. Quarterly and annual cumulations. Price varies. Indexes a wide variety of English language technical, industrial, and engineering periodicals.

NTIS Alerts: Energy. National Technical Information Service. • Semimonthly. $245.00 per year. Provides descriptions of government-sponsored research reports and software, with ordering information. Covers electric power, batteries, fuels, geothermal energy, heating/cooling systems, nuclear technology, solar energy, energy policy, and related subjects. Formerly *Abstract Newsletter.*

ALMANACS AND YEARBOOKS

Agricultural and Mineral Commodities Year Book. Available from Taylor & Francis Group. • Annual. $225.00. Published by Europa Publications. Contains descriptive product profiles, price data, export-import data, and production statistics for major commodities of the world: Includes commodity histories, uses, markets, demand trends, and information about trade agreements and key commodity organizations.

Annual Review of Enviroment and Resources. Annual Reviews. • Annual. Individuals, $89.00. Includes print and online editions. Institutions, $194.00; with online edition, $233.00.

Vital Signs [year]: The Trends That Are Shaping Our Future. Worldwatch Institute. • Annual. $14.95. Provides access to selected indicators showing social, economic, and environmental trends throughout the world. Includes data relating to food, energy, transportation, finance, population, and other topics.

CD-ROM DATABASES

Environment Abstracts on CD-ROM. LEXIS-NEXIS. • Quarterly. $1,295.00 per year. Contains the following CD-ROM databases: *Environment Abstracts, Energy Abstracts,* and *Acid Rain Abstracts.* Length of coverage varies.

OECD Statistical Compendium. Organization for Economic Cooperation and Development. • Semiannual. $1,905.00 per year for 1 to 10 users. CD-ROM contains more than 730,000 monthly, quarterly, and annual time series for OECD countries, 1960 to date. Includes fully searchable data on agriculture, food, economic indicators, national accounts, employment, energy, finance, industry, technology, and foreign trade. Results can be displayed in various forms.

DIRECTORIES

Energy Intelligence Top 100: Ranking the World's Top Oil Companies. Energy Intelligence Group, Inc. • Annual. $775.00. Provides detailed profiles of the world's 100 largest oil companies, with rankings by numerous key criteria. Includes both stockholder-owned and government-owned companies.

Financial Times Business Global Mining Directory. Available from Gale Cengage Learning. • Annual. $355.00. Published by Financial Times Business. Provides detailed information on 1,000 leading mining companies worldwide. Includes financial data

for three years. Formerly *Financial Times Energy Yearbook: Mining.*

Financial Times Business Global Oil & Gas Directory. Available from Gale Cengage Learning. • Annual. $355.00. Published by Financial Times Business. Provides detailed information on 800 leading oil and gas companies worldwide. Includes financial data for three years. Formerly *Financial Times Energy Yearbook: Oil & Gas.*

Institutional Buyers of Energy Stocks. Investment Data Corp. • Annual. $645.00. Provides detailed profiles 555 institutional buyers of petroleum-related and other energy stocks. Includes names of financial analysts and portfolio managers.

Plunkett's Energy Industry Almanac: Complete Profiles on the Energy Industry 500 Companies. Plunkett Research Ltd. • Annual. $199.99. Includes major oil companies, utilities, pipelines, alternative energy companies, etc. Provides information on industry trends.

World Energy and Nuclear Directory. Specialist Journals. • Biennial. $385.00. Lists 5,000 public and private, international research and development organizations functioning in a wide variety of areas related to energy.

ENCYCLOPEDIAS AND DICTIONARIES

Encyclopedia of Energy. Cutler J. Cleveland, editor. Elsevier, Inc. • 2004. $1,560.00. Six volumes. Covers all aspects of energy sources and energy-related environmental issues.

Macmillan Encyclopedia of Energy. Available from Gale Cengage Learning. • 2001. $395.00. Three volumes. Published by Macmillan Reference USA. Covers the business, technology, and history of a wide variety of energy sources.

Wiley Encyclopedia of Energy and the Environment. Attilio Bisio and Sharon Boots. John Wiley and Sons, Inc. • 1996. $285.00. Abriged edition. Two volumes. Covers a wide variety of energy and environmental topics, including legal and policy issues. (Encyclopedia of Energy and the Environment Series: Vol. 2).

HANDBOOKS AND MANUALS

Energy Management Handbook. Wayne C. Turner. Marcel Dekker, Inc. • 2002. $165.00. Fourth edition.

Energy Systems Handbook. McGraw Hill. • 1999. $39.95 (Complete Construction Series).

Handbook of Fuel Cells: Fundamentals, Technology, and Applications. Wolf Vielstich, editor. John Wiley and Sons, Inc. • 2003. $1,225.00. Four volumes. Volume one: *Fundamentals and Survey of Systems.* Volume two: *Fuel Cell Electrocatalysis.* Volumes three and four: *Fuel Cell Technology and Applications.*

Modern Petroleum Technology. Richard A. Dawe, editor. John Wiley and Sons, Inc. • 2000. $600.00. Sixth edition. Two volumes. Volume one, entitled *Upstream,* covers oil rigs and other means of obtaining raw petroleum. Volume two, *Downstream,* covers petroleum refining and end products. Edited for industry technicians, managers, and engineers.

INTERNET DATABASES

U. S. Census Bureau: The Official Statistics. U. S. Bureau of the Census. Phone: (301)763-4100 Fax: (301)763-4794 • URL: http://www.census.gov • Web site is "Your Source for Social, Demographic, and Economic Information." Contains "Current U. S. Population Count," "Current Economic Indicators," and a wide variety of data under "Other Official Statistics." Keyword searching is provided. Fees: Free.

ONLINE DATABASES

Applied Science and Technology Index Online. H. W. Wilson Co. • Provides online indexing of 500 major scientific, technical, industrial, and engineering periodicals. Time period is 1983 to date.

Monthly updates. Inquire as to online cost and availability.

PERIODICALS AND NEWSLETTERS

DOE This Month. Available from U. S. Government Printing Office. • Monthly. $42.00 per year. Describes the U.S. Department of Energy's research and development activities and DOE publications. Includes information on nuclear energy, renewable energy sources, and synthetic fuels.

Energy and Fuels. American Chemical Society. • Bimonthly. Institutions, $852.00 per year; others, price on application. An interdisciplinary technical journal covering non-nuclear energy sources: petroleum, gas, synthetic fuels, etc.

Energy Compass. Energy Intelligence Group. • Description: Focuses on worldwide geopolitical developments and their impact on the oil industry. Also includes marketing and trading information, political risk assessment, and current events and trends. **Remarks:** Available via fax, e-mail, or online.

Energy Conservation News. BCC Research. • Description: Designed to give the industrial energy manager an inside view into current conservation innovations and events in the industrial sector. Covers such topics as effective conservation programs, solar and other energy alternatives, energy efficient building design, financing, utility industry developments, and energy legislation and controls.

Energy Conversion and Management. Elsevier. • 20 times a year. Institutions, $3,457.00 per year. Presents a scholarly approach to alternative or renewable energy sources. Text in English, French and German.

The Energy Daily. King Publishing Group Inc. • Description: Covers the field of energy as it relates to government, policy, and industry. Discusses all forms of energy: nuclear, geothermal, coal, solar, oil, natural gas, wind, shale oil, and wave power. Includes analysis, editorial comment, and hard reporting.

Energy Magazine. Business Communications Co., Inc. • Quarterly. $395.00 per year.

Energy Sources: Recovery, Utilization, and Environmental Effects. Taylor & Francis Group. • Monthly. Individuals, $498.00 per year; institutions, $1,325.00 per year.

Independent Energy: The Power Industry's Business Magazine. PennWell Corp., Industrial Div. • 10 times a year. $127.00 per year. Covers non-utility electric power plants (cogeneration) and other alternative sources of electric energy.

International Journal of Energy Research. John Wiley and Sons, Inc., Journals. • 15 times a year. Individuals, $2,685.00 per year; institutions, $3,500.00 per year. Published in England by John Wiley & Sons Ltd.

Journal of Energy Engineering: The International Journal. American Society of Civil Engineers. • Three times a year. Members, $40.00 per year; with online edition, $46.00 per year; non-members, $60.00 per year; with online edition, $69.00 per year.

Resource and Energy Economics: A Journal Devoted to the Interdisciplinary Studies in the Allocation of Natural Resources. Elsevier. • Quarterly. Individuals, $75.00 per year; institutions, $583.00 per year. Text in English.

World Environment Report: News and Information on International Resource Management. Business Publishers, Inc. • Biweekly. $494.00 per year. Newsletter on international developments having to do with the environment, energy, pollution control, waste management, and toxic substances.

World Watch: Working for a Sustainable Future. Worldwatch Institute. • Bimonthly. $25.00 per year. Emphasis is on environmental trends, including developments in population growth, climate change, human behavior, the role of government, and other factors.

PRICE SOURCES

Energy Prices and Taxes. International Energy Agency. OECD Publications and Information Center. • Quarterly. $385.00 per year. Includes print and online edition. Compiled by the International Energy Agency. Provides data on prices and taxation of petroleum products, natural gas, coal, and electricity. Diskette edition, $800.00. (Published in Paris).

RESEARCH CENTERS AND INSTITUTES

Canadian Energy Research Institute. Canadian Energy Research Institute. 3512 33rd St. NW, No. 150, Calgary, AB, Canada T2L 2A6. Phone: (403)282-1231 Fax: (403)284-4181 E-mail: mmasri@ceri.ca • URL: http://www.ceri.ca • Economic issues relating to all forms of energy, including oil, natural gas, coal, nuclear and hydroelectric power, and alternative energy sources. Develops software such as the World Oil Market Model.

Hawaii Natural Energy Institute. University of Hawaii at Manoa, 2540 Dole St., Holmes Hall 246, Honolulu, HI 96822. Phone: (808)956-8890 Fax: (808)956-2336 E-mail: hnei@hawaii.edu • URL: http://www.soest.hawaii.edu • Research areas include geothermal, wind, solar, hydroelectric, and other energy sources.

Laboratory for Energy and the Environment. Massachusetts Institute of Technology. 77 Massachusetts Ave., Bldg. E40-455, Cambridge, MA 02139-4307. Phone: (617)258-8891 Fax: (617)253-8013 E-mail: jwilmson@mit.edu • URL: http://www.lfee.mit.edu • Formerly Energy Laboratory.

Oak Ridge National Laboratory. Bethel Valley Rd., Oak Ridge, TN 37831-6255. Phone: (865)576-2900 Fax: (865)241-2967 E-mail: madia@ornl.gov • URL: http://www.ornl.gov.

Worldwatch Institute. Worldwatch Institute. 1776 Massachusetts Ave. NW, Washington, DC 20036-1904. Phone: (202)452-1999 or (202)452-1999 Fax: (202)296-7365 E-mail: worldwatch@worldwatch.org • URL: http://www.worldwatch.org • Global trends in the availability and management of both human and natural resources, including research in energy, food policy, population, development, technology, the environment, economics, toxics, and recycling.

STATISTICS SOURCES

Annual Energy Outlook [year], with Projections to [year]. Available from U. S. Government Printing Office. • Annual. $42.00. Issued by the Energy Information Administration, U. S. Department of Energy (http://www.eia.doe.gov). Contains detailed statistics and 20-year projections for electricity, oil, natural gas, coal, and renewable energy. Text provides extensive discussion of energy issues and "Market Trends.".

Annual Energy Review. Available from U. S. Government Printing Office. • Annual. $51.00. Issued by the Energy Information Administration, Office of Energy Markets and End Use, U. S. Department of Energy. Presents long-term historical as well as recent data on production, consumption, stocks, imports, exports, and prices of the principal energy commodities in the U. S.

Datapedia of the United States: American History in Numbers. George T. Kurian, editor. Bernan Press. • 2004. $125.00. Third edition. Based on the Census Bureau publication, *Historical Statistics of the United States.* Provides data from Colonial times to the present on agriculture, business, consumer income, energy, finance, labor, national income, population, and many other subjects. Includes "narrative highlights," maps, charts, and statistical projections.

Electric Power Monthly. Available from U. S. Government Printing Office. • Monthly. $137.00 per year. Issued by the Energy Information Administration, U. S. Department of Energy. Contains statistical data relating to electric utility operation, capability, fuel use, and prices.

Energy Balances of OECD Countries. Organization for Economic Cooperation and Development. Available from OECD Publications and Information Center. • Annual. $115.00. Presents two-year data on the supply and consumption of solid fuels, oil, gas, and electricity, expressed in oil equivalency terms. Historical tables are also provided. Relates to OECD member countries.

Energy Statistics of OECD Countries. Available from OECD Publications Center. • Annual. $110.00. Detailed energy supply and consumption data for OECD member countries.

Energy Statistics Yearbook. United Nations Dept. of Economic and Social Affairs. United Nations Publications. • Annual. $100.00. Text in English and French.

International Energy Annual. Available from U. S. Government Printing Office. • Annual. $34.00. Issued by the Energy Information Administration, U. S. Department of Energy. Provides production, consumption, import, and export data for primary energy commodities in more than 200 countries and areas. In addition to petroleum products and alcohol, renewable energy sources are covered (hydroelectric, geothermal, solar, and wind).

Monthly Bulletin of Statistics. United Nations Publications. • Monthly. $295.00 per year. Provides current data for about 200 countries on a wide variety of economic, industrial, and demographic subjects. Compiled by United Nations Statistical Office.

Monthly Energy Review. Available from U. S. Government Printing Office. • Monthly. $126.00 per year. Issued by the Energy Information Administration, Office of Energy Markets and End Use, U. S. Department of Energy. Contains current and historical statistics on U. S. production, storage, imports, and consumption of petroleum, natural gas, and coal.

Petroleum Supply Annual. Available from U. S. Government Printing Office. • Annual. $78.00. Two volumes. Produced by the Energy Information Administration, U. S. Department of Energy. Contains worldwide data on the petroleum industry and petroleum products.

Petroleum Supply Monthly. Available from U. S. Government Printing Office. • Monthly. Produced by the Energy Information Administration, U. S. Department of Energy. Provides worldwide statistics on a wide variety of petroleum products. Covers production, supplies, exports and imports, transportation, refinery operations, and other aspects of the petroleum industry.

Short-Term Energy Outlook: Quarterly Projections. Available from U. S. Government Printing Office. • Semiannual. Issued by Energy Information Administration, U. S. Department of Energy. Contains forecasts of U. S. energy supply, demand, and prices.

Social Statistics of the United States. Mark S. Littman, editor. Bernan Press. • 2000. $65.00. Includes statistical data on population growth, labor force, occupations, environmental trends, leisure time use, income, poverty, taxes, and other economic or demographic topics.

Statistical Abstract of the United States. Available from U. S. Government Printing Office. • Annual. $51.00. Issued by the U. S. Bureau of the Census.

A Statistical Portrait of the United States: Social Conditions and Trends. Mark S. Littman, editor. Bernan Press. • 1998. $89.00. Covers "social, economic, and environmental trends in the United States over the past 25 years." Includes statistical tables, graphs, and analysis relating to such topics as population, income, poverty, wealth, labor, housing, education, healthcare, air/water quality, and government. (Statistical Portrait of the United States: Social Conditions and Trends Series).

Statistical Yearbook. United Nations Publications. • Annual. $125.00. Contains statistics for about 200 countries on a wide variety of economic, industrial, and demographic topics. Compiled by United Nations Statistical Office.

World Energy Outlook. OECD Publications and Information Center. • Annual. $150.00. Provides detailed, 15-year projections by the International Energy Agency (IEA) for world energy supply and demand.

TRADE/PROFESSIONAL ASSOCIATIONS

International Energy Agency. 9, rue de la Federation, 75739 Paris, France. Phone: 33 1 40576500 Fax: 33 1 40576559 E-mail: info@iea.org • URL: http://www.iea.org • Industrialized oil-consuming countries that carry out an international energy program designed to build and sustain strong energy economies. Seeks to improve energy supply and demand balance. Strives to develop oil-alternative energy sources. Coordinates international oil market information. Maintains an emergency oil sharing system. Compiles statistics.

U.S. Energy Association. 1300 Pennsylvania Ave. NW, Ste. 550, Mailbox 142, Washington, DC 20004-3022. Phone: (202)312-1230 Fax: (202)682-1682 E-mail: kgrover@usea.org • URL: http://www.usea.org • One of 100 national committees representing the energy interests of industry, government, professional and technical societies, educational institutions, and legal and other professional service organizations. Supports World Energy Council objectives, which are: to provide for broad consideration of energy resources, policy, management, technology, use, and conservation as they relate to the total energy picture of the U.S. and the world; to publish data on energy resources and their utilization; to hold conferences and forums for those concerned with surveying, developing, or using energy resources. Conducts special energy seminars.

OTHER SOURCES

Energy Management and Federal Energy Guidelines. CCH, Inc. • Biweekly. $1,827.00 per year. Seven looseleaf volumes. Periodic supplementation. Reports on petroleum allocation rules, conservation efforts, new technology, and other energy concerns.

Major Energy Companies of the World. Available from Gale Cengage Learning. • Annual. $880.00. Published by Graham & Whiteside. Contains detailed information on more than 3,300 important energy companies in various countries. Industries include electricity generation, coal, natural gas, nuclear energy, petroleum, fuel distribution, and equipment for energy production.

ENGINEERING CONSULTANTS

See also: CONSULTANTS; MANAGEMENT CONSULTANTS

DIRECTORIES

American Consulting Engineers Council Membership Directory. American Consulting Engineers Council. • Annual. $140.00. A state-by-state listing of ACEC's 5,200 consulting engineering firms with a total of over 180,000 employees.

Consulting Services. Association of Consulting Chemists and Chemical Engineers Inc. • Covers: about 160 member consultants in chemistry, chemical engineering, metallurgy, etc. Entries include:

Individual name, address, certificate number, qualifications, affiliation, experience, facilities, staff.

Emerson's Directory of Leading U.S. Technology Consulting Firms. Emerson Co. • 2000. $195.00. Provides information on major consulting firms specializing in technology.

HANDBOOKS AND MANUALS

The Consultant's Proposal, Fee, and Contract Problem-Solver. Ronald Tepper. John Wiley and Sons, Inc. • 1993. $29.95. Provides advice for consultants on fees, contracts, proposals, and client communications. Includes case histories in 10 specific fields, such as finance, marketing, engineering, and management.

How to Succeed as an Independent Consultant. Herman Holtz. John Wiley and Sons, Inc. • 1993. $34. 95. Third edition. Covers a wide variety of marketing, financial, professional, and ethical issues for consultants. Includes bibliographic and organizational information.

PERIODICALS AND NEWSLETTERS

Consulting-Specifying Engineer. Reed Business Information. • 13 times a year. $95.90 per year. Formerly *Consulting Engineer.*

The Last Word. American Consulting Engineers Council. • Description: Contains summaries of Council activities and legislative actions of interest to consulting engineers.

STATISTICS SOURCES

Salaries of Scientists, Engineers, and Technicians: A Summary of Salary Surveys. Commission on Professionals in Science and Technology. CPST Publications. • Biennial. $100.00. A summary of salary surveys.

TRADE/PROFESSIONAL ASSOCIATIONS

American Council of Engineering Companies. 1015 15th St., 8th Fl. NW, Washington, DC 20005-2605. Phone: (202)347-7474 Fax: (202)898-0068 E-mail: acec@acec.org • URL: http://www.acec.org • Represents consulting engineering firms engaged in private practice. Conducts programs concerned with public relations, business practices, governmental affairs, international practice and professional liability. Compiles statistics on office practices, insurance, employment, insurance clients served and services provided. Holds professional development seminars. Conducts educational programs; maintains speakers' bureau.

APEC-Automated Procedures for Engineering Consultants, Inc. Talbott Tower, 131 N. Ludlow St., Suite 318, Dayton, OH 45402. Phone: (937)228-2602 Fax: (937)228-5652 E-mail: apecinc@worldnet.att.net.

Association of Consulting Chemists and Chemical Engineers. P.O. Box 297, Sparta, NJ 07871. Phone: (973)729-6671 Fax: (973)729-7088 E-mail: info@chemconsult.org • URL: http://www.chemconsult.org.

ENGINES

See also: LUBRICATION AND LUBRICANTS

DIRECTORIES

Diesel Progress North American Edition: For Engine, Drive and Hydraulic System Engineering and Equipment Management. Diesel and Gas Turbine Publications. • Monthly. $75.00 per year. List of over 1,500 factory-authorized engine distributors and independent service keepers. Formerly *Diesel Progress Engines and Drives?.*

Directory of Marine Diesel Engines. Institute of Marine Engineering, Science, and Technology. • Annual. Price on application. Issued as a supplement to *Marine Engineers Review.*

Fairplay World Shipping Directory. Fairplay Publications Ltd. • Covers: more than 76,000 companies worldwide engaged in some aspect of shipping, including over 10,000 shipowners with fleets totalling over 45,000 vessels, shipbuilders and repairers, marine insurance shipping finance, protection and indemnity associations, marine equipment suppliers, and towing, salvage, and dredging; also lists marine organizations, shipbrokers, and consulting engineers and surveyors. Entries include: Company name, address, phone, fax, e-mail, URL, names of directors and executives, brief description of business; listings may also include associated and subsidiary companies and financial data.

Lloyd's Maritime Directory. Informa PLC. • Covers: Over 40,000 shipowners, managers, and operators with 75,000 vessels. Also includes Marine consultants; towing, salvage, solicitors, P&I clubs; ship building and repair firms; general maritime organizations, banking and finance and more. Entries include: Firm name, address, phone, fax, e-mail, internet; branch offices; names of principal executives; agents; parent and associated companies; and, for shipowners and lines, detailed information on ships owned, type, or capacity, etc. The former second volume of 'International Shipping and Shipbuilding Directory' is now published separately with the title 'Lloyd's List Marine Equipment Buyers' Guide' (see separate entry).

INTERNET DATABASES

Manufacturing Profiles. U. S. Bureau of the Census. Phone: (301)763-4636 E-mail: webmaster@census.gov • URL: http://www.census.gov/prod/www/abs/mfg-prof.html • The Census Bureau makes available free on PDF (Portable Document Format) an annual consolidation of the entire Current Industrial Report series, presenting "all the data compiled." Contains statistics on production, shipments, inventories, consumption, exports, imports, and orders for a wide variety of manufactured products.

PERIODICALS AND NEWSLETTERS

Diesel and Gas Turbine Worldwide: The International Engine Power Systems Magazine. Joseph M. Kane, editor. Diesel & Gas Turbine Publications. • 10 times a year. $65.00 per year.

Gas Turbine World. Pequot Publishing, Inc. • Bimonthly. $90.00 per year.

Lloyd's List. Available from Informa UK Ltd. • Daily. $1,698.00 per year. Published in the UK by Lloyd's List (http://www.lloydslist.com). Marine industry newspaper. Covers a wide variety of maritime topics, including global news, business/insurance, regulation, shipping markets, financial markets, shipping movements, freight logistics, and marine technology. (Also available weekly at $385.00 per year.).

RESEARCH CENTERS AND INSTITUTES

Davidson Laboratory. Stevens Institute of Technology. 711 Hudson St., Hoboken, NJ 07030. Phone: (201)216-5300 Fax: (201)216-8214 E-mail: m1bruno@stevens-tech.edu • URL: http://www.dl.stevens-tech.edu.

Engine Research Center. University of Wisconsin - Madison. 121 Engineering Research Bldg., 1500 Engineering Dr., Madison, WI 53706-1687. Phone: (608)263-2735 Fax: (608)263-9870 E-mail: reitz@engr.wisc.edu • URL: http://www.erc.wisc.edu/.

Mechanical Engineering Department. Stevens Institute of Technology. Castle Point on the Hudson, Hoboken, NJ 07030. Phone: (201)216-5000 • URL: http://www.stevens.edu/maim.

Southwest Research Institute. Southwest Research Institute. PO Box 28510, 6220 Culebra Rd., San Antonio, TX 78228-0510. Phone: (210)684-5111 Fax: (210)522-3547 E-mail: bd@swri.org • URL: http://www.swri.org • Automation, robotics, intelligent systems, space sciences, environmental sciences and engineering, bioengineering, micro encapsulation, chemistry, plant machinery and piping dynamics, radiolocation sciences and development, communications, electromagnetic compatibility, electronic systems, geophysical instrumentation, nondestructive evaluation research, nuclear waste regulatory analysis, fluid dynamics and hydraulics, offshore systems, structural analysis and testing, terminal ballistics and blast effects, materials development, solid mechanics, nonmetallic materials, engine systems engineering, engine emissions analysis and control, fuels and lubricants evaluation, fluids and lubrication technology, alternate energy systems, alternate fuels, mining systems engineering, vehicle and highway safety, and fire research.

STATISTICS SOURCES

Annual Survey of Manufactures. Available from U. S. Government Printing Office. • Annual. Prices vary. Issued by the U. S. Census Bureau as an interim update to the *Census of Manufactures.* Includes data on number of manufacturing establishments in various industries, employment, labor costs, value of shipments, capital expenditures, inventories, energy costs, and assets. (See also Census Bureau home page, http://www.census.gov/.).

World Trade Annual. United Nations Statistical Office. Walker and Co. • Annual. Prices vary.

TRADE/PROFESSIONAL ASSOCIATIONS

Association of Diesel Specialists. 10 Laboratory Dr., Research Triangle Park, NC 27709. Phone: (919)549-4800 Fax: (919)549-4824 E-mail: info@diesel.org • URL: http://www.diesel.org.

Engine Manufacturers Association. 2 N LaSalle St., Ste. 2200, Chicago, IL 60602. Phone: (312)827-8700 Fax: (312)827-8737 E-mail: ema@enginemanufacturers.org • URL: http://www.enginemanufacturers.org • Producers of internal combustion engines for all applications except those used exclusively for automobiles and aircraft. Conducts research and development programs on noise, smoke, and other emissions from internal combustion engines.

ENTERTAINMENT INDUSTRY

See: AMUSEMENT INDUSTRY; SHOW BUSINESS

ENTOMOLOGY, ECONOMIC

See: ECONOMIC ENTOMOLOGY

ENTRANCE REQUIREMENTS

See: COLLEGE ENTRANCE REQUIREMENTS

ENTREPRENEURIAL CAPITAL

See: VENTURE CAPITAL

ENTREPRENEURIAL HISTORY

See: BUSINESS HISTORY

ENTREPRENEURS AND INTRAPRENEURS

See also: WOMEN EXECUTIVES

GENERAL WORKS

Entrepreneurship.com. Tim Burns. Dearborn Trade Publishing, A Kaplan Professional Co. • 2000. $19.

95. Provides basic advice and information on the topic of dot.com startups, including business plan creation and financing.

Hoover's Vision: Original Thinking for Business Success. Gary Hoover. Available from Hoover's, Inc. • 2001. $26.95. Published by Texere. Contains inspirational advice for entrepreneurial achievement. The author is founder of Hoover's, Inc.

Innovation and Entrepreneurship: Practice and Principles. Peter F. Drucker. HarperInformation. • 1993. $16.95.

The Intentional Entrepreneur: Bringing Technology and Engineering to the Real New Economy. David L. Bodde. M. E. Sharpe, Inc. • 2004. $69.95. Covers the "art of entrepreneurship" for engineering and technology professionals. Includes material on marketing, business models, venture capital, and intellectual property.

Is It Too Late to Run Away and Join the Circus? Finding the Life You Really Want. Marti Smye. John Wiley. • 1998. $14.95. Provides philosophical and inspirational advice on leaving corporate life and becoming self-employed as a consultant or whatever. Central theme is dealing with major changes in life style and career objectives.

The Leap: A Memoir of Love and Madness in the Internet Gold Rush. Tom Ashbrook. Houghton Mifflin Co. • 2000. $25.00. The author relates his personal and family tribulations while attempting to obtain financing for an eventually successful e-business startup, HomePortfolio.com.

Recreation Trends and Markets: Info the 21st Century. John R. Kelly and Rodney Warnick. Sagamore Publishing, Inc. • 1999. $25.00. Second edition.

Super Searchers Make It On Their Own: Top Independent Information Professionals Share Their Secrets for Starting and Running a Research Business. Suzanne Sabroski. Information Today, Inc. • 2002. $24.95. Presents discussions by "11 of the world's top research entrepreneurs" on the practical aspects of being in business as an information broker or other information provider. (Super Searchers Series).

Women Entrepreneurs: Moving Beyond the Glass Ceiling. Dorothy P. Moore and E. Holly Buttner. Sage Publications, Inc. • 1997. $79.95. Contains profiles of "129 successful female entrepreneurs who previously worked in corporate environments.".

ABSTRACTS AND INDEXES

Business Periodicals Index. H. W. Wilson Co. • 11 times a year. Quarterly and annual cumulations. Price varies.

BIOGRAPHICAL SOURCES

Leaders of American Business and Industry. Gale Cengage Learning. • 2002. $145.00. Three volumes. Provides popularly written biographies of influential American entrepreneurs and business leaders, past and present. Includes detailed profiles of major companies. (UXL imprint).

Net.people: The Personalities and Passions Behind the Web Sites. Thomas E. Bleier and Eric C. Steinert. Information Today, Inc. • 2000. $19.95. Presents the personal stories of 36 Web "entrepreneurs and visionaries." (CyberAge Books.).

CD-ROM DATABASES

Hoover's Company Capsules on CD-ROM. Hoover's, Inc. • Quarterly. $399.95 per year (single-user). Provides the CD-ROM version of *Hoover's Handbook of American Business, Hoover's Handbook of Emerging Companies, Hoover's Handbook of World Business, Hoover's Guide to Computer Companies, Hoover's Guide to Media Companies, Hoover's Handbook of Private Companies,* and various regional guides. Includes more than 11,000 profiles of companies.

DIRECTORIES

Business Organizations, Agencies, and Publications Directory. Gale Cengage Learning. • 2003. $480.00. 15th edition. Over 40,000 entries describing 39 types of business information sources. Classified by type of organization, publication, or serviceIncludes state, national, and international agencies and organizations. Master index to names and keywords. Also includes e-mail addresses and web site URL's.

Hoover's Handbook of Emerging Companies: Profiles of America's Most Exciting Growth Enterprises. Hoover's, Inc. • Annual. $125.00. Contains detailed profiles of 600 rapidly growing corporations. Includes indexes by industry, location, executive name, company name, and brand name.

Venture Capital Directory (Small Business Administation). Forum Publishing Co. • Annual. $12.95. Over 500 members of the Small Business Administration and the Small Business Investment. Companies that provide funding for small and minority businesses.

ENCYCLOPEDIAS AND DICTIONARIES

Encyclopedia of Small Business. Gale Cengage Learning. • 2002. $450.00. Second edition. Two volumes. Contains about 600 informative entries on a wide variety of topics affecting small business. Arrangement is alphabetical.

HANDBOOKS AND MANUALS

Cyberfinance: Raising Capital for the E-Business. Martin B. Robins. CCH, Inc. • 2001. $79.00. Covers the taxation, financial, and legal aspects of raising money for new Internet-based ("dot.com") companies, including the three stages of startup, growth, and initial public offering. (Solutions for Professional Advisers Series).

Entrepreneur's Guide to Finance and Business: Wealth Creation Techniques for Growing a Business. Steven Rogers. McGraw-Hill. • 2003. $49.95. Coverage includes entrepreneurial financing, business plan development, and structuring a deal.

The Entrepreneur's Guide to Growing Up: Taking Your Small Company to the Next Level. Edna Sheedy. Self-Counsel Press, Inc. • 1993. $8.95. Discusses company structure, delegation, management information requirements, and other topics related to company growth. (Self-Counsel Business Series).

From Executive to Entrepreneur: Making the Transition. Gilbert Z. Zoghlin. AMACOM. • 1991. $24.95. A self-help guide offering psychological and financial advice to corporate employees who wish to go into business for themselves.

Handbook of Entrepreneurial Dynamics. William B. Gartner and others, editors. Sage Publications, Inc. • 2004. $115.00. Covers current academic research in entrepreneurship.

How to Incorporate: A Handbook for Entrepreneurs and Professionals. Michael Diamond and Julia L. Williams. John Wiley and Sons, Inc. • 2000. $24.95. Fourth edition.

Infopreneurs: Turning Data into Dollars. H. Skip Weitzen. John Wiley and Sons, Inc. • 1988. $19.95. Infopreneurs are entrepreneurs who market information. A how-to-do-it manual.

New Venture Creation: Entrepreneurship for the 21st Century. Jeffrey A. Timmons and Stephen Spinelli. McGraw-Hill. • 2003. Sixth edition. Price on application.

Standard Business Forms for the Entrepreneur. Entrepreneur Media, Inc. • Looseleaf. $59.50. A practical collection of forms useful to entrepreneurial small businesses. (Start-Up Business Guide No. E1319.).

Start-Up Business Guides. Entrepreneur Media, Inc.

• Looseleaf. $59.50 each. Practical guides to starting a wide variety of small businesses.

Startup: An Entrepreneur's Guide to Launching and Managing a New Venture. William J. Stolze. Rock Beach Press. • 1989. $24.95.

Venture Capital: An Authoritative Guide for Investors, Entrepreneurs, and Managers. Douglas A. Lindgren. McGraw-Hill. • 1998. $65.00.

INTERNET DATABASES

MBEMAG. Minority Business Entrepreneur Magazine. Phone: (310)540-9398 Fax: (310)792-8263 E-mail: webmaster@mbemag.com • URL: http://www.mbemag.com • Web site's main feature is the "MBE Business Resources Directory." This provides complete mailing addresses, phone, fax, and Web site addresses (URL) for more than 40 organizations and government agencies having information or assistance for ethnic minority and women business owners. Some other links are "Current Events," "Calendar of Events," and "Business Opportunities." Updating is bimonthly. Fees: Free.

ONLINE DATABASES

Wilson Business Abstracts Online. H. W. Wilson Co. • Indexes and abstracts 600 major business periodicals, plus the *Wall Street Journal* and the business section of the *New York Times.* Indexing is from 1982, abstracting from 1990, with the two newspapers included from 1993. Updated weekly. Inquire as to online cost and availability. (*Business Periodicals Index* without abstracts is also available online.).

PERIODICALS AND NEWSLETTERS

Black Enterprise. Earl G. Graves Publishing Co. • Monthly. $17.95 per year. Covers careers, personal finances and leisure.

Business Start-Ups: Smart Ideas for Your Small Business. Entrepreneur Media, Inc. • Monthly. $14.97 per year. Provides advice for starting a small business. Includes business trends, new technology, E-commerce, and case histories ("real-life stories").

Business 2.0. Time Inc. • Monthly. $30.00 per year. General business magazine emphasizing ideas, insight, and innovation.

Chief Executive Officers Newsletter: For the Entrepreneurial Manager and the Pr ofessionals Who Advise Him. Center for Entrepreneurial Management, Inc. • Monthly. $96.00 per year. Looseleaf service. Formerly *Entrepreneurial Manager's Newsletter.*

Entrepreneur: The Small Business Authority. Entrepreneur Media, Inc. • Monthly. $19.97 per year. Contains advice for small business owners and prospective owners. Includes numerous franchise advertisements.

Fast Company: How Smart Business Works. Fast Company, Inc. • Monthly. $12.00 per year. Covers business management, with emphasis on creativity, leadership, innovation, career advancement, teamwork, the global economy, and the "new workplace.".

Home Business Magazine: The Home-Based Entrepreneur's Magazine. United Marketing and Research Co., Inc. • Bimonthly. $15.00 per year. Provides practical advice and ideas relating to the operation of a business in the home. Sections include "Marketing & Sales," "Money Corner" (financing), "Businesses & Opportunities," and "Home Office" (equipment, etc.). Includes an annual directory of more than 250 non-franchised home business opportunities, including start-up costs and information about providers.

Income Opportunities.Com: The Original Small Business - Home Office Magazine. Newline. • Monthly. $31.95 per year.

Inc.: The Magazine for Growing Companies. INC. • 18 times a year. $14.00 per year. Edited for small office and office-in-the-home businesses with from one to 25 employees. Covers management, office technology, and lifestyle. Incorporates *Self-Employed Professional*.

The Journal of Business Venturing. Elsevier. • Bimonthly. Individuals, $148.00 per year; institutions, $768.00 per year.

Minority Business Entrepreneur. • Bimonthly. $16.00 per year. Reports on issues "critical to the growth and development of minority and women-owned firms." Provides information on relevant legislation and profiles successful women and minority entrepreneurs.

RESEARCH CENTERS AND INSTITUTES

Arthur M. Bank Center for Entrepreneurship. Babson College, Babson Park, MA 02459-0310. Phone: (781)239-4623 Fax: (781)239-4178 E-mail: spinelli@babson.edu • URL: http://www.babson.edu/entrep • Sponsors annual Babson College Entrepreneurship Research Conference.

Berkley Center for Entrepreneurial Studies. New York University, Kaufman Management Center, Stern School of Business, 44 W. Fourth St., Ste. 8-180, New York, NY 10012. Phone: (212)998-0070 Fax: (212)995-4211 E-mail: aginsber@stern.nyu.edu • URL: http://www.stern.nyu.edu/bces.

Bureau of Economic and Business Research. University of Illinois at Urbana-Champaign, 1206 S. Sixth St., 403 Wohlers Hall, Champaign, IL 61820. Phone: (217)333-2330 Fax: (217)244-7410 E-mail: g-oldman@uiuc.edu • URL: http://www.business.uiuc.edu/research.

Center for Entrepreneurial Studies and Development, Inc. West Virginia University, College of Engineering and Mineral Resources, 1062 Maple Dr., Morgantown, WV 26506. Phone: (304)293-5551 Fax: (304)293-6707 E-mail: jbyrd@mail.cesd.wvu.edu • URL: http://www.cesd.wvu.edu • Inventory control systems included as a research field.

Center for Private Enterprise. Baylor University, Hankamer School of Business, P.O. Box 98003, Waco, TX 76798-8003. Phone: (254)710-2263 Fax: (254)710-1092 E-mail: jim_truitt@baylor.edu • URL: http://129.62.162.136/enterprise/ • Includes studies of entrepreneurship and women entrepreneurs.

Center for Women's Business Research. 1411 K St. N.W., Ste. 1350, Washington, DC 20005-3407. Phone: (202)638-3060 Fax: (202)638-3064 E-mail: info@womensbusinessresearch.org • URL: http://www.nfwbo.org • Provides research reports and statistical studies relating to various aspects of women-owned business enterprises. Affiliated with the National Association of Women Business Owners.

TRADE/PROFESSIONAL ASSOCIATIONS

Association of African-American Women Business Owners. 3363 Alden Place, N.E., Washington, DC 20019. Phone: (202)399-3645 Fax: (202)399-3645 E-mail: aaawbo@aol.com • URL: http://www.blackpgs.com/aawboa.

Chief Executive Officers Club. 4 W 22nd St., 10th Fl., New York, NY 10010. Phone: (212)925-7911 Fax: (212)925-7463 E-mail: main@ceoclubs.org • URL: http://ceoclubs.org • Serves as a management resource for entrepreneurial managers and their professional advisers. Selects and makes available publications on developing business plans, organizing an entrepreneurial team, attracting venture capital, and obtaining patents, trademarks, and copyrights. Develops, collects, and disseminates information on business trends, new laws and regulations, and tax guidance. Conducts intensive-study courses and seminars. Has identified stages of the entrepreneurial process and, through essays and audiocassettes, addresses problems pertinent to each stage.

National Association of Women Business Owners. 8405 Greensboro Dr., Ste. 800, McLean, VA 22102. Phone: 800-556-2926 or (703)506-3268 Fax: (703)506-3266 E-mail: national@nawbo.org • URL: http://www.nawbo.org • Formerly Association of Women Business Owners.

National Business Incubation Association. 20 E Circle Dr., No. 37198, Athens, OH 45701-3571. Phone: (740)593-4331 Fax: (740)593-1996 E-mail: info@nbia.org • URL: http://www.NBIA.org • Incubator developers and managers; corporate joint venture partners, venture capital investors; economic development professionals. (Incubators are business assistance programs providing business consulting services and financing assistance to start-up and fledgling companies.) Helps newly formed businesses to succeed. Educates businesses and investors on incubator benefits; offers specialized training in incubator formation and management. Conducts research and referral services; compiles statistics; maintains speakers' bureau; publishes information relevant to business incubation and growing companies.

ENVIRONMENT

See also: AIR POLLUTION; ENVIRONMENTAL LAW; WATER POLLUTION

GENERAL WORKS

Crisis Response: Inside Stories on Managing Image Under Siege. Gale Cengage Learning. • 1993. $80.00. Presents first-hand accounts by media relations professionals of major business crises and how they were handled. Topics include the following kinds of crises: environmental, governmental, corporate image, communications, and product.

Environmental Business Management. Klaus North. International Labour Office. • 1997. $31.50. Second edition. (Management Development Series, No. 30).

Environmental Geology: Facing the Challenges of Our Changing Earth. Jon Erickson. Facts on File, Inc. • 2002. Revised edition. (Living Earth Series).

Introduction to Ecological Economics. Robert Costanza and others. Saint Lucie Press. • 1997. $64.95. Advocates environmental policy changes on local, regional, national, and international levels.

The New Economy of Nature: The Quest to Make Conservation Profitable. Gretchen E. Daily and Katherine Ellison. Island Press. • 2002. $25.00. Presents the stories of various individuals who successfully combined the profit motive with conservation of the environment.

Our National Parks and the Search for Sustainability. Bob R. O'Brien. University of Texas Press. • 1999. $40.00. Sustainability is defined as "a balance that allows as many people as possible to visit a park that is kept in as natural a state as possible.".

Pollution: Causes, Effects, and Control. R. M. Harrison. Springer-Verlag. • 2001. $62.00. Fourth edition. Published by The Royal Society of Chemistry. A basic introduction to pollution of air, water, and land. Includes discussions of pollution control technologies.

Recent Advances and Issues in Environmental Science. Joan R. Callahan, editor. Greenwood Publishing Group, Inc. • 1999. $49.95. Includes environmental economic problems, such as saving jobs vs. protecting the environment. (Oryx Frontiers of Science Series.).

Sustainability Perspectives for Resources and Business. Orie L. Loucks and others. Saint Lucie Press. • 1998. $54.95. Discusses the business and economic aspects of environmental protection.

Towards a Sustainable Energy Future. Organization for Economic Cooperation and Development. •

2001. $100.00. Prepared by the International Energy Agency (IEA). Describes various policies for promoting sustainable energy, especially as related to economic development. Discusses "growing concerns about climate change and energy-supply security.".

ABSTRACTS AND INDEXES

Environment Abstracts. Congressional Information Service, Inc. • Monthly. Price varies. Provides multidisciplinary coverage of the world's environmental literature. Incorporates *Acid Rain Abstracts*.

Environment Abstracts Annual: A Guide to the Key Environmental Literature of the Year. Congressional Information Service, Inc. • Annual. $495.00. A yearly cumulation of *Environment Abstracts*.

Environmental Knowledge Base: An Electronic Bibliography Featuring Citations and Abstracts of Scientific and Popular Articles on Environmental Issues, Including Social Policy, Economics, Regulatory, and Legal Topics. Environmental Studies Institute. • Monthly. Price varies. An index to current environmental literature. Formerly *Environmental Periodicals Bibliography*.

Excerpta Medica: Environmental Health and Pollution Control. Elsevier. • 16 times a year. Institutions, $3,246.00 per year. Section 46 of *Excerpta Medica*. Covers air, water, and land pollution and noise control.

NTIS Alerts: Environmental Pollution & Control. National Technical Information Service. • Semimonthly. $245.00 per year. Provides descriptions of government-sponsored research reports and software, with ordering information. Covers the following categories of environmental pollution: air, water, solid wastes, radiation, pesticides, and noise. Formerly *Abstract Newsletter*.

Social Sciences Index. H. W. Wilson Co. • Quarterly, with annual cumulation. Price varies. Indexes more than 400 periodicals covering economics, environmental policy, government, insurance, labor, health care policy, plannning, public administration, public welfare, urban studies, women's issues, criminology, and related topics.

ALMANACS AND YEARBOOKS

Earth Almanac: An Annual Geophysical Review of the State of the Planet. Natalie Goldstein. Greenwood Publishing Group, Inc. • Annual. $69.95. Provides background information, statistics, and a summary of major events relating to the atmosphere, oceans, land, and fresh water.

Environmental Viewpoints. Gale Cengage Learning. • 1993. $195.00. Three volumes. $65.00 per volume. A compendium of excerpts of about 200 articles on a wide variety of environmental topics, selected from both popular and professional periodicals. Arranged alphabetically by topic, with a subject/keyword index.

Gale Environmental Almanac. Gale Cengage Learning. • 1993. $115.00. Contains 15 chapters, each on a broad topic related to the environment, such as "Waste and Recycling." Each chapter has a topical overview, charts, statistics, and illustrations. Includes a glossary of environmental terms and a bibliography.

Land Use and Environment Law Review. West Group. • Annual. $330.00.

State of the World [year]. Worldwatch Institute. • Annual. $16.95. Provides yearly analysis of factors influencing the global environment.

Vital Signs [year]: The Trends That Are Shaping Our Future. Worldwatch Institute. • Annual. $14.95. Provides access to selected indicators showing social, economic, and environmental trends throughout the world. Includes data relating to food, energy, transportation, finance, population, and other topics.

BIBLIOGRAPHIES

The Ecology of Land Use: A Bibliographic Guide. Graham Trelstad. Sage Publications, Inc. • 1994. $10.00.

Using the Agricultural, Environmental, and Food Literature. Barbara S. Hutchinson and Antoinette P. Greider, editors. Marcel Dekker, Inc. • 2002. $125. 00. Serves as a guide to both print and electronic sources of information.

BIOGRAPHICAL SOURCES

World Who is Who and Does What in Environment and Conservation. Nicholas Polunin and Lynn M. Curme. Stylus Publishing, LLC. • 1997. $95.00. Provides biographies of 1,300 individuals considered to be leaders in environmental and conservation areas.

CD-ROM DATABASES

Environment Abstracts on CD-ROM. LEXIS-NEXIS. • Quarterly. $1,295.00 per year. Contains the following CD-ROM databases: *Environment Abstracts, Energy Abstracts,* and *Acid Rain Abstracts.* Length of coverage varies.

Magazine Index Plus. Gale Cengage Learning. • Monthly. $4,000.00 per year (includes InfoTrac workstation). Provides full text on CD-ROM for about 100 popular, general interest magazines and indexing for 300 others. Includes special indexing of reviews and product evaluations. Time period is 1980 to date.

Social Sciences Citation Index. ISI. • Monthly. Price on request. Provides CD-ROM indexing of articles appearing in 1700 leading social science journals worldwide, with additional selections from more than 5700 other journals. Time span is 1992 to date. Coverage includes economics, business, finance, management, communications, demographics, library and information science, political science, sociology, and many other subjects.

Social Sciences Citation Index: Compact Disc Edition with Abstracts. Institute for Scientific Information. • Monthly. Provides CD-ROM indexing and abstracting of "significant articles" from 1,700 social science journals worldwide, with additional selections from 3,200 other journals, 1986 to date. Includes economics, business, finance, management, communications, demographics, information and library science, political science, sociology, and many other subjects.

WILSONDISC: Wilson Social Sciences Abstracts. H. W. Wilson Co. • Monthly. Includes unlimited online access to *Social Sciences Index* through WILSONLINE. Provides CD-ROM indexing from 1983 and abstracting from 1994 of more than 500 periodicals covering economics, area studies, community health, public administration, public welfare, urban studies, and many other topics related to the social sciences.

DIRECTORIES

Gale Environmental Sourcebook: A Guide to Organizations, Agencies, and Publications. Gale Cengage Learning. • 1993. $115.00. Second edition. A directory of print and non-print information sources on a wide variety of environmental topics.

ENCYCLOPEDIAS AND DICTIONARIES

Encyclopedia of Energy. Cutler J. Cleveland, editor. Elsevier, Inc. • 2004. $1,560.00. Six volumes. Covers all aspects of energy sources and energy-related environmental issues.

Encyclopedia of Environmental Science. John Mongillo and Linda Zierdt-Warshaw, editors. Greenwood Publishing Group, Inc. • 2000. $99.95. Provides information on more than 1,000 topics relating to the environment. Includes graphs, tables, maps, illustrations, and 400 Web site addresses.

Encyclopedia of Environmental Science and Engineering. James R. Pfafflin and Edward N. Ziegler, editors. Gordon and Breach Publishing Group. • $798.00. Three volumes.

Encyclopedia of Global Change: Environmental Change and Human Society. Andrew S. Goudie, editor. Oxford University Press. • 2001. $275.00. Two volumes. Contains 300 signed articles on a wide variety of topics relating to changes in the environment and the atmosphere. Includes bibliographies and illustrations.

Encyclopedia of Global Environmental Change. R. E. Munn. John Wiley and Sons, Inc. • 2001. $2,400. 00. Five volumes. Volume five is entitled *Social and Economic Dimensions of Global Environmental Change.*

Environmental Encyclopedia. Gale Cengage Learning. • 2003. $275.00. Third edition. Provides over 1,300 articles on all aspects of the environment. Written in non-technical style.

Macmillan Encyclopedia of the Environment. Stephen R. Kellert, editor. Gale Cengage Learning. • 1997. $400.00. Six volumes.

Pollution A to Z. Gale Cengage Learning. • 2003. $195.00. Two volumes. Provides encyclopedic coverage of many aspects of environmental pollution, including air, water, noise, and soil. (Macmillan Reference USA imprint.).

Unabridged Dictionary of Occupational and Environmental Safety and Health with CD-ROM. Jeffrey W. Vincoli and Kathryn L. Bazan. Lewis Publishers. • 1999. $89.95.

Wiley Encyclopedia of Energy and the Environment. Attilio Bisio and Sharon Boots. John Wiley and Sons, Inc. • 1996. $285.00. Abriged edition. Two volumes. Covers a wide variety of energy and environmental topics, including legal and policy issues. (Encyclopedia of Energy and the Environment Series: Vol. 2).

Wiley Encyclopedia of Environmental Pollution and Cleanup. Robert A. Meyers, editor. John Wiley and Sons, Inc. • 1999. $350.00. Two volumes. Presents generally nontechnical, basic coverage of environmental hazards and methods of detection and cleanup, with consideration of risk assessment, regulatory policy, and economic factors.

HANDBOOKS AND MANUALS

Environmental Accounting: Current Issues, Abstracts, and Bibliography. United Nations Publications. • 1992. Provides guidelines for environmental disclosure in corporate annual reports.

Environmental Engineering. Jeffrey J. Peirce. Elsevier. • 2003. $94.95. Fourth edition.

Environmental Engineering. Joseph A. Salvato and others. John Wiley and Sons, Inc. • 2003. $240.00. Fifth edition. Written for environmental engineers, civil engineers, environmental scientists, public health professionals, and others concerned with the technical aspects of protecting the environment. Covers a wide range of topics, including sanitation management, groundwater contamination, incineration, wastewater treatment, communicable diseases, and noise control.

Handbook of Environmental Health and Safety: Principles and Practices. Herman Koren and Michael S. Bisesi. Lewis Publishers. • 2002. Fourth edition. Two volumes. Price on application.

Industrial Pollution Prevention Handbook. Harry M. Freeman. McGraw-Hill. • 1994. $115.00.

Statistics for the Environment: Statistical Aspects of Health and the Environment. Vic Barnett and others. John Wiley and Sons, Inc. • 1999. $180.00. Two volumes. Vol. 3, $205.00; vol. 4, $225.00. Contains articles on the statistical analysis and interpretation of environmental monitoring and sampling data. Areas covered include meteorology, pollution of the environment, and forest resources. (Statistics for the Environment Series).

INTERNET DATABASES

E: The Environmental Magazine [online]. Earth Action Network, Inc. Phone: (203)854-5559 Fax: (203)866-0602 • URL: http://www.emagazine.com • Web site provides full-text articles from *E: The Environmental Magazine* for a period of about two years. Searching is provided. Alphabetical and subject links are shown for a wide variety of environmental Web sites. Fees: Free.

National Library of Medicine (NLM). National Institutes of Health (NIH). Phone: 888-346-3656 or (301)496-1131 Fax: (301)480-3537 E-mail: access@nlm.nih.gov • URL: http://www.nlm.nih. gov • NLM Web site offers free access through MEDLINE ("PubMed") to about nine million references to articles appearing in some 4,000 biomedical journals, with abstracts. Search interfaces range from "simple keywords to advanced Boolean expressions." The NLM site offers many links to other sources of biomedical and technical information (the National Center for Biotechnology Information, for example). Fees: Free.

ONLINE DATABASES

Aqualine. Cambridge Scientific Abstracts. • Provides online citations and abstracts to a wide variety of literature relating to the aquatic environment, including 400 journals, from 1960 to date. Updating is monthly. Inquire as to online cost and availability.

Newspaper Abstracts Daily. ProQuest Inc. • Provides online coverage (citations and abstracts) of 25 major newspapers. Covers business, economics, current affairs, health, fitness, sports, education, technology, government, consumer affairs, psychology, the arts, and the social sciences. Time period is 1986 to date, with daily updates. Inquire as to online cost and availability.

Wilson Social Sciences Abstracts Online. H. W. Wilson Co. • Provides online abstracting and indexing of more than 500 periodicals covering area studies, community health, public administration, public welfare, urban studies, and many other social science topics. Time period is 1994 to date for abstracts and 1983 to date for indexing, with updates weekly. Inquire as to online cost and availability.

PERIODICALS AND NEWSLETTERS

Amber Waves. Available from U. S. Government Printing Office. • Quarterly. $38.00 per year. Replaces *Agricultural Outlook; Food Review;* and *Rural America.* Provides research and analysis from the U.S. Department of Agriculture's Economic Research Service. Includes economic data on agriculture, food, trade, and environmental factors.

E Magazine: The Environmental. Earth Action Network, Inc. • Bimonthly. $20.00 per year. A popular, consumer magazine providing news, information, and commentary on a wide range of environmental issues.

Ecology. Ecological Society of America. • Monthly. $470.00 per year. All forms of life in relation to environment.

Ecology Law Quarterly. University of California, Berkeley. Boalt Hall School of Law. • Quarterly. Individuals, $30.00 per year; institutions, $54.00 per year; students, $22.00 per year.

EM: A&WMA's Environmental Solutions That Make Good Business Sense. Air and Waste Management Association. • Monthly. Institutions, $299.00 per year; nonprofit and government agencies, $199.00 per year. Newsletter. Provides news of regulations, legislation, and technology relating to the environment, recycling, and waste control. Formerly *Environmental Manager.*

Environment Reporter. The Bureau of National Affairs, Inc. Bureau of National Affairs Inc. • Description: Offers a notification and reference service covering legislative, administrative, judicial, industrial, and technological developments affecting pollution control and environmental protection. Recurring features include columns titled Current Developments, Federal Laws and Regulations, Decisions.

Environment: Where Science and Policy Meet. Scientists' Institute for Public Information. Heldref Publications. • 10 times a year. Individuals, $48.00 per year; institutions, $98.00 per year.

Environmental Business Journal: Strategic Information for a Changing Industry. Environmental Business International, Inc. • Monthly. $495.00 per year. Newsletter. Includes both industrial and financial information relating to individual companies and to the environmental industry in general. Covers air pollution, wat es, U. S. Department of Health and Human Services. Provides conference, workshop, and symposium proceedings, as well as extensive reviews of environmental prospects.

Environmental Health Perspectives. Available from U. S. Government Printing Office. • Monthly. $263.00 per year. Issued by the U.S. Department of Health and Human Services (http://www.dhhs.gov). Contains original research on various aspects of the environment and human health. Includes news of environment-related legislation, regulatory actions, and technological advances.

Environmental Science and Technology. Kluwer Academic Publishers. • Irregular. $120.00.

Journal of Environmental Sciences. Chinese Academy of Sciences, Committee of Environmental Science. IOS Press, Inc. • Six times a year. $470.00 per year.

Journal of Industrial Ecology. Yale University, School of Forestry and Environmental Studies. MIT Press. • Quarterly. Individuals, $55.00 per year; institutions, $140.00 per year. Contains multidisciplinary articles on the relationships between industrial activity and the environment.

Journal of Sustainable Agriculture: Innovations for the Long-Term and Lasting Maintenance of Enhancement of Agricultural Resources, Production and Environmental Quality. Haworth Press, Inc. • Quarterly. Institutions, $285.00 per year. Two volumes. An academic and practical journal concerned with resource depletion and environmental misuse.

Resources. Resources for the Future. • Description: Features articles on renewable resources, energy, climate, quality of the environment, and risk assessment and management. Recurring features include organizational news and book notices.

World Environment Report: News and Information on International Resource Management. Business Publishers, Inc. • Biweekly. $494.00 per year. Newsletter on international developments having to do with the environment, energy, pollution control, waste management, and toxic substances.

World Watch: Working for a Sustainable Future. Worldwatch Institute. • Bimonthly. $25.00 per year. Emphasis is on environmental trends, including developments in population growth, climate change, human behavior, the role of government, and other factors.

RESEARCH CENTERS AND INSTITUTES

Center for Energy and Environmental Studies. Carnegie Mellon University Department of Engineering and Public Policy. Baker Hall 128-A, Pittsburgh, PA 15213. Phone: (412)268-5897 Fax: (412)268-1089 E-mail: rubin@cmu.edu.

Environmental Hazards Management Institute. Environmental Hazards Management Institute. 10 Newmarket Rd., PO Box 932, Durham, NH 03824. Phone: (603)868-1496 Fax: (603)868-1547 E-mail: aborner@ehmi.org • URL: http://www.ehmi.org •

Natural and man-made disasters, global pandemic influenza preparedness or risk avoidance and societal continuity.

Molecular and Environmental Toxicology Center. University of Wisconsin-Madison, Enzyme Institute, Room 290, 1710 University Ave., Madison, WI 53705. Phone: (608)263-5557 Fax: (608)262-5245 E-mail: jefcoate@facstaff.wisc.edu • URL: http://www.wisc.edu/etc/ • Formerly Environmental Toxicology Center.

Urban Land Institute. Urban Land Institute. 1025 Thomas Jefferson St. NW, Ste. 500 W, Washington, DC 20007. Phone: (202)624-7000 Fax: (202)624-7140 E-mail: customerservice@uli.org • URL: http://www.uli.org • Urban land use policy, planning, and development issues, including studies on central city problems, industrial development, new community development, residential developments of all types, taxation, smart growth, shopping center development and economics, metropolitan and urbanized area growth and development, mixed use development, and environmental factors affecting development.

Worldwatch Institute. Worldwatch Institute. 1776 Massachusetts Ave. NW, Washington, DC 20036-1904. Phone: (202)452-1999 or (202)452-1999 Fax: (202)296-7365 E-mail: worldwatch@worldwatch.org • URL: http://www.worldwatch.org • Global trends in the availability and management of both human and natural resources, including research in energy, food policy, population, development, technology, the environment, economics, toxics, and recycling.

STATISTICS SOURCES

Health and Environment in America's Top-Rated Cities: A Statistical Profile. Grey House Publishing. • Biennial. $125.00. Covers 75 U. S. cities. Includes statistical and other data on a wide variety of topics, such as air quality, water quality, recycling, hospitals, physicians, health care costs, death rates, infant mortality, accidents, and suicides.

The Little Green Data Book. The World Bank. • 2003. $15.00. Presents "key environmental data for over 200 countries" in such areas as water quality, air emissions, sanitation, and agriculture.

OECD Environmental Indicators. Organization for Economic Cooperation and Development. • Annual. $27.00. Provides statistical information relating to climate change, air pollution, biodiversity, waste management, water resources, and other environmental topics.

OECD Environmental Outlook. Organization for Economic Cooperation and Development. • Biennial. $65.00. Contains 20-year projections of economic, social, and technological data affecting the environment.

OECD in Figures. Organization for Economic Cooperation and Development. • Annual. $13.00. A "pocket data book" providing a summary of key statistics for OECD countries, including economic growth, employment, education, the environment, and transportation.

Social Statistics of the United States. Mark S. Littman, editor. Bernan Press. • 2000. $65.00. Includes statistical data on population growth, labor force, occupations, environmental trends, leisure time use, income, poverty, taxes, and other economic or demographic topics.

A Statistical Portrait of the United States: Social Conditions and Trends. Mark S. Littman, editor. Bernan Press. • 1998. $89.00. Covers "social, economic, and environmental trends in the United States over the past 25 years." Includes statistical tables, graphs, and analysis relating to such topics as population, income, poverty, wealth, labor, housing, education, healthcare, air/water quality, and government. (Statistical Portrait of the United States: Social Conditions and Trends Series).

Statistical Record of the Environment. Gale Cengage Learning. • 1996. $130.00. Third edition. Provides over 875 charts, tables, and graphs of major environmental statistics, arranged by subject. Covers population growth, hazardous waste, nuclear energy, acid rain, pesticides, and other subjects related to the environment. A keyword index is included. (Gale Environmental Library Series).

U. S. Industry and Trade Outlook. Available from National Technical Information Service. • Annual. $69.95. Produced by the International Trade Administration, U. S. Department of Commerce, in a "public-private" partnership with DRI/McGraw-Hill and Standard & Poor's. Provides basic data, outlook for the current year, and "Long-Term Prospects" (five-year projections) for a wide variety of products and services. Includes high technology industries. Formerly *U. S. Industrial Outlook*.

The World Bank Atlas. World Bank Group. • Annual. $10.00. Contains "color maps, charts, and graphs representing the main social, economic, and environmental indicators for 209 countries and territories" (publisher).

World Development Indicators. The World Bank Group. • Annual. $60.00. Provides data and information on the people, economy, environment, and markets of 148 countries. Emphasis is on statistics relating to major development issues.

TRADE/PROFESSIONAL ASSOCIATIONS

Environmental Management Association. PO Box 610548, Port Huron, MI 48061. Phone: (866)999-4EMA or (810)982-7271 Fax: (313)475-9229 E-mail: bdoetsch@emaweb.org • URL: http://www.emaweb.org • Individuals administering environmental sanitation maintenance programs in industrial plants, commercial and public buildings, institutions, and governmental agencies. Conducts educational programs; operates placement service; compiles statistics.

Friends of the Earth. 1025 Vermont Ave., N.W., Suite 300, Washington, DC 20005. Phone: 877-843-8687 or (202)783-7400 Fax: (202)783-0444 E-mail: foe@foe.org • URL: http://www.foe.org • Promotes protection of the environment and conservation of natural resources. Affiliated with Oceanic Society.

National Association of Environmental Professionals. P.O. Box 2086, Bowie, MD 20718. Phone: (866)251-9902 or (301)860-1140 Fax: (301)860-1141 E-mail: office@naep.org • URL: http://www.naep.org.

OTHER SOURCES

Environment Reporter. BNA, Inc. • Weekly. $3,166.00 per year. 18 looseleaf volumes. Covers legal aspects of wide variety of environmental concerns.

Environmental Law Reporter. Environmental Law Institute. • Monthly. $1,045.00 per year. Seven looseleaf volumes.

ENVIRONMENTAL CONTROL

See: AIR POLLUTION; LAND UTILIZATION; WATER POLLUTION

ENVIRONMENTAL LAW

GENERAL WORKS

Environmental Law in a Nutshell. Roger W. Findley. West Group. • 2000. $23.50. Fifth edition. (Nutshell Series).

Environmental Policy in the 1990s: Reform or Reaction?. Norman Vig and Michael Kraft. CQ Press. • 1996. $43.95 Third edition.

Environmental Politics and Policy. Walter A.

Rosenbaum. CQ Press. • 2001. $31.95. Fifth edition.

Public Policies for Environmental Protection. Paul R. Portney, editor. Resources for the Future. • 2000. $29.95. Second edition. A discussion of issues, progress, and problems in the regulation of air pollution, water pollution, hazardous wastes, and toxic substances. Economic factors are emphasized.

ABSTRACTS AND INDEXES

Current Law Index: Multiple Access to Legal Periodicals. Gale Cengage Learning. • Monthly. $725.00 per year. Produced in cooperation with the American Association of Law Libraries. Indexes more than 900 law journals, legal newspapers, and specialty publications from the U.S., Canada, U.K., Ireland, Australia, and New Zealand.

Environment Abstracts. Congressional Information Service, Inc. • Monthly. Price varies. Provides multidisciplinary coverage of the world's environmental literature. Incorporates *Acid Rain Abstracts.*

Environment Abstracts Annual: A Guide to the Key Environmental Literature of the Year. Congressional Information Service, Inc. • Annual. $495.00. A yearly cumulation of *Environment Abstracts.*

Index to Legal Periodicals and Books. H. W. Wilson Co. • Monthly. $490.00 per year. Quarterly and annual cumulations.

BIBLIOGRAPHIES

Encyclopedia of Legal Information Sources. Gale Cengage Learning. • 1992. $180.00. Second edition. Lists more than 23,000 law-related information sources, including print, nonprint, and organizational.

CD-ROM DATABASES

Environment Abstracts on CD-ROM. LEXIS-NEXIS. • Quarterly. $1,295.00 per year. Contains the following CD-ROM databases: *Environment Abstracts, Energy Abstracts,* and *Acid Rain Abstracts.* Length of coverage varies.

LegalTrac. Gale Cengage Learning. • Monthly. $5,000.00 per year. Price includes workstation. Provides CD-ROM indexing of periodical literature relating to legal matters from 1980 to date. Corresponds to online *Legal Resource Index.*

PAIS on CD-ROM. Public Affairs Information Service, Inc. • Quarterly. $1,995.00 per year. Provides a CD-ROM version of the online service, *PAIS International.* Contains over 500,000 citations to the literature of contemporary social, political, and economic issues.

WILSONDISC: Index to Legal Periodicals and Books. H. W. Wilson Co. • Monthly. Includes unlimited online access to *Index to Legal Periodicals* through WILSONLINE. Contains CD-ROM indexing of more than 1,400 English language legal periodicals from 1981 to date and 2,500 books.

DIRECTORIES

Directory of Environmental Attorneys. Aspen Publishers, Inc. • 1994. $195.00.

Law and Legal Information Directory. Gale Cengage Learning. • Annual. $440.00. Contains a wide range of sources of legal information, such as associations, law schools, courts, federal agencies, referral services, libraries, publishers, and research centers. There is a separate chapter for each of 23 types of information source or service.

Lawyer's Register International by Specialties and Fields of Law Including a Directory of Corporate Counsel. Lawyer's Register Publishing Co. • Annual. $359.00. Three volumes. Referral source for law firms.

HANDBOOKS AND MANUALS

Environmental Compliance Handbook. Jacob I. Bregman and Robert D. Edell. CRC Press LLC. • 2001. $99.95. Second edition. Provides practical information and advice on complying with the National Environmental Policy Act (NEPA) and other federal and state environmental laws and regulations. Includes checklists, glossaries, and references.

INTERNET DATABASES

Lexis.com Research System. Lexis-Nexis Group. Phone: 800-227-4908 or (937)865-6800 Fax: (937)865-6909 E-mail: webmaster@prod.lexis-nexis.com • URL: http://www.lexis.com • Fee-based Web site offers extensive searching of a wide variety of legal sources. Additional features include Daily Opinion Service, lexis.com Bookstore, Career Center, CLE Center, Law Schools, and Practice Pages ("Pages specific to areas of specialty").

ONLINE DATABASES

Environmental Law Reporter [online]. Environmental Law Institute. • Provides full text online of *Environmental Law Reporter,* covering administrative materials, news, pending legislation, statutes, bibliography, etc. Time periods vary. Inquire as to online cost and availability.

Index to Legal Periodicals and Books (Online). H. W. Wilson Co. • Broad coverage of law journals and books 1981 to date. Monthly updates. Inquire as to online cost and availability.

Legal Resource Index. Gale Cengage Learning. • Broad coverage of law literature appearing in legal, business, and other periodicals, 1980 to date. Daily updates. Inquire as to online cost and availability.

PAIS International. Public Affairs Information Service, Inc. • Corresponds to the former printed publications, *PAIS Bulletin* (1976-90) and *PAIS Foreign Language Index* (1972-90), and to the current *PAIS International in Print* (1991 to date). Covers economic, political, and sociological material appearing in periodicals, books, government documents, and other publications. Updating is monthly. Inquire as to online cost and availability.

PERIODICALS AND NEWSLETTERS

Environmental Health Perspectives. Available from U. S. Government Printing Office. • Monthly. $263.00 per year. Issued by the U.S. Department of Health and Human Services (http://www.dhhs.gov). Contains original research on various aspects of the environment and human health. Includes news of environment-related legislation, regulatory actions, and technological advances.

Environmental Policy Alert. Inside Washington Publishers. • Description: Tracks environmental legislation, regulation, and litigation. Recurring features include interviews and news of research.

RESEARCH CENTERS AND INSTITUTES

Environmental Law Institute. Environmental Law Institute. 2000 L St. NW, Ste. 620, Suite 200, Washington, DC 20036. Phone: (202)939-3800 Fax: (202)939-3868 E-mail: carothers@eli.org • URL: http://www2.eli.org/index.cfm • Legal, administrative, economic, scientific, and technical aspects of environmental policy in such areas as enforcement, air and water pollution, toxic substances, hazardous wastes, surface mining, wetlands, and environmental management. Research projects include studies on regulatory enforcement and reform, Superfund implementation, economics, international control strategies and training for professionals, and land use.

Institute for Environmental Negotiation. University of Virginia, P.O. Box 400179, Charlottesville, VA 22904-4179. Phone: (434)924-1970 Fax: (434)924-0231 E-mail: ed7k@virginia.edu • URL: http://www.virginia/edu • Research activities are related to the resolution of environmental disputes through negotiation, mediation, and consensus building.

Natural Resources Defense Council. Natural Resources Defense Council. 40 W 20th St., New York, NY 10011. Phone: (212)727-2700 Fax: (212)727-1773 E-mail: nrdcinfo@nrdc.org • URL: http://www.nrdc.org • Use of the judicial system to enforce environmental protection laws. Environmental policy studies, including studies related to public health and the environment, public lands and the coast, nuclear energy and weapons, energy conservation, and the global environment. Specific concerns include air quality, acid rain, airborne toxic pollutants, metropolitan air pollution, stratospheric ozone loss, solid waste disposal, water pollution, sewage treatment, industrial pollution, hazardous waste disposal, drinking water, pesticide policy, national forest management, agricultural resource conservation, public lands protection, irrigation policy, endangered species conservation, offshore oil leasing, shoreline protection, sea level rise, Nuclear Test Ban verification, nuclear weapons, environmental effects of nuclear production, nuclear winter, energy conservation, energy efficiency of appliances, energy efficient buildings, habitat protection, desertification, deforestation, wetlands conservation, international wildlife trade, international environmental treaties, Russian environmental law exchange, urban issues, environmental justice, Brownfield's redevelopment, and transportation.

TRADE/PROFESSIONAL ASSOCIATIONS

Association of Local Air Pollution Control Officials. 444 N Capitol St., NW, Ste. 307, Washington, DC 20001. Phone: (202)624-7864 Fax: (202)624-7863 E-mail: 4clnair@4cleanair.org • URL: http://www.4cleanairworld.org.

Association of State and Interstate Water Pollution Control Administrators. 750 1st St., NE, Ste. 1010, Washington, DC 20002. Phone: (202)898-0905 Fax: (202)898-0929 E-mail: c.fortier@asiwpca.org • URL: http://www.asiwpca.org.

National Conference of Local Environmental Health Administrators. c/o University of Washington, Dept. of Environmental Health, Campus Box 357234, Seattle, WA 98195-7234. Phone: (206)616-2097 Fax: (206)543-8123 E-mail: ctreser@u.washington.edu • URL: http://www.depts.washington.edu/clehaweb • Affiliated with National Environmental Health Association. Formerly Conference of Local Environmental Health Administrators.

OTHER SOURCES

Environment Reporter. BNA, Inc. • Weekly. $3,166.00 per year. 18 looseleaf volumes. Covers legal aspects of wide variety of environmental concerns.

Environmental Law Reporter. Environmental Law Institute. • Monthly. $1,045.00 per year. Seven looseleaf volumes.

ENVIRONMENTAL POLLUTION

See: AIR POLLUTION; WATER POLLUTION

EQUAL EMPLOYMENT OPPORTUNITY

See also: AFFIRMATIVE ACTION PROGRAMS; EMPLOYMENT OF OLDER WORKERS; EMPLOYMENT OF WOMEN

GENERAL WORKS

Breaking Through the Glass Ceiling: Women in Management. Linda Wirth. International Labour Organization. • 2001. $16.95. Portrays "national and international efforts to improve equal opportunities amd promote gender equality in management." Includes statistical information and discussion of earnings gaps, recruitment of women, education, training, and career-building strategies for women.

EEO Law and Personnel Practices. Arthur Gutman. Sage Publications, Inc. • 2000. $93.95. Second edition. Discusses the practical effect of federal regulations dealing with race, color, religion, sex, national origin, age, and disability. Explains administrative procedures, litigation actions, and penalties. (Management Studies Series).

Employment Equity and Affirmative Action: An International Comparison. Harish C. Jain and others. M. E. Sharpe, Inc. • 2003. $66.95. Describes and compares the affirmative action and employment equity policies of six countries: the U. S., Canada, Great Britain, India, South Africa, and Malaysia.

Labor and Employment Law: Text and Cases. David P. Twomey. South-Western. • 2000. $93.94. 11th edition. (Business Law Series).

Women, Gender, and Work: What is Equality and How Do We Get There?. Martha F. Loutfi, editor. International Labour Organization • 2001. $26.95. A collection of articles from the *International Labour Review* covering such topics as equal opportunity for women, family concerns, legal issues, the glass ceiling, wage inequality, and sexual harassment in the workplace. Includes statistical data.

ABSTRACTS AND INDEXES

Human Resources Abstracts: An International Information Service. Sage Publications, Inc. • Quarterly. Institutions, $968.00 per year; includes print and online editions.

DIRECTORIES

National Directory of Minority-Owned Business Firms. Available from Gale Cengage Learning. • 2003. $295.00. 12th edition. Published by Business Research Services. Includes more than 30,000 minority-owned businesses.

National Directory of Women-Owned Business Firms. Gale Cengage Learning. • 2003. $295.00. 12th edition. Published by Business Research Services. Includes more than 28,000 businesses owned by women.

HANDBOOKS AND MANUALS

Employer's Guide to Discrimination Laws. Maureen F. Moore. LexisNexis Matthew Bender. • 2003. $28.00, including CD-ROM. Edited for business owners and managers. Provides a concise guide to federal discrimination laws relating to race, sex, age, disability, pregnancy, religion, and national origin.

Equal Employment Opportunity Compliance Guide. John F. Buckley. Aspen Publishers, Inc. • 2002. $175.00.

Equality in the Workplace: An Equal Opportunities Handbook for Trainers. Helen Collins. Blackwell Publishing. • 1995. $55.95. (Human Resource Management in Action Series).

Federal Civil Rights Acts. West Group. • Semiannual. $410.00 per year. Two looseleaf volumes. Covers current legislation relating to a wide range of civil rights issues, including discrimination in employment, housing, property rights, and voting.

Investigations in the Workplace. Eugene F. Ferraro. CRC Press. • 2004. $79.95. Written for security professionals, lawyers, and human resource directors. Explains how to properly conduct internal investigations in the private sector and avoid litigation. Such investigations may relate to loss prevention, asset protection, or employee rights issues. (Imprint: Auerbach Publications.).

Manual on Employment Discrimination Law and Civil Rights Action in the Federal Courts. West Group. • Biennial. $236.00. Two looseleaf volumes.

ONLINE DATABASES

Labordoc. International Labour Organization. • Indexing of labor literature and the publications of the International Labour Organization, 1965 to

present. Monthly updates. Inquire as to online cost and availability.

PERIODICALS AND NEWSLETTERS

Employment Practices Update. West Group. • Description: Discusses such topics as employment decisions, willful violations, reduction-in-force terminations, age discrimination, and erroneous credibility determinations.

The Equal Employer. Y. S. Publications, Inc. • Biweekly. $245.00 per year. Newsletter on fair employment practices.

Fair Employment Compliance: A Confidential Letter to Management. Management Resources, Inc. • Semimonthly. $245.00 per year. Newsletter.

Fair Employment Report. Clarity Publishing. • Description: Focuses on developments on the state and national levels regarding employment practices and discrimination. Emphasizes important legal decisions and governmental activities, particularly those of the Equal Employment Opportunity Commission, the Office of Federal Contract Compliance Programs, the Supreme Court, federal courts, Congress, state legislatures, state courts, and state agencies. Covers the efforts of businesses to comply with EEO, affirmative action, and diversity standards.

PE Update. Project Equality. • Quarterly. Membership. Formerly *Project Equality Update.*

RESEARCH CENTERS AND INSTITUTES

Human Resources Institute. University of Alabama. P.O. 870225, Tuscaloosa, AL 35487. Phone: (205)348-8939 Fax: (205)348-6995 E-mail: jcashman@cba.ua.edu • URL: http://www.ua.edu.

Industrial Relations Section. Princeton University, Firestone Library, Pinceton, NJ 08544. Phone: (609)258-4040 Fax: (609)258-2907 • URL: http://www.irs.princeton.edu/ • Fields of research include labor supply, manpower training, unemployment, and equal employment opportunity.

Women Employed Institute. Women Employed Institute. 111 N Wabash, 13th Fl., Chicago, IL 60602. Phone: (312)782-3902 Fax: (312)782-5249 E-mail: info@womenemployed.org • URL: http://www.womenemployed.org • Economic status of working women, working women and the law, sexual harassment in the workplace, equal employment opportunity, women's access to vocational education and job training, comparable worth, working mothers, and career development.

STATISTICS SOURCES

Job Patterns for Minorities and Women in Private Industry. Available from U. S. Government Printing Office. • Annual. $61.00. Issued by the Equal Employment Opportunity Commission (http://www.eeoc.gov). "Provides statistical information on the composition of the United States workforce in private industry by sex, race, and ethnic category.".

TRADE/PROFESSIONAL ASSOCIATIONS

American Association for Affirmative Action. 11250 Roger Bacon Dr., No. 8, Reston, WA 20190. Phone: 800-252-8952 Fax: (703)435-4390 E-mail: execdir@affirmativeaction.org • URL: http://www.affirmativeaction.org.

OTHER SOURCES

BNA Fair Employment Practices. BNA, Inc. • Biweekly. $938.00 per year. Looseleaf service.

Corporate Compliance Series. Joseph E. Murphy and Paul H. Dawes. West Group. • $1,210.00. 12 looseleaf volumes. Covers criminal and civil liability problems for corporations. Includes employee safety, product liability, pension requirements, securities violations, equal employment opportunity issues, intellectual property, employee hiring and firing, and other corporate compliance topics.

EEOC Compliance Manual (Equal Employment Opportunity Commission). BNA, Inc. • Irregular. $316.00 per year. Looseleaf service. Guide to federal Equal Employment Opportunity Commission activities.

Employment Discrimination: Law and Litigation. Lexis Law Publishing. • $185.00 per year. Two looseleaf volumes. Periodic supplementation. Covers employment provisions of the Civil Rights Act, the Equal Pay Act, and related topics.

Human Resources Management Whole. CCH, Inc. • Nine looseleaf volumes. $1,572 per year. Includes monthly updates. Components are *Ideas and Trends Newsletter, Employment Relations, Compensation, Equal Employment Opportunity, Personnel Practices/Communications* and *OSHA Compliance.* Components are available separately.

Larson's Employment Discrimination. LexisNexis Matthew Bender. • $1,487.00. 10 looseleaf volumes. Treatise on both substantive and procedural law governing employment discrimination based on sex, age, race, religion, national origin, etc.

Practical Guide to Equal Employment Opportunity. American Lawyer Media, Inc. • Looseleaf. $199.00. Two volumes. Updated as needed. Serves as a legal manual for EEO compliance. "Volume one analyzes discrimination on the basis of race, religion, sex, age, and physical handicaps including AIDS." Provides information relating to an employer's liability in cases of sexual harassment of employees, including same-sex harassment. Covers affirmative action and reverse discrimination issues. Volume two contains model affirmative action plans, a sample EEO compliance manual, checklists, and other documents. (Law Journal Press).

EQUIPMENT LEASING

See also: RENTAL SERVICES

ABSTRACTS AND INDEXES

Business Periodicals Index. H. W. Wilson Co. • 11 times a year. Quarterly and annual cumulations. Price varies.

CD-ROM DATABASES

WILSONDISC: Wilson Business Abstracts. H. W. Wilson Co. • Monthly. Includes unlimited online access to *Wilson Business Abstracts* through WILSONLINE. Provides CD-ROM "cover-to-cover" abstracting and indexing of over 600 prominent business periodicals. Indexing is from 1982, abstracting from 1990. (*Business Periodicals Index* without abstracts is available on CD-ROM at $1,495 per year.).

DIRECTORIES

Leasing Sourcebook: The Directory of the U. S. Capital Equipment Leasing Industry. Bibliotechnology Systems and Publishing Co. • Every 12-18 months. $135.00. Lists approximately 5,200 capital equipment leasing companies.

HANDBOOKS AND MANUALS

Equipment Leasing. LexisNexis Matthew Bender. • $478.00. Three looseleaf volumes. Periodic supplementation. Covers vital information needed to structure a transaction involving an equipment lease.

Equipment Leasing-Leveraged Leasing. Practising Law Institute. • $350.00. Three looseleaf volumes. Annual revisions. Contains "practical analyses of the legal, tax, accounting, and financial aspects of equipment leasing." Includes forms, agreements, and checklists.

ONLINE DATABASES

Management Contents. Gale Cengage Learning. • Covers a wide range of management, financial, marketing, personnel, and administrative topics. About 150 leading business journals are indexed and abstracted from 1974 to date, with monthly updating. Inquire as to online cost and availability.

Trade & Industry Database. Gale Cengage Learning. • Provides indexing of business periodicals, January 1981 to date. Daily updates. (Full text articles from some periodicals are available online, 1983 to date. Inquire as to online cost and availability).

Wilson Business Abstracts Online. H. W. Wilson Co. • Indexes and abstracts 600 major business periodicals, plus the *Wall Street Journal* and the business section of the *New York Times.* Indexing is from 1982, abstracting from 1990, with the two newspapers included from 1993. Updated weekly. Inquire as to online cost and availability. (*Business Periodicals Index* without abstracts is also available online.).

PERIODICALS AND NEWSLETTERS

Equipment Leasing Newsletter. American Lawyer Media, Inc. • Monthly. $269.00 per year. Newsletter. Covers a wide range of legal topics relating to the leasing of business and industrial equipment, including taxation, insurance, dealing with banks, lease securitization, and letter of credit issues. (A Law Journal Newsletter, formerly published by Leader Publications).

STATISTICS SOURCES

WEFA Industrial Monitor. John Wiley and Sons, Inc. • Annual. $65.00. Prepared by industry analysts at WEFA, an economic forecasting and consulting firm (originally Wharton Econometric Forecasting Associates). Contains discussions of the outlook for major U. S. industries, with many 10-year forecasts (WEFA Web site is http://www.wefa.com).

ERGONOMICS

See: HUMAN ENGINEERING

ESSENTIAL OILS

See: ADDITIVES AND FLAVORINGS; PERFUME INDUSTRY

ESTATE PLANNING

See also: INHERITANCE TAX; TAX PLANNING

GENERAL WORKS

How to Avoid Financial Tangles. American Institute for Economic Research. • 2001. $8.00. Provides basic information and advice on such topics as property ownership, taxes, wills, trusts, insurance, record retention, and professional assistance. (Economic Education Bulletin.).

Smart Questions to Ask Your Financial Advisers. Lynn Brenner. Bloomberg. • 1997. $19.95. Provides practical advice on how to deal with financial planners, stockbrokers, insurance agents, and lawyers. Some of the areas covered are investments, estate planning, tax planning, house buying, prenuptial agreements, divorce arrangements, loss of a job, and retirement. (Bloomberg Personal Bookshelf Series).

Staying Wealthy: Strategies for Protecting Your Assets. Brian H. Breuel. Bloomberg. • 1998. $21.95. Presents ideas for estate planning and personal wealth preservation. Includes case studies. (Bloomberg Personal Bookshelf Series).

ABSTRACTS AND INDEXES

Insurance Periodicals Index. Specials Libraries Association, Insurance and Employees Benefits Div. NILS Publishing Co. • Annual. $250.00. Compiled by the Insurance and Employee Benefits Div., Special Libraries Association. A yearly index of over 15,000 articles from about 35 insurance periodicals. Arrangement is by subject, with an index to authors.

BIBLIOGRAPHIES

Insurance and Employee Benefits Literature. Special Libraries Association, Insurance and Employee Benefits Div. • Bimonthly. $15.00 per year. Lists a wide variety of literature in all branches of the insurance industry. Includes annotations.

CD-ROM DATABASES

Authority Tax and Estate Planning Library. LexisNexis/Matthew Bender. • Periodic revisions. Price on request. CD-ROM contains updated full text of *Bender's Payroll Tax Guide, Depreciation Handbook, Federal Income Taxation of Corporations, Tax Planning for Corporations, Modern Estate Planning, Planning for Large Estates, Murphy's Will Clauses, Tax & Estate Planning for the Elderly*, and 12 other Matthew Bender publications. The Internal Revenue Code is also included.

ENCYCLOPEDIAS AND DICTIONARIES

Dictionary of Finance and Investment Terms. John Downes. Barron's Educational Series, Inc. • 2002. $14.95. Sixth edition. Provides clear explanations of more than 5,000 business, banking, financial, investment, and tax terms. Includes a separate list of financial abbreviations and acronyms. (Business Dictionaries Series).

Encyclopedia of Estate Planning. Robert S. Holzman. Boardroom Books. • 1995. $59.00. Second revised edition.

Glossary of Insurance Policy Terms. Organization for Economic Cooperation and Development. • 1999. $30.00. "The selected topics range from insurance policy regulation/supervision to general trade issues and include technical terms related to issues such as claims, premiums, and provisions." Edited for government, academic, business, and insurance organizations.

FINANCIAL RATIOS

Financial Planning for Older Clients. James E. Pearman. CCH, Inc. • 2000. $49.00. Covers income sources, social security, Medicare, Medicaid, investment planning, estate planning, and other retirement-related topics. Edited for accountants, attorneys, and other financial advisors. (Solutions for Professional Advisors Series).

HANDBOOKS AND MANUALS

Asset Protection Planning Guide: A State-of-the-Art Approach to Integrated Estate Planning. Barry S. Engel and others. CCH, Inc. • 2001. $99.00. Provides advice for attorneys, trust officers, accountants, and others engaged in financial planning for protection of assets.

CCH Financial and Estate Planning. CCH, Inc. • $895.00 per year. Four looseleaf volumes. Semimonthly updates.

CCH Financial and Estate Planning Guide. CCH, Inc. • Annual. $63.00. Contains four main parts: General Principles and Techniques, Special Situations, Building the Estate, and Planning Aids.

The Complete Probate Kit. Jens C. Appel and others. John Wiley and Sons, Inc. • 1991, $35.00. A practical guide to settling estates. Provides summaries of the applicable state laws and definitions of relevant terms.

Estate and Retirement Planning Answer Book. William D. Mitchell. Aspen Publishers, Inc. • 2000. $145.00. Third edition. Basic questions and answers by a lawyer.

Estate Plan Book 2000. William S. Moore. American Institute for Economic Research. • 2000. $10.00. Revision of 1997 edition. Part one: "Basic Estate Planning." Part two: "Reducing Taxes on the Disposition of Your Estate." Part three: "Putting it All Together: Examples of Estate Plans." Provides succinct information on wills, trusts, tax planning, and gifts. (Economic Education Bulletin.).

Estate Planning After The Economic Growth and Tax Relief Reconciliation Act of 2001: A Supplement to The Estate Plan Book 2000. William S. Moore. American Institute for Economic Research. • 2001. Included with *The Estate Plan Book 2000* ($10.00). Contains two sections: "Major Changes Bearing on Estate Planning Under the New Act" and "Estate Planning Under the New Act" (Economic Education Bulletin).

Estate Planning Primer. Ralph G. Miller. ViewPlan, Inc. • 1994. $99.00. Eighth edition. Written for attorneys and other estate planning professionals. Includes tables, sample tax forms, legal documents, and client letters. letters.

How to Save Time and Taxes Preparing Fiduciary Income Tax Returns. LexisNexis Matthew Bender. • Biennial. $272.00 per year. Looseleaf service. Comprehensive coverage of the federal income taxation of trusts and estates.

Individual Retirement Account Answer Book. Donald R. Levy and others. Aspen Publishers, Inc. • 2002. $195.00. Ninth edition. Periodic supplementation available. Questions and answers include information about contributions, distributions, rollovers, Roth IRAs, SIMPLE IRAs (Savings Incentive Match Plans for Employees), Education IRAs, and SEPs (Simplified Employee Pension plans). Chapters are provided on retirement planning, estate planning, and tax planning.

Inheritor's Handbook: A Definitive Guide for Beneficiaries. Dan Rottenberg. Bloomberg. • 1998. $23.95. Covers both financial and emotional issues faced by beneficiaries. (Bloomberg Personal Bookshelf Series.).

Life Insurance Answer Book: For Qualified Plans and Estate Planning. Gary S. Lesser and Lawrence C. Starr, editors. Aspen Publishers, Inc. • 2002. $175.00. Third edition. Four parts by various authors cover life insurance in general, qualified plans, fiduciary responsibility, and estate planning. Includes sample documents, worksheets, and information in Q&A form.

The Living Trust: The Failproof Way to Pass Along Your Estate to Your Heirs Without Lawyers, Courts, or the Probate System. Henry W. Abts. McGraw-Hill. • 2002. $24.95. Third edition.

Modern Estate Planning. Ernest D. Fiore and M. Friedlich. LexisNexis Matthew Bender. • $1,008.00. Five looseleaf volumes. Periodic supplementation.

Tools and Techniques of Financial Planning. Stephan Leimberg and others. National Underwriter Co. • 2004. $74.95.

U. S. Master Estate and Gift Tax Guide. CCH, Inc. • Annual. $55.00. Covers federal estate and gift taxes, including generation-skipping transfer tax plans. Includes tax tables and sample filled-in tax return forms.

INTERNET DATABASES

CCH Essentials: An Internet Tax Research and Primary Source Library. CCH, Inc. Phone: 800-248-3248 or (773)866-6000 Fax: 800-224-8299 or (773)866-3608 E-mail: cust_serv@cch.com • URL: http://tax.cch.com/essentials • Fee-based Web site provides full-text coverage of federal tax law and regulations, including rulings, procedures, tax court decisions, and IRS publications, announcements, notices, and penalties. Includes explanation, analysis, tax planning guides, and a daily tax news service. Searching is offered, including citation search.

PERIODICALS AND NEWSLETTERS

Broker World. Insurance Publications, Inc. • Bimonthly. $6.00 per year. Edited for independent insurance agents and brokers. Special feature issue topics include annuities, disability insurance, estate planning, and life insurance.

Estate Planner's Alert. RIA. • Monthly. $140.00 per year. Newsletter. Covers the tax aspects of personal finance, including home ownership, investments, insurance, retirement planning, and charitable giving. Formerly *Estate and Financial Planners Alert.*

Estate Planning Journal. RIA. • Monthly. $295.00 per year.

Estate Planning Review. CCH Inc. • Description: Monthly newsletter covering estate and financial planning issues for individuals. Includes coverage of retirement planning, insurance planning and investments.

Financial Planning: The Magazine for Financial Service Professionals. Thomson Media. • Monthly. $79.00 per year. Edited for independent financial planners and insurance agents. Covers retirement planning, estate planning, tax planning, and insurance, including long-term healthcare considerations. Special features include a Retirement Planning Issue, Mutual Fund Performance Survey, and Variable Life and Annuity Survey.

Jounal of Finacial Services Professionals. Society of Financial Services Professional. • Bimonthly. $95.00 per year. Provides information on life insurance and financial planning, including estate planning, retirement, tax planning, trusts, business insurance, long-term care insurance, disability insurance, and employee benefits. Formerly (American Society of CLU and Ch F C Journal).

Journal of Practical Estate Planning. CCH, Inc. • Bimonthly. $215.00 per year. Edited for attorneys and other estate planning professionals.

Journal of Retirement Planning. CCH, Inc. • Bimonthly. $179.00 per year. Emphasis is on retirement and estate planning advice provided by lawyers and accountants as part of their practices.

Robb Report Worth: Wealth in Perspective. CurtCo Robb Media. • Monthly. $54.95 per year. Glossy magazine featuring articles for the affluent on personal financial management, investments, estate planning, trusts, private bankers, taxes, travel, yachts, and lifestyle. Formerly *Worth: Financial Intelligence.*

OTHER SOURCES

AACE International. Transactions of the Annual Meetings. American Assoiciation of Cost Engineers. AACE International. • Annual. Price varies. Contains texts of papers presented at AACE meetings.

Estate and Personal Financial Planning. West Group. • Quarterly. $980.00 per year. Newsletter.

Estate Planning. American Lawyer Media, Inc. • Looseleaf. $239.00. Two volumes. Updated as needed. Covers all legal aspects of estate planning, including wills, trusts, taxation, gifts, charitable contributions, family business considerations, and insurance. Includes forms and checklists. (Law Journal Press).

Estate Planning and Taxation Coordinator. RIA. • Biweekly. $1,290.00 per year. Nine looseleaf volumes. Includes *Estate Planner's Alert* and *Lifetime Planning Alert.*

Estate Planning: Inheritance Taxes. Prentice Hall PTR. • Five looseleaf volumes. Periodic supplementation. Price on application.

Estate Planning Program. Prentice Hall PTR. • Two looseleaf volumes. Periodic supplementation. Price on application. Includes checklists and forms.

Estate Planning Strategies After Estate Tax Reform: Insights and Analysis. Charles D. Fox and Thomas W. Aberdroth. CCH, Inc. • 2001. $45.00. Produced by the Estate Planning Department of Schiff, Hardin & Waite. Covers estate planning techniques and opportunities resulting from tax legislation of 2001.

Estate Planning Under the New Law: What You Need to Know. CCH, Inc. • 2001. $7.00. Booklet

summarizes significant changes in estate planning brought about by tax legislation of 2001.

Estate Planning: Wills, Trusts and Forms. RIA. • Looseleaf service. Includes bimonthly updates.

Federal Estate and Gift Tax Reports. CCH, Inc. • Weekly. $578.00. Three looseleaf volumes.

Fiduciary Tax Guide. CCH, Inc. • Monthly. $478.00 per year. Looseleaf service. Covers federal income taxation of estates, trusts, and beneficiaries. Provides information on gift and generation- skipping taxation.

Financial and Estate Planning: Analysis, Strategies and Checklists. CCH, Inc. • 4 looseleaf volumes. Price on application. services.

How to Plan for a Secure Retirement. Elias Zuckerman and others. Consumer Reports Books. • 2000. $29.95. Covers pension plans, health insurance, estate planning, retirement communities, and related topics. (Consumer Reports Money Guide.).

ESTATE TAX

See: INHERITANCE TAX

ESTIMATING

GENERAL WORKS

Cost Estimating. Rodney D. Stewart. John Wiley and Sons, Inc. • 1991. $150.00. Second edition. Discusses high technology engineering cost forecasting, including the estimation of software costs. (New Dimensions in Engineering Series).

Fundamentals of Construction Estimating. David Pratt. Delmar Learning. • 1995. $93.95. (Trade, Technology and Industry Series).

ABSTRACTS AND INDEXES

Business Periodicals Index. H. W. Wilson Co. • 11 times a year. Quarterly and annual cumulations. Price varies.

NTIS Alerts: Building Industry Technology. National Technical Information Service. • Semimonthly. $210.00 per year. Provides descriptions of government-sponsored research reports and software, with ordering information. Covers architecture, construction management, building materials, maintenance, furnishings, and related subjects. Formerly *Abstract Newsletter.*

CD-ROM DATABASES

ABI/INFORM. PROQUEST. • Monthly. Provides CD-ROM indexing and abstracting of worldwide business literature. Archival discs are available from 1971. Formerly *ABI/INFORM OnDisc.*

WILSONDISC: Business Periodicals Index. H. W. Wilson Co. • Monthly. Provides CD-ROM indexing of business periodicals from 1982 to date. Price includes online service.

DIRECTORIES

AACE International-Directory of Members. AACE International. • Annual. $20.00 per year. 6,000 cost engineers, estimators, and cost management professionals worldwide.

HANDBOOKS AND MANUALS

Basic Estimating for Construction. James A. Fatzinger. Prentice Hall PTR. • 2000. $69.95. Covers electrical, plumbing, concrete, masonry, framing, etc. Includes a glossary and typical bid forms.

Construction Contractors' Survival Guide. Thomas C. Schleifer. John Wiley and Sons, Inc. • 1990. $99.00. (Practical Construction Guides Series).

Estimating for Home Builders. Jerry Householder. Builderbooks. • 1998. $30.80. Third edition. Describes the process of developing complete cost estimates-and the shortcut methods-to ensure success in the building business.

Estimating in Building Construction. Frank R. Dagostino and Leslie Feigenbaum. Prentice Hall PTR. • 2003. Sixth edition. Price on application.

Walker's Building Estimator's Reference Book. Frank R. Walker Co. • 2002. $75.00. 27th edition.

ONLINE DATABASES

Trade & Industry Database. Gale Cengage Learning. • Provides indexing of business periodicals, January 1981 to date. Daily updates. (Full text articles from some periodicals are available online, 1983 to date. Inquire as to online cost and availability).

Wilson Business Abstracts Online. H. W. Wilson Co. • Indexes and abstracts 600 major business periodicals, plus the *Wall Street Journal* and the business section of the *New York Times.* Indexing is from 1982, abstracting from 1990, with the two newspapers included from 1993. Updated weekly. Inquire as to online cost and availability. (*Business Periodicals Index* without abstracts is also available online.).

PERIODICALS AND NEWSLETTERS

Cost Engineering: The Journal of Cost Estimating, Cost Control, and Project Management. • Monthly. $60.00 per year. Subjects include cost estimation and cost control.

Design Cost Data: The Cost Estimating Magazine for Architects, Builders and Specifiers. L. M. Rector Corp. • Bimonthly. $64.80 per year. Provides a preliminary cost estimating system for architects, contractors, builders, and developers, utilizing historical data. Includes case studies of actual costs. Formerly *Design Cost and Data.*

The National Estimator. Society of Cost Estimating and Analysis. • Quarterly. $30.00 per year. Covers government contract estimating.

PRICE SOURCES

Means Facilities Construction Cost Data. RSMeans. • Annual. $236.95.. Provides costs for use in building estimating.

Means Interior Cost Data. RSMeans. • Annual. $108.95

Means Repair and Remodeling Cost Data. RSMeans. • Annual. $95.95.

Means Residential Cost Data. RSMeans. • Annual. $95.95.

National Building Cost Manual. Craftsman Book Co. • Annual. $23.00.

National Construction Estimator. Martin Kiley and William Moselle. Craftsman Book Co. • Annual. $47.50.

RESEARCH CENTERS AND INSTITUTES

Construction Industry Institute. Construction Industry Institute. 3925 W Braker Ln., No. R4500, Austin, TX 78759-5316. Phone: (512)232-3000 Fax: (512)499-8101 E-mail: wcrew@mail.utexas.edu • URL: http://construction-institute.org • Management, planning, design, and technology aspects of construction project execution, as well as methods and materials of construction and craft labor techniques. Links owners, contractors, and others directly active in the construction industry with academic resources to develop techniques and databases to improve the cost, schedule, quality and safety of the constructed project, the capital investment process, and total quality of the construction industry. Identifies immediate, long-range, and breakthrough research needs; directs appropriate research and studies; collects information from engineering and construction projects; and provides implementation guides on how to get research into actual engineering and construction projects. Also addresses education needs of the industry and conducts benchmarking studies for "best practices" comparisons.

Construction Research Center. University of Texas

at Arlington, P.O. Box 19347, Arlington, TX 76019. Phone: (817)272-3701 Fax: (817)272-7575 E-mail: matthys@uta.edu • Addresses the needs of the construction industry through construction research and educational programs.

TRADE/PROFESSIONAL ASSOCIATIONS

American Society of Professional Estimators. 11141 Georgia Ave., Suite 412, Wheaton, MD 20902. Phone: 888-378-6283 or (301)929-8848 Fax: (301)929-0231 E-mail: info@aspenational.com • URL: http://www.aspenational.com • Members are construction cost estimators and construction educators.

Professional Construction Estimators Association of America. P.O. Box 680336, Charlotte, NC 28216. Phone: 877-521-7232 or (704)987-9978 Fax: (704)987-9979 E-mail: pcea@pcea.org • URL: http://www.pcea.org • Members are building and construction cost estimators.

Society of Cost Estimating and Analysis. 101 S Whiting St., Ste. 201, Alexandria, VA 22304. Phone: (703)751-3013 Fax: (703)461-7328 E-mail: scea@sceaonline.net • URL: http://www.sceaonline.net • Members are engaged in government contract estimating and pricing.

ETHICAL DRUG INDUSTRY

See: PHARMACEUTICAL INDUSTRY

ETHICS

See: BUSINESS ETHICS; SOCIAL RESPONSIBILITY

ETIQUETTE

HANDBOOKS AND MANUALS

Amy Vanderbilt's Complete Book of Etiquette. Nancy Tuckerman and Nancy Dunnan. Doubleday Publishing. • 1995. $32.00. Revised edition.

Business Etiquette. Marjorie Brody and Barbara Pachter. McGraw-Hill. • 1994. $10.95. (Business Skills Express Series).

Business Etiquette: 101 Ways to Conduct Business with Charm and Savvy. Ann M. Sabath. Career Press, Inc. • 2002. $12.99. Second edition. Topics include business correspondence, e-mail, current attire, telephone etiquette, social situations, and foreign business customs.

Executive Etiquette in the New Workplace. Majabelle Y. Stewart and Marian Faux. Saint Martin's Press. • 1995. $14.95.

Little Black Book of Business Etiquette. Michael C. Thomsett. AMACOM. • 1991. $14.95. Covers company politics, chain of command, business lunches, dress codes, etc. (Little Black Book Series).

EUROCURRENCY

See also: FOREIGN EXCHANGE

INTERNET DATABASES

Gateway to the European Union. European Union. E-mail: pressoffice@eurostat.cec.be • URL: http://www.europa.eu.int • Web site provides access to a wide variety of EU information, including statistics (Eurostat), news, policies, publications, key issues, and official exchange rates for the euro. Includes links to the European Central Bank, the European Investment Bank, and other institutions. Fees: Free.

ONLINE DATABASES

Banking Information Source. PROQUEST. • Provides indexing and abstracting of periodical and

other literature from 1982 to date, with weekly updates. Covers the financial services industry: banks, savings institutions, investment houses, credit unions, insurance companies, and real estate organizations. Emphasis is on marketing and management. Inquire as to online cost and availability. (Formerly *FINIS: Financial Industry Information Service.*).

PERIODICALS AND NEWSLETTERS

American Banker: The Financial Services Daily. Thomson Media. • Daily. $895.00 per year. Provides news of banking, investment products, mortgages, credit unions, finance, bank technology, and legal developments.

Euromoney: The Monthly Journal of International Money and Capital Markets. American Educational Systems. • Monthly. $490.00 per year. Includes print and online editions. Supplement available*Guide to World Equity Markets.*

Financial Times [London]. The Financial Times, Inc. • Daily, except Sunday. $572.88 per year. An international business and financial newspaper, featuring news from London, Paris, Frankfurt, New York, and Tokyo. Includes worldwide stock and bond market data, commodity market data, and monetary/currency exchange information.

International Currency Review. World Reports Ltd. • Quarterly. $475.00 per year.

Rundt's World Business Intelligence. S. J. Rundt and Associates, Inc. • Weekly. $695.00 per year. Formerly *Rundt's Weekly Intelligence.*

U. S. Banker. Thomson Media. • Monthly. $65.00 per year. Edited for bank executives and managers. Covers a wide variety of banking and financial topics.

STATISTICS SOURCES

International Financial Statistics. International Monetary Fund, Publications Services. • Monthly. Individuals, $495.00 per year; students, $247.00 per year. Includes a wide variety of current data for individual countries in Europe and elsewhere. Includes *Annual* issue.

EURODOLLARS

See: EUROCURRENCY

EUROPEAN CONSUMER MARKET

See also: EUROPEAN MARKETS

ABSTRACTS AND INDEXES

Business Periodicals Index. H. W. Wilson Co. • 11 times a year. Quarterly and annual cumulations. Price varies.

CD-ROM DATABASES

ABI/INFORM. PROQUEST. • Monthly. Provides CD-ROM indexing and abstracting of worldwide business literature. Archival discs are available from 1971. Formerly *ABI/INFORM OnDisc.*

WILSONDISC: Business Periodicals Index. H. W. Wilson Co. • Monthly. Provides CD-ROM indexing of business periodicals from 1982 to date. Price includes online service.

World Consumer Markets. Gale Cengage Learning. • Annual. $2,500.00. Pblished by Euromonitor. Provides five- year historical data, current data, and forecasts, on CD-ROM for 330 consumer products in 55 countries. Market data is presented in a standardized format for each country.

World Database of Consumer Brands and Their Owners on CD-ROM. Gale Cengage Learning. • Annual. $3,190.00. Produced by Euromonitor.

Provides detailed information on CD-ROM for about 10,000 companies and 80,000 brands around the world. Covers 1,000 product sectors.

World Marketing Forecasts on CD-ROM. Gale Cengage Learning. • Annual. $2,500.00. Produced by Euromonitor. Provides detailed forecast data for the years to 2012 on CD-ROM for 54 countries in all parts of the world. Covers a wide range of social, demographic, economic, and market factors. Includes specific forecasts for many kinds of consumer products.

DIRECTORIES

Continental Europe Market Guide. Dun and Bradstreet Corp. • Semiannual. $1,600.00 per two volume set. Lists about 220,000 firms in 21 European countries. Includes financial strength and credit ratings. Geographic arrangement.

Directory of Consumer Brands and Their Owners: Eastern Europe. Euromonitor International, Business Reference Div. • 1998. $990.00. Provides information about brands available from major Eastern European companies. Descriptions of companies are also included.

European Food Marketing Directory. Euromonitor International. • Covers: The food marketing industry in Europe, including information sources, retailers, wholesalers, leading companies, and statistics. Entries include: Name, address, phone, fax, telex.

Global Market Share Planner. Euromonitor International. • 2003. $5,900.00. Six volumes. Second edition. Provides detailed profiles and market share rankings of major consumer product companies in North America, Latin America, Europe, South Africa, and the Asia-Pacific region. Covers firms operating in key consumer markets: beverages, food products, household products, and personal care items. (Volumes are available individually.).

Major Market Share Companies: Europe. Available from Gale Cengage Learning. • 2001. $990.00. Published by Euromonitor. Provides consumer market share data and rankings for multinational and regional companies. Covers leading firms in 14 European countries.

Major Performance Rankings. Available from Gale Cengage Learning. • 2003. $1,190.00. Second edition. Published by Euromonitor. Ranks 2,500 leading consumer product companies worldwide by various kinds of business and financial data, such as sales, profit, and market share. Includes international, regional, and country rankings.

Market Share Reporter. Available from Gale Cengage Learning. • 2002. $285.00. Sixth edition. Published by Euromonitor. Provides consumer market share data for leading companies in 30 major countries.

SRDS International Media Guides. SRDS. • Covers: In five volumes (Newspapers worldwide, Consumer magazines worldwide, Business Publications: Asia-Pacific/Middle East/Africa, Business Publications: Europe, Business Publications: The Americas), advertising rates and data for 20,000 newspapers, consumer magazines and business publications worldwide. Entries include: contact names, addresses, phone and fax numbers, and e-mail.

World Retail Directory and Sourcebook. Available from Gale Cengage Learning. • 2003. $1,250.00. Fifth edition. Published by Euromonitor. Provides information on more than 2,400 retailers around the world. Information sources, conferences, trade fairs, and special libraries are also listed.

World's Major Multinationals. Euromonitor International. • Covers: List of major multinational companies. Entries include: Company name, address, phone; performance analysis; list of subsidiaries; market share; net profit and turnover; leading brands; and merger and acquisition information.

HANDBOOKS AND MANUALS

Consumer Price Indices: An ILO Manual. Ralph Turvey and others. International Labour Office. • 1990. $24.75.

The World's Largest Market: A Business Guide to Europe 1992. Robert Williams and others. AMACOM. • 1991. $19.95. Reprint edition. Provides information on agencies, organizations programs, and regulations relevant to the forthcoming 1992 unified European Community.

ONLINE DATABASES

F & S Index. Gale Cengage Learning. • Contains about four million citations to worldwide business, financial, and industrial or consumer product literature appearing from 1972 to date. Weekly updates. Inquire as to online cost and availability.

Globalbase. Gale Cengage Learning. • Provides more than one million online summaries of business, industrial, and economic news reports from more than 1,000 publications worldwide. Covers a wide range of material appearing in international trade journals, professional magazines, and newspapers. Time period is 1984 to date, with weekly updates. Inquire as to online cost and availability.

Market Research Monitor. Euromonitor International. • Contains full-text reports online from *Market Research Europe, Market Research Great Britain, Market Research International,* and *Retail Monitor International.* Time period is 1995 to date, with monthly updates. Inquire as to online cost and availability.

PROMT: Predicasts Overview of Markets and Technology. Gale Cengage Learning. • Companies, products, applied technologies and markets. U.S. and international literature coverage, 1972 to date. Inquire as to online cost and availability. Provides abstracts from more than 1,600 publications. Weekly updates.

Trade & Industry Database. Gale Cengage Learning. • Provides indexing of business periodicals, January 1981 to date. Daily updates. (Full text articles from some periodicals are available online, 1983 to date. Inquire as to online cost and availability).

Wilson Business Abstracts Online. H. W. Wilson Co. • Indexes and abstracts 600 major business periodicals, plus the *Wall Street Journal* and the business section of the *New York Times.* Indexing is from 1982, abstracting from 1990, with the two newspapers included from 1993. Updated weekly. Inquire as to online cost and availability. (*Business Periodicals Index* without abstracts is also available online.).

PERIODICALS AND NEWSLETTERS

Advertising Age's Euromarketing. Crain Communications, Inc. • Weekly. $295.00 per year. Newsletter on European advertising and marketing.

Europa 2000: The American Business Report on Europe. Wolfe Publishing, Inc. • Monthly. $119.00 per year. Newsletter on consumer and industrial marketing in a unified European Economic Community. Includes classified business opportunity advertisements and a listing by country of forthcoming major trade shows in Europe.

Journal of Euromarketing. Haworth Press, Inc. • Quarterly. $435.00 per year; Includes print and online editions.

Journal of International Consumer Marketing. Haworth Press, Inc. • Quarterly. Individuals, $80.00 per year; institutions, $150.00 per year.

Pharma Business: The International Magazine of Pharmaceutical Business and Marketing. Engel Publishing Partners. • Six times a year. $235.00 per year. Circulated mainly in European countries.

Coverage includes worldwide industry news, new drug products, regulations, and research developments.

STATISTICS SOURCES

Consumer Eastern Europe. Available from Gale Cengage Learning. • Annual. $1,250.00. Published by Euromonitor. Provides demographic and consumer market data for the countries of Eastern Europe.

Consumer Europe 2000/2001. Available from Gale Cengage Learning. • Annual. $1,290.00. Published by Euromonitor. Detailed statistical tables furnish five-year data on the production, sales, distribution, consumption, and other aspects of more than 240 consumer product categories. Sixteen countries of Western Europe are included.

European Compendium of Marketing Information. Available from Gale Cengage Learning. • 1996. $350.00. Second edition. Volume two. Published by Euromonitor. Provides marketing and production statistics relating to European consumer products and services.

European Economy, Series A: Recent Economic Trends. Bernan Associates. • Monthly. $65.00 per year. Published by the Commission of the European Communities, Luxembourg.

European Economy, Series B: Business and Consumer Survey Results. Commission of the European Communities. Available from Bernan Associates. • Monthly. $65.00 per year. Published by the Commission of the European Communities, Luxembourg. Editions in English, French, German, and Italian.

European Marketing Data and Statistics. Available from Gale Cengage Learning. • Annual. $530.00. Published by Euromonitor. Presents essential marketing data, including demographics and consumer expenditure patterns, for 31 European countries.

European Marketing Forecasts. Available from Gale Cengage Learning. • Annual. $1,250.00. Published by Euromonitor. Contains demographic, economic, and market forecasts for the countries of Europe to the year 2010. Forecasts include market-size data for 15 consumer product sectors (food, clothing, automobiles, consumer electronics, etc.).

Regions Statistical Yearbook. Bernan Associates. • Annual. $45.00. Published by the Commission of European Communities. Provides data on the social and economic situation in specific European areas. Includes population, employment, migration, industry, living standards, etc.

Retail Trade International. Gale Cengage Learning. • 2002. $1,990.00. 11th edition. Eight volumes. Published by Euromonitor. Presents comprehensive data on retail trends in 52 countries. Includes textual analysis and profiles of major retailers. Covers Europe, Asia, the Middle East, Africa and the Americas.

World Consumer Income and Expenditure Patterns. Available from Gale Cengage Learning. • Annual. $1,090.00. Two volumes. Published by Euromonitor. Provides data for countries worldwide on consumer income, earning power, spending patterns, and savings. Expenditures are detailed for product or service categories.

TRADE/PROFESSIONAL ASSOCIATIONS

Association of International Marketing. PO Box 70, London E13 8BQ, United Kingdom. Phone: 44 208 9867539 Fax: 44 208 9867539 • A multinational organization. Promotes the advancement and exchange of information and ideas in international marketing.

European Marketing Academy. Pl. de Brouckere Plein, 31, B-1000 Brussels, Belgium. Phone: 32 2 2266660 Fax: 32 2 5121929 E-mail: jozsef.beracs@uni-corvinus.hu • URL: http://www.emac-online.

org • Persons involved or interested in teaching or research in the field of marketing. Serves as forum for exchange of information concerning marketing; fosters improved dissemination of information; promotes international exchange in the field of marketing.

Federation of European Direct Marketing. Rue de l'Aurore 4, 439 Ave. de Tervueren, B-1060 Brussels, Belgium. Fax: 32 2 5379984 E-mail: irene.allanson@direxions.be • URL: http://www.fedma.org • A multinational organization. Facilitates contacts and exchange of ideas and techniques among countries and members. Sponsors "Best of Europe" contest, with awards for best direct mail campaigns. Formerly European Direct Marketing Association.

OTHER SOURCES

Disposable Paper Products. Available from MarketResearch.com. • 2001. $5,900.00. Published by Euromonitor Publications Ltd. Provides consumer market data and forecasts to 2004 for the United States, the United Kingdom, Germany, France, and Italy.

Fast Food. Available from MarketResearch.com. • 2001. $5,000.00. Published by Euromonitor Publications Ltd. Provides consumer market data for the United States, the United Kingdom, Germany, France, and Italy.

Frozen Foods. Available from MarketResearch.com. • 2000. $5,000.00. Published by Euromonitor Publications Ltd. Provides consumer market data and forecasts for the United States, the United Kingdom, Germany, France, and Italy. Contains market analyses for many kinds of frozen foods.

Fruit Juices. Available from MarketResearch.com. • 2001. $4,500.00. Published by Euromonitor Publications Ltd. Provides consumer market data and forecasts to 2004 for the United States, the United Kingdom, Germany, France, and Italy. Includes fresh, frozen, bottled, and canned fruit and vegetable juices.

Household Cleaning Agents. Available from MarketResearch.com. • 2001. $5,900.00. Published by Euromonitor Publications Ltd. Provides consumer market data and forecasts to 2005 for the United States, the United Kingdom, Germany, France, and Italy. Covers dishwashing detergents, floor cleaning products, scourers, polishes, bleaching products, etc.

EUROPEAN ECONOMIC COMMUNITY

See: EUROPEAN MARKETS

EUROPEAN MARKETS

See also: EUROPEAN CONSUMER MARKET; INTERNATIONAL BUSINESS

ABSTRACTS AND INDEXES

Business Periodicals Index. H. W. Wilson Co. • 11 times a year. Quarterly and annual cumulations. Price varies.

F & S Index: Europe. Gale Cengage Learning. • Monthly. $1,450.00 per year, including quarterly and annual cumulations. Provides annotated citations to marketing, business, financial, and industrial literature. Coverage of European business activity includes trade journals, financial magazines, business newspapers, and special reports. Formerly *Predicasts F & S Index: Europe.*

ALMANACS AND YEARBOOKS

Economic Survey of Europe. United Nations Publications. • Three times a year. Price varies. Provides yearly analysis and review of the European economy, including Eastern Europe and the USSR. Text in English.

Euroguide Yearbook of the Institutions of the European Union and of the Other European Organiz. Bernan Associates. • Annual. Free. Published by Editions Delta. Information on public and private institutions in the European Union contributing to European integration.

European Union Annual Review of Activities, 2001/ 2002. Geoffrey Edwards and George Wiessala, editors. Blackwell Publishing. • 2002. $39.95.

CD-ROM DATABASES

Baltia Kompass Business Disc. Available from Kompass USA, Inc. • Semiannual. CD-ROM provides information on more than 29,000 companies in Estonia, Latvia, and Lithuania. Classification system covers approximately 50,000 products and services.

Benelux Kompass Business Disc. Available from Kompass USA, Inc. • Semiannual. CD-ROM provides information on more than 52,000 companies in Belgium, Netherlands, and Luxembourg. Classification system covers approximately 50,000 products and services.

East European Kompass on Disc. Available from Kompass USA, Inc. • Semiannual. CD-ROM provides information on more than 350,000 companies in Austria, Azerbaijan, Belarus, Croatia, Czech Republic, Estonia, Hungary, Latvia, Lithuania, Moldova, Poland, Romania, Russia, Slovakia, Slovenia, Ukraine, and Yugoslavia. Classification system covers approximately 50,000 products and services.

European Kompass on Disc. Available from Kompass USA, Inc. • Semiannual. CD-ROM provides information on more than 400,000 companies in Belgium, Denmark, France, Germany, Ireland, Italy, Luxembourg, Netherlands, Norway, Spain, Sweden, and UK. Classification system covers approximately 50,000 products and services.

Hoover's Company Capsules on CD-ROM. Hoover's, Inc. • Quarterly. $399.95 per year (single-user). Provides the CD-ROM version of *Hoover's Handbook of American Business, Hoover's Handbook of Emerging Companies, Hoover's Handbook of World Business, Hoover's Guide to Computer Companies, Hoover's Guide to Media Companies, Hoover's Handbook of Private Companies,* and various regional guides. Includes more than 11,000 profiles of companies.

Kompass CD-ROM Editions. Available from Kompass USA, Inc. • Semiannual or annual. Prices vary. CD-ROM versions of Kompass international trade directories are available for each of 36 major countries and nine world regions. Searching is provided for 50,000 product/service items and for many company details.

Kompass Concord CD-ROM. Available from Kompass USA, Inc. • Semiannual. CD-ROM provides information on more than 280,000 companies in 17 rapidly developing East European countries: Armenia, Azerbaijan, Belarus, Bulgaria, Czech Republic, Estonia, Hungary, Kazakhstan, Kyrgyzstan, Latvia, Lithuania, Moldova, Poland, Romania, Russia, Ukraine, and Uzbekistan. Classification system covers approximately 50,000 products and services.

OECD Statistical Compendium. Organization for Economic Cooperation and Development. • Semiannual. $1,905.00 per year for 1 to 10 users. CD-ROM contains more than 730,000 monthly, quarterly, and annual time series for OECD countries, 1960 to date. Includes fully searchable data on agriculture, food, economic indicators, national accounts, employment, energy, finance, industry, technology, and foreign trade. Results can be displayed in various forms.

Scandinavian Kompass on Disc. Available from Kompass USA, Inc. • Semiannual. CD-ROM provides information on more than 120,000 companies in Denmark, Finland, Norway, and Sweden. Classification system covers approximately 50,000 products and services.

DIRECTORIES

The Directory of EU Information Sources: The Red Book. Euroconfidentiel S. A. • Annual. $230.00. Lists publications, associations, consultants, law firms, diplomats, jounalists, and other sources of information about Europe and the European Union.

Directory of Trade and Professional Associations in the European Union - The Blue Book. Euroconfidentiel S. A. • Annual. $160.00. Includes more than 9,000 EU-related associations.

The EU Institutions' Register. Routledge Reference. • Covers: Over 5,900 key personnel in each of the major institutions, including: European Commission, European Parliament, Economic and Social Committee, Council of the European Union, Court of Justice, European Investment Bank, Court of Auditors, Committee of Regions and EU Agencies. Entries include: Contact information.

European Marketing Information Sourcebook. Euromonitor International. • 2003. $475.00. Lists trade associations, statistical offices, government agencies, special libraries, trade journals, websites, and other sources of business information for the countries of Europe.

European Union Encyclopedia and Directory. Taylor & Francis Group. • Semiannual. $600.00. Published by Europa. Provides directory information for major European Union organizations, with detailed descriptions of various groups or concepts in an "Encyclopedia" section. A statistics section contains a wide variety of data related to business, industry, and economics. Formerly *European Communities Encyclopedia and Directory.*

Europe's Top Quoted Companies: A Comparative Directory from Seventeen European Stock Exchanges. Kogan Page. • Annual. $325.00. Provides detailed, 5-year financial data on 850 major European companies that are publicly traded. Includes company addresses.

Guide to EU Information Sources on the Internet. Euroconfidentiel S. A. • Annual. $210.00. Contains descriptions of more than 1,700 Web sites providing information relating to the European Union and European commerce and industry. Includes a quarterly e-mail newsletter with new sites and address changes.

Hoover's Handbook of World Business: Profiles of Major European, Asian, Latin American, and Canadian Companies. Hoover's, Inc. • Annual. $165.00. Contains detailed profiles for approximately 300 large foreign companies. Includes indexes by industry, location, executive name, company name, and brand name.

International Media Guide Business-Professional Publications: Europe. SRDS. • Annual. $300.00. Describes 6,000 trade journals from Eastern and Western Europe, with advertising rates and circulation data.

Kompass International Trade Directories. Kompass International/Kompass USA, Inc. • Annual. Prices and volumes vary. Kompass directories are published internationally for each of more than 70 countries, from Algeria to Uzbekistan. The Kompass classification system covers more than 50,000 individual product and service categories, with most directories containing a tradename index and company profiles. Total number of companies in Kompass volumes is about two million.

Major Chemical and Petrochemical Companies of Europe. Available from Gale Cengage Learning. • 2003. $880.00. Fifth edition. Two volumes. Published by Graham & Whiteside Ltd., London. Includes financial, personnel, and product information for chemical companies in Western Europe.

Major Companies of Europe. Available from Gale Cengage Learning. • 2003. $1,895.00. Four volumes. Published by Graham & Whiteside. Approximately 24,000 major companies and key executives in European countries in all lines of business.

Major Employers of Europe. Available from Gale Cengage Learning. • Annual. $295.00. Published by Graham & Whiteside. Provides concise information on the top 10,000 companies in Europe, according to number of employees. Firms are indexed by country and by business activity.

Major Financial Institutions of Europe. Available from Gale Cengage Learning. • Annual. $510.00. Contains profiles of over 2,000 financial institutions in Europe such as banks, investment companies, and insurance companies. Formerly *Major Financial Institutions of Continental Europe.*

The Top 5,000 European Companies 2002. Available from Gale Cengage Learning. • 2002. $645.00. Third edition. Published by Graham & Whiteside. In addition to about 5,000 manufacturing and service companies, includes the 500 largest banks in Europe and the 100 largest insurance companies.

Trade Associations amd Professional Bodies of Continental Europe. Available from Gale Cengage Learning. • 2003. $290.00. Second edition. Published by Graham & Whiteside. Provides detailed information on more than 3,600 business and professional organizations in Europe.

ENCYCLOPEDIAS AND DICTIONARIES

Dictionary of the European Union. Available from Taylor & Francis Group. • 2002. $145.00. Published by Europa Publications (http://www. europapublications.com). Provides about 1,000 entries defining and explaining all aspects of the European Union.

Encyclopedia of Business. Gale Cengage Learning. • 2000. $425.00. Second edition. Two volumes. Contains more than 700 signed articles covering major business disciplines and concepts. International in scope. (Encyclopedia of Business Series).

Encyclopedia of the European Union. Desmond Dinan, editor. Lynne Rienner Publishers. • 2000. $110.00. Covers "virtually every aspect" of the EU. Includes "maps, glossaries, appendixes, and a comprehensive index.".

HANDBOOKS AND MANUALS

Access to European Union: Law, Economics, Policies. Euroconfidentiel S. A. • 2001. $62.00. Covers EU legislation and policy in major industrial and commercial sectors. Includes customs policy, the common market, monetary union, taxation, competition, "The EU in the World," and related topics. Contains more than 300 bibliographical references.

Practical Guide to Foreign Direct Investment in the European Union: The Green Book. Euroconfidentiel S. A. • Annual. $240.00. Provides coverage of national and EU business incentives. In addition to 70 charts and tables, includes EU country profiles of taxation, labor costs, and employment regulations.

Transnational Accounting. Dieter Ordelheide and others, editors. Groves Dictionaries, Inc. • 2001. $685.00. Second edition. Three volumes. Published by Macmillan (UK). Provides detailed descriptions of financial accounting principles and practices in 14 major countries (10 European, plus the U. S., Canada, Australia, and Japan). Includes tables, exhibits, index, and a glossary of 244 accounting terms in eight languages.

INTERNET DATABASES

Financial Times: Where Information Becomes Intelligence. FT Group. Phone: 800-628-8088 • URL: http://www.ft.com • Web site provides extensive data and information relating to international business and finance, with daily updates. Includes Markets Today, Company News, Economic Indicators, Equities, Currencies, Capital Markets, Euro Prices, etc. Fees: Free (registration required).

Gateway to the European Union. European Union. E-mail: pressoffice@eurostat.cec.be • URL: http://www.europa.eu.int • Web site provides access to a wide variety of EU information, including statistics (Eurostat), news, policies, publications, key issues, and official exchange rates for the euro. Includes links to the European Central Bank, the European Investment Bank, and other institutions. Fees: Free.

ONLINE DATABASES

Globalbase. Gale Cengage Learning. • Provides more than one million online summaries of business, industrial, and economic news reports from more than 1,000 publications worldwide. Covers a wide range of material appearing in international trade journals, professional magazines, and newspapers. Time period is 1984 to date, with weekly updates. Inquire as to online cost and availability.

Management Contents. Gale Cengage Learning. • Covers a wide range of management, financial, marketing, personnel, and administrative topics. About 150 leading business journals are indexed and abstracted from 1974 to date, with monthly updating. Inquire as to online cost and availability.

PAIS International. Public Affairs Information Service, Inc. • Corresponds to the former printed publications, *PAIS Bulletin* (1976-90) and *PAIS Foreign Language Index* (1972-90), and to the current *PAIS International in Print* (1991 to date). Covers economic, political, and sociological material appearing in periodicals, books, government documents, and other publications. Updating is monthly. Inquire as to online cost and availability.

Trade & Industry Database. Gale Cengage Learning. • Provides indexing of business periodicals, January 1981 to date. Daily updates. (Full text articles from some periodicals are available online, 1983 to date. Inquire as to online cost and availability).

PERIODICALS AND NEWSLETTERS

Business Week International: The World's Only International Newsweekly of Business. McGraw-Hill. • Weekly. $95.00 per year.

Commission European Union Bulletin. Commision of the European Communities. Bernan Associates. • 11 times a year. $210.00 per year. Published by the Office of Official Publications of the European Communities. Covers all main events within the Union. Supplement available. Text in Danish, Dutch, English, French, German, Greek, Italian, Spanish, Portuguese. Formerly *Bulletin of the European Communities.*

Europa 2000: The American Business Report on Europe. Wolfe Publishing, Inc. • Monthly. $119.00 per year. Newsletter on consumer and industrial marketing in a unified European Economic Community. Includes classified business opportunity advertisements and a listing by country of forthcoming major trade shows in Europe.

European Access. European Commission-United Kingdom Offices. Chadwyck-Healey, Inc. • Bimonthly. $195.00 per year. Published in England. A journal providing general coverage of developments and trends within the European Community.

European Management Journal. Elsevier. • Bimonthly. Individuals, $140.00 per year; institutions, $690.00 per year. Covers a wide variety of topics, including management problems of the European Single Market.

EuroWatch. LRP Publications. • Description: Provides news and analysis from European capitals and Washington, D.C. concerning how the United

States' and other business interests are affected by the European Community's program to remove national barriers and create a single market for the trade and movement of goods, services, capital, and labor.

Institutional Investor International Edition: The Magazine for International Finance and Investment. Institutional Investor, Inc., Journals Group. • Monthly. $475.00 per year. Covers the international aspects of professional investing and finance. Emphasis is on Europe, the Far East, and Latin America.

International Economic Scoreboard. The Conference Board Inc. • Description: Provides current data on the business outlook in 11 major industrial countries: Australia, Canada, France, West Germany, Italy, Japan, Korea, New Zealand, Taiwan, the United Kingdom, and the U.S. **Remarks:** A source for additional information on this indicator system and its uses is available at the Center for International Business Cycle Research, Columbia University Business School.

Market: Europe. Edimax. • Description: Profiles European consumers and provides ideas for marketing strategies. Reports on European conferences and summarizes articles from international periodicals. Recurring features include analyses of specific countries and cities.

Market Research Europe. Available from MarketResearch.com. • Monthly. $1,220.00 per year. Published by Euromonitor Publications. Newsletter on consumer spending in Europe.

Wall Street Journal/Europe. Dow Jones & Co., Inc. • Daily. $300.00 per year (air mail). Published in Europe. Text in English.

STATISTICS SOURCES

Basic Statistics of the European Union. Statistical Office of the European Communities. Available from Bernan Associates. • Annual. Provides European demographic, economic, and other basic data. The U. S., Canada, Japan, and the Soviet Union are included for comparative purposes. Text in Dutch, English, French, and German. Formerly *Basic Statistics of the European Community.*

Consumer Europe 2000/2001. Available from Gale Cengage Learning. • Annual. $1,290.00. Published by Euromonitor. Detailed statistical tables furnish five-year data on the production, sales, distribution, consumption, and other aspects of more than 240 consumer product categories. Sixteen countries of Western Europe are included.

The Enlarged European Union: A Statistical Handbook. Euromonitor International. • 2003. $470.00. Presents comparative statistical data for 28 countries (15 EU member states and 13 candidate countries). Covers economics, population, labor, trade, consumer markets, and other topics.

European Economy, Series A: Recent Economic Trends. Bernan Associates. • Monthly. $65.00 per year. Published by the Commission of the European Communities, Luxembourg.

European Economy, Series B: Business and Consumer Survey Results. Commission of the European Communities. Available from Bernan Associates. • Monthly. $65.00 per year. Published by the Commission of the European Communities, Luxembourg. Editions in English, French, German, and Italian.

European Marketing Data and Statistics. Available from Gale Cengage Learning. • Annual. $530.00. Published by Euromonitor. Presents essential marketing data, including demographics and consumer expenditure patterns, for 31 European countries.

European Marketing Forecasts. Available from Gale Cengage Learning. • Annual. $1,250.00. Published by Euromonitor. Contains demographic, economic,

and market forecasts for the countries of Europe to the year 2010. Forecasts include market-size data for 15 consumer product sectors (food, clothing, automobiles, consumer electronics, etc.).

Eurostat Yearbook: A Statistical View on Europe. Available from Bernan Associates. • Annual. $65.00. Published by European Communities (http://www.europa.eu.int/comm/eurostat/). Statistical topics include economics, national income, population, land, agriculture, environment, government, housing, and crime. Covers "every country in Europe and the European Union.".

Handbook of International Economic Statistics. Available from National Technical Information Service. • Annual. $40.00. Prepared by U. S. Central Intelligence Agency. Provides basic statistics for comparing worldwide economic performance, with an emphasis on Europe, including Eastern Europe.

International Financial Statistics. International Monetary Fund, Publications Services. • Monthly. Individuals, $495.00 per year; students, $247.00 per year. Includes a wide variety of current data for individual countries in Europe and elsewhere. Includes *Annual* issue.

OECD in Figures. Organization for Economic Cooperation and Development. • Annual. $13.00. A "pocket data book" providing a summary of key statistics for OECD countries, including economic growth, employment, education, the environment, and transportation.

Panorama of European Business. Available from Bernan Associates. • Annual. $65.00. Presents statistical data for manufacturing and service industries in major European countries. Text in English, French and Spanish.

Regions Statistical Yearbook. Bernan Associates. • Annual. $45.00. Published by the Commission of European Communities. Provides data on the social and economic situation in specific European areas. Includes population, employment, migration, industry, living standards, etc.

TRADE/PROFESSIONAL ASSOCIATIONS

European Union - Delegation of the Commission to the United States. 2300 M St. NW, Washington, DC 20037. Phone: (202)862-9500 Fax: (202)429-1766 E-mail: relex-delusw-help@cec.eu.int • URL: http://www.eurunion.org • Diplomatic delegation of the European Commission in the United States for the European Union, comprising European Community (Common Market); European Coal and Steel Community; and European Atomic Energy Community. Distributes official documents and information brochures of the European Union. Provides speakers' bureau and reference service. Represents the EU to U.S. government, international organizations, trade associations, academia, U.S. industry and the general public. Responds to all public inquiries.

OTHER SOURCES

Common Market Reports. CCH, Inc. • Biweekly. $1,070.00 per year, including weekly *Euromarket News.* Looseleaf service. Four volumes. Periodic supplementation.

The Rome, Maastricht, and Amsterdam Treaties: Comparative Texts. Available from Paul and Co. Publishers Consortium, Inc. • 1997. Price on application. Includes a comprehensive keyword index. Published in Belgium by Euroconfidential.

EUROPEAN UNION

See: EUROPEAN MARKETS

EVALUATION OF PERFORMANCE

See: RATING OF EMPLOYEES

EVENT PLANNING

See: SPECIAL EVENT PLANNING

EXCHANGE, FOREIGN

See: FOREIGN EXCHANGE

EXCHANGE RATES

See: CURRENCY EXCHANGE RATES

EXCHANGES, COMMODITY

See: COMMODITY FUTURES TRADING

EXCHANGES, STOCK

See: STOCK EXCHANGES

EXCISE TAX

HANDBOOKS AND MANUALS
Excise Taxes. Prentice Hall PTR. • Looseleaf. $216. 00. Monthly updates. (Information Services Series).
Internal Revenue Code. RIA. • Annual. $86.50. Provides full text of the Internal Revenue Code (5,000 pages), including procedural and administrative provisions.

INTERNET DATABASES
CCH Essentials: An Internet Tax Research and Primary Source Library. CCH, Inc. Phone: 800-248-3248 or (773)866-6000 Fax: 800-224-8299 or (773)866-3608 E-mail: cust_serv@cch.com • URL: http://tax.cch.com/essentials • Fee-based Web site provides full-text coverage of federal tax law and regulations, including rulings, procedures, tax court decisions, and IRS publications, announcements, notices, and penalties. Includes explanation, analysis, tax planning guides, and a daily tax news service. Searching is offered, including citation search.

PERIODICALS AND NEWSLETTERS
The Journal of Taxation: A National Journal of Current Developments, Analysis and Commentary for Tax Professionals. RIA. • Monthly. $305.00 per year. Analysis of current tax developments for tax specialists.

RESEARCH CENTERS AND INSTITUTES
Office of Tax Policy Research. University of Michigan, 701 Tappan St., Ann Arbor, MI 48109-1234. Phone: (734)763-3068 Fax: (734)763-4032 E-mail: otpr@umich.edu • URL: http://www.taxpolicyresearch.umich.edu/.

Tax Foundation. Tax Foundation. 2001 L St. NW, Ste. 1050, Washington, DC 20036. Phone: (202)464-6200 Fax: (202)464-6201 E-mail: hodge@taxfoundation.org • URL: http://www.taxfoundation.org • Fiscal and management aspects of federal, state, and local government, including studies on government expenditures, the federal budget, taxation, and international competitiveness. Serves as a national information agency for individuals and organizations concerned with problems of government expenditures, taxation, and debt.

EXECUTIVE COMPENSATION

See also: ADMINISTRATION; EXECUTIVES
GENERAL WORKS
Compensation. George T. Milkovich. McGraw-Hill. • 2001. $114.38. Seventh edition.

Compensation. Robert E. Sibson. AMACOM. • 1990. $75.00. Fifth edition. Discusses planning, implementing, and managing employee compensation.
Compensation Management in a Knowledge-Based World. Richard I. Henderson. Prentice Hall PTR. • 2002. $120.00. Ninth edition.
Executive Compensation: A Strategic Guide for the 1990s. John J. McFadden, editor. The American College. • 2001. $54.00. Sixth edition.

ABSTRACTS AND INDEXES
Business Periodicals Index. H. W. Wilson Co. • 11 times a year. Quarterly and annual cumulations. Price varies.

BIBLIOGRAPHIES
Available Pay Survey Reports: An Annotated Bibliography. Abbott, Langer and Associates. • 1995. $610.00. Fourth edition. Two volumes. Vol. 1, $450.00; Vol. 2, $160.00.

HANDBOOKS AND MANUALS
Compensating Executives: Drafting and Managing Tax-Advantaged Arrangements. Arthur H. Kroll. CCH, Inc. • 1998. $115.00. Covers the creation and implementation of executive compensation programs. Includes sample forms, plans, and checklists.
Executive Compensation. Michael Melbinger. CCH, Inc. • 2004. $145.00. "...describes the numerous federal statutes that govern the terms and provisions of executive compensation." Contains various samples, including an employment agreement, offer letter, retirement plan, and stock appreciation rights agreement.
How to Design and Install Management Incentive Compensation Plans: A Practical Guide to Installing Performance Bonus Plans. Dale Arahood. Dale Arahood and Associates. • 1996. $129.00. Revised edition. "This book focuses on how pay should be determined rather than how much should be paid.".
Personnel Management: Compensation. Prentice Hall PTR. • Looseleaf. Periodic supplementation. Price on application.
U. S. Master Compensation Tax Guide. Dennis R. Lassila and Bob G. Kilpatrick. CCH, Inc. • 2001. $57.00. Third edition. Provides concise coverage of taxes on salaries, bonuses, fringe benefits, other current compensation, and deferred compensation (qualified and nonqualified).

INTERNET DATABASES
eComp: The Most Powerful Executive Compensation Online Research Tool. AON Consulting Inc. Phone: (212)441-2047 Fax: (212)441-1944 E-mail: sales@ecomp-online.com • URL: http://www.ecomponline.com • Web site provides free access to executive compensation data by company name or industry. Gives names and titles of top executives for each company, with the following information for each corporate officer: salary, bonus, long-term incentive plan data (LTIP), options granted, options expiration date, dollar value of options, and detailed options exercisable data. More extensive, customized data is available on a fee basis.
U. S. Securities and Exchange Commission. Phone: 800-732-0330 or (202)942-7040 Fax: (202)942-9634 E-mail: webmaster@sec.gov • URL: http://www.sec.gov • SEC Web site offers free access through EDGAR to text of official corporate filings, such as annual reports (10-K), quarterly reports (10-Q), and proxies. (EDGAR is "Electronic Data Gathering, Analysis, and Retrieval System.") An example is given of how to obtain executive compensation data from proxies. Text of the daily *SEC News Digest* is offered, as are links to other government sites, non-government market regulators, and U. S. stock exchanges. Search facilities are extensive. Fees: Free.

Wageweb: Salary Survey Data On-Line. HRPDI: Human Resources Programs Development and Improvement. Phone: (804)363-1792 Fax: (804)594-3721 E-mail: salaries@wageweb.com • URL: http://www.wageweb.com • Web site provides salary information for more than 170 benchmark positions, including (for example) 29 information management jobs. Data shows average minimum, median, and average maximum compensation for each position, based on salary surveys. Fees: Free for national salary data; $169.00 per year for more detailed information (geographic, organization size, specific industries).

ONLINE DATABASES
Disclosure SEC Database. Thomson Financial. • Provides online information from records filed with the Securities and Exchange Commission by more than 12,000 publicly-owned companies in the U.S. Includes about 200 financial data items and information relating to executives. Time span is 1977 to date, with weekly updates. Inquire as to online cost and availability.
EdgarPlus: SEC Basic Filings. Thomson Financial. • Online service provides full text of about 60,000 documents that have been filed with the U.S. Securities and Exchange Commission, 1987 to date, with daily updates. Filings include 6-K, 8-K, 10-K, 10-C, 10-Q, 20-F, and proxy statements. Inquire as to online cost and availability.
Wilson Business Abstracts Online. H. W. Wilson Co. • Indexes and abstracts 600 major business periodicals, plus the *Wall Street Journal* and the business section of the *New York Times.* Indexing is from 1982, abstracting from 1990, with the two newspapers included from 1993. Updated weekly. Inquire as to online cost and availability. (*Business Periodicals Index* without abstracts is also available online.).

PERIODICALS AND NEWSLETTERS
Compensation and Benefits Review: The Journal of Total Compensation Strategies. Sage Publications, Inc. • Institutions, $358.00 per year; includes print and online editions.
Compensation and Benefits Update. RIA. • Monthly. $149.00 per year. Provides information on the latest ideas and developments in the field of employee benefits. In-depth exploration of popular benefits programs. Formerly *Benefits and Compensation Update.*
Tax Management Compensation Planning Journal. BNA Tax Management. • Monthly. $426.00 per year. Formerly *Compensation Planning Journal.*

STATISTICS SOURCES
Compensation Systems in Private Law Firms. Altman Weil Publications, Inc. • Annual. $325.00. Provides legal-office compensation standards arranged by region, firm size, legal specialty, and various other factors. Covers attorneys, paralegals, and other personnel.
Executive Remuneration. American Banker Newsletter, Thomson Financial Media. • Annual.
Project Management Salary Survey. Project Management Institute. • Annual. $129.00. Gives compensation data for key project management positions in North America, according to job title, level of responsibility, number of employees supervised, and various other factors. Includes data on retirement plans and benefits.
Top CEOs: Forbes's Executive Pay Survey. Forbes Magazine. • 2001. $4.95. List of 800 firms. May issue of *Forbes Magazine.*
Top Executive Compensation. The Conference Board. • Annual. Members, $55.00; non-members, $195.00. Provides data on compensation of highest

---

paid executives in major corporations.

TRADE/PROFESSIONAL ASSOCIATIONS

WorldatWork. 14040 N Northsight Blvd., Scottsdale, AZ 85260. Phone: 877-951-9191 or (480)951-9191 Fax: (480)483-8352 E-mail: customerrelations@worldatwork.org • URL: http://www.worldatwork.org • Dedicated to knowledge leadership in compensation, benefits and total rewards, focusing on disciplines associated with attracting, retaining and motivating employees. Offers CCP, CBP, and GRP certification and education programs, conducts surveys, research and provides networking opportunities.

OTHER SOURCES

BNA Policy and Practice Series: Compensation. BNA, Inc. • Weekly. $938.00 per year.

Business Rankings Annual. Gale Cengage Learning. • Annual. $325.00. Two volumes. Compiled by the Business Library Staff of the Brooklyn Public Library. This is a guide to lists and rankings appearing in major business publications. The top ten names are listed in each case.

Executive Compensation. Arthur H. Kroll. Prentice Hall PTR. • Three looseleaf volumes. Periodic supplementation. Price on application. Includes monthly newsletter.

Executive Compensation. American Lawyer Media, Inc. • Looseleaf. $189.00. Updated as needed. Covers many topics relating to the legal aspects of executive compensation, including taxation, securities law, payments in stock, fringe benefits, employment agreements, and severance arrangements. (Law Journal Press).

Executive Compensation and Taxation Coordinator. RIA. • Monthly. $765.00 per year. Three looseleaf volumes.

Executive Compensation for Emerging Companies. Daniel Niehans and Shawn E. Lampron. Glasser Legalworks. • Looseleaf. $225.00, including CD-ROM version. Periodic Supplementation. Covers various aspects of executive compensation, with emphasis on stock option plans and stock ownership. Includes many annotated legal forms. (Emerging Growth Companies Series.).

Executive Stock Options and Stock Appreciation Rights. American Lawyer Media, Inc. • Looseleaf. $189.00. Updated as needed. Coverage includes non-qualified stock options and incentive stock options. Contains sample forms and documents. (Law Journal Press).

EXECUTIVE EDUCATION

See: EXECUTIVE TRAINING AND DEVELOPMENT

EXECUTIVE RATING

See: RATING OF EMPLOYEES

EXECUTIVE RECRUITING

See: RECRUITMENT OF PERSONNEL

EXECUTIVE SALARIES

See: EXECUTIVE COMPENSATION

EXECUTIVE SEARCH SERVICES

See: EMPLOYMENT AGENCIES AND SERVICES; RECRUITMENT OF PERSONNEL

EXECUTIVE SECRETARIES

See: OFFICE PRACTICE

EXECUTIVE STRESS

See: STRESS (ANXIETY)

EXECUTIVE TRAINING AND DEVELOPMENT

See also: ADULT EDUCATION; BUSINESS EDUCATION; TRAINING OF EMPLOYEES

ABSTRACTS AND INDEXES

Business Periodicals Index. H. W. Wilson Co. • 11 times a year. Quarterly and annual cumulations. Price varies.

DIRECTORIES

Bricker's International Directory: Long-Term University- Based Executive Programs. Peterson's. • Annual. $395.00. Presents detailed information about executive education programs offered by 85 universities and nonprofit organizations in the U. S. and around the world. Includes general management and function-specific programs.

Training and Development Organizations Directory. Gale Cengage Learning. • 1994. $415.00. Sixth edition.

HANDBOOKS AND MANUALS

Gower Handbook of Management Development. Alan Mumford, editor. Ashgate Publishing Co. • 1995. $129.95. Fourth edition. Consists of 28 chapters written by various authors. Published by Gower in England.

How to Conduct Training Seminars: A Complete Reference Guide for Training Managers. Lawrence S. Munson. McGraw-Hill. • 1992. $34.95. Second edition.

Studying Your Workforce: Applied Research Methods and Tools for the Training and Development Practitioner. Alan Clardy. Sage Publications, Inc. • 1997. $79.95. Describes how to apply specific research methods to common training problems. Emphasis is on data collection methods: testing, observation, surveys, and interviews. Topics include performance problems and assessment.

ONLINE DATABASES

Wilson Business Abstracts Online. H. W. Wilson Co. • Indexes and abstracts 600 major business periodicals, plus the *Wall Street Journal* and the business section of the *New York Times*. Indexing is from 1982, abstracting from 1990, with the two newspapers included from 1993. Updated weekly. Inquire as to online cost and availability. (*Business Periodicals Index* without abstracts is also available online.).

PERIODICALS AND NEWSLETTERS

Business Education Forum. National Business Education Association. • Four times a year. Libraries, $70.00 per year. Includes *Yearbook* and *Keying In*, a newsletter.

Executive Excellence: The Newsletter of Personal Development, Managerial Effectiveness, and Organizational Productivity. Kenneth M. Shelton, editor. Executive Excellence Publishing. • Monthly. $129.00 per year. Newsletter.

Journal of Management Education. Organizational Behavior Teaching Society. Sage Publications, Inc. • Bimonthly. Institutions, $397.00 per year; includes print and online editions. A scholarly journal dealing with the teaching and training of business students and managers.

T and D Magazine. American Society for Training

and Development. • Monthly. Free to members; non-members, $85.00 per year.

Training: The Magazine of Covering the Human Side of Business. VNU Business Media. • Monthly. $78.00 per year.

TRADE/PROFESSIONAL ASSOCIATIONS

American Society for Training and Development. 1640 King St., Alexandria, VA 22313-2043. Phone: 800-628-2783 or (703)683-8100 Fax: (703)683-1523 • URL: http://www.astd.org.

OTHER SOURCES

Maximizing Law Firm Profitability: Hiring, Training, and Developing Productive Lawyers. American Lawyer Media, Inc. • Looseleaf. $169.00. Updated as needed. (Law Journal Press).

EXECUTIVES

See also: ADMINISTRATION; BUSINESS; CORPORATE DIRECTORS AND OFFICERS

BIBLIOGRAPHIES

Thunderbird International Business Review. Thunderbird American Graduate School of International Management. John Wiley and Sons, Inc., Journals. • Bimonthly. $499.00 per year; with online edition, $532.00 per year. Formerly *International Executive*.

BIOGRAPHICAL SOURCES

American Business Leaders: From Colonial Times to the Present. Neil A. Hamilton. ABC-CLIO, Inc. • 1999. $175.00. Two volumes. Contains biographies of 413 notable business figures. Historical coverage is from the 17th century to the 1990s.

The Highwaymen: Warriors on the Information Superhighway. Ken Auletta. Harcourt Trade Publications. • 1998. $13.00. Revised expanded edition. Contains critical articles about Ted Turner, Rupert Murdoch, Barry Diller, Michael Eisner, and other key figures in electronic communications, entertainment, and information. (Harvest Book Series).

Leaders of American Business and Industry. Gale Cengage Learning. • 2002. $145.00. Three volumes. Provides popularly written biographies of influential American entrepreneurs and business leaders, past and present. Includes detailed profiles of major companies. (UXL imprint).

Newsmakers. Gale Cengage Learning. • Annual. $155.00. Three softbound issues and one hardbound annual. Biographical information on individuals currently in the news. Includes photographs. Formerly *Contemporary Newsmakers*.

Who Knows Who: Networking Through Corporate Boards. Jeannette E. Glynn. Who Knows Who Publishing. • 1998. $165.00. Fifth edition. Shows the connections between the board members of major U. S. corporations and major foundations and nonprofit organizations.

Who's Who in Finance and Industry. Marquis Who's Who. • Biennial. $259.95. Provides over 21,000 concise biographies of business leaders in all fields.

CD-ROM DATABASES

OECD Statistical Compendium. Organization for Economic Cooperation and Development. • Semiannual. $1,905.00 per year for 1 to 10 users. CD-ROM contains more than 730,000 monthly, quarterly, and annual time series for OECD countries, 1960 to date. Includes fully searchable data on agriculture, food, economic indicators, national accounts, employment, energy, finance, industry, technology, and foreign trade. Results can be displayed in various forms.

Profiles in Business and Management: An International Directory of Scholars and Their Research [CD-ROM]. Harvard Business School

Publishing. • Annual. $595.00. Fully searchable CD-ROM version of two-volume printed directory. Contains bibliographic and biographical information for over 5600 business and management experts active in 21 subject areas. Formerly *International Directory of Business and Management Scholars*.

Standard & Poor's Corporations. Available from Dialog OnDisc. • Monthly. Price on application. Produced by Standard & Poor's. Contains three CD-ROM files: Executives, Private Companies, and Public Companies, providing detailed information on more than 70,000 business executives, 55,000 private companies, and 12,000 publicly-traded corporations.

The Tax Directory [CD-ROM]. Tax Analysts. • Quarterly. Provides *The Tax Directory* listings on CD-ROM, covering federal, state, and international tax officials, tax practitioners, and corporate tax executives.

WILSONDISC: Wilson Business Abstracts. H. W. Wilson Co. • Monthly. Includes unlimited online access to *Wilson Business Abstracts* through WILSONLINE. Provides CD-ROM "cover-to-cover" abstracting and indexing of over 600 prominent business periodicals. Indexing is from 1982, abstracting from 1990. (*Business Periodicals Index* without abstracts is available on CD-ROM at $1,495 per year.).

DIRECTORIES

Corporate Yellow Book: Who's Who at the Leading U.S. Companies. Leadership Directions, Inc. • Quarterly. $360.00 per year. Lists names and titles of over 42,000 key executives in major U. S. corporations. Includes four indexes: industry, personnel, geographic by state, and company/subsidiary. Companion volume to *Financial Yellow Book*.

Cyberhound's Guide to People on the Internet. Gale Cengage Learning. • 1996. $79.00. Second edition. Provides descriptions of about 5,500 Internet databases maintained by or for prominent individuals in business, the professions, entertainment, and sports. Indexed by name, subject, and keyword (master index). (Cyberhound's Series).

D and B Million Dollar Directory. • Annual. Commercial institutions, $1,395.00; libraries, $1,275.00. Lease basis.

Directory of Executive Recruiters. Kennedy Information, Inc. • Annual. $49.95. Contains profiles of more than 5,500 executive search firms in the U. S., Canada, and Mexico.

Directory of Outplacement and Career Management Firms. Kennedy Information, Inc. • Annual. $149.95. Contains profiles of more than 390 firms specialize in helping "downsized" executives find new employment. Formerly *Directory of Outplacement Firms*.

Financial Yellow Book: Who's Who at the Leading U. S. Financial Institutions. Leadership Directories, Inc. • Semiannual. $265.00. Gives the names and titles of over 28,000 key executives in financial institutions. Includes the areas of banking, investment, money management, and insurance. Five indexes are provided: institution, executive name, geographic by state, financial service segment, and parent company.

Standard and Poor's Register of Corporations, Directors and Executives. Standard and Poor's. • Annual. $675.00. Looseleaf service. Lease basis. Periodic supplementation. Over 55,000 public and privately held corporations in the U.S.

The Tax Directory. Tax Analysts. • Covers: Volume One--Approximately 15,000 federal and state government tax legislators, policymakers, administrators, and employees; tax regulation attorneys; over 500 international tax officials with central banks, ministries of finance, foreign embassies and consulate, and chambers of commerce; over

300 tax and business journalists and editors working for magazines, journals, newspapers, television, and radio; tax sections of over 100 trade and professional associations; state CPA, bar, and enrolled agent associations. Volume Two--Over 5,000 corporate tax managers of large U.S. and international firms. Entries include: For government and international officials--Name, title, address, phone, fax, email and website. For corporate tax managers--Name, address, phone, fax, email, website, and company name. For journalists--Name, address, phone, fax, email, website, and name of publication/network. For organizations and associations--Name, address, phone, fax, email, website, budget, membership, background information, and description of purpose.

HANDBOOKS AND MANUALS

Kennedy's Pocket Guide to Working with Executive Recruiters. James H. Kennedy, editor. Kennedy Information, Inc. • 2002. $17.95. Second revised editon. Consists of 30 chapters written by various experts. Includes a glossary: "Lexicon of Executive Recruiting.".

INTERNET DATABASES

Business 2.0 Web Guide to the Best Business Links. Business 2.0 Media Inc. Phone: (415)293-4800 E-mail: support@business2.com • URL: http://www.business2.com/webguide • Web site presents an extensive, searchable directory of links to "the best, most informative, and authoritative web pages." Twenty main categories cover business, finance, career, company information, people, and technology topics, with thousands of subtopics, all linking to Web sites recommended by experienced business researchers. Fees: Free.

EBSCO Information Services. Ebsco Publishing. Phone: 800-653-2726 or (978)356-6500 Fax: (978)356-6565 E-mail: ep@epnet.com • URL: http://www.epnet.com • Fee-based Web site providing Internet access to a wide variety of databases, including business-related material. Full text is available for many periodical titles, with daily updates. Fees: Apply.

InSite 2. Intelligence Data/Thomson Financial. Phone: 800-654-0393 or (617)856-1890 Fax: (617)737-3182 E-mail: intelligence.data@tfn.com • URL: http://www.insite2.gale.com/ • Fee-based Web site consolidates information in a "Base Pack" consisting of Business InSite, Market InSite, and Company InSite. Optional databases are Consumer InSite, Health and Wellness InSite, Newsletter In-Site, and Computer InSite. Includes fulltext content from more than 2,500 trade publications, journals, newsletters, newspapers, analyst reports, and other sources. Continuous updating. Formerly produced by The Gale Group.

ProQuest Direct. ProQuest Inc. Phone: 800-889-3358 or (734)761-4700 Fax: (734)662-4554 • URL: http://proquest.com • Fee-based Web site providing Internet access to more than 3,000 periodicals, newspapers, and other publications. Many items are available full-text, with daily updates. Includes extensive corporate and financial information. Fees: Apply.

ONLINE DATABASES

Management Contents. Gale Cengage Learning. • Covers a wide range of management, financial, marketing, personnel, and administrative topics. About 150 leading business journals are indexed and abstracted from 1974 to date, with monthly updating. Inquire as to online cost and availability.

Standard & Poor's Register: Biographical. Standard & Poor's Corp. • Contains brief biographies of approximately 70,000 business executives and directors. Corresponds to the biographical volume of *Standard & Poor's Register of Corporations, Directors, and Executives*.

Updated twice a year. Inquire as to online cost and availability.

Wilson Business Abstracts Online. H. W. Wilson Co. • Indexes and abstracts 600 major business periodicals, plus the *Wall Street Journal* and the business section of the *New York Times*. Indexing is from 1982, abstracting from 1990, with the two newspapers included from 1993. Updated weekly. Inquire as to online cost and availability. (*Business Periodicals Index* without abstracts is also available online.).

PERIODICALS AND NEWSLETTERS

Academy of Management Executive. Academy of Management. • Bimonthly. $125.00 per year. Contains articles relating to the practical application of management principles and theory.

Administrative Science Quarterly. Cornell University, Johnson Graduate School of Management. • Individuals: $65.00 per year; institutions, $130.00 per year.

Business Finance. Penton Technology and Lifestyle Media. • Monthly. $59.00 per year. Covers trends in finance, technology, and economics for corporate financial executives.

Daily Report for Executives. BNA, Inc. • Daily. $7,698.00 per year. Newsletter. Covers legal, regulatory, economic, and tax developments affecting corporations.

Directors & Boards. • Quarterly. $295.00 per year. Edited for corporate board members and senior executive officers.

Director's Monthly. National Association of Corporate Directors. • Description: Reports current issues and events of interest to corporate directors. Covers such topics as director independence, ethics, directors, audit, compensation, nominating committees, and changing regulatory requirements. Recurring features include roundtable discussions and interviews.

Executive Wealth Advisory. National Institute of Business Management. • Description: Provides investment strategies and opportunities to build personal wealth rapidly and safely.

Management Review. American Management Association. • Membership.

TRADE/PROFESSIONAL ASSOCIATIONS

Academy of Management. P.O. Box 3020, Briarcliff Manor, NY 10510-3020. Phone: (914)923-2607 Fax: (914)923-2615 E-mail: academy@pace.edu • URL: http://www.aomonline.edu • Members are university professors of management and selected business executives.

American Association of Industrial Management. Stearns Bldg., Ste. 506, 293 Bridge St., Springfield, MA 01103. Phone: 888-698-1968 or (413)737-9725 or (413)737-8766 Fax: (413)737-9724 E-mail: aaimnmta@aol.com • URL: http://www.aaimnmta.com.

Association of Master of Business Administration Executives. c/o AMBA Center, 388 E Main St., Ste. A, Branford, CT 06405. Phone: (203)315-5221 Fax: (203)483-6186.

Chief Executives Organization. 7920 Norfolk Ave., Ste. 400, Bethesda, MD 20814-2507. Phone: (301)656-9220 Fax: (301)656-9221 E-mail: info@ceo.org • URL: http://www.ceo.org • Invited members of the Young Presidents' Organization who have reached the age of 49, the mandatory "retirement" age for YPO. (Young Presidents' Organization comprises presidents of corporations with gross annual revenue of at least one million dollars and a minimum of 50 employees, of nonindustrial corporations with revenue of two million dollars and 25 employees, or of banking corporations with average deposits of 15 million dollars and 25 employees. Each member must have been elected president of a corporation before reaching the age of 40.) Sponsors educational programs.

International Executive Service Corps. 1900 M St. NW, Ste. 500, Washington, DC 20036. Phone: 800-243-4372 or (202)589-2600 Fax: (202)326-0289 E-mail: iesc@iesc.org • URL: http://www.iesc.org • Provides technical and managerial assistance to enterprises, organizations and government bodies in emerging democracies and developing countries. Focuses on the knowledge, skill and experience of its 12,000 industry experts. Maintains a network of experts that includes high-level professionals drawn from nearly every area of private enterprise, government and non-governmental organizations; Geekcorps division includes experts in communications and information technology and is committed to closing the digital divide.

National Association for Female Executives. P.O. Box 156, Congers, NY 10920-0156. Phone: 800-634-6233 Fax: (212)351-6486 E-mail: nafe@nafe.com • URL: http://www.nafe.com.

National Association of Corporate Directors. 1828 L St., N.W., Ste. 801, Washington, DC 20036. Phone: (202)775-0509 Fax: (202)775-4857 E-mail: info@nacdonline.org • URL: http://www.nacdonline.org.

Tax Analysts. 400 S Maple Ave., Ste. 400, Falls Church, VA 22046. Phone: 800-955-2444 or (703)533-4400 Fax: (703)533-4444 E-mail: cservice@tax.org • URL: http://www.tax.org • Reviews all tax law developments, federal, state, international comprehensively; compiles statistics. **Convention/Meeting:** none.

Young Presidents' Organization. 600 E Las Colinas Blvd., Ste. 1000, 451 S Decker, Ste. 200, Irving, TX 75039. Phone: 800-773-7976 or (972)587-1500 Fax: (972)650-4777 E-mail: membership@ypo.org • URL: http://www.ypo.org • Presidents or chief executive officers of corporations with minimum of 50 employees; each member must have been elected president before his/her 40th birthday and must retire by June 30th the year after his/her 50th birthday. Assists members in becoming better presidents through education and idea exchange. Conducts courses for members and spouses, in business, arts and sciences, world affairs, and family and community life, during a given year at various locations, including graduate business schools.

EXECUTIVES, WOMEN

See: WOMEN EXECUTIVES

EXERCISE EQUIPMENT INDUSTRY

See: FITNESS INDUSTRY

EXHIBITS

See: DISPLAY OF MERCHANDISE; TRADE SHOWS

EXPENSE CONTROL

See: COST CONTROL

EXPERT SYSTEMS

See: ARTIFICIAL INTELLIGENCE

EXPLOSIVES INDUSTRY

ABSTRACTS AND INDEXES
Applied Science and Technology Index. H. W. Wilson Co. • 11 times a year. Quarterly and annual

cumulations. Price varies. Indexes a wide variety of English language technical, industrial, and engineering periodicals.

Engineering Index Monthly: Abstracting and Indexing Services Covering Sources of the World's Engineering Literature. Engineering Information Inc. • Monthly. Institutions, $5,279.00 per year. Provides indexing and abstracting of the world's engineering and technical literature.

F & S Index: United States. Gale Cengage Learning. • Monthly. $1,450.00 per year, including quarterly and annual cumulations. Provides annotated citations to marketing, business, financial, and industrial literature. Coverage of U. S. business activity includes trade journals, financial magazines, business newspapers, and special reports.

IMM Abstracts and Index: A Survey of World Literature on the Economic Geology and Mining of All Minerals (Except Coal), Mineral Processing, and Nonferrous Extraction Metallurgy. Institution of Mining and Metallurgy. • Bimonthly. $500.00 per year. Provides international coverage of the literature of mining and nonferrous metallurgy. Includes mineral economics, tunnelling, and rock mechanics.

CD-ROM DATABASES
WILSONDISC: Applied Science and Technology Abstracts. H. W. Wilson Co. • Monthly. Includes unlimited access to the online version of *Applied Science and Technology Abstracts* through WILSONLINE. Provides CD-ROM indexing and abstracting of 500 prominent scientific, technical, engineering, and industrial periodicals. Indexing coverage is provided from 1983 to date and abstracting from 1993 to date.

HANDBOOKS AND MANUALS
Explosives. Josef Kohler and others. John Wiley and Sons, Inc. • 2002. $200.00. Fifth edition. Provides fundamental information on explosives for chemical engineers and other professionals.

ONLINE DATABASES
Aerospace Database. American Institute of Aeronautics and Astronautics. • Contains abstracts of literature covering all aspects of the aerospace and aircraft industry 1983 to date. Monthly updates. Inquire as to online cost and availability.

Aerospace/Defense Markets and Technology. Gale Cengage Learning. • Abstracts of commerical aerospace/defense related literature, 1982 to date. Also includes information about major defense contracts awarded by the U. S. Department of Defense. International coverage. Inquire as to online cost and availability.

Applied Science and Technology Index Online. H. W. Wilson Co. • Provides online indexing of 500 major scientific, technical, industrial, and engineering periodicals. Time period is 1983 to date. Monthly updates. Inquire as to online cost and availability.

F & S Index. Gale Cengage Learning. • Contains about four million citations to worldwide business, financial, and industrial or consumer product literature appearing from 1972 to date. Weekly updates. Inquire as to online cost and availability.

Trade & Industry Database. Gale Cengage Learning. • Provides indexing of business periodicals, January 1981 to date. Daily updates. (Full text articles from some periodicals are available online, 1983 to date. Inquire as to online cost and availability).

PERIODICALS AND NEWSLETTERS
Journal of Explosives Engineering. International Society of Explosives Engineers. • Bimonthly. $35.00 per year.

RESEARCH CENTERS AND INSTITUTES
Energetic Materials Research and Testing Center. New Mexico Institute of Mining and Technology,

100 South Rd., Socorro, NM 87801. Phone: (505)835-5312 Fax: (505)835-5630 E-mail: collis@emrtc.nmt.edu • URL: http://www.emrtc.nmt • Research areas include the development of industrial applications for explosives as energy sources.

New Mexico Engineering Research Institute. University of New Mexico. 901 University Blvd., S.E., Albuquerque, NM 87106-4339. Phone: (505)272-7200 Fax: (505)272-7203 E-mail: oneil@nmeri.umm.edu • URL: http://www.nmeri.umn.edu.

Rock Mechanics and Explosives Research Center. University of Missouri at Rolla, Rolla, MO 65401-0660. Phone: (573)341-4365 Fax: (573)341-4368 E-mail: vsnelson@umr.edu • URL: http://www.umr.edu.

TRADE/PROFESSIONAL ASSOCIATIONS
Institute of Makers of Explosives. 1120 19th St., N. W., Suite 310, Washington, DC 20036. Phone: (202)429-9280 Fax: (202)293-2420 E-mail: info@ime.org • URL: http://www.ime.org • Members are manufacturers of commercial explosives.

International Society of Explosives Engineers. 30325 Bainbridge Rd., Cleveland, OH 44139. Phone: (440)349-4400 Fax: (440)349-3788 E-mail: isee@isee.org • URL: http://www.isee.org • Formerly Society of Explosives Engineers.

EXPORT-IMPORT TRADE

See also: CUSTOMS HOUSE, U.S. CUSTOMS SERVICE; FOREIGN TRADE

GENERAL WORKS
United States Agricultural Trade: Trends, Policy, and Direction. Larry V. Fedorov, editor. Nova Science Publishers, Inc. • 2003. $59.00. Includes data on the impact of NAFTA on the import and export of farm products.

ALMANACS AND YEARBOOKS
International Monetary Fund. Annual Report on Exchange Arrangements and Exchange Restrictions. International Monetary Fund Publications Services. • Annual. Individuals, $95.00; libraries, $47.50.

CD-ROM DATABASES
OECD Statistical Compendium. Organization for Economic Cooperation and Development. • Semiannual. $1,905.00 per year for 1 to 10 users. CD-ROM contains more than 730,000 monthly, quarterly, and annual time series for OECD countries, 1960 to date. Includes fully searchable data on agriculture, food, economic indicators, national accounts, employment, energy, finance, industry, technology, and foreign trade. Results can be displayed in various forms.

U. S. Exports of Merchandise on CD-ROM. U. S. Bureau of the Census, Foreign Trade Div.,. • Monthly. $1,200 per year. Provides export data in the most extensive detail available, including product, quantity, value, shipping weight, country of destination, customs district of exportation, etc.

U. S. Imports of Merchandise (CD-ROM). U. S. Bureau of the Census, Foreign Trade Division. • Monthly. $1,200 per year. Provides import data in the most extensive detail available, including product, quantity, value, shipping weight, country of origin, customs district of entry, rate provision, etc.

USA Trade. U. S. Department of Commerce. • Monthly. $650.00 per year. Provides over 150,000 trade-related data series on CD-ROM. Includes full text of many government publications. Specific data is included on national income, labor, price indexes, foreign exchange, technical standards, and international markets. Website address is http://www.stat-usa.gov/.

World Trade Analyzer. Statistics Canada,

International Trade Division. • Annual. CD-ROM provides 20 years of export-import data for 800 commodities traded by the 180 member countries of the United Nations.

World Trade Atlas CD-ROM. Global Trade Information Services, Inc. • Monthly. $4,920.00 per year. ($3,650.00 per year with quarterly updates.) Provides government statistics on trade between the U. S. and each of more than 200 countries. Includes import-export data, trade balances, product information, market share, price data, etc. Time period is the most recent three years.

DIRECTORIES

American Export Register. Thomas Publishing Co. • Covers: over 45,000 companies in the United States exporting products and services, United States and foreign government services to exporters and importers, chambers of commerce abroad, embassies and consulates in the U.S., and financial and transportation services such as airlines, steamship lines, freight forwarders, customs brokers, and banks, international cargo carriers and carriers, world trade centers. Entries include: Company name, address, phone, URL address, fax, markets served, contact name, product or service, company description.

Directory of United States Exporters. Piers Publishing Group. • Annual. $2,750. Provides information on about 22,000 exporters located in the U. S.

Directory of United States Importers. Piers Publishing Group. • Annual. $2,750.00. Provides information on about 32,000 importers located in the U. S.

Directory of United States Importers/Directory of United States Exporters. Piers Publishing Group. • Annual. $675.00. Two volumes. $475.00 per volume. Approximately 55,000 firms with import and export interests; export and import managers, agents, and merchants in the United States; World ports; consulates and embassies. Formerly *United States Importers and Exporters Directories.*

International Intertrade Index of New Imported Products. John E. Felber. • Monthly. $45.00 per year. Lists new foreign products being offered to importers. Newsletter available *Foreign Trade Fairs New Products.*

Kelly's Industrial Directory. Kelly's Directories. • Covers: Over 105,000 UK industrial companies. Entries include: Company name, address, phone, fax, telex, product or service.

U.S. Custom House Guide. Commonwealth Business Media Inc. • Publication includes: List of ports having customs facilities, customs officials, port authorities, chambers of commerce, embassies and consulates, foreign trade zones, and other organizations; related trade services. Entries include: For each principal port--Name of organization or agency, address, phone, fax, names and titles of key personnel; description and limitations of port facilities. For service firms--Company name, address, phone, fax. Principal content is U.S. tariff schedules and customs regulations, and a "How to Import" manual.

ENCYCLOPEDIAS AND DICTIONARIES

Exporters' Encyclopedia. Dun and Bradstreet Information Services. • 1995. $495.00. Lease basis.

HANDBOOKS AND MANUALS

Arthur Andersen North American Business Sourcebook: The Most Comprehensive, Authoritative Reference Guide to Expanding Trade in the North American Market. Triumph Books. • 1993. $195.00. Includes statistical, regulatory, economic, and directory information relating to North American trade, including information on the North American Free Trade Agreement (NAFTA). Emphasis is on exporting to Mexico and Canada.

Basic Guide to Exporting. Available from U. S. Government Printing Office. • R999. $19.00. Issued by the International Trade Administration, U. S. Department of Commerce. Discusses the costs, risks, and strategy of exporting. Includes sources of assistance and a glossary of terms used in the export business.

Export Administration Regulations, 2004: Basic Manual. Available from U. S. Government Printing Office. • 2004. $160.00. Looseleaf. Price includes supplements for an indeterminate period. Issued by the Bureau of Export Administration, U. S. Department of Commerce. Includes information on export policies, regulations, boycotted countries, licensing procedures, documentation requirements, and so forth.

Export-Import Financing. Harry M. Vendikian and Gerald A. Warfield. John Wiley and Sons, Inc. • 1996. $79.95. Fourth edition. (Frontiers in Finance Series).

Export Sales and Marketing Manual. Export Institute. • Annual. $315.00. Includes CD-Rom. Provides detailed information on exporting from the U. S. Includes sections on licenses, markets, pricing, agreements, shipping, payment, and other export topics.

Exporting with the Internet. Peter J. Robinson and Jonathan Powell. John Wiley and Sons, Inc. • 1997. $39.95. Explains how the Internet can help with finding overseas buyers and expediting export shipments and payments. (Business Technology Series).

Import and Export. Entrepreneur Media, Inc. • Looseleaf. $59.50. A practical guide to starting an import/ export business. Covers profit potential, start-up costs, market size evaluation, owner's time required, pricing, accounting, advertising promotion, etc. (Start-Up Business Guide No. E1092.).

Importers Manual U. S. A.: The Single Source Reference Encyclopedia for Importied States. Edward G. Hinkelman. World Trade Press. • 1998. $87.00. Third edition. Published by World Trade Press. Covers U. S. customs regulations, letters of credit, contracts, shipping, insurance, and other items relating to importing. Includes 60 essays on practical aspects of importing.

Importing into the United States. Available from U. S. Government Printing Office. • 1998. $10.50. Issued by the U. S. Customs Service, Department of the Treasury. Formerly *Exporting to the United States.* Explains customs organization, entry of goods, invoices, assessment of duty, marking requirements, and other subjects.

International Standards Desk Reference: Your Passport to World Markets. Amy Zuckerman. AMACOM. • 1996. $35.00. Provides information on standards important in export-import trade, such as ISO 9000.

Reference Book for World Traders, 1987. Croner Publications, Inc. • 1990. Price on application. A looseleaf handbook covering information required for planning and executing exports and imports to and from all foreign countries; kept up to date by an amendment service.

United States Export Administration Regulations. Available from U. S. Government Printing Office. • $132.00. Looseleaf. Includes basic manual and supplementary bulletins for one year. Issued by the Bureau of Export Administration, U. S. Department of Commerce (http://www.doc.gov). Consists of export licensing rules and regulations.

INTERNET DATABASES

Business 2.0 Web Guide to the Best Business Links. Business 2.0 Media Inc. Phone: (415)293-4800 E-mail: support@business2.com • URL: http://www.business2.com/webguide • Web site presents an extensive, searchable directory of links to "the best, most informative, and authoritative web pages." Twenty main categories cover business, finance, career, company information, people, and technology topics, with thousands of subtopics, all linking to Web sites recommended by experienced business researchers. Fees: Free.

Fedstats. Federal Interagency Council on Statistical Policy. Phone: (202)395-7254 • URL: http://www.fedstats.gov • Web site features an efficient search facility for full-text statistics produced by more than 100 federal agencies, including the Census Bureau, the Bureau of Economic Analysis, and the Bureau of Labor Statistics. Boolean searches can be made within one agency or for all agencies combined. Links are offered to international statistical bureaus, including the UN, IMF, OECD, UNESCO, Eurostat, and 20 individual countries. Fees: Free.

FreeLunch.com. Economy.com, Inc. Phone: (610)696-8700 Fax: (610)696-1678 • URL: http://www.freelunch.com • Web site provides free access to more than 1.5 million economic and financial data series, covering industry, demographics, labor markets, prices, retail sales, government spending, trade, interest rates, housing starts, the stock market, and many other topics. Data is available for various time periods in either chart or table form. Searching is offered. Fees: Free, but registration required. Economy.com, Inc. also offers fee-based economic analysis at *The Dismal Scientist* site (http://www.dismal.com).

Manufacturing Profiles. U. S. Bureau of the Census. Phone: (301)763-4636 E-mail: webmaster@census.gov • URL: http://www.census.gov/prod/www/abs/mfg-prof.html • The Census Bureau makes available free on PDF (Portable Document Format) an annual consolidation of the entire Current Industrial Report series, presenting "all the data compiled." Contains statistics on production, shipments, inventories, consumption, exports, imports, and orders for a wide variety of manufactured products.

U. S. Business Advisor. Small Business Administration. Phone: (202)205-6600 Fax: (202)205-7064 • URL: http://www.business.gov • Web site provides "a one-stop electronic link to all the information and services government provides for the business community." Covers about 60 federal agencies that exist to assist or regulate business. Detailed information is provided on financial assistance, workplace issues, taxes, regulations, international trade, and other business topics. Searching is offered. Fees: Free.

ONLINE DATABASES

Business and Industry. Gale Cengage Learning. • Contains online citations, abstracts, and selected fulltext from more than 1,000 trade journals, newspapers, and other publications. Provides general coverage of both manufacturing and service industries, including marketing, production, industry trends, key events, and information on specific companies. Time span is 1994 to date. Daily updates. Inquire as to online cost and availability. (Also available in a CD-ROM version.).

Tablebase. Gale Cengage Learning. • Provides online numerical tabular data from a wide variety of business, organization, and government sources, including about 1,000 trade journals. Includes industry and individual company statistics relating to products, market share, sales forecasts, production, exports, market trends, etc. Time span is 1997 to date. Weekly updates. Inquire as to online cost and availability. (Also available in a CD-ROM version.).

PERIODICALS AND NEWSLETTERS

AgExporter. Available from U. S. Government Printing Office. • Monthly. $44.00 per year. Issued by the Foreign Agricultural Service, U. S. Department of Agriculture. Edited for U. S. exporters of farm products. Provides practical information on exporting, including overseas trade opportunities.

Amber Waves. Available from U. S. Government Printing Office. • Quarterly. $38.00 per year. Replaces *Agricultural Outlook; Food Review;* and

Rural America. Provides research and analysis from the U.S. Department of Agriculture's Economic Research Service. Includes economic data on agriculture, food, trade, and environmental factors.

Customs Bulletin and Decisions. Available from U. S. Government Printing Office. • Weekly. $247.00 per year. Issued by U. S. Customs Service, Department of the Treasury. Contains regulations, rulings, decisions, and notices relating to customs laws.

Export America. Available from U. S. Government Printing Office. • Monthly. $61.00 per year. Issued by the International Trade Administration, U. S. Department of Conmmerce (http://www.ita.doc.gov/). Contains articles written to help American exporters penetrate overseas markets. Provides information on opportunities for trade and methods of doing international business. Formerly *Business America.*

Export Today: The Global Business and Technology Magazine. Trade Communications, Inc. • Monthly. $49.00 per year. Edited for corporate executives to provide practical information on international business and exporting.

International Trade Alert. American Association of Exporters and Importers. • Description: Reports on trade issues as they affect importers and exporters. Contains news of actions by Customs, the Federal Drug Administration (FDA), and the Department of Commerce, CITA, CPSC, FTC, and the USDA, as well as other federal agencies and departments; and the status of regulations on imported/exported products. Also contains information on legislative activity affecting importers and exporters.

International Trade Reporter Export Reference Manual. BNA, Inc. • Biweekly. $874.00 per year. Looseleaf service.

The Journal of Commerce. Commonwealth Business Media. • Weekly. $146.00 per year. Topics include transatlantic shipping, domestic shipping, customs brokers, freight forwarders, ports, air freight, containerization, and other aspects of transportation and shipping logistics. Formerly *Journal of Commerce.*

Outlook for United States Agricultural Trade. Available from U. S. Government Printing Office. • Quarterly. $15.00 per year. Issued by the Economic Research Service, U. S. Department of Agriculture.

(Situation and Outlook Reports.).

RESEARCH CENTERS AND INSTITUTES

Division of Business and Economic Research. University of New Orleans. New Orleans, LA 70148. Phone: (504)280-6240 Fax: (504)280-6094.

International Tax Program. Harvard University, 1563 Massachusetts Ave., Pound Hall, Room 400, Cambridge, MA 02138. Phone: (617)495-4406 Fax: (617)495-0423 E-mail: itp@law.harvard.edu • URL: http://www.law.harvard.edu/programs/itp • Studies the worldwide problems of taxation, including tax law and tax administration.

STATISTICS SOURCES

Business Statistics of the United States. Linz Audain and Cornelia J. Strawser. Bernan Associates. • Annual. $147.00. Based on *Business Statistics*, formerly issue by the Bureau of Economic Analysis, U. S. Department of Commerce. Provides basic data for a wide variety of U. S. industries, services, and economic indicators. Most statistics are shown annually for 30 years and monthly for the most recent four years.

FAO Trade Yearbook. Available from Bernan Associates. • Annual. $45.00. Published by the Food and Agriculture Organization (http://www.fao.org). Provides extensive worldwide data on exports and imports of agricultural commodities, fertilizers, tractors, and pesticides. Includes more than 130 tables of detailed statistics.

Foreign Trade of the United States: Including State and Metro Area Export Data, 2000. Courtenay M. Slater. Bernan Press. • 2000. $147.00. 2001 Provides detailed national, state, and local data relating to U. S. exports and imports.

International Trade by Commodities Statistics. Organization for Economic Cooperation and Development. • Five times a year. $605.00 per year. Presents extensive, detailed statistical tables of OECD countries' imports and exports. Products are grouped by Standard International Trade Classification and by country.

International Trade Statistics Yearbook. United Nations Statistical Office. United Nations Publications. • Annual. $135.00. Two volumes.

National Trade Estimate Report on Foreign Trade Barriers [year]. Available from U. S. Government Printing Office. • Annual. $47.00. Issued by the Office of the United States Trade Representative. "Provides quantitative estimates of the impact of

foreign practices on the value of United States exports.".

Survey of Current Business. Available from U. S. Government Printing Office. • Monthly. $63.00 per year. Issued by Bureau of Economic Analysis, U. S. Department of Commerce. Presents a wide variety of business and economic data.

United States Waterborne Exports and General Imports. U.S. Bureau of the Census. • Quarterly and annual.

TRADE/PROFESSIONAL ASSOCIATIONS

American Association of Exporters and Importers. 1200 G St., N.W., Suite 800, Washington, DC 20005. Phone: (202)661-2181 Fax: (202)661-2185 E-mail: hq@aaei.org • URL: http://www.aaei.org.

National Association of Export Companies. Grand Central Station, P.O. Box 3949, New York, NY 10163-3949. Phone: 877-291-4901 Fax: (646)349-9628 E-mail: director@nexco.org • URL: http://www.nexco.org.

National Customs Brokers and Forwarders Association of America. 1200 18th St., N.W., Suite 901, Washington, DC 20036. Phone: (202)466-0222 Fax: (202)466-0226 E-mail: staff@ncbfaa.org • URL: http://www.ncbfaa.org • Formerly Customs Brokers and Forwarders Association of America.

OTHER SOURCES

Customs Regulations of the United States. Available from U. S. Government Printing Office. • Looseleaf. $175.00. Issued by U. S. Customs Service, Department of the Treasury. Reprint of regulations published to carry out customs laws of the U. S. Includes supplementary material for an indeterminate period.

Investing, Licensing, and Trading. Economist Intelligence Unit. • Semiannual. $345.00 per year for each country. Key laws, rules, and licensing provisions are explained for each of 60 countries. Information is provided on political conditions, markets, price policies, foreign exchange practices, labor, and export-import.

EXPOSITIONS

See: CONVENTIONS; FAIRS

EYECARE INDUSTRY

See: CONTACT LENS AND INTRAOCULAR LENS INDUSTRIES; OPHTHALMIC INDUSTRY

F

FABRICS, INDUSTRIAL

See: INDUSTRIAL FABRICS INDUSTRY

FABRICS, NONWOVEN

See: NONWOVEN FABRICS INDUSTRY

FACILITIES MANAGEMENT

See: FACTORY MANAGEMENT

FACSIMILE SYSTEMS

ABSTRACTS AND INDEXES

Applied Science and Technology Index. H. W. Wilson Co. • 11 times a year. Quarterly and annual cumulations. Price varies. Indexes a wide variety of English language technical, industrial, and engineering periodicals.

Business Periodicals Index. H. W. Wilson Co. • 11 times a year. Quarterly and annual cumulations. Price varies.

DIRECTORIES

Better Buys for Business: The Independent Consumer Guide to Office Equipment. What to Buy for Business, Inc. • 10 times a year. $134.00 per year. Each issue is on a particular office product, with detailed evaluation of specific models: 1. Low-Volume Copier Guide, 2. Mid-Volume Copier Guide, 3. High-Volume Copier Guide, 4. Plain Paper Fax and Low-Volume Multifunctional Guide, 5. Mid/High-Volume Multifunctional Guide, 6. Laser Printer Guide, 7. Color Printer and Color Copier Guide, 8. Scan-to-File Guide, 9. Business Phone Systems Guide, 10. Postage Meter Guide, with a Short Guide to Shredders.

FaxUSA: A Directory of Facsimile Numbers for Business and Organizations Nationwide. Omnigraphics, Inc. • 2004. $165.00. 11th edition. Provides more than 118,000 listings, with fax numbers, telephone numbers, and addresses.

National E-Mail and Fax Directory. Gale Cengage Learning. • Annual. $160.00. Provides fax numbers, telephone numbers, and addresses for U. S. companies, organizations, government agencies, and libraries. Includes alphabetic listings and subject listings.

North American Fax Directory. Dial-A-Fax Directories Corp. • Covers: Approximately 209,000 companies that possess facsimile machines. Entries include: Company name, address, phone, subsidiary

and branch names and locations, standard industrial classification (sic) code, fax number. Subscription includes access to a database of over 500,000 firms worldwide with fax numbers.

Telecommunications Directory. Gale. • Covers: Two volumes-North America and International, Cover approximately 6,000 national and international voice and data communications networks, electronic mail services, teleconferencing facilities and services, facsimile services, Internet access providers, videotex and teletext operations, transactional services, local area networks, audiotex services, microwave systems/networkers, satellite facilities, and others involved in telecommunications, including related consultants, advertisers/marketers; associations, regulatory bodies, and publishers. Entries include: Company or organization name, address, phone, fax, year established, name and title of contact, executive officers and board of directors, function or type of service; geographical area served; NAICS and SIC codes; number of employees; general description, including telecommunications-related activities; product/service; specific applications; means of access and equipment required; publications; intended market and availability; pricing; stock exchanges traded and ticker symbols; financial figures.

HANDBOOKS AND MANUALS

Fax Handbook. Gerald V. Quinn. McGraw-Hill. • 1989. $16.95.

Fax Modem Sourcebook. Andrew Margolis. John Wiley and Sons, Inc. • 1995. $90.00. Explains fax modem technology for both the novice and the experienced user. Includes technical programming information and international standards.

The Modem Reference: The Complete Guide to PC Communications. Michael A. Banks. Information Today, Inc. • 2000. $29.95. Fourth edition. Covers personal computer data communications technology, including fax transmissions, computer networks, modems, and the Internet. Popularly written.

ONLINE DATABASES

Applied Science and Technology Index Online. H. W. Wilson Co. • Provides online indexing of 500 major scientific, technical, industrial, and engineering periodicals. Time period is 1983 to date. Monthly updates. Inquire as to online cost and availability.

Wilson Business Abstracts Online. H. W. Wilson Co. • Indexes and abstracts 600 major business periodicals, plus the *Wall Street Journal* and the business section of the *New York Times.* Indexing is from 1982, abstracting from 1990, with the two newspapers included from 1993. Updated weekly.

Inquire as to online cost and availability. (*Business Periodicals Index* without abstracts is also available online.).

PERIODICALS AND NEWSLETTERS

FAX Magazine. Technical Data Publishing Corp. • Quarterly. Price on application.

T W I C E: This Week in Consumer Electronics. Reed Business Information. • 29 times a year. $129.90 per year. Contains marketing and manufacturing news relating to a wide variety of consumer electronic products, including video, audio, telephone, and home office equipment.

FACTORY LOCATION

See: LOCATION OF INDUSTRY

FACTORY MAINTENANCE

See: MAINTENANCE OF BUILDINGS

FACTORY MANAGEMENT

See also: TIME AND MOTION STUDY

GENERAL WORKS

Contemporary Supervision: Managing People and Technology. Betty R. Ricks and others. McGraw-Hill. • 1994. $68.75. Second edition. (Management Series).

ABSTRACTS AND INDEXES

Key Abstracts: Factory Automation. Available from INSPEC, Inc. • Monthly. $250.00 per year. Provides international coverage of journal and proceedings literature, including publications on CAD/CAM, materials handling, robotics, and factory management. Published in England by the Institution of Electrical Engineers (IEE).

ENCYCLOPEDIAS AND DICTIONARIES

Blackwell Encyclopedic Dictionary of Operations Management. Nigel Slack, editor. Blackwell Publishing. • 1997. $130.95. The editor is associated with the University of Warwick, England. Contains definitions of key terms combined with longer articles written by various U. S. and foreign business educators. Includes bibliographies and index. (Blackwell Encyclopedia of Management Series.).

HANDBOOKS AND MANUALS

Effective Supervisor's Handbook. Louis V. Imundo. AMACOM. • 1992. $16.95. Second edition.

Maintenance Engineering Handbook. Lindley R. Higgins and R. Keith Mobley. McGraw-Hill. • 2001. $150.00. Sixth edition. Contains about 60 chapters by various authors in 12 major sections covering all elements of industrial and plant maintenance.

Manager's Tool Kit: Practical Tips for Tackling 100 On-the-Job Problems. Cy Charney. AMACOM. • 1995. $17.95.

Managing Factory Maintenance. Joel Levitt. Industrial Press, Inc. • 1996. $39.95.

Standard Handbook of Plant Engineering. Robert C. Rosaler, editor. McGraw-Hill Professional. • 2002. $125.00. Third edition. (Handbook Series).

PERIODICALS AND NEWSLETTERS

AFE Newsline elsewhere. Association for Facilities Engineering. • Description: Internal newsletter of the association.

IndustryWeek: The Management Resource. Penton Media, Inc. • 22 times a year. Free to qualified personnel; others, $65.00 per year. Edited for industrial and business managers. Covers organizational and technological developments affecting industrial management.

Production. Gardner Publications, Inc. • Monthly. $48.00 per year. Covers the latest manufacturing management issues. Discusses the strategic and financial implications of various tecnologies as they impact factory management, quality and competitiveness.

RESEARCH CENTERS AND INSTITUTES

Carnegie Mellon Research Institute-Computer Automation and Robotics. Carnegie Mellon University, 700 Technology Dr., Pittsburgh, PA 15219. Phone: (412)268-3363 Fax: (412)368-7759 • URL: http://www.cmu.edu/cmri • Multidisciplinary research activities include expert systems applications, minicomputer and microcomputer systems design, genetic engineering, and transportation systems analysis.

Research Program in Takeovers and Corporate Restructuring. University of California, Los Angeles. UCLA-AGSM, 258 Tavistock Ave., Los Angeles, CA 90049-3229. Phone: (310)472-5110 Fax: (310)472-9471 E-mail: jweston@anderson. ucla.edu • URL: http://www.agsm.ucla.edu.

TRADE/PROFESSIONAL ASSOCIATIONS

American Association of Industrial Management. Stearns Bldg., Ste. 506, 293 Bridge St., Springfield, MA 01103. Phone: 888-698-1968 or (413)737-9725 or (413)737-8766 Fax: (413)737-9724 E-mail: aaimnmta@aol.com • URL: http://www.aaimnmta. com.

American Society of Mechanical Engineers. Three Park Ave., New York, NY 10016-5990. Phone: 800-843-2763 or (212)591-7722 Fax: (212)591-7674 E-mail: infocentral@asme.org • URL: http://www. asme.org.

Association for Facilities Engineering. 8180 Corporate Park Dr., Ste. 125, Cincinnati, OH 45242. Phone: (513)489-2473 Fax: (513)247-7422 E-mail: mail@afe.org • URL: http://www.afe.org.

Institute of Industrial Engineers. 3377 Parkway Ln., Ste. 200, Norcross, GA 30092. Phone: 800-494-0460 or (770)449-0460 Fax: (770)441-3295 E-mail: cs@iienet.org • URL: http://www.iienet.org • Formerly American Institute of Industrial Engineers.

Society for Advancement of Management. Texas A&M University-Corpus Christi, College of Business, 6300 Ocean Dr., Corpus Christi, TX 78412. Phone: 888-827-6077 or (361)825-6045 or (361)825-5574 Fax: (361)825-2725 E-mail: moustafa@falcon.tamucc.edu • URL: http://www. enterprise.tamucc.edu/sam/ • Professional organization of management executives in industry, commerce, government and education. Absorbed

Industrial Methods Society.

OTHER SOURCES

First-Line Supervision. American Management Association Extension Institute. • Looseleaf. $139.00. Self-study course. Focuses on the day-to-day concerns of the first line supervisor. A self-study course.

FACTORY SECURITY

See: INDUSTRIAL SECURITY PROGRAMS

FAILURES, BANK

See: BANK FAILURES

FAILURES, BUSINESS

See: BUSINESS FAILURES

FAIR EMPLOYMENT PRACTICES

See: EQUAL EMPLOYMENT OPPORTUNITY; LABOR

FAIR TRADE

See: PRICES AND PRICING

FAIRS

See also: CONCESSIONS; CONVENTIONS

DIRECTORIES

Cavalcade of Acts and Attractions. Amusement Business. • Annual. $85.00. Directory of personal appearance artists, touring shows and other specialized entertainment. Lists promoters, producers, managers and booking agents.

Directory of North American Fairs, Festivals and Expositions. Amusement Business. • Annual. $79.00. Lists over 5,000 fairs, festivals and expositions in the U.S. and Canada which run three days or more.

IAFE Directory. International Association of Fairs and Expositions. • Annual. Free to members; nonmembers, $125.00. Lists more than 1,300 member agricultural fairs in the United States and Canada. Formerly *International Association of Fairs and Expositions Directory.*

IEG Sponsorship Sourcebook. IEG Inc. • Covers: about 5,000 corporate sponsors and 1,600 major sports, events, and organizations worldwide available for commercial sponsorship; companies serving special events and sponsors (sports marketing agencies, fireworks suppliers, public relations firms, etc.). Entries include: For events--Event title, site, dates, name, and address of contact (including year-round phone number), attendance figures, event budget, and major present and past sponsors. For service firms--Company name, address, phone, contact, speciality/services. New sponsorship events are reported in "IEG Sponsorship Report", published every two weeks, which also includes a frequent "In Depth" directory of corporations and their special events contact, budget, priorities, events sponsored, etc.; $445 per year; $370 for nonprofit organizations.

International Association of Amusement Parks and Attractions International Directory and Buyers' Guide. International Association of Amusement Parks and Attractions. • Annual. $83.00. Over 1,800

member amusement parks, attractions and industry suppliers.

PERIODICALS AND NEWSLETTERS

Horseman and Fair World: Devoted to the Trotting and Pacing Horse. Horseman Publishing Co., Insite Communications. • Weekly. $80.00 per year.

IEG's Sponsorship Report: The International Newsletter of Event Sponsorship and Lifestyle Marketing. International Events Group, Inc. • Biweekly. $445.00 per year. Includes print and on-line editions. Newsletter reporting on corporate sponsorship of special events: sports, music, festivals, and the arts. Edited for event producers, directors, and marketing personnel.

TRADE/PROFESSIONAL ASSOCIATIONS

International Association of Fairs and Expositions. 3043 E Cario St., Springfield, MO 65802. Phone: 800-516-0313 or (417)862-5771 Fax: (417)862-0156 E-mail: iafe@fairsandexpos.com • URL: http://www.fairsandexpos.com.

FAMILY CORPORATIONS

See: CLOSELY HELD CORPORATIONS

FAMILY LAW

See also: DIVORCE

GENERAL WORKS

Women, Gender, and Work: What is Equality and How Do We Get There?: Martha F. Loutfi, editor. International Labour Organization. • 2001. $26.95. A collection of articles from the *International Labour Review* covering such topics as equal opportunity for women, family concerns, legal issues, the glass ceiling, wage inequality, and sexual harassment in the workplace. Includes statistical data.

ABSTRACTS AND INDEXES

Current Law Index: Multiple Access to Legal Periodicals. Gale Cengage Learning. • Monthly. $725.00 per year. Produced in cooperation with the American Association of Law Libraries. Indexes more than 900 law journals, legal newspapers, and specialty publications from the U.S., Canada, U.K., Ireland, Australia, and New Zealand.

Readers' Guide to Periodical Literature. H. W. Wilson Co. • Monthly. $345.00 per year. Includes annual *Cumulation.* Indexes about 250 pericdals of general interest.

ALMANACS AND YEARBOOKS

American Law Yearbook. Gale Cengage Learning. • Annual. $165.00. Serves as a yearly supplement to *West's Encyclopedia of American Law.* Describes new legal developments in many subject areas.

BIBLIOGRAPHIES

Encyclopedia of Legal Information Sources. Gale Cengage Learning. • 1992. $180.00. Second edition. Lists more than 23,000 law-related information sources, including print, nonprint, and organizational.

DIRECTORIES

Directory of Judges with Juvenile/Family Law Jurisdiction. National Council of Juvenile and Family Court Judges. • Irregular. $25.00. 1,400 judges who have juvenile, family, or domestic relations jurisdiction.

ENCYCLOPEDIAS AND DICTIONARIES

West's Encyclopedia of American Law. Available from Gale Cengage Learning. • 2003. $1,195.00. Second edition. 12 volumes. Published by West Group. Covers a wide variety of legal topics for the general reader.

HANDBOOKS AND MANUALS

Family Law in a Nutshell. Harry D. Krause. West Publishing Co. • 1995. $25.50. Third edition. (Nutshell Series).

Handbook of Family Law. Stuart J. Faber. Lega Books. • 1987. $56.50. Fifth revised edition. Two volumes.

Women and the Law. Carol H. Lefcourt, editor. West Group. • Annual. $302.00. Looseleaf service. Covers such topics as employment discrimination, pay equity (comparable worth), sexual harassment in the workplace, property rights, and child custody issues.

INTERNET DATABASES

Lexis.com Research System. Lexis-Nexis Group. Phone: 800-227-4908 or (937)865-6800 Fax: (937)865-6909 E-mail: webmaster@prod.lexis-nexis.com • URL: http://www.lexis.com • Fee-based Web site offers extensive searching of a wide variety of legal sources. Additional features include Daily Opinion Service, lexis.com Bookstore, Career Center, CLE Center, Law Schools, and Practice Pages ("Pages specific to areas of specialty").

ONLINE DATABASES

Contemporary Women's Issues. Gale Cengage Learning. • Provides fulltext articles online from 150 periodicals and a wide variety of additional sources relating to economic, legal, social, political, education, health, and other women's issues. Time span is 1992 to date. Weekly updates. Inquire as to online cost and availability. (Also available in a CD-ROM version.).

Readers' Guide Abstracts Online. H. W. Wilson Co. • Indexes and abstracts general interest periodicals, 1983 to date. Weekly updates. Inquire as to online cost and availability.

PERIODICALS AND NEWSLETTERS

Brandeis Law Journal. University of Louisville Louis D. Brandeis School of Law. University of Louisville. • Quarterly. $30.00 per year.

Family Advocate. American Bar Association, Family Law Section. • Quarterly. Members $39.50; non-members, $44.50 per year. Practical advice for attorneys practicing family law.

Family Court Review: An Interdisciplinary Journal. Association of Family and Conciliation Courts. Sage Publications, Inc. • Quarterly. Institutions, $456.00 per year.

Family Law Quarterly. American Bar Association, Family Law Section. • Quarterly. Free to members; non-members, $49.95 per year.

Family Law Reporter. Bureau of National Affairs Inc. • Description: Offers a notification and reference service tracking state and federal developments affecting family law. Covers divorce, adoption, support order enforcement, parental rights termination, taxes, property division, and other topics of interest to lawyers. Recurring features include full text of selected judicial opinions; federal regulations and standards; and columns titled Current Developments, Survey and Analysis, Courts and Legislatures Report, Monographs, Reference File, Practice Aids, State Divorce Laws, and Uniform and Model Acts.

Family Relations: State Capitals. Wakeman-Walworth, Inc. • 50 times a year. $245.00 per year.; print and online editions, $350.00 per year. Newsletter. Formerly *From the State Capitals: Family Relations.*

Journal of Social Welfare and Family Law. Taylor & Francis Group. • Quarterly. Individuals, $99.00 per year; institutions, $385.00 per year.

The Liberator: Male Call. Men's Defense Association. • Monthly. $24.00 per year. Newsletter supporting men's rights in family law. Formerly *Legal Beagle.*

Matrimonial Strategist. American Lawyer Media Inc. • Monthly. $175.00 per year. Newsletter on

legal strategy and matrimonial law.

RESEARCH CENTERS AND INSTITUTES

Center for Governmental Responsibility. University of Florida, College of Law, 230 Bruton-Geer, P.O. Box 117629, Gainesville, FL 32611. Phone: (352)392-2237 Fax: (352)392-1457 • URL: http://www.law.ufl.edu/cgr • Research fields include family law.

TRADE/PROFESSIONAL ASSOCIATIONS

American Academy of Matrimonial Lawyers. 150 N. Michigan Ave., Suite 2040, Chicago, IL 60601. Phone: (312)263-6477 Fax: (312)263-7682 E-mail: aaml@aaml.org • URL: http://www.aaml.org • Members are attorneys specializing in family law.

American College of Counselors. 1124 1/2 S 5th St., Springfield, IL 62703-2314. Phone: (217)726-6220 Fax: (217)726-6220 • Formerly National Alliance for Family Life.

Association for Conflict Resolution. 1527 New Hampshire Ave. NW, 3rd Fl., Washington, DC 20036. Phone: (202)667-9700 Fax: (202)265-1968 E-mail: info@acresolution.org • URL: http://www.acresolution.org • Formerly Academy of Family Mediators.

Association of Family and Conciliation Courts. c/o Ann Milne, 6515 Grand Teton Plz., Ste. 210, Madison, WI 53719-1048. Phone: (608)664-3750 Fax: (608)664-3751 E-mail: afcc@afccnet.org • URL: http://www.afccnet.org • Members are judges, attorneys, and family counselors. Promotes conciliation counseling as a complement to legal procedures.

National Council of Juvenile and Family Court Judges. P.O. Box 8907, Reno, NV 89507. Phone: (775)784-6012 Fax: (775)784-6628 E-mail: admin@ncjfcj.org • URL: http://www.ncjfcj.org/.

NOW Legal Defense and Education Fund. 395 Hudson St., 5th Fl., New York, NY 10014-3684. Phone: (212)925-6635 Fax: (212)226-1066 E-mail: peo@nowldef.org • URL: http://www.nowldef.org • Supersedes NOW Legal Committee.

OTHER SOURCES

Family Law Tax Guide. CCH, Inc. • Monthly. $619.00 per year. Looseleaf service.

FARM BUSINESS

See: AGRIBUSINESS

FARM CREDIT

See: AGRICULTURAL CREDIT

FARM EQUIPMENT INDUSTRY

See: AGRICULTURAL MACHINERY

FARM IMPLEMENTS

See: AGRICULTURAL MACHINERY

FARM INCOME

See: AGRICULTURAL STATISTICS

FARM JOURNALS

See also: BUSINESS JOURNALISM

ABSTRACTS AND INDEXES

Biological and Agricultural Index. H. W. Wilson Co. • 11 times a year. Annual and quarterly cumulations. Price varies.

DIRECTORIES

SRDS Consumer Magazine Advertising Source. SRDS. • Annual. $699.00 per year. Contains

advertising rates and other data for U. S. consumer magazines and agricultural publications. Also provides consumer market data for population, households, income, and retail sales. Formerly *Consumer Magazine and Advertising Source.*

PERIODICALS AND NEWSLETTERS

Agronomy Journal: An International Journal. American Society of Agronomy, Inc. • Bimonthly. Free to members; non-members, $216.00 per year.

Farm Journal: The Magazine of American Agriculture. Farm Journal Corp. • 12 times a year. $19.50 per year. Includes *Supplements.*

TRADE/PROFESSIONAL ASSOCIATIONS

Agricultural Communicators in Education. c/o University of Florida, Mowry Rd., Bldg. 16, Gainesville, FL 32611-0811. Phone: (352)392-9588 Fax: (352)392-7902 E-mail: ace@gnv.ifas.ufl.edu • URL: http://www.aceweb.org.

American Agricultural Editors' Association. PO Box 156, PO Box 156, New Prague, MN 56071. Phone: (952)758-6502 Fax: (952)758-5813 E-mail: ageditors@aol.com • URL: http://www.ageditors.com • Editors and editorial staff members of farm publications; affiliate members are agricultural public relations and advertising personnel, and state and national agricultural officials. Maintains the AAEA Professional Improvement Foundation. Conducts educational programs.

OTHER SOURCES

Bacon's Newspaper and Magazine Directories. Bacon's Information Inc. • Annual. $325.00 per year. Two volumes: Magazines and Newspapers. Covers print media in the United States and Canada. Formerly *Bacon's Publicity Checker.*

FARM LABOR

See: FARMERS; LABOR

FARM MACHINERY

See: AGRICULTURAL MACHINERY

FARM MANAGEMENT

See also: AGRICULTURE

GENERAL WORKS

Farm Management. Ronald D. Kay and others. McGraw-Hill. • 2003. $94.37. Fifth edition. (Science, Engineering and Mathematics Series).

Farm Management: Principles, Budgets, Plans. John Herbst and Duane Erickson. Stipes Publishing L.L.C. • 1996. $25.80. 10th edition.

HANDBOOKS AND MANUALS

Farm Management. Michael D. Boehlje and Vernon R. Eidman. John Wiley and Sons, Inc. • 1984. $107.95.

PERIODICALS AND NEWSLETTERS

Ag Executive. Ag Executive Inc. • Description: Focuses on financial, personnel, and risk management issues for commercial agriculture. Covers business analysis and practical management ideas for improving profitability. Includes such topics as accounting, farm business organization, financing, economic forecasting, resource/risk control, and taxes.

FMRA News. American Society of Farm Managers and Rural Appraisers. • Description: Considers such topics as environmental issues, governmental regulation, technological advances, relative legislation, and other issues pertinent to rural resource properties. Recurring features include news of

Society activities, educational offerings, and membership updates.

Journal of Range Management: Covering the Study, Management, and Use of Rangeland Ecosystems and Range Resources. Society for Range Management. • Bimonthly. Institutions, $95.00 per year. Technical articles oriented towards research in range science and management.

TRADE/PROFESSIONAL ASSOCIATIONS

American Society of Farm Managers and Rural Appraisers. 950 S. Cherry St., Suite 508, Denver, CO 80246-2664. Phone: (303)758-3513 Fax: (303)758-0190 E-mail: asfmra@agri-associations. org • URL: http://www.asfmra.org.

Northwest Farm Managers Association. PO Box 5599, Fargo, ND 58105-5599. Phone: (701)231-8914 Fax: (701)231-5632 E-mail: daakre@ndsuext. nodak.edu • URL: http://www.lib.ndsu.nodak.edu/ ndirs/index.html • Represents manager-operators of commercial farms and agriculturists interested in research in farm management, marketing, and agribusiness.

Society for Range Management. 445 Union Blvd., Ste. 230, Lakewood, CO 80228-1259. Phone: (303)986-3309 Fax: (303)986-3892 E-mail: srmweb@rangelands.org • URL: http://www. rangelands.org • Formerly American Society of Range Management.

OTHER SOURCES

Agricultural Law. LexisNexis Matthew Bender. • Semiannual. $2,501.00. 15 looseleaf volumes. Covers all aspects of state and federal law relating to farms, ranches and other agricultural interests. Includes five volumes dealing with agricultural estate, tax and business planning.

FARM MARKETS

See also: MARKETING

GENERAL WORKS

United States Agricultural Trade: Trends, Policy, and Direction. Larry V. Fedorov, editor. Nova Science Publishers, Inc. • 2003. $59.00. Includes data on the impact of NAFTA on the import and export of farm products.

ALMANACS AND YEARBOOKS

Agricultural and Mineral Commodities Year Book. Available from Taylor & Francis Group. • Annual. $225.00. Published by Europa Publications. Contains descriptive product profiles, price data, export-import data, and production statistics for major commodities of the world. Includes commodity histories, uses, markets, demand trends, and information about trade agreements and key commodity organizations.

Agricultural Policies, Markets, and Trade: Monitoring and Evaluation. Organization for Economic Cooperation and Development. Available from OECD Publications and Information Center. • Annual. $62.00. A yearly report on agricultural and trade policy developments in OECD member countries.

DIRECTORIES

Packer Produce Availability and Merchandising Guide. Vance Publishing Corp., Produce Div. • Annual. $35.00. A buyer's directory giving sources of fresh fruits and vegetables. Shippers are listed by location for each commodity.

ENCYCLOPEDIAS AND DICTIONARIES

Dictionary of Agriculture: From Abaca to Zoonosis. Kathryn L. Lipton. Lynne Rienner Publishers, Inc. • 1995. $75.00. Emphasis is on agricultural economics.

PERIODICALS AND NEWSLETTERS

Agri Marketing: The Magazine for Professionals Selling to the Farm Market. Doane Agricultural

Services. • Monthly. $30.00 per year.

Produce Merchandising: The Packer's Retailing and Merchandising Magazine. Vance Publishing Corp. • Monthly. $35.00 per year. Provides information and advice on the retail marketing and promotion of fresh fruits and vegetalbe.

RESEARCH CENTERS AND INSTITUTES

Giannini Foundation of Agricultural Economics. University of California at Berkeley. 248 Giannini Hall, Berkeley, CA 94720-3310. Phone: (510)642-7121 Fax: (510)643-8911 E-mail: dote@are. berkeley.edu • URL: http://www.are.berkeley.edu/ library.

Texas Agricultural Market Research Center. Texas A & M University. Dept. of Agricultural Economics, College Station, TX 77843-2124. Phone: (979)845-5911 Fax: (979)845-6378 E-mail: tamrc@tamu.edu.

STATISTICS SOURCES

OECD Agricultural Outlook. Organization for Economic Cooperation and Development. • Annual. $34.00. Provides a five-year outlook for agricultural markets in various countries of the world, including the U. S., other OECD countries, and selected non-OECD nations.

TRADE/PROFESSIONAL ASSOCIATIONS

North American Agricultural Marketing Officials. Califorinia Department of Food and Agriculture, 1220 N St., Rm. A270, Sacramento, CA 95814. E-mail: joegaines@state.tn.us • URL: http://www. naamo.org • Affiliated with National Association of Produce Market Managers and the National Association of State Departments of Argicutural. Formerly National Agricultural Marketing Officals.

OTHER SOURCES

Global Seed Markets. Theta Reports. • 2000. $1,040.00. Market research data. Covers the major seed sectors, including cereal crops, legumes, oilseed crops, fibre crops, and beet crops. Provides analysis of biotechnology developments. (Theta Report No. DS208E.).

FARM PRODUCE

See also: AGRICULTURE

GENERAL WORKS

Agricultural Biotechnology: An Economic Perspective. Margriet F. Caswell and others. Nova Science Publishers, Inc. • 2003. $30.00. Considers such factors as consumer demand, producer demand, public policies, regulation, food safety, and research funding.

Agricultural Product Prices. William G. Tomek and Kenneth L. Robinson. Cornell University Press. • 1990. $37.50. Third edition.

ABSTRACTS AND INDEXES

Field Crop Abstracts: Monthly Abstract Journal on World Annual Cereal, Legume, Root, Oilseed and Fibre Crops. Available from CABI Publishing North America. • Monthly. Institutions, $1,775.00 per year. Online edition available, $1,820.00 per year. Published in England by CABI Publishing, formerly Commonwealth Agricultural Bureaux. Provides worldwide coverage of the literature.

CD-ROM DATABASES

AGRICOLA on SilverPlatter. Available from Silver-Platter Information, Inc. • Quarterly. $825.00 per year. Produced by the National Agricultural Library. Provides about three million citations on CD-ROM to the literature of agriculture, agricultural economics, animal sciences, entomology, fertilizer, food, forestry, nutrition, pesticides, plant science, water resources, and other topics. Each quarterly disc covers the past ten years, with archival discs available from 1970.

WILSONDISC: Biological and Agricultural Index. H. W. Wilson Co. • Monthly. Includes unlimited online access to *Biological and Agricultural Index* through WILSONLINE. Provides CD-ROM indexing of over 250 periodicals covering agriculture, agricultural chemicals, biochemistry, biotechnology, entomology, horticulture, and related topics.

DIRECTORIES

Agriculture: Websites and Glossary. Carol Canada. Nova Science Publishers, Inc. • 2003. $29.50. Lists agricultural Web sites according to 24 main categories and 16 subcategories. Includes a glossary and an index.

American Fruit Grower Source Book. Meister Publishing Co. • Annual. $5.00. Manufacturers and distributors of equipment and supplies for the commericial fruit growing industry.

American Vegetable Grower--Source Book. Meister Media Worldwide. • Publication includes: Lists of suppliers of agricultural chemicals and manufacturers and suppliers of other agricultural products, equipment, and services including packaging equipment, transportation services, direct marketing suppliers, plants and seeds, etc. Entries include: Company name, address, phone, fax, e-mail.

ENCYCLOPEDIAS AND DICTIONARIES

Encyclopedia of Agriculture Science. Charles J. Arntzen and Ellen M. Ritter, editors. Elsevier. • 1994. $900.00. Four volumes.

Encyclopedia of Food and Culture. Gale Cengage Learning. • 2002. $395.00. Three volumes. Contains 600 articles covering various aspects of food and its place in society, from agronomy to zucchini. Includes illustrations and a detailed index.

FINANCIAL RATIOS

Annual Statement Studies. The Risk Management Association. • Annual. Median and quartile financial ratios are given for over 400 kinds of manufacturing, wholesale, retail, construction, and consumer finance establishments. Data is sorted by both asset size and sales volume. Includes a clearly written "Definition of Ratios" and an alphabetical industry index.

Annual Statement Studies: Industry Default Probabilities and Cash Flow Measures. The Risk Management Association. • Annual. $145.00. Serves as a companion volume to the original *Annual Statement Studies.* Gives probability of default estimates on a percentage scale for more than 450 industries. Includes changes in position year-by-year for eight financial statement line items and provides percentage measures of cash flow.

HANDBOOKS AND MANUALS

Knott's Handbook for Vegetable Growers. Donald N. Maynard and George J. Hochmuth. John Wiley and Sons, Inc. • 1997. $99.00. Fourth edition. Written for commercial vegetable growers, truck farmers, horticulturists, and other professionals. Covers such topics as spacing of plants, disease control, insect pests, seeds, weeds, water management, and irrigation.

INTERNET DATABASES

USDA. United States Department of Agriculture. Phone: (202)720-2791 E-mail: agsec@usda.gov • URL: http://www.usda.gov • The USDA home page has six sections: News and Information; What's New; About USDA; Agencies; Opportunities; Search and Help. Keyword searching is offered from the USDA home page and from various individual agency home pages. Agencies are the Economic Research Service, Agricultural Marketing Service, National Agricultural Statistics Service, National Agricultural Library, and about 12 others. Updating varies. Fees: Free.

ONLINE DATABASES

Agricola. U.S. National Agricultural Library. • Covers worldwide agricultural literature. Over 3.3 million citations, 1970 to present, with monthly updates. Inquire as to online cost and availability.

CAB Abstracts. CAB Publishing North America. • Contains 46 specialized abstract collections covering over 10,000 journals and monographs in the areas of agriculture, horticulture, forest products, farm products, nutrition, dairy science, poultry, grains, animal health, entomology, etc. Time period is 1972 to date, with monthly updates. Inquire as to online cost and availability. *CAB Abstracts on CD-ROM* also available, with annual updating.

PERIODICALS AND NEWSLETTERS

Agricultural Research. Available from U. S. Government Printing Office. • Monthly. $50.00 per year. Issued by the Agricultural Research Service of the U. S. Department of Agriculture. Presents results of research projects related to a wide variety of farm crops and products.

Barron's: The Dow Jones Business and Financial Weekly. • Weekly. $145.00 per year.

Crop Science: A Journal Serving the International Community. Crop Science Society of America. • Bimonthly. Free to members, non-members, $241.00 per year.

Journal of Crop Improvement. Haworth Press, Inc. • Semiannual. $300.00 per year to libraries; $80.00 per year to individuals. Topics include plant biotechnology, plant genetics, crop productivity, quality, safety, pest control, and environmental concerns. Formerly *Journal of Crop Production.*

RESEARCH CENTERS AND INSTITUTES

California Agricultural Experiment Station. University of California. 1111 Franklin St., 6th Fl., Oakland, CA 94607-5200. Phone: (510)987-0060 Fax: (510)451-2317 E-mail: wr.gomes@ucop.edu • URL: http://www.ucanr.org/aes.

Florida Agricultural Experiment Station. University of Florida. Institute of Food and Agricultural Science, 1022 McCarty Hall, Gainesville, FL 32611. Phone: (352)392-1784 Fax: (352)392-4965 E-mail: rljones@mail.fas.ufl.edu • URL: http://www. research.ifas.ufl.edu.

Kansas Agricultural Experiment Station - Performance Test Program. Kansas State University. Department of Agronomy, Throckmorton Hall, Manhattan, KS 66506. Phone: (785)532-6101 Fax: (785)532-6094 E-mail: dmengel@bear.agron.ksu. edu • URL: http://www.ksu.edu/kscpt.

Michigan Agricultural Experiment Station. Michigan State University. 109 Argricultural Hall, East Lansing, MI 48224-1039. Phone: (517)355-0123 Fax: (517)355-5406 E-mail: maesdir@msu. edu • URL: http://www.maes.msu.edu.

Texas Agricultural Experiment Station at Sonora. Texas A & M University. P.O. Box 918, Sonora, TX 76950. Phone: (915)387-3168 Fax: (915)387-5045 E-mail: angora@sonoratx.net.

STATISTICS SOURCES

Agricultural Statistics. Available from U. S. Government Printing Office. • Annual. $38.00. Produced by the National Agricultural Statistics Service, U. S. Department of Agriculture. Provides a wide variety of statistical data relating to agricultural production, supplies, consumption, prices/price-supports, foreign trade, costs, and returns, as well as farm labor, loans, income, and population. In many cases, historical data is shown annually for 10 years. In addition to farm data, includes detailed fishery statistics.

FAO Production Yearbook. Available from Bernan Associates. • Annual. $45.00. Published by the Food and Agriculture Organization (http://www.fao.org). Contains worldwide data on agriculture, land use, farm crops, livestock, and agricultural prices.

FAO Quarterly Bulletin of Statistics. Food and Agriculture Organization of the United Nations.

Available from UNIPUB. • Quarterly. $20.00 per year. Provides international data on agricultural production, trade, and prices, covering the major commodities of many countries. Text in English, French, and Spanish. Formerly *FAO Monthly Bulletin of Statistics.*

FAO Trade Yearbook. Available from Bernan Associates. • Annual. $45.00. Published by the Food and Agriculture Organization (http://www.fao.org). Provides extensive worldwide data on exports and imports of agricultural commodities, fertilizers, tractors, and pesticides. Includes more than 130 tables of detailed statistics.

United States Census of Agriculture. U.S. Bureau of the Census. • Quinquennial. Results presented in reports, tape, CD-ROM, and Diskette files.

Vegetables and Specialties Situation and Outlook. Available from U. S. Government Printing Office. • Three times a year. Issued by the Economic Research Service of the U. S. Department of Agriculture. Provides current statistical information on supply, demand, and prices.

World Agricultural Supply and Demand Estimates. Available from U. S. Government Printing Office. • Monthly. $52.00 per year. Issued by the Economics and Statistics Service and the Foreign Agricultural Service of the U. S. Department of Agriculture. Consists mainly of statistical data and tables.

TRADE/PROFESSIONAL ASSOCIATIONS

National Association of Produce Market Managers. P.O. Box 291284, Columbia, SC 29229. Phone: (404)675-1782 Fax: (404)362-4564 E-mail: sbrannon@mfca.state.md.us • URL: http://www. napmm.com.

Produce Marketing Association. 1500 Casho Mill Rd., PO Box 6036, Newark, DE 19714-6036. Phone: (302)738-7100 Fax: (302)731-2409 E-mail: bsilbermann@pma.com • URL: http://www.pma. com • Represents marketers of fresh fruits, vegetables, and related products worldwide. Members are involved in the production, distribution, retail, and foodservice sectors of the industry. Works to create a favorable, responsible environment that advances the marketing of produce and floral products and services for North American buyers and sellers and their international partners.

FARMERS

See also: AGRICULTURE; LABOR

ABSTRACTS AND INDEXES

World Agricultural Economics and Rural Sociology Abstracts: Abstracts of World Literature. Available from CABI Publishing, North America. • Monthly. Institutions, $1,425.00 per year. Print and online edition, $1,460.00 per year. Published in England by CABI Publishing. Provides worldwide coverage of the literature.

INTERNET DATABASES

USDA. United States Department of Agriculture. Phone: (202)720-2791 E-mail: agsec@usda.gov • URL: http://www.usda.gov • The USDA home page has six sections: News and Information; What's New; About USDA; Agencies; Opportunities; Search and Help. Keyword searching is offered from the USDA home page and from various individual agency home pages. Agencies are the Economic Research Service, Agricultural Marketing Service, National Agricultural Statistics Service, National Agricultural Library, and about 12 others. Updating varies. Fees: Free.

PERIODICALS AND NEWSLETTERS

Amber Waves. Available from U. S. Government Printing Office. • Quarterly. $38.00 per year. Replaces *Agricultural Outlook; Food Review;* and *Rural America.* Provides research and analysis from

the U.S. Department of Agriculture's Economic Research Service. Includes economic data on agriculture, food, trade, and environmental factors.

Farm Industry News. Primedia Business Magazines and Media. • Monthly. $25.00 per year. Includes new products for farm use.

Farmer's Digest. Heartland Communications Group, Inc. • 10 times a year. $17.95 per year. Current information on all phases of agriculture.

National Farmers Union News. National Farmers Union. • Description: Provides news, legislation, and tax information in relation to the farming industry.

Progressive Farmer. Progressive Farmer, Inc. • 18 times a year. $18.00 per year. 17 regional editions. Includes supplement *Rural Sportsman.*

STATISTICS SOURCES

Agricultural Statistics. Available from U. S. Government Printing Office. • Annual. $38.00. Produced by the National Agricultural Statistics Service, U. S. Department of Agriculture. Provides a wide variety of statistical data relating to agricultural production, supplies, consumption, prices/price-supports, foreign trade, costs, and returns, as well as farm labor, loans, income, and population. In many cases, historical data is shown annually for 10 years. In addition to farm data, includes detailed fishery statistics.

Agriculture Fact Book. Available from U. S. Government Printing Office. • Annual. $26.00. Issued by the Office of Communications, U. S. Department of Agriculture. Includes data on U. S. agriculture, farmers, food, nutrition, and rural America. Programs of the Department of Agriculture in six areas are described: rural economic development, foreign trade, nutrition, the environment, inspection, and education.

FAO Production Yearbook. Available from Bernan Associates. • Annual. $45.00. Published by the Food and Agriculture Organization (http://www.fao.org). Contains worldwide data on agriculture, land use, farm crops, livestock, and agricultural prices.

FAO Trade Yearbook. Available from Bernan Associates. • Annual. $45.00. Published by the Food and Agriculture Organization (http://www.fao.org). Provides extensive worldwide data on exports and imports of agricultural commodities, fertilizers, tractors, and pesticides. Includes more than 130 tables of detailed statistics.

Farm Labor. U.S. Department of Agriculture. • Monthly.

TRADE/PROFESSIONAL ASSOCIATIONS

National Farmers Organization. PO Box 2508, Ames, IA 50010-2000. Phone: 800-247-2110 or (515)292-2000 Fax: (515)292-7106 E-mail: nfo@ nfo.org • URL: http://www.nfo.org • Nonpartisan organization of farmers who bargain collectively to obtain contracts with buyers, processors, and exporters for the sale of farm commodities. Works to continuously improve such contracts. Conducts educational programs; maintains speakers' bureau.

National Farmers Union. 5619 DTC Pkwy., Ste. 300, Greenwood Village, CO 80111-3136. Phone: 800-347-1961 or (303)337-5500 Fax: (303)771-1770 E-mail: tbuis@nfudc.org • URL: http://www. nfu.org • Farm families interested in agricultural welfare. Carries on educational, cooperative and legislative activities. Represents members' interests especially in acquiring a more equitable share of the food dollar. Assists farm families in developing self-help institutions such as cooperatives.

FARMS

See: AGRICULTURE

FASHION INDUSTRY

See also: CLOTHING INDUSTRY; WOMEN'S APPAREL

GENERAL WORKS

Fashion Accessories: The Complete Twentieth Century Sourcebook. John Peacock. Thames Hudson. • 2000. $34.95.

Fashion and Merchandising Fads. Frank W. Hoffmann and William G. Bailey. Haworth Press, Inc. • 1994. $49.95. Contains descriptions of fashion industry fads or promotions from A to Z (Popular Culture Series).

Fashion Merchandising: An Introduction. Elaine Stone. McGraw-Hill. • 1989. $45.72. Fifth edition. (Marketing Series).

CD-ROM DATABASES

Magazine Index Plus. Gale Cengage Learning. • Monthly. $4,000.00 per year (includes InfoTrac workstation). Provides full text on CD-ROM for about 100 popular, general interest magazines and indexing for 300 others. Includes special indexing of reviews and product evaluations. Time period is 1980 to date.

DIRECTORIES

Accessories Resources Directory. Business Journals Inc. • Covers: 1,600 manufacturers, importers, and sales representatives producing or handling belts, gloves, handbags, scarves, hosiery, jewelry, sunglasses, and umbrellas. Entries include: Company, name, address, phone, fax.

Contemporary Fashion. St. James Press. • Publication includes: Contact information for designers featured. Entries include: name, address, phone, and Web site. Principal content of publication is essays evaluating contemporary clothing and accessories designers worldwide.

ENCYCLOPEDIAS AND DICTIONARIES

Fairchild's Dictionary of Fashion. Charlotte Calasibetta. Fairchild Books. • 1998. $45.00. Second revised edition.

Fashion, Fad, and Style. Gale Cengage Learning. • 2003. $250.00. Five volumes. Contains 500 entries covering "human decoration and adornment throughout history." Includes information on clothing, hairstyles, jewelry, and related items. (U-X-L imprint.).

HANDBOOKS AND MANUALS

Fashion Advertising and Promotion. Arthur A. Winters and Stanley Goodman. Fairchild Books. • 1984. $50.00.

PERIODICALS AND NEWSLETTERS

Accessories. Business Journals, Inc. • 11 times a year. $35.00 per year. Covers the merchandising of women's fashion accessories, including handbags, belts, jewelry, gloves, hats, and umbrellas.

Apparel Merchandising. Lebhar-Friedman, Inc. • Eight times a year. $24.00 per year. Reports on fashion trends in women's, men's, and children's clothing. Supplement to (DSN Retailing Today).

DNR: The Men's Fashion Retail Textile Authority. Fairchild Publications. • Daily. $85.00 per year. Formerly *Daily News Record.*

Fashion Market Magazine. Fashion Market Magazine Group, Inc. • Monthly. $59.00 per year. Covers the women's apparel industry, including photographs of "current collections of apparel available on the wholesale market." Includes news of all categories of women's clothing.

GQ: Gentleman's Quarterly for Men. Conde Nast Publications, Inc. • Monthly. $15.00 per year.

Harper's Bazaar. Hearst Corp. • Monthly. $18.00 per year.

Tobe Report. Tobe. • 38 times a year. Price on application. Edited for fashion retailers. Provides detailed information and analysis relating to current trends in the women's, children's, and men's apparel and accessories markets.

Vogue. Conde Nast Publications, Inc. • Monthly. $18.00 per year.

WWD: The Retailer's Daily Newspaper (Women's Wear Daily). Fairchild Publications. • Daily. Individuals, $195.00 per year; retailers, $99.00 per year; manufacturers, $135.00 per year.

TRADE/PROFESSIONAL ASSOCIATIONS

Council of Fashion Designers of America. 1412 Broadway, Suite 2006, New York, NY 10018. Phone: (212)302-1821 Fax: (212)768-0515.

International Association of Clothing Designers and Executives. 475 Park Ave. S, 9th Fl., New York, NY 10016. Fax: (212)545-1709 E-mail: dmschmida@aol.com • Formerly International Associatin of Clothing Designers.

UNITE!-Union of Needletrades, Industrial and Textile Employees. 275 Seventh Ave., New York, NY 10001-6708. Phone: (212)265-7000 Fax: (212)315-3803 E-mail: kkirsch@uniteunion.org • URL: http://www.uniteunion.org.

OTHER SOURCES

Fashion Calendar. Fashion Calendar International. • Bimonthly. $365.00 per year.

FAST FOOD INDUSTRY

See also: FROZEN FOOD INDUSTRY; RESTAURANTS, LUNCHROOMS, ETC.

GENERAL WORKS

Fast Food Nation: The Dark Side of the All-American Meal. Eric Schlosser. Gale Cengage Learning. • 2001. $30.95. Explains how the fast food industry is contributing to obesity, disease, urban sprawl, and other bad things. Special attention is given to the meatpacking industry, *E.coli*, worker injuries, fast food franchise problems, detrimental labor practices, and the effect of fast food diets on children. Companies prominently mentioned are McDonald's, Burger King, Wendy's, Taco Bell, Pizza Hut, Jack in the Box, ConAgra, and Iowa Beef Packers. Includes many research notes, a bibliography, and a detailed index.

DIRECTORIES

Directory of Chain Restaurant Operators. Chain Store Guide. • Annual. $335.00. Includes fast food establishments, and leading chain hotel copanies operating foodservice unit.

FINANCIAL RATIOS

Annual Statement Studies. The Risk Management Association. • Annual. Median and quartile financial ratios are given for over 400 kinds of manufacturing, wholesale, retail, construction, and consumer finance establishments. Data is sorted by both asset size and sales volume. Includes a clearly written "Definition of Ratios" and an alphabetical industry index.

Annual Statement Studies: Industry Default Probabilities and Cash Flow Measures. The Risk Management Association. • Annual. $145.00. Serves as a companion volume to the original *Annual Statement Studies.* Gives probability of default estimates on a percentage scale for more than 450 industries. Includes changes in position year-by-year for eight financial statement line items and provides percentage measures of cash flow.

HANDBOOKS AND MANUALS

Donut Shop. Entrepreneur Media, Inc. • Looseleaf. $59.50. A practical guide to starting a doughnut shop. Covers profit potential, start-up costs, market size evaluation, owner's time required, site selec-

tion, lease negotiation, pricing, accounting, advertising, promotion, etc. (Start-Up Business Guide No. E1126.).

Pizzeria. Entrepreneur Media, Inc. • Looseleaf. $59.50. A practical guide to starting a pizza shop. Covers profit potential, start-up costs, market size evaluation, owner's time required, site selection, lease negotiation, pricing, accounting, advertising, promotion, etc. (Start-Up Business Guide No. E1006.).

Sandwich Shop/Deli. Entrepreneur Media, Inc. • Looseleaf. $59.50. A practical guide to starting a sandwich shop and delicatessen. Covers profit potential, start-up costs, market size evaluation, owner's time required, site selection, lease negotiation, pricing, accounting, advertising, promotion, etc. (Start-Up Business Guide No. E1156.).

PERIODICALS AND NEWSLETTERS

Pizza Today. National Association of Pizza Operators. Pete Lachapelle. • Monthly. $29.95 per year. Covers both practical business topics and food topics for pizza establishments.

QSR: The Magazine of Quick Service Restaurant Success. Journalistic, Inc. • Ten times a year. $30.00 per year. Provides news and management advice for quick-service restaurants, including franchisors and franchisees.

Restaurant Business. VNU Business Media. • Biweekly. $119.00 per year. Formerly *Fast Food.*

TRADE/PROFESSIONAL ASSOCIATIONS

National Association of Pizzaria Operators. PO Box 2132, New Albany, NY 47151. Phone: 800-489-8324 or (216)766-5710 E-mail: webmaster@napa.com • URL: http://www.napo.com • Members are pizza establishment operators, food suppliers, and equipment manufacturers. Affiliated with American Society of Association Executives, Meeting Professionals International and National Restaurant Association.

OTHER SOURCES

Fast Food. Available from MarketResearch.com. • 2001. $5,000.00. Published by Euromonitor Publications Ltd. Provides consumer market data for the United States, the United Kingdom, Germany, France, and Italy.

FASTENER INDUSTRY

See also: HARDWARE INDUSTRY

DIRECTORIES

Assembly Buyers Guide. Reed Business Information. • Annual. $68.00. Lists manufacturers and suppliers of equipment relating to assembly automation, fasteners, adhesives, robotics, and power tools.

Fastener Technology International Buyers' Guide. Initial Publications, Inc. • Annual. $40.00. Lists about 2,000 international manufacturers and distributors of fasteners and precision-formed parts.

Thomas Register of American Manufacturers. Thomas Publishing Co., Inc. • Annual. $149.00. 34 volumes. A three-part system offering information on a wide variety of industrial equipment and supplies. Lists more than 151,000 industrial product and services companies.

HANDBOOKS AND MANUALS

McGraw-Hill Machining and Metalworking Handbook. Ronald A. Walsh. McGraw-Hill. • 1998. $99.95. Second edition. Coverage includes machinery, machining techniques, machine tools, machine design, parts, fastening, and plating.

ONLINE DATABASES

Thomas Register Online. Thomas Publishing Co., Inc. • Provides concise information on approximately 194,000 U. S. companies, mainly manufacturers, with over 50,000 product classifications. Indexes over 115,000 trade names. Information is updated semiannually. Inquire as to online cost and availability.

PERIODICALS AND NEWSLETTERS

Assembly: Design and Manufacturing Technology for Better Assembled Products. Business News Publishing Co. • Monthly. $68.00 per year. Covers assembly, fastening, and joining systems. Includes information on automation and robotics.

Fastener Technology International. Initial Publications. • Bimonthly. $40.00 per year.

Hardware Age. Reed Business Information. • Monthly. $75.00 per year.

STATISTICS SOURCES

U. S. Industry and Trade Outlook. Available from National Technical Information Service. • Annual. $69.95. Produced by the International Trade Administration, U. S. Department of Commerce, in a "public-private" partnership with DRI/McGraw-Hill and Standard & Poor's. Provides basic data, outlook for the current year, and "Long-Term Prospects" (five-year projections) for a wide variety of products and services. Includes high technology industries. Formerly *U. S. Industrial Outlook.*

TRADE/PROFESSIONAL ASSOCIATIONS

ASM International. 9639 Kinsman Rd., Novelty, OH 44073-0002. Phone: 800-336-5152 or (440)338-5151 Fax: (440)338-4634 E-mail: customerservice@asminternational.org • URL: http://asmcommunity.asminternational.org/portal/site/asm • Metallurgists, materials engineers, executives in materials producing and consuming industries; teachers and students. Disseminates technical information about the manufacture, use, and treatment of engineered materials. Offers in-plant, home study, and intensive courses through Materials +Engineering Institute. Conducts career development program. Established ASM Foundation for +Education and Research.

Cold Formed Parts and Machine Institute. 25 N. Broadway, Tarrytown, NY 10591. Phone: (914)332-0040 Fax: (914)332-1541 E-mail: cfpmi@cfpmi.org • URL: http://www.cfpmi.org • Formerly Tubular Rivet and Machine Institute.

Industrial Fasteners Institute. 6363 Oak Tree Blvd., 1717 E. Ninth St., Suite 1105, Independence, OH 44131. Phone: (216)241-1482 Fax: (216)241-5901 E-mail: rharris@indfast.org • URL: http://www.industrial-fasteners.org • Manufacturers of industrial fasteners and formed parts; associate members are suppliers of primary and secondary equipment, raw materials, and services used in the manufacture of fasteners and formed parts. Seeks to advance fastener and formed parts application engineering. Establishes standards and technical practices.

National Fastener Distributors Association. 401 N Michigan Ave., Chicago, IL 60611. Phone: 877-487-6332 or (312)527-6671 Fax: (312)673-6740 E-mail: nfda@nfda-fastener.org • URL: http://www.nfda-fastener.org • Marketers, distributors, manufacturers, and importers of the fastener industry (producers or distributors of screws, bolts, and nuts). Develops new uses for fasteners; collects and disseminates statistics and information for members; conducts membership performance surveys. Assists in the maintenance of sound and equitable relationships among members of the industry, the public, and government. Offers training and educational programs.

Specialty Tools and Fasteners Distributors Association. 500 Elm Grove Rd., Elm Grove, WI 53122. Phone: 800-352-2981 or (262)784-4774 Fax: (262)784-5059 E-mail: info@stafda.org • URL: http://www.stafda.org.

FATS

See: OIL AND FATS INDUSTRY

FAX

See: FACSIMILE SYSTEMS

FEDERAL AID

See also: GRANTS-IN-AID

GENERAL WORKS

From Idea to Funded Project: Grant Proposals that Work. Jane C. Belcher and Julia M. Jacobsen. Greenwood Publishing Group, Inc. • 1992. $26.50. Fourth edition. Formerly *A Process for the Development of Ideas.*

DIRECTORIES

Catalog of Federal Domestic Assistance. U.S. Office of Management and Budget. Available from U.S. Government Printing Office. • Annual. $87.00. Looseleaf service. Includes up-dating service for indeterminate period. Summary of financial and nonfinanacial Federal programs, projects, services and activities that provide assistance or benefits to the American public.

Getting Yours; The Complete Guide to Government Money. Matthew Lesko. Putnam Publishing Group. • 1987. $14.95. Third edition. (Penguin Handbook Series).

Government Assistance Almanac: The Guide to Federal, Domestic, Financial and Other Programs Covering Grants, Loans, Insurance, Personal Payments and Benefits. J. Robert Dumouchel, editor. Omnigraphics, Inc. • Annual. $235.00. Describes more than 1,400 federal assistance programs available from about 50 agencies. Includes statistics, a directory of 3,000 field offices, and comprehensive indexing.

Guide to Federal Funding for Governments and Non-Profits. Government Information Services. • Quarterly. $339.00 per year. Looseleaf service. Contains detailed descriptions of federal grant programs in economic development, housing, transportation, social services, science, etc. Semimonthly *Supplement* available: *Federal Grant Deadline Calendar.*

HANDBOOKS AND MANUALS

Financing Graduate School: How to Get Money for Your Master's or Ph.D. Patricia McWade. Peterson's. • 1996. $16.95. Second revised edition. Discusses the practical aspects of various types of financial aid for graduate students. Includes bibliographic and directory information.

Grants Policy Directives. U.S. Dept. of Health, and Human Services. Available from U.S. Government Printing Office. • $219.00. Periodic supplementation. Provides guidelines on the fiscal and administrative aspects of grant management to all granting agencies of the Dept. of Health and Human Services.

How to Write Proposals that Produce. Joel P. Bowman and Bernadine P. Branchaw. Greenwood Publishing Group, Inc. • 1992. $23.50. An extensive guide to effective proposal writing for both nonprofit organizations and businesses. Covers writing style, intended audience, format, use of graphs, charts, and tables, documentation, evaluation, oral presentation, and related topics.

Proposal Planning and Writing. Lynn E. Miner and Jeremy T. Miner. Greenwood Publishing Group, Inc. • 2003. $39.95. Third edition. Discusses the steps necessary to locate and obtain funding from the federal government, foundations, and corporations.

INTERNET DATABASES

FedWorld: A Program of the United States Department of Commerce. National Technical Information Service. Phone: (703)605-6000 Fax: (703)605-6900 E-mail: webmaster@fedworld.gov • URL: http://www.fedworld.gov • Web site offers "a comprehensive central access point for searching, locating, ordering, and acquiring government and business information." Emphasis is on searching the Web pages, databases, and government reports of a wide variety of federal agencies. Fees: Free.

FirstGov: Your First Click to the U. S. Government. General Services Administration. Phone: 800-333-4636 or (202)501-0705 E-mail: public.affairs@gsa.gov • URL: http://www.firstgov.gov • Free Web site provides extensive links to federal agencies covering a wide variety of topics, such as agriculture, business, consumer safety, education, the environment, government jobs, grants, health, social security, statistics sources, taxes, technology, travel, and world affairs. Also provides links to federal forms, including IRS tax forms. Searching is offered, both keyword and advanced.

U. S. Business Advisor. Small Business Administration. Phone: (202)205-6600 Fax: (202)205-7064 • URL: http://www.business.gov • Web site provides "a one-stop electronic link to all the information and services government provides for the business community." Covers about 60 federal agencies that exist to assist or regulate business. Detailed information is provided on financial assistance, workplace issues, taxes, regulations, international trade, and other business topics. Searching is offered. Fees: Free.

ONLINE DATABASES

GrantSelect. Oryx Press. • Online service provides detailed descriptions of more than 10,000 grants offered by government and organizations in the U. S. Includes grants in a wide variety of subject fields. Contains current information with daily updates. Inquire as to online cost and availability.

PERIODICALS AND NEWSLETTERS

Federal Assistance Monitor: Semi-Monthly Report on Federal and Private Grant Opportunities. Community Development Services. CD Publications. • Semimonthly. $339.00 per year; with online edition, $379.00 per year. Newsletter. Provides news of federal grant and loan programs for social, economic, and community purposes. Monitors grant announcements, funding, and availability. Formerly *Federal Research Report.*

Federal Grants and Contracts Weekly: Funding Opportunities in Research, Training and Services. Aspen Publishers, Inc. • 50 times a year. $450.00 per year. Newsletter.

Grantsmanship Center Magazine: A Compendium of Resources for Nonprofit Organizations. Grantsmanship Center. • Irregular. Free to qualified personnel. Contains a variety of concise articles on grant-related topics, such as program planning, proposal writing, fundraising, non-cash gifts, federal project grants, benchmarking, taxation, etc.

OTHER SOURCES

Retired Activities Branch. • A program of the U.S. Department of the Navy. Assists Navy retirees and survivors with benefits and entitlement information. Maintains speakers' bureau.

FEDERAL AID FOR EDUCATION

See: FEDERAL AID

FEDERAL AID TO RESEARCH

See: FEDERAL AID

FEDERAL BUDGET

See also: NATIONAL DEBT

GENERAL WORKS

Balanced Budgets and American Politics. James D. Savage. Cornell University Press. • 1988. $19.95. States the case for economic growth being more important than a balanced federal budget.

Budget Options. Available from U. S. Government Printing Office. • 2003. $38.00. Issued by the Congressional Budget Office (CBO). Presents both sides of the coin: major proposals to increase spending or cut taxes because of large budget surpluses, or specific options to reduce spending or increase revenues because of large deficits.

Setting National Priorities: Budget Choices for the Next Century. Robert D. Reischauer, editor. Brookings Institution Press. • 1996. $42.95. Contains discussions of the federal budget, economic policy, and government spending policy.

ABSTRACTS AND INDEXES

American Statistics Index: A Comprehensive Guide and Index to the Statistical Publications of the United States Government. Congressional Information Service, Inc. • Monthly. Price varies. Quarterly and annual cumulations.

CD-ROM DATABASES

OECD Statistical Compendium. Organization for Economic Cooperation and Development. • Semiannual. $1,905.00 per year for 1 to 10 users. CD-ROM contains more than 730,000 monthly, quarterly, and annual time series for OECD countries, 1960 to date. Includes fully searchable data on agriculture, food, economic indicators, national accounts, employment, energy, finance, industry, technology, and foreign trade. Results can be displayed in various forms.

ENCYCLOPEDIAS AND DICTIONARIES

International Encyclopedia of Public Policy and Administration. Jay M. Shafritz, editor. Westview Press. • 1997. $550.00. Four volumes. Covers 20 major areas, such as public administration, government budgeting, industrial policy, nonprofit management, organizational theory, public finance, labor relations, and taxation. Includes a brief bibliography for each major entry and a comprehensive index.

FINANCIAL RATIOS

Financial Report of the United States Government. Available from U. S. Government Printing Office. • Annual. $21.00. Issued by the U. S. Treasury Department (http://www.treas.gov). Presents information about the financial condition and operations of the federal government. Program accounting systems of various government agencies provide data for the report.

HANDBOOKS AND MANUALS

Guide to the Federal Budget 2000. Stanley E. Collender. The Century Foundation. • 1999. $22.95. A practical explanation of the federal budget for the most recent fiscal year.

INTERNET DATABASES

Business 2.0 Web Guide to the Best Business Links. Business 2.0 Media Inc. Phone: (415)293-4800 E-mail: support@business2.com • URL: http://www.business2.com/webguide • Web site presents an extensive, searchable directory of links to "the best, most informative, and authoritative web pages." Twenty main categories cover business, finance, career, company information, people, and technology topics, with thousands of subtopics, all linking to Web sites recommended by experienced business researchers. Fees: Free.

Fedstats. Federal Interagency Council on Statistical Policy. Phone: (202)395-7254 • URL: http://www.fedstats.gov • Web site features an efficient search facility for full-text statistics produced by more than 100 federal agencies, including the Census Bureau, the Bureau of Economic Analysis, and the Bureau of Labor Statistics. Boolean searches can be made within one agency or for all agencies combined. Links are offered to international statistical bureaus, including the UN, IMF, OECD, UNESCO, Eurostat, and 20 individual countries. Fees: Free.

FreeLunch.com. Economy.com, Inc. Phone: (610)696-8700 Fax: (610)696-1678 • URL: http://www.freelunch.com • Web site provides free access to more than 1.5 million economic and financial data series, covering industry, demographics, labor markets, prices, retail sales, government spending, trade, interest rates, housing starts, the stock market, and many other topics. Data is available for various time periods in either chart or table form. Searching is offered. Fees: Free, but registration required. Economy.com, Inc. also offers fee-based economic analysis at *The Dismal Scientist* site (http://www.dismal.com).

STATISTICS SOURCES

The AIER Chart Book. AIER Research Staff. American Institute for Economic Research. • Annual. $4.00. A compact compilation of long-range charts ("Purchasing Power of the Dollar," for example, goes back to 1780) covering various aspects of the U. S. economy. Includes inflation, interest rates, debt, gold, taxation, stock prices, etc. (Economic Education Bulletin.).

Budget and Economic Outlook: Fiscal Years [10-year period]. Available from U. S. Government Printing Office. • Annual. $27.00. Issued by the Congressional Budget Office (CBO). Reports on fiscal policy and provides baseline projections of federal budget for 10 years. Also offers "impartial analysis with no recommendations.".

Budget of the United States Government. U.S. Office of Management and Budget. Available from U.S. Government Printing Office. • Annual. $52.00.

Business Statistics of the United States. Linz Audain and Cornelia J. Strawser. Bernan Associates. • Annual. $147.00. Based on *Business Statistics*, formerly issue by the Bureau of Economic Analysis, U. S. Department of Commerce. Provides basic data for a wide variety of U. S. industries, services, and economic indicators. Most statistics are shown annually for 30 years and monthly for the most recent four years.

Citizen's Guide to the Federal Budget. Available from U. S. Government Printing Office. • Annual. $3.25. Issued by the Office of Management and Budget, Executive Office of the President (http://www.whitehouse.gov). Provides basic data for the general public about the budget of the U. S. government.

Combined Statement of Receipts, Outlays, and Balances of the United States Government. Available from U. S. Government Printing Office. • Annual. $54.00. Issued by the Financial Mangement Service, U. S. Treasury Department (http://www.fms.treas.gov). In three parts: "Fiscal Year Summary," "Details of Receipts," and "Details of Appropriations, Outlays, and Balances.".

Economic and Budget Outlook: Fiscal Years 2004-2013. Available from U. S. Government Printing Office. • 2002. $27.00. Issued by the Congressional Budget Office (http://www.cbo.gov). Contains CBO economic projections and federal budget projections annually in billions of dollars. An appendix contains "Historical Budget Data" annually from, including revenues, outlays, deficits, surpluses, and debt held by the public.

Historical Tables, Budget of the United States Government. Available from U. S. Government Printing Office. • Annual. $41.00. Issued by the Office of Management and Budget, Executive Office of the President (http://www.whitehouse.gov). Provides statistical data on the federal budget for an extended period of about 60 years in the past to projections of four years in the future. Includes federal debt and federal employment.

Monthly Treasury Statement of Receipts and Outlays of the United States Government. Available from U. S. Government Printing Office. • Monthly. $58.00 per year. Issued by the Financial Management Service, U. S. Treasury Department.

Survey of Current Business. Available from U. S. Government Printing Office. • Monthly. $63.00 per year. Issued by Bureau of Economic Analysis, U. S. Department of Commerce. Presents a wide variety of business and economic data.

Treasury Bulletin. Available from U. S. Government Printing Office. • Quarterly. $45.00 per year. Issued by the Financial Management Service, U. S. Treasury Department. Provides data on the federal budget, government securities and yields, the national debt, and the financing of the federal government in general.

OTHER SOURCES

Center for Strategic and Budgetary Assessments. • Serves as nonpartisan independent research organization that analyzes military spending and national security policy issues. Provides timely, independent analyses of military budget and defense issues to the media, citizens' organizations, policymakers, and advocacy groups. Conducts research and educational programs. Sponsors briefings and discussions on defense and military issues. Analyzes issues such as the impact of the defense budget on other national spending priorities, the American economy, and the federal deficit; the relationship between defense spending, national security, and the development of alternatives to present national security policies. Maintains internship program.

United States Government Annual Report, Fiscal Year... Available from U. S. Government Printing Office. • Annual. $5.00. Issued by the Financial Management Service, U. S. Treasury Department (http://www.fms.treas.gov). Contains the official report on the receipts and outlays of the federal government. Presents budgetary results at the summary level.

FEDERAL EMPLOYEES

See: BUREAUCRACY; GOVERNMENT EMPLOYEES

FEDERAL GOVERNMENT

GENERAL WORKS

American Government: Readings and Cases. Peter Woll. Longman Publishing Group. • 2003. $38.80. 15th edition.

Moving Power and Money: The Politics of Census Taking. Barbara E. Bryant and William Dunn. New Strategist Publications, Inc. • 1995. $24.95. Barbara Everitt Bryant was Director of the U. S. Census Bureau from 1989 to 1993. She provides a plan for reducing the costs of census taking, improving accuracy, and overcoming public resistance to the census.

ABSTRACTS AND INDEXES

Current Law Index: Multiple Access to Legal Periodicals. Gale Cengage Learning. • Monthly. $725.00 per year. Produced in cooperation with the American Association of Law Libraries. Indexes more than 900 law journals, legal newspapers, and specialty publications from the U.S., Canada, U.K., Ireland, Australia, and New Zealand.

Social Sciences Index. H. W. Wilson Co. • Quarterly, with annual cumulation. Price varies. Indexes more than 400 periodicals covering economics, environmental policy, government, insurance, labor, health care policy, plannning, public administration, public welfare, urban studies, women's issues, criminology, and related topics.

BIBLIOGRAPHIES

Subject Bibliography Index: A Guide to U. S. Government Information. Available from U. S. Government Printing Office. • Annual. Free. Issued by the Superintendent of Documents. Lists currently available subject bibliographies by title and by topic. Each *Subject Bibliography* describes government books, periodicals, posters, pamphlets, and subscription services available for sale from the Government Printing Office.

CD-ROM DATABASES

Leadership Library on CD-ROM: Who's Who in the Leadership of the United States. Leadership Directories, Inc. • Quarterly. Including access to Internet version (weekly updates). Contains all 14 *Yellow Book* personnel directories on CD-ROM, providing contact and brief biographical information for about 400,000 individuals. Covers business, government, financial institutions, news media, law firms, associations, foreign representatives, and nonprofit organizations. Includes photographs.

OECD Statistical Compendium. Organization for Economic Cooperation and Development. • Semiannual. $1,905.00 per year for 1 to 10 users. CD-ROM contains more than 730,000 monthly, quarterly, and annual time series for OECD countries, 1960 to date. Includes fully searchable data on agriculture, food, economic indicators, national accounts, employment, energy, finance, industry, technology, and foreign trade. Results can be displayed in various forms.

Social Sciences Citation Index. ISI. • Monthly. Price on request. Provides CD-ROM indexing of articles appearing in 1700 leading social science journals worldwide, with additional selections from more than 5700 other journals. Time span is 1992 to date. Coverage includes economics, business, finance, management, communications, demographics, library and information science, political science, sociology, and many other subjects.

Social Sciences Citation Index: Compact Disc Edition with Abstracts. Institute for Scientific Information. • Monthly. Provides CD-ROM indexing and abstracting of "significant articles" from 1,700 social science journals worldwide, with additional selections from 3,200 other journals, 1986 to date. Includes economics, business, finance, management, communications, demographics, information and library science, political science, sociology, and many other subjects.

WILSONDISC: Wilson Social Sciences Abstracts. H. W. Wilson Co. • Monthly. Includes unlimited online access to *Social Sciences Index* through WILSONLINE. Provides CD-ROM indexing from 1983 and abstracting from 1994 of more than 500 periodicals covering economics, area studies, community health, public administration, public welfare, urban studies, and many other topics related to the social sciences.

DIRECTORIES

Almanac of the Federal Judiciary. Aspen Publishers, Inc. • Annual. $295.00 per set. Two volumes. Volume one provides information on federal district judges; volume two relates to federal circuit judges.

Carroll's Federal & Federal Regional Directory. Carroll Publishing. • Semiannual. $325.00 per year; with online edition, $1,200 per year. Lists more than 23,000 U. S. government officials throughout the country, including military installations.

Carroll's Federal Directory. Carroll Publishing. • Covers: About 38,000 executive managers in federal government offices in Washington, DC, including executive, congressional and judicial branches;

members of Congress and Congressional committees and staff. Entries include: Agency names, titles, office address (including room numbers), e-mail addresses, and telephone and fax numbers. Also available as part of a "library edition" titled "Federal Directory Annual".

Carroll's Federal Regional Directory. Carroll Publishing. • Covers: Over 32,000 officials in federal congressional, judicial, and executive branch departments and agencies outside the District of Columbia. Entries include: Organization or agency name; names, addresses, and phone numbers of key personnel.

Congressional Directory. Office of Membership Grassroots Management. • Covers: Members of Congress. Entries include: List of members of Congress by state includes member party and home city; alphabetical list by member name includes addresses, phone, fax, e-mail, committee/subcommittee assignments, names of key staff members, and photos.

Federal Agency Profiles for Students. Gale Cengage Learning. • 1999. $115.00. Provides detailed descriptions of more than 175 prominent U.S. government agencies, including major activities, organizational structure, political issues, budget, and history. Includes a glossary, chronology, and index.

Federal Regional Yellow Book: Who's Who in the Federal Government's Departments, Agencies, Military Installations, and Service Academies Outside of Washington, DC. Leadership Directories, Inc. • Semiannual. $265.00 per year. Lists over 35,000 federal officials and support staff at 8,000 regional offices.

Federal Regulatory Directory. CQ Press. • Covers: Over 100 federal regulatory agencies including about 15 major agencies, about 15 smaller independent agencies, and agencies within federal departments. Entries include: For major agencies-- Agency name, address, jurisdiction, description of responsibilities, list of key contacts and phone numbers, breakdown of divisions and offices with names of key officials and their phone numbers, organization chart, information sources within the agency, regional offices, analytical essays on history, recent developments, power, and outlook for agency. For other agencies--Same general information but less detail.

Federal Staff Directory: With Biographical Information on Executive Staff Personnel. CQ Press. • Three times a year. $259.00 per year. Single copies, $149. 00. Lists 35,000 staff members of federal departments and agencies, with biographies of 3,200 key executives. Includes keyword and name indexes.

Government Phone Book USA: Your Comprehensive Guide to Federal, State, County, and Local Government Offices in the United States. Omnigraphics, Inc. • Annual. $265.00. Contains more than 270,000 listings of federal, state, county, and local government offices and personnel, including legislatures. Formerly *Government Directory of Addresses and Phone Numbers.*

The Internet Blue Pages: The Guide to Federal Government Web Sites. Information Today, Inc. • Annual. $34.95. Provides information on more than 1,800 Web sites used by various agencies of the federal government. Includes indexes to agencies and topics. Links to all Web sites listed are available at http://www.fedweb.com. (CyberAge Books.).

Judicial Staff Directory: With Biographical Information on Judges and Key Court Staff. CQ Press. • Semiannual. $450.00. $225.00 per volume. Lists 33,500 federal court personnel, including 1,900 federal judges and their staffs, including biographies of judges and key executives. Includes maps of court jurisdictions.

Judicial Yellow Book: Who's Who in Federal and State Courts. Leadership Directories, Inc. •

Semiannual. $245.00 per year. Lists more than 3,200 judges and staffs in various federal courts and 1,200 judges and staffs in state courts. Includes biographical profiles of judges.

United States Government Manual. National Archives and Records Administration. Office of the Federal Register. • Description: Provides information on the agencies of the executive, judicial, and legislative branches of the Federal government. Contains a section on terminated or transferred agencies.

Washington: A Comprehensive Directory of the Key Institutions and Leaders in th e National Capitol Area. Columbia Books, Inc. • Annual. $149.00. Provides information on about 5,000 Washington, DC key businesses, government offices, non-profit organizations, and cultural institutions, with the names of about 25,000 principal executives. Includes Washington media, law offices, foundations, labor unions, international organizations, clubs, etc.

Washington Information Directory. CQ Press. • Covers: 5,000 governmental agencies, congressional committees, and non-governmental associations considered competent sources of specialized information. Entries include: Name of agency, committee, or association; address, phone, fax, and Internet; annotation concerning function or activities of the office; and name of contact.

HANDBOOKS AND MANUALS

Government Auditing Standards. Available from U. S. Government Printing Office. • 1994. $6.50. Revised edition. Issued by the U. S. General Accounting Office (http://www.gao.gov). Contains standards for CPA firms to follow in financial and performance audits of federal government agencies and programs. Also known as the "Yellow Book.".

INTERNET DATABASES

Business 2.0 Web Guide to the Best Business Links. Business 2.0 Media Inc. Phone: (415)293-4800 E-mail: support@business2.com • URL: http://www.business2.com/webguide • Web site presents an extensive, searchable directory of links to "the best, most informative, and authoritative web pages." Twenty main categories cover business, finance, career, company information, people, and technology topics, with thousands of subtopics, all linking to Web sites recommended by experienced business researchers. Fees: Free.

Fedstats. Federal Interagency Council on Statistical Policy. Phone: (202)395-7254 • URL: http://www.fedstats.gov • Web site features an efficient search facility for full-text statistics produced by more than 100 federal agencies, including the Census Bureau, the Bureau of Economic Analysis, and the Bureau of Labor Statistics. Boolean searches can be made within one agency or for all agencies combined. Links are offered to international statistical bureaus, including the UN, IMF, OECD, UNESCO, Eurostat, and 20 individual countries. Fees: Free.

FedWorld: A Program of the United States Department of Commerce. National Technical Information Service. Phone: (703)605-6000 Fax: (703)605-6900 E-mail: webmaster@fedworld.gov • URL: http://www.fedworld.gov • Web site offers "a comprehensive central access point for searching, locating, ordering, and acquiring government and business information." Emphasis is on searching the Web pages, databases, and government reports of a wide variety of federal agencies. Fees: Free.

FirstGov: Your First Click to the U. S. Government. General Services Administration. Phone: 800-333-4636 or (202)501-0705 E-mail: public.affairs@gsa.gov • URL: http://www.firstgov.gov • Free Web site provides extensive links to federal agencies covering a wide variety of topics, such as agriculture, business, consumer safety, education, the environment, government jobs, grants, health, social security, statistics sources, taxes, technology, travel, and world affairs. Also provides links to federal forms, including IRS tax forms. Searching is offered, both keyword and advanced.

FreeLunch.com. Economy.com, Inc. Phone: (610)696-8700 Fax: (610)696-1678 • URL: http://www.freelunch.com • Web site provides free access to more than 1.5 million economic and financial data series, covering industry, demographics, labor markets, prices, retail sales, government spending, trade, interest rates, housing starts, the stock market, and many other topics. Data is available for various time periods in either chart or table form. Searching is offered. Fees: Free, but registration required. Economy.com, Inc. also offers fee-based economic analysis at *The Dismal Scientist* site (http://www.dismal.com).

Lexis.com Research System. Lexis-Nexis Group. Phone: 800-227-4908 or (937)865-6800 Fax: (937)865-6909 E-mail: webmaster@prod.lexis-nexis.com • URL: http://www.lexis.com • Fee-based Web site offers extensive searching of a wide variety of legal sources. Additional features include Daily Opinion Service, lexis.com Bookstore, Career Center, CLE Center, Law Schools, and Practice Pages ("Pages specific to areas of specialty").

U. S. Census Bureau: The Official Statistics. U. S. Bureau of the Census. Phone: (301)763-4100 Fax: (301)763-4794 • URL: http://www.census.gov • Web site is "Your Source for Social, Demographic, and Economic Information." Contains "Current U. S. Population Count," "Current Economic Indicators," and a wide variety of data under "Other Official Statistics." Keyword searching is provided. Fees: Free.

ONLINE DATABASES

Catalog of U.S. Government Publications. U. S. Government Printing Office. • Contains over 375,000 online citations to U. S. government publications, 1976 to date, with monthly updates. Corresponds to the printed *Monthly Catalog of United States Government Publications.* Inquire as to online cost and availability.

GPO Sales Product Catalog. U. S. Government Printing Office. • An online guide to federal government publications in print (currently for sale), forthcoming, and recently out-of-print. Daily updates. Inquire as to online cost and availability.

Wilson Social Sciences Abstracts Online. H. W. Wilson Co. • Provides online abstracting and indexing of more than 500 periodicals covering area studies, community health, public administration, public welfare, urban studies, and many other social science topics. Time period is 1994 to date for abstracts and 1983 to date for indexing, with updates weekly. Inquire as to online cost and availability.

PERIODICALS AND NEWSLETTERS

Federal Computer Week: The Newspaper for the Government Systems Community. FCW Government Technology Group. • 41 times a year. $95.00 per year.

Government Executive: Federal Government's Business Magazine. National Journal Group, Inc. • Monthly. $48.00 per year. Includes management of computerized information systems in the federal government.

The Information Freeway Report: Free Business and Government Information Via Modem. Washington Researchers, Ltd. • Monthly. $160.00 per year. Newsletter. Provides news of business and government databases that are available free of charge through the Internet or directly. Emphasis is on federal government databases and electronic bulletin boards (Fedworld).

Legal Times: Law and Lobbying in the Nation's Capital. American Lawyer Media, Inc. • Weekly. $318.00 per year. Published in Washington, DC. Provides news relating to lawyers and the federal

government. Special features cover a variety of topics relating to law firm administration.

National Journal: The Weekly on Politics and Government. National Journal Group, Inc. • Weekly $1,499.00 per year. Includes semiannual supplement *Capital Source.* A non-partisan weekly magazine on politics and government.

RESEARCH CENTERS AND INSTITUTES

American Enterprise Institute. American Enterprise Institute. 1150 17th St. NW, Washington, DC 20036. Phone: 800-862-5801 or (202)862-5800 Fax: (202)862-7177 E-mail: cdemuth@aei.org • URL: http://www.aei.org • Economic policy, including domestic taxing, spending, and regulatory programs, and international trade and competitiveness; foreign and defense policy, including the spread of democracy and free enterprise, and the development of stable international security arrangements; social and political studies, including U.S. politics and public opinion, the Constitution and legal policy, and social welfare, educational and cultural issues.

Armed Forces Institute of Pathology. 6825 16th St. NW, Washington, DC 20306-6000. Phone: (202)782-2882 Fax: (202)782-9376 E-mail: telepath@afip.osd.mil • URL: http://www.afip.org • Chartered by the Department of Defense to: maintain a consultation service for the diagnosis of pathologic material; conduct experimental, statistical, and morphological research in pathology; provide instruction in advanced pathology and related subjects; prepare, procure, and duplicate teaching aids; operate the AFIP Repository and Research Services; maintain the National Museum of Health and Medicine and a Visual Information Service for the collection, preparation, duplication, reference, and filing of medical illustrative material. Sponsors a series of courses.

Brookings Institution. Brookings Institution. 1775 Massachusetts Ave. NW, Washington, DC 20036. Phone: (202)797-6000 Fax: (202)797-6004 E-mail: communications@brookings.edu • URL: http://www.brookings.edu/ • Economics, including studies on what economic policies are most conducive to sustained growth of the U.S. economy, how social programs can be made more effective in an era of constrained resources, and how international economic relations can be improved; government, including studies on political institutions, the media, regulation and economic policy, and social policy; and foreign policy, including defense analysis and international economics and trade studies, and U.S. relations with, and regional studies on, the former Soviet Union, East Asia, China, the Middle East, Latin America, and Africa.

RAND. RAND. 1776 Main St., PO Box 2138, Santa Monica, CA 90407-2138. Phone: (310)393-0411 Fax: (310)393-4818 E-mail: correspondence@rand.org • URL: http://www.rand.org/ • Analysis and effective solutions that address the challenges facing the nation and the world, including critical issues surrounding education, homeland security, social security, health care and international development, as well as a range of national security issues.

United States Naval Institute. 291 Wood Rd., Annapolis, MD 21402. Phone: 800-233-8764 or (410)268-6110 Fax: (410)269-7940 E-mail: twilkerson@usni.org • URL: http://www.navalinstitute.org • Regular, reserve, and retired professionals in the Navy, Marine Corps, and Coast Guard; civilians interested in the advancement of the knowledge of sea power and in advancing professional, literary, and scientific knowledge in the naval and maritime services. Conducts oral history and color print program.

STATISTICS SOURCES

Datapedia of the United States: American History in Numbers. George T. Kurian, editor. Bernan Press. • 2004. $125.00. Third edition. Based on the Census

Bureau publication, *Historical Statistics of the United States.* Provides data from Colonial times to the present on agriculture, business, consumer income, energy, finance, labor, national income, population, and many other subjects. Includes "narrative highlights," maps, charts, and statistical projections.

Social Statistics of the United States. Mark S. Littman, editor. Bernan Press. • 2000. $65.00. Includes statistical data on population growth, labor force, occupations, environmental trends, leisure time use, income, poverty, taxes, and other economic or demographic topics.

Statistical Abstract of the United States. Available from U. S. Government Printing Office. • Annual. $51.00. Issued by the U. S. Bureau of the Census.

A Statistical Portrait of the United States: Social Conditions and Trends. Mark S. Littman, editor. Bernan Press. • 1998. $89.00. Covers "social, economic, and environmental trends in the United States over the past 25 years." Includes statistical tables, graphs, and analysis relating to such topics as population, income, poverty, wealth, labor, housing, education, healthcare, air/water quality, and government. (Statistical Portrait of the United States: Social Conditions and Trends Series).

OTHER SOURCES

American Society of Military Comptrollers. • Civilians and military personnel who are now or who have been involved in the overall field of military comptrollership; other interested individuals. Conducts research programs. Compiles statistics; maintains speakers' bureau. Plans to establish library.

Armed Forces Sports. • Persons serving as head of the morale and welfare activities of the U.S. Army, Navy, Marines, and Air Force. Encourages physical fitness in the armed forces through a policy of "sports for all"; has established uniform rules to govern all service sports within its jurisdiction. Conducts interservice sports championship competitions. Develops and encourages spectator interest sports for the individual services. Selects and sends military athletes and teams to national and international competitions; has representative on the Executive Board and House of Delegates of the U.S. Olympic Committee, various U.S. sports governing bodies, and the International Military Sports Council. Compiles statistics.

Carroll's Defense Organization Charts. Carroll Publishing. • Every six weeks. $1,500.00 per year. Provides more than 200 large, fold-out paper charts showing personnel relationships in 2,400 U. S. military offices. Charts are also available online and on CD-ROM.

Carroll's Federal Organization Charts. Carroll Publishing. • Every six weeks. $1,000.00 per year. Provides 200 large, fold-out paper charts showing personnel relationships in 2,100 federal departments and agencies. Charts are also available online and on CD-ROM.

Citizen Soldier. • Individuals concerned with military-civilian relationships within American society. Aims to help Vietnam War veterans who may have been harmed by highly toxic herbicides (including Agent Orange) that were used in Vietnam between 1962 and 1970. Works with veterans who were exposed to low-level radiation at Nevada and South Pacific A-bomb test sites and Persian Gulf War veterans suffering from unexplained chronic ailments. Represents GIs on active duty who are victims of military racism and/or sexism. Assists GIs who have been prosecuted or otherwise punished due to positive results on drug residue urine tests that CS believes to have been inaccurate because of defective laboratory work. Seeks to protect the rights of soldiers testing positive for the AIDS antibody. Advocates for veterans suffering from

Persian Gulf Syndrome. Promotes a public service campaign to inform service members of their legal rights regarding the military's HIV testing program. Works with high school and college youths to address concerns on military recruiting practices. Maintains speakers' bureau. Advises GIs who wish alternatives to service in current Iraqi War.

Defense Advisory Committee on Women in the Services. • Civilians appointed by Secretary of Defense to provide recommendations to optimize utilization and quality of life for women in U.S. armed forces. Assists the Department of Defense by advising on specified matters relating to the recruitment and retention, treatment, employment, integration, and well-being of highly qualified professional women in the Services. Advises on family issues related to the recruitment and retention of a highly qualified professional military.

Inter-University Seminar on Armed Forces and Society. • Individuals from both public and private life in the academic, military, and government fields who are primarily researchers. Promotes the study of armed forces and society; provides a focal point for the exchange of information on the subject; stimulates research in the field on a cross-national basis. Compiles statistics; recommends a scholar to conduct seminars and give lectures.

Marine Corps League. • Represents men and women who are serving or who have served honorably in the United States Marine Corps, and U.S. Navy Corpsmen. Preserves the traditions and promotes the interests of the United States Marine Corps. Promotes the ideals of American freedom and democracy. Preserves the history and memory of the men who have given their lives to the nation. Maintains true allegiance to American institutions. Creates a bond of comradeship between those in the service and those who have returned to civilian life. Renders assistance to all Marines and former Marines as well as to their widows and orphans.

Military Law Task Force. • Counselors, attorneys, and law students concerned with military, selective service, and veterans' law. Purposes are to: assist active-duty personnel, veterans, and those affected by selective service; provide educational and political work focused on these areas of law; offer research assistance in military and veterans law; support networking among attorneys and counselors. Operates speakers' bureau; offers informal referral services and educational materials.

National Committee for Employer Support of the Guard and Reserve. • Provides free education, consultation, and if necessary, mediation for employers of guard and reserve members. Aims to ensure the national security. Promotes cooperation and understanding between reserve component members and their civilian employers and assists in the resolution of conflicts arising from an employee's military commitment. Operates with a network of almost 4,000 volunteers throughout 56 Committees located in each state, commonwealth, territory, and the District of Columbia. Operates an ombudsman program to assist in the informal resolution of employer-employee conflicts resulting from employee participation in the National Guard and Reserve.

National Council of Industrial Naval Air Stations. • Federation of local groups of government civilian employees at Industrial Naval Air Stations.

Naval Intelligence Professionals. • Active duty and former naval intelligence officers; enlisted personnel; civilian professionals; corporations. Objectives are to: improve naval intelligence operations; act as a clearinghouse for information on scientific and technical advances in naval intelligence; provide a forum for the exchange of ideas. Encourages readiness for those who would be involved in a national crisis mobilization.

FEDERAL INSURANCE CONTRIBUTIONS ACT (FICA)

See: SOCIAL SECURITY

FEDERAL REGULATION

See: REGULATION OF INDUSTRY

FEDERAL RESERVE SYSTEM

See also: BANKS AND BANKING

GENERAL WORKS

Federal Reserve System: Background, Analyses, and Bibliography. George B. Grey, editor. Nova Science Publishers, Inc. • 2002. $69.00. Provides articles by various authors on the purposes and functions of the Federal Reserve System.

Tight Money Timing: The Impact of Interest Rates and the Federal Reserve on the Stock Market. Wilfred R. George. Greenwood Publishing Group, Inc. • 1982. $55.00.

BIBLIOGRAPHIES

FED in Print: Economics and Banking Topics. Federal Reserve Bank of Philadelphia. • Semiannual. Free. Business and banking topics.

Federal Reserve Board Publications. U.S. Board of Governors of the Federal Reserve System. • Semiannual. Free.

CD-ROM DATABASES

OECD Statistical Compendium. Organization for Economic Cooperation and Development. • Semiannual. $1,905.00 per year for 1 to 10 users. CD-ROM contains more than 730,000 monthly, quarterly, and annual time series for OECD countries, 1960 to date. Includes fully searchable data on agriculture, food, economic indicators, national accounts, employment, energy, finance, industry, technology, and foreign trade. Results can be displayed in various forms.

HANDBOOKS AND MANUALS

Federal Reserve Regulatory Service. U.S. Federal Reserve System, Board of Governors Publications Services Section, R. • Monthly. $200.00 per year. Looseleaf. Includes four handbooks updated monthly: *Consumer and Community Affairs, Monetary Policy and Reserve Requirements Securities, Credit Transactions and Payment Systems.* Irregular supplements.

Federal Reserve System: Purposes and Functions. U.S. Board of Governors of the Federal Reserve System. • Irregular.

INTERNET DATABASES

Business 2.0 Web Guide to the Best Business Links. Business 2.0 Media Inc. Phone: (415)293-4800 E-mail: support@business2,com • URL: http://www.business2.com/webguide • Web site presents an extensive, searchable directory of links to "the best, most informative, and authoritative web pages." Twenty main categories cover business, finance, career, company information, people, and technology topics, with thousands of subtopics, all linking to Web sites recommended by experienced business researchers. Fees: Free.

Federal Reserve Board Publications and Education Resources. Board of Governors of the Federal Reserve System. Phone: (202)452-3000 Fax: (202)452-3819 • URL: http://www.federalreserve.gov/publications.htm • Web site provides convenient access to statistics, surveys, and research from the Federal Reserve Board. *Federal Reserve Bulletin* articles are available as abstracts or full text

(PDF) currently or from six-year archives. The link "Statistics: Releases and Historical Data" offers daily, weekly, monthly, quarterly, and annual data in great detail for interest rates, foreign exchange, consumer credit, money stock measures, industrial production indexes, bank reserves, and other items. Historical tabulations are available for various time periods. Fees: Free.

Fedstats. Federal Interagency Council on Statistical Policy. Phone: (202)395-7254 • URL: http://www.fedstats.gov • Web site features an efficient search facility for full-text statistics produced by more than 100 federal agencies, including the Census Bureau, the Bureau of Economic Analysis, and the Bureau of Labor Statistics. Boolean searches can be made within one agency or for all agencies combined. Links are offered to international statistical bureaus, including the UN, IMF, OECD, UNESCO, Eurostat, and 20 individual countries. Fees: Free.

FreeLunch.com. Economy.com, Inc. Phone: (610)696-8700 Fax: (610)696-1678 • URL: http://www.freelunch.com • Web site provides free access to more than 1.5 million economic and financial data series, covering industry, demographics, labor markets, prices, retail sales, government spending, trade, interest rates, housing starts, the stock market, and many other topics. Data is available for various time periods in either chart or table form. Searching is offered. Fees: Free, but registration required. Economy.com, Inc. also offers fee-based economic analysis at *The Dismal Scientist* site (http://www.dismal.com).

Summary of Commentary on Current Economic Conditions by Federal Reserve District [the Beige Book]. Board of Governors of the Federal Reserve System. Phone: (202)452-3000 Fax: (202)452-3819 • URL: http://www.federalreserve.gov/fomc/beigebook/2004/ • Free Web site provides current "anecdotal information" eight times a year on economic conditions within each of the 12 Federal Reserve Districts, plus an extensive national *Summary.* Text is based on the opinions of bank officials, business executives, economists, financial market experts, and others. Typically contains views of consumer spending, manufacturing, services, credit, employment, prices, wages, and the economy in general. Usually referred to as the Beige Book.

ONLINE DATABASES

Banking Information Source. PROQUEST. • Provides indexing and abstracting of periodical and other literature from 1982 to date, with weekly updates. Covers the financial services industry: banks, savings institutions, investment houses, credit unions, insurance companies, and real estate organizations. Emphasis is on marketing and management. Inquire as to online cost and availability. (Formerly *FINIS: Financial Industry Information Service.*).

PERIODICALS AND NEWSLETTERS

American Banker: The Financial Services Daily. Thomson Media. • Daily. $895.00 per year. Provides news of banking, investment products, mortgages, credit unions, finance, bank technology, and legal developments.

Central Banking: Policy, Markets, Supervision. Available from European Business Publications, Inc. • Quarterly. $260.00 per year, including annual *Central Banking Directory.* Published in England by Central Banking Publications. Reports and comments on the activities of central banks around the world. Also provides discussions of the International Monetary Fund (IMF), the Organization for Economic Cooperation and Development (OECD), the Bank for International Settlements (BIS), and the World Bank.

InvesTech Market Analyst: Technical and Monetary Investment Analysis. InvesTech Research. • Every three weeks. $190.00 per year. Newsletter. Provides interpretation of monetary statistics and Federal Reserve actions, especially as related to technical analysis of stock market price trends.

U. S. Banker. Thomson Media. • Monthly. $65.00 per year. Edited for bank executives and managers. Covers a wide variety of banking and financial topics.

STATISTICS SOURCES

Business Indexes. Board of Governors of the Federal Reserve System. • Monthly.

Business Statistics of the United States. Linz Audain and Cornelia J. Strawser. Bernan Associates. • Annual. $147.00. Based on *Business Statistics,* formerly issue by the Bureau of Economic Analysis, U. S. Department of Commerce. Provides basic data for a wide variety of U. S. industries, services, and economic indicators. Most statistics are shown annually for 30 years and monthly for the most recent four years.

Consumer Installment Credit. Board of Governors. • Monthly. $5.00 per year.

Federal Reserve Bulletin. U.S. Federal Reserve System. • Monthly. $25.00 per year. Provides statistics on banking and the economy, including interest rates, money supply, and the Federal Reserve Board indexes of industrial production.

Survey of Current Business. Available from U. S. Government Printing Office. • Monthly. $63.00 per year. Issued by Bureau of Economic Analysis, U. S. Department of Commerce. Presents a wide variety of business and economic data.

FEDERAL STATISTICS

See: GOVERNMENT STATISTICS

FEED AND FEEDSTUFFS INDUSTRY

See also: CORN INDUSTRY; FARM PRODUCE

GENERAL WORKS

Feeds and Feeding. Tilden W. Perry. Prentice Hall PTR. • 2002. $100.00. Sixth edition.

ABSTRACTS AND INDEXES

Field Crop Abstracts: Monthly Abstract Journal on World Annual Cereal, Legume, Root, Oilseed and Fibre Crops. Available from CABI Publishing North America. • Monthly. Institutions, $1,775.00 per year. Online edition available, $1,820.00 per year. Published in England by CABI Publishing, formerly Commonwealth Agricultural Bureaux. Provides worldwide coverage of the literature.

Nutrition Abstracts and Reviews, Series B: Livestock Feeds and Feeding. Available from CABI Publishing, North America. • Monthly. Institutions, $1,180.00 per year. Online edition available, $1,215.00 per year. Published in England by CABI Publishing. Provides worldwide coverage of the literature.

ALMANACS AND YEARBOOKS

Agricultural and Mineral Commodities Year Book. Available from Taylor & Francis Group. • Annual. $225.00. Published by Europa Publications. Contains descriptive product profiles, price data, export-import data, and production statistics for major commodities of the world. Includes commodity histories, uses, markets, demand trends, and information about trade agreements and key commodity organizations.

CD-ROM DATABASES

AGRICOLA on SilverPlatter. Available from Silver-Platter Information, Inc. • Quarterly. $825.00 per year. Produced by the National Agricultural Library. Provides about three million citations on CD-ROM to the literature of agriculture, agricultural economics, animal sciences, entomology, fertilizer, food, forestry, nutrition, pesticides, plant science, water resources, and other topics. Each quarterly disc covers the past ten years, with archival discs available from 1970.

DIRECTORIES

Agriculture: Websites and Glossary. Carol Canada. Nova Science Publishers, Inc. • 2003. $29.50. Lists agricultural Web sites according to 24 main categories and 16 subcategories. Includes a glossary and an index.

Feed Industry Red Book: Reference Book and Buyer's Guide for the Manufacturing Industry. Moffat Publishing, Inc. • Annual. $40.00. List of over 200 firms involved in the large animal and pet food manufacturing and distribution business, including sources of feed ingredients and suppliers of feed materials handling equipment.

NFGA Directory-Yearbook. • Annual. Price on application.

ENCYCLOPEDIAS AND DICTIONARIES

Encyclopedia of Agriculture Science. Charles J. Arntzen and Ellen M. Ritter, editors. Elsevier. • 1994. $900.00. Four volumes.

FINANCIAL RATIOS

Annual Statement Studies. The Risk Management Association. • Annual. Median and quartile financial ratios are given for over 400 kinds of manufacturing, wholesale, retail, construction, and consumer finance establishments. Data is sorted by both asset size and sales volume. Includes a clearly written "Definition of Ratios" and an alphabetical industry index.

Annual Statement Studies: Industry Default Probabilities and Cash Flow Measures. The Risk Management Association. • Annual. $145.00. Serves as a companion volume to the original *Annual Statement Studies.* Gives probability of default estimates on a percentage scale for more than 450 industries. Includes changes in position year-by-year for eight financial statement line items and provides percentage measures of cash flow.

INTERNET DATABASES

USDA. United States Department of Agriculture. Phone: (202)720-2791 E-mail: agsec@usda.gov • URL: http://www.usda.gov • The USDA home page has six sections: News and Information; What's New; About USDA; Agencies; Opportunities; Search and Help. Keyword searching is offered from the USDA home page and from various individual agency home pages. Agencies are the Economic Research Service, Agricultural Marketing Service, National Agricultural Statistics Service, National Agricultural Library, and about 12 others. Updating varies. Fees: Free.

ONLINE DATABASES

CAB Abstracts. CAB Publishing North America. • Contains 46 specialized abstract collections covering over 10,000 journals and monographs in the areas of agriculture, horticulture, forest products, farm products, nutrition, dairy science, poultry, grains, animal health, entomology, etc. Time period is 1972 to date, with monthly updates. Inquire as to online cost and availability. *CAB Abstracts on CD-ROM* also available, with annual updating.

PERIODICALS AND NEWSLETTERS

Feed and Feeding Digest. National Grain and Feed Association. • Monthly. Membership.

Feed Bulletin. Jacobsen Publishing Co. • Daily. $750.00 per year.

Livestock and Grain Market News Branch Weekly Summary. U.S. Dept of Agriculture. Livestock and Grain Market News Branch. • Weekly. $85.00 per year. Formerly *Grain and Feed Weekly Summary and Statistics.*

PRICE SOURCES

Feedstuffs: The Weekly Newspaper for Agribusiness. Farm Progress Companies. • Weekly. $135.00 per year. Newsletter.

RESEARCH CENTERS AND INSTITUTES

Food and Feed Grains Institute. Kansas State University. 105 Waters Hall, Manhattan, KS 66506-4030. Phone: (785)532-4056 Fax: (785)532-5861 E-mail: ffgi@ksu.edu • URL: http://www.ksu.edu/ffgi.

Soil and Plant Tissue Testing Laboratory. University of Massachusetts at Amherst. West Experimental Station, Amherst, MA 01003-8020. Phone: (413)545-2311 Fax: (413)545-1931 E-mail: bodine@pssci.umass.edu • URL: http://www.umass.edu/plsoils.

STATISTICS SOURCES

Agricultural Statistics. Available from U. S. Government Printing Office. • Annual. $38.00. Produced by the National Agricultural Statistics Service, U. S. Department of Agriculture. Provides a wide variety of statistical data relating to agricultural production, supplies, consumption, prices/price-supports, foreign trade, costs, and returns, as well as farm labor, loans, income, and population. In many cases, historical data is shown annually for 10 years. In addition to farm data, includes detailed fishery statistics.

Annual Survey of Manufactures. Available from U. S. Government Printing Office. • Annual. Prices vary. Issued by the U. S. Census Bureau as an interim update to the *Census of Manufactures.* Includes data on number of manufacturing establishments in various industries, employment, labor costs, value of shipments, capital expenditures, inventories, energy costs, and assets. (See also Census Bureau home page, http://www.census.gov/.).

FAO Production Yearbook. Available from Bernan Associates. • Annual. $45.00. Published by the Food and Agriculture Organization (http://www.fao.org). Contains worldwide data on agriculture, land use, farm crops, livestock, and agricultural prices.

FAO Trade Yearbook. Available from Bernan Associates. • Annual. $45.00. Published by the Food and Agriculture Organization (http://www.fao.org). Provides extensive worldwide data on exports and imports of agricultural commodities, fertilizers, tractors, and pesticides. Includes more than 130 tables of detailed statistics.

World Agricultural Supply and Demand Estimates. Available from U. S. Government Printing Office. • Monthly. $52.00 per year. Issued by the Economics and Statistics Service and the Foreign Agricultural Service of the U. S. Department of Agriculture. Consists mainly of statistical data and tables.

TRADE/PROFESSIONAL ASSOCIATIONS

American Feed Industry Association - Alfalfa Processors Council. 8810 Craig Rd., Overland Park, KS 66212. Phone: (913)648-6800 Fax: (913)648-2648 E-mail: aapa@cysource.com • URL: http://www.feedsearch.com.

National Grain and Feed Association. 1250 Eye St., N.W., Ste. 1003, Washington, DC 20005-3922. Phone: (202)289-0873 Fax: (202)289-5388 E-mail: ngfa@ngfa.org • URL: http://www.ngfa.org • Formerly Grain and Feed Dealers National Association.

National Hay Association. 102 Treasure Island Causeway, St. Petersburg, FL 33706. Phone: 800-707-0014 or (727)367-9702 Fax: (727)367-9608 E-mail: haynha@aol.com • URL: http://nationalhay.org • Hay shippers, dealers, brokers, producers, and others interested in the hay industry.

U.S. Grains Council. 1400 K St. NW, Ste. 1200, Washington, DC 20005. Phone: (202)789-0789 Fax: (202)898-0522 E-mail: grains@grains.org • URL: http://www.grains.org • Federation of feed grain producer organizations, seed trade associations, and organizations of grain processors, exporters, dealers and related agribusiness manufacturers. Maintains 10 international offices for development of foreign markets in over 80 countries for barley, corn, grain sorghum and related products.

FERTILIZER INDUSTRY

See also: AGRICULTURAL CHEMICALS; POTASH INDUSTRY

ALMANACS AND YEARBOOKS

Association of American Plant Food Control Officials Official Publication. Association of American Plant Food Control Officials, Inc., Div. of Regulatory Services. University of Kentucky. • Annual. $25.00.

CD-ROM DATABASES

AGRICOLA on SilverPlatter. Available from Silver-Platter Information, Inc. • Quarterly. $825.00 per year. Produced by the National Agricultural Library. Provides about three million citations on CD-ROM to the literature of agriculture, agricultural economics, animal sciences, entomology, fertilizer, food, forestry, nutrition, pesticides, plant science, water resources, and other topics. Each quarterly disc covers the past ten years, with archival discs available from 1970.

OECD Statistical Compendium. Organization for Economic Cooperation and Development. • Semiannual. $1,905.00 per year for 1 to 10 users. CD-ROM contains more than 730,000 monthly, quarterly, and annual time series for OECD countries, 1960 to date. Includes fully searchable data on agriculture, food, economic indicators, national accounts, employment, energy, finance, industry, technology, and foreign trade. Results can be displayed in various forms.

DIRECTORIES

Major Chemical and Petrochemical Companies of the World. Available from Gale Cengage Learning. • 2002. $880.00. Sixth edition. Published by Graham & Whiteside. Contains profiles of more than 7,000 important chemical and petrochemical companies in various countries. Subject areas include general chemicals, specialty chemicals, agricultural chemicals, petrochemicals, industrial gases, and fertilizers.

ENCYCLOPEDIAS AND DICTIONARIES

Encyclopedia of Agriculture Science. Charles J. Arntzen and Ellen M. Ritter, editors. Elsevier. • 1994. $900.00. Four volumes.

FINANCIAL RATIOS

Annual Statement Studies. The Risk Management Association. • Annual. Median and quartile financial ratios are given for over 400 kinds of manufacturing, wholesale, retail, construction, and consumer finance establishments. Data is sorted by both asset size and sales volume. Includes a clearly written "Definition of Ratios" and an alphabetical industry index.

Annual Statement Studies: Industry Default Probabilities and Cash Flow Measures. The Risk Management Association. • Annual. $145.00. Serves as a companion volume to the original *Annual Statement Studies.* Gives probability of default estimates on a percentage scale for more than 450 industries. Includes changes in position year-by-year for eight financial statement line items and provides percentage measures of cash flow.

HANDBOOKS AND MANUALS

Agrochemicals: Composition, Production, Toxicology, Applications. Franz Muller, editor. John Wiley

and Sons, Inc. • 2000. $375.00. Coverage includes fertilizers, herbicides, fungicides, insecticides, and biological control agents. Content is both theoretical and practical.

INTERNET DATABASES

Business 2.0 Web Guide to the Best Business Links. Business 2.0 Media Inc. Phone: (415)293-4800 E-mail: support@business2.com • URL: http://www.business2.com/webguide • Web site presents an extensive, searchable directory of links to "the best, most informative, and authoritative web pages." Twenty main categories cover business, finance, career, company information, people, and technology topics, with thousands of subtopics, all linking to Web sites recommended by experienced business researchers. Fees: Free.

Fedstats. Federal Interagency Council on Statistical Policy. Phone: (202)395-7254 • URL: http://www.fedstats.gov • Web site features an efficient search facility for full-text statistics produced by more than 100 federal agencies, including the Census Bureau, the Bureau of Economic Analysis, and the Bureau of Labor Statistics. Boolean searches can be made within one agency or for all agencies combined. Links are offered to international statistical bureaus, including the UN, IMF, OECD, UNESCO, Eurostat, and 20 individual countries. Fees: Free.

FreeLunch.com. Economy.com, Inc. Phone: (610)696-8700 Fax: (610)696-1678 • URL: http://www.freelunch.com • Web site provides free access to more than 1.5 million economic and financial data series, covering industry, demographics, labor markets, prices, retail sales, government spending, trade, interest rates, housing starts, the stock market, and many other topics. Data is available for various time periods in either chart or table form. Searching is offered. Fees: Free, but registration required. Economy.com, Inc. also offers fee-based economic analysis at *The Dismal Scientist* site (http://www.dismal.com).

Manufacturing Profiles. U. S. Bureau of the Census. Phone: (301)763-4636 E-mail: webmaster@census.gov • URL: http://www.census.gov/prod/www/abs/mfg-prof.html • The Census Bureau makes available free on PDF (Portable Document Format) an annual consolidation of the entire Current Industrial Report series, presenting "all the data compiled." Contains statistics on production, shipments, inventories, consumption, exports, imports, and orders for a wide variety of manufactured products.

USDA. United States Department of Agriculture. Phone: (202)720-2791 E-mail: agsec@usda.gov • URL: http://www.usda.gov • The USDA home page has six sections: News and Information; What's New; About USDA; Agencies; Opportunities; Search and Help. Keyword searching is offered from the USDA home page and from various individual agency home pages. Agencies are the Economic Research Service, Agricultural Marketing Service, National Agricultural Statistics Service, National Agricultural Library, and about 12 others. Updating varies. Fees: Free.

ONLINE DATABASES

CAB Abstracts. CAB Publishing North America. • Contains 46 specialized abstract collections covering over 10,000 journals and monographs in the areas of agriculture, horticulture, forest products, farm products, nutrition, dairy science, poultry, grains, animal health, entomology, etc. Time period is 1972 to date, with monthly updates. Inquire as to online cost and availability. *CAB Abstracts on CD-ROM* also available, with annual updating.

PERIODICALS AND NEWSLETTERS

Ag Professional. Doane Agricultural Services. • 10 times a year. Free to qualified personnel. Published to meet the business needs of the retail fertilizer and agrichemical dealer industry. Formerly *Ag Retailer Magazine.*

Better Crops With Plant Food. Potash and Phosphate Institute. • Quarterly. $8.00.

Croplife. Meister Media. • Monthly. $36.00 per year. Formerly *Farm Chemicals.*

Dealer and Applicator. Vance Publishing Corp. • Nine times a year. $35.00 per year. Formerly *Custom Applicator.*

Dealer Progress: How Smart Agribusiness is Growing. Fertilizer Institute. • Bimonthly. Free to qualified personnel; others, $40.00 per year. Published in association with the Fertilizer Institute. Includes information on fertilizers and agricultural chemicals, including farm pesticides. Formerly *Progress.*

PRICE SOURCES

The National Provisioner: Serving Meat, Poultry, and Seafood Processors. Stagnito Communications, Inc. • Monthly. Free to qualified personnel; others, $85.04 per year. Annual *Buyer's Guide* available. Meat, poultry and seafood newsletter.

Prices of Agricultural Products and Selected Inputs in Europe and North America. Economic Commission for Europe. United Nations Publications. • Annual.

RESEARCH CENTERS AND INSTITUTES

Agricultural Research Division. University of Nebraska - Lincoln. 207 Agricultural Hall, Lincoln, NE 68583-0704. Phone: (402)472-2045 Fax: (402)472-9071 E-mail: dnelson1@unl.edu.

California Agricultural Experiment Station. University of California. 1111 Franklin St., 6th Fl., Oakland, CA 94607-5200. Phone: (510)987-0060 Fax: (510)451-2317 E-mail: wr.gomes@ucop.edu • URL: http://www.ucanr.org/aes.

International Fertilizer Development Center. P.O. Box 2040, Muscle Shoals, AL 35662. Phone: (205)381-6600 Fax: (205)381-7408 E-mail: general@ifdc.org • URL: http://www.ifdc.org • Conducts research relating to all aspects of fertilizer production, marketing, and use. Supported by the United Nations, the World Bank, and other international agencies.

Tennessee Agricultural Experiment Station. University of Tennessee, Knoxville. 103 Morgan Hall, Knoxville, TN 37901. Phone: (865)974-6756 Fax: (865)974-6479 E-mail: caspeer@utk.edu • URL: http://www.web.utk.edu/~taescomm/.

STATISTICS SOURCES

Agricultural Statistics. Available from U. S. Government Printing Office. • Annual. $38.00. Produced by the National Agricultural Statistics Service, U. S. Department of Agriculture. Provides a wide variety of statistical data relating to agricultural production, supplies, consumption, prices/price-supports, foreign trade, costs, and returns, as well as farm labor, loans, income, and population. In many cases, historical data is shown annually for 10 years. In addition to farm data, includes detailed fishery statistics.

Annual Survey of Manufactures. Available from U. S. Government Printing Office. • Annual. Prices vary. Issued by the U. S. Census Bureau as an interim update to the *Census of Manufactures.* Includes data on number of manufacturing establishments in various industries, employment, labor costs, value of shipments, capital expenditures, inventories, energy costs, and assets. (See also Census Bureau home page, http://www.census.gov/.).

Business Statistics of the United States. Linz Audain and Cornelia J. Strawser. Bernan Associates. • Annual. $147.00. Based on *Business Statistics,* formerly issue by the Bureau of Economic Analysis, U. S. Department of Commerce. Provides basic data for a wide variety of U. S. industries, services, and economic indicators. Most statistics are shown annually for 30 years and monthly for the most recent four years.

FAO Fertilizer Yearbook. United Nations Food and Agriculture Organization. Bernan Associates. • Annual. $36.00. Text in English, French, and Spanish. Formerly *Annual Fertilizer Review.*

FAO Trade Yearbook. Available from Bernan Associates. • Annual. $45.00. Published by the Food and Agriculture Organization (http://www.fao.org). Provides extensive worldwide data on exports and imports of agricultural commodities, fertilizers, tractors, and pesticides. Includes more than 130 tables of detailed statistics.

Survey of Current Business. Available from U. S. Government Printing Office. • Monthly. $63.00 per year. Issued by Bureau of Economic Analysis, U. S. Department of Commerce. Presents a wide variety of business and economic data.

TRADE/PROFESSIONAL ASSOCIATIONS

Agricultural Retailers Association. 1156 15th St. NW, Ste. 302, Washington, DC 20005. Phone: 800-535-6272 or (202)457-0825 Fax: (202)457-0864 E-mail: ara@aradc.org • URL: http://www.aradc.org • Retailers, manufacturers, and suppliers of fertilizers and agrochemicals; equipment manufacturers; retail affiliations; and state association affiliates.

Association of American Plant Food Control Officials. University of Kentucky, 103 Regulatory Services Bldg., Lexington, KY 40546-0275. Phone: (859)257-2668 Fax: (859)257-9478 E-mail: aafpco@att.net • URL: http://www.aapfco.org.

Fertilizer Industry Round Table. 1701 S Highland Ave., Baltimore, MD 21224. Phone: (410)276-4466 Fax: (410)276-0241 E-mail: peggyl@ajsackett.com • URL: http://www.firt.org • Participants include production, technical, and research personnel in the fertilizer industry. Acts as a forum for discussion of technical and production problems.

The Fertilizer Institute. Union Center Plz., 820 1st St. NE, Ste. 430, Washington, DC 20002. Phone: (202)962-0490 Fax: (202)962-0577 E-mail: informationtfi@tfi.org • URL: http://www.tfi.org • Producers, manufacturers, retailers, trading firms, and equipment manufacturers. Represents members in various legislative, educational, and technical areas. Provides information and public relations programs.

The Sulphur Institute. 1140 Connecticut Ave. NW, Ste. 612, Washington, DC 20036. Phone: (202)331-9660 Fax: (202)293-2940 E-mail: sulphur@sulphurinstitute.org • URL: http://www.sulphurinstitute.org • International organization supported by the sulphur industry to promote and expand the use of sulphur in all forms worldwide.

FESTIVALS

See: ANNIVERSARIES AND HOLIDAYS; FAIRS

FIBER INDUSTRY

See also: COTTON INDUSTRY; JUTE INDUSTRY; SYNTHETIC TEXTILE FIBER INDUSTRY; WOOL AND WORSTED INDUSTRY

ABSTRACTS AND INDEXES

NTIS Alerts: Materials Sciences. National Technical Information Service. • Semimonthly. $220.00 per year. Provides descriptions of government-sponsored research reports and software, with ordering information. Covers ceramics, glass, coatings, composite materials, alloys, plastics, wood, paper, adhesives, fibers, lubricants, and related subjects. Formerly *Abstract Newsletter.*

Textile Technology Digest. Institute of Textile Technology. • Annual. $535.00. Provides indexing and abstracting of a wide variety of textile technology literature.

CD-ROM DATABASES

Textile Technology Digest [CD-ROM]. Textile Information Center, Institute of Textile Technology. • Quarterly. Provides CD-ROM indexing and abstracting of worldwide journals and monographs in various areas of textile technology, production, and management. Covers 1978 to date.

DIRECTORIES

Materials Research Centres: A World Directory of Organizations and Programmes in Materials Science. Specialist Journals. • Biennial. $445.00. Profiles of research centers in 75 countries. Materials include plastics, metals, fibers, etc.

ENCYCLOPEDIAS AND DICTIONARIES

Textile Terms and Definitions. J.E. McIntyre and Paul N. Daniels, editors. Available from State Mutual Book and Periodical Service Ltd. • 1996. $180.00. 10th edition. Published by the Textile Insitute (UK). Includes more than 1,000 definitions of textile processes, fiber types, and end products. Illustrated.

ONLINE DATABASES

Textile Technology Digest [online]. Institute of Textile Technology. • Contains indexing and abstracting of more than 300 worldwide journals and monographs in various areas of textile technology, production, and management. Time period is 1978 to date, with monthly updating. Inquire as to online cost and availability.

World Textiles. Elsevier Science, Inc. • Provides abstracting and indexing from 1970 of worldwide textile literature (periodicals, books, pamphlets, and reports). Includes U. S., European, and British patent information. Updating is monthly. Inquire as to online cost and availability.

PERIODICALS AND NEWSLETTERS

Fibre Market News. Group Interest Enterprises. G.I.E. Media, MC. • Description: Focuses on developments affecting the recycled paper industry and current market trends. Recurring features include news of research and educational opportunities, legislative updates, a calendar of events, and meeting reports.

Journal of Natural Fibers. Haworth Press, Inc. • Quarterly. $400.00 per year to libraries; $45.00 per year to individuals. Covers applications, technology, research, and world markets relating to fibers from silk, wool, cotton, flax, hemp, jute, etc. Previously *Natural Fibres,* published annually.

RESEARCH CENTERS AND INSTITUTES

Herty Foundation: Research and Development Center. 110 Brampton Rd., Savannah, GA 31408. Phone: (912)963-2600 Fax: (912)963-2614 E-mail: mwoodlie@herty.com • URL: http://www.herty.com.

Institute of Textile Technology. 2551 Ivy Rd., Charlottesville, VA 22903-4614. Phone: (434)296-5511 Fax: (434)296-2957 E-mail: library@itt.edu • URL: http://www.itt.edu.

Texas Agricultural Market Research Center. Texas A & M University. Dept. of Agricultural Economics, College Station, TX 77843-2124. Phone: (979)845-5911 Fax: (979)845-6378 E-mail: tamrc@tamu.edu.

Textiles and Materials. Philadelphia University, Schoolhouse Lane and Henry Ave., Philadelphia, PA 19144-5497. Phone: (215)951-2751 Fax: (215)951-2651 E-mail: brooksteind@philau.edu • URL: http://www.philaau.edu/schools • Many research areas, including industrial and nonwoven textiles.

STATISTICS SOURCES

Consumption on the Woolen System and Worsted Combing. U. S. Bureau of the Census. • Quarterly

and annual. Provides data on consumption of fibers in woolen and worsted spinning mills, by class of fibers and end use. (Current Industrial Reports, MQ-22D.).

TRADE/PROFESSIONAL ASSOCIATIONS

American Fiber Manufacturers Association. 1530 Wilson Blvd., Ste. 690, Arlington, VA 22209-2418. Phone: (703)875-0432 Fax: (703)875-0907 E-mail: afma@afma.org • URL: http://www.fibersource.com • Producers of manufactured fibers used in apparel, household goods, industrial materials, and other types of products. Represents the industry in educational, governmental, and foreign trade matters. Distributes a video depicting production and end uses of manufactured fibers.

Fiber Society. North Carolina State University, College of Textiles, 2401 Research Dr., Raleigh, NC 27695-8301. Phone: (919)513-0143 Fax: (919)515-3057 E-mail: ellisom@clemson.edu • URL: http://www.thefibersociety.org • Chemists, physicists, engineers, biologists, mathematicians, and other scientists conducting research in fibers, fiber-based products, and fibrous materials. Sponsors lecture program. Sponsors conferences.

Textile Fibers and By-Products Association. 1531 Industrial Dr., Griffin, GA 30224-0008. Phone: (770)412-2325 or (770)227-9236 Fax: (770)227-6321 E-mail: info@tfbpa.org • URL: http://www.tfbpa.org • Firms purchasing and marketing textile fiber by-products, commonly designated as textile waste.

Textile Institute. St. James's Buildings, 1st Fl., 79 Oxford St., Manchester M1 6FQ, United Kingdom. Phone: 44 161 2371188 Fax: 44 161 2361991 E-mail: tiihq@textileinst.org.uk • URL: http://www.texi.org • Companies and individuals in 100 countries involved in management, science, technology, design, information transfer, and marketing of textiles including clothing and footwear. Promotes interests of the textile industry worldwide; serves professional interests of members; confers qualifications and recognizes achievements in research, application of ideas, education, business, and public affairs. Maintains Information Service to collect information relating to textile industrial and economic conditions in different countries and economic sectors.

FIBER OPTICS INDUSTRY

GENERAL WORKS

Fiber Optic Systems Design: A Practical Guide to Designing, Installing and Maintaining. John M. Simmons. McGraw Hill. • 1991. $59.75.

Fundamentals of Optical Fibers. John A. Buck. John Wiley and Sons, Inc. • 1995. $99.95. (Pure and Applied Optics Series).

Introduction to Glass Science and Technology. Springer-Verlag. • 1997. $49.95. Covers the basics of glass manufacture, including the physical, optical, electrical, chemical, and mechanical properties of glass. (RCS Paperback Series).

ABSTRACTS AND INDEXES

Applied Science and Technology Index. H. W. Wilson Co. • 11 times a year. Quarterly and annual cumulations. Price varies. Indexes a wide variety of English language technical, industrial, and engineering periodicals.

Key Abstracts: Optoelectronics. Available from INSPEC, Inc. • Monthly. $250.00 per year. Provides international coverage of journal and proceedings literature relating to fiber optics, lasers, and optoelectronics in general. Published in England by the Institution of Electrical Engineers (IEE).

BIBLIOGRAPHIES

Encyclopedia of Physical Science and Engineering Information. Gale Cengage Learning. • 1996. $160.

00. Second edition. Includes print, electronic, and other information sources for a wide range of scientific, technical, and engineering topics.

CD-ROM DATABASES

Science Citation Index: Compact Disc Edition. Institute for Scientific Information. • Monthly. Provides CD-ROM indexing of the world's scientific and technical literature. Corresponds to online *Scisearch* and printed *Science Citation Index.*

WILSONDISC: Applied Science and Technology Abstracts. H. W. Wilson Co. • Monthly. Includes unlimited access to the online version of *Applied Science and Technology Abstracts* through WILSONLINE. Provides CD-ROM indexing and abstracting of 500 prominent scientific, technical, engineering, and industrial periodicals. Indexing coverage is provided from 1983 to date and abstracting from 1993 to date.

DIRECTORIES

Fiber Optics Yellow Pages: The International Optical Networks/Fiberoptics Yellow Pages. Information Gatekeepers, Inc. • Annual. $89.95. Includes manufacturers of fiber optics products. Provides a glossary and a discussion of current uses of fiber optics. Formerly *Fiber Optics Yellow Pages.*

Fiberoptic Technology News Buying Guide. Reed Business Information. • Publication includes: Over 500 manufacturers and suppliers of fiber optic products, equipment, and services. Entries include: Company name, address, phone, fax, telex, key personnel, number of employees, years in operation, description of products and services.

Laser Focus World Buyers Guide. Advanced Technology Group. • Covers: over 2,000 manufacturers, suppliers, and consultants in the laser, fiber optic, electro-optic, optic, and related industries, worldwide. Entries include: Company name, address, phone, fax, e-mail, principal executives, number of employees, list of products and services, brief description of company.

Lightwave Buyers Guide. PennWell Corp., Advanced Technology Div. • Annual. $79.00. Lists manufacturers and distributors of fiberoptic systems and components.

ENCYCLOPEDIAS AND DICTIONARIES

Encyclopedia of Materials: Science and Technology. K.H.J. Buschow and others, editors. Elsevier. • 2001. $4,985.00. Eleven volumes. Provides extensive technical information on a wide variety of materials, including metals, ceramics, plastics, optical materials, and building materials. Includes more than 2,000 articles and 5,000 illustrations.

HANDBOOKS AND MANUALS

Fiber Optic Reference Guide. David R. Goff. Elsevier. • 2002. $44.99. Third edition. A basic guide to fiber optics as utilized in telecommunications. Coverage includes fiber optic cables, light emitters, detectors, optical amplifiers, fiber for video, fiber for data transmission, interconnections, system design, testing, and future trends.

Handbook of Fiber Optics: Theory and Applications. Chai Yeh. Elsevier. • 1990. $165.00.

Optical Fibre Sensor Technology. Ken Grattan and Beverley Meggitt. Kluwer Academic Publishers. • 2000. $145.00.

ONLINE DATABASES

Applied Science and Technology Index Online. H. W. Wilson Co. • Provides online indexing of 500 major scientific, technical, industrial, and engineering periodicals. Time period is 1983 to date. Monthly updates. Inquire as to online cost and availability.

F & S Index. Gale Cengage Learning. • Contains about four million citations to worldwide business, financial, and industrial or consumer product literature appearing from 1972 to date. Weekly updates. Inquire as to online cost and availability.

Globalbase. Gale Cengage Learning. • Provides more than one million online summaries of business, industrial, and economic news reports from more than 1,000 publications worldwide. Covers a wide range of material appearing in international trade journals, professional magazines, and newspapers. Time period is 1984 to date, with weekly updates. Inquire as to online cost and availability.

PROMT: Predicasts Overview of Markets and Technology. Gale Cengage Learning. • Companies, products, applied technologies and markets. U.S. and international literature coverage, 1972 to date. Inquire as to online cost and availability. Provides abstracts from more than 1,600 publications. Weekly updates.

Scisearch. Institute for Scientific Information. • Broad, multidisciplinary index to the literature of science and technology, 1974 to present. Inquire as to online cost and availability. Coverage of literature is worldwide, with weekly updates.

PERIODICALS AND NEWSLETTERS

Fiber Optics and Communications. Information Gatekeepers, Inc. • Monthly. $695.00. Emphasis on the use of fiber optics in telecommunications.

Fiber Optics News. PBI Media, LLC. • Weekly. $797.00 per year. Newsletter.

Fiberoptic Product News. Reed Business Information. • Monthly. $167.75 per year. Includes annual *Directory* and five *European Editions.* Provides general coverage of the fiber optics industry, for both producers and users.

FiberSystems International. Available from IOP Publishing, Inc. • Seven times a year. Free to qualified personnel. Published in the UK by the Institute of Physics. "Covering the optical communications marketplace within the Americas and Asia." *Fibre Systems Europe* is also available, covering the business and marketing aspects of fiber optics communications in Europe.

Laser Focus World: The World of Optoelectronics. PennWell Corp., Advanced Technology Div. • Monthly. $165.00 per year. Covers business and technical aspects of electro-optics, including lasers and fiberoptics. Includes *Buyer's Guide.*

Lightwave: Fiber Optics Technology and Applications Worldwide. PennWell Corp., Advaned Technology Div. • Monthly. $105.00 per year. Includes *Buyers Guide.*

Optical Fiber Technology: Materials, Devices, and Systems. Elsevier. • Quarterly. Individuals, $210.00 per year; institutions, $391.00 per year.

Optics and Photonics News. Optical Society of America, Inc. • Monthly. $99.00 per year. Includes print and online editions.

RESEARCH CENTERS AND INSTITUTES

Edward L. Ginzton Laboratory. Stanford University, 450 Via Palou, Stanford, CA 94305-4085. Phone: (650)723-0111 Fax: (650)725-9355 E-mail: dabm@ee.stanford.edu • URL: http://www.stanford.edu/group/ginzton • Research fields include low-temperature physics and superconducting electronics.

Fiber and Electro Optics Research Center. Virginia Polytechnic Institute and State University, Dept. of Electrical Engineering, 106 Plantation Rd., Blacksburg, VA 24061. Phone: (540)231-7203 Fax: (540)231-4561 E-mail: roclaus@vt.edu.

Fiberoptic Materials Research Program. Rutgers University. College of Engineering, 607 Taylor Rd., Piscataway, NJ 08854-8065. Phone: (732)445-4729 Fax: (908)445-4545 E-mail: sigel@alumnia.rutgers.edu • Research fields include the communications and biomedical applications of fiber optics.

Laboratory for Information and Decision Systems. Massachusetts Institute of Technology, 127 Mas-

sachusetts Ave., Bldg. 35, Room 308, Cambridge, MA 02139-4307. Phone: (617)258-8222 Fax: (617)253-3578 E-mail: chan@mit.edu • URL: http://www.justice.mit.edu • Research areas include data communication networks and fiber optic networks.

STATISTICS SOURCES

U. S. Industry and Trade Outlook. Available from National Technical Information Service. • Annual. $69.95. Produced by the International Trade Administration, U. S. Department of Commerce, in a "public-private" partnership with DRI/McGraw-Hill and Standard & Poor's. Provides basic data, outlook for the current year, and "Long-Term Prospects" (five-year projections) for a wide variety of products and services. Includes high technology industries. Formerly *U. S. Industrial Outlook.*

TRADE/PROFESSIONAL ASSOCIATIONS

IEEE Lasers and Electro-Optics Society. c/o IEEE Corporate Center, Three Park Ave., 17th Fl., New York, NY 10016-5997. Phone: (212)419-7900 or (212)752-4929 E-mail: ieeeusa@ieee.org • URL: http://www.ieee.org • Fields of interest include lasers, fiber optics, optoelectronics, and photonics.

Optical Society of America. 2010 Massachusetts Ave., N.W., Washington, DC 20036-1023. Phone: (202)223-8130 Fax: (202)223-1096 E-mail: info@osa.org • URL: http://www.osa.org.

SPIE-The International Society for Optical Engineering. P.O. Box 10, Bellingham, WA 98227-0010. Phone: (360)676-3290 Fax: (360)647-1445 E-mail: spie@spie.org • URL: http://www.spie.org • Formerly Society of Photo-Optical Instrumentation Engineers.

OTHER SOURCES

Fiber Optic Products and Applications. Available from MarketResearch.com. • 2002. $3,950.00. Published by Global Industry Analysts. Provides worldwide market research data, including profiles of major companies in the field.

FICTION, BUSINESS

See: BUSINESS IN FICTION

FILES AND FILING (DOCUMENTS)

See also: LIBRARY MANAGEMENT; OFFICE MANAGEMENT; OFFICE PRACTICE

CD-ROM DATABASES

LISA Plus. Available from Cambridge Scientific Abstracts (CSA). • Quarterly. $2,000.00 per year. CD-ROM version of Library Information and Science Abstracts, providing abstracting and indexing of the world's library and information science literature, 1969 to date. Contains more than 180,000 citations.

ONLINE DATABASES

LISA: Library and Information Science Abstracts. Available from Cambridge Scientific Abstracts (CSA). • Provides abstracting and indexing of the world's library and information science literature, 1969 to date. Covers more than 440 periodicals from 68 countries. Updating is biweekly. Inquire as to online cost and availability.

TRADE/PROFESSIONAL ASSOCIATIONS

National Association of Professional Organizers. 4700 W Lake Ave., Glenview, IL 60025. Phone: (847)375-4746 Fax: (847)734-9236 E-mail: hq@napo.net • URL: http://www.napo.net • Members are concerned with time management, productivity, and the efficient organization of documents and activities. Formerly Association of Professional Organizers.

FILMS, MOTION PICTURE

See: MOTION PICTURE INDUSTRY

FILMSTRIPS

See: AUDIOVISUAL AIDS IN EDUCATION; AUDIOVISUAL AIDS IN INDUSTRY

FILTER INDUSTRY

ABSTRACTS AND INDEXES

Applied Science and Technology Index. H. W. Wilson Co. • 11 times a year. Quarterly and annual cumulations. Price varies. Indexes a wide variety of English language technical, industrial, and engineering periodicals.

Current Contents: Engineering, Computing and Technology. Thomson/ISI. • Weekly. $730.00 per year. Reproductions of contents pages of technical journals. Includes *Author Index, Address Directory, Current Book Contents* and *Title Word Index.* Formerly *Current Contents: Engineering, Technology and Applied Sciences.*

DIRECTORIES

Thomas Register of American Manufacturers. Thomas Publishing Co., Inc. • Annual. $149.00. 34 volumes. A three-part system offering information on a wide variety of industrial equipment and supplies. Lists more than 151,000 industrial product and services companies.

HANDBOOKS AND MANUALS

Filters and Filtration Handbook. T. Christopher Dickenson. Elsevier. • 1997. $265.00. Fourth edition.

ONLINE DATABASES

Applied Science and Technology Index Online. H. W. Wilson Co. • Provides online indexing of 500 major scientific, technical, industrial, and engineering periodicals. Time period is 1983 to date. Monthly updates. Inquire as to online cost and availability.

PROMT: Predicasts Overview of Markets and Technology. Gale Cengage Learning. • Companies, products, applied technologies and markets. U.S. and international literature coverage, 1972 to date. Inquire as to online cost and availability. Provides abstracts from more than 1,600 publications. Weekly updates.

Thomas Register Online. Thomas Publishing Co., Inc. • Provides concise information on approximately 194,000 U. S. companies, mainly manufacturers, with over 50,000 product classifications. Indexes over 115,000 trade names. Information is updated semiannually. Inquire as to online cost and availability.

PERIODICALS AND NEWSLETTERS

Fabric Filter Newsletter. The McIlvaine Co. • Description: Focuses on dry filtration using fabric and granular media filters. Provides information on all applications of dry filtration, from grain handling to power plants.

Filtration News. Eagle Publications, Inc. • Bimonthly. Controlled circulation. Emphasis is on new filtration products for industrial use.

Industrial Equipment News. Thomas Publishing Co., LLC. • Monthly. $65.00 per year. What's new in equipment, parts and materials.

Liquid Filtration Newsletter. The McIlvaine Co. • Description: Focuses on the liquid filtration industry, providing information on technical developments

and reports on individual companies in the field. Recurring features include a calendar of events and a column titled New & Different.

New Equipment Digest. Penton Media, Inc. • Monthly. Free to qualified personnel; others, $60.00 per year. Formerly *Material Handling Engineering.*

New Equipment Reporter: New Products Industrial News. De Roche Publications. • Monthly. Controlled circulation.

Processing. Putman Media. • 14 times a year. $54.00 per year. Emphasis is on descriptions of new products for all areas of industrial processing, including valves, controls, filters, pumps, compressors, fluidics, and instrumentation.

TRADE/PROFESSIONAL ASSOCIATIONS

Filter Manufacturers Council. PO Box 13966, 10 Laboratory Dr., Research Triangle Park, NC 27709-3966. Phone: 800-993-4583 or (919)549-4800 Fax: (919)406-1306 E-mail: jdenton@mema.org • URL: http://www.filtercouncil.org • Worldwide manufacturers of filters for automotive and industrial companies. Keeps members informed of governmental actions relating to the filter industry. Provides regulatory assistance to commercial generators of used vehicular oil filters, and a forum for discussions of issues affecting the industry.

FINANCE

See also: ACCOUNTING; BUSINESS; COMPUTERS IN FINANCE; CORPORATE FINANCE; COUNTY FINANCE; FINANCIAL MANAGEMENT; INTERNATIONAL FINANCE; INVESTMENTS; MUNICIPAL FINANCE

GENERAL WORKS

Accounting and Finance for Non-Specialists. Peter Atrill and Eddie McLaney. Pearson Education. • 2003. $77.00. Fourth edition. Includes the measurement and reporting of financial performance and cash flow.

Case Studies in Finance: Managing for Corporate Value Creation. Robert Bruner. McGraw-Hill. • 2002. $109.69. Fourth edition. (Finance, Insurance and Real Estate Series).

Essentials of Managerial Finance. South-Western. • 2003. $112.95. 13th edition.

Finance for Non-Financial Managers. A. H. Millichamp. Continuum International Publishing Group, Inc. • 2001. $24.95. Third edition. (Letts Higher Education List Series).

Financial History of the United States. Jerry W. Markham. M. E. Sharpe, Inc. • 2002. $349.00. Three volumes. Vol. 1: *From Christopher Columbus to the Robber Barons (1492-1900).* Vol. 2: *From J. P. Morgan to the Institutional Investor (1900-1970).* Vol. 3: *From the Age of Derivatives to the Internet (1970-2000).* Each volume contains name and subject indexes, with cumulative indexes in volume three.

Manias, Panics, and Crashes: A History of Financial Crises. Charles P. Kindleberger. John Wiley and Sons, Inc. • 2000. $19.95. Fourth edition. Provides a history of financial troubles from 1618 to modern times, with greed as a central theme. (Investment Classic Series).

Money, Banking, and Financial Markets. Roger L. Miller and David D. VanHoose. South-Western. • 2003. $102.95. Second edition.

The New Financial Order: Risk in the 21st Century. Robert J. Shiller. Princeton University Press. • 2003. $29.95. By the author of *Irrational Exuberance* (2000). Recommends that risk management schemes be developed for application to the risks of everyday life, as in such chapters as "Insurance for Livelihoods and Home Values," "Inequality Insurance:

Protecting the Distribution of Income," and "Intergenerational Social Security: Sharing Risks Between Young and Old.".

Resumes for Banking and Financial Careers. McGraw-Hill. • 2001. $10.95. Second edition. Contains 100 sample resumes and 20 cover letters. (VGM Professional Resumes Series.).

Winning Numbers: How to Use Business Facts and Figures to Make Your Point and Get Ahead. Michael C. Thomsett. AMACOM. • 1990. $22.95. A short course in financial communication, or finance for the nonfinancial manager.

ABSTRACTS AND INDEXES

Business Periodicals Index. H. W. Wilson Co. • 11 times a year. Quarterly and annual cumulations. Price varies.

Investment Statistics Locator. Linda H. Bentley and Jennifer J. Kiesl, editors. Greenwood Publishing Group, Inc. • 1994. $69.95. Expanded revised edition. Provides detailed subject indexing of more than 50 of the most-used sources of financial and investment data. Includes an annotated bibliography.

NTIS Alerts: Business & Economics. National Technical Information Service. • Text: Semimonthly. $210.00 per year.

BIBLIOGRAPHIES

Using the Financial and Business Literature. Thomas P. Slavens. Marcel Dekker, Inc. • 2004. $165.00. Provides detailed descriptions of both print and electronic information sources. (Books in Library and Information Science Series/64.).

BIOGRAPHICAL SOURCES

Who's Who in Finance and Industry. Marquis Who's Who. • Biennial. $259.95. Provides over 21,000 concise biographies of business leaders in all fields.

CD-ROM DATABASES

OECD Statistical Compendium. Organization for Economic Cooperation and Development. • Semiannual. $1,905.00 per year for 1 to 10 users. CD-ROM contains more than 730,000 monthly, quarterly, and annual time series for OECD countries, 1960 to date. Includes fully searchable data on agriculture, food, economic indicators, national accounts, employment, energy, finance, industry, technology, and foreign trade. Results can be displayed in various forms.

Social Sciences Citation Index. ISI. • Monthly. Price on request. Provides CD-ROM indexing of articles appearing in 1700 leading social science journals worldwide, with additional selections from more than 5700 other journals. Time span is 1992 to date. Coverage includes economics, business, finance, management, communications, demographics, library and information science, political science, sociology, and many other subjects.

Social Sciences Citation Index: Compact Disc Edition with Abstracts. Institute for Scientific Information. • Monthly. Provides CD-ROM indexing and abstracting of "significant articles" from 1,700 social science journals worldwide, with additional selections from 3,200 other journals, 1986 to date. Includes economics, business, finance, management, communications, demographics, information and library science, political science, sociology, and many other subjects.

WILSONDISC: Wilson Business Abstracts. H. W. Wilson Co. • Monthly. Includes unlimited online access to *Wilson Business Abstracts* through WILSONLINE. Provides CD-ROM "cover-to-cover" abstracting and indexing of over 600 prominent business periodicals. Indexing is from 1982, abstracting from 1990. (*Business Periodicals*

Index without abstracts is available on CD-ROM at $1,495 per year.).

DIRECTORIES

Internet Tools of the Profession: A Guide for Information Professionals. Hope N. Tillman, editor. Special Libraries Association. • 1997. $49.00. Second edition. Consists of 14 sections by various authors or compilers. After two introductory articles on searching the Internet, there are 12 annotated lists of useful Web sites, covering the SLA, business and finance, chemistry, education, food and agriculture, information technology, insurance and employee benefits, law, library management, metals and materials, pharmaceuticals, and telecommunications. An index is provided.

Major Financial Institutions of the World 2001. Available from Gale Cengage Learning. • 2003. $880.00. Sixth edition. Two volumes. Published by Graham & Whiteside. Contains detailed information on more than 7,500 important financial institutions in various countries. Includes banks, investment companies, and insurance companies.

Plunkett's On-Line Trading, Finance, and Investment Web Sites Almanac. Plunkett Research, Ltd. • Annual. $149.99. Provides profiles and usefulness rankings of financial Web sites. Sites are rated from 1 to 5 for specific uses. Includes CD-ROM.

ENCYCLOPEDIAS AND DICTIONARIES

The A-Z Vocabulary for Investors. American Institute for Economic Research. • 1997. $7.00. Second half of book is a "General Glossary" of about 400 financial terms "most-commonly used" in investing. First half contains lengthier descriptions of types of banking institutions (commercial banks, thrift institutions, credit unions), followed by succinct explanations of various forms of investment: stocks, bonds, options, futures, commodities, and "Other Investments" (collectibles, currencies, mortgages, precious metals, real estate, charitable trusts). (Economic Education Bulletin.).

Blackwell Encyclopedic Dictionary of Finance. Dean Paxson and Douglas Wood, editors. Blackwell Publishing. • 1997. $110.00. The editors are associated with the University of Manchester. Contains definitions of key terms combined with longer articles written by various U. S. and foreign business educators. Includes bibliographies and index. (Blackwell Encyclopedia of Management Series).

Dictionary of Finance and Investment Terms. John Downes. Barron's Educational Series, Inc. • 2002. $14.95. Sixth edition. Provides clear explanations of more than 5,000 business, banking, financial, investment, and tax terms. Includes a separate list of financial abbreviations and acronyms. (Business Dictionaries Series).

Dictionary of Financial Abbreviations. John Paxton. Routledge. • 2002. $50.00. Provides more than 4,000 abbreviations and acronyms relating to finance, currencies, and financial organizations.

Encyclopedia of Banking and Finance. Charles J. Woelfel. McGraw-Hill. • 1996. $150.00. 10th revised edition. Includes CD-ROM.

Encyclopedia of Business. Gale Cengage Learning. • 2000. $425.00. Second edition. Two volumes. Contains more than 700 signed articles covering major business disciplines and concepts. International in scope. (Encyclopedia of Business Series).

Encyclopedia of Business and Finance. Burton Kaliski, editor. Available from Gale Cengage Learning. • 2001. $275.00. Two volumes. Published by Macmillan Reference USA. Contains articles by various contributors on accounting, business administration, banking, finance, management information systems, and marketing.

International Dictionary of Accounting Acronyms. Thomas W. Morris, editor. Fitzroy Dearborn

Publishers, Inc. • 1999. $45.00. Defines 2,000 acronyms used in worldwide accounting and finance.

Knowledge Exchange Business Encyclopedia: Your Complete Business Advisor. Lorraine Spurge. Knowledge Exchange LLC. • 1998. $45.00. Provides definitions of business terms and financial expressions, profiles of leading industries, tables of economic statistics, biographies of business leaders, and other business information. Includes "A Chronology of Business from 3000 B.C. Through 1995." Contains illustrations and three indexes.

The New Palgrave Dictionary of Money and Finance. Peter Newman and others, editors. Palgrave Macmillan. • 1992. $595.00. Two volumes. Consists of signed essays on over 1,000 financial topics, each with a bibliography. Covers a wide variety of financial, monetary, and investment areas. A detailed subject index is provided.

HANDBOOKS AND MANUALS

Barron's Finance & Investment Handbook. John Downes and Jordan Goodman. Barron's Educational Series, Inc. • 1998. $35.00. Fifth edition. Mainly concerned with personal finance, including advice on stocks, bonds, mutual funds, annuities, life insurance, real estate, futures, and collectibles. Includes a glossary of financial and investment terms.

Financial Investigations: A Forensic Accounting Approach to Detecting and Resolving Crimes. Available from U. S. Government Printing Office. • 2002. $54.00. Two volumes: textbook and workbook. Issued by the Internal Revenue Service (http://www.irs.ustreas.gov). Serves as a text "for courses on conducting financial investigations." (IRS Publications 1714 and 1816.).

Financing Your Small Business. Robert Walter. Barron's Educational Series, Inc. • 2004. $18.95. Explains various sources of capital for small businesses, including bank loans, venture capital, and initial public offerings of stock.

Where to Go When the Bank Says No: Alternatives to Financing Your Business. David R. Evanson. Bloomberg. • 1998. $24.95. Emphasis is on obtaining business financing in the $250,000 to $15,000,000 range. Business plans are discussed. (Bloomberg Small Business Series).

INTERNET DATABASES

BanxQuote Banking, Mortgage, and Finance Center. BanxQuote, Inc. Phone: (914)722-1600 Fax: (914)722-6630 E-mail: info@banx.com • URL: http://www.banx.com • Web site quotes interest rates paid by banks around the country on various savings products, as well as rates paid by consumers for automobile loans, mortgages, credit cards, home equity loans, and personal loans. Also provided: stock quotes, indexes, stock options, futures trading data, economic indicators, and links to many other financial sites. Daily updates. Fees: Free.

Business 2.0 Web Guide to the Best Business Links. Business 2.0 Media Inc. Phone: (415)293-4800 E-mail: support@business2.com • URL: http://www.business2.com/webguide • Web site presents an extensive, searchable directory of links to "the best, most informative, and authoritative web pages." Twenty main categories cover business, finance, career, company information, people, and technology topics, with thousands of subtopics, all linking to Web sites recommended by experienced business researchers. Fees: Free.

Business Week Online. McGraw-Hill. Phone: (212)512-2511 Fax: (684)842-6101 • URL: http://www.businessweek.com • Web site provides complete contents of current issue of *Business Week* plus "BW Daily" with additonal business news, financial market quotes, and corporate information from Standard & Poor's. Includes various features, such as "Banking Center" with mortgage and interest data, and "Interactive Computer Buying Guide."

The "Business Week Archive" is fully searchable back to 1996.

EBSCO Information Services. Ebsco Publishing. Phone: 800-653-2726 or (978)356-6500 Fax: (978)356-6565 E-mail: ep@epnet.com • URL: http://www.epnet.com • Fee-based Web site providing Internet access to a wide variety of databases, including business-related material. Full text is available for many periodical titles, with daily updates. Fees: Apply.

Factiva. Dow Jones Reuters Business Interactive, LLC. Phone: 800-369-7466 or (609)452-1511 Fax: (609)520-5770 E-mail: solutions@factiva.com • URL: http://www.factiva.com • Fee-based Web site provides "global news and business information through Web sites and content integration solutions." Includes Dow Jones and Reuters newswires, The Wall Street Journal, and more than 7,000 other sources of current news, historical articles, market research reports, and investment analysis. Content includes 96 major U. S. newspapers, 900 non-English sources, trade publications, media transcripts, country profiles, news photos, etc.

Fedstats. Federal Interagency Council on Statistical Policy. Phone: (202)395-7254 • URL: http://www.fedstats.gov • Web site features an efficient search facility for full-text statistics produced by more than 100 federal agencies, including the Census Bureau, the Bureau of Economic Analysis, and the Bureau of Labor Statistics. Boolean searches can be made within one agency or for all agencies combined. Links are offered to international statistical bureaus, including the UN, IMF, OECD, UNESCO, Eurostat, and 20 individual countries. Fees: Free.

The Financial Post (Web site). National Post Online. Phone: 800-805-1184 or (244)383-2300 Fax: (416)383-2443 • URL: http://www.nationalpost.com/financialpost/ • Provides a broad range of Canadian business news online, with daily updates. Includes news, opinion, and special reports, as well as "Investing," "Money Rates," "Market Watch," and "Daily Mutual Funds." Allows advanced searching (Boolean operators), with links to various other sites. Fees: Free.

FreeLunch.com. Economy.com, Inc. Phone: (610)696-8700 Fax: (610)696-1678 • URL: http://www.freelunch.com • Web site provides free access to more than 1.5 million economic and financial data series, covering industry, demographics, labor markets, prices, retail sales, government spending, trade, interest rates, housing starts, the stock market, and many other topics. Data is available for various time periods in either chart or table form. Searching is offered. Fees: Free, but registration required. Economy.com, Inc. also offers fee-based economic analysis at *The Dismal Scientist* site (http://www.dismal.com).

InSite 2. Intelligence Data/Thomson Financial. Phone: 800-654-0393 or (617)856-1890 Fax: (617)737-3182 E-mail: intelligence.data@tfn.com • URL: http://www.insite2.gale.com/ • Fee-based Web site consolidates information in a "Base Pack" consisting of Business InSite, Market InSite, and Company InSite. Optional databases are Consumer InSite, Health and Wellness InSite, Newsletter InSite, and Computer InSite. Includes fulltext content from more than 2,500 trade publications, journals, newsletters, newspapers, analyst reports, and other sources. Continuous updating. Formerly produced by The Gale Group.

Nexis.com. Lexis-Nexis Group. Phone: 800-227-4908 or (937)865-6800 Fax: (937)865-6909 E-mail: webmaster@prod.lexis-nexis.com • URL: http://www.nexis.com • Fee-based Web site offers searching of about 2.8 billion documents in some 30,000 news, business, and legal information sources. Features include a subject directory covering 1,200 topics in 34 categories and a Company Dossier containing information on more than 500,000 public and private companies. Boolean searching is offered.

ProQuest Direct. ProQuest Inc. Phone: 800-889-3358 or (734)761-4700 Fax: (734)662-4554 • URL: http://proquest.com • Fee-based Web site providing Internet access to more than 3,000 periodicals, newspapers, and other publications. Many items are available full-text, with daily updates. Includes extensive corporate and financial information. Fees: Apply.

Wall Street Journal Interactive Edition. Dow Jones & Co., Inc. Phone: 800-369-2834 or (212)416-2000 Fax: (212)416-2658 E-mail: inquiries@interactive. wsj.com • URL: http://www.wsj.com • Fee-based Web site providing online searching of worldwide information from the *The Wall Street Journal.* Includes "Company Snapshots," "The Journal's Greatest Hits," "Index to Market Data," "Journal Links," etc. Financial price quotes are available. Fees: $49.00 per year; $29.00 per year to print subscribers.

ONLINE DATABASES

Banking Information Source. PROQUEST. • Provides indexing and abstracting of periodical and other literature from 1982 to date, with weekly updates. Covers the financial services industry: banks, savings institutions, investment houses, credit unions, insurance companies, and real estate organizations. Emphasis is on marketing and management. Inquire as to online cost and availability. (Formerly *FINIS: Financial Industry Information Service.*).

Compustat. Standard and Poor's. • Financial data on publicly held U.S. and some foreign corporations; data held for 20 years. Inquire as to online cost and availability.

EconLit. American Economic Association. • Covers the worldwide literature of economics as contained in selected monographs and about 550 journals. Subjects include microeconomics, macroeconomics, economic history, inflation, money, credit, finance, accounting theory, trade, natural resource economics, and regional economics. Time period is 1969 to present, with monthly updates. Inquire as to online cost and availability.

Wilson Business Abstracts Online. H. W. Wilson Co. • Indexes and abstracts 600 major business periodicals, plus the *Wall Street Journal* and the business section of the *New York Times.* Indexing is from 1982, abstracting from 1990, with the two newspapers included from 1993. Updated weekly. Inquire as to online cost and availability. (*Business Periodicals Index* without abstracts is also available online.).

PERIODICALS AND NEWSLETTERS

American Banker: The Financial Services Daily. Thomson Media. • Daily. $895.00 per year. Provides news of banking, investment products, mortgages, credit unions, finance, bank technology, and legal developments.

Applied Financial Economics. Taylor and Francis Group. • Monthly. Institutions, $1,277.00 per year. Covers practical aspects of financial economics, banking, and monetary economics. Supplement to *Applied Economics.*

Barron's: The Dow Jones Business and Financial Weekly. • Weekly. $145.00 per year.

Business Credit. National Association of Credit Management. • 10 tims a year. $48.00 per year. Formerly *Credit and Financial Management.*

Commercial and Financial Chronicle. William B. Dana Co. • Weekly. $140.00. per year.

Financial History: Chronicling the History of America's Capital Markets. Museum of American Financial History. • Quarterly. Membership. Contains articles on early stock and bond markets and trading in the U. S., with photographs and other illustrations. Current trading in rare and unusual,

obsolete stock and bond certificates is featured. Formerly *Friends or Financial History.*

Financial Markets, Institutions, and Instruments. New York University, Salomon Center. Blackwell Publishing. • Five times a year. Institutions, $338.00 per year. Includes online edition. Edited to "bridge the gap between the academic and professional finance communities." Special fifth issue each year provides surveys of developments in four areas: money and banking, derivative securities, corporate finance, and fixed-income securities.

Fortune Magazine. Time Inc., Business Information Group. • Biweekly. $59.95 per year. Edited for top executives and upper-level managers.

The Journal of Finance. American Finance Association. Blackwell Publishing. • Bimonthly. Institutions, $304.00 per year. Includes online edition.

Journal of Financial and Quantitative Analysis. University of Washington, School of Business Administration. • Quarterly. Individuals, $45.00 per year; libraries, $120.00 per year; students, $25.00 per year.

Journal of Financial Economics. Elsevier. • Monthly. Individuals, $95.00 per year; institutions, $1,881.00 per year; students, $70.00 per year.

Mathematical Finance: An International Journal of Mathematics, Statistics, and Financial Economics. Blackwell Publishing. • Quarterly. Institutions, $683.00 per year. Includes online edition. Covers the use of sophisticated mathematical tools in financial research and practice.

Paytech. American Payroll Association. • Monthly. Membership. Covers the details and technology of payroll administration.

The Quarterly Review of Economics and Finance. University of Illinois at Urbana-Champaign, Bureau of Economics and Business Research. Available from JAI Press, Inc. • Five times a year. Individuals, $95.00 per year; institutions, $426.00 per year. Includes annual *Supplement.* Formerly *Quarterly Review of Economics and Business.*

U. S. Banker. Thomson Media. • Monthly. $65.00 per year. Edited for bank executives and managers. Covers a wide variety of banking and financial topics.

The Wall Street Journal. Dow Jones & Co., Inc. • Daily. $189.00 per year. Covers news and trends relating to business, industry, finance, the economy, and international commerce. Provides extensive price and other data for the securities, commodity, options, futures, foreign exchange, and money markets.

WebFinance. Thomson Media. • Semimonthly. $995.00 per year. Newsletter (also available online at www.webfinance.net). Covers the Internet-based provision of online financial services by banks, on-line brokers, mutual funds, and insurance companies. Provides news stories, analysis, and descriptions of useful resources.

RESEARCH CENTERS AND INSTITUTES

American Institute for Economic Research. P.O. Box 1000, Great Barrington, MA 01230. Phone: (413)528-1216 Fax: (413)528-0103 E-mail: info@aier.org • URL: http://www.aier.org.

Bendheim Center for Finance. Princeton University, 26 Prospect Ave., Princeton, NJ 08540-5296. Phone: (609)258-0770 Fax: (609)258-0771 E-mail: yacine@princeton.edu • URL: http://www. princeton.edu/~bcf/ • Research areas include securities markets, portfolio analysis, credit markets, and corporate finance. Emphasis is on quantitative and mathematical perspectives.

Conference Board, Inc. The Conference Board, Inc. 845 3rd Ave., New York, NY 10022. Phone: (212)339-0345 Fax: (212)980-7014 E-mail: info@conference-board.org • URL: http://www.

conference-board.org • Business management practices worldwide, especially economic, and demographic in nature. Specific concerns include: corporate citizenship, including corporate contributions, diversity, environmental policy and issues, and government relations; corporate governance, including boards of directors, role of chief executives, relations with institutional investors, and shareholder input and influence; economics, including economic and financial forecasts, consumer confidence, leading economic indicators, North American outlook and trends, and global economic environment; human resources and organizational effectiveness, including organization structure and design, compensation and benefits, training and development, and communications; and performance excellence.

Financial Executives Research Foundation. 10 Madison Ave., Morristown, NJ 07962. Phone: (973)898-4600 Fax: (973)898-6636 E-mail: mbace@fei.org • URL: http://www.fei.org/rf.

Salomon Center. New York University. Stern School of Business, 44 W. Fourth St., Ste. 9-60, New York, NY 10012-1126. Phone: (212)998-0707 Fax: (212)995-4220 E-mail: iwalter@stern.nyu.edu • URL: http://www.stern.nyu.edu/salmon/.

STATISTICS SOURCES

Business Statistics of the United States. Linz Audain and Cornelia J. Strawser. Bernan Associates. • Annual. $147.00. Based on *Business Statistics,* formerly issue by the Bureau of Economic Analysis, U. S. Department of Commerce. Provides basic data for a wide variety of U. S. industries, services, and economic indicators. Most statistics are shown annually for 30 years and monthly for the most recent four years.

Economic Report of the President: Together with the Annual Report of the Council of Economic Advisors. Available from U. S. Government Printing Office. • Annual. $32.00. Includes about 130 pages of "Statistical Tables Relating to Income, Employment, and Production." Tables cover national income, employment, wages, productivity, manufacturing, prices, credit, finance (public and private), corporate profits, and foreign trade.

Information, Finance, and Services USA. Gale Cengage Learning. • 2001. $240.00. Replaces *Service Industries USA* and *Finance, Insurance, and Real Estate USA.* Presents statistics and projections relating to economic activity in a wide variety of non-manufacturing areas.

Statistical Information on the Financial Services Industry. American Bankers Association. • Annual. Members, $150.00; non-members, $275.00. Presents a wide variety of data relating to banking and financial services, including consumer economics, personal finance, credit, government loans, capital markets, and international banking.

Survey of Current Business. Available from U. S. Government Printing Office. • Monthly. $63.00 per year. Issued by Bureau of Economic Analysis, U. S. Department of Commerce. Presents a wide variety of business and economic data.

TRADE/PROFESSIONAL ASSOCIATIONS

American Finance Association. University of California, Haas School of Business, 350 Main St., 545 Student Services Bldg., Berkeley, CA 94720-1900. Phone: 800-835-6770 or (781)388-8532 Fax: (781)388-8232 E-mail: pyle@haas.berkeley.edu • URL: http://www.afajof.org • College and university professors of economics and finance, bankers, treasurers, analysts, financiers, and others interested in financial problems; libraries and other institutions. Seeks to improve public understanding of financial problems and to provide for exchange of analytical ideas. Areas of special interest include: corporate finance, investments, banking, and international and public finance.

American Financial Services Association. 919 18th St. NW, Ste. 300, Washington, DC 20006-5517. Phone: (202)296-5544 Fax: (202)223-0321 E-mail: cstinebert@afsamail.org • URL: http://www.afsaonline.org • Represents companies whose business is primarily direct credit lending to consumers and/or the purchase of sales finance paper on consumer goods. Has members that have insurance and retail subsidiaries; some are themselves subsidiaries of highly diversified parent corporations. Encourages the business of financing individuals and families for necessary and useful purposes at reasonable charges, including interest; promotes consumer understanding of basic money management principles as well as constructive uses of consumer credit. Includes educational services such as films, textbooks, and study units for the classroom and budgeting guides for individuals and families. Compiles statistical reports; offers seminars.

American Payroll Association. 660 N Main Ave., Ste. 100, San Antonio, TX 78205-1217. Phone: 800-398-8681 or (210)226-4600 Fax: (210)226-4027 E-mail: apa@americanpayroll.org • URL: http://www.americanpayroll.org • Payroll employees. Works to increase members' skills and professionalism through education and mutual support. Represents the interest of members before legislative bodies. Conducts training courses. Operates speakers' bureau; conducts educational programs. Administers the certified payroll professional program of recognition.

Commercial Finance Association. 370 7th Ave., Ste. 1801, New York, NY 10001-3979. Phone: (212)792-9390 Fax: (212)564-6053 E-mail: info@cfa.com • URL: http://www.cfa.com • Organizations engaged in asset-based financial services including commercial financing and factoring and lending money on a secured basis to small- and medium-sized business firms. Acts as a forum for information and consideration about ideas, opportunities, and legislation concerning asset-based financial services. Seeks to improve the industry's legal and operational procedures. Offers job placement and reference services for members. Sponsors School for Field Examiners and other educational programs. Compiles statistics; conducts seminars and surveys; maintains speakers' bureau and 21 committees.

Financial Executives International. 200 Campus Dr., PO Box 674, Florham Park, NJ 07932-0674. Phone: (973)765-1000 Fax: (973)765-1018 E-mail: mcangemi@financialexecutives.org • URL: http://www.financialexecutives.org • Professional organization of corporate financial executives performing duties of chief financial officer, controller, treasurer, or vice-president-finance. Sponsors research activities through its affiliated Financial Executives Research Foundation. Maintains offices in Toronto, Canada, and Washington, DC.

Government Finance Officers Association of the United States and Canada. 203 N. LaSalle St., Ste. 2700, Chicago, IL 60601. Phone: (312)977-9700 Fax: (312)977-4806 E-mail: membership@gfoa.org • URL: http://www.gfoa.org • Formerly Municipal Finance Officers Association of United States and Canada.

OTHER SOURCES

BNA's Banking Report: Legal and Regulatory Developments in the Financial Services Industry. BNA, Inc. • Weekly. $1,221.00 per year. Two looseleaf volumes. Emphasis on federal regulations.

Business Rankings Annual. Gale Cengage Learning. • Annual. $325.00. Two volumes. Compiled by the Business Library Staff of the Brooklyn Public Library. This is a guide to lists and rankings appearing in major business publications. The top ten names are listed in each case.

Finance and Accounting for Nonfinancial Managers. American Management Association

Extension Institute. • Looseleaf. $159.00. Self-study course. Emphasis is on practical explanations, examples, and problem solving. Quizzes and a case study are included.

FINANCE, BANK

See: BANK LOANS

FINANCE COMPANIES

See also: CREDIT

FINANCIAL RATIOS

Almanac of Business and Industrial Financial Ratios. Leo Troy. Aspen Publishers, Inc. • 2003. $125.95. Includes CD-Rom. Contains financial ratios derived from federal tax returns. Ratios for each of about 200 industries are arranged according to company asset size. (Almanac of Business and Industrial Financial Ratios Series).

HANDBOOKS AND MANUALS

Moody's Bank and Finance Manual. Mergent. • Annual. $1,750.00 per year. Four volumes. Includes biweekly supplements in *Moody's Bank and Finance News Report.*

INTERNET DATABASES

Federal Reserve Board Publications and Education Resources. Board of Governors of the Federal Reserve System. Phone: (202)452-3000 Fax: (202)452-3819 • URL: http://www.federalreserve.gov/publications.htm • Web site provides convenient access to statistics, surveys, and research from the Federal Reserve Board. *Federal Reserve Bulletin* articles are available as abstracts or full text (PDF) currently or from six-year archives. The link "Statistics: Releases and Historical Data" offers daily, weekly, monthly, quarterly, and annual data in great detail for interest rates, foreign exchange, consumer credit, money stock measures, industrial production indexes, bank reserves, and other items. Historical tabulations are available for various time periods. Fees: Free.

PERIODICALS AND NEWSLETTERS

Consumer Credit and Truth-in-Lending Compliance Report. RIA. • Monthly. $183.75 per year. Newsletter. Focuses on the latest regulatory rulings and findings involving consumer lending and credit activity. Incorporates (Consumer Lending Report).

Consumer Finance Newsletter. Financial Publishing Co. • Description: Provides information on effective and pending credit insurance and installment loan regulations on the state and federal levels. Supplies news of potential state changes in regulations.

Credit Executive Letter. American Financial Services Association. • Monthly. Members, $12.00 per year; non-members, $22.00 per year.

Secured Lender. Commercial Finance Association. • Bimonthly. Members, $24.00 per year; non-members, $48.00 per year.

STATISTICS SOURCES

Consumer Installment Credit. Board of Governors. • Monthly. $5.00 per year.

Finance Companies. U. S. Federal Reserve System. • Monthly. $5.00 per year. (Federal Reserve Statistical Release, G.20.).

TRADE/PROFESSIONAL ASSOCIATIONS

American Financial Services Association. 919 18th St. NW, Ste. 300, Washington, DC 20006-5517. Phone: (202)296-5544 Fax: (202)223-0321 E-mail: cstinebert@afsamail.org • URL: http://www.afsaonline.org • Represents companies whose business is primarily direct credit lending to consumers and/or the purchase of sales finance paper on

consumer goods. Has members that have insurance and retail subsidiaries; some are themselves subsidiaries of highly diversified parent corporations. Encourages the business of financing individuals and families for necessary and useful purposes at reasonable charges, including interest; promotes consumer understanding of basic money management principles as well as constructive uses of consumer credit. Includes educational services such as films, textbooks, and study units for the classroom and budgeting guides for individuals and families. Compiles statistical reports; offers seminars.

Commercial Finance Association. 370 7th Ave., Ste. 1801, New York, NY 10001-3979. Phone: (212)792-9390 Fax: (212)564-6053 E-mail: info@cfa.com • URL: http://www.cfa.com • Organizations engaged in asset-based financial services including commercial financing and factoring and lending money on a secured basis to small- and medium-sized business firms. Acts as a forum for information and consideration about ideas, opportunities, and legislation concerning asset-based financial services. Seeks to improve the industry's legal and operational procedures. Offers job placement and reference services for members. Sponsors School for Field Examiners and other educational programs. Compiles statistics; conducts seminars and surveys; maintains speakers' bureau and 21 committees.

National Foundation for Credit Counseling. 801 Roeder Rd., Ste. 900, Silver Spring, MD 20910. Phone: 800-388-2227 or (301)589-5600 Fax: (301)495-5623 • URL: http://www.nfcc.org • Supersedes Retail Credit Institute of America.

FINANCE, COMPUTERS IN

See: COMPUTERS IN FINANCE

FINANCE, CORPORATE

See: CORPORATE FINANCE

FINANCE, INTERNATIONAL

See: INTERNATIONAL FINANCE

FINANCE, PERSONAL

See: PERSONAL FINANCE

FINANCE, PUBLIC

See: PUBLIC FINANCE

FINANCIAL ANALYSIS

See also: COMPUTERS IN FINANCE; FINANCE; FINANCIAL RATIOS; TECHNICAL ANALYSIS (FINANCE)

GENERAL WORKS

Asset Allocation and Financial Market Timing: Techniques for Investment Professionals. Carroll D. Aby and Donald E. Vaughn. Greenwood Publishing Group, Inc. • 1995. $79.95.

Dow 40,000 Portfolio: The Stock to Own to Out Perform Today's Leading Benchmark. David Elias. McGraw Hill. • 2000. $24.95.

The Financial Numbers Game: Detecting Creative Accounting Practices. Charles W. Mulford and Eugene E. Comiskey. John Wiley and Sons, Inc. • 2002. $39.95. Serves as a guide to financial statement analysis for investors. Explains the "creative" schemes used by corporations to boost earnings-per-share data.

Investments: An Introduction to Analysis and Management. Frederick Amling. Pearson Custom Publishing. • 1999. $94.00. Seventh edition.

Market Efficiency: Stock Market Behavior in Theory and Practice. Andrew W. Lo, editor. Edward Elgar Publishing, Inc. • 1997. $465.00. Two volumes. Consists of reprints of 49 articles dating from 1937 to 1993, in five sections: "Theoretical Foundations," "The Random Walk Hypothesis," "Variance Bounds Tests," "Overreaction and Underreaction," and "Anomalies." (International Library of Critical Writings in Financial Economics Series: No. 3).

Modern Portfolio Theory and Investment Analysis and Investment Portfolio Software, Edwin J. Elton. John Wiley and Sons, Inc. • 1998. $88.00. Fifth edition. Includes CD-Rom. The authors' central concern is that of mixing assets to achieve maximum overall return consonant with an acceptable level of risk. (Portfolio Management Series).

Super Searchers on Wall Street: Top Investment Professionals Share Their Online Research Secrets. Amelia Kassel. Information Today, Inc. • 2000. $24.95. Gives the results of interviews with "10 leading financial industry research experts." Explains how online information is used by stock brokers, investment bankers, and individual investors. Includes relevant Web sites and other sources. (Super Searchers Series).

Understanding Financial Statements. Lyn M. Fraser and Aileen Orminston. Prentice Hall PTR. • 2003. $42.67. Seventh edition. Emphasis is on the evaluation and interpretation of financial statements.

ALMANACS AND YEARBOOKS

Advances in Investment Analysis and Portfolio Management. Chung-Few Lee, editor. Elsevier. • Dates vary. Six volumes. Price varies.

CD-ROM DATABASES

InvesText [CD-ROM]. Thomson Financial. • Monthly. Contains full text on CD-ROM of investment research reports from about 630 sources, including leading brokers and investment bankers. Reports are available on both U. S. and international publicly traded corporations. Separate industry reports cover more than 50 industries. Time span is 1982 to date.

DIRECTORIES

Association for Investment Management and Research-Membership Directory. Association for Investment Management and Research. • Annual. $150.00. Lists 38,000 professional investment managers and securities analysts.

Directory of Registered Investment Advisors. Money Market Directories, Inc. • Annual. $510.00. Lists over 12,000 investment advisors and advisory firms. Indicates services offered, personnel, and amount of assets being managed. Formerly *Directory of Registered Investment Advisors with the Securities and Exchange Commission.* .

Institutional Buyers of Bank and Thrift Stocks: A Targeted Directory. Investment Data Corp. • Annual. $645.00. Provides detailed profiles of about 600 institutional buyers of bank and savings and loan stocks. Includes names of financial analysts and portfolio managers.

Institutional Buyers of Energy Stocks. Investment Data Corp. • Annual. $645.00. Provides detailed profiles 555 institutional buyers of petroleum-related and other energy stocks. Includes names of financial analysts and portfolio managers.

Institutional Buyers of Foreign Stocks: A Targeted Directory. Investment Data Corp. • Annual. $595.00. Provides detailed profiles of institutional buyers of international stocks. Includes names of financial analysts and portfolio managers.

Institutional Buyers of REIT Securities. Investment Data Corp. • Semiannual. $995.00 per year. Provides detailed profiles of about 500 institutional buyers of REIT securities. Includes names of financial analysts and portfolio managers.

Institutional Buyers of Small-Cap Stocks. Investment Data Corp. • Annual. $295.00. Provides detailed profiles of more than 837 institutional buyers of small capitalization stocks. Includes names of financial analysts and portfolio managers.

Nelson Information's Directory of Investment Research. Nelson Information. • Annual. $665.00. Three volumes. Provides information on 7,000 investment research analysts at more than 800 firms. Indexes include company name, industry, and name of person.

Zacks Analyst Directory: Listed by Broker. Zacks Investment Research. • Quarterly. $395.00 per year. Lists stockbroker investment analysts and gives the names of major U. S. corporations covered by those analysts.

Zacks Analyst Directory: Listed by Company. Zacks Investment Research. • Quarterly. $395.00 per year. Lists major U. S. corporations and gives the names of stockbroker investment analysts covering those companies.

Zacks EPS Calendar. Zacks Investment Research. • Biweekly. $1,250.00 per year. (Also available monthly at $895.00 per year.) Lists anticipated reporting dates of earnings per share for major U. S. corporations.

HANDBOOKS AND MANUALS

Analysis and Use of Financial Statements. Gerald I. White. John Wiley and Sons, Inc. • 2002. $123.95. Third edition. Includes analysis of financial ratios, cash flow, inventories, assets, debt, etc. Also covered are employee benefits, corporate investments, multinational operations, financial derivatives, and hedging activities.

Analysis of Financial Statements. Leopold A. Bernstein and John J. Wild. McGraw-Hill. • 1999. $65.00. Fifth edition. Includes practical examples of analysis.

Analyst's Handbook: Composite Corporate Per Share Data by Industry. Standard and Poor's. • Annual. $795.00. Monthly updates.

Computational Finance: Numerical Methods for Pricing Financial Instruments. George Levy. Elsevier Butterworth Heinemann. • 2003. $89.95. Explains advanced financial modeling techniques using Windows software.

Convertible Securities: The Latest Instruments, Portfolio Strategies, and Valuation Analysis. John P. Calamos. McGraw-Hill. • 1998. $65.00. Second revised edition. (Irwin Library of Investment and Finance Series).

Corporate Financial Analysis: Decisions in a Global Environment. Diana R. Harrington and Brent D. Wilson. McGraw-Hill. • 1993. $50.00. Fourth edition.

Econometrics of Financial Markets. John Y. Campbell and others. Princeton University Press. • 1996. $70.00. Written for advanced students and industry professionals. Includes chapters on "The Predictability of Asset Returns," "Derivative Pricing Models," and "Fixed-Income Securities." Provides a discussion of the random walk theory of investing and tests of the theory.

Elements of Financial Risk Management. Peter F. Christoffersen. Elsevier Butterworth Heinemann. • 2003. $79.95. Includes material on the various kinds of financial market risk, simulation methods, hedging, options, and evaluation of risk models.

Financial Statement Analysis: A Practitioner's Guide. Martin Fridson and Fernando Alvarez. John Wiley and Sons, Inc. • 2002. $69.95. Third edition. (Finance Series).

Financial Statement Analysis: The Investor's Self Study Guide to Interpreting and Analyzing. Charles J. Woelfel. McGraw-Hill. • 1993. $24.95. Revised edition.

Fixed Income Analytics: State-of-the-Art Analysis and Valuation Modeling. Ravi E. Dattatreya, editor. McGraw-Hill. • 1991. $69.95. Discusses the yield curve, structure and value in corporate bonds, mortgage-backed securities, and other topics. (Institutional Investor Publications).

Guide to Financial Reporting and Analysis. Eugene E. Comiskey and Charles W. Mulford. John Wiley and Sons, Inc. • 2000. $75.00. Provides financial statement examples to illustrate the application of generally accepted accounting principles.

An Introduction to the Mathematics of Financial Derivatives. Salih N. Neftci. Elsevier. • 2000. $64.95. Second edition. Covers the mathematical models underlying the pricing of derivatives. Includes explanations of basic financial calculus for students, derivatives traders, risk managers, and others concerned with derivatives.

Manager's Guide to Financial Statement Analysis. Stephen F. Jablonsky and Noah P. Barsky. John Wiley and Sons, Inc. • 2001. $49.95. Second edition. The two main sections are "Financial Statements and Business Strategy" and "Market Valuation and Business Strategy.".

Mining for Gold on the Internet: How to Find Investment and Financial Information on the Internet. Mary Ellen Bates. McGraw-Hill. • 2000. $24.95. Tells how to effectively search the Internet for financial advice and information. Specific web-sites are discussed.

The Numbers You Need. Gale Cengage Learning. • 1993. $75.00. Contains mathematical equations, formulas, charts, and graphs, including many that are related to business or finance. Explanations, step-by-step directions, and examples of use are provided.

Reliable Financial Reporting and Internal Control: A Global Implementation Guide. Dmitris N. Chorafas. John Wiley and Sons, Inc. • 2000. $75.00. Discusses financial reporting and control as related to doing business internationally.

Techniques of Financial Analysis: A Modern Approach. Erich A. Helfert. McGraw-Hill. • 1996. $32.00. Ninth edition.

INTERNET DATABASES

Mergent Online. Mergent, Inc. Phone: 800-342-5647 or (704)559-7601 Fax: (704)559-6945 E-mail: customerservice@mergent.com • URL: http://www.mergentonline.com • Fee-based Web site provides detailed information on 20,000 publicly-owned companies in 100 foreign countries, as well as more than 10,000 corporations listed on the New York Stock Exchange, American Stock Exchange, NAS-DAQ, and U. S. regional exchanges. Searching is offered on many financial variables and text fields. Weekly updating. Formerly *FIS Online.*

ONLINE DATABASES

Compustat. Standard and Poor's. • Financial data on publicly held U.S. and some foreign corporations; data held for 20 years. Inquire as to online cost and availability.

Disclosure SEC Database. Thomson Financial. • Provides online information from records filed with the Securities and Exchange Commission by more than 12,000 publicly-owned companies in the U.S. Includes about 200 financial data items and information relating to executives. Time span is 1977 to date, with weekly updates. Inquire as to online cost and availability.

EdgarPlus: SEC Basic Filings. Thomson Financial. • Online service provides full text of about 60,000 documents that have been filed with the U.S. Securities and Exchange Commission, 1987 to date, with daily updates. Filings include 6-K, 8-K, 10-K, 10-C,

10-Q, 20-F, and proxy statements. Inquire as to on-line cost and availability.

InvesText. Thomson Financial. • Provides full text online of investment research reports from more than 600 sources, including leading brokers and investment bankers. Reports are available on approximately 60,000 U. S. and international corporations. Separate industry reports cover 54 industries. Time span is 1982 to date, with daily updates. Inquire as to online cost and availability.

PERIODICALS AND NEWSLETTERS

Consensus: National Futures and Financial Weekly. Consensus, Inc. • Weekly. $365.00 per year. Newspaper. Contains news, statistics, and special reports relating to agricultural, industrial, and financial futures markets. Features daily basis price charts, reprints of market advice, and "The Consensus Index of Bullish Market Opinion" (charts show percent bullish of advisors for various futures).

Economics and Portfolio Strategy. Peter L. Bernstein, Inc. • Semimonthly. $1,700.00 per year. Provides financial analysis and insight for "institutional investors and sophisticated individual investors.".

Financial Analysts Journal. Association for Investment Management and Research. • Bimonthly. $220.00 per year.

Institutional Investor: The Premier of Professional Magazine Finance. Institutional Investor, Inc., Journals Group. • Monthly. $445.00 per year. Includes print and online editions. Edited for portfolio managers and other investment professionals. Special feature issues include "Country Credit Ratings," "Fixed Income Trading Ranking," "All-America Research Team," and "Global Banking Ranking.".

MPT Review; Specializing in Modern Portfolio Theory. Navellier and Associates, Inc. • Monthly. $275.00 per year. Newsletter. Provides specific stock selection and model portfolio advice (conservative, moderately aggressive, and aggressive) based on quantitative analysis and modern portfolio theory.

Quantitative Finance. Available from American Institute of Physics. • Bimonthly. $340.00 per year. Print and online edition, $765.00 per year. Published in the UK by the Institute of Physics. A technical journal on the use of quantitative tools and applications in financial analysis and financial engineering. Covers such topics as portfolio theory, derivatives, asset allocation, return on assets, risk management, price volatility, financial econometrics, market anomalies, and trading systems.

Zacks Analyst Watch. Zacks Investment Research. • Biweekly. $250.00 per year. Provides the results of research by stockbroker investment analysts on major U. S. corporations.

Zacks Earnings Forecaster. Zacks Investment Research. • Biweekly. $495.00 per year. (Also available monthly at $375.00 per year.) Provides estimates by stockbroker investment analysts of earnings per share of individual U. S. companies.

Zacks Profit Guide. Zacks Investment Research. • Quarterly. $375.00 per year. Provides analysis of total return and stock price performance of major U. S. companies.

RESEARCH CENTERS AND INSTITUTES

Institute for Quantitative Research in Finance. Church Street Station, P.O. Box 6194, New York, NY 10249-6194. Phone: (212)744-6825 Fax: (212)517-2259 E-mail: daleberman@compuserve • Financial research areas include quantitative methods, securities analysis, and the financial structure of industries. Also known as the "Q Group.".

TRADE/PROFESSIONAL ASSOCIATIONS

Association for Investment Management and Research. 560 Ray C. Hunt Dr., Charlottesville, VA 22903. Phone: 800-247-8132 or (434)951-5499 Fax: (434)951-5262 E-mail: info@aimr.org • URL: http://www.aimr.org • Members are practicing investment analysts.

New York Society of Security Analysts. 1601 Broadway, 11th Floor, New York, NY 10019-7406. Phone: 800-248-0108 or (212)541-4530 Fax: (212)541-4677 E-mail: staff@nyssa.org • URL: http://www.nyssa.org • Members are portfolio managers, financial analysts, investment counselors, and other financial professionals.

FINANCIAL FUTURES TRADING

See also: STOCK INDEX TRADING

GENERAL WORKS

Financial Options: From Theory to Practice. Stephen Figlewski. McGraw-Hill. • 1992. $29.95. Includes options on financial futures.

Futures Markets. A. G. Malliaris, editor. Edward Elgar Publishing, Inc. • 1997. $550.00. Three volumes. Consists of reprints of 70 articles dating from 1959 to 1993, on futures market volatility, speculation, hedging, stock indexes, portfolio insurance, interest rates, and foreign currencies. (International Library of Critical Writings in Financial Economics Series: No. 2).

Getting Started in Futures. Todd Lofton. John Wiley and Sons, Inc. • 2001. $19.95. Fourth edition. A general introduction to commodity and financial futures trading. Includes case studies and a glossary. (Getting Started in.... Series).

Introduction to Futures and Options Markets. John C. Hull. Prentice Hall PTR. • 1997. $110.00. Third edition.

ABSTRACTS AND INDEXES

Business Periodicals Index. H. W. Wilson Co. • 11 times a year. Quarterly and annual cumulations. Price varies.

ALMANACS AND YEARBOOKS

Agricultural and Mineral Commodities Year Book. Available from Taylor & Francis Group. • Annual. $225.00. Published by Europa Publications. Contains descriptive product profiles, price data, export-import data, and production statistics for major commodities of the world. Includes commodity histories, uses, markets, demand trends, and information about trade agreements and key commodity organizations.

DIRECTORIES

Business Organizations, Agencies, and Publications Directory. Gale Cengage Learning. • 2003. $480.00. 15th edition. Over 40,000 entries describing 39 types of business information sources. Classified by type of organization, publication, or serviceIncludes state, national, and international agencies and organizations. Master index to names and keywords. Also includes e-mail addresses and web site URL's.

Futures Magazine SourceBook: The Most Complete List of Exchanges, Companies, Regulators, Organizations, etc., Offering Products and Services to the Futures and Options Industry. Futures Magazine, Inc. • Annual. $19.50. Provides information on commodity futures brokers, trading method services, publications, and other items of interest to futures traders and money managers.

ENCYCLOPEDIAS AND DICTIONARIES

International Encyclopedia of Futures and Options. Fitzroy Dearborn Publishers, Inc. • 2000. $285.00. Two volumes. Covers terminology, concepts, events, individuals, and markets.

HANDBOOKS AND MANUALS

The Bond and Money Markets: Strategy, Trading, Analysis. Moorad Choudhry. Elsevier Butterworth Heinemann. • 2003. $115.00. Serves as a reference work on corporate bonds, government bonds, currency markets, interest-rate futures, convertible securities, various kinds of derivatives, and technical analysis of financial securities.

Derivatives: A Comprehensive Resource for Options, Futures, Interest Rate Swaps, and Mortgage Securities. Fred D. Arditti. Harvard Business School Publishing. • 1996. $60.00. Published by Harvard Business School Press. Provides detailed explanations of various kinds of financial derivatives (options, futures, swaps, etc.) and their trading tactics, uses, and risks. (Financial Management Association Survey and Synthesis Series).

Foreign Exchange Handbook: Managing Risk and Opportunity in Global Currency Markets. Paul Bishop and Don Dixon. McGraw-Hill. • 1992. $69.95. Discusses factors affecting currency value, currency price forecasting, options trading, futures, credit risk, and related subjects.

Handbook of Derivative Instruments: Investment Research, Analysis, and Portfolio Applications. Arsuo Konishi and Ravi Dattatreya, editors. McGraw-Hill. • 1996. $80.00. Second revised edition. Contains 41 chapters by various authors on all aspects of derivative securities, including such esoterica as "Inverse Floaters," "Positive Convexity," "Exotic Options," and "How to Use the Holes in Black-Scholes.".

Handbook of Equity Derivatives. Jack C. Francis and others, editors. John Wiley and Sons, Inc. • 1999. $105.00. Revised edition. Contains 27 chapters by various authors. Covers options (puts and calls), stock index futures, warrants, convertibles, over-the-counter options, swaps, legal issues, taxation, etc. (Financial Engineering Series).

International Guide to Foreign Currency Management. Gary Shoup, editor. Glenlake Publishing Co., Ltd. • 1999. $65.00. Written for corporate financial managers. Covers the market for currencies, price forecasting, exposure of various kinds, and risk management.

Money Management Strategies for Futures Traders. Nauzer J. Balsara. John Wiley and Sons, Inc. • 1992. $75.00. How to limit risk and avoid catastrophic losses. (Finance Series).

Options, Futures, and Other Derivatives. John C. Hull. Prentice Hall PTR. • 2002. $135.00. Fifth edition.

Options: The International Guide to Valuation and Trading Strategies. Gordon Gemmill. McGraw-Hill. • 1992. $37.95. Covers valuation techniques for American, European, and Asian options. Trading strategies are discussed for options on currencies, stock indexes, interest rates, and commodities.

Strategic Trading in the Foreign Exchange Markets. Gary Klopfenstein. Fitzroy Dearborn Publishers, Inc. • 2000. $65.00. Describes the tactics of successful foreign exchange traders.

Trading and Investing in Bond Options: Risk Management, Arbitrage, and Value Investing. M. Anthony Wong. John Wiley and Sons, Inc. • 1991. $55.00. Covers dealing, trading, and investing in U. S. government bond futures options (puts and calls). (Finance Series).

Trading Financial Futures: Markets, Methods, Strategies, and Tactics. John W. Labuszewski and John E. Nyhoff. John Wiley and Sons, Inc. • 1997. $49.95. Second edition. (Finance Series).

Understanding Financial Derivatives: How to Protect Your Investments. Donald Strassheim. McGraw-Hill. • 1996. $40.00. Covers three basic risk management instruments: options, futures, and swaps. Includes advice on equity index options, financial futures contracts, and over-the-counter derivatives markets.

INTERNET DATABASES

BanxQuote Banking, Mortgage, and Finance Center. BanxQuote, Inc. Phone: (914)722-1600 Fax: (914)722-6630 E-mail: info@banx.com • URL: http://www.banx.com • Web site quotes interest rates paid by banks around the country on various savings products, as well as rates paid by consumers for automobile loans, mortgages, credit cards, home equity loans, and personal loans. Also provided: stock quotes, indexes, stock options, futures trading data, economic indicators, and links to many other financial sites. Daily updates. Fees: Free.

Chicago Board of Trade: The World's Leading Futures Exchange. Chicago Board of Trade. Phone: (312)535-3500 Fax: (312)341-3392 E-mail: comments@cbot.com • URL: http://www.cbot.com • Web site provides a wide variety of statistics, commentary, charts, and news relating to both agricultural and financial futures trading. For example, Web page "MarketPlex: Information MarketPlace to the World" offers prices & volume, contract specifications & margins, government reports, etc. Searching is available, with daily updates for current data. Fees: Mostly free (some specialized services are fee-based).

CRB Markets Overview. Commodity Research Bureau. Phone: 800-621-5271 or (312)554-8456 Fax: (312)939-4135 E-mail: info@crbtrader.com • URL: http://www.crbtrader.com/data/ • Web site provides free, detailed, current price quotes for about 100 futures contracts, covering Currencies, Energies, Financials, Grains, Meats, Metals, "Softs" (orange juice, coffee, etc.) and stock price indexes. Includes contract specifications and detailed prices of options on futures.

Futures Online. Futures Magazine Inc. Phone: (312)846-4600 Fax: (312)846-4638 • URL: http://www.futuresmag.com • Web site presents updates of *Futures* magazine and links to other futures-related sites.

ONLINE DATABASES

Wilson Business Abstracts Online. H. W. Wilson Co. • Indexes and abstracts 600 major business periodicals, plus the *Wall Street Journal* and the business section of the *New York Times.* Indexing is from 1982, abstracting from 1990, with the two newspapers included from 1993. Updated weekly. Inquire as to online cost and availability. (*Business Periodicals Index* without abstracts is also available online.).

PERIODICALS AND NEWSLETTERS

Barron's: The Dow Jones Business and Financial Weekly. • Weekly. $145.00 per year.

Futures and Derivatives Law Report: The Journal on the Law of Investment and Risk Management Products. Glasser Legalworks. • Monthly. $305.00 per year. Newsletter. Covers developments in regulation, legislation, and litigation concerning financial derivatives, futures trading, and options trading.

Futures and OTC World (Over the Counter). Russell R. Wasendorf. • Weekly. $435.00 per year. Newsletter. Futures market information. Includes Daily Hotline Information to update advice. Formerly *Futures and Options Factors.*

Futures: News, Analysis, and Strategies for Futures, Options, and Derivatives Traders. Futures Magazine. • Monthly. $39.00 per year. Edited for institutional money managers and traders, brokers, risk managers, and individual investors or speculators. Includes special feature issues on interest rates, technical indicators, currencies, charts, precious metals, hedge funds, and derivatives. Supplements available.

Journal of Fixed Income. Institutional Investor, Inc.,

Journals Group. • Quarterly. $360.00 per year. Includes print and online editions. Covers a wide range of fixed-income investments for institutions, including bonds, interest-rate options, high-yield securities, and mortgages.

SFO: Stocks, Futures & Options. Wasendorf & Associates, Inc. • Monthly. $49.95 per year. Subtitle: *Official Journal for Personal Investing in Stocks, Futures, and Options.* Covers mainly speculative techniques for stocks, commodity futures, financial futures, stock index futures, foreign exchange, short selling, and various kinds of options.

Technical Analysis of Stocks & Commodities: The Traders Magazine. Technical Analysis, Inc. • 13 times a year. $64.95 per year. Covers use of personal computers for stock trading, price movement analysis by means of charts, and other technical trading methods.

The Wall Street Journal. Dow Jones & Co., Inc. • Daily. $189.00 per year. Covers news and trends relating to business, industry, finance, the economy, and international commerce. Provides extensive price and other data for the securities, commodity, options, futures, foreign exchange, and money markets.

PRICE SOURCES

CRB Futures Perspective: Financial Edition. Commodity Research Bureau. • Weekly. $275.00 per year. Service provides comprehensive price charts for more than 50 financial futures, from Australian Bills to Swiss Francs (includes precious metals and oil). Also provides technical analysis of price movements and market commentary. Formerly part of *CRB Futures Chart Service.*

STATISTICS SOURCES

Statistical Annual: Interest Rates, Metals, Stock Indices, Options on Financial Futures, Options on Metals Futures. Chicago Board of Trade. • Annual. Includes historical data on GNMA CDR Futures, Cash-Settled GNMA Futures, U. S. Treasury Bond Futures, U. S. Treasury Note Futures, Options on Treasury Note Futures, NASDAQ-100 Futures, Major Market Index Futures, Major Market Index MAXI Futures, Municipal Bond Index Futures, 1,000-Ounce Silver Futures, Options on Silver Futures, and Kilo Gold Futures.

TRADE/PROFESSIONAL ASSOCIATIONS

Futures Industry Association. 2001 Pennsylvania Ave. NW, Ste. 600, Washington, DC 20006. Phone: (202)466-5460 Fax: (202)296-3184 E-mail: info@futuresindustry.org • URL: http://www.futuresindustry.org • Acts as a principal spokesman for the futures and options industry. Represents all facets of the futures industry, including many international exchanges. Works to preserve the system of free and competitive markets by representing the interests of the industry in connection with legislative and regulatory issues.

National Association of Securities Dealers (NASD). 1735 K St., N.W., Washington, DC 20006-1506. Phone: (202)728-8000 Fax: (202)293-6260 E-mail: waltere@nasd.com • URL: http://www.nasd.com • Formerly National Association of Securities Dealers.

National Futures Association. 300 S Riverside Plaza, No. 1800, Chicago, IL 60606-6615. Phone: 800-621-3570 or (312)781-1300 Fax: (312)781-1467 E-mail: information@nfa.futures.org • URL: http://www.nfa.futures.org • Futures commission merchants; commodity trading advisors; commodity pool operators; brokers and their associated persons. Works to: strengthen and expand industry self-regulation to include all segments of the futures industry; provide uniform standards to eliminate duplication of effort and conflict; remove unnecessary regulatory constraints to aid effective regulation. Conducts member qualification screening, financial surveillance, and registration. Moni-

tors and enforces customer protection rules and uniform business standards. Maintains information center. Arbitrates customer disputes; audits non-exchange member FCM's.

OTHER SOURCES

Managing Financial Risk with Forwards, Futures, Options, and Swaps. American Management Association Extension Institute. • Looseleaf. $159.00. Self-study course. Emphasis is on practical explanations, examples, and problem solving. Quizzes and a case study are included.

FINANCIAL MANAGEMENT

See also: COMPUTERS IN FINANCE; CORPORATE FINANCE; FINANCE

GENERAL WORKS

Analysis for Financial Management. Robert C. Higgins. McGraw-Hill. • 2003. $65.94. Seventh edition. Price on application. (Finance, Insurance and Real Estate Series).

Cases in Financial Mangement: Directed Versions. Eugene Brigham and Louis Gapenski. Dryden Press. • 1993. $32.00.

Financial Management: Theory and Practice. Eugene F. Brigham and Michael C. Ehrhardt. Harcourt College Publishers. • 2002. $119.50. 10th edition. Includes CD-ROM. (Finance Series).

Foundations of Financial Management With +Self Study Software +Powerweb. Stanley R. Block and Geoffrey A. Hirt. McGraw-Hill. • 2002. $110.31. 10th edition. Includes CD-ROM. (Finance, Insurance and Real Estate Series).

Fundamentals of Financial Management. James C. Van Horne and John M. Wachowicz. Prentice Hall PTR. • 2000. $90.67. 11th edition.

Introduction to Financial Management. Bodil Dickerson and others. Dryden Press. • 1994. $43.50. Fourth edition. (Finance Series).

ABSTRACTS AND INDEXES

Business Periodicals Index. H. W. Wilson Co. • 11 times a year. Quarterly and annual cumulations. Price varies.

BIOGRAPHICAL SOURCES

Who's Who in Finance and Industry. Marquis Who's Who. • Biennial. $259.95. Provides over 21,000 concise biographies of business leaders in all fields.

CD-ROM DATABASES

ABI/INFORM. PROQUEST. • Monthly. Provides CD-ROM indexing and abstracting of worldwide business literature. Archival discs are available from 1971. Formerly *ABI/INFORM OnDisc.*

Corporate Affiliations Plus. National Register Publishing, Reed Reference Publishing. • Quarterly. $1,995.00 per year. Provides CD-ROM discs corresponding to *Directory of Corporate Affiliations* and *Corporate Finance Bluebook.* Contains corporate financial services information and worldwide data on subsidiaries and affiliates.

WILSONDISC: Business Periodicals Index. H. W. Wilson Co. • Monthly. Provides CD-ROM indexing of business periodicals from 1982 to date. Price includes online service.

DIRECTORIES

America's Corporate Finance Directory. LexisNexis Group. • Covers: Financial personnel and outside financial services relationships of 5,000 leading United States corporations and their wholly-owned United States subsidiaries. Entries include: Company name, address, phone, fax, telex, e-mail addresses, stock exchange information, earnings, total assets, size of pension/profit-sharing fund portfolio, number of employees, description of business, wholly-owned U.S. Subsidiaries of parent company; name and title of key executives; outside suppliers of financial services.

Financial Management Association: Membership/ Professional Directory. Financial Management Association. • Annual. Membership. Lists 4,800 corporate financial officers and professors of financial management.

Nelson Information's Directory of Investment Managers. Nelson Information. • Annual. $595.00. Three volumes. Provides information on 2,200 investment management firms, both U.S. and foreign.

ENCYCLOPEDIAS AND DICTIONARIES

Blackwell Encyclopedic Dictionary of Finance. Dean Paxson and Douglas Wood, editors. Blackwell Publishing. • 1997. $110.00. The editors are associated with the University of Manchester. Contains definitions of key terms combined with longer articles written by various U. S. and foreign business educators. Includes bibliographies and index. (Blackwell Encyclopedia of Management Series).

HANDBOOKS AND MANUALS

Accountant's Business Manual. American Institute of Certified Public Accountants. • $189.75. Looseleaf. Two volumes. Semiannual updates. Covers a wide variety of topics relating to financial and accounting management, including types of ownership, business planning, financing, cash management, valuation, retirement plans, estate planning, workers' compensation, unemployment insurance, social security, and employee benefits management.

Advanced Strategies in Financial Risk Management. Robert J. Schwartz and Clifford W. Smith. Prentice Hall PTR. • 1993. $65.00. Includes technical discussions of financial swaps and derivatives. (New York Institute of Finance Series).

AMA Management Handbook. John J. Hampton, editor. AMACOM. • 1994. $110.00. Third edition. Provides 200 chapters in 16 major subject areas. Covers a wide variety of business and industrial management topics.

Banking and Finance on the Internet. Mary J. Cronin, editor. John Wiley and Sons, Inc. • 1997. $45.00. Contains articles on Internet services, written by bankers, money mangers, investment analysts, and stockbrokers. Emphasis is on operations management. (Communications Series).

Financial Management Handbook. Philip Vale. Ashgate Publishing Co. • 1988. $93.95. Third edition. Published by Gower in England.

Financial Management Techniques for Small Business. Art R. DeThomas. PSI Research. • 1991. $19.95. (Successful Business Library Series).

Guide to Preparing Financial Statements. John R. Clay and others. Practitioners Publishing Co. • 1998. Three looseleaf volumes. Price on application.

Guide to Preparing Nonprofit Financial Statements. Practitioners Publishing Co. • 2002. Three looseleaf volumes. Price on application.

Managing Finance: A Socially Responsible Approach. David Crowther. Elsevier Butterworth Heinemann. • 2004. $37.50. Explains how to manage an ethical approach to such items as accounting, company reports, profit analysis, costing, budgeting, performance data, and investment appraisal.

McGraw-Hill Pocket Guide to Business Finance: 201 Decision Making Tools for Managers. Joel G. Siegel. McGraw-Hill. • 1992. $14.95. Includes ratios, formulas, models, guidelines, instructions, strategies, and rules of thumb.

Money Manager's Compliance Guide. Thompson Publishing Group, Inc. • $649.00 per year. Two looseleaf volumes. Monthly updates and newletters. Edited for investment advisers and investment companies to help them be in compliance with governmental regulations, including SEC rules,

restrictions based on the Employee Retirement Income Security Act (ERISA), and regulations issued by the Commodity Futures Trading Commission (CFTC).

Swap Literacy. Elizabeth Ungar. Bloomberg. • 1996. $40.00. Written for corporate finance officers. Provides basic information on arbitrage, hedging, and speculation, involving interest rate, currency, and other types of financial swaps. (Bloomberg Professional Library.).

Swaps and Financial Engineering: A Self-Study Guide to Mastering and Applying Swaps and Financial Engineering. McGraw-Hill. • 1994. $55.00.

ONLINE DATABASES

Accounting and Tax Database. PROQUEST. • Provides indexing and abstracting of the literature of accounting, taxation, and financial management, 1971 to date. Updating is weekly. Especially covers accounting, auditing, banking, bankruptcy, employee compensation and benefits, cash management, financial planning, and credit. Inquire as to online cost and availability.

American Banker Full Text. American Banker-Bond Buyer, Database Services. • Provides complete text online of the daily *American Banker.* Inquire as to online cost and availability.

Banking Information Source. PROQUEST. • Provides indexing and abstracting of periodical and other literature from 1982 to date, with weekly updates. Covers the financial services industry: banks, savings institutions, investment houses, credit unions, insurance companies, and real estate organizations. Emphasis is on marketing and management. Inquire as to online cost and availability. (Formerly *FINIS: Financial Industry Information Service.*).

Management Contents. Gale Cengage Learning. • Covers a wide range of management, financial, marketing, personnel, and administrative topics. About 150 leading business journals are indexed and abstracted from 1974 to date, with monthly updating. Inquire as to online cost and availability.

Trade & Industry Database. Gale Cengage Learning. • Provides indexing of business periodicals, January 1981 to date. Daily updates. (Full text articles from some periodicals are available online, 1983 to date. Inquire as to online cost and availability).

Wilson Business Abstracts Online. H. W. Wilson Co. • Indexes and abstracts 600 major business periodicals, plus the *Wall Street Journal* and the business section of the *New York Times.* Indexing is from 1982, abstracting from 1990, with the two newspapers included from 1993. Updated weekly. Inquire as to online cost and availability. (*Business Periodicals Index* without abstracts is also available online.).

PERIODICALS AND NEWSLETTERS

American Banker: The Financial Services Daily. Thomson Media. • Daily. $895.00 per year. Provides news of banking, investment products, mortgages, credit unions, finance, bank technology, and legal developments.

Bank Accounting and Finance. Aspen Publishers, Inc. • Quarterly. $345.00 per year. Emphasis is on the practical aspects of bank accounting and bank financial management.

Business Finance. Penton Technology and Lifestyle Media. • Monthly. $59.00 per year. Covers trends in finance, technology, and economics for corporate financial executives.

CFO: The Magazine for Senior Financial Executives. CFO Publishing Corp. • Monthly. $65.00 per year.

Financial Executive. Financial Executives International. • Nine times a year. $59.00 per year.

Published for corporate financial officers and managers.

Financial Management. Financial Management Association International. • Quarterly. Individuals, $80.00 per year; libraries, $100.00 per year. Covers theory and practice of financial planning, international finance, investment banking, and portfolio management. Includes *Financial Practice* and *Education and Contempory Finance Digest.*

Fund Action. Institutional Investor, Inc., Journals Group. • Weekly. $2,475.00 per year. Newsletter. Includes print and online editions. Edited for mutual fund executives. Covers competition among funds, aggregate statistics, new products, regulations, service providers, and other subjects of interest to fund managers.

Global Finance. Global Finance Media, Inc. • Monthly. $350.00 per year. Edited for corporate financial executives and money managers responsible for "cross-border" financial transactions.

Investment Management Weekly. Thomson Media. • Weekly. $1,370.00 per year. Newsletter. Edited for money managers and other investment professionals. Covers personnel news, investment strategies, and industry trends.

IT Cost Management Strategies: The Planning Assistant for IT Directors. Computer Economics, Inc. • Monthly. $495.00 per year. Newsletter for information technology professionals. Covers data processing costs, budgeting, financial management, and related topics.

Operations Management. Institutional Investor, Inc., Journals Group. • Weekly. $2,105.00 per year. Includes print and online editions. Newsletter. Edited for managers of securities clearance and settlement at financial institutions. Covers new products, technology, legalities, management practices, and other topics related to securities processing.

Robb Report Worth: Wealth in Perspective. CurtCo Robb Media. • Monthly. $54.95 per year. Glossy magazine featuring articles for the affluent on personal financial management, investments, estate planning, trusts, private bankers, taxes, travel, yachts, and lifestyle. Formerly *Worth: Financial Intelligence.*

Strategic Finance. Institute of Management Accountants. • Monthly. Institutions, $140.00 per year; non-profit libraries, $70,00 per year. Provides articles on corporate finance, cost control, cash flow, budgeting, corporate taxes, and other financial management topics.

U. S. Banker. Thomson Media. • Monthly. $65.00 per year. Edited for bank executives and managers. Covers a wide variety of banking and financial topics.

Windows in Financial Services. • Quarterly. $39.00 per year. Covers information technology applications and products for Microsoft Windows users in the financial sector.

RESEARCH CENTERS AND INSTITUTES

Financial Executives Research Foundation. 10 Madison Ave., Morristown, NJ 07962. Phone: (973)898-4600 • Fax: (973)898-6636 E-mail: mbace@fei.org • URL: http://www.fei.org/rf.

Rodney L. White Center for Financial Research. University of Pennsylvania, 3254 Steinberg Hall-Dietrich Hall, Philadelphia, PA 19104. Phone: (215)898-7616 Fax: (215)573-8084 E-mail: rlwtcr@finance.wharton.upenn.edu • URL: http://www.finance.wharton.upenn.edu • Research areas include financial management, money markets, real estate finance, and international finance.

TRADE/PROFESSIONAL ASSOCIATIONS

American Finance Association. University of California, Haas School of Business, 350 Main St., 545 Student Services Bldg., Berkeley, CA 94720-

1900. Phone: 800-835-6770 or (781)388-8532 Fax: (781)388-8232 E-mail: pyle@haas.berkeley.edu • URL: http://www.afajof.org • College and university professors of economics and finance, bankers, treasurers, analysts, financiers, and others interested in financial problems; libraries and other institutions. Seeks to improve public understanding of financial problems and to provide for exchange of analytical ideas. Areas of special interest include: corporate finance, investments, banking, and international and public finance.

Association for Financial Professionals. 7315 Wisconsin Ave., Suite 600 W, Bethesda, MD 20814-3211. Phone: (301)907-2862 Fax: (301)907-2864 E-mail: afp@afponline.org • URL: http://www.afponline.org • Goal is to raise the stature and visibility of the finance profession. Formerly Treasury Management Association.

Financial Executives International. 200 Campus Dr., PO Box 674, Florham Park, NJ 07932-0674. Phone: (973)765-1000 Fax: (973)765-1018 E-mail: mcangemi@financialexecutives.org • URL: http://www.financialexecutives.org • Professional organization of corporate financial executives performing duties of chief financial officer, controller, treasurer, or vice-president-finance. Sponsors research activities through its affiliated Financial Executives Research Foundation. Maintains offices in Toronto, Canada, and Washington, DC.

Financial Management Association International. University of South Florida, College of Business Administration, 4202 E Fowler Ave., BSN 3331, Tampa, FL 33620-5500. Phone: (813)974-2084 Fax: (813)974-3318 E-mail: fma@coba.usf.edu • URL: http://www.fma.org • Professors of financial management; corporate financial officers. Facilitates exchange of ideas among persons involved in financial management or the study thereof. Conducts workshops for comparison of current research projects and development of cooperative ventures in writing and research. Sponsors honorary society for superior students at 300 colleges and universities. Offers placement services.

Financial Managers Society. 100 W Monroe, Ste. 810, Chicago, IL 60603. Phone: 800-275-4367 or (312)578-1300 Fax: (312)578-1308 E-mail: info@fmsinc.org • URL: http://www.fmsinc.org • Works for the needs of finance and accounting professionals from banks, thrifts and credit unions. Offers career-enhancing education, specialized publications, national leadership opportunities, and worldwide connections with other industry professionals.

Financial Women's Association of New York. 215 Park Ave. S., Suite 1713, New York, NY 10003. Phone: (212)533-2141 Fax: (212)982-3008 E-mail: fwaoffice@fwa.org • URL: http://www.fwa.org • Members are professional women in finance. Formerly Young Women's Financial Association of New York.

OTHER SOURCES

Finance and Accounting for Nonfinancial Managers. American Management Association Extension Institute. • Looseleaf. $159.00. Self-study course. Emphasis is on practical explanations, examples, and problem solving. Quizzes and a case study are included.

FINANCIAL PLANNING

See also: ESTATE PLANNING; PERSONAL FINANCE; TAX PLANNING

GENERAL WORKS

Financial Planning for the Utterly Confused. Joel Lerner. McGraw-Hill. • 1998. $12.95. Fifth edition. Covers annuities, certificates of deposit, bonds, mutual funds, insurance, home ownership, retire-

ment, social security, wills, etc.

How to Avoid Financial Tangles. American Institute for Economic Research. • 2001. $8.00. Provides basic information and advice on such topics as property ownership, taxes, wills, trusts, insurance, record retention, and professional assistance. (Economic Education Bulletin.).

Smart Questions to Ask Your Financial Advisers. Lynn Brenner. Bloomberg. • 1997. $19.95. Provides practical advice on how to deal with financial planners, stockbrokers, insurance agents, and lawyers. Some of the areas covered are investments, estate planning, tax planning, house buying, prenuptial agreements, divorce arrangements, loss of a job, and retirement. (Bloomberg Personal Bookshelf Series).

ABSTRACTS AND INDEXES

Business Periodicals Index. H. W. Wilson Co. • 11 times a year. Quarterly and annual cumulations. Price varies.

DIRECTORIES

Business Organizations, Agencies, and Publications Directory. Gale Cengage Learning. • 2003. $480.00. 15th edition. Over 40,000 entries describing 39 types of business information sources. Classified by type of organization, publication, or serviceIncludes state, national, and international agencies and organizations. Master index to names and keywords. Also includes e-mail addresses and web site URL's.

Directory of Registered Investment Advisors. Money Market Directories, Inc. • Annual. $510.00. Lists over 12,000 investment advisors and advisory firms. Indicates services offered, personnel, and amount of assets being managed. Formerly *Directory of Registered Investment Advisors with the Securities and Exchange Commission.*

Plunkett's Financial Services Industry Almanac: The Only Comprehensive Overview of the Banking, Insurance, Credit and Investment Sectors. Plunkett Research, Ltd. • Annual. $229.99. Includes CD-ROM. Discusses important trends in various sectors of the financial industry. Five hundred major banking, credit card, investment, and financial services companies are profiled. (Business, Careers and Internet Reference Tools Series).

FINANCIAL RATIOS

Financial Planning for Older Clients. James E. Pearman. CCH, Inc. • 2000. $49.00. Covers income sources, social security, Medicare, Medicaid, investment planning, estate planning, and other retirement-related topics. Edited for accountants, attorneys, and other financial advisors. (Solutions for Professional Advisors Series).

HANDBOOKS AND MANUALS

Asset Protection Planning Guide: A State-of-the-Art Approach to Integrated Estate Planning. Barry S. Engel and others. CCH, Inc. • 2001. $99.00. Provides advice for attorneys, trust officers, accountants, and others engaged in financial planning for protection of assets.

Best Practices for Financial Advisors. Mary Rowland. Bloomberg. • 1997. $40.00. Provides advice for professional financial advisors on practice management, ethics, marketing, and legal concerns. (Bloomberg Professional Library.).

CCH Financial and Estate Planning Guide. CCH, Inc. • Annual. $63.00. Contains four main parts: General Principles and Techniques, Special Situations, Building the Estate, and Planning Aids.

Ernst & Young's Personal Financial Planning Guide. John Wiley and Sons, Inc. • 2001. $19.95. Fourth edition.

Estate and Retirement Planning Answer Book. William D. Mitchell. Aspen Publishers, Inc. • 2000. $145.00. Third edition. Basic questions and answers by a lawyer.

Financial Planning Applications. Thomas P. Lang-

don and William J. Ruckstuhl. The American College. • 2003. $70.00. 19th edition. Emphasis on annuities and life insurance.

Financial Planning for Libraries. Ann E. Prentice. Scarecrow Press, Inc. • 1996. $36.00. Second edition. Includes examples of budgets for libraries. (Library Administration Series, No. 12).

Getting Started in Investment Planning Services. James E. Grant. CCH, Inc. • 1999. $85.00. Second edition. Provides advice and information for lawyers and accountants who are planning to initiate fee-based investment services.

Personal Financial Planning Handbook: With Forms and Checklists. Warren, Gorham & Lamont/RIA. • $215.00. Looseleaf service. Biennial supplementation. Designed for professional financial planners, accountants, attorneys, insurance marketers, brokers, and bankers.

Personal Financial Planning: The Advisor's Guide. Rolf Austen. CCH, Inc. • 1998. $55.95. Third edition. Covers personal taxes, investments, credit, mortgages, insurance, pensions, social security, estate planning, etc.

Practicing Financial Planning: A Complete Guide for Professionals. Sitansu S. Mittra. R. H. Publishing. • 1993. $29.95. Approved for continuing education of financial planners by the International Board of Standards and Practices for Certified Financial Planners. Covers planning strategies, funds allocation, insurance considerations, risk management, ethics, and other topics.

Protecting Your Practice. Katherine Vessenes. Bloomberg. • 1997. $60.00. Discusses legal compliance issues for financial planners. (Bloomberg Professional Library.).

Retirement Planning Guide. Sidney Kess and Barbara Weltman. CCH, Inc. • 2000. $49.00. Second edition. Presents an overview for attorneys, accountants, and other professionals of the various concepts involved in retirement planning. Includes checklists, tables, forms, and study questions.

The Touche Ross Personal Financial Planning and Investment Workbook. John R. Connell and others. Prentice Hall. • 1989. $39.95. Third edition.

Wall Street Journal Guide to Planning Your Financial Future: The Easy-to-Read Guide to Lifetime Planning for Retirement. Kenneth M. Morris and Virginia B. Morris. Simon & Schuster Trade. • 2002. $15.95. Third edition. (Wall Street Journal Guides Series).

ONLINE DATABASES

Wilson Business Abstracts Online. H. W. Wilson Co. • Indexes and abstracts 600 major business periodicals, plus the *Wall Street Journal* and the business section of the *New York Times*. Indexing is from 1982, abstracting from 1990, with the two newspapers included from 1993. Updated weekly. Inquire as to online cost and availability. (*Business Periodicals Index* without abstracts is also available online.).

PERIODICALS AND NEWSLETTERS

Accounting and Financial Planning for Law Firms. American Lawyer Media, Inc. • Monthly. $225.00 per year. Newsletter. Covers budgeting, liability issues, billing systems, benefits management, and other topics relating to law firm administration. (A Law Journal Newsletter, formerly published by Leader Publications).

Bank Investment Consultant: Sales Strategies for the Financial Adviser. Thomson Media. • Monthly. Controlled circulation. Covers sales and marketing techniques for bank investment and asset management divisions. Formerly *Bank Investment Marketing.*

Estate Planner's Alert. RIA. • Monthly. $140.00 per year. Newsletter. Covers the tax aspects of personal finance, including home ownership, investments,

For publishers addresses, refer to SOURCES CITED section at the back of the book.

insurance, retirement planning, and charitable giving. Formerly *Estate and Financial Planners Alert.*

Financial Counseling and Planning. Association for Financial Counseling and Planning Education. • Semiannual. Members, $60. per year; institutional members, $100.00 per year; libraries, $60.00 per year. Disseminates scholarly research relating to financial planning and counseling .

Financial Management. Financial Management Association International. • Quarterly. Individuals, $80.00 per year; libraries, $100.00 per year. Covers theory and practice of financial planning, international finance, investment banking, and portfolio management. Includes *Financial Practice and Education and Contempory Finance Digest.*

Financial Planning: The Magazine for Financial Service Professionals. Thomson Media. • Monthly. $79.00 per year. Edited for independent financial planners and insurance agents. Covers retirement planning, estate planning, tax planning, and insurance, including long-term healthcare considerations. Special features include a Retirement Planning Issue, Mutual Fund Performance Survey, and Variable Life and Annuity Survey.

Investment Advisor: The Advisor to Advisors. Wicks Business Information. • Monthly. $79.00 per year. Edited for professional investment advisors, financial planners, stock brokers, bankers, and others concerned with the management of assets.

Investment News: The Weekly Newspaper for Financial Advisers. Crain Communications, Inc. • Weekly. $29.00 per year. Edited for both personal and institutional investment advisers, planners, and managers.

Jounal of Finacial Services Professionals. Society of Financial Services Professional. • Bimonthly. $95.00 per year. Provides information on life insurance and financial planning, including estate planning, retirement, tax planning, trusts, business insurance, long-term care insurance, disability insurance, and employee benefits. Formerly (American Society of CLU and Ch F C Journal).

Journal of Financial Planning. Financial Planning Association. • 12 times a year. Free to members; non-members, $90.00 per year. Edited for professional financial and investment planners.

Journal of Retirement Planning. CCH, Inc. • Bimonthly. $179.00 per year. Emphasis is on retirement and estate planning advice provided by lawyers and accountants as part of their practices.

Journal of Taxation of Financial Products. CCH, Inc. • Bimonthly. $249.00 per year.

Journal of Wealth Management. Institutional Investor, Inc., Journals Group. • Quarterly. $410.00 per year. Includes print and online editions. Edited for managers of wealthy individuals' investment portfolios. Formerly *Journal of Private Portfolio Management.*

Money. • 13 times a year. $19.95 per year. Covers all aspects of family finance; investments, careers, shopping, taxes, insurance, consumerism, etc.

On Wall Street. Thomson Media. • Monthly. $96.00 per year. Edited for securities dealers. Includes articles on financial planning, retirement planning, variable annuities, and money management, with special coverage of 401(k) plans and IRAs.

The Practical Accountant: Providing the Competitive Edge. Thomson Media. • Monthly. $65.00 per year. Covers tax planning, financial planning, practice management, client relationships, and related topics.

Private Asset Management. Institutional Investor, Inc., Journals Group. • Biweekly. $2,335.00 per year. Newsletter. Includes print and online editions. Edited for managers investing the private assets of wealthy ("high-net-worth") individuals. Includes

marketing, taxation, regulation, and fee topics.

Treasury Manager's Report: Strategic Information for the Financial Executive. PBI Media, LLC. • Biweekly. $630.00. Newsletter reporting on legal developments affecting the operations of banks, savings institutions, and other financial service organizations. Formerly *Financial Services Law Report.*

RESEARCH CENTERS AND INSTITUTES

American Institute for Economic Research. P.O. Box 1000, Great Barrington, MA 01230. Phone: (413)528-1216 Fax: (413)528-0103 E-mail: info@aier.org • URL: http://www.aier.org.

Center for Financial Responsibility. College of Human Sciences, Box 41162, Texas Tech University, Lubbock, TX 79409-1162. Phone: (806)742-9781 Fax: (806)742-9784 E-mail: bill.gustafson@ttu.edu • URL: http://www.hs.ttu.edu/cfr/ • Research areas include financial preparation for retirement, financial education, determinants of financial satisfaction, risk tolerance, and the career preparation of retirement industry professionals.

TRADE/PROFESSIONAL ASSOCIATIONS

Association for Financial Counseling and Planning Education. 2121 Arlington Ave., Ste. 5, Upper Arlington, OH 43221-4339. Phone: (614)485-9650 Fax: (614)485-9621 • URL: http://www.afcpe.org • Members are researchers, academics, financial counselors and financial planners.

Financial Planning Association. 4100 E Mississippi Ave., Ste. 400, Denver, CO 80246-3053. Phone: 800-322-4237 or (303)759-4910 Fax: (303)759-0749 E-mail: marv.tuttle@fpanet.org • URL: http://www.fpanet.org • Works to support the financial planning process in order to help people achieve their goals and dreams. Believes that everyone needs objective advice to make smart financial decisions and that when seeking the advice of a financial planner, the planner should be a CFP professional.

Investment Counsel Association of America. 1050 17th St., N.W., Suite 725, Washington, DC 20036-5503. Phone: (202)293-4222 Fax: (202)293-4223 E-mail: icaa@icaa.org • URL: http://www.icaa.org.

National Association of Personal Financial Advisors. 3250 N Arlington Heights Rd., Ste. 109, Arlington Heights, IL 60004. Phone: 800-366-2732 or (847)483-5400 or 888-333-6659 Fax: (847)483-5415 E-mail: info@napfa.org • URL: http://www.napfa.org • Members are full-time financial planners who are compensated on a fee-only basis.

OTHER SOURCES

Estate and Personal Financial Planning. West Group. • Quarterly. $980.00 per year. Newsletter.

Financial and Estate Planning: Analysis, Strategies and Checklists. CCH, Inc. • 4 looseleaf volumes. Price on application. services.

FINANCIAL RATIOS

See also: FINANCIAL ANALYSIS

CD-ROM DATABASES

CreditDisk 2.0. Fitch, Inc. • Price and frequency on application. CD-ROM provides credit research and ratings on individual banks throughout the world, with Internet updating. Includes graphic displays of rating histories and financial ratios.

FINANCIAL RATIOS

Almanac of Business and Industrial Financial Ratios. Leo Troy. Aspen Publishers, Inc. • 2003. $125.95. Includes CD-Rom. Contains financial ratios derived from federal tax returns. Ratios for each of about 200 industries are arranged according to company asset size. (Almanac of Business and Industrial Financial Ratios Series).

Annual Statement Studies. The Risk Management Association. • Annual. Median and quartile financial ratios are given for over 400 kinds of manufacturing, wholesale, retail, construction, and consumer finance establishments. Data is sorted by both asset size and sales volume. Includes a clearly written "Definition of Ratios" and an alphabetical industry index.

Annual Statement Studies: Industry Default Probabilities and Cash Flow Measures. The Risk Management Association. • Annual. $145.00. Serves as a companion volume to the original *Annual Statement Studies.* Gives probability of default estimates on a percentage scale for more than 450 industries. Includes changes in position year-by-year for eight financial statement line items and provides percentage measures of cash flow.

Industry Norms and Key Business Ratios. Desk Top Edition. Dun and Bradstreet Corp. • Annual. Five volumes. $475.00 per volume. $1,890.00 per set. Covers over 800 kinds of businesses, arranged by Standard Industrial Classification number. More detailed editions covering longer periods of time are also available.

IRS Corporate Financial Ratios. Available from MarketResearch.com. • 2002. $225.00. Published by Schonfeld & Associates, Inc. Presents 70 key financial ratios for 260 industries. Ratios are calculated from income statement and balance sheet data available from the Internal Revenue Service. Includes four asset size classes.

Quarterly Financial Report for Manufacturing, Mining, and Trade Corporations. U.S. Federal Trade Commission and U.S. Securities and Exchange Commission. Available from U.S. Government Printing Office. • Quarterly. $49.00 per year.

HANDBOOKS AND MANUALS

Analysis and Use of Financial Statements. Gerald I. White. John Wiley and Sons, Inc. • 2002. $123.95. Third edition. Includes analysis of financial ratios, cash flow, inventories, assets, debt, etc. Also covered are employee benefits, corporate investments, multinational operations, financial derivatives, and hedging activities.

Business Ratios and Formulas: A Comprehensive Guide. Steven M. Bragg. John Wiley and Sons, Inc. • 2002. $85.00. Describes and explains a wide variety of ratios used in finance and management.

Dun & Bradstreet/Gale Group Industry Handbooks. Gale Cengage Learning. • 2000. $650.00. Five volumes. $130.00 per volume. Each volume covers two or more major industries: 1. *Entertainment and Hospitality*; 2. *Construction and Agriculture*; 3. *Chemicals and Pharmaceuticals*; 4. *Computers & Software and Broadcasting & Telecommunications*; 5. *Insurance and Health & Medical Services.* The following are included for each industry: overview, statistics, financial ratios, rankings, merger information, company directory, directory of associations, and consultants directory. (Dun and Bradstreet/Gale Industry Reference Handbook Series).

How to Read a Financial Report: Wringing Vital Signs Out of the Numbers. John A. Tracy. John Wiley and Sons, Inc. • 1999. $29.95. Fifth edition.

ONLINE DATABASES

Compustat. Standard and Poor's. • Financial data on publicly held U.S. and some foreign corporations; data held for 20 years. Inquire as to online cost and availability.

STATISTICS SOURCES

By the Numbers: Electronic and Online Publishing. Gale Cengage Learning. • 1997-98. $305.00. Four volumes. $85.00 per volume. Covers "high-interest" industries: 1. *By the Numbers: Electronic and Online Publishing*; 2. *By the Numbers: Emerging Industries*; 3. *By the Numbers: Nonprofits*; 4. *By the*

Numbers: Publishing. Each volume provides about 600 tabulations of industry data on revenues, market share, employment, trends, financial ratios, profits, salaries, and so forth. Citations to data sources are included. (By the Numbers Series).

OTHER SOURCES

Country Risk Monitor. Bank of America, World Information Services, Dept. 3015. • Looseleaf, with semiannual updates. $495.00 per year. Provides rankings of 80 countries according to current and future business risk. Utilizes key economic ratios and benchmarks for countries in a manner similar to financial ratio analysis for industries.

FINANCIAL SERVICES

See: INVESTMENT ADVISORY SERVICES

FINANCIAL STATEMENTS

See: CORPORATION REPORTS; FINANCIAL ANALYSIS

FIRE ALARMS

See: ELECTRONIC SECURITY SYSTEMS

FIRE INSURANCE

See also: INSURANCE

GENERAL WORKS

Smarter Insurance Solutions. Janet Bamford. Bloomberg. • 1996. $19.95. Provides practical advice to consumers, with separate chapters on the following kinds of insurance: automobile, home-owners, health, disability, and life. (Bloomberg Personal Bookshelf Series).

ABSTRACTS AND INDEXES

Insurance Periodicals Index. Specials Libraries Association, Insurance and Employees Benefits Div. NILS Publishing Co. • Annual. $250.00. Compiled by the Insurance and Employee Benefits Div., Special Libraries Association. A yearly index of over 15,000 articles from about 35 insurance periodicals. Arrangement is by subject, with an index to authors.

ALMANACS AND YEARBOOKS

Insurance Almanac: Who, What, When and Where in Insurance. Underwriter Printing and Publishing Co. • Annual. $175.00. Lists insurance agencies and brokerage firms; U.S. and Canadian insurance companies, adjusters, appraisers, auditors, investigators, insurance officials and insurance organizations.

BIBLIOGRAPHIES

Insurance and Employee Benefits Literature. Special Libraries Association, Insurance and Employee Benefits Div. • Bimonthly. $15.00 per year. Lists a wide variety of literature in all branches of the insurance industry. Includes annotations.

CD-ROM DATABASES

U. S. Insurance: Property and Casualty. Sheshunoff Information Services, Inc. • Monthly. Price on application. CD-ROM provides detailed, current financial information on more than 3,200 property and casualty insurance companies.

DIRECTORIES

S & P's Insurance Book. Standard & Poor's Ratings Group, Insurance Rating Services. • Quarterly. Price on application. Contains detailed financial analyses and ratings of various kinds of insurance companies.

S & P's Insurance Digest: Property-Casualty and Reinsurance Edition. Standard & Poor's Ratings Group, Insurance Rating Services. • Quarterly. Contains concise financial analyses and ratings of property-casualty insurance companies.

ENCYCLOPEDIAS AND DICTIONARIES

Dictionary of Insurance Terms. Harvey W. Rubin. Barron's Educational Series, Inc. • 2000. $14.95. Fourth edition. Defines terms in a wide variety of insurance fields. (Business Dictionaries Series).

Glossary of Insurance Policy Terms. Organization for Economic Cooperation and Development. • 1999. $30.00. "The selected topics range from insurance policy regulation/supervision to general trade issues and include technical terms related to issues such as claims, premiums, and provisions." Edited for government, academic, business, and insurance organizations.

Insurance Words and Their Meanings: A Glossary of Insurance Terms. The Rough Notes Co., Inc. • 2001. 17th edition. Price on application.

Rupp's Insurance and Risk Management Glossary. Richard V. Rupp. NILS Publishing Co. • 2001. $35.00. Second edition. Provides definitions of 6,400 insurance words and phrases. Includes a guide to acronyms and abbreviations.

HANDBOOKS AND MANUALS

The Complete Book of Insurance: Protecting Your Life, Health Property, and Income. Ben G. Baldwin. McGraw-Hill. • 1991. $24.95. Provides basic information and advice on various kinds of insurance: life, health, property (fire), disability, long-term care, automobile, liability, and annuities.

ONLINE DATABASES

I.I.I. Data Base Search. Insurance Information Institute. • Provides online citations and abstracts of insurance-related literature in magazines, newspapers, trade journals, and books. Emphasis is on property and casualty insurance issues, including highway safety, product safety, and environmental liability. Inquire as to online cost and availability.

PERIODICALS AND NEWSLETTERS

Fire, Casualty and Surety Bulletin. The National Underwriter Co. • Monthly. $420.00 per year. Five looseleaf volumes.

NAMIC Magazine. National Association of Mutual Insurance Cos. • Bimonthly. $18.00 per year. Formerly *Mutual Insurance Bulletin.*

STATISTICS SOURCES

Best's Aggregates and Averages: Property-Casualty. A.M. Best Co., Inc. • Annual. $335.00. Statistical summary of composite property casualty business. 400 pages of historical data, underwriting expenses and underwriting experience by line.

Property-Casualty Insurance Facts. Insurance Information Institute. • Annual. $22.50. Formerly *Insurance Facts.*

TRADE/PROFESSIONAL ASSOCIATIONS

American Insurance Association. 1130 Connecticut Ave. NW, Ste. 1000, Washington, DC 20036. Phone: 800-242-2302 or (202)828-7100 or (202)828-7183 Fax: (202)293-1219 E-mail: info@aiadc.org • URL: http://www.aiadc.org/aiadotnet • Represents companies providing property and casualty insurance and suretyship. Monitors and reports on economic, political, and social trends; serves as a clearinghouse for ideas, advice, and technical information. Represents members' interests before state and federal legislative and regulatory bodies; coordinates members' litigation.

CPCU Society. 720 Providence Rd., 720 Providence Rd., PO Box 3009, Malvern, PA 19355-3402. Phone: 800-932-2728 or (610)251-2727 Fax: (610)251-2780 E-mail: membercenter@cpcusociety.org • URL: http://www.cpcusociety.org • Serves as a professional society of individuals who have passed national examinations of the American Institute for Chartered Property Casualty Underwriters (see separate entry), have 3 years of work experience, have agreed to be bound by a code of ethics, and have been awarded CPCU designation. Promotes education, research, social responsibility, and professionalism in the field. Holds seminars, symposia, and workshops.

Insurance Services Office (ISO). 545 Washington Blvd., Jersey City, NJ 07310-1686. Phone: 800-888-4476 or (201)469-2000 Fax: (201)748-1472 E-mail: info@iso.com • URL: http://www.iso.com • Provides statistical, actuarial, underwriting, and claims information to property and casualty insurance companies.

OTHER SOURCES

Best's Insurance Reports: Property-Casualty. A.M. Best Co. • Annual. $750.00. Guide to over 3,200 major property/casualty companies.

BestWeek: Insurance News and Analysis. A.M. Best Co. • Weekly. $495.00 per year. Newsletter. Focuses on key areas of the insurance industry.

Fire and Casualty Insurance Law Reports. CCH, Inc. • $870.00 per year. Looseleaf service. Semimonthly updates.

FIRE PREVENTION

See also: FIRE PROTECTION

ABSTRACTS AND INDEXES

Applied Science and Technology Index. H. W. Wilson Co. • 11 times a year. Quarterly and annual cumulations. Price varies. Indexes a wide variety of English language technical, industrial, and engineering periodicals.

ONLINE DATABASES

Applied Science and Technology Index Online. H. W. Wilson Co. • Provides online indexing of 500 major scientific, technical, industrial, and engineering periodicals. Time period is 1983 to date. Monthly updates. Inquire as to online cost and availability.

PERIODICALS AND NEWSLETTERS

Fire and Materials: An International Journal. John Wiley and Sons, Inc., Journals. • Bimonthly. Individuals, $1,215.00 per year; institutions, $1,620.00 per year. Published in England by John Wiley & Sons Ltd. Provides international coverage of subject matter.

Security Letter. Security Letter Inc. • Description: Contains "solution-oriented information on security and protection of assets from loss," particularly for executives concerned about the following: internal checks and controls, personnel practices, management of change, fraud and embezzlement, business crime trends, security, and urban terrorism. Recurring features include news of research, a calendar of events, semiannual FBI crime data, quarterly financial news of major companies in the security industry, book reviews, security and safety pointers, and a question-and-answer feature.

STATISTICS SOURCES

NFPA Journal. National Fire Protection Association. • Bimonthly. Membership. Incorporates *Fire Journal* and *Fire Command.*

FIRE PROTECTION

See also: FIRE PREVENTION

DIRECTORIES

NFPA Journal Buyers'. National Fire Protection Association. • Annual. $30.00. Listing of fire protection equipment manufacturers.

HANDBOOKS AND MANUALS

Fire Protection Handbook. National Fire Protection Association. • Irregular. Members, $112.50; non-members, $125.00.

National Fire Codes. National Fire Protection Association. • Annual. Members, $710.00; non-members, $790.00. Lists over 270 codes.

PERIODICALS AND NEWSLETTERS

Fire Chief: Administration, Training, Operations. Primedia Business Magazines and Media. • Monthly. $54.00 per year.

Fire Engineering: The Journal of Fire Suppression and Protection. PennWell Corp., Industrial Div. • Monthly. $19.95 per year.

Fire International: The Journal of the World's Fire Protection Services. DMG World Media Ltd. • 10 times a year. $158.00 per year. Text in English. Summaries in French, German and Spanish.

Fire Technology: An International Journal of Fire Protection Research and Engineering. National Fire Protection Association. • Quarterly. $199.00 per year.

STATISTICS SOURCES

NFPA Journal. National Fire Protection Association. • Bimonthly. Membership. Incorporates *Fire Journal* and *Fire Command.*

TRADE/PROFESSIONAL ASSOCIATIONS

International Association of Fire Chiefs. 4025 Fair Ridge Dr., Ste. 300, Fairfax, VA 22033-2868. Phone: (703)273-0911 Fax: (703)273-9363 E-mail: membership@iafc.org • URL: http://www.iafc.org.

International Association of Fire Fighters. 1750 New York Ave., N.W., 3rd Fl., Washington, DC 20006-5395. Phone: (202)737-8484 Fax: (202)737-8418 E-mail: pr@iaff.org • URL: http://www.iaff.org.

International Fire Marshals Association. 1 Batterymarch Park, PO Box 9101, Quincy, MA 02169-7471. Phone: (617)984-7423 Fax: (617)984-7056 E-mail: ifma@nfpa.org • URL: http://www.nfpa.org • Municipal, county, state, and provincial fire marshals and fire prevention bureau officials. Works for professional improvement through information exchange, meetings, and conferences. Seeks to minimize the loss of life and property by fire through fire prevention education, enforcement of fire laws, investigation of fire causes, and fire hazard regulation.

International Fire Service Training Association. Oklahoma State University, 930 N Willis, Stillwater, OK 74078-8045. Phone: 800-654-4055 or (405)744-5723 Fax: (405)744-8204 E-mail: customer.service@osufpp.org • URL: http://www.ifsta.org • Educational organization formed to develop training materials for the fire service. Committee members are individuals who represent their respective fire-related fields and are considered leaders or innovators. Association committee members meet annually to validate training material for publication, add new techniques and developments, delete outmoded methods and equipment, and upgrade fire service training in general; actual publication is done for the association by Fire Protection Publications of Oklahoma State University.

National Fire Protection Association (NFPA). 1 Batterymarch Pk., Quincy, MA 02269-9101. Phone: 800-344-3555 or (617)770-3000 Fax: (617)770-0700 E-mail: custserv@nfpa.org • URL: http://www.nfpa.org.

Society of Fire Protection Engineers. 7315 Wisconsin Ave., No. 1225W, Bethesda, MD 20814. Phone: (301)718-2910 Fax: (301)718-2242 E-mail: sfpehqtrs@sfpe.org • URL: http://www.sfpe.org.

FIREARMS INDUSTRY

See also: DEFENSE INDUSTRIES; MILITARY MARKET

DIRECTORIES

Guns Illustrated. Krause Publications Inc. • Publication includes: Lists of national and international firearms associations; manufacturers, importers, and distributors of firearms, shooting equipment, and services. Entries include: For associations--Name, address, phone, area of interest. For manufacturers and distributors--Name, address, phone, product or service provided. Principal content of publication is articles on hunting, handloading, ammunition, ballistics, collecting, gunsmithing, and customizing, as well as other related information.

Law and Order Magazine Police Equipment Buyer's Guide. Hendon, Inc. • Annual. $15.00. Lists manufacturers, dealers, and distributors of equipment and services for police departments.

Law Enforcement Technology Directory. Cygnus Business Media, Inc. • Annual. $60.00 per year. $6.00 per issue; a directory of products, equipment, services, and technology for police professionals. Includes weapons, uniforms, communications equipment, and software.

Shooting Industry-Buyers Guide. Publishers Development Corp. • Annual. $15.00. Manufacturers, wholesalers, and importers of guns and related equipment and supplies.

HANDBOOKS AND MANUALS

Modern Guns: Identification and Values. Russell C. Quertermous and Steven C. Quertermous. Collector Books. • 2000. $14.95. 13th edition. (Modern Guns Series).

PERIODICALS AND NEWSLETTERS

American Firearms Industry. National Association of Federally Licensed Firearms Dealers. AFI Communications Group, Inc. • Monthly. $35.00 per year.

American Rifleman. National Rifle Association of America. NRA Publications. • Monthly. $35.00 per year.

Bureau of Alcohol, Tobacco, and Firearms Quarterly Bulletin. Bureau of Alcohol, Tobacco, and Firearms, U.S. Department of the Treasury. Available from U.S. Government Printing Office. • Quarterly. $25.00 per year. Laws and regulations.

Guns and Ammo. PRIMEDIA Inc. • Monthly. $14.97 per year.

Guns Magazine: Finest in the Firearms Field. Publishers Development Corp. • Monthly. $19.95 per year. Annual *Supplement* available. Formerly *Guns.*

Law and Order Magazine: The Magazine for Police Management. Hendon Publishing Co. • Monthly. $24.95 per year. Edited for law enforcement officials. Includes special issues on communications, technology, weapons, and uniforms and equipment.

Law Enforcement Technology. Cygnus Business Media. • Monthly. $60.00 per year. Covers new products and technologies for police professionals. Includes special issues on weapons, uniforms, communications equipment, computers (hardware-software), vehicles, and enforcement of drug laws.

Shooting Industry. Publishers Development Corp. • Monthly. $25.00 per year.

STATISTICS SOURCES

Annual Survey of Manufactures. Available from U.S. Government Printing Office. • Annual. Prices vary. Issued by the U. S. Census Bureau as an interim update to the *Census of Manufactures.* Includes data on number of manufacturing establishments in various industries, employment, labor costs, value of shipments, capital expenditures, inventories, energy costs, and assets. (See also Census Bureau home page, http://www.census.gov/.).

Statistics on Weapons and Violence: A Selection of Statistical Charts, Graphs and Tables about Weapons and Violence from a Variety of Published Sources with Explanatory Comments. Gale Cengage Learning. • 1995. $85.00. Includes graphs, charts, and tables arranged within subject chapters. Citations to data sources are provided. (Statistics for Students Series).

TRADE/PROFESSIONAL ASSOCIATIONS

National Rifle Association of America. 12810 Gaffney Rd., Silver Spring, MD 20904-3517. Phone: 800-207-8192 or (301)680-0035 Fax: (301)622-1819 E-mail: hq@mynra.com • URL: http://www.mynra.com.

National Shooting Sports Foundation. Flintlock Ridge Office Ctr., 11 Mile Hill Rd., Newtown, CT 06470-2359. Phone: (203)426-1320 Fax: (203)426-1087 E-mail: info@nssf.org • URL: http://www.nssf.org • Represents manufacturers of firearms and ammunition, accessories, components, gun sights, hunting clothes, and other reputable firms that make a profit from hunting and shooting; includes outdoor and gun magazine publishers. Fosters a better understanding of and more active participation in the shooting sports. Promotes firearms safety; works with state and federal agencies in providing additional hunting opportunities. Cooperates with private enterprise to create outdoor recreational facilities. Distributes literature concerning firearms safety, conservation, and recreational shooting. Finances educational programs.

Sporting Arms and Ammunition Manufacturers Institute. 11 Mile Hill Rd., c/o Flintlock Ridge Office Ctr., Newtown, CT 06470-2359. Phone: (203)426-4358 Fax: (203)426-1087 E-mail: info@nssf.org • URL: http://www.nssf.org • Producers of firearms, ammunition and propellants.

FIRING OF EMPLOYEES

See: DISMISSAL OF EMPLOYEES

FISH CULTURE

See: AQUACULTURE

FISH INDUSTRY

See also: SEAFOOD INDUSTRY

ABSTRACTS AND INDEXES

NTIS Alerts: Agriculture & Food. National Technical Information Service. • Semimonthly. $195.00 per year. Provides descriptions of government-sponsored research reports and software, with ordering information. Covers agricultural economics, horticulture, fisheries, veterinary medicine, food technology, and related subjects. Formerly *Abstract Newsletter.*

CD-ROM DATABASES

Food Science and Technology Abstracts [CD-ROM]. Available from SilverPlatter Information, Inc. • Quarterly. Produced by International Food Information Service (home page is http://www.ifis.org). Provides worldwide coverage on CD-ROM of the literature of food technology and production. Various types of publications are indexed, with abstracts, including about 1,800 periodicals. Time period is 1969 to date.

DIRECTORIES

Major Food and Drink Companies of the World. Available from Gale Cengage Learning. • Annual. $880.00. Two volumes. Published by Graham & Whiteside. Contains profiles and trade names for more than 9,800 important food and beverage companies in various countries. In addition to foods, includes both alcoholic and nonalcoholic drink products.

Thomas Food and Beverage Market Place. Grey House Publishing. • 2004. $495.00. Three volumes.

Contains more than 40,000 entries covering food companies, beverages, food equipment, warehouse companies, food brokers, wholesalers, importers, and exporters. Formerly *Thomas Food Industry Register*.

ENCYCLOPEDIAS AND DICTIONARIES

Encyclopedia of Aquaculture. Robert R. Stickney. John Wiley and Sons, Inc. • 2000. $415.00. Includes both economic and biological aspects of aquaculture and fish farming.

INTERNET DATABASES

USDA. United States Department of Agriculture. Phone: (202)720-2791 E-mail: agsec@usda.gov • URL: http://www.usda.gov • The USDA home page has six sections: News and Information; What's New; About USDA; Agencies; Opportunities; Search and Help. Keyword searching is offered from the USDA home page and from various individual agency home pages. Agencies are the Economic Research Service, Agricultural Marketing Service, National Agricultural Statistics Service, National Agricultural Library, and about 12 others. Updating varies. Fees: Free.

ONLINE DATABASES

Food Science and Technology Abstracts [online]. IFIS North American Desk. • Produced by International Food Information Service. Provides about 500,000 online citations, with abstracts, to the international literature of food science, technology, commodities, engineering, and processing. Approximately 2,000 periodicals are covered. Time period is 1969 to date, with monthly updates. Inquire as to online cost and availability.

PERIODICALS AND NEWSLETTERS

Commercial Fisheries News. Compass Publications, Fisheries Division. • Monthly. $21.95 per year. Covers the commercial fishing industry in New England. Includes news of marine technology, boatbuilding, fish and lobster prices, business trends, government regulation, and other topics.

Fisheries. American Fisheries Society. • Monthly. $76.00 per year. Covers the management of fisheries and aquatic resources, including related technology.

North American Journal of Fisheries Management. American Fisheries Society. • Quarterly. $499.00 per year. Covers fisheries management trends and research.

Seafood Business. Diversified Business Communications. • Monthly. $69.00 per year. Edited for a wide range of seafood buyers, including distributors, restaurants, supermarkets, and institutions. Special issues feature information on specific products, such as salmon or lobster.

PRICE SOURCES

Seafood Price-Current. Urner Barry Publications, Inc. • Semiweekly. $295.00 per year.

RESEARCH CENTERS AND INSTITUTES

Darling Marine Center. University of Maine, 193 Clarks Cove Rd., Walpole, ME 04573. Phone: (207)563-3146 Fax: (207)563-3119 E-mail: kevin@ maine.maine.edu • URL: http://www.server.dmc. maine.edu • *Formerly Ira C. Darling Center for Research, Teaching, and Service*.

Institute for Fisheries Research. 212 Museums Annex Bldg., 1109 N. University Ave., Ann Arbor, MI 48109-1084. Phone: (734)663-3554 Fax: (734)663-9399 E-mail: seelbacp@state.mi.us • URL: http:// www.dnr.state.mi.us.

Mote Marine Laboratory. Mote Marine Laboratory. 1600 Ken Thompson Pky., Sarasota, FL 34236-1096. Phone: 800-691-6683 or (941)388-4441 Fax: (941)388-4312 E-mail: president@mote.org • URL: http://www.mote.org • Wetland and estuarine ecology, habitat restoration, toxic organic chemistry, physical chemistry, biochemistry, analytical

chemistry, marine chemistry, fisheries, aquaculture, fish stock enhancement, benthic fauna, phytoplankton, meroplankton, ichthyoplankton, landscape ecology, marine mammals and turtles, sediments, red tide, aerosols, neurobiology, cancer resistance in sharks, elasmobranch immunology and cell culture, bioassays, toxicology, bioactive substances, corals, development of skate as a standardized laboratory animal, and reproductive patterns of sharks, skates and rays.

Scripps Institution of Oceanography-Integrative Oceanography Div. 9500 Gilman Dr., La Jolla, CA 92093-0233. Phone: (858)534-3624 Fax: (858)534-5306 E-mail: scrippsnews@ucsd.edu • URL: http:// www.sio.ucsd.edu.

University of California, San Diego. Scripps Institution of Oceanography, Integrative Oceanography Div., 9500 Gilman Dr., La Jolla, CA 92093-0227. Phone: (858)534-2068 Fax: (858)534-6500 E-mail: evenrick@ucsd.edu • URL: http://www.mlrg.ucsd. edu/ • *Formerly Marine Life Research Group*.

STATISTICS SOURCES

Agricultural Statistics. Available from U. S. Government Printing Office. • Annual. $38.00. Produced by the National Agricultural Statistics Service, U. S. Department of Agriculture. Provides a wide variety of statistical data relating to agricultural production, supplies, consumption, prices/price-supports, foreign trade, costs, and returns, as well as farm labor, loans, income, and population. In many cases, historical data is shown annually for 10 years. In addition to farm data, includes detailed fishery statistics.

Annual Survey of Manufactures. Available from U. S. Government Printing Office. • Annual. Prices vary. Issued by the U. S. Census Bureau as an interim update to the *Census of Manufactures*. Includes data on number of manufacturing establishments in various industries, employment, labor costs, value of shipments, capital expenditures, inventories, energy costs, and assets. (See also Census Bureau home page, http://www.census. gov/.).

FAO Fishery Series. Food and Agriculture Organization of the United States. Available from Bernan Associates. • Irregular. Price varies. Text in English, French, and Spanish. Incorporates *Yearbook of Fishery Statistics*.

Fisheries of the United States. Available from U. S. Government Printing Office. • Annual. $20.00. Issued by the National Marine Fisheries Service, National Oceanic and Atmospheric Administration, U. S. Department of Commerce.

Imports and Exports of Fishery Products. National Marine Fisheries Service. U.S. Department of Commerce. • Annual.

Infrastructure Industries USA. Gale Cengage Learning. • 2001. $260.00. Presents statistics and projections relating to economic activity in a wide variety of natural resource and construction industries.

World Food Data and Statistics. Euromonitor International. • 2004. $650.00. Provides five-year data for a wide variety of food products in 52 countries. Includes market size, consumer expenditures, price indicators, and retail distribution data for many kinds of meat, fish, fruits, vegetables, dairy products, baked goods, condiments, canned food, and frozen food.

TRADE/PROFESSIONAL ASSOCIATIONS

American Fisheries Society. 5410 Grosvenor Ln., Ste. 110, Bethesda, MD 20814-2199. Phone: (301)897-8616 Fax: (301)897-8096 E-mail: main@ fisheries.org • URL: http://www.fisheries.org • International scientific organization of fisheries and aquatic science professionals, including fish culturists, fish biologists, water quality scientists, fish health professionals, fish technologists, educators,

limnologists, and oceanographers. Promotes the development of all branches of fishery science and practice, and the conservation, development, and wise utilization of fisheries, both recreational and commercial. Strengthens professional standards by certifying fisheries scientists, stressing professional ethics, and providing forums for the exchange of scientific and management information. Represents members through written and verbal testimony before legislative and administrative bodies concerning aquatic environmental issues. Maintains over 30 committees.

OTHER SOURCES

The Seafood Market. MarketResearch.com. • 1997. $1,625.00. Market research report. Covers fresh, frozen, and canned seafood. Market projections are provided.

FITNESS INDUSTRY

ABSTRACTS AND INDEXES

Readers' Guide to Periodical Literature. H. W. Wilson Co. • Monthly. $345.00 per year. Includes annual *Cumulation*. Indexes about 250 peridicals of general interest.

CD-ROM DATABASES

WILSONDISC: Readers' Guide to Periodical Literature. H. W. Wilson Co. • Monthly. $1,095.00 per year, including unlimited online access to *Readers' Guide to Periodical Literature* through WILSONLINE. Provides CD-ROM indexing of about 270 general interest periodicals. Covers 1983 to date. (*Readers' Guide Abstracts* also available on CD-ROM at $1,995 per year.).

DIRECTORIES

Club Industry: Buyers Guide. Primedia Business Magazines and Media. • Annual. $25.00. A directory of over 1,000 companies furnishing equipment, supplies, and services to health and fitness clubs.

Fitness Management Products and Services Source Guide. Leisure Publications. • Annual. $24.00. A directory of more than 1,250 fitness equipment manufacturers and suppliers of services. Includes a glossary of terms related to the fitness industry and employee wellness programs.

Looking Fit Buyers Guide. Virgo Publishing, Inc. • Annual. $4.00. Lists suppliers of products and equipment for health clubs, aerobic studios, and tanning salons.

HANDBOOKS AND MANUALS

Children's Fitness Center. Entrepreneur Media, Inc. • Looseleaf. $59.50. A practical guide to starting a physical fitness center for children. Covers profit potential, start-up costs, market size evaluation, owner's time required, site selection, lease negotiation, pricing, accounting, advertising, promotion, etc. (Start-Up Business Guide No. E1351.).

Physical Fitness Center. Entrepreneur Media, Inc. • Looseleaf. $59.50. A practical guide to starting a physical fitness center. Covers profit potential, start-up costs, market size evaluation, owner's time required, site selection, lease negotiation, pricing, accounting, advertising, promotion, etc. (Start-Up Business Guide No. E1172.).

ONLINE DATABASES

Newspaper Abstracts Daily. ProQuest Inc. • Provides online coverage (citations and abstracts) of 25 major newspapers. Covers business, economics, current affairs, health, fitness, sports, education, technology, government, consumer affairs, psychology, the arts, and the social sciences. Time period is 1986 to date, with daily updates. Inquire as to online cost and availability.

PROMT: Predicasts Overview of Markets and Technology. Gale Cengage Learning. • Companies, products, applied technologies and markets. U.S.

and international literature coverage, 1972 to date. Inquire as to online cost and availability. Provides abstracts from more than 1,600 publications. Weekly updates.

Readers' Guide Abstracts Online. H. W. Wilson Co. • Indexes and abstracts general interest periodicals, 1983 to date. Weekly updates. Inquire as to online cost and availability.

PERIODICALS AND NEWSLETTERS

Athletic Business. Athletic Business Publications, Inc. • Monthly. $55.00 per year. Published for those whose responsibility is the business of planning, financing and operating athletic/recreation/fitness programs and facilities.

Fitness Management. Leisure Publications, Inc. • Monthly. $24.00 per year. Published for owners and managers of physical fitness centers, both commercial and corporate.

Looking Fit. Virgo Publishing, Inc. • 14 times a year. $52.00 per year. Covers the business and marketing side of health clubs, aerobic studios, and tanning salons.

RESEARCH CENTERS AND INSTITUTES

Center for Exercise Science. University of Florida, 25 Florida Gym, Gainesville, FL 32611. Phone: (352)392-9575 Fax: (352)392-0316 E-mail: spowers@hhp.ufl.edu • Studies fitness as it relates to the general population and as it relates to athletic performance.

Health Management Research Center. University of Michigan, 1027 E. Huron St., Ann Arbor, MI 48104-1688. Phone: (734)763-2462 Fax: (734)763-2206 E-mail: dwe@umich.edu • URL: http://www.umich.edu/~hmrc.

High Technology Fitness Research Institute. 1510 W. Montana St., Chicago, IL 60614. Phone: (773)528-1000 Fax: (773)528-1043 E-mail: bgoldman@worldhealth.net • URL: http://www.worldhealth.net • Research activities include the analysis of health and fitness products and programs on the market.

Human Power, Biochemechanics, and Robotics Laboratory. Cornell University, Dept. of Theoretical and Applied Mechanics, 306 Kimball Hall, Ithaca, NY 14853-1503. Phone: (607)255-7108 Fax: (607)255-2011 E-mail: ruina@cornell.edu • URL: http://www.tam.cornell.edu/~ruina • Conducts research relating to human muscle-powered machines, such as bicycles and rowers.

National Institute for Fitness and Sport. 250 University Blvd., Indianapolis, IN 46202-5192. Phone: (317)274-3432 Fax: (317)274-7408 • URL: http://www.nifs.org.

STATISTICS SOURCES

Profiles of Success. International Health, Racquet, and Sportsclub Association. • Annual. Members, $125.00; non-members, $500.00. Provides detailed financial statistics for commercial health clubs, sports clubs, and gyms.

United States Census of Service Industries. U.S. Bureau of the Census. • Quinquennial. Various reports available.

TRADE/PROFESSIONAL ASSOCIATIONS

Aerobics and Fitness Association of America. 15250 Ventura Blvd., Suite 200, Sherman Oaks, CA 91403. Phone: 877-968-7263 or 800-446-2322 Fax: (818)788-6301 E-mail: contactafaa@afaa.com • URL: http://www.afaa.com • Members are fitness professionals and aerobic exercise instructors.

American Spa and Health Resort Association. P.O. Box 585, Lake Forest, IL 60045. Phone: (847)234-8851 Fax: (847)295-7790 • Members are owners and operators of health spas.

Association for Worksite Health Promotion. 60 Revere Dr., Suite 500, Northbrook, IL 60062-1577.

Phone: (847)480-9574 Fax: (847)480-9282 E-mail: awhp@awhp.com • URL: http://www.awhp.com • Members are physical fitness professionals hired by major corporations to conduct health and fitness programs. Formerly Association for Fitness in Business.

Fitness Motivation Institute. 26685 Sussex Hwy., Ste. B, Seaford, DE 19973. Phone: 800-538-7790 E-mail: info@fmia.com • URL: http://www.fmia.com • Seeks to motivate, educate, and evaluate individuals in the area of physical fitness. Members are health and fitness professionals.

IDEA, The Health and Fitness Source. 6190 Cornerstone Court E., Suite 204, San Diego, CA 92121-3733. Phone: 800-999-4332 or (619)535-8979 Fax: (619)535-8234 E-mail: member@ideafit.com • URL: http://www.ideafit.com • An educational network and forum for fitness instructors, personal trainers, exercise club owners, and others. Formerly The Health and Fitness Source.

International Health, Racquet and Sportsclub Association. 263 Summer St., Boston, MA 02210. Phone: 800-228-4772 or (617)951-0055 Fax: (617)951-0056 E-mail: info@ihrsa.org • URL: http://www.ihrsa.org • Members are for-profit health clubs, sports clubs, and gyms. Formerly IRSA, The Association of Quality Clubs.

International Physical Fitness Association. 415 W Court St., Flint, MI 48503. Phone: 877-520-IPFA or (810)239-2166 Fax: (810)239-9390 E-mail: contact@ipfa.us • URL: http://www.ipfa.us • Physical fitness centers. Facilitates the transfer of individual memberships from one member club to another.

National Health Club Association. 640 Plaza Dr., Ste. 300, Highlands Ranch, CO 80129. Phone: 800-765-6422 or (303)753-6422 Fax: (303)980-8006 E-mail: haynha@aol.com • URL: http://www.nhcainsurance.com • Fitness centers and health clubs. Provides insurance and financial services to the fitness center/health club industry nationwide. Awards strength and aerobic certification.

National Spa and Pool Institute. 2111 Eisenhower Ave., Alexandria, VA 22314. Phone: (703)838-0083 Fax: (703)549-0493 E-mail: memberservices@nspi.org • URL: http://www.nspi.org • Members include a wide variety of business firms and individuals involved in some way with health spas, swimming pools, or hot tubs. Formerly National Swimming Pool Institute.

National Sports and Fitness Association. 1945 Palo Verde Ave., Suite 202, Long Beach, CA 90815. Phone: (562)799-8333 Fax: (562)799-3355 E-mail: info@nsfa-online.com • URL: http://www.nsfa-online.com • Members are health and fitness professionals. Formerly American Fitness Association.

United States Association of Independent Gymnastic Clubs. 22 River Terrace, Ste. 2D, New York, NY 10282. Phone: 800-480-0201 or (212)227-9792 Fax: (212)227-9793 E-mail: usaigcpsnyz@aol.com • URL: http://www.usaigc.com • Members include gym clubs and manufacturers of gymnastic equipment.

OTHER SOURCES

Consumer Attitudes Toward Physical Fitness. Available from MarketResearch.com. • 2002. $375.00. Published by American Sports Data, Inc. Contains market research information.

The Market for Physical Fitness and Exercise Equipment. MarketResearch.com. • 1999. $3,250.00. Provides consumer and institutional market data, with forecasts to the year 2003.

Superstudy of Sports Participation. Available from MarketResearch.com. • 2002. $700.00. Three volumes. Published by American Sports Data, Inc. Provides market research data on 102 sports and activities. Vol. 1: *Physical Fitness Activities.* Vol. 2:

Recreational Sports. Vol. 3: *Outdoor Activities.* (Volumes are available separately at $295.00.).

Weight Loss and Diet Control Market. Available from MarketResearch.com. • 2002. $795.00. Market research report published by Marketdata Enterprises. Covers commercial diet programs, medical plans, nonprescription appetite suppressants low-calorie foods, artifical sweeteners, health clubs, and diet books. Includes forecasts to the year 2006.

FIXED INCOME SECURITIES

See: BONDS

FLAVORINGS

See: ADDITIVES AND FLAVORINGS

FLOOR COVERINGS

ALMANACS AND YEARBOOKS

Flooring Buying and Resource Guide. Douglas Publications, Inc. • Annual. $42.50. Lists of manufacturers, workroom manufacturers' representatives, and distributors of floor and other interior surfacing products and equipment; carpet inspection servicecompanies' and related trade associations in the United States and Canada. Formerly *Flooring Directory and Buying Guide.*

DIRECTORIES

Floor Covering Weekly--Annual Product Source Guide. FCW. • Publication includes: Lists of manufacturers and importers of carpet, rugs, carpet cushion, fiber, resilient wood, and ceramic floor coverings; separate listing of distributors by state, retail groups and associations. Entries include: For manufacturers--Company name, address, phone, regional sales offices, names and titles of key personnel, local distributors, products. For distributors--Company name, address, phone, manufacturers represented.

ICS Cleaning Specialists Annual Trade Directory and Buying Guide. Business News Publishing Co., II, L.L.C. • Annual. $25.00. Lists about 6,000 manufacturers and distributors of floor covering installation and cleaning equipment. Formerly *Installation and Cleaning Specialists Trade Directory and Buying Guide.*

FINANCIAL RATIOS

Annual Statement Studies. The Risk Management Association. • Annual. Median and quartile financial ratios are given for over 400 kinds of manufacturing, wholesale, retail, construction, and consumer finance establishments. Data is sorted by both asset size and sales volume. Includes a clearly written "Definition of Ratios" and an alphabetical industry index.

Annual Statement Studies: Industry Default Probabilities and Cash Flow Measures. The Risk Management Association. • Annual. $145.00. Serves as a companion volume to the original *Annual Statement Studies.* Gives probability of default estimates on a percentage scale for more than 450 industries. Includes changes in position year-by-year for eight financial statement line items and provides percentage measures of cash flow.

INTERNET DATABASES

Manufacturing Profiles. U. S. Bureau of the Census. Phone: (301)763-4636 E-mail: webmaster@census.gov • URL: http://www.census.gov/prod/www/abs/mfg-prof.html • The Census Bureau makes available free on PDF (Portable Document Format) an annual consolidation of the entire Current Industrial Report series, presenting "all the data compiled."

Contains statistics on production, shipments, inventories, consumption, exports, imports, and orders for a wide variety of manufactured products.

ONLINE DATABASES

F & S Index. Gale Cengage Learning. • Contains about four million citations to worldwide business, financial, and industrial or consumer product literature appearing from 1972 to date. Weekly updates. Inquire as to online cost and availability.

PERIODICALS AND NEWSLETTERS

Carpet and Rug Industry. Rodman Publications. • Monthly. $42.00 per year. Edited for manufacturers and distributors of carpets and rugs.

Carpet Flooring Retail. CMP Information, Ltd. • Biweekly. $92.00 per year. Formerly *Carpet and Floorcoverings Review.*

Dalton Carpet Journal. Daily Citizen-News. • Monthly. $12.00. Covers the international tufted carpet market.

Floor Covering News. Roel Product Inc. • Biweekly. $25.00 per year. For retailers, distributors, contractors, and manufacturers.

Floor Covering Weekly: The Business Newspaper of the Floor Covering Industry. FCW. • 32 times a year. $61.00 per year.

ICS Cleaning Specialist (Installationa and Cleaning Specialist). Business News Publishing Co. • Monthly. Free to qualified personnel. Written for floor covering installers and cleaners. Formerly *Installation and Cleaning Specialist.*

Oriental Rug Review. Oriental Rug Auction Review, Inc. • Bimonthly. $48.00 per year.

Paint and Decorating Retailer. Paint and Decorating Retailers Association. • Monthly. $45.00 per year. Formerly *Decorating Retailer.*

STATISTICS SOURCES

Annual Survey of Manufactures. Available from U. S. Government Printing Office. • Annual. Prices vary. Issued by the U. S. Census Bureau as an interim update to the *Census of Manufactures.* Includes data on number of manufacturing establishments in various industries, employment, labor costs, value of shipments, capital expenditures, inventories, energy costs, and assets. (See also Census Bureau home page, http://www.census.gov/.).

U. S. Industry and Trade Outlook. Available from National Technical Information Service. • Annual. $69.95. Produced by the International Trade Administration, U. S. Department of Commerce, in a "public-private" partnership with DRI/McGraw-Hill and Standard & Poor's. Provides basic data, outlook for the current year, and "Long-Term Prospects" (five-year projections) for a wide variety of products and services. Includes high technology industries. Formerly *U. S. Industrial Outlook.*

United States Census of Manufactures. U.S. Bureau of the Census. • Quinquennial. Results presented in reports, tape, CD-ROM, and Diskette files.

WEFA Industrial Monitor. John Wiley and Sons, Inc. • Annual. $65.00. Prepared by industry analysts at WEFA, an economic forecasting and consulting firm (originally Wharton Econometric Forecasting Associates). Contains discussions of the outlook for major U. S. industries, with many 10-year forecasts (WEFA Web site is http://www.wefa.com).

TRADE/PROFESSIONAL ASSOCIATIONS

Carpet and Rug Institute. 310 Holiday Ave., Dalton, GA 30722. Phone: 800-882-8846 or (706)278-3176 Fax: (706)278-8835 • URL: http://www.carpet-rug.com • Formerly Tufted Textile Manufacturers Association.

Carpet Cushion Council. 23 Courtney Cir., Bryn Mawr, PA 19010. Phone: (610)527-3880 Fax: (610)527-8535 E-mail: carpetcushion@msn.com •

URL: http://www.carpetcushion.org • Works to promote the sale and use of separate carpet cushions; to act as public relations counsel for the industry; to maintain contact with various government agencies; to establish quality and performance standards. Compiles statistics; maintains speakers' bureau.

Jute Carpet Backing Council and Burlap and Jute Association. c/o Textile Bag and Packaging Association, 322 Davis Ave., Dayton, OH 45401. Phone: 800-543-3400 or (937)476-8272 Fax: (937)258-0029 E-mail: tbpa@aol.com • Affiliated with Burlap and Jute Association. Formerly Jute Carpet Backing Council.

OTHER SOURCES

Carpets and Rugs. Available from MarketResearch.com. • 2001. $4,000.00. Market research data. Published by the Freedonia Group. Provides both historical data and forecasts to 2007 for various kinds of carpeting.

Floor Coverings. Available from MarketResearch.com. • 2002. $3,950.00. Published by Global Industry Analysts. Provides worldwide market research data, including profiles of major floor covering companies.

Laminate Flooring. Available from MarketResearch.com. • 1997. $495.00. Market research report published by Specialists in Business Information. Presents laminate flooring market data relative to demographics, sales growth, shipments, exports, imports, price trends, and end-use. Includes company profiles.

U. S. Floor Coverings Industry. Available from MarketResearch.com. • 2000. $1,795.00. Market research report published by Specialists in Business Information. Covers carpets, hardwood flooring, and tile. Presents market data relative to demographics, sales growth, shipments, exports, imports, price trends, and end-use. Includes company profiles.

Vinyl Sheet and Floor Tile. Available from MarketResearch.com. • 1997. $495.00. Market research report published by Specialists in Business Information. Presents vinyl flooring market data relative to demographics, sales growth, shipments, exports, imports, price trends, and end-use. Includes company profiles.

Wood Flooring. Available from MarketResearch.com. • 1999. $2,250.00. Market research report published by Specialists in Business Information. Presents hardwood flooring market data relative to demographics, sales growth, shipments, exports, imports, price trends, and end-use. Includes company profiles.

FLORIST SHOPS

See also: NURSERIES (HORTICULTURAL)

GENERAL WORKS

Retail Florist Business. Peter B. Pfahl and P. Blair Pfahl. Interstate Publishers, Inc. • 1994. $48.75. Fifth edition.

DIRECTORIES

Florist-Buyers Directory. Florist's Transworld Delivery Association. • Annual. $7.00. Lists 1,200 suppliers in floral industry.

Wholesale Florists and Florist Suppliers Association Membership Directory. Wholesale Florists and Florist Suppliers Association. • Free to members; non-members, $100.00.

FINANCIAL RATIOS

Annual Statement Studies. The Risk Management Association. • Annual. Median and quartile financial ratios are given for over 400 kinds of manufacturing, wholesale, retail, construction, and consumer finance establishments. Data is sorted by both asset size and sales volume. Includes a clearly written

"Definition of Ratios" and an alphabetical industry index.

Annual Statement Studies: Industry Default Probabilities and Cash Flow Measures. The Risk Management Association. • Annual. $145.00. Serves as a companion volume to the original *Annual Statement Studies.* Gives probability of default estimates on a percentage scale for more than 450 industries. Includes changes in position year-by-year for eight financial statement line items and provides percentage measures of cash flow.

HANDBOOKS AND MANUALS

Flower Shop. Entrepreneur Media, Inc. • Looseleaf. $59.50. A practical guide to starting a retail flower shop. Covers profit potential, start-up costs, market size evaluation, owner's time required, site selection, lease negotiation, pricing, accounting, advertising, promotion, etc. (Start-Up Business Guide No. E1143.).

PERIODICALS AND NEWSLETTERS

Florafacts. Florafax International, Inc. • Monthly. $15.00 per year.

Florists' Review. Florists' Review Enterprises. • Monthly. $39.00 per year.

Flowers &: The Beautiful Magazine About the Business of Flowers. Teleflora, Inc. • Monthly. $38.95 per year.

STATISTICS SOURCES

United States Census of Retail Trade. U.S. Bureau of the Census. • Quinquennial.

TRADE/PROFESSIONAL ASSOCIATIONS

Society of American Florists. 1601 Duke St., Alexandria, VA 22314-3406. Phone: 800-336-4743 or (703)836-8700 Fax: (703)836-8705 E-mail: memberinfo@safnow.org • URL: http://www.safnow.org • Members are growers, wholesalers, retailers and allied tradesmen in the floral industry. Formerly SAF-The Center for Commercial Floriculture.

Wholesale Florists and Florist Suppliers of America. 147 Old Solomons Island Rd., Suite 302, Annapolis, MD 21401-3838. Phone: (410)573-0400 Fax: (410)573-5001 E-mail: j.wanko@wffsa.org • URL: http://www.wffsa.org • Formerly Wholesale Commission Florists.

FLOUR INDUSTRY

See also: GRAIN INDUSTRY

ABSTRACTS AND INDEXES

Flour Milling and Baking Abstracts. CCFAA Technology Ltd. • Bimonthly. Members, $275.00 per year; non-members, $325.00 per year. Includes print and online editions.

CD-ROM DATABASES

Food Science and Technology Abstracts [CD-ROM]. Available from SilverPlatter Information, Inc. • Quarterly. Produced by International Food Information Service (home page is http://www.ifis.org). Provides worldwide coverage on CD-ROM of the literature of food technology and production. Various types of publications are indexed, with abstracts, including about 1,800 periodicals. Time period is 1969 to date.

OECD Statistical Compendium. Organization for Economic Cooperation and Development. • Semiannual. $1,905.00 per year for 1 to 10 users. CD-ROM contains more than 730,000 monthly, quarterly, and annual time series for OECD countries, 1960 to date. Includes fully searchable data on agriculture, food, economic indicators, national accounts, employment, energy, finance, industry, technology, and foreign trade. Results can

be displayed in various forms.

DIRECTORIES

Major Food and Drink Companies of the World. Available from Gale Cengage Learning. • Annual. $880.00. Two volumes. Published by Graham & Whiteside. Contains profiles and trade names for more than 9,800 important food and beverage companies in various countries. In addition to foods, includes both alcoholic and nonalcoholic drink products.

Thomas Food and Beverage Market Place. Grey House Publishing. • 2004. $495.00. Three volumes. Contains more than 40,000 entries covering food companies, beverages, food equipment, warehouse companies, food brokers, wholesalers, importers, and exporters. Formerly *Thomas Food Industry Register.*

INTERNET DATABASES

Business 2.0 Web Guide to the Best Business Links. Business 2.0 Media Inc. Phone: (415)293-4800 E-mail: support@business2.com • URL: http://www.business2.com/webguide • Web site presents an extensive, searchable directory of links to "the best, most informative, and authoritative web pages." Twenty main categories cover business, finance, career, company information, people, and technology topics, with thousands of subtopics, all linking to Web sites recommended by experienced business researchers. Fees: Free.

Fedstats. Federal Interagency Council on Statistical Policy. Phone: (202)395-7254 • URL: http://www.fedstats.gov • Web site features an efficient search facility for full-text statistics produced by more than 100 federal agencies, including the Census Bureau, the Bureau of Economic Analysis, and the Bureau of Labor Statistics. Boolean searches can be made within one agency or for all agencies combined. Links are offered to international statistical bureaus, including the UN, IMF, OECD, UNESCO, Eurostat, and 20 individual countries. Fees: Free.

FreeLunch.com. Economy.com, Inc. Phone: (610)696-8700 Fax: (610)696-1678 • URL: http://www.freelunch.com • Web site provides free access to more than 1.5 million economic and financial data series, covering industry, demographics, labor markets, prices, retail sales, government spending, trade, interest rates, housing starts, the stock market, and many other topics. Data is available for various time periods in either chart or table form. Searching is offered. Fees: Free, but registration required. Economy.com, Inc. also offers fee-based economic analysis at *The Dismal Scientist* site (http://www.dismal.com).

Manufacturing Profiles. U. S. Bureau of the Census. Phone: (301)763-4636 E-mail: webmaster@census.gov • URL: http://www.census.gov/prod/www/abs/mfg-prof.html • The Census Bureau makes available free on PDF (Portable Document Format) an annual consolidation of the entire Current Industrial Report series, presenting "all the data compiled." Contains statistics on production, shipments, inventories, consumption, exports, imports, and orders for a wide variety of manufactured products.

USDA. United States Department of Agriculture. Phone: (202)720-2791 E-mail: agsec@usda.gov • URL: http://www.usda.gov • The USDA home page has six sections: News and Information; What's New; About USDA; Agencies; Opportunities; Search and Help. Keyword searching is offered from the USDA home page and from various individual agency home pages. Agencies are the Economic Research Service, Agricultural Marketing Service, National Agricultural Statistics Service, National Agricultural Library, and about 12 others. Updating varies. Fees: Free.

ONLINE DATABASES

Food Science and Technology Abstracts [online]. IFIS North American Desk. • Produced by International Food Information Service. Provides about 500,000 online citations, with abstracts, to the international literature of food science, technology, commodities, engineering, and processing. Approximately 2,000 periodicals are covered. Time period is 1969 to date, with monthly updates. Inquire as to online cost and availability.

PRICE SOURCES

Commercial Review. Oregon Feed and Grain Association. Commercial Review, Inc. • Weekly. $35.00 per year.

RESEARCH CENTERS AND INSTITUTES

Food and Feed Grains Institute. Kansas State University. 105 Waters Hall, Manhattan, KS 66506-4030. Phone: (785)532-4056 Fax: (785)532-5861 E-mail: ffgi@ksu.edu • URL: http://www.ksu.edu/ffgi.

Plant Biotechnology Institute. National Research Council of Canada. 110 Gymnasium Place, Saskatoon, SK, Canada S7N 0W9. Phone: (306)975-5248 Fax: (306)975-4839 E-mail: lisa.jategaonkar@nrc.ca • URL: http://www.pbi-ibp.nrc.

STATISTICS SOURCES

Agricultural Statistics. Available from U. S. Government Printing Office. • Annual. $38.00. Produced by the National Agricultural Statistics Service, U. S. Department of Agriculture. Provides a wide variety of statistical data relating to agricultural production, supplies, consumption, prices/price-supports, foreign trade, costs, and returns, as well as farm labor, loans, income, and population. In many cases, historical data is shown annually for 10 years. In addition to farm data, includes detailed fishery statistics.

Annual Survey of Manufactures. Available from U. S. Government Printing Office. • Annual. Prices vary. Issued by the U. S. Census Bureau as an interim update to the *Census of Manufactures.* Includes data on number of manufacturing establishments in various industries, employment, labor costs, value of shipments, capital expenditures, inventories, energy costs, and assets. (See also Census Bureau home page, http://www.census.gov/.).

Business Statistics of the United States. Linz Audain and Cornelia J. Strawser. Bernan Associates. • Annual. $147.00. Based on *Business Statistics,* formerly issue by the Bureau of Economic Analysis, U. S. Department of Commerce. Provides basic data for a wide variety of U. S. industries, services, and economic indicators. Most statistics are shown annually for 30 years and monthly for the most recent four years.

FAO Production Yearbook. Available from Bernan Associates. • Annual. $45.00. Published by the Food and Agriculture Organization (http://www.fao.org). Contains worldwide data on agriculture, land use, farm crops, livestock, and agricultural prices.

FAO Trade Yearbook. Available from Bernan Associates. • Annual. $45.00. Published by the Food and Agriculture Organization (http://www.fao.org). Provides extensive worldwide data on exports and imports of agricultural commodities, fertilizers, tractors, and pesticides. Includes more than 130 tables of detailed statistics.

Flour Milling Products. U. S. Bureau of the Census. • Monthly and annual. Covers production, mill stocks, exports, and imports of wheat and rye flour. (Current Industrial Reports, M20A.).

Survey of Current Business. Available from U. S. Government Printing Office. • Monthly. $63.00 per year. Issued by Bureau of Economic Analysis, U. S. Department of Commerce. Presents a wide variety of business and economic data.

World Food Data and Statistics. Euromonitor International. • 2004. $650.00. Provides five-year data for a wide variety of food products in 52 countries. Includes market size, consumer expenditures, price indicators, and retail distribution data for many kinds of meat, fish, fruits, vegetables, dairy products, baked goods, condiments, canned food, and frozen food.

TRADE/PROFESSIONAL ASSOCIATIONS

American Institute of Baking. 1213 Bakers Way, Manhattan, KS 66505. Phone: 800-633-5137 or (785)537-4750 Fax: (785)537-1493 E-mail: info@aibonline.org • URL: http://www.aibonline.org.

Association of Operative Millers. 5001 College Blvd., Suite 104, Leawood, KS 66211. Phone: (913)338-3377 Fax: (913)338-3553 E-mail: aom@sky.net • URL: http://www.aomillers.org.

National Association of Flour Distributors. c/o David Scruggs, P.O. Box 165067, Little Rock, AR 72216. Phone: (501)372-0636 Fax: (501)372-2468 • Affiliated with National Association of Wholesaler-Distributors.

North American Millers' Association. 600 Maryland Ave. SW, Ste. 825 W, Washington, DC 20024. Phone: (202)484-2200 Fax: (202)488-7416 E-mail: generalinfo@namamillers.org • URL: http://www.namamillers.org • Millers of wheat, corn, oats, durum, and rye flour; members mill 95 percent of total U.S. capacity.

FLUIDICS INDUSTRY

See also: HYDRAULIC ENGINEERING AND MACHINERY

ABSTRACTS AND INDEXES

Applied Science and Technology Index. H. W. Wilson Co. • 11 times a year. Quarterly and annual cumulations. Price varies. Indexes a wide variety of English language technical, industrial, and engineering periodicals.

Current Contents: Engineering, Computing and Technology. Thomson/ISI. • Weekly. $730.00 per year. Reproductions of contents pages of technical journals. Includes *Author Index, Address Directory, Current Book Contents* and *Title Word Index.* Formerly *Current Contents: Engineering, Technology and Applied Sciences.*

Mechanical Engineering Abstracts. CSA. • Bimonthly. $1,620.00 per year. Includes print and online editions. Formerly *ISMEC - Mechanical Engineering Abstracts.*

CD-ROM DATABASES

Science Citation Index: Compact Disc Edition. Institute for Scientific Information. • Monthly. Provides CD-ROM indexing of the world's scientific and technical literature. Corresponds to online *Scisearch* and printed *Science Citation Index.*

DIRECTORIES

Fluid Power Handbook and Directory. Penton Media, Inc. • Biennial. $95.00 per year. Over 1,500 manufacturers and 3,000 distributors of fluid power products in the United States and Canada.

Thomas Register of American Manufacturers. Thomas Publishing Co., Inc. • Annual. $149.00. 34 volumes. A three-part system offering information on a wide variety of industrial equipment and supplies. Lists more than 151,000 industrial product and services companies.

INTERNET DATABASES

Manufacturing Profiles. U. S. Bureau of the Census. Phone: (301)763-4636 E-mail: webmaster@census.gov • URL: http://www.census.gov/prod/www/abs/mfg-prof.html • The Census Bureau makes available free on PDF (Portable Document Format) an annual consolidation of the entire Current Industrial Report series, presenting "all the data compiled." Contains statistics on production, shipments, inventories, consumption, exports, imports, and orders for a wide variety of manufactured products.

ONLINE DATABASES

Applied Science and Technology Index Online. H. W. Wilson Co. • Provides online indexing of 500 major scientific, technical, industrial, and engineering periodicals. Time period is 1983 to date. Monthly updates. Inquire as to online cost and availability.

FLUIDEX. Elsevier Science, Inc. • Produced in the Netherlands by Elsevier Science B.V. Provides indexing and abstracting of the international literature of fluid engineering and technology, 1973 to date, with monthly updates. Also known as *Fluid Engineering Abstracts.* Inquire as to online cost and availability.

PROMT: Predicasts Overview of Markets and Technology. Gale Cengage Learning. • Companies, products, applied technologies and markets. U.S. and international literature coverage, 1972 to date. Inquire as to online cost and availability. Provides abstracts from more than 1,600 publications. Weekly updates.

Scisearch. Institute for Scientific Information. • Broad, multidisciplinary index to the literature of science and technology, 1974 to present. Inquire as to online cost and availability. Coverage of literature is worldwide, with weekly updates.

Thomas Register Online. Thomas Publishing Co., Inc. • Provides concise information on approximately 194,000 U. S. companies, mainly manufacturers, with over 50,000 product classifications. Indexes over 115,000 trade names. Information is updated semiannually. Inquire as to online cost and availability.

PERIODICALS AND NEWSLETTERS

FPDA News. Fluid Power Distributors Association. • Description: Provides sales, marketing tips, and cost-cutting ideas submitted by members. Recurring features include news of the Association and its members, news of research, statistics, a calendar of events, and obituaries.

Hydraulics and Pneumatics: The Magazine of Fluid Power and Motion Control Systems. Penton Media, Inc. • Monthly. $65.00 per year.

Industrial Equipment News. Thomas Publishing Co., LLC. • Monthly. $65.00 per year. What's new in equipment, parts and materials.

National Fluid Power Association--Reporter. National Fluid Power Association. • Description: Includes articles on the fluid power market, manufacturing, people and meetings. Also includes statistics.

New Equipment Digest. Penton Media, Inc. • Monthly. Free to qualified personnel; others, $60.00 per year. Formerly *Material Handling Engineering.*

New Equipment Reporter: New Products Industrial News. De Roche Publications. • Monthly. Controlled circulation.

Processing. Putman Media. • 14 times a year. $54.00 per year. Emphasis is on descriptions of new products for all areas of industrial processing, including valves, controls, filters, pumps, compressors, fluidics, and instrumentation.

RESEARCH CENTERS AND INSTITUTES

Fluid Power Institute. Milwaukee School of Engineering, Milwaukee, WI 53202. Phone: (414)277-7191 Fax: (414)277-7470 E-mail: wanke@msoe.edu • URL: http://www.msoe.edu.

Fluid Power Laboratory. Ohio State University, Mechanical Engineering Department, 206 W. 18th Ave., Columbus, OH 43210. Phone: (614)292-2289 Fax: (614)292-3163 • URL: http://www.mecheng.ohio-state.edu/.

STATISTICS SOURCES

Annual Survey of Manufactures. Available from U. S. Government Printing Office. • Annual. Prices vary. Issued by the U. S. Census Bureau as an interim update to the *Census of Manufactures.* Includes data on number of manufacturing establishments in various industries, employment, labor costs, value of shipments, capital expenditures, inventories, energy costs, and assets. (See also Census Bureau home page, http://www.census.gov/.).

TRADE/PROFESSIONAL ASSOCIATIONS

Fluid Power Distributors Association. PO Box 1420, 1930 East Marlton Pike Ste. A-2, Cherry Hill, NJ 08034-0054. Phone: (856)424-8998 Fax: (856)424-9248 E-mail: info@fpda.org • URL: http://www.fpda.org • Represents wholesalers and manufacturers involved in the distribution of hydraulic and pneumatic equipment. Works to advance the distribution of such equipment; conducts research and educational activities. Compiles statistics.

International Fluid Power Society. PO Box 1420, Cherry Hill, NJ 08034-0054. Phone: 800-303-8520 or (856)489-8983 Fax: (856)424-9248 E-mail: info@ifps.org • URL: http://www.ifps.org • Persons interested in all phases of fluid power and related motion control and its uses. Concerned with research, development, design, installation, operation, maintenance, education, and application to industry, aviation, marine, mobile, material handling, and agricultural equipment. Maintains speakers' bureau. Operates certification programs and placement service for fluid power mechanics, technicians, specialists, and engineers.

National Fluid Power Association. 3333 N Mayfair Rd., Ste. 211, Milwaukee, WI 53222-3219. Phone: (414)778-3344 Fax: (414)778-3361 E-mail: nfpa@nfpa.com • URL: http://www.nfpa.com • Manufacturers of components such as fittings used in transmitting power by hydraulic and pneumatic pumps, valves, cylinders, filters, seals; the components are used in industrial and mobile machinery in the material-handling, automotive, railway, aircraft, marine, aerospace, construction, agricultural, and other industries. Works to develop: American National Standards Institute and International Organization for Standardization (see separate entries); fluid power technical standards; fluid power index (industry sales); management and marketing studies. Compiles statistics. Administers and serves as secretariat to several international project groups and other fluid power organizations.

FLUORESCENT LIGHTING

See: LIGHTING

FLYING

See: AIR PILOTS; AIR TRAVEL; AIRLINE INDUSTRY; BUSINESS AVIATION

FM BROADCASTING

See: RADIO BROADCASTING INDUSTRY

FOCUS GROUPS

See: MARKET RESEARCH; SURVEY METHODS

FOOD ADDITIVES

See: ADDITIVES AND FLAVORINGS

FOOD EQUIPMENT AND MACHINERY

ABSTRACTS AND INDEXES

Applied Science and Technology Index. H. W. Wilson Co. • 11 times a year. Quarterly and annual cumulations. Price varies. Indexes a wide variety of English language technical, industrial, and engineering periodicals.

Food Science and Technology Abstracts. International Food Information Service Publishing. • Monthly. $1,780.00 per year. Provides worldwide coverage of the literature of food technology and food production.

Foods Adlibra: Key to the World's Food Literature. General Mills, Inc. Foods Adlibra Publications. • Semimonthly. $240.00 per year. Provides journal citations and abstracts to the literature of food technology and packaging.

ALMANACS AND YEARBOOKS

Almanac of the Canning, Freezing, Preserving Industries, Vol. Two. Edward E. Judge and Sons, Inc. • Annual. $73.00. Contains U. S. food laws and regulations and detailed production statistics.

CD-ROM DATABASES

Food Science and Technology Abstracts [CD-ROM]. Available from SilverPlatter Information, Inc. • Quarterly. Produced by International Food Information Service (home page is http://www.ifis.org). Provides worldwide coverage on CD-ROM of the literature of food technology and production. Various types of publications are indexed, with abstracts, including about 1,800 periodicals. Time period is 1969 to date.

DIRECTORIES

Food Master. BNP Media. • Covers: over 5,000 manufacturers and distributors of equipment, ingredients, services and supplies for food processing plants. Entries include: Company name, address, phone.

Food Processing Guide and Directory. Putman Media Inc. • Annual. $90.00. Lists over 5,390 food ingredient and equipment manufacturers.

Foodservice Equipment and Supplies Product Source Guide. Reed Business Information. • Annual. $35.00. Nearly 1,700 manufacturers of food service equipment and supplies. Formerly *Foodservice Equipment Buyer's Guide and Product Directory.*

Major Food and Drink Companies of the World. Available from Gale Cengage Learning. • Annual. $880.00. Two volumes. Published by Graham & Whiteside. Contains profiles and trade names for more than 9,800 important food and beverage companies in various countries. In addition to foods, includes both alcoholic and nonalcoholic drink products.

Prepared Foods Sourcebook. Reed Business Information. • Annual. $75.00. Lists approximately 600 food and veverage companies.

Thomas Food and Beverage Market Place. Grey House Publishing. • 2004. $495.00. Three volumes. Contains more than 40,000 entries covering food companies, beverages, food equipment, warehouse companies, food brokers, wholesalers, importers, and exporters. Formerly *Thomas Food Industry Register.*

Thomas Food and Beverage Market Place. Grey House Publishing. • 2004. $495.00. Three volumes. Contains more than 40,000 entries covering food companies, beverages, food equipment, warehouse companies, food brokers, wholesalers, importers, and exporters. Formerly *Thomas Food Industry Register.*

ENCYCLOPEDIAS AND DICTIONARIES

Wiley Encyclopedia of Packaging Technology. Aaron Brody and Kenneth Marsh, editors. John Wiley and Sons, Inc. • 1997. $330.00. Second edition.

ONLINE DATABASES

Food Science and Technology Abstracts [online]. IFIS North American Desk. • Produced by

International Food Information Service. Provides about 500,000 online citations, with abstracts, to the international literature of food science, technology, commodities, engineering, and processing. Approximately 2,000 periodicals are covered. Time period is 1969 to date, with monthly updates. Inquire as to online cost and availability.

FOODS ADLIBRA. General Mills, Inc. • Contains online citations, with abstracts, to the technical and business literature of food processing and packaging. New products and new ingredients are featured. Covers about 250 trade journals and 500 research journals from 1974 to date, with monthly updates. Inquire as to online cost and availability.

PERIODICALS AND NEWSLETTERS

Food Engineering and Ingredients. Reed Business Information. • Bimonthly. Price on application. Formerly *Food Engineering International.*

Food Manufacturing. Reed Business Information. • Monthly. $86.99 per year. Edited for food processing operations managers and food engineering managers. Includes end-of-year *Food Products and Equipment Literature Review.* Formerly *Food Products and Equipment.*

Food Processing. Putman Media. • Monthly. Free to qualified personnel; others, $89.00 per year. Edited for executive and operating personnel in the food processing industry.

Food Production-Management: Monthly Publication of the Canning, Glass-Packing, As eptic, and Frozen Food Industry. CTI Publications, Inc. • Monthly. $35.00 per year.

Foodservice Equipment and Supplies. Reed Business Information. • 13 times a year. $106.90 per year.

RESEARCH CENTERS AND INSTITUTES

Food Industries Center. Ohio State University, Howlett Hall, 2001 Fyffe Court, Columbus, OH 43210-1007. Phone: (614)292-7004 Fax: (614)292-4233 E-mail: bash1@osu.edu • URL: http://www.fst.ohio-state.edu.

Institute of Food Science. Cornell University, 114 Stocking Hall, Ithaca, NY 14853-7201. Phone: (607)255-7900 E-mail: cifs@cornell.edu • URL: http://www.nysaes.cornell.edu/cifs/ • Research areas include the chemistry and processing of food commodities, food processing engineering, food packaging, and nutrition.

National Food Processors Association Research Foundation. 1350 Eye St., N.W., Suite 300, Washington, DC 20005. Phone: (202)639-5900 Fax: (202)639-5932 E-mail: nfpa@nfpa.org • URL: http://www.nfpa-food.org • Conducts research on food processing engineering, chemistry, microbiology, sanitation, preservation aspects, and public health factors.

STATISTICS SOURCES

Annual Survey of Manufactures. Available from U. S. Government Printing Office. • Annual. Prices vary. Issued by the U. S. Census Bureau as an interim update to the *Census of Manufactures.* Includes data on number of manufacturing establishments in various industries, employment, labor costs, value of shipments, capital expenditures, inventories, energy costs, and assets. (See also Census Bureau home page, http://www.census.gov/.).

U. S. Industry and Trade Outlook. Available from National Technical Information Service. • Annual. $69.95. Produced by the International Trade Administration, U. S. Department of Commerce, in a "public-private" partnership with DRI/McGraw-Hill and Standard & Poor's. Provides basic data, outlook for the current year, and "Long-Term Prospects" (five-year projections) for a wide variety of products and services. Includes high technology industries. Formerly *U. S. Industrial Outlook.*

World Food Data and Statistics. Euromonitor International. • 2004. $650.00. Provides five-year data for a wide variety of food products in 52 countries. Includes market size, consumer expenditures, price indicators, and retail distribution data for many kinds of meat, fish, fruits, vegetables, dairy products, baked goods, condiments, canned food, and frozen food.

TRADE/PROFESSIONAL ASSOCIATIONS

Commercial Food Equipment Service Association. 2216 W Meadowview Rd., Ste. 100, Greensboro, NC 27407. Phone: 877-414-4127 or (336)346-4700 Fax: (336)346-4745 E-mail: cstrickland@cfesa.com • URL: http://www.cfesa.com • Represents firms that repair food preparation equipment used by restaurants, hotels, and institutions. Provides training and education for members and their employees.

FISA-Food Industry Suppliers Association. 1207 Sunset Dr., Greensboro, NC 27408. Phone: (336)274-6311 Fax: (336)691-1839 E-mail: stella@fisanet.org • URL: http://www.fisanet.org • Distributorfs and manufacturers of equipment and supplies fro the sanitary processing industry. Formerly Food Industries Suppliers Association.

Food Processing Machinery Association. 200 Daingerfield Rd., Alexandria, VA 22314-2800. Phone: 800-331-8816 or (703)684-1080 Fax: (703)548-6563 E-mail: info@fpmamail.com • URL: http://www.foodprocessingmachinery.com • Represents firms manufacturing machinery and providing services and supplies for the canning, freezing, food, beverage, and pharmaceutical processing industries. Produces annual exposition of food processing equipment, supplies, and services, the International Exposition for Food Processors (IEFP); offers export and marketing services for members.

Foodservice and Packaging Institute. 150 S. Washington St., Ste. 204, Falls Church, VA 22046. Phone: (703)538-2800 Fax: (703)538-2187 E-mail: fpi@fpi.org • URL: http://www.fpi.org • Members are manufacturers of one-time-use food containers. Formerly Single Service Institute.

Foodservice Equipment Distributors Association. 2250 Point Blvd., Ste. 200, Elgin, IL 60123-7887. Phone: 800-677-9605 or (224)293-6500 Fax: (224)293-6505 E-mail: feda@feda.com • URL: http://www.feda.com • Distributors of foodservice equipment, such as ovens, ranges, dishwashing machines, china, utensils, and cutlery for hotels, restaurants, and institutions. Conducts specialized education programs.

International Association of Food Industry Suppliers. 1451 Dolley Madison Blvd., McLean, VA 22101-3850. Phone: (703)761-2600 Fax: (703)761-4334 E-mail: info@iafis.org • URL: http://www.iafis.org • Formerly Dairy and Food Industries Supply Association.

International Foodservice Manufacturers Association. 2 Prudential Plz., 180 N Stetson Ave., Ste. 4400, Chicago, IL 60601. Phone: (312)540-4400 Fax: (312)540-4401 E-mail: ifma@ifmaworld.com • URL: http://www.ifmaworld.com • National and international manufacturers and processors of food, food equipment, and related products for the away-from-home food market. Associate and allied members provide support services to the industry through marketing, publishing, distribution, consulting, promotion, research, advertising, public relations, and brokering. Activities are aimed at marketing, merchandising, sales training, and market research. Compiles statistics.

Manufacturers' Agents for Food Service Industry. 814 Spring Rd., Ste. 211, Atlanta, GA 30339. Phone: (770)433-9844 Fax: (770)433-2450 E-mail: info@mafsi.org • URL: http://www.mafsi.org • Members are independent manufacturers' representatives who sell food service equipment and supplies. Formerly

Marketing Agents for Food Service Industry.

North American Association of Food Equipment Manufacturers. 161 N. Clark St., Ste. 2020, Chicago, IL 60601. Phone: (312)821-0201 Fax: (312)821-0202 E-mail: info@nafem.org • URL: http://www.nafem.org • Formerly Food Equipment Manufacturers Association.

Research and Development Associates for Military Food and Packaging Systems. 16607 Blanco Rd., No. 1506, San Antonio, TX 78232. Phone: (210)493-8024 or (210)493-8025 Fax: (210)493-8036 E-mail: rda50@flash.net • URL: http://www.militaryfood.org • Industrial firms, educational institutions and related groups engged in food, food service, distribution and container research and development.

FOOD INDUSTRY

See also: GROCERY BUSINESS

GENERAL WORKS

Food Safety: Is Anyone Watching?. V. L. Smyth, editor. Nova Science Publishers, Inc. • 2002. $59.00. Provides material by several authors on governmental oversight of the American food industry. Includes a food safety chronology of selected events, 1992-1999.

ABSTRACTS AND INDEXES

Applied Science and Technology Index. H. W. Wilson Co. • 11 times a year. Quarterly and annual cumulations. Price varies. Indexes a wide variety of English language technical, industrial, and engineering periodicals.

Food Science and Technology Abstracts. International Food Information Service Publishing. • Monthly. $1,780.00 per year. Provides worldwide coverage of the literature of food technology and food production.

Foods Adlibra: Key to the World's Food Literature. General Mills, Inc. Foods Adlibra Publications. • Semimonthly. $240.00 per year. Provides journal citations and abstracts to the literature of food technology and packaging.

NTIS Alerts: Agriculture & Food. National Technical Information Service. • Semimonthly. $195.00 per year. Provides descriptions of government-sponsored research reports and software, with ordering information. Covers agricultural economics, horticulture, fisheries, veterinary medicine, food technology, and related subjects. Formerly *Abstract Newsletter.*

Nutrition Abstracts and Reviews, Series A: Human and Experimental. Available from CABI Publishing, North America. • Monthly. Institutions, $1,835.00 per year. Includes single site internet access. Published in England by CABI Publishing. Provides worldwide coverage of the literature.

ALMANACS AND YEARBOOKS

The State of Food and Agriculture. Available from Bernan Associates. • Annual. $55.00. Published by the Food and Agriculture Organization of the United Nations (FAO). A yearly review of world and regional agricultural and food activities. Includes tables and graphs. Text in English.

BIBLIOGRAPHIES

Using the Agricultural, Environmental, and Food Literature. Barbara S. Hutchinson and Antoinette P. Greider, editors. Marcel Dekker, Inc. • 2002. $125.00. Serves as a guide to both print and electronic sources of information.

CD-ROM DATABASES

AGRICOLA on SilverPlatter. Available from SilverPlatter Information, Inc. • Quarterly. $825.00 per year. Produced by the National Agricultural Library. Provides about three million citations on CD-ROM to the literature of agriculture, agricultural economics, animal sciences, entomology, fertilizer, food, forestry, nutrition, pesticides, plant science, water resources, and other topics. Each quarterly disc covers the past ten years, with archival discs available from 1970.

Food Science and Technology Abstracts [CD-ROM]. Available from SilverPlatter Information, Inc. • Quarterly. Produced by International Food Information Service (home page is http://www.ifis.org). Provides worldwide coverage on CD-ROM of the literature of food technology and production. Various types of publications are indexed, with abstracts, including about 1,800 periodicals. Time period is 1969 to date.

OECD Statistical Compendium. Organization for Economic Cooperation and Development. • Semiannual. $1,905.00 per year for 1 to 10 users. CD-ROM contains more than 730,000 monthly, quarterly, and annual time series for OECD countries, 1960 to date. Includes fully searchable data on agriculture, food, economic indicators, national accounts, employment, energy, finance, industry, technology, and foreign trade. Results can be displayed in various forms.

World Marketing Forecasts on CD-ROM. Gale Cengage Learning. • Annual. $2,500.00. Produced by Euromonitor. Provides detailed forecast data for the years to 2012 on CD-ROM for 54 countries in all parts of the world. Covers a wide range of social, demographic, economic, and market factors. Includes specific forecasts for many kinds of consumer products.

DIRECTORIES

Food Business Mergers and Acquisitions. The Food Institute. • Annual. $285.00. Gives names, locations, and industry categories of all companies involved in food business mergers during the previous year.

Food Chemicals News Directory. Food Chemical News. CRC Press LLC. • Semiannual. $497.00. Over 2,000 subsidiaries belonging to nearly 250 corporate parents plus an additional 3,000 independent processors. Formerly *Hereld's 1,500.*

Food Engineering Database. Reed Business Information. • Covers: more than 17,000 food and beverage plants with 20 or more employees; food and beverage research and development facilities; and company headquarters. Entries include: Company name, address, number of employees, phone, Standard Industrial Classification (SIC) code codes.

Food Master. BNP Media. • Covers: over 5,000 manufacturers and distributors of equipment, ingredients, services and supplies for food processing plants. Entries include: Company name, address, phone.

Food Processing Guide and Directory. Putman Media Inc. • Annual. $90.00. Lists over 5,390 food ingredient and equipment manufacturers.

Global Market Share Planner. Euromonitor International. • 2003. $5,900.00. Six volumes. Second edition. Provides detailed profiles and market share rankings of major consumer product companies in North America, Latin America, Europe, South Africa, and the Asia-Pacific region. Covers firms operating in key consumer markets: beverages, food products, household products, and personal care items. (Volumes are available individually.).

Internet Tools of the Profession: A Guide for Information Professionals. Hope N. Tillman, editor. Special Libraries Association. • 1997. $49.00. Second edition. Consists of 14 sections by various authors or compilers. After two introductory articles on searching the Internet, there are 12 annotated lists of useful Web sites, covering the SLA, business and finance, chemistry, education, food and agriculture,

information technology, insurance and employee benefits, law, library management, metals and materials, pharmaceuticals, and telecommunications. An index is provided.

Major Food and Drink Companies of the World. Available from Gale Cengage Learning. • Annual. $880.00. Two volumes. Published by Graham & Whiteside. Contains profiles and trade names for more than 9,800 important food and beverage companies in various countries. In addition to foods, includes both alcoholic and nonalcoholic drink products.

Plunkett's Food Industry Almanac. Plunkett Research Ltd. • Covers: 340 leading companies in the global food industry. Entries include: Name, address, phone, fax, and key executives. Also includes analysis and information on trends, technology, and statistics in the field.

Prepared Foods Sourcebook. Reed Business Information. • Annual. $75.00. Lists approximately 600 food and veverage companies.

Thomas Food and Beverage Market Place. Grey House Publishing. • 2004. $495.00. Three volumes. Contains more than 40,000 entries covering food companies, beverages, food equipment, warehouse companies, food brokers, wholesalers, importers, and exporters. Formerly *Thomas Food Industry Register.*

World Food Marketing Directory. Euromonitor International. • Covers: Over 2,000 retailers and wholesalers, 1,600 manufacturers, over 2,000 international and European organizations, statistical agencies, trade journals and associations, databases, and trade fairs in the grocery and food industries worldwide. Entries include: Company name, address, phone, telex, names of parent company and subsidiaries, number of employees, financial data, products and brand names handled; retailers and wholesalers include type of outlet, names and titles of key personnel.

World Leading Global Brand Owners. Euromonitor International. • 2003. $1,190.00. Second edition. Contains detailed profiles of multinational consumer product companies. Includes sales, market share, brand names, and financial information. (*Global Market Share Planner,* vol. 3.).

ENCYCLOPEDIAS AND DICTIONARIES

Consumers' Guide to Product Grades and Terms: From Grade A to VSOP-Definitions of 8,000 Terms Describing Food Housewares and Other Everyday Terms. Gale Cengage Learning. • 1992. $95.00. Includes product grades and classifications defined by government agencies, such as the Food and Drug Administration (FDA), and by voluntary standards organizations, such as the American National Standards Institute (ANSI).

Dictionary of Agriculture: From Abaca to Zoonosis. Kathryn L. Lipton. Lynne Rienner Publishers, Inc. • 1995. $75.00. Emphasis is on agricultural economics.

Dictionary of Food Ingredients. Robert S. Igoe and Y.H. Hui. Aspen Publishers, Inc. • 2001. $44.00. Fourth edition.

Encyclopedia of Agriculture Science. Charles J. Arntzen and Ellen M. Ritter, editors. Elsevier. • 1994. $900.00. Four volumes.

Encyclopedia of Food and Culture. Gale Cengage Learning. • 2002. $395.00. Three volumes. Contains 600 articles covering various aspects of food and its place in society, from agronomy to zucchini. Includes illustrations and a detailed index.

Encyclopedia of Food Science, Food Technology, and Nutrition. Robert Macrae and others, editors. Elsevier. • 1993. Eight volumes. $3,056.00. $382.00 per volume.

Foods and Nutrition Encyclopedia. Audrey H. Ensminger and others. CRC Press, Inc. • 1993. $309.95.

Second edition. Two volumes.

Oxford Encyclopedia of Food and Drink in America. Andrew F. Smith, editor. Oxford University Press. • 2004. $250.00. Two volumes. Emphasis is on historical and cultural aspects of food and beverages in the U. S.

Wiley Encyclopedia of Food Science and Technology. Frederick J. Francis, editor. John Wiley and Sons, Inc. • 2000. $1,650.00. Second edition. Four volumes. Contains about 400 entries. Coverage includes biotechnology, genetic engineering, nutrition, regulatory matters, food safety, labeling, food substitutes (sugar, fat, dairy), and many other topics.

FINANCIAL RATIOS

Almanac of Business and Industrial Financial Ratios. Leo Troy. Aspen Publishers, Inc. • 2003. $125.95. Includes CD-Rom. Contains financial ratios derived from federal tax returns. Ratios for each of about 200 industries are arranged according to company asset size. (Almanac of Business and Industrial Financial Ratios Series).

Food Marketing Industry Speaks. Food Marketing Institute. • Annual. Members, $30.00; nonmembers, $75.00. Provides data on overall food industry marketing performance, including retail distribution and store operations.

HANDBOOKS AND MANUALS

Progressive Grocer Guidebook. Trade Dimensions. • Annual. $375.00. Over 800 major chain and independent food retailers and wholesalers in the United States and Canada; also includes food brokers, rack jobbers, candy and tobacco distributors, and magazine distributors.

INTERNET DATABASES

Business 2.0 Web Guide to the Best Business Links. Business 2.0 Media Inc. Phone: (415)293-4800 E-mail: support@business2.com • URL: http://www.business2.com/webguide • Web site presents an extensive, searchable directory of links to "the best, most informative, and authoritative web pages." Twenty main categories cover business, finance, career, company information, people, and technology topics, with thousands of subtopics, all linking to Web sites recommended by experienced business researchers. Fees: Free.

Fedstats. Federal Interagency Council on Statistical Policy. Phone: (202)395-7254 • URL: http://www.fedstats.gov • Web site features an efficient search facility for full-text statistics produced by more than 100 federal agencies, including the Census Bureau, the Bureau of Economic Analysis, and the Bureau of Labor Statistics. Boolean searches can be made within one agency or for all agencies combined. Links are offered to international statistical bureaus, including the UN, IMF, OECD, UNESCO, Eurostat, and 20 individual countries. Fees: Free.

FreeLunch.com. Economy.com, Inc. Phone: (610)696-8700 Fax: (610)696-1678 • URL: http://www.freelunch.com • Web site provides free access to more than 1.5 million economic and financial data series, covering industry, demographics, labor markets, prices, retail sales, government spending, trade, interest rates, housing starts, the stock market, and many other topics. Data is available for various time periods in either chart or table form. Searching is offered. Fees: Free, but registration required. Economy.com, Inc. also offers fee-based economic analysis at *The Dismal Scientist* site (http://www.dismal.com).

ONLINE DATABASES

Applied Science and Technology Index Online. H. W. Wilson Co. • Provides online indexing of 500 major scientific, technical, industrial, and engineering periodicals. Time period is 1983 to date. Monthly updates. Inquire as to online cost and availability.

For publishers addresses, refer to SOURCES CITED section at the back of the book.

Food Science and Technology Abstracts [online]. IFIS North American Desk. • Produced by International Food Information Service. Provides about 500,000 online citations, with abstracts, to the international literature of food science, technology, commodities, engineering, and processing. Approximately 2,000 periodicals are covered. Time period is 1969 to date, with monthly updates. Inquire as to online cost and availability.

FOODS ADLIBRA. General Mills, Inc. • Contains online citations, with abstracts, to the technical and business literature of food processing and packaging. New products and new ingredients are featured. Covers about 250 trade journals and 500 research journals from 1974 to date, with monthly updates. Inquire as to online cost and availability.

PERIODICALS AND NEWSLETTERS

Amber Waves. Available from U. S. Government Printing Office. • Quarterly. $38.00 per year. Replaces *Agricultural Outlook; Food Review*; and *Rural America.* Provides research and analysis from the U.S. Department of Agriculture's Economic Research Service. Includes economic data on agriculture, food, trade, and environmental factors.

FDA Consumer. Available from U. S. Government Printing Office. • Bimonthly. $14.00 per year. Issued by the U. S. Food and Drug Administration. Provides consumer information about FDA regulations and product safety.

Food Industry Newsletter: All the Food News That Matters. Newsletters, Inc. • 26 times a year. $245.00 per year. Newsletter. A summary of key industry news for food executives.

The Food Institute Report. American Institute of Food Distribution Inc. • Description: Reports on developments in the food industry, including new products, the food service industry, mergers and acquisitions, current legislation and regulations, judicial decisions, and financial and marketing information.

Food Technology. Institute of Food Technologists. • Monthly. Free to members; non-members, $82.00 per year. Articles cover food product development, food ingredients, production, packaging, research, and regulation.

Journal of Agricultural and Food Information. Haworth Press, Inc. • Quarterly. Institutions, $95.00 per year. A journal for librarians and others concerned with the acquisition of information on food and agriculture.

Journal of Food Products Marketing: Innovations in Food Advertising, Food Promotion, Food Publicity, Food Sales Promotion. Haworth Press, Inc. • Semiannual. $300.00 per year.

Journal of Food Science. Institute of Food Technologists. • Bimonthly. Members, $20.00 per year; non-members, $100.00 per year. A peer-reviewed research journal.

Journal of International Food and Agribusiness Marketing. Haworth Press, Inc. • Semiannual. Institutions, $320.00 per year.

Prepared Foods. Business News Publishing Co. • Monthly. $99.90 per year. Edited for food manufacturing management, marketing, and operations personnel.

Progressive Grocer: The Magazine of Supermarketing. VNU Business Media. • 18 times a year. $129.00 per year.

Seafood Business. Diversified Business Communications. • Monthly. $69.00 per year. Edited for a wide range of seafood buyers, including distributors, restaurants, supermarkets, and institutions. Special issues feature information on specific products, such as salmon or lobster.

The Washington Agricultural Record. Washington Agricultural Record. • Description: Focuses on Washington farm issues and developments, report-

ing international congressional and United States Department of Agriculture (U.S.D.A.) news and international agricultural developments.

RESEARCH CENTERS AND INSTITUTES

Academy of Food Marketing. Saint Joseph's University. 5600 City Ave., Philadelphia, PA 19131. Phone: (610)660-1600 Fax: (610)660-1604 E-mail: cmallowe@sju.edu • URL: http://www.sju.edu.

Institute for Food Laws and Regulations. Michigan State University, 165 National Food Safety and Toxicology Ctr., East Lansing, MI 48224. Phone: (517)355-8295 • URL: http://www.iflr.msu.edu/ • Conducts research on the food industry, including processing, packaging, marketing, and new products.

Monell Chemical Senses Center. Monell Chemical Senses Center. 3500 Market St., Philadelphia, PA 19104-3308. Phone: (267)519-4700 Fax: (267)898-2084 E-mail: beauchamp@monell.org • URL: http://www.monell.org • Mechanisms and functions of the chemical senses (taste, smell, and chemical irritation), including studies in the areas of biochemistry, biophysics, endocrinology, physiology, ethology, neurology, behavior, genetics, psychophysics, nutrition, organic chemistry, chemical ecology, and zoology. Basic research relates to solutions of problems in health and nutrition, aging and neurodegenerative disease, environmental odors, reproduction, disease diagnosis, expansion of world food supply, and alternative means of vertebrate pest control. Projects focus on biochemistry of receptor mechanisms, sensory qualities of food, role of early diet in shaping food preferences, relationship between chemosensory function and nutritional and disease states, role of body volatiles in disease diagnosis, methods of altering salt preference, role of taste and smell in food utilization, effect of aging on taste and smell, information processing in taste and smell, role of genes in determining sensory perception and hedonic responses, and diagnosis and treatment of taste and smell disorders.

Texas Agricultural Market Research Center. Texas A & M University. Dept. of Agricultural Economics, College Station, TX 77843-2124. Phone: (979)845-5911 Fax: (979)845-6378 E-mail: tamrc@tamu.edu.

STATISTICS SOURCES

Agriculture Fact Book. Available from U. S. Government Printing Office. • Annual. $26.00. Issued by the Office of Communications, U. S. Department of Agriculture. Includes data on U. S. agriculture, farmers, food, nutrition, and rural America. Programs of the Department of Agriculture in six areas are described: rural economic development, foreign trade, nutrition, the environment, inspection, and education.

Annual Survey of Manufactures. Available from U. S. Government Printing Office. • Annual. Prices vary. Issued by the U. S. Census Bureau as an interim update to the *Census of Manufactures.* Includes data on number of manufacturing establishments in various industries, employment, labor costs, value of shipments, capital expenditures, inventories, energy costs, and assets. (See also Census Bureau home page, http://www.census.gov/.).

Business Statistics of the United States. Linz Audain and Cornelia J. Strawser. Bernan Associates. • Annual. $147.00. Based on *Business Statistics*, formerly issue by the Bureau of Economic Analysis, U. S. Department of Commerce. Provides basic data for a wide variety of U. S. industries, services, and economic indicators. Most statistics are shown annually for 30 years and monthly for the most recent four years.

Consumer International. Available from Gale Cengage Learning. • Annual. $1,290.00. Published by Euromonitor. Contains extensive consumer market, economic, and demographic data for 25 major, non-

European countries, including the U. S. and Canada. Includes consumer market size (volume and value) for 150 product types in 14 categories (food, clothing, automobiles, cosmetics, appliances, etc.).

European Marketing Forecasts. Available from Gale Cengage Learning. • Annual. $1,250.00. Published by Euromonitor. Contains demographic, economic, and market forecasts for the countries of Europe to the year 2010. Forecasts include market-size data for 15 consumer product sectors (food, clothing, automobiles, consumer electronics, etc.).

International Marketing Forecasts. Available from Gale Cengage Learning. • Annual. $1,250.00. Published by Euromonitor. Contains demographic, economic, and market forecasts to the year 2013 for major, non-European countries, including the U. S. and Canada. Forecasts include market-size data for 15 consumer product sectors, such as food, clothing, and automobiles.

Standard & Poor's Industry Surveys. Standard & Poor's. • Semiannual. $1,800.00. Two looseleaf volumes. Includes monthly *Supplements.* Provides detailed, individual surveys of 52 major industry groups. Each survey is revised on a semiannual basis. Also includes "Monthly Investment Review" (industry group investment analysis) and monthly "Trends & Projections" (economic analysis).

Survey of Current Business. Available from U. S. Government Printing Office. • Monthly. $63.00 per year. Issued by Bureau of Economic Analysis, U. S. Department of Commerce. Presents a wide variety of business and economic data.

WEFA Industrial Monitor. John Wiley and Sons, Inc. • Annual. $65.00. Prepared by industry analysts at WEFA, an economic forecasting and consulting firm (originally Wharton Econometric Forecasting Associates). Contains discussions of the outlook for major U. S. industries, with many 10-year forecasts (WEFA Web site is http://www.wefa.com).

World Food Data and Statistics. Euromonitor International. • 2004. $650.00. Provides five-year data for a wide variety of food products in 52 countries. Includes market size, consumer expenditures, price indicators, and retail distribution data for many kinds of meat, fish, fruits, vegetables, dairy products, baked goods, condiments, canned food, and frozen food.

TRADE/PROFESSIONAL ASSOCIATIONS

American Institute of Food Distribution. One Broadway, 2nd Fl., Elmwood Park, NJ 07407. Phone: (201)791-5570 Fax: (201)791-5222 E-mail: info@foodinstitute.com • URL: http://www. foodinstitute.com.

FISA-Food Industry Suppliers Association. 1207 Sunset Dr., Greensboro, NC 27408. Phone: (336)274-6311 Fax: (336)691-1839 E-mail: stella@ fisanet.org • URL: http://www.fisanet.org • Distributorfs and manufacturers of equipment and supplies fro the sanitary processing industry. Formerly Food Industries Suppliers Association.

Grocery Manufacturers of America, Inc. 2401 Pennsylvania Ave., NW, 2nd Fl., Washington, DC 20037. Phone: (202)337-9400 Fax: (202)337-4508 E-mail: info@gmabrands.com • URL: http://www. gmabrands.com • Absorbed Association of Sales and Marketing Companies.

Institute of Food Technologists. 525 W. Van Buren St., No. 1000, Chicago, IL 60607. Phone: (312)782-8424 Fax: (312)782-8348 E-mail: info@ift.org • URL: http://www.ift.org • A professional society of food scientists active in government, academia, and industry.

United Food and Commercial Workers International Union. 1775 K. St., N.W., Washington, DC 20006.

Phone: (202)223-3111 Fax: (202)466-1562 • URL: http://www.ufcw.org.

OTHER SOURCES

Food Law Reports. CCH, Inc. • Weekly. $1,459.00 per year. Six looseleaf volumes. Covers regulation of adulteration, packaging, labeling, and additives. Formerly *Food Drug Cosmetic Law Reports.*

Healthy Prepared Foods. MarketResearch.com. • 1999. $2,750.00. Consumer market data on foods that are low in calories, fat, cholesterol, sodium, and sugar or high in fiber and calcium, with forecasts to 2003.

The Market for Value-Added Fresh Produce. MarketResearch.com. • 1999. $2,750.00. Market research report. Covers packaged salad mixes, bulk salad mixes, pre-cut fruits, and pre-cut vegetables. Market projections are provided to the year 2003.

Market Share Tracker. Euromonitor International. • 2003. $1,190.00. Second edition. Contains market share rankings of more than 1,800 consumer product companies in 30 countries. Covers 16 kinds of products within "Drinks," "Household and Personal Care," and "Foods." Includes brand shares for leading brands. (*Global Market Share Planner*, vol. 1.).

FOOD MACHINERY

See: FOOD EQUIPMENT AND MACHINERY

FOOD PACKAGING

See: PACKAGING

FOOD, PROCESSED

See: PROCESSED FOOD INDUSTRY

FOOD PROCESSING

See: FOOD INDUSTRY; PROCESSED FOOD INDUSTRY

FOOD SERVICE INDUSTRY

See also: RESTAURANTS, LUNCHROOMS, ETC.

GENERAL WORKS

Fundamentals of Professional Food Preparation: A Laboratory Text-Workbook. Donald V. Laconi. John Wiley and Sons, Inc. • 1995. $60.00.

DIRECTORIES

Directory of Foodservice Distributors. Chain Store Guide. • Annual. $335.00. Available online. Covers distributors of food and equipment to restaurants and institutions.

Foodservice Consultants Society International: Membership Roster. Foodservice Consultants Society International. • Annual. $450.00. About 950 food service consultants.

Foodservice Equipment and Supplies Product Source Guide. Reed Business Information. • Annual. $35.00. Nearly 1,700 manufacturers of food service equipment and supplies. Formerly *Foodservice Equipment Buyer's Guide and Product Directory.*

International Foodservice Manufacturers Association: Membership Directory. International Foodservice Manufacturers Association. • Annual. Membership. Manufacturers of processed foods equipment and supplies for schools, hospitals, hotels, restaurants, and institutions and related services in the foodservice industry.

School Foodservice Who's Who. Information Central Inc. • Covers: about 5,800 food service programs in public and Catholic school systems with enrollments in excess of 1,500 students. Separate listings of the biggest buyers (school districts reporting over $1.5 million/year in foodservice purchases), state school foodservice officials, and co-op buying groups and food management companies involved in food service. Entries include: School district name, address, phone, fax; food service budget, key food service executive, number of meals served daily, types of food and services, food management company, fast food brands.

HANDBOOKS AND MANUALS

Catering Service. Entrepreneur Media, Inc. • Looseleaf. $59.50. A practical guide to starting a food and beverage catering business. Covers profit potential, start-up costs, market size evaluation, owner's time required, site selection, pricing, accounting, advertising, promotion, etc. (Start-Up Business Guide No. E1215.).

Cooking for Fifty: The Complete Reference and Cookbook. Chet Holden. John Wiley and Sons, Inc. • 1993. $95.00. Discusses commercial cooking techniques and includes 300 "contemporary" recipes for institutional and commercial cooks.

Diet and Meal Planning. Entrepreneur Media, Inc. • Looseleaf. $59.50. A practical guide to starting a diet and meal planning service. Covers profit potential, start-up costs, market size evaluation, pricing, accounting, advertising, promotion, etc. (Start-Up Business Guide No. E2333.).

INTERNET DATABASES

Advance Monthly Sales for Retail Trade and Food Services. U. S. Census Bureau. Phone: 800-541-8345 or (301)763-4636 Fax: (301)457-3842 E-mail: rcb@census.gov • URL: http://www.census.gov/svsd/www/fullpub.html • Web pages provide monthly sales figures for a wide range of retail businesses. Advance, preliminary, and final statistics are provided for the latest month available in each case, with a previous-year comparison. Updates are monthly.

ONLINE DATABASES

PROMT: Predicasts Overview of Markets and Technology. Gale Cengage Learning. • Companies, products, applied technologies and markets. U.S. and international literature coverage, 1972 to date. Inquire as to online cost and availability. Provides abstracts from more than 1,600 publications. Weekly updates.

PERIODICALS AND NEWSLETTERS

Chef. Talcott Communications Corp. • Monthly. $24.00 per year. Edited for executive chefs, food and beverage directors, caterers, banquet and club managers, and others responsible for food buying and food service. Special coverage of regional foods is provided.

Food Management: Ideas for Colleges, Healthcare, Schools, and Business Dining. Penton Media, Inc. • Monthly. Free to qualified personel; others.

Foodservice Equipment and Supplies. Reed Business Information. • 13 times a year. $106.90 per year.

Hospitality Technology: Guiding High-Growth Businesses to Best-Choice IT Solutions. Edgell Communications, Inc. • 10 times a year. Price on application. Covers information technology, computer communications, and software for food-service and lodging enterprises.

Journal of Foodservice Business Research. Haworth Press, Inc. • Quarterly. $225.00 per year. Includes print and online editions. Formerly *Journal of Restaurant and Foodservice Marketing.*

Restaurants and Institutions. Reed Business Information. • Semimonthly. $149.00 per year.

Features news, new products, recipes, menu concepts and merchandising ideas from the most successful foodservice operations around the U.S.

STATISTICS SOURCES

Annual Benchmark Report for Retail Trade and Food Services...A Detailed Summary of Retail Sales, Purchases, Accounts Receivable, Inventories, and Food Service Sales. Available from U. S. Government Printing Office. • Annual. $13.00. Issued by the U.S. Census Bureau. Provides detailed annual and monthly retail statistics for the most recent 10 years. Includes data for various kinds of retail outlets, including automobiles, furniture, appliances, building supplies, grocery stores, drug stores, gasoline stations, clothing, sporting goods, department stores, and restaurants.

TRADE/PROFESSIONAL ASSOCIATIONS

American School Food Service Association. 700 S. Washington St., Suite 300, Alexandria, VA 22314. Phone: 800-877-8822 or (703)739-3900 Fax: (703)739-3915 E-mail: servicecenter@asfsa.org • URL: http://www.asfsa.org.

American Society for Healthcare Food Service Administrators. c/o American Hospital Association, One N. Franklin St., Chicago, IL 60606. Phone: (312)422-3840 Fax: (312)422-4581 E-mail: ashfsa@aha.org • URL: http://www.ashfsa.org • Formerly American Society for Hospital Food Service Administrators.

Association of Correctional Food Service Affiliates. 210 N Glenoaks Blvd., Ste. C, Burbank, CA 91502. Phone: (818)843-6608 Fax: (818)843-7423 E-mail: jonnichols@acfsa.org • URL: http://www.acfsa.org • Food service professionals from federal, state and county correctional institutions and vendors that serve them. Works to advance skills and professionalism through education, information and networking.

Convenience Caterers and Food Manufacturers Association. 1205 Spartan Dr., Madison Heights, MI 48071. Phone: 800-620-6422 or (248)982-5379 Fax: (248)582-3268 E-mail: ccfma@sbcglobal.net • URL: http://www.mobilecaterers.com • Firms and corporations engaged in the mobile catering business and in any other business catering to industrial feeding by mobile equipment; associate members are suppliers and manufacturers. Deals with common intra-industry problems through exchange of ideas, advice on legal problems, and safety standards and licensing regulations.

Dietary Managers Association. 406 Surrey Woods Dr., St. Charles, IL 60174. Phone: 800-323-1908 or (630)587-6336 Fax: (630)587-6308 E-mail: info@dmaonline.org • URL: http://www.dmaonline.org • Dietary managers united to maintain a high level of competency and quality in dietary departments through continuing education. Provides educational programs and placement service.

Food Distributors International. 201 Park Washington Ct., Falls Church, VA 22046. Phone: (703)532-9400 Fax: (703)538-4673 E-mail: info@ifps.org • URL: http://www.fdi.org • Comprised of food distribution companies that supply and service independent wholesale grocers and foodservice operations. Goal is to educate and inform members on industry events, government affairs, and technology.

Foodservice and Packaging Institute. 150 S. Washington St., Ste. 204, Falls Church, VA 22046. Phone: (703)538-2800 Fax: (703)538-2187 E-mail: fpi@fpi.org • URL: http://www.fpi.org • Members are manufacturers of one-time-use food containers. Formerly Single Service Institute.

Foodservice Consultants Society International. 455 S 4th St., Ste. 650, Louisville, KY 40202. Phone: (502)583-3783 Fax: (502)589-3602 E-mail: fcsi@fcsi.org • URL: http://www.fcsi.org • Works to promote client usage of services provided by members. Promotes ethical industry practices; disseminates information; develops accreditation programs; conducts educational and research programs; maintains speakers' bureau.

Foodservice Equipment Distributors Association. 2250 Point Blvd., Ste. 200, Elgin, IL 60123-7887. Phone: 800-677-9605 or (224)293-6500 Fax: (224)293-6505 E-mail: feda@feda.com • URL: http://www.feda.com • Distributors of foodservice equipment, such as ovens, ranges, dishwashing machines, china, utensils, and cutlery for hotels, restaurants, and institutions. Conducts specialized education programs.

International Food Service Executives Association. 8155 Briar Cliff Dr., Castle Rock, CO 80108-8215. Phone: 800-893-5499 or (720)733-8001 Fax: (720)733-8999 E-mail: hq@ifsea.com • URL: http://www.ifsea.com • Owners, managers, stewards, caterers, proprietors, purchasing agents, dietitians, and other management-level personnel of hotels, clubs, restaurants, cafeterias, schools, hospitals, institutions, and airlines. Associate members are providers of goods and services to the food service industry. Seeks to raise standards in the food service industry by educating members. Underwrites scholarships; provides assistance to universities and other educational institutions establishing programs for professional food service training. Maintains Certified Food Executive Program, through which individuals in the food service industry who have demonstrated outstanding leadership capabilities receive certification training.

International Foodservice Editorial Council. PO Box 491, Hyde Park, NY 12538-0491. Phone: (845)229-6973 Fax: (845)229-6993 E-mail: info@ifeconline.com • URL: http://www.ifec-is-us.com • Key communicators within the U.S. foodservice industry, including top editors and marketing and public relations personnel for leading food companies and foodservice educational institutions. Organized to sound the marketing directions of the industry on all levels; seeks to improve communications.

International Foodservice Manufacturers Association. 2 Prudential Plz., 180 N Stetson Ave., Ste. 4400, Chicago, IL 60601. Phone: (312)540-4400 Fax: (312)540-4401 E-mail: ifma@ifmaworld.com • URL: http://www.ifmaworld.com • National and international manufacturers and processors of food, food equipment, and related products for the away-from-home food market. Associate and allied members provide support services to the industry through marketing, publishing, distribution, consulting, promotion, research, advertising, public relations, and brokering. Activities are aimed at marketing, merchandising, sales training, and market research. Compiles statistics.

Manufacturers' Agents for Food Service Industry. 814 Spring Rd., Ste. 211, Atlanta, GA 30339. Phone: (770)433-9844 Fax: (770)433-2450 E-mail: info@mafsi.org • URL: http://www.mafsi.org • Members are independent manufacturers' representatives who sell food service equipment and supplies. Formerly Marketing Agents for Food Service Industry.

National Council of Chain Restaurants. 325 Seventh St. N.W., Suite 1000, Washington, DC 20004. Phone: (202)626-8183 Fax: (202)626-8185 E-mail: purviss@nrf.com • URL: http://www.nccr.net • Major multiunit, multistate foodservice, restaurant and lodging companies in the United States.

National Restaurant Association Educational Foundation. 175 W Jackson Blvd., Ste. 1500, Chicago, IL 60604-2702. Phone: 800-765-2122 or (312)715-1010 E-mail: info@restaurant.org • URL: http://www.nraef.org • Serves as an educational foundation supported by the National Restaurant Association and all segments of the foodservice industry including restaurateurs, foodservice companies, food and equipment manufacturers,

distributors, and trade associations. Advances the professional standards of the industry through education and research. Offers video training programs, management courses, and careers information. Conducts research and maintains hall of fame.

Society for Foodservice Management. 304 W Liberty St., Ste. 201, Louisville, KY 40202. Phone: (502)583-3783 Fax: (502)589-3602 E-mail: sfm@hqtrs.com • URL: http://www.sfm-online.org.

FOOD SERVICE, INSTITUTIONAL

See: FOOD SERVICE INDUSTRY

FOOD, SNACK

See: SNACK FOOD INDUSTRY

FOOD, SPECIALTY

See: SPECIALTY FOOD INDUSTRY

FOOTWEAR

See: SHOE INDUSTRY

FORECASTING

See: BUSINESS FORECASTING; FUTURISTICS

FOREIGN AGRICULTURE

See also: AGRICULTURE

GENERAL WORKS
United States Agricultural Trade: Trends, Policy, and Direction. Larry V. Fedorov, editor. Nova Science Publishers, Inc. • 2003. $59.00. Includes data on the impact of NAFTA on the import and export of farm products.

CD-ROM DATABASES
OECD Statistical Compendium. Organization for Economic Cooperation and Development. • Semiannual. $1,905.00 per year for 1 to 10 users. CD-ROM contains more than 730,000 monthly, quarterly, and annual time series for OECD countries, 1960 to date. Includes fully searchable data on agriculture, food, economic indicators, national accounts, employment, energy, finance, industry, technology, and foreign trade. Results can be displayed in various forms.

ONLINE DATABASES
CAB Abstracts. CAB Publishing North America. • Contains 46 specialized abstract collections covering over 10,000 journals and monographs in the areas of agriculture, horticulture, forest products, farm products, nutrition, dairy science, poultry, grains, animal health, entomology, etc. Time period is 1972 to date, with monthly updates. Inquire as to online cost and availability. *CAB Abstracts on CD-ROM* also available, with annual updating.

PERIODICALS AND NEWSLETTERS
AgExporter. Available from U. S. Government Printing Office. • Monthly. $44.00 per year. Issued by the Foreign Agricultural Service, U. S. Department of Agriculture. Edited for U. S. exporters of farm products. Provides practical information on exporting, including overseas trade opportunities.

IFAP Newsletter. International Federation of

Agricultural Producers. • Bimonthly. Price on application.

Outlook for United States Agricultural Trade. Available from U. S. Government Printing Office. • Quarterly. $15.00 per year. Issued by the Economic Research Service, U. S. Department of Agriculture. (Situation and Outlook Reports.).

STATISTICS SOURCES
FAO Production Yearbook. Available from Bernan Associates. • Annual. $45.00. Published by the Food and Agriculture Organization (http://www.fao.org). Contains worldwide data on agriculture, land use, farm crops, livestock, and agricultural prices.

FAO Trade Yearbook. Available from Bernan Associates. • Annual. $45.00. Published by the Food and Agriculture Organization (http://www.fao.org). Provides extensive worldwide data on exports and imports of agricultural commodities, fertilizers, tractors, and pesticides. Includes more than 130 tables of detailed statistics.

World Agricultural Supply and Demand Estimates. Available from U. S. Government Printing Office. • Monthly. $52.00 per year. Issued by the Economics and Statistics Service and the Foreign Agricultural Service of the U. S. Department of Agriculture. Consists mainly of statistical data and tables.

FOREIGN AUTOMOBILES

See also: AUTOMOBILES

DIRECTORIES
Overseas Automotive Council Membership Roster. Overseas Automotive Council. • Annual. $50.00 per year. Lists over 700 U.S. and overseas members. Newsletter.

ONLINE DATABASES
Ward's AutoInfoBank. Ward's Communications, Inc. • Provides weekly, monthly, quarterly, and annual statistical data from 1980 to date for U. S. and imported cars and trucks. Covers production, shipments, sales, inventories, optional equipment, etc. Updating varies by series. Inquire as to online cost and availability.

PERIODICALS AND NEWSLETTERS
Importcar: The Complete Import Service Magazine. Babcox Publications, Inc. • Monthly. $64.00 per year. Includes *Automotive Aftermarket Training Guide.* Formerly *Importcar and Truck.*

TRADE/PROFESSIONAL ASSOCIATIONS
American International Automobile Dealers Association. 211 N Union St., Ste. 300, Alexandria, VA 22314. Phone: 800-GO-AIADA or (703)519-7800 Fax: (703)519-7810 E-mail: goaiada@aiada.org • URL: http://www.aiada.org • Trade association for America's international nameplate automobile dealerships and their employees who sell and service automobiles manufactured in the U.S. and abroad. Works to preserve a free market for international automobiles in the U.S. and is dedicated to increasing public awareness of the benefits the industry provides.

Association of International Automobile Manufacturers. 1001 19th St. N., Suite 1200, Arlington, VA 22209. Phone: (703)525-7788 Fax: (703)525-8817 E-mail: webmaster@aiam.org • URL: http://www.aiam.org.

FOREIGN BUSINESS

See: INTERNATIONAL BUSINESS

FOREIGN COMMERCE

See: FOREIGN TRADE

FOREIGN CREDIT

See also: CREDIT; EXPORT-IMPORT TRADE; FOREIGN EXCHANGE

ABSTRACTS AND INDEXES

PAIS International in Print. Public Affairs Information Service, Inc. • Monthly. $850.00 per year; cumulations three times a year. Provides topical citations to the worldwide literature of public affairs, economics, demographics, sociology, and trade. Text in English; indexed materials in English, French, German, Italian, Portuguese and Spanish.

CD-ROM DATABASES

CreditDisk 2.0. Fitch, Inc. • Price and frequency on application. CD-ROM provides credit research and ratings on individual banks throughout the world, with Internet updating. Includes graphic displays of rating histories and financial ratios.

EconLit. Available from SilverPlatter Information, Inc. • Monthly. Single-user, $1,600.00 per year. Provides CD-ROM citations, with abstracts, to articles from more than 500 economics journals. Time period is 1969 to date. Produced by the American Economic Association.

PAIS on CD-ROM. Public Affairs Information Service, Inc. • Quarterly. $1,995.00 per year. Provides a CD-ROM version of the online service, *PAIS International.* Contains over 500,000 citations to the literature of contemporary social, political, and economic issues.

ONLINE DATABASES

PAIS International. Public Affairs Information Service, Inc. • Corresponds to the former printed publications, *PAIS Bulletin* (1976-90) and *PAIS Foreign Language Index* (1972-90), and to the current *PAIS International in Print* (1991 to date). Covers economic, political, and sociological material appearing in periodicals, books, government documents, and other publications. Updating is monthly. Inquire as to online cost and availability.

PERIODICALS AND NEWSLETTERS

Bondweek: The Newsweekly of Fixed Income and Credit Markets. Institutional Investor, Inc., Journals Group. • Weekly. $2,425.00 per year. Newsletter. Includes print and online editions. Covers taxable, fixed-income securities for professional investors, including corporate, government, foreign, mortgage, and high-yield.

FCIB International Bulletin (Finance, Credit and International Business). Finance, Credit and International Business-National Assoiciation of Credit Management. FCIB - NACM Corp. • Quarterly. Membership.

Grant's Interest Rate Observer. James Grant, editor. Grant's Financial Publishing Inc. • Biweekly. $725.00 per year. Newsletter containing detailed analysis of money-related topics, including interest rate trends, global credit markets, fixed-income investments, bank loan policies, and international money markets.

International Bank Credit Analyst. BCA Publications Ltd. • Monthly. $795.00 per year. "A monthly forecast and analysis of currency movements, interest rates, and stock market developments in the principal countries, based on a continuous appraisal of money and credit trends worldwide." Includes many charts and graphs providing international coverage of money, credit, and securities.

Loan Market Week: The Newsweekly of the Loan Syndication, Trading and Investment Markets. Institutional Investor, Inc., Journals Group. • Weekly. $2,370.00 per year. Newsletter. Includes print and online editions. Covers retail banking, commercial lending, foreign loans, bank technology, government regulations, and other topics related to banking. Formerly *Bank Letter.*

Project Finance Monthly. Infocast Inc. • Description: Provides information about the power industry. Includes industry news, financing, regulation, and contracts.

STATISTICS SOURCES

Statistical Information on the Financial Services Industry. American Bankers Association. • Annual. Members, $150.00; non-members, $275.00. Presents a wide variety of data relating to banking and financial services, including consumer economics, personal finance, credit, government loans, capital markets, and international banking.

TRADE/PROFESSIONAL ASSOCIATIONS

FCIB-NACM Corp. 8840 Columbia 100 Pkwy., Columbia, MD 21045-2158. Phone: 888-256-3242 or (410)423-1840 Fax: (410)423-1845 E-mail: fcib_info@fcibglobal.com • URL: http://www.fcibglobal.com • Provides services to international credit and trade finance professionals, including international receivables management education, products, services and networking. Offers roundtable discussions, international trade surveys, industry groups, conferences, credit hotline, workshops and research services.

Foreign Credit Insurance Association. 125 Park Ave., 14th Fl., New York, NY 10017. Phone: (212)885-1500 Fax: (212)885-1535 E-mail: service@fcia.org • URL: http://www.fcia.com • Represents marine, property, and casualty insurance companies. Insures companies against the risks of nonpayment by buyers for commercial and/or political reasons. Facilitates the financing of term credit sales, thus providing companies with support to meet competitive terms of payment offered by others.

OTHER SOURCES

Country Finance. Economist Intelligence Unit. • Annual $425.00 per year. Discusses banking and financial conditions in each of 47 countries. Includes foreign exchange regulations, the currency outlook, sources of capital, financing techniques, and tax considerations.

FOREIGN EMPLOYMENT

See: EMPLOYMENT IN FOREIGN COUNTRIES

FOREIGN EXCHANGE

See also: CURRENCY EXCHANGE RATES; MONEY; PAPER MONEY

GENERAL WORKS

Currency Risk Management. Gary Shoup, editor. Fitzroy Dearborn Publishers Inc. • 1998. $55.00.

Exchange Rate Determination and Adjustment. Jagdeep S. Bhandari. Greenwood Publishing Group, Inc. • 1982. $70.00.

Financial Institutions and Markets. Meir J. Kohn. Oxford University Press, Inc. • 2003. $115.00. Second edition.

Foreign Exchange Exposure Management: A Portfolio Approach. Niso Abuaf and Stephan Schoess. Executive Enterprises Publications Co. Inc. • 1988. $59.95.

ALMANACS AND YEARBOOKS

International Monetary Fund. Annual Report on Exhange Arrangements and Exchange Restrictions. International Monetary Fund Publications Services. • Annual. Individuals, $95.00; libraries, $47.50.

World Currrency Yearbook. International Currency Analysis, Inc. • Annual. $250.00. Directory of more than 110 central banks worldwide.

HANDBOOKS AND MANUALS

The Bond and Money Markets: Strategy, Trading, Analysis. Moorad Choudhry. Elsevier Butterworth Heinemann. • 2003. $115.00. Serves as a reference work on corporate bonds, government bonds, currency markets, interest-rate futures, convertible securities, various kinds of derivatives, and technical analysis of financial securities.

Foreign Exchange Handbook: Managing Risk and Opportunity in Global Currency Markets. Paul Bishop and Don Dixon. McGraw-Hill. • 1992. $69.95. Discusses factors affecting currency value, currency price forecasting, options trading, futures, credit risk, and related subjects.

International Guide to Foreign Currency Management. Gary Shoup, editor. Glenlake Publishing Co., Ltd. • 1999. $65.00. Written for corporate financial managers. Covers the market for currencies, price forecasting, exposure of various kinds, and risk management.

Strategic Trading in the Foreign Exchange Markets. Gary Klopfenstein. Fitzroy Dearborn Publishers, Inc. • 2000. $65.00. Describes the tactics of successful foreign exchange traders.

INTERNET DATABASES

Factiva. Dow Jones Reuters Business Interactive, LLC. Phone: 800-369-7466 or (609)452-1511 Fax: (609)520-5770 E-mail: solutions@factiva.com • URL: http://www.factiva.com • Fee-based Web site provides "global news and business information through Web sites and content integration solutions." Includes Dow Jones and Reuters newswires, The Wall Street Journal, and more than 7,000 other sources of current news, historical articles, market research reports, and investment analysis. Content includes 96 major U. S. newspapers, 900 non-English sources, trade publications, media transcripts, country profiles, news photos, etc.

Federal Reserve Board Publications and Education Resources. Board of Governors of the Federal Reserve System. Phone: (202)452-3000 Fax: (202)452-3819 • URL: http://www.federalreserve.gov/publications.htm • Web site provides convenient access to statistics, surveys, and research from the Federal Reserve Board. *Federal Reserve Bulletin* articles are available as abstracts or full text (PDF) currently or from six-year archives. The link "Statistics: Releases and Historical Data" offers daily, weekly, monthly, quarterly, and annual data in great detail for interest rates, foreign exchange, consumer credit, money stock measures, industrial production indexes, bank reserves, and other items. Historical tabulations are available for various time periods. Fees: Free.

Financial Times: Where Information Becomes Intelligence. FT Group. Phone: 800-628-8088 • URL: http://www.ft.com • Web site provides extensive data and information relating to international business and finance, with daily updates. Includes Markets Today, Company News, Economic Indicators, Equities, Currencies, Capital Markets, Euro Prices, etc. Fees: Free (registration required).

Gateway to the European Union. European Union. E-mail: pressoffice@eurostat.cec.be • URL: http://www.europa.eu.int • Web site provides access to a wide variety of EU information, including statistics (Eurostat), news, policies, publications, key issues, and official exchange rates for the euro. Includes links to the European Central Bank, the European Investment Bank, and other institutions. Fees: Free.

Nexis.com. Lexis-Nexis Group. Phone: 800-227-4908 or (937)865-6800 Fax: (937)865-6909 E-mail: webmaster@prod.lexis-nexis.com • URL: http://www.nexis.com • Fee-based Web site offers searching of about 2.8 billion documents in some 30,000 news, business, and legal information sources. Features include a subject directory covering 1,200 topics in 34 categories and a Company Dossier containing information on more than 500,000 public and private companies. Boolean searching is offered.

Wall Street Journal Interactive Edition. Dow Jones & Co., Inc. Phone: 800-369-2834 or (212)416-2000 Fax: (212)416-2658 E-mail: inquiries@interactive. wsj.com • URL: http://www.wsj.com • Fee-based Web site providing online searching of worldwide information from the *The Wall Street Journal.* Includes "Company Snapshots," "The Journal's Greatest Hits," "Index to Market Data," "Journal Links," etc. Financial price quotes are available. Fees: $49.00 per year; $29.00 per year to print subscribers.

PERIODICALS AND NEWSLETTERS

American Banker: The Financial Services Daily. Thomson Media. • Daily. $895.00 per year. Provides news of banking, investment products, mortgages, credit unions, finance, bank technology, and legal developments.

Financial Times [London]. The Financial Times, Inc. • Daily, except Sunday. $572.88 per year. An international business and financial newspaper, featuring news from London, Paris, Frankfurt, New York, and Tokyo. Includes worldwide stock and bond market data, commodity market data, and monetary/currency exchange information.

Foreign Exchange Letter. Institutional Investor, Inc., Journals Group. • Biweekly. $1,625.00 per year. Newsletter. Provides information on foreign exchange rates, trends, and opportunities. Edited for banks, multinational corporations, currency traders, and others concerned with money rates.

Foreign Exchange Rates. U.S. Federal Reserve System. • Weekly, $20.00 per year; monthly, $5.00 per year.

International Market Alert. United Communications Group. • Description: Provides a fax service covering financial markets, world economy developments, foreign exchange, and U.S. interest rates.

International Monetary Fund Staff Papers. International Monetary Fund, Publication Services. • Quarterly. Individuals, $56.00 per year; students, $28.00 per year. Contains studies by IMF staff members on balance of payments, foreign exchange, fiscal policy, and related topics. Formerly *International Monetary Fund Staff Papers.*

Rundt's World Business Intelligence. S. J. Rundt and Associates, Inc. • Weekly. $695.00 per year. Formerly *Rundt's Weekly Intelligence.*

U. S. Banker. Thomson Media. • Monthly. $65.00 per year. Edited for bank executives and managers. Covers a wide variety of banking and financial topics.

The Wall Street Journal. Dow Jones & Co., Inc. • Daily. $189.00 per year. Covers news and trends relating to business, industry, finance, the economy, and international commerce. Provides extensive price and other data for the securities, commodity, options, futures, foreign exchange, and money markets.

RESEARCH CENTERS AND INSTITUTES

Institute for International Economics. 1750 Massachusetts Ave., N.W., Washington, DC 20036. Phone: (202)328-9000 Fax: (202)328-5432 E-mail: alreeves@iie.com • URL: http://www.iie.com • Research fields include a wide range of international economic issues, including foreign exchange rates.

STATISTICS SOURCES

Financial Market Trends. Organization for Economic Cooperation and Development. • Quarterly. $80.00 per year. Provides analysis of developments and trends in international and national capital markets. Includes charts and graphs on interest rates, exchange rates, stock market indexes, bank stock indexes, trading volumes, and loans outstanding. Data from OECD countries includes international direct investment, bank profitability, institutional investment, and privatization.

International Financial Statistics. International

Monetary Fund, Publications Services. • Monthly. Individuals, $495.00 per year; students, $247.00 per year. Includes a wide variety of current data for individual countries in Europe and elsewhere. Includes *Annual* issue.

TRADE/PROFESSIONAL ASSOCIATIONS

International Monetary Fund. 700 19th St. NW, Washington, DC 20431. Phone: (202)623-7000 Fax: (202)623-4661 E-mail: publicaffairs@imf.org • URL: http://www.imf.org • Comprises 185 national governments. Works to: facilitate monetary cooperation through consultation and collaboration among member nations; assist in the balanced expansion of trade and thus contribute to the internal development and prosperity of member nations; maintain stability in monetary exchange arrangements, particularly to avoid exchange depreciations; participate in establishing a multilateral system of payments between member nations and in eliminating exchange restrictions that hamper trade; make available the resources of the fund to provide member nations with a means of assuaging economic difficulties. Maintains the IMF Institute, which conducts training courses and seminars and provides lecturers on subjects such as compilation of statistics and formulation and execution of balance of payment policies. Offers technical assistance on monetary matters to member nations and their dependencies and to multinational institutions. Acts as a depository of information and statistical data regarding the economic affairs of member nations. Operates library, in conjunction with the World Bank, on finance and economic development.

FOREIGN INVESTMENTS

See also: FOREIGN TRADE; INTERNATIONAL FINANCE; INVESTMENTS

ALMANACS AND YEARBOOKS

Emerging Markets Analyst. • Monthly. $895.00 per year. Provides an annual overview of the emerging financial markets in 24 countries of Latin America, Asia, and Europe. Includes data on international mutual funds and closed-end funds.

BIBLIOGRAPHIES

Thunderbird International Business Review. Thunderbird American Graduate School of International Management. John Wiley and Sons, Inc., Journals. • Bimonthly. $499.00 per year; with online edition, $532.00 per year. Formerly *International Executive.*

DIRECTORIES

Asia Pacific Securities Handbook. Hoover's Inc. • Covers: stock exchanges and brokers in Australia, Bangladesh, China, Hong Kong, India, Indonesia, Japan, Malaysia, Nepal, New Zealand, Pakistan, Philippines, Singapore, South Korea, Sri Lanka, Taiwan, and Thailand. Entries include: Name, address, phone, fax; exchanges also list market practices, most active and highest capitalized stocks.

Europe's Top Quoted Companies: A Comparative Directory from Seventeen European Stock Exchanges. Kogan Page. • Annual. $325.00. Provides detailed, 5-year financial data on 850 major European companies that are publicly traded. Includes company addresses.

Institutional Buyers of Foreign Stocks: A Targeted Directory. Investment Data Corp. • Annual. $595.00. Provides detailed profiles of institutional buyers of international stocks. Includes names of financial analysts and portfolio managers.

International Centre for Settlement of Investment Disputes - Annual Report. International Centre for Settlement of Investment Disputes. • Annual. Free. Editions available in French and Spanish.

HANDBOOKS AND MANUALS

Global Equity Selection Strategies. Ross P. Bruner, editor. Fitzroy Dearborn Publishers, Inc. • 1999.

$65.00. Written by various professionals in the field of international investments. Contains six major sections covering growth, value, size, price momentum, sector rotation, and country allocation. (Glenlake Business Monographs).

Practical Guide to Foreign Direct Investment in the European Union: The Green Book. Euroconfidentiel S. A. • Annual. $240.00. Provides coverage of national and EU business incentives. In addition to 70 charts and tables, includes EU country profiles of taxation, labor costs, and employment regulations.

INTERNET DATABASES

CANOE: Canadian Online Explorer. Canoe Limited Partnership. Phone: (416)947-2154 Fax: (416)947-2209 • URL: http://www.canoe.ca • Web site provides a wide variety of Canadian news and information, including business and financial data. Includes "Money," "Your Investment," "Technology," and "Stock Quotes." Allows keyword searching, with links to many other sites. Daily updating. Fees: Free.

ETF Connect. Nuveen Investments. Phone: 800-257-8787 • URL: http://www.etfconnect.com • Free Web site makes available extensive, searchable information on individual closed-end investment funds, preferred share funds, and exchange-traded index funds. Information on a particular fund is available by name or as part of a classification (high yield, investment grade, municipal, emerging markets, global equity, etc.). Fund charts are available for various time periods, as is data concerning premiums or discounts, dividends, annualized total return, credit quality, "Top 10 Holdings," and so forth.

ONLINE DATABASES

Worldscope. Thomson Financial. • Online service provides detailed financial and other information on more than 32,000 publicly-owned companies in 50 countries. Includes business description, balance sheets, earnings statements, senior officers, major shareholders, financial ratios, and 20-year historical data. Monthly updates. Inquire as to online cost and availability.

PERIODICALS AND NEWSLETTERS

Emerging Markets Debt Report. Thomson Media. • Weekly. $895.00 per year. Newsletter. Provides information on new and prospective sovereign and corporate bond issues from developing countries. Includes an emerging market bond index and pricing data.

Emerging Markets Quarterly. Institutional Investor, Inc., Journals Group. • Quarterly. Price on application. Newsletter on financial markets in developing areas, such as Africa, Latin America, Southeast Asia, and Eastern Europe. Topics include institutional investment opportunities and regulatory matters. Formerly *Emerging Markets Weekly.*

Global Money Management. Aspen Publishers. • Description: Reports on international fund management, including investment strategies; pension fund searches; hires for consultants, managers, and custodians; performance measurement; developing markets, and significant personnel changes.

Institutional Investor International Edition: The Magazine for International Finance and Investment. Institutional Investor, Inc., Journals Group. • Monthly. $475.00 per year. Covers the international aspects of professional investing and finance. Emphasis is on Europe, the Far East, and Latin America.

Institutional Investor: The Premier of Professional Magazine Finance. Institutional Investor, Inc., Journals Group. • Monthly. $445.00 per year. Includes print and online editions. Edited for portfolio managers and other investment professionals. Special feature issues include "Country Credit Ratings," "Fixed Income Trading

Ranking," "All-America Research Team," and "Global Banking Ranking.".

Journal of Alternative Investments. Institutional Investor, Inc., Journals Group. • Quarterly. $540.00 per year. Includes print and online editions. Covers such items as hedge funds, private equity financing, funds of funds, real estate investment trusts, natural resource investments, foreign exchange, and emerging markets.

STATISTICS SOURCES

Financial Market Trends. Organization for Economic Cooperation and Development. • Quarterly. $80.00 per year. Provides analysis of developments and trends in international and national capital markets. Includes charts and graphs on interest rates, exchange rates, stock market indexes, bank stock indexes, trading volumes, and loans outstanding. Data from OECD countries includes international direct investment, bank profitability, institutional investment, and privatization.

Institutional Investors Statistical Yearbook. Organization for Economic Cooperation and Development. • Annual. $67.00. Provides data relating to institutional saving and investment in OECD countries. Includes investments by insurance companies, pension funds, and investment companies.

International Direct Investment Statistics Yearbook. OECD Publications and Information Center. • Annual. $76.00. Provides direct investment inflow and outflow data for OECD countries.

International Guide to Securities Market Indices. Henry Shilling, editor. Fitzroy Dearborn Publishers, Inc. • 1996. $150.00. Describes 400 stock market, bond market, and other financial price indexes maintained in various countries of the world (300 of the indexes are described in detail, including graphs and 10-year data).

OTHER SOURCES

Investing in Latin America: Best Stocks, Best Funds. Michael Molinski and Constance Anderson. Bloomberg. • 1999. $24.95. Provides Latin American stock and mutual fund recommendations for individual investors. (Bloomberg Personal Bookshelf Series).

Investing, Licensing, and Trading. Economist Intelligence Unit. • Semiannual. $345.00 per year for each country. Key laws, rules, and licensing provisions are explained for each of 60 countries. Information is provided on political conditions, markets, price policies, foreign exchange practices, labor, and export-import.

World Investment Report. United Nations Publications. • Annual. $49.00. Concerned with foreign direct investment, economic development, regional trends, transnational corporations, and globalization.

FOREIGN LANGUAGE PRESS AND NEWSPAPERS

See also: BUSINESS JOURNALISM; NEWSPAPERS

ALMANACS AND YEARBOOKS

Editor and Publisher International Yearbook: Encyclopedia of the Newspaper Industry. Editor and Publisher Co., Inc. • Annual. $150.00. Daily and Sunday newspapers in the United States and Canada.

DIRECTORIES

Bacon's International Directory--Western Europe. Cision US Inc. • Covers: over 16,000 consumer, business, trade, and technical publications, and about 1,000 national and regional newspapers in 12 countries of western Europe. Entries include:

Publication name, address, phone, telex, translation requirements for news releases, code indicating type of publicity in which interested (new products, trade literature, etc.), frequency, circulation.

Benn's Media Directory. Data & Information Services Div. • Covers: over 38,000 daily and weekly newspapers, free newspapers, periodicals, directories, major publishers, television and radio broadcasting stations, media associations, and suppliers of services to the publishing and broadcasting industries. The United Kingdom volume covers all UK media including e-mail and internet addresses; the European and World volumes cover key media in each country in depth and detail. Entries include: For newspapers--Title, year established, affiliated publications, geographical coverage, name and address of publisher, phone, telex, fax, names and titles of key personnel, circulation, frequency. For periodicals--Title, year established and frequency, description of editorial contents, key personnel, address, phone, fax, telex. For broadcasting stations--Firm name, address, phone, waveband, personnel.

Burrelle's Media Directory: Newspapers and Related Media. Burrelle's Information Services. • Annual. $550.00. *Daily Newspapers* volume lists more than 2,200 daily publications in the U. S., Canada, and Mexico. *Non-Daily Newspapers* volume lists more than 10,400 items published no more than three times a week. Provides detailed descriptions, including key personnel.

Hispanic Media and Market Source. SRDS. • Quarterly. $295.00 per year. Provides detailed information on the following Hispanic advertising media in the U. S.: TV, radio, newspapers, magazines, direct mail, outdoor, and special events.

International Media Guide: Newspapers Worldwide. SRDS. • Annual. $350.00. Provides advertising rates, circulation, and other details relating to newspapers in major cities of the world (covers 200 countries, including U. S.).

Willing's Press Guide. Romeike. • Covers: almost 20,000 United Kingdom print media titles, publishers, and broadcasters; over 30,000 periodicals and newspapers in the United Kingdom, with listings for major publications in Europe, the Americas, Australasia, Africa, the Far East, and the Middle East; also includes services and suppliers section to publishers in the United Kingdom. Entries include: For periodicals--Publication title, name of publisher, address, frequency, subscription price, advertising rates, editorial contact names, phone, names and titles of key personnel, circulation. For services--Name, address.

PERIODICALS AND NEWSLETTERS

International Press Journal: International Press News and Views. • Quarterly. $20.00 per year.

World Press Review: News and Views from Around the World. Stanley Foundation. • Monthly. $26.97 per year. International news and information on a wide variety of subjects that do not appear in other American publications.

TRADE/PROFESSIONAL ASSOCIATIONS

Foreign Press Association. 333 E 46th St., Ste. 1K, New York, NY 10017-7425. Phone: (212)370-1054 Fax: (212)370-1058 E-mail: fpanewyork@aol.com • URL: http://www.nyforeignpress.org • Represents foreign print and broadcast correspondents stationed in the U.S.

United Press International. 1510 H St. NW, Washington, DC 20005. Phone: 800-796-4874 or (202)898-8188 Fax: (202)898-8048 E-mail: hguerra@upi.com • URL: http://www.upi.com • Gathers news and photographs of current events to distribute to newspapers, periodicals, cable systems, and radio and television stations throughout the world; maintains 204 local news bureaus in 79 countries. Provides speakers.

FOREIGN LAW

See: INTERNATIONAL LAW AND REGULATION

FOREIGN MARKETS

See: FOREIGN TRADE

FOREIGN OPERATIONS

See: INTERNATIONAL BUSINESS

FOREIGN RADIO AND TELEVISION

See also: FOREIGN LANGUAGE PRESS AND NEWSPAPERS; RADIO BROADCASTING INDUSTRY; TELEVISION BROADCASTING INDUSTRY

DIRECTORIES

International Television and Video Almanac: Reference Tool of the Television and Home Video Industries. Quigley Publishing Co., Inc. • Annual. $130.00.

Media Communications Association International Membership Directory. Media Communications Association International. • Annual. Membership.

PERIODICALS AND NEWSLETTERS

International Broadcast Engineer. DMG World Media Ltd. • Eight times a year. $119.00 per year.

Television International Magazine. TVI Publishing. • Bimonthly. $42.00 per year.

TRADE/PROFESSIONAL ASSOCIATIONS

International Radio and Television Society Foundation. 420 Lexington Ave., Suite 1714, New York, NY 10170. Phone: (212)867-6650 Fax: (212)867-6653 • URL: http://www.irts.org • Affiliated with National Broadcasting Society-Alpha Epsilon Pho. Formerly International Radio and Television Society.

Media Communications Association International. 2810 Crossroads Dr., Ste. 3800, Madison, WI 53718. Phone: (608)443-2464 Fax: (608)443-2474 E-mail: info@mca-i.org • URL: http://www.mca-i.org • Individuals engaged in multimedia communications needs analysis, scriptwriting, producing, directing, consulting, and operations management in the video, multimedia, and film fields. Seeks to advance the benefits and image of media communications professionals.

FOREIGN SERVICE

See: DIPLOMATIC AND CONSULAR SERVICE

FOREIGN STUDY

See: STUDY ABROAD

FOREIGN TRADE

See also: EXPORT-IMPORT TRADE

GENERAL WORKS

From GATT to the WTO: The Multilateral Trading System in the New Millennium. WTO Secretariat, editor. Kluwer Law International. • 2000. $79.50. Published by the World Trade Organization (http://www.wto.org). A collection of essays on the future of world trade, written on the occasion of the 50th anniversary of the multilateral trading system (GATT/WTO). The authors are described as "important academics in international trade.".

Reciprocity, U. S. Trade Policy, and the GATT Regime. Carolyn Rhodes. Cornell University Press. • 1993. $42.50.

U. S. Trade Policy: History, Theory, and the WTO. William A. Lovett and others. M. E. Sharpe, Inc. • 2004. $66.95. Second edition. Discusses the consequences of free trade and the activities of the World Trade Organization. Covers U. S. trade history from colonial times to recent years.

World Trade Issues. Lambert S. Martin, editor. Nova Science Publishers, Inc. • 2002. $69.00. Provides articles by various authors on foreign trade and the influence of globalization, including discussion of the World Trade Organization. Emphasis is on Asian countries and Latin America.

ABSTRACTS AND INDEXES

PAIS International in Print. Public Affairs Information Service, Inc. • Monthly. $850.00 per year; cumulations three times a year. Provides topical citations to the worldwide literature of public affairs, economics, demographics, sociology, and trade. Text in English; indexed materials in English, French, German, Italian, Portuguese and Spanish.

ALMANACS AND YEARBOOKS

Agricultural Policies, Markets, and Trade: Monitoring and Evaluation. Organization for Economic Cooperation and Development. Available from OECD Publications and Information Center. • Annual. $62.00. A yearly report on agricultural and trade policy developments in OECD member countries.

Trade and Development Report and Overview. Available from United Nations Publications. • Annual. $45.00. Yearly overview of trends in international trade, including an analysis of the economic and trade situation in developing countries. Published by the United Nations Conference on Trade and Development (UNCTAD).

BIBLIOGRAPHIES

Global Data Locator. George T. Kurian. Bernan Associates. • 1997. $89.00. Provides detailed descriptions of international statistical sourcebooks and electronic databases. Covers a wide variety of trade, economic, and demographic topics.

Globalization: A Bibliography with Indexes. Marina Elbakidze. Nova Science Publishers, Inc. • 2002. $59.00. Covers various aspects of globalization: effect on society, trade, economics, politics, business, technology, and the environment. Includes author, title, and subject indexes.

CD-ROM DATABASES

OECD Statistical Compendium. Organization for Economic Cooperation and Development. • Semiannual. $1,905.00 per year for 1 to 10 users. CD-ROM contains more than 730,000 monthly, quarterly, and annual time series for OECD countries, 1960 to date. Includes fully searchable data on agriculture, food, economic indicators, national accounts, employment, energy, finance, industry, technology, and foreign trade. Results can be displayed in various forms.

PAIS on CD-ROM. Public Affairs Information Service, Inc. • Quarterly. $1,995.00 per year. Provides a CD-ROM version of the online service, *PAIS International.* Contains over 500,000 citations to the literature of contemporary social, political, and economic issues.

USA Trade. U. S. Department of Commerce. • Monthly. $650.00 per year. Provides over 150,000 trade-related data series on CD-ROM. Includes full text of many government publications. Specific data is included on national income, labor, price indexes,

foreign exchange, technical standards, and international markets. Website address is http://www.stat-usa.gov/.

WILSONDISC: Wilson Business Abstracts. H. W. Wilson Co. • Monthly. Includes unlimited online access to *Wilson Business Abstracts* through WILSONLINE. Provides CD-ROM "cover-to-cover" abstracting and indexing of over 600 prominent business periodicals. Indexing is from 1982, abstracting from 1990. (*Business Periodicals Index* without abstracts is available on CD-ROM at $1,495 per year.).

World Trade Atlas CD-ROM. Global Trade Information Services, Inc. • Monthly. $4,920.00 per year. ($3,650.00 per year with quarterly updates.) Provides government statistics on trade between the U. S. and each of more than 200 countries. Includes import-export data, trade balances, product information, market share, price data, etc. Time period is the most recent three years.

World Trade Organization Trade Policy Review. Bernan Press. • Annual. $95.00. CD-ROM provides detailed trade information for each of 40 countries. Includes search capabilities, hypertext links, charts, tables, and graphs.

DIRECTORIES

Directory of American Firms Operating in Foreign Countries. Uniworld Business Publications. • Biennial. $355.00. Three volumes. Lists approximately 3,000 American companies with more than 34,500 subsidiaries and affiliates in 190 foreign countries.

Directory of Foreign Firms Operating in the United States. Uniworld Business Publications, Inc. • Biennial. $250.00. Lists about 2,400 foreign companies and 5,700 American affiliates. 75 countries are represented.

Internet Resources and Services for International Business: A Global Guide. Lewis-Guodo Liu. Greenwood Publishing Group, Inc. • 1998. $62.95. Describes more than 2,500 business-related Web sites from 176 countries. Includes five major categories: general information, economics, business and trade, business travel, and contacts. Indexed by Web site name, country, and subject.

Principal International Businesses: The World Marketing Directory. • Annual. $5,000. Provides information about 50,000 major businesses located in over 145 countries. Geographic arrangement with company name and product indexes.

Trade Directories of the World. Croner Publications, Inc. • Annual. 100.00. Looseleaf service. Monthly supplements. Lists over 3,300 publications.

U. S. Almanac of International Trade. Bernan Press. • 2000. $225.00. Fifth edition. Provides directory information on individuals and organizations concerned with foreign trade. Contains four sections dealing with: U. S. government, foreign governments, international organizations, and trade-related groups. Formerly *Washington Almanac of International Trade and Business.*

World Business Directory. Gale. • Covers: nearly 140,000 companies in over 180 countries involved in international trade. Entries include: Company name, address, phone, fax, telex, names and titles of key personnel, financial data, number of employees, type of company, fiscal year end, year founded, product description, Standard Industrial Classification (SIC) codes, parent company.

ENCYCLOPEDIAS AND DICTIONARIES

Blackwell Encyclopedic Dictionary of International Management. John J. O'Connell, editor. Blackwell Publishers. • 1999. $130.95. The editor is associated with the American Graduate School of International Management. Contains definitions of key terms combined with longer articles written by various U. S. and foreign business educators. Includes

bibliographies and index. (Encyclopedia of Management Series).

Encyclopedia of Business. Gale Cengage Learning. • 2000. $425.00. Second edition. Two volumes. Contains more than 700 signed articles covering major business disciplines and concepts. International in scope. (Encyclopedia of Business Series).

HANDBOOKS AND MANUALS

Arthur Andersen North American Business Sourcebook: The Most Comprehensive, Authoritative Reference Guide to Expanding Trade in the North American Market. Triumph Books. • 1993. $195.00. Includes statistical, regulatory, economic, and directory information relating to North American trade, including information on the North American Free Trade Agreement (NAFTA). Emphasis is on exporting to Mexico and Canada.

Reference Book for World Traders, 1987. Croner Publications, Inc. • 1990. Price on application. A looseleaf handbook covering information required for planning and executing exports and imports to and from all foreign countries; kept up to date by an amendment service.

INTERNET DATABASES

Bureau of Economic Analysis (BEA). U. S. Department of Commerce, Bureau of Economic Analysis. Phone: (202)606-9900 Fax: (202)606-5310 E-mail: webmaster@bea.doc.gov • URL: http://www.bea.doc.gov • Web site includes "News Release Information" covering national, regional, and international economic estimates from the BEA. Highlights of releases appear online the same day, complete text and tables appear the next day. "Recent News Releases" section provides titles for past nine months, with links. "BEA Data and Methodology" includes "Frequently Requested NIPA Data" (national income and product accounts, such as gross domestic product and personal income). Other statistics are available. Fees: Free.

Business 2.0 Web Guide to the Best Business Links. Business 2.0 Media Inc. Phone: (415)293-4800 E-mail: support@business2.com • URL: http://www.business2.com/webguide • Web site presents an extensive, searchable directory of links to "the best, most informative, and authoritative web pages." Twenty main categories cover business, finance, career, company information, people, and technology topics, with thousands of subtopics, all linking to Web sites recommended by experienced business researchers. Fees: Free.

EBSCO Information Services. Ebsco Publishing. Phone: 800-653-2726 or (978)356-6500 Fax: (978)356-6565 E-mail: ep@epnet.com • URL: http://www.epnet.com • Fee-based Web site providing Internet access to a wide variety of databases, including business-related material. Full text is available for many periodical titles, with daily updates. Fees: Apply.

Fedstats. Federal Interagency Council on Statistical Policy. Phone: (202)395-7254 • URL: http://www.fedstats.gov • Web site features an efficient search facility for full-text statistics produced by more than 100 federal agencies, including the Census Bureau, the Bureau of Economic Analysis, and the Bureau of Labor Statistics. Boolean searches can be made within one agency or for all agencies combined. Links are offered to international statistical bureaus, including the UN, IMF, OECD, UNESCO, Eurostat, and 20 individual countries. Fees: Free.

FedWorld: A Program of the United States Department of Commerce. National Technical Information Service. Phone: (703)605-6000 Fax: (703)605-6900 E-mail: webmaster@fedworld.gov • URL: http://www.fedworld.gov • Web site offers "a comprehensive central access point for searching, locating, ordering, and acquiring government and business information." Emphasis is on searching the

Web pages, databases, and government reports of a wide variety of federal agencies. Fees: Free.

FreeLunch.com. Economy.com, Inc. Phone: (610)696-8700 Fax: (610)696-1678 • URL: http://www.freelunch.com • Web site provides free access to more than 1.5 million economic and financial data series, covering industry, demographics, labor markets, prices, retail sales, government spending, trade, interest rates, housing starts, the stock market, and many other topics. Data is available for various time periods in either chart or table form. Searching is offered. Fees: Free, but registration required. Economy.com, Inc. also offers fee-based economic analysis at *The Dismal Scientist* site (http://www.dismal.com).

InSite 2. Intelligence Data/Thomson Financial. Phone: 800-654-0393 or (617)856-1890 Fax: (617)737-3182 E-mail: intelligence.data@tfn.com • URL: http://www.insite2.gale.com/ • Fee-based Web site consolidates information in a "Base Pack" consisting of Business InSite, Market InSite, and Company InSite. Optional databases are Consumer InSite, Health and Wellness InSite, Newsletter InSite, and Computer InSite. Includes fulltext content from more than 2,500 trade publications, journals, newsletters, newspapers, analyst reports, and other sources. Continuous updating. Formerly produced by The Gale Group.

ProQuest Direct. ProQuest Inc. Phone: 800-889-3358 or (734)761-4700 Fax: (734)662-4554 • URL: http://proquest.com • Fee-based Web site providing Internet access to more than 3,000 periodicals, newspapers, and other publications. Many items are available full-text, with daily updates. Includes extensive corporate and financial information. Fees: Apply.

Trade Show Center. Global Sources/Trade Media Holdings Ltd. [Singapore]. Phone: (656)574-2800 E-mail: service@globalsources.com • URL: http://www.globalsources.com/TRADESHW/TRDSHFRM.HTM • Free Web site provides current, detailed information on more than 1,000 major trade shows worldwide, including events in the U. S., but with an emphasis on "Asia and Greater China." Searching is offered by product, supplier, country, and month of year. Includes links to "Trade Information.".

ONLINE DATABASES

EconLit. American Economic Association. • Covers the worldwide literature of economics as contained in selected monographs and about 550 journals. Subjects include microeconomics, macroeconomics, economic history, inflation, money, credit, finance, accounting theory, trade, natural resource economics, and regional economics. Time period is 1969 to present, with monthly updates. Inquire as to online cost and availability.

PAIS International. Public Affairs Information Service, Inc. • Corresponds to the former printed publications, *PAIS Bulletin* (1976-90) and *PAIS Foreign Language Index* (1972-90), and to the current *PAIS International in Print* (1991 to date). Covers economic, political, and sociological material appearing in periodicals, books, government documents, and other publications. Updating is monthly. Inquire as to online cost and availability.

Wilson Business Abstracts Online. H. W. Wilson Co. • Indexes and abstracts 600 major business periodicals, plus the *Wall Street Journal* and the business section of the *New York Times.* Indexing is from 1982, abstracting from 1990, with the two newspapers included from 1993. Updated weekly. Inquire as to online cost and availability. (*Business Periodicals Index* without abstracts is also available online.).

PERIODICALS AND NEWSLETTERS

Direction of Trade Statistics. International Monetary Fund. International Monetary Fund Publications Services. • Quarterly. Individuals, $128.00 per year; libraries, $89.00 per year. Includes *Yearbook.*

Economic Justice Report: Global Issues of Economic Justice. Ecumenical Coalition for Economic Justice. • Quarterly. Individuals, $30.00 per year; institutions, $40.00 per year. Reports on economic fairness in foreign trade. Formerly *Gatt-Fly Report.*

EuroWatch. LRP Publications. • Description: Provides news and analysis from European capitals and Washington, D.C. concerning how the United States' and other business interests are affected by the European Community's program to remove national barriers and create a single market for the trade and movement of goods, services, capital, and labor.

International Trade Reporter Export Reference Manual. BNA, Inc. • Biweekly. $874.00 per year. Looseleaf service.

The Journal of International Trade and Economic Development. Taylor and Francis Group. • Quarterly. Individuals, $81.00 per year; institutions, $529.00 per year. Emphasizes the effect of trade on the economies of developing nations.

Journal of World Trade. Kluwer Academic Publishers. • Bimonthly. Institutions, $599.00 per year. Includes print and online editions. Formerly *Journal of World Trade Law.*

Project Finance Monthly. Infocast Inc. • Description: Provides information about the power industry. Includes industry news, financing, regulation, and contracts.

World Trade: For U.S. Executives with Global Vision. BNP Media. • Monthly. $24.00 per year. Edited for senior management of U. S. companies engaged in international business and trade.

World Trade Review: Economics, Law, International Institutions. Cambridge University Press. • Three times a year. Individuals, $48.00 pr year; institutions, $200.00 per year. Published in conjunction with the World Trade Organization (http://www.wto.org). Covers "issues of relevance to the multilateral trading system.".

WTO Focus. World Trade Organization, Publications Service. • Newsletter. Free. 10 times a year. Text in English. Provides current news about activities relating to the World Trade Organization (WTO) and the General Agreement on Tariffs and Trade (GATT). Formerly *GATT Focus.*

RESEARCH CENTERS AND INSTITUTES

Conference Board, Inc. The Conference Board, Inc. 845 3rd Ave., New York, NY 10022. Phone: (212)339-0345 Fax: (212)980-7014 E-mail: info@conference-board.org • URL: http://www.conference-board.org • Business management practices worldwide, especially economic, and demographic in nature. Specific concerns include: corporate citizenship, including corporate contributions, diversity, environmental policy and issues, and government relations; corporate governance, including boards of directors, role of chief executives, relations with institutional investors, and shareholder input and influence; economics, including economic and financial forecasts, consumer confidence, leading economic indicators, North American outlook and trends, and global economic environment; human resources and organizational effectiveness, including organization structure and design, compensation and benefits, training and development, and communications; and performance excellence.

International Law Institute. International Law Institute. The Foundry Bldg., 1055 Thomas Jefferson St. NW, Washington, DC 20007. Phone: (202)247-6006 Fax: (202)247-6010 E-mail: kphan@ili.org • URL: http://www.ili.org • Issues of international law and development, including American and international antitrust law; trade agreements; problems of investments in foreign countries and of foreign investments in the U.S.; comparative studies on corporation and labor law, including studies of economic development, foreign investments and loans, transfer of technology, arbitration, petroleum and mining, trade, budgeting, management, and procurement, and contracting. Performs surveys of literature on U.S. trade policy instruments and their implementation, operation, and industry performance implications; also assesses U.S. international economic policy.

STATISTICS SOURCES

Agriculture Fact Book. Available from U. S. Government Printing Office. • Annual. $26.00. Issued by the Office of Communications, U. S. Department of Agriculture. Includes data on U. S. agriculture, farmers, food, nutrition, and rural America. Programs of the Department of Agriculture in six areas are described: rural economic development, foreign trade, nutrition, the environment, inspection, and education.

Business Statistics of the United States. Linz Audain and Cornelia J. Strawser. Bernan Associates. • Annual. $147.00. Based on *Business Statistics,* formerly issue by the Bureau of Economic Analysis, U. S. Department of Commerce. Provides basic data for a wide variety of U. S. industries, services, and economic indicators. Most statistics are shown annually for 30 years and monthly for the most recent four years.

Economic Report of the President: Together with the Annual Report of the Council of Economic Advisors. Available from U. S. Government Printing Office. • Annual. $32.00. Includes about 130 pages of "Statistical Tables Relating to Income, Employment, and Production." Tables cover national income, employment, wages, productivity, manufacturing, prices, credit, finance (public and private), corporate profits, and foreign trade.

Foreign Trade by Commodities (Series C). OECD Publications and Information Center. • Annual. $625.00. Five volumes. Presents detailed five-year export-import data for specific commodities in OECD member countries.

Foreign Trade of the United States: Including State and Metro Area Export Data, 2000. Courtenay M. Slater. Bernan Press. • 2000. $147.00. 2001 Provides detailed national, state, and local data relating to U. S. exports and imports.

Handbook of International Economic Statistics. Available from National Technical Information Service. • Annual. $40.00. Prepared by U. S. Central Intelligence Agency. Provides basic statistics for comparing worldwide economic performance, with an emphasis on Europe, including Eastern Europe.

Handbook of International Trade and Development Statistics. United Nations Publications. • Annual. $80.00. Text in English and French.

International Trade Statistics Yearbook. United Nations Statistical Office. United Nations Publications. • Annual. $135.00. Two volumes.

Monthly Bulletin of Statistics. United Nations Publications. • Monthly. $295.00 per year. Provides current data for about 200 countries on a wide variety of economic, industrial, and demographic subjects. Compiled by United Nations Statistical Office.

Monthly Statistics of International Trade. Organization for Economic Cooperation and Development. • Monthly. $270.00 per year. Provides foreign trade data for OECD countries. Includes statistics by country and by product classification according to Standard International Trade Classification. (Also available on CD-ROM.)

National Trade Estimate Report on Foreign Trade Barriers [year]. Available from U. S. Government Printing Office. • Annual. $47.00. Issued by the Office of the United States Trade Representative.

"Provides quantitative estimates of the impact of foreign practices on the value of United States exports.".

Services: Statistics on International Transactions. Organization for Economic Cooperation and Development. Available from OECD Publications and Information Center. • Annual. $71.00. Presents a compilation and assessment of data on OECD member countries' international trade in services. Covers four major categories for 20 years: travel, transportation, government services, and other services.

State Profiles: The Population and Economy of Each U. S. State. Courtenay Slater and Others. Bernan Press. • 1999. $89.00. Presents charts, tables, and text in an eight-page profile for each state. Covers population, labor force, income, poverty, employment, wages, industry, trade, housing, education, health, taxes, and government finances. (The Population and Economy of Each United States Series).

Statistical Yearbook. United Nations Publications. • Annual. $125.00. Contains statistics for about 200 countries on a wide variety of economic, industrial, and demographic topics. Compiled by United Nations Statistical Office.

Survey of Current Business. Available from U. S. Government Printing Office. • Monthly. $63.00 per year. Issued by Bureau of Economic Analysis, U. S. Department of Commerce. Presents a wide variety of business and economic data.

UNCTAD Handbook of Statistics. United Nations Conference on Trade and Development. United Nations Publications. • Annual. $80.00. Contains a "comprehensive collection of statistical data relevant to the analysis of world trade, investment, and development." Includes rank-orderings, growth rates, and 20-year time series.

World Trade Annual. United Nations Statistical Office. Walker and Co. • Annual. Prices vary.

WTO Annual Report (World Trade Organization). Available from Bernan Associates. • Annual. $80.00. Two volumes ($40.00 per volume). Published by the World Trade Organization. Volume one: *Annual Report.* Volume two: *International Trade Statistics.*

TRADE/PROFESSIONAL ASSOCIATIONS

National Foreign Trade Council. 1625 K St. NW, Ste. 200, Washington, DC 20006. Phone: (202)887-0278 Fax: (202)452-8160 E-mail: nftcinformation@nftc.org • URL: http://www.nftc.org • Manufacturers, exporters, importers, foreign investors, banks, transportation lines, and insurance, communication, law, accounting, service, and publishing firms. Works to promote and protect American foreign trade and investment. Areas of concern include the removal of arbitrary barriers to expansion of international trade and investment; a greater awareness by the government that this expansion is essential to the economic growth of the U.S.; the formation of a cohesive, consistent international economic policy.

World Trade Centers Association. 420 Lexington Ave., Ste. 518, New York, NY 10170. Phone: 800-937-8886 or (212)432-2626 Fax: (212)488-0064 E-mail: wtca@wtca.org • URL: http://world.wtca.org/portal/site/wtcaonline • Regular members are organizations involved in the development or operation of a World Trade Center (WTC). Affiliate members are Chambers of Commerce, clubs, exhibit facilities or other international trade related organizations. Encourages expansion of world trade and international business relationships.

OTHER SOURCES

Foreign Tax and Trade Briefs. LexisNexis Matthew Bender. • Quarterly. $550.00 per year. Two looseleaf volumes. The latest tax and trade information for over 100 foreign countries.

Trade Policy Agenda. Available from U. S. Government Printing Office. • Annual. $45.00. Lists U. S. trade agreements "that afford increased foreign market access or reduce foreign barriers...".

Trade Policy Reviews. Bernan Press. • Annual. Price varies for each country's review (31 are available). Each review describes "trade policies, practices, and macroeconomic situations." Prepared by the Trade Policy Review Board of the World Trade Organization.

World Trade Organization Dispute Settlement Decisions: Bernan's Annotated Reporter. Bernan Press. • Dates vary. $75.00 per volume. Contains all World Trade Organization Panel Reports and Appellate Decisions since the establishment of the WTO in 1995. Includes such cases as "The Importation, Sale, and Distribution of Bananas.".

FOREMEN

See: FACTORY MANAGEMENT

FOREST PRODUCTS

See also: HARDWOOD INDUSTRY; LUMBER INDUSTRY; PAPER INDUSTRY

GENERAL WORKS

Decision-Making in Forest Management. R. W. Williams, editor. State Mutual Book and Periodical Service, Ltd. • 1988. $63.00.

Forest Products and Wood Science: An Introduction. Jim L. Bowyer and others. Blackwell Publishing. • 2002. Fourth edition. Price on application.

Introduction to Forest Science. Scholargy Custom Publishing, Inc. • 2002. $42.57. Looseleaf service.

ABSTRACTS AND INDEXES

Forestry Abstracts: Compiled from World Literature. Available from CABI Publishing North America. • Monthly. Institutions, $1,435.00 per year. Print and online edition, $1,460.00 per year. Published in England by CABI Publishing. Provides worldwide coverage of the literature.

ALMANACS AND YEARBOOKS

Agricultural and Mineral Commodities Year Book. Available from Taylor & Francis Group. • Annual. $225.00. Published by Europa Publications. Contains descriptive product profiles, price data, export-import data, and production statistics for major commodities of the world. Includes commodity histories, uses, markets, demand trends, and information about trade agreements and key commodity organizations.

Wood Technology-Equipment Catalog and Buyers' Guide. CMP Media, Inc. • Annual. $55.00. Formerly *Forest Industries-Lumber Review and Buyers' Guide.*

CD-ROM DATABASES

AGRICOLA on SilverPlatter. Available from SilverPlatter Information, Inc. • Quarterly. $825.00 per year. Produced by the National Agricultural Library. Provides about three million citations on CD-ROM to the literature of agriculture, agricultural economics, animal sciences, entomology, fertilizer, food, forestry, nutrition, pesticides, plant science, water resources, and other topics. Each quarterly disc covers the past ten years, with archival discs available from 1970.

ENCYCLOPEDIAS AND DICTIONARIES

Encyclopedia of Agriculture Science. Charles J. Arntzen and Ellen M. Ritter, editors. Elsevier. • 1994. $900.00. Four volumes.

Encyclopedia of Wood: A Tree by Tree Guide to the World's Most Valuable Resource. Bill Lincoln and

others. Facts on File, Inc. • 1989. $29.95.

FINANCIAL RATIOS

IRS Corporate Financial Ratios. Available from MarketResearch.com. • 2002. $225.00. Published by Schonfeld & Associates, Inc. Presents 70 key financial ratios for 260 industries. Ratios are calculated from income statement and balance sheet data available from the Internal Revenue Service. Includes four asset size classes.

INTERNET DATABASES

USDA. United States Department of Agriculture. Phone: (202)720-2791 E-mail: agsec@usda.gov • URL: http://www.usda.gov • The USDA home page has six sections: News and Information; What's New; About USDA; Agencies; Opportunities; Search and Help. Keyword searching is offered from the USDA home page and from various individual agency home pages. Agencies are the Economic Research Service, Agricultural Marketing Service, National Agricultural Statistics Service, National Agricultural Library, and about 12 others. Updating varies. Fees: Free.

ONLINE DATABASES

Business and Industry. Gale Cengage Learning. • Contains online citations, abstracts, and selected fulltext from more than 1,000 trade journals, newspapers, and other publications. Provides general coverage of both manufacturing and service industries, including marketing, production, industry trends, key events, and information on specific companies. Time span is 1994 to date. Daily updates. Inquire as to online cost and availability. (Also available in a CD-ROM version.).

CAB Abstracts. CAB Publishing North America. • Contains 46 specialized abstract collections covering over 10,000 journals and monographs in the areas of agriculture, horticulture, forest products, farm products, nutrition, dairy science, poultry, grains, animal health, entomology, etc. Time period is 1972 to date, with monthly updates. Inquire as to online cost and availability. *CAB Abstracts on CD-ROM* also available, with annual updating.

PaperChem Database. Information Services Div. • Worldwide coverage of the scientific and technical paper industry chemical literature, including patents, 1967 to present. Weekly updates. Inquire as to online cost and availability.

PIRA. PIRA International Information Centre. • Citations and abstracts pertaining to bookbinding and other pulp, paper, and packaging industries, 1975 to present. Weekly updates. Inquire as to online cost and availability.

Tablebase. Gale Cengage Learning. • Provides online numerical tabular data from a wide variety of business, organization, and government sources, including about 1,000 trade journals. Includes industry and individual company statistics relating to products, market share, sales forecasts, production, exports, market trends, etc. Time span is 1997 to date. Weekly updates. Inquire as to online cost and availability. (Also available in a CD-ROM version.).

PERIODICALS AND NEWSLETTERS

Forest Products Journal. Forest Products Society. • 10 times a year. $145.00 per year.

Journal of Sustainable Forestry. Haworth Press, Inc. • Quarterly. Institutions, $337.50 per year. An academic and practical journal. Topics include forest management, forest economics, and wood science.

PRICE SOURCES

Official Board Markets: "The Yellow Sheet". Mark Arzoumanian. Advanstar Communications. • Weekly. $160.00 per year. Covers the corrugated container, folding carton, rigid box and waste paper industries.

RESEARCH CENTERS AND INSTITUTES

Forintek Canada Corporation. FPInnovations. 2665 E Mall, Vancouver, BC, Canada V6T 1W5. Phone: (604)224-3221 Fax: (604)222-5690 E-mail: info@van.forintek.ca • URL: http://www.forintek.ca • Wood products, including tree quality, wood quality, utilization of damaged trees, sawing for maximum yield, productivity improvement, panel products, adhesive development, quality control, complete resource utilization, sawmill improvement, techno-economic studies, new uses for wood, biotechnology, and treated wood products. Acts as a liaison between international bodies and industry to help develop codes of standards for the forest products industry.

STATISTICS SOURCES

Agricultural Statistics. Available from U. S. Government Printing Office. • Annual. $38.00. Produced by the National Agricultural Statistics Service, U. S. Department of Agriculture. Provides a wide variety of statistical data relating to agricultural production, supplies, consumption, prices/price-supports, foreign trade, costs, and returns, as well as farm labor, loans, income, and population. In many cases, historical data is shown annually for 10 years. In addition to farm data, includes detailed fishery statistics.

Encyclopedia of American Industries. Gale Cengage Learning. • 2000. $560.00. Third edition. Two volumes. $280.00 per volume. Volume one is *Manufacturing Industries* and volume two is *Service and Non-Manufacturing Industries*. Provides the history, development, and recent status of approximately 1,000 industries. Includes statistical graphs, with industry and general indexes.

Infrastructure Industries USA. Gale Cengage Learning. • 2001. $260.00. Presents statistics and projections relating to economic activity in a wide variety of natural resource and construction industries.

Lumber Production and Mill Stocks. U.S. Bureau of the Census. • Annual. (Current Industrial Reports MA-24T).

Standard & Poor's Industry Surveys. Standard & Poor's. • Semiannual. $1,800.00. Two looseleaf volumes. Includes monthly *Supplements.* Provides detailed, individual surveys of 52 major industry groups. Each survey is revised on a semiannual basis. Also includes "Monthly Investment Review" (industry group investment analysis) and monthly "Trends & Projections" (economic analysis).

Timber Bulletin. Economic Commission for Europe. United Nations Publications. • Irregular. Price on application. Contains international statistics on forest products, including price, production, and foreign trade data.

U. S. Industry and Trade Outlook. Available from National Technical Information Service. • Annual. $69.95. Produced by the International Trade Administration, U. S. Department of Commerce, in a "public-private" partnership with DRI/McGraw-Hill and Standard & Poor's. Provides basic data, outlook for the current year, and "Long-Term Prospects" (five-year projections) for a wide variety of products and services. Includes high technology industries. Formerly *U. S. Industrial Outlook.*

United States Timber Production, Trade, Consumption, And Price Statistics. Forest Service. U.S. Department of Agriculture. • Annual.

Yearbook of Forest Products. Food and Agriculture Organization of the United Nations. Available from Bernan Associates. • Annual. $57.00. Test in

English, French, and Spanish.

TRADE/PROFESSIONAL ASSOCIATIONS

American Forest and Paper Association. 1111 19th St., N.W., Ste. 800, Washington, DC 20036. Phone: (202)463-2700 Fax: (202)463-2471 E-mail: info@afandpa.org • URL: http://www.afandpa.org.

American Wood Preservers Institute. 12100 Sunset Hills Rd., Ste. 130, Reston, VA 20190-3221. Phone: 800-356-2974 or (703)204-0500 Fax: (703)204-4610 E-mail: info@awpa.org • URL: http://www.preservedwood.com • Pressure treating plants for the preservative treatment of wood products; manufacturers and distributors of standard chemical preservatives.

Forest Products Society. 2801 Marshall Ct., Madison, WI 53705-2295. Phone: (608)231-1361 Fax: (608)231-2152 E-mail: info@forestprod.org • URL: http://www.forestprod.org • Individuals interested in wood industry research, development, production, utilization, and distribution, from logging operations through finished products and utilization of residue as by-products. Maintains 30 technical committees.

National Hardwood Lumber Association. PO Box 34518, 6830 Raleigh-LaGrange Rd., Memphis, TN 38184-0518. Phone: (901)377-1818 Fax: (901)382-6419 E-mail: info@nhla.com • URL: http://www.nhla.com • United States, Canadian and International hardwood lumber and veneer manufacturers, distributors, and consumers. Inspects hardwood lumber. Maintains inspection training school. Conducts management and marketing seminars for the hardwood industry. Promotes research in hardwood timber management and utilization. Promotes public awareness of the industry.

Wood Products Manufacturers Association. PO Box 761, Westminster, MA 01473-0761. Phone: (978)874-5445 Fax: (978)874-9946 E-mail: wcma@woodcomponents.org • URL: http://www.wpma.org • Manufacturers of component parts, turned and shaped wood products, moulding, mill-work, manufacturer's representatives, wholesalers, suppliers of lumber, machinery, and service providers in the industry.

FORGERIES

See also: COUNTERFEITING; CRIME AND CRIMINALS; FRAUD AND EMBEZZLEMENT

ENCYCLOPEDIAS AND DICTIONARIES

Encyclopedia of White-Collar and Corporate Crime. Lawrence M. Salinger, editor. Sage Publications, Inc. • 2004. $295.00. Two volumes. Covers such items as fraud, kickbacks, price fixing, tax evasion, bribery, forgery, counterfeiting, embezzlement, extortion, graft, bid rigging, and assorted scams and swindles.

ONLINE DATABASES

NCJRS: National Criminal Justice Reference Service. U.S. Department of Justice. • References print and non-print information on law enforcement and criminal justice, 1972 to present. Monthly updates. Inquire as to online cost and availability.

PERIODICALS AND NEWSLETTERS

FBI Law Enforcement Bulletin. Available from U. S. Government Printing Office. • Monthly. $36.00 per year. Issued by Federal Bureau of Investigation, U. S. Department of Justice. Contains articles on a wide variety of law enforcement and crime topics, including computer-related crime.

TRADE/PROFESSIONAL ASSOCIATIONS

American Association of Handwriting Analysts. 1060 Grandview Blvd., No. 622, Huntsville, AL

35824. Phone: (248)262-4850 Fax: (248)262-4851 E-mail: aahaemail@aol.com • URL: http://www.handwriting.org/aaha.

FORGES

See: FOUNDRIES

FORMS AND BLANKS

DIRECTORIES

Business Forms and Systems Manufacturers. Info USA. • Annual. Price on application. Lists more than 800 suppliers and manufacturers of business forms, labels, and related equipment.

ENCYCLOPEDIAS AND DICTIONARIES

Nichols Cyclopedia of Legal Forms: Annotated. West Group. • $1,968.00. 47 volumes. Annual updates. Provides personal and business forms and alternative provisions for more than 250 subjects.

FINANCIAL RATIOS

Annual Statement Studies. The Risk Management Association. • Annual. Median and quartile financial ratios are given for over 400 kinds of manufacturing, wholesale, retail, construction, and consumer finance establishments. Data is sorted by both asset size and sales volume. Includes a clearly written "Definition of Ratios" and an alphabetical industry index.

Annual Statement Studies: Industry Default Probabilities and Cash Flow Measures. The Risk Management Association. • Annual. $145.00. Serves as a companion volume to the original *Annual Statement Studies.* Gives probability of default estimates on a percentage scale for more than 450 industries. Includes changes in position year-by-year for eight financial statement line items and provides percentage measures of cash flow.

HANDBOOKS AND MANUALS

Business Forms on File. Facts on File Staff. Facts on File, Inc. • Annual. $126.00. Update edition, $49.50.

Complete Book of Personal Legal Forms. Daniel Sitarz. Nova Publishing Co. • 2001. $24.95. Third edition. Provides more than 100 forms, including contracts, bills of sale, promissory notes, leases, deeds, receipts, and wills. Forms are also available on IBM or MAC diskettes. (Legal Self-Help Series).

Complete Book of Small Business Legal Forms. Daniel Sitarz. Nova Publishing Co. • 2002. $24.95. Third edition. Includes CD-Rom and basic forms and instructions for use by small businesses in routine legal situations. Forms are also available on IBM or MAC diskettes. (Small Business Library Series).

Legal Forms for Starting and Running a Small Business. Fred Steingold. Nolo Press. • 2004. $29.99. Third edition.

PMI Book of Project Management Forms. Project Management Institute. • 1997. $49.95. Contains more than 100 sample forms for use in project management. Includes checklists, reports, charts, agreements, schedules, requisitions, order forms, and other documents.

Standard Business Forms for the Entrepreneur. Entrepreneur Media, Inc. • Looseleaf. $59.50. A practical collection of forms useful to entrepreneurial small businesses. (Start-Up Business Guide No. E1319.).

Warren's Forms of Agreements. LexisNexis Matthew Bender. • Biennial. $1,110.00. Eight looseleaf volumes. A compact source of forms that business transaction lawyers are most frequently asked to document.

West's Legal Forms. West Group. • $1,938.00. Multivolume set. Annual cumulation.

PERIODICALS AND NEWSLETTERS

Business Forms, Labels and Systems. North American Publishing Co. • Semimonthly. $95.00 per year. Formerly *Business Forms and Systems.*

Print Solutions Magazine. Document Management Industries Association. • Monthly. Members, $29.00 per year; non-members, $49.00 per year. Formerly *Form.*

TRADE/PROFESSIONAL ASSOCIATIONS

Business Forms Management Association. 319 SW Washington, Ste. 710, Portland, OR 97204-2618. Phone: (503)227-3393 Fax: (503)274-7667 E-mail: bfma@bfma.org • URL: http://www.bfma.org • Persons engaged in forms management work, forms procedures analysis, forms design, or in education in this field; customer service firms selling, manufacturing, or servicing forms and supplies. Provides leadership and education to businesses in areas where the forms profession has demonstrated its special competence; promotes a broader function as a component of effective management; encourages, establishes, and maintains high standards of professional education, competence, and performance; provides a means for the sharing of information through study, programs, and research.

Document Management Industries Association. 433 E Monroe Ave., Alexandria, VA 22301-1645. Phone: 800-336-4641 or (703)836-6232 Fax: (703)836-2241 E-mail: dmia@dmia.org • URL: http://www.dmia.org • Independent distributors, manufacturers, and suppliers to the forms, business printing and document management industries. Sponsors educational and channel marketing programs. Compiles statistics.

OTHER SOURCES

Complete Federal Tax Forms. RIA. • $605.00. Three looseleaf volumes. Periodic supplementation. Contains more than 650 reproducible Internal Revenue Service forms, with instructions.

Current Legal Forms with Tax Analysis. LexisNexis Matthew Bender. • Quarterly. $2,183.00 per year. 34 looseleaf volumes.

E-Commerce and Internet Law: Treatise with Forms. Ian C. Ballon. Glasser Legalworks. • Three looseleaf volumes. $595.00. Periodic supplementation. Analyzes Internet legalities, including litigious matters relating to downloading, streaming, music, video, content aggregation, domain names, chatrooms, and search engines. Includes forms, contracts, checklists, sample pleadings, and an extensive glossary.

Employment Forms and Policies. LexisNexis Matthew Bender. • Looseleaf. $120.00, including CD-ROM. Periodic supplementation available. Contains more than 300 forms, policies, and checklists for use by small or medium-sized businesses. Covers such topics as employee selection, payroll issues, benefits, performance appraisal, dress codes, and employee termination.

Fletcher Corporation Forms Annotated. West Group. • Annual. $1,263.00. 26 volumes.

Forms and Agreements for Architects, Engineers and Contractors. Albert Dib. West Group. • Three times a year. $900.00. Five looseleaf volume. Covers evaluation of construction documents and alternative clauses. Includes pleadings for litigation and resolving of claims. (Real Property Law Series).

Forms of Business Agreements and Resolutions-Annotated, Tax Tested. Prentice Hall PTR. • Three looseleaf volumes. Periodic supplementation. Price on application.

Reproducible Copies of Federal Tax Forms and Instructions. Available from U. S. Government Printing Office. • Annual. $54.00. Two looseleaf volumes issued by the Internal Revenue Service (http://www.irs.gov). "Contains the most frequently requested tax forms and instructions," prepared especially for libraries.

FORMS OF ADDRESS

See: ETIQUETTE

FORWARDING COMPANIES

See: FREIGHT TRANSPORT

FORWARDING FREIGHT

See: FREIGHT TRANSPORT

FOUNDATIONS

See also: ARTS MANAGEMENT; FUND-RAISING; GRANTS-IN-AID; NONPROFIT CORPORATIONS

GENERAL WORKS

Foundation Trusteeship: Service in the Public Interest. John Nason. The Foundation Center. • 1989. $19.95. Covers the roles and responsibilities of foundation boards.

ABSTRACTS AND INDEXES

Foundation Grants Index. The Foundation Center. • Irregular. $165.00 per year. Over 73,000 grants of $10,000 or more. Formerly *Foundation Grants Quarterly.*

BIBLIOGRAPHIES

Literature of the Nonprofit Sector: A Bibliography with Abstracts. The Foundation Center. • Dates vary. Six volumes. $45.00 per volume. Covers the literature of philanthropy, foundations, nonprofit organizations, fund-raising, and federal aid.

BIOGRAPHICAL SOURCES

Who Knows Who: Networking Through Corporate Boards. Jeannette E. Glynn. Who Knows Who Publishing. • 1998. $165.00. Fifth edition. Shows the connections between the board members of major U. S. corporations and major foundations and nonprofit organizations.

CD-ROM DATABASES

Leadership Library on CD-ROM: Who's Who in the Leadership of the United States. Leadership Directories, Inc. • Quarterly. Including access to Internet version (weekly updates). Contains all 14 *Yellow Book* personnel directories on CD-ROM, providing contact and brief biographical information for about 400,000 individuals. Covers business, government, financial institutions, news media, law firms, associations, foreign representatives, and nonprofit organizations. Includes photographs.

Prospector's Choice: The Electronic Product Profiling 10,000 Corporate and Foundation Grantmakers. Gale Cengage Learning. • Annual. Provides detailed CD-ROM information on foundations and corporate philanthropies. Also known as *Corporate and Foundation Givers on Disk.*

DIRECTORIES

Corporate Foundation Profiles. Foundation Center. • Covers: 235 corporate foundations in the United States that award at least $1.25 million in grants each year. Entries include: financial data on 1,131 additional corporate foundations that each give at least $66,000 in grants every year. For detailed entries--Foundation name, address, phone, contact name, detailed information on parent company; names of major donors; purpose and activities, fields of interest, giving limitations, application guidelines; names of officers, trustees, and directors;

publications; financial data. For others--Foundation name, state, financial data.

Corporate Giving Directory: Comprehensive Profiles of America's Major Corporate Foundations and Corporate Charitable Giving Programs. Gale Cengage Learning. • Annual. $550.00. Contains detailed descriptions of the philanthropic foundations of over 1,000 major U. S. corporations. Includes grant types, priorities for giving, recent grants, and advice on approaching corporate givers.

Cumulative List of Organizations Described in Section 170(c) of the Internal Revenue Code of 1986. Available from U. S. Government Printing Office. • Annual. $153.00 per year, including quarterly supplements. Lists about 300,000 organizations eligible for contributions deductible for federal income tax purposes. Provides name of each organization and city, but not complete address information. Arranged alphabetically by name of institution. (Office of Employee Plans and Exempt Organizations, Internal Revenue Service.).

Directory of Operating Grants. Richard M. Eckstein. Research Grant Guides. • Annual. $59.50. Contains profiles for approximately 800 foundations that award grants to nonprofit organizations for such operating expenses as salaries, rent, and utilities. Geographical arrangement, with indexes.

The Foundation 1000. Foundation Center. • Covers: the 1,000 largest corporate, community, and private foundations. Entries include: Foundation name, address, phone, name and title of contact, historical background, names and titles of key personnel, publications, detailed statements of policies and programs, application procedures, grant analysis (by subject, type of grant, and type of recipient), and listing of sample grants for latest year available.

Foundation Reporter: Comprehensive Profiles and Giving Analyses of America's Major Private Foundations. The Taft Group. • Annual. $490.00. Provides detailed information on major U. S. foundations. Eight indexes (location, grant type, recipient type, personnel, etc.).

Grants for Libraries and Information Services. The Foundation Center. • Annual. $75.00. Foundations and organizations which have awarded grants made the preceding year for public, academic, research, special, and school libraries; for archives and information centers; for consumer information; and for philanthropy information centers.

International Directory of Corporate Philanthropy. Available from Taylor & Francis Group. • Annual. $295.00. Published by Europa Publications (http://www.europapublications.com). Contains profiles of about 1,000 corporate foundations and "coordinating organizations" in various countries of the world. Provides details of charitable activities and philanthropic expenditures.

International Foundation Directory. Routledge Reference. • Covers: More than 2,300 foundations, charitable and grant-making NGOs, trusts, and similar nonprofit organizations that operate on an international basis, and selected national foundations worldwide spanning over 100 countries. Entries include: Name, address, founding date, brief history and description of activities, names of officers, publications, and other details.

National Directory of Corporate Giving: A Guide to Corporate Giving Programs and Corporate Foundations. The Foundation Center. • Biennial. $195.00. Provides information on 2,895 corporations that maintain philanthropic programs (direct giving programs or company-sponsored foundations).

National Guide to Funding for Libraries and Information Services. The Foundation Center. • 2001. $115.00. Sixth edition. Contains detailed information on about 600 foundations and corporate direct giving programs providing funding to libraries. Includes indexing by type of support, subject field, location, and key personnel.

Nelson Information's Directory of Plan Sponsors. Nelson Information. • Annual. $610.00. Three volumes. Formerly *Nelson's Directory of Plan Sponsors and Tax-Exempt Funds.*

Nonprofit Sector Yellow Book: Who's Who in the Management of the Leading Foundations, Universities, Museums, and Other Nonprofit Organizations. Leadership Directories, Inc. • Semiannual. $265.00 per year. Covers management personnel and board members of about 1,300 prominent, nonprofit organizations: foundations, colleges, museums, performing arts groups, medical institutions, libraries, private preparatory schools, and charitable service organizations.

Washington: A Comprehensive Directory of the Key Institutions and Leaders in th e National Capitol Area. Columbia Books, Inc. • Annual. $149.00. Provides information on about 5,000 Washington, DC key businesses, government offices, non-profit organizations, and cultural institutions, with the names of about 25,000 principal executives. Includes Washington media, law offices, foundations, labor unions, international organizations, clubs, etc.

HANDBOOKS AND MANUALS

Foundation Fundamentals: A Guide for Grantseekers. The Foundation Center. • 1999. $24. 95. Sixth edition.

INTERNET DATABASES

Welcome to the Foundation Center. The Foundation Center. Phone: (212)620-4230 or (212)807-3679 Fax: (212)807-3677 E-mail: mfn@fdncenter.org • URL: http://www.fdncenter.org • Web site provides a wide variety of information about foundations, grants, and philanthropy, with links to philanthropic organizations. "Grantmaker Information" link furnishes descriptions of available funding.

PERIODICALS AND NEWSLETTERS

Foundation News and Commentary: Philanthropy and the Nonprofit Sector. Council on Foundations, Inc. • Bimonthly. $48.00 per year. Formerly *Foundation News.*

Nonprofit Issues. Donald W. Kramer. • Description: Presents legal information for nonprofit executives and their professional advisors.

RESEARCH CENTERS AND INSTITUTES

Foundation Center. Foundation Center. 79 5th Ave./ 16th St., New York, NY 10003-3076. Phone: 800-424-9836 or (212)620-4230 Fax: (212)807-3677 E-mail: communications@foundationcenter.org • URL: http://foundationcenter.org • Strengthens the nonprofit sector by advancing knowledge about U.S. philanthropy, maintains a comprehensive database on U.S. grantmakers and their grants, and operates research, education and training programs designed to advance philanthropy.

STATISTICS SOURCES

Giving U.S.A: The Annual Report on Philanthropy. American Association of Fund-Raising Counsel. AAFRC Trust for Philanthropy. • Annual. $65.00.

TRADE/PROFESSIONAL ASSOCIATIONS

Council on Foundations. 1828 L St. NW, Ste. 300, Washington, DC 20036. Phone: (202)466-6512 Fax: (202)785-3926 E-mail: webmaster@cof.org • URL: http://www.cof.org • Formerly National Council on Community Foundations.

Independent Sector. 1200 18th St. NW, Ste. 200, Washington, DC 20036. Phone: 888-860-8118 or (202)467-6100 Fax: (202)467-6101 E-mail: info@independentsector.org • URL: http://www. independentsector.org • Represents charities and foundations. Organizes corporate giving programs committed to advancement of the common good in

America and around the world. Leads, strengthens, and mobilizes charitable community.

FOUNDRIES

See also: IRON AND STEEL INDUSTRY

DIRECTORIES

Directory of Steel Foundries and Buyers Guide. Steel Founders' Society of America. • Biennial. $400.00. Available only online. Lists approximately 435 steel foundries in the United States, Canada and Mexico. Formerly *Directory of Steel Foundries in the United States, Canada, and Mexico.*

Foundry Directory and Register of Forges. Metal Bulletin PLC. • Biennial. $165.00. Foundries and forges in the United Kingdom and Europe; suppliers of foundry and forging equipment, raw materials and services.

Modern Casting-Buyer's Reference. American Foundry Society, Inc. • Annual. $25.00. About 1,700 manufacturers, suppliers, and distributors of foundry and metal casting equipment and products. Formerly *Modern Castings - Buyer's Guide.*

FINANCIAL RATIOS

Annual Statement Studies. The Risk Management Association. • Annual. Median and quartile financial ratios are given for over 400 kinds of manufacturing, wholesale, retail, construction, and consumer finance establishments. Data is sorted by both asset size and sales volume. Includes a clearly written "Definition of Ratios" and an alphabetical industry index.

Annual Statement Studies: Industry Default Probabilities and Cash Flow Measures. The Risk Management Association. • Annual. $145.00. Serves as a companion volume to the original *Annual Statement Studies.* Gives probability of default estimates on a percentage scale for more than 450 industries. Includes changes in position year-by-year for eight financial statement line items and provides percentage measures of cash flow.

HANDBOOKS AND MANUALS

Foundryman's Handbook: Facts, Figures, Formulae. Elsevier. • 1986. $114.00. Ninth edition.

PERIODICALS AND NEWSLETTERS

Foundry Management and Technology. Penton Media, Inc. • Monthly. Free to qualified personnel; others, $50.00 per year. Coverage includes nonferrous casting technology and production.

Modern Casting. American Foundry Society, Inc. • Monthly. Free to qualified personnel; others, $50.00 per year.

RESEARCH CENTERS AND INSTITUTES

Cast Metals Laboratory. University of Wisconsin-Madison, Dept. of Materials Science and Engineering, 1509 University Ave., Madison, WI 53706-1595. Phone: (608)262-2562 Fax: (608)262-8353 • URL: http://www.engr.wisc.edu/mse.

Metal Casting Laboratory. Pennsylvania State University, 207 Hammond Bldg., University Park, PA 16802. Phone: (814)863-7290 Fax: (814)863-4745 E-mail: rvoight@psu.edu • URL: http://www. tntech.edu/it/metalcastlab.

STATISTICS SOURCES

Nonferrous Castings. U. S. Bureau of the Census. • Annual. (Current Industrial Reports MA-33E.).

TRADE/PROFESSIONAL ASSOCIATIONS

American Foundry Society. 1695 N Penny Ln., Schaumburg, IL 60173-4555. Phone: 800-537-4237 or (847)824-0181 Fax: (847)824-7848 E-mail: jcall@afsinc.org • URL: http://www.afsinc.org • Technical, trade and management association of foundrymen, patternmakers, technologists, and educators. Sponsors foundry training courses

through the Cast +Metals Institute on all subjects pertaining to the castings industry; conducts educational and instructional exhibits of foundry industry; sponsors 10 regional foundry conferences and 400 local foundry technical meetings. Maintains Technical Information Center providing literature searching and document retrieval service; and Metalcasting Abstract Service involving abstracts of the latest metal casting literature. Provides environmental services and testing; conducts research programs; compiles statistics, provides marketing information.

Casting Industry Suppliers Association. 14175 W Indian School Rd., Ste. B4-504, Goodyear, AZ 85395. Phone: (623)547-0920 Fax: (623)536-1486 E-mail: info@cisa.org • URL: http://www.cisa.org • Manufacturers of foundry equipment and supplies such as molding machinery, dust control equipment and systems, blast cleaning machines, tumbling equipment, and related products. Fosters better trade practices; serves as industry representative before the government and the public. Encourages member research into new processes and methods of foundry operation and disseminates reports of progress in these fields. Compiles monthly statistics on booked and billed sales.

Non-Ferrous Founders' Society. 1480 Renaissance Dr., Ste. 310, Park Ridge, IL 60068. Phone: (847)299-0950 Fax: (847)299-3598 E-mail: nffstaff@nffs.org • URL: http://www.nffs.org • Manufacturers of brass, bronze, aluminum, and other nonferrous castings.

Steel Founders' Society of America. 205 Park Ave., Barrington, IL 60010. Phone: (847)382-8240 Fax: (847)382-8287 E-mail: monroe@sfsa.org • URL: http://www.sfsa.org • Manufacturers of steel casting. Provides technical support and research. Abosorbed Alloy Casting Institute.

FOUNTAIN PENS

See: WRITING INSTRUMENTS

401(K) RETIREMENT PLANS

GENERAL WORKS

A Commonsense Guide to Your 401(k). Mary Rowland. Bloomberg. • 1997. $19.95. Explains how to use a 401(k) plan as a foundation for financial planning. (Bloomberg Personal Bookshelf Series.).

Fundamentals of Employee Benefit Programs. Employee Benefit Research Institute. • 1996. $49. 95. Fifth edition. Provides basic explanation of employee benefit programs in both the private and public sectors, including health insurance, pension plans, retirement planning, social security, and long-term care insurance.

Smart Money Guide to Long-Term Investing: How to Build Real Wealth for Retirement and Other Future Goals. Nellie S. Huang and Peter Finch. John Wiley and Sons, Inc. • 2002. $24.95. The authors are associated with *Smart Money* magazine. Their book emphsizes the importance of effective asset allocation through the years and recommends specific stock and bond mutual funds for retirement, including "The Best and Worst Funds for Your 401(k)."

Social Security, Medicare, and Government Pensions: Get the Most Out of Your Retirement and Medical Benefits. Joseph Matthews and Dorothy M. Berman. Nolo. • 2002. $29.99. Eighth edition. In addition to the basic topics, includes practical information on Supplemental Security Income (SSI), disability benefits, veterans benefits, 401(k) plans, Medicare HMOs, medigap insurance, Medicaid, and how to appeal decisions. (Social Security, Medicare and Pensions Series).

Vanguard Retirement Investing Guide: Charting

Your Course to a Secure Retirement. McGraw-Hill. • 1995. $24.95. Second edition. Covers saving and investing for future retirement. Topics include goal setting, investment fundamentals, mutual funds, asset allocation, defined contribution retirement savings plans, social security, and retirement savings strategies. Includes glossary and worksheet for retirement saving.

DIRECTORIES

Business Insurance: Directory of 401(k) Plan Administrators. Crain Communications, Inc. • Annual. $4.00. Provides information on approximately 75 companies that administer 401(k) retirement plans.

HANDBOOKS AND MANUALS

Estate Plan Book 2000. William S. Moore. American Institute for Economic Research. • 2000. $10.00. Revision of 1997 edition. Part one: "Basic Estate Planning." Part two: "Reducing Taxes on the Disposition of Your Estate." Part three: "Putting it All Together: Examples of Estate Plans." Provides succinct information on wills, trusts, tax planning, and gifts. (Economic Education Bulletin.).

401(k) Handbook. Thompson Publishing Group, Inc. • Two looseleaf volumes. $387.00 per year, including monthly updates and newsletters. Provides detailed information on 401(k) retirement plan design, administration, employee communication, rollovers, federal regulations, plan loans, investment vehicles, and related topics. Includes a glossary.

The 401(k) Plan Handbook. Julie Jason. Prentice Hall PTR. • 1997. $79.95. Provides technical, legal, administrative, and investment details of 401(k) retirement plans.

How to Build Wealth with Tax-Sheltered Investments. Kerry Anne Lynch. American Institute for Economic Research. • 2000. $6.00. Provides practical information on conservative tax shelters, including defined-contribution pension plans, individual retirement accounts, Keogh plans, U. S. savings bonds, municipal bonds, and various kinds of annuities: deferred, variable-rate, immediate, and foreign-currency. (Economic Education Bulletin.).

The New Working Woman's Guide to Retirement Planning: Saving and Investing Now for a Secure Future. Martha P. Patterson. University of Pennsylvania Press. • 1999. $19.95. Second edition. Provides retirement advice for employed women, including information on various kinds of IRAs, cash balance and other pension plans, 401(k) plans, and social security. Four case studies are provided to illustrate retirement planning at specific life and career stages.

Pension Plan Fix-It Handbook. Thompson Publishing Group, Inc. • Two looseleaf volumes. $499.00 per year. Two looseleaf volumes. Monthly updates and newsletters. Serves as a comprehensive guide to pension plan administration, taxation, and federal regulation. Includes both defined benefit and defined contribution plans.

Retirement Planning Guide. Sidney Kess and Barbara Weltman. CCH, Inc. • 2000. $49.00. Second edition. Presents an overview for attorneys, accountants, and other professionals of the various concepts involved in retirement planning. Includes checklists, tables, forms, and study questions.

U. S. Master Pension Guide. CCH, Inc. • Annual. $56.95. Explains IRS rules and regulations applying to 401(k) plans, 403(k) plans, ESOPs (employee stock ownership plans), IRAs, SEPs (simplified employee pension plans), Keogh plans, and non-qualified plans.

INTERNET DATABASES

Mutual Funds Interactive. Brill Editorial Services, Inc. Phone: 877-442-7455 • URL: http://www.brill.com • Web site provides specific information on individual funds in addition to general advice on mutual fund investing and 401(k) plans. Searching is provided, including links to moderated newsgroups and a chat page. Fees: Free.

Small Business Retirement Savings Advisor. U. S. Department of Labor. Phone: (202)219-8921 • URL: http://www.dol.gov/elaws/pwbaplan.htm • Web site provides "answers to a variety of commonly asked questions about retirement saving options for small business employers." Includes a comparison chart and detailed descriptions of various plans: 401(k), SEP-IRA, SIMPLE-IRA, Payroll Deduction IRA, Keogh Profit-Sharing, Keogh Money Purchase, and Defined Benefit. Searching is offered. Fees: Free.

PERIODICALS AND NEWSLETTERS

Defined Contribution News. Aspen Publishers. • Description: Covers all aspects of the defined contribution pension plan market from the plan sponsor and vendor points of view. Discusses topics such as searches for investment managers; record keepers, administrators, and trustees; legislative and regulatory developments; plan profiles; sponsor forums; new vendor products; and personnel changes and DC Database.

Financial Planning: The Magazine for Financial Service Professionals. Thomson Media. • Monthly. $79.00 per year. Edited for independent financial planners and insurance agents. Covers retirement planning, estate planning, tax planning, and insurance, including long-term healthcare considerations. Special features include a Retirement Planning Issue, Mutual Fund Performance Survey, and Variable Life and Annuity Survey.

IOMA's Report on Defined Contribution Plan Investing. Institute of Management and Administration, Inc. • Semimonthly. $1,189.90 per year. Newsletter. Edited for 401(k) and other defined contribution retirement plan managers, sponsors, and service providers. Reports on such items as investment manager performance, guaranteed investment contract (GIC) yields, and asset allocation trends.

IOMA's Report on Managing 401(k) Plans. Institute of Management and Administration, Inc. • Monthly. $269.00 per year. Includes print and online editions. Newsletter for retirement plan managers.

On Wall Street. Thomson Media. • Monthly. $96.00 per year. Edited for securities dealers. Includes articles on financial planning, retirement planning, variable annuities, and money management, with special coverage of 401(k) plans and IRAs.

Plan Sponsor. Asset International, Inc. • Monthly. $150.00 per year. Edited for professional pension plan managers and executives. Defined contribution plans are emphasized.

Retirement Plans Bulletin: Practical Explanations for the IRA and Retirement Plan Professional. Universal Pensions, Inc. • Monthly. $99.00 per year. Newsletter. Provides information on the rules and regulations governing qualified (tax-deferred) retirement plans.

RESEARCH CENTERS AND INSTITUTES

Center for Pension and Retirement Research. Miami University, Department of Economics, 109E Laws Hall, Oxford, OH 45056. Phone: (513)529-2850 Fax: (513)529-3308 E-mail: swilliamson@eh.net • URL: http://www.eh.net/cprr • Research areas include pension economics, pension plans, and retirement decisions.

Employee Benefit Research Institute. Employee Benefit Research Institute. 1100 13 St. NW, Ste. 878, Washington, DC 20005. Phone: (202)659-0670 Fax: (202)775-6312 E-mail: salisbury@ebri.org • URL: http://www.ebri.org • Employee benefits in the public and private sectors, including studies on individual retirement accounts, retirement income, flexible benefits, financing health care for the elderly, health care costs, long-term care, employee benefits and federal tax policy, social security, changing benefits, and government regulation of employee benefit plans.

Pension Research Council. University of Pennsylvania, 304 CPC, 3641 Locust Walk, Philadelphia, PA 19104-6218. Phone: (215)898-7620 Fax: (215)898-0310 E-mail: prc@wharton.upenn.edu • URL: http://www.prc.wharton.upenn.edu/prc • Research areas include various types of private sector and public employee pension plans.

STATISTICS SOURCES

EBRI's Databook on Employee Benefits: What is the Promise?. Ken McDonnell and others. Employee Benefit Research Institute. • 1997 $99.00. Fourth edition. Contains more than 350 tables and charts presenting data on employee benefits in the U. S., including pensions, health insurance, social security, and medicare. Includes a glossary of employee benefit terms.

Handbook of U. S. Labor Statistics: Employment, Earnings, Prices, Productivity, and Other Labor Data. Eva E. Jacobs, editor. Bernan Associates. • 1999. $74.00. Based on *Handbook of Labor Statistics,* formerly issued by the Bureau of Labor Statistics, U. S. Department of Labor. Includes the Bureau's projections of employment in the U. S. by industry and occupation. Provides a wide variety of data on the work force, prices, fringe benefits, and consumer expenditures.

Key Indicators of the Labour Market. Available from Routledge. • Biennial. $125.00. Published by the International Labour Office (http://www.ilo.org). Provides data on 20 key indicators in 220 countries. Includes labor force statistics, employment, unemployment, part-time workers, wages, productivity, poverty indicators, and related topics.

Pension Investment Report. Employee Benefit Research Institute. • Irregualr. Membership.

TRADE/PROFESSIONAL ASSOCIATIONS

American Benefits Council. 1212 New York Ave. NW, Ste. 1250, Washington, DC 20005-3987. Phone: (202)289-6700 Fax: (202)289-4582 E-mail: info@abcstaff.org • URL: http://www.americanbenefitscouncil.org • Serves as national trade association for companies concerned about federal legislation and regulations affecting all aspects of the employee benefits system. Represents the entire spectrum of the private employee benefits community and sponsors or administers retirement and health plans covering more than one hundred million Americans.

American Society of Pension Actuaries. 4245 N. Fairfax Dr., Suite 750, Arlington, VA 22203. Phone: (703)516-9300 Fax: (703)516-9308 E-mail: aspa@aspa.org • URL: http://www.aspa.org • Members are involved in the pension and insurance aspects of employee benefits. Includes an Insurance and Risk Management Committee, and sponsors an annual 401(k) Workshop.

Profit Sharing/401(K) Council of America. 10 S. Riverside Plaza, No. 1610, Chicago, IL 60606-3802. Phone: (312)441-8550 Fax: (312)441-8559 E-mail: psca@psca.org • URL: http://www.psca.org • Members are business firms with profit sharing and/or 401(K) plans. Affiliated with the Profit Sharing/401(K) Education Foundation. Formerly Profit Sharing Council of America.

FRAGRANCE INDUSTRY

See: PERFUME INDUSTRY

FRANCHISES

See also: CHAIN STORES; CONCESSIONS

GENERAL WORKS

Fast Food Nation: The Dark Side of the All-American Meal. Eric Schlosser. Gale Cengage

---

Learning. • 2001. $30.95. Explains how the fast food industry is contributing to obesity, disease, urban sprawl, and other bad things. Special attention is given to the meatpacking industry, *E.coli*, worker injuries, fast food franchise problems, detrimental labor practices, and the effect of fast food diets on children. Companies prominently mentioned are McDonald's, Burger King, Wendy's, Taco Bell, Pizza Hut, Jack in the Box, ConAgra, and Iowa Beef Packers. Includes many research notes, a bibliography, and a detailed index.

The Franchise Option: How to Expand Your Business Through Franchising. Kathryn L. Boe and others. International Franchise Association. • 1987. $24.00. Second edition.

Franchising Dreams. Peter M. Birkeland. The University of Chicago Press. • 2002. $22.50. Provides a serious discussion of both the risks and the benefits of franchising.

Franchising: Realities and Remedies. Harold Brown. American Lawyer Media. • Revised edition. Price on application.

Tips and Traps When Buying a Franchise. Mary E. Tomzack. Source Book Publications. • 1999. $19.95. Second edition. Provides specific cautionary advice and information for prospective franchisees.

DIRECTORIES

Bond's Franchise Guide. Todd Publications. • Covers: 2,000 American and 500 Canadian franchisers divided into 54 business categories. Entries include: Company name, address, phone, fax, names and titles of key personnel for 1,500 franchise operations; for all entries: Company history, size, geographic distribution, financial requirements, staff, start-up assistance and training provided, ongoing royalty fees and franchiser services, and more.

Directory of Franchising Organizations. Prima Publishing. • 1998. $12.95. Lists over 700 franchises with description and cost of investment.

Entrepreneur's Annual Franchise 500 Issue. Entrepreneur Media, Inc. • Annual. $4.95. Provides a ranking of 500 "top franchise opportunities," based on a combination of financial strength, growth rate, size, stability, number of years in business, litigation history, and other factors. Includes 17 major business categories, further divided into about 140 very specific groups (22 kinds of fast food, for example).

Franchise Annual. Todd Publications. • Covers: Approximately 5,000 franchises, distributors, licensors and franchise consultants with U.S. or Canadian headquarters, as well as 465 overseas listings. Entries include: Company description, initial and total investment required, and government rules on franchising.

Franchise Opportunities Guide: A Comprehensive Listing of the World's Leading Franchises. International Franchise Association. • Semiannual. $21.00 per year. More than 600 companies which offer franchises.

Franchise Opportunities Handbook. U. S. International Trade Administration. • Covers: over 1,400 franchisors in some 40 lines of business (auto rentals, campgrounds, foods, security systems, etc.). Entries include: Company name, address, name of contact, description of the business operation franchised, number of franchisees, date company began, amount of capital needed, whether financial assistance is available, and what training and managerial assistance are provided. Also includes general information on securing franchises and operating franchised businesses. Users of the directory are cautioned that the Commerce Department

has not verified statements in the listings for the various franchisors.

ENCYCLOPEDIAS AND DICTIONARIES

Encyclopedia of Small Business. Gale Cengage Learning. • 2002. $450.00. Second edition. Two volumes. Contains about 600 informative entries on a wide variety of topics affecting small business. Arrangement is alphabetical.

HANDBOOKS AND MANUALS

Blueprint for Franchising a Business. Steven S. Raab and Gregory Matusky. John Wiley and Sons, Inc. • 1987. $45.00.

Franchising and Licensing: Two Ways to Build Your Business. Andrew Sherman. AMACOM. • 1999. $45.00. Second edition. Written for the business person who wishes to become a franchiser. Tells how to raise capital, create a prototype, structure franchise agreements, develop operations manuals, market the franchise, and maintain good relations with franchisees.

Guide to Franchising. Martin Mendelsohn. Continuum International Publishing Group, Inc. • 1999. $32.95. Sixth edition.

Master Franchising: Selecting, Negotiating, and Operating a Master Franchise. Carl E. Zwisler. CCH, Inc. • 1999. $80.00. Written for franchisees, franchisers, and professional advisors. Emphasis is on international franchise transactions.

PERIODICALS AND NEWSLETTERS

Entrepreneur: The Small Business Authority. Entrepreneur Media, Inc. • Monthly. $19.97 per year. Contains advice for small business owners and prospective owners. Includes numerous franchise advertisements.

Franchise Times. Sparks Publishing & Reporting Corp. • Description: Provides analysis and information on franchising, including trends and legal and financial aspects. Recurring features include domestic and international franchising news, questions and answers, and an editorial column.

Franchising Business and Law Alert. American Lawyer Media, Inc. • Monthly. $199.00 per year. Newsletter. Provides news of legal developments affecting both franchisors and franchisees. (A Law Journal Newsletter, formerly published by Leader Publications).

Franchising World. International Franchise Association. • Eight times a year. $18.00 per year. Formerly *Franchising Opportunities.*

Info Franchise Newsletter. Info Press Inc. • Description: Covers business format franchising in the U.S., Canada, and overseas; reports on trends, legislation and litigation, and on developments in the franchising business scene. Recurring features include lists of new franchisors, including descriptions, contact addresses and telephone numbers for each; and address changes of franchisor headquarters. Spotlights upcoming seminars, conferences and business opportunity shows.

QSR: The Magazine of Quick Service Restaurant Success. Journalistic, Inc. • Ten times a year. $30.00 per year. Provides news and management advice for quick-service restaurants, including franchisors and franchisees.

ReCareering Newsletter: An Idea and Resource Guide to Second Career and Relocation Planning. Publications Plus, Inc. • Monthly. $59.00 per year. Edited for "downsized managers, early retirees, and others in career transition after leaving traditional employment." Offers advice on second careers, franchises, starting a business, finances, education, training, skills assessment, and other matters of interest to the newly unemployed.

TRADE/PROFESSIONAL ASSOCIATIONS

International Franchise Association. 1501 K St. NW, Ste. 350, Washington, DC 20005. Phone: (202)628-

8000 Fax: (202)628-0812 E-mail: ifa@franchise.org • URL: http://www.franchise.org • Firms in 100 countries utilizing the franchise method of distribution for goods and services in all industries.

OTHER SOURCES

Franchising: Realities and Remedies. American Lawyer Media, Inc. • Looseleaf. $189.00. Two volumes. Updated as needed. Provides comprehensive coverage of common legal problems "faced by both franchisors and franchisees." (Law Journal Press).

Product Distribution Law Guide. CCH, Inc. • $199.00. Looseleaf service. Annual updates available. Covers the legal aspects of various methods of product distribution, including franchising.

FRAUD AND EMBEZZLEMENT

See also: CRIME AND CRIMINALS; FORGERIES

GENERAL WORKS

Dirty Business: Exploring Corporate Misconduct: Analysis and Cases. Maurice Punch. Sage Publications, Inc. • 1996. $113.00. Covers organizational misbehavior and white-collar crime. Includes "Ten Cases of Corporate Deviance.".

Web of Deception: Misinformation on the Internet. Anne P. Mintz, editor. Information Today, Inc. • 2002. $24.95. Barbara Quint, Susan M. Detwiler, and others discuss the spread of intentionally misleading or erroneous information by Web sites. Provides advice on the evaluation of Internet sources. (CyberAge Books.).

ABSTRACTS AND INDEXES

Current Law Index: Multiple Access to Legal Periodicals. Gale Cengage Learning. • Monthly. $725.00 per year. Produced in cooperation with the American Association of Law Libraries. Indexes more than 900 law journals, legal newspapers, and specialty publications from the U.S., Canada, U.K., Ireland, Australia, and New Zealand.

ENCYCLOPEDIAS AND DICTIONARIES

Concise Dictionary of Crime and Justice. Mark S. Davis. Sage Publications, Inc. • 2002. $64.95. Contains more than 2,000 definitions of terms relating to the criminal justice system and criminology.

Encyclopedia of Crime and Justice. Available from Gale Cengage Learning. • 2001. $475.00. Second edition. Four volumes. Published by Macmillan Reference USA. Contains extensive information on a wide variety of topics pertaining to crime, criminology, social issues, and the courts. (A complete revision of 1982 edition.).

Encyclopedia of Crime and Punishment. David Levinson, editor. Sage Publications, Inc. • 2002. $600.00. Four volumes. Contains 425 signed entries dealing with civil, criminal, media, corporate, and international issues. Includes material on fraud, police science, correctional institutions, social matters, methodology, national surveys, and crime statistics.

Encyclopedia of White-Collar and Corporate Crime. Lawrence M. Salinger, editor. Sage Publications, Inc. • 2004. $295.00. Two volumes. Covers such items as fraud, kickbacks, price fixing, tax evasion, bribery, forgery, counterfeiting, embezzlement, extortion, graft, bid rigging, and assorted scams and swindles.

World of Criminal Justice. Gale Cengage Learning. • 2002. $160.00. Two volumes. Contains both topical and biographical entries relating to the criminal justice system and criminology.

HANDBOOKS AND MANUALS

Accountant's Handbook of Fraud and Commercial Crime. G. Jack Bologna and others. John Wiley and

Sons, Inc. • 1992. $225.00.

Banking Crimes: Fraud, Money Laundering and Embezzlement. John K. Villa. West Group. • Annual. $280.00. Looseleaf service. Covers fraud and embezzlement.

Corporate Fraud. Michael J. Comer. Ashgate Publishing Co. • 1997. Third edition. $139.95. Examines new risks of corporate fraud related to "electronic commerce, derivatives, computerization, empowerment, downsizing, and other recent developments." Covers fraud detection, prevention, and internal control systems. Published by Gower in England.

Financial Investigations: A Forensic Accounting Approach to Detecting and Resolving Crimes. Available from U. S. Government Printing Office. • 2002. $54.00. Two volumes: textbook and workbook. Issued by the Internal Revenue Service (http://www.irs.ustreas.gov). Serves as a text "for courses on conducting financial investigations." (IRS Publications 1714 and 1816.).

Financial Shenanigans: How to Detect Accounting Gimmicks and Fraud in Financial Reports. Howard M. Schilit. McGraw-Hill. • 2002. $27.95. Second edition. Tells how to interpret the footnotes and fine print in corporate annual and other reports.

Investigations in the Workplace. Eugene F. Ferraro. CRC Press. • 2004. $79.95. Written for security professionals, lawyers, and human resource directors. Explains how to properly conduct internal investigations in the private sector and avoid litigation. Such investigations may relate to loss prevention, asset protection, or employee rights issues. (Imprint: Auerbach Publications.).

Private Investigator. Entrepreneur Media, Inc. • Looseleaf. $59.50. A practical guide to starting a private investigation agency. Covers profit potential, start-up costs, market size evaluation, pricing, accounting, advertising, promotion, etc. (Start-Up Business Guide No. E1320.).

Securities Crimes. West Group. • Annual. $225.00. Two looseleaf volumes. Analyzes the enfo of federal securities laws from the viewpoint of the defendant. Discusses Securities and Exchange Commission (SEC) investigations and federal sentencing guidelines. (Securities Law Series).

U. S. Master Auditing Guide. CCH, Inc. • 2002. $65.00. Covers such topics as auditing standards, audit management, compliance, consulting, governmental audits, forensic auditing, and fraud. Includes checklists, charts, graphs, and sample reports.

INTERNET DATABASES

Lexis.com Research System. Lexis-Nexis Group. Phone: 800-227-4908 or (937)865-6800 Fax: (937)865-6909 E-mail: webmaster@prod.lexisnexis.com • URL: http://www.lexis.com • Fee-based Web site offers extensive searching of a wide variety of legal sources. Additional features include Daily Opinion Service, lexis.com Bookstore, Career Center, CLE Center, Law Schools, and Practice Pages ("Pages specific to areas of specialty").

ONLINE DATABASES

NCJRS: National Criminal Justice Reference Service. U.S. Department of Justice. • References print and non-print information on law enforcement and criminal justice, 1972 to present. Monthly updates. Inquire as to online cost and availability.

PERIODICALS AND NEWSLETTERS

Business Crimes Bulletin. American Lawyer Media, Inc. • Monthly. $229.00 per year. Newsletter. Provides news of the "multifaceted world of financial and white collar crime." Covers such items as foreign corrupt practices, mail fraud, money laundering, tax fraud, securities law violations, environmental crime, and antitrust violations. Includes developments in sentencing guidelines for white collar perpetrators. (A Law Journal Newslet-

ter, formerly published by Leader Publications).

Claims. National Underwriter Co. • Monthly. $46.00 per year. Edited for insurance adjusters, risk managers, and claims professionals. Covers investigation, fraud, insurance law, and other claims-related topics.

FBI Law Enforcement Bulletin. Available from U. S. Government Printing Office. • Monthly. $36.00 per year. Issued by Federal Bureau of Investigation, U. S. Department of Justice. Contains articles on a wide variety of law enforcement and crime topics, including computer-related crime.

Health Care Fraud and Abuse Newsletter. American Lawyer Media, Inc. • Monthly. $195.00 per year. Newsletter. Provides legal news relating mainly to fraudulent or excessive medical billing practices. Covers both civil and criminal proceedings. (A Law Journal Newsletter, formerly published by Leader Publications).

White-Collar Crime Reporter: Information and Analyses Concerning White-Collar Practice. Andrews Publications. • 10 times a year. $550.00 per year. Newsletter. Provides information on trends in white collar crime.

STATISTICS SOURCES

Uniform Crime Reports for the United States. Federal Bureau of Investigation, U.S. Department of Justice. Available from U.S. Government Printing Office. • Annual. $45.00.

TRADE/PROFESSIONAL ASSOCIATIONS

American Society of Criminology. 1314 Kinnear Rd., Suite 212, Columbus, OH 43212-1156. Phone: (614)292-9207 Fax: (614)292-6767 E-mail: asc41@infinet.com • URL: http://www.asc41.com • Formerly Society for the Advancement of Criminology.

OTHER SOURCES

Consumer Protection and the Law. Mary D. Pridgen. West Group. • Annual. $269.00. Looseleaf service. Covers advertising, sales practices, unfair trade practices, consumer fraud, and product warranties.

Forensic Accounting and Financial Fraud. American Management Association Extension Institute. • Looseleaf. $159.00. Self-study course. Emphasis is on practical explanations, examples, and problem solving. Quizzes and a case study are included.

White Collar Crime: Business and Regulatory Offenses. American Lawyer Media, Inc. • Looseleaf. $249.00. Updated as needed. Covers such legal matters as criminal tax cases, securities fraud, computer crime, mail fraud, bank embezzlement, criminal antitrust activities, extortion, perjury, the criminal liability of corporations, and RICO (Racketeer Influenced and Corrupt Organization Act). (Law Journal Press).

FRAUD, COMPUTER

See: COMPUTER CRIME AND SECURITY

FREEDOM OF INFORMATION

GENERAL WORKS

Freedom of Information Act. Christopher L. Henry. Nova Science Publishers, Inc. • 2003. $29.50. Serves as a practical guide to making a freedom of information request to the U.S. Justice Department. Includes copies of forms.

ABSTRACTS AND INDEXES

Index to Legal Periodicals and Books. H. W. Wilson Co. • Monthly. $490.00 per year. Quarterly and annual cumulations.

DIRECTORIES

American Society of Access Professionals-Membership Directory. American Society of Access

Professionals. • Annual. Membership.

HANDBOOKS AND MANUALS

Citizen's Guide on Using the Freedom of Information Act and the Privacy Act of 1974 to Request Government Records. U. S. Government Printing Office. • 1997. $5.00.

Guidebook to the Freedom of Information and Privacy Acts. Robert F. Bouchard and Douglas E. Franklin. West Group. • Semiannual. $291.50 per year. Two looseleaf volumes. Includes procedures for requesting and acquiring business and government data.

ONLINE DATABASES

Index to Legal Periodicals and Books (Online). H. W. Wilson Co. • Broad coverage of law journals and books 1981 to date. Monthly updates. Inquire as to online cost and availability.

Legal Resource Index. Gale Cengage Learning. • Broad coverage of law literature appearing in legal, business, and other periodicals, 1980 to date. Daily updates. Inquire as to online cost and availability.

LEXIS. LEXIS-NEXIS. • The various LEXIS databases provide full text and indexing for a wide variety of legal cases, statutes, orders, and opinions.

PERIODICALS AND NEWSLETTERS

Access Reports: Freedom of Information. Access Reports, Inc. • Biweekly. $350.00 per year. Newsletter.

FTC Freedom of Information Log (Federal Trade Commission). Washington Regulatory Reporting Associates. • Weekly. $451.00 per year. Newsletter listing Freedom of Information Act requests that have been submitted to the Federal Trade Commission.

The IRE Journal (Investigative Reporters and Editors). Investigative Reporters and Editors, Inc. • Bimonthly. Free to members; non-members, $60.00 per year; institutions, $70.00 per year. Contains practical information relating to investigative journalism.

RESEARCH CENTERS AND INSTITUTES

Public Law Education Institute. Public Law Education Institute. 454 New Jersey Ave. SE, Washington, DC 20002. Phone: (202)544-8646 • Investigation and legal analysis of issues relating to military justice, veterans rights and benefits, selective service, federal tort claims, federal judiciary, and freedom of information.

TRADE/PROFESSIONAL ASSOCIATIONS

American Society of Access Professionals. 1441 Eye St. N.W., Suite 700, Washington, DC 20005-6542. Phone: (202)712-9054 Fax: (202)216-9646 E-mail: asap@bostromdc.com • URL: http://www.accesspro.org • Members are individuals concerned with safeguarding freedom of information, privacy, open meetings, and fair credit reporting laws.

Electronic Frontier Foundation. 454 Shotwell St., San Francisco, CA 94110-1914. Phone: (415)436-9333 Fax: (415)436-9993 E-mail: information@eff.org • URL: http://www.eff.org • Promotes the creation of legal and structural approaches to help ease the assimilation of new technologies by society. Seeks to: help policymakers develop a better understanding of issues underlying telecommunications; increase public understanding of the opportunities and challenges posed by computing and telecommunications fields. Fosters awareness of civil liberties issues arising from the advancements in new computer-based communications media and supports litigation to preserve, protect, and extend First Amendment rights in computing and telecommunications technology. Maintains speakers' bureau; conducts educational programs. Encourages and supports the development of tools to endow non-technical users with access to computer-based telecommunications.

Freedom of Information Center. FOI Center, University of Missouri, 133 Neff Annex, Columbia, MO 65211. Phone: (573)882-4856 Fax: (537)884-6204 E-mail: edwardsm@missouri.edu • URL: http://www.foi.missouri.edu.

Investigative Reporters and Editors. School of Journalism, 138 Neff Annex, Columbia, MO 65211. Phone: (573)882-2042 Fax: (573)882-5431 E-mail: info@ire.org • URL: http://www.ire.org • Provides educational services to those engaged in investigative journalism.

Public Citizen/Freedom of Information Clearinghouse. 1600 20th St. NW, Washington, DC 20036. Phone: (202)588-1000 Fax: (202)588-7795 E-mail: member@citizen.org • URL: http://www.citizen.org/litigation/ • Promotes citizen access to government-held information.

Reporters Committee for Freedom of the Press. 1815 N. Fort Meyer Dr., Suite 900, Arlington, VA 22209. Phone: 800-336-4243 or (703)807-2100 Fax: (703)807-2109 E-mail: rcfp@rcfp.org • URL: http://www.rcfp.org/rcfp • Concerned with protecting freedom of information rights for the working press.

FREIGHT, AIR

See: AIR FREIGHT

FREIGHT FORWARDERS

See: FREIGHT TRANSPORT

FREIGHT RATES

See also: FREIGHT TRANSPORT

PERIODICALS AND NEWSLETTERS
International Freighting Weekly; Sea, Air, Rail, Road. Informa UK Limited. • Weekly. $289.00 per year. Looseleaf service.

FREIGHT SHIPS

See: SHIPS, SHIPPING AND SHIPBUILDING

FREIGHT TRANSPORT

See also: AIR FREIGHT; FREIGHT RATES; TRANSPORTATION INDUSTRY

CD-ROM DATABASES
OECD Statistical Compendium. Organization for Economic Cooperation and Development. • Semiannual. $1,905.00 per year for 1 to 10 users. CD-ROM contains more than 730,000 monthly, quarterly, and annual time series for OECD countries, 1960 to date. Includes fully searchable data on agriculture, food, economic indicators, national accounts, employment, energy, finance, industry, technology, and foreign trade. Results can be displayed in various forms.

DIRECTORIES
Air Freight Directory. Air Cargo Inc. • Publication includes: Directory of more than 500 motor carriers contracting with Air Cargo, Inc. for delivery and pick up of freight. Air Cargo is a ground service specialist organization jointly owned by 18 major air carriers. Entries include: Airport city and code, firm name, address, phone, and services offered. Principal content of publication is chart of service points and rates.

American Motor Carrier Directory. Commonwealth Business Media Inc. • Publication includes: Lists of all licensed Less Than Truckload (LTL) general commodity carriers in the United States; includes specialized motor carriers and related services; includes refrigerated carriers, heavy haulers, bulk haulers, riggers, and specified commodity carriers; state and federal regulatory bodies governing the trucking industry; tariff publishing bureaus; freight claim councils; industry associations, etc. Entries include: For carriers and services--Company name, address of headquarters and terminals, phones, tariffs followed, names of executives, insurance, and equipment information, services or commodities handled. Principal content of publication is listing of direct point-to-point services of LTL general commodity carriers throughout the United States and to Canada and Mexico.

National Customs Brokers and Forwarders Association of America Membership Direc tory. National Customs Brokers and Forwarders Association of America. • Annual. $25.00. Lists about 600 customs brokers, international air cargo agents, and freight forwarders in the U.S.

Official Directory of Industrial and Commercial Logistics Executives. Commonwealth Business Media, Inc. • Annual. $205.00. CD-ROM only. About 16,000 U.S. and Canadian commercial firms with full-time or part-time traffic/transportation departments, and 28,000 traffic executives.

Plunkett's Transportation and Logistics Industry Almanac. Plunkett Research, Ltd. • 2004. $249.99. Contains profiles of 300 leading companies in the fields of transportation, logistics, supply chain management, warehousing, distribution, and intermodal shipment systems. Includes industry trends and statistics.

ENCYCLOPEDIAS AND DICTIONARIES
Dictionary of Shipping Terms. Peter Brodie. LLP, Inc. • 1997. Third edition. Price on application. Published in the UK by Lloyd's List (http://www.lloydslist.com). Defines more than 2,000 words, phrases, and abbreviations related to the shipping and maritime industries.

Illustrated Dictionary of Cargo Handling. Peter Brodie. LLP, Inc. • 1991. $90.00. Second edition. Published in the UK by Lloyd's List (http://www.lloydslist.com). Provides definitions of about 600 terms relating to "the vessels and equipment used in modern cargo handling and shipping," including containerization.

Macmillan Encyclopedia of Transportation. Available from Gale Cengage Learning. • 1999. $450.00. Six volumes. Published by Macmillan Reference USA. Covers the business, technology, and history of transportation on land, on water, in the air, and in space. Includes definitions, cross-references, and 200 color illustrations.

FINANCIAL RATIOS
Annual Statement Studies. The Risk Management Association. • Annual. Median and quartile financial ratios are given for over 400 kinds of manufacturing, wholesale, retail, construction, and consumer finance establishments. Data is sorted by both asset size and sales volume. Includes a clearly written "Definition of Ratios" and an alphabetical industry index.

Annual Statement Studies: Industry Default Probabilities and Cash Flow Measures. The Risk Management Association. • Annual. $145.00. Serves as a companion volume to the original *Annual Statement Studies.* Gives probability of default estimates on a percentage scale for more than 450 industries. Includes changes in position year-by-year for eight financial statement line items and provides percentage measures of cash flow.

HANDBOOKS AND MANUALS
The Business of Shipping. James J. Buckley and Lane C. Kendall. Cornell Maritime Press, Inc. • 2001. $50.00. Seventh edition.

Freight Brokerage. Entrepreneur Media, Inc. • Looseleaf. $59.50. A practical guide to freight transportation brokering. Covers profit potential, start-up costs, market size evaluation, pricing, accounting, advertising, promotion, etc. (Start-Up Business Guide No. E1328.).

INTERNET DATABASES
Business 2.0 Web Guide to the Best Business Links. Business 2.0 Media Inc. Phone: (415)293-4800 E-mail: support@business2.com • URL: http://www.business2.com/webguide • Web site presents an extensive, searchable directory of links to "the best, most informative, and authoritative web pages." Twenty main categories cover business, finance, career, company information, people, and technology topics, with thousands of subtopics, all linking to Web sites recommended by experienced business researchers. Fees: Free.

Fedstats. Federal Interagency Council on Statistical Policy. Phone: (202)395-7254 • URL: http://www.fedstats.gov • Web site features an efficient search facility for full-text statistics produced by more than 100 federal agencies, including the Census Bureau, the Bureau of Economic Analysis, and the Bureau of Labor Statistics. Boolean searches can be made within one agency or for all agencies combined. Links are offered to international statistical bureaus, including the UN, IMF, OECD, UNESCO, Eurostat, and 20 individual countries. Fees: Free.

FreeLunch.com. Economy.com, Inc. Phone: (610)696-8700 Fax: (610)696-1678 • URL: http://www.freelunch.com • Web site provides free access to more than 1.5 million economic and financial data series, covering industry, demographics, labor markets, prices, retail sales, government spending, trade, interest rates, housing starts, the stock market, and many other topics. Data is available for various time periods in either chart or table form. Searching is offered. Fees: Free, but registration required. Economy.com, Inc. also offers fee-based economic analysis at *The Dismal Scientist* site (http://www.dismal.com).

PERIODICALS AND NEWSLETTERS
The Journal of Commerce. Commonwealth Business Media. • Weekly. $146.00 per year. Topics include transatlantic shipping, domestic shipping, customs brokers, freight forwarders, ports, air freight, containerization, and other aspects of transportation and shipping logistics. Formerly *Journal of Commerce.*

STATISTICS SOURCES
Business Statistics of the United States. Linz Audain and Cornelia J. Strawser. Bernan Associates. • Annual. $147.00. Based on *Business Statistics,* formerly issue by the Bureau of Economic Analysis, U. S. Department of Commerce. Provides basic data for a wide variety of U. S. industries, services, and economic indicators. Most statistics are shown annually for 30 years and monthly for the most recent four years.

Survey of Current Business. Available from U. S. Government Printing Office. • Monthly. $63.00 per year. Issued by Bureau of Economic Analysis, U. S. Department of Commerce. Presents a wide variety of business and economic data.

TRADE/PROFESSIONAL ASSOCIATIONS
Transportation Institute. 5201 Auth Way, Camp Springs, MD 20746-4211. Phone: (301)423-3335 Fax: (301)423-0634 E-mail: info@trans-inst.org • URL: http://www.trans-inst.org • U.S. deep-sea and inland waters shipping, towing and dredging companies devoted to research and education on a broad range of transportation problems, with emphasis on problems related to the nation's citizen-owned and citizen-manned Merchant Marine. Addresses the need for halting the decline of deep-sea commerce aboard vessels flying the American flag

and the need for full development of waterborne commerce on the Great Lakes. Supports utilizing America's 25,000-mile long network of inland waterways to meet the domestic transportation needs of a growing nation and the need for revitalizing the American fishing industry to halt the incursion of foreign fishing fleets on U.S. spawning grounds. Supports the need for a national oceanographic policy to ensure maximum exploitation of the wealth of the sea. Conducts ongoing research.

OTHER SOURCES

Federal Carriers Reports. CCH, Inc. • Biweekly. $1,484.00 per year. Four looseleaf volumes. Federal rules and regulations for motor carriers, water carriers, and freight forwarders.

FRINGE AREAS

See: CITY PLANNING; URBAN DEVELOPMENT

FRINGE BENEFITS

See also: EMPLOYEE BENEFIT PLANS

ABSTRACTS AND INDEXES

Business Periodicals Index. H. W. Wilson Co. • 11 times a year. Quarterly and annual cumulations. Price varies.

HANDBOOKS AND MANUALS

U. S. Master Compensation Tax Guide. Dennis R. Lassila and Bob G. Kilpatrick. CCH, Inc. • 2001. $57.00. Third edition. Provides concise coverage of taxes on salaries, bonuses, fringe benefits, other current compensation, and deferred compensation (qualified and nonqualified).

ONLINE DATABASES

Wilson Business Abstracts Online. H. W. Wilson Co. • Indexes and abstracts 600 major business periodicals, plus the *Wall Street Journal* and the business section of the *New York Times.* Indexing is from 1982, abstracting from 1990, with the two newspapers included from 1993. Updated weekly. Inquire as to online cost and availability. (*Business Periodicals Index* without abstracts is also available online.).

STATISTICS SOURCES

Compensation and Working Conditions. Available from U. S. Government Printing Office. • Quarterly. Issued by the Bureau of Labor Statistics, U. S. Department of Labor. Presents wage and benefit changes that result from collective bargaining settlements and unilateral management decisions. Includes statistical summaries and special reports on wage trends. Formerly *Current Wage Developments.*

Employee Benefits in Medium and Large Private Establishments. Available from U. S. Government Printing Office. • Biennial. Issued by Bureau of Labor Statistics, U. S. Department of Labor. Provides data on benefits provided by companies with 100 or more employees. Covers benefits for both full-time and part-time workers, including health insurance, pensions, a wide variety of paid time-off policies (holidays, vacations, personal leave, maternity leave, etc.), and other fringe benefits.

Employee Benefits in Small Private Establishments. Available from U. S. Government Printing Office. • Biennial. $12.00. Issued by Bureau of Labor Statistics, U. S. Department of Labor. Supplies data on a wide variety of benefits provided by companies with fewer than 100 employees. Includes statistics for both full-time and part-time workers.

Handbook of U. S. Labor Statistics: Employment,

Earnings, Prices, Productivity, and Other Labor Data. Eva E. Jacobs, editor. Bernan Associates. • 1999. $74.00. Based on *Handbook of Labor Statistics,* formerly issued by the Bureau of Labor Statistics, U. S. Department of Labor. Includes the Bureau's projections of employment in the U. S. by industry and occupation. Provides a wide variety of data on the work force, prices, fringe benefits, and consumer expenditures.

Key Indicators of the Labour Market. Available from Routledge. • Biennial. $125.00. Published by the International Labour Office (http://www.ilo.org). Provides data on 20 key indicators in 220 countries. Includes labor force statistics, employment, unemployment, part-time workers, wages, productivity, poverty indicators, and related topics.

OTHER SOURCES

Executive Compensation. Arthur H. Kroll. Prentice Hall PTR. • Three looseleaf volumes. Periodic supplementation. Price on application. Includes monthly newsletter.

Executive Compensation and Taxation Coordinator. RIA. • Monthly. $765.00 per year. Three looseleaf volumes.

Fringe Benefits Tax Guide. CCH, Inc. • Monthly. $539.00. Looseleaf service.

FROZEN FOOD INDUSTRY

See also: CANNED FOOD INDUSTRY; FAST FOOD INDUSTRY; REFRIGERATION INDUSTRY

ABSTRACTS AND INDEXES

Food Science and Technology Abstracts. International Food Information Service Publishing. • Monthly. $1,780.00 per year. Provides worldwide coverage of the literature of food technology and food production.

Foods Adlibra: Key to the World's Food Literature. General Mills, Inc. Foods Adlibra Publications. • Semimonthly. $240.00 per year. Provides journal citations and abstracts to the literature of food technology and packaging.

ALMANACS AND YEARBOOKS

Almanac of the Canning, Freezing, Preserving Industries, Vol. Two. Edward E. Judge and Sons, Inc. • Annual. $73.00. Contains U. S. food laws and regulations and detailed production statistics.

CD-ROM DATABASES

Food Science and Technology Abstracts [CD-ROM]. Available from SilverPlatter Information, Inc. • Quarterly. Produced by International Food Information Service (home page is http://www.ifis.org). Provides worldwide coverage on CD-ROM of the literature of food technology and production. Various types of publications are indexed, with abstracts, including about 1,800 periodicals. Time period is 1969 to date.

DIRECTORIES

American Frozen Food Institute-Membership Directory and Buyers Guide. American Frozen Food Institute. • Annual. $100.00. 520 member frozen food processors, suppliers, brokers, and distributors.

Judge's Peerless Food Processors. Edward E. Judge & Sons Inc. • Covers: over 4,000 North American plants producing frozen, refrigerated, and shelf-stable foods, fruits, vegetables, juices, preserves, jams and jellies (SIC 2033); canned specialties (SIC 2032); frozen fruits and vegetables (SIC 2037); frozen specialties (SIC 2038); pickles, sauces and salad dressings (SIC 2035); canned and cured seafood (SIC 2091); fresh or frozen packaged fish (SIC 2092); refrigerated canned and frozen meat and poultry (SIC's 2013 and 2015); meat slaughtering (SIC 2011); butler (SIC 2021); cheese (SIC 2022);

ice cream (SIC 2024); fluid milk and dry milk (SIC 2026, 2023). Entries include: Company name, address, phone, divisions, subsidiaries, factories, pack volume, names and titles of key personnel, container sizes, association affiliation, brands, products by factory and process. Plant SIC codes, number of employees for each plant.

Major Food and Drink Companies of the World. Available from Gale Cengage Learning. • Annual. $880.00. Two volumes. Published by Graham & Whiteside. Contains profiles and trade names for more than 9,800 important food and beverage companies in various countries. In addition to foods, includes both alcoholic and nonalcoholic drink products.

National Frozen and Refrigerated Foods Association Membership Directory. National Frozen and Refrigerated Foods Association, Inc. • Annual. $195.00. Lists products, services and personnel.

Plunkett's Food Industry Almanac. Plunkett Research Ltd. • Covers: 340 leading companies in the global food industry. Entries include: Name, address, phone, fax, and key executives. Also includes analysis and information on trends, technology, and statistics in the field.

Quick Frozen Foods Annual Directory of Frozen Food Processors and Buyers' Guide. Saul Beck Publications. • Annual. $140.00. Lists 10,500 frozen food processors; suppliers of freezing and food processing machinery, equipment, and supplies; broker locaters, refrigerated warehouses, truck and rail freight lines, and packaging systems handling frozen food.

Thomas Food and Beverage Market Place. Grey House Publishing. • 2004. $495.00. Three volumes. Contains more than 40,000 entries covering food companies, beverages, food equipment, warehouse companies, food brokers, wholesalers, importers, and exporters. Formerly *Thomas Food Industry Register.*

ENCYCLOPEDIAS AND DICTIONARIES

Wiley Encyclopedia of Food Science and Technology. Frederick J. Francis, editor. John Wiley and Sons, Inc. • 2000. $1,650.00. Second edition. Four volumes. Contains about 400 entries. Coverage includes biotechnology, genetic engineering, nutrition, regulatory matters, food safety, labeling, food substitutes (sugar, fat, dairy), and many other topics.

ONLINE DATABASES

Food Science and Technology Abstracts [online]. IFIS North American Desk. • Produced by International Food Information Service. Provides about 500,000 online citations, with abstracts, to the international literature of food science, technology, commodities, engineering, and processing. Approximately 2,000 periodicals are covered. Time period is 1969 to date, with monthly updates. Inquire as to online cost and availability.

FOODS ADLIBRA. General Mills, Inc. • Contains online citations, with abstracts, to the technical and business literature of food processing and packaging. New products and new ingredients are featured. Covers about 250 trade journals and 500 research journals from 1974 to date, with monthly updates. Inquire as to online cost and availability.

PERIODICALS AND NEWSLETTERS

Quick Frozen Foods International. EW Williams Publications Co. • Quarterly. $42.00 per year. Text in English, summaries in French and German.

STATISTICS SOURCES

Annual Survey of Manufactures. Available from U. S. Government Printing Office. • Annual. Prices vary. Issued by the U. S. Census Bureau as an interim update to the *Census of Manufactures.* Includes data on number of manufacturing establishments in various industries, employment, labor costs, value of shipments, capital expenditures, inventories, energy costs, and assets. (See also Census Bureau home page, http://www.census.gov/.).

Frozen Food Pack Statistics. American Frozen Food Institute. • Annual. Members, $10.00; non-members, $100.00.

World Food Data and Statistics. Euromonitor International. • 2004. $650.00. Provides five-year data for a wide variety of food products in 52 countries. Includes market size, consumer expenditures, price indicators, and retail distribution data for many kinds of meat, fish, fruits, vegetables, dairy products, baked goods, condiments, canned food, and frozen food.

TRADE/PROFESSIONAL ASSOCIATIONS

American Association of Meat Processors. P.O. Box 269, Elizabethtown, PA 17022. Phone: (717)367-1168 Fax: (717)367-9096 E-mail: aamp@aamp.com • URL: http://www.aamp.com.

American Frozen Food Institute. 2000 Corporate Ridge, Ste. 1000, McLean, VA 22102. Phone: (703)821-0770 Fax: (703)821-1350 E-mail: info@affi.com • URL: http://www.affi.com • Frozen food processors and allied industry companies who work for the advancement of the frozen food industry. Seeks to improve consumer understanding and acceptance of frozen foods and to increase sales of frozen products through promotional and communications programs. Sponsors retail trade study, consumer and industry education on care and handling of frozen foods. Promotes a cooperative relationship between frozen food processors, suppliers and marketing associates. Represents the frozen food industry before federal, state and local governments. Conducts research to improve the quality of frozen food products.

National Frozen and Refrigerated Foods Association. 4755 Linglestown Rd., Ste. 300, Harrisburg, PA 17112. Phone: (717)657-8601 Fax: (717)657-9862 E-mail: info@nfraweb.org • URL: http://www.nfraweb.org/ • Absorbed Foodservice Organizations of Distributors. Formerly National Frozen Food Association.

National Prepared Food Association. 485 Kinderkamack Rd., 2nd Fl., Mahwah, NJ 07430. Phone: (201)634-1870 Fax: (201)634-1871 E-mail: star1870@aol.com • Manufacturers, brokers, and distributors involved in food service to restaurants, hotels and insitutions.

OTHER SOURCES

Frozen Foods. Available from MarketResearch.com. • 2000. $5,000.00. Published by Euromonitor Publications Ltd. Provides consumer market data and forecasts for the United States, the United Kingdom, Germany, France, and Italy. Contains market analyses for many kinds of frozen foods.

FRUIT INDUSTRY

See also: APPLE INDUSTRY; BANANA INDUSTRY; CITRUS FRUIT INDUSTRY

ABSTRACTS AND INDEXES

Food Science and Technology Abstracts. International Food Information Service Publishing. • Monthly. $1,780.00 per year. Provides worldwide coverage of the literature of food technology and food production.

Foods Adlibra: Key to the World's Food Literature. General Mills, Inc. Foods Adlibra Publications. • Semimonthly. $240.00 per year. Provides journal citations and abstracts to the literature of food technology and packaging.

Horticultural Abstracts: Compiled from World Literature on Temperate and Tropical Fruits,

Vegetables, Ornaments, Plantation Crops. Available from CABI Publishing North America. • Monthly. $2,010.00 per year. Print and online edition, $2,030.00 per year. Published in England by CABI Publishing. Provides worldwide coverage of the literature of fruits, vegetables, flowers, plants, and all aspects of gardens and gardening.

ALMANACS AND YEARBOOKS

Agricultural and Mineral Commodities Year Book. Available from Taylor & Francis Group. • Annual. $225.00. Published by Europa Publications. Contains descriptive product profiles, price data, export-import data, and production statistics for major commodities of the world. Includes commodity histories, uses, markets, demand trends, and information about trade agreements and key commodity organizations.

CD-ROM DATABASES

AGRICOLA on SilverPlatter. Available from Silver-Platter Information, Inc. • Quarterly. $825.00 per year. Produced by the National Agricultural Library. Provides about three million citations on CD-ROM to the literature of agriculture, agricultural economics, animal sciences, entomology, fertilizer, food, forestry, nutrition, pesticides, plant science, water resources, and other topics. Each quarterly disc covers the past ten years, with archival discs available from 1970.

Food Science and Technology Abstracts [CD-ROM]. Available from SilverPlatter Information, Inc. • Quarterly. Produced by International Food Information Service (home page is http://www.ifis.org). Provides worldwide coverage on CD-ROM of the literature of food technology and production. Various types of publications are indexed, with abstracts, including about 1,800 periodicals. Time period is 1969 to date.

DIRECTORIES

American Fruit Grower Source Book. Meister Publishing Co. • Annual. $5.00. Manufacturers and distributors of equipment and supplies for the commericial fruit growing industry.

Major Food and Drink Companies of the World. Available from Gale Cengage Learning. • Annual. $880.00. Two volumes. Published by Graham & Whiteside. Contains profiles and trade names for more than 9,800 important food and beverage companies in various countries. In addition to foods, includes both alcoholic and nonalcoholic drink products.

Packer Produce Availability and Merchandising Guide. Vance Publishing Corp., Produce Div. • Annual. $35.00. A buyer's directory giving sources of fresh fruits and vegetables. Shippers are listed by location for each commodity.

Thomas Food and Beverage Market Place. Grey House Publishing. • 2004. $495.00. Three volumes. Contains more than 40,000 entries covering food companies, beverages, food equipment, warehouse companies, food brokers, wholesalers, importers, and exporters. Formerly *Thomas Food Industry Register.*

ENCYCLOPEDIAS AND DICTIONARIES

Encyclopedia of Agriculture Science. Charles J. Arntzen and Ellen M. Ritter, editors. Elsevier. • 1994. $900.00. Four volumes.

Encyclopedia of Food and Culture. Gale Cengage Learning. • 2002. $395.00. Three volumes. Contains 600 articles covering various aspects of food and its place in society, from agronomy to zucchini. Includes illustrations and a detailed index.

Foods and Nutrition Encyclopedia. Audrey H. Ensminger and others. CRC Press, Inc. • 1993. $309.95. Second edition. Two volumes.

Wiley Encyclopedia of Food Science and Technology. Frederick J. Francis, editor. John Wiley

and Sons, Inc. • 2000. $1,650.00. Second edition. Four volumes. Contains about 400 entries. Coverage includes biotechnology, genetic engineering, nutrition, regulatory matters, food safety, labeling, food substitutes (sugar, fat, dairy), and many other topics.

INTERNET DATABASES

USDA. United States Department of Agriculture. Phone: (202)720-2791 E-mail: agsec@usda.gov • URL: http://www.usda.gov • The USDA home page has six sections: News and Information; What's New; About USDA; Agencies; Opportunities; Search and Help. Keyword searching is offered from the USDA home page and from various individual agency home pages. Agencies are the Economic Research Service, Agricultural Marketing Service, National Agricultural Statistics Service, National Agricultural Library, and about 12 others. Updating varies. Fees: Free.

ONLINE DATABASES

Food Science and Technology Abstracts [online]. IFIS North American Desk. • Produced by International Food Information Service. Provides about 500,000 online citations, with abstracts, to the international literature of food science, technology, commodities, engineering, and processing. Approximately 2,000 periodicals are covered. Time period is 1969 to date, with monthly updates. Inquire as to online cost and availability.

FOODS ADLIBRA. General Mills, Inc. • Contains online citations, with abstracts, to the technical and business literature of food processing and packaging. New products and new ingredients are featured. Covers about 250 trade journals and 500 research journals from 1974 to date, with monthly updates. Inquire as to online cost and availability.

PERIODICALS AND NEWSLETTERS

American Fruit Grower. Meister Media. • Monthly. $27.47 per year.

American Pomological Society Journal. American Pomological Society. • Quarterly. $30.00 per year. Presents reports and general information on fruit varieties.

Fresh Produce Journal. Lockwood Press, Ltd. • Weekly. $148.00 per year. Formerly *Fruit Trades Journal.*

Journal of Tree Fruit Production. Haworth Press, Inc. • Semiannual. Institutions, $95.00 per year. A research journal for tree fruit growers.

The Packer: Devoted to the Interest of Commericial Growers, Packers, Shippers, Receivers and Retailers of Fruits, Vegetables and Other Products. Vance Publishing Corp., Produce Div. • Weekly. $65.00 per year. *Supplments* available: *Brand Directory* and *Fresh Trends, Packer's Produce Availiability and Merchandising Guide* and *Produce Services Sourcebooks.*

Produce Merchandising: The Packer's Retailing and Merchandising Magazine. Vance Publishing Corp. • Monthly. $35.00 per year. Provides information and advice on the retail marketing and promotion of fresh fruits and vegetalbe.

Small Fruits Review. Haworth Press, Inc. • Quarterly. Institutions $200.00 per year. An academic and practical journal focusing on the marketing of grapes, berries, and other small fruit. Formerly *Journal of Small Fruit and Viticulture.*

Western Fruit Grower: The Business Magazine of the Western Produce Industry. Meister Media. • Monthly. $15.95 per year. Covers the commercial fruit industry in 13 western states.

PRICE SOURCES

PPI Detailed Report. Bureau of Labor Statistics, U.S. Department of Labor. Available from U.S. Government Printing Office. • Monthly. $55.00 per year. Formerly *Producer Price Indexes*.

RESEARCH CENTERS AND INSTITUTES

Agricultural Research Center. Washington State University. PO Box 646240, P.O. Box 646240, Pullman, WA 99164-6240. Phone: (509)335-4563 Fax: (509)335-6751 E-mail: agresearch@wsu.edu • URL: http://arc.wsu.edu • Agriculture and food safety, including economics; biological systems engineering; agronomy and soils; animal sciences; human development; food science and human nutrition; apparel; merchandising; interior design; rural sociology; entomology; natural resource management; horticulture and landscape architecture; plant pathology; veterinary science; plant and animal biotechnology; wood materials; and low-input sustainable agriculture. Performs forage, seed, and minor pesticide testing.

California Agricultural Experiment Station. University of California. 1111 Franklin St., 6th Fl., Oakland, CA 94607-5200. Phone: (510)987-0060 Fax: (510)451-2317 E-mail: wr.gomes@ucop.edu • URL: http://www.ucanr.org/aes.

College of Tropical Agriculture and Human Resources. University of Hawaii at Manoa, 2515 Campus Rd., Miller Hall 110, Honolulu, HI 96822. Phone: (808)956-8105 Fax: (808)956-8105 E-mail: fcs@ctahr.hawaii.edu • URL: http://www.ctahr.hawaii.edu/ • Concerned with the production and marketing of tropical food and ornamental plant products, including pineapples, bananas, coffee, and macadamia nuts.

New York State Agricultural Experiment Station. Cornell University. 630 W. North St., Geneva, NY 14456. Phone: (315)787-2211 Fax: (315)787-2276 E-mail: jeh3@cornell.edu • URL: http://www.nysaes.cornell.edu/.

STATISTICS SOURCES

Agricultural Statistics. Available from U. S. Government Printing Office. • Annual. $38.00. Produced by the National Agricultural Statistics Service, U. S. Department of Agriculture. Provides a wide variety of statistical data relating to agricultural production, supplies, consumption, prices/price-supports, foreign trade, costs, and returns, as well as farm labor, loans, income, and population. In many cases, historical data is shown annually for 10 years. In addition to farm data, includes detailed fishery statistics.

FAO Production Yearbook. Available from Bernan Associates. • Annual. $45.00. Published by the Food and Agriculture Organization (http://www.fao.org). Contains worldwide data on agriculture, land use, farm crops, livestock, and agricultural prices.

FAO Quarterly Bulletin of Statistics. Food and Agriculture Organization of the United Nations. Available from UNIPUB. • Quarterly. $20.00 per year. Provides international data on agricultural production, trade, and prices, covering the major commodities of many countries. Text in English, French, and Spanish. Formerly *FAO Monthly Bulletin of Statistics*.

FAO Trade Yearbook. Available from Bernan Associates. • Annual. $45.00. Published by the Food and Agriculture Organization (http://www.fao.org). Provides extensive worldwide data on exports and imports of agricultural commodities, fertilizers, tractors, and pesticides. Includes more than 130 tables of detailed statistics.

World Agricultural Supply and Demand Estimates. Available from U. S. Government Printing Office. • Monthly. $52.00 per year. Issued by the Economics and Statistics Service and the Foreign Agricultural Service of the U. S. Department of Agriculture. Consists mainly of statistical data and tables.

World Food Data and Statistics. Euromonitor International. • 2004. $650.00. Provides five-year data for a wide variety of food products in 52 countries. Includes market size, consumer expenditures, price indicators, and retail distribution data for many kinds of meat, fish, fruits, vegetables, dairy products, baked goods, condiments, canned food, and frozen food.

TRADE/PROFESSIONAL ASSOCIATIONS

National Association of Flavors and Food Ingredient Systems. 3301 Rte. 66, Ste. 205, Bldg. C, Neptune, NJ 07753. Phone: (732)922-3218 Fax: (732)922-3590 E-mail: info@naffs.org • URL: http://www.naffs.org • Manufacturers of fruit and syrup toppings, flavors and stabilizers for the food industry. Formerly National Association of Fruits, Flavors and Syrups.

Tampa Bay Rare Fruit Council International. c/o Charles Novak, 2812 N Wilder Rd., Plant City, FL 33565-2669. URL: http://www.rarefruit.org • Individuals in 34 countries interested in propagating and raising tropical fruit plants. Formerly Rare Fruit Council.

United Fresh Fruit and Vegetable Association. 1901 Pennsylvania Ave. NW, Ste. 1100, Washington, DC 20006. Phone: (202)303-3400 Fax: (202)303-3433 E-mail: united@uffva.org • URL: http://www.uffva.org.

OTHER SOURCES

The Market for Value-Added Fresh Produce. MarketResearch.com. • 1999. $2,750.00. Market research report. Covers packaged salad mixes, bulk salad mixes, pre-cut fruits, and pre-cut vegetables. Market projections are provided to the year 2003.

FRUIT JUICE INDUSTRY

See: BEVERAGE INDUSTRY; CITRUS FRUIT INDUSTRY

FUEL

GENERAL WORKS

Biofuels. OECD Publications and Information Center. • 1994. $28.00. Produced by the International Energy Agency (IEA). Analyzes costs and greenhouse gas emissions resulting from the production and use of ethanol fuel. In addition to ethanol from corn, wheat, and sugar beets, consideration is given to diesel fuel from rapeseed oil and methanol from wood.

ABSTRACTS AND INDEXES

NTIS Alerts: Energy. National Technical Information Service. • Semimonthly. $245.00 per year. Provides descriptions of government-sponsored research reports and software, with ordering information. Covers electric power, batteries, fuels, geothermal energy, heating/cooling systems, nuclear technology, solar energy, energy policy, and related subjects. Formerly *Abstract Newsletter*.

ALMANACS AND YEARBOOKS

Agricultural and Mineral Commodities Year Book. Available from Taylor & Francis Group. • Annual. $225.00. Published by Europa Publications. Contains descriptive product profiles, price data, export-import data, and production statistics for major commodities of the world. Includes commodity histories, uses, markets, demand trends, and information about trade agreements and key commodity organizations.

CD-ROM DATABASES

Environment Abstracts on CD-ROM. LEXIS-NEXIS. • Quarterly. $1,295.00 per year. Contains the following CD-ROM databases: *Environment Abstracts, Energy Abstracts,* and *Acid Rain Abstracts*. Length of coverage varies.

DIRECTORIES

Financial Times Business Global Oil & Gas Directory. Available from Gale Cengage Learning. • Annual. $355.00. Published by Financial Time's Business. Provides detailed information on 800 leading oil and gas companies worldwide. Includes financial data for three years. Formerly *Financial Times Energy Yearbook: Oil & Gas*.

ENCYCLOPEDIAS AND DICTIONARIES

Encyclopedia of Energy. Cutler J. Cleveland, editor. Elsevier, Inc. • 2004. $1,560.00. Six volumes. Covers all aspects of energy sources and energy-related environmental issues.

Macmillan Encyclopedia of Energy. Available from Gale Cengage Learning. • 2001. $395.00. Three volumes. Published by Macmillan Reference USA. Covers the business, technology, and history of a wide variety of energy sources.

HANDBOOKS AND MANUALS

Modern Petroleum Technology. Richard A. Dawe, editor. John Wiley and Sons, Inc. • 2000. $600.00. Sixth edition. Two volumes. Volume one, entitled *Upstream*, covers oil rigs and other means of obtaining raw petroleum. Volume two, *Downstream*, covers petroleum refining and end products. Edited for industry technicians, managers, and engineers.

PERIODICALS AND NEWSLETTERS

Barron's: The Dow Jones Business and Financial Weekly. • Weekly. $145.00 per year.

Energy and Fuels. American Chemical Society. • Bimonthly. Institutions, $852.00 per year; others, price on application. An interdisciplinary technical journal covering non-nuclear energy sources: petroleum, gas, synthetic fuels, etc.

Fuel: Science and Technology of Fuel and Energy. Elsevier. • 15 times a year. Qualified personnel, $98.00 per year; institutions, $2,765.00 per year.

International Journal of Energy Research. John Wiley and Sons, Inc., Journals. • 15 times a year. Individuals, $2,685.00 per year; institutions, $3,500.00 per year. Published in England by John Wiley & Sons Ltd.

Journal of Energy Engineering: The International Journal. American Society of Civil Engineers. • Three times a year. Members, $40.00 per year; with online edition, $46.00 per year; non-members, $60.00 per year; with online edition, $69.00 per year.

PRICE SOURCES

Energy Prices and Taxes. Organization for Economic Cooperation and Development. • Quarterly. $355.00 per year. Includes both industrial and consumer prices for oil products, natural gas, coal, and electricity in various countries. (Also available on CD-ROM.).

RESEARCH CENTERS AND INSTITUTES

Acoustic and Ultrasonic Laboratory. Argonne National Laboratory. Bldg. 308, Rm. D135, 9700 S Cass Ave., Argonne, IL 60439. Phone: (630)252-2000 Fax: (630)252-3250 E-mail: raptis@anl.gov • URL: http://www.anl.gov • Acoustic and ultrasonic technology, developing sensors and instrumentation and solving difficult applications problems. Also develops NDE techniques for material characterizations.

Energy and Environmental Research Center. University of North Dakota. P.O. Box 9018, Grand Forks, ND 58202-9018. Phone: (701)777-5000 Fax: (701)777-5181 E-mail: ggroenewold@undeerc.org • URL: http://www.undeerc.org.

Laboratory for Energy and the Environment. Massachusetts Institute of Technology. 77 Massachusetts Ave., Bldg. E40-455, Cambridge, MA 02139-4307. Phone: (617)258-8891 Fax: (617)253-8013 E-mail: jwilmson@mit.edu • URL: http://www.lfee.mit.edu • Formerly Energy Laboratory.

Southwest Research Institute. Southwest Research Institute. PO Box 28510, 6220 Culebra Rd., San

Antonio, TX 78228-0510. Phone: (210)684-5111 Fax: (210)522-3547 E-mail: bd@swri.org • URL: http://www.swri.org • Automation, robotics, intelligent systems, space sciences, environmental sciences and engineering, bioengineering, micro encapsulation, chemistry, plant machinery and piping dynamics, radiolocation sciences and development, communications, electromagnetic compatibility, electronic systems, geophysical instrumentation, nondestructive evaluation research, nuclear waste regulatory analysis, fluid dynamics and hydraulics, offshore systems, structural analysis and testing, terminal ballistics and blast effects, materials development, solid mechanics, nonmetallic materials, engine systems engineering, engine emissions analysis and control, fuels and lubricants evaluation, fluids and lubrication technology, alternate energy systems, alternate fuels, mining systems engineering, vehicle and highway safety, and fire research.

STATISTICS SOURCES

Annual Energy Outlook [year], with Projections to [year]. Available from U. S. Government Printing Office. • Annual. $42.00. Issued by the Energy Information Administration, U. S. Department of Energy (http://www.eia.doe.gov). Contains detailed statistics and 20-year projections for electricity, oil, natural gas, coal, and renewable energy. Text provides extensive discussion of energy issues and "Market Trends.".

Energy Statistics Yearbook. United Nations Dept. of Economic and Social Affairs. United Nations Publications. • Annual. $100.00. Text in English and French.

International Energy Annual. Available from U. S. Government Printing Office. • Annual. $34.00. Issued by the Energy Information Administration, U. S. Department of Energy. Provides production, consumption, import, and export data for primary energy commodities in more than 200 countries and areas. In addition to petroleum products and alcohol, renewable energy sources are covered (hydroelectric, geothermal, solar, and wind).

Oil, Gas, Coal, and Electricity: Quarterly Statistics. Organization for Economic Cooperation and Development. • Quarterly. $355.00 per year. Provides detailed data for OECD countries. Covers crude oil, nine oil product groups, hard coal, brown coal (lignite), natural gas, and electric power.

Oil Information. Organization for Economic Cooperation and Development. • Annual. $150.00. Contains international data for major petroleum product groups. Includes statistics on supply, demand, trade, production, prices, and consumption for individual OECD countries and regions. Various time series cover about 30 years. (Also available on CD-ROM.).

Petroleum Statement, Annual Energy Report. Energy Information Administration. U.S. Department of Energy. • Annual.

Steam Electric Market Analysis. National Mining Association. • Monthly. Free to members; nonmembers, $300.00 per year. Covers 400 major electric power plants, with detailed data on coal consumption and stockpiles. Shows percent of power generated by fuel type. (Publisher formerly National Coal Association.).

OTHER SOURCES

Major Energy Companies of the World. Available from Gale Cengage Learning. • Annual. $880.00. Published by Graham & Whiteside. Contains detailed information on more than 3,300 important energy companies in various countries. Industries include electricity generation, coal, natural gas, nuclear energy, petroleum, fuel distribution, and equipment for energy production.

FUEL CELLS

See: BATTERY INDUSTRY

FUEL OIL INDUSTRY

CD-ROM DATABASES

OECD Statistical Compendium. Organization for Economic Cooperation and Development. • Semiannual. $1,905.00 per year for 1 to 10 users. CD-ROM contains more than 730,000 monthly, quarterly, and annual time series for OECD countries, 1960 to date. Includes fully searchable data on agriculture, food, economic indicators, national accounts, employment, energy, finance, industry, technology, and foreign trade. Results can be displayed in various forms.

FINANCIAL RATIOS

Annual Statement Studies. The Risk Management Association. • Annual. Median and quartile financial ratios are given for over 400 kinds of manufacturing, wholesale, retail, construction, and consumer finance establishments. Data is sorted by both asset size and sales volume. Includes a clearly written "Definition of Ratios" and an alphabetical industry index.

Annual Statement Studies: Industry Default Probabilities and Cash Flow Measures. The Risk Management Association. • Annual. $145.00. Serves as a companion volume to the original *Annual Statement Studies*. Gives probability of default estimates on a percentage scale for more than 450 industries. Includes changes in position year-by-year for eight financial statement line items and provides percentage measures of cash flow.

HANDBOOKS AND MANUALS

Modern Petroleum Technology. Richard A. Dawe, editor. John Wiley and Sons, Inc. • 2000. $600.00. Sixth edition. Two volumes. Volume one, entitled *Upstream*, covers oil rigs and other means of obtaining raw petroleum. Volume two, *Downstream*, covers petroleum refining and end products. Edited for industry technicians, managers, and engineers.

INTERNET DATABASES

Advance Monthly Sales for Retail Trade and Food Services. U. S. Census Bureau. Phone: 800-541-8345 or (301)763-4636 Fax: (301)457-3842 E-mail: rcb@census.gov • URL: http://www.census.gov/svsd/www/fullpub.html • Web pages provide monthly sales figures for a wide range of retail businesses. Advance, preliminary, and final statistics are provided for the latest month available in each case, with a previous-year comparison. Updates are monthly.

Business 2.0 Web Guide to the Best Business Links. Business 2.0 Media Inc. Phone: (415)293-4800 E-mail: support@business2.com • URL: http://www.business2.com/webguide • Web site presents an extensive, searchable directory of links to "the best, most informative, and authoritative web pages." Twenty main categories cover business, finance, career, company information, people, and technology topics, with thousands of subtopics, all linking to Web sites recommended by experienced business researchers. Fees: Free.

Fedstats. Federal Interagency Council on Statistical Policy. Phone: (202)395-7254 • URL: http://www.fedstats.gov • Web site features an efficient search facility for full-text statistics produced by more than 100 federal agencies, including the Census Bureau, the Bureau of Economic Analysis, and the Bureau of Labor Statistics. Boolean searches can be made within one agency or for all agencies combined. Links are offered to international statistical bureaus, including the UN, IMF, OECD, UNESCO, Eurostat, and 20 individual countries. Fees: Free.

FreeLunch.com. Economy.com, Inc. Phone: (610)696-8700 Fax: (610)696-1678 • URL: http://www.freelunch.com • Web site provides free access to more than 1.5 million economic and financial data series, covering industry, demographics, labor markets, prices, retail sales, government spending, trade, interest rates, housing starts, the stock market, and many other topics. Data is available for various time periods in either chart or table form. Searching is offered. Fees: Free, but registration required. Economy.com, Inc. also offers fee-based economic analysis at *The Dismal Scientist* site (http://www.dismal.com).

PERIODICALS AND NEWSLETTERS

Oil and Gas Journal. PennWell Corp., Industrial Div. • Weekly. $84.00 per year.

Oilheating: Journal of Indoor Comfort Marketing. Industry Publications, Inc. • Monthly. $30.00 per year. Formerly *Fueloil and Oil Heat with Air Conditioning*.

STATISTICS SOURCES

Annual Benchmark Report for Retail Trade and Food Services...A Detailed Summary of Retail Sales, Purchases, Accounts Receivable, Inventories, and Food Service Sales. Available from U. S. Government Printing Office. • Annual. $13.00. Issued by the U.S. Census Bureau. Provides detailed annual and monthly retail statistics for the most recent 10 years. Includes data for various kinds of retail outlets, including automobiles, furniture, appliances, building supplies, grocery stores, drug stores, gasoline stations, clothing, sporting goods, department stores, and restaurants.

Business Statistics of the United States. Linz Audain and Cornelia J. Strawser. Bernan Associates. • Annual. $147.00. Based on *Business Statistics*, formerly issue by the Bureau of Economic Analysis, U. S. Department of Commerce. Provides basic data for a wide variety of U. S. industries, services, and economic indicators. Most statistics are shown annually for 30 years and monthly for the most recent four years.

Fuel Oil News: Source Book. • Annual. $28.00. Provides fuel (heating) oil industry data.

Petroleum Supply Annual. Available from U. S. Government Printing Office. • Annual. $78.00. Two volumes. Produced by the Energy Information Administration, U. S. Department of Energy. Contains worldwide data on the petroleum industry and petroleum products.

Petroleum Supply Monthly. Available from U. S. Government Printing Office. • Monthly. Produced by the Energy Information Administration, U. S. Department of Energy. Provides worldwide statistics on a wide variety of petroleum products. Covers production, supplies, exports and imports, transportation, refinery operations, and other aspects of the petroleum industry.

Survey of Current Business. Available from U. S. Government Printing Office. • Monthly. $63.00 per year. Issued by Bureau of Economic Analysis, U. S. Department of Commerce. Presents a wide variety of business and economic data.

TRADE/PROFESSIONAL ASSOCIATIONS

Petroleum Marketers Association of America. 1901 N Fort Meyer Dr., Ste. 1200, Arlington, VA 22209. Phone: (703)351-8000 Fax: (703)351-9160 E-mail: info@pmaa.org • URL: http://www.pmaa.org • Absorbed National Oil Fuel Institute and Oil Heat Institute of America. Formerly National Jobbers Council.

FUEL, SYNTHETIC

See: SYNTHETIC FUELS

388

For publishers addresses, refer to SOURCES CITED section at the back of the book.

FUND-RAISING

See also: FEDERAL AID; FOUNDATIONS; GRANTS-IN-AID

GENERAL WORKS

Complete Guide to Corporate Fund Raising. Joseph Dermer and Stephen Wertheimer, editors. Fund Raising Institute. • 1991. $19.95. Discusses the art of obtaining grants from corporate sources. Written by nine fund raising counselors.

Fund Raising: The Guide to Raising Money from Private Sources. Thomas Broce. University of Oklahoma Press. • 1986. $27.95. Second enlarged revised edition.

BIBLIOGRAPHIES

The Non-Profit Handbook: Everything You Need to Know to Start and Run Your Nonprofit Organization. Gary M. Grobman. Chronicle of Higher Education, Inc. • 2002. $29.95. Third edition.

DIRECTORIES

Charitable Organizations of the U. S.: A Descriptive and Financial Information Guide. Gale Cengage Learning. • 1991. $180.00. Second edition. Describes nearly 800 nonprofit groups active in soliciting funds from the American public. Includes nearly 800 data on sources of income, administrative expenses, and payout.

Foundation Reporter: Comprehensive Profiles and Giving Analyses of America's Major Private Foundations. The Taft Group. • Annual. $490.00. Provides detailed information on major U. S. foundations. Eight indexes (location, grant type, recipient type, personnel, etc.).

Funding Sources for Community and Economic Development 2003-2004: A Guide to Current Sources for Local Programs and Projects. Greenwood Publishing Group, Inc. • 2003. $64.95. Sixth edition. Provides information on 2,600 funding sources. Includes "A Guide to Proposal Planning." (Funding Sources for Community and Economic Development Series).

Guide to Federal Funding for Governments and Non-Profits. Government Information Services. • Quarterly. $339.00 per year. Looseleaf service. Contains detailed descriptions of federal grant programs in economic development, housing, transportation, social services, science, etc. Semimonthly *Supplement* available: *Federal Grant Deadline Calendar.*

HANDBOOKS AND MANUALS

The Art of Asking: How to Solicit Philanthropic Gifts. Paul H. Schneiter. Fund Raising Institute. • 1985. $25.00.

The Art of Fund Raising. Irving R. Warner. Fund Raising Institute. • 1991. $19.95. Third edition. Includes case histories.

Becoming a Fundraiser: The Principles and Practice of Library Development. Victoria Steele and Stephen D. Elder. American Library Association. • 2000. $38.00. Second edition.

The Business of Special Events: Fundraising Strategies for Changing Times. Harry A. Freedman and Karen Feldman. Pineapple Press, Inc. • 1998. $21.95.

Conducting a Successful Capital Campaign. Kent E. Dove. John Wiley and Sons, Inc. • 1999. $55.00. Second expanded revised edition. (Nonprofit and Public Management Series).

Fundraising: Hands-On Tactics for Nonprofit Groups. L. Peter Edles. McGraw-Hill. • 1992. $16.95. Covers fundamental premises, soliciting major gifts, small gift prospecting, canvassing, telephone appeals, creating publications, direct mail, and other fund-raising topics for nonprofit organizations.

How to Write Proposals that Produce. Joel P. Bowman and Bernadine P. Branchaw. Greenwood Publishing Group, Inc. • 1992. $23.50. An extensive guide to effective proposal writing for both nonprofit organizations and businesses. Covers writing style, intended audience, format, use of graphs, charts, and tables, documentation, evaluation, oral presentation, and related topics.

The Law of Fundraising. Bruce R. Hopkins. John Wiley and Sons, Inc. • 2002. $170.00. Third edition. Annual supplements available. Covers all aspects of state and federal nonprofit fund-raising law. Includes summaries of the relevant laws and regulations of each state. (Nonprofit Law, Finance and Management Series).

The Nonprofit Entrepreneur: Creating Ventures to Earn Income. Edward Skloot, editor. The Foundation Center. • 1988. $19.95. Advice on earning income through fees and service charges.

Raise More Money for Your Nonprofit Organization: A Guide to Evaluating and Improving Your Fundraising. Anne L. New. The Foundation Center. • 1991. $14.95.

INTERNET DATABASES

Welcome to the Foundation Center. The Foundation Center. Phone: (212)620-4230 or (212)807-3679 Fax: (212)807-3677 E-mail: mfn@fdncenter.org • URL: http://www.fdncenter.org • Web site provides a wide variety of information about foundations, grants, and philanthropy, with links to philanthropic organizations. "Grantmaker Information" link furnishes descriptions of available funding.

PERIODICALS AND NEWSLETTERS

DM News: The Newspaper of Direct Marketing. Courtenay Communications Corp. • 48 times a year. $49.00 per year. Includes special feature issues on catalog marketing, telephone marketing, database marketing, and fundraising. Includes monthly supplements, *DM News International*, *DRTV News*, and *TeleServices.*

FRM Weekly (Fund Raising Management). Hoke Communications, Inc. • Weekly. $115.00 per year.

Giving USA Update. American Association of Fund-Raising Counsel. AAFRC Trust for Philanthropy. • Quarterly. $110.00 per year. Legal, economic and social essays on philanthropy.

Grantsmanship Center Magazine: A Compendium of Resources for Nonprofit Organizations. Grantsmanship Center. • Irregular. Free to qualified personnel. Contains a variety of concise articles on grant-related topics, such as program planning, proposal writing, fundraising, non-cash gifts, federal project grants, benchmarking, taxation, etc.

NSFRE-News. National Society of Fund Raising Executives. • Description: Covers tax-related issues affecting nonprofit organizations, conference and seminar information, educational opportunities, and chapter news.

Taft Monthly Portfolio. Taft Group. • Monthly. $75.00 per year. New ideas and proven techniques used by universitites, hospitals and a wide range of other nonprofit organizations to raise philanthropic gifts. Formerly *FRI Monthly Portfolio.*

RESEARCH CENTERS AND INSTITUTES

Foundation Center. Foundation Center. 79 5th Ave./16th St., New York, NY 10003-3076. Phone: 800-424-9836 or (212)620-4230 Fax: (212)807-3677 E-mail: communications@foundationcenter.org • URL: http://foundationcenter.org • Strengthens the nonprofit sector by advancing knowledge about U.S. philanthropy, maintains a comprehensive database on U.S. grantmakers and their grants, and operates research, education and training programs designed to advance philanthropy.

STATISTICS SOURCES

Giving U.S.A: The Annual Report on Philanthropy. American Association of Fund-Raising Counsel. AAFRC Trust for Philanthropy. • Annual. $65.00.

United Way Annual Report. United Way of America. • Annual. Price on application.

TRADE/PROFESSIONAL ASSOCIATIONS

Alliance of Nonprofit Mailers. 1211 Connecticut Ave., No. 620, Washington, DC 20036. Phone: (202)462-5132 Fax: (202)462-0423 E-mail: alliance@nonprofitmailers.org • URL: http://www.nonprofitmailers.org.

American Association of Fund-Raising Counsel. 10293 N. Meridian St., Suite 175, Indianapolis, IN 46290-1130. Phone: (317)816-1613 Fax: (317)816-1633 E-mail: info@aafrc.org • URL: http://www.aafrc.org.

Association of Fundraising Professionals. 1101 King St., Ste. 700, Alexandria, VA 22314-2967. Phone: 800-666-3863 or (703)684-0410 Fax: (703)684-0540 • URL: http://www.afpnet.org • Formerly National Society of Fundraising Executives.

DMA Nonprofit Federation. 1615 L St. NW, Ste. 1100, Washington, DC 20036. Phone: (202)628-4380 Fax: (202)628-4383 E-mail: nonprofitfederation@the-dma.org • URL: http://www.the-dma.org/nonprofitfederation • Trade and lobbying group for non-profit organizations that use direct and online marketing to raise funds and communicate with members. Sponsors professional development conferences and seminars, lobbies on state and federal legislation, regulation, and standards related to direct marketing and related issues. Provides information about and participants in litigation affecting non-profits. Promotes the overall welfare of non-profits. Represents health care charities, social service agencies, religious groups, colleges and universities and fraternal organizations.

OTHER SOURCES

Charitable Giving and Solicitation. RIA. • $495.00 per year. Looseleaf service. Updates 13 times a year. Bulletin discusses federal tax rules pertaining to charitable contributions.

FUNDS, COMMUNITY

See: COMMUNITY FUNDS

FUNDS, MUTUAL

See: INVESTMENT COMPANIES

FUNERAL HOMES AND DIRECTORS

DIRECTORIES

American Blue Book of Funeral Directors. Kates-Boylston Publications, Inc. • Biennial. $75.00. About 24,000 funeral homes primarily in the United States and Canada.

NFDA Directory of Members and Resource Guide. NFDA Publications, Inc. • Annual. $75.00. 14,000 members of state funeral director associations affiliated with the National Funeral Directors Association. Formerly *National Funeral Directors Association-Membership Listing and Resources.*

FINANCIAL RATIOS

Annual Statement Studies. The Risk Management Association. • Annual. Median and quartile financial ratios are given for over 400 kinds of manufacturing, wholesale, retail, construction, and consumer finance establishments. Data is sorted by both asset size and sales volume. Includes a clearly written "Definition of Ratios" and an alphabetical industry index.

Annual Statement Studies: Industry Default Probabilities and Cash Flow Measures. The Risk Management Association. • Annual. $145.00. Serves as a companion volume to the original *Annual Statement Studies.* Gives probability of default estimates on a percentage scale for more than 450 industries. Includes changes in position year-by-year for eight financial statement line items and provides percentage measures of cash flow.

HANDBOOKS AND MANUALS

Dealing Creatively with Death: A Manual of Death Education and Simple Burial. Ernest Morgan and Jennifer Morgan. Upper Access, Inc. • 2001. $14.95. 14th revised edition. A humanistic approach to dying and grieving; pursuing economy, simplicity and greater sensitivity in funeral practices.

PERIODICALS AND NEWSLETTERS

American Funeral Director. Kates-Boylston Publications, Inc. • Monthly. $32.00 per year.

The Director. National Funeral Directors Association. NFDA Publications, Inc. • Monthly. $30.00 per year.

Funeral Service "Insider". Jean DeSapio, editor. United Communications Group. • Description: Covers the latest trends in funeral service education, legislation, franchising, marketing, and consumer purchasing. Recurring features include editorials, news of research, letters to the editor, and a calendar of events.

TRADE/PROFESSIONAL ASSOCIATIONS

Funeral Consumers Alliance. 33 Patchen Rd., South Burlington, VT 05403. Phone: 800-765-0107 or (802)865-8300 Fax: (802)865-2626 E-mail: fca@funerals.org • URL: http://www.funerals.org • Promotes a consumer's right to choose a dignified, meaningful, affordable funeral. Provides educational material to the public and affiliates. Monitors the funeral and cemetery industry for consumers nationwide. Responds to consumer complaints. Maintains speakers' bureau.

National Funeral Directors and Morticians Association. 3951 Snapfinger Parkway, Suite 570, Omega World Center, Decatur, GA 30035. Phone: 800-434-0958 or (404)286-6680 Fax: (404)286-6573 E-mail: nfdma@nfdma.com • URL: http://www.nfdma.com.

National Funeral Directors Association. 13625 Bishop's Dr., 13625 Bishops Dr., Brookfield, WI 53005-6607. Phone: 800-228-6332 or (262)789-1880 Fax: (262)789-6977 E-mail: nfda@nfda.org • URL: http://www.nfda.org • Federation of state funeral directors' associations with individual membership of funeral directors. Seeks to enhance the funeral service profession and promote quality services to the consumers. Conducts professional education seminars and home study courses. Compiles statistics.

Selected Independent Funeral Homes. 500 Lake Cook Rd., Ste. 205, Deerfield, IL 60015. Phone: 800-323-4219 or (847)236-9401 Fax: (847)236-9968 E-mail: info@selectedfuneralhomes.org • URL: http://www.selectedfuneralhomes.org • Funeral directors. Aims to study, develop, and establish a standard of service for the benefit of its consumers. Provides a continuing forum for the exchange, development and dissemination of knowledge and information beneficial to members and the public.

OTHER SOURCES

The U. S. Market for Funeral and Cremation Services. Available from MarketResearch.com. • 1997. $1,375.00. Market research report published by Packaged Facts. Includes information on multinational funeral service chains.

FUR INDUSTRY

DIRECTORIES

Blue Book of Fur Farming. • Annual. $20.00. Lists manufacturers and suppliers of equipment and materials used in the raising of fur-bearing animals for the fur industry.

PERIODICALS AND NEWSLETTERS

Fur Rancher. Becker Publishing. • Quarterly. Controlled circulation. Includes *Blue Book of Fur Farming.* Covers the farm raising of animals for fur.

TRADE/PROFESSIONAL ASSOCIATIONS

Fur Information Council of America. 8424 A Santa Monica Blvd., No. 860, West Hollywood, CA 90069. Phone: (323)848-7940 Fax: (323)848-2931 E-mail: info@fur.org • URL: http://www.fur.org • Formerly American Fur Industry.

OTHER SOURCES

Fur World: The Newsmagazine of Fur and Better Outerware. Creative Marketing Plus, Inc. • Semimonthly. $50.00 per year. Edited for fur retailers, ranchers, pelt dealers, and manufacturers. Provides news and statistics relating to the retail and wholesale fur business.

FURNISHINGS (MEN'S CLOTHING)

See: MEN'S CLOTHING INDUSTRY

FURNITURE INDUSTRY

See also: OFFICE FURNITURE INDUSTRY

ABSTRACTS AND INDEXES

NTIS Alerts: Building Industry Technology. National Technical Information Service. • Semimonthly. $210.00 per year. Provides descriptions of government-sponsored research reports and software, with ordering information. Covers architecture, construction management, building materials, maintenance, furnishings, and related subjects. Formerly *Abstract Newsletter.*

BIOGRAPHICAL SOURCES

Who's Who in the Southern Furniture Industry. American Furniture Manufacturers Association. • Annual. $50.00. Lists about 400 manufacturers of furniture and their suppliers.

CD-ROM DATABASES

OECD Statistical Compendium. Organization for Economic Cooperation and Development. • Semiannual. $1,905.00 per year for 1 to 10 users. CD-ROM contains more than 730,000 monthly, quarterly, and annual time series for OECD countries, 1960 to date. Includes fully searchable data on agriculture, food, economic indicators, national accounts, employment, energy, finance, industry, technology, and foreign trade. Results can be displayed in various forms.

World Marketing Forecasts on CD-ROM. Gale Cengage Learning. • Annual. $2,500.00. Produced by Euromonitor. Provides detailed forecast data for the years to 2012 on CD-ROM for 54 countries in all parts of the world. Covers a wide range of social, demographic, economic, and market factors. Includes specific forecasts for many kinds of consumer products.

DIRECTORIES

Directory of Home Furnishings Retailers. Chain Store Guide. • Annual. $335.00. Online edition, $775.00. Includes more than 5,500 furniture retailers and wholesalers. Covers United States and Canada.

FDM--The Source--Woodworking Industry

Directory. Reed Business Information. • Publication includes: List of over 1,800 suppliers to secondary woodworking industry; coverage includes Canada. Entries include: Company name, address, phone, fax, product lines.

Wood Digest-Showcase. Cygnus Business Media. • Publication includes: List of suppliers of materials, machinery, tools, and services for woodworking, cabinetry, casegoods, and furniture manufacturing processes (SIC 24, 25, 37, and 39). Entries include: Company name, phone number, photograph of product, services.

FINANCIAL RATIOS

Almanac of Business and Industrial Financial Ratios. Leo Troy. Aspen Publishers, Inc. • 2003. $125.95. Includes CD-Rom. Contains financial ratios derived from federal tax returns. Ratios for each of about 200 industries are arranged according to company asset size. (Almanac of Business and Industrial Financial Ratios Series).

Industry Norms and Key Business Ratios. Desk Top Edition. Dun and Bradstreet Corp. • Annual. Five volumes. $475.00 per volume. $1,890.00 per set. Covers over 800 kinds of businesses, arranged by Standard Industrial Classification number. More detailed editions covering longer periods of time are also available.

HANDBOOKS AND MANUALS

PVC Furniture Manufacturing. Entrepreneur Media, Inc. • Looseleaf. $59.50. A practical guide to starting a business for the manufacture of plastic furniture. Covers profit potential, start-up costs, market size evaluation, owner's time required, site selection, lease negotiation, pricing, accounting, advertising, promotion, etc. (Start-Up Business Guide No. E1262.).

INTERNET DATABASES

Advance Monthly Sales for Retail Trade and Food Services. U. S. Census Bureau. Phone: 800-541-8345 or (301)763-4636 Fax: (301)457-3842 E-mail: rcb@census.gov • URL: http://www.census.gov/svsd/www/fullpub.html • Web pages provide monthly sales figures for a wide range of retail businesses. Advance, preliminary, and final statistics are provided for the latest month available in each case, with a previous-year comparison. Updates are monthly.

Business 2.0 Web Guide to the Best Business Links. Business 2.0 Media Inc. Phone: (415)293-4800 E-mail: support@business2.com • URL: http://www.business2.com/webguide • Web site presents an extensive, searchable directory of links to "the best, most informative, and authoritative web pages." Twenty main categories cover business, finance, career, company information, people, and technology topics, with thousands of subtopics, all linking to Web sites recommended by experienced business researchers. Fees: Free.

Fedstats. Federal Interagency Council on Statistical Policy. Phone: (202)395-7254 • URL: http://www.fedstats.gov • Web site features an efficient search facility for full-text statistics produced by more than 100 federal agencies, including the Census Bureau, the Bureau of Economic Analysis, and the Bureau of Labor Statistics. Boolean searches can be made within one agency or for all agencies combined. Links are offered to international statistical bureaus, including the UN, IMF, OECD, UNESCO, Eurostat, and 20 individual countries. Fees: Free.

FreeLunch.com. Economy.com, Inc. Phone: (610)696-8700 Fax: (610)696-1678 • URL: http://www.freelunch.com • Web site provides free access to more than 1.5 million economic and financial data series, covering industry, demographics, labor markets, prices, retail sales, government spending, trade, interest rates, housing starts, the stock market, and many other topics. Data is available for various time periods in either chart or table form. Searching is offered. Fees: Free, but registration required. Economy.com, Inc. also offers fee-based economic analysis at *The Dismal Scientist* site (http://www.dismal.com).

PERIODICALS AND NEWSLETTERS

FDM: For Builders of Cabinets, Fixtures, Furniture, Millwork Furniture Design a nd Manufacturing. Chartwell Communications, Inc. • Monthly. Free to qualified personnel. Edited for furniture executives, production managers, and designers. Covers the manufacturing of household, office, and institutional furniture, store fixtures, and kitchen and bathroom cabinets.

Furniture-Today: The Weekly Business Newspaper of the Furniture Industry. Reed Business Information. • Weekly. $159.97 per year.

Furniture World. Towse Publishing Co. • Monthly. $19.00 per year. Formerly *Furniture World and Furniture Buyer and Decorator*.

HFN (Home Furnishing Network): The Newsweekly of Home Products Retailing. Fairchild Publications. • Weekly. Individuals, $99.00 per year; institutions, $295.00 per year. Formerly *H F D-Home Furnishing Daily*.

RESEARCH CENTERS AND INSTITUTES

Wood Research Laboratory. Purdue University, Department of Forestry and Natural Resources, West Lafayette, IN 47907-1200. Phone: (765)494-3615 Fax: (765)496-1344 E-mail: mhunt@fnr.purdue.edu • URL: http://www.fnr.purdue.edu.

STATISTICS SOURCES

Annual Benchmark Report for Retail Trade and Food Services...A Detailed Summary of Retail Sales, Purchases, Accounts Receivable, Inventories, and Food Service Sales. Available from U. S. Government Printing Office. • Annual. $13.00. Issued by the U.S. Census Bureau. Provides detailed annual and monthly retail statistics for the most recent 10 years. Includes data for various kinds of retail outlets, including automobiles, furniture, appliances, building supplies, grocery stores, drug stores, gasoline stations, clothing, sporting goods, department stores, and restaurants.

Annual Survey of Manufactures. Available from U. S. Government Printing Office. • Annual. Prices vary. Issued by the U. S. Census Bureau as an interim update to the *Census of Manufactures*. Includes data on number of manufacturing establishments in various industries, employment, labor costs, value of shipments, capital expenditures, inventories, energy costs, and assets. (See also Census Bureau home page, http://www.census.gov/.).

Business Statistics of the United States. Linz Audain and Cornelia J. Strawser. Bernan Associates. • Annual. $147.00. Based on *Business Statistics*, formerly issue by the Bureau of Economic Analysis, U. S. Department of Commerce. Provides basic data for a wide variety of U. S. industries, services, and economic indicators. Most statistics are shown annually for 30 years and monthly for the most recent four years.

Consumer International. Available from Gale Cengage Learning. • Annual. $1,290.00. Published by Euromonitor. Contains extensive consumer market, economic, and demographic data for 25 major, non-European countries, including the U. S. and Canada. Includes consumer market size (volume and value) for 150 product types in 14 categories (food, clothing, automobiles, cosmetics, appliances, etc.).

European Marketing Forecasts. Available from Gale Cengage Learning. • Annual. $1,250.00. Published by Euromonitor. Contains demographic, economic, and market forecasts for the countries of Europe to the year 2010. Forecasts include market-size data for 15 consumer product sectors (food, clothing, automobiles, consumer electronics, etc.).

International Marketing Forecasts. Available from Gale Cengage Learning. • Annual. $1,250.00. Published by Euromonitor. Contains demographic, economic, and market forecasts to the year 2013 for major, non-European countries, including the U. S. and Canada. Forecasts include market-size data for 15 consumer product sectors, such as food, clothing, and automobiles.

Survey of Current Business. Available from U. S. Government Printing Office. • Monthly. $63.00 per year. Issued by Bureau of Economic Analysis, U. S. Department of Commerce. Presents a wide variety of business and economic data.

WEFA Industrial Monitor. John Wiley and Sons, Inc. • Annual. $65.00. Prepared by industry analysts at WEFA, an economic forecasting and consulting firm (originally Wharton Econometric Forecasting Associates). Contains discussions of the outlook for major U. S. industries, with many 10-year forecasts (WEFA Web site is http://www.wefa.com).

TRADE/PROFESSIONAL ASSOCIATIONS

American Home Furnishings Alliance. 317 W High Ave., 10th Fl., High Point, NC 27260. Phone: (336)884-5000 Fax: (336)884-5303 E-mail: pbowling@ahfa.us • URL: http://www.ahfa.us • Furniture manufacturers seeking to provide a unified voice for the furniture industry and to aid in the development of industry personnel. Provides: market research data; industrial relations services; costs and operating statistics; transportation information; general management and information services. Compiles statistics; develops quarterly Econometric Forecast.

International Home Furnishings Representatives Association. PO Box 670, High Point, NC 27261. Phone: 800-889-3920 or (336)889-3375 Fax: (336)883-8245 E-mail: ihfra@aol.com • URL: http://www.ihfra.org • Formerly National Home Furnishings Representatives Association.

National Home Furnishings Association. 3910 Tinsley Dr., Ste. 101, High Point, NC 27265-3610. Phone: 800-888-9590 or (336)886-6100 Fax: (336)801-6102 E-mail: info@nhfa.org • URL: http://www.nhfa.org • Provides business services to help retailers of home furnishings grow their businesses. Provides educational programs for retail sales managers and trainers, for middle management, for owners and executives, and for family businesses.

United Furniture Workers Insurance Fund. 1910 Air Lane Dr., PO Box 100037, Nashville, TN 37210. Phone: (615)889-8860 Fax: (615)889-8860 E-mail: info@gs1us.org • URL: http://ufwip.com • AFL-CIO. A division of International Union of Electronic, Electrical, Salaried, Machine, and Furniture Workers.

FUTURES, FINANCIAL

See: FINANCIAL FUTURES TRADING

FUTURES TRADING

See: COMMODITY FUTURES TRADING

FUTURISTICS

GENERAL WORKS

The Age of Spiritual Machines: When Computers Exceed Human Intelligence. Ray Kurzweil. Penguin Group. • 1998. $25.95. Provides speculation on the future of artificial intelligence and "computer consciousness.".

The Art of the Long View: Planning for the Future in an Uncertain World. Peter Schwartz. Doubleday. • 1996. $30.95. Covers strategic planning for corpora-

tions and smaller firms. Includes "The World in 2005: Three Scenarios.".

Being Digital. Nicholas Negroponte. Knopf Publishing Group. • 1995. $30.00. A kind of history of multimedia, with visions of future technology and public participation. Predicts how computers will affect society in years to come.

Cyberquake: How the Internet will Erase Profits, Topple Market Leaders, and Shatter Business Models. Michael Sullivan-Trainor. John Wiley and Sons, Inc. • 1997. $26.95. Predicts that the Internet will cause "an overwhelming shift in control of the worldwide marketplace" in the early 21st century. (Business Technology Series).

Data Smog: Surviving the Information Glut. David Shenk. HarperSanFrancisco. • 1997. $14.00. A critical view of both the electronic and print information industries. Emphasis is on information overload.

Dow 100,000: Fact or Fiction. Charles W. Kadlec. Prentice Hall PTR. • 1999. $25.00. Predicts a level of 100,000 for the Dow Jones Industrial Average in the year 2020, based mainly on a technological revolution.

The 500 Year Delta: What Happens After What Comes Next. Jim Taylor and others. HarperInformation. • 1998. $14.00. Provides analysis of major corporate and political trends.

The Fortune Sellers: The Big Business of Buying and Selling Predictions. William A. Sherden. John Wiley and Sons, Inc. • 1997. $29.95. The author states that predictions are notoriously unreliable in any field, including the stock market, the economy, and the weather. (Forecasters in all areas don't have to be right; they just have to be interesting.).

The Future of Money. Organization for Economic Cooperation and Development. • 2002. $19.00. Discusses the inevitable trend in money from the physical to the abstract (digital or virtual money). Will cash disappear? Will virtual money threaten control of the money supply? - and so forth.

Libraries and the Future: Essays on the Library in the Twenty-First Century. F. W. Lancaster, editor. Haworth Press, Inc. • 1994. $49.95. Emphasis is on information services in libraries of the future. (Original Book Series).

Megatrends Two Thousand: Ten New Directions for the 1990's. John Naisbitt and Patricia Aburdene. Morrow Avon. • 1991. $6.99. Social forecasting to the year 2000 and into the 21st century.

Predicting the Future: An Introduction to the Theory of Forecasting. Nicholas Rescher. State University of New York Press. • 1997. $24.50. Provides a general theory of prediction, including the principles and methodology of forecasting. Includes "The Evaluation of Predictions and Predictors.".

Preparing for the Twenty-First Century. Paul Kennedy. Random House, Inc. • 1993. $16.00. A somber view of the future.

Probable Tomorrows: How Science and Technology Will Transform Our Lives in the Next Twenty Years. Marvin J. Cetron and Owen L. Davies. Saint Martin's Press. • 1997. $24.95. Predicts the developments in technological products, services, and "everyday conveniences" by the year 2017. Covers such items as personal computers, artificial intelligence, telecommunications, highspeed railroads, and healthcare.

Recreation Trends and Markets: Info the 21st Century. John R. Kelly and Rodney Warnick. Sagamore Publishing, Inc. • 1999. $25.00. Second edition.

A Short History of the Future. W. Warren Wagar. The University of Chicago Press. • 1999. $19.00. Third edition.

What Will Be: How the New World of Information Will Change Our Lives. Michael L. Dertouzos. DIANE Publishing Co. • 1997. $25.00. A discussion of the "information market place" of the future, including telecommuting, virtual reality, and computer recognition of speech. The author is director of the MIT Laboratory for Computer Science.

The World in 2020: Power, Culture, and Prosperity. Hamish McRae. Harvard Business School Publishing. • 1995. $14.95. States that the best predictor of economic success will be a nation's creativity and social responsibility.

ABSTRACTS AND INDEXES

Future Survey: A Monthly Abstract of Books, Articles, and Reports Concerning Trends, Forecasts, and Ideas About the Future. World Future Society. • Monthly. Individuals, $98.00 per year; libraries, $145.00 per year. Includes author and subject indexes.

ALMANACS AND YEARBOOKS

Vital Signs [year]: The Trends That Are Shaping Our Future. Worldwatch Institute. • Annual. $14.95. Provides access to selected indicators showing social, economic, and environmental trends throughout the world. Includes data relating to food, energy, transportation, finance, population, and other topics.

BIBLIOGRAPHIES

Future Survey Annual: A Guide to the Recent Literature of Trends, Forecasts, and Policy Proposals. World Future Society. • Annual. $35.00.

DIRECTORIES

World Futures Studies Federation Membership Directory. World Futures Studies Federation. • Publication includes: List of over 700 member individuals and 60 institutions with an interest in the study of the world's future. Entries include: Name, address, phone, fax, e-mail.

PERIODICALS AND NEWSLETTERS

Futures Research Quarterly. World Future Society. • Quarterly. Members, $77.00 per year; others, $99.00 per year.

Futuretech. Technical Insights/John Wiley & Sons Inc. • Description: Contains briefings on newly emerging technologies and the markets that they will create. Each issue focuses on one technology, analyzes its market impact, and provides access to developers looking for partners, licenses, or marketing agreements.

The Futurist: A Journal of Forecasts, Trends, and Ideas About the Future. World Future Society. • Bimonthly. Free to members; libraries and institutions, $55.00 per year.

The Trends Journal: The Authority on Trends Management. Gerald Celente, editor. Trends Research Institute. • Quarterly. $185.00 per year. Newsletter. Provides forecasts on a wide variety of economic, social, and political topics. Includes "Hot Trends to Watch.".

21.C: Scanning the Future: A Magazine of Culture, Technology, and Science. International Publishers Distributors. • Quarterly. $24.00 per year. Contains multidisciplinary articles relating to the 21st century.

World Watch: Working for a Sustainable Future. Worldwatch Institute. • Bimonthly. $25.00 per year. Emphasis is on environmental trends, including developments in population growth, climate change, human behavior, the role of government, and other factors.

RESEARCH CENTERS AND INSTITUTES

Institute for Alternative Futures. 100 N. Pitt St., Suite 235, Alexandria, VA 22314. Phone: (703)684-5880 Fax: (703)684-0640 E-mail: futurist@altfutures.com • URL: http://www.altfutures.com • Conducts studies in the future of communications, health care, bioengineering, the legal system, etc.

Worldwatch Institute. Worldwatch Institute. 1776 Massachusetts Ave. NW, Washington, DC 20036-1904. Phone: (202)452-1999 or (202)452-1999 Fax: (202)296-7365 E-mail: worldwatch@worldwatch.org • URL: http://www.worldwatch.org • Global

trends in the availability and management of both human and natural resources, including research in energy, food policy, population, development, technology, the environment, economics, toxics, and recycling.

TRADE/PROFESSIONAL ASSOCIATIONS

Academy of Arts and Sciences of the Americas. 9450 Old Cutler Rd., Miami, FL 33156. Phone: (305)663-9897 Fax: (305)667-5600 E-mail: atsworld@bellsouth.net • Seeks an interdisciplinary approach to the 21st century.

Institute for the Future. 2744 Sand Hill Rd., Menlo Park, CA 94025-7020. Phone: (650)854-6322 Fax: (650)854-7850 E-mail: info@iftf.org • URL: http://www.iftf.org • Assists organizations, businesses, industry and the government in conducting long-term futures research.

World Future Society. 7910 Woodmont Ave., Ste. 450, Bethesda, MD 20814. Phone: 800-989-8274 or (301)656-8274 Fax: (301)951-0394 E-mail: info@wfs.org • URL: http://www.wfs.org • Helps individuals, organizations, and communities see, understand, and respond appropriately and effectively to change. Raises awareness of change and encourages development of creative solutions through media, meetings, and dialogue among its members. Serves as a neutral forum for exploring possible, probable, and preferable futures.

World Futures Studies Federation. 2nd Floor, Main Administration Bldg., University of St. La Salle, La Salle Ave., PO Box 249, Bacolod City 6100, Philippines. Phone: 34 4353857 Fax: 34 4353857 E-mail: secretariat@worldfutures.org • URL: http://www.worldfutures.org • Institutions, scholars, policymakers, and individuals involved in futures studies. Promotes futures studies and innovative interdisciplinary analyses. Encourages the exchange of information and opinion through organized research projects.

G

GAMBLING INDUSTRY

DIRECTORIES

International Gaming Resource Guide. Gem Communications. • Publication includes: Lists of 1,800 organizations concerned with gaming and wagering establishments, including casinos, lotteries, racing commissions, race tracks, jai alai frontons, etc.; and regulatory agencies. Entries include: Listings in the 'Corporate Profiles' section (which expand selected other listings) include name, parent company name, address, mailing address (if different), phone, names and titles of key personnel. Other listings show name, address, and phone only.

Plunkett's Airline, Hotel, and Travel Industry Almanac. Plunkett Research, Ltd. • Annual. $249.95. Contains profiles of 300 leading companies, including airlines, hotels, travel agencies, theme parks, cruise lines, casinos, and car rental companies.

ENCYCLOPEDIAS AND DICTIONARIES

Dictionary of Gambling and Gaming. Thomas L. Clark. Lexik House Publishers. • 1988. $48.00.

Encyclopedia of Emerging Industries. Gale Cengage Learning. • 2001. $320.00. Fourth edition. Provides detailed information on 115 "newly flourishing" industries. Includes historical background, organizational structure, significant individuals, current conditions, major companies, work force, technology trends, research developments, and other industry facts.

HANDBOOKS AND MANUALS

Casino and Gaming Market Research Handbook. Available from MarketResearch.com. • 2003. $375.00. Published by Terri C. Walker Consulting, Inc. Includes analysis and statistical data on casinos, lotteries, table games, electronic gaming machines, bingo, and online gambling.

Managing Casinos: A Guide for Entrepreneurs, Management Personnel, and Aspiring Managers. Ruben Martinez. Barricade Books, Inc. • 1995. $75.00. Covers such topics as the installation of profitable games, providing credit to players, casino business math, and understanding odds.

ONLINE DATABASES

PAIS International. Public Affairs Information Service, Inc. • Corresponds to the former printed publications, *PAIS Bulletin* (1976-90) and *PAIS Foreign Language Index* (1972-90), and to the current *PAIS International in Print* (1991 to date). Covers economic, political, and sociological material appearing in periodicals, books, government documents, and other publications. Updating is monthly.

Inquire as to online cost and availability.

PERIODICALS AND NEWSLETTERS

Bottomline. Hospitality Financial and Technology Professionals. • Bimonthly. Free to members, educational institutions and libraries; non-members, $50.00 per year. Contains articles on accounting, finance, information technology, and management for hotels, resorts, casinos, clubs, and other hospitality businesses.

Casino Chronicle: A Weekly Newsletter Focusing on the Gaming Industry. Ben Borowsky. • 48 times a year. $175.00 per year. Newsletter focusing on the Atlantic City gambling industry.

Gambling Times Magazine. Gambling Times, Inc. • Monthly. $44.00 per year.

Hospitality Technology: Guiding High-Growth Businesses to Best-Choice IT Solutions. Edgell Communications, Inc. • 10 times a year. Price on application. Covers information technology, computer communications, and software for food-service and lodging enterprises.

International Gaming and Wagering Business. Gem Communications. • Monthly. $113.00 per year.

STATISTICS SOURCES

Standard & Poor's Industry Surveys. Standard & Poor's. • Semiannual. $1,800.00. Two looseleaf volumes. Includes monthly *Supplements.* Provides detailed, individual surveys of 52 major industry groups. Each survey is revised on a semiannual basis. Also includes "Monthly Investment Review" (industry group investment analysis) and monthly "Trends & Projections" (economic analysis).

TRADE/PROFESSIONAL ASSOCIATIONS

American Amusement Machine Association. 450 E Higgins Rd., Ste. 201, Elk Grove Village, IL 60007. Phone: (866)372-5190 or (847)290-9088 Fax: (847)290-9121 E-mail: information@coin-op.org • URL: http://www.coin-op.org • Manufacturers and distributors of coin machines; parts suppliers and others interested in promoting and protecting the amusement machine industry. Seeks solutions to the problem of copyright infringement by foreign manufacturers, and legislative and regulatory problems facing the industry and manufacturers. Works to improve the image of the coin-operated amusement industry. Presents views to governmental decision-makers. Operates American +Amusement Machine +Charitable Foundation.

Gam-Anon International Service Office. PO Box 157, Whitestone, NY 11357. Phone: (718)352-1671 Fax: (718)746-2571 E-mail: info3@gam-anon.org • URL: http://www.gam-anon.org • Represents husbands, wives, relatives, and close friends of compulsive gamblers. Seeks to help members better understand the compulsive gambler and learn to cope with the problems involved. Conducts regularly scheduled meetings throughout the world to allow members to share experiences, strength, and hope, recover from the effects of compulsive gambling, and achieve a normal way of thinking and living. Maintains speakers' bureau. Sponsors social activities. Conducts open, topic, recognition, and special focus meetings.

Gamblers Anonymous. PO Box 17173, Los Angeles, CA 90017. Phone: 888-424-3577 or (213)386-8789 Fax: (213)386-0030 E-mail: isomain@gamblersanonymous.org • URL: http://www.gamblersanonymous.org • Men and women who have joined together in order to stop gambling and to help other compulsive gamblers do the same; is self-supporting, declines outside contributions, and neither opposes nor endorses outside causes.

Hospitality Financial and Technology Professionals. 11709 Boulder Lane, Suite 110, Austin, TX 78726. Phone: 800-646-4387 or (512)249-5333 Fax: (512)249-1533 E-mail: frank.wolfe@hftp.org • URL: http://www.hftp.org • Members are accounting and finance officers in the hotel, motel, casino, club, and other areas of the hospitality industry. Formerly International Association of Hospitality Accountants.

National Association of Off-Track Betting. 978 Park Pl., Pomona, NY 10970. Phone: (845)362-0400 Fax: (845)362-0419 E-mail: naotb@betsrus.com.

National Council on Problem Gambling. 208 G St. NE, Washington, DC 20002. Phone: 800-522-4700 or (202)547-9204 Fax: (202)547-9206 E-mail: ncpg@ncpgambling.org • URL: http://www.ncpgambling.org • Advocates for programs and services to assist problem gamblers and their families. Formerly National Council on Compulsive Gambling.

GAMES

See: TOY INDUSTRY

GAMES, MANAGEMENT

See: MANAGEMENT GAMES

GARAGES

See: GASOLINE SERVICE STATIONS

GARBAGE DISPOSAL

See: SANITATION INDUSTRY

GARDEN SUPPLY INDUSTRY

See also: LAWN CARE INDUSTRY

DIRECTORIES

Yard and Garden. Cygnus Business Media, Inc. • Nine times a year. $48.00. Includes retailers and distributors of lawn and garden power equipment, lawn and plant care products, patio furniture, etc. Arranged by type of product. Includes a *Product* issue.

STATISTICS SOURCES

U. S. Industry and Trade Outlook. Available from National Technical Information Service. • Annual. $69.95. Produced by the International Trade Administration, U. S. Department of Commerce, in a "public-private" partnership with DRI/McGraw-Hill and Standard & Poor's. Provides basic data, outlook for the current year, and "Long-Term Prospects" (five-year projections) for a wide variety of products and services. Includes high technology industries. Formerly *U. S. Industrial Outlook.*

OTHER SOURCES

Lawn and Garden Market. Available from MarketResearch.com. • 2003. $3,000.00. Published by Packaged Facts. Provides market data on garden equipment, fertilizers and other substances, and professional lawn care services.

GARMENT INDUSTRY

See: CLOTHING INDUSTRY

GAS AND OIL ENGINES

See: ENGINES

GAS APPLIANCES

DIRECTORIES

AM-Appliance Manufacturer Directory. Business News Publishing Co. • Annual. $25.00. Formerly *Appliance Manufacturer Directory.*

Appliance - Appliance Industry Purchasing Directory. Dana Chase Publications, Inc. • Annual. $40.00. Suppliers to manufacturers of consumer, commercial, and business appliances.

Kitchen and Bath Business Buyers' Guide. CMP Books. • Annual. $7.00. Guide to kitchen and bath products, supplies and services. Formerly *Kitchen and Bath Business and Buyers' Guide/Almanac.*

PERIODICALS AND NEWSLETTERS

Appliance. Dana Chase Publications, Inc. • Monthly. $75.00 per year.

Appliance Manufacturer. Business News Publishing Co. • Monthly. $55.00 per year.

TRADE/PROFESSIONAL ASSOCIATIONS

American Society of Gas Engineers. 2805 Barranca Pky., Irvine, CA 92606. Phone: (949)733-4304 Fax: (949)733-4320 E-mail: jerry.moore@csa-international.org • URL: http://www.asge-national.org.

Gas Appliance Manufacturers Association. 2107 Wilson Blvd., Ste. 600, Arlington, VA 22201-3042. Phone: (703)525-7060 Fax: (703)525-6790 E-mail: membership@gamanet.org • URL: http://www.ahrinet.org • Composed of manufacturers of gas, oil, and electric space heating and water heating equipment for residential, commercial, and industrial applications, and associated components and accessories. Scope includes gas and oil central furnaces and boilers; gas, oil, and electric water heaters; gas space heaters; gas-fired commercial cooking equipment; gas-fired industrial heating equipment; and equipment used in the production,

transmission, and distribution of natural gas.

GAS COMPANIES

See: PUBLIC UTILITIES

GAS ENGINES

See: ENGINES

GAS INDUSTRY

See also: NATURAL GAS; PROPANE AND BUTANE GAS INDUSTRY; PUBLIC UTILITIES

CD-ROM DATABASES

OECD Statistical Compendium. Organization for Economic Cooperation and Development. • Semiannual. $1,905.00 per year for 1 to 10 users. CD-ROM contains more than 730,000 monthly, quarterly, and annual time series for OECD countries, 1960 to date. Includes fully searchable data on agriculture, food, economic indicators, national accounts, employment, energy, finance, industry, technology, and foreign trade. Results can be displayed in various forms.

DIRECTORIES

American Public Gas Association--Directory. American Public Gas Association. • Covers: about 1,000 municipally owned gas systems throughout the United States. Entries include: Name of system, address, phone, contact name, number of meters, number of employees, name of supplier of natural gas, miles of transmission and distribution lines, and date it became a municipal utility.

Brown's Directory of North American and International Gas Companies. Advanstar Communications. • Annual. $345.00.

Gas Industry Training Directory. American Gas Association. • Covers: over 600 programs available from gas transmission and distribution companies, manufacturers of gas-fired equipment, consultants, etc., and from gas associations. Entries include: Name, address, phone of source of program, name of contact, program description.

Gas Utility Industry Worldwide. Midwest Publishing Co. • Covers: Approximately 8,000 utility companies, contractors, engineering firms, equipment manufacturers, supply companies, underground natural gas storage facilities, regulatory agencies; international coverage. Entries include: Company name, address, phone, names and titles of key personnel, description of services.

Major Chemical and Petrochemical Companies of the World. Available from Gale Cengage Learning. • 2002. $880.00. Sixth edition. Published by Graham & Whiteside. Contains profiles of more than 7,000 important chemical and petrochemical companies in various countries. Subject areas include general chemicals, specialty chemicals, agricultural chemicals, petrochemicals, industrial gases, and fertilizers.

Plunkett's Energy Industry Almanac: Complete Profiles on the Energy Industry 500 Companies. Plunkett Research Ltd. • Annual. $199.99. Includes major oil companies, utilities, pipelines, alternative energy companies, etc. Provides information on industry trends.

ENCYCLOPEDIAS AND DICTIONARIES

Manual of Oil and Gas Terms. LexisNexis Matthew Bender. • $109.00. 12th edition. Defines technical, legal, and tax terms relating to the oil and gas industry.

FINANCIAL RATIOS

Almanac of Business and Industrial Financial Ratios. Leo Troy. Aspen Publishers, Inc. • 2003.

$125.95. Includes CD-Rom. Contains financial ratios derived from federal tax returns. Ratios for each of about 200 industries are arranged according to company asset size. (Almanac of Business and Industrial Financial Ratios Series).

HANDBOOKS AND MANUALS

Ernst and Young's Oil and Gas Federal Income Taxation. John R. Braden and others. CCH, Inc. • Annual. $92.95. Formerly *Miller's Oil and Gas Federal Income Taxation.*

Moody's Public Utility Manual. Mergent, Inc. • Annual. $1,995.00. Updated weekly online. Contains financial and other information concerning publicly-held utility companies (electric, gas, telephone, water).

World Gas Handbook. Energy Intelligence Group, Inc. • Annual. $1,250.00. Contains the gas industry structure, policies, markets, and production data for each of about 50 countries. Also includes detailed profiles of 56 major gas producers.

INTERNET DATABASES

Business 2.0 Web Guide to the Best Business Links. Business 2.0 Media Inc. Phone: (415)293-4800 E-mail: support@business2.com • URL: http://www.business2.com/webguide • Web site presents an extensive, searchable directory of links to "the best, most informative, and authoritative web pages." Twenty main categories cover business, finance, career, company information, people, and technology topics, with thousands of subtopics, all linking to Web sites recommended by experienced business researchers. Fees: Free.

Fedstats. Federal Interagency Council on Statistical Policy. Phone: (202)395-7254 • URL: http://www.fedstats.gov • Web site features an efficient search facility for full-text statistics produced by more than 100 federal agencies, including the Census Bureau, the Bureau of Economic Analysis, and the Bureau of Labor Statistics. Boolean searches can be made within one agency or for all agencies combined. Links are offered to international statistical bureaus, including the UN, IMF, OECD, UNESCO, Eurostat, and 20 individual countries. Fees: Free.

FreeLunch.com. Economy.com, Inc. Phone: (610)696-8700 Fax: (610)696-1678 • URL: http://www.freelunch.com • Web site provides free access to more than 1.5 million economic and financial data series, covering industry, demographics, labor markets, prices, retail sales, government spending, trade, interest rates, housing starts, the stock market, and many other topics. Data is available for various time periods in either chart or table form. Searching is offered. Fees: Free, but registration required. Economy.com, Inc. also offers fee-based economic analysis at *The Dismal Scientist* site (http://www.dismal.com).

ONLINE DATABASES

F & S Index. Gale Cengage Learning. • Contains about four million citations to worldwide business, financial, and industrial or consumer product literature appearing from 1972 to date. Weekly updates. Inquire as to online cost and availability.

PERIODICALS AND NEWSLETTERS

American Gas. American Gas Association. • 11 times a year. $59.00 per year. Formerly *AGA Monthly.*

American Public Gas Association Public Gas News. American Public Gas Association. • Biweekly. $45.00 per year. Formerly, *American Public Gas Association Newsletter.*

Gas Utility Manager. James Informational Media, Inc. • Monthly. $24.00 per year. Formerly *Gas Utility and Pipeline Industries.*

Oil and Gas Journal. PennWell Corp., Industrial Div. • Weekly. $84.00 per year.

Oil, Gas and Energy Quarterly. LexisNexis Matthew Bender. • Quarterly. $234.00 per year. Covers latest tax ideas, techniques, and practice pointers in oil and gas taxation and accounting features.

PRICE SOURCES

AGA Rate Service. American Gas Association. • Semiannual. Members, $175.00 per year; non-members, $300.00 per year. Looseleaf service.

STATISTICS SOURCES

Business Statistics of the United States. Linz Audain and Cornelia J. Strawser. Bernan Associates. • Annual. $147.00. Based on *Business Statistics*, formerly issue by the Bureau of Economic Analysis, U. S. Department of Commerce. Provides basic data for a wide variety of U. S. industries, services, and economic indicators. Most statistics are shown annually for 30 years and monthly for the most recent four years.

Energy Balances of OECD Countries. Organization for Economic Cooperation and Development. Available from OECD Publications and Information Center. • Annual. $115.00. Presents two-year data on the supply and consumption of solid fuels, oil, gas, and electricity, expressed in oil equivalency terms. Historical tables are also provided. Relates to OECD member countries.

Gas Facts. American Gas Association. • Annual. Members, $48.00; non-members, $120.00.

Gas Facts: A Statistical Record of the Gas Utility Industry. American Gas Association, Dept. of Statistics. • Annual. Members, $40.00; non-members, $80.00.

Infrastructure Industries USA. Gale Cengage Learning. • 2001. $260.00. Presents statistics and projections relating to economic activity in a wide variety of natural resource and construction industries.

Standard & Poor's Industry Surveys. Standard & Poor's. • Semiannual. $1,800.00. Two looseleaf volumes. Includes monthly *Supplements*. Provides detailed, individual surveys of 52 major industry groups. Each survey is revised on a semiannual basis. Also includes "Monthly Investment Review" (industry group investment analysis) and monthly "Trends & Projections" (economic analysis).

Survey of Current Business. Available from U. S. Government Printing Office. • Monthly. $63.00 per year. Issued by Bureau of Economic Analysis, U. S. Department of Commerce. Presents a wide variety of business and economic data.

TRADE/PROFESSIONAL ASSOCIATIONS

American Gas Association. 400 N Capitol St. NW, Ste. 450, Washington, DC 20001. Phone: (202)824-7000 Fax: (202)824-7115 E-mail: dparker@aga.org • URL: http://www.aga.org • Advocates for local natural gas utility companies; provides a broad range of programs and services for member natural gas pipelines, marketers, gatherers, international gas companies and industry associates.

American Public Gas Association. 201 Massachusetts Ave. NE, Ste. C-4, Washington, DC 20002. Phone: 800-927-4204 or (202)464-2742 Fax: (202)464-0246 E-mail: bkalisch@apga.org • URL: http://www.apga.org • Publicly owned gas systems; private corporations, persons or firms dealing with public gas systems are associate members. Promotes efficiency among public gas systems and protects the interests of the gas consumer. Provides information service on federal developments affecting natural gas; surveys municipal systems.

Gas Technology Institute. 1700 S Mt. Prospect Rd., Des Plaines, IL 60018-1804. Phone: (847)768-0500 Fax: (847)768-0501 E-mail: businessdevelopmentinfo@gastechnology.org • URL: http://www.gastechnology.org • Educational and research facility sponsored by companies engaged in the production, processing, transmission, and distribution of natural gas and related fuels;

engineering firms; large energy consumers. Conducts contract research for government and industry in the field of non-nuclear energy technology. Offers short courses in gas production, transmission, distribution, economics, and marketing. Sponsors symposia on current topics in non-nuclear energy.

Interstate Natural Gas Association of America. 10 G St., NE, Ste. 700, Washington, DC 20002. Phone: (202)216-5900 Fax: (202)216-0877 • URL: http://www.ingaa.org • Formerly Independent Natural Gas Association of America.

National Propane Gas Association. 1150 17th St. NW, Ste. 310, Washington, DC 20036-4623. Phone: (202)466-7200 Fax: (202)466-7205 E-mail: info@npga.org • URL: http://www.npga.org • Represents the propane industry, including small businesses and large corporations engaged in the retail marketing of propane gas and appliances, producers and wholesalers of propane gas and equipment, manufacturers and fabricators of propane gas cylinders and tanks, propane transporters, and manufacturer's representatives. Works to promote the safe and increased use of propane; advocates in Congress and federal regulatory agencies for favorable environment for production, distributing, and marketing of propane gas. Develops safety standards and training materials for the safe use and distribution of propane gas.

OTHER SOURCES

Federal Taxation of Oil and Gas Transactions. LexisNexis Matthew Bender. • Semiannual. $414.00 per year. Two looseleaf volumes.

GAS, LIQUEFIED PETROLEUM

See: PROPANE AND BUTANE GAS INDUSTRY

GAS, NATURAL

See: NATURAL GAS

GAS PIPELINES

See: PIPELINE INDUSTRY

GAS RATES

See: GAS INDUSTRY

GASOHOL

See: FUEL

GASOLINE ENGINES

See: ENGINES

GASOLINE INDUSTRY

See also: GAS INDUSTRY; PETROLEUM INDUSTRY

CD-ROM DATABASES

OECD Statistical Compendium. Organization for Economic Cooperation and Development. • Semiannual. $1,905.00 per year for 1 to 10 users. CD-ROM contains more than 730,000 monthly, quarterly, and annual time series for OECD countries, 1960 to date. Includes fully searchable

data on agriculture, food, economic indicators, national accounts, employment, energy, finance, industry, technology, and foreign trade. Results can be displayed in various forms.

DIRECTORIES

Financial Times Business Global Oil & Gas Directory. Available from Gale Cengage Learning. • Annual. $355.00. Published by Financial Times Business. Provides detailed information on 800 leading oil and gas companies worldwide. Includes financial data for three years. Formerly *Financial Times Energy Yearbook: Oil & Gas.*

The Geophysical Directory. Claudia LaCalli, editor. Geophysical Directory Inc. • Covers: about 4,000 companies that provide geophysical equipment, supplies, or services, and mining and petroleum companies that use geophysical techniques; international coverage. Entries include: Company name, address, phone, fax, names of principal executives, operations, and sales personnel; similar information for branch locations.

Worldwide Refining and Gas Processing Directory. PennWell Corp., Petroeum Div. • Annual. $165.00. Lists over 1,000 crude oil refineries, 1,300 gas processing plants and over 600 engineering and construction firms which build and service these plants; worldwide coverage.

ENCYCLOPEDIAS AND DICTIONARIES

Encyclopedia of Energy. Cutler J. Cleveland, editor. Elsevier, Inc. • 2004. $1,560.00. Six volumes. Covers all aspects of energy sources and energy-related environmental issues.

HANDBOOKS AND MANUALS

Modern Petroleum Technology. Richard A. Dawe, editor. John Wiley and Sons, Inc. • 2000. $600.00. Sixth edition. Two volumes. Volume one, entitled *Upstream*, covers oil rigs and other means of obtaining raw petroleum. Volume two, *Downstream*, covers petroleum refining and end products. Edited for industry technicians, managers, and engineers.

INTERNET DATABASES

Business 2.0 Web Guide to the Best Business Links. Business 2.0 Media Inc. Phone: (415)293-4800 E-mail: support@business2.com • URL: http://www.business2.com/webguide • Web site presents an extensive, searchable directory of links to "the best, most informative, and authoritative web pages." Twenty main categories cover business, finance, career, company information, people, and technology topics, with thousands of subtopics, all linking to Web sites recommended by experienced business researchers. Fees: Free.

Fedstats. Federal Interagency Council on Statistical Policy. Phone: (202)395-7254 • URL: http://www.fedstats.gov • Web site features an efficient search facility for full-text statistics produced by more than 100 federal agencies, including the Census Bureau, the Bureau of Economic Analysis, and the Bureau of Labor Statistics. Boolean searches can be made within one agency or for all agencies combined. Links are offered to international statistical bureaus, including the UN, IMF, OECD, UNESCO, Eurostat, and 20 individual countries. Fees: Free.

FreeLunch.com. Economy.com, Inc. Phone: (610)696-8700 Fax: (610)696-1678 • URL: http://www.freelunch.com • Web site provides free access to more than 1.5 million economic and financial data series, covering industry, demographics, labor markets, prices, retail sales, government spending, trade, interest rates, housing starts, the stock market, and many other topics. Data is available for various time periods in either chart or table form. Searching is offered. Fees: Free, but registration required. Economy.com, Inc. also offers fee-based economic analysis at *The Dismal Scientist* site (http://www. dismal.com).

PERIODICALS AND NEWSLETTERS

American Petroleum Institute. Division of Statistics. Weekly Statistical Bulletin. American Petroleum Institute. • Weekly. $115.00 per year. Includes *Monthly Statistical Report.*

Barron's: The Dow Jones Business and Financial Weekly. • Weekly. $145.00 per year.

International Oil News. William F. Bland Co. • Description: Covers "timely and significant developments in the international oil business, including exploration, production, transportation, refining, and marketing.".

Lundberg Letter. Lundberg Survey, Incorporated. • Description: Provides statistics and analysis of U.S. oil marketing primary data. Includes an in-depth single-subject profile of a development in the petroleum market in each issue. Discusses such topics as retail/wholesale pricing, market shares, and station characteristics nationwide and regionally.

Oil and Gas Journal. PennWell Corp., Industrial Div. • Weekly. $84.00 per year.

PRICE SOURCES

CPI Detailed Report: Consumer Price Index. Available from U.S. Government Printing Office. • Monthly. $45.00 per year. Cost of living data.

Energy Prices and Taxes. Organization for Economic Cooperation and Development. • Quarterly. $355.00 per year. Includes both industrial and consumer prices for oil products, natural gas, coal, and electricity in various countries. (Also available on CD-ROM.).

STATISTICS SOURCES

Annual Energy Outlook [year], with Projections to [year]. Available from U.S. Government Printing Office. • Annual. $42.00. Issued by the Energy Information Administration, U.S. Department of Energy (http://www.eia.doe.gov). Contains detailed statistics and 20-year projections for electricity, oil, natural gas, coal, and renewable energy. Text provides extensive discussion of energy issues and "Market Trends.".

Business Statistics of the United States. Linz Audain and Cornelia J. Strawser. Bernan Associates. • Annual. $147.00. Based on *Business Statistics*, formerly issue by the Bureau of Economic Analysis, U.S. Department of Commerce. Provides basic data for a wide variety of U.S. industries, services, and economic indicators. Most statistics are shown annually for 30 years and monthly for the most recent four years.

International Energy Annual. Available from U.S. Government Printing Office. • Annual. $34.00. Issued by the Energy Information Administration, U.S. Department of Energy. Provides production, consumption, import, and export data for primary energy commodities in more than 200 countries and areas. In addition to petroleum products and alcohol, renewable energy sources are covered (hydroelectric, geothermal, solar, and wind).

Oil, Gas, Coal, and Electricity: Quarterly Statistics. Organization for Economic Cooperation and Development. • Quarterly. $355.00 per year. Provides detailed data for OECD countries. Covers crude oil, nine oil product groups, hard coal, brown coal (lignite), natural gas, and electric power.

Oil Information. Organization for Economic Cooperation and Development. • Annual. $150.00. Contains international data for major petroleum product groups. Includes statistics on supply, demand, trade, production, prices, and consumption for individual OECD countries and regions. Various time series cover about 30 years. (Also available on CD-ROM.).

Petroleum Supply Annual. Available from U.S.

Government Printing Office. • Annual. $78.00. Two volumes. Produced by the Energy Information Administration, U.S. Department of Energy. Contains worldwide data on the petroleum industry and petroleum products.

Petroleum Supply Monthly. Available from U.S. Government Printing Office. • Monthly. Produced by the Energy Information Administration, U.S. Department of Energy. Provides worldwide statistics on a wide variety of petroleum products. Covers production, supplies, exports and imports, transportation, refinery operations, and other aspects of the petroleum industry.

Standard & Poor's Industry Surveys. Standard & Poor's. • Semiannual. $1,800.00. Two looseleaf volumes. Includes monthly *Supplements.* Provides detailed, individual surveys of 52 major industry groups. Each survey is revised on a semiannual basis. Also includes "Monthly Investment Review" (industry group investment analysis) and monthly "Trends & Projections" (economic analysis).

Survey of Current Business. Available from U.S. Government Printing Office. • Monthly. $63.00 per year. Issued by Bureau of Economic Analysis, U.S. Department of Commerce. Presents a wide variety of business and economic data.

Weekly Petroleum Status Report. Energy Information Administration. Available from U.S. Government Printing Office. • Weekly. Current statistics in the context of both historical information and selected prices and forecasts.

TRADE/PROFESSIONAL ASSOCIATIONS

Federation of Tax Administrators. 444 N. Capitol St., Suite 348, Washington, DC 20001. Phone: (202)624-5890 Fax: (202)624-7888 E-mail: fta@ taxadmin.org • URL: http://www.taxadmin.org.

Society of Independent Gasoline Marketers of America. 11911 Freedom Dr., Ste. 590, Reston, VA 20190. Phone: (703)709-7000 Fax: (703)709-7007 E-mail: sigma@sigma.org • URL: http://www. sigma.org • Chain gasoline marketers, wholesale and retail.

GASOLINE SERVICE STATIONS

See also: GASOLINE INDUSTRY

CD-ROM DATABASES

OECD Statistical Compendium. Organization for Economic Cooperation and Development. • Semiannual. $1,905.00 per year for 1 to 10 users. CD-ROM contains more than 730,000 monthly, quarterly, and annual time series for OECD countries, 1960 to date. Includes fully searchable data on agriculture, food, economic indicators, national accounts, employment, energy, finance, industry, technology, and foreign trade. Results can be displayed in various forms.

FINANCIAL RATIOS

Almanac of Business and Industrial Financial Ratios. Leo Troy. Aspen Publishers, Inc. • 2003. $125.95. Includes CD-Rom. Contains financial ratios derived from federal tax returns. Ratios for each of about 200 industries are arranged according to company asset size. (Almanac of Business and Industrial Financial Ratios Series).

Annual Statement Studies. The Risk Management Association. • Annual. Median and quartile financial ratios are given for over 400 kinds of manufacturing, wholesale, retail, construction, and consumer finance establishments. Data is sorted by both asset size and sales volume. Includes a clearly written "Definition of Ratios" and an alphabetical industry index.

Annual Statement Studies: Industry Default Prob-

abilities and Cash Flow Measures. The Risk Management Association. • Annual. $145.00. Serves as a companion volume to the original *Annual Statement Studies.* Gives probability of default estimates on a percentage scale for more than 450 industries. Includes changes in position year-by-year for eight financial statement line items and provides percentage measures of cash flow.

INTERNET DATABASES

Advance Monthly Sales for Retail Trade and Food Services. U.S. Census Bureau. Phone: 800-541-8345 or (301)763-4636 Fax: (301)457-3842 E-mail: rcb@census.gov • URL: http://www.census.gov/ svsd/www/fullpub.html • Web pages provide monthly sales figures for a wide range of retail businesses. Advance, preliminary, and final statistics are provided for the latest month available in each case, with a previous-year comparison. Updates are monthly.

Business 2.0 Web Guide to the Best Business Links. Business 2.0 Media Inc. Phone: (415)293-4800 E-mail: support@business2.com • URL: http:// www.business2.com/webguide • Web site presents an extensive, searchable directory of links to "the best, most informative, and authoritative web pages." Twenty main categories cover business, finance, career, company information, people, and technology topics, with thousands of subtopics, all linking to Web sites recommended by experienced business researchers. Fees: Free.

Fedstats. Federal Interagency Council on Statistical Policy. Phone: (202)395-7254 • URL: http://www. fedstats.gov • Web site features an efficient search facility for full-text statistics produced by more than 100 federal agencies, including the Census Bureau, the Bureau of Economic Analysis, and the Bureau of Labor Statistics. Boolean searches can be made within one agency or for all agencies combined. Links are offered to international statistical bureaus, including the UN, IMF, OECD, UNESCO, Eurostat, and 20 individual countries. Fees: Free.

FreeLunch.com. Economy.com, Inc. Phone: (610)696-8700 Fax: (610)696-1678 • URL: http:// www.freelunch.com • Web site provides free access to more than 1.5 million economic and financial data series, covering industry, demographics, labor markets, prices, retail sales, government spending, trade, interest rates, housing starts, the stock market, and many other topics. Data is available for various time periods in either chart or table form. Searching is offered. Fees: Free, but registration required. Economy.com, Inc. also offers fee-based economic analysis at *The Dismal Scientist* site (http://www. dismal.com).

PERIODICALS AND NEWSLETTERS

Motor Age: For the Professional Automotive Import and Domestic Service Industry. Reed Business Information. • Monthly. $49.00 per year. Published for independent automotive repair shops and gasoline service stations.

Oil Express: Inside Report on Trends in Petroleum Marketing Without the Influ nce of Advertising. United Communications Group. • 50 times a year. $337.00 per year. Newsletter. Provides news of trends in petroleum marketing and convenience store operations. Includes *U.S. Oil Week's Price Monitor* (petroleum product prices) and *C-Store Digest* (news concerning convenience stores operated by the major oil companies) and *Fuel Oil Update.* Formerly *U.S. Oil Week.*

STATISTICS SOURCES

Annual Benchmark Report for Retail Trade and Food Services...A Detailed Summary of Retail Sales, Purchases, Accounts Receivable, Inventories, and Food Service Sales. Available from U.S. Government Printing Office. • Annual. $13.00. Issued by the U.S. Census Bureau. Provides detailed annual and monthly retail statistics for the most recent 10 years. Includes data for various kinds of retail outlets, including automobiles, furniture, appliances, building supplies, grocery stores, drug stores, gasoline stations, clothing, sporting goods, department stores, and restaurants.

Business Statistics of the United States. Linz Audain and Cornelia J. Strawser. Bernan Associates. • Annual. $147.00. Based on *Business Statistics*, formerly issue by the Bureau of Economic Analysis, U. S. Department of Commerce. Provides basic data for a wide variety of U. S. industries, services, and economic indicators. Most statistics are shown annually for 30 years and monthly for the most recent four years.

Survey of Current Business. Available from U. S. Government Printing Office. • Monthly. $63.00 per year. Issued by Bureau of Economic Analysis, U. S. Department of Commerce. Presents a wide variety of business and economic data.

United States Census of Service Industries. U.S. Bureau of the Census. • Quinquennial. Various reports available.

TRADE/PROFESSIONAL ASSOCIATIONS

Automotive Service Association. PO Box 929, PO Box 929, Bedford, TX 76095-0929. Phone: 800-272-7467 or (817)283-6205 Fax: (817)685-0225 E-mail: asainfo@asashop.org • URL: http://www.asashop.org • Automotive service businesses including body, paint, and trim shops, engine rebuilders, radiator shops, brake and wheel alignment services, transmission shops, tune-up services, and air conditioning services; associate members are manufacturers and wholesalers of automotive parts, and the trade press. Represents independent business owners and managers before private agencies and national and state legislative bodies. Promotes confidence between consumer and the automotive service industry, safety inspection of motor vehicles, and better highways.

Gasoline and Automotive Service Dealers Association. 9520 Seaview Ave., Brooklyn, NY 11236. Phone: (718)241-1111 Fax: (718)763-6589 E-mail: gasdal@cs.com • Members are owners and operators of automobile service stations and repair shops. Formerly Gasoline Merchants.

GATT

See: GENERAL AGREEMENT ON TARIFFS AND TRADE (GATT)

GAUGES

See: TOOL INDUSTRY

GEAR INDUSTRY

See also: MACHINERY

ABSTRACTS AND INDEXES

Applied Science and Technology Index. H. W. Wilson Co. • 11 times a year. Quarterly and annual cumulations. Price varies. Indexes a wide variety of English language technical, industrial, and engineering periodicals.

Engineering Index Monthly: Abstracting and Indexing Services Covering Sources ofthe World's Engineering Literature. Engineering Information Inc. • Monthly. Institutions, $5,279.00 per year. Provides indexing and abstracting of the world's engineering and technical literature.

F & S Index: United States. Gale Cengage Learning. • Monthly. $1,450.00 per year, including quarterly and annual cumulations. Provides annotated citations to marketing, business, financial, and industrial literature. Coverage of U. S. business activity

includes trade journals, financial magazines, business newspapers, and special reports.

NTIS Alerts: Manufacturing Technology. National Technical Information Service. • Semimonthly. $265.00 per year. Provides descriptions of government-sponsored research reports and software, with ordering information. Covers computer-aided design and manufacturing (CAD/CAM), engineering materials, quality control, machine tools, robots, lasers, productivity, and related subjects. Formerly *Abstract Newsletter*.

CD-ROM DATABASES

WILSONDISC: Applied Science and Technology Abstracts. H. W. Wilson Co. • Monthly. Includes unlimited access to the online version of *Applied Science and Technology Abstracts* through WILSONLINE. Provides CD-ROM indexing and abstracting of 500 prominent scientific, technical, engineering, and industrial periodicals. Indexing coverage is provided from 1983 to date and abstracting from 1993 to date.

ENCYCLOPEDIAS AND DICTIONARIES

Encyclopedic Dictionary of Gears and Gearing. David W. South. McGraw-Hill • 1994. $54.50.

HANDBOOKS AND MANUALS

Mechanical Engineer's Reference Book. E. H. Smith, editor. Society of Automotive Engineers. • 1994. $135.00. 12th edition. Covers mechanical engineering principles, computer integrated engineering systems, design standards, materials, power transmission, and many other engineering topics. (Authored Series).

ONLINE DATABASES

Applied Science and Technology Index Online. H. W. Wilson Co. • Provides online indexing of 500 major scientific, technical, industrial, and engineering periodicals. Time period is 1983 to date. Monthly updates. Inquire as to online cost and availability.

F & S Index. Gale Cengage Learning. • Contains about four million citations to worldwide business, financial, and industrial or consumer product literature appearing from 1972 to date. Weekly updates. Inquire as to online cost and availability.

Trade & Industry Database. Gale Cengage Learning. • Provides indexing of business periodicals, January 1981 to date. Daily updates. (Full text articles from some periodicals are available online, 1983 to date. Inquire as to online cost and availability).

PERIODICALS AND NEWSLETTERS

American Gear Manufacturers Association--News Digest. American Gear Manufacturers Association. • Description: Carries information of interest to gear manufacturers and suppliers. Recurring features include news of research, a calendar of events, reports of meetings, news of educational opportunities, and columns titled Economic Review, President's Corner, and Executive Director's View.

Gear Technology: The Journal of Gear Manufacturing. Randall Publishing, Inc. • Bimonthly. $45.00 per year. Edited for manufacturers, engineers, and designers of gears.

RESEARCH CENTERS AND INSTITUTES

Gear Dynamics and Gear Noise Research Laboratory. Ohio State University, 1009 Robinson Laboratory, 206 W. 18th Ave., Columbus, OH 43210. Phone: (614)292-5860 Fax: (614)292-3163 E-mail: houser.4@osu.edu • URL: http://www.gearlab.org.

TRADE/PROFESSIONAL ASSOCIATIONS

American Gear Manufacturers Association. 500 Montgomery St., Ste. 350, Alexandria, VA 22314-1581. Phone: (703)684-0211 Fax: (703)684-0242 E-mail: webmaster@agma.org • URL: http://www.

agma.org • Represents manufacturers of gears, geared speed changers, and related equipment; manufacturers of gear cutting and checking equipment; teachers of mechanical engineering and gearing. Conducts educational and research programs; compiles statistics and financial data. Develops technical standards for domestic and international industry.

GEMS AND GEMSTONES

See also: JEWELRY BUSINESS

GENERAL WORKS

Gemstones of the World. Walter Schumann. Sterling Publishing Co., Inc. • 2000. $24.95. Expanded revised edition.

HANDBOOKS AND MANUALS

Gem Identification Made Easy: A Hands-on Guide to More Confident Buying and Selling. Antoinette L. Matlins and Antonio C. Bonanno. GemStone Press. • 1997. $34.95. Second revised edition.

Gemstone Buying Guide. Renee Newman and John Raimo. International Jewelry Publications. • 2003. $19.95. Second edition. Serves as a guide for evaluating, identifying, selecting, and buying gemstones of various types and colors. Includes supplier information and 281 color photographs.

Handbook of Gem Identification. Richard T. Liddicoat, Jr. Gemological Institute of America. • 1987. $47.50. 12th edition.

Jewelry and Gems: The Buying Guide: How to Buy Diamonds, Pearls, Precious and Other Popular Gems with Confidence and Knowledge. Antoinette L. Matlins and Antonio C. Bonanno. GemStone Press. • 2001. $24.95. Fifth edition.

ONLINE DATABASES

GEOREF. American Geological Institute. • Bibliography and index of geology and geosciences literature, 1785 to present. Inquire as to online cost and availability.

PERIODICALS AND NEWSLETTERS

Gems and Gemology. Gemological Institute of America. • Quarterly. $69.95 per year.

Lapidary Journal. Primedia Enthusiast Group. • Monthly. $29.95.

Modern Jeweler. Cygnus Business Media. • Monthly. $60.00 per year. Edited for retail jewelers. Covers the merchandising of jewelry, gems, and watches. Supersedes in part *Modern Jeweler*.

Spectra. National Communication Association. • Description: Discusses forensics, interpretation, interpersonal communication, rhetoric and public address, communication theory, mass media, theater, speech and language sciences, and job advertising. Recurring features include official business of the Association, news briefs concerning members, and notices of available materials.

STATISTICS SOURCES

Mineral Commodity Summaries. Available from U. S. Government Printing Office. • Annual. $26.00. Published by the U. S. Geological Survey, Department of the Interior (http://www.usgs.gov). Contains detailed, five-year data for about 90 nonfuel minerals. Covers a wide range of statistics, including production, imports, exports, consumption, reserves, prices, tariff information, and industry employment. (Two pages are devoted to each mineral.).

TRADE/PROFESSIONAL ASSOCIATIONS

American Gem and Mineral Suppliers Association. 475 Smith St., Middletown, CT 06457. 475 Smith St.,.

American Gem Society. 8881 W Sahara Ave., Las Vegas, NV 89117. Phone: (866)805-6500 or

(702)255-6500 Fax: (702)255-7420 E-mail: info@ags.org • URL: http://www.americangemsociety.org • Represents 1,600 retail and manufacturer jewelry firms in North America dedicated to proven ethics, knowledge and consumer protection. Encourages members to pursue studies in gemology; confers titles of Registered Jeweler, Registered Supplier, Certified Gemologist, and Certified Gemologist Appraiser upon those taking recognized courses and passing extensive examinations. Sponsors national promotional programs. Conducts educational programs.

American Gem Trade Association. 3030 LBJ Fwy., Ste. 840, 3030 LBJ Freeway, Ste. 840, Dallas, TX 75234. Phone: 800-972-1162 or (214)742-4367 Fax: (214)742-7334 E-mail: info@agta.org • URL: http://www.agta.org • Represents suppliers of natural colored gemstones; retail jewelers and jewelry manufacturers. Promotes natural colored gemstones; encourages high ethical standards among members and within the industry. Seeks to establish closer communication within the industry; works to protect consumers from fraud and to create a greater awareness of natural colored gemstones. Conducts seminars; maintains speakers' bureau.

Gemological Institute of America. 5345 Armada Dr., Carlsbad, CA 92008. Phone: 800-421-7250 or (760)603-4000 Fax: (760)603-4080 E-mail: president@gia.edu • URL: http://www.gia.edu.

GENERAL AGREEMENT ON TARIFFS AND TRADE (GATT)

GENERAL WORKS

From GATT to the WTO: The Multilateral Trading System in the New Millennium. WTO Secretariat, editor. Kluwer Law International. • 2000. $79.50. Published by the World Trade Organization (http://www.wto.org). A collection of essays on the future of world trade, written on the occasion of the 50th anniversary of the multilateral trading system (GATT/WTO). The authors are described as "important academics in international trade.".

Reciprocity, U. S. Trade Policy, and the GATT Regime. Carolyn Rhodes. Cornell University Press. • 1993. $42.50.

PERIODICALS AND NEWSLETTERS

Economic Justice Report: Global Issues of Economic Justice. Ecumenical Coalition for Economic Justice. • Quarterly. Individuals, $30.00 per year; institutions, $40.00 per year. Reports on economic fairness in foreign trade. Formerly *Gatt-Fly Report.*

WTO Focus. World Trade Organization, Publications Service. • Newsletter. Free. 10 times a year. Text in English. Provides current news about activities relating to the World Trade Organization (WTO) and the General Agreement on Tariffs and Trade (GATT). Formerly *GATT Focus.*

RESEARCH CENTERS AND INSTITUTES

Institute for International Economics. 1750 Massachusetts Ave., N.W., Washington, DC 20036. Phone: (202)328-9000 Fax: (202)328-5432 E-mail: alreeves@iie.com • URL: http://www.iie.com • Research fields include a wide range of international economic issues, including foreign exchange rates.

STATISTICS SOURCES

WTO Annual Report (World Trade Organization). Available from Bernan Associates. • Annual. $80.00. Two volumes ($40.00 per volume). Published by the World Trade Organization. Volume one: *Annual Report.* Volume two: *International Trade Statistics.*

OTHER SOURCES

Copyright Law in Business and Practice. John W. Hazard. West Group. • Semiannual. $274.00 per year. Two looseleaf volumes.

GENERAL AVIATION

See: BUSINESS AVIATION

GENERATORS, ELECTRIC

See: ELECTRICAL EQUIPMENT INDUSTRY

GENERIC DRUG INDUSTRY

See also: PHARMACEUTICAL INDUSTRY

ABSTRACTS AND INDEXES

Business Periodicals Index. H. W. Wilson Co. • 11 times a year. Quarterly and annual cumulations. Price varies.

International Pharmaceutical Abstracts: Key to the World's Literature of Pharmacy. American Society of Health-System Pharmacists. • Semimonthly. $565.50 per year.

CD-ROM DATABASES

ABI/INFORM. PROQUEST. • Monthly. Provides CD-ROM indexing and abstracting of worldwide business literature. Archival discs are available from 1971. Formerly *ABI/INFORM OnDisc.*

International Pharmaceutical Abstracts [CD-ROM]. American Society of Health-System Pharmacists. • Monthly. $1,795.00 per year. Contains CD-ROM indexing and abstracting of international pharmaceutical literature from 1970 to date.

Mosby's GenRx [year]. CME, Inc. • Quarterly. $250.00. CD-ROM contains detailed monographs for more than 45,000 generic and brand name prescription drugs. Includes color pill images and customizable patient education handouts.

Physicians' Desk Reference Library on CD-ROM. Medical Economics. • Three times a year. Contains the CD-ROM equivalent of *Physicians' Desk Reference (PDR), Physicians' Desk Reference for Nonprescription Drugs, Physicians' Desk Reference for Opthalmology,* and other PDR publications.

WILSONDISC: Wilson Business Abstracts. H. W. Wilson Co. • Monthly. Includes unlimited online access to *Wilson Business Abstracts* through WILSONLINE. Provides CD-ROM "cover-to-cover" abstracting and indexing of over 600 prominent business periodicals. Indexing is from 1982, abstracting from 1990. (*Business Periodicals Index* without abstracts is available on CD-ROM at $1,495 per year.).

DIRECTORIES

Major Pharmaceutical Companies of the World. Available from Gale Cengage Learning. • 2003. $880.00. Fifth edition. Published by Graham & Whiteside. Contains detailed information and trade names for more than 2,500 important pharmaceutical companies in various countries.

Mosby's GenRx: The Complete Reference for Generic and Brand Drugs. Mosby, Inc. • 2000. $72.95. 11th edition. Provides detailed information on a wide variety of generic and brand name prescription drugs. Includes color identification pictures, prescribing data, and price comparisons. (Mosby's Physicians GenRx Series).

Red Book. American Monument Association. • Covers: 7,000 retail monument dealers, suppliers of granite and marble, wholesalers, quarriers, funeral homes and cemeteries. Entries include: company; name, address, phone, fax; trade classification, names of owner or corporate officers and their titles. Available only to members of The American Monument Association.

HANDBOOKS AND MANUALS

Approved Drug Products, with Therapeutic Equivalence Evaluations. Available from U. S.

Government Printing Office. • $108.00 for basic manual and supplemental material for an indeterminate period. Issued by the Food and Drug Administration, U. S. Department of Health and Human Services. Lists prescription drugs that have been approved by the FDA. Includes therapeutic equivalents to aid in containment of health costs and to serve State drug selection laws.

Physicians' Desk Reference. Medical Economics Co. • Annual. $82.95. Generally known as "PDR". Provides detailed descriptions, effects, and adverse reactions for about 4,000 prescription drugs. Includes data on more than 250 drug manufacturers, with brand name and generic name indexes and drug identification photographs. Discontinued drugs are also listed.

INTERNET DATABASES

National Library of Medicine (NLM). National Institutes of Health (NIH). Phone: 888-346-3656 or (301)496-1131 Fax: (301)480-3537 E-mail: access@nlm.nih.gov • URL: http://www.nlm.nih.gov • NLM Web site offers free access through MEDLINE ("PubMed") to about nine million references to articles appearing in some 4,000 biomedical journals, with abstracts. Search interfaces range from "simple keywords to advanced Boolean expressions." The NLM site offers many links to other sources of biomedical and technical information (the National Center for Biotechnology Information, for example). Fees: Free.

RxList: The Internet Drug Index. Neil Sandow. Phone: (707)746-8754 E-mail: info@rxlist.com • URL: http://www.rxlist.com • Web site features detailed information (cost, usage, dosage, side effects, etc.) from Mosby, Inc. for about 300 major pharmaceutical products, representing two thirds of prescriptions filled in the U. S. (3,700 other products are listed). The "Top 200" drugs are ranked by number of prescriptions filled. Keyword searching is provided. Fees: Free.

ONLINE DATABASES

Derwent Drug File. Derwent, Inc. • Provides indexing and abstracting of the world's pharmaceutical journal literature since 1964, with weekly updates. Formerly *RINGDOC.* Inquire as to online cost and availability.

F & S Index. Gale Cengage Learning. • Contains about four million citations to worldwide business, financial, and industrial or consumer product literature appearing from 1972 to date. Weekly updates. Inquire as to online cost and availability.

F-D-C Reports. FDC Reports, Inc. • An online version of "The Gray Sheet" (medical devices), "The Pink Sheet" (pharmaceuticals), "The Rose Sheet" (cosmetics), "The Blue Sheet" (biomedical), and "The Tan Sheet" (nonprescription). Contains full-text information on legal, technical, corporate, financial, and marketing developments from 1987 to date, with weekly updates. Inquire as to online cost and availability.

International Pharmaceutical Abstracts [online]. American Society of Health-System Pharmacists. • Provides online indexing and abstracting of the world's pharmaceutical literature from 1970 to date. Monthly updates. Inquire as to online cost and availability.

Pharmaceutical News Index. ProQuest Inc. • Indexes major pharmaceutical industry newsletters, 1974 to present. Weekly updates. Inquire as to online cost and availability.

PROMT: Predicasts Overview of Markets and Technology. Gale Cengage Learning. • Companies, products, applied technologies and markets. U.S. and international literature coverage, 1972 to date. Inquire as to online cost and availability. Provides abstracts from more than 1,600 publications. Weekly updates.

Trade & Industry Database. Gale Cengage

Learning. • Provides indexing of business periodicals, January 1981 to date. Daily updates. (Full text articles from some periodicals are available online, 1983 to date. Inquire as to online cost and availability).

Wilson Business Abstracts Online. H. W. Wilson Co. • Indexes and abstracts 600 major business periodicals, plus the *Wall Street Journal* and the business section of the *New York Times.* Indexing is from 1982, abstracting from 1990, with the two newspapers included from 1993. Updated weekly. Inquire as to online cost and availability. (*Business Periodicals Index* without abstracts is also available online.).

PERIODICALS AND NEWSLETTERS

Drug Store News Continuing Education Quarterly. Lebhar-Friedman, Inc. • Quarterly. $59.95 per year. Formerly *Drug Store News Chain Pharmacy.*

Generic Line. Scitec Services Inc. • Description: Focuses on the pharmaceutical industry, emphasizing generic products. Discusses regulatory, legislative, technical, and business developments of interest to generic and small pharmaceutical manufacturers. Recurring features include reports on current research and actions of pharmaceutical companies.

The Pink Sheet: Prescription Pharmaceuticals and Biotechnology. F-D-C Reports, Inc. • 51 times a year. Institutions, $1,431.00 per year. Newsletter covering business and regulatory developments affecting the pharmaceutical and biotechnology industries. Provides information on generic drug approvals and includes a drug sector stock index.

Worst Pills Best Pills News. Public Citizen. • Monthly. $20.00 per year. Newsletter. Provides pharmaceutical news and information for consumers, with an emphasis on harmful drug interactions.

PRICE SOURCES

First DataBank Blue Book. Hearst Corp. • Annual. $65.00. List of manufacturers of prescription and over-the-counter drugs, sold in retail drug stores. Formerly *American Druggist Blue Book.*

RESEARCH CENTERS AND INSTITUTES

Pharmaceutical Marketing and Management Research Program. University of Mississippi, Waller Lab Complex, Room 101, University, MS 38677. Phone: (662)915-5948 Fax: (662)915-5262 E-mail: mkolassa@olemiss.edu • URL: http://www.olemiss.edu/depts/rips.

STATISTICS SOURCES

Industry Profile and Healthcare Factbook. Healthcare Distribution Management Association. • Annual. $349.00. Provides 266 statistical tables in three sections: "Industry Profile" (financial ratios related to drug distribution), "Pharmaceutical and Healthcare Distribution Trends and Facts," and "Healthcare Factbook" (expenditures, insurance utilization, company/product rankings, drug price inflation, generics, OTC, drug store data, hospital statistics, healthcare consumer summaries, etc.). Also known as *HDMA Factbook.* The Healthcare Distribution Management Association was formerly the National Wholesale Druggists' Association.

TRADE/PROFESSIONAL ASSOCIATIONS

Generic Pharmaceutical Association. 2300 Clarendon Blvd., Ste. 400, Arlington, VA 22201. Phone: (703)647-2480 Fax: (703)647-2481 E-mail: info@gphaonline.org • URL: http://www.gphaonline.org • Promotes the common interests of the members and the general welfare of the pharmaceutical industry; prepares and disseminates among members and others, accurate and reliable information concerning the industry, products, needs and requirements; participates in international, federal, state and municipal legislative, regulatory and administrative proceedings with respect to law, rules and orders af-

fecting the pharmaceutical industry; participates in scientific research and product development with intent to increase consumer access to generic products; and raises awareness and visibility of the significant benefits and value of generic drugs to the consumers.

OTHER SOURCES

The Market for Generic Drugs. MarketResearch.com. • 2000. $3,250.00. Market research data. Includes a discussion of current trends in the use of generic prescription drugs to reduce healthcare costs, with forcasts to 2004.

GENERIC PRODUCTS

See: PRIVATE LABEL PRODUCTS

GENETIC ENGINEERING

See also: BIOTECHNOLOGY

GENERAL WORKS

Altered Fates: The Genetic Re-Engineering of Human Life. Jeff Lyon and Peter Gorner. W. W. Norton & Co., Inc. • 1995. $27.50. A discussion of recent progress in genetic engineering.

ABSTRACTS AND INDEXES

Applied Science and Technology Index. H. W. Wilson Co. • 11 times a year. Quarterly and annual cumulations. Price varies. Indexes a wide variety of English language technical, industrial, and engineering periodicals.

Excerpta Medica: Human Genetics. Elsevier. • Semimonthly. Qualified personnel, $409.00 per year; institutions, $4,140.00 per year. Section 22 of *Excerpta Medica.*

Genetics Abstracts. CSA. • 11 times a year. $1,595.00 per year. Includes print and online editions.

NTIS Alerts: Biomedical Technology & Human Factors Engineering. National Technical Information Service. • Semimonthly. $210.00 per year. Provides descriptions of government-sponsored research reports and software, with ordering information. Covers biotechnology, ergonomics, bionics, artificial intelligence, prosthetics, and related subjects. Formerly *Abstract Newsletter.*

CD-ROM DATABASES

Biotechnology Abstracts on CD-ROM. Thomson Derwent, Inc. • Quarterly. Price on application. Provides CD-ROM indexing and abstracting of the world's biotechnology journal literature since 1982, including genetic engineering topics.

DIRECTORIES

BioScan: The Worldwide Biotech Industry Reporting Service. Greenwood Publishing Group, Inc. • Annual. $975.00 per year. Bimonthly updates. Provides detailed information on over 1,000 U.S. and foreign companies broadly classified as biotechnological. In addition to medical technology and advanced pharmaceutical firms, includes firms doing research in food processing, waste management, agriculture, and veterinary science.

Genetic Engineering and Biotechnology Firms Worldwide Directory. Mega-Type Publishing. • Annual. $299.00. About 6,000 firms, including major firms with biotechnology divisions as well as small independent firms.

Plunkett's Biotech and Genetics Industry Almanac. Plunkett Research, Ltd. • Annual. $249.99. Provides detailed profiles of 400 leading biotech corporations. Includes information on current trends and research in the field of biotechnology/genetics.

ENCYCLOPEDIAS AND DICTIONARIES

Encyclopedia of Emerging Industries. Gale Cengage Learning. • 2001. $320.00. Fourth edition. Provides

detailed information on 115 "newly flourishing" industries. Includes historical background, organizational structure, significant individuals, current conditions, major companies, work force, technology trends, research developments, and other industry facts.

Wiley Encyclopedia of Food Science and Technology. Frederick J. Francis, editor. John Wiley and Sons, Inc. • 2000. $1,650.00. Second edition. Four volumes. Contains about 400 entries. Coverage includes biotechnology, genetic engineering, nutrition, regulatory matters, food safety, labeling, food substitutes (sugar, fat, dairy), and many other topics.

ONLINE DATABASES

Applied Science and Technology Index Online. H. W. Wilson Co. • Provides online indexing of 500 major scientific, technical, industrial, and engineering periodicals. Time period is 1983 to date. Monthly updates. Inquire as to online cost and availability.

CSA Life Sciences Collection. Cambridge Scientific Abstracts. • Includes online versions of *Biotechnology Research Abstracts, Entomology Abstracts, Genetics Abstracts,* and about 20 other abstract collections. Time period is 1978 to date, with monthly updates. Inquire as to online cost and availability.

Derwent Biotechnology Abstracts. Derwent, Inc. • Provides indexing and abstracting of the world's biotechnology journal literature since 1982, including genetic engineering topics. Monthly updates. Inquire as to online cost and availability.

PROMT: Predicasts Overview of Markets and Technology. Gale Cengage Learning. • Companies, products, applied technologies and markets. U.S. and international literature coverage, 1972 to date. Inquire as to online cost and availability. Provides abstracts from more than 1,600 publications. Weekly updates.

PERIODICALS AND NEWSLETTERS

Applied Genetics News. BCC Research. • Description: Concerned primarily with the application of genetic research to industry and technology. Evaluates ongoing research in the areas of aging, cancer, disease, and cell differentiation. Discusses research funding and finances. Analyzes new developments in venture capital and stock price movement.

BioWorld Today: The Daily Biotechnology Newspaper. American Health Consultants, Inc., BioWorld Publishing Group. • Daily. $1,897.00 per year; with online edition, $1,927.00 per year. Covers news of the biotechnology and genetic engineering industries, with emphasis on finance, investments, and marketing.

BioWorld Week: The Weekly Biotechnology Report. American Health Consultants, Inc., BioWorld Publishing Group. • Weekly. $789.00 per year. Newsletter. Provides a weekly summary of business and financial news relating to the biotechnology and genetic engineering industries.

Genetic Engineering News: The Information Source of the Biotechnology Industry. Mary Ann Liebert, Inc. • 21 times a year. Institutions, $666.00 per year. Newsletter. Business and financial coverage.

Genetic Technology News. Technical Insights/John Wiley & Sons Inc. • Description: Informs corporate development and research managers of advances in genetic engineering with applications in medical, agricultural, chemical, food, and other businesses. Covers areas such as recombinant DNA, monoclonal antibodies, and interferon. Recurring features include news of research, company reports, a calendar of events, and supplements titled Market Forecasts, Patent Update, and Strategic Partners. **Remarks:** Also available as part of Biotechnology Information Package, which includes Industrial Bioprocessing (see separate listings).

Health Policy and Biomedical Research: The Blue Sheet. F-D-C Reports, Inc. • 51 times a year. $716.00 per year. Newsletter. Emphasis is on news of medical research agencies and institutions, especially the National Institutes of Health (NIH).

Washington Drug Letter. Washington Business Information Inc. • Description: Focuses on regulation and legislation affecting prescription and proprietary drugs. Monitors Food & Drug Administration (FDA) actions and new drug applications, manufacturing procedures, advertising and labeling, compliance cases, research, and testing rules.

RESEARCH CENTERS AND INSTITUTES

Carnegie Mellon Research Institute-Computer Automation and Robotics. Carnegie Mellon University, 700 Technology Dr., Pittsburgh, PA 15219. Phone: (412)268-3363 Fax: (412)368-7759 • URL: http://www.cmu.edu/cmri • Multidisciplinary research activities include expert systems applications, minicomputer and microcomputer systems design, genetic engineering, and transportation systems analysis.

Department of Molecular and Human Genetics. Baylor College of Medicine, One Baylor Plaza, Rm. T619, Houston, TX 77030. Phone: (713)798-6522 Fax: (713)798-7773 E-mail: abeaudet@bcm.tmc. edu • URL: http://www.imgen.bcm.tmc.edu.

Environmental Research Institute. University of Idaho, Food Research Center 103, Moscow, ID 83844-1052. Phone: (208)885-6580 Fax: (208)885-5741 E-mail: crawford@uidaho.edu • URL: http://www.image.fs.uidaho.edu • Formerly Environmental Biotechnology Institute.

TRADE/PROFESSIONAL ASSOCIATIONS

American Genetic Association. 2030 SE Marine Science Dr., Newport, OR 97365. Phone: (541)867-0334 Fax: (301)695-9292 E-mail: agajoh@oregonstate.edu • URL: http://www.theaga.org • Represents biologists, zoologists, geneticists, botanists, and others engaged in basic and applied research in genetics. Explores transmission genetics of plants and animals.

Council for Responsible Genetics. Five Upland Rd., Suite 3, Cambridge, MA 02140. Phone: (617)868-0870 Fax: (617)491-5344 E-mail: crg@gene-watch.org • URL: http://www.gene-watch.org • Concerned with the social implications of genetic engineering. Affiliated with Biotechnology Industry Organization. Formerly Committee for Responsible Genetics.

Genetics Society of America. 9650 Rockville Pike, Bethesda, MD 20814-3998. Phone: (866)486-4363 or (301)634-7300 Fax: (301)634-7079 E-mail: estrass@genetics-gsa.org • URL: http://www.genetics-gsa.org • Members are individuals and organizations with an interest in genetics.

OTHER SOURCES

New and Breaking Technologies in the Pharmaceutical and Medical Device Industries. Theta Reports. • 1999. $1,695.00. Contains market research predictions of medical technology trends over the next 5 to 10 years (2004-2009), including developments in biotechnology, genetic engineering, medical device technology, therapeutic vaccines, non-invasive diagnostics, and minimally-invasive surgery. (Theta Report No. 931.).

GEOTHERMAL ENERGY

GENERAL WORKS

Renewables for Power Generation: Status and Prospect. Organization for Economic Cooperation and Development. • 2003. $75.00. Presents the global outlook for electrical power generation from renewable sources, including water power, wind power, solar power, and geothermal power.

ABSTRACTS AND INDEXES

Applied Science and Technology Index. H. W. Wilson Co. • 11 times a year. Quarterly and annual cumulations. Price varies. Indexes a wide variety of English language technical, industrial, and engineering periodicals.

Engineering Index Monthly: Abstracting and Indexing Services Covering Sources of the World's Engineering Literature. Engineering Information Inc. • Monthly. Institutions, $5,279.00 per year. Provides indexing and abstracting of the world's engineering and technical literature.

Environment Abstracts. Congressional Information Service, Inc. • Monthly. Price varies. Provides multidisciplinary coverage of the world's environmental literature. Incorporates *Acid Rain Abstracts.*

Environment Abstracts Annual: A Guide to the Key Environmental Literature of the Year. Congressional Information Service, Inc. • Annual. $495.00. A yearly cumulation of *Environment Abstracts.*

NTIS Alerts: Energy. National Technical Information Service. • Semimonthly. $245.00 per year. Provides descriptions of government-sponsored research reports and software, with ordering information. Covers electric power, batteries, fuels, geothermal energy, heating/cooling systems, nuclear technology, solar energy, energy policy, and related subjects. Formerly *Abstract Newsletter.*

ALMANACS AND YEARBOOKS

Earth Almanac: An Annual Geophysical Review of the State of the Planet. Natalie Goldstein. Greenwood Publishing Group, Inc. • Annual. $69.95. Provides background information, statistics, and a summary of major events relating to the atmosphere, oceans, land, and fresh water.

CD-ROM DATABASES

Environment Abstracts on CD-ROM. LEXIS-NEXIS. • Quarterly. $1,295.00 per year. Contains the following CD-ROM databases: *Environment Abstracts, Energy Abstracts,* and *Acid Rain Abstracts.* Length of coverage varies.

WILSONDISC: Applied Science and Technology Abstracts. H. W. Wilson Co. • Monthly. Includes unlimited access to the online version of *Applied Science and Technology Abstracts* through WILSONLINE. Provides CD-ROM indexing and abstracting of 500 prominent scientific, technical, engineering, and industrial periodicals. Indexing coverage is provided from 1983 to date and abstracting from 1993 to date.

DIRECTORIES

The International Competitive Power Industry Directory. PennWell Corp. • Publication includes: List of 1,400 companies active in the global power industry, providing information on developers, financial firms, law firms, engineering and construction firms, fuel suppliers, consultants, manufacturers and other suppliers of products, equipment at the hydro, geothermal, solar and wind industries. Entries include: Company name, address, phone, fax; contact name; business area or tyope; technology used; region covered; products.

ENCYCLOPEDIAS AND DICTIONARIES

Encyclopedia of Energy. Cutler J. Cleveland, editor. Elsevier, Inc. • 2004. $1,560.00. Six volumes. Covers all aspects of energy sources and energy-related environmental issues.

Macmillan Encyclopedia of Energy. Available from Gale Cengage Learning. • 2001. $395.00. Three volumes. Published by Macmillan Reference USA. Covers the business, technology, and history of a wide variety of energy sources.

Wiley Encyclopedia of Energy and the Environment. Attilio Bisio and Sharon Boots. John Wiley and Sons, Inc. • 1996. $285.00. Abriged edition. Two volumes. Covers a wide variety of energy and environmental topics, including legal and policy issues. (Encyclopedia of Energy and the Environment Series: Vol. 2).

ONLINE DATABASES

Applied Science and Technology Index Online. H. W. Wilson Co. • Provides online indexing of 500 major scientific, technical, industrial, and engineering periodicals. Time period is 1983 to date. Monthly updates. Inquire as to online cost and availability.

Current Contents Connect. Institute for Scientific Information. • Provides online abstracts of articles listed in the tables of contents of about 7,500 journals. Coverage is very broad, including science, social science, life science, technology, engineering, industry, agriculture, the environment, economics, and arts and humanities. Time period is two years, with weekly updates. Inquire as to online cost and availability.

PROMT: Predicasts Overview of Markets and Technology. Gale Cengage Learning. • Companies, products, applied technologies and markets. U.S. and international literature coverage, 1972 to date. Inquire as to online cost and availability. Provides abstracts from more than 1,600 publications. Weekly updates.

PERIODICALS AND NEWSLETTERS

Energy Conversion and Management. Elsevier. • 20 times a year. Institutions, $3,457.00 per year. Presents a scholarly approach to alternative or renewable energy sources. Text in English, French and German.

Geothermics: International Journal of Geothermal Research and Its Applications. Elsevier. • Bimonthly. Institutions, $1,124.00 per year. Covers theory, exploration, development, and utilization of geothermal energy. Text and summaries in English and French.

Independent Energy: The Power Industry's Business Magazine. PennWell Corp., Industrial Div. • 10 times a year. $127.00 per year. Covers non-utility electric power plants (cogeneration) and other alternative sources of electric energy.

RESEARCH CENTERS AND INSTITUTES

Geothermal Laboratory. Southern Methodist University, 217 Heroy Bldg., 3225 Daniels Ave., Dallas, TX 75206-0395. Phone: (214)768-2749 Fax: (214)768-2701 E-mail: blackwel@passion.isem.smu.edu • URL: http://www.smu.edu/geothermal.

Hawaii Natural Energy Institute. University of Hawaii at Manoa, 2540 Dole St., Holmes Hall 246, Honolulu, HI 96822. Phone: (808)956-8890 Fax: (808)956-2336 E-mail: hnei@hawaii.edu • URL: http://www.soest.hawaii.edu • Research areas include geothermal, wind, solar, hydroelectric, and other energy sources.

STATISTICS SOURCES

Annual Energy Outlook [year], with Projections to [year]. Available from U. S. Government Printing Office. • Annual. $42.00. Issued by the Energy Information Administration, U. S. Department of Energy (http://www.eia.doe.gov). Contains detailed statistics and 20-year projections for electricity, oil, natural gas, coal, and renewable energy. Text provides extensive discussion of energy issues and "Market Trends.".

International Energy Annual. Available from U. S. Government Printing Office. • Annual. $34.00. Issued by the Energy Information Administration, U. S. Department of Energy. Provides production, consumption, import, and export data for primary energy commodities in more than 200 countries and areas. In addition to petroleum products and alcohol, renewable energy sources are covered (hydroelectric, geothermal, solar, and wind).

TRADE/PROFESSIONAL ASSOCIATIONS

Geothermal Resources Council. PO Box 1350, Davis, CA 95617. Phone: (530)758-2360 Fax: (530)758-2839 E-mail: grc@geothermal.org • URL: http://www.geothermal.org • Encourages research, exploration, and development of geothermal energy; promotes establishment of criteria for the development of geothermal resources compatible with the natural environment. Provides information for the public and encourages the collection and dissemination of geothermal information and data. Cooperates and communicates with national and international governmental, institutional, and private agencies. Holds technical training workshops and annual meeting. Maintains largest geothermal technical library in existence.

OTHER SOURCES

Major Energy Companies of the World. Available from Gale Cengage Learning. • Annual. $880.00. Published by Graham & Whiteside. Contains detailed information on more than 3,300 important energy companies in various countries. Industries include electricity generation, coal, natural gas, nuclear energy, petroleum, fuel distribution, and equipment for energy production.

GIFT BUSINESS

DIRECTORIES

Directory of Discount and General Merchandise Stores. Chain Store Guide. • Annual. $327.00. On-line edition, $747.00. Includes retailers and wholesalers of housewares, giftwares, novelties, toys, hobby materials, crafts, and stationery.

Gift, Housewares and Home Textiles Buyers Directory. Douglas Publications, Inc. • Annual. $259.00. Lists more than 7,300 companies with names of over 15,200 buyers.

FINANCIAL RATIOS

Annual Statement Studies. The Risk Management Association. • Annual. Median and quartile financial ratios are given for over 400 kinds of manufacturing, wholesale, retail, construction, and consumer finance establishments. Data is sorted by both asset size and sales volume. Includes a clearly written "Definition of Ratios" and an alphabetical industry index.

Annual Statement Studies: Industry Default Probabilities and Cash Flow Measures. The Risk Management Association. • Annual. $145.00. Serves as a companion volume to the original *Annual Statement Studies.* Gives probability of default estimates on a percentage scale for more than 450 industries. Includes changes in position year-by-year for eight financial statement line items and provides percentage measures of cash flow.

HANDBOOKS AND MANUALS

Gift/Specialty Store. Entrepreneur Media, Inc. • Looseleaf. $59.50. A practical guide to starting a gift shop. Covers profit potential, start-up costs, market size evaluation, owner's time required, site selection, lease negotiation, pricing, accounting, advertising, promotion, etc. (Start-Up Business Guide No. E1218.).

PERIODICALS AND NEWSLETTERS

Fancy Food and Culinary Products. Talcott Communications Corp. • Monthly. $34.00 per year. Emphasizes new specialty food products and the business management aspects of the specialty food and confection industries. Includes special issues on wine, cheese, candy, "upscale" cookware, and gifts. Formerly (Fancy Foods).

Gifts and Decorative Accessories: The International Business Magazine of Gifts, Tabletop, Gourmet, Home Accessories, Greeting Card and Social Stationery. Reed Business Information. • Monthly. $53.95 per year. Includes *Annual Directory.*

Gifts and Tablewares. Business Information Group. • Seven times a year. $47.95 per year. Includes annual *Trade Directory.*

Giftware News: The International Magazine for Gifts, China and Glass, Stationery and Home Accessories. Talcott Communications Corp. • Monthly. $36.00 per year. Includes annual *Directory.*

Gourmet News: The Business Newspaper for the Gourmet Industry. United Publications, Inc. • Monthly. $60.00 per year. Provides news of the gourmet food industry, including specialty food stores, upscale cookware shops, and gift shops.

TRADE/PROFESSIONAL ASSOCIATIONS

Gift Association of America. 172 White Pine Way, Harleysville, PA 19426-2851. Phone: (610)584-3108 Fax: (610)584-7860 E-mail: info@giftassn.com • URL: http://www.giftassn.com • Formerly Gift and Decorative Accessories Association of America.

Souvenir and Gift Novelty Trade Association. 7000 Terminal Sq., Ste. 210, Upper Darby, PA 19082. Phone: (610)734-2420 Fax: (610)734-2423 E-mail: souvnovmag@aol.com • Formerly Souvenir and Novelty Trade Association.

OTHER SOURCES

Gifts and Decorative Accessories Market. Available from MarketResearch.com. • 2001. $2,250.00. Published by Unity Marketing. Market research report covering growth trends and projections.

GIFT TAX

GENERAL WORKS

How to Make Tax-Saving Gifts. William S. Moore. American Institute for Economic Research. • 1999. $3.00. Provides practical advice on the tax consequences of gifts, including gifts for college tuition expenses, gifts of real estate, charitable gifts, and the use of life insurance trusts. (Economic Education Bulletin.).

HANDBOOKS AND MANUALS

Corporate, Partnership, Estate, and Gift Taxation 1997. James W. Pratt and William Kulsrud, editors. McGraw-Hill. • 1996. $71.25. 10th edition.

Federal Estate and Gift Taxation. RIA. • Three times a year. $425.0 per year. Clarification and guidance on estate tax laws.

Federal Estate and Gift Taxes: Code and Regulations, Including Related Income Tax Provisions. CCH, Inc. • 2000. $47.00. Revised edition. Provides full text of estate, gift, and generation-skipping tax provisions of the Internal Revenue Code.

Federal Tax Course. Aspen Publishers, Inc. • Annual. $210.00. Provides basic reference and training for various forms of federal taxation: individual, business, corporate, partnership, estate, gift, etc.

Internal Revenue Code. RIA. • Annual. $86.50. Provides full text of the Internal Revenue Code (5,000 pages), including procedural and administrative provisions.

U. S. Master Estate and Gift Tax Guide. CCH, Inc. • Annual. $55.00. Covers federal estate and gift taxes, including generation-skipping transfer tax plans. Includes tax tables and sample filled-in tax return forms.

INTERNET DATABASES

ACGA: Partners in Philanthropy. American Council on Gift Annuities. Phone: (317)269-6271 Fax: (317)269-6276 E-mail: acga@acga-web.org • URL: http://www.acga-web.org • Web site provides detailed information on gift annuities, including suggested charitable gift annuity rates for use by charities and their donors. Rates for immediate and deferred annuities are presented in the form of tables for ages 20 to 90 (and over), for both "Single Life" and "Two Lives - Joint and Survivor." Other items covered include the philosophy of gift annuities, state regulations, "What's New," and a search site. Fees: Free.

Internal Revenue Service IRS.gov. Internal Revenue Service. Phone: 800-829-1040 or (202)622-5000 Fax: (202)622-5844 • URL: http://www.irs.gov • Web site provides a wide variety of tax information, including IRS forms and publications. Searching is available. Fees: Free.

Tax Analysts [Web site]. Tax Analysts. Phone: 800-955-3444 or (703)533-4400 Fax: (703)533-4444 • URL: http://www.tax.org • The three main sections of Tax Analysts home page are "Tax News" (Today's Tax News, Feature of the Week, Tax Snapshots, Tax Calendar); "Products & Services" (Product Catalog, Press Releases); and "Public Interest" (Discussion Groups, Tax Clinic, Tax History Project). Fees: Free for coverage of current tax events; fee-based for comprehensive information. Daily updating.

PERIODICALS AND NEWSLETTERS

Highlights and Documents. Tax Analysts. • Daily. $2,249.00 per year, including monthly indexes. Newsletter. Provides daily coverage of IRS, congressional, judicial, state, and international tax developments. Includes abstracts and citations for "all tax documents released within the previous 24 to 48 hours." Annual compilation available *Highlights and Documents on Microfiche.*

The Journal of Taxation: A National Journal of Current Developments, Analysis and Commentary for Tax Professionals. RIA. • Monthly. $305.00 per year. Analysis of current tax developments for tax specialists.

Tax Notes: The Weekly Tax Service. Tax Analysts. • Weekly. $1,699.00 per year. Includes an *Annual* and 1985-1996 compliations on CD-ROM. Newsletter. Covers "tax news from all federal sources," including congressional committees, tax courts, and the Internal Revenue Service. Each issue contains "summaries of every document that pertains to federal tax law," with citations. Commentary is provided.

Tax Practice. Tax Analysts. • Weekly. $199.00 per year. Newsletter. Covers news affecting tax practitioners and litigators, with emphasis on federal court decisions, rules and regulations, and tax petitions. Provides a guide to Internal Revenue Service audit issues.

RESEARCH CENTERS AND INSTITUTES

Office of Tax Policy Research. University of Michigan, 701 Tappan St., Ann Arbor, MI 48109-1234. Phone: (734)763-3068 Fax: (734)763-4032 E-mail: otpr@umich.edu • URL: http://www.taxpolicyresearch.umich.edu/.

Tax Foundation. Tax Foundation. 2001 L St. NW, Ste. 1050, Washington, DC 20036. Phone: (202)464-6200 Fax: (202)464-6201 E-mail: hodge@taxfoundation.org • URL: http://www.taxfoundation.org • Fiscal and management aspects of federal, state, and local government, including studies on government expenditures, the federal budget, taxation, and international competitiveness. Serves as a national information agency for individuals and organizations concerned with problems of government expenditures, taxation, and debt.

TRADE/PROFESSIONAL ASSOCIATIONS

National Tax Association-Tax Institute of America. 725 15th St., N.W., No. 600, Washington, DC 20005-2109. Phone: (202)737-3325 Fax: (202)737-

7308 E-mail: natltax@aol.com • URL: http://www. ntanet.org.

OTHER SOURCES

Fiduciary Tax Guide. CCH, Inc. • Monthly. $478.00 per year. Looseleaf service. Covers federal income taxation of estates, trusts, and beneficiaries. Provides information on gift and generation- skipping taxation.

GIRLS' CLOTHING

See: CHILDREN'S APPAREL INDUSTRY

GLASS CONTAINER INDUSTRY

See also: CONTAINER INDUSTRY; GLASS INDUSTRY; GLASSWARE INDUSTRY

CD-ROM DATABASES

OECD Statistical Compendium. Organization for Economic Cooperation and Development. • Semiannual. $1,905.00 per year for 1 to 10 users. CD-ROM contains more than 730,000 monthly, quarterly, and annual time series for OECD countries, 1960 to date. Includes fully searchable data on agriculture, food, economic indicators, national accounts, employment, energy, finance, industry, technology, and foreign trade. Results can be displayed in various forms.

ENCYCLOPEDIAS AND DICTIONARIES

Wiley Encyclopedia of Packaging Technology. Aaron Brody and Kenneth Marsh, editors. John Wiley and Sons, Inc. • 1997. $330.00. Second edition.

INTERNET DATABASES

Business 2.0 Web Guide to the Best Business Links. Business 2.0 Media Inc. Phone: (415)293-4800 E-mail: support@business2.com • URL: http://www.business2.com/webguide • Web site presents an extensive, searchable directory of links to "the best, most informative, and authoritative web pages." Twenty main categories cover business, finance, career, company information, people, and technology topics, with thousands of subtopics, all linking to Web sites recommended by experienced business researchers. Fees: Free.

Fedstats. Federal Interagency Council on Statistical Policy. Phone: (202)395-7254 • URL: http://www.fedstats.gov • Web site features an efficient search facility for full-text statistics produced by more than 100 federal agencies, including the Census Bureau, the Bureau of Economic Analysis, and the Bureau of Labor Statistics. Boolean searches can be made within one agency or for all agencies combined. Links are offered to international statistical bureaus, including the UN, IMF, OECD, UNESCO, Eurostat, and 20 individual countries. Fees: Free.

FreeLunch.com. Economy.com, Inc. Phone: (610)696-8700 Fax: (610)696-1678 • URL: http://www.freelunch.com • Web site provides free access to more than 1.5 million economic and financial data series, covering industry, demographics, labor markets, prices, retail sales, government spending, trade, interest rates, housing starts, the stock market, and many other topics. Data is available for various time periods in either chart or table form. Searching is offered. Fees: Free, but registration required. Economy.com, Inc. also offers fee-based economic analysis at *The Dismal Scientist* site (http://www.dismal.com).

STATISTICS SOURCES

Business Statistics of the United States. Linz Audain and Cornelia J. Strawser. Bernan Associates. • Annual. $147.00. Based on *Business Statistics,* formerly issue by the Bureau of Economic Analysis, U. S. Department of Commerce. Provides basic data for a wide variety of U. S. industries, services, and economic indicators. Most statistics are shown annually for 30 years and monthly for the most recent four years.

Survey of Current Business. Available from U. S. Government Printing Office. • Monthly. $63.00 per year. Issued by Bureau of Economic Analysis, U. S. Department of Commerce. Presents a wide variety of business and economic data.

TRADE/PROFESSIONAL ASSOCIATIONS

American Scientific Glassblowers Society. PO Box 778, Madison, NC 27025. Phone: (336)427-2406 Fax: (336)427-2496 E-mail: natl-office@asgs-glass.org • URL: http://www.asgs-glass.org • Glassblowers with more than 5 years' experience in making scientific glass apparatus (condensers, distillation apparatus, glass-to-metal seals, and vacuum devices); junior members are glassblowers with less than 5 years' professional experience; associates are persons connected with the manufacture or use of glass or glassblowing equipment in scientific work. Seeks to gather and disseminate information concerning scientific glassblowing, apparatus, equipment, and materials.

Glass Molders, Pottery, Plastics, and Allied Workers International Union. 608 E. Baltimore Pike, Media, PA 19063. Phone: (610)565-5051 Fax: (610)565-0983 E-mail: gmpiu@ix.netcom.com • URL: http://www.gmpiu.org.

Glass Packaging Institute. 700 N Fairfax St., Ste. 510, Alexandria, VA 22314. Phone: (703)684-6359 Fax: (703)299-1543 E-mail: info@gpi.org • URL: http://www.gpi.org • Glass container manufacturers and suppliers. Promotes the manufacture, use, and recycling of glass containers and closures. Develops and evaluates testing procedures and equipment; conducts experimental activities in glass packaging; develops designs and specifications for glass containers and finishes; conducts advertising and promotional campaigns for the generic products; develops and maintains constructive relationships with various public and government agencies at the local, regional, state, and national levels.

National Association of Container Distributors. 1900 Arch St., Philadelphia, PA 19103-1498. Phone: (215)564-3484 Fax: (215)564-2175 E-mail: nacd@fernley.com • URL: http://www.nacd.net.

GLASS INDUSTRY

See also: GLASS CONTAINER INDUSTRY; GLASSWARE INDUSTRY; TABLEWARE

GENERAL WORKS

Glass Science. Robert H. Doremus. John Wiley and Sons, Inc. • 1994. $120.00. Second edition.

Introduction to Glass Science and Technology. Springer-Verlag. • 1997. $49.95. Covers the basics of glass manufacture, including the physical, optical, electrical, chemical, and mechanical properties of glass. (RCS Paperback Series).

ABSTRACTS AND INDEXES

NTIS Alerts: Materials Sciences. National Technical Information Service. • Semimonthly. $220.00 per year. Provides descriptions of government-sponsored research reports and software, with ordering information. Covers ceramics, glass, coatings, composite materials, alloys, plastics, wood, paper, adhesives, fibers, lubricants, and related subjects. Formerly *Abstract Newsletter.*

CD-ROM DATABASES

OECD Statistical Compendium. Organization for Economic Cooperation and Development. • Semiannual. $1,905.00 per year for 1 to 10 users. CD-ROM contains more than 730,000 monthly, quarterly, and annual time series for OECD countries, 1960 to date. Includes fully searchable data on agriculture, food, economic indicators, national accounts, employment, energy, finance, industry, technology, and foreign trade. Results can be displayed in various forms.

DIRECTORIES

Glass Digest--Buyers' Guide. Ashlee Publishing Company Inc. • Covers: manufacturers, importers, and other suppliers who furnish the products and services used by fabricators, distributors, retailers, and installers of flat glass, architectural metal, and related products. Entries include: Supplier name, address, phone, and, when furnished, cable address, TWX, fax, and telex.

Glass Factory Directory of North America. • Annual. $30.00. Lists over 600 glass factory locations in the U.S., Canada and Mexico.

U. S. Glass, Metal, and Glazing: Buyers Guide. Key Communications, Inc. • Annual. $25.00. A directory of about 3,000 supplies and equipment for the glass fabrication and installation industry.

FINANCIAL RATIOS

Almanac of Business and Industrial Financial Ratios. Leo Troy. Aspen Publishers, Inc. • 2003. $125.95. Includes CD-Rom. Contains financial ratios derived from federal tax returns. Ratios for each of about 200 industries are arranged according to company asset size. (Almanac of Business and Industrial Financial Ratios Series).

Annual Statement Studies. The Risk Management Association. • Annual. Median and quartile financial ratios are given for over 400 kinds of manufacturing, wholesale, retail, construction, and consumer finance establishments. Data is sorted by both asset size and sales volume. Includes a clearly written "Definition of Ratios" and an alphabetical industry index.

Annual Statement Studies: Industry Default Probabilities and Cash Flow Measures. The Risk Management Association. • Annual. $145.00. Serves as a companion volume to the original *Annual Statement Studies.* Gives probability of default estimates on a percentage scale for more than 450 industries. Includes changes in position year-by-year for eight financial statement line items and provides percentage measures of cash flow.

HANDBOOKS AND MANUALS

ASM Engineered Materials Reference Book. Michael L. Bauccio, editor. ASM International. • 1994. $155.00. Third edition. Provides information on a wide range of materials, with special sections on ceramics, industrial glass products, and plastics.

The Handbook of Glass Manufacture. Fay V. Tooley, editor. Ashlee Publishing Co., Inc. • 1985. 195.00. Revised edition. Two volumes.

INTERNET DATABASES

Business 2.0 Web Guide to the Best Business Links. Business 2.0 Media Inc. Phone: (415)293-4800 E-mail: support@business2.com • URL: http://www.business2.com/webguide • Web site presents an extensive, searchable directory of links to "the best, most informative, and authoritative web pages." Twenty main categories cover business, finance, career, company information, people, and technology topics, with thousands of subtopics, all linking to Web sites recommended by experienced business researchers. Fees: Free.

Fedstats. Federal Interagency Council on Statistical Policy. Phone: (202)395-7254 • URL: http://www.fedstats.gov • Web site features an efficient search facility for full-text statistics produced by more than 100 federal agencies, including the Census Bureau, the Bureau of Economic Analysis, and the Bureau of Labor Statistics. Boolean searches can be made within one agency or for all agencies combined.

Links are offered to international statistical bureaus, including the UN, IMF, OECD, UNESCO, Eurostat, and 20 individual countries. Fees: Free.

FreeLunch.com. Economy.com, Inc. Phone: (610)696-8700 Fax: (610)696-1678 • URL: http://www.freelunch.com • Web site provides free access to more than 1.5 million economic and financial data series, covering industry, demographics, labor markets, prices, retail sales, government spending, trade, interest rates, housing starts, the stock market, and many other topics. Data is available for various time periods in either chart or table form. Searching is offered. Fees: Free, but registration required. Economy.com, Inc. also offers fee-based economic analysis at *The Dismal Scientist* site (http://www.dismal.com).

Manufacturing Profiles. U. S. Bureau of the Census. Phone: (301)763-4636 E-mail: webmaster@census.gov • URL: http://www.census.gov/prod/www/abs/mfg-prof.html • The Census Bureau makes available free on PDF (Portable Document Format) an annual consolidation of the entire Current Industrial Report series, presenting "all the data compiled." Contains statistics on production, shipments, inventories, consumption, exports, imports, and orders for a wide variety of manufactured products.

PERIODICALS AND NEWSLETTERS

Glass Digest: Trade Magazine Serving the Flat Glass, Architectural Metal an d Allied Products Industry. Ashlee Publishing Co., Inc. • Monthly. $40.00 per year.

Glass Magazine. National Glass Association. • Monthly. $34.95 per year.

U. S. Glass, Metal, and Glazing. Key Communications, Inc. • Monthly. $35.00 per year. Edited for glass fabricators, glaziers, distributors, and retailers. Special feature issues are devoted to architectural glass, mirror glass, windows, storefronts, hardware, machinery, sealants, and adhesives. Regular topics include automobile glass and fenestration (window design and placement).

RESEARCH CENTERS AND INSTITUTES

Physics Research Center and Vitreous State Laboratory. Catholic University of America. 620 Michigan Ave., N.E., 200 Hannan Hall, Washington, DC 20064. Phone: (202)319-5315 Fax: (202)319-4448 E-mail: adm_phys@cua.edu • URL: http://www.arts-sciences.cua.edu/phys.

STATISTICS SOURCES

Annual Survey of Manufactures. Available from U. S. Government Printing Office. • Annual. Prices vary. Issued by the U. S. Census Bureau as an interim update to the *Census of Manufactures.* Includes data on number of manufacturing establishments in various industries, employment, labor costs, value of shipments, capital expenditures, inventories, energy costs, and assets. (See also Census Bureau home page, http://www.census.gov/.).

Business Statistics of the United States. Linz Audain and Cornelia J. Strawser. Bernan Associates. • Annual. $147.00. Based on *Business Statistics,* formerly issue by the Bureau of Economic Analysis, U. S. Department of Commerce. Provides basic data for a wide variety of U. S. industries, services, and economic indicators. Most statistics are shown annually for 30 years and monthly for the most recent four years.

Survey of Current Business. Available from U. S. Government Printing Office. • Monthly. $63.00 per year. Issued by Bureau of Economic Analysis, U. S. Department of Commerce. Presents a wide variety of business and economic data.

TRADE/PROFESSIONAL ASSOCIATIONS

Glass Association of North America. 2945 S.W. Wanamaker Dr., Suite A, Topeka, KS 66614. Phone: (785)271-0208 Fax: (785)271-0166 E-mail: gana@glasswebsite.com • URL: http://www.glasswebsite.com • Flat Glass Jobbers Association.

National Glass Association. 8200 Greensboro Dr., Ste. 302, McLean, VA 22102-3881. Phone: (866)DIAL-NGA or (703)442-4890 Fax: (703)442-0630 E-mail: pjames@glass.org • URL: http://www.glass.org • Manufacturers, installers, retailers, distributors, and fabricators of flat, architectural, automotive, and specialty glass and metal products, mirrors, shower and patio doors, windows, and tabletops. Provides informational, educational and technical services.

Sealed Insulating Glass Manufacturers Association. 401 N. Michigan Ave., Chicago, IL 60611-4267. Phone: (312)644-6610 Fax: (312)527-6783 E-mail: sigma@sba.com • URL: http://www.sigmaonline.org • Manufacturers of insulating glass; suppliers to the industry.

United Steelworkers of America. Aluminum, Brick and Glassworkers Division. c/o Unitrd Steelworkers of America, Five Gateway Center, Pittsburgh, PA 15222. Phone: (412)562-2400 E-mail: webmaster@uswa.org • URL: http://www.uswa.org.

US Workders Flint Glass Conference. c/o United Steelworkers of America, Five Gateway Ctr., Pittsburgh, PA 15222. Phone: (412)562-2400 E-mail: webmaster@uswa.org • URL: http://www.uswa.org.

OTHER SOURCES

Glass and Glass Products. Available from MarketResearch.com. • 2002. $3,850.00. Published by Global Industry Analysts. Provides worldwide market research data, including profiles of major glass and glass products companies.

GLASSWARE INDUSTRY

See also: GLASS CONTAINER INDUSTRY; GLASS INDUSTRY; TABLEWARE

INTERNET DATABASES

Manufacturing Profiles. U. S. Bureau of the Census. Phone: (301)763-4636 E-mail: webmaster@census.gov • URL: http://www.census.gov/prod/www/abs/mfg-prof.html • The Census Bureau makes available free on PDF (Portable Document Format) an annual consolidation of the entire Current Industrial Report series, presenting "all the data compiled." Contains statistics on production, shipments, inventories, consumption, exports, imports, and orders for a wide variety of manufactured products.

STATISTICS SOURCES

Annual Survey of Manufactures. Available from U. S. Government Printing Office. • Annual. Prices vary. Issued by the U. S. Census Bureau as an interim update to the *Census of Manufactures.* Includes data on number of manufacturing establishments in various industries, employment, labor costs, value of shipments, capital expenditures, inventories, energy costs, and assets. (See also Census Bureau home page, http://www.census.gov/.).

TRADE/PROFESSIONAL ASSOCIATIONS

Associated Glass and Pottery Manufacturers. 912 Country Club Dr., Greensburg, PA 15601. Phone: (724)837-9451 Fax: (724)523-2022 E-mail: robrupp@helicon.net.

Glass Association of North America. 2945 S.W. Wanamaker Dr., Suite A, Topeka, KS 66614. Phone: (785)271-0208 Fax: (785)271-0166 E-mail: gana@glasswebsite.com • URL: http://www.glasswebsite.com • Flat Glass Jobbers Association.

National Glass Association. 8200 Greensboro Dr., Ste. 302, McLean, VA 22102-3881. Phone: (866)DIAL-NGA or (703)442-4890 Fax: (703)442-0630 E-mail: pjames@glass.org • URL: http://www.glass.org • Manufacturers, installers, retailers, distributors, and fabricators of flat, architectural, automotive, and specialty glass and metal products, mirrors, shower and patio doors, windows, and tabletops. Provides informational, educational and technical services.

Stained Glass Association of America. 10009 E 62nd St., Raytown, MO 64133. Phone: 800-888-7422 or (816)737-2090 Fax: (816)737-2801 E-mail: sgaa@stainedglass.org • URL: http://www.stainedglass.org • Formerly National Ornamental Glass Manufacturers Association.

OTHER SOURCES

The Tabletop Market. Available from MarketResearch.com. • 2000. $2,750.00. Published by Packaged Facts. Provides market data on dinnerware, glassware, and flatware, with projections to 2002.

GLOVE INDUSTRY

See also: CHILDREN'S APPAREL INDUSTRY; MEN'S CLOTHING INDUSTRY; WOMEN'S APPAREL

GENERAL WORKS

Fashion Accessories: The Complete Twentieth Century Sourcebook. John Peacock. Thames Hudson. • 2000. $34.95.

DIRECTORIES

Accessories Resources Directory. Business Journals Inc. • Covers: 1,600 manufacturers, importers, and sales representatives producing or handling belts, gloves, handbags, scarves, hosiery, jewelry, sunglasses, and umbrellas. Entries include: Company, name, address, phone, fax.

INTERNET DATABASES

Manufacturing Profiles. U. S. Bureau of the Census. Phone: (301)763-4636 E-mail: webmaster@census.gov • URL: http://www.census.gov/prod/www/abs/mfg-prof.html • The Census Bureau makes available free on PDF (Portable Document Format) an annual consolidation of the entire Current Industrial Report series, presenting "all the data compiled." Contains statistics on production, shipments, inventories, consumption, exports, imports, and orders for a wide variety of manufactured products.

PERIODICALS AND NEWSLETTERS

Accessories. Business Journals, Inc. • 11 times a year. $35.00 per year. Covers the merchandising of women's fashion accessories, including handbags, belts, jewelry, gloves, hats, and umbrellas.

STATISTICS SOURCES

Annual Survey of Manufactures. Available from U. S. Government Printing Office. • Annual. Prices vary. Issued by the U. S. Census Bureau as an interim update to the *Census of Manufactures.* Includes data on number of manufacturing establishments in various industries, employment, labor costs, value of shipments, capital expenditures, inventories, energy costs, and assets. (See also Census Bureau home page, http://www.census.gov/.).

TRADE/PROFESSIONAL ASSOCIATIONS

International Hand Protection Association. PO Box 146, Brookville, PA 15825. Phone: (814)328-5208 Fax: (814)328-5208 E-mail: burdge@key-net.com • Formerly Work Glove Manufacturers Association.

OTHER SOURCES

Medical Gloves. Available from MarketResearch.com. • 2002. $3,850.00. Published by Global Industry Analysts. Provides worldwide market research data, including profiles of major medical glove companies.

GLUE INDUSTRY

See: ADHESIVES

GOING PUBLIC

See: NEW ISSUES (FINANCE)

GOLD

See also: COINS AS AN INVESTMENT;
MONEY

GENERAL WORKS

How to Invest Wisely. Lawrence S. Pratt. American Institute for Economic Research. • 2002. $12.00. Presents a conservative policy of investing, with emphasis on dividend-paying common stocks. Gold and other inflation hedges are compared. Includes a reprint of *Toward an Optimal Stock Selection Strategy* (1997). (Economic Education Bulletin.).

Money: Its Origins, Development, Debasement, and Prospects. John H. Wood. American Institute for Economic Research. • 1999. $10.00. A politically conservative view of monetary history, the gold standard, banking systems, and inflation. Includes a list of references. (Economic Education Bulletin.).

The Power of Gold: The History of an Obsession. Peter L. Bernstein. John Wiley and Sons, Inc. • 2000. $27.95. Covers the economic and financial history of gold from ancient times to the present.

ALMANACS AND YEARBOOKS

Agricultural and Mineral Commodities Year Book. Available from Taylor & Francis Group. • Annual. $225.00. Published by Europa Publications. Contains descriptive product profiles, price data, export-import data, and production statistics for major commodities of the world. Includes commodity histories, uses, markets, demand trends, and information about trade agreements and key commodity organizations.

World Currrency Yearbook. International Currency Analysis, Inc. • Annual. $250.00. Directory of more than 110 central banks worldwide.

CD-ROM DATABASES

OECD Statistical Compendium. Organization for Economic Cooperation and Development. • Semiannual. $1,905.00 per year for 1 to 10 users. CD-ROM contains more than 730,000 monthly, quarterly, and annual time series for OECD countries, 1960 to date. Includes fully searchable data on agriculture, food, economic indicators, national accounts, employment, energy, finance, industry, technology, and foreign trade. Results can be displayed in various forms.

DIRECTORIES

Financial Times Business Global Mining Directory. Available from Gale Cengage Learning. • Annual. $355.00. Published by Financial Times Business. Provides detailed information on 1,000 leading mining companies worldwide. Includes financial data for three years. Formerly *Financial Times Energy Yearbook: Mining.*

Futures Magazine SourceBook: The Most Complete List of Exchanges, Companies, Regulators, Organizations, etc., Offering Products and Services to the Futures and Options Industry. Futures Magazine, Inc. • Annual. $19.50. Provides information on commodity futures brokers, trading method services, publications, and other items of interest to futures traders and money managers.

HANDBOOKS AND MANUALS

Gold: Progress in Chemistry, Biotechnology, and Technology. Hubert Schmidbaur. John Wiley and Sons, Inc. • 1999. $330.00. Covers various uses of gold, as in jewelry, decoration, electronics, and medicine. Includes detailed information on the history, chemistry, and metallurgical aspects of gold.

Jake Bernstein's New Guide to Investing in Metals. Jacob Bernstein. John Wiley and Sons, Inc. • 1991. $34.95. Covers bullion, coins, futures, options, mining stocks, and precious metal mutual funds. Includes the history of metals as an investment.

Looking for Gold: The Modern Prospector's Handbook. Bradford Angier. Stackpole Books, Inc. • 1995. $16.95.

INTERNET DATABASES

Business 2.0 Web Guide to the Best Business Links. Business 2.0 Media Inc. Phone: (415)293-4800 E-mail: support@business2.com • URL: http://www.business2.com/webguide • Web site presents an extensive, searchable directory of links to "the best, most informative, and authoritative web pages." Twenty main categories cover business, finance, career, company information, people, and technology topics, with thousands of subtopics, all linking to Web sites recommended by experienced business researchers. Fees: Free.

Fedstats. Federal Interagency Council on Statistical Policy. Phone: (202)395-7254 • URL: http://www.fedstats.gov • Web site features an efficient search facility for full-text statistics produced by more than 100 federal agencies, including the Census Bureau, the Bureau of Economic Analysis, and the Bureau of Labor Statistics. Boolean searches can be made within one agency or for all agencies combined. Links are offered to international statistical bureaus, including the UN, IMF, OECD, UNESCO, Eurostat, and 20 individual countries. Fees: Free.

FreeLunch.com. Economy.com, Inc. Phone: (610)696-8700 Fax: (610)696-1678 • URL: http://www.freelunch.com • Web site provides free access to more than 1.5 million economic and financial data series, covering industry, demographics, labor markets, prices, retail sales, government spending, trade, interest rates, housing starts, the stock market, and many other topics. Data is available for various time periods in either chart or table form. Searching is offered. Fees: Free, but registration required. Economy.com, Inc. also offers fee-based economic analysis at *The Dismal Scientist* site (http://www.dismal.com).

Futures Online. Futures Magazine Inc. Phone: (312)846-4600 Fax: (312)846-4638 • URL: http://www.futuresmag.com • Web site presents updates of *Futures* magazine and links to other futures-related sites.

ONLINE DATABASES

GEOREF. American Geological Institute. • Bibliography and index of geology and geosciences literature, 1785 to present. Inquire as to online cost and availability.

PERIODICALS AND NEWSLETTERS

Bullion Advisory. Moneypower. • Monthly. $36.00 per year. Specializes in gold, silver and platinum.

Canadian Resources and PennyMines Analyst: The Canadian Newsletter for Penny-Mines Investors Who Insist on Geological Value. MPL Communications, Inc. • Weekly. $145.00 per year. Newsletter. Mainly on Canadian gold mine stocks. Formerly *Canadian PennyMines Analyst.*

Futures: News, Analysis, and Strategies for Futures, Options, and Derivatives Traders. Futures Magazine. • Monthly. $39.00 per year. Edited for institutional money managers and traders, brokers, risk managers, and individual investors or speculators. Includes special feature issues on interest rates, technical indicators, currencies, charts, precious metals, hedge funds, and derivatives. Supplements available.

Gold Newsletter. Jefferson Financial Inc. • Description: Reports on the relationship between gold and the economic system. Covers news of the "world gold markets, other precious metals markets, monetary reform, international economics, inflation, deflation, future of gold prices," and related economic and political matters. **Remarks:** Also available via e-mail.

Powell Monetary Analyst. Larson M. Powell, editor. Reserve Research Ltd. • Description: Offers investment advice concentrating on precious metals, gold coins, currencies, and mining stocks.

PRICE SOURCES

Platt's Metals Week. Platt's. • Weekly. $770.00 per year.

STATISTICS SOURCES

The AIER Chart Book. AIER Research Staff. American Institute for Economic Research. • Annual. $4.00. A compact compilation of long-range charts ("Purchasing Power of the Dollar," for example, goes back to 1780) covering various aspects of the U. S. economy. Includes inflation, interest rates, debt, gold, taxation, stock prices, etc. (Economic Education Bulletin.).

Business Statistics of the United States. Linz Audain and Cornelia J. Strawser. Bernan Associates. • Annual. $147.00. Based on *Business Statistics,* formerly issue by the Bureau of Economic Analysis, U. S. Department of Commerce. Provides basic data for a wide variety of U. S. industries, services, and economic indicators. Most statistics are shown annually for 30 years and monthly for the most recent four years.

London Currency Report. World Reports Ltd. • 10 times a year. $950.00 per year. Formerly *Gold and Silver Survey.*

Mineral Commodity Summaries. Available from U. S. Government Printing Office. • Annual. $26.00. Published by the U. S. Geological Survey, Department of the Interior (http://www.usgs.gov). Contains detailed, five-year data for about 90 nonfuel minerals. Covers a wide range of statistics, including production, imports, exports, consumption, reserves, prices, tariff information, and industry employment. (Two pages are devoted to each mineral.).

Non-Ferrous Metal Data Yearbook. American Bureau of Metal Statistics. • Annual. $405.00. Provides worldwide data on approximately about 200 statistical tables covering many nonferrous metals. Includes production, consumption, inventories, exports, imports, and other data.

Standard & Poor's Industry Surveys. Standard & Poor's. • Semiannual. $1,800.00. Two looseleaf volumes. Includes monthly *Supplements.* Provides detailed, individual surveys of 52 major industry groups. Each survey is revised on a semiannual basis. Also includes "Monthly Investment Review" (industry group investment analysis) and monthly "Trends & Projections" (economic analysis).

Statistical Annual: Interest Rates, Metals, Stock Indices, Options on Financial Futures, Options on Metals Futures. Chicago Board of Trade. • Annual. Includes historical data on GNMA CDR Futures, Cash-Settled GNMA Futures, U. S. Treasury Bond Futures, U. S. Treasury Note Futures, Options on Treasury Note Futures, NASDAQ-100 Futures, Major Market Index Futures, Major Market Index MAXI Futures, Municipal Bond Index Futures, 1,000-Ounce Silver Futures, Options on Silver Futures, and Kilo Gold Futures.

Survey of Current Business. Available from U. S. Government Printing Office. • Monthly. $63.00 per year. Issued by Bureau of Economic Analysis, U. S. Department of Commerce. Presents a wide variety of business and economic data.

United States Census of Mineral Industries. Bureau of the Census, U.S. Department of Commerce.

Available from U.S. Government Printing Office. • Quinquennial.

TRADE/PROFESSIONAL ASSOCIATIONS

American Bureau of Metal Statistics. P.O. Box 805, Chatham, NJ 07928. Phone: (973)701-2299 Fax: (973)701-2152 E-mail: info@abms.com • URL: http://www.abms.com • Members are metal companies. Compiles and publishes detailed statistical data on a wide variety of nonferrous metals: aluminum, copper, gold, lead, nickel, platinum, silver, tin, titanium, uranium, zinc, and others.

Gold Institute. 1112 16th St. NW, Ste. 240, 101 Constitution Ave., Ste. 500E, Washington, DC 20036. Phone: (202)835-0185 Fax: (202)835-0155 E-mail: info@goldinstitute.org • URL: http://www.goldinstitute.org • Miners, refiners, bullion suppliers, manufacturers of gold products, wholesalers of gold investment products. Promotes the common business interests of the gold industry as a whole by providing members with relevant, current statistical data and other information on the gold industry. Also provides early indentification of changes in the operating climate for the industry, and information and statistics on the gold industry for the media and the public. Acts as a spokesperson for the industry.

GOLF INDUSTRY

GENERAL WORKS

Careers in Golf: An Insider's Guide to Careers in the Golf Industry. Nancy Berkley. National Golf Foundation. • 2001. $19.95. Information on careers in golf product manufacturing, retailing, tour management, public relations, event management, course design, and instruction. Includes CD-ROM.

DIRECTORIES

Directory of Golf. National Golf Foundation. • Annual $60.00. Lists golf course architects, contractors, builders, appraisers, and consulting firms. Golf equipment manufacturers are also included.

Golf Course Directory. National Golf Foundation. • Annual. Free to members; non-members, $199.00. Three volumes. Lists about 15,000 public and private golf facilities, with information as to size, number of holes, year opened, and practice ranges.

Golf Index. Ingledue Travel Publications. • Semiannual. $40.00 per year. Provides directory listings of golf courses and resorts around the world. Contains information on golf travel packages, tour operators, and tournaments.

Golf Magazine Buyers' Guide. Times4 Media Inc. • Annual. Price on application. Lists golf club manufacturers, with description of products and prices.

Golf U.S.A.: A Guide to the Best Golf Courses and Resorts. Corey Sandler. McGraw-Hill. • 2001. $16.95. Second edition. Describes 2,500 public and private golf courses. (Econoguides Series).

Golf World Business--Buyers' Guide. Advance Magazine Publishers Inc. • Publication includes: List of companies supplying golfing equipment, components, and apparel, accessories, golf shoes, balls, and bags, shafts, clubs, club fitting programs. Entries include: Company name and address; descriptions of products available, including model names, component materials, and suggested retail prices.

The NGF's Executive and Par-3 Golf Course Directory. National Golf Foundation. • Covers: More than 1,800 executive and par-3 golf courses in the United States. Entries include: Mailing address, telephone number, contact names, type of course, fee information, and number of holes.

Resorts and Parks Purchasing Guide. Klevens Publications, Inc. • Annual. $85.00. Lists suppliers of products and services for resorts and parks, including national parks, amusement parks, dude ranches, golf resorts, ski areas, and national monument areas.

HANDBOOKS AND MANUALS

Human Resource Management for Golf Course Superintendents. Robert A. Milligan and Thomas R. Maloney. John Wiley and Sons, Inc. • 1996. $34.95. Covers various personnel topics as related to golf course management, including organizational structure, recruitment, employee selection, training, motivation, and discipline.

PERIODICALS AND NEWSLETTERS

AGS Quarterly. The Association for Gravestone Studies. • Description: Concerned with the study and preservation of national and international gravestones: folk art carvings, lettering, epitaphs, shapes, materials used, and symbolism. Recurring features include articles on conservation procedures, Association news, book reviews, news of research, and regional news.

Golf Course Management. Golf Course Superintendents Association of America. • Monthly. $48.00 per year. Contains articles on golf course maintenance, equipment, landscaping, renovation, and management.

Golf Course News: The Newspaper for the Golf Course Industry. United Publications, Inc. • Monthly. $60.00 per year. Edited for golf course superintendents, managers, architects, and developers.

Golf Digest: How to Play, What to Play, Where to Play. The Golf Digest Companies. • Monthly. $14.97 per year. A high circulation consumer magazine for golfers. Editions available in various languages. Supplement available *Golf Digest Woman.*

Golf Magazine. Time Inc. • Monthly. $19.95 per year. Popular consumer magazine for golfers.

Golf World Business. The Golf Digest Companies. • Nine times a year. $72.00 per year. Edited for retailers of golf equipment. Formerly *Golf Shop Operations.*

Golfdom. Elsevier. • Monthly. $30.00 per year. Covers marketing, financing, insurance, human resources, maintenance, environmental factors, and other aspects of golf course management. *Formerly Golf Business.*

Golfweek: America's Golf Newspaper. Turnstile Publishing Co. • Weekly. $69.95 per year. Includes biweekly supplement, *Golfweek's Strictly Business,* covering business and marketing for the golfing industry.

RESEARCH CENTERS AND INSTITUTES

National Golf Foundation. National Golf Foundation. 1150 S U.S. Hwy. 1, Ste. 401, Jupiter, FL 33477. Phone: (561)744-6006 Fax: 800-733-6006 or (561)744-6107 E-mail: general@ngf.org • URL: http://www.ngf.org • Golf consumers, golf courses, range operations and maintenance, industry sales, and golf facility development.

STATISTICS SOURCES

U. S. Industry and Trade Outlook. Available from National Technical Information Service. • Annual. $69.95. Produced by the International Trade Administration, U. S. Department of Commerce, in a "public-private" partnership with DRI/McGraw-Hill and Standard & Poor's. Provides basic data, outlook for the current year, and "Long-Term Prospects" (five-year projections) for a wide variety of products and services. Includes high technology industries. Formerly *U. S. Industrial Outlook.*

TRADE/PROFESSIONAL ASSOCIATIONS

American Recreational Golf Association. 7300 W Fullerton Ave., PO Box 35215, Chicago, IL 60707-0215. Phone: (708)453-0080 Fax: (708)453-0083 E-mail: concido@concido.com • URL: http://rentamark.com/arga/ • Initiated by the American Recreational Sports Association. Evaluates golf equipment for the sporting goods industry and offers equipment certification program. Studies trends in the golf industry. Maintains a hall of fame; sponsors competitions; conducts charitable and educational programs.

American Society of Golf Course Architects. 111 E Wacher Dr., 18th Fl., Chicago, IL 60601. Phone: (312)372-7090 Fax: (312)372-6160 E-mail: asgca@publicis-usa.com • URL: http://www.golfdesign.org • Members are professional designers and architects of golf courses.

Association of Golf Merchandisers. P.O. Box 19899, Fountain Hills, AZ 85269-9899. Phone: (480)836-8250 Fax: (480)836-8251 E-mail: info@aol.com • URL: http://www.agmgolf.org • Members are vendors of gold equipment and merchandise.

Golf Course Builders Association of America. 727 O St., Lincoln, NE 68503-1323. Phone: (402)476-4444 Fax: (402)476-4489 E-mail: gcbaa@aol.com • URL: http://www.gcbaa.org • Members are golf course builders, designers, and suppliers. Formerly Golf Course Builders Association.

Golf Course Superintendents Association of America. 1421 Research Park Dr., Lawrence, KS 66049-3859. Phone: 800-472-7878 or (785)841-2240 or (785)832-4430 Fax: (785)832-4488 E-mail: infobox@gcsaa.org • URL: http://www.gcsaa.org • Members are golf course superintendents and others concerned with golf course maintenance and improvement. Formerly National Greenkeepimg Superintendents Association.

Golf Manufacturers and Distributors Association. 4925 Bonnie Rd., Kettering, OH 45440-2126. Phone: (440)460-3977 • Members are exhibitors at the Professional Golfers' Association annual trade show. Seeks to improve the "business habits" of professional golfers.

Ladies Professional Golf Association. 100 International Golf Dr., Daytona Beach, FL 32124-1092. Phone: (386)274-6200 Fax: (386)274-1099 E-mail: feedback@lpga.com • URL: http://www.lpga.com • Represents and promotes women golfers, teachers and competitors. Compiles statistics on tournaments, money winnings, and scoring.

National Golf Course Owners Association. 291 Seven Farms Dr., Charleston, SC 29492. Phone: 800-933-4262 or (843)881-9956 Fax: (843)881-9958 E-mail: info@ngcoa.org • URL: http://www.ngcoa.org • Owners and operators of privately owned golf courses. Assist members to develop more productive, efficient, and profitable golf operations. Provides information on taxation, destination golf, community relations, environmental regulations, and marketing. Offers group purchasing opportunities. Conducts educational seminars. Compiles statistics.

PGA TOUR Tournaments Association. 13000 Sawgrass Village Cir., Ste. 36, Ponte Vedra Beach, FL 32082. Phone: (904)285-4222 Fax: (904)273-5726 E-mail: suzanne@pgatta.org • URL: http://pgatta.org • Sponsors major professional golf tournaments held on the regular PGA Tour in the United States and Canada each year. Provides forum for exchange of information and ideas.

Professional Golfers' Association of America. 100 Ave. of Champions, Palm Beach Gardens, FL 33410-9601. Phone: (561)624-8400 Fax: (561)624-8430 E-mail: info@pga.com • URL: http://www.pga.com/.

United States Golf Association (USGA). P.O. Box 708, Far Hills, NJ 07931. Phone: (908)234-2300 Fax: (908)234-9687 E-mail: usga@usga.org • URL: http://www.usga.org • Members are established golf courses and clubs. Serves as governing body for golf in the U. S. and provides rules and regulations. Affiliated with USGA Green Section.

OTHER SOURCES

Golf Participation in the U. S. Available from MarketResearch.com. • 1998. $250.00. Published by the National Golf Foundation. Market research report on consumer attitudes and industry statistics.

Superstudy of Sports Participation. Available from MarketResearch.com. • 2002. $700.00. Three volumes. Published by American Sports Data, Inc. Provides market research data on 102 sports and activities. Vol. 1: *Physical Fitness Activities.* Vol. 2: *Recreational Sports.* Vol. 3: *Outdoor Activities.* (Volumes are available separately at $295.00.).

GOURMET FOODS

See: SPECIALTY FOOD INDUSTRY

GOVERNMENT ACCOUNTING

GENERAL WORKS

Accounting for Governmental and Non-Profit Entities. Earl R. Wilson and Susan C. Kattleus. McGraw-Hill. • 2003. 13th edition. Price on application.

Essentials of Accounting for Governmental and Not-for-Profit Organizations. John H. Engstrom and Paul Coley. McGraw-Hill. • 2003. $66.88. Seventh edition.

ABSTRACTS AND INDEXES

Accounting and Tax Index. UMI. • Quarterly. Price on application. Annual cumulation. Indexes accounting, auditing, and taxation literature appearing in journals, books, pamphlets, conference proceedings, and newsletters.

Accounting Articles. CCH, Inc. • Monthly. $624.00 per year. Looseleaf service.

PAIS International in Print. Public Affairs Information Service, Inc. • Monthly. $850.00 per year; cumulations three times a year. Provides topical citations to the worldwide literature of public affairs, economics, demographics, sociology, and trade. Text in English; indexed materials in English, French, German, Italian, Portuguese and Spanish.

Sage Public Administration Abstracts. Sage Publications, Inc. • Quarterly. Institutions, $785.00 per year.

ALMANACS AND YEARBOOKS

Research in Governmental and Nonprofit Accounting. Elsevier. • Dates vary. Price varies. 10 volumes.

CD-ROM DATABASES

PAIS on CD-ROM. Public Affairs Information Service, Inc. • Quarterly. $1,995.00 per year. Provides a CD-ROM version of the online service, *PAIS International.* Contains over 500,000 citations to the literature of contemporary social, political, and economic issues.

HANDBOOKS AND MANUALS

GAAP for Governments: Interpretation and Application of Generally Accepted Accounting Principles for State and Local Governments. John Wiley and Sons, Inc. • Annual. $134.00. (Includes CD-ROM.).

Government Auditing Standards. Available from U. S. Government Printing Office. • 1994. $6.50. Revised edition. Issued by the U. S. General Accounting Office (http://www.gao.gov). Contains standards for CPA firms to follow in financial and performance audits of federal government agencies and programs. Also known as the "Yellow Book.".

Managerial Accounting for Libraries and Other Not-for-Profit Organizations. G. Stevenson Smith. American Library Association. • 2002. $55.00.

Coverage includes responsibility accounting, life cycle costing, and activity-based accounting, as opposed to traditional cost accounting for profit-based organizations.

INTERNET DATABASES

Rutgers Accounting Web (RAW). Rutgers University Accounting Research Center. Phone: (973)353-5172 Fax: (973)353-1283 • URL: http://www.rutgers.edu/accounting • RAW Web site provides extensive links to sources of national and international accounting information, such as the Big Six accounting firms, the Financial Accounting Standards Board (FASB), SEC filings (EDGAR), journals, publishers, software, the International Accounting Network, and "Internet's largest list of accounting firms in USA." Searching is offered. Fees: Free.

ONLINE DATABASES

Accounting and Tax Database. PROQUEST. • Provides indexing and abstracting of the literature of accounting, taxation, and financial management, 1971 to date. Updating is weekly. Especially covers accounting, auditing, banking, bankruptcy, employee compensation and benefits, cash management, financial planning, and credit. Inquire as to online cost and availability.

PAIS International. Public Affairs Information Service, Inc. • Corresponds to the former printed publications, *PAIS Bulletin* (1976-90) and *PAIS Foreign Language Index* (1972-90), and to the current *PAIS International in Print* (1991 to date). Covers economic, political, and sociological material appearing in periodicals, books, government documents, and other publications. Updating is monthly. Inquire as to online cost and availability.

PERIODICALS AND NEWSLETTERS

Governing: The States and Localities. • Monthly. $39.95 per year. Edited for state and local government officials. Covers finance, office management, computers, telecommunications, environmental concerns, etc.

The Journal of Government Financial Management. Association of Government Accountants. • Quarterly. $90.00 per year. Formerly *Government Accountants Journal.*

TRADE/PROFESSIONAL ASSOCIATIONS

Association of Government Accountants. 2208 Mount Vernon Ave., Alexandria, VA 22301-1314. Phone: 800-242-7211 or (703)684-6931 Fax: (703)548-9367 E-mail: agamembers@agacgfm.org • URL: http://www.agacgfm.org • Members are employed by federal, state, county, and city government agencies. Includes accountants, auditors, budget officers, and other government finance administrators and officials.

GOVERNMENT ADMINISTRATION

See: PUBLIC ADMINISTRATION

GOVERNMENT AGENCIES

See: FEDERAL GOVERNMENT; MUNICIPAL GOVERNMENT; STATE GOVERNMENT

GOVERNMENT AID

See: FEDERAL AID

GOVERNMENT AND BUSINESS

See: REGULATION OF INDUSTRY

GOVERNMENT BONDS

See also: BONDS; MUNICIPAL BONDS

GENERAL WORKS

Financial Institutions and Markets. Meir J. Kohn. Oxford University Press, Inc. • 2003. $115.00. Second edition.

OECD Public Debt Markets: Trends and Recent Structural Changes. Organization for Economic Cooperation and Development. • 2002. $49.00. Provides information on North American, Asian-Pacific, and European government bond markets. Contains chapters on individual countries, with discussion of debt management policies and techniques.

ALMANACS AND YEARBOOKS

Fixed Income Almanac: The Bond Investor's Compendium of Key Market, Product, and Performance Data. Livingston G. Douglas. McGraw-Hill. • 1993. $75.00. Presents 20 years of data in 350 graphs and charts. Covers bond market volatility, yield spreads, high-yield (junk) corporate bonds, default rates, and other items, such as Federal Reserve policy.

CD-ROM DATABASES

OECD Statistical Compendium. Organization for Economic Cooperation and Development. • Semiannual. $1,905.00 per year for 1 to 10 users. CD-ROM contains more than 730,000 monthly, quarterly, and annual time series for OECD countries, 1960 to date. Includes fully searchable data on agriculture, food, economic indicators, national accounts, employment, energy, finance, industry, technology, and foreign trade. Results can be displayed in various forms.

DIRECTORIES

Mergent Municipal and Government Manual. Mergent, Inc. • Annual. $3,250.00 per year. Updated weekly online.

ENCYCLOPEDIAS AND DICTIONARIES

Dictionary of Finance and Investment Terms. John Downes. Barron's Educational Series, Inc. • 2002. $14.95. Sixth edition. Provides clear explanations of more than 5,000 business, banking, financial, investment, and tax terms. Includes a separate list of financial abbreviations and acronyms. (Business Dictionaries Series).

HANDBOOKS AND MANUALS

Fixed Income Analytics: State-of-the-Art Analysis and Valuation Modeling. Ravi E. Dattatreya, editor. McGraw-Hill. • 1991. $69.95. Discusses the yield curve, structure and value in corporate bonds, mortgage-backed securities, and other topics. (Institutional Investor Publications).

Fixed Income Mathematics: Analytical and Statistical Techniques. Frank J. Fabozzi. McGraw-Hill. • 1996. $65.00. Third edition. Covers the basics of fixed income analysis, as well as more advanced techniques used for complex securities.

How to Build Wealth with Tax-Sheltered Investments. Kerry Anne Lynch. American Institute for Economic Research. • 2000. $6.00. Provides practical information on conservative tax shelters, including defined-contribution pension plans, individual retirement accounts, Keogh plans, U. S. savings bonds, municipal bonds, and various kinds of annuities: deferred, variable-rate, immediate, and foreign-currency. (Economic Education Bulletin.).

Trading and Investing in Bond Options: Risk Management, Arbitrage, and Value Investing. M. Anthony Wong. John Wiley and Sons, Inc. • 1991. $55.00. Covers dealing, trading, and investing in U. S. government bond futures options (puts and calls). (Finance Series).

INTERNET DATABASES

Business 2.0 Web Guide to the Best Business Links. Business 2.0 Media Inc. Phone: (415)293-4800

E-mail: support@business2.com • URL: http://
www.business2.com/webguide • Web site presents
an extensive, searchable directory of links to "the
best, most informative, and authoritative web
pages." Twenty main categories cover business,
finance, career, company information, people, and
technology topics, with thousands of subtopics, all
linking to Web sites recommended by experienced
business researchers. Fees: Free.

Factiva. Dow Jones Reuters Business Interactive,
LLC. Phone: 800-369-7466 or (609)452-1511 Fax:
(609)520-5770 E-mail: solutions@factiva.com •
URL: http://www.factiva.com • Fee-based Web site
provides "global news and business information
through Web sites and content integration solutions."
Includes Dow Jones and Reuters newswires, The
Wall Street Journal, and more than 7,000 other
sources of current news, historical articles, market
research reports, and investment analysis. Content
includes 96 major U. S. newspapers, 900 non-
English sources, trade publications, media
transcripts, country profiles, news photos, etc.

Fedstats. Federal Interagency Council on Statistical
Policy. Phone: (202)395-7254 • URL: http://www.
fedstats.gov • Web site features an efficient search
facility for full-text statistics produced by more than
100 federal agencies, including the Census Bureau,
the Bureau of Economic Analysis, and the Bureau of
Labor Statistics. Boolean searches can be made
within one agency or for all agencies combined.
Links are offered to international statistical bureaus,
including the UN, IMF, OECD, UNESCO, Eurostat,
and 20 individual countries. Fees: Free.

FreeLunch.com. Economy.com, Inc. Phone:
(610)696-8700 Fax: (610)696-1678 • URL: http://
www.freelunch.com • Web site provides free access
to more than 1.5 million economic and financial data
series, covering industry, demographics, labor
markets, prices, retail sales, government spending,
trade, interest rates, housing starts, the stock market,
and many other topics. Data is available for various
time periods in either chart or table form. Searching
is offered. Fees: Free, but registration required.
Economy.com, Inc. also offers fee-based economic
analysis at *The Dismal Scientist* site (http://www.
dismal.com).

Nexis.com. Lexis-Nexis Group. Phone: 800-227-
4908 or (937)865-6800 Fax: (937)865-6909 E-mail:
webmaster@prod.lexis-nexis.com • URL: http://
www.nexis.com • Fee-based Web site offers searching of about 2.8 billion documents in some 30,000
news, business, and legal information sources.
Features include a subject directory covering 1,200
topics in 34 categories and a Company Dossier
containing information on more than 500,000 public
and private companies. Boolean searching is offered.

Wall Street Journal Interactive Edition. Dow Jones
& Co., Inc. Phone: 800-369-2834 or (212)416-2000
Fax: (212)416-2658 E-mail: inquiries@interactive.
wsj.com • URL: http://www.wsj.com • Fee-based
Web site providing online searching of worldwide
information from the *The Wall Street Journal.*
Includes "Company Snapshots," "The Journal's
Greatest Hits," "Index to Market Data," "Journal
Links," etc. Financial price quotes are available.
Fees: $49.00 per year; $29.00 per year to print
subscribers.

PERIODICALS AND NEWSLETTERS

American Banker: The Financial Services Daily.
Thomson Media. • Daily. $895.00 per year. Provides
news of banking, investment products, mortgages,
credit unions, finance, bank technology, and legal
developments.

The Bond Buyer. Veronis, Suhler and Associates Inc.
• Daily edition, $1,897 per year. Weekly edition,
$525.00 per year. Reports on new municipal bond
issues.

Bondweek: The Newsweekly of Fixed Income and

Credit Markets. Institutional Investor, Inc., Journals
Group. • Weekly. $2,425.00 per year. Newsletter.
Includes print and online editions. Covers taxable,
fixed-income securities for professional investors,
including corporate, government, foreign, mortgage,
and high-yield.

Journal of Fixed Income. Institutional Investor, Inc.,
Journals Group. • Quarterly. $360.00 per year.
Includes print and online editions. Covers a wide
range of fixed-income investments for institutions,
including bonds, interest-rate options, high-yield
securities, and mortgages.

Moody's Bond Survey. Moody's Investors Service
Inc. • Description: Presents statistical information
and analysis of corporate, municipal, government,
federal agency, and international bonds, preferred
stock, and commercial paper. Includes ratings
changes and withdrawals, calendars of recent and
prospective bond offerings, and Moody's bond and
preferred stock yield averages.

U. S. Banker. Thomson Media. • Monthly. $65.00
per year. Edited for bank executives and managers.
Covers a wide variety of banking and financial
topics.

The Wall Street Journal. Dow Jones & Co., Inc. •
Daily. $189.00 per year. Covers news and trends
relating to business, industry, finance, the economy,
and international commerce. Provides extensive
price and other data for the securities, commodity,
options, futures, foreign exchange, and money
markets.

STATISTICS SOURCES

Business Statistics of the United States. Linz Audain
and Cornelia J. Strawser. Bernan Associates. •
Annual. $147.00. Based on *Business Statistics*,
formerly issue by the Bureau of Economic Analysis,
U. S. Department of Commerce. Provides basic data
for a wide variety of U. S. industries, services, and
economic indicators. Most statistics are shown annually for 30 years and monthly for the most recent
four years.

*Daily Treasury Statement: Cash and Debt Opera-
tions of the United States Treasury.* Available from
U. S. Government Printing Office. • Daily, except
Saturdays, Sundays, and holidays. (Financial
Management Service, U. S. Treasury Department.).

*Statistical Annual: Interest Rates, Metals, Stock
Indices, Options on Financial Futures, Options on
Metals Futures.* Chicago Board of Trade. • Annual.
Includes historical data on GNMA CDR Futures,
Cash-Settled GNMA Futures, U. S. Treasury Bond
Futures, U. S. Treasury Note Futures, Options on
Treasury Note Futures, NASDAQ-100 Futures,
Major Market Index Futures, Major Market Index
MAXI Futures, Municipal Bond Index Futures,
1,000-Ounce Silver Futures, Options on Silver
Futures, and Kilo Gold Futures.

Stocks, Bonds, Bills, and Inflation Yearbook. Ibbotson Associates. • Annual. $92.00. Provides detailed
data from 1926 to the present on inflation and the
returns from various kinds of financial investments,
such as small-cap stocks and long-term government
bonds.

Survey of Current Business. Available from U. S.
Government Printing Office. • Monthly. $63.00 per
year. Issued by Bureau of Economic Analysis, U. S.
Department of Commerce. Presents a wide variety
of business and economic data.

Treasury Bulletin. Available from U. S. Government
Printing Office. • Quarterly. $45.00 per year. Issued
by the Financial Management Service, U. S.
Treasury Department. Provides data on the federal
budget, government securities and yields, the

national debt, and the financing of the federal
government in general.

OTHER SOURCES

Fitch Insights. Fitch Investors Service, Inc. •
Biweekly. $1,040.00 per year. Includes bond rating
actions and explanation of actions. Provides commentary and Fitch's view of the financial markets.

*Tables of Redemption Values for United States Sav-
ings Bonds, Series EE and Series E.* Available from
U. S. Government Printing Office. • Semiannual.
$12.00 per year. Issued by the Public Debt Bureau,
U. S. Treasury Department.

GOVERNMENT BUDGET

See: FEDERAL BUDGET

GOVERNMENT, COMPUTERS IN

See: COMPUTERS IN GOVERNMENT

GOVERNMENT CONTRACTS

See also: CONTRACTS; GOVERNMENT
PURCHASING

GENERAL WORKS

*Government Contracts and Subcontract Leads
Directory.* Government Data Publications, Inc. •
1992. $89.50. Firms which received prime contracts
for production of goods or services from federal
government agencies during the preceeding twelve
months. Formerly *Government Contracts Directory.*

ABSTRACTS AND INDEXES

*Current Law Index: Multiple Access to Legal
Periodicals.* Gale Cengage Learning. • Monthly.
$725.00 per year. Produced in cooperation with the
American Association of Law Libraries. Indexes
more than 900 law journals, legal newspapers, and
specialty publications from the U.S., Canada, U.K.,
Ireland, Australia, and New Zealand.

DIRECTORIES

Government Prime Contractors Directory. Government Data Publications Inc. • Covers: Organizations
that received government prime contracts during the
previous two years. Entries include: Contractor
name and address, product/service; contractors with
contracts of more than $500,000 are marked.

HANDBOOKS AND MANUALS

Contracting with the Federal Government. Margaret
M. Worthington and Louis P. Goldsman. John Wiley
and Sons, Inc. • 1998. $165.00. Fourth edition. Tells
how to acquire federal contracts and execute them
profitably.

Cost Accounting Standards Board Regulations.
CCH, Inc. • 2002. $27.00. Covers Federal Acquisi-
tion Regulation (FAR) cost accounting standards for
both defense and civilian government contracts.
Provides the rules for estimating and reporting costs
for contracts of more than $500,000.

How to Obtain Government Contracts. Entrepreneur
Media, Inc. • Looseleaf. $59.50. A practical guide to
acquiring and negotiating government contracts.
(Start-Up Business Guide No. E1227.).

Win Government Contracts for Your Small Business.
John DiGiacomo and James Kleckner. CCH, Inc. •
2003. $24.95. Second edition. Provides 10 "easy-to-
understand steps" to obtain government contracts.
Appendices include a glossary, sample forms, and
other information.

INTERNET DATABASES

Lexis.com Research System. Lexis-Nexis Group.
Phone: 800-227-4908 or (937)865-6800 Fax:

(937)865-6909 E-mail: webmaster@prod.lexis-nexis.com • URL: http://www.lexis.com • Fee-based Web site offers extensive searching of a wide variety of legal sources. Additional features include Daily Opinion Service, lexis.com Bookstore, Career Center, CLE Center, Law Schools, and Practice Pages ("Pages specific to areas of specialty").

PERIODICALS AND NEWSLETTERS

Commerce Business Daily. Industry and Trade Administration, U.S. Department of Commerce. U.S. Department of Commerce. • Description: Lists notices of proposed government procurement actions, contract awards, sales of government property, and contract procurement information. Includes 500-1,000 notices in each edition; notices appear in the publication only once.

Federal Grants and Contracts Weekly: Funding Opportunities in Research, Training and Services. Aspen Publishers, Inc. • 50 times a year. $450.00 per year. Newsletter.

Government Contractor. West DC Editorial. • Weekly. $1,700.00 per year.

Government Contracts Update: How to Target, Win, and Perform Government Contracts. United Communications Group (UCG). • Biweekly. $277.00 per year. Newsletter.

Government Primecontracts Monthly. Government Data Publications, Inc. • Monthly. $96.00 per year.

MBI: The National Report on Minority, Women-Owned and Disadvantaged Business. Community Development Services, Inc. CD Publications. • Semimonthly. $379.00 per year. Newsletter. Provides news of affirmative action, government contracts, minority business employment, and education/training for minorities in business. Formerly *Minorities in Business.*

The National Estimator. Society of Cost Estimating and Analysis. • Quarterly. $30.00 per year. Covers government contract estimating.

TRADE/PROFESSIONAL ASSOCIATIONS

Contract Services Association of America. 1000 Wilson Blvd., Ste. 1800, Arlington, VA 20009. Phone: (703)243-2020 Fax: (703)243-3601 E-mail: info@csa-dc.org • URL: http://www.csa-dc.org • Formerly National Council of Technical Services Industries.

National Contract Management Association. 21740 Beaumeade Cir., Ste. 125, Ashburn, VA 20147. Phone: 800-344-8096 or (571)382-0082 Fax: (703)448-0939 E-mail: couture@ncmahq.org • URL: http://www.ncmahq.org • Professional individuals concerned with administration, procurement, acquisition, negotiation and management of contracts and subcontracts. Works for the education, improvement and professional development of members and nonmembers through national and chapter programs, symposia and educational materials. Offers certification in Contract Management (CPCM, CFCM, and CCCM) designations as well as a credential program. Operates speakers' bureau.

Society of Cost Estimating and Analysis. 101 S Whiting St., Ste. 201, Alexandria, VA 22304. Phone: (703)751-3013 Fax: (703)461-7328 E-mail: scea@sceaonline.net • URL: http://www.sceaonline.net • Members are engaged in government contract estimating and pricing.

OTHER SOURCES

Federal Contracts Report. BNA, Inc. • Weekly. $1,453.00 per year. Two looseleaf volumes. Developments affecting federal contracts and grants.

Government Contracts; Law, Administration and Procedure. LexisNexis Matthew Bender. • Quarterly. $1,329.00 per year. 17 looseleaf volumes. Coverage of important aspects of government contracts.

Government Contracts Reports. CCH, Inc. •

Weekly. $2,600.00 per year. 10 looseleaf volumes. Laws and regulations affecting government contracts.

GOVERNMENT DOCUMENTS

See: GOVERNMENT PUBLICATIONS

GOVERNMENT EMPLOYEES

See also: BUREAUCRACY; CIVIL SERVICE; PUBLIC ADMINISTRATION

GENERAL WORKS

Opportunities in Government Careers. Neale J. Baxter. McGraw-Hill. • 2001. $15.95. Edited for students and job seekers. Includes education requirements and salary data. (VGM Career Books.).

Performance Management in Government: Contemporary Illustrations. David Shand. OECD Publications and Information Center. • 1996. (Public Management Occasional Papers: No. 9).

CD-ROM DATABASES

Leadership Library on CD-ROM: Who's Who in the Leadership of the United States. Leadership Directories, Inc. • Quarterly. Including access to Internet version (weekly updates). Contains all 14 *Yellow Book* personnel directories on CD-ROM, providing contact and brief biographical information for about 400,000 individuals. Covers business, government, financial institutions, news media, law firms, associations, foreign representatives, and nonprofit organizations. Includes photographs.

OECD Statistical Compendium. Organization for Economic Cooperation and Development. • Semiannual. $1,905.00 per year for 1 to 10 users. CD-ROM contains more than 730,000 monthly, quarterly, and annual time series for OECD countries, 1960 to date. Includes fully searchable data on agriculture, food, economic indicators, national accounts, employment, energy, finance, industry, technology, and foreign trade. Results can be displayed in various forms.

The Tax Directory [CD-ROM]. Tax Analysts. • Quarterly. Provides *The Tax Directory* listings on CD-ROM, covering federal, state, and international tax officials, tax practitioners, and corporate tax executives.

DIRECTORIES

The Almanac of the Executive Branch. Maximov Publications. • Annual. $149.00. Provides detailed information on more than 830 key staff memebers of the executive branch of the federal government. Includes educational background, previous employment, job responsibilities, etc.

Almanac of the Unelected: Staff of the U. S. Congress. Bernan Associates. • Annual. $275.00. Provides detailed information on key staff members of the legislative branch of the federal government. Includes educational background, previous employment, job responsibilities, etc.

Carroll's County Directory. Carroll Publishing. • Covers: Over 57,000 officials in more than 3,000 counties; includes elected, appointed, and career office holders. Entries include: County seat, locator phone, address, population, officials' names, titles, addresses, and phone numbers. Available as part of a "library volume" titled "Municipal/County Directory Annual Edition" (see separate entry).

Carroll's Federal & Federal Regional Directory. Carroll Publishing. • Semiannual. $325.00 per year; with online edition, $1,200 per year. Lists more than 23,000 U. S. government officials throughout the country, including military installations.

Carroll's Federal Directory. Carroll Publishing. • Covers: About 38,000 executive managers in federal

government offices in Washington, DC, including executive, congressional and judicial branches; members of Congress and Congressional committees and staff. Entries include: Agency names, titles, office address (including room numbers), e-mail addresses, and telephone and fax numbers. Also available as part of a "library edition" titled "Federal Directory Annual".

Carroll's Federal Regional Directory. Carroll Publishing. • Covers: Over 32,000 officials in federal congressional, judicial, and executive branch departments and agencies outside the District of Columbia. Entries include: Organization or agency name; names, addresses, and phone numbers of key personnel.

Carroll's Municipal/County Directory. Carroll Publishing. • Annual. $250.00 per year. Provides listings of about 90,000 city, town, and county officials in the U. S.

Carroll's Municipal Directory. Carroll Publishing. • Covers: about 50,000 officials in more than 7,900 cities towns and villages: includes top elected council or elected board members. Entries include: Name, county name, locator phone, address, population; officials' names, titles, addresses, and phone numbers.

Carroll's State Directory. Carroll Publishing. • Covers: about 73,000 state government officials in all branches of government; officers, committees and members of state legislatures; managers of boards and authorities. Entries include: Name, address, phone, fax, title.

Carroll's State Directory: CD-ROM Edition. Carroll Publishing. • Three times a year. $325.00 per year. Provides CD-ROM listings of about 43,000 state officials, plus the text of all state constitutions and biographies of all governors. Also available online.

Congressional Directory. Office of Membership Grassroots Management. • Covers: Members of Congress. Entries include: List of members of Congress by state includes member party and home city; alphabetical list by member name includes addresses, phone, fax, e-mail, committee/subcommittee assignments, names of key staff members, and photos.

Congressional Staff Directory: With Biographical Information on Members and Key Congressional Staff. CQ Press. • Three times a year. $225.00 per year. Contains more than 3,200 detailed biographies of members of Congress and their staffs. Includes committees and subcommittees. Keyword and name indexes are provided.

Federal Regional Yellow Book: Who's Who in the Federal Government's Departments, Agencies, Military Installations, and Service Academies Outside of Washington, DC. Leadership Directories, Inc. • Semiannual. $265.00 per year. Lists over 35,000 federal officials and support staff at 8,000 regional offices.

Federal Staff Directory: With Biographical Information on Executive Staff Personnel. CQ Press. • Three times a year. $259.00 per year. Single copies, $149.00. Lists 35,000 staff members of federal departments and agencies, with biographies of 3,200 key executives. Includes keyword and name indexes.

The Tax Directory. Tax Analysts. • Covers: Volume One--Approximately 15,000 federal and state government tax legislators, policymakers, administrators, and employees; tax regulation attorneys; over 500 international tax officials with central banks, ministries of finance, foreign embassies and consulate, and chambers of commerce; over 300 tax and business journalists and editors working for magazines, journals, newspapers, television, and radio; tax sections of over 100 trade and professional associations; state CPA, bar, and enrolled agent associations. Volume Two--Over 5,000 corporate tax managers of large U.S. and international firms. Entries include: For government and international officials--Name, title, address, phone, fax, email and website. For corporate tax managers--Name, address, phone, fax, email, website, and company name. For journalists--Name, address, phone, fax, email, website, and name of publication/network. For organizations and associations--Name, address, phone, fax, email, website, budget, membership, background information, and description of purpose.

United States Government Manual. National Archives and Records Administration. Office of the Federal Register. • Description: Provides information on the agencies of the executive, judicial, and legislative branches of the Federal government. Contains a section on terminated or transferred agencies.

Worldwide Government Directory. MacFarlane Management Services Inc. • Covers: 32,000 key elected and appointed government officials in 196 nations and 100 international agencies. Entries include: Head of state, key government ministers, address, phone, and areas of responsibility.

ENCYCLOPEDIAS AND DICTIONARIES

International Encyclopedia of Public Policy and Administration. Jay M. Shafritz, editor. Westview Press. • 1997. $550.00. Four volumes. Covers 20 major areas, such as public administration, government budgeting, industrial policy, nonprofit management, organizational theory, public finance, labor relations, and taxation. Includes a brief bibliography for each major entry and a comprehensive index.

HANDBOOKS AND MANUALS

The Federal Manager's Handbook: A Guide to Rehabilitating or Removing the Problem Employee. G. Jerry Shaw and William L. Bransford. FPMI Communications, Inc. • 1997. $29.95. Third revised edition.

INTERNET DATABASES

Business 2.0 Web Guide to the Best Business Links. Business 2.0 Media Inc. Phone: (415)293-4800 E-mail: support@business2.com • URL: http://www.business2.com/webguide • Web site presents an extensive, searchable directory of links to "the best, most informative, and authoritative web pages." Twenty main categories cover business, finance, career, company information, people, and technology topics, with thousands of subtopics, all linking to Web sites recommended by experienced business researchers. Fees: Free.

Fedstats. Federal Interagency Council on Statistical Policy. Phone: (202)395-7254 • URL: http://www.fedstats.gov • Web site features an efficient search facility for full-text statistics produced by more than 100 federal agencies, including the Census Bureau, the Bureau of Economic Analysis, and the Bureau of Labor Statistics. Boolean searches can be made within one agency or for all agencies combined. Links are offered to international statistical bureaus, including the UN, IMF, OECD, UNESCO, Eurostat, and 20 individual countries. Fees: Free.

FreeLunch.com. Economy.com, Inc. Phone: (610)696-8700 Fax: (610)696-1678 • URL: http://www.freelunch.com • Web site provides free access to more than 1.5 million economic and financial data series, covering industry, demographics, labor markets, prices, retail sales, government spending, trade, interest rates, housing starts, the stock market, and many other topics. Data is available for various time periods in either chart or table form. Searching is offered. Fees: Free, but registration required. Economy.com, Inc. also offers fee-based economic analysis at *The Dismal Scientist* site (http://www.dismal.com).

U. S. Census Bureau: The Official Statistics. U. S. Bureau of the Census. Phone: (301)763-4100 Fax: (301)763-4794 • URL: http://www.census.gov •

Web site is "Your Source for Social, Demographic, and Economic Information." Contains "Current U. S. Population Count," "Current Economic Indicators," and a wide variety of data under "Other Official Statistics." Keyword searching is provided. Fees: Free.

PERIODICALS AND NEWSLETTERS

AFSCME Public Employee. American Federation of State, County, and Municipal Employees. • Bimonthly. Membership. Newsletter. Formerly *Public Employee Magazine.*

Employee Policy for the Private and Public Sector: State Capitals. Wakeman-Walworth, Inc. • Weekly. $245.00 per year; print and online editions, $350.00 per year. Newsletter. Formerly *From the State Capitals: Employee Policy for the Private and Public Sector.*

The Federal Employee. National Federation of Federal Employees. • Description: Provides news and information on issues (legislative and regulatory) affecting federal employees.

Federal Employee News Digest. Federal Employee News Digest, Inc. • Weekly. $59.00 per year. Provides essential information for federal employees.

Federal Human Resources Week: News, Strategies and Best Practices for the HR Professional. LRP Publications. • 48 times a year. $350.00 per year. Newsletter. Covers federal personnel issues, including legislation, benefits, budgets, and downsizing.

Federal Jobs Digest. • Biweekly. Individuals, $125.00 per year; libraries, $112.50 per year. Lists 15,000 immediate job openings within the federal government in each issue.

Government Standard. American Federation of Government Employees. • Bimonthly. Membership.

Government Union Review and Public Policy Digest. Public Service Research Foundation. • Quarterly. $20.00 per year. Academic quarterly covering the labor relations field. Formerly *Government Union Review.*

RESEARCH CENTERS AND INSTITUTES

Office of Government Programs. Louisiana State University. Pleasant Hall, Room 379, Baton Rouge, LA 70803. Phone: (225)578-6746 Fax: (225)578-6200 E-mail: ogp@doce.lsu.edu • URL: http://www.doce.lsu.edu/government.

STATISTICS SOURCES

Business Statistics of the United States. Linz Audain and Cornelia J. Strawser. Bernan Associates. • Annual. $147.00. Based on *Business Statistics,* formerly issue by the Bureau of Economic Analysis, U. S. Department of Commerce. Provides basic data for a wide variety of U. S. industries, services, and economic indicators. Most statistics are shown annually for 30 years and monthly for the most recent four years.

Datapedia of the United States: American History in Numbers. George T. Kurian, editor. Bernan Press. • 2004. $125.00. Third edition. Based on the Census Bureau publication, *Historical Statistics of the United States.* Provides data from Colonial times to the present on agriculture, business, consumer income, energy, finance, labor, national income, population, and many other subjects. Includes "narrative highlights," maps, charts, and statistical projections.

Handbook of U. S. Labor Statistics: Employment, Earnings, Prices, Productivity, and Other Labor Data. Eva E. Jacobs, editor. Bernan Associates. • 1999. $74.00. Based on *Handbook of Labor Statistics,* formerly issued by the Bureau of Labor Statistics, U. S. Department of Labor. Includes the Bureau's projections of employment in the U. S. by industry and occupation. Provides a wide variety of data on the work force, prices, fringe benefits, and consumer expenditures.

Historical Tables, Budget of the United States Government. Available from U. S. Government Printing Office. • Annual. $41.00. Issued by the Office of Management and Budget, Executive Office of the President (http://www.whitehouse.gov). Provides statistical data on the federal budget for an extended period of about 60 years in the past to projections of four years in the future. Includes federal debt and federal employment.

Key Indicators of the Labour Market. Available from Routledge. • Biennial. $125.00. Published by the International Labour Office (http://www.ilo.org). Provides data on 20 key indicators in 220 countries. Includes labor force statistics, employment, unemployment, part-time workers, wages, productivity, poverty indicators, and related topics.

Public Employment. Bureau of the Census, U.S. Department of Commerce. Available from U.S. Government Printing Office. • Annual.

Social Statistics of the United States. Mark S. Littman, editor. Bernan Press. • 2000. $65.00. Includes statistical data on population growth, labor force, occupations, environmental trends, leisure time use, income, poverty, taxes, and other economic or demographic topics.

Statistical Abstract of the United States. Available from U. S. Government Printing Office. • Annual. $51.00. Issued by the U. S. Bureau of the Census.

A Statistical Portrait of the United States: Social Conditions and Trends. Mark S. Littman, editor. Bernan Press. • 1998. $89.00. Covers "social, economic, and environmental trends in the United States over the past 25 years." Includes statistical tables, graphs, and analysis relating to such topics as population, income, poverty, wealth, labor, housing, education, healthcare, air/water quality, and government. (Statistical Portrait of the United States: Social Conditions and Trends Series).

Survey of Current Business. Available from U. S. Government Printing Office. • Monthly. $63.00 per year. Issued by Bureau of Economic Analysis, U. S. Department of Commerce. Presents a wide variety of business and economic data.

TRADE/PROFESSIONAL ASSOCIATIONS

American Federation of Government Employees. 80 F St., N.W., Washington, DC 20001. Phone: (202)737-8700 or (202)639-6419 Fax: (202)639-6441 E-mail: comments@afge.org • URL: http://www.afge.org • Affiliated with AFL-CIO.

American Federation of State, County and Municipal Employees. 1625 L St., N.W., Washington, DC 20036-5687. Phone: (202)429-1000 or (202)659-0446 Fax: (202)429-1293 E-mail: education@afscme.org • URL: http://www.afscme.org.

Civil Service Employees Association. PO Box 7125, Capitol Sta., Box 7125, Albany, NY 12224-0125. Phone: 800-342-4146 or (518)257-1000 Fax: (518)462-3639 E-mail: donohue@cseainc.org • URL: http://www.csealocal1000.org • AFL-CIO. Represents state and local government employees from all public employee classifications. Negotiates work contracts; represents members in grievances; provides legal assistance for on-the-job problems; provides advice and assistance on federal, state, and local laws affecting public employees. Conducts research, training and education programs. Compiles statistics.

National Association of Government Employees. 159 Burgin Parkway, Quincy, MA 02169-4213. Phone: (617)376-0220 Fax: (617)376-0285 • URL: http://www.nage.org • Supersedes Federal Employees Veterans Association.

National Federation of Federal Employees. 1016 16th St., N.W., Suite 300, Washington, DC 20036. Phone: (202)862-4400 Fax: (202)862-4432 E-mail: rcrandall@nffe.org • URL: http://www.nffe.org.

Tax Analysts. 400 S Maple Ave., Ste. 400, Falls Church, VA 22046. Phone: 800-955-2444 or (703)533-4400 Fax: (703)533-4444 E-mail: cservice@tax.org • URL: http://www.tax.org • Reviews all tax law developments, federal, state, international comprehensively; compiles statistics. **Convention/Meeting:** none.

OTHER SOURCES

Carroll's Federal Organization Charts. Carroll Publishing. • Every six weeks. $1,000.00 per year. Provides 200 large, fold-out paper charts showing personnel relationships in 2,100 federal departments and agencies. Charts are also available online and on CD-ROM.

Government Discrimination: Equal Protection Law and Litigation. James A. Kushner. West Group. • Semiannual. $244.00 per year. Looseleaf service. Covers discrimination in employment, housing, and other areas by local, state, and federal offices or agencies. (Civil Rights Series).

Government Employee Relations Report. BNA, Inc. • Weekly. $1,144.00 per year. Three looseleaf volumes. Concerned with labor relations in the public sector.

GOVERNMENT EXPENDITURES

See: FEDERAL BUDGET

GOVERNMENT FINANCE

See: PUBLIC FINANCE

GOVERNMENT HOUSING PROJECTS

See: HOUSING

GOVERNMENT INVESTIGATIONS

GENERAL WORKS

Congressional Investigations: Law and Practice. John C. Grabow. Aspen Publishers, Inc. • $95.00. Looseleaf service. Periodic supplementation.

ABSTRACTS AND INDEXES

PAIS International in Print. Public Affairs Information Service, Inc. • Monthly. $850.00 per year; cumulations three times a year. Provides topical citations to the worldwide literature of public affairs, economics, demographics, sociology, and trade. Text in English; indexed materials in English, French, German, Italian, Portuguese and Spanish.

CD-ROM DATABASES

PAIS on CD-ROM. Public Affairs Information Service, Inc. • Quarterly. $1,995.00 per year. Provides a CD-ROM version of the online service, *PAIS International.* Contains over 500,000 citations to the literature of contemporary social, political, and economic issues.

ENCYCLOPEDIAS AND DICTIONARIES

Encyclopedia of Crime and Justice. Available from Gale Cengage Learning. • 2001. $475.00. Second edition. Four volumes. Published by Macmillan Reference USA. Contains extensive information on a wide variety of topics pertaining to crime, criminology, social issues, and the courts. (A complete revision of 1982 edition.).

Encyclopedia of Crime and Punishment. David Levinson, editor. Sage Publications, Inc. • 2002. $600.00. Four volumes. Contains 425 signed entries

dealing with civil, criminal, media, corporate, and international issues. Includes material on fraud, police science, correctional institutions, social matters, methodology, national surveys, and crime statistics.

Encyclopedia of Governmental Advisory Organizations. Gale Cengage Learning. • 2003. $685.00. 18th edition. Contains more than 7,300 entries describing activities and personnel. Complete contact information.

World of Criminal Justice. Gale Cengage Learning. • 2002. $160.00. Two volumes. Contains both topical and biographical entries relating to the criminal justice system and criminology.

ONLINE DATABASES

Newspaper Abstracts Daily. ProQuest Inc. • Provides online coverage (citations and abstracts) of 25 major newspapers. Covers business, economics, current affairs, health, fitness, sports, education, technology, government, consumer affairs, psychology, the arts, and the social sciences. Time period is 1986 to date, with daily updates. Inquire as to online cost and availability.

PAIS International. Public Affairs Information Service, Inc. • Corresponds to the former printed publications, *PAIS Bulletin* (1976-90) and *PAIS Foreign Language Index* (1972-90), and to the current *PAIS International in Print* (1991 to date). Covers economic, political, and sociological material appearing in periodicals, books, government documents, and other publications. Updating is monthly. Inquire as to online cost and availability.

TRADE/PROFESSIONAL ASSOCIATIONS

Federal Criminal Investigators Association. PO Box 23400, Washington, DC 20026. Phone: 800-403-3374 or (630)969-8537 Fax: 800-528-3492 or 800-528-3492 E-mail: fcianat@aol.com • URL: http://www.fedcia.org • Serves as professional fraternal organization dedicated to the advancement of federal law enforcement officers and the citizens they serve. Aims to ensure law enforcement professionals have the tools and support network to meet the challenges of future criminal investigations while becoming more community oriented. Intends to pursue mission by promoting professionalism, enhancing the image of federal officers, fostering cooperation among all law enforcement professionals, providing a fraternal environment for the advancement of the membership and community. Helps charitable programs and organizations.

Society of Professional Investigators. PO Box 1128, Baltimore, MD 11710. Phone: (516)781-1000 Fax: (516)783-0000 E-mail: info@spionline.org • URL: http://www.spionline.org.

GOVERNMENT OFFICIALS

See: BUREAUCRACY; GOVERNMENT EMPLOYEES

GOVERNMENT PROCUREMENT

See: GOVERNMENT PURCHASING

GOVERNMENT PUBLICATIONS

See also: CENSUS REPORTS

ABSTRACTS AND INDEXES

U. S. Government Periodicals Index. Congressional Information Service, Inc. • Quarterly. $995.00 per year; with annual cumulation, $1,295.00 per year. An index to approximately 180 periodicals issued by

various agencies of the federal government.

BIBLIOGRAPHIES

Bibliographic Guide to Government Publications: U. S. Available from Gale Cengage Learning. • Annual. $650.00. Two volumes. Published by G. K. Hall & Co. Lists U. S. government publications.

Bibliographic Guide to Government Publications: United States. Available from Gale Cengage Learning. • Annual. $680.00. Two volumes. Published by G. K. Hall & Co. Lists government publications from countries other than the U. S.

Lesko's Info-PowerIII: Over 45,000 Free and Low Cost Sources of Information. Information U.S.A. Inc. • 1996. $39.95. Third edition.

Monthly Catalog of United States Government Publications. U. S. Government Printing Office. • Monthly. $52.00 per year. Modified in 1996. Print edition now consists of very brief entries, indexed only by key words in titles.

Subject Bibliography Index: A Guide to U. S. Government Information. Available from U. S. Government Printing Office. • Annual. Free. Issued by the Superintendent of Documents. Lists currently available subject bibliographies by title and by topic. Each *Subject Bibliography* describes government books, periodicals, posters, pamphlets, and subscription services available for sale from the Government Printing Office.

U. S. Government Books: Publications for Sale by the Government Printing Office. U. S. Government Printing Office. • Quarterly. Free. Describes best selling government documents and "new titles that reflect today's news and consumer issues.".

U. S. Government Information Catalog of New and Popular Titles. U. S. Government Printing Office. • Irregular. Free. Includes recently issued and popular publications, periodicals, and electronic products.

U. S. Government Information for Business. U. S. Government Printing Office. • Annual. Free. A selected list of currently available publications, periodicals, and electronic products on business, trade, labor, federal regulations, economics, and other topics. Also known as *Business Catalog.*

U.S. Government Subscriptions. U. S. Government Printing Office. • Quarterly. Free. Includes agency and subject indexes.

DIRECTORIES

Congressional Directory. Office of Membership Grassroots Management. • Covers: Members of Congress. Entries include: List of members of Congress by state includes member party and home city; alphabetical list by member name includes addresses, phone, fax, e-mail, committee/subcommittee assignments, names of key staff members, and photos.

Directory of Federal Libraries. William R. Evinger, editor. Greenwood Publishing Group, Inc. • 1997. $99.50. Third edition. (Directory of Federal Library Series).

Directory of Government Document Collections and Librarians. Government Documents Roundtable. American Library Association. • Triennial. $57.50. A guide to federal, state, local, foreign, and international document collections in the U.S. Includes name of librarians and other government document professionals.

The Internet Blue Pages: The Guide to Federal Government Web Sites. Information Today, Inc. • Annual. $34.95. Provides information on more than 1,800 Web sites used by various agencies of the federal government. Includes indexes to agencies and topics. Links to all Web sites listed are available at http://www.fedweb.com. (CyberAge Books.).

National Five Digit Zip Code and Post Office Directory. U.S. Postal Service. • Annual. Two volumes. Formerly *National Zip Code and Post Office Directory-.*

United States Government Manual. National Archives and Records Administration. Office of the Federal Register. • Description: Provides information on the agencies of the executive, judicial, and legislative branches of the Federal government. Contains a section on terminated or transferred agencies.

HANDBOOKS AND MANUALS

Guide to U. S. Government Publications. Gale Cengage Learning. • Annual. $230.00. Catalogs "important series, periodicals, and reference tools" published annually by the federal government. Includes references to annual reports of various agencies.

Standard Industrial Classification Manual. U.S. Department of Commerce, Bureau of the Census. Available from U.S. Government Printing Office. • 1987. $36.00.

Tapping the Government Grapevine: The User-Friendly Guide to U. S. Government Information Sources. Judith S. Robinson, editor. Greenwood Publishing Group, Inc. • 1998. $47.95. Third edition. Includes source information on statistics, regulations, patents, technology, nonprint items, bibliographies, and indexes. A special chapter by Karen Smith covers "Foreign and International Documents.".

United States Government Printing Office Style Manual. U. S. Government Printing Office. • 2000. $41.00. 29th edition. Supersedes the 1984 edition (28th). Designed to achieve uniformity in the style and form of government printing.

Using Government Documents: A How-To-Do-It Manual for School Librarians. Melody S. Kelly. Neal-Schuman Publishers, Inc. • 1992. $27.50. (How-to-Do-It Manuals Series).

Using Government Information Sources, Electronic and Print. Marilyn K. Moody and Jean L. Sears. Greenwood Publishing Group, Inc. • 2001. $125.00. Third edition. Contains detailed information in four sections on subject searches, agency searches, statistical searches, and special techniques for searching. Appendixes give selected agency and publisher addresses, telephone numbers, and computer communications numbers.

INTERNET DATABASES

FedWorld: A Program of the United States Department of Commerce. National Technical Information Service. Phone: (703)605-6000 Fax: (703)605-6900 E-mail: webmaster@fedworld.gov • URL: http://www.fedworld.gov • Web site offers "a comprehensive central access point for searching, locating, ordering, and acquiring government and business information." Emphasis is on searching the Web pages, databases, and government reports of a wide variety of federal agencies. Fees: Free.

FirstGov: Your First Click to the U. S. Government. General Services Administration. Phone: 800-333-4636 or (202)501-0705 E-mail: public.affairs@gsa.gov • URL: http://www.firstgov.gov • Free Web site provides extensive links to federal agencies covering a wide variety of topics, such as agriculture, business, consumer safety, education, the environment, government jobs, grants, health, social security, statistics sources, taxes, technology, travel, and world affairs. Also provides links to federal forms, including IRS tax forms. Searching is offered, both keyword and advanced.

GPO Access. U. S. Government Printing Office Sales Program, Bibliographic Systems Branch. Phone: 888-293-6498 or (202)512-1530 Fax: (202)512-1262 E-mail: gpoaccess@gpo.gov • URL: http://www.access.gpo.gov • Web site provides searching of the GPO's Sales Product Catalog (SPC), also known as Publications Reference File (PRF). Covers all "Government information products currently offered for sale by the Superintendent of Documents." There are also

specialized search pages for individual databases, such as the *Code of Federal Regulations*, the *Federal Register*, and *Commerce Business Daily*. Updated daily. Fees: Free.

ONLINE DATABASES

Catalog of U.S. Government Publications. U. S. Government Printing Office. • Contains over 375,000 online citations to U. S. government publications, 1976 to date, with monthly updates. Corresponds to the printed *Monthly Catalog of United States Government Publications*. Inquire as to online cost and availability.

GPO Sales Product Catalog. U. S. Government Printing Office. • An online guide to federal government publications in print (currently for sale), forthcoming, and recently out-of-print. Daily updates. Inquire as to online cost and availability.

PERIODICALS AND NEWSLETTERS

D T T P (Documents to the People). Government Documents Round Table. American Library Association. • Quarterly. $30.00 per year. Formerly-*Documents to the People*.

Federal Register. Office of the Federal Register. Available from U.S. Government Printing Office. • Daily except Saturday and Sunday. $764.00 per year. Publishes regulations and legal notices issued by federal agencies, including executive orders and presidential proclamations. Issued by the National Archives and Records Administration (http://www.nara.gov).

Government Publications News. Bernan Associates. • Monthly. Free. Controlled circulation newsletter providing information on recent publications from the U. S. Government Printing Office and selected international agencies.

Internet Connection: Your Guide to Government Resources. Glasser Legalworks. • 10 times a year. $89.00 per year. Newsletter (print) devoted to finding free or low-cost U. S. Government information on the Internet. Provides detailed descriptions of government Web sites.

Journal of Government Information: An International Review of Policy, Issues an d Resources. Elsevier. • Bimonthly. Institutions, $653.00 per year.

GOVERNMENT PURCHASING

See also: GOVERNMENT CONTRACTS; GOVERNMENT PUBLICATIONS

DIRECTORIES

United States Government Manual. National Archives and Records Administration. Office of the Federal Register. • Description: Provides information on the agencies of the executive, judicial, and legislative branches of the Federal government. Contains a section on terminated or transferred agencies.

United States Government Purchasing and Sales Directory. U.S. Small Business Administration. Available from U.S. Government Printing Office. • 1994. $24.00.

PERIODICALS AND NEWSLETTERS

Commerce Business Daily. Industry and Trade Administration, U.S. Department of Commerce. U.S. Department of Commerce. • Description: Lists notices of proposed government procurement actions, contract awards, sales of government property, and other procurement information. Includes 500-1,000 notices in each edition; notices appear in the publication only once.

Federal Register. Office of the Federal Register. Available from U.S. Government Printing Office. • Daily except Saturday and Sunday. $764.00 per

year. Publishes regulations and legal notices issued by federal agencies, including executive orders and presidential proclamations. Issued by the National Archives and Records Administration (http://www.nara.gov).

Government Contracts Update: How to Target, Win, and Perform Government Contracts. United Communications Group (UCG). • Biweekly. $277.00 per year. Newsletter.

Government Product News. Penton Media, Inc. • 13 times a year. $50.00 per year.

Navy Supply Corps Newsletter. Available from U. S. Government Printing Office. • Bimonthly. $30.00 per year. Newsletter issued by U. S. Navy Supply Systems Command. Provides news of Navy supplies and stores activities.

TRADE/PROFESSIONAL ASSOCIATIONS

National Association of State Procurement Officials. c/o Association Management Resources, 167 W. Main St., Suite 600, Lexington, KY 40507. Phone: (859)231-1877 or (606)231-1963 Fax: (859)514-9188 E-mail: msisler@amrinc.net • URL: http://www.naspo.org • Purchasing officials of the states and territories. Formerly National Association of State Purchasing Officials.

National Institute of Government Purchasing. 151 Spring St., Herndon, VA 20170. Phone: 800-367-6447 or (703)736-8900 Fax: (703)736-9644 E-mail: membership@nigp.org • URL: http://www.nigp.org.

OTHER SOURCES

Federal Contracts Report. BNA, Inc. • Weekly. $1,453.00 per year. Two looseleaf volumes. Developments affecting federal contracts and grants.

Government Contracts Reports. CCH, Inc. • Weekly. $2,600.00 per year. 10 looseleaf volumes. Laws and regulations affecting government contracts.

GOVERNMENT REGULATION OF INDUSTRY

See: REGULATION OF INDUSTRY

GOVERNMENT REGULATION OF RAILROADS

See: INTERSTATE COMMERCE

GOVERNMENT RESEARCH

See also: GOVERNMENT PUBLICATIONS; GOVERNMENT STATISTICS

ABSTRACTS AND INDEXES

NTIS Alerts: Business & Economics. National Technical Information Service. • Text: Semimonthly. $210.00 per year.

NTIS Alerts: Government Inventions for Licensing. National Technical Information Service. • Semimonthly. $270.00 per year. Identifies new inventions available from various government agencies. Covers a wide variety of industrial and technical areas. Formerly *Abstract Newsletter*.

PAIS International in Print. Public Affairs Information Service, Inc. • Monthly. $850.00 per year; cumulations three times a year. Provides topical citations to the worldwide literature of public affairs, economics, demographics, sociology, and trade. Text in English; indexed materials in English, French, German, Italian, Portuguese and Spanish.

CD-ROM DATABASES

PAIS on CD-ROM. Public Affairs Information Service, Inc. • Quarterly. $1,995.00 per year.

Provides a CD-ROM version of the online service, *PAIS International*. Contains over 500,000 citations to the literature of contemporary social, political, and economic issues.

DIRECTORIES

Government Research Directory. Gale. • Covers: About 6,000 research and development facilities operated or sponsored by the United States or Canadian governments, including research centers, bureaus, and institutes; testing and experiment stations; data collection and analysis centers; government-supported user facilities; cooperative research programs; and major research-supporting service units. Entries include: Unit name, address, phone, fax, mail address, e-mail addresses, name of director, staff, year founded, parent agencies, description of activities and fields of research, special research facilities, publications, public services, and library collections.

GRA Professional Directory of Who's Who in Governmental Research. Governmental Research Association, Inc. • Annual. $50.00. Lists information on governmental research organization throughout the country.

Unique 3-in-1 Research and Development Directory. Government Data Publications, Inc. • Annual. $15.00. Government contractors in the research and development fields. Included with subscription to *R and D Contracts Monthly*. Formerly *Research and Development Directory*.

ENCYCLOPEDIAS AND DICTIONARIES

Encyclopedia of Governmental Advisory Organizations. Gale Cengage Learning. • 2003. $685.00. 18th edition. Contains more than 7,300 entries describing activities and personnel. Complete contact information.

HANDBOOKS AND MANUALS

Using Government Information Sources, Electronic and Print. Marilyn K. Moody and Jean L. Sears. Greenwood Publishing Group, Inc. • 2001. $125.00. Third edition. Contains detailed information in four sections on subject searches, agency searches, statistical searches, and special techniques for searching. Appendixes give selected agency and publisher addresses, telephone numbers, and computer communications numbers.

INTERNET DATABASES

FedWorld: A Program of the United States Department of Commerce. National Technical Information Service. Phone: (703)605-6000 Fax: (703)605-6900 E-mail: webmaster@fedworld.gov • URL: http://www.fedworld.gov • Web site offers "a comprehensive central access point for searching, locating, ordering, and acquiring government and business information." Emphasis is on searching the Web pages, databases, and government reports of a wide variety of federal agencies. Fees: Free.

FirstGov: Your First Click to the U. S. Government. General Services Administration. Phone: 800-333-4636 or (202)501-0705 E-mail: public.affairs@gsa.gov • URL: http://www.firstgov.gov • Free Web site provides extensive links to federal agencies covering a wide variety of topics, such as agriculture, business, consumer safety, education, the environment, government jobs, grants, health, social security, statistics sources, taxes, technology, travel, and world affairs. Also provides links to federal forms, including IRS tax forms. Searching is offered, both keyword and advanced.

ONLINE DATABASES

NTIS Database. National Technical Information Service. • Contains citations and abstracts to unrestricted reports of government-sponsored research, 1964 to date. Covers a wide range of technical, engineering, business, and social science topics. Monthly updates. Inquire as to online cost and availability.

PAIS International. Public Affairs Information Service, Inc. • Corresponds to the former printed publications, *PAIS Bulletin* (1976-90) and *PAIS Foreign Language Index* (1972-90), and to the current *PAIS International in Print* (1991 to date). Covers economic, political, and sociological material appearing in periodicals, books, government documents, and other publications. Updating is monthly. Inquire as to online cost and availability.

Research Centers and Services Directories. Gale Cengage Learning. • Contains profiles of about 30,000 research centers, organizations, laboratories, and agencies in 147 countries. Corresponds to the printed *Research Centers Directory, International Research Centers Directory, Government Research Directory*, and *Research Services Directory*. Updating is semiannual. Inquire as to online cost and availability.

PERIODICALS AND NEWSLETTERS

Federal Assistance Monitor: Semi-Monthly Report on Federal and Private Grant Opportunities. Community Development Services. CD Publications. • Semimonthly. $339.00 per year; with online edition, $379.00 per year. Newsletter. Provides news of federal grant and loan programs for social, economic, and community purposes. Monitors grant announcements, funding, and availability. Formerly *Federal Research Report*.

GRA Reporter. Governmental Research Association. • Description: Provides a research bibliography and news of members and their organizations. Recurring features include news of research, reports of meetings, and notices of publications available.

The Information Freeway Report: Free Business and Government Information Via Modem. Washington Researchers, Ltd. • Monthly. $160.00 per year. Newsletter. Provides news of business and government databases that are available free of charge through the Internet or directly. Emphasis is on federal government databases and electronic bulletin boards (Fedworld).

R and D Contracts Monthly (Research and Development): A Continuously Up-dated Sales and R and D Tool For All Research Organizations and Manufacturers. Government Data Publications, Inc. • Monthly. $96.00 per year. Lists recently awarded government contracts. Annual *Directory* available.

RESEARCH CENTERS AND INSTITUTES

Bureau of Governmental Research. University of Maryland. 4511 Knox Rd., Ste. 301, College Park, MD 20742. Phone: (301)403-4403 Fax: (301)403-4404 E-mail: bgr@bgr.umd.edu • URL: http://www.bgr.umd.edu/.

Division of Government Research. University of New Mexico. 1920 Lomas Blvd., N.E., Albuquerque, NM 87131. Phone: (505)277-3305 Fax: (505)277-6540 E-mail: dgrint@unm.edu • URL: http://www.unm.edu/~dgrint.

Inter-University Consortium for Political and Social Research. University of Michigan. P.O. Box 1248, Ann Arbor, MI 48106-1248. Phone: (734)998-9900 Fax: (734)998-9889 E-mail: netmail@icpsr.umich.edu • URL: http://www.icpsr.umich.edu.

TRADE/PROFESSIONAL ASSOCIATIONS

Governmental Research Association. PO Box 292300, Birmingham, AL 35229. Phone: (205)726-2482 Fax: (205)726-2900 E-mail: rancoble@nccppr.org • URL: http://www.graonline.org • Individuals professionally engaged in governmental research. Furthers research that will improve government in the public interest. Encourages development and use of effective methods of administration in government and standards for judging the results.

GOVERNMENT RESEARCH SUPPORT

See: FEDERAL AID

GOVERNMENT SERVICE

See: CIVIL SERVICE

GOVERNMENT, STATE

See: STATE GOVERNMENT

GOVERNMENT STATISTICS

See also: BUSINESS STATISTICS; GOVERNMENT PUBLICATIONS; STATISTICS SOURCES

ABSTRACTS AND INDEXES

American Statistics Index: A Comprehensive Guide and Index to the Statistical Publications of the United States Government. Congressional Information Service, Inc. • Monthly. Price varies. Quarterly and annual cumulations.

Current Index to Statistics: Applications, Methods, and Theory. American Statistical Association. • Annual. Price on application. An index to journal articles on statistical applications and methodology.

CD-ROM DATABASES

OECD Statistical Compendium. Organization for Economic Cooperation and Development. • Semiannual. $1,905.00 per year for 1 to 10 users. CD-ROM contains more than 730,000 monthly, quarterly, and annual time series for OECD countries, 1960 to date. Includes fully searchable data on agriculture, food, economic indicators, national accounts, employment, energy, finance, industry, technology, and foreign trade. Results can be displayed in various forms.

DIRECTORIES

Government Information on the Internet. Greg R. Notess. Bernan Associates. • Annual. $38.50. directory of publicly-accessible Internet sites maintained by the U. S. Government. Also includes selected foreign government sites, state sites, and non-government sites containing government-provided data.

HANDBOOKS AND MANUALS

Guide to Everyday Economic Statistics. Gary E. Clayton and Martin G. Giesbrecht. McGraw-Hill. • 2001. $19.90. Fifth edition. Contains clear explanations of the commonly used economic indicators.

Using Government Information Sources, Electronic and Print. Marilyn K. Moody and Jean L. Sears. Greenwood Publishing Group, Inc. • 2001. $125.00. Third edition. Contains detailed information in four sections on subject searches, agency searches, statistical searches, and special techniques for searching. Appendixes give selected agency and publisher addresses, telephone numbers, and computer communications numbers.

INTERNET DATABASES

Business 2.0 Web Guide to the Best Business Links. Business 2.0 Media Inc. Phone: (415)293-4800 E-mail: support@business2.com • URL: http://www.business2.com/webguide • Web site presents an extensive, searchable directory of links to "the best, most informative, and authoritative web pages." Twenty main categories cover business, finance, career, company information, people, and technology topics, with thousands of subtopics, all linking to Web sites recommended by experienced business researchers. Fees: Free.

Fedstats. Federal Interagency Council on Statistical Policy. Phone: (202)395-7254 • URL: http://www.fedstats.gov • Web site features an efficient search facility for full-text statistics produced by more than 100 federal agencies, including the Census Bureau, the Bureau of Economic Analysis, and the Bureau of

Labor Statistics. Boolean searches can be made within one agency or for all agencies combined. Links are offered to international statistical bureaus, including the UN, IMF, OECD, UNESCO, Eurostat, and 20 individual countries. Fees: Free.

FedWorld: A Program of the United States Department of Commerce. National Technical Information Service. Phone: (703)605-6000 Fax: (703)605-6900 E-mail: webmaster@fedworld.gov • URL: http://www.fedworld.gov • Web site offers "a comprehensive central access point for searching, locating, ordering, and acquiring government and business information." Emphasis is on searching the Web pages, databases, and government reports of a wide variety of federal agencies. Fees: Free.

FirstGov: Your First Click to the U. S. Government. General Services Administration. Phone: 800-333-4636 or (202)501-0705 E-mail: public.affairs@gsa.gov • URL: http://www.firstgov.gov • Free Web site provides extensive links to federal agencies covering a wide variety of topics, such as agriculture, business, consumer safety, education, the environment, government jobs, grants, health, social security, statistics sources, taxes, technology, travel, and world affairs. Also provides links to federal forms, including IRS tax forms. Searching is offered, both keyword and advanced.

FreeLunch.com. Economy.com, Inc. Phone: (610)696-8700 Fax: (610)696-1678 • URL: http://www.freelunch.com • Web site provides free access to more than 1.5 million economic and financial data series, covering industry, demographics, labor markets, prices, retail sales, government spending, trade, interest rates, housing starts, the stock market, and many other topics. Data is available for various time periods in either chart or table form. Searching is offered. Fees: Free, but registration required. Economy.com, Inc. also offers fee-based economic analysis at *The Dismal Scientist* site (http://www.dismal.com).

STATISTICS SOURCES

Internal Revenue Service Data Book. Available from U. S. Government Printing Office. • Annual. $8.00. "Contains statistical tables and organizational information previously included in the Internal Revenue Service annual report." (Internal Revenue Service Publication, 55B.).

Revenue Statistics. OECD Publications and Information Center. • Annual. $65.00. Presents data on government revenues in OECD countries, classified by type of tax and level of government. Text in English and French.

Social Statistics of the United States. Mark S. Littman, editor. Bernan Press. • 2000. $65.00. Includes statistical data on population growth, labor force, occupations, environmental trends, leisure time use, income, poverty, taxes, and other economic or demographic topics.

Standard & Poor's Statistical Service. Current Statistics. Standard & Poor's. • Monthly. $688.00 per year. Includes 10 *Basic Statistics* sections, *Current Statistics Supplements* and *Annual Security Price Index Record.*

Statistical Abstract of the United States. Available from U. S. Government Printing Office. • Annual. $51.00. Issued by the U. S. Bureau of the Census.

A Statistical Portrait of the United States: Social Conditions and Trends. Mark S. Littman, editor. Bernan Press. • 1998. $89.00. Covers "social, economic, and environmental trends in the United States over the past 25 years." Includes statistical tables, graphs, and analysis relating to such topics as population, income, poverty, wealth, labor, housing, education, healthcare, air/water quality, and government. (Statistical Portrait of the United

States: Social Conditions and Trends Series).

TRADE/PROFESSIONAL ASSOCIATIONS

American Statistical Association. 732 N Washington St., Alexandria, VA 22314-1943. Phone: 888-231-3473 or (703)684-1221 Fax: (703)684-2037 E-mail: asainfo@amstat.org • URL: http://www.amstat.org • Professional society of persons interested in the theory, methodology, and application of statistics to all fields of human endeavor.

National Association for Public Health Statistics and Information Systems. 801 Roeder Rd., Ste. 650, Silver Spring, MD 20910. Phone: (301)563-6001 Fax: (301)563-6012 E-mail: hq@napshsis.org • URL: http://www.naphsis.org • Members are officials of state and local health agencies.

GOVERNMENT SURPLUS

See: SURPLUS PRODUCTS

GRADUATE WORK IN UNIVERSITIES

See also: ADULT EDUCATION; BUSINESS EDUCATION; COLLEGES AND UNIVERSITIES

GENERAL WORKS

Gravy Training: Inside the Real World of Business Schools. Stuart Crainer and Des Dearlove. Jossey-Bass. • 1999. $25.00. Provides a critical look at major American business schools. (Business and Management Series).

Overeducated Worker? The Economics of Skill Utilization. Lex Borghans and Andries De Grip. Edward Elgar Publishing, Inc. • 2000. $95.00.

ABSTRACTS AND INDEXES

Current Index to Journals in Education (CIJE). Oryx Press. • Monthly. $245.00 per year. Semiannual cumulations, $475.00.

Education Index. H. W. Wilson Co. • 10 times a year. Quarterly and annual cumulations. Price varies.

Educational Administration Abstracts. Sage Publication, Inc. • Quarterly. Institutions, $722.00 per year.

CD-ROM DATABASES

College Blue Book CD-ROM. Available from Gale Cengage Learning. • Annual. $250.00. Produced by Macmillan Reference USA. Serves as electronic version of printed *College Blue Book.* Provides detailed information on programs, degrees, and financial aid sources in the U.S. and Canada.

DIRECTORIES

AACSB: The International Association for Management Education Membership Directory. AACSB-The Association to Advance Collegiate Schools of Business. • Annual. $15.00. Lists over 800 member institutions offering instructional programs in business administration at the college level.

American Universities and Colleges. American Council on Education USA. Walter de Gruyter, Inc. • Quadrennial. $249.50. Two volumes. Produced in collaboration with the American Council on Education. Provides full descriptions of more than 1,900 institutions of higher learning, including details of graduate and professional programs.

Barron's Guide to Graduate Business Schools. Barron's Educational Series. • Biennial. Contains profiles of more than 600 business schools offering graduate business degrees in the U. S. and Canada. Includes advice on choosing a school.

Faculty White Pages. Gale Cengage Learning. • 1991. $135.00. 91st edition. "Telephone book" clas-

sified arrangement of over 537,000 U. S. college faculty members in 41 subject sections. A roster of institutions is included.

Peterson's Computer Science and Electrical Engineering Programs. Peterson's. • 1996. $24.95. A guide to 900 accredited graduate degree programs related to computers or electrical engineering at colleges and universities in the U. S. and Canada.

Peterson's Graduate and Professional Programs: Business, Education, Health, Information Studies, Law, and Social Work. Peterson's. • 2002. $49.95. Provides details of graduate and professional programs in business, law, information, and other fields at colleges and universities. (Peterson's Graduate and Professional Program Series). Formerly *Peterson's Guide to Graduate Programs in Business, Education, Health, Information Studies, Law and Social Work.*

Peterson's Graduate and Professional Programs in Engineering and Applied Sciences. Peterson's. • Annual. $49.95. Provides details of more than 3,400 graduate and professional programs in engineering and related fields at colleges and universities. (Peterson's Graduate in Professional Programs Series). Formerly *Peterson's Guide to Graduate Programs in Engineering and Professional Sciences.*

Peterson's Guide to Graduate and Professional Programs: An Overview. Peterson's. • Annual. $49.95. Provide details for more than 31,000 graduate programs at 1,700 colleges and universities. (Peterson's Graduate and Professinal Program Series).

Peterson's Guide to MBA Programs: The Most Comprehensive Guide to U. S., Canadian, and International Business Schools. Peterson's. • 2002. $29.95. Provides detailed information on about 850 graduate programs in business at 700 colleges and universities in the U. S., Canada, and other countries.

Peterson's Professional Degree Programs in the Visual and Performing Arts. Peterson's. • Annual. $21.95. A directory of more than 900 degree programs in art, music, theater, and dance at 600 colleges and professional schools.

The World of Learning. Available from Taylor and Francis, Inc. • Annual. $525.00. Covers about 30,000 colleges, libraries, museums, learned societies, academies, and research institutions throughout the world. Published by Europa Publications.

HANDBOOKS AND MANUALS

Directory of Graduate Programs. National Communication Association. • Irregular. Available only online. Accredited institutions that offer advanced deree in 84 graduate program areas. Degrees not included are J.D., D.D.S., M.D. and some other professional degrees.

Financing Graduate School: How to Get Money for Your Master's or Ph.D. Patricia McWade. Peterson's. • 1996. $16.95. Second revised edition. Discusses the practical aspects of various types of financial aid for graduate students. Includes bibliographic and directory information.

Official Guide for GMAT Review (Graduate Management Admission Test). Graduate Management Admissions Council. Educational Testing Service. • 2003. 10th edition. Price on application. Provides sample tests, answers, and explanations for the Graduate Management Admission Test (GMAT).

ONLINE DATABASES

Dissertation Abstracts Online. PROQUEST. • Citations to all dissertations accepted for doctoral degrees by accredited U.S. educational institutions, 1861 to date. Includes British theses, 1988 to date. Inquire as to online cost and availability.

Education Index Online. H. W. Wilson Co. • Indexes a wide variety of periodicals related to schools, colleges, and education, 1984 to date. Monthly updates.

Inquire as to online cost and availability.

PERIODICALS AND NEWSLETTERS

AACSB Newsline. AACSB--American Assembly of Collegiate Schools of Business. • Description: Covers issues and events affecting management education, and Association projects and activities. Recurring features include notices of publications available and news of educational opportunities.

Journal of Higher Education. Ohio State University Press. • Bimonthly. Individuals, $50.00 per year; institutions, $110.00 per year. Issues important to faculty administrators and program managers in higher education.

Resources in Education. Educational Resources Information Center. Available from U.S. Government Printing Office. • Monthly. Reports on educational research.

RESEARCH CENTERS AND INSTITUTES

Center for the Study of Higher Education. Pennsylvania State University. 400 Rackley Bldg., University Park, PA 16802. Phone: (814)865-6346 Fax: (814)865-3638 E-mail: cshe@psu.edu • URL: http://www.ed.psu.edu/cshe.

ERIC Clearinghouse on Higher Education. George Washington University. Graduate School of Education and Human Development, One Dupont Circle, Suite 630, Washington, DC 20036. Phone: 800-773-3742 or (202)296-2597 Fax: (202)452-1844 E-mail: wcummings@eric-he.edu • URL: http://www.eriche.org.

STATISTICS SOURCES

Degrees and Other Awards Conferred by Institutions of Higher Education. Available from U. S. Government Printing Office. • Annual. Issued by the National Center for Education Statistics, U. S. Department of Education. Provides data on the number of degrees awarded at the associate's, bachelor's, master's, and doctor's levels. Includes fields of study and racial-ethnic-sex data by major field or discipline.

Digest of Education Statistics. Available from U. S. Government Printing Office. • Annual. $51.00. Covers all areas of education from kindergarten through graduate school. Includes data from both government and private sources. Compiled by National Center for Education Statistics, U. S. Department of Education.

Occupational Projections and Training Data. Available from U. S. Government Printing Office. • Biennial. $21.00. Issued by Bureau of Labor Statistics, U. S. Department of Labor. Contains projections of employment change and job openings over the next 15 years for about 500 specific occupations. Also includes the number of associate, bachelor's, master's, doctoral, and professional degrees awarded in a recent year for about 900 specific fields of study.

School Enrollment, Social and Economic Characteristics of Students. Available from U. S. Government Printing Office. • Annual. $2.25. Issued by the U. S. Bureau of the Census. Presents detailed tabulations of data on school enrollment of the civilian noninstitutional population three years old and over. Covers nursery school, kindergarten, elementary school, high school, college, and graduate school. Information is provided on age, race, sex, family income, marital status, employment, and other characteristics.

Survey of Salaries. AACSB International-The Association to Advance Collegiate Schools of Business. • Annual. $25.00, Reports aggregate salary data of business school administrators and faculty. Text in English and Spanish.

TRADE/PROFESSIONAL ASSOCIATIONS

AACSB International - The Association to Advance Collegiate Schools of Business. 600 Emerson Rd.,

Suite 300, St. Louis, MO 63141-6762. Phone: (314)872-8481 Fax: (314)872-8495 E-mail: webmaster@aacsb.edu • URL: http://www.aacsb.edu • Formerly AACSB - International Association for Management Education.

Association of Graduate Schools in Association of American Universities. 1200 New York Ave., Suite 550, Washington, DC 20005. Phone: (202)408-7500 Fax: (202)408-8184 E-mail: matt_owens@aau.edu.

Association of Master of Business Administration Executives. c/o AMBA Center, 388 E Main St., Ste. A, Branford, CT 06405. Phone: (203)315-5221 Fax: (203)483-6186.

Consortium for Graduate Study in Management. 5585 Pershing, Ste. 240, Saint Louis, MO 63112-4621. Phone: 888-658-6814 or (314)877-5500 Fax: (314)877-5505 E-mail: frontdesk@cgsm.org • URL: http://www.cgsm.org.

Council of Graduate Schools. One Dupont Circle, N.W., Suite 430, Washington, DC 20036-1173. Phone: (202)223-3791 Fax: (202)331-7157 E-mail: cflagg@cgs.nche.edu • URL: http://www.cgsnet.org • Formerly Council of Graduate Schools in the United States.

Graduate Management Admission Council. 1600 Tysons Blvd., Ste. 1400, McLean, VA 22102. Phone: (866)505-6559 or (703)749-0131 Fax: (703)749-0169 E-mail: webmaster1@gmac.com • URL: http://www.gmac.com • Graduate schools of management and business administration. Works to establish criteria for use in admission to graduate management programs. Provides professional development for academic administrators and seminars for admissions officers. Maintains Graduate +Management Admission Search Service, a program that provides institutions with the names of qualified students with desirable characteristics. Employs Educational Testing Service to develop and administer the Graduate Management Admission Test. Conducts research on student selection issues and political and social issues related to graduate management education.

Graduate Record Examinations Board. PO Box 6000, 225 Phillips Blvd., PO Box 6000, Princeton, NJ 08541-6000. Phone: (866)473-4373 or (609)771-7670 Fax: (610)290-8975 E-mail: gre-info@rosedale.org • URL: http://www.ets.org/gre • Participants are appointees of the Association of Graduate Schools in Association of American Universities, the Council of Graduate Schools, and the GRE Board. Has responsibility for the Graduate Record Examinations Program (GRE) to assist in graduate school selection. Seeks to ensure that the program is carried out in the best interests of graduate education, the students, and the schools. Educational Testing Service provides technical advice, research expertise, professional counsel, and administers the GRE. Graduate Record Examinations, first administered in 1937, were initiated as a joint venture of the Carnegie Foundation for the Advancement of Teaching and the graduate school deans of four eastern U.S. universities. The examination and programs in which they were used became the responsibility of ETS when it began operating in 1948, until 1966, when the present structure was formed in order to give broader representation to the graduate education community.

OTHER SOURCES

Educational Rankings Annual: A Compilation of Approximately 3,500 Published Rankings and Lists on Every Aspect of Education. Gale Cengage Learning. • Annual. $265.00. Provides national, regional, local, and international rankings of a wide variety of educational institutions, including business and professional schools.

GRAFT (POLITICS)

See: CRIME AND CRIMINALS

GRAIN DEALERS

See: GRAIN INDUSTRY

GRAIN ELEVATORS

See: GRAIN INDUSTRY

GRAIN INDUSTRY

ABSTRACTS AND INDEXES

Field Crop Abstracts: Monthly Abstract Journal on World Annual Cereal, Legume, Root, Oilseed and Fibre Crops. Available from CABI Publishing North America. • Monthly. Institutions, $1,775.00 per year. Online edition available, $1,820.00 per year. Published in England by CABI Publishing, formerly Commonwealth Agricultural Bureaux. Provides worldwide coverage of the literature.

Food Science and Technology Abstracts. International Food Information Service Publishing. • Monthly. $1,780.00 per year. Provides worldwide coverage of the literature of food technology and food production.

Foods Adlibra: Key to the World's Food Literature. General Mills, Inc. Foods Adlibra Publications. • Semimonthly. $240.00 per year. Provides journal citations and abstracts to the literature of food technology and packaging.

ALMANACS AND YEARBOOKS

Agricultural and Mineral Commodities Year Book. Available from Taylor & Francis Group. • Annual. $225.00. Published by Europa Publications. Contains descriptive product profiles, price data, export-import data, and production statistics for major commodities of the world. Includes commodity histories, uses, markets, demand trends, and information about trade agreements and key commodity organizations.

CD-ROM DATABASES

AGRICOLA on SilverPlatter. Available from SilverPlatter Information, Inc. • Quarterly. $825.00 per year. Produced by the National Agricultural Library. Provides about three million citations on CD-ROM to the literature of agriculture, agricultural economics, animal sciences, entomology, fertilizer, food, forestry, nutrition, pesticides, plant science, water resources, and other topics. Each quarterly disc covers the past ten years, with archival discs available from 1970.

Food Science and Technology Abstracts [CD-ROM]. Available from SilverPlatter Information, Inc. • Quarterly. Produced by International Food Information Service (home page is http://www.ifis.org). Provides worldwide coverage on CD-ROM of the literature of food technology and production. Various types of publications are indexed, with abstracts, including about 1,800 periodicals. Time period is 1969 to date.

OECD Statistical Compendium. Organization for Economic Cooperation and Development. • Semiannual. $1,905.00 per year for 1 to 10 users. CD-ROM contains more than 730,000 monthly, quarterly, and annual time series for OECD countries, 1960 to date. Includes fully searchable data on agriculture, food, economic indicators, national accounts, employment, energy, finance, industry, technology, and foreign trade. Results can be displayed in various forms.

DIRECTORIES

Agriculture: Websites and Glossary. Carol Canada. Nova Science Publishers, Inc. • 2003. $29.50. Lists agricultural Web sites according to 24 main categories and 16 subcategories. Includes a glossary and an index.

Grain and Milling Annual. Sosland Publishing Co. • Annual. $100.00. Features listings of the major grain facilities in the U.S. and Canada. Provides an annual overview of the U.S. grain industry and a complete reference to equipment and service suppliers. Formerly *North American Grain and Milling Annual.*

Major Food and Drink Companies of the World. Available from Gale Cengage Learning. • Annual. $880.00. Two volumes. Published by Graham & Whiteside. Contains profiles and trade names for more than 9,800 important food and beverage companies in various countries. In addition to foods, includes both alcoholic and nonalcoholic drink products.

NFGA Directory-Yearbook. • Annual. Price on application.

Thomas Food and Beverage Market Place. Grey House Publishing. • 2004. $495.00. Three volumes. Contains more than 40,000 entries covering food companies, beverages, food equipment, warehouse companies, food brokers, wholesalers, importers, and exporters. Formerly *Thomas Food Industry Register.*

ENCYCLOPEDIAS AND DICTIONARIES

Encyclopedia of Agriculture Science. Charles J. Arntzen and Ellen M. Ritter, editors. Elsevier. • 1994. $900.00. Four volumes.

Encyclopedia of Food and Culture. Gale Cengage Learning. • 2002. $395.00. Three volumes. Contains 600 articles covering various aspects of food and its place in society, from agronomy to zucchini. Includes illustrations and a detailed index.

FINANCIAL RATIOS

Almanac of Business and Industrial Financial Ratios. Leo Troy. Aspen Publishers, Inc. • 2003. $125.95. Includes CD-Rom. Contains financial ratios derived from federal tax returns. Ratios for each of about 200 industries are arranged according to company asset size. (Almanac of Business and Industrial Financial Ratios Series).

Annual Statement Studies. The Risk Management Association. • Annual. Median and quartile financial ratios are given for over 400 kinds of manufacturing, wholesale, retail, construction, and consumer finance establishments. Data is sorted by both asset size and sales volume. Includes a clearly written "Definition of Ratios" and an alphabetical industry index.

Annual Statement Studies: Industry Default Probabilities and Cash Flow Measures. The Risk Management Association. • Annual. $145.00. Serves as a companion volume to the original *Annual Statement Studies.* Gives probability of default estimates on a percentage scale for more than 450 industries. Includes changes in position year-by-year for eight financial statement line items and provides percentage measures of cash flow.

INTERNET DATABASES

Business 2.0 Web Guide to the Best Business Links. Business 2.0 Media Inc. Phone: (415)293-4800 E-mail: support@business2.com • URL: http://www.business2.com/webguide • Web site presents an extensive, searchable directory of links to "the best, most informative, and authoritative web pages." Twenty main categories cover business, finance, career, company information, people, and technology topics, with thousands of subtopics, all linking to Web sites recommended by experienced business researchers. Fees: Free.

Fedstats. Federal Interagency Council on Statistical Policy. Phone: (202)395-7254 • URL: http://www.fedstats.gov • Web site features an efficient search facility for full-text statistics produced by more than 100 federal agencies, including the Census Bureau, the Bureau of Economic Analysis, and the Bureau of Labor Statistics. Boolean searches can be made

within one agency or for all agencies combined. Links are offered to international statistical bureaus, including the UN, IMF, OECD, UNESCO, Eurostat, and 20 individual countries. Fees: Free.

FreeLunch.com. Economy.com, Inc. Phone: (610)696-8700 Fax: (610)696-1678 • URL: http://www.freelunch.com • Web site provides free access to more than 1.5 million economic and financial data series, covering industry, demographics, labor markets, prices, retail sales, government spending, trade, interest rates, housing starts, the stock market, and many other topics. Data is available for various time periods in either chart or table form. Searching is offered. Fees: Free, but registration required. Economy.com, Inc. also offers fee-based economic analysis at *The Dismal Scientist* site (http://www.dismal.com).

USDA. United States Department of Agriculture. Phone: (202)720-2791 E-mail: agsec@usda.gov • URL: http://www.usda.gov • The USDA home page has six sections: News and Information; What's New; About USDA; Agencies; Opportunities; Search and Help. Keyword searching is offered from the USDA home page and from various individual agency home pages. Agencies are the Economic Research Service, Agricultural Marketing Service, National Agricultural Statistics Service, National Agricultural Library, and about 12 others. Updating varies. Fees: Free.

ONLINE DATABASES

Agricola. U.S. National Agricultural Library. • Covers worldwide agricultural literature. Over 3.3 million citations, 1970 to present, with monthly updates. Inquire as to online cost and availability.

CAB Abstracts. CAB Publishing North America. • Contains 46 specialized abstract collections covering over 10,000 journals and monographs in the areas of agriculture, horticulture, forest products, farm products, nutrition, dairy science, poultry, grains, animal health, entomology, etc. Time period is 1972 to date, with monthly updates. Inquire as to online cost and availability. *CAB Abstracts on CD-ROM* also available, with annual updating.

Food Science and Technology Abstracts [online]. IFIS North American Desk. • Produced by International Food Information Service. Provides about 500,000 online citations, with abstracts, to the international literature of food science, technology, commodities, engineering, and processing. Approximately 2,000 periodicals are covered. Time period is 1969 to date, with monthly updates. Inquire as to online cost and availability.

FOODS ADLIBRA. General Mills, Inc. • Contains online citations, with abstracts, to the technical and business literature of food processing and packaging. New products and new ingredients are featured. Covers about 250 trade journals and 500 research journals from 1974 to date, with monthly updates. Inquire as to online cost and availability.

PERIODICALS AND NEWSLETTERS

Amber Waves. Available from U. S. Government Printing Office. • Quarterly. $38.00 per year. Replaces *Agricultural Outlook; Food Review*; and *Rural America*. Provides research and analysis from the U.S. Department of Agriculture's Economic Research Service. Includes economic data on agriculture, food, trade, and environmental factors.

Livestock and Grain Market News Branch Weekly Summary. U.S. Dept of Agriculture. Livestock and Grain Market News Branch. • Weekly. $85.00 per year. Formerly *Grain and Feed Weekly Summary and Statistics.*

Milling and Baking News. Sosland Publishing Co. •

Weekly. $128.00 per year. News magazine for the breadstuffs industry.

PRICE SOURCES

Commercial Review. Oregon Feed and Grain Association. Commercial Review, Inc. • Weekly. $35.00 per year.

Nebraska Farmer. Farm Progress Companies. • 15 times a year. $23.95 per year.

RESEARCH CENTERS AND INSTITUTES

Cereal Disease Laboratory-U.S. Department of Agricultural Research Service. University of Minnesota, 1551 Lindig St., St. Paul, MN 55108. Phone: (612)625-6299 Fax: (612)649-5054 E-mail: markh@cdl.umn.edu • URL: http://www.cdl.umn.edu/.

Food and Feed Grains Institute. Kansas State University. 105 Waters Hall, Manhattan, KS 66506-4030. Phone: (785)532-4056 Fax: (785)532-5861 E-mail: ffgi@ksu.edu • URL: http://www.ksu.edu/ffgi.

STATISTICS SOURCES

Agricultural Statistics. Available from U. S. Government Printing Office. • Annual. $38.00. Produced by the National Agricultural Statistics Service, U. S. Department of Agriculture. Provides a wide variety of statistical data relating to agricultural production, supplies, consumption, prices/price-supports, foreign trade, costs, and returns, as well as farm labor, loans, income, and population. In many cases, historical data is shown annually for 10 years. In addition to farm data, includes detailed fishery statistics.

Business Statistics of the United States. Linz Audain and Cornelia J. Strawser. Bernan Associates. • Annual. $147.00. Based on *Business Statistics*, formerly issue by the Bureau of Economic Analysis, U. S. Department of Commerce. Provides basic data for a wide variety of U. S. industries, services, and economic indicators. Most statistics are shown annually for 30 years and monthly for the most recent four years.

FAO Production Yearbook. Available from Bernan Associates. • Annual. $45.00. Published by the Food and Agriculture Organization (http://www.fao.org). Contains worldwide data on agriculture, land use, farm crops, livestock, and agricultural prices.

FAO Quarterly Bulletin of Statistics. Food and Agriculture Organization of the United Nations. Available from UNIPUB. • Quarterly. $20.00 per year. Provides international data on agricultural production, trade, and prices, covering the major commodities of many countries. Text in English, French, and Spanish. Formerly *FAO Monthly Bulletin of Statistics.*

FAO Trade Yearbook. Available from Bernan Associates. • Annual. $45.00. Published by the Food and Agriculture Organization (http://www.fao.org). Provides extensive worldwide data on exports and imports of agricultural commodities, fertilizers, tractors, and pesticides. Includes more than 130 tables of detailed statistics.

Statistical Annual: Grains, Options on Agricultural Futures. Chicago Board of Trade. • Annual. Includes historical data on Wheat Futures, Options on Wheat Futures, Corn Futures, Options on Corn Futures, Oats Futures, Soybean Futures, Options on Soybean Futures, Soybean Oil Futures, Soybean Meal Futures.

Survey of Current Business. Available from U. S. Government Printing Office. • Monthly. $63.00 per year. Issued by Bureau of Economic Analysis, U. S. Department of Commerce. Presents a wide variety of business and economic data.

United States Census of Agriculture. U.S. Bureau of the Census. • Quinquennial. Results presented in reports, tape, CD-ROM, and Diskette files.

World Agricultural Supply and Demand Estimates.

Available from U. S. Government Printing Office. • Monthly. $52.00 per year. Issued by the Economics and Statistics Service and the Foreign Agricultural Service of the U. S. Department of Agriculture. Consists mainly of statistical data and tables.

World Food Data and Statistics. Euromonitor International. • 2004. $650.00. Provides five-year data for a wide variety of food products in 52 countries. Includes market size, consumer expenditures, price indicators, and retail distribution data for many kinds of meat, fish, fruits, vegetables, dairy products, baked goods, condiments, canned food, and frozen food.

TRADE/PROFESSIONAL ASSOCIATIONS

Commodity Markets Council. 1300 L St. NW, Ste. 1020, Washington, DC 20005. Phone: (202)842-0400 Fax: (202)789-7223 E-mail: ccochran@cmcmarkets.org • URL: http://cmcmarkets.org • Represents and supports grain exchanges, boards of trade, grain companies, milling and processing companies, transportation companies, futures commission merchants, and banks.

Grain Elevator and Processing Society. 301 Fourth Ave., S., Ste. 365, Minneapolis, MN 55415-0026. Phone: (612)339-4625 Fax: (612)339-4644 E-mail: info@geaps.com • URL: http://www.geaps.com • Formerly Society of Grain Elevator Superintendents.

National Grain and Feed Association. 1250 Eye St., N.W., Ste. 1003, Washington, DC 20005-3922. Phone: (202)289-0873 Fax: (202)289-5388 E-mail: ngfa@ngfa.org • URL: http://www.ngfa.org • Formerly Grain and Feed Dealers National Association.

North American Export Grain Association. 1250 I St. NW, Ste. 1003, Washington, DC 20005-3939. Phone: (202)682-4030 Fax: (202)682-4033 E-mail: info@naega.org • URL: http://www.naega.org • U.S. and Canadian exporters of grain and oilseeds from the United States.

Transportation, Elevator and Grain Merchants Association. 1300 L St. NW, Ste. 1020, Washington, DC 20005. Phone: (202)842-0400 Fax: (202)789-7223 E-mail: jkinnaird@ngtc.org • URL: http://www.grainnet.com • Formerly Terminal Elevator Grain Association.

U.S. Grains Council. 1400 K St. NW, Ste. 1200, Washington, DC 20005. Phone: (202)789-0789 Fax: (202)898-0522 E-mail: grains@grains.org • URL: http://www.grains.org • Federation of feed grain producer organizations, seed trade associations, and organizations of grain processors, exporters, dealers and related agribusiness manufacturers. Maintains 10 international offices for development of foreign markets in over 80 countries for barley, corn, grain sorghum and related products.

GRANITE

See: QUARRYING

GRANTS-IN-AID

See also: ARTS MANAGEMENT; FEDERAL AID; FOUNDATIONS

GENERAL WORKS

A Casebook of Grant Proposals in the Humanities. William Coleman and others, editors. Neal-Schuman Publishers, Inc. • 1982. $45.00.

From Idea to Funded Project: Grant Proposals that Work. Jane C. Belcher and Julia M. Jacobsen. Greenwood Publishing Group, Inc. • 1992. $26.50. Fourth edition. Formerly *A Process for the Development of Ideas.*

Grants for Arts, Culture, and the Humanities. The Foundation Center. • 1997. $75.00. (Grants Guides Series).

ABSTRACTS AND INDEXES

Foundation Grants Index. The Foundation Center. • Irregular. $165.00 per year. Over 73,000 grants of $10,000 or more. Formerly *Foundation Grants Quarterly.*

DIRECTORIES

Annual Register of Grant Support: A Directory of Funding Sources. Information Today, Inc. • Annual. $229.00. Contains information on more than 3,500 corporate, private, and public organizations that provide grants in 11 major subject areas, including 61 specific sub-categories.

Big Book of Library Grant Money 2002-2003: Profiles of Private and Corporate Foundations and Direct Corporate Givers Receptive to Library Grant Proposals. American Library Association. • 2002. $250.00. Provides profiles, contacts, past contributions data, application procedures, and biographical information on foundation personnel. (Prepared by the Taft Group for the American Library Association.).

Directory of Operating Grants. Richard M. Eckstein. Research Grant Guides. • Annual. $59.50. Contains profiles for approximately 800 foundations that award grants to nonprofit organizations for such operating expenses as salaries, rent, and utilities. Geographical arrangement, with indexes.

Directory of Research Grants. Greenwood Publishing Group, Inc. • Annual. $135.00. More than 5,100 research grants available from government, business, foundation and private sources.

Foundation Grants to Individuals. The Foundation Center. • Biennial. $65.00. Over 3,200 foundations that make grants to individuals.

Foundation Reporter: Comprehensive Profiles and Giving Analyses of America's Major Private Foundations. The Taft Group. • Annual. $490.00. Provides detailed information on major U. S. foundations. Eight indexes (location, grant type, recipient type, personnel, etc.).

Government Assistance Almanac: The Guide to Federal, Domestic, Financial and Other Programs Covering Grants, Loans, Insurance, Personal Payments and Benefits. J. Robert Dumouchel, editor. Omnigraphics, Inc. • Annual. $235.00. Describes more than 1,400 federal assistance programs available from about 50 agencies. Includes statistics, a directory of 3,000 field offices, and comprehensive indexing.

Grants for Libraries and Information Services. The Foundation Center. • Annual. $75.00. Foundations and organizations which have awarded grants made the preceding year for public, academic, research, special, and school libraries; for archives and information centers; for consumer information; and for philanthropy information centers.

Grants Register. Palgrave Macmillan Ltd. • Covers: over 3,500 sources in the United Kingdom, Ireland, Australia, Canada, the United States, and other English-speaking areas which award financial aid for graduate study, research, or travel, including scholarships, fellowships, grants, awards for creative work, etc. Many are not available to United States nationals. Entries include: Name of awarding organization, name of award, address, subjects, purpose, number of awards offered and their value, place and duration of tenancy, eligibility requirements, application procedure.

Guide to Federal Funding for Governments and Non-Profits. Government Information Services. • Quarterly. $339.00 per year. Looseleaf service. Contains detailed descriptions of federal grant programs in economic development, housing, transportation, social services, science, etc.

Semimonthly *Supplement* available: *Federal Grant Deadline Calendar.*

Peterson's Scholarships, Grants, and Prizes: Your Complete Guide to College Aid from Private Sources. Peterson's. • 1998. $26.95. Third edition.

HANDBOOKS AND MANUALS

Foundation Fundamentals: A Guide for Grantseekers. The Foundation Center. • 1999. $24.95. Sixth edition.

How to Write Proposals that Produce. Joel P. Bowman and Bernadine P. Branchaw. Greenwood Publishing Group, Inc. • 1992. $23.50. An extensive guide to effective proposal writing for both nonprofit organizations and businesses. Covers writing style, intended audience, format, use of graphs, charts, and tables, documentation, evaluation, oral presentation, and related topics.

Proposal Planning and Writing. Lynn E. Miner and Jeremy T. Miner. Greenwood Publishing Group, Inc. • 2003. $39.95. Third edition. Discusses the steps necessary to locate and obtain funding from the federal government, foundations, and corporations.

INTERNET DATABASES

FedWorld: A Program of the United States Department of Commerce. National Technical Information Service. Phone: (703)605-6000 Fax: (703)605-6900 E-mail: webmaster@fedworld.gov • URL: http://www.fedworld.gov • Web site offers "a comprehensive central access point for searching, locating, ordering, and acquiring government and business information." Emphasis is on searching the Web pages, databases, and government reports of a wide variety of federal agencies. Fees: Free.

FirstGov: Your First Click to the U. S. Government. General Services Administration. Phone: 800-333-4636 or (202)501-0705 E-mail: public.affairs@gsa.gov • URL: http://www.firstgov.gov • Free Web site provides extensive links to federal agencies covering a wide variety of topics, such as agriculture, business, consumer safety, education, the environment, government jobs, grants, health, social security, statistics sources, taxes, technology, travel, and world affairs. Also provides links to federal forms, including IRS tax forms. Searching is offered, both keyword and advanced.

Welcome to the Foundation Center. The Foundation Center. Phone: (212)620-4230 or (212)807-3679 Fax: (212)807-3677 E-mail: mfn@fdncenter.org • URL: http://www.fdncenter.org • Web site provides a wide variety of information about foundations, grants, and philanthropy, with links to philanthropic organizations. "Grantmaker Information" link furnishes descriptions of available funding.

ONLINE DATABASES

GrantSelect. Oryx Press. • Online service provides detailed descriptions of more than 10,000 grants offered by government and organizations in the U. S. Includes grants in a wide variety of subject fields. Contains current information with daily updates. Inquire as to online cost and availability.

PERIODICALS AND NEWSLETTERS

Federal Assistance Monitor: Semi-Monthly Report on Federal and Private Grant Opportunities. Community Development Services. CD Publications. • Semimonthly. $339.00 per year; with online edition, $379.00 per year. Newsletter. Provides news of federal grant and loan programs for social, economic, and community purposes. Monitors grant announcements, funding, and availability. Formerly *Federal Research Report.*

Federal Grants and Contracts Weekly: Funding Opportunities in Research, Training and Services. Aspen Publishers, Inc. • 50 times a year. $450.00 per year. Newsletter.

Grants for Libraries Hotline. Quinlan Publishing Group. • Monthly. $129.00 per year. Newsletter.

Provides news of grants and awards specifically for libraries (http://www.grantshotline.com). Includes "Deadline Update," a list of awarding agencies or programs, approximate dollar amounts available, deadlines, contacts (telephone numbers), and dates of newsletter profiles.

Grantsmanship Center Magazine: A Compendium of Resources for Nonprofit Organizations. Grantsmanship Center. • Irregular. Free to qualified personnel. Contains a variety of concise articles on grant-related topics, such as program planning, proposal writing, fundraising, non-cash gifts, federal project grants, benchmarking, taxation, etc.

RESEARCH CENTERS AND INSTITUTES

Foundation Center. Foundation Center. 79 5th Ave./16th St., New York, NY 10003-3076. Phone: 800-424-9836 or (212)620-4230 Fax: (212)807-3677 E-mail: communications@foundationcenter.org • URL: http://foundationcenter.org • Strengthens the nonprofit sector by advancing knowledge about U.S. philanthropy, maintains a comprehensive database on U.S. grantmakers and their grants, and operates research, education and training programs designed to advance philanthropy.

TRADE/PROFESSIONAL ASSOCIATIONS

Council for Aid to Education. 212 Lexington Ave., 21st Fl., New York, NY 10016. Phone: (212)661-5800 Fax: (212)661-9766 E-mail: akaplan@cae.org • URL: http://www.cae.org.

National Association of Student Financial Aid Administrators. 1129 20th St., N.W., Suite 400, Washington, DC 20036-5020. Phone: (202)785-0453 Fax: (202)785-1487 E-mail: ask@nasfaa.org • URL: http://www.nsfaa.org • Serves as a national forum for matters related to student aid.

National Grants Management Association. 11654 Plaza America Dr., No. 609, Reston, VA 20190-4700. Phone: (703)648-9023 Fax: (703)648-9024 E-mail: info@ngma.org • URL: http://www.ngma.org • Strengthens the relationship between grant-making agencies and grant recipients by empowering both sides with knowledge through training, seminars, workshops, and conferences. Focuses on federal, state, and local governments and private foundations that provide grants, grants-in-aid, cooperative agreements, and subsidies.

GRAPE INDUSTRY

See: FRUIT INDUSTRY

GRAPHIC ARTS INDUSTRY

See also: COMMERCIAL ART; DESIGN IN INDUSTRY; LITHOGRAPHY; PRINTING AND PRINTING EQUIPMENT INDUSTRIES

GENERAL WORKS

Institute of Paper Science and Technology Graphic Arts Bulletin. Cengage Learning. • Monthly. $400.00 per volume. Formerly *Graphic Arts Literature Abstracts.*

The Visual Display of Quantitative Information. Edward R. Tufte. Graphics Press. • 2001. $40.00. Second edition. A classic work on the graphic display of numerical data, including many illustrations. The two parts are "Graphical Practice," and "Theory of Data Graphics.".

ABSTRACTS AND INDEXES

Art Index. H. W. Wilson Co. • Quarterly. Annual cumulations. Price varies. Subject and author index to periodicals in art, architecture, industrial design, city planning, photography, and various related topics.

GATF World. Graphic Arts Technical Foundation. • Bimonthly. $75.00 per year. Technical articles of interest to the graphic communications industry. Incorporates *Graphic Arts Abstracts.*

DIRECTORIES

Graphic Arts Blue Book. Reed Business Information. • Covers: printing plants, bookbinders, imagesetters, platemakers, paper merchants, paper manufacturers, printing machinery manufacturers and dealers, and others serving the graphic arts industry (Standard Industrial Classification (SIC) code 2600, 2700). Eight editions: New York edition (7,000 establishments) covers metropolitan New York and the state of New Jersey; Southeastern edition (10,500 establishments) covers Kentucky, Tennessee, Alabama, Mississippi, Virginia (except Washington suburbs), North Carolina, South Carolina, Georgia, and Florida; Northeastern edition (6,000 establishments) covers Connecticut, Maine, Massachusetts, New Hampshire, New York (upstate only), Rhode Island, and Vermont and the eastern Canadian provinces; Delaware Valley-Ohio edition (8,500 establishments) covers Pennsylvania, Maryland, Delaware, District of Columbia and its Virginia suburbs, and Ohio; Midwestern edition (13,000 establishments) covers Illinois, Indiana, Iowa, Michigan, Minnesota, Missouri, Wisconsin, North and South Dakota; Southwestern edition (5,500 establishments) covers Arizona, southern California, Hawaii, southern Nevada; Pacific Northwestern edition (5,500 establishments), covers northern California, northern Nevada, Oregon, Washington, Montana, Idaho, Wyoming, Utah, Alaska, and the western provinces of Canada. Texas central edition (8000 establishments) covering Texas, Colorado, New Mexico, Oklahoma, Louisiana, Kansas, Missouri, and Nebraska. Entries include: Company name, address, phone, names and titles of executives, name of buyer, list of products or services, year established.

ENCYCLOPEDIAS AND DICTIONARIES

Graphically Speaking: An Illustrated Guide to the Working Language of Design and Publishing. Mark Beach. Coast to Coast Books. • 1992. $29.50. Provides practical definitions of 2,800 terms used in printing, graphic design, publishing, and desktop publishing. Over 300 illustrations are included, about 40 in color.

FINANCIAL RATIOS

Annual Statement Studies. The Risk Management Association. • Annual. Median and quartile financial ratios are given for over 400 kinds of manufacturing, wholesale, retail, construction, and consumer finance establishments. Data is sorted by both asset size and sales volume. Includes a clearly written "Definition of Ratios" and an alphabetical industry index.

Annual Statement Studies: Industry Default Probabilities and Cash Flow Measures. The Risk Management Association. • Annual. $145.00. Serves as a companion volume to the original *Annual Statement Studies.* Gives probability of default estimates on a percentage scale for more than 450 industries. Includes changes in position year-by-year for eight financial statement line items and provides percentage measures of cash flow.

PIA Financial Ratio Studies. Printing Industries of America, Inc. • Annual. $3,582.00. 18 volumes. $199.00 per volume.

HANDBOOKS AND MANUALS

Getting It Printed: How to Work with Printers and Graphic Arts Services to Assure Quality, Stay on Schedule, and Control Costs. Mark Beach and Eric Kenly. F and W. Publications, Inc. • 1999. $32.99. Third edition.

Graphic Artists Guild Handbook of Pricing and Ethical Guidelines: Pricing and Ethical Guidelines. Graphic Artists Guild. • 2001. $34.95. 10th edition.

Graphic Designer's Production Handbook. Norman Sanders and William Bevington. Hastings House Daytrips Publishers. • 1982. $12.95. Ninth edition. (Visual Communication Books Series).

Newspaper Designer's Handbook. Timothy Harrower. McGraw-Hill. • 2001. $50.00. Fifth edition. Includes CD-ROM. (Humanities, Social Sciences and World Language Series).

ONLINE DATABASES

Art Index Online. H. W. Wilson Co. • Indexes a wide variety of art-related periodicals, 1984 to date. Monthly updates. Inquire as to online cost and availability.

PERIODICALS AND NEWSLETTERS

Color Publishing. PennWell Corp., Advanced Technology Div. • Bimonthly. $29.70 per year.

Graphic Arts Monthly: The Magazine of the Printing Industry. Reed Business Information. • Monthly. Free to qualified personnel; others, $142.99 per year.

In-Plant Graphics. North American Publishing Co. • Monthly. Free. Formerly *In-Plant Reproductions.*

The Magazine for Electronic Publishing Professionals. Publish Media. • Monthly. $39.90 per year. Edited for professional publishers, graphic designers, and industry service providers. Covers new products and emerging technologies for the electronic publishing industry.

Step Inside Design: The World of Design from Inside Out. Dynamic Graphics, Inc. • Bimonthly. $42.00 per year. Formerly *Step-by-Step Graphics.*

TAGA Newsletter. Technical Association of the Graphic Arts. • Description: Disseminates information in the graphic arts industry to members which is international in scope. Recurring features include interviews, news of research, reports of meetings, news of educational opportunities, and standards updates.

RESEARCH CENTERS AND INSTITUTES

Chester F. Carlson Center for Imaging Science. Rochester Institute of Technology, 54 Lomb Memorial Dr., Rochester, NY 14623. Phone: 800-724-2536 or (716)475-5944 Fax: (716)475-5988 E-mail: garley@cis.rit.edu • URL: http://www.cis.rit.edu/.

Design Research Unit. Massachusetts College of Art, 621 Huntington Ave., Boston, MA 02115. Phone: (617)879-7733 Fax: (617)566-4034 E-mail: rstreit@massart.edu • URL: http://www.babel.massart.edu/dru • Conducts research related to the design of printed matter, including annual reports, letterheads, posters, and brochures.

TRADE/PROFESSIONAL ASSOCIATIONS

American Institute of Graphic Arts. 164 Fifth Ave., New York, NY 10010. Phone: 800-548-1634 or (212)807-1990 Fax: (212)807-1799 E-mail: comments@aiga.org • URL: http://www.aiga.org.

Design Management Institute. 101 Tremont St., Ste. 300, Boston, MA 02108. Phone: (617)338-6380 Fax: (617)338-6570 E-mail: dmistaff@dmi.org • URL: http://www.dmi.org • In-house design groups and consultant design firms; individuals involved in the management of designers with in-house corporate design groups or consultant design firms. Aims to share management techniques as applied to design groups, and to facilitate better understanding by business management of the role design can play in achieving business goals. Design disciplines included are: architecture, advertising, communications, exhibit design, graphics, interior design, packaging and product design. Develops and distributes design management education materials. Sponsors seminars for design professionals. Identifies critical areas of design management study; conducts surveys and research on corporate design management. Maintains design management archive. Operates Center for Research, Center for Education, and Center for +Design and Management Resources.

Graphic Artists Guild. 32 Broadway, Ste. 1114, New York, NY 10004-1612. Phone: (212)791-3400 Fax: (212)791-0333 E-mail: admin@gag.org • URL: http://gag.org • Professional graphic artists who work in the disciplines of illustration, graphic design, surface design, computer graphics, and cartoons, and create work for national magazines, newspaper syndicates, books, television, advertising, corporate and promotional materials. Aims to: raise the business and ethical standards in the industry; provide legal and educational services to members; increase public appreciation of graphic artists as professionals. Maintains professional discipline meetings and provides professional education services for each chapter.

Graphic Arts Technical Foundation. 200 Deer Run Rd., Sewickley, PA 15143-2600. Phone: 800-910-4283 or (412)741-6860 Fax: (412)741-2311 E-mail: gain@piagatf.org • URL: http://www.gain.net • Scientific, research, technical, and educational organization serving the international graphic communications industries. Conducts research in all graphic processes and their commercial applications. Conducts seminars, workshops, and forums on graphic arts and environmental subjects. Conducts educational programs, including the publishing of graphic arts textbooks and learning modules, videotapes and CD-ROMs and broadcast video seminars. Conducts training and certification program in sheet-fed offset press operating, Web Offset press operating, Image Assembly, and desktop publishing. Produces test images and quality control devices for the industry. Performs technical services for the graphic arts industry, including problem-solving, material evaluation, and plant audits.

Graphic Communications Conference of the International Brotherhood of Teamsters. 1900 L St. NW, Washington, DC 20036. Phone: (202)462-1400 Fax: (202)721-0600 E-mail: webmessenger@gciu. org • URL: http://www.gciu.org • AFL-CIO; Serves as a Canadian Labour Congress.

Research and Engineering Council of NAPL. 816 Rappahannock Dr., White Stone, VA 22578. Phone: (804)436-9922 Fax: (804)436-9511 E-mail: recouncil@rivnet.com • URL: http://www. recouncil.org.

Society of American Graphic Artists. 32 Union Square, Room 1214, New York, NY 10003. Phone: (212)260-5706 • URL: http://www.clt.astate.edu • Formerly Society of American Erchers, Engravers, Lithographers and Woodcutters.

Technical Association of the Graphic Arts. 68 Lomb Memorial Dr., Rochester, NY 14623-5604. Phone: (585)475-7470 Fax: (585)475-2250 E-mail: tagaofc@aol.com • URL: http://www.taga.org • Formerly Technical Association of the Lithographic Industry.

GRAPHICS, COMPUTER

See: COMPUTER GRAPHICS

GRAPHS AND CHARTS

GENERAL WORKS
The Visual Display of Quantitative Information. Edward R. Tufte. Graphics Press. • 2001. $40.00. Second edition. A classic work on the graphic display of numerical data, including many illustrations. The two parts are "Graphical Practice," and "Theory of Data Graphics.".

ENCYCLOPEDIAS AND DICTIONARIES
Information Graphics: A Comprehensive Illustrated Reference: Visual Tools for Analyzing, Managing, and Communicating. Robert L. Harris. Oxford University Press. • 2000. $50.00. Provides more

than 850 alphabetical entries and about 4,000 illustrations. Covers the practical application of charts, graphs, maps, diagrams, and tables.

PERIODICALS AND NEWSLETTERS
Harvard Management Communication Letter. Harvard Business School Publishing. • Description: Provides information and techniques for managers on effective communication.

Presentations: Technology and Techniques for Effective Communication. VNU Business Media. • Monthly. Free to qualified personnel; others, $69.00 per year. Covers the use of presentation hardware and software, including audiovisual equipment and computerized display systems. Includes an annual "Buyers Guide to Presentation Products.".

GRAPHITE

See: MINES AND MINERAL RESOURCES

GRAVEL INDUSTRY

See: QUARRYING

GREASE

See: LUBRICATION AND LUBRICANTS

GREETING CARD INDUSTRY

TRADE/PROFESSIONAL ASSOCIATIONS
Greeting Card Association. 1156 15th St. NW, Ste. 900, Washington, DC 20005-1717. Phone: (202)393-1778 Fax: (202)331-2714 E-mail: info@ greetingcard.org • URL: http://www.greetingcard. org • Publishers of greeting cards and suppliers of materials.

OTHER SOURCES
Greeting Cards. Available from MarketResearch. com. • 2002. $3,950.00. Published by Global Industry Analysts. Provides worldwide market research data, including profiles of major greeting card companies.

GRINDING AND POLISHING

See: ABRASIVES INDUSTRY

GROCERY BUSINESS

See also: CHAIN STORES; FOOD INDUSTRY; SUPERMARKETS

CD-ROM DATABASES
OECD Statistical Compendium. Organization for Economic Cooperation and Development. • Semiannual. $1,905.00 per year for 1 to 10 users. CD-ROM contains more than 730,000 monthly, quarterly, and annual time series for OECD countries, 1960 to date. Includes fully searchable data on agriculture, food, economic indicators, national accounts, employment, energy, finance, industry, technology, and foreign trade. Results can be displayed in various forms.

DIRECTORIES
Directory of Supermarket, Grocery, and Convenience Store Chains. Chain Store Guide. • Annual. $327.00. Online edition, $747.00. Provides information on about 3,300 food store chains operating 120,000 individual stores. Store locations are given.

Directory of Wholesale Grocers. Chain Store Guide. • Annual. $327.00. Online edition, $747.00. Profiles

over 1,100 cooperatives, voluntaries, non-sponsoring wholesalers, cash and carry warehouses, and nearly 220 service merchandisers. Covers United States and Canada.

Grocery Headquarters: The Newspaper for the Food Industry. Trend Publishing. • Monthly. $80.00 per year. Covers the sale and distribution of food products and other items sold in supermarkets and grocery stores. Edited mainly for retailers and wholesalers. Incorporates (Grocery Distribution).

International Private Label Directory. E. W. Williams Publications Co. • Annual. $75.00. Provides information on over 2,000 suppliers of a wide variety of private label and generic products: food, over-the-counter health products, personal care items, and general merchandise. Formerly *Private Label Directory.*

Plunkett's Food Industry Almanac. Plunkett Research Ltd. • Covers: 340 leading companies in the global food industry. Entries include: Name, address, phone, fax, and key executives. Also includes analysis and information on trends, technology, and statistics in the field.

Thomas Food and Beverage Market Place. Grey House Publishing. • 2004. $495.00. Three volumes. Contains more than 40,000 entries covering food companies, beverages, food equipment, warehouse companies, food brokers, wholesalers, importers, and exporters. Formerly *Thomas Food Industry Register.*

Trade Dimensions' Market Scope. Trade Dimensions. • Covers: Market share for over 1,400 supermarket chains and wholesalers. Entries include: Company name, location, number of stores in the area, market share. Syndicated market areas include 52 AC Nielsen Scantrack markets, all 64 IRI InfoScan markets, all 205 DMAs (Designated Market Areas) and 100 MSAs (government-defined), plus 48 Trad Dimensions markets.

FINANCIAL RATIOS
Almanac of Business and Industrial Financial Ratios. Leo Troy. Aspen Publishers, Inc. • 2003. $125.95. Includes CD-Rom. Contains financial ratios derived from federal tax returns. Ratios for each of about 200 industries are arranged according to company asset size. (Almanac of Business and Industrial Financial Ratios Series).

Food Marketing Industry Speaks. Food Marketing Institute. • Annual. Members, $30.00; non-members, $75.00. Provides data on overall food industry marketing performance, including retail distribution and store operations.

Operations Review. Food Marketing Institute. • Quarterly. $50.00 per year. Includes operating ratios for food retailing companies.

HANDBOOKS AND MANUALS
Convenience Food Store. Entrepreneur Media, Inc. • Looseleaf. $59.50. A practical guide to starting a convenience food store. Covers profit potential, start-up costs, market size evaluation, owner's time required, site selection, lease negotiation, pricing, accounting, advertising, promotion, etc. (Start-Up Business Guide No. E1173.).

Progressive Grocer Guidebook. Trade Dimensions. • Annual. $375.00. Over 800 major chain and independent food retailers and wholesalers in the United States and Canada; also includes food brokers, rack jobbers, candy and tobacco distributors, and magazine distributors.

INTERNET DATABASES
Advance Monthly Sales for Retail Trade and Food Services. U. S. Census Bureau. Phone: 800-541-8345 or (301)763-4636 Fax: (301)457-3842 E-mail: rcb@census.gov • URL: http://www.census.gov/svsd/www/fullpub.html • Web pages provide monthly sales figures for a wide range of retail businesses. Advance, preliminary, and final statistics

are provided for the latest month available in each case, with a previous-year comparison. Updates are monthly.

Business 2.0 Web Guide to the Best Business Links. Business 2.0 Media Inc. Phone: (415)293-4800 E-mail: support@business2.com • URL: http://www.business2.com/webguide • Web site presents an extensive, searchable directory of links to "the best, most informative, and authoritative web pages." Twenty main categories cover business, finance, career, company information, people, and technology topics, with thousands of subtopics, all linking to Web sites recommended by experienced business researchers. Fees: Free.

Fedstats. Federal Interagency Council on Statistical Policy. Phone: (202)395-7254 • URL: http://www.fedstats.gov • Web site features an efficient search facility for full-text statistics produced by more than 100 federal agencies, including the Census Bureau, the Bureau of Economic Analysis, and the Bureau of Labor Statistics. Boolean searches can be made within one agency or for all agencies combined. Links are offered to international statistical bureaus, including the UN, IMF, OECD, UNESCO, Eurostat, and 20 individual countries. Fees: Free.

FreeLunch.com. Economy.com, Inc. Phone: (610)696-8700 Fax: (610)696-1678 • URL: http://www.freelunch.com • Web site provides free access to more than 1.5 million economic and financial data series, covering industry, demographics, labor markets, prices, retail sales, government spending, trade, interest rates, housing starts, the stock market, and many other topics. Data is available for various time periods in either chart or table form. Searching is offered. Fees: Free, but registration required. Economy.com, Inc. also offers fee-based economic analysis at *The Dismal Scientist* site (http://www.dismal.com).

PERIODICALS AND NEWSLETTERS

Food Industry Newsletter: All the Food News That Matters. Newsletters, Inc. • 26 times a year. $245.00 per year. Newsletter. A summary of key industry news for food executives.

Food Trade News. Best-Met Publishing Co., Inc. • Monthly. $36.00 per year. Reports on the retail food industry in Pennsylvania, Delaware, southern New Jersey and northern Maryland.

Modern Grocer. GC Publishing Co. • Monthly. $45.00 per year. Formerly *Modern Grocer.*

Produce Merchandising: The Packer's Retailing and Merchandising Magazine. Vance Publishing Corp. • Monthly. $35.00 per year. Provides information and advice on the retail marketing and promotion of fresh fruits and vegetalbe.

Progressive Grocer: The Magazine of Supermarketing. VNU Business Media. • 18 times a year. $129.00 per year.

STATISTICS SOURCES

Annual Benchmark Report for Retail Trade and Food Services...A Detailed Summary of Retail Sales, Purchases, Accounts Receivable, Inventories, and Food Service Sales. Available from U. S. Government Printing Office. • Annual. $13.00. Issued by the U.S. Census Bureau. Provides detailed annual and monthly retail statistics for the most recent 10 years. Includes data for various kinds of retail outlets, including automobiles, furniture, appliances, building supplies, grocery stores, drug stores, gasoline stations, clothing, sporting goods, department stores, and restaurants.

Business Statistics of the United States. Linz Audain and Cornelia J. Strawser. Bernan Associates. • Annual. $147.00. Based on *Business Statistics,* formerly issue by the Bureau of Economic Analysis, U. S. Department of Commerce. Provides basic data for a wide variety of U. S. industries, services, and economic indicators. Most statistics are shown an-

nually for 30 years and monthly for the most recent four years.

Survey of Current Business. Available from U. S. Government Printing Office. • Monthly. $63.00 per year. Issued by Bureau of Economic Analysis, U. S. Department of Commerce. Presents a wide variety of business and economic data.

WEFA Industrial Monitor. John Wiley and Sons, Inc. • Annual. $65.00. Prepared by industry analysts at WEFA, an economic forecasting and consulting firm (originally Wharton Econometric Forecasting Associates). Contains discussions of the outlook for major U. S. industries, with many 10-year forecasts (WEFA Web site is http://www.wefa.com).

TRADE/PROFESSIONAL ASSOCIATIONS

Food Distributors International. 201 Park Washington Ct., Falls Church, VA 22046. Phone: (703)532-9400 Fax: (703)538-4673 E-mail: info@ifps.org • URL: http://www.fdi.org • Comprised of food distribution companies that supply and service independent wholesale grocers and foodservice operations. Goal is to educate and inform members on industry events, government affairs, and technology.

Food Marketing Institute. 2345 Crystal Dr., Ste. 800, Arlington, VA 22202-4801. Phone: (202)452-8444 Fax: (202)429-4519 E-mail: info@ifps.org • URL: http://www.fmi.org • Grocery retailers and wholesalers. Maintains liaison with government and consumers. Conducts 30 educational conferences and seminars per year. Conducts research programs; compiles statistics.

Food Products Association. 1350 I St. NW, Ste. 300, Washington, DC 20005. Phone: 800-355-0983 or (202)639-5900 Fax: (202)639-5932 E-mail: membership@fpa-food.org • URL: http://www.fpa-food.org • Leading authority on food science and food safety for the food industry. Members produce processed and packaged fruits and vegetables, meat and poultry, seafood, cereals, dairy products, drinks, juices, and other specialty items or provides supplies and services to food manufacturers.

Grocery Manufacturers of America. 1010 Wisconsin Ave., N.W., Suite 900, Washington, DC 20007. Phone: (202)337-9400 Fax: (202)337-4508 E-mail: info@gmabrands.com • URL: http://www.gmabrands.com • Members are global manufacturers of food and nonfood products sold in the United States.

Grocery Manufacturers of America, Inc. 2401 Pennsylvania Ave., NW, 2nd Fl., Washington, DC 20037. Phone: (202)337-9400 Fax: (202)337-4508 E-mail: info@gmabrands.com • URL: http://www.gmabrands.com • Absorbed Association of Sales and Marketing Companies.

National Grocers Association. 1005 N Glebe Rd., Ste. 250, Arlington, VA 22201-5758. Phone: (703)516-0700 Fax: (703)516-0115 E-mail: info@nationalgrocers.org • URL: http://www.nationalgrocers.org • Independent food retailers; wholesale food distributors servicing 29,000 food stores. Promotes industry interests and works to advance understanding, trade, and cooperation among all sectors of the food industry. Represents members' interests before the government. Aids in the development of programs designed to improve the productivity and efficiency of the food distribution industry. Offers services in areas such as store planning and engineering, personnel selection and training, operations, and advertising. Sponsors seminars and in-house training. Maintains liaison with Women Grocers of America (see separate entry), which serves as an advisory arm.

GROSS NATIONAL PRODUCT

See also: NATIONAL ACCOUNTING

CD-ROM DATABASES

OECD Statistical Compendium. Organization for Economic Cooperation and Development. • Semiannual. $1,905.00 per year for 1 to 10 users. CD-ROM contains more than 730,000 monthly, quarterly, and annual time series for OECD countries, 1960 to date. Includes fully searchable data on agriculture, food, economic indicators, national accounts, employment, energy, finance, industry, technology, and foreign trade. Results can be displayed in various forms.

ENCYCLOPEDIAS AND DICTIONARIES

Worldmark Encyclopedia of National Economies. Gale Cengage Learning. • 2002. $325.00. Four volumes. Covers both the current and historical development of the economies of 200 foreign nations. Includes analysis and statistics.

INTERNET DATABASES

Bureau of Economic Analysis (BEA). U. S. Department of Commerce, Bureau of Economic Analysis. Phone: (202)606-9900 Fax: (202)606-5310 E-mail: webmaster@bea.doc.gov • URL: http://www.bea.doc.gov • Web site includes "News Release Information" covering national, regional, and international economic estimates from the BEA. Highlights of releases appear online the same day, complete text and tables appear the next day. "Recent News Releases" section provides titles for past nine months, with links. "BEA Data and Methodology" includes "Frequently Requested NIPA Data" (national income and product accounts, such as gross domestic product and personal income). Other statistics are available. Fees: Free.

Business 2.0 Web Guide to the Best Business Links. Business 2.0 Media Inc. Phone: (415)293-4800 E-mail: support@business2.com • URL: http://www.business2.com/webguide • Web site presents an extensive, searchable directory of links to "the best, most informative, and authoritative web pages." Twenty main categories cover business, finance, career, company information, people, and technology topics, with thousands of subtopics, all linking to Web sites recommended by experienced business researchers. Fees: Free.

Fedstats. Federal Interagency Council on Statistical Policy. Phone: (202)395-7254 • URL: http://www.fedstats.gov • Web site features an efficient search facility for full-text statistics produced by more than 100 federal agencies, including the Census Bureau, the Bureau of Economic Analysis, and the Bureau of Labor Statistics. Boolean searches can be made within one agency or for all agencies combined. Links are offered to international statistical bureaus, including the UN, IMF, OECD, UNESCO, Eurostat, and 20 individual countries. Fees: Free.

FreeLunch.com. Economy.com, Inc. Phone: (610)696-8700 Fax: (610)696-1678 • URL: http://www.freelunch.com • Web site provides free access to more than 1.5 million economic and financial data series, covering industry, demographics, labor markets, prices, retail sales, government spending, trade, interest rates, housing starts, the stock market, and many other topics. Data is available for various time periods in either chart or table form. Searching is offered. Fees: Free, but registration required. Economy.com, Inc. also offers fee-based economic analysis at *The Dismal Scientist* site (http://www.dismal.com).

STATISTICS SOURCES

Business Statistics of the United States. Linz Audain and Cornelia J. Strawser. Bernan Associates. • Annual. $147.00. Based on *Business Statistics,* formerly issue by the Bureau of Economic Analysis, U. S. Department of Commerce. Provides basic data for a wide variety of U. S. industries, services, and economic indicators. Most statistics are shown annually for 30 years and monthly for the most recent four years.

Economic Indicators Handbook: Time Series, Conversions, Documentation. Gale Cengage Learning. • 2002. $205.00. Sixth edition. Provides data for about 175 U. S. economic indicators, such as the consumer price index (CPI), gross national product (GNP), and the rate of inflation. Values for series are given since inception, in both original form and adjusted for inflation. A bibliography of sources is included.

Nations of the World: A Political, Economic, and Business Handbook. Grey House Publishing. • 2002. $135.00. Third edition. Includes descriptive data on economic characteristics, population, gross domestic product (GDP), banking, inflation, agriculture, tourism, and other factors. Covers "all the nations of the world.".

Survey of Current Business. Available from U. S. Government Printing Office. • Monthly. $63.00 per year. Issued by Bureau of Economic Analysis, U. S. Department of Commerce. Presents a wide variety of business and economic data.

The World Economy: A Millennial Perspective. Angus Maddison. Organization for Economic Cooperation and Development. • 2001. $63.00. "...covers the development of the entire world economy over the past 2000 years," including data on world population and gross domestic product (GDP) since the year 1000, and exports since 1820. Focuses primarily on the disparity in economic performance among nations over the very long term. More than 200 statistical tables and figures are provided.

TRADE/PROFESSIONAL ASSOCIATIONS

Institute for Economic Analysis. c/o John S. Atlee, Four High St., No. 3, Brattleboro, VT 05301. Phone: (802)254-0089 Fax: (802)254-0089 E-mail: jatlee@ sover.net • URL: http://www.iea-macro-economics. org.

GROUP INSURANCE

See: HEALTH INSURANCE

GROUP MEDICAL PRACTICE

See also: HEALTH CARE INDUSTRY; MEDICAL ECONOMICS (PRACTICE MANAGEMENT)

ABSTRACTS AND INDEXES

NTIS Alerts: Health Care. National Technical Information Service. • Semimonthly. $210.00 per year. Provides descriptions of government-sponsored research reports and software, with ordering information. Covers a wide variety of health care topics, including quality assurance, delivery organization, economics (costs), technology, and legislation. Formerly *Abstract Newsletter.*

CD-ROM DATABASES

Authority Health Care Law Library. LexisNexis/ Matthew Bender. • Periodic updates. Price on request. Full text CD-ROM provides legal information, case law, and analysis relating to health care facilities, health insurance, longterm care, Medigap, and Medicare.

DIRECTORIES

AHA Integrated Delivery Network Directory: U.S. Health Care Systems, Networks, and Alliances.

American Hospital Association. • Annual. $250.00. Provides information about a wide variety of U.S. health care groups and affiliations, including hospitals, nursing homes, rehabilitation centers, psychiatric facilities, home health care agencies, clinical laboratories, outpatient facilities, and diagnostic imaging centers. Includes names of more than 8,000 key executives.

Directory of Physician Groups and Networks. Dorland Healthcare Information. • Annual. $495.00. Available only online. Approximately 8,000 independent practice associations (IPAs), physician hospital organizations (PHOs), management service organizations (MSOs), physician practice management companies (PPMCs), and group practices having 20 or more physicians.

Dorland's Directory of Health Plans. Dorland Healthcare Information. • Annual. $195.00. Published in association with the American Association of Health Plans (http://www.aahp.org). Lists more than 2,400 health plans, including Health Maintenance Organizations (HMOs), Preferred Provider Organizations (PPOs), and Point of Service plans (POS). Includes the names of about 9,000 health plan executives.

Medical Group Management Association-- Directory. Medical Group Management Association. • Database covers: more than 20,000 representing over 185,000 physicians. Entries include: Group or clinic name, address, phone, size, services provided, types of specialties, statistical data; name, title, and biographical data of administrator(s).

ENCYCLOPEDIAS AND DICTIONARIES

Guidebook to Managed Care and Practice Management Terminology. Norman Winegar and L. Michelle Hayter. Haworth Press, Inc. • 1998. $39. 95. Provides definitions of managed care "terminology, jargon, and concepts.".

HANDBOOKS AND MANUALS

Healthcare Finance for the Non-Financial Manager: Basic Guide to Financial Analysis & Control. Louis Gapenski. McGraw-Hill. • 1994. $47.50.

Managed Care Handbook: How to Prepare Your Medical Practice for the Managed Care Revolution. James R. Lyle and Hoyt Torras. Practice Management Information Corp. • 1994. $49.95. Second edition. A management guide for physicians in private practice.

PERIODICALS AND NEWSLETTERS

AHA News. American Hospital Association. HealthForum. • Description: Highlights major news affecting hospitals and the health care field. Reports on legislation and regulation, court cases, surveys, and federal programs. Carries information on individual hospitals and allied hospital associations.

Group Practice Journal. American Medical Group Practice Association. • 10 times a year. Institutions, $75.00 per year.

Health Forum Journal: Leadership Strategies for Healthcare Executives. Health Forum. • Biweekly. $65.00 per year. Covers the general management of hospitals, nursing homes, and managed care organizations. Formerly *HospitalsHealthNetworks.*

Healthplan. America Association of Health Plans. • Bimonthly. $75.00 per year.

MGMA Connexion. Medical Group Management Association. • 10 times a year. Individuals, $95.00 per year; institutions, $175.00 per year. Formerly

Medical Group Management Journal.

Modern Physician: Essential Business News for the Executive Physician. Crain Communications, Inc. • Monthly. $45.00. Edited for physicians responsible for business decisions at hospitals, clinics, HMOs, and other health groups. Includes special issues on managed care, practice management, legal issues, and finance.

TRADE/PROFESSIONAL ASSOCIATIONS

American College of Medical Practice Executives. 104 Inverness Terrace E., Englewood, CO 80112-5306. Phone: 877-275-6442 Fax: (303)643-4439 E-mail: acmpe@mgma.com • URL: http://www. mgma.com/acmpe • Formerly American College of Medical Group Administrators.

American Medical Group Association. 1422 Duke St., Alexandria, VA 22314-3403. Phone: (703)838-0033 Fax: (703)548-1890 E-mail: dfisher@amga. org • URL: http://www.amga.org • Represents the interests of medical groups. Advocates for the medical groups and patients through innovation and information sharing, benchmarking, developing leadership, and improving patient care. Provides political advocacy, educational and networking programs and publications, benchmarking data services, and financial and operations assistance.

Medical Group Management Association. 104 Inverness Terr. E, Englewood, CO 80112-5306. Phone: 877-275-6462 or (303)799-1111 or (303)799-1111 Fax: (303)643-4439 E-mail: service@mgma.com • URL: http://www.mgma.com • Represents professionals involved in the management of medical group practices and administration of other ambulatory healthcare facilities. Provides products and services that includes education, benchmarking, surveys, national advocacy and networking opportunities for members.

GROWTH STOCKS

See: STOCKS

GUARANTEED WAGES

See: WAGES AND SALARIES

GUIDANCE

See: COUNSELING; VOCATIONAL GUIDANCE

GUIDED MISSILES

See: ROCKET INDUSTRY

GUMS AND RESINS

See: NAVAL STORES

GUNS

See: FIREARMS INDUSTRY

H

HABERDASHERY

See: MEN'S CLOTHING INDUSTRY

HAIR CARE PRODUCTS

See: COSMETICS INDUSTRY

HAIRDRESSERS

See: BARBER AND BEAUTY SHOPS

HALF-TONE PROCESS

See: PHOTOENGRAVING

HANDICAPPED WORKERS

See also: EQUAL EMPLOYMENT OP-
PORTUNITY

GENERAL WORKS

The Americans with Disabilities Act: Overview, Regulations, and Interpretations. Nancy L. Jones. Nova Science Publishers, Inc. • 2003. $29.50. Serves as a basic guide to the legal ramifications of the Act.

New Technologies and the Employment of Disabled Persons. H. Allan Hunt and Monroe Berkowitz, editors. International Labour Office. • 1992. $18.00. Discusses the development and use of new technologies to create job opportunities for the disabled in various countries.

DIRECTORIES

Complete Directory for People with Disabilities. Grey House Publishing. • Annual. $195.00. Provides information on a wide variety of products, goods, services, and facilities, including job training programs, rehabilitation services, and funding sources. Indexed by organization name, disability/need, and location.

Directory of Grants for Organizations Serving People with Disabilities: A Guide to Sources of Funding in the United States for Programs and Services for Personswith Disabilities. Richard M. Eckstein. Research Grant Guides. • Biennial. $59. 50. Lists over 800 foundations, associations, and government agencies that grant funds to non-profit organizations for projects related to handicapped persons. Formerly *Handicapped Funding Directory.*

HANDBOOKS AND MANUALS

ADA Compliance Guide. Thompson Publishing Group, Inc. • Two looseleaf volumes. $329.00 per year, including monthly updates and newslettrs. Provides detailed information for employers and others on complying with the Americans With Disabilities Act (ADA). Includes material on employment discrimination, transportation accessibility, accessibility in public accommodations, and state disability laws.

Americans with Disabilities Act: A Practical and Legal Guide to Impact, Enforcement, and Compliance. BNA, Inc. • 1990. $95.00. (Special Report Series).

Americans with Disabilities Act Handbook. Henry H. Perritt. Aspen Publishers, Inc. • 2003. Fourth edition. Price on application.

Employer's Guide to Discrimination Laws. Maureen F. Moore. LexisNexis Matthew Bender. • 2003. $28.00, including CD-ROM. Edited for business owners and managers. Provides a concise guide to federal discrimination laws relating to race, sex, age, disability, pregnancy, religion, and national origin.

Employment Law Guide to the Americans with Disabilities Act. Mark Daniels. Prentice Hall PTR. • 1992. $95.00.

Handbook of Services for the Handicapped. Alfred H. Katz and Knute Martin. Greenwood Publishing Group Inc. • 1982. $68.50.

Managing Disability in the Workplace: An ILO Code of Practice. International Labour Organization. • 2002. $6.95. Provides concise "guidelines for employers in the management of disability-related issues in the workplace." Outlines responsibilities for improving the employment prospects of people with disabilities.

PERIODICALS AND NEWSLETTERS

GDL Alert. RIA. • Monthly. $110.98 per year. Newsletter. Covers current legal developments of interest to employers. Formerly *Disabilities in the Workplace Alert.*

RESEARCH CENTERS AND INSTITUTES

Rehabilitation Program. University of Arizona. College of Education, P.O. Box 210069, Tucson, AZ 85721. Phone: (520)621-0941 Fax: (520)621-3821 E-mail: sales@u.arizona.edu.

Vocational and Rehabilitation Research Institute. 3304 33rd St., N.W., Calgary, AB, Canada T2L 2A6. Phone: (403)284-1121 Fax: (403)284-1146 E-mail: vrri@cadvision.com • URL: http://www.vrri.org • Associated with University of Calgary.

TRADE/PROFESSIONAL ASSOCIATIONS

Disability Rights Center. PO Box 2007, Augusta, ME 04338-2007. Phone: 800-452-1948 or (207)626-2774 Fax: (207)621-1419 E-mail: advocate@drcme. org • URL: http://www.drcme.org • Represents public interest research group committed on educat-ing society about the disability rights movement. Aims to inform the public, political activists, consumer activists, advocates, and students on the disability movement. Seeks to involve as many disabled citizens as possible in processes that directly affect their lives, to work closely with other disability-related, consumer-based advocacy groups, and to educate the public in the legitimate demands and needs of the disabled. Compiles statistics.

Goodwill Industries International, Inc. 1850 Indianola Dr., Rockville, MD 20814. Phone: 800-664-6577 or (301)530-6500 Fax: (301)530-1516 • URL: http://www.goodwill.org.

National Association of the Physically Handicapped. 1375 Dewitt St., Akron, OH 44316. Phone: 800-743-5008 E-mail: trumanjm@aol.com • URL: http://www.naph.net.

Special Interest Group on Computers and the Physically Handicapped. c/o Association for Computing Machinery, 1515 Broadway, New York, NY 10036. Phone: 800-342-6626 or (212)869-7440 Fax: (212)944-1318 E-mail: acmhelp@acm.org • URL: http://www.acm.org/sigcaph • Members are physically disabled computer professionals.

OTHER SOURCES

ADA Compliance Manual for Employers. LexisNexis Matthew Bender. • Looseleaf. $95.00. Periodic supplementation available. "Every business with more than 15 employees must comply with the Amricans with Disabilities Act." This guide provides practical advice on job requirements, accessibility, employee selection, reasonable accomodations, termination issues, and other matters.

Disability and Rehabilitation Products Markets. Theta Reports/PJB Medical Publications, Inc. • 1999. $1,295.00. Market research data. Covers the market for products designed to help differently-abled people lead more active lives. Includes such items as adaptive computers, augmentative communication devices, lifts/vans, and bath/home products. Profiles of leading suppliers are included. (Theta Report No. 800.).

HANDICRAFTS

See: GIFT BUSINESS; HOBBY INDUSTRY

HANDLING OF MATERIALS

See: MATERIALS HANDLING

HARASSMENT, SEXUAL

See: SEXUAL HARASSMENT IN THE WORKPLACE

HARBORS

See: PORTS

HARD FIBERS INDUSTRY

See: FIBER INDUSTRY

HARDWARE INDUSTRY

See also: FASTENER INDUSTRY; SAW INDUSTRY; TOOL INDUSTRY

DIRECTORIES

Directory of Home Center Operators and Hardware Chains. Chain Store Guide. • Annual. $327.00. Online edition, $747.00. Nearly 4,700 home center operators, paint and home decorating chains, and lumber and building materials companies. Covers United States and Canada.

ProSales Buyer's Guide. Hanley-Wood, LLC. • Annual. Price on application. A directory of equipment for professional builders.

Thomas Register of American Manufacturers. Thomas Publishing Co., Inc. • Annual. $149.00. 34 volumes. A three-part system offering information on a wide variety of industrial equipment and supplies. Lists more than 151,000 industrial product and services companies.

Tools of the Trade Annual Buyers Guide. Hanley-Wood, LLC. • Annual. Price on application. A directory of tools for the construction industry.

FINANCIAL RATIOS

Almanac of Business and Industrial Financial Ratios. Leo Troy. Aspen Publishers, Inc. • 2003. $125.95. Includes CD-Rom. Contains financial ratios derived from federal tax returns. Ratios for each of about 200 industries are arranged according to company asset size. (Almanac of Business and Industrial Financial Ratios Series).

Annual Statement Studies. The Risk Management Association. • Annual. Median and quartile financial ratios are given for over 400 kinds of manufacturing, wholesale, retail, construction, and consumer finance establishments. Data is sorted by both asset size and sales volume. Includes a clearly written "Definition of Ratios" and an alphabetical industry index.

Annual Statement Studies: Industry Default Probabilities and Cash Flow Measures. The Risk Management Association. • Annual. $145.00. Serves as a companion volume to the original *Annual Statement Studies.* Gives probability of default estimates on a percentage scale for more than 450 industries. Includes changes in position year-by-year for eight financial statement line items and provides percentage measures of cash flow.

National Retail Hardware Association Management Report: Cost of Doing Business Study. National Retail Hardware Association. • Annual. Members, $49.00; non-members, $98.00.

INTERNET DATABASES

Advance Monthly Sales for Retail Trade and Food Services. U. S. Census Bureau. Phone: 800-541-8345 or (301)763-4636 Fax: (301)457-3842 E-mail: rcb@census.gov • URL: http://www.census.gov/svsd/www/fullpub.html • Web pages provide monthly sales figures for a wide range of retail businesses. Advance, preliminary, and final statistics are provided for the latest month available in each case, with a previous-year comparison. Updates are monthly.

ONLINE DATABASES

Thomas Register Online. Thomas Publishing Co., Inc. • Provides concise information on ap-

proximately 194,000 U. S. companies, mainly manufacturers, with over 50,000 product classifications. Indexes over 115,000 trade names. Information is updated semiannually. Inquire as to online cost and availability.

PERIODICALS AND NEWSLETTERS

Building Products. Hanley-Wood, LLC. • Quarterly. $36.00 per year. Covers building products and materials for the construction industry, including new products.

Do-it-Yourself Retailing: Serving Hardware, Home Center and Building Material Retailers. National Retail Hardware Association. • Monthly. $50.00 per year. Formerly *DIY Retailing.*

Doors and Hardware. Door and Hardware Institute. • Monthly. $49.00 per year.

Hardware Age. Reed Business Information. • Monthly. $75.00 per year.

Journal of Light Construction. Hanley-Wood, LLC. • Monthly. $35.95 per year. Provides jobsite tips, techniques, and product advice for builders and contractors.

Tools of the Trade. Hanley-Wood, LLC. • Five times a year. $19.80 per year. Provides advice and information on tools for the construction industry. Includes product tests and evaluations.

STATISTICS SOURCES

Annual Benchmark Report for Retail Trade and Food Services...A Detailed Summary of Retail Sales, Purchases, Accounts Receivable, Inventories, and Food Service Sales. Available from U. S. Government Printing Office. • Annual. $13.00. Issued by the U.S. Census Bureau. Provides detailed annual and monthly retail statistics for the most recent 10 years. Includes data for various kinds of retail outlets, including automobiles, furniture, appliances, building supplies, grocery stores, drug stores, gasoline stations, clothing, sporting goods, department stores, and restaurants.

TRADE/PROFESSIONAL ASSOCIATIONS

American Hardware Manufacturers Association. 801 N Plaza Dr., Schaumburg, IL 60173. Phone: (847)605-1025 Fax: (847)605-1030 E-mail: info@ahma.org • URL: http://www.ahma.org • Represents the hardware, home improvement, lawn and garden, paint and decorating, and related industries.

Builders Hardware Manufacturers Association. 355 Lexington Ave., 15th Fl., New York, NY 10017. Phone: (212)297-2122 Fax: (212)370-9047 E-mail: bhma@kellencompany.com • URL: http://www.buildershardware.com • Manufacturers of builders' hardware, both contract and stock. Provides statistical services; maintains standardization program; sponsors certification programs for locks, latches, door closers, and cabinet hardware. Maintains 12 product sections.

Door and Hardware Institute. 14150 Newbrook Dr., Suite 200, Chantilly, VA 20151-2232. Phone: (703)222-2010 Fax: (703)222-2410 E-mail: info@dhi.org • URL: http://www.dhi.org.

North American Retail Hardware Association. 5822 W 74th St., Indianapolis, IN 46278-1787. Phone: 800-772-4424 or (317)290-0338 Fax: (317)328-4354 E-mail: contact@nrha.org • URL: http://www.nrha.org • Represents independent family-owned hardware/home improvement retailers. Sponsors correspondence courses in hardware and building materials retailing; conducts annual cost-of-doing-business study.

OTHER SOURCES

Door Hardware. Available from MarketResearch.com. • 1997. $495.00. Market research report published by Specialists in Business Information. Covers locks, closers, doorknobs, security devices, and other door hardware. Presents market data relative to demographics, sales growth, shipments,

exports, imports, price trends, and end-use. Includes company profiles.

The Home Improvement Market. Available from MarketResearch.com. • 1999. $2,750.00. Market research report published by Packaged Facts. Covers the market for lumber, finishing materials, tools, hardware, etc.

HARDWOOD INDUSTRY

See also: LUMBER INDUSTRY

GENERAL WORKS

Forest Products and Wood Science: An Introduction. Jim L. Bowyer and others. Blackwell Publishing. • 2002. Fourth edition. Price on application.

ABSTRACTS AND INDEXES

Forest Products Abstracts. CABI Publishing North America. • Bimonthly. $770.00 per year; with online edition, $805.00 per year. Published in England by CABI Publishing. Provides worldwide coverage of forest products literature.

ALMANACS AND YEARBOOKS

Agricultural and Mineral Commodities Year Book. Available from Taylor & Francis Group. • Annual. $225.00. Published by Europa Publications. Contains descriptive product profiles, price data, export-import data, and production statistics for major commodities of the world. Includes commodity histories, uses, markets, demand trends, and information about trade agreements and key commodity organizations.

CD-ROM DATABASES

AGRICOLA on SilverPlatter. Available from SilverPlatter Information, Inc. • Quarterly. $825.00 per year. Produced by the National Agricultural Library. Provides about three million citations on CD-ROM to the literature of agriculture, agricultural economics, animal sciences, entomology, fertilizer, food, forestry, nutrition, pesticides, plant science, water resources, and other topics. Each quarterly disc covers the past ten years, with archival discs available from 1970.

OECD Statistical Compendium. Organization for Economic Cooperation and Development. • Semiannual. $1,905.00 per year for 1 to 10 users. CD-ROM contains more than 730,000 monthly, quarterly, and annual time series for OECD countries, 1960 to date. Includes fully searchable data on agriculture, food, economic indicators, national accounts, employment, energy, finance, industry, technology, and foreign trade. Results can be displayed in various forms.

WILSONDISC: Biological and Agricultural Index. H. W. Wilson Co. • Monthly. Includes unlimited online access to *Biological and Agricultural Index* through WILSONLINE. Provides CD-ROM indexing of over 250 periodicals covering agriculture, agricultural chemicals, biochemistry, biotechnology, entomology, horticulture, and related topics.

DIRECTORIES

Hardwood Manufacturers Association: Membership Directory. Hardwood Manufacturers Association. • Annual. Lists over 100 companies. Price on application.

National Hardwood Lumber Association Membership Directory. National Hardwood Lumber Association. • Annual. $500.00. Members are hardwood lumber and veneer manufacturers, distributors, and users.

Where to Buy Hardwood Plywood, Veneer, and Engineered Hardwood Flooring. Hardwood Plywood and Veneer Association. • Annual. Free. Lists about 190 member manufacturers, prefinishers, and suppliers of hardwood veneer and plywood.

ENCYCLOPEDIAS AND DICTIONARIES

Encyclopedia of Agriculture Science. Charles J. Arntzen and Ellen M. Ritter, editors. Elsevier. • 1994. $900.00. Four volumes.

Encyclopedia of Wood. U.S. Dept. of Forestry Staff. Sterling Publishing Co., Inc. • 1989. $24.95. Revised edition.

Encyclopedia of Wood: A Tree by Tree Guide to the World's Most Valuable Resource. Bill Lincoln and others. Facts on File, Inc. • 1989. $29.95.

FINANCIAL RATIOS

Annual Statement Studies. The Risk Management Association. • Annual. Median and quartile financial ratios are given for over 400 kinds of manufacturing, wholesale, retail, construction, and consumer finance establishments. Data is sorted by both asset size and sales volume. Includes a clearly written "Definition of Ratios" and an alphabetical industry index.

Annual Statement Studies: Industry Default Probabilities and Cash Flow Measures. The Risk Management Association. • Annual. $145.00. Serves as a companion volume to the original *Annual Statement Studies.* Gives probability of default estimates on a percentage scale for more than 450 industries. Includes changes in position year-by-year for eight financial statement line items and provides percentage measures of cash flow.

Industry Norms and Key Business Ratios. Desk Top Edition. Dun and Bradstreet Corp. • Annual. Five volumes. $475.00 per volume. $1,890.00 per set. Covers over 800 kinds of businesses, arranged by Standard Industrial Classification number. More detailed editions covering longer periods of time are also available.

INTERNET DATABASES

Business 2.0 Web Guide to the Best Business Links. Business 2.0 Media Inc. Phone: (415)293-4800 E-mail: support@business2.com • URL: http:// www.business2.com/webguide • Web site presents an extensive, searchable directory of links to "the best, most informative, and authoritative web pages." Twenty main categories cover business, finance, career, company information, people, and technology topics, with thousands of subtopics, all linking to Web sites recommended by experienced business researchers. Fees: Free.

Fedstats. Federal Interagency Council on Statistical Policy. Phone: (202)395-7254 • URL: http://www. fedstats.gov • Web site features an efficient search facility for full-text statistics produced by more than 100 federal agencies, including the Census Bureau, the Bureau of Economic Analysis, and the Bureau of Labor Statistics. Boolean searches can be made within one agency or for all agencies combined. Links are offered to international statistical bureaus, including the UN, IMF, OECD, UNESCO, Eurostat, and 20 individual countries. Fees: Free.

FreeLunch.com. Economy.com, Inc. Phone: (610)696-8700 Fax: (610)696-1678 • URL: http:// www.freelunch.com • Web site provides free access to more than 1.5 million economic and financial data series, covering industry, demographics, labor markets, prices, retail sales, government spending, trade, interest rates, housing starts, the stock market, and many other topics. Data is available for various time periods in either chart or table form. Searching is offered. Fees: Free, but registration required. Economy.com, Inc. also offers fee-based economic analysis at *The Dismal Scientist* site (http://www. dismal.com).

Manufacturing Profiles. U. S. Bureau of the Census. Phone: (301)763-4636 E-mail: webmaster@census. gov • URL: http://www.census.gov/prod/www/abs/ mfg-prof.html • The Census Bureau makes available free on PDF (Portable Document Format) an annual consolidation of the entire Current Industrial Report series, presenting "all the data compiled." Contains statistics on production, shipments, inventories, consumption, exports, imports, and orders for a wide variety of manufactured products.

USDA. United States Department of Agriculture. Phone: (202)720-2791 E-mail: agsec@usda.gov • URL: http://www.usda.gov • The USDA home page has six sections: News and Information; What's New; About USDA; Agencies; Opportunities; Search and Help. Keyword searching is offered from the USDA home page and from various individual agency home pages. Agencies are the Economic Research Service, Agricultural Marketing Service, National Agricultural Statistics Service, National Agricultural Library, and about 12 others. Updating varies. Fees: Free.

ONLINE DATABASES

Agricola. U.S. National Agricultural Library. • Covers worldwide agricultural literature. Over 3.3 million citations, 1970 to present, with monthly updates. Inquire as to online cost and availability.

CAB Abstracts. CAB Publishing North America. • Contains 46 specialized abstract collections covering over 10,000 journals and monographs in the areas of agriculture, horticulture, forest products, farm products, nutrition, dairy science, poultry, grains, animal health, entomology, etc. Time period is 1972 to date, with monthly updates. Inquire as to online cost and availability. *CAB Abstracts on CD-ROM* also available, with annual updating.

Globalbase. Gale Cengage Learning. • Provides more than one million online summaries of business, industrial, and economic news reports from more than 1,000 publications worldwide. Covers a wide range of material appearing in international trade journals, professional magazines, and newspapers. Time period is 1984 to date, with weekly updates. Inquire as to online cost and availability.

PROMT: Predicasts Overview of Markets and Technology. Gale Cengage Learning. • Companies, products, applied technologies and markets. U.S. and international literature coverage, 1972 to date. Inquire as to online cost and availability. Provides abstracts from more than 1,600 publications. Weekly updates.

PERIODICALS AND NEWSLETTERS

Hardwood Floors. National Wood Flooring Association. Athletic Business Publications, Inc. • Bimonthly. $36.00 per year. Covers the marketing and installation of hardwood flooring. Published for contractors and retailers.

National Hardwood Magazine. Miller Publishing Co. • Monthly. $45.00 per year.

NHLA Newsletter. National Hardwood Lumber Association. • Monthly. Membership. Newsletter on hardwood products, industry trends, and legislation.

RESEARCH CENTERS AND INSTITUTES

Wood and Paper Science. North Carolina State University, P.O. Box 8005, Raleigh, NC 27695. Phone: (919)515-5807 Fax: (919)515-6302 E-mail: mike_kocurek@ncsu.edu • URL: http://www.cfr. ncsu.edu/wps/ • Studies the mechanical and engineering properties of wood, wood finishing, wood anatomy, wood chemistry, etc.

Wood Research Laboratory. Purdue University, Department of Forestry and Natural Resources, West Lafayette, IN 47907-1200. Phone: (765)494-3615 Fax: (765)496-1344 E-mail: mhunt@fnr.purdue.edu • URL: http://www.fnr.purdue.edu.

STATISTICS SOURCES

AF and PA Statistical Roundup. American Forest and Paper Association. • Monthly. Members, $57.00 per year; non-members, $157.00 per year. Contains monthly statistical data for hardwood and softwood products. Formerly *NFPA Statistical Roundup.*

Agricultural Statistics. Available from U. S. Government Printing Office. • Annual. $38.00. Produced by the National Agricultural Statistics Service, U. S. Department of Agriculture. Provides a wide variety of statistical data relating to agricultural production, supplies, consumption, prices/price-supports, foreign trade, costs, and returns, as well as farm labor, loans, income, and population. In many cases, historical data is shown annually for 10 years. In addition to farm data, includes detailed fishery statistics.

Annual Survey of Manufactures. Available from U. S. Government Printing Office. • Annual. Prices vary. Issued by the U. S. Census Bureau as an interim update to the *Census of Manufactures.* Includes data on number of manufacturing establishments in various industries, employment, labor costs, value of shipments, capital expenditures, inventories, energy costs, and assets. (See also Census Bureau home page, http://www.census. gov/.).

Business Statistics of the United States. Linz Audain and Cornelia J. Strawser. Bernan Associates. • Annual. $147.00. Based on *Business Statistics,* formerly issue by the Bureau of Economic Analysis, U. S. Department of Commerce. Provides basic data for a wide variety of U. S. industries, services, and economic indicators. Most statistics are shown annually for 30 years and monthly for the most recent four years.

Survey of Current Business. Available from U. S. Government Printing Office. • Monthly. $63.00 per year. Issued by Bureau of Economic Analysis, U. S. Department of Commerce. Presents a wide variety of business and economic data.

TRADE/PROFESSIONAL ASSOCIATIONS

American Forest and Paper Association. 1111 19th St., N.W., Ste. 800, Washington, DC 20036. Phone: (202)463-2700 Fax: (202)463-2471 E-mail: info@ afandpa.org • URL: http://www.afandpa.org.

American Walnut Manufacturers Association. 6516 Linchmere Ln., Dublin, OH 43017. Phone: (614)923-4421 Fax: (614)923-4421 E-mail: bshardwoods1@yahoo.com • URL: http://www. walnutassociation.org • Manufacturers of hardwood veneer and lumber, especially American black walnut. Seeks to improve the sale of products made from hardwoods through advertising, promotion, sales education, and product improvement; also promotes good forest management.

Appalachian Hardwood Manufacturers, Inc. PO Box 427, High Point, NC 27261. Phone: (336)885-8315 Fax: (336)886-8865 E-mail: info@ appalachianwood.org • URL: http://www. appalachianwood.org • Promotes Appalachian hardwoods.

Hardwood Distributor's Association. 2559 S Damen Ave., Chicago, IL 60608. Phone: (773)847-7444 Fax: (773)847-7833 E-mail: gaspamerica@aol.com • URL: http://www.hardwooddistributors.net • Promotes the interests of Hardwood distributors.

Hardwood Manufacturers Association. 400 Penn Center Blvd., Ste. 530, Pittsburgh, PA 15235. Phone: 800-373-9663 or (412)829-0770 Fax: (412)829-0844 E-mail: info@hardwood.org • URL: http:// www.hardwoodinfo.com • Represents manufacturers of hardwood lumber and hardwood products. Conducts promotion program; compiles statistics.

Hardwood Plywood and Veneer Association. 1825 Michael Faraday Dr., Reston, VA 20195-0789. Phone: (703)435-2900 Fax: (703)435-2537 E-mail: hpva@hpva.org • URL: http://www.hpva.org • Formerly Hardwood Plywood Manufactures Association.

National Hardwood Lumber Association. PO Box 34518, 6830 Raleigh-LaGrange Rd., Memphis, TN 38184-0518. Phone: (901)377-1818 Fax: (901)382-

6419 E-mail: info@nhla.com • URL: http://www.nhla.com • United States, Canadian and International hardwood lumber and veneer manufacturers, distributors, and consumers. Inspects hardwood lumber. Maintains inspection training school. Conducts management and marketing seminars for the hardwood industry. Promotes research in hardwood timber management and utilization. Promotes public awareness of the industry.

Wood Component Manufacturers Association. 741 Butlers Gate, Ste. 100, Marietta, GA 30068. Phone: (770)565-6660 Fax: (770)565-6663 E-mail: wcma@woodcomponents.org • URL: http://www.woodcomponents.org • Manufacturers of wood parts for the furniture, kitchen cabinet, and building industries, including interior trim moldings, stair treads and risers, thresholds, and paneling; industrial users. Establishes grading rules and standards. Offers seminars in cost accounting, marketing, and production techniques. Conducts plant tours among members.

OTHER SOURCES

U. S. Floor Coverings Industry. Available from MarketResearch.com. • 2000. $1,795.00. Market research report published by Specialists in Business Information. Covers carpets, hardwood flooring, and tile. Presents market data relative to demographics, sales growth, shipments, exports, imports, price trends, and end-use. Includes company profiles.

Wood Flooring. Available from MarketResearch.com. • 1999. $2,250.00. Market research report published by Specialists in Business Information. Presents hardwood flooring market data relative to demographics, sales growth, shipments, exports, imports, price trends, and end-use. Includes company profiles.

HARVESTING MACHINERY

See: AGRICULTURAL MACHINERY

HAT INDUSTRY

See: MEN'S CLOTHING INDUSTRY; MILLINERY INDUSTRY

HAY INDUSTRY

See: FEED AND FEEDSTUFFS INDUSTRY

HAZARDOUS MATERIALS

See also: INDUSTRIAL HYGIENE; WASTE MANAGEMENT

GENERAL WORKS

Hazardous Waste Management. Michael D. La Gregor and others. McGraw-Hill. • 2000. $113.75. Second edition. (Environmental Engineering and Water Resources Series).

Management of Hazardous Materials and Wastes: Treatment, Minimization, and Environmental Impacts. Shyamal K. Majumdar and others, editors. Pennsylvania Academy of Science. • 1989. $45.00.

Safety in Tunnels: Transport of Dangerous Goods Through Road Tunnels. Organization for Economic Cooperation and Development. • 2001. $19.00. Discusses risks in road tunnels and the consequences of incidents.

Understanding Toxicology: Chemicals, Their Benefits and Uses. Bruno H. Schiefer and others. CRC Press LLC. • 1997. $39.95. Provides a basic introduction to chemical interactions and toxicology for the general reader.

ABSTRACTS AND INDEXES

Applied Science and Technology Index. H. W. Wilson Co. • 11 times a year. Quarterly and annual cumulations. Price varies. Indexes a wide variety of English language technical, industrial, and engineering periodicals.

Current Contents: Engineering, Computing and Technology. Thomson/ISI. • Weekly. $730.00 per year. Reproductions of contents pages of technical journals. Includes *Author Index, Address Directory, Current Book Contents* and *Title Word Index.* Formerly *Current Contents: Engineering, Technology and Applied Sciences.*

Health and Safety Science Abstracts. Institute of Safety and Systems Management. Cambridge Information Group. • Monthly. Online edition, $850.00 year. Formerly *Safety Science Abstracts Journal.*

NTIS Alerts: Environmental Pollution & Control. National Technical Information Service. • Semimonthly. $245.00 per year. Provides descriptions of government-sponsored research reports and software, with ordering information. Covers the following categories of environmental pollution: air, water, solid wastes, radiation, pesticides, and noise. Formerly *Abstract Newsletter.*

CD-ROM DATABASES

Hazardous Substances Data Bank. SilverPlatter Information, Inc. • Provides CD-ROM information on hazardous substances, including 140,000 chemicals in the *Registry of Toxic Effects of Chemical Substances* and 60,000 materials covered by the *Toxic Substances Control Act Initial Inventory.*

OSH-ROM: Occupational Safety and Health Information on CD-ROM. Available from SilverPlatter Information, Inc. • Price and frequency on application. Produced in Geneva by the International Occupational Safety and Health Information Centre, International Labour Organization (http://www.ilo.org). Provides about two million citations and abstracts to the worldwide literature of industrial safety, industrial hygiene, hazardous materials, and accident prevention. Material is included from journals, technical reports, books, government publications, and other sources. Time span varies.

DIRECTORIES

Best's Safety and Security Directory. A.M. Best Co. • Annual. Free to members; non-members, $295.00. A manual of current industrial safety practices with a directory of manufacturers and distributors of plant safety, security and industrial hygiene products and services listed by hazard. Formerly *Best's Safety Directory.*

EI Environmental Services Directory. Environmental Information Ltd. • Covers: Over 8,000 environmental services businesses, including waste-handling facilities, transportation firms, spill response firms, consultants, laboratories, soil boring/well drilling firms; also includes incineration services, polychlorinated biphenyl (PCB) detoxification and mobile solvent-recovery services, asbestos services and underground tank services, summaries of states' regulatory programs. Entries include: Company name, address, phone, description of services, regulatory status, on and off site processes used, type of waste handled.

Hazardous Substances Resource Guide. Gale. • Publication includes: Organizations and research centers involved with hazardous substances treatment. Principal content of publication is a guide to approximately 1,200 hazardous materials and their handling, use, disposal, and health risks.

Hazardous Waste Consultant Directory of Commercial Hazardous Waste Management Facilities. Elsevier. • Annual. $115.00. List of 170 facilities that process, store, and dispose of hazardous waste materials.

Pollution Equipment News Buyer's Guide. Rimbach Publishing, Inc. • Annual. $100.00. Over 3,000 manufacturers of pollution control equipment and products.

Waste Age Buyers' Guide. Primedia Business Magazines and Media. • Annual. $64.95. Manufacturers of equipment and supplies for the waste management industry.

ENCYCLOPEDIAS AND DICTIONARIES

Encyclopedia of Occupational Health and Safety. International Labour Organization. • 1998. $990.00. Fourth edition. Four volumes. Includes CD-ROM. Covers safety engineering, industrial medicine, ergonomics, hygiene, epidemiology, toxicology, industrial psychology, and related topics. Includes material related to specific chemical, textile, transport, construction, manufacturing, and other industries. Indexed by subject, chemical name, and author, with a "Directory of Experts.".

Hazardous Materials Dictionary. Ronald Coleman. CRC Press LLC. • 1994. $99.95. Second revised edition. Looseleaf service.

Wiley Encyclopedia of Environmental Pollution and Cleanup. Robert A. Meyers, editor. John Wiley and Sons, Inc. • 1999. $350.00. Two volumes. Presents generally nontechnical, basic coverage of environmental hazards and methods of detection and cleanup, with consideration of risk assessment, regulatory policy, and economic factors.

HANDBOOKS AND MANUALS

Comprehensive Guide to the Hazardous Properties of Chemical Substances. Pradyot Patnaik. John Wiley and Sons, Inc. • 1999. $210.00. Second edition.

A Guide to Hazardous Materials Management: Physical Characteristics, Federal Regulations, and Response Alternatives. Aileen Schumacher. Greenwood Publishing Group Inc. • 1988. $72.95.

Handbook of Industrial Toxicology. E. R. Plunkett, editor. Chemical Publishing Co., Inc. • 1987. $100.00.

Hazardous and Toxic Materials: Safe Handling and Disposal. Howard H. Fawcett, editor. John Wiley and Sons, Inc. • 1988. $160.00. Second edition.

Hazardous Chemicals Desk Reference. Richard J. Lewis. John Wiley and Sons, Inc. • 2002. $185.00. Fifth edition. Summarizes the hazardous properties of about 5,000 chemical substances.

Hazardous Waste Management in Small Businesses: Regulating and Assisting the Smaller Generator. Robert E. Deyle. Greenwood Publishing Group, Inc. • 1989. $59.95. Emphasis on legal aspects.

Patty's Industrial Hygiene and Toxicology. Robert L. Harris. John Wiley and Sons, Inc. • 2001. $3,290.00. Fifth edition. Provides broad coverage of environmental factors and stresses affecting the health of workers. Contains detailed information on the effects of specific substances.

Recommendations on the Transport of Dangerous Goods. United Nations Publications. • 1999. $120.00. 11th edition. Covers regulations imposed by various governments and international organizations.

Sax's Dangerous Properties of Industrial Materials. Richard J. Lewis. John Wiley and Sons, Inc. • 1999. $545.00. 10th edition. Three volumes. Provides detailed information on the chemical, physical, and toxicity characteristics of more than 22,000 industrial materials. Hazard ratings and safety profiles are specified. Includes CD-ROM.

Standard Handbook of Hazardous Waste Treatment and Disposal. Harry M. Freeman, editor. McGraw-Hill. • 1997. $140.00. Second expanded revised edition.

Toxic Substances Controls Guide. Mary D. Worobec and Cheryl Hogue. BNA, Inc. • 1992. 45.00. Second edition. Emphasis on legal aspects.

ONLINE DATABASES

Applied Science and Technology Index Online. H. W. Wilson Co. • Provides online indexing of 500 major scientific, technical, industrial, and engineering periodicals. Time period is 1983 to date. Monthly updates. Inquire as to online cost and availability.

NIOSHTIC: National Institute for Occupational Safety and Health Technical Information Center Database. National Institute for Occupational Safety and Health, Technical Information Bra. • Provides citations and abstracts of technical literature in the areas of industrial safety, industrial hygiene, and toxicology. Covers 1890 to date, but mostly 1973 to date. Monthly updates. (Database is also known as *Occupational Safety and Health.*) Inquire as to online cost and availability.

PROMT: Predicasts Overview of Markets and Technology. Gale Cengage Learning. • Companies, products, applied technologies and markets. U.S. and international literature coverage, 1972 to date. Inquire as to online cost and availability. Provides abstracts from more than 1,600 publications. Weekly updates.

PERIODICALS AND NEWSLETTERS

AIHA Journal: Journal for the Science of Occupational and Environmental Health. American Industrial Hygiene Association. • Bimonthly. Institutions, $185.00 per year.

Environment Advisor. J.J. Keller & Associates, Inc. • Monthly. $90.00 per year. Newsletter. Formerly *Hazardous Substances Advisor.*

Environmental Science and Technology. Kluwer Academic Publishers. • Irregular. $120.00.

Golob's Environmental Business Report. World Information Systems. • Description: Provides news and analysis on environmental business, hazardous materials, waste management, and pollution prevention and control. Covers regulations, legislation and court decisions, new technology, contract opportunities and awards, and conferences.

Hazardous Materials Newsletter. John R. Cashman. • Description: Focuses on response to and control of hazardous materials emergencies, particularly appropriate tools, equipment, materials, methods, procedures, strategies, and lessons learned. Addresses leak, fire, and spill control for incident commanders and experienced responders, including incident causes, prevention, and remedial actions; decisionmaking; scene management; control and containment; response teams; and product identification and hazards. Recurring features include incident reports, a calendar of events, description of public safety agency/commercial/industrial response team operations, coverage of research sources and resources, networking ideas, and chemical and biological agents.

Hazardous Waste Consultant. Elsevier. • Seven times a year. $798.00 per year. Discusses the technical, regulatory and legal aspects of the hazardous waste industry.

Hazardous Waste/Superfund Week. Business Publishers Inc. • Description: Examines issues and developments in the hazardous waste management industry. Covers legislative and regulatory actions, technology research and development, disposal site controversies, Superfund contracting, and other news of interest. Recurring features include columns titled Slants & Trends, Business and Technology News, Grants and Contracts, calendar, Around the States, Market News, and Industrial Waste Focus.

Nuclear Waste News: Generation-Packaging-Transportation-Processing-Disposal. Business Publishers, Inc. • Weekly. $867.00. per year. Newsletter.

OSHA Required Safety Training for Supervisors. Occupational Safety and Health Administration. Business and Legal Reports, Inc. • Monthly. $99.00 per year. Newsletter. Formerly *Safetyworks for Supervisors.*

Pollution Engineering: Magazine of Environmental Control. Business News Publishing Co. • 13 times a year. $85.90 per year.

Sludge Newsletter: The Newsletter on Municipal Wastewater and Biosolids. Business Publishers, Inc. • Biweekly. $409.00 per year. per year. Newsletter. Monitors sludge management developments in Washington and around the country.

Waste Management: Industrial-Radioactive-Hazardous. Elsevier. • 10 times a year.Individuals, $120.00 per year; institutions, $1,646.00 per year. Formerly *Nuclear and Chemical Waste Management.*

World Environment Report: News and Information on International Resource Management. Business Publishers, Inc. • Biweekly. $494.00 per year. Newsletter on international developments having to do with the environment, energy, pollution control, waste management, and toxic substances.

RESEARCH CENTERS AND INSTITUTES

Battelle Memorial Institute. Battelle Memorial Institute. 505 King Ave., Columbus, OH 43201. Phone: 800-201-2011 or (614)424-5853 Fax: (614)424-5263 E-mail: solutions@battelle.org • URL: http://www.battelle.org/ • Environment and energy; national security; transportation; health and life sciences; medical, pharmaceutical, agrochemical, and consumer product development. Conducts marine research at three coastal locations: Florida Marine Research Facility (Daytona Beach), Northwest Marine Research Laboratory (Sequim, Washington), and the Ocean Sciences Laboratory (Duxbury, Massachusetts). Specialized facilities and units include: Aviation Safety Reporting System Office; the Breakthrough Center for Strategic Product Development; the Human Engineering, Ergonomics, and Organizational Research Center; and the William R. Wiley Environmental Molecular Sciences Laboratory.

Concurrent Technologies Corporation. 100 CTC Dr., Johnstown, PA 15904. Phone: 800-282-4392 or (412)269-6888 Fax: (814)262-6500 E-mail: ctc@ctc.com • URL: http://www.ctc.com • Formerly Center for Hazardous Materials Research.

Environmental Hazards Management Institute. Environmental Hazards Management Institute. 10 Newmarket Rd., PO Box 932, Durham, NH 03824. Phone: (603)868-1496 Fax: (603)868-1547 E-mail: aborner@ehmi.org • URL: http://www.ehmi.org • Natural and man-made disasters, global pandemic influenza preparedness or risk avoidance and societal continuity.

Hazardous Substance Management Research Center. New Jersey Institute of Technology, 138 Warren St., Newark, NJ 07102-1982. Phone: (973)596-3233 Fax: (973)642-7170 E-mail: watts@admin.njit.edu • URL: http://www.hsmrc.org.

Molecular and Environmental Toxicology Center. University of Wisconsin-Madison, Enzyme Institute, Room 290, 1710 University Ave., Madison, WI 53705. Phone: (608)263-5557 Fax: (608)262-5245 E-mail: jefcoate@facstaff.wisc.edu • URL: http://www.wisc.edu/etc/ • Formerly Environmental Toxicology Center.

STATISTICS SOURCES

Health, United States, 1999: Health and Aging Chartbook. Available from U. S. Government Printing Office. • 1999. $43.00. Issued by the National Center for Health Statistics, U. S. Department of Health and Human Services. Contains 34 bar charts in color, with related statistical tables. Provides detailed data on persons over 65 years of age, including population, living arrangements, life expectancy, nursing home residence, poverty, health status, assistive devices, health insurance, and health care expenditures.

Statistical Record of the Environment. Gale Cengage Learning. • 1996. $130.00. Third edition.

Provides over 875 charts, tables, and graphs of major environmental statistics, arranged by subject. Covers population growth, hazardous waste, nuclear energy, acid rain, pesticides, and other subjects related to the environment. A keyword index is included. (Gale Environmental Library Series).

TRADE/PROFESSIONAL ASSOCIATIONS

American Conference of Governmental Industrial Hygienists. 1330 Kemper Meadow Dr., Ste. 600, Cincinnati, OH 45240. Phone: (513)742-2020 or (513)742-6163 Fax: (513)742-3355 E-mail: mail@acgih.org • URL: http://www.acgih.org • Members are government employees. Formerly National Conference of Governmental Industrial Hygients.

American Industrial Hygiene Association. 2700 Prosperity Ave., Ste. 250, Fairfax, VA 22031. Phone: (703)849-8888 Fax: (703)207-3561 E-mail: infonet@aiha.org • URL: http://www.aiha.org • Professional society of industrial hygienists. Promotes the study and control of environmental factors affecting the health and well-being of workers. Sponsors continuing education courses in industrial hygiene, government affairs program, and public relations. Accredits laboratories. Maintains 40 technical committees and a foundation. Operates placement service. Conducts educational and research programs.

Conference on Safe Transportation of Hazardous Articles. 7803 Hill House Ct., Fairfax Station, VA 22039. Phone: (703)451-4031 Fax: (703)451-4207 E-mail: mail@costha.com • URL: http://www.costha.com • Members are shipper associations concerned with the legal aspects of transporting hazardous materials.

Dangerous Goods Advisory Council. 1100 H St. NW, Ste. 740, Washington, DC 20005-5484. Phone: (202)289-4550 Fax: (202)289-4074 E-mail: info@dgac.org • URL: http://www.dgac.org • Represents shippers, carriers, and container manufacturers of hazardous materials, substances, and wastes, shipper and carrier associations. Works to promote safe transportation of these materials; provides assistance in answering regulatory questions, guidance to appropriate governmental resources, and advice in establishing corporate compliance and safety programs. Conducts seminars on domestic and international hazardous materials packaging and transporting; sponsors educational programs. Provides training courses.

National Solid Wastes Management Association. 4301 Connecticut Ave. NW, Ste. 300, 4301 Connecticut Ave., N.W., Suite 300, Washington, DC 20008-2304. Phone: 800-424-2869 or (202)244-4700 Fax: (202)966-4824 E-mail: membership@envasns.org • URL: http://www.nswma.org • Commercial firms that collect and dispose solid wastes. Acts as a forum for the discussion of specific aspects of hazardous waste transport. Promotes professionalism in the industry to minimize the risks to public health and safety. Aids in the development of industry laws and regulations. Fosters public understanding of waste transport and disposal through educational programs. Urges members to: comply with federal liability insurance requirements; employ drivers who have completed a comprehensive training program and obtained their Department of Transportation commercial vehicle operator's license and medical evaluation certificate; set limits on drivers' hours of service; and maintain transport vehicles in accordance with federal motor carrier safety regulations.

OTHER SOURCES

Hazardous Waste Litigation Reporter: The National Journal of Record of Hazardous Waste-Related Litigation. Andrews Publications. • Semimonthly. $875.00 per year. Newsletter. Reports on hazardous waste legal cases.

HEALTH CARE INDUSTRY

See also: HEALTH INSURANCE; HEALTH MAINTENANCE ORGANIZATIONS; HOME HEALTH CARE INDUSTRY; HOSPITAL ADMINISTRATION; MEDICARE; NURSING HOMES

GENERAL WORKS

Fundamentals of Strategic Planning for Healthcare Organizations. Stan Williamson and others. Haworth Press, Inc. • 1996. $49.95.

Health Care Economics. Paul J. Feldstein. Delmar Learning. • 1998. $98.95. Fifth edition.

Marketing Health Care into the Twenty-First Century: The Changing Dynamic. Alan K. Vitberg. Haworth Press, Inc. • 1996. $39.95. (Marketing Resources Series).

Medical Care, Medical Costs: The Search for a Health Insurance Policy. Rashi Fein. Replica Books. • 1999. $29.00.

Oxymorons: The Myth of the U.S. Health Care System. J. D. Kleinke. John Wiley and Sons, Inc. • 2001. $35.00. The author is a healthcare economist who states that managed care has "left in the rubble bewildered consumers, disappointed employers, enraged patients, embittered physicians, and a raft of lawsuits." (Jossey-Bass Health Series).

Super Searchers on Health and Medicine: The Online Secrets of Top Health and Medical Researchers. Susan M. Detwiler. Information Today, Inc. • 2000. $24.95. Provides the results of interviews with 10 experts in online searching for medical research data and healthcare information. Discusses both traditional sources and Web sites. (Super Searchers Series).

ABSTRACTS AND INDEXES

Business Periodicals Index. H. W. Wilson Co. • 11 times a year. Quarterly and annual cumulations. Price varies.

Cumulative Index to Nursing and Allied Health Literature. CINAHL Information Systems. • Quarterly. $365.00 per year. Includes annual *Cumulation Index.*

Index Medicus. National Library of Medicine. Available from U. S. Government Printing Office. • Monthly. $620.00 per year. Bibliographic listing of references to current articles from approximately 3,000 of the world's biomedical journals.

NTIS Alerts: Health Care. National Technical Information Service. • Semimonthly. $210.00 per year. Provides descriptions of government-sponsored research reports and software, with ordering information. Covers a wide variety of health care topics, including quality assurance, delivery organization, economics (costs), technology, and legislation. Formerly *Abstract Newsletter.*

Science Citation Index. Thomson/ISI. • Bimonthly. $15,020.00 per year. Annual cumulation. Includes *Source Index, Citation Index, Permuterm Subject Index,* and *Corporate Index.*

Social Sciences Index. H. W. Wilson Co. • Quarterly, with annual cumulation. Price varies. Indexes more than 400 periodicals covering economics, environmental policy, government, insurance, labor, health care policy, plannning, public administration, public welfare, urban studies, women's issues, criminology, and related topics.

ALMANACS AND YEARBOOKS

Annual Review of Medicine: Selected Topics in the Clinical Sciences. Annual Reviews. • Annual. Individuals, $74.00. Includes print and online editions. INstitutions, $168.00; with online edition, $202.00.

Annual Review of Public Health. Annual Reviews. • Annual. Individuals, $74.00. Includes print and on-line editions. Institutions, $163.00; with online edidtion, $215.00.

BIBLIOGRAPHIES

Encyclopedia of Health Information Sources. Gale Cengage Learning. • 1993. $180.00. Second edition. Both print and nonprint sources of information are listed for 450 health-related topics.

Long-Term Care: An Annotated Bibliography. Theodore H. Koff. Greenwood Publishing Group, Inc. • 1995. $59.95. (Bibliographies and Indexes in Gerontology Series: No. 25).

Medical and Health Care Books and Serials in Print: An Index to Literature in Health Sciences. R. R. Bowker. • Annual. $359.00. Two volumes.

Vital and Health Statistics. Available from U. S. Government Printing Office. • Annual. Free. Lists government publications. (GPO Subject Bibliography Number 121).

BIOGRAPHICAL SOURCES

Dictionary of American Medical Biography. Joseph Carvalho and others. Greenwood Publishing Group Inc. • 1984. $210.00. Two volumes. Vol. one, $110.00; vol. two, $110.00.

CD-ROM DATABASES

Authority Health Care Law Library. LexisNexis/Matthew Bender. • Periodic updates. Price on request. Full text CD-ROM provides legal information, case law, and analysis relating to health care facilities, health insurance, longterm care, Medigap, and Medicare.

Healthcare QuickDisc. American Hospital Association. • Annual. AHA members, $2,800.00. Non-members, $3,750.00. CD-ROM corresponds to the printed *AHA Guide,* with additional material and extensive search capabilities (400 data fields). Provides detailed information on 6,000 hospitals and hospital systems, including utilization data.

Social Sciences Citation Index. ISI. • Monthly. Price on request. Provides CD-ROM indexing of articles appearing in 1700 leading social science journals worldwide, with additional selections from more than 5700 other journals. Time span is 1992 to date. Coverage includes economics, business, finance, management, communications, demographics, library and information science, political science, sociology, and many other subjects.

Social Sciences Citation Index: Compact Disc Edition with Abstracts. Institute for Scientific Information. • Monthly. Provides CD-ROM indexing and abstracting of "significant articles" from 1,700 social science journals worldwide, with additional selections from 3,200 other journals, 1986 to date. Includes economics, business, finance, management, communications, demographics, information and library science, political science, sociology, and many other subjects.

WILSONDISC: Wilson Social Sciences Abstracts. H. W. Wilson Co. • Monthly. Includes unlimited online access to *Social Sciences Index* through WILSONLINE. Provides CD-ROM indexing from 1983 and abstracting from 1994 of more than 500 periodicals covering economics, area studies, community health, public administration, public welfare, urban studies, and many other topics related to the social sciences.

DIRECTORIES

AHA Integrated Delivery Network Directory: U.S. Health Care Systems, Networks, and Alliances. American Hospital Association. • Annual. $250.00. Provides information about a wide variety of U.S. health care groups and affiliations, including hospitals, nursing homes, rehabilitation centers, psychiatric facilities, home health care agencies, clinical laboratories, outpatient facilities, and diagnostic imaging centers. Includes names of more than 8,000 key executives.

BioScan: The Worldwide Biotech Industry Reporting Service. Greenwood Publishing Group, Inc. • Annual. $975.00 per year. Bimonthly updates. Provides detailed information on over 1,000 U.S. and foreign companies broadly classified as biotechnological. In addition to medical technology and advanced pharmaceutical firms, includes firms doing research in food processing, waste management, agriculture, and veterinary science.

Business Organizations, Agencies, and Publications Directory. Gale Cengage Learning. • 2003. $480.00. 15th edition. Over 40,000 entries describing 39 types of business information sources. Classified by type of organization, publication, or service Includes state, national, and international agencies and organizations. Master index to names and keywords. Also includes e-mail addresses and web site URL's.

Buyers' Guide for the Health Care Market: A Directory of Products and Services for Health Care Institutions. Health Forum. • Annual. $17.95. Lists 1,200 suppliers and manufacturers of health care products and services for hospitals, nursing homes, and related organizations.

Detwiler's Directory of Health and Medical Resources. S. M. Detwiler and Associates. Information Today, Inc. • Biennial. $203.00. Lists sources of information relating to the healthcare industry, including government agencies, medical experts, directories, newsletters, research groups, associations, and mailing list producers. Four indexes are provided: subject, publication, service, and acronym.

Detwiler's Directory of Health and Medical Resources. S.M. Detwiler and Associates. • Biennial. $195.00. Lists a wide range of healthcare information resources, including more than 2,000 corporations, associations, government agencies, publishers, licensure organizations, market research firms, foundations, and institutes, as well as 6,000 publications. Indexed by type of information, publication, acronym, and 600 subject categories.

Directory of Physician Groups and Networks. Dorland Healthcare Information. • Annual. $495.00. Available only online. Approximately 8,000 independent practice associations (IPAs), physician hospital organizations (PHOs), management service organizations (MSOs), physician practice management companies (PPMCs), and group practices having 20 or more physicians.

Directory of Physicians in the United States. American Medical Association. • Biennial. $695.00. Four volumes. Brief information for more than 850,000 physicians. Formerly *American Medical Directory.*

Encyclopedia of Medical Organizations and Agencies. Gale Cengage Learning. • 2001. $295.00. 11th edition. Information on over 18,000 public and private organizations in medicine and related fields.

The HCEA Directory of Healthcare Meetings and Conventions. Healthcare Convention Exhibitors Association. • Semiannual. Free to members; nonmembers, $245.00 per year. Lists more than 6,000 health care meetings, most of which have an exhibit program. Formerly *Handbook-A Directory of Health Care Meetings and Conventions.*

Health Devices Sourcebook. ECRI. • Covers: Over 6,800 suppliers of patient care equipment, medical and surgical instruments, implants, clinical laboratory equipment and supplies, medical and hospital disposable supplies, and testing instruments; also lists companies that service, recondition, lease, or buy and sell used equipment; coverage includes U.S. and Canada. Entries include: Company name, address, phone, toll-free phone, fax, toll-free fax, URL, e-mail, total sales, names of key executives and contacts, product categories handled, trade names, methods of distribution, typical pricing, annual volume. Price of directory includes custom updates upon request.

Health Industry Buyers Guide. Lippincott Williams & Wilkins. • Covers: 4,000 manufacturers of hospital and physician's supplies and equipment, including medical laboratory, oxygen therapy, and X-ray supplies, home health care products, and orthopedic appliances. Entries include: Manufacturer name, address, phone, fax, full product line.

Medical and Health Information Directory. Gale Cengage Learning. • 2002. $675.00. Three volumes. 14th edition. Three volumes. $285.00 per volume. Vol. one covers medical organizations, agencies, and institutions; vol. two includes bibliographic, library, and database information; vol. three is a guide to services available for various medical and health problems.

Medical and Healthcare Marketplace Guide. IDD, Inc. • Annual. $595.00. Two volumes. Provides market survey summaries for about 500 specific product and service categories (volume one: "Research Reports"). Contains profiles of nearly 5,500 pharmaceutical, medical product, and health-care service companies (volume two: "Company Profiles").

Medical Research Centres: A World Directory of Organizations and Programmes. FT Healthcare. • Biennial. $470.00. Two volumes. Contains profiles of more than 7,000 medical research facilities around the world. Includes medical, dental, nursing, pharmaceutical, psychiatric, and surgical research centers.

National Health Directory. Aspen Publishers Inc. • Covers: about 10,000 public health-care officials at policy-making levels. Covers federal and state agencies, and members of congress and key health committees and county and city health officials. Entries include: Agency name, address; names, titles, addresses, and phone numbers of key personnel.

Plunkett's Health Care Industry Almanac: The Only Complete Guide to the Health Care Industry in America. Plunkett Research, Ltd. • Biennial. $229.99. Includes CD-ROM. Includes detailed profiles of 500 large companies providing health care products or services, with indexes by products, services, and location. Provides statistical and trend information for the health insurance industry, HMOs, hospital utilization, Medicare, medical technology, and national health expenditures.

Telehealth Buyer's Guide. Miller Freeman. • Annual. $10.00. Lists sources of telecommunications and information technology products and services for the health care industry.

ENCYCLOPEDIAS AND DICTIONARIES

Encyclopedia of Health Care Management. Michael Stahl, editor. Sage Publications, Inc. • 2004. $150.00. Contains 600 entries covering "the business of health care.".

Encyclopedic Guide to Searching and Finding Health Information on the Web. P. F. Anderson and Nancy J. Allee, editors. Neal-Schuman Publishers. • 2004. $395.00. Three volumes. Comprehensive guide to searching the Web for reliable information on hundreds of specific diseases, disorders, and health issues. Volume three covers Search Strategies and provides a Cumulative Index. (Published in conjunction with the Medical Library Association.).

FINANCIAL RATIOS

Industry Norms and Key Business Ratios. Desk Top Edition. Dun and Bradstreet Corp. • Annual. Five volumes. $475.00 per volume. $1,890.00 per set. Covers over 800 kinds of businesses, arranged by Standard Industrial Classification number. More

detailed editions covering longer periods of time are also available.

HANDBOOKS AND MANUALS

Advertising Handbook for Health Care Services. William J. Winston, editor. The Haworth Press, Inc. • 1986. $8.95. (Health Marketing Quarterly Series: Supplement No. 1).

The Consumer Health Information Source Book. Alan Rees, editor. Greenwood Publishing Group, Inc. • 2003. $65.00. Seventh edition. Bibliography of current literature and guide to organizations.

Consumers' Guide to Health Plans. Center for the Study of Services. • 1996. $14.95. Revised edition. Presents the results of a consumer survey on satisfaction with specific managed care health insurance plans, and related information. Includes "Top-Rated Plans," "Health Plans That Chose Not to Have Their Members Surveyed," and other lists. General advice is provided on choosing a plan, finding a good doctor, getting good care, etc.

Dun & Bradstreet/Gale Group Industry Handbooks. Gale Cengage Learning. • 2000. $650.00. Five volumes. $130.00 per volume. Each volume covers two or more major industries: 1. *Entertainment and Hospitality*; 2. *Construction and Agriculture*; 3. *Chemicals and Pharmaceuticals*; 4. *Computers & Software and Broadcasting & Telecommunications*; 5. *Insurance and Health & Medical Services*. The following are included for each industry: overview, statistics, financial ratios, rankings, merger information, company directory, directory of associations, and consultants directory. (Dun and Bradstreet/Gale Industry Reference Handbook Series).

Health Law Handbook. Alice G. Gosfield. West Group. • Annual. $246.00.

Healthcare Finance for the Non-Financial Manager: Basic Guide to Financial Analysis & Control. Louis Gapenski. McGraw-Hill. • 1994. $47.50.

Indexing Specialties: Medicine. L. Pilar Wyman, editor. Information Today, Inc. • 1999. $35.00. Published in conjunction with the American Society of Indexers (ASI). Includes chapters by professional medical indexers on book indexing, database indexing, reviews of published indexes, and details of such specialties as nutrition, nursing, and general medicine.

Long Term Care Administration; The Management of Institutional and Non-Institutional Components of the Continuum of Care. Ben Abramovice. The Haworth Press, Inc. • 1987. $39.95. Explores the multidisciplinary nature of long-term care. (Marketing and Health Services Administration: No. 1).

Management Accounting for Healthcare Organizations. Bruce R. Neumann and Keith E. Boles. Teach'em. • 1998. $65.00. Fifth revised edition.

INTERNET DATABASES

National Center for Health Statistics: Monitoring the Nation's Health. National Center for Health Statistics, Centers for Disease Control and Preventio.. Phone: (301)458-4000 E-mail: nchsquery@cdc.gov • URL: http://www.cdc.gov/nchswww • Web site provides detailed data on diseases, vital statistics, and health care in the U. S. Includes a search facility and links to many other health-related Web sites. "Fastats A to Z" offers quick data on hundreds of topics from Accidents to Work-Loss Days, with links to Comprehensive Data and related sources. Frequent updates. Fees: Free.

National Library of Medicine (NLM). National Institutes of Health (NIH). Phone: 888-346-3656 or (301)496-1131 Fax: (301)480-3537 E-mail: access@nlm.nih.gov • URL: http://www.nlm.nih.gov • NLM Web site offers free access through MEDLINE ("PubMed") to about nine million references to articles appearing in some 4,000 biomedi-

cal journals, with abstracts. Search interfaces range from "simple keywords to advanced Boolean expressions." The NLM site offers many links to other sources of biomedical and technical information (the National Center for Biotechnology Information, for example). Fees: Free.

ONLINE DATABASES

Embase. Elsevier Science, Inc. • Worldwide medical literature, 1974 to present. Weekly updates. Inquire as to online cost and availability.

F-D-C Reports. FDC Reports, Inc. • An online version of "The Gray Sheet" (medical devices), "The Pink Sheet" (pharmaceuticals), "The Rose Sheet" (cosmetics), "The Blue Sheet" (biomedical), and "The Tan Sheet" (nonprescription). Contains full-text information on legal, technical, corporate, financial, and marketing developments from 1987 to date, with weekly updates. Inquire as to online cost and availability.

Globalbase. Gale Cengage Learning. • Provides more than one million online summaries of business, industrial, and economic news reports from more than 1,000 publications worldwide. Covers a wide range of material appearing in international trade journals, professional magazines, and newspapers. Time period is 1984 to date, with weekly updates. Inquire as to online cost and availability.

Healthstar. Medlars Management Section. • Provides indexing and abstracting of non-clinical literature relating to health care delivery, 1975 to date. Monthly updates. Inquire as to online cost and availability.

Marketing and Advertising Reference Service (MARS). Gale Cengage Learning. • Provides abstracts of literature relating to consumer marketing and advertising, including all forms of advertising media. Time period is 1984 to date. Daily updates. Inquire as to online cost and availability.

Medline. Medlars Management Section. • Provides indexing and abstracting of worldwide medical literature, 1966 to date. Weekly updates. Inquire as to online cost and availability.

Newspaper Abstracts Daily. ProQuest Inc. • Provides online coverage (citations and abstracts) of 25 major newspapers. Covers business, economics, current affairs, health, fitness, sports, education, technology, government, consumer affairs, psychology, the arts, and the social sciences. Time period is 1986 to date, with daily updates. Inquire as to online cost and availability.

PAIS International. Public Affairs Information Service, Inc. • Corresponds to the former printed publications, *PAIS Bulletin* (1976-90) and *PAIS Foreign Language Index* (1972-90), and to the current *PAIS International in Print* (1991 to date). Covers economic, political, and sociological material appearing in periodicals, books, government documents, and other publications. Updating is monthly. Inquire as to online cost and availability.'

PROMT: Predicasts Overview of Markets and Technology. Gale Cengage Learning. • Companies, products, applied technologies and markets. U.S. and international literature coverage, 1972 to date. Inquire as to online cost and availability. Provides abstracts from more than 1,600 publications. Weekly updates.

Scisearch. Institute for Scientific Information. • Broad, multidisciplinary index to the literature of science and technology, 1974 to present. Inquire as to online cost and availability. Coverage of literature is worldwide, with weekly updates.

Wilson Business Abstracts Online. H. W. Wilson Co. • Indexes and abstracts 600 major business periodicals, plus the *Wall Street Journal* and the business section of the *New York Times*. Indexing is from 1982, abstracting from 1990, with the two newspapers included from 1993. Updated weekly.

Inquire as to online cost and availability. (*Business Periodicals Index* without abstracts is also available online.).

Wilson Social Sciences Abstracts Online. H. W. Wilson Co. • Provides online abstracting and indexing of more than 500 periodicals covering area studies, community health, public administration, public welfare, urban studies, and many other social science topics. Time period is 1994 to date for abstracts and 1983 to date for indexing, with updates weekly. Inquire as to online cost and availability.

PERIODICALS AND NEWSLETTERS

AHA News. American Hospital Association. HealthForum. • Description: Highlights major news affecting hospitals and the health care field. Reports on legislation and regulation, court cases, surveys, and federal programs. Carries information on individual hospitals and allied hospital associations.

American Dental Association Journal. American Dental Association. • Monthly. Free to members; non-members, $100.00 per year; institutions, $121.00 per year.

American Health Care Association: Provider. American Health Care Association. • Monthly. $48.00 per year. Formerly *American Health Care Association Journal.*

American Journal of Nursing. American Nurses Association. Lippincott Williams and Wilkins. • Monthly. Individuals, $39.00 per year; institutions, $129.00 per year. For registered nurses. Emphasis on the latest technological advances affecting nursing care.

American Medical News. American Medical Association. • 48 times a year. Members, $95.00 per year; non-members, $145.00 per year; institutions, $325.00 per year. Economic and legal news for the medical profession.

The BBI Newsletter: A Perceptive Analysis of the Healthcare Industry and Marketplace Focusing on New Technology, Strategic Planning, and Marketshare Projections. American Health Consultants. • Monthly. $827.00 per year.

The Gray Sheet Reports: Medical Devices, Diagnostics and Instrumentation. F-D-C Reports, Inc. • Weekly. Institutions, $1,172.00 per year. Newsletter. Provides industry and financial news, including a medical sector stock index. Monitors regulatory developments at the Center for Devices and Radiological Health of the U. S. Food and Drug Administration.

Health Care Financing Review. Available from U. S. Government Printing Office. • Quarterly. $48.00 per year. Issued by the Health Care Financing Administration, U. S. Department of Health and Human Services. Presents articles by professionals in the areas of health care costs and financing.

Health Care Fraud and Abuse Newsletter. American Lawyer Media, Inc. • Monthly. $195.00 per year. Newsletter. Provides legal news relating mainly to fraudulent or excessive medical billing practices. Covers both civil and criminal proceedings. (A Law Journal Newsletter, formerly published by Leader Publications).

Health Care Strategic Management: The Newsletter for Hospital Strategies. Business Word, Inc. • Monthly. $284.00 per year. Planning, marketing and resource allocation.

Health Facilities Management. American Hospital Association. American Hospital Publishing, Inc. • Monthly. $40.00 per year. Covers building maintenance and engineering for hospitals and nursing homes.

Health Forum Journal: Leadership Strategies for Healthcare Executives. Health Forum. • Biweekly. $65.00 per year. Covers the general management of hospitals, nursing homes, and managed care organizations. Formerly *HospitalsHealthNetworks.*

Health Forum Journal: Leadership Strategies for Healthcare Executives. Healthcare Forum. • Bimonthly. $65.00 per year.

Health Grants and Contracts Weekly: Selected Federal Project Opportunities. Aspen Publishers, Inc. • 50 times a year. $459.00 per year. Newsletter. Lists new health-related federal contracts and grants.

Health Industry Today: The Market Letter for Health Care Industry Vendors. Business Word, Inc. • Monthly. $360.00 per year; online edition, $420.00 per year.

The Health Letter. Sidney M. Wolfe, editor. North America Syndicate. • Description: Addresses health topics, with discussion of cause and effect, practical counsel, and information on normal variations. Carries news of research, briefings from current medical literature, and highlights of conferences and other events.

Health Management Technology. Nelson Publishing, Inc. • Monthly. $38.00 per year. Formerly *Computers in Healthcare.*

Health Marketing Quarterly. The Haworth Press, Inc. • Quarterly. $580.00 per year.

Health News Daily. F-D-C Reports Inc. • Description: Tracks developments in health care policy, legislation and regulation, insurance, pharmaceuticals, delivery, manufacturing, technology and treatment, funding, and research.

Health Policy and Biomedical Research: The Blue Sheet. F-D-C Reports, Inc. • 51 times a year. $716.00 per year. Newsletter. Emphasis is on news of medical research agencies and institutions, especially the National Institutes of Health (NIH).

Healthcare Executive. American College of Healthcare Executives. • Bimonthly. $70.00 per year. Focuses on critical management issues.

Healthcare Financial Management. Healthcare Financial Management Association. • Monthly. $102.00 per year.

Healthcare Informatics: The Business of Healthcare Information Technology. McGraw-Hill. • Monthly. $39.95 per year. Covers various aspects of information and computer technology for the health care industry.

Healthcare Marketing Report. HMR Publication Group. • Monthly. Price on application.

Healthcare Risk Management. American Health Consultants Inc. • Description: Analyzes specific legal cases and trends relevant to healthcare liability. Discusses malpractice, liability for patients, staff and visitor injury, injury prevention, biomedical engineering, and medical staff credentials. Also covers high-risk areas of hospitals, hospital-owned home health and physician practices, accreditation, Medicare reimbursement, physician liability, medical records, and claims management. Recurring features include interviews, statistics, news of research, guest columns, legal briefs, and commentaries.

HealthLeaders, Inc. • Bimonthly. $49.95 per year. Provides broad coverage of finance, marketing, management, and technology for executives in the health care industry. Includes "Roundtable" discussions of particular health care issues. F ormerly *Healthcare Business.*

International Journal of Health Planning and Management. John Wiley and Sons, Inc., Journals. • Quarterly. Individuals, $960.00 per year; institutions, $1,280.00 per year. Published in England by John Wiley and Sons Ltd.

JAMA: The Journal of the American Medical Association. American Medical Association. • 48 times a year. Institutions, $365.00 per year. Includes online edition.

Marketing Health Services. American Marketing Association. • Quarterly. Members, $45.00 per year; non-members, $70.00 per year; institutions, $90.00

per year. Formerly *Journal of Health Care Marketing.*

Medical Malpractice Law and Strategy. American Lawyer Media, Inc. • Monthly. $189.00 per year. Newsletter. Covers malpractice legal issues for lawyers representing physicians and for lawyers representing patients. Includes news of judicial, legislative, and medical developments affecting malpractice strategies. (A Law Journal Newsletter, formerly published by Leader Publications).

Medical Marketing and Media. Haymarket Media, Inc. • Monthly. Individuals, $96.00 per year; institutions, $108.00 per person. Contains articles on marketing, direct marketing, advertising media, and sales personnel for the healthcare and pharmaceutical industries.

Medical Reference Services Quarterly. Haworth Press, Inc. • Quarterly. Institutions, $275.00 per year. An academic and practical journal for medical reference librarians.

MGMA Connexion. Medical Group Management Association. • 10 times a year. Individuals, $95.00 per year; institutions, $175.00 per year. Formerly *Medical Group Management Journal.*

The Milbank Quarterly: A Journal of Public Health and Health Care Policy. Milbank Memorial Fund. Blackwell Publishing. • Quarterly. Institutions, $142.00 per year. Includes print and online editions. Formerly *Health and Society.*

Modern Healthcare: The Newsmagazine for Administrators and Managers in Hospitals and Other Healthcare Institutions. Crain Communications, Inc. • Weekly. $145.00 per year; students, $63.00 per year.

Modern Physician: Essential Business News for the Executive Physician. Crain Communications, Inc. • Monthly. $45.00. Edited for physicians responsible for business decisions at hospitals, clinics, HMOs, and other health groups. Includes special issues on managed care, practice management, legal issues, and finance.

New England Journal of Medicine. Massachusetts Medical Society, Publishing Div. • Weekly. Individuals, $139.00 per year; institutions, $489.00 per year. The offical journal of the Massachusetts Medical Society.

Physicians & Computers. Moorhead Publications Inc. • Monthly. $40.00 per year. Includes material on computer diagnostics, online research, medical and non-medical software, computer equipment, and practice management.

Public Relations. PBI Media, LLC. • Biweekly. $397.00 per year. Newsletter on public relations and client communications for the healthcare industry. Incorporates (Healthcare PR and Marketing News).

Services Marketing Quarterly. Haworth Press, Inc. • Quarterly. Institutions, $425.00 per year. Two volumes. Supplies "how to" marketing tools for specific sectors of the expanding service sector of the economy. Formerly *Journal of Professional Services Marketing.*

Strategic Health Care Marketing. Health Care Communications. • Description: Provides news and analysis on health care services marketing, and business development. Covers strategies and techniques used by marketing innovators. Recurring features include interviews, news of research, a calendar of events, reports of meetings, and notices of publications available.

RESEARCH CENTERS AND INSTITUTES

Bureau of Economic and Business Research. University of Illinois at Urbana-Champaign, 1206 S. Sixth St., 403 Wohlers Hall, Champaign, IL 61820. Phone: (217)333-2330 Fax: (217)244-7410 E-mail: g-oldman@uiuc.edu • URL: http://www.business.uiuc.edu/research.

Center for Health Administration Studies.

University of Chicago, 969 E. 60th St., Chicago, IL 60637. Phone: (773)702-7104 Fax: (773)702-7222 E-mail: chas@uchichago.edu • URL: http://www.chas.uchicago.edu.

Center for Health Policy Law and Management. Duke University, 125 Old Chemistry Bldg., Durham, NC 27708. Phone: (919)684-3023 Fax: (919)684-6246 E-mail: fsloan@hpolicy.duke.edu • URL: http://www.hpolicy.duke.edu.

Center for Health Research. Wayne State University, College of Nursing, 5557 Cass Ave., Detroit, MI 48202-3515. Phone: (313)577-4134 Fax: (313)577-5777 E-mail: nursinginfo@wayne.edu • URL: http://www.nursing.wayne.edu • Studies innovation in health care organization and financing.

ECRI: Emergency Care Research Institute. 5200 Butler Pike, Plymouth Meeting, PA 19462-1298. Phone: (610)825-6000 Fax: (610)834-1275 E-mail: info@ecri.org • URL: http://www.ecri.org • Major research area is health care technology.

Health Policy Institute. University of Texas-Houston Health Science Center, 1200 Herman Pressler Dr., Suite 301, Houston, TX 77030. Phone: (713)500-9485 Fax: (713)500-9493.

Institute for Health, Health Care Policy, and Aging Research. Rutgers University, 30 College Ave., New Brunswick, NJ 08901-1293. Phone: (732)932-8413 Fax: (732)932-6872 E-mail: caboyer@rci.rutgers.edu • URL: http://www.ihhcpar.rutgers.edu/ • Areas of study include HMO use by older adults.

Institute for Health Services Research and Policy Studies. Northwestern University, 629 Noyes St., Evanston, IL 60208-4170. Phone: (847)491-5643 Fax: (847)491-2202 E-mail: ihsrps@northwestern.edu • URL: http://www.northwestern.edu/ihsrps.

Leonard Davis Institute of Health Economics. University of Pennsylvania, 3641 Locust Walk, Philadelphia, PA 19104-6218. Phone: (215)898-1655 Fax: (215)898-0229 E-mail: levyj@wharton.upenn.edu • URL: http://www.upenn.edu/ldi/ • Research fields include health care management and cost-quality trade-offs.

Malcolm Wiener Center for Social Policy. Harvard University, John F. Kennedy School of Government, 79 John F. Kennedy St., Cambridge, MA 02138. Phone: (617)495-1461 Fax: (617)496-9053 E-mail: julie_wilson@harvard.edu • URL: http://www.ksg.harvard.edu/socpol • Does multidisciplinary research on health care access and financing.

STATISTICS SOURCES

Health and Environment in America's Top-Rated Cities: A Statistical Profile. Grey House Publishing. • Biennial. $125.00. Covers 75 U. S. cities. Includes statistical and other data on a wide variety of topics, such as air quality, water quality, recycling, hospitals, physicians, health care costs, death rates, infant mortality, accidents, and suicides.

Health Care Costs. DRI/McGraw-Hill. • Quarterly. Price on application. Cost indexes for hospitals, nursing homes, and home healthcare agencies.

Industry Profile and Healthcare Factbook. Healthcare Distribution Management Association. • Annual. $349.00. Provides 266 statistical tables in three sections: "Industry Profile" (financial ratios related to drug distribution), "Pharmaceutical and Healthcare Distribution Trends and Facts," and "Healthcare Factbook" (expenditures, insurance utilization, company/product rankings, drug price inflation, generics, OTC, drug store data, hospital statistics, healthcare consumer summaries, etc.). Also known as *HDMA Factbook.* The Healthcare Distribution Management Association was formerly the National Wholesale Druggists' Association.

Social Statistics of the United States. Mark S. Littman, editor. Bernan Press. • 2000. $65.00. Includes statistical data on population growth, labor force, occupations, environmental trends, leisure time use,

income, poverty, taxes, and other economic or demographic topics.

Social Trends and Indicators USA. Monique D. Magee, editor. Gale Cengage Learning. • 2003. $450.00. Four volumes. Includes data on labor, economics, the health care industry, crime, leisure, population, education, social security, and many other topics. Sources include various government agencies and major publications.

Standard & Poor's Industry Surveys. Standard & Poor's. • Semiannual. $1,800.00. Two looseleaf volumes. Includes monthly *Supplements.* Provides detailed, individual surveys of 52 major industry groups. Each survey is revised on a semiannual basis. Also includes "Monthly Investment Review" (industry group investment analysis) and monthly "Trends & Projections" (economic analysis).

Statistical Forecasts of the United States. Gale Cengage Learning. • 1995. $115.00. Second edition. Provides both long-term and short-term statistical forecasts relating to basic items in the U. S.: population, employment, labor, crime, education, and health care. Data in the form of charts, graphs, and tables has been taken from a wide variety of government and private sources. Includes a subject index and an "Index of Forecast by Year.".

A Statistical Portrait of the United States: Social Conditions and Trends. Mark S. Littman, editor. Bernan Press. • 1998. $89.00. Covers "social, economic, and environmental trends in the United States over the past 25 years." Includes statistical tables, graphs, and analysis relating to such topics as population, income, poverty, wealth, labor, housing, education, healthcare, air/water quality, and government. (Statistical Portrait of the United States: Social Conditions and Trends Series).

U. S. Industry and Trade Outlook. Available from National Technical Information Service. • Annual. $69.95. Produced by the International Trade Administration, U. S. Department of Commerce, in a "public-private" partnership with DRI/McGraw-Hill and Standard & Poor's. Provides basic data, outlook for the current year, and "Long-Term Prospects" (five-year projections) for a wide variety of products and services. Includes high technology industries. Formerly *U. S. Industrial Outlook.*

The Universal Healthcare Almanac: A Complete Guide for the Healthcare Professional - Facts, Figures, Analysis. Silver & Cherner, Ltd. • $195.00 per year. Looseleaf service. Quarterly updates. Includes a wide variety of health care statistics: national expenditures, hospital data, health insurance, health professionals, vital statistics, demographics, etc. Years of coverage vary, with long range forecasts provided in some cases.

WEFA Industrial Monitor. John Wiley and Sons, Inc. • Annual. $65.00. Prepared by industry analysts at WEFA, an economic forecasting and consulting firm (originally Wharton Econometric Forecasting Associates). Contains discussions of the outlook for major U. S. industries, with many 10-year forecasts (WEFA Web site is http://www.wefa.com).

TRADE/PROFESSIONAL ASSOCIATIONS

Advanced Medical Technology Association. 701 Pennsylvania Ave. NW, Ste. 800, Washington, DC 20004-2654. Phone: (202)783-8700 Fax: (202)783-8750 E-mail: info@advamed.org • URL: http://www.advamed.org • Represents domestic (including U.S. territories and possessions) manufacturers of medical devices, diagnostic products, and healthcare information systems. Develops programs and activities on economic, technical, medical, and scientific matters affecting the industry. Gathers and disseminates information concerning the United States and international developments in legislative, regulatory, scientific or standards-making areas. Conducts scientific and educational seminars and programs.

American Academy of Medical Administrators. 701 Lee St., Ste. 600, Des Plaines, IL 60016. Phone: (847)759-8601 Fax: (847)759-8602 E-mail: info@aameda.org • URL: http://www.aameda.org • Members are executives and middle managers in health care administration.

American Association for Continuity of Care. P.O. Box 532, Dunedin, FL 34697. Phone: (727)738-1030 Fax: (727)738-8099 • URL: http://www.continuityofcare.com • Members are professionals concerned with continuity of care, health care after hospital discharge, and home health care.

American Association of Health Plans. 1129 20th St., N.W., Suite 600, Washington, DC 20036-3421. Phone: (202)728-3200 Fax: (202)331-7487 E-mail: aahp@aahp.org • URL: http://www.aahp.org • Supports the managed health care industry.

American Association of Healthcare Consultants. Five Revere Dr., Suite 200, Northbrook, IL 60062. Phone: 888-350-2242 E-mail: info@aahc.net • URL: http://www.aahc.net • Members are professional consultants who specialize in the health care industry. Formerly American Association of Hospital Consultants.

American Board of Medical Specialties. 1007 Church St., Suite 404, Evanston, IL 60201-5913. Phone: (847)491-9091 Fax: (847)328-3596 E-mail: info@abms.org • URL: http://www.abms.org/abms • Functions as the parent organization for U. S. medical specialty boards. Supersedes Advisory Board for Medical Specialties.

American College of Health Care Administrators. 300 N. Lee St., No. 301, Alexandria, VA 22314. Phone: 888-882-2422 or (703)739-7900 Fax: (703)739-7901 E-mail: mtn@achca.org • URL: http://www.achca.org • Formerly American College of Nursing Home Administrators.

American College of Healthcare Executives. One N. Franklin, St., Suite 1700, Chicago, IL 60606-3491. Phone: (312)424-2800 Fax: (312)424-0023 E-mail: ache@ache.org • URL: http://www.ache.org • Formerly American College of Hospital Administrators.

American Dental Association. 211 E Chicago Ave., Chicago, IL 60611-2678. Phone: (312)440-2500 Fax: (312)440-2800 E-mail: publicinfo@ada.org • URL: http://www.ada.org • Professional society of dentists. Encourages the improvement of the health of the public and promotes the art and science of dentistry in matters of legislation and regulations. Inspects and accredits dental schools and schools for dental hygienists, assistants, and laboratory technicians. Conducts research programs at ADA Foundation +Research Institute. Produces dental health education material used in the U.S. Sponsors National Children's Dental Health Month and Give Kids a Smile Day. Compiles statistics on personnel, practice, and dental care needs and attitudes of patients with regard to dental health. Sponsors 13 councils.

American Health Care Association. 1201 L St. NW, Washington, DC 20005. Phone: (202)842-4444 Fax: (202)842-3860 E-mail: hr@ahca.org • URL: http://www.ahcancal.org/Pages/Default.aspx • Federation of state associations of long-term health care facilities. Promotes standards for professionals in long-term health care delivery and quality care for patients and residents in a safe environment. Focuses on issues of availability, quality, affordability, and fair payment. Operates as liaison with governmental agencies, Congress, and professional associations. Compiles statistics.

American Hospital Association. 1 N Franklin, Chicago, IL 60606-3421. Phone: (312)422-3000 Fax: (312)422-4796 E-mail: info@highways.org • URL: http://www.aha.org • Represents health care provider organizations. Seeks to advance the health of individuals and communities. Leads, represents, and serves health care provider organizations that are accountable to the community and committed to health improvement.

American Medical Association. 515 N State St., Chicago, IL 60610. Phone: 800-621-8335 or (312)464-5000 Fax: (312)464-4184 E-mail: msc@ama-assn.org • URL: http://www.ama-assn.org • Represents county medical societies and physicians. Disseminates scientific information to members and the public. Informs members on significant medical and health legislation on state and national levels and represents the profession before Congress and governmental agencies. Cooperates in setting standards for medical schools, hospitals, residency programs, and continuing medical education courses. Offers physician placement service and counseling on practice management problems. Operates library that lends material and provides specific medical information to physicians. Maintains Ad-hoc committees for such topics as health care planning and principles of medical ethics.

American Nurses Association. 8515 Georgia Ave., Ste. 400, Silver Spring, MD 20910. Phone: 800-274-4262 or (301)628-5000 Fax: (301)628-5001 E-mail: memberinfo@ana.org • URL: http://www.nursingworld.org • Serves as membership association representing registered nurses. Advances the nursing profession by fostering high standards of nursing practice, promoting the rights of nurses in the workplace, projecting a positive and realistic view of nursing, and by lobbying the Congress and regulatory agencies on health care issues affecting nurses and the public.

American Pharmaceutical Association-Academy of Pharmacy Practice and Management. c/o Anne Burns, 2215 Constitution Ave., N.W., Washington, DC 20037-2895. Phone: 800-237-2742 or (202)628-4410 Fax: (202)783-2351 E-mail: apha-appm@mail.aphanet.org • URL: http://www.aphanet.org • Pharmacists concerned with rendering professional services directly to the public, without regard for status of employment or environment of practice. Formerly Academy of Pharmacy Practice and Management.

Health Industry Distributors Association. 310 Montgomery St., Alexandria, VA 22314-1516. Phone: 800-549-4432 or (703)549-4432 Fax: (703)549-6495 E-mail: rowan@hida.org • URL: http://www.hida.org • Represents distributors of medical, laboratory, surgical, and other health care equipment and supplies to hospitals, physicians, nursing homes, and industrial medical departments. Conducts sales training, management seminars, and research through the HIDA Educational Foundation.

Health Industry Representatives Association. 7315 E 5th Ave. Pkwy., Denver, CO 80230. Phone: (303)756-8115 Fax: (303)341-0282 E-mail: hirainfo@comcast.net • URL: http://www.hira.org • Represents manufacturers who operate independent marketing firms under contract to manufacturers of non-competing lines and manufacturers within the healthcare industry who market through independent marketing firms. Conducts special surveys at regular intervals for members. Provides panel discussions and special discounts for member firms on advertising and reference publications.

Healthcare Convention and Exhibitors Association. 5775 Peachtree-Dunwoody Rd., Bldg. G, Ste. 500, Atlanta, GA 30342. Phone: (404)252-3663 Fax: (404)252-0774 E-mail: hcea@kellencompnay.com • URL: http://www.hcea.org • Promotes more effective display of health care products at professional conventions. Formerly Health Care Exhibitors Association.

Healthcare Financial Management Association. 2 Westbrook Corporate Ctr., Ste. 700, Westchester, IL 60154. Phone: 800-252-4362 or (708)531-9600 Fax: (708)531-0032 E-mail: memberservices@hfma.org

• URL: http://www.hfma.org • Financial management professionals employed by hospitals and long-term care facilities, public accounting and consulting firms, insurance companies, medical groups, managed care organizations, government agencies, and other organizations. Conducts conferences, including annual conference in late June and audio teleconferences. Publishes books on healthcare financial issues. A Fellowship in Healthcare Financial Management (FHFMA) as well as the Certified Healthcare Professional (CHFP) in Finance and Accounting, Financial Management of Physician Practices, Managed Care, and Patient Financial Services are offered.

Independent Medical Distributors Association. 5204 Fairmount Ave., Downers Grove, IL 60515. Phone: (866)463-2937 or (630)655-9280 Fax: (630)463-0798 E-mail: imda@imda.org • URL: http://www.imda.org • Represents sales, marketing and distribution organizations focused on bringing innovative medical technologies to market. Employs salespeople who are technically sophisticated, and who enjoy long-standing relationships with clinicians in their territories.

Medical Group Management Association. 104 Inverness Terr. E, Englewood, CO 80112-5306. Phone: 877-275-6462 or (303)799-1111 or (303)799-1111 Fax: (303)643-4439 E-mail: service@mgma.com • URL: http://www.mgma.com • Represents professionals involved in the management of medical group practices and administration of other ambulatory healthcare facilities. Provides products and services that includes education, benchmarking, surveys, national advocacy and networking opportunities for members.

People's Medical Society. PO Box 868, Allentown, PA 18105-0868. Phone: 800-624-8773 or (610)770-1670 Fax: (610)770-0607 E-mail: cbi@peoplesmed.org • URL: http://www.peoplesmed.org • Promotes citizen involvement in the cost, quality, and management of the American health care system. Seeks to: train and encourage individuals to study local health care systems, practitioners, and institutions and promote preventive health care and medical cost control by these groups; address major policy issues and control health costs; encourage more preventive practice and research; promote self-care and alternative health care procedures; launch an information campaign to assist individuals in maintaining personal health and to prepare them for appointments with medical professionals. **Convention/Meeting:** none.

Pharmaceutical Research and Manufacturers Association. 1100 15th St., N.W., Suite 900, Washington, DC 20005. Phone: (202)835-3400 Fax: (202)835-3429 • URL: http://www.phrma.org • Formerly Pharmaceutical Manufacturers Association.

OTHER SOURCES

HMO Competitive Edge. InterStudy Publications. • Semiannual. Price on application. Provides highly detailed statistical, directory, and market information on U. S. health maintenance organizations. Consists of three parts: *The HMO Directory, The HMO Industry Report*, and *The Regional Market Analysis.*

HEALTH CLUB INDUSTRY

See: FITNESS INDUSTRY

HEALTH FOOD INDUSTRY

See also: DIET; FOOD INDUSTRY; HERBS; VITAMINS

GENERAL WORKS

Dietary Supplements: Current Issues. Donna V. Porter. Nova Science Publishers, Inc. • 2003. $29.

50. Covers the legislative and regulatory status of vitamin and mineral supplements.

ABSTRACTS AND INDEXES

Nutrition Abstracts and Reviews, Series A: Human and Experimental. Available from CABI Publishing, North America. • Monthly. Institutions, $1,835.00 per year. Includes single site internet access. Published in England by CABI Publishing. Provides worldwide coverage of the literature.

DIRECTORIES

Health Products Business Purchasing Guide. Cygnus Business Media. • Annual. $10.00. Listing of manufacturers, importers, exclusive distributors, brokers, and wholesalers of health food products, publishers of health food related books and magazines, and associations interested in the health foods industry. Formerly*Health Foods Business Purchasing Guide.*

ENCYCLOPEDIAS AND DICTIONARIES

Dictionary of Natural Products. George M. Hocking. Available from Information Today, Inc. • 1997. $139.50. Published by Plexus Publishing (http://www.plexuspublishing.com). Explains terms relating to the raw materials and products used in natural, folk, or alternative medicine.

FINANCIAL RATIOS

Annual Statement Studies. The Risk Management Association. • Annual. Median and quartile financial ratios are given for over 400 kinds of manufacturing, wholesale, retail, construction, and consumer finance establishments. Data is sorted by both asset size and sales volume. Includes a clearly written "Definition of Ratios" and an alphabetical industry index.

Annual Statement Studies: Industry Default Probabilities and Cash Flow Measures. The Risk Management Association. • Annual. $145.00. Serves as a companion volume to the original *Annual Statement Studies*. Gives probability of default estimates on a percentage scale for more than 450 industries. Includes changes in position year-by-year for eight financial statement line items and provides percentage measures of cash flow.

HANDBOOKS AND MANUALS

Health Food/Vitamin Store. Entrepreneur Media, Inc. • Looseleaf. $59.50. A practical guide to starting a health food store. Covers profit potential, start-up costs, market size evaluation, owner's time required, site selection, lease negotiation, pricing, accounting, advertising, promotion, etc. (Start-Up Business Guide No. E1296.).

Herbal Drugs and Phytopharmaceuticals. Max Wichtl and Norman G. Bisset, editors. CRC Press LLC. • 1994. $190.00. Provides a scientific approach to the medicinal use of herbs. (English translation of original German edition.).

PERIODICALS AND NEWSLETTERS

Health Products Business: The Business Publication of the Natural Foods In dustry. Cygnus Business Media. • Monthly. $60.00 per year.

Journal of Dietary Supplements. Haworth Press, Inc. • Quarterly. $175.00 per year to libraries; $50.00 per year to individuals. Edited with a view to both academic research and industry concerns. Sections of the journal are dedicated to health professionals, educators, dieticians, and an "Industry Spotlight." Includes book reviews and short reviews of research appearing elsewhere. Formerly *Journal of Nutraceuticals, Functional & Medical Foods.*

Natural Business: The Journal of Business and Financial News for the Natural Products Industry. Natural Business Communications. • Monthly. $279.00 per year. Covers the business aspects of natural and organic products and dietary supplements, including information about private and public companies in the industry.

OTHER SOURCES

The Health and Natural Product Store Market. Available from MarketResearch.com. • 1999. $2,750.00. Published by Packaged Facts. Contains market research data.

Healthy Prepared Foods. MarketResearch.com. • 1999. $2,750.00. Consumer market data on foods that are low in calories, fat, cholesterol, sodium, and sugar or high in fiber and calcium, with forecasts to 2003.

Market for Healthy Snacks. MarketResearch.com. • 1996. $3,250.00. Provides market data on granola bars, dried fruit, trail mix, rice cakes, etc.

HEALTH, INDUSTRIAL

See: INDUSTRIAL HYGIENE

HEALTH INSURANCE

See also: ACCIDENT INSURANCE; HEALTH MAINTENANCE ORGANIZATIONS; INSURANCE; LIFE INSURANCE; LONG-TERM CARE INSURANCE; MEDICARE

GENERAL WORKS

Compulsory Health Insurance: The Continuing American Debate. Ronald L. Numbers, editor. Greenwood Publishing Group Inc. • 1982. $57.95. (Contributions in Medical History Series: No.11).

Fundamentals of Employee Benefit Programs. Employee Benefit Research Institute. • 1996. $49.95. Fifth edition. Provides basic explanation of employee benefit programs in both the private and public sectors, including health insurance, pension plans, retirement planning, social security, and long-term care insurance.

Health Insurance: Current Issues and Background. William S. Stevens, editor. Nova Science Publishers, Inc. • 2003. $59.00. Provides articles by various authors on the health insurance situation in America, with emphasis on the health problems of the uninsured. Includes statistical data.

Medical Care, Medical Costs: The Search for a Health Insurance Policy. Rashi Fein. Replica Books. • 1999. $29.00.

Medicare Made Easy: Everything You Need to Know to Make Medicare Work for You. Charles B. Inlander and Michael A. Danio. Fine Communications. • 1999. $19.98. Revised edition. Provides basic information on Medicare claims processing and the manner in which Medicare relates to other health insurance. The author is a consumer advocate and president of the People's Medical Society.

Smarter Insurance Solutions. Janet Bamford. Bloomberg. • 1996. $19.95. Provides practical advice to consumers, with separate chapters on the following kinds of insurance: automobile, homeowners, health, disability, and life. (Bloomberg Personal Bookshelf Series).

ABSTRACTS AND INDEXES

Insurance Periodicals Index. Specials Libraries Association, Insurance and Employees Benefits Div. NILS Publishing Co. • Annual. $250.00. Compiled by the Insurance and Employee Benefits Div., Special Libraries Association. A yearly index of over 15,000 articles from about 35 insurance periodicals. Arrangement is by subject, with an index to authors.

ALMANACS AND YEARBOOKS

Insurance Almanac: Who, What, When and Where in Insurance. Underwriter Printing and Publishing Co. • Annual. $175.00. Lists insurance agencies and brokerage firms; U.S. and Canadian insurance companies, adjusters, appraisers, auditors, investiga-

tors, insurance officials and insurance organizations.

BIBLIOGRAPHIES

Insurance and Employee Benefits Literature. Special Libraries Association, Insurance and Employee Benefits Div. • Bimonthly. $15.00 per year. Lists a wide variety of literature in all branches of the insurance industry. Includes annotations.

List of Worthwhile Life and Health Insurance Books. American Council of Life Insurance. • Annual. Free. Books in print on life and health insurance and closely related subjects.

CD-ROM DATABASES

Magazine Index Plus. Gale Cengage Learning. • Monthly. $4,000.00 per year (includes InfoTrac workstation). Provides full text on CD-ROM for about 100 popular, general interest magazines and indexing for 300 others. Includes special indexing of reviews and product evaluations. Time period is 1980 to date.

U. S. Insurance: Life, Accident, and Health. Sheshunoff Information Services, Inc. • Monthly. Price on application. CD-ROM provides detailed, current information on the financial characteristics of more than 2,300 life, accident, and health insurance companies.

DIRECTORIES

Business Insurance-Directory of HMOs, POSs and PPOs. Crain Communications. • Annual. $40.00. Provides detailed information on more than 600 managed care providers in the U. S., chiefly health maintenance organizations (HMOs) and preferred provider organizations (PPOs).

Who Writes What in Life and Health Insurance. The National Underwriter Co. • Annual. $9.95.

ENCYCLOPEDIAS AND DICTIONARIES

Dictionary of Insurance Terms. Harvey W. Rubin. Barron's Educational Series, Inc. • 2000. $14.95. Fourth edition. Defines terms in a wide variety of insurance fields. (Business Dictionaries Series).

Glossary of Insurance Policy Terms. Organization for Economic Cooperation and Development. • 1999. $30.00. "The selected topics range from insurance policy regulation/supervision to general trade issues and include technical terms related to issues such as claims, premiums, and provisions." Edited for government, academic, business, and insurance organizations.

Health Insurance Terminology: A Glossary of Health Insurance Terms. Margaret Lynch, editor. Health Insurance Association of America. • 1992. $10.00.

Insurance Words and Their Meanings: A Glossary of Insurance Terms. The Rough Notes Co., Inc. • 2001. 17th edition. Price on application.

Rupp's Insurance and Risk Management Glossary. Richard V. Rupp. NILS Publishing Co. • 2001. $35.00. Second edition. Provides definitions of 6,400 insurance words and phrases. Includes a guide to acronyms and abbreviations.

HANDBOOKS AND MANUALS

The Complete Book of Insurance: Protecting Your Life, Health Property, and Income. Ben G. Baldwin. McGraw-Hill. • 1991. $24.95. Provides basic information and advice on various kinds of insurance: life, health, property (fire), disability, long-term care, automobile, liability, and annuities.

How to Cover the Gaps in Medicare: Health Insurance and Long-Term Care Options for the Retired. Robert A. Gilmour. American Institute for Economic Research. • 2003. $10.00. Four parts: "The Medicare Quandry," "How to Protect Yourself Against the Medigap," "Long-Term Care Options", and "End-of-Life Decisions" (living wills). Includes discussions of long-term care insurance, retirement communities, and HMO Medicare insurance.

Insurance Handbook for the Medical Offices. Marilyn T. Fordney. Elsevier. • 2001. $55.00. Seventh edition.

Life and Health Insurance Law. Muriel L. Crawford. McGraw Hill. • 1997. $118.88. Eighth edition. Covers the legal aspects of life, health, and accident insurance.

McGill's Life Insurance. Edward E. Graves, editor. The American College. • 2002. $80.00. Fourth edition. Contains chapters by various authors on diverse kinds of life insurance, as well as annuities, disability insurance, long-term care insurance, risk management, reinsurance, and other insurance topics. (Huebner School Series).

Medical Claims Processing. Entrepreneur Media, Inc. • Looseleaf. $59.50. A practical guide to starting a medical claims processing service. Covers profit potential, start-up costs, market size evaluation, owner's time required, site selection, pricing, accounting, advertising, promotion, etc. (Start-Up Business Guide No. E1345.).

Medicare and Medicaid Claims and Procedures. Harvey L. McCormick. West Publishing Co. • 2001. Two volumes. Third edition. Price on application.

Medicare: Employer Health Plans. Available from Consumer Information Center. • Free. Published by the U. S. Department of Health and Human Services. Explains the special rules that apply to Medicare beneficiaries who have employer group health plan coverage. (Publication No. 520-Y.).

Medicare Explained. CCH, Inc. • Annual. $37.50.

Source Book of Health Insurance Data, 1997-1998. Health Insurance Association of America. • 1998. $35.00. Data on health insurance, medical care costs, morbidity and health manpower in the U. S.

INTERNET DATABASES

InsWeb. InsWeb Corp. Phone: (916)853-3300 E-mail: info@insweb.com • URL: http://www.insweb.com • Web site offers a wide variety of advice and information on automobile, life, health, and "other" insurance. Includes glossaries of insurance terms, Standard & Poor's ratings of individual insurance companies, and "Financial Needs Estimators." Searching is available. Fees: Free.

National Center for Health Statistics: Monitoring the Nation's Health. National Center for Health Statistics, Centers for Disease Control and Preventio. Phone: (301)458-4000 E-mail: nchsquery@cdc.gov • URL: http://www.cdc.gov/nchswww • Web site provides detailed data on diseases, vital statistics, and health care in the U. S. Includes a search facility and links to many other health-related Web sites. "Fastats A to Z" offers quick data on hundreds of topics from Accidents to Work-Loss Days, with links to Comprehensive Data and related sources. Frequent updates. Fees: Free.

ONLINE DATABASES

Healthstar. Medlars Management Section. • Provides indexing and abstracting of non-clinical literature relating to health care delivery, 1975 to date. Monthly updates. Inquire as to online cost and availability.

I.I.I. Data Base Search. Insurance Information Institute. • Provides online citations and abstracts of insurance-related literature in magazines, newspapers, trade journals, and books. Emphasis is on property and casualty insurance issues, including highway safety, product safety, and environmental liability. Inquire as to online cost and availability.

PERIODICALS AND NEWSLETTERS

Advisor Today. National Association of Insurance and Finacial Advisors. • Monthly. Free to members; non-members, $7.00 per year. Edited for individual life and health insurance agents. Among the topics included are disability insurance and long-term care insurance. Formerly Life Association News.

Best's Review: Inurance Issues and Analysis. A.M.

Best Co. • Monthly. $25.00 per year. Editorial coverage of significant industry trends, developments, and important events. Formerly Best's Review: Property-Casualty Insurance.

Contingencies: The Magazine of the Actuarial Profession. American Academy of Actuaries. • Bimonthly. $30.00 per year. Provides non-technical articles on the actuarial aspects of insurance, employee benefits, and pensions.

Drug Benefit Trends: For Pharmacy Managers and Managed HealthCare Professionals. Cliggott Publishing Co. • Monthly. Individuals, $95.00 per year; libraries, $120.00 per year; students, $40.00 per year. Covers the business of managed care drug benefits.

Guide to HMOs and Health Insurers: A Quarterly Compilation of Health Insurance Company Ratings and Analysis. Weiss Ratings, Inc. • Quarterly. $438.00 per year. Emphasis is on rating of financial safety and relative risk. Includes annual summary.

Guide to Life, Health, and Annuity Insurers: A Quarterly Compilation of Insurance Company Ratings and Analysis. Weiss Ratings, Inc. • Quarterly. $438.00 per year. Emphasis is on rating of financial safety and relative risk. Includes annual summary.

Health Care Financing Review. Available from U. S. Government Printing Office. • Quarterly. $48.00 per year. Issued by the Health Care Financing Administration, U. S. Department of Health and Human Services. Presents articles by professionals in the areas of health care costs and financing.

Health Data Management. Thomson Media. • Monthly. $98.00 per year. Covers the management and automation of clinical data and health care insurance claims. Provides news and analysis of various aspects of health care information technology for administrators of hospitals, clinics, and managed care plans.

Health Insurance Underwriter. National Association of Health Underwriters. • Monthly. $25.00 per year. Includes special feature issues on long-term care insurance, disability insurance, managed health care, and insurance office management.

Health News Daily. F-D-C Reports Inc. • Description: Tracks developments in health care policy, legislation and regulation, insurance, pharmaceuticals, delivery, manufacturing, technology and treatment, funding, and research.

Healthcare Risk Management. American Health Consultants Inc. • Description: Analyzes specific legal cases and trends relevant to healthcare liability. Discusses malpractice, liability for patients, staff and visitor injury, injury prevention, biomedical engineering, and medical staff credentials. Also covers high-risk areas of hospitals, hospital-owned home health and physician practices, accreditation, Medicare reimbursement, physician liability, medical records, and claims management. Recurring features include interviews, statistics, news of research, guest columns, legal briefs, and commentaries.

Healthplan: The Magazine of Trends, Insights, and Best Practices. American Association of Health Plans. • Bimonthly. $75.00 per year. Edited for managed care executives.

Inquiry: The Journal of Health Care Organization, Provision, and Financing. Blue Cross and Blue Shield Association of the Rochester Area. • Quarterly. Individuals, $53.00 per year; institutions, $75.00 per year.

Insurance and Technology. CMP Media LLC. • Monthly. $65.00 per year. Covers information technology and systems management as applied to the operation of life, health, casualty, and property insurance companies.

Insurance Forum: For the Unfettered Exchange of Ideas About Insurance. Joseph M. Belth, editor.

Insurance Forum, Inc. • Monthly. $90.00 per year. Newsletter. Provides analysis of the insurance business, including occasional special issues showing the ratings of about 1,600 life-health insurance companies, as determined by four major rating services: Duff & Phelps Credit Rating Co., Moody's Investors Service, Standard & Poor's Corp., and Weiss Research, Inc.

Risk and Insurance. LRP Publications. • 15 times a year. Price on application. Topics include risk management, workers' compensation, reinsurance, employee benefits, and managed care.

RESEARCH CENTERS AND INSTITUTES

Division of Health Services Research and Policy. University of Minnesota, Mayo Memorial Bldg., Minneapolis, MN 55455. Phone: (612)624-6151 Fax: (612)624-2196 E-mail: foote003@tc.umn.edu • URL: http://www.hsr.umn.edu • Fields of research include health insurance, consumer choice of health plans, quality of care, and long-term care.

Employee Benefit Research Institute. Employee Benefit Research Institute. 1100 13 St. NW, Ste. 878, Washington, DC 20005. Phone: (202)659-0670 Fax: (202)775-6312 E-mail: salisbury@ebri.org • URL: http://www.ebri.org • Employee benefits in the public and private sectors, including studies on individual retirement accounts, retirement income, flexible benefits, financing health care for the elderly, health care costs, long-term care, employee benefits and federal tax policy, social security, changing benefits, and government regulation of employee benefit plans.

Office of Academic Affairs, School of Public Health. University of Michigan, 109 S. Observatory St., 3537 SPH 1, Ann Arbor, MI 48109-2029. Phone: (734)764-5425 Fax: (734)763-5455 E-mail: sph.inquiries@umich.edu • URL: http://www.sph.umich.edu/ • Research fields include health care economics, health insurance, and long-term care.

Social Welfare Research Institute. Boston College. 140 Commonwealth Ave., McGuinn Hall, Room 515, Chestnut Hill, MA 02167. Phone: (617)552-4070 Fax: (617)552-3903 E-mail: swri508@bc.edu • URL: http://www.bc.edu/swri

STATISTICS SOURCES

DRG Handbook. HCIA-Sachs, Inc. • Annual. $399.00. Presents summary data for all 477 DRGs (diagnosis-related groups) and the 23 MDCs (major diagnostic categories), based on information from more than 11 million Medicare patients. Ranks DRG information for 100 hospital groups according to number of beds, payor mix, case-mix, system affiliation, and profitability. Emphasis is financial. Formerly *Medicare DRG Handbook.*

EBRI's Databook on Employee Benefits: What is the Promise?. Ken McDonnell and others. Employee Benefit Research Institute. • 1997 $99.00. Fourth edition. Contains more than 350 tables and charts presenting data on employee benefits in the U. S., including pensions, health insurance, social security, and medicare. Includes a glossary of employee benefit terms.

Employee Benefits in Medium and Large Private Establishments. Available from U. S. Government Printing Office. • Biennial. Issued by Bureau of Labor Statistics, U. S. Department of Labor. Provides data on benefits provided by companies with 100 or more employees. Covers benefits for both full-time and part-time workers, including health insurance, pensions, a wide variety of paid time-off policies (holidays, vacations, personal leave, maternity leave, etc.), and other fringe benefits.

Employee Benefits in Small Private Establishments. Available from U. S. Government Printing Office. • Biennial. $12.00. Issued by Bureau of Labor Statistics, U. S. Department of Labor. Supplies data on a wide variety of benefits provided by companies

with fewer than 100 employees. Includes statistics for both full-time and part-time workers.

Handbook of U. S. Labor Statistics: Employment, Earnings, Prices, Productivity, and Other Labor Data. Eva E. Jacobs, editor. Bernan Associates. • 1999. $74.00. Based on *Handbook of Labor Statistics,* formerly issued by the Bureau of Labor Statistics, U. S. Department of Labor. Includes the Bureau's projections of employment in the U. S. by industry and occupation. Provides a wide variety of data on the work force, prices, fringe benefits, and consumer expenditures.

Health Insurance Company Financial Data. The National Underwriter Co. • Annual.

Health, United States, 1999: Health and Aging Chartbook. Available from U. S. Government Printing Office. • 1999. $43.00. Issued by the National Center for Health Statistics, U. S. Department of Health and Human Services. Contains 34 bar charts in color, with related statistical tables. Provides detailed data on persons over 65 years of age, including population, living arrangements, life expectancy, nursing home residence, poverty, health status, assistive devices, health insurance, and health care expenditures.

Insurance Statistics Yearbook, 1991-1998. OECD Publications and Information Center. • 2000. $75.00. Presents detailed statistics on insurance premiums collected in OECD countries, by type of insurance.

Key Indicators of the Labour Market. Available from Routledge. • Biennial. $125.00. Published by the International Labour Office (http://www.ilo.org). Provides data on 20 key indicators in 220 countries. Includes labor force statistics, employment, unemployment, part-time workers, wages, productivity, poverty indicators, and related topics.

Standard & Poor's Industry Surveys. Standard & Poor's. • Semiannual. $1,800.00. Two looseleaf volumes. Includes monthly *Supplements.* Provides detailed, individual surveys of 52 major industry groups. Each survey is revised on a semiannual basis. Also includes "Monthly Investment Review" (industry group investment analysis) and monthly "Trends & Projections" (economic analysis).

TRADE/PROFESSIONAL ASSOCIATIONS

Blue Cross and Blue Shield Association. 225 N. Michigan Ave., Chicago, IL 60611. Phone: (312)297-6000 Fax: (312)297-6609 • URL: http://www.bluecares.com.

Health Insurance Association of America. 1201 F St., N.W., No. 500, Washington, DC 20004. Phone: (202)824-1600 Fax: (202)824-1722 E-mail: jbalda@hiaa.org • URL: http://www.hiaa.org • Members are commercial health insurers. Includes a Disability Insurance Committee, a Medicare Administration Committee, and a Long-Term Care Committee.

National Association of Professional Insurance Agents. 400 N. Washington St., Alexandria, VA 22314. Phone: (703)836-9340 Fax: (703)836-1279 E-mail: piaweb@pianet.org • URL: http://www.pianet.com • Members are independent agents in various fields of insurance. Formerly National Association of Mutual Insurance Agents.

OTHER SOURCES

Best's Insurance Reports. A.M. Best Co. • Annual. $1495.00. Life-health insurance covering about 1,750 companies, and property-casualty insurance covering over 3,200 companies. Includes one year subscription to both *Best's Review* and *Best's Insurance Management Reports.*

Health Care Benefits Law. American Lawyer Media, Inc. • Looseleaf. $169.00. Updated as needed. Covers the legal compliance aspects of employer health care plans. Includes checklists and sample forms. (Law Journal Press).

Life, Health, and Accident Insurance Law Reports.
CCH, Inc. • $835.00 per year. Looseleaf service.
Monthly updates.

The Long-Term Care Market. MarketResearch.com.
• 1999. $3,250.00. Market data with forecasts to the
year 2005. Emphasis is on the over-85 age group.
Covers health insurance, the nursing home industry,
pharmaceuticals, healthcare supplies, etc.

HEALTH MAINTENANCE ORGANIZATIONS

See also: HEALTH CARE INDUSTRY;
HEALTH INSURANCE

GENERAL WORKS

Choosing and Using an HMO. Ellyn Spragins.
Bloomberg. • 1998. $19.95. Includes advice on find-
ing a doctor, going outside the plan, and avoiding
excess costs. (Bloomberg Personal Bookshelf
Series.).

*Health Against Wealth: HMOs and the Breakdown
of Medical Trust.* George Anders. Gale Cengage
Learning. • 1997. $26.95. The author, a *Wall Street
Journal* reporter, presents the negative side of HMO
cost cutting.

*Social Security, Medicare, and Government Pen-
sions: Get the Most Out of Your Retirement and
Medical Benefits.* Joseph Matthews and Dorothy M.
Berman. Nolo. • 2002. $29.99. Eighth edition. In ad-
dition to the basic topics, includes practical information on Supplemental Security Income (SSI), disability benefits, veterans benefits, 401(k) plans,
Medicare HMOs, medigap insurance, Medicaid, and
how to appeal decisions. (Social Security, Medicare
and Pensions Series).

BIBLIOGRAPHIES

AAHSA Resource Catalog. American Association of
Homes and Services for the Aging. • Annual. Free.
Provides descriptions of material relating to managed care, senior housing, assisted living, continuing care retirement communities (CCRCs), nursing
facilities, and home health care. Publishers are
AAHSA and others.

Encyclopedia of Health Information Sources. Gale
Cengage Learning. • 1993. $180.00. Second edition.
Both print and nonprint sources of information are
listed for 450 health-related topics.

CD-ROM DATABASES

Authority Health Care Law Library. LexisNexis/
Matthew Bender. • Periodic updates. Price on
request. Full text CD-ROM provides legal information, case law, and analysis relating to health care
facilities, health insurance, longterm care, Medigap,
and Medicare.

DIRECTORIES

*AHA Integrated Delivery Network Directory: U.S.
Health Care Systems, Networks, and Alliances.*
American Hospital Association. • Annual. $250.00.
Provides information about a wide variety of U.S.
health care groups and affiliations, including
hospitals, nursing homes, rehabilitation centers,
psychiatric facilities, home health care agencies,
clinical laboratories, outpatient facilities, and
diagnostic imaging centers. Includes names of more
than 8,000 key executives.

*Business Insurance-Directory of HMOs, POSs and
PPOs.* Crain Communications. • Annual. $40.00.
Provides detailed information on more than 600
managed care providers in the U. S., chiefly health
maintenance organizations (HMOs) and preferred
provider organizations (PPOs).

Dorland's Directory of Health Plans. Dorland
Healthcare Information. • Annual. $195.00.
Published in association with the American Associa-
tion of Health Plans (http://www.aahp.org). Lists

more than 2,400 health plans, including Health
Maintenance Organizations (HMOs), Preferred
Provider Organizations (PPOs), and Point of Service
plans (POS). Includes the names of about 9,000
health plan executives.

*Encyclopedia of Medical Organizations and
Agencies.* Gale Cengage Learning. • 2001. $295.00.
11th edition. Information on over 18,000 public and
private organizations in medicine and related fields.

*Health Maintenance Organization (HMO) Direc-
tory and Market Report.* Firstmark. • Annual. $630.
00. Three looseleaf volumes. Contains information
relating to over 700 HMOs. Relevant market data is
also provided.

Medical and Health Information Directory. Gale
Cengage Learning. • 2002. $675.00. Three volumes.
14th edition. Three volumes. $285.00 per volume.
Vol. one covers medical organizations, agencies, and
institutions; vol. two includes bibliographic, library,
and database information; vol. three is a guide to
services available for various medical and health
problems.

National Directory of HMOs. American Association
of Health Plans. • Annual. $125.00. Includes names
of key personnel and benefit options.

ENCYCLOPEDIAS AND DICTIONARIES

Encyclopedia of Health Care Management. Michael
Stahl, editor. Sage Publications, Inc. • 2004. $150.
00. Contains 600 entries covering "the business of
health care.".

*Guidebook to Managed Care and Practice Manage-
ment Terminology.* Norman Winegar and L.
Michelle Hayter. Haworth Press, Inc. • 1998. $39.
95. Provides definitions of managed care "terminology, jargon, and concepts.".

HANDBOOKS AND MANUALS

Consumers' Guide to Health Plans. Center for the
Study of Services. • 1996. $14.95. Revised edition.
Presents the results of a consumer survey on
satisfaction with specific managed care health insurance plans, and related information. Includes "Top-
Rated Plans," "Health Plans That Chose Not to Have
Their Members Surveyed," and other lists. General
advice is provided on choosing a plan, finding a
good doctor, getting good care, etc.

*Healthcare Finance for the Non-Financial
Manager: Basic Guide to Financial Analysis &
Control.* Louis Gapenski. McGraw-Hill. • 1994.
$47.50.

*How to Cover the Gaps in Medicare: Health Insur-
ance and Long-Term Care Options for the Retired.*
Robert A. Gilmour. American Institute for Economic
Research. • 2003. $10.00. Four parts: "The Medicare
Quandry," "How to Protect Yourself Against the
Medigap," "Long-Term Care Options," and "End-of-
Life Decisions" (living wills). Includes discussions
of long-term care insurance, retirement communi-
ties, and HMO Medicare insurance.

*The Managed Care Contracting Handbook: Plan-
ning and Negotiating the Managed Care
Relationship.* Maria K. Todd. Available from
McGraw Hill Higher Education. • 1996. $65.00. Co-
published by McGraw-Hill Healthcare Education
Group and the Healthcare Financial Management
Association. Covers managed care planning,
proposals, strategy, negotiation, and contract law.
Written for healthcare providers.

*Managed Care Handbook: How to Prepare Your
Medical Practice for the Managed Care Revolution.*
James R. Lyle and Hoyt Torras. Practice Management Information Corp. • 1994. $49.95. Second
edition. A management guide for physicians in
private practice.

Medicare and Coordinated Care Plans. Available
from Consumer Information Center. • Free.
Published by the U. S. Department of Health and
Human Services. Contains detailed information on

services to Medicare beneficiaries from health
maintenance organizations (HMOs). (Publication
No. 509-X.).

INTERNET DATABASES

InsWeb. InsWeb Corp. Phone: (916)853-3300
E-mail: info@insweb.com • URL: http://www.
insweb.com • Web site offers a wide variety of
advice and information on automobile, life, health,
and "other" insurance. Includes glossaries of insurance terms, Standard & Poor's ratings of individual
insurance companies, and "Financial Needs
Estimators." Searching is available. Fees: Free.

PERIODICALS AND NEWSLETTERS

AHA News. American Hospital Association.
HealthForum. • Description: Highlights major news
affecting hospitals and the health care field. Reports
on legislation and regulation, court cases, surveys,
and federal programs. Carries information on
individual hospitals and allied hospital associations.

*Drug Benefit Trends: For Pharmacy Managers and
Managed HealthCare Professionals.* Cliggott
Publishing Co. • Monthly. Individuals, $95.00 per
year; libraries, $120.00 per year; students, $40.00
per year. Covers the business of managed care drug
benefits.

Effective Clinical Practice. American College of
Physicians. • Bimonthly. Individuals, $54.00 per
year; institutions, $70.00 per year. Formerly *HMO
Practice*.

Group Practice Journal. American Medical Group
Practice Association. • 10 times a year. Institutions,
$75.00 per year.

*Guide to HMOs and Health Insurers: A Quarterly
Compilation of Health Insurance Company Ratings
and Analysis.* Weiss Ratings, Inc. • Quarterly.
$438.00 per year. Emphasis is on rating of financial
safety and relative risk. Includes annual summary.

*Health Forum Journal: Leadership Strategies for
Healthcare Executives.* Health Forum. • Biweekly.
$65.00 per year. Covers the general management of
hospitals, nursing homes, and managed care
organizations. Formerly *HospitalsHealthNetworks*.

Health Insurance Underwriter. National Association
of Health Underwriters. • Monthly. $25.00 per year.
Includes special feature issues on long-term care
insurance, disability insurance, managed health care,
and insurance office management.

Healthcare Executive. American College of Healthcare Executives. • Bimonthly. $70.00 per year.
Focuses on critical management issues.

Healthplan. America Association of Health Plans. •
Bimonthly. $75.00 per year.

*Healthplan: The Magazine of Trends, Insights, and
Best Practices.* American Association of Health
Plans. • Bimonthly. $75.00 per year. Edited for man-
aged care executives.

Managed Care: A Guide for Physicians. MediMedia
USA, Inc. • Monthly. $93.00 per year. Edited for
physicians and managed care administrators.
Includes advice on careers and the business aspects
of managed care.

*Managed Care Interface: Today's Experts Tomor-
row's Health Care.* Medicom International, Inc. •
Monthly. Individuals, $80.00 per year; institutions,
$100.00 per year. Provides news and information on
all aspects of the managed health care industry.

Managed Care Marketing. Engel Publishing
Partners. • Quarterly. $24.00 per year. Edited for
executives of managed health care companies and
organizations.

*Managed Care Outlook: The Insider's Business
Briefing on Managed Health Care.* Aspen Publish-
ers, Inc. • 50 times a year. $632.00 per year.
Newsletter relating to health maintenance organiza-
tions (HMOs), preferred provider organizations
(PPOs), and other managed care systems.

For publishers addresses, refer to SOURCES CITED section at the back of the book.

Managed Healthcare Executive: The News Magazine for Managers of Healthcare Costs and Quality. Advantstar Communications. • Individuals, $75.00 per year; students, $35.00 per year. Edited for managers of HMOs and other managed care organizations. Covers outcomes, quality assurance, technology, long term care, and trends in the health care industry. Formerly *Managed Healthcare.*

Medical Benefits. Aspen Publishers Inc. • Description: Focuses on key developments, statistics, and studies relating to the health care system. Covers eight major topic areas: cost containment, employee benefits, employee health/wellness, quality of care, delivery systems, government in health care, legal issues, and health care expenditure data.

Modern Physician: Essential Business News for the Executive Physician. Crain Communications, Inc. • Monthly. $45.00. Edited for physicians responsible for business decisions at hospitals, clinics, HMOs, and other health groups. Includes special issues on managed care, practice management, legal issues, and finance.

RESEARCH CENTERS AND INSTITUTES

Center for Health Administration Studies. University of Chicago, 969 E. 60th St., Chicago, IL 60637. Phone: (773)702-7104 Fax: (773)702-7222 E-mail: chas@uchicago.edu • URL: http://www.chas.uchicago.edu.

Center for Health Economics Research. 411 Waverly Oaks Rd., Suite 330, Waltham, MA 02452. Phone: (781)788-8100 Fax: (781)788-8101 E-mail: jmitchell@cher.org • URL: http://www.her-cher.org • A social science research company.

Center for Health Policy Law and Management. Duke University, 125 Old Chemistry Bldg., Durham, NC 27708. Phone: (919)684-3023 Fax: (919)684-6246 E-mail: fsloan@hpolicy.duke.edu • URL: http://www.hpolicy.duke.edu.

Center for Health Research. Wayne State University, College of Nursing, 5557 Cass Ave., Detroit, MI 48202-3515. Phone: (313)577-4134 Fax: (313)577-5777 E-mail: nursinginfo@wayne.edu • URL: http://www.nursing.wayne.edu • Studies innovation in health care organization and financing.

Health Services Research and Development Center. Johns Hopkins University, 624 N. Broadway, Room 482, Baltimore, MD 21205-1996. Phone: (410)955-3625 Fax: (410)614-9152 E-mail: dsteinwa@jhsph.edu.

Institute for Health, Health Care Policy, and Aging Research. Rutgers University, 30 College Ave., New Brunswick, NJ 08901-1293. Phone: (732)932-8413 Fax: (732)932-6872 E-mail: caboyer@rci.rutgers.edu • URL: http://www.ihhcpar.rutgers.edu/ • Areas of study include HMO use by older adults.

MGMA Center for Research. 104 Inverness Terrace E., Englewood, CO 80112-5306. Phone: (303)397-7879 Fax: (303)397-1827 E-mail: npiland@mgma.com • URL: http://www.mgma.com/research • Fields of research include medical group practice management. Formerly Center for Research in Ambulatory Health Care Administration.

Stratis Health. 2901 Metro Dr., Suite 400, Bloomington, MN 55425-1525. Phone: (952)854-3306 Fax: (952)853-8503 E-mail: info@stratishealth.org • URL: http://www.stratishealth.org.

STATISTICS SOURCES

Standard & Poor's Industry Surveys. Standard & Poor's. • Semiannual. $1,800.00. Two looseleaf volumes. Includes monthly *Supplements.* Provides detailed, individual surveys of 52 major industry groups. Each survey is revised on a semiannual basis. Also includes "Monthly Investment Review" (industry group investment analysis) and monthly

"Trends & Projections" (economic analysis).

TRADE/PROFESSIONAL ASSOCIATIONS

American Association of Health Plans. 1129 20th St., N.W., Suite 600, Washington, DC 20036-3421. Phone: (202)728-3200 Fax: (202)331-7487 E-mail: aahp@aahp.org • URL: http://www.aahp.org • Supports the managed health care industry.

American Association of Preferred Provider Organizations. PO Box 429, Jeffersonville, IN 47131-0429. Phone: 800-642-2515 or (812)246-4376 Fax: (812)246-4630 E-mail: kgreenrose@aappo.org • URL: http://www.aappo.org • Formerly Association of Managed Healthcare Organizations.

American Medical Group Association. 1422 Duke St., Alexandria, VA 22314-3403. Phone: (703)838-0033 Fax: (703)548-1890 E-mail: dfisher@amga.org • URL: http://www.amga.org • Represents the interests of medical groups. Advocates for the medical groups and patients through innovation and information sharing, benchmarking, developing leadership, and improving patient care. Provides political advocacy, educational and networking programs and publications, benchmarking data services, and financial and operations assistance.

OTHER SOURCES

HMO Competitive Edge. InterStudy Publications. • Semiannual. Price on application. Provides highly detailed statistical, directory, and market information on U. S. health maintenance organizations. Consists of three parts: *The HMO Directory, The HMO Industry Report,* and *The Regional Market Analysis.*

The Managed Medicare and Medicaid Market. MarketResearch.com. • 2003. $2,195.00. Market research report on medicare HMOs. Includes analysis of legal issues and the impact of managed care on older consumers. Providers such as Kaiser Permanente, Humana, and U. S. Healthcare are profiled.

HEALTH OF EMPLOYEES

See: EMPLOYEE WELLNESS PROGRAMS

HEATING AND VENTILATION

See also: AIR CONDITIONING INDUSTRY

ABSTRACTS AND INDEXES

NTIS Alerts: Energy. National Technical Information Service. • Semimonthly. $245.00 per year. Provides descriptions of government-sponsored research reports and software, with ordering information. Covers electric power, batteries, fuels, geothermal energy, heating/cooling systems, nuclear technology, solar energy, energy policy, and related subjects. Formerly *Abstract Newsletter.*

DIRECTORIES

Air Conditioning, Heating, and Refrigeration News-Directory. Business News Publishing Co. • Annual. $35.00.

The Wholesaler "The Wholesaling 100". TMB Publishing, Inc. • Annual. $25.00. Provides information on the 100 leading wholesalers of plumbing, piping, heating, and air conditioning equipment.

ENCYCLOPEDIAS AND DICTIONARIES

Encyclopedia of Energy. Cutler J. Cleveland, editor. Elsevier, Inc. • 2004. $1,560.00. Six volumes. Covers all aspects of energy sources and energy-related environmental issues.

Macmillan Encyclopedia of Energy. Available from Gale Cengage Learning. • 2001. $395.00. Three volumes. Published by Macmillan Reference USA.

Covers the business, technology, and history of a wide variety of energy sources.

FINANCIAL RATIOS

American Supply Association Operating Performance Report. American Supply Association. • Annual. Members, $45.00; non-members, $150.00.

Annual Statement Studies. The Risk Management Association. • Annual. Median and quartile financial ratios are given for over 400 kinds of manufacturing, wholesale, retail, construction, and consumer finance establishments. Data is sorted by both asset size and sales volume. Includes a clearly written "Definition of Ratios" and an alphabetical industry index.

Annual Statement Studies: Industry Default Probabilities and Cash Flow Measures. The Risk Management Association. • Annual. $145.00. Serves as a companion volume to the original *Annual Statement Studies.* Gives probability of default estimates on a percentage scale for more than 450 industries. Includes changes in position year-by-year for eight financial statement line items and provides percentage measures of cash flow.

HANDBOOKS AND MANUALS

Guide to Energy Efficient Commercial Equipment. Margaret Suozzo and others. American Council for an Energy Efficient Economy. • 1997. $25.00. Provides information on specifying and purchasing energy-saving systems for buildings (heating, air conditioning, lighting, and motors).

No-Regrets Remodeling: Creating a Comfortable, Healthy Home That Saves Energy. Home Energy. • 1997. $19.95. Edited by *Home Energy* magazine. Serves as a home remodeling guide to efficient heating, cooling, ventilation, water heating, insulation, lighting, and windows.

INTERNET DATABASES

Manufacturing Profiles. U. S. Bureau of the Census. Phone: (301)763-4636 E-mail: webmaster@census.gov • URL: http://www.census.gov/prod/www/abs/mfg-prof.html • The Census Bureau makes available free on PDF (Portable Document Format) an annual consolidation of the entire Current Industrial Report series, presenting "all the data compiled." Contains statistics on production, shipments, inventories, consumption, exports, imports, and orders for a wide variety of manufactured products.

PERIODICALS AND NEWSLETTERS

Air Conditioning, Heating, and Refrigeration News: The HVACR Contractor's Weekly Newsmagazine. Business News Publishing Co. • Weekly. $87.00 per year. Includes *Supplement.*

ASHRAE Journal: The Magazine of the American Society of Heating, Refrigeration, Air-Conditioning, Ventilation. American Society of Heating, Refrigerating and Air Conditioning Engineers, Inc. • Monthly. Free to members; non-members, $59.00 per year.

Heating/Piping/Air Conditioning Engineering: The Magazine of Mechanical Systems Engineering. Penton Media, Inc. • Monthly. $65.00 per year. Covers design, specification, installation, operation, and maintenance for systems in industrial, commercial, and institutional buildings. Formerly (Heating, Piping and Air Conditioning).

The Wholesaler. TMB Publishing, Inc. • Monthly. $75.00 per year. Edited for wholesalers and distributors of plumbing, piping, heating, and air conditioning equipment.

RESEARCH CENTERS AND INSTITUTES

Ray W. Herrick Laboratories. Purdue University, 1077 Ray W. Herrick Laboratories, West Lafayette, IN 47907-1077. Phone: (765)494-2132 Fax: (765)494-0787 E-mail: rhlab@ecn.purdue.edu •

URL: http://www.herrick.ecn.purdue.edu.

STATISTICS SOURCES

Annual Survey of Manufactures. Available from U. S. Government Printing Office. • Annual. Prices vary. Issued by the U. S. Census Bureau as an interim update to the *Census of Manufactures*. Includes data on number of manufacturing establishments in various industries, employment, labor costs, value of shipments, capital expenditures, inventories, energy costs, and assets. (See also Census Bureau home page, http://www.census. gov/.).

Refrigeration, Air Conditioning, and Warm Air Heating Equipment. U. S. Bureau of the Census. • Annual. Provides data on quantity and value of shipments by manufacturers. Formerly *Air Conditioning and Refrigeration Equipment*. (Current Industrial Reports, MA-35M.).

TRADE/PROFESSIONAL ASSOCIATIONS

American Society of Heating, Refrigerating and Air Conditioning Engineers. c/o Frank Coda, 1791 Tullie Circle, N.E., Atlanta, GA 30329. Phone: 800-527-4723 or (404)636-8400 Fax: (404)321-5478 E-mail: ashrae@ashrae.org • URL: http://www. ashrae.org.

Industrial Heating Equipment Association. PO Box 54172, Cincinnati, OH 45254. Phone: (513)231-5613 Fax: (513)624-0601 E-mail: ihea@ihea.org • URL: http://www.ihea.org • Manufacturers of industrial furnaces, ovens, combustion equipment, atmosphere generators, induction and dielectric heating equipment, industrial heaters, process controls, fuel saving and heating devices, and heat recovery equipment.

International District Energy Association. 24 Lyman St., Ste. 230, Westborough, MA 01581-2841. Phone: (508)366-9339 Fax: (508)366-0019 E-mail: idea@ districtenergy.org • URL: http://www.districtenergy. org • Suppliers of space heating by means of steam and hot water, and air conditioning by means of steam and chilled water, via piping systems from a central station to groups of buildings.

OTHER SOURCES

Heating Systems. Available from MarketResearch. com. • 2002. $3,950.00. Published by Global Industry Analysts. Provides worldwide market research data, including profiles of major heating system companies.

HPAC Techlit Selector (Heating, Piping, Air Conditioning). Penton Media, Inc. • Semiannual. Free to qualified personnel. Manufacturers' catalogs and technical literature.

Major Energy Companies of the World. Available from Gale Cengage Learning. • Annual. $880.00. Published by Graham & Whiteside. Contains detailed information on more than 3,300 important energy companies in various countries. Industries include electricity generation, coal, natural gas, nuclear energy, petroleum, fuel distribution, and equipment for energy production.

HELICOPTERS

See also: AEROSPACE INDUSTRY; AVIATION INDUSTRY

DIRECTORIES

The Helicopter Annual. Helicopter Association International. • Covers: Private and corporate members of the Helicopter Association International, as well as manufacturers in the helicopter industry; international coverage. Entries include: For members--Personal or company name, address, phone, fax, name and title of contact, description of services, fleet size. For manufacturers--Company name, address, phone, fax, technical description of products.

Military Helicopter Handbook. The Shephard Press Ltd. • Annual. $110.00. Data includes specifications of fighter helicopters, inventory of world helicopter forces, government contacts, directory of services & products, and listing of exhibits & conferences. Coverage is international.

Vertiflite-American Helicopter Society Membership Directory. American Helicopter Society, Inc. • Annual. $45.00. Lists over 6,000 individuals and 150 companies concerned with vertical take off and landing craft.

ENCYCLOPEDIAS AND DICTIONARIES

Macmillan Encyclopedia of Transportation. Available from Gale Cengage Learning. • 1999. $450.00. Six volumes. Published by Macmillan Reference USA. Covers the business, technology, and history of transportation on land, on water, in the air, and in space. Includes definitions, cross-references, and 200 color illustrations.

HANDBOOKS AND MANUALS

Operations and Management, Guide/Safety Manual. Helicopter Association International. • Annual.

PERIODICALS AND NEWSLETTERS

American Helicopter Society Journal. American Helicopter Society, Inc. • Quarterly. $60.00 per year.

Defence & Public Service Helicopter. Shephard Press Ltd. • Monthly. $130.00 per year. Provides international coverage of both the public service (police, emergency, etc.) and military helicopter industries and markets. Includes technical, piloting, and safety topics. Formerly *Defence Helicopter*.

Helicopter News. Access Intelligence L.L.C. • Description: Reports to company executives, military leaders, and ancillary industries on the state of the helicopter industry. Tracks buying and selling information, news of contracts, and new programs. Also concerned with related issues, including EMS (Emergency Mission Support) and insurance. Recurring features include interviews and news of technology and new products. **Remarks:** Also available online and via e-mail.

Journal of Aircraft: Devoted to Aeronautical Science and Technology. American Institute of Aeronautics and Astronautics, Inc. • Bimonthly. Members, $55.00 per year; institutions, $520.00 per year. Online edition available.

Rotor and Wing: Serving the Worldwide Helicopter Industry. PBI Media, LLC. • Monthly. Free to qualified personnel; others, $49.00 per year. Includes supplement *World Helicopter Resources*. Formerly *Rotor and Wing International*.

Vertiflite. American Helicopter Society, Inc. • Quarterly. $55.00 per year.

RESEARCH CENTERS AND INSTITUTES

Flight Mechanics Laboratory. Texas A & M University, College Station, TX 77843-3141. Phone: (979)845-1685 Fax: (979)845-6051 E-mail: valasek@aero.tamu.edu • URL: http://www.flutie. tamu.edu.

OAI. 22800 Cedar Point Rd., Cleveland, OH 44142. Phone: (440)962-3000 Fax: (440)962-3120 E-mail: michaelsalkind@oai.org • URL: http://www.oai.org • Aerospace-related research, education, and technology transfers. Formerly Ohio Aerospace Institute.

STATISTICS SOURCES

Aerospace Facts and Figures. Aerospace Industries Association of America. • Annual. $35.00. Includes financial data for the aerospace industries.

TRADE/PROFESSIONAL ASSOCIATIONS

AHS International - The Vertical Flight Society. 217 N. Washington St., Alexandria, VA 22314-2520. Phone: (703)684-6777 Fax: (703)739-9279 E-mail: staff@vtol.org • URL: http://www.vtol.org.

Helicopter Association International. 1635 Prince St., Alexandria, VA 22314-2818. Phone: 800-435-4976 or (703)683-4646 Fax: (703)683-4745 E-mail: questions@rotor.com • URL: http://www.rotor.com • Owners, operators, helicopter enthusiasts, and affiliated companies in the civil helicopter industry. Receives and disseminates information concerning the use, operation, hiring, contracting, and leasing of helicopters. Maintains a collection of current helicopter service bulletins and technical data; organizes safety seminars, continuing education courses, and helicopter operator management courses; and maintains a maintenance malfunction information database.

HENS

See: POULTRY INDUSTRY

HERBS

See also: DIET; HEALTH FOOD INDUSTRY

ALMANACS AND YEARBOOKS

Herbarist. Herb Society of America, Inc. • Annual. Free to members; non-members, $10.00.

CD-ROM DATABASES

Pharmacopeia of Herbs. CME, Inc. • $149.00. Frequently updated CD-ROM provides searchable data on a wide variety of herbal medicines, vitamins, and amino acids. Includes information on clinical studies, contraindications, side-effects, phytoactivity, and 534 therapeutic use categories. Contains a 1,000 word glossary.

ENCYCLOPEDIAS AND DICTIONARIES

Dictionary of Natural Products. George M. Hocking. Available from Information Today, Inc. • 1997. $139.50. Published by Plexus Publishing (http://www.plexuspublishing.com). Explains terms relating to the raw materials and products used in natural, folk, or alternative medicine.

HANDBOOKS AND MANUALS

Herb Farming. Entrepreneur Media, Inc. • Looseleaf. $59.50. A practical guide to the business side of herb farming. Covers profit potential, start-up costs, market size evaluation, owner's time required, pricing, accounting, advertising, promotion, etc. (Start-Up Business Guide No. E1282.).

Herbal Drugs and Phytopharmaceuticals. Max Wichtl and Norman G. Bisset, editors. CRC Press LLC. • 1994. $190.00. Provides a scientific approach to the medicinal use of herbs. (English translation of original German edition.).

The Herbalist. Michael Katz. University Press of America. • 1992. $38.50.

The Honest Herbal: A Sensible Guide to the Use of Herbs and Related Remedies. Varro E. Tyler. The Haworth Press, Inc. • 1993. $49.95. Third edition.

PERIODICALS AND NEWSLETTERS

Herb Quarterly. EGW Publishing Co. • Quarterly. $19.97 per year. A magazine for herb enthusiasts covering all aspects of herb uses.

HSR: Health Supplement Retailer. Virgo Publishing, Inc. • Monthly. $50.00 per year. Covers all aspects of the vitamin and health supplement market, including new products. Includes an annual buyer's guide, an annual compilation of industry statistics, and annual guides to vitamins and herbs.

Journal of Dietary Supplements. Haworth Press, Inc. • Quarterly. $175.00 per year to libraries; $50.00 per year to individuals. Edited with a view to both academic research and industry concerns. Sections of the journal are dedicated to health professionals, educators, dieticians, and an "Industry Spotlight." Includes book reviews and short reviews of research appearing elsewhere. Formerly *Journal of Nutraceu-*

ticals, Functional & Medical Foods.

Journal of Herbs, Spices and Medicinal Plants. Haworth Press, Inc. • Quarterly. $285.00 per year. An academic and practical journal on production, marketing, and other aspects of herbs and spices.

Natural Business: The Journal of Business and Financial News for the Natural Products Industry. Natural Business Communications. • Monthly. $279.00 per year. Covers the business aspects of natural and organic products and dietary supplements, including information about private and public companies in the industry.

Nutrition Industry Executive. Vitamin Retailer Magazine, Inc. • 10 times a year. $50.00 per year. Edited for manufacturers of vitamins and other dietary supplements. Covers marketing, new products, industry trends, regulations, manufacturing procedures, and related topics. Includes a directory of suppliers to the industry.

Vitamin Retailer: The Dietary Supplement Industry's Leading Magazine. Vitamin Retailer Magazine, Inc. • Monthly. $60.00 per year. Edited for retailers of vitamins, herbal remedies, minerals, antioxidants, essential fatty acids, and other food supplements.

TRADE/PROFESSIONAL ASSOCIATIONS

Herb Society of America. 9019 Kirtland-Chardon Rd., Kirtland, OH 44094. Phone: (440)256-0514 Fax: (440)256-0541 E-mail: herbs@herbsociety.org • URL: http://www.herbsociety.org.

OTHER SOURCES

U. S. Herbal Supplement Market. Available from MarketResearch.com. • 2001. $2,750.00. Market research data published by Packaged Facts. Includes forecasts to 2005.

HIDE INDUSTRY

See: CATTLE INDUSTRY

HIGH BLOOD PRESSURE

See: HYPERTENSION

HIGH FIDELITY/STEREO

See also: RADIO EQUIPMENT INDUSTRY; SOUND RECORDERS AND RECORDING

GENERAL WORKS

Sound and Recording: An Introduction. Francis Rumsey and Tim McCormick. Elsevier. • 2002. $42.99. Fourth edition. Covers the theory and principles of sound recording and reproduction, with chapters on amplifiers, microphones, mixers, and other components. (Music Technology Series).

DIRECTORIES

Directory of Computer and Consumer Electronics Retailers. Chain Store Guide. • Annual. $335.00. Online edition, $775.00. Lists 4,500 United States and Canada companies operating almost 59,000 stores with at least $1,000,000 in sales.

Pro Audio Review Gear Guide. IMAS Publishing, Inc. • Annual. Issued as February issue of *Pro Audio Review.* Contains detailed product listings of professional audio equipment and recording gear. Includes prices, specifications, and addresses of manufacturers.

HANDBOOKS AND MANUALS

Audio Electronics. John L. Hood. Elsevier. • 1998. $54.95. Second edition.

Audio Engineer's Reference Book. Michael Talbot-Smith, editor. Elsevier. • 2001. $84.95. Second edition.

Audio Recording and Reproduction: Practical Measures for Audio Enthusiasts. Michael Talbot-Smith. Elsevier. • 1994. $29.95.

Handbook for Sound Engineers. Glen M. Ballou, editor. Elsevier. • 2002. $120.00. Third edition. Covers fundamentals of sound, sound-system design, loudspeaker building, sound recording, audio circuits, and computer-generated music.

Home Entertainment Installation. Entrepreneur Media, Inc. • Looseleaf. $59.50. A practical guide to starting a home entertainment installation service. Covers profit potential, start-up costs, market size evaluation, owner's time required, pricing, accounting, advertising, promotion, etc. (Start-Up Business Guide No. E1349.).

Master Handbook of Acoustics. F. Alton Everest. McGraw-Hill. • 2001. $39.95. Fourth edition. Covers the theory of acoustics and practical applications of acoustics, as in the design of audio control rooms, recording studios, and listening rooms for the home. (Tab Electronics Series).

Principles of Digital Audio. Ken C. Pohlmann. McGraw-Hill. • 2000. $54.95. Fourth edition. Includes the details of digital audio recording, reproduction, error correction, compact disc technology, DVD, minidiscs, Internet audio, and related topics. (Video/Audio Engineering Series).

Standard Handbook of Audio and Radio Engineering. Jerry C. Whitaker and K. Blair Benson. McGraw-Hill. • 2002. $125.00. Second edition. Emphasis is on audio. Covers such topics as DVD, MP3, sound reproduction, amplification, noise reduction, and Internet audio.

PERIODICALS AND NEWSLETTERS

The Absolute Sound: The High End Journal of Audio and Music. Harry Pearson, editor. Absolute Multimedia Inc. • Six times a year. $36.00 per year.

Audio Week: The Authoritative News Service of the Audio Consumer Electronics Industry. Warren Publishing, Inc. • Weekly. $663.00. Newsletter. Provdies audio industry news, company news, and new product information.

High Performance Review: Definitive Magazine for Audiophiles and Music Lovers. High Performance Review Publishing. • Quarterly. $15.00 per year.

Poptronics. Gernsback Publications, Inc. • Monthly. $19.99 per year. Incorporates *Electronics Now.*

Pro Audio Review: The Industry's Equipment Authority. IMAS Publishing, Inc. • Monthly. $35.00 per year. Provides critical product reviews of professional audio equipment and recording gear, including bench tests and user reports.

Robb Report Home Entertaining & Design. CurtCo Robb Media. • Nine times a year. $21.95 per year. Covers "high end" home theaters, audio, video, wireless home networks, and custom installations.

Sensible Sound: Helping Audiophiles and Music Lovers to Spend Less and Get More. • Bimonthly. $29.00 per year. High fidelity equipment review.

Sound & Vision: Home Theater- Audio- Video-MultimediaMovies- Music. Hachette Filipacchi Media U.S., Inc. • 10 times a year. $24.00 per year. Popular magazine providing explanatory articles and critical reviews of equipment and media (CD-ROM, DVD, videocassettes, etc.). Supplement available *Stero Review's Sound and Vision Buyers Guide.* Replaces *Stereo Review* and *Video Magazine.*

Stereophile: For the High Fidelity Stereo Perfectionist. PRIMEDIA Inc. • Monthly. $12.97 per year. Review of high-end audio products.

T W I C E: This Week in Consumer Electronics. Reed Business Information. • 29 times a year. $129.90 per year. Contains marketing and manufacturing news relating to a wide variety of consumer electronic products, including video, audio, telephone, and home office equipment.

PRICE SOURCES

Audio. Orion Research Corp. • Annual. $179.00. Quotes retail and wholesale prices of used audio equipment. Original list prices and years of manufacture are also shown.

Car Stereo. Orion Research Corp. • Annual. $144.00. Quotes retail and wholesale prices of used stereo sound equipment for automobiles. Original list prices and years of manufacture are also shown.

Guitars and Musical Instruments. Orion Research Corp. • Annual. $179.00. List of manufacturers of guitars and musical instruments. Original list prices and years of manufacture are also shown.

TRADE/PROFESSIONAL ASSOCIATIONS

Electronic Industries Alliance. 2500 Wilson Blvd., Arlington, VA 22201. Phone: (703)907-7500 Fax: (703)907-7501 E-mail: mflanigan@eia.org • URL: http://www.eia.org • Seeks for the competitiveness of the American producer, represents all companies involved in the design and manufacture of electronic components, parts, systems and equipment for communications, industrial, government and consumer uses.

OTHER SOURCES

U. S. Home Theater Market. Available from MarketResearch.com. • 1997. $1,3750.00. Market research report published by Packaged Facts. Covers big-screen TV, high definition TV, audio equipment, and video sources. Market projections are provided.

HIGH TECHNOLOGY

See: TECHNOLOGY

HIGH YIELD BONDS

See: JUNK BOND FINANCING

HIGHER EDUCATION

See: COLLEGES AND UNIVERSITIES

HIGHWAY ACCIDENTS

See: TRAFFIC ACCIDENTS AND TRAFFIC SAFETY

HIGHWAYS

See: ROADS AND HIGHWAYS

HIRE PURCHASE PLAN

See: INSTALLMENT PLAN PURCHASING

HISPANIC MARKETS

See: MINORITY MARKETS

HISTORY, BUSINESS

See: BUSINESS HISTORY

HMOS

See: HEALTH MAINTENANCE ORGANIZATIONS

HOBBY INDUSTRY

DIRECTORIES

CNA Trade Directory (Craft and Needlework Age). Krause Publications, Inc. • Annual. $35.00. Lists of about 300 manufacturers and 50 publishers of books and periodicals in the craft and needlework industry.

Directory of Discount and General Merchandise Stores. Chain Store Guide. • Annual. $327.00. On-line edition, $747.00. Includes retailers and wholesalers of housewares, giftwares, novelties, toys, hobby materials, crafts, and stationery.

FINANCIAL RATIOS

Annual Statement Studies. The Risk Management Association. • Annual. Median and quartile financial ratios are given for over 400 kinds of manufacturing, wholesale, retail, construction, and consumer finance establishments. Data is sorted by both asset size and sales volume. Includes a clearly written "Definition of Ratios" and an alphabetical industry index.

Annual Statement Studies: Industry Default Probabilities and Cash Flow Measures. The Risk Management Association. • Annual. $145.00. Serves as a companion volume to the original *Annual Statement Studies*. Gives probability of default estimates on a percentage scale for more than 450 industries. Includes changes in position year-by-year for eight financial statement line items and provides percentage measures of cash flow.

HANDBOOKS AND MANUALS

Collectibles Broker. Entrepreneur Media, Inc. • Looseleaf. $59.50. A practical guide to starting a brokerage service for collectibles. Covers profit potential, start-up costs, market size evaluation, owner's time required, pricing, accounting, advertising, promotion, etc. (Start-Up Business Guide No. E1360.).

Craft Businesses. Entrepreneur Media, Inc. • Looseleaf. $59.50. A practical guide to starting a handicrafts-related business. Covers profit potential, start-up costs, market size evaluation, owner's time required, site selection, lease negotiation, pricing, accounting, advertising, promotion, etc. (Start-Up Business Guide No. E1304.).

Hobby Shop. Entrepreneur Media, Inc. • Looseleaf. $59.50. A practical guide to starting a hobby shop. Covers profit potential, start-up costs, market size evaluation, owner's time required, site selection, lease negotiation, pricing, accounting, advertising, promotion, etc. (Start-Up Business Guide No. E1132.).

Start and Run a Successful Craft Business: A Step-by-Step Business Plan. William G. Hynes. Self-Counsel Press, Inc. • 2002. $14.95. Seventh revised edition. (Start and Run a Profitable Series: Vol. 6).

PERIODICALS AND NEWSLETTERS

Antiques and Collecting Magazine. Lightner Publishing Corp. • Monthly. $32.00 per year.

International Journal: The News and Views Paper for the Hobbyist. Levine Publications. • Quarterly. $52.50.

PRICE SOURCES

Kovels' on Antiques and Collectibles: The Newsletter for Dealers, Collectors, and Investors. Antiques Inc. • Monthly. $46.00 per year.

Pictorial Price Guide to American Antiques: 2002-2003. Dorothy Hammond. Antique Collectors Club. • 2002 $19.95 (Pictorial Price Guide to American Antiques Series).

STATISTICS SOURCES

SRDS Lifestyle Market Analyst. SRDS. • Annual. $440.00. Published in conjunction with EQUIFAX. Provides extensive lifestyle data on interests, activities, and hobbies within specific geographic and demographic markets. Formerly *Lifestyle Market Analyst.*

TRADE/PROFESSIONAL ASSOCIATIONS

Association of American Military Uniform Collectors. PO Box 1876, Elyria, OH 44036. Phone: (440)365-5321 E-mail: aamucfl@comcast.net • URL: http://www.naples.net/clubs/aamuc • Collectors of American military and naval uniforms (1776-present). Promotes interest in uniform preservation and heritage along with patriotic interest in the U.S. armed forces. Loans uniform displays by members to various groups, including Boy Scouts of America, Girl Scouts of the U.S.A., American Legion, and Veterans of Foreign Wars of the U.S.A. branches, public schools, libraries, and public exhibitions. Reviews the books on U.S. military uniforms. **Convention/Meeting:** none.

Hobby Industry Association. 319 E. 54th St., Elmwood Park, NJ 07407. Phone: (201)794-1133 Fax: (201)797-0657 E-mail: hia@hobby.org • URL: http://www.hobby.org • Formerly Hobby Industry Association of America.

Society of Craft Designers. P.O. Box 3388, Zanesville, OH 43702-3388. Phone: (740)452-4541 Fax: (740)452-2552 E-mail: scd@offinger.com • URL: http://www.craftdesigners.org.

OTHER SOURCES

American Society of Military Insignia Collectors. • Represents oldest military insignia collectors group in the U.S. Promotes the collection and preservation of U.S. and foreign military insignia. Disseminates information on the symbolism and historical significance of insignia. Assists veterans and individuals in search of insignia.

HOG INDUSTRY

See: LIVESTOCK INDUSTRY; SWINE INDUSTRY

HOISTING MACHINERY

See: CONVEYING MACHINERY; ELEVATORS

HOLIDAYS

See: ANNIVERSARIES AND HOLIDAYS

HOME APPLIANCES

See: ELECTRIC APPLIANCE INDUSTRY

HOME-BASED BUSINESSES

See: SELF-EMPLOYMENT

HOME BUILDING INDUSTRY

See: BUILDING INDUSTRY

HOME COMPUTERS

See: MICROCOMPUTERS AND MINICOMPUTERS

HOME DECORATION

See: INTERIOR DECORATION

HOME EDUCATION

See: CORRESPONDENCE SCHOOLS AND COURSES

HOME FREEZERS

See: FROZEN FOOD INDUSTRY

HOME FURNISHINGS

See: FLOOR COVERINGS; FURNITURE INDUSTRY; INTERIOR DECORATION

HOME FURNITURE INDUSTRY

See: FURNITURE INDUSTRY

HOME HEALTH CARE INDUSTRY

See also: HEALTH CARE INDUSTRY

GENERAL WORKS

Caring for Frail Elderly People: New Directions in Care. OECD Publications and Information Center. • 1994. $27.00. Discusses the problem in OECD countries of providing good quality care to the elderly at manageable cost. Includes trends in family care, housing policies, and private financing.

Long-Term Care and Its Alternatives. Charles B. Inlander and others. People's Medical Society. • 1996. $16.95. Provides practical advice on the financing of long-term health care. The author is a consumer advocate and president of the People's Medical Society.

Who Cares for Them? Workers in the Home Care Industry. Penny H. Feldman and others. Greenwood Publishing Group, Inc. • 1990. $67.95. (Contributions to the Study of Aging Series: No.16).

BIBLIOGRAPHIES

AAHSA Resource Catalog. American Association of Homes and Services for the Aging. • Annual. Free. Provides descriptions of material relating to managed care, senior housing, assisted living, continuing care retirement communities (CCRCs), nursing facilities, and home health care. Publishers are AAHSA and others.

Encyclopedia of Health Information Sources. Gale Cengage Learning. • 1993. $180.00. Second edition. Both print and nonprint sources of information are listed for 450 health-related topics.

CD-ROM DATABASES

Authority Health Care Law Library. LexisNexis/Matthew Bender. • Periodic updates. Price on request. Full text CD-ROM provides legal information, case law, and analysis relating to health care facilities, health insurance, longterm care, Medigap, and Medicare.

DIRECTORIES

AHA Integrated Delivery Network Directory: U.S. Health Care Systems, Networks, and Alliances. American Hospital Association. • Annual. $250.00. Provides information about a wide variety of U.S. health care groups and affiliations, including hospitals, nursing homes, rehabilitation centers, psychiatric facilities, home health care agencies, clinical laboratories, outpatient facilities, and diagnostic imaging centers. Includes names of more than 8,000 key executives.

Encyclopedia of Medical Organizations and

Agencies. Gale Cengage Learning. • 2001. $295.00. 11th edition. Information on over 18,000 public and private organizations in medicine and related fields.

Health Devices Sourcebook. ECRI. • Covers: Over 6,800 suppliers of patient care equipment, medical and surgical instruments, implants, clinical laboratory equipment and supplies, medical and hospital disposable supplies, and testing instruments; also lists companies that service, recondition, lease, or buy and sell used equipment; coverage includes U.S. and Canada. Entries include: Company name, address, phone, toll-free phone, fax, toll-free fax, URL, e-mail, total sales, names of key executives and contacts, product categories handled, trade names, methods of distribution, typical pricing, annual volume. Price of directory includes custom updates upon request.

Health Industry Buyers Guide. Lippincott Williams & Wilkins. • Covers: 4,000 manufacturers of hospital and physician's supplies and equipment, including medical laboratory, oxygen therapy, and X-ray supplies, home health care products, and orthopedic appliances. Entries include: Manufacturer name, address, phone, fax, full product line.

Home Health Agencies Report and Directory. SMG Marketing Group, Inc. • Annual. $575.00. Lists over 13,000 home healthcare agencies and corporations. Includes a market analysis and growth projections.

Home Healthcare Agency Chains Directory. Firstmark Inc. • Description: Includes operational statistics and other data on 240 chains which own or manage home healthcare agencies. Entries include: Headquarter name, address, phone, agencies belonging to the chain, ownership type, number of employees.

HomeCare Magazine Buyers' Guide. Primedia Business. • Publication includes: List of about 800 manufacturers and distributors of home health care and rehabilitation products, as well as service providers. Entries include: Company name, address, phone, fax, web site, e-mail, names and titles of key personnel, trade names, product or service provided; also by product category.

FINANCIAL RATIOS

Annual Statement Studies. The Risk Management Association. • Annual. Median and quartile financial ratios are given for over 400 kinds of manufacturing, wholesale, retail, construction, and consumer finance establishments. Data is sorted by both asset size and sales volume. Includes a clearly written "Definition of Ratios" and an alphabetical industry index.

Annual Statement Studies: Industry Default Probabilities and Cash Flow Measures. The Risk Management Association. • Annual. $145.00. Serves as a companion volume to the original *Annual Statement Studies.* Gives probability of default estimates on a percentage scale for more than 450 industries. Includes changes in position year-by-year for eight financial statement line items and provides percentage measures of cash flow.

HANDBOOKS AND MANUALS

Administrator's Handbook for Community Health and Home Care Services. Anne S. Smith. National League for Nursing Press. • 1988. $175.00.

Home Health Care Management. Lazelle E. Benefield. Prentice Hall PTR. • 1988. $50.00.

An Insider's Guide to Home Health Care. Tova Navarra and Margaret Ferrer. SLACK, Inc. • 1996. $28.00. Covers "unexpected situations, cultural differences, and potential comflicts" for professionals in the home health care field. Emphasizes teamwork for optimal care management.

PERIODICALS AND NEWSLETTERS

Caring. Manitoba Association of Licensed Practical Nurses. • Description: Contains educational articles,

reports, and surveys pertinent to the nursing profession. Recurring features include letters to the editor, a calendar of events, reports of meetings, news of educational opportunities, board meeting highlights, and a licensed practical nurse (LPN) page.

Continuing Care News: Supporting the Transition into Post Hospital Care. Stevenson Publishing Corp. • Monthly. $99.00 per year. Topics include insurance, legal issues, health business news, ethics, and case management. Includes annual *Buyer's Guide.*

HME News (Home Medical Equipment). United Publications, Inc. • Monthly. Free to qualified personnel; others, $60.00 per year. Covers the home medical equipment business for dealers and manufacturers. Provides information on a wide variety of home health care supplies and equipment.

Home Health Care Dealer-Provider. Curant Communications, Inc. • Bimonthly. Free. For home care dealer and home care pharmacies. Formerly *Home Health Care Dealer - Supplier.*

Home Health Care Services Quarterly: The Journal of Community Care. Haworth Press, Inc. • Quarterly. $535.00 per year. An academic and practical journal focusing on the marketing and administration of home care.

Home Health Line: The Home Care Industry's National Independent Newsletter. • 48 times a year. $399.00 per year. Newsletter on legislation and regulations affecting the home health care industry, with an emphasis on federal funding and Medicare programs.

Home Health Products. Stevens Publishing Corp. • 10 times a year. $99.00 per year. Covers new medical equipment products for the home care industry.

Home Healthcare Nurse: The Journal for the Home Care and Hospice Professional. The Home Healthcare Nurses Association. Lippincott Williams and Wilkins. • 10 times a year. Individuals, $52.95 per year; institutions, $202.95 per year. For professional nurses in the home health care field.

Homecare Magazine: The Business Magazine of the Home Health Industry. Primedia Business Magazines and Media. • Monthly. $69.00 per year. Edited for dealers and suppliers of home medical equipment, including pharmacies and chain stores. Includes information on new products.

Homecare News. National Association for Home Care. • Description: Reports on National Association for Home Care news plus home care industry developments for the entire industry.

Hospital Home Health: The Monthly Updates for Executives and Health Care Professionals. American Health Consultants, Inc. • Monthly. $399.00 per year. Newsletter for hospital-based home health agencies.

RESEARCH CENTERS AND INSTITUTES

Stratis Health. 2901 Metro Dr., Suite 400, Bloomington, MN 55425-1525. Phone: (952)854-3306 Fax: (952)853-8503 E-mail: info@stratishealth.org • URL: http://www.stratishealth.org.

STATISTICS SOURCES

Health Care Costs. DRI/McGraw-Hill. • Quarterly. Price on application. Cost indexes for hospitals, nursing homes, and home healthcare agencies.

Health, United States, 1999: Health and Aging Chartbook. Available from U. S. Government Printing Office. • 1999. $43.00. Issued by the National Center for Health Statistics, U. S. Department of Health and Human Services. Contains 34 bar charts in color, with related statistical tables. Provides detailed data on persons over 65 years of age, including population, living arrangements, life expectancy, nursing home residence, poverty, health

status, assistive devices, health insurance, and health care expenditures.

TRADE/PROFESSIONAL ASSOCIATIONS

American Association for Continuity of Care. P.O. Box 532, Dunedin, FL 34697. Phone: (727)738-1030 Fax: (727)738-8099 • URL: http://www.continuityofcare.com • Members are professionals concerned with continuity of care, health care after hospital discharge, and home health care.

American Federation of Home Health Agencies. 1320 Fenwick Lane,, Suite 100, Silver Spring, MD 20910. Fax: (301)588-4732 E-mail: afhha@his.com • URL: http://www.aft.org • Promotes home health care.

National Association for Home Care. 228 Seventh St., S.E., Washington, DC 20003. Phone: (202)547-7424 Fax: (202)547-3540 E-mail: exec@nahc.org • URL: http://www.nahc.org • Promotes high standards of patient care in home care services. Members are durable medical providers, medical equipment and oxygen suppliers, mainly for home health care.

OTHER SOURCES

Disability and Rehabilitation Products Markets. Theta Reports/PJB Medical Publications, Inc. • 1999. $1,295.00. Market research data. Covers the market for products designed to help differently-abled people lead more active lives. Includes such items as adaptive computers, augmentative communication devices, lifts/vans, and bath/home products. Profiles of leading suppliers are included. (Theta Report No. 800.).

Home Care Products Market. MarketResearch.com. • 2001. $3,500.00. Market data with projections to 2005. Covers a wide variety of products: wheelchairs, crutches, beds, monitoring equipment, etc.

Home Care Services Market. MarketResearch.com. • 1999. $3,250.00. Market data with projections. Covers a wide variety of services: primary nursing, respiratory, dialysis, infusion, etc.

The U. S. Market for Home Medical Tests. Available from MarketResearch.com. • 1997. $1,375.00. Market research report published by Packaged Facts. Covers the market for diagnostic products used in the home and the effect of regulation.

HOME IMPROVEMENT INDUSTRY

See also: BUILDING INDUSTRY

DIRECTORIES

Builder: Buyer's Guide. Hanley-Wood, LLC. • Annual. $10.00. A directory of products and services for the home building and remodeling industry.

Directory of Home Center Operators and Hardware Chains. Chain Store Guide. • Annual. $327.00. On-line edition, $747.00. Nearly 4,700 home center operators, paint and home decorating chains, and lumber and building materials companies. Covers United States and Canada.

Remodeling--Product Guide. Hanley-Wood L.L.C. • Publication includes: List of more than 2,000 manufacturers and suppliers serving the remodeling contracting industry; list of industry-related associations. Entries include: For manufacturers and suppliers--Company name, address, phone, name and title of contact, product line, geographical area served. For associations--Association name, address, phone, director.

ENCYCLOPEDIAS AND DICTIONARIES

Illustrated Dictionary of Building Materials and Techniques: An Invaluable Sourcebook to the Tools, Terms, Materials, and Techniques Used by Building Professionals. Paul Bianchina. John Wiley and Sons,

Inc. • 1993. $19.95. Contains 4,000 definitions of building and building materials terms, with 500 illustrations. Includes materials grades, measurements, and specifications.

HANDBOOKS AND MANUALS

No-Regrets Remodeling: Creating a Comfortable, Healthy Home That Saves Energy. Home Energy. • 1997. $19.95. Edited by *Home Energy* magazine. Serves as a home remodeling guide to efficient heating, cooling, ventilation, water heating, insulation, lighting, and windows.

Profiting from Real Estate Rehab. Sandra M. Brassfield. John Wiley and Sons, Inc. • 1992. $42.95. How to fix up old houses and sell them at a profit.

PERIODICALS AND NEWSLETTERS

Builder: The Voice of America's Housing Industry. National Association of Home Builders of the United States, Economics, Mortgage Finance and Housing Policy Div. Hanley-Wood, LLC. • Monthly. $29.95 per year. Covers the home building and remodeling industry in general, including design, construction, and marketing.

Building Material Dealer. National Lumber and Building Material Dealers Association. • Monthly. $48.00 per year. Includes special feature issues on hand and power tools, lumber, roofing, kitchens, flooring, windows and doors, and insulation. Formerly *Builder Material Retailer.*

National Home Center News: News and Analysis for the Home Improvement, Building Material Industry. Lebhar-Friedman, Inc. • 22 times a year. $99.00 per year. Includes special feature issues on hardware and tools, building materials, millwork, electrical supplies, lighting, and kitchens.

Remodeling: Excellence in Professional Remodeling. Hanley-Wood, LLC. • Monthly. $44.95 per year. Covers new products, construction, management, and marketing for remodelers.

STATISTICS SOURCES

Expenditures for Residential Improvements and Repairs. Available from U. S. Government Printing Office. • Quarterly. $16.00 per year. Bureau of the Census Construction Report, C50. Provides estimates of spending for housing maintenance, repairs, additions, alterations, and major replacements.

TRADE/PROFESSIONAL ASSOCIATIONS

National Association of the Remodeling Industry. 780 Lee St., Suite 200, Des Plaines, IL 60016. Phone: 800-611-6274 or (847)298-9200 Fax: (847)298-9225 E-mail: info@nari.org • URL: http://www.nari.org.

OTHER SOURCES

The Home Improvement Market. Available from MarketResearch.com. • 1999. $2,750.00. Market research report published by Packaged Facts. Covers the market for lumber, finishing materials, tools, hardware, etc.

HOME OWNERSHIP

See also: PERSONAL FINANCE

GENERAL WORKS

How to Sell Your Home for Top Dollar. Michael C. Thomsett. McGraw-Hill. • 1989. $13.00. (One Hour Guides Series).

A New Housing Policy for America: Recapturing the American Dream. Richard C. Ferlauto and others. Temple University Press. • 1988. $24.95.

CD-ROM DATABASES

Magazine Index Plus. Gale Cengage Learning. • Monthly. $4,000.00 per year (includes InfoTrac workstation). Provides full text on CD-ROM for about 100 popular, general interest magazines and indexing for 300 others. Includes special indexing of reviews and product evaluations. Time period is 1980 to date.

WILSONDISC: Readers' Guide to Periodical Literature. H. W. Wilson Co. • Monthly. $1,095.00 per year, including unlimited online access to *Readers' Guide to Periodical Literature* through WILSONLINE. Provides CD-ROM indexing of about 270 general interest periodicals. Covers 1983 to date. (*Readers' Guide Abstracts* also available on CD-ROM at $1,995 per year.).

ENCYCLOPEDIAS AND DICTIONARIES

Dictionary of Real Estate Terms. Jack P. Friedman and others. Barron's Educational Series, Inc. • 2004. $13.95. Sixth edition. Defines more than 2,500 terms relating to real estate business, including mortgages, financing, leasing, insurance, and home buying.

HANDBOOKS AND MANUALS

Complete Guide to Your Real Estate Closing: Answers to All Your Questions from Opening Escrow to Negotiating Fees to Signing Closing Papers. Sandy Gadow. McGraw-Hill. • Date not set. $19.95. Includes sample forms and work sheets, with specific real estate closing information for all 50 states. (Teach Yourself Series).

Home Inspection Service. Entrepreneur Media, Inc. • Looseleaf. $59.50. A practical guide to starting a home inspection service. Covers profit potential, start-up costs, market size evaluation, owner's time required, pricing, accounting, advertising, promotion, etc. (Start-Up Business Guide No. E1334.).

Homeowner or Tenant? How to Make a Wise Choice. Lawrence S. Pratt. American Institute for Economic Research. • 2002. $8.00. Provides detailed information for making rent or buy decisions. Includes "Mortgage Arithmetic," "Hints for Buyers, Sellers, and Renters," worksheets, mortgage loan interest tables, and other data. (Economic Education Bulletin.).

How to Buy a House, Condo, or Co-op. Jean C. Thomsett. Consumers Union of the United States, Inc. • 1996. $84.75. Fifth edition.

Your Dream Home: A Comprehensive Guide to Buying a House, Condo, or Co-op. Marguerite Smith. Warner Books, Inc. • 1997. $10.99. (Money, America's Financial Advisor Series).

ONLINE DATABASES

PAIS International. Public Affairs Information Service, Inc. • Corresponds to the former printed publications, *PAIS Bulletin* (1976-90) and *PAIS Foreign Language Index* (1972-90), and to the current *PAIS International in Print* (1991 to date). Covers economic, political, and sociological material appearing in periodicals, books, government documents, and other publications. Updating is monthly. Inquire as to online cost and availability.

Readers' Guide Abstracts Online. H. W. Wilson Co. • Indexes and abstracts general interest periodicals, 1983 to date. Weekly updates. Inquire as to online cost and availability.

PERIODICALS AND NEWSLETTERS

Ledger Quarterly: A Financial Review for Community Association Practitioners. Community Associations Institute. • Quarterly. $67.00 per year. Newsletter. Provides current information on issues affecting the finances of condominium, cooperative, homeowner, apartment, and other community housing associations.

Metropolitan Home: Style for Our Generation. Hachette Filipacchi Media U.S., Inc. • Bimonthly. $17.94 per year.

Taunton's Fine Homebuilding. Taunton Press, Inc. • Bimonthly $37.95. Special interest magazine written by builders for builders - professional and homeowners. Formerly *Fine Homebuilding.*

Unique Homes: The Global Resource of Luxury Real Estate. Unique Homes, Inc. • Six times a year. $29.97 per year. Homes for sale.

STATISTICS SOURCES

American Housing Survey for the United States in [year]. Available from U. S. Government Printing Office. • Biennial. $51.00. Issued by the U. S. Census Bureau (http://www.census.gov). Covers both owner-occupied and renter-occupied housing. Includes data on such factors as condition of building, type of mortgage, utility costs, and housing occupied by minorities. (Current Housing Reports, H150.).

Current Population Reports: Household Economic Studies, Series P-70. Available from U. S. Government Printing Office. • Irregular. $21.00 per year. Issued by the U.S. Bureau of the Census (http://www.census.gov). Each issue covers a special topic relating to household socioeconomic characteristics.

Housing Statistics of the United States. Patrick A. Simmons. Bernan Press. • 2000. $89.00. Third edition. (Housing Statistics of the United States Series).

New One-Family Houses Sold. Available from U. S. Government Printing Office. • Monthly. $45.00 per year. Bureau of the Census Construction Report, C25. Provides data on new, privately-owned, one-family homes sold during the month and for sale at the end of the month.

ULI Market Profiles: North America. Urban Land Institute. • Annual. Members, $249.95; nonmembers, $299.95. Provides real estate marketing data for residential, retail, office, and industrial sectors. Covers 76 U. S. metropolitan areas and 13 major foreign metropolitan areas.

TRADE/PROFESSIONAL ASSOCIATIONS

Community Associations Institute. 225 Reinekers Ln., Ste. 300, Alexandria, VA 22314. Phone: 888-CAI-4321 or (703)548-8600 Fax: (703)684-1581 E-mail: caidirect@caionline.org • URL: http://www.caionline.org • Condominium and homeowner associations, cooperatives, and association-governed planned communities of all sizes and architectural types; community or property managers and management firms; individual homeowners; community association managers and management firms; public officials; and lawyers, accountants, engineers, reserve specialists, builder/developers and other providers of professional services and products for CAs. Seeks to educate and represent America's 250,000 residential condominium, cooperative and homeowner associations and related professionals and service providers. Aims to foster vibrant, responsive, competent community associations that promote harmony, community and responsible leadership.

National Foundation of Manufactured Home Owners. 62 Hawthorne Cir., 62 Hawthorne Circle, Willow Street, PA 17584. Phone: (717)284-4520 Fax: (717)284-4520 E-mail: pamhoa@aol.com • URL: http://www.manhousingfoundation.org • Represents 20,000,000 owners of mobile/manufactured homes. Serves as a unified national voice for mobile/manufactured homeowners and to improve communications among members, and research problems homeowners can experience. Maintains resources, include extensive collection of material, clearinghouse of information, especially on the purchase, set-up and maintenance of homes.

National Homeowners Association. PO Box 221225, Chantilly, VA 20153. Phone: (703)581-1515 Fax: (703)581-1234 E-mail: info@nhfa.org • Advocacy organization for individual homeowners. Promotes a political and economic climate favorable to American homeowners; provides legislative/regulatory liaison. Conducts political, educational, and consumer programs. Topics researched include: taxes, insurance, energy savings, home maintenance and repairs, mortgage and financing options, crime and safety precautions, and real estate practices. **Convention/Meeting:** none.

National Housing Conference. 1801 K St. NW, Ste. M-100, Washington, DC 20006-1301. Phone: (202)466-2121 Fax: (202)466-2122 E-mail: cegan@ nhc.org • URL: http://www.nhc.org • Housing authority officials, community development specialists, builders, bankers, lawyers, accountants, owners, residents, insurers, architects and planners, religious organizations, labor groups, and national housing and housing related organizations. Mobilizes support for effective programs in housing and community development as well as affordable and accessible housing for all Americans. Holds educational programs.

National Rural Housing Coalition. 1250 Eye St. NW, Ste. 902, Washington, DC 20005. Phone: (202)393-5229 Fax: (202)393-3034 E-mail: nrhc@ nrhcweb.org • URL: http://www.nrhcweb.org • Advocates for improved government and private housing programs for people in small towns and rural areas. Develops informational and educational material; gives and coordinates testimony before congressional committees; seeks improved administrative procedures within the executive branch of the federal government. Lobbies for low-income rural housing and community facilities.

HOME TEXTILES

See: LINEN INDUSTRY

HOMES FOR THE AGED

See: NURSING HOMES

HONEY INDUSTRY

GENERAL WORKS
World History of Beekeeping and Honey Hunting. Eva Crane. Taylor & Francis. • 1999. $140.00. Provides a wide variety of information on beekeeping and the honey industry.

ABSTRACTS AND INDEXES
Apicultural Abstracts. International Bee Research Association. • Quarterly. $295.00 per year. Up-to-date summary of world literature on bees and beekeeping.

Bee Culture: The Magazine of American Beekeeping. A. I. Root Co. • Monthly. $20.00 per year. Articles, reports and stories about beekeeping market. Latest industry news. Formerly *Gleanings in Bee Culture.*

ALMANACS AND YEARBOOKS
Agricultural and Mineral Commodities Year Book. Available from Taylor & Francis Group. • Annual. $225.00. Published by Europa Publications. Contains descriptive product profiles, price data, export-import data, and production statistics for major commodities of the world. Includes commodity histories, uses, markets, demand trends, and information about trade agreements and key commodity organizations.

INTERNET DATABASES
USDA. United States Department of Agriculture. Phone: (202)720-2791 E-mail: agsec@usda.gov • URL: http://www.usda.gov • The USDA home page has six sections: News and Information; What's New; About USDA; Agencies; Opportunities; Search and Help. Keyword searching is offered from the USDA home page and from various individual agency home pages. Agencies are the Economic Research Service, Agricultural Marketing Service, National Agricultural Statistics Service, National

Agricultural Library, and about 12 others. Updating varies. Fees: Free.

ONLINE DATABASES
CAB Abstracts. CAB Publishing North America. • Contains 46 specialized abstract collections covering over 10,000 journals and monographs in the areas of agriculture, horticulture, forest products, farm products, nutrition, dairy science, poultry, grains, animal health, entomology, etc. Time period is 1972 to date, with monthly updates. Inquire as to online cost and availability. *CAB Abstracts on CD-ROM* also available, with annual updating.

F & S Index. Gale Cengage Learning. • Contains about four million citations to worldwide business, financial, and industrial or consumer product literature appearing from 1972 to date. Weekly updates. Inquire as to online cost and availability.

PERIODICALS AND NEWSLETTERS
American Bee Journal. Dadant and Sons, Inc. • Monthly. $22.25 per year. Magazine for hobbyist and professional beekeepers.

American Beekeeping Federation Newsletter. American Beekeeping Federation, Inc. • Bimonthly. $25.00 per year. Newsletter.

Bee Craft: The Official Journal of the British Bee-Keepers' Association. British Bee-Keepers Association. Bee Craft Ltd. • Monthly. $51.00 per year.

Bee World. International Bee Research Association. • Quarterly. $85.00 per year. Authoritative articles and reviews about recent scientific and technological developments.

Beekeeping. Devon Beekeepers Association. • Ten times a year. Free to members; non-members, $11.50 per year.

Journal of Apicultural Research. International Bee Research Association. • Quarterly. $225.00 per year. Primary research.

RESEARCH CENTERS AND INSTITUTES
Bee Biology and Systematics Laboratory. Utah State University. 5310 Old Main Hill, Logan, UT 84322-5310. Phone: (435)797-2524 Fax: (435)797-0461 • URL: http://www.loganbeelab.usu.edu.

Honey Bee Research Unit. U.S. Department of Agricultural Research Service, Carl Hayden Bee Research Center, 2000 E. Allen Rd., Tucson, AZ 85719. Phone: (520)670-6380 Fax: (520)670-6493 E-mail: gdhoff@aol.com • URL: http://www.gears. tucson.ars.ag.gov.

Kika de la Garza Subtropical Agricultural Research Center. USDA Agricultural Research Center, 2413 E. Highway 83, BIRU Bldg. 200, Welasco, TX 78596. Phone: (956)447-6301 Fax: (956)447-6345 E-mail: jquisenberry@welasco.ars.usda.gov • URL: http://www.welasco.ars.usda.gov.

Northeast Research and Extension Center. University of Arkansas. P.O. Box 48, Keiser, AR 72351. Phone: (870)526-2199 Fax: (870)526-2582 E-mail: fbourland@uaex.edu.

STATISTICS SOURCES
Agricultural Statistics. Available from U. S. Government Printing Office. • Annual. $38.00. Produced by the National Agricultural Statistics Service, U. S. Department of Agriculture. Provides a wide variety of statistical data relating to agricultural production, supplies, consumption, prices/price-supports, foreign trade, costs, and returns, as well as farm labor, loans, income, and population. In many cases, historical data is shown annually for 10 years. In addition to farm data, includes detailed fishery statistics.

FAO Production Yearbook. Available from Bernan Associates. • Annual. $45.00. Published by the Food and Agriculture Organization (http://www.fao.org). Contains worldwide data on agriculture, land use,

farm crops, livestock, and agricultural prices.

FAO Trade Yearbook. Available from Bernan Associates. • Annual. $45.00. Published by the Food and Agriculture Organization (http://www.fao.org). Provides extensive worldwide data on exports and imports of agricultural commodities, fertilizers, tractors, and pesticides. Includes more than 130 tables of detailed statistics.

Honey Production, Annual Summary. U.S. Department of Agriculture. • Annual.

Sugar and Sweetener Situation and Outlook. Available from U. S. Government Printing Office. • Three times per year. $18.00 per year. Issued by Economic Research Service, U. S. Department of Agriculture. Provides current statistical information on supply, demand, and prices.

TRADE/PROFESSIONAL ASSOCIATIONS
American Beekeeping Federation. PO Box 1337, Jesup, GA 31598-1038. Phone: (912)427-4233 Fax: (912)427-8447 E-mail: info@abfnet.org • URL: http://www.abfnet.org • Commercial and avocational beekeepers, suppliers, bottlers, packers, and others affiliated with the honey industry. Promotes the industry and serves as an representative before legislative bodies; makes recommendations and helps secure appropriations for research programs. Operates the Honey Defense Fund, which works to insure the purity of honey marketed in the U.S. Sponsors American Honey Queen Program.

International Bee Research Association. 18 North Rd., Cardiff CF1 3DT, United Kingdom. Phone: (999)44 2920 372409 Fax: (999)44 2920 665522 E-mail: mail@ibra.org.uk • URL: http://www.ibra. org.uk • Individuals, beekeeping societies, and research organizations in 130 countries. Promotes and coordinates bee research work and research on pollination. Provides worldwide information service through publications, correspondence, and journals. Aids beekeepers and promotes beekeeping as a sustainable activity in developing countries.

International Federation of Beekeepers' Associations. c/o Apimondia, Corso Vittorio Emanuele 101, I-00186 Rome, Italy. Phone: 39 6 6852286 Fax: 39 6 6852286 E-mail: apimondia@mclink.it • URL: http://www.apimondia.org.

National Honey Packers and Dealers Association. 3301 Rte. 66, Ste. 205, Bldg. C, Neptune, NJ 07753. Phone: (732)922-3008 Fax: (732)922-3590 E-mail: info@nhpda.org • URL: http://www.nhpda.org.

HONG KONG

See: ASIAN MARKETS

HONORARY DEGREES

See: ACADEMIC DEGREES

HOPS

See: BREWING INDUSTRY

HOROLOGY

See: CLOCK AND WATCH INDUSTRY

HORTICULTURE

See: NURSERIES (HORTICULTURAL)

HOSIERY INDUSTRY

See also: CHILDREN'S APPAREL INDUSTRY; CLOTHING INDUSTRY; WOMEN'S APPAREL; TEXTILE INDUSTRY

CD-ROM DATABASES
OECD Statistical Compendium. Organization for Economic Cooperation and Development. •

Semiannual. $1,905.00 per year for 1 to 10 users. CD-ROM contains more than 730,000 monthly, quarterly, and annual time series for OECD countries, 1960 to date. Includes fully searchable data on agriculture, food, economic indicators, national accounts, employment, energy, finance, industry, technology, and foreign trade. Results can be displayed in various forms.

DIRECTORIES

Accessories Resources Directory. Business Journals Inc. • Covers: 1,600 manufacturers, importers, and sales representatives producing or handling belts, gloves, handbags, scarves, hosiery, jewelry, sunglasses, and umbrellas. Entries include: Company, name, address, phone, fax.

HANDBOOKS AND MANUALS

Sock Shop. Entrepreneur Media, Inc. • Looseleaf. $59.50. A practical guide to starting a store that sells stockings of various kinds. Covers profit potential, start-up costs, market size evaluation, owner's time required, site selection, lease negotiation, pricing, accounting, advertising, etc. (Start-Up Business Guide No. E1340.).

INTERNET DATABASES

Business 2.0 Web Guide to the Best Business Links. Business 2.0 Media Inc. Phone: (415)293-4800 E-mail: support@business2.com • URL: http://www.business2.com/webguide • Web site presents an extensive, searchable directory of links to "the best, most informative, and authoritative web pages." Twenty main categories cover business, finance, career, company information, people, and technology topics, with thousands of subtopics, all linking to Web sites recommended by experienced business researchers. Fees: Free.

Fedstats. Federal Interagency Council on Statistical Policy. Phone: (202)395-7254 • URL: http://www.fedstats.gov • Web site features an efficient search facility for full-text statistics produced by more than 100 federal agencies, including the Census Bureau, the Bureau of Economic Analysis, and the Bureau of Labor Statistics. Boolean searches can be made within one agency or for all agencies combined. Links are offered to international statistical bureaus, including the UN, IMF, OECD, UNESCO, Eurostat, and 20 individual countries. Fees: Free.

FreeLunch.com. Economy.com, Inc. Phone: (610)696-8700 Fax: (610)696-1678 • URL: http://www.freelunch.com • Web site provides free access to more than 1.5 million economic and financial data series, covering industry, demographics, labor markets, prices, retail sales, government spending, trade, interest rates, housing starts, the stock market, and many other topics. Data is available for various time periods in either chart or table form. Searching is offered. Fees: Free, but registration required. Economy.com, Inc. also offers fee-based economic analysis at *The Dismal Scientist* site (http://www.dismal.com).

PERIODICALS AND NEWSLETTERS

Hosiery News. Hosiery Association. • Monthly. Membership. Hosiery-related news including new offerings for retail, industry changes, legislative updates of hosiery-impacting laws, foreign trade and statistical information.

STATISTICS SOURCES

Business Statistics of the United States. Linz Audain and Cornelia J. Strawser. Bernan Associates. • Annual. $147.00. Based on *Business Statistics*, formerly issue by the Bureau of Economic Analysis, U. S. Department of Commerce. Provides basic data for a wide variety of U. S. industries, services, and economic indicators. Most statistics are shown annually for 30 years and monthly for the most recent four years.

Hosiery Statistics. Hosiery Association. • Annual.

Free to members; non-members, $50.00.

Survey of Current Business. Available from U. S. Government Printing Office. • Monthly. $63.00 per year. Issued by Bureau of Economic Analysis, U. S. Department of Commerce. Presents a wide variety of business and economic data.

TRADE/PROFESSIONAL ASSOCIATIONS

The Hosiery Association. 7421 Carmel Executive Park, Ste. 200, Charlotte, NC 28226. Phone: (704)365-0913 Fax: (704)362-2056 E-mail: thainfo@hosieryassociation.com • URL: http://www.hosieryassociation.com • Hosiery manufacturers and suppliers. Develops standards for hosiery measurement. Sponsors annual "Celebrate Hosiery" to educate consumers on hosiery varieties. Conducts field visitations for assistance in technical areas. Compiles statistics; conducts research programs. Operates Group Purchasing Program.

Unite!-The Union of Needletrades, Industrial and Textile Employees. 1710 Broadway, New York, NY 10019. Phone: (212)265-7000 Fax: (212)315-3803 E-mail: kkirsch@uniteunion.org • URL: http://www.uniteunion.org.

HOSPITAL ADMINISTRATION

See also: ADMINISTRATION; HEALTH CARE INDUSTRY; HOSPITAL EQUIPMENT

GENERAL WORKS

The Financial Management of Hospitals and Healthcare Organizations. Michael Nowicki. Health Administration Press. • 2001. $52.00. Second edition.

Fundamentals of Strategic Planning for Healthcare Organizations. Stan Williamson and others. Haworth Press, Inc. • 1996. $49.95.

Introduction to Hospital Accounting. L. Vann Seawell. Healthcare Financial Management Educational Foundation. • 1992. $45.00. Third edition.

Predicting Successful Hospital Mergers and Acquisitions: A Financial and Analytical Marketing Tool. David P. Angrisani and Robert L. Goldman. Haworth Press, Inc. • 1997. $49.95.

ABSTRACTS AND INDEXES

Excerpta Medica: Health Policy, Economics and Management. Elsevier. • Bimonthly. Qualified personnel, $336.00 per year; institutions, $1,719.00 per year. Section 36 of *Excerpta Medica*.

CD-ROM DATABASES

Authority Health Care Law Library. LexisNexis/Matthew Bender. • Periodic updates. Price on request. Full text CD-ROM provides legal information, case law, and analysis relating to health care facilities, health insurance, longterm care, Medigap, and Medicare.

Healthcare QuickDisc. American Hospital Association. • Annual. AHA members, $2,800.00. Non-members, $3,750.00. CD-ROM corresponds to the printed *AHA Guide*, with additional material and extensive search capabilities (400 data fields). Provides detailed information on 6,000 hospitals and hospital systems, including utilization data.

DIRECTORIES

AHA Guide to the Health Care Field. American Hospital Association. • Annual. $295.00. A directory of hospitals and health care systems.

AHA Integrated Delivery Network Directory: U.S. Health Care Systems, Networks, and Alliances. American Hospital Association. • Annual. $250.00. Provides information about a wide variety of U.S. health care groups and affiliations, including hospitals, nursing homes, rehabilitation centers,

psychiatric facilities, home health care agencies, clinical laboratories, outpatient facilities, and diagnostic imaging centers. Includes names of more than 8,000 key executives.

Directory of Hospital Personnel. Medical Economics Co. • Annual. $325.00. Lists over 200,000 healthcare professionals in 7,000 U. S. hospitals. Geographic arrangement, with indexes by personnel, hospital name, and bed size.

Directory of Physician Groups and Networks. Dorland Healthcare Information. • Annual. $495.00. Available only online. Approximately 8,000 independent practice associations (IPAs), physician hospital organizations (PHOs), management service organizations (MSOs), physician practice management companies (PPMCs), and group practices having 20 or more physicians.

Directory of Privately-Owned Hospitals,Residential Treatment Facilities and Centers, Hospital Management Companies, and Health Systems. Federation of American Health Systems. • Annual. $125.00. Lists approximately 1,700 privately-owned hospitals and over 80 hospital management companies in the United States, Puerto Rico, and internationally.

Plunkett's Health Care Industry Almanac: The Only Complete Guide to the Health Care Industry in America. Plunkett Research, Ltd. • Biennial. $229.99. Includes CD-ROM. Includes detailed profiles of 500 large companies providing health care products or services, with indexes by products, services, and location. Provides statistical and trend information for the health insurance industry, HMOs, hospital utilization, Medicare, medical technology, and national health expenditures.

Profiles of U. S. Hospitals. Dorland Healthcare Information. • Annual. $299.00. Contains profiles of more than 6,000 community, teaching, children's, specialty, psychiatric, and rehabilitation hospitals. Emphasis is on 50 key financial and performance measures. Annual CD-ROM version with key word searching is available at $395.00.

Society for Health Strategy and Market Development-Directory of Membership and Services. Society for Healthcare Strategy and Market Development. American Hospital Association. • Annual. Membership.

ENCYCLOPEDIAS AND DICTIONARIES

Encyclopedia of Health Care Management. Michael Stahl, editor. Sage Publications, Inc. • 2004. $150.00. Contains 600 entries covering "the business of health care.".

FINANCIAL RATIOS

Almanac of Business and Industrial Financial Ratios. Leo Troy. Aspen Publishers, Inc. • 2003. $125.95. Includes CD-Rom. Contains financial ratios derived from federal tax returns. Ratios for each of about 200 industries are arranged according to company asset size. (Almanac of Business and Industrial Financial Ratios Series).

Hospital Finance Almanac. Healthcare Financial Management Association. • Annual. $350.00. Provides five-year data relating to the financial and operating performance of the U. S. hospital industry. A consolidation of the former *Financial Report of the Hospital Industry* and *Performance Report of the Hospital Industry*.

HANDBOOKS AND MANUALS

Healthcare Finance for the Non-Financial Manager: Basic Guide to Financial Analysis & Control. Louis Gapenski. McGraw-Hill. • 1994. $47.50.

Hospital Cost Management. Prentice Hall PTR. • Looseleaf. Periodic supplementation. Price on application.

The Managed Care Contracting Handbook: Planning and Negotiating the Managed Care Relationship. Maria K. Todd. Available from

McGraw Hill Higher Education. • 1996. $65.00. Co-published by McGraw-Hill Healthcare Education Group and the Healthcare Financial Management Association. Covers managed care planning, proposals, strategy, negotiation, and contract law. Written for healthcare providers.

Management Accounting for Healthcare Organizations. Bruce R. Neumann and Keith E. Boles. Teach'em. • 1998. $65.00. Fifth revised edition.

ONLINE DATABASES

Healthstar. Medlars Management Section. • Provides indexing and abstracting of non-clinical literature relating to health care delivery, 1975 to date. Monthly updates. Inquire as to online cost and availability.

PERIODICALS AND NEWSLETTERS

AHA News. American Hospital Association. HealthForum. • Description: Highlights major news affecting hospitals and the health care field. Reports on legislation and regulation, court cases, surveys, and federal programs. Carries information on individual hospitals and allied hospital associations.

Health Data Management. Thomson Media. • Monthly. $98.00 per year. Covers the management and automation of clinical data and health care insurance claims. Provides news and analysis of various aspects of health care information technology for administrators of hospitals, clinics, and managed care plans.

Health Facilities Management. American Hospital Association. American Hospital Publishing, Inc. • Monthly. $40.00 per year. Covers building maintenance and engineering for hospitals and nursing homes.

Health Forum Journal: Leadership Strategies for Healthcare Executives. Health Forum. • Biweekly. $65.00 per year. Covers the general management of hospitals, nursing homes, and managed care organizations. Formerly *HospitalsHealthNetworks.*

Healthcare Risk Management. American Health Consultants Inc. • Description: Analyzes specific legal cases and trends relevant to healthcare liability. Discusses malpractice, liability for patients, staff and visitor injury, injury prevention, biomedical engineering, and medical staff credentials. Also covers high-risk areas of hospitals, hospital-owned home health and physician practices, accreditation, Medicare reimbursement, physician liability, medical records, and claims management. Recurring features include interviews, statistics, news of research, guest columns, legal briefs, and commentaries.

Hospital Pharmacist Report. Thomson Medical Economics. • Monthly. $39.00 per year. Covers both business and clinical topics for hospital pharmacists.

Journal of Healthcare Management. Foundation of the American College of Healthcare Executives. Health Administration Press. • Bimonthly. $85.00 per year. Information on the latest trends, developments and innovations in the industry. Formerly (Hospital and Health Services Administration).

Journal of Hospital Marketing and Public Relations. Haworth Press, Inc. • Semiannual. $390.00 per year. Formerly *Journal of Hospital Marketing.*

Modern Physician: Essential Business News for the Executive Physician. Crain Communications, Inc. • Monthly. $45.00. Edited for physicians responsible for business decisions at hospitals, clinics, HMOs, and other health groups. Includes special issues on managed care, practice management, legal issues, and finance.

Public Relations. PBI Media, LLC. • Biweekly. $397.00 per year. Newsletter on public relations and client communications for the healthcare industry. Incorporates (Healthcare PR and Marketing News).

Report on Healthcare Information Management. Capital Publications, Inc. • Monthly. $358.00 per year. Newsletter. Covers management information sytems for hospitals and physicicans' groups.

Solid Waste Report: Resource Recovery-Recycling-Collection-Disposal. Business Publishers, Inc. • Weekly. $627.00 per year. Newsletter. Covers regulation, business news, technology, and international events relating to solid waste management.

Trustee: The Magazine for Hospital Governing Boards. American Hospital Association. American Hospital Publishing, Inc. • 10 times a year. $40.00 per year. Emphasis is on community health care.

RESEARCH CENTERS AND INSTITUTES

Center for Health Administration Studies. University of Chicago, 969 E. 60th St., Chicago, IL 60637. Phone: (773)702-7104 Fax: (773)702-7222 E-mail: chas@uchichago.edu • URL: http://www.chas.uchicago.edu.

Health Services Research and Development Center. Johns Hopkins University, 624 N. Broadway, Room 482, Baltimore, MD 21205-1996. Phone: (410)955-3625 Fax: (410)614-9152 E-mail: dsteinwa@jhsph.edu.

STATISTICS SOURCES

AHA Hospital Statistics. American Hospital Association. American Hospital Publishing, Inc. • Annual. Members, $59.00 per year; non-members $139.00 per year. Provides detailed statistical data on the nation's hospitals, including revenues, expenses, utilization, and personnel. Formerly *Hospital Statistics.*

Economic Trends. American Hospital Association. American Hospital Publishing. • Quarterly. Members, $85.00 per year; non-members $135.00 per year. Provides statistical data on the nation's hospitals, including revenues, expenses.

Health and Environment in America's Top-Rated Cities: A Statistical Profile. Grey House Publishing. • Biennial. $125.00. Covers 75 U. S. cities. Includes statistical and other data on a wide variety of topics, such as air quality, water quality, recycling, hospitals, physicians, health care costs, death rates, infant mortality, accidents, and suicides.

Health Care Costs. DRI/McGraw-Hill. • Quarterly. Price on application. Cost indexes for hospitals, nursing homes, and home healthcare agencies.

Lilly Hospital Pharmacy Survey. Eli Lilly and Co. • Annual. $30.00. Includes financial data for drug stores located in hospitals.

Standard & Poor's Industry Surveys. Standard & Poor's. • Semiannual. $1,800.00. Two looseleaf volumes. Includes monthly *Supplements.* Provides detailed, individual surveys of 52 major industry groups. Each survey is revised on a semiannual basis. Also includes "Monthly Investment Review" (industry group investment analysis) and monthly "Trends & Projections" (economic analysis).

TRADE/PROFESSIONAL ASSOCIATIONS

American College of Healthcare Executives. One N. Franklin, St., Suite 1700, Chicago, IL 60606-3491. Phone: (312)424-2800 Fax: (312)424-0023 E-mail: ache@ache.org • URL: http://www.ache.org • Formerly American College of Hospital Administrators.

American Hospital Association. 1 N Franklin, Chicago, IL 60606-3421. Phone: (312)422-3000 Fax: (312)422-4796 E-mail: info@highways.org • URL: http://www.aha.org • Represents health care provider organizations. Seeks to advance the health of individuals and communities. Leads, represents, and serves health care provider organizations that are accountable to the community and committed to health improvement.

American Society of Health System Pharmacists.

7272 Wisconsin Ave., Bethesda, MD 20814. Phone: (301)657-3000 Fax: (301)664-8867 E-mail: ahfs@ashp.org • URL: http://www.ashp.org • Affiliated with American Hospital Association and American Nurses Association.

Healthcare Financial Management Association. 2 Westbrook Corporate Ctr., Ste. 700, Westchester, IL 60154. Phone: 800-252-4362 or (708)531-9600 Fax: (708)531-0032 E-mail: memberservices@hfma.org • URL: http://www.hfma.org • Financial management professionals employed by hospitals and long-term care facilities, public accounting and consulting firms, insurance companies, medical groups, managed care organizations, government agencies, and other organizations. Conducts conferences, including annual conference in late June and audio teleconferences. Publishes books on healthcare financial issues. A Fellowship in Healthcare Financial Management (FHFMA) as well as the Certified Healthcare Professional (CHFP) in Finance and Accounting, Financial Management of Physician Practices, Managed Care, and Patient Financial Services are offered.

Healthcare Information and Management Systems Society. 230 E. Ohio St., Suite 500, Chicago, IL 60611-3269. Phone: (312)664-4467 Fax: (312)664-6143 E-mail: himss@himss.org • URL: http://www.himss.org • Absorbed Center for Hospital Management Engineering. Formerly Hospital Management Systems Society.

OTHER SOURCES

Hospital Liability. American Lawyer Media, Inc. • Looseleaf. $189.00. Updated as needed. Written for attorneys representing either hospitals or patients of hospitals. Covers a wide variety of legal topics relating to hospital/physician malpractice, including the expansion of HMO liability. (Law Journal Press).

HOSPITAL EQUIPMENT

See also: SURGICAL INSTRUMENTS INDUSTRY; X-RAY EQUIPMENT INDUSTRY

CD-ROM DATABASES

Health Devices Alerts [CD-ROM]. ECRI. • Weekly. $2,450.00 per year. Provides CD-ROM reports of medical equipment defects, problems, failures, misuses, and recalls.

DIRECTORIES

Association for the Advancement of Medical Instrumentation Membership Directory. c/o AAMI Foundation. • Annual. Membership. List 6,500 physicians, clinical engineers, biomedical engineersand technicians and nurses, researchers, and medical equipment manufacturers.

Buyers' Guide for the Health Care Market: A Directory of Products and Services for Health Care Institutions. Health Forum. • Annual. $17.95. Lists 1,200 suppliers and manufacturers of health care products and services for hospitals, nursing homes, and related organizations.

Health Devices Sourcebook. ECRI. • Covers: Over 6,800 suppliers of patient care equipment, medical and surgical instruments, implants, clinical laboratory equipment and supplies, medical and hospital disposable supplies, and testing instruments; also lists companies that service, recondition, lease, or buy and sell used equipment; coverage includes U.S. and Canada. Entries include: Company name, address, phone, toll-free phone, fax, toll-free fax, URL, e-mail, total sales, names of key executives and contacts, product categories handled, trade names, methods of distribution, typical pricing, annual volume. Price of directory includes custom updates upon request.

Medical and Healthcare Marketplace Guide. IDD,

Inc. • Annual. $595.00. Two volumes. Provides market survey summaries for about 500 specific product and service categories (volume one: "Research Reports"). Contains profiles of nearly 5,500 pharmaceutical, medical product, and health-care service companies (volume two: "Company Profiles").

Society for Health Strategy and Market Development-Directory of Membership and Services. Society for Healthcare Strategy and Market Development. American Hospital Association. • Annual. Membership.

INTERNET DATABASES

National Library of Medicine (NLM). National Institutes of Health (NIH). Phone: 888-346-3656 or (301)496-1131 Fax: (301)480-3537 E-mail: access@nlm.nih.gov • URL: http://www.nlm.nih.gov • NLM Web site offers free access through MEDLINE ("PubMed") to about nine million references to articles appearing in some 4,000 biomedical journals, with abstracts. Search interfaces range from "simple keywords to advanced Boolean expressions." The NLM site offers many links to other sources of biomedical and technical information (the National Center for Biotechnology Information, for example). Fees: Free.

ONLINE DATABASES

F-D-C Reports. FDC Reports, Inc. • An online version of "The Gray Sheet" (medical devices), "The Pink Sheet" (pharmaceuticals), "The Rose Sheet" (cosmetics), "The Blue Sheet" (biomedical), and "The Tan Sheet" (nonprescription). Contains full-text information on legal, technical, corporate, financial, and marketing developments from 1987 to date, with weekly updates. Inquire as to online cost and availability.

Health Devices Alerts [online]. ECRI. • Provides online reports of medical equipment defects, problems, failures, misuses, and recalls. Time period is 1977 to date, with weekly updates. Inquire as to online cost and availability.

PERIODICALS AND NEWSLETTERS

The Gray Sheet Reports: Medical Devices, Diagnostics and Instrumentation. F-D-C Reports, Inc. • Weekly. Institutions, $1,172.00 per year. Newsletter. Provides industry and financial news, including a medical sector stock index. Monitors regulatory developments at the Center for Devices and Radiological Health of the U. S. Food and Drug Administration.

Health Devices Alerts: A Summary of Reported Problems, Hazards, Recalls, and Updates. ECRI (Emergency Care Research Institute). • Weekly. $3,649.40 per year. Looseleaf service. Contains reviews of health equipment problems. Includes *Health Devices Alerts Action Items, Health Devices Alerts Abstracts, Health Devices Alerts FDA Data, Health Devices Alerts Implants, Health Devices Alerts Hazards Bulletin.*

Healthcare Purchasing News: A Magazine for Hospital Materials Management Central Service, Infection Control Practitioners. Thomson/Medical Economics. • Monthly. $47.95 per year. Edited for personnel responsible for the purchase of medical, surgical, and hospital equipment and supplies. Features new purchasing techniques and new products. Includes news of the activities of two major purchasing associations, Health Care Material Management Society and International Association of Healthcare Central Service Materiel Management.

Medical Industry Information Report. Nicholas Communications, Inc. • Quarterly. $48.00 per year. Edited for executives in medical products industries, including medical devices and equipment, hospital supplies, and pharmaceuticals. Covers major trends and developments, with an emphasis on information technology.

Medical Product Manufacturing News. Canon Communications LLC. • 10 times a year. Free to qualified personnel; others, $150.00 per year. Directed at manufacturers of medical devices and medical electronic equipment. Covers industry news, service news, and new products.

Surgical Products. Reed Business Information. • Monthly. $41.90 per year. Covers new Technology and products for surgeons and operation rooms.

STATISTICS SOURCES

Electromedical Equipment and Irradiation Equipment, Including X-Ray. U. S. Bureau of the Census. • Annual. Contains shipment quantity, value of shipment, export, and import data. (Current Industrial Report No. MA-38R.).

Standard & Poor's Industry Surveys. Standard & Poor's. • Semiannual. $1,800.00. Two looseleaf volumes. Includes monthly *Supplements.* Provides detailed, individual surveys of 52 major industry groups. Each survey is revised on a semiannual basis. Also includes "Monthly Investment Review" (industry group investment analysis) and monthly "Trends & Projections" (economic analysis).

TRADE/PROFESSIONAL ASSOCIATIONS

Advanced Medical Technology Association. 701 Pennsylvania Ave. NW, Ste. 800, Washington, DC 20004-2654. Phone: (202)783-8700 Fax: (202)783-8750 E-mail: info@advamed.org • URL: http://www.advamed.org • Represents domestic (including U.S. territories and possessions) manufacturers of medical devices, diagnostic products, and healthcare information systems. Develops programs and activities on economic, technical, medical, and scientific matters affecting the industry. Gathers and disseminates information concerning the United States and international developments in legislative, regulatory, scientific or standards-making areas. Conducts scientific and educational seminars and programs.

Association for Healthcare Resource and Materials Management. c/o American Hospital Association, One N Franklin St., Chicago, IL 60606-3420. Phone: (312)422-3840 Fax: (312)422-4573 E-mail: ahrmm@aha.org • URL: http://www.ahrmm.org • Members are involved with the purchasing and distribution of supplies and equipment for hospitals and other healthcare establishments. Formerly American Society for Healthcare Materials Management.

International Association of Healthcare Central Service Materiel Management. 213 W. Institute Place, Suite 307, Chicago, IL 60610. Phone: 800-962-8274 or (312)440-0078 Fax: (312)440-9474 E-mail: mailbox@iahcsmm.com • URL: http://www.iahcsmm.com • Members are professional personnel responsible for management and distribution of supplies from a central service material management (purchasing) department of a hospital. Formerly International Association of Hospital Central Service Management.

National Association for Home Care. 228 Seventh St., S.E., Washington, DC 20003. Phone: (202)547-7424 Fax: (202)547-3540 E-mail: exec@nahc.org • URL: http://www.nahc.org • Promotes high standards of patient care in home care services. Members are durable medical providers, medical equipment and oxygen suppliers, mainly for home health care.

OTHER SOURCES

Disposable Medical Supplies. Available from MarketResearch.com. • 2001. $3,500.00. Published by the Freedonia Group. Market data with forecasts to 2007. Includes disposable syringes, catheters, kits, trays, etc.

Medical Gloves. Available from MarketResearch.com. • 2002. $3,850.00. Published by Global Industry Analysts. Provides worldwide market research data, including profiles of major medical glove companies.

New and Breaking Technologies in the Pharmaceutical and Medical Device Industries. Theta Reports. • 1999. $1,695.00. Contains market research predictions of medical technology trends over the next 5 to 10 years (2004-2009), including developments in biotechnology, genetic engineering, medical device technology, therapeutic vaccines, non-invasive diagnostics, and minimally-invasive surgery. (Theta Report No. 931.).

Nonwoven Disposables. Theta Reports. • 1999. $1,495.00. Provides market research data, including sales projections. Covers hospital disposable items, such as surgical drapes, masks, head covers, patient gowns, and incontinence products. (Theta Report No. 922.).

HOSPITALITY INDUSTRY

See: HOTEL AND MOTEL INDUSTRY; RESTAURANTS, LUNCHROOMS, ETC.; TRAVEL INDUSTRY

HOSPITALS

See: HOSPITAL ADMINISTRATION

HOTEL AND MOTEL INDUSTRY

See also: TRAVEL INDUSTRY

GENERAL WORKS

How Consumers Pick a Hotel: Strategic Segmentation and Target Marketing. Dennis J. Cahill. The Haworth Press, Inc. • 1997. $39.95.

The Lodging and Food Service Industry. Gerald W. Lattin and others. Educational Institute of the American Hotel & Motel Association. • 1998. $60.95. Fourth revised edition. General survey of the hospitality industry.

Marketing Management for the Hospitality Industry: A Strategic Approach. Allen Z. Reich. John Wiley and Sons, Inc. • 1997. $65.00.

ABSTRACTS AND INDEXES

Leisure, Recreation, and Tourism Abstracts. Available from CABI Publishing North America. • Quarterly. Members, $280.00 per year; Institutions, $610.00 per year. Includes single site internet access. Published in England by CABI Publishing. Provides coverage of the worldwide literature of travel, recreation, sports, and the hospitality industry. Emphasis is on research.

Lodging, Restaurant and Tourism Index. Distance Learning Service. Purdue University, Consumer and Family Sciences Library. • Quarterly. $265.00 per year. Provides subject indexing to 52 periodicals related to the hospitality industry. Annual bound cumulations are available. Formerly *Lodging and Restaurant Index.*

CD-ROM DATABASES

OECD Statistical Compendium. Organization for Economic Cooperation and Development. • Semiannual. $1,905.00 per year for 1 to 10 users. CD-ROM contains more than 730,000 monthly, quarterly, and annual time series for OECD countries, 1960 to date. Includes fully searchable data on agriculture, food, economic indicators, national accounts, employment, energy, finance, industry, technology, and foreign trade. Results can be displayed in various forms.

DIRECTORIES

Almanac. Penton Media Inc. • Annual. $50.00. Lists equipment, products, and services for the hotel and motel industry.

Directory of Hotel and Lodging Companies. American Hotel and Lodging Association. • Annual. $82.00. Contains listings of suppliers of products and services for the lodging industry.

Directory of Hotel and Motel Companies. HealthForum. • Annual. $79.00 per year. Lists more than 1,025 hotel, motel and resort chain companies. International coverage.

Hotel and Travel Index: The World Wide Hotel Directory. Northstar Travel Media. • Quarterly. $185.00 per year. $60.00 per issue. Contains concise information on more than 41,000 hotels in the U. S. and around the world. Includes 400 maps showing location of hotels and airports.

OAG Business Travel Planner: North America. OAG. • Quarterly. $142.00 per year. $55.00 per issue. Arranged according to more than 14,500 destinations in the U. S., Canada, Mexico, and the Caribbean. Lists more than 31,500 hotels, with AAA ratings where available. Provides information on airports, ground transportation, coming events, and climate. Includes maps.

OAG Travel Planner: Europe Worldwide. OAG. • Quarterly. $149.00 per year. Arranged according to more than 13,850 destinations in Europe. Lists more than 14,700 hotels, with information on airports, ground transportation, coming events, and climate.

OAG Travel Planner Hotel and Motel Redbook: Asia Pacific. OAG. • Quarterly. $130.00 per year. Arranged according to more than 5,000 destinations throughout Asia and the Pacific. Lists about 3,000 hotels, with information on airports, ground transportation, coming events, and climate.

Official Hotel Guide. Northstar Travel Media L.L.C. • Covers: in four volumes, 29,000 hotels, motels, and resorts worldwide. Volume 1 covers most of the U.S. ; Volume 2 covers the rest of the U.S. and the Western Hemisphere; Volume 3 covers Europe, the Middle East, Asia, and Africa. Volume 4 specialty travel guide includes listings of golf resorts and tennis resorts; health spas, dude ranches, bed and breakfasts, and casino & hotels in the United States; also includes lists of hotels in the Caribbean with golf, tennis, casinos, and all-inclusive. Entries include: Hotel/motel/resort name, address, phone, fax, CRS's, number of rooms or units, rates, brief description of facilities, ratings, codes indicating credit cards accepted, email and website addresses, and travel agent's commission, if any.

Plunkett's Airline, Hotel, and Travel Industry Almanac. Plunkett Research, Ltd. • Annual. $249. 95. Contains profiles of 300 leading companies, including airlines, hotels, travel agencies, theme parks, cruise lines, casinos, and car rental companies.

Resorts and Parks Purchasing Guide. Klevens Publications, Inc. • Annual. $85.00. Lists suppliers of products and services for resorts and parks, including national parks, amusement parks, dude ranches, golf resorts, ski areas, and national monument areas.

Star Service: The Critical Guide to Hotels and Cruise Ships. New Concepts Canada. • $210.00. Looseleaf. Quarterly updates. Provides "honest and unbiased descriptions of accommodations, facilities, amenities, ambience, appearance, and service" for more than 10,000 hotels worldwide and 150 cruise ships. Ship information includes history, passenger profiles, crew profiles, and other data.

ENCYCLOPEDIAS AND DICTIONARIES

Uniform System of Accounts for the Lodging Industry. Timothy J. Eaton, editor. Educational Institute of the American Hotel & Motel Association. • 1996. $55.95. 9th revised edition.

FINANCIAL RATIOS

Almanac of Business and Industrial Financial Ratios. Leo Troy. Aspen Publishers, Inc. • 2003.

$125.95. Includes CD-Rom. Contains financial ratios derived from federal tax returns. Ratios for each of about 200 industries are arranged according to company asset size. (Almanac of Business and Industrial Financial Ratios Series).

Annual Statement Studies. The Risk Management Association. • Annual. Median and quartile financial ratios are given for over 400 kinds of manufacturing, wholesale, retail, construction, and consumer finance establishments. Data is sorted by both asset size and sales volume. Includes a clearly written "Definition of Ratios" and an alphabetical industry index.

Annual Statement Studies: Industry Default Probabilities and Cash Flow Measures. The Risk Management Association. • Annual. $145.00. Serves as a companion volume to the original *Annual Statement Studies*. Gives probability of default estimates on a percentage scale for more than 450 industries. Includes changes in position year-by-year for eight financial statement line items and provides percentage measures of cash flow.

HANDBOOKS AND MANUALS

Check-In-Check-Out. Principles of Effective Front Office Management. Gary K. Vallen and Jerome J. Vallen. Brown and Benchmark. • $44.75. Looseleaf service.

Dun & Bradstreet/Gale Group Industry Handbooks. Gale Cengage Learning. • 2000. $650.00. Five volumes. $130.00 per volume. Each volume covers two or more major industries: 1. *Entertainment and Hospitality*; 2. *Construction and Agriculture*; 3. *Chemicals and Pharmaceuticals*; 4. *Computers & Software and Broadcasting & Telecommunications*; 5. *Insurance and Health & Medical Services*. The following are included for each industry: overview, statistics, financial ratios, rankings, merger information, company directory, directory of associations, and consultants directory. (Dun and Bradstreet/Gale Industry Reference Handbook Series).

Hotel Development. Urban Land Institute. • 1996. $39.95. Provides practical information on developing, acquiring, and renovating hotels in urban areas. Covers market analysis, financing, construction, and management. Includes case studies.

Management of People in Hotels and Restaurants. Donald E. Lundberg and James P. Armatas. Brown and Benchmark. • 1992. $36.50. Fifth edition.

Managing Front Office Operations. Michael L. Kasavana and Richard M. Brooks. Educational Institute of the American Hotel & Motel Association. • 2001. $66.95. Sixth edition. Covers all aspects of the front office. Includes computer appliations throughout all phases of the guest cycle.

Professional Management of Housekeeping Operations. Robert J. Martin and Tom Jones. John Wiley and Sons, Inc. • 1998. $75.00. Third edition. For hotels and motels.

Resort Development Handbook. Urban Land Institute. • 1997. $89.95. Covers a wide range of resort settings and amenities, with details of development, market analysis, financing, design, and operations. Includes color photographs and case studies. (ULI Development Handbook Series).

Strategic Hotel Motel Marketing. Christopher W. L. Hart and David Troy. Educational Institute of the American Hotel & Motel Association. • 1998. $59. 95. Third edition.

Supervision in the Hospitality Industry. Jack E. Miller and others. John Wiley and Sons, Inc. • 2002. $70.00. Fourth edition. Principles of communication, motivation, recruiting, training, etc.

INTERNET DATABASES

Business 2.0 Web Guide to the Best Business Links. Business 2.0 Media Inc. Phone: (415)293-4800 E-mail: support@business2.com • URL: http://www.business2.com/webguide • Web site presents

an extensive, searchable directory of links to "the best, most informative, and authoritative web pages." Twenty main categories cover business, finance, career, company information, people, and technology topics, with thousands of subtopics, all linking to Web sites recommended by experienced business researchers. Fees: Free.

Fedstats. Federal Interagency Council on Statistical Policy. Phone: (202)395-7254 • URL: http://www.fedstats.gov • Web site features an efficient search facility for full-text statistics produced by more than 100 federal agencies, including the Census Bureau, the Bureau of Economic Analysis, and the Bureau of Labor Statistics. Boolean searches can be made within one agency or for all agencies combined. Links are offered to international statistical bureaus, including the UN, IMF, OECD, UNESCO, Eurostat, and 20 individual countries. Fees: Free.

FreeLunch.com. Economy.com, Inc. Phone: (610)696-8700 Fax: (610)696-1678 • URL: http://www.freelunch.com • Web site provides free access to more than 1.5 million economic and financial data series, covering industry, demographics, labor markets, prices, retail sales, government spending, trade, interest rates, housing starts, the stock market, and many other topics. Data is available for various time periods in either chart or table form. Searching is offered. Fees: Free, but registration required. Economy.com, Inc. also offers fee-based economic analysis at *The Dismal Scientist* site (http://www.dismal.com).

PERIODICALS AND NEWSLETTERS

Bottomline. Hospitality Financial and Technology Professionals. • Bimonthly. Free to members, educational institutions and libraries; non-members, $50.00 per year. Contains articles on accounting, finance, information technology, and management for hotels, resorts, casinos, clubs, and other hospitality businesses.

The Cornell Hotel and Restaurant Administration Quarterly. Cornell University School of Hotel Administration. Sage Publications, Inc. • Bimonthly. Individuals, $113.00 per year; institutions, $319.00 per year.

Hospitality Technology: Guiding High-Growth Businesses to Best-Choice IT Solutions. Edgell Communications, Inc. • 10 times a year. Price on application. Covers information technology, computer communications, and software for food-service and lodging enterprises.

Hotel and Motel Management: The Global News Magazine of the Hospitality Industry. Advanstar Communications. • 21 times a year. $49.00 per year.

Hotel Business. ICD Publications. • Semimonthly. Free to qualified personnel; others, $150.00 per year. Covers management, technology, design, business trends, new products, finance, and other topics for the hotel-motel industry.

International Journal of Hospitality and Tourism Administration: A Multinationaland Cross-Cultural Journal of Applied Research. Haworth Press, Inc. • Quarterly. $200.00 per year. Includes print and on-line editions. An academic journal with articles relating to lodging, food service, travel, tourism, and the hospitality/leisure industries in general. Formerly *Journal of International Hospitality, Leisure, and Tourism Management.*

Journal of Hospitality and Leisure Marketing: The International Forum for Research, Theory and Practice. Haworth Press, Inc. • Quarterly. $315.00 per year. An academic and practical journal covering various aspects of hotel, restaurant, and recreational marketing.

Lodging. American Hotel and Lodging Association. • Monthly. Membership. Editorial sections include news, finance, technology, foodservice, new products, human resources, marketing, design, and renovation.

Lodging Hospitality: Management Magazine for Hotels, Motels and Resorts. Penton Media, Inc. • 16 times a year. $70.00 per year. Covers a wide variety of topics relating to hotels, motels, and resorts, including management, marketing, finance, operations, and technology.

Resort Management and Operations: The Resort Resource. Finan Publishing Co., Inc. • Bimonthly. Price on application. Edited for hospitality professionals at both large and small resort facilities.

Restaurant Hospitality. Penton Media, Inc. • Monthly. $70.00 per year.

STATISTICS SOURCES

Business Statistics of the United States. Linz Audain and Cornelia J. Strawser. Bernan Associates. • Annual. $147.00. Based on *Business Statistics,* formerly issue by the Bureau of Economic Analysis, U. S. Department of Commerce. Provides basic data for a wide variety of U. S. industries, services, and economic indicators. Most statistics are shown annually for 30 years and monthly for the most recent four years.

Outlook for Travel and Tourism. Travel Industry Association of America. • Annual. Members, $100.00; non-members, $175.00. Contains forecasts of the performance of the U. S. travel industry, including air travel, business travel, recreation (attractions), and accomodations.

Standard & Poor's Industry Surveys. Standard & Poor's. • Semiannual. $1,800.00. Two looseleaf volumes. Includes monthly *Supplements.* Provides detailed, individual surveys of 52 major industry groups. Each survey is revised on a semiannual basis. Also includes "Monthly Investment Review" (industry group investment analysis) and monthly "Trends & Projections" (economic analysis).

Survey of Current Business. Available from U. S. Government Printing Office. • Monthly. $63.00 per year. Issued by Bureau of Economic Analysis, U. S. Department of Commerce. Presents a wide variety of business and economic data.

Trends in the Hotel Industry. PKF Consulting. • Quarterly. $150.00 per year.

Trends in the Hotel Industry: U.S.A. Edition. PKF Consulting. • Annual. $225.00. Provides detailed financial analysis of hotel operations in the U. S. (PKF is Pannell Kerr Forster.).

TRADE/PROFESSIONAL ASSOCIATIONS

Hospitality Financial and Technology Professionals. 11709 Boulder Lane, Suite 110, Austin, TX 78726. Phone: 800-646-4387 or (512)249-5333 Fax: (512)249-1533 E-mail: frank.wolfe@hftp.org • URL: http://www.hftp.org • Members are accounting and finance officers in the hotel, motel, casino, club, and other areas of the hospitality industry. Formerly International Association of Hospitality Accountants.

Hospitality Sales and Marketing Association International. 8201 Greensboro Dr., Ste. 300, Mclean, VA 22102. Phone: (703)610-9024 Fax: (703)610-9005 • URL: http://www.hsmai.org.

OTHER SOURCES

The Laws of Innkeepers: For Hotels, Motels, Restaurants, and Clubs. John E. Sherry. Cornell University Press. • 1993. $49.95. Third edition.

HOUSE BUYING AND SELLING

See: HOME OWNERSHIP

HOUSE DECORATION

See: INTERIOR DECORATION

HOUSE OF REPRESENTATIVES

See: UNITED STATES CONGRESS

HOUSE ORGANS

See also: BUSINESS JOURNALISM; EDITORS AND EDITING; JOURNALISM; NEWSLETTERS

ALMANACS AND YEARBOOKS

Editor and Publisher International Yearbook: Encyclopedia of the Newspaper Industry. Editor and Publisher Co., Inc. • Annual. $150.00. Daily and Sunday newspapers in the United States and Canada.

DIRECTORIES

Working Press of the Nation. R. R. Bowker. • Annual. $530.00. $295.00 per volume. Three volumes: (1) *Newspaper Directory;* (2) *Magazine and Internal Publications Directory;* (3) *Radio and Television Directory.* Includes names of editors and other personnel.

HANDBOOKS AND MANUALS

Personnel Management: Communications. Prentice Hall PTR. • Looseleaf. Periodic supplementation. Price on application. Includes how to write effectively and how to prepare employee publications.

HOUSE-TO-HOUSE SELLING

See: DIRECT MARKETING

HOUSEHOLD APPLIANCES

See: ELECTRIC APPLIANCE INDUSTRY

HOUSEHOLD FURNISHINGS

See: FURNITURE INDUSTRY

HOUSEHOLD PRODUCTS INDUSTRY

See: CLEANING PRODUCTS INDUSTRY

HOUSES, PREFABRICATED

See: PREFABRICATED HOUSE INDUSTRY

HOUSEWARES INDUSTRY

DIRECTORIES

Directory of Discount and General Merchandise Stores. Chain Store Guide. • Annual. $327.00. Online edition, $747.00. Includes retailers and wholesalers of housewares, giftwares, novelties, toys, hobby materials, crafts, and stationery.

Gift, Housewares and Home Textiles Buyers Directory. Douglas Publications, Inc. • Annual. $259.00. Lists more than 7,300 companies with names of over 15,200 buyers.

Housewares Retail Directory. infoUSA Inc. • Number of listings: 2,992. Entries include: Name, address, phone, size of advertisement, name of owner or manager, number of employees, year first in "Yellow Pages." Compiled from telephone

company "Yellow Pages," nationwide.

PERIODICALS AND NEWSLETTERS

Fancy Food and Culinary Products. Talcott Communications Corp. • Monthly. $34.00 per year. Emphasizes new specialty food products and the business management aspects of the specialty food and confection industries. Includes special issues on wine, cheese, candy, "upscale" cookware, and gifts. Formerly (Fancy Foods).

Gourmet News: The Business Newspaper for the Gourmet Industry. United Publications, Inc. • Monthly. $60.00 per year. Provides news of the gourmet food industry, including specialty food stores, upscale cookware shops, and gift shops.

Gourmet Retailer. VNU Business Media. • Monthly. Free to qualified personnel; others, $75.00 per year. Covers upscale food and housewares, including confectionery items, bakery operations, and coffee.

TRADE/PROFESSIONAL ASSOCIATIONS

Cookware Manufacturers Association. PO Box 531335, P.O. Box 531335, Birmingham, AL 35253-1335. Phone: (205)823-3448 Fax: (205)823-3449 E-mail: hrushing@usit.net • URL: http://www.cookware.org • Represents manufacturers of cooking utensils and cooking accessories. Compiles statistics.

International Housewares Association. 6400 Shafer Ct., Ste. 650, Rosemont, IL 60018. Phone: 800-843-6462 or (847)292-4200 Fax: (847)292-4211 E-mail: pbrandl@housewares.org • URL: http://www.housewares.org • Manufacturers and distributors of housewares and small appliances. Conducts annual market research survey of the housewares industry. Manages the international housewares show.

OTHER SOURCES

Silverware, Plateware & Cutlery. Available from MarketResearch.com. • 2002. $3,950.00. Published by Global Industry Analysts. Provides worldwide market research data, including profiles of major tableware companies.

HOUSING

See also: APARTMENT HOUSES; BUILDING INDUSTRY; CONDOMINIUMS; PREFABRICATED HOUSE INDUSTRY; REAL ESTATE BUSINESS

GENERAL WORKS

Housing the Poor: An Overview. Morton J. Schussheim. Nova Science Publishers, Inc. • 2003. $29.50. Discusses currrent and emerging housing problems affecting the poor. Covers housing rehabilitation programs, community development block grants, and other programs for low-income households.

A New Housing Policy for America: Recapturing the American Dream. Richard C. Ferlauto and others. Temple University Press. • 1988. $24.95.

Rethinking Rental Housing. John I. Gilderbloom and Richard P. Applebaum. Temple University Press. • 1987. $44.95. Emphasis on social and political factors.

6,000 Years of Housing. Norbert Schoenauer. W. W. Norton & Co., Inc. • 2000. $50.00. Revised edition. Presents the story of housing from early nomadic societies to the present.

BIBLIOGRAPHIES

AAHSA Resource Catalog. American Association of Homes and Services for the Aging. • Annual. Free. Provides descriptions of material relating to managed care, senior housing, assisted living, continuing care retirement communities (CCRCs), nursing facilities, and home health care. Publishers are AAHSA and others.

CD-ROM DATABASES

Newspaper Abstracts Ondisc. PROQUEST. • Monthly. $2,950.00 per year (covers 1989 to date;

archival discs are available for 1985-88). Provides cover-to-cover CD-ROM indexing and abstracting of 19 major newspapers, including the *New York Times, Wall Street Journal, Washington Post, Chicago Tribune,* and *Los Angeles Times.*

OECD Statistical Compendium. Organization for Economic Cooperation and Development. • Semiannual. $1,905.00 per year for 1 to 10 users. CD-ROM contains more than 730,000 monthly, quarterly, and annual time series for OECD countries, 1960 to date. Includes fully searchable data on agriculture, food, economic indicators, national accounts, employment, energy, finance, industry, technology, and foreign trade. Results can be displayed in various forms.

Sourcebooks America CD-ROM. CACI Marketing Systems. • Annual. $1,250.00. Provides the CD-ROM version of *The Sourcebook of ZIP Code Demographics: Census Edition* and *The Sourcebook of County Demographics: Census Edition.*

DIRECTORIES

Directory of Retirement Facilities. Solucient. • Biennial. $125.00. Provides information on more than 14,000 "senior citizen residential alternative facilities," including both assisted living settings and independent living communities.

NAHRO Directory of Local Agencies and Resource Guide. NAHRO. • 1995. Members, $85.00; non-members, $100.00. Formerly *Directory of Local Agencies: Housing, Community Development, Redevelopment.*

ENCYCLOPEDIAS AND DICTIONARIES

Encyclopedia of Homelessness. David Levinson, editor. Sage Publications, Inc. • 2004. $295.00. Two volumes. Topics relating to homelessness include Causes, Health Issues, History in the United States, Legal Issues, and Organizations. Contains about 150 entries, arranged alphabetically, by various contributors. Appendices provide additional features, such as examples of homelessness in film and literaure. Includes extensive bibliographic information.

Encyclopedia of Housing. Willem van Vliet, editor. Sage Publications, Inc. • 1998. $216.00. Contains 500 entries covering all aspects of housing. Includes index of names and subjects.

HANDBOOKS AND MANUALS

Federal Civil Rights Acts. West Group. • Semiannual. $410.00 per year. Two looseleaf volumes. Covers current legislation relating to a wide range of civil rights issues, including discrimination in employment, housing, property rights, and voting.

INTERNET DATABASES

Business 2.0 Web Guide to the Best Business Links. Business 2.0 Media Inc. Phone: (415)293-4800 E-mail: support@business2.com • URL: http://www.business2.com/webguide • Web site presents an extensive, searchable directory of links to "the best, most informative, and authoritative web pages." Twenty main categories cover business, finance, career, company information, people, and technology topics, with thousands of subtopics, all linking to Web sites recommended by experienced business researchers. Fees: Free.

Fedstats. Federal Interagency Council on Statistical Policy. Phone: (202)395-7254 • URL: http://www.fedstats.gov • Web site features an efficient search facility for full-text statistics produced by more than 100 federal agencies, including the Census Bureau, the Bureau of Economic Analysis, and the Bureau of Labor Statistics. Boolean searches can be made within one agency or for all agencies combined. Links are offered to international statistical bureaus, including the UN, IMF, OECD, UNESCO, Eurostat, and 20 individual countries. Fees: Free.

FreeLunch.com. Economy.com, Inc. Phone:

(610)696-8700 Fax: (610)696-1678 • URL: http://www.freelunch.com • Web site provides free access to more than 1.5 million economic and financial data series, covering industry, demographics, labor markets, prices, retail sales, government spending, trade, interest rates, housing starts, the stock market, and many other topics. Data is available for various time periods in either chart or table form. Searching is offered. Fees: Free, but registration required. Economy.com, Inc. also offers fee-based economic analysis at *The Dismal Scientist* site (http://www.dismal.com).

U. S. Census Bureau: The Official Statistics. U. S. Bureau of the Census. Phone: (301)763-4100 Fax: (301)763-4794 • URL: http://www.census.gov • Web site is "Your Source for Social, Demographic, and Economic Information." Contains "Current U. S. Population Count," "Current Economic Indicators," and a wide variety of data under "Other Official Statistics." Keyword searching is provided. Fees: Free.

ONLINE DATABASES

Information Bank Abstracts. New York Times Index Dept. • Provides indexing and abstracting of current affairs, primarily from the final late edition of *The New York Times* and the Eastern edition of *The Wall Street Journal.* Time period is 1969 to present, with daily updates. Inquire as to online cost and availability.

PERIODICALS AND NEWSLETTERS

Affordable Housing Finance. Alexander & Edwards Publishing. • Ten times a year. $119.00 per year. Provides advice and information on obtaining financing for lower-cost housing. Covers both government and private sources.

Builder: The Voice of America's Housing Industry. National Association of Home Builders of the United States, Economics, Mortgage Finance and Housing Policy Div. Hanley-Wood, LLC. • Monthly. $29.95 per year. Covers the home building and remodeling industry in general, including design, construction, and marketing.

Custom Home. Hanley-Wood, LLC. • Seven times a year. $36.00 per year. Edited for "top of the market" custom builders, designers, and architects.

Housing Affairs Letter: The Weekly Washington Report on Housing. Community Development Services, Inc. CD Publications. • Weekly. $473.00 per year. Newsletter. Covers mortgage activity news, including forecasts of mortgage rates.

Journal of Housing and Community Development. National Association of Housing and Redevelopment Officials (NAHRO). • Bimonthly. $33.00 per year. Formerly *Journal of Housing.*

Journal of Housing Economics. Elsevier. • Quarterly. Individuals, $50.00 per year; institutions, $299.00 per year.

Journal of Light Construction. Hanley-Wood, LLC. • Monthly. $35.95 per year. Provides jobsite tips, techniques, and product advice for builders and contractors.

Regional Economics and Markets: A Quarterly Analysis from the Conference Board. The Conference Board. • Quarterly. Members, $145.00 per year; non-members, $295.00 per year. Summarizes economic trends and prospects for nine geographic regions of the U. S. Provides data on key predictive indexes, including employment, housing permits, retail sales, consumer confidence, and help-wanted advertising. Charts and graphs are included.

Residential Architect: Exclusively Housing. Hanley-Wood, LLC. • Monthly. $39.95 per year. Edited for architects specializing in home design.

RESEARCH CENTERS AND INSTITUTES

Building Research Council. University of Illinois at Urbana-Champaign. One E. Saint Mary's Rd., Champaign, IL 61820. Phone: 800-336-0616 or

(217)333-1801 Fax: (217)244-2204 • Integral unit of School of Architecture.

Center for Finance and Real Estate. University of California, Los Angeles, John E. Anderson Graduate School of Management, 110 Westwood Plaza, Los Angeles, CA 90095-1481. Phone: (310)206-5455 Fax: (310)206-5455 E-mail: wtorous@anderson.ucla.edu • URL: http://www.agsm.ucla.edu.

National Association of Home Builders Research Center. 400 Prince George's Blvd., Upper Marlboro, MD 20774. Phone: 800-638-8556 or (301)249-4000 Fax: (301)430-6180 • URL: http://www.nahbrc.org.

National Economic Development and Law Center. 2201 Broadway, Suite 815, Oakland, CA 94612. Phone: (510)251-2600 Fax: (510)251-0600 E-mail: james@nedlc.org • URL: http://www.nedlc.org.

Urban Institute. Urban Institute. 2100 M St. NW, Washington, DC 20037. Phone: (202)833-7200 Fax: (202)728-0232 E-mail: paffairs@ui.urban.org • URL: http://www.urban.org • Domestic, social, and economic affairs, including multidisciplinary studies and government program evaluations in the areas of tax and budget reform, education policy, health policy, crime and justice, housing and community development, labor and human services, income security and retirement, welfare reform, international activities, nonprofit sector and philanthropy, public finance, productivity and economic development, social services, and immigration. Also conducts research programs on employment and training, children's issues and family policy, minorities and social policy, poverty, state and local governments, and community impact and demography.

STATISTICS SOURCES

American Housing Survey for the United States in [year]. Available from U. S. Government Printing Office. • Biennial. $51.00. Issued by the U. S. Census Bureau (http://www.census.gov). Covers both owner-occupied and renter-occupied housing. Includes data on such factors as condition of building, type of mortgage, utility costs, and housing occupied by minorities. (Current Housing Reports, H150.).

Annual Bulletin of Housing and Building Statistics for Europe and North America. United Nations Publications. • Annual. $25.00. Provides basic data on housing and construction in European countries, Canada, and the U. S., including non-residential buildings, value of construction, building materials, prices, costs, and rents. Includes base years of 1990 and 1995 and recent calendar years.

Business Statistics of the United States. Linz Audain and Cornelia J. Strawser. Bernan Associates. • Annual. $147.00. Based on *Business Statistics,* formerly issue by the Bureau of Economic Analysis, U. S. Department of Commerce. Provides basic data for a wide variety of U. S. industries, services, and economic indicators. Most statistics are shown annually for 30 years and monthly for the most recent four years.

County and City Data Book 2000: A Statistical Abstract Supplement. Available from U. S. Government Printing Office. • 2002. $68.00. 13th edition. Issued by the U. S. Bureau of the Census (http://www.census.gov). Contains a wide variety of data on 3,141 U.S. counties, 1,078 cities, and 11,097 places of 2,500 or more inhabitants. Includes statistical information on retailing, manufacturing, banking, service industries, income, employment, housing, education, crime, and population. Updated metropolitan areas are included.

County and City Extra: Annual Metro, City and County Data Book. Deirdre A. Gaquin and Mark S. Littman. Bernan Press. • 2001. $120.00. Updates and augments data published irregularly in print form by the U. S. Census Bureau in *County and City Data Book.* Covers "every state, county, metropolitan area, and congressional district in the United States, as well as all U. S. cities with a 1990 population of 25,000 or more." Contains a wide range tic maps.

County and City Extra: Special Decennial Census Edition. Deidre A. Gaquin and Katherine A. De-Brandt, editors. Bernan Press. • 2002. $95.00. Presents conveniently arranged population, housing, and other data from the 2000 census, with many 1980 and 1990 comparisons. Includes maps and tables with rankings of about 20 items for various geographic locations. Complements the annual *County and City Extra.*

Datapedia of the United States: American History in Numbers. George T. Kurian, editor. Bernan Press. • 2004. $125.00. Third edition. Based on the Census Bureau publication, *Historical Statistics of the United States.* Provides data from Colonial times to the present on agriculture, business, consumer income, energy, finance, labor, national income, population, and many other subjects. Includes "narrative highlights," maps, charts, and statistical projections.

Expenditures for Residential Improvements and Repairs. Available from U. S. Government Printing Office. • Quarterly. $16.00 per year. Bureau of the Census Construction Report, C50. Provides estimates of spending for housing maintenance, repairs, additions, alterations, and major replacements.

Gale Country and World Rankings Reporter. Gale Cengage Learning. • 1997. $160.00. Second edition. Provides about 3,000 statistical ranking tables and charts covering more than 235 nations. Sources include the United Nations and various government publications.

Gale State Rankings Reporter. Gale Cengage Learning. • 1996. $130.00. Second edition Provides 3,000 ranked lists of states under 35 subject headings. Sources are newspapers, periodicals, books, research institute publications, and government publications.

Housing Market Report: Forecasting Home Sales and Construction Trends Since 1976. Community Development Services, Inc. • Semimonthly. $399.00 per year. Real estate outlook for U.S. housing markets.

Housing Starts. U.S. Bureau of the Census. Available from U.S. Government Printing Office. • Monthly. Construction Reports: C-20.

Housing Statistics of the United States. Patrick A. Simmons. Bernan Press. • 2000. $89.00. Third edition. (Housing Statistics of the United States Series).

Monthly Bulletin of Statistics. United Nations Publications. • Monthly. $295.00 per year. Provides current data for about 200 countries on a wide variety of economic, industrial, and demographic subjects. Compiled by United Nations Statistical Office.

New One-Family Houses Sold. Available from U. S. Government Printing Office. • Monthly. $45.00 per year. Bureau of the Census Construction Report, C25. Provides data on new, privately-owned, one-family homes sold during the month and for sale at the end of the month.

Social Statistics of the United States. Mark S. Littman, editor. Bernan Press. • 2000. $65.00. Includes statistical data on population growth, labor force, occupations, environmental trends, leisure time use, income, poverty, taxes, and other economic or demographic topics.

State Profiles: The Population and Economy of Each U. S. State. Courtenay Slater and Others. Bernan Press. • 1999. $89.00. Presents charts, tables, and text in an eight-page profile for each state. Covers population, labor force, income, poverty, employment, wages, industry, trade, housing, education,

health, taxes, and government finances. (The Population and Economy of Each United States Series)

Statistical Abstract of the United States. Available from U. S. Government Printing Office. • Annual. $51.00. Issued by the U. S. Bureau of the Census.

A Statistical Portrait of the United States: Social Conditions and Trends. Mark S. Littman, editor. Bernan Press. • 1998. $89.00. Covers "social, economic, and environmental trends in the United States over the past 25 years." Includes statistical tables, graphs, and analysis relating to such topics as population, income, poverty, wealth, labor, housing, education, healthcare, air/water quality, and government. (Statistical Portrait of the United States: Social Conditions and Trends Series).

Statistical Yearbook. United Nations Publications. • Annual. $125.00. Contains statistics for about 200 countries on a wide variety of economic, industrial, and demographic topics. Compiled by United Nations Statistical Office.

Survey of Current Business. Available from U. S. Government Printing Office. • Monthly. $63.00 per year. Issued by Bureau of Economic Analysis, U. S. Department of Commerce. Presents a wide variety of business and economic data.

U. S. Housing Markets. Hanley-Wood, LLC. • Monthly. $345.00 per year. Includes eight interim reports. Provides data on residential building permits, apartment building completions, rental vacancy rates, sales of existing homes, average home prices, housing affordability, etc. All major U. S. cities and areas are covered.

TRADE/PROFESSIONAL ASSOCIATIONS

Building Systems Councils of NAHB. 1201 15th St., N.W., Washington, DC 20005. Phone: 800-368-5242 or (202)822-0576 Fax: (202)861-2141 E-mail: bsc@nahb.com • URL: http://www. buildingsystems.org • Formerly Home Manufacturers Councils of NAHB.

National Association of Home Builders. 1201 15th St., N.W., Washington, DC 20005. Phone: 800-368-5242 or (202)266-8200 • URL: http://www.nahb. com • Members are single and multifamily home builders, commercial builders and others associated with the building industry.

National Association of Housing and Redevelopment Officials. 630 Eye St., N.W., Washington, DC 20001. Phone: 877-866-2476 or (202)289-3500 Fax: (202)289-8181 E-mail: nahro@nahro.org • URL: http://www.nahro.org • Formerly National Association of Housing Officials.

National Center for Housing Management. 1010 N Glebe Rd., No. 160, Arlington, VA 22201. Phone: 800-368-5625 or (703)516-4070 Fax: (703)516-4069 E-mail: service@nchm.org • URL: http:// www.nchm.org.

National Housing Conference. 1801 K St. NW, Ste. M-100, Washington, DC 20006-1301. Phone: (202)466-2121 Fax: (202)466-2122 E-mail: cegan@ nhc.org • URL: http://www.nhc.org • Housing authority officials, community development specialists, builders, bankers, lawyers, accountants, owners, residents, insurers, architects and planners, religious organizations, labor groups, and national housing and housing related organizations. Mobilizes support for effective programs in housing and community development as well as affordable and accessible housing for all Americans. Holds educational programs.

OTHER SOURCES

Housing Discrimination: Law and Litigation. Robert G. Schwemm. West Group. • Annual. $256. 00. Looseleaf service. Covers provisions of the Fair Housing Act and related topics.

HOUSING MANAGEMENT

See: PROPERTY MANAGEMENT

HUMAN ENGINEERING

GENERAL WORKS

Designing the User Interface: Strategies for Effective Human-Computer Interaction. Ben Shneiderman. Addison-Wesley. • 2002. $70.00. Third edition. Provides an introduction to computer user-interface design. Covers usability testing, dialog boxes, menus, command languages, interaction devices, tutorials, printed user manuals, and related subjects.

The Ergonomics Edge: Improving Safety, Quality, and Productivity. Dan MacLeod. John Wiley and Sons, Inc. • 1995. $110.00. (Industrial Health and Safety Series).

ABSTRACTS AND INDEXES

NTIS Alerts: Biomedical Technology & Human Factors Engineering. National Technical Information Service. • Semimonthly. $210.00 per year. Provides descriptions of government-sponsored research reports and software, with ordering information. Covers biotechnology, ergonomics, bionics, artificial intelligence, prosthetics, and related subjects. Formerly *Abstract Newsletter.*

ENCYCLOPEDIAS AND DICTIONARIES

Encyclopedia of Occupational Health and Safety. International Labour Organization. • 1998. $990.00. Fourth edition. Four volumes. Includes CD-ROM. Covers safety engineering, industrial medicine, ergonomics, hygiene, epidemiology, toxicology, industrial psychology, and related topics. Includes material related to specific chemical, textile, transport, construction, manufacturing, and other industries. Indexed by subject, chemical name, and author, with a "Directory of Experts.".

HANDBOOKS AND MANUALS

Handbook of Human Factors and Ergonomics. Gavriel Salvendy. John Wiley and Sons, Inc. • 1997. $275.00. Second edition.

Human Factors Design Handbook. Wesley E. Woodson and others. McGraw-Hill. • 1992. $150. 00. Second edition.

PERIODICALS AND NEWSLETTERS

Applied Ergonomics: Human Factors in Technology and Society. Elsevier. • Bimonthly. Qualified personnel, $228.00 per year; institutions, $941.00 per year.

Ergonomics: An International Journal of Research and Practice in Human Factors and Ergonomics. Taylor and Francis Group. • 15 times per year. Individuals, $1,210.00 per year; institutions, $2,472.00 per year.

Human Factors and Ergonomics in Manufacturing. John Wiley and Sons, Inc., Journals. • Quarterly. $649.00 per year; with online edition, $682.00 per year. Published in England by John Wiley and Sons Ltd. Formerly *International Journal of Human Factors in Manufacturing.*

RESEARCH CENTERS AND INSTITUTES

Ergonomics and Engineering Controls Reaearch Laboratory. University of Cincinnati. Industrial Engineering Dept., Cincinnati, OH 45221-0116. Phone: (513)556-2652 Fax: (513)556-4999 E-mail: anil.mital@uc.edu • Formerly Human Factors/ Ergonomics Laboratory.

TRADE/PROFESSIONAL ASSOCIATIONS

Human Factors and Ergonomics Society. P.O. Box 1369, Santa Monica, CA 90406-1369. Phone: (310)394-1811 Fax: (310)394-2410 E-mail: info@

hfes.org • URL: http://www.hfes.org • Formerly Human Factors Society.

The MTM Association for Standards and Research. 1111 E. Touhy Ave., Des Plaines, IL 60018. Phone: (847)299-1111 Fax: (847)299-3509 E-mail: webmaster@mtm.org • URL: http://www.mtm.org.

HUMAN MOTIVATION

See: MOTIVATION (PSYCHOLOGY)

HUMAN RELATIONS

See also: INDUSTRIAL PSYCHOLOGY; INDUSTRIAL RELATIONS; PERSONNEL MANAGEMENT

GENERAL WORKS

Coping with Difficult People. Robert N. Bramson. Bantam Dell Publishing Group. • 1981. $7.50.

Dinosaur Brains: Dealing with All Those Impossible People at Work. Albert J. Bernstein and Sydney C. Rozen. John Wiley and Sons, Inc. • 1989. $29.95. How to cope with "lizard logic" and overcome the "reptile response." That is, how to deal with irrational, impulsive, and self-destructive work behavior. Covers problem bosses, manipulators, self-promoters, the old boy network, etc.

Human Behavior at Work. O. Jeff Harris and Sandra Hartman. West Publishing Co. • 1991. $55.50.

Human Relations. Marie Dalton and others. South-Western. • 2000. $49.95. Second edition.

ABSTRACTS AND INDEXES

Current Contents: Social and Behavioral Sciences. Thomson/ISI. • Weekly. $730.00 per year. Includes *Author Index.*

Personnel Management Abstracts. • Quarterly. $190.00 per year. Includes annual cumulation.

Psychological Abstracts. American Psychological Association. • Monthly. Members, $815.00 per year; individuals and institutions, $1,207.00 per year. Covers the international literature of psychology and the behavioral sciences. Includes journals, technical reports, dissertations, and other sources.

Social Sciences Index. H. W. Wilson Co. • Quarterly, with annual cumulation. Price varies. Indexes more than 400 periodicals covering economics, environmental policy, government, insurance, labor, health care policy, plannning, public administration, public welfare, urban studies, women's issues, criminology, and related topics.

Sociological Abstracts. Cambridge Information Group. • Bimonthly. $720.00 per year; with cumulative index, $860.00 per year. Includes print and online editions. A compendium of non-evaluative abstracts covering the field of sociology and related disciplines.

CD-ROM DATABASES

Magazine Index Plus. Gale Cengage Learning. • Monthly. $4,000.00 per year (includes InfoTrac workstation). Provides full text on CD-ROM for about 100 popular, general interest magazines and indexing for 300 others. Includes special indexing of reviews and product evaluations. Time period is 1980 to date.

Social Sciences Citation Index. ISI. • Monthly. Price on request. Provides CD-ROM indexing of articles appearing in 1700 leading social science journals worldwide, with additional selections from more than 5700 other journals. Time span is 1992 to date. Coverage includes economics, business, finance, management, communications, demographics, library and information science, political science, sociology, and many other subjects.

Social Sciences Citation Index: Compact Disc Edi-

tion with Abstracts. Institute for Scientific Information. • Monthly. Provides CD-ROM indexing and abstracting of "significant articles" from 1,700 social science journals worldwide, with additional selections from 3,200 other journals, 1986 to date. Includes economics, business, finance, management, communications, demographics, information and library science, political science, sociology, and many other subjects.

WILSONDISC: Wilson Social Sciences Abstracts. H. W. Wilson Co. • Monthly. Includes unlimited online access to *Social Sciences Index* through WILSONLINE. Provides CD-ROM indexing from 1983 and abstracting from 1994 of more than 500 periodicals covering economics, area studies, community health, public administration, public welfare, urban studies, and many other topics related to the social sciences.

ENCYCLOPEDIAS AND DICTIONARIES

Encyclopedia of Human Behavior. Vangipuram S. Ramachandran, editor. Elsevier. • 1994. $1,000.00. Four volumes. Contains signed articles on aptitude testing, arbitration, career development, consumer psychology, crisis management, decision making, economic behavior, group dynamics, leadership, motivation, negotiation, organizational behavior, planning, problem solving, stress, work efficiency, and other human behavior topics applicable to business situations.

The Gale Encyclopedia of Psychology. Gale Cengage Learning. • 2001. $155.00. Second edition. Includes bibliographies arranged by topic and a glossary. More than 650 topics are covered.

HANDBOOKS AND MANUALS

Human Resource Skills for the Project Manager: The Human Aspects of Project Management, Volume Two. Vijay K. Verma. Project Management Institute. • 1996. $32.95. (Human Aspects of Project Management Series).

Managing the Project Team: The Human Aspects of Project Management, Volume Three. Vijay K. Verma. Project Management Institute. • 1997. $32. 95. (Human Aspects of Project Management Series: Vol. 3).

Negotiating and Influencing Skills: The Art of Creating and Claiming Value. Brad McRae. Sage Publications, Inc. • 1997. $79.95. Presents a practical approach to various circumstances, based on the Harvard Project on Negotiation. Chapters include "Dealing with Difficult People and Difficult Situations." Contains a bibliography and glossary of terms.

Organizing Projects for Success: The Human Aspects of Project Management, Volume One. Vijay K. Verma. Project Management Institute. • 1995. $32.95. (Human Aspects of Project Management Series: Vol. 1).

Sexual Orientation in the Workplace: Gays, Lesbians, Bisexuals and Heterosexuals Working Together. Amy J. Zuckerman and George F. Simons. Sage Publications, Inc. • 1994. $34.95. A workbook containing "a variety of simple tools and exercises" to provide skills for "working realistically and effectively with diverse colleagues.".

ONLINE DATABASES

Newspaper Abstracts Daily. ProQuest Inc. • Provides online coverage (citations and abstracts) of 25 major newspapers. Covers business, economics, current affairs, health, fitness, sports, education, technology, government, consumer affairs, psychology, the arts, and the social sciences. Time period is 1986 to date, with daily updates. Inquire as to online cost and availability.

PsycINFO. American Psychological Association. • Provides indexing and abstracting of the worldwide literature of psychology and the behavioral sciences. Time period is 1967 to date, with monthly updates.

Inquire as to online cost and availability.

Wilson Social Sciences Abstracts Online. H. W. Wilson Co. • Provides online abstracting and indexing of more than 500 periodicals covering area studies, community health, public administration, public welfare, urban studies, and many other social science topics. Time period is 1994 to date for abstracts and 1983 to date for indexing, with updates weekly. Inquire as to online cost and availability.

PERIODICALS AND NEWSLETTERS

American Behavioral Scientist. Sage Publications, Inc. • Monthly. Institutions, $1,139.00 per year.

Communication Briefings: A Monthly Idea Source for Decision Makers. Briefings Publishing Group. • Monthly. $139.00 per year. Newsletter. Presents useful ideas for communication, public relations, customer service, human resources, and employee training.

Human Communication Research. International Communication Association. Oxford University Press, Journals. • Quarterly. Institutions, $294.00 per year; with online edition, $309.00 per year. A scholarly journal of interpersonal communication.

Human Relations: Towards the Integration of Social Sciences. Tavistock Institute of Human Relations. Sage Publications, Inc. • Monthly. Institutions, $1,158.00 per year.

Journal of Applied Behavioral Science. Sage Publications, Inc. • Quarterly. Institutions, $493.00 per year. Includes print and online editions.

Journal of Organizational Behavior Management. Haworth Press, Inc. • Quarterly. $485.00 per year.

Organizational Dynamics: A Quarterly Review of Organizational Behavior for Management Executives. American Management Association. • Quarterly. Individuals, $77.00 per year; institutions, $171.00 per year. Covers the application of behavioral sciences to business management.

People to People. American Public Power Association. • Description: Reports on public sector labor and personnel issues, especially those concerning the electric utility industry. Summarizes case studies in public labor relations.

Teamwork: Your Personal Guide to Working Successfully with People. Dartnell Corp. • Biweekly. $76.70 per year. Provides advice for employees on human relations, motivation, and team spirit.

RESEARCH CENTERS AND INSTITUTES

Committee on Human Development. University of Chicago. 1126 E. 59th St., Chicago, IL 60637. Phone: (773)702-1234 Fax: (773)702-0320 • URL: http://www.humdev.uchicago.edu.

OTHER SOURCES

How to Manage Conflict in the Organization. American Management Association Extension Institute. • Looseleaf. $139.00. Self-study course. Emphasis is on practical explanations, examples, and problem solving. Quizzes and a case study are included.

HUMAN RESOURCES MANAGEMENT

See: PERSONNEL MANAGEMENT

HUMAN RIGHTS

See: CIVIL RIGHTS

HUMOR AND JOKES

See also: PUBLIC SPEAKING; TOASTS
GENERAL WORKS
The New Yorker Book of Business Cartoons. Robert Mankoff, editor. Bloomberg. • 1998. $21.95.

Contains reprints of 110 cartoons relating to business and finance. Artists are Charles Addams, George Booth, Roz Chast, William Hamilton, Edward Sorel, and other *New Yorker* cartoonists.

ENCYCLOPEDIAS AND DICTIONARIES

Encyclopedia of 20th Century American Humor: Patterns, Trends and Connections. Alleen P. Nilsen and Don L. F. Nilsen. Greenwood Publishing Group, Inc. • 2000. $69.95. Provides an A-to-Z consideration of American humor in its various forms, from early vaudeville to the Internet. Includes a bibliography, subject index, illustrations, and numerous humorous examples.

HANDBOOKS AND MANUALS

Laffirmations: 1001 Ways to Add Humor to Your Life and Work. Joel Goodman. Health Communications, Inc. • 1995. $8.95. The author is director of the Humor Project, a private company promoting humor in the corporate workplace.

PERIODICALS AND NEWSLETTERS

Studies in American Humor. American Human Studies Association. • Annual. Membership.

TRADE/PROFESSIONAL ASSOCIATIONS

American Humor Studies Association. St. Louis University, Department of English, 3800 Lindell Blvd., St. Louis, MO 63108-3414. Phone: (314)977-3068 Fax: (314)977-1514 E-mail: mcintire@slu.edu • URL: http://www.americanhumor.org • Academics, general readers, and professional humorists. Encourages the study and appreciation of American humor from interdisciplinary perspectives.

International Association of Professional Bureaucrats. c/o Dr. James H. Boren, 2400 Jolinda, Whitesboro, TX 76273. Phone: (903)564-9290 Fax: (903)564-9430 E-mail: jimboren@cox-intenet.com • URL: http://www.jimboren.com/inataprobu • Motto of Association: "When in doubt, mumble.".

International Save the Pun Foundation. Station A, P.O. Box 5040, Toronto, ON, Canada M5W 1N4. Phone: (416)736-7126 Fax: (416)736-7116 E-mail: punpunpun@rogers.com • URL: http://www.punpunpun.com.

International Training in Communication. 2519 Woodland Dr., Anaheim, CA 92801-2637. Phone: (714)995-3660 Fax: (714)995-6974 E-mail: itcintl@mediamatters.co.nz • URL: http://www.itcintl.com • Members are interested in speech improvement, communication, lexicology, leadership training and skill in organizational techniques and self-development.

Puns Corps. c/o Robert L. Birch. 3108 Dashiell Rd., Box 2364, Falls Church, VA 22042. Phone: (304)947-5991 E-mail: wjones@pinechemicals.org • Promotes the humorous treatment of "precocious senility in bureaucratic and other contexts." Believes that the creative ambiguity inherent in puns can be used in triggering the creative imagination. Encourages training in mnemonics and other memory improvement techniques, particularly for nursing home patients. Sponsors Compliment-Your-Mirror Day and Memory Day. **Convention/Meeting:** none.

Toastmasters International. PO Box 9052, PO Box 9052, Mission Viejo, CA 92690-9052. Phone: 800-993-7732 or (949)858-8255 Fax: (949)858-1207 E-mail: tminfo@toastmasters.org • URL: http://www.toastmasters.org • Men and women who wish to improve their communication and leadership skills. Sponsors clubs in corporate, government, and military facilities, as well as local communities in over 90 countries. Sponsors annual World Championship of Public Speaking. Special activities include: advanced communication and leadership program; youth leadership programs for junior and senior high school students; Gavel Clubs in schools, prisons, and other institutions.

HYDRAULIC ENGINEERING AND MACHINERY

See also: CIVIL ENGINEERING; FLUIDICS INDUSTRY

GENERAL WORKS

Fundamentals of Hydraulic Engineering Systems. Ned H. Hwang and R.J. Houghtalen. Prentice Hall PTR. • 1995. $115.00. Third edition.

Industrial Hydraulics. William V. Vockroth. Delmar Learning. • 1994. $37.00.

ABSTRACTS AND INDEXES

Fluid Abstracts: Civil Engineering. Elsevier. • Monthly. Institutions, $1,709.00 per year. Includes annual cumulation. Includes the literature of coastal structures.Published in England by Elsevier Science Publishing Ltd. Formerly *Civil Engineering Hydraulics Abstracts.*

ENCYCLOPEDIAS AND DICTIONARIES

Dictionary of Hydraulic Machinery. A. T. Troskolanski. Elsevier. • 1986. $233.00. Text in English, French, German, Italian, and Russian.

HANDBOOKS AND MANUALS

Handbook of Hydraulics. Ernest F. Brater. McGraw-Hill. • 1996. $84.95. Seventh edition.

Hydraulic Engineering. Hsieh Wen Shen and others, editors. American Society of Civil Engineers. • 1993. $210.00. Two volumes.

ONLINE DATABASES

FLUIDEX. Elsevier Science, Inc. • Produced in the Netherlands by Elsevier Science B.V. Provides indexing and abstracting of the international literature of fluid engineering and technology, 1973 to date, with monthly updates. Also known as *Fluid Engineering Abstracts.* Inquire as to online cost and availability.

PERIODICALS AND NEWSLETTERS

Hydraulics and Pneumatics: The Magazine of Fluid Power and Motion Control Systems. Penton Media, Inc. • Monthly. $65.00 per year.

Journal of Hydraulic Research. International Association for Hydraulic Research. • Bimonthly. $340.00 per year. Text in English; summaries in English and French.

RESEARCH CENTERS AND INSTITUTES

Environmental Fluid Mechanics Laboratory. Stanford University. Dept. of Civil Engineering, Campus Box 4020, Stanford, CA 94305-4020. Phone: (650)723-4372 Fax: (650)725-3133 E-mail: monismit@ce.stanford.edu.

Foundation for Cross-Connection Control and Hydraulic Research. University of Southern California. Kaprielian 200, Los Angeles, CA 90089-2531. Phone: (213)740-2032 Fax: (213)740-8399 E-mail: fccchr@usc.edu • URL: http://www.usc.edu/dept/fccchr/.

IIHR-Hyrdroscience and Engineering. University of Iowa. 107 Hydraulics Laboratory, Iowa City, IA 52242-1585. Phone: (319)335-5237 Fax: (319)335-5238 E-mail: v-cpatel@uiowa.edu • URL: http://www.iihr.uiowa.edu.

TRADE/PROFESSIONAL ASSOCIATIONS

Hydraulic Institute. 9 Sylvan Way, Parsippany, NJ 07054. Phone: 888-786-7744 or (973)267-9700 or (973)267-9700 Fax: (973)267-9055 E-mail: info@pumps.org • URL: http://www.pumps.org • Manufacturers of pumps and products used with pumps. Compiles industry statistics, develops technical standards and meetings for pump manufacturers, creates educational programs for members and pump users worldwide and focuses on energy-savings with pumps and pumping systems through its Pump Systems Matter market

transformation initiative. Provides education and tools for the effective application, testing, installation, operation and maintenance of pumps and pumping systems.

Hydraulic Tool Manufacturers Association. PO Box 5416, 198 N Brandon Dr., 198 N. Brandon Dr., Glendale Heights, IL 60139-5416. Phone: (630)893-7755 Fax: (630)790-2626 E-mail: kpolifka@wachsco.com • URL: http://www.htma.net • Manufacturers of hydraulic tools. Seeks to promote the use of portable hydraulic tools through market education, tool classification, and standardization. Has established a system for the classification of hydraulic tools based on rate of flow. Cooperates with related industry groups and standards committees; represents members to appropriate agencies or officials of the federal government. Develops research and educational programs; conducts demonstrations.

International Association of Hydraulic Engineering and Research. Paseo Bajo Virgen del Puerto 3, 28005 Madrid, Spain. Phone: 34 91 3357908 Fax: 34 91 3357935 E-mail: iahr@iahr.org • URL: http://www.iahr.net • Formerly International Association for Hydraulic Research.

International Fluid Power Society. PO Box 1420, Cherry Hill, NJ 08034-0054. Phone: 800-303-8520 or (856)489-8983 Fax: (856)424-9248 E-mail: info@ifps.org • URL: http://www.ifps.org • Persons interested in all phases of fluid power and related motion control and its uses. Concerned with research, development, design, installation, operation, maintenance, education, and application to industry, aviation, marine, mobile, material handling, and agricultural equipment. Maintains speakers' bureau. Operates certification programs and placement service for fluid power mechanics, technicians, specialists, and engineers.

National Fluid Power Association. 3333 N Mayfair Rd., Ste. 211, Milwaukee, WI 53222-3219. Phone: (414)778-3344 Fax: (414)778-3361 E-mail: nfpa@nfpa.com • URL: http://www.nfpa.com • Manufacturers of components such as fittings used in transmitting power by hydraulic and pneumatic pumps, valves, cylinders, filters, seals; the components are used in industrial and mobile machinery in the material-handling, automotive, railway, aircraft, marine, aerospace, construction, agricultural, and other industries. Works to develop: American National Standards Institute and International Organization for Standardization (see separate entries); fluid power technical standards; fluid power index (industry sales); management and marketing studies. Compiles statistics. Administers and serves as secretariat to several international project groups and other fluid power organizations.

HYDROCARBONS

See: PETROLEUM INDUSTRY

HYDROELECTRIC INDUSTRY

GENERAL WORKS

Renewables for Power Generation: Status and Prospect. Organization for Economic Cooperation and Development. • 2003. $75.00. Presents the global outlook for electrical power generation from renewable sources, including water power, wind power, solar power, and geothermal power.

DIRECTORIES

Hydro Review Worldwide Industry Directory. HCI Publications. • Annual. $20.00. Lists more than 250 manufacturers and suppliers of products and services to the hydroelectric industry worldwide. Formerly *Hydro Review-Industry Directory.*

The International Competitive Power Industry Directory. PennWell Corp. • Publication includes: List of 1,400 companies active in the global power industry, providing information on developers, financial firms, law firms, engineering and construction firms, fuel suppliers, consultants, manufacturers and other suppliers of products, equipment ot the hydro, geothermal, solar and wind industries. Entries include: Company name, address, phone, fax; contact name; business area or tyope; technology used; region covered; products.

ENCYCLOPEDIAS AND DICTIONARIES

Wiley Encyclopedia of Energy and the Environment. Attilio Bisio and Sharon Boots. John Wiley and Sons, Inc. • 1996. $285.00. Abriged edition. Two volumes. Covers a wide variety of energy and environmental topics, including legal and policy issues. (Encyclopedia of Energy and the Environment Series: Vol. 2).

PERIODICALS AND NEWSLETTERS

Hydro Review: A Magazine Covering the North American Hydroelectric Industry. HCI Publications. • Eight times a year. $65.00 per year. Covers hydroelectric power generation in North America. Supplement available *Industry Directory.*

RESEARCH CENTERS AND INSTITUTES

Canadian Energy Research Institute. Canadian Energy Research Institute. 3512 33rd St. NW, No. 150, Calgary, AB, Canada T2L 2A6. Phone: (403)282-1231 Fax: (403)284-4181 E-mail: mmasri@ceri.ca • URL: http://www.ceri.ca • Economic issues relating to all forms of energy, including oil, natural gas, coal, nuclear and hydroelectric power, and alternative energy sources. Develops software such as the World Oil Market Model.

Hawaii Natural Energy Institute. University of Hawaii at Manoa, 2540 Dole St., Holmes Hall 246, Honolulu, HI 96822. Phone: (808)956-8890 Fax: (808)956-2336 E-mail: hnei@hawaii.edu • URL: http://www.soest.hawaii.edu • Research areas include geothermal, wind, solar, hydroelectric, and other energy sources.

STATISTICS SOURCES

Annual Energy Outlook [year], with Projections to [year]. Available from U. S. Government Printing Office. • Annual. $42.00. Issued by the Energy Information Administration, U. S. Department of Energy (http://www.eia.doe.gov). Contains detailed statistics and 20-year projections for electricity, oil, natural gas, coal, and renewable energy. Text provides extensive discussion of energy issues and "Market Trends.".

TRADE/PROFESSIONAL ASSOCIATIONS

National Hydropower Association. One Massachusetts Ave. NW, Ste. 850, Washington, DC 20001. Phone: (202)682-1700 Fax: (202)682-9478 E-mail: help@hydro.org • URL: http://www.hydro.org • Represents hydrodevelopers, dam site owners, manufacturers, utilities and municipalities, individuals from the financial community (such as bankers, brokers, and investors), civil contracting firms, architects, engineering firms, and others actively involved in the promotion and development of hydropower. Promotes the development of hydroelectric energy. Participates in the regulatory process on issues such as simplified licensing procedures, purchase power rates, removal of regulatory barriers, and timely implementation of previously adopted legislation. Informs the government about the potential of hydropower and also monitors and drafts new legislation to government regulatory and legislative bodies.

HYGIENE

See: INDUSTRIAL HYGIENE

HYPERTENSION

See also: STRESS (ANXIETY)

GENERAL WORKS

Hypertension Sourcebook. Mary P. McGowan and Jo McGowan Chopra. McGraw-Hill. • 2001. $17.95. Emphasizes recent research relating to the control and prevention of high blood pressure.

Mayo Clinic on High Blood Pressure. Sheldon G. Sheps, editor. Mason Crest Publishers. • 2002. $29.95. Covers diet, medications, exercise, monitoring, and alternative therapies. (Mayo Clinic on Health Series)

CD-ROM DATABASES

Consumers Reference Disc. National Information Services Corp. • Quarterly. Provides the CD-ROM version of *Consumer Health and Nutrition Index* from Oryx Press and *Consumers Index to Product Evaluations and Information Sources* from Pierian Press. Contains citations to consumer health articles and consumer product evaluations, tests, warnings, and recalls.

HANDBOOKS AND MANUALS

Personal Health Reporter. Gale Cengage Learning. • 1992. $150.00. Two volumes. Volume one, $115.00; volume two, $115.00. Presents a collection of professional and popular articles on 150 topics relating to physical and mental health conditions and treatments.

INTERNET DATABASES

National Library of Medicine (NLM). National Institutes of Health (NIH). Phone: 888-346-3656 or (301)496-1131 Fax: (301)480-3537 E-mail: access@nlm.nih.gov • URL: http://www.nlm.nih.gov • NLM Web site offers free access through MEDLINE ("PubMed") to about nine million references to articles appearing in some 4,000 biomedical journals, with abstracts. Search interfaces range from "simple keywords to advanced Boolean expressions." The NLM site offers many links to other sources of biomedical and technical information (the National Center for Biotechnology Information, for example). Fees: Free.

PERIODICALS AND NEWSLETTERS

Hypertension. American Heart Association. Available from Lippincott Williams and Wilkins. • Individuals, $256.00 per year; institutions, $401.00 per year.

RESEARCH CENTERS AND INSTITUTES

Division of Hypertension. Cornell University. New York Hospital-Cornell Medical Center, 520 E. 70th St., New York, NY 10021. Phone: (212)746-2210 Fax: (212)746-8277 E-mail: paugust@med.cornell.edu.

Hypertension Research Center. Indiana University-Purdue University at Indianapolis. 541 Clinical Dr., Room 423, Indianapolis, IN 46202-5111. Phone: (317)274-8153 Fax: (317)278-0673 E-mail: mweinbe@iupui.edu.

TRADE/PROFESSIONAL ASSOCIATIONS

National Institute of Hypertension Studies-Institute of Hypertension School of Research. P.O. Box 02006, Detroit, MI 48202. Phone: (313)872-0505 Fax: (313)872-0505 • Formerly Institute of Hypertension Studies-Institute of Hypertension School of Research.

450

For publishers addresses, refer to SOURCES CITED section at the back of the book.

I

ICE CREAM INDUSTRY

See also: DAIRY INDUSTRY

ABSTRACTS AND INDEXES

Food Science and Technology Abstracts. International Food Information Service Publishing. • Monthly. $1,780.00 per year. Provides worldwide coverage of the literature of food technology and food production.

Foods Adlibra: Key to the World's Food Literature. General Mills, Inc. Foods Adlibra Publications. • Semimonthly. $240.00 per year. Provides journal citations and abstracts to the literature of food technology and packaging.

CD-ROM DATABASES

Food Science and Technology Abstracts [CD-ROM]. Available from SilverPlatter Information, Inc. • Quarterly. Produced by International Food Information Service (home page is http://www.ifis.org). Provides worldwide coverage on CD-ROM of the literature of food technology and production. Various types of publications are indexed, with abstracts, including about 1,800 periodicals. Time period is 1969 to date.

DIRECTORIES

Dairy Foods Market Directory. Gorman Publishing Co. • Covers: Manufacturers of equipment, supplies and ingredients in the dairy foods industry. Entries include: Contact information.

Major Food and Drink Companies of the World. Available from Gale Cengage Learning. • Annual. $880.00. Two volumes. Published by Graham & Whiteside. Contains profiles and trade names for more than 9,800 important food and beverage companies in various countries. In addition to foods, includes both alcoholic and nonalcoholic drink products.

National Dipper Yellow Pages. • Annual. $10.00. Special directory issue of *The National Dipper.* Lists products and services for the ice cream retail industry.

Thomas Food and Beverage Market Place. Grey House Publishing. • 2004. $495.00. Three volumes. Contains more than 40,000 entries covering food companies, beverages, food equipment, warehouse companies, food brokers, wholesalers, importers, and exporters. Formerly *Thomas Food Industry Register.*

HANDBOOKS AND MANUALS

Ice Cream Store. Entrepreneur Media, Inc. • Looseleaf. $59.50. A practical guide to starting an ice cream shop. Covers profit potential, start-up costs, market size evaluation, owner's time required,

site selection, lease negotiation, pricing, accounting, advertising, promotion, etc. (Start-Up Business Guide No. E1187.).

ONLINE DATABASES

Food Science and Technology Abstracts [online]. IFIS North American Desk. • Produced by International Food Information Service. Provides about 500,000 online citations, with abstracts, to the international literature of food science, technology, commodities, engineering, and processing. Approximately 2,000 periodicals are covered. Time period is 1969 to date, with monthly updates. Inquire as to online cost and availability.

FOODS ADLIBRA. General Mills, Inc. • Contains online citations, with abstracts, to the technical and business literature of food processing and packaging. New products and new ingredients are featured. Covers about 250 trade journals and 500 research journals from 1974 to date, with monthly updates. Inquire as to online cost and availability.

PERIODICALS AND NEWSLETTERS

Dairy Field: Helping Processors Manage the Changing Industry. Stagnito Publishing Co. • Monthly. Free to qualified personnel; others, $85.03 per year. Annual *Buyers Guide* available.

Dairy Foods: Innovative Ideas and Technologies for Dairy Processors. Business News Publishing Co. • Monthly. $99.90 per year. Provides broad coverage of new developments in the dairy industry, including cheese and ice cream products. Includes an annual *Supplement.*

Ice Cream Reporter: The Newsletter for Ice Cream Executives. MarketResearch.com. • Monthly. $395.00 per year. Covers new products, mergers, research, packaging, etc.

The National Dipper: The Magazine for Ice Cream Retailers. • Bimonthly. $55.00 per year. Edited for ice cream store owners and managers. Includes industry news, new product information, statistics, and feature articles.

PRICE SOURCES

Supermarket News: The Industry's Weekly Newspaper. Fairchild Publications. • Weekly. Individuals, $196.00 per year; retailers, $45.00 per year; manufacturers, $89.00 per year.

STATISTICS SOURCES

World Food Data and Statistics. Euromonitor International. • 2004. $650.00. Provides five-year data for a wide variety of food products in 52 countries. Includes market size, consumer expenditures, price indicators, and retail distribution data for many kinds of meat, fish, fruits, vegetables,

dairy products, baked goods, condiments, canned food, and frozen food.

TRADE/PROFESSIONAL ASSOCIATIONS

International Ice Cream Association. 1250 H St., N.W., Suite 900, Washington, DC 20005. Phone: (202)737-4332 Fax: (202)331-7820 • URL: http://www.idfa.org.

National Ice Cream Retailers Association. 1028 W Devon Ave., Elk Grove Village, IL 60007. Phone: (847)301-7500 Fax: (847)301-8402 E-mail: info@nicyra.org • URL: http://www.nicyra.org • Represents frozen dessert retailers that operate ice cream and frozen yogurt dipping stores or parlors. Provides free and frank exchange of information among members so that all may improve their operations, increase profits and prosper.

OTHER SOURCES

The Ice Cream Market. MarketResearch.com. • 2002. $3,000.00. Market data and forecasts to 2004 on ice cream and related products (ice milk, frozen yogurt, etc.).

The Market for Ice Cream and Other Frozen Desserts. MarketResearch.com. • 2000. $2,750.00. Provides market data and discusses the impact on the ice cream industry of new technology and the Nutrition Labeling and Education Act. Includes sales projections to 2004.

IDENTIFICATION SYSTEMS, AUTOMATIC

See: AUTOMATIC IDENTIFICATION SYSTEMS

ILLEGAL ALIENS

See: IMMIGRATION AND EMIGRATION

IMAGE, CORPORATE

See: CORPORATE IMAGE

IMMIGRATION AND EMIGRATION

See also: CITIZENSHIP

GENERAL WORKS

Mass Immigration and the National Interest: Policy Directions for the New Century. Vernon M. Briggs. M. E. Sharpe, Inc. • 2003. $69.95. Third edition.

Discusses needed reforms in U. S. immigration policy, with historical background.

U. S. Immigration and Migration Reference Library. Gale Cengage Learning. • 2003. $250.00. Five volumes. Includes *Almanac* (2 vols.), *Biographies* (2 vols.), and *Primary Sources*. Provides detailed history and information relating to U. S. immigration from "earliest times" to the present. (U-X-L imprint.).

ABSTRACTS AND INDEXES

Current Law Index: Multiple Access to Legal Periodicals. Gale Cengage Learning. • Monthly. $725.00 per year. Produced in cooperation with the American Association of Law Libraries. Indexes more than 900 law journals, legal newspapers, and specialty publications from the U.S., Canada, U.K., Ireland, Australia, and New Zealand.

BIBLIOGRAPHIES

International Migration of the Highly Qualified: A Bibliographic and Conceptual Itinerary. Jacques Gaillard and Anne-Marie Gaillard. Center for Migration Studies. • 1998. $29.95. Includes more than 1,800 references from 1954 to 1995 on the migration patterns of skilled or highly qualified workers. (CMS Bibliographies and Documentation Series).

CD-ROM DATABASES

Authority Immigration Law Library. LexisNexis/ Matthew Bender. • Periodic revisions. Price on request. CD-ROM contains updated full text of *Immigration Case Reporter, Immigration Law and Procedure Treatise, INS Regulations*, and other immigration law publications issued by Matthew Bender.

HANDBOOKS AND MANUALS

Immigration Fundamentals: A Guide to Law and Practice. Practising Law Institute. • $195.00. 4th edition. Includes the legal aspects of employment-based immigration, family-sponsored immigration, nonimmigrants, refugees, deportation, naturalization, and citizenship. (Basic Practice Skills Series).

Immigration Procedures Handbook; A How-To Guide for Legal and Business Professionals. West Group. • 2004. $330.00. Two volumes. How to bring foreign nationals to the U. S. on a temporary or permanent basis.

United States Immigration Laws, General Information. U.S. Immigration and Naturalization Service. Available from U.S. Government Printing Office. • Irregular.

INTERNET DATABASES

Lexis.com Research System. Lexis-Nexis Group. Phone: 800-227-4908 or (937)865-6800 Fax: (937)865-6909 E-mail: webmaster@prod.lexis-nexis.com • URL: http://www.lexis.com • Fee-based Web site offers extensive searching of a wide variety of legal sources. Additional features include Daily Opinion Service, lexis.com Bookstore, Career Center, CLE Center, Law Schools, and Practice Pages ("Pages specific to areas of specialty").

PERIODICALS AND NEWSLETTERS

Immigration Law Report. Austin T. Fragomen and Steven C. Bell. West Group. • Description: Reports on U.S. immigration and nationality laws. Presents arguments that can be used in preparing Immigration and Naturalization Service (INS) cases and federal court cases. Carries analysis of material not readily available, such as internal INS policy statements and unpublished cases. Recurring features include reviews of recent decisions and regulations.

International Migration Review: A Quarterly Studying Sociological, Demographic, Economic, Historical, and Legislative Aspects of Human Migration Movements and Ethnic Group Relations. Center for Migration Studies. • Quarterly. Individuals, $39.00 per year; institutions, $80.00 per year.

Migration World: A Bimonthly Magazine Focusing on the Newest Immigrant and Refugee Groups; Policy and Legislation; Resources. Center for Migration Studies. • Five times a year. Individuals, $31.00 per year; institutions, $50.00 per year.

RESEARCH CENTERS AND INSTITUTES

Center for Migration Studies. 209 Flagg Place, Staten Island, NY 10304-1122. Phone: (718)351-8800 Fax: (718)667-4598 E-mail: cms@cmsny.org • URL: http://www.cmsny.org • A nonprofit institute "committed to encourage and facilitate the study of sociodemographic, economic, political..aspects of human migration and refugee movement.".

Immigration History Research Center. University of Minnesota. 222 21st Ave., S., 311 Andersen Library, St. Paul, MN 55455. Phone: (612)625-4800 Fax: (612)626-0018 E-mail: ihrc@umn.edu • URL: http://www.umn.edu/ihrc.

STATISTICS SOURCES

Statistical Yearbook of the Immigration and Naturalization Service. Available from U. S. Government Printing Office. • Annual. $40.00. Provides data on legal immigrants, deportable aliens, refugees, persons naturalized, political asylum cases, foreign tourists, and foreign students.

Trends in International Migration. Organization for Economic Cooperation and Development. • 2001. $59.00. Contains detailed data on population migration flows, channels of immigration, and migrant nationalities. Includes demographic analysis.

TRADE/PROFESSIONAL ASSOCIATIONS

American Immigration Lawyers Association. 918 F St. NW, Washington, DC 20004-1400. Phone: (202)216-2400 Fax: (202)783-7853 E-mail: executive@aila.org • URL: http://www.aila.org • Lawyers specializing in the field of immigration and nationality law. Fosters and promotes the administration of justice with particular reference to the immigration and nationality laws of the United States.

Hebrew Immigrant Aid Society. 333 7th Ave., 16th Fl., New York, NY 10001-5004. Phone: 800-HIAS-714 or (212)967-4100 Fax: (212)967-4483 E-mail: info@hias.org • URL: http://www.hias.org • Assists refugees and migrants from Europe, North Africa, the Middle East, and other trouble areas resettle in the United States, Canada, Latin America, and Australia. Maintains offices and committees around the world to: help locate relatives and friends; prepare documents; arrange for transportation; provide reception and resettlement services. Is involved in assistance to refugees at the request of the U.S. government. Compiles statistics.

National Immigration Forum. 50 F St. NW, Ste. 300, Washington, DC 20001. Phone: (202)347-0040 Fax: (202)347-0058 E-mail: info@nicyra.org • URL: http://www.immigrationforum.org • Dedicated to extending and defending America's tradition as a nation of immigrants. Supports the reunification of families, the rescue and resettlement of refugees fleeing persecution, and the equitable treatment of immigrants under the law. Encourages immigrants to become U.S. citizens and promote cooperation and understanding between immigrants and other Americans.

OTHER SOURCES

Board of Immigration Appeals Interim Decisions. U.S. Immigration and Naturalization Service. Available from U.S. Government Printing Office. • Irregular.

Business Immigration Law: Strategies for Employing Foreign Nationals. American Lawyer Media, Inc. • Looseleaf. $169.00. Updated as needed. Provides step-by-step employment procedures relating to the law and regulations of the State Department, the Immigration and Naturalization Service, specific visa programs, and the Labor Department.

Includes guidelines and samples of forms. (Law Journal Press).

Immigration Law and Business. Sam Bernsen. West Group. • Three times a year. $435.00 per year. Three looseleaf volumes. Covers labor certification, temporary workers, applications, petitions, etc.

Immigration Law and Crimes. Dan Kesselbrenner and Lory D. Rosenberg. West Group. • Semiannual. $250.00 per year. Looseleaf service. Covers legal representation of the foreign-born criminal defendant.

Immigration Law and Defense. National Lawyers Guild. West Group. • Semiannual. $295.00 per year. Two looseleaf volumes. Covers legal defense of immigrants and aliens.

Immigration Law and Procedure. LexisNexis Matthew Bender. • $1,888.00. 20 looseleaf volumes. Periodic supplementation.

World Migration Report. United Nations Publications. • Annual. $39.00. Analyzes major trends in world migration, including individual country profiles.

IMPORT TRADE

See: EXPORT-IMPORT TRADE

INCANDESCENT LAMPS

See: LIGHTING

INCENTIVE

See: MOTIVATION (PSYCHOLOGY)

INCENTIVE MERCHANDISING

See: PREMIUMS

INCOME

GENERAL WORKS

Money: Who Has How Much and Why. Andrew Hacker. Simon & Schuster Trade. • 1997. $24.50. A discourse on the distribution of wealth in America, with emphasis on the gap between rich and poor.

The New Financial Order: Risk in the 21st Century. Robert J. Shiller. Princeton University Press. • 2003. $29.95. By the author of *Irrational Exuberance* (2000). Recommends that risk management schemes be developed for application to the risks of everyday life, as in such chapters as "Insurance for Livelihoods and Home Values," "Inequality Insurance: Protecting the Distribution of Income," and "Intergenerational Social Security: Sharing Risks Between Young and Old.".

ALMANACS AND YEARBOOKS

National Accounts Statistics: Main Aggregates and Detailed Tables. United Nations Publications. • Annual. $160.00.

CD-ROM DATABASES

OECD Statistical Compendium. Organization for Economic Cooperation and Development. • Semiannual. $1,905.00 per year for 1 to 10 users. CD-ROM contains more than 730,000 monthly, quarterly, and annual time series for OECD countries, 1960 to date. Includes fully searchable data on agriculture, food, economic indicators, national accounts, employment, energy, finance, industry, technology, and foreign trade. Results can be displayed in various forms.

Sourcebook America. Gale Cengage Learning. • Annual. $995.00. Produced by CACI Marketing Systems. A combination on CD-ROM of *The Sourcebook of ZIP Code Demographics* and *The Sourcebook of County Demographics*. Provides detailed population and socio-economic data (about 75 items) for each of 3,141 U. S. counties and approximately 30,000 ZIP codes, plus states, metropolitan areas, and media market areas. Includes forecasts to the year 2004.

Sourcebooks America CD-ROM. CACI Marketing Systems. • Annual. $1,250.00. Provides the CD-ROM version of *The Sourcebook of ZIP Code Demographics: Census Edition* and *The Sourcebook of County Demographics: Census Edition*.

INTERNET DATABASES

Bureau of Economic Analysis (BEA). U. S. Department of Commerce, Bureau of Economic Analysis. Phone: (202)606-9900 Fax: (202)606-5310 E-mail: webmaster@bea.doc.gov • URL: http://www.bea.doc.gov • Web site includes "News Release Information" covering national, regional, and international economic estimates from the BEA. Highlights of releases appear online the same day, complete text and tables appear the next day. "Recent News Releases" section provides titles for past nine months, with links. "BEA Data and Methodology" includes "Frequently Requested NIPA Data" (national income and product accounts, such as gross domestic product and personal income). Other statistics are available. Fees: Free.

Business 2.0 Web Guide to the Best Business Links. Business 2.0 Media Inc. Phone: (415)293-4800 E-mail: support@business2.com • URL: http://www.business2.com/webguide • Web site presents an extensive, searchable directory of links to "the best, most informative, and authoritative web pages." Twenty main categories cover business, finance, career, company information, people, and technology topics, with thousands of subtopics, all linking to Web sites recommended by experienced business researchers. Fees: Free.

Fedstats. Federal Interagency Council on Statistical Policy. Phone: (202)395-7254 • URL: http://www.fedstats.gov • Web site features an efficient search facility for full-text statistics produced by more than 100 federal agencies, including the Census Bureau, the Bureau of Economic Analysis, and the Bureau of Labor Statistics. Boolean searches can be made within one agency or for all agencies combined. Links are offered to international statistical bureaus, including the UN, IMF, OECD, UNESCO, Eurostat, and 20 individual countries. Fees: Free.

FreeLunch.com. Economy.com, Inc. Phone: (610)696-8700 Fax: (610)696-1678 • URL: http://www.freelunch.com • Web site provides free access to more than 1.5 million economic and financial data series, covering industry, demographics, labor markets, prices, retail sales, government spending, trade, interest rates, housing starts, the stock market, and many other topics. Data is available for various time periods in either chart or table form. Searching is offered. Fees: Free, but registration required. Economy.com, Inc. also offers fee-based economic analysis at *The Dismal Scientist* site (http://www.dismal.com).

ONLINE DATABASES

EconLit. American Economic Association. • Covers the worldwide literature of economics as contained in selected monographs and about 550 journals. Subjects include microeconomics, macroeconomics, economic history, inflation, money, credit, finance, accounting theory, trade, natural resource economics, and regional economics. Time period is 1969 to present, with monthly updates. Inquire as to online cost and availability.

PERIODICALS AND NEWSLETTERS

Review of Income and Wealth. International Association for Research in Income and Wealth. • Quarterly. Institutions, $200.00 per year. Includes print and online editions.

Review of Social Economy. Association for Social Economics. Taylor and Francis Group. • Quarterly. Individuals, $78.00 per year; institutions, $211.00 per year. Subject matter is concerned with the relationships between social values and economics. Includes articles on income distribution, poverty, labor, and class.

STATISTICS SOURCES

American Business Climate and Economic Profiles. Priscilla C. Geahigan. Gale Cengage Learning. • 1993. $170.00. Provides business, industrial, demographic, and economic figures for all states and 300 metropolitan areas. Includes production, taxation, population, growth rates, labor force data, incomes, total sales, etc.

Benefits and Wages: OECD Indicators. Organization for Economic Cooperation and Development. • Biennial. $19.00. Provides data for 28 countries on unemployment benefits and related welfare benefits. Includes a cross-country comparison of family incomes, in work and out of work. Formerly *Benefit Systems and Work Incentives.*

Business Statistics of the United States. Linz Audain and Cornelia J. Strawser. Bernan Associates. • Annual. $147.00. Based on *Business Statistics,* formerly issue by the Bureau of Economic Analysis, U. S. Department of Commerce. Provides basic data for a wide variety of U. S. industries, services, and economic indicators. Most statistics are shown annually for 30 years and monthly for the most recent four years.

Comparative Guide to American Suburbs, 2003/2004. Grey House Publishing. • 2003. $130.00. Third edition. Contains detailed profiles of 1,800 suburban communities having a population of 10,000 or more and located within the 50 largest metropolitan areas. Includes ranking tables for income, unemployment, new housing permits, home prices, and crime, as well as information on school districts. (Universal Reference Publications.).

County and City Data Book 2000: A Statistical Abstract Supplement. Available from U. S. Government Printing Office. • 2002. $68.00. 13th edition. Issued by the U. S. Bureau of the Census (http://www.census.gov). Contains a wide variety of data on 3,141 U.S. counties, 1,078 cities, and 11,097 places of 2,500 or more inhabitants. Includes statistical information on retailing, manufacturing, banking, service industries, income, employment, housing, education, crime, and population. Updated metropolitan areas are included.

County and City Extra: Annual Metro, City and County Data Book. Deirdre A. Gaquin and Mark S. Littman. Bernan Press. • 2001. $120.00. Updates and augments data published irregularly in print form by the U. S. Census Bureau in *County and City Data Book.* Covers "every state, county, metropolitan area, and congressional district in the United States, as well as all U. S. cities with a 1990 population of 25,000 or more." Contains a wide range tic maps.

County and City Extra: Special Decennial Census Edition. Deidre A. Gaquin and Katherine A. DeBrandt, editors. Bernan Press. • 2002. $95.00. Presents conveniently arranged population, housing, and other data from the 2000 census, with many 1980 and 1990 comparisons. Includes maps and tables with rankings of about 20 items for various geographic locations. Complements the annual *County and City Extra.*

Current Population Reports: Household Economic

Studies, Series P-70. Available from U. S. Government Printing Office. • Irregular. $21.00 per year. Issued by the U.S. Bureau of the Census (http://www.census.gov). Each issue covers a special topic relating to household socioeconomic characteristics.

Current Population Reports: Population Characteristics, Special Studies, and Consumer Income, Series P-20, P-23, and P-60. Available from U. S. Government Printing Office. • Irregular. $80.00 per year. Issued by the U.S. Bureau of the Census (http://www.census.gov). Each issue covers a special topic relating to population or income. Series P-20, *Population Characteristics,* provides statistical studies on such items as mobility, fertility, education, and marital status. Series P-23, *Special Studies,* consists of occasional reports on methodology. Series P-60, *Consumer Income,* publishes reports on income in relation to age, sex, education, occupation, family size, etc.

Datapedia of the United States: American History in Numbers. George T. Kurian, editor. Bernan Press. • 2004. $125.00. Third edition. Based on the Census Bureau publication, *Historical Statistics of the United States.* Provides data from Colonial times to the present on agriculture, business, consumer income, energy, finance, labor, national income, population, and many other subjects. Includes "narrative highlights," maps, charts, and statistical projections.

Demographics USA: County Edition. Trade Dimensions. • Annual. $435.00. Contains 200 statistical series for each of 3,000 counties. Includes population, household income, employment, retail sales, and consumer expenditures. Also provides Effective Buying Income, Buying Power Index, and data summaries by Metro Market, Media Market, and State. (CD-ROM version is available.).

Demographics USA: ZIP Edition. Trade Dimensions. • Annual. $435.00. Contains 50 statistical series for each of 40,000 ZIP codes. Includes population, household income, employment, retail sales, and consumer expenditures. Also provides Effective Buying Income, Business Characteristics, and data summaries by state, region, and the first three digits of ZIP codes. (CD-ROM version is available.).

Economic Report of the President: Together with the Annual Report of the Council of Economic Advisors. Available from U. S. Government Printing Office. • Annual. $32.00. Includes about 130 pages of "Statistical Tables Relating to Income, Employment, and Production." Tables cover national income, employment, wages, productivity, manufacturing, prices, credit, finance (public and private), corporate profits, and foreign trade.

Gale Country and World Rankings Reporter. Gale Cengage Learning. • 1997. $160.00. Second edition. Provides about 3,000 statistical ranking tables and charts covering more than 235 nations. Sources include the United Nations and various government publications.

Gale State Rankings Reporter. Gale Cengage Learning. • 1996. $130.00. Second edition Provides 3,000 ranked lists of states under 35 subject headings. Sources are newspapers, periodicals, books, research institute publications, and government publications.

Handbook of U. S. Labor Statistics: Employment, Earnings, Prices, Productivity, and Other Labor Data. Eva E. Jacobs, editor. Bernan Associates. • 1999. $74.00. Based on *Handbook of Labor Statistics,* formerly issued by the Bureau of Labor Statistics, U. S. Department of Labor. Includes the Bureau's projections of employment in the U. S. by industry and occupation. Provides a wide variety of data on the work force, prices, fringe benefits, and consumer expenditures.

Household Spending: Who Spends How Much On

For publishers addresses, refer to SOURCES CITED section at the back of the book.

What. New Strategist Publications, Inc. • 1999. $94.95. Fifth edition. Gives facts about the buying habits of U. S. consumers according to income, age, household type, and household size. Includes spending data for about 1,000 products and services.

Income of the Population 55 and Older. Available from U. S. Government Printing Office. • Biennial. $23.00. Issued by the Social Security Administration (http://www.ssa.gov). Covers major sources and amounts of income for the 55 and older population in the U. S., "with special emphasis on some aspects of the income of the population 65 and older.".

Individual Income Tax Returns. U.S. Department of the Treasury, Internal Revenue Service. Available from U.S. Government Printing Office. • Annual. $22.00.

Key Indicators of the Labour Market. Available from Routledge. • Biennial. $125.00. Published by the International Labour Office (http://www.ilo.org). Provides data on 20 key indicators in 220 countries. Includes labor force statistics, employment, unemployment, part-time workers, wages, productivity, poverty indicators, and related topics.

Money Income in the United States. Available from U. S. Government Printing Office. • Annual. $5.50. Issued by the U. S. Bureau of the Census. Presents data on consumer income in current and constant dollars, both totals and averages (means, medians, distributions). Includes figures for a wide variety of demographic and occupational characteristics. (Current Population Reports.).

Social Statistics of the United States. Mark S. Littman, editor. Bernan Press. • 2000. $65.00. Includes statistical data on population growth, labor force, occupations, environmental trends, leisure time use, income, poverty, taxes, and other economic or demographic topics.

Sourcebook of Zip Code Demographics. ESRI Business Information Solutions. • 2002. $495.00. 16th edition. Provides data on 75 demographic and socioeconomic characteristics for each ZIP code in the U. S.

State Profiles: The Population and Economy of Each U. S. State. Courtenay Slater and Others. Bernan Press. • 1999. $89.00. Presents charts, tables, and text in an eight-page profile for each state. Covers population, labor force, income, poverty, employment, wages, industry, trade, housing, education, health, taxes, and government finances. (The Population and Economy of Each United States Series).

Statistical Abstract of the World. Gale Cengage Learning. • 1997. $85.00. Third edition. Provides data on a wide variety of economic, social, and political topics for about 200 countries. Arranged by country.

Statistical Handbook on Consumption and Wealth in the United States. Greenwood Publishing Group, Inc. • 1999. $69.95. Provides more than 400 graphs, tables, and charts dealing with basic income levels, income inequalities, spending patterns, taxation, subsidies, etc. (Statistical Handbook Series).

Statistics of Income Bulletin. Available from U.S. Government Printing Office. • Quarterly. $44.00 per year. Current data compiled from tax returns relating to income, assets, and expenses of individuals and businesses. (U. S. Internal Revenue Service.).

Statistics of Income: Corporation Income Tax Returns. U.S. Internal Revenue Service. Available from U.S. Government Printing Office. • Annual. $26.00.

Survey of Current Business. Available from U. S. Government Printing Office. • Monthly. $63.00 per year. Issued by Bureau of Economic Analysis, U. S. Department of Commerce. Presents a wide variety of business and economic data.

Working Americans, 1880-1999, Volume One: The

Working Class. Scott Derks, editor. Grey House Publishing. • 2000. $375.00. Provides detailed information on the lifestyles and economic life of working class families in the 12 decades from 1880 to 1999. Includes such items as selected consumer prices, income, family finances, budgets, life at home, jobs, and working conditions. (Universal Reference Publications.).

Working Americans, 1880-1999, Volume Two: The Middle Class. Scott Derks, editor. Grey House Publishing. • 2000. $135.00. Three volumes. Furnishes details of the social and economic lives of middle class Americans during the years 1880 to 1999. Describes such items as selected consumer prices, income, family finances, budgets, life at home, jobs, and working conditions. (Universal Reference Publications.).

World Consumer Income and Expenditure Patterns. Available from Gale Cengage Learning. • Annual. $1,090.00. Two volumes. Published by Euromonitor. Provides data for countries worldwide on consumer income, earning power, spending patterns, and savings. Expenditures are detailed for product or service categories.

World Consumer Income Patterns. Euromonitor International. • 2003. $1,190.00. Provides detailed data on household income in 71 countries (10-year statistics). Covers income by age, sex, and level of education, with further data on savings, earnings, and average taxes.

TRADE/PROFESSIONAL ASSOCIATIONS

International Association for Research in Income and Wealth. c/o New York University, Dept. of Economics, Rm. 700, 269 Mercer St., New York, NY 10003. Phone: (212)924-4386 Fax: (212)366-5067 E-mail: iariw@nyu.edu • URL: http://www.econ.nyu.edu/iariw • Specialists in the field of national income accounting.

INCOME TAX

See also: CORPORATE INCOME TAX; STATE TAXES; TAX PLANNING; TAX SHELTERS; TAXATION

GENERAL WORKS

The Decline (and Fall?) of the Income Tax: How to Make Sense of the American Tax Mess and the Flat-Tax Cures That Are Supposed to Fix It. Michael J. Graetz. W. W. Norton & Co., Inc. • 1997. $27.50. The author, a former U. S. Treasury official, proposes a value-added tax (VAT) to augment federal income tax. He reviews recent tax history and provides entertaining tax anecdotes.

The Flat Tax. Robert E. Hall and Alvin Rabushka. Hoover Institution Press. • 1995. $14.95. Second edition. A favorable view of a flat tax as a replacement for the graduated federal income tax. (Publication Series: No. 423).

How to Avoid Financial Tangles. American Institute for Economic Research. • 2001. $8.00. Provides basic information and advice on such topics as property ownership, taxes, wills, trusts, insurance, record retention, and professional assistance. (Economic Education Bulletin.).

What the IRS Doesn't Want You to Know: A CPA Reveals the Tricks of the Trade. Martin Kaplan. John Wiley and Sons, Inc. • 2003. $18.95. Ninth edition. Explains how to legally pay as little income tax as possible.

ABSTRACTS AND INDEXES

Accounting and Tax Index. UMI. • Quarterly. Price on application. Annual cumulation. Indexes accounting, auditing, and taxation literature appearing

in journals, books, pamphlets, conference proceedings, and newsletters.

ALMANACS AND YEARBOOKS

Tax Year in Review. CCH, Inc. • Annual. Covers the year's "major new legislative and regulatory changes.".

CD-ROM DATABASES

Authority Tax and Estate Planning Library. LexisNexis/Matthew Bender. • Periodic revisions. Price on request. CD-ROM contains updated full text of *Bender's Payroll Tax Guide, Depreciation Handbook, Federal Income Taxation of Corporations, Tax Planning for Corporations, Modern Estate Planning, Planning for Large Estates, Murphy's Will Clauses, Tax & Estate Planning for the Elderly,* and 12 other Matthew Bender publications. The Internal Revenue Code is also included.

Federal Tax Products. Available from U. S. Government Printing Office. • Annual. $27.00. CD-ROM issued by the Internal Revenue Service (http://www.irs.treas.gov/forms_pubs/). Provides current tax forms, instructions, and publications. Also includes older tax forms beginning with 1991.

OECD Statistical Compendium. Organization for Economic Cooperation and Development. • Semiannual. $1,905.00 per year for 1 to 10 users. CD-ROM contains more than 730,000 monthly, quarterly, and annual time series for OECD countries, 1960 to date. Includes fully searchable data on agriculture, food, economic indicators, national accounts, employment, energy, finance, industry, technology, and foreign trade. Results can be displayed in various forms.

The Tax Directory [CD-ROM]. Tax Analysts. • Quarterly. Provides *The Tax Directory* listings on CD-ROM, covering federal, state, and international tax officials, tax practitioners, and corporate tax executives.

U. S. Master Tax Guide on CD-ROM. CCH, Inc. • Annual. CD-ROM version of the printed *U. S. Master Tax Guide.* Includes search commands, link commands, and on-screen prompts.

WILSONDISC: Wilson Business Abstracts. H. W. Wilson Co. • Monthly. Includes unlimited online access to *Wilson Business Abstracts* through WILSONLINE. Provides CD-ROM "cover-to-cover" abstracting and indexing of over 600 prominent business periodicals. Indexing is from 1982, abstracting from 1990. (*Business Periodicals Index* without abstracts is available on CD-ROM at $1,495 per year.).

DIRECTORIES

Cumulative List of Organizations Described in Section 170(c) of the Internal Revenue Code of 1986. Available from U. S. Government Printing Office. • Annual. $153.00 per year, including quarterly supplements. Lists about 300,000 organizations eligible for contributions deductible for federal income tax purposes. Provides name of each organization and city, but not complete address information. Arranged alphabetically by name of institution. (Office of Employee Plans and Exempt Organizations, Internal Revenue Service.).

The Tax Directory. Tax Analysts. • Covers: Volume One--Approximately 15,000 federal and state government tax legislators, policymakers, administrators, and employees; tax regulation attorneys; over 500 international tax officials with central banks, ministries of finance, foreign embassies and consulate, and chambers of commerce; over 300 tax and business journalists and editors working for magazines, journals, newspapers, television, and radio; tax sections of over 100 trade and professional associations; state CPA, bar, and enrolled agent associations. Volume Two--Over 5,000 corporate tax managers of large U.S. and international firms. Entries include: For government and international officials--Name, title, address, phone, fax, email and website. For corporate tax managers--Name, address, phone, fax, email, website, and company name. For journalists--Name, address, phone, fax, email, website, and name of publication/network. For organizations and associations--Name, address, phone, fax, email, website, budget, membership, background information, and description of purpose.

ENCYCLOPEDIAS AND DICTIONARIES

Dictionary of 1040 Deductions. LexisNexis Matthew Bender. • Annual. $75.00. Organized by schedule and supported by thousands of citations. Designed to quickly answer all questions about deductions.

HANDBOOKS AND MANUALS

Bender's Payroll Tax Guide. LexisNexis Matthew Bender. • Annual. $149.00. Guide to payroll tax planning. Includes procedures, forms, and examples.

Bender's Tax Return Manual. Ernest D. Fiore and others. LexisNexis Matthew Bender. • Annual. $91.00. One looseleaf volume. Periodic supplementation. Includes all major federal tax forms and schedules.

Business Taxpayer Information Publications. Available from U. S. Government Printing Office. • Annual. $63.00. Two volumes, consisting of *Circular E, Employer's Tax Guide* and *Employer's Supplemental Tax Guide.* Issued by the Internal Revenue Service (http://www.irs.ustreas.gov). Includes a wide variety of business-related tax information, including withholding tables, tax calendars, self-employment issues, partnership matters, corporation topics, depreciation, and bankruptcy.

CCH Analysis of Top Tax Issues. CCH, Inc. • Annual. $49.00. Covers yearly tax changes affecting business and personal transactions, planning, and returns.

CCH Guide to Car, Travel, Entertainment, and Home Office Deductions. CCH, Inc. • Annual. $45.00. Explains how to claim maximum tax deductions for common business expenses. Includes automobile depreciation tables, lease value tables, worksheets, and examples of filled-in tax forms.

Ernst & Young Tax Guide 2002: The Official IRS Tax Guide and Usable Forms, Plus Easy-to-Use Explanation and Tax Saving Tips from America's Leading Big Six Accountants. Ernst & Young Staff. John Wiley and Sons, Inc. • Annual. $16.95. (Ernst and Young Tax Guide Series).

Essentials of Federal Income Taxation for Individuals and Business. CCH, Inc. • Annual. $72.00. Covers basic tax planning and tax reduction strategies as affected by tax law changes and IRS interpretations. Includes sample filled-in forms.

Estate Plan Book 2000. William S. Moore. American Institute for Economic Research. • 2000. $10.00. Revision of 1997 edition. Part one: "Basic Estate Planning." Part two: "Reducing Taxes on the Disposition of Your Estate." Part three: "Putting it All Together: Examples of Estate Plans." Provides succinct information on wills, trusts, tax planning, and gifts. (Economic Education Bulletin.).

Federal Tax Course. Aspen Publishers, Inc. • Annual. $210.00. Provides basic reference and training for various forms of federal taxation: individual, business, corporate, partnership, estate, gift, etc.

Federal Tax Manual. CCH, Inc. • Monthly. $342.00 per year. Looseleaf service. Covers "basic federal tax rules and forms affecting individuals and businesses." Includes a copy of *Annuity, Depreciation, and Withholding Tables.*

Federal Taxation Practice and Procedure Problem Supplement. Robert E. Meldman and Richard J. Sideman. CCH, Inc. • 1998. $40.00. Provides information on the administrative structure of the

Internal Revenue Service. Includes discussions of penalties, ethical duties, statute of limitations, litigation, and IRS collection procedures. Contains IRS standardized letters and notices.

Federal Withholding Tax Tables. CCH, Inc. • Annual. $18.00.

H & R Block 2003 Income Tax Guide: Preparing America's Taxes for Over 40 Years. Simon & Schuster Trade. • 2002. $16.00. (H&R Block Income Tax Guide Series).

How to Practice Before the New IRS. Robert S. Schriebman. CCH, Inc. • 1999. $115.00. Reflects changes made by the IRS Restructuring and Reform Act of 1998. Covers audits, appeals, tax court basics, refunds, penalties, etc., for tax professionals.

Income Tax Regulations. CCH, Inc. • Annual. $119.00. Six volumes. Contains full text of official Internal Revenue Code regulations.

Individual Tax Return Guide. RIA. • 2003. $20.00.

Individual Taxation. James W. Pratt and William N. Kulsrud. McGraw-Hill. • 1996. $69.95. Tenth edition. Focuses on the federal income tax.

Individual Taxes 2002-2003: Worldwide Summaries. John Wiley and Sons, Inc. • 2002. $105.00. Two volumes. Summarizes the personal tax regulations of more than 125 countries. Provides information useful for international tax planning and foreign investments.

Individuals' Filled-In Tax Return Forms. CCH, Inc. • 2002. $34.00.

Internal Revenue Code. RIA. • Annual. $86.50. Provides full text of the Internal Revenue Code (5,000 pages), including procedural and administrative provisions.

IRS Tax Collection Procedures. CCH, Inc. • $195.00. Looseleaf service. Periodic supplementation. Covers IRS collection personnel, payment arrangements, penalties, abatements, summons, liens, etc.

J. K. Lasser's Your Income Tax, 2004: For Preparing Your 2003 Tax Return. J. K. Lasser Tax Institute Staff. John Wiley and Sons, Inc. • 2003. $18.95.

1040 Preparation. Sidney Kess and others. CCH, Inc. • 2001. How to prepare individual federal income tax returns.

Practical Guide to Tax Issues in Employment. Julia K. Brazelton. CCH, Inc. • 1999. $95.00. Covers income taxation as related to labor law and tax law, including settlements and awards. Written for tax professionals.

Tax Guide for Small Business. U.S. Department of the Treasury, Internal Revenue Service. Available from U.S. Government Printing Office. • Annual. $8.00.

Tax Preparation Service. Entrepreneur Media, Inc. • Looseleaf. $59.50. A practical guide to starting a business for the preparation of income tax returns. Covers profit potential, start-up costs, market size evaluation, owner's time required, site selection, lease negotiation, pricing, accounting, advertising, promotion, etc. (Start-Up Business Guide No. E2332.).

U. S. Master Compensation Tax Guide. Dennis R. Lassila and Bob G. Kilpatrick. CCH, Inc. • 2001. $57.00. Third edition. Provides concise coverage of taxes on salaries, bonuses, fringe benefits, other current compensation, and deferred compensation (qualified and nonqualified).

U. S. Master Tax Guide. CCH, Inc. • $184.00. Looseleaf service. Periodic supplementation. Provides concise information on personal and business income tax, with cross-references to the Internal Revenue Code and Income Tax Regulations.

Your Federal Income Tax. U.S. Department of the Treasury, Internal Revenue Service. Available from U.S. Government Printing Office. • Annual. $25.00.

Layman's guide to income tax preparation.

INTERNET DATABASES

Business 2.0 Web Guide to the Best Business Links. Business 2.0 Media Inc. Phone: (415)293-4800 E-mail: support@business2.com • URL: http://www.business2.com/webguide • Web site presents an extensive, searchable directory of links to "the best, most informative, and authoritative web pages." Twenty main categories cover business, finance, career, company information, people, and technology topics, with thousands of subtopics, all linking to Web sites recommended by experienced business researchers. Fees: Free.

CCH Essentials: An Internet Tax Research and Primary Source Library. CCH, Inc. Phone: 800-248-3248 or (773)866-6000 Fax: 800-224-8299 or (773)866-3608 E-mail: cust_serv@cch.com • URL: http://tax.cch.com/essentials • Fee-based Web site provides full-text coverage of federal tax law and regulations, including rulings, procedures, tax court decisions, and IRS publications, announcements, notices, and penalties. Includes explanation, analysis, tax planning guides, and a daily tax news service. Searching is offered, including citation search.

Factiva. Dow Jones Reuters Business Interactive, LLC. Phone: 800-369-7466 or (609)452-1511 Fax: (609)520-5770 E-mail: solutions@factiva.com • URL: http://www.factiva.com • Fee-based Web site provides "global news and business information through Web sites and content integration solutions." Includes Dow Jones and Reuters newswires, The Wall Street Journal, and more than 7,000 other sources of current news, historical articles, market research reports, and investment analysis. Content includes 96 major U. S. newspapers, 900 non-English sources, trade publications, media transcripts, country profiles, news photos, etc.

Fedstats. Federal Interagency Council on Statistical Policy. Phone: (202)395-7254 • URL: http://www.fedstats.gov • Web site features an efficient search facility for full-text statistics produced by more than 100 federal agencies, including the Census Bureau, the Bureau of Economic Analysis, and the Bureau of Labor Statistics. Boolean searches can be made within one agency or for all agencies combined. Links are offered to international statistical bureaus, including the UN, IMF, OECD, UNESCO, Eurostat, and 20 individual countries. Fees: Free.

FedWorld: A Program of the United States Department of Commerce. National Technical Information Service. Phone: (703)605-6000 Fax: (703)605-6900 E-mail: webmaster@fedworld.gov • URL: http://www.fedworld.gov • Web site offers "a comprehensive central access point for searching, locating, ordering, and acquiring government and business information." Emphasis is on searching the Web pages, databases, and government reports of a wide variety of federal agencies. Fees: Free.

FirstGov: Your First Click to the U. S. Government. General Services Administration. Phone: 800-333-4636 or (202)501-0705 E-mail: public.affairs@gsa.gov • URL: http://www.firstgov.gov • Free Web site provides extensive links to federal agencies covering a wide variety of topics, such as agriculture, business, consumer safety, education, the environment, government jobs, grants, health, social security, statistics sources, taxes, technology, travel, and world affairs. Also provides links to federal forms, including IRS tax forms. Searching is offered, both keyword and advanced.

FreeLunch.com. Economy.com, Inc. Phone: (610)696-8700 Fax: (610)696-1678 • URL: http://www.freelunch.com • Web site provides free access to more than 1.5 million economic and financial data series, covering industry, demographics, labor markets, prices, retail sales, government spending, trade, interest rates, housing starts, the stock market, and many other topics. Data is available for various time periods in either chart or table form. Searching is offered. Fees: Free, but registration required. Economy.com, Inc. also offers fee-based economic analysis at *The Dismal Scientist* site (http://www.dismal.com).

Internal Revenue Service IRS.gov. Internal Revenue Service. Phone: 800-829-1040 or (202)622-5000 Fax: (202)622-5844 • URL: http://www.irs.gov • Web site provides a wide variety of tax information, including IRS forms and publications. Searching is available. Fees: Free.

Nexis.com. Lexis-Nexis Group. Phone: 800-227-4908 or (937)865-6800 Fax: (937)865-6909 E-mail: webmaster@prod.lexis-nexis.com • URL: http://www.nexis.com • Fee-based Web site offers searching of about 2.8 billion documents in some 30,000 news, business, and legal information sources. Features include a subject directory covering 1,200 topics in 34 categories and a Company Dossier containing information on more than 500,000 public and private companies. Boolean searching is offered.

Rutgers Accounting Web (RAW). Rutgers University Accounting Research Center. Phone: (973)353-5172 Fax: (973)353-1283 • URL: http://www.rutgers.edu/accounting • RAW Web site provides extensive links to sources of national and international accounting information, such as the Big Six accounting firms, the Financial Accounting Standards Board (FASB), SEC filings (EDGAR), journals, publishers, software, the International Accounting Network, and "Internet's largest list of accounting firms in USA." Searching is offered. Fees: Free.

Tax Analysts [Web site]. Tax Analysts. Phone: 800-955-3444 or (703)533-4400 Fax: (703)533-4444 • URL: http://www.tax.org • The three main sections of Tax Analysts home page are "Tax News" (Today's Tax News, Feature of the Week, Tax Snapshots, Tax Calendar); "Products & Services" (Product Catalog, Press Releases); and "Public Interest" (Discussion Groups, Tax Clinic, Tax History Project). Fees: Free for coverage of current tax events; fee-based for comprehensive information. Daily updating.

ONLINE DATABASES

Accounting and Tax Database. PROQUEST. • Provides indexing and abstracting of the literature of accounting, taxation, and financial management, 1971 to date. Updating is weekly. Especially covers accounting, auditing, banking, bankruptcy, employee compensation and benefits, cash management, financial planning, and credit. Inquire as to online cost and availability.

Wilson Business Abstracts Online. H. W. Wilson Co. • Indexes and abstracts 600 major business periodicals, plus the *Wall Street Journal* and the business section of the *New York Times.* Indexing is from 1982, abstracting from 1990, with the two newspapers included from 1993. Updated weekly. Inquire as to online cost and availability. (*Business Periodicals Index* without abstracts is also available online.).

PERIODICALS AND NEWSLETTERS

Highlights and Documents. Tax Analysts. • Daily. $2,249.00 per year, including monthly indexes. Newsletter. Provides daily coverage of IRS, congressional, judicial, state, and international tax developments. Includes abstracts and citations for "all tax documents released within the previous 24 to 48 hours." Annual compilation available *Highlights and Documents on Microfiche.*

Internal Revenue Bulletin. Research Institute of America. • Description: Presents new treasury and IRS releases in full official text. Contains rulings and decisions, releases on treaties, tax legislation, administrative and procedural releases, disbarment and suspensions.

Internal Revenue Cumulative Bulletin. Available from U. S. Government Printing Office. • Semiannual. Issued by the Internal Revenue Service.

Cumulates all items of a "permanent nature" appearing in the weekly *Internal Revenue Bulletin.*

Journal of Tax Practice and Procedure. CCH, Inc. • Bimonthly. $215.00 per year. Covers the representation of taxpayers before the IRS, "from initial contact through litigation.".

Practical Tax Strategies. RIA. • Monthly. $275.00. per year. Emphasis is on current tax developments as they affect accountants and their clients. Includes advice on tax software and computers. Formerly *Taxation for Accountants.*

State Income Tax Alert. State Taxation Institute. • Description: Features updates on state income tax issues. Recurring features include a calendar of events, book reviews, and news of educational opportunities.

Tax Notes: The Weekly Tax Service. Tax Analysts. • Weekly. $1,699.00 per year. Includes an *Annual* and 1985-1996 compliations on CD-ROM. Newsletter. Covers "tax news from all federal sources," including congressional committees, tax courts, and the Internal Revenue Service. Each issue contains "summaries of every document that pertains to federal tax law," with citations. Commentary is provided.

Tax Practice. Tax Analysts. • Weekly. $199.00 per year. Newsletter. Covers news affecting tax practitioners and litigators, with emphasis on federal court decisions, rules and regulations, and tax petitions. Provides a guide to Internal Revenue Service audit issues.

RESEARCH CENTERS AND INSTITUTES

Office of Tax Policy Research. University of Michigan, 701 Tappan St., Ann Arbor, MI 48109-1234. Phone: (734)763-3068 Fax: (734)763-4032 E-mail: otpr@umich.edu • URL: http://www.taxpolicyresearch.umich.edu/.

Tax Foundation. Tax Foundation. 2001 L St. NW, Ste. 1050, Washington, DC 20036. Phone: (202)464-6200 Fax: (202)464-6201 E-mail: hodge@taxfoundation.org • URL: http://www.taxfoundation.org • Fiscal and management aspects of federal, state, and local government, including studies on government expenditures, the federal budget, taxation, and international competitiveness. Serves as a national information agency for individuals and organizations concerned with problems of government expenditures, taxation, and debt.

STATISTICS SOURCES

Business Statistics of the United States. Linz Audain and Cornelia J. Strawser. Bernan Associates. • Annual. $147.00. Based on *Business Statistics,* formerly issue by the Bureau of Economic Analysis, U. S. Department of Commerce. Provides basic data for a wide variety of U. S. industries, services, and economic indicators. Most statistics are shown annually for 30 years and monthly for the most recent four years.

Individual Income Tax Returns. U.S. Department of the Treasury, Internal Revenue Service. Available from U.S. Government Printing Office. • Annual. $22.00.

Internal Revenue Service Data Book. Available from U. S. Government Printing Office. • Annual. $8.00. "Contains statistical tables and organizational information previously included in the Internal Revenue Service annual report." (Internal Revenue Service Publication, 55B.).

Statistics of Income: Corporation Income Tax Returns. U.S. Internal Revenue Service. Available from U.S. Government Printing Office. • Annual. $26.00.

Survey of Current Business. Available from U. S. Government Printing Office. • Monthly. $63.00 per year. Issued by Bureau of Economic Analysis, U. S. Department of Commerce. Presents a wide variety of business and economic data.

Taxing Wages. Organization for Economic Cooperation and Development. • Annual. $52.00. Contains data on income tax and social security levies collected from employees and employers in OECD countries. Includes marginal and effective tax burden figures for various family income levels and statistics on cash transfers paid as family benefits.

TRADE/PROFESSIONAL ASSOCIATIONS

Institute of Tax Consultants. 7500 212th St., S.W., No. 205, Edmonds, WA 98026. Phone: (425)774-3521 Fax: (425)672-0461 E-mail: kraemerc@juno.com • URL: http://www.taxprofessionals.homestead.com.

National Taxpayers Union. 108 N Alfred St., Alexandria, VA 22314. Phone: 800-829-4258 or (703)683-5700 Fax: (703)683-5722 E-mail: ntu@ntu.org • URL: http://www.ntu.org • Seeks to: reduce government spending; cut taxes; protect the rights of taxpayers. Claims to have helped generate federal budget cuts of over 120 billion dollars. Activities include research programs and an intense lobbying campaign in Washington, DC; has been a leader in the fights against government ventures such as: social security tax; guaranteed income; congressional and bureaucratic pay raises; federal subsidies; foreign aid; national health insurance. Works for a balanced federal budget/tax limitation constitutional amendment; federal pension reform; reduction of capital gains and personal income tax; social security reform. Has worked for airline deregulation; indexing of federal income tax, California's Proposition 13, Massachusetts Proposition 2 1/2, and other state tax cutting initiatives. Conducts annual voting study of congressmen and senators, rating their votes on spending and tax issues and presenting awards for best and worst records.

Tax Analysts. 400 S Maple Ave., Ste. 400, Falls Church, VA 22046. Phone: 800-955-2444 or (703)533-4400 Fax: (703)533-4444 E-mail: cservice@tax.org • URL: http://www.tax.org • Reviews all tax law developments, federal, state, international comprehensively; compiles statistics. **Convention/Meeting:** none.

OTHER SOURCES

Complete Federal Tax Forms. RIA. • $605.00. Three looseleaf volumes. Periodic supplementation. Contains more than 650 reproducible Internal Revenue Service forms, with instructions.

Executive Compensation and Taxation Coordinator. RIA. • Monthly. $765.00 per year. Three looseleaf volumes.

Federal Income, Gift and Estate Taxation. LexisNexis Matthew Bender. • $1,220.00. Seven looseleaf volumes. Periodic supplementation.

Federal Tax Coordinator Library. RIA. • $2,125.00 per year. Available only online.

Federal Tax Forms. CCH, Inc. • Irregular. $370.00. Looseleaf service. Three volumes. Actual size reproductions of federal income tax forms.

Federal Tax Guide. CCH, Inc. • Monthly. $929.00 per year. Eight looseleaf volumes. For everyday business and personal federal income tax questions. Explanation of federal tax system, income tax regulations, check lists, withholding tables, and charts.

Federal Tax Guide: Internal Revenue Code. Prentice Hall PTR. • Looseleaf. Periodic supplementation. Price on application.

Federal Taxes: Internal Memoranda of the IRS. Prentice Hall PTR. • Looseleaf. Periodic supplementation. Price on application.

Internal Revenue Manual: Audit and Administration. CCH, Inc. • Irregular. $1,254.00. Six looseleaf volumes. Reproduces IRS tax administration provisions and procedures.

IRS Publications. CCH, Inc. • Irregular. $352.00.

For publishers addresses, refer to SOURCES CITED section at the back of the book.

Three looseleaf volumes. Periodic supplementation. Photographic reproductions of current Internal Revenue Service tax publications intended for public use.

Reproducible Copies of Federal Tax Forms and Instructions. Available from U. S. Government Printing Office. • Annual. $54.00. Two looseleaf volumes issued by the Internal Revenue Service (http://www.irs.gov). "Contains the most frequently requested tax forms and instructions," prepared especially for libraries.

Tax Legislation 2001: Law, Explanation, and Analysis. CCH, Inc. • 2001. $42.50. Provides explanation and interpretation of federal tax legislation enacted in 2001.

Tax Legislation 2002: Highlights. CCH, Inc. • 2002. $7.00. Booklet summarizes significant changes in U. S. tax law resulting from the legislation of 2001.

Tax Planning for Individuals and Small Businesses. Sidney Kess. CCH, Inc. • 2002. $52.00. Second edition. Includes illustrations, charts, and sample client letters. Edited primarily for accountants and lawyers.

INCOME TAX, STATE

See: STATE TAXES

INCORPORATION

See also: CORPORATION LAW AND REGULATION

ABSTRACTS AND INDEXES
Business Periodicals Index. H. W. Wilson Co. • 11 times a year. Quarterly and annual cumulations. Price varies.

Current Law Index: Multiple Access to Legal Periodicals. Gale Cengage Learning. • Monthly. $725.00 per year. Produced in cooperation with the American Association of Law Libraries. Indexes more than 900 law journals, legal newspapers, and specialty publications from the U.S., Canada, U.K., Ireland, Australia, and New Zealand.

Index to Legal Periodicals and Books. H. W. Wilson Co. • Monthly. $490.00 per year. Quarterly and annual cumulations.

ALMANACS AND YEARBOOKS
American Law Yearbook. Gale Cengage Learning. • Annual. $165.00. Serves as a yearly supplement to *West's Encyclopedia of American Law.* Describes new legal developments in many subject areas.

CD-ROM DATABASES
WILSONDISC: Index to Legal Periodicals and Books. H. W. Wilson Co. • Monthly. Includes unlimited online access to *Index to Legal Periodicals* through WILSONLINE. Contains CD-ROM indexing of more than 1,400 English language legal periodicals from 1981 to date and 2,500 books.

WILSONDISC: Wilson Business Abstracts. H. W. Wilson Co. • Monthly. Includes unlimited online access to *Wilson Business Abstracts* through WILSONLINE. Provides CD-ROM "cover-to-cover" abstracting and indexing of over 600 prominent business periodicals. Indexing is from 1982, abstracting from 1990. (*Business Periodicals Index* without abstracts is available on CD-ROM at $1,495 per year.).

ENCYCLOPEDIAS AND DICTIONARIES
Encyclopedia of Business. Gale Cengage Learning. • 2000. $425.00. Second edition. Two volumes. Contains more than 700 signed articles covering major business disciplines and concepts. International in scope. (Encyclopedia of Business Series).

West's Encyclopedia of American Law. Available from Gale Cengage Learning. • 2003. $1,195.00. Second edition. 12 volumes. Published by West Group. Covers a wide variety of legal topics for the general reader.

HANDBOOKS AND MANUALS
Financing the Corporation. Richard A. Booth. West Group. • Annual. $160.00. Looseleaf service. Covers a wide variety of corporate finance legal topics, from initial capital structure to public sale of securities.

How to Form a Nonprofit Corporation. Anthony Mancuso. Nolo. • 2002. $44.99. Fifth edition.

How to Incorporate: A Handbook for Entrepreneurs and Professionals. Michael Diamond and Julia L. Williams. John Wiley and Sons, Inc. • 2000. $24.95. Fourth edition.

Incorporate in Any State. W. Dean Brown. Corporate Publishing, Co. • Annual. $24.95. Available in separate editions for every state and the District of Columbia. Includes specific instructions for creating a simple corporation in a particular state, with legal forms and sample stock certificates.

Incorporate Your Business: The National Corporation Kit. Daniel Sitarz. Nova Publishing Co. • 2001. $29.95. Third edition. IncludesCD-ROM and basic forms and instructions for incorporating a small business in any state. Forms are also available on IBM or MAC diskettes. (Small Business Library Series).

Inc. Yourself: How to Profit by Setting Up Your Own Corporation. Judith H. McQuown. Career Press, Inc. • 2002. $27.99. 10th revised edition. Includes information on current tax laws and other legislation affecting small corporations and individuals. Provides a step-by-step guide to forming a corporation.

INTERNET DATABASES
Lexis.com Research System. Lexis-Nexis Group. Phone: 800-227-4908 or (937)865-6800 Fax: (937)865-6909 E-mail: webmaster@prod.lexis-nexis.com • URL: http://www.lexis.com • Fee-based Web site offers extensive searching of a wide variety of legal sources. Additional features include Daily Opinion Service, lexis.com Bookstore, Career Center, CLE Center, Law Schools, and Practice Pages ("Pages specific to areas of specialty").

ONLINE DATABASES
Index to Legal Periodicals and Books (Online). H. W. Wilson Co. • Broad coverage of law journals and books 1981 to date. Monthly updates. Inquire as to online cost and availability.

Management Contents. Gale Cengage Learning. • Covers a wide range of management, financial, marketing, personnel, and administrative topics. About 150 leading business journals are indexed and abstracted from 1974 to date, with monthly updating. Inquire as to online cost and availability.

Wilson Business Abstracts Online. H. W. Wilson Co. • Indexes and abstracts 600 major business periodicals, plus the *Wall Street Journal* and the business section of the *New York Times.* Indexing is from 1982, abstracting from 1990, with the two newspapers included from 1993. Updated weekly. Inquire as to online cost and availability. (*Business Periodicals Index* without abstracts is also available online.).

OTHER SOURCES
Formation and Financing of Emerging Companies. Daniel E. O'Connor and others. Glasser Legalworks. • Looseleaf. $225.00, including CD-ROM version. Periodic Supplementation. Covers incorporation, bylaws, indemnification, intellectual property, financing sources, venture capital, due diligence, bridge loans, investor rights, compliance, and other legal issues associated with company formation. (Emerging Growth Companies Series.).

How to Form Your Own Corporation Without a Lawyer for Under $75.00. Ted Nicholas and Sean P. Melvin. Dearborn Trade Publishing, A Kaplan Professional Co. • 1999. $19.95. 26th edition.

Start-Up and Emerging Companies: Planning, Financing, and Operating the Successful Business, with Forms on Disk. American Lawyer Media, Inc. • Looseleaf. $289.00. Two volumes. Updated as needed. Covers a wide variety of business and legal topics relating to new enterprises. Provides information on venture financing, formation of corporations, tax laws, limited liability companies, employee benefits, contracts, and accounting. Includes a CD-ROM containing more than 75 sample legal forms, clauses, agreements, organizational resolutions, and checklists. (Law Journal Press).

INDEPENDENT SCHOOLS

See: PRIVATE SCHOOLS

INDEX TRADING

See: STOCK INDEX TRADING

INDEXING

See also: FILES AND FILING (DOCUMENTS)

GENERAL WORKS
The Amazing Internet Challenge: How Leading Projects Use Library Skills to Organize the Web. Amy T. Wells and others. American Library Association. • 1999. $45.00. Presents profiles of 12 digital libraries, such as the Agriculture Network Information Center and the Social Science Information Gateway. Emphasis is on how online indexes were created.

Explorations in Indexing and Abstracting: Pointing, Virtue, and Power. Brian C. O'Connor. Libraries Unlimited, Inc. • 1996. $40.00. Presents a philosophy of indexing. (Library and Information Science Text Series).

Introduction to Indexing and Abstracting. Donald B. Cleveland and Ana D. Cleveland. Libraries Unlimited. • 2000. $45.00. Third edition. Covers a wide variety of topics relating to indexing, including new developments and career possibilities. Includes a bibliography and a glossary.

BIBLIOGRAPHIES
Can You Recommend a Good Book on Indexing?. Bella H. Weinberg. Information Today, Inc. • 1998. $39.50. Contains reviews of books on indexing, classified of general works, theory, book indexing, databases, thesauri, and computer-assisted (automatic) indexing. (CyberAge Books).

CD-ROM DATABASES
LISA Plus. Available from Cambridge Scientific Abstracts (CSA). • Quarterly. $2,000.00 per year. CD-ROM version of Library Information and Science Abstracts, providing abstracting and indexing of the world's library and information science literature, 1969 to date. Contains more than 180,000 citations.

DIRECTORIES
Indexer Locater. American Society of Indexers, Inc. • Annual. Members, $10.00; non-members, $15.00. Lists over 200 free-lance indexers in the U. S. and their subject specialties. Formerly *Register of Indexers.*

ENCYCLOPEDIAS AND DICTIONARIES
Glossary of Terminology in Abstracting, Classification, Indexing, and Thesaurus Construction. Hans

H. Wellisch. Information Today, Inc. • 2000. $20.00. Second edition. Published in conjunction with the American Society of Indexers (ASI). In addition to terms related to indexing, includes terms for the most common types of documents and their parts.

HANDBOOKS AND MANUALS

Beyond Book Indexing: How to Get Started in Web Indexing, Embedded Indexing, and Other Computer-Based Media. Information Today, Inc. • 1999. $31.25. Published for the American Society of Indexers. Contains 12 chapters written by professional indexers. Part one discusses making an index by marking items in an electronic document (embedded indexing); part two is on indexing to make Web pages more accessible; part three covers CD-ROM and multimedia indexing; part four provides career and promotional advice for professionals in the field. Includes an index by Janet Perlman and a glossary.

Indexer's Guide to the Internet. Lori Lathrop. Information Today, Inc. • 1999. $31.25. Second edition. Published in conjunction with the American Society of Indexers (ASI). Includes advice on useful Web sites, service providers, Web site design, and the use of search engines.

Indexing and Abstracting in Theory and Practice. F. Wilfrid Lancaster. University of Illinois at Urbana-Champaign. • 1998. $47.50. Second revised edition. Includes indexing and abstracting exercises.

Indexing from A to Z. Hans H. Wellisch. H. W. Wilson Co. • 1996. $60.00. Second enlarged revised edition. A practical guide to the indexing of books, periodicals, and non-print materials. Covers such technical topics as exhaustivity, specificity, thesauri, and keywords, and such mundane topics as contracts and fees.

Indexing Specialties: Law. Peter Kendrick and Enid L. Zafran, editors. Information Today, Inc. • 2001. $35.00. Published in conjunction with the American Society of Indexers (ASI). Includes chapters by professional legal indexers on legal cases, statutory materials, new methodologies, careers in legal indexing, and related topics.

Indexing Specialties: Medicine. L. Pilar Wyman, editor. Information Today, Inc. • 1999. $35.00. Published in conjunction with the American Society of Indexers (ASI). Includes chapters by professional medical indexers on book indexing, database indexing, reviews of published indexes, and details of such specialties as nutrition, nursing, and general medicine.

Indexing Specialties: Psychology. Becky Hornyak, editor. Information Today, Inc. • 2002. $25.00. Published in conjunction with the American Society of Indexers (ASI). Contains articles written by specialists in the area of "indexing textbooks and books aimed at clinical practitioners in the field of psychology." Includes an annotated bibliography.

Indexing: The Manual of Good Practice. Pat Booth. Available from Gale Cengage Learning. • 2001. $99.00. Published by K. G. Saur. Covers indexing of books, serials, graphic images, and audio sources, in addition to providing a discussion of the principles of effective indexing.

Marketing Your Indexing Services. Anne Leach, editor. Information Today, Inc. • 1998. $20.00. Second edition. Published in conjunction with the American Society of Indexers (ASI). Provides a collection of useful articles from *Key Words*, the newsletter of the American Society of Indexers.

Running an Indexing Business. Janet Perlman, editor. Information Today, Inc. • 2001. $31.25. Published in conjunction with the American Society of Indexers (ASI). Experienced indexers provide advice on fees, proposals, subcontractors, taxes, and other business matters.

Software for Indexing. Sandi Schroeder, editor. Information Today, Inc. • 2003. $35.00. Published in conjunction with the American Society of Index-

ers (ASI). Material by professional indexers covers dedicated indexing programs, embedded software, online indexing, Web indexing, database software, customized software, automatic indexing, and other indexing software topics.

Starting an Indexing Business. Enid L. Zafran, editor. Information Today, Inc. • 2000. $30.00. Third edition. Published in conjunction with the American Society of Indexers (ASI). Covers fees, contractual forms, indexing as a business in the home, publisher expectations, career concerns, and related topics.

Subject Indexing: An Introductory Guide. Trudi Bellardo. Special Libraries Association. • 1991. $85.00. A self-study guide to creating subject indices for a variety of materials and formats.

ONLINE DATABASES

LISA: Library and Information Science Abstracts. Available from Cambridge Scientific Abstracts (CSA). • Provides abstracting and indexing of the world's library and information science literature, 1969 to date. Covers more than 440 periodicals from 68 countries. Updating is biweekly. Inquire as to online cost and availability.

PERIODICALS AND NEWSLETTERS

The Indexer: The International Journal of Indexing. American Society of Indexers. • Semiannual. Free to members; non-members, $65.00 per year. Devoted specifically to all aspects of indexing.

Keywords. SPSS Inc. • Description: Intended for users of SPSS, Inc. computer software. Offers advice and technical information on using SPSS products and carries data on new products. Recurring features include training schedules and publications ordering information.

TRADE/PROFESSIONAL ASSOCIATIONS

American Society of Indexers. 10200 W. 44th Ave., Suite 304, Wheat Ridge, CO 80033. Phone: (303)463-2887 Fax: (303)422-8894 E-mail: info@asindexing.org • URL: http://www.asindexing.org • Affiliated with the American Library Association, the American Society for Information Science, and other organizations.

National Federation of Abstracting and Information Services. 1518 Walnut St., Suite 307, Philadelphia, PA 19102-3403. Phone: (215)893-1561 Fax: (215)893-1564 E-mail: nfais@nfais.org • URL: http://www.nfais.org • Formerly National Federation of Abstracting and Indexing Services.

Society of Indexers. Blades Enterprise, John St., Sheffield S2 4SU, England. Phone: 44 114 2922350 Fax: 44 114 2922351 E-mail: admin@indexers.org.uk • URL: http://www.socind.demon.co.uk.

INDICATORS, ECONOMIC

See: ECONOMIC INDICATORS

INDIVIDUAL RETIREMENT ACCOUNTS

GENERAL WORKS

Fundamentals of Employee Benefit Programs. Employee Benefit Research Institute. • 1996. $49.95. Fifth edition. Provides basic explanation of employee benefit programs in both the private and public sectors, including health insurance, pension plans, retirement planning, social security, and long-term care insurance.

Vanguard Retirement Investing Guide: Charting Your Course to a Secure Retirement. McGraw-Hill. • 1995. $24.95. Second edition. Covers saving and investing for future retirement. Topics include goal setting, investment fundamentals, mutual funds, asset allocation, defined contribution retirement savings plans, social security, and retirement savings

strategies. Includes glossary and worksheet for retirement saving.

HANDBOOKS AND MANUALS

Estate Plan Book 2000. William S. Moore. American Institute for Economic Research. • 2000. $10.00. Revision of 1997 edition. Part one: "Basic Estate Planning." Part two: "Reducing Taxes on the Disposition of Your Estate." Part three: "Putting it All Together: Examples of Estate Plans." Provides succinct information on wills, trusts, tax planning, and gifts. (Economic Education Bulletin.).

How to Build Wealth with Tax-Sheltered Investments. Kerry Anne Lynch. American Institute for Economic Research. • 2000. $6.00. Provides practical information on conservative tax shelters, including defined-contribution pension plans, individual retirement accounts, Keogh plans, U. S. savings bonds, municipal bonds, and various kinds of annuities: deferred, variable-rate, immediate, and foreign-currency. (Economic Education Bulletin.).

Individual Retirement Account Answer Book. Donald R. Levy and others. Aspen Publishers, Inc. • 2002. $195.00. Ninth edition. Periodic supplementation available. Questions and answers include information about contributions, distributions, rollovers, Roth IRAs, SIMPLE IRAs (Savings Incentive Match Plans for Employees), Education IRAs, and SEPs (Simplified Employee Pension plans). Chapters are provided on retirement planning, estate planning, and tax planning.

IRA Basics. The Institute of Financial Education. • 1997. $34.95. Seventh edition. A guide for bank personnel.

The New Working Woman's Guide to Retirement Planning: Saving and Investing Now for a Secure Future. Martha P. Patterson. University of Pennsylvania Press. • 1999. $19.95. Second edition. Provides retirement advice for employed women, including information on various kinds of IRAs, cash balance and other pension plans, 401(k) plans, and social security. Four case studies are provided to illustrate retirement planning at specific life and career stages.

Retirement Planning Guide. Sidney Kess and Barbara Weltman. CCH, Inc. • 2000. $49.00. Second edition. Presents an overview for attorneys, accountants, and other professionals of the various concepts involved in retirement planning. Includes checklists, tables, forms, and study questions.

U. S. Master Pension Guide. CCH, Inc. • Annual. $56.95. Explains IRS rules and regulations applying to 401(k) plans, 403(k) plans, ESOPs (employee stock ownership plans), IRAs, SEPs (simplified employee pension plans), Keogh plans, and non-qualified plans.

INTERNET DATABASES

Internal Revenue Service IRS.gov. Internal Revenue Service. Phone: 800-829-1040 or (202)622-5000 Fax: (202)622-5844 • URL: http://www.irs.gov • Web site provides a wide variety of tax information, including IRS forms and publications. Searching is available. Fees: Free.

Small Business Retirement Savings Advisor. U. S. Department of Labor. Phone: (202)219-8921 • URL: http://www.dol.gov/elaws/pwbaplan.htm • Web site provides "answers to a variety of commonly asked questions about retirement saving options for small business employers." Includes a comparison chart and detailed descriptions of various plans: 401(k), SEP-IRA, SIMPLE-IRA, Payroll Deduction IRA, Keogh Profit-Sharing, Keogh Money Purchase, and Defined Benefit. Searching is offered. Fees: Free.

PERIODICALS AND NEWSLETTERS

Financial Planning: The Magazine for Financial Service Professionals. Thomson Media. • Monthly. $79.00 per year. Edited for independent financial planners and insurance agents. Covers retirement planning, estate planning, tax planning, and insurance, including long-term healthcare considerations. Special features include a Retirement Planning Issue, Mutual Fund Performance Survey, and Variable Life and Annuity Survey.

The IRA Reporter (Individual Retirement Account). Universal Pensions, Inc. • Monthly. $115.00 per year. Newsletter. Edited for financial planners. Provides information on the rules and regulations of individual retirement accounts (IRAs).

On Wall Street. Thomson Media. • Monthly. $96.00 per year. Edited for securities dealers. Includes articles on financial planning, retirement planning, variable annuities, and money management, with special coverage of 401(k) plans and IRAs.

Retirement Plans Bulletin: Practical Explanations for the IRA and Retirement Plan Professional. Universal Pensions, Inc. • Monthly. $99.00 per year. Newsletter. Provides information on the rules and regulations governing qualified (tax-deferred) retirement plans.

RESEARCH CENTERS AND INSTITUTES

Employee Benefit Research Institute. Employee Benefit Research Institute. 1100 13 St. NW, Ste. 878, Washington, DC 20005. Phone: (202)659-0670 Fax: (202)775-6312 E-mail: salisbury@ebri.org • URL: http://www.ebri.org • Employee benefits in the public and private sectors, including studies on individual retirement accounts, retirement income, flexible benefits, financing health care for the elderly, health care costs, long-term care, employee benefits and federal tax policy, social security, changing benefits, and government regulation of employee benefit plans.

STATISTICS SOURCES

EBRI's Databook on Employee Benefits: What is the Promise?. Ken McDonnell and others. Employee Benefit Research Institute. • 1997 $99.00. Fourth edition. Contains more than 350 tables and charts presenting data on employee benefits in the U. S., including pensions, health insurance, social security, and medicare. Includes a glossary of employee benefit terms.

INDUSTRIAL ADVERTISING

See also: ADVERTISING; INDUSTRIAL MARKETING

CD-ROM DATABASES

Advertiser and Agency Red Books Plus. National Register Publishing. • Quarterly. $1,295.00 per year. The CD-ROM version of *Standard Directory of Advertisers, Standard Directory of Advertising Agencies,* and *Standard Directory of International Advertisers and Agencies.*

DIRECTORIES

Business Marketing Association and Resource Directory. Business Marketing Association. • Annual. $100.00. Lists professionals in business and industrial advertising and marketing. Available online.

SRDS Business Publication Advertising Source. SRDS. • Monthly. $714.00 per year. Issued in three parts: (1) U. S. Business Publications, (2) U. S. Healthcare Publications, and (3) International Publications. Provides detailed advertising rates, profiles of editorial content, management names, "Multiple Publications Publishers," circulation data, and other trade journal information. Formerly *Business Publication Advertising Source.*

Standard Directory of Advertisers: Business Classifications Edition. National Register Publishing. • Annual $799.00; with supplements, $899.00. Arranged by product or service. Provides information on the advertising programs of over 14,000 companies, including advertising/marketing person-

nel and the names of advertising agencies used.

Standard Directory of Advertisers: Geographic Edition. National Register Publishing. • Annual $659.00; with supplements, $759.00. Arranged geographically by state. Provides information on the advertising programs of over 20,000 companies, including advertising/marketing personnel and the names of advertising agencies used. Includes *Advertiser/Agency* supplement.

ENCYCLOPEDIAS AND DICTIONARIES

Advertising Age Encyclopedia of Advertising. John McDonough and others, editors. Fitzroy Dearborn Publishers. • 2002. $385.00. Three volumes. Contains 600 entries in alphabetical order covering a wide variety of advertising and market research topics. Includes bibliographies.

HANDBOOKS AND MANUALS

Business to Business Advertising: A Marketing Management Approach. Charles Patti and others. McGraw-Hill. • 1994. $39.95. (NTC Business Books Series).

PERIODICALS AND NEWSLETTERS

Adweek Magazines' Technology Marketing. VNU Business Media. • Monthly. $55.00 per year. Edited for marketing executives in high technology industries. Covers both advertising and marketing. Formerly *MC Technology Marketing Intelligence.*

B to B: The Magazine for Marketing and E-Commerce Strategists. Crain Communications, Inc. • 26 times a year. $59.00 per year. Formerly *Advertising Age's Business Marketing.*

TRADE/PROFESSIONAL ASSOCIATIONS

Association of National Advertisers. 708 3rd Ave., New York, NY 10017-4270. Phone: (212)697-5950 Fax: (212)661-8057 • URL: http://www.ana.net.

Business Market Association. 4131 N. Central Expy., Ste. 720, Dallas, TX 75204. Phone: 800-664-4262 or (312)822-0005 Fax: (312)822-0054 E-mail: rh@udel.edu • URL: http://www.marketing.org • Small- and medium-sized businesses. Works to bring large corporate lobbying and benefits to companies who do not have the workforce to achieve those benefits.

INDUSTRIAL ARBITRATION

See: ARBITRATION; INDUSTRIAL RELATIONS

INDUSTRIAL COATINGS

See also: CORROSION CONTROL INDUSTRY; PAINT AND PAINTING

GENERAL WORKS

The Chemistry and Physics of Coatings. Alastair R. Marrion, editor. Springer-Verlag. • 1994. $46.95. Published by The Royal Society of Chemistry. Provides an overview of paint science and technology, including environmental considerations.

ABSTRACTS AND INDEXES

Applied Science and Technology Index. H. W. Wilson Co. • 11 times a year. Quarterly and annual cumulations. Price varies. Indexes a wide variety of English language technical, industrial, and engineering periodicals.

Corrosion Abstracts: Abstracts of the World's Literature on Corrosion and Corrosion Mitigation. National Association of Corrosion Engineers. CSA. • Bimonthly. Individuals, $240.00 per year; institutions, $340.00 per year. Includes print and online editions. Provides abstracts of the worldwide literature of corrosion and corrosion control. Also available on CD-ROM.

CPI Digest: Key to World Literature Serving the Coatings, Plastics, Fibers, Adhesives, and Related Industries (Chemical Process Industries). CPI Information Services. • Monthly. $397.00 per year. Abstracts of business and technical articles for polymer-based, chemical process industries. Includes a monthly list of relevant U. S. patents. International coverage.

Current Contents: Engineering, Computing and Technology. Thomson/ISI. • Weekly. $730.00 per year. Reproductions of contents pages of technical journals. Includes *Author Index, Address Directory, Current Book Contents* and *Title Word Index.* Formerly *Current Contents: Engineering, Technology and Applied Sciences.*

NTIS Alerts: Materials Sciences. National Technical Information Service. • Semimonthly. $220.00 per year. Provides descriptions of government-sponsored research reports and software, with ordering information. Covers ceramics, glass, coatings, composite materials, alloys, plastics, wood, paper, adhesives, fibers, lubricants, and related subjects. Formerly *Abstract Newsletter.*

Surface Finishing Technology. ASM International. • Monthly. Members, $130.00 per year; non-members, $160.00 per year. Provides abstracts of the international literature of metallic and nonmetallic industrial coating and finishing. Formerly *Cleaning-Finishing-Coating Digest.*

DIRECTORIES

Federation of Societies for Coatings Technology: Year Book and Membership Directory. Federation of Societies for Coatings Technology. • Annual. $150.00. About 7,500 chemists, technicians, and supervisory production personnel in the decorative and protective coatings industry who are members of the 27 constituent societies of the federation.

Industrial Paint and Powder Buyer's Guide. Business News Publishing. • Annual. Free to qualified personnel; others, $15.00. List of about 2,000 manufacturers of finishing and formulating products. Formerly *Industrial Finishing Buyer's Guide.*

McCutcheon's Functional Materials Volumes 2. MC Publishing Co. • Annual. $170.00. Edited for product development, quality control and research and development chemists.

Thomas Register of American Manufacturers. Thomas Publishing Co., Inc. • Annual. $149.00. 34 volumes. A three-part system offering information on a wide variety of industrial equipment and supplies. Lists more than 151,000 industrial product and services companies.

HANDBOOKS AND MANUALS

Industrial Coatings: Properties, Applications, Quality, and Environmental Compliance: Proceedings of ASM and ESD Conference. ASM International. • 1992. $90.00.

Maintenance Engineering Handbook. Lindley R. Higgins and R. Keith Mobley. McGraw-Hill. • 2001. $150.00. Sixth edition. Contains about 60 chapters by various authors in 12 major sections covering all elements of industrial and plant maintenance.

Uhlig's Corrosion Handbook. R. Winston Revie and Herbert H. Uhlig, editors. John Wiley and Sons, Inc. • 2000. $248.00. Second edition. Covers the basics of corrosion science and the use of modern materials for corrosion control. (Electrochemical Society Series, vol. 39).

ONLINE DATABASES

Applied Science and Technology Index Online. H. W. Wilson Co. • Provides online indexing of 500 major scientific, technical, industrial, and engineering periodicals. Time period is 1983 to date. Monthly updates. Inquire as to online cost and availability.

PROMT: Predicasts Overview of Markets and Technology. Gale Cengage Learning. • Companies, products, applied technologies and markets. U.S. and international literature coverage, 1972 to date. Inquire as to online cost and availability. Provides abstracts from more than 1,600 publications. Weekly updates.

Thomas Register Online. Thomas Publishing Co., Inc. • Provides concise information on approximately 194,000 U. S. companies, mainly manufacturers, with over 50,000 product classifications. Indexes over 115,000 trade names. Information is updated semiannually. Inquire as to online cost and availability.

World Surface Coatings Abstracts [Online]. Paint Research Association of Great Britain. • Indexing and abstracting of the literature of paint and surface coatings, 1976 to present. Monthly updates. Inquire as to online cost and availability.

PERIODICALS AND NEWSLETTERS

Advanced Coatings and Surface Technology. Technical Insights. • Institutions. Monthly. $650.00 per year. Newsletter on technical developments relating to industrial coatings.

Corrosion: Journal of Science and Engineering. National Association of Corrosion Engineers. NACE International. • Monthly. Individuals, $160.00 per year; institutions, $290.00 per year. Covers corrosion control science, theory, engineering, and practice.

eCoatings. National Paint & Coatings Association. • Description: Covers legislative, regulatory, and judicial issues affecting the paint and coatings industry. Recurring features include news of research, a calendar of events, notices of publications available, reports of meetings, and editorials.

Industrial Equipment News. Thomas Publishing Co., LLC. • Monthly. $65.00 per year. What's new in equipment, parts and materials.

Industrial Paint and Powder: Coatings Manufacturing and Application. Reed Business Information. • Monthly. $72.90 per year. Supplement available, *Annual Buyer's Guide.* Formerly *Industrial Finishing.*

JCT:Journal of Coatings Technology. Federation of Societies for Coatings Technology. • Monthly. Free to members; non-members, $150.00 per year.

Journal of Industrial Textiles. Sage Publications. • Quarterly. Institutions, $708.00 per year. Includes print and online editions. Formerly *Journal of Coated Fabrics.*

Materials Performance: Articles on Corrosion Science and Engineering Solutions for Corrosion Problems. National Association of Corrosion Engineers. NACE International. • Monthly. Individuals, $115.00 per year; institutions, $205.00 per year. Covers the protection and performance of materials in corrosive environments. Includes information on new materials and industrial coatings.

Modern Paint and Coatings. Chemical Week Associates. • Monthly. $52.00 per year.

New Equipment Digest. Penton Media, Inc. • Monthly. Free to qualified personnel; others, $60.00 per year. Formerly *Material Handling Engineering.*

New Equipment Reporter: New Products Industrial News. De Roche Publications. • Monthly. Controlled circulation.

Paint and Coatings Industry. Business News Publishing Co. • Monthly. Free to members, non-members, $55.00 per year. Includes annual *Raw Material* and *Equipment Directory and Buyers Guide.*

RESEARCH CENTERS AND INSTITUTES

Emulsion Polymers Institute. Lehigh University, Iacocca Hall, 111 Research Dr., Bethlehem, PA 18015. Phone: (610)758-3590 Fax: (610)758-5880 E-mail: mse0@lehigh.edu • URL: http://www.lehigh.edu/ •

Includes latex paint research.

Fontana Corrosion Center. Ohio State University, 477 Watts Halls, 2041 College Rd., Columbus, OH 43210. Phone: (614)292-9857 Fax: (614)292-9857 E-mail: fcc@osu.edu/ • URL: http://www.mse.eng.ohio-state.edu • Research areas include metal coatings and corrosion of alloys.

International Coatings and Formulation Institute. University of Southern Mississippi, School of Polymers and High Performance Materials, P.O. Box 10037, Hattiesburg, MS 39406-0037. Phone: (601)266-4080 Fax: (601)266-5880 E-mail: shelby.f.thames@usm.edu • URL: http://www.psrc.usm.edu/icfi.

STATISTICS SOURCES

Paint, Varnish, and Lacquer. U. S. Bureau of the Census. • Quarterly and annual. Provides data on shipments: value, quantity, imports, and exports. Includes paint, varnish, lacquer, product finishes, and special purpose coatings. (Current Industrial Reports, MQ-28F.).

U. S. Industry and Trade Outlook. Available from National Technical Information Service. • Annual. $69.95. Produced by the International Trade Administration, U. S. Department of Commerce, in a "public-private" partnership with DRI/McGraw-Hill and Standard & Poor's. Provides basic data, outlook for the current year, and "Long-Term Prospects" (five-year projections) for a wide variety of products and services. Includes high technology industries. Formerly *U. S. Industrial Outlook.*

TRADE/PROFESSIONAL ASSOCIATIONS

American Electroplaters and Surface Finishers Society. 12644 Research Parkway, Orlando, FL 32826-3298. Phone: (407)281-6441 Fax: (407)281-6446 E-mail: aesf@aesf.org • URL: http://www.aesf.org.

Association for Finishing Processes of the Society of Manufacturing Engineers. One SME Dr., Dearborn, MI 48121. Phone: 800-733-4863 or (313)271-1500 Fax: (313)240-8255 E-mail: johnbar@sme.org • URL: http://www.sme.org.

Association of Industrial Metallizers, Coaters and Laminators. 2166 Gold Hill Rd, Fort Mill, SC 29708. Phone: (803)802-7820 Fax: (803)802-7821 E-mail: aimcal@aimcal.org • URL: http://www.aimcal.org.

Chemical Coaters Association International. PO Box 54316, Cincinnati, OH 45254. Phone: 800-926-2848 or (513)624-6767 Fax: (513)624-0601 E-mail: aygoyer@one.net • URL: http://www.ccaiweb.com • Industrial users of organic finishing systems; suppliers of chemicals, equipment, and paints. Works toward the improvement of decorative, functional, and performance standards of chemical coatings. Encourages members to continue improvements in application technology. Provides coating industry with representation to public authorities and government agencies. Sponsors research and educational programs to control environmental pollution. Maintains placement service. Provides speaker's bureau.

Federation of Societies for Coatings Technology. 492 Norristown Rd., Blue Bell, PA 19422-2350. Phone: (610)940-0777 Fax: (610)940-0292 E-mail: fsct@coatingstech.org • URL: http://ww.coatingstech.org • Formerly Federation of Societies for Paint Technology.

NACE International: The Corrosion Society. 1440 S Creek Dr., Houston, TX 77084-4906. Phone: 800-797-6223 or (281)228-6200 Fax: (281)228-6300 E-mail: firstservice@nace.org • URL: http://www.nace.org • Serves as professional technical society dedicated to reducing the economic impact of corrosion, promoting public safety, and protecting the environment by advancing the knowledge of corrosion engineering and science. Conducts programs for technical training, sponsors technical confer-

ences, and produces standards, publications, and software. Maintains certification program for engineers, technicians, and coating inspectors.

National Association of Metal Finishers. 21165 Whitfield Pl., Ste. 105, Potomac Falls, VA 20165. Phone: (703)433-2522 Fax: (703)433-0369 E-mail: namf@erols.com • URL: http://www.namf.org • Members are management personnel of metal and plastic finishing companies. Finishing includes plating, coating, polishing, rustproofing, and other processes.

National Paint and Coatings Association. 1500 Rhode Island Ave., N.W., Washington, DC 20005-5597. Phone: (202)462-6272 Fax: (202)462-8549 E-mail: npca@paint.org • URL: http://www.paint.org • Formerly National Paint, Varnish and Lacquer Association.

Powder Coating Institute. 2121 Eisenhower Ave., Ste. 401, Alexandria, VA 22314. Phone: 800-988-COAT or (703)684-1770 Fax: (703)684-1771 E-mail: pci-info@powdercoating.org • URL: http://www.powdercoating.org • Individuals and businesses that manufacture, sell, or develop powder coating materials and equipment. Promotes the application and use of powder coating technology among industrial finishers; disseminates information to both consumers and the industry on the value and performance of powder coating; supports educational programs in the industrial coating/finishing field; updates members, governmental departments, and regulatory agencies on the activities and developments concerning the manufacture, application, and proper handling of powder coatings. Presents technical papers at conferences of related organizations and prepares articles for the media on the powder coating industry.

Society of Vacuum Coaters. 71 Pinon Hill Place N.E., Albuquerque, NM 87122-1914. Phone: (505)856-7188 Fax: (505)856-6716 E-mail: svcinfo@svc.org • URL: http://www.svc.org.

INDUSTRIAL CONTROLS

See: CONTROL EQUIPMENT INDUSTRY

INDUSTRIAL COUNSELING

See: PERSONNEL MANAGEMENT; VOCATIONAL GUIDANCE

INDUSTRIAL DESIGN

See: DESIGN IN INDUSTRY

INDUSTRIAL DEVELOPMENT

See also: DEVELOPING AREAS; ECONOMIC DEVELOPMENT; LOCATION OF INDUSTRY

DIRECTORIES

Site Selection. Conway Data, Inc. • Bimonthly. Six volumes, $22.00 per volume. $85.00 per set. Each of the six issues per year is a separate directory: *Geo-Corporate* (facility planners), *Geo-Economic* (area development officials), *Geo-Labor* (labor force data), *Geo-Life* (quality of life information), *GeoPolitical* (government agencies), and *Geo-Sites* (industrial/office parks). Formerly *Site Selection and Industrial Development.*

PERIODICALS AND NEWSLETTERS

Area Development Sites and Facility Planning: The Executive Magazine of Sites and Facility Planning. Halcyon Business Publications, Inc. • Monthly. Free to the business trade; others, $65.00 per year. Site selection, facility planning, and plant relocation. Formerly *Area Development Magazines.*

Economic Development Monitor. Whitaker Newsletters, Inc. • Biweekly. $247.00 per year. Newsletter. Covers the news of U. S. economic and industrial development, including legislation, regulation, planning, and financing.

Plants, Sites, and Parks. Reed Business Information. • Seven times a year. Free to qualified personnel; others, $43.90 per year. Covers economic development, site location, industrial parks, and industrial development programs.

Sales Prospector. Sales Prospector. • Description: Reports on planned construction of new plants, plant additions, shopping centers, commercial and institutional buildings, relocations, mergers, acquisitions, and government contracts to provide sales leads for salesmen and other businessmen. Provides name of company, location of construction, purpose, approximate dates of start and completion, name of contractor, architect, or developer, and estimate of amount of investment. Published in 28 separate editions each month for different areas of the country, plus two editions for Canada.

RESEARCH CENTERS AND INSTITUTES

Center for International Policy. 1755 Massachusetts Ave., N. W., Ste. 550, Washington, DC 20036. Phone: (202)232-3317 Fax: (202)232-3440 E-mail: cip@ciponline.org • URL: http://www.ciponline.org • Research subjects include the International Monetary Fund, the World Bank, and other international financial institutions. Analyzes the impact of policies on social and economic conditions in developing countries.

Urban Land Institute. Urban Land Institute. 1025 Thomas Jefferson St. NW, Ste. 500 W, Washington, DC 20007. Phone: (202)624-7000 Fax: (202)624-7140 E-mail: customerservice@uli.org • URL: http://www.uli.org • Urban land use policy, planning, and development issues, including studies on central city problems, industrial development, new community development, residential developments of all types, taxation, smart growth, shopping center development and economics, metropolitan and urbanized area growth and development, mixed use development, and environmental factors affecting development.

STATISTICS SOURCES

Handbook of International Economic Statistics. Available from National Technical Information Service. • Annual. $40.00. Prepared by U. S. Central Intelligence Agency. Provides basic statistics for comparing worldwide economic performance, with an emphasis on Europe, including Eastern Europe.

Industrial Commodity Statistics Yearbook. United Nations Dept. of Economic and Social Affairs. United Nations Publications. • Annual.

TRADE/PROFESSIONAL ASSOCIATIONS

CoreNet Global. 260 Peachtree St., Ste. 1500, Atlanta, GA 30303-1237. Phone: 800-726-8111 or (404)589-3200 Fax: (404)589-3201 E-mail: mark.tamburro@nokia.com • URL: http://www.corenetglobal.org • Executives, attorneys, real estate department heads, architects, engineers, analysts, researchers, and anyone responsible for the management, administration, and operation of national and regional real estate departments of national and international corporations. Encourages professionalism within corporate real estate through education and communication; protects the interests of corporate realty in dealing with adversaries, public or private; maintains contact with other real estate organizations; publicizes the availability of fully qualified members to the job market. Conducts seminars, including concentrated workshops on the corporate real estate field. Compiles statistics; spon-

sors competitions; maintains biographical archives and placement service.

International Economic Development Council. 734 15th St. NW, Ste. 900, Washington, DC 20005. Phone: (202)223-7800 Fax: (202)223-4745 E-mail: cziegler@iedconline.org • URL: http://www.iedconline.org • Works to help economic development professionals improve the quality of life in their communities. Represents all levels of government, academia, and private industry; provides a broad range of member services including research, advisory services, conferences, professional certification, professional development, publications, legislative tracking and more.

National Association of Industrial and Office Properties. 2201 Cooperative Way, 3rd Fl., Herndon, VA 20171. Phone: 800-666-6780 or (703)904-7100 Fax: (703)904-7942 E-mail: naiop@naiop.org • URL: http://www.naiop.org • Members are owners and developers of business, industrial, office, and retail properties. Formerly NAIOP - The Association of Commercial Real Estate.

INDUSTRIAL DIAMONDS

ABSTRACTS AND INDEXES

Industrial Diamond Review. De Beers Industrial Diamond Div. • Quarterly. Free to qualified personnel. Incorporating *Industrial Diamond Abstracts.*

STATISTICS SOURCES

Mineral Commodity Summaries. Available from U. S. Government Printing Office. • Annual. $26.00. Published by the U. S. Geological Survey, Department of the Interior (http://www.usgs.gov). Contains detailed, five-year data for about 90 nonfuel minerals. Covers a wide range of statistics, including production, imports, exports, consumption, reserves, prices, tariff information, and industry employment. (Two pages are devoted to each mineral.).

TRADE/PROFESSIONAL ASSOCIATIONS

Industrial Diamond Association. PO Box 29460, Columbus, OH 43229. Phone: (614)797-2265 Fax: (614)797-2264 E-mail: tkane-ida@insight.rr.com • URL: http://www.superabrasives.org • Represents industrial diamond, CBN, CVD diamond and polycrystalline and other superabrasive manufacturers, toolmakers, end users, contractors, machine tool builders and related suppliers.

INDUSTRIAL DIRECTORIES

See: CATALOGS AND DIRECTORIES

INDUSTRIAL DISPUTES

See: ARBITRATION; STRIKES AND LOCKOUTS

INDUSTRIAL DISTRIBUTION

See: DISTRIBUTION

INDUSTRIAL EFFICIENCY

See: TIME AND MOTION STUDY

INDUSTRIAL ENGINEERING

See also: INDUSTRIAL MANAGEMENT

GENERAL WORKS

Lessons to be Learned Just in Time. James J. Cammarano. Engineering and Management Press. •

1997. $34.95. Discusses the background, theory, and practical application of just-in-time (JIT) inventory control in manufacturing.

ABSTRACTS AND INDEXES

Applied Science and Technology Index. H. W. Wilson Co. • 11 times a year. Quarterly and annual cumulations. Price varies. Indexes a wide variety of English language technical, industrial, and engineering periodicals.

Business Periodicals Index. H. W. Wilson Co. • 11 times a year. Quarterly and annual cumulations. Price varies.

Engineering Index Monthly: Abstracting and Indexing Services Covering Sources ofthe World's Engineering Literature. Engineering Information Inc. • Monthly. Institutions, $5,279.00 per year. Provides indexing and abstracting of the world's engineering and technical literature.

BIBLIOGRAPHIES

Encyclopedia of Physical Science and Engineering Information. Gale Cengage Learning. • 1996. $160.00. Second edition. Includes print, electronic, and other information sources for a wide range of scientific, technical, and engineering topics.

CD-ROM DATABASES

WILSONDISC: Applied Science and Technology Abstracts. H. W. Wilson Co. • Monthly. Includes unlimited access to the online version of *Applied Science and Technology Abstracts* through WILSONLINE. Provides CD-ROM indexing and abstracting of 500 prominent scientific, technical, engineering, and industrial periodicals. Indexing coverage is provided from 1983 to date and abstracting from 1993 to date.

WILSONDISC: Business Periodicals Index. H. W. Wilson Co. • Monthly. Provides CD-ROM indexing of business periodicals from 1982 to date. Price includes online service.

DIRECTORIES

NAEDA Equipment Dealer Buyer's Guide. North American Equipment Dealers Association. • Annual. $28.00. List of manufacturers and suppliers of agricultural, lawn and garden, and light industrial machinery.

ENCYCLOPEDIAS AND DICTIONARIES

Blackwell Encyclopedic Dictionary of Operations Management. Nigel Slack, editor. Blackwell Publishing. • 1997. $130.95. The editor is associated with the University of Warwick, England. Contains definitions of key terms combined with longer articles written by various U. S. & foreign business educators. Includes bibliographies and index. (Blackwell Encyclopedia of Management Series.).

Industrial Engineering Terminology. Institute of Industrial Engineering Staff. McGraw-Hill. • 1992. $80.95. Revised edition.

HANDBOOKS AND MANUALS

Handbook of Industrial Engineering: Technology and Operations Management. Gavriel Salvendy, editor. John Wiley and Sons, Inc. • 2001. $275.00. Third edition.

Handbook of Systems Engineering and Management. Andrew P. Sage and William B. Rouse, editors. John Wiley and Sons, Inc. • 1999. $200.00. Emphasis is on information technology and systems software.

Maynard's Industrial Engineering Handbook. Kjell B. Zandin. McGraw-Hill. • 2001. $150.00. Fifth edition. (Standard Handbooks Series).

Standard Handbook of Plant Engineering. Robert C. Rosaler, editor. McGraw-Hill Professional. • 2002. $125.00. Third edition. (Handbook Series).

ONLINE DATABASES

Applied Science and Technology Index Online. H. W. Wilson Co. • Provides online indexing of 500 major scientific, technical, industrial, and engineering periodicals. Time period is 1983 to date. Monthly updates. Inquire as to online cost and availability.

Wilson Business Abstracts Online. H. W. Wilson Co. • Indexes and abstracts 600 major business periodicals, plus the *Wall Street Journal* and the business section of the *New York Times.* Indexing is from 1982, abstracting from 1990, with the two newspapers included from 1993. Updated weekly. Inquire as to online cost and availability. (*Business Periodicals Index* without abstracts is also available online.).

PERIODICALS AND NEWSLETTERS

Computers and Industrial Engineering: An International Journal. Elsevier. • Eight times a year. Qualified personnel, $83.00 per year; institutions, $2,576.00 per year.

IEE Solutions. Institute of Industrial Engineers. • Monthly. Free to members; non-members, $66.00 per year. Features articles on material handling, computers, quality control, production and inventory control, engineering economics, worker motivation, management strategies, and factory automation. Formerly *Industrial Engineers.*

Manufacturing Computer Solutions: The Management Magazine of Integrated Manufacturing. Findlay Publications Ltd. • Monthly. $88.00 per year.

NAEDA Equipment Dealer. North American Equipment Dealers Association. • Monthly. $40.00 per year. Covers power equipment for farm, outdoor, and industrial use. Formerly *Farm and Power Equipment Dealer.*

Production. Gardner Publications, Inc. • Monthly. $48.00 per year. Covers the latest manufacturing management issues. Discusses the strategic and financial implications of various tecnologies as they impact factory management, quality and competitiveness.

RESEARCH CENTERS AND INSTITUTES

Center for Quality and Productivity Improvement. University of Wisconsin-Madison, 610 N. Walnut St., 575 WARF Bldg., Madison, WI 53705. Phone: (608)263-2520 Fax: (608)263-1425 E-mail: quality@engr.wisc.edu • URL: http://www.engr.wisc.edu/centers/cqpi • Research areas include quality management and industrial engineering.

Engineering and Industrial Experiment Station. University of Florida, College of Engineering, Gainesville, FL 32611. Phone: (352)392-6000 Fax: (352)392-9673 E-mail: johan@eng.ufl.edu • URL: http://www.eng.ufl.edu • Research fields include chemical, civil, electrical, industrial, mechanical, and other types of engineering.

Engineering Dean's Office. University of California at Berkeley, 308 Mclaughin Hall, MC. 1702, Berkeley, CA 94720-1706. Phone: (510)642-7594 Fax: (510)643-8653 E-mail: dma@coe.berkeley.edu • Research fields include civil, electrical, industrial, mechanical, and other types of engineering.

Engineering Experiment Station. Purdue University, West Lafayette, IN 47907. Phone: (765)494-5340 Fax: (765)494-9321 E-mail: richard.j.schwartz@purdue.edu • URL: http://www.ecn.purdue.edu • Research fields include chemical, civil, electrical, industrial, mechanical, and other types of engineering.

STATISTICS SOURCES

United States Census of Service Industries. U.S. Bureau of the Census. • Quinquennial. Various reports available.

TRADE/PROFESSIONAL ASSOCIATIONS

Institute of Industrial Engineers. 3377 Parkway Ln., Ste. 200, Norcross, GA 30092. Phone: 800-494-0460 or (770)449-0460 Fax: (770)441-3295 E-mail: cs@iienet.org • URL: http://www.iienet.org •

Formerly American Institute of Industrial Engineers.

SAVE International. 136 S Keowee St., Dayton, OH 45402. Phone: (937)224-7283 Fax: (937)222-5794 E-mail: info@value-eng.org • URL: http://www.value-eng.org • Value engineers and analysts. Works to promote advancement of value engineering and value analysis and its application to the research, design, development, test, evaluation, engineering, production, purchasing and distribution phases in government, private industry, and commerce. Sponsors competitions.

SOLE-The International Society of Logistics. 8100 Professional Pl., Ste. 111, Hyattsville, MD 20785. Phone: (301)459-8446 Fax: (301)459-1522 E-mail: solehq@sosle.org • URL: http://www.sole.org • Concerned with designing, supplying, and maintaining resources to support objectives, plans, and operations. Formerly Society of Logistics Engineers.

INDUSTRIAL EQUIPMENT INDUSTRY

DIRECTORIES

My Little Salesman Heavy Equipment Catalog; New and Used Equipment Guide. My Little Salesman. • Monthly. $24.95 per year.

Thomas Register of American Manufacturers. Thomas Publishing Co., Inc. • Annual. $149.00. 34 volumes. A three-part system offering information on a wide variety of industrial equipment and supplies. Lists more than 151,000 industrial product and services companies.

ONLINE DATABASES

PROMT: Predicasts Overview of Markets and Technology. Gale Cengage Learning. • Companies, products, applied technologies and markets. U.S. and international literature coverage, 1972 to date. Inquire as to online cost and availability. Provides abstracts from more than 1,600 publications. Weekly updates.

Thomas Register Online. Thomas Publishing Co., Inc. • Provides concise information on approximately 194,000 U. S. companies, mainly manufacturers, with over 50,000 product classifications. Indexes over 115,000 trade names. Information is updated semiannually. Inquire as to online cost and availability.

PERIODICALS AND NEWSLETTERS

IEEE Industry Applications Magazine. Institute of Electrical and Electronics Engineers. • Bimonthly. $190.00 per year. Covers new industrial applications of power conversion, drives, lighting, and control. Emphasis is on the petroleum, chemical, rubber, plastics, textile, and mining industries.

Industrial Distribution: For Industrial Distributors and Their Sales Personnel. Reed Business Information. • Monthly. $109.90 per year.

Industrial Equipment News. Thomas Publishing Co., LLC. • Monthly. $65.00 per year. What's new in equipment, parts and materials.

New Equipment Digest. Penton Media, Inc. • Monthly. Free to qualified personnel; others, $60.00 per year. Formerly *Material Handling Engineering.*

STATISTICS SOURCES

U. S. Industry and Trade Outlook. Available from National Technical Information Service. • Annual. $69.95. Produced by the International Trade Administration, U. S. Department of Commerce, in a "public-private" partnership with DRI/McGraw-Hill and Standard & Poor's. Provides basic data, outlook for the current year, and "Long-Term Prospects" (five-year projections) for a wide variety of products and services. Includes high technology

industries. Formerly *U. S. Industrial Outlook.*

TRADE/PROFESSIONAL ASSOCIATIONS

Industrial Distribution Association. 1277 Lenox Pk. Blvd., Ste. 275, Atlanta, GA 30319. Phone: 877-591-6210 or (404)266-3991 Fax: 877-664-5398 or 877-664-5398 E-mail: idainc@ida-assoc.com • URL: http://www.ida-assoc.org • Distributors of industrial equipment and supplies. Conducts seminars on sales management training, inventory management, purchasing paperwork, industrial marketing, and sales profitability analysis. Maintains speakers' bureau; compiles statistics.

Industrial Supply Manufacturers Association. 1300 Sumner Ave., Cleveland, OH 44115-2851. Phone: (216)241-7333 Fax: (216)241-0105 E-mail: isma@ismaonline.org • URL: http://www.ismaonline.org • Formerly Industrial Supply and Machinery Manufacturers Association.

OTHER SOURCES

Factory Automation-Related Equipment and Accessories. Available from MarketResearch.com. • 2002. $3,850.00. Published by Global Industry Analysts. Provides worldwide market research data, including profiles of major automation equipment and software companies.

Industrial Pumps and Pumping Equipment. Available from MarketResearch.com. • 1997. $1,195.00. Market research report published by Specialists in Business Information. Covers centrifugal, rotary, turbine, reciprocating, and other types of pumps. Presents market data relative to sales growth, shipments, exports, imports, and end-use. Includes company profiles.

INDUSTRIAL EQUIPMENT LEASING

See: RENTAL SERVICES

INDUSTRIAL FABRICS INDUSTRY

See also: NONWOVEN FABRICS INDUSTRY

ABSTRACTS AND INDEXES

Applied Science and Technology Index. H. W. Wilson Co. • 11 times a year. Quarterly and annual cumulations. Price varies. Indexes a wide variety of English language technical, industrial, and engineering periodicals.

Textile Technology Digest. Institute of Textile Technology. • Annual. $535.00. Provides indexing and abstracting of a wide variety of textile technology literature.

CD-ROM DATABASES

Textile Technology Digest [CD-ROM]. Textile Information Center, Institute of Textile Technology. • Quarterly. Provides CD-ROM indexing and abstracting of worldwide journals and monographs in various areas of textile technology, production, and management. Covers 1978 to date.

DIRECTORIES

Davison's Textile Blue Book. Davison Publishing Company L.L.C. • Covers: Over 8,400 companies in the textile industry in the United States, Canada, and Mexico including about 4,400 textile plants. Covers mills, manufacturers, dyers, bleachers, finishers, dealers, importers, exporters, brokers, shippers, and agents for various textiles, fibers, yarns, and cordage. Also includes supplies of equipment, materials and services. Entries include: Company name, address, phone, fax, e-mail, website addresses, names of executives, description of product/service, and trade names. Mill and other production facility listings include data on equipment and capacity.

Industrial Fabric Products Review Buyer's Guide: The Encyclopedia of Industrial Fabrics. Industrial Fabrics Association International. • Annual. $40.00. Includes manufacturers of fabrics, fibers, and end products. Included with subscriptions to *Industrial Fabric Products Review.*

Industrial Fabrics Association International Membership Directory. Industrial Fabrics Association International. • Annual. Free to members; non-members, $40.00.

ENCYCLOPEDIAS AND DICTIONARIES

Textile Terms and Definitions. J.E. McIntyre and Paul N. Daniels, editors. Available from State Mutual Book and Periodical Service Ltd. • 1996. $180.00. 10th edition. Published by the Textile Insitute (UK). Includes more than 1,000 definitions of textile processes, fiber types, and end products. Illustrated.

FINANCIAL RATIOS

Industry Norms and Key Business Ratios. Desk Top Edition. Dun and Bradstreet Corp. • Annual. Five volumes. $475.00 per volume. $1,890.00 per set. Covers over 800 kinds of businesses, arranged by Standard Industrial Classification number. More detailed editions covering longer periods of time are also available.

HANDBOOKS AND MANUALS

Industrial Dyes: Chemistry, Properties, Applications. Klaus Hunger, editor. John Wiley and Sons, Inc. • 2003. $185.00. Covers textile dyeing, nontextile dyeing, functional dyes, and optical brighteners. Includes health and safety aspects and examples of commercially available dyes.

ONLINE DATABASES

Applied Science and Technology Index Online. H. W. Wilson Co. • Provides online indexing of 500 major scientific, technical, industrial, and engineering periodicals. Time period is 1983 to date. Monthly updates. Inquire as to online cost and availability.

Textile Technology Digest [online]. Institute of Textile Technology. • Contains indexing and abstracting of more than 300 worldwide journals and monographs in various areas of textile technology, production, and management. Time period is 1978 to date, with monthly updating. Inquire as to online cost and availability.

World Textiles. Elsevier Science, Inc. • Provides abstracting and indexing from 1970 of worldwide textile literature (periodicals, books, pamphlets, and reports). Includes U. S., European, and British patent information. Updating is monthly. Inquire as to online cost and availability.

PERIODICALS AND NEWSLETTERS

Industrial Fabric Products Review. Industrial Fabrics Association International. • Monthly. $47.00 per year. Includes *Buyers Guide.*

International Textile Bulletin: Nonwovens and Industrial Textiles Edition. ITS Publishing, International Textile Service. • Quarterly. $170.00 per year. Editions in Chinese, English, French, German, Italian and Spanish.

Journal of Industrial Textiles. Sage Publications. • Quarterly. Institutions, $708.00 per year. Includes print and online editions. Formerly *Journal of Coated Fabrics.*

RESEARCH CENTERS AND INSTITUTES

Fibrous Materials Research Center. Drexel University, Dept. of Materials Engineering, 31st and Market St., Philadelphia, PA 19104. Phone: (215)895-1640 Fax: (215)895-6684 E-mail: fko@coe.drexel.edu • URL: http://www.fmac.coe.drexel.edu • Research fields include computer-aided design

of nonwoven fabrics and design curves for industrial fibers.

Institute of Textile Technology. 2551 Ivy Rd., Charlottesville, VA 22903-4614. Phone: (434)296-5511 Fax: (434)296-2957 E-mail: library@itt.edu • URL: http://www.itt.edu.

International Textile Center. Texas Tech University. P.O. Box 45019, Lubbock, TX 79409-5019. Phone: (806)747-3790 Fax: (806)747-3796 E-mail: itc@ttu.edu • URL: http://www.depts.ttu.edu/itc.

Textiles and Materials. Philadelphia University, Schoolhouse Lane and Henry Ave., Philadelphia, PA 19144-5497. Phone: (215)951-2751 Fax: (215)951-2651 E-mail: brooksteind@philau.edu • URL: http://www.philaau.edu/schools • Many research areas, including industrial and nonwoven textiles.

TRI/Princeton. TRI/Princeton. 601 Prospect Ave., PO Box 625, Princeton, NJ 08542. Phone: (609)430-4820 Fax: (609)683-7149 E-mail: info@triprinceton.org • URL: http://www.triprinceton.org • Physics, chemistry, and engineering as related to raw materials, processes, and products of polymer, fiber, and textile systems with special strengths in: surface physics and chemistry; micro and nano structure characterization; fluid flow in porous materials; resins and composites; process-structure-property relationships; human hair chemistry, physics, and mechanics; on-line monitoring of spin finish; dye transport; fabric wear and soiling; modeling of sorption and transport phenomena; and instrument design and development.

STATISTICS SOURCES

Broadwoven Fabrics (Gray). U.S. Bureau of the Census. • Quarterly. Provides statistical data on production, value, shipments, and consumption. Includes woolen and worsted fabrics, tire fabrics, cotton broadwoven fabrics, etc. (Current Industrial Reports, MQ-22T.)

TRADE/PROFESSIONAL ASSOCIATIONS

Industrial Fabrics Association International. 1801 County Rd. B W, Roseville, MN 55113-4061. Phone: 800-225-4324 or (651)222-2508 Fax: (651)631-9334 E-mail: generalinfo@ifai.com • URL: http://www.ifai.com • Fiber producers, weavers, non-woven producers, coaters, laminators, finishers, and producers and manufacturers of canvas and specialty fabric end products in more than 36 countries. Provides technical, marketing, production, governmental and public relations services.

Textile Institute. St. James's Buildings, 1st Fl., 79 Oxford St., Manchester M1 6FQ, United Kingdom. Phone: 44 161 2371188 Fax: 44 161 2361991 E-mail: tiihq@textileinst.org.uk • URL: http://www.texi.org • Companies and individuals in 100 countries involved in management, science, technology, design, information transfer, and marketing of textiles including clothing and footwear. Promotes interests of the textile industry worldwide; serves professional interests of members; confers qualifications and recognizes achievements in research, application of ideas, education, business, and public affairs. Maintains Information Service to collect information relating to textile industrial and economic conditions in different countries and economic sectors.

INDUSTRIAL FASTENERS

See: FASTENER INDUSTRY

INDUSTRIAL HYGIENE

See also: INDUSTRIAL MEDICINE; INDUSTRIAL SAFETY

GENERAL WORKS

Industrial Safety and Health Management. C. Ray Asfahl. Prentice Hall PTR. • 2003. $92.33. Fifth

edition. (Prentice Hall International Industrial and Systems Series).

Principles of Health and Hygiene in the Workplace. Timothy J. Key and Michael A. Mueller. Lewis Publishers. • Date not set. $69.95.

Understanding Toxicology: Chemicals, Their Benefits and Uses. Bruno H. Schiefer and others. CRC Press LLC. • 1997. $39.95. Provides a basic introduction to chemical interactions and toxicology for the general reader.

ABSTRACTS AND INDEXES

Safety and Health at Work. International Labour Office. • Bimonthly. $240.00 per year. Formerly *Occupational Safety and Health Abstracts.*

DIRECTORIES

Industrial Hygiene News Buyer's Guide. Rimbach Publishing, Inc. • Annual. $50.00. Lists about 1,000 manufacturers and suppliers of products, equipment, and services to the occupational health, industrial hygiene, and high-tech safety industry.

ENCYCLOPEDIAS AND DICTIONARIES

Encyclopedia of Occupational Health and Safety. International Labour Organization. • 1998. $990.00. Fourth edition. Four volumes. Includes CD-ROM. Covers safety engineering, industrial medicine, ergonomics, hygiene, epidemiology, toxicology, industrial psychology, and related topics. Includes material related to specific chemical, textile, transport, construction, manufacturing, and other industries. Indexed by subject, chemical name, and author, with a "Directory of Experts.".

Encyclopedia of Occupational Health and Safety. Jeanne M. Stellman. International Labour Office. • 1998. $990.00. Fourth edition. Four volumes. Includes CD-Rom.

Unabridged Dictionary of Occupational and Environmental Safety and Health with CD-ROM. Jeffrey W. Vincoli and Kathryn L. Bazan. Lewis Publishers. • 1999. $89.95.

HANDBOOKS AND MANUALS

Fundamental Principles of Occupational Health and Safety. Benjamin Alli. International Labour Organization. • 2001. $14.95. A practical guide to health and safety policies in the workplace. Covers legal issues, enforcement, health surveillance, protective measures, education, and training. Includes a glossary.

Handbook of Industrial Toxicology. E. R. Plunkett, editor. Chemical Publishing Co., Inc. • 1987. $100.00.

Handbook of Toxic and Hazardous Chemicals and Carcinogens. Marshall Sittig. Noyes Data Corp. • 2001. $495.00. Fourth edition. Two volumes.

Hazardous and Toxic Materials: Safe Handling and Disposal. Howard H. Fawcett, editor. John Wiley and Sons, Inc. • 1988. $160.00. Second edition.

Hazardous Chemicals Desk Reference. Richard J. Lewis. John Wiley and Sons, Inc. • 2002. $185.00. Fifth edition. Summarizes the hazardous properties of about 5,000 chemical substances.

Patty's Industrial Hygiene and Toxicology. Robert L. Harris. John Wiley and Sons, Inc. • 2001. $3,290.00. Fifth edition. Provides broad coverage of environmental factors and stresses affecting the health of workers. Contains detailed information on the effects of specific substances.

INTERNET DATABASES

National Center for Health Statistics: Monitoring the Nation's Health. National Center for Health Statistics, Centers for Disease Control and Preventio. Phone: (301)458-4000 E-mail: nchsquery@cdc.gov • URL: http://www.cdc.gov/nchswww • Web site provides detailed data on diseases, vital statistics, and health care in the U. S. Includes a search facility and links to many other health-related Web sites. "Fastats A to Z" offers quick data on hundreds of topics from Accidents to Work-Loss Days, with links to Comprehensive Data and related sources. Frequent updates. Fees: Free.

ONLINE DATABASES

Embase. Elsevier Science, Inc. • Worldwide medical literature, 1974 to present. Weekly updates. Inquire as to online cost and availability.

Toxline. National Library of Medicine. • Abstracting service covering human and animal toxicity studies, 1965 to present (older studies available in *Toxback* file). Monthly updates. Inquire as to online cost and availability.

PERIODICALS AND NEWSLETTERS

AIHA Journal: Journal for the Science of Occupational and Environmental Health. American Industrial Hygiene Association. • Bimonthly. Institutions, $185.00 per year.

Archives of Environmental Health: An International Journal. Helen Dwight Reid Educational Foundation. Heldref Publications. • Monthly. $382.00 per year. Objective documentation of the effects of environmental agents on human health.

BNA's SafetyNet. Bureau of National Affairs Inc. • Description: Designed to help employers deal with occupational safety and health regulations, policies, standards, and practices, and to understand the effects of compliance on employee relations. Covers the establishment, management, evaluation, maintenance, and administration of health and safety programs. Carries information on recordkeeping, inspections, enforcement, employer defenses, and training.

Environmental Toxicology: An International Journal. John Wiley and Sons, Inc. Journals. • Bimonthly. $700.00 per year; with online edition, $735.00 per year. Formerly *Environmental Toxicology and Water Quality.*

Industrial Hygiene News. Rimbach Publishing, Inc. • Seven times a year. Free to qualified personnel.

Management OHS and E. Stevens Publishing Corp. • Monthly. Free to qualified personnel; others, $150.00 per year. Includes news, interviews, feature articles, legal developments, and reviews of literature. Includes *Buyer's Guide.*

Occupational Health and Safety Letter...Towards Productivity and Peace of Mind. Business Publishers, Inc. • Biweekly. $317.00 per year.

RESEARCH CENTERS AND INSTITUTES

Michigan Institute for Environmental and Health Sciences. School of Public Health, University of Michigan, 1420 Washington Heights, Ann Arbor, MI 48109-2029. Phone: (734)764-3188 Fax: (734)936-7283 E-mail: jhv@umich.edu.

TRADE/PROFESSIONAL ASSOCIATIONS

American Industrial Hygiene Association. 2700 Prosperity Ave., Ste. 250, Fairfax, VA 22031. Phone: (703)849-8888 Fax: (703)207-3561 E-mail: infonet@aiha.org • URL: http://www.aiha.org • Professional society of industrial hygienists. Promotes the study and control of environmental factors affecting the health and well-being of workers. Sponsors continuing education courses in industrial hygiene, government affairs program, and public relations. Accredits laboratories. Maintains 40 technical committees and a foundation. Operates placement service. Conducts educational and research programs.

OTHER SOURCES

Practical Guide to the Occupational Safety and Health Act. American Lawyer Media, Inc. • Looseleaf. $149.00. Updated as needed. Covers the practical aspects of doing business while complying with OSHA regulations. Covers inspections, enforcement, rights of employees, the possibility of

criminal prosecution, and related issues. (Law Journal Press).

INDUSTRIAL JOURNALISM

See: BUSINESS JOURNALISM

INDUSTRIAL LOCATION

See: LOCATION OF INDUSTRY

INDUSTRIAL MANAGEMENT

See also: ADMINISTRATION; FACTORY MANAGEMENT; INDUSTRIAL ENGINEERING; PROJECT MANAGEMENT; RECORDS MANAGEMENT; SALES MANAGEMENT; SYSTEMS IN MANAGEMENT; TRAFFIC MANAGEMENT (INDUSTRIAL)

GENERAL WORKS

Chaos on the Shop Floor: A Worker's View of Quality, Productivity, and Management. Tom Juravich. Temple University Press. • 1988. $19.95. (Labor and Social Change Series).

Contemporary Supervision: Managing People and Technology. Betty R. Ricks and others. McGraw-Hill. • 1994. $68.75. Second edition. (Management Series).

Fundamentals of Management. James H. Donnelly and others. McGraw-Hill. • 1997. $60.50. 10th edition.

Management: Concepts, Practice, and Skills. R. Wayne Mondy and Shane R. Premeaux. Cengage Learning. • 2000. $61.95.

Management: Skills and Application. Lloyd L. Byars. McGraw-Hill. • 2002. 10th edition. Price on application. An introductory text covering the principles of successful management. Arranged according to the following "Skills:" Planning, Organizing, Staffing, Directing, and Controlling. Includes a glossary of key terms and three indexes. (Irwin Professional Publishing.).

A Manager's Guide to Creative Cost Cutting: 101 Ways to Build the Bottom Line. David W. Young. McGraw-Hill. • 2002. $16.95. Mainly concerned with reducing expenses without reducing staff. (Teach Yourself Series).

Managing the Small to Mid-Sized Company: Concepts and Cases. James C. Collins and William C. Lazier. McGraw-Hill. • 1994. $92.50.

Psychology for Leaders: Using Motivation, Conflict, and Power to Manage More Effectively. Dean Tjosvold and Mary Tjosvold. John Wiley and Sons, Inc. • 1995. $32.95. (Portable MBA Series).

Reengineering Management: The Mandate for New Leadership. James Champy. DIANE Publishing Co. • 1998. $25.00.

Reengineering the Corporation: A Manifesto for Business Revolution. Michael Hammer and James Champy. HarperInformation. • 2001. $16.00. Revised edition.

ABSTRACTS AND INDEXES

Business Periodicals Index. H. W. Wilson Co. • 11 times a year. Quarterly and annual cumulations. Price varies.

CD-ROM DATABASES

WILSONDISC: Wilson Business Abstracts. H. W. Wilson Co. • Monthly. Includes unlimited online access to *Wilson Business Abstracts* through WILSONLINE. Provides CD-ROM "cover-to-cover" abstracting and indexing of over 600 prominent business periodicals. Indexing is from 1982, abstracting from 1990. (*Business Periodicals*

Index without abstracts is available on CD-ROM at $1,495 per year.).

DIRECTORIES

Reference Book of Corporate Managements. • Annual. Libraries, $650.00 per year; others, $795.00 per year. Lease basis. Management executives at over 12,000 leading United States companies.

ENCYCLOPEDIAS AND DICTIONARIES

Blackwell Encyclopedic Dictionary of Operations Management. Nigel Slack, editor. Blackwell Publishing. • 1997. $130.95. The editor is associated with the University of Warwick, England. Contains definitions of key terms combined with longer articles written by various U. S. and foreign business educators. Includes bibliographies and index. (Blackwell Encyclopedia of Management Series.).

Every Manager's Guide to Information Technology: A Glossary of Key Terms and Concepts for Today's Business Leader. Peter G. W. Keen. Harvard Business School Publishing. • 1994. $18.95. Second edition. Provides definitions of terms related to computers, data communications, and information network systems. (Harvard Business Reference Series).

International Encyclopedia of Business and Management. Malcolm Warner, editor. Cengage Learning. • 2001. $1,899.00.Second edition. Eight volumes. Contains more than 500 articles on global management issues. Includes extensive bibliographies, cross references, and an index of key words and phrases.

HANDBOOKS AND MANUALS

AMA Management Handbook. John J. Hampton, editor. AMACOM. • 1994. $110.00. Third edition. Provides 200 chapters in 16 major subject areas. Covers a wide variety of business and industrial management topics.

Effective Supervisor's Handbook. Louis V. Imundo. AMACOM. • 1992. $16.95. Second edition.

Handbook of Systems Engineering and Management. Andrew P. Sage and William B. Rouse, editors. John Wiley and Sons, Inc. • 1999. $200.00. Emphasis is on information technology and systems software.

How To Be a Manager: A Practical Guide to Tips and Techniques. Robert W. Gallant. Lewis Publishers. • 1991. $69.95. A concise handbook of principles, techniques, and methods of problem solving. Covers negotiation, discipline, management ethics, training, and other subjects.

Management: Skills and Application With Powerweb. Leslie W. Rue and Lloyd L. Byars. McGraw-Hill. • 2002. 10th edition. Price on application.

Manager's Tool Kit: Practical Tips for Tackling 100 On-the-Job Problems. Cy Charney. AMACOM. • 1995. $17.95.

Managing More Effectively: A Professional Approach to Get the Best Out of People. Madhurendra K. Varma. Sage Publications, Inc. • 2001. $37.95. Second edition. Focuses on the daily and practical application of management principles.

Organization Charts: Structures of More Than 200 Businesses and Non-Profit Organizations. Gale Cengage Learning. • 1999. $180.00. Third edition. Includes an introductory discussion of the history and use of such charts.

Production and Operations Management. Richard B. Chase. McGraw-Hill. • 2002. $39.69. Ninth edition. Covers capacity planning, facility location, process design, inventory planning, personnel scheduling, etc.

Reengineering Revolution: A Handbook. Michael Hammer and Steven Stanton. HarperInformation. • 1995. $17.95.

Teambuilding and Total Quality: A Guidebook to TQM Success. Gene Milas. Engineering and Management Press. • 1997. $29.95. A practical, how-to-do-it guide to total quality management in industry. The importance of employee involvement is stressed.

Work Simplification: An Analyst's Handbook. Pierre Theriault. Engineering and Management Press. • 1996. $25.00. A basic guide to work simplification as an industrial management technique.

ONLINE DATABASES

Business and Management Practices. Gale Cengage Learning. • Provides fulltext of management articles appearing in more than 350 relevant publications. Emphasis is on "the processes, methods, and strategies of managing a business." Time span is 1995 to date. Inquire as to online cost and availability. (Also available in a CD-ROM version.).

Management Contents. Gale Cengage Learning. • Covers a wide range of management, financial, marketing, personnel, and administrative topics. About 150 leading business journals are indexed and abstracted from 1974 to date, with monthly updating. Inquire as to online cost and availability.

Wilson Business Abstracts Online. H. W. Wilson Co. • Indexes and abstracts 600 major business periodicals, plus the *Wall Street Journal* and the business section of the *New York Times*. Indexing is from 1982, abstracting from 1990, with the two newspapers included from 1993. Updated weekly. Inquire as to online cost and availability. (*Business Periodicals Index* without abstracts is also available online.).

PERIODICALS AND NEWSLETTERS

Executive Excellence: The Newsletter of Personal Development, Managerial Effectiveness, and Organizational Productivity. Kenneth M. Shelton, editor. Executive Excellence Publishing. • Monthly. $129.00 per year. Newsletter.

Hard at Work. Professional Training Associates, Inc. • Monthly. $89.00 per year. Newsletter on common personnel problems of supervisors and office managers. Formerly *Practical Supervision.*

Harvard Management Update. Harvard Business School Publishing. • Description: Provides information on current management techniques and trends.

Human Factors and Ergonomics in Manufacturing. John Wiley and Sons, Inc., Journals. • Quarterly. $649.00 per year; with online edition, $682.00 per year. Published in England by John Wiley and Sons Ltd. Formerly *International Journal of Human Factors in Manufacturing.*

IEE Solutions. Institute of Industrial Engineers. • Monthly. Free to members; non-members, $66.00 per year. Features articles on material handling, computers, quality control, production and inventory control, engineering economics, worker motivation, management strategies, and factory automation. Formerly *Industrial Engineers.*

IndustryWeek: The Management Resource. Penton Media, Inc. • 22 times a year. Free to qualified personnel; others, $65.00 per year. Edited for industrial and business managers. Covers organizational and technological developments affecting industrial management.

Journal of Economics and Management Strategy. MIT Press. • Quarterly. Institutions, $195.00 per year. Includes print and online editions. Covers "theoretical and empirical industrial organization, applied game theory, and management strategy.".

The Manager's Intelligence Report: An Insider's Fast Track to Better Management. Lawrence Ragan Communications, Inc. • Monthly. $129.00 per year. Newsletter on various aspects of management, including strategy, employee morale, and time management.

MIT Sloan Management Review. Sloan Management Review Association. Massachusetts Institute of Technology. • Quarterly. Individuals, $89.00 per year; institutions, $148.00 per year. Formerly *Sloan Management Review.*.

Production and Operations Management. Production and Operations Management Society. • Quarterly. Individuals, $70.00 per year; libraries, $200.00 per year.

The Professional Manager. Institute of Industrial Engineers. • Bimonthly. Free to members; non-members, $24.00 per year. Features articles on the latest problem-solving techniques and trends available to industrial managers. Formerly *Industrial Management.*

Research-Technology Management: International Journal of Research Management. Industrial Research Institute. • Bimonthly. Individuals, $65.00 per year; institutions, $150.00 per year. Covers both theoretical and practical aspects of the management of industrial research and development.

RESEARCH CENTERS AND INSTITUTES

Board of Research. Babson College, 204 Babson, Babson Park, MA 02457-0310. Phone: (718)239-5339 Fax: (718)239-6416 E-mail: chern@babson.edu • URL: http://www.babson.edu/bor • Research areas include management, entrepreneurial characteristics, and multi-product inventory analysis.

TRADE/PROFESSIONAL ASSOCIATIONS

American Association of Industrial Management. Stearns Bldg., Ste. 506, 293 Bridge St., Springfield, MA 01103. Phone: 888-698-1968 or (413)737-9725 or (413)737-8766 Fax: (413)737-9724 E-mail: aaimnmta@aol.com • URL: http://www.aaimnmta.com.

American Management Association. 1601 Broadway, New York, NY 10019-7420. Phone: 800-262-9699 or (212)586-8100 Fax: (212)903-8168 E-mail: membership@amanet.org • URL: http://www.amanet.org • Provides educational forums worldwide where members and their colleagues learn superior, practical business skills and explore best practices of world-class organizations through interaction with each other and expert faculty practitioners. Maintains a publishing program providing tools individuals use to extend learning beyond the classroom in a process of life-long professional growth and development through education.

Institute of Industrial Engineers. 3377 Parkway Ln., Ste. 200, Norcross, GA 30092. Phone: 800-494-0460 or (770)449-0460 Fax: (770)441-3295 E-mail: cs@iienet.org • URL: http://www.iienet.org • Formerly American Institute of Industrial Engineers.

International Management Council of the YMCA. 7502 Maple St., Omaha, NE 68134-6602. Phone: 800-688-9622 or (402)330-6310 Fax: (402)330-7424 E-mail: imcoffice@msn.com • URL: http://www.imc-ymca.org • Formerly International Management Council.

National Management Association. 2210 Arbor Blvd., Dayton, OH 45439. Phone: (937)294-0421 Fax: (937)294-2374 E-mail: nma@nma1.org • URL: http://www.nma1.org • Business and industrial management personnel; membership comes from supervisory level, with the remainder from middle management and above. Seeks to develop and recognize management as a profession and to promote the free enterprise system. Prepares chapter programs on basic management, management policy and practice, communications, human behavior, industrial relations, economics, political education, and liberal education. Maintains speakers' bureau and hall of fame. Maintains educational, charitable, and research programs. Sponsors charitable programs.

Production and Operations Management Society. Florida International University, College of Engineering, 10555 W. Flagle St., EAS 2460, Miami, FL 33174. Phone: (305)348-1413 Fax: (305)348-6890 E-mail: poms@eng.fiu.edu • URL: http://www.poms.org • Members are professionals and educators in fields related to operations management and production.

Society for Advancement of Management. Texas A&M University-Corpus Christi, College of Business, 6300 Ocean Dr., Corpus Christi, TX 78412. Phone: 888-827-6077 or (361)825-6045 or (361)825-5574 Fax: (361)825-2725 E-mail: moustafa@falcon.tamucc.edu • URL: http://www.enterprise.tamucc.edu/sam/ • Professional organization of management executives in industry, commerce, government and education. Absorbed Industrial Methods Society.

OTHER SOURCES

First-Line Supervision. American Management Association Extension Institute. • Looseleaf. $139.00. Self-study course. Focuses on the day-to-day concerns of the first line supervisor. A self-study course.

INDUSTRIAL MARKETING

See also: INDUSTRIAL ADVERTISING; MARKETING

GENERAL WORKS

Business Marketing. McGraw-Hill. • 2001. $68.00. Second edition.

Business Marketing Management. Frank G. Bingham. McGraw-Hill. • 1997. $71.95.

Defining Your Market: Winning Strategies for High-Tech, Industrial, and Service Firms. Art Weinstein. Haworth Press, Inc. • 1998. $39.95. Includes "models, frameworks, and processes" for effective industrial marketing.

Industrial Marketing Strategy. Frederick E. Webster. John Wiley and Sons, Inc. • 1995. $44.95. Third edition. (Marketing Management Series).

BIBLIOGRAPHIES

Marketing Information Revolution. Robert C. Blattberg, editor. McGraw-Hill. • 1993. $39.95. Third edition. Includes a wide variety of sources for specific kinds of marketing.

DIRECTORIES

Business Marketing Association and Resource Directory. Business Marketing Association. • Annual. $100.00. Lists professionals in business and industrial advertising and marketing. Available online.

Directory of Business-to-Business Catalogs. Grey House Publishing. • Annual. $165.00. Provides over 6,000 listings of U. S. mail order companies selling business or industrial products and services.

ENCYCLOPEDIAS AND DICTIONARIES

Blackwell Encyclopedic Dictionary of Marketing. Dale Littler and Barbara R. Lewis, editors. Blackwell Publishers. • 1997. $38.95. The editors are associated with the Manchester School of Management. Contains definitions of key terms combined with longer articles written by various U. S. and foreign business educators. Includes bibliographies and index. (Blackwell Encyclopedia of Management Series.).

Field Guide to Marketing: A Glossary to Essential Tools and Concepts for Today's Manager. McGraw-Hill. • 1993. $29.95. Defines fundamental terms.

HANDBOOKS AND MANUALS

Marketing Manager's Handbook. Sidney J. Levy and others. Prentice Hall PTR. • 2000. Price on application. Contains 71 chapters by various authors on a wide variety of marketing topics, including market segmentation, market research, international marketing, industrial marketing, survey methods, customer service, advertising, pricing, planning, strategy, and ethics.

ONLINE DATABASES

PROMT: Predicasts Overview of Markets and Technology. Gale Cengage Learning. • Companies, products, applied technologies and markets. U.S. and international literature coverage, 1972 to date. Inquire as to online cost and availability. Provides abstracts from more than 1,600 publications. Weekly updates.

PERIODICALS AND NEWSLETTERS

Adweek Magazines' Technology Marketing. VNU Business Media. • Monthly. $55.00 per year. Edited for marketing executives in high technology industries. Covers both advertising and marketing. Formerly *MC Technology Marketing Intelligence.*

Industrial Marketing Management: The International Journal of Marketing for Industrial and High-Tech Firms. Elsevier. • Eight times a year. Qualified personnel, $127.00 per year; institutions, $816.00 per year.

Journal of Business-to-Business Marketing: Innovations in Basic and Applied Research for Industrial Marketing. Haworth Press, Inc. • Quarterly. Institutions, $285.00 per year. For buyers and sellers.

RESEARCH CENTERS AND INSTITUTES

Institute for the Study of Business Markets. Pennsylvania State University, 402 Business Administration Bldg., University Park, PA 16802-3004. Phone: (814)863-2782 Fax: (814)863-0413 E-mail: isbm@psu.edu • URL: http://www.smeal.psu.edu/isbm/ • Research areas include international distribution channels.

TRADE/PROFESSIONAL ASSOCIATIONS

Business Market Association. 4131 N. Central Expy., Ste. 720, Dallas, TX 75204. Phone: 800-664-4262 or (312)822-0005 Fax: (312)822-0054 E-mail: rh@udel.edu • URL: http://www.marketing.org • Small- and medium-sized businesses. Works to bring large corporate lobbying and benefits to companies who do not have the workforce to achieve those benefits.

INDUSTRIAL MEDICINE

See also: INDUSTRIAL HYGIENE

GENERAL WORKS

Principles of Health and Hygiene in the Workplace. Timothy J. Key and Michael A. Mueller. Lewis Publishers. • Date not set. $69.95.

ABSTRACTS AND INDEXES

Excerpta Medica: Occupational Health and Industrial Medicine. Elsevier. • Monthly. Institutions, $2,375.00 per year. Section 35 of *Excerpta Medica.*

DIRECTORIES

American College of Occupational and Environmental Medicine-Membership Directory. • Annual. $195.00. Lists 6,500 medical directories and plant physicians specializing in occupational medicine and surgery; coverage includes Canada and other foreign countries. Geographically arranged.

ENCYCLOPEDIAS AND DICTIONARIES

Attorneys' Dictionary of Medicine. J. E. Schmidt. LexisNexis Matthew Bender. • Irregular. $673.00. Over 57,000 definitions of medical terms. Includes common lay words that lead to correct medical terms.

Encyclopedia of Occupational Health and Safety. International Labour Organization. • 1998. $990.00. Fourth edition. Four volumes. Includes CD-ROM.

Covers safety engineering, industrial medicine, ergonomics, hygiene, epidemiology, toxicology, industrial psychology, and related topics. Includes material related to specific chemical, textile, transport, construction, manufacturing, and other industries. Indexed by subject, chemical name, and author, with a "Directory of Experts.".

HANDBOOKS AND MANUALS

Patty's Industrial Hygiene and Toxicology. Robert L. Harris. John Wiley and Sons, Inc. • 2001. $3,290.00. Fifth edition. Provides broad coverage of environmental factors and stresses affecting the health of workers. Contains detailed information on the effects of specific substances.

INTERNET DATABASES

National Library of Medicine (NLM). National Institutes of Health (NIH). Phone: 888-346-3656 or (301)496-1131 Fax: (301)480-3537 E-mail: access@nlm.nih.gov • URL: http://www.nlm.nih.gov • NLM Web site offers free access through MEDLINE ("PubMed") to about nine million references to articles appearing in some 4,000 biomedical journals, with abstracts. Search interfaces range from "simple keywords to advanced Boolean expressions." The NLM site offers many links to other sources of biomedical and technical information (the National Center for Biotechnology Information, for example). Fees: Free.

ONLINE DATABASES

Embase. Elsevier Science, Inc. • Worldwide medical literature, 1974 to present. Weekly updates. Inquire as to online cost and availability.

Medline. Medlars Management Section. • Provides indexing and abstracting of worldwide medical literature, 1966 to date. Weekly updates. Inquire as to online cost and availability.

PERIODICALS AND NEWSLETTERS

American Journal of Industrial Medicine. John Wiley and Sons, Inc., Journals. • Monthly. Institutions, $3,220.00 per year; with online edition, $3,381.00 per year.

Environmental Epidemiology and Toxicology. Nature Publishing Group. • Quarterly. Individuals, $365.00 per year; institutions, $430.00 per year. Formerly *Environmental Epidemiology and Toxicology.*

OTHER SOURCES

Attorneys' Textbook of Medicine. LexisNexis Matthew Bender. • Quarterly. $3,145.00 per year. 23 looseleaf volumes. Medico-legal material.

Society of Air Force Physicians. • Air Force internists, family practitioners, and specialists in emergency medicine, dermatology, allergy/immunology, and neurology. Seeks to foster advancement of the art and science of medicine in the Air Force; encourage clinical and laboratory investigation; disseminate information.

Society of Medical Consultants to the Armed Forces. • Professional society of physicians and surgeons who have been in active military service and who have acted as consultants to the Surgeons General of the Army, Navy, or Air Force. Preserves and encourages the association of civilian consultants and military medical personnel and assists in the development and maintenance of the highest standards of medical practice in the Armed Forces.

Society of Military Orthopaedic Surgeons. • Orthopedic surgeons who have served in the active or reserve military. Seeks to stimulate scholarly contribution by military medical residents; act as clearinghouse; provides opportunities for consultation with and contributions of surgeons who are retired from the military; furthers the continuing education of orthopedic surgeons and residents. Presents scientific papers at annual meeting.

Society of Military Otolaryngologists - Head and

Neck Surgeons. • Otolaryngologists, head and neck surgeons and residents in training of the U.S. Army, Air Force, Navy, and former active duty members. Purposes are to further the social and professional contacts of military otolaryngologists and to advance the science and art of the field.

Uniformed Services Academy of Family Physicians. • Family physicians, teachers of family medicine, medical students, and residents in the armed services, public health service, or Indian health service. Sponsors continuing education program. Sponsors educational programs.

INDUSTRIAL MORALE

See: HUMAN RELATIONS

INDUSTRIAL PARKS

See: INDUSTRIAL DEVELOPMENT

INDUSTRIAL PHOTOGRAPHY

See: COMMERCIAL PHOTOGRAPHY

INDUSTRIAL PRODUCTIVITY

See: PRODUCTIVITY

INDUSTRIAL PSYCHOLOGY

See also: MENTAL HEALTH; PSYCHOLOGICAL TESTING; STRESS (ANXIETY)

GENERAL WORKS

Introduction to Industrial-Organization Psychology. Addison-Wesley. • 2000. Third edition. Price on application.

Managing Workplace Stress. Cary L. Cooper and Susan Cartwright. Sage Publications, Inc. • 1996. $70.95. Includes references and indexes. *Advanced Topics in Organizational Behavior Series, vol. 1.*

Psychology for Leaders: Using Motivation, Conflict, and Power to Manage More Effectively. Dean Tjosvold and Mary Tjosvold. John Wiley and Sons, Inc. • 1995. $32.95. (Portable MBA Series).

Psychology in Industrial Organizations. Norman R. Maier and Trudy G. Verser. Houghton Mifflin Co. • 1982. $101.56. Five volumes. Fifth edition.

ABSTRACTS AND INDEXES

Business Periodicals Index. H. W. Wilson Co. • 11 times a year. Quarterly and annual cumulations. Price varies.

Psychological Abstracts. American Psychological Association. • Monthly. Members, $815.00 per year; individuals and institutions, $1,207.00 per year. Covers the international literature of psychology and the behavioral sciences. Includes journals, technical reports, dissertations, and other sources.

ALMANACS AND YEARBOOKS

International Review of Industrial and Organizational Psychology. John Wiley and Sons, Inc., Journals. • Annual. $150.00. Published in England by John Wiley and Sons Ltd.

DIRECTORIES

Tests: A Comprehensive Reference for Assessments in Psychology, Education and Business. Available from Gale Cengage Learning. • 2003. $96.00. Fifth edition. List nearly 200 publishers for over 2,000 tests. Published by Pro-Ed Inc.

ENCYCLOPEDIAS AND DICTIONARIES

Blackwell Encyclopedic Dictionary of Organizational Behavior. Nigel Nicholson, editor. Blackwell Publishing. • 1997. $130.95. The editor is associated with the London Business School. Contains definitions of key terms combined with longer articles written by various U. S. and foreign business educators. Includes bibliographies and index. *Blackwell Encyclopedia of Management Series.*

Encyclopedia of Human Behavior. Vangipuram S. Ramachandran, editor. Elsevier. • 1994. $1,000.00. Four volumes. Contains signed articles on aptitude testing, arbitration, career development, consumer psychology, crisis management, decision making, economic behavior, group dynamics, leadership, motivation, negotiation, organizational behavior, planning, problem solving, stress, work efficiency, and other human behavior topics applicable to business situations.

Encyclopedia of Occupational Health and Safety. International Labour Organization. • 1998. $990.00. Fourth edition. Four volumes. Includes CD-ROM. Covers safety engineering, industrial medicine, ergonomics, hygiene, epidemiology, toxicology, industrial psychology, and related topics. Includes material related to specific chemical, textile, transport, construction, manufacturing, and other industries. Indexed by subject, chemical name, and author, with a "Directory of Experts.".

Encyclopedia of Psychological Assessment. Rocio Fernandez-Ballesteros, editor. Sage Publications, Inc. • 2003. $525.00. Two volumes. Contains about 235 alphabetically arranged entries covering various areas of applied psychology and testing.

The Gale Encyclopedia of Psychology. Gale Cengage Learning. • 2001. $155.00. Second edition. Includes bibliographies arranged by topic and a glossary. More than 650 topics are covered.

HANDBOOKS AND MANUALS

Comprehensive Handbook of Psychological Assessment. Michel Hersen, editor. John Wiley and Sons, Inc. • 2003. $500.00. Four volumes. Covers psychological testing and evaluation. Volume one: *Intellectual and Neuropsychological Assessment.* Volume two: *Personality Assessment.* Volume three: *Behavioral Assessment.* Volume four: *Industrial/Organizational Assessment.* (Individual volumes are available at $150.00.).

Handbook of Mental Health in the Workplace. Jay C. Thomas and Michael Hersen, editors. Sage Publications, Inc. • 2002. $99.95. The five parts deal with general issues, working conditions, psychopathology, disruptive behavior, and organizational practice.

Industrial and Organizational Psychology: Research and Practice. Paul E. Spector. John Wiley and Sons, Inc. • 2002. $96.95. Third edition.

Stress and Well-Being at Work: Assessments and Interventions for Occupational Mental Health. James C. Quick and others, editors. American Psychological Association. • 1992. $19.95.

ONLINE DATABASES

Mental Health Abstracts. IFI/Plenum Data Corp. • Provides indexing and abstracting of mental health and mental illness literature appearing in more than 1,200 journals and other sources from 1969 to date. Monthly updates. Inquire as to online cost and availability.

PsycINFO. American Psychological Association. • Provides indexing and abstracting of the worldwide literature of psychology and the behavioral sciences. Time period is 1967 to date, with monthly updates.

Inquire as to online cost and availability.

PERIODICALS AND NEWSLETTERS

Journal of Business and Psychology. Business Psychology Research Institute. Kluwer Academic Publishers. • Quarterly. Institutions, $614.00 per year; with online edition, $736.80 per year.

Journal of Occupational and Organizational Psychology. The British Psychological Society. • Quarterly. Individuals, $72.00 per year; institutions, $265.00 per year. Formerly *Journal of Occupational Psychology.*

INDUSTRIAL PURCHASING

See: PURCHASING

INDUSTRIAL REAL ESTATE

See also: PROPERTY TAX; TAX SHELTERS

ABSTRACTS AND INDEXES

Business Periodicals Index. H. W. Wilson Co. • 11 times a year. Quarterly and annual cumulations. Price varies.

DIRECTORIES

Executive Guide to Specialists in Industrial and Office Real Estate. Society of Industrial and Office Realtors. • Annual. $70.00. Approximately 1,800 specialist in industrial real estate.

Plunkett's Real Estate and Construction Industry Almanac. Plunkett Research, Ltd. • 2004. $249.99. Contains profiles of 300 leading firms concerned with real estate or construction. Specialties include architecture, development, mortgages, building engineering, real estate sales, etc. Also covers industry trends and statistical data.

U.S. Real Estate Register. Barry Inc. • Covers: real estate departments of large national companies, industrial economic/development organizations, utilities, real estate brokers, and railroads involved in commercial and industrial real estate development. Entries include: Company or organization name, address; many listings include name of contact.

ONLINE DATABASES

Wilson Business Abstracts Online. H. W. Wilson Co. • Indexes and abstracts 600 major business periodicals, plus the *Wall Street Journal* and the business section of the *New York Times.* Indexing is from 1982, abstracting from 1990, with the two newspapers included from 1993. Updated weekly. Inquire as to online cost and availability. (*Business Periodicals Index* without abstracts is also available online.).

PERIODICALS AND NEWSLETTERS

Area Development Sites and Facility Planning: The Executive Magazine of Sites and Facility Planning. Halcyon Business Publications, Inc. • Monthly. Free to the business trade; others, $65.00 per year. Site selection, facility planning, and plant relocation. Formerly *Area Development Magazines.*

Buildings: The Source for Facilities Decision-Makers. Stamats Communications, Inc. • Monthly. $70.00 per year. Serves professional building ownership/management organizations.

Business Facilities: The Location Advisor. Group C Communications, Inc. • Monthly. Free to qualified personnel; others, $30.00 per year. Facility planning and site selection.

Commercial Leasing Law and Strategy. American Lawyer Media, Inc. • Monthly. $215.00 per year. Newsletter. Covers commercial real estate leasing developments relating to large retailers, tenant inducements, tax consequences, unbilled rent obligations, and other matters. (A Law Journal

Newsletter, formerly published by Leader Publications).

Development Magazine. National Association of Industrial and Office Properties. • Quarterly. Free to members; non-members, $65.00 per year. Focuses on issues, trends and new ideas affecting the commercial and industrial real estate development industry.

Marketscore. CB Richard Ellis. • Quarterly. Price on application. Newsletter. Provides proprietary forecasts of commercial real estate performance in metropolitan areas.

Quarterly Market Report. Property and Portfolio Research. • Quarterly. $1,000.00 per year for one property type; 2,000 per year for six property types. Newsletter. Reviews current prices, rents, capitalization rates, and occupancy trends for commercial real estate.

Real Estate Finance. Institutional Investor, Inc., Journals Group. • Bimonthly. $350.00 per year. Covers real estate for professional investors. Provides information on complex financing, legalities, and industry trends.

Real Estate Finance and Investment. Institutional Investor, Inc., Journals Group. • Weekly. $2,275.00 per year. Includes print and online editions. Newsletter for professional investors in commercial real estate. Includes information on financing, restructuring, strategy, and regulation.

Real Estate Forum: America's Premier Real Estate Business Magazine. Real Estate Media, Inc. • Monthly. $59.95 per year. Emphasis on corporate and industrial real estate.

PRICE SOURCES

National Real Estate Index. CB Richard Ellis. • Price and frequency on application. Provides reports on commercial real estate prices, rents, capitalization rates, and trends in more than 65 metropolitan areas. Time span is 12 years. Includes urban office buildings, suburban offices, warehouses, retail properties, and apartments.

RESEARCH CENTERS AND INSTITUTES

Center for Real Estate Studies. University of Florida. College of Business Administration, P.O. Box 117168, Gainesville, FL 32611-7168. Phone: (352)392-9307 Fax: (352)392-0381 E-mail: archer@notes.cba.ufl.edu • URL: http://www.ufrealestate.com • Formerly Real Estate Research Center.

Office of Real Estate Research. University of Illinois at Urbana-Champaign, 1407 W. Gregory Dr., 304 David Kinley Hall, Urbana, IL 61801. Phone: (217)333-1185 Fax: (217)244-9867 E-mail: orer@uiuc.edu • URL: http://www.cba.uiuc.edu/orer.

STATISTICS SOURCES

Comparative Statistics of Industrial Office Real Estate Markets. Society of Industrial and Office Realtors. • Annual. $100.00. Includes review and forecast section. Formerly *Guide to Industrial and Office Real Estate Markets.*

ULI Market Profiles: North America. Urban Land Institute. • Annual. Members, $249.95; non-members, $299.95. Provides real estate marketing data for residential, retail, office, and industrial sectors. Covers 76 U. S. metropolitan areas and 13 major foreign metropolitan areas.

TRADE/PROFESSIONAL ASSOCIATIONS

American Industrial Real Estate Association. 700 S. Flower St., Suite 600, Los Angeles, CA 90017. Phone: (213)687-8777 Fax: (213)687-8616 E-mail: thayes@airea.com • URL: http://www.airea.com.

National Association of Industrial and Office Properties. 2201 Cooperative Way, 3rd Fl., Herndon, VA 20171. Phone: 800-666-6780 or (703)904-7100 Fax: (703)904-7942 E-mail: naiop@naiop.org • URL: http://www.naiop.org • Members are own-

---

ers and developers of business, industrial, office, and retail properties. Formerly NAIOP - The Association of Commercial Real Estate.

OTHER SOURCES

Shopping Center and Store Leases. American Lawyer Media, Inc. • Looseleaf. $195.00. Two volumes. Updated as needed. Provides analysis of retail leases, financing, construction issues, insurance, taxation, bankruptcy, and condemnation of property. Includes detailed information about the shopping-center business and fast-food restaurants, with many examples of lease clauses. (Law Journal Press).

INDUSTRIAL RECREATION

ABSTRACTS AND INDEXES

Leisure, Recreation, and Tourism Abstracts. Available from CABI Publishing North America. • Quarterly. Members, $280.00 per year; Institutions, $610.00 per year. Includes single site internet access. Published in England by CABI Publishing. Provides coverage of the worldwide literature of travel, recreation, sports, and the hospitality industry. Emphasis is on research.

DIRECTORIES

Membership and Peer Network Directory. ESM Association. • Annual. Membership. Lists more than 4,500 personnel managers, recreation directors and certified administrators in employee recreation, fitness and services. Formerly *National Employee Services and Recreation Association-Membership and Peer Network Directory.*

PERIODICALS AND NEWSLETTERS

Employee Services Management: The Journal of Employee Services Recreation, Heal th and Education. Employee Services Management. • Bimonthly. Free to members; non-members, $52.00 per year.

TRADE/PROFESSIONAL ASSOCIATIONS

Employee Services Management Association. 568 Spring Rd., Ste. D, Elmhurst, IL 60126-3896. Phone: (630)559-0020 Fax: (630)559-0025 E-mail: esmahq@esmassn.org • URL: http://www.esmassn. org • Corporations and governmental agencies that sponsor recreation, fitness, and service programs for their employees; associate members are manufacturers and suppliers in the employee recreation market and distributors of consumer products and services. Serves as an information resource network for members nationwide. Implements and maintains a diverse range of employee services; believes that employee services, as practical solutions to work/ life issues, are essential to sound business management. Conducts programs that improves relations between employees and management, increases overall productivity, boosts morale, and reduces absenteeism and turnover. Covers the 10 Components of a Well-Rounded Employee Services Program such as employee stores, convenience services, recognition programs, recreation programs, travel services, and special events.

INDUSTRIAL RELATIONS

See also: NEGOTIATION

GENERAL WORKS

Labor-Management Relations. Daniel Q. Mills. McGraw-Hill. • 1993. $112.50. Fifth edition. (Management Series).

Labor Relations. Arthur A. Sloan and Fred Witney. Prentice Hall PTR. • 2000. $115.00. 10th edition. Emphasizes collective bargaining and arbitration.

Labor Relations: Development, Structure, Process.

John A. Fossum. McGraw-Hill. • 2001. $112.50. Eighth edition.

ABSTRACTS AND INDEXES

Business Periodicals Index. H. W. Wilson Co. • 11 times a year. Quarterly and annual cumulations. Price varies.

Human Resources Abstracts: An International Information Service. Sage Publications, Inc. • Quarterly. Institutions, $968.00 per year; includes print and online editions.

Index to Legal Periodicals and Books. H. W. Wilson Co. • Monthly. $490.00 per year. Quarterly and annual cumulations.

Personnel Management Abstracts. • Quarterly. $190.00 per year. Includes annual cumulation.

BIBLIOGRAPHIES

Labor Arbitration: An Annotated Bibliography, 1991-1996. Charles J. Coleman and others, editors. Cornell Universtiy Press. • 1997. $27.50. (ILR Bibliography Series, No. 18).

BIOGRAPHICAL SOURCES

Biographical Dictionary of American Labor. Gary M. Fink, editor. Greenwood Publishing Group Inc. • 1984. $120.00.

DIRECTORIES

Directory of U. S. Labor Organizations. BNA, Inc. . • Annual. $105.00. More than 150 national unions and professional and state employees associations engaged in labor representation.

ENCYCLOPEDIAS AND DICTIONARIES

International Encyclopedia of Public Policy and Administration. Jay M. Shafritz, editor. Westview Press. • 1997. $550.00. Four volumes. Covers 20 major areas, such as public administration, government budgeting, industrial policy, nonprofit management, organizational theory, public finance, labor relations, and taxation. Includes a brief bibliography for each major entry and a comprehensive index.

HANDBOOKS AND MANUALS

AMA Management Handbook. John J. Hampton, editor. AMACOM. • 1994. $110.00. Third edition. Provides 200 chapters in 16 major subject areas. Covers a wide variety of business and industrial management topics.

Labor Management Relations: Strikes, Lockouts, and Boycotts. West Group. • Annual. $165.00. Looseleaf service. Covers legal issues involved in labor-management confrontations. Includes recent decisions of the National Labor Relations Board (NLRB).

ONLINE DATABASES

Index to Legal Periodicals and Books (Online). H. W. Wilson Co. • Broad coverage of law journals and books 1981 to date. Monthly updates. Inquire as to online cost and availability.

Legal Resource Index. Gale Cengage Learning. • Broad coverage of law literature appearing in legal, business, and other periodicals, 1980 to date. Daily updates. Inquire as to online cost and availability.

LEXIS. LEXIS-NEXIS. • The various LEXIS databases provide full text and indexing for a wide variety of legal cases, statutes, orders, and opinions.

Wilson Business Abstracts Online. H. W. Wilson Co. • Indexes and abstracts 600 major business periodicals, plus the *Wall Street Journal* and the business section of the *New York Times.* Indexing is from 1982, abstracting from 1990, with the two newspapers included from 1993. Updated weekly. Inquire as to online cost and availability. (*Business Periodicals Index* without abstracts is also available online.).

PERIODICALS AND NEWSLETTERS

Berkeley Journal of Employment and Labor Law. University of California. • Biennial. Individuals,

$36.00 per year; institutions, $47.00 per year. Formerly *Industrial Relations Law Journal.*

HR Magazine (Human Resources): Strategies and Solutions for Human Resource Professionals. Society for Human Resource Management. • Monthly. Free to members; non-members, $70.00 per year. Formerly *Personnel Administrator.*

Industrial and Labor Relations Review. Cornell University, New York State School of Industrial and Labor Relations. • Quarterly. Individuals, $32.00 per year; institutions, $52.00 per year; students, $16.00 per year.

Industrial Relations: A Journal of Economy and Society. University of California at Berkeley. Blackwell Publishing. • Bimonthly. Institutions, $862.00 per year. Includes online edition.

IRRA Newsletter. Labor and Employment Relations Association. • Description: Presents news of meetings, elections, and programs of this Association of business, labor, and government leaders interested in researching labor and management relationships.

Weekly Summary of the National Labor Relations Board Cases. Available from U. S. Government Printing Office. • Weekly. $237.00 per year. Issued by the Division of Information, National Labor Relations Board.

RESEARCH CENTERS AND INSTITUTES

Center for Human Resources. University of Pennsylvania, The Wharton School, 309 Vance Hall, 3733 Spruce St., Philadelphia, PA 19104-6358. Phone: (215)898-2722 Fax: (215)898-5908 E-mail: cappelli@wharton.upenn.edu • URL: http://www. management.wharton.upenn.edu/.

Industrial Relations Research Institute. University of Wisconsin-Madison, 4226 Social Science Bldg., Madison, WI 53706-1393. Phone: (608)262-1882 Fax: (608)265-4591 E-mail: irri@mhub.facstaff. wisc.edu • URL: http://www.wisc.edu/irr.

Industrial Relations Section. Princeton University, Firestone Library, Pinceton, NJ 08544. Phone: (609)258-4040 Fax: (609)258-2907 • URL: http:// www.irs.princeton.edu/ • Fields of research include labor supply, manpower training, unemployment, and equal employment opportunity.

Industrial Relations Section. Massachusetts Institute of Technology. Sloan School of Management, 50 Memorial Dr., E 52-586, Cambridge, MA 02142. Phone: (617)253-2667 Fax: (617)253-7696 E-mail: osterman@mit.edu.

Institute of Industrial Relations. University of California at Berkeley, 2521 Channing Way, No. 5555, Berkeley, CA 94720-5555. Phone: (510)642-5452 Fax: (510)642-6432 E-mail: lincoln@haas. berkeley.edu • URL: http://www.violet.berkeley. edu/.

Institute of Labor and Industrial Relations. University of Michigan, Victor Vaughn Bldg., 1111 E. Catherine St., Ann Arbor, MI 48109-2054. Phone: (734)763-3116 Fax: (734)763-0913 E-mail: swines@umich.edu • URL: http://www.ilir.umich. edu.

TRADE/PROFESSIONAL ASSOCIATIONS

Council of Communication Management. 65 Enterprise, Aliso Viejo, CA 92656. Phone: (866)463-6226 Fax: (949)715-6931 E-mail: membership@ccmconnection.com • URL: http:// www.ccmconnection.com/ • Formerly Industrial Communication Council.

Industrial Relations Research Association. University of Illinois, 121 LIR, 504 E. Armory Ave., Champaign, IL 61820. Phone: (217)333-0072 Fax: (217)265-5130 E-mail: irra@uiuc.edu • URL: http:// www.irra.uiuc.edu.

Society for Human Resource Management. 1800 Duke St., Alexandria, VA 22314. Phone: 800-283-7476 or (703)548-3440 Fax: (703)535-6490 • URL: http://www.shrm.org • Affiliated with Human

Resource Certification Institute; Media Human Resources Association and SHRM Global Forum. Formerly American Society for Personnel Administration.

OTHER SOURCES

How to Manage Conflict in the Organization. American Management Association Extension Institute. • Looseleaf. $139.00. Self-study course. Emphasis is on practical explanations, examples, and problem solving. Quizzes and a case study are included.

Labor Relations Reporter. BNA, Inc. • Weekly. $4,998.00 per year. Looseleaf service.

INDUSTRIAL RESEARCH

See also: RESEARCH AND DEVELOPMENT

GENERAL WORKS

Industry's Future: Changing Patterns of Industrial Research. Herbert I. Fusfeld. American Chemical Society. • 1994. $45.00.

The Innovator's Dilemma: When New Technologies Cause Great Firms to Fail. Clayton M. Christensen. Harvard Business School Publishing. • 1997. $27. 50. Discusses management myths relating to innovation, change, and research and development. (Mangement of Innovation and Change Series).

ABSTRACTS AND INDEXES

Applied Science and Technology Index. H. W. Wilson Co. • 11 times a year. Quarterly and annual cumulations. Price varies. Indexes a wide variety of English language technical, industrial, and engineering periodicals.

CD-ROM DATABASES

Profiles in Business and Management: An International Directory of Scholars and Their Research [CD-ROM]. Harvard Business School Publishing. • Annual. $595.00. Fully searchable CD-ROM version of two-volume printed directory. Contains bibliographic and biographical information for over 5600 business and management experts active in 21 subject areas. Formerly *International Directory of Business and Management Scholars.*

Science Citation Index: Compact Disc Edition. Institute for Scientific Information. • Monthly. Provides CD-ROM indexing of the world's scientific and technical literature. Corresponds to online *Scisearch* and printed *Science Citation Index.*

DIRECTORIES

Directory of American Research and Technology: Organizations Active in Product Development for Business. Information Today. • Annual. $359.95. Lists over 13,000 publicly and privately owned research facilities. Formerly *Industrial Research Laboratories of the U.S.*

Plunkett's Engineering and Research Industry Almanac. Plunkett Research, Ltd. • Annual. $179. 99. Contains detailed profiles of major engineering and technology corporations. Includes CD-ROM.

Unique 3-in-1 Research and Development Directory. Government Data Publications, Inc. • Annual. $15.00. Government contractors in the research and development fields. Included with subscription to *R and D Contracts Monthly.* Formerly *Research and Development Directory.*

ENCYCLOPEDIAS AND DICTIONARIES

Blackwell Encyclopedic Dictionary of Operations Management. Nigel Slack, editor. Blackwell Publishing. • 1997. $130.95. The editor is associated with the University of Warwick, England. Contains definitions of key terms combined with longer articles written by various U. S. and foreign business educators. Includes bibliographies and index. (Blackwell Encyclopedia of Management Series.).

ONLINE DATABASES

Applied Science and Technology Index Online. H. W. Wilson Co. • Provides online indexing of 500 major scientific, technical, industrial, and engineering periodicals. Time period is 1983 to date. Monthly updates. Inquire as to online cost and availability.

Current Contents Connect. Institute for Scientific Information. • Provides online abstracts of articles listed in the tables of contents of about 7,500 journals. Coverage is very broad, including science, social science, life science, technology, engineering, industry, agriculture, the environment, economics, and arts and humanities. Time period is two years, with weekly updates. Inquire as to online cost and availability.

NTIS Database. National Technical Information Service. • Contains citations and abstracts to unrestricted reports of government-sponsored research, 1964 to date. Covers a wide range of technical, engineering, business, and social science topics. Monthly updates. Inquire as to online cost and availability.

Scisearch. Institute for Scientific Information. • Broad, multidisciplinary index to the literature of science and technology, 1974 to present. Inquire as to online cost and availability. Coverage of literature is worldwide, with weekly updates.

Who's Who in Technology [Online]. Gale Cengage Learning. • Provides online biographical profiles of over 25,000 American scientists, engineers, and others in technology-related occupations. Inquire as to online cost and availability.

PERIODICALS AND NEWSLETTERS

Industrial and Engineering Chemistry Research. American Chemical Society. • Monthly. Members, $169.00 per year; institutions, $1,445.00 per year; students, $127.00 per year. Available on line . Fomerly *Industrial and Engineering Chemistry Product Research and Development.*

Research and Development: The Voice of the Research and Development Community. Reed Business Information. • 13 times a year. $81.90 per year.

RESEARCH CENTERS AND INSTITUTES

Center for Industrial Research and Service. Iowa State University of Science and Technology. 2272 Howe Hall, No. 2620, Ames, IA 50011-2272. Phone: (515)294-3420 Fax: (515)294-4925 E-mail: info@ciras.iastate.edu • URL: http://www.ciras.iastate. edu.

STATISTICS SOURCES

Research and Development Expenditures in Industry. Organization for Economic Cooperation and Development. • Annual. $51.00. Presents research and development expenditures for OECD countries and the European Union zone. Includes about 60 industrial sectors.

TRADE/PROFESSIONAL ASSOCIATIONS

Industrial Research Institute. 2200 Clarendon Blvd., Ste. 1102, Arlington, VA 22201. Phone: (703)647-2580 Fax: (703)647-2581 E-mail: bernstein@iriinc. org • URL: http://www.iriinc.org • Manufacturers and industrial firms maintaining industrial research laboratories. Identifies and promotes effective techniques for the organization and management of research, development, and engineering in support of technological innovation.

Society of Research Administrators International. 1901 N Moore St., Ste. 1004, Arlington, VA 22209. Phone: (703)741-0140 Fax: (703)741-0142 E-mail: info@srainternational.org • URL: http://www. srainternational.org • Dedicated to advancing the profession and improving the efficiency and effectiveness of research administration.

INDUSTRIAL ROBOTS

See: ROBOTS

INDUSTRIAL SAFETY

See also: INDUSTRIAL HYGIENE; SAFETY

GENERAL WORKS

Industrial Safety and Health Management. C. Ray Asfahl. Prentice Hall PTR. • 2003. $92.33. Fifth edition. (Prentice Hall International Industrial and Systems Series).

ABSTRACTS AND INDEXES

Health and Safety Science Abstracts. Institute of Safety and Systems Management. Cambridge Information Group. • Monthly. Online edition, $850.00 year. Formerly *Safety Science Abstracts Journal.*

Safety and Health at Work. International Labour Office. • Bimonthly. $240.00 per year. Formerly *Occupational Safety and Health Abstracts.*

CD-ROM DATABASES

Authority Worker's Compensation Library. LexisNexis/Matthew Bender. • Periodic revisions. Price on request. CD-ROM contains updated full text of *Larson's Workmen's Compensation, Occupational Injuries and Illnesses,* and other Matthew Bender publications relating to the law of worker's compensation.

OSH-ROM: Occupational Safety and Health Information on CD-ROM. Available from Silver-Platter Information, Inc. • Price and frequency on application. Produced in Geneva by the International Occupational Safety and Health Information Centre, International Labour Organization (http://www.ilo. org). Provides about two million citations and abstracts to the worldwide literature of industrial safety, industrial hygiene, hazardous materials, and accident prevention. Material is included from journals, technical reports, books, government publications, and other sources. Time span varies.

DIRECTORIES

Best's Safety and Security Directory. A.M. Best Co. • Annual. Free to members; non-members, $295.00. A manual of current industrial safety practices with a directory of manufacturers and distributors of plant safety, security and industrial hygiene products and services listed by hazard. Formerly *Best's Safety Directory.*

ENCYCLOPEDIAS AND DICTIONARIES

Encyclopedia of Occupational Health and Safety. International Labour Organization. • 1998. $990.00. Fourth edition. Four volumes. Includes CD-ROM. Covers safety engineering, industrial medicine, ergonomics, hygiene, epidemiology, toxicology, industrial psychology, and related topics. Includes material related to specific chemical, textile, transport, construction, manufacturing, and other industries. Indexed by subject, chemical name, and author, with a "Directory of Experts.".

Encyclopedia of Occupational Health and Safety. Jeanne M. Stellman. International Labour Office. • 1998. $990.00. Fourth edition. Four volumes. Includes CD-Rom.

Unabridged Dictionary of Occupational and Environmental Safety and Health with CD-ROM. Jeffrey W. Vincoli and Kathryn L. Bazan. Lewis Publishers. • 1999. $89.95.

HANDBOOKS AND MANUALS

Fundamental Principles of Occupational Health and Safety. Benjamin Alli. International Labour Organization. • 2001. $14.95. A practical guide to health and safety policies in the workplace. Covers legal issues, enforcement, health surveillance, protective measures, education, and training. Includes a glossary.

Handbook of Occupational Safety and Health. Louis J. DiBerardinis. John Wiley and Sons, Inc. • 1998. $170.00. Second edition.

Managing Worker's Compensation: A Guide to Injury Reduction and Effective Claim Management. Keith Wertz and others. Lewis Publishers. • 2000. $69.95. (Occupation Safety and Health Guide Series).

Occupational Safety and Health Law. Randy S. Rabinowitz. BNA Books. • 2002. $265.00. Third edition.

Occupational Safety and Health Standards for General Industry. CCH, Inc. • 1999. $42.95.

Sax's Dangerous Properties of Industrial Materials. Richard J. Lewis. John Wiley and Sons, Inc. • 1999. $545.00. 10th edition. Three volumes. Provides detailed information on the chemical, physical, and toxicity characteristics of more than 22,000 industrial materials. Hazard ratings and safety profiles are specified. Includes CD-ROM.

ONLINE DATABASES

NIOSHTIC: National Institute for Occupational Safety and Health Technical Information Center Database. National Institute for Occupational Safety and Health, Technical Information Bra. • Provides citations and abstracts of technical literature in the areas of industrial safety, industrial hygiene, and toxicology. Covers 1890 to date, but mostly 1973 to date. Monthly updates. (Database is also known as *Occupational Safety and Health.*) Inquire as to online cost and availability.

PERIODICALS AND NEWSLETTERS

BNA's SafetyNet. Bureau of National Affairs Inc. • Description: Designed to help employers deal with occupational safety and health regulations, policies, standards, and practices, and to understand the effects of compliance on employee relations. Covers the establishment, management, evaluation, maintenance, and administration of health and safety programs. Carries information on recordkeeping, inspections, enforcement, employer defenses, and training.

Industrial Safety and Hygiene News: News of Safety, Health and Hygiene, Environmental, Fire, Security and Emergency Protection Equipment. Business News Publishing Co. • Monthly. Free to qualified personnel; others, $120.00 per year.

Job Safety and Health Quarterly. Available from U. S. Government Printing Office. • Quarterly. $17.00 per year. Issued by the Occupational Safety and Health Administration (OSHA), U. S. Department of Labor. Contains articles on employee safety and health, with information on current OSHA activities.

Occupational Hazards: Magazine of Health and Environment. Penton Media, Inc. • Monthly. $55.00 per year. Industrial safety and security management.

Professional Safety. American Society of Safety Engineers. • Monthly. Free to members; nonmembers, $60.00 per year. Emphasis is on research and technology in the field of accident prevention.

Safety and Health: The International Safety, Health and Environment Magazine. National Safety Council,. • Monthly. Members, $45.00 per year; non-members, $58.50 per year. Formerly *National Safety and Health News.*

RESEARCH CENTERS AND INSTITUTES

Institute for Advanced Safety Studies. 5950 W. Touhy Ave., Niles, IL 60714. Phone: (847)647-1101 Fax: (847)647-2047 E-mail: iass@tridyne.com.

National Safe Workplace Institute/Safeplaces.com. P.O. Box 2841, Monroe, NC 28110. Phone: (704)282-1111 Fax: (704)289-6601 E-mail: info@

safespaces.com • URL: http://www.safespaces.com.

STATISTICS SOURCES

Report on the American Workforce. Available from U. S. Government Printing Office. • Annual. Issued by the U. S. Department of Labor (http://www.dol.gov). Appendix contains tabular statistics, including employment, unemployment, price indexes, consumer expenditures, employee benefits (retirement, insurance, vacation, etc.), wages, productivity, hours of work, and occupational injuries. Annual figures are shown for up to 50 years.

Yearbook of Labour Statistics. Available from Bernan Associates. • Annual. $168.00. Published by the International Labour Organizaton (http://www.ilo.org). Provides data for more than 180 countries on employment, unemployment, wages, hours of work, cost of labor, strikes, industrial accidents, and consumer prices.

TRADE/PROFESSIONAL ASSOCIATIONS

American Society of Safety Engineers. 1800 E. Oakton St., Des Plaines, IL 60018. Phone: (847)699-2929 Fax: (847)768-3434 E-mail: customerservice@asse.org • URL: http://www.asse.org.

International Association of Industrial Accident Boards and Commissions. 5610 Medical Ctr, Ste. 24, Madison, WI 53719. Phone: (608)663-6355 Fax: (608)663-1546 E-mail: fhowe@iaiabc.org • URL: http://www.iaiabc.org • Members are government agencies, insurance companies, lawyers, unions, self-insurers, and others with an interest in industrial safety and the administration of workers' compensation laws.

National Safety Council. 1121 Spring Lake Dr., Itasca, IL 60143-3201. Phone: 800-621-7619 or (630)285-1121 Fax: (630)285-1613 E-mail: nrhc@nrhcweb.org • URL: http://www.nsc.org • Individuals whose professional activities are related to the safety of employees and college or university students.

Safety Equipment Dealers Association. 2105 Laurel Bush Rd., Suite 200, Bel Air, MD 21015. Phone: (443)640-1065 Fax: (443)640-1031 E-mail: steve@ksgroup.org • URL: http://www.safetycentral.org.

OTHER SOURCES

Corporate Compliance Series. Joseph E. Murphy and Paul H. Dawes. West Group. • $1,210.00. 12 looseleaf volumes. Covers criminal and civil liability problems for corporations. Includes employee safety, product liability, pension requirements, securities violations, equal employment opportunity issues, intellectual property, employee hiring and firing, and other corporate compliance topics.

Human Resources Management Whole. CCH, Inc. • Nine looseleaf volumes. $1,572 per year. Includes monthly updates. Components are *Ideas and Trends Newsletter, Employment Relations, Compensation, Equal Employment Opportunity, Personnel Practices/Communications* and *OSHA Compliance.* Components are available separately.

Occupational Safety and Health Handbook: An Employer's Guide to OSHA Laws. LexisNexis Matthew Bender. • Looseleaf. $115.00. Periodic supplementation available. Covers inspections, violations, the citation process, ergonomics, hazards, equipment, and other topics relating to the law enforced by the federal Occupational Safety and Health Administration (OSHA).

Practical Guide to the Occupational Safety and Health Act. American Lawyer Media, Inc. • Looseleaf. $149.00. Updated as needed. Covers the practical aspects of doing business while complying with OSHA regulations. Covers inspections, enforcement, rights of employees, the possibility of criminal prosecution, and related issues. (Law Journal Press).

INDUSTRIAL SECURITY PROGRAMS

See also: ELECTRONIC SECURITY SYSTEMS; LOCKS AND KEYS

DIRECTORIES

Security: Product Service Suppliers Guide. Reed Business Information. • Annual. $50.00 Includes computer and information protection products. Formerly *Security World Product Directory.*

HANDBOOKS AND MANUALS

Effective Physical Security: Design, Equipment, and Operations. Lawrence J. Fennelly, editor. Elsevier. • 1996. $44.99. Second edition. Contains chapters written by various U. S. security equipment specialists. Covers architectural considerations, locks, safes, alarms, intrusion detection systems, closed circuit television, identification systems, etc.

Investigations in the Workplace. Eugene F. Ferraro. CRC Press. • 2004. $79.95: Written for security professionals, lawyers, and human resource directors. Explains how to properly conduct internal investigations in the private sector and avoid litigation. Such investigations may relate to loss prevention, asset protection, or employee rights issues. (Imprint: Auerbach Publications.).

National Industrial Security Program Operating Manual. U.S. Department of Defense. Available from U.S. Government Printing Office. • 1995.

Office Building Safety and Health. Charles D. Reese. CRC Press. • 2004. $89.95. Covers a wide variety of topics relating to office building safety, including management of emergencies, common hazards, accident prevention, environmental health issues, and security.

Private Investigator. Entrepreneur Media, Inc. • Looseleaf. $59.50. A practical guide to starting a private investigation agency. Covers profit potential, start-up costs, market size evaluation, pricing, accounting, advertising, promotion, etc. (Start-Up Business Guide No. E1320.).

PERIODICALS AND NEWSLETTERS

CSO: The Resource for Security Executives. CXO Media, Inc. • Monthly. $64.95 per year. Edited for corporate chief security officers (CSOs). Covers a wide variety of business security issues, including computer security, identity theft, spam, physical security, loss prevention, risk management, privacy, and investigations.

Homeland Security and Defense: Weekly Intelligence for the Global Homeland Security and Defense Community. Aviation Week Business Intelligence Services. • Weekly. $595.00 per year. Newsletter. Emphasis is on airline and airport programs (federal, state, and local). Also covers counterterrorism, protection of military units, Department of Homeland Security activities, industrial security, communications equipment, and other topics related to homeland security.

Security Letter. Security Letter Inc. • Description: Contains "solution-oriented information on security and protection of assets from loss," particularly for executives concerned about the following: internal checks and controls, personnel practices, management of change, fraud and embezzlement, business crime trends, security, and urban terrorism. Recurring features include news of research, a calendar of events, semiannual FBI crime data, quarterly financial news of major companies in the security industry, book reviews, security and safety pointers, and a question-and-answer feature.

Security Management. American Society for Industrial Security. • Monthly. Members, $38.00 per year; non-members, $48.00 per year. Articles cover the protection of corporate assets, including personnel property and information security.

TRADE/PROFESSIONAL ASSOCIATIONS

American Society for Industrial Security. 1625 Prince St., Alexandria, VA 22314-2818. Phone: (703)519-6200 Fax: (703)519-6299 E-mail: asis@ asisonline • URL: http://www.asisonline.org.

International Security Management Association. PO Box 623, Buffalo, IA 52728. Phone: 800-368-1894 or (563)381-4008 Fax: 800-568-1894 or (563)381-4283 E-mail: isma3@aol.com • URL: http://www.ismanet.com • Senior security executives of multinational business firms and chief executive officers of full service security services companies. Aims to assist senior security executives in coordinating and exchanging information about security management and to establish high business and professional standards.

INDUSTRIAL STATISTICS

See: BUSINESS STATISTICS; STATISTICAL METHODS

INDUSTRIAL TOXICOLOGY

See: INDUSTRIAL HYGIENE

INDUSTRIAL WELFARE

See: EMPLOYEE BENEFIT PLANS

INDUSTRY

See also: BUSINESS; CORPORATIONS

GENERAL WORKS

How Products Are Made. Gale Cengage Learning. • 2002. Three volumes. $115.00. Previous volumes available. Provides easy-to-read, step-by-step descriptions of how approximately 100 different products are manufactured. Items are of all kinds, both mechanical and non-mechanical.

Industrial Revolution Reference Library. Gale Cengage Learning. • 2003. $165.00. Three volumes. Individual volumes are available at $55.00. Includes *Industrial Revolution: Almanac; Industrial Revolution: Biographies* and *Industrial Revolution: Primary Sources.* (UXL imprint).

The Organization of Industry. William F. Shughart. Cengage Learning Custom Publishing. • 1997. $77.95. Second edition.

ABSTRACTS AND INDEXES

Applied Science and Technology Index. H. W. Wilson Co. • 11 times a year. Quarterly and annual cumulations. Price varies. Indexes a wide variety of English language technical, industrial, and engineering periodicals.

ALMANACS AND YEARBOOKS

Irwin Business and Investment Almanac, 1994: Dow Jones and Company Edition. Summer N. Levine and Caroline Levine. McGraw-Hill. • 1994. $75.00. 18th edition. A review of last year's business activity. Covers a wide variety of business and economic data: stock market statistics, industrial information, commodity futures information, art market trends, comparative living costs for U. S. metropolitan areas, foreign stock market data, etc. Formerly *Business One Irwin Business and Investment Almanac.*

BIOGRAPHICAL SOURCES

Who's Who in Finance and Industry. Marquis Who's Who. • Biennial. $259.95. Provides over

21,000 concise biographies of business leaders in all fields.

CD-ROM DATABASES

D & B Business Locator. Dun & Bradstreet, Inc. • Quarterly. $2,495.00 per year. CD-ROM provides concise information on more than 10 million U. S. companies or businesses. Includes data on number of employees.

Hoover's Company Capsules on CD-ROM. Hoover's, Inc. • Quarterly. $399.95 per year (single-user). Provides the CD-ROM version of *Hoover's Handbook of American Business, Hoover's Handbook of Emerging Companies, Hoover's Handbook of World Business, Hoover's Guide to Computer Companies, Hoover's Guide to Media Companies, Hoover's Handbook of Private Companies,* and various regional guides. Includes more than 11,000 profiles of companies.

OECD Statistical Compendium. Organization for Economic Cooperation and Development. • Semiannual. $1,905.00 per year for 1 to 10 users. CD-ROM contains more than 730,000 monthly, quarterly, and annual time series for OECD countries, 1960 to date. Includes fully searchable data on agriculture, food, economic indicators, national accounts, employment, energy, finance, industry, technology, and foreign trade. Results can be displayed in various forms.

16 Million Businesses Phone Directory. Info USA. • Annual. $29.95. Provides more than 16 million yellow pages telephone directory listings on CD-ROM for all ZIP Code areas of the U. S.

Statistical Abstract of the United States on CD-ROM. Hoover's, Inc. • Annual. $49.95. Provides all statistics from official print version, plus expanded historical data, greater detail, and keyword searching features.

USA Trade. U. S. Department of Commerce. • Monthly. $650.00 per year. Provides over 150,000 trade-related data series on CD-ROM. Includes full text of many government publications. Specific data is included on national income, labor, price indexes, foreign exchange, technical standards, and international markets. Website address is http://www.stat-usa.gov/.

DIRECTORIES

American Big Businesses Directory. infoUSA Inc. • Covers: 218,000 U.S. businesses with more than 100 employees, and 500,000 key executives and directors. CD-ROM version contains 160,000 top firms and 431,000 key executives. Entries include: Name, address, phone, names and titles of key personnel, number of employees, sales volume, Standard Industrial Classification (SIC) codes, subsidiaries and parent company names, stock exchanges on which traded.

American Manufacturers Directory. infoUSA Inc. • Covers: more than 150,000 manufacturing companies with 20 or more employees. CD-ROM version lists all 531,000 U.S. manufacturers, in all employee size ranges. Entries include: Company name, address, phone, contact name, Standard Industrial Classification (SIC) codes, number of employees, sales volume code, credit rating scores.

America's Corporate Families. Dun & Bradstreet Corp. • Covers: Approximately 12,700 U.S. corporations. Ultimate companies must meet all of the following criteria for inclusion: two or more business locations, 250 or more employees at that location or in excess of $25 million in sales volume or a tangible net worth greater than $500,000, and controlling interest in one or more subsidiary company. Entries include: D&B D-U-N-S number, company name, address, phone, state of incorporation, line of business, primary/secondary SIC codes, sales volume, net worth, number of employees, current ownership date, year started, number of sites, key executives' names/titles, directors and than of-

ficers, primary bank and accounting firm, import/ export designation, stock exchange symbol and indicator for publicly owned companies, parent company and location.

Canadian Trade Index. MacRae's Blue Book. • Covers: in one volume, over 30,000 manufacturers in Canada. Also includes distributors, service companies, and exporters. Entries include: Company name, address, names and titles of key personnel, products, trademarks, number of employees, annual sales, non-manufacturing locations, subsidiaries and associates, foreign representatives, headquarters phone, ISO information, export regions.

The Corporate Directory of U.S. Public Companies. Walker's Research, LLC. • Annual. $360.00. Two volumes. Contains information on more than 10,000 publicly-traded companies, including names of executives and major subsidiaries. Includes financial and stock data.

D and B Million Dollar Directory. • Annual. Commercial institutions, $1,395.00; libraries, $1,275.00. Lease basis.

Dun's Industrial Guide: The Metalworking Directory. Dun and Bradstreet Corp. • Annual. Libraries, $485; commercial institutions, $795.00. Lease basis. Three volumes. Lists about 65,000 U. S. manufacturing plants using metal and suppliers of metalworking equipment and materials. Includes names and titles of key personnel. Products, purchases, and processes are indicated.

Harris Manufacturers Directory 2000: National Edition. Harris InfoSource. • Annual. $565.00. Two volumes. Provides statistical and descriptive information for about 47,062 U.S. industrial firms having 100 or more employees.

Headquarters USA: A Directory of Contact Information for Headquarters and Other Central Offices of Major Businesses and Organizations Nationwide. Omnigraphics, Inc. • Annual. $185.00. Two volumes. Volume one is alphabetical by name of business or organization. Volume two is classified by subject. Includes more than 112,000 businesses, organizations, agencies, institutions, and "high-profile" individuals. Listings include addresses, telephone numbers, fax numbers, and toll-free numbers and Web addresses where available. Formerly *Business Phone Book USA.*

Hoover's Masterlist of Major U. S. Companies. Hoover's, Inc. • 2003. $275.00. Provides brief information, including annual sales, number of employees, and chief executive, for about 5,000 U. S. companies, both public and private.

Kompass USA. Kompass International/Kompass USA, Inc. • Annual. Price on application. Two volumes. Includes information on about 125,000 U.S. companies. Classification system covers approximately 50,000 products and services. Product and tradename indexes are provided.

Standard and Poor's Register of Corporations, Directors and Executives. Standard and Poor's. • Annual. $675.00. Looseleaf service. Lease basis. Periodic supplementation. Over 55,000 public and privately held corporations in the U.S.

Thomas Register of American Manufacturers. Thomas Publishing Co., Inc. • Annual. $149.00. 34 volumes. A three-part system offering information on a wide variety of industrial equipment and supplies. Lists more than 151,000 industrial product and services companies.

Ward's Business Directory of U. S. Private and Public Companies. Gale Cengage Learning. • 2002. $2,765.00. 45th edition. Eight volumes. *Ward's* contains basic information on about 120,000 business firms, of which 90 percent are private companies. Includes mid-year *Supplement.* Volumes

For publishers addresses, refer to SOURCES CITED section at the back of the book.

471

available individually. Prices vary.

ENCYCLOPEDIAS AND DICTIONARIES

Encyclopedia of Emerging Industries. Gale Cengage Learning. • 2001. $320.00. Fourth edition. Provides detailed information on 115 "newly flourishing" industries. Includes historical background, organizational structure, significant individuals, current conditions, major companies, work force, technology trends, research developments, and other industry facts.

Knowledge Exchange Business Encyclopedia: Your Complete Business Advisor. Lorraine Spurge. Knowledge Exchange LLC. • 1998. $45.00. Provides definitions of business terms and financial expressions, profiles of leading industries, tables of economic statistics, biographies of business leaders, and other business information. Includes "A Chronology of Business from 3000 B.C. Through 1995." Contains illustrations and three indexes.

Oxford Encyclopedia of Economic History. Joel Mokyr, editor. Oxford University Press. • 2003. $695.00. Five volumes. Provides extensive coverage of a wide variety of topics relating to business, industrial, and economic history.

FINANCIAL RATIOS

IRS Corporate Financial Ratios. Available from MarketResearch.com. • 2002. $225.00. Published by Schonfeld & Associates, Inc. Presents 70 key financial ratios for 260 industries. Ratios are calculated from income statement and balance sheet data available from the Internal Revenue Service. Includes four asset size classes.

HANDBOOKS AND MANUALS

Career Guide to Industries. Available from U. S. Government Printing Office. • 2002. $32.00. Issued by the Bureau of Labor Statistics, U. S. Department of Labor (http://www.bls.gov). Presents background career information (text) and statistics for the 40 industries that account for 70 percent of wage and salary jobs in the U. S. Includes nature of the industry, employment data, working conditions, training, earnings, rate of job growth, outlook, and other career factors. (BLS Bulletin 2541.).

Dun & Bradstreet/Gale Group Industry Handbooks. Gale Cengage Learning. • 2000. $650.00. Five volumes. $130.00 per volume. Each volume covers two or more major industries: 1. *Entertainment and Hospitality*; 2. *Construction and Agriculture*; 3. *Chemicals and Pharmaceuticals*; 4. *Computers & Software & Broadcasting & Telecommunications*; 5. *Insurance and Health & Medical Services.* The following are included for each industry: overview, statistics, financial ratios, rankings, merger information, company directory, directory of associations, and consultants directory. (Dun and Bradstreet/Gale Industry Reference Handbook Series).

Industry and Product Classification Manual (SIC Basis). Available from National Technical Information Service. • 1992. Issued by U. S. Bureau of the Census. Contains extended Standard Industrial Classification (SIC) numbers used by the Census Bureau to allow a more detailed classification of industry, services, and agriculture.

Manufacturing Processes Reference Guide. R. H. Todd and others. Industrial Press, Inc. • 1994. $46.95. Describes 130 manufacturing processes used in industry.

North American Industry Classification System (NAICS). Available from Bernan Press. • 2002. $45.00. Issued by the Executive Office of the President, Office of Management and Budget (OMB).

Standard Industrial Classification Manual. U.S. Department of Commerce, Bureau of the Census.

Available from U.S. Government Printing Office. • 1987. $36.00.

INTERNET DATABASES

Bureau of Economic Analysis (BEA). U. S. Department of Commerce, Bureau of Economic Analysis. Phone: (202)606-9900 Fax: (202)606-5310 E-mail: webmaster@bea.doc.gov • URL: http://www.bea.doc.gov • Web site includes "News Release Information" covering national, regional, and international economic estimates from the BEA. Highlights of releases appear online the same day, complete text and tables appear the next day. "Recent News Releases" section provides titles for past nine months, with links. "BEA Data and Methodology" includes "Frequently Requested NIPA Data" (national income and product accounts, such as gross domestic product and personal income). Other statistics are available. Fees: Free.

Business 2.0 Web Guide to the Best Business Links. Business 2.0 Media Inc. Phone: (415)293-4800 E-mail: support@business2.com • URL: http://www.business2.com/webguide • Web site presents an extensive, searchable directory of links to "the best, most informative, and authoritative web pages." Twenty main categories cover business, finance, career, company information, people, and technology topics, with thousands of subtopics, all linking to Web sites recommended by experienced business researchers. Fees: Free.

EBSCO Information Services. Ebsco Publishing. Phone: 800-653-2726 or (978)356-6500 Fax: (978)356-6565 E-mail: ep@epnet.com • URL: http://www.epnet.com • Fee-based Web site providing Internet access to a wide variety of databases, including business-related material. Full text is available for many periodical titles, with daily updates. Fees: Apply.

Factiva. Dow Jones Reuters Business Interactive, LLC. Phone: 800-369-7466 or (609)452-1511 Fax: (609)520-5770 E-mail: solutions@factiva.com • URL: http://www.factiva.com • Fee-based Web site provides "global news and business information through Web sites and content integration solutions." Includes Dow Jones and Reuters newswires, The Wall Street Journal, and more than 7,000 other sources of current news, historical articles, market research reports, and investment analysis. Content includes 96 major U. S. newspapers, 900 non-English sources, trade publications, media transcripts, country profiles, news photos, etc.

Federal Reserve Board Publications and Education Resources. Board of Governors of the Federal Reserve System. Phone: (202)452-3000 Fax: (202)452-3819 • URL: http://www.federalreserve.gov/publications.htm • Web site provides convenient access to statistics, surveys, and research from the Federal Reserve Board. *Federal Reserve Bulletin* articles are available as abstracts or full text (PDF) currently or from six-year archives. The link "Statistics: Releases and Historical Data" offers daily, weekly, monthly, quarterly, and annual data in great detail for interest rates, foreign exchange, consumer credit, money stock measures, industrial production indexes, bank reserves, and other items. Historical tabulations are available for various time periods. Fees: Free.

Fedstats. Federal Interagency Council on Statistical Policy. Phone: (202)395-7254 • URL: http://www.fedstats.gov • Web site features an efficient search facility for full-text statistics produced by more than 100 federal agencies, including the Census Bureau, the Bureau of Economic Analysis, and the Bureau of Labor Statistics. Boolean searches can be made within one agency or for all agencies combined. Links are offered to international statistical bureaus, including the UN, IMF, OECD, UNESCO, Eurostat, and 20 individual countries. Fees: Free.

FreeLunch.com. Economy.com, Inc. Phone: (610)696-8700 Fax: (610)696-1678 • URL: http://

www.freelunch.com • Web site provides free access to more than 1.5 million economic and financial data series, covering industry, demographics, labor markets, prices, retail sales, government spending, trade, interest rates, housing starts, the stock market, and many other topics. Data is available for various time periods in either chart or table form. Searching is offered. Fees: Free, but registration required. Economy.com, Inc. also offers fee-based economic analysis at *The Dismal Scientist* site (http://www.dismal.com).

InSite 2. Intelligence Data/Thomson Financial. Phone: 800-654-0393 or (617)856-1890 Fax: (617)737-3182 E-mail: intelligence.data@tfn.com • URL: http://www.insite2.gale.com/ • Fee-based Web site consolidates information in a "Base Pack" consisting of Business InSite, Market InSite, and Company InSite. Optional databases are Consumer InSite, Health and Wellness InSite, Newsletter InSite, and Computer InSite. Includes fulltext content from more than 2,500 trade publications, journals, newsletters, newspapers, analyst reports, and other sources. Continuous updating. Formerly produced by The Gale Group.

Manufacturing Profiles. U. S. Bureau of the Census. Phone: (301)763-4636 E-mail: webmaster@census.gov • URL: http://www.census.gov/prod/www/abs/mfg-prof.html • The Census Bureau makes available free on PDF (Portable Document Format) an annual consolidation of the entire Current Industrial Report series, presenting "all the data compiled." Contains statistics on production, shipments, inventories, consumption, exports, imports, and orders for a wide variety of manufactured products.

Nexis.com. Lexis-Nexis Group. Phone: 800-227-4908 or (937)865-6800 Fax: (937)865-6909 E-mail: webmaster@prod.lexis-nexis.com • URL: http://www.nexis.com • Fee-based Web site offers searching of about 2.8 billion documents in some 30,000 news, business, and legal information sources. Features include a subject directory covering 1,200 topics in 34 categories and a Company Dossier containing information on more than 500,000 public and private companies. Boolean searching is offered.

1997 NAICS and 1987 SIC Correspondence Tables. U. S. Census Bureau. Phone: (301)457-4100 Fax: (301)457-1296 E-mail: naics@census.gov • URL: http://www.census.gov/epcd/www/naicstab.htm • Web site provides detailed tables for converting four-digit Standard Industrial Classification (SIC) numbers to the six-digit North American Industrial Classification System (NAICS) or vice versa: "1987 SIC Matched to 1997 NAICS" or "1997 NAICS Matched to 1987 SIC." Fees: Free.

ProQuest Direct. ProQuest Inc. Phone: 800-889-3358 or (734)761-4700 Fax: (734)662-4554 • URL: http://proquest.com • Fee-based Web site providing Internet access to more than 3,000 periodicals, newspapers, and other publications. Many items are available full-text, with daily updates. Includes extensive corporate and financial information. Fees: Apply.

Summary of Commentary on Current Economic Conditions by Federal Reserve District [the Beige Book]. Board of Governors of the Federal Reserve System. Phone: (202)452-3000 Fax: (202)452-3819 • URL: http://www.federalreserve.gov/fomc/beigebook/2004/ • Free Web site provides current "anecdotal information" eight times a year on economic conditions within each of the 12 Federal Reserve Districts, plus an extensive national *Summary.* Text is based on the opinions of bank officials, business executives, economists, financial market experts, and others. Typically contains views of consumer spending, manufacturing, services, credit, employment, prices, wages, and the economy in general. Usually referred to as the Beige Book.

Switchboard. Switchboard, Inc. Phone: (508)898-8000 Fax: (508)898-1755 E-mail: webmaster@

switchboard.com • URL: http://www.switchboard. com • Web site provides telephone numbers and street addresses for more than 100 million business locations and residences in the U. S. Broad industry categories are available. Fees: Free.

U. S. Census Bureau: The Official Statistics. U. S. Bureau of the Census. Phone: (301)763-4100 Fax: (301)763-4794 • URL: http://www.census.gov • Web site is "Your Source for Social, Demographic, and Economic Information." Contains "Current U. S. Population Count," "Current Economic Indicators," and a wide variety of data under "Other Official Statistics." Keyword searching is provided. Fees: Free.

Wall Street Journal Interactive Edition. Dow Jones & Co., Inc. Phone: 800-369-2834 or (212)416-2000 Fax: (212)416-2658 E-mail: inquiries@interactive. wsj.com • URL: http://www.wsj.com • Fee-based Web site providing online searching of worldwide information from the *The Wall Street Journal.* Includes "Company Snapshots," "The Journal's Greatest Hits," "Index to Market Data," "Journal Links," etc. Financial price quotes are available. Fees: $49.00 per year; $29.00 per year to print subscribers.

ONLINE DATABASES

Applied Science and Technology Index Online. H. W. Wilson Co. • Provides online indexing of 500 major scientific, technical, industrial, and engineering periodicals. Time period is 1983 to date. Monthly updates. Inquire as to online cost and availability.

Business and Industry. Gale Cengage Learning. • Contains online citations, abstracts, and selected fulltext from more than 1,000 trade journals, newspapers, and other publications. Provides general coverage of both manufacturing and service industries, including marketing, production, industry trends, key events, and information on specific companies. Time span is 1994 to date. Daily updates. Inquire as to online cost and availability. (Also available in a CD-ROM version.).

F & S Index. Gale Cengage Learning. • Contains about four million citations to worldwide business, financial, and industrial or consumer product literature appearing from 1972 to date. Weekly updates. Inquire as to online cost and availability.

Industry Insider. Thomson Financial. • Contains full-text online industry research reports from more than 200 leading trade associations, covering 50 specific industries. Reports include extensive statistics and market research data. Inquire as to online cost and availability.

Market Share Reporter (MSR) [online]. Gale Cengage Learning. • Provides online market share data for individual companies, products, and services, covering all industries. Sources include various publications, trade journals, associations, government agencies, corporate reports, investment research reports, etc. Time period is 1991 to date, with annual updates. Inquire as to online cost and availability.

PROMT: Predicasts Overview of Markets and Technology. Gale Cengage Learning. • Companies, products, applied technologies and markets. U.S. and international literature coverage, 1972 to date. Inquire as to online cost and availability. Provides abstracts from more than 1,600 publications. Weekly updates.

Tablebase. Gale Cengage Learning. • Provides online numerical tabular data from a wide variety of business, organization, and government sources, including about 1,000 trade journals. Includes industry and individual company statistics relating to products, market share, sales forecasts, production, exports, market trends, etc. Time span is 1997 to date. Weekly updates. Inquire as to online cost

and availability. (Also available in a CD-ROM version.).

Thomas Register Online. Thomas Publishing Co., Inc. • Provides concise information on approximately 194,000 U. S. companies, mainly manufacturers, with over 50,000 product classifications. Indexes over 115,000 trade names. Information is updated semiannually. Inquire as to online cost and availability.

Trade & Industry Database. Gale Cengage Learning. • Provides indexing of business periodicals, January 1981 to date. Daily updates. (Full text articles from some periodicals are available online, 1983 to date. Inquire as to online cost and availability).

PERIODICALS AND NEWSLETTERS

American Industry. Publications for Industry. • Description: Provides new product releases and information on brochures and catalogs available to industrial plant managers in the largest firms in the U.S. Recurring features include interviews, news of research, and successful use of reports.

Fortune Magazine. Time Inc., Business Information Group. • Biweekly. $59.95 per year. Edited for top executives and upper-level managers.

IEEE Industry Applications Magazine. Institute of Electrical and Electronics Engineers. • Bimonthly. $190.00 per year. Covers new industrial applications of power conversion, drives, lighting, and control. Emphasis is on the petroleum, chemical, rubber, plastics, textile, and mining industries.

Industries in Transition; A Newsletter Written for Growth Directed Management and Business Planners. Business Communications Co., Inc. • Monthly. $375.00 per year. Newsletter. Formerly *Growth Industry News.*

IndustryWeek: The Management Resource. Penton Media, Inc. • 22 times a year. Free to qualified personnel; others, $65.00 per year. Edited for industrial and business managers. Covers organizational and technological developments affecting industrial management.

Journal of Industrial Ecology. Yale University, School of Forestry and Environmental Studies. MIT Press. • Quarterly. Individuals, $55.00 per year; institutions, $140.00 per year. Contains multidisciplinary articles on the relationships between industrial activity and the environment.

The Levy Institute Forecast. Forecasting Center. • Description: Provides analyses and forecasts of U.S. business conditions. Reports on production, sales, inflation, corporate profits, and interest rates.

The Wall Street Journal. Dow Jones & Co., Inc. • Daily. $189.00 per year. Covers news and trends relating to business, industry, finance, the economy, and international commerce. Provides extensive price and other data for the securities, commodity, options, futures, foreign exchange, and money markets.

RESEARCH CENTERS AND INSTITUTES

Conference Board, Inc. The Conference Board, Inc. 845 3rd Ave., New York, NY 10022. Phone: (212)339-0345 Fax: (212)980-7014 E-mail: info@ conference-board.org • URL: http://www. conference-board.org • Business management practices worldwide, especially economic, and demographic in nature. Specific concerns include: corporate citizenship, including corporate contributions, diversity, environmental policy and issues, and government relations; corporate governance, including boards of directors, role of chief executives, relations with institutional investors, and shareholder input and influence; economics, including economic and financial forecasts, consumer confidence, leading economic indicators, North American outlook and trends, and global economic environment; human resources and organizational

effectiveness, including organization structure and design, compensation and benefits, training and development, and communications; and performance excellence.

National Center for Manufacturing Sciences. 3025 Boardwalk St., Ann Arbor, MI 48108. Phone: (734)995-0300 Fax: (734)995-4004 E-mail: johnd@ ncms.org • URL: http://www.ncms.org • Research areas include process technology and control, machine mechanics, sensors, testing methods, and quality assurance.

STATISTICS SOURCES

American Business Climate and Economic Profiles. Priscilla C. Geahigan. Gale Cengage Learning. • 1993. $170.00. Provides business, industrial, demographic, and economic figures for all states and 300 metropolitan areas. Includes production, taxation, population, growth rates, labor force data, incomes, total sales, etc.

Annual Survey of Manufactures. Available from U. S. Government Printing Office. • Annual. Prices vary. Issued by the U. S. Census Bureau as an interim update to the *Census of Manufactures.* Includes data on number of manufacturing establishments in various industries, employment, labor costs, value of shipments, capital expenditures, inventories, energy costs, and assets. (See also Census Bureau home page, http://www.census. gov/.).

Business Statistics of the United States. Linz Audain and Cornelia J. Strawser. Bernan Associates. • Annual. $147.00. Based on *Business Statistics,* formerly issue by the Bureau of Economic Analysis, U. S. Department of Commerce. Provides basic data for a wide variety of U. S. industries, services, and economic indicators. Most statistics are shown annually for 30 years and monthly for the most recent four years.

By the Numbers: Electronic and Online Publishing. Gale Cengage Learning. • 1997-98. $305.00. Four volumes. $85.00 per volume. Covers "high-interest" industries: 1. *By the Numbers: Electronic and Online Publishing*; 2. *By the Numbers: Emerging Industries*; 3. *By the Numbers: Nonprofits*; 4. *By the Numbers: Publishing.* Each volume provides about 600 tabulations of industry data on revenues, market share, employment, trends, financial ratios, profits, salaries, and so forth. Citations to data sources are included. (By the Numbers Series).

County Business Patterns. Available from U. S. Government Printing Office. • Irregular. 52 issues containing annual data for each state, the District of Columbia, and a U. S. Summary. Produced by U.S. Bureau of the Census (http://www.census.gov). Provides local establishment and employment statistics by industry.

Datapedia of the United States: American History in Numbers. George T. Kurian, editor. Bernan Press. • 2004. $125.00. Third edition. Based on the Census Bureau publication, *Historical Statistics of the United States.* Provides data from Colonial times to the present on agriculture, business, consumer income, energy, finance, labor, national income, population, and many other subjects. Includes "narrative highlights," maps, charts, and statistical projections.

Dun's Census of American Business. Dun and Bradstreet Corp. • Annual. $325.00.

Economic Report of the President: Together with the Annual Report of the Council of Economic Advisors. Available from U. S. Government Printing Office. • Annual. $32.00. Includes about 130 pages of "Statistical Tables Relating to Income, Employment, and Production." Tables cover national income, employment, wages, productivity, manufacturing, prices, credit, finance (public and private), corporate profits, and foreign trade.

Encyclopedia of American Industries. Gale Cengage

Learning. • 2000. $560.00. Third edition. Two volumes. $280.00 per volume. Volume one is *Manufacturing Industries* and volume two is *Service and Non-Manufacturing Industries*. Provides the history, development, and recent status of approximately 1,000 industries. Includes statistical graphs, with industry and general indexes.

Encyclopedia of Global Industries. Gale Cengage Learning. • 2002. $450.00. Third edition. Provides detailed statistical information on 115 industries. Coverage is international, with country and subject indexes.

Federal Reserve Bulletin. U.S. Federal Reserve System. • Monthly. $25.00 per year. Provides statistics on banking and the economy, including interest rates, money supply, and the Federal Reserve Board indexes of industrial production.

Handbook of North American Industry: NAFTA and the Economies of its Member Nations. John E. Cremeans. Bernan Press. • 1999. $115.00. Second revised edition. Provides detailed industry statistics for the U.S., Canada, and Mexico.

Handbook of U. S. Labor Statistics: Employment, Earnings, Prices, Productivity, and Other Labor Data. Eva E. Jacobs, editor. Bernan Associates. • 1999. $74.00. Based on *Handbook of Labor Statistics*, formerly issued by the Bureau of Labor Statistics, U. S. Department of Labor. Includes the Bureau's projections of employment in the U. S. by industry and occupation. Provides a wide variety of data on the work force, prices, fringe benefits, and consumer expenditures.

Indicators of Industrial and Services. OECD Publications and Information Center. • 2001-2004. Information on production, deliveries, orders, prices and employment for 17 industrial sectors in selected OECD member countries.

Industrial Commodity Statistics Yearbook. United Nations Dept. of Economic and Social Affairs. United Nations Publications. • Annual.

Key Indicators of the Labour Market. Available from Routledge. • Biennial. $125.00. Published by the International Labour Office (http://www.ilo.org). Provides data on 20 key indicators in 220 countries. Includes labor force statistics, employment, unemployment, part-time workers, wages, productivity, poverty indicators, and related topics.

Manufacturers' Shipments, Inventories, and Orders. Available from U. S. Government Printing Office. • Monthly. $79.00 per year. Issued by Bureau of the Census, U. S. Department of Commerce. Includes monthly *Advance Report on Durable Goods*. Provides data on production, value, shipments, and consumption for a wide variety of manufactured products. (Current Industrial Reports, M3-1.).

Manufacturing and Distribution USA. Gale Cengage Learning. • 2002. $395.00. Second edition. Three volumes. Presents statistics and projections relating to economic activity in more than 500 business classifications.

Manufacturing Worldwide: Industry Analysis Statistics. Gale Cengage Learning. • 1999. $240.00. Third edition. A guide to worldwide economic activity in 500 product lines within 119 countries. Includes 37 detailed industry profiles. Name, address, phone, fax, employment, and ranking are shown for major companies worldwide in each industry sector.

Monthly Bulletin of Statistics. United Nations Publications. • Monthly. $295.00 per year. Provides current data for about 200 countries on a wide variety of economic, industrial, and demographic subjects. Compiled by United Nations Statistical Office.

Panorama of European Business. Available from Bernan Associates. • Annual. $65.00. Presents statistical data for manufacturing and service industries in major European countries. Text in English, French and Spanish.

Social Statistics of the United States. Mark S. Littman, editor. Bernan Press. • 2000. $65.00. Includes statistical data on population growth, labor force, occupations, environmental trends, leisure time use, income, poverty, taxes, and other economic or demographic topics.

SRC Green Book of 5 Trend 35-Year Charts. Securities Research Co. • Annual. $150.00. Chart book presents statistical information on the stocks of 400 leading companies over a 35-year period. Each full page chart is in semi-log format to avoid visual distortion. Also includes charts of 12 leading market averages or indexes and 39 major industry groups.

Standard & Poor's Industry Surveys. Standard & Poor's. • Semiannual. $1,800.00. Two looseleaf volumes. Includes monthly *Supplements*. Provides detailed, individual surveys of 52 major industry groups. Each survey is revised on a semiannual basis. Also includes "Monthly Investment Review" (industry group investment analysis) and monthly "Trends & Projections" (economic analysis).

State Profiles: The Population and Economy of Each U. S. State. Courtenay Slater and Others. Bernan Press. • 1999. $89.00. Presents charts, tables, and text in an eight-page profile for each state. Covers population, labor force, income, poverty, employment, wages, industry, trade, housing, education, health, taxes, and government finances. (The Population and Economy of Each United States Series)

Statistical Abstract of the United States. Available from U. S. Government Printing Office. • Annual. $51.00. Issued by the U. S. Bureau of the Census.

A Statistical Portrait of the United States: Social Conditions and Trends. Mark S. Littman, editor. Bernan Press. • 1998. $89.00. Covers "social, economic, and environmental trends in the United States over the past 25 years." Includes statistical tables, graphs, and analysis relating to such topics as population, income, poverty, wealth, labor, housing, education, healthcare, air/water quality, and government. (Statistical Portrait of the United States: Social Conditions and Trends Series).

Statistical Yearbook. United Nations Publications. • Annual. $125.00. Contains statistics for about 200 countries on a wide variety of economic, industrial, and demographic topics. Compiled by United Nations Statistical Office.

Structural Statistics for Industry and Services: Core Data. Organization for Economic Cooperation and Development. • Annual. $63.00. Provides annual data for eight years for both industrial and service sectors. Industries include mining, manufacturing, utilities, and construction. Statistics for OECD countries cover production, value added, investment, employment, wages, hours worked, and number of establishments.

Survey of Current Business. Available from U. S. Government Printing Office. • Monthly. $63.00 per year. Issued by Bureau of Economic Analysis, U. S. Department of Commerce. Presents a wide variety of business and economic data.

U. S. Industry and Trade Outlook. Available from National Technical Information Service. • Annual. $69.95. Produced by the International Trade Administration, U. S. Department of Commerce, in a "public-private" partnership with DRI/McGraw-Hill and Standard & Poor's. Provides basic data, outlook for the current year, and "Long-Term Prospects" (five-year projections) for a wide variety of products and services. Includes high technology industries. Formerly *U. S. Industrial Outlook*.

U. S. Industry Profiles: The Leading 100. Gale Cengage Learning. • 1998. $130.00. Second edition. Contains detailed profiles, with statistics, of 100 industries in the areas of manufacturing, construc-

tion, transportation, wholesale trade, retail trade, and entertainment.

U. S. Market Trends and Forecasts. Gale Cengage Learning. • 2002. $325.00. Third edition. Provides graphic representation of market statistics by means of pie charts and tables for each of 30 major industries and 400 market segments. Includes market forecasts and historical overviews.

United States Census of Manufactures. U.S. Bureau of the Census. • Quinquennial. Results presented in reports, tape, CD-ROM, and Diskette files.

TRADE/PROFESSIONAL ASSOCIATIONS

National Association of Manufacturers. 1331 Pennsylvania Ave., NW, Suite 600, Washington, DC 20004-1790. Phone: 800-814-8468 or (202)637-3000 Fax: (202)637-3182 E-mail: manufacturing@nam.org • URL: http://www.nam.org.

OTHER SOURCES

Business Rankings Annual. Gale Cengage Learning. • Annual. $325.00. Two volumes. Compiled by the Business Library Staff of the Brooklyn Public Library. This is a guide to lists and rankings appearing in major business publications. The top ten names are listed in each case.

World Business Rankings Annual. Gale Cengage Learning. • 1998. $189.00. Provides 2,500 ranked lists of international companies, compiled from a variety of published sources. Each list shows the "top ten" in a particular category. Keyword indexing, a country index, and citations are provided.

INDUSTRY, REGULATION OF

See: REGULATION OF INDUSTRY

INFANTS WEAR

See: CHILDREN'S APPAREL INDUSTRY

INFLATION

See also: MONEY; PRICES AND PRICING

GENERAL WORKS

Financial Institutions and Markets. Meir J. Kohn. Oxford University Press, Inc. • 2003. $115.00. Second edition.

Great Inflations of the 20th Century: Theories, Policies, and Evidence. Pierre L. Siklos, editor. Edward Elgar Publishing, Inc. • 1995. $100.00. Contains reprints of papers on the history and economic analysis of major inflations.

How to Invest Wisely. Lawrence S. Pratt. American Institute for Economic Research. • 2002. $12.00. Presents a conservative policy of investing, with emphasis on dividend-paying common stocks. Gold and other inflation hedges are compared. Includes a reprint of *Toward an Optimal Stock Selection Strategy* (1997). (Economic Education Bulletin.).

Inflation, Exchange Rates, and the World Economy: Lectures on International Monetary Economics. Warner M. Corden. The University of Chicago Press. • 1986. $22.50. Third edition. (Studies in Business and Society Series).

Money: Its Origins, Development, Debasement, and Prospects. John H. Wood. American Institute for Economic Research. • 1999. $10.00. A politically conservative view of monetary history, the gold standard, banking systems, and inflation. Includes a list of references. (Economic Education Bulletin.).

Reducing Inflation: Motivation and Strategy. Christina Romer and David Romer. The University of Chicago Press. • 1997. $58.00. Consists of 10 essays and comments by various economists on strategies for controlling inflation. (NBER Studies in Business Cycles Series: Vol. 30).

ABSTRACTS AND INDEXES

Business Periodicals Index. H. W. Wilson Co. • 11 times a year. Quarterly and annual cumulations. Price varies.

Social Sciences Index. H. W. Wilson Co. • Quarterly, with annual cumulation. Price varies. Indexes more than 400 periodicals covering economics, environmental policy, government, insurance, labor, health care policy, plannning, public administration, public welfare, urban studies, women's issues, criminology, and related topics.

CD-ROM DATABASES

Magazine Index Plus. Gale Cengage Learning. • Monthly. $4,000.00 per year (includes InfoTrac workstation). Provides full text on CD-ROM for about 100 popular, general interest magazines and indexing for 300 others. Includes special indexing of reviews and product evaluations. Time period is 1980 to date.

OECD Statistical Compendium. Organization for Economic Cooperation and Development. • Semiannual. $1,905.00 per year for 1 to 10 users. CD-ROM contains more than 730,000 monthly, quarterly, and annual time series for OECD countries, 1960 to date. Includes fully searchable data on agriculture, food, economic indicators, national accounts, employment, energy, finance, industry, technology, and foreign trade. Results can be displayed in various forms.

Social Sciences Citation Index. ISI. • Monthly. Price on request. Provides CD-ROM indexing of articles appearing in 1700 leading social science journals worldwide, with additional selections from more than 5700 other journals. Time span is 1992 to date. Coverage includes economics, business, finance, management, communications, demographics, library and information science, political science, sociology, and many other subjects.

Social Sciences Citation Index: Compact Disc Edition with Abstracts. Institute for Scientific Information. • Monthly. Provides CD-ROM indexing and abstracting of "significant articles" from 1,700 social science journals worldwide, with additional selections from 3,200 other journals, 1986 to date. Includes economics, business, finance, management, communications, demographics, information and library science, political science, sociology, and many other subjects.

WILSONDISC: Wilson Social Sciences Abstracts. H. W. Wilson Co. • Monthly. Includes unlimited online access to *Social Sciences Index* through WILSONLINE. Provides CD-ROM indexing from 1983 and abstracting from 1994 of more than 500 periodicals covering economics, area studies, community health, public administration, public welfare, urban studies, and many topics related to the social sciences.

INTERNET DATABASES

Business 2.0 Web Guide to the Best Business Links. Business 2.0 Media Inc. Phone: (415)293-4800 E-mail: support@business2.com • URL: http://www.business2.com/webguide • Web site presents an extensive, searchable directory of links to "the best, most informative, and authoritative web pages." Twenty main categories cover business, finance, career, company information, people, and technology topics, with thousands of subtopics, all linking to Web sites recommended by experienced business researchers. Fees: Free.

Fedstats. Federal Interagency Council on Statistical Policy. Phone: (202)395-7254 • URL: http://www.fedstats.gov • Web site features an efficient search facility for full-text statistics produced by more than 100 federal agencies, including the Census Bureau, the Bureau of Economic Analysis, and the Bureau of

Labor Statistics. Boolean searches can be made within one agency or for all agencies combined. Links are offered to international statistical bureaus, including the UN, IMF, OECD, UNESCO, Eurostat, and 20 individual countries. Fees: Free.

FreeLunch.com. Economy.com, Inc. Phone: (610)696-8700 Fax: (610)696-1678 • URL: http://www.freelunch.com • Web site provides free access to more than 1.5 million economic and financial data series, covering industry, demographics, labor markets, prices, retail sales, government spending, trade, interest rates, housing starts, the stock market, and many other topics. Data is available for various time periods in either chart or table form. Searching is offered. Fees: Free, but registration required. Economy.com, Inc. also offers fee-based economic analysis at *The Dismal Scientist* site (http://www.dismal.com).

ONLINE DATABASES

EconLit. American Economic Association. • Covers the worldwide literature of economics as contained in selected monographs and about 550 journals. Subjects include microeconomics, macroeconomics, economic history, inflation, money, credit, finance, accounting theory, trade, natural resource economics, and regional economics. Time period is 1969 to present, with monthly updates. Inquire as to online cost and availability.

Wilson Business Abstracts Online. H. W. Wilson Co. • Indexes and abstracts 600 major business periodicals, plus the *Wall Street Journal* and the business section of the *New York Times.* Indexing is from 1982, abstracting from 1990, with the two newspapers included from 1993. Updated weekly. Inquire as to online cost and availability. (*Business Periodicals Index* without abstracts is also available online.).

Wilson Social Sciences Abstracts Online. H. W. Wilson Co. • Provides online abstracting and indexing of more than 500 periodicals covering area studies, community health, public administration, public welfare, urban studies, and many other social science topics. Time period is 1994 to date for abstracts and 1983 to date for indexing, with updates weekly. Inquire as to online cost and availability.

PERIODICALS AND NEWSLETTERS

Blue Chip Financial Forecasts: What Top Analysts are Saying About U. S. and Foreign Interest Rates, Monetary Policy, Inflation, and Economic Growth. Aspen Publishers, Inc. • Monthly. $665.00 per year. Newsletter. Gives forecasts about a year in advance for interest rates, inflation, currency exchange rates, monetary policy, and economic growth rates.

Forecasts and Strategies. PBI Media, LLC. • Monthly. $99.00 per year. Covers inflation, taxes and government controls.

Personal Finance. KCI Communications Inc. • Description: Contains articles on subjects of interest to those investigating personal finance strategies. Provides news, information, and suggestions on investment decisions. Covers stock and growth stock activity, individual retirement accounts, market trends and developments, and real estate. Recurring features include columns titled Capsule Advisory and Answers to Your Money Questions.

PRICE SOURCES

CPI Detailed Report: Consumer Price Index. Available from U.S. Government Printing Office. • Monthly. $45.00 per year. Cost of living data.

The Value of a Dollar: Millennium Edition, 1860-1999. Grey House Publishing. • 1999. $135.00. Second edition. Shows the actual prices of thousands of items available to consumers from the Civil War era to recent years. Includes selected data on consumer expenditures, investments, income,

and jobs. (Universal Reference Publications.).

STATISTICS SOURCES

ACCRA Cost of Living Index (Association for Applied Community Reseach). ACCRA. • Quarterly. $130.00 per year. Compares price levels for 280-310 U.S. cities.

The AIER Chart Book. AIER Research Staff. American Institute for Economic Research. • Annual. $4.00. A compact compilation of long-range charts ("Purchasing Power of the Dollar," for example, goes back to 1780) covering various aspects of the U. S. economy. Includes inflation, interest rates, debt, gold, taxation, stock prices, etc. (Economic Education Bulletin.).

American Cost of Living Survey. Gale Cengage Learning. • 2001. $245.00. Third edition. Cost of living data is provided for 455 U.S. cities and metropolitan areas.

Business Statistics of the United States. Linz Audain and Cornelia J. Strawser. Bernan Associates. • Annual. $147.00. Based on *Business Statistics,* formerly issue by the Bureau of Economic Analysis, U. S. Department of Commerce. Provides basic data for a wide variety of U. S. industries, services, and economic indicators. Most statistics are shown annually for 30 years and monthly for the most recent four years.

Economic Indicators Handbook: Time Series, Conversions, Documentation. Gale Cengage Learning. • 2002. $205.00. Sixth edition. Provides data for about 175 U. S. economic indicators, such as the consumer price index (CPI), gross national product (GNP), and the rate of inflation. Values for series are given since inception, in both original form and adjusted for inflation. A bibliography of sources is included.

Nations of the World: A Political, Economic, and Business Handbook. Grey House Publishing. • 2002. $135.00. Third edition. Includes descriptive data on economic characteristics, population, gross domestic product (GDP), banking, inflation, agriculture, tourism, and other factors. Covers "all the nations of the world.".

Prices and Earnings Around the Globe. Union Bank of Switzerland. • Triennial. Free. Published in Zurich. Compares prices and purchasing power in 48 major cities of the world. Wages and hours are also compared.

Stocks, Bonds, Bills, and Inflation Yearbook. Ibbotson Associates. • Annual. $92.00. Provides detailed data from 1926 to the present on inflation and the returns from various kinds of financial investments, such as small-cap stocks and long-term government bonds.

Survey of Current Business. Available from U. S. Government Printing Office. • Monthly. $63.00 per year. Issued by Bureau of Economic Analysis, U. S. Department of Commerce. Presents a wide variety of business and economic data.

The Value of a Dollar: Millenium Edition. Scott Derks, editor. Grey House Publishing, Inc. • 1999. $135.00. Second edition.

World Cost of Living Survey. Gale Cengage Learning. • 1999. $275.00. Second edition. Arranged by country and then by city within each country. Provides cost of living data for many products and services. Includes indexes and an annotated bibliography.

INFORMATION BROKERS

See: INFORMATION INDUSTRY

INFORMATION, FREEDOM OF

See: FREEDOM OF INFORMATION

INFORMATION INDUSTRY

See also: ONLINE INFORMATION SYSTEMS

GENERAL WORKS

Economic Perspectives on the Internet. Alan E. Wiseman. Nova Science Publishers, Inc. • 2003. $59.00. Discusses the pricing of Internet access, pricing of goods and services sold through the Internet, network effects, and Internet taxation.

Economics of Information: A Guide to Economic and Cost-Benefit Analysis for Information Professionals. Bruce R. Kingma. Libraries Unlimited. • 2001. $45.00. Second edition. A technical discussion of market forces affecting the information industry. (Library and Information Science Text Series).

Essentials of Knowledge Management. Bryan Bergeron. John Wiley and Sons, Inc. • 2003. $29.95. Covers current strategies, trends, and technologies in knowledge management. Includes examples of best practices. (Essentials Series).

Expanding Technologies, Expanding Careers: Librarianship in Transition. Ellis Mount, editor. Special Libraries Association. • 1997. $45.00. Contains articles on alternative, non-traditional career paths for librarians, whether as entrepreneurs or employees. All the careers are related to computer-based, information retrieval and technology.

Future Libraries: Dreams, Madness, and Reality. Walt Crawford and Michael Gorman. American Library Association. • 1995. $28.00. Discusses the "over-hyped virtual library" and electronic-publishing "fantasies." Presents the argument for the importance of books, physical libraries, and library personnel.

Highway of Dreams: A Critical View Along the Information Superhighway. A. Michael Noll. Lawrence Erlbaum Associates, Inc. • 1996. $49.95. States that such factors as consumer needs and finance are often of more importance to the information industry than technological utopia. Includes such chapter headings as "Historical Perspective," "History Repeats," "Business Considerations," and "The Internet Exposed." (LEA's Telecommunications Series).

Information Imagineering: Meeting at the Interface. Milton T. Wolf and others, editors. American Library Association. • 1997. $36.00. A collection of articles on the effect of information technology on libraries, museums, and other institutions.

Information Management for the Intelligent Organization: The Art of Scanning the Environment. Chun Wei Choo. Information Today, Inc. • 2001. $39.50. Third edition. Published on behalf of the American Society for Information Science (ASIS). Covers the general principles of acquiring, creating, organizing, and using information within organizations.

Interface Culture: How New Technology Transforms the Way We Create and Communicate. Steven Johnson. HarperSanFrancisco. • 1997. $24.00. A discussion of how computer interfaces and online technology ("cyberspace") affect society in general.

Introductory Concepts in Information Science. Melanie J. Norton, editor. Information Today, Inc. • 2000. $39.50. Covers the basic concepts of information science and retrieval, both practical and theoretical. Published in conjunction with the American Society for Information Science and Technology. (ASIS Monograph Series).

Knowledge Management for the Information Professional. T. Kanti Srikantaiah and Michael Koenig. Information Today, Inc. • 2000. $44.50. Contains articles by 26 contributors on the concept of "knowledge management." (ASIS Monograph Series).

Knowledge Management Lessons Learned: What Works and What Doesn't. Michael Koenig and T. Kanti Srikantaiah, editors. Information Today, Inc. • 2003. $44.50. Contains more than 30 articles by KM experts, covering recent applications, innovations, strategy, implementation, cost analysis, training, content management, and other topics related to knowledge management. (ASIS Management Series).

The Quintessential Searcher: The Wit and Wisdom of Barbara Quint. Marylaine Block, editor. Information Today, Inc. • 2001. $19.95. Presents the sayings of Barbara Quint, editor of *Searcher* magazine, who is often critical of the online information industry. (CyberAge Books.).

Silicon Snake Oil: Second Thoughts on the Information Highway. Clifford Stoll. Doubleday Publishing. • 1996. $14.00. The author discusses the extravagant claims being made for online networks and multimedia.

Super Searchers Make It On Their Own: Top Independent Information Professionals Share Their Secrets for Starting and Running a Research Business. Suzanne Sabroski. Information Today, Inc. • 2002. $24.95. Presents discussions by "11 of the world's top research entrepreneurs" on the practical aspects of being in business as an information broker or other information provider. (Super Searchers Series).

Super Searchers on Competitive Intelligence: The Online and Offline Secrets of Top CI Researchers. Margaret M. Carr. Information Today, Inc. • 2003. $24.95. Presents the views of business intelligence experts from 15 major corporations and organizations. Contains information on sources for "monitoring competitive forces." (Super Searchers Series).

Valuating Information Intangibles: Measuring the Bottom Line Contribution of Librarians and Information Professionals. Frank H. Portugal. Special Libraries Association. • 2000. $79.00. Focuses on the importance of the intangible aspects of appraising information resources and services.

ABSTRACTS AND INDEXES

Applied Science and Technology Index. H. W. Wilson Co. • 11 times a year. Quarterly and annual cumulations. Price varies. Indexes a wide variety of English language technical, industrial, and engineering periodicals.

Business Periodicals Index. H. W. Wilson Co. • 11 times a year. Quarterly and annual cumulations. Price varies.

Computer and Information Systems Abstracts Journal: An Abstract Journal Pertaining to the Theory, Design, Fabrication and Application of Computer and Information Systems. CSA. • 11 times a year. $1,750 per year.

Computer Literature Index: A Subject/Author Index to Computer and Data Processing Literature. EBSCO Publishing. • Quarterly, with annual cumulation. $245.00 per year. Contains brief abstracts of book and periodical literature covering all phases of computing, including approximately 70 specific application areas.

Information Science Abstracts. American Society for Information Science. Information Today, Inc. • Nine times a year. $789.00 per year.

Internet and Personal Computing Abstracts [print edition]. EBSCO Publishing. • Quarterly. $269.00 per year, including cumulative index. Provides more than 10,000 abstracts annually from both trade and academic publications. Covers computer hardware, software, product reviews, Web topics, e-commerce, networks, corporate news, security, and related topics. Formerly *Microcomputer Abstracts.*

Library Literature and Information Science Index.

H. W. Wilson Co. • Quarterly. Annual cumulation. Price varies.

LISA: Library and Information Science Abstracts. R. R. Bowker. • 13 times a year. $1,055.00 per year; includes print and online editions.

Social Sciences Citation Index. Thomson/ISI. • Three times a year. $6,900 per year. Annual cumulation. Includes *Source Index, Citation Index, Permuterm Subject Index,* and *Corporate Index.*

ALMANACS AND YEARBOOKS

Annual Society for Information Science and Technology, Information and Business Div. Martha E. Williams, editor. Information Today, Inc. • Annual. Members, $79.95; non-members, $99.95. Published on behalf of the American Society for Information Science (ASIS). Covers trends in planning, basic techniques, applications, and the information profession in general.

Information Technology Outlook. OECD Publications and Information Center. • Biennial. $57.00. A review of recent developments in international markets for computer hardware, software, and services. Also examines current legal provisions for information systems security and privacy in OECD countries.

BIBLIOGRAPHIES

Knowledge Management: The Bibliography. Paul Burden and others. Information Today, Inc. • 2000. $22.50. Provides citations to more than 1,500 articles, 150 Web sites, and 400 books. Arranged according to specific KM topics, such as "KM and E-Commerce." Published in conjunction with the American Society for Information Science and Technology (ASIST).

CD-ROM DATABASES

Computer Database. Gale Cengage Learning. • Provides one year of full-text on CD-ROM for 150 leading computer-related publications. Also includes 70,000 product specifications and brief profiles of 13,000 computer product vendors and manufacturers.

LISA Plus. Available from Cambridge Scientific Abstracts (CSA). • Quarterly. $2,000.00 per year. CD-ROM version of Library Information and Science Abstracts, providing abstracting and indexing of the world's library and information science literature, 1969 to date. Contains more than 180,000 citations.

Social Sciences Citation Index. ISI. • Monthly. Price on request. Provides CD-ROM indexing of articles appearing in 1700 leading social science journals worldwide, with additional selections from more than 5700 other journals. Time span is 1992 to date. Coverage includes economics, business, finance, management, communications, demographics, library and information science, political science, sociology, and many other subjects.

Social Sciences Citation Index: Compact Disc Edition with Abstracts. Institute for Scientific Information. • Monthly. Provides CD-ROM indexing and abstracting of "significant articles" from 1,700 social science journals worldwide, with additional selections from 3,200 other journals, 1986 to date. Includes economics, business, finance, management, communications, demographics, information and library science, political science, sociology, and many other subjects.

WILSONDISC: Library Literature and Information Science Index. H. W. Wilson Co. • Quarterly. Includes unlimited access to the online version of *Library Literature.* Provides CD-ROM indexing of about 300 periodicals, covering a wide range of topics having to do with libraries, library management, and the information industry.

DIRECTORIES

Burwell World Directory of Information Brokers. Helen P. Burwell, editor. Burwell Enterprises. •

Annual. $59.50. Lists more than 1,000 information brokers, document delivery firms, free-lance librarians, and fee-based library services. Provides U. S. and international coverage (46 countries). Formerly *Directory of Fee-Based Information Services.*

Data Sources: The Comprehensive Guide to the Data Processing Industry: Hardware, Data Communications Products, Software, Company Profiles. Gale Cengage Learning. • Semiannual. $455.00 per year. Two volumes. Describes hardware and software for all computer operating sysems, including prices and technical details. Lists about 75,000 products from 14,000 suppliers. Industry-specific software applications are described.

Gale Directory of Databases. Gale Cengage Learning. • 2003. $490.00. Two volumes. Volume 1, $315.00; volume 2, $195.00. *Volume 1: Online Databases* and *Volume 2: CD-ROM, Diskette, Magnetic Tape, Handheld, and Batch Access Database Products.*

Information Industry Directory. Gale. • Covers: Approximately 11,000 organizations, systems, and services involved in the production and distribution of information in electronic form: database producers and their products online host services, transactional services, library and information networks, bibliographic utilities, library management systems, information retrieval software, mailing list services, fee-based information on demand services, document delivery sources, data collection and analysis centers and firms, and related consultants, service companies, professional and trade associations, publishers, and research activities. Entries include: Name of parent organization, name of system of service, address, phone, toll-free phone, fax, telex, email address, year founded name of unit head, size of staff, names of any affiliated organizations, financial information. Internet access information, general description of electronic product, system, or service, subjects covered or areas of service offered, sources of data for the system, type and quantity of stored information in all forms, publications and microform products and services, computer-based products and services, other services, clientele served, availability and restrictions, name of contact.

Information Sources: The Annual Directory of the Information Industry Association. Software and Information Industry Association. • Annual. Members, $75.00; non-members, $125.00.

Internet Tools of the Profession: A Guide for Information Professionals. Hope N. Tillman, editor. Special Libraries Association. • 1997. $49.00. Second edition. Consists of 14 sections by various authors or compilers. After two introductory articles on searching the Internet, there are 12 annotated lists of useful Web sites, covering the SLA, business and finance, chemistry, education, food and agriculture, information technology, insurance and employee benefits, law, library management, metals and materials, pharmaceuticals, and telecommunications. An index is provided.

KMWorld Buyer's Guide. Knowledge Asset Media. • Semiannual. Controlled circulation as part of *KMWorld*. Contains corporate and product profiles related to various aspects of knowledge management and information systems. (Knowledge Asset Media is a an affiliate of Information Today, Inc.).

Major Information Technology Companies of the World 2001. Available from Gale Cengage Learning. • Annual. $880.00. Published by Graham & Whiteside. Contains profiles of more than 3,100 leading information technology companies in various countries.

Peterson's Graduate and Professional Programs: Business, Education, Health, Information Studies, Law, and Social Work. Peterson's. • 2002. $49.95. Provides details of graduate and professional programs in business, law, information, and other

fields at colleges and universities. (Peterson's Graduate and Professional Program Series). Formerly *Peterson's Guide to Graduate Programs in Business, Education, Health, Information Studies, Law and Social Work.*

Plunkett's InfoTech Industry Almanac: Complete Profiles on the InfoTech 500-the Leading Firms in the Movement and Management of Voice, Data, and Video. Plunkett Research, Ltd. • Biennial. $229.99. Includes CD-ROM. Five hundred major information companies are profiled, with corporate culture aspects. Discusses major trends in various sectors of the computer and information industry, including data on careers and job growth. Includes several indexes.

Research Services Directory: Commercial & Corporate Research Centers. Grey House Publishing. • 2003. $495.00. Ninth edition. Lists more than 8,000 independent commercial research centers and laboratories offering contract or fee-based services. Includes corporate research departments, market research companies, and information brokers.

A S I S Handbook and Directory. American Society for Information Science. • Annual. Members, $25.00; non-members, $100.00.

ENCYCLOPEDIAS AND DICTIONARIES

Acronyms of Computer Science and Communications: A Comprehensive Acronym Dictionary and Illustrated Encyclopedia. Enjob Kajan and Ejub Kajan. Springer Verlag. • 2002. $49.95. Explains more than 4,000 "broadly used" computer, telecommunications, and information technology acronyms. Includes illustrations and Web addresses, where applicable.

Dictionary of Bibliometrics. Virgil Diodato. Haworth Press, Inc. • 1994. $39.95. Contains detailed explanations of 225 terms, with references. (Bibliometrics is "the application of mathematical and statistical techniques to the study of publishing and professional communication.").

Dictionary of Computing. Valerie Illingworth, editor. Oxford University Press. • 1997. $18.00. Fourth edition.

Dictionary of Information Technology and Computer Science. Tony Gunton. Blackwell Publishing. • 1994. $62.95. Second edition. Covers key words, phrases, abbreviations, and acronyms used in computing and data communications.

Encyclopedia of Communication and Information. Available from Gale Cengage Learning. • 2001. $395.00. Three volumes. Published by Macmillan Reference USA.

Encyclopedia of Emerging Industries. Gale Cengage Learning. • 2001. $320.00. Fourth edition. Provides detailed information on 115 "newly flourishing" industries. Includes historical background, organizational structure, significant individuals, current conditions, major companies, work force, technology trends, research developments, and other industry facts.

Encyclopedia of Information Systems. Hossein Bidgoli, editor. Elsevier. • 2002. $1,200.00. Four volumes. Contains a wide range of articles relating to computers, databases, communication, and information technology. The 200 topics include coverage of hardware, software, artificial intelligence, the Internet, networks, knowledge management, electronic commerce, search engines, and systems design.

Encyclopedia of Library and Information Science. Allen Kent and others, editors. Marcel Dekker, Inc. • 73 volumes. Dates vary. Prices vary.

Every Manager's Guide to Information Technology: A Glossary of Key Terms and Concepts for Today's Business Leader. Peter G. W. Keen. Harvard Business School Publishing. • 1994. $18.95. Second

edition. Provides definitions of terms related to computers, data communications, and information network systems. (Harvard Business Reference Series).

World Encyclopedia of Library and Information Services. Robert Wedgeworth, editor. American Library Association. • 1993. $200.00. Third edition. Contains about 340 articles from various contributors.

HANDBOOKS AND MANUALS

Building and Running a Successful Research Business: A Guide for the Independent Information Professional. Mary Ellen Bates. Information Today, Inc. • 2003. $29.95. Provides practical advice for information brokers. Includes material on such topics as organization of the business, marketing, and sales promotion. (CyberAge Books).

Coyle's Information Highway Handbook: A Practical File on the New Information Order. Karen Coyle. American Library Association. • 1997. $30.00. Provides useful "essays on copyright, access, privacy, censorship, and the information marketplace.".

How to Avoid Liability: The Information Professionals' Guide to Negligence and Warrant Risks. T. R. Halvorson. Burwell Enterprises. • 1998. $24.50. Second edition. Provides legal advice, cases, and decisions relating to information brokers and others in the information business.

Infopreneurs: Turning Data into Dollars. H. Skip Weitzen. John Wiley and Sons, Inc. • 1988. $19.95. Infopreneurs are entrepreneurs who market information. A how-to-do-it manual.

Information Broker. Entrepreneur Media, Inc. • Looseleaf. $59.50. A practical guide to starting an information retrieval business. Covers profit potential, start-up costs, market size evaluation, pricing, accounting, advertising, promotion, etc. (Start-Up Business Guide No. E1237.).

Information Brokering: How to Make Money Selling Information Services. Florence M. Mason and Chris Dobson. Neal-Schuman Publishers, Inc. • 1998. $45.00. A practical guide to business plans, location, costs, fees, billing, marketing, accounting, taxes, and legal issues. Covers information brokering as a small business enterprise.(How-To-Do-It Manuals Series).

Information for Sale: How to Start and Operate Your Own Data Research Service. John H. Everett and Elizabeth P. Crowe. McGraw-Hill. • 1988. $15.95. Second edition. A revision of *The Information Broker's Handbook.*

The Information Professional's Guide to Career Development Online. Sarah L. Nesbeitt and Rachel S. Gordon. Information Today, Inc. • 2001. $29.50. Provides advice to librarians and other information professionals about using online sources for career advancement. The Career Development Online Web Page (http://www.lisjobs.com/careerdev/) contains links to relevant resources.

Legal Liability Problems in Cyberspace: Craters in the Information Highway. T. R. Halvorson. Burwell Enterprises. • 1998. $24.50. Covers the legal risks and liabilities involved in doing online research as a paid professional. Includes a table of cases.

Position Descriptions in Special Libraries. Del Sweeney and Karin Zilla, editors. Special Libraries Association. • 1996. $41.00. Third revised edition. Provides 87 descriptions of library and information management positions.

Recruiter's Research Blue Book: A How-To Guide for Researchers, Consultants, Corporate Recruiters, Small Business Owners, Venture Capitalists, and Line Executives. Andrea A. Jupina. Kennedy Information, Inc. • 2000. $179.00. Second edition. Provides detailed coverage of the role that research plays in executive recruiting. Includes such practical items as "Telephone Interview Guide," "Legal Issues in Executive Search," and "How to Create an Executive Search Library." Covers both person-to-person research and research using printed and on-line business information sources. Includes an extensive directory of recommended sources. Formerly *Handbook of Executive Search Research*.

Sawyer's Success Tactics for Information Businesses. Deborah C. Sawyer. Burwell Enterprises. • 1998. $24.50. Covers such items as pricing, costs, and service for information brokers and others in the fee-based information business.

Sawyer's Survival Guide for Information Brokers. Deborah C. Sawyer. Burwell Enterprises. • 1995. $39.50. Provides practical advice for information entrepreneurs.

Statistical Methods for the Information Professional: A Practical, Painless Approach to Understanding, Using, and Interpreting Statistics. Liwen Vaughan. Information Today, Inc. • 2001. $39.50. Published in conjunction with the American Society for Information Science and Technology (ASIST).

Trade Secret Protection in an Information Age. Gale R. Peterson. Glasser LegalWorks. • Looseleaf. $149.00, including sample forms on disk. Periodic supplementation available. Covers trade secret law relating to computer software, online databases, and multimedia products. Explanations are based on more than 1,000 legal cases. Sample forms on disk include work-for-hire examples and covenants not to compete.

INTERNET DATABASES

InfoTech Trends. Data Analysis Group. Phone: (925)462-1202 Fax: (925)462-1225 E-mail: support@infotechtrends.com • URL: http://www.infotechtrends.com • Web site provides both free and fee-based market research data on the information technology industry, including computers, peripherals, telecommunications, the Internet, software, CD-ROM/DVD, e-commerce, and workstations. Fees: Free for current (most recent year) data; more extensive information has various fee structures. Formerly *Computer Industry Forecasts*.

Wired News. Lycos, Inc. Phone: (415)276-8400 Fax: (415)276-8500 E-mail: newsfeedback@wired.com • URL: http://www.wired.com • Provides summaries and full-text of "Top Stories" relating to the Internet, computers, multimedia, telecommunications, and the electronic information industry in general. These news stories are placed in the broad categories of Politics, Business, Culture, and Technology. Affiliated with *Wired* magazine. Fees: Free.

ONLINE DATABASES

Applied Science and Technology Index Online. H. W. Wilson Co. • Provides online indexing of 500 major scientific, technical, industrial, and engineering periodicals. Time period is 1983 to date. Monthly updates. Inquire as to online cost and availability.

Gale Directory of Databases [online]. Gale Cengage Learning. • Presents the online version of the printed *Gale Directory of Databases, Volume 1: Online Databases* and *Gale Directory of Databases, Volume 2: CD-ROM, Diskette, Magnetic Tape, Handheld, and Batch Access Database Products*. Semiannual updates. Inquire as to online cost and availability.

Information Science Abstracts [online]. Information Today, Inc. • Provides indexing and abstracting of the international literature of information science, including library science, from 1966 to date. Monthly updates. Inquire as to online cost and availability.

INSPEC. Institution of Electrical Engineers (IEE). • Provides online citations, with abstracts, to the world literature of electrical engineering, electronics, optoelectronics, telecommunications, industrial controls, instrumentation, computer technology, information technology, and physics. Coverage includes more than 4,000 technical and scientific journals from 1969 to date, with weekly updating. (INSPEC is Information Services in Physics, Electronics, and Computing.) Inquire as to online cost and availability.

LISA: Library and Information Science Abstracts. Available from Cambridge Scientific Abstracts (CSA). • Provides abstracting and indexing of the world's library and information science literature, 1969 to date. Covers more than 440 periodicals from 68 countries. Updating is biweekly. Inquire as to online cost and availability.

PROMT: Predicasts Overview of Markets and Technology. Gale Cengage Learning. • Companies, products, applied technologies and markets. U.S. and international literature coverage, 1972 to date. Inquire as to online cost and availability. Provides abstracts from more than 1,600 publications. Weekly updates.

Scisearch. Institute for Scientific Information. • Broad, multidisciplinary index to the literature of science and technology, 1974 to present. Inquire as to online cost and availability. Coverage of literature is worldwide, with weekly updates.

Social Scisearch. Institute for Scientific Information. • Broad, multidisciplinary index to the literature of the social sciences, 1972 to present. Weekly updates. Worldwide coverage. Inquire as to online cost and availability.

Wilson Business Abstracts Online. H. W. Wilson Co. • Indexes and abstracts 600 major business periodicals, plus the *Wall Street Journal* and the business section of the *New York Times*. Indexing is from 1982, abstracting from 1990, with the two newspapers included from 1993. Updated weekly. Inquire as to online cost and availability. (*Business Periodicals Index* without abstracts is also available online.).

PERIODICALS AND NEWSLETTERS

Aslib Proceedings: New Information Perspectives. Available from Information Today, Inc. • Ten times a year. $349.00 per year. Published in London by Aslib Covers a wide variety of information industry and library management topics.

CIO: The Magazine for Chief Information Officers. CXO Media, Inc. • 23 times a year. $150.00 per year. Edited for chief information officers. Includes a monthly "Web Business" section (incorporates the former *WebMaster* periodical) and a monthly "Enterprise" section for company executives other than CIOs.

EContent: Digital Content Strategies and Resources. Online, Inc. • Monthly. $110.00 per year. Emphasis is on the business management and financial aspects of the digital content industry. (Formerly published by Online, Inc.)

Electronic Information Report: Empowering Industry Decision Makers Since 1979. SIMBA Information. • 46 times a year. $649.00 per year. Newsletter. Provides business and financial news and trends for online services, electronic publishing, storage media, multimedia, and voice services. Includes information on relevant IPOs (initial public offerings) and mergers. Formerly *Electronic Information Week*.

The Electronic Library: The International Journal for the Application of Technology in Information Environments. Sage Publications, Inc. • Bimonthly. $469.00 per year. Incorporated*Library Computing*.

The Gray Sheet. F-D-C Reports Inc. • Description: Monitors the complex regulatory environment for devices, instrumentation, and diagnostics. Topics include device-related Congressional activity, Medicare reimbursement policies, international regulatory intiatives, enforcement and premarket approval programs at FDA's Center for Devices and Radiological Health. Recurring features include device approvals, 510(k) clearances, FDA recalls and seizures, mergers and acquisitions, and sales and earnings.

Healthcare Informatics: The Business of Healthcare Information Technology. McGraw-Hill. • Monthly. $39.95 per year. Covers various aspects of information and computer technology for the health care industry.

InForm. Victor O. Schinnerer & Company Inc. • Description: Reports national and state developments affecting architects and engineers.

Information Broker. Helen P. Burwell, editor. Burwell Enterprises Inc. • Description: Covers companies that offer fee-based information services and issues related to "the business" of information brokering.

Information Hotline. Science Associates/International Inc. • Description: "The oldest, most respected, continuously published newsletter." Devoted to objective coverage of trends, policy, analysis, and opinion in the information field.

Information Outlook: The Monthly Magazine of the Special Libraries Association. Special Libraries Association. • Monthly. $65.00 per year. Topics include information technology, the Internet, copyright, research techniques, library management, and professional development. Replaces *Special Libraries* and *SpeciaList*.

Information Services and Use: An International Journal. IOS Press, Inc. • Quarterly. Institutions, $296.00 per year.

The Information Society: An International Journal. Taylor & Francis Group. • Five times a year. Individuals, $105.00 per year; institutions, $285.00 per year.

Information Standards Quarterly: News About Library, Information Sciences, and Publishing Standards. National Information Standards Organization (NISO). • Quarterly. $80.00 per year. Newsletter. Reports on activities of the National Information Standards Organization.

Information Times. Software and Information Industry Association. • Monthly. Membership. Formerly *Friday Memo*.

Information Today: The Newspaper for Users and Producers of Electronic Information Services. Information Today, Inc. • 11 times a year. $68.95 per year.

Information Week: Business Innovation Powered by Technology. CMP Publications, Inc. • Weekly. $199.00 per year. The magazine for information systems management.

InfoWorld: Defining Technology for Business. InfoWorld Publishing. • Weekly. $195.00 per year. For personal computing professionals.

Journal of Organizational Excellence. Society of Competitive Intelligence Professionals. John Wiley and Sons, Inc. Journals. • Quarterly. Institutions, $425.00 per year; with online edition, $447.00 per year. Formerly *Competitive Intelligence Review*.

Journal of the American Society for Information Science and Tehnology. John Wiley and Sons, Inc., Journals. • 14 times a year. $1,600.00 per year; with online edition, $1,680.00 per year.

KM World: Creating and Managing the Knowledge-Based Enterprise (Knowledge Management). Asset Media. • 10 times a year. Free to qualified personnel; others, $63.95 per year. Provides articles on knowledge management, including business intelligence, multimedia content management, document management, e-business, and intellectual property. Emphasis is on business-to-business information technology. (Knowledge Asset Media is a an affiliate of Information Today, Inc.).

Online Newsletter. Information Intelligence Inc. • Description: Tracks developments in the fields of CD-ROM and online services. Contains news of online/CD-ROM developments and events, mergers and acquisitions, personnel movements, telecommunications and networks, new equipment and developments, microcomputer hardware and software, new and forthcoming databases, forthcoming meetings, and publications and user aids.

Report on Electronic Commerce: Online Business, Financial and Consumer Strategies and Trends. Aspen Publishers. • Biweekly. $1,789.00 per year. Newsletter. Includes *Daily Multimedia News Service.* Incorporates *Interactive Services Report.*

The Seybold Report (Analyzing Publishing Technologies). Seybold Publications. • Semimonthly. $595.00 per year. Newsletter. Formerly *Seybold Report on Publishing Systems.*

Telematics and Informatics: An International Journal on Telecommunications and Internet Technology. Elsevier. • Four times a year. Institutions, $938.00 per year.

Upgrade. Software and Information Industry Association. • Monthly. $79.00 per year. Covers news and trends relating to the software, information, and Internet industries. Formerly *SPA News* from Software Publisers Association.

Wired. Wired Ventures Ltd. • Monthly. $10.00 per year. Edited for creators and managers in various areas of electronic information and entertainment, including multimedia, the Internet, and video. Often considered to be the primary publication of the "digital generation.".

RESEARCH CENTERS AND INSTITUTES

Library Research Center. University of Illinois at Urbana-Champaign. 501 E. Daniel, Room 321, Champaign, IL 61820-6212. Phone: (217)333-1980 Fax: (217)244-3302 E-mail: lrc@uiuc.edu • URL: http://www.alexia.lis.uiuc.edu.

STATISTICS SOURCES

By the Numbers: Electronic and Online Publishing. Gale Cengage Learning. • 1997-98. $305.00. Four volumes. $85.00 per volume. Covers "high-interest" industries: 1. *By the Numbers: Electronic and Online Publishing*; 2. *By the Numbers: Emerging Industries*; 3. *By the Numbers: Nonprofits*; 4. *By the Numbers: Publishing.* Each volume provides about 600 tabulations of industry data on revenues, market share, employment, trends, financial ratios, profits, salaries, and so forth. Citations to data sources are included. (By the Numbers Series).

Information, Finance, and Services USA. Gale Cengage Learning. • 2001. $240.00. Replaces *Service Industries USA* and *Finance, Insurance, and Real Estate USA.* Presents statistics and projections relating to economic activity in a wide variety of nonmanufacturing areas.

Information Systems Spending: An Analysis of Trends and Strategies. Computer Economics, Inc. • Annual. $1,595.00. Three volumes. Based on "in-depth surveys of public and private companies amd government organizations." Provides detailed data on management information systems spending, budgeting, and benchmarks. Includes charts, graphs, and analysis.

OECD Information Technology Outlook 2000: ICTs, E-Commerce and the Information Economy. Organization for Economic Cooperation and Development. • 2000. $72.00. Provides data on information and communications technology (ICT) and electronic commerce in 11 OECD nations (includes U. S.). Coverage includes network infrastructure, electronic payment systems, financial transaction technologies, intelligent agents, global navigation systems, and portable flat panel display technologies.

U. S. Industry and Trade Outlook. Available from National Technical Information Service. • Annual. $69.95. Produced by the International Trade Administration, U. S. Department of Commerce, in a "public-private" partnership with DRI/McGraw-Hill and Standard & Poor's. Provides basic data, outlook for the current year, and "Long-Term Prospects" (five-year projections) for a wide variety of products and services. Includes high technology industries. Formerly *U. S. Industrial Outlook.*

TRADE/PROFESSIONAL ASSOCIATIONS

American Society for Information Science and Technology. 1320 Fenwick Lane, No. 510, Silver Spring, MD 20910. Phone: (301)495-0900 Fax: (301)495-0810 E-mail: asis@asis.org • URL: http://www.asis.org • Members are information managers, scientists, librarians, and others who are interested in the storage, retrieval, and use of information.

Association of Independent Information Professionals. 8550 United Plz. Blvd., Ste. 1001, Baton Rouge, IL 70809. Phone: 888-544-2447 or (225)408-4400 Fax: (225)922-4611 E-mail: info@aiip.org • URL: http://www.aiip.org • Members are information brokers, document providers, librarians, consultants, database designers, webmasters, and other information professionals. Formerly International Association of Independent Information Brokers.

Association of Information and Dissemination Centers. P.O. Box 3212, Maple Glen, PA 19002-8212. Phone: (215)654-9129 Fax: (215)654-9129 E-mail: info@asidic.org • URL: http://www.asidic.org.

Library and Information Technology Association. 50 E. Huron St., Chicago, IL 60611. Phone: 800-545-2433 or (312)280-4270 Fax: (312)280-3257 E-mail: lita@ala.org • URL: http://www.lita.org • Affiliated with the American Library Association. Formerly Information Science and Automation Division of ALA.

National Federation of Abstracting and Information Services. 1518 Walnut St., Suite 307, Philadelphia, PA 19102-3403. Phone: (215)893-1561 Fax: (215)893-1564 E-mail: nfais@nfais.org • URL: http://www.nfais.org • Formerly National Federation of Abstracting and Indexing Services.

National Information Standards Organization. 1 N Charles St., Ste. 1905, Baltimore, MD 21201. Phone: (866)957-1593 or (301)654-2512 Fax: (301)654-1721 E-mail: nisohq@niso.org • URL: http://www.niso.org • Identifies, develops, maintains, and publishes technical standards to manage information in the changing environment used by libraries, publishers, and information services. Supports open access to NISO standards. Standards available at website.

Society of Competitive Intelligence Professionals. 1700 Diagonal Rd., Suite 600, Alexandria, VA 22314. Phone: (703)739-0696 Fax: (703)739-2524 E-mail: info@scip.org • URL: http://www.scip.org • Members are professionals involved in competitor intelligence and analysis. Formerly Society of Competitor Intelligence Professionals.

Software and Information Industry Association. 1090 Vermont Ave. NW, 6th Fl., Washington, DC 20005. Phone: (202)289-7442 Fax: (202)289-7097 • URL: http://www.siia.net • A trade association for the software and digital content industry. Affiliated with Massachusetts Software and Internet Council.

Special Interest Group on Information Retrieval. c/o Association for Computing Machinery, 1515 Broadway, New York, NY 10036-5701. Phone: 800-342-6626 or (212)869-7440 Fax: (212)944-1318 E-mail: sigs@acm.org • URL: http://www.acm.org/sigir/.

OTHER SOURCES

E-Commerce and Internet Law: Treatise with Forms. Ian C. Ballon. Glasser Legalworks. • Three looseleaf volumes. $595.00. Periodic supplementation. Analyzes Internet legalities, including litigious matters relating to downloading, streaming, music, video, content aggregation, domain names, chatrooms, and search engines. Includes forms, contracts, checklists, sample pleadings, and an extensive glossary.

Information and Image Management: The State of the Industry. AIIM-The Enterprise Content Management Association. • Annual. $130.00. Market data with five-year forecasts. Covers electronic imaging, micrographics supplies and equipment, software, and records management services.

INFORMATION MANAGEMENT SYSTEMS

See: MANAGEMENT INFORMATION SYSTEMS

INFORMATION RETRIEVAL (DOCUMENTATION)

See: ONLINE INFORMATION SYSTEMS

INFORMATION SOURCES

See also: STATISTICS SOURCES

BIBLIOGRAPHIES

Analyzing Your Competition: Simple, Low-Cost Techniques for Intelligence Gathering. Michael Strenges. MarketResearch.com. • 1997. $95.00. Third edition. Mainly an annotated listing of specific, business information sources, but also contains concise discussions of information-gathering techniques. Indexed by publisher and title.

The Basic Business Library: Core Resources. Rashells S. Karp and Bernard S. Schlessinger. Greenwood Publishing Group, Inc. • 2002. $64.95. Fourth edition. Consists of three parts: (1) "Core List of Printed Business Reference Sources," (2) "The Literature of Business Reference and Business Libraries: 1976-1994," and (3) "Business Reference Sources and Services: Essays." Part one lists 200 basic titles, with annotations and evaluations.

Booklist. American Library Association. • 22 times a year. $79.95. Reviews library materials for school and public libraries. Incorporates *Reference Books Bulletin.*

Business Information: How to Find It, How to Use It. Michael R. Lavin. Greenwood Publishing Group, Inc. • 2001. $61.00. Third edition. Combines discussions of business research techniques with detailed descriptions of major business publications and databases. Includes title and subject indexes.

Business Research Handbook: Methods and Sources for Lawyers and Business Professionals. Kathy E. Shimpock. Aspen Publishers, Inc. • $155.00. Looseleaf service. Periodic supplementation. Provides detailed advice on how to find business information. Describes a wide variety of data sources, both private and government.

Data Sources for Business and Market Analysis. John Ganly. Scarecrow Press, Inc. • 1994. $60.00. Fourth edition. Emphasis is on sources of statistics for market research, especially government sources. Relevant directories, periodicals, and research aids are included.

Encyclopedia of Health Information Sources. Gale Cengage Learning. • 1993. $180.00. Second edition. Both print and nonprint sources of information are listed for 450 health-related topics.

Encyclopedia of Legal Information Sources. Gale Cengage Learning. • 1992. $180.00. Second edition. Lists more than 23,000 law-related information sources, including print, nonprint, and organizational.

Guide to Reference Books. Robert Balay and others. American Library Association. • 1996. $275.00. 11th edition.

How to Find Chemical Information: A Guide for Practicing Chemists, Educators, and Students. Robert E. Maizell. John Wiley and Sons, Inc. • 1998. $89.95. Third edition.

International Business Information: How to Find It, How to Use It. Ruth A. Pagell and Michael Halperin. Glenlake Publishing Co., Ltd. • 2000. $65.00.

Legal Information: How to Find It, How to Use It. Kent Olson. Greenwood Publishing Group, Inc. • 1998. $64.95. Includes CD-ROM. Recommends sources for various kinds of legal information.

Lesko's Info-PowerIII: Over 45,000 Free and Low Cost Sources of Information. Information U.S.A. Inc. • 1996. $39.95. Third edition.

Public Library Catalog: Guide to Reference Books and Adult Nonfiction. Juliette Yaakov, editor. H. W. Wilson Co. • 1999. $350.00. 11th revised edition. Contains annotations for 8,000 of the "best" reference and other nonfiction books in English. Covers a wide range of topics, including many that are related to business, economics, finance, or industry. (Standard Catalog Series).

Reference Books Bulletin: A Compilation of Evaluations. Mary Ellen Quinn, editor. American Library Association. • Annual. $79.95. Contains reference book reviews that appeared during the year in *Booklist*.

Reference Sources for Small and Medium-sized Libraries. Scott E. Kennedy, editor. American Library Association. • 1999. $60.00. Sixth edition. Includes alternative (electronic) formats for reference works.

Statistics Sources: A Subject Guide to Data on Industrial, Business, Social, Educational, Financial and Other Topics for the U. S. and Selected Foreign Countries. Gale Cengage Learning. • 2003. $515.00. 27th edition. Two volumes. Lists sources of statistical information for more than 20,000 topics.

Subject Encyclopedias: User's Guide, Review Citations, and Keyword Index. Allan N. Mirwis. Greenwood Publishing Group, Inc. • 1999. $300.00. Two volumes. $150.00 per volume. Volume one describes 1,000 subject encyclopedias; volume two provides a keyword index to articles appearing in 100 selected encyclopedias.

Topical Reference Books: Authoritative Evaluations of Recommended Resources in Specialized Subject Areas. Marion Sader, editor. Greenwood Publishing Group, Inc. • 1991. $109.00. Ranks 2,000 reference books ("Core Titles," "New and Noteworthy," "Supplementary"). (Buying Guide Series).

U. S. Government Information for Business. U. S. Government Printing Office. • Annual. Free. A selected list of currently available publications, periodicals, and electronic products on business, trade, labor, federal regulations, economics, and other topics. Also known as *Business Catalog.*

Using the Agricultural, Environmental, and Food Literature. Barbara S. Hutchinson and Antoinette P. Greider, editors. Marcel Dekker, Inc. • 2002. $125.00. Serves as a guide to both print and electronic sources of information.

Using the Financial and Business Literature. Thomas P. Slavens. Marcel Dekker, Inc. • 2004. $165.00. Provides detailed descriptions of both print and electronic information sources. (Books in Library and Information Science Series/64.).

CD-ROM DATABASES

World Database of Business Information Sources on CD-ROM. Gale Cengage Learning. • Annual. Produced by Euromonitor. Presents Euromonitor's entire information source database on CD-ROM.

Contains a worldwide total of about 35,000 publications, organizations, libraries, trade fairs, and online databases.

DIRECTORIES

Asian Marketing Information Sourcebook. Euromonitor International. • 2003. $475.00. Lists trade associations, statistical offices, government agencies, special libraries, trade journals, websites, and other sources of business information for the countries of Asia.

Business Organizations, Agencies, and Publications Directory. Gale Cengage Learning. • 2003. $480.00. 15th edition. Over 40,000 entries describing 39 types of business information sources. Classified by type of organization, publication, or serviceIncludes state, national, and international agencies and organizations. Master index to names and keywords. Also includes e-mail addresses and web site URL's.

CD-ROMS in Print. Gale Cengage Learning. • 2003. $185.00. 17th edition. Describes more than 20,000 currrenly available reference and multimedia CD-ROM titles and provides contact information for about 4,000 CD-ROM publishing and distribution companies. Includes several indexes.

Detwiler's Directory of Health and Medical Resources. S.M. Detwiler and Associates. • Biennial. $195.00. Lists a wide range of healthcare information resources, including more than 2,000 corporations, associations, government agencies, publishers, licensure organizations, market research firms, foundations, and institutes, as well as 6,000 publications. Indexed by type of information, publication, acronym, and 600 subject categories.

Directories in Print. Gale Cengage Learning. • Annual. $565.00. Two volumes. *Midyear Supplement*, $440.00. Two volumes. An annotated guide to approximately 15,500 business, industrial, professional, and scientific directories. Formerly *Directory of Directories.*

The Directory of Business Information Resources: Associations, Newsletters, Magazine Trade Shows. Grey House Publishing, Inc. • Annual. $250.00. Provides concise information on associations, newsletters, magazines, and trade shows for each of 90 major industry groups. An "Entry & Company Index" serves as a guide to titles, publishers, and organizations.

The Directory of EU Information Sources: The Red Book. Euroconfidentiel S. A. • Annual. $230.00. Lists publications, associations, consultants, law firms, diplomats, jounalists, and other sources of information about Europe and the European Union.

Directory of Special Libraries and Information Centers. Gale Cengage Learning. • 2003. $975.00. 28th edition. Three volumes. Two available separately: volume one,*Directory of Special Libraries and Information Centers*, $740.00; volume two *Geographic and Personnel Indexes*, $560.00. Contains 34,000 entries from the U.S., Canada, and 80 other countries. A detailed subject index is included in volume one.

European Marketing Information Sourcebook. Euromonitor International. • 2003. $475.00. Lists trade associations, statistical offices, government agencies, special libraries, trade journals, websites, and other sources of business information for the countries of Europe.

Findex: The Worldwide Directory of Market Research Reports, Studies, and Surveys. MarketResearch.com. • Annual. $425.00. Provides brief annotations of market research reports and related publications from about 1,000 publishers, arranged by topic. Back of book includes Report Titles by Publisher, Publishers/Distributors Directory, Subject Index, Geography Index, and Company Index. (Formerly published by Cambridge Information Group.).

Fulltext Sources Online. Information Today Inc. •

Covers: over 21,000 periodicals, newspapers, newsletters, newswires; and tv/radio transcripts available in full text online. Entries include: Name of file, online services through which available, dates of coverage, lag time if applicable. Separate list gives online service address and phone; indicates degree of online coverage and selection policy. Internet url's listed where applicable.

Gale Guide to Internet Databases. Gale Cengage Learning. • 1999. $125.00. Sixth edition. Presents critical descriptions and ratings of more than 5,000 useful Internet databases (especially World Wide Web sites). Includes a glossary of Internet terms, a bibliography, and five indexes.

Great Scouts! CyberGuides to Subject Searching on the Web. Margot Williams and others. Information Today, Inc. • 1999. $24.95. Contains descriptions of selected Web sites, arranged by subject. Covers business, investments, computers, travel, the environment, health, social issues, etc. (CyberAge Books.).

Information Sources: The Annual Directory of the Information Industry Association. Software and Information Industry Association. • Annual. Members, $75.00; non-members, $125.00.

Internet Plus Directory of Express Library Services. Steve Coffman and others, editors. American Library Association. • 1998. $55.00. Covers fee-based services of various U. S., Canadian, and international libraries. Paid services include online searches, faxed documents, and specialized professional research. Price ranges are quoted. (A joint production of FISCAL, the ALA/ACRL Discussion Group of Fee-Based Information Service Centers in Academic Libraries, and FYI, the Professional Research and Rapid Information Delivery Service of the County of Los Angeles Public Library.) Formerly *FISCAL Directory of Fee-Based Information Services in Libraries.*

Latin American Marketing Information Sourcebook. Euromonitor International. • 2003. $475.00. Lists trade associations, statistical offices, government agencies, special libraries, trade journals, websites, and other sources of business information for the countries of Latin America.

Library Journal: Reference [year]: Print, CD-ROM, Online. Reed Business Information. • Annual. Issued in November as a supplement to *Library Journal.* Lists new and updated reference material, including general and trade print titles, directories, annuals, CD-ROM titles, and online sources. Includes material from more than 200 publishers, arranged by company name, with an index by subject. Addresses include e-mail and Web information.

Library Journal Sourcebook. Reed Business Information. • Publication includes: List of over 600 suppliers of products and services used by libraries from abstracting to word processing equipment. Entries include: Company name, address, phone, list of products or services. Complete listings for more than 100 architectural firms; Disaster planning for librarians.

Subject Collections: A Guide to Special Book Collections and Subject Emphasis in Libraries. Lee Ash and William G. Miller, editors. R. R. Bowker. • Irregular. $275.00. Two volumes. A guide to special book collections and subject emphases as reported by university, college, public and special libraries in th United States and Canada.

Subject Directory of Special Libraries and Information Centers. Gale Cengage Learning. • Annual. $960.00. Three volumes, available separately: volume one, *Business, Government, and Law Libraries*, $375.00; volume two, *Computer, Engineering, and Law Libraries*, $375.00; volume three, *Health Sciences Libraries*, $375.00. Altogether, 14,000 entries from the *Directory of Special Libraries and Information Centers* are arranged in 14 subject chapters.

The World Directory of Business Information Libraries. Available from Gale Cengage Learning. • 2003. $650.00. Fifth edition. Published by Euromonitor. Provides detailed information on 2,000 major business libraries in 180 countries. Emphasis is on collections relevant to consumer goods and services markets.

World Directory of Business Information Web Sites. Available from Gale Cengage Learning. • 2003. $690.00. Sixth edition. Published by Euromonitor. Provides detailed descriptions of a wide variety of business-related Web sites. More than 1,500 sites are included from around the world. Covers statistics sources, market research, company information, rankings, surveys, economic data, etc.

World Directory of Marketing Information Sources. Available from Gale Cengage Learning. • 2003. $650.00. Fourth edition. Published by Euromonitor. Provides details on approximately 6,000 sources of marketing information, including publications, libraries, associations, market research companies, online databases, and governmental organizations. Coverage is worldwide.

HANDBOOKS AND MANUALS

Best Bet Internet: Reference and Research When You Don't Have Time to Mess Around. Shirley D. Kennedy. American Library Association. • 1997. $35.00. Provides advice for librarians and others on the effective use of World Wide Web information sources.

Business Information Handbook. David Mort. Available from Gale Cengage Learning. • 2003. $140.00. Published by K. G. Saur. Serves as a general guide to the world of business information.

The Business Library and How to Use It: A Guide to Sources and Research Strategies for Information on Business and Management. Elizabeth Wood and others, editors. Omnigraphics, Inc. • 1996. $28.00. Sixth edition. Explains library research methods and describes specific sources of business information. A revision of *How to Use the Business Library*, by H. Webster Johnson and others.

Guide to the Use of Libraries and Information Sources. Jean K. Gates. McGraw-Hill. • 1994. $36.56. Seventh edition. (Humanities, Social Sciences and World Languages Series).

Introduction to Reference Work. William A. Katz. McGraw-Hill. • 2001. $58.60. Eighth edition. Two volumes. (Introduction to Reference Works Series).

The Invisible Web: Uncovering Information Sources Search Engines Can't See. Chris Sherman and Gary Price. Information Today, Inc. • 2001. $29.95. A guide to Web sites from universities, libraries, associations, government agencies, and other sources that are inadequately covered by conventional search engines (see also http://www.invisible-web.net). (CyberAge Books.).

Researching Company Financial Information. Washington Researchers, Ltd. • 2002. $59.00.

The Skeptical Business Searcher: The Information Advisor's Guide to Evaluating Web Data, Sites, and Sources. Robert Berkman. Information Today, Inc. • 2003. $29.95. Covers free Internet sources of company backgrounds, sales data, earnings, SEC documents, competitive intelligence information, poll data, business news, economic statistics, etc. The author is editor of *The Information Advisor* newsletter. (CyberAge Books).

Using Government Information Sources, Electronic and Print. Marilyn K. Moody and Jean L. Sears. Greenwood Publishing Group, Inc. • 2001. $125.00. Third edition. Contains detailed information in four sections on subject searches, agency searches, statistical searches, and special techniques for searching. Appendixes give selected agency and publisher addresses, telephone numbers, and computer communications numbers.

INTERNET DATABASES

EBSCO Information Services. Ebsco Publishing. Phone: 800-653-2726 or (978)356-6500 Fax: (978)356-6565 E-mail: ep@epnet.com • URL: http://www.epnet.com • Fee-based Web site providing Internet access to a wide variety of databases, including business-related material. Full text is available for many periodical titles, with daily updates. Fees: Apply.

GPO Access. U. S. Government Printing Office Sales Program, Bibliographic Systems Branch. Phone: 888-293-6498 or (202)512-1530 Fax: (202)512-1262 E-mail: gpoaccess@gpo.gov • URL: http://www.access.gpo.gov • Web site provides searching of the GPO's Sales Product Catalog (SPC), also known as Publications Reference File (PRF). Covers all "Government information products currently offered for sale by the Superintendent of Documents." There are also specialized search pages for individual databases, such as the *Code of Federal Regulations*, the *Federal Register*, and *Commerce Business Daily*. Updated daily. Fees: Free.

InSite 2. Intelligence Data/Thomson Financial. Phone: 800-654-0393 or (617)856-1890 Fax: (617)737-3182 E-mail: intelligence.data@tfn.com • URL: http://www.insite2.gale.com/ • Fee-based Web site consolidates information in a "Base Pack" consisting of Business InSite, Market InSite, and Company InSite. Optional databases are Consumer InSite, Health and Wellness InSite, Newsletter InSite, and Computer InSite. Includes fulltext content from more than 2,500 trade publications, journals, newsletters, newspapers, analyst reports, and other sources. Continuous updating. Formerly produced by The Gale Group.

Intelligence Data. Thomson Financial. Phone: 800-654-0393 Fax: (617)824-2477 • URL: http://www.intelligencedata.com • Fee-based Web site provides a wide variety of information relating to competitive intelligence, strategic planning, business development, mergers, acquisitions, sales, and marketing. "Intelliscope" feature offers searching of other Thomson units, such as Investext, MarkIntel, InSite 2, and Industry Insider. Weekly updating.

ProQuest Direct. ProQuest Inc. Phone: 800-889-3358 or (734)761-4700 Fax: (734)662-4554 • URL: http://proquest.com • Fee-based Web site providing Internet access to more than 3,000 periodicals, newspapers, and other publications. Many items are available full-text, with daily updates. Includes extensive corporate and financial information. Fees: Apply.

PubList.com: The Internet Directory of Publications. Bowes & Associates, Inc. Phone: (781)792-0999 Fax: (781)792-0988 E-mail: info@publist.com • URL: http://www.publist.com • "The premier online global resource for information about print and electronic publications." Provides online searching for information on more than 150,000 magazines, journals, newsletters, e-journals, and monographs. Database entries generally include title, publisher, format, address, editor, circulation, subject, and International Standard Serial Number (ISSN). Fees: Free.

Ulrichsweb.com. R. R. Bowker. Phone: 888-269-5372 or (908)464-6800 Fax: (908)464-3553 E-mail: info@bowker.com • URL: http://www.ulrichsweb.com • Web site provides fee-based access to about 250,000 serials records from the *Ulrich's International Periodicals Directory* database. Includes periodical evaluations from *Library Journal* and *Magazines for Libraries*. Monthly updates.

WilsonWeb Periodicals Databases. H. W. Wilson. Phone: 800-367-6770 or (718)588-8400 Fax: 800-590-1617 or (718)992-8003 E-mail: custserv@hwwilson.com • URL: http://www.hwwilson.com/ • Web sites provide fee-based access to *Wilson Business Full Text*, *Applied Science & Technology Full Text*, *Biological & Agricultural Index*, *Library Literature & Information Science Full Text*, and *Readers' Guide Full Text, Mega Edition*. Daily updates.

ONLINE DATABASES

Catalog of U.S. Government Publications. U. S. Government Printing Office. • Contains over 375,000 online citations to U. S. government publications, 1976 to date, with monthly updates. Corresponds to the printed *Monthly Catalog of United States Government Publications*. Inquire as to online cost and availability.

GPO Sales Product Catalog. U. S. Government Printing Office. • An online guide to federal government publications in print (currently for sale), forthcoming, and recently out-of-print. Daily updates. Inquire as to online cost and availability.

LC MARC: Books. U. S. Library of Congress. • Contains online bibliographic records for over five million books cataloged by the Library of Congress since 1968. Updating is weekly or monthly. Inquire as to online cost and availability. (MARC is machine readable cataloging.).

Newsletter Database. Gale Cengage Learning. • Contains the full text of about 600 U. S. and international newsletters covering a wide range of business and industrial topics. Time period is 1988 to date, with daily updates. Inquire as to online cost and availability.

PERIODICALS AND NEWSLETTERS

Business Information Alert: Sources, Strategies and Signposts for Information Professionals. Alert Publications, Inc. • 10 times per year. Libraries, $162.00 per year. Newsletter for business librarians and information specialists.

The Information Advisor: Tips and Techniques for Smart Information Users. MarketResearch.com. • Monthly. $159.00 per year. Newsletter. Evaluates and discusses online, CD-ROM, and published sources of business, financial, and market research information.

The Information Report. Washington Researchers. • Description: Contains 40-140 items in each issue identifying little-known sources of information. Lists and describes directories, special libraries, booklets, seminars, studies, and other research sources available on markets, competition, federal regulation, and economic conditions. Covers government as well as corporate sources, trade, and professional organizations.

Internet Reference Services Quarterly: A Journal of Innovative Information Practice, Technologies, and Resources. Haworth Press, Inc. • Quarterly. $110.00 per year. Covers both theoretical research and practical applications.

Reference and User Services Quarterly. American Library Association, Reference and Adult Services Div. • Quarterly. $50.00 per year. In addition to articles, includes reviews of databases, reference books, and library professional material. Formerly *RQ*.

Reference Services Review: Information on All Aspects of the Reference Function. Emerald (North America). • Quarterly. $319.00 per year. Covers automation of library reference services, user needs, reference source evaluation, service delivery models, and related topics.

TRADE/PROFESSIONAL ASSOCIATIONS

Association of Information and Dissemination Centers. P.O. Box 3212, Maple Glen, PA 19002-8212. Phone: (215)654-9129 Fax: (215)654-9129

E-mail: info@asidic.org • URL: http://www.asidic.org.

OTHER SOURCES

Business Information Desk Reference: Where to Find Answers to Your Business Questions. Melvyn N. Freed and Virgil P. Diodato. Prentice Hall PTR. • 1992. $20.00. Offers a unique, question and answer approach to business information sources. Covers print sources, online databases, trade associations, and government agencies.

Business Rankings Annual. Gale Cengage Learning. • Annual. $325.00. Two volumes. Compiled by the Business Library Staff of the Brooklyn Public Library. This is a guide to lists and rankings appearing in major business publications. The top ten names are listed in each case.

The Information Catalog. MarketResearch.com. • Bimonthly. Free. Mainly a catalog of market research reports from various publishers, but also includes business and marketing reference sources. Includes keyword title index. Formerly *The Information Catalog: Marketing Intelligence Studies, Competitor Reports, Business and Marketing Sources.*

INFORMATION SYSTEMS, MANAGEMENT

See: MANAGEMENT INFORMATION SYSTEMS

INFORMATION SYSTEMS, ONLINE

See: ONLINE INFORMATION SYSTEMS

INHERITANCE TAX

See also: ESTATE PLANNING

HANDBOOKS AND MANUALS

Corporate, Partnership, Estate, and Gift Taxation 1997. James W. Pratt and William Kulsrud, editors. McGraw-Hill. • 1996. $71.25. 10th edition.

Estate Plan Book 2000. William S. Moore. American Institute for Economic Research. • 2000. $10.00. Revision of 1997 edition. Part one: "Basic Estate Planning." Part two: "Reducing Taxes on the Disposition of Your Estate." Part three: "Putting it All Together: Examples of Estate Plans." Provides succinct information on wills, trusts, tax planning, and gifts. (Economic Education Bulletin.).

Federal Estate and Gift Taxation. RIA. • Three times a year. $425.0 per year. Clarification and guidance on estate tax laws.

Federal Estate and Gift Taxes: Code and Regulations, Including Related Income Tax Provisions. CCH, Inc. • 2000. $47.00. Revised edition. Provides full text of estate, gift, and generation-skipping tax provisions of the Internal Revenue Code.

Federal Income Taxes of Decedents, Estates, and Trusts. CCH, Inc. • 2001. $48.00. 20th revised edition. Provides rules for preparing a decedent's final income tax return. Includes discussions of fiduciary duties, grantor trusts, and bankruptcy estates.

Federal Tax Course. Aspen Publishers, Inc. • Annual. $210.00. Provides basic reference and training for various forms of federal taxation: individual, business, corporate, partnership, estate, gift, etc.

How to Save Time and Taxes Preparing Fiduciary Income Tax Returns. LexisNexis Matthew Bender. • Biennial. $272.00 per year. Looseleaf service. Comprehensive coverage of the federal income

taxation of trusts and estates.

Inheritor's Handbook: A Definitive Guide for Beneficiaries. Dan Rottenberg. Bloomberg. • 1998. $23.95. Covers both financial and emotional issues faced by beneficiaries. (Bloomberg Personal Bookshelf Series.).

Internal Revenue Code. RIA. • Annual. $86.50. Provides full text of the Internal Revenue Code (5,000 pages), including procedural and administrative provisions.

Law of Federal Estate and Gift Taxation-Code Commentary. West Group. • Annual. $177.00. Looseleaf service.

The Living Trust: The Failproof Way to Pass Along Your Estate to Your Heirs Without Lawyers, Courts, or the Probate System. Henry W. Abts. McGraw-Hill. • 2002. $24.95. Third edition.

Trust Administration and Taxation. LexisNexis Matthew Bender. • Semiannual. $1,007.00. Four looseleaf volumes. Text on establishment, administration, and taxation of trusts.

U. S. Master Estate and Gift Tax Guide. CCH, Inc. • Annual. $55.00. Covers federal estate and gift taxes, including generation-skipping transfer tax plans. Includes tax tables and sample filled-in tax return forms.

INTERNET DATABASES

CCH Essentials: An Internet Tax Research and Primary Source Library. CCH, Inc. Phone: 800-248-3248 or (773)866-6000 Fax: 800-224-8299 or (773)866-3608 E-mail: cust_serv@cch.com • URL: http://tax.cch.com/essentials • Fee-based Web site provides full-text coverage of federal tax law and regulations, including rulings, procedures, tax court decisions, and IRS publications, announcements, notices, and penalties. Includes explanation, analysis, tax planning guides, and a daily tax news service. Searching is offered, including citation search.

Internal Revenue Service IRS.gov. Internal Revenue Service. Phone: 800-829-1040 or (202)622-5000 Fax: (202)622-5844 • URL: http://www.irs.gov • Web site provides a wide variety of tax information, including IRS forms and publications. Searching is available. Fees: Free.

Tax Analysts [Web site]. Tax Analysts. Phone: 800-955-3444 or (703)533-4400 Fax: (703)533-4444 • URL: http://www.tax.org • The three main sections of Tax Analysts home page are "Tax News" (Today's Tax News, Feature of the Week, Tax Snapshots, Tax Calendar); "Products & Services" (Product Catalog, Press Releases); and "Public Interest" (Discussion Groups, Tax Clinic, Tax History Project). Fees: Free for coverage of current tax events; fee-based for comprehensive information. Daily updating.

PERIODICALS AND NEWSLETTERS

Estate Planner's Alert. RIA. • Monthly. $140.00 per year. Newsletter. Covers the tax aspects of personal finance, including home ownership, investments, insurance, retirement planning, and charitable giving. Formerly *Estate and Financial Planners Alert.*

Highlights and Documents. Tax Analysts. • Daily. $2,249.00 per year, including monthly indexes. Newsletter. Provides daily coverage of IRS, congressional, judicial, state, and international tax developments. Includes abstracts and citations for "all tax documents released within the previous 24 to 48 hours." Annual compilation available *Highlights and Documents on Microfiche.*

Tax Notes: The Weekly Tax Service. Tax Analysts. • Weekly. $1,699.00 per year. Includes an *Annual* and 1985-1996 compliations on CD-ROM. Newsletter. Covers "tax news from all federal sources," including congressional committees, tax courts, and the Internal Revenue Service. Each issue contains "summaries of every document that pertains to federal tax

law," with citations. Commentary is provided.

Tax Practice. Tax Analysts. • Weekly. $199.00 per year. Newsletter. Covers news affecting tax practitioners and litigators, with emphasis on federal court decisions, rules and regulations, and tax petitions. Provides a guide to Internal Revenue Service audit issues.

OTHER SOURCES

Estate Planning and Taxation Coordinator. RIA. • Biweekly. $1,290.00 per year. Nine looseleaf volumes. Includes *Estate Planner's Alert* and *Lifetime Planning Alert.*

Estate Planning: Inheritance Taxes. Prentice Hall PTR. • Five looseleaf volumes. Periodic supplementation. Price on application.

Estate Planning Strategies After Estate Tax Reform: Insights and Analysis. Charles D. Fox and Thomas W. Aberdroth. CCH, Inc. • 2001. $45.00. Produced by the Estate Planning Department of Schiff, Hardin & Waite. Covers estate planning techniques and opportunities resulting from tax legislation of 2001.

Estate Planning Under the New Law: What You Need to Know. CCH, Inc. • 2001. $7.00. Booklet summarizes significant changes in estate planning brought about by tax legislation of 2001.

Federal Estate and Gift Tax Reports. CCH, Inc. • Weekly. $578.00. Three looseleaf volumes.

Federal Income, Gift and Estate Taxation. LexisNexis Matthew Bender. • $1,220.00. Seven looseleaf volumes. Periodic supplementation.

Fiduciary Tax Guide. CCH, Inc. • Monthly. $478.00 per year. Looseleaf service. Covers federal income taxation of estates, trusts, and beneficiaries. Provides information on gift and generation- skipping taxation.

INITIAL PUBLIC OFFERINGS

See: NEW ISSUES (FINANCE)

INJURIES

See: ACCIDENTS

INK

See: PRINTING INK INDUSTRY

INLAND MARINE INSURANCE

See: MARINE INSURANCE

INLAND WATERWAYS

See: WATERWAYS

INNOVATION, BUSINESS

See: BUSINESS INNOVATION

INNOVATION IN PRODUCTS

See: NEW PRODUCTS

INSECTICIDES

See: PESTICIDE INDUSTRY

INSECTS

See: ECONOMIC ENTOMOLOGY

INSERVICE TRAINING

See: TRAINING OF EMPLOYEES

INSIDER TRADING

See also: STOCKHOLDERS

ABSTRACTS AND INDEXES

Business Periodicals Index. H. W. Wilson Co. • 11 times a year. Quarterly and annual cumulations. Price varies.

Index to Legal Periodicals and Books. H. W. Wilson Co. • Monthly. $490.00 per year. Quarterly and annual cumulations.

HANDBOOKS AND MANUALS

Insider Trading Regulation, Enforcement and Prevention. Donald C. Langevoort. West Group. • Annual. $216.00. Two looseleaf volumes. (Securities Law Series).

Responsibilities of Corporate Officers and Directors Under Federal Securities Law. CCH, Inc. • Annual. $79.00. Includes discussions of indemnification, "D & O" insurance, corporate governance, and insider liability.

INTERNET DATABASES

U. S. Securities and Exchange Commission. Phone: 800-732-0330 or (202)942-7040 Fax: (202)942-9634 E-mail: webmaster@sec.gov • URL: http://www.sec.gov • SEC Web site offers free access through EDGAR to text of official corporate filings, such as annual reports (10-K), quarterly reports (10-Q), and proxies. (EDGAR is "Electronic Data Gathering, Analysis, and Retrieval System.") An example is given of how to obtain executive compensation data from proxies. Text of the daily *SEC News Digest* is offered, as are links to other government sites, non-government market regulators, and U. S. stock exchanges. Search facilities are extensive. Fees: Free.

ONLINE DATABASES

Index to Legal Periodicals and Books (Online). H. W. Wilson Co. • Broad coverage of law journals and books 1981 to date. Monthly updates. Inquire as to online cost and availability.

Legal Resource Index. Gale Cengage Learning. • Broad coverage of law literature appearing in legal, business, and other periodicals, 1980 to date. Daily updates. Inquire as to online cost and availability.

LEXIS. LEXIS-NEXIS. • The various LEXIS databases provide full text and indexing for a wide variety of legal cases, statutes, orders, and opinions.

Vickers On-Line. Vickers Stock Research Corp. • Provides detailed online information relating to insider trading and the securities holdings of institutional investors. Daily updates. Inquire as to online cost and availability.

Wilson Business Abstracts Online. H. W. Wilson Co. • Indexes and abstracts 600 major business periodicals, plus the *Wall Street Journal* and the business section of the *New York Times.* Indexing is from 1982, abstracting from 1990, with the two newspapers included from 1993. Updated weekly. Inquire as to online cost and availability. (*Business Periodicals Index* without abstracts is also available online.).

PERIODICALS AND NEWSLETTERS

Barron's: The Dow Jones Business and Financial Weekly. • Weekly. $145.00 per year.

Vickers Weekly Insider Report. Vickers Stock

Research Corp. • Description: Reports on stock insider transactions and maintains portfolios based on insider buy signals-96 up 68%.

RESEARCH CENTERS AND INSTITUTES

Center for Research in Security Prices. University of Chicago, 725 S. Wells St., Suite 800, Chicago, IL 60607. Phone: (773)834-4610 Fax: (773)702-3036 E-mail: custom@crsp.uchicago.edu • URL: http://gsbwww.uchicago.edu/research/crsp.

Glucksman Institute. New York University. Salomon Center, Stern School of Business, 44 W. Fourth St., Room 9-65, New York, NY 10012-0267. Phone: (212)998-0714 Fax: (212)995-4220 E-mail: wsilber@stern.nyu.edu.

Rodney L. White Center for Financial Research. University of Pennsylvania, 3254 Steinberg Hall-Dietrich Hall, Philadelphia, PA 19104. Phone: (215)898-7616 Fax: (215)573-8084 E-mail: rlwtcr@finance.wharton.upenn.edu • URL: http://www.finance.wharton.upenn.edu • Research areas include financial management, money markets, real estate finance, and international finance.

TRADE/PROFESSIONAL ASSOCIATIONS

American Stock Exchange. 86 Trinity Pl., New York, NY 10006. Phone: (866)422-2639 or (212)306-1000 Fax: (212)306-1218 E-mail: amexfeedback@amex.com • URL: http://www.amex.com • Represents domestic and international equities and derivative securities market. Provides an auction marketplace that integrates service and information programs for its listed companies.

National Association of Securities Dealers (NASD). 1735 K St., N.W., Washington, DC 20006-1506. Phone: (202)728-8000 Fax: (202)293-6260 E-mail: waltere@nasd.com • URL: http://www.nasd.com • Formerly National Association of Securities Dealers.

New York Stock Exchange. 11 Wall St., New York, NY 10005. Phone: (212)656-3000 Fax: (212)656-3939 E-mail: boardofdirectors@nyse.com • URL: http://www.nyse.com • Aims to "add value to the capital-raising and asset-management process by providing the highest-quality and most cost-effective self-regulated marketplace for the trading of financial instruments, promote confidence in and understanding of that process, and serve as a forum for discussion of relevant national and international policy issues".

North American Securities Administrators Association. 750 1st St. NE, Ste. 1140, Washington, DC 20002-8034. Phone: 800-84-NASAA or (202)737-0900 Fax: (202)783-3571 E-mail: info@nasaa.org • URL: http://www.nasaa.org • Represents the interests of the state, provincial and territorial securities administrators in the U.S., Canada, Mexico and Puerto Rico. Provides support to its members in government relations and with federal regulators, industry SROs and other groups.

Securities Industry and Financial Markets Association. 120 Broadway, 35th Fl., New York, NY 10271-0080. Phone: (212)313-1200 Fax: (212)313-1301 E-mail: rbrockhaus@sifma.org • URL: http://www.sifma.org • Represents more than 650 member firms of all sizes, in all financial markets in the U.S. and around the world. Enhances the public's trust and confidence in the markets, delivering an efficient, enhanced member network of access and forward-looking services, as well as premiere educational resources for the professionals in the industry and the investors whom they serve. Maintains offices in New York City and Washington, DC.

OTHER SOURCES

Ferrara on Insider Trading and The Wall. Ralph C. Ferrara. American Lawyer Media, Inc. • Looseleaf. $179.00. Updated as needed. Demonstrates how firms can use "Chinese Walls" and other devices to

control the dissemination of material, nonpublic information by employees. Includes "suggested guidelines for deterring insider trading by employees." (Law Journal Press).

Securities Litigation and Regulation Reporter: The National Journal of Record of Commodities Litigation. Andrews Publications. • Semimonthly. $1,250.00 per year. Newsletter. Provides reports on litigation involving the rules and decisions of the Commodity Futures Trading Commission. Formerly *Securities and Commodities Litigation Reporter.*

INSOLVENCY

See: BANKRUPTCY

INSTALLMENT PLAN PURCHASING

See also: CONSUMER CREDIT; FINANCE COMPANIES

PERIODICALS AND NEWSLETTERS

Consumer Finance Newsletter. Financial Publishing Co. • Description: Provides information on effective and pending credit insurance and installment loan regulations on the state and federal levels. Supplies news of potential state changes in regulations.

OTHER SOURCES

Consumer and Commercial Credit: Installment Sales. Prentice Hall PTR. • Three looseleaf volumes. Periodic supplementation. Price on application. Covers secured transactions under the Uniform Commercial Code and the Uniform Consumer Credit Code. Includes retail installment sales, home improvement loans, higher education loans, and other kinds of installment loans.

INSTITUTIONAL FOOD SERVICE

See: FOOD SERVICE INDUSTRY

INSTITUTIONAL INVESTMENTS

See also: INVESTMENTS; TRUSTS AND TRUSTEES

GENERAL WORKS

Asset Allocation and Financial Market Timing: Techniques for Investment Professionals. Carroll D. Aby and Donald E. Vaughn. Greenwood Publishing Group, Inc. • 1995. $79.95.

Asset Allocation: Balancing Financial Risk. Roger C. Gibson. McGraw-Hill. • 2000. $55.00. Third edition. Provides a scholarly discussion of the fine points of investment asset allocation and financial risk management.

Beyond Junk Bonds: Expanding High Yield Markets. Glenn Yago. Oxford University Press. • 2003. $45.00. Describes the "broadening and deepening of the high yield market over the past decade..." Indicates there are now thousands of institutional buyers of lower-rated bonds, including many mutual funds.

Cases in Portfolio Management. John W. Peavy and Katrina F. Sherrerd. Association of Investment Management and Research. • 1991. $30.00.

Financial Markets and Institutions. Frederic S. Mishkin and Stanley G. Eakins. Addison-Wesley. • 2002. $118.00. Fourth edition.

Investments: An Introduction to Analysis and Management. Frederick Amling. Pearson Custom

Publishing. • 1999. $94.00. Seventh edition.

Market Efficiency: Stock Market Behavior in Theory and Practice. Andrew W. Lo, editor. Edward Elgar Publishing, Inc. • 1997. $465.00. Two volumes. Consists of reprints of 49 articles dating from 1937 to 1993, in five sections: "Theoretical Foundations," "The Random Walk Hypothesis," "Variance Bounds Tests," "Overreaction and Underreaction," and "Anomalies." (International Library of Critical Writings in Financial Economics Series: No. 3).

Modern Portfolio Theory and Investment Analysis and Investment Portfolio Software. Edwin J. Elton. John Wiley and Sons, Inc. • 1998. $88.00. Fifth edition. Includes CD-Rom. The authors' central concern is that of mixing assets to achieve maximum overall return consonant with an acceptable level of risk. (Portfolio Management Series).

Portfolio Management in Practice. Christine Brentani. Elsevier Butterworth Heinemann. • 2003. $40.00. Serves as a basic text on portfolio management. Among the topics covered are portfolio theory, portfolio construction, valuation methodologies, measuring returns, financial statement analysis, and financial ratios. Includes a glossary.

Portfolio Selection: Efficient Diversification of Investments. Harry M. Markowitz. Blackwell Publishing. • 1991. $66.95. Second edition. A standard work on diversification of investments for institutions. Provides a mathematical approach.

The Strategic Bond Investor: Strategies and Tools to Unlock the Power of the Bond Market. Anthony Crescenzi. McGraw-Hill. • 2002. $29.95. Covers management strategies for fixed-income investment portfolios. (Teach Yourself Series).

Super Searchers on Wall Street: Top Investment Professionals Share Their Online Research Secrets. Amelia Kassel. Information Today, Inc. • 2000. $24.95. Gives the results of interviews with "10 leading financial industry research experts." Explains how online information is used by stock brokers, investment bankers, and individual investors. Includes relevant Web sites and other sources. (Super Searchers Series).

ALMANACS AND YEARBOOKS

Advances in Investment Analysis and Portfolio Management. Chung-Few Lee, editor. Elsevier. • Dates vary. Six volumes. Price varies.

CD-ROM DATABASES

Compact D/SEC. Thomson Financial. • Monthly. Provides 200 financial data items for 12,000 U. S. publicly-held corporations filing reports with the Securities and Exchange Commission. Includes company profiles.

InvesText [CD-ROM]. Thomson Financial. • Monthly. Contains full text on CD-ROM of investment research reports from about 630 sources, including leading brokers and investment bankers. Reports are available on both U. S. and international publicly traded corporations. Separate industry reports cover more than 50 industries. Time span is 1982 to date.

DIRECTORIES

Association for Investment Management and Research-Membership Directory. Association for Investment Management and Research. • Annual. $150.00. Lists 38,000 professional investment managers and securities analysts.

Directory of Trust Banking. Thomson Financial Publishing. • Annual. $344.00. Contains profiles of bank affiliated trust companies, independent trust companies, trust investment advisors, and trust fund managers. Provides contact information for professional personnel at more than 3,000 banking and other financial institutions.

Financial Yellow Book: Who's Who at the Leading U. S. Financial Institutions. Leadership Directories,

Inc. • Semiannual. $265.00. Gives the names and titles of over 28,000 key executives in financial institutions. Includes the areas of banking, investment, money management, and insurance. Five indexes are provided: institution, executive name, geographic by state, financial service segment, and parent company.

Futures Magazine SourceBook: The Most Complete List of Exchanges, Companies, Regulators, Organizations, etc., Offering Products and Services to the Futures and Options Industry. Futures Magazine, Inc. • Annual. $19.50. Provides information on commodity futures brokers, trading method services, publications, and other items of interest to futures traders and money managers.

HedgeWorld Annual Compendium: The Hedge Fund Industry's Definitive Reference Guide. HedgeWorld USA. • Annual. $499.00. Contains profiles of 500 domestic and offshore hedge funds with more than $50 million in assets under management. Includes articles on "The Basics of Investing in Hedge Funds," "Beyond the Basics," and other information.

HedgeWorld Service Provider League Tables & Analyses. HedgeWorld USA. • Annual. $595.00. Provides quantitative and qualitative information on firms providing services to hedge funds: accountants/auditors, administrators, custodians, legal counsel, and prime brokers. Detailed categories cover banks, clearing services, consultants, derivatives business, investment companies, wealth management services, etc.

Institutional Buyers of Bank and Thrift Stocks: A Targeted Directory. Investment Data Corp. • Annual. $645.00. Provides detailed profiles of about 600 institutional buyers of bank and savings and loan stocks. Includes names of financial analysts and portfolio managers.

Institutional Buyers of Energy Stocks. Investment Data Corp. • Annual. $645.00. Provides detailed profiles 555 institutional buyers of petroleum-related and other energy stocks. Includes names of financial analysts and portfolio managers.

Institutional Buyers of Foreign Stocks: A Targeted Directory. Investment Data Corp. • Annual. $595.00. Provides detailed profiles of institutional buyers of international stocks. Includes names of financial analysts and portfolio managers.

Institutional Buyers of REIT Securities. Investment Data Corp. • Semiannual. $995.00 per year. Provides detailed profiles of about 500 institutional buyers of REIT securities. Includes names of financial analysts and portfolio managers.

Institutional Buyers of Small-Cap Stocks. Investment Data Corp. • Annual. $295.00. Provides detailed profiles of more than 837 institutional buyers of small capitalization stocks. Includes names of financial analysts and portfolio managers.

Major Financial Institutions of the World 2001. Available from Gale Cengage Learning. • 2003. $880.00. Sixth edition. Two volumes. Published by Graham & Whiteside. Contains detailed information on more than 7,500 important financial institutions in various countries. Includes banks, investment companies, and insurance companies.

Money Market Directory of Pension Funds and Their Investment Managers. Money Market Directories, Inc. • Annual. $1,150.00. Institutional funds and managers.

Nelson Information's Directory of Institutional Real Estate. Nelson Information. • Annual. $400.00. Includes real estate investment managers, service firms, consultants, real estate investment trusts (REITs), and various institutional investors in real estate. Formerly *Nelson's Directory of Real Estate Investments.*

Nelson Information's Directory of Investment Managers. Nelson Information. • Annual. $595.00. Three volumes. Provides information on 2,200

investment management firms, both U.S. and foreign.

Nelson Information's Directory of Investment Research. Nelson Information. • Annual. $665.00. Three volumes. Provides information on 7,000 investment research analysts at more than 800 firms. Indexes include company name, industry, and name of person.

Nelson Information's Directory of Pension Fund Consultants. Nelson Information. • Annual. $610.00. Covers the pension plan sponsor industry. More than 325 worldwide consulting firms are described. Formerly *Nelson's Guide to Pension Fund Consultants.*

Nelson Information's Directory of Plan Sponsors. Nelson Information. • Annual. $610.00. Three volumes. Formerly *Nelson's Directory of Plan Sponsors and Tax-Exempt Funds.*

Plunkett's Financial Services Industry Almanac: The Only Comprehensive Overview of the Banking, Insurance, Credit and Investment Sectors. Plunkett Research, Ltd. • Annual. $229.99. Includes CD-ROM. Discusses important trends in various sectors of the financial industry. Five hundred major banking, credit card, investment, and financial services companies are profiled. (Business, Careers and Internet Reference Tools Series).

Vickers Directory of Institutional Investors. Vickers Stock Research Corp. • Semiannual. $195.00 per year. Detailed alphabetical listing of more than 4,000 U. S., Canadian, and foreign institutional investors. Includes insurance companies, banks, endowment funds, and investment companies. Formerly *Directory of Institutional Investors.*

Zacks Analyst Directory: Listed by Broker. Zacks Investment Research. • Quarterly. $395.00 per year. Lists stockbroker investment analysts and gives the names of major U. S. corporations covered by those analysts.

Zacks Analyst Directory: Listed by Company. Zacks Investment Research. • Quarterly. $395.00 per year. Lists major U. S. corporations and gives the names of stockbroker investment analysts covering those companies.

Zacks EPS Calendar. Zacks Investment Research. • Biweekly. $1,250.00 per year. (Also available monthly at $895.00 per year.) Lists anticipated reporting dates of earnings per share for major U. S. corporations.

ENCYCLOPEDIAS AND DICTIONARIES

Blackwell Encyclopedic Dictionary of Finance. Dean Paxson and Douglas Wood, editors. Blackwell Publishing. • 1997. $110.00. The editors are associated with the University of Manchester. Contains definitions of key terms combined with longer articles written by various U. S. and foreign business educators. Includes bibliographies and index. (Blackwell Encyclopedia of Management Series).

Dictionary of Finance and Investment Terms. John Downes. Barron's Educational Series, Inc. • 2002. $14.95. Sixth edition. Provides clear explanations of more than 5,000 business, banking, financial, investment, and tax terms. Includes a separate list of financial abbreviations and acronyms. (Business Dictionaries Series).

International Encyclopedia of Futures and Options. Fitzroy Dearborn Publishers, Inc. • 2000. $285.00. Two volumes. Covers terminology, concepts, events, individuals, and markets.

The New Palgrave Dictionary of Money and Finance. Peter Newman and others, editors. Palgrave Macmillan. • 1992. $595.00. Two volumes. Consists of signed essays on over 1,000 financial topics, each with a bibliography. Covers a wide variety of financial, monetary, and investment areas.

A detailed subject index is provided.

HANDBOOKS AND MANUALS

Active Portfolio Management: Quantitative Theory and Applications. Richard C. Grinold and Ronald N. Kahn. McGraw-Hill. • 1999. $75.00. Second edition.

Advanced Fixed Income Analysis. Moorad Choudhry. Elsevier Butterworth Heinemann. • 2004. $60.00. Edited for "experienced practitioners in the corporate bond markets." Covers trading, hedging, interest rate models, corporate bond default risk, the yield curve, long bond yields, and other topics.

Bank Investments and Funds Management. Gerald O. Hatler. American Bankers Association. • 1991. $49.00. Second edition. Focuses on portfolio management, risk analysis, and investment strategy.

The Bond and Money Markets: Strategy, Trading, Analysis. Moorad Choudhry. Elsevier Butterworth Heinemann. • 2003. $115.00. Serves as a reference work on corporate bonds, government bonds, currency markets, interest-rate futures, convertible securities, various kinds of derivatives, and technical analysis of financial securities.

Computational Finance: Numerical Methods for Pricing Financial Instruments. George Levy. Elsevier Butterworth Heinemann. • 2003. $89.95. Explains advanced financial modeling techniques using Windows software.

Convertible Securities: The Latest Instruments, Portfolio Strategies, and Valuation Analysis. John P. Calamos. McGraw-Hill. • 1998. $65.00. Second revised edition. (Irwin Library of Investment and Finance Series).

Derivatives: A Comprehensive Resource for Options, Futures, Interest Rate Swaps, and Mortgage Securities. Fred D. Arditti. Harvard Business School Publishing. • 1996. $60.00. Published by Harvard Business School Press. Provides detailed explanations of various kinds of financial derivatives (options, futures, swaps, etc.) and their trading tactics, uses, and risks. (Financial Management Association Survey and Synthesis Series).

Econometrics of Financial Markets. John Y. Campbell and others. Princeton University Press. • 1996. $70.00. Written for advanced students and industry professionals. Includes chapters on "The Predictability of Asset Returns," "Derivative Pricing Models," and "Fixed-Income Securities." Provides a discussion of the random walk theory of investing and tests of the theory.

Elements of Financial Risk Management. Peter F. Christoffersen. Elsevier Butterworth Heinemann. • 2003. $79.95. Includes material on the various kinds of financial market risk, simulation methods, hedging, options, and evaluation of risk models.

Global Equity Selection Strategies. Ross P. Bruner, editor. Fitzroy Dearborn Publishers, Inc. • 1999. $65.00. Written by various professionals in the field of international investments. Contains six major sections covering growth, value, size, price momentum, sector rotation, and country allocation. (Glenlake Business Monographs).

Handbook of Alternative Investment Strategies. Thomas Schneeweis and Joseph F. Pescatore, editors. Institutional Investor, Inc., Journals Group. • 1999. $95.00. Covers various forms of alternative investment, including hedge funds, managed futures, derivatives, venture capital, and natural resource financing.

Handbook of Derivative Instruments: Investment Research, Analysis, and Portfolio Applications. Arsuo Konishi and Ravi Dattatreya, editors. McGraw-Hill. • 1996. $80.00. Second revised edition. Contains 41 chapters by various authors on all aspects of derivative securities, including such esoterica as "Inverse Floaters," "Positive Convexity,"

"Exotic Options," and "How to Use the Holes in Black-Scholes.".

Handbook of Fixed Income Securities. Frank J. Fabozzi. McGraw-Hill. • 2000. $99.95. Sixth edition. Topics include risk measurement, valuation techniques, and portfolio strategy.

Indexing for Maximum Investment Results. Albert S. Neuberg. Fitzroy Dearborn Publishers, Inc. • 1998. $65.00. Covers the Standard & Poor's 500 and other indexing strategies for both individual and institutional investors.

Interest Rate Risk Measurement and Management. Sanjay K. Nawalkha and Donald R. Chambers, editors. Institutional Investor, Inc. • 1999. $95.00. Provides interest rate risk models for fixed-income derivatives and for investments by various kinds of financial institutions.

An Introduction to the Mathematics of Financial Derivatives. Salih N. Neftci. Elsevier. • 2000. $64.95. Second edition. Covers the mathematical models underlying the pricing of derivatives. Includes explanations of basic financial calculus for students, derivatives traders, risk managers, and others concerned with derivatives.

Money Manager's Compliance Guide. Thompson Publishing Group, Inc. • $649.00 per year. Two looseleaf volumes. Monthly updates and newletters. Edited for investment advisers and investment companies to help them be in compliance with governmental regulations, including SEC rules, restrictions based on the Employee Retirement Income Security Act (ERISA), and regulations issued by the Commodity Futures Trading Commission (CFTC).

Pension Fund Investment Management: A Handbook for Sponsors and Their Advisors. Fran K. Fabozzi, editor. John Wiley and Sons, Inc. • 1997. $95.00. Second revised edition. (Frank K. Fabozzi Series: Vol. 25).

Portfolio Management Formulas: Mathematical Trading Methods for the Futures, Options, and Stock Markets. Ralph Vince. John Wiley and Sons, Inc. • 1990. $90.00. Discusses optimization of trading systems by exploiting the rules of probability and making use of the principles of modern portfolio management theory. Computer programs are included. (Finance Series).

Real Estate Investment Trusts: Structure, Performance, and Investment Opportunities. Su Han Chan. Oxford University Press. • 2002. $45.00. Covers the history of REITs, organizational structure, institutional investing, dividends, debt, and "existing scholarly research." An appendix provides "Monthly Stock Returns and Performance Index of All Publicly Traded REITs (1962-2000 and 2001-2002)." (Financial Management Association Survey and Synthesis Series).

Risk Management, Speculation, and Derivative Securities. Geoffrey Poitras. Elsevier Butterworth Heinemann. • 2002. $99.95. In addition to "Risk Management Concepts" and "Speculative Concepts," topics include financial futures, forward contracts, arbitrage, spread trading, hedging, and diversification. Three appendices are devoted to mathematical concepts and calculations.

Trading and Exchanges: Market Microstructure for Practitioners. Larry Harris. Oxford University Press. • 2002. $95.00. Explains the function and workings of modern stock markets. Covers such topics as liquidity, volatility, speculation, market efficiency, stock indexes, and the structure of trading. (Financial Management Association Survey and Synthesis Series).

INTERNET DATABASES

Derivatives. Imagine Software Inc. Phone: (212)317-7600 Fax: (212)317-7601 • URL: http://www.derivatives.com • Web site mainly promotes proprietary software for the use of derivatives in risk

management, but also provides free access to articles on a variety of derivatives-related topics.

ETF Connect. Nuveen Investments. Phone: 800-257-8787 • URL: http://www.etfconnect.com • Free Web site makes available extensive, searchable information on individual closed-end investment funds, preferred share funds, and exchange-traded index funds. Information on a particular fund is available by name or as part of a classification (high yield, investment grade, municipal, emerging markets, global equity, etc.). Fund charts are available for various time periods, as is data concerning premiums or discounts, dividends, annualized total return, credit quality, "Top 10 Holdings," and so forth.

Futures Online. Futures Magazine Inc. Phone: (312)846-4600 Fax: (312)846-4638 • URL: http://www.futuresmag.com • Web site presents updates of *Futures* magazine and links to other futures-related sites.

ONLINE DATABASES

Banking Information Source. PROQUEST. • Provides indexing and abstracting of periodical and other literature from 1982 to date, with weekly updates. Covers the financial services industry: banks, savings institutions, investment houses, credit unions, insurance companies, and real estate organizations. Emphasis is on marketing and management. Inquire as to online cost and availability. (Formerly *FINIS: Financial Industry Information Service.*).

First Call Consensus Earnings Estimates. Thomson Financial. • Online service provides corporate earnings estimates for more than 2,500 U. S. companies, based on data from leading brokerage firms. Weekly updates. Inquire as to online cost and availability.

Fitch Ratings Delivery Service. Fitch Inc. • Provides online delivery of Fitch financial ratings in three sectors: "Corporate Finance" (corporate bonds, insurance companies), "Structured Finance" (asset-backed securities), and "U.S. Public Finance" (municipal bonds). Daily updates. Inquire as to online cost and availability.

InvesText. Thomson Financial. • Provides full text online of investment research reports from more than 600 sources, including leading brokers and investment bankers. Reports are available on approximately 60,000 U. S. and international corporations. Separate industry reports cover 54 industries. Time span is 1982 to date, with daily updates. Inquire as to online cost and availability.

Vickers On-Line. Vickers Stock Research Corp. • Provides detailed online information relating to insider trading and the securities holdings of institutional investors. Daily updates. Inquire as to online cost and availability.

Zacks Earnings Estimates. Zacks Investment Research. • Provides online earnings projections for about 6,000 U. S. corporations, based on investment analysts' reports. Data is mainly from 200 major brokerage firms. Time span varies according to online provider, with daily or weekly updates. Inquire as to online cost and availability.

PERIODICALS AND NEWSLETTERS

American Banker: The Financial Services Daily. Thomson Media. • Daily. $895.00 per year. Provides news of banking, investment products, mortgages, credit unions, finance, bank technology, and legal developments.

Bank Investment Consultant: Sales Strategies for the Financial Adviser. Thomson Media. • Monthly. Controlled circulation. Covers sales and marketing techniques for bank investment and asset management divisions. Formerly *Bank Investment Marketing.*

Bloomberg Markets. Bloomberg. • Monthly. Free to

qualified personnel. Edited for securities dealers and investment managers.

Bondweek: The Newsweekly of Fixed Income and Credit Markets. Institutional Investor, Inc., Journals Group. • Weekly. $2,425.00 per year. Newsletter. Includes print and online editions. Covers taxable, fixed-income securities for professional investors, including corporate, government, foreign, mortgage, and high-yield.

Commercial Lending Review. American Bankers Association. Aspen Publishers, Inc. • Quarterly. $315.00 per year. Edited for senior-level lending officers. Includes specialized lending techniques, management issues, legal developments, and reviews of specific industries.

Derivatives Quarterly. Institutional Investor, Inc., Journals Group. • Quarterly. Price on application. Emphasis is on the practical use of derivatives. Includes case studies to demonstrate "real-life" risks and benefits.

Economics and Portfolio Strategy. Peter L. Bernstein, Inc. • Semimonthly. $1,700.00 per year. Provides financial analysis and insight for "institutional investors and sophisticated individual investors.".

Emerging Markets Debt Report. Thomson Media. • Weekly. $895.00 per year. Newsletter. Provides information on new and prospective sovereign and corporate bond issues from developing countries. Includes an emerging market bond index and pricing data.

Emerging Markets Quarterly. Institutional Investor, Inc., Journals Group. • Quarterly. Price on application. Newsletter on financial markets in developing areas, such as Africa, Latin America, Southeast Asia, and Eastern Europe. Topics include institutional investment opportunities and regulatory matters. Formerly *Emerging Markets Weekly.*

Financial Management. Financial Management Association International. • Quarterly. Individuals, $80.00 per year; libraries, $100.00 per year. Covers theory and practice of financial planning, international finance, investment banking, and portfolio management. Includes *Financial Practice* and *Education and Contempory Finance Digest.*

Financial Markets, Institutions, and Instruments. New York University, Salomon Center. Blackwell Publishing. • Five times a year. Institutions, $338.00 per year. Includes online edition. Edited to "bridge the gap between the academic and professional finance communities." Special fifth issue each year provides surveys of developments in four areas: money and banking, derivative securities, corporate finance, and fixed-income securities.

Futures: News, Analysis, and Strategies for Futures, Options, and Derivatives Traders. Futures Magazine. • Monthly. $39.00 per year. Edited for institutional money managers and traders, brokers, risk managers, and individual investors or speculators. Includes special feature issues on interest rates, technical indicators, currencies, charts, precious metals, hedge funds, and derivatives. Supplements available.

Global Money Management. Aspen Publishers. • Description: Reports on international fund management, including investment strategies; pension fund searches; hires for consultants, managers, and custodians; performance measurement; developing markets, and significant personnel changes.

Guide to Stock Mutual Funds: A Quarterly Compilation of Mutual Fund Ratings and Analysis Covering Equity and Balanced Funds. Weiss Ratings, Inc. • Quarterly. $438.00 per year. Emphasis is on rating of financial safety and relative risk. Includes annual summary.

High Yield Report. American Banker/Bond Buyer Inc. • Description: Examines markets for high-yield corporate bonds, work-outs, bankruptcies, and

secondary markets for distressed securities. Contains pricing information for primary and secondary markets and analysis of the high-yield sector. Reports on developments affecting the senior and subordinated debt of companies in bankruptcy or working their way out of debt, detailing proposed financial restructurings. Tracks regulatory decisions affecting trade of distressed debt and funds purchased and sold. **Remarks:** Incorporates the former Distressed Debt Report.

Institutional Investor International Edition: The Magazine for International Finance and Investment. Institutional Investor, Inc., Journals Group. • Monthly. $475.00 per year. Covers the international aspects of professional investing and finance. Emphasis is on Europe, the Far East, and Latin America.

Institutional Investor: The Premier of Professional Magazine Finance. Institutional Investor, Inc., Journals Group. • Monthly. $445.00 per year. Includes print and online editions. Edited for portfolio managers and other investment professionals. Special feature issues include "Country Credit Ratings," "Fixed Income Trading Ranking," "All-America Research Team," and "Global Banking Ranking.".

Insurance Finance and Investment. Institutional Investor, Inc., Journals Group. • Biweekly. $1,960.00 per year. Newsletter. Edited for insurance company investment managers.

Investment Advisor: The Advisor to Advisors. Wicks Business Information. • Monthly. $79.00 per year. Edited for professional investment advisors, financial planners, stock brokers, bankers, and others concerned with the management of assets.

Investment Dealers' Digest. Thomson Media. • Weekly. $750.00 per year. Covers financial news, trends, new products, people, private placements, new issues of securities, and other aspects of the investment business. Includes feature stories.

Investment Management Weekly. Thomson Media. • Weekly. $1,370.00 per year. Newsletter. Edited for money managers and other investment professionals. Covers personnel news, investment strategies, and industry trends.

Investment News: The Weekly Newspaper for Financial Advisers. Crain Communications, Inc. • Weekly. $29.00 per year. Edited for both personal and institutional investment advisers, planners, and managers.

Investor Relations Business. Thomson Media. • Semimonthly. $495.00 per year. Covers the issues affecting stockholder relations, corporate public relations, and institutional investor relations.

IOMA's Report on Defined Contribution Plan Investing. Institute of Management and Administration, Inc. • Semimonthly. $1,189.90 per year. Newsletter. Edited for 401(k) and other defined contribution retirement plan managers, sponsors, and service providers. Reports on such items as investment manager performance, guaranteed investment contract (GIC) yields, and asset allocation trends.

Journal of Alternative Investments. Institutional Investor, Inc., Journals Group. • Quarterly. $540.00 per year. Includes print and online editions. Covers such items as hedge funds, private equity financing, funds of funds, real estate investment trusts, natural resource investments, foreign exchange, and emerging markets.

Journal of Derivatives. Institutional Investor, Inc., Journals Group. • Quarterly. $365.00 per year. Includes print and online editions. Covers the structure and management of financial derivatives. Includes graphs, equations, and detailed analyses.

Journal of Fixed Income. Institutional Investor, Inc., Journals Group. • Quarterly. $360.00 per year. Includes print and online editions. Covers a wide

range of fixed-income investments for institutions, including bonds, interest-rate options, high-yield securities, and mortgages.

Journal of Investing. Institutional Investor, Inc., Journals Group. • Quarterly. $350.00 per year. Includes print and online editions. Edited for professional investors. Topics include equities, fixed-income securities, derivatives, asset allocation, and other institutional investment subjects.

Journal of Portfolio Management: The Journal for Investment Professionals. Institutional Investor, Inc., Journals Group. • Quarterly. $410.00 per year. Includes print and online editions. Edited for professional portfolio managers. Contains articles on investment practice, theory, and models.

Journal of Private Equity: Strategies and Techniques for Venture Investing. Institutional Investor, Inc., Journals Group. • Quarterly. $450.00 per year. Includes print and online editions. Includes venture capital case histories, financial applications, foreign opportunities, industry analysis, management methods, etc.

Journal of Risk Finance: The Convergence of Financial Products and Insurance. Institutional Investor, Inc., Journals Group. • Quarterly. $500.00 per year. Includes print and online editions. Covers the field of customized risk management, including securitization, insurance, hedging, derivatives, and credit arbitrage.

Journal of Structured and Project Finance. Institutional Investor, Inc., Journals Group. • Quarterly. $365.00 per year. Includes print and online editions. Covers the financing of large-scale construction projects, such as power plants and convention centers. Formerly *Journal of Project Finance.*

Journal of Wealth Management. Institutional Investor, Inc., Journals Group. • Quarterly. $410.00 per year. Includes print and online editions. Edited for managers of wealthy individuals' investment portfolios. Formerly *Journal of Private Portfolio Management.*

Latin Fund Management. Thomson Media. • Monthly. $495.00 per year. Newsletter (also available online at www.latinfund.net). Provides news and analysis of Latin American mutual funds, pension funds, and annuities.

Money Management Letter: Bi-Weekly Newsletter Covering the Pensions and Money Maagement Industry. Institutional Investor, Inc., Journals Group. • Biweekly. $2,440.00 per year. Newsletter. Includes print and online editions. Edited for pension fund investment managers.

Mortgage-Backed Securities Letter. Securities Data Publishing. • Description: Covers developments in the structured finance markets. Analyzes transactions and their collateral; follows litigation, refinancing opportunities, and market conditions.

MPT Review; Specializing in Modern Portfolio Theory. Navellier and Associates, Inc. • Monthly. $275.00 per year. Newsletter. Provides specific stock selection and model portfolio advice (conservative, moderately aggressive, and aggressive) based on quantitative analysis and modern portfolio theory.

Outstanding Investor Digest: Perspectives and Activities of the Nation's Most Successful Money Managers. Outstanding Investor Digest, Inc. • $395.00 for 10 issues. Newsletter. Each issue features interviews with leading money managers.

Private Equity Week. Thomson Financial. • Weekly. $1,495.00 per year. Provides detailed information on both prospective and completed private equity transactions. Includes news, data, commentary, trends, developments, and analysis.

Project Finance: The Magazine for Global Development. American Educational Systems. • 11 times a year. $740.00 per year. Includes print and online editions. Provides articles on the financing of the infrastructure (transportation, utilities, communications, the environment, etc). Coverage is international. Supplements available *World Export Credit Guide* and *Project Finance Book of Lists*. Formed by the merger of *Infrastructure Finance* and *Project and Trade Finance*.

Quantitative Finance. Available from American Institute of Physics. • Bimonthly. $340.00 per year. Print and online edition, $765.00 per year. Published in the UK by the Institute of Physics. A technical journal on the use of quantitative tools and applications in financial analysis and financial engineering. Covers such topics as portfolio theory, derivatives, asset allocation, return on assets, risk management, price volatility, financial econometrics, market anomalies, and trading systems.

Real Estate Finance and Investment. Institutional Investor, Inc., Journals Group. • Weekly. $2,275.00 per year. Includes print and online editions. Newsletter for professional investors in commercial real estate. Includes information on financing, restructuring, strategy, and regulation.

Traders Magazine. Thomson Media. • Monthly. $60.00 per year. Edited for institutional buy side and sell side equity traders. Covers industry news, market trends, regulatory developments, and personnel news. Serves as the official publication of the Security Traders Association.

U. S. Banker. Thomson Media. • Monthly. $65.00 per year. Edited for bank executives and managers. Covers a wide variety of banking and financial topics.

Zacks Analyst Watch. Zacks Investment Research. • Biweekly. $250.00 per year. Provides the results of research by stockbroker investment analysts on major U. S. corporations.

Zacks Earnings Forecaster. Zacks Investment Research. • Biweekly. $495.00 per year. (Also available monthly at $375.00 per year.) Provides estimates by stockbroker investment analysts of earnings per share of individual U. S. companies.

Zacks Profit Guide. Zacks Investment Research. • Quarterly. $375.00 per year. Provides analysis of total return and stock price performance of major U. S. companies.

RESEARCH CENTERS AND INSTITUTES

Bendheim Center for Finance. Princeton University, 26 Prospect Ave., Princeton, NJ 08540-5296. Phone: (609)258-0770 Fax: (609)258-0771 E-mail: yacine@princeton.edu • URL: http://www.princeton.edu/~bcf/ • Research areas include securities markets, portfolio analysis, credit markets, and corporate finance. Emphasis is on quantitative and mathematical perspectives.

Institute for Quantitative Research in Finance. Church Street Station, P.O. Box 6194, New York, NY 10249-6194. Phone: (212)744-6825 Fax: (212)517-2259 E-mail: daleberman@compuserve • Financial research areas include quantitative methods, securities analysis, and the financial structure of industries. Also known as the "Q Group.".

STATISTICS SOURCES

Financial Market Trends. Organization for Economic Cooperation and Development. • Quarterly. $80.00 per year. Provides analysis of developments and trends in international and national capital markets. Includes charts and graphs on interest rates, exchange rates, stock market indexes, bank stock indexes, trading volumes, and loans outstanding. Data from OECD countries includes international direct investment, bank profitability, institutional investment, and privatization.

Institutional Investors Statistical Yearbook. Organization for Economic Cooperation and Development. • Annual. $67.00. Provides data relat-

ing to institutional saving and investment in OECD countries. Includes investments by insurance companies, pension funds, and investment companies.

Life Insurance Fact Book. American Council of Life Insurers. • Biennial. $37.50 per year; with diskette, $55.00 per year.

The New Finance: The Case Against Efficient Markets. Prentice Hall PTR. • 1998. $36.00. Second edition.

Pension Investment Report. Employee Benefit Research Institute. • Irregualr. Membership.

TRADE/PROFESSIONAL ASSOCIATIONS

Association for Investment Management and Research. 560 Ray C. Hunt Dr., Charlottesville, VA 22903. Phone: 800-247-8132 or (434)951-5499 Fax: (434)951-5262 E-mail: info@aimr.org • URL: http://www.aimr.org • Members are practicing investment analysts.

Council of Institutional Investors. 1730 Rhode Island Ave., N. W., Suite 512, Washington, DC 20036. Phone: (202)822-0800 Fax: (202)822-0801 E-mail: info@cii.org • URL: http://www.cii.org • Members are nonprofit organization pension plans and other nonprofit institutional investors.

Investment Counsel Association of America. 1050 17th St., N.W., Suite 725, Washington, DC 20036-5503. Phone: (202)293-4222 Fax: (202)293-4223 E-mail: icaa@icaa.org • URL: http://www.icaa.org.

New York Society of Security Analysts. 1601 Broadway, 11th Floor, New York, NY 10019-7406. Phone: 800-248-0108 or (212)541-4530 Fax: (212)541-4677 E-mail: staff@nyssa.org • URL: http://www.nyssa.org • Members are portfolio managers, financial analysts, investment counselors, and other financial professionals.

INSTRUCTION OF EMPLOYEES

See: TRAINING OF EMPLOYEES

INSTRUCTION, PROGRAMMED

See: PROGRAMMED LEARNING

INSTRUMENTS, MUSICAL

See: MUSICAL INSTRUMENTS INDUSTRY

INSTRUMENTS, SCIENTIFIC

See: SCIENTIFIC APPARATUS AND INSTRUMENT INDUSTRIES

INSTRUMENTS, SURGICAL

See: SURGICAL INSTRUMENTS INDUSTRY

INSULATION

See also: BUILDING INDUSTRY

HANDBOOKS AND MANUALS

No-Regrets Remodeling: Creating a Comfortable, Healthy Home That Saves Energy. Home Energy. • 1997. $19.95. Edited by *Home Energy* magazine. Serves as a home remodeling guide to efficient heating, cooling, ventilation, water heating, insulation, lighting, and windows.

PERIODICALS AND NEWSLETTERS

Building Material Dealer. National Lumber and Building Material Dealers Association. • Monthly.

$48.00 per year. Includes special feature issues on hand and power tools, lumber, roofing, kitchens, flooring, windows and doors, and insulation. Formerly *Builder Material Retailer*.

Journal of Thermal Enevelope and Building Science. Sage Publications, Inc. • Quarterly. Institutions, $765.00 per year; includes print and online editions. Formerly *Journal of Thermal Insulation and Building Envelopes*.

RSI (Roofing, Siding, Insulation). Advanstar Communications. • Monthly. $44.00 per year.

TRADE/PROFESSIONAL ASSOCIATIONS

Insulation Contractors Association of America. 1321 Duke St., Suite 303, Alexandria, VA 22314. Phone: (703)739-0356 Fax: (703)739-0412 E-mail: icca@insulate.org • URL: http://www.insulate.org.

National Fenestration Rating Council. 6305 Ivy Ln., Ste. 140, Greenbelt, MD 20770. Phone: (301)589-1776 Fax: (301)589-3884 E-mail: info@nfrc.org • URL: http://www.nfrc.org • Individuals, organizations, and corporations interested in production, regulation, promotion, and development of technology related to fenestration products. Develops national voluntary energy performance rating system for fenestration products; coordinates certification and labeling activities to ensure uniform rating application. Promotes consumer awareness of fenestration ratings in an effort to encourage informed purchase of windows, doors, and skylights. Conducts efficiency testing. Maintains speakers' bureau; conducts educational and research programs.

National Insulation Association. 99 Canal Center Plz., Ste. 222, Alexandria, VA 22314. Phone: (703)683-6422 Fax: (703)549-4838 E-mail: mjones@insulation.org • URL: http://www.insulation.org • Insulation contractors, distributors, and manufacturers.

North American Insulation Manufacturers Association. 44 Canal Center Plz., Ste. 310, Alexandria, VA 22314. Phone: (703)684-0084 Fax: (703)684-0427 E-mail: insulation@naima.org • URL: http://www.naima.org • Manufacturers of fiberglass, rock wool, and slag wool insulation products. Promotes energy efficiency and environmental preservation through the use of fiberglass, rock wool, and slag wool insulation products. Encourages safe production and use of insulation materials.

INSURANCE

See also: ACCIDENT INSURANCE; AUTOMOBILE INSURANCE; BUSINESS INTERRUPTION INSURANCE; CASUALTY INSURANCE; CREDIT INSURANCE; DISABILITY INSURANCE; FIRE INSURANCE; HEALTH INSURANCE; LIFE INSURANCE; LONG-TERM CARE INSURANCE; MARINE INSURANCE; PROPERTY AND LIABILITY INSURANCE; RISK MANAGEMENT; UNEMPLOYMENT INSURANCE

GENERAL WORKS

How to Avoid Financial Tangles. American Institute for Economic Research. • 2001. $8.00. Provides basic information and advice on such topics as property ownership, taxes, wills, trusts, insurance, record retention, and professional assistance. (Economic Education Bulletin.).

Smarter Insurance Solutions. Janet Bamford. Bloomberg. • 1996. $19.95. Provides practical advice to consumers, with separate chapters on the following kinds of insurance: automobile, homeowners, health, disability, and life. (Bloomberg Personal Bookshelf Series).

ABSTRACTS AND INDEXES

Business Periodicals Index. H. W. Wilson Co. • 11 times a year. Quarterly and annual cumulations. Price varies.

Insurance Periodicals Index. Specials Libraries Association, Insurance and Employees Benefits Div. NILS Publishing Co. • Annual. $250.00. Compiled by the Insurance and Employee Benefits Div., Special Libraries Association. A yearly index of over 15,000 articles from about 35 insurance periodicals. Arrangement is by subject, with an index to authors.

Social Sciences Citation Index. Thomson/ISI. • Three·times a year. $6,900 per year. Annual cumulation. Includes *Source Index, Citation Index, Permuterm Subject Index,* and *Corporate Index.*

Social Sciences Index. H. W. Wilson Co. • Quarterly, with annual cumulation. Price varies. Indexes more than 400 periodicals covering economics, environmental policy, government, insurance, labor, health care policy, plannning, public administration, public welfare, urban studies, women's issues, criminology, and related topics.

ALMANACS AND YEARBOOKS

Insurance Almanac: Who, What, When and Where in Insurance. Underwriter Printing and Publishing Co. • Annual. $175.00. Lists insurance agencies and brokerage firms; U.S. and Canadian insurance companies, adjusters, appraisers, auditors, investigators, insurance officials and insurance organizations.

BIBLIOGRAPHIES

Insurance and Employee Benefits Literature. Special Libraries Association, Insurance and Employee Benefits Div. • Bimonthly. $15.00 per year. Lists a wide variety of literature in all branches of the insurance industry. Includes annotations.

CD-ROM DATABASES

Assecuranz Compass CD-ROM. Available from Kompass USA, Inc. • Annual. CD-ROM provides detailed financial and other information on more than 21,000 insurance companies in 209 countries worldwide. Includes listings of 47,000 insurance company executives.

OECD Statistical Compendium. Organization for Economic Cooperation and Development. • Semiannual. $1,905.00 per year for 1 to 10 users. CD-ROM contains more than 730,000 monthly, quarterly, and annual time series for OECD countries, 1960 to date. Includes fully searchable data on agriculture, food, economic indicators, national accounts, employment, energy, finance, industry, technology, and foreign trade. Results can be displayed in various forms.

Social Sciences Citation Index. ISI. • Monthly. Price on request. Provides CD-ROM indexing of articles appearing in 1700 leading social science journals worldwide, with additional selections from more than 5700 other journals. Time span is 1992 to date. Coverage includes economics, business, finance, management, communications, demographics, library and information science, political science, sociology, and many other subjects.

Social Sciences Citation Index: Compact Disc Edition with Abstracts. Institute for Scientific Information. • Monthly. Provides CD-ROM indexing and abstracting of "significant articles" from 1,700 social science journals worldwide, with additional selections from 3,200 other journals, 1986 to date. Includes economics, business, finance, management, communications, demographics, information and library science, political science, sociology, and many other subjects.

U. S. Insurance: Life, Accident, and Health. Sheshunoff Information Services, Inc. • Monthly. Price on application. CD-ROM provides detailed, current information on the financial characteristics of more than 2,300 life, accident, and health insurance companies.

U. S. Insurance: Property and Casualty. Sheshunoff Information Services, Inc. • Monthly. Price on application. CD-ROM provides detailed, current financial information on more than 3,200 property

and casualty insurance companies.

WILSONDISC: Wilson Business Abstracts. H. W. Wilson Co. • Monthly. Includes unlimited online access to *Wilson Business Abstracts* through WILSONLINE. Provides CD-ROM "cover-to-cover" abstracting and indexing of over ·600 prominent business periodicals. Indexing is from 1982, abstracting from 1990. (*Business Periodicals Index* without abstracts is available on CD-ROM at $1,495 per year.).

WILSONDISC: Wilson Social Sciences Abstracts. H. W. Wilson Co. • Monthly. Includes unlimited online access to *Social Sciences Index* through WILSONLINE. Provides CD-ROM indexing from 1983 and abstracting from .1994 of more than 500 periodicals covering economics, area studies, community health, public administration, public welfare, urban studies, and many other topics related to the social sciences.

DIRECTORIES

America's Corporate Finance Directory. LexisNexis Group. • Covers: Financial personnel and outside financial services relationships of 5,000 leading United States corporations and their wholly-owned United States subsidiaries. Entries include: Company name, address, phone, fax, telex, e-mail addresses, stock exchange information, earnings, total assets, size of pension/profit-sharing fund portfolio, number of employees, description of business, wholly-owned U.S. Subsidiaries of parent company; name and title of key executives; outside suppliers of financial services.

Best's Directory of Recommended Insurance Attorneys and Adjusters. A.M. Best Co. • Annual. $1,175.00. More than 5,000 American, Canadian, and foreign insurance defense law firms; lists 1,200 national and international insurance adjusting firms. Formerly *Best's Recommended Insurance Adjusters.*

Financial Yellow Book: Who's Who at the Leading U. S. Financial Institutions. Leadership Directories, Inc. • Semiannual. $265.00, Gives the names and titles of over 28,000 key executives in financial institutions. Includes the areas of banking, investment, money management, and insurance. Five indexes are provided: institution, executive name, geographic by state, financial service segment, and parent company.

Hine's Directory of Insurance Adjusters, Investigators, and Appraisers. Hine's, Inc. • Annual. $20.00. Lists selected independent insurance adjusters in the United States and Canada.

Insurance Marketplace: The Agents and Brokers Guide to Non-Standard and Special ty Lines, Aviation, Marine and International Insurance. The Rough Notes Co., Inc. • Annual. Included in subscription to *Rough Notes Magazine*; others, $15.95. Lists specialty, excess, and surplus insurance lines.

Internet Tools of the Profession: A Guide for Information Professionals. Hope N. Tillman, editor. Special Libraries Association. • 1997. $49.00. Second edition. Consists of 14 sections by various authors or compilers. After two introductory articles on searching the Internet, there are 12 annotated lists of useful Web sites, covering the SLA, business and finance, chemistry, education, food and agriculture, information technology, insurance and employee benefits, law, library management, metals and materials, pharmaceuticals, and telecommunications. An index is provided.

Major Financial Institutions of Europe. Available from Gale Cengage Learning. • Annual. $510.00. Contains profiles of over 2,000 financial institutions in Europe such as banks, investment companies, and insurance companies. Formerly *Major Financial Institutions of Continental Europe.*

Major Financial Institutions of the World 2001.

Available from Gale Cengage Learning. • 2003. $880.00. Sixth edition. Two volumes. Published by Graham & Whiteside. Contains detailed information on more than 7,500 important financial institutions in various countries. Includes banks, investment companies, and insurance companies.

S & P's Insurance Book. Standard & Poor's Ratings Group, Insurance Rating Services. • Quarterly. Price on application. Contains detailed financial analyses and ratings of various kinds of insurance companies.

S & P's Insurance Digest: Life Insurance Edition. Standard & Poor's Ratings Group, Insurance Rating Services. • Quarterly. Contains concise financial analyses and ratings of life insurance companies.

The Top 5,000 European Companies 2002. Available from Gale Cengage Learning. • 2002. $645.00. Third edition. Published by Graham & Whiteside. In addition to about 5,000 manufacturing and service companies, includes the 500 largest banks in Europe and the 100 largest insurance companies.

The Top 5,000 Global Companies 2002. Available from Gale Cengage Learning. • 2002. $730.00. Third edition. Published by Graham & Whiteside. Includes about 5,000 manufacturing and service companies worldwide, plus the world's 500 largest banks and 100 largest insurance companies.

Who Writes What in Life and Health Insurance. The National Underwriter Co. • Annual. $9.95.

ENCYCLOPEDIAS AND DICTIONARIES

Dictionary of Insurance Terms. Harvey W. Rubin. Barron's Educational Series, Inc. • 2000. $14.95. Fourth edition. Defines terms in a wide variety of insurance fields. (Business Dictionaries Series).

Glossary of Insurance Policy Terms. Organization for Economic Cooperation and Development. • 1999. $30.00. "The selected topics range from insurance policy regulation/supervision to general trade issues and include technical terms related to issues such as claims, premiums, and provisions." Edited for government, academic, business, and insurance organizations.

Insurance Words and Their Meanings: A Glossary of Insurance Terms. The Rough Notes Co., Inc. • 2001. 17th edition. Price on application.

Rupp's Insurance and Risk Management Glossary. Richard V. Rupp. NILS Publishing Co. • 2001. $35.00. Second edition. Provides definitions of 6,400 insurance words and phrases. Includes a guide to acronyms and abbreviations.

FINANCIAL RATIOS

Almanac of Business and Industrial Financial Ratios. Leo Troy. Aspen Publishers, Inc. • 2003. $125.95. Includes CD-Rom. Contains financial ratios derived from federal tax returns. Ratios for each of about 200 industries are arranged according to company asset size. (Almanac of Business and Industrial Financial Ratios Series).

HANDBOOKS AND MANUALS

Barron's Finance & Investment Handbook. John Downes and Jordan Goodman. Barron's Educational Series, Inc. • 1998. $35.00. Fifth edition. Mainly concerned with personal finance, including advice on stocks, bonds, mutual funds, annuities, life insurance, real estate, futures, and collectibles. Includes a glossary of financial and investment terms.

The Complete Book of Insurance: Protecting Your Life, Health Property, and Income. Ben G. Baldwin. McGraw-Hill. • 1991. $24.95. Provides basic information and advice on various kinds of insurance: life, health, property (fire), disability, long-term care, automobile, liability, and annuities.

Dun & Bradstreet/Gale Group Industry Handbooks. Gale Cengage Learning. • 2000. $650.00. Five volumes. $130.00 per volume. Each volume covers two or more major industries: 1. *Entertainment and Hospitality*; 2. *Construction and Agriculture*; 3.

Chemicals and Pharmaceuticals; 4. *Computers & Software and Broadcasting & Telecommunications*; 5. *Insurance and Health & Medical Services*. The following are included for each industry: overview, statistics, financial ratios, rankings, merger information, company directory, directory of associations, and consultants directory. (Dun and Bradstreet/Gale Industry Reference Handbook Series).

Insuring Your Business: What You Need to Know to Get the Best Insurance Coverage for Your Business. Sean Mooney. Insurance Information Institute. • 1992. $22.50.

INTERNET DATABASES

Business 2.0 Web Guide to the Best Business Links. Business 2.0 Media Inc. Phone: (415)293-4800 E-mail: support@business2.com • URL: http://www.business2.com/webguide • Web site presents an extensive, searchable directory of links to "the best, most informative, and authoritative web pages." Twenty main categories cover business, finance, career, company information, people, and technology topics, with thousands of subtopics, all linking to Web sites recommended by experienced business researchers. Fees: Free.

InsWeb. InsWeb Corp. Phone: (916)853-3300 E-mail: info@insweb.com • URL: http://www.insweb.com • Web site offers a wide variety of advice and information on automobile, life, health, and "other" insurance. Includes glossaries of insurance terms, Standard & Poor's ratings of individual insurance companies, and "Financial Needs Estimators." Searching is available. Fees: Free.

ONLINE DATABASES

Banking Information Source. PROQUEST. • Provides indexing and abstracting of periodical and other literature from 1982 to date, with weekly updates. Covers the financial services industry: banks, savings institutions, investment houses, credit unions, insurance companies, and real estate organizations. Emphasis is on marketing and management. Inquire as to online cost and availability. (Formerly *FINIS: Financial Industry Information Service*.).

Fitch Ratings Delivery Service. Fitch Inc. • Provides online delivery of Fitch financial ratings in three sectors: "Corporate Finance" (corporate bonds, insurance companies), "Structured Finance" (asset-backed securities), and "U.S. Public Finance" (municipal bonds). Daily updates. Inquire as to online cost and availability.

I.I.I. Data Base Search. Insurance Information Institute. • Provides online citations and abstracts of insurance-related literature in magazines, newspapers, trade journals, and books. Emphasis is on property and casualty insurance issues, including highway safety, product safety, and environmental liability. Inquire as to online cost and availability.

Social Scisearch. Institute for Scientific Information. • Broad, multidisciplinary index to the literature of the social sciences, 1972 to present. Weekly updates. Worldwide coverage. Inquire as to online cost and availability.

Wilson Business Abstracts Online. H. W. Wilson Co. • Indexes and abstracts 600 major business periodicals, plus the *Wall Street Journal* and the business section of the *New York Times.* Indexing is from 1982, abstracting from 1990, with the two newspapers included from 1993. Updated weekly. Inquire as to online cost and availability. (*Business Periodicals Index* without abstracts is also available online.).

Wilson Social Sciences Abstracts Online. H. W. Wilson Co. • Provides online abstracting and indexing of more than 500 periodicals covering area studies, community health, public administration, public welfare, urban studies, and many other social science topics. Time period is 1994 to date for abstracts and 1983 to date for indexing, with updates weekly.

Inquire as to online cost and availability.

PERIODICALS AND NEWSLETTERS

American Banker: The Financial Services Daily. Thomson Media. • Daily. $895.00 per year. Provides news of banking, investment products, mortgages, credit unions, finance, bank technology, and legal developments.

Bank Investment Product News. Institutional Investor, Inc., Journals Group. • Weekly. $1,195.00 per year. Newsletter. Edited for bank executives. Covers the marketing and regulation of financial products sold through banks, such as mutual funds, stock brokerage services, and insurance.

Chartered Property and Casualty Underwriters Society Journal. Chartered Property and Casualty Underwriters Society. • Quarterly. $30.00 per year. Published by the Chartered Property and Casualty Underwriters Society (CPCU). Edited for professional insurance underwriters and agents.

Claims. National Underwriter Co. • Monthly. $46.00 per year. Edited for insurance adjusters, risk managers, and claims professionals. Covers investigation, fraud, insurance law, and other claims-related topics.

Contingencies: The Magazine of the Actuarial Profession. American Academy of Actuaries. • Bimonthly. $30.00 per year. Provides non-technical articles on the actuarial aspects of insurance, employee benefits, and pensions.

Guide to Life, Health, and Annuity Insurers: A Quarterly Compilation of Insurance Company Ratings and Analysis. Weiss Ratings, Inc. • Quarterly. $438.00 per year. Emphasis is on rating of financial safety and relative risk. Includes annual summary.

Guide to Property and Casualty Insurers: A Quarterly Compilation of Insurance Company Ratings and Analysis. Weiss Ratings, Inc. • Quarterly. $438.00 per year. Emphasis is on rating of financial safety and relative risk. Includes annual summary.

Guide to Property and Casualty Insurers: A Quarterly Compilation of Insurance Company Ratings and Analysis. Weiss Ratings, Inc. • Quarterly. $438.00 per year. Emphasis is on rating of financial safety and relative risk. Includes annual summary.

Insurance Advocate. Emanuel Levy, editor. Shea-Haarmann Cos. • Weekly. $59.00 per year. News and features on all aspects of insurance business for industry professionals.

Insurance and Technology. CMP Media LLC. • Monthly. $65.00 per year. Covers information technology and systems management as applied to the operation of life, health, casualty, and property insurance companies.

Insurance Day. Available from Informa Publishing Group Ltd. • Three times a week. $440.00 per year. Published in the UK by Lloyd's List (http://www.lloydslist.com). A newspaper providing international coverage of property/casualty/liability insurance, reinsurance, and risk, with an emphasis on marine insurance.

Insurance Finance and Investment. Institutional Investor, Inc., Journals Group. • Biweekly. $1,960.00 per year. Newsletter. Edited for insurance company investment managers.

Insurance Forum: For the Unfettered Exchange of Ideas About Insurance. Joseph M. Belth, editor. Insurance Forum, Inc. • Monthly. $90.00 per year. Newsletter. Provides analysis of the insurance business, including occasional special issues showing the ratings of about 1,600 life-health insurance companies, as determined by four major rating services: Duff & Phelps Credit Rating Co., Moody's Investors Service, Standard & Poor's Corp., and Weiss Research, Inc.

Insurance Networking: Strategies and Solutions for Electronic Commerce. Thomson Media. • 10 times a year. Price on application. Covers information

technology for the insurance industry, with emphasis on computer communications and the Internet.

InsuranceWeek. I.W. Publications, Inc. • Weekly. $30.00 per year.

Journal of Risk Finance: The Convergence of Financial Products and Insurance. Institutional Investor, Inc., Journals Group. • Quarterly. $500.00 per year. Includes print and online editions. Covers the field of customized risk management, including securitization, insurance, hedging, derivatives, and credit arbitrage.

Martin Weiss' Safe Money Report. Weiss Ratings, Inc. • Monthly. $189.00 per year. Newsletter. Provides financial advice and current safety ratings of various banks, savings and loan companies, insurance companies, and securities dealers. Formerly (The Safe Money Report).

Risk and Insurance. LRP Publications. • 15 times a year. Price on application. Topics include risk management, workers' compensation, reinsurance, employee benefits, and managed care.

Risk Management. Risk and Insurance Management Society. Risk Management Society Publishing, Inc. • Monthly. $59.00 per year.

U. S. Banker. Thomson Media. • Monthly. $65.00 per year. Edited for bank executives and managers. Covers a wide variety of banking and financial topics.

RESEARCH CENTERS AND INSTITUTES

Center for Risk Management and Insurance Research. Georgia State University, P.O. Box 4036, Atlanta, GA 30302-4036. Phone: (404)651-4250 Fax: (404)651-4219 E-mail: rwklein@gsu.edu • URL: http://www.rmi.gsu.edu.

S. S. Huebner Foundation. University of Pennsylvania, 3733 Spruce St., Vance Hall, Suite 430, Philadelphia, PA 19104-6301. Phone: (215)898-9631 Fax: (215)573-2218 E-mail: cummins@wharton.upenn.edu • URL: http://www.rider.wharton.upenn.edu/ • Awards grants for research in various areas of insurance.

STATISTICS SOURCES

Information, Finance, and Services USA. Gale Cengage Learning. • 2001. $240.00. Replaces *Service Industries USA* and *Finance, Insurance, and Real Estate USA.* Presents statistics and projections relating to economic activity in a wide variety of non-manufacturing areas.

Insurance Statistics Yearbook, 1991-1998. OECD Publications and Information Center. • 2000. $75.00. Presents detailed statistics on insurance premiums collected in OECD countries, by type of insurance.

Property-Casualty Insurance Facts. Insurance Information Institute. • Annual. $22.50. Formerly *Insurance Facts.*

Standard & Poor's Industry Surveys. Standard & Poor's. • Semiannual. $1,800.00. Two looseleaf volumes. Includes monthly *Supplements.* Provides detailed, individual surveys of 52 major industry groups. Each survey is revised on a semiannual basis. Also includes "Monthly Investment Review" (industry group investment analysis) and monthly "Trends & Projections" (economic analysis).

U. S. Industry and Trade Outlook. Available from National Technical Information Service. • Annual. $69.95. Produced by the International Trade Administration, U. S. Department of Commerce, in a "public-private" partnership with DRI/McGraw-Hill and Standard & Poor's. Provides basic data, outlook for the current year, and "Long-Term Prospects" (five-year projections) for a wide variety of products and services. Includes high technology industries. Formerly *U. S. Industrial Outlook.*

TRADE/PROFESSIONAL ASSOCIATIONS

American Risk and Insurance Association. 716 Providence Rd., Malvern, PA 19355-0728. Phone:

(610)640-1997 or (610)644-2100 Fax: (610)725-1007 E-mail: aria@cpcuiia.org • URL: http://www.aria.org • Promotes education and research in the science of risk and insurance.

Insurance Services Office (ISO). 545 Washington Blvd., Jersey City, NJ 07310-1686. Phone: 800-888-4476 or (201)469-2000 Fax: (201)748-1472 E-mail: info@iso.com • URL: http://www.iso.com • Provides statistical, actuarial, underwriting, and claims information to property and casualty insurance companies.

National Association of Independent Insurers. 2600 River Rd., Des Plaines, IL 60018. Phone: (847)297-7800 Fax: (847)297-5064 E-mail: naiinet@naii.org • URL: http://www.naii.org.

National Association of Insurance Women International. 1847 E 15th St., Tulsa, OK 74104. Phone: 800-766-6249 Fax: (918)743-1968 E-mail: joinnaiw@naiw.org • URL: http://www.naiw.org • Formerly Nationl Assoiciation of Insurance Women.

National Association of Mutual Insurance Companies. 3601 Vincennes Rd., Indianapolis, IN 46268. Phone: 800-336-2642 or (317)875-5250 Fax: (317)879-8408 E-mail: services@naminc.org • URL: http://www.namic.org • Affiliated with Crop Insurance Research Bureau and the Insurance Loss Control Association.

National Insurance Association. 411 Chapel Hill St., Durham, NC 27701. E-mail: nia1921@aol.com • Conducts annual Institute in +Agency +Management and Institute in +Home Office Operations. Sponsors National Insurance Week.

Risk and Insurance Management Society. 655 Third Ave., 2nd Fl., New York, NY 10017. Phone: (212)286-9292 Fax: (212)986-9716 E-mail: jwaldman@rims.org • URL: http://www.rims.org • Formerly American Society of Insurance Management.

OTHER SOURCES

Best's Insurance Reports. A.M. Best Co. • Annual. $1495.00. Life-health insurance covering about 1,750 companies, and property-casualty insurance covering over 3,200 companies. Includes one year subscription to both *Best's Review* and *Best's Insurance Management Reports.*

Best's Insurance Reports: Property-Casualty. A.M. Best Co. • Annual. $750.00. Guide to over 3,200 major property/casualty companies.

Federal Taxation of Insurance Companies. Dennis P. Van Mieghem and others. Prentice Hall PTR. • $447.00 per year. Looseleaf service. Biweekly updates.

Fire and Casualty Insurance Law Reports. CCH, Inc. • $870.00 per year. Looseleaf service. Semimonthly updates.

Life, Health, and Accident Insurance Law Reports. CCH, Inc. • $835.00 per year. Looseleaf service. Monthly updates.

INSURANCE, ACCIDENT

See: ACCIDENT INSURANCE

INSURANCE ACTUARIES

See: ACTUARIAL SCIENCE

INSURANCE AGENTS

GENERAL WORKS

Smart Questions to Ask Your Financial Advisers. Lynn Brenner. Bloomberg. • 1997. $19.95. Provides practical advice on how to deal with financial planners, stockbrokers, insurance agents, and lawyers. Some of the areas covered are investments, estate planning, tax planning, house buying, prenuptial agreements, divorce arrangements, loss of a job, and retirement. (Bloomberg Personal Bookshelf Series).

BIOGRAPHICAL SOURCES

Who's Who in Insurance. Underwriter Printing and Publishing Co. • Annual. $150.00. Contains over 5,000 biographies of insurance officials, leading agents and brokers, and high-ranking company officials.

FINANCIAL RATIOS

Almanac of Business and Industrial Financial Ratios. Leo Troy. Aspen Publishers, Inc. • 2003. $125.95. Includes CD-Rom. Contains financial ratios derived from federal tax returns. Ratios for each of about 200 industries are arranged according to company asset size. (Almanac of Business and Industrial Financial Ratios Series).

Annual Statement Studies. The Risk Management Association. • Annual. Median and quartile financial ratios are given for over 400 kinds of manufacturing, wholesale, retail, construction, and consumer finance establishments. Data is sorted by both asset size and sales volume. Includes a clearly written "Definition of Ratios" and an alphabetical industry index.

Annual Statement Studies: Industry Default Probabilities and Cash Flow Measures. The Risk Management Association. • Annual. $145.00. Serves as a companion volume to the original *Annual Statement Studies.* Gives probability of default estimates on a percentage scale for more than 450 industries. Includes changes in position year-by-year for eight financial statement line items and provides percentage measures of cash flow.

HANDBOOKS AND MANUALS

Responsibilities of Insurance Agents and Brokers. LexisNexis Matthew Bender. • Semiannual. $886.00. Four looseleaf volumes. Covers legal responsibilities of agents and federal tax consequences of insurance arrangements.

PERIODICALS AND NEWSLETTERS

Broker World. Insurance Publications, Inc. • Bimonthly. $6.00 per year. Edited for independent insurance agents and brokers. Special feature issue topics include annuities, disability insurance, estate planning, and life insurance.

Financial Planning: The Magazine for Financial Service Professionals. Thomson Media. • Monthly. $79.00 per year. Edited for independent financial planners and insurance agents. Covers retirement planning, estate planning, tax planning, and insurance, including long-term healthcare considerations. Special features include a Retirement Planning Issue, Mutual Fund Performance Survey, and Variable Life and Annuity Survey.

GAMA International Journal. GAMA International. • Bimonthly. Members, $4.00 per year; non-members, $20.00 per year. Contains practical articles on the management of life insurance agencies.

Health Insurance Underwriter. National Association of Health Underwriters. • Monthly. $25.00 per year. Includes special feature issues on long-term care insurance, disability insurance, managed health care, and insurance office management.

Independent Agent. Independent Insurance Agents of North America. • Monthly. $24.00 per year.

Insurance Marketing: The Ins and Outs of Recruiting and Retaining More Agents. Agent Media Corp. • Bimonthly. Controlled circulation. Provides practical advice for insurance companies on how to hire and keep sales personnel.

Resource: LOMA's Magazine for Insurance and Financial Services Management. LOMA. • Monthly. Free to qualified personnel. Covers management topics for life insurance home and field office personnel.

Today's Insurance Professionals. National Association of Insurance Women. • Quarterly. Free to members; non-members, $15.00 per year. Provides advice on professional and personal development in the insurance business. Formerly *Today's Insurance Woman.*

TRADE/PROFESSIONAL ASSOCIATIONS

American Association of Managing General Agents. 150 S. Warner Rd., Suite 156, King of Prussia, PA 19406. Phone: (610)225-1999 Fax: (610)225-1996 E-mail: bernie.heinze@aamga.org • URL: http://www.aamga.org.

GAMA International. 2901 Telestar Ct., Ste. 140, Falls Church, VA 22042-1205. Phone: 800-345-2687 or (703)770-8184 Fax: (703)770-8182 E-mail: gamamail@gamaweb.com • URL: http://www.gamaweb.com • Provides world-class education and training resources for individuals, companies and organizations involved with the recruitment and development of field managers, representatives and staff in the life insurance and financial services industry; advocates of the value-added role of field management and representatives in the ethical distribution of life insurance and financial products and services industry.

Independent Insurance Agents and Brokers of America. 127 S. Peyton, Alexandria, VA 22314. Phone: 800-221-7917 or (703)683-4422 Fax: (703)683-7556 E-mail: info@iiaba.org • URL: http://www.independentagent.com • Formerly Independent Insurance Agents and Brokers of America.

National Association of Professional Insurance Agents. 400 N. Washington St., Alexandria, VA 22314. Phone: (703)836-9340 Fax: (703)836-1279 E-mail: piaweb@pianet.org • URL: http://www.pianet.com • Members are independent agents in various fields of insurance. Formerly National Association of Mutual Insurance Agents.

INSURANCE, AUTOMOBILE

See: AUTOMOBILE INSURANCE

INSURANCE, BUSINESS INTERRUPTION

See: BUSINESS INTERRUPTION INSURANCE

INSURANCE, CASUALTY

See: CASUALTY INSURANCE

INSURANCE, DISABILITY

See: DISABILITY INSURANCE

INSURANCE, FIRE

See: FIRE INSURANCE

INSURANCE, HEALTH

See: HEALTH INSURANCE

INSURANCE LAW AND REGULATION

ABSTRACTS AND INDEXES

Current Law Index: Multiple Access to Legal Periodicals. Gale Cengage Learning. • Monthly.

$725.00 per year. Produced in cooperation with the American Association of Law Libraries. Indexes more than 900 law journals, legal newspapers, and specialty publications from the U.S., Canada, U.K., Ireland, Australia, and New Zealand.

Index to Legal Periodicals and Books. H. W. Wilson Co. • Monthly. $490.00 per year. Quarterly and annual cumulations.

ALMANACS AND YEARBOOKS

American Law Yearbook. Gale Cengage Learning. • Annual. $165.00. Serves as a yearly supplement to *West's Encyclopedia of American Law.* Describes new legal developments in many subject areas.

CD-ROM DATABASES

WILSONDISC: Index to Legal Periodicals and Books. H. W. Wilson Co. • Monthly. Includes unlimited online access to *Index to Legal Periodicals* through WILSONLINE. Contains CD-ROM indexing of more than 1,400 English language legal periodicals from 1981 to date and 2,500 books.

DIRECTORIES

Best's Directory of Recommended Insurance Attorneys and Adjusters. A.M. Best Co. • Annual. $1,175.00. More than 5,000 American, Canadian, and foreign insurance defense law firms; lists 1,200 national and international insurance adjusting firms. Formerly *Best's Recommended Insurance Adjusters.*

Hine's Insurance Counsel. Hine's Inc. • Covers: 2,500 law firms in the United States and Canada that handle defense in litigation involving insurance and transportation companies. Entries include: Firm name, address, phone, type of practice, names of partners and associates, clients, memberships in trial organizations. An insurance law list. See separate listing, "Law Lists. ".

Insurance Bar Directory. Bar Listing Publishing Co. • Covers: law firms that handle defense insurance litigation, and general insurance practice matters. Entries include: Firm name, address, phone, names and titles of key personnel, specialty, list of clients.

ENCYCLOPEDIAS AND DICTIONARIES

West's Encyclopedia of American Law. Available from Gale Cengage Learning. • 2003. $1,195.00. Second edition. 12 volumes. Published by West Group. Covers a wide variety of legal topics for the general reader.

INTERNET DATABASES

Lexis.com Research System. Lexis-Nexis Group. Phone: 800-227-4908 or (937)865-6800 Fax: (937)865-6909 E-mail: webmaster@prod.lexisnexis.com • URL: http://www.lexis.com • Fee-based Web site offers extensive searching of a wide variety of legal sources. Additional features include Daily Opinion Service, lexis.com Bookstore, Career Center, CLE Center, Law Schools, and Practice Pages ("Pages specific to areas of specialty").

ONLINE DATABASES

Index to Legal Periodicals and Books (Online). H. W. Wilson Co. • Broad coverage of law journals and books 1981 to date. Monthly updates. Inquire as to online cost and availability.

PERIODICALS AND NEWSLETTERS

Defense Counsel Journal. International Association of Defense Counsel. • Quarterly. $65.00 per year. Scholarly and practical articles dealing with defense of civil cases, particularly those involving insurance.

Federation of Insurance and Corporate Counsel Quarterly. • Quarterly. Individuals, $40.00 per year; libraries, $34.00 per year. A journal dealing with the legal aspects of insurance.

Insurance Coverage Law Bulletin. American Lawyer Media, Inc. • Monthly. $199.00 per year. Newsletter. Provides news of property insurance claims management and coverage disputes. Edited

for both legal and non-legal insurance professionals. (A Law Journal Newsletter, formerly published by Leader Publications).

Insurance Regulation: State Capitals. Wakeman-Walworth, Inc. • 50 times a year. $245.00 per year; print and online editions, $350.00 per year. Formerly *From the State Capitals: Insurance Regulation.*

Journal of Insurance Regulation. National Association of Insurance Commissioners. • Quarterly. $65.00 per year.

NAIC News. National Association of Insurance Commissioners. • Monthly. $200.00 per year. Newsletter covering insurance legislation and regulation.

National Insurance Law Review. NILS Publishing Co. • Quarterly. $95.00 per year. Contains insurance-related articles from major law reviews.

STATISTICS SOURCES

Property-Casualty Insurance Facts. Insurance Information Institute. • Annual. $22.50. Formerly *Insurance Facts.*

TRADE/PROFESSIONAL ASSOCIATIONS

Association of Defense Trial Attorneys. 1300 Liberty Bldg., Buffalo, NY 14202-3614. Phone: (304)340-1000 E-mail: scrislip@jacksonkelly.com • URL: http://www.adtalaw.com.

Association of Life Insurance Counsel. 1300 Clinton St., Fort Wayne, IN 46801. Phone: 800-659-5589 or (219)455-2000 Fax: (219)455-4503 E-mail: membersupport@legalstaff.com • URL: http://www.legalstaff.com • Members are attorneys for life insurance companies.

Federation of Defense and Corporate Counsel, Inc. c/o Martha J. Streeper, 11812-A N 56th St., Tampa, MA 33617. Phone: (813)983-0022 Fax: (813)988-5837 E-mail: mmg@gte.net • URL: http://www.thefederation.org • Members are insurance lawyers and insurance company executives. Formerly Federation of Insurance and Corporate Counsel.

International Association for Insurance Law in the United States. PO Box 9001, Mount Vernon, NY 10552. Phone: (914)699-2020 Fax: (914)699-2025 • URL: http://www.aida.org • Members are attorneys and others concerned with the international aspects of insurance law. Affiliated with International Association for Insurance Law-United Kingdom.

International Association of Defense Counsel. 1 N Franklin St., Ste. 1205, Chicago, IL 60606. Phone: (312)368-1494 Fax: (312)368-1854 E-mail: office@iadclaw.org • URL: http://www.iadclaw.org • Affiliated with Defense Research Institute. Formerly International Association of Insurance Counsel.

National Association of Insurance Commissioners. 2301 McGee St., Ste. 800, Kansas City, MO 64108-2604. Phone: (816)842-3600 Fax: (816)783-8175 E-mail: pubdjst@naic.org • URL: http://www.naic.org • Members are state officials involved in the regulation of insurance companies. Formerly National Convention of Insurance Commissioners.

INSURANCE, LIABILITY

See: PROPERTY AND LIABILITY INSURANCE

INSURANCE, LIFE

See: LIFE INSURANCE

INSURANCE, LONG-TERM CARE

See: LONG-TERM CARE INSURANCE

INSURANCE, MARINE

See: MARINE INSURANCE

INSURANCE, PROPERTY

See: PROPERTY AND LIABILITY INSURANCE

INSURANCE, SOCIAL

See: SOCIAL SECURITY

INSURANCE, TITLE

See: TITLE INSURANCE

INSURANCE UNDERWRITERS

PERIODICALS AND NEWSLETTERS

Jounal of Finacial Services Professionals. Society of Financial Services Professional. • Bimonthly. $95.00 per year. Provides information on life insurance and financial planning, including estate planning, retirement, tax planning, trusts, business insurance, long-term care insurance, disability insurance, and employee benefits. Formerly (American Society of CLU and Ch F C Journal).

National Underwriter. The National Underwriter Co. • Weekly. Two editions: *Life* or *Health.* $86.00 per year, each edition.

TRADE/PROFESSIONAL ASSOCIATIONS

American Institute for CPCU. 720 Providence Rd., Malvern, PA 19355-0716. Phone: 800-644-2101 or (610)644-2100 Fax: (610)640-9576 E-mail: cserv@cpuiia.org • URL: http://www.aicpcu.com.

American Insurance Association. 1130 Connecticut Ave. NW, Ste. 1000, Washington, DC 20036. Phone: 800-242-2302 or (202)828-7100 or (202)828-7183 Fax: (202)293-1219 E-mail: info@aiadc.org • URL: http://www.aiadc.org/aiadotnet • Represents companies providing property and casualty insurance and suretyship. Monitors and reports on economic, political, and social trends; serves as a clearinghouse for ideas, advice, and technical information. Represents members' interests before state and federal legislative and regulatory bodies; coordinates members' litigation.

CPCU Society. 720 Providence Rd., 720 Providence Rd., PO Box 3009, Malvern, PA 19355-3402. Phone: 800-932-2728 or (610)251-2727 Fax: (610)251-2780 E-mail: membercenter@cpcusociety.org • URL: http://www.cpcusociety.org • Serves as a professional society of individuals who have passed national examinations of the American Institute for Chartered Property Casualty Underwriters (see separate entry), have 3 years of work experience, have agreed to be bound by a code of ethics, and have been awarded CPCU designation. Promotes education, research, social responsibility, and professionalism in the field. Holds seminars, symposia, and workshops.

Inland Marine Underwriters Association. 14 Wall St., 8th Fl., New York, NY 10005. Phone: (212)233-0550 Fax: (212)227-5102 E-mail: rthornton@imua.org • URL: http://www.imua.org • Insurance companies transacting commercial inland marine insurance in the U.S. Purposes are to provide a forum for the discussion of insurance problems of common concern; to develop underwriting and loss prevention guidelines for the protection of property; to advise with respect to legislation affecting the business. Conducts specialized education programs nationwide.

Insurance Services Office (ISO). 545 Washington Blvd., Jersey City, NJ 07310-1686. Phone: 800-888-4476 or (201)469-2000 Fax: (201)748-1472 E-mail: info@iso.com • URL: http://www.iso.com • Provides statistical, actuarial, underwriting, and claims information to property and casualty insurance companies.

National Association of Insurance and Financial Advisors. 2901 Telestar Court, Falls Church, VA 22042-1205. Phone: 877-866-2432 or (703)770-8100 Fax: (703)770-8142 E-mail: membersupport@naifa.org • URL: http://www.naifa.org • Affiliated with Association for Advanced Life Underwriting. Formerly National Association of Life Underwriters.

Society of Financial Service Professionals. 270 S. Bryn Mawr Ave., Bryn Mawr, PA 19010-2195. Phone: 800-392-6900 or (610)526-2500 Fax: (610)527-4010 E-mail: custserv@financialpro.org • URL: http://www.financialpro.org.

INSURANCE, UNEMPLOYMENT

See: UNEMPLOYMENT INSURANCE

INTEGRATED CIRCUITS

See: SEMICONDUCTOR INDUSTRY

INTEGRATED SYSTEMS

See: SYSTEMS INTEGRATION

INTELLECTUAL PROPERTY

See also: COPYRIGHT; LICENSING AGREEMENTS; TRADE SECRETS

GENERAL WORKS

Essentials of Knowledge Management. Bryan Bergeron. John Wiley and Sons, Inc. • 2003. $29.95. Covers current strategies, trends, and technologies in knowledge management. Includes examples of best practices. (Essentials Series).

The Intentional Entrepreneur: Bringing Technology and Engineering to the Real New Economy. David L. Bodde. M. E. Sharpe, Inc. • 2004. $69.95. Covers the "art of entrepreneurship" for engineering and technology professionals. Includes material on marketing, business models, venture capital, and intellectual property.

Knowledge Management Lessons Learned: What Works and What Doesn't. Michael Koenig and T. Kanti Srikantaiah, editors. Information Today, Inc. • 2003. $44.50. Contains more than 30 articles by KM experts, covering recent applications, innovations, strategy, implementation, cost analysis, training, content management, and other topics related to knowledge management. (ASIS Management Series).

Modern Intellectual Property. Michael A. Epstein. Aspen Publishers, Inc. • 1995. Third edition. Price on application.

ABSTRACTS AND INDEXES

Current Law Index: Multiple Access to Legal Periodicals. Gale Cengage Learning. • Monthly. $725.00 per year. Produced in cooperation with the American Association of Law Libraries. Indexes more than 900 law journals, legal newspapers, and specialty publications from the U.S., Canada, U.K., Ireland, Australia, and New Zealand.

Index to Legal Periodicals and Books. H. W. Wilson Co. • Monthly. $490.00 per year. Quarterly and annual cumulations.

ALMANACS AND YEARBOOKS

Intellectual Property Law Review. West Group. • 1999. $299.00. Patent, trademark, and copyright practices.

IP Almanac. American Lawyer Media, Inc. • Annual. $20.00. Provides a digest of the year's most important developments in the area of intellectual property. (Also included with subscription to *IP Law and Business*).

BIBLIOGRAPHIES

Knowledge Management: The Bibliography. Paul Burden and others. Information Today, Inc. • 2000. $22.50. Provides citations to more than 1,500 articles, 150 Web sites, and 400 books. Arranged according to specific KM topics, such as "KM and E-Commerce." Published in conjunction with the American Society for Information Science and Technology (ASIST).

CD-ROM DATABASES

Authority Computer and Telecommunications Law Library. LexisNexis/Matthew Bender. • Quarterly. Price on request. Full text CD-ROM provides cases, analysis, sample agreements, and other information relating to computer law, telecommunications regulation (cable, broadcasting, satellite, Internet), international computer law, and computer contracts.

Authority Intellectual Property Library. LexisNexis/Matthew Bender. • Quarterly. Price on request. CD-ROM contains updated full text of *Intellectual Property Counseling and Litigation, Computer Law, International Computer Law, Nimmer on Copyright, Milgrim on Trade Secrets, Patent Litigation, Patent Licensing Transactions, Trademark Protection and Practice,* and other Matthew Bender publications relating to the law of intellectual property.

DIRECTORIES

Attorneys and Agents Registered to Practice Before United States Patent and Trademark Office. U.S. Patent and Trademark Office. Available from U.S. Government Printing Office. • Annual. $56.00.

Directory of Intellectual Property Attorneys, 1995. Aspen Publishers, Inc. • 1994. $195.00.

KMWorld Buyer's Guide. Knowledge Asset Media. • Semiannual. Controlled circulation as part of *KMWorld.* Contains corporate and product profiles related to various aspects of knowledge management and information systems. (Knowledge Asset Media is a an affiliate of Information Today, Inc.).

ENCYCLOPEDIAS AND DICTIONARIES

McCarthy's Desk Encyclopedia of Intellectual Property. J. Thomas McCarthy. BNA, Inc. • 1995. $75.00.Second edition. Defines legal terms relating to patents, trademarks, copyrights, trade secrets, entertainment, and the computer industry.

HANDBOOKS AND MANUALS

Antitrust-Intellectual Property Handbook. Alan J. Weinschel. Glasser Legalworks. • Looseleaf. $175.00. Periodic supplementation. Covers patent licensing, patent antitrust issues, innovation markets, intervention by government agencies, standard-setting activities, royalty arrangements, and related intellectual property/antitrust topics. Provides explanations, legal guidance, and historical background.

Clearance and Copyright: Everything the Independent Filmmaker Needs to Know. Michael C. Donaldson. Silman-James Press. • 1996. $26.95. Covers film rights problems in pre-production, production, post-production, and final release. Includes sample contracts and forms.

Intellectual Property in the International Marketplace. Melvi Simensky and others. John Wiley and Sons, Inc. • 1999. $350.00. Second edition. Two volumes. Volume one: *Valuation, Protection, and Electronic Commerce.* Volume two: *Exploitation and Country-by-Country Profiles.* Includes contributions from lawyers and consultants in various countries. (Intellectual Property-General, Law, Accounting and Finance, Management, Licensing, Special Topics Series).

Intellectual Property Infringement Damages: A Litigation Support Handbook 2003 Cumulative Supplement. Russell L. Parr. John Wiley and Sons, Inc. • 2003. $78.00. Second edition. Describes how to calculate damages for patent, trademark, and copyright infringement. (Intellectual Property-General, Law, Accounting and Finance, Management, Licensing and Special Topics Series).

Intellectual Property Primary Law Soucebook. LexisNexis Matthew Bender. • Annual. $88.00. Provides federal copyright, patent, and trademark statutes and regulations.

Librarian's Guide to Intellectual Property in the Digital Age: Copyrights, Patents, and Trademarks. Timothy L. Wherry. American Library Association. • 2002. $38.00. Includes lists of patent and trademark depositories, relevant Web sites, and questions & answers.

Patent, Copyright, and Trademark: An Intellectual Property Desk Reference. Stephen Elias. Nolo. • 2003. $39.99. Sixth revised edition. Contains practical explanations of the legalities of patents, copyrights, trademarks, and trade secrets. Includes examples of relevant legal forms. A 1985 version was called *Nolo's Intellectual Property Law Dictionary.* (Nolo Press Self-Help Law Series).

Patent, Trademark, and Copyright Laws, 2003. Jeffrey Samuels, editor. BNA, Inc. • 2003. $115.00. Contains text of "all pertinent intellectual property legislation to date.".

Protecting Trade Secrets, Patents, Copyrights, and Trademarks. Robert C. Dorr and Christopher H. Munch. Aspen Publishers, Inc. • $165.00. Looseleaf service.

What Corporate and General Practitioners Should Know About Intellectual Property Litigation. Raphael V. Lupo and Donna M. Tanguay. American Law Institute-American Bar Association. • 1991. $34.00. A lawyer's guide to patents, trademarks, copyrights, and trade secrets.

INTERNET DATABASES

Lexis.com Research System. Lexis-Nexis Group. Phone: 800-227-4908 or (937)865-6800 Fax: (937)865-6909 E-mail: webmaster@prod.lexis-nexis.com • URL: http://www.lexis.com • Fee-based Web site offers extensive searching of a wide variety of legal sources. Additional features include Daily Opinion Service, lexis.com Bookstore, Career Center, CLE Center, Law Schools, and Practice Pages ("Pages specific to areas of specialty").

ONLINE DATABASES

Index to Legal Periodicals and Books (Online). H. W. Wilson Co. • Broad coverage of law journals and books 1981 to date. Monthly updates. Inquire as to online cost and availability.

Legal Resource Index. Gale Cengage Learning. • Broad coverage of law literature appearing in legal, business, and other periodicals, 1980 to date. Daily updates. Inquire as to online cost and availability.

LEXIS. LEXIS-NEXIS. • The various LEXIS databases provide full text and indexing for a wide variety of legal cases, statutes, orders, and opinions.

PERIODICALS AND NEWSLETTERS

BNA's Patent, Trademark and Copyright Journal. BNA, Inc. • Weekly. $1,495.00 per year. Looseleaf service.

Intellectual Property Newsletter. L L Professional Publishing. • Monthly. $261.00 per year.

Intellectual Property Strategist. American Lawyer

Media, Inc. • Monthly. $229.00 per year. Newsletter. Covers "business and litigation tactics" in the field of intellectual property law, including international issues. (A Law Journal Newsletter, formerly published by Leader Publications).

Intellectual Property Today. • Monthly. $96.00 per year. Covers legal developments in copyright, patents, trademarks, and licensing. Emphasizes the effect of new technology on intellectual property. Formerly *Law Works.*

IP Law and Business. American Lawyer Media, Inc. • Monthly. $125.00 per year. Covers intellectual property litigation and business issues. Includes annual *IP Almanac.*

KM World: Creating and Managing the Knowledge-Based Enterprise (Knowledge Management). Asset Media. • 10 times a year. Free to qualified personnel; others, $63.95 per year. Provides articles on knowledge management, including business intelligence, multimedia content management, document management, e-business, and intellectual property. Emphasis is on business-to-business information technology. (Knowledge Asset Media is a an affiliate of Information Today, Inc.).

RESEARCH CENTERS AND INSTITUTES

PTC Research Foundation. 24 Warren St., Concord, NH 03301. Phone: (603)228-4530 Fax: (603)228-4730 E-mail: anharr@cybertours.com • URL: http://www.ptcforum.org.

TRADE/PROFESSIONAL ASSOCIATIONS

American Intellectual Property Law Association. 241 18th St. S, Ste. 700, Arlington, VA 22202. Phone: (703)415-0780 Fax: (703)415-0786 E-mail: aipla@aipla.org • URL: http://www.aipla.org • Voluntary bar association of lawyers practicing in the fields of patents, trademarks, copyrights, and trade secrets. Aids in the operation and improvement of U.S. patent, trademark, and copyright systems, including the laws by which they are governed and rules and regulations under which federal agencies administer those laws. Sponsors moot court and legal writing competitions.

Intellectual Property Owners Association. 1255 23rd St. NW, Ste. 200, Washington, DC 20037. Phone: (202)466-2396 Fax: (202)466-2893 E-mail: info@ipo.org • URL: http://www.ipo.org • Corporations, lawyers, and individuals interested in intellectual property (patents, trademarks, copyrights, and trade secrets). Seeks to support and strengthen the patent, trademark, copyright, and trade secret laws. Monitors related legislative activities.

International Intellectual Property Alliance. 2101 L St. NW, Ste. 1000, Washington, DC 20037. Phone: (202)833-4198 Fax: (202)331-3101 E-mail: info@iipa.com • URL: http://www.iipa.com • Comprised of six trade associations, each representing a significant segment of the U.S. copyright community. Represents over 1,300 U.S. companies producing and distributing materials protected by copyright laws globally: computer software which includes business applications software and entertainment software (such as videogame CDs and cartridges, personal computer CD-ROMs and multimedia products); theatrical films, television programs, home videos and digital representations of audiovisual works, music, records, CDs, and audiocassettes; and textbooks, tradebooks, reference and professional publications and journals (in both electronic and print media).

International Intellectual Property Association. 1255 23rd St. NW, Ste. 200, Washington, DC 20037. Phone: (202)466-2396 Fax: (202)466-2893 E-mail: herb@ipo.org • URL: http://www.ipo.org • Lawyers who have professional qualifications and interest in the international protection of patents, designs, trademarks, copyrights, and other intellectual property rights. American group of the International Association for the Protection of Industrial Property.

Monitors international developments that may affect industrial property and related rights. Studies, discusses, and reports on proposed national and foreign legislation treaties and conventions that are likely to affect national and international intellectual property interests.

International Licensing Industry Merchandisers' Association. 350 Fifth Ave., Suite 1408, New York, NY 10118. Phone: (212)244-1944 Fax: (212)563-6552 E-mail: info@licensing.org • URL: http://www.licensing.org • Promotes the legal protection of licensed properties.

Licensing Executives Society. 1800 Diagonal Rd., Ste. 280, Alexandria, VA 22314. Phone: (703)836-3106 Fax: (703)836-3107 E-mail: info@les.org • URL: http://www.usa-canada.les.org • U.S. and foreign businessmen, scientists, engineers, and lawyers having direct responsibility for the transfer of technology. Maintains placement service.

OTHER SOURCES

Corporate Compliance Series. Joseph E. Murphy and Paul H. Dawes. West Group. • $1,210.00. 12 looseleaf volumes. Covers criminal and civil liability problems for corporations. Includes employee safety, product liability, pension requirements, securities violations, equal employment opportunity issues, intellectual property, employee hiring and firing, and other corporate compliance topics.

Cyberlaw: Intellectual Property in the Digital Millennium. American Lawyer Media, Inc. • Looseleaf. $159.00. Updated as needed. A basic guide to copyright as applied to the Internet and other electronic sources. (Law Journal Press).

E-Commerce and Internet Law: Treatise with Forms. Ian C. Ballon. Glasser Legalworks. • Three looseleaf volumes. $595.00. Periodic supplementation. Analyzes Internet legalities, including litigious matters relating to downloading, streaming, music, video, content aggregation, domain names, chatrooms, and search engines. Includes forms, contracts, checklists, sample pleadings, and an extensive glossary.

Intellectual Property and Antitrust Law. William C. Holmes. West Group. • Semiannual. $389.00 per year. Two looseleaf volumes. Includes patent, trademark, and copyright practices.

Intellectual Property Law: Commercial, Creative, and Industrial Property. American Lawyer Media, Inc. • Looseleaf. $229.00. Two volumes. Updated as needed. Covers the legal aspects of patents, trade secrets, copyright, technology protection, software protection, databases, etc. Also "compares the basic principles of U.S. law with those of Asian and European law." (Law Journal Press).

Licensing of Intellectual Property. American Lawyer Media, Inc. • Looseleaf. $169.00. Updated as needed. Includes such licensing topics as royalties, infringement, antitrust, trade secrets, and patent agreements. Examples of licensing agreements and sample forms (on CD-ROM) are included. (Law Journal Press).

INTELLIGENCE, ARTIFICIAL

See: ARTIFICIAL INTELLIGENCE

INTERACTIVE MEDIA

See also: MULTIMEDIA

GENERAL WORKS

Interactive Marketing: The Future Present. Edward Forrest and Richard Mizerski, editors. McGraw-Hill. • 1995. $47.95. Contains articles on the collection and analysis of interactive marketing data,

database management, interactive media, marketing research strategies, and related topics.(NTC Business Book Series).

Interactive Television Demystified. Jerry C. Whitaker. McGraw-Hill. • 2001. $49.95. Discusses the current applications and future possibilities of interactive TV, including business models. Case histories are provided. (Demystified Series).

Interface Culture: How New Technology Transforms the Way We Create and Communicate. Steven Johnson. HarperSanFrancisco. • 1997. $24.00. A discussion of how computer interfaces and online technology ("cyberspace") affect society in general.

ABSTRACTS AND INDEXES

Internet and Personal Computing Abstracts [print edition]. EBSCO Publishing. • Quarterly. $269.00 per year, including cumulative index. Provides more than 10,000 abstracts annually from both trade and academic publications. Covers computer hardware, software, product reviews, Web topics, e-commerce, networks, corporate news, security, and related topics. Formerly *Microcomputer Abstracts.*

ALMANACS AND YEARBOOKS

Communication Technology Update. Elsevier. • 2000. $36.95. 7th edition. A yearly review of developments in electronic media, telecommunications, and the Internet.

CD-ROM DATABASES

Computer Database. Gale Cengage Learning. • Provides one year of full-text on CD-ROM for 150 leading computer-related publications. Also includes 70,000 product specifications and brief profiles of 13,000 computer product vendors and manufacturers.

Hoover's Company Capsules on CD-ROM. Hoover's, Inc. • Quarterly. $399.95 per year (single-user). Provides the CD-ROM version of *Hoover's Handbook of American Business, Hoover's Handbook of Emerging Companies, Hoover's Handbook of World Business, Hoover's Guide to Computer Companies, Hoover's Guide to Media Companies, Hoover's Handbook of Private Companies,* and various regional guides. Includes more than 11,000 profiles of companies.

DIRECTORIES

AV Market Place: The Complete Business Directory of Audio, Audio Visual, Computer Systems, Film, Video, and Programming, with Industry Yellow Pages. Information Today, Inc. • Annual. $195.00. Provides information on "more than 7,500 companies that create, apply, or distribute AV equipment and services for business, education, science, and government." Multimedia, virtual reality, presentation software, and interactive video are among the categories. Formerly published by R. R. Bowker.

Data Sources: The Comprehensive Guide to the Data Processing Industry: Hardware, Data Communications Products, Software, Company Profiles. Gale Cengage Learning. • Semiannual. $455.00 per year. Two volumes. Describes hardware and software for all computer operating sysems, including prices and technical details. Lists about 75,000 products from 14,000 suppliers. Industry-specific software applications are described.

DV Buyer's Guide. CMP Media LLC. • Annual. $10.00. A directory of professional video products, including digital cameras, monitors, editing systems, and software.

Interactive TV Investor Buyer's Guide and Directory. Paul Kagan Associates Inc. • Annual. Price on application. (A special issue of the periodical *Convergence.*).

Plunkett's InfoTech Industry Almanac: Complete Profiles on the InfoTech 500-the Leading Firms in the Movement and Management of Voice, Data, and

Video. Plunkett Research, Ltd. • Biennial. $229.99. Includes CD-ROM. Five hundred major information companies are profiled, with corporate culture aspects. Discusses major trends in various sectors of the computer and information industry, including data on careers and job growth. Includes several indexes.

ENCYCLOPEDIAS AND DICTIONARIES

Acronyms of Computer Science and Communications: A Comprehensive Acronym Dictionary and Illustrated Encyclopedia. Enjob Kajan and Ejub Kajan. Springer Verlag. • 2002. $49.95. Explains more than 4,000 "broadly used" computer, telecommunications, and information technology acronyms. Includes illustrations and Web addresses, where applicable.

Encyclopedia of Emerging Industries. Gale Cengage Learning. • 2001. $320.00. Fourth edition. Provides detailed information on 115 "newly flourishing" industries. Includes historical background, organizational structure, significant individuals, current conditions, major companies, work force, technology trends, research developments, and other industry facts.

Encyclopedia of Information Systems. Hossein Bidgoli, editor. Elsevier. • 2002. $1,200.00. Four volumes. Contains a wide range of articles relating to computers, databases, communication, and information technology. The 200 topics include coverage of hardware, software, artificial intelligence, the Internet, networks, knowledge management, electronic commerce, search engines, and systems design.

Encyclopedia of New Media: An Essential Reference to Communication and Technology. Steve Jones, editor. Sage Publications, Inc. • 2003. $125.00. Contains more than 250 entries dealing with such areas as multimedia, broadband access, information communication technology (ICT), content filtering, wireless networks, and cyberethics.

New Hacker's Dictionary. Eric S. Raymond. MIT Press. • 1996. $65.00. Third edition. Includes three classifications of hacker communication: slang, jargon, and "techspeak.".

HANDBOOKS AND MANUALS

Creating Digital Content: A Video Production for Web, Broadcast, and Cinema. John Rice and Brian McKernan. McGraw-Hill. • 2001. $49.95. Discusses the technicalities of digital content with a light touch, as in "Throw Another Analog on the Digital Fire." Other chapter titles are "Digital Recording," "Datacasting," "Coming to a Theatre Near You: Digital Cinema," and "The Promise of Digital Interactive Television.".

Interactive Music Handbook: The Definitive Guide to Internet Music Strategies, Enhanced CD Production and Business Development. Jodi Summers. Allworth Press. • 1996. $19.95. Covers interactive or enhanced music CD-ROMs and online music for producers, audio technicians, and musicians. Includes case studies and interviews.

INTERNET DATABASES

InfoTech Trends. Data Analysis Group. Phone: (925)462-1202 Fax: (925)462-1225 E-mail: support@infotechtrends.com • URL: http://www.infotechtrends.com • Web site provides both free and fee-based market research data on the information technology industry, including computers, peripherals, telecommunications, the Internet, software, CD-ROM/DVD, e-commerce, and workstations. Fees: Free for current (most recent year) data; more extensive information has various fee structures. Formerly *Computer Industry Forecasts.*

Wired News. Lycos, Inc. Phone: (415)276-8400 Fax: (415)276-8500 E-mail: newsfeedback@wired.com • URL: http://www.wired.com • Provides sum-

maries and full-text of "Top Stories" relating to the Internet, computers, multimedia, telecommunications, and the electronic information industry in general. These news stories are placed in the broad categories of Politics, Business, Culture, and Technology. Affiliated with *Wired* magazine. Fees: Free.

PERIODICALS AND NEWSLETTERS

Convergence: The Journal of Research Into New Media Technologies. Reed Business Information. • Monthly. Individuals, $40.00 per year; institutions, $160.00 per year. Covers the merging of communications technologies. Includes telecommunications networks, interactive TV, multimedia, wireless phone service, and electronic information services.

Digital Video. CMP Media LLC. • Monthly. $60.00 per year. Edited for professionals in the field of digital video production. Covers such topics as operating systems, videography, digital video cameras, audio, workstations, web video, software development, and interactive television.

Digital Video Magazine. CMP Media LLC. • Monthly. $29.97 per year. Edited for producers and creators of digital media. Includes topics relating to video, audio, animation, multimedia, interactive design, and special effects. Covers both hardware and software, with product reviews. Formerly *Digital Video Magazine.*

InterActive Consumers. MarketResearch.com. • Monthly. $395.00 per year. Newsletter. Covers the emerging markets for digital content, products, and services. Includes market information on telecommuting, online services, the Internet, online investing, and other areas of electronic commerce.

Interactive Content: Consumer Media Strategies Monthly. Jupitermedia. • Monthly. $675.00 per year; with online edition, $775.00 per year. Newsletter. Covers the broad field of providing content (information, news, entertainment) for the Internet/ World Wide Web.

Interactive Update. Alexander & Associates. • Description: Provides information on the interactive entertainment industry, focusing on software.

Maximum PC (Personal Computer). Imagine Media, Inc. • Quarterly. $29.95 per year. Provides articles and reviews relating to multimedia hardware and software. Each issue includes a CD-ROM sampler (emphasis is on games). Formed by the merger of *Home PC* and *Boot.*

Smart TV and Sound: Interactive Television and DVD-MP3-Internet Audio and Video-Satellite Television. York Publishing. • Semiannual. $14.97 per year. Consumer magazine covering WebTV, PC/TV appliances, DVD players, "Smart TV," advanced VCRs, and other topics relating to interactive television, the Internet, and multimedia. Formerly *Smart TV.*

Sound & Vision: Home Theater- Audio- Video-MultimediaMovies- Music. Hachette Filipacchi Media U.S., Inc. • 10 times a year. $24.00 per year. Popular magazine providing explanatory articles and critical reviews of equipment and media (CD-ROM, DVD, videocassettes, etc.). Supplement available *Stero Review's Sound and Vision Buyers Guide.* Replaces *Stereo Review* and *Video Magazine.*

PRICE SOURCES

Opportunities in Interactive TV Applications & Services: An Analysis of Market Interest & Price Sensitivity. Available from MarketResearch.com. • 2001. $1,395. Published by TechTrends, Inc. Market research data. Includes an analysis of how much consumers are willing to pay per month for each application.

RESEARCH CENTERS AND INSTITUTES

Electronic Visualization Laboratory. University of Illinois at Chicago, Engineering Research Facility,

842 W. Taylor St., Room 2032, Chicago, IL 60607-7053. Phone: (312)996-3002 Fax: (312)413-7585 E-mail: tom@uic.edu • URL: http://www.evl.uic.edu • Research areas include computer graphics, virtual reality, multimedia, and interactive techniques.

Graphics, Visualization, and Usability Center. Georgia Institute of Technology. GVU Center, 801 Atlantic Dr., Atlanta, GA 30332-0280. Phone: (404)894-4488 Fax: (404)894-0673 E-mail: afb@cc.gatech.edu • URL: http://www.cc.gatech.edu/gvu/ • Research areas include computer graphics, multimedia, image recognition, interactive graphics systems, animation, and virtual realities.

Institute for Studies in the Arts. Arizona State University, College of Fine Arts, P.O. Box 873302, Tempe, AZ 85287-3302. Phone: (480)965-9438 Fax: (480)965-0961 E-mail: trikakis@asu.edu • URL: http://www.isa.asu.edu • Research areas include the fine arts aspects of interactive media.

Integrated Media Systems Center. University of Southern California, 3740 McClintock Ave., Suite 131, Los Angeles, CA 90089-2561. Phone: (213)740-0877 Fax: (213)740-8931 E-mail: imsc@imsc.usc.edu • URL: http://www.imsc.usc.edu • Media areas for research include education, mass communication, and entertainment.

Inter-Arts Center. San Francisco State University, School of Creative Arts, 1600 Holloway Ave., San Francisco, CA 94132. Phone: (415)338-1478 Fax: (415)338-6159 E-mail: jimdavis@sfsu.edu • URL: http://www.sfsu.edu/~iac • Research areas include multimedia, computerized experimental arts processes, and digital sound.

International Data Corp. (IDC). Five Speen St., Framingham, MA 01701. Phone: (508)872-8200 Fax: (508)935-4015 E-mail: leads@idc.com • URL: http://www.idc.com • Private research firm specializing in market research related to computers, multimedia, and telecommunications.

Media Laboratory. Massachusetts Institute of Technology, 20 Ames St., Room E-15, Cambridge, MA 02139-4307. Phone: (617)253-0300 Fax: (617)258-6264 E-mail: casr@media.mit.edu • URL: http://www.media.mit.edu • Research areas include electronic publishing, spatial imaging, human-machine interface, computer vision, and advanced television.

Multimedia Communications Laboratory. Boston University, Eight Saint Mary's St., PHO 445, Boston, MA 02215. Phone: (617)353-8042 Fax: (617)353-6440 E-mail: mcl@spiderman.bu.edu • URL: http://www.hulk.bu.edu • Research areas include interactive multimedia applications.

Studio for Creative Inquiry. Carnegie Mellon University, College of Fine Arts, Pittsburgh, PA 15213-3890. Phone: (412)268-3454 Fax: (412)268-2829 E-mail: mmbm@andrew.cmu.edu • URL: http://www.cmu.edu/studio/ • Research areas include artificial intelligence, virtual reality, hypermedia, multimedia, and telecommunications, in relation to the arts.

STATISTICS SOURCES

DMA Statistical Fact Book. Direct Marketing Association. Library and Resource Center. • Annual. Members, $79.95; non-members, $104.95. Provides data in five sections covering direct response advertising, media, mailing lists, market applications, and "Practical Management Information." Includes material on interactive/online marketing. (Cover title: *Direct Marketing Association's Statistical Fact Book.*).

TRADE/PROFESSIONAL ASSOCIATIONS

Association for Interactive Marketing. 1430 Broadway, 8th Fl., New York, NY 10018. Phone: 888-337-0008 or (212)790-1408 Fax: (212)391-9233 • URL: http://www.interactivehq.org • Members are companies engaged in various interactive enterprises, utilizing the internet, interactive television, computer communications and multimedia. Formerly Association for Interactive Media.

Association of Internet Professionals. 2929 Main St., No. 136, Santa Monica, CA 90405. Phone: (866)247-9700 or (501)423-2248 Fax: (501)423-2248 E-mail: info@association.org • URL: http://www.iproa.org • Members are interactive media professionals concerned with intetractive arts and technologies. Formerly International Interactive Communications Society.

Entertainment Software Association. 575 7th St. NW, Ste. 300, Washington, DC 20004. Phone: (202)223-2400 E-mail: esa@theesa.com • URL: http://www.theesa.com • Represents the interactive entertainment software publishing industry. Established an autonomous rating board to rate interactive entertainment software. Established a program to combat piracy in the United States and around the world. Represents members on industry issues at the federal and state level. Provides market research and information. **Publications:** none.

Internet Alliance. 1111 19th St. NW, Ste. 1100, Washington, DC 20035-5782. Phone: (202)861-2476 Fax: (202)955-8081 E-mail: info@internetalliance.org • URL: http://www.internetalliance.org • Companies offering Internet services. Seeks to "build the confidence and trust necessary for the Internet to become the global mass market medium of the 21st century". Represents members' commercial and regulatory interests; conducts promotional activities; facilitates communication and cooperation among members.

OTHER SOURCES

DVD Assessment, No. 3. Julie B. Schwerin and Theodore A. Pine. InfoTech, Inc. • 1998. $1,295.00. Third edition. Provides detailed market research data on Digital Video Discs (also known as Digital Versatile Discs). Includes history of DVD, technical specifications, DVD publishing outlook, "Industry Overview," "Market Context," "Infrastructure Analysis," "Long-Range Forecast to 2005," and emerging technologies.

The Market for Interactive Television. MarketResearch.com. • 2000. $995.00. Market research data.

North American Interactive Television Markets. Available from MarketResearch.com. • 1999. $3,450.00. Published by Frost & Sullivan. Contains market research data on growth, end-user trends, and market strategies. Company profiles are included.

Optical Publishing Industry Assessment. Julie B. Schwerin and Theodore A. Pine. InfoTech, Inc. • 1997. $1,295.00. Ninth edition. Provides market research data and forecasts to 2005 for DVD-ROM, "Hybrid ROM/Online Media," and other segments of the interactive entertainment, digital information, and consumer electronics industries. Covers both software (content) and hardware. Includes Video-CD, DVD- Video, CD-Audio, DVD-Audio, DVD-ROM, PC-Desktop, TV Set-Top, CD-R, CD-RW, DVD-R and DVD-RAM.

INTERACTIVE TELEVISION

See: INTERACTIVE MEDIA; VIDEOTEX/TELETEXT

INTEREST

See also: MONEY

GENERAL WORKS

Futures Markets. A. G. Malliaris, editor. Edward Elgar Publishing, Inc. • 1997. $550.00. Three volumes. Consists of reprints of 70 articles dating from 1959 to 1993, on futures market volatility, speculation, hedging, stock indexes, portfolio insurance, interest rates, and foreign currencies. (International Library of Critical Writings in Financial Economics Series: No. 2).

History of Interest Rates. Sidney Homer and Richard Sylla. Rutgers University Press. • 1996. $79.00. Third revised edition.

CD-ROM DATABASES

OECD Statistical Compendium. Organization for Economic Cooperation and Development. • Semiannual. $1,905.00 per year for 1 to 10 users. CD-ROM contains more than 730,000 monthly, quarterly, and annual time series for OECD countries, 1960 to date. Includes fully searchable data on agriculture, food, economic indicators, national accounts, employment, energy, finance, industry, technology, and foreign trade. Results can be displayed in various forms.

ENCYCLOPEDIAS AND DICTIONARIES

Blackwell Encyclopedic Dictionary of Finance. Dean Paxson and Douglas Wood, editors. Blackwell Publishing. • 1997. $110.00. The editors are associated with the University of Manchester. Contains definitions of key terms combined with longer articles written by various U. S. and foreign business educators. Includes bibliographies and index. (Blackwell Encyclopedia of Management Series).

HANDBOOKS AND MANUALS

Advanced Fixed Income Analysis. Moorad Choudhry. Elsevier Butterworth Heinemann. • 2004. $60.00. Edited for "experienced practitioners in the corporate bond markets." Covers trading, hedging, interest rate models, corporate bond default risk, the yield curve, long bond yields, and other topics.

Advanced Strategies in Financial Risk Management. Robert J. Schwartz and Clifford W. Smith. Prentice Hall PTR. • 1993. $65.00. Includes technical discussions of financial swaps and derivatives. (New York Institute of Finance Series).

The Bond and Money Markets: Strategy, Trading, Analysis. Moorad Choudhry. Elsevier Butterworth Heinemann. • 2003. $115.00. Serves as a reference work on corporate bonds, government bonds, currency markets, interest-rate futures, convertible securities, various kinds of derivatives, and technical analysis of financial securities.

Derivatives: A Comprehensive Resource for Options, Futures, Interest Rate Swaps, and Mortgage Securities. Fred D. Arditti. Harvard Business School Publishing. • 1996. $60.00. Published by Harvard Business School Press. Provides detailed explanations of various kinds of financial derivatives (options, futures, swaps, etc.) and their trading tactics, uses, and risks. (Financial Management Association Survey and Synthesis Series).

Fibonacci Applications and Strategies for Traders. Robert Fischer. John Wiley and Sons, Inc. • 1993. $60.00. Provides a new look at the Elliott Wave Theory and Fibonacci numbers as applied to commodity prices, business cycles, and interest rate movements. (Traders Advantage Series).

Fixed Income Analytics: State-of-the-Art Analysis and Valuation Modeling. Ravi E. Dattatreya, editor. McGraw-Hill. • 1991. $69.95. Discusses the yield curve, structure and value in corporate bonds, mortgage-backed securities, and other topics. (Institutional Investor Publications).

Interest Rate Risk Measurement and Management. Sanjay K. Nawalkha and Donald R. Chambers, editors. Institutional Investor, Inc. • 1999. $95.00. Provides interest rate risk models for fixed-income derivatives and for investments by various kinds of financial institutions.

Options, Futures, and Other Derivatives. John C. Hull. Prentice Hall PTR. • 2002. $135.00. Fifth edition.

Swap and Derivative Financing: The Global Reference to Products Pricing Applications and Markets. Satyajit Das. McGraw-Hill. • 1993. $99.95. Second revised edition.

Swap Literacy. Elizabeth Ungar. Bloomberg. • 1996. $40.00. Written for corporate finance officers. Provides basic information on arbitrage, hedging, and speculation, involving interest rate, currency, and other types of financial swaps. (Bloomberg Professional Library.).

Swaps and Financial Engineering: A Self-Study Guide to Mastering and Applying Swaps and Financial Engineering. McGraw-Hill. • 1994. $55.00.

INTERNET DATABASES

BanxQuote Banking, Mortgage, and Finance Center. BanxQuote, Inc. Phone: (914)722-1600 Fax: (914)722-6630 E-mail: info@banx.com • URL: http://www.banx.com • Web site quotes interest rates paid by banks around the country on various savings products, as well as rates paid by consumers for automobile loans, mortgages, credit cards, home equity loans, and personal loans. Also provided: stock quotes, indexes, stock options, futures trading data, economic indicators, and links to many other financial sites. Daily updates. Fees: Free.

Bondtalk.com: Live Talk & Analysis on the Bond Market & the Economy. Miller Tabak & Co., LLC. Phone: (212)370-0040 E-mail: acrescenzi@bondtalk.com • URL: http://www.bondtalk.com • Web site provides extensive, free data on the fixed income securities market, including individual bond prices, yields, interest rates, Federal Reserve information, charts, bond market news, and economic analysis. Also offered on a fee basis is "Bondtalkpro.com: The New and Enhanced Service for Market Professionals.".

Bureau of Economic Analysis (BEA). U. S. Department of Commerce, Bureau of Economic Analysis. Phone: (202)606-9900 Fax: (202)606-5310 E-mail: webmaster@bea.doc.gov • URL: http://www.bea.doc.gov • Web site includes "News Release Information" covering national, regional, and international economic estimates from the BEA. Highlights of releases appear online the same day, complete text and tables appear the next day. "Recent News Releases" section provides titles for past nine months, with links. "BEA Data and Methodology" includes "Frequently Requested NIPA Data" (national income and product accounts, such as gross domestic product and personal income). Other statistics are available. Fees: Free.

Business 2.0 Web Guide to the Best Business Links. Business 2.0 Media Inc. Phone: (415)293-4800 E-mail: support@business2.com • URL: http://www.business2.com/webguide • Web site presents an extensive, searchable directory of links to "the best, most informative, and authoritative web pages." Twenty main categories cover business, finance, career, company information, people, and technology topics, with thousands of subtopics, all linking to Web sites recommended by experienced business researchers. Fees: Free.

Business Week Online. McGraw-Hill. Phone: (212)512-2511 Fax: (684)842-6101 • URL: http://www.businessweek.com • Web site provides complete contents of current issue of *Business Week* plus "BW Daily" with additonal business news, financial market quotes, and corporate information from Standard & Poor's. Includes various features, such as "Banking Center" with mortgage and interest data, and "Interactive Computer Buying Guide." The "Business Week Archive" is fully searchable back to 1996.

Federal Reserve Board Publications and Education Resources. Board of Governors of the Federal Reserve System. Phone: (202)452-3000 Fax: (202)452-3819 • URL: http://www.federalreserve.

gov/publications.htm • Web site provides convenient access to statistics, surveys, and research from the Federal Reserve Board. *Federal Reserve Bulletin* articles are available as abstracts or full text (PDF) currently or from six-year archives. The link "Statistics: Releases and Historical Data" offers daily, weekly, monthly, quarterly, and annual data in great detail for interest rates, foreign exchange, consumer credit, money stock measures, industrial production indexes, bank reserves, and other items. Historical tabulations are available for various time periods. Fees: Free.

Fedstats. Federal Interagency Council on Statistical Policy. Phone: (202)395-7254 • URL: http://www. fedstats.gov • Web site features an efficient search facility for full-text statistics produced by more than 100 federal agencies, including the Census Bureau, the Bureau of Economic Analysis, and the Bureau of Labor Statistics. Boolean searches can be made within one agency or for all agencies combined. Links are offered to international statistical bureaus, including the UN, IMF, OECD, UNESCO, Eurostat, and 20 individual countries. Fees: Free.

FreeLunch.com. Economy.com, Inc. Phone: (610)696-8700 Fax: (610)696-1678 • URL: http:// www.freelunch.com • Web site provides free access to more than 1.5 million economic and financial data series, covering industry, demographics, labor markets, prices, retail sales, government spending, trade, interest rates, housing starts, the stock market, and many other topics. Data is available for various time periods in either chart or table form. Searching is offered. Fees: Free, but registration required. Economy.com, Inc. also offers fee-based economic analysis at *The Dismal Scientist* site (http://www. dismal.com).

ONLINE DATABASES

Banking Information Source. PROQUEST. • Provides indexing and abstracting of periodical and other literature from 1982 to date, with weekly updates. Covers the financial services industry: banks, savings institutions, investment houses, credit unions, insurance companies, and real estate organizations. Emphasis is on marketing and management. Inquire as to online cost and availability. (Formerly *FINIS: Financial Industry Information Service.*).

PERIODICALS AND NEWSLETTERS

American Banker: The Financial Services Daily. Thomson Media. • Daily. $895.00 per year. Provides news of banking, investment products, mortgages, credit unions, finance, bank technology, and legal developments.

Bank Rate Monitor: The Weekly Financial Rate Reporter. Advertising News Service, Inc. • Weekly. $895.00 per year. Newsletter. Includes online addition and monthly supplement. Provides detailed information on interest rates currently paid by U. S. banks and savings institutions.

Barron's: The Dow Jones Business and Financial Weekly. • Weekly. $145.00 per year.

BCA Interest Rate Forecast: A Monthly Analysis and Forecast of U.S. Bond and Money Market Trends. BCA Publications. • Monthly. $695.00 per year. Formerly *Interest Rate Forecast.*

Blue Chip Financial Forecasts: What Top Analysts are Saying About U. S. and Foreign Interest Rates, Monetary Policy, Inflation, and Economic Growth. Aspen Publishers, Inc. • Monthly. $665.00 per year. Newsletter. Gives forecasts about a year in advance for interest rates, inflation, currency exchange rates, monetary policy, and economic growth rates.

Grant's Interest Rate Observer. James Grant, editor. Grant's Financial Publishing Inc. • Biweekly. $725.00 per year. Newsletter containing detailed analysis of money-related topics, including interest rate trends, global credit markets, fixed-income

investments, bank loan policies, and international money markets.

Interest Rate Service. World Reports Ltd. • 10 times a year. $950.00 per year.

Journal of Fixed Income. Institutional Investor, Inc., Journals Group. • Quarterly. $360.00 per year. Includes print and online editions. Covers a wide range of fixed-income investments for institutions, including bonds, interest-rate options, high-yield securities, and mortgages.

Jumbo Rate News. BauerFinancial, Inc. • Description: Reports on high-yielding, insured Jumbo CD (Certificate of Deposit) rates nationwide. Analyzes each institution by current credit-worthiness, and lists current assets and capital ratios. Provides phone numbers, contacts, methods of computation, and information on how interest is paid. Also contains financial news, insights, and commentary of interest to Jumbo CD investors. Recurring features include editorials and news of interest.

Money Reporter: The Insider's Letter for Investors Whose Interest is More Interest. MPL Communications, Inc. • Biweekly. $185.00 per year. Newsletter. Supplement available, *Monthly Key Investment.* Canadian interest-bearing deposits and investments.

Moneyletter. Agora Inc. • Description: "Provides assertive, do-it-yourself, individual investors with a unique market timing system, specific buy and sell recommendations, and portfolio allocation advice on no-load mutual funds. Features updates on economic and financial market, fund profiles, and articles on non-mutual fund financial planning issues.".

One Hundred Highest Yields. Advertising News Service, Inc. • Weekly. $124.00 per year. Newsletter. List CD's and money markets offered by federally insured banks. National coverage.

StraightTalk. The Conference Board. • 10 times a year. Members, $195.00 per year; non-members, $395.00 per year. Newsletter. Provides analysis of domestic and international economic issues. Includes coverage of interest rate trends and the currency exchange outlook.

U. S. Banker. Thomson Media. • Monthly. $65.00 per year. Edited for bank executives and managers. Covers a wide variety of banking and financial topics.

STATISTICS SOURCES

The AIER Chart Book. AIER Research Staff. American Institute for Economic Research. • Annual. $4.00. A compact compilation of long-range charts ("Purchasing Power of the Dollar," for example, goes back to 1780) covering various aspects of the U. S. economy. Includes inflation, interest rates, debt, gold, taxation, stock prices, etc. (Economic Education Bulletin.).

Business Statistics of the United States. Linz Audain and Cornelia J. Strawser. Bernan Associates. • Annual. $147.00. Based on *Business Statistics*, formerly issue by the Bureau of Economic Analysis, U. S. Department of Commerce. Provides basic data for a wide variety of U. S. industries, services, and economic indicators. Most statistics are shown annually for 30 years and monthly for the most recent four years.

Federal Reserve Bulletin. U.S. Federal Reserve System. • Monthly. $25.00 per year. Provides statistics on banking and the economy, including interest rates, money supply, and the Federal Reserve Board indexes of industrial production.

Financial Market Trends. Organization for Economic Cooperation and Development. • Quarterly. $80.00 per year. Provides analysis of developments and trends in international and national capital markets. Includes charts and graphs on interest rates, exchange rates, stock market indexes, bank stock indexes, trading volumes, and loans outstanding. Data from OECD countries

includes international direct investment, bank profitability, institutional investment, and privatization.

Selected Interest Rates. U.S. Federal Reserve System. • Weekly release, $20.00 per year.

Statistical Annual: Interest Rates, Metals, Stock Indices, Options on Financial Futures, Options on Metals Futures. Chicago Board of Trade. • Annual. Includes historical data on GNMA CDR Futures, Cash-Settled GNMA Futures, U. S. Treasury Bond Futures, U. S. Treasury Note Futures, Options on Treasury Note Futures, NASDAQ-100 Futures, Major Market Index Futures, Major Market Index MAXI Futures, Municipal Bond Index Futures, 1,000-Ounce Silver Futures, Options on Silver Futures, and Kilo Gold Futures.

Survey of Current Business. Available from U. S. Government Printing Office. • Monthly. $63.00 per year. Issued by Bureau of Economic Analysis, U. S. Department of Commerce. Presents a wide variety of business and economic data.

Treasury Bulletin. Available from U. S. Government Printing Office. • Quarterly. $45.00 per year. Issued by the Financial Management Service, U. S. Treasury Department. Provides data on the federal budget, government securities and yields, the national debt, and the financing of the federal government in general.

INTERIOR DECORATION

See also: WINDOW COVERING INDUSTRY

GENERAL WORKS

Professional Practice for Interior Design. Christine M. Piotrowski. John Wiley and Sons, Inc. • 2001. $75.00. Third edition. (Interior Design Series).

ABSTRACTS AND INDEXES

Art Index. H. W. Wilson Co. • Quarterly. Annual cumulations. Price varies. Subject and author index to periodicals in art, architecture, industrial design, city planning, photography, and various related topics.

DIRECTORIES

ASID Professional Designer. American Society of Interior Designers. • Bimonthly. Membership.

Decorating Registry. Paint and Decorating Retailers Association. • Publication includes: List of about 1,500 manufacturers, manufacturers' representatives, distributors, and suppliers of decorating merchandise; a comprehensive trademark and brand name directory; associations, societies, and trade shows related to the home decorating industry. Entries include: For companies and manufacturer representatives--Firm name, address, phone, fax, name and title of contact, trademark, brand names. For associations--Name, address, phone, statement of purpose or description of service, key personnel, trade shows sponsored with dates and locations. Principal content of publication is decorative products (coatings, wallcoverings, window treatments, flooring, sundries).

Directory of Home Furnishings Retailers. Chain Store Guide. • Annual. $335.00. Online edition, $775.00. Includes more than 5,500 furniture retailers and wholesalers. Covers United States and Canada.

Home Fashions: Buyer's Guide. Fairchild Publications. • Annual. $10.00. Lists manufacturers, importers, and regional sales representatives supplying bed, bath, kitchen, and table linens; window treatments; wall coverings; and fibers and fabrics.

IDH--Interior Decorators Handbook. E.W. Williams Publications Co. • Covers: Over 3,000 manufacturers and distributors of furniture, accessories, floor coverings, fabrics, wall coverings and services related to these products. Entries include: Manufacturer or distributor name, address, phone, fax, brands carried. Similar information for importers, jobbers and agents.

Interior Design Buyers Guide. Reed Business Information. • Annual. $16.95. Included with subscription to *Interior Design.*

Interiors and Sources: Directory and Buyer's Guide. L. C. Clark Publishing Co., Inc. • Annual. $10.00. Lists sources of surface materials, furniture, lighting, etc., for interior designers.

ENCYCLOPEDIAS AND DICTIONARIES

Design Encyclopedia. Mel Byars. John Wiley and Sons, Inc. • 1994. $60.00. Contains more than 3,000 entries covering various aspects of design and decoration since the 19th century.

Encyclopedia of Interior Design. Joanna Banham, editor. Fitzroy Dearborn Publishers, Inc. • 1997. $295.00. Two volumes. Contains more than 500 essays on interior design topics. Includes bibliographies.

HANDBOOKS AND MANUALS

Interior Designer. Entrepreneur Media, Inc. • Looseleaf. $59.50. A practical guide to starting an interior design and decoration business. Covers profit potential, start-up costs, market size evaluation, owner's time required, pricing, accounting, advertising, promotion, etc. (Start-Up Business Guide No. E1314.).

Interior Graphic Standards. Maryrose T. McGowan. John Wiley and Sons, Inc. • 2003. $175.00. Provides guidelines for the planning and detailing of commercial and residential interiors. Includes more than 3,000 architectural drawings.

Office Interior Design Guide: An Introduction for Facility and Design. Julie K. Rayfield. John Wiley and Sons, Inc. • 1997. $70.00. (Professional Series).

ONLINE DATABASES

Art Index Online. H. W. Wilson Co. • Indexes a wide variety of art-related periodicals, 1984 to date. Monthly updates. Inquire as to online cost and availability.

Avery Architectural Periodicals Index. Avery Architectural and Fine Arts Library. • Indexes a wide range of periodicals related to architecture and design. Subjects include building design, building materials, interior design, housing, land use, and city planning. Time span: 1977 to date. *bul* URL: http://www-rlg.stanford.edu/cit-ave.html.

PERIODICALS AND NEWSLETTERS

Contract: The Business Magazine of Commercial and Institutional Interior Design, and Architecture, Planning and Construction. VNU Business Media. • Monthly. $94.00 per year. Firms engaged in specifying furniture and furnishings for commercial installations. Formerly *Contract Design.*

Interior Design. Reed Business Information. • Monthly. $64.95 per year. For the professional designed, provides information on trends and new products.

Interiors and Sources. L. C. Clark Publishing Co., Inc. • Bimonthly. $27.00 per year. Promotes professionalism for interior designers and design firms. Includes special features on office systems, work stations, and office furniture.

Paint and Decorating Retailer. Paint and Decorating Retailers Association. • Monthly. $45.00 per year. Formerly *Decorating Retailer.*

Waland Window Trends. Cygnus Business Media, Inc. • Monthly $36.00 per year. Edited for retailers of interior decoration products, with an emphasis on

wallcoverings. Formerly *Wallcoverings, Windows and Interior Fashion.*

RESEARCH CENTERS AND INSTITUTES

Interior Design Laboratory. Lambuth University, 7051 Lambuth Blvd., Jackson, TN 38301. Phone: 800-526-2884.

TRADE/PROFESSIONAL ASSOCIATIONS

American Society of Interior Designers. 608 Massachusetts Ave., N.E., Washington, DC 20002. Phone: (202)546-3480 Fax: (202)546-3240 E-mail: asid@asid.org • URL: http://www.interiors.org.

International Interior Design Association. 222 Merchandise Mart Plz., Ste. 567, Chicago, IL 60654. Phone: 888-799-4432 or (312)467-1950 or (312)467-1950 Fax: (312)467-0779 E-mail: iidahq@iida.org • URL: http://www.iida.org • Represents professional interior designers, including designers of commercial, healthcare, hospitality, government, retail, residential facilities; educators; researchers; representatives of allied manufacturing sources. Conducts research, student programs, and continuing education programs for members. Has developed a code of ethics for the professional design membership.

INTERNAL AUDITING

See also: AUDITING

ABSTRACTS AND INDEXES

Business Periodicals Index. H. W. Wilson Co. • 11 times a year. Quarterly and annual cumulations. Price varies.

DIRECTORIES

Business Organizations, Agencies, and Publications Directory. Gale Cengage Learning. • 2003. $480.00. 15th edition. Over 40,000 entries describing 39 types of business information sources. Classified by type of organization, publication, or serviceIncludes state, national, and international agencies and organizations. Master index to names and keywords. Also includes e-mail addresses and web site URL's.

ENCYCLOPEDIAS AND DICTIONARIES

Blackwell Encyclopedic Dictionary of Accounting. Rashad Abdel-khalik. Blackwell Publishing. • 1997. $38.95. The editor is associated with the University of Florida. Contains definitions of key terms combined with longer articles written by various U. S. and foreign business educators. Includes bibliographies and index. (Blackwell Encyclopedia of Management Series).

Dictionary of Accounting Terms. Joel G. Siegel. Barron's Educational Series, Inc. • 2000. $13.95. Third edition. (Business Dictionaries Series).

HANDBOOKS AND MANUALS

Accountants' Handbook. Douglas R. Carmichael and Paul Rosenfeld. John Wiley and Sons, Inc. • 2003. $160.00. 10th edition. Two volumes. Vol. one, $95.00; vol. two, $95.00. Chapters are written by various accounting and auditing specialists.

Brink's Modern Internal Auditing. Robert R. Moeller and others. John Wiley and Sons, Inc. • 1999. $168.00. Fifth edition.

Corporate Fraud. Michael J. Comer. Ashgate Publishing Co. • 1997. Third edition. $139.95. Examines new risks of corporate fraud related to "electronic commerce, derivatives, computerization, empowerment, downsizing, and other recent developments." Covers fraud detection, prevention, and internal control systems. Published by Gower in England.

Internal Auditing Manual. RIA. • Annual. $260.00. Available online.

Internal Auditor's Handbook. Paul E. Heeschen. Institute of Internal Auditors, Inc. • 1984. $43.75.

Reliable Financial Reporting and Internal Control: A Global Implementation Guide. Dmitris N. Chorafas. John Wiley and Sons, Inc. • 2000. $75.00. Discusses financial reporting and control as related to doing business internationally.

INTERNET DATABASES

Rutgers Accounting Web (RAW). Rutgers University Accounting Research Center. Phone: (973)353-5172 Fax: (973)353-1283 • URL: http://www.rutgers.edu/accounting • RAW Web site provides extensive links to sources of national and international accounting information, such as the Big Six accounting firms, the Financial Accounting Standards Board (FASB), SEC filings (EDGAR), journals, publishers, software, the International Accounting Network, and "Internet's largest list of accounting firms in USA." Searching is offered. Fees: Free.

ONLINE DATABASES

Wilson Business Abstracts Online. H. W. Wilson Co. • Indexes and abstracts 600 major business periodicals, plus the *Wall Street Journal* and the business section of the *New York Times.* Indexing is from 1982, abstracting from 1990, with the two newspapers included from 1993. Updated weekly. Inquire as to online cost and availability. (*Business Periodicals Index* without abstracts is also available online.).

PERIODICALS AND NEWSLETTERS

Internal Auditing Alert. Warren, Gorham & Lamont Inc. • Description: Presents unique coverage that includes reviews and explanations of current Institute of Internal Auditors releases, appraisals of new audit techniques, and highlights of successful audit management practices.

Internal Auditor. Institute of Internal Auditors, Inc. • Bimonthly. $60.00 per year.

TRADE/PROFESSIONAL ASSOCIATIONS

Institute of Internal Auditors. 247 Maitland Ave., Altamonte Springs, FL 32701-4201. Phone: (407)937-1100 Fax: (407)937-1101 E-mail: iia@theiia.org • URL: http://www.theiia.org.

INTERNAL PUBLICATIONS

See: HOUSE ORGANS

INTERNAL REVENUE SERVICE

See: INCOME TAX

INTERNATIONAL AGENCIES

See also: ASSOCIATIONS; ORGANIZATION FOR ECONOMIC COOPERATION AND DEVELOPMENT; UNITED NATIONS

GENERAL WORKS

From GATT to the WTO: The Multilateral Trading System in the New Millennium. WTO Secretariat, editor. Kluwer Law International. • 2000. $79.50. Published by the World Trade Organization (http://www.wto.org). A collection of essays on the future of world trade, written on the occasion of the 50th anniversary of the multilateral trading system (GATT/WTO). The authors are described as "important academics in international trade.".

ABSTRACTS AND INDEXES

PAIS International in Print. Public Affairs Information Service, Inc. • Monthly. $850.00 per year; cumulations three times a year. Provides topical citations to the worldwide literature of public affairs, economics, demographics, sociology, and trade. Text in English; indexed materials in English,

French, German, Italian, Portuguese and Spanish.

UNDOC: Current Index (United Nations Documents). United Nations Publications. • Quarterly. $150.00. Annual cumulation on microfiche. Text in English.

BIBLIOGRAPHIES

Monthly Bibliography. United Nations Publications. • Monthly. $125.00 per year. Text in English and French.

CD-ROM DATABASES

PAIS on CD-ROM. Public Affairs Information Service, Inc. • Quarterly. $1,995.00 per year. Provides a CD-ROM version of the online service, *PAIS International.* Contains over 500,000 citations to the literature of contemporary social, political, and economic issues.

World Database of Business Information Sources on CD-ROM. Gale Cengage Learning. • Annual. Produced by Euromonitor. Presents Euromonitor's entire information source database on CD-ROM. Contains a worldwide total of about 35,000 publications, organizations, libraries, trade fairs, and online databases.

Yearbook of International Organizations PLUS. R. R. Bowker. • Annual. Compiled by the Union of International Organizations, Brussels. Includes the *Yearbook of International Organizations* and *Who's Who in International Organizations.*

DIRECTORIES

Encyclopedia of Associations: International Organizations. Gale Cengage Learning. • Annual. $695.00. Two volumes. Includes detailed information on approximately 24,000 international nonprofit membership organizations.

The EU Institutions' Register. Routledge Reference. • Covers: Over 5,900 key personnel in each of the major institutions, including: European Commission, European Parliament, Economic and Social Committee, Council of the European Union, Court of Justice, European Investment Bank, Court of Auditors, Committee of Regions and EU Agencies. Entries include: Contact information.

Europa Directory of International Organizations. Available from Taylor & Francis Group. • 2001. $250.00. Published by Europa Publications (http://www.europapublications.com). Describes about 1,700 associations and other organizations around the world.

Europa World Year Book. Routledge Reference. • Covers: Background and statistical information on recent history, government, economic affairs, geography and the current situation in every country of the world as well as providing an extensive listing of national key organizations and firms and about 1,650 international organization. Entries include: For international organizations--Name, address, principal officials, organization, function, activities, financial structure. For national organizations--Lists with names, addresses, officials, and key facts as appropriate, for the government, religious bodies, newspapers, radio and television stations, banks, trade associations, transport industry, tourism and cultural organizations, universities, research institutes.

Trade Associations amd Professional Bodies of Continental Europe. Available from Gale Cengage Learning. • 2003. $290.00. Second edition. Published by Graham & Whiteside. Provides detailed information on more than 3,600 business and professional organizations in Europe.

Washington: A Comprehensive Directory of the Key Institutions and Leaders in th e National Capitol Area. Columbia Books. • Annual. $149.00. Provides information on about 5,000 Washington, DC key businesses, government offices, non-profit organizations, and cultural institutions, with the names of about 25,000 principal executives.

Includes Washington media, law offices, foundations, labor unions, international organizations, clubs, etc.

World Directory of Marketing Information Sources. Available from Gale Cengage Learning. • 2003. $650.00. Fourth edition. Published by Euromonitor. Provides details on approximately 6,000 sources of marketing information, including publications, libraries, associations, market research companies, online databases, and governmental organizations. Coverage is worldwide.

World Directory of Trade and Business Associations. Available from Gale Cengage Learning. • 2003. $650.00. Fourth edition. Published by Euromonitor. Provides detailed information on approximately 3,000 trade associations in various countries of the world. Includes subject and geographic indexes.

Yearbook of International Organizations. Available from Gale Cengage Learning. • Annual. $1,460,00. Five volumes. Vol. 1 *Organization Descriptions and Cross-References*; Vol. 2 *Geographic*; Vol. 4 *Bibliographic*; Vol. 5 *Statistics, Visualizations and Patterns.* Published by K. G. Saur.

INTERNET DATABASES

Fedstats. Federal Interagency Council on Statistical Policy. Phone: (202)395-7254 • URL: http://www.fedstats.gov • Web site features an efficient search facility for full-text statistics produced by more than 100 federal agencies, including the Census Bureau, the Bureau of Economic Analysis, and the Bureau of Labor Statistics. Boolean searches can be made within one agency or for all agencies combined. Links are offered to international statistical bureaus, including the UN, IMF, OECD, UNESCO, Eurostat, and 20 individual countries. Fees: Free.

Publishers' Catalogues Home Page. EBSCO Publishing. Phone: (306)931-0020 Fax: (306)931-7667 E-mail: info@lights.com • URL: http://www.lights.com/publisher • Provides links to the Web home pages of about 1,700 U. S. publishers (including about 80 University presses) and publishers in 48 foreign countries. "International/Multinational Publishers" are included, such as the International Monetary Fund, the World Bank, and the World Trade Organization. Publishers are arranged in convenient alphabetical lists. Searching is offered. Fees: Free.

ONLINE DATABASES

Encyclopedia of Associations [Online]. Gale Cengage Learning. • Provides detailed information on about 170,000 U. S. and International non-profit organizations. Semiannual updates. Inquire as to online cost and availability.

PAIS International. Public Affairs Information Service, Inc. • Corresponds to the former printed publications, *PAIS Bulletin* (1976-90) and *PAIS Foreign Language Index* (1972-90), and to the current *PAIS International in Print* (1991 to date). Covers economic, political, and sociological material appearing in periodicals, books, government documents, and other publications. Updating is monthly. Inquire as to online cost and availability.

Research Centers and Services Directories. Gale Cengage Learning. • Contains profiles of about 30,000 research centers, organizations, laboratories, and agencies in 147 countries. Corresponds to the printed *Research Centers Directory, International Research Centers Directory, Government Research Directory,* and *Research Services Directory.* Updating is semiannual. Inquire as to online cost and availability.

PERIODICALS AND NEWSLETTERS

Government Publications News. Bernan Associates. • Monthly. Free. Controlled circulation newsletter providing information on recent publications from the U. S. Government Printing Office and selected international agencies.

World Trade Review: Economics, Law, International Institutions. Cambridge University Press. • Three times a year. Individuals, $48.00 pr year; institutions, $200.00 per year. Published in conjunction with the World Trade Organization (http://www.wto.org). Covers "issues of relevance to the multilateral trading system.".

STATISTICS SOURCES

WTO Annual Report (World Trade Organization). Available from Bernan Associates. • Annual. $80.00. Two volumes ($40.00 per volume). Published by the World Trade Organization. Volume one: *Annual Report.* Volume two: *International Trade Statistics.*

TRADE/PROFESSIONAL ASSOCIATIONS

United States Council for International Business. 1212 Ave. of the Americas, 21st Fl., New York, NY 10036. Phone: (212)354-4480 Fax: (212)575-0327 E-mail: info@uscib.org • URL: http://www.uscib.org • Formerly United States Council of the International Chamber of Commerce.

World Trade Centers Association. 420 Lexington Ave., Ste. 518, New York, NY 10170. Phone: 800-937-8886 or (212)432-2626 Fax: (212)488-0064 E-mail: wtca@wtca.org • URL: http://world.wtca.org/portal/site/wtcaonline • Regular members are organizations involved in the development or operation of a World Trade Center (WTC). Affiliate members are Chambers of Commerce, clubs, exhibit facilities or other international trade related organizations. Encourages expansion of world trade and international business relationships.

OTHER SOURCES

World Trade Organization Dispute Settlement Decisions: Bernan's Annotated Reporter. Bernan Press. • Dates vary. $75.00 per volume. Contains all World Trade Organization Panel Reports and Appellate Decisions since the establishment of the WTO in 1995. Includes such cases as "The Importation, Sale, and Distribution of Bananas.".

INTERNATIONAL ASSOCIATIONS

See: INTERNATIONAL AGENCIES

INTERNATIONAL BUSINESS

See also: EUROPEAN MARKETS; FOREIGN INVESTMENTS; FOREIGN TRADE; INTERNATIONAL MARKETING; MULTINATIONAL CORPORATIONS

GENERAL WORKS

Bargaining Across Borders: How to Conduct Business Successfully Anywhere in the World. Dean A. Foster. McGraw-Hill. • 1992. $14.95. Includes a consideration of non-negotiable cultural differences.

Building Parterships: Cooperarion Between the United Nations System and the Private Sector. United Nations Publications. • 2002. $27.50. Describes "the main types of cooperation between the UN and business." (A joint initiative of the UN Global Compact and the UN Department of Public Information in cooperation with the Prince of Wales International Business Leaders Forum).

Doing Business Internationally: The Guide to Cross Cultural Success. Danielle Walker and Thomas Walker. McGraw-Hill. • 2002. $29.95. Second edition.

International Business. Shenkar. John Wiley and Sons, Inc. • 2003. $88.95.

International Business and Multinational Enterprises. Stefan H. Robock and Kenneth Simmonds. McGraw-Hill. • 1988. $68.50. Fourth edition.

International Marketing. Philip R. Cateora and John Graham. McGraw-Hill. • 2001. $94.69. 11th edition. (Marketing Series).

Managing Globally: A Complete Guide to Competing Worldwide. Carl A. Nelson. McGraw-Hill. • 1993. $65.00. Emphasis is on global strategic management and tactics.

Successful Mergers, Acquisitions, and Strategic Alliances: How to Bridge Corporate Cultures. Irene Rodgers and others. McGraw-Hill. • 2002. $39.95. Provides advice on mergers involving companies in different countries.

Super Searchers Cover the World: The Online Secrets of International Business Researchers. Mary E. Bates. Information Today, Inc. • 2001. $24.95. Presents interviews with 15 experts in the area of online searching for international business information. (Super Searchers Series).

ABSTRACTS AND INDEXES

F & S Index: Europe. Gale Cengage Learning. • Monthly. $1,450.00 per year, including quarterly and annual cumulations. Provides annotated citations to marketing, business, financial, and industrial literature. Coverage of European business activity includes trade journals, financial magazines, business newspapers, and special reports. Formerly *Predicasts F & S Index: Europe.*

F & S Index: International. Gale Cengage Learning. • Monthly. $1,450.00 per year, including quarterly and annual cumulations. Provides annotated citations to marketing, business, financial, and industrial literature. Coverage of international business activity includes trade journals, financial magazines, business newspapers, and special reports. Areas included are Asia, Latin America, Africa, the Middle East, Oceania, and Canada.

NTIS Alerts: Business & Economics. National Technical Information Service. • Text: Semimonthly. $210.00 per year.

ALMANACS AND YEARBOOKS

Countries of the World and Their Leaders Yearbook. Gale Cengage Learning. • 2003. $260.00. Two volumes. Based on U. S. State Department data covering nearly 170 countries. Features "Background Notes on countries of the world." Also includes the CIA's list of "Chiefs of State and Cabinet Members of Foreign Governments," as well as key officers at U.S. embassies and other information.

Political Risk Yearbook. The PRS Group, Inc. • Annual. $2,415.00. Seven regional volumes; $345.00 per volume. Each volume covers a separate region of the world and assesses economic and political conditions as they relate to the risk of doing business.

Research in International Business and Finance. Elsevier. • Three times a year. Individuals, $50.00 per year; institutions, $195.00 per year.

BIBLIOGRAPHIES

International Business Finance: A Bibliography of Selected Business and Academic Sources. Raj Aggarwal. Greenwood Publishing Group, Inc. • 1984. $72.50.

International Business Information: How to Find It, How to Use It. Ruth A. Pagell and Michael Halperin. Glenlake Publishing Co., Ltd. • 2000. $65.00.

CD-ROM DATABASES

Asia Pacific Kompass on Disc. Available from Kompass USA, Inc. • Annual. CD-ROM provides information on more than 200,000 companies in Australia, China, Hong Kong, India, Korea, Malaysia, New Zealand, Philippines, Singapore, Thailand, and Taiwan. Classification system covers approximately 50,000 products and services.

Baltia Kompass Business Disc. Available from Kompass USA, Inc. • Semiannual. CD-ROM provides information on more than 29,000 companies in Estonia, Latvia, and Lithuania. Classification system covers approximately 50,000 products and services.

Benelux Kompass Business Disc. Available from Kompass USA, Inc. • Semiannual. CD-ROM provides information on more than 52,000 companies in Belgium, Netherlands, and Luxembourg. Classification system covers approximately 50,000 products and services.

Corporate Affiliations Plus. National Register Publishing, Reed Reference Publishing. • Quarterly. $1,995.00 per year. Provides CD-ROM discs corresponding to *Directory of Corporate Affiliations* and *Corporate Finance Bluebook.* Contains corporate financial services information and worldwide data on subsidiaries and affiliates.

East European Kompass on Disc. Available from Kompass USA, Inc. • Semiannual. CD-ROM provides information on more than 350,000 companies in Austria, Azerbaijan, Belarus, Croatia, Czech Republic, Estonia, Hungary, Latvia, Lithuania, Moldova, Poland, Romania, Russia, Slovakia, Slovenia, Ukraine, and Yugoslavia. Classification system covers approximately 50,000 products and services.

European Kompass on Disc. Available from Kompass USA, Inc. • Semiannual. CD-ROM provides information on more than 400,000 companies in Belgium, Denmark, France, Germany, Ireland, Italy, Luxembourg, Netherlands, Norway, Spain, Sweden, and UK. Classification system covers approximately 50,000 products and services.

Hoover's Company Capsules on CD-ROM. Hoover's, Inc. • Quarterly. $399.95 per year (single-user). Provides the CD-ROM version of *Hoover's Handbook of American Business, Hoover's Handbook of Emerging Companies, Hoover's Handbook of World Business, Hoover's Guide to Computer Companies, Hoover's Guide to Media Companies, Hoover's Handbook of Private Companies,* and various regional guides. Includes more than 11,000 profiles of companies.

Kompass CD-ROM Editions. Available from Kompass USA, Inc. • Semiannual or annual. Prices vary. CD-ROM versions of Kompass international trade directories are available for each of 36 major countries and nine world regions. Searching is provided for 50,000 product/service items and for many company details.

Kompass Concord CD-ROM. Available from Kompass USA, Inc. • Semiannual. CD-ROM provides information on more than 280,000 companies in 17 rapidly developing East European countries: Armenia, Azerbaijan, Belarus, Bulgaria, Czech Republic, Estonia, Hungary, Kazakhstan, Kyrgyzstan, Latvia, Lithuania, Moldova, Poland, Romania, Russia, Ukraine, and Uzbekistan. Classification system covers approximately 50,000 products and services.

Middle-East/Africa Kompass on Disc. Available from Kompass USA, Inc. • Annual. CD-ROM provides information on more than 140,000 companies in Algeria, Bahrain, Cyprus, Egypt, Lebanon, Mauritania, Morocco, Oman, Saudi Arabia, South Africa, Tunisia, and United Arab Emirates. Classification system covers approximately 50,000 products and services.

OECD Statistical Compendium. Organization for Economic Cooperation and Development. • Semiannual. $1,905.00 per year for 1 to 10 users. CD-ROM contains more than 730,000 monthly, quarterly, and annual time series for OECD countries, 1960 to date. Includes fully searchable data on agriculture, food, economic indicators, national accounts, employment, energy, finance, industry, technology, and foreign trade. Results can be displayed in various forms.

Scandinavian Kompass on Disc. Available from Kompass USA, Inc. • Semiannual. CD-ROM provides information on more than 120,000 companies in Denmark, Finland, Norway, and Sweden. Classification system covers approximately 50,000 products and services.

World Database of Business Information Sources on CD-ROM. Gale Cengage Learning. • Annual. Produced by Euromonitor. Presents Euromonitor's entire information source database on CD-ROM. Contains a worldwide total of about 35,000 publications, organizations, libraries, trade fairs, and online databases.

World Database of Consumer Brands and Their Owners on CD-ROM. Gale Cengage Learning. • Annual. $3,190.00. Produced by Euromonitor. Provides detailed information on CD-ROM for about 10,000 companies and 80,000 brands around the world. Covers 1,000 product sectors.

DIRECTORIES

China: A Directory and Sourcebook. Euromonitor International, Business Referene Div. • 1998. $590.00. Second edition. Describes about 500 companies in both China and Hong Kong. Sourcebook section provides 1,000 information sources.

Directory of American Firms Operating in Foreign Countries. Uniworld Business Publications. • Biennial. $355.00. Three volumes. Lists approximately 3,000 American companies with more than 34,500 subsidiaries and affiliates in 190 foreign countries.

Directory of Foreign Firms Operating in the United States. Uniworld Business Publications, Inc. • Biennial. $250.00. Lists about 2,400 foreign companies and 5,700 American affiliates. 75 countries are represented.

Energy Intelligence Top 100: Ranking the World's Top Oil Companies. Energy Intelligence Group, Inc. • Annual. $775.00. Provides detailed profiles of the world's 100 largest oil companies, with rankings by numerous key criteria. Includes both stockholder-owned and government-owned companies.

Hoover's Handbook of World Business: Profiles of Major European, Asian, Latin American, and Canadian Companies. Hoover's, Inc. • Annual. $165.00. Contains detailed profiles for approximately 300 large foreign companies. Includes indexes by industry, location, executive name, company name, and brand name.

Internet Resources and Services for International Business: A Global Guide. Lewis-Guodo Liu. Greenwood Publishing Group, Inc. • 1998. $62.95. Describes more than 2,500 business-related Web sites from 176 countries. Includes five major categories: general information, economics, business and trade, business travel, and contacts. Indexed by Web site name, country, and subject.

Japan Trade Directory. Japan External Trade Organization. • Covers: nearly 2,000 Japanese firms; trade and industrial associations. Entries include: For companies--Name, address, cable address, fax, e-mail, URL, name of chief executive officer, year established, line of business, amount of capital, annual sales, number of employees, bank references, office hours, trade names, whether catalog is available, languages spoken, countries with which business relationship is desired, products desired and those available for export, contact name and phone.

Kelly's Industrial Directory. Kelly's Directories. • Covers: Over 105,000 UK industrial companies. Entries include: Company name, address, phone, fax, telex, product or service.

Kompass International Trade Directories. Kompass International/Kompass USA, Inc. • Annual. Prices and volumes vary. Kompass directories are published internationally for each of more than 70 countries, from Algeria to Uzbekistan. The Kompass classification system covers more than 50,000 individual product and service categories, with most directories containing a tradename index and company profiles. Total number of companies in Kompass volumes is about two million.

Major Companies of Europe. Available from Gale Cengage Learning. • 2003. $1,895.00. Four volumes. Published by Graham & Whiteside. Approximately 24,000 major companies and key executives in European countries in all lines of business.

Major Companies of South West Asia. Available from Gale Cengage Learning. • 2001. $570.00. Fifth edition. Published by Graham and Whiteside. Provides information on 6,000 leading businesses in India, Turkey, Pakistan, Iran and other countries of the region.

Major Companies of the Arab World. Available from Gale Cengage Learning. • Annual. $955.00. Contains basic information on companies. Published by Graham & Whiteside, London.

Major Companies of the Far East and Australasia. Gale Cengage Learning. • Annual. $1,595.00. Three volumes. Published by Graham & Whiteside. Volume one: *South East Asia,* volume two: *East Asia,* volume three: *Australia, New Zealand, and Papua New Guinea.* Includes a total of 13,000 leading companies, with the names of 81,000 senior executives. (Volumes are available individually.).

Major Performance Rankings. Available from Gale Cengage Learning. • 2003. $1,190.00. Second edition. Published by Euromonitor. Ranks 2,500 leading consumer product companies worldwide by various kinds of business and financial data, such as sales, profit, and market share. Includes international, regional, and country rankings.

Mergent International Manual and News Reports. Mergent, Inc. • Annual. Price on application. Financial and other information about 3,000 publicly-owned corporations in 100 countries. Formerly *Moody's International Manual and News Reports.*

Principal International Businesses: The World Marketing Directory. • Annual. $5,000. Provides information about 50,000 major businesses located in over 145 countries. Geographic arrangement with company name and product indexes.

Standard Directory of International Advertisers and Agencies: The International Red Book. National Register Publishing. • Annual. $629.00. Includes more than 5,000 foreign companies and their advertising agencies. Geographic, company name, personal name, and trade name indexes are provided.

The Top 5,000 European Companies 2002. Available from Gale Cengage Learning. • 2002. $645.00. Third edition. Published by Graham & Whiteside. In addition to about 5,000 manufacturing and service companies, includes the 500 largest banks in Europe and the 100 largest insurance companies.

The Top 5,000 Global Companies 2002. Available from Gale Cengage Learning. • 2002. $730.00. Third edition. Published by Graham & Whiteside. Includes about 5,000 manufacturing and service companies worldwide, plus the world's 500 largest banks and 100 largest insurance companies.

Trade Directories of the World. Croner Publications, Inc. • Annual. 100.00. Looseleaf service. Monthly supplements. Lists over 3,300 publications.

Who Owns Whom. Dun & Bradstreet Corp. • Covers: In four regional volumes, approximately 320,000 company affiliates and subsidiaries of more than 23,000 companies in Australia and the Far East, North America, the United Kingdom and Ireland, and Continental Europe. Entries include: Ultimate parent and country, parent name, address, phone, place of incorporation, Standard Industrial Classification (SIC) code, trade investments, direct subsidiaries.

World Business Directory 2001. Gale Cengage Learning. • 2003. $645.00. Four volumes. 11th edition. Covers about 136,000 companies in 180 countries.

World Retail Directory and Sourcebook. Available from Gale Cengage Learning. • 2003. $1,250.00. Fifth edition. Published by Euromonitor. Provides information on more than 2,400 retailers around the world. Information sources, conferences, trade fairs, and special libraries are also listed.

ENCYCLOPEDIAS AND DICTIONARIES

Blackwell Encyclopedic Dictionary of International Management. John J. O'Connell, editor. Blackwell Publishers. • 1999. $130.95. The editor is associated with the American Graduate School of International Management. Contains definitions of key terms combined with longer articles written by various U. S. and foreign business educators. Includes bibliographies and index. (Encyclopedia of Management Series).

Dictionary of International Business Terms. John J. Capela. Barron's Educational Series, Inc. • 2000. $14.95. Second edition. (Business Dictionaries Series).

International Encyclopedia of Business and Management. Malcolm Warner, editor. Cengage Learning. • 2001. $1,899.00.Second edition. Eight volumes. Contains more than 500 articles on global management issues. Includes extensive bibliographies, cross references, and an index of key words and phrases.

HANDBOOKS AND MANUALS

Business Information Handbook. David Mort. Available from Gale Cengage Learning. • 2003. $140.00. Published by K. G. Saur. Serves as a general guide to the world of business information.

Handbook of International Management. John Wiley and Sons, Inc. • 1988. $280.00.

Handbook of the Nations: A Brief Guide to the Economy, Government, Land, Demographics, Communications, and National Defense Establishments of Each of 206 Nations and Other Political Entities. Gale Cengage Learning. • 2003. $180.00. 22nd edition. Includes maps and tables.

International Business Handbook. Vishnu H. Kirpalani, editor. Haworth Press, Inc. • 1990. $89.95. (International Business Series: No. 1).

International Business Information on the Web: Searcher Magazine's Guide to Sites and Strategies for Global Business Research. Sheri R. Lanza. Information Today, Inc. • 2001. $29.95. (CyberAge Books.).

INTERNET DATABASES

Ebusiness Forum: Global Business Intelligence for the Digital Age. Economist Intelligence Unit (EIU), Economist Group. Phone: 800-938-4685 or (212)554-0600 Fax: (212)586-0248 E-mail: newyork@eiu.com • URL: http://www. ebusinessforum.com • Web site provides information relating to multinational business, with an emphasis on activities in specific countries. Includes rankings of countries for "e-business readiness," additional data on the political, economic, and business environment in 180 nations ("Doing Business in.."), and "Today's News Analysis." Fees: Free, but registration is required for access to all content. Daily updates.

Factiva. Dow Jones Reuters Business Interactive, LLC. Phone: 800-369-7466 or (609)452-1511 Fax: (609)520-5770 E-mail: solutions@factiva.com • URL: http://www.factiva.com • Fee-based Web site provides "global news and business information through Web sites and content integration solutions." Includes Dow Jones and Reuters newswires, The Wall Street Journal, and more than 7,000 other sources of current news, historical articles, market research reports, and investment analysis. Content

includes 96 major U. S. newspapers, 900 non-English sources, trade publications, media transcripts, country profiles, news photos, etc.

FedWorld: A Program of the United States Department of Commerce. National Technical Information Service. Phone: (703)605-6000 Fax: (703)605-6900 E-mail: webmaster@fedworld.gov • URL: http://www.fedworld.gov • Web site offers "a comprehensive central access point for searching, locating, ordering, and acquiring government and business information." Emphasis is on searching the Web pages, databases, and government reports of a wide variety of federal agencies. Fees: Free.

Financial Times: Where Information Becomes Intelligence. FT Group. Phone: 800-628-8088 • URL: http://www.ft.com • Web site provides extensive data and information relating to international business and finance, with daily updates. Includes Markets Today, Company News, Economic Indicators, Equities, Currencies, Capital Markets, Euro Prices, etc. Fees: Free (registration required).

Nexis.com. Lexis-Nexis Group. Phone: 800-227-4908 or (937)865-6800 Fax: (937)865-6909 E-mail: webmaster@prod.lexis-nexis.com • URL: http://www.nexis.com • Fee-based Web site offers searching of about 2.8 billion documents in some 30,000 news, business, and legal information sources. Features include a subject directory covering 1,200 topics in 34 categories and a Company Dossier containing information on more than 500,000 public and private companies. Boolean searching is offered.

Trade Show Center. Global Sources/Trade Media Holdings Ltd. [Singapore]. Phone: (656)574-2800 E-mail: service@globalsources.com • URL: http://www.globalsources.com/TRADESHW/TRDSHFRM.HTM • Free Web site provides current, detailed information on more than 1,000 major trade shows worldwide, including events in the U. S., but with an emphasis on "Asia and Greater China." Searching is offered by product, supplier, country, and month of year. Includes links to "Trade Information.".

Wall Street Journal Interactive Edition. Dow Jones & Co., Inc. Phone: 800-369-2834 or (212)416-2000 Fax: (212)416-2658 E-mail: inquiries@interactive.wsj.com • URL: http://www.wsj.com • Fee-based Web site providing online searching of worldwide information from the *The Wall Street Journal.* Includes "Company Snapshots," "The Journal's Greatest Hits," "Index to Market Data," "Journal Links," etc. Financial price quotes are available. Fees: $49.00 per year; $29.00 per year to print subscribers.

ONLINE DATABASES

Country Report Services. The PRS Group. • Provides full text of reports describing the business risks and opportunities currently existing in more than 150 countries of the world. Contains a wide variety of statistics and forecasts relating to economics political and social conditions. Also includes demographics, tax, and currency information. Updated monthly. Inquire as to online cost and availability.

Globalbase. Gale Cengage Learning. • Provides more than one million online summaries of business, industrial, and economic news reports from more than 1,000 publications worldwide. Covers a wide range of material appearing in international trade journals, professional magazines, and newspapers. Time period is 1984 to date, with weekly updates. Inquire as to online cost and availability.

Moody's Corporate News: International. Moody's Investors Service, Inc. • Provides financial and other business news relating to over 5,000 corporations in 100 countries, excluding the U. S. Time period is

1983 to date, with weekly updates. Inquire as to on-line cost and availability.

Worldscope. Thomson Financial. • Online service provides detailed financial and other information on more than 32,000 publicly-owned companies in 50 countries. Includes business description, balance sheets, earnings statements, senior officers, major shareholders, financial ratios, and 20-year historical data. Monthly updates. Inquire as to online cost and availability.

PERIODICALS AND NEWSLETTERS

Acquisitions Monthly. Thomson Financial. • Monthly. $790.00 per year. Published in London. Provides detailed information, commentary, and statistics on merger, acquisition, and buyout activity in Europe, the U.S., and Asia.

Business Week International: The World's Only International Newsweekly of Business. McGraw-Hill. • Weekly. $95.00 per year.

Canadian Business. Canadian Business Media. • Biweekly. $64.95 per year. Edited for corporate managers and executives, this is a major periodical in Canada covering a variety of business, economic, and financial topics. Emphasis is on the top 500 Canadian corporations.

The Economist. Economist Intelligence Unit. • 51 times a year. $125.00 per year.

Energy Compass. Energy Intelligence Group. • Description: Focuses on worldwide geopolitical developments and their impact on the oil industry. Also includes marketing and trading information, political risk assessment, and current events and trends. **Remarks:** Available via fax, e-mail, or online.

EuroWatch. LRP Publications. • Description: Provides news and analysis from European capitals and Washington, D.C. concerning how the United States' and other business interests are affected by the European Community's program to remove national barriers and create a single market for the trade and movement of goods, services, capital, and labor.

Export Today: The Global Business and Technology Magazine. Trade Communications, Inc. • Monthly. $49.00 per year. Edited for corporate executives to provide practical information on international business and exporting.

International Market Alert. United Communications Group. • Description: Provides a fax service covering financial markets, world economy developments, foreign exchange, and U.S. interest rates.

Journal of Global Marketing. Haworth Press, Inc. • Quarterly. $460.00 per year. Includes print and on-line editions.

Journal of International Consumer Marketing. Haworth Press, Inc. • Quarterly. Individuals, $80.00 per year; institutions, $150.00 per year.

Journal of International Marketing. American Marketing Association. • Members $45.00; non-members, $80.00 per year institutions, $150.00 per year.

Journal of Teaching in International Business. Haworth Press, Inc. • Quarterly. Institutions, $315.00 per year.

Journal of World Business. Columbia University, Trustees of Columbia University. Elsevier. • Quarterly. Individuals, $131.00 per year; institutions, $315.00 per year.

Political Risk Letter. The PRS Group. • Description: Offers concise political and economic forecasts for both 18 month and 5 year time spans. Provides country risk forecasts and analysis on 100 countries around the world and provides indepth coverage on 20 countries.

The Wall Street Journal. Dow Jones & Co., Inc. • Daily. $189.00 per year. Covers news and trends

relating to business, industry, finance, the economy, and international commerce. Provides extensive price and other data for the securities, commodity, options, futures, foreign exchange, and money markets.

World Trade: For U.S. Executives with Global Vision. BNP Media. • Monthly. $24.00 per year. Edited for senior management of U. S. companies engaged in international business and trade.

RESEARCH CENTERS AND INSTITUTES

Bureau of Economic and Business Research. University of Illinois at Urbana-Champaign, 1206 S. Sixth St., 403 Wohlers Hall, Champaign, IL 61820. Phone: (217)333-2330 Fax: (217)244-7410 E-mail: g-oldman@uiuc.edu • URL: http://www.business. uiuc.edu/research.

International Business Institute. University of Toledo, 1040 Stranaham Hall, 2801 W. Bancroft St., Toledo, OH 43606. Phone: (419)530-2068 Fax: (419)530-2101.

Mack Center on Managing Technological Innovation. University of Pennsylvania, 3620 Locust Walk, Suite 1400, Philadelphia, PA 19104. Phone: (215)898-2104 Fax: (215)573-2129 E-mail: dayg@wharton.upenn.edu • URL: http://www. emertech.wharton.upenn.edu • Conducts research related to international business. Formerly Huntsman Center for Global Competition and Innovation.

STATISTICS SOURCES

Consumer Asia. Available from Gale Cengage Learning. • Annual. $1,090.00. Published by Euromonitor. Provides statistical andanalytical surveys of factors affecting Asian consumer markets: energy, labor, population, finance, debt, tourism, consumer expenditures, household characteristics, etc. Emphasis is on Hong Kong, Singapore, Taiwan, South Korea, Indonesia, and Malaysia.

Country Data Forecasts. Bank of America, World Information Services, Dept. 3015. • Looseleaf, with semiannual updates. $495.00 per year. Provides detailed statistical tables for 80 countries, showing historical data and five-year forecasts of 23 key economic series. Includes population, inflation figures, debt, per capita income, foreign trade, exchange rates, and other data.

Encyclopedia of Global Industries. Gale Cengage Learning. • 2002. $450.00. Third edition. Provides detailed statistical information on 115 industries. Coverage is international, with country and subject indexes.

International Marketing Data and Statistics. Available from Gale Cengage Learning. • Annual. $530. 00. Published by Euromonitor. Contains statistics on population, economic factors, energy, consumer expenditures, prices, and other items affecting marketing in 158 countries of the world.

International Survey of Business Expectations. Dun & Bradstreet Corp., Economic Analysis Dept. • Quarterly. $40.00 per year. A survey of international business executives regarding their quarterly expectations for sales, profits, prices, inventories, employment, and new orders. Results are given for each of 14 major foreign countries and the U. S.

International Trade Statistics Yearbook. United Nations Statistical Office. United Nations Publications. • Annual. $135.00. Two volumes.

Manufacturing Worldwide: Industry Analysis Statistics. Gale Cengage Learning. • 1999. $240.00. Third edition. A guide to worldwide economic activity in 500 product lines within 119 countries. Includes 37 detailed industry profiles. Name, address, phone, fax, employment, and ranking are shown for major companies worldwide in each industry sector.

OECD Information Technology Outlook 2000: ICTs, E-Commerce and the Information Economy.

Organization for Economic Cooperation and Development. • 2000. $72.00. Provides data on information and communications technology (ICT) and electronic commerce in 11 OECD nations (includes U. S.). Coverage includes network infrastructure, electronic payment systems, financial transaction technologies, intelligent agents, global navigation systems, and portable flat panel display technologies.

Panorama of European Business. Available from Bernan Associates. • Annual. $65.00. Presents statistical data for manufacturing and service industries in major European countries. Text in English, French and Spanish.

Retail Trade International. Gale Cengage Learning. • 2002. $1,990.00. 11th edition. Eight volumes. Published by Euromonitor. Presents comprehensive data on retail trends in 52 countries. Includes textual analysis and profiles of major retailers. Covers Europe, Asia, the Middle East, Africa and the Americas.

Services: Statistics on Value Added and Employment. Organization for Economic Cooperation and Development. • 2000. $69.00. Provides 10-year data on service industry employment and output (value added) for all OECD countries. Covers such industries as telecommunications, business services, and information technology services.

Structural Statistics for Industry and Services: Core Data. Organization for Economic Cooperation and Development. • Annual. $63.00. Provides annual data for eight years for both industrial and service sectors. Industries include mining, manufacturing, utilities, and construction. Statistics for OECD countries cover production, value added, investment, employment, wages, hours worked, and number of establishments.

TRADE/PROFESSIONAL ASSOCIATIONS

International Executive Service Corps. 1900 M St. NW, Ste. 500, Washington, DC 20036. Phone: 800-243-4372 or (202)589-2600 Fax: (202)326-0289 E-mail: iesc@iesc.org • URL: http://www.iesc.org • Provides technical and managerial assistance to enterprises, organizations and government bodies in emerging democracies and developing countries. Focuses on the knowledge, skill and experience of its 12,000 industry experts. Maintains a network of experts that includes high-level professionals drawn from nearly every area of private enterprise, government and non-governmental organizations; Geek-corps division includes experts in communications and information technology and is committed to closing the digital divide.

OTHER SOURCES

Country Finance. Economist Intelligence Unit. • Annual $425.00 per year. Discusses banking and financial conditions in each of 47 countries. Includes foreign exchange regulations, the currency outlook, sources of capital, financing techniques, and tax considerations.

Country Forecasts. The PRS Group. • Semiannual. $695.00 per year per country. $375.00 per volume. Five-year forecasts are provided for each of 62 countries. Analyzes economic, political, and business prospects.

Country Reports. Economist Intelligence Unit. • Quarterly. $455.00 per year per country or country group. Comprehensive economic and political information is presented for 180 countries in 99 *Country Reports*, with 12 to 18 month forecasts. Each subscription includes an annual *Country Profile* containing statistical tables.

Country Risk Monitor. Bank of America, World Information Services, Dept. 3015. • Looseleaf, with semiannual updates. $495.00 per year. Provides rankings of 80 countries according to current and future business risk. Utilizes key economic ratios and benchmarks for countries in a manner similar to financial ratio analysis for industries.

Country Risk Service. Economist Intelligence Unit. • Quarterly. $695.00 per year per country. Two-year risk forecasts are provided for each of 82 countries. Business, political, economic, and credit risks are analyzed.

Foreign Labor Trends. Available from U. S. Government Printing Office. • Irregular (50 to 60 issues per year, each on an individual country). $95.00 per year. Prepared by various American Embassies. Issued by the Bureau of International Labor Affairs, U. S. Department of Labor. Covers labor developments in important foreign countries, including trends in wages, working conditions, labor supply, employment, and unemployment.

Foreign Tax and Trade Briefs. LexisNexis Matthew Bender. • Quarterly. $550.00 per year. Two looseleaf volumes. The latest tax and trade information for over 100 foreign countries.

International Business Planning: Law and Taxation (United States). William P. Streng and Jeswald W. Salacuse. LexisNexis Matthew Bender. • $1,483.00. Six looseleaf volumes. Periodic supplementation.

International Country Risk Guide. The PRS Group, Inc. • Monthly. $3,795.00 per year. Each issue provides detailed analysis of a group of countries, covering financial risks, political trends, and economic developments. More than 130 countries are covered during the course of a year, with specific business risk point ratings assigned.

International Tax Planning Manual-Corporations. CCH, Inc. • Two looseleaf volumes. Periodic supplementation. Price on application. Tax strategies for doing business in 38 major countries.

Investing, Licensing, and Trading. Economist Intelligence Unit. • Semiannual. $345.00 per year for each country. Key laws, rules, and licensing provisions are explained for each of 60 countries. Information is provided on political conditions, markets, price policies, foreign exchange practices, labor, and export-import.

World Business Rankings Annual. Gale Cengage Learning. • 1998. $189.00. Provides 2,500 ranked lists of international companies, compiled from a variety of published sources. Each list shows the "top ten" in a particular category. Keyword indexing, a country index, and citations are provided.

INTERNATIONAL CORPORATIONS

See: MULTINATIONAL CORPORATIONS

INTERNATIONAL DEVELOPMENT

See: DEVELOPING AREAS

INTERNATIONAL ECONOMICS

See also: ECONOMICS; INTERNATIONAL BUSINESS

GENERAL WORKS

Economic and Social Survey of Asia and the Pacific. United Nations Publications. • Annual. $65.00. Emphasis is on trends in economic policy and economic development strategies.

Global Employment Trends. Claire Harasty and Dorothea Schmidt. International Labour Organization. • 2003. $22.95. Provides an analysis of "current labour market trends around the world." Emphasis is on how the "global economic downturn" has af-

fected various regions and economic groups.

International Economics. Dennis R. Appleyard and Alfred J. Field. McGraw-Hill. • 2000. $105.00. Fourth edition.

Managing World Economic Change: International Political Economy. Prentice Hall PTR. • 2000. Third edition. Price on application.

Modern International Economics. Wilfred Ethier. W. W. Norton & Co., Inc. • 1995. $106.50. Third edition.

The World in 2020: Power, Culture, and Prosperity. Hamish McRae. Harvard Business School Publishing. • 1995. $14.95. States that the best predictor of economic success will be a nation's creativity and social responsibility.

ABSTRACTS AND INDEXES

PAIS International in Print. Public Affairs Information Service, Inc. • Monthly. $850.00 per year; cumulations three times a year. Provides topical citations to the worldwide literature of public affairs, economics, demographics, sociology, and trade. Text in English; indexed materials in English, French, German, Italian, Portuguese and Spanish.

ALMANACS AND YEARBOOKS

Economic Survey of Europe. United Nations Publications. • Three times a year. Price varies. Provides yearly analysis and review of the European economy, including Eastern Europe and the USSR. Text in English.

State of the World [year]. Worldwatch Institute. • Annual. $16.95. Provides yearly analysis of factors influencing the global environment.

Worldmark Yearbook. Gale Cengage Learning. • 2001. $295.00. Three volumes. Covers economic, social, and political events in about 230 countries. Includes statistical data, directories, and a bibliography.

BIBLIOGRAPHIES

Globalization: A Bibliography with Indexes. Marina Elbakidze. Nova Science Publishers, Inc. • 2002. $59.00. Covers various aspects of globalization: effect on society, trade, economics, politics, business, technology, and the environment. Includes author, title, and subject indexes.

International Bibliography of the Social Sciences: Economics. British Library of Political and Economic Science. Routledge. • 1995. $250.00. (International Bibliography of the Social Sciences Series).

OECD Catalogue of Publications. Organization for Economic Cooperation and Development. Available from OECD Publications and Information Center. • Online only. No print edition.

CD-ROM DATABASES

EconLit. Available from SilverPlatter Information, Inc. • Monthly. Single-user, $1,600.00 per year. Provides CD-ROM citations, with abstracts, to articles from more than 500 economics journals. Time period is 1969 to date. Produced by the American Economic Association.

OECD Statistical Compendium. Organization for Economic Cooperation and Development. • Semiannual. $1,905.00 per year for 1 to 10 users. CD-ROM contains more than 730,000 monthly, quarterly, and annual time series for OECD countries, 1960 to date. Includes fully searchable data on agriculture, food, economic indicators, national accounts, employment, energy, finance, industry, technology, and foreign trade. Results can be displayed in various forms.

PAIS on CD-ROM. Public Affairs Information Service, Inc. • Quarterly. $1,995.00 per year. Provides a CD-ROM version of the online service, *PAIS International.* Contains over 500,000 citations to the literature of contemporary social, political, and economic issues,

USA Trade. U. S. Department of Commerce. • Monthly. $650.00 per year. Provides over 150,000 trade-related data series on CD-ROM. Includes full text of many government publications. Specific data is included on national income, labor, price indexes, foreign exchange, technical standards, and international markets. Website address is http://www.stat-usa.gov/.

DIRECTORIES

Capital for Shipping. Available from Informa Publishing Group Ltd. • Annual. $128.00. Published in the UK by Lloyd's List (http://www.lloydslist.com). Consists of a "Financial Directory" and a "Legal Directory," listing international ship finance providers and international law firms specializing in shipping. (Included with subscription to *Lloyd's Shipping Economist.*).

ENCYCLOPEDIAS AND DICTIONARIES

Blackwell Encyclopedic Dictionary of Managerial Economics. Robert McAuliffe, editor. Blackwell Publishers. • 1999. $138.95. The editor is associated with Boston College. Contains definitions of key terms combined with longer articles written by various U. S. and foreign business educators. Includes bibliographies and index. *Blackwell Encyclopedia of Management Series.*

Worldmark Encyclopedia of National Economies. Gale Cengage Learning. • 2002. $325.00. Four volumes. Covers both the current and historical development of the economies of 200 foreign nations. Includes analysis and statistics.

INTERNET DATABASES

Gateway to the European Union. European Union. E-mail: pressoffice@eurostat.cec.be • URL: http://www.europa.eu.int • Web site provides access to a wide variety of EU information, including statistics (Eurostat), news, policies, publications, key issues, and official exchange rates for the euro. Includes links to the European Central Bank, the European Investment Bank, and other institutions. Fees: Free.

ONLINE DATABASES

EconLit. American Economic Association. • Covers the worldwide literature of economics as contained in selected monographs and about 550 journals. Subjects include microeconomics, macroeconomics, economic history, inflation, money, credit, finance, accounting theory, trade, natural resource economics, and regional economics. Time period is 1969 to present, with monthly updates. Inquire as to online cost and availability.

OECD Main Economic Indicators. Organization for Economic Cooperation and Development. • International statistics provided by OECD, 1960 to date. Monthly updates. Inquire as to online cost and availability.

PAIS International. Public Affairs Information Service, Inc. • Corresponds to the former printed publications, *PAIS Bulletin* (1976-90) and *PAIS Foreign Language Index* (1972-90), and to the current *PAIS International in Print* (1991 to date). Covers economic, political, and sociological material appearing in periodicals, books, government documents, and other publications. Updating is monthly. Inquire as to online cost and availability.

PERIODICALS AND NEWSLETTERS

Asia Pacific Economic Review: Bridging Pacific Rim Business and Society. Zencore, Inc. • Monthly. $35.00 per year. Includes special issues on individual countries: Taiwan, Malayasia, China/Hong Kong, Japan, and Korea.

The Economist. Economist Intelligence Unit. • 51 times a year. $125.00 per year.

Financial Times Currency Forecaster: Consensus Forecasts of the Worldwide Currency and Economic Outlook. Briefings Publishing Group. • Monthly. $695.00 per year. Newsletter. Provides forecasts of foreign currency exchange rates and economic conditions. Supplement available: *Mid-Month Global Financial Report.*

The George Washington International Law Review. George Washington University, National Law Center. • Quarterly. $28.00 per year. Articles dealing with a variety of topics within the area of private international comparative law and economics. Formerly *George Washington Journal of International Law and Economics.*

International Economic Scoreboard. The Conference Board Inc. • Description: Provides current data on the business outlook in 11 major industrial countries: Australia, Canada, France, West Germany, Italy, Japan, Korea, New Zealand, Taiwan, the United Kingdom, and the U.S. **Remarks:** A source for additional information on this indicator system and its uses is available at the Center for International Business Cycle Research, Columbia University Business School.

International Review of Applied Economics. Routledge. • Quarterly. Individuals, $310.00 per year; institutions, $1,007.00 per year.

The Journal of International Trade and Economic Development. Taylor and Francis Group. • Quarterly. Individuals, $81.00 per year; institutions, $529.00 per year. Emphasizes the effect of trade on the economies of developing nations.

Review of International Political Economy. Taylor and Francis Group. • Quarterly. Individuals, $86.00 per year; institutions, $346.00 per year. Includes articles on international trade, finance, production, and consumption.

World Trade Review: Economics, Law, International Institutions. Cambridge University Press. • Three times a year. Individuals, $48.00 pr year; institutions, $200.00 per year. Published in conjunction with the World Trade Organization (http://www.wto.org). Covers "issues of relevance to the multilateral trading system.".

RESEARCH CENTERS AND INSTITUTES

Institute for International Economics. 1750 Massachusetts Ave., N.W., Washington, DC 20036. Phone: (202)328-9000 Fax: (202)328-5432 E-mail: alreeves@iie.com • URL: http://www.iie.com • Research fields include a wide range of international economic issues, including foreign exchange rates.

STATISTICS SOURCES

Country Outlooks. Pyramid Research. • Looseleaf. $495.00 per year. Covers 81 major countries, with each country updated quarterly. Provides detailed economic data and financial forecasts, including tables of key economic indicators.

Country Profile: Annual Survey of Political and Economic Background. Economist Intelligence Unit. • Annual. $245.00 per country or country group. Contains statistical tables "showing the last 6 year run of macro-economic indicators, and an overview of a country's politics, economy and industry." Covers 180 countries in 115 annual editions.

Economic Survey of Latin America and the Caribbean. United Nations Publications. • Annual. $50.00. Includes reports on economic trends in 20 Latin American countries.

Eurostat Yearbook: A Statistical View on Europe. Available from Bernan Associates. • Annual. $65.00. Published by European Communities (http://www.europa.eu.int/comm/eurostat/). Statistical topics include economics, national income, population, land, agriculture, environment, government, housing, and crime. Covers "every country in Europe and the European Union.".

Handbook of International Economic Statistics. Available from National Technical Information Service. • Annual. $40.00. Prepared by U. S. Central Intelligence Agency. Provides basic statistics for

comparing worldwide economic performance, with an emphasis on Europe, including Eastern Europe.

The Little Data Book. The World Bank. • 2003. $15.00. Contains "key development data for 208 countries," including country profiles and 54 statistical indicators relating to such factors as population, economics, trade, technology, finance, and environment.

Main Economic Indicators. OECD Publication and Information Center. • Monthly. $450.00 per year. "The essential source of timely statistics for OECD member countries." Includes a wide variety of business, economic, and industrial data for the 29 OECD nations.

Main Economic Indicators: Historical Statistics. OECD Publications and Information Center. • Annual. $475.00. Includes online edition.

Measuring Globalisation: The Role of Multinationals in OECD Economies. Organization for Economic Cooperation and Development. • Biennial. $85.00. Two volumes. Volume one provides extensive statistics for the multinational corporate manufacturing sector. Volume two covers the services sector.

MiniAtlas of Global Development. The World Bank. • 2003. $7.00. Presents concise data for 208 countries, based on the *World Bank Atlas* and other World Bank publications. Includes maps, tables, and graphs summarizing social, economic, and environmental statistics.

Nations of the World: A Political, Economic, and Business Handbook. Grey House Publishing. • 2002. $135.00. Third edition. Includes descriptive data on economic characteristics, population, gross domestic product (GDP), banking, inflation, agriculture, tourism, and other factors. Covers "all the nations of the world.".

OECD Economic Outlook. OECD Publications and Information Center. • Semiannual. Price on application. $95.00 per year. Contains a wide range of economic and monetary data relating to the member countries of the Organization for Economic Cooperation and Development. Includes about 100 statistical tables and graphs, with 24-month forecasts for each of the OECD countries. Provides extensive review and analysis of recent economic trends.

OECD Economic Surveys. OECD Publications and Information Center. • Annual. $26.00 each. These are separate, yearly reviews for each of the economies of the industrialized nations that comprise the OECD. Each edition includes forecasts, analyses, and detailed statistical tables for the country being surveyed. (The combined series, one annual volume for each nation, is available at $485.00.).

OECD in Figures. Organization for Economic Cooperation and Development. • Annual. $13.00. A "pocket data book" providing a summary of key statistics for OECD countries, including economic growth, employment, education, the environment, and transportation.

Services: Statistics on International Transactions. Organization for Economic Cooperation and Development. Available from OECD Publications and Information Center. • Annual. $71.00. Presents a compilation and assessment of data on OECD member countries' international trade in services. Covers four major categories for 20 years: travel, transportation, government services, and other services.

Source OECD. Economic Outlook Statistics. • 2000. $325.00. Includes country and global forecasts of over 170 economic and business variables. Actual data is shown for two years, with forecasts up to ten years.

Statistical Handbook on Poverty in the Developing World. Chandrika Kaul. Greenwood Publishing

Group, Inc. • 1999. $69.95. Provides international coverage, including special sections on women and children, and on selected cities. (Statistical Handbooks Series).

UNCTAD Handbook of Statistics. United Nations Conference on Trade and Development. United Nations Publications. • Annual. $80.00. Contains a "comprehensive collection of statistical data relevant to the analysis of world trade, investment, and development." Includes rank-orderings, growth rates, and 20-year time series.

The World Economic Factbook. Available from Gale Cengage Learning. • Annual. $530.00. Published by Euromonitor. Presents key economic facts and figures for each of 200 countries, including details of chief industries, export-import trade, currency, political risk, household expenditures, and the economic situation in general.

World Economic Outlook: A Survey by the Staff of the International Monetary Fund. International Monetary Fund, Publications Services. • Semiannual. $78.00 per year. Presents international statistics combined with forecasts and analyses of the world economy.

World Economic Prospects: A Planner's Guide to International Market Conditions. Available from Gale Cengage Learning. • 2002. $490.00. Second edition. Published by Euromonitor. Ranks countries by specific economic characteristics, such as gross domestic product (GDP) per capita and short term growth prospects. Discusses the economic situation, prospects, and market potential of each of the countries.

The World Economy: A Millennial Perspective. Angus Maddison. Organization for Economic Cooperation and Development. • 2001. $63.00. "...covers the development of the entire world economy over the past 2000 years," including data on world population and gross domestic product (GDP) since the year 1000, and exports since 1820. Focuses primarily on the disparity in economic performance among nations over the very long term. More than 200 statistical tables and figures are provided.

World Factbook. U.S. National Technical Information Service. • Annual. $83.00. Prepared by the Central Intelligence Agency. For all countries of the world, provides current economic, demographic, geographic, communications, government, defense force, and illicit drug trade information (where applicable).

TRADE/PROFESSIONAL ASSOCIATIONS

Organisation for Economic Co-Operation and Development. 2, rue Andre Pascal, F-75775 Paris Cedex 16, France. Phone: 33 1 45248200 E-mail: webmaster@oecd.org • URL: http://www.oecd.org.

OTHER SOURCES

Consensus Forecasts: A Worldwide Survey. Consensus Economics Inc. • Monthly. $565.00 per year. Provides a survey of more than 200 "prominent" financial and economic forecasters, covering 20 major countries. Two-year forecasts for each country include future growth, inflation, interest rates, and exchange rates. Each issue contains analysis of business conditions in various countries.

World Economic and Social Survey: Trends and Policies in the World Economy. United Nations Publications. • Annual. $55.00. Includes discussion and "an extensive statistical annex of economic, trade, and financial indicators, incorporating current data and forecasts.".

World Economic Situation and Prospects. United Nations Publications. • Annual. $15.00. Serves as a supplement and update to the UN *World Economic and Social Survey.*

INTERNATIONAL FINANCE

See also: FOREIGN EXCHANGE; FOREIGN INVESTMENTS; INTERNATIONAL MONETARY FUND (IMF); MONEY

GENERAL WORKS

Cases in International Finance. Gunter Duffey. Addison-Wesley. • 2001. 3rd edition. Price on application.

A Guide to the World Bank. The World Bank. • 2003. $15.00. Covers history of the World Bank, with its organization, mission, and purpose.

OECD Public Debt Markets: Trends and Recent Structural Changes. Organization for Economic Cooperation and Development. • 2002. $49.00. Provides information on North American, Asian-Pacific, and European government bond markets. Contains chapters on individual countries, with discussion of debt management policies and techniques.

ABSTRACTS AND INDEXES

World Banking Abstracts: The International Journal of the Financial Services Industry. Institution of European Finance. Blackwell Publishing Ltd. • Bimonthly. Institutions, $1,393.00 per year. Includes print and online editions. Provides worldwide coverage of articles appearing in over 400 financial publications.

ALMANACS AND YEARBOOKS

Bankers' Almanac. Reed Business Information. • Semiannual. $1,170.00. Six volumes. Lists more than 27,000 financial institutions; international coverage. Formerly *Bankers' Almanac and Yearbook.*

Emerging Markets Analyst. • Monthly. $895.00 per year. Provides an annual overview of the emerging financial markets in 24 countries of Latin America, Asia, and Europe. Includes data on international mutual funds and closed-end funds.

International Monetary Fund. Annual Report on Exchange Arrangements and Exchange Restrictions. International Monetary Fund Publications Services. • Annual. Individuals, $95.00; libraries, $47.50.

National Accounts Statistics: Main Aggregates and Detailed Tables. United Nations Publications. • Annual. $160.00.

BIOGRAPHICAL SOURCES

Who's Who in International Banking. Bowker-Saur. • Irregular. $400.00. Contains biographical sketches of about 4,000 bankers. Worldwide coverage.

CD-ROM DATABASES

InvesText [CD-ROM]. Thomson Financial. • Monthly. Contains full text on CD-ROM of investment research reports from about 630 sources, including leading brokers and investment bankers. Reports are available on both U. S. and international publicly traded corporations. Separate industry reports cover more than 50 industries. Time span is 1982 to date.

Leadership Library on CD-ROM: Who's Who in the Leadership of the United States. Leadership Directories, Inc. • Quarterly. Including access to Internet version (weekly updates). Contains all 14 *Yellow Book* personnel directories on CD-ROM, providing contact and brief biographical information for about 400,000 individuals. Covers business, government, financial institutions, news media, law firms, associations, foreign representatives, and nonprofit organizations. Includes photographs.

OECD Statistical Compendium. Organization for Economic Cooperation and Development. • Semiannual. $1,905.00 per year for 1 to 10 users. CD-ROM contains more than 730,000 monthly, quarterly, and annual time series for OECD countries, 1960 to date. Includes fully searchable

data on agriculture, food, economic indicators, national accounts, employment, energy, finance, industry, technology, and foreign trade. Results can be displayed in various forms.

DIRECTORIES

Europe's Top Quoted Companies: A Comparative Directory from Seventeen European Stock Exchanges. Kogan Page. • Annual. $325.00. Provides detailed, 5-year financial data on 850 major European companies that are publicly traded. Includes company addresses.

Foreign Representatives in the U. S. Yellow Book: Who's Who in the U. S. Offices of Foreign Corporations, Foreign Nations, the Foreign Press, and Intergovernmental Organizations. Leadership Directories, Inc. • Annual. $265.00 per year. Lists executives located in the U. S. for 1,200 foreign companies, 300 foreign banks and other financial institutions, 175 embassies and consulates, and 375 foreign press outlets. Includes five indexes.

Major Financial Institutions of Europe. Available from Gale Cengage Learning. • Annual. $510.00. Contains profiles of over 2,000 financial institutions in Europe such as banks, investment companies, and insurance companies. Formerly *Major Financial Institutions of Continental Europe.*

Morgan Stanley Central Bank Directory. Central Banking Publications Ltd. • 2003. $160.00. Provides detailed information on over 160 central banks around the world. A full page is devoted to each country included. Included in subscription to *Central Banking.*

Morningstar American Depositary Receipts. Morningstar, Inc. • Biweekly. $195.00 per year. Looseleaf. Provides detailed profiles of 700 foreign companies having shares traded in the U. S. through American Depositary Receipts (ADRs).

Thomson Bank Directory. Accuity. • Covers: in five volumes, about 11,000 banks and 50,000 branches of United States banks, and 60,000 foreign banks and branches engaged in foreign banking; Federal Reserve system and other United States government and state government banking agencies; 500 largest North American and International commercial banks; paper and automated clearinghouses. Volumes 1 and 2 contain North American listings; volumes 3 and 4, international listings (also cited as 'Thomson International Bank Directory'); volume 5, Worldwide Correspondents Guide containing key correspondent data to facilitate funds transfer. Entries include: For domestic banks--Bank name, address, phone, telex, cable, date established, routing number, charter type, bank holding company affiliation, memberships in Federal Reserve System and other banking organizations, principal officers by function performed, principal correspondent banks, and key financial data (deposits, etc.). For international banks--Bank name, address, phone, fax, telex, cable, SWIFT address, transit or sort codes within home country, ownership, financial data, names and titles of key personnel, branch locations. For branches--Bank name, address, phone, charter type, ownership and other details comparable to domestic bank listings.

Thomson World Bank Directory. Accuity. • Covers: Over 10,000 international banks and their branches in around 200 countries around the globe, including the top 1,000 U.S. Banks. Entries include: Institution name, address, phone, fax, key banking officers by functional title, directors, data established, expanded statement of condition, including a profit and loss account and historic performance ratios.

ENCYCLOPEDIAS AND DICTIONARIES

Blackwell Encyclopedic Dictionary of Finance. Dean Paxson and Douglas Wood, editors. Blackwell Publishing. • 1997. $110.00. The editors are associated with the University of Manchester. Contains definitions of key terms combined with longer

articles written by various U. S. and foreign business educators. Includes bibliographies and index. (Blackwell Encyclopedia of Management Series).

Encyclopedic Dictionary of International Finance and Banking. Jae K. Shim and Michael Constas. CRC Press. • 2001. $64.95. Contains 550 detailed entries covering multinational business, international finance, money, investments, financial planning, financial economics, and banking. Includes statistics, charts, exhibits, diagrams, rules-of-thumb and checklists.

International Dictionary of Accounting Acronyms. Thomas W. Morris, editor. Fitzroy Dearborn Publishers, Inc. • 1999. $45.00. Defines 2,000 acronyms used in worldwide accounting and finance.

HANDBOOKS AND MANUALS

IAS: Interpretation and Application of International Accounting Standards. John Wiley and Sons, Inc. • Annual. $71.00. (Also available on CD-ROM.).

International Banking. Peter K. Oppenheim. American Bankers Association. • 1991. $51.00. Sixth edition. Covers letters of credit, money transfers, collections, and other aspects of global banking.

Library of Investment Banking. Robert L. Kuhn, editor. McGraw-Hill. • 1990. $475.00. Seven volumes: 1. Investing and Risk Management; 2. Capital Raising and Financial Structure; 3. Corporate and Municipal Securities; 4. Mergers, Acquisitions, and Leveraged Buyouts; 5. Mortgage and Asset Securitization; 6. International Finance and Investing; 7. Index.

Miller European Accounting Guide. Aspen Publishers. • Annual. $159.00. Presents analysis of accounting standards in 25 European and Eastern European countries.

Miller International Accounting Standards Guide. Aspen Publishers. • Annual. $139.00. Covers all current International Financial Reporting Standards (IFRS), International Accounting Standards (IAS), and related interpretations issued by the International Accounting Standards Board (IASB).

Options: The International Guide to Valuation and Trading Strategies. Gordon Gemmill. McGraw-Hill. • 1992. $37.95. Covers valuation techniques for American, European, and Asian options. Trading strategies are discussed for options on currencies, stock indexes, interest rates, and commodities.

Reliable Financial Reporting and Internal Control: A Global Implementation Guide. Dmitris N. Chorafas. John Wiley and Sons, Inc. • 2000. $75.00. Discusses financial reporting and control as related to doing business internationally.

Swap and Derivative Financing: The Global Reference to Products Pricing Applications and Markets. Satyajit Das. McGraw-Hill. • 1993. $99.95. Second revised edition.

Transnational Accounting. Dieter Ordelheide and others, editors. Groves Dictionaries, Inc. • 2001. $685.00. Second edition. Three volumes. Published by Macmillan (UK). Provides detailed descriptions of financial accounting principles and practices in 14 major countries (10 European, plus the U. S., Canada, Australia, and Japan). Includes tables, exhibits, index, and a glossary of 244 accounting terms in eight languages.

INTERNET DATABASES

Financial Times: Where Information Becomes Intelligence. FT Group. Phone: 800-628-8088 • URL: http://www.ft.com • Web site provides extensive data and information relating to international business and finance, with daily updates. Includes Markets Today, Company News, Economic Indicators, Equities, Currencies, Capital Markets, Euro Prices, etc. Fees: Free (registration required).

Gateway to the European Union. European Union. E-mail: pressoffice@eurostat.cec.be • URL: http://www.europa.eu.int • Web site provides access to a wide variety of EU information, including statistics (Eurostat), news, policies, publications, key issues, and official exchange rates for the euro. Includes links to the European Central Bank, the European Investment Bank, and other institutions. Fees: Free.

ONLINE DATABASES

Banking Information Source. PROQUEST. • Provides indexing and abstracting of periodical and other literature from 1982 to date, with weekly updates. Covers the financial services industry: banks, savings institutions, investment houses, credit unions, insurance companies, and real estate organizations. Emphasis is on marketing and management. Inquire as to online cost and availability. (Formerly *FINIS: Financial Industry Information Service.*).

InvesText. Thomson Financial. • Provides full text online of investment research reports from more than 600 sources, including leading brokers and investment bankers. Reports are available on approximately 60,000 U. S. and international corporations. Separate industry reports cover 54 industries. Time span is 1982 to date, with daily updates. Inquire as to online cost and availability.

PERIODICALS AND NEWSLETTERS

American Banker: The Financial Services Daily. Thomson Media. • Daily. $895.00 per year. Provides news of banking, investment products, mortgages, credit unions, finance, bank technology, and legal developments.

Applied Financial Economics. Taylor and Francis Group. • Monthly. Institutions, $1,277.00 per year. Covers practical aspects of financial economics, banking, and monetary economics. Supplement to *Applied Economics.*

The Asian Wall Street Journal. Dow Jones & Co., Inc. • Daily. $970.00 per year (air mail). Published in Hong Kong. Also available in a weekly edition at $259.00 per year: *Asian Wall Street Journal Weekly.*

Central Banking: Policy, Markets, Supervision. Available from European Business Publications, Inc. • Quarterly. $260.00 per year, including annual *Central Banking Directory.* Published in England by Central Banking Publications. Reports and comments on the activities of central banks around the world. Also provides discussions of the International Monetary Fund (IMF), the Organization for Economic Cooperation and Development (OECD), the Bank for International Settlements (BIS), and the World Bank.

The Economist. Economist Intelligence Unit. • 51 times a year. $125.00 per year.

Emerging Markets Debt Report. Thomson Media. • Weekly. $895.00 per year. Newsletter. Provides information on new and prospective sovereign and corporate bond issues from developing countries. Includes an emerging market bond index and pricing data.

Emerging Markets Quarterly. Institutional Investor, Inc., Journals Group. • Quarterly. Price on application. Newsletter on financial markets in developing areas, such as Africa, Latin America, Southeast Asia, and Eastern Europe. Topics include institutional investment opportunities and regulatory matters. Formerly *Emerging Markets Weekly.*

Euromoney: The Monthly Journal of International Money and Capital Markets. American Educational Systems. • Monthly. $490.00 per year. Includes print and online editions. Supplement available *Guide to World Equity Markets.*

Finance and Development. International Monetary Fund, Publication Services. • Quarterly. Free.

Financial Flows and the Developing Countries. The World Bank Group. • Quarterly. $150.00 per year.

Concerned mainly with debt, capital markets, and foreign direct investment. Includes statistical tables.

Financial Management. Financial Management Association International. • Quarterly. Individuals, $80.00 per year; libraries, $100.00 per year. Covers theory and practice of financial planning, international finance, investment banking, and portfolio management. Includes *Financial Practice and Education* and *Contempory Finance Digest.*

Financial Times [London]. The Financial Times, Inc. • Daily, except Sunday. $572.88 per year. An international business and financial newspaper, featuring news from London, Paris, Frankfurt, New York, and Tokyo. Includes worldwide stock and bond market data, commodity market data, and monetary/currency exchange information.

Global Finance. Global Finance Media, Inc. • Monthly. $350.00 per year. Edited for corporate financial executives and money managers responsible for "cross-border" financial transactions.

Institutional Investor International Edition: The Magazine for International Finance and Investment. Institutional Investor, Inc., Journals Group. • Monthly. $475.00 per year. Covers the international aspects of professional investing and finance. Emphasis is on Europe, the Far East, and Latin America.

Institutional Investor: The Premier of Professional Magazine Finance. Institutional Investor, Inc., Journals Group. • Monthly. $445.00 per year. Includes print and online editions. Edited for portfolio managers and other investment professionals. Special feature issues include "Country Credit Ratings," "Fixed Income Trading Ranking," "All-America Research Team," and "Global Banking Ranking.".

International Bank Credit Analyst. BCA Publications Ltd. • Monthly. $795.00 per year. "A monthly forecast and analysis of currency movements, interest rates, and stock market developments in the principal countries, based on a continuous appraisal of money and credit trends worldwide." Includes many charts and graphs providing international coverage of money, credit, and securities.

International Currency Review. World Reports Ltd. • Quarterly. $475.00 per year.

International Financial Law Review. American Educational Systems. • Monthly. $750.00 per year. Includes print and online editions.

International Monetary Fund Staff Papers. International Monetary Fund, Publication Services. • Quarterly. Individuals, $56.00 per year; students, $28.00 per year. Contains studies by IMF staff members on balance of payments, foreign exchange, fiscal policy, and related topics. Formerly *International Monetary Fund Staff Papers.*

LatinFinance. Latin American Financial Publications, Inc. • 10 times a year. $235.00 per year. Includes print and online editions. Covers finance, investment, venture capital, and banking in Latin America.

Project Finance Monthly. Infocast Inc. • Description: Provides information about the power industry. Includes industry news, financing, regulation, and contracts.

Standard and Poor's Ratings Handbook. Standard & Poor's. • Monthly. $275.00 per year. Newsletter. Provides news and analysis of international credit markets, including information on new bond issues. Formerly *Credit Week International Ratings.*

U. S. Banker. Thomson Media. • Monthly. $65.00 per year. Edited for bank executives and managers. Covers a wide variety of banking and financial topics.

The Wall Street Journal. Dow Jones & Co., Inc. • Daily. $189.00 per year. Covers news and trends relating to business, industry, finance, the economy,

and international commerce. Provides extensive price and other data for the securities, commodity, options, futures, foreign exchange, and money markets.

Wall Street Journal/Europe. Dow Jones & Co., Inc. • Daily. $300.00 per year (air mail). Published in Europe. Text in English.

RESEARCH CENTERS AND INSTITUTES

International Economics Section. Princeton University. Dept. of Economics, Fisher Hall, Princeton, NJ 08544-1021. Phone: (609)258-5715 Fax: (609)258-6419 E-mail: ies@princeton.edu • URL: http://www.princeton.edu • Formerly International Finance Section.

Rodney L. White Center for Financial Research. University of Pennsylvania, 3254 Steinberg Hall-Dietrich Hall, Philadelphia, PA 19104. Phone: (215)898-7616 Fax: (215)573-8084 E-mail: rlwtcr@finance.wharton.upenn.edu • URL: http://www.finance.wharton.upenn.edu • Research areas include financial management, money markets, real estate finance, and international finance.

STATISTICS SOURCES

Bank Profitability: Financial Statements of Banks. Organization for Economic Cooperation and Development. Available from OECD Publications and Information Center. • Annual. $85.00. Presents data for 10 years on bank profitability in OECD member countries.

Emerging Stock Markets Factbook 1999. International Finance Corp. • 1998. $150.00. Provides statistical profiles for emerging stock markets in various countries of the world. Includes regional, composite, and industry indexes.

Financial Market Trends. Organization for Economic Cooperation and Development. • Quarterly. $80.00 per year. Provides analysis of developments and trends in international and national capital markets. Includes charts and graphs on interest rates, exchange rates, stock market indexes, bank stock indexes, trading volumes, and loans outstanding. Data from OECD countries includes international direct investment, bank profitability, institutional investment, and privatization.

Global Development Finance. The World Bank Group. • Annual. $400.00.

Institutional Investors Statistical Yearbook. Organization for Economic Cooperation and Development. • Annual. $67.00. Provides data relating to institutional saving and investment in OECD countries. Includes investments by insurance companies, pension funds, and investment companies.

International Direct Investment Statistics Yearbook. OECD Publications and Information Center. • Annual. $76.00. Provides direct investment inflow and outflow data for OECD countries.

International Financial Statistics. International Monetary Fund, Publications Services. • Monthly. Individuals, $495.00 per year; students, $247.00 per year. Includes a wide variety of current data for individual countries in Europe and elsewhere. Includes *Annual* issue.

International Guide to Securities Market Indices. Henry Shilling, editor. Fitzroy Dearborn Publishers, Inc. • 1996. $150.00. Describes 400 stock market, bond market, and other financial price indexes maintained in various countries of the world (300 of the indexes are described in detail, including graphs and 10-year data).

Statistical Information on the Financial Services Industry. American Bankers Association. • Annual. Members, $150.00; non-members, $275.00. Presents a wide variety of data relating to banking and financial services, including consumer economics, personal finance, credit, government loans, capital markets, and international banking.

TRADE/PROFESSIONAL ASSOCIATIONS

International Monetary Fund. 700 19th St. NW, Washington, DC 20431. Phone: (202)623-7000 Fax: (202)623-4661 E-mail: publicaffairs@imf.org • URL: http://www.imf.org • Comprises 185 national governments. Works to: facilitate monetary cooperation through consultation and collaboration among member nations; assist in the balanced expansion of trade and thus contribute to the internal development and prosperity of member nations; maintain stability in monetary exchange arrangements, particularly to avoid exchange depreciations; participate in establishing a multilateral system of payments between member nations and in eliminating exchange restrictions that hamper trade; make available the resources of the fund to provide member nations with a means of assuaging economic difficulties. Maintains the IMF Institute, which conducts training courses and seminars and provides lecturers on subjects such as compilation of statistics and formulation and execution of balance of payment policies. Offers technical assistance on monetary matters to member nations and their dependencies and to multinational institutions. Acts as a depository of information and statistical data regarding the economic affairs of member nations. Operates library, in conjunction with the World Bank, on finance and economic development.

World Bank Group. 1818 H St. NW, Washington, DC 20433. Phone: (202)473-1000 or (202)473-1000 Fax: (202)477-6391 E-mail: wbannualreport@worldbank.org • URL: http://www.worldbank.org • Comprises of the International Bank for Reconstruction and Development, the International Development Association, International Finance Corporation and the Multilateral Investment Guarantee Agency. Established by the United Nations to assist in raising the standards of living in developing countries by channeling financial resources from developed countries. Emphasis is placed on investments which foster active participation in the development process. Programs concentrate on rural and urban development, agriculture, and education. Activities include improving water and sewage facilities, building low-cost housing, and increasing the productivity of small industries. Assists organizations with identifying, designing, and executing development projects; offers financial aid to national development institutions. Encourages discussion on common development problems such as income distribution, rural poverty, unemployment, excessive population growth, and rapid urbanization. Conducts research programs on topics including economic planning and public utilities. Works in association with the United Nations Development Program and executes many UNDP projects.

OTHER SOURCES

Country Finance. Economist Intelligence Unit. • Annual $425.00 per year. Discusses banking and financial conditions in each of 47 countries. Includes foreign exchange regulations, the currency outlook, sources of capital, financing techniques, and tax considerations.

International Capital Markets and Securities Regulation. Harold S. Bloomenthal. West Group. • $1,083.00. Nine looseleaf volumes. Periodic supplementation. Securities regulation in industrialized nations. (Securities Law Series).

World Investment Report. United Nations Publications. • Annual. $49.00. Concerned with foreign direct investment, economic development, regional trends, transnational corporations, and globalization.

INTERNATIONAL INSTITUTIONS

See: INTERNATIONAL AGENCIES

INTERNATIONAL INVESTMENTS

See: FOREIGN INVESTMENTS

INTERNATIONAL LAW AND REGULATION

GENERAL WORKS

Business Law: Ethical, International and E-Commerce Environment. Henry R. Cheesman. Prentice Hall PTR. • 2000. $140.00. Fourth edition.

ABSTRACTS AND INDEXES

Current Law Index: Multiple Access to Legal Periodicals. Gale Cengage Learning. • Monthly. $725.00 per year. Produced in cooperation with the American Association of Law Libraries. Indexes more than 900 law journals, legal newspapers, and specialty publications from the U.S., Canada, U.K., Ireland, Australia, and New Zealand.

Index to Foreign Legal Periodicals. American Association of Law Libraries. University of California Press, Journals Div. • Quarterly. $725.00 per year. Annual cumulation.

Index to Legal Periodicals and Books. H. W. Wilson Co. • Monthly. $490.00 per year. Quarterly and annual cumulations.

ALMANACS AND YEARBOOKS

British Year Book of International Law. Oxford University Press. • Annual. Price varies.

Yearbook of the International Law Commission. Available from United Nations Publications. • Annual. $90.00. Two volumes. Volume one, $35.00; volume two, $55.00.

BIBLIOGRAPHIES

Basic Documents in International Law. Ian Brownlie, editor. Oxford University Press. • 2002. $35.00. Fifth edition.

CD-ROM DATABASES

WILSONDISC: Index to Legal Periodicals and Books. H. W. Wilson Co. • Monthly. Includes unlimited online access to *Index to Legal Periodicals* through WILSONLINE. Contains CD-ROM indexing of more than 1,400 English language legal periodicals from 1981 to date and 2,500 books.

DIRECTORIES

Martindale-Hubbell Law Directory. Martindale-Hubbell Inc. • Covers: lawyers and law firms in the United States, its possessions, and Canada, plus leading law firms worldwide; includes a biographical section by firm, and a separate list of patent lawyers, attorneys in government service, in-house counsel, and services, suppliers, and consultants to the legal profession. Entries include: For non-subscribing lawyers--Name, year of birth and of first admission to bar, code indicating college and law school attended and first degree, firm name (or other affiliation, if any) and relationship to firm, whether practicing other than as individual or in partnership. For subscribing lawyers--Above information plus complete address, phone, fax, e-mail and URL, type of practice, clients, plus additional personal details (education, certifications, etc.). A general law list. See separate listing, 'Law Lists'.

Worldwide Government Directory. MacFarlane Management Services Inc. • Covers: 32,000 key elected and appointed government officials in 196 nations and 100 international agencies. Entries

include: Head of state, key government ministers, address, phone, and areas of responsibility.

ENCYCLOPEDIAS AND DICTIONARIES

Legal Systems of the World: A Political, Social, and Cultural Encyclopedia. Herbert M. Kritzer, editor. ABC-CLIO, Inc. • 2002. $385.00. Four volumes. Describes how the courts and legal systems operate in many different countries.

HANDBOOKS AND MANUALS

ABC of Women Workers' Rights and Gender Equality. International Labour Organization. • 2000. $12.95. Second edition. Provides a concise guide to international laws and agreements relating to the rights of women workers.

Access to European Union: Law, Economics, Policies. Euroconfidentiel S. A. • 2001. $62.00. Covers EU legislation and policy in major industrial and commercial sectors. Includes customs policy, the common market, monetary union, taxation, competition, "The EU in the World," and related topics. Contains more than 300 bibliographical references.

INTERNET DATABASES

Lexis.com Research System. Lexis-Nexis Group. Phone: 800-227-4908 or (937)865-6800 Fax: (937)865-6909 E-mail: webmaster@prod.lexis-nexis.com • URL: http://www.lexis.com • Fee-based Web site offers extensive searching of a wide variety of legal sources. Additional features include Daily Opinion Service, lexis.com Bookstore, Career Center, CLE Center, Law Schools, and Practice Pages ("Pages specific to areas of specialty").

ONLINE DATABASES

Index to Legal Periodicals and Books (Online). H. W. Wilson Co. • Broad coverage of law journals and books 1981 to date. Monthly updates. Inquire as to online cost and availability.

PERIODICALS AND NEWSLETTERS

American Journal of International Law. • Quarterly. $140.00 per year.

International and Comparative Law Quarterly. Oxford University Press, Journals. • Quarterly. Institutions, $236.00 per year; with online edition, $248.00 per year.

International Financial Law Review. American Educational Systems. • Monthly. $750.00 per year. Includes print and online editions.

International Lawyer. American Bar Association, International Law and Practice Section. • Quarterly. Free to members; non-members, $60.00 per year.

International Legal Materials. American Society of International Law. • Bimonthly. $190.00 per year.

World Trade Review: Economics, Law, International Institutions. Cambridge University Press. • Three times a year. Individuals, $48.00 pr year; institutions, $200.00 per year. Published in conjunction with the World Trade Organization (http://www.wto.org). Covers "issues of relevance to the multilateral trading system.".

RESEARCH CENTERS AND INSTITUTES

International Law Institute. International Law Institute. The Foundry Bldg., 1055 Thomas Jefferson St. NW, Washington, DC 20007. Phone: (202)247-6006 Fax: (202)247-6010 E-mail: kphan@ili.org • URL: http://www.ili.org • Issues of international law and development, including American and international antitrust law; trade agreements; problems of investments in foreign countries and of foreign investments in the U.S.; comparative studies on corporation and labor law, including studies of economic development, foreign investments and loans, transfer of technology, arbitration, petroleum and mining, trade, budgeting, management, and procurement, and contracting. Performs surveys of literature on U.S. trade policy instruments and their implementation, operation, and industry performance implications; also assesses U.S. international economic policy.

TRADE/PROFESSIONAL ASSOCIATIONS

American Society of International Law. 2223 Massachusetts Ave., N.W., Washington, DC 20008-2864. Phone: (202)939-6000 Fax: (202)797-7133 E-mail: services@asil.org • URL: http://www.asil.org.

International Bar Association. 1 Stephen St., 10th Fl., London W1T 1AT, United Kingdom. Phone: 44 20 76916868 Fax: 44 20 76916544 E-mail: member@int-bar.org • URL: http://www.ibanet.org • National bar associations and individual members of the legal profession working in the field of international law in 183 countries. Works to advance the science of jurisprudence; promotes uniformity in related legal fields and administration of justice under law. Seeks to establish and maintain friendly relations among members of the legal profession worldwide. Supports the legal principles and aims of the United Nations.

International Center for Law in Development. 777 United Nations Plaza, 7 E., New York, NY 10017. Phone: (212)687-0036 Fax: (212)370-9844.

International Law Association. Charles Clore House, 17 Russell Sq., London WC1B 5DR, United Kingdom. Phone: 44 20 73232978 Fax: 44 20 73233580 E-mail: info@ila-hq.org • URL: http://www.ila-hq.org • Lawyers and representatives in 85 countries active in the shipping, commercial, and banking industries. Fosters interest in the study, advancement and unification of international public and private law and comparative law, and in resolving legal conflicts. Conducts seminars.

OTHER SOURCES

International Capital Markets and Securities Regulation. Harold S. Bloomenthal. West Group. • $1,083.00. Nine looseleaf volumes. Periodic supplementation. Securities regulation in industrialized nations. (Securities Law Series).

The Rome, Maastricht, and Amsterdam Treaties: Comparative Texts. Available from Paul and Co. Publishers Consortium, Inc. • 1997. Price on application. Includes a comprehensive keyword index. Published in Belgium by Euroconfidential.

World Trade Organization Dispute Settlement Decisions: Bernan's Annotated Reporter. Bernan Press. • Dates vary. $75.00 per volume. Contains all World Trade Organization Panel Reports and Appellate Decisions since the establishment of the WTO in 1995. Includes such cases as "The Importation, Sale, and Distribution of Bananas.".

INTERNATIONAL MARKETING

See also: ASIAN MARKETS; CANADIAN MARKETS; EUROPEAN CONSUMER MARKET; LATIN AMERICAN MARKETS

GENERAL WORKS

Applying Telecommunications and Technology from a Global Business Perspective. Jay J. Zajas and Olive D. Church. Haworth Press, Inc. • 1997. $29.95. Provides an international, multicultural perspective.

Global Economic Prospects 2004. The World Bank Group. • 2003. $38.00. "..offers an in-depth analysis of the economic prospects of developing countries.." Emphasis is on the impact of recessions and financial crises. Regional statistical data is included.

International Advertising: Realities and Myths. John P. Jones, editor. Sage Publications, Inc. • 1999. $95.95. Includes articles by advertising professionals in 10 different countries. (Advertising Series).

Marketing in the Third World. Denise M. Johnson and Erdener Kaynak, editors. Haworth Press, Inc. • 1996. $29.95. Various authors discuss marketing, advertising, government regulations, and other topics relating to business promotion in developing countries. (Also published in the *Journal of Global Marketing*, vol. 9, no. 4).

ABSTRACTS AND INDEXES

Business Periodicals Index. H. W. Wilson Co. • 11 times a year. Quarterly and annual cumulations. Price varies.

F & S Index: Europe. Gale Cengage Learning. • Monthly. $1,450.00 per year, including quarterly and annual cumulations. Provides annotated citations to marketing, business, financial, and industrial literature. Coverage of European business activity includes trade journals, financial magazines, business newspapers, and special reports. Formerly *Predicasts F & S Index: Europe.*

F & S Index: International. Gale Cengage Learning. • Monthly. $1,450.00 per year, including quarterly and annual cumulations. Provides annotated citations to marketing, business, financial, and industrial literature. Coverage of international business activity includes trade journals, financial magazines, business newspapers, and special reports. Areas included are Asia, Latin America, Africa, the Middle East, Oceania, and Canada.

NTIS Alerts: Business & Economics. National Technical Information Service. • Text: Semimonthly. $210.00 per year.

PAIS International in Print. Public Affairs Information Service, Inc. • Monthly. $850.00 per year; cumulations three times a year. Provides topical citations to the worldwide literature of public affairs, economics, demographics, sociology, and trade. Text in English; indexed materials in English, French, German, Italian, Portuguese and Spanish.

ALMANACS AND YEARBOOKS

World Development Report 2004. The World Bank Group. • Annual. $26.00. Covers history, conditions, and trends relating to economic globalization and localization. Includes selected data from *World Development Indicators* for 132 countries or economies. Key indicators are provided for 78 additional countries or economies.

CD-ROM DATABASES

PAIS on CD-ROM. Public Affairs Information Service, Inc. • Quarterly. $1,995.00 per year. Provides a CD-ROM version of the online service, *PAIS International.* Contains over 500,000 citations to the literature of contemporary social, political, and economic issues.

WILSONDISC: Wilson Business Abstracts. H. W. Wilson Co. • Monthly. Includes unlimited online access to *Wilson Business Abstracts* through WILSONLINE. Provides CD-ROM "cover-to-cover" abstracting and indexing of over 600 prominent business periodicals. Indexing is from 1982, abstracting from 1990. (*Business Periodicals Index* without abstracts is available on CD-ROM at $1,495 per year.).

World Consumer Markets. Gale Cengage Learning. • Annual. $2,500.00. Pblished by Euromonitor. Provides five- year historical data, current data, and forecasts, on CD-ROM for 330 consumer products in 55 countries. Market data is presented in a standardized format for each country.

World Development Report [CD-ROM]. The World Bank, Office of the Publisher. • Annual. CD-ROM includes the current edition of *World Development Report* and 21 previous editions.

World Marketing Data and Statistics on CD-ROM. Gale Cengage Learning. • Annual. $1,750.00. Published by Euromonitor. Provides demographic, marketing, socioeconomic, and political data on CD-ROM for each of 209 countries.

World Marketing Forecasts on CD-ROM. Gale Cengage Learning. • Annual. $2,500.00. Produced by Euromonitor. Provides detailed forecast data for the years to 2012 on CD-ROM for 54 countries in all parts of the world. Covers a wide range of social, demographic, economic, and market factors. Includes specific forecasts for many kinds of consumer products.

DIRECTORIES

Directory of Consumer Brands and Their Owners: Asia Pacific. Euromonitor International, Business Reference Div. • 1998. $990.00. Provides information about brands available from major Asia Pacific companies. Descriptions of companies are also included.

Directory of Consumer Brands and Their Owners: Eastern Europe. Euromonitor International, Business Reference Div. • 1998. $990.00. Provides information about brands available from major Eastern European companies. Descriptions of companies are also included.

Directory of Consumer Brands and Their Owners: Latin America. Euromonitor International, Business Reference Div. • 1999. $990.00. Provides information about brands available from major Latin American companies. Descriptions of companies are also included.

Global Market Share Planner. Euromonitor International. • 2003. $5,900.00. Six volumes. Second edition. Provides detailed profiles and market share rankings of major consumer product companies in North America, Latin America, Europe, South Africa, and the Asia-Pacific region. Covers firms operating in key consumer markets: beverages, food products, household products, and personal care items. (Volumes are available individually.).

International Media Guide: Business-Professional: Asia/Pacific, Middle East, Africa. SRDS. • Annual. $300.00. Provides information on 14,000 trade journals "from Africa to the Pacific Rim," including advertising rates and circulation data.

International Media Guide Business-Professional Publications: Europe. SRDS. • Annual. $300.00. Describes 6,000 trade journals from Eastern and Western Europe, with advertising rates and circulation data.

International Media Guide: Business/Professional Publications: The Americas. SRDS. • Annual. $300.00. Describes trade journals from North, South, and Central America, with advertising rates and circulation data.

International Media Guide: Newspapers Worldwide. SRDS. • Annual. $350.00. Provides advertising rates, circulation, and other details relating to newspapers in major cities of the world (covers 200 countries, including U. S.).

Major Market Share Companies: The Americas. Available from Gale Cengage Learning. • 2003. $990.00. Second edition. Published by Euromonitor. Provides consumer market share data and rankings for multinational and regional companies. Covers leading firms in the U.S., Canada, Mexico, Brazil, Argentina, Venezuela, and Chile.

Market Share Reporter. Available from Gale Cengage Learning. • 2002. $285.00. Sixth edition. Published by Euromonitor. Provides consumer market share data for leading companies in 30 major countries.

MRA Blue Book Research Services Directory. Marketing Research Association. • Covers: over 1,200 marketing research companies and field interviewing services. Entries include: Company name, address, phone, names of executives, services, facilities, special interviewing capabilities.

SRDS International Media Guides. SRDS. • Covers: In five volumes (Newspapers worldwide,

---

Consumer magazines worldwide, Business Publications: Asia-Pacific/Middle East/Africa, Business Publications: Europe, Business Publications: The Americas), advertising rates and data for 20,000 newspapers, consumer magazines and business publications worldwide. Entries include: contact names, addresses, phone and fax numbers, and e-mail.

World Directory of Marketing Information Sources. Available from Gale Cengage Learning. • 2003. $650.00. Fourth edition. Published by Euromonitor. Provides details on approximately 6,000 sources of marketing information, including publications, libraries, associations, market research companies, online databases, and governmental organizations. Coverage is worldwide.

ENCYCLOPEDIAS AND DICTIONARIES

Blackwell Encyclopedic Dictionary of Marketing. Dale Littler and Barbara R. Lewis, editors. Blackwell Publishers. • 1997. $38.95. The editors are associated with the Manchester School of Management. Contains definitions of key terms combined with longer articles written by various U. S. and foreign business educators. Includes bibliographies and index. (Blackwell Encyclopedia of Management Series.).

Encyclopedia of Business. Gale Cengage Learning. • 2000. $425.00. Second edition. Two volumes. Contains more than 700 signed articles covering major business disciplines and concepts. International in scope. (Encyclopedia of Business Series).

Field Guide to Marketing: A Glossary to Essential Tools and Concepts for Today's Manager. McGraw-Hill. • 1993. $29.95. Defines fundamental terms.

HANDBOOKS AND MANUALS

Marketing Manager's Handbook. Sidney J. Levy and others. Prentice Hall PTR. • 2000. Price on application. Contains 71 chapters by various authors on a wide variety of marketing topics, including market segmentation, market research, international marketing, industrial marketing, survey methods, customer service, advertising, pricing, planning, strategy, and ethics.

ONLINE DATABASES

F & S Index. Gale Cengage Learning. • Contains about four million citations to worldwide business, financial, and industrial or consumer product literature appearing from 1972 to date. Weekly updates. Inquire as to online cost and availability.

Globalbase. Gale Cengage Learning. • Provides more than one million online summaries of business, industrial, and economic news reports from more than 1,000 publications worldwide. Covers a wide range of material appearing in international trade journals, professional magazines, and newspapers. Time period is 1984 to date, with weekly updates. Inquire as to online cost and availability.

Management Contents. Gale Cengage Learning. • Covers a wide range of management, financial, marketing, personnel, and administrative topics. About 150 leading business journals are indexed and abstracted from 1974 to date, with monthly updating. Inquire as to online cost and availability.

Market Research Monitor. Euromonitor International. • Contains full-text reports online from *Market Research Europe, Market Research Great Britain, Market Research International,* and *Retail Monitor International.* Time period is 1995 to date, with monthly updates. Inquire as to online cost and availability.

MarkIntel. Thomson Financial. • Provides the current full text online of more than 50,000 market research reports covering 54 industries, from 85 leading research firms worldwide. Reports include extensive forecasts and market analysis. Inquire as

to online cost and availability.

PAIS International. Public Affairs Information Service, Inc. • Corresponds to the former printed publications, *PAIS Bulletin* (1976-90) and *PAIS Foreign Language Index* (1972-90), and to the current *PAIS International in Print* (1991 to date). Covers economic, political, and sociological material appearing in periodicals, books, government documents, and other publications. Updating is monthly. Inquire as to online cost and availability.

PROMT: Predicasts Overview of Markets and Technology. Gale Cengage Learning. • Companies, products, applied technologies and markets. U.S. and international literature coverage, 1972 to date. Inquire as to online cost and availability. Provides abstracts from more than 1,600 publications. Weekly updates.

Wilson Business Abstracts Online. H. W. Wilson Co. • Indexes and abstracts 600 major business periodicals, plus the *Wall Street Journal* and the business section of the *New York Times*. Indexing is from 1982, abstracting from 1990, with the two newspapers included from 1993. Updated weekly. Inquire as to online cost and availability. (*Business Periodicals Index* without abstracts is also available online.).

PERIODICALS AND NEWSLETTERS

Advertising Age's Euromarketing. Crain Communications, Inc. • Weekly. $295.00 per year. Newsletter on European advertising and marketing.

Journal of International Marketing. American Marketing Association. • Members $45.00; nonmembers, $80.00 per year institutions, $150.00 per year.

Pharma Business: The International Magazine of Pharmaceutical Business and Marketing. Engel Publishing Partners. • Six times a year. $235.00 per year. Circulated mainly in European countries. Coverage includes worldwide industry news, new drug products, regulations, and research developments.

RESEARCH CENTERS AND INSTITUTES

Institute for the Study of Business Markets. Pennsylvania State University, 402 Business Administration Bldg., University Park, PA 16802-3004. Phone: (814)863-2782 Fax: (814)863-0413 E-mail: isbm@psu.edu • URL: http://www.smeal.psu.edu/isbm/ • Research areas include international distribution channels.

STATISTICS SOURCES

Consumer International. Available from Gale Cengage Learning. • Annual. $1,290.00. Published by Euromonitor. Contains extensive consumer market, economic, and demographic data for 25 major, non-European countries, including the U. S. and Canada. Includes consumer market size (volume and value) for 150 product types in 14 categories (food, clothing, automobiles, cosmetics, appliances, etc.).

The Enlarged European Union: A Statistical Handbook. Euromonitor International. • 2003. $470.00. Presents comparative statistical data for 28 countries (15 EU member states and 13 candidate countries). Covers economics, population, labor, trade, consumer markets, and other topics.

European Marketing Forecasts. Available from Gale Cengage Learning. • Annual. $1,250.00. Published by Euromonitor. Contains demographic, economic, and market forecasts for the countries of Europe to the year 2010. Forecasts include market-size data for 15 consumer product sectors (food, clothing, automobiles, consumer electronics, etc.).

Gale Country and World Rankings Reporter. Gale Cengage Learning. • 1997. $160.00. Second edition. Provides about 3,000 statistical ranking tables and charts covering more than 235 nations. Sources include the United Nations and various government publications.

International Marketing Forecasts. Available from Gale Cengage Learning. • Annual. $1,250.00. Published by Euromonitor. Contains demographic, economic, and market forecasts to the year 2013 for major, non-European countries, including the U. S. and Canada. Forecasts include market-size data for 15 consumer product sectors, such as food, clothing, and automobiles.

The World Bank Atlas. World Bank Group. • Annual. $10.00. Contains "color maps, charts, and graphs representing the main social, economic, and environmental indicators for 209 countries and territories" (publisher).

World Consumer Expenditure Patterns. Euromonitor International. • 2003. $1,190.00. Contains detailed consumer expenditure data for 71 countries. Covers 70 specific categories within the areas of food, beverages, tobacco, clothing, housing, appliances, health, transportation, leisure, etc. Provides 10 years of data and includes consumer price indexes.

World Consumer Income and Expenditure Patterns. Available from Gale Cengage Learning. • Annual. $1,090.00. Two volumes. Published by Euromonitor. Provides data for countries worldwide on consumer income, earning power, spending patterns, and savings. Expenditures are detailed for product or service categories.

World Consumer Income Patterns. Euromonitor International. • 2003. $1,190.00. Provides detailed data on household income in 71 countries (10-year statistics). Covers income by age, sex, and level of education, with further data on savings, earnings, and average taxes.

World Consumer Lifestyles Databook: Key Trends. Euromonitor International. • 2003. $1,190.00. Second edition. Covers 71 countries. Presents statistical data relating to such consumer lifestyle characteristics as family size, household income, family expenditures, home ownership, shopping habits, eating habits, drinking habits, savings, transportation, travel, health characteristics, and education.

World Development Indicators. The World Bank Group. • Annual. $60.00. Provides data and information on the people, economy, environment, and markets of 148 countries. Emphasis is on statistics relating to major development issues.

World Market Share Reporter: A Compilation of Reported World Market Share Data and Rankngs on Companies, Products, and Services. Gale Cengage Learning. • 2001. $340.00. Fifth edition. Provides market share data for companies, products, and industries in countries or regions other than North America and Mexico.

INTERNATIONAL MONETARY FUND (IMF)

GENERAL WORKS

Financial Institutions and Markets. Meir J. Kohn. Oxford University Press, Inc. • 2003. $115.00. Second edition.

International Monetary Fund: Overview, Issues, and Bibliography. Elisabeth P. McLellan, editor. Nova Science Publishers, Inc. • 2002. $69.00. Provides articles by various authors on the basics of the IMF. Includes an extensive bibliography with author, title, and subject indexes.

ABSTRACTS AND INDEXES

PAIS International in Print. Public Affairs Information Service, Inc. • Monthly. $850.00 per year; cumulations three times a year. Provides topical citations to the worldwide literature of public affairs, economics, demographics, sociology, and trade. Text in English; indexed materials in English,

French, German, Italian, Portuguese and Spanish.

BIBLIOGRAPHIES

International Monetary Fund: A Selected Bibliography. Anne C. Salda. Transaction Publishers. • 1992. $64.95.

CD-ROM DATABASES

PAIS on CD-ROM. Public Affairs Information Service, Inc. • Quarterly. $1,995.00 per year. Provides a CD-ROM version of the online service, *PAIS International*. Contains over 500,000 citations to the literature of contemporary social, political, and economic issues.

ONLINE DATABASES

PAIS International. Public Affairs Information Service, Inc. • Corresponds to the former printed publications, *PAIS Bulletin* (1976-90) and *PAIS Foreign Language Index* (1972-90), and to the current *PAIS International in Print* (1991 to date). Covers economic, political, and sociological material appearing in periodicals, books, government documents, and other publications. Updating is monthly. Inquire as to online cost and availability.

PERIODICALS AND NEWSLETTERS

Central Banking: Policy, Markets, Supervision. Available from European Business Publications, Inc. • Quarterly. $260.00 per year, including annual *Central Banking Directory*. Published in England by Central Banking Publications. Reports and comments on the activities of central banks around the world. Also provides discussions of the International Monetary Fund (IMF), the Organization for Economic Cooperation and Development (OECD), the Bank for International Settlements (BIS), and the World Bank.

IMF Survey. International Monetary Fund. • Description: Timely news on topics of general interest in the fields of international finance, country economics, trade, and commodities. Contains information on the IMF's activities, including press releases, major management speeches, and lending activity data rates.

International Monetary Fund Staff Papers. International Monetary Fund, Publication Services. • Quarterly. Individuals, $56.00 per year; students, $28.00 per year. Contains studies by IMF staff members on balance of payments, foreign exchange, fiscal policy, and related topics. Formerly *International Monetary Fund Staff Papers*.

RESEARCH CENTERS AND INSTITUTES

Center for International Policy. 1755 Massachusetts Ave., N. W., Ste. 550, Washington, DC 20036. Phone: (202)232-3317 Fax: (202)232-3440 E-mail: cip@ciponline.org • URL: http://www.ciponline.org • Research subjects include the International Monetary Fund, the World Bank, and other international financial institutions. Analyzes the impact of policies on social and economic conditions in developing countries.

TRADE/PROFESSIONAL ASSOCIATIONS

Bretton Woods Committee. 1726 M St. NW, Ste. 200, Washington, DC 20036. Phone: (202)331-1616 Fax: (202)785-9423 E-mail: info@brettonwoods. org • URL: http://www.brettonwoods.org • Corporate CEOs, university administrators, former government officials, state governors, association and trade union executives, and bankers. Seeks to inform and educate the public regarding the activities of the World Bank, International Monetary Fund, and other Multinational Development Banks (MDB). Promotes U.S. participation in MDBs.

International Monetary Fund. 700 19th St. NW, Washington, DC 20431. Phone: (202)623-7000 Fax: (202)623-4661 E-mail: publicaffairs@imf.org • URL: http://www.imf.org • Comprises 185 national governments. Works to: facilitate monetary cooperation through consultation and collaboration among

member nations; assist in the balanced expansion of trade and thus contribute to the internal development and prosperity of member nations; maintain stability in monetary exchange arrangements, particularly to avoid exchange depreciations; participate in establishing a multilateral system of payments between member nations and in eliminating exchange restrictions that hamper trade; make available the resources of the fund to provide member nations with a means of assuaging economic difficulties. Maintains the IMF Institute, which conducts training courses and seminars and provides lecturers on subjects such as compilation of statistics and formulation and execution of balance of payment policies. Offers technical assistance on monetary matters to member nations and their dependencies and to multinational institutions. Acts as a depository of information and statistical data regarding the economic affairs of member nations. Operates library, in conjunction with the World Bank, on finance and economic development.

INTERNATIONAL ORGANIZATIONS

See: INTERNATIONAL AGENCIES

INTERNATIONAL TAXATION

See also: MULTINATIONAL CORPORATIONS; TAX SHELTERS

GENERAL WORKS

Improving Access to Bank Information for Tax Purposes. Organization for Economic Cooperation and Development. • 2000. $66.00. Discusses ways to improve the international exchange of bank account information for tax determinations.

ABSTRACTS AND INDEXES

Accounting and Tax Index. UMI. • Quarterly. Price on application. Annual cumulation. Indexes accounting, auditing, and taxation literature appearing in journals, books, pamphlets, conference proceedings, and newsletters.

Business Periodicals Index. H. W. Wilson Co. • 11 times a year. Quarterly and annual cumulations. Price varies.

Index to Legal Periodicals and Books. H. W. Wilson Co. • Monthly. $490.00 per year. Quarterly and annual cumulations.

PAIS International in Print. Public Affairs Information Service, Inc. • Monthly. $850.00 per year; cumulations three times a year. Provides topical citations to the worldwide literature of public affairs, economics, demographics, sociology, and trade. Text in English; indexed materials in English, French, German, Italian, Portuguese and Spanish.

CD-ROM DATABASES

PAIS on CD-ROM. Public Affairs Information Service, Inc. • Quarterly. $1,995.00 per year. Provides a CD-ROM version of the online service, *PAIS International*. Contains over 500,000 citations to the literature of contemporary social, political, and economic issues.

The Tax Directory [CD-ROM]. Tax Analysts. • Quarterly. Provides *The Tax Directory* listings on CD-ROM, covering federal, state, and international tax officials, tax practitioners, and corporate tax executives.

DIRECTORIES

The Tax Directory. Tax Analysts. • Covers: Volume One--Approximately 15,000 federal and state government tax legislators, policymakers, administrators, and employees; tax regulation attorneys; over 500 international tax officials with

central banks, ministries of finance, foreign embassies and consulate, and chambers of commerce; over 300 tax and business journalists and editors working for magazines, journals, newspapers, television, and radio; tax sections of over 100 trade and professional associations; state CPA, bar, and enrolled agent associations. Volume Two--Over 5,000 corporate tax managers of large U.S. and international firms. Entries include: For government and international officials--Name, title, address, phone, fax, email and website. For corporate tax managers--Name, address, phone, fax, email, website, and company name. For journalists--Name, address, phone, fax, email, website, and name of publication/network. For organizations and associations--Name, address, phone, fax, email, website, budget, membership, background information, and description of purpose.

ENCYCLOPEDIAS AND DICTIONARIES

Dictionary of Taxation. Simon James. Edward Elgar Publishing, Inc. • 1998. $65.00. Provides detailed definitions of terms relating to "various aspects of taxes and tax systems throughout the world.".

HANDBOOKS AND MANUALS

Corporate Taxes: Worldwide Summaries. John Wiley and Sons, Inc. • 2003. $105.00. Summarizes the corporate tax regulations of more than 125 countries. Provides information useful for international tax planning and foreign investments.

Individual Taxes 2002-2003: Worldwide Summaries. John Wiley and Sons, Inc. • 2002. $105. 00. Two volumes. Summarizes the personal tax regulations of more than 125 countries. Provides information useful for international tax planning and foreign investments.

International Income Taxation: Code and Regulations, Selected Sections. CCH, Inc. • Annual. $77. 00. Covers U. S. taxation of foreign entities and U. S. taxation of domestic entities having foreign income.

Practical Guide to U. S. Taxation of International Transactions. Robert E. Meldman and Michael S. Schadewald. CCH, Inc. • 2000. $99.00. Third edition. Contains three parts: Basic Principles, U. S. Taxation of Foreign Income, and U. S. Taxation of Foreign Persons.

INTERNET DATABASES

TAXNET.PRO. Carswell. Phone: 800-387-5164 or (416)609-3800 Fax: (416)298-5082 E-mail: orders@carswell.com • URL: http://www.carswell. com/taxnetpro.asp • Fee-based Web site provides complete coverage of Canadian tax law and regulation, including income tax, provincial taxes, accounting, and payrolls. Daily updates. Base price varies according to product.

ONLINE DATABASES

Index to Legal Periodicals and Books (Online). H. W. Wilson Co. • Broad coverage of law journals and books 1981 to date. Monthly updates. Inquire as to online cost and availability.

Legal Resource Index. Gale Cengage Learning. • Broad coverage of law literature appearing in legal, business, and other periodicals, 1980 to date. Daily updates. Inquire as to online cost and availability.

LEXIS. LEXIS-NEXIS. • The various LEXIS databases provide full text and indexing for a wide variety of legal cases, statutes, orders, and opinions.

PAIS International. Public Affairs Information Service, Inc. • Corresponds to the former printed publications, *PAIS Bulletin* (1976-90) and *PAIS Foreign Language Index* (1972-90), and to the current *PAIS International in Print* (1991 to date). Covers economic, political, and sociological material appearing in periodicals, books, government documents, and other publications. Updating is monthly. Inquire as to online cost and availability.

Wilson Business Abstracts Online. H. W. Wilson Co. • Indexes and abstracts 600 major business periodicals, plus the *Wall Street Journal* and the business section of the *New York Times.* Indexing is from 1982, abstracting from 1990, with the two newspapers included from 1993. Updated weekly. Inquire as to online cost and availability. (*Business Periodicals Index* without abstracts is also available online.).

PERIODICALS AND NEWSLETTERS

Highlights and Documents. Tax Analysts. • Daily. $2,249.00 per year, including monthly indexes. Newsletter. Provides daily coverage of IRS, congressional, judicial, state, and international tax developments. Includes abstracts and citations for "all tax documents released within the previous 24 to 48 hours." Annual compilation available *Highlights and Documents on Microfiche.*

International Tax Journal. Aspen Publishers. • Quarterly. $297.00 per year. Articles, columns and tax notes pertaining to the international tax market.

International Tax Report: Maximizing Tax Opportunities Worldwide. Informa Group PLC. • Monthly. $1,100.00 per year.

Journal of International Taxation. RIA. • Monthly. $260.00 per year.

Journal of Taxation of Global Transactions. CCH, Inc. • Quarterly. $215.00 per year. Covers tax laws affecting international business activity.

Tax Management International Forum. BNA, Inc. • Quarterly. $370.00 per year.

Tax Management International Journal: A Monthly Professional Review of Current International Tax Developments. BNA Tax Management. • Monthly. $426.00 per year. Semiannual *Index.*

Tax Notes International. Tax Analysts. • Weekly. $949.00 per year. Newsletter. Provides "news and in-depth reports on a variety of international tax topics." Summarizes tax statutes, regulations, rulings, court decisions, and treaties from various countries of the world.

RESEARCH CENTERS AND INSTITUTES

International Tax Program. Harvard University, 1563 Massachusetts Ave., Pound Hall, Room 400, Cambridge, MA 02138. Phone: (617)495-4406 Fax: (617)495-0423 E-mail: itp@law.harvard.edu • URL: http://www.law.harvard.edu/programs/itp • Studies the worldwide problems of taxation, including tax law and tax administration.

STATISTICS SOURCES

Revenue Statistics. OECD Publications and Information Center. • Annual. $65.00. Presents data on government revenues in OECD countries, classified by type of tax and level of government. Text in English and French.

Taxing Wages. Organization for Economic Cooperation and Development. • Annual. $52.00. Contains data on income tax and social security levies collected from employees and employers in OECD countries. Includes marginal and effective tax burden figures for various family income levels and statistics on cash transfers paid as family benefits.

TRADE/PROFESSIONAL ASSOCIATIONS

Tax Analysts. 400 S Maple Ave., Ste. 400, Falls Church, VA 22046. Phone: 800-955-2444 or (703)533-4400 Fax: (703)533-4444 E-mail: cservice@tax.org • URL: http://www.tax.org • Reviews all tax law developments, federal, state, international comprehensively; compiles statistics. **Convention/Meeting:** none.

OTHER SOURCES

Foreign Tax and Trade Briefs. LexisNexis Matthew Bender. • Quarterly. $550.00 per year. Two looseleaf volumes. The latest tax and trade information for over 100 foreign countries.

International Tax Agreements. United Nations Publications. • Irregular. Price varies. Looseleaf.

Manufacturers' Tax Alert. CCH, Inc. • Monthly $297.00 per year. Newsletter. Covers the major tax issues affecting manufacturing companies. Includes current developments in various kind of federal, state, and international taxes: sales, use, franchise, property, and corporate income.

INTERNATIONAL TRADE

See: FOREIGN TRADE

INTERNET

See also: COMPUTER COMMUNICATIONS; ONLINE INFORMATION SYSTEMS; ELECTRONIC COMMERCE

GENERAL WORKS

Accidental Webmaster. Julie M. Still. Information Today, Inc. • 2003. $29.50. Covers the practical aspects of designing and maintaining a successful Web site. Written for librarians and others without previous Webmaster experience.

The Amazing Internet Challenge: How Leading Projects Use Library Skills to Organize the Web. Amy T. Wells and others. American Library Association. • 1999. $45.00. Presents profiles of 12 digital libraries, such as the Agriculture Network Information Center and the Social Science Information Gateway. Emphasis is on how online indexes were created.

Creating Web-Accessible Databases: Case Studies for Libraries, Museums, and Other Non-Profits. Julie M. Still, editor. Information Today, Inc. • 2001. $39.50. Presents case studies of successful Web projects in libraries and other institutions.

Cyberquake: How the Internet will Erase Profits, Topple Market Leaders, and Shatter Business Models. Michael Sullivan-Trainor. John Wiley and Sons, Inc. • 1997. $26.95. Predicts that the Internet will cause "an overwhelming shift in control of the worldwide marketplace" in the early 21st century. (Business Technology Series).

Digital Literacy: Personal Preparation for the Internet Age. Paul Gilster. John Wiley and Sons, Inc. • 1997. $22.95. Provides practical advice for the online consumer on how to evaluate various aspects of the Internet ("digital literacy" is required, as well as "print literacy").

Economic Perspectives on the Internet. Alan E. Wiseman. Nova Science Publishers, Inc. • 2003. $59.00. Discusses the pricing of Internet access, pricing of goods and services sold through the Internet, network effects, and Internet taxation.

The Emperor's Virtual Clothes: The Naked Truth About Internet Culture. Dinty Moore. Algonquin Books of Chapel Hill. • 1995. $17.95. A readable consideration of both positive and negative aspects of the Internet.

The Evolving Virtual Library: Practical and Philosophical Perspectives. Laverna M. Saunders, editor. Information Today, Inc. • 1999. $39.50. Various authors cover trends in library and school use of the Internet, intranets, extranets, and electronic databases.

Highway of Dreams: A Critical View Along the Information Superhighway. A. Michael Noll. Lawrence Erlbaum Associates, Inc. • 1996. $49.95. States that such factors as consumer needs and finance are often of more importance to the information industry than technological utopia. Includes such chapter headings as "Historical Perspective," "History Repeats," "Business Considerations," and "The Internet Exposed." (LEA's Telecommunications Series).

History of the Internet: A Chronology, 1843 to the Present. Christos J. P. Moschovitis and others. ABC-CLIO, Inc. • 1999. $65.00. Early entries cover the history of the computer. Includes biographical information, bibliography, and glossary.

The Individual Investor's Revolution: Unlock the Secrets of Wall Street and Invest Like a Pro. Charles B. Carlson. McGraw-Hill. • 2000. $15.95. Emphasizes the growing importance of the individual investor, especially with regard to online trading (e-trading). Includes the author's favorite websites for investors and traders.

Interface Culture: How New Technology Transforms the Way We Create and Communicate. Steven Johnson. HarperSanFrancisco. • 1997. $24.00. A discussion of how computer interfaces and online technology ("cyberspace") affect society in general.

The Internet Bubble: Inside the Overvalued World of High-Tech Stocks, and What You Should Know to Avoid the Coming Catastrophe. Anthony Perkins and Michael C. Perkins. HarperInformation. • 2001. $28.00. Revised edition. The authors predict a shakeout in e-commerce stocks and other Internet-related investments. (HarperBusiness.).

The Internet Initiative: Libraries Providing Internet Services and How They Plan, Pay, and Manage. Edward J. Valauskas and others. American Library Association. • 1995. $27.00. Provides 18 reports on Internet services in various kinds of libraries.

Internet Taxation. Albert Tokin, editor. Nova Science Publishers, Inc. • 2003. $29.50. Several authors discuss the controversial issue of local taxation of e-commerce transactions.

Law of the Super Searchers: The Online Secrets of Top Legal Researchers. T. R. Halvorson. Information Today, Inc. • 1999. $24.95. Eight law researchers explain how to find useful legal information online. (Super Searchers Series).

Management Information Systems: With Application Cases and Internet Primer. Stephen Haag and others. McGraw-Hill. • 2001. $107.19. Third edition. Includes CD-ROM.

Marketing on the Internet: Multimedia Strategies for the World Wide Web. Jill Ellsworth and Matthew Ellsworth. John Wiley and Sons, Inc. • 1996. $29.99. Second expanded revised edition.

Mastering Online Investing: How to Use the Internet to Become a More Successful Investor. Michael C. Thomsett. Dearborn Trading Publishing, A Kaplan Professional Co. • 2001. $19.95. Emphasis is on the Internet as an information source for intelligent investing, avoiding "speculation and fads.".

Net Curriculum: An Educator's Guide to Using the Internet. Linda Joseph. Information Today, Inc. • 1999. $29.95. Covers various educational aspects of the Internet. Written for K-12 teachers, librarians, and media specialists by a columnist for *Multimedia Schools.* (CyberAge Books.).

Net Effects: How Librarians Can Manage the Unintended Consequences of the Internet. Marylaine Block, editor. Information Today, Inc. • 2003. $39.50. Contains about 50 articles by librarians on the "side effects" of Internet use in libraries, such as technology stress, threats to print sources, retraining problems, new budget demands, and legal controversies.

Net Income: Cut Costs, Boost Profits, and Enhance Operations Online. Wally Bock and Jeff Senne. John Wiley and Sons, Inc. • 1997. $29.95. "Net Income" in this case is hoped-for Internet income. Promotes the use of the Internet, intranet, and extranet to improve business operations or start new businesses. The authors take a nontechnical, business strategy approach.

Online Competitive Intelligence: Move Your Business to the Top Using Cyber-Intelligence. Helen P. Burwell. Facts on Demand Press. • 1999. $25.95.

Covers the selection and use of online sources for competitive intelligence. Includes descriptions of many Internet Web sites, classified by subject. (Online Ease Series).

The Quintessential Searcher: The Wit and Wisdom of Barbara Quint. Marylaine Block, editor. Information Today, Inc. • 2001. $19.95. Presents the sayings of Barbara Quint, editor of *Searcher* magazine, who is often critical of the online information industry. (CyberAge Books.).

Silicon Snake Oil: Second Thoughts on the Information Highway. Clifford Stoll. Doubleday Publishing. • 1996. $14.00. The author discusses the extravagant claims being made for online networks and multimedia.

Super Searcher, Author, Scribe: Successful Writers Share Their Internet Research Secrets. Loraine Page. Information Today, Inc. • 2002. $24.95. Presents the results of interviews with 14 leading journalists, book authors, writing teachers, and professional literary researchers. Tips, techniques, and sources for searching the Web are featured. (Super Searchers Series).

Super Searchers Cover the World: The Online Secrets of International Business Researchers. Mary E. Bates. Information Today, Inc. • 2001. $24.95. Presents interviews with 15 experts in the area of online searching for international business information. (Super Searchers Series).

Super Searchers Go to the Source: The Interviewing and Hands-On Information Strategies of Top Primary Researchers - Online, On the Phone, and In Person. Risa Sacks. Information Today, Inc. • 2001. $24.95. Explains how information-search experts use various print, electronic, and live sources for competitive intelligence and other purposes. (Super Searchers Series).

Super Searchers in the News: The Online Secrets of Journalists and News Researchers. Paula J. Hane. Information Today, Inc. • 2000. $24.95. Contains online searching advice from 10 professional news researchers and fact checkers. (Super Searchers Series).

Super Searchers on Health and Medicine: The Online Secrets of Top Health and Medical Researchers. Susan M. Detwiler. Information Today, Inc. • 2000. $24.95. Provides the results of interviews with 10 experts in online searching for medical research data and healthcare information. Discusses both traditional sources and Web sites. (Super Searchers Series).

Super Searchers on Mergers & Acquisitions: The Online Secrets of Top Corporate Researchers and M & A Professionals. Jan Tudor. Information Today, Inc. • 2001. $24.95. Presents the results of interviews with 13 "top M & A information pros." Covers the finding, evaluating, and delivering of relevant data on companies and industries. (Super Searchers Series).

Super Searchers on Wall Street: Top Investment Professionals Share Their Online Research Secrets. Amelia Kassel. Information Today, Inc. • 2000. $24.95. Gives the results of interviews with "10 leading financial industry research experts." Explains how online information is used by stock brokers, investment bankers, and individual investors. Includes relevant Web sites and other sources. (Super Searchers Series).

The Web Library: Building a World Class Personal Library with Free Web Resources. Nicholas G. Tomaiuolo. Information Today, Inc. • 2003. $24.95. Provides advice on obtaining free, useful information and literature by way of the Internet. (CyberAge Books).

Web of Deception: Misinformation on the Internet. Anne P. Mintz, editor. Information Today, Inc. • 2002. $24.95. Barbara Quint, Susan M. Detwiler, and others discuss the spread of intentionally misleading or erroneous information by Web sites. Provides advice on the evaluation of Internet sources. (CyberAge Books.).

Wired Neighborhood. Stephen Doheny-Farina. Yale University Press. • 1996. $40.00. The author examines both the hazards and the advantages of "making the computer the center of our public and private lives," as exemplified by the Internet and telecommuting.

ABSTRACTS AND INDEXES

Business Periodicals Index. H. W. Wilson Co. • 11 times a year. Quarterly and annual cumulations. Price varies.

Computer Literature Index: A Subject/Author Index to Computer and Data Processing Literature. EBSCO Publishing. • Quarterly, with annual cumulation. $245.00 per year. Contains brief abstracts of book and periodical literature covering all phases of computing, including approximately 70 specific application areas.

F & S Index: United States. Gale Cengage Learning. • Monthly. $1,450.00 per year, including quarterly and annual cumulations. Provides annotated citations to marketing, business, financial, and industrial literature. Coverage of U. S. business activity includes trade journals, financial magazines, business newspapers, and special reports.

Internet and Personal Computing Abstracts [print edition]. EBSCO Publishing. • Quarterly. $269.00 per year, including cumulative index. Provides more than 10,000 abstracts annually from both trade and academic publications. Covers computer hardware, software, product reviews, Web topics, e-commerce, networks, corporate news, security, and related topics. Formerly *Microcomputer Abstracts.*

Key Abstracts: Computer Communications and Storage. Available from INSPEC, Inc. • Monthly. $250.00 per year. Provides international coverage of journal and proceedings literature, including material on optical disks and networks. Published in England by the Institution of Electrical Engineers (IEE).

Library Literature and Information Science Index. H. W. Wilson Co. • Quarterly. Annual cumulation. Price varies.

ALMANACS AND YEARBOOKS

Annual Society for Information Science and Technology, Information and Business Div. Martha E. Williams, editor. Information Today, Inc. • Annual. Members, $79.95; non-members, $99.95. Published on behalf of the American Society for Information Science (ASIS). Covers trends in planning, basic techniques, applications, and the information profession in general.

Communication Technology Update. Elsevier. • 2000. $36.95. 7th edition. A yearly review of developments in electronic media, telecommunications, and the Internet.

BIOGRAPHICAL SOURCES

Net.people: The Personalities and Passions Behind the Web Sites. Thomas E. Bleier and Eric C. Steinert. Information Today, Inc. • 2000. $19.95. Presents the personal stories of 36 Web "entrepreneurs and visionaries." (CyberAge Books.).

CD-ROM DATABASES

Authority Computer and Telecommunications Law Library. LexisNexis/Matthew Bender. • Quarterly. Price on request. Full text CD-ROM provides cases, analysis, sample agreements, and other information relating to computer law, telecommunications regulation (cable, broadcasting, satellite, Internet), international computer law, and computer contracts.

Computer Database. Gale Cengage Learning. • Provides one year of full-text on CD-ROM for 150 leading computer-related publications. Also includes 70,000 product specifications and brief profiles of 13,000 computer product vendors and manufacturers.

Hoover's Company Capsules on CD-ROM. Hoover's, Inc. • Quarterly. $399.95 per year (single-user). Provides the CD-ROM version of *Hoover's Handbook of American Business, Hoover's Handbook of Emerging Companies, Hoover's Handbook of World Business, Hoover's Guide to Computer Companies, Hoover's Guide to Media Companies, Hoover's Handbook of Private Companies,* and various regional guides. Includes more than 11,000 profiles of companies.

OECD Statistical Compendium. Organization for Economic Cooperation and Development. • Semiannual. $1,905.00 per year for 1 to 10 users. CD-ROM contains more than 730,000 monthly, quarterly, and annual time series for OECD countries, 1960 to date. Includes fully searchable data on agriculture, food, economic indicators, national accounts, employment, energy, finance, industry, technology, and foreign trade. Results can be displayed in various forms.

WILSONDISC: Library Literature and Information Science Index. H. W. Wilson Co. • Quarterly. Includes unlimited access to the online version of *Library Literature.* Provides CD-ROM indexing of about 300 periodicals, covering a wide range of topics having to do with libraries, library management, and the information industry.

WILSONDISC: Wilson Business Abstracts. H. W. Wilson Co. • Monthly. Includes unlimited online access to *Wilson Business Abstracts* through WILSONLINE. Provides CD-ROM "cover-to-cover" abstracting and indexing of over 600 prominent business periodicals. Indexing is from 1982, abstracting from 1990. (*Business Periodicals Index* without abstracts is available on CD-ROM at $1,495 per year.).

DIRECTORIES

Agriculture: Websites and Glossary. Carol Canada. Nova Science Publishers, Inc. • 2003. $29.50. Lists agricultural Web sites according to 24 main categories and 16 subcategories. Includes a glossary and an index.

The Core Business Web: A Guide to Key Information Sources. Gary W. White, editor. Haworth Press, Inc. • 2003. $49.95. Business librarians select Web sites in 25 areas of business, such as banking, e-commerce, investments, tourism, and small business.

Cyberhound's Guide to Companies on the Internet. Gale Cengage Learning. • 1996. $79.00. Presents critical descriptions and ratings of more than 2,000 company or corporate Internet databases. Includes a glossary of Internet terms, a bibliography, and indexes. (Cyberhound's Series).

Cyberhound's Guide to Internet Libraries. Gale Cengage Learning. • 1996. 79.00. Presents critical descriptions and ratings of more than 2,000 library Internet databases. Includes a glossary of Internet terms, a bibliography, and indexes. (Cyberhound's Series).

Cyberhound's Guide to People on the Internet. Gale Cengage Learning. • 1996. $79.00. Second edition. Provides descriptions of about 5,500 Internet databases maintained by or for prominent individuals in business, the professions, entertainment, and sports. Indexed by name, subject, and keyword (master index). (Cyberhound's Series).

Cyberhound's Guide to Publications on the Internet. Gale Cengage Learning. • 1996. $79.00. Presents critical descriptions and ratings of more than 3,400 Internet databases of journals, newspapers, newsletters, and other publications. Includes a glossary of Internet terms, a bibliography, and three indexes. (Cyberhound's Series).

Data Sources: The Comprehensive Guide to the Data Processing Industry: Hardware, Data Com-

munications Products, Software, Company Profiles. Gale Cengage Learning. • Semiannual. $455.00 per year. Two volumes. Describes hardware and software for all computer operating sysems, including prices and technical details. Lists about 75,000 products from 14,000 suppliers. Industry-specific software applications are described.

Essential Guide to the Best (and Worst) Legal Sites on the Web. Robert J. Ambrogi. American Lawyer Media, Inc. • 2001. $34.95. Sites are classified according to 25 legal subject areas and assigned 1-to-5 star ratings.

Fulltext Sources Online. Information Today Inc. • Covers: over 21,000 periodicals, newspapers, newsletters, newswires; and tv/radio transcripts available in full text online. Entries include: Name of file, online services through which available, dates of coverage, lag time if applicable. Separate list gives online service address and phone; indicates degree of online coverage and selection policy. Internet url's listed where applicable.

Gale Guide to Internet Databases. Gale Cengage Learning. • 1999. $125.00. Sixth edition. Presents critical descriptions and ratings of more than 5,000 useful Internet databases (especially World Wide Web sites). Includes a glossary of Internet terms, a bibliography, and five indexes.

Government Information on the Internet. Greg R. Notess. Bernan Associates. • Annual. $38.50. directory of publicly-accessible Internet sites maintained by the U. S. Government. Also includes selected foreign government sites, state sites, and non-government sites containing government-provided data.

Great Scouts! CyberGuides to Subject Searching on the Web. Margot Williams and others. Information Today, Inc. • 1999. $24.95. Contains descriptions of selected Web sites, arranged by subject. Covers business, investments, computers, travel, the environment, health, social issues, etc. (CyberAge Books.).

Guide to EU Information Sources on the Internet. Euroconfidentiel S. A. • Annual. $210.00. Contains descriptions of more than 1,700 Web sites providing information relating to the European Union and European commerce and industry. Includes a quarterly e-mail newsletter with new sites and address changes.

Handbook of Internet Stocks. Mergent. • Annual. $19.95. Contains detailed financial information on more than 200 Internet-related corporations, including e-commerce firms and telecommunications hardware manufacturers. Lists and rankings are provided.

Harley Hahn's Internet and Web Yellow Pages. Harley Hahn. Osborne/McGraw-Hill. • Annual. $34.99. Lists World Wide Web sites in more than 100 categories.

The Internet Blue Pages: The Guide to Federal Government Web Sites. Information Today, Inc. • Annual. $34.95. Provides information on more than 1,800 Web sites used by various agencies of the federal government. Includes indexes to agencies and topics. Links to all Web sites listed are available at http://www.fedweb.com. (CyberAge Books.).

The Internet Compendium: Guide to Resources by Subject: Subject Guides to Health and Science Resources. Joseph Janes and others, editors. Neal-Schuman Publishers, Inc. • 1995. $82.50. Editors are with the University of Michigan Internet Clearinghouse. Provides direct location access to "thousands" of Internet addresses, in a detailed subject arrangement, with critical analysis of content. Contains information databases, text archives, library catalogs, bulletin boards, newsletters, forums, etc. Includes topics in medicine, agriculture, biology, chemistry, mathematics, physics, engineering, computers, and science in general.

The Internet Compendium: Guide to Resources by Subject: Subject Guides to Social Sciences, Business, and Law Resources. Joseph Janes and others, editors. Neal-Schuman Publishers, Inc. • 1995. $82. 50. Editors are with the University of Michigan Internet Clearinghouse. Provides direct location access to "thousands" of Internet addresses, in a detailed subject arrangement, with critical analysis of content. Contains information databases, text archives, library catalogs, bulletin boards, newsletters, forums, etc. Includes topics in economics, finance, taxation, history, population, civil rights law, law careers, women's studies, and so forth.

The Internet Compendium: Guide to Resources by Subject: Subject Guides to the Humanities. Joseph Janes. Neal-Schuman Publishers, Inc. • 1995. $82. 50. Editors are with the University of Michigan Internet Clearinghouse. Provides direct location access to "thousands" of Internet addresses, in a detailed subject arrangement, with critical analysis of content. Contains information databases, text archives, library catalogs, bulletin boards, newsletters, forums, etc. Includes topics in literature, art, religion, philosophy, music, education, library science, games, magic, and the humanities in general.

Internet Resources: A Subject Guide. Available from American Library Association. • 1995. $18.00. Published by Association of College and Research Libraries. Provides updated versions of Internet subject directories appearing originally in *College and Research Libraries News.*

Internet Resources and Services for International Business: A Global Guide. Lewis-Guodo Liu. Greenwood Publishing Group, Inc. • 1998. $62.95. Describes more than 2,500 business-related Web sites from 176 countries. Includes five major categories: general information, economics, business and trade, business travel, and contacts. Indexed by Web site name, country, and subject.

Internet Tools of the Profession: A Guide for Information Professionals. Hope N. Tillman, editor. Special Libraries Association. • 1997. $49.00. Second edition. Consists of 14 sections by various authors or compilers. After two introductory articles on searching the Internet, there are 12 annotated lists of useful Web sites, covering the SLA, business and finance, chemistry, education, food and agriculture, information technology, insurance and employee benefits, law, library management, metals and materials, pharmaceuticals, and telecommunications. An index is provided.

Library Journal: Reference [year]: Print, CD-ROM, Online. Reed Business Information. • Annual. Issued in November as a supplement to *Library Journal.* Lists new and updated reference material, including general and trade print titles, directories, annuals, CD-ROM titles, and online sources. Includes material from more than 200 publishers, arranged by company name, with an index by subject. Addresses include e-mail and Web information.

Library Journal Sourcebook. Reed Business Information. • Publication includes: List of over 600 suppliers of products and services used by libraries from abstracting to word processing equipment. Entries include: Company name, address, phone, list of products or services. Complete listings for more than 100 architectural firms; Disaster planning for librarians.

Major Information Technology Companies of the World 2001. Available from Gale Cengage Learning. • Annual. $880.00. Published by Graham & Whiteside. Contains profiles of more than 3,100 leading information technology companies in various countries.

New Riders' Official World Wide Web Yellow Pages. New Riders Publishing. • 1998. $34.99. Sixth edition. A broadly classified listing of Web sites, with brief descriptions of sites and a subject index to narrower topics. Includes a guide to using the Inter-

net and a separate, alphabetical listing of more than 1,500 college and university Web sites, both U. S. and foreign. Includes CD-ROM.

Plunkett's E-Commerce and Internet Business Almanac. Plunkett Research, Ltd. • Annual. $249. 99. Contains detailed profiles of 250 large companies engaged in various areas of Internet commerce, including e-business Web sites, communications equipment manufacturers, and Internet service providers. Includes CD-ROM.

Plunkett's Employers' Internet Sites with Careers Information. Plunkett Research, Ltd. • Annual. $199.99. Includes diskette.

Plunkett's InfoTech Industry Almanac: Complete Profiles on the InfoTech 500-the Leading Firms in the Movement and Management of Voice, Data, and Video. Plunkett Research, Ltd. • Biennial. $229.99. Includes CD-ROM. Five hundred major information companies are profiled, with corporate culture aspects. Discusses major trends in various sectors of the computer and information industry, including data on careers and job growth. Includes several indexes.

Plunkett's On-Line Trading, Finance, and Investment Web Sites Almanac. Plunkett Research, Ltd. • Annual. $149.99. Provides profiles and usefulness rankings of financial Web sites. Sites are rated from 1 to 5 for specific uses. Includes CD-ROM.

The Software Encyclopedia: A Guide for Personal, Professional, and Business Users. Gale. • Annual. $335.00. Two volumes. Volume one lists software programs by title and producer. Volume two provides information on programs according to application and operating system. Includes prices and requirements for hardware and memory.

SRDS Interactive Advertising Source. SRDS. • Quarterly. $569.00 per year. Provides descriptive profiles, rates, audience, personnel, etc., for producers of various forms of interactive or multimedia advertising: online/Internet, CD-ROM, interactive TV, interactive cable, interactive telephone, interactive kiosk, and others.

Telehealth Buyer's Guide. Miller Freeman. • Annual. $10.00. Lists sources of telecommunications and information technology products and services for the health care industry.

Web Site Source Book: A Guide to Major U. S. Businesses, Organizations, Agencies, Institutions, and Other Information Resources on the World Wide Web. Omnigraphics, Inc. • 2004. $150.00. Ninth edition. About 84,000 Web sites are arranged alphabetically by business or organization and by 1,350 subject categories. Surface mail addresses, phone numbers, fax numbers, and e-mail addresses are included.

World Directory of Business Information Web Sites. Available from Gale Cengage Learning. • 2003. $690.00. Sixth edition. Published by Euromonitor. Provides detailed descriptions of a wide variety of business-related Web sites. More than 1,500 sites are included from around the world. Covers statistics sources, market research, company information, rankings, surveys, economic data, etc.

ENCYCLOPEDIAS AND DICTIONARIES

Acronyms of Computer Science and Communications: A Comprehensive Acronym Dictionary and Illustrated Encyclopedia. Enjob Kajan and Ejub Kajan. Springer Verlag. • 2002. $49.95. Explains more than 4,000 "broadly used" computer, telecommunications, and information technology acronyms. Includes illustrations and Web addresses, where applicable.

Business Internet and Intranets: A Manager's Guide to Key Terms and Concepts. McGraw-Hill. • 1998. $39.95. Defines more than 100 words and phrases relating to the Internet or corporate intranets.

CyberDictionary: Your Guide to the Wired World.

Spurge ink!. • 1996. $17.95. Includes many illustrations.

Cyberspace Lexicon: An Illustrated Dictionary of Terms from Multimedia to Virtual Reality. Bob Cotton and Richard Oliver. Phaidon Press. • 1994. $29.95. Defines more than 800 terms, with manyillustrations. Includes a bibliography.

Encyclopedia of Information Systems. Hossein Bidgoli, editor. Elsevier. • 2002. $1,200.00. Four volumes. Contains a wide range of articles relating to computers, databases, communication, and information technology. The 200 topics include coverage of hardware, software, artificial intelligence, the Internet, networks, knowledge management, electronic commerce, search engines, and systems design.

Encyclopedia of New Media: An Essential Reference to Communication and Technology. Steve Jones, editor. Sage Publications, Inc. • 2003. $125.00. Contains more than 250 entries dealing with such areas as multimedia, broadband access, information communication technology (ICT), content filtering, wireless networks, and cyberethics.

Encyclopedic Guide to Searching and Finding Health Information on the Web. P. F. Anderson and Nancy J. Allee, editors. Neal-Schuman Publishers. • 2004. $395.00. Three volumes. Comprehensive guide to searching the Web for reliable information on hundreds of specific diseases, disorders, and health issues. Volume three covers Search Strategies and provides a Cumulative Index. (Published in conjunction with the Medical Library Association.).

Every Manager's Guide to Information Technology: A Glossary of Key Terms and Concepts for Today's Business Leader. Peter G. W. Keen. Harvard Business School Publishing. • 1994. $18.95. Second edition. Provides definitions of terms related to computers, data communications, and information network systems. (Harvard Business Reference Series).

Internet Encyclopedia. Hossein Bidgoli, editor. John Wiley and Sons, Inc. • 2003. $750.00. Four volumes. Covers various aspects of the Internet, including information technology, electronic business, and telecommunications.

Multimedia and the Web from A to Z. David C. Leonard and Patrick M. Dillon. Greenwood Publishing Group, Inc. • 1998. $42.95. Second enlarged revised edition. Defines more than 1,500 terms relating to software and hardware in the areas of computing, online technology, telecommunications, audio, video, motion pictures, CD-ROM, and the Internet. Includes acronyms and an annotated bibliography. Formerly *Multimedia Technology from A to Z* (1994).

New Hacker's Dictionary. Eric S. Raymond. MIT Press. • 1996. $65.00. Third edition. Includes three classifications of hacker communication: slang, jargon, and "techspeak.".

HANDBOOKS AND MANUALS

Banking and Finance on the Internet. Mary J. Cronin, editor. John Wiley and Sons, Inc. • 1997. $45.00. Contains articles on Internet services, written by bankers, money mangers, investment analysts, and stockbrokers. Emphasis is on operations management. (Communications Series).

Basic Internet for Busy Librarians: A Quick Course for Catching Up. Laura K. Murray. American Library Association. • 1998. $26.00. A "practical crash-course primer" for learning how to effectively navigate the Internet and the World Wide Web.

Best Bet Internet: Reference and Research When You Don't Have Time to Mess Around. Shirley D. Kennedy. American Library Association. • 1997. $35.00. Provides advice for librarians and others on the effective use of World Wide Web information sources.

Beyond Book Indexing: How to Get Started in Web Indexing, Embedded Indexing, and Other Computer-Based Media. Information Today, Inc. • 1999. $31.25. Published for the American Society of Indexers. Contains 12 chapters written by professional indexers. Part one discusses making an index by marking items in an electronic document (embedded indexing); part two is on indexing to make Web pages more accessible; part three covers CD-ROM and multimedia indexing; part four provides career and promotional advice for professionals in the field. Includes an index by Janet Perlman and a glossary.

Building the Service-Based Library Web Site: A Step-by-Step Guide to Design and Options. Kristen L. Garlock and Sherry Piontek. American Library Association. • 1996. $30.00. Provides practical information for libraries planning a World Wide Web home page. (ALA Editions Series).

Business Statistics on the Web: Find Them Fast, at Little or No Cost. Paula Berinstein. Information Today, Inc. • 2003. $29.95. Serves as a practical guide to finding and evaluating business data through the Internet. Includes advice on the organization and presentation of business statistics. (CyberAge Books).

Click Here! Internet Advertising: How the Pros Attract, Design, Price, Place, and Measure Ads Online. Eugene Marlow. John Wiley and Sons, Inc. • 1997. $29.95. Covers pricing, effectiveness, Web site selection, content, and other aspects of Internet advertising. (Business Technology Series).

Columbia Guide to Digital Publishing: In Print and On the Web. William E. Kasdorf, editor. Columbia University Press. • 2002. $65.00. Covers the practical production of both written and graphic material in digital format, including archives, new technology, "information architecture," and copyright.

The Cybrarian's Manual. Pat Ensor, editor. American Library Association. • 2000. $45.00. Second edition. Provides information for librarians concerning the Internet, expert systems, computer networks, client/server architecture, Web pages, multimedia, information industry careers, and other "cyberspace" topics.

Electronic Selling: Twenty-Three Steps to E-Selling Profits. Brian Jamison and others. McGraw-Hill. • 1997. $24.95. Covers selling on the World Wide Web, including security and payment issues. Provides a glossary and directory information. The authors are consultants specializing in Web site production.

Electronic Styles: A Handbook of Citing Electronic Information. Xia Li and Nancy Crane. Information Today, Inc. • 1996. $19.99. Second edition. Covers the citing of text-based information, electronic journals, Web sites, CD-ROM items, multimedia products, and online documents.

The Essential Guide to Bulletin Board Systems. Patrick R. Dewey. Information Today, Inc. • 1998. $39.50. Provides details on the setup and operation of online bulletin board systems. Covers both hardware and software.

Exporting with the Internet. Peter J. Robinson and Jonathan Powell. John Wiley and Sons, Inc. • 1997. $39.95. Explains how the Internet can help with finding overseas buyers and expediting export shipments and payments. (Business Technology Series).

The Extreme Searcher's Guide to Web Search Engines: A Handbook for the Serious Searcher. Randolph Hock. Information Today, Inc. • 2001. $24.95. Second expanded revised edition. Provides detailed information and advice on effective use of the major Internet search engines. (CyberAge Books).

The Extreme Searcher's Internet Handbook: A Guide for the Serious Searcher. Randolph Hock. Information Today, Inc. • 2004. $24.95. Provides information on "all major areas of Internet content."

Edited for both beginning and experienced searchers. (CyberAge Books).

Find It Online: The Complete Guide to Online Research. Alan M. Schlein. Facts on Demand Press. • 2002. $19.95. Third edition. Presents the general principles of online searching for information about people, phone numbers, public records, news, business, investments, etc. Covers both free and fee-based sources. (On Line Ease Series).

Finding It on the Internet: The Internet Navigator's Guide to Search Tools and Techniques. Paul Gilster. John Wiley and Sons, Inc. • 1996. $24.95. Second expanded revised edition. A basic guide to efficient use of the World Wide Web, search engines, e-mail, hypertext, and the Internet in general. Includes such programs or systems as Gopher, Archie, Veronica, and Jughead, with emphasis on information searching.

Finding Market Research on the Web: Best Practices of Professional Researchers. Robert I. Berkman. MarketResearch.com. • 2003. $279.00. Provides tips and techniques for locating useful market research data through the Internet.

Finding Statistics Online: How to Locate the Elusive Numbers You Need. Paula Berinstein. Information Today, Inc. • 1998. $29.95. Provides advice on efficient searching when looking for statistical data on the World Wide Web or from commercial online services and database producers. (CyberAge Books.).

Handbook of Digital Publishing. Michael L. Kleper. Prentice Hall PTR. • 2001. $129.99. Two volumes. Edited for the digital publishing industry. Covers print publishing, electronic documents, and Internet (Web) publishing, including basic desktop procedures. Provides information on typography, design, layout, image creation, and page creation.

Hot Text: Web Writing That Works. Jonathan Price and Lisa Price. New Riders Publishing. • 2002. $40.00. Provides practical advice on writing text for Web sites, including such details as headlines and menu design. As the attention span of many Web surfers is limited, clarity and brevity become of great importance.

How to Start a Home-Based Web Design Business. Jim Smith. Globe Pequot Press. • 2004. $17.95. Second edition. Covers planning, marketing, subcontracting, setting fees, customer presentations, and other topics related to starting a freelance, web design business at home. Includes a sample customer contract. (Home-Based Business Series).

Indexer's Guide to the Internet. Lori Lathrop. Information Today, Inc. • 1999. $31.25. Second edition. Published in conjunction with the American Society of Indexers (ASI). Includes advice on useful Web sites, service providers, Web site design, and the use of search engines.

The Information Professional's Guide to Career Development Online. Sarah L. Nesbeitt and Rachel S. Gordon. Information Today, Inc. • 2001. $29.50. Provides advice to librarians and other information professionals about using online sources for career advancement. The Career Development Online Web Page (http://www.lisjobs.com/careerdev/) contains links to relevant resources.

International Business Information on the Web: Searcher Magazine's Guide to Sites and Strategies for Global Business Research. Sheri R. Lanza. Information Today, Inc. • 2001. $29.95. (CyberAge Books.).

Internet Book: Everything You Need to Know About Computer Networking and How the Internet Works. Douglas Comer. Prentice Hall PTR. • 2000. $34.80. Third edition.

Internet Business Intelligence: How to Build a Big Company System on a Small Company Budget. David Vine. Information Today, Inc. • 2000. $29.95. Covers the obtaining of valuable business intelligence data through use of the Internet.

Internet Insider. Ruffin Prevost. Osborne/McGraw-Hill. • 1995. $14.95. A colorful presentation. (Internet Series).

Internet Literacy. Fred Hofstetter. McGraw-Hill. • 2002. $38.75. Third edition. Provides practical information on a wide variety of topics relating to Web creation and electronic publishing.

Internet Research Guide: A Concise, Friendly, and Practical Handbook for Anyone Researching in the Wide World of Cyberspace. Timothy K. Maloy. Allworth Press. • 1997. $18.95. Second revised edition. Provides "hype-free" advice on practical use of the World Wide Web.

The Invisible Web: Uncovering Information Sources Search Engines Can't See. Chris Sherman and Gary Price. Information Today, Inc. • 2001. $29.95. A guide to Web sites from universities, libraries, associations, government agencies, and other sources that are inadequately covered by conventional search engines (see also http://www.invisible-web.net). (CyberAge Books.).

Journalism Online. Mike Ward and Andy Dickinson. Elsevier. • 2002. $39.95. Covers the basic journalism skills needed for identifying, collecting, selecting, and presenting news and information for the World Wide Web.

Learning Web Design: A Beginner's Guide to HTML, Graphics, and Beyond. Jennifer Niederst. O'Reilly & Associates, Inc. • 2001. $34.95. Written for beginners who have no previous knowledge of how Web design works.

Legal Liability Problems in Cyberspace: Craters in the Information Highway. T. R. Halvorson. Burwell Enterprises. • 1998. $24.50. Covers the legal risks and liabilities involved in doing online research as a paid professional. Includes a table of cases.

The Librarian's Internet Survival Guide: Strategies for the High-Tech Reference Desk. Irene E. McDermott. Information Today, Inc. • 2002. $29.50. Provides practical advice relating to Web reference sources, information management strategies, Internet training issues, library Web pages, and patron relations.

Managing Public-Access Computers: A How-To-Do-It Manual for Librarians. Donald A. Barclay. Neal-Schuman Publishers, Inc. • 2000. $59.95. Part one covers hardware, software, and other components. Part two discusses computers users. Part three is about systems management, library policy, and legal issues. (How-to-Do-It Manuals Series).

Mining for Gold on the Internet: How to Find Investment and Financial Information on the Internet. Mary Ellen Bates. McGraw-Hill. • 2000. $24.95. Tells how to effectively search the Internet for financial advice and information. Specific websites are discussed.

Naked in Cyberspace: How to Find Personal Information Online. Carole A. Lane. Information Today, Inc. • 2002. $29.95. Second edition. Covers the availability of personal records on the Internet, including competitive intelligence data, customer characteristics, employee information, backgrounds of experts, public records, criminal records, and genealogical data. From an opposite viewpoint, advice is offered relative to the maintenance of privacy. Includes a Web directory with about 1,000 sources of information. (CyberAge Books.).

Net Crimes and Misdemeanors: Outmaneuvering the Spammers, Swindlers, and Stalkers Who Are Targeting You Online. Jayne Hitchcock. Information Today, Inc. • 2002. $24.95. Provides specific strategies and techniques for dealing with a wide range of online abusive practices. (CyberAge Books.).

The Official America Online Tour Guide. Jennifer Watson and Dave Marx. John Wiley and Sons, Inc.

• 2000. $24.99.Fifth edition. Provides a detailed explanation of the various features of versio of America Online, including electronic mail procedures and "Using the Internet.".

Online Deskbook: Online Magazine's Essential Desk Reference for Online and Internet Searchers. Mary E. Bates. Information Today, Inc. • 1995. $29.95. Covers the World Wide Web, as well as America Online, CompuServe, Dialog, Lexis-Nexis, and all other major online services. (Pemberton Press Books.).

Online Marketing Handbook: How to Promote, Advertise and Sell, Your Products and Services on the Internet. Daniel S. Janal. John Wiley and Sons, Inc. • 1999. $29.95. Revised edition. Provides step-by-step instructions for utilizing online publicity, advertising, and sales promotion. Contains chapters on interactive marketing, online crisis communication, and Web home page promotion, with numerous examples and checklists. (Business Technology Series).

Secrets of the Super Net Searchers: The Reflections, Revelations and Hard-Won Wisdom of 35 of the World's Top Internet Researchers. Reva Basch. Information Today, Inc. • 1996. $29.95. Tells how to find "cyber-gems" among the "cyber-junk." (Cyber Age Books.).

The Skeptical Business Searcher: The Information Advisor's Guide to Evaluating Web Data, Sites, and Sources. Robert Berkman. Information Today, Inc. • 2003. $29.95. Covers free Internet sources of company backgrounds, sales data, earnings, SEC documents, competitive intelligence information, poll data, business news, economic statistics, etc. The author is editor of *The Information Advisor* newsletter. (CyberAge Books).

Software for Indexing. Sandi Schroeder, editor. Information Today, Inc. • 2003. $35.00. Published in conjunction with the American Society of Indexers (ASI). Material by professional indexers covers dedicated indexing programs, embedded software, online indexing, Web indexing, database software, customized software, automatic indexing, and other indexing software topics.

Web Style Guide: Basic Design Principles for Creating Web Sites. Patrick J. Lynch and Sarah Horton. Yale University Press. • 2002. $35.00. Second edition. Covers design of content, interface, page layout, graphics, and multimedia aspects.

INTERNET DATABASES

Business 2.0 Web Guide to the Best Business Links. Business 2.0 Media Inc. Phone: (415)293-4800 E-mail: support@business2.com • URL: http://www.business2.com/webguide • Web site presents an extensive, searchable directory of links to "the best, most informative, and authoritative web pages." Twenty main categories cover business, finance, career, company information, people, and technology topics, with thousands of subtopics, all linking to Web sites recommended by experienced business researchers. Fees: Free.

InfoTech Trends. Data Analysis Group. Phone: (925)462-1202 Fax: (925)462-1225 E-mail: support@infotechtrends.com • URL: http://www.infotechtrends.com • Web site provides both free and fee-based market research data on the information technology industry, including computers, peripherals, telecommunications, the Internet, software, CD-ROM/DVD, e-commerce, and workstations. Fees: Free for current (most recent year) data; more extensive information has various fee structures. Formerly *Computer Industry Forecasts*.

Internet.com: The E-Business and Internet Technology Network. Jupitermedia. Phone: (203)226-6967 Fax: (203)454-5840 E-mail: info@internet.com • URL: http://www.internet.com • Web site provides a wide variety of information relating to Internet

commerce, search engines, news, Web design, servers, browsers, Java, service providers, advertising, marketing, etc. Online searching is offered. Fees: Free. (Formerly produced by Mecklermedia Corp.).

SAEGIS Internet Search. Thomson & Thomson. Phone: 800-692-8833 or (617)479-1600 Fax: (617)786-8273 E-mail: support@thomson-thomson.com • URL: http://www.thomson-thomson.com • Fee-based Web site provides extensive, common law screening of the World Wide Web for trademarks. Searches are performed offline, with final report delivered to user's "SAEGIS Inbox." Context of trademark within each relevant Web site is indicated, and links are provided.

Search Engine Watch. Internet.com Corp. Phone: (203)662-2800 Fax: (203)655-4686 • URL: http://www.searchenginewatch.com • Web site offers information on various aspects of search engines, including new developments, indexing systems, technology, ratings and reviews of major operators, specialty services, tutorials, news, history, "Search Engine EKGs," "Facts and Fun," etc. Online searching is provided. Formerly *A Webmaster's Guide to Search Engines.*

Wired News. Lycos, Inc. Phone: (415)276-8400 Fax: (415)276-8500 E-mail: newsfeedback@wired.com • URL: http://www.wired.com • Provides summaries and full-text of "Top Stories" relating to the Internet, computers, multimedia, telecommunications, and the electronic information industry in general. These news stories are placed in the broad categories of Politics, Business, Culture, and Technology. Affiliated with *Wired* magazine. Fees: Free.

ONLINE DATABASES

F & S Index. Gale Cengage Learning. • Contains about four million citations to worldwide business, financial, and industrial or consumer product literature appearing from 1972 to date. Weekly updates. Inquire as to online cost and availability.

Globalbase. Gale Cengage Learning. • Provides more than one million online summaries of business, industrial, and economic news reports from more than 1,000 publications worldwide. Covers a wide range of material appearing in international trade journals, professional magazines, and newspapers. Time period is 1984 to date, with weekly updates. Inquire as to online cost and availability.

Internet and Personal Computing Abstracts. Information Today, Inc. • Contains abstracts covering a wide variety of personal and business microcomputer literature appearing in more than 100 journals and popular magazines. Time period is 1981 to date, with monthly updates. Formerly *Microcomputer Index.* Inquire as to online cost and availability.

PROMT: Predicasts Overview of Markets and Technology. Gale Cengage Learning. • Companies, products, applied technologies and markets. U.S. and international literature coverage, 1972 to date. Inquire as to online cost and availability. Provides abstracts from more than 1,600 publications. Weekly updates.

Wilson Business Abstracts Online. H. W. Wilson Co. • Indexes and abstracts 600 major business periodicals, plus the *Wall Street Journal* and the business section of the *New York Times.* Indexing is from 1982, abstracting from 1990, with the two newspapers included from 1993. Updated weekly. Inquire as to online cost and availability. (*Business Periodicals Index* without abstracts is also available online.).

PERIODICALS AND NEWSLETTERS

Boardwatch: Analysis of Telecom Software, Services and Strategy. Light Reading, Inc. • Monthly. $72.00 per year. Covers World Wide Web publishing, internet technology, educational aspects of online communication, internet legalities, and other computer communication topics.

Broadband Solutions. North American Publishing Co. • Monthly. Controlled circulation. Covers the high-bandwidth telecommunications industry, including new products and emerging technologies.

Broadband Week. Reed Business Information. • 51 times a year. $139.00 per year. Provides news and trends for all parts of the evolving broadband industry, including operations, marketing, finance, and technology. Incorporates *Broadband.*

CIO: The Magazine for Chief Information Officers. CXO Media, Inc. • 23 times a year. $150.00 per year. Edited for chief information officers. Includes a monthly "Web Business" section (incorporates the former *WebMaster* periodical) and a monthly "Enterprise" section for company executives other than CIOs.

The CyberSkeptic's Guide to Internet Research. Information Today, Inc. • 10 times a year. Individuals, $159.00 per year; nonprofit organizations, $134.00 per year. Newsletter. Presents critical reviews of World Wide Web sites and databases, written by information professionals. Includes "Late Breaking News" of Web sites.

Cyberspace Lawyer. Glasser Legalworks. • 11 times a year. $300.00 per year. Newsletter. Covers various legal topics pertaining to use of the Internet. Includes advice on legal research via the Web.

Fat Pipe: The Business of Marketing Broadband Services. Dagda Mor Media, Inc. • Monthly. Controlled circulation. Edited for those who plan, develop, and market broadband Internet and telecommunications services.

InfoAlert: Your Expert Guide to Online Business Information. Economics Press, Inc. • Monthly. $129.00 per year. Newsletter. Provides information on recommended World Wide Web sites in various business, marketing, industrial, and financial areas.

The Information Freeway Report: Free Business and Government Information Via Modem. Washington Researchers, Ltd. • Monthly. $160.00 per year. Newsletter. Provides news of business and government databases that are available free of charge through the Internet or directly. Emphasis is on federal government databases and electronic bulletin boards (Fedworld).

Information Outlook: The Monthly Magazine of the Special Libraries Association. Special Libraries Association. • Monthly. $65.00 per year. Topics include information technology, the Internet, copyright, research techniques, library management, and professional development. Replaces *Special Libraries* and *SpeciaList.*

Information Standards Quarterly: News About Library, Information Sciences, and Publishing Standards. National Information Standards Organization (NISO). • Quarterly. $80.00 per year. Newsletter. Reports on activities of the National Information Standards Organization.

InterActive Consumers. MarketResearch.com. • Monthly. $395.00 per year. Newsletter. Covers the emerging markets for digital content, products, and services. Includes market information on telecommuting, online services, the Internet, online investing, and other areas of electronic commerce.

Interactive Content: Consumer Media Strategies Monthly. Jupitermedia. • Monthly. $675.00 per year; with online edition, $775.00 per year. Newsletter. Covers the broad field of providing content (information, news, entertainment) for the Internet/World Wide Web.

Interactive Home: Consumer Technology Monthly. Jupiter Communications. • Monthly. $625.00 per year; with online edition, $725.00 per year. Newsletter on devices to bring the Internet into the average American home. Covers TV set-top boxes, game

devices, telephones with display screens, handheld computer communication devices, the usual PCs, etc.

Interactive Marketing and P R News: News and Practical Advice on Using Interactive Advertising and Marketing to Sell Your Products. PBI Media, LLC. • Biweekly. $495.00 per year. Newsletter. Provides information and guidance on merchandising via CD-ROM ("multimedia catalogs"), the Internet, and interactive TV. Topics include "cybermoney", addresses for e-mail marketing, "virtual malls," and other interactive subjects. Formerly *Interactive Marketing News.*

Internet and Electronic Commerce Strategies: Using Technology to Improve Your Bottom Line. Computer Economics, Inc. • Monthly. Price on application. Newsletter on management strategies for making money from the Internet. Compares on-line marketing with traditional marketing.

Internet Business Report: Software, Tools and Platforms. Jupitermedia. • Semimonthly. $695.00 per year; with electronic software, $795.00 per year. Newsletter. Covers Internet advertising, fee collection, and attempts in general to make the Internet/World Wide Web profitable. Includes news of how businesses are using the Internet for sales promotion and public relations.

Internet Connection: Your Guide to Government Resources. Glasser Legalworks. • 10 times a year. $89.00 per year. Newsletter (print) devoted to finding free or low-cost U. S. Government information on the Internet. Provides detailed descriptions of government Web sites.

Internet Industry Magazine. Jonas Publishing. • Semiannual. Price on application. Lists products and services for Internet service providers. Includes Internet-related articles and interviews.

Internet Law and Strategy. American Lawyer Media, Inc. • Monthly. $199.00 per year. Newsletter. Primarily concerned with doing legal research online. Contains reviews of the best Web sites for lawyers. (A Law Journal Newsletter, formerly published by Leader Publications.).

Internet Law Researcher. Glasser Legalworks. • 11 times a year. $200.00 per year. Newsletter for legal professionals on how to search the Web efficiently. Provides detailed information on individual Web sites.

Internet Marketing and Technology Report: Advising Marketing, Sales, and Corporate Executives on Online Opportunities. Computer Economics, Inc. • Monthly. $387.00 per year. Newsletter. Covers strategic marketing, sales, advertising, public relations, and corporate communications, all in relation to the Internet. Includes information on "cutting-edge technology" for the Internet.

Internet Marketing Report: News and Advice to Help Companies Harness the Power of the Internet to Achieve Business Objectives. Progressive Business Publications. • Semimonthly. $299.00 per year. Newsletter. Covers Internet marketing strategy, site traffic, success stories, technology, cost control, and other Web site advertising and marketing topics.

Internet Reference Services Quarterly: A Journal of Innovative Information Practice, Technologies, and Resources. Haworth Press, Inc. • Quarterly. $110.00 per year. Covers both theoretical research and practical applications.

Internet Retailer: E-Business Strategies. Thomson Financial. • 10 times a year. $98.00 per year. Trade journal on the selling of retail merchandise through the Internet. Provides information on pricing, payment systems, order management, fraud, digital imaging, advertising, Web trends, and other topics.

Internet World: Magazine. Semimonthly. $160.00 per year. Edited for "Internet professionals." Includes industry news, new products, e-business

news, and technical developments. (Formerly *WebWeek.*).

Journal of Internet Cataloging: The International Quarterly of Digital Organization, Classification, and Access. Haworth Press, Inc. • Quarterly. $165.00 per year.

Journal of Internet Law. Aspen Publishers, Inc. • Monthly. $360.00 per year. Covers such Internet and e-commerce topics as domain name disputes, copyright protection, Uniform Commercial Code issues, international law, privacy regulation, electronic records, digital signatures, liability, and security.

Journal of Website Promotion: Innovations in Internet Business Research, Theory, and Practice. Haworth Press, Inc. • Semiannual. $250.00 per year to libraries; $45.00 per year to individuals. Presents a scholarly view of such items as spam, banner ads, pop-ups, click rates, and the use of search engines for advertising.

Multimedia Schools: A Practical Journal of Technology for Education including Multimedia, CD-ROM, Online and Internet and Hardware in K-12. Information Today, Inc. • Six times a year. $39.95 per year. Edited for school librarians, media center directors, computer coordinators, and others concerned with educational multimedia. Coverage includes the use of CD-ROM sources, the Internet, online services, and library technology.

Network World: The Newsweekly of Enterprise Network Computing. Network World Inc. • Weekly. $129.00 per year. Includes special feature issues on enterprise Internets, network operating systems, network management, high-speed modems, LAN management systems, and Internet access providers.

New Architecture: Solutions for Internet and World Wide Web Developers. CMP Media LLC. • Monthly. $34.95 per year. A technical magazine edited for Internet and World Wide Web professionals. Formerly *Web Techniques.*

Online Marketplace. Jupiter Communications. • Description: Keeps abreast of the fast-emerging developments in the digital marketplace and emerging interactive technologies. Reports on players and devices to provide the "inside scoop" on this marketplace. Topics include screen phones, interactive television, and smart cards, to name a few. Recurring features include interviews, and columns titled Tool Watch, Site Watch, and News Digest.

Online: The Leading Magazine for Information Professionals. Information Today, Inc. • Bimonthly. $110.00 per year. Edited for librarians, Webmasters, site designers, content managers, and others concerned with knowledge/information management. Includes critical reviews of Web sites, software, search engines, and information services. (Formerly published by Online, Inc.).

U.S. Banker. IMG Media. • Monthly. $79.00 per year. Covers technology innovation for the banking industry, including online banking. Incorporates *Future Banker.*

Upgrade. Software and Information Industry Association. • Monthly. $79.00 per year. Covers news and trends relating to the software, information, and Internet industries. Formerly *SPA News* from Software Publishers Association.

Web Feet: The Internet Traveler's Desk Reference. RockHill Communications. • Monthly. $165.00 per year. Looseleaf service. Serves as a subject guide to the "best" Web sites.

Web Marketing Update: Quick, Actionable, Internet Intelligence for Marketing Executives. Computer Economics, Inc. • Monthly. $347.00 per year. Newsletter on various aspects of promoting or selling products and services through an Internet Web site: technology, advertising, strategy, customer base, cost projections, search engines, etc.

WebFinance. Thomson Media. • Semimonthly. $995.00 per year. Newsletter (also available online at www.webfinance.net). Covers the Internet-based provision of online financial services by banks, on-line brokers, mutual funds, and insurance companies. Provides news stories, analysis, and descriptions of useful resources.

Wired. Wired Ventures Ltd. • Monthly. $10.00 per year. Edited for creators and managers in various areas of electronic information and entertainment, including multimedia, the Internet, and video. Often considered to be the primary publication of the "digital generation.".

Wireless Review: Intelligence for Competitive Providers. Primedia Business Magazines and Media. • Semimonthly. $48.00 per year. Covers business and technology developments for wireless service providers. Includes special issues on a wide variety of wireless topics. Formed by merger of *Cellular Business* and *Wireless World.*

RESEARCH CENTERS AND INSTITUTES

Advanced Networking Research Group. Washington University, One Brookings Dr., St. Louis, MO 63130-4899. Phone: (314)935-6160 Fax: (314)935-7302 E-mail: jst@cs.wustl.edu • Research fields include the design of high speed internetworks and the design of host interfaces.

Bibliographical Center for Research, Inc., Rocky Mountain Region. 14394 E. Evans Ave., Aurora, CO 80014-1478. Phone: 800-397-1552 or (303)751-6277 Fax: (303)751-9787 E-mail: dbrunell@bcr.org • URL: http://www.bcr.org • Fields of research include information retrieval systems, Internet technology, CD-ROM technology, document delivery, and library automation.

Columbia Institute for Tele-Information. Columbia University, Columbia Business School, 3022 Broadway, Uris Hall, Suite 1A, New York, NY 10027. Phone: (212)854-4222 Fax: (212)932-1471 E-mail: webmaster@vii.org • URL: http://www.vii.org • Areas of research include private and public networking, the economics of networks, pricing of network access, and economics of technology adoption in the public network.

Information Sciences Institute. University of Southern California, 4676 Admiralty Way, Suite 1001, Marina del Rey, CA 90292-6695. Phone: (310)822-1511 Fax: (310)823-6714 E-mail: schorr@isis.edu • URL: http://www.isi.edu • Research fields include online information and computer science, with emphasis on the World Wide Web.

STATISTICS SOURCES

Inter-NOT: Online & Internet Statistics Reality Check. Bruce Kushnick. New Networks Institute. • Annual. $495.00. Compares, analyzes, and criticizes statistics issued by Nielsen Media, Forrester Research, FIND/SVP, Yankelovich Partners and many others relating to online and Internet activities. For example, estimates of the number of Internet users have ranged from about 40 million down to six million. Topics include "Adjusting for the Puffery" and "The Most Plausible Statistics.".

OECD Information Technology Outlook 2000: ICTs, E-Commerce and the Information Economy. Organization for Economic Cooperation and Development. • 2000. $72.00. Provides data on information and communications technology (ICT) and electronic commerce in 11 OECD nations (includes U. S.). Coverage includes network infrastructure, electronic payment systems, financial transaction technologies, intelligent agents, global navigation systems, and portable flat panel display technologies.

Standard & Poor's Industry Surveys. Standard & Poor's. • Semiannual. $1,800.00. Two looseleaf volumes. Includes monthly *Supplements.* Provides detailed, individual surveys of 52 major industry groups. Each survey is revised on a semiannual basis. Also includes "Monthly Investment Review" (industry group investment analysis) and monthly "Trends & Projections" (economic analysis).

Statistical Handbook on Technology. Paula Bernstein. Greenwood Publishing Group, Inc. • 1999. $69.95. Provides statistical data on such items as the Internet, online services, computer technology, recycling, patents, prescription drug sales, telecommunications, and aerospace. Includes charts, tables, and graphs. Edited for the general reader. (Statistical Handbook Series).

TRADE/PROFESSIONAL ASSOCIATIONS

Association for Interactive Marketing. 1430 Broadway, 8th Fl., New York, NY 10018. Phone: 888-337-0008 or (212)790-1408 Fax: (212)391-9233 • URL: http://www.interactivehq.org • Members are companies engaged in various interactive enterprises, utilizing the internet, interactive television, computer communications and multimedia. Formerly Association for Interactive Media. /

Electronic Frontier Foundation. 454 Shotwell St., San Francisco, CA 94110-1914. Phone: (415)436-9333 Fax: (415)436-9993 E-mail: information@eff.org • URL: http://www.eff.org • Promotes the creation of legal and structural approaches to help ease the assimilation of new technologies by society. Seeks to: help policymakers develop a better understanding of issues underlying telecommunications; increase public understanding of the opportunities and challenges posed by computing and telecommunications fields. Fosters awareness of civil liberties issues arising from the advancements in new computer-based communications media and supports litigation to preserve, protect, and extend First Amendment rights in computing and telecommunications technology. Maintains speakers' bureau; conducts educational programs. Encourages and supports the development of tools to endow non-technical users with access to computer-based telecommunications.

Internet Alliance. 1111 19th St. NW, Ste. 1100, Washington, DC 20035-5782. Phone: (202)861-2476 Fax: (202)955-8081 E-mail: info@internetalliance.org • URL: http://www.internetalliance.org • Companies offering Internet services. Seeks to "build the confidence and trust necessary for the Internet to become the global mass market medium of the 21st century". Represents members' commercial and regulatory interests; conducts promotional activities; facilitates communication and cooperation among members.

Internet Society. 1775 Wiehle Ave., Ste. 102, Reston, VA 20190-5109. Phone: (703)439-2120 Fax: (703)326-9881 E-mail: isoc@isoc.org • URL: http://www.isoc.org • Technologists, developers, educators, researchers, government representatives, and business people. Seeks to ensure global cooperation and coordination for the Internet and related internetworking technologies and applications. Supports the development and dissemination of standards for the Internet. Promotes the growth of Internet architecture and Internet-related education and research. Encourages assistance to technologically developing countries in implementing local Internet infrastructures.

National Information Standards Organization. 1 N Charles St., Ste. 1905, Baltimore, MD 21201. Phone: (866)957-1593 or (301)654-2512 Fax: (301)654-1721 E-mail: nisohq@niso.org • URL: http://www.niso.org • Identifies, develops, maintains, and publishes technical standards to manage information in the changing environment used by libraries, publishers, and information services. Supports open access to NISO standards. Standards available at website.

Software and Information Industry Association. 1090 Vermont Ave. NW, 6th Fl., Washington, DC 20005. Phone: (202)289-7442 Fax: (202)289-7097 • URL: http://www.siia.net • A trade association for the software and digital content industry. Affiliated with Massachusetts Software and Internet Council.

Special Interest Group on Hypertext, Hypermedia, and Web. c/o Association for Computing Machinery, 1515 Broadway, New York, NY 10036. Phone: 800-342-6626 or (212)869-7440 Fax: (212)944-1318 E-mail: acmhelp@acm.org • URL: http://www.acm.org/sigweb • Concerned with the design, use, and evaluation of hypertext and hypermedia systems. Provides a multi-disciplinary forum for the promotion, dissemination, and exchange of ideas relating to research technologies and applications. Publishes the *SIGWEB Newsletter* three times a year.

OTHER SOURCES

Consumer Online Services Report. JupiterMedia. • Annual. $1,895.00. Market research report. Provides analysis of trends in the online information industry, with projections of growth in future years (five-year forecasts). Contains profiles of electronic media companies.

Cyberlaw: Intellectual Property in the Digital Millennium. American Lawyer Media, Inc. • Looseleaf. $159.00. Updated as needed. A basic guide to copyright as applied to the Internet and other electronic sources. (Law Journal Press).

E-Business, Internet, and Online Transactions. Michael L. Taviss and others. Glasser Legalworks. • Looseleaf. $225.00, including CD-ROM version. Periodic Supplementation. Covers the legal aspects of online content, marketing, advertising, domain names, software licensing, and other Internet issues. Includes many sample forms. (Emerging Growth Companies Series.).

E-Commerce and Internet Law: Treatise with Forms. Ian C. Ballon. Glasser Legalworks. • Three looseleaf volumes. $595.00. Periodic supplementation. Analyzes Internet legalities, including litigious matters relating to downloading, streaming, music, video, content aggregation, domain names, chatrooms, and search engines. Includes forms, contracts, checklists, sample pleadings, and an extensive glossary.

eAdvertising Report. Available from MarketResearch.com. • 2001. $495.00. Market research data published by eMarketer. Covers the growth of the Internet online advertising market. Includes future trends and Internet users' attitudes.

Internet Payments Report. JupiterMedia. • Annual. $1,095.00. Market research report. Provides data, comment, and forecasts on the collection of electronic payments ("e-money") for goods and services offered through the Internet.

Key Note Market Report: Home Shopping. Jupitermedia. • 2001. $400.00. Market research report. Covers "interactive retailing," mainly through the Internet and television, with predictions of future trends. Formerly *Key Note Report: Home Shopping.*

Online Banking. MarketResearch.com. • 2000. $3,000.00. Market research report. Includes demographics relating to the users and nonusers of online banking services. Provides market forecasts.

Telecommunications Regulation: Cable, Broadcasting, Satellite, and the Internet. LexisNexis Matthew Bender. • Semiannual. $826.00. Four looseleaf volumes. Covers local, state, and federal regulation, with emphasis on the Telecommunications Act of 1996. Includes regulation of television, telephone, cable, satellite, computer communication, and online services. Formerly *Cable Television Law.*

World Online Markets. JupiterMedia. • Annual. $1,895.00. Market research report. Provides broad coverage of worldwide Internet and online information business activities, including country-by-country data. Includes company profiles and five-year forecasts or trend projections.

INTERNET COMMERCE

See: ELECTRONIC COMMERCE

INTERNSHIP PROGRAMS

DIRECTORIES

Internship Bible. The Princeton Review. • Covers: Approximately 850 internship programs. Entries include: Selectivity of applicant pool, compensation, location, fields of employment, duration of internship, how to apply and deadline information, organization description, and internship perks.

Peterson's Internships. Peterson's. • Covers: 50,000 career-oriented internship positions with over 2,000 organizations in the U.S. ranging from business to theater, communications to science. Entries include: Company name, address, phone, name and title of contact, types of internships available, number of internships offered, salary where applicable, qualifications, how to apply.

Yale Daily News Guide to Internships 2000: The Essential Guide to Landing an Internship that Launches Your Career. John Anselmi and others. Simon & Schuster Trade. • 1999. Annual. $25.00. Lists internships in various fields.

TRADE/PROFESSIONAL ASSOCIATIONS

National Society for Experiential Education. 9001 Braddock Rd., Ste. 380, Springfield, VA 22151. Phone: 800-803-4170 or (703)426-4268 Fax: (703)426-8400 E-mail: info@nsee.org • URL: http://www.nsee.org • Members include representatives of internship programs. Formerly National Society for Internships and Experential Education.

INTERPERSONAL RELATIONS

See: HUMAN RELATIONS

INTERSTATE COMMERCE

See also: MOTOR VEHICLE LAW AND REGULATION

ENCYCLOPEDIAS AND DICTIONARIES

Macmillan Encyclopedia of Transportation. Available from Gale Cengage Learning. • 1999. $450.00. Six volumes. Published by Macmillan Reference USA. Covers the business, technology, and history of transportation on land, on water, in the air, and in space. Includes definitions, cross-references, and 200 color illustrations.

TRADE/PROFESSIONAL ASSOCIATIONS

Logistics Management - The Association for Transportation Law, Logistics, and Policy. 19564 Club House Rd., Montgomery Village, MD 20886-3002. Phone: (410)267-0023 Fax: (301)670-6735 E-mail: atllp@aol.com • URL: http://www.transportlink.com/atllp.

OTHER SOURCES

Federal Carriers Reports. CCH, Inc. • Biweekly. $1,484.00 per year. Four looseleaf volumes. Federal rules and regulations for motor carriers, water carriers, and freight forwarders.

INTERVIEWING

See also: COUNSELING

GENERAL WORKS

Encyclopedia of Careers and Vocational Guidance. Holli Cosgrove. Fact on File Inc. • 2002. 12th edition. Price on application.

Human Resources. Richard B. Renckly. Barron's Educational Series, Inc. • 2004. $18.95. Second edition. Emphasis is on investigating, interviewing, hiring, and evaluating employees.

The Perfect Interview: How to Get the Job You Really Want. John D. Drake. AMACOM. • 1996. $17.95. Second edition. Contains advice for jobseekers on how to control an interview and deal with difficult questions. Includes examples of both successful and unsuccessful interviews.

Super Searchers Go to the Source: The Interviewing and Hands-On Information Strategies of Top Primary Researchers - Online, On the Phone, and In Person. Risa Sacks. Information Today, Inc. • 2001. $24.95. Explains how information-search experts use various print, electronic, and live sources for competitive intelligence and other purposes. (Super Searchers Series).

Sweaty Palms: The Neglected Art of Being Interviewed. H. Anthony Medley. Ten Speed Press. • 1992. $12.95. Revised edition.

ABSTRACTS AND INDEXES

Psychological Abstracts. American Psychological Association. • Monthly. Members, $815.00 per year; individuals and institutions, $1,207.00 per year. Covers the international literature of psychology and the behavioral sciences. Includes journals, technical reports, dissertations, and other sources.

HANDBOOKS AND MANUALS

Fair, Square, and Legal: Safe Hiring, Managing, and Firing Practices to Keep You and Your Company Out of Court. Donald Weiss. AMACOM. • 1999. $29.95. Third edition. Covers recruiting, interviewing, sexual discrimination, evaluation of employees, disipline, defamation charges, and wrongful discharge.

The Five Minute Interview: A New and Powerful Approach to Interviewing. Richard H. Beatty. John Wiley and Sons, Inc. • 2002. $16.95. Third edition. Advice for job applicants.

Hiring Right: A Practical Guide. Susan J. Herman. Sage Publications, Inc. • 1994. $77.95. A practical manual covering job definition, recruitment, interviewing, testing, and checking of references.

How to Get Results from Interviewing: A Practical Guide for Operating Management. James M. Black. Krieger Publishing Co. • 1982. $22.00. Reprint of 1970 edition.

Recruiter's Research Blue Book: A How-To Guide for Researchers, Consultants, Corporate Recruiters, Small Business Owners, Venture Capitalists, and Line Executives. Andrea A. Jupina. Kennedy Information, Inc. • 2000. $179.00. Second edition. Provides detailed coverage of the role that research plays in executive recruiting. Includes such practical items as "Telephone Interview Guide," "Legal Issues in Executive Search," and "How to Create an Execuive Search Library." Covers both person-to-person research and research using printed and online business information sources. Includes an extensive directory of recommended sources. Formerly *Handbook of Executive Search Research.*

Recruiting, Interviewing, Selecting, and Orienting New Employees. Diane Arthur. AMACOM. • 1998. $59.95. Third edition. A practical guide to the basics of hiring, including legal considerations and sample forms.

Studying Your Workforce: Applied Research Methods and Tools for the Training and Development Practitioner. Alan Clardy. Sage Publications, Inc. • 1997. $79.95. Describes how to apply specific research methods to common training problems. Emphasis is on data collection methods: testing, observation, surveys, and interviews. Topics include

performance problems and assessment.

ONLINE DATABASES

PsycINFO. American Psychological Association. • Provides indexing and abstracting of the worldwide literature of psychology and the behavioral sciences. Time period is 1967 to date, with monthly updates. Inquire as to online cost and availability.

INTRANETS (COMPUTER NETWORKS)

GENERAL WORKS

The Evolving Virtual Library: Practical and Philosophical Perspectives. Laverna M. Saunders, editor. Information Today, Inc. • 1999. $39.50. Various authors cover trends in library and school use of the Internet, intranets, extranets, and electronic databases.

ABSTRACTS AND INDEXES

Internet and Personal Computing Abstracts [print edition]. EBSCO Publishing. • Quarterly. $269.00 per year, including cumulative index. Provides more than 10,000 abstracts annually from both trade and academic publications. Covers computer hardware, software, product reviews, Web topics, e-commerce, networks, corporate news, security, and related topics. Formerly *Microcomputer Abstracts.*

ENCYCLOPEDIAS AND DICTIONARIES

Acronyms of Computer Science and Communications: A Comprehensive Acronym Dictionary and Illustrated Encyclopedia. Enjob Kajan and Ejub Kajan. Springer Verlag. • 2002. $49.95. Explains more than 4,000 "broadly used" computer, telecommunications, and information technology acronyms. Includes illustrations and Web addresses, where applicable.

Business Internet and Intranets: A Manager's Guide to Key Terms and Concepts. McGraw-Hill. • 1998. $39.95. Defines more than 100 words and phrases relating to the Internet or corporate intranets.

Encyclopedia of Information Systems. Hossein Bidgoli, editor. Elsevier. • 2002. $1,200.00. Four volumes. Contains a wide range of articles relating to computers, databases, communication, and information technology. The 200 topics include coverage of hardware, software, artificial intelligence, the Internet, networks, knowledge management, electronic commerce, search engines, and systems design.

HANDBOOKS AND MANUALS

The Corporate Intranet: Create and Manage an Internal Web for your Organization. Ryan Bernard. John Wiley and Sons, Inc. • 1997. $29.99. Second edition.

The Modem Reference: The Complete Guide to PC Communications. Michael A. Banks. Information Today, Inc. • 2000. $29.95. Fourth edition. Covers personal computer data communications technology, including fax transmissions, computer networks, modems, and the Internet. Popularly written.

Windows XP Professional Network Administration. Toby J. Velte. McGraw-Hill. • 2002. $49.99. Covers design, implementation, administration, configuration, networking, functionality, remote desktop assistance, and other matters. (Networking Series).

INTERNET DATABASES

InfoTech Trends. Data Analysis Group. Phone: (925)462-1202 Fax: (925)462-1225 E-mail: support@infotechtrends.com • URL: http://www.infotechtrends.com • Web site provides both free and fee-based market research data on the information technology industry, including computers, peripherals, telecommunications, the Internet, software, CD-ROM/DVD, e-commerce, and workstations. Fees: Free for current (most recent year) data; more extensive information has various fee structures. Formerly *Computer Industry Forecasts*.

PERIODICALS AND NEWSLETTERS

Business Communications Review. Key3Media Group, Inc. • Monthly. $45.00 per year. Edited for communications managers in large end-user companies and institutions. Includes special feature issues on intranets and network management.

Communications News: Solutions for Today's Networking Decision Managers. Nelson Publishing, Inc. • Monthly. Free to qualified personnel; others, $84.00 per year. Includes coverage of "Internetworking" and "Intrenetworking." Emphasis is on emerging telecommunications technologies.

Computer Economics Networking Strategies Report: Advising IT Decision Maker ractices and Current Trends. Computer Economics, Inc. • Monthly. $395.00 per year. Newsletter. Edited for information technology managers. Covers news and trends relating to a variety of corporate computer network and management information systems topics. Emphasis is on costs. Formerly *Intranet and Networking Strategies Report*.

IntraNet Professional: IntraNet Applications and Knowledge Management for Libraries and Information Professionals. Information Today, Inc. • Bimonthly. $89.95 per year. Newsletter on the use of Internet technology for local library networks.

Wireless Review: Intelligence for Competitive Providers. Primedia Business Magazines and Media. • Semimonthly. $48.00 per year. Covers business and technology developments for wireless service providers. Includes special issues on a wide variety of wireless topics. Formed by merger of *Cellular Business* and *Wireless World*.

OTHER SOURCES

On-the-Job Research: How Usable are Corporate Research Intranets?. Alison J. Head and Shannon Staley. Special Libraries Association. • 2002. Members, $100.00; non-members, $135.00. Presents the results of a survey of how employees at seven major corporations make use of company intranets for news and information research. Searching by individual employees generally had a success rate of less than 50 percent.

INTRAOCULAR LENS INDUSTRY

See: CONTACT LENS AND INTRAOCULAR LENS INDUSTRIES

INTRAPRENEURS

See: ENTREPRENEURS AND INTRAPRENEURS

INVENTIONS

See also: NEW PRODUCTS; PATENTS

GENERAL WORKS

World of Invention: History's Most Significant Inventions and the People Beh ind Them. Gale Cengage Learning. • 1999. $115.00. Second edition.

ABSTRACTS AND INDEXES

Index of Patents Issued from the United States Patent and Trademark Office, Part One: List of Patentees. Available from U. S. Government Printing Office. • Annual. $160.00. Lists patentees and reissue patentees for each year.

Index of Patents Issued from the United States

Patent and Trademark Office, Part Two: Index to Subjects of Invention. Available from U. S. Government Printing Office. • Annual. $71.00. A subject index to patents issued each year, arranged by class and subclass numbers. Includes a list of patent and tradmark depository libraries.

NTIS Alerts: Government Inventions for Licensing. National Technical Information Service. • Semimonthly. $270.00 per year. Identifies new inventions available from various government agencies. Covers a wide variety of industrial and technical areas. Formerly *Abstract Newsletter*.

HANDBOOKS AND MANUALS

Inventing and Patenting Sourcebook. Gale Cengage Learning. • 1992. $120.00. Second edition. A general guide for inventors. Contains how-to-do-it text, information sources, and sample forms.

INTERNET DATABASES

United States Patent and Trademark Office. U. S. Department of Commerce. Phone: 800-786-9199 or (703)308-4357 Fax: (703)305-7786 • URL: http://www.uspto.gov • Web site provides extensive information about patents and trademarks, with advanced search facilities for specific documents or names. "Special Pages" are available for "How to Search," "Trademarks-Logos-Brands," "Inventor Resources," and other topics. A complete fee schedule is available for filing applications, appeals, copies, etc.

PERIODICALS AND NEWSLETTERS

Official Gazette of the United States Patent and Trademark Office: Patents. Available from U. S. Government Printing Office. • Weekly. Contains the Patents, Patent Office Notices, and Designs issued each week (http://www.uspto.gov). Annual indexes are sold separately.

TRADE/PROFESSIONAL ASSOCIATIONS

American Society of Inventors. P.O. Box 58426, Philadelphia, PA 19102. Phone: (215)546-6601 E-mail: info@asoi.org • URL: http://www.americaninventor.org.

and Entrepreneurs Workshop International. 1029 Castillo St., Santa Barbara, CA 93101-3736. Phone: (805)962-5722 Fax: (805)899-5722 E-mail: info@inventorsworkshop.org • URL: http://www.inventorsworkshop.org • Formerly Inventors Workshop International.

INVENTORY CONTROL

See also: PRODUCTION CONTROL

GENERAL WORKS

Inventory Control and Management. C. D. Waters. John Wiley and Sons, Inc. • 2003. $50.00. Second edition.

Lessons to be Learned Just in Time. James J. Cammarano. Engineering and Management Press. • 1997. $34.95. Discusses the background, theory, and practical application of just-in-time (JIT) inventory control in manufacturing.

Principles of Inventory and Materials Management. Richard J. Tersine. Prentice Hall PTR. • 1993. $45. 50. Fourth edition. Includes material on just-in-time inventory systems.

ABSTRACTS AND INDEXES

Business Periodicals Index. H. W. Wilson Co. • 11 times a year. Quarterly and annual cumulations. Price varies.

ENCYCLOPEDIAS AND DICTIONARIES

Blackwell Encyclopedic Dictionary of Operations Management. Nigel Slack, editor. Blackwell Publishing. • 1997. $130.95. The editor is associated with the University of Warwick, England. Contains definitions of key terms combined with

longer articles written by various U. S. and foreign business educators. Includes bibliographies and index. (Blackwell Encyclopedia of Management Series.).

ONLINE DATABASES

Wilson Business Abstracts Online. H. W. Wilson Co. • Indexes and abstracts 600 major business periodicals, plus the *Wall Street Journal* and the business section of the *New York Times*. Indexing is from 1982, abstracting from 1990, with the two newspapers included from 1993. Updated weekly. Inquire as to online cost and availability. (*Business Periodicals Index* without abstracts is also available online.).

PERIODICALS AND NEWSLETTERS

Journal of Supply Chain Management: A Global Review of Purchasing and Supply. Institute for Supply Management. • Quarterly. $59.00 per year. Text in English. Summaries in French, German and Spanish. Formerly *International Journal of Purchasing and Materials Management*.

Production and Inventory Management Journal. A P I C S: The Educational Society for Resource Management. • Quarterly. Members, $64.00 per year; non-members, $80.00 per year.

RESEARCH CENTERS AND INSTITUTES

Board of Research. Babson College, 204 Babson, Babson Park, MA 02457-0310. Phone: (718)239-5339 Fax: (718)239-6416 E-mail: chern@babson.edu • URL: http://www.babson.edu/bor • Research areas include management, entrepreneurial characteristics, and multi-product inventory analysis.

Center for Business and Industrial Studies. University of Missouri-St. Louis, School of Business Administration, 8001 Natural Bridge Rd., St. Louis, MO 63121. Phone: (314)516-5000 • URL: http://www.umsl.edu/ • Research fields include inventory and management control. Specific projects also include development of computer software for operations in public transit systems.

Center for Entrepreneurial Studies and Development, Inc. West Virginia University, College of Engineering and Mineral Resources, 1062 Maple Dr., Morgantown, WV 26506. Phone: (304)293-5551 Fax: (304)293-6707 E-mail: jbyrd@mail.cesd.wvu.edu • URL: http://www.cesd.wvu.edu • Inventory control systems included as a research field.

Engineering Systems Research Center. University of California at Berkeley. 3115 Etcheverry Hall, MC 1750, Berkeley, CA 94720-1750. Phone: (510)643-9150 Fax: (510)643-0966 E-mail: esrc@esrc.berkeley.edu • URL: http://www.esrc.berkeley.edu/.

TRADE/PROFESSIONAL ASSOCIATIONS

APICS-The Educational Society for Resource Management. 5301 Shawnee Rd., Alexandria, VA 22312-2317. Phone: 800-444-2742 or (703)354-8851 Fax: (703)354-8106 E-mail: webmaster@apicshq.org • URL: http://www.apics.org • Members are professional resource managers.

INVESTMENT ADVISORY SERVICES

See also: INVESTMENTS; STOCKS

GENERAL WORKS

The Fortune Sellers: The Big Business of Buying and Selling Predictions. William A. Sherden. John Wiley and Sons, Inc. • 1997. $29.95. The author states that predictions are notoriously unreliable in any field, including the stock market, the economy, and the weather. (Forecasters in all areas don't have to be right; they just have to be interesting.).

DIRECTORIES

Directory of Registered Investment Advisors. Money Market Directories, Inc. • Annual. $510.00. Lists over 12,000 investment advisors and advisory firms. Indicates services offered, personnel, and amount of assets being managed. Formerly *Directory of Registered Investment Advisors with the Securities and Exchange Commission.*

Investment Council of American Directory of Member Firms. Investment Counsel Association of America. • Annual. Free.

Money Market Directory of Pension Funds and Their Investment Managers. Money Market Directories, Inc. • Annual. $1,150.00. Institutional funds and managers.

SIE Investment Advisory Guide. George H. Wein, editor. Select Information Exchange. • Annual. $2.00. Provides descriptions and prices of about 100 financial newsletters covering stocks, bonds, mutual funds, commodity futures, options, gold, and foreign investments. Offers subscription services, including short trials of any 20 investment newsletters for a total of $11.95.

HANDBOOKS AND MANUALS

Mining for Gold on the Internet: How to Find Investment and Financial Information on the Internet. Mary Ellen Bates. McGraw-Hill. • 2000. $24.95. Tells how to effectively search the Internet for financial advice and information. Specific websites are discussed.

ONLINE DATABASES

F & S Index. Gale Cengage Learning. • Contains about four million citations to worldwide business, financial, and industrial or consumer product literature appearing from 1972 to date. Weekly updates. Inquire as to online cost and availability.

PERIODICALS AND NEWSLETTERS

Bull and Bear Financial Newspaper. • Monthly. $36.00 per year. Each issue includes a digest of advice from investment advisory newsletters.

Dick Davis Digest. Dick Davis Publishing. • Description: Carries excerpts from over 400 stock market letters and stock, bond, and mutual fund recommendations from leading analysts on Wall Street. Provides overview of general market trends and news of specific industries and companies. Recurring features include columns titled Personal Note, Spotlight Stock, Where's the Market Going, and The Last Word.

Hulbert Financial Digest. Hulbert Financial Digest. • Description: Provides performance ratings on more than 400 portfolios recommended by more than 145 financial newsletters, calculated on the basis of model portfolios constructed according to each newsletter's advice. Includes a timing scoreboard, analysis of newsletter performance, list of mutual funds most frequently recommended for sale or purchase, a stock market sentiment index, and a question and answer section.

Investors Intelligence. Michael Burke, editor. Chartcraft Inc. • Description: Serves as a "comprehensive and authoritative Stock Market Advisory Service dedicated to bringing the investor facts, original projections, and a cross section of the recommendations of other leading Services.".

The Moneypaper. Temper of the Times Communications, Inc. Temper of the Times Communications Inc. • Description: Contains strategies to minimize stock sales costs and articles on investing and market trends. Includes a summary of monthly financial news drawn from over 70 financial publications and advisory services. Recurring features include columns titled Summing Up, Market Outlook, and Stocktrack.

The Wall Street Digest. Donald H. Rowe. • Description: Covers major investment areas, including stocks and bonds; foreign currencies; gold, silver, and other precious metals; real estate; tax shelters; and estate planning. Recurring features include "a digest of the month's best" investment and financial

seminars, newsletter reviews, and statistics.

TRADE/PROFESSIONAL ASSOCIATIONS

Association for Investment Management and Research. 560 Ray C. Hunt Dr., Charlottesville, VA 22903. Phone: 800-247-8132 or (434)951-5499 Fax: (434)951-5262 E-mail: info@aimr.org • URL: http://www.aimr.org • Members are practicing investment analysts.

Investment Counsel Association of America. 1050 17th St., N.W., Suite 725, Washington, DC 20036-5503. Phone: (202)293-4222 Fax: (202)293-4223 E-mail: icaa@icaa.org • URL: http://www.icaa.org.

INVESTMENT ANALYSIS

See: FINANCIAL ANALYSIS

INVESTMENT BANKING

BIOGRAPHICAL SOURCES

Who's Who in Finance and Industry. Marquis Who's Who. • Biennial. $259.95. Provides over 21,000 concise biographies of business leaders in all fields.

Who's Who in the Securities Industry. Economist Publishing Co. • Annual. $15.00. Lists about 1,000 investment bankers.

CD-ROM DATABASES

Buyout Financing Sources/M & A Intermediaries. Thomson Media. • Annual. $895.00. Provides the CD-ROM combination of *Directory of Buyout Financing Sources* and *Directory of M & A Intermediaries.* Contains information on more than 1,000 financing sources (banks, insurance companies, venture capital firms, etc.) and 850 intermediaries (corporate acquirers, valuation firms, lawyers, accountants, etc.). Also includes back issues of *Buyouts Newsletter* and *Mergers & Acquisitions Report.* Fully searchable.

DIRECTORIES

Directory of Buyout Financing Sources. Thomson Financial. • Annual. $445.00. Describes more than 1,000 U. S. and foreign sources of financing for buyout deals. Indexed by personnel, company, industry, and location.

Directory of M & A Intermediaries. Thomson Financial. • Annual. $360.00. Lists more than 850 dealmakers for mergers and acquisitions, including investment banks, business brokers, and commercial banks.

Plunkett's Financial Services Industry Almanac: The Only Comprehensive Overview of the Banking, Insurance, Credit and Investment Sectors. Plunkett Research, Ltd. • Annual. $229.99. Includes CD-ROM. Discusses important trends in various sectors of the financial industry. Five hundred major banking, credit card, investment, and financial services companies are profiled. (Business, Careers and Internet Reference Tools Series).

Securities Industry Yearbook. Securities Industry and Financial Markets Association. • Covers: over 600 member securities firms, with about 480 of them covered in detail. Entries include: For firms covered in detail--Company name, name of parent company, address, phone, capital position and rank, number of offices and type, number of employees, area of specialization, names and titles of key personnel, number of registered representatives, departments with name of department head, dollar volume of underwriting and syndication by type, other financial data. For other firms--Company name, address, name of delegated liaison to the association.

ENCYCLOPEDIAS AND DICTIONARIES

Blackwell Encyclopedic Dictionary of Finance. Dean Paxson and Douglas Wood, editors. Blackwell

Publishing. • 1997. $110.00. The editors are associated with the University of Manchester. Contains definitions of key terms combined with longer articles written by various U. S. and foreign business educators. Includes bibliographies and index. (Blackwell Encyclopedia of Management Series).

HANDBOOKS AND MANUALS

Investment Banking Handbook. J. Peter Williamson. John Wiley and Sons, Inc. • 1988. $270.00. (Frontiers in Finance Series).

Library of Investment Banking. Robert L. Kuhn, editor. McGraw-Hill. • 1990. $475.00. Seven volumes: 1. Investing and Risk Management; 2. Capital Raising and Financial Structure; 3. Corporate and Municipal Securities; 4. Mergers, Acquisitions, and Leveraged Buyouts; 5. Mortgage and Asset Securitization; 6. International Finance and Investing; 7. Index.

PERIODICALS AND NEWSLETTERS

Corporate Financing Week: The Newsweekly of Corporate Finance, Investment Banking and M and A. Institutional Investor, Inc., Journals Group. • Weekly. $2,550.00 per year. Includes print and online editions. Newsletter for corporate finance officers. Emphasis is on debt and equity financing, mergers, leveraged buyouts, investment banking, and venture capital.

Financial Management. Financial Management Association International. • Quarterly. Individuals, $80.00 per year; libraries, $100.00 per year. Covers theory and practice of financial planning, international finance, investment banking, and portfolio management. Includes *Financial Practice and Education and Contempory Finance Digest.*

Investment Management Weekly. Thomson Media. • Weekly. $1,370.00 per year. Newsletter. Edited for money managers and other investment professionals. Covers personnel news, investment strategies, and industry trends.

TRADE/PROFESSIONAL ASSOCIATIONS

National Association of Securities Dealers (NASD). 1735 K St., N.W., Washington, DC 20006-1506. Phone: (202)728-8000 Fax: (202)293-6260 E-mail: waltere@nasd.com • URL: http://www.nasd.com • Formerly National Association of Securities Dealers.

Securities Industry and Financial Markets Association. 120 Broadway, 35th Fl., New York, NY 10271-0080. Phone: (212)313-1200 Fax: (212)313-1301 E-mail: rbrockhaus@sifma.org • URL: http://www.sifma.org • Represents more than 650 member firms of all sizes, in all financial markets in the U.S. and around the world. Enhances the public's trust and confidence in the markets, delivering an efficient, enhanced member network of access and forward-looking services, as well as premiere educational resources for the professionals in the industry and the investors whom they serve. Maintains offices in New York City and Washington, DC.

INVESTMENT CLUBS

HANDBOOKS AND MANUALS

Investors' Manuals. National Association of Investors Corporation. • Provides stock study tools and procedures for do-it-yourself equity investors.

PERIODICALS AND NEWSLETTERS

Better Investing. National Association of Investors Corp. • Description: Features investment information on various corporations as seen by 10 different columnists.

TRADE/PROFESSIONAL ASSOCIATIONS

National Association of Investors Corporation. P.O. Box 220, Royal Oak, MI 48068. Phone: 877-275-6242 or (248)583-6242 Fax: (248)583-4880 E-mail:

service@better-investing.org • URL: http://www.
better-investing.org • Affiliated with Investment
Education Institute. Formerly National Association
of Investment Clubs.

INVESTMENT COMPANIES

See also: CLOSED-END FUNDS

GENERAL WORKS

All About Index Funds: A Guidebook to Investment Success. Richard A. Ferri. McGraw-Hill. • 2002. $16.95. States that index mutual funds "routinely outperform 80 percent of managed funds." (All About Series).

Beating the Street: The Best-Selling Author of "One Up on Wall Street" Shows You How to Pick Winning Stocks and Mutual Funds. Peter Lynch and John Rothchild. Simon & Schuster Trade. • 1993. $23.00.

Bogle on Mutual Funds: New Perspectives for the Intelligent Investor. John C. Bogle. McGraw-Hill. • 1993. $25.00.

Common Sense on Mutual Funds: New Imperatives for the Intelligent Investor. John C. Bogle. John Wiley and Sons, Inc. • 1999. $29.95. Provides practical, conservative advice for the average investor. Topics include asset allocation, index funds, global investing, fund selection, and taxes.

Getting Started in Mutual Funds. Alvin D. Hall. John Wiley and Sons, Inc. • 1999. $18.95. (Getting Started in... Series).

Morningstar Guide to Mutual Funds: 5-Star Strategies for Success. Christine Benz and others. Morningstar, Inc. • 2003. $24.95. Contains general advice on mutual funds for the small investor, including "How to Pick Mutual Funds," "How to Build a Portfolio," and "How to Monitor Your Portfolio." (Also available from John Wiley & Sons.).

The New Commonsense Guide to Mutual Funds. Mary Rowland. Bloomberg. • 1998. $15.95. Revised edition. Includes "Do's and Don'ts" for mutual fund investors. (Bloomberg Personal Bookshelf Series).

One Up on Wall Street: How to Use What You Already Know to Make Money in the Market. Peter Lynch and John Rothchild. Simon and Schuster. • 2000. $14.00.

The Only Investment Guide You'll Ever Need. Andrew Tobias. Harcourt Trade Publishers. • 1999. $14.00. Expanded revised edition. An entertaining, optimistic look at investing, written for the "average" investor. Provides generally conservative advice, favoring no-load, low-expense index funds.

Straight Talk on Investing: What You Need to Know. Jack Brennan. John Wiley and Sons, Inc. • 2002. $22.95. Provides basic, conservative advice for the small investor. Emphasis is on long-term goals and investment planning.

What You Need to Know About Mutual Funds. Kenneth M. Lefkowitz. American Institute for Economic Research. • 2001. $6.00. Provides conservative advice on investing in mutual funds, unit investment trusts, closed-end investment companies, and other funds. Includes a glossary and lists of recommended information sources.

Yes, You Can Achieve Financial Independence. James E. Stowers and others. Stowers Innovations, Inc. • 2000. $34.00. Third revised edition.

ALMANACS AND YEARBOOKS

Emerging Markets Analyst. • Monthly. $895.00 per year. Provides an annual overview of the emerging financial markets in 24 countries of Latin America, Asia, and Europe. Includes data on international mutual funds and closed-end funds.

Investment Company Yearbook. Thomson Financial. • Annual. $310.00. Provides an "entire history of

recent events in the mutual funds industry," with emphasis on changes during the past year. About 100 pages are devoted to general information and advice for fund investors. Includes 600 full-page profiles of popular mutual funds, with brief descriptions of 10,000 others, plus 7,000 variable annuities and 500 closed-end funds. Contains a glossary of technical terms, a Web site index, and an overall book index. Also known as *Wiesenberger Investment Companies Yearbook.*

DIRECTORIES

HedgeWorld Annual Compendium: The Hedge Fund Industry's Definitive Reference Guide. HedgeWorld USA. • Annual. $499.00. Contains profiles of 500 domestic and offshore hedge funds with more than $50 million in assets under management. Includes articles on "The Basics of Investing in Hedge Funds," "Beyond the Basics," and other information.

HedgeWorld Service Provider League Tables & Analyses. HedgeWorld USA. • Annual. $595.00. Provides quantitative and qualitative information on firms providing services to hedge funds: accountants/auditors, administrators, custodians, legal counsel, and prime brokers. Detailed categories cover banks, clearing services, consultants, derivatives business, investment companies, wealth management services, etc.

Major Financial Institutions of Europe. Available from Gale Cengage Learning. • Annual. $510.00. Contains profiles of over 2,000 financial institutions in Europe such as banks, investment companies, and insurance companies. Formerly *Major Financial Institutions of Continental Europe.*

Major Financial Institutions of the World 2001. Available from Gale Cengage Learning. • 2003. $880.00. Sixth edition. Two volumes. Published by Graham & Whiteside. Contains detailed information on more than 7,500 important financial institutions in various countries. Includes banks, investment companies, and insurance companies.

Morningstar Closed-End Fund 250. McGraw-Hill. • 1996. $35.00. Second edition. Provides detailed information on 50 actively traded closed-end investment companies. Past data is included for up to 12 years, depending on life of the fund.

Morningstar Mutual Funds. Morningstar, Inc. • Biweekly. $395.00 per year. Looseleaf service. Contains detailed information and risk-adjusted ratings on over 1,240 load and no-load, equity and fixed-income mutual funds. Annual returns are provided for up to 12 years for each fund.

Mutual Fund Profiles. Standard & Poor's. • Quarterly. $158.00 per year. Produced jointly with Lipper Analytical Services. Provides detailed information on approximately 800 of the largest stock funds and taxable bond funds. In addition, contains concise data on about 2,400 smaller funds and municipal bond funds.

Nelson Information's Directory of Investment Managers. Nelson Information. • Annual. $595.00. Three volumes. Provides information on 2,200 investment management firms, both U.S. and foreign.

Value Line Mutual Fund Survey. Value Line Publishing, Inc. • Every three weeks. $345.00 per year. Looseleaf service. Provides ratings and detailed performance information for 2,300 equity and fixed income funds.

Vickers Directory of Institutional Investors. Vickers Stock Research Corp. • Semiannual. $195.00 per year. Detailed alphabetical listing of more than 4,000 U. S., Canadian, and foreign institutional investors. Includes insurance companies, banks, endowment funds, and investment companies.

Formerly *Directory of Institutional Investors.*

FINANCIAL RATIOS

Almanac of Business and Industrial Financial Ratios. Leo Troy. Aspen Publishers, Inc. • 2003. $125.95. Includes CD-Rom. Contains financial ratios derived from federal tax returns. Ratios for each of about 200 industries are arranged according to company asset size. (Almanac of Business and Industrial Financial Ratios Series).

HANDBOOKS AND MANUALS

Handbook for No-Load Fund Investors: Everything You Need for Successful Investing Without Brokers. Sheldon Jacobs. McGraw-Hill. • 1999. $40.00. 16th edition. Includes data on individual funds.

Indexing for Maximum Investment Results. Albert S. Neuberg. Fitzroy Dearborn Publishers, Inc. • 1998. $65.00. Covers the Standard & Poor's 500 and other indexing strategies for both individual and institutional investors.

Money Manager's Compliance Guide. Thompson Publishing Group, Inc. • $649.00 per year. Two looseleaf volumes. Monthly updates and newletters. Edited for investment advisers and investment companies to help them be in compliance with governmental regulations, including SEC rules, restrictions based on the Employee Retirement Income Security Act (ERISA), and regulations issued by the Commodity Futures Trading Commission (CFTC).

Moody's Bank and Finance Manual. Mergent. • Annual. $1,750.00 per year. Four volumes. Includes biweekly supplements in *Moody's Bank and Finance News Report.*

Mutual Fund Buyer's Guide: Performance Ratings, Five Year Projections, Safety Ratings, Sales. Norman G. Fosback. McGraw-Hill. • 1994. $17.95.

INTERNET DATABASES

The Financial Post (Web site). National Post Online. Phone: 800-805-1184 or (244)383-2300 Fax: (416)383-2443 • URL: http://www.nationalpost.com/financialpost/ • Provides a broad range of Canadian business news online, with daily updates. Includes news, opinion, and special reports, as well as "Investing," "Money Rates," "Market Watch," and "Daily Mutual Funds." Allows advanced searching (Boolean operators), with links to various other sites. Fees: Free.

FundAlarm. Roy Weitz. Phone: (818)345-7516 Fax: (818)776-1562 • URL: http://www.fundalarm.com • Web site subtitle: "Know when to hold'em, know when to fold'em, know when to walk away, know when to run." Provides lists of underperforming mutual funds ("3-ALARM Funds") and severely underperforming funds ("Most Alarming 3-ALARM Funds"). Performance is based on various benchmarks. Site also provides mutual fund news, recent manager changes, and basic data for each of about 2,100 funds. Monthly updates. Fees: Free.

Morningstar.com: Your First Second Opinion. Morningstar, Inc. Phone: 800-735-0700 or (312)696-6000 Fax: (312)696-6001 E-mail: productsupport@morningstar.com • URL: http://www.morningstar.com • Web site provides a broad selection of information and advice on both mutual funds and individual stocks, including financial news and articles on investment fundamentals. Basic service is free, with "Premium Membership" available at $109.00 per year. Annual fee provides personal portfolio analysis, screening tools, and more extensive profiles of funds and stocks.

Mutual Funds Interactive. Brill Editorial Services, Inc. Phone: 877-442-7455 • URL: http://www.brill.com • Web site provides specific information on individual funds in addition to general advice on mutual fund investing and 401(k) plans. Searching is provided, including links to moderated newsgroups and a chat page. Fees: Free.

TheStreet.com: Your Insider's Look at Wall Street. TheStreet.com, Inc. Phone: 800-562-9571 or (212)321-5000 Fax: (212)321-5016 • URL: http://www.thestreet.com • Web site offers "Free Sections" and "Premium Sections" ($24.95 per month). Both sections offer iconoclastic advice and comment on the stock market, but premium service displays a more comprehensive selection of news and analysis. There are many by-lined articles. "Search the Site" is included.

U. S. Securities and Exchange Commission. Phone: 800-732-0330 or (202)942-7040 Fax: (202)942-9634 E-mail: webmaster@sec.gov • URL: http://www.sec.gov • SEC Web site offers free access through EDGAR to text of official corporate filings, such as annual reports (10-K), quarterly reports (10-Q), and proxies. (EDGAR is "Electronic Data Gathering, Analysis, and Retrieval System.") An example is given of how to obtain executive compensation data from proxies. Text of the daily *SEC News Digest* is offered, as are links to other government sites, non-government market regulators, and U. S. stock exchanges. Search facilities are extensive. Fees: Free.

ONLINE DATABASES

Vickers On-Line. Vickers Stock Research Corp. • Provides detailed online information relating to insider trading and the securities holdings of institutional investors. Daily updates. Inquire as to online cost and availability.

PERIODICALS AND NEWSLETTERS

Bank Investment Product News. Institutional Investor, Inc., Journals Group. • Weekly. $1,195.00 per year. Newsletter. Edited for bank executives. Covers the marketing and regulation of financial products sold through banks, such as mutual funds, stock brokerage services, and insurance.

Barron's: The Dow Jones Business and Financial Weekly. • Weekly. $145.00 per year.

The Cabot Market Letter. Cabot Heritage Corp. • Description: Analyzes and recommends stock investments. Emphasizes that "optimum profits depend upon good market timing and good stock selection." Each issue follows a model portfolio made up of 12 stocks from lesser known companies chosen for their high potential for rapid, long-term growth.

Financial Planning: The Magazine for Financial Service Professionals. Thomson Media. • Monthly. $79.00 per year. Edited for independent financial planners and insurance agents. Covers retirement planning, estate planning, tax planning, and insurance, including long-term healthcare considerations. Special features include a Retirement Planning Issue, Mutual Fund Performance Survey, and Variable Life and Annuity Survey.

The Financial Post: Canadian's Business Voice. Financial Post Datagroup. • Daily. $200.00 per year. Provides Canadian business, economic, financial, and investment news. Features extensive price quotes from all major Canadian markets: stocks, bonds, mutual funds, commodities, and currencies. Supplement available: *Financial Post 500.* Includes annual supplement.

Fund Action. Institutional Investor, Inc., Journals Group. • Weekly. $2,475.00 per year. Newsletter. Includes print and online editions. Edited for mutual fund executives. Covers competition among funds, aggregate statistics, new products, regulations, service providers, and other subjects of interest to fund managers.

Growth Fund Guide: The Investor's Guide to Dynamic Growth Funds. Growth Fund Research, Inc. • Monthly. $99.00 per year. Newsletter. Covers no-load growth mutual funds.

Guide to Stock Mutual Funds: A Quarterly Compilation of Mutual Fund Ratings and Analysis Covering Equity and Balanced Funds. Weiss Ratings, Inc. •

Quarterly. $438.00 per year. Emphasis is on rating of financial safety and relative risk. Includes annual summary.

InvesTech Mutual Fund Advisor: Professional Portfolio Allocation. InvesTech Research. • Every three weeks. $190.00 per year. Newsletter. Contains model portfolio for mutual fund investing.

Latin Fund Management. Thomson Media. • Monthly. $495.00 per year. Newsletter (also available online at www.latinfund.net). Provides news and analysis of Latin American mutual funds, pension funds, and annuities.

Louis Rukeyser's Mutual Funds. Louis Rukeyser's Wall Street Club. • Monthly. $79.00 per year. Newsletter. Provides conservative advice on mutual fund investing.

Moneyletter. Agora Inc. • Description: "Provides assertive, do-it-yourself, individual investors with a unique market timing system, specific buy and sell recommendations, and portfolio allocation advice on no-load mutual funds. Features updates on economic and financial market, fund profiles, and articles on non-mutual fund financial planning issues.".

Morningstar FundInvestor. Morningstar, Inc. • Monthly. $89.00 per year. Newsletter. Provides tables of statistical data and star ratings for leading mutual funds ("The Morningstar 500"). News of funds and financial planning advice for investors is also included.

Mutual Fund Advisor: The Top Performing Mutual Funds. Mutual Fund Advisor, Inc. • Monthly. Price on application. Newsletter.

Mutual Fund Letter. Investment Information Services, Inc. • Monthly. $125.00 per year. Newsletter. Provides mutual fund recommendations.

Mutual Fund Market News. Dalbar Publishing Inc. • Description: Provides persons in the mutual fund industry with critical information, breaking news, industry developments, new product analyses, and changes in market share. Covers all major changes of distribution for mutual funds and related products, with emphasis on banks, broker/dealers, captive sales forces, corporate and nonprofit pensions, and direct markets. Recurring features include portfolio management strategies, letters to the editor, a calendar of events and conferences, reports of industry meetings, and columns titled Hot Off the Wire, On the Move, and Newly Registered Funds.

Mutual Fund Strategies. Progressive Investing, Inc. • Monthly. $127.00 per year. Newsletter.

Mutual Fund Trends. Growth Fund Research Inc. • Description: Provides high quality semi-log charts with multiple moving averages and relative strength line on approximately 180 top performing funds. Statistics include lows to current time and high to low. Market indicators with good records. Includes weekly telephone hot line.

Mutual Funds Update. Thomson Financial. • Monthly. $325.00 per year. Provides recent performance information and statistics for approximately 10,000 mutual funds and closed-end funds as compiled from the CDA/Wiesenberger database. Includes commentary and analysis relating to the mutual fund industry. Information is provided on new funds, name changes, mergers, and liquidations.

The No-Load Fund Investor. No-Load Fund Investor Inc. • Description: Predicts which no-load and low-load funds will perform best overall in the coming year. Provides performance data for 995 no- and low-loads and recommends funds and analyzes promising new funds. Recurring features include a listing of the top 20 no-loads plus 18 model portfolios. **Remarks:** Published in conjuction with the Handbook for No-Load Investors.

The Wall Street Journal. Dow Jones & Co., Inc. • Daily. $189.00 per year. Covers news and trends

relating to business, industry, finance, the economy, and international commerce. Provides extensive price and other data for the securities, commodity, options, futures, foreign exchange, and money markets.

STATISTICS SOURCES

Mutual Fund Fact Book: Industry Trends and Statistics. Investment Company Institute. • 1997. $25.00. 37th edition. Industry trends and statistics.

Standard & Poor's Stock and Bond Guide. McGraw-Hill. • Annual. $24.95. Contains concise data on 6,000 stocks, 7,000 bonds, and 700 mutual funds. Includes year-end prices, earnings estimates for stocks, and debt ratings for bonds.

Statistical Information on the Financial Services Industry. American Bankers Association. • Annual. Members, $150.00; non-members, $275.00. Presents a wide variety of data relating to banking and financial services, including consumer economics, personal finance, credit, government loans, capital markets, and international banking.

Trends in Mutual Fund Activity. Investment Company Institute. • Monthly. $225.00 per year. Contains statistical tables showing fund industry sales, redemptions, assets, cash, and other data.

U. S. Industry and Trade Outlook. Available from National Technical Information Service. • Annual. $69.95. Produced by the International Trade Administration, U. S. Department of Commerce, in a "public-private" partnership with DRI/McGraw-Hill and Standard & Poor's. Provides basic data, outlook for the current year, and "Long-Term Prospects" (five-year projections) for a wide variety of products and services. Includes high technology industries. Formerly *U. S. Industrial Outlook.*

TRADE/PROFESSIONAL ASSOCIATIONS

Investment Company Institute. 1401 H St. NW, 12th Fl., Washington, DC 20005. Phone: (202)326-5800 Fax: (202)326-8309 E-mail: memberservices@ici.org • URL: http://www.ici.org • Represents open-end and closed-end investment companies registered under Investment Company Act of 1940; investment advisers to, and underwriters of, such companies; unit investment trust sponsors; interested others. Represents members in matters of legislation, taxation, regulation, economic research marketing, and public information. Provides a clearinghouse for information on the mutual fund industry. Compiles statistics.

Mutual Fund Education Alliance (The Association of No-Load Funds). 100 N.W. Englewood Rd., No. 130, Kansas City, MO 64118. Phone: (816)454-9422 Fax: (816)454-9322 E-mail: mfeamail@mfea.com • URL: http://www.mea.com • Formerly No-Load Mutual Fund Association.

National Association of Real Estate Investment Trusts. 1875 Eye St., N.W., Washington, DC 20006. Phone: 800-362-7348 or (202)739-9400 Fax: (202)739-9401 E-mail: info@nareit.org • URL: http://www.nareit.com • Formerly National Association of Real Estste Investment Funds.

OTHER SOURCES

Fund Governance: Legal Duties of Investment Company Directors. American Lawyer Media, Inc. • Looseleaf. $159.00. Updated as needed. Covers the legal obligations of directors of mutual funds and closed-end funds. (Law Journal Press).

IBC's Money Fund Report. i MoneyNet Inc. • Weekly. $1,095.00 per year. Looseleaf. Contains detailed information on about 1,000 U. S. money market funds, including portfolios and yields. Formerly *Money Fund Report.*

Mergent's Annual Dividend Record. Mergent, Inc. • Annual. $49.00. Provides detailed dividend data, including tax information, for 12,000 stocks and 18,000 mutual funds. Covers the most recent year. Formerly *Moody's Annual Dividend Record.*

Quarterly Report on Money Fund Performance. IBC-Donoghue, Inc. • Quarterly. $525.00 per year. Provides expense ratio and yield data for about 1,000 money market funds in the U. S.

The Winning Portfolio: Choosing Your 10 Best Mutual Funds. Paul B. Farrell. Bloomberg. • 1999. $15.95. Tells how to select 10 from among the 10,000 mutual funds that are available. (Bloomberg Personal Bookshelf Series).

INVESTMENT COMPANIES, CLOSED-END

See: CLOSED-END FUNDS

INVESTMENT DEALERS

See: STOCK BROKERS

INVESTMENT SERVICES

See: INVESTMENT ADVISORY SERVICES

INVESTMENT TRUSTS

See: INVESTMENT COMPANIES

INVESTMENTS

GENERAL WORKS

The Bear Book: Survive and Profit in Ferocious Markets. John Rothchild. John Wiley and Sons, Inc. • 1998. $24.95. Tells how to invest when the stock market is sinking.

Don't Die Broke: How to Turn Your Retirement Savings into Lasting Income. Margaret A. Malaspina. Bloomberg. • 1999. $21.95. Provides advice on such matters as retirement portfolio asset allocation and retirement spending accounts. (Bloomberg Personal Bookshelf Series).

Education of a Speculator. Victor Niederhoffer. John Wiley and Sons, Inc. • 1998. $18.95. An autobiography providing basic advice on speculation, investment, and the commodity futures market.

Everyone's Money Book: Everything You Need to Know About Investing Wisely, Buying a Home... Jordan E. Goodman. Dearborn Trade Publishing, A Kaplan Professional Co. • 2001. $30.00. Third edition. Covers investing, taxes, mortgages, retirement planning and other personal finance topics. Jordan E. Goodman is a writer for *Money* magazine.

The Five Rules for Successful Stock Investing: Morningstar's Guide to Building Wealth and Winning in the Market. Pat Dorsey. John Wiley and Sons, Inc. • 2004. $24.95. Provides conservative investment advice from Morningstar's Director of Stock Analysis.

Fundamentals of Investing. Lawrence J. Gitman and Michael D. Joehnk. Addison-Wesley. • 2003. $101. 33. Eighth edition.

How to Invest Wisely. Lawrence S. Pratt. American Institute for Economic Research. • 2002. $12.00. Presents a conservative policy of investing, with emphasis on dividend-paying common stocks. Gold and other inflation hedges are compared. Includes a reprint of *Toward an Optimal Stock Selection Strategy* (1997). (Economic Education Bulletin.).

The Individual Investor's Revolution: Unlock the Secrets of Wall Street and Invest Like a Pro. Charles B. Carlson. McGraw-Hill. • 2000. $15.95. Emphasizes the growing importance of the individual investor, especially with regard to online trading (e-trading). Includes the author's favorite

websites for investors and traders.

The Intelligent Asset Allocator: How to Build Your Portfolio to Maximize Returns and Minimize Risk. William J. Bernstein. McGraw-Hill. • 2000. $29.95. Contains popularly written, conservative advice for the average investor. Explains such items as portfolio theory, market efficiency, stock valuation models, and index investing.

Investments: An Introduction to Analysis and Management. Frederick Amling. Pearson Custom Publishing. • 1999. $94.00. Seventh edition.

Investments: Analysis and Management. Charles P. Jones. John Wiley and Sons, Inc. • 2001. $118.95. Eighth edition.

Keys to Investing in Common Stocks. Barbara Apostolou and Nicholas Apostolou. Barron's Educational Series, Inc. • 2004. $7.95. Fourth edition. Provides basic information for the average small investor. Covers investing in both individual stocks and mutual funds.

Learn to Earn: An Introduction to the Basics of Investing and Business. Peter Lynch and John Rothchild. Simon & Schuster Trade. • 1996. $14.00.

Mastering Online Investing: How to Use the Internet to Become a More Successful Investor. Michael C. Thomsett. Dearborn Trading Publishing, A Kaplan Professional Co. • 2001. $19.95. Emphasis is on the Internet as an information source for intelligent investing, avoiding "speculation and fads.".

Never Call Your Broker on Monday: And 300 Other Financial Lessons You Can't Afford Not to Know. Nancy Dunnan. HarperInformation. • 1997. $8.50. Presents a wide range of personal finance advice, covering investments, insurance, wills, credit, real estate, etc.

The Only Investment Guide You'll Ever Need. Andrew Tobias. Harcourt Trade Publishers. • 1999. $14.00. Expanded revised edition. An entertaining, optimistic look at investing, written for the "average" investor. Provides generally conservative advice, favoring no-load, low-expense index funds.

A Random Walk Down Wall Street: The Best Investment Advice for the New Century. Burton G. Malkiel. W. W. Norton & Co., Inc. • 1999. $29.95. Seventh revised edition.

A Short History of Financial Euphoria. John Kenneth Galbraith. Penguin Group. • 1994. $13.00. An analysis of speculative euphoria and subsequent crashes, from the Holland tulip mania in 1637 to the 1987 unpleasantness in the U. S. stock market. (Whittle Series).

Smart Money Guide to Long-Term Investing: How to Build Real Wealth for Retirement and Other Future Goals. Nellie S. Huang and Peter Finch. John Wiley and Sons, Inc. • 2002. $24.95. The authors are associated with *Smart Money* magazine. Their book emphsizes the importance of effective asset allocation through the years and recommends specific stock and bond mutual funds for retirement, including "The Best and Worst Funds for Your 401(k).".

Smart Questions to Ask Your Financial Advisers. Lynn Brenner. Bloomberg. • 1997. $19.95. Provides practical advice on how to deal with financial planners, stockbrokers, insurance agents, and lawyers. Some of the areas covered are investments, estate planning, tax planning, house buying, prenuptial agreements, divorce arrangements, loss of a job, and retirement. (Bloomberg Personal Bookshelf Series).

Stocks for the Long Run: The Definitive Guide to Financial Market Returns and Long-Term Investment Strategies. Jeremy J. Siegel. McGraw-Hill. • 2002. $29.95. Third revised edition. A favorable view of a buy-and-hold strategy for stock market investors. (Teach Yourself Series).

Straight Talk on Investing: What You Need to Know. Jack Brennan. John Wiley and Sons, Inc. • 2002. $22.95. Provides basic, conservative advice for the

small investor. Emphasis is on long-term goals and investment planning.

Super Searchers on Wall Street: Top Investment Professionals Share Their Online Research Secrets. Amelia Kassel. Information Today, Inc. • 2000. $24. 95. Gives the results of interviews with "10 leading financial industry research experts." Explains how online information is used by stock brokers, investment bankers, and individual investors. Includes relevant Web sites and other sources. (Super Searchers Series).

Vanguard Retirement Investing Guide: Charting Your Course to a Secure Retirement. McGraw-Hill. • 1995. $24.95. Second edition. Covers saving and investing for future retirement. Topics include goal setting, investment fundamentals, mutual funds, asset allocation, defined contribution retirement savings plans, social security, and retirement savings strategies. Includes glossary and worksheet for retirement saving.

What Works on Wall Street: A Guide to the Best Performing Investment Strategies of All Time. James P. O'Shaughnessy. McGraw-Hill. • 1998. $49.95. Second revised edition. Examines investment strategies over a 43-year period and concludes that large capitalization, high-dividend-yield stocks produce the best results. Includes digital audio.

Yes, You Can Time the Market!. Ben Stein and Phil DeMuth. John Wiley and Sons, Inc. • 2003. $24.95. Despite the title, provides generally conservative advice for investors. Timing, in this case, relates to longterm trends and valuations.

ABSTRACTS AND INDEXES

Investment Statistics Locator. Linda H. Bentley and Jennifer J. Kiesl, editors. Greenwood Publishing Group, Inc. • 1994. $69.95. Expanded revised edition. Provides detailed subject indexing of more than 50 of the most-used sources of financial and investment data. Includes an annotated bibliography.

ALMANACS AND YEARBOOKS

Advances in Investment Analysis and Portfolio Management. Chung-Few Lee, editor. Elsevier. • Dates vary. Six volumes. Price varies.

Irwin Business and Investment Almanac, 1994: Dow Jones and Company Edition. Summer N. Levine and Caroline Levine. McGraw-Hill. • 1994. $75.00. 18th edition. A review of last year's business activity. Covers a wide variety of business and economic data: stock market statistics, industrial information, commodity futures information, art market trends, comparative living costs for U. S. metropolitan areas, foreign stock market data, etc. Formerly *Business One Irwin Business and Investment Almanac.*

CD-ROM DATABASES

InvesText [CD-ROM]. Thomson Financial. • Monthly. Contains full text on CD-ROM of investment research reports from about 630 sources, including leading brokers and investment bankers. Reports are available on both U. S. and international publicly traded corporations. Separate industry reports cover more than 50 industries. Time span is 1982 to date.

WILSONDISC: Wilson Business Abstracts. H. W. Wilson Co. • Monthly. Includes unlimited online access to *Wilson Business Abstracts* through WILSONLINE. Provides CD-ROM "cover-to-cover" abstracting and indexing of over 600 prominent business periodicals. Indexing is from 1982, abstracting from 1990. (*Business Periodicals Index* without abstracts is available on CD-ROM at $1,495 per year.).

DIRECTORIES

Association for Investment Management and Research-Membership Directory. Association for Investment Management and Research. • Annual. $150.00. Lists 38,000 professional investment managers and securities analysts.

Major Financial Institutions of the World 2001. Available from Gale Cengage Learning. • 2003. $880.00. Sixth edition. Two volumes. Published by Graham & Whiteside. Contains detailed information on more than 7,500 important financial institutions in various countries. Includes banks, investment companies, and insurance companies.

Mergent International Manual and News Reports. Mergent, Inc. • Annual. Price on application. Financial and other information about 3,000 publicly-owned corporations in 100 countries. Formerly *Moody's International Manual and News Reports.*

Plunkett's On-Line Trading, Finance, and Investment Web Sites Almanac. Plunkett Research, Ltd. • Annual. $149.99. Provides profiles and usefulness rankings of financial Web sites. Sites are rated from 1 to 5 for specific uses. Includes CD-ROM.

ENCYCLOPEDIAS AND DICTIONARIES

The A-Z Vocabulary for Investors. American Institute for Economic Research. • 1997. $7.00. Second half of book is a "General Glossary" of about 400 financial terms "most-commonly used" in investing. First half contains lengthier descriptions of types of banking institutions (commercial banks, thrift institutions, credit unions), followed by succinct explanations of various forms of investment: stocks, bonds, options, futures, commodities, and "Other Investments" (collectibles, currencies, mortgages, precious metals, real estate, charitable trusts). (Economic Education Bulletin.).

Blackwell Encyclopedic Dictionary of Finance. Dean Paxson and Douglas Wood, editors. Blackwell Publishing. • 1997. $110.00. The editors are associated with the University of Manchester. Contains definitions of key terms combined with longer articles written by various U. S. and foreign business educators. Includes bibliographies and index. (Blackwell Encyclopedia of Management Series).

Dictionary of Finance and Investment Terms. John Downes. Barron's Educational Series, Inc. • 2002. $14.95. Sixth edition. Provides clear explanations of more than 5,000 business, banking, financial, investment, and tax terms. Includes a separate list of financial abbreviations and acronyms. (Business Dictionaries Series).

Knowledge Exchange Business Encyclopedia: Your Complete Business Advisor. Lorraine Spurge. Knowledge Exchange LLC. • 1998. $45.00. Provides definitions of business terms and financial expressions, profiles of leading industries, tables of economic statistics, biographies of business leaders, and other business information. Includes "A Chronology of Business from 3000 B.C. Through 1995." Contains illustrations and three indexes.

The New Palgrave Dictionary of Money and Finance. Peter Newman and others, editors. Palgrave Macmillan. • 1992. $595.00. Two volumes. Consists of signed essays on over 1,000 financial topics, each with a bibliography. Covers a wide variety of financial, monetary, and investment areas. A detailed subject index is provided.

HANDBOOKS AND MANUALS

Barron's Finance & Investment Handbook. John Downes and Jordan Goodman. Barron's Educational Series, Inc. • 1998. $35.00. Fifth edition. Mainly concerned with personal finance, including advice on stocks, bonds, mutual funds, annuities, life insurance, real estate, futures, and collectibles. Includes a glossary of financial and investment terms.

The 401(k) Plan Handbook. Julie Jason. Prentice Hall PTR. • 1997. $79.95. Provides technical, legal, administrative, and investment details of 401(k) retirement plans.

Getting Started in Investment Planning Services. James E. Grant. CCH, Inc. • 1999. $85.00. Second

edition. Provides advice and information for lawyers and accountants who are planning to initiate fee-based investment services.

Handbook of Alternative Investment Strategies. Thomas Schneeweis and Joseph F. Pescatore, editors. Institutional Investor, Inc., Journals Group. • 1999. $95.00. Covers various forms of alternative investment, including hedge funds, managed futures, derivatives, venture capital, and natural resource financing.

Indexing for Maximum Investment Results. Albert S. Neuberg. Fitzroy Dearborn Publishers, Inc. • 1998. $65.00. Covers the Standard & Poor's 500 and other indexing strategies for both individual and institutional investors.

The Prudent Speculator: Al Frank on Investing. Al Frank. McGraw-Hill. • 1989. $30.00. How to be a sensible investor or speculator. Includes advice on the use of margin accounts and stock market timing.

Venture Capital: An Authoritative Guide for Investors, Entrepreneurs, and Managers. Douglas A. Lindgren. McGraw-Hill. • 1998. $65.00.

Wall Street Journal Guide to Planning Your Financial Future: The Easy-to-Read Guide to Lifetime Planning for Retirement. Kenneth M. Morris and Virginia B. Morris. Simon & Schuster Trade. • 2002. $15.95. Third edition. (Wall Street Journal Guides Series).

INTERNET DATABASES

ETF Connect. Nuveen Investments. Phone: 800-257-8787 • URL: http://www.etfconnect.com • Free Web site makes available extensive, searchable information on individual closed-end investment funds, preferred share funds, and exchange-traded index funds. Information on a particular fund is available by name or as part of a classification (high yield, investment grade, municipal, emerging markets, global equity, etc.). Fund charts are available for various time periods, as is data concerning premiums or discounts, dividends, annualized total return, credit quality, "Top 10 Holdings," and so forth.

Factiva. Dow Jones Reuters Business Interactive, LLC. Phone: 800-369-7466 or (609)452-1511 Fax: (609)520-5770 E-mail: solutions@factiva.com • URL: http://www.factiva.com • Fee-based Web site provides "global news and business information through Web sites and content integration solutions." Includes Dow Jones and Reuters newswires, The Wall Street Journal, and more than 7,000 other sources of current news, historical articles, market research reports, and investment analysis. Content includes 96 major U. S. newspapers, 900 non-English sources, trade publications, media transcripts, country profiles, news photos, etc.

Morningstar.com: Your First Second Opinion. Morningstar, Inc. Phone: 800-735-0700 or (312)696-6000 Fax: (312)696-6001 E-mail: productsupport@morningstar.com • URL: http://www.morningstar.com • Web site provides a broad selection of information and advice on both mutual funds and individual stocks, including financial news and articles on investment fundamentals. Basic service is free, with "Premium Membership" available at $109.00 per year. Annual fee provides personal portfolio analysis, screening tools, and more extensive profiles of funds and stocks.

Nexis.com. Lexis-Nexis Group. Phone: 800-227-4908 or (937)865-6800 Fax: (937)865-6909 E-mail: webmaster@prod.lexis-nexis.com • URL: http://www.nexis.com • Fee-based Web site offers searching of about 2.8 billion documents in some 30,000 news, business, and legal information sources. Features include a subject directory covering 1,200 topics in 34 categories and a Company Dossier containing information on more than 500,000 public and private companies. Boolean searching is offered.

TheStreet.com: Your Insider's Look at Wall Street.

TheStreet.com, Inc. Phone: 800-562-9571 or (212)321-5000 Fax: (212)321-5016 • URL: http://www.thestreet.com • Web site offers "Free Sections" and "Premium Sections" ($24.95 per month). Both sections offer iconoclastic advice and comment on the stock market, but premium service displays a more comprehensive selection of news and analysis. There are many by-lined articles. "Search the Site" is included.

ONLINE DATABASES

InvesText. Thomson Financial. • Provides full text online of investment research reports from more than 600 sources, including leading brokers and investment bankers. Reports are available on approximately 60,000 U. S. and international corporations. Separate industry reports cover 54 industries. Time span is 1982 to date, with daily updates. Inquire as to online cost and availability.

Wilson Business Abstracts Online. H. W. Wilson Co. • Indexes and abstracts 600 major business periodicals, plus the *Wall Street Journal* and the business section of the *New York Times.* Indexing is from 1982, abstracting from 1990, with the two newspapers included from 1993. Updated weekly. Inquire as to online cost and availability. (*Business Periodicals Index* without abstracts is also available online.).

PERIODICALS AND NEWSLETTERS

AAII Journal. American Association of Individual Investors. • 10 times a year. $49.00 per year. Covers strategy and investment techniques.

Bank Credit Analyst. BCA Publications Ltd. • Monthly. $695.00 per year. "The independent monthly forecast and analysis of trends in business conditions and major investment markets based on a continuous appraisal of money and credit flows." Includes many charts and graphs relating to money, credit, and securities in the U. S.

Bank Investment Consultant: Sales Strategies for the Financial Adviser. Thomson Media. • Monthly. Controlled circulation. Covers sales and marketing techniques for bank investment and asset management divisions. Formerly *Bank Investment Marketing.*

Bank Rate Monitor: The Weekly Financial Rate Reporter. Advertising News Service, Inc. • Weekly. $895.00 per year. Newsletter. Includes online addition and monthly supplement. Provides detailed information on interest rates currently paid by U. S. banks and savings institutions.

Barron's: The Dow Jones Business and Financial Weekly. • Weekly. $145.00 per year.

Commercial and Financial Chronicle. William B. Dana Co. • Weekly. $140.00. per year.

Financial Sentinel: Your Beacon to the World of Investing. Gulf Atlantic Publishing, Inc. • Monthly. $29.95 per year. Provides "The only complete listing of all OTC Bulletin Board stocks traded, with all issues listed on the Nasdaq SmallCap Market, the Toronto, and Vancouver Stock Exchanges." Also includes investment advice and recommendations of small capitalization stocks.

Forbes. Forbes, Inc. • Biweekly. $59.95 per year. Includes supplements: *Forbes ASAP* and *Forbes FYI.*

Investment Advisor: The Advisor to Advisors. Wicks Business Information. • Monthly. $79.00 per year. Edited for professional investment advisors, financial planners, stock brokers, bankers, and others concerned with the management of assets.

Investment Dealers' Digest. Thomson Media. • Weekly. $750.00 per year. Covers financial news, trends, new products, people, private placements, new issues of securities, and other aspects of the investment business. Includes feature stories.

Investment Guide. American Investment Services Inc. • Description: Contains analyses of stock market activity and strategies for investment. Recurring features include market statistics, Dow high-yield stock investing.

Investment News: The Weekly Newspaper for Financial Advisers. Crain Communications, Inc. • Weekly. $29.00 per year. Edited for both personal and institutional investment advisers, planners, and managers.

The Investment Reporter. MPL Communications Inc. • Description: Profiles specific companies and market trends and developments, making recommendations to assist in formulating investment strategies. Includes short articles offering advice on investment decisions.

Investor's Business Daily. Investor's Business Daily, Inc. • Daily. $295.00 per year. Newspaper.

Journal of Alternative Investments. Institutional Investor, Inc., Journals Group. • Quarterly. $540.00 per year. Includes print and online editions. Covers such items as hedge funds, private equity financing, funds of funds, real estate investment trusts, natural resource investments, foreign exchange, and emerging markets.

Journal of Wealth Management. Institutional Investor, Inc., Journals Group. • Quarterly. $410.00 per year. Includes print and online editions. Edited for managers of wealthy individuals' investment portfolios. Formerly *Journal of Private Portfolio Management.*

Louis Rukeyser's Wall Street. Louis Rukeyser's Wall Street Club. • Monthly. $39.50 per year. Newsletter. Gives recommendations for personal investing.

One Hundred Highest Yields. Advertising News Service, Inc. • Weekly. $124.00 per year. Newsletter. List CD's and money markets offered by federally insured banks. National coverage.

Online Investor: Personal Investing for the Digital Age. Stock Trends, Inc. • Monthly. $14.95 per year. Provides advice and Web site reviews for online traders.

Outstanding Investor Digest: Perspectives and Activities of the Nation's Most Successful Money Managers. Outstanding Investor Digest, Inc. • $395.00 for 10 issues. Newsletter. Each issue features interviews with leading money managers.

Predictions: Specific Investment Forecasts and Recommendations from the World's Top Financial Experts. Lee Euler, editor. Agora, Inc. • Monthly. $78.00 per year. Newsletter.

Profit Investor Portfolio: The International Magazine of Money and Style. Profit Publications, Inc. • Bimonthly. $29.95 per year. A glossy consumer magazine featuring specific investment recommendations and articles on upscale travel and shopping.

Profitable Investing. Richard E. Band, editor. Profitable Investing. • Description: Advises individuals seeking low-risk growth by providing "a wealth of information." Discusses various stocks, mutual funds, interest income, and tax issues. Contains lists of best investments.

Richard C. Young's Intelligence Report. Access Intelligence L.L.C. • Description: Provides information for "serious, conservative investors (buy and hold as opposed to active traders)." Features investing advice and recommendations for best funds, stocks, and bonds for current or retirement income.

Robb Report Worth: Wealth in Perspective. CurtCo Robb Media. • Monthly. $54.95 per year. Glossy magazine featuring articles for the affluent on personal financial management, investments, estate planning, trusts, private bankers, taxes, travel, yachts, and lifestyle. Formerly *Worth: Financial Intelligence.*

SmartMoney: The Wall Street Journal Magazine of Personal Business. Hearst Communications, Inc. •

Monthly. $15.00 per year. Includes *Stock Trader's Almanac.*

Stanger Report: A Guide to Partnership Investing. Robert A. Stanger and Co. • Quarterly. $447.00 per year. Newsletter providing analysis of limited partnership investments.

The Wall Street Journal. Dow Jones & Co., Inc. • Daily. $189.00 per year. Covers news and trends relating to business, industry, finance, the economy, and international commerce. Provides extensive price and other data for the securities, commodity, options, futures, foreign exchange, and money markets.

Wall Street Transcript: A Professional Publication for the Business and Financial Community. Wall Street Transcript Corp. • Weekly. $1,890.00. per year. Provides reprints of investment research reports.

PRICE SOURCES

Bank and Quotation Record. William B. Dana Co. • Monthly. $130.00 per year.

RESEARCH CENTERS AND INSTITUTES

Bendheim Center for Finance. Princeton University, 26 Prospect Ave., Princeton, NJ 08540-5296. Phone: (609)258-0770 Fax: (609)258-0771 E-mail: yacine@princeton.edu • URL: http://www.princeton.edu/~bcf/ • Research areas include securities markets, portfolio analysis, credit markets, and corporate finance. Emphasis is on quantitative and mathematical perspectives.

STATISTICS SOURCES

Standard & Poor's Industry Surveys. Standard & Poor's. • Semiannual. $1,800.00. Two looseleaf volumes. Includes monthly *Supplements.* Provides detailed, individual surveys of 52 major industry groups. Each survey is revised on a semiannual basis. Also includes "Monthly Investment Review" (industry group investment analysis) and monthly "Trends & Projections" (economic analysis).

Standard & Poor's Stock and Bond Guide. McGraw-Hill. • Annual. $24.95. Contains concise data on 6,000 stocks, 7,000 bonds, and 700 mutual funds. Includes year-end prices, earnings estimates for stocks, and debt ratings for bonds.

TRADE/PROFESSIONAL ASSOCIATIONS

American Association of Individual Investors. 625 N. Michigan Ave., Suite 1900, Chicago, IL 60611. Phone: 800-428-2244 or (312)280-0170 Fax: (312)280-9883 E-mail: members@aaii.com • URL: http://www.aaii.com.

Association for Investment Management and Research. 560 Ray C. Hunt Dr., Charlottesville, VA 22903. Phone: 800-247-8132 or (434)951-5499 Fax: (434)951-5262 E-mail: info@aimr.org • URL: http://www.aimr.org • Members are practicing investment analysts.

National Association of Securities Dealers (NASD). 1735 K St., N.W., Washington, DC 20006-1506. Phone: (202)728-8000 Fax: (202)293-6260 E-mail: waltere@nasd.com • URL: http://www.nasd.com • Formerly National Association of Securities Dealers.

National Investor Relations Institute. 8020 Towers Crescent Dr., Ste. 250, Vienna, VA 22182. Phone: (703)506-3570 Fax: (703)506-3571 E-mail: info@niri.org • URL: http://www.niri.org • Executives engaged in investor relations. Identifies the role of the investor relations practitioner; protects a free and open market with equity and access to investors of all kinds; improves communication between corporate management and shareholders, present and future. Holds professional development seminars and conducts research programs.

Maintains placement service and speakers' bureau; compiles statistics.

OTHER SOURCES

The Value Line Investment Survey. Value Line Publishing, Inc. • Weekly. $570.00 per year. Newsletter. Provides detailed information and ratings for 1,700 stocks actively-traded in the U. S.

INVESTMENTS, INSTITUTIONAL

See: INSTITUTIONAL INVESTMENTS

INVESTMENTS, REAL ESTATE

See: REAL ESTATE INVESTMENTS

IRAS

See: INDIVIDUAL RETIREMENT ACCOUNTS

IRON AND STEEL INDUSTRY

See also: FOUNDRIES; METAL INDUSTRY

CD-ROM DATABASES

METADEX Materials Collection: Metals-Polymers-Ceramics. Cambridge Scientific Abstracts. • Quarterly. Provides CD-ROM citations to the worldwide literature of materials science and metallurgy. Corresponds to *Metals Abstracts, Alloys Index, Steels Alert, Nonferrous Alert, Polymers/Ceramics/Composites Alert,* and *Engineered Materials Abstracts.* (Formerly produced by ASM International.).

OECD Statistical Compendium. Organization for Economic Cooperation and Development. • Semiannual. $1,905.00 per year for 1 to 10 users. CD-ROM contains more than 730,000 monthly, quarterly, and annual time series for OECD countries, 1960 to date. Includes fully searchable data on agriculture, food, economic indicators, national accounts, employment, energy, finance, industry, technology, and foreign trade. Results can be displayed in various forms.

DIRECTORIES

Directory of Iron and Steel Plants (The Black Book). Association of Iron and Steel Engineers. • Biennial. $75.00. Lists executives and officials in the United States and selected overseas steel companies and plants.

Directory of Steel Foundries and Buyers Guide. Steel Founders' Society of America. • Biennial. $400.00. Available only online. Lists approximately 435 steel foundries in the United States, Canada and Mexico. Formerly *Directory of Steel Foundries in the United States, Canada, and Mexico.*

FINANCIAL RATIOS

Annual Statement Studies. The Risk Management Association. • Annual. Median and quartile financial ratios are given for over 400 kinds of manufacturing, wholesale, retail, construction, and consumer finance establishments. Data is sorted by both asset size and sales volume. Includes a clearly written "Definition of Ratios" and an alphabetical industry index.

Annual Statement Studies: Industry Default Probabilities and Cash Flow Measures. The Risk Management Association. • Annual. $145.00. Serves as a companion volume to the original *Annual Statement Studies.* Gives probability of default estimates on a percentage scale for more than 450 industries. Includes changes in position year-by-year for eight financial statement line items and provides percentage measures of cash flow.

HANDBOOKS AND MANUALS

Corrosion of Stainless Steels. A. John Sedriks. John Wiley and Sons, Inc. • 1996. $105.00. Second edition. Covers the corrosion and corrosion control of stainless steels used in a variety of applications. (Corrosion Monograph Series).

Stainless Steels, 87: Proceedings of Conference, University of York, 14-16 September, 87. Available from Ashgate Publishing Co. • 1988. $94.50. Published by Institute of Materials.

INTERNET DATABASES

Business 2.0 Web Guide to the Best Business Links. Business 2.0 Media Inc. Phone: (415)293-4800 E-mail: support@business2.com • URL: http://www.business2.com/webguide • Web site presents an extensive, searchable directory of links to "the best, most informative, and authoritative web pages." Twenty main categories cover business, finance, career, company information, people, and technology topics, with thousands of subtopics, all linking to Web sites recommended by experienced business researchers. Fees: Free.

Fedstats. Federal Interagency Council on Statistical Policy. Phone: (202)395-7254 • URL: http://www.fedstats.gov • Web site features an efficient search facility for full-text statistics produced by more than 100 federal agencies, including the Census Bureau, the Bureau of Economic Analysis, and the Bureau of Labor Statistics. Boolean searches can be made within one agency or for all agencies combined. Links are offered to international statistical bureaus, including the UN, IMF, OECD, UNESCO, Eurostat, and 20 individual countries. Fees: Free.

FreeLunch.com. Economy.com, Inc. Phone: (610)696-8700 Fax: (610)696-1678 • URL: http://www.freelunch.com • Web site provides free access to more than 1.5 million economic and financial data series, covering industry, demographics, labor markets, prices, retail sales, government spending, trade, interest rates, housing starts, the stock market, and many other topics. Data is available for various time periods in either chart or table form. Searching is offered. Fees: Free, but registration required. Economy.com, Inc. also offers fee-based economic analysis at *The Dismal Scientist* site (http://www.dismal.com).

Manufacturing Profiles. U. S. Bureau of the Census. Phone: (301)763-4636 E-mail: webmaster@census.gov • URL: http://www.census.gov/prod/www/abs/mfg-prof.html • The Census Bureau makes available free on PDF (Portable Document Format) an annual consolidation of the entire Current Industrial Report series, presenting "all the data compiled." Contains statistics on production, shipments, inventories, consumption, exports, imports, and orders for a wide variety of manufactured products.

ONLINE DATABASES

Materials Business File. Cambridge Scientific Abstracts. • Provides online abstracts and citations to worldwide materials literature, covering the business and industrial aspects of metals, plastics, ceramics, and composites. Corresponds to *Steels Alert, Nonferrous Metals Alert,* and *Polymers/Ceramics/Composites Alert.* Time period is 1985 to date, with monthly updates. (Formerly produced by ASM International.) Inquire as to online cost and availability.

METADEX. Cambridge Scientific Abstracts. • Covers the worldwide literature of metals, metallurgy, and materials science, 1966 to date. Includes detailed alloys indexing from 1974. Biweekly updating. Inquire as to online cost and availability. (Formerly produced by ASM International.).

PROMT: Predicasts Overview of Markets and Technology. Gale Cengage Learning. • Companies, products, applied technologies and markets. U.S. and international literature coverage, 1972 to date. Inquire as to online cost and availability. Provides abstracts from more than 1,600 publications. Weekly updates.

PERIODICALS AND NEWSLETTERS

Advanced Materials and Processes. ASM International. • Monthly. Free to members; institutions, $325.00 per year. Incorporates *Metal Progress.*Technical information and reports on new developments in the technology of engineered materials and manufacturing processes.

AISE Steel Technology. Association of Iron and Steel Engineers. • Monthly. $58.00 per year. Formerly *Iron and Steel Engineer.*

Metal Bulletin. Metal Bulletin, Inc. • Semiweekly. $1,378 per year. Provides news of international trends, prices, and market conditions for both steel and non-ferrous metal industries. (Published in England.).

Metal Bulletin Monthly. Metal Bulletin, Inc. • Monthly. Price on application. Edited for international metal industry business executives and senior technical personnel. Covers business, economic, and technical developments. (Published in England.).

Modern Casting. American Foundry Society, Inc. • Monthly. Free to qualified personnel; others, $50.00 per year.

Steel Times International. DMG World Media Ltd. • Bimonthly. $182.00 per year. Includes *Iron and Steel Directory.*

33 Metalproducing: For Primary Producers of Steel, Aluminum, and Copper-Base Alloys. Penton Media, Inc. • Monthly. $65.00 per year. Covers metal production technology and methods and industry news. Includes a bimonthly *Nonferrous Supplement.*

STATISTICS SOURCES

American Iron and Steel Annual Statistical Report. American Iron and Steel Institute. • Annual. $100.00 per year.

Annual Bulletin of Steel Statistics for Europe, America, and Asia. United Nations Publications. • Annual. $90.00. Presents detailed steel data for European countries, Canada, Japan, and the U. S. Includes statistics on production, trade, raw materials, scrap, deliveries, and energy use.

Annual Survey of Manufactures. Available from U. S. Government Printing Office. • Annual. Prices vary. Issued by the U. S. Census Bureau as an interim update to the *Census of Manufactures.* Includes data on number of manufacturing establishments in various industries, employment, labor costs, value of shipments, capital expenditures, inventories, energy costs, and assets. (See also Census Bureau home page, http://www.census.gov/.).

Business Statistics of the United States. Linz Audain and Cornelia J. Strawser. Bernan Associates. • Annual. $147.00. Based on *Business Statistics,* formerly issue by the Bureau of Economic Analysis, U. S. Department of Commerce. Provides basic data for a wide variety of U. S. industries, services, and economic indicators. Most statistics are shown annually for 30 years and monthly for the most recent four years.

Iron and Steel Industry in [year]. Organization for Economic Cooperation and Development. • Annual. $28.00. Contains yearly statistics on steel production, consumption, industry employment, investment expenditures, trade, and prices. Covers both OECD and developing countries.

Mineral Commodity Summaries. Available from U. S. Government Printing Office. • Annual. $26.00. Published by the U. S. Geological Survey, Department of the Interior (http://www.usgs.gov). Contains detailed, five-year data for about 90 nonfuel minerals. Covers a wide range of statistics, including production, imports, exports, consumption, reserves, prices, tariff information, and industry employment. (Two pages are devoted to each mineral.).

OECD Iron and Steel Industry. Organization for Economic Cooperation and Development. Available from OECD Publications and Information Center. • Annual. $34.00. Data for orders, production, manpower, imports, exports, consumption, prices and investment in the iron and steel industry in OECD member countries. Text in English and French.

OECD Steel Market and Outlook. Organization for Economic Cooperation and Development. OECD Publications and Information Center. • Annual. Price varies.

Standard & Poor's Industry Surveys. Standard & Poor's. • Semiannual. $1,800.00. Two looseleaf volumes. Includes monthly *Supplements.* Provides detailed, individual surveys of 52 major industry groups. Each survey is revised on a semiannual basis. Also includes "Monthly Investment Review" (industry group investment analysis) and monthly "Trends & Projections" (economic analysis).

Statistics of World Trade in Steel. United Nations Economic Commission for Europe. Available from United Nations Publications. • Annual. $90.00.

Steel Mill Products. U.S. Bureau of the Census. • Annual. (Current Industrial Reports MA-33B).

Survey of Current Business. Available from U. S. Government Printing Office. • Monthly. $63.00 per year. Issued by Bureau of Economic Analysis, U. S. Department of Commerce. Presents a wide variety of business and economic data.

WEFA Industrial Monitor. John Wiley and Sons, Inc. • Annual. $65.00. Prepared by industry analysts at WEFA, an economic forecasting and consulting firm (originally Wharton Econometric Forecasting Associates). Contains discussions of the outlook for major U. S. industries, with many 10-year forecasts (WEFA Web site is http://www.wefa.com).

TRADE/PROFESSIONAL ASSOCIATIONS

American Foundry Society. 1695 N Penny Ln., Schaumburg, IL 60173-4555. Phone: 800-537-4237 or (847)824-0181 Fax: (847)824-7848 E-mail: jcall@afsinc.org • URL: http://www.afsinc.org • Technical, trade and management association of foundrymen, patternmakers, technologists, and educators. Sponsors foundry training courses through the Cast +Metals Institute on all subjects pertaining to the castings industry; conducts educational and instructional exhibits of foundry industry; sponsors 10 regional foundry conferences and 400 local foundry technical meetings. Maintains Technical Information Center providing literature searching and document retrieval service; and Metalcasting Abstract Service involving abstracts of the latest metal casting literature. Provides environmental services and testing; conducts research programs; compiles statistics, provides marketing information.

American Iron and Steel Institute. 1140 Connecticut Ave. NW, Ste. 705, Washington, DC 20036. Phone: (202)452-7100 Fax: (202)463-6573 • URL: http://www.steel.org.

Association for Iron and Steel Technology. 186 Thorn Hill Rd., Warrendale, PA 15086-7528. Phone: (724)776-6040 Fax: (724)776-1880 E-mail: info@aist.org • URL: http://www.aistech.org • Formerly Iron and Steel Society.

Association of Steel Distributors. 401 N. Michigan Ave., Chicago, IL 60611. Phone: (312)644-6610 Fax: (312)527-6705 E-mail: asd@ssba.com • URL: http://www.steeldistributors.org/asd/.

Institute of Scrap Recycling Industries. 1325 G St., NW, Ste. 1000, Washington, DC 20005-3104. Phone: (202)737-1770 Fax: (202)626-0900 E-mail: isri@isri.org • URL: http://www.isri.org.

Metals Service Center Institute. 4201 Euclid Ave., Rolling Meadows, IL 60008-2025. Phone: (847)485-3000 Fax: (847)485-3001 E-mail: info@msci.org • URL: http://www.msci.org • Wholesalers of industrial steel products; associate members include companies manufacturing these products. Seeks to improve distribution and management performance standards of member companies through research, statistical, promotional, and public relations activities.

Steel Founders' Society of America. 205 Park Ave., Barrington, IL 60010. Phone: (847)382-8240 Fax: (847)382-8287 E-mail: monroe@sfsa.org • URL: http://www.sfsa.org • Manufacturers of steel casting. Provides technical support and research. Abosorbed Alloy Casting Institute.

IRON AND STEEL SCRAP METAL INDUSTRY

CD-ROM DATABASES

OECD Statistical Compendium. Organization for Economic Cooperation and Development. • Semiannual. $1,905.00 per year for 1 to 10 users. CD-ROM contains more than 730,000 monthly, quarterly, and annual time series for OECD countries, 1960 to date. Includes fully searchable data on agriculture, food, economic indicators, national accounts, employment, energy, finance, industry, technology, and foreign trade. Results can be displayed in various forms.

DIRECTORIES

North American Scrap Metals Directory. Recycling Today Media Group. • Covers: Suppliers of scrap metal materials in North America. Entries include: Contact information.

INTERNET DATABASES

Business 2.0 Web Guide to the Best Business Links. Business 2.0 Media Inc. Phone: (415)293-4800 E-mail: support@business2.com • URL: http://www.business2.com/webguide • Web site presents an extensive, searchable directory of links to "the best, most informative, and authoritative web pages." Twenty main categories cover business, finance, career, company information, people, and technology topics, with thousands of subtopics, all linking to Web sites recommended by experienced business researchers. Fees: Free.

Fedstats. Federal Interagency Council on Statistical Policy. Phone: (202)395-7254 • URL: http://www.fedstats.gov • Web site features an efficient search facility for full-text statistics produced by more than 100 federal agencies, including the Census Bureau, the Bureau of Economic Analysis, and the Bureau of Labor Statistics. Boolean searches can be made within one agency or for all agencies combined. Links are offered to international statistical bureaus, including the UN, IMF, OECD, UNESCO, Eurostat, and 20 individual countries. Fees: Free.

FreeLunch.com. Economy.com, Inc. Phone: (610)696-8700 Fax: (610)696-1678 • URL: http://www.freelunch.com • Web site provides free access to more than 1.5 million economic and financial data series, covering industry, demographics, labor markets, prices, retail sales, government spending, trade, interest rates, housing starts, the stock market, and many other topics. Data is available for various time periods in either chart or table form. Searching is offered. Fees: Free, but registration required. Economy.com, Inc. also offers fee-based economic analysis at *The Dismal Scientist* site (http://www.dismal.com).

PERIODICALS AND NEWSLETTERS

Scrap. Institute of Scrap Recycling Industries, Inc. • Bimonthly. Free to members; non-members, $32.95 per year. Formerly *Scrap Processing and Recycling.*

STATISTICS SOURCES

Business Statistics of the United States. Linz Audain and Cornelia J. Strawser. Bernan Associates. • Annual. $147.00. Based on *Business Statistics,* formerly issue by the Bureau of Economic Analysis, U. S. Department of Commerce. Provides basic data for a wide variety of U. S. industries, services, and economic indicators. Most statistics are shown annually for 30 years and monthly for the most recent four years.

Survey of Current Business. Available from U. S. Government Printing Office. • Monthly. $63.00 per year. Issued by Bureau of Economic Analysis, U. S. Department of Commerce. Presents a wide variety of business and economic data.

TRADE/PROFESSIONAL ASSOCIATIONS

Institute of Scrap Recycling Industries. 1325 G St., NW, Ste. 1000, Washington, DC 20005-3104. Phone: (202)737-1770 Fax: (202)626-0900 E-mail: isri@isri.org • URL: http://www.isri.org.

IRON FOUNDRIES

See: FOUNDRIES

IRRIGATION

ABSTRACTS AND INDEXES

Environment Abstracts. Congressional Information Service, Inc. • Monthly. Price varies. Provides multidisciplinary coverage of the world's environmental literature. Incorporates *Acid Rain Abstracts.*

Environment Abstracts Annual: A Guide to the Key Environmental Literature of the Year. Congressional Information Service, Inc. • Annual. $495.00. A yearly cumulation of *Environment Abstracts.*

Irrigation and Drainage Abstracts. Available from CABI Publishing, North America. • Quarterly. Institutions, $770.00 per year; with online edition, $785.00 per year. Published in England by CABI Publishing. Provides worldwide coverage of the literature.

CD-ROM DATABASES

Environment Abstracts on CD-ROM. LEXIS-NEXIS. • Quarterly. $1,295.00 per year. Contains the following CD-ROM databases: *Environment Abstracts, Energy Abstracts,* and *Acid Rain Abstracts.* Length of coverage varies.

DIRECTORIES

Irrigation Association Membership Directory and Industry Buyers' Guide. The Irrigation Association. • Annual. Free to members; non-members, $25.00. Includes manufacturing, distribution, contracting, consultation, research and educational information.

HANDBOOKS AND MANUALS

Knott's Handbook for Vegetable Growers. Donald N. Maynard and George J. Hochmuth. John Wiley and Sons, Inc. • 1997. $99.00. Fourth edition. Written for commercial vegetable growers, truck farmers, horticulturists, and other professionals. Covers such topics as spacing of plants, disease control, insect pests, seeds, weeds, water management, and irrigation.

ONLINE DATABASES

CAB Abstracts. CAB Publishing North America. • Contains 46 specialized abstract collections covering over 10,000 journals and monographs in the areas of agriculture, horticulture, forest products, farm products, nutrition, dairy science, poultry, grains, animal health, entomology, etc. Time period is 1972 to date, with monthly updates. Inquire as to online cost and availability. *CAB Abstracts on CD-ROM* also available, with annual updating.

STATISTICS SOURCES

FAO Production Yearbook. Available from Bernan Associates. • Annual. $45.00. Published by the Food and Agriculture Organization (http://www.fao.org). Contains worldwide data on agriculture, land use, farm crops, livestock, and agricultural prices.

TRADE/PROFESSIONAL ASSOCIATIONS

Irrigation Association. 6540 Arlington Blvd., Falls Church, VA 22042-6638. Phone: (703)536-7080 Fax: (703)536-7019 E-mail: deborah@irrigation.org • URL: http://www.irrigation.org • Manufacturers, distributors, dealers, designers, engineers, technicians, students, educators, sports facility managers, park and university grounds managers, golf course/resort designers and managers, government administrators, and contractors. Offers government relations, education courses, and certification programs.

National Water Resources Association. 3800 N Fairfax Dr., Ste. 4, Arlington, VA 22203. Phone: (703)524-1544 Fax: (703)524-1548 E-mail: nwra@nwra.org • URL: http://www.nwra.org • Officers of irrigation districts, canal companies, businesses, and others interested in the development, control, conservation, and utilization of water resources in the reclamation states (17 western states). Conducts legislative tracking and provides updates.

U.S. Committee on Irrigation and Drainage. 1616 17th St., No. 483, Denver, CO 80202. Phone: (303)628-5430 Fax: (303)628-5431 E-mail: stephens@uscid.org • URL: http://www.uscid.org • Formerly U.S. Committee on Irrigation, Drainage and Flood Control.

ISO 9000 STANDARDS

See: TOTAL QUALITY MANAGEMENT (TQM)

ISOTOPES

GENERAL WORKS

Isotopes for Medicine and the Life Sciences. S. James Adelstein and Frederick J. Manning, editors. National Academy Press. • 1995. $30.00. Includes bibliographical references and a glossary.

PERIODICALS AND NEWSLETTERS

Applied Radiation and Isotopes. Elsevier. • Monthly. Individuals, $374.00 per year; institutions, $2,546.00 per year.

RESEARCH CENTERS AND INSTITUTES

Radioisotope Laboratory. Louisiana State University. 3960 W. Lakeshore House, Baton Rouge, LA 70803. Phone: (225)578-8654 E-mail: urelat1@lsu.edu.

J

JANITORIAL SERVICES

See: MAINTENANCE OF BUILDINGS

JAPAN

See: ASIAN MARKETS

JAVA (COMPUTER PROGRAM LANGUAGE)

GENERAL WORKS

Learning Java. Patrick Niemeyer and Jonathon Knudsen. O'Reilly & Associates, Inc. • 2002. $44.95. Second edition. Includes CD-ROM. Covers the essentials for programmers beginning to use Java.

Teach Yourself Java. Chris Wright. McGraw-Hill. • 2001. $12.95. Second edition. Covers the basics of designing websites and interactive pages.

ABSTRACTS AND INDEXES

Internet and Personal Computing Abstracts [print edition]. EBSCO Publishing. • Quarterly. $269.00 per year, including cumulative index. Provides more than 10,000 abstracts annually from both trade and academic publications. Covers computer hardware, software, product reviews, Web topics, e-commerce, networks, corporate news, security, and related topics. Formerly *Microcomputer Abstracts.*

ENCYCLOPEDIAS AND DICTIONARIES

Acronyms of Computer Science and Communications: A Comprehensive Acronym Dictionary and Illustrated Encyclopedia. Enjob Kajan and Ejub Kajan. Springer Verlag. • 2002. $49.95. Explains more than 4,000 "broadly used" computer, telecommunications, and information technology acronyms. Includes illustrations and Web addresses, where applicable.

Encyclopedia of Information Systems. Hossein Bidgoli, editor. Elsevier. • 2002. $1,200.00. Four volumes. Contains a wide range of articles relating to computers, databases, communication, and information technology. The 200 topics include coverage of hardware, software, artificial intelligence, the Internet, networks, knowledge management, electronic commerce, search engines, and systems design.

HANDBOOKS AND MANUALS

Bitter Java. Bruce A. Tate. Manning Publications Co. • 2002. $44.95. A guide that describes common errors in Java programming.

Developing Java Software. Russel Winder and Graham Roberts. John Wiley and Sons, Inc. • 2002.

$55.00. Second edition. (Worldwide Computer Science Series).

Introduction to Object-Oriented Programming with Java with Code Warrior. C. Thomas Wu. McGraw-Hill. • 2001. $82.81. Second edition. Includes CD-ROM. (Science, Engineering and Mathematics Series).

Java Cookbook: Solutions and Examples for Java Developers. Ian Darwin. O'Reilly & Associates, Inc. • 2001. $44.95. Presents a "comprehensive collection of problems, solutions, and practical examples" for Java developers.

Java FAQs. Clifford J. Berg. Prentice Hall PTR. • 2001. $26.95.

Java for Students. Douglas Bell and Mike Parr. Prentice Hall PTR. • 2001. $77.33. Third edition. A basic introduction to Java.

Java in a Nutshell. David Flanagan. O'Reilly & Associates, Inc. • 2002. $39.95. Fourth edition. (In a Nutshell Series).

Java in 60 Minutes a Day. R. F. Raposa. John Wiley and Sons, Inc. • 2003. $50.00. "Includes thirty one-hour lessons that recreate a typical week-long introductory seminar." A companion Web site is offered.

Java Tutorial: A Short Course on the Basics. Mary Campione and Others. Addison-Wesley. • 2000. $44.99. Third edition. Presents a self-guided tour of the Java programming language. CD-ROM included. (Java Tutorial Series).

Understanding Object-Oriented Programming with Java. Timothy Budd. Addison-Wesley. • 1999. $85.00. Second revised edition.

PERIODICALS AND NEWSLETTERS

Java Developer's Journal. Sys-Con Media. • Monthly. $69.99 per year. Provides technical information for Java professionals.

Java Pro. Fawcette Technical Publications. • Monthly. $29.95 per year. Contains technical articles for Java developers.

JET PROPULSION

See: ROCKET INDUSTRY

JEWELRY BUSINESS

See also: GEMS AND GEMSTONES

DIRECTORIES

Jewelers' Circular/Keystone-Jewelers' Directory. Reed Business Information. • Annual. $33.95. About 8,500 manufacturers, importers and

wholesale jewelers providing merchandise and supplies to the jewelry retailing industry; and related trade organizations. Included with subscription to *Jewelers' Circular Keystone.*

Manufacturing Jewelers Buyers' Guide. Manufacturing Jewelers and Suppliers of America. • Biennial. Free to members; non-members, $125.00. Lists manufacturers and suppliers and has cross-reference by products listed.

ENCYCLOPEDIAS AND DICTIONARIES

Illustrated Dictionary of Jewelry. Harold Newman. Thames Hudson. • 1994. $29.95.

FINANCIAL RATIOS

Annual Statement Studies. The Risk Management Association. • Annual. Median and quartile financial ratios are given for over 400 kinds of manufacturing, wholesale, retail, construction, and consumer finance establishments. Data is sorted by both asset size and sales volume. Includes a clearly written "Definition of Ratios" and an alphabetical industry index.

Annual Statement Studies: Industry Default Probabilities and Cash Flow Measures. The Risk Management Association. • Annual. $145.00. Serves as a companion volume to the original *Annual Statement Studies.* Gives probability of default estimates on a percentage scale for more than 450 industries. Includes changes in position year-by-year for eight financial statement line items and provides percentage measures of cash flow.

HANDBOOKS AND MANUALS

Diamond Ring Buying Guide: How to Evaluate, Identify, and Select Diamonds and Diamond Jewelry. Renee Newman. International Jewelry Publications. • 2003. $17.95. Sixth edition. A well known gemologist explains diamond "cut, color, clarity, and carat." Color photographs are included, as well as information on diamond settings.

Jewelry and Gems: The Buying Guide: How to Buy Diamonds, Pearls, Precious and Other Popular Gems with Confidence and Knowledge. Antoinette L. Matlins and Antonio C. Bonanno. GemStone Press. • 2001. $24.95. Fifth edition.

INTERNET DATABASES

Advance Monthly Sales for Retail Trade and Food Services. U. S. Census Bureau. Phone: 800-541-8345 or (301)763-4636 Fax: (301)457-3842 E-mail: rcb@census.gov • URL: http://www.census.gov/svsd/www/fullpub.html • Web pages provide monthly sales figures for a wide range of retail businesses. Advance, preliminary, and final statistics are provided for the latest month available in each case, with a previous-year comparison. Updates are monthly.

ONLINE DATABASES

PROMT: Predicasts Overview of Markets and Technology. Gale Cengage Learning. • Companies, products, applied technologies and markets. U.S. and international literature coverage, 1972 to date. Inquire as to online cost and availability. Provides abstracts from more than 1,600 publications. Weekly updates.

PERIODICALS AND NEWSLETTERS

Accessories. Business Journals, Inc. • 11 times a year. $35.00 per year. Covers the merchandising of women's fashion accessories, including handbags, belts, jewelry, gloves, hats, and umbrellas.

AJM: Authority on Jewelry Manufacturing. Manufacturing Jewelers and Silversmiths of America, Inc. Skies America Publishing Co. • Monthly. $42.00 per year.

JCK (Jewelers' Circular Keystone). Reed Business Information. • Monthly. $90.00 per year.

Modern Jeweler. Cygnus Business Media. • Monthly. $60.00 per year. Edited for retail jewelers. Covers the merchandising of jewelry, gems, and watches. Supersedes in part *Modern Jeweler.*

National Jeweler. VNU Business Media. • Bimonthly. $65.00 per year. For jewelry retailers.

STATISTICS SOURCES

Annual Benchmark Report for Retail Trade and Food Services...A Detailed Summary of Retail Sales, Purchases, Accounts Receivable, Inventories, and Food Service Sales. Available from U. S. Government Printing Office. • Annual. $13.00. Issued by the U.S. Census Bureau. Provides detailed annual and monthly retail statistics for the most recent 10 years. Includes data for various kinds of retail outlets, including automobiles, furniture, appliances, building supplies, grocery stores, drug stores, gasoline stations, clothing, sporting goods, department stores, and restaurants.

U. S. Industry and Trade Outlook. Available from National Technical Information Service. • Annual. $69.95. Produced by the International Trade Administration, U. S. Department of Commerce, in a "public-private" partnership with DRI/McGraw-Hill and Standard & Poor's. Provides basic data, outlook for the current year, and "Long-Term Prospects" (five-year projections) for a wide variety of products and services. Includes high technology industries. Formerly *U. S. Industrial Outlook.*

TRADE/PROFESSIONAL ASSOCIATIONS

Gemological Institute of America. 5345 Armada Dr., Carlsbad, CA 92008. Phone: 800-421-7250 or (760)603-4000 Fax: (760)603-4080 E-mail: president@gia.edu • URL: http://www.gia.edu.

The Jewelers Board of Trade. 95 Jefferson Blvd., Providence, RI 02940. Phone: (401)467-0055 Fax: (401)467-1199 E-mail: jbtinfo@jewelersboard.com • URL: http://www.jewelersboard.com • A credit reporting and collection organization for the jewelry business.

Jewelers of America. 52 Vanderbilt Ave., 19th Fl., New York, NY 10017. Phone: 800-223-0673 or (646)658-0246 Fax: (646)658-0256 E-mail: info@jewelers.org • URL: http://www.jewelers.org • Formerly Retail Jewelers of America.

Jewelers Security Alliance of the U.S. Six E. 45th St., New York, NY 10017. Phone: 800-537-0067 or (212)687-0328 Fax: (212)808-9168 E-mail: jsa2@jewelerssecurity.org • URL: http://www.jewelerssecurity.org • Formerly Jewelers Security Alliance of U.S.

Jewelers Vigilance Committee. 25 W 45th St., Ste. 1406, New York, NY 10036. Phone: 800-JOI-NJVC or (212)997-2002 Fax: (212)997-9148 E-mail: clg@jvclegal.org • URL: http://www.jvclegal.org •

Represents manufacturers, importers, wholesalers, and retailers. Combats deceptive trade practices and misleading advertising. Aims to develop and maintain high trade standards. Provides advice on markings and assists in prosecution of violations of marking, advertising, and related jewelry industry laws.

Jewelry Information Center. 52 Vanderbilt Ave., 19th Fl., New York, NY 10017. Phone: 800-459-0130 or (646)658-0240 Fax: (646)658-0245 E-mail: info@jic.org • URL: http://www.jic.org • Represents retailers, wholesalers, and manufacturers of fine jewelry products. Conducts industry-wide promotional and educational programs; sponsors marketing seminars and consumer-oriented programs on radio, television, and print media.

Manufacturing Jewelers and Suppliers of America. 45 Royal Little Dr., Providence, RI 02904-5305. Phone: 800-444-6572 or (401)274-3840 Fax: (401)274-0265 E-mail: mjsa@mjsainc.com • URL: http://www.mjsanic.com • Formerly Manufacturing Jewelers and Silversmiths of America.

OTHER SOURCES

Confidential Reference Book of the Jewelers Board of Trade. Jewelers Board of Trade. • Supplied on loan basis only to members of the Jewelers Board of Trade. Jewelry and allied product manufacturers, wholesalers and retailers; complete address, phone number and credit rating.

JOB DESCRIPTIONS

See also: OCCUPATIONS

ENCYCLOPEDIAS AND DICTIONARIES

BLR Encyclopedia of Prewritten Job Descriptions. Stephen D. Bruce. Business and Legal Reports, Inc. • $159.95. Looseleaf service. Two volumes. Covers all levels "from president to mail clerk.".

HANDBOOKS AND MANUALS

Complete Guide to Performance Standards for Library Personnel. Carol F. Goodson. Neal-Schuman Publishers, Inc. • 1997. $55.00. Provides specific job descriptions and performance standards for both professional and paraprofessional library personnel. Includes a bibliography of performance evaluation literature, with annotations.

Hiring Right: A Practical Guide. Susan J. Herman. Sage Publications, Inc. • 1994. $77.95. A practical manual covering job definition, recruitment, interviewing, testing, and checking of references.

Position Descriptions in Special Libraries. Del Sweeney and Karin Zilla, editors. Special Libraries Association. • 1996. $41.00. Third revised edition. Provides 87 descriptions of library and information management positions.

Standard Occupational Classification Manual. Available from Bernan Associates. • 2000. $38.00. Replaces the *Dictionary of Occupational Titles.* Produced by the federal Office of Management and Budget, Executive Office of the President. "Occupations are classified based on the work performed, and on the required skills, education, training, and credentials for each one." Six-digit codes contain elements for 23 Major Groups, 96 Minor Groups, 451 Broad Occupations, and 820 Detailed Occupations. Designed to reflect the occupational structure currently existing in the U. S.

JOB HUNTING

See also: EMPLOYMENT AGENCIES AND SERVICES; JOB RESUMES

GENERAL WORKS

Encyclopedia of Careers and Vocational Guidance. Holli Cosgrove. Fact on File Inc. • 2002. 12th

edition. Price on application.

What Color is Your Parachute? 2003: A Practical Manual for Job Hunters and Career Changers. Richard N. Bolles. Ten Speed Press. • 2002. $27.95. Revised edition. Features non-traditional job searching methods. (What Color is Your Parachute? Series).

When You Lose Your Job: Laid Off, Fired, Early Retired, Relocated, Demoted. Cliff Hakim. Berrett-Koehler Publishers, Inc. • 1993. $14.95. A guide to overcoming job loss. Covers emotional responses, as well as practical matters such as networking, resumes, and preparing for interviews.

ABSTRACTS AND INDEXES

Business Periodicals Index. H. W. Wilson Co. • 11 times a year. Quarterly and annual cumulations. Price varies.

Readers' Guide to Periodical Literature. H. W. Wilson Co. • Monthly. $345.00 per year. Includes annual *Cumulation.* Indexes about 250 peridicals of general interest.

BIBLIOGRAPHIES

Job & Career Books. Kennedy Information. • Annual. Free. Contains descriptions of selected books from various publishers on job searching and choice of career.

Job Hunter's Sourcebook: Where to Find Employment Leads and Other Job Search Resources. Gale Cengage Learning. • 2002. $125.00. Fifth edition. Covers 206 professions and occupations.

Jobs-Careers-Professions: A Bibliography with Indexes. Leon V. Werner. Nova Science Publishers, Inc. • 2001. $59.00. Contains more than 1,500 citations to books and periodical articles on job hunting, compensation, career choice, education, mobility, supply-demand factors, and other job topics. Includes author, title, and subject indexes.

CD-ROM DATABASES

Magazine Index Plus. Gale Cengage Learning. • Monthly. $4,000.00 per year (includes InfoTrac workstation). Provides full text on CD-ROM for about 100 popular, general interest magazines and indexing for 300 others. Includes special indexing of reviews and product evaluations. Time period is 1980 to date.

OECD Statistical Compendium. Organization for Economic Cooperation and Development. • Semiannual. $1,905.00 per year for 1 to 10 users. CD-ROM contains more than 730,000 monthly, quarterly, and annual time series for OECD countries, 1960 to date. Includes fully searchable data on agriculture, food, economic indicators, national accounts, employment, energy, finance, industry, technology, and foreign trade. Results can be displayed in various forms.

DIRECTORIES

Computing and Software Career Directory. Gale Cengage Learning. • 1993. $39.00. Includes career information relating to programmers, software engineers, technical writers, systems experts, and other computer specialists. Provides advice from "insiders," resume suggestions, a directory of companies that may offer entry-level positions, and a directory of career information sources. (Career Advisor Series.).

D and B Employment Opportunities Directory Career Guide. • Annual. Libraries, $495.00. Lists more than 5,000 companies that have career opportunities in various fields. A Dun & Bradstreet publication.

Job Seeker's Guide to Private and Public Companies. Gale Cengage Learning. • 1993. $390. 00. Second edition. $99.00 per volume. Four regional volumes: *The West, The Midwest, The Northeast,* and *The South.* Covers about 15,000 companies, providing information on personnel department contacts, corporate officials, company benefits, application procedures, etc.

Magazines Career Directory: A Practical One-Stop Guide to Getting a Job in Publ c Relations. Visible Ink Press. • 1993. $39.00. Fifth edition. Includes information on magazine publishing careers in art, editing, sales, and business management. Provides advice from "insiders," resume suggestions, a directory of companies that may offer entry-level positions, and a directory of career information sources. (Career Advisor Series).

NACE Directory: Who's Who in Career Services and HR/Staffing t. National Association of Colleges and Employers. • Annual. Free to members; nonmembers, $47.95. Lists over 2,200 college placement offices and about 2,000 companies interested in recruiting college graduates. Gives names of placement and recruitment personnel. Formerly *CPC National Dierctory.*

Peterson's Internships. Peterson's. • Covers: 50,000 career-oriented internship positions with over 2,000 organizations in the U.S. ranging from business to theater, communications to science. Entries include: Company name, address, phone, name and title of contact, types of internships available, number of internships offered, salary where applicable, qualifications, how to apply.

Peterson's Job Opportunities for Business Majors. Peterson's. • 1999. $18.95. Provides career information for the 2,000 largest U. S. employers in various industries.

Plunkett's Employers' Internet Sites with Careers Information. Plunkett Research, Ltd. • Annual. $199.99. Includes diskette.

HANDBOOKS AND MANUALS

Career Guide to Industries. Available from U. S. Government Printing Office. • 2002. $32.00. Issued by the Bureau of Labor Statistics, U. S. Department of Labor (http://www.bls.gov). Presents background career information (text) and statistics for the 40 industries that account for 70 percent of wage and salary jobs in the U. S. Includes nature of the industry, employment data, working conditions, training, earnings, rate of job growth, outlook, and other career factors. (BLS Bulletin 2541.).

The Information Professional's Guide to Career Development Online. Sarah L. Nesbeitt and Rachel S. Gordon. Information Today, Inc. • 2001. $29.50. Provides advice to librarians and other information professionals about using online sources for career advancement. The Career Development Online Web Page (http://www.lisjobs.com/careerdev/) contains links to relevant resources.

Job Search: The Total System. Kenneth Dawson and Sheryl N. Dawson. John Wiley and Sons, Inc. • 1988. $24.95. Second edition.

The Only Job-Hunting Guide You'll Ever Need: The Most Comprehensive Guide for Job Hunters and Career Switchers. Kathryn Petras and Ross Petras. Simon & Schuster Trade. • 1995. $15.00. Revised edition.

INTERNET DATABASES

Business 2.0 Web Guide to the Best Business Links. Business 2.0 Media Inc. Phone: (415)293-4800 E-mail: support@business2.com • URL: http://www.business2.com/webguide • Web site presents an extensive, searchable directory of links to "the best, most informative, and authoritative web pages." Twenty main categories cover business, finance, career, company information, people, and technology topics, with thousands of subtopics, all linking to Web sites recommended by experienced business researchers. Fees: Free.

ONLINE DATABASES

Readers' Guide Abstracts Online. H. W. Wilson Co. • Indexes and abstracts general interest periodicals,

1983 to date. Weekly updates. Inquire as to online cost and availability.

Wilson Business Abstracts Online. H. W. Wilson Co. • Indexes and abstracts 600 major business periodicals, plus the *Wall Street Journal* and the business section of the *New York Times.* Indexing is from 1982, abstracting from 1990, with the two newspapers included from 1993. Updated weekly. Inquire as to online cost and availability. (*Business Periodicals Index* without abstracts is also available online.).

PERIODICALS AND NEWSLETTERS

Corporate Jobs Outlook!. Plunkett Research Ltd. • Description: Provides information about corporate employment opportunities. Includes salaries, benefits, and hiring policies.

ReCareering Newsletter: An Idea and Resource Guide to Second Career and Relocation Planning. Publications Plus, Inc. • Monthly. $59.00 per year. Edited for "downsized managers, early retirees, and others in career transition after leaving traditional employment." Offers advice on second careers, franchises, starting a business, finances, education, training, skills assessment, and other matters of interest to the newly unemployed.

RESEARCH CENTERS AND INSTITUTES

National Institute for Work and Learning. Academy for Educational Development, 1875 Connecticut Ave., N.W., Washington, DC 20009-5721. Phone: (202)884-8186 Fax: (202)884-8422 E-mail: niwl@aed.org • URL: http://www.niwl.org • Research areas include adult education, training, unemployment insurance, and career development.

Women Employed Institute. Women Employed Institute. 111 N Wabash, 13th Fl., Chicago, IL 60602. Phone: (312)782-3902 Fax: (312)782-5249 E-mail: info@womenemployed.org • URL: http://www.womenemployed.org • Economic status of working women, working women and the law, sexual harassment in the workplace, equal employment opportunity, women's access to vocational education and job training, comparable worth, working mothers, and career development.

TRADE/PROFESSIONAL ASSOCIATIONS

Association of Executive Search Consultants. 500 Fifth Ave., Suite 930, New York, NY 10110-0999. Phone: 877-843-2372 or (212)398-9556 Fax: (212)398-9560 E-mail: aesc@aesc.org • URL: http://www.aesc.org.

Council on Career Development for Minorities. PO Box 560987, Dallas, TX 75356-0987. Phone: (214)631-3677 Fax: (214)905-2046 E-mail: ccm35@aol.com • URL: http://www.ccdm.-inc.org • Seeks to improve career counseling and placement services for minority college students.

International Association of Personnel in Employment Security. 1801 Louisville Rd., Frankfort, KY 40601. Phone: 888-898-9960 or (502)223-4459 Fax: (502)233-4127 E-mail: iapes@iapes.org • URL: http://www.iapes.org • Formerly International Association of Public Employment Services.

National Association of Personnel Services. 10905 Fort Washington Rd., Ste. 400, Fort Washington, MD 20744. Phone: (301)203-6700 Fax: (301)203-4346 E-mail: conrad.taylor@recrutinglife.com • URL: http://www.napsweb.org • Members are private employment agencies. Formerly National Association of Personnel Consultants.

National Center for Disablty Services. 201 I.U. Willets Rd., Albertson, NY 11507. Phone: (516)465-1400 Fax: (516)747-5400 • URL: http://www.ncds.org • Seeks to improve employment opportunities for persons with disabilities.

The National Council on Aging. 300 D St., NW, Ste. 801, Washington, DC 20024. Phone: (202)479-1200 or (202)479-6674 Fax: (202)479-0735 E-mail: info@ncoa.org • URL: http://www.ncoa.org •

Dedicated to improving the health and independence of older people.

Options. 225 S 15th St., Ste. 1635, Philadelphia, PA 19102-3916. Phone: (215)735-2202 Fax: (215)735-8097 E-mail: ola@ola-labs.org • URL: http://www.optionscareers.org • Career advising and human resource consulting service. Provides consulting and training programs on the changing workforce and workplace. Offers counseling on career issues such as job searches, career changes, and career management. Provides consultation in the areas of managing change, career management, mentoring, sexual harassment prevention gender sensitivity counseling, outplacement, managing diversity, and spouse employment assistance. Offers training to professionals. Conducts studies on employment-related issues; maintains speakers' bureau.

JOB INTERVIEWS

See: INTERVIEWING

JOB PERFORMANCE

See: RATING OF EMPLOYEES

JOB RESUMES

See also: EMPLOYMENT AGENCIES AND SERVICES; JOB HUNTING

GENERAL WORKS

Resumes for Banking and Financial Careers. McGraw-Hill. • 2001. $10.95. Second edition. Contains 100 sample resumes and 20 cover letters. (VGM Professional Resumes Series.).

HANDBOOKS AND MANUALS

How to Write Better Resumes and Cover Letters. Pat Criscito. Barron's Educational Series, Inc. • 2003. $14.95.

McGraw-Hill's Big Red Book of Resumes. McGraw-Hill. • 2002. $16.95. Contains 350 sample resumes using various approaches and styles. Includes examples of cover letters.

101 Best Resumes for Grads. Jay A. Block. McGraw-Hill. • 2002. $11.95. Contains sample resumes for recent graduates lacking significant work history or job experience. Covers 70 job categories and includes sample cover letters. (Teach Yourself Series).

175 High-Impact Cover Letters. Richard H. Beatty. John Wiley and Sons, Inc. • 2002. $14.95. Third edition. Provides samples of cover letters for resumes.

Power Resumes. Ronald Tepper. John Wiley and Sons, Inc. • 1998. $14.95. Third edition. Offers 71 techniques for more effective resumes.

Professional Resumes for Accounting, Tax, Finance and Law: A Special Gallery of Best Resumes by Professional Resume Writers. David H. Noble. JIST Publishing. • 1999. $19.95. Written for accounting, tax, law, and finance professionals. In addition to advice, provides 335 sample resumes and 22 cover letters.

The Resume Kit. Richard H. Beatty. John Wiley and Sons, Inc. • 2003. $14.95. Fifth edition. Includes information on the linear resume, a form said to be favored by outplacement firms.

Resume Writing: A Comprehensive How-To-Do-It Guide. Burdette Bostwick. John Wiley and Sons, Inc. • 1990. $14.95. Fourth edition.

Resume Writing and Career Counseling. Entrepreneur Media, Inc. • Looseleaf. $59.50. A practical guide to starting a resume writing and career counseling service. Covers profit potential, start-up costs, market size evaluation, owner's time required, site selection, pricing, accounting, advertising, promotion, etc. (Start-Up Business Guide No. E1260.).

Resumes That Work: How to Sell Yourself on Paper. Lorretta D. Foxman. John Wiley. • 1992. $14.95. Ninth edition.

Sure-Hire Resumes. Robbie M. Kaplan. Impact Publications. • 1998. $14.95. Second edition. Includes sample cover letters and 25 sample resumes.

JOB SEARCHING

See: JOB HUNTING

JOB TRAINING

See: TRAINING OF EMPLOYEES

JOBBERS

See: RACK JOBBERS; WHOLESALE TRADE

JOBBERS, RACK

See: RACK JOBBERS

JOBLESS COMPENSATION

See: UNEMPLOYMENT INSURANCE

JOBS IN FOREIGN COUNTRIES

See: EMPLOYMENT IN FOREIGN COUNTRIES

JOKES

See: HUMOR AND JOKES

JOURNALISM

See also: EDITORS AND EDITING; NEWSPAPERS

GENERAL WORKS

Opportunities in Journalism Careers. Jim Patten and Donald L. Ferguson. McGraw-Hill. • 2001. $15.95. Edited for students and job seekers. Includes education requirements and salary data. (Opportunities in....Series).

Super Searcher, Author, Scribe: Successful Writers Share Their Internet Research Secrets. Loraine Page. Information Today, Inc. • 2002. $24.95. Presents the results of interviews with 14 leading journalists, book authors, writing teachers, and professional literary researchers. Tips, techniques, and sources for searching the Web are featured. (Super Searchers Series).

Super Searchers in the News: The Online Secrets of Journalists and News Researchers. Paula J. Hane. Information Today, Inc. • 2000. $24.95. Contains online searching advice from 10 professional news researchers and fact checkers. (Super Searchers Series).

ALMANACS AND YEARBOOKS

Editor and Publisher International Yearbook: Encyclopedia of the Newspaper Industry. Editor and Publisher Co., Inc. • Annual. $150.00. Daily and Sunday newspapers in the United States and Canada.

BIOGRAPHICAL SOURCES

Biographical Dictionary of American Journalism. Joseph P. McKerns, editor. Greenwood Publishing Group Inc. • 1989. $92.95. Covers major mass media: newspapers, radio, television, and magazines. Includes reporters, editors, columnists, cartoonists, commentators, etc.

Major 20th-Century Writers: A Selection of Sketches from Contemporary Authors. Gale Cengage Learning. • 1998. $355.00. Second edition. Five volumes. Includes important nonfiction writers and journalists.

DIRECTORIES

Accredited Journalism and Mass Communication Education. School of Journalism. Accrediting Council on Education for Journalism and Mass Communications. • Annual. Free. Lists about 109 accredited schools.

Editor and Publisher Journalism Awards and Fellowship Directory. Editor and Publisher Co., Inc. • Annual. $8.00. Over 500 cash prizes scholarships, fellowships, and grants available to journalists and students for work on special subjects or in specific fields.

Journalism and Mass Communication Directory. Association for Education in Journalism and Mass Communication. • Annual $35.00. Schools and departments of journalism and mass communication.

Journalist's Road to Success: Career and Scholarship Guide. Dow Jones Newspaper Fund, Inc. • Annual. $300.00. Lists more than 400 colleges and universities offering journalism/mass communications; general journalism career information; section of minority scholarships and special training programs; section on fellowships for continuing education. Formerly *Journalism Career and Scholarship Guide.*

Working Press of the Nation. R. R. Bowker. • Annual. $530.00. $295.00 per volume. Three volumes: (1) *Newspaper Directory*; (2) *Magazine and Internal Publications Directory*; (3) *Radio and Television Directory*. Includes names of editors and other personnel.

ENCYCLOPEDIAS AND DICTIONARIES

World Press Encyclopedia. Gale Cengage Learning. • 2003. $325.00. Second edition. Two volumes. Comprehensive essays cover the background and economic framework of newspapers and other news media in about 200 countries. Covers relevant legal issues, censorship, government relations, education in journalism, status of news agencies, cable, Internet, and other media topics.

HANDBOOKS AND MANUALS

Journalism Online. Mike Ward and Andy Dickinson. Elsevier. • 2002. $39.95. Covers the basic journalism skills needed for identifying, collecting, selecting, and presenting news and information for the World Wide Web.

PERIODICALS AND NEWSLETTERS

Columbia Journalism Review. Columbia University, Graduate School of Journalism. • Bimonthly. $19.95 per year. Critical review of news media.

Editor and Publisher - The Newsmagazine of the Fourth Estate Since 1894. Editor and Publisher Co., Inc. • Weekly. $99.00 per year. Includes print and online edition. Trade journal of the newspaper industry.

The IRE Journal (Investigative Reporters and Editors). Investigative Reporters and Editors, Inc. • Bimonthly. Free to members; non-members, $60.00 per year; institutions, $70.00 per year. Contains

practical information relating to investigative journalism.

Journalism and Mass Communication Quarterly: Devoted to Research and Commentary in Journalism and Mass Communication. Association for Education in Journalism and Mass Communication. • Quarterly. Individuals, $50.00 per year; institutions, $70.00 per year. Formerly *Journalism Quarterly.*

Quill: The Magazine for Journalists. Society of Professional Journalists, Eugene S. Pullman Nationalo Journalism Center. • Monthly. $35.00 per year.

RESEARCH CENTERS AND INSTITUTES

Institute for Communications Research. Texas Tech University, P.O. Box 43082, Lubbock, TX 79409-3082. Phone: (806)742-3385 Fax: (806)742-1085 E-mail: jerry.hudson@ttu.edu • URL: http://www.mcom.ttu.edu/icr.

Knight Center for Specialized Journalism. University of Maryland, 1117 Cole Field House, College Park, MD 20742-1024. Phone: (301)405-4817 E-mail: knight@umail.umd.edu • URL: http://www.knightcenter.umd.edu/ • Research area is media coverage of complex subjects, such as economics, law, science, and medicine.

Northwestern University-Media Management Center. 1007 Church St., No. 500, Evanston, IL 60201-5981. Phone: (847)491-4900 Fax: (847)491-5619 E-mail: mediamanagement@mmc.northwestern.edu • URL: http://www.mediamanagement.northwestern.edu • Research areas are related to various business aspects of the newspaper industry: management, marketing, personnel, planning, accounting, and finance. A joint activity of the J. L. Kellogg Graduate School of Management and the Medill School of Journalism.

TRADE/PROFESSIONAL ASSOCIATIONS

Accrediting Council on Education in Journalism and Mass Communications. University of Kansas. School of Journalism, Stauffer-Flint Hall, Lawrence, KS 66045-7575. Phone: (785)864-3973 Fax: (785)864-5225 E-mail: sshaw@ukans.edu • URL: http://www.ukans.edu/~acejmc.

Association for Education in Journalism and Mass Communication. 234 Outlet Pointe Blvd., Suite A, Columbia, SC 29210. Phone: (803)798-0271 Fax: (803)772-3509 E-mail: aejmc@aejmc.org • URL: http://www.aejmc.org.

Foreign Press Association. 333 E 46th St., Ste. 1K, New York, NY 10017-7425. Phone: (212)370-1054 Fax: (212)370-1058 E-mail: fpanewyork@aol.com • URL: http://www.nyforeignpress.org • Represents foreign print and broadcast correspondents stationed in the U.S.

Investigative Reporters and Editors. School of Journalism, 138 Neff Annex, Columbia, MO 65211. Phone: (573)882-2042 Fax: (573)882-5431 E-mail: info@ire.org • URL: http://www.ire.org • Provides educational services to those engaged in investigative journalism.

National Press Club. National Press Bldg., 529 14th St. NW, 14th Fl., Washington, DC 20045. Phone: (202)662-7500 Fax: (202)662-7512 E-mail: info@press.org • URL: http://www.press.org • Reporters, writers, and news people employed by newspapers, wire services, magazines, radio and television stations, and other forms of news media; former news people and associates of news people are nonvoting members. Sponsors sports, travel, and cultural events, rap sessions with news figures and authors, and newsmaker breakfasts and luncheons. Offers monthly training.

Society of Professional Journalists. 3909 N. Meridian St., Indianapolis, IN 46208-4011. Phone: (317)927-8000 Fax: (317)920-4789 E-mail: questions@spj.org • URL: http://www.spj.org • Affiliated with Sigma Delta Chi Foundation. Absorbed Economics News Broadcaster Association.

JOURNALISM, BUSINESS

See: BUSINESS JOURNALISM

JOURNALS, TRADE

See: TRADE JOURNALS

JUDICIARY

See: COURTS

JUICE INDUSTRY

See: BEVERAGE INDUSTRY; CITRUS FRUIT INDUSTRY

JUKE BOXES

See: VENDING MACHINES

JUNIOR COLLEGES

DIRECTORIES

American Association of Community Colleges Directory. American Association of Community Colleges. • Annual. $35.00. Formerly *Community, Junior and Technical College Directory.*

Patterson's Schools Classified. Educational Directories Inc. • Covers: Over 7,000 accredited colleges, universities, community colleges, junior colleges, career schools and teaching hospitals. Entries include: School name, address, phone, URL, e-mail, name of administrator or admissions officer, description, professional accreditation (where applicable). Updated from previous year's edition of 'Patterson's American Education' (see separate entry).

Peterson's Guide to Two-Year Colleges. Peterson's. • Annual. $26.95. Provides information on more than 1,700 U. S. academic institutions granting associate degrees.

PERIODICALS AND NEWSLETTERS

Community and Junior College Libraries: The Journal for Learning Resources Centers. Haworth Press, Inc. • Quarterly. $85.00 per year.

Community College Journal. American Association of Community Colleges. • Bimonthly. $28.00 per year. Formerly *Community, Technical and Junior College Journal.*

Community College Review. Dept. of Adult and Community College Education. North Carolina State University. • Quarterly. $55.00 per year.

Community College Week: The Independent Voice Serving Community, Technical and Junior Colleges. Cox, Matthews & Associates, Inc. • Biweekly. $40.00 per year. Covers a wide variety of current topics relating to the administration and operation of community colleges.

STATISTICS SOURCES

Digest of Education Statistics. Available from U. S. Government Printing Office. • Annual. $51.00. Covers all areas of education from kindergarten through graduate school. Includes data from both government and private sources. Compiled by National Center for Education Statistics, U. S. Department of Education.

TRADE/PROFESSIONAL ASSOCIATIONS

American Association of Community Colleges. One Dupont Circle, N.W., Suite 410, Washington, DC 20036-1176. Phone: (202)728-0200 Fax: (202)833-2467 E-mail: gboggs@aacc.nche.edu • URL: http://www.aacc.nche.edu.

JUNK

See: WASTE PRODUCTS

JUNK BOND FINANCING

See also: BONDS; FINANCE; LEVERAGED BUYOUTS

GENERAL WORKS

Advances and Innovations in the Bond and Mortgage Markets. Frank J. Fabozzi, editor. McGraw-Hill. • 1989. $65.00.

Beyond Junk Bonds: Expanding High Yield Markets. Glenn Yago. Oxford University Press. • 2003. $45.00. Describes the "broadening and deepening of the high yield market over the past decade..." Indicates there are now thousands of institutional buyers of lower-rated bonds, including many mutual funds.

The First Junk Bond: A Story of Corporate Boom and Bust. Harlan D. Platt. M. E. Sharpe, Inc. • 1994. $80.95. Relates the development and history of Michael Milken's first low-quality bond issue at high interest rates. Includes a chapter, "What Have We Learned?".

The High Yield Debt Market: Investment Performance and Economic Impact. Edward I. Altman, editor. McGraw-Hill. • 1990. $55.00.

Junk Bonds: How High Yield Securities Restructured Corporate America. Glenn Yago. Oxford University Press. • 1990. $35.00.

The Predator's Ball: The Inside Story of Drexel Burnham and the Rise of the Junk Bond Raiders. Connie Bruck. Penguin Group. • 1989. $15.00.

Understanding Corporate Bonds. Harold Kerzner. McGraw-Hill. • 1991. $24.95. A general introduction to investing in corporate bonds. Includes a discussion of high-risk (junk) bonds.

ABSTRACTS AND INDEXES

Business Periodicals Index. H. W. Wilson Co. • 11 times a year. Quarterly and annual cumulations. Price varies.

ALMANACS AND YEARBOOKS

Fixed Income Almanac: The Bond Investor's Compendium of Key Market, Product, and Performance Data. Livingston G. Douglas. McGraw-Hill. • 1993. $75.00. Presents 20 years of data in 350 graphs and charts. Covers bond market volatility, yield spreads, high-yield (junk) corporate bonds, default rates, and other items, such as Federal Reserve policy.

DIRECTORIES

Standard and Poor's Security Dealers of North America. Standard & Poor's. • Semiannual. $480.00 per year; with *Supplements* every six weeks. Geographical listing of over 12,000 stock, bond, and commodity dealers.

HANDBOOKS AND MANUALS

Advanced Fixed Income Analysis. Moorad Choudhry. Elsevier Butterworth Heinemann. • 2004. $60.00. Edited for "experienced practitioners in the corporate bond markets." Covers trading, hedging, interest rate models, corporate bond default risk, the yield curve, long bond yields, and other topics.

Bond Markets: Analysis and Stratgies. Frank J. Fabozzi. Prentice Hall PTR. • 1999. $115.00. Fourth edition.

Corporate Financial Distress and Bankruptcy: A Complete Guide to Predicting and Avoiding Distress and Profiting from Bankruptcy. Edward I. Altman. John Wiley and Sons, Inc. • 1993. $110.00. Second edition. Provides practical advice on analyzing the financial position of a corporation, with case studies. Includes a discussion of the junk bond market. (Finance Series).

Fixed Income Analytics: State-of-the-Art Analysis and Valuation Modeling. Ravi E. Dattatreya, editor. McGraw-Hill. • 1991. $69.95. Discusses the yield curve, structure and value in corporate bonds, mortgage-backed securities, and other topics. (Institutional Investor Publications).

Fixed Income Mathematics: Analytical and Statistical Techniques. Frank J. Fabozzi. McGraw-Hill. • 1996. $65.00. Third edition. Covers the basics of fixed income analysis, as well as more advanced techniques used for complex securities.

INTERNET DATABASES

ETF Connect. Nuveen Investments. Phone: 800-257-8787 • URL: http://www.etfconnect.com • Free Web site makes available extensive, searchable information on individual closed-end investment funds, preferred share funds, and exchange-traded index funds. Information on a particular fund is available by name or as part of a classification (high yield, investment grade, municipal, emerging markets, global equity, etc.). Fund charts are available for various time periods, as is data concerning premiums or discounts, dividends, annualized total return, credit quality, "Top 10 Holdings," and so forth.

ONLINE DATABASES

Wilson Business Abstracts Online. H. W. Wilson Co. • Indexes and abstracts 600 major business periodicals, plus the *Wall Street Journal* and the business section of the *New York Times.* Indexing is from 1982, abstracting from 1990, with the two newspapers included from 1993. Updated weekly. Inquire as to online cost and availability. (*Business Periodicals Index* without abstracts is also available online.).

PERIODICALS AND NEWSLETTERS

The Bond Buyer. Veronis, Suhler and Associates Inc. • Daily edition, $1,897 per year. Weekly edition, $525.00 per year. Reports on new municipal bond issues.

Bondweek: The Newsweekly of Fixed Income and Credit Markets. Institutional Investor, Inc., Journals Group. • Weekly. $2,425.00 per year. Newsletter. Includes print and online editions. Covers taxable, fixed-income securities for professional investors, including corporate, government, foreign, mortgage, and high-yield.

CreditWeek. Standard & Poor's. • Description: Standard & Poor's flagship print information and news publication that covers the global credit markets. Includes insightful feature articles on market events and trends, plus columns titled Rating News and Credit Watch.

High Yield Report. American Banker/Bond Buyer Inc. • Description: Examines markets for high-yield corporate bonds, work-outs, bankruptcies, and secondary markets for distressed securities. Contains pricing information for primary and secondary markets and analysis of the high-yield sector. Reports on developments affecting the senior and subordinated debt of companies in bankruptcy or working their way out of debt, detailing proposed financial restructurings. Tracks regulatory decisions affecting trade of distressed debt and funds purchased and sold. **Remarks:** Incorporates the former Distressed Debt Report.

Journal of Fixed Income. Institutional Investor, Inc., Journals Group. • Quarterly. $360.00 per year. Includes print and online editions. Covers a wide range of fixed-income investments for institutions, including bonds, interest-rate options, high-yield securities, and mortgages.

Moody's Bond Survey. Moody's Investors Service Inc. • Description: Presents statistical information and analysis of corporate, municipal, government, federal agency, and international bonds, preferred stock, and commercial paper. Includes ratings changes and withdrawals, calendars of recent and prospective bond offerings, and Moody's bond and preferred stock yield averages.

PRICE SOURCES

National Bond Summary. Pink Sheets LLC. • Monthly, with semiannual cumulations. $504.00 per year. Includes price quotes for both active and inactive issues, with transfer agents, market makers (brokers), capital changes, name changes, and other corporate information. Formerly published by the National Quotation Bureau.

RESEARCH CENTERS AND INSTITUTES

Glucksman Institute. New York University. Salomon Center, Stern School of Business, 44 W. Fourth St., Room 9-65, New York, NY 10012-0267. Phone: (212)998-0714 Fax: (212)995-4220 E-mail: wsilber@stern.nyu.edu.

Institute for Quantitative Research in Finance. Church Street Station, P.O. Box 6194, New York, NY 10249-6194. Phone: (212)744-6825 Fax: (212)517-2259 E-mail: daleberman@compuserve • Financial research areas include quantitative methods, securities analysis, and the financial structure of industries. Also known as the "Q Group.".

Investor Responsibility Research Center, Inc. Investor Responsibility Research Center. 1350 Connecticut Ave. NW, Ste. 700, Washington, DC 20036-1702. Phone: (202)833-0700 Fax: (202)833-3555 E-mail: marketing@irrc.com • URL: http://www.irrc.org • Social, public policy, and corporate governance issues and their impact on major corporations and institutional investors. Issues studied have included anti-takeover measures, board and compensation practices, energy and the environment, the electric utility industry, military contracting, executive compensation, business in Northern Ireland, plant closings, global shareholder rights, animal testing, and voting and other actions by

institutional investors. Also offers consulting and contract research.

Rodney L. White Center for Financial Research. University of Pennsylvania, 3254 Steinberg Hall-Dietrich Hall, Philadelphia, PA 19104. Phone: (215)898-7616 Fax: (215)573-8084 E-mail: rlwtcr@finance.wharton.upenn.edu • URL: http://www.finance.wharton.upenn.edu • Research areas include financial management, money markets, real estate finance, and international finance.

TRADE/PROFESSIONAL ASSOCIATIONS

Securities Industry and Financial Markets Association. 120 Broadway, 35th Fl., New York, NY 10271-0080. Phone: (212)313-1200 Fax: (212)313-1301 E-mail: rbrockhaus@sifma.org • URL: http://www.sifma.org • Represents more than 650 member firms of all sizes, in all financial markets in the U.S. and around the world. Enhances the public's trust and confidence in the markets, delivering an efficient, enhanced member network of access and forward-looking services, as well as premiere educational resources for the professionals in the industry and the investors whom they serve. Maintains offices in New York City and Washington, DC.

OTHER SOURCES

Fitch Insights. Fitch Investors Service, Inc. • Biweekly. $1,040.00 per year. Includes bond rating actions and explanation of actions. Provides commentary and Fitch's view of the financial markets.

JURIES

See: TRIALS AND JURIES

JURISTS

See: LAWYERS

JURORS

See: COURTS

JUTE INDUSTRY

HANDBOOKS AND MANUALS

Handbook on Jute. Available from Bernan Associates. • 1984. $30.00. Published by the Food and Agriculture Organization (http://www.fao.org). (FAO Plant Production and Protection Paper, No. 51.).

PERIODICALS AND NEWSLETTERS

Journal of Natural Fibers. Haworth Press, Inc. • Quarterly. $400.00 per year to libraries; $45.00 per year to individuals. Covers applications, technology, research, and world markets relating to fibers from silk, wool, cotton, flax, hemp, jute, etc. Previously *Natural Fibres*, published annually.

Jute and Jute Fabrics-Bangladesh. Bangladesh Jute Research Institute. • Monthly. $5.00 per year. Text in English.

STATISTICS SOURCES

FAO Production Yearbook. Available from Bernan Associates. • Annual. $45.00. Published by the Food and Agriculture Organization (http://www.fao.org). Contains worldwide data on agriculture, land use, farm crops, livestock, and agricultural prices.

FAO Trade Yearbook. Available from Bernan Associates. • Annual. $45.00. Published by the Food and Agriculture Organization (http://www.fao.org). Provides extensive worldwide data on exports and imports of agricultural commodities, fertilizers, tractors, and pesticides. Includes more than 130 tables of detailed statistics.

TRADE/PROFESSIONAL ASSOCIATIONS

Burlap and Jute Association. c/o Susan Spiegel, Drawer 8, Dayton, OH 45401. Phone: 800-543-3400 or (937)476-8272 Fax: (937)258-0029 E-mail: tbpa@aol.com.

OTHER SOURCES

International Agreement on Jute and Jute Products. United Nations Publications. • 1992. Second revised edition. An international trade agreement.

JUVENILES

See: YOUTH MARKET

K

KEOGH PLANS

See also: SELF-EMPLOYMENT; TAX
SHELTERS

ABSTRACTS AND INDEXES

Business Periodicals Index. H. W. Wilson Co. • 11
times a year. Quarterly and annual cumulations.
Price varies.

HANDBOOKS AND MANUALS

*How to Build Wealth with Tax-Sheltered
Investments.* Kerry Anne Lynch. American Institute
for Economic Research. • 2000. $6.00. Provides
practical information on conservative tax shelters,
including defined-contribution pension plans,
individual retirement accounts, Keogh plans, U. S.
savings bonds, municipal bonds, and various kinds
of annuities: deferred, variable-rate, immediate, and
foreign-currency. (Economic Education Bulletin.).

Pension Plan Fix-It Handbook. Thompson Publishing Group, Inc. • Two looseleaf volumes. $499.00
per year. Two looseleaf volumes. Monthly updates
and newsletters. Serves as a comprehensive guide to
pension plan administration, taxation, and federal
regulation. Includes both defined benefit and defined
contribution plans.

U. S. Master Pension Guide. CCH, Inc. • Annual.
$56.95. Explains IRS rules and regulations applying
to 401(k) plans, 403(k) plans, ESOPs (employee
stock ownership plans), IRAs, SEPs (simplified
employee pension plans), Keogh plans, and non-
qualified plans.

INTERNET DATABASES

Small Business Retirement Savings Advisor. U. S.
Department of Labor. Phone: (202)219-8921 • URL:
http://www.dol.gov/elaws/pwbaplan.htm • Web site
provides "answers to a variety of commonly asked
questions about retirement saving options for small
business employers." Includes a comparison chart
and detailed descriptions of various plans: 401(k),
SEP-IRA, SIMPLE-IRA, Payroll Deduction IRA,
Keogh Profit-Sharing, Keogh Money Purchase, and
Defined Benefit. Searching is offered. Fees: Free.

ONLINE DATABASES

Wilson Business Abstracts Online. H. W. Wilson Co.
• Indexes and abstracts 600 major business
periodicals, plus the *Wall Street Journal* and the
business section of the *New York Times.* Indexing is
from 1982, abstracting from 1990, with the two
newspapers included from 1993. Updated weekly.
Inquire as to online cost and availability. (*Business
Periodicals Index* without abstracts is also available
online.).

PERIODICALS AND NEWSLETTERS

Small Business Tax News. Inside Mortgage Finance
Publications. • Monthly. $175.00 per year.

Newsletter. Formerly *Small Business Tax Control.*
The Small Business Tax Review. A/N Group Inc. •
Description: Reports tax news on such topics as new
laws, court cases, IRS rulings, fringe benefits, and
business and individual taxes, with emphasis on
smaller businesses. Advises on financial planning
and technical aspects of small business
management.

OTHER SOURCES

Tax Strategies for the Self-Employed. Alan D.
Campbell and others. CCH, Inc. • 2000. $95.00.
Covers accounting methods, start-up expenses,
transportation deductions, depreciation, pension
deductions, tax penalties, and other topics related to
tax planning for the self-employed.

KEYLESS DATA ENTRY

See: AUTOMATIC IDENTIFICATION
SYSTEMS

KEYS

See: LOCKS AND KEYS

KITCHENS

DIRECTORIES

*FDM--The Source--Woodworking Industry
Directory.* Reed Business Information. • Publication
includes: List of over 1,800 suppliers to secondary
woodworking industry; coverage includes Canada.
Entries include: Company name, address, phone,
fax, product lines.

FINANCIAL RATIOS

*Kitchen Cabinet Manufacturers Association Income
and Expense Study.* Kitchen Cabinet Manufacturers
Association. • Annual. Membership.

PERIODICALS AND NEWSLETTERS

Building Material Dealer. National Lumber and
Building Material Dealers Association. • Monthly.
$48.00 per year. Includes special feature issues on
hand and power tools, lumber, roofing, kitchens,
flooring, windows and doors, and insulation.
Formerly *Builder Material Retailer.*

*FDM: For Builders of Cabinets, Fixtures, Furniture,
Millwork Furniture Design a nd Manufacturing.*
Chartwell Communications, Inc. • Monthly. Free to
qualified personnel. Edited for furniture executives,
production managers, and designers. Covers the
manufacturing of household, office, and institutional

furniture, store fixtures, and kitchen and bathroom
cabinets.

Kitchen and Bath Business. VNU Business Media. •
Monthly. $79.00 per year.

*National Home Center News: News and Analysis for
the Home Improvement, Building Material Industry.*
Lebhar-Friedman, Inc. • 22 times a year. $99.00 per
year. Includes special feature issues on hardware and
tools, building materials, millwork, electrical supplies, lighting, and kitchens.

TRADE/PROFESSIONAL ASSOCIATIONS

Kitchen Cabinet Manufacturers Association. 1899
Preston White Dr., Reston, VA 20191-5435. Phone:
(703)264-1690 Fax: (703)620-6530 E-mail: info@
kcma.org • URL: http://www.kcma.org • Serves as
a national trade association representing cabinet and
countertop manufacturers and suppliers to the
industry. Promotes the cabinet manufacturing
industry, develops standards for the industry,
administers a testing and certification program,
conducts education programs and meetings,
provides management information and industry
data, and engages in activities on behalf of members
on legislative and regulatory issues.

National Kitchen and Bath Association. 687 Willow
Grove St., Hackettstown, NJ 07840. Phone:
(908)852-0033 Fax: (908)852-1695 E-mail:
feeback@nkba.org • URL: http://www.nkba.org •
Formerly American Institute of Kitchen Dealers.

OTHER SOURCES

Kitchen Cabinets and Countertops. Available from
MarketResearch.com. • 2002. $2,250.00. Market
research report published by Catalina Research.
Covers both custom and stock cabinets. Presents
market data relative to demographics, sales growth,
shipments, exports, imports, price trends, and end-
use. Includes company profiles.

KNIT GOODS INDUSTRY

See also: TEXTILE INDUSTRY

ABSTRACTS AND INDEXES

Textile Technology Digest. Institute of Textile
Technology. • Annual. $535.00. Provides indexing
and abstracting of a wide variety of textile technology literature.

CD-ROM DATABASES

Textile Technology Digest [CD-ROM]. Textile
Information Center, Institute of Textile Technology.
• Quarterly. Provides CD-ROM indexing and
abstracting of worldwide journals and monographs
in various areas of textile technology, production,

533

and management. Covers 1978 to date.

DIRECTORIES

American Sportswear and Knitting Times Buyers' Guide. National Knitwear and Sportswear Association. • Annual. $25.00. Formerly *Knitting Times Buyers' Guide.*

ENCYCLOPEDIAS AND DICTIONARIES

Textile Terms and Definitions. J.E. McIntyre and Paul N. Daniels, editors. Available from State Mutual Book and Periodical Service Ltd. • 1996. $180.00. 10th edition. Published by the Textile Insitute (UK). Includes more than 1,000 definitions of textile processes, fiber types, and end products. Illustrated.

FINANCIAL RATIOS

Annual Statement Studies. The Risk Management Association. • Annual. Median and quartile financial ratios are given for over 400 kinds of manufacturing, wholesale, retail, construction, and consumer finance establishments. Data is sorted by both asset size and sales volume. Includes a clearly written "Definition of Ratios" and an alphabetical industry index.

Annual Statement Studies: Industry Default Probabilities and Cash Flow Measures. The Risk Management Association. • Annual. $145.00. Serves as a companion volume to the original *Annual Statement Studies.* Gives probability of default estimates on a percentage scale for more than 450 industries. Includes changes in position year-by-year for eight financial statement line items and provides percentage measures of cash flow.

INTERNET DATABASES

Manufacturing Profiles. U. S. Bureau of the Census. Phone: (301)763-4636 E-mail: webmaster@census. gov • URL: http://www.census.gov/prod/www/abs/ mfg-prof.html • The Census Bureau makes available free on PDF (Portable Document Format) an annual consolidation of the entire Current Industrial Report series, presenting "all the data compiled." Contains statistics on production, shipments, inventories, consumption, exports, imports, and orders for a wide variety of manufactured products.

ONLINE DATABASES

Textile Technology Digest [online]. Institute of Textile Technology. • Contains indexing and abstracting of more than 300 worldwide journals and monographs in various areas of textile technology, production, and management. Time period is 1978 to date, with monthly updating. Inquire as to online cost and availability.

World Textiles. Elsevier Science, Inc. • Provides abstracting and indexing from 1970 of worldwide textile literature (periodicals, books, pamphlets, and reports). Includes U. S., European, and British patent information. Updating is monthly. Inquire as to online cost and availability.

PERIODICALS AND NEWSLETTERS

American Sportswear and Knitting Times. National Knitwear and Sportswear Association. • Monthly. $40.00 per year. Includes *American Sportswear and Knitting Times Buyer's Guide.* Formerly *Knitting Times.*

DNR: The Men's Fashion Retail Textile Authority. Fairchild Publications. • Daily. $85.00 per year. Formerly *Daily News Record.*

STATISTICS SOURCES

Annual Survey of Manufactures. Available from U. S. Government Printing Office. • Annual. Prices vary. Issued by the U. S. Census Bureau as an interim update to the *Census of Manufactures.* Includes data on number of manufacturing establishments in various industries, employment, labor costs, value of shipments, capital expenditures, inventories, energy costs, and assets. (See also Census Bureau home page, http://www.census. gov/.).

Knit Fabric Production. U.S. Bureau of the Census. • Annual. (Current Industrial Reports MA-22K.).

U. S. Industry and Trade Outlook. Available from National Technical Information Service. • Annual. $69.95. Produced by the International Trade Administration, U. S. Department of Commerce, in a "public-private" partnership with DRI/McGraw-Hill and Standard & Poor's. Provides basic data, outlook for the current year, and "Long-Term Prospects" (five-year projections) for a wide variety of products and services. Includes high technology industries. Formerly *U. S. Industrial Outlook.*

WEFA Industrial Monitor. John Wiley and Sons, Inc. • Annual. $65.00. Prepared by industry analysts at WEFA, an economic forecasting and consulting firm (originally Wharton Econometric Forecasting Associates). Contains discussions of the outlook for major U. S. industries, with many 10-year forecasts (WEFA Web site is http://www.wefa.com).

TRADE/PROFESSIONAL ASSOCIATIONS

Knitwear Division - American Apparel Manufacturers Association. 1601 N. Kent St., Ste. 1200, Arlington, VA 22209-2105. • Formerly National Knitwear Manufacturers Association.

National Knitwear and Sportswear Association. 386

Park Ave. S, New York, NY 10016. Phone: (212)683-7520 Fax: (212)532-0766 E-mail: nksa@ pop.interport.net • URL: http://www.rtwear.com • Formerly National Knitted Outerwear Association.

Textile Institute. St. James's Buildings, 1st Fl., 79 Oxford St., Manchester M1 6FQ, United Kingdom. Phone: 44 161 2371188 Fax: 44 161 2361991 E-mail: tiihq@textileinst.org.uk • URL: http://www. texi.org • Companies and individuals in 100 countries involved in management, science, technology, design, information transfer, and marketing of textiles including clothing and footwear. Promotes interests of the textile industry worldwide; serves professional interests of members; confers qualifications and recognizes achievements in research, application of ideas, education, business, and public affairs. Maintains Information Service to collect information relating to textile industrial and economic conditions in different countries and economic sectors.

KOSHER FOODS INDUSTRY

DIRECTORIES

Directory of Delicatessen Products. Pacific Rim Publishing Co. • Annual. Included with February issue of *Deli News.* Lists suppliers of cheeses, lunch meats, packaged fresh meats, kosher foods, gourmet-specialty items, and bakery products.

Kosher Directory :Directory of Kosher Products and Services. Union of Orthodox Jewish Congregations of America (Orthodox Union). • Annual. $15.00. Over 10,000 consumer, institutional and industrial products and services produced under the rabbinical supervision of the Union.

PERIODICALS AND NEWSLETTERS

Deli News. Delicatessen Council of Southern California, Inc. Pacific Rim Publishing Co. • Monthly. $25.00 per year. Includes product news and comment related to cheeses, lunch meats, packaged fresh meats, kosher foods, gourmet-specialty items, and bakery products.

Di Yiddishe Heim/Jewish Home. Chabad Lubavitch. • Quarterly. $8.00 per year. Text in English and Yiddishe.

TRADE/PROFESSIONAL ASSOCIATIONS

Union of Orthodox Jewish Congregations of America. 11 Broadway, New York, NY 10004. Phone: (212)563-4000 Fax: (212)564-9058 E-mail: info@ou.org • URL: http://www.ou.org.

L

LABELS AND LABELING

See also: PACKAGING

DIRECTORIES

Business Forms and Systems Manufacturers. Info USA. • Annual. Price on application. Lists more than 800 suppliers and manufacturers of business forms, labels, and related equipment.

ENCYCLOPEDIAS AND DICTIONARIES

Consumers' Guide to Product Grades and Terms: From Grade A to VSOP-Definitions of 8,000 Terms Describing Food Housewares and Other Everyday Terms. Gale Cengage Learning. • 1992. $95.00. Includes product grades and classifications defined by government agencies, such as the Food and Drug Administration (FDA), and by voluntary standards organizations, such as the American National Standards Institute (ANSI).

ONLINE DATABASES

PIRA. PIRA International Information Centre. • Citations and abstracts pertaining to bookbinding and other pulp, paper, and packaging industries, 1975 to present. Weekly updates. Inquire as to online cost and availability.

PERIODICALS AND NEWSLETTERS

PackagePrinting: For Printers and Converters of Labels, Flexible Packaging and Folding Cartons. North American Publishing Co. • Monthly. Free to qualified personnel; others, $59.00 per year. Formerly *Package Printing and Converting.*

TRADE/PROFESSIONAL ASSOCIATIONS

Label Printing Industries of America. 100 Daingerfield Rd., Alexandria, VA 22314. Phone: (703)519-8100 Fax: (703)548-3227 E-mail: gain@printing.org • URL: http://www.gain.org • Affiliated with Printing Industries of America.

Tag and Label Manufacturers Institute. 40 Shuman Blvd., Suite 295, Naperville, IL 60563. Phone: 800-533-8564 or (630)357-9222 Fax: (630)357-0192 E-mail: office@tlmi.com • URL: http://www.tlmi.com • Formerly Tag Manufacturers Institute.

OTHER SOURCES

Food Law Reports. CCH, Inc. • Weekly. $1,459.00 per year. Six looseleaf volumes. Covers regulation of adulteration, packaging, labeling, and additives. Formerly *Food Drug Cosmetic Law Reports.*

Labels. Available from MarketResearch.com. • 2002. $3,900.00. Market research report published by the Freedonia Group. Covers types of label materials, methods of application, printing technology, and end-use markets. Includes company profiles and forecasts to the year 2006.

LABOR

See also: INDUSTRIAL RELATIONS; LABOR LAW AND REGULATION; LABOR UNIONS

GENERAL WORKS

Labor-Management Relations. Daniel Q. Mills. McGraw-Hill. • 1993. $112.50. Fifth edition. (Management Series).

Labor Relations. Arthur A. Sloan and Fred Witney. Prentice Hall PTR. • 2000. $115.00. 10th edition. Emphasizes collective bargaining and arbitration.

Labor Relations: Development, Structure, Process. John A. Fossum. McGraw-Hill. • 2001. $112.50. Eighth edition.

ABSTRACTS AND INDEXES

Social Sciences Citation Index. Thomson/ISI. • Three times a year. $6,900 per year. Annual cumulation. Includes *Source Index, Citation Index, Permuterm Subject Index,* and *Corporate Index.*

Social Sciences Index. H. W. Wilson Co. • Quarterly, with annual cumulation. Price varies. Indexes more than 400 periodicals covering economics, environmental policy, government, insurance, labor, health care policy, plannning, public administration, public welfare, urban studies, women's issues, criminology, and related topics.

ALMANACS AND YEARBOOKS

Advances in Industrial and Labor Relations. David B. Lipsky and David Levin, editors. Elsevier. • Dates vary. 12 volumes. Prices vary.

World Labour Report. International Labour Office. • Irregular. Price varies. Volume eight. International coverage. Reviews significant recent events and labor policy developments in the following areas: employment, human rights, labor relations, and working conditions.

CD-ROM DATABASES

Social Sciences Citation Index. ISI. • Monthly. Price on request. Provides CD-ROM indexing of articles appearing in 1700 leading social science journals worldwide, with additional selections from more than 5700 other journals. Time span is 1992 to date. Coverage includes economics, business, finance, management, communications, demographics, library and information science, political science, sociology, and many other subjects.

Social Sciences Citation Index: Compact Disc Edition with Abstracts. Institute for Scientific Information. • Monthly. Provides CD-ROM indexing and abstracting of "significant articles" from 1,700 social science journals worldwide, with additional selections from 3,200 other journals, 1986 to date. Includes economics, business, finance,

management, communications, demographics, information and library science, political science, sociology, and many other subjects.

WILSONDISC: Wilson Business Abstracts. H. W. Wilson Co. • Monthly. Includes unlimited online access to *Wilson Business Abstracts* through WILSONLINE. Provides CD-ROM "cover-to-cover" abstracting and indexing of over 600 prominent business periodicals. Indexing is from 1982, abstracting from 1990. (*Business Periodicals Index* without abstracts is available on CD-ROM at $1,495 per year.).

WILSONDISC: Wilson Social Sciences Abstracts. H. W. Wilson Co. • Monthly. Includes unlimited online access to *Social Sciences Index* through WILSONLINE. Provides CD-ROM indexing from 1983 and abstracting from 1994 of more than 500 periodicals covering economics, area studies, community health, public administration, public welfare, urban studies, and many other topics related to the social sciences.

DIRECTORIES

D1rectory of U. S. Labor Organizations. BNA, Inc. . • Annual. $105.00. More than 150 national unions and professional and state employees associations engaged in labor representation.

ENCYCLOPEDIAS AND DICTIONARIES

Encyclopedia of Labor History Worldwide. Gale Cengage Learning. • 2003. $295.00. Two volumes. Cover 300 key events, national and international, that took place in labor history over the past 200 years. Includes illustrations, maps, a glossary, a bibliography, and indexes. (St. James Press imprint.).

Roberts' Dictionary of Industrial Relations. BNA, Inc. • 1993. $85.00. Fourth edition.

Work in America: An Encyclopedia of History, Policy, and Society. Carl E. Van Horn and Herbert A. Schaffner. ABC-CLIO, Inc. • 2003. $185.00. Two volumes. Contains 265 A-Z entries covering work in the U. S. from the Industrial Revolution to modern times. Covers labor-related topics in economics, history, law, welfare, employment policy, and other areas.

HANDBOOKS AND MANUALS

Guidebook to Labor Relations. CCH, Inc. • Annual. $12.00.

Personnel Management: Labor Relations Guide. Prentice Hall PTR. • Three looseleaf volumes. Periodic supplementation. Price on application.

Primer of Labor Relations. Linda G. Kahn. BNA, Inc. • 1994. $45.00. 25th edition.

Standard Occupational Classification Manual. Available from Bernan Associates. • 2000. $38.00.

Replaces the *Dictionary of Occupational Titles*. Produced by the federal Office of Management and Budget, Executive Office of the President. "Occupations are classified based on the work performed, and on the required skills, education, training, and credentials for each one." Six-digit codes contain elements for 23 Major Groups, 96 Minor Groups, 451 Broad Occupations, and 820 Detailed Occupations. Designed to reflect the occupational structure currently existing in the U. S.

ONLINE DATABASES

Labordoc. International Labour Organization. • Indexing of labor literature and the publications of the International Labour Organization, 1965 to present. Monthly updates. Inquire as to online cost and availability.

Social Scisearch. Institute for Scientific Information. • Broad, multidisciplinary index to the literature of the social sciences, 1972 to present. Weekly updates. Worldwide coverage. Inquire as to online cost and availability.

Wilson Business Abstracts Online. H. W. Wilson Co. • Indexes and abstracts 600 major business periodicals, plus the *Wall Street Journal* and the business section of the *New York Times.* Indexing is from 1982, abstracting from 1990, with the two newspapers included from 1993. Updated weekly. Inquire as to online cost and availability. (*Business Periodicals Index* without abstracts is also available online.).

Wilson Social Sciences Abstracts Online. H. W. Wilson Co. • Provides online abstracting and indexing of more than 500 periodicals covering area studies, community health, public administration, public welfare, urban studies, and many other social science topics. Time period is 1994 to date for abstracts and 1983 to date for indexing, with updates weekly. Inquire as to online cost and availability.

PERIODICALS AND NEWSLETTERS

Daily Labor Report. Bureau of National Affairs Inc. • Description: Covers labor developments in Congress, the courts, federal agencies, unions, management, and the National Labor Relations Board.

International Labour Review. International Labour Office. ILO Publications Center. • Bimonthly. $80.00. Editions in English, French and Spanish.

People to People. American Public Power Association. • Description: Reports on public sector labor and personnel issues, especially those concerning the electric utility industry. Summarizes case studies in public labor relations.

Review of Social Economy. Association for Social Economics. Taylor and Francis Group. • Quarterly. Individuals, $78.00 per year; institutions, $211.00 per year. Subject matter is concerned with the relationships between social values and economics. Includes articles on income distribution, poverty, labor, and class.

RESEARCH CENTERS AND INSTITUTES

Council on Employee Relations. University of Pennsylvania. 309 Vance Hall, 3733 Spruce St., Philadelphia, PA 19104-6358. Phone: (215)898-5605 Fax: (215)898-5908 E-mail: cappelli@wharton.upenn.edu • URL: http://www.management.wharton.upenn.edu/chrl.

Institute of Labor and Industrial Relations. University of Michigan, Victor Vaughn Bldg., 1111 E. Catherine St., Ann Arbor, MI 48109-2054. Phone: (734)763-3116 Fax: (734)763-0913 E-mail: swines@umich.edu • URL: http://www.ilir.umich.edu.

Labor Research Association. Labor Research Association. 330 W 42nd St., 13th Fl., New York, NY 10001. Phone: (212)714-1677 Fax: (212)714-1674 E-mail: info@lra-ny.com • URL: http://www.laborresearch.org/about.php • Economic, social, and

political conditions, focusing on labor relations.

STATISTICS SOURCES

Bulletin of Labour Statistics: Supplementing the Annual Data Presented in the Year Book of Labour Statistics. International Labour Ofice. • Quarterly. $84.00 per year. Includes five *Supplements.* A supplement to *Yearbook of Labour Statistics.* Provides current labor and price index statistics for over 130 countries. Generally includes data for the most recent four years. Text in English, French and Spanish.

Gale Book of Averages. Gale Cengage Learning. • 1994. $75.00. Contains 1,100-1,200 statistical averages on a variety of topics, with references to published sources. Subjects include business, labor, consumption, crime, and other areas of contemporary society.

Handbook of U. S. Labor Statistics: Employment, Earnings, Prices, Productivity, and Other Labor Data. Eva E. Jacobs, editor. Bernan Associates. • 1999. $74.00. Based on *Handbook of Labor Statistics,* formerly issued by the Bureau of Labor Statistics, U. S. Department of Labor. Includes the Bureau's projections of employment in the U. S. by industry and occupation. Provides a wide variety of data on the work force, prices, fringe benefits, and consumer expenditures.

Key Indicators of the Labour Market. Available from Routledge. • Biennial. $125.00. Published by the International Labour Office (http://www.ilo.org). Provides data on 20 key indicators in 220 countries. Includes labor force statistics, employment, unemployment, part-time workers, wages, productivity, poverty indicators, and related topics.

Monthly Labor Review. Available from U. S. Government Printing Office. • Monthly. $49.00 per year. Issued by the Bureau of Labor Statistics, U. S. Department of Labor. Contains data on the labor force, wages, work stoppages, price indexes, productivity, economic growth, and occupational injuries and illnesses.

Social Trends and Indicators USA. Monique D. Magee, editor. Gale Cengage Learning. • 2003. $450.00. Four volumes. Includes data on labor, economics, the health care industry, crime, leisure, population, education, social security, and many other topics. Sources include various government agencies and major publications.

Statistical Forecasts of the United States. Gale Cengage Learning. • 1995. $115.00. Second edition. Provides both long-term and short-term statistical forecasts relating to basic items in the U. S.: population, employment, labor, crime, education, and health care. Data in the form of charts, graphs, and tables has been taken from a wide variety of government and private sources. Includes a subject index and an "Index of Forecast by Year.".

Yearbook of Labour Statistics. Available from Bernan Associates. • Annual. $168.00. Published by the International Labour Organizaton (http://www.ilo.org). Provides data for more than 180 countries on employment, unemployment, wages, hours of work, cost of labor, strikes, industrial accidents, and consumer prices.

TRADE/PROFESSIONAL ASSOCIATIONS

AFL-CIO. 815 16th St. NW, Washington, DC 20006. Phone: (202)637-5137 Fax: (202)637-5058 E-mail: info@workingamerica.org • URL: http://www.aflcio.org • Federation of national unions, state federations, city central bodies, and directly affiliated local unions.

Labor Policy Association. 1015 15th St., NW, Ste. 1200, Washington, DC 20005. Phone: (202)789-8670 Fax: (202)789-0064 E-mail: hrpolicy.org •

URL: http://www.hrpolicy.org.

OTHER SOURCES

Labor Relations Reporter. BNA, Inc. • Weekly. $4,998.00 per year. Looseleaf service.

LABOR ARBITRATION

See: ARBITRATION

LABOR DISCIPLINE

See: EMPLOYEE DISCIPLINE

LABOR DISPUTES

See: ARBITRATION; STRIKES AND LOCKOUTS

LABOR FORCE

See: LABOR SUPPLY

LABOR LAW AND REGULATION

GENERAL WORKS

Child Labor: An American History. Hugh D. Hindman. M. E. Sharpe, Inc. • 2002. $88.95.

Labor and Employment Law: Text and Cases. David P. Twomey. South-Western. • 2000. $93.94. 11th edition. (Business Law Series).

ABSTRACTS AND INDEXES

Current Law Index: Multiple Access to Legal Periodicals. Gale Cengage Learning. • Monthly. $725.00 per year. Produced in cooperation with the American Association of Law Libraries. Indexes more than 900 law journals, legal newspapers, and specialty publications from the U.S., Canada, U.K., Ireland, Australia, and New Zealand.

Index to Legal Periodicals and Books. H. W. Wilson Co. • Monthly. $490.00 per year. Quarterly and annual cumulations.

ALMANACS AND YEARBOOKS

American Law Yearbook. Gale Cengage Learning. • Annual. $165.00. Serves as a yearly supplement to *West's Encyclopedia of American Law.* Describes new legal developments in many subject areas.

CD-ROM DATABASES

WILSONDISC: Index to Legal Periodicals and Books. H. W. Wilson Co. • Monthly. Includes unlimited online access to *Index to Legal Periodicals* through WILSONLINE. Contains CD-ROM indexing of more than 1,400 English language legal periodicals from 1981 to date and 2,500 books.

ENCYCLOPEDIAS AND DICTIONARIES

West's Encyclopedia of American Law. Available from Gale Cengage Learning. • 2003. $1,195.00. Second edition. 12 volumes. Published by West Group. Covers a wide variety of legal topics for the general reader.

HANDBOOKS AND MANUALS

ABC of Women Workers' Rights and Gender Equality. International Labour Organization. • 2000. $12.95. Second edition. Provides a concise guide to international laws and agreements relating to the rights of women workers.

Employee and Union Member Guide to Labor Law. National Lawyers Guild. West Group. • Semiannual. $366.00 per year. Three looseleaf volumes. Labor law for union members.

Employer's Guide to Discrimination Laws. Maureen F. Moore. LexisNexis Matthew Bender. • 2003. $28.00, including CD-ROM. Edited for business owners and managers. Provides a concise guide to federal discrimination laws relating to race, sex, age, disability, pregnancy, religion, and national origin.

Guidebook to Labor Relations. CCH, Inc. • Annual. $12.00.

Labor Management Relations: Strikes, Lockouts, and Boycotts. West Group. • Annual. $165.00. Looseleaf service. Covers legal issues involved in labor-management confrontations. Includes recent decisions of the National Labor Relations Board (NLRB).

Law of the Workplace: Rights of Employers and Employees. James Hunt and Patricia Strongin. BNA, Inc. • 1994. $45.00. Third edition. Wages, hours, working conditions, benefits, and so forth.

Practical Guide to Tax Issues in Employment. Julia K. Brazelton. CCH, Inc. • 1999. $95.00. Covers income taxation as related to labor law and tax law, including settlements and awards. Written for tax professionals.

INTERNET DATABASES

Lexis.com Research System. Lexis-Nexis Group. Phone: 800-227-4908 or (937)865-6800 Fax: (937)865-6909 E-mail: webmaster@prod.lexisnexis.com • URL: http://www.lexis.com • Fee-based Web site offers extensive searching of a wide variety of legal sources. Additional features include Daily Opinion Service, lexis.com Bookstore, Career Center, CLE Center, Law Schools, and Practice Pages ("Pages specific to areas of specialty").

ONLINE DATABASES

Index to Legal Periodicals and Books (Online). H. W. Wilson Co. • Broad coverage of law journals and books 1981 to date. Monthly updates. Inquire as to online cost and availability.

Instant Computer Arbitration Search. LRP Publications. • Provides citations to U. S. labor arbitration cases and a detailed directory of about 2,500 public and private labor arbitrators. Weekly updates. Cases date from 1970. Inquire as to online cost and availability.

PERIODICALS AND NEWSLETTERS

Bender's Labor and Employment Bulletin. LexisNexis Matthew Bender. • Monthly. $296.00 per year. Newsletter.

The Canadian Employer. MPL Communications Inc. • Description: Provides information regarding Canadian employment laws.

Daily Labor Report. Bureau of National Affairs Inc. • Description: Covers labor developments in Congress, the courts, federal agencies, unions, management, and the National Labor Relations Board.

Employee Policy for the Private and Public Sector: State Capitals. Wakeman-Walworth, Inc. • Weekly. $245.00 per year; print and online editions, $350.00 per year. Newsletter. Formerly *From the State Capitals: Employee Policy for the Private and Public Sector.*

Employment Law Strategist. Law Journal Newsletter. • Monthly. 279 individuals for print version per year. Covers employment law topics, including immigration laws, repetitive stress claims, workplace violence, liability of actions of intoxicated employees, record keeping, liability for fetal injury, independent contractor, and employee issues. Monthly. 229 individuals electronic edition. Description: Reports on legal strategy and substantive developments in the area of matrimonial law, including such topics as tax considerations, custody, visitation, division of property, and valuation. Recurring features include litigation roundup and a legislative update.

Federal Register. Office of the Federal Register.

Available from U.S. Government Printing Office. • Daily except Saturday and Sunday. $764.00 per year. Publishes regulations and legal notices issued by federal agencies, including executive orders and presidential proclamations. Issued by the National Archives and Records Administration (http://www.nara.gov).

Labor and Employment Law. Labor and Employment Law Section. American Bar Association. • Quarterly. Membership.

Labor Law Journal: To Promote Sound Thinking on Labor Law Problems. CCH, Inc. • Monthly. $189.00 per year.

Weekly Summary of the National Labor Relations Board Cases. Available from U. S. Government Printing Office. • Weekly. $237.00 per year. Issued by the Division of Information, National Labor Relations Board.

OTHER SOURCES

Contingent Workforce: Business and Legal Strategies. American Lawyer Media, Inc. • Looseleaf. $169.00. Updated as needed. Covers the legal, employee benefit, and taxation aspects of alternative work arrangements (temporary employees, independent contractors, outsourcing). (Law Journal Press).

Employment Forms and Policies. LexisNexis Matthew Bender. • Looseleaf. $120.00, including CD-ROM. Periodic supplementation available. Contains more than 300 forms, policies, and checklists for use by small or medium-sized businesses. Covers such topics as employee selection, payroll issues, benefits, performance appraisal, dress codes, and employee termination.

Labor Relations. CCH, Inc. • $2,589.00 per year. Seven looseleaf volumes. Weekly updates. Covers labor relations, wages and hours, state labor laws, and employment practices. Supplement available, *Labor Law Reports.* Summary Newsletter.

Labor Relations Reporter. BNA, Inc. • Weekly. $4,998.00 per year. Looseleaf service.

Occupational Safety and Health Handbook: An Employer's Guide to OSHA Laws. LexisNexis Matthew Bender. • Looseleaf. $115.00. Periodic supplementation available. Covers inspections, violations, the citation process, ergonomics, hazards, equipment, and other topics relating to the law enforced by the federal Occupational Safety and Health Administration (OSHA).

LABOR MARKET

See: LABOR SUPPLY

LABOR ORGANIZATION

See: LABOR UNIONS

LABOR PRODUCTIVITY

See: PRODUCTIVITY

LABOR RELATIONS

See: INDUSTRIAL RELATIONS; LABOR

LABOR SUPPLY

GENERAL WORKS

Global Employment Trends. Claire Harasty and Dorothea Schmidt. International Labour Organization. • 2003. $22.95. Provides an analysis of "current labour market trends around the world." Emphasis is

on how the "global economic downturn" has affected various regions and economic groups.

Welfare, the Working Poor, and Labor. Louise Simmons, editor. M. E. Sharpe, Inc. • 2004. $66.95. Presents material by various authors on poverty, welfare reform, and the market for low-wage labor.

ALMANACS AND YEARBOOKS

OECD Employment Outlook. OECD Publications and Information Center. • 2000. $48.00. Outlines the employment prospects for the coming year in OECD countries. Also discusses labor force growth, job creation, labor standards, and collective bargaining.

BIBLIOGRAPHIES

International Migration of the Highly Qualified: A Bibliographic and Conceptual Itinerary. Jacques Gaillard and Anne-Marie Gaillard. Center for Migration Studies. • 1998. $29.95. Includes more than 1,800 references from 1954 to 1995 on the migration patterns of skilled or highly qualified workers. (CMS Bibliographies and Documentation Series).

CD-ROM DATABASES

OECD Statistical Compendium. Organization for Economic Cooperation and Development. • Semiannual. $1,905.00 per year for 1 to 10 users. CD-ROM contains more than 730,000 monthly, quarterly, and annual time series for OECD countries, 1960 to date. Includes fully searchable data on agriculture, food, economic indicators, national accounts, employment, energy, finance, industry, technology, and foreign trade. Results can be displayed in various forms.

Sourcebooks America CD-ROM. CACI Marketing Systems. • Annual. $1,250.00. Provides the CD-ROM version of *The Sourcebook of ZIP Code Demographics: Census Edition* and *The Sourcebook of County Demographics: Census Edition.*

HANDBOOKS AND MANUALS

WARN Act: A Manager's Compliance Guide to Workforce Reductions. Joseph A. Brislin. BNA, Inc. • 1990. $195.00.

INTERNET DATABASES

Bureau of Economic Analysis (BEA). U. S. Department of Commerce, Bureau of Economic Analysis. Phone: (202)606-9900 Fax: (202)606-5310 E-mail: webmaster@bea.doc.gov • URL: http://www.bea.doc.gov • Web site includes "News Release Information" covering national, regional, and international economic estimates from the BEA. Highlights of releases appear online the same day, complete text and tables appear the next day. "Recent News Releases" section provides titles for past nine months, with links. "BEA Data and Methodology" includes "Frequently Requested NIPA Data" (national income and product accounts, such as gross domestic product and personal income). Other statistics are available. Fees: Free.

Business 2.0 Web Guide to the Best Business Links. Business 2.0 Media Inc. Phone: (415)293-4800 E-mail: support@business2.com • URL: http://www.business2.com/webguide • Web site presents an extensive, searchable directory of links to "the best, most informative, and authoritative web pages." Twenty main categories cover business, finance, career, company information, people, and technology topics, with thousands of subtopics, all linking to Web sites recommended by experienced business researchers. Fees: Free.

Fedstats. Federal Interagency Council on Statistical Policy. Phone: (202)395-7254 • URL: http://www.fedstats.gov • Web site features an efficient search facility for full-text statistics produced by more than 100 federal agencies, including the Census Bureau, the Bureau of Economic Analysis, and the Bureau of Labor Statistics. Boolean searches can be made within one agency or for all agencies combined.

Links are offered to international statistical bureaus, including the UN, IMF, OECD, UNESCO, Eurostat, and 20 individual countries. Fees: Free.

FreeLunch.com. Economy.com, Inc. Phone: (610)696-8700 Fax: (610)696-1678 • URL: http://www.freelunch.com • Web site provides free access to more than 1.5 million economic and financial data series, covering industry, demographics, labor markets, prices, retail sales, government spending, trade, interest rates, housing starts, the stock market, and many other topics. Data is available for various time periods in either chart or table form. Searching is offered. Fees: Free, but registration required. Economy.com, Inc. also offers fee-based economic analysis at *The Dismal Scientist* site (http://www.dismal.com).

PERIODICALS AND NEWSLETTERS

Journal of Human Resources: Education, Manpower and Welfare Economics. University of Wisconsin at Madison, Industrial Relations Research Institute. University of Wisconsin Press. • Quarterly. Individuals, $60.00 per year; institutions, $150.00 per year. Articles on manpower, health and welfare policies as they relate to the labor market and to economic and social development.

Regional Economics and Markets: A Quarterly Analysis from the Conference Board. The Conference Board. • Quarterly. Members, $145.00 per year; non-members, $295.00 per year. Summarizes economic trends and prospects for nine geographic regions of the U. S. Provides data on key predictive indexes, including employment, housing permits, retail sales, consumer confidence, and help-wanted advertising. Charts and graphs are included.

Work and Occupations: An International Sociological Journal. Sage Publications, Inc. • Quarterly. $499.00 per year. Includes print and online editions.

Working USA: The Journal of Labor and Society. M. E. Sharpe, Inc. • Quarterly. $160.00 per year to institutions; $45.00 to individuals. Provides a wide range of material on employment, labor markets, societal issues, and present-day labor unions.

RESEARCH CENTERS AND INSTITUTES

Industrial Relations Section. Princeton University, Firestone Library, Pinceton, NJ 08544. Phone: (609)258-4040 Fax: (609)258-2907 • URL: http://www.irs.princeton.edu/ • Fields of research include labor supply, manpower training, unemployment, and equal employment opportunity.

Office of Manpower Studies. Purdue University. School of Technology, Knoy Hall, West Lafayette, IN 47907-1410. Phone: (765)494-2558 Fax: (765)494-0486 E-mail: jplisack@tech.purdue.edu • URL: http://www.tech.purdue.edu.

W. E. Upjohn Institute for Employment Research. 300 S. Westnedge Ave., Kalamazoo, MI 49007-4686. Phone: (616)343-5541 Fax: (616)343-3308 E-mail: eberts@we.upjohninst.org • URL: http://www.upjohninst.org • Research fields include unemployment, unemployment insurance, worker's compensation, labor productivity, profit sharing, the labor market, economic development, earnings, training, and other areas related to employment.

STATISTICS SOURCES

American Business Climate and Economic Profiles. Priscilla C. Geahigan. Gale Cengage Learning. • 1993. $170.00. Provides business, industrial, demographic, and economic figures for all states and 300 metropolitan areas. Includes production, taxation, population, growth rates, labor force data, incomes, total sales, etc.

Business Statistics of the United States. Linz Audain and Cornelia J. Strawser. Bernan Associates. • Annual. $147.00. Based on *Business Statistics,* formerly issue by the Bureau of Economic Analysis, U. S. Department of Commerce. Provides basic data for a wide variety of U. S. industries, services, and

economic indicators. Most statistics are shown annually for 30 years and monthly for the most recent four years.

Employment and Earnings. Available from U. S. Government Printing Office. • Monthly. $50.00 per year, including annual supplement. Produced by the Bureau of Labor Statistics, U. S. Department of Labor. Provides current data on employment, hours, and earnings for the U. S. as a whole, for states, and for more than 200 local areas.

Geographic Profile of Employment and Unemployment. Available from U. S. Government Printing Office. • Annual. $23.00. Issued by Bureau of Labor Statistics, U. S. Department of Labor. Presents detailed, annual average employment, unemployment, and labor force data for regions, states, and metropolitan areas. Characteristics include sex, age, race, Hispanic origin, marital status, occupation, and type of industry.

Job Patterns for Minorities and Women in Private Industry. Available from U. S. Government Printing Office. • Annual. $61.00. Issued by the Equal Employment Opportunity Commission (http://www.eeoc.gov). "Provides statistical information on the composition of the United States workforce in private industry by sex, race, and ethnic category.".

Labour Force Statistics. Organization for Economic Cooperation and Development. Available from OECD Publications and Information Center. • Annual. $98.00. Provides 21 years of data for OECD member countries on population, employment, unemployment, civilian labor force, armed forces, and other labor factors.

Monthly Bulletin of Statistics. United Nations Publications. • Monthly. $295.00 per year. Provides current data for about 200 countries on a wide variety of economic, industrial, and demographic subjects. Compiled by United Nations Statistical Office.

Monthly Labor Review. Available from U. S. Government Printing Office. • Monthly. $49.00 per year. Issued by the Bureau of Labor Statistics, U. S. Department of Labor. Contains data on the labor force, wages, work stoppages, price indexes, productivity, economic growth, and occupational injuries and illnesses.

Quarterly Labour Force Statistics. Organization for Economic Cooperation and Development. Available from OECD Publications and Information Center. • Quarterly. $90.00 per year. Provides current data for OECD member countries on population, employment, unemployment, civilian labor force, armed forces, and other labor factors.

Report on the American Workforce. Available from U. S. Government Printing Office. • Annual. Issued by the U. S. Department of Labor (http://www.dol.gov). Appendix contains tabular statistics, including employment, unemployment, price indexes, consumer expenditures, employee benefits (retirement, insurance, vacation, etc.), wages, productivity, hours of work, and occupational injuries. Annual figures are shown for up to 50 years.

Social Statistics of the United States. Mark S. Littman, editor. Bernan Press. • 2000. $65.00. Includes statistical data on population growth, labor force, occupations, environmental trends, leisure time use, income, poverty, taxes, and other economic or demographic topics.

State Profiles: The Population and Economy of Each U. S. State. Courtenay Slater and Others. Bernan Press. • 1999. $89.00. Presents charts, tables, and text in an eight-page profile for each state. Covers population, labor force, income, poverty, employment, wages, industry, trade, housing, education, health, taxes, and government finances. (The Population and Economy of Each United States Series).

Statistical Handbook of Working America. Gale

Cengage Learning. • 1997. $130.00. Second edition. Provides statistics, rankings, and forecasts relating to a wide variety of careers, occupations, and working conditions.

Statistical Yearbook. United Nations Publications. • Annual. $125.00. Contains statistics for about 200 countries on a wide variety of economic, industrial, and demographic topics. Compiled by United Nations Statistical Office.

Survey of Current Business. Available from U. S. Government Printing Office. • Monthly. $63.00 per year. Issued by Bureau of Economic Analysis, U. S. Department of Commerce. Presents a wide variety of business and economic data.

OTHER SOURCES

Foreign Labor Trends. Available from U. S. Government Printing Office. • Irregular (50 to 60 issues per year, each on an individual country). $95.00 per year. Prepared by various American Embassies. Issued by the Bureau of International Labor Affairs, U. S. Department of Labor. Covers labor developments in important foreign countries, including trends in wages, working conditions, labor supply, employment, and unemployment.

LABOR TURNOVER

GENERAL WORKS

Handle with Care: Motivating and Retaining Employees - Creative, Low-Cost Ways to Raise Morale, Increase Commitment, and Reduce Turnover. Barbara A. Glanz. McGraw-Hill. • 2002. $16.95. (Teach Yourself Series).

LABOR UNIONS

See also: COLLECTIVE BARGAINING

GENERAL WORKS

The Changing Role of Unions: New Forms of Representation. Phanindra V. Wunnava, editor. M. E. Sharpe, Inc. • 2004. $74.95. Contains articles by labor economists on the future of labor unions in the U. S.

Labor Relations: Development, Structure, Process. John A. Fossum. McGraw-Hill. • 2001. $112.50. Eighth edition.

DIRECTORIES

DIrectory of U. S. Labor Organizations. BNA, Inc. . • Annual. $105.00. More than 150 national unions and professional and state employees associations engaged in labor representation.

Profiles of American Labor Unions. Gale Cengage Learning. • 1998. $315.00. Second edition. Provides detailed information on more than 280 national labor unions. Includes descriptions of about 800 bargaining agreements and biographies of more than 170 union officials. Local unions are also listed. Four indexes. Formerly *American Directory of Organized Labor* (1992).

Trade Union World. International Confederation of Free Trade Unions. • Monthly. $60.00 per year. Formerly *Free Labour World.*

Washington: A Comprehensive Directory of the Key Institutions and Leaders in th e National Capitol Area. Columbia Books, Inc. • Annual. $149.00. Provides information on about 5,000 Washington, DC key businesses, government offices, non-profit organizations, and cultural institutions, with the names of about 25,000 principal executives. Includes Washington media, law offices, foundations, labor unions, international organizations, clubs, etc.

ENCYCLOPEDIAS AND DICTIONARIES

Encyclopedia of Labor History Worldwide. Gale Cengage Learning. • 2003. $295.00. Two volumes.

Cover 300 key events, national and international, that took place in labor history over the past 200 years. Includes illustrations, maps, a glossary, a bibliography, and indexes. (St. James Press imprint.).

Roberts' Dictionary of Industrial Relations. BNA, Inc. • 1993. $85.00. Fourth edition.

HANDBOOKS AND MANUALS

Employee and Union Member Guide to Labor Law. National Lawyers Guild. West Group. • Semiannual. $366.00 per year. Three looseleaf volumes. Labor law for union members.

PERIODICALS AND NEWSLETTERS

America at Work. AFL-CIO, Public Affairs Dept. • Monthly. Membership. Formerly *AFL-CIO News.*

Union Labor Report. Bureau of National Affairs Inc. • Description: Covers legal, legislative, and regulatory developments and trends affecting management and labor in the workplace.

Working USA: The Journal of Labor and Society. M. E. Sharpe, Inc. • Quarterly. $160.00 per year to institutions; $45.00 to individuals. Provides a wide range of material on employment, labor markets, societal issues, and present-day labor unions.

TRADE/PROFESSIONAL ASSOCIATIONS

AFL-CIO. 815 16th St. NW, Washington, DC 20006. Phone: (202)637-5137 Fax: (202)637-5058 E-mail: info@workingamerica.org • URL: http://www.aflcio.org • Federation of national unions, state federations, city central bodies, and directly affiliated local unions.

OTHER SOURCES

Labor Relations Reporter. BNA, Inc. • Weekly. $4,998.00 per year. Looseleaf service.

LABORATORIES

See also: CLINICAL LABORATORY INDUSTRY; RESEARCH AND DEVELOPMENT

CD-ROM DATABASES

Science Citation Index: Compact Disc Edition. Institute for Scientific Information. • Monthly. Provides CD-ROM indexing of the world's scientific and technical literature. Corresponds to online *Scisearch* and printed *Science Citation Index.*

DIRECTORIES

American Laboratory Buyers' Guide. International Scientific Communications, Inc. • Annual. $25.00. Manufacturers of and dealers in scientific instruments, equipment, apparatus, and chemicals worldwide.

Directory of American Research and Technology: Organizations Active in Product Development for Business. Information Today. • Annual. $359.95. Lists over 13,000 publicly and privately owned research facilities. Formerly *Industrial Research Laboratories of the U.S.*

Directory of Standards Laboratories. NCSL International. • Biennial. Available only online. Lists about 1,500 measurement standards laboratories.

Research Services Directory: Commercial & Corporate Research Centers. Grey House Publishing. • 2003. $495.00. Ninth edition. Lists more than 8,000 independent commercial research centers and laboratories offering contract or fee-based services. Includes corporate research departments, market research companies, and information brokers.

ONLINE DATABASES

Research Centers and Services Directories. Gale Cengage Learning. • Contains profiles of about 30,000 research centers, organizations, laboratories,

and agencies in 147 countries. Corresponds to the printed *Research Centers Directory, International Research Centers Directory, Government Research Directory,* and *Research Services Directory.* Updating is semiannual. Inquire as to online cost and availability.

Scisearch. Institute for Scientific Information. • Broad, multidisciplinary index to the literature of science and technology, 1974 to present. Inquire as to online cost and availability. Coverage of literature is worldwide, with weekly updates.

PERIODICALS AND NEWSLETTERS

American Laboratory. International Scientific Communications, Inc. • Monthly. $235.00 per year. Includes annual *Buyers' Guide.*

Laboratory Equipment. Reed Business Information. • 12 times a year. $105.90 per year.

Today's Chemist at Work. American Chemical Society. • Monthly. Institutions, $200.00 per year; others, price on application. Provide practical information for chemists on day-to-day operations. Product coverage includes chemicals, equipment, apparatus, instruments, and supplies.

TRADE/PROFESSIONAL ASSOCIATIONS

American Council of Independent Laboratories. 1629 K St., N.W. Suite 400, Washington, DC 20006-1633. Phone: (202)887-5872 Fax: (202)887-0021 E-mail: info@acil.org • URL: http://www.acil.org.

LABORATORIES, CLINICAL

See: CLINICAL LABORATORY INDUSTRY

LABORATORY EQUIPMENT

See: SCIENTIFIC APPARATUS AND INSTRUMENT INDUSTRIES

LACE INDUSTRY

ABSTRACTS AND INDEXES

Textile Technology Digest. Institute of Textile Technology. • Annual. $535.00. Provides indexing and abstracting of a wide variety of textile technology literature.

CD-ROM DATABASES

Textile Technology Digest [CD-ROM]. Textile Information Center, Institute of Textile Technology. • Quarterly. Provides CD-ROM indexing and abstracting of worldwide journals and monographs in various areas of textile technology, production, and management. Covers 1978 to date.

DIRECTORIES

Lace and Embroideries Directory. Schiffli Lace and Embroidery Manufacturers Association. • Annual. $5.00. Embroidery and lace product merchandisers, producers, and industry service providers in the United States with limited international coverage. Formerly *Embroidery Directory.*

ENCYCLOPEDIAS AND DICTIONARIES

Textile Terms and Definitions. J.E. McIntyre and Paul N. Daniels, editors. Available from State Mutual Book and Periodical Service Ltd. • 1996. $180.00. 10th edition. Published by the Textile Insitute (UK). Includes more than 1,000 definitions of textile processes, fiber types, and end products. Illustrated.

ONLINE DATABASES

Textile Technology Digest [online]. Institute of Textile Technology. • Contains indexing and abstracting of more than 300 worldwide journals and monographs in various areas of textile technology, production, and management. Time period is 1978

to date, with monthly updating. Inquire as to online cost and availability.

World Textiles. Elsevier Science, Inc. • Provides abstracting and indexing from 1970 of worldwide textile literature (periodicals, books, pamphlets, and reports). Includes U. S., European, and British patent information. Updating is monthly. Inquire as to online cost and availability.

PERIODICALS AND NEWSLETTERS

Embroidery News. Schiffli Lace and Embroidery Manufacturers Association. • Description: Features articles of interest to manufacturers of machine-made lace, embroideries, eyelets, appliques, etc. Focuses on the concerns of the industry. Recurring features include a calendar of events, reports, notices of publications available, and columns titled Dropped Stitches and Thoughts to Think About.

TRADE/PROFESSIONAL ASSOCIATIONS

Schiffli Embroidery Manufacturers Promotion Fund. 22 Industrial Ave., Fairview, NJ 07022. Phone: (201)943-7757 Fax: (201)943-7793 E-mail: info@schiffli.org • URL: http://www.schiffli.org • Represents embroidery firms contributing to promotional activities to increase demand for laces, embroideries, emblems, and motifs manufactured on Schiffli embroidery machines. Serves as promotional arm of the Schiffli lace and embroidery industry.

Textile Institute. St. James's Buildings, 1st Fl., 79 Oxford St., Manchester M1 6FQ, United Kingdom. Phone: 44 161 2371188 Fax: 44 161 2361991 E-mail: tiihq@textileinst.org.uk • URL: http://www.texi.org • Companies and individuals in 100 countries involved in management, science, technology, design, information transfer, and marketing of textiles including clothing and footwear. Promotes interests of the textile industry worldwide; serves professional interests of members; confers qualifications and recognizes achievements in research, application of ideas, education, business, and public affairs. Maintains Information Service to collect information relating to textile industrial and economic conditions in different countries and economic sectors.

LACQUER AND LACQUERING

See: PAINT AND PAINTING

LAMB INDUSTRY

See: SHEEP INDUSTRY

LAMPS

See: LIGHTING

LAND COMPANIES

See: REAL ESTATE BUSINESS

LAND UTILIZATION

GENERAL WORKS

Recent Advances and Issues in Environmental Science. Joan R. Callahan, editor. Greenwood Publishing Group, Inc. • 1999. $49.95. Includes environmental economic problems, such as saving jobs vs. protecting the environment. (Oryx Frontiers of Science Series.).

Urban Economics and Land Use in America: The Transformation of Cities in the Twentieth Century.

Alan Rabinowitz. M. E. Sharpe, Inc. • 2004. $72.95. Covers suburbanization and its problems from 1900 to modern times.

ABSTRACTS AND INDEXES

Environment Abstracts. Congressional Information Service, Inc. • Monthly. Price varies. Provides multidisciplinary coverage of the world's environmental literature. Incorporates *Acid Rain Abstracts*.

Environment Abstracts Annual: A Guide to the Key Environmental Literature of the Year. Congressional Information Service, Inc. • Annual. $495.00. A yearly cumulation of *Environment Abstracts*.

Environmental Knowledge Base: An Electronic Bibliography Featuring Citations and Abstracts of Scientific and Popular Articles on Environmental Issues, Including Social Policy, Economics, Regulatory, and Legal Topics. Environmental Studies Institute. • Monthly. Price varies. An index to current environmental literature. Formerly *Environmental Periodicals Bibliography*.

ALMANACS AND YEARBOOKS

Earth Almanac: An Annual Geophysical Review of the State of the Planet. Natalie Goldstein. Greenwood Publishing Group, Inc. • Annual. $69.95. Provides background information, statistics, and a summary of major events relating to the atmosphere, oceans, land, and fresh water.

Institute on Planning, Zoning and Eminent Domain. LexisNexis. • 1971. $199.00.

Land Use and Environment Law Review. West Group. • Annual. $330.00.

BIBLIOGRAPHIES

The Ecology of Land Use: A Bibliographic Guide. Graham Trelstad. Sage Publications, Inc. • 1994. $10.00.

NIMBYS and LULUs (Not-in-My-Back-Yard and Locally-Unwanted-Land-Uses). Jan Horah and Heather Scott. Sage Publications, Inc. • 1993. $10.00.

CD-ROM DATABASES

Environment Abstracts on CD-ROM. LEXIS-NEXIS. • Quarterly. $1,295.00 per year. Contains the following CD-ROM databases: *Environment Abstracts, Energy Abstracts,* and *Acid Rain Abstracts*. Length of coverage varies.

ENCYCLOPEDIAS AND DICTIONARIES

Encyclopedia of Global Change: Environmental Change and Human Society. Andrew S. Goudie, editor. Oxford University Press. • 2001. $275.00. Two volumes. Contains 300 signed articles on a wide variety of topics relating to changes in the environment and the atmosphere. Includes bibliographies and illustrations.

PERIODICALS AND NEWSLETTERS

Housing and Commercial Real Estate News Roundup. ULI/Urban Land Institute. • Description: Summarizes current developments in land use, real estate development, and related areas.

Land Use Law and Zoning Digest. American Planning Association. • Monthly. $275.00 per year. Covers judicial decisions and state laws affecting zoning and land use. Edited for city planners and lawyers. Monthly supplement available *Zoning News*.

Land Use Law Report. Business Publishers Inc. • Description: Provides up-to-date information on court decisions, legislation, and regulations that impact today's most pressing land-use policy, planning, and legal issues. Readers receive in-depth coverage on zoning and planning policies, regulatory takings, undesirable land uses, environmental legislation, and much more. **Remarks:** Also available via e-mail.

STATISTICS SOURCES

FAO Production Yearbook. Available from Bernan Associates. • Annual. $45.00. Published by the Food and Agriculture Organization (http://www.fao.org). Contains worldwide data on agriculture, land use, farm crops, livestock, and agricultural prices.

OTHER SOURCES

American Land Planning Law. John Taylor and Norma Williams. West Group. • $780.00. Eight volumes. Annual cumulative updates. (Real Property and Zoning Series).

Federal Land Use Law: Limitations, Procedures, Remedies. West Group. • Annual. $205.00 per year. Looseleaf service.

LANDLORD AND TENANT

See: APARTMENT HOUSES; PROPERTY MANAGEMENT; REAL ESTATE BUSINESS

LANDSCAPE ARCHITECTURE

GENERAL WORKS

Landscape Architecture: An Illustrated History in Timelines, Site Plans, and Biography. William A. Mann. John Wiley and Sons, Inc. • 1993. $75.00. Includes illustrations of notable site plans and biographies of people important to landscape architecture history.

ABSTRACTS AND INDEXES

Art Index. H. W. Wilson Co. • Quarterly. Annual cumulations. Price varies. Subject and author index to periodicals in art, architecture, industrial design, city planning, photography, and various related topics.

DIRECTORIES

American Society of Landscape Architects Members' Handbook. American Society of Landscape Architects. • Annual. Members, $25.00; non-members, $250.00.

ENCYCLOPEDIAS AND DICTIONARIES

Penguin Dictionary of Architecture and Landscape Architecture. Nikolas Pevsner and others. Penguin Group. • 2000. $16.95. Fifth edition. (Penguin Reference Series).

FINANCIAL RATIOS

Annual Statement Studies. The Risk Management Association. • Annual. Median and quartile financial ratios are given for over 400 kinds of manufacturing, wholesale, retail, construction, and consumer finance establishments. Data is sorted by both asset size and sales volume. Includes a clearly written "Definition of Ratios" and an alphabetical industry index.

Annual Statement Studies: Industry Default Probabilities and Cash Flow Measures. The Risk Management Association. • Annual. $145.00. Serves as a companion volume to the original *Annual Statement Studies*. Gives probability of default estimates on a percentage scale for more than 450 industries. Includes changes in position year-by-year for eight financial statement line items and provides percentage measures of cash flow.

HANDBOOKS AND MANUALS

Landscape Planning: Environmental Applications. William M. Marsh. John Wiley and Sons, Inc. • 1997. $62.95. Third edition. A handbook on environmental problems associated with landscape design, land planning, and land use. Includes techniques for obtaining data.

ONLINE DATABASES

Art Index Online. H. W. Wilson Co. • Indexes a wide variety of art-related periodicals, 1984 to date. Monthly updates. Inquire as to online cost and availability.

PERIODICALS AND NEWSLETTERS

Landscape Architecture. American Society of Landscape Architects. • Monthly. $49.00 per year.

Landscape Architecture News Digest. American Society of Landscape Architects. • 10 times a year. Free to members; non-members, $32.00 per year. Looseleaf service.

Landscape Journal: Design, Planning, and Management of the Land. Council of Education in Landscape Architecture. University of Wisconsin Press, Journal Div. • Semiannual. Individuals, $42.00 per year; institutions, $135.00 per year.

Landscape Maintenance News. Landscape Information Services. • Description: Provides landscape service companies with information to help them manage their services; covers changes and events in the industry. Covers image, customer service, advertising and marketing, estimating, mowing, poweraking, fertilization, weed control, maintenance, and miscellaneous services. Discusses trade shows, products and services, associations, and franchise opportunities. Recurring features include news of research, news of educational opportunities, book reviews, and notices of publications available.

Landscape Management: Commercial Magazine for Lawn, Landscape and Grounds Managers. Advanstar Communications. • Monthly. $41.00 per year.

RESEARCH CENTERS AND INSTITUTES

Landscape Architecture Foundation. Landscape Architecture Foundation. 818 18th St. NW, Ste. 810, Washington, DC 20006. Phone: (202)331-7070 Fax: (202)331-7079 E-mail: rfigura@lafoundation.org • URL: http://www.lafoundation.org • Landscape planning, land use planning and design, environmental planning, landscape change, landscape intervention, place-based land use planning, public participation processes.

TRADE/PROFESSIONAL ASSOCIATIONS

American Society of Landscape Architects. 636 Eye St., N.W., Washington, DC 20001-3736. Phone: 888-999-2752 or (202)898-2444 Fax: (202)898-1185 • URL: http://www.asla.org/.

LAN

See: LOCAL AREA NETWORKS

LAPTOP COMPUTERS

See: PORTABLE COMPUTERS

LARD INDUSTRY

See: OIL AND FATS INDUSTRY

LASERDISKS

See: OPTICAL DISK STORAGE DEVICES

LASERS

GENERAL WORKS

Introduction to Laser Technology. C. Breck Hitz and others. John Wiley and Sons, Inc. • 2001. $79.95. Third edition. Published by the Institute of Electrical and Electronics Engineers (IEEE) (http://www.ieee.org). Provides basic information about a wide variety of commercial lasers. Edited for "professionals, students, and non-engineer executives interested in the design, sales, or applications of the laser and electro-optics industry.".

Photonics. Ralf Menzel. Springer-Verlag. • 2001. $89.95. "...covers the fundamental properties and the description of single photons and light beams, experimentally and theoretically." Provides basic information about modern lasers. Edited for graduate students and scientists.

ABSTRACTS AND INDEXES

Journal of Current Laser Abstracts. PennWell Corp., Advanced Technology Div. • Monthly. $495.00 per year. Covers the world's literature of lasers: industrial, medical, and military. Subscription includes annual subject and author index.

Key Abstracts: Optoelectronics. Available from INSPEC, Inc. • Monthly. $250.00 per year. Provides international coverage of journal and proceedings literature relating to fiber optics, lasers, and optoelectronics in general. Published in England by the Institution of Electrical Engineers (IEE).

NTIS Alerts: Manufacturing Technology. National Technical Information Service. • Semimonthly. $265.00 per year. Provides descriptions of government-sponsored research reports and software, with ordering information. Covers computer-aided design and manufacturing (CAD/CAM), engineering materials, quality control, machine tools, robots, lasers, productivity, and related subjects. Formerly *Abstract Newsletter*.

Solid State and Superconductivity Abstracts. CSA. • Bimonthly. $1,695.00 per year. Includes print and online editions. Formerly *Solid State Abstracts Journal*.

BIBLIOGRAPHIES

Lasers: A Guide to the Book Literature. Charles Blain. Nova Science Publishers, Inc. • 2002. $49.00. Provides citations to books on various kinds of lasers: chemical, dye, far infrared, tree-electron, gas, ruby, semiconductor, solid-state, and tunable. Includes author, title, and subject indexes.

DIRECTORIES

Industrial Laser Buyers Guide. PennWell Corp., Advanced Technology Div. • Annual. $104.00. Lists industrial laser suppliers by category and geographic location. (Included with subscription to *Industrial Laser Solutions*.).

Laser Focus World Buyers Guide. Advanced Technology Group. • Covers: over 2,000 manufacturers, suppliers, and consultants in the laser, fiber optic, electro-optic, optic, and related industries, worldwide. Entries include: Company name, address, phone, fax, e-mail, principal executives, number of employees, list of products and services, brief description of company.

HANDBOOKS AND MANUALS

Handbook of Lasers. Marvin J. Weber. CRC Press LLC. • 2000. $169.95. (Laser and Optical Science and Technology Series).

PERIODICALS AND NEWSLETTERS

Industrial Laser Solutions for Manufacturing. PennWell Corp., Advanced Technology Div. • Monthly. $300.00 per year. Covers industrial laser technology, especially machine tool applications.

Laser Focus World: The World of Optoelectronics. PennWell Corp., Advanced Technology Div. • Monthly. $165.00 per year. Covers business and technical aspects of electro-optics, including lasers and fiberoptics. Includes *Buyer's Guide*.

Lasers in Surgery and Medicine. John Wiley and Sons, Inc., Journals. • 11 times a year. $1,425.00 per year; with online edition, $1,497.00 per year. Original articles in laser surgery and medicine.

Medical Laser Report. PennWell Corp. • Description: Presents news on the medical laser industry, technology, research, and markets. Recurring features include news of research, business news and product introductions.

Optics and Laser Technology. Elsevier. • Eight times a year. Institutions, $1,196.00 per year. Published in United Kingdom.

RESEARCH CENTERS AND INSTITUTES

Center for Laser Applications. UT Space Institute Research Park, University of Tennessee, 411 B.H.

Goethert Pky., Tullahoma, TN 37388. Phone: (931)393-7485 Fax: (931)454-2271 E-mail: dkeefer@utsi.edu • URL: http://www.cla.utsi.edu • In addition to research, provides technical assistance relating to the industrial use of lasers.

Center for Research and Education in Optics and Lasers. University of Central Florida, School of Optics, 4000 Central Florida Blvd., Orlando, FL 32816-2700. Phone: (407)823-6800 Fax: (407)823-6880 E-mail: ewvs@creol.ucf.edu • URL: http://www.creol.ucf.edu.

Laser Biomedical Research Center. Massachusetts Institute of Technology, 77 Massachusetts Ave., Cambridge, MA 02139. Phone: (617)253-7700 Fax: (617)253-4513 E-mail: msfeld@mit.edu • Concerned with the medical use of lasers.

TRADE/PROFESSIONAL ASSOCIATIONS

IEEE Lasers and Electro-Optics Society. c/o IEEE Corporate Center, Three Park Ave., 17th Fl., New York, NY 10016-5997. Phone: (212)419-7900 or (212)752-4929 E-mail: ieeeusa@ieee.org • URL: http://www.ieee.org • Fields of interest include lasers, fiber optics, optoelectronics, and photonics.

Laser Institute of America. 13501 Ingenuity Dr., No. 128, Orlando, FL 32826. Phone: 800-345-2737 or (407)380-1553 Fax: (407)380-5588 E-mail: webmaster@laserinstitute.org • URL: http://www.laserinstitute.org • Formerly Laser Industry Association.

Optical Society of America. 2010 Massachusetts Ave., N.W., Washington, DC 20036-1023. Phone: (202)223-8130 Fax: (202)223-1096 E-mail: info@osa.org • URL: http://www.osa.org.

OTHER SOURCES

Commercial Diode Lasers. Available from MarketResearch.com. • 2001. Price on application. Published by Global Industry Analysts. Provides market research data relating to commercial diode lasers, including market projections to 2005.

Commercial Nondiode Lasers. Available from MarketResearch.com. • 2001. Price on application. Published by Global Industry Analysts. Provides market research data relating to commercial non-diode lasers.

LATHING

See: PLASTER AND PLASTERING

LATIN AMERICAN MARKETS

See also: NORTH AMERICAN FREE TRADE AGREEMENT

GENERAL WORKS

Latin America's Economy: Diversity, Trends, and Conflicts. Eliana Cardoso and Ann Helwege. MIT Press. • 1995. $30.00.

World Trade Issues. Lambert S. Martin, editor. Nova Science Publishers, Inc. • 2002. $69.00. Provides articles by various authors on foreign trade and the influence of globalization, including discussion of the World Trade Organization. Emphasis is on Asian countries and Latin America.

ABSTRACTS AND INDEXES

Business Periodicals Index. H. W. Wilson Co. • 11 times a year. Quarterly and annual cumulations. Price varies.

F & S Index: International. Gale Cengage Learning. • Monthly. $1,450.00 per year, including quarterly and annual cumulations. Provides annotated citations to marketing, business, financial, and industrial literature. Coverage of international business activity includes trade journals, financial magazines,

business newspapers, and special reports. Areas included are Asia, Latin America, Africa, the Middle East, Oceania, and Canada.

Hispanic American Periodicals Index. University of California, Los Angeles. Latin American Studies Center Publications. • Annual. $400.00. Indexes about 250 periodicals that regularly include material on Latin America. Supplement available.

PAIS International in Print. Public Affairs Information Service, Inc. • Monthly. $850.00 per year; cumulations three times a year. Provides topical citations to the worldwide literature of public affairs, economics, demographics, sociology, and trade. Text in English; indexed materials in English, French, German, Italian, Portuguese and Spanish.

ALMANACS AND YEARBOOKS

Emerging Markets Analyst. • Monthly. $895.00 per year. Provides an annual overview of the emerging financial markets in 24 countries of Latin America, Asia, and Europe. Includes data on international mutual funds and closed-end funds.

CD-ROM DATABASES

Hoover's Company Capsules on CD-ROM. Hoover's, Inc. • Quarterly. $399.95 per year (single-user). Provides the CD-ROM version of *Hoover's Handbook of American Business, Hoover's Handbook of Emerging Companies, Hoover's Handbook of World Business, Hoover's Guide to Computer Companies, Hoover's Guide to Media Companies, Hoover's Handbook of Private Companies*, and various regional guides. Includes more than 11,000 profiles of companies.

Latin American Studies, Volume I: Multidisciplinary. National Information Services Corp. • Semiannual. Provides more than 700,000 CD-ROM citations to scholarly literature on a wide variety of Latin American topics, including agriculture, business, demography, economics, government, and politics. Producers are the University of Texas, the University of California, and the Library of Congress.

Latin American Studies, Volume II: Current Affairs and Law. National Information Services Corp. • Semiannual. Contains a wide variety of information on CD-ROM, from various producers, relating to Latin American business, current events, and legislation. Includes periodical citations and abstracts in *INFO-SOUTH*; the full-text newsletters, *Chronicle of Latin American Economic Affairs, Central America Update,* and *SourceMex*; and other databases. Time periods are typically 1986, 1988, or 1990 to date.

PAIS on CD-ROM. Public Affairs Information Service, Inc. • Quarterly. $1,995.00 per year. Provides a CD-ROM version of the online service, *PAIS International.* Contains over 500,000 citations to the literature of contemporary social, political, and economic issues.

WILSONDISC: Wilson Business Abstracts. H. W. Wilson Co. • Monthly. Includes unlimited online access to *Wilson Business Abstracts* through WILSONLINE. Provides CD-ROM "cover-to-cover" abstracting and indexing of over 600 prominent business periodicals. Indexing is from 1982, abstracting from 1990. (*Business Periodicals Index* without abstracts is available on CD-ROM at $1,495 per year.).

World Consumer Markets. Gale Cengage Learning. • Annual. $2,500.00. Pblished by Euromonitor. Provides five- year historical data, current data, and forecasts, on CD-ROM for 330 consumer products in 55 countries. Market data is presented in a standardized format for each country.

World Database of Consumer Brands and Their Owners on CD-ROM. Gale Cengage Learning. • Annual. $3,190.00. Produced by Euromonitor. Provides detailed information on CD-ROM for about 10,000 companies and 80,000 brands around the world. Covers 1,000 product sectors.

World Marketing Forecasts on CD-ROM. Gale Cengage Learning. • Annual. $2,500.00. Produced by Euromonitor. Provides detailed forecast data for the years to 2012 on CD-ROM for 54 countries in all parts of the world. Covers a wide range of social, demographic, economic, and market factors. Includes specific forecasts for many kinds of consumer products.

DIRECTORIES

Brazil Company Handbook: Data on Major Listed Companies. Hoovers, Inc. • Annual. $59.95. Contains profiles of approximately 54 publicly traded companies in Brazil. Includes information on local stock exchanges and the nation's economic situation.

Directory of Consumer Brands and Their Owners: Latin America. Euromonitor International, Business Reference Div. • 1999. $990.00. Provides information about brands available from major Latin American companies. Descriptions of companies are also included.

Global Market Share Planner. Euromonitor International. • 2003. $5,900.00. Six volumes. Second edition. Provides detailed profiles and market share rankings of major consumer product companies in North America, Latin America, Europe, South Africa, and the Asia-Pacific region. Covers firms operating in key consumer markets: beverages, food products, household products, and personal care items. (Volumes are available individually.).

Hoover's Handbook of World Business: Profiles of Major European, Asian, Latin American, and Canadian Companies. Hoover's, Inc. • Annual. $165.00. Contains detailed profiles for approximately 300 large foreign companies. Includes indexes by industry, location, executive name, company name, and brand name.

International Media Guide: Business/Professional Publications: The Americas. SRDS. • Annual. $300.00. Describes trade journals from North, South, and Central America, with advertising rates and circulation data.

Latin American Marketing Information Sourcebook. Euromonitor International. • 2003. $475.00. Lists trade associations, statistical offices, government agencies, special libraries, trade journals, websites, and other sources of business information for the countries of Latin America.

Major Companies of Latin America and the Caribbean 2001. Available from Gale Cengage Learning. • Annual. $850.00. Published by Graham & Whiteside, London. Contains detailed information on 9,000 major companies in Central and South America and the Caribbean. Includes manufacturers, exporters, importers, service companies, and financial institutions.

Major Market Share Companies: The Americas. Available from Gale Cengage Learning. • 2003. $990.00. Second edition. Published by Euromonitor. Provides consumer market share data and rankings for multinational and regional companies. Covers leading firms in the U.S., Canada, Mexico, Brazil, Argentina, Venezuela, and Chile.

Trade Directory of Mexico. Available from Hoovers, Inc. • Annual. $99.95. Published by IMF Editora. Contains profiles of 6,000 Mexican companies involved in foreign trade. Includes profile of Mexico and of the individual states.

Trade Directory of Mexico. Mexican Foreign Trade Bank. • Annual. $100.00. Provides information on more than 6,000 Mexican companies involved in foreign trade. Lists forwarding agencies, customs brokers, consulting groups, transportation companies, and other trade-related Mexican organizations.

Venezuela Company Handbook: Data on Major Listed Companies. Hoovers, Inc. • Annual. $29.95. Published by IMF Editora. Contains profiles of publicly traded companies in Venezuela. Includes information on local stock exchanges and the nation's economic situation. Text in English.

ENCYCLOPEDIAS AND DICTIONARIES

Encyclopedia of Business. Gale Cengage Learning. • 2000. $425.00. Second edition. Two volumes. Contains more than 700 signed articles covering major business disciplines and concepts. International in scope. (Encyclopedia of Business Series).

HANDBOOKS AND MANUALS

Investing and Selling in Latin America. Judith Evans and others. Morning Light Publishing Co. • 1995. $60.00. Consists of one chapter for each of 12 Latin American countries. Covers a wide variety of legal, economic, and practical information relating to doing business in the region.

Mexico Business: The Portable Encyclopedia for Doing Business with Mexico. World Trade Press. • 1994. $24.95. Covers economic data, import/export possibilities, basic tax and trade laws, travel information, and other useful facts for doing business with Mexico. Includes a special section on NAFTA. (Country Business Guides Series).

ONLINE DATABASES

Chronicle of Latin American Economic Affairs [online]. Latin America Data Base. • Contains the complete text online of the weekly newsletter, *Chronicle of Latin American Economic Affairs.* Provides news and analysis of trade and economic developments in Latin America, including Caribbean countries. Time period is 1986 to date, with weekly updates. Inquire as to online cost and availability.

F & S Index. Gale Cengage Learning. • Contains about four million citations to worldwide business, financial, and industrial or consumer product literature appearing from 1972 to date. Weekly updates. Inquire as to online cost and availability.

Globalbase. Gale Cengage Learning. • Provides more than one million online summaries of business, industrial, and economic news reports from more than 1,000 publications worldwide. Covers a wide range of material appearing in international trade journals, professional magazines, and newspapers. Time period is 1984 to date, with weekly updates. Inquire as to online cost and availability.

NotiCen: Central American & Caribbean Affairs. Latin America Data Base. • An online newsletter covering economic, trade, political, and social issues in Central America. Time period is 1986 to date, with weekly updates. Inquire as to online cost and availability. Formerly EcoCentral.

PAIS International. Public Affairs Information Service, Inc. • Corresponds to the former printed publications, *PAIS Bulletin* (1976-90) and *PAIS Foreign Language Index* (1972-90), and to the current *PAIS International in Print* (1991 to date). Covers economic, political, and sociological material appearing in periodicals, books, government documents, and other publications. Updating is monthly. Inquire as to online cost and availability.

PROMT: Predicasts Overview of Markets and Technology. Gale Cengage Learning. • Companies, products, applied technologies and markets. U.S. and international literature coverage, 1972 to date. Inquire as to online cost and availability. Provides abstracts from more than 1,600 publications. Weekly updates.

SourceMex. Latin America Data Base. • An online newsletter covering economic conditions in Mexico, including foreign trade, public finances, foreign debt, agriculture, and the oil industry. Time period is

1990 to date, with weekly updates. Inquire as to online cost and availability.

Wilson Business Abstracts Online. H. W. Wilson Co. • Indexes and abstracts 600 major business periodicals, plus the *Wall Street Journal* and the business section of the *New York Times.* Indexing is from 1982, abstracting from 1990, with the two newspapers included from 1993. Updated weekly. Inquire as to online cost and availability. (*Business Periodicals Index* without abstracts is also available online.).

PERIODICALS AND NEWSLETTERS

Business Latin America: Weekly Report to Managers of Latin American Operations. Economist Intelligence Unit. • Weekly. $1,250.00 per year. Newsletter covering Latin American business trends, politics, regulations, exchange rates, economics, and finance. Provides statistical data on foreign debt, taxes, labor costs, gross domestic product (GDP), and inflation rates.

Business Week International: The World's Only International Newsweekly of Business. McGraw-Hill. • Weekly. $95.00 per year.

Caribbean Business. Casiano Communications. • Weekly. $45.00 per year. Text in English.

Economic and Social Progress in Latin America. Inter-American Development Bank. • Monthly. $24.95 per year. Covers developments in Latin America affecting business and trade. Text in Spanish.

Emerging Markets Quarterly. Institutional Investor, Inc., Journals Group. • Quarterly. Price on application. Newsletter on financial markets in developing areas, such as Africa, Latin America, Southeast Asia, and Eastern Europe. Topics include institutional investment opportunities and regulatory matters. Formerly *Emerging Markets Weekly.*

Institutional Investor International Edition: The Magazine for International Finance and Investment. Institutional Investor, Inc., Journals Group. • Monthly. $475.00 per year. Covers the international aspects of professional investing and finance. Emphasis is on Europe, the Far East, and Latin America.

International Economic Scoreboard. The Conference Board Inc. • Description: Provides current data on the business outlook in 11 major industrial countries: Australia, Canada, France, West Germany, Italy, Japan, Korea, New Zealand, Taiwan, the United Kingdom, and the U.S. **Remarks:** A source for additional information on this indicator system and its uses is available at the Center for International Business Cycle Research, Columbia University Business School.

Latin American Business Review. Monterrey Institute of Technology. kGraduate School of Business Administration and Leadership. Haworth Press, Inc. • Quarterly. Institutions, $200.00 per year.

Latin Fund Management. Thomson Media. • Monthly. $495.00 per year. Newsletter (also available online at www.latinfund.net). Provides news and analysis of Latin American mutual funds, pension funds, and annuities.

Latin Trade: Your Business Source for Latin America. Freedom Publications, Inc. • Monthly. $36.00 per year. English and Spanish editions. Covers various aspects of Latin American business and trade, including economic indicators, export-import, finance, commodity news, company profiles, and political developments. Formerly *U.S.-Latin Trade.*

LatinFinance. Latin American Financial Publications, Inc. • 10 times a year. $235.00 per year. Includes print and online editions. Covers finance, investment, venture capital, and banking in Latin America.

Market: Latin America. The PRS Group, Inc. • Monthly. $397.00 per year ($198.00 to academic institutions). Newsletter. Provides market trend information and demographic data for Latin American countries. Includes sales trend projections for various products and services, with consumer household buying patterns and industrial expenditures. Formerly published by Market Newsletters.

Twin Plant News: The Magazine of the Maquiladora Industry. Nibbe, Hernandez and Associates, Inc. • Monthly. $85.00 per year. Focuses on Mexican labor laws, taxes, economics, industrial trends, and culture. Industries featured include electronic components, plastics, automotive supplies, metals, communications, and packaging.

Vision: Revista Latinoamericana. Vision, Inc. • Semimonthly. $124.00 per year. A popular newsmagazine covering Latin American politics, economics, business, and culture. Text in Spanish.

RESEARCH CENTERS AND INSTITUTES

Center for Latin American Studies. University of Chicago, 5848 S. University Ave., K308, Chicago, IL 60637. Phone: (773)702-8420 Fax: (773)702-1755 E-mail: clas@uchicago.edu • URL: http://www.clas.uchicago.edu • Includes economic inquiry on Latin America.

International Studies and Overseas Programs-Latin American Center, University of California, Los Angeles. 10343 Bunche Hall, Los Angeles, CA 90095-1447. Phone: (310)825-4571 Fax: (310)206-6859 E-mail: nmoss@isop.ucla.edu • URL: http://www.isop.ucla.edu/lac.

Latin American and Caribbean Center-Intercultural Dance and Music Institute. Florida International University, University Park, DM 353, Miami, FL 33199. Phone: (305)348-2894 Fax: (305)348-3593 E-mail: seidel@fiu.edu • URL: http://www.lacc.fiu.edu • Research fields include economic development and trade.

STATISTICS SOURCES

Consumer International. Available from Gale Cengage Learning. • Annual. $1,290.00. Published by Euromonitor. Contains extensive consumer market, economic, and demographic data for 25 major, non-European countries, including the U. S. and Canada. Includes consumer market size (volume and value) for 150 product types in 14 categories (food, clothing, automobiles, cosmetics, appliances, etc.).

Consumer Latin America. Available from Gale Cengage Learning. • Annual. $1,090.00. Published by Euromonitor. Contains a wide variety of consumer market data relating to the countries of Latin America. Includes market forecasts.

Economic and Social Progress in Latin America Report. Inter-American Development Bank. • Annual. $24.95. Includes surveys of economic conditions in individual Latin American countries. Text in English.

Economic Survey of Latin America and the Caribbean. United Nations Publications. • Annual. $50.00. Includes reports on economic trends in 20 Latin American countries.

Emerging Stock Markets Factbook 1999. International Finance Corp. • 1998. $150.00. Provides statistical profiles for emerging stock markets in various countries of the world. Includes regional, composite, and industry indexes.

Gale Country and World Rankings Reporter. Gale Cengage Learning. • 1997. $160.00. Second edition. Provides about 3,000 statistical ranking tables and charts covering more than 235 nations. Sources include the United Nations and various government publications.

International Marketing Forecasts. Available from Gale Cengage Learning. • Annual. $1,250.00. Published by Euromonitor. Contains demographic, economic, and market forecasts to the year 2013 for major, non-European countries, including the U. S.

and Canada. Forecasts include market-size data for 15 consumer product sectors, such as food, clothing, and automobiles.

Latin America in Graphs 1994-95: Demographic and Economic Trends. Inter-American Development Bank. • 1995. $8.00.

Latin American Market Data and Statistics. Euromonitor International. • 2003. $430.00. Provides demographic, economic, and lifestyle statistics for 43 Latin American countries.

Retail Trade International. Gale Cengage Learning. • 2002. $1,990.00. 11th edition. Eight volumes. Published by Euromonitor. Presents comprehensive data on retail trends in 52 countries. Includes textual analysis and profiles of major retailers. Covers Europe, Asia, the Middle East, Africa and the Americas.

Statistical Abstract of Latin America. University of California, Los Angeles. • Annual. $325.00. Two volumes.

Statistical Yearbook for Latin America and the Caribbean. Available from United Nations Publications. • Annual. $79.00. Issued by the Economic Commission for Latin America and the Caribbean. Includes a wide variety of economic, industrial, and trade data for Latin American nations. Text in English and Spanish.

TRADE/PROFESSIONAL ASSOCIATIONS

The Americas Society--Council of the Americas. 680 Park Ave., New York, NY 10021. Phone: (212)628-3200 Fax: (212)249-1880 E-mail: inforequest@as-coa.org • URL: http://www.americas-society.org • Members are U. S. corporations with business interests in Latin America. Formerly Council of the Americas.

Association of American Chambers of Commerce in Latin America. 1615 H St., N.W., Washington, DC 20062. Phone: (202)463-5485 Fax: (202)463-3126 E-mail: inbox@aaccla.org • URL: http://www.aaccla.org • Umbrella organization for American chambers of commerce in Latin America. Affiliated with U.S. Chamber of Commerce.

Brazilian-American Chamber of Commerce. 509 W. Madison Ave., Suite 304, New York, NY 10022. Phone: (212)751-4691 Fax: (212)751-7692 E-mail: info@brazilcham.com • URL: http://www.brazilcham.com • Promotes trade between Brazil and the U. S.

Brazilian Trade Bureau of the Consulate General of Brazil in New York. 1185 Avenue of the Americas, 21st Fl., New York, NY 10036. Phone: (917)777-7777 Fax: (212)827-0225 E-mail: trade@brazilny.org • URL: http://www.braziltradeny.com • Offers assistance to American firms wishing to purchase Brazilian products, and promotes Brazilian firms and their exports. Formerly Brazilian Government Trade Bureau.

Colombian American Association. 30 Vesey St., Ste. 506, New York, NY 10007. Phone: (212)233-7776 Fax: (212)233-7779 E-mail: andean@nyct.net • URL: http://www.colombianamerican.org • Facilitates commerce and trade between the Republic of Colombia and the U.S. Fosters and advances cultural relations and goodwill between the two nations. Encourages sound investments in Colombia by Americans and in the U.S. by Colombians. Disseminates information in the U.S. concerning Colombia.

Coltrade: Colombian Government Trade Bureau. 1901 L St. NW, Ste. 700, Washington, DC 20036. Phone: (202)887-9000 Fax: (202)223-0526 E-mail: coltrade@coltrade.org • URL: http://www.coltrade.org • Promotes Colombian exports to the U. S.

Inter-American Development Bank. 1300 New York Ave. NW, Washington, DC 20577. Phone: (202)623-1000 Fax: (202)623-3096 E-mail: webmaster@iadb.org • URL: http://www.iadb.org • Western

Hemisphere countries; other interested countries. Seeks to help accelerate the economic and social development of members in Latin America and the Caribbean. Works to: promote the investment of public and private capital in the region; use its own capital, as well as funds raised in financial markets and other available resources, for financing high-priority projects; supplement private investment when capital is not available on reasonable terms and conditions; encourage members to direct their policies toward better use of their natural resources while fostering growth of their foreign trade and development of complementary economies in Latin America; provide technical cooperation for the preparation, financing, and execution of development plans and projects, including the study of priorities and formulation of specific project proposals; contribute to the strengthening of the institutional base of lesser-developed member countries. Fosters equitable distribution of benefits of development. Sponsors projects which alleviate poverty, expand agricultural production, finance energy projects, promote modernization, develop industry, urban renewal, and health and education, and improve development institutions. Operates Fund for Special Operations, which is used to make long-term, low-interest loans to less-developed Latin American countries and a microenterprise division, which provides financing and technical support to low-income individuals and groups who ordinarily do not have access to public or commercial credit. Also administers the Venezuelan +Trust Fund and the Social Progress +Trust Fund. Cooperates with other development and financial institutions with similar goals. Offers technical training and seminars. Operates Speakers' Bureau.

United States-Mexico Chamber of Commerce. 1300 Pennsylvania Ave., Suite 270, Washington, DC 20004-3021. Phone: 800-876-2624 or (202)371-8680 Fax: (202)371-8686 E-mail: news-hq@usmc.org • URL: http://www.usmoc.org • Works to promote trade and investment between the U. S. and Mexico.

Venezuelan American Association of the United States. 30 Vesey St., Rm. 506, New York, NY 10007. Phone: (212)233-7776 Fax: (212)233-7779 E-mail: andean@nyct.net • URL: http://www.venezuelanamerican.org • Facilitates trade and investment between the U.S. and Venezuela. Formerly Venezuelan Chamber of Commerce of the United States.

OTHER SOURCES

Investing in Latin America: Best Stocks, Best Funds. Michael Molinski and Constance Anderson. Bloomberg. • 1999. $24.95. Provides Latin American stock and mutual fund recommendations for individual investors. (Bloomberg Personal Bookshelf Series).

Latin America and the Caribbean in the World Economy. United Nations Publications. • 1999. $25.00. Discusses trade policy, trade activity, regional integration, and environmental protection issues.

Latin American Market Planning Report. Available from MarketResearch.com. • 2000. $750.00. Market research report published by Strategy Research Corporation. Provides results of U. S. Hispanic Market Study covering demographics, product usage, media usage, public opinion issues, and other items.

LAUNDRY INDUSTRY

See also: CLEANING INDUSTRY

ABSTRACTS AND INDEXES

Textile Technology Digest. Institute of Textile Technology. • Annual. $535.00. Provides indexing and abstracting of a wide variety of textile technology literature.

CD-ROM DATABASES

Textile Technology Digest [CD-ROM]. Textile Information Center, Institute of Textile Technology. • Quarterly. Provides CD-ROM indexing and abstracting of worldwide journals and monographs in various areas of textile technology, production, and management. Covers 1978 to date.

DIRECTORIES

Coin Laundry Association Supplier Directory. Coin Laundry Association. • Covers: about 500 manufacturers and suppliers of products and services to the coin laundry and dry cleaning industries. Entries include: Name of firm, address, phone, e-mail, URL, products or services; distributors show area served.

ENCYCLOPEDIAS AND DICTIONARIES

Textile Terms and Definitions. J.E. McIntyre and Paul N. Daniels, editors. Available from State Mutual Book and Periodical Service Ltd. • 1996. $180.00. 10th edition. Published by the Textile Insitute (UK). Includes more than 1,000 definitions of textile processes, fiber types, and end products. Illustrated.

FINANCIAL RATIOS

Annual Statement Studies. The Risk Management Association. • Annual. Median and quartile financial ratios are given for over 400 kinds of manufacturing, wholesale, retail, construction, and consumer finance establishments. Data is sorted by both asset size and sales volume. Includes a clearly written "Definition of Ratios" and an alphabetical industry index.

Annual Statement Studies: Industry Default Probabilities and Cash Flow Measures. The Risk Management Association. • Annual. $145.00. Serves as a companion volume to the original *Annual Statement Studies.* Gives probability of default estimates on a percentage scale for more than 450 industries. Includes changes in position year-by-year for eight financial statement line items and provides percentage measures of cash flow.

HANDBOOKS AND MANUALS

Diaper Delivery Service. Entrepreneur Media, Inc. • Looseleaf. $59.50. A practical guide to starting a service for the laundering and delivery of all-cotton diapers. Covers profit potential, start-up costs, market size evaluation, owner's time required, site selection, pricing, accounting, advertising, promotion, etc. (Start-Up Business Guide No. E1364.).

Laundromat. Entrepreneur Media, Inc. • Looseleaf. $59.50. A practical guide to starting a coin-operated, self-service laundry business. Covers profit potential, start-up costs, market size evaluation, owner's time required, site selection, lease negotiation, pricing, accounting, advertising, promotion, etc. (Start-Up Business Guide No. E1162.).

ONLINE DATABASES

Textile Technology Digest [online]. Institute of Textile Technology. • Contains indexing and abstracting of more than 300 worldwide journals and monographs in various areas of textile technology, production, and management. Time period is 1978 to date, with monthly updating. Inquire as to online cost and availability.

PERIODICALS AND NEWSLETTERS

American Coin-Op: The Magazine for Coin-Operated Laundry and Drycleaning Businessmen. Crain Communications, Inc. • Monthly. Free.

American Laundry News. Crain Communications, Inc. • Monthly. Free. Formerly *Laundry News.*

Journal of the Coin Laundry and Drycleaning Industry. Coin Laundry Association. • Monthly.

$24.00 per year. Edited for owners and operators of coinoperated laundries.

TRADE/PROFESSIONAL ASSOCIATIONS

Coin Laundry Association. 1315 Butterfield Rd., Ste. 212, Downers Grove, IL 60515. Phone: 877-CLA-IDEA or (630)963-5547 Fax: (630)963-5864 E-mail: info@coinlaundry.org • URL: http://www.coinlaundry.org • Manufacturers of equipment or supplies used in self-service (coin-operated) laundry or dry cleaning establishments; distributors of equipment services and supplies; owners and operators of self-service laundry and/or dry cleaning stores. Compiles statistics.

International Fabricare Institute. 14700 Sweitzer Ln., Laurel, MD 20707. Phone: 800-638-2627 or (301)622-1900 Fax: (240)295-0685 E-mail: techline@ifi.org • URL: http://www.ifi.org • Retail and industrial drycleaners, hospital laundries, linen supply and drapery services, distributors and manufacturers of supplies and machinery, dry-cleaning and laundry associations, and individual launders in 43 countries. Provides washability and dry-cleanability testing for manufacturers of fabrics and related products; offers quality testing and consulting services; conducts research for members. Organizes courses in dry-cleaning, laundering, management, and maintenance. Maintains consulting service, speakers' bureau, research facilities, and library.

Multi-Housing Laundry Association. 1500 Sunday Dr., Ste. 102, Raleigh, NC 27607. Phone: 800-380-3652 or (919)861-5579 Fax: (919)787-4916 E-mail: nshore@mla-online.com • URL: http://www.mla-online.com • Operating and supplier companies. Strives to provide tenants with professionally operated laundry facilities. Sponsors annual convention and trade show.

National Association of Institutional Linen Management. 2130 Lexington Rd., Suite H, Richmond, KY 40475. Phone: 800-669-0863 or (859)624-0177 Fax: (859)624-3580 E-mail: linda@nlmnet.org • URL: http://www.nlmnet.org • Formerly National Assoiciation of Institutional Laundry Managers.

Textile Care Allied Trades Association. 271 Rte. 46 W, No. D203, Fairfield, NJ 07004. Phone: (973)244-1790 Fax: (973)244-4455 E-mail: info@tcata.org • URL: http://www.tcata.org • Represents Manufacturers and distributors of laundry and dry-cleaning machinery, and supplies.

Textile Institute. St. James's Buildings, 1st Fl., 79 Oxford St., Manchester M1 6FQ, United Kingdom. Phone: 44 161 2371188 Fax: 44 161 2361991 E-mail: tiihq@textileinst.org.uk • URL: http://www.texi.org • Companies and individuals in 100 countries involved in management, science, technology, design, information transfer, and marketing of textiles including clothing and footwear. Promotes interests of the textile industry worldwide; serves professional interests of members; confers qualifications and recognizes achievements in research, application of ideas, education, business, and public affairs. Maintains Information Service to collect information relating to textile industrial and economic conditions in different countries and economic sectors.

Uniform and Textile Service Association. 1300 N. 17th St., Suite 750, Arlington, VA 22209. Phone: (703)247-2600 Fax: (703)841-4750 E-mail: info@utsa.com • URL: http://www.utsa.com • Formerly Institute of Industrial Launderers.

LAW

GENERAL WORKS

Introduction to Law and the Legal System. Frank A. Schubert. Houghton Mifflin Co. • 2000. Seventh edition. Price on application.

Law of the Super Searchers: The Online Secrets of Top Legal Researchers. T. R. Halvorson. Information Today, Inc. • 1999. $24.95. Eight law researchers explain how to find useful legal information online. (Super Searchers Series).

ABSTRACTS AND INDEXES

Current Law Index: Multiple Access to Legal Periodicals. Gale Cengage Learning. • Monthly. $725.00 per year. Produced in cooperation with the American Association of Law Libraries. Indexes more than 900 law journals, legal newspapers, and specialty publications from the U.S., Canada, U.K., Ireland, Australia, and New Zealand.

Index to Foreign Legal Periodicals. American Association of Law Libraries. University of California Press, Journals Div. • Quarterly. $725.00 per year. Annual cumulation.

Index to Legal Periodicals and Books. H. W. Wilson Co. • Monthly. $490.00 per year. Quarterly and annual cumulations.

Index to Periodical Articles Related to Law. Glanville Publishers, Inc. • Quarterly. $95.00 per year. Selected from journals not included in the *Index to Legal Periodicals, Current Law Index, Index to Foreign Legal Periodicals, Legal Resolve Index or Legaltrac.*

ALMANACS AND YEARBOOKS

American Law Yearbook. Gale Cengage Learning. • Annual. $165.00. Serves as a yearly supplement to *West's Encyclopedia of American Law.* Describes new legal developments in many subject areas.

BIBLIOGRAPHIES

Bibliographic Guide to Law. Available from Gale Cengage Learning. • Annual. $575.00. Two volumes. Published by G. K. Hall & Co. Lists legal publications cataloged by the New York Public Library and the Library of Congress.

Criminal Justice Information: How to Find It, How to Use It. Dennis C. Benamati and others. Greenwood Publishing Group, Inc. • 1997. $64.95. A guide to print, electronic, and online criminal justice information resources. Includes statistical reports, directories, periodicals, monographs, databases, and other sources.

Encyclopedia of Legal Information Sources. Gale Cengage Learning. • 1992. $180.00. Second edition. Lists more than 23,000 law-related information sources, including print, nonprint, and organizational.

Law Books in Print: Law Books in English Published Throughout the World. Glanville Publishers, Inc. • Triennial. $750.00.

Legal Information: How to Find It, How to Use It. Kent Olson. Greenwood Publishing Group, Inc. • 1998. $64.95. Includes CD-ROM. Recommends sources for various kinds of legal information.

Pimsleur's Checklists of Basic American Legal Publications. American Association of Law Libraries. Fred B. Rothman and Co. • Irregular. $265.00. Looseleaf service.

CD-ROM DATABASES

LegalTrac. Gale Cengage Learning. • Monthly. $5,000.00 per year. Price includes workstation. Provides CD-ROM indexing of periodical literature relating to legal matters from 1980 to date. Corresponds to online *Legal Resource Index.*

WILSONDISC: Index to Legal Periodicals and Books. H. W. Wilson Co. • Monthly. Includes unlimited online access to *Index to Legal Periodicals* through WILSONLINE. Contains CD-ROM indexing of more than 1,400 English language legal periodicals from 1981 to date and 2,500 books.

DIRECTORIES

Essential Guide to the Best (and Worst) Legal Sites on the Web. Robert J. Ambrogi. American Lawyer

Media, Inc. • 2001. $34.95. Sites are classified according to 25 legal subject areas and assigned 1-to-5 star ratings.

Internet Tools of the Profession: A Guide for Information Professionals. Hope N. Tillman, editor. Special Libraries Association. • 1997. $49.00. Second edition. Consists of 14 sections by various authors or compilers. After two introductory articles on searching the Internet, there are 12 annotated lists of useful Web sites, covering the SLA, business and finance, chemistry, education, food and agriculture, information technology, insurance and employee benefits, law, library management, metals and materials, pharmaceuticals, and telecommunications. An index is provided.

Law and Legal Information Directory. Gale Cengage Learning. • Annual. $440.00. Contains a wide range of sources of legal information, such as associations, law schools, courts, federal agencies, referral services, libraries, publishers, and research centers. There is a separate chapter for each of 23 types of information source or service.

Peterson's Graduate and Professional Programs: Business, Education, Health, Information Studies, Law, and Social Work. Peterson's. • 2002. $49.95. Provides details of graduate and professional programs in business, law, information, and other fields at colleges and universities. (Peterson's Graduate and Professional Program Series). Formerly *Peterson's Guide to Graduate Programs in Business, Education, Health, Information Studies, Law and Social Work.*

ENCYCLOPEDIAS AND DICTIONARIES

Black's Law Dictionary. Bryan A. Garner, editor. West Group. • 1999. $59.95. Seventh edition. Contains a total of 30,000 legal definitions, including 4,500 new terms, 2,200 legal maxims, and 2,000 illustrative quotations from scholarly works.

Black's Law Dictionary. Thomas Black, editor. Kluwer Law International. • 2001. $147.00. Seventh edition. Definitions of the terms and phrases of American and English jurisprudence, ancient and modern.

Communicating with Legal Databases: Terms and Abbreviations for the Legal Researcher. Anne L. McDonald. Neal-Schuman Publishers, Inc. • 1987. $82.50.

Encyclopedia of Crime and Justice. Available from Gale Cengage Learning. • 2001. $475.00. Second edition. Four volumes. Published by Macmillan Reference USA. Contains extensive information on a wide variety of topics pertaining to crime, criminology, social issues, and the courts. (A complete revision of 1982 edition.).

Encyclopedia of Crime and Punishment. David Levinson, editor. Sage Publications, Inc. • 2002. $600.00. Four volumes. Contains 425 signed entries dealing with civil, criminal, media, corporate, and international issues. Includes material on fraud, police science, correctional institutions, social matters, methodology, national surveys, and crime statistics.

Law Dictionary for Non-Lawyers. Daniel Oran. Delmar Learning. • 1999. $31.95. Fourth edition.

Legal Thesaurus-Dictionary. William P. Statsky. West Publishing Co., College and School Div. • 1985. $37.75. Second edition.

World of Criminal Justice. Gale Cengage Learning. • 2002. $160.00. Two volumes. Contains both topical and biographical entries relating to the criminal justice system and criminology.

HANDBOOKS AND MANUALS

Indexing Specialties: Law. Peter Kendrick and Enid L. Zafran, editors. Information Today, Inc. • 2001. $35.00. Published in conjunction with the American Society of Indexers (ASI). Includes chapters by professional legal indexers on legal cases, statutory

materials, new methodologies, careers in legal indexing, and related topics.

Restatement of the Law. American Law Institute-American Bar Association Committee on Continuing Professional Education. • Multivolume set. Periodic supplementation. Price varies. Statements of the common law-an overview, clarification, and simplification of American law.

INTERNET DATABASES

Law.com: First in Legal News and Information. American Lawyer Media, Inc. Phone: 800-888-8300 or (212)779-9200 Fax: (212)481-8110 • URL: http://www.law.com • Web site provides free, law-related, current news (National News Sites and Regional News Sites). Free searching of martindale.com lawyer locator is offered, including lawyer ratings. Fee-based premium services for the legal profession are also available.

Lexis.com Research System. Lexis-Nexis Group. Phone: 800-227-4908 or (937)865-6800 Fax: (937)865-6909 E-mail: webmaster@prod.lexis-nexis.com • URL: http://www.lexis.com • Fee-based Web site offers extensive searching of a wide variety of legal sources. Additional features include Daily Opinion Service, lexis.com Bookstore, Career Center, CLE Center, Law Schools, and Practice Pages ("Pages specific to areas of specialty").

ONLINE DATABASES

Index to Legal Periodicals and Books (Online). H. W. Wilson Co. • Broad coverage of law journals and books 1981 to date. Monthly updates. Inquire as to online cost and availability.

Legal Resource Index. Gale Cengage Learning. • Broad coverage of law literature appearing in legal, business, and other periodicals, 1980 to date. Daily updates. Inquire as to online cost and availability.

PERIODICALS AND NEWSLETTERS

American Journal of Comparative Law. University of California, Berkeley. • Quarterly. $30.00 per year.

Harvard Law Review. Harvard Law Review Association. • Eight times a year. $45.00 per year.

Journal of Internet Law. Aspen Publishers, Inc. • Monthly. $360.00 per year. Covers such Internet and e-commerce topics as domain name disputes, copyright protection, Uniform Commercial Code issues, international law, privacy regulation, electronic records, digital signatures, liability, and security.

Law and Contemporary Problems. Duke University, School of Law. • Quarterly. $48.00 per year.

Legal Information Alert: What's New in Legal Publications, Databases, and Research Techniques. Donna T. Heroy, editor. Alert Publications, Inc. • 10 times per year. $179.00 per year. Newsletter for law librarians and legal information specialists.

Legal Reference Services Quarterly. Haworth Press, Inc. • Quarterly. Institutions, $225.00 per year.

Legal Times. American Lawyer Media, L.P. • Weekly. Individuals, $249.00 per year; institutions, $635.00 per year.

National Law Journal: The Weekly Newspaper for the Profession. American Lawyer Media Inc. • Weekly. $158.00 per year. News and analysis of the latest developments in the law and the law profession.

United States Law Week: A National Survey of Current Law. BNA, Inc. • Weekly. $1,152.00 per year. Covers U.S. Supreme Court proceedings and gives full text of decisions. Also provides detailed reports on important legislative and regulatory actions.

Yale Law Journal. Yale Journal Co., Inc. • Eight times a year. $40.00 per year.

RESEARCH CENTERS AND INSTITUTES

Center for the Study of Law, Science, and Technology. Arizona State University, College of

Law, P.O. Box 877906, Tempe, AZ 85287-7906. Phone: (480)965-2554 Fax: (480)965-2427 E-mail: gary.marchant@asu.edu • URL: http://www.law.asu.edu • Studies the legal problems created by technological advances.

Morin Center for Banking and Financial Law. Boston University, School of Law, 765 Commonwealth Ave., Boston, MA 02215. Phone: (617)353-3023 Fax: (617)353-2444 E-mail: banklaw@bu.edu • URL: http://www.web.bu.edu/law • Research fields include banking law, regulation of depository institutions, and deposit insurance.

STATISTICS SOURCES

Statistics on Crime, Justice, and Punishment. Gale Cengage Learning. • 1996. $850.00. Volume three. Includes graphs, charts, and tables arranged within subject chapters. Citations to data sources are provided. (Statistics on...Series: vol. 3).

TRADE/PROFESSIONAL ASSOCIATIONS

American Bar Association. 321 N Clark St., Chicago, IL 60610. Phone: 800-285-2221 or (312)988-5000 Fax: (312)988-5522 E-mail: askaba@abanet.org • URL: http://www.abanet.org • Attorneys in good standing of the bar of any state. Conducts research and educational projects and activities to: encourage professional improvement; provide public services; improve the administration of civil and criminal justice; increase the availability of legal services to the public. Sponsors Law Day USA. Administers numerous standing and special committees such as Committee on +Soviet and +East +European +Law, providing seminars and newsletters. Operates 25 sections, including Criminal Justice, Economics of Law Practice, and Family Law. Sponsors essay competitions. Maintains library.

American Law Institute. 4025 Chestnut St., Philadelphia, PA 19104-3099. Phone: 800-253-6397 or (215)243-1600 Fax: (215)243-1636 E-mail: ali@ali.org • URL: http://www.ali.org • Judges, law teachers, and lawyers. Promotes the clarification and simplification of the law and its better adaptation to social needs by continuing work on the Restatement of the Law, model and uniform codes, and model statutes. Conducts a program of continuing legal education jointly with the American Bar Association called "ALI-ABA" (see separate entry).

American Society of Comparative Law. Williamette University, College of Law, c/o Dr. David S. Clark, 245 Winter SE, Salem, OR 97301. Phone: (503)370-6403 Fax: (503)370-6375 E-mail: symeon@williamette.edu • URL: http://www.comparativelaw.org.

Practising Law Institute. 810 7th Ave., New York, NY 10019-5818. Phone: 800-260-4754 or (212)824-5710 Fax: (212)581-4670 E-mail: info@pli.edu • URL: http://www.pli.edu • Provides through publications, videotapes, forums, and live and on-line seminars, training for lawyers throughout the country in new developments in the law and new legal techniques. Presents over 250 seminars annually.

LAW, BUSINESS

See: BUSINESS LAW

LAW, COMPUTER

See: COMPUTER LAW

LAW ENFORCEMENT INDUSTRIES

See also: CRIME AND CRIMINALS

DIRECTORIES

Directory of Juvenile and Adult Correctional Departments, Institutions, Agencies, Parole Authori-

ties, and Probation. American Correctional Association. • Annual. $90.00. Provides information on more than 4,000 correctional agencies and institutions in the U. S. and Canada. Formerly *Directory of Juvenile and Adult Correctional Agencies of the United States and Canada.*

Jane's Police and Security Equipment: The Complete Source on Worldwide Law Enforcement Equipment. Jane's Information Group. • Annual. $557.00; CD-ROM edition, $1,370.00; online edition, $1,478.00. Provides information on sources of more than 2,000 items of law enforcement equipment. Covers traffic control, riot control, communications, personal protection, surveillance, and other equipment categories. Includes detailed product descriptions.

Law and Order Magazine Police Equipment Buyer's Guide. Hendon, Inc. • Annual. $15.00. Lists manufacturers, dealers, and distributors of equipment and services for police departments.

Law Enforcement Technology Directory. Cygnus Business Media, Inc. • Annual. $60.00 per year. $6.00 per issue; a directory of products, equipment, services, and technology for police professionals. Includes weapons, uniforms, communications equipment, and software.

National Directory of Law Enforcement Administrators, Correctional Institutio ns and Related Agencies. National Public Safety Information Bureau. • Annual. $129.00. Lists a wide variety of law enforcement administrators and institutions, including city police departments, sheriffs, prosecutors, state agencies, federal agencies, correctional institutions, college campus police departments, airport police, and harbor police. Formerly *National Directory of Law Enforcement Administrators and Correctional Institutions.*

Police: Buyer's Guide. Bobit Publications. • Annual. $3.00. Lists suppliers of products and services for police departments.

Police Chief: Buyer's Guide. Bobit Publishing. • Annual. $3.00. Contains a list of suppliers of equipment and services for police departments.

ENCYCLOPEDIAS AND DICTIONARIES

Encyclopedia of American Prisons. Carl Sifakis. Facts on File Inc. • 2002. $75.00. Crime Library.

Encyclopedia of Crime and Punishment. David Levinson, editor. Sage Publications, Inc. • 2002. $600.00. Four volumes. Contains 425 signed entries dealing with civil, criminal, media, corporate, and international issues. Includes material on fraud, police science, correctional institutions, social matters, methodology, national surveys, and crime statistics.

Encyclopedia of Law Enforcement. Larry E. Sullivan, editor. Sage Publications, Inc. • 2004. $295.00. Two volumes. Contains more than 400 entries by 250 contributors. Covers a wide variety of topics relating to local, state, federal, and international law enforcement and investigation.

Encyelopedia of Prisons and Correctional Facilities. Mary Bosworth, editor. Sage Publications, Inc. • 2004. $295.00. Two volumes. Contains 400 entries by various "recognized authorities." Appendix includes detailed information about every federal prison in the U.S.

PERIODICALS AND NEWSLETTERS

Correctional News. Emlen Publications, Inc. • Bimonthly. Free to qualified personnel. Only available online.

Corrections Today. American Correctional Association. • Bimonthly. Free to members; nonmembers, $35.00 per year. Includes "Annual Architecture, Construction, and Design Issue" on prisons and other correctional facilities.

Law and Order Magazine: The Magazine for Police Management. Hendon Publishing Co. • Monthly.

$24.95 per year. Edited for law enforcement officials. Includes special issues on communications, technology, weapons, and uniforms and equipment.

Law Enforcement Product News. General Communications, Inc. • Bimonthly. Free. Covers new products and equipment for police departments and other law enforcement and correctional agencies.

Law Enforcement Technology. Cygnus Business Media. • Monthly. $60.00 per year. Covers new products and technologies for police professionals. Includes special issues on weapons, uniforms, communications equipment, computers (hardware-software), vehicles, and enforcement of drug laws.

9-1-1 Magazine: Public Safety Communications and Response. Official Publications, Inc. • Bimonthly. $29.95 per year. Covers technical information and applications for public safety communications personnel.

Police Chief: Professional Voice of Law Enforcement. International Association of Chiefs of Police. • Monthly. $25.00 per year. Subject matter includes information on law enforcement technology and new products.

Police Science and Technology Review. Jane's Information Group. • Quarterly. $57.00 per year. Includes detailed information on technology relating to surveillance, forensics, and fingerprints.

Police: The Law Officer's Magazine. Bobit Publications. • Monthly. $25.00 per year. Edited for law enforcement professionals. Includes information on new technology and equipment.

RESEARCH CENTERS AND INSTITUTES

Municipal Technical Advisory Service Library. University of Tennessee, Knoxville, Conference Center Bldg., 600 Henley St., Ste. 120, Knoxville, TN 37996-4105. Phone: (865)974-0411 Fax: (865)974-0423 E-mail: schwartzr@tennessee.edu • URL: http://www.mtas.utk.edu/library • Research areas include municipal finance, police administration, and public works.

Police Executive Research Forum. Police Executive Research Forum. 1120 Connecticut Ave. NW, Ste. 930, Washington, DC 20036. Phone: 877-576-5423 or (202)466-7820 Fax: (202)466-7826 E-mail: cwexler@policeforum.org • URL: http://www. policeforum.org • Policing, including studies on community policing, operational and administrative procedures, police management, police response strategies, criminal investigations, drug abuse and enforcement, problem-oriented policing.

STATISTICS SOURCES

Crime in America's Top-Rated Cities: A Statistical Profile. Grey House Publishing. • 2000. $155.00. Third edition. Contains 20-year data for major crime categories in 76 cities, suburbs, metropolitan areas, and the U. S. Also includes statistics on correctional facilities, inmates, hate crimes, illegal drugs, and other crime-related matters.

Sourcebook of Criminal Justice Statistics. Available from U. S. Government Printing Office. • Annual. $56.00. Issued by the Bureau of Justice Statistics, U. S. Department of Justice (http://www.usdoj.gov/bjs). Contains both crime data and corrections statistics.

TRADE/PROFESSIONAL ASSOCIATIONS

American Correctional Association. 206 N Washington St., Ste. 200, Alexandria, VA 22314. Phone: 800-222-5646 or (301)918-1800 Fax: (301)918-0557 E-mail: execoffice@aca.org • URL: http://www.aca.org • Correctional administrators, wardens, superintendents, members of prison and parole boards, probation officers, psychologists, educators, sociologists, and other individuals; institutions and associations involved in the correctional field. Promotes improved correctional standards, including selection of personnel, care,

supervision, education, training, employment, treatment, and post-release adjustment of inmates. Studies causes of crime and juvenile delinquency and methods of crime control and prevention through grants and contracts. Compiles statistics. Conducts research programs and training of correctional professionals. Offers accreditation of institutions and certification for correctional executive, manager, supervisor, and officer.

International Association of Chiefs of Police (IACP). 515 N. Washington St., Alexandria, VA 22314. Phone: 800-843-4227 or (703)836-6767 Fax: (703)836-4543 E-mail: information@theiacp.org • URL: http://www.theiacp.org • The IACP Law Enforcement Information Management Section is concerned with law enforcement management information systems, including data processing, telecommunications, and automated systems. Formerly Chiefs of Police of the United States and Canada.

International Security Management Association. PO Box 623, Buffalo, IA 52728. Phone: 800-368-1894 or (563)381-4008 Fax: 800-568-1894 or (563)381-4283 E-mail: isma3@aol.com • URL: http://www. ismanet.com • Senior security executives of multinational business firms and chief executive officers of full service security services companies. Aims to assist senior security executives in coordinating and exchanging information about security management and to establish high business and professional standards.

National Correctional Industries Association. 1202 N Charles St., Baltimore, MD 21201. Phone: 888-553-4210 or (410)230-3972 Fax: (410)230-3981 E-mail: info@nationalcia.org • URL: http://www. nationalcia.org • Professional correctional industry managers, supervisors, superintendents, and others employed in the industry. Seeks to improve the effectiveness of industrial programs as they relate to the correctional process by providing a forum for the development and exchange of ideas and by providing professional reaction and guidance concerning projected ideas and programs related to correctional industry trends. Compiles statistics.

OTHER SOURCES

The Corrections Market. Available from MarketResearch.com. • 1996. $1,375.00. Market research report published by Packaged Facts. Covers the markets for prison food service, health care, private management, and telecommunications. Includes market growth projections.

Police Markets of North America and the European Union. Charles LeMesurier and Marc Arnold. Jane's Information Group, Inc. • 1997. $695.00. Provides detailed market research data relative to the police and security industry. Covers a wide range of equipment and vehicle markets geographically for U. S. states, Canadian provinces, and countries. (Law Enforcement Series).

LAW, ENVIRONMENTAL

See: ENVIRONMENTAL LAW

LAW, FAMILY

See: FAMILY LAW

LAW FIRMS

See: LAWYERS

LAW, STATE

See: STATE LAW

LAWN CARE INDUSTRY

See also: GARDEN SUPPLY INDUSTRY

ABSTRACTS AND INDEXES

Horticultural Abstracts: Compiled from World Literature on Temperate and Tropical Fruits, Vegetables, Ornaments, Plantation Crops. Available from CABI Publishing North America. • Monthly. $2,010.00 per year. Print and online edition, $2,030.00 per year. Published in England by CABI Publishing. Provides worldwide coverage of the literature of fruits, vegetables, flowers, plants, and all aspects of gardens and gardening.

Readers' Guide to Periodical Literature. H. W. Wilson Co. • Monthly. $345.00 per year. Includes annual *Cumulation.* Indexes about 250 periodicals of general interest.

CD-ROM DATABASES

AGRICOLA on SilverPlatter. Available from Silver-Platter Information, Inc. • Quarterly. $825.00 per year. Produced by the National Agricultural Library. Provides about three million citations on CD-ROM to the literature of agriculture, agricultural economics, animal sciences, entomology, fertilizer, food, forestry, nutrition, pesticides, plant science, water resources, and other topics. Each quarterly disc covers the past ten years, with archival discs available from 1970.

WILSONDISC: Biological and Agricultural Index. H. W. Wilson Co. • Monthly. Includes unlimited online access to *Biological and Agricultural Index* through WILSONLINE. Provides CD-ROM indexing of over 250 periodicals covering agriculture, agricultural chemicals, biochemistry, biotechnology, entomology, horticulture, and related topics.

WILSONDISC: Readers' Guide to Periodical Literature. H. W. Wilson Co. • Monthly. $1,095.00 per year, including unlimited online access to *Readers' Guide to Periodical Literature* through WILSONLINE. Provides CD-ROM indexing of about 270 general interest periodicals. Covers 1983 to date. (*Readers' Guide Abstracts* also available on CD-ROM at $1,995 per year.).

DIRECTORIES

Yard and Garden. Cygnus Business Media, Inc. • Nine times a year. $48.00. Includes retailers and distributors of lawn and garden power equipment, lawn and plant care products, patio furniture, etc. Arranged by type of product. Includes a *Product* issue.

ENCYCLOPEDIAS AND DICTIONARIES

Encyclopedia of Agriculture Science. Charles J. Arntzen and Ellen M. Ritter, editors. Elsevier. • 1994. $900.00. Four volumes.

HANDBOOKS AND MANUALS

Lawn Care Service. Entrepreneur Media, Inc. • Looseleaf. $59.50. A practical guide to starting a lawn care business. Covers profit potential, start-up costs, market size evaluation, owner's time required, pricing, accounting, advertising, promotion, etc. (Start-Up Business Guide No. E1198.).

ONLINE DATABASES

Agricola. U.S. National Agricultural Library. • Covers worldwide agricultural literature. Over 3.3 million citations, 1970 to present, with monthly updates. Inquire as to online cost and availability.

CAB Abstracts. CAB Publishing North America. • Contains 46 specialized abstract collections covering over 10,000 journals and monographs in the areas of agriculture, horticulture, forest products, farm products, nutrition, dairy science, poultry, grains, animal health, entomology, etc. Time period is 1972 to date, with monthly updates. Inquire as to online cost and availability. *CAB Abstracts on CD-ROM* also available, with annual updating.

Globalbase. Gale Cengage Learning. • Provides more than one million online summaries of business, industrial, and economic news reports from more than 1,000 publications worldwide. Covers a wide range of material appearing in international trade journals, professional magazines, and newspapers. Time period is 1984 to date, with weekly updates. Inquire as to online cost and availability.

PROMT: Predicasts Overview of Markets and Technology. Gale Cengage Learning. • Companies, products, applied technologies and markets. U.S. and international literature coverage, 1972 to date. Inquire as to online cost and availability. Provides abstracts from more than 1,600 publications. Weekly updates.

Readers' Guide Abstracts Online. H. W. Wilson Co. • Indexes and abstracts general interest periodicals, 1983 to date. Weekly updates. Inquire as to online cost and availability.

PERIODICALS AND NEWSLETTERS

Landscape Management: Commercial Magazine for Lawn, Landscape and Grounds Managers. Advanstar Communications. • Monthly. $41.00 per year.

Lawn and Landscape Magazine. Group Interest Enterprises. G.I.E., Publishers Inc. • Monthly. $30.00 per year. Supplement available. Formerly *Lawn and Landscape Maintenance.*

PRO. Cygnus Business Media. • Seven times a year. $48.00 per year. For owners and operators of lawn maintenance service firms. Includes annual *Product* issue.

RESEARCH CENTERS AND INSTITUTES

Landscape Architecture Foundation. Landscape Architecture Foundation. 818 18th St. NW, Ste. 810, Washington, DC 20006. Phone: (202)331-7070 Fax: (202)331-7079 E-mail: rfigura@lafoundation.org • URL: http://www.lafoundation.org • Landscape planning, land use planning and design, environmental planning, landscape change, landscape intervention, place-based land use planning, public participation processes.

TRADE/PROFESSIONAL ASSOCIATIONS

Lawn Institute. 2 E Main St., East Dundee, IL 60118. Phone: 800-405-8873 or (847)649-5555 Fax: (847)649-5678 E-mail: info@thelawninstitue.org • URL: http://www.lawninstitute.com • Producers of lawn seed and lawn products. "Seeks to help bridge the gap between professional research and an increasingly sophisticated consumer." Promotes better lawns through use of quality materials, research, and education.

Outdoor Power Equipment Institute. 341 S Patrick St., Old Town, Alexandria, VA 22314. Phone: (703)549-7600 Fax: (703)549-7604 E-mail: kreamy@opei.org • URL: http://www.opei.org • Manufacturers of lawn mowers, garden tractors, snow throwers, utility vehicles, chainsaws, motor tillers, shredder/grinders, edger/trimmers, leaf vacuums, log splitters, stump cutters, chippers and sprayers, and major components. Compiles statistics and forecasting information; sponsors industry trade shows; produces comprehensive consumer education materials on safety and other industry issues; hosts' annual member meeting; represents members' interests on important legislative and regulatory issues.

Professional Lawn Care Association of America. 1000 Johnson Ferry Rd., Suite C-135, Marietta, GA 30068-6071. Phone: 800-458-3466 or (770)977-5222 Fax: (770)578-6071 E-mail: plcaa@plcaa.org • URL: http://www.plcaa.org • Members are active in the business of treating lawns with chemicals.

LAWS

See also: LAW

GENERAL WORKS

How Our Laws Are Made. Available from U. S. Government Printing Office. • 2000. $3.75. 22nd edition. Issued by U. S. House of Representatives.

Lawmaking and the Legislative Process: Committees, Connections, and Compromises. Greenwood Publishing Group, Inc. • 1996. $29.95. Explains how bills are enacted into laws through the state legislative process. Provides step-by-step examples, using fictitious bills.

ABSTRACTS AND INDEXES

Congressional Index. CCH, Inc. • Weekly when Congress is in session. $1,283.00 per year. Index to action on Public Bills from introduction to final disposition. Subject, author, and bill number indexes.

Current Law Index: Multiple Access to Legal Periodicals. Gale Cengage Learning. • Monthly. $725.00 per year. Produced in cooperation with the American Association of Law Libraries. Indexes more than 900 law journals, legal newspapers, and specialty publications from the U.S., Canada, U.K., Ireland, Australia, and New Zealand.

ALMANACS AND YEARBOOKS

Advertising Law: Year in Review. CCH, Inc. • Annual. $85.00. Summarizes the year's significant legal and regulatory developments.

Securities, Commodities, and Federal Banking: 1999 in Review. CCH, Inc. • Irregular. $57.00. Summarizes the year's significant legal and regulatory developments.

Suggested State Legislation. Council of State Governments. • Annual. $59.00. A source of legislative ideas and drafting assistance for state government officials.

DIRECTORIES

Federal Regulatory Directory. CQ Press. • Covers: Over 100 federal regulatory agencies including about 15 major agencies, about 15 smaller independent agencies, and agencies within federal departments. Entries include: For major agencies--Agency name, address, jurisdiction, description of responsibilities, list of key contacts and phone numbers, breakdown of divisions and offices with names of key officials and their phone numbers, organization chart, information sources within the agency, regional offices, analytical essays on history, recent developments, power, and outlook for agency. For other agencies--Same general information but less detail.

Martindale-Hubbell Law Directory. Martindale-Hubbell Inc. • Covers: lawyers and law firms in the United States, its possessions, and Canada, plus leading law firms worldwide; includes a biographical section by firm, and a separate list of patent lawyers, attorneys in government service, in-house counsel, and services, suppliers, and consultants to the legal profession. Entries include: For non-subscribing lawyers--Name, year of birth and of first admission to bar, code indicating college and law school attended and first degree, firm name (or other affiliation, if any) and relationship to firm, whether practicing other than as individual or in partnership. For subscribing lawyers--Above information plus complete address, phone, fax, e-mail and URL, type of practice, clients, plus additional personal details (education, certifications, etc.). A general law list. See separate listing, 'Law Lists'.

ENCYCLOPEDIAS AND DICTIONARIES

Gale Encyclopedia of Everyday Law. Gale Cengage Learning. • 2002. $250.00. Two volumes. Contains about 200 entries providing profiles of important U.

S. laws and regulations, with historical background. Includes bibliographies.

HANDBOOKS AND MANUALS

Code of Federal Regulations. Office of the Federal Register, U.S. General Services Administration. Available from U.S. Government Printing Office. • $1,094.00 per year. Complete service.

National Survey of State Laws. Gale Cengage Learning. • 2002. $105.00. Fourth edition. Provides concise state-by-state comparisons of current state laws on a wide variety of topics. Includes references to specific codes or statutes.

United States Code. U.S. Congress. Available from U.S. Government Printing Office. • Continual supplements. Price varies. Permanent and general public law of the United States from 1789 to the codification date.

United States Code Annotated: Crimes and Criminal Procedures. West Group. • $3,125.00. 15 volumes. Annual cumulation. Arranged in parallel fashion to *United States Code.* Gives abstracts of relevant federal and state court decisions pertaining to each section of the code. Supplemented by annual pocket parts.

United States Statutes at Large. U.S. Office of the Federal Register. Available from U.S. Government Printing Office. • Annual. Price varies. Congressional acts and presidential proclamations issued during the Congressional session. For all laws in force at a specific date, refer to *United States Code.*

INTERNET DATABASES

FindLaw: Internet Legal Resources. FindLaw, Inc. Phone: (650)940-4300 E-mail: info@findlaw.com • URL: http://www.findlaw.com • Web site provides a wide variety of information and links relating to laws, law schools, professional development, lawyers, the U. S. Supreme Court, consultants (experts), law reviews, legal news, etc. Online searching is provided. Fees: Free.

Lexis.com Research System. Lexis-Nexis Group. Phone: 800-227-4908 or (937)865-6800 Fax: (937)865-6909 E-mail: webmaster@prod.lexis-nexis.com • URL: http://www.lexis.com • Fee-based Web site offers extensive searching of a wide variety of legal sources. Additional features include Daily Opinion Service, lexis.com Bookstore, Career Center, CLE Center, Law Schools, and Practice Pages ("Pages specific to areas of specialty").

PERIODICALS AND NEWSLETTERS

Congressional Record. U.S. Congress. Available from U.S. Government Printing Office. • Daily. Indexes give names, subjects, and history of bills. Texts of bills not included.

Congressional Record Scanner. Congressional Quarterly. • Description: Contains abstracts of the Congressional Record.

Federal Register. Office of the Federal Register. Available from U.S. Government Printing Office. • Daily except Saturday and Sunday. $764.00 per year. Publishes regulations and legal notices issued by federal agencies, including executive orders and presidential proclamations. Issued by the National Archives and Records Administration (http://www.nara.gov).

United States Law Week: A National Survey of Current Law. BNA, Inc. • Weekly. $1,152.00 per year. Covers U.S. Supreme Court proceedings and gives full text of decisions. Also provides detailed reports on important legislative and regulatory actions.

STATISTICS SOURCES

Property-Casualty Insurance Facts. Insurance Information Institute. • Annual. $22.50. Formerly *Insurance Facts.*

LAWS, ADVERTISING

See: ADVERTISING LAW AND REGULATION

LAWS, BANKING

See: BANKING LAW AND REGULATION

LAWYERS

See also: WOMEN LAWYERS

GENERAL WORKS

The Betrayed Profession: Lawyering at the End of the Twentieth Century. Sol M. Linowitz and Martin Mayer. John Hopkins University Press. • 1996. $18.95. Reprint edition. A critical view of present-day lawyers and law firms.

Full Disclosure: The New Lawyer's Must-Read Career Guide. Christen C. Carey. American Lawyer Media, Inc. • 2001. $19.95. "All the Things Lawyers Wish They Had Known at the Beginning of Their Careers, Rather Than at the End." Covers such topics as job hunting, job interviews, summer associate programs, law firm economics, life as a law firm associate, and gender in law firms.

Gender on Trial: Sexual Stereotypes and Work/Life Balance in the Legal Workplace. Holly English. American Lawyer Media, Inc. • 2003. $44.95. Provides an "oral history" of legal profession employment practices, based on interviews with lawyers from around the U.S., psychologists, consultants, and recruiters. Contains recommendations for "new models to help firms and individuals achieve a workplace free of gender bias for both men and women." (ALM Publishing).

Smart Questions to Ask Your Financial Advisers. Lynn Brenner. Bloomberg. • 1997. $19.95. Provides practical advice on how to deal with financial planners, stockbrokers, insurance agents, and lawyers. Some of the areas covered are investments, estate planning, tax planning, house buying, prenuptial agreements, divorce arrangements, loss of a job, and retirement. (Bloomberg Personal Bookshelf Series).

ALMANACS AND YEARBOOKS

The Lawyer's Almanac; An Encyclopedia of Information about Law, Lawyers, and the Profession. Aspen Law. • Annual. $144.00. List of the 250 largest law firms.

BIOGRAPHICAL SOURCES

Who's Who in American Law. Marquis Who's Who. • Biennial. $295.00. Contains over 23,000 concise biographies of American lawyers, judges, and others in the legal field.

CD-ROM DATABASES

Martindale-Hubbell Law Directory on CD-ROM. Martindale-Hubbell, Reed Reference Publishing. • Quarterly. $995.00 per year. Provides CD-ROM information on over 900,000 lawyers. International coverage.

The Tax Directory [CD-ROM]. Tax Analysts. • Quarterly. Provides *The Tax Directory* listings on CD-ROM, covering federal, state, and international tax officials, tax practitioners, and corporate tax executives.

DIRECTORIES

American Bar Association--Directory. American Bar Association. • Covers: Approximately 7,500 lawyers active in the affairs of the Association, including officers, members of Boards of Governors and House of Delegates, section officers and council members, committee leaders, headquarters staff, state and local bars, affiliated and other legal organizations. Entries include: Section, council, or other unit name; names, addresses, and phone numbers of officers or chairpersons and members.

Best's Directory of Recommended Insurance Attorneys and Adjusters. A.M. Best Co. • Annual. $1,175.00. More than 5,000 American, Canadian, and foreign insurance defense law firms; lists 1,200 national and international insurance adjusting firms. Formerly *Best's Recommended Insurance Adjusters.*

Campbell's List. Campbell's List Inc. • Covers: about 1,000 law firms in general practice that will handle referrals; international coverage. Entries include: Firm name, address, phone, and whether collection cases are accepted. A general law list. See separate listing, 'Law Lists.' Also includes court reporters and process servers by geographical arrangement.

Capital for Shipping. Available from Informa Publishing Group Ltd. • Annual. $128.00. Published in the UK by Lloyd's List (http://www.lloydslist.com). Consists of a "Financial Directory" and a "Legal Directory," listing international ship finance providers and international law firms specializing in shipping. (Included with subscription to *Lloyd's Shipping Economist*.).

Directory of Environmental Attorneys. Aspen Publishers, Inc. • 1994. $195.00.

Directory of Intellectual Property Attorneys, 1995. Aspen Publishers, Inc. • 1994. $195.00.

Directory of Litigation Attorneys, 1995-1996. Aspen Publishers, Inc. • 1993. $450.00. Two volumes. Includes about 40,000 attorneys, 15,000 law firms, and 100 areas of litigation specialization.

Emerson's Directory of Leading U.S. Law Firms. Emerson Co. • 2000. $195.00. Provides information on major law firms in the United States.

Law Firms Yellow Book: Who's Who in the Management of the Leading U. S. Law Firms. Leadership Directories, Inc. • Semiannual. $265.00 per year. Provides detailed information on more than 850 major U. S. law firms. Includes domestic offices, foreign offices, subsidiaries, and affiliates. There are seven indexes: geographic, subject specialty, management, administrative, law school attended, personnel, and law firm.

Lawyers' List. Commercial Publishing Company Inc. • Covers: about 2,500 lawyers in general, corporate, trial, patent, trademark, and copywrite practices internationally. Entries include: Firm name, address, phone, fax, e-mail, website, areas of practice, branch offices, names of representative clients, names of partners and associates. A general law list. See separate listing, 'Law Lists'.

Lawyer's Register International by Specialties and Fields of Law Including a Directory of Corporate Counsel. Lawyer's Register Publishing Co. • Annual. $359.00. Three volumes. Referral source for law firms.

Martindale-Hubbell Bar Register of Preeminent Lawyers. Martindale-Hubbell. • Annual. $195.00. Lists over 9,700 "outstanding members of the bar" in general practice and in 28 specific fields. Covers the U. S. and Canada.

Martindale-Hubbell Law Directory. Martindale-Hubbell Inc. • Covers: lawyers and law firms in the United States, its possessions, and Canada, plus leading law firms worldwide; includes a biographical section by firm, and a separate list of patent lawyers, attorneys in government service, in-house counsel, and services, suppliers, and consultants to the legal profession. Entries include: For non-subscribing lawyers--Name, year of birth and of first admission to bar, code indicating college and law school attended and first degree, firm name (or other affiliation, if any) and relationship to firm, whether practicing other than as individual or in partnership. For subscribing lawyers--Above information plus complete address, phone, fax, e-mail and URL, type of practice, clients, plus additional personal details (education, certifications, etc.). A general law list. See separate listing, 'Law Lists'.

National Directory of Minority Attorneys. American Lawyer Media, Inc. • Annual. $35.00. Contains 500 listings in four sections, covering minority-owned law firms, minority lawyers at other law firms, minority corporate (in-house) lawyers, and minority lawyers in government agencies. (Minority Law Journal).

NLADA Directory of Legal Aid and Defender Offices in the United States and Territories. National Legal Aid and Defender Association. • Biennial. $70.00. Geographical list of approximately 3,600 legal aid and defender offices and their branches. Formerly *Directory Legal Aid and Defender Offices in the United States.*

The Tax Directory. Tax Analysts. • Covers: Volume One--Approximately 15,000 federal and state government tax legislators, policymakers, administrators, and employees; tax regulation attorneys; over 500 international tax officials with central banks, ministries of finance, foreign embassies and consulate, and chambers of commerce; over 300 tax and business journalists and editors working for magazines, journals, newspapers, television, and radio; tax sections of over 100 trade and professional associations; state CPA, bar, and enrolled agent associations. Volume Two--Over 5,000 corporate tax managers of large U.S. and international firms. Entries include: For government and international officials--Name, title, address, phone, fax, email and website. For corporate tax managers--Name, address, phone, fax, email, website, and company name. For journalists--Name, address, phone, fax, email, website, and name of publication/network. For organizations and associations--Name, address, phone, fax, email, website, budget, membership, background information, and description of purpose.

Washington: A Comprehensive Directory of the Key Institutions and Leaders in th e National Capitol Area. Columbia Books, Inc. • Annual. $149.00. Provides information on about 5,000 Washington, DC key businesses, government offices, non-profit organizations, and cultural institutions, with the names of about 25,000 principal executives. Includes Washington media, law offices, foundations, labor unions, international organizations, clubs, etc.

FINANCIAL RATIOS

Almanac of Business and Industrial Financial Ratios. Leo Troy. Aspen Publishers, Inc. • 2003. $125.95. Includes CD-Rom. Contains financial ratios derived from federal tax returns. Ratios for each of about 200 industries are arranged according to company asset size. (Almanac of Business and Industrial Financial Ratios Series).

Annual Statement Studies. The Risk Management Association. • Annual. Median and quartile financial ratios are given for over 400 kinds of manufacturing, wholesale, retail, construction, and consumer finance establishments. Data is sorted by both asset size and sales volume. Includes a clearly written "Definition of Ratios" and an alphabetical industry index.

Annual Statement Studies: Industry Default Probabilities and Cash Flow Measures. The Risk Management Association. • Annual. $145.00. Serves as a companion volume to the original *Annual Statement Studies.* Gives probability of default estimates on a percentage scale for more than 450 industries. Includes changes in position year-by-year for eight financial statement line items and provides percentage measures of cash flow.

HANDBOOKS AND MANUALS

ABA/BNA Lawyer's Manual on Professional Conduct. American Bar Association. BNA, Inc. •

Bimonthly. $595.00 per year. Looseleaf service. Covers American Bar Association's model rules governing ethical practice of law.

The Business of Law: A Handbook on How to Manage Law Firms. Aspen Publishers, Inc. • $95.00. Looseleaf service. Periodic supplementation.

Career Legal Secretary. National Association of Legal Secretaries. West Publishing Co. • 1997. $35. 50. Fourth edition.

Getting Started in Investment Planning Services. James E. Grant. CCH, Inc. • 1999. $85.00. Second edition. Provides advice and information for lawyers and accountants who are planning to initiate fee-based investment services.

How to Manage Your Law Office. LexisNexis Matthew Bender. • Annual. $254.00. A practical guide with cutting edge information about effective techniques in law office administration.

Legal Assistant's Handbook. Thomas W. Brunner and others. BNA, Inc. • 1988. $44.00. Second edition.

Legal Ethics in the Practice of Law. Richard A. Zitrin and Carol M. Langford. LexisNexis Matthew Bender. • 2002. $57.00. Provides "real-life examples of ethical dilemmas" occurring in the law profession.

Legal Malpractice: Liability, Prevention, Litigation, Insurance. Ronald E. Mallen and Jeffrey M. Smith. West Group. • 2000. Fifth edition. Five volumes. Periodic supplementation.

Managing People in Today's Law Firm: The Human Resources Approach to Surviving Change. Ellen Weisbord and others. Greenwood Publishing Group, Inc. • 1995. $64.95.

Manual for Managing the Law Office. Prentice Hall PTR. • Looseleaf service. Price on application. (Information Services Series).

Professional Resumes for Accounting, Tax, Finance and Law: A Special Gallery of Best Resumes by Professional Resume Writers. David H. Noble. JIST Publishing. • 1999. $19.95. Written for accounting, tax, law, and finance professionals. In addition to advice, provides 335 sample resumes and 22 cover letters.

Professional's Guide to Successful Management: The Eight Essentials for Running Your Firm, Practice, or Partnership. Carol A. O'Connor. McGraw-Hill. • 1994. Price on application.

Valuing Professional Practices: A Practitioner's Guide. Robert Reilly and Robert Schweihs. CCH, Inc. • 1997. $99.00. Provides a basic introduction to estimating the dollar value of practices in various professional fields.

INTERNET DATABASES

FindLaw: Internet Legal Resources. FindLaw, Inc. Phone: (650)940-4300 E-mail: info@findlaw.com • URL: http://www.findlaw.com • Web site provides a wide variety of information and links relating to laws, law schools, professional development, lawyers, the U. S. Supreme Court, consultants (experts), law reviews, legal news, etc. Online searching is provided. Fees: Free.

Law.com: First in Legal News and Information. American Lawyer Media, Inc. Phone: 800-888-8300 or (212)779-9200 Fax: (212)481-8110 • URL: http://www.law.com • Web site provides free, law-related, current news (National News Sites and Regional News Sites). Free searching of martindale. com lawyer locator is offered, including lawyer ratings. Fee-based premium services for the legal profession are also available.

PERIODICALS AND NEWSLETTERS

ABA Journal: The Lawyer's Magazine. American Bar Association. • Monthly. Individuals, $75.00 per year; institutions, $120.00 per year. Includes five regular sections: news affecting lawyers, practical applications of court decisions, pratice management advice, feature articles, and lifestyle stories.

Accounting and Financial Planning for Law Firms. American Lawyer Media, Inc. • Monthly. $225.00 per year. Newsletter. Covers budgeting, liability issues, billing systems, benefits management, and other topics relating to law firm administration. (A Law Journal Newsletter, formerly published by Leader Publications).

The American Lawyer. American Lawyer Media Inc. • 10 times a year. $149.00 per year. General information for American attorneys.

Corporate Counselor. American Lawyer Media, Inc. • Monthly. $229.00 per year. Newsletter. Covers issues involved with managing the legal department of a corporation, including relations with outside counsel. (A Law Journal Newsletter, formerly published by Leader Publications).

Cyberspace Lawyer. Glasser Legalworks. • 11 times a year. $300.00 per year. Newsletter. Covers various legal topics pertaining to use of the Internet. Includes advice on legal research via the Web.

Internet Law and Strategy. American Lawyer Media, Inc. • Monthly. $199.00 per year. Newsletter. Primarily concerned with doing legal research online. Contains reviews of the best Web sites for lawyers. (A Law Journal Newsletter, formerly published by Leader Publications.).

Internet Law Researcher. Glasser Legalworks. • 11 times a year. $200.00 per year. Newsletter for legal professionals on how to search the Web efficiently. Provides detailed information on individual Web sites.

Journal of Electronic Resources in Law Libraries. Haworth Press, Inc. • Quarterly. $300.00 per year to libraries; $48.00 per year to individuals.

Law Firm Governance: Journal of Practice Management, Development, and Technology. Aspen Publishers, Inc. • Quarterly. $196.00 per year. Covers project management, strategic planning, compensation systems, advertising, etc. Regular columns include "Best Practices," "Technology Trends," and "Professional Development." Formerly *Law Governance Review.*

Law Firm Inc. American Lawyer Media, Inc. • Quarterly. $49.95 per year. Covers human resources, insurance, financing, marketing, compensation, recruitment, etc., as related to law firm management.

Law Firm Partnership and Benefits Report. American Lawyer Media, Inc. • Monthly. $215.00 per year. Newsletter. Covers personnel issues for law firms, including compensation, partnership agreements, malpractice, employment discrimination, training, health insurance, pension plans, and other matters relating to human resources management. (A Law Journal Newsletter, formerly published by Leader Publications).

Law Technology News: Products, Systems, and Services for Legal Professionals. American Lawyer Media, Inc. • Monthly. $69.00 per year. Features descriptions of new technology products and services of interest to the legal profession.

The Lawyers Competitive Edge: The Journal of Law Office Economics and Management. West Group. • Monthly. $322.00 per year. Newsletter.

Legal Times: Law and Lobbying in the Nation's Capital. American Lawyer Media, Inc. • Weekly. $318.00 per year. Published in Washington, DC. Provides news relating to lawyers and the federal government. Special features cover a variety of topics relating to law firm administration.

Marketing for Lawyers. American Lawyer Media. • Monthly. $195.00 per year. Newsletter. Provides advice for law firms on attracting new clients and providing good service to present clients.

Marketing the Law Firm. American Lawyer Media, Inc. • Monthly. $199.00 per year. Newsletter. Focuses on actions that lawyers can take to find more clients and do more business. (A Law Journal

Newsletter, formerly published by Leader Publications under the title *Marketing for Lawyers*).

National Law Journal: The Weekly Newspaper for the Profession. American Lawyer Media Inc. • Weekly. $158.00 per year. News and analysis of the latest developments in the law and the law profession.

Of Counsel: The Monthly Legal Practice Report. Aspen Law and Business. • 12 times a year. $445.00 per year. Newsletter on the management, marketing, personnel, and compensation of law firms.

The Practical Lawyer. Committee on Continuing Professional Education. American Law Institute-American Bar Association Committee on Continuing Professional Education. • Eight times a year. $49.00 per year.

The Practical Real Estate Lawyer. Committee on Continuing Professional Education. American Law Institute-American Bar Association Committee on Continuing Professional Education. • Bimonthly. $49.00 per year. Frequently includes legal forms for use in real estate practice.

Tax Practice. Tax Analysts. • Weekly. $199.00 per year. Newsletter. Covers news affecting tax practitioners and litigators, with emphasis on federal court decisions, rules and regulations, and tax petitions. Provides a guide to Internal Revenue Service audit issues.

Wallstreetlawyer.com: Securities in the Electronic Age. Glasser Legalworks. • Monthly. $345.00 per year. Newsletter. Covers the latest regulatory developments in capital raising, disclosure, and enforcement.

STATISTICS SOURCES

Compensation Systems in Private Law Firms. Altman Weil Publications, Inc. • Annual. $325.00. Provides legal-office compensation standards arranged by region, firm size, legal specialty, and various other factors. Covers attorneys, paralegals, and other personnel.

Small Law Firm Economic Survey. Altman Weil Publications, Inc. • Annual. $395.00. Provides aggregate data (benchmarks) on the economics, finances, billing, and staffing of law offices in the U. S. having "less than 12 lawyers.".

Survey of Law Firm Economics: A Management and Planning Tool. Altman Weil Publications, Inc. • Annual. $995.00. Provides aggregate economic statistics and financial data (benchmarks) relating to the legal profession in the U. S. Includes income, expenses, hourly rates, billable hours, compensation, staffing, data by states, and trends. Most information is arranged by region, firm size, years of experience, and other factors.

U. S. Industry and Trade Outlook. Available from National Technical Information Service. • Annual. $69.95. Produced by the International Trade Administration, U. S. Department of Commerce, in a "public-private" partnership with DRI/McGraw-Hill and Standard & Poor's. Provides basic data, outlook for the current year, and "Long-Term Prospects" (five-year projections) for a wide variety of products and services. Includes high technology industries. Formerly *U. S. Industrial Outlook*.

WEFA Industrial Monitor. John Wiley and Sons, Inc. • Annual. $65.00. Prepared by industry analysts at WEFA, an economic forecasting and consulting firm (originally Wharton Econometric Forecasting Associates). Contains discussions of the outlook for major U. S. industries, with many 10-year forecasts (WEFA Web site is http://www.wefa.com).

TRADE/PROFESSIONAL ASSOCIATIONS

American Bar Association. 321 N Clark St., Chicago, IL 60610. Phone: 800-285-2221 or (312)988-5000 Fax: (312)988-5522 E-mail: askaba@abanet.org • URL: http://www.abanet.org • Attorneys in good standing of the bar of any state.

Conducts research and educational projects and activities to: encourage professional improvement; provide public services; improve the administration of civil and criminal justice; increase the availability of legal services to the public. Sponsors Law Day USA. Administers numerous standing and special committees such as Committee on +Soviet and +East +European +Law, providing seminars and newsletters. Operates 25 sections, including Criminal Justice, Economics of Law Practice, and Family Law. Sponsors essay competitions. Maintains library.

American College of Trial Lawyers. 19900 MacArthur Blvd., Ste. 610, Irvine, CA 92712-8405. Phone: (949)752-1801 Fax: (949)752-1674 E-mail: nationaloffice@actl.com • URL: http://www.actl.com.

Defense Research Institute. 150 N Michigan Ave., Ste. 300, Chicago, IL 60601. Phone: 800-667-8108 or (312)795-1101 Fax: (312)795-0747 E-mail: dri@dri.org • URL: http://www.dri.org • Lawyers, claims people, adjusters, insurance companies, trade associations, corporations, and "target" defendants in civil litigation, such as doctors, pharmacists, engineers, manufacturers, and other professional and skilled personnel. Seeks to increase the knowledge and improve the skills of defense lawyers and to improve the adversary system of justice. Maintains research facilities, including files of speeches, briefs, and names of expert witnesses in various fields. Maintains Expert Witness Index.

National Lawyers Guild. 132 Nassau St., Rm. 922, New York, NY 10038. Phone: (212)679-5100 Fax: (212)679-2811 E-mail: nlgno@nlg.org • URL: http://www.nlg.org • Lawyers, law students, legal workers, and jailhouse lawyers dedicated to seek economic justice, social equality, and the right to political dissent. Serves as national center for progressive legal work providing training programs to both members and nonmembers. Sponsors skills seminars in different areas of law. Maintains speakers' bureau and offers legal referrals.

National Legal Aid and Defender Association. 1625 K St., N.W., Suite 800, Washington, DC 20006-1604. Phone: (202)452-0620 Fax: (202)872-1031 E-mail: info@nlada.org • URL: http://www.nlada.org.

Tax Analysts. 400 S Maple Ave., Ste. 400, Falls Church, VA 22046. Phone: 800-955-2444 or (703)533-4400 Fax: (703)533-4444 E-mail: cservice@tax.org • URL: http://www.tax.org • Reviews all tax law developments, federal, state, international comprehensively; compiles statistics. **Convention/Meeting:** none.

OTHER SOURCES

Andrews' Professional Liability Litigation Reporter. Andrews Publications. • Monthly. $550.00 per year. Provides reports on lawsuits against attorneys, accountants, and investment professionals.

Avoiding Tax Malpractice. CCH, Inc. • 2000. $75.00. Covers malpractice considerations for professional tax practitioners.

Marketing the Law Firm: Business Development Techniques. American Lawyer Media, Inc. • Looseleaf. $189.00. Updated as needed. Covers client surveys, brochures, direct mail, Web sites, seminars, newsletters, proposals, trade shows, and other marketing avenues for both large and small law firms. (Law Journal Press).

Maximizing Law Firm Profitability: Hiring, Training, and Developing Productive Lawyers. American Lawyer Media, Inc. • Looseleaf. $169.00. Updated as needed. (Law Journal Press).

LAYOFFS

See: DISMISSAL OF EMPLOYEES

LEAD INDUSTRY

ABSTRACTS AND INDEXES

IMM Abstracts and Index: A Survey of World Literature on the Economic Geology and Mining of All Minerals (Except Coal), Mineral Processing, and Nonferrous Extraction Metallurgy. Institution of Mining and Metallurgy. • Bimonthly. $500.00 per year. Provides international coverage of the literature of mining and nonferrous metallurgy. Includes mineral economics, tunnelling, and rock mechanics.

Leadscan: A Review of Recent Technical Literature on the Uses of lead and its Products. Clive Larson,ed. C and C Associates. • Quarterly. $110.00 per year. Provides technical articles and abstracts of recent technical and market related literature on lead and its uses.

ALMANACS AND YEARBOOKS

Agricultural and Mineral Commodities Year Book. Available from Taylor & Francis Group. • Annual. $225.00. Published by Europa Publications. Contains descriptive product profiles, price data, export-import data, and production statistics for major commodities of the world. Includes commodity histories, uses, markets, demand trends, and information about trade agreements and key commodity organizations.

CD-ROM DATABASES

METADEX Materials Collection: Metals-Polymers-Ceramics. Cambridge Scientific Abstracts. • Quarterly. Provides CD-ROM citations to the worldwide literature of materials science and metallurgy. Corresponds to *Metals Abstracts, Alloys Index, Steels Alert, Nonferrous Alert, Polymers/Ceramics/Composites Alert,* and *Engineered Materials Abstracts*. (Formerly produced by ASM International.).

ONLINE DATABASES

Materials Business File. Cambridge Scientific Abstracts. • Provides online abstracts and citations to worldwide materials literature, covering the business and industrial aspects of metals, plastics, ceramics, and composites. Corresponds to *Steels Alert, Nonferrous Metals Alert,* and *Polymers/Ceramics/Composites Alert*. Time period is 1985 to date, with monthly updates. (Formerly produced by ASM International.) Inquire as to online cost and availability.

METADEX. Cambridge Scientific Abstracts. • Covers the worldwide literature of metals, metallurgy, and materials science, 1966 to date. Includes detailed alloys indexing from 1974. Biweekly updating. Inquire as to online cost and availability. (Formerly produced by ASM International.).

STATISTICS SOURCES

Lead and Zinc Statistics. International Lead and Zinc Study Group. • Monthly. $390.00 per year. Supplement available *Advance Data Service*. Text in English and French.

Mineral Commodity Summaries. Available from U. S. Government Printing Office. • Annual. $26.00. Published by the U. S. Geological Survey, Department of the Interior (http://www.usgs.gov). Contains detailed, five-year data for about 90 nonfuel minerals. Covers a wide range of statistics, including production, imports, exports, consumption, reserves, prices, tariff information, and industry employment. (Two pages are devoted to each mineral.).

Non-Ferrous Metal Data Yearbook. American Bureau of Metal Statistics. • Annual. $405.00. Provides worldwide data on approximately about 200 statistical tables covering many nonferrous metals. Includes production, consumption, inventories, exports, imports, and other data.

U. S. Industry and Trade Outlook. Available from

National Technical Information Service. • Annual. $69.95. Produced by the International Trade Administration, U. S. Department of Commerce, in a "public-private" partnership with DRI/McGraw-Hill and Standard & Poor's. Provides basic data, outlook for the current year, and "Long-Term Prospects" (five-year projections) for a wide variety of products and services. Includes high technology industries. Formerly *U. S. Industrial Outlook*.

WEFA Industrial Monitor. John Wiley and Sons, Inc. • Annual. $65.00. Prepared by industry analysts at WEFA, an economic forecasting and consulting firm (originally Wharton Econometric Forecasting Associates). Contains discussions of the outlook for major U. S. industries, with many 10-year forecasts (WEFA Web site is http://www.wefa.com).

TRADE/PROFESSIONAL ASSOCIATIONS

American Bureau of Metal Statistics. P.O. Box 805, Chatham, NJ 07928. Phone: (973)701-2299 Fax: (973)701-2152 E-mail: info@abms.com • URL: http://www.abms.com • Members are metal companies. Compiles and publishes detailed statistical data on a wide variety of nonferrous metals: aluminum, copper, gold, lead, nickel, platinum, silver, tin, titanium, uranium, zinc, and others.

International Lead Zinc Research Organization. 2525 Meridian Pkwy., Ste. 100, Durham, NC 27713. Phone: (919)361-4647 Fax: (919)361-1957 E-mail: rputnam@ilzro.org • URL: http://www.ilzro.org • Seeks to develop new applications for lead and zinc. Improves current uses of lead and zinc; compiles technical information on these metals. Directs approximately 150 research programs through its contracts with universities, governments, independent laboratories, industrial companies, and member companies. Research and development projects deal with die castings, wrought zinc, alloys, galvanized steel, plating, welding, lead and zinc chemistry, environmental studies, batteries, lead for architectural uses, and other subjects. Acts as a Research organization sponsored by major producers, smelters, and refiners of lead and/or zinc from 15 countries.

Non-Ferrous Metals Producers Committee. 2030 M St. NW, Ste. 800, 2030 M St. NW, Ste. 800, 2030 M. St., N.W., Suite 800, Washington, DC 20036. Phone: (202)466-7720 Fax: (202)466-2710 E-mail: nffstaff@nffs.org • URL: http://www.arcat.com/arcatcos/cos37/arc37679.cfm • Represents domestic copper, lead, and zinc producers. Promotes the interests of copper, lead, and zinc mining and metal industries in the U.S. with emphasis on tariffs, laws, regulations, and government policies affecting international trade and foreign imports.

LEADERSHIP

GENERAL WORKS

The Art and Science of Leadership. Afsaneh Nahavandi. Prentice Hall PTR. • 2002. $73.33. Third edition. Includes a discussion of participative management. Emphasis is on strategic leadership.

The Extraordinary Leader: Turning Good Managers into Great Leaders. John H. Zenger and Joseph Folkman. McGraw-Hill. • 2002. $27.95. Presents a new model of leadership featuring 16 competencies.

Innovation: Leadership Strategies for the Competitive Edge. Thomas D. Kuczmarski. McGraw-Hill. • 1995. $37.95. (NTC Business Books Series).

The Leader of the Future: New Essays by World-Class Leaders and Thinkers. Frances Hesselbein. John Wiley and Sons, Inc. • 2000. $16.50. Contains articles on leadership by "executives, consultants, and commentators." (Management Series).

Leadership: Theory and Practice. Peter G. Northouse. Sage Publications, Inc. • 2003. $42.95. Third edition. Considers the strengths and criticisms of specific leadership approaches, such as trait, style,

situational, transformational, psychodynamic, path-goal, and others.

Project Leadership. James P. Lewis. McGraw-Hill. • 2002. $29.95. Provides detailed advice for project managers in a leadership role. (Teach Yourself Series).

Psychology for Leaders: Using Motivation, Conflict, and Power to Manage More Effectively. Dean Tjosvold and Mary Tjosvold. John Wiley and Sons, Inc. • 1995. $32.95. (Portable MBA Series).

Why Leaders Can't Lead: The Unconscious Conspiracy Continues. Warren Bennis. John Wiley and Sons, Inc. • 1997. $22.95.

ENCYCLOPEDIAS AND DICTIONARIES

Blackwell Encyclopedic Dictionary of Organizational Behavior. Nigel Nicholson, editor. Blackwell Publishing. • 1997. $130.95. The editor is associated with the London Business School. Contains definitions of key terms combined with longer articles written by various U. S. and foreign business educators. Includes bibliographies and index. *Blackwell Encyclopedia of Management Series*.

Encyclopedia of Human Behavior. Vangipuram S. Ramachandran, editor. Elsevier. • 1994. $1,000.00. Four volumes. Contains signed articles on aptitude testing, arbitration, career development, consumer psychology, crisis management, decision making, economic behavior, group dynamics, leadership, motivation, negotiation, organizational behavior, planning, problem solving, stress, work efficiency, and other human behavior topics applicable to business situations.

Encyclopedia of Leadership. George R. Goethals and Georgia Sorenson, editors. Sage Publications, Inc. • 2004. $595.00. Four volumes. Contains articles written by "400 leading scholars and experts from 17 countries, exploring leadership theories and leadership practice." Includes many case studies and biographical essays.

HANDBOOKS AND MANUALS

Tough-Minded Leadership. Joe D. Batten. AMACOM. • 1989. $15.95.

PERIODICALS AND NEWSLETTERS

Executive Excellence: The Newsletter of Personal Development, Managerial Effectiveness, and Organizational Productivity. Kenneth M. Shelton, editor. Executive Excellence Publishing. • Monthly. $129.00 per year. Newsletter.

Fast Company: How Smart Business Works. Fast Company, Inc. • Monthly. $12.00 per year. Covers business management, with emphasis on creativity, leadership, innovation, career advancement, teamwork, the global economy, and the "new workplace.".

Leader to Leader. Peter F. Drucker Foundation for Nonprofit Management. Jossey-Bass. • Quarterly. Institutions, $199.00 per year. Contains articles on "management, leadership, and strategy" written by "leading executives, thinkers, and consultants." Covers both business and nonprofit issues.

Leadership Strategies: The Tools to Help You Lead Effectively. Briefings Publishing Group. • Monthly. Free to qualified personnel. Newsletter. Includes concise articles on change management, delegation of authority, team building, conflict resolution, and other leadership topics.

Perspective. Magna Publications Inc. • Description: Provides administrators with guidelines for keeping their schools out of court. Examines current trends in law related to higher education, as well as past and future legal issues affecting students, faculty, administrators and the public. Recurring features include columns titled Key Case Review, Follow-Up, Resources, Legislative Note, Outside the Courts, Cross-Examination, and Cases Noted.

Positive Leadership: Improving Performance

Through Value-Centered Management. Lawrence Ragan Communications, Inc. • Monthly. $99.00 per year. Newsletter. Emphasis is on employee motivation, family issues, ethics, and community relations.

TRADE/PROFESSIONAL ASSOCIATIONS

Future Business Leaders of America-Phi Beta Lambda. 1912 Association Dr., Reston, VA 22091-1591. Phone: 800-325-2946 or (703)860-3334 Fax: (703)758-0749 E-mail: general@fbla.org • URL: http://www.fbla-pbl.org.

OTHER SOURCES

First-Level Leadership: Supervising in the New Organization. American Management Association Extension Institute. • Looseleaf. $139.00. Self-study course. Emphasis is on practical explanations, examples, and problem solving. Quizzes and a case study are included.

LEADING INDICATORS

See: ECONOMIC INDICATORS

LEARNING, PROGRAMMED

See: PROGRAMMED LEARNING

LEASING SERVICES

See: AUTOMOBILE LEASE AND RENTAL SERVICES; EQUIPMENT LEASING; RENTAL SERVICES

LEATHER INDUSTRY

See also: LUGGAGE INDUSTRY; SHOE INDUSTRY; TANNING INDUSTRY

CD-ROM DATABASES

OECD Statistical Compendium. Organization for Economic Cooperation and Development. • Semiannual. $1,905.00 per year for 1 to 10 users. CD-ROM contains more than 730,000 monthly, quarterly, and annual time series for OECD countries, 1960 to date. Includes fully searchable data on agriculture, food, economic indicators, national accounts, employment, energy, finance, industry, technology, and foreign trade. Results can be displayed in various forms.

DIRECTORIES

American Leather Chemists Association--Membership Directory. American Leather Chemists Association. • Covers: about 500 chemists, leather technologists, and educators concerned with the tanning and leather industry. Entries include: Personal name, address; company name, address, phone, fax.

Leather Manufacturer Directory. Shoe Trades Publishing Co. • Covers: Tanneries, leather finishers, and hide processors and their suppliers in the United States and Canada. Entries include: Company name, address, phone, names of executives, list of products or services and over 300 companies classified by their goods and services.

Travelware Suppliers Directory. Business Journals Inc. • Covers: 500 manufacturers and importers that supply hardware, leather, fabrics, and other components to the luggage and leather goods industry (SIC 3161). Entries include: Company name, address, phone, fax, telex, name of principal executive, sales offices/showrooms/reps, email, URL.

FINANCIAL RATIOS

Annual Statement Studies. The Risk Management Association. • Annual. Median and quartile financial ratios are given for over 400 kinds of manufacturing, wholesale, retail, construction, and consumer finance establishments. Data is sorted by both asset size and sales volume. Includes a clearly written "Definition of Ratios" and an alphabetical industry index.

Annual Statement Studies: Industry Default Probabilities and Cash Flow Measures. The Risk Management Association. • Annual. $145.00. Serves as a companion volume to the original *Annual Statement Studies.* Gives probability of default estimates on a percentage scale for more than 450 industries. Includes changes in position year-by-year for eight financial statement line items and provides percentage measures of cash flow.

INTERNET DATABASES

Business 2.0 Web Guide to the Best Business Links. Business 2.0 Media Inc. Phone: (415)293-4800 E-mail: support@business2.com • URL: http://www.business2.com/webguide • Web site presents an extensive, searchable directory of links to "the best, most informative, and authoritative web pages." Twenty main categories cover business, finance, career, company information, people, and technology topics, with thousands of subtopics, all linking to Web sites recommended by experienced business researchers. Fees: Free.

Fedstats. Federal Interagency Council on Statistical Policy. Phone: (202)395-7254 • URL: http://www.fedstats.gov • Web site features an efficient search facility for full-text statistics produced by more than 100 federal agencies, including the Census Bureau, the Bureau of Economic Analysis, and the Bureau of Labor Statistics. Boolean searches can be made within one agency or for all agencies combined. Links are offered to international statistical bureaus, including the UN, IMF, OECD, UNESCO, Eurostat, and 20 individual countries. Fees: Free.

FreeLunch.com. Economy.com, Inc. Phone: (610)696-8700 Fax: (610)696-1678 • URL: http://www.freelunch.com • Web site provides free access to more than 1.5 million economic and financial data series, covering industry, demographics, labor markets, prices, retail sales, government spending, trade, interest rates, housing starts, the stock market, and many other topics. Data is available for various time periods in either chart or table form. Searching is offered. Fees: Free, but registration required. Economy.com, Inc. also offers fee-based economic analysis at *The Dismal Scientist* site (http://www.dismal.com).

PERIODICALS AND NEWSLETTERS

American Leather Chemists Association Journal. American Leather Chemists Association. • Monthly. Members, $8.50 per year; non-members, $115.00 per year.

Leather Manufacturer. Shoe Trades Publishing Co. • Monthly. $40.00 per year. Edited for hide processors, tanners and leather finishers in the U.S. and Canada.

RESEARCH CENTERS AND INSTITUTES

Leather Research Laboratory. University of Cincinnati, 5997 Center Hill Ave., Bldg. C, Cincinnati, OH 45224. Phone: (513)242-6300 Fax: (513)242-9797 E-mail: corynj@uc.edu • URL: http://www.leatherusa.com.

STATISTICS SOURCES

Annual Survey of Manufactures. Available from U. S. Government Printing Office. • Annual. Prices vary. Issued by the U. S. Census Bureau as an interim update to the *Census of Manufactures.* Includes data on number of manufacturing establishments in various industries, employment, labor costs, value of shipments, capital expenditures, inventories, energy costs, and assets. (See also Census Bureau home page, http://www.census.gov/.).

Business Statistics of the United States. Linz Audain

and Cornelia J. Strawser. Bernan Associates. • Annual. $147.00. Based on *Business Statistics,* formerly issue by the Bureau of Economic Analysis, U. S. Department of Commerce. Provides basic data for a wide variety of U. S. industries, services, and economic indicators. Most statistics are shown annually for 30 years and monthly for the most recent four years.

Leather Industries Statistics. Leather Industries of America. • Annual. Free to members; non-members, $30.00. Provides detailed analysis of domestic and foreign trade.

Survey of Current Business. Available from U. S. Government Printing Office. • Monthly. $63.00 per year. Issued by Bureau of Economic Analysis, U. S. Department of Commerce. Presents a wide variety of business and economic data.

TRADE/PROFESSIONAL ASSOCIATIONS

American Leather Chemists Association. 1314 50th St., Ste. 103; P.O. Box 45300, Lubbock, TX 79412-2940. Phone: (806)744-1798 Fax: (806)744-1785 E-mail: alca@leatherchemists.org • URL: http://www.leatherchemists.org • Chemists, leather technologists, and educators concerned with the tanning and leather industry. Works to devise and perfect methods for the analysis and testing of leathers and materials used in leather manufacture. Promotes advancement of chemistry and other sciences, especially their application to problems confronting the leather industry.

Leather Industries of America. 1900 L St., NW, Ste 710, Washington, DC 20036. Phone: (202)296-4806 Fax: (202)296-7882 E-mail: info@leatherusa.com • URL: http://www.leatherusa.com • Formerly Tanners' Council of America.

United States Hide, Skin and Leather Association. 1700 N. Moore St., Suite 1600, Arlington, VA 22209. Phone: (703)841-5485 Fax: (703)841-9656 E-mail: lcondon@ushsla.org • URL: http://www.meatami.org • Affiliated with American Meat Institute.

LEGAL FORMS

See: FORMS AND BLANKS

LEGAL HOLIDAYS

See: ANNIVERSARIES AND HOLIDAYS

LEGAL PROFESSION

See: LAWYERS

LEGAL RIGHTS

See: CIVIL RIGHTS

LEGATIONS

See: DIPLOMATIC AND CONSULAR SERVICE

LEGISLATION

See: LAWS

LEGISLATIVE INVESTIGATIONS

See: GOVERNMENT INVESTIGATIONS

LEGISLATIVE PROCEDURE

GENERAL WORKS

American Legislative Process: Congress and the States. William J. Keefe and Morris Ogul, editors. Prentice Hall PTR. • 2000. $60.00. 10th edition.

How Our Laws Are Made. Available from U. S. Government Printing Office. • 2000. $3.75. 22nd edition. Issued by U. S. House of Representatives.

Legislative Process. Abner J. Mikva and Eric Lane. Aspen Publishers, Inc. • 2002. $56.00. Second edition.

ABSTRACTS AND INDEXES

Current Law Index: Multiple Access to Legal Periodicals. Gale Cengage Learning. • Monthly. $725.00 per year. Produced in cooperation with the American Association of Law Libraries. Indexes more than 900 law journals, legal newspapers, and specialty publications from the U.S., Canada, U.K., Ireland, Australia, and New Zealand.

BIBLIOGRAPHIES

Legislative Reference Services and Sources. Kathleen Low. Haworth Press, Inc. • 1994. $39.95. Describes more than 100 reference sources that are frequently consulted in providing information to legislators and their staffs. Includes a discussion of online services used for legislative reference. (Library and Information Science Series).

INTERNET DATABASES

Lexis.com Research System. Lexis-Nexis Group. Phone: 800-227-4908 or (937)865-6800 Fax: (937)865-6909 E-mail: webmaster@prod.lexis-nexis.com • URL: http://www.lexis.com • Fee-based Web site offers extensive searching of a wide variety of legal sources. Additional features include Daily Opinion Service, lexis.com Bookstore, Career Center, CLE Center, Law Schools, and Practice Pages ("Pages specific to areas of specialty").

RESEARCH CENTERS AND INSTITUTES

Harvard Legislative Research Bureau. Harvard University, Harvard Law School, 1541 Massachusetts Ave., Cambridge, MA 02138. Phone: (617)495-4400 Fax: (617)495-1110 E-mail: pgowder@law.harvard.edu • Concerned with federal and state legislation in all fields.

LEGISLATURES

GENERAL WORKS

Lawmaking and the Legislative Process: Committees, Connections, and Compromises. Greenwood Publishing Group, Inc. • 1996. $29.95. Explains how bills are enacted into laws through the state legislative process. Provides step-by-step examples, using fictitious bills.

ALMANACS AND YEARBOOKS

Suggested State Legislation. Council of State Governments. • Annual. $59.00. A source of legislative ideas and drafting assistance for state government officials.

BIOGRAPHICAL SOURCES

Who's Who in American Politics. Marquis Who's Who. • Biennial. $275.00. Two volumes. Contains about 27,000 biographical sketches of local, state, and national elected or appointed individuals.

DIRECTORIES

CSG State Directories, I. Council of State Governments. • Covers: About 8,000 state legislators, elected state executive branch officials, and state supreme court judges. Entries include: Name, title, address, district, party affiliation, fax and facts about each state-motto, flower, bird, nickname, capitol address, bill status phone, land area, population, D. C. Liaison, term limits, election and session dates.

Directory of State Legislatures. National Conference of State Legislatures. • Annual. $85.00. Provides names, addresses, telephone numbers, and e-mail addresses of state legislators and executive officials. Available only online. Formerly *Election Results Directory.*

PERIODICALS AND NEWSLETTERS

State Legislatures. National Conference of State Legislatures. • Description: Provides a national perspective on government and policy in the each state. Features articles on public policy issues.

TRADE/PROFESSIONAL ASSOCIATIONS

Council of State Governments. 2760 Research Park Dr., Lexington, KY 40578-1910. Phone: 800-800-1910 or (859)244-8000 Fax: (859)244-8001 E-mail: web_editor@csg.org • URL: http://www.csg.org • Supersedes American Legislator Association.

National Conference of State Legislatures. 1560 Broadway, Ste. 700, 7700 E First Pl., Denver, CO 80230. Phone: (303)364-7700 Fax: (303)364-7800 E-mail: info@ncsl.org • URL: http://www.ncsl.org • Affiliated with Council of State Governments.

LEISURE INDUSTRY

See: AMUSEMENT INDUSTRY; RECREATION INDUSTRY; SHOW BUSINESS; SPORTS BUSINESS

LEMONS

See: CITRUS FRUIT INDUSTRY

LENSES, CONTACT

See: CONTACT LENS AND INTRAOCULAR LENS INDUSTRIES

LENSES, INTRAOCULAR

See: CONTACT LENS AND INTRAOCULAR LENS INDUSTRIES

LETTER WRITING

See: BUSINESS CORRESPONDENCE

LEVERAGED BUYOUTS

See also: JUNK BOND FINANCING; MERGERS AND ACQUISITIONS

GENERAL WORKS

Cases in Corporate Acquisitions, Buyouts, Mergers, and Takeovers. Gale Cengage Learning. • 1999. $350.00. Reviews and analyzes about 300 cases of both success and failure in corporate acquisitiveness.

Mergers, Acquisitions, and Corporate Restructurings. Patrick A. Gaughan. John Wiley and Sons, Inc. • 2001. $75.00. Third edition. Covers mergers, acquisitions, divestitures, internal reorganizations, joint ventures, leveraged buyouts, bankruptcy workouts, and recapitalizations.

ABSTRACTS AND INDEXES

Business Periodicals Index. H. W. Wilson Co. • 11 times a year. Quarterly and annual cumulations. Price varies.

CD-ROM DATABASES

Buyout Financing Sources/M & A Intermediaries. Thomson Media. • Annual. $895.00. Provides the CD-ROM combination of *Directory of Buyout*

Financing Sources and *Directory of M & A Intermediaries.* Contains information on more than 1,000 financing sources (banks, insurance companies, venture capital firms, etc.) and 850 intermediaries (corporate acquirers, valuation firms, lawyers, accountants, etc.). Also includes back issues of *Buyouts Newsletter* and *Mergers & Acquisitions Report.* Fully searchable.

DIRECTORIES

Directory of Buyout Financing Sources. Thomson Financial. • Annual. $445.00. Describes more than 1,000 U. S. and foreign sources of financing for buyout deals. Indexed by personnel, company, industry, and location.

HANDBOOKS AND MANUALS

The Art of M & A: A Merger-Acquisition-Buyout Guide. Stanley F. Reed and Aleandra R. Lajoux. McGraw-Hill. • 1998. $125.00. Third edition. A how-to-do-it guide for merger and acquisition ventures. Emphasis is on legal issues.

Corporate Acquisitions, Mergers, and Divestitures. Lewis D. Solomon. Prentice Hall PTR. • Looseleaf. Periodic supplementation. Price on application. Includes how to buy a company with its own assets or earnings.

A Management Guide to Leveraged Buyouts. Edward K. Crawford. John Wiley and Sons, Inc. • 1987. $175.00. (Frontiers in Finance Series).

ONLINE DATABASES

Wilson Business Abstracts Online. H. W. Wilson Co. • Indexes and abstracts 600 major business periodicals, plus the *Wall Street Journal* and the business section of the *New York Times.* Indexing is from 1982, abstracting from 1990, with the two newspapers included from 1993. Updated weekly. Inquire as to online cost and availability. (*Business Periodicals Index* without abstracts is also available online.).

PERIODICALS AND NEWSLETTERS

Acquisitions Monthly. Thomson Financial. • Monthly. $790.00 per year. Published in London. Provides detailed information, commentary, and statistics on merger, acquisition, and buyout activity in Europe, the U.S., and Asia.

Buyouts: The Newsletter for Management Buyouts, Leveraged Aquisitions, and Special Situations. Thomson Financial. • Biweekly. $1,595.00 per year. Newsletter. Covers news and trends for the buyout industry. Provides information on deal makers and current buyout activity.

Corporate Acquisitions. ARCH Group. • Description: Summaries of trends and analysis of transactions in corporate mergers and acquisitions. Recurring features include interviews, reports of meetings, book reviews, and companies listed for sale.

Corporate Control Alert; A Report on Current Changes for Corporate Control. American Lawyer Media Inc. • Monthly. $1,595 per year. A monthly mergers and acquisitions newsletter.

Corporate Financing Week: The Newsweekly of Corporate Finance, Investment Banking and M and A. Institutional Investor, Inc., Journals Group. • Weekly. $2,550.00 per year. Includes print and online editions. Newsletter for corporate finance officers. Emphasis is on debt and equity financing, mergers, leveraged buyouts, investment banking, and venture capital.

Corporate Growth. Princeton Research Institute. • Monthly. $198.00 per year.

Corporate Growth Report. NVST Inc. • Description: Reports merger, acquisition, and divestiture activity, including in-depth analysis of major transactions. Publishes statistics on seller's and buyer's sales, profits, net worth, book value and earnings per share, and multiples of earnings, sales,

and net worth compared with purchase price.

RESEARCH CENTERS AND INSTITUTES

Bradley Policy Research Center. University of Rochester, William E. Simon Graduate School of Business Administration, Rochester, NY 14627. Phone: (585)275-2668 Fax: (585)275-0095 E-mail: hansen@simon.rochester.edu • URL: http://www.ssb.rochester.edu • Corporate control and corporate takeovers are among the research areas covered.

Investor Responsibility Research Center, Inc. Investor Responsibility Research Center. 1350 Connecticut Ave. NW, Ste. 700, Washington, DC 20036-1702. Phone: (202)833-0700 Fax: (202)833-3555 E-mail: marketing@irrc.com • URL: http://www.irrc.org • Social, public policy, and corporate governance issues and their impact on major corporations and institutional investors. Issues studied have included anti-takeover measures, board and compensation practices, energy and the environment, the electric utility industry, military contracting, executive compensation, business in Northern Ireland, plant closings, global shareholder rights, animal testing, and voting and other actions by institutional investors. Also offers consulting and contract research.

Rodney L. White Center for Financial Research. University of Pennsylvania, 3254 Steinberg Hall-Dietrich Hall, Philadelphia, PA 19104. Phone: (215)898-7616 Fax: (215)573-8084 E-mail: rlwtcr@finance.wharton.upenn.edu • URL: http://www.finance.wharton.upenn.edu • Research areas include financial management, money markets, real estate finance, and international finance.

Weidenbaum Center on the Economy, Government, and Public Policy. Washington University in Saint Louis. One Brookings Dr., CB 1027, St. Louis, MO 63130-4899. Phone: (314)935-5630 Fax: (314)935-5688 • URL: http://www.wc.wustl.edu • Research activity includes the study of corporate takeovers. Formerly Center for the Study of American Business.

TRADE/PROFESSIONAL ASSOCIATIONS

International Merger and Acquisition Professionals. 525 SW Fifth St., Des Moines, IA 50309. Phone: (515)282-8192 Fax: (515)282-9117 E-mail: info@imap.com • URL: http://www.imap.com • Mainly concerned with medium-sized businesses having annual sales of less than 50 million dollars.

OTHER SOURCES

Going Private. American Lawyer Media, Inc. • Looseleaf. $169.00. Updated as needed. Discusses the legal ramifications of a publicly-owned company "going private" by way of a sale, leveraged buyout, reverse stock split, or merger. (Law Journal Press).

LIABILITY INSURANCE

See: PROPERTY AND LIABILITY INSURANCE; PROFESSIONAL LIABILITY

LIABILITY, PRODUCT

See: PRODUCT SAFETY AND LIABILITY

LIABILITY, PROFESSIONAL

See: PROFESSIONAL LIABILITY

LIBRARIANS

GENERAL WORKS

Accidental Systems Librarian. Rachel S. Gordon. Information Today, Inc. • 2003. $29.50. Provides practical advice for librarians with newly-assigned, computer systems technology responsibilities.

Accidental Webmaster. Julie M. Still. Information Today, Inc. • 2003. $29.50. Covers the practical aspects of designing and maintaining a successful Web site. Written for librarians and others without previous Webmaster experience.

Expanding Technologies, Expanding Careers: Librarianship in Transition. Ellis Mount, editor. Special Libraries Association. • 1997. $45.00. Contains articles on alternative, non-traditional career paths for librarians, whether as entrepreneurs or employees. All the careers are related to computer-based, information retrieval and technology.

Extending the Librarian's Domain: A Survey of Emerging Occupational Opportunities for Librarians and Information Professionals. Forest W. Horton. Special Libraries Association. • 1994. $38.00. An examination of non-traditional career possibilities for special librarians. (Occasional Papers: No. 4).

First Have Something to Say: Writing for the Library Profession. Walt Crawford. American Library Association. • 2003. $29.00. Provides practical advice for librarian-writers on such matters as copyright, contracts, and getting published.

Net Effects: How Librarians Can Manage the Unintended Consequences of the Internet. Marylaine Block, editor. Information Today, Inc. • 2003. $39.50. Contains about 50 articles by librarians on the "side effects" of Internet use in libraries, such as technology stress, threats to print sources, retraining problems, new budget demands, and legal controversies.

Opening New Doors: Alternative Careers for Librarians. Ellis Mount, editor. Special Libraries Association. • 1992. $39.00. Information professionals in careers outside the library field discuss the nature of their work, qualifications, rewards, finding a job, etc.

Stress and Burnout in Library Service. Janette S. Caputo. Greenwood Publishing Group, Inc. • 1991. $24.95. Discusses symptoms of stress in library staff members and ways of dealing with stress. Includes self-help checklists and a list of references for further information.

Valuating Information Intangibles: Measuring the Bottom Line Contribution of Librarians and Information Professionals. Frank H. Portugal. Special Libraries Association. • 2000. $79.00. Focuses on the importance of the intangible aspects of appraising information resources and services.

The Visible Librarian: Asserting Your Value with Marketing and Advocacy. Judith A. Siess. American Library Association. • 2003. $34.00. Contains practical advice on library public relations and marketing of services. The author is editor of *The One-Person Library: A Newsletter for Librarians and Management.*

ABSTRACTS AND INDEXES

Library Literature and Information Science Index. H. W. Wilson Co. • Quarterly. Annual cumulation. Price varies.

BIOGRAPHICAL SOURCES

The Best of Times: A Personal and Occupational Odyssey. Paul Wasserman. Omnigraphics, Inc. • 2000. $35.00. Autobiography of a well known librarian, educator, and reference book editor. Foreward by Frederick G. Ruffner.

CD-ROM DATABASES

Leadership Library on CD-ROM: Who's Who in the Leadership of the United States. Leadership Directories, Inc. • Quarterly. Including access to Internet version (weekly updates). Contains all 14 *Yellow Book* personnel directories on CD-ROM, providing contact and brief biographical information for about 400,000 individuals. Covers business,

government, financial institutions, news media, law firms, associations, foreign representatives, and nonprofit organizations. Includes photographs.

LISA Plus. Available from Cambridge Scientific Abstracts (CSA). • Quarterly. $2,000.00 per year. CD-ROM version of Library Information and Science Abstracts, providing abstracting and indexing of the world's library and information science literature, 1969 to date. Contains more than 180,000 citations.

WILSONDISC: Library Literature and Information Science Index. H. W. Wilson Co. • Quarterly. Includes unlimited access to the online version of *Library Literature.* Provides CD-ROM indexing of about 300 periodicals, covering a wide range of topics having to do with libraries, library management, and the information industry.

DIRECTORIES

American Library Association Handbook of Organization and Membership Directory. American Library Association. • Annual. $30.00. Lists about 52,000 librarians. Formerly *American Library Association Membership Directory.*

Burwell World Directory of Information Brokers. Helen P. Burwell, editor. Burwell Enterprises. • Annual. $59.50. Lists more than 1,000 information brokers, document delivery firms, free-lance librarians, and fee-based library services. Provides U. S. and international coverage (46 countries). Formerly *Directory of Fee-Based Information Services.*

Guide to Employment Sources in the Library and Information Professions. American Library Association. • Annual. Free. Associations and agencies offering library placement services.

Nonprofit Sector Yellow Book: Who's Who in the Management of the Leading Foundations, Universities, Museums, and Other Nonprofit Organizations. Leadership Directories, Inc. • Semiannual. $265.00 per year. Covers management personnel and board members of about 1,300 prominent, nonprofit organizations: foundations, colleges, museums, performing arts groups, medical institutions, libraries, private preparatory schools, and charitable service organizations.

Who's Who in Special Libraries. Special Libraries Association. • Annual. $125.00. Available only online. About 14,000 librarians of libraries and special collections having a specific subject focus.

HANDBOOKS AND MANUALS

Complete Guide to Performance Standards for Library Personnel. Carol F. Goodson. Neal-Schuman Publishers, Inc. • 1997. $55.00. Provides specific job descriptions and performance standards for both professional and paraprofessional library personnel. Includes a bibliography of performance evaluation literature, with annotations.

Evaluating Library Staff: A Performance Appraisal System. Patricia Belcastro. American Library Association. • 1998. $35.00. Provides information on an appraisal system applicable to a wide variety of jobs in all types of libraries. Includes guidelines, performance appraisal forms, sample employee profiles, and a "Code of Service.".

How to Avoid Liability: The Information Professionals' Guide to Negligence and Warrant Risks. T. R. Halvorson. Burwell Enterprises. • 1998. $24.50. Second edition. Provides legal advice, cases, and decisions relating to information brokers and others in the information business.

Information Brokering: How to Make Money Selling Information Services. Florence M. Mason and Chris Dobson. Neal-Schuman Publishers, Inc. • 1998. $45.00. A practical guide to business plans, location, costs, fees, billing, marketing, accounting, taxes, and legal issues. Covers information brokering as a small business enterprise. (How-To-Do-It Manuals Series).

The Information Professional's Guide to Career Development Online. Sarah L. Nesbeitt and Rachel S. Gordon. Information Today, Inc. • 2001. $29.50. Provides advice to librarians and other information professionals about using online sources for career advancement. The Career Development Online Web Page (http://www.lisjobs.com/careerdev/) contains links to relevant resources.

Legal Liability Problems in Cyberspace: Craters in the Information Highway. T. R. Halvorson. Burwell Enterprises. • 1998. $24.50. Covers the legal risks and liabilities involved in doing online research as a paid professional. Includes a table of cases.

Position Descriptions in Special Libraries. Del Sweeney and Karin Zilla, editors. Special Libraries Association. • 1996. $41.00. Third revised edition. Provides 87 descriptions of library and information management positions.

Recruiting Library Staff: A How-To-Do-It Manual for Librarians. Kathleen Low. Neal-Schuman Publishers, Inc. • 1999. $45.00. Includes position description forms, sample announcements, and checklists. Discusses job fairs and other career events. (How-To-Do-It Manual for Librarians Series).

Sawyer's Success Tactics for Information Businesses. Deborah C. Sawyer. Burwell Enterprises. • 1998. $24.50. Covers such items as pricing, costs, and service for information brokers and others in the fee-based information business.

Sawyer's Survival Guide for Information Brokers. Deborah C. Sawyer. Burwell Enterprises. • 1995. $39.50. Provides practical advice for information entrepreneurs.

The SOLO Librarian's Sourcebook. Judith A. Siess. Information Today, Inc. • 1997. $39.50. Covers management and other aspects of one-librarian libraries.

Virtual Reference Training: The Complete Guide to Providing Anytime, Anywhere Answers. Buff Hirko and Mary Bucher Ross. American Library Association. • 2004. $42.00. Serves as a guide to effective, online library reference service. Emphasis is on staff training and "14 core competencies.".

ONLINE DATABASES

LISA: Library and Information Science Abstracts. Available from Cambridge Scientific Abstracts (CSA). • Provides abstracting and indexing of the world's library and information science literature, 1969 to date. Covers more than 440 periodicals from 68 countries. Updating is biweekly. Inquire as to online cost and availability.

PERIODICALS AND NEWSLETTERS

American Libraries. American Library Association. • 11 times a year. Institutions, $60.00 per year. Current news and information concerning the library industry.

Information Broker. Helen P. Burwell, editor. Burwell Enterprises Inc. • Description: Covers companies that offer fee-based information services and issues related to "the business" of information brokering.

Library Administrator's Digest. Baltimore County Public Library Foundation Inc. • Description: Designed to keep library administrators abreast of new ideas and developments, particularly in the public library field. Recurring features include editorials and letters to the editor.

Library Hotline: Breaking News for Library and Information Decision Makers. Reed Business Information. • 50 times a year. $109.00 per year. Newsletter. News and developments affecting libraries and librarians.

Library Personnel News. Office for Library Personnel Resources. American Library Association. • Quarterly. $20.00 per year. Newsletter covering personnel trends and issues.

For publishers addresses, refer to SOURCES CITED section at the back of the book.

The One-Person Library: A Newsletter for Librarians and Management. Information Bridges International, Inc. • Monthly. $85.00 per year. Newsletter for librarians working alone or with minimal assistance. Contains reports on library literature, management advice, case studies, book reviews, and general information.

School Library Journal: The Magazine of Children Young Adults and School Librarians. Reed Business Information. • Monthly. $124.00 per year. Provides news, information and reviews for librarians and media specialists who serve children and young adults in school and public libraries.

The Unabashed Librarian: The "How I Run My Library Good" Letter. Maurice J. Freedman. • Quarterly. $57.50 per year. Newsletter. Provides practical library management ideas and library humor.

STATISTICS SOURCES

ALA Survey of Librarian Salaries. American Library Association. • Annual. $55.00. Provides data on salaries paid to librarians in academic and public libraries. Position categories range from beginning librarian to director.

SLA Annual Salary Survey. Special Libraries Association. • Annual. Members, $45.00; non-members, $125.00. Provides data on salaries for special librarians in the U. S. and Canada, according to location, job title, industry, budget, and years of experience.

TRADE/PROFESSIONAL ASSOCIATIONS

American Association of School Librarians. 50 E. Huron St., Chicago, IL 60611. Phone: 800-545-2433 or (312)280-4386 Fax: (312)664-7459 E-mail: aasl@ala.org • URL: http://www.ala.org/aasl • A division of the American Library Association.

American Library Association. 50 E Huron St., Chicago, IL 60611. Phone: 800-545-2433 or (312)944-6780 Fax: (312)440-9374 E-mail: ala@ala.org • URL: http://www.ala.org • Librarians, libraries, trustees, friends of libraries, and others interested in the responsibilities of libraries in the educational, social, and cultural needs of society. Promotes and improves library service and librarianship. Establishes standards of service, support, education, and welfare for libraries and library personnel; promotes the adoption of such standards in libraries of all kinds; safeguards the professional status of librarians; encourages the recruiting of competent personnel for professional careers in librarianship; promotes popular understanding and public acceptance of the value of library service and librarianship. Works in liaison with federal agencies to initiate the enactment and administration of legislation that will extend library services. Offers placement services.

American Library Association Gay, Lesbian, Bisexual and Transgendered Roundtable. 50 E Huron St., Chicago, IL 60611. Phone: 800-545-2433 E-mail: amoore@library.umass.edu • URL: http://www.ala.org • Promotes gay, lesbian, bisexual and transgendered professionals.

Asia/Pacific American Librarians Association. MIT Humanities Library, 77 Massachusetts Ave., Rm. 14S-222, Cambridge, MA 02139. Phone: 800-545-2433 or (617)253-9352 Fax: (617)253-3109 E-mail: baildon@mit.edu • URL: http://www.apalaweb.org • Librarians and information specialists of Asian Pacific descent working in the U.S.; interested persons. Provides a forum for discussing problems and concerns; supports and encourages library services to Asian Pacific communities; recruits and supports Asian Pacific Americans in the library and information science professions. Offers placement service; compiles statistics. Conducts fundraising for scholarships.

Association of Independent Information Professionals. 8550 United Plz. Blvd., Ste. 1001, Baton Rouge, IL 70809. Phone: 888-544-2447 or (225)408-4400 Fax: (225)922-4611 E-mail: info@aiip.org • URL: http://www.aiip.org • Members are information brokers, document providers, librarians, consultants, database designers, webmasters, and other information professionals. Formerly International Association of Independent Information Brokers.

Black Caucus of the American Library Association. c/o Bobby Player, Howard University Libraries, Washington, DC 20059. Phone: (202)806-7255 Fax: (202)806-7271 E-mail: bplayer@howard.edu • URL: http://www.bcala.org.

Catholic Library Association. 100 North St., Ste. 224, Pittsfield, MA 01201-5109. Phone: (413)443-2252 Fax: (413)442-2252 E-mail: cla@cathla.org • URL: http://www.cathla.org • Librarians, teachers, and booksellers concerned with Catholic libraries and their specialized problems and the writing, publishing, and distribution of Catholic literature. Members represent lay and clergy in both Catholic and non-Catholic institutions.

Chinese American Librarians Association. California State University Sacramento, 2000 State University Dr. E, 605 Agriculture Dr., Mailcode 6632, Sacramento, CA 95819. Fax: (949)857-1988 E-mail: dora4ala@yahoo.com • URL: http://www.cala-web.org • Promotes better communication among Chinese American librarians in the U.S., serves as a forum for the discussion of mutual problems, and supports the development and promotion of librarianship. Maintains placement referral service.

Italian American Librarians Caucus. 6 Peter Cooper Rd., Apt. 11G, New York, NY 10010. Phone: (212)228-8438 E-mail: deborah@irrigation.org • Political and national Italian and non-Italian American organizations; business, government, public, and academic information scientists. Provides guidelines and studies, for use by libraries and information centers, on Italian and Italian American materials and populations. Conducts educational, research, and charitable programs. Maintains speakers' bureau; compiles statistics.

Middle East Librarians Association. University of Pennsylvania Library, 3420 Walnut St., University of Washington Libraries, Philadelphia, PA 19104-6206. Phone: (215)898-2196 Fax: (215)898-0559 E-mail: secretary@mela.us • URL: http://www.mela.us • Librarians and others interested in aspects of librarianship that support the study or dissemination of information about the Middle East since the rise of Islam. Facilitates communication among members through meetings and publications. Improves the quality of area librarianship through the development of standards for the profession and education of Middle East library specialists. Compiles and disseminates information concerning Middle East libraries and collections and represents the judgment of the members in matters affecting them. Encourages cooperation among members and Middle East libraries, especially in the acquisition of materials and the development of bibliographic controls.

Special Libraries Association. 331 S Patrick St., Alexandria, VA 22314-3501. Phone: (703)647-4900 Fax: (703)647-4901 E-mail: sla@sla.org • URL: http://www.sla.org • International association of information professionals who work in special libraries serving business, research, government, universities, newspapers, museums, and institutions that use or produce specialized information. Seeks to advance the leadership role of special librarians. Offers consulting services to organizations that wish to establish or expand a library or information services. Conducts strategic learning and development courses, public relations, and government relations programs. Provides employment services. Operates knowledge exchange on topics pertaining to the development and management of special libraries. Maintains Hall of Fame.

LIBRARIES

See also: LIBRARY MANAGEMENT

GENERAL WORKS

Creating Web-Accessible Databases: Case Studies for Libraries, Museums, and Other Non-Profits. Julie M. Still, editor. Information Today, Inc. • 2001. $39.50. Presents case studies of successful Web projects in libraries and other institutions.

The Enduring Library: Technology, Tradition, and the Quest for Balance. Michael Gorman. American Library Association. • 2003. $35.00. Considers the fundamental mission of libraries, as affected by new information technologies.

Future Libraries: Dreams, Madness, and Reality. Walt Crawford and Michael Gorman. American Library Association. • 1995. $28.00. Discusses the "over-hyped virtual library" and electronic-publishing "fantasies." Presents the argument for the importance of books, physical libraries, and library personnel.

Introduction to Librarianship. Jean K. Gates. Neal-Schuman Publishers, Inc. • 2004. $38.50. Fourth edition.

Libraries and the Future: Essays on the Library in the Twenty-First Century. F. W. Lancaster, editor. Haworth Press, Inc. • 1994. $49.95. Emphasis is on information services in libraries of the future. (Original Book Series).

Library: An Unquiet History. Matthew Battles. W. W. Norton & Co., Inc. • 2003. $24.95. A colorful history of libraries from very early times to the present.

ABSTRACTS AND INDEXES

Library Literature and Information Science Index. H. W. Wilson Co. • Quarterly. Annual cumulation. Price varies.

LISA: Library and Information Science Abstracts. R. R. Bowker. • 13 times a year. $1,055.00 per year; includes print and online editions.

ALMANACS AND YEARBOOKS

The Bowker Annual: Library and Book Trade Almanac. Information Today, Inc. • Annual. $199.00. Reviews key trends and events and provides basic statistical information. Includes financial averages: library expenditures, salaries, and book prices. Contains lists of "best books, literary prizes, winners, and bestsellers." Formerly published by R. R. Bowker.

CD-ROM DATABASES

ERIC on SilverPlatter. Available from SilverPlatter Information, Inc. • Quarterly. $700.00 per year. Produced by the Office of Educational Research and Improvement, U. S. Dept. of Education. Provides CD-ROM indexing and abstracting of a wide variety of literature relating to education. Archival discs are available from 1966.

LISA Plus. Available from Cambridge Scientific Abstracts (CSA). • Quarterly. $2,000.00 per year. CD-ROM version of Library Information and Science Abstracts, providing abstracting and indexing of the world's library and information science literature, 1969 to date. Contains more than 180,000 citations.

WILSONDISC: Library Literature and Information Science Index. H. W. Wilson Co. • Quarterly. Includes unlimited access to the online version of *Library Literature.* Provides CD-ROM indexing of about 300 periodicals, covering a wide range of topics having to do with libraries, library management, and the information industry.

DIRECTORIES

ALA Handbook of Organization. American Library Association. • Annual. Free to members; non-members, $30.00. Includes information on ALA officers, committees, divisions, sections, round tables, and state chapters. (Issued as a supplement to *American Libraries*.).

American Library Directory. Information Today Inc. • Covers: Over 37,000 U.S. and Canadian academic, public, county, provincial, and regional libraries; library systems; medical, law, and other special libraries; and libraries for the blind and physically handicapped. Separate section lists over 350 library networks and consortia and 220 accredited and un-accredited library school programs. Entries include: For libraries--Name, supporting or affiliated institution or firm name, address, phone, fax, electronic mail address, Standard Address Number (SANs), names of librarian and department heads, income, collection size, special collections, computer hardware, automated functions, and type of catalog. For library systems--Name, location. For library schools--Name, address, phone, fax, electronic mail address, director, type of training and degrees, admission requirements, tuition, faculty size. For networks and consortia--Name, address, phone, names of affiliates, name of director, function.

Big Book of Library Grant Money 2002-2003: Profiles of Private and Corporate Foundations and Direct Corporate Givers Receptive to Library Grant Proposals. American Library Association. • 2002. $250.00. Provides profiles, contacts, past contributions data, application procedures, and biographical information on foundation personnel. (Prepared by the Taft Group for the American Library Association.)

Cyberhound's Guide to Internet Libraries. Gale Cengage Learning. • 1996. 79.00. Presents critical descriptions and ratings of more than 2,000 library Internet databases. Includes a glossary of Internet terms, a bibliography, and indexes. (Cyberhound's Series).

Directory of Government Document Collections and Librarians. Government Documents Roundtable. American Library Association. • Triennial. $57.50. A guide to federal, state, local, foreign, and international document collections in the U.S. Includes name of librarians and other government document professionals.

Grants for Libraries and Information Services. The Foundation Center. • Annual. $75.00. Foundations and organizations which have awarded grants made the preceding year for public, academic, research, special, and school libraries; for archives and information centers; for consumer information; and for philanthropy information centers.

National Guide to Funding for Libraries and Information Services. The Foundation Center. • 2001. $115.00. Sixth edition. Contains detailed information on about 600 foundations and corporate direct giving programs providing funding to libraries. Includes indexing by type of support, subject field, location, and key personnel.

Subject Collections: A Guide to Special Book Collections and Subject Emphasis in Libraries. Lee Ash and William G. Miller, editors. R. R. Bowker. • Irregular. $275.00. Two volumes. A guide to special book collections and subject emphases as reported by university, college, public and special libraries in th United States and Canada.

Who's Who in Special Libraries. Special Libraries Association. • Annual. $125.00. Available only online. About 14,000 librarians of libraries and special collections having a specific subject focus.

World Guide to Libraries. Available from Gale Cengage Learning. • 2003. $465.00. 17th edition. Two volumes. Provides information on more than 43,000 academic, government, and public libraries in 200 countries. Published by K. G. Saur.

ENCYCLOPEDIAS AND DICTIONARIES

Encyclopedia of Library and Information Science. Allen Kent and others, editors. Marcel Dekker, Inc. • 73 volumes. Dates vary. Prices vary.

World Encyclopedia of Library and Information Services. Robert Wedgeworth, editor. American Library Association. • 1993. $200.00. Third edition. Contains about 340 articles from various contributors.

HANDBOOKS AND MANUALS

Buying Books: A How-To-Do-It Manual for Librarians. Audrey Eaglen. Neal-Schuman Publishers, Inc. • 2000. $45.00. Second edition. Discusses vendor selection and book ordering in the age of electronic commerce. Covers both print and electronic bibliographic sources. (How-to-Do-It Manuals Series).

Buying Serials: A How-To-Do-It Manual for Librarians. N. Bernard Basch and Judy McQueen. Neal-Schuman Publishers, Inc. • 1990. $49.95. (How-to-Do-It Manuals Series).

Checklist of Library Building Design Considerations. William W. Sannwald and others. American Library Association. • 2001. $38.00. Fourth edition.

Copyright Primer for Librarians and Educators. Janis H. Bruwelheide. American Library Association. • 1995. $25.00. Second edition.

Coyle's Information Highway Handbook: A Practical File on the New Information Order. Karen Coyle. American Library Association. • 1997. $30.00. Provides useful "essays on copyright, access, privacy, censorship, and the information marketplace.".

Creating Newsletters, Brochures, and Pamphlets: A How-To-Do-It Manual for Librarians. Barbara A. Radke and Barbara Stein. Neal-Schuman Publishers, Inc. • 1992. $39.95. Includes desktop publishing. (How-to-Do-It Manuals Series).

Friends of Libraries Sourcebook. Sandy Dolnick. American Library Association. • 1996. $35.00. Third edition. Provides information and guidance relating to Friends of Libraries support groups.

Going Live: Starting and Running a Virtual Reference Service. Steve Coffman. American Library Association. • 2003. $42.00. Serves as a practical manual for libraries wishing to start a Web-based, always available reference service. Includes a bibliography by Bernie Sloan.

Interior Design for Libraries: Drawing on Function and Appeal. Carol R. Brown. American Library Association. • 2002. $45.00. Covers furniture, lighting, signs, acoustics, and other items important to interior design. Contains many illustrations of library interiors, including color plates.

The OPL Sourcebook: A Guide for Solo and Small Libraries. Judith A. Siess. Information Today, Inc. • 2001. $39.50. The editor of *The One-Person Library* newsletter covers a wide variety of practical topics for improving the management and efficiency of OPLs.

INTERNET DATABASES

WilsonWeb Periodicals Databases. H. W. Wilson. Phone: 800-367-6770 or (718)588-8400 Fax: 800-590-1617 or (718)992-8003 E-mail: custserv@hwwilson.com • URL: http://www.hwwilson.com/ • Web sites provide fee-based access to *Wilson Business Full Text, Applied Science & Technology Full Text, Biological & Agricultural Index, Library Literature & Information Science Full Text,* and *Readers' Guide Full Text, Mega Edition.* Daily updates.

ONLINE DATABASES

American Library Directory Online. Information Today, Inc. • Provides information on more than 30,000 public, college, and special libraries in the U.S. and Canada, with annual updates. Includes library networks, consortia, organizations, and schools. Inquire as to online cost and availability.

ERIC. Educational Resources Information Center. • Funded by the U. S. Department of Education, Institute of Education Sciences (formerly Office of Educational Research and Improvement). Provides access to more than one million online records covering education-related journal and report literature, 1966 to date. Updating is monthly. Inquire as to online cost and availability.

Information Science Abstracts [online]. Information Today, Inc. • Provides indexing and abstracting of the international literature of information science, including library science, from 1966 to date. Monthly updates. Inquire as to online cost and availability.

LC MARC: Books. U. S. Library of Congress. • Contains online bibliographic records for over five million books cataloged by the Library of Congress since 1968. Updating is weekly or monthly. Inquire as to online cost and availability. (MARC is machine readable cataloging.).

LISA: Library and Information Science Abstracts. Available from Cambridge Scientific Abstracts (CSA). • Provides abstracting and indexing of the world's library and information science literature, 1969 to date. Covers more than 440 periodicals from 68 countries. Updating is biweekly. Inquire as to online cost and availability.

PERIODICALS AND NEWSLETTERS

American Libraries. American Library Association. • 11 times a year. Institutions, $60.00 per year. Current news and information concerning the library industry.

Grants for Libraries Hotline. Quinlan Publishing Group. • Monthly. $129.00 per year. Newsletter. Provides news of grants and awards specifically for libraries (http://www.grantshotline.com). Includes "Deadline Update," a list of awarding agencies or programs, approximate dollar amounts available, deadlines, contacts (telephone numbers), and dates of newsletter profiles.

The Journal of Academic Librarianship: Articles, Features, and Book Reviews for the Academic Library Professional. Elsevier. • Bimonthly. Qualified personnel, $101.00 per year; institutions, $253.00 per year.

Journal of Library and Information Services in Distance Learning. Haworth Press, Inc. • Quarterly. $150.00 per year to libraries; $48.00 per year to individuals.

Library Hotline: Breaking News for Library and Information Decision Makers. Reed Business Information. • 50 times a year. $109.00 per year. Newsletter. News and developments affecting libraries and librarians.

Library Journal. Reed Business Information. • 20 times a year. $134.00 per year. Includes *Buyer's Guide*, six *Supplements* and weekly *Newswire*.

The Library Quarterly: A Journal of Investigation and Discussion in the Field of Library Science. University of Chicago Graduate Library School. The University of Chicago Press, Journals Div. • Quarterly. Individuals, $40.00 per year; includes print and online editions. Institutions, $120.00 per year; includes print and online editions.

Library Trends. University of Illinois at Urbana-Champaign, Graduate School of Library and Information Science. University of Illinois Press. • Quarterly. Individuals, $70.00 per year; institutions; $100.00 per year.

Public Library Quarterly. The Haworth Press, Inc. •

Quarterly. Institutions, $250.00 per year.

RESEARCH CENTERS AND INSTITUTES

Library Research Center. University of Illinois at Urbana-Champaign. 501 E. Daniel, Room 321, Champaign, IL 61820-6212. Phone: (217)333-1980 Fax: (217)244-3302 E-mail: lrc@uiuc.edu • URL: http://www.alexia.lis.uiuc.edu.

STATISTICS SOURCES

Digest of Education Statistics. Available from U. S. Government Printing Office. • Annual. $51.00. Covers all areas of education from kindergarten through graduate school. Includes data from both government and private sources. Compiled by National Center for Education Statistics, U. S. Department of Education.

Librarian's Companion: A Handbook of Thousands of Facts on Libraries, Librarians, Books, Newspapers, Publishers, Booksellers. Vladimir F. Wertsman. Greenwood Publishing Group, Inc. • 1996. $69.95. Provides international statistics on libraries and publishing. Includes directory and biographical information.

UNESCO Statistical Yearbook. Bernan Press. • 1998. $95.00. Co-published by Bernan Press and the United Nations Educational, Scientific, and Cultural Organization (http://www.unesco.org). Presents statistical data from more than 200 countries on education, technology, research, broadcasting, cinema, book publishing, newspapers, libraries, museums, and population. Includes charts, maps, and graphs.

TRADE/PROFESSIONAL ASSOCIATIONS

American Library Association. 50 E Huron St., Chicago, IL 60611. Phone: 800-545-2433 or (312)944-6780 Fax: (312)440-9374 E-mail: ala@ala.org • URL: http://www.ala.org • Librarians, libraries, trustees, friends of libraries, and others interested in the responsibilities of libraries in the educational, social, and cultural needs of society. Promotes and improves library service and librarianship. Establishes standards of service, support, education, and welfare for libraries and library personnel; promotes the adoption of such standards in libraries of all kinds; safeguards the professional status of librarians; encourages the recruiting of competent personnel for professional careers in librarianship; promotes popular understanding and public acceptance of the value of library service and librarianship. Works in liaison with federal agencies to initiate the enactment and administration of legislation that will extend library services. Offers placement services.

Special Libraries Association. 331 S Patrick St., Alexandria, VA 22314-3501. Phone: (703)647-4900 Fax: (703)647-4901 E-mail: sla@sla.org • URL: http://www.sla.org • International association of information professionals who work in special libraries serving business, research, government, universities, newspapers, museums, and institutions that use or produce specialized information. Seeks to advance the leadership role of special librarians. Offers consulting services to organizations that wish to establish or expand a library or information services. Conducts strategic learning and development courses, public relations, and government relations programs. Provides employment services. Operates knowledge exchange on topics pertaining to the development and management of special libraries. Maintains Hall of Fame.

OTHER SOURCES

Advances in Librarianship. Elsevier. • Irregular. Prices vary.

LIBRARIES, COLLEGE AND UNIVERSITY

See: COLLEGE AND UNIVERSITY LIBRARIES

LIBRARIES, PUBLIC

See: LIBRARIES

LIBRARIES, SPECIAL

See: SPECIAL LIBRARIES

LIBRARY AUTOMATION

See also: ONLINE INFORMATION SYSTEMS

GENERAL WORKS

Accidental Systems Librarian. Rachel S. Gordon. Information Today, Inc. • 2003. $29.50. Provides practical advice for librarians with newly-assigned, computer systems technology responsibilities.

Accidental Webmaster. Julie M. Still. Information Today, Inc. • 2003. $29.50. Covers the practical aspects of designing and maintaining a successful Web site. Written for librarians and others without previous Webmaster experience.

The Amazing Internet Challenge: How Leading Projects Use Library Skills to Organize the Web. Amy T. Wells and others. American Library Association. • 1999. $45.00. Presents profiles of 12 digital libraries, such as the Agriculture Network Information Center and the Social Science Information Gateway. Emphasis is on how online indexes were created.

Electronic Library: The Promise and the Process. Kenneth E. Dowlin. Neal-Schuman Publishers, Inc. • 1984. $45.00. (Applications in Information Management and Technology Series).

The Evolving Virtual Library: Practical and Philosophical Perspectives. Laverna M. Saunders, editor. Information Today, Inc. • 1999. $39.50. Various authors cover trends in library and school use of the Internet, intranets, extranets, and electronic databases.

Information Imagineering: Meeting at the Interface. Milton T. Wolf and others, editors. American Library Association. • 1997. $36.00. A collection of articles on the effect of information technology on libraries, museums, and other institutions.

Introduction to Automation for Librarians. William Saffady. American Library Association. • 1999. $60.00. Fourth edition. Provides basic information on electronic technology (computers, telecommunications) and library applications of technology.

Towards Electronic Journals: Realities for Scientists, Librarians, and Publishers. Carol Tenopir and Donald W. King. Special Libraries Association. • 2000. $59.00. Discusses journals in electronic form vs. traditional (paper) scholarly journals, including the impact of subscription prices.

The Ultimate Digital Library: Where the New Information Players Meet. Andrew K. Pace. American Library Association. • 2003. $35.00. Discusses how libraries can remain competitive within the new digital information world.

Wired for the Future: Developing Your Library Technology Plan. Diane Mayo and others. American Library Association. • 1998. $38.00. Describes various technologies and applications available to libraries.

ABSTRACTS AND INDEXES

Information Science Abstracts. American Society for Information Science. Information Today, Inc. • Nine times a year. $789.00 per year.

Library Literature and Information Science Index. H. W. Wilson Co. • Quarterly. Annual cumulation. Price varies.

LISA: Library and Information Science Abstracts. R. R. Bowker. • 13 times a year. $1,055.00 per year;

includes print and online editions.

CD-ROM DATABASES

LISA Plus. Available from Cambridge Scientific Abstracts (CSA). • Quarterly. $2,000.00 per year. CD-ROM version of Library Information and Science Abstracts, providing abstracting and indexing of the world's library and information science literature, 1969 to date. Contains more than 180,000 citations.

WILSONDISC: Library Literature and Information Science Index. H. W. Wilson Co. • Quarterly. Includes unlimited access to the online version of *Library Literature.* Provides CD-ROM indexing of about 300 periodicals, covering a wide range of topics having to do with libraries, library management, and the information industry.

DIRECTORIES

Computers in Libraries: Buyer's Guide and Consultant Directory. Mecklermedia Corp. • Annual. $30.00.

Directory of Library Automation Software, Systems, and Services. Information Today, Inc. • Biennial. $89.00. Provides detailed descriptions of about 330 software programs and software services for libraries.

The Librarian's Yellow Pages: Publications, Products, and Services for Libraries and Information Centers. • Irregular. Free to librarians in the United States; others, $15.00. A classified compilation of advertisements. for library items from more than 1,000 U. S. and Canadian companies. Major sections cover audio, automation, books, CD-ROMs, periodicals, and video. Subject and company indexes are included.

Library Journal Sourcebook. Reed Business Information. • Publication includes: List of over 600 suppliers of products and services used by libraries from abstracting to word processing equipment. Entries include: Company name, address, phone, list of products or services. Complete listings for more than 100 architectural firms; Disaster planning for librarians.

Library Resource Guide: A Catalog of Services and Suppliers for the Library Community. Information Today, Inc. • Annual. Free to libraries. An advertising directory listing several hundred manufacturers or distributors of library supplies, services, and equipment in such areas as audiovisual, automation, bar codes, binding, furniture, microfilm, shelving, and storage. Some book dealers, document delivery services, online services, and publishers are also included (http://www.libraryresource.com). Formerly published by R. R. Bowker.

A S I S Handbook and Directory. American Society for Information Science. • Annual. Members, $25.00; non-members, $100.00.

303 Software Programs to Use in Your Library: Descriptions, Evaluations, and Practical Advice. Patrick R. Dewey. American Library Association. • 1997. $36.00. Contains profiles of a wide variety of software (21 categories) that may be useful in libraries. Includes prices, company addresses, glossary, bibliography, and an index.(101 Micro Series).

HANDBOOKS AND MANUALS

Basic Internet for Busy Librarians: A Quick Course for Catching Up. Laura K. Murray. American Library Association. • 1998. $26.00. A "practical crash-course primer" for learning how to effectively navigate the Internet and the World Wide Web.

Building the Service-Based Library Web Site: A Step-by-Step Guide to Design and Options. Kristen L. Garlock and Sherry Piontek. American Library Association. • 1996. $30.00. Provides practical information for libraries planning a World Wide Web home page. (ALA Editions Series).

Buying and Maintaining Personal Computers: A How-To-Do-It Manual for Librarians with

Companion Web Site. Norman Howden. Neal-Schuman Publishers, Inc. • 2000. $45.00. Covers various aspects of buying PCs or MACs for library use, including choice of hardware, software selection, warranties, backup systems, staffing, and dealing with vendors. (How-To-Do-It Manuals Series).

CD-ROM Primer: The ABC's of CD-ROM. Cheryl LaGuardia. Neal-Schuman Publishers, Inc. • 1994. $49.95. Provides advice for librarians and others on CD-ROM equipment, selection, collecting, and maintenance. Includes a glossary, bibliography, and directory of suppliers.

The Cybrarian's Manual. Pat Ensor, editor. American Library Association. • 2000. $45.00. Second edition. Provides information for librarians concerning the Internet, expert systems, computer networks, client/server architecture, Web pages, multimedia, information industry careers, and other "cyberspace" topics.

Developing and Managing Electronic Journal Collections: A How-To-DoIt Manual forLibrarians. Donnelyn Curtis and others. Neal-Schuman Publishers, Inc. • 2000. $55.00. Covers the acquisition, management, and integration of journals published in electronic form. (How-To-Do-It Manuals Series).

Improving Online Public Access Catalogs. Martha M. Yee and Sara S. Layne. American Library Association. • 1998. $48.00. A practical guide to developing user-friendly online catalogs (OPACs).

Introduction to the Use of Computers in Libraries: A Textbook for the Non-Technical Student. Harold C. Ogg. Information Today, Inc. • 1997. $42.50. Provides basic information on computer programs for libraries, including spreadsheets, database applications, desktop publishing, automated circulation systems, and public access online catalogs.

The Librarian's Internet Survival Guide: Strategies for the High-Tech Reference Desk. Irene E. McDermott. Information Today, Inc. • 2002. $29.50. Provides practical advice relating to Web reference sources, information management strategies, Internet training issues, library Web pages, and patron relations.

The Library Administrator's Automation Handbook. Richard Boss. Information Today, Inc. • 1997. $39.50. Covers the library administrator's role in the planning, selection, and implementation of hardware and software for automated library systems.

Managing Public-Access Computers: A How-To-Do-It Manual for Librarians. Donald A. Barclay. Neal-Schuman Publishers, Inc. • 2000. $59.95. Part one covers hardware, software, and other components. Part two discusses computers users. Part three is about systems management, library policy, and legal issues. (How-to-Do-It Manuals Series).

Online Deskbook: Online Magazine's Essential Desk Reference for Online and Internet Searchers. Mary E. Bates. Information Today, Inc. • 1995. $29.95. Covers the World Wide Web, as well as America Online, CompuServe, Dialog, Lexis-Nexis, and all other major online services. (Pemberton Press Books.).

PC Management: A How-To-Do-It Manual for Librarians. Michael Schuyler and Jake Hoffman. Neal-Schuman Publishers, Inc. • 1990. $45.00. Covers the use of personal computers for library routines. Includes evaluations of software. (How-to-Do-It Manuals Series).

Using Desktop Publishing to Create Newsletters, Library Guides, and Web Pages: A How-To-Do-It Manual for Librarians. John Maxymuk. Neal-Schuman Publishers, Inc. • 1997. $55.00. Includes more than 90 illustrations. (How-to-Do-It Manuals Series).

Using Windows for Library Administration. Kenneth E. Marks and Steven P. Nielson. Information Today, Inc. • 1997. $34.95. Contains details on the use of Microsoft Windows software applications for library management: spreadsheets, desktop publishing, project planning, forms, etc.

ONLINE DATABASES

Information Science Abstracts [online]. Information Today, Inc. • Provides indexing and abstracting of the international literature of information science, including library science, from 1966 to date. Monthly updates. Inquire as to online cost and availability.

LISA: Library and Information Science Abstracts. Available from Cambridge Scientific Abstracts (CSA). • Provides abstracting and indexing of the world's library and information science literature, 1969 to date. Covers more than 440 periodicals from 68 countries. Updating is biweekly. Inquire as to online cost and availability.

PERIODICALS AND NEWSLETTERS

Aslib Proceedings: New Information Perspectives. Available from Information Today, Inc. • Ten times a year. $349.00 per year. Published in London by Aslib Covers a wide variety of information industry and library management topics.

Computers in Libraries. Information Today, Inc. • 10 times a year. $98.95 per year.

The Electronic Library: The International Journal for the Application of Technology in Information Environments. Sage Publications, Inc. • Bimonthly. $469.00 per year. Incorporated*Library Computing.*

Information Processing and Management: An International Journal. Elsevier Science. • Bimonthly. Qualified personnel, $301.00 per year; institutions, $1,196.00 per year. Text in English, French, German and Italian.

Information Standards Quarterly: News About Library, Information Sciences, and Publishing Standards. National Information Standards Organization (NISO). • Quarterly. $80.00 per year. Newsletter. Reports on activities of the National Information Standards Organization.

IntraNet Professional: IntraNet Applications and Knowledge Management for Libraries and Information Professionals. Information Today, Inc. • Bimonthly. $89.95 per year. Newsletter on the use of Internet technology for local library networks.

Journal of Internet Cataloging: The International Quarterly of Digital Organization, Classification, and Access. Haworth Press, Inc. • Quarterly. $165.00 per year.

Library Hi Tech News: The First in the Field to Identify the "Hot Topics" of Library Technology. Emerald (North America). • Quarterly. $319.00 per year. Provides detailed information on current and emerging library technologies.

Library Hi Tech News: Up to Date News on the Latest Developments in Library Automation. Emerald (North America). • 10 times a year. $389.00 per year. Newsletter. Contains news of library products and procedures, including software, hardware, and network-related items. Covers forthcoming events internationally.

Multimedia Schools: A Practical Journal of Technology for Education including Multimedia, CD-ROM, Online and Internet and Hardware in K-12. Information Today, Inc. • Six times a year. $39.95 per year. Edited for school librarians, media center directors, computer coordinators, and others concerned with educational multimedia. Coverage includes the use of CD-ROM sources, the Internet, online services, and library technology.

Online Libraries and Microcomputers. Information Intelligence, Inc. • Ten times a year. Individuals $43.75 per year; libraries. $62.50 per year. Newsletter. Covers library automation and electronic information (online, CD-ROM). Reviews or describes new computer hardware and software for library use.

Online: The Leading Magazine for Information Professionals. Information Today, Inc. • Bimonthly. $110.00 per year. Edited for librarians, Webmasters, site designers, content managers, and others concerned with knowledge/information management. Includes critical reviews of Web sites, software, search engines, and information services. (Formerly published by Online, Inc.).

Program: Electronic Library and Information Systems. Available from Information Today, Inc. • Quarterly. $339.00 per year. Published in London by Aslib: The Association for Information Management. Discusses computer applications for libraries.

Reference Services Review: Information on All Aspects of the Reference Function. Emerald (North America). • Quarterly. $319.00 per year. Covers automation of library reference services, user needs, reference source evaluation, service delivery models, and related topics.

Smart Libraries Newsletter: An Innovative Overview of Library Automation. American Library Association. • Monthly. $144.00 per year. Articles and news briefs covering all aspects of library automation. Formerly *Library Systems Newsletter.*

Technical Services Quarterly: New Trends in Computers, Automation, and Advanced Technologies in the Technical Operation of Libraries and Information Centers. Haworth Press, Inc. • Quarterly. Institutions, $375.00 per year.

RESEARCH CENTERS AND INSTITUTES

Bibliographical Center for Research, Inc., Rocky Mountain Region. 14394 E. Evans Ave., Aurora, CO 80014-1478. Phone: 800-397-1552 or (303)751-6277 Fax: (303)751-9787 E-mail: dbrunell@bcr.org • URL: http://www.bcr.org • Fields of research include information retrieval systems, Internet technology, CD-ROM technology, document delivery, and library automation.

Center for Study of Librarianship. Kent State University, P.O. Box 5190, Kent, OH 44242-0001. Phone: (330)672-2782 Fax: (330)672-7965 E-mail: rrubin1@kent.edu • URL: http://www.techtrans.kent.edu.

TRADE/PROFESSIONAL ASSOCIATIONS

American Society for Information Science and Technology. 1320 Fenwick Lane, No. 510, Silver Spring, MD 20910. Phone: (301)495-0900 Fax: (301)495-0810 E-mail: asis@asis.org • URL: http://www.asis.org • Members are information managers, scientists, librarians, and others who are interested in the storage, retrieval, and use of information.

Association for Library Collections and Technical Services. c/o American Library Association, 50 E. Huron St., Chicago, IL 60611. Phone: 800-545-2433 or (312)280-5308 Fax: (312)280-5033 E-mail: alcts@ala.org • URL: http://www.ala.org/alcts/.

Library and Information Technology Association. 50 E. Huron St., Chicago, IL 60611. Phone: 800-545-2433 or (312)280-4270 Fax: (312)280-3257 E-mail: lita@ala.org • URL: http://www.lita.org • Affiliated with the American Library Association. Formerly Information Science and Automation Division of ALA.

National Information Standards Organization. 1 N Charles St., Ste. 1905, Baltimore, MD 21201. Phone: (866)957-1593 or (301)654-2512 Fax: (301)654-1721 E-mail: nisohq@niso.org • URL: http://www.niso.org • Identifies, develops, maintains, and publishes technical standards to manage information in the changing environment used by libraries, publishers, and information services. Supports open access to NISO standards. Standards available at website.

Public Library Association; Technology Committee. c/o American Library Association, 50 E. Huron St., Chicago, IL 60611. Phone: 800-545-2433 or

(312)280-5028 Fax: (312)280-5029 E-mail: pla@pla.org • URL: http://www.pla.org • Affiliated with the American Library Association. Formerly Public Libraries Division.

Reference and User Services Association of American Library Association: Machine Assisted Reference Section. c/o American Library Association, 50 E Huron St., Chicago, IL 60611. Phone: 800-545-2433 or (312)280-4398 Fax: (312)944-8085 E-mail: rusa@ala.org • URL: http://www.ala.org/rusa • Affiliated with American Library Association. Formerly Reference and Adult Services Division of American Library Association.

Special Libraries Association; Information Technology Division. 1700 18th St., N.W., Washington, DC 20009-2514. Phone: (202)234-4700 Fax: (202)265-9317 E-mail: sla@sla.org • URL: http://www.sla.org/.

OTHER SOURCES

Library Technology Reports: Expert Guides to Library Systems and Services. American Library Association. • Bimonthly. $315.00 per year. Looseleaf service.

LIBRARY MANAGEMENT

See also: LIBRARIES

GENERAL WORKS

Administration of the Small Public Library. Darlene E. Weingand. American Library Association. • 2001. $45.00. Fourth edition.

The Best of OPL, II: Selected Readings from the One-Person Library: 1990-1994. Andrew Berner and Guy St. Clair. Special Libraries Association. • 1996. $36.00. Contains reprints of useful material from *The One-Person Library: A Newsletter for Librarians and Management.*

Corporate Library Excellence. James M. Matarazzo. Special Libraries Association. • 1990. $28.00.

Creating Policies for Results: From Chaos to Clarity. Sandra Nelson and June Garcia. American Library Association. • 2003. $50.00. Explains how to create clear, non-ambivalent public and staff policies for libraries. Covers policies relating to library organization, management, and service to patrons (Public Library Association Results Series).

Future-Driven Library Marketing. Darlene E. Weingand. American Library Association. • 1998. $25.00. The author discusses progressive marketing strategies for libraries. An annotated bibliography is included.

Human Resource Management in Libraries: Theory and Practice. Richard Rubin. Neal-Schuman Publishers, Inc. • 1991. $55.00. Covers such topics as performance rating, pay equity, and collective bargaining.

Management Strategies for Libraries: A Basic Reader. Beverly Lynch, editor. Neal-Schuman Publishers, Inc. • 1985. $55.00.

Net Effects: How Librarians Can Manage the Unintended Consequences of the Internet. Marylaine Block, editor. Information Today, Inc. • 2003. $39.50. Contains about 50 articles by librarians on the "side effects" of Internet use in libraries, such as technology stress, threats to print sources, retraining problems, new budget demands, and legal controversies.

Organizational Structure of Libraries. Lowell A. Martin. Scarecrow Press, Inc. • 1996. $42.00. Second edition. (Library Administration: No. 12).

Personnel Administration in Libraries. Sheila Creth and Frederick Duda. Neal-Schuman Publishers, Inc. • 1989. $55.00. Second edition.

Practical Strategies for Library Managers. Joan Giesecke. American Library Association. • 2001.

$32.00. Covers such basic items as decision making, team-building, and effective communication with staff members.

Special Libraries: A Guide for Management. Cathy A. Porter and Elin B. Christianson. Special Libraries Association. • 1997. $42.00. Fourth edition. Provides basic information for the managers of business and other organizations on starting, staffing, and maintaining a special library.

Strategic Management for Today's Libraries. Marilyn G. Mason. American Library Association. • 1999. $35.00. (ALA Editions Series).

The Visible Librarian: Asserting Your Value with Marketing and Advocacy. Judith A. Siess. American Library Association. • 2003. $34.00. Contains practical advice on library public relations and marketing of services. The author is editor of *The One-Person Library: A Newsletter for Librarians and Management.*

ABSTRACTS AND INDEXES

Library Literature and Information Science Index. H. W. Wilson Co. • Quarterly. Annual cumulation. Price varies.

ALMANACS AND YEARBOOKS

Advances in Library Administration and Organization. JAI Press, Inc. • Annual. Price varies. 20 volumes.

CD-ROM DATABASES

Leadership Library on CD-ROM: Who's Who in the Leadership of the United States. Leadership Directories, Inc. • Quarterly. Including access to Internet version (weekly updates). Contains all 14 *Yellow Book* personnel directories on CD-ROM, providing contact and brief biographical information for about 400,000 individuals. Covers business, government, financial institutions, news media, law firms, associations, foreign representatives, and nonprofit organizations. Includes photographs.

LISA Plus. Available from Cambridge Scientific Abstracts (CSA). • Quarterly. $2,000.00 per year. CD-ROM version of Library Information and Science Abstracts, providing abstracting and indexing of the world's library and information science literature, 1969 to date. Contains more than 180,000 citations.

WILSONDISC: Library Literature and Information Science Index. H. W. Wilson Co. • Quarterly. Includes unlimited access to the online version of *Library Literature.* Provides CD-ROM indexing of about 300 periodicals, covering a wide range of topics having to do with libraries, library management, and the information industry.

DIRECTORIES

Internet Tools of the Profession: A Guide for Information Professionals. Hope N. Tillman, editor. Special Libraries Association. • 1997. $49.00. Second edition. Consists of 14 sections by various authors or compilers. After two introductory articles on searching the Internet, there are 12 annotated lists of useful Web sites, covering the SLA, business and finance, chemistry, education, food and agriculture, information technology, insurance and employee benefits, law, library management, metals and materials, pharmaceuticals, and telecommunications. An index is provided.

Nonprofit Sector Yellow Book: Who's Who in the Management of the Leading Foundations, Universities, Museums, and Other Nonprofit Organizations. Leadership Directories, Inc. • Semiannual. $265.00 per year. Covers management personnel and board members of about 1,300 prominent, nonprofit organizations: foundations, colleges, museums, performing arts groups, medical institutions, librar-

ies, private preparatory schools, and charitable service organizations.

HANDBOOKS AND MANUALS

Accounting for Libraries and Other Not-for-Profit Organizations. G. Stevenson Smith. American Library Association. • 1999. $82.00. Second edition. Covers accounting fundamentals for nonprofit organizations. Includes a glossary.

Assessing Service Quality: Satisfying the Expectations of Library Customers. Peter Hernon and Ellen Altman. American Library Association. • 1998. $40.00. Discusses surveys, focus groups, and other data collection methods for measuring the quality of library service. Includes sample forms and an annotated bibliography.

Becoming a Fundraiser: The Principles and Practice of Library Development. Victoria Steele and Stephen D. Elder. American Library Association. • 2000. $38.00. Second edition.

Budgeting: A How-to-Do-it Manual for Librarians. Alice S. Warner. Neal-Schuman Publishers, Inc. • 1998. $49.95. Explains six forms of budgeting suitable for various kinds of libraries. Includes a bibliography. (How-to-Do-It Manuals Series).

Buying Books: A How-To-Do-It Manual for Librarians. Audrey Eaglen. Neal-Schuman Publishers, Inc. • 2000. $45.00. Second edition. Discusses vendor selection and book ordering in the age of electronic commerce. Covers both print and electronic bibliographic sources. (How-to-Do-It Manuals Series).

Complete Guide to Performance Standards for Library Personnel. Carol F. Goodson. Neal-Schuman Publishers, Inc. • 1997. $55.00. Provides specific job descriptions and performance standards for both professional and paraprofessional library personnel. Includes a bibliography of performance evaluation literature, with annotations.

Countdown to a New Library: Managing the Building Project. Jeannette Woodward. American Library Association. • 2000. $48.00. Explains how to work in harmony with builders and architects.

Creating a Financial Plan: A How-To-Do-It Manual for Librarians. Betty J. Turock amd Andrea Pedolsky. Neal-Schuman Publishers, Inc. • 1992. $49.95. (How-to-Do-It Manuals Series).

Customer Service Excellence: A Concise Guide for Librarians. Darlene E. Weingand. American Library Association. • 1997. $30.00. Includes information on quality of service benchmarks, teamwork, patron-librarian conflict management, "customer service language," and other library service topics. (ALA Editions Series).

Descriptive Statistical Techniques for Librarians. Arthur W. Hafner. American Library Association. • 1997. $55.00 Second edition.

Developing a Compensation Plan for Your Library. Paula M. Singer. American Library Association. • 2002. $38.00. Discusses a variety of pay plans for libraries, with checklists, questionnaires, case studies, and frequently asked questions. Includes samples of forms, work plans, and spreadsheets.

Evaluating Library Staff: A Performance Appraisal System. Patricia Belcastro. American Library Association. • 1998. $35.00. Provides information on an appraisal system applicable to a wide variety of jobs in all types of libraries. Includes guidelines, performance appraisal forms, sample employee profiles, and a "Code of Service.".

Financial Planning for Libraries. Ann E. Prentice. Scarecrow Press, Inc. • 1996. $36.00. Second edition. Includes examples of budgets for libraries. (Library Administration Series, No. 12).

The Library Administrator's Automation Handbook. Richard Boss. Information Today, Inc. • 1997. $39.50. Covers the library administrator's role in the planning, selection, and implementation of hardware and software for automated library systems.

Library Displays Handbook. Mark Schaeffer. H. W. Wilson Co. • 1991. $65.00. Provides detailed instructions for signs, posters, wall displays, bulletin boards, and exhibits.

Library Forms Illustrated Handbook. Elizabeth Futas. Neal-Schuman Publishers, Inc. • $125.00 per year. Looseleaf service Contains forms for acquisition, cataloging, circulation, reference, online searching, interlibrary loan, bibliographic instruction, personnel, administration, budgets, software control, hardware control, statistics, and special collections.

Library Manager's Deskbook: 102 Expert Solutions to 101 Common Dilemmas. Paula P. Carson and others. American Library Association. • 1995. $32.00. "..focuses on issues relevant to today's administrators and supervisors in all types and sizes of libraries.".

Library Personnel Administration. Lowell A. Martin. Scarecrow Press, Inc. • 1994. $35.00. (Library Administration Series: No. 11).

Library Space Planning: A How-To-Do-It Manual for Assessing, Allocating and Recognizing Collections, Resources, and Physical Facilities. Ruth A. Fraley and Carol Lee Anderson. Neal-Schuman Publishers, Inc. • 1990. $45.00. Second edition.

The Library's Legal Answer Book. Mary Minow and Tomas A. Lipinski. American Library Association. • 2003. $48.00. Includes detailed answers to more than 600 legal questions relating to libraries. Covers Internet content filters, copyright, fair use, employment issues, library liability, and other legal matters.

Managerial Accounting for Libraries and Other Not-for-Profit Organizations. G. Stevenson Smith. American Library Association. • 2002. $55.00. Coverage includes responsibility accounting, life cycle costing, and activity-based accounting, as opposed to traditional cost accounting for profit-based organizations.

Managing Public-Access Computers: A How-To-Do-It Manual for Librarians. Donald A. Barclay. Neal-Schuman Publishers, Inc. • 2000. $59.95. Part one covers hardware, software, and other components. Part two discusses computers users. Part three is about systems management, library policy, and legal issues. (How-to-Do-It Manuals Series).

Marketing: A How-To-Do-It Manual for Librarians. Suzanne Walters. Neal-Schuman Publishers, Inc. • 2003. Second edition. Price on application. Includes a sample library marketing plan with worksheets. Covers market research, strategies, tactics, and evaluation. (How-to-Do-It Manuals Series).

Moving and Reorganizing a Library. Marianna Wells and Rosemary Young. Ashgate Publishing Co. • 1997. $79.95. "This book provides detailed guidance on how to plan, design, prepare, and implement the move of a small or medium sized library from the time of the project's inception to its completion." Includes a case study and checklists. Published by Gower in England.

The OPL Sourcebook: A Guide for Solo and Small Libraries. Judith A. Siess. Information Today, Inc. • 2001. $39.50. The editor of *The One-Person Library* newsletter covers a wide variety of practical topics for improving the management and efficiency of OPLs.

Performance Analysis and Appraisal: A How-To-Do-It Manual for Librarians. Robert D. Stueart and Maureen Sullivan. Neal-Schuman Publishers, Inc. • 1991. $49.95. (How-to-Do-It Manuals Series).

Powerful Public Relations: A How-To Guide for Libraries. Rashelle S. Karp, editor. American Library Association. • 2002. $32.00. Provides concise coverage of library press releases, public service announcements, brochures, special events,

exhibits, and use of multimedia.

Recruiting Library Staff: A How-To-Do-It Manual for Librarians. Kathleen Low. Neal-Schuman Publishers, Inc. • 1999. $45.00. Includes position description forms, sample announcements, and checklists. Discusses job fairs and other career events. (How-To-Do-It Manual for Librarians Series).

Small Libraries: A Handbook for Successful Management. Sally Gardner. McFarland and Co., Inc., Publishers. • 2002. $35.00. Second revised edition. Covers personnel (including volunteers), buildings, collections, service policies, community politics, and other topics.

Staffing for Results: A Guide to Working Smarter. Diane Mayo and Jeanne Goodrich. American Library Association. • 2002. $42.00. Written for the Public Library Association. Emphasizes work measurement in libraries for the sake of efficiency and productivity.

Strategic Management for Academic Libraries: A Handbook. Robert M. Hayes. Greenwood Publishing Group, Inc. • 1993. $69.95. (Library Management Collection).

Strategic Management for Public Libraries: A Handbook. Robert M. Hayes and Virginia A. Walter. Greenwood Publishing Group, Inc. • 1996. $69.95. (Greenwood Library Management Collection).

Strategic Planning: A How-To-Do-It Manual for Librarians. M. E. Jacob. Neal-Schuman Publishers, Inc. • 1990. $45.00. (How-to-Do-It Manuals Series).

Using Windows for Library Administration. Kenneth E. Marks and Steven P. Nielson. Information Today, Inc. • 1997. $34.95. Contains details on the use of Microsoft Windows software applications for library management: spreadsheets, desktop publishing, project planning, forms, etc.

ONLINE DATABASES

LISA: Library and Information Science Abstracts. Available from Cambridge Scientific Abstracts (CSA). • Provides abstracting and indexing of the world's library and information science literature, 1969 to date. Covers more than 440 periodicals from 68 countries. Updating is biweekly. Inquire as to online cost and availability.

PERIODICALS AND NEWSLETTERS

The Bottom Line: Managing Library Finances. Emerald. • Quarterly. $1,039.00 per year. Provides articles on the financial management of libraries: budgeting, funding, cost analysis, etc.

Collection Management: A Quarterly Journal Devoted to the Management of Library Collections. Haworth Press, Inc. • Quarterly. $235.00 per year.

The Electronic Library: The International Journal for the Application of Technology in Information Environments. Sage Publications, Inc. • Bimonthly. $469.00 per year. Incorporated *Library Computing*.

Information Management Report: An International Newsletter for Information Professionals and Librarians. R. R. Bowker. • Monthly. $505.00 per year; includes print and online editions. Incorporates *Outlook on Research Libraries*.

Information Outlook: The Monthly Magazine of the Special Libraries Association. Special Libraries Association. • Monthly. $65.00 per year. Topics include information technology, the Internet, copyright, research techniques, library management, and professional development. Replaces *Special Libraries* and *SpeciaList*.

Journal of Library Administration. Haworth Press, Inc. • Quarterly. $265.00 per year. Two volumes. Supplement available *Monographic*. Demonstrates the application of theory to everyday problems faced by library administrators.

MLS: Marketing Library Services. Information Today Inc. • Description: Tells librarians and information professionals how to actively market

their services to gain clients and to justify their existence. Discusses marketing, communication skills, fundraising, promotional events, publicity, and advocacy. Recurring features include how-to articles, case studies, news, a Customer-Based Marketing column, and book reviews.

The One-Person Library: A Newsletter for Librarians and Management. Information Bridges International, Inc. • Monthly. $85.00 per year. Newsletter for librarians working alone or with minimal assistance. Contains reports on library literature, management advice, case studies, book reviews, and general information.

Smart Libraries Newsletter: An Innovative Overview of Library Automation. American Library Association. • Monthly. $144.00 per year. Articles and news briefs covering all aspects of library automation. Formerly *Library Systems Newsletter*.

The Unabashed Librarian: The "How I Run My Library Good" Letter. Maurice J. Freedman. • Quarterly. $57.50 per year. Newsletter. Provides practical library management ideas and library humor.

TRADE/PROFESSIONAL ASSOCIATIONS

Library Administration and Management Association. 50 E Huron St., Chicago, IL 60611-2795. Phone: 800-545-2433 or (312)280-5036 Fax: (312)280-5033 E-mail: lama@ala.org • URL: http://www.ala.org/lama • Affiliated with American Library Association. Formerly Library Administration Division of ALA.

OTHER SOURCES

Legal Research and Law Library Management. American Lawyer Media, Inc. • Looseleaf. $169.00. Updated as needed. Covers the planning and operation of libraries for law firms, including personnel selection and selection of books, periodicals, online services, microforms, and other materials. (Law Journal Press).

LIBRARY RESEARCH

See also: ONLINE INFORMATION SYSTEMS

GENERAL WORKS

Doing Exemplary Research. Ralph E. Stablein. Sage Publications, Inc. • 1992. $43.95. Contains discussions of research methodologies.

Super Searchers Make It On Their Own: Top Independent Information Professionals Share Their Secrets for Starting and Running a Research Business. Suzanne Sabroski. Information Today, Inc. • 2002. $24.95. Presents discussions by "11 of the world's top research entrepreneurs" on the practical aspects of being in business as an information broker or other information provider. (Super Searchers Series).

Surviving Your Dissertation: A Comprehensive Guide to Content and Process. Kjell E. Rudestam and Rae R. Newton. Sage Publications, Inc. • 2000. $72.95. Second edition. Provides general advice on how to successfully complete a dissertation or thesis.

The Ultimate Digital Library: Where the New Information Players Meet. Andrew K. Pace. American Library Association. • 2003. $35.00. Discusses how libraries can remain competitive within the new digital information world.

BIBLIOGRAPHIES

American Reference Books Annual. Bohdan S. Wynar, editor. Libraries Unlimited, Inc. • Annual. $125.00.

The Basic Business Library: Core Resources. Rashells S. Karp and Bernard S. Schlessinger. Greenwood Publishing Group, Inc. • 2002. $64.95. Fourth edition. Consists of three parts: (1) "Core List of Printed Business Reference Sources," (2) "The Literature of Business Reference and Business Libraries: 1976-1994," and (3) "Business Reference Sources and Services: Essays." Part one lists 200 basic titles, with annotations and evaluations.

Fundamental Reference Sources. James S. Sweetland and Frances N. Cheney. American Library Association. • 2001. $75.00. Third edition. Describes "the best available materials in all media for general library collections.".

Reference Books Bulletin: A Compilation of Evaluations. Mary Ellen Quinn, editor. American Library Association. • Annual. $79.95. Contains reference book reviews that appeared during the year in *Booklist*.

Reference Sources for Small and Medium-sized Libraries. Scott E. Kennedy, editor. American Library Association. • 1999. $60.00. Sixth edition. Includes alternative (electronic) formats for reference works.

Subject Encyclopedias: User's Guide, Review Citations, and Keyword Index. Allan N. Mirwis. Greenwood Publishing Group, Inc. • 1999. $300.00. Two volumes. $150.00 per volume. Volume one describes 1,000 subject encyclopedias; volume two provides a keyword index to articles appearing in 100 selected encyclopedias.

Topical Reference Books: Authoritative Evaluations of Recommended Resources in Specialized Subject Areas. Marion Sader, editor. Greenwood Publishing Group, Inc. • 1991. $109.00. Ranks 2,000 reference books ("Core Titles," "New and Noteworthy," "Supplementary"). (Buying Guide Series).

DIRECTORIES

The Core Business Web: A Guide to Key Information Sources. Gary W. White, editor. Haworth Press, Inc. • 2003. $49.95. Business librarians select Web sites in 25 areas of business, such as banking, e-commerce, investments, tourism, and small business.

Directory of Special Libraries and Information Centers. Gale Cengage Learning. • 2003. $975.00. 28th edition. Three volumes. Two available separately: volume one, *Directory of Special Libraries and Information Centers*, $740.00; volume two *Geographic and Personnel Indexes*, $560.00. Contains 34,000 entries from the U.S., Canada, and 80 other countries. A detailed subject index is included in volume one.

Internet Plus Directory of Express Library Services. Steve Coffman and others, editors. American Library Association. • 1998. $55.00. Covers fee-based services of various U. S., Canadian, and international libraries. Paid services include online searches, faxed documents, and specialized professional research. Price ranges are quoted. (A joint production of FISCAL, the ALA/ACRL Discussion Group of Fee-Based Information Service Centers in Academic Libraries, and FYI, the Professional Research and Rapid Information Delivery Service of the County of Los Angeles Public Library.) Formerly *FISCAL Directory of Fee-Based Information Services in Libraries.*

Library Journal: Reference [year]: Print, CD-ROM, Online. Reed Business Information. • Annual. Issued in November as a supplement to *Library Journal*. Lists new and updated reference material, including general and trade print titles, directories, annuals, CD-ROM titles, and online sources. Includes material from more than 200 publishers, arranged by company name, with an index by subject. Addresses include e-mail and Web information.

Library Journal Sourcebook. Reed Business Information. • Publication includes: List of over 600 suppliers of products and services used by libraries from abstracting to word processing equipment. Entries include: Company name, address, phone, list of products or services. Complete listings for more

than 100 architectural firms; Disaster planning for librarians.

Subject Directory of Special Libraries and Information Centers. Gale Cengage Learning. • Annual. $960.00. Three volumes, available separately: volume one, *Business, Government, and Law Libraries*, $375.00; volume two, *Computer, Engineering, and Law Libraries*, $375.00; volume three, *Health Sciences Libraries*, $375.00. Altogether, 14,000 entries from the *Directory of Special Libraries and Information Centers* are arranged in 14 subject chapters.

ENCYCLOPEDIAS AND DICTIONARIES

Encyclopedic Guide to Searching and Finding Health Information on the Web. P. F. Anderson and Nancy J. Allee, editors. Neal-Schuman Publishers. • 2004. $395.00. Three volumes. Comprehensive guide to searching the Web for reliable information on hundreds of specific diseases, disorders, and health issues. Volume three covers Search Strategies and provides a Cumulative Index. (Published in conjunction with the Medical Library Association.).

HANDBOOKS AND MANUALS

Best Bet Internet: Reference and Research When You Don't Have Time to Mess Around. Shirley D. Kennedy. American Library Association. • 1997. $35.00. Provides advice for librarians and others on the effective use of World Wide Web information sources.

Building the Reference Collection: A How-To-Do-It Manual for School and Public Librarians. Neal-Schuman Publishers, Inc. • 1992. $38.50. Includes a list of 300 basic reference sources. (How-to-Do-It Manuals Series).

Complete Copyright: An Everyday Guide for Librarians. Carrie Russell. American Library Association. • 2004. $50.00. Covers the fundamentals of U. S. copyright law, including the Digital Millennium Copyright Act (DMCA, 1998) and the Technology, Education, and Copyright Harmonization Act (the TEACH Act, 2002). The author is copyright specialist for the ALA Office for Information Technology Policy.

Developing Reference Collections and Services in an Electronic Age: A How-To-Do-It Manual for Librarians. Kay A. Cassell. Neal-Schuman Publishers, Inc. • 1999. $55.00. Discusses print vs. electronic media for library reference services. (How-To-Do-It Manuals Series).

Electronic Styles: A Handbook of Citing Electronic Information. Xia Li and Nancy Crane. Information Today, Inc. • 1996. $19.99. Second edition. Covers the citing of text-based information, electronic journals, Web sites, CD-ROM items, multimedia products, and online documents.

Going Live: Starting and Running a Virtual Reference Service. Steve Coffman. American Library Association. • 2003. $42.00. Serves as a practical manual for libraries wishing to start a Web-based, always available reference service. Includes a bibliography by Bernie Sloan.

Guide to the Use of Libraries and Information Sources. Jean K. Gates. McGraw-Hill. • 1994. $36.56. Seventh edition. (Humanities, Social Sciences and World Languages Series).

Information Broker. Entrepreneur Media, Inc. • Looseleaf. $59.50. A practical guide to starting an information retrieval business. Covers profit potential, start-up costs, market size evaluation, pricing, accounting, advertising, promotion, etc. (Start-Up Business Guide No. E1237.).

Introduction to Reference Work. William A. Katz. McGraw-Hill. • 2001. $58.60. Eighth edition. Two volumes. (Introduction to Reference Works Series).

Introductory CD-ROM Searching: The Key to Effective Ondisc Searching. Joseph Meloche. Haworth Press, Inc. • 1994. $49.95. Covers basic search

strategies, with specific suggestions for Dialog On-Disc, Silverplatter, Wilsondisc, UMI, and others.

The Invisible Web: Uncovering Information Sources Search Engines Can't See. Chris Sherman and Gary Price. Information Today, Inc. • 2001. $29.95. A guide to Web sites from universities, libraries, associations, government agencies, and other sources that are inadequately covered by conventional search engines (see also http://www.invisible-web.net). (CyberAge Books.).

The Librarian's Internet Survival Guide: Strategies for the High-Tech Reference Desk. Irene E. McDermott. Information Today, Inc. • 2002. $29.50. Provides practical advice relating to Web reference sources, information management strategies, Internet training issues, library Web pages, and patron relations.

Oxford Guide to Library Research. Thomas Mann. Oxford University Press. • 1998. $35.00. Covers print sources, electronic sources, and "nine research methods.".

Recruiter's Research Blue Book: A How-To Guide for Researchers, Consultants, Corporate Recruiters, Small Business Owners, Venture Capitalists, and Line Executives. Andrea A. Jupina. Kennedy Information, Inc. • 2000. $179.00. Second edition. Provides detailed coverage of the role that research plays in executive recruiting. Includes such practical items as "Telephone Interview Guide," "Legal Issues in Executive Search," and "How to Create an Executive Search Library." Covers both person-to-person research and research using printed and online business information sources. Includes an extensive directory of recommended sources. Formerly *Handbook of Executive Search Research.*

Teaching Information Literacy: 35 Practical, Standards-based Exercises for College Students. Joanna M. Burkhardt and others. American Library Association. • 2003. $35.00. Provides a step-by-step guide for teaching students the intricacies of library and online research.

Virtual Reference Training: The Complete Guide to Providing Anytime, Anywhere Answers. Buff Hirko and Mary Bucher Ross. American Library Association. • 2004. $42.00. Serves as a guide to effective, online library reference service. Emphasis is on staff training and "14 core competencies.".

Working with Faculty to Design Undergraduate Information Literacy Programs: A How-To-Do-It Manual for Librarians. Rosemary M. Young and Stephana Harmony. Neal-Schuman Publishers, Inc. • 1999. $45.00. Includes sample forms, surveys, evaluations, and assignments for credit courses or single sessions. (How-to-Do-It Manuals Series).

PERIODICALS AND NEWSLETTERS

College and Research Libraries (CRL). Association of College and Research Libraries. American Library Association. • Bimonthly. $60.00 per year. Supplement available *C and R L News.*

College and Research Libraries News. Association of College and Research Libraries. American Library Association. • 11 times per year. Free to members; non-members, $40.00 per year. Supplement to *College and Research Libraries.*

The CyberSkeptic's Guide to Internet Research. Information Today, Inc. • 10 times a year. Individuals, $159.00 per year; nonprofit organizations, $134.00 per year. Newsletter. Presents critical reviews of World Wide Web sites and databases, written by information professionals. Includes "Late Breaking News" of Web sites.

Focus: On the Center for Research Libraries. Center for Research Libraries. • Bimonthly. Free. Newsletter. Provides news of Center activites.

Internet Reference Services Quarterly: A Journal of Innovative Information Practice, Technologies, and Resources. Haworth Press, Inc. • Quarterly. $110.00

per year. Covers both theoretical research and practical applications.

Journal of Electronic Resources in Law Libraries. Haworth Press, Inc. • Quarterly. $300.00 per year to libraries; $48.00 per year to individuals.

Journal of Electronic Resources in Medical Libraries. Haworth Press, Inc. • Quarterly. $240.00 per year to libraries; $75.00 per year to individuals.

Reference and User Services Quarterly. American Library Association, Reference and Adult Services Div. • Quarterly. $50.00 per year. In addition to articles, includes reviews of databases, reference books, and library professional material. Formerly *RQ.*

The Reference Librarian. Haworth Press, Inc. • Semiannual. Institutions, $325.00 per year. Two volumes.

Reference Services Review: Information on All Aspects of the Reference Function. Emerald (North America). • Quarterly. $319.00 per year. Covers automation of library reference services, user needs, reference source evaluation, service delivery models, and related topics.

Research Strategies: A Journal of Library Concepts and Instruction. Elsevier. • Quarterly. Individuals, $76.00 per year; institutions, $152.00 per year. Edited for librarians involved in bibliographic or library instruction.

LICENSE PLATES

See: MOTOR VEHICLE LAW AND REGULATION

LICENSES

GENERAL WORKS

From Red Tape to Smart Tape: Administrative Simplification in OECD Countries. Organization for Economic Cooperation and Development. • 2003. $58.00. "This report looks at a set of tools and practices commonly used by governments to make administrative regulations simpler and less burdensome to comply with." Includes information on one-stop facilitation, license/permit simplification, decision-making time limits, small business assistance, and the use of information technology (IT) for administrative simplification.

DIRECTORIES

Professional and Occupational Licensing Directory. Gale Cengage Learning. • 1996. $125.00. Second edition. Provides detailed national and state information on the requirements for obtaining a license in each of about 500 occupations. Information needed to contact the appropriate licensing agency or organization is included in each case.

PERIODICALS AND NEWSLETTERS

CLEAR News. Council of Licensure, Enforcement, and Regulation. Council of State Governments. • Description: Concentrates on professional licensing. Addresses such issues as reciprocity, alternatives to individual licensure, sunset, antitrust, and administrative rule-making. Recurring features include news of members, conferences, committees, programs, and legislation, and a column titled State Lines.

The Licensing Letter. EPM Communications Inc. • Description: Concerned with all aspects of licensed merchandising, "the business of associating someone's name, likeness or creation with someone else's product or service, for a consideration." Recurring features include statistics, research, events, mechanics, available properties, and identification of licensors, licensing agents, and licensees.

TRADE/PROFESSIONAL ASSOCIATIONS

Council on Licensure, Enforcement and Regulation. 403 Marquis Ave., Ste. 100, Lexington, KY 40502.

Phone: (859)269-1289 Fax: (859)231-1943 E-mail: sburke@mis.net • URL: http://www.clearhq.org/ • Members are state government occupational and professional licensing officials. Formerly National Clearinghouse on Licensure, Enforcement and Regulation.

OTHER SOURCES

Broker-Dealer Regulation. David A. Lipton. West Group. • Semiannual. $429.00 per year. Looseleaf service. Focuses on the basics of stockbroker license application procedure, registration, regulation, and responsibilities. (Securities Law Series).

LICENSING AGREEMENTS

See also: INTELLECTUAL PROPERTY

ABSTRACTS AND INDEXES

Current Law Index: Multiple Access to Legal Periodicals. Gale Cengage Learning. • Monthly. $725.00 per year. Produced in cooperation with the American Association of Law Libraries. Indexes more than 900 law journals, legal newspapers, and specialty publications from the U.S., Canada, U.K., Ireland, Australia, and New Zealand.

Index to Legal Periodicals and Books. H. W. Wilson Co. • Monthly. $490.00 per year. Quarterly and annual cumulations.

NTIS Alerts: Government Inventions for Licensing. National Technical Information Service. • Semimonthly. $270.00 per year. Identifies new inventions available from various government agencies. Covers a wide variety of industrial and technical areas. Formerly *Abstract Newsletter.*

DIRECTORIES

Licensing Executives Society--Membership Directory. Licensing Executives Society Intl. • Covers: About 10,000 U.S. and foreign business executives, scientists, engineers, lawyers, and new-idea scouts having direct responsibility for the licensing of technology, patents, trade marks, and know-how. Entries include: Name, address, telephone, fax, email, website.

HANDBOOKS AND MANUALS

Antitrust-Intellectual Property Handbook. Alan J. Weinschel. Glasser Legalworks. • Looseleaf. $175.00. Periodic supplementation. Covers patent licensing, patent antitrust issues, innovation markets, intervention by government agencies, standard-setting activities, royalty arrangements, and related intellectual property/antitrust topics. Provides explanations, legal guidance, and historical background.

Licensing Law Handbook. West Group. • $299.00. Periodic supplementation.

INTERNET DATABASES

Lexis.com Research System. Lexis-Nexis Group. Phone: 800-227-4908 or (937)865-6800 Fax: (937)865-6909 E-mail: webmaster@prod.lexis-nexis.com • URL: http://www.lexis.com • Fee-based Web site offers extensive searching of a wide variety of legal sources. Additional features include Daily Opinion Service, lexis.com Bookstore, Career Center, CLE Center, Law Schools, and Practice Pages ("Pages specific to areas of specialty").

ONLINE DATABASES

Index to Legal Periodicals and Books (Online). H. W. Wilson Co. • Broad coverage of law journals and books 1981 to date. Monthly updates. Inquire as to online cost and availability.

Legal Resource Index. Gale Cengage Learning. • Broad coverage of law literature appearing in legal, business, and other periodicals, 1980 to date. Daily updates. Inquire as to online cost and availability.

LEXIS. LEXIS-NEXIS. • The various LEXIS

databases provide full text and indexing for a wide variety of legal cases, statutes, orders, and opinions.

PERIODICALS AND NEWSLETTERS

Intellectual Property Today. • Monthly. $96.00 per year. Covers legal developments in copyright, patents, trademarks, and licensing. Emphasizes the effect of new technology on intellectual property. Formerly *Law Works.*

International New Product Newsletter. International New Product Newsletter. • Description: Provides "advance news of new products and processes, primarily from sources outside the U.S." Emphasizes new products which can cut costs and improve efficiency. Recurring features include the column Special Licensing Opportunities which lists new products and processes that are available for manufacture under license, or are for sale or import.

Les Nouvelles. Licensing Executives Society International. • Description: Concerned with technological licensing and related subjects. Covers technology, patents, trademarks, and licensing "know-how" world-wide.

The Licensing Book. Adventure Publishing. • Monthly. $36.00 per year. Contains articles about licensed product merchandising.

TRADE/PROFESSIONAL ASSOCIATIONS

International Licensing Industry Merchandisers' Association. 350 Fifth Ave., Suite 1408, New York, NY 10118. Phone: (212)244-1944 Fax: (212)563-6552 E-mail: info@licensing.org • URL: http://www.licensing.org • Promotes the legal protection of licensed properties.

Licensing Executives Society. 1800 Diagonal Rd., Ste. 280, Alexandria, VA 22314. Phone: (703)836-3106 Fax: (703)836-3107 E-mail: info@les.org • URL: http://www.usa-canada.les.org • U.S. and foreign businessmen, scientists, engineers, and lawyers having direct responsibility for the transfer of technology. Maintains placement service.

OTHER SOURCES

Investing, Licensing, and Trading. Economist Intelligence Unit. • Semiannual. $345.00 per year for each country. Key laws, rules, and licensing provisions are explained for each of 60 countries. Information is provided on political conditions, markets, price policies, foreign exchange practices, labor, and export-import.

Licensing of Intellectual Property. American Lawyer Media, Inc. • Looseleaf. $169.00. Updated as needed. Includes such licensing topics as royalties, infringement, antitrust, trade secrets, and patent agreements. Examples of licensing agreements and sample forms (on CD-ROM) are included. (Law Journal Press).

LIFE INSURANCE

See also: ACCIDENT INSURANCE; HEALTH INSURANCE; INSURANCE

GENERAL WORKS

Smarter Insurance Solutions. Janet Bamford. Bloomberg. • 1996. $19.95. Provides practical advice to consumers, with separate chapters on the following kinds of insurance: automobile, homeowners, health, disability, and life. (Bloomberg Personal Bookshelf Series).

ABSTRACTS AND INDEXES

Insurance Periodicals Index. Specials Libraries Association, Insurance and Employees Benefits Div. NILS Publishing Co. • Annual. $250.00. Compiled by the Insurance and Employee Benefits Div., Special Libraries Association. A yearly index of over 15,000 articles from about 35 insurance periodicals. Arrangement is by subject, with an index to authors.

BIBLIOGRAPHIES

Insurance and Employee Benefits Literature. Special Libraries Association, Insurance and Employee

Benefits Div. • Bimonthly. $15.00 per year. Lists a wide variety of literature in all branches of the insurance industry. Includes annotations.

List of Worthwhile Life and Health Insurance Books. American Council of Life Insurance. • Annual. Free. Books in print on life and health insurance and closely related subjects.

CD-ROM DATABASES

U. S. Insurance: Life, Accident, and Health. Sheshunoff Information Services, Inc. • Monthly. Price on application. CD-ROM provides detailed, current information on the financial characteristics of more than 2,300 life, accident, and health insurance companies.

DIRECTORIES

Ratings Guide to Life, Health and Annuity Insurers. Weiss Ratings, Inc. • Quarterly. $438.00 per year. Rates life insurance companies for overall safety and financial stability.

S & P's Insurance Book. Standard & Poor's Ratings Group, Insurance Rating Services. • Quarterly. Price on application. Contains detailed financial analyses and ratings of various kinds of insurance companies.

S & P's Insurance Digest: Life Insurance Edition. Standard & Poor's Ratings Group, Insurance Rating Services. • Quarterly. Contains concise financial analyses and ratings of life insurance companies.

Who Writes What in Life and Health Insurance. The National Underwriter Co. • Annual. $9.95.

ENCYCLOPEDIAS AND DICTIONARIES

Dictionary of Insurance Terms. Harvey W. Rubin. Barron's Educational Series, Inc. • 2000. $14.95. Fourth edition. Defines terms in a wide variety of insurance fields. (Business Dictionaries Series).

Glossary of Insurance Policy Terms. Organization for Economic Cooperation and Development. • 1999. $30.00. "The selected topics range from insurance policy regulation/supervision to general trade issues and include technical terms related to issues such as claims, premiums, and provisions." Edited for government, academic, business, and insurance organizations.

Insurance Words and Their Meanings: A Glossary of Insurance Terms. The Rough Notes Co., Inc. • 2001. 17th edition. Price on application.

Rupp's Insurance and Risk Management Glossary. Richard V. Rupp. NILS Publishing Co. • 2001. $35.00. Second edition. Provides definitions of 6,400 insurance words and phrases. Includes a guide to acronyms and abbreviations.

FINANCIAL RATIOS

Almanac of Business and Industrial Financial Ratios. Leo Troy. Aspen Publishers, Inc. • 2003. $125.95. Includes CD-Rom. Contains financial ratios derived from federal tax returns. Ratios for each of about 200 industries are arranged according to company asset size. (Almanac of Business and Industrial Financial Ratios Series).

HANDBOOKS AND MANUALS

The Complete Book of Insurance: Protecting Your Life, Health Property, and Income. Ben G. Baldwin. McGraw-Hill. • 1991. $24.95. Provides basic information and advice on various kinds of insurance: life, health, property (fire), disability, long-term care, automobile, liability, and annuities.

Financial Planning Applications. Thomas P. Langdon and William J. Ruckstuhl. The American College. • 2003. $70.00. 19th edition. Emphasis on annuities and life insurance.

Life and Health Insurance Law. Muirel L. Crawford. McGraw Hill. • 1997. $118.88. Eighth edition. Covers the legal aspects of life, health, and accident insurance.

Life Insurance Answer Book: For Qualified Plans and Estate Planning. Gary S. Lesser and Lawrence

C. Starr, editors. Aspen Publishers, Inc. • 2002. $175.00. Third edition. Four parts by various authors cover life insurance in general, qualified plans, fiduciary responsibility, and estate planning. Includes sample documents, worksheets, and information in Q&A form.

Life Insurance from the Buyer's Point of View. American Institute for Economic Research. • Annual. $8.00.

McGill's Life Insurance. Edward E. Graves, editor. The American College. • 2002. $80.00. Fourth edition. Contains chapters by various authors on diverse kinds of life insurance, as well as annuities, disability insurance, long-term care insurance, risk management, reinsurance, and other insurance topics. (Huebner School Series).

INTERNET DATABASES

InsWeb. InsWeb Corp. Phone: (916)853-3300 E-mail: info@insweb.com • URL: http://www. insweb.com • Web site offers a wide variety of advice and information on automobile, life, health, and "other" insurance. Includes glossaries of insurance terms, Standard & Poor's ratings of individual insurance companies, and "Financial Needs Estimators." Searching is available. Fees: Free.

PERIODICALS AND NEWSLETTERS

Advisor Today. National Association of Insurance and Finacial Advisors. • Monthly. Free to members; non-members, $7.00 per year. Edited for individual life and health insurance agents. Among the topics included are disability insurance and long-term care insurance. Formerly Life Association News.

Annuity and Life Insurance Shopper. United States Annuities. • Semiannual. $25.00 per year. Provides information on rates and performance for fixed annuities, variable annuities, and term life policies issued by more than 250 insurance companies.

Best's Review: Inurance Issues and Analysis. A.M. Best Co. • Monthly. $25.00 per year. Editorial coverage of significant industry trends, developments, and important events. Formerly Best's Review: Property-Casualty Insurance.

Broker World. Insurance Publications, Inc. • Bimonthly. $6.00 per year. Edited for independent insurance agents and brokers. Special feature issue topics include annuities, disability insurance, estate planning, and life insurance.

Contingencies: The Magazine of the Actuarial Profession. American Academy of Actuaries. • Bimonthly. $30.00 per year. Provides non-technical articles on the actuarial aspects of insurance, employee benefits, and pensions.

GAMA International Journal. GAMA International. • Bimonthly. Members, $4.00 per year; non-members, $20.00 per year. Contains practical articles on the management of life insurance agencies.

Guide to Life, Health, and Annuity Insurers: A Quarterly Compilation of Insurance Company Ratings and Analysis. Weiss Ratings, Inc. • Quarterly. $438.00 per year. Emphasis is on rating of financial safety and relative risk. Includes annual summary.

Insurance and Technology. CMP Media LLC. • Monthly. $65.00 per year. Covers information technology and systems management as applied to the operation of life, health, casualty, and property insurance companies.

Insurance Forum: For the Unfettered Exchange of Ideas About Insurance. Joseph M. Belth, editor. Insurance Forum, Inc. • Monthly. $90.00 per year. Newsletter. Provides analysis of the insurance business, including occasional special issues showing the ratings of about 1,600 life-health insurance companies, as determined by four major rating services: Duff & Phelps Credit Rating Co., Moody's Investors Service, Standard & Poor's Corp., and Weiss Research, Inc.

Insurance Marketing: The Ins and Outs of Recruiting and Retaining More Agents. Agent Media Corp. • Bimonthly. Controlled circulation. Provides practical advice for insurance companies on how to hire and keep sales personnel.

Jounal of Finacial Services Professionals. Society of Financial Services Professional. • Bimonthly. $95.00 per year. Provides information on life insurance and financial planning, including estate planning, retirement, tax planning, trusts, business insurance, long-term care insurance, disability insurance, and employee benefits. Formerly (American Society of CLU and Ch F C Journal).

Martin Weiss' Safe Money Report. Weiss Ratings, Inc. • Monthly. $189.00 per year. Newsletter. Provides financial advice and current safety ratings of various banks, savings and loan companies, insurance companies, and securities dealers. Formerly (The Safe Money Report).

National Underwriter. The National Underwriter Co. • Weekly. Two editions: Life or Health. $86.00 per year, each edition.

Resource: LOMA's Magazine for Insurance and Financial Services Management. LOMA. • Monthly. Free to qualified personnel. Covers management topics for life insurance home and field office personnel.

RESEARCH CENTERS AND INSTITUTES

S. S. Huebner Foundation. University of Pennsylvania, 3733 Spruce St., Vance Hall, Suite 430, Philadelphia, PA 19104-6301. Phone: (215)898-9631 Fax: (215)573-2218 E-mail: cummins@wharton.upenn.edu • URL: http://www. rider.wharton.upenn.edu/ • Awards grants for research in various areas of insurance.

STATISTICS SOURCES

Information, Finance, and Services USA. Gale Cengage Learning. • 2001. $240.00. Replaces Service Industries USA and Finance, Insurance, and Real Estate USA. Presents statistics and projections relating to economic activity in a wide variety of non-manufacturing areas.

Insurance Statistics Yearbook, 1991-1998. OECD Publications and Information Center. • 2000. $75.00. Presents detailed statistics on insurance premiums collected in OECD countries, by type of insurance.

Life Insurance Fact Book. American Council of Life Insurers. • Biennial. $37.50 per year; with diskette, $55.00 per year.

Standard & Poor's Industry Surveys. Standard & Poor's. • Semiannual. $1,800.00. Two looseleaf volumes. Includes monthly Supplements. Provides detailed, individual surveys of 52 major industry groups. Each survey is revised on a semiannual basis. Also includes "Monthly Investment Review" (industry group investment analysis) and monthly "Trends & Projections" (economic analysis).

Statistical Information on the Financial Services Industry. American Bankers Association. • Annual. Members, $150.00; non-members, $275.00. Presents a wide variety of data relating to banking and financial services, including consumer economics, personal finance, credit, government loans, capital markets, and international banking.

U. S. Industry and Trade Outlook. Available from National Technical Information Service. • Annual. $69.95. Produced by the International Trade Administration, U. S. Department of Commerce, in a "public-private" partnership with DRI/McGraw-Hill and Standard & Poor's. Provides basic data, outlook for the current year, and "Long-Term Prospects" (five-year projections) for a wide variety of products and services. Includes high technology industries. Formerly *U. S. Industrial Outlook.*

TRADE/PROFESSIONAL ASSOCIATIONS

American Council of Life Insurance. 101 Constitution Ave. NW, Washington, DC 20001-2133. Phone: (202)624-2000 • URL: http://www.acli.com.

Association of Life Insurance Counsel. 1300 Clinton St., Fort Wayne, IN 46801. Phone: 800-659-5589 or (219)455-2000 Fax: (219)455-4503 E-mail: membersupport@legalstaff.com • URL: http://www.legalstaff.com • Members are attorneys for life insurance companies.

GAMA International. 2901 Telestar Ct., Ste. 140, Falls Church, VA 22042-1205. Phone: 800-345-2687 or (703)770-8184 Fax: (703)770-8182 E-mail: gamamail@gamaweb.com • URL: http://www.gamaweb.com • Provides world-class education and training resources for individuals, companies and organizations involved with the recruitment and development of field managers, representatives and staff in the life insurance and financial services industry; advocates of the value-added role of field management and representatives in the ethical distribution of life insurance and financial products and services industry.

Life Communicators Association. c/o Carol Morgan, PO Box 387, East Rutherford, NJ 07073. Phone: (201)939-4739 E-mail: cmorgan@comcast.net • Formerly Life Insurance Advertisers.

LIMRA International. 300 Day Hill Rd., Windsor, CT 06095. Phone: 800-235-4672 or (860)688-3358 Fax: (860)298-9555 E-mail: webmaster@limra.com • URL: http://www.limra.com • Life insurance and financial services companies. Conducts market, consumer, economic, financial, and human resources research; monitors industry distribution systems and product and service developments. Provides executive and field management development schools and seminars. Offers human resource development consulting services, including needs analysis and program design, evaluation, and implementation.

LOMA. 2300 Windy Ridge Pkwy., Ste. 600, Atlanta, GA 30339-8443. Phone: 800-275-5662 or (770)951-1770 Fax: (770)984-0441 E-mail: askloma@loma.org • URL: http://www.loma.org • Life and health insurance companies and financial services in the U.S. and Canada; and overseas in 45 countries; affiliate members are firms that provide professional support to member companies. Provides research, information, training, and educational activities in areas of operations and systems, human resources, financial planning and employee development. Administers FLMI Insurance Education Program, which awards FLMI (Fellow, Life Management Institute) designation to those who complete the ten-examination program.

National Association of Insurance and Financial Advisors. 2901 Telestar Court, Falls Church, VA 22042-1205. Phone: 877-866-2432 or (703)770-8100 Fax: (703)770-8142 E-mail: membersupport@naifa.org • URL: http://www.naifa.org • Affiliated with Association for Advanced Life Underwriting. Formerly National Association of Life Underwriters.

National Association of Professional Insurance Agents. 400 N. Washington St., Alexandria, VA 22314. Phone: (703)836-9340 Fax: (703)836-1279 E-mail: piaweb@pianet.org • URL: http://www.pianet.com • Members are independent agents in various fields of insurance. Formerly National Association of Mutual Insurance Agents.

Society of Financial Service Professionals. 270 S. Bryn Mawr Ave., Bryn Mawr, PA 19010-2195. Phone: 800-392-6900 or (610)526-2500 Fax: (610)527-4010 E-mail: custserv@financialpro.org • URL: http://www.financialpro.org.

OTHER SOURCES

Best's Insurance Reports. A.M. Best Co. • Annual. $1495.00. Life-health insurance covering about 1,750 companies, and property-casualty insurance covering over 3,200 companies. Includes one year subscription to both *Best's Review* and *Best's Insurance Management Reports.*

Federal Income Taxation of Life Insurance Companies. LexisNexis Matthew Bender. • Annual. $743.00. Three looseleaf volumes.

Life, Health, and Accident Insurance Law Reports. CCH, Inc. • $835.00 per year. Looseleaf service. Monthly updates.

LIFT TRUCKS

See: MATERIALS HANDLING

LIGHTING

DIRECTORIES

Home Lighting and Accessories Suppliers Directory. Doctorow Communications, Inc. • Semiannual. $6.00 per issue. Lists almost 1,000 suppliers of residential lighting fixtures and accessories.

L D + A: Lighting Equipment Accessories Directory. Illuminating Engineering Society of North America. • Annual. $10.00. Lists over 800 manufacturers of lighting fixtures, controls, components, mounting devices, maintenance equipment, etc.

FINANCIAL RATIOS

Annual Statement Studies. The Risk Management Association. • Annual. Median and quartile financial ratios are given for over 400 kinds of manufacturing, wholesale, retail, construction, and consumer finance establishments. Data is sorted by both asset size and sales volume. Includes a clearly written "Definition of Ratios" and an alphabetical industry index.

Annual Statement Studies: Industry Default Probabilities and Cash Flow Measures. The Risk Management Association. • Annual. $145.00. Serves as a companion volume to the original *Annual Statement Studies.* Gives probability of default estimates on a percentage scale for more than 450 industries. Includes changes in position year-by-year for eight financial statement line items and provides percentage measures of cash flow.

HANDBOOKS AND MANUALS

I.E.S. Lighting Handbook. Illuminating Engineering Society of North America. • Quadrennial. $389.00.

Lighting Design: An Introductory Guide for Professionals. Carl Gardner and Barry Hannaford. Ashgate Publishing Co. • 1993. $109.95. Includes project case studies and product/effect examples. Emphasis is on commercial interior and exterior lighting. Published by Design Council Books in England.

No-Regrets Remodeling: Creating a Comfortable, Healthy Home That Saves Energy. Home Energy. • 1997. $19.95. Edited by *Home Energy* magazine. Serves as a home remodeling guide to efficient heating, cooling, ventilation, water heating, insulation, lighting, and windows.

INTERNET DATABASES

Manufacturing Profiles. U. S. Bureau of the Census. Phone: (301)763-4636 E-mail: webmaster@census.gov • URL: http://www.census.gov/prod/www/abs/mfg-prof.html • The Census Bureau makes available free on PDF (Portable Document Format) an annual consolidation of the entire Current Industrial Report series, presenting "all the data compiled." Contains statistics on production, shipments, inventories, consumption, exports, imports, and orders for a wide variety of manufactured products.

PERIODICALS AND NEWSLETTERS

Home Lighting and Accessories. Doctorow Communications, Inc. • Monthly. $30.00 per year. Trade magazine of the residential lighting industry for retailers, distributors, designers, architects, specifiers, manufacturers and all lighting professionals.

IEEE Industry Applications Magazine. Institute of Electrical and Electronics Engineers. • Bimonthly. $190.00 per year. Covers new industrial applications of power conversion, drives, lighting, and control. Emphasis is on the petroleum, chemical, rubber, plastics, textile, and mining industries.

LD & A: (Lighting Design and Application). Illuminating Engineering Society of North America. • Monthly. $39.00 per year. Information on current events, products, projects and people in the lighting industry.

National Home Center News: News and Analysis for the Home Improvement, Building Material Industry. Lebhar-Friedman, Inc. • 22 times a year. $99.00 per year. Includes special feature issues on hardware and tools, building materials, millwork, electrical supplies, lighting, and kitchens.

STATISTICS SOURCES

Annual Survey of Manufactures. Available from U. S. Government Printing Office. • Annual. Prices vary. Issued by the U. S. Census Bureau as an interim update to the *Census of Manufactures.* Includes data on number of manufacturing establishments in various industries, employment, labor costs, value of shipments, capital expenditures, inventories, energy costs, and assets. (See also Census Bureau home page, http://www.census.gov/.).

Electric Lamps. U. S. Bureau of the Census. • Quarterly and annual. Provides data on shipments: value, quantity, imports, and exports. (Current Industrial Reports, MQ-36B.).

U. S. Industry and Trade Outlook. Available from National Technical Information Service. • Annual. $69.95. Produced by the International Trade Administration, U. S. Department of Commerce, in a "public-private" partnership with DRI/McGraw-Hill and Standard & Poor's. Provides basic data, outlook for the current year, and "Long-Term Prospects" (five-year projections) for a wide variety of products and services. Includes high technology industries. Formerly *U. S. Industrial Outlook.*

TRADE/PROFESSIONAL ASSOCIATIONS

American Lighting Association. PO Box 420288, 2050 Stemmons Fwy., PO Box 420288, Dallas, TX 75342-0288. Phone: 800-274-4448 or (214)698-9898 or (214)274-4484 Fax: (214)698-9899 E-mail: dupton@americanlightingassoc.com • URL: http://www.americanlightingassoc.com • Manufacturers, manufacturers' representatives, distributors, and retailers of residential lighting fixtures, portable lamps, component parts, accessories, and bulbs. Trains and certifies lighting consultants; conducts showroom sales seminars; disseminates marketing and merchandising information. Compiles statistics.

Illuminating Engineering Society of North America. 120 Wall St., 17th Fl., New York, NY 10005-4001. Phone: (212)248-5000 Fax: (212)248-5017 E-mail: iesna@iesna.org • URL: http://www.iesna.org • Members are lighting engineers, designers, architects, and manufacturers.

OTHER SOURCES

Lighting Equipment and Fixtures. Available from MarketResearch.com. • 2002. $4,450.00. Published by Global Industry Analysts. Provides worldwide market research data, including profiles of major lighting equipment companies.

LIMESTONE INDUSTRY

See also: QUARRYING

FINANCIAL RATIOS

Annual Statement Studies. The Risk Management Association. • Annual. Median and quartile financial

ratios are given for over 400 kinds of manufacturing, wholesale, retail, construction, and consumer finance establishments. Data is sorted by both asset size and sales volume. Includes a clearly written "Definition of Ratios" and an alphabetical industry index.

Annual Statement Studies: Industry Default Probabilities and Cash Flow Measures. The Risk Management Association. • Annual. $145.00. Serves as a companion volume to the original *Annual Statement Studies.* Gives probability of default estimates on a percentage scale for more than 450 industries. Includes changes in position year-by-year for eight financial statement line items and provides percentage measures of cash flow.

PERIODICALS AND NEWSLETTERS

Building Stone Magazine. Building Stone Institute. • Bimonthly. $65.00 per year.

TRADE/PROFESSIONAL ASSOCIATIONS

National Stone, Sand and Gravel Association. 2101 Wilson Blvd., Ste. 100, Arlington, VA 22201. Phone: 800-342-1415 or (703)525-8788 Fax: (703)525-7782 E-mail: info@nssga.org • URL: http://www.aggregates.org • Formerly National Stone Association.

LIMITED PARTNERSHIPS

See: PARTNERSHIP

LINEAR PROGRAMMING

GENERAL WORKS

Applied Calculus with Linear Programming for Business, Economics, Life Sciences, and Social Science. Michael R. Ziegler and Raymond A. Barnett. Pearson Custom Publishing. • 1999. $80.00. Fifth edition.

Critical Path Analysis and Linear Programming. Mik Wisniewski and Jonathan Klein. Palgrave Macmillan Ltd. • 2001. f29.99. Contains "Book 1: Linear Programming" and "Book 2: Critical Path Analysis." Chapters include "Linear Programming in the Real World" and "Critical Path Analysis Techniques." Emphasis is on software applications, with a non-mathematical orientation.

Elementary Linear Programming with Applications. Bernard Kolman and Robert E. Beck. Elsevier. • 1995. $44.95. Second edition. Covers the basics of linear programming, with examples of practical applications in commerce. (Computer Science and Scientific Computing Series).

Introduction to Linear Programming. Leonid N. Vaserstein and others. Prentice Hall. • 2002. $81.00. Publisher: "...enables those with little mathematical background to learn to use linear programming in their respective fields (business, economics, operations research, etc.).".

An Introduction to Linear Programming and Theory. Paul R. Thie. John Wiley and Sons, Inc. • 1988. $104.95. Second edition.

Introduction to Practical Linear Programming. David J. Pannell. John Wiley and Sons, Inc. • 1996. $105.00. Explains how to apply linear programming to real-world situations in various areas, such as agriculture, manufacturing, finance, and advertising. Includes an IBM PC diskette containing "user-friendly" software.

ONLINE DATABASES

INSPEC. Institution of Electrical Engineers (IEE). • Provides online citations, with abstracts, to the world literature of electrical engineering, electronics, optoelectronics, telecommunications, industrial controls, instrumentation, computer technology, information technology, and physics. Coverage

includes more than 4,000 technical and scientific journals from 1969 to date, with weekly updating. (INSPEC is Information Services in Physics, Electronics, and Computing.) Inquire as to online cost and availability.

LINEN INDUSTRY

ABSTRACTS AND INDEXES

Textile Technology Digest. Institute of Textile Technology. • Annual. $535.00. Provides indexing and abstracting of a wide variety of textile technology literature.

CD-ROM DATABASES

Textile Technology Digest [CD-ROM]. Textile Information Center, Institute of Textile Technology. • Quarterly. Provides CD-ROM indexing and abstracting of worldwide journals and monographs in various areas of textile technology, production, and management. Covers 1978 to date.

DIRECTORIES

Gift, Housewares and Home Textiles Buyers Directory. Douglas Publications, Inc. • Annual. $259.00. Lists more than 7,300 companies with names of over 15,200 buyers.

LDB Interior Textiles Annual Buyers' Guide. E.W. Williams Publications Co. • Covers: Over 3,000 manufacturers, importers, and suppliers of home fashions products and services, decorative fabric converters, and alternative window coverings; fabricators; manufacturer's representatives; and others allied to the home fashions trade. Entries include: For manufacturers, importers, converters, fabricators, and suppliers--Company name, address, phone, fax, contact, product line. For manufacturer's representatives--Name, address, phone, contact, lines carried. For others--Name, address, phone, fax.

ENCYCLOPEDIAS AND DICTIONARIES

Textile Terms and Definitions. J.E. McIntyre and Paul N. Daniels, editors. Available from State Mutual Book and Periodical Service Ltd. • 1996. $180.00. 10th edition. Published by the Textile Insitute (UK). Includes more than 1,000 definitions of textile processes, fiber types, and end products. Illustrated.

INTERNET DATABASES

Manufacturing Profiles. U. S. Bureau of the Census. Phone: (301)763-4636 E-mail: webmaster@census.gov • URL: http://www.census.gov/prod/www/abs/mfg-prof.html • The Census Bureau makes available free on PDF (Portable Document Format) an annual consolidation of the entire Current Industrial Report series, presenting "all the data compiled." Contains statistics on production, shipments, inventories, consumption, exports, imports, and orders for a wide variety of manufactured products.

ONLINE DATABASES

Textile Technology Digest [online]. Institute of Textile Technology. • Contains indexing and abstracting of more than 300 worldwide journals and monographs in various areas of textile technology, production, and management. Time period is 1978 to date, with monthly updating. Inquire as to online cost and availability.

World Textiles. Elsevier Science, Inc. • Provides abstracting and indexing from 1970 of worldwide textile literature (periodicals, books, pamphlets, and reports). Includes U. S., European, and British patent information. Updating is monthly. Inquire as to online cost and availability.

PERIODICALS AND NEWSLETTERS

LDB Interior Textiles. EW Williams Publications Co. • Monthly. $66.00 per year. Supplement available *Linens, Domestics and Baths-Interior Textile*

Annual Buyer's Guide. Formerly *Interior Textiles.*

STATISTICS SOURCES

Annual Survey of Manufactures. Available from U. S. Government Printing Office. • Annual. Prices vary. Issued by the U. S. Census Bureau as an interim update to the *Census of Manufactures.* Includes data on number of manufacturing establishments in various industries, employment, labor costs, value of shipments, capital expenditures, inventories, energy costs, and assets. (See also Census Bureau home page, http://www.census.gov/.).

TRADE/PROFESSIONAL ASSOCIATIONS

Textile Institute. St. James's Buildings, 1st Fl., 79 Oxford St., Manchester M1 6FQ, United Kingdom. Phone: 44 161 2371188 Fax: 44 161 2361991 E-mail: tiihq@textileinst.org.uk • URL: http://www.texi.org • Companies and individuals in 100 countries involved in management, science, technology, design, information transfer, and marketing of textiles including clothing and footwear. Promotes interests of the textile industry worldwide; serves professional interests of members; confers qualifications and recognizes achievements in research, application of ideas, education, business, and public affairs. Maintains Information Service to collect information relating to textile industrial and economic conditions in different countries and economic sectors.

LINGERIE INDUSTRY

See: UNDERWEAR INDUSTRY

LIQUEFIED PETROLEUM GAS

See: PROPANE AND BUTANE GAS INDUSTRY

LIQUOR INDUSTRY

See: DISTILLING INDUSTRY

LIQUOR LAW AND REGULATION

ABSTRACTS AND INDEXES

Current Law Index: Multiple Access to Legal Periodicals. Gale Cengage Learning. • Monthly. $725.00 per year. Produced in cooperation with the American Association of Law Libraries. Indexes more than 900 law journals, legal newspapers, and specialty publications from the U.S., Canada, U.K., Ireland, Australia, and New Zealand.

Index to Legal Periodicals and Books. H. W. Wilson Co. • Monthly. $490.00 per year. Quarterly and annual cumulations.

ALMANACS AND YEARBOOKS

American Law Yearbook. Gale Cengage Learning. • Annual. $165.00. Serves as a yearly supplement to *West's Encyclopedia of American Law.* Describes new legal developments in many subject areas.

CD-ROM DATABASES

WILSONDISC: Index to Legal Periodicals and Books. H. W. Wilson Co. • Monthly. Includes unlimited online access to *Index to Legal Periodicals* through WILSONLINE. Contains CD-ROM indexing of more than 1,400 English language legal periodicals from 1981 to date and 2,500 books.

ENCYCLOPEDIAS AND DICTIONARIES

West's Encyclopedia of American Law. Available from Gale Cengage Learning. • 2003. $1,195.00.

Second edition. 12 volumes. Published by West Group. Covers a wide variety of legal topics for the general reader.

INTERNET DATABASES

Lexis.com Research System. Lexis-Nexis Group. Phone: 800-227-4908 or (937)865-6800 Fax: (937)865-6909 E-mail: webmaster@prod.lexis-nexis.com • URL: http://www.lexis.com • Fee-based Web site offers extensive searching of a wide variety of legal sources. Additional features include Daily Opinion Service, lexis.com Bookstore, Career Center, CLE Center, Law Schools, and Practice Pages ("Pages specific to areas of specialty").

ONLINE DATABASES

Index to Legal Periodicals and Books (Online). H. W. Wilson Co. • Broad coverage of law journals and books 1981 to date. Monthly updates. Inquire as to online cost and availability.

PERIODICALS AND NEWSLETTERS

Alcoholic Beverage Control: State Capitals. Wakeman-Walworth Inc. • 50 times a year. $245.00 per year; print and online editions, $350.00 per year. Formerly *From the State Capitals: Alcoholic Beverage Control.*

STATISTICS SOURCES

Statistical Reports. National Alcoholic Beverage Control Association. • Monthly. Price on application. Includes quarterly and annual cumulations.

Uniform Crime Reports for the United States. Federal Bureau of Investigation, U.S. Department of Justice. Available from U.S. Government Printing Office. • Annual. $45.00.

TRADE/PROFESSIONAL ASSOCIATIONS

Joint Committee of the States. c/o National Alcoholic Beverage Control Association, 4216 King St., W, Alexandria, VA 22302. Phone: (703)578-4200 Fax: (703)820-3551 • Formerly Joint Committee of the States to study Alcoholic Beverage Laws.

National Alcohol Beverage Control Association. 4401 Ford Ave., Ste. 700, Alexandria, VA 22302-1473. Phone: (703)578-4200 Fax: (703)820-3551 E-mail: info@nabca.org • URL: http://www.nabca.org • State agencies controlling the purchase, distribution, and sale of alcoholic beverages under the control system; distillery firms and trade associations are associate members.

National Conference of State Liquor Administrators. c/o Jeffrey J. Green, State of Rhode Island, Division of Commercial Licensing, Liquor Control Section, 233 Richmond St., Ste. 230, Providence, RI 02903. Phone: (401)222-2416 Fax: (401)222-6654 E-mail: jgreen@ncsla.org • URL: http://www.ncsla.org.

OTHER SOURCES

Liquor Control Law Reporter: Federal and All States. CCH, Inc. • Biweekly. $3,649.00 per year. Nine looseleaf volumes. Federal and state regulation and taxation of alcoholic beverages.

LIQUOR STORES

FINANCIAL RATIOS

Almanac of Business and Industrial Financial Ratios. Leo Troy. Aspen Publishers, Inc. • 2003. $125.95. Includes CD-Rom. Contains financial ratios derived from federal tax returns. Ratios for each of about 200 industries are arranged according to company asset size. (Almanac of Business and Industrial Financial Ratios Series).

Annual Statement Studies. The Risk Management Association. • Annual. Median and quartile financial ratios are given for over 400 kinds of manufacturing, wholesale, retail, construction, and consumer finance establishments. Data is sorted by both asset size and sales volume. Includes a clearly written

"Definition of Ratios" and an alphabetical industry index.

Annual Statement Studies: Industry Default Probabilities and Cash Flow Measures. The Risk Management Association. • Annual. $145.00. Serves as a companion volume to the original *Annual Statement Studies.* Gives probability of default estimates on a percentage scale for more than 450 industries. Includes changes in position year-by-year for eight financial statement line items and provides percentage measures of cash flow.

INTERNET DATABASES

Advance Monthly Sales for Retail Trade and Food Services. U. S. Census Bureau. Phone: 800-541-8345 or (301)763-4636 Fax: (301)457-3842 E-mail: rcb@census.gov • URL: http://www.census.gov/svsd/www/fullpub.html • Web pages provide monthly sales figures for a wide range of retail businesses. Advance, preliminary, and final statistics are provided for the latest month available in each case, with a previous-year comparison. Updates are monthly.

PRICE SOURCES

Beverage Media. Beverage Network. Beverage Media, Ltd. • Monthly. $78.00 per year. Wholesale prices.

STATISTICS SOURCES

Annual Benchmark Report for Retail Trade and Food Services...A Detailed Summary of Retail Sales, Purchases, Accounts Receivable, Inventories, and Food Service Sales. Available from U. S. Government Printing Office. • Annual. $13.00. Issued by the U.S. Census Bureau. Provides detailed annual and monthly retail statistics for the most recent 10 years. Includes data for various kinds of retail outlets, including automobiles, furniture, appliances, building supplies, grocery stores, drug stores, gasoline stations, clothing, sporting goods, department stores, and restaurants.

TRADE/PROFESSIONAL ASSOCIATIONS

American Beverage Licensees. 5101 River Rd., Ste. 108, Bethesda, MD 20816-1560. Phone: 888-656-3241 or (301)656-1494 Fax: (301)656-7539 E-mail: wiles@ablusa.org • URL: http://www.ablusa.org • Federation of associations of alcohol beverage retailers.

LITERARY AGENTS

See: WRITERS AND WRITING

LITERARY PROPERTY

See: COPYRIGHT

LITERATURE SEARCHING, ONLINE

See: ONLINE INFORMATION SYSTEMS

LITHOGRAPHY

See also: GRAPHIC ARTS INDUSTRY; PRINTING AND PRINTING EQUIPMENT INDUSTRIES

FINANCIAL RATIOS

PIA Financial Ratio Studies. Printing Industries of America, Inc. • Annual. $3,582.00. 18 volumes. $199.00 per volume.

ONLINE DATABASES

PIRA. PIRA International Information Centre. • Citations and abstracts pertaining to bookbinding

and other pulp, paper, and packaging industries, 1975 to present. Weekly updates. Inquire as to online cost and availability.

PERIODICALS AND NEWSLETTERS

American Printer: The Graphic Arts Manager Magazine. Primedia Business Magazines and Media. • Monthly. Free to qualified personnel; others, $73.00 per year. Serves the printing and lithographic industries and allied manufacturing and service segments.

TRADE/PROFESSIONAL ASSOCIATIONS

National Association for Printing Leadership. 75 W. Century Rd., Paramus, NJ 07652-1408. Phone: 800-642-6275 or (201)634-9600 Fax: (201)634-0325 E-mail: info@napl.org • URL: http://www.napl.org • Text: Formerly National Association of Printers and Lithographers.

LIVESTOCK INDUSTRY

See also: CATTLE INDUSTRY; MEAT INDUSTRY; SWINE INDUSTRY

ABSTRACTS AND INDEXES

Animal Breeding Abstracts: A Monthly Abstract of World Literature. Available from CABI Publishing North America. • Monthly. Institutions, $1,305.00 per year. Online edition available. Published in England by CABI Publishing. Provides worldwide coverage of the literature.

Index Veterinarius: Comprehensive Monthly Subject and Author Index to the World's Veterinary Literature. Availabe in Print and on the Internet. Available from CABI Publishing North America. • Monthly. Institutions, $1,660.00 per year. Annual cumulation. Includes single site internet access. Published in England by CABI Publishing. Provides worldwide coverage of the literature.

Nutrition Abstracts and Reviews, Series B: Livestock Feeds and Feeding. Available from CABI Publishing, North America. • Monthly. Institutions, $1,180.00 per year. Online edition available, $1,215.00 per year. Published in England by CABI Publishing. Provides worldwide coverage of the literature.

CD-ROM DATABASES

OECD Statistical Compendium. Organization for Economic Cooperation and Development. • Semiannual. $1,905.00 per year for 1 to 10 users. CD-ROM contains more than 730,000 monthly, quarterly, and annual time series for OECD countries, 1960 to date. Includes fully searchable data on agriculture, food, economic indicators, national accounts, employment, energy, finance, industry, technology, and foreign trade. Results can be displayed in various forms.

HANDBOOKS AND MANUALS

Stockman's Handbook. R. M. Ensminger. Prentice Hall. • 2002. $85.00. Seventh edition.

INTERNET DATABASES

BEEF. National Cattlemen's Beef Association. Phone: (303)694-0305 Fax: (303)694-2851 E-mail: cows@beef.org • URL: http://www.beef.org • Web site provides detailed information from the "Cattle and Beef Handbook," including "Beef Economics" (production, sales, consumption, retail value, foreign competition, etc.). Text of monthly newsletter is also available: "The Beef Brief-Issues & Trends in the Cattle Industry." Keyword searching is offered. Fees: Free.

Business 2.0 Web Guide to the Best Business Links. Business 2.0 Media Inc. Phone: (415)293-4800 E-mail: support@business2.com • URL: http://www.business2.com/webguide • Web site presents an extensive, searchable directory of links to "the best, most informative, and authoritative web pages." Twenty main categories cover business, finance, career, company information, people, and technology topics, with thousands of subtopics, all linking to Web sites recommended by experienced business researchers. Fees: Free.

Fedstats. Federal Interagency Council on Statistical Policy. Phone: (202)395-7254 • URL: http://www. fedstats.gov • Web site features an efficient search facility for full-text statistics produced by more than 100 federal agencies, including the Census Bureau, the Bureau of Economic Analysis, and the Bureau of Labor Statistics. Boolean searches can be made within one agency or for all agencies combined. Links are offered to international statistical bureaus, including the UN, IMF, OECD, UNESCO, Eurostat, and 20 individual countries. Fees: Free.

FreeLunch.com. Economy.com, Inc. Phone: (610)696-8700 Fax: (610)696-1678 • URL: http:// www.freelunch.com • Web site provides free access to more than 1.5 million economic and financial data series, covering industry, demographics, labor markets, prices, retail sales, government spending, trade, interest rates, housing starts, the stock market, and many other topics. Data is available for various time periods in either chart or table form. Searching is offered. Fees: Free, but registration required. Economy.com, Inc. also offers fee-based economic analysis at *The Dismal Scientist* site (http://www. dismal.com).

USDA. United States Department of Agriculture. Phone: (202)720-2791 E-mail: agsec@usda.gov • URL: http://www.usda.gov • The USDA home page has six sections: News and Information; What's New; About USDA; Agencies; Opportunities; Search and Help. Keyword searching is offered from the USDA home page and from various individual agency home pages. Agencies are the Economic Research Service, Agricultural Marketing Service, National Agricultural Statistics Service, National Agricultural Library, and about 12 others. Updating varies. Fees: Free.

ONLINE DATABASES

CAB Abstracts. CAB Publishing North America. • Contains 46 specialized abstract collections covering over 10,000 journals and monographs in the areas of agriculture, horticulture, forest products, farm products, nutrition, dairy science, poultry, grains, animal health, entomology, etc. Time period is 1972 to date, with monthly updates. Inquire as to online cost and availability. *CAB Abstracts on CD-ROM* also available, with annual updating.

PERIODICALS AND NEWSLETTERS

Doane's Agricultural Report. Doane Agricultural Services. • Description: Covers the marketing of commodities (such as cattle, hogs, corn, wheat, and soybeans), as well as providing agricultural, economic, management, and production information. Discusses such topics as profit management, prices, outlook, machinery, buildings, equipment, taxes, social security, law, and government.

Journal of Animal Science. American Society of Animal Science. • Monthly. $400.00 per year.

Livestock Production Science. Elsevier. • 21 times a year. Qualified personnel, $111.00 per year; institutions, $1,571.00 per year.

PRICE SOURCES

The National Provisioner: Serving Meat, Poultry, and Seafood Processors. Stagnito Communications, Inc. • Monthly. Free to qualified personnel; others, $85.04 per year. Annual *Buyer's Guide* available. Meat, poultry and seafood newsletter.

STATISTICS SOURCES

Agricultural Statistics. Available from U. S. Government Printing Office. • Annual. $38.00. Produced by the National Agricultural Statistics Service, U. S. Department of Agriculture. Provides a wide variety of statistical data relating to agricultural production,

supplies, consumption, prices/price-supports, foreign trade, costs, and returns, as well as farm labor, loans, income, and population. In many cases, historical data is shown annually for 10 years. In addition to farm data, includes detailed fishery statistics.

Business Statistics of the United States. Linz Audain and Cornelia J. Strawser. Bernan Associates. • Annual. $147.00. Based on *Business Statistics*, formerly issue by the Bureau of Economic Analysis, U. S. Department of Commerce. Provides basic data for a wide variety of U. S. industries, services, and economic indicators. Most statistics are shown annually for 30 years and monthly for the most recent four years.

FAO Production Yearbook. Available from Bernan Associates. • Annual. $45.00. Published by the Food and Agriculture Organization (http://www.fao.org). Contains worldwide data on agriculture, land use, farm crops, livestock, and agricultural prices.

FAO Trade Yearbook. Available from Bernan Associates. • Annual. $45.00. Published by the Food and Agriculture Organization (http://www.fao.org). Provides extensive worldwide data on exports and imports of agricultural commodities, fertilizers, tractors, and pesticides. Includes more than 130 tables of detailed statistics.

Livestock, Meat, Wool, Market News. U.S. Department of Agriculture. • Weekly.

Survey of Current Business. Available from U. S. Government Printing Office. • Monthly. $63.00 per year. Issued by Bureau of Economic Analysis, U. S. Department of Commerce. Presents a wide variety of business and economic data.

WEFA Industrial Monitor. John Wiley and Sons, Inc. • Annual. $65.00. Prepared by industry analysts at WEFA, an economic forecasting and consulting firm (originally Wharton Econometric Forecasting Associates). Contains discussions of the outlook for major U. S. industries, with many 10-year forecasts (WEFA Web site is http://www.wefa.com).

TRADE/PROFESSIONAL ASSOCIATIONS

American Society of Animal Science. 111 N Dunlap St., Savoy, IL 61874-9604. Phone: (217)356-9050 Fax: (217)398-4119 E-mail: asas@assochq.org • URL: http://www.asas.org.

Livestock Marketing Association. 10510 NW Ambassador Dr., Kansas City, MO 64153. Phone: 800-821-2048 or (816)891-0502 Fax: (816)891-7926 E-mail: lmainfo@lmaweb.com • URL: http:// www.lmaweb.com • Livestock marketing businesses and livestock dealers. Sponsors annual World Livestock Auctioneer Championships. Offers management and promotional services.

National Cattlemen's Beef Association. 9110 E Nichols Ave., Ste. 300, Centennial, CO 80112. Phone: (866)233-3872 or (303)694-0305 Fax: (303)694-2851 E-mail: membership@beef.org • URL: http://www.beefusa.org • Represents 149 organizations of livestock marketers, growers, meat packers, food retailers, and food service firms. Conducts extensive program of promotion, education and information about beef, veal, and associated meat products. Conducts projects such as recipe testing and development, food demonstrations, food photography, educational service to colleges, experimental meat cutting methods, merchandising programs, and preparation of materials for newspapers, magazines, radio, and television.

LOAN COMPANIES

See: FINANCE COMPANIES; SAVINGS AND LOAN ASSOCIATIONS

LOANS

See: BANK LOANS; CONSUMER CREDIT; CREDIT

LOANS, BANK

See: BANK LOANS

LOANS, COMMERCIAL

See: COMMERCIAL LENDING

LOANS, STUDENT

See: SCHOLARSHIPS AND STUDENT AID

LOBBYING

See: PRESSURE GROUPS

LOBSTER INDUSTRY

See also: SHELLFISH INDUSTRY

ABSTRACTS AND INDEXES

Oceanic Abstracts. CSA. • 11 times a year. $1,645.00 per year. Includes print and online editions. Covers oceanography, marine biology, ocean shipping, and a wide range of other marine-related subject areas.

ONLINE DATABASES

Oceanic Abstracts (Online). Cambridge Scientific Abstracts. • Oceanographic and other marine-related technical literature, 1981 to present. Monthly updates. Inquire as to online cost and availability.

PERIODICALS AND NEWSLETTERS

Commercial Fisheries News. Compass Publications, Fisheries Division. • Monthly. $21.95 per year. Covers the commercial fishing industry in New England. Includes news of marine technology, boatbuilding, fish and lobster prices, business trends, government regulation, and other topics.

Seafood Business. Diversified Business Communications. • Monthly. $69.00 per year. Edited for a wide range of seafood buyers, including distributors, restaurants, supermarkets, and institutions. Special issues feature information on specific products, such as salmon or lobster.

STATISTICS SOURCES

Fisheries of the United States. Available from U. S. Government Printing Office. • Annual. $20.00. Issued by the National Marine Fisheries Service, National Oceanic and Atmospheric Administration, U. S. Department of Commerce.

TRADE/PROFESSIONAL ASSOCIATIONS

Maine Lobstermen's Association. 21 Western Ave., Ste. 1, Kennebunk, ME 04043. Phone: (207)967-4555 or (207)363-6783 Fax: (866)407-3770 E-mail: info@mainelobstermen.org • URL: http://www. mainelobstermen.org • Licensed lobstermen and supporting business. Gives Maine's lobstermen a voice and influence at the highest levels of government.

LOCAL AREA NETWORKS

See also: COMPUTER COMMUNICATIONS; MICROCOMPUTERS AND MINICOMPUTERS

GENERAL WORKS

Computer Networks. Andrew S. Tanenbaum. Prentice Hall PTR. • 2002. $89.00. Fourth edition.

Local Area Networks. Gerd Keiser. McGraw Hill. •

2001. $76.00. Second edition.

ABSTRACTS AND INDEXES

Business Periodicals Index. H. W. Wilson Co. • 11 times a year. Quarterly and annual cumulations. Price varies.

Computer and Control Abstracts. Available from INSPEC, Inc. • Monthly. $2,400.00 per year. Section C of *Science Abstracts*.

Computer and Information Systems Abstracts Journal: An Abstract Journal Pertaining to the Theory, Design, Fabrication and Application of Computer and Information Systems. CSA. • 11 times a year. $1,750 per year.

Computer Literature Index: A Subject/Author Index to Computer and Data Processing Literature. EBSCO Publishing. • Quarterly, with annual cumulation. $245.00 per year. Contains brief abstracts of book and periodical literature covering all phases of computing, including approximately 70 specific application areas.

Key Abstracts: Computer Communications and Storage. Available from INSPEC, Inc. • Monthly. $250.00 per year. Provides international coverage of journal and proceedings literature, including material on optical disks and networks. Published in England by the Institution of Electrical Engineers (IEE).

CD-ROM DATABASES

Datapro on CD-ROM: Communications Analyst. Gartner Group, Inc. • Monthly. Price on application. Provides detailed information on products and services for communications systems, including local area networks and voice systems.

DIRECTORIES

Network Buyers Guide. CMP Media LLC. • Annual. $5.00. Lists suppliers of products for local and wide area computer networks. Formerly *LAN Buyers Guide Issue*.

ENCYCLOPEDIAS AND DICTIONARIES

Dictionary of Information Technology and Computer Science. Tony Gunton. Blackwell Publishing. • 1994. $62.95. Second edition. Covers key words, phrases, abbreviations, and acronyms used in computing and data communications.

Every Manager's Guide to Information Technology: A Glossary of Key Terms and Concepts for Today's Business Leader. Peter G. W. Keen. Harvard Business School Publishing. • 1994. $18.95. Second edition. Provides definitions of terms related to computers, data communications, and information network systems. (Harvard Business Reference Series).

HANDBOOKS AND MANUALS

Hacker's Handbook: The Strategy Behind Breaking Into and Defending Networks. Susan Young and Dave Aitel. CRC Press. • 2003. $79.95. Reveals "the technical aspects of hacking that are least understood by network administrators." Practical defenses are outlined. (Imprint: Auerbach Publications.).

Local Area Networks in Information Management. Harry M. Kibrige. Greenwood Publishing Group, Inc. • 1989. $60.00. (New Directions in Information Management Series).

ONLINE DATABASES

Internet and Personal Computing Abstracts. Information Today, Inc. • Contains abstracts covering a wide variety of personal and business microcomputer literature appearing in more than 100 journals and popular magazines. Time period is 1981 to date, with monthly updates. Formerly *Microcomputer Index*. Inquire as to online cost and availability.

PROMT: Predicasts Overview of Markets and Technology. Gale Cengage Learning. • Companies, products, applied technologies and markets. U.S. and international literature coverage, 1972 to date. Inquire as to online cost and availability. Provides abstracts from more than 1,600 publications. Weekly updates.

Wilson Business Abstracts Online. H. W. Wilson Co. • Indexes and abstracts 600 major business periodicals, plus the *Wall Street Journal* and the business section of the *New York Times*. Indexing is from 1982, abstracting from 1990, with the two newspapers included from 1993. Updated weekly. Inquire as to online cost and availability. (*Business Periodicals Index* without abstracts is also available online.).

PERIODICALS AND NEWSLETTERS

Computer Economics Networking Strategies Report: Advising IT Decision Maker ractices and Current Trends. Computer Economics, Inc. • Monthly. $395.00 per year. Newsletter. Edited for information technology managers. Covers news and trends relating to a variety of corporate computer network and management information systems topics. Emphasis is on costs. Formerly *Intranet and Networking Strategies Report*.

Computer Reseller News: The Newsweekly for Builders of Technology Solutions. CMP Worldwide Media Networks. • Weekly. $199.00 per year. Includes bimonthly supplement. Incorporates *Computer Reseller Sources and Macintosh News.* Formerly *Computer Retailer News*.

EDP Weekly: The Leading Weekly Computer News Summary. Computer Age and EDP News Services. • Weekly. $495.00 per year. Newsletter. Summarizes news from all areas of the computer and microcomputer industries.

Exploring Windows NT for Professionals. Element K Journals. • Monthly. $139.00 per year. Newsletter on the Windows operating system for networks. Formerly *Exploring Windows NT*.

Industrial Computing. Industrial Computing Society. ISA Services, Inc. • Monthly. Members $100.00 per year; non-members, $80.00 per year. Published by the Instrument Society of America. Edited for engineering managers and systems integrators. Subject matter includes industrial software, programmable controllers, artificial intelligence systems, and industrial computer networking systems.

Insurance Networking: Strategies and Solutions for Electronic Commerce. Thomson Media. • 10 times a year. Price on application. Covers information technology for the insurance industry, with emphasis on computer communications and the Internet.

Managing Automation. Thomas Publishing Co., LLC. • Monthly. Free to qualified personnel; others, $60.00 per year. Coverage includes software for manufacturing, systems planning, integration in process industry automation, computer integrated manufacturing (CIM), computer networks for manufacturing, management problems, industry news, and new products.

Network Computing: Computing in a Network Environment. CMP Publications, Inc. • Semimonthly. Free to qualified personnel.

Network: Strategies and Solutions for the Network Professional. CMP Media LLC. • 13 times a year. Free to qualified personnel. Covers network products and peripherals for computer professionals. Includes annual network managers salary survey and annual directory issue. Formerly *LAN: The Network Solutions Magazine*.

Network World: The Newsweekly of Enterprise Network Computing. Network World Inc. • Weekly. $129.00 per year. Includes special feature issues on enterprise Internets, network operating systems, network management, high-speed modems, LAN management systems, and Internet access providers.

SAN/LAN: Newsletter Covering Worldwide Technology Trends, Applications and Markets (Storage Area Network/Local Area Network). Information Gatekeepers, Inc. • Monthly. $695.00 per year. Cover new developments, new products, and marketing. Formerly *Local Area Networks*.

Wireless Data News. Access Intelligence L.L.C. • Description: Provides analysis of technology, applications, marketing, and competition in the mobile communications industry. Scope is international. Recurring features include news of research.

RESEARCH CENTERS AND INSTITUTES

Center for Advanced Technology in Information Management. Columbia University, Vanderbilt Clinic, 622 W 168th St., 5th Fl., New York, NY 10032. Phone: (212)305-2944 Fax: (212)305-0196 E-mail: shortliffe@dmi.columbia.edu • URL: http://www.dmi.columbia.edu/cat.

Laboratory for Information and Decision Systems. Massachusetts Institute of Technology, 127 Massachusetts Ave., Bldg. 35, Room 308, Cambridge, MA 02139-4307. Phone: (617)258-8222 Fax: (617)253-3578 E-mail: chan@mit.edu • URL: http://www.justice.mit.edu • Research areas include data communication networks and fiber optic networks.

STATISTICS SOURCES

Standard & Poor's Industry Surveys. Standard & Poor's. • Semiannual. $1,800.00. Two looseleaf volumes. Includes monthly *Supplements*. Provides detailed, individual surveys of 52 major industry groups. Each survey is revised on a semiannual basis. Also includes "Monthly Investment Review" (industry group investment analysis) and monthly "Trends & Projections" (economic analysis).

U. S. Industry and Trade Outlook. Available from National Technical Information Service. • Annual. $69.95. Produced by the International Trade Administration, U. S. Department of Commerce, in a "public-private" partnership with DRI/McGraw-Hill and Standard & Poor's. Provides basic data, outlook for the current year, and "Long-Term Prospects" (five-year projections) for a wide variety of products and services. Includes high technology industries. Formerly *U. S. Industrial Outlook*.

TRADE/PROFESSIONAL ASSOCIATIONS

Computer and Communications Industry Association. 666 11th St., N.W., Suite 600, Washington, DC 20001. Phone: (202)783-0070 Fax: (202)783-0534 E-mail: asteinem@ccianet.org • URL: http://www.ccianet.org • Formerly Computer Industry Association.

Instrumentation Systems and Automation Society. 67 Alexander Dr., Research Triangle Park, NC 27709. Phone: (919)549-8411 Fax: (919)549-8288 E-mail: info@isa.org • URL: http://www.isa.org • Members are engineers and others concerned with industrial instrumentation, systems, computers, and automation. Formerly Instrument Society of America.

International Council for Computer Communication. P.O. Box 9745, Washington, DC 20016-9745. Phone: (703)836-7787 Fax: (703)836-7787 E-mail: office@icccgovernors.org • URL: http://www.icccgovernors.org • Affiliated with International Federation for Information Processing.

LOCAL GOVERNMENT

See: COUNTY GOVERNMENT; MUNICIPAL GOVERNMENT; STATE GOVERNMENT

LOCATION OF INDUSTRY

See also: INDUSTRIAL DEVELOPMENT
GENERAL WORKS
Industrial Location: Principles and Policies. J.W. Harrington and Barney Warf. Routledge. • 1995.

$100.00. Second revised edition.

DIRECTORIES

Site Selection. Conway Data, Inc. • Bimonthly. Six volumes, $22.00 per volume. $85.00 per set. Each of the six issues per year is a separate directory: *Geo-Corporate* (facility planners), *Geo-Economic* (area development officials), *Geo-Labor* (labor force data), *Geo-Life* (quality of life information), *GeoPolitical* (government agencies), and *Geo-Sites* (industrial/office parks). Formerly *Site Selection and Industrial Development.*

PERIODICALS AND NEWSLETTERS

Area Development Sites and Facility Planning: The Executive Magazine of Sites and Facility Planning. Halcyon Business Publications, Inc. • Monthly. Free to the business trade; others, $65.00 per year. Site selection, facility planning, and plant relocation. Formerly *Area Development Magazines.*

Business Facilities: The Location Advisor. Group C Communications, Inc. • Monthly. Free to qualified personnel; others, $30.00 per year. Facility planning and site selection.

Expansion Management: Growth Strategies for Companies on the Move. Penton Media Inc., Industry Div. • Monthly. Free to qualified personnel; others, $40.00 per year. Subject matter is concerned with expansion and relocation of industrial facilities.

Insulation Outlook: Business Solutions for Expanding or Relocating Companies. National Insulation Association. • $45.00 per year. Covers site selection and related topics.

New Plant Report. Conway Data Inc. • Description: Covers new plants and plant expansions. Provides project location, company name, product to be manufactured or service performed, NAICS code, type of facility, stage of development, and (as available) number of employees, square footage, investment amount, and contact name. **Remarks:** Also available on disk and via e-mail.

Plants, Sites, and Parks. Reed Business Information. • Seven times a year. Free to qualified personnel; others, $43.90 per year. Covers economic development, site location, industrial parks, and industrial development programs.

STATISTICS SOURCES

Ernst & Young Almanac and Guide to U. S. Business Cities: 65 Leading Places to Do Business. John Wiley and Sons, Inc. • 1994. $16.95. Provides demographic, business, economic, and site selection data for 65 major U. S. cities.

LOCKOUTS

See: STRIKES AND LOCKOUTS

LOCKS AND KEYS

See also: INDUSTRIAL SECURITY PROGRAMS

DIRECTORIES

Locksmith Ledger's Security Register. Locksmith Publishing Corp. • Publication includes: Lists of about 1,300 manufacturers, wholesalers, and distributors of security products; and nearly 80 trade associations. Entries include: For manufacturers and distributors--Company name; address, phone, name of contact, names of key personnel, products manufactured or lines handled. For trade associations--Name, address.

HANDBOOKS AND MANUALS

Effective Physical Security: Design, Equipment, and Operations. Lawrence J. Fennelly, editor. Elsevier. • 1996. $44.99. Second edition. Contains chapters

written by various U. S. security equipment specialists. Covers architectural considerations, locks, safes, alarms, intrusion detection systems, closed circuit television, identification systems, etc.

PERIODICALS AND NEWSLETTERS

Keynotes. USA Section/International College of Dentists. • Description: Contains news of the activities and projects of the organization, which provides networking and educational opportunities for professionals in the dental field. Recurring features include a calendar of events, reports of meetings, news of educational opportunities, and a column titled the History Corner.

Locksmith Ledger International. Locksmith Publishing Corp. • Monthly. $38.00 per year. Includes *Directory* issue. Formerly *Locksmith Ledger.*

National Locksmith. National Publishing Co. • Monthly. $41.00.

TRADE/PROFESSIONAL ASSOCIATIONS

Associated Locksmiths of America. 3003 Live Oak St., Dallas, TX 75204. Phone: 800-532-2562 or (214)827-1701 Fax: (214)827-1810 E-mail: aloa@ aloa.org • URL: http://www.aloa.org.

Security Hardware Distributors Association. 1900 Arch St., Philadelphia, PA 19103-1498. Phone: (215)564-3484 Fax: (215)564-2175 E-mail: shda@ fernley.com • URL: http://www.shda.org • Formerly National Locksmith Suppliers Association.

LOCOMOTIVES

See: RAILROADS

LOGGING

See: LUMBER INDUSTRY

LOGISTIC RESEARCH

See: OPERATIONS RESEARCH

LOGOS

See: CORPORATE IMAGE; TRADEMARKS AND TRADE NAMES

LONG-TERM CARE INSURANCE

See also: HEALTH INSURANCE; NURSING HOMES

GENERAL WORKS

Caring for Frail Elderly People: New Directions in Care. OECD Publications and Information Center. • 1994. $27.00. Discusses the problem in OECD countries of providing good quality care to the elderly at manageable cost. Includes trends in family care, housing policies, and private financing.

Fundamentals of Employee Benefit Programs. Employee Benefit Research Institute. • 1996. $49.95. Fifth edition. Provides basic explanation of employee benefit programs in both the private and public sectors, including health insurance, pension plans, retirement planning, social security, and long-term care insurance.

J. K. Lasser's Choosing the Right Long-Term Care Insurance. Benjamin Lipson. John Wiley and Sons, Inc. • 2002. $16.95. Provides practical, consumer-oriented information, with advice to be skeptical of media hype and insurance company promotions. (Practical Guides for All Your Financial Needs Series).

Long-Term Care and Its Alternatives. Charles B. Inlander and others. People's Medical Society. • 1996. $16.95. Provides practical advice on the financing of long-term health care. The author is a consumer advocate and president of the People's Medical Society.

Planning for Long Term Care. McGraw-Hill. • 2002. $14.95. Provides detailed information for consumers on long-term care insurance.

Sharing the Burden: Strategies for Public and Private Long-Term Care Insurance. Joshua M. Wiener and others. Brookings Institution Press. • 1994. $42.95.

A Shopper's Guide to Long-Term Care Insurance. Barry Leonard, editor. DIANE Publishing Co. • 1995. $15.00. Revised edition. Provides impartial, consumer-oriented information and advice on long-term care insurance policies. Includes worksheets.

ABSTRACTS AND INDEXES

Insurance Periodicals Index. Specials Libraries Association, Insurance and Employees Benefits Div. NILS Publishing Co. • Annual. $250.00. Compiled by the Insurance and Employee Benefits Div., Special Libraries Association. A yearly index of over 15,000 articles from about 35 insurance periodicals. Arrangement is by subject, with an index to authors.

Readers' Guide to Periodical Literature. H. W. Wilson Co. • Monthly. $345.00 per year. Includes annual *Cumulation.* Indexes about 250 peridicals of general interest.

BIBLIOGRAPHIES

Insurance and Employee Benefits Literature. Special Libraries Association, Insurance and Employee Benefits Div. • Bimonthly. $15.00 per year. Lists a wide variety of literature in all branches of the insurance industry. Includes annotations.

Long-Term Care: An Annotated Bibliography. Theodore H. Koff. Greenwood Publishing Group, Inc. • 1995. $59.95. (Bibliographies and Indexes in Gerontology Series: No. 25).

CD-ROM DATABASES

Authority Health Care Law Library. LexisNexis/ Matthew Bender. • Periodic updates. Price on request. Full text CD-ROM provides legal information, case law, and analysis relating to health care facilities, health insurance, longterm care, Medigap, and Medicare.

ENCYCLOPEDIAS AND DICTIONARIES

Rupp's Insurance and Risk Management Glossary. Richard V. Rupp. NILS Publishing Co. • 2001. $35.00. Second edition. Provides definitions of 6,400 insurance words and phrases. Includes a guide to acronyms and abbreviations.

HANDBOOKS AND MANUALS

The Complete Book of Insurance: Protecting Your Life, Health Property, and Income. Ben G. Baldwin. McGraw-Hill. • 1991. $24.95. Provides basic information and advice on various kinds of insurance: life, health, property (fire), disability, long-term care, automobile, liability, and annuities.

How to Cover the Gaps in Medicare: Health Insurance and Long-Term Care Options for the Retired. Robert A. Gilmour. American Institute for Economic Research. • 2003. $10.00. Four parts: "The Medicare Quandry," "How to Protect Yourself Against the Medigap," "Long-Term Care Options," and "End-of-Life Decisions" (living wills). Includes discussions of long-term care insurance, retirement communities, and HMO Medicare insurance.

The Managed Care Contracting Handbook: Planning and Negotiating the Managed Care Relationship. Maria K. Todd. Available from McGraw Hill Higher Education. • 1996. $65.00. Co-published by McGraw-Hill Healthcare Education Group and the Healthcare Financial Management Association. Covers managed care planning, proposals, strategy, negotiation, and contract law. Written for healthcare providers.

INTERNET DATABASES

InsWeb. InsWeb Corp. Phone: (916)853-3300 E-mail: info@insweb.com • URL: http://www. insweb.com • Web site offers a wide variety of advice and information on automobile, life, health, and "other" insurance. Includes glossaries of insurance terms, Standard & Poor's ratings of individual insurance companies, and "Financial Needs Estimators." Searching is available. Fees: Free.

ONLINE DATABASES

Ageline. American Association of Retired Persons. • Provides indexing and abstracting of the literature of social gerontology, including consumer aspects, financial planning, employment, housing, health care services, mental health, social security, and retirement. Time period is 1978 to date. Inquire as to online cost and availability.

Readers' Guide Abstracts Online. H. W. Wilson Co. • Indexes and abstracts general interest periodicals, 1983 to date. Weekly updates. Inquire as to online cost and availability.

PERIODICALS AND NEWSLETTERS

Advisor Today. National Association of Insurance and Finacial Advisors. • Monthly. Free to members; non-members, $7.00 per year. Edited for individual life and health insurance agents. Among the topics included are disability insurance and long-term care insurance. Formerly Life Association News.

Financial Planning: The Magazine for Financial Service Professionals. Thomson Media. • Monthly. $79.00 per year. Edited for independent financial planners and insurance agents. Covers retirement planning, estate planning, tax planning, and insurance, including long-term healthcare considerations. Special features include a Retirement Planning Issue, Mutual Fund Performance Survey, and Variable Life and Annuity Survey.

Health Insurance Underwriter. National Association of Health Underwriters. • Monthly. $25.00 per year. Includes special feature issues on long-term care insurance, disability insurance, managed health care, and insurance office management.

Jounal of Finacial Services Professionals. Society of Financial Services Professional. • Bimonthly. $95.00 per year. Provides information on life insurance and financial planning, including estate planning, retirement, tax planning, trusts, business insurance, long-term care insurance, disability insurance, and employee benefits. Formerly (American Society of CLU and Ch F C Journal).

RESEARCH CENTERS AND INSTITUTES

Division of Health Services Research and Policy. University of Minnesota, Mayo Memorial Bldg., Minneapolis, MN 55455. Phone: (612)624-6151 Fax: (612)624-2196 E-mail: foote003@tc.umn.edu • URL: http://www.hsr.umn.edu • Fields of research include health insurance, consumer choice of health plans, quality of care, and long-term care.

Employee Benefit Research Institute. Employee Benefit Research Institute. 1100 13 St. NW, Ste. 878, Washington, DC 20005. Phone: (202)659-0670 Fax: (202)775-6312 E-mail: salisbury@ebri.org • URL: http://www.ebri.org • Employee benefits in the public and private sectors, including studies on individual retirement accounts, retirement income, flexible benefits, financing health care for the elderly, health care costs, long-term care, employee benefits and federal tax policy, social security, changing benefits, and government regulation of employee benefit plans.

Institute for Health Policy Research. Health Science Center, University of Florida, P.O. Box 100177, Gainesville, FL 32610-0177. Phone: (352)395-8035 Fax: (352)395-8047 E-mail: admin@hpe.ufl.edu •

URL: http://www.hpe.ufl.edu • Research areas include health economics, financing, and long-term care considerations.

Office of Academic Affairs, School of Public Health. University of Michigan, 109 S. Observatory St., 3537 SPH 1, Ann Arbor, MI 48109-2029. Phone: (734)764-5425 Fax: (734)763-5455 E-mail: sph. inquiries@umich.edu • URL: http://www.sph. umich.edu/ • Research fields include health care economics, health insurance, and long-term care.

STATISTICS SOURCES

EBRI's Databook on Employee Benefits: What is the Promise?. Ken McDonnell and others. Employee Benefit Research Institute. • 1997 $99.00. Fourth edition. Contains more than 350 tables and charts presenting data on employee benefits in the U. S., including pensions, health insurance, social security, and medicare. Includes a glossary of employee benefit terms.

TRADE/PROFESSIONAL ASSOCIATIONS

Families U. S. A. Foundation. 1334 G St., N. W., Washington, DC 20005. Phone: (202)628-3030 Fax: (202)347-2417 E-mail: info@familiesusa.org • URL: http://www.familiesusa.org • Fields of interest are health care and long-term health care, including insurance. Formerly Villers Foundation.

Health Insurance Association of America. 1201 F St., N.W., No. 500, Washington, DC 20004. Phone: (202)824-1600 Fax: (202)824-1722 E-mail: jbalda@hiaa.org • URL: http://www.hiaa.org • Members are commercial health insurers. Includes a Disability Insurance Committee, a Medicare Administration Committee, and a Long-Term Care Committee.

Long Term Care Campaign. PO Box 27394, Washington, DC 20038. Phone: (202)434-3744 or (202)434-3829 Fax: (202)434-6403 E-mail: lmainfo@lmaweb.com • URL: http://www. ltccampaign.org • Consumer, provider, business, labor, older adult, and disability groups. Works to make long term health care accessible and affordable for all families.

National Association of Health Underwriters. 200 N. 14th St., Suite. 450, Arlington, VA 22201. Phone: (703)276-0220 Fax: (703)841-7797 E-mail: info@ nahu.org • URL: http://www.nahu.org • Members are engaged in the sale of health and disability insurance. Formerly International Association of Health Underwriters.

National Association of Insurance and Financial Advisors. 2901 Telestar Court, Falls Church, VA 22042-1205. Phone: 877-866-2432 or (703)770-8100 Fax: (703)770-8142 E-mail: membersupport@ naifa.org • URL: http://www.naifa.org • Affiliated with Association for Advanced Life Underwriting. Formerly National Association of Life Underwriters.

National Institute on Community-Based Long-Term Care. c/o National Council on the Aging, 409 Third St., S.W., Washington, DC 20024. Phone: 800-424-9046 or (202)479-1200 Fax: (202)479-0735 E-mail: info@ncoa.org • URL: http://www.ncoa.org • A division of the National Council on the Aging. Seeks to promote and develop a comprehensive long-term health care system.

OTHER SOURCES

The Long-Term Care Market. MarketResearch.com. • 1999. $3,250.00. Market data with forecasts to the year 2005. Emphasis is on the over-85 age group. Covers health insurance, the nursing home industry, pharmaceuticals, healthcare supplies, etc.

LONG-TERM HEALTH CARE INDUSTRY

See: HEALTH CARE INDUSTRY; NURSING HOMES

LOW TEMPERATURE TECHNOLOGY

See: CRYOGENICS

LUBRICATION AND LUBRICANTS

See also: PETROLEUM INDUSTRY

ABSTRACTS AND INDEXES

NLGI Spokesman. National Lubricating Grease Institute. • Monthly. $24.00 per year. Information about the lubricating grease industry.

NTIS Alerts: Materials Sciences. National Technical Information Service. • Semimonthly. $220.00 per year. Provides descriptions of government-sponsored research reports and software, with ordering information. Covers ceramics, glass, coatings, composite materials, alloys, plastics, wood, paper, adhesives, fibers, lubricants, and related subjects. Formerly *Abstract Newsletter.*

DIRECTORIES

McCutcheon's Functional Materials Volumes 2. MC Publishing Co. • Annual. $170.00. Edited for product development, quality control and research and development chemists.

FINANCIAL RATIOS

Annual Statement Studies. The Risk Management Association. • Annual. Median and quartile financial ratios are given for over 400 kinds of manufacturing, wholesale, retail, construction, and consumer finance establishments. Data is sorted by both asset size and sales volume. Includes a clearly written "Definition of Ratios" and an alphabetical industry index.

Annual Statement Studies: Industry Default Probabilities and Cash Flow Measures. The Risk Management Association. • Annual. $145.00. Serves as a companion volume to the original *Annual Statement Studies.* Gives probability of default estimates on a percentage scale for more than 450 industries. Includes changes in position year-by-year for eight financial statement line items and provides percentage measures of cash flow.

HANDBOOKS AND MANUALS

Maintenance Engineering Handbook. Lindley R. Higgins and R. Keith Mobley. McGraw-Hill. • 2001. $150.00. Sixth edition. Contains about 60 chapters by various authors in 12 major sections covering all elements of industrial and plant maintenance.

PERIODICALS AND NEWSLETTERS

Journal of Tribology. ASME International. • Quarterly. Members, $50.00 per year; includes print and online editions. Non-members, $275.00 per year; includes print and online editons. Details lubrication and lubricants.

Lubrication Engineering. Society of Tribiologists and Lubrication Engineers. • Monthly. $70.00 per year.

Tribology International; The Practice and Technology of Lubrication, Wear Prevention and Friction Control. Elsevier. • Monthly. Qualified personnel, $173.00 per year; institutions, $1,528.00 per year.

TRADE/PROFESSIONAL ASSOCIATIONS

National Lubricating Grease Institute. 4635 Wyandotte St., Kansas City, MO 64112-1509. Phone: (816)931-9480 Fax: (816)753-5026 E-mail: nlgi@ nlgi.org • URL: http://www.nlgi.org • Companies manufacturing or selling all types of lubricating greases; suppliers to such companies; technical and educational organizations. Promotes research and testing for the development of better lubricating greases and improved grease lubrication engineering service to industry. Collects and disseminates technical data; conducts forums and educational program. Operates the National Lubricating +Grease Institute Research Fund.

Society of Tribologists and Lubrication Engineers. 840 Busse Hwy., Park Ridge, IL 60068-2376. Phone: (847)825-5536 Fax: (847)825-1456 E-mail: information@sstle.org • URL: http://www.stle.org • Formerly American Society of Lubrication Engineers.

LUGGAGE INDUSTRY

DIRECTORIES

Travelware Resources Directory. Business Journals, Inc. • Annual. $20.00. Manufacturers of trunks, luggage, brief cases, and personal leather goods are listed. Formerly *Luggage and Travelware Directory.*

FINANCIAL RATIOS

Annual Statement Studies. The Risk Management Association. • Annual. Median and quartile financial ratios are given for over 400 kinds of manufacturing, wholesale, retail, construction, and consumer finance establishments. Data is sorted by both asset size and sales volume. Includes a clearly written "Definition of Ratios" and an alphabetical industry index.

Annual Statement Studies: Industry Default Probabilities and Cash Flow Measures. The Risk Management Association. • Annual. $145.00. Serves as a companion volume to the original *Annual Statement Studies.* Gives probability of default estimates on a percentage scale for more than 450 industries. Includes changes in position year-by-year for eight financial statement line items and provides percentage measures of cash flow.

Annual Statement Studies: Industry Default Probabilities and Cash Flow Measures. The Risk Management Association. • Annual. $145.00. Serves as a companion volume to the original *Annual Statement Studies.* Gives probability of default estimates on a percentage scale for more than 450 industries. Includes changes in position year-by-year for eight financial statement line items and provides percentage measures of cash flow.

PERIODICALS AND NEWSLETTERS

Newsbreak. Leather Industries of America. • Free to members and other qualified personnel. Reports on issues and events in the luggage industry.

Travelware. Business Journals, Inc. • Seven times a year. $32.00. Formerly *Luggage and Travelware.*

STATISTICS SOURCES

U. S. Industry and Trade Outlook. Available from National Technical Information Service. • Annual. $69.95. Produced by the International Trade Administration, U. S. Department of Commerce, in a "public-private" partnership with DRI/McGraw-Hill and Standard & Poor's. Provides basic data, outlook for the current year, and "Long-Term Prospects" (five-year projections) for a wide variety of products and services. Includes high technology industries. Formerly *U. S. Industrial Outlook.*

TRADE/PROFESSIONAL ASSOCIATIONS

Luggage and Leather Goods Manufacturers of America. Five Vaughn Dr., Ste. 105, Princeton, NJ 08540-6313. Phone: 800-826-4224 or (212)695-2340 Fax: (212)643-8021 E-mail: llgma@llgma.org • URL: http://www.llgma.org.

National Luggage Dealers Association. 1817 Elmdale Ave., Glenview, IL 60025-1355. Phone: (847)998-6869 Fax: (847)998-6884 E-mail: inquiry@nlda.com • URL: http://www.nlda.com • Represents retailers of luggage, leather goods, gifts, and handbags. Buying group producing promotional materials.

LUMBER INDUSTRY

See also: FOREST PRODUCTS; HARDWOOD INDUSTRY; PLYWOOD INDUSTRY; WOODWORKING INDUSTRIES

ABSTRACTS AND INDEXES

Forest Products Abstracts. CABI Publishing North America. • Bimonthly. $770.00 per year; with on-line edition, $805.00 per year. Published in England by CABI Publishing. Provides worldwide coverage of forest products literature.

Forestry Abstracts: Compiled from World Literature. Available from CABI Publishing North America. • Monthly. Institutions, $1,435.00 per year. Print and online edition, $1,460.00 per year. Published in England by CABI Publishing. Provides worldwide coverage of the literature.

ALMANACS AND YEARBOOKS

Agricultural and Mineral Commodities Year Book. Available from Taylor & Francis Group. • Annual. $225.00. Published by Europa Publications. Contains descriptive product profiles, price data, export-import data, and production statistics for major commodities of the world. Includes commodity histories, uses, markets, demand trends, and information about trade agreements and key commodity organizations.

CD-ROM DATABASES

OECD Statistical Compendium. Organization for Economic Cooperation and Development. • Semiannual. $1,905.00 per year for 1 to 10 users. CD-ROM contains more than 730,000 monthly, quarterly, and annual time series for OECD countries, 1960 to date. Includes fully searchable data on agriculture, food, economic indicators, national accounts, employment, energy, finance, industry, technology, and foreign trade. Results can be displayed in various forms.

DIRECTORIES

Lumbermens Red Book: Reference Book of the Lumbermens Credit Association. Lumbermens Credit Association. • Semiannual $2,140.00 per year. Weekly supplements. Lists approximately 39,000 United States firms in the lumber and woodworking industries, with credit ratings. Available online.

Timber Harvesting--Logger's Resource Guide. Hatton-Brown Publishers Inc. • Publication includes: List manufacturers and distributors of equipment used in harvesting and handling timber, logging trade organizations and trade associations. Entries include: Firm name, division or subsidiary name, address, fax, phone, e-mail, website, year company established, names and titles of key personnel.

ENCYCLOPEDIAS AND DICTIONARIES

Encyclopedia of Wood: A Tree by Tree Guide to the World's Most Valuable Resource. Bill Lincoln and others. Facts on File, Inc. • 1989. $29.95.

Illustrated Dictionary of Building Materials and Techniques: An Invaluable Sourcebook to the Tools, Terms, Materials, and Techniques Used by Building Professionals. Paul Bianchina. John Wiley and Sons, Inc. • 1993. $19.95. Contains 4,000 definitions of building and building materials terms, with 500 illustrations. Includes materials grades, measurements, and specifications.

FINANCIAL RATIOS

Almanac of Business and Industrial Financial Ratios. Leo Troy. Aspen Publishers, Inc. • 2003. $125.95. Includes CD-Rom. Contains financial ratios derived from federal tax returns. Ratios for each of about 200 industries are arranged according to company asset size. (Almanac of Business and Industrial Financial Ratios Series).

HANDBOOKS AND MANUALS

Timber Construction Manual. American Institute of Timber Construction. John Wiley and Sons, Inc. •

1994. $160.00. Fourth edition.

INTERNET DATABASES

Business 2.0 Web Guide to the Best Business Links. Business 2.0 Media Inc. Phone: (415)293-4800 E-mail: support@business2.com • URL: http://www.business2.com/webguide • Web site presents an extensive, searchable directory of links to "the best, most informative, and authoritative web pages." Twenty main categories cover business, finance, career, company information, people, and technology topics, with thousands of subtopics, all linking to Web sites recommended by experienced business researchers. Fees: Free.

Fedstats. Federal Interagency Council on Statistical Policy. Phone: (202)395-7254 • URL: http://www.fedstats.gov • Web site features an efficient search facility for full-text statistics produced by more than 100 federal agencies, including the Census Bureau, the Bureau of Economic Analysis, and the Bureau of Labor Statistics. Boolean searches can be made within one agency or for all agencies combined. Links are offered to international statistical bureaus, including the UN, IMF, OECD, UNESCO, Eurostat, and 20 individual countries. Fees: Free.

FreeLunch.com. Economy.com, Inc. Phone: (610)696-8700 Fax: (610)696-1678 • URL: http://www.freelunch.com • Web site provides free access to more than 1.5 million economic and financial data series, covering industry, demographics, labor markets, prices, retail sales, government spending, trade, interest rates, housing starts, the stock market, and many other topics. Data is available for various time periods in either chart or table form. Searching is offered. Fees: Free, but registration required. Economy.com, Inc. also offers fee-based economic analysis at *The Dismal Scientist* site (http://www.dismal.com).

Manufacturing Profiles. U. S. Bureau of the Census. Phone: (301)763-4636 E-mail: webmaster@census.gov • URL: http://www.census.gov/prod/www/abs/mfg-prof.html • The Census Bureau makes available free on PDF (Portable Document Format) an annual consolidation of the entire Current Industrial Report series, presenting "all the data compiled." Contains statistics on production, shipments, inventories, consumption, exports, imports, and orders for a wide variety of manufactured products.

USDA. United States Department of Agriculture. Phone: (202)720-2791 E-mail: agsec@usda.gov • URL: http://www.usda.gov • The USDA home page has six sections: News and Information; What's New; About USDA; Agencies; Opportunities; Search and Help. Keyword searching is offered from the USDA home page and from various individual agency home pages. Agencies are the Economic Research Service, Agricultural Marketing Service, National Agricultural Statistics Service, National Agricultural Library, and about 12 others. Updating varies. Fees: Free.

ONLINE DATABASES

PROMT: Predicasts Overview of Markets and Technology. Gale Cengage Learning. • Companies, products, applied technologies and markets. U.S. and international literature coverage, 1972 to date. Inquire as to online cost and availability. Provides abstracts from more than 1,600 publications. Weekly updates.

PERIODICALS AND NEWSLETTERS

Building Material Dealer. National Lumber and Building Material Dealers Association. • Monthly. $48.00 per year. Includes special feature issues on hand and power tools, lumber, roofing, kitchens, flooring, windows and doors, and insulation. Formerly *Builder Material Retailer.*

Lumber Co-Operator. Northeastern Retail Lumber Association. • Bimonthly. Members, $35.00 per year; non-members, $40.00 per year.

Random Lengths: The Weekly Report on North

American Forest Products Markets. Random Lengths Publications, Inc. • Weekly. $265.00 per year. Newsletter. Information covering the wood products industry. Supplement available *Random Lengths Midweek Market Report.*

Southern Lumberman. Hatton-Brown Publishers, Inc. • Monthly. $23.00 per year. Controlled circulation. A magazine for the sawmill industry.

Timber Harvesting. Hatton Brown Publishers, Inc. • 10 times a year. $40.00 per year.

Wood and Wood Products: Furniture, Cabinets, Woodworking and Allied Products Management and Operations. Vance Publishing Corp. • 13 times a year. $55.00 per year.

STATISTICS SOURCES

Agricultural Statistics. Available from U. S. Government Printing Office. • Annual. $38.00. Produced by the National Agricultural Statistics Service, U. S. Department of Agriculture. Provides a wide variety of statistical data relating to agricultural production, supplies, consumption, prices/price-supports, foreign trade, costs, and returns, as well as farm labor, loans, income, and population. In many cases, historical data is shown annually for 10 years. In addition to farm data, includes detailed fishery statistics.

Annual Survey of Manufactures. Available from U. S. Government Printing Office. • Annual. Prices vary. Issued by the U. S. Census Bureau as an interim update to the *Census of Manufactures.* Includes data on number of manufacturing establishments in various industries, employment, labor costs, value of shipments, capital expenditures, inventories, energy costs, and assets. (See also Census Bureau home page, http://www.census. gov/.).

Business Statistics of the United States. Linz Audain and Cornelia J. Strawser. Bernan Associates. • Annual. $147.00. Based on *Business Statistics,* formerly issue by the Bureau of Economic Analysis, U. S. Department of Commerce. Provides basic data for a wide variety of U. S. industries, services, and economic indicators. Most statistics are shown annually for 30 years and monthly for the most recent four years.

Lumber Production and Mill Stocks. U.S. Bureau of the Census. • Annual. (Current Industrial Reports MA-24T).

Survey of Current Business. Available from U. S. Government Printing Office. • Monthly. $63.00 per year. Issued by Bureau of Economic Analysis, U. S. Department of Commerce. Presents a wide variety of business and economic data.

Timber Bulletin. Economic Commission for Europe. United Nations Publications. • Irregular. Price on application. Contains international statistics on forest products, including price, production, and foreign trade data.

WEFA Industrial Monitor. John Wiley and Sons, Inc. • Annual. $65.00. Prepared by industry analysts at WEFA, an economic forecasting and consulting firm (originally Wharton Econometric Forecasting Associates). Contains discussions of the outlook for major U. S. industries, with many 10-year forecasts (WEFA Web site is http://www.wefa.com).

TRADE/PROFESSIONAL ASSOCIATIONS

American Hardware Export Council. 1111 19th St., N.W., Suite 800, Washington, DC 20036. Phone: (202)463-2720 Fax: (202)463-2787 E-mail: andrew_roberts@afandpa.org • URL: http://www.ahec.org.

American Lumber Standards Committee. P.O. Box 210, Germantown, MD 20875. Phone: (301)972-1700 Fax: (301)540-8004 E-mail: alsc@alsc.org • URL: http://www.alsc.org.

National Hardwood Lumber Association. PO Box 34518, 6830 Raleigh-LaGrange Rd., Memphis, TN 38184-0518. Phone: (901)377-1818 Fax: (901)382-6419 E-mail: info@nhla.com • URL: http://www.nhla.com • United States, Canadian and International hardwood lumber and veneer manufacturers, distributors, and consumers. Inspects hardwood lumber. Maintains inspection training school. Conducts management and marketing seminars for the hardwood industry. Promotes research in hardwood timber management and utilization. Promotes public awareness of the industry.

National Lumber and Building Materials Dealers Association. 40 Ivy St., S.E., Washington, DC 20003. Phone: 800-634-8645 or (202)547-2230 Fax: (202)547-7640 E-mail: nikki@dealer.org • URL: http://www.dealer.org • Formerly National Retail Lumber Dealers Association.

LUNCHROOMS

See: RESTAURANTS, LUNCHROOMS, ETC.

LUNCHROOMS, EMPLOYEE

See: EMPLOYEE LUNCHROOMS AND CAFETERIAS

M

MACARONI

PRICE SOURCES
Supermarket News: The Industry's Weekly Newspaper. Fairchild Publications. • Weekly. Individuals, $196.00 per year; retailers, $45.00 per year; manufacturers, $89.00 per year.

TRADE/PROFESSIONAL ASSOCIATIONS
National Pasta Association. 1156 15th St. NW, Ste. 900, Washington, DC 20005. Phone: (202)637-5888 Fax: (202)223-9741 E-mail: info@ilovepasta.org • URL: http://www.ilovepasta.org • Manufacturers of pasta in the U.S. and suppliers to the industry. Seeks to improve manufacturer and supplier efficiency. Conducts agricultural and technical research programs. Sponsors U.S. pasta product public relations program and pasta/durum wheat technical course.

MACHINE DESIGN

See also: MECHANICAL ENGINEERING

HANDBOOKS AND MANUALS
Design of Machine Elements and Machines. J.A. Collins. John Wiley and Sons, Inc. • 2002. $122.95. Seventh edition.

McGraw-Hill Machining and Metalworking Handbook. Ronald A. Walsh. McGraw-Hill. • 1998. $99.95. Second edition. Coverage includes machinery, machining techniques, machine tools, machine design, parts, fastening, and plating.

Mechanical Engineering Design. Joseph Shigley and others. McGraw-Hill. • 2003. Seventh edition. Price on application.

Mechanical Engineer's Reference Book. E. H. Smith, editor. Society of Automotive Engineers. • 1994. $135.00. 12th edition. Covers mechanical engineering principles, computer integrated engineering systems, design standards, materials, power transmission, and many other engineering topics. (Authored Series).

PERIODICALS AND NEWSLETTERS
Advanced Manufacturing Technology: Monthly Report. Technical Insights. • Monthly. Institutions, $695.00 per year. Newsletter. Covers technological developments relating to robotics, computer graphics, automation, computer-integrated manufacturing, and machining.

International Journal of Machine Tools and Manufacture: Design, Research and Application. Elsevier. • 15 times a year. Institutions, $2,772.00 per year.

Journal of Mechanical Design. ASME International.

• Quarterly. Members, $50.00 per year. Formerly *Journal of Mechanisms, Transmissions and Automation in Design.*

Machine Design: Magazine of Applied Technology for Design Engineering. Penton Media, Inc. • 21 times a year. $110.00 per year. Includes *Machine Design Reference Issues* and *Penton Executive Network.*

Mechanism and Machine Theory. Elsevier. • Monthly. Qualified personnel, $99.00 per year; institutions, $2,568.00 per year.

MACHINE SHOPS

DIRECTORIES
Dun's Industrial Guide: The Metalworking Directory. Dun and Bradstreet Corp. • Annual. Libraries, $485; commercial institutions, $795.00. Lease basis. Three volumes. Lists about 65,000 U. S. manufacturing plants using metal and suppliers of metalworking equipment and materials. Includes names and titles of key personnel. Products, purchases, and processes are indicated.

FINANCIAL RATIOS
Annual Statement Studies. The Risk Management Association. • Annual. Median and quartile financial ratios are given for over 400 kinds of manufacturing, wholesale, retail, construction, and consumer finance establishments. Data is sorted by both asset size and sales volume. Includes a clearly written "Definition of Ratios" and an alphabetical industry index.

Annual Statement Studies: Industry Default Probabilities and Cash Flow Measures. The Risk Management Association. • Annual. $145.00. Serves as a companion volume to the original *Annual Statement Studies.* Gives probability of default estimates on a percentage scale for more than 450 industries. Includes changes in position year-by-year for eight financial statement line items and provides percentage measures of cash flow.

HANDBOOKS AND MANUALS
Machine Shop Fundamentals. Stephen F. Krar. Delmar Learning. • 1997. $37.95. (Machine Tool Series).

McGraw-Hill Machining and Metalworking Handbook. Ronald A. Walsh. McGraw-Hill. • 1998. $99.95. Second edition. Coverage includes machinery, machining techniques, machine tools, machine design, parts, fastening, and plating.

PERIODICALS AND NEWSLETTERS
Modern Machine Shop. Gardner Publications, Inc. • Monthly. $50.00 per year.

MACHINE TOOL INDUSTRY

See also: TOOL INDUSTRY

ABSTRACTS AND INDEXES
Cutting Technology. Penton Media, Inc. • Seven times a year. Free to qualified personnel; others, $55.00 per year. Provides abstracts of the international literature of metal cutting and machining. Formerly *Cutting Tool-Machine Digest.*

NTIS Alerts: Manufacturing Technology. National Technical Information Service. • Semimonthly. $265.00 per year. Provides descriptions of government-sponsored research reports and software, with ordering information. Covers computer-aided design and manufacturing (CAD/ CAM), engineering materials, quality control, machine tools, robots, lasers, productivity, and related subjects. Formerly *Abstract Newsletter.*

CD-ROM DATABASES
OECD Statistical Compendium. Organization for Economic Cooperation and Development. • Semiannual. $1,905.00 per year for 1 to 10 users. CD-ROM contains more than 730,000 monthly, quarterly, and annual time series for OECD countries, 1960 to date. Includes fully searchable data on agriculture, food, economic indicators, national accounts, employment, energy, finance, industry, technology, and foreign trade. Results can be displayed in various forms.

DIRECTORIES
Dun's Industrial Guide: The Metalworking Directory. Dun and Bradstreet Corp. • Annual. Libraries, $485; commercial institutions, $795.00. Lease basis. Three volumes. Lists about 65,000 U. S. manufacturing plants using metal and suppliers of metalworking equipment and materials. Includes names and titles of key personnel. Products, purchases, and processes are indicated.

Industrial Laser Buyers Guide. PennWell Corp., Advanced Technology Div. • Annual. $104.00. Lists industrial laser suppliers by category and geographic location. (Included with subscription to *Industrial Laser Solutions*.).

Modern Machine Shop Material Working Technology Guide. Gardner Publications, Inc. • Annual. $15.00. Lists products and services for the metalworking industry. Formerly *Modern Machine Shop CNC and Software Guide.*

FINANCIAL RATIOS
Annual Statement Studies. The Risk Management Association. • Annual. Median and quartile financial ratios are given for over 400 kinds of manufacturing, wholesale, retail, construction, and consumer

finance establishments. Data is sorted by both asset size and sales volume. Includes a clearly written "Definition of Ratios" and an alphabetical industry index.

Annual Statement Studies: Industry Default Probabilities and Cash Flow Measures. The Risk Management Association. • Annual. $145.00. Serves as a companion volume to the original *Annual Statement Studies.* Gives probability of default estimates on a percentage scale for more than 450 industries. Includes changes in position year-by-year for eight financial statement line items and provides percentage measures of cash flow.

HANDBOOKS AND MANUALS

Machine Tool Practices. Richard R. Kibbe. Prentice Hall PTR. • 2001. $95.00. Seventh edition.

INTERNET DATABASES

Business 2.0 Web Guide to the Best Business Links. Business 2.0 Media Inc. Phone: (415)293-4800 E-mail: support@business2.com • URL: http://www.business2.com/webguide • Web site presents an extensive, searchable directory of links to "the best, most informative, and authoritative web pages." Twenty main categories cover business, finance, career, company information, people, and technology topics, with thousands of subtopics, all linking to Web sites recommended by experienced business researchers. Fees: Free.

Fedstats. Federal Interagency Council on Statistical Policy. Phone: (202)395-7254 • URL: http://www.fedstats.gov • Web site features an efficient search facility for full-text statistics produced by more than 100 federal agencies, including the Census Bureau, the Bureau of Economic Analysis, and the Bureau of Labor Statistics. Boolean searches can be made within one agency or for all agencies combined. Links are offered to international statistical bureaus, including the UN, IMF, OECD, UNESCO, Eurostat, and 20 individual countries. Fees: Free.

FreeLunch.com. Economy.com, Inc. Phone: (610)696-8700 Fax: (610)696-1678 • URL: http://www.freelunch.com • Web site provides free access to more than 1.5 million economic and financial data series, covering industry, demographics, labor markets, prices, retail sales, government spending, trade, interest rates, housing starts, the stock market, and many other topics. Data is available for various time periods in either chart or table form. Searching is offered. Fees: Free, but registration required. Economy.com, Inc. also offers fee-based economic analysis at *The Dismal Scientist* site (http://www.dismal.com).

ONLINE DATABASES

PROMT: Predicasts Overview of Markets and Technology. Gale Cengage Learning. • Companies, products, applied technologies and markets. U.S. and international literature coverage, 1972 to date. Inquire as to online cost and availability. Provides abstracts from more than 1,600 publications. Weekly updates.

PERIODICALS AND NEWSLETTERS

Industrial Laser Solutions for Manufacturing. PennWell Corp., Advanced Technology Div. • Monthly. $300.00 per year. Covers industrial laser technology, especially machine tool applications.

International Journal of Machine Tools and Manufacture: Design, Research and Application. Elsevier. • 15 times a year. Institutions, $2,772.00 per year.

Manufacturing Engineering. Society of Manufacturing Engineers. • Monthly. $100.00 per year.

RESEARCH CENTERS AND INSTITUTES

Advanced Manufacturing Engineering Institute. University of Hartford, United Technologies Hall, Room 215, West Hartford, CT 06117. Phone: 800-678-4844 or (860)768-4615 Fax: (860)768-5073

E-mail: shetty@mail.hartford.edu..

STATISTICS SOURCES

Annual Survey of Manufactures. Available from U. S. Government Printing Office. • Annual. Prices vary. Issued by the U. S. Census Bureau as an interim update to the *Census of Manufactures.* Includes data on number of manufacturing establishments in various industries, employment, labor costs, value of shipments, capital expenditures, inventories, energy costs, and assets. (See also Census Bureau home page, http://www.census.gov/.).

Business Statistics of the United States. Linz Audain and Cornelia J. Strawser. Bernan Associates. • Annual. $147.00. Based on *Business Statistics,* formerly issue by the Bureau of Economic Analysis, U. S. Department of Commerce. Provides basic data for a wide variety of U. S. industries, services, and economic indicators. Most statistics are shown annually for 30 years and monthly for the most recent four years.

Survey of Current Business. Available from U. S. Government Printing Office. • Monthly. $63.00 per year. Issued by Bureau of Economic Analysis, U. S. Department of Commerce. Presents a wide variety of business and economic data.

TRADE/PROFESSIONAL ASSOCIATIONS

American Machine Tool Distributors' Association. 1445 Research Blvd., Ste. 450, Rockville, MD 20850. Phone: 800-878-2683 or (301)738-1200 Fax: (301)738-9499 E-mail: pborden@amtda.org • URL: http://www.amtda.org • Distributors and builders of manufacturing technology. Offers technical training, sales training and management. Compiles statistics.

ASM International. 9639 Kinsman Rd., Novelty, OH 44073-0002. Phone: 800-336-5152 or (440)338-5151 Fax: (440)338-4634 E-mail: customerservice@asminternational.org • URL: http://asmcommunity.asminternational.org/portal/site/asm • Metallurgists, materials engineers, executives in materials producing and consuming industries; teachers and students. Disseminates technical information about the manufacture, use, and treatment of engineered materials. Offers in-plant, home study, and intensive courses through Materials +Engineering Institute. Conducts career development program. Established ASM Foundation for +Education and Research.

National Tooling and Machining Association. 9300 Livingston Rd., Fort Washington, MD 20744-4998. Phone: 800-248-6862 Fax: (301)248-7104 • URL: http://www.ntma.org.

Society of Manufacturing Engineers. One SME Dr., Dearborn, MI 48121. Phone: 800-733-4763 or (313)271-1500 Fax: (313)271-2861 E-mail: service@sme.org • URL: http://www.sme.org.

MACHINE TRANSLATING

ALMANACS AND YEARBOOKS

Translating and the Computer. Available from Information Today, Inc. • Annual. Members, $50.00; non-members, $57.50. Published in London by Aslib: The Association for Information Management. Includes papers from the annual International Conference on Translating and the Computer.

PERIODICALS AND NEWSLETTERS

Computational Linguistics. Association for Computational Linguistics. MIT Press. • Quarterly. Institutions, $150.00 per year. Includes print and online editions. Covers developments in research and applications of natural language processing.

TRADE/PROFESSIONAL ASSOCIATIONS

Association for Computational Linguistics. c/o Pricilla Rasmussen, 75 Paterson St., Suite 9, New

Burnswick, NJ 08901. Phone: (732)342-9100 Fax: (732)342-9339 E-mail: acl@aclweb.org • URL: http://www.cs.columbia.edu.

MACHINE VISION

See also: AUTOMATION; ROBOTS

ABSTRACTS AND INDEXES

Applied Science and Technology Index. H. W. Wilson Co. • 11 times a year. Quarterly and annual cumulations. Price varies. Indexes a wide variety of English language technical, industrial, and engineering periodicals.

CompuMath Citation Index. Institute for Scientific Information. • Three times a year. $1,090.00 per year. Provides citations to the worldwide literature of computer science and mathematics.

Computer and Information Systems Abstracts Journal: An Abstract Journal Pertaining to the Theory, Design, Fabrication and Application of Computer and Information Systems. CSA. • 11 times a year. $1,750 per year.

Computer Literature Index: A Subject/Author Index to Computer and Data Processing Literature. EBSCO Publishing. • Quarterly, with annual cumulation. $245.00 per year. Contains brief abstracts of book and periodical literature covering all phases of computing, including approximately 70 specific application areas.

Engineering Index Monthly: Abstracting and Indexing Services Covering Sources ofthe World's Engineering Literature. Engineering Information Inc. • Monthly. Institutions, $5,279.00 per year. Provides indexing and abstracting of the world's engineering and technical literature.

Internet and Personal Computing Abstracts [print edition]. EBSCO Publishing. • Quarterly. $269.00 per year, including cumulative index. Provides more than 10,000 abstracts annually from both trade and academic publications. Covers computer hardware, software, product reviews, Web topics, e-commerce, networks, corporate news, security, and related topics. Formerly *Microcomputer Abstracts.*

Key Abstracts: Machine Vision. Available from INSPEC, Inc. • Monthly. $250.00 per year. Provides international coverage of journal and proceedings literature on optical noncontact sensing. Published in England by the Institution of Electrical Engineers (IEE).

NTIS Alerts: Computers, Control & Information Theory. National Technical Information Service. • Semimonthly. $235.00 per year. Provides descriptions of government-sponsored research reports and software, with ordering information. Covers computer hardware, software, control systems, pattern recognition, image processing, and related subjects. Formerly *Abstract Newsletter.*

NTIS Alerts: Manufacturing Technology. National Technical Information Service. • Semimonthly. $265.00 per year. Provides descriptions of government-sponsored research reports and software, with ordering information. Covers computer-aided design and manufacturing (CAD/CAM), engineering materials, quality control, machine tools, robots, lasers, productivity, and related subjects. Formerly *Abstract Newsletter.*

CD-ROM DATABASES

Computer Database. Gale Cengage Learning. • Provides one year of full-text on CD-ROM for 150 leading computer-related publications. Also includes 70,000 product specifications and brief profiles of 13,000 computer product vendors and manufacturers.

WILSONDISC: Applied Science and Technology Abstracts. H. W. Wilson Co. • Monthly. Includes unlimited access to the online version of *Applied*

Science and Technology Abstracts through WILSONLINE. Provides CD-ROM indexing and abstracting of 500 prominent scientific, technical, engineering, and industrial periodicals. Indexing coverage is provided from 1983 to date and abstracting from 1993 to date.

DIRECTORIES

Data Sources: The Comprehensive Guide to the Data Processing Industry: Hardware, Data Communications Products, Software, Company Profiles. Gale Cengage Learning. • Semiannual. $455.00 per year. Two volumes. Describes hardware and software for all computer operating sysems, including prices and technical details. Lists about 75,000 products from 14,000 suppliers. Industry-specific software applications are described.

Frontline Solutions Buyer's Guide. Advanstar Communications. • Publication includes: List of manufacturers, suppliers, consultants, value added resellers, and dealers/distributors of automatic identification and data capture software, technology, equipment, and products for bar code, biometric identification, electronic data interchange, machine vision, magnetic stripe, optical character recognition, radio frequency data communications, radio frequency identification, smart cards, and voice data entry; also includes related organizations, and sources for industry standards. Entries include: Company name, address, phone, e-mail, web address, products or services.

Machine Vision and Robotics Industry Directory. Society of Manufacturing Engineers. • Biennial. $25.00. Provides information on suppliers of machine vision systems, services, and equipment. Formerly *Machine Vision Industry Directory.*

Manufacturing Systems: Buyers Guide. Reed Business Information. • Annual. Price on application. Contains information on companies manufacturing or supplying materials handling systems, CAD/CAM systems, specialized software for manufacturing, programmable controllers, machine vision systems, and automatic identification systems.

Sensors Buyers Guide. Advanstar Communications. • Covers: Lists manufacturers and vendors of sensors and transducers for use in high-technology applications engineering. Also covers related products and services. Entries include: Company name, address, phone, fax, e-mail, URL, contact person, type of sensors manufactured and/or physical, chemical, or biological characteristics utilized in sensing.

ENCYCLOPEDIAS AND DICTIONARIES

Acronyms of Computer Science and Communications: A Comprehensive Acronym Dictionary and Illustrated Encyclopedia. Enjob Kajan and Ejub Kajan. Springer Verlag. • 2002. $49.95. Explains more than 4,000 "broadly used" computer, telecommunications, and information technology acronyms. Includes illustrations and Web addresses, where applicable.

Encyclopedia of Information Systems. Hossein Bidgoli, editor. Elsevier. • 2002. $1,200.00. Four volumes. Contains a wide range of articles relating to computers, databases, communication, and information technology. The 200 topics include coverage of hardware, software, artificial intelligence, the Internet, networks, knowledge management, electronic commerce, search engines, and systems design.

HANDBOOKS AND MANUALS

Handbook of Machine Vision Engineering. Michael Burke. John Wiley and Sons, Inc. • 1996. $159.95. Two volumes. Volume two, $79.95; volume three, $79.95.

ONLINE DATABASES

Applied Science and Technology Index Online. H. W. Wilson Co. • Provides online indexing of 500 major scientific, technical, industrial, and engineering periodicals. Time period is 1983 to date. Monthly updates. Inquire as to online cost and availability.

Current Contents Connect. Institute for Scientific Information. • Provides online abstracts of articles listed in the tables of contents of about 7,500 journals. Coverage is very broad, including science, social science, life science, technology, engineering, industry, agriculture, the environment, economics, and arts and humanities. Time period is two years, with weekly updates. Inquire as to online cost and availability.

PROMT: Predicasts Overview of Markets and Technology. Gale Cengage Learning. • Companies, products, applied technologies and markets. U.S. and international literature coverage, 1972 to date. Inquire as to online cost and availability. Provides abstracts from more than 1,600 publications. Weekly updates.

PERIODICALS AND NEWSLETTERS

IEEE Transactions on Visualization and Computer Graphics. Institute of Electrical and Electronics Engineers, Inc. • Quarterly. $676.00 per year. Topics include computer vision, computer graphics, image processing, signal processing, computer-aided design, animation, and virtual reality.

International Journal of Intelligent Systems. John Wiley and Sons, Inc., Journals. • Monthly. $1,925.00 per year; with online edition, $2,022.00 per year.

Manufacturing Computer Solutions. • Monthly. $88.00 per year. Edited for managers of factory automation, emphasizing the integration of systems in manufacturing. Subjects include materials handling, CAD/CAM, specialized software for manufacturing, programmable controllers, machine vision, and automatic identification systems. Formerly *Manufacturing Systems.*

Sensors: Your Resource for Sensing, Communications, and Control. Advanstar Communications. • Monthly. $70.00 per year. Edited for design, production, and manufacturing engineers involved with sensing systems. Emphasis is on emerging technology.

RESEARCH CENTERS AND INSTITUTES

Alliance for Innovative Manufacturing. Stanford University, Bldg.02-530, Rm. 225, Stanford, CA 94305-3036. Phone: (650)723-9038 Fax: (650)723-5034 E-mail: cborn@stanford.edu • URL: http://www.stanford.edu/group/aim • Development of new products and processing. Formerly Stanford Integrated Manufacturing Association.

Computer Vision Laboratory. University of Arizona, Department of Electrical and Computer Engineering, ECE Bldg. 104, Room 230, Tucson, AZ 85721. Phone: (520)621-6191 Fax: (520)621-8076 E-mail: strickland@ece.arizona.edu • URL: http://www.ece.arizona.edu • Research areas include computer vision and speech synthesis.

Digital Image Analysis Laboratory. University of Arizona, Dept. of Electrical and Computer Engineering, Tucson, AZ 85721. Phone: (520)621-2706 Fax: (520)621-8076 E-mail: schowengerdt@ece.arizona.edu • URL: http://www.ece.arizona.edu/ • Research fields include image processing, computer vision, and artificial intelligence.

Image Science Research Group. Worcester Polytechnic Institute, Computer Science Dept., 100 Institute Rd., Worcester, MA 01609-2208. Phone: (508)831-5357 Fax: (508)831-5776 E-mail: matt@wpi.edu • URL: http://www.cs.wpi.edu/research/isrg • Areas of research include image processing, computer graphics, and computational vision.

Imaging and Computer Vision Center. Drexel University, 32nd and Market Sts., Room 110-7, Philadelphia, PA 19104. Phone: (215)895-2279 Fax: (215)895-4987 E-mail: icvc-support@cbis.ece.

drexel.edu • URL: http://www.cbis.ece.drexel.edu/icvc • Fields of research include computer vision, robot vision, and expert systems.

Imaging Systems Laboratory. Carnegie Mellon University, Robotics Institute, 5000 Forbes Ave., Pittsburgh, PA 15213. Phone: (412)268-3824 Fax: (412)683-3763 E-mail: rht@cs.cmu.edu • Fields of research include computer vision and document interpretation.

Media Laboratory. Massachusetts Institute of Technology, 20 Ames St., Room E-15, Cambridge, MA 02139-4307. Phone: (617)253-0300 Fax: (617)258-6264 E-mail: casr@media.mit.edu • URL: http://www.media.mit.edu • Research areas include electronic publishing, spatial imaging, human-machine interface, computer vision, and advanced television.

TRADE/PROFESSIONAL ASSOCIATIONS

AIM Global. 125 Warrendale-Bayne Rd., Ste. 100, Warrendale, PA 15086. Phone: (724)934-4470 Fax: (724)934-4495 E-mail: dan@aimglobal.org • URL: http://www.aimglobal.org • Serves as a trade association for the automatic identification data captures technology industry.

AIM, Inc. 125 Warrendale Bayne Rd., Warrendale, PA 15086. Phone: 800-338-0206 or (724)934-4470 Fax: (724)934-4495 E-mail: info@aimglobal.org • URL: http://www.aimglobal.org • Members are companies concerned with automatic identification and data capture, including bar code systems, magnetic stripes, machine vision, voice technology, optical character recognition, and systems integration technology.

Automated Imaging Association. PO Box 3724, PO Box 3724, Ann Arbor, MI 48106. Phone: 800-994-6099 or (734)994-6088 Fax: (734)994-3338 E-mail: dwhalls@robotics.org • URL: http://www.machinevisiononline.org • Represents manufacturers of machine vision components and systems, users, system integrators, universities and non-profit research groups, and financial firms that track the machine vision industry. Promotes the use and understanding of image capture and analysis technology.

Machine Vision Association of the Society of Manufacturing Engineers. 1 SME Dr., Dearborn, MI 48121. Phone: 800-733-4763 or (313)271-1500 Fax: (313)425-3400 E-mail: service@sme.org • URL: http://www.sme.org/mva • Members are professional engineers, managers, and students. Promotes the effective use of machine vision (optical sensing of actual scenes for use in machine control).

MACHINERY

ABSTRACTS AND INDEXES

Applied Science and Technology Index. H. W. Wilson Co. • 11 times a year. Quarterly and annual cumulations. Price varies. Indexes a wide variety of English language technical, industrial, and engineering periodicals.

CD-ROM DATABASES

OECD Statistical Compendium. Organization for Economic Cooperation and Development. • Semiannual. $1,905.00 per year for 1 to 10 users. CD-ROM contains more than 730,000 monthly, quarterly, and annual time series for OECD countries, 1960 to date. Includes fully searchable data on agriculture, food, economic indicators, national accounts, employment, energy, finance, industry, technology, and foreign trade. Results can be displayed in various forms.

DIRECTORIES

Dun's Industrial Guide: The Metalworking Directory. Dun and Bradstreet Corp. • Annual. Libraries, $485; commercial institutions, $795.00. Lease basis. Three volumes. Lists about 65,000 U.

S. manufacturing plants using metal and suppliers of metalworking equipment and materials. Includes names and titles of key personnel. Products, purchases, and processes are indicated.

Machinery Buyers' Guide: The Annual Directory of Engineering and Products Services (United Kingdom). Findlay Publications Ltd. • Annual. $200.00. About 6,000 firms offering machine tool, engineering products, machinery, industrial equipment and services worldwide.

Thomas Register of American Manufacturers. Thomas Publishing Co., Inc. • Annual. $149.00. 34 volumes. A three-part system offering information on a wide variety of industrial equipment and supplies. Lists more than 151,000 industrial product and services companies.

Used Equipment Directory. Penton Technology and Lifestyle Media Inc. • Publication includes: List of 800 dealers in used metalworking, electrical, power, process, and material handling equipment, woodworking and machine tools. Entries include: Company name, address, phone; principal executive; types of equipment handled; description of machinery offered. Principal content is approximately 30,000 paid listings of used equipment for sale, classified by type.

FINANCIAL RATIOS

Almanac of Business and Industrial Financial Ratios. Leo Troy. Aspen Publishers, Inc. • 2003. $125.95. Includes CD-Rom. Contains financial ratios derived from federal tax returns. Ratios for each of about 200 industries are arranged according to company asset size. (Almanac of Business and Industrial Financial Ratios Series).

Annual Statement Studies. The Risk Management Association. • Annual. Median and quartile financial ratios are given for over 400 kinds of manufacturing, wholesale, retail, construction, and consumer finance establishments. Data is sorted by both asset size and sales volume. Includes a clearly written "Definition of Ratios" and an alphabetical industry index.

Annual Statement Studies: Industry Default Probabilities and Cash Flow Measures. The Risk Management Association. • Annual. $145.00. Serves as a companion volume to the original *Annual Statement Studies.* Gives probability of default estimates on a percentage scale for more than 450 industries. Includes changes in position year-by-year for eight financial statement line items and provides percentage measures of cash flow.

IRS Corporate Financial Ratios. Available from MarketResearch.com. • 2002. $225.00. Published by Schonfeld & Associates, Inc. Presents 70 key financial ratios for 260 industries. Ratios are calculated from income statement and balance sheet data available from the Internal Revenue Service. Includes four asset size classes.

HANDBOOKS AND MANUALS

Machinery's Handbook. Macauley and others. Industrial Press, Inc. • 2001. $149.95. 26th edition. Reference book for the mechanical engineer, draftsman, toolmaker, and machinist. Includes CD-ROM.

INTERNET DATABASES

Business 2.0 Web Guide to the Best Business Links. Business 2.0 Media Inc. Phone: (415)293-4800 E-mail: support@business2.com • URL: http://www.business2.com/webguide • Web site presents an extensive, searchable directory of links to "the best, most informative, and authoritative web pages." Twenty main categories cover business, finance, career, company information, people, and technology topics, with thousands of subtopics, all linking to Web sites recommended by experienced business researchers. Fees: Free.

Fedstats. Federal Interagency Council on Statistical Policy. Phone: (202)395-7254 • URL: http://www.

fedstats.gov • Web site features an efficient search facility for full-text statistics produced by more than 100 federal agencies, including the Census Bureau, the Bureau of Economic Analysis, and the Bureau of Labor Statistics. Boolean searches can be made within one agency or for all agencies combined. Links are offered to international statistical bureaus, including the UN, IMF, OECD, UNESCO, Eurostat, and 20 individual countries. Fees: Free.

FreeLunch.com. Economy.com, Inc. Phone: (610)696-8700 Fax: (610)696-1678 • URL: http://www.freelunch.com • Web site provides free access to more than 1.5 million economic and financial data series, covering industry, demographics, labor markets, prices, retail sales, government spending, trade, interest rates, housing starts, the stock market, and many other topics. Data is available for various time periods in either chart or table form. Searching is offered. Fees: Free, but registration required. Economy.com, Inc. also offers fee-based economic analysis at *The Dismal Scientist* site (http://www.dismal.com).

ONLINE DATABASES

Applied Science and Technology Index Online. H. W. Wilson Co. • Provides online indexing of 500 major scientific, technical, industrial, and engineering periodicals. Time period is 1983 to date. Monthly updates. Inquire as to online cost and availability.

Business and Industry. Gale Cengage Learning. • Contains online citations, abstracts, and selected fulltext from more than 1,000 trade journals, newspapers, and other publications. Provides general coverage of both manufacturing and service industries, including marketing, production, industry trends, key events, and information on specific companies. Time span is 1994 to date. Daily updates. Inquire as to online cost and availability. (Also available in a CD-ROM version.).

Tablebase. Gale Cengage Learning. • Provides online numerical tabular data from a wide variety of business, organization, and government sources, including about 1,000 trade journals. Includes industry and individual company statistics relating to products, market share, sales forecasts, production, exports, market trends, etc. Time span is 1997 to date. Weekly updates. Inquire as to online cost and availability. (Also available in a CD-ROM version.).

Thomas Register Online. Thomas Publishing Co., Inc. • Provides concise information on approximately 194,000 U. S. companies, mainly manufacturers, with over 50,000 product classifications. Indexes over 115,000 trade names. Information is updated semiannually. Inquire as to online cost and availability.

PERIODICALS AND NEWSLETTERS

American Machinist: Strategies and Innovations for Competitive Manufacturing. Penton Media Inc. • Monthly. Free to qualified personnel; others, $75.00 per year.

Processing. Putman Media. • 14 times a year. $54.00 per year. Emphasis is on descriptions of new products for all areas of industrial processing, including valves, controls, filters, pumps, compressors, fluidics, and instrumentation.

RESEARCH CENTERS AND INSTITUTES

National Center for Manufacturing Sciences. 3025 Boardwalk St., Ann Arbor, MI 48108. Phone: (734)995-0300 Fax: (734)995-4004 E-mail: johnd@ncms.org • URL: http://www.ncms.org • Research areas include process technology and control, machine mechanics, sensors, testing methods, and quality assurance.

STATISTICS SOURCES

Annual Survey of Manufactures. Available from U. S. Government Printing Office. • Annual. Prices

vary. Issued by the U. S. Census Bureau as an interim update to the *Census of Manufactures.* Includes data on number of manufacturing establishments in various industries, employment, labor costs, value of shipments, capital expenditures, inventories, energy costs, and assets. (See also Census Bureau home page, http://www.census.gov/.).

Business Statistics of the United States. Linz Audain and Cornelia J. Strawser. Bernan Associates. • Annual. $147.00. Based on *Business Statistics,* formerly issue by the Bureau of Economic Analysis, U. S. Department of Commerce. Provides basic data for a wide variety of U. S. industries, services, and economic indicators. Most statistics are shown annually for 30 years and monthly for the most recent four years.

Encyclopedia of American Industries. Gale Cengage Learning. • 2000. $560.00. Third edition. Two volumes. $280.00 per volume. Volume one is *Manufacturing Industries* and volume two is *Service and Non-Manufacturing Industries.* Provides the history, development, and recent status of approximately 1,000 industries. Includes statistical graphs, with industry and general indexes.

Survey of Current Business. Available from U. S. Government Printing Office. • Monthly. $63.00 per year. Issued by Bureau of Economic Analysis, U. S. Department of Commerce. Presents a wide variety of business and economic data.

United States Census of Manufactures. U.S. Bureau of the Census. • Quinquennial. Results presented in reports, tape, CD-ROM, and Diskette files.

WEFA Industrial Monitor. John Wiley and Sons, Inc. • Annual. $65.00. Prepared by industry analysts at WEFA, an economic forecasting and consulting firm (originally Wharton Econometric Forecasting Associates). Contains discussions of the outlook for major U. S. industries, with many 10-year forecasts (WEFA Web site is http://www.wefa.com).

TRADE/PROFESSIONAL ASSOCIATIONS

Industrial Supply Manufacturers Association. 1300 Sumner Ave., Cleveland, OH 44115-2851. Phone: (216)241-7333 Fax: (216)241-0105 E-mail: isma@ismaonline.org • URL: http://www.ismaonline.org • Formerly Industrial Supply and Machinery Manufacturers Association.

Machinery Dealers National Association. 315 S Patrick St., Alexandria, VA 22314. Phone: 800-872-7807 or (703)836-9300 Fax: (703)836-9303 E-mail: office@mdna.org • URL: http://www.mdna.org • Dealers in used, rebuilt, and reconditioned industrial machinery.

Manufacturers Alliance/MAPI. 1600 Wilson Blvd., Ste. 1100, Arlington, VA 22209-2594. Phone: (703)841-9000 Fax: (703)841-9514 E-mail: info@mapi.net • URL: http://www.mapi.net • Manufacturing and related business service companies. Membership concentrated in the following sectors: aerospace; automotive; scientific instruments; electronics; computers and telecommunication equipment; high technology; chemicals/pharmaceuticals; oil and oil-related equipment; electrical equipment farm, construction, food, material handling, and other machinery; primary and fabricated metals. Provides member services through councils and research programs. Produces a variety of research, including economic, policy, and benchmark work to assist members in their planning, compliance, and process improvement efforts.

MACHINERY, USED

See: SURPLUS PRODUCTS

MAGAZINE CIRCULATION

See: CIRCULATION MANAGEMENT (PUBLISHING)

MAGAZINES

See: PERIODICALS

MAGNESIUM INDUSTRY

DIRECTORIES

International Magnesium Association--Buyer's Guide. International Magnesium Association. • Covers: Companies involved in the magnesium industry, including producers, die caster, processors, researchers, and suppliers. Entries include: Company name, address, phone, fax, plant locations, products and services offered.

STATISTICS SOURCES

Mineral Commodity Summaries. Available from U. S. Government Printing Office. • Annual. $26.00. Published by the U. S. Geological Survey, Department of the Interior (http://www.usgs.gov). Contains detailed, five-year data for about 90 nonfuel minerals. Covers a wide range of statistics, including production, imports, exports, consumption, reserves, prices, tariff information, and industry employment. (Two pages are devoted to each mineral.).

Non-Ferrous Metal Data Yearbook. American Bureau of Metal Statistics. • Annual. $405.00. Provides worldwide data on approximately about 200 statistical tables covering many nonferrous metals. Includes production, consumption, inventories, exports, imports, and other data.

Nonferrous Castings. U. S. Bureau of the Census. • Annual. (Current Industrial Reports MA-33E.).

TRADE/PROFESSIONAL ASSOCIATIONS

American Bureau of Metal Statistics. P.O. Box 805, Chatham, NJ 07928. Phone: (973)701-2299 Fax: (973)701-2152 E-mail: info@abms.com • URL: http://www.abms.com • Members are metal companies. Compiles and publishes detailed statistical data on a wide variety of nonferrous metals: aluminum, copper, gold, lead, nickel, platinum, silver, tin, titanium, uranium, zinc, and others.

International Magnesium Association. 1000 N Rand Rd., Ste. 214, Wauconda, IL 60084. Phone: (847)526-2010 Fax: (847)526-3993 E-mail: info@ intlmag.org • URL: http://www.intlmag.org • Represents manufacturers, processors, users, suppliers, and recyclers of magnesium. Works to promote the magnesium industry; develops and increases the use of magnesium and its alloys; publicizes and promotes new uses of the metal to end-use markets. Conducts research programs, compiles statistics and offers educational programs.

MAGNETIC RECORDS AND RECORDINGS

See: SOUND RECORDERS AND RECORD-ING

MAIL ORDER BUSINESS

See also: DIRECT MAIL ADVERTISING

CD-ROM DATABASES

MediaFinder CD-ROM: Oxbridge Directories of Print Media and Catalogs. Oxbridge Communications, Inc. • Quarterly. $1,995.00 per year. CD-ROM includes about 100,000 listings from *Standard Periodical Directory, National Directory of Catalogs, National Directory of British Mail Order Catalogs, National Directory of German Mail Order Catalogs, Oxbridge Directory of Newsletters, National Directory of Mailing Lists, College Media Directory,* and *National Directory of Magazines.*

DIRECTORIES

Catalog Age--Direct Sourcebook. Primedia Business. • Publication includes: List of approximately 300 suppliers of equipment, products, and services to the direct marketing industry; related trade associations. Entries include: Name, address, phone, key personnel, geographical area covered, description of products or services, branch offices or subsidiary names and locations.

Directory of Business-to-Business Catalogs. Grey House Publishing. • Annual. $165.00. Provides over 6,000 listings of U. S. mail order companies selling business or industrial products and services.

Directory of Mail Order Catalogs. Grey House Publishing. • Annual. $165.00. Contains 12,000 entries for mail order companies selling consumer products throughout the U.S.

Drop Shipping Source Directory of Major Consumer Product Lines. Consolidated Marketing Services, Inc. • Irregular. $15.00. Lists over 700 firms of a wide variety of consumer products that can be drop shipped.

Mail Order Business Directory. B. Klein Publications. • Covers: 5,000 firms in the United States and doing business by mail order and catalogs. Entries include: Name, address, phone, name of owner or contact, and products or services.

The National Directory of Catalogs. Oxbridge Communications. • Annual. $645.00. Describes over 9,000 United States and Canadian catalogs within 78 subject areas.

FINANCIAL RATIOS

Annual Statement Studies. The Risk Management Association. • Annual. Median and quartile financial ratios are given for over 400 kinds of manufacturing, wholesale, retail, construction, and consumer finance establishments. Data is sorted by both asset size and sales volume. Includes a clearly written "Definition of Ratios" and an alphabetical industry index.

Annual Statement Studies: Industry Default Probabilities and Cash Flow Measures. The Risk Management Association. • Annual. $145.00. Serves as a companion volume to the original *Annual Statement Studies.* Gives probability of default estimates on a percentage scale for more than 450 industries. Includes changes in position year-by-year for eight financial statement line items and provides percentage measures of cash flow.

HANDBOOKS AND MANUALS

Building a Mail Order Business: A Complete Manual for Success. William A. Cohen. John Wiley and Sons, Inc. • 1996. $42.95. Fourth edition.

Drop Shipping as a Marketing Function: A Handbook of Methods and Policies. Nicholas T. Scheel. Greenwood Publishing Group, Inc. • 1990. $64.95.

Mail Order Business. Entrepreneur Media, Inc. • Looseleaf. $59.50. A practical guide to starting a mail order business. Covers profit potential, start-up costs, pricing, market size evaluation, accounting, advertising, promotion, etc. (Start-Up Business Guide No. E1015.).

INTERNET DATABASES

Advance Monthly Sales for Retail Trade and Food Services. U. S. Census Bureau. Phone: 800-541-8345 or (301)763-4636 Fax: (301)457-3842 E-mail: rcb@census.gov • URL: http://www.census.gov/ svsd/www/fullpub.html • Web pages provide monthly sales figures for a wide range of retail businesses. Advance, preliminary, and final statistics are provided for the latest month available in each case, with a previous-year comparison. Updates are monthly.

PERIODICALS AND NEWSLETTERS

Catalog Age. PRIMEDIA Business Magazine and Media. • 13 times a year. Free to qualified personnel; others, $85.00 per year. Edited for catalog marketing and management personnel.

The Catalog Marketer. Maxwell Sroge Publishing Inc. • Description: Provides information about producing catalogs. Topics include marketing, photography, news, and telephone marketing.

DM News: The Newspaper of Direct Marketing. Courtenay Communications Corp. • 48 times a year. $49.00 per year. Includes special feature issues on catalog marketing, telephone marketing, database marketing, and fundraising. Includes monthly supplements, *DM News International, DRTV News,* and *TeleServices.*

Drop Shipping News. • Monthly. Price on application. Newsletter.

Non- Store Marketing Report. Maxwell Sroge Publishing Inc. • Description: Source of analyses of key trends and key happeningsin the mail order, Internet, and interactive shopping business. order companies. Recurring features include an semiannual insert titled Trendwatch, which assesses the performance of publicly owned direct selling businesses, and company profiles on direct marketing businesses in the news.

STATISTICS SOURCES

Annual Benchmark Report for Retail Trade and Food Services...A Detailed Summary of Retail Sales, Purchases, Accounts Receivable, Inventories, and Food Service Sales. Available from U. S. Government Printing Office. • Annual. $13.00. Issued by the U.S. Census Bureau. Provides detailed annual and monthly retail statistics for the most recent 10 years. Includes data for various kinds of retail outlets, including automobiles, furniture, appliances, building supplies, grocery stores, drug stores, gasoline stations, clothing, sporting goods, department stores, and restaurants.

WEFA Industrial Monitor. John Wiley and Sons, Inc. • Annual. $65.00. Prepared by industry analysts at WEFA, an economic forecasting and consulting firm (originally Wharton Econometric Forecasting Associates). Contains discussions of the outlook for major U. S. industries, with many 10-year forecasts (WEFA Web site is http://www.wefa.com).

TRADE/PROFESSIONAL ASSOCIATIONS

Mail Order Association of America. 1877 Bourne Court, Wantagh, NY 11793. Phone: (516)221-8257 Fax: (516)221-5697.

OTHER SOURCES

Mail Service Pharmacy Market. MarketResearch. com. • 1999. $3,250.00. Provides detailed market data, with forecasts to the year 2003.

The U. S. Market for Catalog Shopping. Available from MarketResearch.com. • 1997. $1,375.00. Market research report published by Packaged Facts. Includes analysis of catalog shopping market by age, ethnic groups, and income.

MAIL SERVICE

See: POSTAL SERVICES

MAILING LISTS

See also: DIRECT MAIL ADVERTISING

CD-ROM DATABASES

MediaFinder CD-ROM: Oxbridge Directories of Print Media and Catalogs. Oxbridge Communications, Inc. • Quarterly. $1,995.00 per year. CD-

ROM includes about 100,000 listings from *Standard Periodical Directory, National Directory of Catalogs, National Directory of British Mail Order Catalogs, National Directory of German Mail Order Catalogs, Oxbridge Directory of Newsletters, National Directory of Mailing Lists, College Media Directory,* and *National Directory of Magazines.*

DIRECTORIES

Directory of Mailing List Companies. Todd Publications. • Biennial. $75.00. Lists and describes approximately 1,000 of the most active list brokers, owners, managers and compilers.

SRDS Direct Marketing List Source. SRDS. • Bimonthly. $561.00 per year. Provides detailed information and rates for business, farm, and consumer mailing lists (U. S., Canadian, and international). Includes current postal information and directories of list brokers, compilers, and managers. Formerly *Direct Mail List Source.*

PERIODICALS AND NEWSLETTERS

Database Marketer. SIMBA Information. • Monthly. $329.00 per year.

Direct Marketing: Using Direct Response Advertising to Enhance Marketing Database. Hoke Communications, Inc. • Monthly. $65.00 per year. Direct marketing to consumers and business.

Target Marketing: The Leading Magazine for Integrated Database Marketing. North American Publishing Co. • Monthly. $65.00 per year. Dedicated to direct marketing excellence. Formerly *Zip Target Marketing.*

STATISTICS SOURCES

DMA Statistical Fact Book. Direct Marketing Association. Library and Resource Center. • Annual. Members, $79.95; non-members, $104.95. Provides data in five sections covering direct response advertising, media, mailing lists, market applications, and "Practical Management Information." Includes material on interactive/online marketing. (Cover title: *Direct Marketing Association's Statistical Fact Book.*).

MAINTENANCE OF BUILDINGS

See also: BUILDING INDUSTRY

DIRECTORIES

ICS Cleaning Specialists Annual Trade Directory and Buying Guide. Business News Publishing Co., II, L.L.C. • Annual. $25.00. Lists about 6,000 manufacturers and distributors of floor covering installation and cleaning equipment. Formerly *Installation and Cleaning Specialists Trade Directory and Buying Guide.*

Maintenance Supplies Buyers' Guide. Cygnus Business Media, Inc. • Annual. $15.00. Approximately 1,000 manufacturers and associations for commercial, industrial, and institutional janitorial supplies; international coverage. Formerly *Maintenance Supplies Annual.*

Sanitary Maintenance Buyers' Guide. Trade Press Publishing Corp. • Annual. $20.00. For distributors and wholesalers of sanitary supplies.

FINANCIAL RATIOS

Annual Statement Studies. The Risk Management Association. • Annual. Median and quartile financial ratios are given for over 400 kinds of manufacturing, wholesale, retail, construction, and consumer finance establishments. Data is sorted by both asset size and sales volume. Includes a clearly written "Definition of Ratios" and an alphabetical industry index.

Annual Statement Studies: Industry Default Probabilities and Cash Flow Measures. The Risk

Management Association. • Annual. $145.00. Serves as a companion volume to the original *Annual Statement Studies.* Gives probability of default estimates on a percentage scale for more than 450 industries. Includes changes in position year-by-year for eight financial statement line items and provides percentage measures of cash flow.

HANDBOOKS AND MANUALS

Carpet Cleaning Service. Entrepreneur Media, Inc. • Looseleaf. $59.50. A practical guide to starting a carpet cleaning business. Covers profit potential, start-up costs, market size evaluation, owner's time required, pricing, accounting, advertising, promotion, etc. (Start-Up Business Guide No. E1053.).

Everything You Need to Know to Start a House Cleaning Service. Mary P. Johnson. Cleaning Consultant Services, Inc. • 1999. $38.00. Revised edition.

Home Inspection Service. Entrepreneur Media, Inc. • Looseleaf. $59.50. A practical guide to starting a home inspection service. Covers profit potential, start-up costs, market size evaluation, owner's time required, pricing, accounting, advertising, promotion, etc. (Start-Up Business Guide No. E1334.).

House Painting. Entrepreneur Media, Inc. • Looseleaf. $59.50. A practical guide to starting a house painting business. Covers profit potential, start-up costs, market size evaluation, owner's time required, pricing, accounting, advertising, promotion, etc. (Start-Up Business Guide No. E1249.).

Janitorial Service. Entrepreneur Media, Inc. • Looseleaf. $59.50. A practical guide to starting a janitorial service business. Covers profit potential, start-up costs, market size evaluation, owner's time required, site selection, lease negotiation, pricing, accounting, advertising, promotion, etc. (Start-Up Business Guide No. E1034.).

Maintenance Engineering Handbook. Lindley R. Higgins and R. Keith Mobley. McGraw-Hill. • 2001. $150.00. Sixth edition. Contains about 60 chapters by various authors in 12 major sections covering all elements of industrial and plant maintenance.

Managing Factory Maintenance. Joel Levitt. Industrial Press, Inc. • 1996. $39.95.

Window Washing Service. Entrepreneur Media, Inc. • Looseleaf. $59.50. A practical guide to starting a window cleaning business. Covers profit potential, start-up costs, market size evaluation, owner's time required, pricing, accounting, advertising, promotion, etc. (Start-Up Business Guide No. E1012.).

PERIODICALS AND NEWSLETTERS

Building Operating Management: The National Magazine for Commercial and Institutional Buildings Construction, Renovation, Facility Management. Trade Press Publishing Corp. • Monthly. Free to qualified personnel.

Cleaning Business: Published Monthly for the Self-Employed Cleaning and Maintenance Professionals. William R. Griffin, Publisher. • Monthly. $20.00 per year. Formerly *Service Business.*

ICS Cleaning Specialist (Installationa and Cleaning Specialist). Business News Publishing Co. • Monthly. Free to qualified personnel. Written for floor covering installers and cleaners. Formerly *Installation and Cleaning Specialist.*

Industrial Maintenance and Plant Operation. Reed Business Information. • Monthly. $95.99 per year.

Maintenance Supplies. Cygnus Business Media. • Monthly. $60.00 per year. Geared to distributors of sanitary supplies, maintenance equipment, etc.

Plant Services. Putman Media Inc. • Monthly. Free to qualified personnel.

Sanitary Maintenance: The Journal of the Sanitary Supply Industry. Trade Press Publishing Corp. •

Monthly. Free to qualified personnel.

TRADE/PROFESSIONAL ASSOCIATIONS

Building Service Contractors Association International. 401 N Michigan Ave., 22nd Fl., Chicago, IL 60611-4267. Phone: 800-368-3414 or (312)321-5167 Fax: (312)673-6735 E-mail: info@bscai.org • URL: http://www.bscai.org • Firms and corporations in 40 countries engaged in contracting building maintenance services including the provision of labor, purchasing materials, and janitorial cleaning and maintenance of a building or its surroundings; associate members are manufacturers of cleaning supplies and equipment. Seeks to provide a unified voice for building service contractors and to promote increased recognition by government, property owners, and the general business and professional public. Conducts continuing study and action, through committees and special task groups on areas such as public affairs, costs and ratios, uniform accounting, industrial relations and personnel, marketing and sales, contract improvement, research and planning, materials and supplies sources, group insurance, management training, statistics collection, safety, and insurance costs. Has developed a certification program for building service executives, and a registration program for building service managers.

International Maintenance Institute. PO Box 751896, Houston, TX 77275-1896. Phone: 888-207-1773 or (281)481-0869 Fax: (281)481-8337 E-mail: iminst@swbell.net • URL: http://www.imionline.org • Persons directly engaged in maintenance in a key position (superintendent, supervisor, foreman, or manager) for chemical refineries, manufacturing firms, government agencies, institutions, and other organizations; associate members are persons indirectly engaged in maintenance in sales, service, consulting, or publications capacities. Seeks to promote the professionalism of maintenance personnel and keep members informed of developments in the field. Assembles and disseminates maintenance information related to modern cost-saving methods, processes, and equipment. Conducts plant tours; local chapters sponsor monthly meetings, lectures, and discussions on such topics as preventive maintenance, electrical specification and maintenance, purchasing procedures, painting, heating, and grounds maintenance. Maintains hall of fame.

OTHER SOURCES

U. S. Commercial and Residential Cleaning Services Industry. Available from MarketResearch.com. • 2001. $2,025.00. Market research report published by Marketdata Enterprises. Covers commercial contract cleaning services and residential services. Provides actual industry and market statistics and forecasts to the year 2005.

MALLS, SHOPPING

See: SHOPPING CENTERS

MALPRACTICE

See: PROFESSIONAL LIABILITY

MANAGED CARE

See: HEALTH INSURANCE; HEALTH MAINTENANCE ORGANIZATIONS

MANAGEMENT

See: ADMINISTRATION; FACTORY MANAGEMENT; FINANCIAL MANAGEMENT; INDUSTRIAL MANAGEMENT; MANAGEMENT THEORY; OFFICE MANAGEMENT; PUBLIC ADMINISTRATION; SALES MANAGEMENT

MANAGEMENT, BANK

See: BANK MANAGEMENT

MANAGEMENT BY OBJECTIVES

See: INDUSTRIAL MANAGEMENT

MANAGEMENT CONSULTANTS

See also: CONSULTANTS

ABSTRACTS AND INDEXES

Business Periodicals Index. H. W. Wilson Co. • 11 times a year. Quarterly and annual cumulations. Price varies.

BIBLIOGRAPHIES

Management Consultant Books. Kennedy Information. • Annual. Free. Contains descriptions of selected books from various publishers on management consulting.

DIRECTORIES

Consultants and Consulting Organizations Directory. Gale Cengage Learning. • 2003. $840.00. 25th edition. Three volumes. Includes mid-year *Supplement.* Lists more than 27,000 firms and individuals covering 14 general fields of consulting activity.

Directory of Management Consultants. Kennedy Information, Inc. • Biennial. $295.00. Contains profiles of more than 2,100 general and specialty management consulting firms in the U. S., Canada, and Mexico.

FINANCIAL RATIOS

Annual Statement Studies. The Risk Management Association. • Annual. Median and quartile financial ratios are given for over 400 kinds of manufacturing, wholesale, retail, construction, and consumer finance establishments. Data is sorted by both asset size and sales volume. Includes a clearly written "Definition of Ratios" and an alphabetical industry index.

Annual Statement Studies: Industry Default Probabilities and Cash Flow Measures. The Risk Management Association. • Annual. $145.00. Serves as a companion volume to the original *Annual Statement Studies.* Gives probability of default estimates on a percentage scale for more than 450 industries. Includes changes in position year-by-year for eight financial statement line items and provides percentage measures of cash flow.

HANDBOOKS AND MANUALS

The Consultant's Proposal, Fee, and Contract Problem-Solver. Ronald Tepper. John Wiley and Sons, Inc. • 1993. $29.95. Provides advice for consultants on fees, contracts, proposals, and client communications. Includes case histories in 10 specific fields, such as finance, marketing, engineering, and management.

Consulting Business. Entrepreneur Media, Inc. • Looseleaf. $59.50. A practical guide to becoming a business consultant. Covers profit potential, start-up costs, market size evaluation, pricing, accounting, advertising, promotion, etc. (Start-Up Business Guide No. E1151.).

How to Become a Successful Consultant in Your Own Field. Hubert Bermont. Prima Publishing. • 2000. $14.00. Third editon.

How to Succeed as an Independent Consultant. Herman Holtz. John Wiley and Sons, Inc. • 1993. $34.95. Third edition. Covers a wide variety of marketing, financial, professional, and ethical issues for

consultants. Includes bibliographic and organizational information.

Management Consulting: A Guide to the Profession. Milan Kubr. International Labour Organization. • 2002. $85.00. Fourth edition. Serves as a complete guide to managememt consulting, including such practical matters as contracts, client relationships, report-writing, fees, and the management of a management consulting firm.

ONLINE DATABASES

Wilson Business Abstracts Online. H. W. Wilson Co. • Indexes and abstracts 600 major business periodicals, plus the *Wall Street Journal* and the business section of the *New York Times.* Indexing is from 1982, abstracting from 1990, with the two newspapers included from 1993. Updated weekly. Inquire as to online cost and availability. (*Business Periodicals Index* without abstracts is also available online.).

PERIODICALS AND NEWSLETTERS

Consultants News: Independent Commentary on Management Consulting Since 1970. Kennedy Information, Inc. • Monthly. $295.00 per year. Newsletter. News and ideas for management consultants.

STATISTICS SOURCES

U. S. Industry and Trade Outlook. Available from National Technical Information Service. • Annual. $69.95. Produced by the International Trade Administration, U. S. Department of Commerce, in a "public-private" partnership with DRI/McGraw-Hill and Standard & Poor's. Provides basic data, outlook for the current year, and "Long-Term Prospects" (five-year projections) for a wide variety of products and services. Includes high technology industries. Formerly *U. S. Industrial Outlook.*

TRADE/PROFESSIONAL ASSOCIATIONS

Association of Management Consulting Firms. 380 Lexington Ave., No. 1700, New York, NY 10168-0002. Phone: (212)551-7887 Fax: (212)551-7934 E-mail: info@amcf.org • URL: http://www.amcf.org • Members are management consultants. One of the two divisions of the Council of Consulting Organizations.

Institute of Management Consultants. 2025 M St., NW, Ste. 800, Washington, DC 20036-3309. Phone: 800-221-2557 or (202)367-1134 Fax: (202)367-2134 E-mail: office@imcusa.org • URL: http://www.imcusa.org • Provides professional services and certification to management consultants. Affiliated with Association of Management Consulting Firms.

MANAGEMENT DEVELOPMENT

See: EXECUTIVE TRAINING AND DEVELOPMENT

MANAGEMENT, FINANCIAL

See: FINANCIAL MANAGEMENT

MANAGEMENT GAMES

GENERAL WORKS

Games, Strategies, and Managers: How Managers Can Use Game Theory to Make Better Business Decisions. John McMillan. Oxford University Press. • 1992. $19.95.

HANDBOOKS AND MANUALS

Business Policy Game: An International Simulation. Richard V. Cotter and David J. Fritzsche. Prentice Hall PTR. • 1995. $53.33. Fourth edition.

Handbook of Management Games and Simulations. Chris Elgood, editor. Ashgate Publishing Co. • 1997. $109.95. Sixth edition. Published by Gower in England.

Imaginative Events: A Sourcebook of Innovative Simulations, Exercises, Puzzles, and Games. Ken Jones. McGraw-Hill. • 1992. $110.00. Two volumes. Vol. 1, $65.00; vol. 2, $65.00. (Training Series).

PERIODICALS AND NEWSLETTERS

Journal of Economics and Management Strategy. MIT Press. • Quarterly. Institutions, $195.00 per year. Includes print and online editions. Covers "theoretical and empirical industrial organization, applied game theory, and management strategy.".

Simulation & Gaming: An International Journal of Theory, Design and Research. Sage Publications, Inc. • Quarterly. Institutions, $5155.00 per year; includes print and online editions.

TRADE/PROFESSIONAL ASSOCIATIONS

Association for Business Simulation and Experiential Learning. c/o Hugh M. Cannon, Dept. of Marketing, Wayne State University, 5201 Cass Ave., Suite 300, Detroit, MI 48202-3930. Phone: (313)577-4551 Fax: (313)577-5486 E-mail: hughcannon@email.com • URL: http://www.towson.edu/~absel/.

North American Simulation and Gaming Association. P.O. Box 78636, Indianapolis, IN 46278. Phone: 888-432-4263 or (317)387-1424 Fax: (317)387-1921 E-mail: info@nasaga.org • URL: http://www.nasaga.org • Members are professionals interested in the use of games and simulations for problem solving and decision-making in all types of organizations. Formerly National Gaming Council.

MANAGEMENT INFORMATION SYSTEMS

See also: COMPUTERS; SYSTEMS IN MANAGEMENT

GENERAL WORKS

Cases in the Management of Information Systems and Information Technology. Richard Lorette and Howard Walton. McGraw-Hill. • 1994. $40.95.

Essentials of Knowledge Management. Bryan Bergeron. John Wiley and Sons, Inc. • 2003. $29.95. Covers current strategies, trends, and technologies in knowledge management. Includes examples of best practices. (Essentials Series).

Information Management for the Intelligent Organization: The Art of Scanning the Environment. Chun Wei Choo. Information Today, Inc. • 2001. $39.50. Third edition. Published on behalf of the American Society for Information Science (ASIS). Covers the general principles of acquiring, creating, organizing, and using information within organizations.

Information Systems Concept Management. Henry C. Lucas. McGraw-Hill. • 1994. $25.00. Fifth edition.

Introduction to Information Systems. James A. O'Brien. McGraw-Hill. • 2000. $87.81. 10th edition.

Knowledge Management for the Information Professional. T. Kanti Srikantaiah and Michael Koenig. Information Today, Inc. • 2000. $44.50. Contains articles by 26 contributors on the concept of "knowledge management." (ASIS Mongraph Series).

Knowledge Management Lessons Learned: What Works and What Doesn't. Michael Koenig and T. Kanti Srikantaiah, editors. Information Today, Inc. • 2003. $44.50. Contains more than 30 articles by KM experts, covering recent applications, innovations, strategy, implementation, cost analysis, training, content management, and other topics related to knowledge management. (ASIS Management Series).

Management Information Systems. Raymond McLeod and George Schell. Prentice Hall PTR. • 2000. $116.67. Eighth edition.

Management Information Systems: Managing Information. Fritz J. Erickson and James A. O'Brien. McGraw-Hill. • 1996. $72.25. Third edition.

Management Information Systems: Solving Business Problems with Information Technology. Gerald V. Post and David Anderson. McGraw-Hill. • 2002. $75.25. Third edition. Emphasizes the use of databases in practical business applications.

Management Information Systems: With Application Cases and Internet Primer. Stephen Haag and others. McGraw-Hill. • 2001. $107.19. Third edition. Includes CD-ROM.

ABSTRACTS AND INDEXES

Business Periodicals Index. H. W. Wilson Co. • 11 times a year. Quarterly and annual cumulations. Price varies.

Internet and Personal Computing Abstracts [print edition]. EBSCO Publishing. • Quarterly. $269.00 per year, including cumulative index. Provides more than 10,000 abstracts annually from both trade and academic publications. Covers computer hardware, software, product reviews, Web topics, e-commerce, networks, corporate news, security, and related topics. Formerly *Microcomputer Abstracts.*

BIBLIOGRAPHIES

Knowledge Management: The Bibliography. Paul Burden and others. Information Today, Inc. • 2000. $22.50. Provides citations to more than 1,500 articles, 150 Web sites, and 400 books. Arranged according to specific KM topics, such as "KM and E-Commerce." Published in conjunction with the American Society for Information Science and Technology (ASIST).

CD-ROM DATABASES

Computer Database. Gale Cengage Learning. • Provides one year of full-text on CD-ROM for 150 leading computer-related publications. Also includes 70,000 product specifications and brief profiles of 13,000 computer product vendors and manufacturers.

Datapro on CD-ROM: Computer Systems Analyst. Gartner Group, Inc. • Monthly. Price on application. Includes detailed information on specific computer hardware and software products, such as peripherals, security systems, document imaging systems, and UNIX-related products.

DIRECTORIES

Data Sources: The Comprehensive Guide to the Data Processing Industry: Hardware, Data Communications Products, Software, Company Profiles. Gale Cengage Learning. • Semiannual. $455.00 per year. Two volumes. Describes hardware and software for all computer operating sysems, including prices and technical details. Lists about 75,000 products from 14,000 suppliers. Industry-specific software applications are described.

KMWorld Buyer's Guide. Knowledge Asset Media. • Semiannual. Controlled circulation as part of *KMWorld.* Contains corporate and product profiles related to various aspects of knowledge management and information systems. (Knowledge Asset Media is a an affiliate of Information Today, Inc.).

Major Information Technology Companies of the World 2001. Available from Gale Cengage Learning. • Annual. $880.00. Published by Graham & Whiteside. Contains profiles of more than 3,100

leading information technology companies in various countries.

ENCYCLOPEDIAS AND DICTIONARIES

Acronyms of Computer Science and Communications: A Comprehensive Acronym Dictionary and Illustrated Encyclopedia. Enjob Kajan and Ejub Kajan. Springer Verlag. • 2002. $49.95. Explains more than 4,000 "broadly used" computer, telecommunications, and information technology acronyms. Includes illustrations and Web addresses, where applicable.

Blackwell Encyclopedic Dictionary of Management of Information Systems. Gordon B. Davis, editor. Blackwell Publishers. • 1999. $38.95. The editor is associated with the University of Minnesota. Contains definitions of key terms combined with longer articles written by various U. S. and foreign business educators. Includes bibliographies and index. (Blackwell Encyclopedia of Management Series).

Encyclopedia of Business and Finance. Burton Kaliski, editor. Available from Gale Cengage Learning. • 2001. $275.00. Two volumes. Published by Macmillan Reference USA. Contains articles by various contributors on accounting, business administration, banking, finance, management information systems, and marketing.

Encyclopedia of Information Systems. Hossein Bidgoli, editor. Elsevier. • 2002. $1,200.00. Four volumes. Contains a wide range of articles relating to computers, databases, communication, and information technology. The 200 topics include coverage of hardware, software, artificial intelligence, the Internet, networks, knowledge management, electronic commerce, search engines, and systems design.

INTERNET DATABASES

InfoTech Trends. Data Analysis Group. Phone: (925)462-1202 Fax: (925)462-1225 E-mail: support@infotechtrends.com • URL: http://www.infotechtrends.com • Web site provides both free and fee-based market research data on the information technology industry, including computers, peripherals, telecommunications, the Internet, software, CD-ROM/DVD, e-commerce, and workstations. Fees: Free for current (most recent year) data; more extensive information has various fee structures. Formerly *Computer Industry Forecasts.*

ONLINE DATABASES

SoftBase: Reviews, Companies, and Products. Information Sources, Inc. • Describes and reviews business software packages. Inquire as to online cost and availability.

Wilson Business Abstracts Online. H. W. Wilson Co. • Indexes and abstracts 600 major business periodicals, plus the *Wall Street Journal* and the business section of the *New York Times.* Indexing is from 1982, abstracting from 1990, with the two newspapers included from 1993. Updated weekly. Inquire as to online cost and availability. (*Business Periodicals Index* without abstracts is also available online.).

PERIODICALS AND NEWSLETTERS

CIO: The Magazine for Chief Information Officers. CXO Media, Inc. • 23 times a year. $150.00 per year. Edited for chief information officers. Includes a monthly "Web Business" section (incorporates the former *WebMaster* periodical) and a monthly "Enterprise" section for company executives other than CIOs.

Computer Economics Networking Strategies Report: Advising IT Decision Maker ractices and Current Trends. Computer Economics, Inc. • Monthly. $395.00 per year. Newsletter. Edited for information technology managers. Covers news and trends relating to a variety of corporate computer

network and management information systems topics. Emphasis is on costs. Formerly *Intranet and Networking Strategies Report.*

Computer Economics Report: The Financial Advisor of Data Processing Users. Computer Economics, Inc. • Monthly. $595.00 per year. Newsletter on lease/purchase decisions, prices, discounts, residual value forecasts, personnel allocation, cost control, and other corporate computer topics. Edited for information technology (IT) executives.

Computerworld: Newsweekly for Information Technology Leaders. Computerworld, Inc. • Weekly. $190.00 per year.

DM Review: The Premier Publication for Business Intelligence and Analytics. Thomson Media. • Monthly. $49.00 per year. Edited for corporate executives and information technology personnel. Covers data management, business intelligence, data warehousing, systems management, data integration, knowledge management, data mining, and related topics.

Information and Management; International Journal of Information Systems Applications. Elsevier. • Eight times a year. Institutions, $646.00 per year.

Information Executive: A Monthly Publication for DPMA and the Information Systems Profession. AITP-Association of Information Technology Professional. • Monthly. $45.00 per year. Articles reporting developmental and technical aspects of EDP services, supplies, equipment, accessories and related contemporary trends and issues. Formerly *Inside DPMA.*

Information Strategy: The Executive's Journal. Auerbach Publications. • Quarterly. $195.00 per year.

Information Systems; Data Bases: Their Creation, Management and Utilization. Elsevier. • Eight times a year. Institutions, $1,554.00 per year.

Information Systems Management. Auerbach Publications. • Quarterly. $175.00 per year. Formerly *Journal of Information Systems Management.*

Information Week: Business Innovation Powered by Technology. CMP Publications, Inc. • Weekly. $199.00 per year. The magazine for information systems management.

IT Cost Management Strategies: The Planning Assistant for IT Directors. Computer Economics, Inc. • Monthly. $495.00 per year. Newsletter for information technology professionals. Covers data processing costs, budgeting, financial management, and related topics.

Journal of Management Information Systems. M. E. Sharpe, Inc. • Quarterly. Individuals, $88.00 per year; institutions, $599.00 per year. Includes print and online edtions. Analysis, case studies, and current research.

KM World: Creating and Managing the Knowledge-Based Enterprise (Knowledge Management). Asset Media. • 10 times a year. Free to qualified personnel; others, $63.95 per year. Provides articles on knowledge management, including business intelligence, multimedia content management, document management, e-business, and intellectual property. Emphasis is on business-to-business information technology. (Knowledge Asset Media is a an affiliate of Information Today, Inc.).

Manufacturing Computer Solutions: The Management Magazine of Integrated Manufacturing. Findlay Publications Ltd. • Monthly. $88.00 per year.

MIS Quarterly (Management Information Systems). University of Minnesota, School of Management. MIS Research Center, Carlson School of Management. • Quarterly. $75.00 per year.

Network Computing: Computing in a Network Environment. CMP Publications, Inc. •

For publishers addresses, refer to SOURCES CITED section at the back of the book.

Semimonthly. Free to qualified personnel.

Report on Healthcare Information Management. Capital Publications, Inc. • Monthly. $358.00 per year. Newsletter. Covers management information sytems for hospitals and physicans' groups.

Systems User. Caulfield Publishing Ltd. • Monthly. $62.00 per year.

RESEARCH CENTERS AND INSTITUTES

Center for Information Systems Research. Massachusetts Institute of Technology. Sloan School of Management, Three Cambridge Ctr., NE20-336, Cambridge, MA 02142. Phone: (617)253-2348 Fax: (617)253-4424 E-mail: cisr@mit.edu • URL: http://www.web.mit.edu/cisr.

Management Information Systems Research Center. University of Minnesota. Carlson School of Management, 321 19th Ave. S., Minneapolis, MN 55455-0430. Phone: (612)624-6565 Fax: (612)624-2056 E-mail: misrc@csom.umn.edu • URL: http://www.misrc.umn.edu.

STATISTICS SOURCES

Information Systems Spending: An Analysis of Trends and Strategies. Computer Economics, Inc. • Annual. $1,595.00. Three volumes. Based on "in-depth surveys of public and private companies amd government organizations." Provides detailed data on management information systems spending, budgeting, and benchmarks. Includes charts, graphs, and analysis.

TRADE/PROFESSIONAL ASSOCIATIONS

AFCOM. 742 E Chapman Ave., Orange, CA 92866. Phone: (714)997-7966 Fax: (714)997-9743 E-mail: afcom@afcom.com • URL: http://www.afcom.com • Data center, networking and enterprise systems management professionals from medium and large scale mainframe, midrange and client/server data centers worldwide. Works to meet the professional needs of the enterprise system management community. Provides information and support through educational events, research and assistance hotlines, and surveys.

Government Management Information Sciences. 8315 SW 183rd Ter., P.O. Box 421, Palmetto Bay, FL 33157. Phone: 800-460-7454 or (973)632-0470 Fax: (786)242-3925 E-mail: headquarters@gmis.org • URL: http://www.gmis.org • Represents state and local government agencies involved in Information Technology; while member agencies differ in many aspects, it is a homogenous group with similar interests dedicated to sharing with each other. Provides organizational support to eighteen state chapters. State chapters enable member agencies within a geographical area to develop close relationships and to foster the spirit and intent through cooperation, assistance and mutual support. Affiliated with five international sister organizations of local governments: KommITS in Sweden, SOCITM in United Kingdom, VIAG in the Netherlands, MISA in Canada, and ALGIM in New Zealand.

Institute for the Management of Information Systems. Five Kingfisher House, New Mill Rd., Orpington, Kent BR5 3QG, England. Phone: 44 70 00023456 Fax: 44 70 00023023 E-mail: central@imis.org.uk • URL: http://www.imis.org.uk • Formerly Institute of Data Processing Management.

Society for Information Management. 401 N. Michigan Ave., Chicago, IL 60621-4267. Phone: 800-387-9746 or (312)527-6734 or (312)644-6610 Fax: (312)245-1081 E-mail: info@simnet.org • URL: http://www.simnet.org • Formerly Society for Management Information Systems.

Special Interest Group on Management of Data. c/o Association for Computing Machinery, 1515 Broadway, New York, NY 10036. Phone: 800-342-6626 or (212)869-7440 Fax: (212)944-1318 E-mail: acmhelp@acm.org • URL: http://www.acm.org/sigmod • Focuses on network architecture,

protocols, and distributed systems. Publishes a quarterly newsletter *Computer Communication Review.* Formerly Special Interest Group on Data Communication.

MANAGEMENT OF FACTORIES

See: FACTORY MANAGEMENT

MANAGEMENT, OPERATIONS

See: OPERATIONS MANAGEMENT

MANAGEMENT, PARTICIPATIVE

See: PARTICIPATIVE MANAGEMENT

MANAGEMENT, PRODUCTION

See: OPERATIONS MANAGEMENT

MANAGEMENT, SCIENTIFIC

See: TIME AND MOTION STUDY

MANAGEMENT SYSTEMS

See: SYSTEMS IN MANAGEMENT

MANAGEMENT THEORY

See also: ADMINISTRATION

GENERAL WORKS

Designing Organizations to Create Value: From Strategy to Structure. Jerry Zimmerman and others. McGraw-Hill. • 2002. $29.95. Describes a process for "identifying the critical aspects of an organization's internal structure" and making administrative enhancements.

The Logic of Organizations. Bengt Abrahamsson. Sage Publications, Inc. • 1992. $39.95. Consists of two major sections: "The Emergence of Bureaucracy.." and "Administration Theory..".

Modern Organizations: Theory and Practice. Ali Farazmand, editor. Greenwood Publishing Group, Inc. • 2002. $67.95. Second edition.

A Primer on Organizational Behavior. James L. Bowditch and Anthony F. Buono. John Wiley and Sons, Inc. • 2000. $50.95. Fifth edition. Includes a discussion of participative management. Emphasis is on research and the theory of organizations. (Management Series).

Rethinking Organization: New Directions in Organization Theory and Analysis. Michael Reed and Michael Hughes. Sage Publications, Inc. • 1992. $37.95.

ABSTRACTS AND INDEXES

Business Periodicals Index. H. W. Wilson Co. • 11 times a year. Quarterly and annual cumulations. Price varies.

Social Sciences Citation Index. Thomson/ISI. • Three times a year. $6,900 per year. Annual cumulation. Includes *Source Index, Citation Index, Permuterm Subject Index,* and *Corporate Index.*

Social Sciences Index. H. W. Wilson Co. • Quarterly,

with annual cumulation. Price varies. Indexes more than 400 periodicals covering economics, environmental policy, government, insurance, labor, health care policy, plannning, public administration, public welfare, urban studies, women's issues, criminology, and related topics.

CD-ROM DATABASES

Profiles in Business and Management: An International Directory of Scholars and Their Research [CD-ROM]. Harvard Business School Publishing. • Annual. $595.00. Fully searchable CD-ROM version of two-volume printed directory. Contains bibliographic and biographical information for over 5600 business and management experts active in 21 subject areas. Formerly *International Directory of Business and Management Scholars.*

Social Sciences Citation Index. ISI. • Monthly. Price on request. Provides CD-ROM indexing of articles appearing in 1700 leading social science journals worldwide, with additional selections from more than 5700 other journals. Time span is 1992 to date. Coverage includes economics, business, finance, management, communications, demographics, library and information science, political science, sociology, and many other subjects.

Social Sciences Citation Index: Compact Disc Edition with Abstracts. Institute for Scientific Information. • Monthly. Provides CD-ROM indexing and abstracting of "significant articles" from 1,700 social science journals worldwide, with additional selections from 3,200 other journals, 1986 to date. Includes economics, business, finance, management, communications, demographics, information and library science, political science, sociology, and many other subjects.

WILSONDISC: Wilson Social Sciences Abstracts. H. W. Wilson Co. • Monthly. Includes unlimited online access to *Social Sciences Index* through WILSONLINE. Provides CD-ROM indexing from 1983 and abstracting from 1994 of more than 500 periodicals covering economics, area studies, community health, public administration, public welfare, urban studies, and many other topics related to the social sciences.

ENCYCLOPEDIAS AND DICTIONARIES

Blackwell Encyclopedic Dictionary of Organizational Behavior. Nigel Nicholson, editor. Blackwell Publishing. • 1997. $130.95. The editor is associated with the London Business School. Contains definitions of key terms combined with longer articles written by various U. S. and foreign business educators. Includes bibliographies and index. *Blackwell Encyclopedia of Management Series.*

International Encyclopedia of Business and Management. Malcolm Warner, editor. Cengage Learning. • 2001. $1,899.00.Second edition. Eight volumes. Contains more than 500 articles on global management issues. Includes extensive bibliographies, cross references, and an index of key words and phrases.

International Encyclopedia of Public Policy and Administration. Jay M. Shafritz, editor. Westview Press. • 1997. $550.00. Four volumes. Covers 20 major areas, such as public administration, government budgeting, industrial policy, nonprofit management, organizational theory, public finance, labor relations, and taxation. Includes a brief bibliography for each major entry and a comprehensive index.

HANDBOOKS AND MANUALS

Theories of Macro-Organizational Behavior: A Handbook of Ideas and Explanations. Conor Vibert. M. E. Sharpe, Inc. • 2004. $64.95. Presents summaries of 30 major theories of organizational behavior and economic organization.

ONLINE DATABASES

Business and Management Practices. Gale Cengage Learning. • Provides fulltext of management articles appearing in more than 350 relevant publications. Emphasis is on "the processes, methods, and strategies of managing a business." Time span is 1995 to date. Inquire as to online cost and availability. (Also available in a CD-ROM version.).

Management Contents. Gale Cengage Learning. • Covers a wide range of management, financial, marketing, personnel, and administrative topics. About 150 leading business journals are indexed and abstracted from 1974 to date, with monthly updating. Inquire as to online cost and availability.

Social Scisearch. Institute for Scientific Information. • Broad, multidisciplinary index to the literature of the social sciences, 1972 to present. Weekly updates. Worldwide coverage. Inquire as to online cost and availability.

Wilson Business Abstracts Online. H. W. Wilson Co. • Indexes and abstracts 600 major business periodicals, plus the *Wall Street Journal* and the business section of the *New York Times.* Indexing is from 1982, abstracting from 1990, with the two newspapers included from 1993. Updated weekly. Inquire as to online cost and availability. (*Business Periodicals Index* without abstracts is also available online.).

Wilson Social Sciences Abstracts Online. H. W. Wilson Co. • Provides online abstracting and indexing of more than 500 periodicals covering area studies, community health, public administration, public welfare, urban studies, and many other social science topics. Time period is 1994 to date for abstracts and 1983 to date for indexing, with updates weekly. Inquire as to online cost and availability.

PERIODICALS AND NEWSLETTERS

Academy of Management Executive. Academy of Management. • Bimonthly. $125.00 per year. Contains articles relating to the practical application of management principles and theory.

Academy of Management Journal. Academy of Management. • Bimonthly. $125.00 per year. Presents research papers on management-related topics.

Academy of Management Review. Academy of Management. • Quarterly. $105.00 per year. A scholarly journal concerned with the theory of management and organizations.

Administrative Science Quarterly. Cornell University, Johnson Graduate School of Management. • Individuals: $65.00 per year; institutions, $130.00 per year.

Chief Executive Magazine. Chief Executive Group, Inc. • Monthly. $95.00 per year.

Harvard Business Review. Harvard University, Graduate School of Business Administration. Harvard Business School Publishing. • Monthly. $118.00 per year.

The Journal of Business. The University of Chicago Press, Journals Div. • Quarterly. Individuals, $31.00 per year; institutions, $125.00 per year; students, $25.00 per year.

Journal of Economics and Management Strategy. MIT Press. • Quarterly. Institutions, $195.00 per year. Includes print and online editions. Covers "theoretical and empirical industrial organization, applied game theory, and management strategy.".

Management Review. American Management Association. • Membership.

Management Science. INFORMS. • Monthly. Individuals, $185.00 per year; institutions, $488.00 per year. Includes print and online editions. Provides an interchange of information between management and management scientists in industry, academia, the military and go vernment.

MIT Sloan Management Review. Sloan Management Review Association. Massachusetts Institute of Technology. • Quarterly. Individuals, $89.00 per

year; institutions, $148.00 per year. Formerly *Sloan Management Review.*.

Organizational Dynamics: A Quarterly Review of Organizational Behavior for Management Executives. American Management Association. • Quarterly. Individuals, $77.00 per year; institutions, $171.00 per year. Covers the application of behavioral sciences to business management.

RESEARCH CENTERS AND INSTITUTES

Board of Research. Babson College, 204 Babson, Babson Park, MA 02457-0310. Phone: (718)239-5339 Fax: (718)239-6416 E-mail: chern@babson.edu • URL: http://www.babson.edu/bor • Research areas include management, entrepreneurial characteristics, and multi-product inventory analysis.

Bureau of Economic and Business Research. University of Illinois at Urbana-Champaign, 1206 S. Sixth St., 403 Wohlers Hall, Champaign, IL 61820. Phone: (217)333-2330 Fax: (217)244-7410 E-mail: g-oldman@uiuc.edu • URL: http://www.business.uiuc.edu/research.

Executive Education. University of Wisconsin-Madison, School of Business, 601 University Ave., Madison, WI 53706-1035. Phone: 800-292-8964 or (608)441-7357 Fax: (608)441-7325 E-mail: dantonioni@bus.wisc.edu • URL: http://www.uwexeced.com.

SEI Center for Advanced Studies in Management. University of Pennsylvania, 1400 Steinberg Hall-Dietrich Hall, 3620 Locust Walk, Philadelphia, PA 19104-6371. Phone: (215)898-2349 Fax: (215)898-1703 E-mail: seicenter@wharton.upenn.edu • URL: http://www.seicenter.wharton.upenn.edu/seicenter • Conducts interdisciplinary management studies.

TRADE/PROFESSIONAL ASSOCIATIONS

Academy of Management. P.O. Box 3020, Briarcliff Manor, NY 10510-3020. Phone: (914)923-2607 Fax: (914)923-2615 E-mail: academy@pace.edu • URL: http://www.aomonline.edu • Members are university professors of management and selected business executives.

American Management Association. 1601 Broadway, New York, NY 10019-7420. Phone: 800-262-9699 or (212)586-8100 Fax: (212)903-8168 E-mail: membership@amanet.org • URL: http://www.amanet.org • Provides educational forums worldwide where members and their colleagues learn superior, practical business skills and explore best practices of world-class organizations through interaction with each other and expert faculty practitioners. Maintains a publishing program providing tools individuals use to extend learning beyond the classroom in a process of life-long professional growth and development through education.

Society for Advancement of Management. Texas A&M University-Corpus Christi, College of Business, 6300 Ocean Dr., Corpus Christi, TX 78412. Phone: 888-827-6077 or (361)825-6045 or (361)825-5574 Fax: (361)825-2725 E-mail: moustafa@falcon.tamucc.edu • URL: http://www.enterprise.tamucc.edu/sam/ • Professional organization of management executives in industry, commerce, government and education. Absorbed Industrial Methods Society.

MANPOWER

See: LABOR SUPPLY

MANUALS, PROCEDURE

See: PROCEDURE MANUALS

MANUFACTURED HOUSING

See: PREFABRICATED HOUSE INDUSTRY

MANUFACTURERS

See: CORPORATIONS; INDUSTRY; PRIVATE COMPANIES

MANUFACTURERS' AGENTS

DIRECTORIES

Manufacturers' Agents National Association - Directory of Manufacturers' Sales Agencies. Manufacturers' Agents National Association. • Annual. $249.00. Lists over 4,000 independent agents and firms. Price includes one year subscription to *Agency Sales Magazines.* Formerly *Manufacturers' Agents National Association-Directory of Members.*

HANDBOOKS AND MANUALS

Sales Representative Law Guide. CCH, Inc. • $195.00 per year. Looseleaf service. Semiannual updates. Covers state laws on independent sales representation. Includes checklists and forms.

PERIODICALS AND NEWSLETTERS

Agency Sales: The Marketing Magazine for Manufacturers' Agencies and Their Principals. Manufacturers' Agents National Association. • Monthly. $49.00 per year.

Rep-Letter. Manufacturers' Agents National Association. • Monthly. $37.50. A bound-in monthly feature of *Agency Sales Magazine.*

TRADE/PROFESSIONAL ASSOCIATIONS

Manufacturers' Agents National Association. 1 Spectrum Pointe, Ste. 150, Lake Forest, CA 92630-2283. Phone: 877-626-2776 or (949)859-4040 Fax: (949)855-2973 E-mail: mana@manaonline.org • URL: http://www.manaonline.org • Manufacturers' agents in all fields representing two or more manufacturers on a commission basis; associate members are manufacturers and others interested in improving the agent-principal relationship. Maintains code of ethics and rules of business and professional conduct; issues model standard form of agreement.

MANUFACTURING

See: INDUSTRY

MANUFACTURING, COMPUTER-AIDED

See: COMPUTER-AIDED DESIGN AND MANUFACTURING (CAD/CAM)

MAPS

GENERAL WORKS

World Cartography. United Nations, Department of Economic and Social Affairs. United Nations Publications. • Various volumes. Price on application.

ABSTRACTS AND INDEXES

Geographical Abstracts: Human and Physical Geography. Elsevier. • Monthly. Institutions, $4,213.00 per year. *Human Geography* $1,822.00 per year. Annual cumulation. *Physical Geography* $2,391.00 per year. Annual cumulation.

BIBLIOGRAPHIES

Bibliographic Guide to Maps and Atlases. Available from Gale Cengage Learning. • Anual. $430.00. Published by G. K. Hall & Co. Lists maps and atlases cataloged by the New York Public Library and the Library of Congress.

HANDBOOKS AND MANUALS

Map Librarianship: An Introduction. Mary L. Larsgaard. Libraries Unlimited, Inc. • 1998. $68.50. Third edition.

The Map Library in the New Millennium. R. B. Parry and others, editors. American Library Association. • 2001. $75.00. Coverage includes new technologies, standards, geographical information systems, conservation, and intellectual property rights.

ONLINE DATABASES

GEOARCHIVE. Geosystems. • Citations to literature on geoscience and water. 1974 to present. Monthly updates. Inquire as to online cost and availability.

PERIODICALS AND NEWSLETTERS

Cartography and Geographic Information Science. American Congress on Surveying and Mapping. • Quarterly. Free to members; non-members, $110.00 per year.

Surveying and Land Information Systems: Devoted to the Advancement of the Sciences of Surveying and Mapping. American Congress on Surveying and Mapping. • Quarterly. Free to members; non-members, $110.00 per year. Formerly *Surveying and Mapping.*

STATISTICS SOURCES

The World Bank Atlas. World Bank Group. • Annual. $10.00. Contains "color maps, charts, and graphs representing the main social, economic, and environmental indicators for 209 countries and territories" (publisher).

TRADE/PROFESSIONAL ASSOCIATIONS

American Congress on Surveying and Mapping. Six Montgomery Village Ave., Ste. 403, Gaithersburg, MD 20879-3546. Phone: (240)632-9716 Fax: (240)632-1321 E-mail: csumner@acsm.net • URL: http://www.acsm.net.

OTHER SOURCES

Atlas & Gazetteer Series. DeLorme Mapping Co. • Dates vary. $983.50 complete ($19.95 region). Consists of 50 volumes covering all areas of the U. S. Includes detailed maps, as well as descriptions of attractions, natural areas, and historic sites. (CD-ROM versions available.).

Columbia Gazetteer of North America. Saul B. Cohen, editor. Columbia University Press. • 2000. $250.00. Contains information on 50,000 places within the U. S., Canada, Mexico, and the Caribbean. Includes 24 pages of color maps. Provides brief descriptions of natural resources and industrial activities.

Columbia Gazetteer of the World. Saul B. Cohen, editor. Columbia University Press. • 1998. $750.00. Three volumes. Also available online (http://www. columbiagazetteer.org) and on CD-ROM.

Commercial Atlas and Marketing Guide. Rand McNally. • Annual. $395.00. Includes maps and marketing data: population, transportation, communication, and local area business statistics. Provides information on more than 128,000 U.S. locations. (Commercial Atlas and Marketing Guide series).

Lloyd's Maritime Atlas. Available from Informa UK Limited. • Biennial. $119.00. Contains more than 70 pages of world, ocean, regional, and port maps in color. Provides additional information for the planning of world shipping routes, including data on distances, port facilities, recurring weather hazards at sea, international load line zones, and sailing times.

Maps on File. Facts on File. • Annual. $195.00. Update, $45.00. 300 country and other maps in looseleaf binder.

Township Atlas of the United States. Gale Cengage Learning. • 2000. $85.00. Fourth edition. Covers the 48 contiguous states. Includes state maps, county maps, townships, subdivisions, and indexes.

Zip Code Mapbook of Metropolitan Areas. ESRI Business Information Solutions. • 1992. $195.00. Second edition. Contains Zip Code two-color maps of 326 metropolitan areas. Includes summary statistical profiles of each area: population characteristics, employment, housing, and income.

MARBLE

See also: QUARRYING

PERIODICALS AND NEWSLETTERS

Building Stone Magazine. Building Stone Institute. • Bimonthly. $65.00 per year.

TRADE/PROFESSIONAL ASSOCIATIONS

International Cast Polymer Association. 304 Bell Park Dr., Woodstock, GA 30188-1660. Phone: 800-414-4272 or (770)928-2252 Fax: (770)874-7540 E-mail: dirk@intlmarbleindustries.com • URL: http://www.icpa-hq.org • Firms and corporations that make cast polymer products (such as cast marble vanity tops and solid surface countertops); firms and corporations that supply raw materials and production equipment to manufacturers of cast polymer products. Promotes the merits of cast polymer products to their markets; works to expand these markets for the benefit of manufacturers, suppliers, and sellers of these products; firms that fabricate/install cast polymer products. Develops and promotes industry-wide standards of product quality and acceptability for the protection of purchasers of cast polymer products. Represents the cast polymer industry before government, code bodies, and regulatory agencies of all types. Defends the industry against unwarranted regulations and seeks to guarantee its source and supply of raw materials; helps members improve their skills as businessmen; educates the public on how the industry sells its products. Works to develop reliable industry-wide market data to guide members in planning operations; strives to advance the interests of the industry and of members within the boundaries set by law. Participates in standards, product testing, technical exchange, marketing and business educational activities, production data, and informal exchanges. Conducts research programs; compiles statistics.

Marble Institute of America. 28901 Clemens Rd., Ste. 100, Cleveland, OH 44145. Phone: (440)250-9222 Fax: (440)250-9223 E-mail: info@marble-institute.com • URL: http://www.marble-institute.com.

MARGARINE INDUSTRY

ALMANACS AND YEARBOOKS

Agricultural and Mineral Commodities Year Book. Available from Taylor & Francis Group. • Annual. $225.00. Published by Europa Publications. Contains descriptive product profiles, price data, export-import data, and production statistics for major commodities of the world. Includes commodity histories, uses, markets, demand trends, and information about trade agreements and key commodity organizations.

CD-ROM DATABASES

Food Science and Technology Abstracts [CD-ROM]. Available from SilverPlatter Information, Inc. • Quarterly. Produced by International Food Information Service (home page is http://www.ifis. org). Provides worldwide coverage on CD-ROM of the literature of food technology and production. Various types of publications are indexed, with

abstracts, including about 1,800 periodicals. Time period is 1969 to date.

DIRECTORIES

Major Food and Drink Companies of the World. Available from Gale Cengage Learning. • Annual. $880.00. Two volumes. Published by Graham & Whiteside. Contains profiles and trade names for more than 9,800 important food and beverage companies in various countries. In addition to foods, includes both alcoholic and nonalcoholic drink products.

Thomas Food and Beverage Market Place. Grey House Publishing. • 2004. $495.00. Three volumes. Contains more than 40,000 entries covering food companies, beverages, food equipment, warehouse companies, food brokers, wholesalers, importers, and exporters. Formerly *Thomas Food Industry Register.*

INTERNET DATABASES

USDA. United States Department of Agriculture. Phone: (202)720-2791 E-mail: agsec@usda.gov • URL: http://www.usda.gov • The USDA home page has six sections: News and Information; What's New; About USDA; Agencies; Opportunities; Search and Help. Keyword searching is offered from the USDA home page and from various individual agency home pages. Agencies are the Economic Research Service, Agricultural Marketing Service, National Agricultural Statistics Service, National Agricultural Library, and about 12 others. Updating varies. Fees: Free.

ONLINE DATABASES

Food Science and Technology Abstracts [online]. IFIS North American Desk. • Produced by International Food Information Service. Provides about 500,000 online citations, with abstracts, to the international literature of food science, technology, commodities, engineering, and processing. Approximately 2,000 periodicals are covered. Time period is 1969 to date, with monthly updates. Inquire as to online cost and availability.

STATISTICS SOURCES

Agricultural Statistics. Available from U. S. Government Printing Office. • Annual. $38.00. Produced by the National Agricultural Statistics Service, U. S. Department of Agriculture. Provides a wide variety of statistical data relating to agricultural production, supplies, consumption, prices/price-supports, foreign trade, costs, and returns, as well as farm labor, loans, income, and population. In many cases, historical data is shown annually for 10 years. In addition to farm data, includes detailed fishery statistics.

FAO Production Yearbook. Available from Bernan Associates. • Annual. $45.00. Published by the Food and Agriculture Organization (http://www.fao.org). Contains worldwide data on agriculture, land use, farm crops, livestock, and agricultural prices.

FAO Trade Yearbook. Available from Bernan Associates. • Annual. $45.00. Published by the Food and Agriculture Organization (http://www.fao.org). Provides extensive worldwide data on exports and imports of agricultural commodities, fertilizers, tractors, and pesticides. Includes more than 130 tables of detailed statistics.

World Food Data and Statistics. Euromonitor International. • 2004. $650.00. Provides five-year data for a wide variety of food products in 52 countries. Includes market size, consumer expenditures, price indicators, and retail distribution data for many kinds of meat, fish, fruits, vegetables, dairy products, baked goods, condiments, canned food, and frozen food.

TRADE/PROFESSIONAL ASSOCIATIONS

National Association of Margarine Manufacturers. 1101 15th St., N.W., Suite 202, Washington, DC

20005. Phone: (202)785-3232 Fax: (202)223-9741 E-mail: namm@assnhq.com • URL: http://www.margarine.org.

MARINAS

ABSTRACTS AND INDEXES

Fluid Abstracts: Civil Engineering. Elsevier. • Monthly. Institutions, $1,709.00 per year. Includes annual cumulation. Includes the literature of coastal structures.Published in England by Elsevier Science Publishing Ltd. Formerly *Civil Engineering Hydraulics Abstracts.*

Oceanic Abstracts. CSA. • 11 times a year. $1,645.00 per year. Includes print and online editions. Covers oceanography, marine biology, ocean shipping, and a wide range of other marine-related subject areas.

Readers' Guide to Periodical Literature. H. W. Wilson Co. • Monthly. $345.00 per year. Includes annual *Cumulation.* Indexes about 250 peridicals of general interest.

CD-ROM DATABASES

WILSONDISC: Readers' Guide to Periodical Literature. H. W. Wilson Co. • Monthly. $1,095.00 per year, including unlimited online access to *Readers' Guide to Periodical Literature* through WILSONLINE. Provides CD-ROM indexing of about 270 general interest periodicals. Covers 1983 to date. (*Readers' Guide Abstracts* also available on CD-ROM at $1,995 per year.).

DIRECTORIES

Waterway Guide--The Yachtman's Bible. Primedia Business. • Covers: inland and coastal waterways in the eastern half of the United States; published in three editions. Northern edition covers coastal waterways from the Delaware Bay to the U.S.-Canadian border; plus New York canals, Champlain Waterways, and St. Lawrence River; Middle Atlantic edition covers waterways from the Chesapeake Bay to the Florida-Georgia line; Southern edition covers intracoastal waterways from the Florida-Georgia line to the Texas-Mexico border and the Bahamas. Entries include: Name of marine facility, location, navigation information and courses, points of interest, anchorages.

ONLINE DATABASES

Oceanic Abstracts (Online). Cambridge Scientific Abstracts. • Oceanographic and other marine-related technical literature, 1981 to present.Monthly updates. Inquire as to online cost and availability.

Readers' Guide Abstracts Online. H. W. Wilson Co. • Indexes and abstracts general interest periodicals, 1983 to date. Weekly updates. Inquire as to online cost and availability.

PERIODICALS AND NEWSLETTERS

Boating Industry Buyers Guide and Directory. Ehlert Publishing Group. • Monthly. $38.00 per year.

Marina Dock Age. Preston Publications, Inc. • Eight times a year. $35.00 per year. Published for owners and managers of marinas and boatyards.

RESEARCH CENTERS AND INSTITUTES

National Ports and Waterways Institute. University of New Orleans, 2300 Claredon Blvd., Suite 300, Arlington, VA 22201. Phone: (703)276-7101 Fax: (703)276-7102 E-mail: npwi@seas.gwu.edu • URL: http://www.members.tripod.com/npwi.

TRADE/PROFESSIONAL ASSOCIATIONS

American Boat Builders and Repairers Association. 50 Water St., Warren, RI 02885. Phone: (401)247-0318 Fax: (401)247-0074 • URL: http://www.abbra.org.

MARINE ENGINEERING

ABSTRACTS AND INDEXES

NTIS Alerts: Ocean Sciences and Technology. National Technical Information Service. •

Semimonthly. $210.00 per year. Provides descriptions of government-sponsored research reports and software, with ordering information. Formerly *Abstract Newsletter.*

DIRECTORIES

Directory of Marine Diesel Engines. Institute of Marine Engineering, Science, and Technology. • Annual. Price on application. Issued as a supplement to *Marine Engineers Review.*

Fairplay World Shipping Directory. Fairplay Publications Ltd. • Covers: more than 76,000 companies worldwide engaged in some aspect of shipping, including over 10,000 shipowners with fleets totalling over 45,000 vessels, shipbuilders and repairers, marine insurance shipping finance, protection and indemnity associations, marine equipment suppliers, and towing, salvage, and dredging; also lists marine organizations, shipbrokers, and consulting engineers and surveyors. Entries include: Company name, address, phone, fax, e-mail, URL, names of directors and executives, brief description of business; listings may also include associated and subsidiary companies and financial data.

Lloyd's Marine Equipment Buyers' Guide. Available from Informa UK Ltd. • Annual. $270.00. Published in the UK by Lloyd's List (http://www.lloydslist.com). Lists more than 6,000 companies worldwide supplying over 2,000 types of marine products and services, including offshore equipment.

Lloyd's Maritime Directory. Informa PLC. • Covers: Over 40,000 shipowners, managers, and operators with 75,000 vessels. Also includes Marine consultants; towing, salvage, solicitors, P&I clubs; ship building and repair firms; general maritime organizations, banking and finance and more. Entries include: Firm name, address, phone, fax, e-mail, internet; branch offices; names of principal executives; agents; parent and associated companies; and, for shipowners and lines, detailed information on ships owned, type, or capacity, etc. The former second volume of 'International Shipping and Shipbuilding Directory' is now published separately with the title 'Lloyd's List Marine Equipment Buyers' Guide' (see separate entry).

Motor Ship Directory of Shipowners and Shipbuilders. Reed Business Information. • Annual. $120.00. Formerly *Directory of Shipowners and Shipbuilders.*

ENCYCLOPEDIAS AND DICTIONARIES

Illustrated Dictionary of Cargo Handling. Peter Brodie. LLP, Inc. • 1991. $90.00. Second edition. Published in the UK by Lloyd's List (http://www.lloydslist.com). Provides definitions of about 600 terms relating to "the vessels and equipment used in modern cargo handling and shipping," including containerization.

PERIODICALS AND NEWSLETTERS

Journal of Offshore Technology. Institute of Marine Engineering, Science, and Technology. • Bimonthly. Free to members; non-members, $100.00 per year. Covers the latest technological developments and trends for senior offshore engineers.

Journal of Ship Research. Society of Naval Architects and Marine Engineers. • Quarterly. Individuals, $25.00 per year; institutions, $98.00 per year.

Lloyd's List. Available from Informa UK Ltd. • Daily. $1,698.00 per year. Published in the UK by Lloyd's List (http://www.lloydslist.com). Marine industry newspaper. Covers a wide variety of maritime topics, including global news, business/insurance, regulation, shipping markets, financial markets, shipping movements, freight logistics, and marine technology. (Also available weekly at $385.00 per year.).

Lloyd's Ship Manager. LLP Inc. • 10 times a year.

$478.00 per year, including annual supplementary guides and directories. Published in the UK by Lloyd's List (http://www.lloydslist.com). Covers all management, technical, and operational aspects of ocean-going shipping.

Marine Engineers Review (MER). Institute of Marine Engineering, Science, and Technology (IMarEST). • Monthly. Free to members; non-members, $150.00 per year. Covers marine engineering, offshore industries, and ocean shipping.

Marine Log. Simmons-Boardman Publishing Corp. • Monthly. $35.00 per year. Formerly *Marine Engineering-Log.*

Marine Management Holdings: Transactions. Available from Information Today, Inc. • Bimonthly. $220.00 per year. Published in London by Marine Management Holdings Ltd. Contains technical and regulatory material on a wide variety of marine and offshore topics. Formerly *Institute of Marine Engineers: Transactions.*

Marine Technology and SNAME News. Society of Naval Architects and Marine Engineers. • Quarterly. Individuals, $25.00 per year; institutions, $98.00 per year. Formerly *Marine Technology.*

Maritime IT & Electronics. Institute of Marine Engineering, Science, and Technology. • Bimonthly. $65.00 per year. Covers modern electronic technology as applied to all areas of the maritime industry. Includes navigation systems, communications, control systems, monitoring, diagnostics, and software.

Maritime Reporter and Engineering News. Maritime Activity Reports, Inc. • Monthly. $44.00 per year.

Naval Engineers Journal. American Society of Naval Engineers, Inc. • Bimonthly. $100 per year.

Satellite News. Access Intelligence L.L.C. • Description: Provides business insights and analysis into the commercial satellite industry including new satellite applications, developing technologies, and unfolding partnerships. Recurring features include columns titled Satellite Spotlight, DBS News, Satellite News, Newsmaker Interiews, Satellite Circuit, and Satellite News Financial Ticker.

Workboat. Diversified Business Communications. • Monthly. $49.00 per year. Covers equipment, products, and services for commercial boats such as tugboats, ferries, fireboats, fishing boats, and excursion boats.

TRADE/PROFESSIONAL ASSOCIATIONS

American Society of Naval Engineers. 1452 Duke St., Alexandria, VA 22314. Phone: (703)836-6727 Fax: (703)836-7491 E-mail: asnehq@navalengineers.org • URL: http://www.navalengineers.org.

Institute of Marine Engineers, Science and Technology. 80 Coleman St., London EC2R 5BJ, United Kingdom. Phone: 44 207 3822600 Fax: 44 207 3822670 E-mail: keith.read@imarest.org • URL: http://www.imarest.org • An international organization of marine engineers, offshore engineers, and naval architects.

Marine Technology Society. 5565 Sterrett Pl., Ste. 108, Columbia, MD 21044. Phone: (410)884-5330 Fax: (410)884-9060 E-mail: membership@mtsociety.org • URL: http://www.mtsociety.org • Scientists, engineers, educators, and others with professional interest in the marine sciences or related fields; includes institutional and corporate members. Disseminates marine scientific and technical information, including institutional, environmental, physical, and biological aspects; fosters a deeper understanding of the world's seas and attendant technologies. Maintains 13 sections and 29 professional committees. Conducts tutorials.

Society of Naval Architects and Marine Engineers. 601 Pavonia Ave., Jersey City, NJ 07306. Phone: 800-798-2188 or (201)798-4800 Fax: (201)798-

4975 E-mail: ccali-poutre@sname.org • URL: http://www.sname.org.

MARINE INSURANCE

BIBLIOGRAPHIES

Insurance and Employee Benefits Literature. Special Libraries Association, Insurance and Employee Benefits Div. • Bimonthly. $15.00 per year. Lists a wide variety of literature in all branches of the insurance industry. Includes annotations.

CD-ROM DATABASES

U. S. Insurance: Property and Casualty. Sheshunoff Information Services, Inc. • Monthly. Price on application. CD-ROM provides detailed, current financial information on more than 3,200 property and casualty insurance companies.

DIRECTORIES

Fairplay World Shipping Directory. Fairplay Publications Ltd. • Covers: more than 76,000 companies worldwide engaged in some aspect of shipping, including over 10,000 shipowners with fleets totalling over 45,000 vessels, shipbuilders and repairers, marine insurance shipping finance, protection and indemnity associations, marine equipment suppliers, and towing, salvage, and dredging; also lists marine organizations, shipbrokers, and consulting engineers and surveyors. Entries include: Company name, address, phone, fax, e-mail, URL, names of directors and executives, brief description of business; listings may also include associated and subsidiary companies and financial data.

Lloyd's Maritime Directory. Informa PLC. • Covers: Over 40,000 shipowners, managers, and operators with 75,000 vessels. Also includes Marine consultants; towing, salvage, solicitors, P&I clubs; ship building and repair firms; general maritime organizations, banking and finance and more. Entries include: Firm name, address, phone, fax, e-mail, internet; branch offices; names of principal executives; agents; parent and associated companies; and, for shipowners and lines, detailed information on ships owned, type, or capacity, etc. The former second volume of 'International Shipping and Shipbuilding Directory' is now published separately with the title 'Lloyd's List Marine Equipment Buyers' Guide' (see separate entry).

ENCYCLOPEDIAS AND DICTIONARIES

Glossary of Insurance Policy Terms. Organization for Economic Cooperation and Development. • 1999. $30.00. "The selected topics range from insurance policy regulation/supervision to general trade issues and include technical terms related to issues such as claims, premiums, and provisions." Edited for government, academic, business, and insurance organizations.

ONLINE DATABASES

I.I.I. Data Base Search. Insurance Information Institute. • Provides online citations and abstracts of insurance-related literature in magazines, newspapers, trade journals, and books. Emphasis is on property and casualty insurance issues, including highway safety, product safety, and environmental liability. Inquire as to online cost and availability.

PERIODICALS AND NEWSLETTERS

Business Insurance: News Magazine for Corporate Risk, Employee Benefit and Financial Executives. Crain Communications, Inc. • Weekly. $95.00 per year. Covers a wide variety of business insurance topics, including risk management, employee benefits, workers compensation, marine insurance, and casualty insurance.

Insurance Day. Available from Informa Publishing Group Ltd. • Three times a week. $440.00 per year. Published in the UK by Lloyd's List (http://www.lloydslist.com). A newspaper providing international coverage of property/casualty/liability insurance, reinsurance, and risk, with an emphasis on marine insurance.

Lloyd's List. Available from Informa UK Ltd. • Daily. $1,698.00 per year. Published in the UK by Lloyd's List (http://www.lloydslist.com). Marine industry newspaper. Covers a wide variety of maritime topics, including global news, business/insurance, regulation, shipping markets, financial markets, shipping movements, freight logistics, and marine technology. (Also available weekly at $385.00 per year.).

STATISTICS SOURCES

Property-Casualty Insurance Facts. Insurance Information Institute. • Annual. $22.50. Formerly *Insurance Facts.*

TRADE/PROFESSIONAL ASSOCIATIONS

American Institute of Marine Underwriters. 14 Wall St., New York, NY 10005. Phone: (212)233-0550 Fax: (212)227-5102 E-mail: aimu@aimu.org • URL: http://www.aimu.org.

MARINE LAW

See: MARITIME LAW AND REGULATION

MARITIME INDUSTRY

See: SHIPS, SHIPPING AND SHIPBUILDING

MARITIME LAW AND REGULATION

ABSTRACTS AND INDEXES

Index to Legal Periodicals and Books. H. W. Wilson Co. • Monthly. $490.00 per year. Quarterly and annual cumulations.

BIBLIOGRAPHIES

Law of the Sea: A Select Bibliography. United Nations Publications. • Annual. $17.00. Includes 23 subject categories.

Law of the Sea Bulletin. United Nations Publications. • Three times per year. $15.00 per issue. $40.00 per year.

DIRECTORIES

Capital for Shipping. Available from Informa Publishing Group Ltd. • Annual. $128.00. Published in the UK by Lloyd's List (http://www.lloydslist.com). Consists of a "Financial Directory" and a "Legal Directory," listing international ship finance providers and international law firms specializing in shipping. (Included with subscription to *Lloyd's Shipping Economist*).

Fairplay World Shipping Directory. Fairplay Publications Ltd. • Covers: more than 76,000 companies worldwide engaged in some aspect of shipping, including over 10,000 shipowners with fleets totalling over 45,000 vessels, shipbuilders and repairers, marine insurance shipping finance, protection and indemnity associations, marine equipment suppliers, and towing, salvage, and dredging; also lists marine organizations, shipbrokers, and consulting engineers and surveyors. Entries include: Company name, address, phone, fax, e-mail, URL, names of directors and executives, brief description of business; listings may also include associated and subsidiary companies and financial data.

Lloyd's Maritime Directory. Informa PLC. • Covers: Over 40,000 shipowners, managers, and operators with 75,000 vessels. Also includes Marine consultants; towing, salvage, solicitors, P&I clubs; ship building and repair firms; general maritime organizations, banking and finance and more. Entries include: Firm name, address, phone, fax,

e-mail, internet; branch offices; names of principal executives; agents; parent and associated companies; and, for shipowners and lines, detailed information on ships owned, type, or capacity, etc. The former second volume of 'International Shipping and Shipbuilding Directory' is now published separately with the title 'Lloyd's List Marine Equipment Buyers' Guide' (see separate entry).

ENCYCLOPEDIAS AND DICTIONARIES

Dictionary of Shipping Terms. Peter Brodie. LLP, Inc. • 1997. Third edition. Price on application. Published in the UK by Lloyd's List (http://www.lloydslist.com). Defines more than 2,000 words, phrases, and abbreviations related to the shipping and maritime industries.

HANDBOOKS AND MANUALS

Cruise Ship Law. LexisNexis Matthew Bender. • 2003. $198.00. Provides analysis of federal cruise ship law, relevant international treaties, and court forms. Covers the law relating to passengers, crew members, stowaways, concessionaires, shipboard medical care, cruise line bankruptcies, and other items.

PERIODICALS AND NEWSLETTERS

American Maritime Cases. American Maritime Cases, Inc. • 10 times a year. $654.50 per year.

Journal of Maritime Law and Commerce. Jefferson Law Book Co. • Quarterly. Individuals, $195.00 per year; institutions, $245.00 per year.

Lloyd's List. Available from Informa UK Ltd. • Daily. $1,698.00 per year. Published in the UK by Lloyd's List (http://www.lloydslist.com). Marine industry newspaper. Covers a wide variety of maritime topics, including global news, business/insurance, regulation, shipping markets, financial markets, shipping movements, freight logistics, and marine technology. (Also available weekly at $385.00 per year.).

Lloyd's Maritime and Commercial Law Quarterly. Available from LLP Inc. • Quarterly. $255.00 per year. Published in the UK by Lloyd's List (http://www.lloydslist.com). Provides international coverage of relevant cases, decisions, and developments.

Lloyd's Maritime Law News Letter North American Edition. Informa UK Ltd. • Biweekly. $630.00 per year. Newsletter. Published in the UK by Lloyd's List (http://www.lloydslist.com). Provides "in-depth analysis of developments in U. S. maritimne law and maritime trends.".

Ocean Development and International Law; The Journal of Marine Affairs. Taylor & Francis Group. • Quarterly. Individuals, $225.00 per year; institutions, $454.00 per year.

Tulane Maritime Law Journal. Tulane University, School of Law, John Giffen Weinmann Hall. • Semiannual. $28.00 per year. Formerly *Maritime Lawyer.*

United States Coast Guard Marine Safety Council Proceedings. U.S. Coast Guard. • Bimonthly.

TRADE/PROFESSIONAL ASSOCIATIONS

Maritime Law Association of the U.S. 45 Broadway, Ste. 1500, New York, NY 10005-1759. Phone: (212)425-1900 Fax: (212)425-1901 E-mail: rhayden@hillrivkins.com • URL: http://www.mlaus.org.

OTHER SOURCES

Benedict on Admiralty. LexisNexis Matthew Bender. • Three times a year. $3,138.00. 27 looseleaf volumes. Periodic supplementation. Covers American law of the sea and shipping.

MARKET RESEARCH

See also: CONSUMER SURVEYS;
INTERVIEWING; MARKET STATISTICS;
MARKETING; MOTIVATION (PSYCHOL-
OGY); STATISTICS SOURCES; SURVEY
METHODS

GENERAL WORKS

Breaking Up America: Advertisers and the New Media World. Joseph Turow. The University of Chicago Press. • 1997. $22.50. A social criticism of target marketing, market segmentation, and customized media.

Exploring Marketing Research. William G. Zikmund. South-Western. • 2002. $115.95. Eighth edition.

How Consumers Pick a Hotel: Strategic Segmentation and Target Marketing. Dennis J. Cahill. The Haworth Press, Inc. • 1997. $39.95.

Interactive Marketing: The Future Present. Edward Forrest and Richard Mizerski, editors. McGraw-Hill. • 1995. $47.95. Contains articles on the collection and analysis of interactive marketing data, database management, interactive media, marketing research strategies, and related topics.(NTC Business Book Series).

Marketing Research. Alvin Burns and Ronald Bush. John Wiley and Sons, Inc. • 1998. $115.00. Second edition.

Marketing Research: An Applied Approach. Naresh K. Malhotra and David F. Birks. Prentice Hall. • 2003. $75.00. Second edition.

Marketing Research in a Marketing Environment. William R. Dillion and others. McGraw-Hill. • 1993. $67.50. Third edition.

Marketing Research Process. Len T. Wright and Margaret Crimp. Prentice Hall PTR. • 2000. Fifth edition. Price on application.

Marketing Research That Pays Off: Case Histories of Marketing Research Leading to Success in the Marketplace. Larry Percy, editor. Haworth Press, Inc. • 1997. $49.95.

Super Searchers on Madison Avenue: Top Advertising and Marketing Professionals Share Their Online Research Strategies. Grace A. Villamora. Information Today, Inc. • 2003. $24.95. Provides research "tips, techniques, and resources" from 13 information professionals working in advertising and marketing. (Super Searchers Series).

What's in a Name? Advertising and the Concept of Brands. John P. Jones and Jan S. Slater. M. E. Sharpe, Inc. • 2003. $79.95. Second edition. Covers brand identity and loyalty from the viewpoint of modern marketing theory.

ALMANACS AND YEARBOOKS

Research Alert Yearbook: Vital Facts on Consumer Behavior and Attitudes. EPM Communications, Inc. • Annual. $295.00. Provides summaries of consumer market research from the newsletters *Research Alert, Youth Markets Alert, and Minority Markets Alert.* Includes tables, charts, graphs, and textual summaries for 41 subject categories. Sources include reports, studies, polls, and focus groups.

Research in Marketing: An Annual Compilation of Research. Jagdish N. Sheth, editor. Elsevier. • Annual. Price on application.

BIBLIOGRAPHIES

Data Sources for Business and Market Analysis. John Ganly. Scarecrow Press, Inc. • 1994. $60.00. Fourth edition. Emphasis is on sources of statistics for market research, especially government sources. Relevant directories, periodicals, and research aids are included.

Marketing Power: Your Guide to Successful Research. American Demographics, Inc. •

Quarterly. Issued as a supplement to *American Demographics* and *Marketing Tools.* Describes a wide variety of current market research material issued by various publishers and available from American Demographics, Inc.

CD-ROM DATABASES

FINDEX [cd-rom]. Available from SilverPlatter Information, Inc. • Quarterly. Produced by Cambridge Scientific Abstracts. Serves as the CD-ROM version of *Findex: The Worldwide Directory of Market Research Reports, Studies, and Surveys.*

OECD Statistical Compendium. Organization for Economic Cooperation and Development. • Semiannual. $1,905.00 per year for 1 to 10 users. CD-ROM contains more than 730,000 monthly, quarterly, and annual time series for OECD countries, 1960 to date. Includes fully searchable data on agriculture, food, economic indicators, national accounts, employment, energy, finance, industry, technology, and foreign trade. Results can be displayed in various forms.

Profiles in Business and Management: An International Directory of Scholars and Their Research [CD-ROM]. Harvard Business School Publishing. • Annual. $595.00. Fully searchable CD-ROM version of two-volume printed directory. Contains bibliographic and biographical information for over 5600 business and management experts active in 21 subject areas. Formerly *International Directory of Business and Management Scholars.*

DIRECTORIES

Asian Marketing Information Sourcebook. Euromonitor International. • 2003. $475.00. Lists trade associations, statistical offices, government agencies, special libraries, trade journals, websites, and other sources of business information for the countries of Asia.

Bradford's International Directory of Marketing Research Agencies. Business Research Services, Inc. • Annual. $95.00. Over 1,700 marketing research agencies and management consultants in market research. Formerly *Bradford's Directory of Marketing Research of the United States and the World.*

European Marketing Information Sourcebook. Euromonitor International. • 2003. $475.00. Lists trade associations, statistical offices, government agencies, special libraries, trade journals, websites, and other sources of business information for the countries of Europe.

Findex: The Worldwide Directory of Market Research Reports, Studies, and Surveys. MarketResearch.com. • Annual. $425.00. Provides brief annotations of market research reports and related publications from about 1,000 publishers, arranged by topic. Back of book includes Report Titles by Publisher, Publishers/Distributors Directory, Subject Index, Geography Index, and Company Index. (Formerly published by Cambridge Information Group.).

GreenBook. New York AMA. • Annual. $100.00. Contains information on companies offering focus group facilities, including recruiting, moderating, and transcription services.

GreenBook Worldwide Directory of Marketing Research Companies and Services. New York AMA-Green Book. • Annual. $250.00. Contains information in 300 categories on more than 2,500 market research companies, consultants, field services, computer services, survey research companies, etc. Indexed by specialty, industry, company, computer program, and personnel. Available online. Formerly *Greenbook Worldwide International Directory of Marketing Research Companies and Services.*

Latin American Marketing Information Sourcebook. Euromonitor International. • 2003. $475.00. Lists trade associations, statistical offices, government

agencies, special libraries, trade journals, websites, and other sources of business information for the countries of Latin America.

Medical and Healthcare Marketplace Guide. IDD, Inc. • Annual. $595.00. Two volumes. Provides market survey summaries for about 500 specific product and service categories (volume one: "Research Reports"). Contains profiles of nearly 5,500 pharmaceutical, medical product, and health-care service companies (volume two: "Company Profiles").

MRA Blue Book Research Services Directory. Marketing Research Association. • Covers: over 1,200 marketing research companies and field interviewing services. Entries include: Company name, address, phone, names of executives, services, facilities, special interviewing capabilities.

Research Services Directory: Commercial & Corporate Research Centers. Grey House Publishing. • 2003. $495.00. Ninth edition. Lists more than 8,000 independent commercial research centers and laboratories offering contract or fee-based services. Includes corporate research departments, market research companies, and information brokers.

World Directory of Marketing Information Sources. Available from Gale Cengage Learning. • 2003. $650.00. Fourth edition. Published by Euromonitor. Provides details on approximately 6,000 sources of marketing information, including publications, libraries, associations, market research companies, online databases, and governmental organizations. Coverage is worldwide.

ENCYCLOPEDIAS AND DICTIONARIES

Advertising Age Encyclopedia of Advertising. John McDonough and others, editors. Fitzroy Dearborn Publishers. • 2002. $385.00. Three volumes. Contains 600 entries in alphabetical order covering a wide variety of advertising and market research topics. Includes bibliographies.

Blackwell Encyclopedic Dictionary of Marketing. Dale Littler and Barbara R. Lewis, editors. Blackwell Publishers. • 1997. $38.95. The editors are associated with the Manchester School of Management. Contains definitions of key terms combined with longer articles written by various U. S. and foreign business educators. Includes bibliographies and index. (Blackwell Encyclopedia of Management Series.).

HANDBOOKS AND MANUALS

Do-it-Yourself Marketing Research. George Breen and Albert B. Blankenship. Replica Books. • 1998. $44.95. Third edition.

Finding Market Research on the Web: Best Practices of Professional Researchers. Robert I. Berkman. MarketResearch.com. • 2003. $279.00. Provides tips and techniques for locating useful market research data through the Internet.

Focus Group Kit. David L. Morgan and Richard A. Krueger. Sage Publications, Inc. • 1997. $150.00. Six volumes. Various authors cover the basics of focus group research, including planning, developing questions, moderating, and analyzing results. (Focus Group Kit Series).

Focus Groups: A Practical Guide for Applied Research. Richard A. Krueger and Mary Anne Casey. Sage Publications, Inc. • 2000. $81.95. Third edition. A step-by-step guide to obtaining useful research data from a focus group.

Handbook for Focus Group Research. Thomas L. Greenbaum. Sage Publications, Inc. • 1998. $97.95. Second edition. Includes glossary and index.

Handbook of Marketing. Barton A. Weitz and Robin Wensley, editors. Sage Publications, Inc. • 2003. $99.95. Features summaries of current research in various areas of marketing.

How to Find Market Research on the Web.

MarketResearch.com. • 2001. $239.00. Analyzes and compares the online products of 80 market research publishers. Describes popular Internet search engines and provides information on useful World Wide Web sites.

Market Research Toolbox: A Concise Guide for Beginners. Edward F. McQuarrie. Sage Publications, Inc. • 1996. $35.95.

Marketing Manager's Handbook. Sidney J. Levy and others. Prentice Hall PTR. • 2000. Price on application. Contains 71 chapters by various authors on a wide variety of marketing topics, including market segmentation, market research, international marketing, industrial marketing, survey methods, customer service, advertising, pricing, planning, strategy, and ethics.

Marketing Research Guide. Robert E. Stevens and others. Haworth Press, Inc. • 1997. $79.95. A practical guide to the preparation of a market research report, including worksheets, sample proposals, questionnaires, and an example of a final report. (Marketing Resources Series).

Marketing Research Project Manual. Glen R. Jarboe. South-Western. • 1998. $32.95. Fourth edition. Covers the methodology of market research surveys. (Marketing Series).

The New Direct Marketing: How to Implement a Profit-Driven Database Marketing Strategy. McGraw-Hill. • 1999. $79.95. Third edition. Discusses the construction, analysis, practical use, and evaluation of direct marketing databases containing primary and/or secondary data.

Survey Research Handbook: Guidelines and Strategies for Conducting a Survey. Pamela L. Alreck and Robert B. Settle. McGraw-Hill. • 1994. $50.00. Second edition. Consists of four major parts: 1. Planning and Designing the Survey, 2. Developing Survey Instruments, 3. Collecting and Processing Data, 4. Interpreting and Reporting Results. Includes a glossary and index. (Marketing Series).

INTERNET DATABASES

Business 2.0 Web Guide to the Best Business Links. Business 2.0 Media Inc. Phone: (415)293-4800 E-mail: support@business2.com • URL: http:// www.business2.com/webguide • Web site presents an extensive, searchable directory of links to "the best, most informative, and authoritative web pages." Twenty main categories cover business, finance, career, company information, people, and technology topics, with thousands of subtopics, all linking to Web sites recommended by experienced business researchers. Fees: Free.

Factiva. Dow Jones Reuters Business Interactive, LLC. Phone: 800-369-7466 or (609)452-1511 Fax: (609)520-5770 E-mail: solutions@factiva.com • URL: http://www.factiva.com • Fee-based Web site provides "global news and business information through Web sites and content integration solutions." Includes Dow Jones and Reuters newswires, The Wall Street Journal, and more than 7,000 other sources of current news, historical articles, market research reports, and investment analysis. Content includes 96 major U. S. newspapers, 900 non-English sources, trade publications, media transcripts, country profiles, news photos, etc.

InSite 2. Intelligence Data/Thomson Financial. Phone: 800-654-0393 or (617)856-1890 Fax: (617)737-3182 E-mail: intelligence.data@tfn.com • URL: http://www.insite2.gale.com/ • Fee-based Web site consolidates information in a "Base Pack" consisting of Business InSite, Market InSite, and Company InSite. Optional databases are Consumer InSite, Health and Wellness InSite, Newsletter InSite, and Computer InSite. Includes fulltext content from more than 2,500 trade publications, journals, newsletters, newspapers, analyst reports, and other sources. Continuous updating. Formerly produced by The Gale Group.

Intelligence Data. Thomson Financial. Phone: 800-654-0393 Fax: (617)824-2477 • URL: http://www.intelligencedata.com • Fee-based Web site provides a wide variety of information relating to competitive intelligence, strategic planning, business development, mergers, acquisitions, sales, and marketing. "Intelliscope" feature offers searching of other Thomson units, such as Investext, MarkIntel, InSite 2, and Industry Insider. Weekly updating.

ONLINE DATABASES

Frost & Sullivan Market Research Reports. Frost & Sullivan. • Contains full text of Frost & Sullivan market research reports on various industries and products. Each report includes a five-year forecast.

Market Research Monitor. Euromonitor International. • Contains full-text reports online from *Market Research Europe, Market Research Great Britain, Market Research International,* and *Retail Monitor International.* Time period is 1995 to date, with monthly updates. Inquire as to online cost and availability.

Market Research Reports. MarketResearch.com. • Provides online full text of market research reports produced by FIND/SVP, Packaged Facts, Specialists in Business Information and others. Contains market data for a wide variety of industries, products, and services, including market size, forecasts, trends, structure, and opportunities. Inquire as to online cost and availability.

MarkIntel. Thomson Financial. • Provides the current full text online of more than 50,000 market research reports covering 54 industries, from 85 leading research firms worldwide. Reports include extensive forecasts and market analysis. Inquire as to online cost and availability.

National Consumer Survey. Simmons Market Research Bureau. • Market and media survey data relating to the American consumer. Inquire as to online cost and availability.

PROMT: Predicasts Overview of Markets and Technology. Gale Cengage Learning. • Companies, products, applied technologies and markets. U.S. and international literature coverage, 1972 to date. Inquire as to online cost and availability. Provides abstracts from more than 1,600 publications. Weekly updates.

PERIODICALS AND NEWSLETTERS

American Demographics: Consumer Trends for Business Leaders. Media Central. • Monthly. $58.00 per year.

Brandweek: The Newsweekly of Marketing Communications. VNU Business Media. • 46 times a year. $149.00 per year. Includes articles and case studies on mass marketing and mass media. Formerly *Adweek's Marketing Week.*

Database Marketer. SIMBA Information. • Monthly. $329.00 per year.

The Information Advisor: Tips and Techniques for Smart Information Users. MarketResearch.com. • Monthly. $159.00 per year. Newsletter. Evaluates and discusses online, CD-ROM, and published sources of business, financial, and market research information.

Journal of Consumer Research; An Interdisciplinary Quarterly. The University of Chicago Press, Journals Div. • Quarterly. Members, $62.00 per year; non-members, $145.00 per year; institutions, $152.00 per year; students, $25.00. Covers various aspects of consumer behavior.

Journal of Marketing Research. American Marketing Association. • Quarterly. Members, $45.00 per year; non-members, $80.00 per year; institutions, $200.00 per year. Provides analysis of marketing research theory and practice.

Marketing Research: A Magazine of Management and Applications. American Marketing Association. • Quarterly. Members, $45.00 per year; non-

members, $70.00 per year; institutions, $120.00 per year.

Marketing to the Emerging Minorities. EPM Communications, Inc. • Monthly. $295.00 per year. Newsletter on market research relating to African American, Asian American, and U. S. Hispanic populations.

Research Alert: A Bi-Weekly Report of Consumer Marketing Studies. EPM Communications, Inc. • Biweekly. $369.00 per year. Newsletter. Provides descriptions (abstracts) of new, consumer market research reports from private, government, and academic sources. Includes sample charts and tables.

Youth Markets Alert. EPM Communications Inc. • Description: Features information and research results related to young consumers from elementary school through high school.

STATISTICS SOURCES

DMA Statistical Fact Book. Direct Marketing Association. Library and Resource Center. • Annual. Members, $79.95; non-members, $104.95. Provides data in five sections covering direct response advertising, media, mailing lists, market applications, and "Practical Management Information." Includes material on interactive/online marketing. (Cover title: *Direct Marketing Association's Statistical Fact Book.*).

TRADE/PROFESSIONAL ASSOCIATIONS

American Marketing Association. 311 S Wacker Dr., Ste. 5800, Chicago, IL 60606. Phone: 800-262-1150 or (312)542-9000 Fax: (312)542-9001 E-mail: info@ama.org • URL: http://www.marketingpower.com • Serves as a professional society of marketing and market research executives, sales and promotion managers, advertising specialists, academics, and others interested in marketing. Fosters research; sponsors seminars, conferences, and student marketing clubs; provides educational placement service and doctoral consortium.

Marketing Research Association. 110 National Dr., 2nd Fl., PO Box 230, Glastonbury, CT 06033-1212. Phone: (860)682-1000 Fax: (860)682-1010 E-mail: larry.brownell@mra-net.org • URL: http://www.mra-net.org • Companies and individuals involved in any area of opinion and marketing research, such as data collection, research, or as an end-user.

Sales and Marketing Executives International. PO Box 1390, Sumas, WA 98295-1390. Phone: 800-999-1414 or (312)893-0751 Fax: (604)855-0165 E-mail: smei@smei.org • URL: http://www.smei.org • Formerly Sales and Marketing Executives.

OTHER SOURCES

The Information Catalog. MarketResearch.com. • Bimonthly. Free. Mainly a catalog of market research reports from various publishers, but also includes business and marketing reference sources. Includes keyword title index. Formerly *The Information Catalog: Marketing Intelligence Studies, Competitor Reports, Business and Marketing Sources.*

MARKET STATISTICS

See also: BUSINESS STATISTICS; MARKET RESEARCH; MARKETING; PURCHASING POWER; STATISTICS SOURCES

GENERAL WORKS

Global Economic Prospects 2004. The World Bank Group. • 2003. $38.00. "..offers an in-depth analysis of the economic prospects of developing countries.." Emphasis is on the impact of recessions and financial crises. Regional statistical data is included.

ALMANACS AND YEARBOOKS

World Development Report 2004. The World Bank Group. • Annual. $26.00. Covers history, condi-

---

tions, and trends relating to economic globalization and localization. Includes selected data from *World Development Indicators* for 132 countries or economies. Key indicators are provided for 78 additional countries or economies.

BIBLIOGRAPHIES

Data Sources for Business and Market Analysis. John Ganly. Scarecrow Press, Inc. • 1994. $60.00. Fourth edition. Emphasis is on sources of statistics for market research, especially government sources. Relevant directories, periodicals, and research aids are included.

Global Data Locator. George T. Kurian. Bernan Associates. • 1997. $89.00. Provides detailed descriptions of international statistical sourcebooks and electronic databases. Covers a wide variety of trade, economic, and demographic topics.

Statistics Sources: A Subject Guide to Data on Industrial, Business, Social, Educational, Financial and Other Topics for the U. S. and Selected Foreign Countries. Gale Cengage Learning. • 2003. $515. 00. 27th edition. Two volumes. Lists sources of statistical information for more than 20,000 topics.

World Directory of Non-Official Statistical Sources. Gale Group, Inc. • 2002. $650.00. Fourth edition. Provides detailed descriptions of more than 4,000 regularly published, non-governmental statistics sources. Includes surveys, studies, market research reports, trade journals, databank compilations, and other print sources. Coverage is international, with four indexes.

CD-ROM DATABASES

Sourcebook America. Gale Cengage Learning. • Annual. $995.00. Produced by CACI Marketing Systems. A combination on CD-ROM of *The Sourcebook of ZIP Code Demographics* and *The Sourcebook of County Demographics.* Provides detailed population and socio-economic data (about 75 items) for each of 3,141 U. S. counties and approximately 30,000 ZIP codes, plus states, metropolitan areas, and media market areas. Includes forecasts to the year 2004.

Sourcebooks America CD-ROM. CACI Marketing Systems. • Annual. $1,250.00. Provides the CD-ROM version of *The Sourcebook of ZIP Code Demographics: Census Edition* and *The Sourcebook of County Demographics: Census Edition.*

World Consumer Markets. Gale Cengage Learning. • Annual. $2,500.00. Pblished by Euromonitor. Provides five- year historical data, current data, and forecasts, on CD-ROM for 330 consumer products in 55 countries. Market data is presented in a standardized format for each country.

World Development Report [CD-ROM]. The World Bank, Office of the Publisher. • Annual. CD-ROM includes the current edition of *World Development Report* and 21 previous editions.

World Marketing Data and Statistics on CD-ROM. Gale Cengage Learning. • Annual. $1,750.00. Published by Euromonitor. Provides demographic, marketing, socioeconomic, and political data on CD-ROM for each of 209 countries.

World Marketing Forecasts on CD-ROM. Gale Cengage Learning. • Annual. $2,500.00. Produced by Euromonitor. Provides detailed forecast data for the years to 2012 on CD-ROM for 54 countries in all parts of the world. Covers a wide range of social, demographic, economic, and market factors. Includes specific forecasts for many kinds of consumer products.

DIRECTORIES

Editor and Publisher Market Guide. Editor and Publisher Co., Inc. • Annual. $150.00. More than 1,700 newspaper markets in the United States and Canada.

Major Performance Rankings. Available from Gale Cengage Learning. • 2003. $1,190.00. Second

edition. Published by Euromonitor. Ranks 2,500 leading consumer product companies worldwide by various kinds of business and financial data, such as sales, profit, and market share. Includes international, regional, and country rankings.

Marketing Know-How: Your Guide to the Best Marketing Tools and Sources. Primedia Business Magazines and Media. • 1996. $49.95. Describes more than 700 public and private sources of consumer marketing data. Also discusses market trends and provides information on such marketing techniques as cluster analysis, focus groups, and geodemographic analysis.

HANDBOOKS AND MANUALS

Finding Statistics Online: How to Locate the Elusive Numbers You Need. Paula Berinstein. Information Today, Inc. • 1998. $29.95. Provides advice on efficient searching when looking for statistical data on the World Wide Web or from commercial online services and database producers. (CyberAge Books.).

ONLINE DATABASES

F & S Index. Gale Cengage Learning. • Contains about four million citations to worldwide business, financial, and industrial or consumer product literature appearing from 1972 to date. Weekly updates. Inquire as to online cost and availability.

Industry Insider. Thomson Financial. • Contains full-text online industry research reports from more than 200 leading trade associations, covering 50 specific industries. Reports include extensive statistics and market research data. Inquire as to online cost and availability.

Market Share Reporter (MSR) [online]. Gale Cengage Learning. • Provides online market share data for single companies, products, and services, covering all industries. Sources include various publications, trade journals, associations, government agencies, corporate reports, investment research reports, etc. Time period is 1991 to date, with annual updates. Inquire as to online cost and availability.

PROMT: Predicasts Overview of Markets and Technology. Gale Cengage Learning. • Companies, products, applied technologies and markets. U.S. and international literature coverage, 1972 to date. Inquire as to online cost and availability. Provides abstracts from more than 1,600 publications. Weekly updates.

Tablebase. Gale Cengage Learning. • Provides online numerical tabular data from a wide variety of business, organization, and government sources, including about 1,000 trade journals. Includes industry and individual company statistics relating to products, market share, sales forecasts, production, exports, market trends, etc. Time span is 1997 to date. Weekly updates. Inquire as to online cost and availability. (Also available in a CD-ROM version.).

PERIODICALS AND NEWSLETTERS

Regional Economics and Markets: A Quarterly Analysis from the Conference Board. The Conference Board. • Quarterly. Members, $145.00 per year; non-members, $295.00 per year. Summarizes economic trends and prospects for nine geographic regions of the U. S. Provides data on key predictive indexes, including employment, housing permits, retail sales, consumer confidence, and help-wanted advertising. Charts and graphs are included.

STATISTICS SOURCES

American Business Climate and Economic Profiles. Priscilla C. Geahigan. Gale Cengage Learning. • 1993. $170.00. Provides business, industrial, demographic, and economic figures for all states and 300 metropolitan areas. Includes production, taxation, population, growth rates, labor force data, incomes, total sales, etc.

Consumer International. Available from Gale Cengage Learning. • Annual. $1,290.00. Published by Euromonitor. Contains extensive consumer market, economic, and demographic data for 25 major, non-European countries, including the U. S. and Canada. Includes consumer market size (volume and value) for 150 product types in 14 categories (food, clothing, automobiles, cosmetics, appliances, etc.).

Consumer Power: How Americans Spend. Margaret Ambry. McGraw-Hill. • 1992. $27.50. Contains detailed statistics on consumer income and spending. Nine major categories of products and services are covered, with spending data and dollar size of market for each item.

Consumer USA. Available from Gale Cengage Learning. • Annual. $1,090.00. Fifth edition. Published by Euromonitor. Provides demographic and consumer market data for the United States. Forecasts to the year 2005.

County and City Data Book, a Statistical Abstract Supplement. U.S. Bureau of the Census. Available from U.S. Government Printing Office. • 1994. $60. 00.

Current Population Reports: Household Economic Studies, Series P-70. Available from U. S. Government Printing Office. • Irregular. $21.00 per year. Issued by the U.S. Bureau of the Census (http://www.census.gov). Each issue covers a special topic relating to household socioeconomic characteristics.

Demographics USA: County Edition. Trade Dimensions. • Annual. $435.00. Contains 200 statistical series for each of 3,000 counties. Includes population, household income, employment, retail sales, and consumer expenditures. Also provides Effective Buying Income, Buying Power Index, and data summaries by Metro Market, Media Market, and State. (CD-ROM version is available.).

Demographics USA: ZIP Edition. Trade Dimensions. • Annual. $435.00. Contains 50 statistical series for each of 40,000 ZIP codes. Includes population, household income, employment, retail sales, and consumer expenditures. Also provides Effective Buying Income, Business Characteristics, and data summaries by state, region, and the first three digits of ZIP codes. (CD-ROM version is available.).

European Marketing Data and Statistics. Available from Gale Cengage Learning. • Annual. $530.00. Published by Euromonitor. Presents essential marketing data, including demographics and consumer expenditure patterns, for 31 European countries.

European Marketing Forecasts. Available from Gale Cengage Learning. • Annual. $1,250.00. Published by Euromonitor. Contains demographic, economic, and market forecasts for the countries of Europe to the year 2010. Forecasts include market-size data for 15 consumer product sectors (food, clothing, automobiles, consumer electronics, etc.).

Gale Country and World Rankings Reporter. Gale Cengage Learning. • 1997. $160.00. Second edition. Provides about 3,000 statistical ranking tables and charts covering more than 235 nations. Sources include the United Nations and various government publications.

Gale State Rankings Reporter. Gale Cengage Learning. • 1996. $130.00. Second edition Provides 3,000 ranked lists of states under 35 subject headings. Sources are newspapers, periodicals, books, research institute publications, and government publications.

Geographic Reference Report: Annual Report of Costs, Wages, Salaries, and Human Resource Statistics for the United States and Canada. ERI (Economic Research Institute). • Annual. $389.00. Provides demographic and other data for each of 298 North American metropolian areas, including local salaries, wage differentials, cost-of-living, housing costs, income taxation, employment, unemployment, population, major employers, crime rates, weather, etc.

Household Spending: Who Spends How Much On What. New Strategist Publications, Inc. • 1999. $94. 95. Fifth edition. Gives facts about the buying habits of U. S. consumers according to income, age, household type, and household size. Includes spending data for about 1,000 products and services.

International Marketing Data and Statistics. Available from Gale Cengage Learning. • Annual. $530. 00. Published by Euromonitor. Contains statistics on population, economic factors, energy, consumer expenditures, prices, and other items affecting marketing in 158 countries of the world.

International Marketing Forecasts. Available from Gale Cengage Learning. • Annual. $1,250.00. Published by Euromonitor. Contains demographic, economic, and market forecasts to the year 2013 for major, non-European countries, including the U. S. and Canada. Forecasts include market-size data for 15 consumer product sectors, such as food, clothing, and automobiles.

Market Share Reporter: An Annual Compilation of Reported Market Share Data on Companies, Products, and Services. Gale Cengage Learning. • Annual. $285.00. Contains summaries of market share reports. Actual data is given, with many charts and graphs. List more than 2,000 entries.

Moving and Relocation Sourcebook and Directory: Reference Guide to the 120 Largest Metropolitan Areas in the United States. Omnigraphics, Inc. • Annual. $225.00 Provides extensive statistical and other descriptive data for the 120 largest metropolitan areas in the U. S. Includes maps and a discussion of factors to be considered when relocating.

Sales and Marketing Management Survey of Buying Power. VNU Business Media. • Annual. $150.00.

The Sourcebook of ZIP Code Demographics. Available from Gale Cengage Learning. • Annual. $495. 00. Published by ESRI Business Information Systems. Presents detailed statistical profiles of every ZIP code in America. Each profile contains data on more than 70 variables with 2003 updates and 2008 forecasts.

Sourcebook of Zip Code Demographics. ESRI Business Information Solutions. • 2002. $495.00. 16th edition. Provides data on 75 demographic and socioeconomic characteristics for each ZIP code in the U. S.

SRDS Lifestyle Market Analyst. SRDS. • Annual. $440.00. Published in conjunction with EQUIFAX. Provides extensive lifestyle data on interests, activities, and hobbies within specific geographic and demographic markets. Formerly *Lifestyle Market Analyst.*

Statistical Handbook on Consumption and Wealth in the United States. Greenwood Publishing Group, Inc. • 1999. $69.95. Provides more than 400 graphs, tables, and charts dealing with basic income levels, income inequalities, spending patterns, taxation, subsidies, etc. (Statistical Handbook Series).

U. S. Market Trends and Forecasts. Gale Cengage Learning. • 2002. $325.00. Third edition. Provides graphic representation of market statistics by means of pie charts and tables for each of 30 major industries and 400 market segments. Includes market forecasts and historical overviews.

The World Bank Atlas. World Bank Group. • Annual. $10.00. Contains "color maps, charts, and graphs representing the main social, economic, and environmental indicators for 209 countries and territories" (publisher).

World Consumer Expenditure Patterns. Euromonitor International. • 2003. $1,190.00. Contains detailed consumer expenditure data for 71 countries.

Covers 70 specific categories within the areas of food, beverages, tobacco, clothing, housing, appliances, health, transportation, leisure, etc. Provides 10 years of data and includes consumer price indexes.

World Consumer Income and Expenditure Patterns. Available from Gale Cengage Learning. • Annual. $1,090.00. Two volumes. Published by Euromonitor. Provides data for countries worldwide on consumer income, earning power, spending patterns, and savings. Expenditures are detailed for product or service categories.

World Consumer Income Patterns. Euromonitor International. • 2003. $1,190.00. Provides detailed data on household income in 71 countries (10-year statistics). Covers income by age, sex, and level of education, with further data on savings, earnings, and average taxes.

World Consumer Lifestyles Databook: Key Trends. Euromonitor International. • 2003. $1,190.00. Second edition. Covers 71 countries. Presents statistical data relating to such consumer lifestyle characteristics as family size, household income, family expenditures, home ownership, shopping habits, eating habits, drinking habits, savings, transportation, travel, health characteristics, and education.

World Development Indicators. The World Bank Group. • Annual. $60.00. Provides data and information on the people, economy, environment, and markets of 148 countries. Emphasis is on statistics relating to major development issues.

The World Economic Factbook. Available from Gale Cengage Learning. • Annual. $530.00. Published by Euromonitor. Presents key economic facts and figures for each of 200 countries, including details of chief industries, export-import trade, currency, political risk, household expenditures, and the economic situation in general.

World Economic Prospects: A Planner's Guide to International Market Conditions. Available from Gale Cengage Learning. • 2002. $490.00. Second edition. Published by Euromonitor. Ranks countries by specific economic characteristics, such as gross domestic product (GDP) per capita and short term growth prospects. Discusses the economic situation, prospects, and market potential of each of the countries.

World Market Share Reporter: A Compilation of Reported World Market Share Data and Rankngs on Companies, Products, and Services. Gale Cengage Learning. • 2001. $340.00. Fifth edition. Provides market share data for companies, products, and industries in countries or regions other than North America and Mexico.

OTHER SOURCES

Commercial Atlas and Marketing Guide. Rand McNally. • Annual. $395.00. Includes maps and marketing data: population, transportation, communication, and local area business statistics. Provides information on more than 128,000 U.S. locations. (Commercial Atlas and Marketing Guide series).

Market Share Tracker. Euromonitor International. • 2003. $1,190.00. Second edition. Contains market share rankings of more than 1,800 consumer product companies in 30 countries. Covers 16 kinds of products within "Drinks," "Household and Personal Care," and "Foods." Includes brand shares for leading brands. (*Global Market Share Planner*, vol. 1.).

Zip Code Mapbook of Metropolitan Areas. ESRI Business Information Solutions. • 1992. $195.00. Second edition. Contains Zip Code two-color maps of 326 metropolitan areas. Includes summary statistical profiles of each area: population characteristics, employment, housing, and income.

MARKET SURVEYS

See: CONSUMER SURVEYS; MARKET RESEARCH; SURVEY METHODS

MARKET TESTING OF NEW PRODUCTS

See: CONSUMER SURVEYS; MARKET RESEARCH

MARKETING

See also: CHAIN STORES; DISTRIBUTION; MARKET RESEARCH; MARKET STATISTICS; SALESMEN AND SALESMANSHIP

GENERAL WORKS

Cases in Marketing Management. Kenneth L. Bernhardt and Thomas C. Kinnear. McGraw-Hill. • 1997. Ninth edition. Price on application.

Cases in Strategic Marketing: An Integrated Approach. Strickland. McGraw-Hill. • 2000. $41. 25. 12th edition.

Cyberquake: How the Internet will Erase Profits, Topple Market Leaders, and Shatter Business Models. Michael Sullivan-Trainor. John Wiley and Sons, Inc. • 1997. $26.95. Predicts that the Internet will cause "an overwhelming shift in control of the worldwide marketplace" in the early 21st century. (Business Technology Series).

Future-Driven Library Marketing. Darlene E. Weingand. American Library Association. • 1998. $25.00. The author discusses progressive marketing strategies for libraries. An annotated bibliography is included.

Gonzo Marketing: Winning Through Worst Practices. Christopher Locke. John Wiley and Sons, Inc. • 2001. $29.95. An iconoclastic, entertaining view of e-commerce advertising and marketing (banners, pop-ups, spam, etc.). States the obvious: most Web advertising is more annoying than effective.

International Marketing. Philip R. Cateora and John Graham. McGraw-Hill. • 2001. $94.69. 11th edition. (Marketing Series).

Marketing. Damico Zikmund. Cengage Learning. • 2000. $65.00 Seventh edition. (SWC-General Business Series).

Marketing. Bruce J. Walker. McGraw-Hill. • 2003. 13th edition. Price on application.

Marketing: Contemporary Concepts and Practices. William F. Schoell. Allyn and Bacon, Inc. • 1995. $110.00. Sixth edition.

Marketing Management: Knowledge and Skills. J. Paul Peter and James H. Donnelly. McGraw-Hill. • 2003. $120.70 Seventh edition. (Marketing Series).

Marketing Management: Text and Cases. Robert Dolan. McGraw Hill. • 2001. $108.75. (Marketing Series).

Marketing on the Internet: Multimedia Strategies for the World Wide Web. Jill Ellsworth and Matthew Ellsworth. John Wiley and Sons, Inc. • 1996. $29. 99. Second expanded revised edition.

Marketing Planning: A Step-by-Step Guide. James W. Taylor. Prentice Hall PTR. • 1996. $49.95.

Marketing: Principles and Perspectives. William Bearden and others. McGraw-Hill. • 2004. Fourth edition. Price on application. (Marketing Series).

Marketing Strategy. Orville C. Walker and others. McGraw Hill. • 1998. $73.13. Third edition.

A Preface to Marketing Management. J. Paul Peter and James H. Donnelly. McGraw-Hill. • 2002. $57.

81. Ninth edition. (Marketing Series).

Reinventing the Bazaar: A Natural History of Markets. John McMillan. W. W. Norton & Co., Inc. • 2002. $25.05. Covers marketing from early times to modern times. Takes the viewpoint that markets are desirable, occur naturally, and require intelligent regulation.

Strategic Market Management. David A. Aaker. John Wiley and Sons, Inc. • 2001. $57.95. Sixth edition.

Strategic Marketing. David W. Cravens and Nigel Percy. McGraw-Hill. • 2002. $110.00. Seventh edition. (Marketing Series).

Strategic Marketing Problems: Cases and Comments. Roger A. Kerin and Robert A. Peterson. Prentice Hall PTR. • 2003. $113.33. 10th edition.

ABSTRACTS AND INDEXES

Business Periodicals Index. H. W. Wilson Co. • 11 times a year. Quarterly and annual cumulations. Price varies.

NTIS Alerts: Business & Economics. National Technical Information Service. • Text: Semimonthly. $210.00 per year.

What's New in Advertising and Marketing. Special Libraries Association, Advertising and Marketing Div. • Quarterly. Non-profit organizations, $20.00 per year; corporations, $30.00 per year. Lists and briefly describes a wide variety of free or inexpensive material relating to advertising, marketing, and media.

ALMANACS AND YEARBOOKS

Major Marketing Campaigns Annual. Gale Cengage Learning. • 1999. $160.00. Describes in detail "100 major marketing initiatives of the previous calendar year." Includes illustrations.

BIBLIOGRAPHIES

Marketing Information Revolution. Robert C. Blattberg, editor. McGraw-Hill. • 1993. $39.95. Third edition. Includes a wide variety of sources for specific kinds of marketing.

CD-ROM DATABASES

WILSONDISC: Wilson Business Abstracts. H. W. Wilson Co. • Monthly. Includes unlimited online access to *Wilson Business Abstracts* through WILSONLINE. Provides CD-ROM "cover-to-cover" abstracting and indexing of over 600 prominent business periodicals. Indexing is from 1982, abstracting from 1990. (*Business Periodicals Index* without abstracts is available on CD-ROM at $1,495 per year.).

DIRECTORIES

AMA International Member and Marketing Services Guide. American Marketing Association. • Annual. $150.00. Lists professional members of the American Marketing Association. Also contains information on providers of marketing support services and products, including software, communications, direct marketing, promotion, research, and consulting companies. Includes geographical and alphabetical indexes. Formerly *Marketing Yellow Pages and AMA International Membership Directory.*

Incentive's Buyer's Guide. VNU Business Media. • Publication includes: List of 1,500 merchandise suppliers, hotels, cruise lines, airlines, and other companies that provide services to companies offering incentive travel and merchandise programs. Entries include: Company name, address, phone, name of sales contact, description of facilities (for hotels).

The PROMO 100 Promotion Agency Ranking. PROMO Magazine. • Covers: Ranking of the top 100 U.S. Promotion agencies. Entries include: Name, address, phone, financial data, client lists,

rate of growth, name of CEO, and description of product/service.

ENCYCLOPEDIAS AND DICTIONARIES

Blackwell Encyclopedic Dictionary of Marketing. Dale Littler and Barbara R. Lewis, editors. Blackwell Publishers. • 1997. $38.95. The editors are associated with the Manchester School of Management. Contains definitions of key terms combined with longer articles written by various U. S. and foreign business educators. Includes bibliographies and index. (Blackwell Encyclopedia of Management Series.).

Dictionary of Marketing and Advertising. Jerry M. Rosenberg. John Wiley and Sons, Inc. • 1995. $145.00. (Business Dictionary Series).

Dictionary of Marketing Communications. Norman A. P. Govoni. Sage Publications, Inc. • 2003. $69.95. Contains more than 4,000 concise definitions of terms relating to advertising, sales promotion, public relations, direct marketing, and selling.

Dictionary of Marketing Terms. Betsy-Ann Toffler. Barron's Educational Series, Inc. • 2000. $13.95. Third edition. (Business Dictionaries Series).

Encyclopedia of Business. Gale Cengage Learning. • 2000. $425.00. Second edition. Two volumes. Contains more than 700 signed articles covering major business disciplines and concepts. International in scope. (Encyclopedia of Business Series).

Encyclopedia of Business and Finance. Burton Kaliski, editor. Available from Gale Cengage Learning. • 2001. $275.00. Two volumes. Published by Macmillan Reference USA. Contains articles by various contributors on accounting, business administration, banking, finance, management information systems, and marketing.

Encyclopedia of Major Marketing Campaigns. Gale Cengage Learning. • 2000. $285.00. Covers 500 major marketing and advertising campaigns "of the 20th century." Examines historical context, target market, expectations, competition, strategy, development, and outcomes. Includes illustrations.

Field Guide to Marketing: A Glossary to Essential Tools and Concepts for Today's Manager. McGraw-Hill. • 1993. $29.95. Defines fundamental terms.

HANDBOOKS AND MANUALS

Creating Winning Marketing Plans: What Today's Managers Must Do to Succeed. Sidney J. Levy, editor. Dartnell Corp. • 1996. $39.95. Consists of articles by 25 "Top Experts." Covers marketing objectives, customer needs, market segmentation, database marketing, consumer scanning, and other topics.

Handbook of Marketing. Barton A. Weitz and Robin Wensley, editors. Sage Publications, Inc. • 2003. $99.95. Features summaries of current research in various areas of marketing.

Hispanic Market Handbook. Gale Cengage Learning. • 1995. $95.00. Provides advice on marketing consumer items to Hispanic Americans. Includes case studies and demographic profiles. (Professional Library).

How to Write a Successful Marketing Plan: A Disciplined and Comprehensive Approach. Roman G. Hiebing. Prentice Hall PTR. • 1999. $79.95. Second edition. The four main sections cover marketing background, the marketing plan, plan execution, and evaluation. Includes worksheets and formats.

Marketer's Guide to E-Commerce: Everything You Need to Know to Successfully Sell, Promote, and Market Your Business, Product, or Service Online. Arthur Bell and Vincent Leger. McGraw-Hill. • 2001. $39.95. Covers website marketing strategies, including guidelines and examples. (NTC Business Books Series).

Marketing Manager's Handbook. Sidney J. Levy

and others. Prentice Hall PTR. • 2000. Price on application. Contains 71 chapters by various authors on a wide variety of marketing topics, including market segmentation, market research, international marketing, industrial marketing, survey methods, customer service, advertising, pricing, planning, strategy, and ethics.

Marketing Planning Guide. Robert E. Stevens and others. Haworth Press, Inc. • 1997. $49.95. Second edition. Covers market segmentation, product positioning, and other marketing planning topics.

Marketing Plans: How to Prepare Them, How to Use Them. Malcolm H. McDonald. Elsevier. • 2002. $49.99. Fifth edition.

Marketing Without Advertising. Michael Phillips and Salli Rasberry. Nolo. • 2001. $24.00. Fourth edition. How to market a small business economically.

Mastering the Art of Marketing Professional Services: A Step-by-Step Best Practices Guide. Allan S. Boress and Michael G. Cummings. American Institute of Certified Public Accountants. • 2002. $74.00. Discusses recommended marketing practices for accounting firms, including networking, advertising, press release writing, public speaking, seminar planning, and use of trade shows.

Online Marketing Handbook: How to Promote, Advertise and Sell, Your Products and Services on the Internet. Daniel S. Janal. John Wiley and Sons, Inc. • 1999. $29.95. Revised edition. Provides step-by-step instructions for utilizing online publicity, advertising, and sales promotion. Contains chapters on interactive marketing, online crisis communication, and Web home page promotion, with numerous examples and checklists. (Business Technology Series).

Promotional Marketing. Entrepreneur Media, Inc. • Looseleaf. $59.50. A practical guide to sales promotion and marketing for small businesses. (Start-Up Business Guide No. E1111.).

INTERNET DATABASES

EBSCO Information Services. Ebsco Publishing. Phone: 800-653-2726 or (978)356-6500 Fax: (978)356-6565 E-mail: ep@epnet.com • URL: http://www.epnet.com • Fee-based Web site providing Internet access to a wide variety of databases, including business-related material. Full text is available for many periodical titles, with daily updates. Fees: Apply.

InSite 2. Intelligence Data/Thomson Financial. Phone: 800-654-0393 or (617)856-1890 Fax: (617)737-3182 E-mail: intelligence.data@tfn.com • URL: http://www.insite2.gale.com/ • Fee-based Web site consolidates information in a "Base Pack" consisting of Business InSite, Market InSite, and Company InSite. Optional databases are Consumer InSite, Health and Wellness InSite, Newsletter InSite, and Computer InSite. Includes fulltext content from more than 2,500 trade publications, journals, newsletters, newspapers, analyst reports, and other sources. Continuous updating. Formerly produced by The Gale Group.

ProQuest Direct. ProQuest Inc. Phone: 800-889-3358 or (734)761-4700 Fax: (734)662-4554 • URL: http://proquest.com • Fee-based Web site providing Internet access to more than 3,000 periodicals, newspapers, and other publications. Many items are available full-text, with daily updates. Includes extensive corporate and financial information. Fees: Apply.

ONLINE DATABASES

Business and Industry. Gale Cengage Learning. • Contains online citations, abstracts, and selected fulltext from more than 1,000 trade journals, newspapers, and other publications. Provides general coverage of both manufacturing and service industries, including marketing, production, industry trends, key events, and information on specific companies. Time span is 1994 to date. Daily updates. Inquire as to online cost and availability. (Also available in a CD-ROM version.).

Management Contents. Gale Cengage Learning. • Covers a wide range of management, financial, marketing, personnel, and administrative topics. About 150 leading business journals are indexed and abstracted from 1974 to date, with monthly updating. Inquire as to online cost and availability.

Marketing and Advertising Reference Service (MARS). Gale Cengage Learning. • Provides abstracts of literature relating to consumer marketing and advertising, including all forms of advertising media. Time period is 1984 to date. Daily updates. Inquire as to online cost and availability.

Wilson Business Abstracts Online. H. W. Wilson Co. • Indexes and abstracts 600 major business periodicals, plus the *Wall Street Journal* and the business section of the *New York Times.* Indexing is from 1982, abstracting from 1990, with the two newspapers included from 1993. Updated weekly. Inquire as to online cost and availability. (*Business Periodicals Index* without abstracts is also available online.).

PERIODICALS AND NEWSLETTERS

Adweek Magazines' Technology Marketing. VNU Business Media. • Monthly. $55.00 per year. Edited for marketing executives in high technology industries. Covers both advertising and marketing. Formerly *MC Technology Marketing Intelligence.*

Database Marketer. SIMBA Information. • Monthly. $329.00 per year.

Entertainment Marketing Letter. EPM Communications Inc. • Description: Reports on techniques used in the marketing of films, music, videos, television, radio, and cable features. Covers tie-in campaigns, sponsorship, in-theatre advertising, and interactive telephone promotions.

iMarketing News: The Newspaper of E-Business and Internet Marketing. Courtenay Communications. • Monthly. Controlled circulation.

Incentive: Managing and Marketing Through Motivation. VNU Business Media. • Monthly. $59.00 per year.

Interactive Marketing and P R News: News and Practical Advice on Using Interactive Advertising and Marketing to Sell Your Products. PBI Media, LLC. • Biweekly. $495.00 per year. Newsletter. Provides information and guidance on merchandising via CD-ROM ("multimedia catalogs"), the Internet, and interactive TV. Topics include "cybermoney", addresses for e-mail marketing, "virtual malls," and other interactive subjects. Formerly *Interactive Marketing News.*

Internet Marketing Report: News and Advice to Help Companies Harness the Power of the Internet to Achieve Business Objectives. Progressive Business Publications. • Semimonthly. $299.00 per year. Newsletter. Covers Internet marketing strategy, site traffic, success stories, technology, cost control, and other Web site advertising and marketing topics.

Journal of Global Marketing. Haworth Press, Inc. • Quarterly. $460.00 per year. Includes print and online editions.

Journal of International Consumer Marketing. Haworth Press, Inc. • Quarterly. Individuals, $80.00 per year; institutions, $150.00 per year.

Journal of International Marketing. American Marketing Association. • Members $45.00; nonmembers, $80.00 per year institutions, $150.00 per year.

Journal of Internet Commerce. Haworth Press, Inc. • Quarterly. $285.00 per year to libraries; $48.00 per year to individuals. Presents scholarly articles on marketing and other aspects of electronic commerce.

Journal of Marketing. American Marketing Association. • Quarterly. Members, $45.00; per

year; non-members, $80.00 per year; institutions, $200.00 per year. Covers both marketing theory and marketing practice.

Journal of Marketing Channels: Distribution Systems, Strategy, and Management. Haworth Press, Inc. • Quarterly. $315.00 per year. Subject matter has to do with the management of product distribution systems.

Journal of Public Policy and Marketing. American Marketing Association. • Semiannual. Members, $45.00 per year; non-members, $70.00 per year; institutions, $100.00 per year. Devoted to the social and cultural impact of marketing activities.

The Licensing Letter. EPM Communications Inc. • Description: Concerned with all aspects of licensed merchandising, "the business of associating someone's name, likeness or creation with someone else's product or service, for a consideration." Recurring features include statistics, research, events, mechanics, available properties, and identification of licensors, licensing agents, and licensees.

Marketing Magazine: Canada's Weekly Newspaper for Marketing, Advertising and Sales Executives. Rogers Media Publishing. • Weekly. $95.00 per year. "Canada's national weekly publication dedicated to the businesses of marketing, advertising, and media." Includes annual Marketing Awards, quarterly Digital Marketing (emerging technology), Promo Marketing, and PR Quarterly (special issues on public relations).

Marketing Management: Shaping the Profession of Marketing. American Marketing Association. • Quarterly. Members, $45.00 per year; non-members, $70.00 per year; institutions, $90.00 per year. Covers trends in the management of marketing, sales, and distribution.

Marketing News: Reporting on Marketing and Its Association. American Marketing Association. • Biweekly. Free to members; non-members, $100.00 per year; institutions, $130.00 per year.

The Marketing Report: The Best Time-Saving Information Source for Marketing Execcutives. Progressive Business Publications. • Semimonthly. $264.00 per year. Newsletter. Covers marketing ideas, problem solving, and new product development. Includes case histories.

Marketing the Law Firm. American Lawyer Media, Inc. • Monthly. $199.00 per year. Newsletter. Focuses on actions that lawyers can take to find more clients and do more business. (A Law Journal Newsletter, formerly published by Leader Publications under the title *Marketing for Lawyers*).

Marketing Times. Sales and Marketing Executives International. • Quarterly. Membership. Newsletter.

Potentials: Ideas and Products that Motivate. VNU Business Media. • Monthly. $59.00 per year. Covers incentives, premiums, awards, and gifts as related to promotional activities. Formerly *Potentials in Marketing.*

PROMO: Promotion Marketing Worldwide. Primedia Business Magazines and Media. • Monthly. $65.00 per year. Edited for companies and agencies that utilize couponing, point-of-purchase advertising, special events, games, contests, premiums, product samples, and other unique promotional items.

Psychology and Marketing. John Wiley and Sons, Inc., Journals. • Eight times a year. $999.00 per year; with online edition, $1,049.00 per year. Spots the latest social, economic, and cultural trends that affect marketing decisions.

Sales and Marketing Management. VNU Business Media. • Monthly. $48.00 per year.

Sales & Marketing Report: Practical Ideas for Successful Selling. Lawrence Ragan Communications, Inc. • Monthly. $119.00 per year. Newsletter.

Emphasis is on sales training, staff morale, and marketing productivity.

Web Marketing Update: Quick, Actionable, Internet Intelligence for Marketing Executives. Computer Economics, Inc. •. Monthly. $347.00 per year. Newsletter on various aspects of promoting or selling products and services through an Internet Web site: technology, advertising, strategy, customer base, cost projections, search engines, etc.

RESEARCH CENTERS AND INSTITUTES

Marketing Science Institute. Marketing Science Institute. 1000 Massachusetts Ave., Cambridge, MA 02138-5396. Phone: (617)491-2060 Fax: (617)491-2065 E-mail: mclippinger@msi.org • URL: http://www.msi.org • Marketing, including studies on marketing management and strategy, international/global marketing, impact of information technology on marketing, marketing models and methods, advertising, sales promotion, sales force, channels of distribution, consumer services marketing, business-to-business marketing, and marketing of consumer durables and packaged goods.

TRADE/PROFESSIONAL ASSOCIATIONS

American Marketing Association. 311 S Wacker Dr., Ste. 5800, Chicago, IL 60606. Phone: 800-262-1150 or (312)542-9000 Fax: (312)542-9001 E-mail: info@ama.org • URL: http://www.marketingpower.com • Serves as a professional society of marketing and market research executives, sales and promotion managers, advertising specialists, academics, and others interested in marketing. Fosters research; sponsors seminars, conferences, and student marketing clubs; provides educational placement service and doctoral consortium.

OTHER SOURCES

Marketing the Law Firm: Business Development Techniques. American Lawyer Media, Inc. • Looseleaf. $189.00. Updated as needed. Covers client surveys, brochures, direct mail, Web sites, seminars, newsletters, proposals, trade shows, and other marketing avenues for both large and small law firms. (Law Journal Press).

MARKETING, BANK

See: BANK MARKETING

MARKETING, CHEMICAL

See: CHEMICAL MARKETING

MARKETING, DIRECT

See: DIRECT MARKETING

MARKETING, INDUSTRIAL

See: INDUSTRIAL MARKETING

MARKETING, INTERNATIONAL

See: INTERNATIONAL MARKETING

MARKETING, MULTILEVEL

See: MULTILEVEL MARKETING

MARKING MACHINES

DIRECTORIES

Marking Products and Equipment Buyer's Guide. Marking Devices Publishing Co. • Annual. $30.00.

Included in subscription to *Marking Industry Magazine*.

PERIODICALS AND NEWSLETTERS

Marking Industry Magazine, Marking Devices Publishing Co. • Monthly. $44.00 per year. Includes annual buyer's guide *Marking Products and Equipment*.

MASONRY

DIRECTORIES

Masonry Construction Buyers' Guide. Mason Contractors Association of America. • Annual. $3.00. Lists manufacturers or suppliers of products and services related to masonry construction.

FINANCIAL RATIOS

Annual Statement Studies. The Risk Management Association. • Annual. Median and quartile financial ratios are given for over 400 kinds of manufacturing, wholesale, retail, construction, and consumer finance establishments. Data is sorted by both asset size and sales volume. Includes a clearly written "Definition of Ratios" and an alphabetical industry index.

Annual Statement Studies: Industry Default Probabilities and Cash Flow Measures. The Risk Management Association. • Annual. $145.00. Serves as a companion volume to the original *Annual Statement Studies*. Gives probability of default estimates on a percentage scale for more than 450 industries. Includes changes in position year-by-year for eight financial statement line items and provides percentage measures of cash flow.

PERIODICALS AND NEWSLETTERS

Masonry. Mason Contractors Association of America. • Bimonthly. $20.00 per year.

Masonry Construction. Hanley-Wood, LLC. • 10 times a year. $30.00 per year. Covers masonry design, materials, equipment, and techniques.

Masonry Design West. Pleasanton Publishing Co. • Bimonthly. Price on application.

TRADE/PROFESSIONAL ASSOCIATIONS

International Masonry Institute. The James Brice House, 42 East St., Annapolis, MD 21401. Phone: 800-803-0295 or (410)280-1305 Fax: (301)261-2855 E-mail: masonryquestions@imiweb.org • URL: http://www.imiweb.org • Joint labor/management trust fund of the International Union of Bricklayers and Allied Craftworkers and union masonry contractors. Aims for the advancement of quality masonry construction through national and regional training, promotion, advertising and labor management relations programs in the U.S. and Canada. Provides support and materials for local/regional masonry promotion groups in the U.S. and Canada, and cooperates with national groups and organizations promoting the industry. Sponsors craft training and research programs. Offers educational programs. Maintains museum.

Mason Contractors Association of America. 33 S Rosell Rd., Schaumburg, IL 60193. Phone: 800-536-2225 or (847)301-0001 Fax: (847)301-1110 • URL: http://www.masoncontractors.com.

National Concrete Masonry Association. 13750 Sunrise Valley Dr., Herndon, VA 20171-4662. Phone: (703)713-1900 Fax: (703)713-1910 E-mail: ncma@ncma.org • URL: http://www.ncma.org • Manufacturers of concrete masonry units (concrete blocks), segmental retaining wall units and paving block; associate members are machinery, cement, and aggregate manufacturers. Conducts testing and research on masonry units and masonry assemblies. Compiles statistics.

MASS MEDIA

See also: ADVERTISING MEDIA; MEDIA RESEARCH

GENERAL WORKS

Breaking Up America: Advertisers and the New Media World. Joseph Turow. The University of Chicago Press. • 1997. $22.50. A social criticism of target marketing, market segmentation, and customized media.

Crisis Response: Inside Stories on Managing Image Under Siege. Gale Cengage Learning. • 1993. $80.00. Presents first-hand accounts by media relations professionals of major business crises and how they were handled. Topics include the following kinds of crises: environmental, governmental, corporate image, communications, and product.

Interface Culture: How New Technology Transforms the Way We Create and Communicate. Steven Johnson. HarperSanFrancisco. • 1997. $24.00. A discussion of how computer interfaces and online technology ("cyberspace") affect society in general.

The Media Monopoly. Ben H. Bagdikian. Beacon Press. • 2000. $18.50. Sixth edition.

Media Systems Society: Understanding Industries, Strategies and Power. Joseph Turow. Addison-Wesley. • 1996. $74.00. Second edition. Provides commentary on the role of U.S. mass media in a global economy.

ABSTRACTS AND INDEXES

Business Periodicals Index. H. W. Wilson Co. • 11 times a year. Quarterly and annual cumulations. Price varies.

Communication Abstracts: An International Information Service. Sage Publications, Inc. • Bimonthly. Institutions, $1,150.00 per year. Provides broad coverage of the literature of communications, including broadcasting and advertising.

Readers' Guide to Periodical Literature. H. W. Wilson Co. • Monthly. $345.00 per year. Includes annual *Cumulation*. Indexes about 250 periodicals of general interest.

What's New in Advertising and Marketing. Special Libraries Association, Advertising and Marketing Div. • Quarterly. Non-profit organizations, $20.00 per year; corporations, $30.00 per year. Lists and briefly describes a wide variety of free or inexpensive material relating to advertising, marketing, and media.

BIBLIOGRAPHIES

Communication Booknotes Quarterly : Recent Titles in Telecommunications, Information, and Media. Lawrence Erlbaum Associates, Inc. • Bimonthly. Institutions, $395.00 per year; with online edition, $325.00 per year. Contains descriptive reviews of new publications.

BIOGRAPHICAL SOURCES

The Highwaymen: Warriors on the Information Superhighway. Ken Auletta. Harcourt Trade Publications. • 1998. $13.00. Revised expanded edition. Contains critical articles about Ted Turner, Rupert Murdoch, Barry Diller, Michael Eisner, and other key figures in electronic communications, entertainment, and information. (Harvest Book Series).

CD-ROM DATABASES

ABI/INFORM. PROQUEST. • Monthly. Provides CD-ROM indexing and abstracting of worldwide business literature. Archival discs are available from 1971. Formerly *ABI/INFORM OnDisc*.

Authority Computer and Telecommunications Law Library. LexisNexis/Matthew Bender. • Quarterly. Price on request. Full text CD-ROM provides cases, analysis, sample agreements, and other information relating to computer law, telecommunications regulation (cable, broadcasting, satellite, Internet), international computer law, and computer contracts.

Hoover's Company Capsules on CD-ROM. Hoover's, Inc. • Quarterly. $399.95 per year (single-user). Provides the CD-ROM version of *Hoover's Handbook of American Business, Hoover's Handbook of Emerging Companies, Hoover's Handbook of World Business, Hoover's Guide to Computer Companies, Hoover's Guide to Media Companies, Hoover's Handbook of Private Companies*, and various regional guides. Includes more than 11,000 profiles of companies.

Leadership Library on CD-ROM: Who's Who in the Leadership of the United States. Leadership Directories, Inc. • Quarterly. Including access to Internet version (weekly updates). Contains all 14 *Yellow Book* personnel directories on CD-ROM, providing contact and brief biographical information for about 400,000 individuals. Covers business, government, financial institutions, news media, law firms, associations, foreign representatives, and nonprofit organizations. Includes photographs.

PAIS on CD-ROM. Public Affairs Information Service, Inc. • Quarterly. $1,995.00 per year. Provides a CD-ROM version of the online service, *PAIS International*. Contains over 500,000 citations to the literature of contemporary social, political, and economic issues.

WILSONDISC: Business Periodicals Index. H. W. Wilson Co. • Monthly. Provides CD-ROM indexing of business periodicals from 1982 to date. Price includes online service.

WILSONDISC: Readers' Guide to Periodical Literature. H. W. Wilson Co. • Monthly. $1,095.00 per year, including unlimited online access to *Readers' Guide to Periodical Literature* through WILSONLINE. Provides CD-ROM indexing of about 270 general interest periodicals. Covers 1983 to date. (*Readers' Guide Abstracts* also available on CD-ROM at $1,995 per year.).

DIRECTORIES

Burrelle's Media Directory: Broadcast Media. Burrelle's Information Services. • Annual. $550.00. Approximately 48,000 print and electronic media in North America. Provides detailed descriptions, including programming and key personnel.

Burrelle's Media Directory: Magazines and Newsletters. Burrelle's Information Services. • Annual. $550.00. Provides detailed descriptions of more than 13,500 magazines and newsletters published in the U.S., Canada, and Mexico. Categories are professional, consumer, trade, and college. Semiannual *Updates*. Includes CD-ROM.

Burrelle's Media Directory: Newspapers and Related Media. Burrelle's Information Services. • Annual. $550.00. *Daily Newspapers* volume lists more than 2,200 daily publications in the U.S., Canada, and Mexico. *Non-Daily Newspapers* volume lists more than 10,400 items published no more than three times a week. Provides detailed descriptions, including key personnel.

Gale Directory of Publications and Broadcast Media. Gale Cengage Learning. • Annual. $770.00. Five volumes. *Interedition Supplement*, Free. A guide to publications and broadcasting stations in the U.S. and Canada, including newspapers, magazines, journals, radio stations, television stations, and cable systems. Geographic arrangement. Volume three consists of statistical tables, maps, subject indexes, and title index.

Gale's Guide to the Media: A Gale Ready Reference Handbook. Gale Cengage Learning. • 2000. $125.00. Provides profiles of a wide variety of media-related organizations, publications, broadcasters, agencies, and databases, of interest to nonprofit groups. Contains three indexes and a glossary.

News Media Yellow Book: Who's Who Among

Reporters, Writers, Editors, and Producers in the Leading National News Media. Leadership Directories, Inc. • Quarterly. $360.00 per year. Lists the staffs of major newspapers and news magazines, TV and radio networks, news services and bureaus, and feature syndicates. Includes syndicated columnists and programs. Seven specialized indexes are provided.

Power Media Yearbook. Broadcast Interview Source. • Covers: Approximately 3,000 media contacts throughout the United States, including newswire services, syndicates, syndicated columnists, national newspapers, magazines, radio and television talk shows, etc. Entries include: Outlet name, address, phone, fax, names and titles of key personnel, geographical area served, and branch offices.

VNU Business Media. ADWEEK Directories. • Annual. $100.00. Presents cost, circulation, and audience statistics for various mass media segments, including television, radio, magazines, newspapers, telephone yellow pages, and cinema.

Washington: A Comprehensive Directory of the Key Institutions and Leaders in th e National Capitol Area. Columbia Books, Inc. • Annual. $149.00. Provides information on about 5,000 Washington, DC key businesses, government offices, non-profit organizations, and cultural institutions, with the names of about 25,000 principal executives. Includes Washington media, law offices, foundations, labor unions, international organizations, clubs, etc.

ENCYCLOPEDIAS AND DICTIONARIES

Advertising Age Encyclopedia of Advertising. John McDonough and others, editors. Fitzroy Dearborn Publishers. • 2002. $385.00. Three volumes. Contains 600 entries in alphabetical order covering a wide variety of advertising and market research topics. Includes bibliographies.

Encyclopedia of Communication and Information. Available from Gale Cengage Learning. • 2001. $395.00. Three volumes. Published by Macmillan Reference USA.

Encyclopedia of New Media: An Essential Reference to Communication and Technology. Steve Jones, editor. Sage Publications, Inc. • 2003. $125.00. Contains more than 250 entries dealing with such areas as multimedia, broadband access, information communication technology (ICT), content filtering, wireless networks, and cyberethics.

World Press Encyclopedia. Gale Cengage Learning. • 2003. $325.00. Second edition. Two volumes. Comprehensive essays cover the background and economic framework of newspapers and other news media in about 200 countries. Covers relevant legal issues, censorship, government relations, education in journalism, status of news agencies, cable, Internet, and other media topics.

HANDBOOKS AND MANUALS

Mass Media Law. Donald R. Pember. McGraw Hill. • 2000. $62.50 12th edition. Includes CD-ROM. (Humanities, Social Sciences and World Languages Series).

Media for Business. Robert H. Amend and Michael A. Schrader. Elsevier. • 1991. $44.95.

INTERNET DATABASES

Pew Research Center for the People and the Press. Pew Charitable Trusts. Phone: (202)293-3126 Fax: (202)293-2569 E-mail: mailprc@people-press.org • URL: http://www.people-press.org • Free Web site includes public opinion poll "Reports by Topic." Five broad subject areas cover business, social issues, foreign policy, news media, and politics. Searching is offered within each of these broad areas, and there are links to other major sources of public opinion poll results ("FYI Other Polls").

Wired News. Lycos, Inc. Phone: (415)276-8400 Fax:

(415)276-8500 E-mail: newsfeedback@wired.com • URL: http://www.wired.com • Provides summaries and full-text of "Top Stories" relating to the Internet, computers, multimedia, telecommunications, and the electronic information industry in general. These news stories are placed in the broad categories of Politics, Business, Culture, and Technology. Affiliated with *Wired* magazine. Fees: Free.

ONLINE DATABASES

Globalbase. Gale Cengage Learning. • Provides more than one million online summaries of business, industrial, and economic news reports from more than 1,000 publications worldwide. Covers a wide range of material appearing in international trade journals, professional magazines, and newspapers. Time period is 1984 to date, with weekly updates. Inquire as to online cost and availability.

Marketing and Advertising Reference Service (MARS). Gale Cengage Learning. • Provides abstracts of literature relating to consumer marketing and advertising, including all forms of advertising media. Time period is 1984 to date. Daily updates. Inquire as to online cost and availability.

PAIS International. Public Affairs Information Service, Inc. • Corresponds to the former printed publications, *PAIS Bulletin* (1976-90) and *PAIS Foreign Language Index* (1972-90), and to the current *PAIS International in Print* (1991 to date). Covers economic, political, and sociological material appearing in periodicals, books, government documents, and other publications. Updating is monthly. Inquire as to online cost and availability.

Readers' Guide Abstracts Online. H. W. Wilson Co. • Indexes and abstracts general interest periodicals, 1983 to date. Weekly updates. Inquire as to online cost and availability.

Trade & Industry Database. Gale Cengage Learning. • Provides indexing of business periodicals, January 1981 to date. Daily updates. (Full text articles from some periodicals are available online, 1983 to date. Inquire as to online cost and availability).

Wilson Business Abstracts Online. H. W. Wilson Co. • Indexes and abstracts 600 major business periodicals, plus the *Wall Street Journal* and the business section of the *New York Times*. Indexing is from 1982, abstracting from 1990, with the two newspapers included from 1993. Updated weekly. Inquire as to online cost and availability. (*Business Periodicals Index* without abstracts is also available online.).

PERIODICALS AND NEWSLETTERS

Brandweek: The Newsweekly of Marketing Communications. VNU Business Media. • 46 times a year. $149.00 per year. Includes articles and case studies on mass marketing and mass media. Formerly *Adweek's Marketing Week.*

Media Industry Newsletter. Access Intelligence L.L.C. • Description: Covers the media industry, including advertising, marketing, publishing, radio, and television. Recurring features include weekly box scores of advertising pages in major magazines, salaries of top executives, earnings reports, and news of people in the industry.

Mediaweek: The News Magazine of the Media. VNU Business Media. • 47 times a year. Weekly. $149.00 per year. Published for advertising media buyers and managers.

NewsInc.: The Business of the Newspaper Business. The Cole Group. • Biweekly. $425.00 per year. Newsletter. Reports on trends in mass media, especially with regard to newspaper publishing. Articles on cable TV and other competitive media are included.

Wired. Wired Ventures Ltd. • Monthly. $10.00 per

year. Edited for creators and managers in various areas of electronic information and entertainment, including multimedia, the Internet, and video. Often considered to be the primary publication of the "digital generation.".

RESEARCH CENTERS AND INSTITUTES

Center for Mass Media Research. Marquette University, 1131 W. Wisconsin Ave., Milwaukee, WI 53233. Phone: (414)288-3453 E-mail: robert. griffin@marquette.edu.

Freedom Forum First Amendment Center. Vanderbilt Univ., 1207 18th Ave. S., Nashville, TN 37212. Phone: (615)727-1600 Fax: (615)727-1319 E-mail: info@facorg • URL: http://www.freedomforum.org • Research fields include mass communication and technological change, including mass media and the public trust.

Integrated Media Systems Center. University of Southern California, 3740 McClintock Ave., Suite 131, Los Angeles, CA 90089-2561. Phone: (213)740-0877 Fax: (213)740-8931 E-mail: imsc@ imsc.usc.edu • URL: http://www.imsc.usc.edu • Media areas for research include education, mass communication, and entertainment.

Mass Communications Research Center. University of Wisconsin-Madison, 821 University Ave., 5050 Vilas Hall, Madison, WI 53706. Phone: (608)263-3381 Fax: (608)262-1361 E-mail: rhawkins@wisc. edu.

STATISTICS SOURCES

Media Market Guide. Media Market Resources. • Quarterly. $675.00 per year. Presents circulation and cost data for television, radio, magazines, newspapers and outdoor markets.

UNESCO Statistical Yearbook. Bernan Press. • 1998. $95.00. Co-published by Bernan Press and the United Nations Educational, Scientific, and Cultural Organization (http://www.unesco.org). Presents statistical data from more than 200 countries on education, technology, research, broadcasting, cinema, book publishing, newspapers, libraries, museums, and population. Includes charts, maps, and graphs.

TRADE/PROFESSIONAL ASSOCIATIONS

Accuracy in Media. 4455 Connecticut Ave., N.W.,, Suite 330, Washington, DC 20008. Phone: 800-787-0044 or (202)364-4401 Fax: (202)364-4098 E-mail: ar1@aim.org • URL: http://www.aim.org • A nonpartisan organization that receives and researches complaints from the public relating to factual errors made by the news media. Affiliated with Accuracy in Academia.

Association of Schools of Journalism and Mass Communication. c/o Jennifer H. McGill, 234 Outlet Pointe Blvd., Columbia, SC 29210-5667. Phone: (803)798-0271 Fax: (803)772-3509 E-mail: aejmchq@aol.com • URL: http://www.aejmc.org.

Foundation for American Communications. 85 S. Grand Ave., Pasadena, CA 91105-1602. Phone: (626)584-0010 Fax: (626)568-0627 E-mail: facs@ facsnet.org • URL: http://www.facsnet.org.

Minorities in Media. P.O. Box 9198, Petersburg, VA 23806. Phone: (804)524-5935 Fax: (804)524-5757 E-mail: vthota@vsu.edu • Members are minority media professionals.

MASS TRANSPORTATION

See: PUBLIC TRANSPORTATION; TRANSPORTATION INDUSTRY

MATERIALS

ABSTRACTS AND INDEXES

Engineered Materials Abstracts. Cambridge Information Group. • Monthly. $995.00 per year.

Provides citations to the technical and engineering literature of plastic, ceramic, and composite materials.

Key Abstracts: Advanced Materials. Available from INSPEC, Inc. • Monthly. $250.00 per year. Provides international coverage of journal and proceedings literature, including publications on ceramics and composite materials. Published in England by the Institution of Electrical Engineers (IEE).

NTIS Alerts: Manufacturing Technology. National Technical Information Service. • Semimonthly. $265.00 per year. Provides descriptions of government-sponsored research reports and software, with ordering information. Covers computer-aided design and manufacturing (CAD/CAM), engineering materials, quality control, machine tools, robots, lasers, productivity, and related subjects. Formerly *Abstract Newsletter.*

NTIS Alerts: Materials Sciences. National Technical Information Service. • Semimonthly. $220.00 per year. Provides descriptions of government-sponsored research reports and software, with ordering information. Covers ceramics, glass, coatings, composite materials, alloys, plastics, wood, paper, adhesives, fibers, lubricants, and related subjects. Formerly *Abstract Newsletter.*

ALMANACS AND YEARBOOKS

Progress in Materials Science: An International Review Journal. Elsevier. • Bimonthly. $1,120.00 per year.

BIBLIOGRAPHIES

ASTM List of Publications. American Society for Testing and Materials (ASTM). • Annual.

CD-ROM DATABASES

METADEX Materials Collection: Metals-Polymers-Ceramics. Cambridge Scientific Abstracts. • Quarterly. Provides CD-ROM citations to the worldwide literature of materials science and metallurgy. Corresponds to *Metals Abstracts, Alloys Index, Steels Alert, Nonferrous Alert, Polymers/Ceramics/Composites Alert,* and *Engineered Materials Abstracts.* (Formerly produced by ASM International.).

Plastics Digest on CD-ROM. Global Engineering Documents. • Semiannual. CD-ROM index version (technical data only), $695.00 per year or $495.00 per disc. CD-ROM image version (technical data and specification sheet images), $1,295.00 per year or $995.00 per disc. Provides detailed information on the properties of 20,000 types of plastic, both current and obsolete. Time period is 1977 to date. Includes trade names and supplier names and addresses.

DIRECTORIES

Internet Tools of the Profession: A Guide for Information Professionals. Hope N. Tillman, editor. Special Libraries Association. • 1997. $49.00. Second edition. Consists of 14 sections by various authors or compilers. After two introductory articles on searching the Internet, there are 12 annotated lists of useful Web sites, covering the SLA, business and finance, chemistry, education, food and agriculture, information technology, insurance and employee benefits, law, library management, metals and materials, pharmaceuticals, and telecommunications. An index is provided.

Materials Research Centres: A World Directory of Organizations and Programmes in Materials Science. Specialist Journals. • Biennial. $445.00. Profiles of research centers in 75 countries. Materials include plastics, metals, fibers, etc.

ENCYCLOPEDIAS AND DICTIONARIES

ASM Materials Engineering Dictionary. Joseph R. Davis, editor. ASM International. • 1992. $166.00. Contains 10,000 entries, 700 illustrations, and 150 tables relating to metals, plastics, ceramics,

composites, and adhesives. Includes "Technical Briefs" on 64 key material groups.

Encyclopedia of Advanced Materials. David Bloor and others. Elsevier. • 1994. $1,534.00. Four volumes.

Encyclopedia of Materials: Science and Technology. K.H.J. Buschow and others, editors. Elsevier. • 2001. $4,985.00. Eleven volumes. Provides extensive technical information on a wide variety of materials, including metals, ceramics, plastics, optical materials, and building materials. Includes more than 2,000 articles and 5,000 illustrations.

Encyclopedia of Smart Materials. Mel Schwartz, editor. John Wiley and Sons, Inc. • 2002. $725.00. Three volumes. Covers materials "that combine two or more functions in a single material or element.".

Materials Science and Technology: A Comprehensive Treatment. R. W. Cahn and others, editors. John Wiley and Sons, Inc. • 1997. $4,250.00. 18 volumes. Each volume covers a particular area of high-performance materials technology.

HANDBOOKS AND MANUALS

ASM Engineered Materials Reference Book. Michael L. Bauccio, editor. ASM International. • 1994. $155.00. Third edition. Provides information on a wide range of materials, with special sections on ceramics, industrial glass products, and plastics.

Handbook of Materials Selection. Myer Kutz. John Wiley and Sons, Inc. • 2002. $225.00. First section of handbook covers materials relative to the type of engineering application. Second section deals with the specific properties of materials. Covers both traditional materials and high-tech composites.

Industrial Polymers Handbook: Products, Processes, Applications. Edward S. Wilks, editor. John Wiley and Sons, Inc. • 2001. $1,400.00. Four volumes. Covers both naturally occurring and synthetic polymers that have industrial uses.

Materials Handbook. John A. Vaccari and others. McGraw-Hill. • 2002. $99.95. 15th edition. (Handbook Series).

Polymer Handbook. Johannes Brandup and others, editors. John Wiley and Sons, Inc. • 2003. $197.50. Fifth edition. Emphasis is on advances in polymer science since 1989 and descriptions of polymeric materials. (Polymer Handbook Series).

ONLINE DATABASES

Engineered Materials Abstracts [online]. Cambridge Scientific Abstracts. • Provides online citations to the technical and engineering literature of plastic, ceramic, and composite materials. Time period is 1986 to date, with monthly updates. (Formerly produced by ASM International.) Inquire as to online cost and availability.

Materials Business File. Cambridge Scientific Abstracts. • Provides online abstracts and citations to worldwide materials literature, covering the business and industrial aspects of metals, plastics, ceramics, and composites. Corresponds to *Steels Alert, Nonferrous Metals Alert,* and *Polymers/Ceramics/Composites Alert.* Time period is 1985 to date, with monthly updates. (Formerly produced by ASM International.) Inquire as to online cost and availability.

METADEX. Cambridge Scientific Abstracts. • Covers the worldwide literature of metals, metallurgy, and materials science, 1966 to date. Includes detailed alloys indexing from 1974. Biweekly updating. Inquire as to online cost and availability. (Formerly produced by ASM International.).

METADEX. Cambridge Scientific Abstracts. • Covers the worldwide literature of metals, metallurgy, and materials science, 1966 to date. Includes detailed alloys indexing from 1974. Biweekly updating. Inquire as to online cost and availability.

(Formerly produced by ASM International.).

PERIODICALS AND NEWSLETTERS

ASTM Standardization News. American Society for Testing and Materials. • Monthly. $18.00 per year.

High-Tech Materials Alert: Advanced Materials: Their Uses and Manufacture. Technical Insights. • Monthly. Institutions, $695.00 per year. Newsletter on technical developments relating to high-performance materials, including metals and ceramics. Includes market forecasts.

International Materials Review. ASM International. • Bimonthly. $865.00 per year. Provides technical and research coverage of metals, alloys, and advanced materials. Formerly *International Metals Review.*

Journal of Advanced Materials. Society for the Advancement of Material and Process Engineering. • Quarterly. Individuals, $60.00 per year; institutions, $150.00 per year. Contains technical and research articles. Formerly *SAMPE Quarterly.*

Journal of Materials Research. Materials Research Society. • Monthly. $785.00 per year. Includes print and online editions. Covers the preparation, properties, and processing of advanced materials.

Materials Evaluation. American Society for Nondestructive Testing. • Monthly. $105.00 per year. Provides up-to-date information about NDT applications and technical articles addressing nondestructive testing applications.

Materials Performance: Articles on Corrosion Science and Engineering Solutions for Corrosion Problems. National Association of Corrosion Engineers. NACE International. • Monthly. Individuals, $115.00 per year; institutions, $205.00 per year. Covers the protection and performance of materials in corrosive environments. Includes information on new materials and industrial coatings.

Metallurgical and Materials Transactions A: Physical Metallurgy and Materials Sc. ASM International. • 13 times a year. $1,617.00 per year. Formerly *Metallurgical Transactions A- Physical Metallurgy and Materials Science.*

SAMPE Journal. Society for the Advancement of Material and Process Engineering. • Bimonthly. Members, $78.00 per year; non-members, $80.00 per year. Provides technical information.

RESEARCH CENTERS AND INSTITUTES

Center for Advanced Materials Research. Brown University. 182 Hope St., Providence, RI 02912. Phone: (401)863-1386 Fax: (401)863-1387 E-mail: clyde_briant@brown.edu.

Materials Processing Center. Massachusetts Institute of Technology, 77 Massachusetts Ave., Room 12-007, Cambridge, MA 02139-4307. Phone: (617)253-5179 Fax: (617)258-6900 E-mail: fmpage@.mit.edu • URL: http://www.web.mit.edu/mpc • Conducts processing, engineering, and economic research in ferrous and nonferrous metals, ceramics, polymers, photonic materials, superconductors, welding, composite materials, and other materials.

Materials Research Center. Lehigh University. Five E. Packer Ave., Bethlehem, PA 18015. Phone: (610)758-3850 Fax: (610)758-3526 E-mail: mph2@ lehigh.edu • URL: http://www.lehigh.edu/~inmre/mrc.

Materials Science Center. University of Wisconsin - Madison. 1509 University Ave., Madison, WI 53706. Phone: (608)263-1795 Fax: (608)262-8353 E-mail: tfkelly@engr.wisc.edu.

TRADE/PROFESSIONAL ASSOCIATIONS

ASM International. 9639 Kinsman Rd., Novelty, OH 44073-0002. Phone: 800-336-5152 or (440)338-5151   Fax: (440)338-4634   E-mail: customerservice@asminternational.org • URL: http://asmcommunity.asminternational.org/portal/

site/asm • Metallurgists, materials engineers, executives in materials producing and consuming industries; teachers and students. Disseminates technical information about the manufacture, use, and treatment of engineered materials. Offers in-plant, home study, and intensive courses through Materials +Engineering Institute. Conducts career development program. Established ASM Foundation for +Education and Research.

Materials Research Society. 506 Keystone Dr., Warrendale, PA 15086-7573. Phone: (724)779-3003 Fax: (724)779-8313 E-mail: info@mrs.org • URL: http://www.mrs.org • Represents the interests of materials researchers from academia, industry, and government that promotes communication for the advancement of interdisciplinary materials research to improve the quality of life. Fosters interaction among researchers working on different classes of inorganic and organic materials and to promote interdisciplinary basic research on materials. Provides forum for industry, government, and university cooperation; conducts technical conferences, tutorial lectures. Maintains speakers' bureau.

Minerals, Metals and Materials Society. 184 Thorn Hill Dr., Warrendale, PA 15086-7514. Phone: (724)776-9000 Fax: (724)776-3770 E-mail: tmsgeneral@tms.org • URL: http://www.tms.org • Members are metallurgists, metallurgical engineers, and materials scientists. Divisions include Light Metals and Electronic, Magnetic, and Photonic Materials. Formerly The Metallurigical Society.

National Materials Advisory Board. 500 5th St. NW, 500 5th St. NW, MS 932, Washington, DC 20001-2736. Phone: (202)334-3505 Fax: (202)334-3718 E-mail: nmab@nas.edu • URL: http://www7.nationalacademies.org/nmab • Represents members of the board and its committees and panels appointed by the chairman of the National Research Council (see separate entry); industry, universities, research institutes, and government. Promotes the advancement of materials science and engineering in the national interest. Conducts studies on materials problem, potential approaches, and policy issues.

Society for the Advancement of Material and Process Engineering. 1161 Parkview Dr., Covina, CA 91722-3748. Phone: 800-562-7360 or (626)331-0616 Fax: (626)332-8929 E-mail: sampeibo@sampe.org • URL: http://www.sampe.org • Formerly Society of Aerospace Material and Process Engineers.

MATERIALS, BUILDING

See: BUILDING MATERIALS INDUSTRY

MATERIALS, COMPOSITE

See: COMPOSITE MATERIALS

MATERIALS HANDLING

ABSTRACTS AND INDEXES

Key Abstracts: Factory Automation. Available from INSPEC, Inc. • Monthly. $250.00 per year. Provides international coverage of journal and proceedings literature, including publications on CAD/CAM, materials handling, robotics, and factory management. Published in England by the Institution of Electrical Engineers (IEE).

CD-ROM DATABASES

OECD Statistical Compendium. Organization for Economic Cooperation and Development. • Semiannual. $1,905.00 per year for 1 to 10 users. CD-ROM contains more than 730,000 monthly, quarterly, and annual time series for OECD countries, 1960 to date. Includes fully searchable

data on agriculture, food, economic indicators, national accounts, employment, energy, finance, industry, technology, and foreign trade. Results can be displayed in various forms.

DIRECTORIES

Manufacturing Systems: Buyers Guide. Reed Business Information. • Annual. Price on application. Contains information on companies manufacturing or supplying materials handling systems, CAD/CAM systems, specialized software for manufacturing, programmable controllers, machine vision systems, and automatic identification systems.

Modern Materials Handling Casebook Directory. Reed Business Information. • Annual. $25.00. Lists about 2,300 manufacturers of equipment and supplies in the materials handling industry. Supplement to *Modern Materials Handling.*

ENCYCLOPEDIAS AND DICTIONARIES

Illustrated Dictionary of Cargo Handling. Peter Brodie. LLP, Inc. • 1991. $90.00. Second edition. Published in the UK by Lloyd's List (http://www.lloydslist.com). Provides definitions of about 600 terms relating to "the vessels and equipment used in modern cargo handling and shipping," including containerization.

HANDBOOKS AND MANUALS

Plant Layout and Materials Handling. James M. Apple. Krieger Publishing Co. • 1991. $59.50. Reprint edition.

World Class Warehousing and Material Handling. Edward Frazelle. McGraw-Hill. • 2001. $49.95. (Logistics Management Library).

INTERNET DATABASES

Business 2.0 Web Guide to the Best Business Links. Business 2.0 Media Inc. Phone: (415)293-4800 E-mail: support@business2.com • URL: http://www.business2.com/webguide • Web site presents an extensive, searchable directory of links to "the best, most informative, and authoritative web pages." Twenty main categories cover business, finance, career, company information, people, and technology topics, with thousands of subtopics, all linking to Web sites recommended by experienced business researchers. Fees: Free.

Fedstats. Federal Interagency Council on Statistical Policy. Phone: (202)395-7254 • URL: http://www.fedstats.gov • Web site features an efficient search facility for full-text statistics produced by more than 100 federal agencies, including the Census Bureau, the Bureau of Economic Analysis, and the Bureau of Labor Statistics. Boolean searches can be made within one agency or for all agencies combined. Links are offered to international statistical bureaus, including the UN, IMF, OECD, UNESCO, Eurostat, and 20 individual countries. Fees: Free.

FreeLunch.com. Economy.com, Inc. Phone: (610)696-8700 Fax: (610)696-1678 • URL: http://www.freelunch.com • Web site provides free access to more than 1.5 million economic and financial data series, covering industry, demographics, labor markets, prices, retail sales, government spending, trade, interest rates, housing starts, the stock market, and many other topics. Data is available for various time periods in either chart or table form. Searching is offered. Fees: Free, but registration required. Economy.com, Inc. also offers fee-based economic analysis at *The Dismal Scientist* site (http://www.dismal.com).

PERIODICALS AND NEWSLETTERS

Manufacturing Computer Solutions. • Monthly. $88.00 per year. Edited for managers of factory automation, emphasizing the integration of systems in manufacturing. Subjects include materials handling, CAD/CAM, specialized software for manufacturing, programmable controllers, machine vision, and automatic identification systems.

Formerly *Manufacturing Systems.*

Material Handling Management: Educating Industry on Product Handling, Flow Strategies, and Automation Technology. Penton Media, Inc. • 13 times a year. Free to qualified personnel; others, $50.00 per year. Formerly *Material Handling Engineering.*

Modern Materials Handling. Reed Business Information. • 14 times a year. $99.90 per year. For managers and engineers who buy or specify equipment used to move, store, control and protect products throughout the manufacturing and warehousing cycles. Includes *Casebook Directory* and *Planning Guide.* Also includes *ADC News and Solutions.*

STATISTICS SOURCES

Business Statistics of the United States. Linz Audain and Cornelia J. Strawser. Bernan Associates. • Annual. $147.00. Based on *Business Statistics,* formerly issue by the Bureau of Economic Analysis, U. S. Department of Commerce. Provides basic data for a wide variety of U. S. industries, services, and economic indicators. Most statistics are shown annually for 30 years and monthly for the most recent four years.

Survey of Current Business. Available from U. S. Government Printing Office. • Monthly. $63.00 per year. Issued by Bureau of Economic Analysis, U. S. Department of Commerce. Presents a wide variety of business and economic data.

TRADE/PROFESSIONAL ASSOCIATIONS

Industrial Truck Association. 1750 K St. NW, Ste. 460, Washington, DC 20006. Phone: (202)296-9880 Fax: (202)296-9884 E-mail: bernstein@iriinc.org • URL: http://www.indtrk.org • Manufacturers of powered industrial lift trucks, electric storage batteries, tires, engines, attachments, and hydraulic systems for powered industrial lift trucks.

Material Handling Equipment Distributors Association. 201 U.S. Hwy. 45, Vernon Hills, IL 60061-2398. Phone: (847)680-3500 Fax: (847)362-6989 E-mail: connect@mheda.org • URL: http://www.mheda.org • Distributors and manufacturers of material handling equipment. Aims to improve the proficiency of independent material handling distributors.

Material Handling Industry of America. 8720 Red Oak Blvd., Suite 201, Charlotte, NC 28217. Phone: 800-345-1815 or (704)676-1190 Fax: (704)676-1199 E-mail: jnofsinger@mhia.org • URL: http://www.mhia.org • Formerly Material Handling Industry.

Materials Handling and Management Society. 8720 Red Oak Blvd., Suite 201, Charlotte, NC 28217. Phone: 800-345-1815 or (704)676-1183 Fax: (704)676-1199 E-mail: bcurtis@mhia.org • URL: http://www.mhia.org/mhms • Formerly International Material Management Society.

MATERIALS, HAZARDOUS

See: HAZARDOUS MATERIALS

MATHEMATICAL STATISTICS

See: STATISTICAL METHODS

MATHEMATICS, BUSINESS

See: BUSINESS MATHEMATICS

MATURE CONSUMER MARKET

GENERAL WORKS

Ageless Marketing: Strategies for Reaching the Hearts and Minds of the New Customer Majority.

David Wolfe and Robert Snyder. Dearborn Trade Publishing. • 2003. $25.00. Explains how to create marketing campaigns that will attract older comsumers.

Direct Marketing, Direct Selling, and the Mature Consumer: A Research Study. James R. Lumpkin and others. Greenwood Publishing Group, Inc. • 1989. $64.95. A study of older consumers and their use of mail order, telephone shopping, party-plans, etc.

Marketing Strategies for the Mature Market. George P. Moschis. Greenwood Publishing Group, Inc. • 1994. $64.95.

ABSTRACTS AND INDEXES

Business Periodicals Index. H. W. Wilson Co. • 11 times a year. Quarterly and annual cumulations. Price varies.

Readers' Guide to Periodical Literature. H. W. Wilson Co. • Monthly. $345.00 per year. Includes annual *Cumulation.* Indexes about 250 peridicals of general interest.

ALMANACS AND YEARBOOKS

Older Americans Information Directory. Grey House Publshing, Inc. • 2002. $165.00. Fourth edition. Presents articles (text) and sources of information on a wide variety of aging and retirement topics. Includes an index to personal names, organizations, and subjects.

CD-ROM DATABASES

ABI/INFORM. PROQUEST. • Monthly. Provides CD-ROM indexing and abstracting of worldwide business literature. Archival discs are available from 1971. Formerly *ABI/INFORM OnDisc.*

WILSONDISC: Business Periodicals Index. H. W. Wilson Co. • Monthly. Provides CD-ROM indexing of business periodicals from 1982 to date. Price includes online service.

WILSONDISC: Readers' Guide to Periodical Literature. H. W. Wilson Co. • Monthly. $1,095.00 per year, including unlimited online access to *Readers' Guide to Periodical Literature* through WILSONLINE. Provides CD-ROM indexing of about 270 general interest periodicals. Covers 1983 to date. (*Readers' Guide Abstracts* also available on CD-ROM at $1,995 per year.).

ENCYCLOPEDIAS AND DICTIONARIES

Encyclopedia of Aging. David J. Ekerdt, editor. Available from Gale Cengage Learning. • 2002. $450.00. Four volumes. Published by Macmillan Reference USA. Includes articles relating to the financial aspects of aging, such as housing, long-term care insurance, pensions, social security, individual retirement accounts, savings, and retirement planning.

HANDBOOKS AND MANUALS

Marketing to Older Consumers: A Handbook of Information for Strategy Development. George P. Moschis. Greenwood Publishing Group, Inc. • 1992. $74.95.

ONLINE DATABASES

Ageline. American Association of Retired Persons. • Provides indexing and abstracting of the literature of social gerontology, including consumer aspects, financial planning, employment, housing, health care services, mental health, social security, and retirement. Time period is 1978 to date. Inquire as to online cost and availability.

Globalbase. Gale Cengage Learning. • Provides more than one million online summaries of business, industrial, and economic news reports from more than 1,000 publications worldwide. Covers a wide range of material appearing in international trade journals, professional magazines, and newspapers. Time period is 1984 to date, with weekly updates. Inquire as to online cost and availability.

Marketing and Advertising Reference Service (MARS). Gale Cengage Learning. • Provides abstracts of literature relating to consumer marketing and advertising, including all forms of advertising media. Time period is 1984 to date. Daily updates. Inquire as to online cost and availability.

PROMT: Predicasts Overview of Markets and Technology. Gale Cengage Learning. • Companies, products, applied technologies and markets. U.S. and international literature coverage, 1972 to date. Inquire as to online cost and availability. Provides abstracts from more than 1,600 publications. Weekly updates.

Readers' Guide Abstracts Online. H. W. Wilson Co. • Indexes and abstracts general interest periodicals, 1983 to date. Weekly updates. Inquire as to online cost and availability.

Trade & Industry Database. Gale Cengage Learning. • Provides indexing of business periodicals, January 1981 to date. Daily updates. (Full text articles from some periodicals are available online, 1983 to date. Inquire as to online cost and availability).

Wilson Business Abstracts Online. H. W. Wilson Co. • Indexes and abstracts 600 major business periodicals, plus the *Wall Street Journal* and the business section of the *New York Times.* Indexing is from 1982, abstracting from 1990, with the two newspapers included from 1993. Updated weekly. Inquire as to online cost and availability. (*Business Periodicals Index* without abstracts is also available online.).

PERIODICALS AND NEWSLETTERS

Selling to Seniors: The Monthly Report on the Mature Market. Community Development Services, Inc. CD Publications. • Monthly. $249.00 per year. Newsletter on effective ways to reach the "over 50" market.

RESEARCH CENTERS AND INSTITUTES

Center for Mature Consumer Studies. Robinson College of Business, MSC4 A1370, 33 Gilmer St., Unit 4, Atlanta, GA 30303-3083. Phone: (404)651-2740 Fax: (404)651-4198 E-mail: gmoschis@gsu.edu • URL: http://www.cba.gsu.edu/ • Serves as an information resource, assisting in strategy development for reaching the mature consumer market.

Consumer Research Center. Conference Board, Inc., 845 Third Ave., New York, NY 10022. Phone: (212)339-0304 Fax: (212)836-9714 E-mail: crc@conference-board.org • URL: http://www.crc-conquest.org • Conducts research on the consumer market, including elderly and working women segments.

STATISTICS SOURCES

Income of the Population 55 and Older. Available from U. S. Government Printing Office. • Biennial. $23.00. Issued by the Social Security Administration (http://www.ssa.gov). Covers major sources and amounts of income for the 55 and older population in the U. S., "with special emphasis on some aspects of the income of the population 65 and older.".

The Sourcebook of County Demographics. Available from Gale Cengage Learning. • Annual. $395.00. Published by ESRI Business Information Solutions. Contains demographic and socio-economic data (70 characteristics) for each U. S. county.

The Sourcebook of ZIP Code Demographics. Available from Gale Cengage Learning. • Annual. $495.00. Published by ESRI Business Information Systems. Presents detailed statistical profiles of every ZIP code in America. Each profile contains data on more than 70 variables with 2003 updates and 2008 forecasts.

Statistical Handbook on Aging Americans. Renee Schick. Greenwood Publishing Group, Inc. • 1994. $69.95. Second edition. Provides data on demographics, social characteristics, health,

employment, economic conditions, income, pensions, and social security. Includes bibliographic information and a glossary. (Statistical Handbook Series).

Statistical Record of Older Americans. Gale Cengage Learning. • 1996. $130.00. Second edition. Includes income and pension data.

OTHER SOURCES

Active Seniors Market. MarketResearch.com. • 2002. $2,100.00. Published by Packaged Facts. Provides market research data contrasting the consumer-oriented interests of age groups defined as conventionally working (under 55), young mature (55-64), active seniors (65-74), and elderly (75 and over). Covers finances, computer use, cars, housing, leisure activities, sports, and other items.

MEASURES

See: WEIGHTS AND MEASURES

MEAT INDUSTRY

See also: CATTLE INDUSTRY; LIVESTOCK INDUSTRY; SHEEP INDUSTRY; SWINE INDUSTRY

GENERAL WORKS

Fast Food Nation: The Dark Side of the All-American Meal. Eric Schlosser. Gale Cengage Learning. • 2001. $30.95. Explains how the fast food industry is contributing to obesity, disease, urban sprawl, and other bad things. Special attention is given to the meatpacking industry, *E.coli*, worker injuries, fast food franchise problems, detrimental labor practices, and the effect of fast food diets on children. Companies prominently mentioned are McDonald's, Burger King, Wendy's, Taco Bell, Pizza Hut, Jack in the Box, ConAgra, and Iowa Beef Packers. Includes many research notes, a bibliography, and a detailed index.

ABSTRACTS AND INDEXES

Food Science and Technology Abstracts. International Food Information Service Publishing. • Monthly. $1,780.00 per year. Provides worldwide coverage of the literature of food technology and food production.

Foods Adlibra: Key to the World's Food Literature. General Mills, Inc. Foods Adlibra Publications. • Semimonthly. $240.00 per year. Provides journal citations and abstracts to the literature of food technology and packaging.

ALMANACS AND YEARBOOKS

Agricultural and Mineral Commodities Year Book. Available from Taylor & Francis Group. • Annual. $225.00. Published by Europa Publications. Contains descriptive product profiles, price data, export-import data, and production statistics for major commodities of the world. Includes commodity histories, uses, markets, demand trends, and information about trade agreements and key commodity organizations.

CD-ROM DATABASES

Food Science and Technology Abstracts [CD-ROM]. Available from SilverPlatter Information, Inc. • Quarterly. Produced by International Food Information Service (home page is http://www.ifis.org). Provides worldwide coverage on CD-ROM of the literature of food technology and production. Various types of publications are indexed, with abstracts, including about 1,800 periodicals. Time period is 1969 to date.

OECD Statistical Compendium. Organization for Economic Cooperation and Development. • Semiannual. $1,905.00 per year for 1 to 10 users.

CD-ROM contains more than 730,000 monthly, quarterly, and annual time series for OECD countries, 1960 to date. Includes fully searchable data on agriculture, food, economic indicators, national accounts, employment, energy, finance, industry, technology, and foreign trade. Results can be displayed in various forms.

DIRECTORIES

Directory of Delicatessen Products. Pacific Rim Publishing Co. • Annual. Included with February issue of *Deli News.* Lists suppliers of cheeses, lunch meats, packaged fresh meats, kosher foods, gourmet-specialty items, and bakery products.

Major Food and Drink Companies of the World. Available from Gale Cengage Learning. • Annual. $880.00. Two volumes. Published by Graham & Whiteside. Contains profiles and trade names for more than 9,800 important food and beverage companies in various countries. In addition to foods, includes both alcoholic and nonalcoholic drink products.

Meat and Poultry Inspection Directory. U.S. Department of Agriculture. Available from U.S. Government Printing Office. • Semiannual. $49.00 per year.

Meat Processing-Buyer's Guide-North American Edition. Watt Publishing Co. • Annual. $12.00. In-depth statistical review of the meat, poultry, and seafood industries with graphs and tables; governmental phonebook; listing of meat associations, list of suppliers to the industry; list of equipment, services, and supplies, list of meat processors and their respective products.

Specialty Food Industry Directory. Phoenix Media Network, Inc. • Annual. Included in subscription to Food Distribution Magazine. Lists manufacturers and suppliers of specialty foods, and services and equipment for the specialty food industry. Featured food products include legumes, sauces, spices, upscale cheese, specialty beverages, snack foods, baked goods, ethnic foods, and specialty meats.

Thomas Food and Beverage Market Place. Grey House Publishing. • 2004. $495.00. Three volumes. Contains more than 40,000 entries covering food companies, beverages, food equipment, warehouse companies, food brokers, wholesalers, importers, and exporters. Formerly *Thomas Food Industry Register.*

ENCYCLOPEDIAS AND DICTIONARIES

Foods and Nutrition Encyclopedia. Audrey H. Ensminger and others. CRC Press, Inc. • 1993. $309.95. Second edition. Two volumes.

Wiley Encyclopedia of Food Science and Technology. Frederick J. Francis, editor. John Wiley and Sons, Inc. • 2000. $1,650.00. Second edition. Four volumes. Contains about 400 entries. Coverage includes biotechnology, genetic engineering, nutrition, regulatory matters, food safety, labeling, food substitutes (sugar, fat, dairy), and many other topics.

FINANCIAL RATIOS

Almanac of Business and Industrial Financial Ratios. Leo Troy. Aspen Publishers, Inc. • 2003. $125.95. Includes CD-Rom. Contains financial ratios derived from federal tax returns. Ratios for each of about 200 industries are arranged according to company asset size. (Almanac of Business and Industrial Financial Ratios Series).

Annual Statement Studies. The Risk Management Association. • Annual. Median and quartile financial ratios are given for over 400 kinds of manufacturing, wholesale, retail, construction, and consumer finance establishments. Data is sorted by both asset size and sales volume. Includes a clearly written "Definition of Ratios" and an alphabetical industry index.

Annual Statement Studies: Industry Default Probabilities and Cash Flow Measures. The Risk

Management Association. • Annual. $145.00. Serves as a companion volume to the original *Annual Statement Studies.* Gives probability of default estimates on a percentage scale for more than 450 industries. Includes changes in position year-by-year for eight financial statement line items and provides percentage measures of cash flow.

HANDBOOKS AND MANUALS

Meat and Poultry Inspection Regulations. U.S. Department of Agriculture. Available from U.S. Government Printing Office. • Looseleaf. Regulations for slaughter and processing of livestock and poultry as well as for certain voluntary services and humane slaughter.

INTERNET DATABASES

BEEF. National Cattlemen's Beef Association. Phone: (303)694-0305 Fax: (303)694-2851 E-mail: cows@beef.org • URL: http://www.beef.org • Web site provides detailed information from the "Cattle and Beef Handbook," including "Beef Economics" (production, sales, consumption, retail value, foreign competition, etc.). Text of monthly newsletter is also available: "The Beef Brief-Issues & Trends in the Cattle Industry." Keyword searching is offered. Fees: Free.

Business 2.0 Web Guide to the Best Business Links. Business 2.0 Media Inc. Phone: (415)293-4800 E-mail: support@business2.com • URL: http://www.business2.com/webguide • Web site presents an extensive, searchable directory of links to "the best, most informative, and authoritative web pages." Twenty main categories cover business, finance, career, company information, people, and technology topics, with thousands of subtopics, all linking to Web sites recommended by experienced business researchers. Fees: Free.

Fedstats. Federal Interagency Council on Statistical Policy. Phone: (202)395-7254 • URL: http://www.fedstats.gov • Web site features an efficient search facility for full-text statistics produced by more than 100 federal agencies, including the Census Bureau, the Bureau of Economic Analysis, and the Bureau of Labor Statistics. Boolean searches can be made within one agency or for all agencies combined. Links are offered to international statistical bureaus, including the UN, IMF, OECD, UNESCO, Eurostat, and 20 individual countries. Fees: Free.

FreeLunch.com. Economy.com, Inc. Phone: (610)696-8700 Fax: (610)696-1678 • URL: http://www.freelunch.com • Web site provides free access to more than 1.5 million economic and financial data series, covering industry, demographics, labor markets, prices, retail sales, government spending, trade, interest rates, housing starts, the stock market, and many other topics. Data is available for various time periods in either chart or table form. Searching is offered. Fees: Free, but registration required. Economy.com, Inc. also offers fee-based economic analysis at *The Dismal Scientist* site (http://www.dismal.com).

USDA. United States Department of Agriculture. Phone: (202)720-2791 E-mail: agsec@usda.gov • URL: http://www.usda.gov • The USDA home page has six sections: News and Information; What's New; About USDA; Agencies; Opportunities; Search and Help. Keyword searching is offered from the USDA home page and from various individual agency home pages. Agencies are the Economic Research Service, Agricultural Marketing Service, National Agricultural Statistics Service, National Agricultural Library, and about 12 others. Updating varies. Fees: Free.

ONLINE DATABASES

Food Science and Technology Abstracts [online]. IFIS North American Desk. • Produced by International Food Information Service. Provides about 500,000 online citations, with abstracts, to the international literature of food science, technology,

commodities, engineering, and processing. Approximately 2,000 periodicals are covered. Time period is 1969 to date, with monthly updates. Inquire as to online cost and availability.

FOODS ADLIBRA. General Mills, Inc. • Contains online citations, with abstracts, to the technical and business literature of food processing and packaging. New products and new ingredients are featured. Covers about 250 trade journals and 500 research journals from 1974 to date, with monthly updates. Inquire as to online cost and availability.

PERIODICALS AND NEWSLETTERS

Deli News. Delicatessen Council of Southern California, Inc. Pacific Rim Publishing Co. • Monthly. $25.00 per year. Includes product news and comment related to cheeses, lunch meats, packaged fresh meats, kosher foods, gourmet-specialty items, and bakery products.

Food Distribution Magazine. Phoenix Media Network, Inc. • Monthly. $49.00 per year. Edited for marketers and buyers of domestic and imported, specialty or gourmet food products, including ethnic foods, seasonings, and bakery items.

Meat and Poultry: The Business Journal of the Meat and Poultry Industry. Sosland Publishing Co. • Monthly. $42.00 per year.

Meat Processing: North American Edition. Watt Publishing Co. • Monthly. $54.00 per year.

PRICE SOURCES

The National Provisioner: Serving Meat, Poultry, and Seafood Processors. Stagnito Communications, Inc. • Monthly. Free to qualified personnel; others, $85.04 per year. Annual *Buyer's Guide* available. Meat, poultry and seafood newsletter.

STATISTICS SOURCES

Agricultural Statistics. Available from U. S. Government Printing Office. • Annual. $38.00. Produced by the National Agricultural Statistics Service, U. S. Department of Agriculture. Provides a wide variety of statistical data relating to agricultural production, supplies, consumption, prices/price-supports, foreign trade, costs, and returns, as well as farm labor, loans, income, and population. In many cases, historical data is shown annually for 10 years. In addition to farm data, includes detailed fishery statistics.

Annual Survey of Manufactures. Available from U. S. Government Printing Office. • Annual. Prices vary. Issued by the U. S. Census Bureau as an interim update to the *Census of Manufactures.* Includes data on number of manufacturing establishments in various industries, employment, labor costs, value of shipments, capital expenditures, inventories, energy costs, and assets. (See also Census Bureau home page, http://www.census. gov/.).

Business Statistics of the United States. Linz Audain and Cornelia J. Strawser. Bernan Associates. • Annual. $147.00. Based on *Business Statistics*, formerly issue by the Bureau of Economic Analysis, U. S. Department of Commerce. Provides basic data for a wide variety of U. S. industries, services, and economic indicators. Most statistics are shown annually for 30 years and monthly for the most recent four years.

FAO Production Yearbook. Available from Bernan Associates. • Annual. $45.00. Published by the Food and Agriculture Organization (http://www.fao.org). Contains worldwide data on agriculture, land use, farm crops, livestock, and agricultural prices.

FAO Trade Yearbook. Available from Bernan Associates. • Annual. $45.00. Published by the Food and Agriculture Organization (http://www.fao.org). Provides extensive worldwide data on exports and imports of agricultural commodities, fertilizers, tractors, and pesticides. Includes more than 130 tables of detailed statistics.

Livestock, Meat, Wool, Market News. U.S. Department of Agriculture. • Weekly.

Meat Balances in OECD Countries. Organization for Economic Cooperation and Development. Available from OECD Publications and Information Center. • Irregular. Price varies. Presents data for seven years on meat production, trade, and consumption. Covers various categories of meat in OECD member countries. Text in French.

Survey of Current Business. Available from U. S. Government Printing Office. • Monthly. $63.00 per year. Issued by Bureau of Economic Analysis, U. S. Department of Commerce. Presents a wide variety of business and economic data.

World Food Data and Statistics. Euromonitor International. • 2004. $650.00. Provides five-year data for a wide variety of food products in 52 countries. Includes market size, consumer expenditures, price indicators, and retail distribution data for many kinds of meat, fish, fruits, vegetables, dairy products, baked goods, condiments, canned food, and frozen food.

TRADE/PROFESSIONAL ASSOCIATIONS

American Meat Institute. 1150 Connecticut Ave. NW, 12th Fl., Washington, DC 20036. Phone: (202)587-4200 Fax: (202)587-4300 E-mail: memberservices@meatami.com • URL: http://www.meatami.com • Represents the interests of packers and processors of beef, pork, lamb, veal, and turkey products and their suppliers throughout North America. Provides legislative, regulatory, and public relations services. Conducts scientific research. Offers marketing and technical assistance. Sponsors educational programs.

Meat Industry Suppliers Association. 201 Park Washington Ct., Falls Church, VA 22046-4527. Phone: (703)533-0251 Fax: (703)241-5603 E-mail: mbittle@asmii.com • URL: http://www.asmii.com • Firms supplying products and services to the meat, poultry, and seafood processing industries. Members include manufacturers and distributors of machinery, casings, seasonings, material handling and packaging equipment and materials, and other items used in slaughterhouses, packaging plants, processing plants, and supermarkets.

National Cattlemen's Beef Association. 9110 E Nichols Ave., Ste. 300, Centennial, CO 80112. Phone: (866)233-3872 or (303)694-0305 Fax: (303)694-2851 E-mail: membership@beef.org • URL: http://www.beefusa.org • Represents 149 organizations of livestock marketers, growers, meat packers, food retailers, and food service firms. Conducts extensive program of promotion, education and information about beef, veal, and associated meat products. Conducts projects such as recipe testing and development, food demonstrations, food photography, educational service to colleges, experimental meat cutting methods, merchandising programs, and preparation of materials for newspapers, magazines, radio, and television.

North American Meat Processors Association. 1910 Association Dr., Reston, VA 20191. Phone: 800-368-3043 or (703)758-1900 Fax: (703)758-8001 E-mail: pkimball@namp.com • URL: http://www.namp.com • Represents wholesalers of meats and meat products to hotels, restaurants, schools, hospitals, and institutions. Conducts technical seminars.

MEAT PACKING INDUSTRY

See: MEAT INDUSTRY

MECHANICAL DRAWING

GENERAL WORKS

Fundamentals of Engineering Drawing and Design. Cecil H. Jensen and Jay D. Helsel. Glencoe/ McGraw-Hill. • 1995. $73.56. 5th edition.

PERIODICALS AND NEWSLETTERS

Engineering Design Graphics Journal. American Society for Engineering Education. • Three times a year. Free to members; Non-members, $24.00 per year. Concerned with engineering graphics, computer graphics, geometric modeling, computer-aided drafting, etc.

TRADE/PROFESSIONAL ASSOCIATIONS

American Design Drafting Association. 105 E Main St., Newbern, TN 38059. Phone: (731)627-0802 Fax: (731)627-9321 E-mail: cadboss@gmail.com • URL: http://www.adda.org • Designers, drafters, drafting managers, chief drafters, supervisors, administrators, instructors, and students of design and drafting. Encourages a continued program of education for self-improvement and professionalism in design and drafting and computer-aided design/ drafting. Informs members of effective techniques and materials used in drawings and other graphic presentations. Evaluates curriculum of educational institutions through certification program; sponsors drafter certification program.

MECHANICAL ENGINEERING

See also: MACHINE DESIGN

ABSTRACTS AND INDEXES

Applied Mechanics Reviews: An Assessment of World Literature in Engineering Sciences. ASME International. • Monthly. Members, $138.00 per year; non-members, $741.00 per year. Includes print and online editions.

Engineering Index Monthly: Abstracting and Indexing Services Covering Sources of the World's Engineering Literature. Engineering Information Inc. • Monthly. Institutions, $5,279.00 per year. Provides indexing and abstracting of the world's engineering and technical literature.

Mechanical Engineering Abstracts. CSA. • Bimonthly. $1,620.00 per year. Includes print and online editions. Formerly *ISMEC - Mechanical Engineering Abstracts.*

BIBLIOGRAPHIES

Encyclopedia of Physical Science and Engineering Information. Gale Cengage Learning. • 1996. $160.00. Second edition. Includes print, electronic, and other information sources for a wide range of scientific, technical, and engineering topics.

BIOGRAPHICAL SOURCES

Who's Who in Science and Engineering. Marquis Who's Who. • Biennial. $269.00. Provides concise biographical information on 35,000 prominent engineers and scientists. International coverage, with geographical and professional indexes.

DIRECTORIES

Peterson's Graduate and Professional Programs in Engineering and Applied Sciences. Peterson's. • Annual. $49.95. Provides details of more than 3,400 graduate and professional programs in engineering and related fields at colleges and universities. (Peterson's Graduate in Professional Programs Series). Formerly *Peterson's Guide to Graduate Programs in Engineering and Professional Sciences.*

HANDBOOKS AND MANUALS

Mechanical Engineering Design. Joseph Shigley and others. McGraw-Hill. • 2003. Seventh edition. Price on application.

Mechanical Engineers' Handbook. Myer P. Kutz. John Wiley and Sons, Inc. • 1998. $250.00. Second edition.

Mechanical Engineer's Reference Book. E. H. Smith, editor. Society of Automotive Engineers. • 1994. $135.00. 12th edition. Covers mechanical engineering principles, computer integrated engineering systems, design standards, materials, power transmission, and many other engineering topics. (Authored Series).

ONLINE DATABASES

NTIS Database. National Technical Information Service. • Contains citations and abstracts to unrestricted reports of government-sponsored research, 1964 to date. Covers a wide range of technical, engineering, business, and social science topics. Monthly updates. Inquire as to online cost and availability.

Who's Who in Technology [Online]. Gale Cengage Learning. • Provides online biographical profiles of over 25,000 American scientists, engineers, and others in technology-related occupations. Inquire as to online cost and availability.

PERIODICALS AND NEWSLETTERS

International Journal of Mechanical Sciences. Elsevier. • Monthly. Qualified personnel, $228.00 per year; institutions, $2,678.00 per year.

Journal of Applied Mechanics. ASME International. • Bimonthly. Members, $60.00 per year; non-members, $300.00 per year. Subscription includes online edition.

Journal of Heat Transfer. ASME International. • Quarterly. Members, $60.00 per year; non-members, $300.00 per year. Subscription includes online edition.

Journal of Turbomachinery. ASME International. • Quarterly. Members, $50.00 per year; includes print and online editions. Non-members, $250.00 per year; includes print and online editions.

Mechanical Engineering. ASME International. • Monthly. Members, $25.00 per year; non-members, $123.00 per year.

RESEARCH CENTERS AND INSTITUTES

Engineering Dean's Office. University of California at Berkeley, 308 Mclaughin Hall, MC. 1702, Berkeley, CA 94720-1706. Phone: (510)642-7594 Fax: (510)643-8653 E-mail: dma@coe.berkeley.edu • Research fields include civil, electrical, industrial, mechanical, and other types of engineering.

TRADE/PROFESSIONAL ASSOCIATIONS

American Society of Mechanical Engineers. Three Park Ave., New York, NY 10016-5990. Phone: 800-843-2763 or (212)591-7722 Fax: (212)591-7674 E-mail: infocentral@asme.org • URL: http://www.asme.org.

MECHANICAL POWER TRANSMISSION

See: POWER (MECHANICAL)

MEDIA, INTERACTIVE

See: INTERACTIVE MEDIA

MEDIA LAW

See: ADVERTISING LAW AND REGULATION; MASS MEDIA

MEDIA, MASS

See: MASS MEDIA

MEDIA RESEARCH

See also: ADVERTISING RESEARCH; MASS MEDIA

GENERAL WORKS

Electronic Media Ratings. Karen Buzzard. Elsevier. • 1992. $22.95. Provides basic information about

TV and radio audience-rating techniques. Includes glossary and bibliography. (Electronic Media Guide Series).

ABSTRACTS AND INDEXES

Business Periodicals Index. H. W. Wilson Co. • 11 times a year. Quarterly and annual cumulations. Price varies.

Communication Abstracts: An International Information Service. Sage Publications, Inc. • Bimonthly. Institutions, $1,150.00 per year. Provides broad coverage of the literature of communications, including broadcasting and advertising.

Electronics and Communications Abstracts Journal: Comprehensive Coverage of Essential Scientific Literature. CSA. • Monthly. $1,665.00 per year. Includes print and online editions.

DIRECTORIES

VNU Business Media. ADWEEK Directories. • Annual. $100.00. Presents cost, circulation, and audience statistics for various mass media segments, including television, radio, magazines, newspapers, telephone yellow pages, and cinema.

ENCYCLOPEDIAS AND DICTIONARIES

Advertising Age Encyclopedia of Advertising. John McDonough and others, editors. Fitzroy Dearborn Publishers. • 2002. $385.00. Three volumes. Contains 600 entries in alphabetical order covering a wide variety of advertising and market research topics. Includes bibliographies.

Encyclopedia of New Media: An Essential Reference to Communication and Technology. Steve Jones, editor. Sage Publications, Inc. • 2003. $125.00. Contains more than 250 entries dealing with such areas as multimedia, broadband access, information communication technology (ICT), content filtering, wireless networks, and cyberethics.

INTERNET DATABASES

Pew Research Center for the People and the Press. Pew Charitable Trusts. Phone: (202)293-3126 Fax: (202)293-2569 E-mail: mailprc@people-press.org • URL: http://www.people-press.org • Free Web site includes public opinion poll "Reports by Topic." Five broad subject areas cover business, social issues, foreign policy, news media, and politics. Searching is offered within each of these broad areas, and there are links to other major sources of public opinion poll results ("FYI Other Polls").

ONLINE DATABASES

Marketing and Advertising Reference Service (MARS). Gale Cengage Learning. • Provides abstracts of literature relating to consumer marketing and advertising, including all forms of advertising media. Time period is 1984 to date. Daily updates. Inquire as to online cost and availability.

National Consumer Survey. Simmons Market Research Bureau. • Market and media survey data relating to the American consumer. Inquire as to online cost and availability.

Nielsen Station Index. Nielsen Media Research. • Measures local television station audiences in about 220 U. S. geographic areas. Includes current and some historical data. Inquire as to online cost and availability.

Nielsen Television Index. Nielsen Media Research. • Measures national television program audiences by sampling approximately 4,000 U. S. households. Time period is 1970 to date, with weekly updates.

Wilson Business Abstracts Online. H. W. Wilson Co. • Indexes and abstracts 600 major business periodicals, plus the *Wall Street Journal* and the business section of the *New York Times*. Indexing is from 1982, abstracting from 1990, with the two newspapers included from 1993. Updated weekly. Inquire as to online cost and availability. (*Business*

Periodicals Index without abstracts is also available online.).

PERIODICALS AND NEWSLETTERS

American Demographics: Consumer Trends for Business Leaders. Media Central. • Monthly. $58.00 per year.

Journal of Advertising Research. Advertising Research Foundation. • Quarterly. Individuals, $155.00 per year; institutions, $275.00 per year.

Journal of Applied Communication Research. National Communication Association. • Quarterly. $110.00 per year.

The Marketing Pulse: The Exclusive Insight Provider to the Entertainment, Marketing, Advertising and Media Industries. Unlimited Positive Communications, Inc. • Bimonthly. $300.00 per year. Newsletter concerned with advertising media forecasts and analyses. Emphasis is on TV and radio.

Mediaweek: The News Magazine of the Media. VNU Business Media. • 47 times a year. Weekly. $149.00 per year. Published for advertising media buyers and managers.

RESEARCH CENTERS AND INSTITUTES

Center for Communication Research. University of Wisconsin-Madison, 821 University Ave., Madison, WI 53706. Phone: (608)262-2543 Fax: (608)262-9953 E-mail: jdillard@facstaff.wisc.edu.

Center for Media and Public Affairs. 2100 L St., N. W., Suite 300, Washington, DC 20037. Phone: (202)223-2942 Fax: (202)872-4014 E-mail: cmpamm@aol.com • URL: http://www.cmpa.com.

Integrated Media Systems Center. University of Southern California, 3740 McClintock Ave., Suite 131, Los Angeles, CA 90089-2561. Phone: (213)740-0877 Fax: (213)740-8931 E-mail: imsc@imsc.usc.edu • URL: http://www.imsc.usc.edu • Media areas for research include education, mass communication, and entertainment.

Knight Center for Specialized Journalism. University of Maryland, 1117 Cole Field House, College Park, MD 20742-1024. Phone: (301)405-4817 E-mail: knight@umail.umd.edu • URL: http://www.knightcenter.umd.edu/ • Research area is media coverage of complex subjects, such as economics, law, science, and medicine.

Mass Communications Research Center. University of Wisconsin-Madison, 821 University Ave., 5050 Vilas Hall, Madison, WI 53706. Phone: (608)263-3381 Fax: (608)262-1361 E-mail: rhawkins@wisc.edu.

TRADE/PROFESSIONAL ASSOCIATIONS

American Marketing Association. 311 S Wacker Dr., Ste. 5800, Chicago, IL 60606. Phone: 800-262-1150 or (312)542-9000 Fax: (312)542-9001 E-mail: info@ama.org • URL: http://www.marketingpower.com • Serves as a professional society of marketing and market research executives, sales and promotion managers, advertising specialists, academics, and others interested in marketing. Fosters research; sponsors seminars, conferences, and student marketing clubs; provides educational placement service and doctoral consortium.

ARF - Advertising Research Foundation. 432 Park Ave. S, New York, NY 10016. Phone: (212)751-5656 Fax: (212)319-5265 E-mail: info@thearf.org • URL: http://www.thearf.org • Advertisers, advertising agencies, research organizations, associations, and the media are regular members of the foundation; colleges and universities are associate members. Objectives are to: further scientific practices and promote greater effectiveness of advertising and marketing by means of objective and impartial research; develop new research methods and techniques; analyze and evaluate existing methods and techniques, and define proper applications; establish research standards, criteria, and

reporting methods. Compiles statistics and conducts research programs.

Marketing Research Association. 110 National Dr., 2nd Fl., PO Box 230, Glastonbury, CT 06033-1212. Phone: (860)682-1000 Fax: (860)682-1010 E-mail: larry.brownell@mra-net.org • URL: http://www.mra-net.org • Companies and individuals involved in any area of opinion and marketing research, such as data collection, research, or as an end-user.

MEDIATION

See: ARBITRATION

MEDICAL CARE INDUSTRY

See: HEALTH CARE INDUSTRY

MEDICAL ECONOMICS (PRACTICE MANAGEMENT)

See also: GROUP MEDICAL PRACTICE; HEALTH CARE INDUSTRY

BIBLIOGRAPHIES

Medical and Health Care Books and Serials in Print: An Index to Literature in Health Sciences. R. R. Bowker. • Annual. $359.00. Two volumes.

DIRECTORIES

Directory of Physician Groups and Networks. Dorland Healthcare Information. • Annual. $495.00. Available only online. Approximately 8,000 independent practice associations (IPAs), physician hospital organizations (PHOs), management service organizations (MSOs), physician practice management companies (PPMCs), and group practices having 20 or more physicians.

Encyclopedia of Medical Organizations and Agencies. Gale Cengage Learning. • 2001. $295.00. 11th edition. Information on over 18,000 public and private organizations in medicine and related fields.

Medical and Health Information Directory. Gale Cengage Learning. • 2002. $675.00. Three volumes. 14th edition. Three volumes. $285.00 per volume. Vol. one covers medical organizations, agencies, and institutions; vol. two includes bibliographic, library, and database information; vol. three is a guide to services available for various medical and health problems.

Society of Medical-Dental Management Consultants: Membership Directory. Society of Medical-Dental Management Consultants. • Annual. Free. About 100 consultants in business and financial aspects of the management of medical and dental practices.

ENCYCLOPEDIAS AND DICTIONARIES

Encyclopedia of Health Care Management. Michael Stahl, editor. Sage Publications, Inc. • 2004. $150.00. Contains 600 entries covering "the business of health care.".

Guidebook to Managed Care and Practice Management Terminology. Norman Winegar and L. Michelle Hayter. Haworth Press, Inc. • 1998. $39.95. Provides definitions of managed care "terminology, jargon, and concepts.".

FINANCIAL RATIOS

Almanac of Business and Industrial Financial Ratios. Leo Troy. Aspen Publishers, Inc. • 2003. $125.95. Includes CD-Rom. Contains financial ratios derived from federal tax returns. Ratios for each of about 200 industries are arranged according to company asset size. (Almanac of Business and Industrial Financial Ratios Series).

Annual Statement Studies. The Risk Management

Association. • Annual. Median and quartile financial ratios are given for over 400 kinds of manufacturing, wholesale, retail, construction, and consumer finance establishments. Data is sorted by both asset size and sales volume. Includes a clearly written "Definition of Ratios" and an alphabetical industry index.

Annual Statement Studies: Industry Default Probabilities and Cash Flow Measures. The Risk Management Association. • Annual. $145.00. Serves as a companion volume to the original *Annual Statement Studies.* Gives probability of default estimates on a percentage scale for more than 450 industries. Includes changes in position year-by-year for eight financial statement line items and provides percentage measures of cash flow.

Industry Norms and Key Business Ratios. Desk Top Edition. Dun and Bradstreet Corp. • Annual. Five volumes. $475.00 per volume. $1,890.00 per set. Covers over 800 kinds of businesses, arranged by Standard Industrial Classification number. More detailed editions covering longer periods of time are also available.

HANDBOOKS AND MANUALS

Healthcare Finance for the Non-Financial Manager: Basic Guide to Financial Analysis & Control. Louis Gapenski. McGraw-Hill. • 1994. $47.50.

Managed Care Handbook: How to Prepare Your Medical Practice for the Managed Care Revolution. James R. Lyle and Hoyt Torras. Practice Management Information Corp. • 1994. $49.95. Second edition. A management guide for physicians in private practice.

ONLINE DATABASES

Healthstar. Medlars Management Section. • Provides indexing and abstracting of non-clinical literature relating to health care delivery, 1975 to date. Monthly updates. Inquire as to online cost and availability.

PERIODICALS AND NEWSLETTERS

Dental Economics. Pennwell Publishing Co., Dental Economics Div. • Monthly. $88.00 per year.

Dental Practice and Finance. MEDEC Dental Communications. • Bimonthly. $55.00 per year. Covers practice management and financial topics for dentists. Includes investment advice.

Group Practice Journal. American Medical Group Practice Association. • 10 times a year. Institutions, $75.00 per year.

Health Care Strategic Management: The Newsletter for Hospital Strategies. Business Word, Inc. • Monthly. $284.00 per year. Planning, marketing and resource allocation.

Health Marketing Quarterly. The Haworth Press, Inc. • Quarterly. $580.00 per year.

Journal of Medical Practice Management. Greenbranch Publishing. • Bimonthly. Individuals, $169.00 per year; institutions, $213.00 per year.

Medical Economics. Advanstar Medical. • Semimonthly. $109.00 per year. Covers the financial, economic, insurance, administrative, and other non-clinical aspects of private medical practice. Provides investment and estate planning advice.

Medical Economics General Surgery-Orthopedic Surgery. Thomson Medical Economics. • Monthly. $65.00 per year. Provides information and advice on practice management (non-clinical) for surgeons. Formerly *Medical Economics for Surgeons.*

Medicare Compliance Alert. United Communications Group. • Description: Procvides news and guidance to help keep health care practices on the right side of fraud and abuse laws and regulations.

MGMA Connexion. Medical Group Management Association. • 10 times a year. Individuals, $95.00 per year; institutions, $175.00 per year. Formerly *Medical Group Management Journal.*

Modern Physician: Essential Business News for the Executive Physician. Crain Communications, Inc. • Monthly. $45.00. Edited for physicians responsible for business decisions at hospitals, clinics, HMOs, and other health groups. Includes special issues on managed care, practice management, legal issues, and finance.

Nursing Economics: The Journal for Health Care Leaders. Jannetti Publications, Inc. • Bimonthly. Individuals, $54.00 per year; institutions, $70.00 per year.

Nursing Management. Springhouse Corp. Lippincott Williams and Wilkins. • Monthly. Individuals, $39.95 per year; institutions, $139.00 per year. Non-clinical subject matter.

Optometric Management: The Business and Marketing Magazine for Optometry. Boucher Communications, Inc. • Monthly. $37.00 per year. Provides information and advice for optometrists on practice management and marketing.

Physicians & Computers. Moorhead Publications Inc. • Monthly. $40.00 per year. Includes material on computer diagnostics, online research, medical and non-medical software, computer equipment, and practice management.

Physicians Financial News. • Monthly. $105.00 per year.

Physician's Marketing and Management. American Health Consultants, Inc. • Monthly. Individuals, $299.00 per year; institutions, $323.00 per year. Newsletter. Formerly *Physician's Marketing.*

Podiatry Management. Kane Communications, Inc. • Nine times a year. $30.00 per year. Non-clinical subject matter.

Private Practice. Congress of County Medical Societies (CCMS) Publishing Co. • Monthly. $18.00 per year.

Resident and Staff Physician. Romaine Pierson Publishers, Inc. • Monthly. Individuals, $83.00 per year institutions, $149.00 per year; students, $50.00 per year.

Services Marketing Quarterly. Haworth Press, Inc. • Quarterly. Institutions, $425.00 per year. Two volumes. Supplies "how to" marketing tools for specific sectors of the expanding service sector of the economy. Formerly *Journal of Professional Services Marketing.*

TRADE/PROFESSIONAL ASSOCIATIONS

American Academy of Dental Group Practice. 2525 E. Arizona Biltmore Circle, Ste. 127, Phoenix, AZ 85016. Phone: (602)381-1185 Fax: (602)381-1093 E-mail: info@aadgp.org • URL: http://www.aadgp. org.

American Academy of Dental Practice Administration. c/o Kathleen Uebel, 1063 Whippoorwill Lane, Palatine, IL 60067-7064. Phone: (847)934-4404 Fax: (847)934-4410 E-mail: aadpa@ aol.com • URL: http://www.aadpa.org • Professional society of dentists interested in efficient administration of dental practice. Offers educational programs.

American Academy of Family Physicians. 11400 Tomahawk Creek Parkway, Leawood, MO 66211-2672. Phone: 800-274-2237 or (913)906-6000 Fax: (913)906-6077 E-mail: fp@aafp.org • URL: http:// www.aafp.org • Formerly American Academy of General Practice.

American College of Medical Practice Executives. 104 Inverness Terrace E., Englewood, CO 80112-5306. Phone: 877-275-6442 Fax: (303)643-4439 E-mail: acmpe@mgma.com • URL: http://www. mgma.com/acmpe • Formerly American College of Medical Group Administrators.

American Medical Association. 515 N State St.,

Chicago, IL 60610. Phone: 800-621-8335 or (312)464-5000 Fax: (312)464-4184 E-mail: msc@ ama-assn.org • URL: http://www.ama-assn.org • Represents county medical societies and physicians. Disseminates scientific information to members and the public. Informs members on significant medical and health legislation on state and national levels and represents the profession before Congress and governmental agencies. Cooperates in setting standards for medical schools, hospitals, residency programs, and continuing medical education courses. Offers physician placement service and counseling on practice management problems. Operates library that lends material and provides specific medical information to physicians. Maintains Ad-hoc committees for such topics as health care planning and principles of medical ethics.

American Medical Group Association. 1422 Duke St., Alexandria, VA 22314-3403. Phone: (703)838-0033 Fax: (703)548-1890 E-mail: dfisher@amga. org • URL: http://www.amga.org • Represents the interests of medical groups. Advocates for the medical groups and patients through innovation and information sharing, benchmarking, developing leadership, and improving patient care. Provides political advocacy, educational and networking programs and publications, benchmarking data services, and financial and operations assistance.

American Professional Practice Association. Association Member Service Center, Hillsboro Executive Center N, 350 Fairway Dr., Ste. 200, Deerfield Beach, FL 33441-1834. Phone: 800-221-2168 or (954)571-1877 Fax: (954)571-8582 E-mail: membership@assnservices.com • URL: http://www. appa-assn.com • Provides physicians with economic benefits and financial services including the following: unsecured loan plans, mortgage loans, group insurance discounts, accounts receivable collections, office supplies, wealth protection and a vision and dental plan.

Medical Group Management Association. 104 Inverness Terr. E, Englewood, CO 80112-5306. Phone: 877-275-6462 or (303)799-1111 or (303)799-1111 Fax: (303)643-4439 E-mail: service@mgma.com • URL: http://www.mgma.com • Represents professionals involved in the management of medical group practices and administration of other ambulatory healthcare facilities. Provides products and services that includes education, benchmarking, surveys, national advocacy and networking opportunities for members.

Society of Medical-Dental Management Consultants. 3646 E. Ray Rd., B16-45, Phoenix, AZ 85044. Phone: 800-826-2264 Fax: (602)759-3530 E-mail: chuck@smdmc.org • URL: http://www. smdmc.org.

MEDICAL ELECTRONICS

See also: MEDICAL TECHNOLOGY

ABSTRACTS AND INDEXES

Applied Science and Technology Index. H. W. Wilson Co. • 11 times a year. Quarterly and annual cumulations. Price varies. Indexes a wide variety of English language technical, industrial, and engineering periodicals.

Excerpta Medica: Biophysics, Bioengineering, and Medical Instrumentation. Elsevier. • 16 times a year. Institutions, $2,859 per year. Section 27 of *Excerpta Medica.*

NTIS Alerts: Biomedical Technology & Human Factors Engineering. National Technical Information Service. • Semimonthly. $210.00 per year. Provides descriptions of government-sponsored research reports and software, with ordering information. Covers biotechnology, ergonomics, bionics, artificial intelligence, prosthetics, and related subjects. Formerly *Abstract Newsletter*.

CD-ROM DATABASES

Health Devices Alerts [CD-ROM]. ECRI. • Weekly. $2,450.00 per year. Provides CD-ROM reports of medical equipment defects, problems, failures, misuses, and recalls.

WILSONDISC: Applied Science and Technology Abstracts. H. W. Wilson Co. • Monthly. Includes unlimited access to the online version of *Applied Science and Technology Abstracts* through WILSONLINE. Provides CD-ROM indexing and abstracting of 500 prominent scientific, technical, engineering, and industrial periodicals. Indexing coverage is provided from 1983 to date and abstracting from 1993 to date.

DIRECTORIES

Health Devices Sourcebook. ECRI. • Covers: Over 6,800 suppliers of patient care equipment, medical and surgical instruments, implants, clinical laboratory equipment and supplies, medical and hospital disposable supplies, and testing instruments; also lists companies that service, recondition, lease, or buy and sell used equipment; coverage includes U.S. and Canada. Entries include: Company name, address, phone, toll-free phone, fax, toll-free fax, URL, e-mail, total sales, names of key executives and contacts, product categories handled, trade names, methods of distribution, typical pricing, annual volume. Price of directory includes custom updates upon request.

Medical Product Manufacturing News Buyers Guide. Canon Communications LLC. • Annual. Price on application. A directory of over 3,000 medical device and medical electronic equipment. Formerly *Medical Product Manufacturing News-Buyer's Guide and Designer's Sourcebook*.

ENCYCLOPEDIAS AND DICTIONARIES

Wiley Encyclopedia of Electrical and Electronics Engineering. John G. Webster, editor. John Wiley and Sons, Inc. • 1999. $9,630.00. 25 volumes. Includes *Supplement I* and *Supplement II*. Contains about 1,400 articles, each with bibliography. Arrangement is according to 64 categories.

INTERNET DATABASES

Manufacturing Profiles. U. S. Bureau of the Census. Phone: (301)763-4636 E-mail: webmaster@census. gov • URL: http://www.census.gov/prod/www/abs/ mfg-prof.html • The Census Bureau makes available free on PDF (Portable Document Format) an annual consolidation of the entire Current Industrial Report series, presenting "all the data compiled." Contains statistics on production, shipments, inventories, consumption, exports, imports, and orders for a wide variety of manufactured products.

ONLINE DATABASES

Applied Science and Technology Index Online. H. W. Wilson Co. • Provides online indexing of 500 major scientific, technical, industrial, and engineering periodicals. Time period is 1983 to date. Monthly updates. Inquire as to online cost and availability.

Current Contents Connect. Institute for Scientific Information. • Provides online abstracts of articles listed in the tables of contents of about 7,500 journals. Coverage is very broad, including science, social science, life science, technology, engineering, industry, agriculture, the environment, economics, and arts and humanities. Time period is two years, with weekly updates. Inquire as to online cost and availability.

F-D-C Reports. FDC Reports, Inc. • An online version of "The Gray Sheet" (medical devices), "The Pink Sheet" (pharmaceuticals), "The Rose Sheet" (cosmetics), "The Blue Sheet" (biomedical), and "The Tan Sheet" (nonprescription). Contains full-text information on legal, technical, corporate,

financial, and marketing developments from 1987 to date, with weekly updates. Inquire as to online cost and availability.

Health Devices Alerts [online]. ECRI. • Provides online reports of medical equipment defects, problems, failures, misuses, and recalls. Time period is 1977 to date, with weekly updates. Inquire as to online cost and availability.

INSPEC. Institution of Electrical Engineers (IEE). • Provides online citations, with abstracts, to the world literature of electrical engineering, electronics, optoelectronics, telecommunications, industrial controls, instrumentation, computer technology, information technology, and physics. Coverage includes more than 4,000 technical and scientific journals from 1969 to date, with weekly updating. (INSPEC is Information Services in Physics, Electronics, and Computing.) Inquire as to online cost and availability.

PROMT: Predicasts Overview of Markets and Technology. Gale Cengage Learning. • Companies, products, applied technologies and markets. U.S. and international literature coverage, 1972 to date. Inquire as to online cost and availability. Provides abstracts from more than 1,600 publications. Weekly updates.

PERIODICALS AND NEWSLETTERS

Health Devices Alerts: A Summary of Reported Problems, Hazards, Recalls, and Updates. ECRI (Emergency Care Research Institute). • Weekly. $3,649.40 per year. Looseleaf service. Contains reviews of health equipment problems. Includes *Health Devices Alerts Action Items, Health Devices Alerts Abstracts, Health Devices Alerts FDA Data, Health Devices Alerts Implants, Health Devices Alerts Hazards Bulletin*.

Medical Laser Report. PennWell Corp. • Description: Presents news on the medical laser industry, technology, research, and markets. Recurring features include news of research, business news and product introductions.

Medical Product Manufacturing News. Canon Communications LLC. • 10 times a year. Free to qualified personnel; others, $150.00 per year. Directed at manufacturers of medical devices and medical electronic equipment. Covers industry news, service news, and new products.

MEEN Imaging Technology News. Reilly Publishing Co. • Bimonthly. Free to qualified personnel. Provides medical electronics industry news and new product information. Formerly *Medical Electronics and Equipment News*.

Physicians & Computers. Moorhead Publications Inc. • Monthly. $40.00 per year. Includes material on computer diagnostics, online research, medical and non-medical software, computer equipment, and practice management.

RESEARCH CENTERS AND INSTITUTES

Laboratory of Electronics. Rockefeller University, 1230 York Ave., New York, NY 10021. Phone: (212)327-8613 Fax: (212)327-7613 E-mail: ros@ rockvax.rockefeller.edu • Studies the application of computer engineering and electronics to biomedicine.

Medical Electronics Laboratory. University of Wisconsin-Madison, 1300 University Ave., Madison, WI 53706. Phone: (608)262-1326 Fax: (608)262-2327 E-mail: yee@physiology.wisc.edu • Develops electronic instrumentation for medical and biological research.

STATISTICS SOURCES

Annual Survey of Manufactures. Available from U. S. Government Printing Office. • Annual. Prices vary. Issued by the U. S. Census Bureau as an interim update to the *Census of Manufactures*. Includes data on number of manufacturing establishments in various industries, employment, labor

costs, value of shipments, capital expenditures, inventories, energy costs, and assets. (See also Census Bureau home page, http://www.census. gov/.).

U. S. Industry and Trade Outlook. Available from National Technical Information Service. • Annual. $69.95. Produced by the International Trade Administration, U. S. Department of Commerce, in a "public-private" partnership with DRI/McGraw-Hill and Standard & Poor's. Provides basic data, outlook for the current year, and "Long-Term Prospects" (five-year projections) for a wide variety of products and services. Includes high technology industries. Formerly *U. S. Industrial Outlook*.

TRADE/PROFESSIONAL ASSOCIATIONS

Advanced Medical Technology Association. 701 Pennsylvania Ave. NW, Ste. 800, Washington, DC 20004-2654. Phone: (202)783-8700 Fax: (202)783-8750 E-mail: info@advamed.org • URL: http:// www.advamed.org • Represents domestic (including U.S. territories and possessions) manufacturers of medical devices, diagnostic products, and health-care information systems. Develops programs and activities on economic, technical, medical, and scientific matters affecting the industry. Gathers and disseminates information concerning the United States and international developments in legislative, regulatory, scientific or standards-making areas. Conducts scientific and educational seminars and programs.

Association for the Advancement of Medical Instrumentation. 1110 N. Glebe Rd., No. 220, Arlington, VA 22201-4795. Phone: 800-332-2264 or (703)525-4890 Fax: (703)525-1424 • URL: http:// www.aami.org • Members are engineers, technicians, physicians, manufacturers, and others with an interest in medical instrumentation.

IEEE Engineering in Medicine and B iology Society. c/o IEEE Corporate Office, 3 Park Ave., 17th Fl., New York, NY 10016-5997. Phone: 800-678-4333 or (212)419-7900 Fax: (212)752-4929 E-mail: ieeeusa@ieee.org • URL: http://www.ieee. org • Members are engineers, technicians, physicians, manufacturers and others with an interest in medical instrumentation.

OTHER SOURCES

Digital X-Ray Markets: Imaging in the 21st Century. Theta Reports/PJB Medical Publications, Inc. • 2000. $1,995.00. Market research data. Covers digital filmless radiography as a replacement for traditional x-ray technology. (Theta Report No. 1027.).

MEDICAL EQUIPMENT

See: HOSPITAL EQUIPMENT; SURGICAL INSTRUMENTS INDUSTRY

MEDICAL INSURANCE

See: HEALTH INSURANCE

MEDICAL LABORATORIES

See: CLINICAL LABORATORY INDUSTRY

MEDICAL LIABILITY

See: PROFESSIONAL LIABILITY

MEDICAL SERVICE, INDUSTRIAL

See: INDUSTRIAL MEDICINE

MEDICAL TECHNOLOGY

See also: MEDICAL TECHNOLOGY; SURGICAL INSTRUMENTS INDUSTRY; X-RAY EQUIPMENT INDUSTRY

GENERAL WORKS

Health Care, Technology, and the Competitive Environment. Henry P. Brehm and Ross M. Mullner, editors. Greenwood Publishing Group, Inc. • 1989. $74.95.

Super Searchers on Health and Medicine: The Online Secrets of Top Health and Medical Researchers. Susan M. Detwiler. Information Today, Inc. • 2000. $24.95. Provides the results of interviews with 10 experts in online searching for medical research data and healthcare information. Discusses both traditional sources and Web sites. (Super Searchers Series).

ABSTRACTS AND INDEXES

Excerpta Medica: Biophysics, Bioengineering, and Medical Instrumentation. Elsevier. • 16 times a year. Institutions, $2,859 per year. Section 27 of *Excerpta Medica.*

BIBLIOGRAPHIES

Encyclopedia of Physical Science and Engineering Information. Gale Cengage Learning. • 1996. $160.00. Second edition. Includes print, electronic, and other information sources for a wide range of scientific, technical, and engineering topics.

CD-ROM DATABASES

NTIS on SilverPlatter. Available from SilverPlatter Information, Inc. • Quarterly. $2,850.00 per year. Produced by the National Technical Information Service. Provides a CD-ROM guide to over 500,000 government reports on a wide variety of technical, industrial, and business topics.

DIRECTORIES

Association for the Advancement of Medical Instrumentation Membership Directory. c/o AAMI Foundation. • Annual. Membership. List 6,500 physicians, clinical engineers, biomedical engineersand technicians and nurses, researchers, and medical equipment manufacturers.

BioScan: The Worldwide Biotech Industry Reporting Service. Greenwood Publishing Group, Inc. • Annual. $975.00 per year. Bimonthly updates. Provides detailed information on over 1,000 U.S. and foreign companies broadly classified as biotechnology. In addition to medical technology and advanced pharmaceutical firms, includes firms doing research in food processing, waste management, agriculture, and veterinary science.

Health Devices Sourcebook. ECRI. • Covers: Over 6,800 suppliers of patient care equipment, medical and surgical instruments, implants, clinical laboratory equipment and supplies, medical and hospital disposable supplies, and testing instruments; also lists companies that service, recondition, lease, or buy and sell used equipment; coverage includes U.S. and Canada. Entries include: Company name, address, phone, toll-free phone, fax, toll-free fax, URL, e-mail, total sales, names of key executives and contacts, product categories handled, trade names, methods of distribution, typical pricing, annual volume. Price of directory includes custom updates upon request.

Medical and Healthcare Marketplace Guide. IDD, Inc. • Annual. $595.00. Two volumes. Provides market survey summaries for about 500 specific product and service categories (volume one: "Research Reports"). Contains profiles of nearly 5,500 pharmaceutical, medical product, and healthcare service companies (volume two: "Company Profiles").

Medical Device Register. Canon Communications L.L.C. • Covers: More than 65,000 U.S.

Manufacturers of medical devices and clinical laboratory products; includes OEM manufacturers. Entries include: For manufacturers--Company name, address, phone, fax, telex, names and titles of key personnel, ownership, medical product sales volume, number of employees, method of distribution, medical product subsidiaries; public company listings include annual revenues and net income.

Plunkett's Health Care Industry Almanac: The Only Complete Guide to the Health Care Industry in America. Plunkett Research, Ltd. • Biennial. $229.99. Includes CD-ROM. Includes detailed profiles of 500 large companies providing health care products or services, with indexes by products, services, and location. Provides statistical and trend information for the health insurance industry, HMOs, hospital utilization, Medicare, medical technology, and national health expenditures.

FINANCIAL RATIOS

Industry Norms and Key Business Ratios. Desk Top Edition. Dun and Bradstreet Corp. • Annual. Five volumes. $475.00 per volume. $1,890.00 per set. Covers over 800 kinds of businesses, arranged by Standard Industrial Classification number. More detailed editions covering longer periods of time are also available.

HANDBOOKS AND MANUALS

Physicians' Desk Reference for Ophthalmology. Medical Economics Co. • Annual. $49.95. Provides detailed descriptions of ophthalmological instrumentation, equipment, supplies, lenses, and prescription drugs. Indexed by manufacturer, product name, product category, active drug ingredient, and instrumentation. Editorial discussion is included.

INTERNET DATABASES

National Library of Medicine (NLM). National Institutes of Health (NIH). Phone: 888-346-3656 or (301)496-1131 Fax: (301)480-3537 E-mail: access@nlm.nih.gov • URL: http://www.nlm.nih.gov • NLM Web site offers free access through MEDLINE ("PubMed") to about nine million references to articles appearing in some 4,000 biomedical journals, with abstracts. Search interfaces range from "simple keywords to advanced Boolean expressions." The NLM site offers many links to other sources of biomedical and technical information (the National Center for Biotechnology Information, for example). Fees: Free.

ONLINE DATABASES

F-D-C Reports. FDC Reports, Inc. • An online version of "The Gray Sheet" (medical devices), "The Pink Sheet" (pharmaceuticals), "The Rose Sheet" (cosmetics), "The Blue Sheet" (biomedical), and "The Tan Sheet" (nonprescription). Contains full-text information on legal, technical, corporate, financial, and marketing developments from 1987 to date, with weekly updates. Inquire as to online cost and availability.

Globalbase. Gale Cengage Learning. • Provides more than one million online summaries of business, industrial, and economic news reports from more than 1,000 publications worldwide. Covers a wide range of material appearing in international trade journals, professional magazines, and newspapers. Time period is 1984 to date, with weekly updates. Inquire as to online cost and availability.

NTIS Database. National Technical Information Service. • Contains citations and abstracts to unrestricted reports of government-sponsored research, 1964 to date. Covers a wide range of technical, engineering, business, and social science topics. Monthly updates. Inquire as to online cost and availability.

PROMT: Predicasts Overview of Markets and Technology. Gale Cengage Learning. • Companies,

products, applied technologies and markets. U.S. and international literature coverage, 1972 to date. Inquire as to online cost and availability. Provides abstracts from more than 1,600 publications. Weekly updates.

Who's Who in Technology [Online]. Gale Cengage Learning. • Provides online biographical profiles of over 25,000 American scientists, engineers, and others in technology-related occupations. Inquire as to online cost and availability.

PERIODICALS AND NEWSLETTERS

The BBI Newsletter: A Perceptive Analysis of the Healthcare Industry and Marketplace Focusing on New Technology, Strategic Planning, and Market-share Projections. American Health Consultants. • Monthly. $827.00 per year.

Biomedical Products. Reed Business Information. • Monthly. $55.90 per year. Features new products and services. Formerly *Biomedical Products.*

Biomedical Technology Information Service. Lippincott Williams & Wilkins. • Description: Monitors latest advances in medical technology, including developments in medical devices and electronics. Recurring features include new technology, computer applications, legislation and regulations, new inventions, and professional activities. Also includes book reviews, letters to the editor, and a calendar of events.

The Gray Sheet Reports: Medical Devices, Diagnostics and Instrumentation. F-D-C Reports, Inc. • Weekly. Institutions, $1,172.00 per year. Newsletter. Provides industry and financial news, including a medical sector stock index. Monitors regulatory developments at the Center for Devices and Radiological Health of the U. S. Food and Drug Administration.

Health Devices Alerts: A Summary of Reported Problems, Hazards, Recalls, and Updates. ECRI (Emergency Care Research Institute). • Weekly. $3,649.40 per year. Looseleaf service. Contains reviews of health equipment problems. Includes *Health Devices Alerts Action Items, Health Devices Alerts Abstracts, Health Devices Alerts FDA Data, Health Devices Alerts Implants, Health Devices Alerts Hazards Bulletin.*

Health News Daily. F-D-C Reports Inc. • Description: Tracks developments in health care policy, legislation and regulation, insurance, pharmaceuticals, delivery, manufacturing, technology and treatment, funding, and research.

Healthcare Informatics: The Business of Healthcare Information Technology. McGraw-Hill. • Monthly. $39.95 per year. Covers various aspects of information and computer technology for the health care industry.

HME News (Home Medical Equipment). United Publications, Inc. • Monthly. Free to qualified personnel; others, $60.00 per year. Covers the home medical equipment business for dealers and manufacturers. Provides information on a wide variety of home health care supplies and equipment.

IEEE Engineering in Medicine and Biology Magazine. Institute of Electrical and Electronics Engineers, Inc. • Six times a year, $250.00 per year. Published for biomedical engineers.

Medical Design Technology: New Productsd, Materials and Components for Medical Device Designers. Reed Business Information. • 10 times a year. $92.99 per year. Edited for medical technology personnel. Includes new product introductions and applications.

Medical Device and Diagnostic Industry. Canon Communications LLC. • Monthly. Free to qualified personnel; others, $150.00 per year.

Medical Device Technology. Elsevier. • Ten times a year. Free to qualified personnel; others, $100.00 per year.

Medical Industry Information Report. Nicholas Communications, Inc. • Quarterly. $48.00 per year. Edited for executives in medical products industries, including medical devices and equipment, hospital supplies, and pharmaceuticals. Covers major trends and developments, with an emphasis on information technology.

Medical Product Manufacturing News. Canon Communications LLC. • 10 times a year. Free to qualified personnel; others, $150.00 per year. Directed at manufacturers of medical devices and medical electronic equipment. Covers industry news, service news, and new products.

Medical Technology Stock Letter. Medical Technology Stock Letter. • Description: Specializes in investments in biotechnology companies. Offers news of the industry and recommendations for buying, selling, and holding stocks. Recurring features include news of research, a model portfolio reflecting the editors' investment strategy, and columns titled Pulse of the Market and Industry Scan. **Remarks:** Also available through e-mail.

MEEN Imaging Technology News. Reilly Publishing Co. • Bimonthly. Free to qualified personnel. Provides medical electronics industry news and new product information. Formerly*Medical Electronics and Equipment News.*

Pharmaceutical and Medical Device Law Bulletin. American Lawyer Media, Inc. • Monthly. $199.00 per year. Newsletter. Edited for lawyers concerned with drug product or medical device litigation. Contains industry news items of special interest, reports on new products, legal case summaries, Food and Drug Administration actions, patent issues, and related news reports. (A Law Journal Newsletter, formerly published by Leader Publications).

Seminars in Ultrasound, CT, and MR (Computerized Tomography and Magnetic Resonance. W.B. Saunders Co. • Bimonthly. Individuals, $212.00 per year; institutions, $316.00 per year.

Surgical Products. Reed Business Information. • Monthly. $41.90 per year. Covers new Technology and products for surgeons and operation rooms.

RESEARCH CENTERS AND INSTITUTES

ECRI: Emergency Care Research Institute. 5200 Butler Pike, Plymouth Meeting, PA 19462-1298. Phone: (610)825-6000 Fax: (610)834-1275 E-mail: info@ecri.org • URL: http://www.ecri.org • Major research area is health care technology.

Medical Electronics Laboratory. University of Wisconsin-Madison, 1300 University Ave., Madison, WI 53706. Phone: (608)262-1326 Fax: (608)262-2327 E-mail: yee@physiology.wisc.edu • Develops electronic instrumentation for medical and biological research.

Medical Instrumentation Laboratory. University of Wisconsin-Madison, 1415 Engineering Dr., Madison, WI 53706. Phone: (608)263-1574 Fax: (608)265-9239 E-mail: webster@engr.wisc.edu • URL: http://www.engr.wisc.edu • Research subjects include medical electrodes, medical amplifiers, bio-impedance techniques, and miniature tactile pressure sensors.

STATISTICS SOURCES

Electromedical Equipment and Irradiation Equipment, Including X-Ray. U. S. Bureau of the Census. • Annual. Contains shipment quantity, value of shipment, export, and import data. (Current Industrial Report No. MA-38R.).

TRADE/PROFESSIONAL ASSOCIATIONS

Advanced Medical Technology Association. 701 Pennsylvania Ave. NW, Ste. 800, Washington, DC 20004-2654. Phone: (202)783-8700 Fax: (202)783-8750 E-mail: info@advamed.org • URL: http://www.advamed.org • Represents domestic (including U.S. territories and possessions) manufacturers of medical devices, diagnostic products, and health-

care information systems. Develops programs and activities on economic, technical, medical, and scientific matters affecting the industry. Gathers and disseminates information concerning the United States and international developments in legislative, regulatory, scientific or standards-making areas. Conducts scientific and educational seminars and programs.

American Institute for Medical and Biological Engineering. 1901 Pennsylvania Ave., N.W., Suite 401, Washington, DC 20006. Phone: (202)496-9660 Fax: (202)466-8489 E-mail: info@aimbe.org • URL: http://www.aimbe.org.

Association for the Advancement of Medical Instrumentation. 1110 N. Glebe Rd., No. 220, Arlington, VA 22201-4795. Phone: 800-332-2264 or (703)525-4890 Fax: (703)525-1424 • URL: http://www.aami.org • Members are engineers, technicians, physicians, manufacturers, and others with an interest in medical instrumentation.

OTHER SOURCES

Computer Assisted Surgery: Automation, Virtual Reality, Robotics, and Radiosurgery. Theta Reports/PJB Medical Publications, Inc. • 2000. $2,295.00. Contains market research data relating to surgical systems technology. (Theta Report No. 1105.).

New and Breaking Technologies in the Pharmaceutical and Medical Device Industries. Theta Reports. • 1999. $1,695.00. Contains market research predictions of medical technology trends over the next 5 to 10 years (2004-2009), including developments in biotechnology, genetic engineering, medical device technology, therapeutic vaccines, non-invasive diagnostics, and minimally-invasive surgery. (Theta Report No. 931.).

New Ophthalmology: Treatments and Technologies. Theta Reports. • 2000. $1,695. Provides market research data relating to eye surgery, including LASIK, cataract surgery, and associated technology. (Theta Report No. 911.).

Pharmaceutical Litigation Reporter: The National Journal of Record of Pharmaceutical Litigation. Andrews Publications. • Monthly. $775.00 per year. Newsletter. Reports on a wide variety of legal cases involving the pharmaceutical and medical device industries. Includes product liability lawsuits.

MEDICARE

See also: HEALTH CARE INDUSTRY; HEALTH INSURANCE; SOCIAL SECURITY

GENERAL WORKS

Medical Care, Medical Costs: The Search for a Health Insurance Policy. Rashi Fein. Replica Books. • 1999. $29.00.

Medicare Made Easy: Everything You Need to Know to Make Medicare Work for You. Charles B. Inlander and Michael A. Danio. Fine Communications. • 1999. $19.98. Revised edition. Provides basic information on Medicare claims processing and the manner in which Medicare relates to other health insurance. The author is a consumer advocate and president of the People's Medical Society.

Social Security, Medicare, and Government Pensions: Get the Most Out of Your Retirement and Medical Benefits. Joseph Matthews and Dorothy M. Berman. Nolo. • 2002. $29.99. Eighth edition. In addition to the basic topics, includes practical information on Supplemental Security Income (SSI), disability benefits, veterans benefits, 401(k) plans, Medicare HMOs, medigap insurance, Medicaid, and how to appeal decisions. (Social Security, Medicare and Pensions Series).

ABSTRACTS AND INDEXES

NTIS Alerts: Health Care. National Technical Information Service. • Semimonthly. $210.00 per

year. Provides descriptions of government-sponsored research reports and software, with ordering information. Covers a wide variety of health care topics, including quality assurance, delivery organization, economics (costs), technology, and legislation. Formerly *Abstract Newsletter.*

Readers' Guide to Periodical Literature. H. W. Wilson Co. • Monthly. $345.00 per year. Includes annual *Cumulation.* Indexes about 250 peridicals of general interest.

BIBLIOGRAPHIES

Encyclopedia of Health Information Sources. Gale Cengage Learning. • 1993. $180.00. Second edition. Both print and nonprint sources of information are listed for 450 health-related topics.

CD-ROM DATABASES

Authority Health Care Law Library. LexisNexis/Matthew Bender. • Periodic updates. Price on request. Full text CD-ROM provides legal information, case law, and analysis relating to health care facilities, health insurance, longterm care, Medigap, and Medicare.

WILSONDISC: Readers' Guide to Periodical Literature. H. W. Wilson Co. • Monthly. $1,095.00 per year, including unlimited online access to *Readers' Guide to Periodical Literature* through WILSONLINE. Provides CD-ROM indexing of about 270 general interest periodicals. Covers 1983 to date. (*Readers' Guide Abstracts* also available on CD-ROM at $1,995 per year.).

DIRECTORIES

Encyclopedia of Medical Organizations and Agencies. Gale Cengage Learning. • 2001. $295.00. 11th edition. Information on over 18,000 public and private organizations in medicine and related fields.

Medical and Health Information Directory. Gale Cengage Learning. • 2002. $675.00. Three volumes. 14th edition. Three volumes. $285.00 per volume. Vol. one covers medical organizations, agencies, and institutions; vol. two includes bibliographic, library, and database information; vol. three is a guide to services available for various medical and health problems.

Plunkett's Health Care Industry Almanac: The Only Complete Guide to the Health Care Industry in America. Plunkett Research, Ltd. • Biennial. $229.99. Includes CD-ROM. Includes detailed profiles of 500 large companies providing health care products or services, with indexes by products, services, and location. Provides statistical and trend information for the health insurance industry, HMOs, hospital utilization, Medicare, medical technology, and national health expenditures.

ENCYCLOPEDIAS AND DICTIONARIES

Rupp's Insurance and Risk Management Glossary. Richard V. Rupp. NILS Publishing Co. • 2001. $35.00. Second edition. Provides definitions of 6,400 insurance words and phrases. Includes a guide to acronyms and abbreviations.

HANDBOOKS AND MANUALS

All About Medicare. The National Underwriter Co. • Annual. $16.95.

Complete and Easy Guide to Social Security, Healthcare Rights and Government Benefits. Faustin Jehle. Emerson-Adams Press, Inc. • 2000. $18.95. 16th unabridged edition.

How to Cover the Gaps in Medicare: Health Insurance and Long-Term Care Options for the Retired. Robert A. Gilmour. American Institute for Economic Research. • 2003. $10.00. Four parts: "The Medicare Quandry," "How to Protect Yourself Against the Medigap," "Long-Term Care Options", and "End-of-Life Decisions" (living wills). Includes discussions of long-term care insurance, retirement communities, and HMO Medicare insurance.

Medical Claims Processing. Entrepreneur Media,

Inc. • Looseleaf. $59.50. A practical guide to starting a medical claims processing service. Covers profit potential, start-up costs, market size evaluation, owner's time required, site selection, pricing, accounting, advertising, promotion, etc. (Start-Up Business Guide No. E1345.).

Medicare and Coordinated Care Plans. Available from Consumer Information Center. • Free. Published by the U. S. Department of Health and Human Services. Contains detailed information on services to Medicare beneficiaries from health maintenance organizations (HMOs). (Publication No. 509-X.).

Medicare: Employer Health Plans. Available from Consumer Information Center. • Free. Published by the U. S. Department of Health and Human Services. Explains the special rules that apply to Medicare beneficiaries who have employer group health plan coverage. (Publication No. 520-Y.).

Medicare Explained. CCH, Inc. • Annual. $37.50.

Medicare Handbook. Available from U. S. Government Printing Office. • Annual. $3.00. Issued by the Health Care Financing Administration, U. S. Department of Health and Human Services. Provides information on Medicare hospital insurance and medical insurance, including benefits, options, and rights. Discusses the functions of Medigap insurance, managed care plans, peer review organizations, and Medicare insurance carriers. Formerly *Medicare Handbook.*

Nursing Home Regulations Manual. Thompson Publishing Group, Inc. • $295.00 per year. Looseleaf service. Includes monthly updates, newsletters and internet access. Serves as a comprehensive guide to the Nursing Home Reform Act, federal regulations, resident assessment, deficiency findings, Medicare, Medicaid, Health Care Financing Administration (HCFA) policies, and related topics for nursing home and assisted living facility owners and managers.

Social Security Handbook. Available from U. S. Government Printing Office. • Annual. $53.00. Issued by the Social Security Administration (http://www.ssa.gov). Provides detailed information about social security programs, including Medicare, with brief descriptions of related programs administered by agencies other than the Social Security Administration.

INTERNET DATABASES

InsWeb. InsWeb Corp. Phone: (916)853-3300 E-mail: info@insweb.com • URL: http://www.insweb.com • Web site offers a wide variety of advice and information on automobile, life, health, and "other" insurance. Includes glossaries of insurance terms, Standard & Poor's ratings of individual insurance companies, and "Financial Needs Estimators." Searching is available. Fees: Free.

Medicare: The Official U. S. Government Site for Medicare Information. Centers for Medicare and Medicaid Services. Phone: (202)690-6726 • URL: http://www.medicare.gov • Web site provides extensive information on Medicare health plans, publications, fraud, nursing homes, top 20 questions and answers, etc. Includes access to the National Nursing Home Database, providing summary compliance information on "every Medicare and Medicaid certified nursing home in the country." Online searching is offered. Fees: Free.

Social Security Online: The Official Web Site of the Social Security Administration. U. S. Social Security Administration. Phone: 800-772-1213 or (410)965-7700 • URL: http://www.ssa.gov • Web site provides a wide variety of online information relating to social security and Medicare. Topics include benefits, disability, employer wage reporting, personal earnings statements, statistics, government

financing, social security law, and public welfare reform legislation.

ONLINE DATABASES

Readers' Guide Abstracts Online. H. W. Wilson Co. • Indexes and abstracts general interest periodicals, 1983 to date. Weekly updates. Inquire as to online cost and availability.

PERIODICALS AND NEWSLETTERS

American Health Care Association: Provider. American Health Care Association. • Monthly. $48.00 per year. Formerly *American Health Care Association Journal.*

Health Care Financing Review. Available from U. S. Government Printing Office. • Quarterly. $48.00 per year. Issued by the Health Care Financing Administration, U. S. Department of Health and Human Services. Presents articles by professionals in the areas of health care costs and financing.

Health Policy and Biomedical Research: The Blue Sheet. F-D-C Reports, Inc. • 51 times a year. $716.00 per year. Newsletter. Emphasis is on news of medical research agencies and institutions, especially the National Institutes of Health (NIH).

Home Health Line: The Home Care Industry's National Independent Newsletter. • 48 times a year. $399.00 per year. Newsletter on legislation and regulations affecting the home health care industry, with an emphasis on federal funding and Medicare programs.

Medical Benefits. Aspen Publishers Inc. • Description: Focuses on key developments, statistics, and studies relating to the health care system. Covers eight major topic areas: cost containment, employee benefits, employee health/wellness, quality of care, delivery systems, government in health care, legal issues, and health care expenditure data.

Medicare Compliance Alert. United Communications Group. • Description: Procvides news and guidance to help keep health care practices on the right side of fraud and abuse laws and regulations.

Older Americans Report. Business Publishers Inc. • Description: Features brief articles on legislative, judicial, and federal agency activities concerning older Americans. Covers news of developments in such areas as Social Security, social services, Medicare, programs for retirement and pension funds, research projects, and the Older Americans Act. Recurring features include book reviews and a calendar of events.

RESEARCH CENTERS AND INSTITUTES

Center for Health Administration Studies. University of Chicago, 969 E. 60th St., Chicago, IL 60637. Phone: (773)702-7104 Fax: (773)702-7222 E-mail: chas@uchichago.edu • URL: http://www.chas.uchichago.edu.

Center for Health Economics Research. 411 Waverly Oaks Rd., Suite 330, Waltham, MA 02452. Phone: (781)788-8100 Fax: (781)788-8101 E-mail: jmitchell@cher.org • URL: http://www.her-cher.org • A social science research company.

Center for Health Research. Wayne State University, College of Nursing, 5557 Cass Ave., Detroit, MI 48202-3515. Phone: (313)577-4134 Fax: (313)577-5777 E-mail: nursinginfo@wayne.edu • URL: http://www.nursing.wayne.edu • Studies innovation in health care organization and financing.

Center for the Study of Aging. University of Bridgeport, Carlson Hall, 303 University Ave., Division of Counseling and Human Resources, Bridgeport, CT 06601. Phone: (203)576-4175 Fax: (203)576-4200 E-mail: kaplin@bridgeport.edu • Research activities include the study of Medicare and Medicaid.

Health Services Research and Development Center. Johns Hopkins University, 624 N. Broadway, Room 482, Baltimore, MD 21205-1996. Phone: (410)955-

3625 Fax: (410)614-9152 E-mail: dsteinwa@jhsph.edu.

Institute for Health, Health Care Policy, and Aging Research. Rutgers University, 30 College Ave., New Brunswick, NJ 08901-1293. Phone: (732)932-8413 Fax: (732)932-6872 E-mail: caboyer@rci.rutgers.edu • URL: http://www.ihhcpar.rutgers.edu/ • Areas of study include HMO use by older adults.

Malcolm Wiener Center for Social Policy. Harvard University, John F. Kennedy School of Government, 79 John F. Kennedy St., Cambridge, MA 02138. Phone: (617)495-1461 Fax: (617)496-9053 E-mail: julie_wilson@harvard.edu • URL: http://www.ksg.harvard.edu/socpol • Does multidisciplinary research on health care access and financing.

Michigan Health and Social Security Research Institute. 8000 E. Jefferson Ave., Detroit, MI 48214-2699. Phone: (313)926-5321 Fax: (313)824-7220 • Studies the health and social security problems of trade union members.

National Center for Policy Analysis. 12655 N. Central Expressway, Suite 720, Dallas, TX 75243-1739. Phone: (214)386-6272 Fax: (214)386-0924 E-mail: jcgoodman@ncpa.org • URL: http://www.ncpa.org • Includes studies on medicare.

Stratis Health. 2901 Metro Dr., Suite 400, Bloomington, MN 55425-1525. Phone: (952)854-3306 Fax: (952)853-8503 E-mail: info@stratishealth.org • URL: http://www.stratishealth.org.

Thomas A. Roe Institute for Economic Policy Studies. Heritage Foundation, 214 Massachusetts Ave., N. E., Washington, DC 20002. Phone: (202)546-4400 Fax: (202)544-8328 E-mail: staff@heritage.org • URL: http://www.heritage.org/department/roe • Concerned with the financing of Medicare.

STATISTICS SOURCES

DRG Handbook. HCIA-Sachs, Inc. • Annual. $399.00. Presents summary data for all 477 DRGs (diagnosis-related groups) and the 23 MDCs (major diagnostic categories), based on information from more than 11 million Medicare patients. Ranks DRG information for 100 hospital groups according to number of beds, payor mix, case-mix, system affiliation, and profitability. Emphasis is financial. Formerly *Medicare DRG Handbook.*

Health, United States, 1999: Health and Aging Chartbook. Available from U. S. Government Printing Office. • 1999. $43.00. Issued by the National Center for Health Statistics, U. S. Department of Health and Human Services. Contains 34 bar charts in color, with related statistical tables. Provides detailed data on persons over 65 years of age, including population, living arrangements, life expectancy, nursing home residence, poverty, health status, assistive devices, health insurance, and health care expenditures.

Statistical Handbook on Aging Americans. Renee Schick. Greenwood Publishing Group, Inc. • 1994. $69.95. Second edition. Provides data on demographics, social characteristics, health, employment, economic conditions, income, pensions, and social security. Includes bibliographic information and a glossary. (Statistical Handbook Series).

TRADE/PROFESSIONAL ASSOCIATIONS

Health Insurance Association of America. 1201 F St., N.W., No. 500, Washington, DC 20004. Phone: (202)824-1600 Fax: (202)824-1722 E-mail: jbalda@hiaa.org • URL: http://www.hiaa.org • Members are commercial health insurers. Includes a Disability Insurance Committee, a Medicare Administration Committee, and a Long-Term Care Committee.

National Association for Home Care. 228 Seventh St., S.E., Washington, DC 20003. Phone: (202)547-7424 Fax: (202)547-3540 E-mail: exec@nahc.org •

URL: http://www.nahc.org • Promotes high standards of patient care in home care services. Members are durable medical providers, medical equipment and oxygen suppliers, mainly for home health care.

National Committee to Preserve Social Security and Medicare. 10 G St., N.E., Ste. 600, Washington, DC 20002-4215. Phone: 800-966-1935 or (202)216-0420 Fax: (202)216-0451 E-mail: mailto@ncpssm. org • URL: http://www.ncpssm.org • Members are individuals concerned with Medicare and social security programs. Formerly National Committe to Preserve Social Security.

OTHER SOURCES

The Managed Medicare and Medicaid Market. MarketResearch.com • 2003. $2,195.00. Market research report on medicare HMOs. Includes analysis of legal issues and the impact of managed care on older consumers. Providers such as Kaiser Permanente, Humana, and U. S. Healthcare are profiled.

MEDICINE, INDUSTRIAL

See: INDUSTRIAL MEDICINE

MEETING MANAGEMENT

ABSTRACTS AND INDEXES

Business Periodicals Index. H. W. Wilson Co. • 11 times a year. Quarterly and annual cumulations. Price varies.

CD-ROM DATABASES

ABI/INFORM. PROQUEST. • Monthly. Provides CD-ROM indexing and abstracting of worldwide business literature. Archival discs are available from 1971. Formerly *ABI/INFORM OnDisc.*

WILSONDISC: Business Periodicals Index. H. W. Wilson Co. • Monthly. Provides CD-ROM indexing of business periodicals from 1982 to date. Price includes online service.

DIRECTORIES

Association Meeting and Event Planners Directory. Douglas Publications, Inc. • Annual. $650.00. Lists planners of meetings for over 8,000 national associations. Provides past and future convention locations, dates held, number of attendees, exhibit space required, and other convention information. Formerly *Association Meeting Planners.*

Corporate Meeting and Event Planners. Douglas Publications L.L.C. • Covers: Approximately 11,200 corporations that hold regular, off-site meetings arranged by nearly 14,300 corporate meeting planners. Includes companies in the United States, Puerto Rico, the Virgin Islands, and Canada. Entries include: Company name, address, phone, fax; e-mail; URL; names and titles of key personnel; geographical area served; branch/subsidiary office name and address; products and/or services provided; type of business; number of meetings; months when meetings are held; number of attendees; type of facility used; whether company utilizes services of professional speakers or entertainers.

Protocol (Corporate Meetings, Entertainment, and Special Events). Protocol Directory, Inc. • Annual. $48.00. Provides information for about 4,000 suppliers of products and services for special events, shows (entertainment), and business meetings. Geographic arrangement.

HANDBOOKS AND MANUALS

How to Develop and Promote Successful Seminars and Workshops: A Definitive Guide to Creating and Marketing Seminars, Workshops, Classes, and Conferences. Howard L. Shenson. John Wiley and Sons, Inc. • 1990. $34.95.

How to Run Better Business Meetings: A Reference Guide for Managers. McGraw-Hill. • 1987. Price on application. Compiled by the 3M Meeting Management Team. Covers the planning, formatting, and executing of various kinds of business meetings. Charts, checklists, diagrams, and case studies are included.

Little Black Book of Business Meetings. Michael C. Thomsett. AMACOM. • 1989. $14.95. How to run a business meeting. (Little Black Book Series).

Running a Meeting That Works. Robert F. Miller and Marilyn Pincus. Barron's Educational Series, Inc. • 2004. $8.95. Third edition. A concise guide to the organization and management of effective business meetings.

Seminar Promoting. Entrepreneur Media, Inc. • Looseleaf. $59.50. A practical guide to starting a seminar promotion business. Covers profit potential, start-up costs, market size evaluation, owner's time required, site selection, pricing, accounting, advertising, promotion, etc. (Start-Up Business Guide No. E1071.).

INTERNET DATABASES

Trade Show Center. Global Sources/Trade Media Holdings Ltd. [Singapore]. Phone: (656)574-2800 E-mail: service@globalsources.com • URL: http://www.globalsources.com/TRADESHW/TRDSHFRM.HTM • Free Web site provides current, detailed information on more than 1,000 major trade shows worldwide, including events in the U. S., but with an emphasis on "Asia and Greater China." Searching is offered by product, supplier, country, and month of year. Includes links to "Trade Information.".

ONLINE DATABASES

Management Contents. Gale Cengage Learning. • Covers a wide range of management, financial, marketing, personnel, and administrative topics. About 150 leading business journals are indexed and abstracted from 1974 to date, with monthly updating. Inquire as to online cost and availability.

Trade & Industry Database. Gale Cengage Learning. • Provides indexing of business periodicals, January 1981 to date. Daily updates. (Full text articles from some periodicals are available online, 1983 to date. Inquire as to online cost and availability).

Wilson Business Abstracts Online. H. W. Wilson Co. • Indexes and abstracts 600 major business periodicals, plus the *Wall Street Journal* and the business section of the *New York Times.* Indexing is from 1982, abstracting from 1990, with the two newspapers included from 1993. Updated weekly. Inquire as to online cost and availability. (*Business Periodicals Index* without abstracts is also available online.).

PERIODICALS AND NEWSLETTERS

Harvard Management Communication Letter. Harvard Business School Publishing. • Description: Provides information and techniques for managers on effective communication.

Journal of Convention and Event Tourism. Haworth Press, Inc. • Quarterly. $165.00 per year. Formerly *Journal of Convention and Exhibition Management.*

Meeting and Conference Executives Alert. MCEA. • Monthly. $99.00 per year. Newsletter. Formerly *Meeting Planners Alert.*

The Meeting Professional. Meeting Professionals International. • Monthly. $50.00 per year. Published for professionals in the meeting and convention industry. Contains news, features, and how-to's for domestic and international meetings management. Formerly *Meeting Manager.*

TRADE/PROFESSIONAL ASSOCIATIONS

Meeting Professionals International. 3030 Lyndon B. Johnson Fwy., Ste. 1700, Dallas, TX 75234-2759. Phone: (972)702-3000 Fax: (972)702-3070 E-mail: feedback@mpiweb.org • URL: http://www.mpiweb.org • Meeting planners, full meeting consultants, and suppliers of goods and services. Works to: improve meeting method education; create an "open platform" for research and experimentation. Provides survey results, statistics, supply sources, and technical information; offers members assistance with specific problems; encourages information and idea exchange. Maintains professional code; standardizes terminology; monitors legislation affecting the industry. Maintains resource center. Conducts educational, charitable, and research programs.

Society of Corporate Meeting Professionals. 217 Ridgemount Ave., San Antonio, TX 78209. Phone: (210)822-6522 Fax: (210)822-9838 E-mail: info@scmp.org • URL: http://www.scmp.org • Members are company and corporate meeting planners. Formerly Society of Company Meeting Planners.

Society of Government Meeting Professionals. 908 King St., Alexandria, VA 22314. Phone: 800-827-8916 or (703)549-8916 Fax: (703)549-0708 E-mail: membership@sgmp.org • URL: http://www.sgmp.org • Members are individuals involved in the planning of government meetings. Formerly Society of Government Meeting Professionals.

MEETINGS

See: CONFERENCES, WORKSHOPS, AND SEMINARS

MEETINGS, SALES

See: SALES CONVENTIONS

MEN'S CLOTHING INDUSTRY

CD-ROM DATABASES

OECD Statistical Compendium. Organization for Economic Cooperation and Development. • Semiannual. $1,905.00 per year for 1 to 10 users. CD-ROM contains more than 730,000 monthly, quarterly, and annual time series for OECD countries, 1960 to date. Includes fully searchable data on agriculture, food, economic indicators, national accounts, employment, energy, finance, industry, technology, and foreign trade. Results can be displayed in various forms.

DIRECTORIES

Garment Manufacturers Index. Klevens Publications Inc. • Covers: about 8,000 manufacturers and suppliers of products and services such as fabrics, trimmings, factory equipment, and sewing contractors used in the manufacture of apparel. Publication includes: fabrics, trimmings, supplies, services, equipment, and contractors. Entries include: Company name, address, phone, fax, list of products or services, brief description of product.

Hat Life Directory. Mint Publishing. • Covers: About 1,000 hat manufacturers, wholesalers, renovators, and importers of men's headwear, plus trade suppliers listed (SIC 2253, 2352, 5036); includes about 120 Canadian manufacturers. Entries include: Company name, address, phone, fax, trade and brand names.

Men's and Boys' Wear Buyers Directory. Douglas Publications, Inc. • Annual. $329.00. About 6,800 retail stores selling men's and boys' clothing, sportswear, furnishings, and accessories; coverage does not include New York metropolitan area. *Salesman's Guide Directories.*

FINANCIAL RATIOS

Annual Statement Studies. The Risk Management Association. • Annual. Median and quartile financial

ratios are given for over 400 kinds of manufacturing, wholesale, retail, construction, and consumer finance establishments. Data is sorted by both asset size and sales volume. Includes a clearly written "Definition of Ratios" and an alphabetical industry index.

Annual Statement Studies: Industry Default Probabilities and Cash Flow Measures. The Risk Management Association. • Annual. $145.00. Serves as a companion volume to the original *Annual Statement Studies*. Gives probability of default estimates on a percentage scale for more than 450 industries. Includes changes in position year-by-year for eight financial statement line items and provides percentage measures of cash flow.

INTERNET DATABASES

Advance Monthly Sales for Retail Trade and Food Services. U. S. Census Bureau. Phone: 800-541-8345 or (301)763-4636 Fax: (301)457-3842 E-mail: rcb@census.gov • URL: http://www.census.gov/svsd/www/fullpub.html • Web pages provide monthly sales figures for a wide range of retail businesses. Advance, preliminary, and final statistics are provided for the latest month available in each case, with a previous-year comparison. Updates are monthly.

Business 2.0 Web Guide to the Best Business Links. Business 2.0 Media Inc. Phone: (415)293-4800 E-mail: support@business2.com • URL: http://www.business2.com/webguide • Web site presents an extensive, searchable directory of links to "the best, most informative, and authoritative web pages." Twenty main categories cover business, finance, career, company information, people, and technology topics, with thousands of subtopics, all linking to Web sites recommended by experienced business researchers. Fees: Free.

Fedstats. Federal Interagency Council on Statistical Policy. Phone: (202)395-7254 • URL: http://www.fedstats.gov • Web site features an efficient search facility for full-text statistics produced by more than 100 federal agencies, including the Census Bureau, the Bureau of Economic Analysis, and the Bureau of Labor Statistics. Boolean searches can be made within one agency or for all agencies combined. Links are offered to international statistical bureaus, including the UN, IMF, OECD, UNESCO, Eurostat, and 20 individual countries. Fees: Free.

FreeLunch.com. Economy.com, Inc. Phone: (610)696-8700 Fax: (610)696-1678 • URL: http://www.freelunch.com • Web site provides free access to more than 1.5 million economic and financial data series, covering industry, demographics, labor markets, prices, retail sales, government spending, trade, interest rates, housing starts, the stock market, and many other topics. Data is available for various time periods in either chart or table form. Searching is offered. Fees: Free, but registration required. Economy.com, Inc. also offers fee-based economic analysis at *The Dismal Scientist* site (http://www.dismal.com).

Manufacturing Profiles. U. S. Bureau of the Census. Phone: (301)763-4636 E-mail: webmaster@census.gov • URL: http://www.census.gov/prod/www/abs/mfg-prof.html • The Census Bureau makes available free on PDF (Portable Document Format) an annual consolidation of the entire Current Industrial Report series, presenting "all the data compiled." Contains statistics on production, shipments, inventories, consumption, exports, imports, and orders for a wide variety of manufactured products.

ONLINE DATABASES

PROMT: Predicasts Overview of Markets and Technology. Gale Cengage Learning. • Companies, products, applied technologies and markets. U.S. and international literature coverage, 1972 to date. Inquire as to online cost and availability. Provides

abstracts from more than 1,600 publications. Weekly updates.

PERIODICALS AND NEWSLETTERS

Apparel Merchandising. Lebhar-Friedman, Inc. • Eight times a year. $24.00 per year. Reports on fashion trends in women's, men's, and children's clothing. Supplement to (DSN Retailing Today).

DNR: The Men's Fashion Retail Textile Authority. Fairchild Publications. • Daily. $85.00 per year. Formerly *Daily News Record.*

GQ: Gentleman's Quarterly for Men. Conde Nast Publications, Inc. • Monthly. $15.00 per year.

Tobe Report. Tobe. • 38 times a year. Price on application. Edited for fashion retailers. Provides detailed information and analysis relating to current trends in the women's, children's, and men's apparel and accessories markets.

STATISTICS SOURCES

Annual Benchmark Report for Retail Trade and Food Services...A Detailed Summary of Retail Sales, Purchases, Accounts Receivable, Inventories, and Food Service Sales. Available from U. S. Government Printing Office. • Annual. $13.00. Issued by the U.S. Census Bureau. Provides detailed annual and monthly retail statistics for the most recent 10 years. Includes data for various kinds of retail outlets, including automobiles, furniture, appliances, building supplies, grocery stores, drug stores, gasoline stations, clothing, sporting goods, department stores, and restaurants.

Annual Survey of Manufactures. Available from U. S. Government Printing Office. • Annual. Prices vary. Issued by the U. S. Census Bureau as an interim update to the *Census of Manufactures.* Includes data on number of manufacturing establishments in various industries, employment, labor costs, value of shipments, capital expenditures, inventories, energy costs, and assets. (See also Census Bureau home page, http://www.census.gov/.).

Business Statistics of the United States. Linz Audain and Cornelia J. Strawser. Bernan Associates. • Annual. $147.00. Based on *Business Statistics,* formerly issue by the Bureau of Economic Analysis, U. S. Department of Commerce. Provides basic data for a wide variety of U. S. industries, services, and economic indicators. Most statistics are shown annually for 30 years and monthly for the most recent four years.

Survey of Current Business. Available from U. S. Government Printing Office. • Monthly. $63.00 per year. Issued by Bureau of Economic Analysis, U. S. Department of Commerce. Presents a wide variety of business and economic data.

TRADE/PROFESSIONAL ASSOCIATIONS

Bureau of Wholesale Sales Representatives. 1100 Spring St. N.W., Suite 700, Atlanta, GA 30309. Phone: 800-877-1808 or (404)870-7600 Fax: (404)870-7601 E-mail: info@bwsr.com • URL: http://www.bwsr.com • Formerly Bureau of Salesmen's National Association.

Clothing Manufacturers Association of the U.S.A. 730 Broadway, 10th Fl., New York, NY 10003. Phone: (212)529-0823 Fax: (212)529-1443.

MENTAL HEALTH

See also: INDUSTRIAL PSYCHOLOGY; STRESS (ANXIETY)

GENERAL WORKS

Psychological Symptoms. Frank J. Bruno. John Wiley and Sons, Inc. • 1994. $29.95. Explains the meaning of common mental symptoms, what may cause them, and how to deal with them.

ABSTRACTS AND INDEXES

Psychological Abstracts. American Psychological Association. • Monthly. Members, $815.00 per year;

individuals and institutions, $1,207.00 per year. Covers the international literature of psychology and the behavioral sciences. Includes journals, technical reports, dissertations, and other sources.

CD-ROM DATABASES

Consumers Reference Disc. National Information Services Corp. • Quarterly. Provides the CD-ROM version of *Consumer Health and Nutrition Index* from Oryx Press and *Consumers Index to Product Evaluations and Information Sources* from Pierian Press. Contains citations to consumer health articles and consumer product evaluations, tests, warnings, and recalls.

DIRECTORIES

Complete Mental Health Directory. Grey House Publishing. • Covers: mental health resources including government agencies, professional meetings and seminars, clinic and hospital management companies, and pharmaceutical companies and their mental health product lines.

ENCYCLOPEDIAS AND DICTIONARIES

Encyclopedia of Mental Health. Ada P. Kahn and Jan Fawcett. Facts on File, Inc. • 2001. $71.50. Second edition. Provides basic explanations of about 1,000 terms relating to mental health and mental disorders. Library of Health and Living.

Encyclopedia of Psychological Assessment. Rocio Fernandez-Ballesteros, editor. Sage Publications, Inc. • 2003. $525.00. Two volumes. Contains about 235 alphabetically arranged entries covering various areas of applied psychology and testing.

The Gale Encyclopedia of Psychology. Gale Cengage Learning. • 2001. $155.00. Second edition. Includes bibliographies arranged by topic and a glossary. More than 650 topics are covered.

HANDBOOKS AND MANUALS

Comprehensive Handbook of Psychological Assessment. Michel Hersen, editor. John Wiley and Sons, Inc. • 2003. $500.00. Four volumes. Covers psychological testing and evaluation. Volume one: *Intellectual and Neuropsychological Assessment.* Volume two: *Personality Assessment.* Volume three: *Behavioral Assessment.* Volume four: *Industrial/Organizational Assessment.* (Individual volumes are available at $150.00.).

Handbook of Mental Health in the Workplace. Jay C. Thomas and Michael Hersen, editors. Sage Publications, Inc. • 2002. $99.95. The five parts deal with general issues, working conditions, psychopathology, disruptive behavior, and organizational practice.

International Handbook on Mental Health Policy. Donna R. Kemp, editor. Greenwood Publishing Group, Inc. • 1993. $134.95. Provides information on critical mental health issues in 20 countries.

PDR Drug Guide for Mental Health Professionals. Thomson Medical Economics. • Annual. $39.95. Contains detailed profiles of more than 70 "common psychotropic drugs organized by brand name." Also contains information on the psychological side effects of about 1,000 other prescription drugs.

Personal Health Reporter. Gale Cengage Learning. • 1992. $150.00. Two volumes. Volume one, $115.00; volume two, $115.00. Presents a collection of professional and popular articles on 150 topics relating to physical and mental health conditions and treatments.

Stress and Well-Being at Work: Assessments and Interventions for Occupational Mental Health. James C. Quick and others, editors. American Psychological Association. • 1992. $19.95.

INTERNET DATABASES

National Library of Medicine (NLM). National Institutes of Health (NIH). Phone: 888-346-3656 or (301)496-1131 Fax: (301)480-3537 E-mail: access@nlm.nih.gov • URL: http://www.nlm.nih.

gov • NLM Web site offers free access through MEDLINE ("PubMed") to about nine million references to articles appearing in some 4,000 biomedical journals, with abstracts. Search interfaces range from "simple keywords to advanced Boolean expressions." The NLM site offers many links to other sources of biomedical and technical information (the National Center for Biotechnology Information, for example). Fees: Free.

ONLINE DATABASES

Mental Health Abstracts. IFI/Plenum Data Corp. • Provides indexing and abstracting of mental health and mental illness literature appearing in more than 1,200 journals and other sources from 1969 to date. Monthly updates. Inquire as to online cost and availability.

Newspaper Abstracts Daily. ProQuest Inc. • Provides online coverage (citations and abstracts) of 25 major newspapers. Covers business, economics, current affairs, health, fitness, sports, education, technology, government, consumer affairs, psychology, the arts, and the social sciences. Time period is 1986 to date, with daily updates. Inquire as to online cost and availability.

PsycINFO. American Psychological Association. • Provides indexing and abstracting of the worldwide literature of psychology and the behavioral sciences. Time period is 1967 to date, with monthly updates. Inquire as to online cost and availability.

PERIODICALS AND NEWSLETTERS

Employee Assistance Quarterly. Haworth Press, Inc. • Quarterly. $535.00 per year. An academic and practical journal focusing on employee alcoholism and mental health problems. Formerly *Labor-Management Alcoholism Journal.*

Journal of Behavioral Health Services and Research. Association of Behaviorial Healthcare Management. Lippincott Williams and Wilkins. • Quarterly. Individuals, $81.95 per year; institutions, $231.95 per year. Pertains to the financing and organization of behavioral health services. Formerly *Journal of Mental Health Administration.*

Journal of Business and Psychology. Business Psychology Research Institute. Kluwer Academic Publishers. • Quarterly. Institutions, $614.00 per year; with online edition, $736.80 per year.

Journal of Mental Health Counseling. American Counseling Association. • Quarterly. $175.00 per year. The official journal of the American Mental Health Counselors Association.

Mental Health Law Reporter. Business Publishers Inc. • Description: Provides news and coverage of court cases pertaining to legal issues affecting mental health professionals.

Occupational Therapy in Mental Health: A Journal of Psychosocial Practice and Research. Haworth Press, Inc. • Quarterly. Institutions, $385.00 per year.

Psychology Today. Sussex Publishers Inc. • Bimonthly. $18.00 per year.

TRADE/PROFESSIONAL ASSOCIATIONS

American Mental Health Counselors Association. 801 N Fairfax St., Ste. 304, Alexandria, VA 22314. Phone: 800-326-2642 or (703)548-6002 Fax: (703)548-4775 E-mail: mhamilton@amhca.org • URL: http://www.amhca.org • Professional counselors employed in mental health services; students. Aims to: deliver quality mental health services to children, youth, adults, families, and organizations; improve the availability and quality of counseling services through licensure and certification, training standards, and consumer advocacy. Supports specialty and special interest networks. Fosters communication among members. A division of the American Counseling Association (see separate entry).

Mental Health America. 2000 N Beauregard St., 6th Fl., Alexandria, VA 22311. Phone: 800-969-6642 or (703)684-7722 Fax: (703)684-5968 E-mail: infoctr@nmha.org • URL: http://www. mentalhealthamerica.net • Addresses all aspects of mental health and mental illness and is dedicated to improving mental health, preventing mental disorders, and achieving victory over mental illnesses. Accomplishes its mission through advocacy, public education, research, and service in partnership with more than 340 affiliates across the country.

MENTAL INSTITUTIONS

ABSTRACTS AND INDEXES

Psychological Abstracts. American Psychological Association. • Monthly. Members, $815.00 per year; individuals and institutions, $1,207.00 per year. Covers the international literature of psychology and the behavioral sciences. Includes journals, technical reports, dissertations, and other sources.

CD-ROM DATABASES

Authority Health Care Law Library. LexisNexis/ Matthew Bender. • Periodic updates. Price on request. Full text CD-ROM provides legal information, case law, and analysis relating to health care facilities, health insurance, longterm care, Medigap, and Medicare.

DIRECTORIES

AHA Integrated Delivery Network Directory: U.S. Health Care Systems, Networks, and Alliances. American Hospital Association. • Annual. $250.00. Provides information about a wide variety of U.S. health care groups and affiliations, including hospitals, nursing homes, rehabilitation centers, psychiatric facilities, home health care agencies, clinical laboratories, outpatient facilities, and diagnostic imaging centers. Includes names of more than 8,000 key executives.

Buyers' Guide for the Health Care Market: A Directory of Products and Services for Health Care Institutions. Health Forum. • Annual. $17.95. Lists 1,200 suppliers and manufacturers of health care products and services for hospitals, nursing homes, and related organizations.

ONLINE DATABASES

PsycINFO. American Psychological Association. • Provides indexing and abstracting of the worldwide literature of psychology and the behavioral sciences. Time period is 1967 to date, with monthly updates. Inquire as to online cost and availability.

PERIODICALS AND NEWSLETTERS

AHA News. American Hospital Association. HealthForum. • Description: Highlights major news affecting hospitals and the health care field. Reports on legislation and regulation, court cases, surveys, and federal programs. Carries information on individual hospitals and allied hospital associations.

Health Facilities Management. American Hospital Association. American Hospital Publishing, Inc. • Monthly. $40.00 per year. Covers building maintenance and engineering for hospitals and nursing homes.

Health Forum Journal: Leadership Strategies for Healthcare Executives. Health Forum. • Biweekly. $65.00 per year. Covers the general management of hospitals, nursing homes, and managed care organizations. Formerly *HospitalsHealthNetworks.*

Psychiatric Services. American Psychiatric Association. American Psychiatric Publishing, Inc. • Monthly. Members, $60.00 per year; students, Non-members, $73.00 per year; institutions, $161.00 per year; Students, $40.00 per year. Includes online edition. Formerly *Hospital and Community Psychiatry.*

TRADE/PROFESSIONAL ASSOCIATIONS

National Association of Psychiatric Health System. 325 Seventh St., N.W., Ste. 625, Washington, DC 20004-2802. Phone: (202)393-6700 Fax: (202)783-6041 E-mail: naphs@naphs.org • URL: http://www. naphs.org • Formerly National Association of Private Psychiatric Hospitals.

National Association of State Mental Health Program Directors. 66 Canal Center Plaza, Suite 302, Alexandria, VA 22314. Phone: (703)739-9333 Fax: (703)548-9517 • URL: http://www.nasmhpd. org.

Section for Psychiatric and Substance Abuse Services. c/o American Hospital Association, 1 N Franklin St., Chicago, IL 60606-3421. Phone: 800-242-4890 or (312)422-3000 Fax: (312)422-4796 E-mail: hromero@aha.org • URL: http://www.aha. org.

MERCHANDISING

See: MARKETING; RETAIL TRADE

MERCHANT MARINE

See: SHIPS, SHIPPING AND SHIPBUILDING

MERCHANTS

See: RETAIL TRADE

MERGERS AND ACQUISITIONS

See also: LEVERAGED BUYOUTS

GENERAL WORKS

Cases in Corporate Acquisitions, Buyouts, Mergers, and Takeovers. Gale Cengage Learning. • 1999. $350.00. Reviews and analyzes about 300 cases of both success and failure in corporate acquisitiveness.

Mergers, Acquisitions, and Corporate Restructurings. Patrick A. Gaughan. John Wiley and Sons, Inc. • 2001. $75.00. Third edition. Covers mergers, acquisitions, divestitures, internal reorganizations, joint ventures, leveraged buyouts, bankruptcy workouts, and recapitalizations.

Predicting Successful Hospital Mergers and Acquisitions: A Financial and Analytical Marketing Tool. David P. Angrisani and Robert L. Goldman. Haworth Press, Inc. • 1997. $49.95.

Successful Mergers, Acquisitions, and Strategic Alliances: How to Bridge Corporate Cultures. Irene Rodgers and others. McGraw-Hill. • 2002. $39.95. Provides advice on mergers involving companies in different countries.

Super Searchers on Mergers & Acquisitions: The Online Secrets of Top Corporate Researchers and M & A Professionals. Jan Tudor. Information Today, Inc. • 2001. $24.95. Presents the results of interviews with 13 "top M & A information pros." Covers the finding, evaluating, and delivering of relevant data on companies and industries. (Super Searchers Series).

ALMANACS AND YEARBOOKS

Merger Yearbook. Thomson Media. • Annual. $595. 00. Provides detailed information on mergers and acquisitions announced or completed during the year. Includes many charts.

CD-ROM DATABASES

Buyout Financing Sources/M & A Intermediaries. Thomson Media. • Annual. $895.00. Provides the CD-ROM combination of *Directory of Buyout Financing Sources* and *Directory of M & A Intermediaries.* Contains information on more than

1,000 financing sources (banks, insurance companies, venture capital firms, etc.) and 850 intermediaries (corporate acquirers, valuation firms, lawyers, accountants, etc.). Also includes back issues of *Buyouts Newsletter* and *Mergers & Acquisitions Report*. Fully searchable.

Corporate Affiliations Plus. National Register Publishing, Reed Reference Publishing. • Quarterly. $1,995.00 per year. Provides CD-ROM discs corresponding to *Directory of Corporate Affiliations* and *Corporate Finance Bluebook.* Contains corporate financial services information and worldwide data on subsidiaries and affiliates.

DIRECTORIES

Directory of M & A Intermediaries. Thomson Financial. • Annual. $360.00. Lists more than 850 dealmakers for mergers and acquisitions, including investment banks, business brokers, and commercial banks.

Mergerstat Transaction Roster. FactSet Mergerstat LLC. • Annual. $299.00. A directory of all U. S. companies that were involved in merger and acquisition activity during the year covered. Includes details of each transaction.

HANDBOOKS AND MANUALS

The Art of M & A: A Merger-Acquisition-Buyout Guide. Stanley F. Reed and Aleandra R. Lajoux. McGraw-Hill. • 1998. $125.00. Third edition. A how-to-do-it guide for merger and acquisition ventures. Emphasis is on legal issues.

Corporate Acquisitions and Mergers. LexisNexis Matthew Bender. • $1,286.00. Only available on CD-ROM. Four looseleaf volumes. Periodic supplementation. A guide to the antiturst, tax, corporate, securities and financial aspects of business combinations. Includes extensive forms, charts and tables.

Corporate Acquisitions, Mergers, and Divestitures. Lewis D. Solomon. Prentice Hall PTR. • Looseleaf. Periodic supplementation. Price on application. Includes how to buy a company with its own assets or earnings.

Library of Investment Banking. Robert L. Kuhn, editor. McGraw-Hill. • 1990. $475.00. Seven volumes: 1. Investing and Risk Management; 2. Capital Raising and Financial Structure; 3. Corporate and Municipal Securities; 4. Mergers, Acquisitions, and Leveraged Buyouts; 5. Mortgage and Asset Securitization; 6. International Finance and Investing; 7. Index.

Mergers, Acquisitions, and Other Restructuring Activities: An Integrated Approach to Process, Tools, Cases, and Solutions. Donald DePamphilis. Elsevier Butterworth Heinemann. • 2003. $99.95. Second edition. Includes 18 case studies.

Mergers and Acquisitions Handbook. Milton L. Rock and others. McGraw-Hill. • 1994. $84.95. Second edition. The first and last word on successful mergers and acquisitions, from putting together an m&a team and targeting acquistion candidates to merging managements and benefits plans-and every step in between.

INTERNET DATABASES

InSite 2. Intelligence Data/Thomson Financial. Phone: 800-654-0393 or (617)856-1890 Fax: (617)737-3182 E-mail: intelligence.data@tfn.com • URL: http://www.insite2.gale.com/ • Fee-based Web site consolidates information in a "Base Pack" consisting of Business InSite, Market InSite, and Company InSite. Optional databases are Consumer InSite, Health and Wellness InSite, Newsletter InSite, and Computer InSite. Includes fulltext content from more than 2,500 trade publications, journals, newsletters, newspapers, analyst reports, and other sources. Continuous updating. Formerly produced by The Gale Group.

Intelligence Data. Thomson Financial. Phone: 800-

654-0393 Fax: (617)824-2477 • URL: http://www. intelligencedata.com • Fee-based Web site provides a wide variety of information relating to competitive intelligence, strategic planning, business development, mergers, acquisitions, sales, and marketing. "Intelliscope" feature offers searching of other Thomson units, such as Investext, MarkIntel, InSite 2, and Industry Insider. Weekly updating.

PERIODICALS AND NEWSLETTERS

Acquisitions Monthly. Thomson Financial. • Monthly. $790.00 per year. Published in London. Provides detailed information, commentary, and statistics on merger, acquisition, and buyout activity in Europe, the U.S., and Asia.

Bank Mergers & Acquisitions: The Authoritative Newsletter Providing In-Depth Analysis of the Restructuring of American Banking. SNL Financial LLC. • Monthly. $795.00 per year. Newsletter. Includes information on transactions assisted by the Federal Deposit Insurance Corporation (FDIC) for commercial banks or by the Resolution Trust Corporation (RTC) for savings and loan institutions.

Business and Acquisition Newsletter. Newsletters International, Inc. • Monthly. $300.00 per year. Information about firms that want to buy or sell companies, divisions, subsidiaries, product lines, patents, etc.

Business Strategies Bulletin. CCH Inc. • Description: Reports tax and business planning information for all sizes of business, with emphasis on small to mid-sized business advisors.

Mergers and Acquisitions Advisor: Issues, Trends, and Strategies for Successful Mergers and Acquisitions. Mergers and Acquisitions Advisor, Inc. • Monthly. $595.00 per year. Newsletter. Discusses anticipated transactions, major trends, and the economic climate for merger activity.

Mergers & Acquisitions Report. Thomson Media. • Weekly. $1,295.00 per year. Newsletter. Covers pending and ongoing mergers, acquisitions, restructurings, and bankruptcies.

Mergers & Acquisitions: The Dealmaker's Journal. Thomson Media. • Bimonthly. $475.00 per year. Provides articles on various aspects of M & A, including valuation, pricing, taxes, and strategy. Current M & A deals are listed and described.

Mergerstat Quarterly Reports. Houlihan Lokey Howard & Zukin. • Quarterly. $100.00 per year. Newsletter. Provides details and analysis of recent corporate merger activity. Includes "Top deals year-to-date" and rankings of financial and legal advisors.

STATISTICS SOURCES

Mergerstat Review. FactSet Mergerstat LLC. • Annual. $299.00. Provides analysis of merger and acquisition activity and trends during the year. Contains statistical, industry, and geographical data, including a 25-year historical review.

OTHER SOURCES

Acquisitions and Mergers: Negotiated and Contested Transactions. Joy M. Bryan and Simone M. Lorne. West Group. • Three times a year. $1,172.00 per year. Five looseleaf volumes. Includes legal forms and documents. (Securities Law Series).

Business Strategies. CCH, Inc. • Semimonthly. $795.00 per year. Four looseleaf volumes. Semimonthly updates. Legal, tax, and accounting aspects of business planning and decision-making. Provides information on start-ups, forms of ownership (partnerships, corporations), failing businesses, reorganizations, acquisitions, and so forth. Includes *Business Strategies Bulletin,* a monthly newsletter.

Capital Changes Reports. CCH, Inc. • Weekly. $1,395.00. Six looseleaf volumes. Arranged alphabetically by company. This service presents a chronological capital history that includes reorganizations, mergers and consolidations. Recent actions are found in Volume One - "New Matters.".

Mergers & Acquisitions. Glasser Legalworks. • Looseleaf. $225.00, including CD-ROM version. Periodic Supplementation. Includes explanations of M & A legal procedures, with annotated forms. (Emerging Growth Companies Series.).

Savings Institutions: Mergers, Acquisitions, and Conversions. American Lawyer Media, Inc. • Looseleaf. $169.00. Updated as needed. Provides detailed information on the legal complexities of mergers and acquisitions involving savings institutions. (Law Journal Press).

MERIT RATING

See: RATING OF EMPLOYEES

METAL FINISHING

ABSTRACTS AND INDEXES

Surface Finishing Technology. ASM International. • Monthly. Members, $130.00 per year; nonmembers, $160.00 per year. Provides abstracts of the international literature of metallic and nonmetallic industrial coating and finishing. Formerly *Cleaning-Finishing-Coating Digest.*

Surface Treatment Technology Abstracts. Finishing Publications Ltd. • Bimonthly. $880.00 per year. Includes *Printed Circuits* and *Electronics Coating Abstracts.*

DIRECTORIES

AESF Shop Guide-A Directory of Surface Finishing Shops. American Electroplaters' and Surface Finishers Society, Inc. • Annual. Price on application. List of over 1,200 electroplating, coating, and other surface finishing firms.

Dun's Industrial Guide: The Metalworking Directory. Dun and Bradstreet Corp. • Annual. Libraries, $485; commercial institutions, $795.00. Lease basis. Three volumes. Lists about 65,000 U. S. manufacturing plants using metal and suppliers of metalworking equipment and materials. Includes names and titles of key personnel. Products, purchases, and processes are indicated.

Metal Finishing Guidebook and Directory. Elsevier. • Annual. Free to qualified personnel; others, $60. 00. Included with subscription to *Metal Finishing.* Lists manufacturers and suppliers to the industry.

Products Finishing Directory. Gardner Publications Inc. • Publication includes: List of suppliers of products used in electroplating, painting, polishing, buffing, powder coating, cleaning, degreasing, and other metal finishing processes. Entries include: Company name, address, phone, e-mail, URL.

HANDBOOKS AND MANUALS

McGraw-Hill Machining and Metalworking Handbook. Ronald A. Walsh. McGraw-Hill. • 1998. $99.95. Second edition. Coverage includes machinery, machining techniques, machine tools, machine design, parts, fastening, and plating.

PERIODICALS AND NEWSLETTERS

Finishers' Management. Publication Management, Inc. • 10 times a year. $35.00 per year.

Industrial Paint and Powder: Coatings Manufacturing and Application. Reed Business Information. • Monthly. $72.90 per year. Supplement available, *Annual Buyer's Guide.* Formerly *Industrial Finishing.*

Metal Finishing: Devoted Exclusively to Metallic Surface Treatments. Elsevier. • Monthly. Institutions, $190.00 per year. Includes annual *Metal Finishing Guidebook and Directory.*

Modern Metals. Trend Publishing, Inc. • Monthly. $85.00 per year. Covers management and production for plants that fabricate and finish metals of various kinds.

Plating and Surface Finishing: Electroplating,

Finishing of Metals, Organic Finishing. American Electroplaters and Surface Finishers Society, Inc. • Monthly. Members, $16.00 per year; non-members, $60.00 per year.

Products Finishing. Gardner Publications, Inc. • Monthly. $40.00 per year.

TRADE/PROFESSIONAL ASSOCIATIONS

American Electroplaters and Surface Finishers Society. 12644 Research Parkway, Orlando, FL 32826-3298. Phone: (407)281-6441 Fax: (407)281-6446 E-mail: aesf@aesf.org • URL: http://www. aesf.org.

National Association for Surface Finishing. 1155 15th St. NW, Ste. 500, Washington, DC 20005. Phone: (202)457-8404 Fax: (202)530-0659 E-mail: jflatley@nasf.org • URL: http://www.nasf.org • Companies manufacturing metal finishing equipment, materials, and processes, including basic metals, chemicals, and compounds; suppliers of services for metal finishing of all types; distributors. Sponsors metal finishing clinics for industrial groups; promotes the use of established standards to acquaint buyers of plated and finished products with the means of specifying a high-quality finish.

National Association of Metal Finishers. 21165 Whitfield Pl., Ste. 105, Potomac Falls, VA 20165. Phone: (703)433-2522 Fax: (703)433-0369 E-mail: namf@erols.com • URL: http://www.namf.org • Members are management personnel of metal and plastic finishing companies. Finishing includes plating, coating, polishing, rustproofing, and other processes.

METAL INDUSTRY

ABSTRACTS AND INDEXES

IMM Abstracts and Index: A Survey of World Literature on the Economic Geology and Mining of All Minerals (Except Coal), Mineral Processing, and Nonferrous Extraction Metallurgy. Institution of Mining and Metallurgy. • Bimonthly. $500.00 per year. Provides international coverage of the literature of mining and nonferrous metallurgy. Includes mineral economics, tunnelling, and rock mechanics.

Metals Abstracts. CSA. • Monthly. $3,575.00 per year. Includes print and online editions.

ALMANACS AND YEARBOOKS

Agricultural and Mineral Commodities Year Book. Available from Taylor & Francis Group. • Annual. $225.00. Published by Europa Publications. Contains descriptive product profiles, price data, export-import data, and production statistics for major commodities of the world. Includes commodity histories, uses, markets, demand trends, and information about trade agreements and key commodity organizations.

CD-ROM DATABASES

OECD Statistical Compendium. Organization for Economic Cooperation and Development. • Semiannual. $1,905.00 per year for 1 to 10 users. CD-ROM contains more than 730,000 monthly, quarterly, and annual time series for OECD countries, 1960 to date. Includes fully searchable data on agriculture, food, economic indicators, national accounts, employment, energy, finance, industry, technology, and foreign trade. Results can be displayed in various forms.

DIRECTORIES

Dun's Industrial Guide: The Metalworking Directory. Dun and Bradstreet Corp. • Annual. Libraries, $485; commercial institutions, $795.00. Lease basis. Three volumes. Lists about 65,000 U.S. manufacturing plants using metal and suppliers of metalworking equipment and materials. Includes names and titles of key personnel. Products,

purchases, and processes are indicated.

Internet Tools of the Profession: A Guide for Information Professionals. Hope N. Tillman, editor. Special Libraries Association. • 1997. $49.00. Second edition. Consists of 14 sections by various authors or compilers. After two introductory articles on searching the Internet, there are 12 annotated lists of useful Web sites, covering the SLA, business and finance, chemistry, education, food and agriculture, information technology, insurance and employee benefits, law, library management, metals and materials, pharmaceuticals, and telecommunications. An index is provided.

Materials Research Centres: A World Directory of Organizations and Programmes in Materials Science. Specialist Journals. • Biennial. $445.00. Profiles of research centers in 75 countries. Materials include plastics, metals, fibers, etc.

North American Scrap Metals Directory. Recycling Today Media Group. • Covers: Suppliers of scrap metal materials in North America. Entries include: Contact information.

ENCYCLOPEDIAS AND DICTIONARIES

ASM Materials Engineering Dictionary. Joseph R. Davis, editor. ASM International. • 1992. $166.00. Contains 10,000 entries, 700 illustrations, and 150 tables relating to metals, plastics, ceramics, composites, and adhesives. Includes "Technical Briefs" on 64 key material groups.

Encyclopedia of Materials: Science and Technology. K.H.J. Buschow and others, editors. Elsevier. • 2001. $4,985.00. Eleven volumes. Provides extensive technical information on a wide variety of materials, including metals, ceramics, plastics, optical materials, and building materials. Includes more than 2,000 articles and 5,000 illustrations.

FINANCIAL RATIOS

Almanac of Business and Industrial Financial Ratios. Leo Troy. Aspen Publishers, Inc. • 2003. $125.95. Includes CD-Rom. Contains financial ratios derived from federal tax returns. Ratios for each of about 200 industries are arranged according to company asset size. (Almanac of Business and Industrial Financial Ratios Series).

IRS Corporate Financial Ratios. Available from MarketResearch.com. • 2002. $225.00. Published by Schonfeld & Associates, Inc. Presents 70 key financial ratios for 260 industries. Ratios are calculated from income statement and balance sheet data available from the Internal Revenue Service. Includes four asset size classes.

HANDBOOKS AND MANUALS

ASM Metals Reference Book. Michael L. Bauccio, editor. ASM International. • 1993. $155.00. Third edition. Includes glossary, tables, formulas, and diagrams. Covers a wide range of ferrous and nonferrous metals.

Handbook of Materials Selection. Myer Kutz. John Wiley and Sons, Inc. • 2002. $225.00. First section of handbook covers materials relative to the type of engineering application. Second section deals with the specific properties of materials. Covers both traditional materials and high-tech composites.

INTERNET DATABASES

Business 2.0 Web Guide to the Best Business Links. Business 2.0 Media Inc. Phone: (415)293-4800 E-mail: support@business2.com • URL: http:// www.business2.com/webguide • Web site presents an extensive, searchable directory of links to "the best, most informative, and authoritative web pages." Twenty main categories cover business, finance, career, company information, people, and technology topics, with thousands of subtopics, all linking to Web sites recommended by experienced business researchers. Fees: Free.

Fedstats. Federal Interagency Council on Statistical

Policy. Phone: (202)395-7254 • URL: http://www. fedstats.gov • Web site features an efficient search facility for full-text statistics produced by more than 100 federal agencies, including the Census Bureau, the Bureau of Economic Analysis, and the Bureau of Labor Statistics. Boolean searches can be made within one agency or for all agencies combined. Links are offered to international statistical bureaus, including the UN, IMF, OECD, UNESCO, Eurostat, and 20 individual countries. Fees: Free.

FreeLunch.com. Economy.com, Inc. Phone: (610)696-8700 Fax: (610)696-1678 • URL: http:// www.freelunch.com • Web site provides free access to more than 1.5 million economic and financial data series, covering industry, demographics, labor markets, prices, retail sales, government spending, trade, interest rates, housing starts, the stock market, and many other topics. Data is available for various time periods in either chart or table form. Searching is offered. Fees: Free, but registration required. Economy.com, Inc. also offers fee-based economic analysis at *The Dismal Scientist* site (http://www. dismal.com).

ONLINE DATABASES

Business and Industry. Gale Cengage Learning. • Contains online citations, abstracts, and selected fulltext from more than 1,000 trade journals, newspapers, and other publications. Provides general coverage of both manufacturing and service industries, including marketing, production, industry trends, key events, and information on specific companies. Time span is 1994 to date. Daily updates. Inquire as to online cost and availability. (Also available in a CD-ROM version.).

Materials Business File. Cambridge Scientific Abstracts. • Provides online abstracts and citations to worldwide materials literature, covering the business and industrial aspects of metals, plastics, ceramics, and composites. Corresponds to *Steels Alert, Nonferrous Metals Alert,* and *Polymers/ Ceramics/Composites Alert.* Time period is 1985 to date, with monthly updates. (Formerly produced by ASM International.) Inquire as to online cost and availability.

METADEX. Cambridge Scientific Abstracts. • Covers the worldwide literature of metals, metallurgy, and materials science, 1966 to date. Includes detailed alloys indexing from 1974. Biweekly updating. Inquire as to online cost and availability. (Formerly produced by ASM International.).

PROMT: Predicasts Overview of Markets and Technology. Gale Cengage Learning. • Companies, products, applied technologies and markets. U.S. and international literature coverage, 1972 to date. Inquire as to online cost and availability. Provides abstracts from more than 1,600 publications. Weekly updates.

Tablebase. Gale Cengage Learning. • Provides online numerical tabular data from a wide variety of business, organization, and government sources, including about 1,000 trade journals. Includes industry and individual company statistics relating to products, market share, sales forecasts, production, exports, market trends, etc. Time span is 1997 to date. Weekly updates. Inquire as to online cost and availability. (Also available in a CD-ROM version.).

PERIODICALS AND NEWSLETTERS

Advanced Materials and Processes. ASM International. • Monthly. Free to members; institutions, $325.00 per year. Incorporates *Metal Progress.*Technical information and reports on new developments in the technology of engineered materials and manufacturing processes.

JOM: The Member Journal of the Minerals, Metals and Materials Society. Minerals, Metals, and Materials Society. • Four times a year. Membership.

A scholarly journal covering all phases of metals and metallurgy.

Metal Bulletin. Metal Bulletin, Inc. • Semiweekly. $1,378 per year. Provides news of international trends, prices, and market conditions for both steel and non-ferrous metal industries. (Published in England.).

Metal Bulletin Monthly. Metal Bulletin, Inc. • Monthly. Price on application. Edited for international metal industry business executives and senior technical personnel. Covers business, economic, and technical developments. (Published in England.).

Metal Center News. Sackett Business Media Inc. • Quadriennial 13 times a year. $99.00 per year.

Modern Metals. Trend Publishing, Inc. • Monthly. $85.00 per year. Covers management and production for plants that fabricate and finish metals of various kinds.

33 Metalproducing: For Primary Producers of Steel, Aluminum, and Copper-Base Alloys. Penton Media, Inc. • Monthly. $65.00 per year. Covers metal production technology and methods and industry news. Includes a bimonthly *Nonferrous Supplement.*

PRICE SOURCES

Platt's Metals Week. Platt's. • Weekly. $770.00 per year.

STATISTICS SOURCES

Annual Survey of Manufactures. Available from U. S. Government Printing Office. • Annual. Prices vary. Issued by the U. S. Census Bureau as an interim update to the *Census of Manufactures.* Includes data on number of manufacturing establishments in various industries, employment, labor costs, value of shipments, capital expenditures, inventories, energy costs, and assets. (See also Census Bureau home page, http://www.census. gov/.).

Business Statistics of the United States. Linz Audain and Cornelia J. Strawser. Bernan Associates. • Annual. $147.00. Based on *Business Statistics,* formerly issue by the Bureau of Economic Analysis, U. S. Department of Commerce. Provides basic data for a wide variety of U. S. industries, services, and economic indicators. Most statistics are shown annually for 30 years and monthly for the most recent four years.

Encyclopedia of American Industries. Gale Cengage Learning. • 2000. $560.00. Third edition. Two volumes. $280.00 per volume. Volume one is *Manufacturing Industries* and volume two is *Service and Non-Manufacturing Industries.* Provides the history, development, and recent status of approximately 1,000 industries. Includes statistical graphs, with industry and general indexes.

Metal Statistics. Reed Business Information. • Annual. $250.00. Provides statistical data on a wide variety of metals, metal products, ores, alloys, and scrap metal. Includes data on prices, production, consumption, shipments, imports, and exports.

Mineral Commodity Summaries. Available from U. S. Government Printing Office. • Annual. $26.00. Published by the U. S. Geological Survey, Department of the Interior (http://www.usgs.gov). Contains detailed, five-year data for about 90 nonfuel minerals. Covers a wide range of statistics, including production, imports, exports, consumption, reserves, prices, tariff information, and industry employment. (Two pages are devoted to each mineral.).

Non-Ferrous Metal Data Yearbook. American Bureau of Metal Statistics. • Annual. $405.00. Provides worldwide data on approximately about 200 statistical tables covering many nonferrous metals. Includes production, consumption, inventories, exports, imports, and other data.

Standard & Poor's Industry Surveys. Standard & Poor's. • Semiannual. $1,800.00. Two looseleaf volumes. Includes monthly *Supplements.* Provides detailed, individual surveys of 52 major industry groups. Each survey is revised on a semiannual basis. Also includes "Monthly Investment Review" (industry group investment analysis) and monthly "Trends & Projections" (economic analysis).

Survey of Current Business. Available from U. S. Government Printing Office. • Monthly. $63.00 per year. Issued by Bureau of Economic Analysis, U. S. Department of Commerce. Presents a wide variety of business and economic data.

World Metal Statistics. World Bureau of Metal Statistics. • Monthly. $980.00 per year.

TRADE/PROFESSIONAL ASSOCIATIONS

American Bureau of Metal Statistics. P.O. Box 805, Chatham, NJ 07928. Phone: (973)701-2299 Fax: (973)701-2152 E-mail: info@abms.com • URL: http://www.abms.com • Members are metal companies. Compiles and publishes detailed statistical data on a wide variety of nonferrous metals: aluminum, copper, gold, lead, nickel, platinum, silver, tin, titanium, uranium, zinc, and others.

ASM International. 9639 Kinsman Rd., Novelty, OH 44073-0002. Phone: 800-336-5152 or (440)338-5151 Fax: (440)338-4634 E-mail: customerservice@asminternational.org • URL: http://asmcommunity.asminternational.org/portal/ site/asm • Metallurgists, materials engineers, executives in materials producing and consuming industries; teachers and students. Disseminates technical information about the manufacture, use, and treatment of engineered materials. Offers inplant, home study, and intensive courses through Materials +Engineering Institute. Conducts career development program. Established ASM Foundation for +Education and Research.

METAL INDUSTRY, NONFERROUS

See: NONFERROUS METAL INDUSTRY

METAL PLATING

See: METAL FINISHING

METAL POWDERS

See: POWDER METALLURGY INDUSTRY

METAL WORKING INDUSTRY

See also: MACHINE TOOL INDUSTRY

ABSTRACTS AND INDEXES

Cutting Technology. Penton Media, Inc. • Seven times a year. Free to qualified personnel; others, $55.00 per year. Provides abstracts of the international literature of metal cutting and machining. Formerly *Cutting Tool-Machine Digest.*

Metalforming Digest. CSA. • Monthly. Price on application. Provides abstracts of the international literature of metal forming, including powder metallurgy, stamping, extrusion, forging, etc.

DIRECTORIES

Dun's Industrial Guide: The Metalworking Directory. Dun and Bradstreet Corp. • Annual. Libraries, $485; commercial institutions, $795.00. Lease basis. Three volumes. Lists about 65,000 U. S. manufacturing plants using metal and suppliers of

metalworking equipment and materials. Includes names and titles of key personnel. Products, purchases, and processes are indicated.

Who's Who in Metal Forming and Fabricating. Fabricators and Manufacturers Association International. • Annual. Free to members; nonmembers, $200.00. Lists members of the Fabricators and Manufacturers Association (FMA), International; and members of the Tube and Pipe Association. Includes five indexes. Formerly *FMA Member Resource Directory.*

HANDBOOKS AND MANUALS

McGraw-Hill Machining and Metalworking Handbook. Ronald A. Walsh. McGraw-Hill. • 1998. $99.95. Second edition. Coverage includes machinery, machining techniques, machine tools, machine design, parts, fastening, and plating.

INTERNET DATABASES

Manufacturing Profiles. U. S. Bureau of the Census. Phone: (301)763-4636 E-mail: webmaster@census. gov • URL: http://www.census.gov/prod/www/abs/ mfg-prof.html • The Census Bureau makes available free on PDF (Portable Document Format) an annual consolidation of the entire Current Industrial Report series, presenting "all the data compiled." Contains statistics on production, shipments, inventories, consumption, exports, imports, and orders for a wide variety of manufactured products.

PERIODICALS AND NEWSLETTERS

The Fabricator. Fabricators and Manufacturers Association International. • Monthly. $75.00 per year. Covers the manufacture of sheet, coil, tube, pipe, and structural metal shapes.

Production Technology News. Reed Business Information. • Monthly. $57.99. Includes *MBuyer's Guide.* Formerly *Metalworking Digest.*

RESEARCH CENTERS AND INSTITUTES

Advanced Manufacturing Engineering Institute. University of Hartford, United Technologies Hall, Room 215, West Hartford, CT 06117. Phone: 800-678-4844 or (860)768-4615 Fax: (860)768-5073 E-mail: shetty@mail.hartford.edu.

Institute for Metal Forming. Lehigh University. Materials Science and Engineering Dept., Five E. Packer Ave., Bethlehem, PA 18015. Phone: (610)758-4252 Fax: (610)758-4244 E-mail: wzm2@lehigh.edu.

STATISTICS SOURCES

Annual Survey of Manufactures. Available from U. S. Government Printing Office. • Annual. Prices vary. Issued by the U. S. Census Bureau as an interim update to the *Census of Manufactures.* Includes data on number of manufacturing establishments in various industries, employment, labor costs, value of shipments, capital expenditures, inventories, energy costs, and assets. (See also Census Bureau home page, http://www.census. gov/.).

U. S. Industry and Trade Outlook. Available from National Technical Information Service. • Annual. $69.95. Produced by the International Trade Administration, U. S. Department of Commerce, in a "public-private" partnership with DRI/McGraw-Hill and Standard & Poor's. Provides basic data, outlook for the current year, and "Long-Term Prospects" (five-year projections) for a wide variety of products and services. Includes high technology industries. Formerly *U. S. Industrial Outlook.*

TRADE/PROFESSIONAL ASSOCIATIONS

American Machine Tool Distributors' Association. 1445 Research Blvd., Ste. 450, Rockville, MD 20850. Phone: 800-878-2683 or (301)738-1200 Fax: (301)738-9499 E-mail: pborden@amtda.org • URL: http://www.amtda.org • Distributors and builders of manufacturing technology. Offers technical training, sales training and management. Compiles statistics.

Fabricators and Manufacturers Association, International. 833 Featherstone Rd., Rockford, IL 61107-6302. Phone: (815)399-8700 Fax: (815)484-7701 E-mail: info@fmanet.org • URL: http://www.fmanet.org • Members are individuals concerned with metal forming, cutting, and fabricating. Includes a Sheet Metal Division and the Tube and Pipe Fabricators Association. Formerly Fabricating Manufacturers Association.

Precision Metalforming Association. 6363 Oak Tree Blvd., Independence, OH 44131-2556. Phone: (216)901-8800 Fax: (216)901-9190 E-mail: pma@pma.org • URL: http://www.metalforming.com • Represents the metalforming industry of North America; the industry that creates precision metal products using stamping, fabricating and other value-added processes. Its member companies include metal stampers, fabricators, spinners, slide formers and roll formers, as well as suppliers of equipment, materials and services to the industry. Members are located in 30 countries, with the majority found in North America; in 41 states of the United States as well as Canada and Mexico. Conducts technical and educational programs, compiles statistics, offers training systems, and provides legislative and regulatory assistance to members.

METALLURGY

See also: METAL INDUSTRY; POWDER METALLURGY INDUSTRY

ABSTRACTS AND INDEXES

Alloys Index. CSA. • Monthly. $775.00 per year. Includes print and online editions.

Applied Science and Technology Index. H. W. Wilson Co. • 11 times a year. Quarterly and annual cumulations. Price varies. Indexes a wide variety of English language technical, industrial, and engineering periodicals.

IMM Abstracts and Index: A Survey of World Literature on the Economic Geology and Mining of All Minerals (Except Coal), Mineral Processing, and Nonferrous Extraction Metallurgy. Institution of Mining and Metallurgy. • Bimonthly. $500.00 per year. Provides international coverage of the literature of mining and nonferrous metallurgy. Includes mineral economics, tunnelling, and rock mechanics.

Metals Abstracts. CSA. • Monthly. $3,575.00 per year. Includes print and online editions.

NTIS Alerts: Materials Sciences. National Technical Information Service. • Semimonthly. $220.00 per year. Provides descriptions of government-sponsored research reports and software, with ordering information. Covers ceramics, glass, coatings, composite materials, alloys, plastics, wood, paper, adhesives, fibers, lubricants, and related subjects. Formerly *Abstract Newsletter.*

CD-ROM DATABASES

METADEX Materials Collection: Metals-Polymers-Ceramics. Cambridge Scientific Abstracts. • Quarterly. Provides CD-ROM citations to the worldwide literature of materials science and metallurgy. Corresponds to *Metals Abstracts, Alloys Index, Steels Alert, Nonferrous Alert, Polymers/Ceramics/Composites Alert,* and *Engineered Materials Abstracts.* (Formerly produced by ASM International.).

ENCYCLOPEDIAS AND DICTIONARIES

Encyclopedia of Materials: Science and Technology. K.H.J. Buschow and others, editors. Elsevier. • 2001. $4,985.00. Eleven volumes. Provides extensive technical information on a wide variety of materials, including metals, ceramics, plastics, optical materials, and building materials. Includes more than 2,000 articles and 5,000 illustrations.

HANDBOOKS AND MANUALS

Fundamentals of Metallurgical Processes. L. Coudurier and others. Available from Franklin Book Co., Inc. • 1985. $187.00. Second edition. (International Monographs on Materials and Technology Series: Volume 27).

Smithells Metals Reference Book. William F. Gale and Terry C. Totemeier. Elsevier. • 2003. $195.00. Eighth edition.

ONLINE DATABASES

Applied Science and Technology Index Online. H. W. Wilson Co. • Provides online indexing of 500 major scientific, technical, industrial, and engineering periodicals. Time period is 1983 to date. Monthly updates. Inquire as to online cost and availability.

METADEX. Cambridge Scientific Abstracts. • Covers the worldwide literature of metals, metallurgy, and materials science, 1966 to date. Includes detailed alloys indexing from 1974. Biweekly updating. Inquire as to online cost and availability. (Formerly produced by ASM International.).

PERIODICALS AND NEWSLETTERS

ACTA Materialia: An International Journal for the Science of Materials. Elsevier. • 20 times a year. $2,475.00 per year. Text in English, French and German. Formerly *ACTA Metallutgical et Materialia.*

High-Tech Materials Alert: Advanced Materials: Their Uses and Manufacture. Technical Insights. • Monthly. Institutions, $695.00 per year. Newsletter on technical developments relating to high-performance materials, including metals and ceramics. Includes market forecasts.

International Materials Review. ASM International. • Bimonthly. $865.00 per year. Provides technical and research coverage of metals, alloys, and advanced materials. Formerly *International Metals Review.*

JOM: The Member Journal of the Minerals, Metals and Materials Society. Minerals, Metals, and Materials Society. • Four times a year. Membership. A scholarly journal covering all phases of metals and metallurgy.

Metallurgia, The Journal of Metals Technology, Metal Forming and Thermal Processing. British Forging Industry Association. DMG World Media Ltd. • Monthly. $157.00 per year.

Metallurgical and Materials Transactions A: Physical Metallurgy and Materials Sc. ASM International. • 13 times a year. $1,617.00 per year. Formerly *Metallurgical Transactions A- Physical Metallurgy and Materials Science.*

Metallurgical and Materials Transactions B: Process Metallurgy and Materials Processing Science. ASM International. • Bimonthly. $1,277.00 per year. Formerly *Metallurgical Transactions B: Process Metallurgy.*

Scripta Materialia. Acta Metallurgica, Inc. Elsevier. • Semimonthly. $1,358.00 per year.

RESEARCH CENTERS AND INSTITUTES

Basic Metals Processing Research Institute. University of Pittsburgh, School of Engineering, 848 Benedum Hall, Pittsburgh, PA 15261. Phone: (412)624-9737 Fax: (412)624-8069 E-mail: deardo@pitt.edu.

Cooperative Program in Metallurgy. Pennsylvania State University, Dept. of Materials and Engineering, 124 Steidle Bldg., University Park, PA 16802. Phone: (814)865-4882 Fax: (814)865-2917.

Materials Processing Center. Massachusetts Institute of Technology, 77 Massachusetts Ave., Room 12-007, Cambridge, MA 02139-4307. Phone: (617)253-5179 Fax: (617)258-6900 E-mail: fmpage@.mit.edu • URL: http://www.web.mit.edu/mpc • Conducts processing, engineering, and economic research in ferrous and nonferrous metals, ceramics, polymers, photonic materials, superconductors, welding, composite materials, and other materials.

TRADE/PROFESSIONAL ASSOCIATIONS

ASM International. 9639 Kinsman Rd., Novelty, OH 44073-0002. Phone: 800-336-5152 or (440)338-5151 Fax: (440)338-4634 E-mail: customerservice@asminternational.org • URL: http://asmcommunity.asminternational.org/portal/site/asm • Metallurgists, materials engineers, executives in materials producing and consuming industries; teachers and students. Disseminates technical information about the manufacture, use, and treatment of engineered materials. Offers in-plant, home study, and intensive courses through Materials +Engineering Institute. Conducts career development program. Established ASM Foundation for +Education and Research.

Minerals, Metals and Materials Society. 184 Thorn Hill Dr., Warrendale, PA 15086-7514. Phone: (724)776-9000 Fax: (724)776-3770 E-mail: tmsgeneral@tms.org • URL: http://www.tms.org • Members are metallurgists, metallurgical engineers, and materials scientists. Divisions include Light Metals and Electronic, Magnetic, and Photonic Materials. Formerly The Metallurigical Society.

Mining and Metallurgical Society of America. 476 Wilson Ave., Novato, CA 94947-4236. Fax: (415)899-0262 E-mail: info@mmsa.net • URL: http://www.mmsa.net.

Society for Mining, Metallurgy, and Exploration. 8307 Shaeffer Pky., Littleton, CO 80127. Phone: 800-763-3132 or (303)973-9550 or (303)948-4210 Fax: (303)973-3845 E-mail: sme@smenet.org • URL: http://www.smenet.org • Affiliated with American Institute of Mining and the Mettallurgical and Petroleum Engineers. Formerly Society of Mining Engineers.

METALS, PRECIOUS

See: GOLD; METAL INDUSTRY; PLATINUM INDUSTRY; SILVER INDUSTRY

METALS, RARE EARTH

See: RARE EARTH METALS

METEOROLOGY

See: WEATHER AND WEATHER FORECASTING

METRIC SYSTEM

See: WEIGHTS AND MEASURES

METROPOLITAN AREAS

See: CITIES AND TOWNS; CITY PLANNING; MARKET STATISTICS; URBAN DEVELOPMENT

MEXICO

See: LATIN AMERICAN MARKETS

MICROCOMPUTERS AND MINICOMPUTERS

See also: ARTIFICIAL INTELLIGENCE; COMPUTER COMMUNICATIONS; COMPUTER CRIME AND SECURITY; COMPUTER PERIPHERALS AND ACCESSORIES; COMPUTER SOFTWARE INDUSTRY; COMPUTERS; COMPUTERS IN EDUCATION; DESKTOP PUBLISHING; OPTICAL DISK STORAGE DEVICES; PORTABLE COMPUTERS; WORD PROCESSING

GENERAL WORKS

Using Computers: A Gateway to Information. Gary B. Shelley and others. Course Technology. • 1995. $44.00. Second edition.

ABSTRACTS AND INDEXES

Applied Science and Technology Index. H. W. Wilson Co. • 11 times a year. Quarterly and annual cumulations. Price varies. Indexes a wide variety of English language technical, industrial, and engineering periodicals.

Business Periodicals Index. H. W. Wilson Co. • 11 times a year. Quarterly and annual cumulations. Price varies.

Computer and Control Abstracts. Available from INSPEC, Inc. • Monthly. $2,400.00 per year. Section C of *Science Abstracts.*

Computer and Information Systems Abstracts Journal: An Abstract Journal Pertaining to the Theory, Design, Fabrication and Application of Computer and Information Systems. CSA. • 11 times a year. $1,750 per year.

Computer Literature Index: A Subject/Author Index to Computer and Data Processing Literature. EBSCO Publishing. • Quarterly, with annual cumulation. $245.00 per year. Contains brief abstracts of book and periodical literature covering all phases of computing, including approximately 70 specific application areas.

Current Contents: Engineering, Computing and Technology. Thomson/ISI. • Weekly. $730.00 per year. Reproductions of contents pages of technical journals. Includes *Author Index, Address Directory, Current Book Contents* and *Title Word Index.* Formerly *Current Contents: Engineering, Technology and Applied Sciences.*

Internet and Personal Computing Abstracts [print edition]. EBSCO Publishing. • Quarterly. $269.00 per year, including cumulative index. Provides more than 10,000 abstracts annually from both trade and academic publications. Covers computer hardware, software, product reviews, Web topics, e-commerce, networks, corporate news, security, and related topics. Formerly *Microcomputer Abstracts.*

LAMP (Literature Analysis of Microcomputer Publications). Soft Images. • Bimonthly. $89.95 per year. Annual cumulation.

Science Citation Index. Thomson/ISI. • Bimonthly. $15,020.00 per year. Annual cumulation. Includes *Source Index, Citation Index, Permuterm Subject Index,* and *Corporate Index.*

ALMANACS AND YEARBOOKS

Computer Industry Almanac. Egil Juliussen and Karen Petska, editors. Computer Industry Almanac, Inc. • Annual. $53.00. Analyzes recent trends in various segments of the computer industry, with forecasts, employment data and industry salary information. Includes directories of computer companies, industry organizations, and publications.

Information Technology Outlook. OECD Publications and Information Center. • Biennial. $57.00. A review of recent developments in international markets for computer hardware, software, and services. Also examines current legal provisions for information systems security and privacy in OECD countries.

BIBLIOGRAPHIES

Computer Book Review. • Quarterly. $30.00 per year. Includes annual index. Reviews new computer books. Back issues available.

CD-ROM DATABASES

Computer Database. Gale Cengage Learning. • Provides one year of full-text on CD-ROM for 150 leading computer-related publications. Also includes 70,000 product specifications and brief profiles of 13,000 computer product vendors and manufacturers.

Datapro on CD-ROM: Computer Systems Hardware and Software. Gartner Group, Inc. • Monthly. Price on application. CD-ROM provides product specifications, product reports, user surveys, and market forecasts for a wide range of computer hardware and software.

Hoover's Company Capsules on CD-ROM. Hoover's, Inc. • Quarterly. $399.95 per year (single-user). Provides the CD-ROM version of *Hoover's Handbook of American Business, Hoover's Handbook of Emerging Companies, Hoover's Handbook of World Business, Hoover's Guide to Computer Companies, Hoover's Guide to Media Companies, Hoover's Handbook of Private Companies,* and various regional guides. Includes more than 11,000 profiles of companies.

WILSONDISC: Wilson Business Abstracts. H. W. Wilson Co. • Monthly. Includes unlimited online access to *Wilson Business Abstracts* through WILSONLINE. Provides CD-ROM "cover-to-cover" abstracting and indexing of over 600 prominent business periodicals. Indexing is from 1982, abstracting from 1990. (*Business Periodicals Index* without abstracts is available on CD-ROM at $1,495 per year.).

DIRECTORIES

Computing and Software Career Directory. Gale Cengage Learning. • 1993. $39.00. Includes career information relating to programmers, software engineers, technical writers, systems experts, and other computer specialists. Provides advice from "insiders," resume suggestions, a directory of companies that may offer entry-level positions, and a directory of career information sources. (Career Advisor Series.).

Control Engineering Buyers Guide. Reed Business Information. • Annual. Price on application. Contains specifications, prices, and manufacturers' listings for computer software, as related to control engineering.

Data Sources: The Comprehensive Guide to the Data Processing Industry: Hardware, Data Communications Products, Software, Company Profiles. Gale Cengage Learning. • Semiannual. $455.00 per year. Two volumes. Describes hardware and software for all computer operating sysems, including prices and technical details. Lists about 75,000 products from 14,000 suppliers. Industry-specific software applications are described.

MicroLeads Vendor Directory on Disk (Personal Computer Industry). Chromatic Communications Enterprises, Inc. • Annual. $495.00. Includes computer hardware manufacturers, software producers, book-periodical publishers, and franchised or company-owned chains of personal computer equipment retailers, support services and accessory manufacturers. Formerly *MicroLeads U.S. Vender Directory.*

The Software Encyclopedia: A Guide for Personal, Professional, and Business Users. Gale. • Annual. $335.00. Two volumes. Volume one lists software programs by title and producer. Volume two provides information on programs according to application and operating system. Includes prices and requirements for hardware and memory.

ENCYCLOPEDIAS AND DICTIONARIES

Acronyms of Computer Science and Communications: A Comprehensive Acronym Dictionary and Illustrated Encyclopedia. Enjob Kajan and Ejub Kajan. Springer Verlag. • 2002. $49.95. Explains more than 4,000 "broadly used" computer, telecommunications, and information technology acronyms. Includes illustrations and Web addresses, where applicable.

Dictionary of Computing. Valerie Illingworth, editor. Oxford University Press. • 1997. $18.00. Fourth edition.

Dictionary of Information Technology and Computer Science. Tony Gunton. Blackwell Publishing. • 1994. $62.95. Second edition. Covers key words, phrases, abbreviations, and acronyms used in computing and data communications.

Encyclopedia of Information Systems. Hossein Bidgoli, editor. Elsevier. • 2002. $1,200.00. Four volumes. Contains a wide range of articles relating to computers, databases, communication, and information technology. The 200 topics include coverage of hardware, software, artificial intelligence, the Internet, networks, knowledge management, electronic commerce, search engines, and systems design.

Encyclopedia of Microcomputers. Allen Kent and James G. Williams, editors. Marcel Dekker, Inc. • 27 volumes. $5,265.00. $195.00 per volume. Dates vary. Contains scholarly articles written by microcomputer experts. Includes bibliographies.

Encyclopedia of Software Engineering. John J. Marciniak, editor. John Wiley and Sons, Inc. • 2002. $695.00. Second edition. Two volumes. Contains more than 500 entries covering 35 software classifications.

Illustrated Dictionary of Microcomputers. Michael Hordeski. McGraw Hill. • 1990. $19.95. Third edition.

New Hacker's Dictionary. Eric S. Raymond. MIT Press. • 1996. $65.00. Third edition. Includes three classifications of hacker communication: slang, jargon, and "techspeak.".

1001 Computer Words You Need to Know. Jerry Pournelle. Oxford University Press. • 2004. $17.95.

World of Computer Science. Gale Cengage Learning. • 2002. $160.00. Alphabetical arrangement. Contains 650 entries covering discoveries, theories, concepts, issues, ethics, and people in the broad area of computer science and technology.

FINANCIAL RATIOS

Industry Norms and Key Business Ratios. Desk Top Edition. Dun and Bradstreet Corp. • Annual. Five volumes. $475.00 per volume. $1,890.00 per set. Covers over 800 kinds of businesses, arranged by Standard Industrial Classification number. More detailed editions covering longer periods of time are also available.

HANDBOOKS AND MANUALS

Buying and Maintaining Personal Computers: A How-To-Do-It Manual for Librarians with Companion Web Site. Norman Howden. Neal-Schuman Publishers, Inc. • 2000. $45.00. Covers various aspects of buying PCs or MACs for library use, including choice of hardware, software selection, warranties, backup systems, staffing, and dealing with vendors. (How-To-Do-It Manuals Series).

Computer Repair Service. Entrepreneur Media, Inc. • Looseleaf. $59.50. A practical guide to starting a computer repair service. Covers profit potential, start-up costs, market size evaluation, owner's time required, site selection, lease negotiation, pricing, accounting, advertising, promotion, etc. (Start-Up Business Guide No. E1256.).

Computer Science Handbook. Allen B. Tucker. CRC Press. • 2004. $139.95. Second edition. Provides 70 chapters on 11 computer subject areas. Includes material from 150 contributing authors.

Dun & Bradstreet/Gale Group Industry Handbooks. Gale Cengage Learning. • 2000. $650.00. Five volumes. $130.00 per volume. Each volume covers two or more major industries: 1. *Entertainment and Hospitality*; 2. *Construction and Agriculture*; 3. *Chemicals and Pharmaceuticals*; 4. *Computers & Software and Broadcasting & Telecommunications*; 5. *Insurance and Health & Medical Services.* The following are included for each industry: overview, statistics, financial ratios, rankings, merger information, company directory, directory of associations, and consultants directory. (Dun and Bradstreet/Gale Industry Reference Handbook Series).

Microcomputer Engineering. Gene H. Miller. Prentice Hall PTR. • 1998. $113.00. Second edition.

The Modem Reference: The Complete Guide to PC Communications. Michael A. Banks. Information Today, Inc. • 2000. $29.95. Fourth edition. Covers personal computer data communications technology, including fax transmissions, computer networks, modems, and the Internet. Popularly written.

INTERNET DATABASES

InfoTech Trends. Data Analysis Group. Phone: (925)462-1202 Fax: (925)462-1225 E-mail: support@infotechtrends.com • URL: http://www. infotechtrends.com • Web site provides both free and fee-based market research data on the information technology industry, including computers, peripherals, telecommunications, the Internet, software, CD-ROM/DVD, e-commerce, and workstations. Fees: Free for current (most recent year) data; more extensive information has various fee structures. Formerly *Computer Industry Forecasts.*

Wired News. Lycos, Inc. Phone: (415)276-8400 Fax: (415)276-8500 E-mail: newsfeedback@wired.com • URL: http://www.wired.com • Provides summaries and full-text of "Top Stories" relating to the Internet, computers, multimedia, telecommunications, and the electronic information industry in general. These news stories are placed in the broad categories of Politics, Business, Culture, and Technology. Affiliated with *Wired* magazine. Fees: Free.

ONLINE DATABASES

Applied Science and Technology Index Online. H. W. Wilson Co. • Provides online indexing of 500 major scientific, technical, industrial, and engineering periodicals. Time period is 1983 to date. Monthly updates. Inquire as to online cost and availability.

Globalbase. Gale Cengage Learning. • Provides more than one million online summaries of business, industrial, and economic news reports from more than 1,000 publications worldwide. Covers a wide range of material appearing in international trade journals, professional magazines, and newspapers. Time period is 1984 to date, with weekly updates. Inquire as to online cost and availability.

Internet and Personal Computing Abstracts. Information Today, Inc. • Contains abstracts covering a wide variety of personal and business microcomputer literature appearing in more than 100 journals and popular magazines. Time period is 1981 to date, with monthly updates. Formerly *Microcomputer Index.* Inquire as to online cost and availability.

PROMT: Predicasts Overview of Markets and Technology. Gale Cengage Learning. • Companies, products, applied technologies and markets. U.S. and international literature coverage, 1972 to date. Inquire as to online cost and availability. Provides

abstracts from more than 1,600 publications. Weekly updates.

Scisearch. Institute for Scientific Information. • Broad, multidisciplinary index to the literature of science and technology, 1974 to present. Inquire as to online cost and availability. Coverage of literature is worldwide, with weekly updates.

Wilson Business Abstracts Online. H. W. Wilson Co. • Indexes and abstracts 600 major business periodicals, plus the *Wall Street Journal* and the business section of the *New York Times.* Indexing is from 1982, abstracting from 1990, with the two newspapers included from 1993. Updated weekly. Inquire as to online cost and availability. (*Business Periodicals Index* without abstracts is also available online.).

PERIODICALS AND NEWSLETTERS

Computer Shopper: The Computer Magazine for Direct Buyers. Media Inc. • Monthly. $14.99 per year. Nationwide marketplace for computer equipment.

Computerworld: Newsweekly for Information Technology Leaders. Computerworld, Inc. • Weekly. $190.00 per year.

EDP Weekly: The Leading Weekly Computer News Summary. Computer Age and EDP News Services. • Weekly. $495.00 per year. Newsletter. Summarizes news from all areas of the computer and microcomputer industries.

Forbes-Andrew Seybold's Wireless Outlook: A Monthly Perspective of Issues Affecting the Mobile C Computer and Communications Industries. Andrew Seybold's Outlook, Inc. • Monthly. $299.00 per year. Newsletter. Provides analysis of the computer industry to corporate buyers and to end users. Reports on hardware, software trends and future products. Formerly *Andrew Seybold's Outlook.*

The Gray Sheet. F-D-C Reports Inc. • Description: Monitors the complex regulatory environment for devices, instrumentation, and diagnostics. Topics include device-related Congressional activity, Medicare reimbursement policies, international regulatory intiatives, enforcement and premarket approval programs at FDA's Center for Devices and Radiological Health. Recurring features include device approvals, 510(k) clearances, FDA recalls and seizures, mergers and acquisitions, and sales and earnings.

IEEE Micro. Institute of Electrical and Electronics Engineers, Inc. • Bimonthly. $650.00 per year.

InfoWorld: Defining Technology for Business. InfoWorld Publishing. • Weekly. $195.00 per year. For personal computing professionals.

Macworld: The Macintosh Magazine for the Network Professional. Mac Publishing, L.L.C. • Monthly. $19.97 per year. For Macintosh personal computer users.

Microprocessor Report: The Insiders' Guide to Microprocessor Hardware. Reed Business Information. • 12 times a year. $695.00 per year. Newsletter. Covers the technical aspects of microprocessors from Intel, IBM, Cyrix, Motorola, and others.

Online Libraries and Microcomputers. Information Intelligence, Inc. • Ten times a year. Individuals $43.75 per year; libraries. $62.50 per year. Newsletter. Covers library automation and electronic information (online, CD-ROM). Reviews or describes new computer hardware and software for library use.

PC Magazine: The Independent Guide to Personal Computing and the Internet. Media Inc. • Biweekly. $49.97 per year.

PC World: The No. 1 Source for Definitive How-to-Buy, How-to-Use Advice on Personal Computing

Systems and Software. IDG Communications, Inc. • Monthly. $29.90 per year.

PlugIn Datamation: Profit and Value from Information Technology. EarthWeb. • Monthly. Price on application. Technical, semi-technical and general news covering EDP topics.

Release 1.0 Esther Dysons Monthly Report. EDventure Holdings Inc. • Description: Reports on technology, communications, and the Internet. Reviews and analyzes the technology business. Recurring features include a calendar of events.

Smart Computing. Sandhills Publishing Co. • Monthly. $29.00 per year. Provides basic computer advice "in plain English." Includes reviews of hardware and software.

Software Magazine. Wiesner Publishing, Inc. • Monthly. Free to qualified personnel; others, $42.00 per year.

PRICE SOURCES

Computer. Orion Research Corp. • Quarterly. $516.00 per year. $129.00 per issue. Quotes retail and wholesale prices of used computers and equipment. Original list prices and years of manufacture are also shown.

Computer Price Guide: The Blue Book of Used IBM Computer Prices. Computer Economics, Inc. • Quarterly. $140.00 per year. Provides average prices of used IBM computer equipment, including "complete lists of obsolete IBM equipment." Includes a newsletter on trends in the used computer market. Edited for dealers, leasing firms, and business computer buyers.

RESEARCH CENTERS AND INSTITUTES

Battelle Memorial Institute. Battelle Memorial Institute. 505 King Ave., Columbus, OH 43201. Phone: 800-201-2011 or (614)424-5853 Fax: (614)424-5263 E-mail: solutions@battelle.org • URL: http://www.battelle.org/ • Environment and energy; national security; transportation; health and life sciences; medical, pharmaceutical, agrochemical, and consumer product development. Conducts marine research at three coastal locations: Florida Marine Research Facility (Daytona Beach), Northwest Marine Research Laboratory (Sequim, Washington), and the Ocean Sciences Laboratory (Duxbury, Massachusetts). Specialized facilities and units include: Aviation Safety Reporting System Office; the Breakthrough Center for Strategic Product Development; the Human Engineering, Ergonomics, and Organizational Research Center; and the William R. Wiley Environmental Molecular Sciences Laboratory.

Carnegie Mellon Research Institute-Computer Automation and Robotics. Carnegie Mellon University, 700 Technology Dr., Pittsburgh, PA 15219. Phone: (412)268-3363 Fax: (412)368-7759 • URL: http://www.cmu.edu/cmri • Multidisciplinary research activities include expert systems applications, minicomputer and microcomputer systems design, genetic engineering, and transportation systems analysis.

Center for Advanced Technology in Information Management. Columbia University, Vanderbilt Clinic, 622 W 168th St., 5th Fl., New York, NY 10032. Phone: (212)305-2944 Fax: (212)305-0196 E-mail: shortliffe@dmi.columbia.edu • URL: http://www.dmi.columbia.edu/cat.

Center for Microelectronic and Computer Engineering. Rochester Institute of Technology, 82 Lomb Memorial Dr., Rochester, NY 14623-5604. Phone: (716)475-2035 Fax: (716)475-5041 E-mail: lffeee@rit.edu • URL: http://www.microe.rit.edu • Facilities include digital computer organization/ microcomputer laboratory.

Technology Based Learning and Research. Arizona State University, College of Education, Community Service Center, Tempe, AZ 85287-0908. Phone:

(480)965-4960 Fax: (480)946-1423 E-mail: bitter@ asu.edu • URL: http://tblr.ed.asu.edu/ • Research activities are related to computer literacy.

STATISTICS SOURCES

Computers and Office and Accounting Machines. U. S. Bureau of the Census. • Annual. Provides data on shipments: value, quantity, imports, and exports. (Current Industrial Reports, MA-35R.).

Standard & Poor's Industry Surveys. Standard & Poor's. • Semiannual. $1,800.00. Two looseleaf volumes. Includes monthly *Supplements.* Provides detailed, individual surveys of 52 major industry groups. Each survey is revised on a semiannual basis. Also includes "Monthly Investment Review" (industry group investment analysis) and monthly "Trends & Projections" (economic analysis).

U. S. Industry and Trade Outlook. Available from National Technical Information Service. • Annual. $69.95. Produced by the International Trade Administration, U. S. Department of Commerce, in a "public-private" partnership with DRI/McGraw-Hill and Standard & Poor's. Provides basic data, outlook for the current year, and "Long-Term Prospects" (five-year projections) for a wide variety of products and services. Includes high technology industries. Formerly *U. S. Industrial Outlook.*

TRADE/PROFESSIONAL ASSOCIATIONS

Association of Minicomputer Users. 363 E Central St., Franklin, MA 02038. Phone: (508)520-1555 • URL: http://www.arcat.com/arcatcos36.

Computing Technology Industry Association. 1815 S Meyers Rd., Ste. 300, Oakbrook Terrace, IL 60181-5228. Phone: (630)678-8300 Fax: (630)678-8384 E-mail: information@comptia.org • URL: http://www.comptia.org • Trade association of more than 19,000 companies and professional IT members in the rapidly converging computing and communications market. Has members in more than 89 countries and provides a unified voice for the industry in the areas of e-commerce standards, vendor-neutral certification, service metrics, public policy and workforce development. Serves as information clearinghouse and resource for the industry; sponsors educational programs.

IEEE Computer Society. 1828 L St. NW, Ste. 1202, Washington, DC 20036. Phone: (202)371-0101 Fax: (202)728-9614 E-mail: help@computer.org • URL: http://www.computer.org • Computer professionals. Promotes the development of computer and information sciences and fosters communication within the information processing community. Sponsors conferences, symposia, workshops, tutorials, technical meetings, and seminars. Operates Computer Society Press. Presents scholarships; bestows technical achievement and service awards and certificates.

Information Technology Association of America. 1401 Wilson Blvd., Suite 1100, Arlington, VA 22209. Phone: (703)522-5055 Fax: (703)525-2279 E-mail: hmiller@itaa.org • URL: http://www.itaa. org • Members are computer software and services companies. Maintains an Information Systems Integration Services Section. Formerly Software Industry Division of ADAPSO.

Society for Computer Simulation International. PO Box 17900, San Diego, CA 92177-1810. Phone: (858)277-3888 Fax: (858)277-3930 E-mail: info@ scs.org • URL: http://www.scs.org • Formerly Society for Computer Simulation.

MICROFICHE

See: MICROFORMS

MICROFILM

See: MICROFORMS

MICROFORMS

See also: DOCUMENT IMAGING

BIBLIOGRAPHIES

Guide to Microforms in Print: Author-Title. Gale Group. • Annual. $450.00. Lists 166,000 publications from 417 publishers and distributors around the world. *Subject Guide,* $450.00. *Supplement* available, $185.00.

Guide to Microforms in Print: Subject Guide. Available from Gale Cengage Learning. • Annual. $450. 00. Two volumes. Provides international coverage under 135 subject headings. Published by K. G. Saur.

Micropublishers' Trade List Annual. Chadwyck-Healey, Inc. • Annual. $375.00. Over 250 publishers of microfilm and microfiche and their catalogs. Worldwide coverage.

CD-ROM DATABASES

LISA Plus. Available from Cambridge Scientific Abstracts (CSA). • Quarterly. $2,000.00 per year. CD-ROM version of Library Information and Science Abstracts, providing abstracting and indexing of the world's library and information science literature, 1969 to date. Contains more than 180,000 citations.

DIRECTORIES

AIIM Buying Guide. Association for Information and Image Management International Headquarters. • Publication includes: List of approximately 460 manufacturers, software developers, suppliers, service companies, consultants, and system integrators in the document management industry. Entries include: Company name, address, phone, product/ service provided, product or sales contact, business descriptions, number of employees. Organization was formerly called National Micrographics Association.

ONLINE DATABASES

LISA: Library and Information Science Abstracts. Available from Cambridge Scientific Abstracts (CSA). • Provides abstracting and indexing of the world's library and information science literature, 1969 to date. Covers more than 440 periodicals from 68 countries. Updating is biweekly. Inquire as to on-line cost and availability.

Scisearch. Institute for Scientific Information. • Broad, multidisciplinary index to the literature of science and technology, 1974 to present. Inquire as to online cost and availability. Coverage of literature is worldwide, with weekly updates.

PERIODICALS AND NEWSLETTERS

InForm. Victor O. Schinnerer & Company Inc. • Description: Reports national and state developments affecting architects and engineers.

Microform and Imaging Review. R. R. Bowker. • Quarterly. $198.00 per year. Evaluates scholarly micropublications for libraries. Includes articles on microform management. Text in German.

Micrographics and Hybrid Imaging Systems Newsletter: Monthly Report for Busines Excutives Who Use or Market Microfilm Services and Hybrid Imaging Services and Equipment. Microfilm Publishing. Inc. • Monthly. $198.00 per year. A report for business executives who use or market microfilm services and equipment. Formerly *Micrographics Newsletter.*

TRADE/PROFESSIONAL ASSOCIATIONS

AIIM - The Enterprise Content Management Association. 1100 Wayne Ave., Ste. 1100, Silver Spring, MD 20910. Phone: 800-477-2446 or (301)587-8202 Fax: (301)587-2711 E-mail: aiim@ aiim.org • URL: http://www.aiim.org • Manufacturers, vendors, and individual users of information and image management equipment, products, and

services. Holds special meetings for trade members and companies. Maintains speakers' bureau. Operates resource center. Compiles statistics.

International Information Management Congress. 1100 Wayne Ave., Ste. 1100, Silver Spring, MD 20910-5603. Phone: (301)587-8202 Fax: (301)587-2711 E-mail: aiim@aiim.org • URL: http://www. iimc.org • Trade association for the document imaging/management industry. Seeks to communicate document-based technologies and applications to an international audience through conferences, exhibitions, publications, and various membership interactions. Promotes understanding and cooperation among organizations engaged in furthering the progress and application of document-based information systems.

OTHER SOURCES

Information and Image Management: The State of the Industry. AIIM-The Enterprise Content Management Association. • Annual. $130.00. Market data with five-year forecasts. Covers electronic imaging, micrographics supplies and equipment, software, and records management services.

MICROGRAPHICS

See: MICROFORMS

MICROPHOTOGRAPHY

See: MICROFORMS

MICROPROCESSORS

See: MICROCOMPUTERS AND MINICOMPUTERS

MICROSOFT WINDOWS

See: WINDOWS (SOFTWARE)

MICROWAVES

ABSTRACTS AND INDEXES

Key Abstracts: Microwave Technology. Available from INSPEC, Inc. • Monthly. $250.00 per year. Provides international coverage of journal and proceedings literature. Published in England by the Institution of Electrical Engineers (IEE).

DIRECTORIES

Microwaves and RF Product Data Directory (Radio Frequency). Penton Technology and Lifestyle Media. • Annual. $106.00. About 2,000 manufacturers of high frequency equipment components. International coverage.

PERIODICALS AND NEWSLETTERS

Journal of Microwave Power and Electromagnetic Energy. International Microwave Power Institute. • Quarterly. $195.00 per year. Formerly *Journal of Microwave Power.*

Microwave and Optical Technology Letters. John Wiley and Sons, Inc., Journals. • 24 times a year. $1,690.00 per year; with online edition, $1,775.00 per year. Four volumes.

Microwave Journal. Horizon House Publications, Inc. • Monthly. Free to qualified personnel. International coverage.

Wireless Week. Reed Business Information. • 50 times a year. $99.00 per year. Covers news of cellular telephones, mobile radios, communications satellites, microwave transmission, and the wireless industry in general. Includes annual *Directory*.

RESEARCH CENTERS AND INSTITUTES

Microwave Device and Physical Electronics Laboratory. University of Utah. Electrical and Computing Engineering Dept., 50 S. Central Campus Dr., Room 3280 MEB, Salt Lake City, UT 84112-9206. Phone: (801)581-6941 Fax: (801)581-5281 E-mail: bodson@ece.utah.edu • URL: http://www.elen.utah.edu/general/electromagnetics.

STATISTICS SOURCES

Electronic Market Data Book. Consumer Electronics Association. • Annual. Price on application.

U. S. Industry and Trade Outlook. Available from National Technical Information Service. • Annual. $69.95. Produced by the International Trade Administration, U. S. Department of Commerce, in a "public-private" partnership with DRI/McGraw-Hill and Standard & Poor's. Provides basic data, outlook for the current year, and "Long-Term Prospects" (five-year projections) for a wide variety of products and services. Includes high technology industries. Formerly *U. S. Industrial Outlook.*

TRADE/PROFESSIONAL ASSOCIATIONS

International Microwave Power Institute. 7076 Drinkard Way, Mechanicsville, VA 23111-5007. Phone: (804)559-6667 Fax: (804)559-4087 E-mail: info@impi.org • URL: http://www.impi.org • Scientists from 31 countries interested in microwave power for non-communications purposes, particularly in its applications to industrial heating processes, biomedicine, and microwave cooking and ovens. Promotes university research; provides speakers to public affairs conferences and government organizations. Offers short courses.

MIGRATION

See: IMMIGRATION AND EMIGRATION

MIGRATION OF INDUSTRY

See: LOCATION OF INDUSTRY

MILITARY ASSOCIATIONS

GENERAL WORKS

Adjutants General Association of the United States. • Adjutants General (National Guard) of the states and territories.

DIRECTORIES

National Guard Executive Directors Association. • Provides a forum for the exchange of information of common interest to members and the organizations they represent; encourages states to organize and maintain a National Guard association; participates in improving the operational readiness, training and image of the National Guard on both state and national levels.

TRADE/PROFESSIONAL ASSOCIATIONS

Air Force Association. 1501 Lee Hwy., Arlington, VA 22209-1198. Phone: 800-727-3337 or (703)247-5800 Fax: (703)247-5853 E-mail: polcom@afa.org • URL: http://www.afa.org • Promotes public understanding of aerospace power and the pivotal role it plays in the security of the nation.

Air Force Sergeants Association. R 5211 Authl Rd., Suitland, MD 20746. Phone: 800-638-0594 or (301)899-3500 Fax: (301)899-8136 E-mail: staff@afsahq.org • URL: http://www.afsahq.org • Any enlisted man or woman, active or retired, in the Air Force, Air National Guard, Air Force Reserve, Army Air Corps, or Army Air Forces; ladies auxiliaries. Works to: promote, preserve, and uphold fair and equitable legislation as it pertains to the welfare of

the airmen who served and are serving in the U.S.A. F.; maintain the highest professional standards and integrity among members; promote the interests of members, the U.S., and the rest of the "free world"; promote religious, educational, and recreational activities among members, in order to develop a better understanding and mutual respect. Sponsors educational seminars, Air Force training, JOBCAP - a job placement service, and programs for retired members. Provides congressional representation, insurance, and other services.

American Logistics Association. R 1133 15th St. NW, Ste. 640, Washington, DC 20005. Phone: (202)466-2520 Fax: (202)296-4419 E-mail: alanb@ala-national.org • URL: http://www.ala-national.org • Promotes, protects and ensures the continued viability of the military resale (Commissary and Exchange Benefits) and Morale, Welfare and Recreations (MWR Benefits) industries. Acts as liaison between manufacturers and the Armed Forces' purchasing agencies. Promotes cooperation between the Congress, Defense Department and the industries with which it conducts business.

American Retirees Association. PO Box 2333, Redlands, CA 92373-0781. Phone: (909)557-0107 Fax: (909)335-2711 E-mail: contactara@aol.com • URL: http://www.americanretireesassociation.org • Active, reserve, and retired members of the uniformed military services of the United States. Seeks to address what the group feels are inequities in the Uniformed Services Former Spouses' Protection Act (USFSPA). Provides advisory services to military retirees and second families adversely affected by these laws; lobbies for amendments to the USFSPA.

Armed Forces Communications and Electronics Association. 4400 Fair Lakes Ct., Fairfax, VA 22033. Phone: 800-336-4583 or (703)631-6100 Fax: (703)631-6169 E-mail: promo@afcea.org • URL: http://www.afcea.org • Serves as a bridge between government requirements and industry capabilities. Represents top government, industry, and military professionals in the fields of communications, intelligence, information systems, imaging, and multimedia. Aims for the continuing education of its members and for peace through civil government effectiveness and military and industrial preparedness. Supports global security by providing an ethical environment encouraging a close cooperative relationship among civil government agencies, the military and industry.

Armed Forces Hostess Association. The Pentagon, Rm. ID110, 6604 Army Pentagon, Washington, DC 20310-6604. Phone: (703)614-0350 Fax: (703)697-5542 E-mail: promo@afcea.org • URL: http://www.army.mil/afha/main.html • Information office operated by volunteer wives of the armed forces. Assists in welcoming service families to the Washington, DC area; provides information on living conditions at all U.S. installations in the U.S. and overseas. Maintains information files on topics ranging from animal care and camps to universities and local vacation areas.

Army Aviation Association of America. 755 Main St., Ste. 4D, Monroe, CT 06468-2830. Phone: (203)268-2450 Fax: (203)268-5870 E-mail: aaaa@quad-a.org • URL: http://www.quad-a.org • Commissioned officers, warrant officers, and enlisted personnel serving in U.S. Army aviation assignments in the active U.S. Army, Army National Guard, and Army Reserve; Department of Army civilian personnel and industry representatives affiliated with army aviation. Fosters fellowship among military and civilian persons connected with army aviation, past or present; seeks to advance status, overall esprit, and general knowledge of professionals engaged in army aviation. Activities include locator and placement services, technical assistance, and biographical archives. Sponsors speakers' bureau; maintains hall of fame.

Army Nurse Corps Association. PO Box 39235, Serna Sta., San Antonio, TX 78218-1235. Phone: (210)650-3534 Fax: (210)650-3494 E-mail: membership@e-anca.org • URL: http://e-anca.org • Army Nurse Corps officers from active, or retiree status or those serving honorably for shorter periods, or reserve duty. Provides educational and social opportunities for members; disseminates information to the public. Seeks to preserve history of the U.S. Army Nurse Corps.

Association of Graduates. 3116 Academy Dr., 3116 Academy Dr., USAF Academy, CO 80840-4475. Phone: 800-232-GRAD or (719)472-0300 Fax: (719)333-4194 E-mail: aog@usafa.org • URL: http://www.usafa.org • Graduates of the United States Military Academy (West Point); membership currently includes all graduates still living. Promotes the welfare of, and raises money for the academy; helps to improve the education and training of the cadets by providing funds beyond the minimum normal appropriations. Has approximately 120 local and state chapters known as West Point Societies. Compiles statistics; offers career advisory services.

Association of Military Colleges and Schools of the United States. 3604 Glenbrook Rd., Fairfax, VA 22031. Phone: (703)272-8406 E-mail: amcsus@cox.net • URL: http://www.amcsus.org • Comprises of military colleges and secondary schools.

Association of Military Surgeons of the U.S. 9320 Old Georgetown Rd., Bethesda, MD 20814-1653. Phone: 800-761-9320 or (301)897-8800 Fax: (301)530-5446 E-mail: amsus@amsus.org • URL: http://www.amsus.org • Physicians, dentists, veterinarians, nurses, pharmacists, dietitians, therapists, and others of commissioned rank (or grades E5 through E9) or equivalent in the Army, Navy, Air Force, Public Health Service, and Veterans Administration; Reserve and National Guard officers are also eligible for membership. Advances all phases of federal medicine and allied sciences related to federal health services. Provides group insurance.

Association of Naval Aviation. 2550 Huntington Ave., Ste. 201, Alexandria, VA 22303-1499. Phone: (703)960-2490 Fax: (703)960-4490 E-mail: ana@anahq.org • URL: http://www.anahq.org • Active or former officers and enlisted men of the aeronautical organizations of the U.S. Navy, Marines, Coast Guard, or other service personnel and civilians; industrial associates. Objectives are to stimulate and extend appreciation of naval aviation; to help the active and reserve military establishment; to merge the various diverse elements of the military, particularly in relation to problems associated with maritime aviation; to promote greater communication among the military, academic, and business communities on issues of maritime aviation. Sponsors film and videotape programs for U.S. Navy and public service television use.

Association of NROTC Colleges and Universities. University of Rochester, 33A Wallis Hall, PO Box 270041, Rochester, NY 14627-0041. Phone: (585)275-2096 Fax: (585)275-8531 E-mail: jennifer.ashbaugh@rochester.edu • URL: http://www.conferences.rochester.edu/NROTCconstitution.html • Representatives from colleges and universities that have Naval Reserve Officers Training Corps units on their campuses. Promotes NROTC training and coordinates the efforts of institutions offering this service.

Association of the United States Army. 2425 Wilson Blvd., Arlington, VA 22201. Phone: 800-336-4570 or (703)841-4300 Fax: (703)525-9039 E-mail: ausa-info@ausa.org • URL: http://www.ausa.org • Professional society of: active, retired, and reserve military personnel; West Point and Army ROTC cadets; civilians interested in national defense. Seeks to advance the security of the United States and consolidate the efforts of all who support the

United States Army as an indispensable instrument of national security. Conducts industrial symposia for manufacturers of Army weapons and equipment, and those in the Department of the Army who plan, develop, test, and use weapons and equipment. Symposia subjects have included guided missiles, army aviation, electronics and communication, telemedicine, vehicles, and armor. Sponsors monthly PBS TV series America's Army.

Chief Warrant and Warrant Officers Association, United States Coast Guard. 200 V St. SW, Washington, DC 20024. Phone: (202)554-7753 Fax: (202)484-0641 E-mail: cwoauscg@verizon.net • URL: http://www.cwoauscg.org • Individuals who currently hold or once held the rank of Warrant Officer or Chief Warrant Officer on the active, retired, and reserve rolls of the U.S. Coast Guard. Works to aid members in advancing their professional abilities. Seeks to enhance their value, loyalty, and devotion to the service; promotes its unity and morale through social association.

Civil Affairs Association. 10130 Hyla Brook Rd., Columbia, MD 21044-1705. Phone: (410)992-7724 Fax: (410)740-5046 E-mail: civilaffairs@earthlink.net • URL: http://www.civilaffairsassoc.org • U.S. Army active and reserve officers and enlisted personnel serving in Army or Marine Corps civil affairs units or in civil affairs staff positions in major military headquarters, and international members. Advocates and promotes a strong U.S. military civil affairs capability.

Enlisted Association of National Guard of the United States. 3133 Mt. Vernon Ave., Alexandria, VA 22305-2640. Phone: 800-234-EANG or (703)519-3846 Fax: (703)519-3849 E-mail: eangus@eangus.org • URL: http://www.memberconnections.com/eangus • Active and retired members of the U.S. National Guard. Conducts educational, legislative and charitable programs.

Escort Carrier Sailors and Airmen Association. 13114 Blue Bonnet Dr., Sun City, AZ 85375. Phone: (623)584-4794 Fax: (952)935-5454 E-mail: pyzzaz@earthlink.net • URL: http://www.escortcarriers.com • Promotes knowledge and interest in the vital role played by escort carriers during World War II and the Korean War.

Judge Advocates Association. 8109 Overlake Ct., Fairfax Station, VA 22039. Phone: (703)474-7691 Fax: (202)628-0080 E-mail: jaa@jaa.org • URL: http://www.jaa.org • Active, reserve, retired and former Judge Advocates of the Army, Navy, Air Force, Marine Corps, Coast Guard and practitioners of military and veterans law. Assists in the development of military law and an efficient military and veterans legal and judicial system.

Marine Corps Association. 715 Broadway St., Quantico, VA 22134. Phone: 800-336-0291 or (703)640-6161 Fax: (703)640-0823 E-mail: mca@mca-marine.org • URL: http://www.mca-marines.org • Represents active duty, reserve, retired, Fleet Reserve, honorably discharged Marines, and members of other services who have served with Marine Corps units. Disseminates information about the military arts and sciences to members; assists members' professional advancement; fosters the spirit and works to preserve the traditions of the United States Marine Corps. Maintains discount book service and group insurance plan for members. Association founded by members of the Second Provisional Marine Brigade at Guantanamo Bay, Cuba.

Marine Corps Aviation Association. PO Box 296, 715 Broadway St., Quantico, VA 22134. Phone: 800-280-3001 or (703)630-1903 Fax: (703)630-2713 E-mail: mcaa@flymcaa.org • URL: http://www.flymcaa.org • Members and former members of U.S. Marine aviation units and others with an interest in Marine Corps aviation; aerospace

corporations. Aims to: perpetuate camaraderie in marine aviation; foster and encourage professional excellence and recognize important achievements in marine aviation. Conducts charitable programs.

Marine Corps Reserve Association. 8626 Lee Hwy., Fairfax, VA 22031-2135. Phone: 800-287-8780 or (703)289-1204 Fax: (703)289-1206 E-mail: mcrahq@usmcra.org • URL: http://www.usmcra.org • Marines who have served on active duty in peace or war. Seeks to: advance the professional skills of marines; represent and assist individual members; promote the interests of the U.S. Marine Corps in order to advance the welfare and preserve the security of the United States. Maintains speakers' bureau and placement service.

Military Impacted Schools Association. 1600 Hwy. 370, Bellevue, NE 68005. Phone: 800-291-MISA or (402)293-4000 E-mail: rlindner@ngat.org • URL: http://www.militaryimpactedschoolsassociation.org • Provides the educational needs of military families, including quality of life initiatives, community and school district support, and aid funding.

Military Vehicle Preservation Association. PO Box 520378, Independence, MO 64052. Phone: 800-365-5798 or (816)833-6872 Fax: (816)833-5115 E-mail: hq@mvpa.org • URL: http://www.mvpa.org • Represents individuals and groups interested in the preservation, restoration, maintenance, and enjoyment of historic military vehicles. Informs the public of the historical value of collectible military vehicles; serves as a clearinghouse for technical and historical information.

Montford Point Marine Association. PO Box 1070, Sharon Hill, PA 19079. Phone: (202)387-8722 E-mail: info@montfordpointmarines.com • URL: http://www.montfordpointmarines.com • Represents veterans and active members of all branches of the U.S. Armed Forces. Aims to support educational assistance programs, veterans programs and promotion of community services. Works to improve the social conditions of veterans, local families, youth and the growing population of senior citizens; named after Montford Point, New River, Camp Lejeune, NC, the only base in America used for the recruit or "Boot Camp" training of black Marines, 1942-49.

National Association for Uniformed Services. 5535 Hempstead Way, Springfield, VA 22151-4094. Phone: 800-842-3451 or (703)750-1342 Fax: (703)354-4380 E-mail: info@naus.org • URL: http://www.naus.org • Members of the uniformed military services, active, retired or reserve, veteran, enlisted and officers, and their spouses or widows. Develops and supports legislation that upholds the security of the U.S., sustains the morale of the uniformed services, and provides fair and equitable consideration for all service people. Protects and improves compensation, entitlements, and benefits. Provides discount rates on travel, insurance, auto rentals, charge cards, prescription medicine, and legal services.

National Association of Superintendents of U.S. Naval Shore Establishments. 89 Pine Legde Dr., Wells, ME 04090. Phone: (207)646-7316 E-mail: admin@nasnse.org • URL: http://nasnse.org • Superintendents of production, maintenance, and public works branches of naval shore establishments. Promotes the general welfare of members professionally, intellectually, and socially; cultivates high standards of professional ethics.

National Defense Industrial Association. 2111 Wilson Blvd., No. 400, Arlington, VA 22201-3061. Phone: (703)522-1820 Fax: (703)522-1825 E-mail: info@ndia.org • URL: http://www.adpa.org • Concerned citizens, military and government personnel, and defense-related industry workers interested in industrial preparedness for the national defense of the United States. Operates Technology Services which provides a forum for discussion of

defense industry programs and issues. Conducts 55 technical meetings per year.

National Defense Transportation Association. 50 S Pickett St., Ste. 220, Alexandria, VA 22304-7296. Phone: (703)751-5011 Fax: (703)823-8761 E-mail: info@ndtahq.com • URL: http://www.ndtahq.com • Men and women in the field of transportation, travel logistics and related areas in the Armed Forces, federal government, private industry and the academic sector. Dedicated to fostering a strong and efficient transportation system in support of national defense. Serves as link between government and industry on transportation matters. Operates a job placement service for members.

National Guard Association of the United States. 1 Massachusetts Ave. NW, Washington, DC 20001. Phone: (202)789-0031 Fax: (202)682-9358 E-mail: ngaus@ngaus.org • URL: http://www.ngaus.org • Active and Retired Officers and Warrant Officers of the Army National Guard and Air National Guard of the States, Commonwealth of Puerto Rico, the District of Columbia, Guam, and the Virgin Islands. Goals include: adequate national security and a strong Army National Guard and Air National Guard of the United States as components of the armed forces. Sponsors public affairs competition for National Guard personnel. Maintains the Museum of the National Guard, containing rare art and artifacts relating to the militia and National Guard.

National Naval Officers Association. PO Box 10871, Alexandria, VA 22310-0871. Phone: (703)997-1068 Fax: (703)997-1068 E-mail: webmaster@nnoa.org • URL: http://www.nnoa.org • Active, reserve, and retired Navy, Marine, and Coast Guard officers and students in college and military sea service programs. Promotes and assists recruitment, retention, and career development of minority officers in the naval service. Conducts specialized education; maintains counseling, referral, and mentorship. Makes available non-ROTC grants-in-aid. Sponsors competitions; operates charitable program.

Naval Civilian Managers Association. PO Box 215, Portsmouth, VA 23705. Phone: (757)396-2265 Fax: (757)396-7743 E-mail: clifford.elder@navy.mil • Upper echelon civilian personnel in a naval organizational entity. Encourages improvement of administration and management of U.S. Navy. Compiles statistics. Maintains speakers' bureau, museum, and hall of fame.

Naval Enlisted Reserve Association. 6703 Farragut Ave., Falls Church, VA 22042-2189. Phone: 800-776-9020 or (703)534-1329 Fax: (703)534-3617 E-mail: members@nera.org • URL: http://www.nera.org • Enlisted personnel of the U.S. Naval Reserve, Marine Corps Reserve, and Coast Guard Reserve on active duty, inactive duty, or retired. Works to promote career enlisted service in the "seagoing" branches of the armed services; concerned with the readiness, training, morale, and well-being of all Reservists; obtains fair and proper recognition of the contributions made by Reservists to the national defense and to obtain protection and extension of benefits and entitlements for those Reservists who are currently serving and for those who have already served satisfactorily and have retired. Works with Congress and military leaders for legislation and proposals designed to improve and enhance the effectiveness of Reserve programs; also works to provide a communications link with the public.

Naval Reserve Association. 1619 King St., Alexandria, VA 22314-2793. Phone: (866)672-4968 or (703)548-5800 Fax: (703)683-3647 E-mail: membership@navy-reserve.org • URL: http://www.navy-reserve.org • Naval officers on active or inactive duty or retired. Maintains involvement with legislation affecting U.S. Navy and Naval Reserve. Provides Naval Officer Promotion Record Reviews. Sponsors Naval Reserve Junior Officer of the Year

Programs. Offers professional education; sponsors competitions; maintains speakers' bureau.

Non Commissioned Officers Association of the United States of America. 10635 IH 35 N, San Antonio, TX 78233. Phone: 800-662-2620 or (210)653-6161 Fax: (210)637-3337 E-mail: natdir@ncoausa.org • URL: http://www.ncoausa.org • Noncommissioned and petty officers of the United States military serving in grades E1 through E9 from all five branches of the U.S. Armed Forces; includes active duty and retired personnel, members of the Reserve and National Guard components, and personnel who held the rank of NCO/PO at the time of separation from active duty under honorable conditions. Formed for patriotic, fraternal, social, and benevolent purposes. Offers veterans job assistance, legislative representation, and grants. Conducts charitable programs.

Reserve Officers Association of the United States. 1 Constitution Ave. NE, Washington, DC 20002-5618. Phone: 800-809-9448 or (202)479-2200 Fax: (202)547-1641 E-mail: dmccarthy@roa.org • URL: http://www.roa.org • Represents reserve members of the seven United States Uniformed Services-Army, Navy, Air Force, Marines, Coast Guard, Public Health Service, and National Oceanic and Atmospheric Administration Corps. Aims to "support and promote the development and execution of a military policy for the United States that will provide adequate National Security".

State Guard Association of the United States. PO Box 1416, Fayetteville, GA 30214-1416. Phone: (770)460-1215 Fax: (770)261-9099 E-mail: director@sgaus.org • URL: http://www.sgaus.org • Active and retired officers and enlisted personnel of State Defense Forces (SDF) including State Guard, State Military Reserve, National Reserve, Defense Force, Guard Reserve, and other militia. Promotes the SDF in states where they exist; lobbies on behalf of SDF before state and federal governments; fosters exchange among states to keep members abreast of changes in laws pertaining to the SDF. Seeks to educate the public and disseminates information on the history and mission of the militia and to advocate a viable state militia system.

Tailhook Association. 9696 Businesspark Ave., San Diego, CA 92131. Phone: 800-322-4665 or (858)689-9223 Fax: (858)578-8839 E-mail: thookassn@aol.com • URL: http://www.tailhook.org • Individuals who have been designated as Naval Aviators or Naval Flight Officers and have made carrier landings; other individuals who have made carrier landings or who have the background and interest to support the objectives of the association. Seeks to foster, develop, study, and support U.S. aircraft carriers and aircrews, and their role in the nation's defense system.

U.S. Armor Association. PO Box 607, Fort Knox, KY 40121-0607. Phone: (502)942-8624 Fax: (502)942-6219 E-mail: mgavula@bellsouth.net • URL: http://www.usarmor-assn.org • U.S. Army officers, noncommissioned officers, enlisted men, and veterans of all components. Disseminates professional knowledge of military art and science, especially mobile ground warfare.

United States Army Warrant Officers Association. 462 Herndon Pkwy., Ste. 207, Herndon, VA 20170-5235. Phone: 800-587-2962 or (703)742-7727 Fax: (703)742-7728 E-mail: usawoa@cavtel.net • URL: http://www.penfed.org/usawoa • Active duty, National Guard, Reserve, and retired U.S. Army warrant officers. Promotes the technical and social welfare of warrant officers. Recommends Army improvement programs. Circulates professional information among warrant officers. Stimulates patriotism, devotion to duty, and comradeship among members.

United States Marine Corps Drill Instructors Association. PO Box 5401, Parris Island, SC 29905.

Phone: (912)632-4557 Fax: (912)632-4557 E-mail: usmcdia@atc.cc • URL: http://www.usmcdiassn.com • Present and former U.S. Marine Corps drill instructors. Fosters a spirit of comradery through social and recreational activities. Promotes the welfare of elderly, disabled, and needy veterans; sponsors patriotic, charitable, and educational programs. Maintains living memorial monument fund; conducts blood drives and active participants' toys 4 tots.

OTHER SOURCES

American Military Society. • Active or retired members of the armed services (Army, Navy, Air Force, Marine Corps, and Coast Guard), and civilians. Develops and supports activities which promote the general well-being of the members; upholds and defends the Constitution; supports national defense; and preserves the memories and traditions of the Armed Forces.

Navy League of the United States. • Civilian organization that supports U.S. capability to keep the sea lanes open through a strong, viable Navy, Marine Corps, Coast Guard, and Merchant Marine. Seeks to awaken interest and cooperation of U.S. citizens in matters serving to aid, improve, and develop the efficiency of U.S. naval and maritime forces and equipment; acquires and disseminates information concerning the conditions of U.S. naval and maritime forces and equipment.

Society of the Fifth Division. • Works to perpetuate and memorialize the valiant acts and patriotic deeds of the Fifth Division.

MILITARY COMMISSARIES

See: POST EXCHANGES

MILITARY MARKET

See also: DEFENSE INDUSTRIES

BIBLIOGRAPHIES

Defense and Security. Available from U. S. Government Printing Office. • Annual. Free. Issued by the Superintendent of Documents. A list of government publications on defense and related topics. Formerly *Defense Supply and Logistics.* (Subject Bibliography No. 153.).

DIRECTORIES

ECN's Electronic Industry Telephone Directory. Reed Business Information. • Covers: 30,000 electronics manufacturers, distributors, and representatives. Entries include: Company name, address, phone, fax, and type of establishment.

Military Retailing Directory. Military Retailing Publisher. • Semiannual. $95.00 per year. Edited for use by military commissaries in making purchasing decisions. Lists sources of goods and sevices, with official military department and retail order numbers.

FINANCIAL RATIOS

Industry Norms and Key Business Ratios. Desk Top Edition. Dun and Bradstreet Corp. • Annual. Five volumes. $475.00 per volume. $1,890.00 per set. Covers over 800 kinds of businesses, arranged by Standard Industrial Classification number. More detailed editions covering longer periods of time are also available.

HANDBOOKS AND MANUALS

International Defense Electronic Systems Handbook. Primedia Business Magazines and Media. • Annual. $195.00. Includes information concerning federal budget for electronic military equipment. Gives descriptions of equipment.

ONLINE DATABASES

Aerospace America [online]. American Institute of Aeronautics and Astronautics. • Provides complete

text of the periodical, *Aerospace America*, 1984 to date, with monthly updates. Also includes news from the *AIAA Bulletin*. Inquire as to online cost and availability.

Aerospace Database. American Institute of Aeronautics and Astronautics. • Contains abstracts of literature covering all aspects of the aerospace and aircraft industry 1983 to date. Monthly updates. Inquire as to online cost and availability.

Aerospace/Defense Markets and Technology. Gale Cengage Learning. • Abstracts of commerical aerospace/defense related literature, 1982 to date. Also includes information about major defense contracts awarded by the U. S. Department of Defense. International coverage. Inquire as to online cost and availability.

PAIS International. Public Affairs Information Service, Inc. • Corresponds to the former printed publications, *PAIS Bulletin* (1976-90) and *PAIS Foreign Language Index* (1972-90), and to the current *PAIS International in Print* (1991 to date). Covers economic, political, and sociological material appearing in periodicals, books, government documents, and other publications. Updating is monthly. Inquire as to online cost and availability.

PERIODICALS AND NEWSLETTERS

Aerospace America. American Institute of Aeronautics and Astronautics, Inc. • Monthly. Free to members; non-members, $140.00 per year. Provides coverage of key issues affecting the aerospace field.

Aviation Week and Space Technology. McGraw-Hill Aviation Week Group. • Monthly. $92.00 per year.

Defense Electronics. Primedia Business Magazines and Media. • Monthly. $52.00 per year.

Defense Systems Review and Military Communications. Cosgriff-Martin Publishing Group, Inc. • Monthly. $35.00 per year.

Flight International. Reed Business Information. • Weekly. $140.00 per year. Technical aerospace coverage.

Inside R and D: A Weekly Report on Technical Innovation. Technical Insights. • Weekly. Institutions, $840.00 per year. Concentrates on new and significant developments. Formerly *Technolog Transfer Week.*

Interservice. American Logistics Association. • Quarterly. $20.00 per year. Official Journal of the American Logistics Association.

Journal of Electronic Defense. Association of Old Crows. Horizon House Publications. • Monthly. Free to members; non-members, $115.00 per year.

Military Grocer. Downey Communications, Inc. • Five times a year. $30.00 per year. Edited for managers and employees of supermarkets on military bases. (These are supermarkets administered by the Defense Commissary Agency.).

National Defense: NDIA's Business and Technology Journal. National Defense Industrial Association. • 10 times a year. $35.00 per year.

Navy Supply Corps Newsletter. Available from U. S. Government Printing Office. • Bimonthly. $30.00 per year. Newsletter issued by U. S. Navy Supply Systems Command. Provides news of Navy supplies and stores activities.

TRADE/PROFESSIONAL ASSOCIATIONS

Aerospace Industries Association of America. 1250 Eye St., N.W., Ste. 1200, Washington, DC 20005-3924. Phone: (202)371-8400 Fax: (202)371-8470 E-mail: neale@aia-aerospace.org • URL: http://www.aia-aerospace.org.

American Institute of Aeronautics and Astronautics. 1801 Alexander Bell Dr., Suite 500, c/o Michael Lewis, Reston, VA 20191-4344. Phone: 800-639-2422 or (703)264-7500 Fax: (703)264-7551 E-mail: custserv@aiaa.org • URL: http://www.aiaa.org.

American Logistics Association. 1133 15th St. NW, Ste. 640, Washington, DC 20005. Phone: (202)466-2520 Fax: (202)296-4419 E-mail: membership@ala-national.org • URL: http://www.ala-national.org • Promotes, protects and ensures the continued viability of the military resale (Commissary and Exchange Benefits) and Morale, Welfare and Recreations (MWR Benefits) industries. Acts as liaison between manufacturers and the Armed Forces' purchasing agencies. Promotes cooperation between the Congress, Defense Department and the industries which it conducts business.

National Defense Industrial Association. 2111 Wilson Blvd., Ste. 400, Arlington, VA 22201-3061. Phone: (703)522-1820 or (703)247-2589 Fax: (703)522-1885 E-mail: info@ndia.org • URL: http://www.adpa.org • Concerned citizens, military and government personnel, and defense-related industry workers interested in industrial preparedness for the national defense of the United States. Operates Technology Services that provides a forum for discussion of defense industry programs and issues. Conducts 55 technical meetings per year.

Research and Development Associates for Military Food and Packaging Systems. 16607 Blanco Rd., No. 1506, San Antonio, TX 78232. Phone: (210)493-8024 or (210)493-8025 Fax: (210)493-8036 E-mail: rda50@flash.net • URL: http://www.militaryfood.org • Industrial firms, educational institutions and related groups engged in food, food service, distribution and container research and development.

OTHER SOURCES

Carroll's Defense Organization Charts. Carroll Publishing. • Every six weeks. $1,500.00 per year. Provides more than 200 large, fold-out paper charts showing personnel relationships in 2,400 U. S. military offices. Charts are also available online and on CD-ROM.

Jane's All the World's Aircraft. Jane's Information Group, Inc. • Annual. $630.00; CD-ROM edition, $1,455.00; online edition, $1,566.00; microfiche edition, $3,075.00. Lists civil and military aircraft, helicopters, airships, and aero engines.

MILK INDUSTRY

See: DAIRY INDUSTRY

MILLERS AND MILLING

See: FLOUR INDUSTRY

MILLINERY INDUSTRY

DIRECTORIES

Contemporary Fashion. St. James Press. • Publication includes: Contact information for designers featured. Entries include: name, address, phone, and Web site. Principal content of publication is essays evaluating contemporary clothing and accessories designers worldwide.

Garment Manufacturers Index. Klevens Publications Inc. • Covers: about 8,000 manufacturers and suppliers of products and services such as fabrics, trimmings, factory equipment, and sewing contractors used in the manufacture of apparel. Publication includes: fabrics, trimmings, supplies, services, equipment, and contractors. Entries include: Company name, address, phone, fax, list of products or services, brief description of product.

HANDBOOKS AND MANUALS

Women's Accessories Store. Entrepreneur Media, Inc. • Looseleaf. $59.50. A practical guide to starting a women's clothing accessories shop. Covers profit potential, start-up costs, market size evaluation, owner's time required, site selection, lease negotiation, pricing, accounting, advertising, promotion, etc. (Start-Up Business Guide No. E1333.).

PERIODICALS AND NEWSLETTERS

Accessories. Business Journals, Inc. • 11 times a year. $35.00 per year. Covers the merchandising of women's fashion accessories, including handbags, belts, jewelry, gloves, hats, and umbrellas.

TRADE/PROFESSIONAL ASSOCIATIONS

Headwear Information Bureau. 302 W 12th St., PHC, New York, NY 10014. Phone: (212)627-8333 Fax: (212)627-0067 E-mail: milicase@aol.com • URL: http://www.hatsworldwide.com • Headwear and Millinery manufacturers, importers, and suppliers for men and women's hats. Promotes the wearing of hats by women and men of all ages. Disseminates fashion information; conducts promotional and educational campaigns; handles press relations and designer store appearances. Operates speakers' bureau and charitable program; compiles statistics.

MILLWORK

See: WOODWORKING INDUSTRIES

MINERALOGY

See also: METALLURGY; MINES AND MINERAL RESOURCES

ABSTRACTS AND INDEXES

Mineralogical Abstracts: A Quarterly Journal of Abstracts in English, Covering the World Literature of Mineralogy and Related Subjects. Mineralogical Society. • Quarterly. $393.00 per year.

HANDBOOKS AND MANUALS

Dana's New Mineralogy: The System of Mineralogy of James Dwight Dana and Edward Salisbury Dana. Richard V. Gaines and others. John Wiley and Sons, Inc. • 1997. $375.00. Eighth edition. Provides descriptions of more than 3,650 "recognized mineral species.".

Field Guide to Rocks and Minerals. Roger T. Peterson and Frederick H. Pough. Houghton Mifflin Co. • 1998. $20.00. Fifth edition. Data on where to find rocks and minerals, how to collect them, physical properties and various types. (Peterson Field Guide Series).

Manual of Mineralogy:With Minerals and Rock Exercises in Crystallography Mineralogy and Hand Speciman Petrology. Cornelius Klein and Cornelius Hurlburt. John Wiley and Sons, Inc. • 1994. $69.95. 21st revised edition.

ONLINE DATABASES

Scisearch. Institute for Scientific Information. • Broad, multidisciplinary index to the literature of science and technology, 1974 to present. Inquire as to online cost and availability. Coverage of literature is worldwide, with weekly updates.

PERIODICALS AND NEWSLETTERS

American Mineralogist: An International Journal of Earth and Planetary Materials. Mineralogical Society of America. • Eight times a year. $580.00 per year.

Rocks and Minerals: Mineralogy, Geology, Lapidary. Helen Dwight Reid Educational Foundation. Heldref Publications. • Bimonthly. $37. 00. per year.

TRADE/PROFESSIONAL ASSOCIATIONS

American Federation of Mineralogical Societies. 270 Lascassas Pke., Murfreesboro, TN 37130-1540. Phone: (615)893-8270 E-mail: central_office@amfed.org • URL: http://www.ammfed.org.

Mineralogical Society of America. 1015 18th St., NW, Ste. 601, Washington, DC 20036-5212. Phone: (202)775-4344 Fax: (202)775-0018 E-mail: business@minsocam.org • URL: http://www.minsocam.org.

Minerals, Metals and Materials Society. 184 Thorn Hill Dr., Warrendale, PA 15086-7514. Phone: (724)776-9000 Fax: (724)776-3770 E-mail: tmsgeneral@tms.org • URL: http://www.tms.org • Members are metallurgists, metallurgical engineers, and materials scientists. Divisions include Light Metals and Electronic, Magnetic, and Photonic Materials. Formerly The Metallurigical Society.

MINES AND MINERAL RESOURCES

See also: MINERALOGY; NATURAL RESOURCES

ABSTRACTS AND INDEXES

IMM Abstracts and Index: A Survey of World Literature on the Economic Geology and Mining of All Minerals (Except Coal), Mineral Processing, and Nonferrous Extraction Metallurgy. Institution of Mining and Metallurgy. • Bimonthly. $500.00 per year. Provides international coverage of the literature of mining and nonferrous metallurgy. Includes mineral economics, tunnelling, and rock mechanics.

ALMANACS AND YEARBOOKS

Agricultural and Mineral Commodities Year Book. Available from Taylor & Francis Group. • Annual. $225.00. Published by Europa Publications. Contains descriptive product profiles, price data, export-import data, and production statistics for major commodities of the world. Includes commodity histories, uses, markets, demand trends, and information about trade agreements and key commodity organizations.

BIOGRAPHICAL SOURCES

Mining Engineering. Society for Mining, Metallurgy and Exploration. • Monthly. $125.00 per year. Includes *Who's Who in Mining Engineering*.

CD-ROM DATABASES

Environment Abstracts on CD-ROM. LEXIS-NEXIS. • Quarterly. $1,295.00 per year. Contains the following CD-ROM databases: *Environment Abstracts*, *Energy Abstracts*, and *Acid Rain Abstracts*. Length of coverage varies.

OECD Statistical Compendium. Organization for Economic Cooperation and Development. • Semiannual. $1,905.00 per year for 1 to 10 users. CD-ROM contains more than 730,000 monthly, quarterly, and annual time series for OECD countries, 1960 to date. Includes fully searchable data on agriculture, food, economic indicators, national accounts, employment, energy, finance, industry, technology, and foreign trade. Results can be displayed in various forms.

DIRECTORIES

Canadian Mines Handbook. Scott's Directories. • Covers: About 2,400 mining companies in Canada, plus smelters, refineries, trade associations, related government agencies, and similar organizations. Entries include: For mining companies--Name, address, phone, names and titles of officers and directors, stock exchange and symbol, date and province of incorporation, locations of mines and other properties, description of exploration and development, ore reserves, production statistics, financial data.

Engineering and Mining Journal Annual Buyers' Guide. Primedia Business Magazines and Media. •

Annual. Free to qualified subscribers; others, $69.00. List of manufacturers and suppliers of mining equipment; international coverage. Formerly *Engineering and Mining Journal Buying Directory*.

Financial Times Business Global Mining Directory. Available from Gale Cengage Learning. • Annual. $355.00. Published by Financial Times Business. Provides detailed information on 1,000 leading mining companies worldwide. Includes financial data for three years. Formerly *Financial Times Energy Yearbook: Mining*.

FINANCIAL RATIOS

Almanac of Business and Industrial Financial Ratios. Leo Troy. Aspen Publishers, Inc. • 2003. $125.95. Includes CD-Rom. Contains financial ratios derived from federal tax returns. Ratios for each of about 200 industries are arranged according to company asset size. (Almanac of Business and Industrial Financial Ratios Series).

Quarterly Financial Report for Manufacturing, Mining, and Trade Corporations. U.S. Federal Trade Commission and U.S. Securities and Exchange Commission. Available from U.S. Government Printing Office. • Quarterly. $49.00 per year.

INTERNET DATABASES

Business 2.0 Web Guide to the Best Business Links. Business 2.0 Media Inc. Phone: (415)293-4800 E-mail: support@business2.com • URL: http://www.business2.com/webguide • Web site presents an extensive, searchable directory of links to "the best, most informative, and authoritative web pages." Twenty main categories cover business, finance, career, company information, people, and technology topics, with thousands of subtopics, all linking to Web sites recommended by experienced business researchers. Fees: Free.

Fedstats. Federal Interagency Council on Statistical Policy. Phone: (202)395-7254 • URL: http://www.fedstats.gov • Web site features an efficient search facility for full-text statistics produced by more than 100 federal agencies, including the Census Bureau, the Bureau of Economic Analysis, and the Bureau of Labor Statistics. Boolean searches can be made within one agency or for all agencies combined. Links are offered to international statistical bureaus, including the UN, IMF, OECD, UNESCO, Eurostat, and 20 individual countries. Fees: Free.

FreeLunch.com. Economy.com, Inc. Phone: (610)696-8700 Fax: (610)696-1678 • URL: http://www.freelunch.com • Web site provides free access to more than 1.5 million economic and financial data series, covering industry, demographics, labor markets, prices, retail sales, government spending, trade, interest rates, housing starts, the stock market, and many other topics. Data is available for various time periods in either chart or table form. Searching is offered. Fees: Free, but registration required. Economy.com, Inc. also offers fee-based economic analysis at *The Dismal Scientist* site (http://www.dismal.com).

Manufacturing Profiles. U. S. Bureau of the Census. Phone: (301)763-4636 E-mail: webmaster@census.gov • URL: http://www.census.gov/prod/www/abs/mfg-prof.html • The Census Bureau makes available free on PDF (Portable Document Format) an annual consolidation of the entire Current Industrial Report series, presenting "all the data compiled." Contains statistics on production, shipments, inventories, consumption, exports, imports, and orders for a wide variety of manufactured products.

NMA. National Mining Association. Phone: (202)463-2600 Fax: (202)463-2666 • URL: http://www.nma.org • Web site provides information on the U. S. coal and mineral industries. Includes "Salient Statistics of the Mining Industry," showing a wide variety of annual data (six years) for coal and non-fuel minerals. Publications of the National Min-

ing Association are described and links are provided to other sites. (National Mining Association formerly known as National Coal Association.) Fees: Free.

ONLINE DATABASES

GEOARCHIVE. Geosystems. • Citations to literature on geoscience and water. 1974 to present. Monthly updates. Inquire as to online cost and availability.

GEOREF. American Geological Institute. • Bibliography and index of geology and geosciences literature, 1785 to present. Inquire as to online cost and availability.

PERIODICALS AND NEWSLETTERS

Canadian Resources and PennyMines Analyst: The Canadian Newsletter for Penny-Mines Investors Who Insist on Geological Value. MPL Communications, Inc. • Weekly. $145.00 per year. Newsletter. Mainly on Canadian gold mine stocks. Formerly *Canadian PennyMines Analyst*.

Colorado School of Mines Quarterly Review. Colorado School of Mines Press. • Quarterly. $65.00 per year.

Earth and Mineral Sciences. College of Earth and Mineral Sciences. Pennsylvania State University. • Semiannual. Free. Current research in material science, mineral engineering, geosciences, meteorology, geography and mineral economics.

Mines Magazine. Colorado School of Mines Alumni Association and the Colorado School of Mines. • Quarterly. $30.00 per year.

The Mining Record. The Mining Record. • Description: Discusses a myriad of issues within the mining industry, particularly exploration, development, production, and milling.

Mining Week. National Mining Association. • Weekly. Free to members; non-members, $100.00 per year. Newsletter. Covers legislative, business, research, and other developments of interest to the mining industry.

The Northern Miner: Devoted to the Mineral Resources Industry of Canada. Business Information Group. • Monthly. $91.50 per year.

RESEARCH CENTERS AND INSTITUTES

Colorado School of Mines. Office of Research Development, 1500 Illinois St., Golden, CO 80401. Phone: (303)273-3255 Fax: (303)273-3244 E-mail: graddean@mines.edu • URL: http://www.mines.edu/research/ord.

STATISTICS SOURCES

Annual Survey of Manufactures. Available from U. S. Government Printing Office. • Annual. Prices vary. Issued by the U. S. Census Bureau as an interim update to the *Census of Manufactures*. Includes data on number of manufacturing establishments in various industries, employment, labor costs, value of shipments, capital expenditures, inventories, energy costs, and assets. (See also Census Bureau home page, http://www.census.gov/.)

Business Statistics of the United States. Linz Audain and Cornelia J. Strawser. Bernan Associates. • Annual. $147.00. Based on *Business Statistics*, formerly issue by the Bureau of Economic Analysis, U. S. Department of Commerce. Provides basic data for a wide variety of U. S. industries, services, and economic indicators. Most statistics are shown annually for 30 years and monthly for the most recent four years.

Infrastructure Industries USA. Gale Cengage Learning. • 2001. $260.00. Presents statistics and projections relating to economic activity in a wide variety of natural resource and construction industries.

Mineral Commodity Summaries. Available from U.

S. Government Printing Office. • Annual. $26.00. Published by the U. S. Geological Survey, Department of the Interior (http://www.usgs.gov). Contains detailed, five-year data for about 90 nonfuel minerals. Covers a wide range of statistics, including production, imports, exports, consumption, reserves, prices, tariff information, and industry employment. (Two pages are devoted to each mineral.).

Minerals Yearbook. Available from U.S. Government Printing Office. • Annual. Three volumes.

Mining Machinery and Equipment. U.S. Bureau of the Census. • Annual. (Current Industrial Reports MA35F.).

Monthly Bulletin of Statistics. United Nations Publications. • Monthly. $295.00 per year. Provides current data for about 200 countries on a wide variety of economic, industrial, and demographic subjects. Compiled by United Nations Statistical Office.

Quarterly Mining Review. National Mining Association. • Quarterly. $300.00 per year. Contains detailed data on production, shipments, consumption, stockpiles, and trade for coal and various minerals. (Publisher formerly National Coal Association.).

Statistical Yearbook. United Nations Publications. • Annual. $125.00. Contains statistics for about 200 countries on a wide variety of economic, industrial, and demographic topics. Compiled by United Nations Statistical Office.

Structural Statistics for Industry and Services: Core Data. Organization for Economic Cooperation and Development. • Annual. $63.00. Provides annual data for eight years for both industrial and service sectors. Industries include mining, manufacturing, utilities, and construction. Statistics for OECD countries cover production, value added, investment, employment, wages, hours worked, and number of establishments.

Survey of Current Business. Available from U. S. Government Printing Office. • Monthly. $63.00 per year. Issued by Bureau of Economic Analysis, U. S. Department of Commerce. Presents a wide variety of business and economic data.

United States Census of Mineral Industries. Bureau of the Census, U.S. Department of Commerce. Available from U.S. Government Printing Office. • Quinquennial.

WEFA Industrial Monitor. John Wiley and Sons, Inc. • Annual. $65.00. Prepared by industry analysts at WEFA, an economic forecasting and consulting firm (originally Wharton Econometric Forecasting Associates). Contains discussions of the outlook for major U. S. industries, with many 10-year forecasts (WEFA Web site is http://www.wefa.com).

TRADE/PROFESSIONAL ASSOCIATIONS

Mining and Metallurgical Society of America. 476 Wilson Ave., Novato, CA 94947-4236. Fax: (415)899-0262 E-mail: info@mmsa.net • URL: http://www.mmsa.net.

Society for Mining, Metallurgy, and Exploration. 8307 Shaeffer Pky., Littleton, CO 80127. Phone: 800-763-3132 or (303)973-9550 or (303)948-4210 Fax: (303)973-3845 E-mail: sme@smenet.org • URL: http://www.smenet.org • Affiliated with American Institute of Mining and the Mettallurgical and Petroleum Engineers. Formerly Society of Mining Engineers.

OTHER SOURCES

American Law of Mining. Rocky Mountain Mineral Law Institute. LexisNexis Matthew Bender. • $768.00. Six looseleaf volumes. Periodic supplementation.

MINICOMPUTERS

See: MICROCOMPUTERS AND
MINICOMPUTERS

MINING

See: MINES AND MINERAL RESOURCES

MINISTERS OF STATE

See: DIPLOMATIC AND CONSULAR
SERVICE

MINORITY BUSINESS

GENERAL WORKS

The History of Black Business in America: Capitalism, Race, Entrepreneurship. Juliet E. Walker. Available from Gale Cengage Learning. • 1998. $50.00. Published by Twayne Publishers. Includes profiles of African American business pioneers. (Evolution of Modern Business Series.).

In the Black: A History of African Americans on Wall Street. Gregory S. Bell. John Wiley and Sons, Inc. • 2001. $24.95. Written by the son of Travers Bell, co-founder of Daniels Bell stockbrokers, the first black-owned New York Stock Exchange member firm.

Minority Broadcast Ownership. Gregory L. Rohde. Nova Science Publishers, Inc. • 2002. $29.50. Provides discussion and statistical data relating to minority ownership of radio and television stations in the U.S.

Women Entrepreneurs: Moving Beyond the Glass Ceiling. Dorothy P. Moore and E. Holly Buttner. Sage Publications, Inc. • 1997. $79.95. Contains profiles of "129 successful female entrepreneurs who previously worked in corporate environments.".

ABSTRACTS AND INDEXES

NTIS Alerts: Business & Economics. National Technical Information Service. • Text: Semimonthly. $210.00 per year.

BIOGRAPHICAL SOURCES

African-American Business Leaders and Entrepreneurs. Rachel Kranz. Facts on File, Inc. • 2004. $44.00. (A to Z of African Americans Series).

Who's Who Among African Americans. Gale Cengage Learning. • 2002. $195.00. 15th edition. Includes many business leaders.

DIRECTORIES

Black Enterprise: Top Black Businesses. Earl G. Graves Publishing Co. • Annual. $3.95. Lists of 100 black-owned businesses, banks, savings and loan associations, and insurance companies.

DIR National Minority and Women-Owned Business Directory. Diversity Information Resources Inc. • Covers: Over 9,000 minority-owned companies capable of supplying their goods and services on national or regional levels. Entries include: Company name, address, phone, fax, e-mail, Web site, number of employees, year established, products or services, certification status, minority identification, annual sales, NAICS code.

National Directory of Minority Attorneys. American Lawyer Media, Inc. • Annual. $35.00. Contains 500 listings in four sections, covering minority-owned law firms, minority lawyers at other law firms, minority corporate (in-house) lawyers, and minority lawyers in government agencies. (Minority Law Journal).

National Directory of Minority-Owned Business Firms. Available from Gale Cengage Learning. • 2003. $295.00. 12th edition. Published by Business

Research Services. Includes more than 30,000 minority-owned businesses.

INTERNET DATABASES

MBDA: Minority Business Development Agency. U. S. Department of Commerce. Phone: 888-324-1551 E-mail: help@mbda.gov • URL: http://www.mbda.gov • Web site provides links to a wide variety of advice and information for minority businesses. Main headings are Access to Markets, Access to Capital, Management & Technical Assistance, and Education & Training. An MBDA Resource Locator helps to locate sources of assistance in specific cities. Fees: Free. (Additional "business contracting and assistance tools" are offered to those who register with the site.).

MBEMAG. Minority Business Entrepreneur Magazine. Phone: (310)540-9398 Fax: (310)792-8263 E-mail: webmaster@mbemag.com • URL: http://www.mbemag.com • Web site's main feature is the "MBE Business Resources Directory." This provides complete mailing addresses, phone, fax, and Web site addresses (URL) for more than 40 organizations and government agencies having information or assistance for ethnic minority and women business owners. Some other links are "Current Events," "Calendar of Events," and "Business Opportunities." Updating is bimonthly. Fees: Free.

PERIODICALS AND NEWSLETTERS

Black Enterprise. Earl G. Graves Publishing Co. • Monthly. $17.95 per year. Covers careers, personal finances and leisure.

MBI: The National Report on Minority, Women-Owned and Disadvantaged Business. Community Development Services, Inc. CD Publications. • Semimonthly. $379.00 per year. Newsletter. Provides news of affirmative action, government contracts, minority business employment, and education/training for minorities in business. Formerly *Minorities in Business.*

Minority Business Entrepreneur. • Bimonthly. $16.00 per year. Reports on issues "critical to the growth and development of minority and women-owned firms." Provides information on relevant legislation and profiles successful women and minority entrepreneurs.

Minority Business News USA: America's Monthly News Magazine About Minority Business Enterprise and Diversity. Minority Business News. • Monthly. $18.00 per year. "Topics discussed include minority business certification, corporate purchasing trends, and management tips for business owners and professionals.".

STATISTICS SOURCES

Job Patterns for Minorities and Women in Private Industry. Available from U. S. Government Printing Office. • Annual. $61.00. Issued by the Equal Employment Opportunity Commission (http://www.eeoc.gov). "Provides statistical information on the composition of the United States workforce in private industry by sex, race, and ethnic category.".

TRADE/PROFESSIONAL ASSOCIATIONS

Diversity Information Resources. 2105 Central Ave. NE, Minneapolis, MN 55418. Phone: (612)781-6819 Fax: (612)781-0109 E-mail: info@diversityinforesources.com • URL: http://www.diversityinforesources.com • Promotes businesses with minority, women, veteran, service-disabled veteran and HUBZone ownership. Compiles and publishes minority and women-owned business directories to acquaint major corporations and government purchasing agents with the products and services of minority and women-owned firms. Sponsors national supplier diversity seminars.

Interracial Council for Business Opportunity. 350 5th Ave., Ste. 2202, New York, NY 10118. URL: http://www.mbda.gov • Provides technical and financial assistance to minority business people.

National Minority Supplier Development Council. 1040 Ave. of the Americas, 2nd Fl., New York, NY 10018. Phone: (212)944-2430 Fax: (212)719-9611 E-mail: nmsdc1@aol.com • URL: http://www.nmsdc.org • Provides a direct link between its 3,500 corporate members and minority-owned businesses (Black, Hispanic, Asian and Native American) and increases procurement and business opportunities for minority businesses of all sizes.

MINORITY MARKETS

ALMANACS AND YEARBOOKS

Research Alert Yearbook: Vital Facts on Consumer Behavior and Attitudes. EPM Communications, Inc. • Annual. $295.00. Provides summaries of consumer market research from the newsletters *Research Alert, Youth Markets Alert,* and *Minority Markets Alert.* Includes tables, charts, graphs, and textual summaries for 41 subject categories. Sources include reports, studies, polls, and focus groups.

HANDBOOKS AND MANUALS

Hispanic Market Handbook. Gale Cengage Learning. • 1995. $95.00. Provides advice on marketing consumer items to Hispanic Americans. Includes case studies and demographic profiles. (Professional Library).

PERIODICALS AND NEWSLETTERS

Marketing to the Emerging Minorities. EPM Communications, Inc. • Monthly. $295.00 per year. Newsletter on market research relating to African American, Asian American, and U. S. Hispanic populations.

STATISTICS SOURCES

Statistical Handbook on U. S. Hispanics. Frank L. Schick and Renee Schick, editors. Greenwood Publishing Group, Inc. • 1991. $69.95. Includes data on demographics, employment, income, assets, etc. (Statistical Handbooks Series).

Statistical Record of Black Americans. Gale Cengage Learning. • 1996. $130.00. Fourth edition. Contains more than 1,000 statistical graphs, tables, and lists arranged in 16 broad subject chapters. Covers population, housing, business, income, education, etc. Includes an extensive bibliography and a detailed subject index.

TRADE/PROFESSIONAL ASSOCIATIONS

National Minority Supplier Development Council. 1040 Ave. of the Americas, 2nd Fl., New York, NY 10018. Phone: (212)944-2430 Fax: (212)719-9611 E-mail: nmsdc1@aol.com • URL: http://www.nmsdc.org • Provides a direct link between its 3,500 corporate members and minority-owned businesses (Black, Hispanic, Asian and Native American) and increases procurement and business opportunities for minority businesses of all sizes.

OTHER SOURCES

The African American Market. Available from MarketResearch.com. • 2002. $3,000.00. Published by Packaged Facts. Provides consumer market data and demographics, with projections to 2006.

The Hispanic Market. Available from MarketResearch.com. • 2001. $2,750.00. Published by Packaged Facts. Provides consumer market data and demographics, with projections to 2006.

The U. S. Asian American Market. Available from MarketResearch.com. • 2002. $2,700.00. Published by Packaged Facts. Provides market research data pertaining to Asian American consumers: Chinese, Japanese, Korean, Vietnamese, Filipino, and Asian Indian.

MINORITY NEWSPAPERS

CD-ROM DATABASES

Newspaper Abstracts Ondisc. PROQUEST. • Monthly. $2,950.00 per year (covers 1989 to date;

archival discs are available for 1985-88). Provides cover-to-cover CD-ROM indexing and abstracting of 19 major newspapers, including the *New York Times, Wall Street Journal, Washington Post, Chicago Tribune,* and *Los Angeles Times.*

DIRECTORIES

Hispanic Media and Market Source. SRDS. • Quarterly. $295.00 per year. Provides detailed information on the following Hispanic advertising media in the U. S.: TV, radio, newspapers, magazines, direct mail, outdoor, and special events.

TRADE/PROFESSIONAL ASSOCIATIONS

National Newspaper Publishers Association. 3200 13th St. NW, Washington, DC 20010. Phone: (202)588-8764 Fax: (202)588-5302 E-mail: chairman@nnpa.org • URL: http://www.nnpa.org • Represents publishers of daily and weekly newspapers. Maintains Hall of Fame.

MISSILE INDUSTRY

See: ROCKET INDUSTRY

MOBILE HOME INDUSTRY

See also: PREFABRICATED HOUSE INDUSTRY; RECREATIONAL VEHICLE INDUSTRY

CD-ROM DATABASES

OECD Statistical Compendium. Organization for Economic Cooperation and Development. • Semiannual. $1,905.00 per year for 1 to 10 users. CD-ROM contains more than 730,000 monthly, quarterly, and annual time series for OECD countries, 1960 to date. Includes fully searchable data on agriculture, food, economic indicators, national accounts, employment, energy, finance, industry, technology, and foreign trade. Results can be displayed in various forms.

Sourcebooks America CD-ROM. CACI Marketing Systems. • Annual. $1,250.00. Provides the CD-ROM version of *The Sourcebook of ZIP Code Demographics: Census Edition* and *The Sourcebook of County Demographics: Census Edition.*

DIRECTORIES

Manufactured Home Merchandiser Manufactured Home Producers Guide. RLD Group, Inc. • Annual. $20.00. Lists about 163 manufacturers of mobil homes, modular homes and other types of manufactured housing. Includes trade associations. Formerly *Mobile/Manufactured Home Merchandiser Manufactured Home Producers Guide.*

FINANCIAL RATIOS

Annual Statement Studies. The Risk Management Association. • Annual. Median and quartile financial ratios are given for over 400 kinds of manufacturing, wholesale, retail, construction, and consumer finance establishments. Data is sorted by both asset size and sales volume. Includes a clearly written "Definition of Ratios" and an alphabetical industry index.

Annual Statement Studies: Industry Default Probabilities and Cash Flow Measures. The Risk Management Association. • Annual. $145.00. Serves as a companion volume to the original *Annual Statement Studies.* Gives probability of default estimates on a percentage scale for more than 450 industries. Includes changes in position year-by-year for eight financial statement line items and provides percentage measures of cash flow.

INTERNET DATABASES

Business 2.0 Web Guide to the Best Business Links. Business 2.0 Media Inc. Phone: (415)293-4800

E-mail: support@business2.com • URL: http://www.business2.com/webguide • Web site presents an extensive, searchable directory of links to "the best, most informative, and authoritative web pages." Twenty main categories cover business, finance, career, company information, people, and technology topics, with thousands of subtopics, all linking to Web sites recommended by experienced business researchers. Fees: Free.

Fedstats. Federal Interagency Council on Statistical Policy. Phone: (202)395-7254 • URL: http://www.fedstats.gov • Web site features an efficient search facility for full-text statistics produced by more than 100 federal agencies, including the Census Bureau, the Bureau of Economic Analysis, and the Bureau of Labor Statistics. Boolean searches can be made within one agency or for all agencies combined. Links are offered to international statistical bureaus, including the UN, IMF, OECD, UNESCO, Eurostat, and 20 individual countries. Fees: Free.

FreeLunch.com. Economy.com, Inc. Phone: (610)696-8700 Fax: (610)696-1678 • URL: http://www.freelunch.com • Web site provides free access to more than 1.5 million economic and financial data series, covering industry, demographics, labor markets, prices, retail sales, government spending, trade, interest rates, housing starts, the stock market, and many other topics. Data is available for various time periods in either chart or table form. Searching is offered. Fees: Free, but registration required. Economy.com, Inc. also offers fee-based economic analysis at *The Dismal Scientist* site (http://www.dismal.com).

PRICE SOURCES

NADA Appraisal Guides. National Automobile Dealers Association. • Prices and frequencies vary. Guides to prices of used cars, old used cars, motorcycles, mobile homes, recreational vehicles, and mopeds.

STATISTICS SOURCES

Business Statistics of the United States. Linz Audain and Cornelia J. Strawser. Bernan Associates. • Annual. $147.00. Based on *Business Statistics,* formerly issue by the Bureau of Economic Analysis, U. S. Department of Commerce. Provides basic data for a wide variety of U. S. industries, services, and economic indicators. Most statistics are shown annually for 30 years and monthly for the most recent four years.

Survey of Current Business. Available from U. S. Government Printing Office. • Monthly. $63.00 per year. Issued by Bureau of Economic Analysis, U. S. Department of Commerce. Presents a wide variety of business and economic data.

TRADE/PROFESSIONAL ASSOCIATIONS

Manufactured Housing Institute. 2101 Wilson Blvd., Ste. 610, Arlington, VA 22201-3062. Phone: 800-505-5500 or (703)558-0400 Fax: (703)558-0401 E-mail: info@mfghome.org • URL: http://www.manufacturedhousing.org • Manufacturers of manufactured homes; suppliers of equipment, components, furnishings and services, financial services companies, state association organizations, retailers and community owners. Promotes sales of manufactured homes through programs and services in six key areas: government relations, technical activities, financing, public relations, site development, and community operations. Conducts research and educational programs; provides statistics.

MOBILE TELEPHONE INDUSTRY

ABSTRACTS AND INDEXES

Applied Science and Technology Index. H. W. Wilson Co. • 11 times a year. Quarterly and annual cumulations. Price varies. Indexes a wide variety of

English language technical, industrial, and engineering periodicals.

DIRECTORIES

Major Telecommunications Companies of the World. Available from Gale Cengage Learning. • 2003. $885.00. Sixth edition. Published by Graham & Whiteside. Contains detailed information and trade names for more than 3,500 important telecommunications companies in various countries.

Phillips Wireless Industry Directory. Access Intelligence L.L.C. • Covers: Approximately 6,000 national and international cellular telephone companies, PCS companies, paging services, specialized mobile radio operators, and other manufacturers and distributors of products and services to the wireless communications industry. Also includes a listing of all of the PCS, MSA, and MSA license holders. Provides over 13,000 industry contacts. Entries include: For carriers--Carrier name, address, phone, names and titles of key personnel, products or services provided, geographic area covered, branch office names and locations; paging and mobile channels (in a separate list). For suppliers--Company name, address, phone, fax, names and titles of key personnel, products and services. For cellular operators--Company name, address, phone, fax, name and title of contact, plant equipment, CGSA, number of cells, description, cellular frequency, MSA/RSA name, ownership and service area.

Telecommunications Directory. Gale. • Covers: Two volumes-North America and International, Cover approximately 6,000 national and international voice and data communications networks, electronic mail services, teleconferencing facilities and services, facsimile services, Internet access providers, videotex and teletext operations, transactional services, local area networks, audiotex services, microwave systems/networkers, satellite facilities, and others involved in telecommunications, including related consultants, advertisers/marketers; associations, regulatory bodies, and publishers. Entries include: Company or organization name, address, phone, fax, year established, name and title of contact, executive officers and board of directors, function or type of service; geographical area served; NAICS and SIC codes; number of employees; general description, including telecommunications-related activities; product/service; specific applications; means of access and equipment required; publications; intended market and availability; pricing; stock exchanges traded and ticker symbols; financial figures.

HANDBOOKS AND MANUALS

Cellular Phone Service. Entrepreneur Media, Inc. • Looseleaf. $59.50. A practical guide to starting a business for the servicing of cellular (mobile) telephones. Covers profit potential, start-up costs, market size evaluation, owner's time required, site selection, lease negotiation, pricing, accounting, advertising, promotion, etc. (Start-Up Business Guide No. E1268.).

ONLINE DATABASES

Applied Science and Technology Index Online. H. W. Wilson Co. • Provides online indexing of 500 major scientific, technical, industrial, and engineering periodicals. Time period is 1983 to date. Monthly updates. Inquire as to online cost and availability.

PERIODICALS AND NEWSLETTERS

Convergence: The Journal of Research Into New Media Technologies. Reed Business Information. • Monthly. Individuals, $40.00 per year; institutions, $160.00 per year. Covers the merging of communications technologies. Includes telecommunications networks, interactive TV, multimedia, wireless phone service, and electronic information services.

Handheld Computing: The Number One Guide to Handheld Devices. Mobile Media Group. • Nine times a year. $18.95 per year. Covers handheld devices for consumers, including PDAs, cell phones, digital cameras, MP3 players, tablet PCs, accessories, and software. Includes product reviews.

Laptop: Mobile Solutions for Business and Life. Bedford Communications. • Monthly. $18.00 per year. Consumer magazine containing articles and product reviews for notebook/laptop computers, handheld computers, tablet devices, cell phones, digital cameras, and other consumer electronic products.

Mobile PC. Future Network USA. • Monthly. $20.00 per year. Provides information and detailed product reviews for consumers. Covers notebook/laptop computers, personal digital assistants (PDAs), wireless network equipment, cell phones, digital cameras, and other electronic products.

Mobility: Handheld and Wireless Solutions for Today's Business. Mobile Media Group. • Quarterly. $14.95 per year. Edited for business users of wireless handheld devices and notebook computers.

PICA Bulletin: News and Analysis for the Personal Communication Industry. Personal Communications Industry Association. • Weekly. $550.00 per year.

RCR Wireless News: The Newspaper for the Wireless Communications Industry. Crain Communications. • Weekly. $64.00 per year. Covers news of the wireless communications industry, including business and financial developments. Formerly *RCR*.

Wireless Business and Technology: Your Source for Unwired Technology. SYS-CON Media, Inc. • Monthly. $49.99 per year. Trade journal for mobile radio and telephone dealers.

Wireless Review: Intelligence for Competitive Providers. Primedia Business Magazines and Media. • Semimonthly. $48.00 per year. Covers business and technology developments for wireless service providers. Includes special issues on a wide variety of wireless topics. Formed by merger of *Cellular Business* and *Wireless World*.

Wireless Week. Reed Business Information. • 50 times a year. $99.00 per year. Covers news of cellular telephones, mobile radios, communications satellites, microwave transmission, and the wireless industry in general. Includes annual *Directory*.

STATISTICS SOURCES

U. S. Industry and Trade Outlook. Available from National Technical Information Service. • Annual. $69.95. Produced by the International Trade Administration, U. S. Department of Commerce, in a "public-private" partnership with DRI/McGraw-Hill and Standard & Poor's. Provides basic data, outlook for the current year, and "Long-Term Prospects" (five-year projections) for a wide variety of products and services. Includes high technology industries. Formerly *U. S. Industrial Outlook.*

TRADE/PROFESSIONAL ASSOCIATIONS

CTIA - The Wireless Association. 1400 16th St. NW, Ste. 600, Washington, DC 20036. Phone: (202)785-0081 Fax: (202)785-0721 E-mail: memberservices@ctia.org • URL: http://www.ctia.org • Individuals and organizations actively engaged in cellular radiotelephone communications, including: telephone companies and corporations providing radio communications; lay firms; engineering firms; consultants and manufacturers. (A cellular radiotelephone is a mobile communications device. An area is geographically divided into low frequency cells monitored by a computer that switches callers from one frequency to another as they move from cell to cell.) Objectives are to: promote, educate, and facilitate the professional interests, needs, and concerns of members with respect to the development and commercial applications of cellular technology; provide an opportunity

for exchanging experience and concerns; broaden the understanding and importance of cellular communication technology. Conducts discussions, studies, and courses.

Personal Communications Industry Association. 500 Montgomery St., Suite 700, Alexandria, VA 22314-1561. Phone: 800-759-0300 or (703)739-0300 Fax: (703)836-1608 E-mail: ebrahiml@pcia.com • URL: http://www.pcia.com • Promotes development of industry standards for mobile telephone systems. Also concerned with the advertising and marketing of mobile telephones. Formerly National Mobile Radio System.

Wireless Dealers Association. 9746 Tappenbeck Dr., Houston, TX 77055-4102. Phone: 800-624-6918 or (713)467-0077 Fax: 800-820-2284 or 800-820-2284 E-mail: topbox@wirelessindustry.com • URL: http://www.wirelessdealers.com • Individuals involved in the cellular mobile telephone industry including agents, carriers, dealers, distributors, manufacturers, and consultants. Works to: foster members' financial and professional success in the cellular industry; make available skills improvement and educational materials necessary for professional growth; develop a more professional structure conducive to career success. Promotes benefits of cellular telephones and services to current and prospective cellular users. Conducts marketing and sales training seminars. Offers customized primary training materials.

OTHER SOURCES

Cellular Telephones and Communication Equipment. Available from MarketResearch.com. • 2002. $4,450.00. Published by Global Industry Analysts. Provides worldwide market research data, including profiles of major cell phone manufacturers and service providers.

Wireless Data Networks. Gupta. Prentice Hall PTR. • 2000. Price on application. Presents market research information relating to cellular data networks, paging networks, packet radio networks, satellite systems, and other areas of wireless communication. Contains "summaries of recent developments and trends in wireless markets.".

MODEMS

See: COMPUTER COMMUNICATIONS

MODULAR CONSTRUCTION

See: PREFABRICATED HOUSE INDUSTRY

MOLASSES INDUSTRY

INTERNET DATABASES

USDA. United States Department of Agriculture. Phone: (202)720-2791 E-mail: agsec@usda.gov • URL: http://www.usda.gov • The USDA home page has six sections: News and Information; What's New; About USDA; Agencies; Opportunities; Search and Help. Keyword searching is offered from the USDA home page and from various individual agency home pages. Agencies are the Economic Research Service, Agricultural Marketing Service, National Agricultural Statistics Service, National Agricultural Library, and about 12 others. Updating varies. Fees: Free.

PERIODICALS AND NEWSLETTERS

Molasses Market News. Livestock and Seed Div. • Description: Provides the market news on molasses and its import and export.

PRICE SOURCES

Feedstuffs: The Weekly Newspaper for Agribusiness. Farm Progress Companies. • Weekly. $135.00 per year. Newsletter.

STATISTICS SOURCES

Agricultural Statistics. Available from U. S. Government Printing Office. • Annual. $38.00. Produced by

the National Agricultural Statistics Service, U. S. Department of Agriculture. Provides a wide variety of statistical data relating to agricultural production, supplies, consumption, prices/price-supports, foreign trade, costs, and returns, as well as farm labor, loans, income, and population. In many cases, historical data is shown annually for 10 years. In addition to farm data, includes detailed fishery statistics.

FAO Trade Yearbook. Available from Bernan Associates. • Annual. $45.00. Published by the Food and Agriculture Organization (http://www.fao.org). Provides extensive worldwide data on exports and imports of agricultural commodities, fertilizers, tractors, and pesticides. Includes more than 130 tables of detailed statistics.

Sugar and Sweetener Situation and Outlook. Available from U. S. Government Printing Office. • Three times per year. $18.00 per year. Issued by Economic Research Service, U. S. Department of Agriculture. Provides current statistical information on supply, demand, and prices.

MONETARY POLICY

See: ECONOMIC POLICY; MONEY

MONEY

See also: COINS AS AN INVESTMENT; FOREIGN EXCHANGE; INFLATION; INTEREST; PAPER MONEY

GENERAL WORKS

Financial Institutions and Markets. Meir J. Kohn. Oxford University Press, Inc. • 2003. $115.00. Second edition.

The Future of Money. Organization for Economic Cooperation and Development. • 2002. $19.00. Discusses the inevitable trend in money from the physical to the abstract (digital or virtual money). Will cash disappear? Will virtual money threaten control of the money supply? - and so forth.

Manias, Panics, and Crashes: A History of Financial Crises. Charles P. Kindleberger. John Wiley and Sons, Inc. • 2000. $19.95. Fourth edition. Provides a history of financial troubles from 1618 to modern times, with greed as a central theme. (Investment Classic Series).

Money, Banking, and Financial Markets. Roger L. Miller and David D. VanHoose. South-Western. • 2003. $102.95. Second edition.

Money, Banking, and the Economy. Thomas Mayer and others. W. W. Norton & Co., Inc. • 1996. $92.45. Sixth edition.

Money: Its Origins, Development, Debasement, and Prospects. John H. Wood. American Institute for Economic Research. • 1999. $10.00. A politically conservative view of monetary history, the gold standard, banking systems, and inflation. Includes a list of references. (Economic Education Bulletin.).

Money Madness: Strange Manias and Extraordinary Schemes On and Off Wall Street. John M. Waggoner. McGraw-Hill. • 1990. $26.00.

Money: Who Has How Much and Why. Andrew Hacker. Simon & Schuster Trade. • 1997. $24.50. A discourse on the distribution of wealth in America, with emphasis on the gap between rich and poor.

ABSTRACTS AND INDEXES

Business Periodicals Index. H. W. Wilson Co. • 11 times a year. Quarterly and annual cumulations. Price varies.

ALMANACS AND YEARBOOKS

World Currrency Yearbook. International Currency Analysis, Inc. • Annual. $250.00. Directory of more than 110 central banks worldwide.

CD-ROM DATABASES

EconLit. Available from SilverPlatter Information, Inc. • Monthly. Single-user, $1,600.00 per year. Provides CD-ROM citations, with abstracts, to articles from more than 500 economics journals. Time period is 1969 to date. Produced by the American Economic Association.

OECD Statistical Compendium. Organization for Economic Cooperation and Development. • Semiannual. $1,905.00 per year for 1 to 10 users. CD-ROM contains more than 730,000 monthly, quarterly, and annual time series for OECD countries, 1960 to date. Includes fully searchable data on agriculture, food, economic indicators, national accounts, employment, energy, finance, industry, technology, and foreign trade. Results can be displayed in various forms.

DIRECTORIES

Futures Magazine SourceBook: The Most Complete List of Exchanges, Companies, Regulators, Organizations, etc., Offering Products and Services to the Futures and Options Industry. Futures Magazine, Inc. • Annual. $19.50. Provides information on commodity futures brokers, trading method services, publications, and other items of interest to futures traders and money managers.

Major Financial Institutions of the World 2001. Available from Gale Cengage Learning. • 2003. $880.00. Sixth edition. Two volumes. Published by Graham & Whiteside. Contains detailed information on more than 7,500 important financial institutions in various countries. Includes banks, investment companies, and insurance companies.

Money Market Directory of Pension Funds and Their Investment Managers. Money Market Directories, Inc. • Annual. $1,150.00. Institutional funds and managers.

Plunkett's Financial Services Industry Almanac: The Only Comprehensive Overview of the Banking, Insurance, Credit and Investment Sectors. Plunkett Research, Ltd. • Annual. $229.99. Includes CD-ROM. Discusses important trends in various sectors of the financial industry. Five hundred major banking, credit card, investment, and financial services companies are profiled. (Business, Careers and Internet Reference Tools Series).

ENCYCLOPEDIAS AND DICTIONARIES

Blackwell Encyclopedic Dictionary of Finance. Dean Paxson and Douglas Wood, editors. Blackwell Publishing. • 1997. $110.00. The editors are associated with the University of Manchester. Contains definitions of key terms combined with longer articles written by various U. S. and foreign business educators. Includes bibliographies and index. (Blackwell Encyclopedia of Management Series).

Dictionary of Finance and Investment Terms. John Downes. Barron's Educational Series, Inc. • 2002. $14.95. Sixth edition. Provides clear explanations of more than 5,000 business, banking, financial, investment, and tax terms. Includes a separate list of financial abbreviations and acronyms. (Business Dictionaries Series).

Encyclopedia of Banking and Finance. Charles J. Woelfel. McGraw-Hill. • 1996. $150.00. 10th revised edition. Includes CD-ROM.

Encyclopedic Dictionary of International Finance and Banking. Jae K. Shim and Michael Constas. CRC Press. • 2001. $64.95. Contains 550 detailed entries covering multinational business, international finance, money, investments, financial planning, financial economics, and banking. Includes statistics, charts, exhibits, diagrams, rules-of-thumb and checklists.

The New Palgrave Dictionary of Money and Finance. Peter Newman and others, editors. Palgrave Macmillan. • 1992. $595.00. Two volumes.

Consists of signed essays on over 1,000 financial topics, each with a bibliography. Covers a wide variety of financial, monetary, and investment areas. A detailed subject index is provided.

HANDBOOKS AND MANUALS

The Bond and Money Markets: Strategy, Trading, Analysis. Moorad Choudhry. Elsevier Butterworth Heinemann. • 2003. $115.00. Serves as a reference work on corporate bonds, government bonds, currency markets, interest-rate futures, convertible securities, various kinds of derivatives, and technical analysis of financial securities.

Derivatives: A Comprehensive Resource for Options, Futures, Interest Rate Swaps, and Mortgage Securities. Fred D. Arditti. Harvard Business School Publishing. • 1996. $60.00. Published by Harvard Business School Press. Provides detailed explanations of various kinds of financial derivatives (options, futures, swaps, etc.) and their trading tactics, uses, and risks. (Financial Management Association Survey and Synthesis Series).

Monetary Policy and Reserve Requirements Handbook. U.S. Federal Reserve System. Board of Governors Publications Services, Room MS-1. • Annual.

INTERNET DATABASES

BanxQuote Banking, Mortgage, and Finance Center. BanxQuote, Inc. Phone: (914)722-1600 Fax: (914)722-6630 E-mail: info@banx.com • URL: http://www.banx.com • Web site quotes interest rates paid by banks around the country on various savings products, as well as rates paid by consumers for automobile loans, mortgages, credit cards, home equity loans, and personal loans. Also provided: stock quotes, indexes, stock options, futures trading data, economic indicators, and links to many other financial sites. Daily updates. Fees: Free.

Bureau of Economic Analysis (BEA). U. S. Department of Commerce, Bureau of Economic Analysis. Phone: (202)606-9900 Fax: (202)606-5310 E-mail: webmaster@bea.doc.gov • URL: http://www.bea.doc.gov • Web site includes "News Release Information" covering national, regional, and international economic estimates from the BEA. Highlights of releases appear online the same day, complete text and tables appear the next day. "Recent News Releases" section provides titles for past nine months, with links. "BEA Data and Methodology" includes "Frequently Requested NIPA Data" (national income and product accounts, such as gross domestic product and personal income). Other statistics are available. Fees: Free.

Business 2.0 Web Guide to the Best Business Links. Business 2.0 Media Inc. Phone: (415)293-4800 E-mail: support@business2.com • URL: http://www.business2.com/webguide • Web site presents an extensive, searchable directory of links to "the best, most informative, and authoritative web pages." Twenty main categories cover business, finance, career, company information, people, and technology topics, with thousands of subtopics, all linking to Web sites recommended by experienced business researchers. Fees: Free.

Factiva. Dow Jones Reuters Business Interactive, LLC. Phone: 800-369-7466 or (609)452-1511 Fax: (609)520-5770 E-mail: solutions@factiva.com • URL: http://www.factiva.com • Fee-based Web site provides "global news and business information through Web sites and content integration solutions." Includes Dow Jones and Reuters newswires, The Wall Street Journal, and more than 7,000 other sources of current news, historical articles, market research reports, and investment analysis. Content includes 96 major U. S. newspapers, 900 non-English sources, trade publications, media transcripts, country profiles, news photos, etc.

Federal Reserve Board Publications and Education Resources. Board of Governors of the Federal

Reserve System. Phone: (202)452-3000 Fax: (202)452-3819 • URL: http://www.federalreserve.gov/publications.htm • Web site provides convenient access to statistics, surveys, and research from the Federal Reserve Board. *Federal Reserve Bulletin* articles are available as abstracts or full text (PDF) currently or from six-year archives. The link "Statistics: Releases and Historical Data" offers daily, weekly, monthly, quarterly, and annual data in great detail for interest rates, foreign exchange, consumer credit, money stock measures, industrial production indexes, bank reserves, and other items. Historical tabulations are available for various time periods. Fees: Free.

Fedstats. Federal Interagency Council on Statistical Policy. Phone: (202)395-7254 • URL: http://www.fedstats.gov • Web site features an efficient search facility for full-text statistics produced by more than 100 federal agencies, including the Census Bureau, the Bureau of Economic Analysis, and the Bureau of Labor Statistics. Boolean searches can be made within one agency or for all agencies combined. Links are offered to international statistical bureaus, including the UN, IMF, OECD, UNESCO, Eurostat, and 20 individual countries. Fees: Free.

The Financial Post (Web site). National Post Online. Phone: 800-805-1184 or (244)383-2300 Fax: (416)383-2443 • URL: http://www.nationalpost.com/financialpost/ • Provides a broad range of Canadian business news online, with daily updates. Includes news, opinion, and special reports, as well as "Investing," "Money Rates," "Market Watch," and "Daily Mutual Funds." Allows advanced searching (Boolean operators), with links to various other sites. Fees: Free.

FreeLunch.com. Economy.com, Inc. Phone: (610)696-8700 Fax: (610)696-1678 • URL: http://www.freelunch.com • Web site provides free access to more than 1.5 million economic and financial data series, covering industry, demographics, labor markets, prices, retail sales, government spending, trade, interest rates, housing starts, the stock market, and many other topics. Data is available for various time periods in either chart or table form. Searching is offered. Fees: Free, but registration required. Economy.com, Inc. also offers fee-based economic analysis at *The Dismal Scientist* site (http://www.dismal.com).

Futures Online. Futures Magazine Inc. Phone: (312)846-4600 Fax: (312)846-4638 • URL: http://www.futuresmag.com • Web site presents updates of *Futures* magazine and links to other futures-related sites.

Nexis.com. Lexis-Nexis Group. Phone: 800-227-4908 or (937)865-6800 Fax: (937)865-6909 E-mail: webmaster@prod.lexis-nexis.com • URL: http://www.nexis.com • Fee-based Web site offers searching of about 2.8 billion documents in some 30,000 news, business, and legal information sources. Features include a subject directory covering 1,200 topics in 34 categories and a Company Dossier containing information on more than 500,000 public and private companies. Boolean searching is offered.

Wall Street Journal Interactive Edition. Dow Jones & Co., Inc. Phone: 800-369-2834 or (212)416-2000 Fax: (212)416-2658 E-mail: inquiries@interactive.wsj.com • URL: http://www.wsj.com • Fee-based Web site providing online searching of worldwide information from the *The Wall Street Journal.* Includes "Company Snapshots," "The Journal's Greatest Hits," "Index to Market Data," "Journal Links," etc. Financial price quotes are available. Fees: $49.00 per year; $29.00 per year to print subscribers.

ONLINE DATABASES

Banking Information Source. PROQUEST. • Provides indexing and abstracting of periodical and other literature from 1982 to date, with weekly updates. Covers the financial services industry:

---

banks, savings institutions, investment houses, credit unions, insurance companies, and real estate organizations. Emphasis is on marketing and management. Inquire as to online cost and availability. (Formerly *FINIS: Financial Industry Information Service.*).

EconLit. American Economic Association. • Covers the worldwide literature of economics as contained in selected monographs and about 550 journals. Subjects include microeconomics, macroeconomics, economic history, inflation, money, credit, finance, accounting theory, trade, natural resource economics, and regional economics. Time period is 1969 to present, with monthly updates. Inquire as to online cost and availability.

Wilson Business Abstracts Online. H. W. Wilson Co. • Indexes and abstracts 600 major business periodicals, plus the *Wall Street Journal* and the business section of the *New York Times.* Indexing is from 1982, abstracting from 1990, with the two newspapers included from 1993. Updated weekly. Inquire as to online cost and availability. (*Business Periodicals Index* without abstracts is also available online.).

PERIODICALS AND NEWSLETTERS

American Banker: The Financial Services Daily. Thomson Media. • Daily. $895.00 per year. Provides news of banking, investment products, mortgages, credit unions, finance, bank technology, and legal developments.

Applied Financial Economics. Taylor and Francis Group. • Monthly. Institutions, $1,277.00 per year. Covers practical aspects of financial economics, banking, and monetary economics. Supplement to *Applied Economics.*

Bank Credit Analyst. BCA Publications Ltd. • Monthly. $695.00 per year. "The independent monthly forecast and analysis of trends in business conditions and major investment markets based on a continuous appraisal of money and credit flows." Includes many charts and graphs relating to money, credit, and securities in the U. S.

Bank Rate Monitor: The Weekly Financial Rate Reporter. Advertising News Service, Inc. • Weekly. $895.00 per year. Newsletter. Includes online addition and monthly supplement. Provides detailed information on interest rates currently paid by U. S. banks and savings institutions.

Blue Chip Financial Forecasts: What Top Analysts are Saying About U. S. and Foreign Interest Rates, Monetary Policy, Inflation, and Economic Growth. Aspen Publishers, Inc. • Monthly. $665.00 per year. Newsletter. Gives forecasts about a year in advance for interest rates, inflation, currency exchange rates, monetary policy, and economic growth rates.

Financial Markets, Institutions, and Instruments. New York University, Salomon Center. Blackwell Publishing. • Five times a year. Institutions, $338.00 per year. Includes online edition. Edited to "bridge the gap between the academic and professional finance communities." Special fifth issue each year provides surveys of developments in four areas: money and banking, derivative securities, corporate finance, and fixed-income securities.

Financial Times [London]. The Financial Times, Inc. • Daily, except Sunday. $572.88 per year. An international business and financial newspaper, featuring news from London, Paris, Frankfurt, New York, and Tokyo. Includes worldwide stock and bond market data, commodity market data, and monetary/currency exchange information.

Futures: News, Analysis, and Strategies for Futures, Options, and Derivatives Traders. Futures Magazine. • Monthly. $39.00 per year. Edited for institutional money managers and traders, brokers, risk managers, and individual investors or speculators. Includes special feature issues on interest rates, technical indicators, currencies, charts,

precious metals, hedge funds, and derivatives. Supplements available.

Global Finance. Global Finance Media, Inc. • Monthly. $350.00 per year. Edited for corporate financial executives and money managers responsible for "cross-border" financial transactions.

Grant's Interest Rate Observer. James Grant, editor. Grant's Financial Publishing Inc. • Biweekly. $725.00 per year. Newsletter containing detailed analysis of money-related topics, including interest rate trends, global credit markets, fixed-income investments, bank loan policies, and international money markets.

IMF Survey. International Monetary Fund. • Description: Timely news on topics of general interest in the fields of international finance, country economics, trade, and commodities. Contains information on the IMF's activities, including press releases, major management speeches, and lending activity data rates.

International Bank Credit Analyst. BCA Publications Ltd. • Monthly. $795.00 per year. "A monthly forecast and analysis of currency movements, interest rates, and stock market developments in the principal countries, based on a continuous appraisal of money and credit trends worldwide." Includes many charts and graphs providing international coverage of money, credit, and securities.

International Currency Review. World Reports Ltd. • Quarterly. $475.00 per year.

International Market Alert. United Communications Group. • Description: Provides a fax service covering financial markets, world economy developments, foreign exchange, and U.S. interest rates.

InvesTech Market Analyst: Technical and Monetary Investment Analysis. InvesTech Research. • Every three weeks. $190.00 per year. Newsletter. Provides interpretation of monetary statistics and Federal Reserve actions, especially as related to technical analysis of stock market price trends.

Journal of Money, Credit and Banking. Ohio State University Press. • Quarterly. $210.00 per year, with online edition, $294.00 per year. Reports major findings in the study of financial markets, monetary and fiscal policy credit markets, money and banking, portfolio management and related subjects.

Money. • 13 times a year. $19.95 per year. Covers all aspects of family finance; investments, careers, shopping, taxes, insurance, consumerism, etc.

Money Reporter: The Insider's Letter for Investors Whose Interest is More Interest. MPL Communications, Inc. • Biweekly. $185.00 per year. Newsletter. Supplement available, *Monthly Key Investment.* Canadian interest-bearing deposits and investments.

Moneyletter. Agora Inc. • Description: "Provides assertive, do-it-yourself, individual investors with a unique market timing system, specific buy and sell recommendations, and portfolio allocation advice on no-load mutual funds. Features updates on economic and financial market, fund profiles, and articles on non-mutual fund financial planning issues.".

One Hundred Highest Yields. Advertising News Service, Inc. • Weekly. $124.00 per year. Newsletter. List CD's and money markets offered by federally insured banks. National coverage.

Powell Monetary Analyst. Larson M. Powell, editor. Reserve Research Ltd. • Description: Offers investment advice concentrating on precious metals, gold coins, currencies, and mining stocks.

U. S. Banker. Thomson Media. • Monthly. $65.00 per year. Edited for bank executives and managers. Covers a wide variety of banking and financial topics.

The Wall Street Journal. Dow Jones & Co., Inc. • Daily. $189.00 per year. Covers news and trends relating to business, industry, finance, the economy, and international commerce. Provides extensive

price and other data for the securities, commodity, options, futures, foreign exchange, and money markets.

PRICE SOURCES

The Value of a Dollar: Millennium Edition, 1860-1999. Grey House Publishing. • 1999. $135.00. Second edition. Shows the actual prices of thousands of items available to consumers from the Civil War era to recent years. Includes selected data on consumer expenditures, investments, income, and jobs. (Universal Reference Publications.).

RESEARCH CENTERS AND INSTITUTES

Ludwig Von Mises Institute for Austrian Economics. 518 W. Magnolia Ave., Auburn, AL 36832-4528. Phone: (334)321-2100 Fax: (334)321-2119 E-mail: mail@mises.org • URL: http://www.mises.org.

Rodney L. White Center for Financial Research. University of Pennsylvania, 3254 Steinberg Hall-Dietrich Hall, Philadelphia, PA 19104. Phone: (215)898-7616 Fax: (215)573-8084 E-mail: rlwtcr@finance.wharton.upenn.edu • URL: http://www.finance.wharton.upenn.edu • Research areas include financial management, money markets, real estate finance, and international finance.

STATISTICS SOURCES

The AIER Chart Book. AIER Research Staff. American Institute for Economic Research. • Annual. $4.00. A compact compilation of long-range charts ("Purchasing Power of the Dollar," for example, goes back to 1780) covering various aspects of the U. S. economy. Includes inflation, interest rates, debt, gold, taxation, stock prices, etc. (Economic Education Bulletin.).

Business Statistics of the United States. Linz Audain and Cornelia J. Strawser. Bernan Associates. • Annual. $147.00. Based on *Business Statistics*, formerly issue by the Bureau of Economic Analysis, U. S. Department of Commerce. Provides basic data for a wide variety of U. S. industries, services, and economic indicators. Most statistics are shown annually for 30 years and monthly for the most recent four years.

Daily Treasury Statement: Cash and Debt Operations of the United States Treasury. Available from U. S. Government Printing Office. • Daily, except Saturdays, Sundays, and holidays. (Financial Management Service, U. S. Treasury Department.).

Federal Reserve Bulletin. U.S. Federal Reserve System. • Monthly. $25.00 per year. Provides statistics on banking and the economy, including interest rates, money supply, and the Federal Reserve Board indexes of industrial production.

International Financial Statistics. International Monetary Fund, Publications Services. • Monthly. Individuals, $495.00 per year; students, $247.00 per year. Includes a wide variety of current data for individual countries in Europe and elsewhere. Includes *Annual* issue.

Money Stock Liquid Assets, and Debt Measures, in Billions of Dollars. U.S. Federal Reserve System. U.S. Board of Governors. • Weekly. $35.00 per year.

Selected Interest Rates. U.S. Federal Reserve System. • Weekly release, $20.00 per year.

Survey of Current Business. Available from U. S. Government Printing Office. • Monthly. $63.00 per year. Issued by Bureau of Economic Analysis, U. S. Department of Commerce. Presents a wide variety of business and economic data.

Treasury Bulletin. Available from U. S. Government Printing Office. • Quarterly. $45.00 per year. Issued by the Financial Management Service, U. S. Treasury Department. Provides data on the federal budget, government securities and yields, the national debt, and the financing of the federal government in general.

TRADE/PROFESSIONAL ASSOCIATIONS
International Monetary Fund. 700 19th St. NW, Washington, DC 20431. Phone: (202)623-7000 Fax: (202)623-4661 E-mail: publicaffairs@imf.org • URL: http://www.imf.org • Comprises 185 national governments. Works to: facilitate monetary cooperation through consultation and collaboration among member nations; assist in the balanced expansion of trade and thus contribute to the internal development and prosperity of member nations; maintain stability in monetary exchange arrangements, particularly to avoid exchange depreciations; participate in establishing a multilateral system of payments between member nations and in eliminating exchange restrictions that hamper trade; make available the resources of the fund to provide member nations with a means of assuaging economic difficulties. Maintains the IMF Institute, which conducts training courses and seminars and provides lecturers on subjects such as compilation of statistics and formulation and execution of balance of payment policies. Offers technical assistance on monetary matters to member nations and their dependencies and to multinational institutions. Acts as a depository of information and statistical data regarding the economic affairs of member nations. Operates library, in conjunction with the World Bank, on finance and economic development.

OTHER SOURCES
IBC's Money Fund Report. i MoneyNet Inc. • Weekly. $1,095.00 per year. Looseleaf. Contains detailed information on about 1,000 U. S. money market funds, including portfolios and yields. Formerly *Money Fund Report.*

Quarterly Report on Money Fund Performance. IBC-Donoghue, Inc. • Quarterly. $525.00 per year. Provides expense ratio and yield data for about 1,000 money market funds in the U. S.

MONEY MARKET

See: MONEY

MONEY MARKET FUNDS

See: INVESTMENT COMPANIES

MONEY RAISING

See: BUSINESS START-UP PLANS AND PROPOSALS; FUND-RAISING; VENTURE CAPITAL

MONEY RATES

See: INTEREST

MONOPOLIES

See: ANTITRUST ACTIONS

MORALE, INDUSTRIAL

See: HUMAN RELATIONS

MORTALITY

See: VITAL STATISTICS

MORTGAGE BANKS

See also: MORTGAGES

DIRECTORIES
Crittenden Directory of Real Estate Financing. Crittenden Research, Inc. • Semiannual. $399.00 per year. Includes weekly *Newsletter.* Provides information on major U. S. real estate lenders.

Directory of State and Local Mortgage Bankers Association. Mortgage Bankers Association of America. • Irregular. $50.00.

HANDBOOKS AND MANUALS
Residential Mortgage Lending: From Application to Servicing. The Institute of Financial Education. • 1998. $64.95. Fifth edition. A guide for bankers.

PERIODICALS AND NEWSLETTERS
Crittenden Report Real Estate Financing: The Nation's Leading Weekly Newslett er on Real Estate Finance. Crittenden Research, Inc. • Weekly. $395.00 per year. Newsletter on real estate lending and mortgages. Includes semiannual *Crittenden Directory of Real Estate Financing.*

Mortgage Banking: The Magazine of Real Estate Finance Managers and Employees. Mortgage Bankers Association of America. • Monthly. $45.00 per year.

Origination News: For Mortgage Brokers, Correspondents, Lenders, and Wholesalers. Thomson Media. • Monthly. $78.00 per year. Edited for executives responsible for the origination and subsequent sale of mortgage loans.

STATISTICS SOURCES
Information, Finance, and Services USA. Gale Cengage Learning. • 2001. $240.00. Replaces *Service Industries USA* and *Finance, Insurance, and Real Estate USA.* Presents statistics and projections relating to economic activity in a wide variety of non-manufacturing areas.

TRADE/PROFESSIONAL ASSOCIATIONS
Mortgage Bankers Association of America. 1919 Pennsylvania Ave., NW, Washington, DC 20006. Phone: (202)557-2700 E-mail: membership@mbaa.org • URL: http://www.mbaa.org.

MORTGAGES

See also: MORTGAGE BANKS; REAL ESTATE INVESTMENTS

GENERAL WORKS
Real Estate Finance and Investments. William B. Brueggeman and Jeffrey Fisher. McGraw-Hill. • 2001. 11th edition. Price on application. Covers mortgage loans, financing, risk analysis, income properties, land development, real estate investment trusts, and related topics. (Finance, Insurance and Real Estate Series).

Tips and Traps When Mortgage Hunting. Robert Irwin. McGraw-Hill. • 1998. $14.95. Second revised edition. Contains practical advice for home buyers and small real estate investors.

CD-ROM DATABASES
OECD Statistical Compendium. Organization for Economic Cooperation and Development. • Semiannual. $1,905.00 per year for 1 to 10 users. CD-ROM contains more than 730,000 monthly, quarterly, and annual time series for OECD countries, 1960 to date. Includes fully searchable data on agriculture, food, economic indicators, national accounts, employment, energy, finance, industry, technology, and foreign trade. Results can be displayed in various forms.

DIRECTORIES
Crittenden Directory of Real Estate Financing. Crittenden Research, Inc. • Semiannual. $399.00 per

year. Includes weekly *Newsletter.* Provides information on major U. S. real estate lenders.

Mortgage & Asset-Based Desk Reference: U. S. Buyside and Sellside Profiles. Capital Access International. • Annual. $395.00. Provides "detailed buyside and sellside profiles and contacts" for the mortgage and asset-based securities market.

National Mortgage Directory: Lenders, Brokers & Servicers. Thomson Media. • Annual. $479.00. Covers both residential and commercial sectors. Includes the top 400 lenders, 300 servicers, 150 mortgage brokers, commercial lenders, subprime lenders and other listings, with rankings and statistical tables.

ENCYCLOPEDIAS AND DICTIONARIES
Dictionary of Real Estate. Jae K. Shim and others. John Wiley and Sons, Inc. • 1995. $145.00. Contains 3,000 definitions of commercial and residential real estate terms. Covers appraisal, escrow, investment, finance, mortgages, property management, construction, legal aspects, etc. Includes illustrations and formulas. (Business Dictionary Series).

Dictionary of Real Estate Terms. Jack P. Friedman and others. Barron's Educational Series, Inc. • 2004. $13.95. Sixth edition. Defines more than 2,500 terms relating to real estate business, including mortgages, financing, leasing, insurance, and home buying.

Real Estate Dictionary. Barbara Cox and others. South-Western. • 2002. $33.95.

HANDBOOKS AND MANUALS
Derivatives: A Comprehensive Resource for Options, Futures, Interest Rate Swaps, and Mortgage Securities. Fred D. Arditti. Harvard Business School Publishing. • 1996. $60.00. Published by Harvard Business School Press. Provides detailed explanations of various kinds of financial derivatives (options, futures, swaps, etc.) and their trading tactics, uses, and risks. (Financial Management Association Survey and Synthesis Series).

Handbook of Mortgage-Backed Securities. Frank J. Fabozzi. McGraw-Hill. • 2001. $95.00. Fifth edition.

Homeowner or Tenant? How to Make a Wise Choice. Lawrence S. Pratt. American Institute for Economic Research. • 2002. $8.00. Provides detailed information for making rent or buy decisions. Includes "Mortgage Arithmetic," "Hints for Buyers, Sellers, and Renters," worksheets, mortgage loan interest tables, and other data. (Economic Education Bulletin.).

Monthly Payment Direct Reduction Loan Schedules. Financial Publishing Co. • $75.00. 13th edition. Supplement available, $30.00.

Mortgage-Backed Securities: Developments and Trends in the Secondary Mortgage Market. Cameron L. Cowan and Kenneth G. Lore. West Group. • 2003. $275.00. (Securities Handbook Series).

Mortgage Loan Disclosure Handbook: A Step-by-Step Guide with Forms. West Group. • Annual. $363.00. Covers disclosure requirements that lenders must meet under federal laws and regulations. Discusses the Truth-in-Lending Act, RESPA (Real Estate Settlement Procedures Act), the Equal Credit Opportunity Act, and the Fair Credit Reporting Act. (Real Property Law Series).

Real Estate Finance and Investment Manual: A Guide to Money Making Strategies. Jack Cummings. Prentice Hall PTR. • 1997. $34.95. Second edition.

Real Estate Taxation: A Practitioner's Guide. David F. Windish. CCH, Inc. • Date not set. $125.00. Second edition. Serves as a guide to the federal tax consequences of real estate ownership and operation. Covers mortgages, rental agreements, interest, landlord income, forms of ownership, and other tax-oriented topics.

Secondary Mortgage Market: Strategies for Surviv-

ing and Thriving in Today's Challenging Markets. Jess Lederman. McGraw-Hill. • 1992. $70.00. Revised edition.

INTERNET DATABASES

BanxQuote Banking, Mortgage, and Finance Center. BanxQuote, Inc. Phone: (914)722-1600 Fax: (914)722-6630 E-mail: info@banx.com • URL: http://www.banx.com • Web site quotes interest rates paid by banks around the country on various savings products, as well as rates paid by consumers for automobile loans, mortgages, credit cards, home equity loans, and personal loans. Also provided: stock quotes, indexes, stock options, futures trading data, economic indicators, and links to many other financial sites. Daily updates. Fees: Free.

Business 2.0 Web Guide to the Best Business Links. Business 2.0 Media Inc. Phone: (415)293-4800 E-mail: support@business2.com • URL: http://www.business2.com/webguide • Web site presents an extensive, searchable directory of links to "the best, most informative, and authoritative web pages." Twenty main categories cover business, finance, career, company information, people, and technology topics, with thousands of subtopics, all linking to Web sites recommended by experienced business researchers. Fees: Free.

Business Week Online. McGraw-Hill. Phone: (212)512-2511 Fax: (684)842-6101 • URL: http://www.businessweek.com • Web site provides complete contents of current issue of *Business Week* plus "BW Daily" with additonal business news, financial market quotes, and corporate information from Standard & Poor's. Includes various features, such as "Banking Center" with mortgage and interest data, and "Interactive Computer Buying Guide." The "Business Week Archive" is fully searchable back to 1996.

Fedstats. Federal Interagency Council on Statistical Policy. Phone: (202)395-7254 • URL: http://www.fedstats.gov • Web site features an efficient search facility for full-text statistics produced by more than 100 federal agencies, including the Census Bureau, the Bureau of Economic Analysis, and the Bureau of Labor Statistics. Boolean searches can be made within one agency or for all agencies combined. Links are offered to international statistical bureaus, including the UN, IMF, OECD, UNESCO, Eurostat, and 20 individual countries. Fees: Free.

FreeLunch.com. Economy.com, Inc. Phone: (610)696-8700 Fax: (610)696-1678 • URL: http://www.freelunch.com • Web site provides free access to more than 1.5 million economic and financial data series, covering industry, demographics, labor markets, prices, retail sales, government spending, trade, interest rates, housing starts, the stock market, and many other topics. Data is available for various time periods in either chart or table form. Searching is offered. Fees: Free, but registration required. Economy.com, Inc. also offers fee-based economic analysis at *The Dismal Scientist* site (http://www.dismal.com).

PERIODICALS AND NEWSLETTERS

Affordable Housing Finance. Alexander & Edwards Publishing. • Ten times a year. $119.00 per year. Provides advice and information on obtaining financing for lower-cost housing. Covers both government and private sources.

Apartment Finance Today. Alexander & Edwards Publishing. • Bimonthly. $29.00 per year. Covers mortgages and financial services for apartment developers, builders, and owners.

Broker: The Sales and Management Resource for Mortgage Originators. Thomson Media. • Bimonthly. $48.00 per year. Edited for mortgage brokers. Emphasis is on marketing, leads to new business, and profitability.

Crittenden Report Real Estate Financing: The Nation's Leading Weekly Newslett er on Real Estate

Finance. Crittenden Research, Inc. • Weekly. $395.00 per year. Newsletter on real estate lending and mortgages. Includes semiannual *Crittenden Directory of Real Estate Financing.*

Housing Affairs Letter: The Weekly Washington Report on Housing. Community Development Services, Inc. CD Publications. • Weekly. $473.00 per year. Newsletter. Covers mortgage activity news, including forecasts of mortgage rates.

Journal of Fixed Income. Institutional Investor, Inc., Journals Group. • Quarterly. $360.00 per year. Includes print and online editions. Covers a wide range of fixed-income investments for institutions, including bonds, interest-rate options, high-yield securities, and mortgages.

Mortgage and Real Estate Executives Report. West Group. • Biweekly. $368.00 per year. Newsletter. Source of ideas and new updates. Covers the latest opportunities and developments.

Mortgage-Backed Securities Letter. Securities Data Publishing. • Description: Covers developments in the structured finance markets. Analyzes transactions and their collateral; follows litigation, refinancing opportunities, and market conditions.

Mortgage Servicing News: For Residential amd Commercial Servicers. Thomson Media. • Monthly. $98.00 per year. Edited for personnel involved with processing and handling of mortgage loan payments and disbursements for such items as insurance and taxes.

Mortgage Technology. Thomson Media. • Eight times a year. $78.00 per year. Covers the use of computers, software, automation, and technology in the mortgage industry. Includes reviews of new hardware and software products.

Real Estate Finance. Institutional Investor, Inc., Journals Group. • Bimonthly. $350.00 per year. Covers real estate for professional investors. Provides information on complex financing, legalities, and industry trends.

Real Estate Finance and Investment. Institutional Investor, Inc., Journals Group. • Weekly. $2,275.00 per year. Includes print and online editions. Newsletter for professional investors in commercial real estate. Includes information on financing, restructuring, strategy, and regulation.

RESEARCH CENTERS AND INSTITUTES

Center for Finance and Real Estate. University of California, Los Angeles, John E. Anderson Graduate School of Management, 110 Westwood Plaza, Los Angeles, CA 90095-1481. Phone: (310)206-5455 Fax: (310)206-5455 E-mail: wtorous@anderson.ucla.edu • URL: http://www.agsm.ucla.edu.

STATISTICS SOURCES

American Housing Survey for the United States in [year]. Available from U. S. Government Printing Office. • Biennial. $51.00. Issued by the U. S. Census Bureau (http://www.census.gov). Covers both owner-occupied and renter-occupied housing. Includes data on such factors as condition of building, type of mortgage, utility costs, and housing occupied by minorities. (Current Housing Reports, H150.).

Business Statistics of the United States. Linz Audain and Cornelia J. Strawser. Bernan Associates. • Annual. $147.00. Based on *Business Statistics,* formerly issue by the Bureau of Economic Analysis, U. S. Department of Commerce. Provides basic data for a wide variety of U. S. industries, services, and economic indicators. Most statistics are shown annually for 30 years and monthly for the most recent four years.

Housing Statistics of the United States. Patrick A. Simmons. Bernan Press. • 2000. $89.00. Third edition. (Housing Statistics of the United States Series).

MBA National Delinquency Survey. Mortgage Bank-

ers Association of America. • Quarterly. $30.00 per year. Newsletter. Provides delinquency and foreclosure data for single-family mortgage loans.

Statistical Information on the Financial Services Industry. American Bankers Association. • Annual. Members, $150.00; non-members, $275.00. Presents a wide variety of data relating to banking and financial services, including consumer economics, personal finance, credit, government loans, capital markets, and international banking.

Survey of Current Business. Available from U. S. Government Printing Office. • Monthly. $63.00 per year. Issued by Bureau of Economic Analysis, U. S. Department of Commerce. Presents a wide variety of business and economic data.

Survey of Mortgage Lending Activity. U.S. Department of Housing and Urban Development. • Monthly.

TRADE/PROFESSIONAL ASSOCIATIONS

Mortgage Insurance Companies of America. 727 15th St., N.W., 12th Fl., Washington, DC 20005. Phone: (202)393-5566 Fax: (202)393-5557 E-mail: jess@mica.dc.org • URL: http://www.privatemi.com.

OTHER SOURCES

Real Estate Financing, with Forms on Disk. American Lawyer Media, Inc. • Looseleaf. $179.00. Updated as needed. Includes forms on two diskettes. Covers loan modifications, wraparound mortgage loans, loans for condos, co-ops, and time shares, sale-leasebacks, installment sales, sales of mortgage loans, and various related topics. (Law Journal Press).

MOTEL INDUSTRY

See: HOTEL AND MOTEL INDUSTRY

MOTION PICTURE CAMERAS

See: CAMERA INDUSTRY

MOTION PICTURE INDUSTRY

See also: MOTION PICTURE PHOTOGRAPHY; MOTION PICTURE THEATERS

GENERAL WORKS

Movie Money: Understanding Hollywood's (Creative) Accounting Practices. Bill Daniels. Silman-James Press. • 1998. $29.95. Explains the numerous amd mysterious accounting methods used by the film industry to arrive at gross and net profit figures. The authors also discuss profit participation, audits, claims, and negotiating.

ALMANACS AND YEARBOOKS

Annual Index to Motion Picture Credits. Academy of Motion Picture Arts and Sciences. • Annual. $50.00.

International Motion Picture Almanac: Reference Tool of the Film Industry. Quigley Publishing Co., Inc. • Annual. $130.00. Reference covering the motion picture industry.

Magill's Cinema Annual. Gale Cengage Learning. • Annual. $125.00. Provides reviews and facts for new films released each year in the United States. Typically covers about 300 movies, with nine indexes to title, director, screenwriter, actor, music, etc. Includes awards, obituaries, and "up-and- coming" performers of the year.

The Motion Picture Guide Annual. CineBooks. •

Annual. $99.95. Provides detailed information on every domestic and foreign film released theatrically in the U. S. during the year covered. Includes annual Academy Award listings and film industry obituaries. Yearly volumes are available for older movies, beginning with the 1987 edition for films of 1986.

BIBLIOGRAPHIES

Films and Audiovisual Information. Available from U. S. Government Printing Office. • Annual. Free. Issued by the Superintendent of Documents. A list of government publications on motion picture and audiovisual topics. Formerly *Motion Pictures, Films and Audiovisual Information.* (Subject Bibliography No. 73.).

BIOGRAPHICAL SOURCES

Biographical Encyclopedia of Hollywood Film Actors. Barry Monush. Applause Theatre & Cinema Books. • 2000. $85.00. Contains detailed information on more than 1,000 film actors "from Bud Abbott to Pia Zadora." Includes film, stage, and TV credits. The author is Associate Editor of the annual, *Screen World,* and provides critical assessments.

Celebrity Register. Gale Cengage Learning. • 1990. $115.00. 90th edition. Compiled by Celebrity Services International (Earl Blackwell). Contains profiles of 1,300 famous individuals in the performing arts, sports, politics, business, and other fields.

The Highwaymen: Warriors on the Information Superhighway. Ken Auletta. Harcourt Trade Publications. • 1998. $13.00. Revised expanded edition. Contains critical articles about Ted Turner, Rupert Murdoch, Barry Diller, Michael Eisner, and other key figures in electronic communications, entertainment, and information. (Harvest Book Series).

CD-ROM DATABASES

Bowker's Complete Video Directory on Disc. Bowker Electronic Publishing. • Quarterly. $520.00 per year. An extensive CD-ROM directory of video tapes and laserdisks. Includes film reviews from *Variety.*

Hoover's Company Capsules on CD-ROM. Hoover's, Inc. • Quarterly. $399.95 per year (single-user). Provides the CD-ROM version of *Hoover's Handbook of American Business, Hoover's Handbook of Emerging Companies, Hoover's Handbook of World Business, Hoover's Guide to Computer Companies, Hoover's Guide to Media Companies, Hoover's Handbook of Private Companies,* and various regional guides. Includes more than 11,000 profiles of companies.

DIRECTORIES

Celebrity Locator: How to Reach Over 6,000 Movie, TV Stars and Other Famous Ce lebrities. Axiom Information Resources. • Biennial. $39.95. Stars, agents, networks, studios, and other celebrities. Gives names and addresses.

Directors Guild of America Directory of Members. Directors Guild of America Inc. • Annual. $22.00.

Hollywood Creative Directory: Below-the-Line Talent. IFILMpro. • Annual. $80.00. Lists more than 6,000 cinematographers, production designers, costume designers, film editors, set decorators, and art directors and their associated 15,000 film titles.

Hollywood Creative Directory: Film Actors. • Annual. $85.00. Lists more than 6,000 film actors and their associated 15,000 film titles.

Hollywood Creative Directory: Film Directors. Annual. $95.00. Lists more than 5,500 film directors and their associated 43,000 film titles. Includes Canadian, British, European, and Japanese directors.

Hollywood Creative Directory: Film Writers. IFILMpro. • Annual. $85.00. Lists more than 8,000 screenwriters and their associated 35,000 film titles. Includes projects in development and unsold screenplays.

Hollywood Creative Directory: International Film Buyers. • Annual. $59.95. Lists more than 1,750 film and television buyers. Worldwide coverage.

Hollywood Creative Directory: The Phone Book to Hollywood. IFILM Publishing. • Semiannual. $149.95 per year. Three issues per year. Single issue, $59.95. Lists about 9,900 talent agents, personal managers, and casting directors.

Index to AV Producers and Distributors (Educational Audiovisual Materials). National Information Center for Educational Media. c/o Plexus Publishing, Inc. • Biennial. $89.00. A directory listing about 23,300 producers and distributors of all types of audiovisual educational materials.

International Dictionary of Film and Filmmakers. Saint James Press. • 2001. $595.00. Fourth edition. Four volumes. Vol. 1: *Films.* Vol. 2: *Directors.* Vol. 3: *Actors and Actresses.* Vol. 4: *Writers and Production Artists.*

International Film Guide. Variety. • Publication includes: Lists of new films, film production companies, distributors, organizations, and government agencies concerned with film in over 70 countries of the world. Also includes film festivals, film archives, services for the industry, and film schools. Entries include: All entries include company or organization name and address; listings for festivals and other categories in foregoing list include additional details.

Producers Directory. IFILM Publishing. • Covers: over 1,700 film and TV production companies, studios, networks, and TV shows, and over 7,700 creative executives within those companies. Majority of listings are located in Los Angeles and New York. Entries include: Company name, staff names and titles, address, phone, fax, e-mail address, web site address, company type, studio deals, and select credits.

Variety International Film Guide. Peter Cowie, editor. Silman-James Press. • Annual. $24.95. Covers the "who, what, where, and when of the international film scene." Includes information from 70 countries on film festivals, top-grossing films, awards, schools, etc.

ENCYCLOPEDIAS AND DICTIONARIES

Film Finance and Distribution: A Dictionary of Terms. John W. Cones. Silman-James Press. • 1992. $24.95. Includes commentary on practical approaches to financing and distribution for novice filmmakers.

Filmmaker's Dictionary. Ralph S. Singleton and James Conrad. Lone Eagle Publishing Co., LLC. • 2000. $22.95. Second edition. Defines technical terms, legal terms, industry jargon, and film slang.

International Film, Television, and Video Acronyms. Matthew Stevens, editor. Greenwood Publishing Group, Inc. • 1993. $85.00. A guide to 3,400 acronyms and 1,400 technical terms.

Multimedia and the Web from A to Z. David C. Leonard and Patrick M. Dillon. Greenwood Publishing Group, Inc. • 1998. $42.95. Second enlarged revised edition. Defines more than 1,500 terms relating to software and hardware in the areas of computing, online technology, telecommunications, audio, video, motion pictures, CD-ROM, and the Internet. Includes acronyms and an annotated bibliography. Formerly *Multimedia Technology from A to Z* (1994).

FINANCIAL RATIOS

Almanac of Business and Industrial Financial Ratios. Leo Troy. Aspen Publishers, Inc. • 2003. $125.95. Includes CD-Rom. Contains financial ratios derived from federal tax returns. Ratios for each of about 200 industries are arranged according to company asset size. (Almanac of Business and Industrial Financial Ratios Series).

Annual Statement Studies. The Risk Management Association. • Annual. Median and quartile financial ratios are given for over 400 kinds of manufacturing, wholesale, retail, construction, and consumer finance establishments. Data is sorted by both asset size and sales volume. Includes a clearly written "Definition of Ratios" and an alphabetical industry index.

Annual Statement Studies: Industry Default Probabilities and Cash Flow Measures. The Risk Management Association. • Annual. $145.00. Serves as a companion volume to the original *Annual Statement Studies.* Gives probability of default estimates on a percentage scale for more than 450 industries. Includes changes in position year-by-year for eight financial statement line items and provides percentage measures of cash flow.

The Biz: The Basic Business, Legal, and Financial Aspects of the Film Industry. Schuyler M. Moore. Silman-James Press. • 2000. $26.95. Provides information for independent filmmakers on raising money, business structure, budgeting, loans, legalities, taxation, industry jargon, and other topics. The author is an entertainment industry lawyer.

HANDBOOKS AND MANUALS

Clearance and Copyright: Everything the Independent Filmmaker Needs to Know. Michael C. Donaldson. Silman-James Press. • 1996. $26.95. Covers film rights problems in pre-production, production, post-production, and final release. Includes sample contracts and forms.

Contracts for the Film and Television Industry. Mark Litwak. Silman-James Press. • 1999. $35.95. Second expanded edition. Contains a wide variety of sample entertainment contracts. Includes material on rights, employment, joint ventures, music, financing, production, distribution, merchandising, and the retaining of attorneys.

Creativity Rules! A Writer's Workbook. John Vorhaus. Silman-James Press. • 1999. $15.95. Covers the practical process of conceiving, outlining, and developing a story, especially for TV or film scripts. Includes "tactics and exercises.".

Digital Filmmaking 101: An Essential Guide to Producing Low-Budget Movies. Dale Newton and John Gaspard. Michael Wiese Productions. • 2001. $24.95. Using a light touch, covers the essentials of making a low-budget film, including scripting, budgeting, funding, equipping, casting, and recruiting a crew.

Entertainment Law: Legal Concepts and Business Practices. West Group. • Annual. $560.00. Five looseleaf volumes.

Film and Video Budgets. Deke Simon and Michael Wiese. Michael Wiese Productions. • 2001. $26.95. Third edition. Contains detailed, sample budgets for a wide variety of productions from shoestring documentaries to expensive feature films. Includes practical explanations and information.

Independent Film and Videomaker's Guide. Michael Wiese. Michael Wiese Productions. • 1999. $29.95. Second edition. Covers many aspects of the business side of independent filmmaking, such as business plan writing, financing, production, market research, distribution, presentations, and prospectus writing.

Screenwriting 101: The Essential Craft of Feature Film Writing. Neill D. Hicks. Michael Wiese Productions. • 1999. $16.95. Covers both the mechanics of screenwriting and the "practicalities of the business.".

ONLINE DATABASES

PROMT: Predicasts Overview of Markets and Technology. Gale Cengage Learning. • Companies, products, applied technologies and markets. U.S. and international literature coverage, 1972 to date. Inquire as to online cost and availability. Provides

---

abstracts from more than 1,600 publications. Weekly updates.

PERIODICALS AND NEWSLETTERS

Daily Variety: News of the Entertainment Industry. Reed Business Information. • Daily. $297.00 per year. Covers entire scope of the entertainment business on the East and West coast.

Entertainment Law and Finance. American Lawyer Media, Inc. • Monthly. $229.00 per year. Newsletter. Covers contracts, royalties, litigation, copyright, taxation, etc., for the music industry, motion pictures, broadcasting, publishing, video, and related media. (A Law Journal Newsletter, formerly published by Leader Publications.).

Film Journal International. VNU Business Media. • Monthly. $65.00 per year. Formerly *Film Journal.*

Film Quarterly: Quarterly of Film, Radio and Television. University of California Press, Journals Div. • Quarterly. Institutions, $102.00 per year; includes print and online editions.

The Hollywood Reporter. • Daily. $219.00 per year. Covers the latest news in film, TV, cable, multimedia, music, and theatre. Includes box office grosses and entertainment industry financial data.

SMPTE Motion Imaging Journal. Society of Motion Picture and Television Engineers. • Monthly. Membership. Formerly *SMPTE Journal.*

Variety: The International Entertainment Weekly. Reed Business Information. • 50 times a year. $259.00 per year. Contains national and international news of show business, with emphasis on motion pictures and television. Includes *Market* and *Special Focus* issues.

RESEARCH CENTERS AND INSTITUTES

Wisconsin Center for Film and Theater Research. University of Wisconsin-Madison, 816 State St., Madison, WI 53706. Phone: (608)264-6466 Fax: (608)264-6472 • URL: http://www.shsw.wisc.edu/archives/wcftr • Studies the performing arts in America, including theater, cinema, radio, and television.

STATISTICS SOURCES

Standard & Poor's Industry Surveys. Standard & Poor's. • Semiannual. $1,800.00. Two looseleaf volumes. Includes monthly *Supplements.* Provides detailed, individual surveys of 52 major industry groups. Each survey is revised on a semiannual basis. Also includes "Monthly Investment Review" (industry group investment analysis) and monthly "Trends & Projections" (economic analysis).

U. S. Industry and Trade Outlook. Available from National Technical Information Service. • Annual. $69.95. Produced by the International Trade Administration, U. S. Department of Commerce, in a "public-private" partnership with DRI/McGraw-Hill and Standard & Poor's. Provides basic data, outlook for the current year, and "Long-Term Prospects" (five-year projections) for a wide variety of products and services. Includes high technology industries. Formerly *U. S. Industrial Outlook.*

UNESCO Statistical Yearbook. Bernan Press. • 1998. $95.00. Co-published by Bernan Press and the United Nations Educational, Scientific, and Cultural Organization (http://www.unesco.org). Presents statistical data from more than 200 countries on education, technology, research, broadcasting, cinema, book publishing, newspapers, libraries, museums, and population. Includes charts, maps, and graphs.

TRADE/PROFESSIONAL ASSOCIATIONS

Academy of Motion Picture Arts and Sciences. 8949 Wilshire Blvd., Beverly Hills, CA 90211-1972. Phone: (310)247-3000 Fax: (310)859-9351 E-mail: ampas@oscars.org • URL: http://www.oscars.org.

Alliance of Motion Picture and Television Producers. 15503 Ventura Blvd., Encino, CA 91436-

3140. Phone: (818)995-3600 Fax: (818)382-1793 E-mail: info@tw.amptp.org • URL: http://www.amptp.org.

Association of Cinema and Video Laboratories. c/o Rob Monaco, Monaco Labs and Video, 234 Ninth St., San Francisco, CA 15205. Phone: (415)864-5350 Fax: (415)864-5682 E-mail: usc7153@email.msn.com • URL: http://www.acvl.org.

Directors Guild of America. 7920 Sunset Blvd., Hollywood, CA 90046. Phone: 800-420-4173 or (310)289-2000 Fax: (310)289-2029 E-mail: dga@dga.org • URL: http://www.dga.org • Negogiates agreements for members.

Motion Picture Association of America. 15503 Ventura Blvd., Encino, CA 91436. Phone: (818)995-6600 • URL: http://www.mpaa.org • Affiliated with Alliance of Motion Picture and Television Producers and the Motion Picture Association. Formerly Motion Picture Producers and Distributors of America.

Producers Guild of America. 8530 Wilshire Blvd., No. 450, Beverly Hills, CA 90211. Phone: (310)358-9020 Fax: (310)358-9520 E-mail: info@producersguild.org • URL: http://www.producersguild.org.

Society of Motion Picture and Television Engineers. 595 W Hartsdale Ave., White Plains, NY 10607. Phone: (914)761-1100 Fax: (914)761-3115 E-mail: smpte@smpte.org • URL: http://www.smpte.org • Professional engineers and technicians in motion poctures, television, motion imaging and allied arts and sciences.

OTHER SOURCES

Sports and Entertainment Litigation Reporter. Andrews Publications. • Monthly. $899.00 per year. Newsletter. Provides reports on lawsuits involving films, TV, cable broadcasting, stage productions, radio, and other areas of the entertainment business. Formerly *Sports and Entertainment Litigation Reporter.*

Videolog. Muze, Inc. • Annual. $250.00. Five volumes. Provides detailed information on more than 170,000 VHS and DVD video titles. Includes a "Directory of Stars and Directors" and 13 category sections.

MOTION PICTURE PHOTOGRAPHY

See also: CAMERA INDUSTRY; PHOTOGRAPHIC INDUSTRY

ABSTRACTS AND INDEXES

Art Index. H. W. Wilson Co. • Quarterly. Annual cumulations. Price varies. Subject and author index to periodicals in art, architecture, industrial design, city planning, photography, and various related topics.

BIBLIOGRAPHIES

Films and Audiovisual Information. Available from U. S. Government Printing Office. • Annual. Free. Issued by the Superintendent of Documents. A list of government publications on motion picture and audiovisual topics. Formerly *Motion Pictures, Films and Audiovisual Information.* (Subject Bibliography No. 73.).

DIRECTORIES

Hollywood Creative Directory: Below-the-Line Talent. IFILMpro. • Annual. $80.00. Lists more than 6,000 cinematographers, production designers, costume designers, film editors, set decorators, and art directors and their associated 15,000 film titles.

The SHOOT Directory for Commercial Production and Postproduction. SHOOT. • Annual. $79.00. Lists production companies, advertising agencies, and sources of professional television, motion

picture, and audio equipment.

ENCYCLOPEDIAS AND DICTIONARIES

Focal Encyclopedia of Photography. Leslie Stroebel and Richard D. Zakia, editors. Elsevier. • 1996. $69.95. Third edition.

HANDBOOKS AND MANUALS

American Cinematographer Manual. • 1993. $49.95. Seventh edition. A pocket size encyclopedia of practical information about cameras, lenses, films, exposure, depth of field, lighting, special effects, etc.

Digital Filmmaking 101: An Essential Guide to Producing Low-Budget Movies. Dale Newton and John Gaspard. Michael Wiese Productions. • 2001. $24.95. Using a light touch, covers the essentials of making a low-budget film, including scripting, budgeting, funding, equipping, casting, and recruiting a crew.

ONLINE DATABASES

Art Index Online. H. W. Wilson Co. • Indexes a wide variety of art-related periodicals, 1984 to date. Monthly updates. Inquire as to online cost and availability.

PERIODICALS AND NEWSLETTERS

American Cinematographer: The International Journal of Motion Picture ProductionTechniques. American Society of Cinematographers. • Monthly. $50.00 per year.

SHOOT: The Leading Newsweekly for Commercial Production and Postproduction. VNU Business Media. • Weekly. $125.00 per year. Covers animation, music, sound design, computer graphics, visual effects, cinematography, and other aspects of television and motion picture production, with emphasis on TV commercials.

SMPTE Motion Imaging Journal. Society of Motion Picture and Television Engineers. • Monthly. Membership. Formerly *SMPTE Journal.*

Videography. United Entertainment Media. • Monthly. $72.00 per year. Edited for the professional video production industry. Covers trends in technique and technology.

TRADE/PROFESSIONAL ASSOCIATIONS

American Society of Cinematographers. 5700 Wilshire Blvd., Ste. 600, Los Angeles, CA 90036. Phone: 800-448-0145 or (323)634-3400 Fax: (323)634-3550 E-mail: an.tran@creativeplanet.com • URL: http://www.cinematograher.com.

Society of Motion Picture and Television Engineers. 595 W Hartsdale Ave., White Plains, NY 10607. Phone: (914)761-1100 Fax: (914)761-3115 E-mail: smpte@smpte.org • URL: http://www.smpte.org • Professional engineers and technicians in motion poctures, television, motion imaging and allied arts and sciences.

MOTION PICTURE THEATERS

DIRECTORIES

Motion Picture TV and Theatre Directory: For Services and Products. Motion Picture Enterprises Publications, Inc. • Semiannual. $16.20. Companies providing products and services to the motion picture and television industries.

FINANCIAL RATIOS

Almanac of Business and Industrial Financial Ratios. Leo Troy. Aspen Publishers, Inc. • 2003. $125.95. Includes CD-Rom. Contains financial ratios derived from federal tax returns. Ratios for each of about 200 industries are arranged according to company asset size. (Almanac of Business and Industrial Financial Ratios Series).

Annual Statement Studies. The Risk Management Association. • Annual. Median and quartile financial

ratios are given for over 400 kinds of manufacturing, wholesale, retail, construction, and consumer finance establishments. Data is sorted by both asset size and sales volume. Includes a clearly written "Definition of Ratios" and an alphabetical industry index.

Annual Statement Studies: Industry Default Probabilities and Cash Flow Measures. The Risk Management Association. • Annual. $145.00. Serves as a companion volume to the original *Annual Statement Studies.* Gives probability of default estimates on a percentage scale for more than 450 industries. Includes changes in position year-by-year for eight financial statement line items and provides percentage measures of cash flow.

PERIODICALS AND NEWSLETTERS

Boxoffice: The Business Magazine of the Global Motion Picture Industry. RLD Communication. • Monthly. $40.00 per year. Provides national and local news about theater management and operations, industry trends about film production and distribution.

Film Journal International. VNU Business Media. • Monthly. $65.00 per year. Formerly *Film Journal.*

TRADE/PROFESSIONAL ASSOCIATIONS

International Cinema Technology Association. 770 Broadway, 5th Fl., New York, NY 10003-9522. Phone: (646)654-7680 Fax: (646)654-7694 E-mail: edith.malijan@nielsen.com • URL: http://www. internationalcinematechnologyassociation.com • Individuals in the theatre equipment industry.

National Association of Theatre Owners. 4605 Lankershim Blvd., Suite 340, North Hollywood, CA 91602. Phone: (818)506-1778 Fax: (818)506-0269 E-mail: nato@mindspring.com • URL: http://www. natoonline.org.

MOTION PICTURES IN EDUCATION

See: AUDIOVISUAL AIDS IN EDUCATION

MOTION PICTURES IN INDUSTRY

See: AUDIOVISUAL AIDS IN INDUSTRY

MOTION STUDY

See: TIME AND MOTION STUDY

MOTIVATION (PSYCHOLOGY)

See also: INDUSTRIAL PSYCHOLOGY

GENERAL WORKS

Contemporary Sales Force Management. Tony Carter. Haworth Press, Inc. • 1997. $49.95. Emphasis is on motivation of sales personnel. Includes case studies.

Handle with Care: Motivating and Retaining Employees - Creative, Low-Cost Ways to Raise Morale, Increase Commitment, and Reduce Turnover. Barbara A. Glanz. McGraw-Hill. • 2002. $16.95. (Teach Yourself Series).

ABSTRACTS AND INDEXES

Psychological Abstracts. American Psychological Association. • Monthly. Members, $815.00 per year; individuals and institutions, $1,207.00 per year. Covers the international literature of psychology and the behavioral sciences. Includes journals, technical reports, dissertations, and other sources.

ENCYCLOPEDIAS AND DICTIONARIES

Blackwell Encyclopedic Dictionary of Organizational Behavior. Nigel Nicholson, editor. Blackwell Publishing. • 1997. $130.95. The editor is associated with the London Business School. Contains definitions of key terms combined with longer articles written by various U. S. and foreign business educators. Includes bibliographies and index. *Blackwell Encyclopedia of Management Series.*

Encyclopedia of Human Behavior. Vangipuram S. Ramachandran, editor. Elsevier. • 1994. $1,000.00. Four volumes. Contains signed articles on aptitude testing, arbitration, career development, consumer psychology, crisis management, decision making, economic behavior, group dynamics, leadership, motivation, negotiation, organizational behavior, planning, problem solving, stress, work efficiency, and other human behavior topics applicable to business situations.

HANDBOOKS AND MANUALS

Why This Horse Won't Drink: How to Win and Keep Employee Commitment. Ken Mateja. AMACOM. • 1990. $22.95. How to set up programs to build trust and change behavior.

ONLINE DATABASES

PsycINFO. American Psychological Association. • Provides indexing and abstracting of the worldwide literature of psychology and the behavioral sciences. Time period is 1967 to date, with monthly updates. Inquire as to online cost and availability.

PERIODICALS AND NEWSLETTERS

Incentive: Managing and Marketing Through Motivation. VNU Business Media. • Monthly. $59.00 per year.

Learning and Motivation. Elsevier. • Quarterly. Individuals, $241.00 per year; institutions, $519.00 per year; students, $121.00 per year.

Motivation and Emotion. Kluwer Academic Publishers. • Quarterly. Institutions, $569.00 per year; with online edition, $682.80 per year.

Motivational Manager: Strategies to Increase Morale and Productivity in the Workplace. Lawrence Ragan Communications, Inc. • Monthly. $119.00 per year. Newsletter. Emphasis is on participative management.

Positive Leadership: Improving Performance Through Value-Centered Management. Lawrence Ragan Communications, Inc. • Monthly. $99.00 per year. Newsletter. Emphasis is on employee motivation, family issues, ethics, and community relations.

Teamwork: Your Personal Guide to Working Successfully with People. Dartnell Corp. • Biweekly. $76.70 per year. Provides advice for employees on human relations, motivation, and team spirit.

MOTIVATION PAMPHLETS

See: PAMPHLETS

MOTIVATION POSTERS

See: POSTERS

MOTOR BUS LINES TIME TABLES

See: TIMETABLES

MOTOR BUSES

See also: TRANSPORTATION INDUSTRY

DIRECTORIES

Official Bus Guide. Russells Guides Inc. • Publication includes: List of about 475 intercity bus companies in the U.S., Canada, and Mexico. Entries include: Company name, address, phone, executives' names and titles, list of terminals and stations with terminal managers' names. Principal content of publication is intercity operating timetables.

ENCYCLOPEDIAS AND DICTIONARIES

Macmillan Encyclopedia of Transportation. Available from Gale Cengage Learning. • 1999. $450.00. Six volumes. Published by Macmillan Reference USA. Covers the business, technology, and history of transportation on land, on water, in the air, and in space. Includes definitions, cross-references, and 200 color illustrations.

FINANCIAL RATIOS

Annual Statement Studies. The Risk Management Association. • Annual. Median and quartile financial ratios are given for over 400 kinds of manufacturing, wholesale, retail, construction, and consumer finance establishments. Data is sorted by both asset size and sales volume. Includes a clearly written "Definition of Ratios" and an alphabetical industry index.

Annual Statement Studies: Industry Default Probabilities and Cash Flow Measures. The Risk Management Association. • Annual. $145.00. Serves as a companion volume to the original *Annual Statement Studies.* Gives probability of default estimates on a percentage scale for more than 450 industries. Includes changes in position year-by-year for eight financial statement line items and provides percentage measures of cash flow.

ONLINE DATABASES

TRIS: Transportation Research Information Service. National Research Council. • Contains abstracts and citations to a wide range of transportation literature, 1968 to present, with monthly updates. Includes references to the literature of air transportation, highways, ships and shipping, railroads, trucking, and urban mass transportation. Formerly *TRIS-ONLINE.* Inquire as to online cost and availability.

PERIODICALS AND NEWSLETTERS

Bus Ride. Friendship Publications, Inc. • 10 times a year. $35.00 per year.

Commercial Carrier Journal. Randall Publishing Co. • Monthly. $45.00 per year.

Fleet Owner. Primedia Business Magazines and Media. • Monthly. $45.00 per year.

School Bus Fleet. Bobit Publishing Corp. • Monthly. $25.00 per year. Includes *Factbook.*

STATISTICS SOURCES

Transit Fact Book. American Public Transportation Association. • Annual. Free.

Transportation Statistics Annual Report. Available from U. S. Government Printing Office. • Annual. $43.00. Issued by the U. S. Bureau of Transportation Statistics, Transportation Department (http://www.bts.gov). Summarizes national data for various forms of transportation, including airlines, railroads, and motor vehicles. Information on the use of roads and highways is included.

TRADE/PROFESSIONAL ASSOCIATIONS

American Bus Association. 700 13th St. NW, Ste. 575, Washington, DC 20005-5923. Phone: 800-283-2877 or (202)842-1645 Fax: (202)842-0850 E-mail: abainfo@buses.org • URL: http://www.buses.org • Privately owned bus-operating firms engaged in intercity, local, charter, and tour service; state associations; motor bus manufacturers; oil, gas and tire distributors and other suppliers; travel/tourism industry destinations, attractions and organizations. Represents almost 900 motorcoach and tour operators in the United States and Canada. Its members operate charter, tour, regular route, airport express, special operations and some contract services (commuter, school transit). Another 2,400 member organizations represent the travel and tourism industry and supplies of bus products and services that work in partnership with the North American motorcoach industry. Delineates the business concerns of both U.S. and Canadian, privately owned motorcoach and tour operators. Serves the U.S. bus industry in Washington, DC and supports the government affairs activities of its Canadian members and counterpart associations. Facilitates relationships between the North American motorcoach industry and all related segments of the travel and supplier industry. In addition, it creates awareness of the motorcoach industry among consumers in North America (USA, Canada and Mexico), and communicates publicly on important issues like motorcoach and highway safety.

MOTOR CARS

See: AUTOMOBILES

MOTOR HOME INDUSTRY

See: MOBILE HOME INDUSTRY; RECREATIONAL VEHICLE INDUSTRY

MOTOR TRANSPORT

See: TRUCKING INDUSTRY

MOTOR TRUCK INDUSTRY

See: TRUCKING INDUSTRY

MOTOR TRUCK TRAILERS

See: TRUCK TRAILERS

MOTOR TRUCKS

See: TRUCKS (MANUFACTURING)

MOTOR VEHICLE EQUIPMENT INDUSTRY

See: AUTOMOBILE EQUIPMENT INDUSTRY

MOTOR VEHICLE LAW AND REGULATION

See also: INTERSTATE COMMERCE

GENERAL WORKS
What Your Car Really Costs: How to Keep a Financially Safe Driving Record. American Institute for Economic Research. • 2002. $6.00. Contains "Should You Buy or Lease?," "Should You Buy New or Used?," "Dealer Trade-in or Private Sale?," "Lemon Laws," and other car buying information. Includes rankings of specific models for resale value, 1995 to 2001. (Economic Education Bulletin.).

ABSTRACTS AND INDEXES
Current Law Index: Multiple Access to Legal Periodicals. Gale Cengage Learning. • Monthly. $725.00 per year. Produced in cooperation with the American Association of Law Libraries. Indexes more than 900 law journals, legal newspapers, and specialty publications from the U.S., Canada, U.K.,

Ireland, Australia, and New Zealand.

DIRECTORIES
American Association of Motor Vehicle Administrators: Membership Directory. American Association of Motor Vehicle Administrators. • Annual. $100.00.

INTERNET DATABASES
Lexis.com Research System. Lexis-Nexis Group. Phone: 800-227-4908 or (937)865-6800 Fax: (937)865-6909 E-mail: webmaster@prod.lexis-nexis.com • URL: http://www.lexis.com • Fee-based Web site offers extensive searching of a wide variety of legal sources. Additional features include Daily Opinion Service, lexis.com Bookstore, Career Center, CLE Center, Law Schools, and Practice Pages ("Pages specific to areas of specialty").

PERIODICALS AND NEWSLETTERS
AAMVA Bulletin. American Association of Motor Vehicle Administrators. • Description: Provides news and legislative information for motor vehicle administrators. Recurring features include news of research, announcements, and legislative information.

Motor Vehicle Regulation: State Capitals. Wakeman-Walworth, Inc. • 50 times a year. $245.00 per year; print and online editions, $350.00 per year. Formerly *From the State Capitals: Motor Vehicle Regulation.*

TRADE/PROFESSIONAL ASSOCIATIONS
American Association of Motor Vehicle Administrators. 4301 Wilson Blvd., Suite 400, Arlington, VA 22203-1800. Phone: 888-226-8280 or (703)522-4200 Fax: (703)522-1553 E-mail: llewis@aamva.org • URL: http://www.aamva.org.

National Committee on Uniform Traffic Laws and Ordinances. 107 S. West St., No. 110, Alexandria, VA 22314. Phone: 800-807-5290 or (540)465-4701 Fax: (540)465-5383 E-mail: ncutloceo@rica.net • URL: http://www.ncutlo.org • Formerly National Conference on Street and Highway Safety.

OTHER SOURCES
Federal Carriers Reports. CCH, Inc. • Biweekly. $1,484.00 per year. Four looseleaf volumes. Federal rules and regulations for motor carriers, water carriers, and freight forwarders.

MOTOR VEHICLE LICENSES

See: MOTOR VEHICLE LAW AND REGULATION

MOTOR VEHICLE PARKING

See: PARKING

MOTOR VEHICLE PARTS INDUSTRY

See: AUTOMOBILE EQUIPMENT INDUSTRY

MOTOR VEHICLES

See: AUTOMOBILES; MOTOR BUSES; TRUCKS (MANUFACTURING)

MOTOR VEHICLES, FOREIGN

See: FOREIGN AUTOMOBILES

MOTOR VEHICLES, USED

See: USED CAR INDUSTRY

MOTORCYCLES

DIRECTORIES
Dealernews--Buyers Guide. Advanstar Communications. • Publication includes: List of manufacturers, distributors, OEMs, and service organizations serving the motorcycle, all-terrain vehicle, and watercraft industries. Entries include: Company name, address, phone, fax, name and title of contact, years in business, number of employees, annual sales, brand names of products; distributor entries also include territories served and branch locations.

Motorcycle Product News Special Buyers Guide. A.B. Publications, Inc. • Annual. $45.00. Provides information on companies related to the motorcycle business. Formerly*Motorcycle Product News Trade Directory.*

PERIODICALS AND NEWSLETTERS
American Motorcyclist. American Motorcyclist Association. • Monthly. $12.50 per year.

Cycle World. Hachette Filipacchi Media U.S., Inc. • Monthly. $12.97 per year. Incorporates *Cycle.*

Dealernews: The Voice of the Powersports Vehicle Industry. Advanstar Communications. • 13 times a year. $40.00 per year. News concerning the power sports motor vehicle industry.

Motorcycle Product News. Athletic Business Publications, Inc. • Monthly. $55.00 per year. Edited for wholesalers and retailers of motorcycles and supplies.

Motorcycle Shopper: The Source for Motorcycles, Parts, Accessories, Sidecars, Tools, Clubs, Events, and More. Payne Corp. • Monthly. $19.95 per year. Contains consumer advertisements for buying, selling, and trading motorcycles and parts.

Motorcyclist. PRIMEDIA Inc. • Monthly. $10.00 per year.

Robb Report Motorcycling. CurtCo Robb Media. • Semiannual. Price on application. Contains reviews of the "newest high-quality motorcycles.".

PRICE SOURCES
NADA Appraisal Guides. National Automobile Dealers Association. • Prices and frequencies vary. Guides to prices of used cars, old used cars, motorcycles, mobile homes, recreational vehicles, and mopeds.

STATISTICS SOURCES
U. S. Industry and Trade Outlook. Available from National Technical Information Service. • Annual. $69.95. Produced by the International Trade Administration, U. S. Department of Commerce, in a "public-private" partnership with DRI/McGraw-Hill and Standard & Poor's. Provides basic data, outlook for the current year, and "Long-Term Prospects" (five-year projections) for a wide variety of products and services. Includes high technology industries. Formerly *U. S. Industrial Outlook.*

TRADE/PROFESSIONAL ASSOCIATIONS
American Motorcyclist Association. 13515 Yarmouth Dr., Pickerington, OH 43147-8214. Phone: 800-262-5646 or (614)856-1900 Fax: (614)856-1920 E-mail: ama@ama-cycle.org • URL: http://www.ama-cycle.org • Represents motorcycle enthusiasts. Acts as a rulemaking body for motorcycle competition. Promotes highway safety. Maintains museum and hall of fame.

Motorcycle Industry Council. 2 Jenner St., Ste. 150, Irvine, CA 92618-3806. Phone: (949)727-4211 Fax: (949)727-3313 E-mail: ciannello@mic.org • URL: http://www.mic.org • Manufacturers and distributors of motorcycles and allied industries. Maintains liaison with state and federal governments. Operates collection of research documents, federal and state government documents, and trade publications. Compiles statistics.

MOTORS

See: ENGINES

MOVING OF EMPLOYEES

See: RELOCATION OF EMPLOYEES

MOVING PICTURE INDUSTRY

See: MOTION PICTURE INDUSTRY

MULTIFAMILY HOUSING

See: APARTMENT HOUSES; CONDOMINIUMS

MULTILEVEL MARKETING

ABSTRACTS AND INDEXES

Business Periodicals Index. H. W. Wilson Co. • 11 times a year. Quarterly and annual cumulations. Price varies.

HANDBOOKS AND MANUALS

Get Rich Through Multi-Level Selling: Build Your Own Sales and Distribution Organization. Gini G. Scott. Self-Counsel Press, Inc. • 1998. $19.95. Third revised edition. (Self Counsel Business Series).

How to Develop Multilevel Marketing Sales. Entrepreneur Media, Inc. • Looseleaf. $59.50. A practical guide to starting a multilevel marketing business. Covers profit potential, start-up costs, owner's time required, pricing, accounting, advertising, market size evaluation, promotion, etc. (Start-Up Business Guide No. E1222.).

ONLINE DATABASES

Marketing and Advertising Reference Service (MARS). Gale Cengage Learning. • Provides abstracts of literature relating to consumer marketing and advertising, including all forms of advertising media. Time period is 1984 to date. Daily updates. Inquire as to online cost and availability.

Wilson Business Abstracts Online. H. W. Wilson Co. • Indexes and abstracts 600 major business periodicals, plus the *Wall Street Journal* and the business section of the *New York Times.* Indexing is from 1982, abstracting from 1990, with the two newspapers included from 1993. Updated weekly. Inquire as to online cost and availability. (*Business Periodicals Index* without abstracts is also available online.).

MULTIMEDIA

See also: ELECTRONIC PUBLISHING; INTERACTIVE MEDIA; OPTICAL DISK STORAGE DEVICES

GENERAL WORKS

Being Digital. Nicholas Negroponte. Knopf Publishing Group. • 1995. $30.00. A kind of history of multimedia, with visions of future technology and public participation. Predicts how computers will affect society in years to come.

Essentials of Knowledge Management. Bryan Bergeron. John Wiley and Sons, Inc. • 2003. $29.

95. Covers current strategies, trends, and technologies in knowledge management. Includes examples of best practices. (Essentials Series).

Future Libraries: Dreams, Madness, and Reality. Walt Crawford and Michael Gorman. American Library Association. • 1995. $28.00. Discusses the "over-hyped virtual library" and electronic-publishing "fantasies." Presents the argument for the importance of books, physical libraries, and library personnel.

Interface Culture: How New Technology Transforms the Way We Create and Communicate. Steven Johnson. HarperSanFrancisco. • 1997. $24.00. A discussion of how computer interfaces and online technology ("cyberspace") affect society in general.

Knowledge Management Lessons Learned: What Works and What Doesn't. Michael Koenig and T. Kanti Srikantaiah, editors. Information Today, Inc. • 2003. $44.50. Contains more than 30 articles by KM experts, covering recent applications, innovations, strategy, implementation, cost analysis, training, content management, and other topics related to knowledge management. (ASIS Management Series).

Marketing on the Internet: Multimedia Strategies for the World Wide Web. Jill Ellsworth and Matthew Ellsworth. John Wiley and Sons, Inc. • 1996. $29. 99. Second expanded revised edition.

Multimedia: Concepts and Practice. Stephen McGloughlin. Prentice Hall Books. • 2000. $73.33. Includes audio compact disk. Provides basic information and instruction on multimedia graphic design, animation, video editing, sound editing, authoring, product creation, and other multimedia topics.

Net Curriculum: An Educator's Guide to Using the Internet. Linda Joseph. Information Today, Inc. • 1999. $29.95. Covers various educational aspects of the Internet. Written for K-12 teachers, librarians, and media specialists by a columnist for *Multimedia Schools.* (CyberAge Books.).

Silicon Snake Oil: Second Thoughts on the Information Highway. Clifford Stoll. Doubleday Publishing. • 1996. $14.00. The author discusses the extravagant claims being made for online networks and multimedia.

ABSTRACTS AND INDEXES

Business Periodicals Index. H. W. Wilson Co. • 11 times a year. Quarterly and annual cumulations. Price varies.

Computer Literature Index: A Subject/Author Index to Computer and Data Processing Literature. EBSCO Publishing. • Quarterly, with annual cumulation. $245.00 per year. Contains brief abstracts of book and periodical literature covering all phases of computing, including approximately 70 specific application areas.

F & S Index: United States. Gale Cengage Learning. • Monthly. $1,450.00 per year, including quarterly and annual cumulations. Provides annotated citations to marketing, business, financial, and industrial literature. Coverage of U. S. business activity includes trade journals, financial magazines, business newspapers, and special reports.

Internet and Personal Computing Abstracts [print edition]. EBSCO Publishing. • Quarterly. $269.00 per year, including cumulative index. Provides more than 10,000 abstracts annually from both trade and academic publications. Covers computer hardware, software, product reviews, Web topics, e-commerce, networks, corporate news, security, and related topics. Formerly *Microcomputer Abstracts.*

Library Literature and Information Science Index. H. W. Wilson Co. • Quarterly. Annual cumulation. Price varies.

Readers' Guide to Periodical Literature. H. W. Wilson Co. • Monthly. $345.00 per year. Includes

annual *Cumulation.* Indexes about 250 periodicals of general interest.

ALMANACS AND YEARBOOKS

Communication Technology Update. Elsevier. • 2000. $36.95. 7th edition. A yearly review of developments in electronic media, telecommunications, and the Internet.

BIBLIOGRAPHIES

Knowledge Management: The Bibliography. Paul Burden and others. Information Today, Inc. • 2000. $22.50. Provides citations to more than 1,500 articles, 150 Web sites, and 400 books. Arranged according to specific KM topics, such as "KM and E-Commerce." Published in conjunction with the American Society for Information Science and Technology (ASIST).

BIOGRAPHICAL SOURCES

The Highwaymen: Warriors on the Information Superhighway. Ken Auletta. Harcourt Trade Publications. • 1998. $13.00. Revised expanded edition. Contains critical articles about Ted Turner, Rupert Murdoch, Barry Diller, Michael Eisner, and other key figures in electronic communications, entertainment, and information. (Harvest Book Series).

CD-ROM DATABASES

Computer Database. Gale Cengage Learning. • Provides one year of full-text on CD-ROM for 150 leading computer-related publications. Also includes 70,000 product specifications and brief profiles of 13,000 computer product vendors and manufacturers.

Hoover's Company Capsules on CD-ROM. Hoover's, Inc. • Quarterly. $399.95 per year (single-user). Provides the CD-ROM version of *Hoover's Handbook of American Business, Hoover's Handbook of Emerging Companies, Hoover's Handbook of World Business, Hoover's Guide to Computer Companies, Hoover's Guide to Media Companies, Hoover's Handbook of Private Companies,* and various regional guides. Includes more than 11,000 profiles of companies.

WILSONDISC: Library Literature and Information Science Index. H. W. Wilson Co. • Quarterly. Includes unlimited access to the online version of *Library Literature.* Provides CD-ROM indexing of about 300 periodicals, covering a wide range of topics having to do with libraries, library management, and the information industry.

WILSONDISC: Wilson Business Abstracts. H. W. Wilson Co. • Monthly. Includes unlimited online access to *Wilson Business Abstracts* through WILSONLINE. Provides CD-ROM "cover-to-cover" abstracting and indexing of over 600 prominent business periodicals. Indexing is from 1982, abstracting from 1990. (*Business Periodicals Index* without abstracts is available on CD-ROM at $1,495 per year.).

DIRECTORIES

Advanced Imaging Buyers Guide: The Most Comprehensive Worldwide Directory of Imaging Product and Equipment Vendors. Cygnus Business Media. • Annual. $19.95. Lists 800 electronic imaging companies and their products.

AV Market Place: The Complete Business Directory of Audio, Audio Visual, Computer Systems, Film, Video, and Programming, with Industry Yellow Pages. Information Today, Inc. • Annual. $195.00. Provides information on "more than 7,500 companies that create, apply, or distribute AV equipment and services for business, education, science, and government." Multimedia, virtual reality, presentation software, and interactive video are among the categories. Formerly published by R. R. Bowker.

CD-ROMS in Print. Gale Cengage Learning. • 2003.

For publishers addresses, refer to SOURCES CITED section at the back of the book.

$185.00. 17th edition. Describes more than 20,000 currrently available reference and multimedia CD-ROM titles and provides contact information for about 4,000 CD-ROM publishing and distribution companies. Includes several indexes.

Data Sources: The Comprehensive Guide to the Data Processing Industry: Hardware, Data Communications Products, Software, Company Profiles. Gale Cengage Learning. • Semiannual. $455.00 per year. Two volumes. Describes hardware and software for all computer operating sysems, including prices and technical details. Lists about 75,000 products from 14,000 suppliers. Industry-specific software applications are described.

KMWorld Buyer's Guide. Knowledge Asset Media. • Semiannual. Controlled circulation as part of *KMWorld.* Contains corporate and product profiles related to various aspects of knowledge management and information systems. (Knowledge Asset Media is a an affiliate of Information Today, Inc.).

Music Technology Buyer's Guide. United Entertainment Media. • $6.95. Annual. Lists more than 4,000 hardware and software music production products from 350 manufacturers. Includes synthesizers, MIDI hardware and software, mixers, microphones, music notation software, etc. Produced by the editorial staffs of *Keyboard* and *EQ* magazines.

Peterson's Guide to Distance Learning Programs. Peterson's. • 2002. $26.95. Second revised edition. Provides detailed information on accredited college and university programs available through television, radio, computer, videocassette, and audiocassette resources. Covers U. S. and Canadian institutions.

Plunkett's InfoTech Industry Almanac: Complete Profiles on the InfoTech 500-the Leading Firms in the Movement and Management of Voice, Data, and Video. Plunkett Research, Ltd. • Biennial. $229.99. Includes CD-ROM. Five hundred major information companies are profiled, with corporate culture aspects. Discusses major trends in various sectors of the computer and information industry, including data on careers and job growth. Includes several indexes.

The Software Encyclopedia: A Guide for Personal, Professional, and Business Users. Gale. • Annual. $335.00. Two volumes. Volume one lists software programs by title and producer. Volume two provides information on programs according to application and operating system. Includes prices and requirements for hardware and memory.

SRDS Interactive Advertising Source. SRDS. • Quarterly. $569.00 per year. Provides descriptive profiles, rates, audience, personnel, etc., for producers of various forms of interactive or multimedia advertising: online/Internet, CD-ROM, interactive TV, interactive cable, interactive telephone, interactive kiosk, and others.

ENCYCLOPEDIAS AND DICTIONARIES

Acronyms of Computer Science and Communications: A Comprehensive Acronym Dictionary and Illustrated Encyclopedia. Enjob Kajan and Ejub Kajan. Springer Verlag. • 2002. $49.95. Explains more than 4,000 "broadly used" computer, telecommunications, and information technology acronyms. Includes illustrations and Web addresses, where applicable.

CyberDictionary: Your Guide to the Wired World. Spurge ink!. • 1996. $17.95. Includes many illustrations.

Cyberspace Lexicon: An Illustrated Dictionary of Terms from Multimedia to Virtual Reality. Bob Cotton and Richard Oliver. Phaidon Press. • 1994. $29.95. Defines more than 800 terms, with manyillustrations. Includes a bibliography.

Dictionary of Multimedia: Terms and Acronyms. Brad Hansen, editor. Fitzroy Dearborn Publishers, Inc. • 2002. $55.00. Third edition.

Encyclopedia of Information Systems. Hossein Bidgoli, editor. Elsevier. • 2002. $1,200.00. Four volumes. Contains a wide range of articles relating to computers, databases, communication, and information technology. The 200 topics include coverage of hardware, software, artificial intelligence, the Internet, networks, knowledge management, electronic commerce, search engines, and systems design.

Encyclopedia of New Media: An Essential Reference to Communication and Technology. Steve Jones, editor. Sage Publications, Inc. • 2003. $125.00. Contains more than 250 entries dealing with such areas as multimedia, broadband access, information communication technology (ICT), content filtering, wireless networks, and cyberethics.

Every Manager's Guide to Information Technology: A Glossary of Key Terms and Concepts for Today's Business Leader. Peter G. W. Keen. Harvard Business School Publishing. • 1994. $18.95. Second edition. Provides definitions of terms related to computers, data communications, and information network systems. (Harvard Business Reference Series).

Multimedia and the Web from A to Z. David C. Leonard and Patrick M. Dillon. Greenwood Publishing Group, Inc. • 1998. $42.95. Second enlarged revised edition. Defines more than 1,500 terms relating to software and hardware in the areas of computing, online technology, telecommunications, audio, video, motion pictures, CD-ROM, and the Internet. Includes acronyms and an annotated bibliography. Formerly *Multimedia Technology from A to Z* (1994).

New Hacker's Dictionary. Eric S. Raymond. MIT Press. • 1996. $65.00. Third edition. Includes three classifications of hacker communication: slang, jargon, and "techspeak.".

HANDBOOKS AND MANUALS

Business Multimedia Explained: A Manager's Guide to Key Terms and Concepts. Peter G. W. Keen. Harvard Business School Publishing. • 1997. $39.95.

The Cybrarian's Manual. Pat Ensor, editor. American Library Association. • 2000. $45.00. Second edition. Provides information for librarians concerning the Internet, expert systems, computer networks, client/server architecture, Web pages, multimedia, information industry careers, and other "cyberspace" topics.

Digital Audio and Compact Disk Technology. Baert Theunisse and Luc Theunisse. Elsevier. • 1995. $57.95. Third edition.

Electronic Media Management. William E. McCavitt and others. Elsevier. • 1999. $59.95. Fourth edition.

Interactive Computer Systems: Videotex and Multimedia. Antone F. Alber. Perseus Publishing. • 1993. $79.50.

Learning Web Design: A Beginner's Guide to HTML, Graphics, and Beyond. Jennifer Niederst. O'Reilly & Associates, Inc. • 2001. $34.95. Written for beginners who have no previous knowledge of how Web design works.

Principles of Digital Audio. Ken C. Pohlmann. McGraw-Hill. • 2000. $54.95. Fourth edition. Includes the details of digital audio recording, reproduction, error correction, compact disc technology, DVD, minidiscs, Internet audio, and related topics. (Video/Audio Engineering Series).

Standard Handbook of Audio and Radio Engineering. Jerry C. Whitaker and K. Blair Benson. McGraw-Hill. • 2002. $125.00. Second edition. Emphasis is on audio. Covers such topics as DVD, MP3, sound reproduction, amplification, noise reduction, and Internet audio.

Trade Secret Protection in an Information Age. Gale

R. Peterson. Glasser LegalWorks. • Looseleaf. $149.00, including sample forms on disk. Periodic supplementation available. Covers trade secret law relating to computer software, online databases, and multimedia products. Explanations are based on more than 1,000 legal cases. Sample forms on disk include work-for-hire examples and covenants not to compete.

INTERNET DATABASES

InfoTech Trends. Data Analysis Group. Phone: (925)462-1202 Fax: (925)462-1225 E-mail: support@infotechtrends.com • URL: http://www.infotechtrends.com • Web site provides both free and fee-based market research data on the information technology industry, including computers, peripherals, telecommunications, the Internet, software, CD-ROM/DVD, e-commerce, and workstations. Fees: Free for current (most recent year) data; more extensive information has various fee structures. Formerly *Computer Industry Forecasts.*

Wired News. Lycos, Inc. Phone: (415)276-8400 Fax: (415)276-8500 E-mail: newsfeedback@wired.com • URL: http://www.wired.com • Provides summaries and full-text of "Top Stories" relating to the Internet, computers, multimedia, telecommunications, and the electronic information industry in general. These news stories are placed in the broad categories of Politics, Business, Culture, and Technology. Affiliated with *Wired* magazine. Fees: Free.

ONLINE DATABASES

F & S Index. Gale Cengage Learning. • Contains about four million citations to worldwide business, financial, and industrial or consumer product literature appearing from 1972 to date. Weekly updates. Inquire as to online cost and availability.

Gale Directory of Databases [online]. Gale Cengage Learning. • Presents the online version of the printed *Gale Directory of Databases, Volume 1: Online Databases* and *Gale Directory of Databases, Volume 2: CD-ROM, Diskette, Magnetic Tape, Handheld, and Batch Access Database Products.* Semiannual updates. Inquire as to online cost and availability.

Globalbase. Gale Cengage Learning. • Provides more than one million online summaries of business, industrial, and economic news reports from more than 1,000 publications worldwide. Covers a wide range of material appearing in international trade journals, professional magazines, and newspapers. Time period is 1984 to date, with weekly updates. Inquire as to online cost and availability.

Internet and Personal Computing Abstracts. Information Today, Inc. • Contains abstracts covering a wide variety of personal and business microcomputer literature appearing in more than 100 journals and popular magazines. Time period is 1981 to date, with monthly updates. Formerly *Microcomputer Index.* Inquire as to online cost and availability.

PROMT: Predicasts Overview of Markets and Technology. Gale Cengage Learning. • Companies, products, applied technologies and markets. U.S. and international literature coverage, 1972 to date. Inquire as to online cost and availability. Provides abstracts from more than 1,600 publications. Weekly updates.

Readers' Guide Abstracts Online. H. W. Wilson Co. • Indexes and abstracts general interest periodicals, 1983 to date. Weekly updates. Inquire as to online cost and availability.

Wilson Business Abstracts Online. H. W. Wilson Co. • Indexes and abstracts 600 major business periodicals, plus the *Wall Street Journal* and the business section of the *New York Times.* Indexing is from 1982, abstracting from 1990, with the two newspapers included from 1993. Updated weekly. Inquire as to online cost and availability. (*Business Periodicals Index* without abstracts is also available online.).

PERIODICALS AND NEWSLETTERS

Advanced Imaging: Solutions for the Electronic Imaging Professional. Cygnus Business Media. • Monthly. $60.00 per year Covers document-based imaging technologies, products, systems, and services. Coverage is also devoted to multimedia and electronic printing and publishing.

Computer Music Journal. MIT Press. • Quarterly. Individuals, $77.00 per year; instutitions, $215.00 per year. Includes print and online editions. Covers digital soound and the musical applications of computers.

Desktop Video Communications. BCR Enterprises, Inc,. • Bimonthly. Free per year. Covers multimedia technologies, with emphasis on video conferencing and the "virtual office.".

Digital Imaging: The Magazine for the Imaging Professional. Cygnus Business Media, Inc. • Bimonthly. $24.95 per year. Edited for business and professional users of electronic publishing products and services. Topics covered include document imaging, CD-ROM publishing, digital video, and multimedia services. Formerly *Micro Publishing News.*

Digital Video Magazine. CMP Media LLC. • Monthly. $29.97 per year. Edited for producers and creators of digital media. Includes topics relating to video, audio, animation, multimedia, interactive design, and special effects. Covers both hardware and software, with product reviews. Formerly *Digital Video Magazine.*

EContent: Digital Content Strategies and Resources. Online, Inc. • Monthly. $110.00 per year. Emphasis is on the business management and financial aspects of the digital content industry. (Formerly published by Online, Inc.).

Educational Marketer: The Educational Publishing Industry's Voice of Authority Since 1968. SIMBA Information. • Three times a month. $599.00 per year. Newsletter. Edited for suppliers of educational materials to schools and colleges at all levels. Covers print and electronic publishing, software, audiovisual items, and multimedia. Includes corporate news and educational statistics.

Electronic Information Report: Empowering Industry Decision Makers Since 1979. SIMBA Information. • 46 times a year. $649.00 per year. Newsletter. Provides business and financial news and trends for online services, electronic publishing, storage media, multimedia, and voice services. Includes information on relevant IPOs (initial public offerings) and mergers. Formerly *Electronic Information Week.*

eMedia: The Digital Studio Magazine. Online, Inc. • Monthly. $98.00 per year. Covers video production equipment, digital video editing, electronic publishing, digital content streaming, encoding, and other topics related to digital content creation and multimedia. (Formerly published by Online, Inc.).

EQ: The Project Recording and Sound Magazine. United Entertainment Media, Inc. • Monthly. $24.95 per year. Provides advice on professional music recording equipment and technique.

IEEE Multimedia Magazine. Institute of Electrical and Electronic Engineers, Inc. • Quarterly. $560.00 per year. Provides a wide variety of technical information relating to multimedia systems and applications. Articles cover research, advanced applications, working systems, and theory.

Interactive Content: Consumer Media Strategies Monthly. Jupitermedia. • Monthly. $675.00 per year; with online edition, $775.00 per year. Newsletter. Covers the broad field of providing content

(information, news, entertainment) for the Internet/World Wide Web.

KM World: Creating and Managing the Knowledge-Based Enterprise (Knowledge Management). Asset Media. • 10 times a year. Free to qualified personnel; others, $63.95 per year. Provides articles on knowledge management, including business intelligence, multimedia content management, document management, e-business, and intellectual property. Emphasis is on business-to-business information technology. (Knowledge Asset Media is a an affiliate of Information Today, Inc.)

Maximum PC (Personal Computer). Imagine Media, Inc. • Quarterly. $29.95 per year. Provides articles and reviews relating to multimedia hardware and software. Each issue includes a CD-ROM sampler (emphasis is on games). Formed by the merger of *Home PC* and *Boot.*

Media Device Report. Jon Peddie Associates. • Description: Covers media and electronic devices and companies, as well as business information for those devices and companies. Recurring features include a company profile, editorial articles, technology briefs, IPO's, stocks, and stock indices.

Multimedia Schools: A Practical Journal of Technology for Education including Multimedia, CD-ROM, Online and Internet and Hardware in K-12. Information Today, Inc. • Six times a year. $39.95 per year. Edited for school librarians, media center directors, computer coordinators, and others concerned with educational multimedia. Coverage includes the use of CD-ROM sources, the Internet, online services, and library technology.

Sound & Vision: Home Theater- Audio- Video-MultimediaMovies- Music. Hachette Filipacchi Media U.S., Inc. • 10 times a year. $24.00 per year. Popular magazine providing explanatory articles and critical reviews of equipment and media (CD-ROM, DVD, videocassettes, etc.). Supplement available *Stero Review's Sound and Vision Buyers Guide.* Replaces *Stereo Review* and *Video Magazine.*

Syllabus: New Directions in Educational Technology. Syllabus Press. • 10 times a year. $24.00 per year. Covers the use of advanced technology in higher education systems, including video, multimedia, the Internet, distance learning systems, and electronic publishing.

Upgrade. Software and Information Industry Association. • Monthly. $79.00 per year. Covers news and trends relating to the software, information, and Internet industries. Formerly *SPA News* from Software Publisers Association.

Video Librarian: The Video Review Magazine. Video Librarian. • Bimonthly. $64.00 per year. $99.00 per year with online access to archives (15,000 reviews). Edited for public and school libraries. Each issue includes reviews of hundreds of video DVDs or cassettes, in various subject areas.

Wired. Wired Ventures Ltd. • Monthly. $10.00 per year. Edited for creators and managers in various areas of electronic information and entertainment, including multimedia, the Internet, and video. Often considered to be the primary publication of the "digital generation.".

RESEARCH CENTERS AND INSTITUTES

Electronic Visualization Laboratory. University of Illinois at Chicago, Engineering Research Facility, 842 W. Taylor St., Room 2032, Chicago, IL 60607-7053. Phone: (312)996-3002 Fax: (312)413-7585 E-mail: tom@uic.edu • URL: http://www.evl.uic.edu • Research areas include computer graphics, virtual reality, multimedia, and interactive techniques.

Graphics, Visualization, and Usability Center. Georgia Institute of Technology. GVU Center, 801 Atlantic Dr., Atlanta, GA 30332-0280. Phone: (404)894-4488 Fax: (404)894-0673 E-mail: afb@

cc.gatech.edu • URL: http://www.cc.gatech.edu/gvu/ • Research areas include computer graphics, multimedia, image recognition, interactive graphics systems, animation, and virtual realities.

Integrated Media Systems Center. University of Southern California, 3740 McClintock Ave., Suite 131, Los Angeles, CA 90089-2561. Phone: (213)740-0877 Fax: (213)740-8931 E-mail: imsc@imsc.usc.edu • URL: http://www.imsc.usc.edu • Media areas for research include education, mass communication, and entertainment.

Inter-Arts Center. San Francisco State University, School of Creative Arts, 1600 Holloway Ave., San Francisco, CA 94132. Phone: (415)338-1478 Fax: (415)338-6159 E-mail: jimdavis@sfsu.edu • URL: http://www.sfsu.edu/~iac • Research areas include multimedia, computerized experimental arts processes, and digital sound.

International Data Corp. (IDC). Five Speen St., Framingham, MA 01701. Phone: (508)872-8200 Fax: (508)935-4015 E-mail: leads@idc.com • URL: http://www.idc.com • Private research firm specializing in market research related to computers, multimedia, and telecommunications.

Media Laboratory. Massachusetts Institute of Technology, 20 Ames St., Room E-15, Cambridge, MA 02139-4307. Phone: (617)253-0300 Fax: (617)258-6264 E-mail: casr@media.mit.edu • URL: http://www.media.mit.edu • Research areas include electronic publishing, spatial imaging, human-machine interface, computer vision, and advanced television.

Multimedia Communications Laboratory. Boston University, Eight Saint Mary's St., PHO 445, Boston, MA 02215. Phone: (617)353-8042 Fax: (617)353-6440 E-mail: mcl@spiderman.bu.edu • URL: http://www.hulk.bu.edu • Research areas include interactive multimedia applications.

Studio for Creative Inquiry. Carnegie Mellon University, College of Fine Arts, Pittsburgh, PA 15213-3890. Phone: (412)268-3454 Fax: (412)268-2829 E-mail: mmbm@andrew.cmu.edu/ • URL: http://www.cmu.edu/studio/ • Research areas include artificial intelligence, virtual reality, hypermedia, multimedia, and telecommunications, in relation to the arts.

TRADE/PROFESSIONAL ASSOCIATIONS

Association for Interactive Marketing. 1430 Broadway, 8th Fl., New York, NY 10018. Phone: 888-337-0008 or (212)790-1408 Fax: (212)391-9233 • URL: http://www.interactivehq.org • Members are companies engaged in various interactive enterprises, utilizing the internet, interactive television, computer communications and multimedia. Formerly Association for Interactive Media.

Association of Internet Professionals. 2929 Main St., No. 136, Santa Monica, CA 90405. Phone: (866)247-9700 or (501)423-2248 Fax: (501)423-2248 E-mail: info@association.org • URL: http://www.iproa.org • Members are interactive media professionals concerned with intetractive arts and technologies. Formerly International Interactive Communications Society.

Internet Alliance. 1111 19th St. NW, Ste. 1100, Washington, DC 20035-5782. Phone: (202)861-2476 Fax: (202)955-8081 E-mail: info@internetalliance.org • URL: http://www.internetalliance.org • Companies offering Internet services. Seeks to "build the confidence and trust necessary for the Internet to become the global mass market medium of the 21st century". Represents members' commercial and regulatory interests; conducts promotional activities; facilitates communication and cooperation among members.

Software and Information Industry Association. 1090 Vermont Ave. NW, 6th Fl., Washington, DC 20005. Phone: (202)289-7442 Fax: (202)289-7097 •

URL: http://www.siia.net • A trade association for the software and digital content industry. Affiliated with Massachusetts Software and Internet Council.

Special Interest Group on Electronic Sound Technology. c/o Association for Computing Machinery, 1515 Broadway, New York, NY 10036. Phone: 800-342-6626 or (212)626-0603 Fax: (212)944-1318 E-mail: barish@acm.org • URL: http://www.acm.org/sigsound • Concerned with software, algorithms, hardware, and applications relating to digitally generated audio.

Special Interest Group on Multimedia. c/o Association for Computing Machinery, 1515 Broadway, New York, NY 10036. Phone: 800-342-6626 or (212)626-0500 Fax: (212)305-5826 E-mail: sigs@acm.org • URL: http://www.acm.org/sigmm • Concerned with multimedia computing, communication, storage, and applications.

OTHER SOURCES

Consumer Online Services Report. JupiterMedia. • Annual. $1,895.00. Market research report. Provides analysis of trends in the online information industry, with projections of growth in future years (five-year forecasts). Contains profiles of electronic media companies.

DVD Assessment, No. 3. Julie B. Schwerin and Theodore A. Pine. InfoTech, Inc. • 1998. $1,295.00. Third edition. Provides detailed market research data on Digital Video Discs (also known as Digital Versatile Discs). Includes history of DVD, technical specifications, DVD publishing outlook, "Industry Overview," "Market Context," "Infrastructure Analysis," "Long-Range Forecast to 2005," and emerging technologies.

Keyboard: The World's Leading Music Technology Magazine. United Entertainment Media, Inc. • Monthly. $25.95 per year. Emphasis is on recording systems, keyboard technique, and computer-assisted music (MIDI) systems.

Optical Publishing Industry Assessment. Julie B. Schwerin and Theodore A. Pine. InfoTech, Inc. • 1997. $1,295.00. Ninth edition. Provides market research data and forecasts to 2005 for DVD-ROM, "Hybrid ROM/Online Media," and other segments of the interactive entertainment, digital information, and consumer electronics industries. Covers both software (content) and hardware. Includes Video-CD, DVD- Video, CD-Audio, DVD-Audio, DVD-ROM, PC-Desktop, TV Set-Top, CD-R, CD-RW, DVD-R and DVD-RAM.

MULTINATIONAL CORPORATIONS

See also: CORPORATIONS;
INTERNATIONAL BUSINESS;
INTERNATIONAL TAXATION

GENERAL WORKS

International Business and Multinational Enterprises. Stefan H. Robock and Kenneth Simmonds. McGraw-Hill. • 1988. $68.50. Fourth edition.

Successful Mergers, Acquisitions, and Strategic Alliances: How to Bridge Corporate Cultures. Irene Rodgers and others. McGraw-Hill. • 2002. $39.95. Provides advice on mergers involving companies in different countries.

ABSTRACTS AND INDEXES

Business Periodicals Index. H. W. Wilson Co. • 11 times a year. Quarterly and annual cumulations. Price varies.

BIBLIOGRAPHIES

Globalization: A Bibliography with Indexes. Marina Elbakidze. Nova Science Publishers, Inc. • 2002. $59.00. Covers various aspects of globalization: ef-

fect on society, trade, economics, politics, business, technology, and the environment. Includes author, title, and subject indexes.

CD-ROM DATABASES

Corporate Affiliations Plus. National Register Publishing, Reed Reference Publishing. • Quarterly. $1,995.00 per year. Provides CD-ROM discs corresponding to *Directory of Corporate Affiliations* and *Corporate Finance Bluebook.* Contains corporate financial services information and worldwide data on subsidiaries and affiliates.

Hoover's Company Capsules on CD-ROM. Hoover's, Inc. • Quarterly. $399.95 per year (single-user). Provides the CD-ROM version of *Hoover's Handbook of American Business, Hoover's Handbook of Emerging Companies, Hoover's Handbook of World Business, Hoover's Guide to Computer Companies, Hoover's Guide to Media Companies, Hoover's Handbook of Private Companies,* and various regional guides. Includes more than 11,000 profiles of companies.

InvesText [CD-ROM]. Thomson Financial. • Monthly. Contains full text on CD-ROM of investment research reports from about 630 sources, including leading brokers and investment bankers. Reports are available on both U. S. and international publicly traded corporations. Separate industry reports cover more than 50 industries. Time span is 1982 to date.

Leadership Library on CD-ROM: Who's Who in the Leadership of the United States. Leadership Directories, Inc. • Quarterly. Including access to Internet version (weekly updates). Contains all 14 *Yellow Book* personnel directories on CD-ROM, providing contact and brief biographical information for about 400,000 individuals. Covers business, government, financial institutions, news media, law firms, associations, foreign representatives, and nonprofit organizations. Includes photographs.

Newspaper Abstracts Ondisc. PROQUEST. • Monthly. $2,950.00 per year (covers 1989 to date; archival discs are available for 1985-88). Provides cover-to-cover CD-ROM indexing and abstracting of 19 major newspapers, including the *New York Times, Wall Street Journal, Washington Post, Chicago Tribune,* and *Los Angeles Times.*

DIRECTORIES

American Big Businesses Directory. infoUSA Inc. • Covers: 218,000 U.S. businesses with more than 100 employees, and 500,000 key executives and directors. CD-ROM version contains 160,000 top firms and 431,000 key executives. Entries include: Name, address, phone, names and titles of key personnel, number of employees, sales volume, Standard Industrial Classification (SIC) codes, subsidiaries and parent company names, stock exchanges on which traded.

America's Corporate Families. Dun & Bradstreet Corp. • Covers: Approximately 12,700 U.S. corporations. Ultimate companies must meet all of the following criteria for inclusion: two or more business locations, 250 or more employees at that location or in excess of $25 million in sales volume or a tangible net worth greater than $500,000, and controlling interest in one or more subsidiary company. Entries include: D&B D-U-N-S number, company name, address, phone, state of incorporation, line of business, primary/secondary SIC codes, sales volume, net worth, number of employees, current ownership date, year started, number of sites, key executives' names/titles, directors and than officers, primary bank and accounting firm, import/export designation, stock exchange symbol and indicator for publicly owned companies, parent company and location.

Business Organizations, Agencies, and Publications Directory. Gale Cengage Learning. • 2003. $480.00. 15th edition. Over 40,000 entries describing 39

types of business information sources. Classified by type of organization, publication, or serviceIncludes state, national, and international agencies and organizations. Master index to names and keywords. Also includes e-mail addresses and web site URL's.

Directory of American Firms Operating in Foreign Countries. Uniworld Business Publications. • Biennial. $355.00. Three volumes. Lists approximately 3,000 American companies with more than 34,500 subsidiaries and affiliates in 190 foreign countries.

Directory of Foreign Firms Operating in the United States. Uniworld Business Publications, Inc. • Biennial. $250.00. Lists about 2,400 foreign companies and 5,700 American affiliates. 75 countries are represented.

Directory of Multinationals. Available from Gale Cengage Learning. • 2001. $775.00. Sixth edition. Two volumes. Published by Waterlow Specialist Information Publishing. Provides detailed information on multinational firms with total annual sales in excess of one billion dollars and overseas sales in excess of $500 million. Includes narrative company descriptions and statistical data.

Foreign Representatives in the U. S. Yellow Book: Who's Who in the U. S. Offices of Foreign Corporations, Foreign Nations, the Foreign Press, and Intergovernmental Organizations. Leadership Directories, Inc. • Annual. $265.00 per year. Lists executives located in the U. S. for 1,200 foreign companies, 300 foreign banks and other financial institutions, 175 embassies and consulates, and 375 foreign press outlets. Includes five indexes.

Global Market Share Planner. Euromonitor International. • 2003. $5,900.00. Six volumes. Second edition. Provides detailed profiles and market share rankings of major consumer product companies in North America, Latin America, Europe, South Africa, and the Asia-Pacific region. Covers firms operating in key consumer markets: beverages, food products, household products, and personal care items. (Volumes are available individually.).

Hoover's Handbook of World Business: Profiles of Major European, Asian, Latin American, and Canadian Companies. Hoover's, Inc. • Annual. $165.00. Contains detailed profiles for approximately 300 large foreign companies. Includes indexes by industry, location, executive name, company name, and brand name.

Major Market Share Companies: Asia Pacific. Available from Gale Cengage Learning. • 2003. $990.00. Second edition. Published by Euromonitor. Provides consumer market share data and rankings for multinational and regional companies. Covers leading firms in Japan, China, Australia, South Korea, Indonesia, Malaysia, Philippines, and Thailand.

Major Market Share Companies: Europe. Available from Gale Cengage Learning. • 2001. $990.00. Published by Euromonitor. Provides consumer market share data and rankings for multinational and regional companies. Covers leading firms in 14 European countries.

Major Market Share Companies: The Americas. Available from Gale Cengage Learning. • 2003. $990.00. Second edition. Published by Euromonitor. Provides consumer market share data and rankings for multinational and regional companies. Covers leading firms in the U.S., Canada, Mexico, Brazil, Argentina, Venezuela, and Chile.

Major Performance Rankings. Available from Gale Cengage Learning. • 2003. $1,190.00. Second edition. Published by Euromonitor. Ranks 2,500 leading consumer product companies worldwide by various kinds of business and financial data, such as sales, profit, and market share. Includes international, regional, and country rankings.

Market Share Reporter. Available from Gale Cengage Learning. • 2002. $285.00. Sixth edition. Published by Euromonitor. Provides consumer market share data for leading companies in 30 major countries.

Morningstar American Depositary Receipts. Morningstar, Inc. • Biweekly. $195.00 per year. Looseleaf. Provides detailed profiles of 700 foreign companies having shares traded in the U. S. through American Depositary Receipts (ADRs).

Standard Directory of International Advertisers and Agencies: The International Red Book. National Register Publishing. • Annual. $629.00. Includes more than 5,000 foreign companies and their advertising agencies. Geographic, company name, personal name, and trade name indexes are provided.

World Leading Global Brand Owners. Euromonitor International. • 2003. $1,190.00. Second edition. Contains detailed profiles of multinational consumer product companies. Includes sales, market share, brand names, and financial information. (*Global Market Share Planner*, vol. 3.).

World's Major Multinationals. Euromonitor International. • Covers: List of major multinational companies. Entries include: Company name, address, phone; performance analysis; list of subsidiaries; market share; net profit and turnover; leading brands; and merger and acquisition information.

Worldwide Branch Location of Multinational Companies. Gale Cengage Learning. • 1993. $270.00. A guide to subsidiaries, sales offices, manufacturing facilities, and other corporate units operating outside the headquarters country. Includes over 500 leading multinational companies and their 20,000 branch locations.

ENCYCLOPEDIAS AND DICTIONARIES

Blackwell Encyclopedic Dictionary of International Management. John J. O'Connell, editor. Blackwell Publishers. • 1999. $130.95. The editor is associated with the American Graduate School of International Management. Contains definitions of key terms combined with longer articles written by various U. S. and foreign business educators. Includes bibliographies and index. (Encyclopedia of Management Series).

HANDBOOKS AND MANUALS

International Business Handbook. Vishnu H. Kirpalani, editor. Haworth Press, Inc. • 1990. $89.95. (International Business Series: No. 1).

Multinational Financial Management. Alan C. Shapiro. John Wiley and Sons, Inc. • 2002. $106.95. Seventh edition.

INTERNET DATABASES

EBSCO Information Services. Ebsco Publishing. Phone: 800-653-2726 or (978)356-6500 Fax: (978)356-6565 E-mail: ep@epnet.com • URL: http://www.epnet.com • Fee-based Web site providing Internet access to a wide variety of databases, including business-related material. Full text is available for many periodical titles, with daily updates. Fees: Apply.

Ebusiness Forum: Global Business Intelligence for the Digital Age. Economist Intelligence Unit (EIU), Economist Group. Phone: 800-938-4685 or (212)554-0600 Fax: (212)586-0248 E-mail: newyork@eiu.com • URL: http://www.ebusinessforum.com • Web site provides information relating to multinational business, with an emphasis on activities in specific countries. Includes rankings of countries for "e-business readiness," additional data on the political, economic, and business environment in 180 nations ("Doing Business in.."), and "Today's News Analysis." Fees: Free, but registration is required for access to all content. Daily updates.

Factiva. Dow Jones Reuters Business Interactive,

LLC. Phone: 800-369-7466 or (609)452-1511 Fax: (609)520-5770 E-mail: solutions@factiva.com • URL: http://www.factiva.com • Fee-based Web site provides "global news and business information through Web sites and content integration solutions." Includes Dow Jones and Reuters newswires, The Wall Street Journal, and more than 7,000 other sources of current news, historical articles, market research reports, and investment analysis. Content includes 96 major U. S. newspapers, 900 non-English sources, trade publications, media transcripts, country profiles, news photos, etc.

InSite 2. Intelligence Data/Thomson Financial. Phone: 800-654-0393 or (617)856-1890 Fax: (617)737-3182 E-mail: intelligence.data@tfn.com • URL: http://www.insite2.gale.com/ • Fee-based Web site consolidates information in a "Base Pack" consisting of Business InSite, Market InSite, and Company InSite. Optional databases are Consumer InSite, Health and Wellness InSite, Newsletter InSite, and Computer InSite. Includes fulltext content from more than 2,500 trade publications, journals, newsletters, newspapers, analyst reports, and other sources. Continuous updating. Formerly produced by The Gale Group.

Nexis.com. Lexis-Nexis Group. Phone: 800-227-4908 or (937)865-6800 Fax: (937)865-6909 E-mail: webmaster@prod.lexis-nexis.com • URL: http://www.nexis.com • Fee-based Web site offers searching of about 2.8 billion documents in some 30,000 news, business, and legal information sources. Features include a subject directory covering 1,200 topics in 34 categories and a Company Dossier containing information on more than 500,000 public and private companies. Boolean searching is offered.

ProQuest Direct. ProQuest Inc. Phone: 800-889-3358 or (734)761-4700 Fax: (734)662-4554 • URL: http://proquest.com • Fee-based Web site providing Internet access to more than 3,000 periodicals, newspapers, and other publications. Many items are available full-text, with daily updates. Includes extensive corporate and financial information. Fees: Apply.

ONLINE DATABASES

Information Bank Abstracts. New York Times Index Dept. • Provides indexing and abstracting of current affairs, primarily from the final late edition of *The New York Times* and the Eastern edition of *The Wall Street Journal*. Time period is 1969 to present, with daily updates. Inquire as to online cost and availability.

InvesText. Thomson Financial. • Provides full text online of investment research reports from more than 600 sources, including leading brokers and investment bankers. Reports are available on approximately 60,000 U. S. and international corporations. Separate industry reports cover 54 industries. Time span is 1982 to date, with daily updates. Inquire as to online cost and availability.

Wilson Business Abstracts Online. H. W. Wilson Co. • Indexes and abstracts 600 major business periodicals, plus the *Wall Street Journal* and the business section of the *New York Times*. Indexing is from 1982, abstracting from 1990, with the two newspapers included from 1993. Updated weekly. Inquire as to online cost and availability. (*Business Periodicals Index* without abstracts is also available online.).

Worldscope. Thomson Financial. • Online service provides detailed financial and other information on more than 32,000 publicly-owned companies in 50 countries. Includes business description, balance sheets, earnings statements, senior officers, major shareholders, financial ratios, and 20-year historical

data. Monthly updates. Inquire as to online cost and availability.

PERIODICALS AND NEWSLETTERS

Business Week International: The World's Only International Newsweekly of Business. McGraw-Hill. • Weekly. $95.00 per year.

Canadian Business. Canadian Business Media. • Biweekly. $64.95 per year. Edited for corporate managers and executives, this is a major periodical in Canada covering a variety of business, economic, and financial topics. Emphasis is on the top 500 Canadian corporations.

Chief Executive Magazine. Chief Executive Group, Inc. • Monthly. $95.00 per year.

Financial Times [London]. The Financial Times, Inc. • Daily, except Sunday. $572.88 per year. An international business and financial newspaper, featuring news from London, Paris, Frankfurt, New York, and Tokyo. Includes worldwide stock and bond market data, commodity market data, and monetary/currency exchange information.

Fortune Magazine. Time Inc., Business Information Group. • Biweekly. $59.95 per year. Edited for top executives and upper-level managers.

Global Finance. Global Finance Media, Inc. • Monthly. $350.00 per year. Edited for corporate financial executives and money managers responsible for "cross-border" financial transactions.

Harvard Business Review. Harvard University, Graduate School of Business Administration. Harvard Business School Publishing. • Monthly. $118.00 per year.

International Trade and Investment Letter: Trends in U.S Policies, Trade Finance and Trading Operations. International Business Affairs Corp. • Monthly. $240.00 per year. Newsletter.

Journal of Transnational Management Development: The Official Publication of the International Management Development Association. International Management Development Association. Haworth Press, Inc. • Quarterly. Institutions, $375.00 per year.

Multinational Monitor. Essential Information. • Monthly. Individuals, $25.00 per year; non-profit organizations, $30.00 per year; corporations, $40.00 per year. Track the activities of multinational corporations and their effects on the Third World, labor and the environment.

The New Information Report: The International Industry Dossier. Washington Researchers, Ltd. • Looseleaf service. $160.00 per year. Monthly updates. Formerly *The International Information Report.*

Transnational Corporations. United Nations Conference on Trade and Development. United Nations Publications. • Three times a year. $45.00 per year. Reports on both governmental and non-governmental aspects of multinational corporations. Issued by the United Nations Centre on Transnational Corporations (UNCTC). Formerly *CTC Reporter.*

Washington International Business Report: An Analytical Review and Outlook on Major Government Developments Impacting International Trade and Investment. International Business-Government Counsellors, Inc. • Monthly. $288.00 per year. Newsletter.

RESEARCH CENTERS AND INSTITUTES

Center for Human Resources. University of Pennsylvania, The Wharton School, 309 Vance Hall, 3733 Spruce St., Philadelphia, PA 19104-6358. Phone: (215)898-2722 Fax: (215)898-5908 E-mail: cappelli@wharton.upenn.edu • URL: http://www.management.wharton.upenn.edu/.

Conference Board, Inc. The Conference Board, Inc. 845 3rd Ave., New York, NY 10022. Phone: (212)339-0345 Fax: (212)980-7014 E-mail: info@

conference-board.org • URL: http://www. conference-board.org • Business management practices worldwide, especially economic, and demographic in nature. Specific concerns include: corporate citizenship, including corporate contributions, diversity, environmental policy and issues, and government relations; corporate governance, including boards of directors, role of chief executives, relations with institutional investors, and shareholder input and influence; economics, including economic and financial forecasts, consumer confidence, leading economic indicators, North American outlook and trends, and global economic environment; human resources and organizational effectiveness, including organization structure and design, compensation and benefits, training and development, and communications; and performance excellence.

STATISTICS SOURCES

Manufacturing Worldwide: Industry Analysis Statistics. Gale Cengage Learning. • 1999. $240.00. Third edition. A guide to worldwide economic activity in 500 product lines within 119 countries. Includes 37 detailed industry profiles. Name, address, phone, fax, employment, and ranking are shown for major companies worldwide in each industry sector.

Measuring Globalisation: The Role of Multinationals in OECD Economies. Organization for Economic Cooperation and Development. • Biennial. $85.00. Two volumes. Volume one provides extensive statistics for the multinational corporate manufacturing sector. Volume two covers the services sector.

TRADE/PROFESSIONAL ASSOCIATIONS

United States Council for International Business. 1212 Ave. of the Americas, 21st Fl., New York, NY 10036. Phone: (212)354-4480 Fax: (212)575-0327 E-mail: info@uscib.org • URL: http://www.uscib. org • Formerly United States Council of the International Chamber of Commerce.

OTHER SOURCES

Market Share Tracker. Euromonitor International. • 2003. $1,190.00. Second edition. Contains market share rankings of more than 1,800 consumer product companies in 30 countries. Covers 16 kinds of products within "Drinks," "Household and Personal Care," and "Foods." Includes brand shares for leading brands. (*Global Market Share Planner*, vol. 1.).

World Business Rankings Annual. Gale Cengage Learning. • 1998. $189.00. Provides 2,500 ranked lists of international companies, compiled from a variety of published sources. Each list shows the "top ten" in a particular category. Keyword indexing, a country index, and citations are provided.

World Investment Report. United Nations Publications. • Annual. $49.00. Concerned with foreign direct investment, economic development, regional trends, transnational corporations, and globalization.

MULTIPLE DWELLINGS

See: APARTMENT HOUSES; CONDOMINIUMS

MUNICIPAL BONDS

See also: BONDS; MUNICIPAL FINANCE

ALMANACS AND YEARBOOKS

Fixed Income Almanac: The Bond Investor's Compendium of Key Market, Product, and Performance Data. Livingston G. Douglas. McGraw-Hill. • 1993. $75.00. Presents 20 years of data in 350 graphs and charts. Covers bond market

volatility, yield spreads, high-yield (junk) corporate bonds, default rates, and other items, such as Federal Reserve policy.

CD-ROM DATABASES

OECD Statistical Compendium. Organization for Economic Cooperation and Development. • Semiannual. $1,905.00 per year for 1 to 10 users. CD-ROM contains more than 730,000 monthly, quarterly, and annual time series for OECD countries, 1960 to date. Includes fully searchable data on agriculture, food, economic indicators, national accounts, employment, energy, finance, industry, technology, and foreign trade. Results can be displayed in various forms.

DIRECTORIES

Mergent Municipal and Government Manual. Mergent, Inc. • Annual. $3,250.00 per year. Updated weekly online.

ENCYCLOPEDIAS AND DICTIONARIES

Dictionary of Finance and Investment Terms. John Downes. Barron's Educational Series, Inc. • 2002. $14.95. Sixth edition. Provides clear explanations of more than 5,000 business, banking, financial, investment, and tax terms. Includes a separate list of financial abbreviations and acronyms. (Business Dictionaries Series).

HANDBOOKS AND MANUALS

Fixed Income Analytics: State-of-the-Art Analysis and Valuation Modeling. Ravi E. Dattatreya, editor. McGraw-Hill. • 1991. $69.95. Discusses the yield curve, structure and value in corporate bonds, mortgage-backed securities, and other topics. (Institutional Investor Publications).

Fixed Income Mathematics: Analytical and Statistical Techniques. Frank J. Fabozzi. McGraw-Hill. • 1996. $65.00. Third edition. Covers the basics of fixed income analysis, as well as more advanced techniques used for complex securities.

Fundamentals of Municipal Bonds: A Basic, Definitive Text on the Municipal Securities Market. John Wiley & Sons, Inc. • 2001. $65.00. Fifth edition. (Finance Series).

Handbook for Muni Bond Issuers. Joe Mysak. Bloomberg. • 1998. $40.00. Written primarily for the officers and attorneys of municipalities. Provides a practical explanation of the municipal bond market. (Bloomberg Professional Library.).

How to Build Wealth with Tax-Sheltered Investments. Kerry Anne Lynch. American Institute for Economic Research. • 2000. $6.00. Provides practical information on conservative tax shelters, including defined-contribution pension plans, individual retirement accounts, Keogh plans, U. S. savings bonds, municipal bonds, and various kinds of annuities: deferred, variable-rate, immediate, and foreign-currency. (Economic Education Bulletin.).

Municipal Bonds: The Comprehensive Review of Municipal Securities and Public Finance. Robert Lamb and Stephen Rappaport. McGraw-Hill. • 1987. $34.95. Second edition.

INTERNET DATABASES

Business 2.0 Web Guide to the Best Business Links. Business 2.0 Media Inc. Phone: (415)293-4800 E-mail: support@business2.com • URL: http:// www.business2.com/webguide • Web site presents an extensive, searchable directory of links to "the best, most informative, and authoritative web pages." Twenty main categories cover business, finance, career, company information, people, and technology topics, with thousands of subtopics, all linking to Web sites recommended by experienced business researchers. Fees: Free.

ETF Connect. Nuveen Investments. Phone: 800-257-8787 • URL: http://www.etfconnect.com • Free Web site makes available extensive, searchable information on individual closed-end investment

funds, preferred share funds, and exchange-traded index funds. Information on a particular fund is available by name or as part of a classification (high yield, investment grade, municipal, emerging markets, global equity, etc.). Fund charts are available for various time periods, as is data concerning premiums or discounts, dividends, annualized total return, credit quality, "Top 10 Holdings," and so forth.

Factiva. Dow Jones Reuters Business Interactive, LLC. Phone: 800-369-7466 or (609)452-1511 Fax: (609)520-5770 E-mail: solutions@factiva.com • URL: http://www.factiva.com • Fee-based Web site provides "global news and business information through Web sites and content integration solutions." Includes Dow Jones and Reuters newswires, The Wall Street Journal, and more than 7,000 other sources of current news, historical articles, market research reports, and investment analysis. Content includes 96 major U. S. newspapers, 900 non-English sources, trade publications, media transcripts, country profiles, news photos, etc.

Fedstats. Federal Interagency Council on Statistical Policy. Phone: (202)395-7254 • URL: http://www. fedstats.gov • Web site features an efficient search facility for full-text statistics produced by more than 100 federal agencies, including the Census Bureau, the Bureau of Economic Analysis, and the Bureau of Labor Statistics. Boolean searches can be made within one agency or for all agencies combined. Links are offered to international statistical bureaus, including the UN, IMF, OECD, UNESCO, Eurostat, and 20 individual countries. Fees: Free.

FreeLunch.com. Economy.com, Inc. Phone: (610)696-8700 Fax: (610)696-1678 • URL: http:// www.freelunch.com • Web site provides free access to more than 1.5 million economic and financial data series, covering industry, demographics, labor markets, prices, retail sales, government spending, trade, interest rates, housing starts, the stock market, and many other topics. Data is available for various time periods in either chart or table form. Searching is offered. Fees: Free, but registration required. Economy.com, Inc. also offers fee-based economic analysis at *The Dismal Scientist* site (http://www. dismal.com).

Nexis.com. Lexis-Nexis Group. Phone: 800-227-4908 or (937)865-6800 Fax: (937)865-6909 E-mail: webmaster@prod.lexis-nexis.com • URL: http:// www.nexis.com • Fee-based Web site offers searching of about 2.8 billion documents in some 30,000 news, business, and legal information sources. Features include a subject directory covering 1,200 topics in 34 categories and a Company Dossier containing information on more than 500,000 public and private companies. Boolean searching is offered.

Wall Street Journal Interactive Edition. Dow Jones & Co., Inc. Phone: 800-369-2834 or (212)416-2000 Fax: (212)416-2658 E-mail: inquiries@interactive. wsj.com • URL: http://www.wsj.com • Fee-based Web site providing online searching of worldwide information from the *The Wall Street Journal*. Includes "Company Snapshots," "The Journal's Greatest Hits," "Index to Market Data," "Journal Links," etc. Financial price quotes are available. Fees: $49.00 per year; $29.00 per year to print subscribers.

ONLINE DATABASES

Fitch Ratings Delivery Service. Fitch Inc. • Provides online delivery of Fitch financial ratings in three sectors: "Corporate Finance" (corporate bonds, insurance companies), "Structured Finance" (asset-backed securities), and "U.S. Public Finance" (municipal bonds). Daily updates. Inquire as to online cost and availability.

PERIODICALS AND NEWSLETTERS

The Bond Buyer. Veronis, Suhler and Associates Inc. • Daily edition, $1,897 per year. Weekly edition,

$525.00 per year. Reports on new municipal bond issues.

CreditWeek (Municipal Edition). Standard and Poor's. • Weekly. Price on application. Provides news and analysis of the municipal bond market, including information on new issues.

The Lynch Municipal Bond Advisory. James F. Lynch., editor. The Lynch Municipal Bond Advisory. • Description: Addresses the municipal bond market.

The Wall Street Journal. Dow Jones & Co., Inc. • Daily. $189.00 per year. Covers news and trends relating to business, industry, finance, the economy, and international commerce. Provides extensive price and other data for the securities, commodity, options, futures, foreign exchange, and money markets.

PRICE SOURCES

Bank and Quotation Record. William B. Dana Co. • Monthly. $130.00 per year.

STATISTICS SOURCES

Business Statistics of the United States. Linz Audain and Cornelia J. Strawser. Bernan Associates. • Annual. $147.00. Based on *Business Statistics*, formerly issue by the Bureau of Economic Analysis, U. S. Department of Commerce. Provides basic data for a wide variety of U. S. industries, services, and economic indicators. Most statistics are shown annually for 30 years and monthly for the most recent four years.

S & P's Municipal Bond Book, with Notes, Commercial Paper, & IRBs. Standard & Poor's. • Bimonthly. $965.00 per year. Includes ratings and statistical information for about 20,000 municipal bonds, notes, commercial paper issues, and industrial revenue bonds (IRBs). The creditworthiness ("Rationales") of 200 selected municipalities and other issuers is discussed. Securities "under surveillance" by S & P are listed.

Statistical Annual: Interest Rates, Metals, Stock Indices, Options on Financial Futures, Options on Metals Futures. Chicago Board of Trade. • Annual. Includes historical data on GNMA CDR Futures, Cash-Settled GNMA Futures, U. S. Treasury Bond Futures, U. S. Treasury Note Futures, Options on Treasury Note Futures, NASDAQ-100 Futures, Major Market Index Futures, Major Market Index MAXI Futures, Municipal Bond Index Futures, 1,000-Ounce Silver Futures, Options on Silver Futures, and Kilo Gold Futures.

Survey of Current Business. Available from U. S. Government Printing Office. • Monthly. $63.00 per year. Issued by Bureau of Economic Analysis, U. S. Department of Commerce. Presents a wide variety of business and economic data.

TRADE/PROFESSIONAL ASSOCIATIONS

Bond Market Association. 360 Madison Ave., New York, NY 10017-7111. Phone: (646)637-9200 Fax: (646)637-9126 E-mail: membership@bondmarkets. com • URL: http://www.bondmarkets.com • Represents securities firms and banks that underwrite, trade and sell debt securities, both domestically and internationally.

OTHER SOURCES

Blue List of Current Municipal and Corporate Offerings. Standard and Poor's. • Daily. $940.00 per year. Compendium of municipal and corporate bond offers.

Fitch Insights. Fitch Investors Service, Inc. • Biweekly. $1,040.00 per year. Includes bond rating actions and explanation of actions. Provides commentary and Fitch's view of the financial markets.

MUNICIPAL EMPLOYEES

See: CIVIL SERVICE; MUNICIPAL GOVERNMENT

MUNICIPAL FINANCE

See also: MUNICIPAL BONDS; MUNICIPAL GOVERNMENT; PUBLIC FINANCE

ONLINE DATABASES

Social Scisearch. Institute for Scientific Information. • Broad, multidisciplinary index to the literature of the social sciences, 1972 to present. Weekly updates. Worldwide coverage. Inquire as to online cost and availability.

PERIODICALS AND NEWSLETTERS

Government Finance Review. Government Finance Officers Association. • Bimonthly. $30.00. per year.

Journal of Structured and Project Finance. Institutional Investor, Inc., Journals Group. • Quarterly. $365.00 per year. Includes print and online editions. Covers the financing of large-scale construction projects, such as power plants and convention centers. Formerly *Journal of Project Finance.*

Municipal Finance Journal. Civic Research Institute. • Quarterly. $302.00 per year. Recent tax and legal trends affecting both large and small state municipalities.

Nation's Cities Weekly. National League of Cities. • Description: Presents news on the latest developments in Congress, the White House, federal agencies, and other public interest groups which may affect the nation's cities.

Project Finance: The Magazine for Global Development. American Educational Systems. • 11 times a year. $740.00 per year. Includes print and online editions. Provides articles on the financing of the infrastructure (transportation, utilities, communications, the environment, etc) Coverage is international. Supplements available *World Export Credit Guide* and *Project Finance Book of Lists.* Formed by the merger of *Infrastructure Finance* and *Project and Trade Finance.*

Public Finance Review. Sage Publications, Inc. • Bimonthly. Institutions, $599.00 per year; includes print and online editions. Formerly *Public Finance Quarterly.*

RESEARCH CENTERS AND INSTITUTES

Municipal Technical Advisory Service Library. University of Tennessee, Knoxville, Conference Center Bldg.., 600 Henley St., Ste. 120, Knoxville, TN 37996-4105. Phone: (865)974-0411 Fax: (865)974-0423 E-mail: schwartzr@tennessee.edu • URL: http://www.mtas.utk.edu/library • Research areas include municipal finance, police administration, and public works.

Urban Institute. Urban Institute. 2100 M St. NW, Washington, DC 20037. Phone: (202)833-7200 Fax: (202)728-0232 E-mail: paffairs@ui.urban.org • URL: http://www.urban.org • Domestic, social, and economic affairs, including multidisciplinary studies and government program evaluations in the areas of tax and budget reform, education policy, health policy, crime and justice, housing and community development, labor and human services, income security and retirement, welfare reform, international activities, nonprofit sector and philanthropy, public finance, productivity and economic development, social services, and immigration. Also conducts research programs on employment and training, children's issues and family policy, minorities and social policy, poverty, state and local governments, and community impact and demography.

STATISTICS SOURCES

County and City Data Book 2000: A Statistical Abstract Supplement. Available from U. S. Government Printing Office. • 2002. $68.00. 13th edition. Issued by the U. S. Bureau of the Census (http://www.census.gov). Contains a wide variety of data on 3,141 U.S. counties, 1,078 cities, and 11,097 places of 2,500 or more inhabitants. Includes statistical information on retailing, manufacturing, banking, service industries, income, employment, housing, education, crime, and population. Updated metropolitan areas are included.

County and City Extra: Annual Metro, City and County Data Book. Deirdre A. Gaquin and Mark S. Littman. Bernan Press. • 2001. $120.00. Updates and augments data published irregularly in print form by the U. S. Census Bureau in *County and City Data Book.* Covers "every state, county, metropolitan area, and congressional district in the United States, as well as all U. S. cities with a 1990 population of 25,000 or more." Contains a wide range tic maps.

County and City Extra: Special Decennial Census Edition. Deirdre A. Gaquin and Katherine A. De-Brandt, editors. Bernan Press. • 2002. $95.00. Presents conveniently arranged population, housing, and other data from the 2000 census, with many 1980 and 1990 comparisons. Includes maps and tables with rankings of about 20 items for various geographic locations. Complements the annual *County and City Extra.*

Facts and Figures on Government Finance. Tax Foundation. • Annual. $45.00.

S & P's Municipal Bond Book, with Notes, Commercial Paper, & IRBs. Standard & Poor's. • Bimonthly. $965.00 per year. Includes ratings and statistical information for about 20,000 municipal bonds, notes, commercial paper issues, and industrial revenue bonds (IRBs). The creditworthiness ("Rationales") of 200 selected municipalities and other issuers is discussed. Securities "under surveillance" by S & P are listed.

TRADE/PROFESSIONAL ASSOCIATIONS

Association of Government Accountants. 2208 Mount Vernon Ave., Alexandria, VA 22301-1314. Phone: 800-242-7211 or (703)684-6931 Fax: (703)548-9367 E-mail: agamembers@agacgfm.org • URL: http://www.agacgfm.org • Members are employed by federal, state, county, and city government agencies. Includes accountants, auditors, budget officers, and other government finance administrators and officials.

Government Finance Officers Association of the United States and Canada. 203 N. LaSalle St., Ste. 2700, Chicago, IL 60601. Phone: (312)977-9700 Fax: (312)977-4806 E-mail: membership@gfoa.org • URL: http://www.gfoa.org • Formerly Municipal Finance Officers Association of United States and Canada.

MUNICIPAL GOVERNMENT

See also: CITIES AND TOWNS; CITY PLANNING; COUNTY GOVERNMENT; PUBLIC ADMINISTRATION

GENERAL WORKS

Performance Budgeting for State and Local Government. Janet M. Kelly and William C. Rivenbark. M. E. Sharpe, Inc. • 2003. $69.95. Covers performance-based management as applied to local government budgeting.

ABSTRACTS AND INDEXES

Social Sciences Citation Index. Thomson/ISI. • Three times a year. $6,900 per year. Annual cumulation. Includes *Source Index*, *Citation Index*, *Permuterm Subject Index*, and *Corporate Index.*

Social Sciences Index. H. W. Wilson Co. • Quarterly, with annual cumulation. Price varies. Indexes more than 400 periodicals covering economics, environmental policy, government, insurance, labor, health care policy, plannning, public administration, public welfare, urban studies, women's issues, criminology, and related topics.

ALMANACS AND YEARBOOKS

Municipal Year Book. International City-County Management Association. • Annual. $84.95. An authoritative resume of activities and statistical data of American cities.

BIOGRAPHICAL SOURCES

Who's Who in American Politics. Marquis Who's Who. • Biennial. $275.00. Two volumes. Contains about 27,000 biographical sketches of local, state, and national elected or appointed individuals.

CD-ROM DATABASES

Social Sciences Citation Index. ISI. • Monthly. Price on request. Provides CD-ROM indexing of articles appearing in 1700 leading social science journals worldwide, with additional selections from more than 5700 other journals. Time span is 1992 to date. Coverage includes economics, business, finance, management, communications, demographics, library and information science, political science, sociology, and many other subjects.

Social Sciences Citation Index: Compact Disc Edition with Abstracts. Institute for Scientific Information. • Monthly. Provides CD-ROM indexing and abstracting of "significant articles" from 1,700 social science journals worldwide, with additional selections from 3,200 other journals, 1986 to date. Includes economics, business, finance, management, communications, demographics, information and library science, political science, sociology, and many other subjects.

WILSONDISC: Wilson Social Sciences Abstracts. H. W. Wilson Co. • Monthly. Includes unlimited online access to *Social Sciences Index* through WILSONLINE. Provides CD-ROM indexing from 1983 and abstracting from 1994 of more than 500 periodicals covering economics, area studies, community health, public administration, public welfare, urban studies, and many other topics related to the social sciences.

DIRECTORIES

American City and County Municipal Index: Purchasing Guide for City, Township, County Officials and Consulting Engineers. Primedia Business Magazines and Media. • Annual. $61.95. Includes a directory of city and county governments with populations of 10,000 or more. Names and telephone numbers of municipal purchasing officials are listed. Also includes a directory of manufacturers and suppliers of materials, equipment, and services for municipalities.

Carroll's Municipal/County Directory. Carroll Publishing. • Annual. $250.00 per year. Provides listings of about 90,000 city, town, and county officials in the U. S.

Carroll's Municipal Directory. Carroll Publishing. • Covers: about 50,000 officials in more than 7,900 cities towns and villages: includes top elected council or elected board members. Entries include: Name, county name, locator phone, address, population; officials' names, titles, addresses, and phone numbers.

Government Phone Book USA: Your Comprehensive Guide to Federal, State, County, and Local Government Offices in the United States. Omnigraphics, Inc. • Annual. $265.00. Contains more than 270,000 listings of federal, state, county, and local government offices and personnel, including legislatures. Formerly *Government Directory of Addresses and Phone Numbers.*

Mayors of America's Principal Cities. United States Conference of Mayors. • Semiannual. About 1,000 mayors of cities with populations of 30,000 or more.

Mergent Municipal and Government Manual. Mergent, Inc. • Annual. $3,250.00 per year. Updated weekly online.

Municipal Yellow Book: Who's Who in the Leading City and County Governments and Local Authorities. Leadership Directories, Inc. • Annual. $265.00 per year. Lists approximately 30,000 key personnel in city and county departments, agencies, subdivisions, and branches.

HANDBOOKS AND MANUALS

Municipal Management Series. International City-County Management Association. • 14 volumes. Various dates, 1968 to 1988. Finance, planning, training, public relations, and other subjects.

ONLINE DATABASES

Social Scisearch. Institute for Scientific Information. • Broad, multidisciplinary index to the literature of the social sciences, 1972 to present. Weekly updates. Worldwide coverage. Inquire as to online cost and availability.

Wilson Social Sciences Abstracts Online. H. W. Wilson Co. • Provides online abstracting and indexing of more than 500 periodicals covering area studies, community health, public administration, public welfare, urban studies, and many other social science topics. Time period is 1994 to date for abstracts and 1983 to date for indexing, with updates weekly. Inquire as to online cost and availability.

PERIODICALS AND NEWSLETTERS

American City and County: Administration, Engineering and Operations in Relation to Local Government. Primedia Business Magazines and Media. • Monthly. Free to qualified personnel. Edited for mayors, city managers, and other local officials. Emphasis is on equipment and basic services.

Current Municipal Problems. West Group. • Quarterly. $287.50 per year. Full text journal articles on municipal law and administration. Indexing included.

Governing: The States and Localities. • Monthly. $39.95 per year. Edited for state and local government officials. Covers finance, office management, computers, telecommunications, environmental concerns, etc.

Government Technology: Solutions for State and Local Government in the Information Age. E. Republic Inc. • Monthly. Free to qualified personnel.

ICMA Newsletter. International City/County Management Association. • Description: Discusses local government, professional management, and federal regulation. Publishes news of Association activities. Recurring features include news of members; reports of publications, educational workshops, positions open in public management; and two main supplements titled Nuts & Bolts and ICMA University.

National Civic Review. National Civic League, Inc. Jossey-Bass. • Quarterly. Institutions, $115.00 per year; with online edition, $120.75 per year. Presents civic strategies for improving local government operations and community life.

Nation's Cities Weekly. National League of Cities. • Description: Presents news on the latest developments in Congress, the White House, federal agencies, and other public interest groups which may affect the nation's cities.

Public Management: Devoted to the Conduct of Local Government. International City-County Management Association. • Monthly. $34.00 per year.

Public Risk. Public Risk Management Association. • 10 times a year. $125.00 per year. Covers risk management for state and local governments, including various kinds of liabilities.

U.S. Mayor. U.S. Conference of Mayors. • Description: Provides a national forum for issues that affect cities in the U.S. Contains ideas in public programs and coverage of innovative projects. Recurring features include letters to the editor, interviews, a

calendar of events, and reports of meetings.

STATISTICS SOURCES

County and City Data Book, a Statistical Abstract Supplement. U.S. Bureau of the Census. Available from U.S. Government Printing Office. • 1994. $60.00.

Facts About the Cities. Allan Carpenter and Carl Provorse. H. W. Wilson Co. • 1996. $100.00. Second edition. Contains a wide variety of information on 300 American cities, including cities in Puerto Rico, Guam, and the U. S. Virgin Islands. Data is provided on the workplace, taxes, revenues, cost of living, population, climate, housing, transportation, etc.

TRADE/PROFESSIONAL ASSOCIATIONS

International City/County Management Association. 777 N Capitol St. NE, Ste. 500, Washington, DC 20002-4201. Phone: 800-745-8780 or (202)289-4262 or (202)962-3680 Fax: (202)962-3500 E-mail: roneill@icma.org • URL: http://icma.org • International professional and educational organization for appointed administrators and assistant administrators serving cities, counties, districts, and regions. Provides publications, training, and management assistance to help local government professionals improve their skills and increase their knowledge. Collects data on local governments.

International Institute of Municipal Clerks. 8331 Utica Ave., Ste. 200, Rancho Cucamonga, CA 91730. Phone: 800-251-1639 or (909)944-4162 Fax: (909)944-8545 E-mail: hq@iimc.com • URL: http://www.iimc.com.

International Municipal Lawyers Association. 1110 Vermont Ave. NW, Ste. 200, Washington, DC 20005. Phone: (202)466-5424 Fax: (202)785-1052 E-mail: info@imla.org • URL: http://www.imla.org • Seeks to promote and advance the development of local government law and. Serves as a clearinghouse of local law materials; collects and disseminates information; assists government agencies to prepare for litigation and develop new local laws; provides legal research and writing services; offers continuing legal education opportunities; conducts research programs.

National Civic League. 1640 Logan St., 1445 Market, Ste. 300, Denver, CO 80203. Phone: 800-864-8622 or (303)571-4343 Fax: (303)571-4404 E-mail: ncl@ncl.org • URL: http://www.ncl.org • Community leaders, civic leaders, educators, public officials, civic organizations, libraries, nonprofits and businesses interested in community building, transforming democratic institutions and developing techniques of citizen action and participation. Serves as a clearinghouse for information on healthy communities, community renewal, local campaign, finance reform, All-American cities, city and county charters, election systems and techniques of citizen participation.

National League of Cities. 1301 Pennsylvania Ave. NW, Washington, DC 20004-1763. Phone: (202)626-3000 Fax: (202)626-3043 E-mail: inet@nlc.org • URL: http://www.nlc.org • Formerly American Municipal Association.

Public Risk Management Association. 500 Montgomery St., Ste. 750, Alexandria, VA 22314. Phone: (703)528-7701 Fax: (703)739-0200 E-mail: info@primacentral.org • URL: http://www.primacentral.org • Public agency risk, insurance, human resources, attorneys, and/or safety managers from cities, counties, villages, towns, school boards, and other related areas. Provides an information clearinghouse and communications network for public risk managers to share resources, ideas, and experiences. Offers information on risk, insurance, and safety management. Monitors state and federal legislative actions and court decisions that deal with immunity, tort liability, and intergovernmental risk pools. Maintains library containing current reports from governmental units on their insurance procedures, self-insurance plans, and loss control and safety programs; and copies of policy statements, job descriptions, contractual arrangements, and indemnification clauses.

United States Conference of Mayors. 1620 Eye St., N. W., Washington, DC 20006. Phone: (202)293-7330 Fax: (202)293-2352 E-mail: info@usmayors. org • URL: http://www.usmayors.org • Promotes improved municipal government, with emphasis on federal cooperation.

OTHER SOURCES

Local Government Law. Chester J. Antieau. LexisNexis Matthew Bender. • $1,113.00. Six looseleaf volumes. Periodic supplementation. States the principle of law for all types of local governments, and backs those principles with case citations from all jurisdictions. Examines the laws and their impact in three primary cases.

MUSHROOM INDUSTRY

ALMANACS AND YEARBOOKS

Agricultural and Mineral Commodities Year Book. Available from Taylor & Francis Group. • Annual. $225.00. Published by Europa Publications. Contains descriptive product profiles, price data, export-import data, and production statistics for major commodities of the world. Includes commodity histories, uses, markets, demand trends, and information about trade agreements and key commodity organizations.

INTERNET DATABASES

USDA. United States Department of Agriculture. Phone: (202)720-2791 E-mail: agsec@usda.gov • URL: http://www.usda.gov • The USDA home page has six sections: News and Information; What's New; About USDA; Agencies; Opportunities; Search and Help. Keyword searching is offered from the USDA home page and from various individual agency home pages. Agencies are the Economic Research Service, Agricultural Marketing Service, National Agricultural Statistics Service, National Agricultural Library, and about 12 others. Updating varies. Fees: Free.

PERIODICALS AND NEWSLETTERS

Mushroom Journal. Mushroom Growers' Association. • Monthly. Membership.

Mushroom News. American Mushroom Institute. • Monthly. $275.00. Includes *News Flash.*

STATISTICS SOURCES

Agricultural Statistics. Available from U. S. Government Printing Office. • Annual. $38.00. Produced by the National Agricultural Statistics Service, U. S. Department of Agriculture. Provides a wide variety of statistical data relating to agricultural production, supplies, consumption, prices/price-supports, foreign trade, costs, and returns, as well as farm labor, loans, income, and population. In many cases, historical data is shown annually for 10 years. In addition to farm data, includes detailed fishery statistics.

FAO Production Yearbook. Available from Bernan Associates. • Annual. $45.00. Published by the Food and Agriculture Organization (http://www.fao.org). Contains worldwide data on agriculture, land use, farm crops, livestock, and agricultural prices.

FAO Trade Yearbook. Available from Bernan Associates. • Annual. $45.00. Published by the Food and Agriculture Organization (http://www.fao.org). Provides extensive worldwide data on exports and imports of agricultural commodities, fertilizers, tractors, and pesticides. Includes more than 130 tables of detailed statistics.

TRADE/PROFESSIONAL ASSOCIATIONS

American Mushroom Institute. Washington, D.C. Office, 1 Massachusetts Ave. NW, Ste. 800,

Washington, DC 20001. Phone: (202)842-4344 Fax: (202)408-7763 E-mail: ami@mwmlaw.com • URL: http://www.americanmushroom.org • Mushroom growers, processors, suppliers, and researchers united to promote the growing and marketing of cultivated mushrooms. Aims to: increase cultivated mushroom consumption; develop better and more economical methods of growing and marketing mushrooms; collect and disseminate the latest statistics and other information; foster research programs beneficial to the industry; aid members with any problems. Supports a short course on mushroom science at Penn State University and an international congress on mushroom science.

MUSIC INDUSTRY

See also: MUSICAL INSTRUMENTS INDUSTRY; PHONOGRAPH AND PHONOGRAPH RECORD INDUSTRIES

ABSTRACTS AND INDEXES

Music Index: A Subject-Author Guide to Music Periodical Literature. Harmonie Park Press. • Quarterly. $2,195.00 per year. Annual cummulation. Supplement available: *Music Index Subject Heading List.* Guide to current periodicals. Entries are in language of country issuing the index.

BIOGRAPHICAL SOURCES

Celebrity Register. Gale Cengage Learning. • 1990. $115.00. 90th edition. Compiled by Celebrity Services International (Earl Blackwell). Contains profiles of 1,300 famous individuals in the performing arts, sports, politics, business, and other fields.

Contemporary Musicians: Profiles of the People in Music. Available from Gale Cengage Learning. • Annual. $4,305.00. 41 volumes in print. $105.00 per volume.

DIRECTORIES

Billboard's International Buyer's Guide. VNU Business Media. • Covers: record companies; music publishers; record and tape wholesalers; services and supplies for the music-record-tape-video industry; record and tape dealer accessories, fixtures, and merchandising products; includes United States and over 65 other countries. Entries include: Company name, address, phone, names of principal executives, trade and brand names and/or list of products and services.

The Grey House Performing Arts Directory. Grey House Publishing. • Covers: More than 9,000 dance companies, instrumental music programs, opera companies, choral groups, theatre companies, performing arts series, and performing arts facilities. Entries include: Mailing address, telephone and fax numbers, e-mail addresses, Web sites, mission statement, key management contacts, and facility information such as capacity, season, and attendance.

Music Technology Buyer's Guide. United Entertainment Media. • $6.95. Annual. Lists more than 4,000 hardware and software music production products from 350 manufacturers. Includes synthesizers, MIDI hardware and software, mixers, microphones, music notation software, etc. Produced by the editorial staffs of *Keyboard* and *EQ* magazines.

Musical America International Directory of the Performing Arts. Commonwealth Business Media, Inc. • Annual. $115.00. Covers United States and Canada.

Peterson's Professional Degree Programs in the Visual and Performing Arts. Peterson's. • Annual. $21.95. A directory of more than 900 degree programs in art, music, theater, and dance at 600 colleges and professional schools.

Purchasers Guide to the Music Industries. Music Trades Corp. • Annual. Available with subscription to *Music Trades.*

Recording Industry Sourcebook. Thomson Course Technology PTR. • Covers: 14,000 contacts in the music industry in over 65 categories, including record producers, publishers, promoters, attorneys, major and independent record labels, and music production facilities. Entries include: Name, address, phone, fax, name and title of contact, subsidiary and branch names and locations, background information, email, web address.

ENCYCLOPEDIAS AND DICTIONARIES

Encyclopedia of Popular Music. Colin Larkin, editor. Available from Groves Dictionaries, Inc. • 1998. $500.00. Third edition. Eight volumes. Covers a wide variety of music forms and pop culture. Includes bibliography and index.

HANDBOOKS AND MANUALS

All You Need to Know About the Music Business: Revised and Updated for the 21st Century. Donald S. Passman. The Free Press. • 2003. $30.00. Covers the practical and legal aspects of record contracts, music publishing, management agreements, touring, and other music business topics.

Entertainment Law. Jeffrey A. Helewitz and Leah K. Edwards. Delmar Learning. • 2003. $52.95. (West Legal Studies).

Entertainment Law: Legal Concepts and Business Practices. West Group. • Annual. $560.00. Five looseleaf volumes.

Interactive Music Handbook: The Definitive Guide to Internet Music Strategies, Enhanced CD Production and Business Development. Jodi Summers. Allworth Press. • 1996. $19.95. Covers interactive or enhanced music CD-ROMs and online music for producers, audio technicians, and musicians. Includes case studies and interviews.

ONLINE DATABASES

PROMT: Predicasts Overview of Markets and Technology. Gale Cengage Learning. • Companies, products, applied technologies and markets. U.S. and international literature coverage, 1972 to date. Inquire as to online cost and availability. Provides abstracts from more than 1,600 publications. Weekly updates.

PERIODICALS AND NEWSLETTERS

Billboard: The International Newsweekly of Music, Video, and Home Entertainment. VNU Business Media. • 51 times a year. $299.00 per year. Newsweekly for the music and home entertainment industries.

BMI: Music World. Broadcast Music, Inc. • Quarterly. Free to qualified personnel. Formerly *BMI: The Many Worlds of Music.*

Cash Box: The International Music-Record Weekly. Cash Box Publishing Co., Inc. • Weekly. $185.00 per year.

Computer Music Journal. MIT Press. • Quarterly. Individuals, $77.00 per year; instutitions, $215.00 per year. Includes print and online editions. Covers digital sosund and the musical applications of computers.

Down Beat: Jazz, Blues and Beyond. Maher Publications, Inc. • Monthly. $34.95 per year. Contemporary music.

Entertainment Law and Finance. American Lawyer Media, Inc. • Monthly. $229.00 per year. Newsletter. Covers contracts, royalties, litigation, copyright, taxation, etc., for the music industry, motion pictures, broadcasting, publishing, video, and related media. (A Law Journal Newsletter, formerly published by Leader Publications.).

Entertainment Marketing Letter. EPM Communications Inc. • Description: Reports on techniques used in the marketing of films, music, videos, television, radio, and cable features. Covers tie-in campaigns, sponsorship, in-theatre advertising, and interactive telephone promotions.

EQ: The Project Recording and Sound Magazine. United Entertainment Media, Inc. • Monthly. $24.95 per year. Provides advice on professional music recording equipment and technique.

Mix Magazine: Professional Recording, Sound, and Music Production. Primedia Business Magazine and Media. • Monthly. $34.97 per year.

Music Inc. Maher Publications, Inc. • 11 times a year. $16.00. per year. Music and sound retailing. Formerly *Up Beat Monthly.*

Music Journal. Incorporated Society of Musicians. • Monthly. $60.00 per year.

Music Reference Services Quarterly. Haworth Press, Inc. • Quarterly. Institutions, $95.00 per year. An academic journal for music librarians.

Music Trades. Music Trades Corp. • Monthly. $14.00 per year. Includes *Purchaser's Guide to the Music Industries.*

Radio & Records. Radio & Records, Inc. • Weekly. $325.00 per year. Provides news and information relating to the record industry and to regional and national radio broadcasting. Special features cover specific types of programming, such as "classic rock," "adult alternative," "oldies," "country," and "news/talk." Radio station business and management topics are included.

Sound & Vision: Home Theater- Audio- Video-MultimediaMovies- Music. Hachette Filipacchi Media U.S., Inc. • 10 times a year. $24.00 per year. Popular magazine providing explanatory articles and critical reviews of equipment and media (CD-ROM, DVD, videocassettes, etc.). Supplement available *Stero Review's Sound and Vision Buyers Guide.* Replaces *Stereo Review* and *Video Magazine.*

STATISTICS SOURCES

U. S. Industry and Trade Outlook. Available from National Technical Information Service. • Annual. $69.95. Produced by the International Trade Administration, U. S. Department of Commerce, in a "public-private" partnership with DRI/McGraw-Hill and Standard & Poor's. Provides basic data, outlook for the current year, and "Long-Term Prospects" (five-year projections) for a wide variety of products and services. Includes high technology industries. Formerly *U. S. Industrial Outlook.*

TRADE/PROFESSIONAL ASSOCIATIONS

American Society of Composers, Authors and Publishers. One Lincoln Plaza, New York, NY 10023. Phone: (212)621-6000 Fax: (212)724-9064 E-mail: info@ascap.com • URL: http://www.ascap.com.

Broadcast Music, Inc. 320 W 57th St., New York, NY 10019-3790. Phone: (212)586-2000 Fax: (212)956-2059 E-mail: newyork@bmi.com • URL: http://bmi.com • Consists of more than 90,000 writers and 50,000 publisher affiliates. Acts as steward for the performing rights of the works of its affiliates by collecting license fees from music users and making payments to the creators of the music used (based on a published schedule of payments). Maintains reciprocal agreements with 41 sister licensing organizations worldwide.

Music Industry Conference. 1806 Robert Fulton Dr., 1806 Robert Fulton Dr., Reston, VA 20191. Phone: 800-336-3768 or (703)860-4000 Fax: (703)860-1531 E-mail: geobev@consolidated.net • URL: http://www.menc.org/industry • Instrument manufacturers, music publishers, music retailers, music textbook publishers, and other music-related suppliers. Facilitates communication between MENC: The National Association for Music Education (see separate entry) and the industry; provides displays of musical instruments, publications, and other music-related products for MENC conventions.

NAMM, The International Music Products Association. 5790 Armada Dr., Carlsbad, CA 92008. Phone: 800-767-6266 or (760)438-8001 Fax: (760)438-7327 E-mail: info@namm.com • URL: http://www.namm.com.

OTHER SOURCES

Keyboard: The World's Leading Music Technology Magazine. United Entertainment Media, Inc. • Monthly. $25.95 per year. Emphasis is on recording systems, keyboard technique, and computer-assisted music (MIDI) systems.

Lindey on Entertainment, Publishing and the Arts: Agreements and the Law. Alexander Lindey, editor. West Group. • $935.00 per year. Six looseleaf volumes. Periodic supplementation. Provides basic forms, applicable law, and guidance.

Phonolog. Muze, Inc. • Annual. $550.00. 10 volumes. Provides detailed information on more than 370,000 titles of commercially available and out-of-print music recordings. Includes popular, jazz, and classical titles.

MUSICAL INSTRUMENTS INDUSTRY

See also: MUSIC INDUSTRY

DIRECTORIES

Musical Merchandise Review: Directory of Musical Instrument Dealers. Larkin Publications LLC. • Annual. $125.00. Lists retailers of musical instruments and supplies.

Musical Merchandise Review: Music Industry Directory. Larkin Publications. • Annual. $25.00. Lists about 1,500 manufacturers and distributors of musical instruments and supplies. Includes indexes to products and trade names.

Purchasers.Guide to the Music Industries. Music Trades Corp. • Annual. Available with subscription to *Music Trades.*

FINANCIAL RATIOS

Annual Statement Studies. The Risk Management Association. • Annual. Median and quartile financial ratios are given for over 400 kinds of manufacturing, wholesale, retail, construction, and consumer finance establishments. Data is sorted by both asset size and sales volume. Includes a clearly written "Definition of Ratios" and an alphabetical industry index.

Annual Statement Studies: Industry Default Probabilities and Cash Flow Measures. The Risk Management Association. • Annual. $145.00. Serves as a companion volume to the original *Annual Statement Studies.* Gives probability of default estimates on a percentage scale for more than 450 industries. Includes changes in position year-by-year for eight financial statement line items and provides percentage measures of cash flow.

HANDBOOKS AND MANUALS

Sound Synthesis and Sampling. Martin Russ. Elsevier, Inc. • 2004. $44.95. Second edition. Covers "the underlying principles and practical techniques applied to both commercial and research synthesizers." Includes software examples, examples of representative instruments, a glossary, and a "jargon guide." (Imprint: Focal Press.).

PERIODICALS AND NEWSLETTERS

Electronic Musician. Primedia Business Magazines and Media. • Monthly. $23.97 per year.

Instrumentalist: A Magazine for School and College Band and Orchestra Directors, Professional Instrumentalist, Teacher-Training Specialists in Instrumental Music Education and Instrumental Teachers. The Instrumentalist Co. • Monthly. $22.00

per year. Professional journal for school band and orchestra directors and teachers of instruments in those ensembles.

Music and Sound Retailer: The Newsmagazine for Musical Instrument and Sound Product Merchandisers. Testa Communications, Inc. • Monthly. Free to qualified personnel; others, $18.00 per year. Provides news and advice on the retailing of a wide range of music and sound products, including musical instruments, electronic keyboards, sound amplification systems, music software, and recording equipment.

Music Trades. Music Trades Corp. • Monthly. $14.00 per year. Includes *Purchaser's Guide to the Music Industries.*

Musical Merchandise Review: Pianos, Musical Instruments, Organs, Accessories. Larkin Publications, Inc. • Monthly. $32.00 per year. Edited for musical instrument dealers selling pianos, organs, band/orchestra instruments, electronic keyboards, guitars, music amplifiers, microphones, sheet music, and other musical merchandise.

PRICE SOURCES

Guitars and Musical Instruments. Orion Research Corp. • Annual. $179.00. List of manufacturers of guitars and musical instruments. Original list prices and years of manufacture are also shown.

STATISTICS SOURCES

U. S. Industry and Trade Outlook. Available from National Technical Information Service. • Annual. $69.95. Produced by the International Trade Administration, U. S. Department of Commerce, in a "public-private" partnership with DRI/McGraw-Hill and Standard & Poor's. Provides basic data, outlook for the current year, and "Long-Term Prospects" (five-year projections) for a wide variety of products and services. Includes high technology industries. Formerly *U. S. Industrial Outlook.*

TRADE/PROFESSIONAL ASSOCIATIONS

American Music Conference. 5790 Armada Dr., Carlsbad, CA 92008-4391. Phone: 800-767-6266 or (760)431-9124 or (760)366-5260 Fax: (760)438-7327 E-mail: info@amc-music.org • URL: http://www.amc-music.org • Represents associations, companies, and individuals supported by instrument manufacturers, publishers, wholesalers and retailers, educators, music industry and educator associations and other interested individuals. Promotes the importance of music, music making and music education to the general public.

International Band and Orchestra Products Association. 262 W. 38th St., Room 1506, New York, NY 10018-5815. Phone: (212)302-0803 Fax: (212)302-0783 E-mail: assnhdqs@earthlink.net.

Music Distributors Association. 1026 Northwood Dr., 262 W 38th St., Rm. 1506, Effingham, IL 62401. Phone: (217)347-6699 Fax: (217)347-6699 E-mail: geobev@consolidated.net • URL: http://www.musicdistributors.org • International distributors and suppliers of musical instruments, sheet music, and allied merchandise; manufacturers of musical merchandise.

NAMM, The International Music Products Association. 5790 Armada Dr., Carlsbad, CA 92008. Phone: 800-767-6266 or (760)438-8001 Fax: (760)438-7327 E-mail: info@namm.com • URL: http://www.namm.com.

MUTUAL FUNDS

See: INVESTMENT COMPANIES

MUTUAL SAVINGS BANKS

See: SAVINGS BANKS

N

NAFTA

See: NORTH AMERICAN FREE TRADE
AGREEMENT

NARCOTICS

See also: DRUG ABUSE AND TRAFFIC;
PHARMACEUTICAL INDUSTRY

GENERAL WORKS

A Brief History of Cocaine. Steven B. Karch. CRC
Press LLC. • 1997. $29.95. Emphasizes the societal
effects of cocaine abuse in various regions of the
world.

*The Chemistry of Mind-Altering Drugs: History,
Pharmacology, and Cultural Context.* Daniel M.
Perrine. American Chemical Society. • 1996. $45.
00. Contains detailed descriptions of the
pharmacological and psychological effects of a wide
variety of drugs, "from alcohol to zopiclone.".

*Drugs, Alcohol, and Tobacco: Learning About Ad-
dictive Behavior.* Gale Cengage Learning. • 2002.
$295.00. Three volumes. Contains 200 articles on
various aspects of addiction. Includes color illustrations, a glossary, and comprehensive indexing.
(Macmillan Reference USA imprint.).

Drugs of Abuse. Available from U. S. Government
Printing Office. • 2003. $9.00. Issued by the Drug
Enforcement Administration, U. S. Department of
Justice (http://www.usdoj.gov). Provides detailed
information on various kinds of narcotics, depres-
sants, stimulants, hallucinogens, cannabis, steroids,
and inhalants. Contains many color illustrations and
a detailed summary of the Controlled Substances
Act.

ALMANACS AND YEARBOOKS

*Report of the International Narcotics Control Board
on Its Work.* United Nations Publications. • Annual.
$20.00.

CD-ROM DATABASES

*International Pharmaceutical Abstracts [CD-
ROM].* American Society of Health-System
Pharmacists. • Monthly. $1,795.00 per year.
Contains CD-ROM indexing and abstracting of
international pharmaceutical literature from 1970 to
date.

ENCYCLOPEDIAS AND DICTIONARIES

*Drugs and Controlled Substances: Information for
Students.* Gale Cengage Learning. • 2002. $115.00.
Arranged alphabetically by drug name. Provides
detailed information on the psychological and physi-
ological effects of addictive drugs and substances.

Includes illegal drugs, addictive prescription drugs,
and over-the-counter items.

*Encyclopedia of Drugs, Alcohol, and Addictive
Behavior.* Available from Gale Cengage Learning. •
2001. $425.00. Second edition. Four volumes.
Published by Macmillan Reference USA. Covers the
social, economic, political, and medical aspects of
addiction.

HANDBOOKS AND MANUALS

Drug Abuse and the Law Sourcebook. Victor G.
Haddox and Gerald G. Haddox. West Group. •
Annual. $419.00. Two looseleaf volumes. Covers
drugs of abuse, criminal responsibility, possessory
offenses, trafficking offenses, and related topics.
(Criminal Law Series).

Drug Abuse Handbook. Steven B. Karch, editor.
CRC Press LLC. • 1997. $129.95. Provides
comprehensive coverage of drug abuse issues and
trends. Edited for healthcare professionals.

Narcotics and Drug Abuse A to Z. Croner
Publications. • 1990. Three volumes. Price on
application. Lists treatment centers.

Substance Abuse: A Comprehensive Textbook. Joyce
Lowinson and others. Lippincott Williams and
Wilkins. • 1997. $179.00. Third edition. Covers the
medical, psychological, socioeconomic, and public
health aspects of drug and alcohol abuse.

ONLINE DATABASES

International Pharmaceutical Abstracts [online].
American Society of Health-System Pharmacists. •
Provides online indexing and abstracting of the
world's pharmaceutical literature from 1970 to date.
Monthly updates. Inquire as to online cost and
availability.

Pharmaceutical News Index. ProQuest Inc. •
Indexes major pharmaceutical industry newsletters,
1974 to present. Weekly updates. Inquire as to online cost and availability.

Toxline. National Library of Medicine. • Abstracting
service covering human and animal toxicity studies,
1965 to present (older studies available in *Toxback*
file). Monthly updates. Inquire as to online cost and
availability.

PERIODICALS AND NEWSLETTERS

Bulletin on Narcotics. United Nations Publications.
• Quarterly. $10.00 per issue. Editions in Chinese,
French, Russian and Spanish.

STATISTICS SOURCES

Narcotic Drugs: Estimated World Requirements.
International Narcotics Control Board. United Nations Publications. • Annual. $38.00. Includes
production and utilization data relating to legal
narcotics. Text in French, English and Spanish.

Psychotropic Substances. United Nations
Publications. • Annual. $42.00.

*Statistics on Alcohol, Drug, and Tobacco Use: A
Selection of Statistical Charts, Graphs and Tables
about Alcohol, Drug and Tobacco Use from a
Variety of Published Sources with Explanatory
Comments.* Gale Cengage Learning. • 1995. $85.00.
Includes graphs, charts, and tables arranged within
subject chapters. Citations to data sources are
provided. (Statistics on...Series: vol. 1).

TRADE/PROFESSIONAL ASSOCIATIONS

Health Connection. 55 W Oak Ridge Dr., Hagerstown, MD 21740. Phone: 800-548-8700 or
(301)393-3290 Fax: 888-294-8405 or 888-294-8405
E-mail: sales@healthconnection.org • URL: http://
www.healthconnection.org • Promotes nationwide
education for the prevention of drug addiction and
alcoholism through direct mailings of materials to
schools, churches, and civic organizations.
Participates, through exhibits, in conferences and
conventions of teachers and school personnel.

OTHER SOURCES

Defense of Narcotics Cases. David Bernheim. LexisNexis Matthew Bender. • $696.00. Three looseleaf
volumes. Periodic supplementation. Up-to-date
coverage of all aspects of narcotics cases and related
matters.

NATIONAL ACCOUNTING

See also: ECONOMIC POLICY; ECONOMIC
STATISTICS; ECONOMICS

ABSTRACTS AND INDEXES

Social Sciences Index. H. W. Wilson Co. • Quarterly,
with annual cumulation. Price varies. Indexes more
than 400 periodicals covering economics,
environmental policy, government, insurance, labor,
health care policy, plannning, public administration,
public welfare, urban studies, women's issues,
criminology, and related topics.

ALMANACS AND YEARBOOKS

*National Accounts Statistics: Main Aggregates and
Detailed Tables.* United Nations Publications. •
Annual. $160.00.

CD-ROM DATABASES

EconLit. Available from SilverPlatter Information,
Inc. • Monthly. Single-user, $1,600.00 per year.
Provides CD-ROM citations, with abstracts, to
articles from more than 500 economics journals.
Time period is 1969 to date. Produced by the
American Economic Association.

OECD Statistical Compendium. Organization for

Economic Cooperation and Development. • Semiannual. $1,905.00 per year for 1 to 10 users. CD-ROM contains more than 730,000 monthly, quarterly, and annual time series for OECD countries, 1960 to date. Includes fully searchable data on agriculture, food, economic indicators, national accounts, employment, energy, finance, industry, technology, and foreign trade. Results can be displayed in various forms.

Social Sciences Citation Index. ISI. • Monthly. Price on request. Provides CD-ROM indexing of articles appearing in 1700 leading social science journals worldwide, with additional selections from more than 5700 other journals. Time span is 1992 to date. Coverage includes economics, business, finance, management, communications, demographics, library and information science, political science, sociology, and many other subjects.

Social Sciences Citation Index: Compact Disc Edition with Abstracts. Institute for Scientific Information. • Monthly. Provides CD-ROM indexing and abstracting of "significant articles" from 1,700 social science journals worldwide, with additional selections from 3,200 other journals, 1986 to date. Includes economics, business, finance, management, communications, demographics, information and library science, political science, sociology, and many other subjects.

WILSONDISC: Wilson Social Sciences Abstracts. H. W. Wilson Co. • Monthly. Includes unlimited online access to *Social Sciences Index* through WILSONLINE. Provides CD-ROM indexing from 1983 and abstracting from 1994 of more than 500 periodicals covering economics, area studies, community health, public administration, public welfare, urban studies, and many other topics related to the social sciences.

ENCYCLOPEDIAS AND DICTIONARIES

System of National Accounts Glossary. Organization for Economic Cooperation and Development. • 2000. $24.00. Contains "precise definitions of the terms commonly used in national accounting.".

INTERNET DATABASES

Business 2.0 Web Guide to the Best Business Links. Business 2.0 Media Inc. Phone: (415)293-4800 E-mail: support@business2.com • URL: http://www.business2.com/webguide • Web site presents an extensive, searchable directory of links to "the best, most informative, and authoritative web pages." Twenty main categories cover business, finance, career, company information, people, and technology topics, with thousands of subtopics, all linking to Web sites recommended by experienced business researchers. Fees: Free.

Fedstats. Federal Interagency Council on Statistical Policy. Phone: (202)395-7254 • URL: http://www.fedstats.gov • Web site features an efficient search facility for full-text statistics produced by more than 100 federal agencies, including the Census Bureau, the Bureau of Economic Analysis, and the Bureau of Labor Statistics. Boolean searches can be made within one agency or for all agencies combined. Links are offered to international statistical bureaus, including the UN, IMF, OECD, UNESCO, Eurostat, and 20 individual countries. Fees: Free.

FreeLunch.com. Economy.com, Inc. Phone: (610)696-8700 Fax: (610)696-1678 • URL: http://www.freelunch.com • Web site provides free access to more than 1.5 million economic and financial data series, covering industry, demographics, labor markets, prices, retail sales, government spending, trade, interest rates, housing starts, the stock market, and many other topics. Data is available for various time periods in either chart or table form. Searching is offered. Fees: Free, but registration required. Economy.com, Inc. also offers fee-based economic analysis at *The Dismal Scientist* site (http://www.dismal.com).

U. S. Census Bureau: The Official Statistics. U. S. Bureau of the Census. Phone: (301)763-4100 Fax: (301)763-4794 • URL: http://www.census.gov • Web site is "Your Source for Social, Demographic, and Economic Information." Contains "Current U. S. Population Count," "Current Economic Indicators," and a wide variety of data under "Other Official Statistics." Keyword searching is provided. Fees: Free.

ONLINE DATABASES

EconLit. American Economic Association. • Covers the worldwide literature of economics as contained in selected monographs and about 550 journals. Subjects include microeconomics, macroeconomics, economic history, inflation, money, credit, finance, accounting theory, trade, natural resource economics, and regional economics. Time period is 1969 to present, with monthly updates. Inquire as to online cost and availability.

Wilson Social Sciences Abstracts Online. H. W. Wilson Co. • Provides online abstracting and indexing of more than 500 periodicals covering area studies, community health, public administration, public welfare, urban studies, and many other social science topics. Time period is 1994 to date for abstracts and 1983 to date for indexing, with updates weekly. Inquire as to online cost and availability.

STATISTICS SOURCES

Business Statistics of the United States. Linz Audain and Cornelia J. Strawser. Bernan Associates. • Annual. $147.00. Based on *Business Statistics*, formerly issue by the Bureau of Economic Analysis, U. S. Department of Commerce. Provides basic data for a wide variety of U. S. industries, services, and economic indicators. Most statistics are shown annually for 30 years and monthly for the most recent four years.

Datapedia of the United States: American History in Numbers. George T. Kurian, editor. Bernan Press. • 2004. $125.00. Third edition. Based on the Census Bureau publication, *Historical Statistics of the United States*. Provides data from Colonial times to the present on agriculture, business, consumer income, energy, finance, labor, national income, population, and many other subjects. Includes "narrative highlights," maps, charts, and statistical projections.

Monthly Bulletin of Statistics. United Nations Publications. • Monthly. $295.00 per year. Provides current data for about 200 countries on a wide variety of economic, industrial, and demographic subjects. Compiled by United Nations Statistical Office.

National Accounts of OECD Countries. OECD Publications and Information Center. • Annual. Two volumes. Price varies.

Quarterly National Accounts. OECD Publications and Information Center. • Quarterly. $125.00 per year. National accounts data of OECD countries.

Social Statistics of the United States. Mark S. Littman, editor. Bernan Press. • 2000. $65.00. Includes statistical data on population growth, labor force, occupations, environmental trends, leisure time use, income, poverty, taxes, and other economic or demographic topics.

Statistical Abstract of the United States. Available from U. S. Government Printing Office. • Annual. $51.00. Issued by the U. S. Bureau of the Census.

A Statistical Portrait of the United States: Social Conditions and Trends. Mark S. Littman, editor. Bernan Press. • 1998. $89.00. Covers "social, economic, and environmental trends in the United States over the past 25 years." Includes statistical tables, graphs, and analysis relating to such topics as population, income, poverty, wealth, labor, housing, education, healthcare, air/water quality, and government. (Statistical Portrait of the United States: Social Conditions and Trends Series)

Statistical Yearbook. United Nations Publications. • Annual. $125.00. Contains statistics for about 200 countries on a wide variety of economic, industrial, and demographic topics. Compiled by United Nations Statistical Office.

Survey of Current Business. Available from U. S. Government Printing Office. • Monthly. $63.00 per year. Issued by Bureau of Economic Analysis, U. S. Department of Commerce. Presents a wide variety of business and economic data.

NATIONAL BRANDS

See: TRADEMARKS AND TRADE NAMES

NATIONAL DEBT

See also: FEDERAL BUDGET

GENERAL WORKS

Financial Institutions and Markets. Meir J. Kohn. Oxford University Press, Inc. • 2003. $115.00. Second edition.

OECD Public Debt Markets: Trends and Recent Structural Changes. Organization for Economic Cooperation and Development. • 2002. $49.00. Provides information on North American, Asian-Pacific, and European government bond markets. Contains chapters on individual countries, with discussion of debt management policies and techniques.

ABSTRACTS AND INDEXES

Business Periodicals Index. H. W. Wilson Co. • 11 times a year. Quarterly and annual cumulations. Price varies.

Readers' Guide to Periodical Literature. H. W. Wilson Co. • Monthly. $345.00 per year. Includes annual *Cumulation*. Indexes about 250 peridicals of general interest.

CD-ROM DATABASES

International Development Statistics. Organization for Economic Cooperation and Development. • Annual. $71.00. Issued by the OECD Development Assistance Committee. CD-ROM contains data on aid to more than 180 recipient countries, including amount, origin, type, and recipients' external debt.

OECD Statistical Compendium. Organization for Economic Cooperation and Development. • Semiannual. $1,905.00 per year for 1 to 10 users. CD-ROM contains more than 730,000 monthly, quarterly, and annual time series for OECD countries, 1960 to date. Includes fully searchable data on agriculture, food, economic indicators, national accounts, employment, energy, finance, industry, technology, and foreign trade. Results can be displayed in various forms.

INTERNET DATABASES

Business 2.0 Web Guide to the Best Business Links. Business 2.0 Media Inc. Phone: (415)293-4800 E-mail: support@business2.com • URL: http://www.business2.com/webguide • Web site presents an extensive, searchable directory of links to "the best, most informative, and authoritative web pages." Twenty main categories cover business, finance, career, company information, people, and technology topics, with thousands of subtopics, all linking to Web sites recommended by experienced business researchers. Fees: Free.

Fedstats. Federal Interagency Council on Statistical Policy. Phone: (202)395-7254 • URL: http://www.fedstats.gov • Web site features an efficient search facility for full-text statistics produced by more than 100 federal agencies, including the Census Bureau, the Bureau of Economic Analysis, and the Bureau of Labor Statistics. Boolean searches can be made within one agency or for all agencies combined.

Links are offered to international statistical bureaus, including the UN, IMF, OECD, UNESCO, Eurostat, and 20 individual countries. Fees: Free.

FreeLunch.com. Economy.com, Inc. Phone: (610)696-8700 Fax: (610)696-1678 • URL: http://www.freelunch.com • Web site provides free access to more than 1.5 million economic and financial data series, covering industry, demographics, labor markets, prices, retail sales, government spending, trade, interest rates, housing starts, the stock market, and many other topics. Data is available for various time periods in either chart or table form. Searching is offered. Fees: Free, but registration required. Economy.com, Inc. also offers fee-based economic analysis at *The Dismal Scientist* site (http://www.dismal.com).

ONLINE DATABASES

Readers' Guide Abstracts Online. H. W. Wilson Co. • Indexes and abstracts general interest periodicals, 1983 to date. Weekly updates. Inquire as to online cost and availability.

Wilson Business Abstracts Online. H. W. Wilson Co. • Indexes and abstracts 600 major business periodicals, plus the *Wall Street Journal* and the business section of the *New York Times*. Indexing is from 1982, abstracting from 1990, with the two newspapers included from 1993. Updated weekly. Inquire as to online cost and availability. (*Business Periodicals Index* without abstracts is also available online.).

PERIODICALS AND NEWSLETTERS

OMB Watcher (Office of Management and Budget). O M B Watch. • Bimonthly. Individuals, $35.00 per year. Monitors operations of the federal Office of Management and Budget.

RESEARCH CENTERS AND INSTITUTES

League of Women Voters Education Fund. 1730 M St., N. W., Suite 1000, Washington, DC 20036-4508. Phone: (202)429-1965 Fax: (202)429-0854 E-mail: lwv@lwv.org • URL: http://www.lwv.org • Research fields include federal deficit issues.

Tax Foundation. Tax Foundation. 2001 L St. NW, Ste. 1050, Washington, DC 20036. Phone: (202)464-6200 Fax: (202)464-6201 E-mail: hodge@taxfoundation.org • URL: http://www.taxfoundation.org • Fiscal and management aspects of federal, state, and local government, including studies on government expenditures, the federal budget, taxation, and international competitiveness. Serves as a national information agency for individuals and organizations concerned with problems of government expenditures, taxation, and debt.

STATISTICS SOURCES

The AIER Chart Book. AIER Research Staff. American Institute for Economic Research. • Annual. $4.00. A compact compilation of long-range charts ("Purchasing Power of the Dollar," for example, goes back to 1780) covering various aspects of the U. S. economy. Includes inflation, interest rates, debt, gold, taxation, stock prices, etc. (Economic Education Bulletin.).

Business Statistics of the United States. Linz Audain and Cornelia J. Strawser. Bernan Associates. • Annual. $147.00. Based on *Business Statistics,* formerly issue by the Bureau of Economic Analysis, U. S. Department of Commerce. Provides basic data for a wide variety of U. S. industries, services, and economic indicators. Most statistics are shown annually for 30 years and monthly for the most recent four years.

Combined Statement of Receipts, Outlays, and Balances of the United States Government. Available from U. S. Government Printing Office. • Annual. $54.00. Issued by the Financial Mangement Service, U. S. Treasury Department (http://www.fms.treas.gov). In three parts: "Fiscal Year Summary," "Details of Receipts," and "Details of Appropriations, Outlays, and Balances.".

Daily Treasury Statement: Cash and Debt Operations of the United States Treasury. Available from U. S. Government Printing Office. • Daily, except Saturdays, Sundays, and holidays. (Financial Management Service, U. S. Treasury Department.).

Economic and Budget Outlook: Fiscal Years 2004-2013. Available from U. S. Government Printing Office. • 2002. $27.00. Issued by the Congressional Budget Office (http://www.cbo.gov). Contains CBO economic projections and federal budget projections annually in billions of dollars. An appendix contains "Historical Budget Data" annually from, including revenues, outlays, deficits, surpluses, and debt held by the public.

Historical Tables, Budget of the United States Government. Available from U. S. Government Printing Office. • Annual. $41.00. Issued by the Office of Management and Budget, Executive Office of the President (http://www.whitehouse.gov). Provides statistical data on the federal budget for an extended period of about 60 years in the past to projections of four years in the future. Includes federal debt and federal employment.

Monthly Statement of the Public Debt of the United States. U. S. Dept. of the Treasury, Public Debt Bureau. Available from U. S. Government Printing Office. • Monthly. $42.00 per year.

Survey of Current Business. Available from U. S. Government Printing Office. • Monthly. $63.00 per year. Issued by Bureau of Economic Analysis, U. S. Department of Commerce. Presents a wide variety of business and economic data.

Treasury Bulletin. Available from U. S. Government Printing Office. • Quarterly. $45.00 per year. Issued by the Financial Management Service, U. S. Treasury Department. Provides data on the federal budget, government securities and yields, the national debt, and the financing of the federal government in general.

TRADE/PROFESSIONAL ASSOCIATIONS

Committee for a Responsible Federal Budget. 220 1/2 E St., NE, Washington, DC 20002. Phone: (202)547-4484 Fax: (202)547-4476 E-mail: crfb@aol.com • URL: http://www.crfb.org • Members are corporations and others seeking to improve the federal budget process.

Private Sector Council. 1100 New York Ave. NW, Ste. 1090 E, Washington, DC 20005. Phone: (202)775-9111 Fax: (202)775-8885 E-mail: bramati@ourpublicservice.org • URL: http://www.ourpublicservice.org/psc • Serves as a nonpartisan, public service organization dedicated to improving the productivity, efficiency, and management of the federal government through a cooperative sharing of knowledge between the public and private sectors.

NATIONAL HOLIDAYS

See: ANNIVERSARIES AND HOLIDAYS

NATIONAL INCOME

See: INCOME; NATIONAL ACCOUNTING

NATIONAL LABOR GROUP

OTHER SOURCES

Democracy International. • Seeks to build a movement of individuals dedicated to practical action on behalf of common commitments to human rights and pluralistic democracy including freedom of speech and press, religious liberty, free political parties, and the right to contest elections. Works to develop political and economic self-determination of citizens allowing them to control their resources, choose their social systems, and end discrimination. Aims to: revive democracy where it has been destroyed; encourage and sustain democrats trying to bring democracy to dictatorships. Calls upon democracies to: increase help for democratic leaders and politicians in the Third World; provide economic sustenance to relieve human suffering; strengthen democracy where it exists. Provides a forum for democrats to express solidarity and to help each other; encourages membership in an effort to build an international force of people working to make the cause of democracy an enduring ideal. Publicizes the efforts of democratic movements in dictatorships; attempts to increase the amount of uncensored information to closed societies. **Convention/Meeting:** none.

Environmental Action. • National political lobby organization. Prime focuses are: solid waste; toxic substances; recycling; global warming; utility policy; ozone and acid rain. Coordinated efforts on Clean Air Act, Clean Water Act, Occupational Safety and Health Act, Toxic Substances Control Act, Resource Conservation and Recovery Act in Congress, and Superfund. Engages in educational activities and community organizing. **Convention/Meeting:** none.

National Toxics Campaign. • National labor, environmental, and citizens' groups. Purposes are to: obtain support for stronger laws against chemical contamination through canvassing and petition drives in 280 congressional districts; monitor government enforcement practices; provide legislative advocacy. Goal is to win legislation and enforcement that guarantees all Americans the right to be safe from harmful exposure to toxic substances. Maintains speakers' bureau; compiles statistics.

Urban Environment Conference. • National labor, minority, and environmental organizations. Lobbies in Washington, DC, and at a grass roots level for strong environmental and occupational health laws. Offers educational programs to enable minorities, workers, and others to participate more effectively in decisions affecting their health and interests.

NATIONAL LABOR ORGANIZATION

OTHER SOURCES

International Union, UAW - Community Action Program. • Serves as a program of the International Union, United Automobile, Aerospace and Agricultural Implement Workers of America (UAW) (see separate entry). Informs UAW members through political education programs on topics including lobbying, the relationship between collective bargaining and the ballot box, and voluntary fundraising for political contributions. Maintains speakers' bureau; compiles statistics.

Political Department of the AFL-CIO. • AFL-CIO members and others interested in helping to elect progressive and pro-labor candidates to public office.

Twentieth Anniversary Mobilization. • Civil rights, labor, and peace organizations and others joined together in a national effort to concentrate on three key issues: jobs, peace, and freedom. Sponsored a March on Washington on Aug. 27, 1983 commemorating the 20th anniversary of Martin Luther King's "I Have a Dream" speech. Works for legislative passage designating January 15 as a national holiday honoring Martin Luther King's birthday. Promotes the work of the coalition on state and local levels.

NATIONAL PLANNING

See: ECONOMIC POLICY

NATIONAL PRODUCT

See: GROSS NATIONAL PRODUCT

NATIONS, LAW OF

See: INTERNATIONAL LAW AND REGULATION

NATURAL GAS

See also: GAS INDUSTRY; PETROLEUM INDUSTRY; PROPANE AND BUTANE GAS INDUSTRY

ALMANACS AND YEARBOOKS

Agricultural and Mineral Commodities Year Book. Available from Taylor & Francis Group. • Annual. $225.00. Published by Europa Publications. Contains descriptive product profiles, price data, export-import data, and production statistics for major commodities of the world. Includes commodity histories, uses, markets, demand trends, and information about trade agreements and key commodity organizations.

DIRECTORIES

Brown's Directory of North American and International Gas Companies. Advanstar Communications. • Annual. $345.00.

Financial Times Business Global Oil & Gas Directory. Available from Gale Cengage Learning. • Annual. $355.00. Published by Financial Times Business. Provides detailed information on 800 leading oil and gas companies worldwide. Includes financial data for three years. Formerly *Financial Times Energy Yearbook: Oil & Gas.*

Refining and Gas Processing Industry Worldwide. Midwest Publishing Co. • Annual. $145.00. Over 5,200 refineries, gas processing plants, engineering contractors, equipment manufacturers, supply companies and liquid terminals. Formerly *Refining and Gas Processing.*

ENCYCLOPEDIAS AND DICTIONARIES

Encyclopedia of Energy. Cutler J. Cleveland, editor. Elsevier, Inc. • 2004. $1,560.00. Six volumes. Covers all aspects of energy sources and energy-related environmental issues.

HANDBOOKS AND MANUALS

Modern Petroleum Technology. Richard A. Dawe, editor. John Wiley and Sons, Inc. • 2000. $600.00. Sixth edition. Two volumes. Volume one, entitled *Upstream,* covers oil rigs and other means of obtaining raw petroleum. Volume two, *Downstream,* covers petroleum refining and end products. Edited for industry technicians, managers, and engineers.

ONLINE DATABASES

Tulsa (Petroleum Abstracts). Information Services. • Worldwide literature in the petroleum and natural gas areas, 1965 to present. Inquire as to online cost and availability. Includes petroleum exploration patents. Updated weekly.

PERIODICALS AND NEWSLETTERS

American Gas. American Gas Association. • 11 times a year. $59.00 per year. Formerly *AGA Monthly.*

Energy and Fuels. American Chemical Society. • Bimonthly. Institutions, $852.00 per year; others, price on application. An interdisciplinary technical journal covering non-nuclear energy sources:

petroleum, gas, synthetic fuels, etc.

Gas Digest: The Magazine of Gas Operations. T-P Graphics. • Quarterly. Free. Articles and data relating to operations and management phases of natural gas operations.

Gas Utility Manager. James Informational Media, Inc. • Monthly. $24.00 per year. Formerly *Gas Utility and Pipeline Industries.*

Natural Gas and Electricity: The Monthly Journal for Producers, Marketers, Pipels and End Users. John Wiley and Sons, Inc. • Monthly. Institution, $949.00 per year. Newsletter. Covers business, economic, regulatory, and high-technology news relating to the natural gas industry.

Natural Gas Week. Energy Intelligence Group Inc. • Description: Covers natural gas economics, news, and analysis of gas/electric convergence.

The Oilman Weekly Newsletter. PennWell Corp., Petroleum Div. • Weekly. $1,990.00 per year. Newsletter. Provides news of developments concerning the North Sea and European oil and gas businesses. Each issue contains four pages of statistical data.

PRICE SOURCES

AGA Rate Service. American Gas Association. • Semiannual. Members, $175.00 per year; non-members, $300.00 per year. Looseleaf service.

Energy Prices and Taxes. International Energy Agency. OECD Publications and Information Center. • Quarterly. $385.00 per year. Includes print and online edition. Compiled by the International Energy Agency. Provides data on prices and taxation of petroleum products, natural gas, coal, and electricity. Diskette edition, $800.00. (Published in Paris).

Energy Prices and Taxes. Organization for Economic Cooperation and Development. • Quarterly. $355.00 per year. Includes both industrial and consumer prices for oil products, natural gas, coal, and electricity in various countries. (Also available on CD-ROM.).

RESEARCH CENTERS AND INSTITUTES

Canadian Energy Research Institute. Canadian Energy Research Institute. 3512 33rd St. NW, No. 150, Calgary, AB, Canada T2L 2A6. Phone: (403)282-1231 Fax: (403)284-4181 E-mail: mmasri@ceri.ca • URL: http://www.ceri.ca • Economic issues relating to all forms of energy, including oil, natural gas, coal, nuclear and hydroelectric power, and alternative energy sources. Develops software such as the World Oil Market Model.

STATISTICS SOURCES

Annual Energy Outlook [year], with Projections to [year]. Available from U. S. Government Printing Office. • Annual. $42.00. Issued by the Energy Information Administration, U. S. Department of Energy (http://www.eia.doe.gov). Contains detailed statistics and 20-year projections for electricity, oil, natural gas, coal, and renewable energy. Text provides extensive discussion of energy issues and "Market Trends.".

Annual Energy Review. Available from U. S. Government Printing Office. • Annual. $51.00. Issued by the Energy Information Administration, Office of Energy Markets and End Use, U. S. Department of Energy. Presents long-term historical as well as recent data on production, consumption, stocks, imports, exports, and prices of the principal energy commodities in the U. S.

Energy Balances of OECD Countries. Organization for Economic Cooperation and Development. Available from OECD Publications and Information Center. • Annual. $115.00. Presents two-year data on the supply and consumption of solid fuels, oil, gas, and electricity, expressed in oil equivalency

terms. Historical tables are also provided. Relates to OECD member countries.

Gas Facts: A Statistical Record of the Gas Utility Industry. American Gas Association, Dept. of Statistics. • Annual. Members, $40.00; non-members, $80.00.

Infrastructure Industries USA. Gale Cengage Learning. • 2001. $260.00. Presents statistics and projections relating to economic activity in a wide variety of natural resource and construction industries.

International Energy Annual. Available from U. S. Government Printing Office. • Annual. $34.00. Issued by the Energy Information Administration, U. S. Department of Energy. Provides production, consumption, import, and export data for primary energy commodities in more than 200 countries and areas. In addition to petroleum products and alcohol, renewable energy sources are covered (hydroelectric, geothermal, solar, and wind).

Monthly Energy Review. Available from U. S. Government Printing Office. • Monthly. $126.00 per year. Issued by the Energy Information Administration, Office of Energy Markets and End Use, U. S. Department of Energy. Contains current and historical statistics on U. S. production, storage, imports, and consumption of petroleum, natural gas, and coal.

Natural Gas Information. Organization for Economic Cooperation and Development. • Annual. $150.00. Includes international statistics relating to natural gas reserves, storage capacity, prices, consumption, trade, and pipelines. Contains detailed data for individual countries. (Also available on CD-ROM.).

Natural Gas Monthly. Energy Information Administration. Available from U.S. Government Printing Office. • Monthly. State and national data on production, storage, imports, exports and consumption of natural gas.

Oil, Gas, Coal, and Electricity: Quarterly Statistics. Organization for Economic Cooperation and Development. • Quarterly. $355.00 per year. Provides detailed data for OECD countries. Covers crude oil, nine oil product groups, hard coal, brown coal (lignite), natural gas, and electric power.

Petroleum Supply Annual. Available from U. S. Government Printing Office. • Annual. $78.00. Two volumes. Produced by the Energy Information Administration, U. S. Department of Energy. Contains worldwide data on the petroleum industry and petroleum products.

Petroleum Supply Monthly. Available from U. S. Government Printing Office. • Monthly. Produced by the Energy Information Administration, U. S. Department of Energy. Provides worldwide statistics on a wide variety of petroleum products. Covers production, supplies, exports and imports, transportation, refinery operations, and other aspects of the petroleum industry.

Standard & Poor's Industry Surveys. Standard & Poor's. • Semiannual. $1,800.00. Two looseleaf volumes. Includes monthly *Supplements.* Provides detailed, individual surveys of 52 major industry groups. Each survey is revised on a semiannual basis. Also includes "Monthly Investment Review" (industry group investment analysis) and monthly "Trends & Projections" (economic analysis).

U. S. Industry and Trade Outlook. Available from National Technical Information Service. • Annual. $69.95. Produced by the International Trade Administration, U. S. Department of Commerce, in a "public-private" partnership with DRI/McGraw-Hill and Standard & Poor's. Provides basic data, outlook for the current year, and "Long-Term Prospects" (five-year projections) for a wide variety of products and services. Includes high technology industries. Formerly *U. S. Industrial Outlook.*

WEFA Industrial Monitor. John Wiley and Sons, Inc. • Annual. $65.00. Prepared by industry analysts at WEFA, an economic forecasting and consulting firm (originally Wharton Econometric Forecasting Associates). Contains discussions of the outlook for major U. S. industries, with many 10-year forecasts (WEFA Web site is http://www.wefa.com).

TRADE/PROFESSIONAL ASSOCIATIONS

American Gas Association. 400 N Capitol St. NW, Ste. 450, Washington, DC 20001. Phone: (202)824-7000 Fax: (202)824-7115 E-mail: dparker@aga.org • URL: http://www.aga.org • Advocates for local natural gas utility companies; provides a broad range of programs and services for member natural gas pipelines, marketers, gatherers, international gas companies and industry associates.

Gas Technology Institute. 1700 S Mt. Prospect Rd., Des Plaines, IL 60018-1804. Phone: (847)768-0500 Fax: (847)768-0501 E-mail: businessdevelopmentinfo@gastechnology.org • URL: http://www.gastechnology.org • Educational and research facility sponsored by companies engaged in the production, processing, transmission, and distribution of natural gas and related fuels; engineering firms; large energy consumers. Conducts contract research for government and industry in the field of non-nuclear energy technology. Offers short courses in gas production, transmission, distribution, economics, and marketing. Sponsors symposia on current topics in non-nuclear energy.

Interstate Natural Gas Association of America. 10 G St., NE, Ste. 700, Washington, DC 20002. Phone: (202)216-5900 Fax: (202)216-0877 • URL: http://www.ingaa.org • Formerly Independent Natural Gas Association of America.

Natural Energy Services Association. 6430 F.M. 1960 W, No. 213, Houston, TX 77069. Phone: (713)856-6525 Fax: (713)856-6199 E-mail: trice@nesanet.org • URL: http://www.nesanet.org.

NATURAL RESOURCES

See also: FOREST PRODUCTS; GAS INDUSTRY; MINES AND MINERAL RESOURCES; PETROLEUM INDUSTRY; RECYCLING

GENERAL WORKS

The New Economy of Nature: The Quest to Make Conservation Profitable. Gretchen E. Daily and Katherine Ellison. Island Press. • 2002. $25.00. Presents the stories of various individuals who successfully combined the profit motive with conservation of the environment.

ALMANACS AND YEARBOOKS

Environmental Viewpoints. Gale Cengage Learning. • 1993. $195.00. Three volumes. $65.00 per volume. A compendium of excerpts of about 200 articles on a wide variety of environmental topics, selected from both popular and professional periodicals. Arranged alphabetically by topic, with a subject/keyword index.

Gale Environmental Almanac. Gale Cengage Learning. • 1993. $115.00. Contains 15 chapters, each on a broad topic related to the environment, such as "Waste and Recycling." Each chapter has a topical overview, charts, statistics, and illustrations. Includes a glossary of environmental terms and a bibliography.

BIBLIOGRAPHIES

Resources for the Future: An International Annotated Bibliography. Alan J. Mayne. Greenwood Publishing Group, Inc. • 1993. $83.50. (Bibliographies and Indexes in Economics and Economic History Series, No 13).

BIOGRAPHICAL SOURCES

World Who is Who and Does What in Environment and Conservation. Nicholas Polunin and Lynn M. Curme. Stylus Publishing, LLC. • 1997. $95.00. Provides biographies of 1,300 individuals considered to be leaders in environmental and conservation areas.

CD-ROM DATABASES

Environment Abstracts on CD-ROM. LEXIS-NEXIS. • Quarterly. $1,295.00 per year. Contains the following CD-ROM databases: *Environment Abstracts, Energy Abstracts,* and *Acid Rain Abstracts.* Length of coverage varies.

DIRECTORIES

Conservation Directory: A Listing of Organizations, Agencies and Officials Concerned with Natural Resource Use and Management. National Wildlife Federation. • Annual. $70.00. Lists agencies and private organizations in U.S. and Canada concerned with conservation and natural resource management.

ENCYCLOPEDIAS AND DICTIONARIES

Encyclopedia of Global Change: Environmental Change and Human Society. Andrew S. Goudie, editor. Oxford University Press. • 2001. $275.00. Two volumes. Contains 300 signed articles on a wide variety of topics relating to changes in the environment and the atmosphere. Includes bibliographies and illustrations.

Environmental Encyclopedia. Gale Cengage Learning. • 2003. $275.00. Third edition. Provides over 1,300 articles on all aspects of the environment. Written in non-technical style.

HANDBOOKS AND MANUALS

Statistics for the Environment: Statistical Aspects of Health and the Environment. Vic Barnett and others. John Wiley and Sons, Inc. • 1999. $180.00. Two volumes. Vol. 3, $205.00; vol. 4, $225.00. Contains articles on the statistical analysis and interpretation of environmental monitoring and sampling data. Areas covered include meteorology, pollution of the environment, and forest resources. (Statistics for the Environment Series).

INTERNET DATABASES

U. S. Census Bureau: The Official Statistics. U. S. Bureau of the Census. Phone: (301)763-4100 Fax: (301)763-4794 • URL: http://www.census.gov • Web site is "Your Source for Social, Demographic, and Economic Information." Contains "Current U. S. Population Count," "Current Economic Indicators," and a wide variety of data under "Other Official Statistics." Keyword searching is provided. Fees: Free.

PERIODICALS AND NEWSLETTERS

Energy Conservation News. BCC Research. • Description: Designed to give the industrial energy manager an inside view into current conservation innovations and events in the industrial sector. Covers such topics as effective conservation programs, solar and other energy alternatives, energy efficient building design, financing, utility industry developments, and energy legislation and controls.

Environmental Business Journal: Strategic Information for a Changing Industry. Environmental Business International, Inc. • Monthly. $495.00 per year. Newsletter. Includes both industrial and financial information relating to individual companies and to the environmental industry in general. Covers air pollution, wat es, U. S. Department of Health and Human Services. Provides conference, workshop, and symposium proceedings, as well as extensive reviews of environmental prospects.

The Natural Resources Journal. University of New Mexico, School of Law. • Quarterly. $40.00 per year.

Resources Policy; The International Journal on the Economics, Planning and Use of Non-Renewable Resources. Elsevier. • Quarterly. Institutions, $789.00 per year.

World Environment Report: News and Information on International Resource Management. Business Publishers, Inc. • Biweekly. $494.00 per year. Newsletter on international developments having to do with the environment, energy, pollution control, waste management, and toxic substances.

RESEARCH CENTERS AND INSTITUTES

Natural Resources Defense Council. Natural Resources Defense Council. 40 W 20th St., New York, NY 10011. Phone: (212)727-2700 Fax: (212)727-1773 E-mail: nrdcinfo@nrdc.org • URL: http://www.nrdc.org • Use of the judicial system to enforce environmental protection laws. Environmental policy studies, including studies related to public health and the environment, public lands and the coast, nuclear energy and weapons, energy conservation, and the global environment. Specific concerns include air quality, acid rain, airborne toxic pollutants, metropolitan air pollution, stratospheric ozone loss, solid waste disposal, water pollution, sewage treatment, industrial pollution, hazardous waste disposal, drinking water, pesticide policy, national forest management, agricultural resource conservation, public lands protection, irrigation policy, endangered species conservation, offshore oil leasing, shoreline protection, sea level rise, Nuclear Test Ban verification, nuclear weapons, environmental effects of nuclear production, nuclear winter, energy conservation, energy efficiency of appliances, energy efficient buildings, habitat protection, desertification, deforestation, wetlands conservation, international wildlife trade, international environmental treaties, Russian environmental law exchange, urban issues, environmental justice, Brownfield's redevelopment, and transportation.

STATISTICS SOURCES

Datapedia of the United States: American History in Numbers. George T. Kurian, editor. Bernan Press. • 2004. $125.00. Third edition. Based on the Census Bureau publication, *Historical Statistics of the United States.* Provides data from Colonial times to the present on agriculture, business, consumer income, energy, finance, labor, national income, population, and many other subjects. Includes "narrative highlights," maps, charts, and statistical projections.

Social Statistics of the United States. Mark S. Littman, editor. Bernan Press. • 2000. $65.00. Includes statistical data on population growth, labor force, occupations, environmental trends, leisure time use, income, poverty, taxes, and other economic or demographic topics.

Statistical Abstract of the United States. Available from U. S. Government Printing Office. • Annual. $51.00. Issued by the U. S. Bureau of the Census.

A Statistical Portrait of the United States: Social Conditions and Trends. Mark S. Littman, editor. Bernan Press. • 1998. $89.00. Covers "social, economic, and environmental trends in the United States over the past 25 years." Includes statistical tables, graphs, and analysis relating to such topics as population, income, poverty, wealth, labor, housing, education, healthcare, air/water quality, and government. (Statistical Portrait of the United States: Social Conditions and Trends Series).

TRADE/PROFESSIONAL ASSOCIATIONS

Friends of the Earth. 1025 Vermont Ave., N.W., Suite 300, Washington, DC 20005. Phone: 877-843-8687 or (202)783-7400 Fax: (202)783-0444 E-mail: foe@foe.org • URL: http://www.foe.org • Promotes protection of the environment and conservation of natural resources. Affiliated with Oceanic Society.

National Wildlife Federation. 11100 Wildlife Center Dr., Reston, VA 20190-5362. Phone: 800-822-9919 or (703)438-6000 E-mail: info@hdmanet.org • URL: http://www.nwf.org • Serves as a member-supported conservation group, with over four million members and supporters. Federation of state and territorial affiliates, associate members and individual conservationist-contributors. Seeks to educate, inspire and assist individuals and organizations of diverse cultures to conserve wildlife and other natural resources and to protect the earth's environment in order to achieve a peaceful, equitable and sustainable future. Encourages the intelligent management of the life-sustaining resources of the earth and promotes greater appreciation of wild places, wildlife and the natural resources shared by all. Publishes educational materials and conservation periodicals.

OTHER SOURCES

Energy Management and Federal Energy Guidelines. CCH, Inc. • Biweekly. $1,827.00 per year. Seven looseleaf volumes. Periodic supplementation. Reports on petroleum allocation rules, conservation efforts, new technology, and other energy concerns.

NAVAL LAW

See: MARITIME LAW AND REGULATION

NAVAL STORES

PERIODICALS AND NEWSLETTERS

Forest Chemicals Review. Kriedt Enterprises Ltd. • Bimonthly. $98.00 per year. Formerly *Naval Stores Review.*

NAVY

CD-ROM DATABASES

Leadership Library on CD-ROM: Who's Who in the Leadership of the United States. Leadership Directories, Inc. • Quarterly. Including access to Internet version (weekly updates). Contains all 14 *Yellow Book* personnel directories on CD-ROM, providing contact and brief biographical information for about 400,000 individuals. Covers business, government, financial institutions, news media, law firms, associations, foreign representatives, and nonprofit organizations. Includes photographs.

DIRECTORIES

Carroll's Federal & Federal Regional Directory. Carroll Publishing. • Semiannual. $325.00 per year; with online edition, $1,200 per year. Lists more than 23,000 U. S. government officials throughout the country, including military installations.

Carroll's Federal Regional Directory. Carroll Publishing. • Covers: Over 32,000 officials in federal congressional, judicial, and executive branch departments and agencies outside the District of Columbia. Entries include: Organization or agency name; names, addresses, and phone numbers of key personnel.

Directory of U.S. Military Bases Worldwide. William R. Evinger, editor. Greenwood Publishing Group, Inc. • 1998. $125.00. Third edition.

Federal Regional Yellow Book: Who's Who in the Federal Government's Departments, Agencies, Military Installations, and Service Academies Outside of Washington, DC. Leadership Directories, Inc. • Semiannual. $265.00 per year. Lists over 35,000 federal officials and support staff at 8,000 regional offices.

Jane's Fighting Ships. Jane's Information Group Ltd. • Covers: 164 navies of the world and ship details, weapons fits, specifications. Foreword includes an annual review of worldwide naval developments. Entries include: Major command personnel, diplomatic representatives, naval bases, shipyards, strength of fleets, etc. ; details of personnel and units; technical information about each type of ship, weapons fitted to each class.

Ships and Aircraft of the United States Fleet. U.S. Naval Institute. • Irregular. $85.00.

HANDBOOKS AND MANUALS

Division Officer's Guide. James Stavridis. Naval Institute Press. • 1995. $21.95. 10th revised edition.

Watch Officer's Guide: A Handbook for All Deck Watch Offices. James Stavridis. U.S. Naval Institute. • 1999. $21.95. 14th edition.

PERIODICALS AND NEWSLETTERS

All Hands: Magazine of the United States Navy. Available from U. S. Government Printing Office. • Monthly. $42.00 per year. Contains articles of general interest concerning the U. S. Navy (http://www.navy.mil).

Armed Forces Journal International. Armed Forces Journal International, Inc. • Monthly. $45.00 per year. A defense magazine for career military officers and industry executives. Covers defense events, plans, policies, budgets, and innovations.

Naval Affairs: In the Interest of the Enlisted Active Duty Reserve, and Retired Personnel of the U.S. Navy, Marine Corps and Coast Guard. Fleet Reserve Association. • Free to members; non-members, $7.00 per year.

Naval Aviation News. Chief of Naval Operations Bureau of Aeronautics. Available from U.S. Government Printing Office. • Bimonthly. $23.00 per year. Articles on all phases on Navy and Marine activity.

Naval Engineers Journal. American Society of Naval Engineers, Inc. • Bimonthly. $100 per year.

Naval Research Logistics: An International Journal. John Wiley and Sons, Inc. • Eight times a year. $1,235.00 per year; with online edition, $1,297.00 per year.

Naval Review: Annual Review of World Seapower. U.S. Naval Institute. • Annual. Price on application. Covers the previous year's events. May issue of *U.S. Naval Institute Proceedings.*

Navy Supply Corps Newsletter. Available from U. S. Government Printing Office. • Bimonthly. $30.00 per year. Newsletter issued by U. S. Navy Supply Systems Command. Provides news of Navy supplies and stores activities.

Navy Times: Marine Corps, Navy, Coast Guard. Army Times Publishing Co. • Weekly. $52.00 per year. In two editions: Domestic and International. *Supplement* available.

Sea Power. Navy League of the United States. • Monthly. Free to members; non-members $25.00 per year. Includes annual *Almanac of Seapower.*

STATISTICS SOURCES

Annual Report of the Secretary of Defense. U.S. Department of Defense, Office of the Secretary. • Annual.

Budget of the United States Government. U.S. Office of Management and Budget. Available from U.S. Government Printing Office. • Annual. $52.00.

TRADE/PROFESSIONAL ASSOCIATIONS

Fleet Reserve Association. 125 N West St., Alexandria, VA 22314-2709. Phone: 800-FRA-1924 or (703)683-1400 Fax: (703)549-6610 E-mail: news-fra@fra.org • URL: http://www.fra.org • Active duty enlisted personnel in the U.S. Navy, Marine Corps, Coast Guard, Fleet Reserves of the Navy, and Fleet Marine Corps and Coast Guard; retired members of these services.

Naval Historical Foundation. 1306 Dahlgren Ave. SE, Washington Navy Yard, Washington, DC 20374-5055. Phone: 888-880-0102 or (202)678-4333 or (202)678-4431 Fax: (202)889-3565 E-mail: nhfwny@navyhistory.org • URL: http://www.navyhistory.org • Dedicated to preserving and promoting the Navy's proud heritage, including the principal donation point for personal papers relating to naval history, a dynamic nationwide oral history program, a means for supporting the Navy's historical collections and programs, especially the Navy Museum. Provides historic research, and document and photo reproduction services.

Navy Club of the United States of America. 5473 S Jones Blvd., Ste. 1099, Las Vegas, NV 89118-0550. Phone: 800-628-7265 or (702)897-8729 Fax: (702)897-1939 E-mail: navyclubnet@cs.com • URL: http://www.navyclubusa.com.

Navy League of the United States. 2300 Wilson Blvd., Arlington, VA 22201. Phone: 800-356-5760 or (703)528-1775 Fax: (703)528-2333 E-mail: execdirector@navyleague.org • URL: http://www.navyleague.org.

United States Naval Institute. 291 Wood Rd., Annapolis, MD 21402. Phone: 800-233-8764 or (410)268-6110 Fax: (410)571-1703 E-mail: customer@usni.org • URL: http://www.navalinstitute.org • Regular, reserve, and retired professionals in the Navy, Marine Corps, and Coast Guard; civilians interested in the advancement of the knowledge of sea power and in advancing professional, literary, and scientific knowledge in the naval and maritime services. Conducts oral history and color print program.

OTHER SOURCES

Carroll's Defense Organization Charts. Carroll Publishing. • Every six weeks. $1,500.00 per year. Provides more than 200 large, fold-out paper charts showing personnel relationships in 2,400 U. S. military offices. Charts are also available online and on CD-ROM.

Department of the Navy Annual Report to the Congress. U.S. Department of the Navy. • Annual.

NEGOTIATION

See also: INDUSTRIAL RELATIONS

GENERAL WORKS

Bargaining Across Borders: How to Conduct Business Successfully Anywhere in the World. Dean A. Foster. McGraw-Hill. • 1992. $14.95. Includes a consideration of non-negotiable cultural differences.

Business Negotiating Basics: International Edition. Peter Economy. McGraw-Hill. • 1994. $13.95. (Briefcase Books Series).

Negotiation. Edward F. Sherman and others. Foundation Press. • 2001. $39.95. Second edition. (University Casebook Series).

Negotiation Basics: Concepts, Skills, and Exercises. Ralph A. Johnson. Sage Publications, Inc. • 1992. $77.95. Topics include goal building, the role of information, cost-benefit decision making, strategy, and creating a positive negotiating climate.

Win-Win Negotiating: Turning Conflict into Agreement. Fred E. Jandt. John Wiley and Sons, Inc. • 1987. $24.95. (Sound Business Cassette Books).

ABSTRACTS AND INDEXES

Index to Legal Periodicals and Books. H. W. Wilson Co. • Monthly. $490.00 per year. Quarterly and annual cumulations.

Personnel Management Abstracts. • Quarterly. $190.00 per year. Includes annual cumulation.

ENCYCLOPEDIAS AND DICTIONARIES

Blackwell Encyclopedic Dictionary of Strategic Management. Derek F. Channon, editor. Blackwell Publishing. • 1997. $128.95. The editor is associated with Imperial College, London. Contains definitions of key terms combined with longer articles written by various U. S. and foreign business educators. Includes bibliographies and index. (Blackwell Encyclopedia of Management Series.).

Field Guide to Negotiation: A Glossary of Essential

Tools and Concepts for Today's Manager. Gavin Kennedy. McGraw-Hill. • 1993. $29.95. Defines fundamental terms.

HANDBOOKS AND MANUALS

Game, Set, Match: Winning the Negotiations Game - A Step-by-Step Approach to Getting What You Want From Any Negotiation. Henry S. Kramer. American Lawyer Media, Inc. • 2001. $19.95. Contains examples of successful negotiation, imcluding "tips, tricks, and traps.".

Manager's Negotiating Answer Book. George Fuller. DIANE Publishing Co. • 1999. $40.00.

Negotiating and Influencing Skills: The Art of Creating and Claiming Value. Brad McRae. Sage Publications, Inc. • 1997. $79.95. Presents a practical approach to various circumstances, based on the Harvard Project on Negotiation. Chapters include "Dealing with Difficult People and Difficult Situations." Contains a bibliography and glossary of terms.

Negotiating for Business Results. Judith E. Fisher. McGraw-Hill. • 1993. $10.95. (Business Skills Express Series).

Negotiating to Settlement in Divorce. Sanford N. Katz, editor. Aspen Publishers, Inc. • $75.00. Looseleaf service. Periodic supplementation.

Selling Through Negotiation: The Handbook of Sales Negotiation. Homer B. Smith. Marketing Education Associates. • 1988. $14.95.

ONLINE DATABASES

Index to Legal Periodicals and Books (Online). H. W. Wilson Co. • Broad coverage of law journals and books 1981 to date. Monthly updates. Inquire as to online cost and availability.

Legal Resource Index. Gale Cengage Learning. • Broad coverage of law literature appearing in legal, business, and other periodicals, 1980 to date. Daily updates. Inquire as to online cost and availability.

LEXIS. LEXIS-NEXIS. • The various LEXIS databases provide full text and indexing for a wide variety of legal cases, statutes, orders, and opinions.

PERIODICALS AND NEWSLETTERS

Inside Negotiations. EFR Corp. • Monthly. $98.00 per year. Newsletter. Labor negotiations.

Negotiation Journal: On the Process of Dispute Settlement. Program on Negotiation. Blackwell Publishing. • Quarterly. $495.00 per year. Includes print and online editions.

RESEARCH CENTERS AND INSTITUTES

Center for Negotiation and Conflict Resolution. Rutgers University, Bloustein School of Planning and Public Policy, 33 Livingston Ave., Ste. 104, New Brunswick, NJ 08901-1981. Phone: (732)932-5475 • URL: http://www.policy.rutgers.edu/.

Harvard Negotiation Project. Harvard University. Harvard Law School, Pound Hall Room 500, Cambridge, MA 02138. Phone: (617)495-1684 Fax: (617)495-7818 E-mail: info@pon.law.harvard.edu • Seeks to improve the theory and practice of negotiation.

OTHER SOURCES

How to Negotiate the Sale from Start to Finish. American Management Association Extension Institute. • Looseleaf. $155.00. Self-study course. Emphasis is on practical explanations, examples, and problem solving. Quizzes and a case study are included.

NETWORKS, COMPUTER

See: COMPUTER COMMUNICATIONS; LOCAL AREA NETWORKS

NEW ISSUES (FINANCE)

GENERAL WORKS

Financial Institutions and Markets. Meir J. Kohn. Oxford University Press, Inc. • 2003. $115.00. Second edition.

Investing in IPOs: Version 2.0. Tom Taulli. Bloomberg. • 2001. $24.95. Second revised edition. Explains how individual investors can invest profitably in new stock offerings. (Bloomberg Personal Bookshelf Series).

Investing in the Over-the-Counter Markets: Stocks, Bonds, IPOs. Alvin D. Hall. John Wiley and Sons, Inc. • 1995. $29.95. Provides advice and information on investing in "unlisted" or NASDAQ (National Association of Securities Dealers Automated Quotation System) stocks, bonds, and initial public offerings (IPOs).

HANDBOOKS AND MANUALS

Cyberfinance: Raising Capital for the E-Business. Martin B. Robins. CCH, Inc. • 2001. $79.00. Covers the taxation, financial, and legal aspects of raising money for new Internet-based ("dot.com") companies, including the three stages of startup, growth, and initial public offering. (Solutions for Professional Advisers Series).

Financing the Corporation. Richard A. Booth. West Group. • Annual. $160.00. Looseleaf service. Covers a wide variety of corporate finance legal topics, from initial capital structure to public sale of securities.

Financing Your Small Business. Robert Walter. Barron's Educational Series, Inc. • 2004. $18.95. Explains various sources of capital for small businesses, including bank loans, venture capital, and initial public offerings of stock.

Going Public Handbook: Going Public, the Integrated Disclosure System, and Exempt Financing. Harold S. Bloomenthal. West Group. • 2003. $304.00. Covers public financing from initiation of underwriting to closing. (Securities Handbook Series).

Going Public in Good Times and Bad: A Legal and Business Guide. Robert G. Heim. American Lawyer Media, Inc. • 2002. $29.95. Provides practical advice for corporate officers and attorneys. Covers such items as underwriter selection, registration statements, relevant securities laws, and liability concerns. Contains examples of forms needed at various stages of taking a company public.

Initial Public Offerings: All You Need to Know About Taking a Company Public. David Sutton and M. William Benedetto. McGraw-Hill. • 1990. $24. 95. (Entrepreneur's Guide Series).

Securities: Public and Private Offerings, 2d. William W. Prifti. West Group. • Semiannual. $389.00. Three looseleaf volumes. How to issue securities. (Securities Law Series).

Small Business IPOs: From Concept to Closing. Robert W. Walter. CCH, Inc. • 2004. $85.00. Edited mainly for lawyers. Provides a step-by-step guide to taking a relatively small firm public. Covers use of investment bankers, valuation, letter of intent, due diligence, dealing with the SEC, and other topics. Appendices include samples of various forms, letters, and agreements.

INTERNET DATABASES

Business Week Online. McGraw-Hill. Phone: (212)512-2511 Fax: (684)842-6101 • URL: http://www.businessweek.com • Web site provides complete contents of current issue of *Business Week* plus "BW Daily" with additonal business news, financial market quotes, and corporate information from Standard & Poor's. Includes various features, such as "Banking Center" with mortgage and interest data, and "Interactive Computer Buying Guide." The "Business Week Archive" is fully searchable back to 1996.

IPOfn. IPO Financial Network. Phone: (973)379-5100 Fax: (973)379-1696 E-mail: info@ipofinancial.com • URL: http://www.ipofinancial.com • Web site provides free information on initial public offerings: "Pricing Recap" (price performance), "Calendar Update" (weekly listing of new offerings), "Company Roster" (Web sites), "Stock Brokers" (IPO dealers), and "Brokerage Firms" (underwriters). Fees: Basic data is free. Extensive analysis and recommendations are available through fee-based telephone, fax, and database services. Daily updates.

PERIODICALS AND NEWSLETTERS

The Bond Buyer. Veronis, Suhler and Associates Inc. • Daily edition, $1,897 per year. Weekly edition, $525.00 per year. Reports on new municipal bond issues.

Investment Dealers' Digest. Thomson Media. • Weekly. $750.00 per year. Covers financial news, trends, new products, people, private placements, new issues of securities, and other aspects of the investment business. Includes feature stories.

Medical Technology Stock Letter. Medical Technology Stock Letter. • Description: Specializes in investments in biotechnology companies. Offers news of the industry and recommendations for buying, selling, and holding stocks. Recurring features include news of research, a model portfolio reflecting the editors' investment strategy, and columns titled Pulse of the Market and Industry Scan. **Remarks:** Also available through e-mail.

Wallstreetlawyer.com: Securities in the Electronic Age. Glasser Legalworks. • Monthly. $345.00 per year. Newsletter. Covers the latest regulatory developments in capital raising, disclosure, and enforcement.

TRADE/PROFESSIONAL ASSOCIATIONS

National Association of Securities Dealers (NASD). 1735 K St., N.W., Washington, DC 20006-1506. Phone: (202)728-8000 Fax: (202)293-6260 E-mail: waltere@nasd.com • URL: http://www.nasd.com • Formerly National Association of Securities Dealers.

Securities Industry and Financial Markets Association. 120 Broadway, 35th Fl., New York, NY 10271-0080. Phone: (212)313-1200 Fax: (212)313-1301 E-mail: rbrockhaus@sifma.org • URL: http://www.sifma.org • Represents more than 650 member firms of all sizes, in all financial markets in the U.S. and around the world. Enhances the public's trust and confidence in the markets, delivering an efficient, enhanced member network of access and forward-looking services, as well as premiere educational resources for the professionals in the industry and the investors whom they serve. Maintains offices in New York City and Washington, DC.

OTHER SOURCES

Going Public and the Public Corporation. Harold S. Bloomenthal and Samuel Wolff. West Group. • Semiannual. $803.50 per year. Seven looseleaf volumes. Includes legal forms and documents. (Securities Law Series).

Initial Public Offerings. Glasser Legalworks. • Looseleaf. $225.00, including CD-ROM version. Periodic Supplementation. Includes explanations of legal procedures for IPOs, with annotated forms. (Emerging Growth Companies Series.).

NEW PRODUCTS

See also: INVENTIONS; PATENTS

HANDBOOKS AND MANUALS

Design and Marketing of New Products. Glen Urban and John R. Hauser. Prentice Hall PTR. • 1993. $120.00. Second edition.

Faster New Product Development: Getting the Right Product to Market Quickly. Milton D. Rosenau. AMACOM. • 1990. $55.00. A guide to new product development for companies of all sizes and kinds.

New Product Development and Marketing: A Practical Guide. Italo S. Servi. Greenwood Publishing Group, Inc. • 1990. $55.00. A practical guide to the creation, testing, and marketing of a new product.

New Product Development Checklists: From Mission to Market. George Gruenwald. McGraw-Hill. • 1994. $22.95. (NTC Business Books Series).

New Products Management. C. Merle Crawford and C. Anthony Di Benedetto. McGraw-Hill • 1999. $97.81. Sixth edition.

INTERNET DATABASES

InSite 2. Intelligence Data/Thomson Financial. Phone: 800-654-0393 or (617)856-1890 Fax: (617)737-3182 E-mail: intelligence.data@tfn.com • URL: http://www.insite2.gale.com/ • Fee-based Web site consolidates information in a "Base Pack" consisting of Business InSite, Market InSite, and Company InSite. Optional databases are Consumer InSite, Health and Wellness InSite, Newsletter InSite, and Computer InSite. Includes fulltext content from more than 2,500 trade publications, journals, newsletters, newspapers, analyst reports, and other sources. Continuous updating. Formerly produced by The Gale Group.

ONLINE DATABASES

New Product Announcements Plus. Gale Cengage Learning. • Contains the full text of new product and corporate activity press releases, with special emphasis on high technology and emerging industries. Covers 1985 to date. Weekly updates. Inquire as to online cost and availability.

PROMT: Predicasts Overview of Markets and Technology. Gale Cengage Learning. • Companies, products, applied technologies and markets. U.S. and international literature coverage, 1972 to date. Inquire as to online cost and availability. Provides abstracts from more than 1,600 publications. Weekly updates.

PERIODICALS AND NEWSLETTERS

Industrial Equipment News. Thomas Publishing Co., LLC. • Monthly. $65.00 per year. What's new in equipment, parts and materials.

International New Product Newsletter. International New Product Newsletter. • Description: Provides "advance news of new products and processes, primarily from sources outside the U.S." Emphasizes new products which can cut costs and improve efficiency. Recurring features include the column Special Licensing Opportunities which lists new products and processes that are available for manufacture under license, or are for sale or import.

Journal of Product Innovation Management: An International Publication of the Product Development and Management Association. Product Development and Management Association. Elsevier. • Bimonthly. $535.00 per year. Institutions. Includes print and online editions. Covers new product planning and development.

New Equipment Digest. Penton Media, Inc. • Monthly. Free to qualified personnel; others, $60.00 per year. Formerly *Material Handling Engineering.*

New Equipment Reporter: New Products Industrial News. De Roche Publications. • Monthly. Controlled circulation.

Potentials: Ideas and Products that Motivate. VNU Business Media. • Monthly. $59.00 per year. Covers incentives, premiums, awards, and gifts as related to promotional activities. Formerly *Potentials in Marketing.*

Product Design and Development. Reed Business Information. • Monthly. Free to qualified personnel; others, $114.90 per year.

NEW YORK STOCK EXCHANGE

See: STOCK EXCHANGES

NEWSLETTERS

See also: INVESTMENT ADVISORY SERVICES; PERIODICALS

CD-ROM DATABASES

MediaFinder CD-ROM: Oxbridge Directories of Print Media and Catalogs. Oxbridge Communications, Inc. • Quarterly. $1,995.00 per year. CD-ROM includes about 100,000 listings from *Standard Periodical Directory, National Directory of Catalogs, National Directory of British Mail Order Catalogs, National Directory of German Mail Order Catalogs, Oxbridge Directory of Newsletters, National Directory of Mailing Lists, College Media Directory,* and *National Directory of Magazines.*

DIRECTORIES

Books and Periodicals Online: The Guide to Business and Legal Information on Databases and CD-ROM's. Nuchine Nobari, editor. Library Technology Alliance, Ltd. • Annual. $379.00. Two volumes. 119,000 periodicals available as part of online and CD-ROM databases; international coverage.

Burrelle's Media Directory: Magazines and Newsletters. Burrelle's Information Services. • Annual. $550.00. Provides detailed descriptions of more than 13,500 magazines and newsletters published in the U. S., Canada, and Mexico. Categories are professional, consumer, trade, and college. Semiannual *Updates.* Includes CD-ROM.

The Directory of Business Information Resources: Associations, Newsletters, Magazine Trade Shows. Grey House Publishing, Inc. • Annual. $250.00. Provides concise information on associations, newsletters, magazines, and trade shows for each of 90 major industry groups. An "Entry & Company Index" serves as a guide to titles, publishers, and organizations.

Hudson's Subscription Newsletter Directory. Newsletter Clearinghouse. • Covers: about 4,800 newsletters available by subscription. Entries include: Title, publisher, parent company or institution, address, phone, fax, names of editor and publisher, frequency, subscription price, year founded, circulation, field or subjects.

Newsletters in Print. Gale Cengage Learning. • 2003. $315.00. 17th edition. Details 12,000 sources of information on a wide range of topics.

Oxbridge Directory of Newsletters. Oxbridge Communications, Inc. • Annual. $845.00. Lists approximately 20,000 newsletters in the United States and Canada.

SIE Investment Advisory Guide. George H. Wein, editor. Select Information Exchange. • Annual. $2.00. Provides descriptions and prices of about 100 financial newsletters covering stocks, bonds, mutual funds, commodity futures, options, gold, and foreign investments. Offers subscription services, including short trials of any 20 investment newsletters for a total of $11.95.

HANDBOOKS AND MANUALS

Creating Newsletters, Brochures, and Pamphlets: A How-To-Do-It Manual for Librarians. Barbara A. Radke and Barbara Stein. Neal-Schuman Publishers, Inc. • 1992. $39.95. Includes desktop publishing. (How-to-Do-It Manuals Series).

How to Produce Creative Advertising: Traditional Techniques and Computer Applications. Thomas Bivins and Ann Keding. McGraw Hill. • 1993. $37.95. Covers copywriting, advertising design, and the use of desktop publishing techniques in advertising.

(NTC Business Books Series).

How to Produce Creative Publications: Traditional Techniques and Computer Applications. Thomas Bivins and Ann Keding. McGraw-Hill. • 1993. $37.95. A practical guide to the writing, designing, and production of magazines, annual reports, brochures, and newsletters by traditional methods and by desktop publishing. (NTC Business Books Series).

Newsletter Publishing. Entrepreneur Media, Inc. • Looseleaf. $59.50. A practical guide to starting a newsletter. Covers profit potential, start-up costs, market size evaluation, pricing, accounting, advertising, promotion, etc. (Start-Up Business Guide No. E1067.).

Using Desktop Publishing to Create Newsletters, Library Guides, and Web Pages: A How-To-Do-It Manual for Librarians. John Maxymuk. Neal-Schuman Publishers, Inc. • 1997. $55.00. Includes more than 90 illustrations. (How-to-Do-It Manuals Series).

INTERNET DATABASES

PubList.com: The Internet Directory of Publications. Bowes & Associates, Inc. Phone: (781)792-0999 Fax: (781)792-0988 E-mail: info@publist.com • URL: http://www.publist.com • "The premier online global resource for information about print and electronic publications." Provides online searching for information on more than 150,000 magazines, journals, newsletters, e-journals, and monographs. Database entries generally include title, publisher, format, address, editor, circulation, subject, and International Standard Serial Number (ISSN). Fees: Free.

Ulrichsweb.com. R. R. Bowker. Phone: 888-269-5372 or (908)464-6800 Fax: (908)464-3553 E-mail: info@bowker.com • URL: http://www.ulrichsweb.com • Web site provides fee-based access to about 250,000 serials records from the *Ulrich's International Periodicals Directory* database. Includes periodical evaluations from *Library Journal* and *Magazines for Libraries.* Monthly updates.

ONLINE DATABASES

Gale Database of Publications and Broadcast Media. Gale Cengage Learning. • An online directory containing detailed information on over 67,000 periodicals, newspapers, broadcast stations, cable systems, directories, and newsletters. Corresponds to the following print sources: *Gale Directory of Publications and Broadcast Media; Directories in Print; City and State Directories in Print; Newsletters in Print.* Semiannual updates. Inquire as to online cost and availability.

Newsletter Database. Gale Cengage Learning. • Contains the full text of about 600 U. S. and international newsletters covering a wide range of business and industrial topics. Time period is 1988 to date, with daily updates. Inquire as to online cost and availability.

PERIODICALS AND NEWSLETTERS

Circulation Management. Media Central. • Monthly. $39.00 per year. Edited for circulation professionals in the magazine and newsletter publishing industry. Covers marketing, planning, promotion, management, budgeting, and related topics.

Hulbert Financial Digest. Hulbert Financial Digest. • Description: Provides performance ratings on more than 400 portfolios recommended by more than 145 financial newsletters, calculated on the basis of model portfolios constructed according to each newsletter's advice. Includes a timing scoreboard, analysis of newsletter performance, list of mutual funds most frequently recommended for sale or purchase, a stock market sentiment index, and a question and answer section.

Ideas Unlimited: For Editors. Omniprint, Inc. •

Monthly. $195.00 per year. Includes CD-Rom. Contains fillers for company newsletters: articles, cartoons, jokes, seasonal items, etc.

Newsletter on Newsletters: News, Views, Trends and Techniques for the Newsletter and Specilized Information Professional. • Bimonthly. $196.00 per year. Newsletter.

STATISTICS SOURCES

Computer Publishing Market Forecast. SIMBA Information. • Biennial. $1,895.00. Provides market data on computer-related books, magazines, newsletters, and other publications. Includes profiles of major publishers of computer-related material.

TRADE/PROFESSIONAL ASSOCIATIONS

Newsletter and Electronic Publishers Association. 1501 Wilson Blvd., Suite 509, Arlington, VA 22209-2403. Phone: 800-356-9302 or (703)527-2333 Fax: (703)841-0629 E-mail: nepa@newsletter.org • URL: http://www.newsletter.org • Formerly Newsletter Publishers Association.

NEWSPAPER CLIPPINGS

See: CLIPPING SERVICES

NEWSPAPER MARKET RESEARCH

See also: MARKET RESEARCH

DIRECTORIES

Editor and Publisher Market Guide. Editor and Publisher Co., Inc. • Annual. $150.00. More than 1,700 newspaper markets in the United States and Canada.

TRADE/PROFESSIONAL ASSOCIATIONS

International Newspaper Marketing Association. 10300 N Central Expy., Ste. 467, Dallas, TX 75231-8654. Phone: (214)373-9111 Fax: (214)373-9112 E-mail: broke.bode@inma.org • URL: http://www.inma.org • Represents individuals engaged in marketing, circulation, research, and public relations of newspapers. Conducts conferences; holds newspaper executives marketing and strategic planning seminars.

NEWSPAPER WORK

See: JOURNALISM

NEWSPAPERS

See also: COLLEGE AND SCHOOL NEWSPAPERS; FOREIGN LANGUAGE PRESS AND NEWSPAPERS; JOURNALISM; MINORITY NEWSPAPERS

GENERAL WORKS

Super Searchers in the News: The Online Secrets of Journalists and News Researchers. Paula J. Hane. Information Today, Inc. • 2000. $24.95. Contains online searching advice from 10 professional news researchers and fact checkers. (Super Searchers Series).

ABSTRACTS AND INDEXES

Newsbank. Newsbank, Inc. • Monthly. Price varies. Quarterly and annual cumulations. Index to articles of current interest from over 500 U.S. newspapers. Full text available on microfiche.

ALMANACS AND YEARBOOKS

Editor and Publisher International Yearbook: Encyclopedia of the Newspaper Industry. Editor and Publisher Co., Inc. • Annual. $150.00. Daily and

Sunday newspapers in the United States and Canada.

BIOGRAPHICAL SOURCES

Biographical Dictionary of American Journalism. Joseph P. McKerns, editor. Greenwood Publishing Group Inc. • 1989. $92.95. Covers major mass media: newspapers, radio, television, and magazines. Includes reporters, editors, columnists, cartoonists, commentators, etc.

CD-ROM DATABASES

Leadership Library on CD-ROM: Who's Who in the Leadership of the United States. Leadership Directories, Inc. • Quarterly. Including access to Internet version (weekly updates). Contains all 14 *Yellow Book* personnel directories on CD-ROM, providing contact and brief biographical information for about 400,000 individuals. Covers business, government, financial institutions, news media, law firms, associations, foreign representatives, and nonprofit organizations. Includes photographs.

MediaFinder CD-ROM: Oxbridge Directories of Print Media and Catalogs. Oxbridge Communications, Inc. • Quarterly. $1,995.00 per year. CD-ROM includes about 100,000 listings from *Standard Periodical Directory, National Directory of Catalogs, National Directory of British Mail Order Catalogs, National Directory of German Mail Order Catalogs, Oxbridge Directory of Newsletters, National Directory of Mailing Lists, College Media Directory,* and *National Directory of Magazines.*

Newspaper Abstracts Ondisc. PROQUEST. • Monthly. $2,950.00 per year (covers 1989 to date; archival discs are available for 1985-88). Provides cover-to-cover CD-ROM indexing and abstracting of 19 major newspapers, including the *New York Times, Wall Street Journal, Washington Post, Chicago Tribune,* and *Los Angeles Times.*

DIRECTORIES

Burrelle's Media Directory: Newspapers and Related Media. Burrelle's Information Services. • Annual. $550.00. *Daily Newspapers* volume lists more than 2,200 daily publications in the U. S., Canada, and Mexico. *Non-Daily Newspapers* volume lists more than 10,400 items published no more than three times a week. Provides detailed descriptions, including key personnel.

CARD The Media Information Network. Rogers Media Publishing. • Covers: Radio and television stations and networks; daily and weekend newspapers; consumer, farm, and business publications; advertising agencies and international media representatives; advertising, marketing, and media associations; and transportation and out-of-home advertising. Entries include: For publications--Title, company name, address, phone, frequency, names and titles of key personnel, advertising rates, discounts, mechanical requirements, copy regulations, circulation, closing and publication dates. For broadcasting stations--Call letters, name of owning company, address, phone, name of firm or individual representing station for advertising, special features, format, facilities, affiliations, rates, participation programs. For agencies and associations--Name, address, phone, personnel.

Cyberhound's Guide to Publications on the Internet. Gale Cengage Learning. • 1996. $79.00. Presents critical descriptions and ratings of more than 3,400 Internet databases of journals, newspapers, newsletters, and other publications. Includes a glossary of Internet terms, a bibliography, and three indexes. (Cyberhound's Series).

Fulltext Sources Online. Information Today Inc. • Covers: over 21,000 periodicals, newspapers, newsletters, newswires; and tv/radio transcripts available in full text online. Entries include: Name of file, online services through which available, dates of coverage, lag time if applicable. Separate list gives online service address and phone; indicates

degree of online coverage and selection policy. Internet url's listed where applicable.

Gale Directory of Publications and Broadcast Media. Gale Cengage Learning. • Annual. $770.00. Five volumes. *Interedition Supplement*, Free. A guide to publications and broadcasting stations in the U. S. and Canada, including newspapers, magazines, journals, radio stations, television stations, and cable systems. Geographic arrangement. Volume three consists of statistical tables, maps, subject indexes, and title index.

International Media Guide: Newspapers Worldwide. SRDS. • Annual. $350.00. Provides advertising rates, circulation, and other details relating to newspapers in major cities of the world (covers 200 countries, including U. S.).

National Directory of Community Newspapers. American Newspaper Representatives, Inc. • Annual. $105.00. Supersedes *National Directory of Weekly Newspapers.*

News Media Yellow Book: Who's Who Among Reporters, Writers, Editors, and Producers in the Leading National News Media. Leadership Directories, Inc. • Quarterly. $360.00 per year. Lists the staffs of major newspapers and news magazines, TV and radio networks, news services and bureaus, and feature syndicates. Includes syndicated columnists and programs. Seven specialized indexes are provided.

SRDS Community Publication Advertising Source. SRDS. • Semiannual. $186.00 per year. Provides advertising rates for weekly community newspapers, shopping guides, and religious newspapers, with circulation data and other information.

SRDS Newspaper Advertising Source. SRDS. • Monthly. $700.00 per year. Lists newspapers geographically, with detailed information on advertising rates, special features, personnel, circulation, etc. Includes a section on college newspapers. Also provides consumer market data for population, households, income, and retail sales. Formerly *Newspaper Advertising Source.*

SRDS Print Media Production Source. SRDS. • Quarterly. $808.00 per year. Contains details of printing and mechanical production requirements for advertising in specific trade journals, consumer magazines, and newspapers. Formerly *Print Media Production Source.*

Working Press of the Nation. R. R. Bowker. • Annual. $530.00. $295.00 per volume. Three volumes: (1) *Newspaper Directory*; (2) *Magazine and Internal Publications Directory*; (3) *Radio and Television Directory.* Includes names of editors and other personnel.

ENCYCLOPEDIAS AND DICTIONARIES

World Press Encyclopedia. Gale Cengage Learning. • 2003. $325.00. Second edition. Two volumes. Comprehensive essays cover the background and economic framework of newspapers and other news media in about 200 countries. Covers relevant legal issues, censorship, government relations, education in journalism, status of news agencies, cable, Internet, and other media topics.

FINANCIAL RATIOS

Almanac of Business and Industrial Financial Ratios. Leo Troy. Aspen Publishers, Inc. • 2003. $125.95. Includes CD-Rom. Contains financial ratios derived from federal tax returns. Ratios for each of about 200 industries are arranged according to company asset size. (Almanac of Business and Industrial Financial Ratios Series).

Annual Statement Studies. The Risk Management Association. • Annual. Median and quartile financial ratios are given for over 400 kinds of manufacturing, wholesale, retail, construction, and consumer finance establishments. Data is sorted by both asset size and sales volume. Includes a clearly written

"Definition of Ratios" and an alphabetical industry index.

Annual Statement Studies: Industry Default Probabilities and Cash Flow Measures. The Risk Management Association. • Annual. $145.00. Serves as a companion volume to the original *Annual Statement Studies.* Gives probability of default estimates on a percentage scale for more than 450 industries. Includes changes in position year-by-year for eight financial statement line items and provides percentage measures of cash flow.

HANDBOOKS AND MANUALS

Newspaper Designer's Handbook. Timothy Harrower. McGraw-Hill. • 2001. $50.00. Fifth edition. Includes CD-ROM. (Humanities, Social Sciences and World Language Series).

INTERNET DATABASES

Factiva. Dow Jones Reuters Business Interactive, LLC. Phone: 800-369-7466 or (609)452-1511 Fax: (609)520-5770 E-mail: solutions@factiva.com • URL: http://www.factiva.com • Fee-based Web site provides "global news and business information through Web sites and content integration solutions." Includes Dow Jones and Reuters newswires, The Wall Street Journal, and more than 7,000 other sources of current news, historical articles, market research reports, and investment analysis. Content includes 96 major U. S. newspapers, 900 non-English sources, trade publications, media transcripts, country profiles, news photos, etc.

Nexis.com. Lexis-Nexis Group. Phone: 800-227-4908 or (937)865-6800 Fax: (937)865-6909 E-mail: webmaster@prod.lexis-nexis.com • URL: http://www.nexis.com • Fee-based Web site offers searching of about 2.8 billion documents in some 30,000 news, business, and legal information sources. Features include a subject directory covering 1,200 topics in 34 categories and a Company Dossier containing information on more than 500,000 public and private companies. Boolean searching is offered.

Wall Street Journal Interactive Edition. Dow Jones & Co., Inc. Phone: 800-369-2834 or (212)416-2000 Fax: (212)416-2658 E-mail: inquiries@interactive.wsj.com • URL: http://www.wsj.com • Fee-based Web site providing online searching of worldwide information from the *The Wall Street Journal.* Includes "Company Snapshots," "The Journal's Greatest Hits," "Index to Market Data," "Journal Links," etc. Financial price quotes are available. Fees: $49.00 per year; $29.00 per year to print subscribers.

ONLINE DATABASES

Gale Database of Publications and Broadcast Media. Gale Cengage Learning. • An online directory containing detailed information on over 67,000 periodicals, newspapers, broadcast stations, cable systems, directories, and newsletters. Corresponds to the following print sources: *Gale Directory of Publications and Broadcast Media; Directories in Print; City and State Directories in Print; Newsletters in Print.* Semiannual updates. Inquire as to online cost and availability.

Information Bank Abstracts. New York Times Index Dept. • Provides indexing and abstracting of current affairs, primarily from the final late edition of *The New York Times* and the Eastern edition of *The Wall Street Journal.* Time period is 1969 to present, with daily updates. Inquire as to online cost and availability.

National Newspaper Index. Gale Cengage Learning. • Citations to news items in five major newspapers, 1970 to present. Weekly updates. Inquire as to online cost and availability.

Newspaper Abstracts Daily. ProQuest Inc. • Provides online coverage (citations and abstracts) of 25 major newspapers. Covers business, economics, current affairs, health, fitness, sports, education,

technology, government, consumer affairs, psychology, the arts, and the social sciences. Time period is 1986 to date, with daily updates. Inquire as to online cost and availability.

PERIODICALS AND NEWSLETTERS

Editor and Publisher - The Newsmagazine of the Fourth Estate Since 1894. Editor and Publisher Co., Inc. • Weekly. $99.00 per year. Includes print and online edition. Trade journal of the newspaper industry.

NewsInc.: The Business of the Newspaper Business. The Cole Group. • Biweekly. $425.00 per year. Newsletter. Reports on trends in mass media, especially with regard to newspaper publishing. Articles on cable TV and other competitive media are included.

Newspaper Financial Executives Journal. International Newspaper Financial Executives. • Quarterly. $100.00. Provides financially related information to newspaper executives.

Publishers' Auxiliary. National Newspaper Association. • Biweekly. $85.00 per year.

The Wall Street Journal. Dow Jones & Co., Inc. • Daily. $189.00 per year. Covers news and trends relating to business, industry, finance, the economy, and international commerce. Provides extensive price and other data for the securities, commodity, options, futures, foreign exchange, and money markets.

RESEARCH CENTERS AND INSTITUTES

Northwestern University-Media Management Center. 1007 Church St., No. 500, Evanston, IL 60201-5981. Phone: (847)491-4900 Fax: (847)491-5619 E-mail: mediamanagement@mmc.northwestern.edu • URL: http://www.mediamanagement.northwestern.edu • Research areas are related to various business aspects of the newspaper industry: management, marketing, personnel, planning, accounting, and finance. A joint activity of the J. L. Kellogg Graduate School of Management and the Medill School of Journalism.

STATISTICS SOURCES

SRDS Circulation [year]. SRDS. • Annual. $297.00. Contains detailed statistical analysis of newspaper circulation by metropolitan area or county and data on television viewing by area. Includes maps. Formerly *Circulation Year.*

U. S. Industry and Trade Outlook. Available from National Technical Information Service. • Annual. $69.95. Produced by the International Trade Administration, U. S. Department of Commerce, in a "public-private" partnership with DRI/McGraw-Hill and Standard & Poor's. Provides basic data, outlook for the current year, and "Long-Term Prospects" (five-year projections) for a wide variety of products and services. Includes high technology industries. Formerly *U. S. Industrial Outlook.*

UNESCO Statistical Yearbook. Bernan Press. • 1998. $95.00. Co-published by Bernan Press and the United Nations Educational, Scientific, and Cultural Organization (http://www.unesco.org). Presents statistical data from more than 200 countries on education, technology, research, broadcasting, cinema, book publishing, newspapers, libraries, museums, and population. Includes charts, maps, and graphs.

TRADE/PROFESSIONAL ASSOCIATIONS

American Society of Newspaper Editors. 11690B Sunrise Valley Dr., Reston, VA 20191-1409. Phone: (703)453-1122 Fax: (703)453-1133 E-mail: asne@asne.org • URL: http://www.asne.org.

International Newspaper Financial Executives. 21525 Ridgetop Cir., Ste. 200, Sterling, VA 20166. Phone: (703)421-4060 Fax: (703)421-4068 E-mail: infehq@infe.org • URL: http://www.infe.org • Controllers, chief accountants, auditors, business

managers, treasurers, secretaries and related newspaper executives, educators, and public accountants. Conducts research projects on accounting methods and procedures for newspapers. Offers placement service; maintains speakers' bureau. Produces conferences and seminars.

National Federation of Press Women. P.O. Box 5556, Arlington, VA 22205-0056. Phone: 800-780-2715 or (703)534-2500 Fax: (703)534-5731 E-mail: presswomen@aol.com • URL: http://www.nfpw.org.

National Newspaper Association. PO Box 7540, PO Box 7540, Columbia, MO 65205-7540. Phone: 800-829-4662 or (573)882-5800 Fax: (573)884-5490 E-mail: briansteffens@nna.org • URL: http://www.nna.org • Aims to protect, promote, and enhance community newspapers. Represents community newspapers across America; represents the industry before legislators, agencies and departments in Washington, D.C. that enact laws, rules and regulations, or conduct business, and that affect community newspapers. Promotes quality journalism and business practices at its annual convention, through its various contests and awards, and various other educational programs.

National Press Club. National Press Bldg., 529 14th St. NW, 14th Fl., Washington, DC 20045. Phone: (202)662-7500 Fax: (202)662-7512 E-mail: info@press.org • URL: http://www.press.org • Reporters, writers, and news people employed by newspapers, wire services, magazines, radio and television stations, and other forms of news media; former news people and associates of news people are nonvoting members. Sponsors sports, travel, and cultural events, rap sessions with news figures and authors, and newsmaker breakfasts and luncheons. Offers monthly training.

Newsletter and Electronic Publishers Association. 1501 Wilson Blvd., Suite 509, Arlington, VA 22209-2403. Phone: 800-356-9302 or (703)527-2333 Fax: (703)841-0629 E-mail: nepa@newsletter.org • URL: http://www.newsletter.org • Formerly Newsletter Publishers Association.

The Newspaper Guild. 501 3rd St. NW, 6th Fl., Washington, DC 20001-2760. Phone: 800-585-5TNG or (202)434-7177 Fax: (202)434-1472 E-mail: guild@cwa-union.org • URL: http://www.newsguild.org • AFL-CIO; Canadian Labour Congress, and International Federation of Journalists. Sponsors Newspaper Guild International Pension Fund that provides retirement benefits to persons employed in the news industry.

NEWSPAPERS, SCHOOL

See: COLLEGE AND SCHOOL NEWSPAPERS

NEWSPRINT PAPER INDUSTRY

See: PAPER INDUSTRY

NICKEL INDUSTRY

See: METAL INDUSTRY

NOISE CONTROL

ABSTRACTS AND INDEXES

Environment Abstracts. Congressional Information Service, Inc. • Monthly. Price varies. Provides multidisciplinary coverage of the world's environmental literature. Incorporates *Acid Rain Abstracts.*

Environment Abstracts Annual: A Guide to the Key

Environmental Literature of the Year. Congressional Information Service, Inc. • Annual. $495.00. A yearly cumulation of *Environment Abstracts.*

Environmental Knowledge Base: An Electronic Bibliography Featuring Citations and Abstracts of Scientific and Popular Articles on Environmental Issues, Including Social Policy, Economics, Regulatory, and Legal Topics. Environmental Studies Institute. • Monthly. Price varies. An index to current environmental literature. Formerly *Environmental Periodicals Bibliography.*

Excerpta Medica: Environmental Health and Pollution Control. Elsevier. • 16 times a year. Institutions, $3,246.00 per year. Section 46 of *Excerpta Medica.* Covers air, water, and land pollution and noise control.

NTIS Alerts: Environmental Pollution & Control. National Technical Information Service. • Semimonthly. $245.00 per year. Provides descriptions of government-sponsored research reports and software, with ordering information. Covers the following categories of environmental pollution: air, water, solid wastes, radiation, pesticides, and noise. Formerly *Abstract Newsletter.*

Pollution Abstracts. Cambridge Information Group. • Monthly. $1,390.00 per year. Includes print and online editions; with index, $1,515.00 per year.

CD-ROM DATABASES

Environment Abstracts on CD-ROM. LEXIS-NEXIS. • Quarterly. $1,295.00 per year. Contains the following CD-ROM databases: *Environment Abstracts, Energy Abstracts,* and *Acid Rain Abstracts.* Length of coverage varies.

DIRECTORIES

Sound and Vibration Buyer's Guide. • Annual. Free to qualified personnel. Lists of manufacturers of products for noise and vibration control, dynamic measurements instrumentation, and dynamic testing equipment.

ENCYCLOPEDIAS AND DICTIONARIES

Pollution A to Z. Gale Cengage Learning. • 2003. $195.00. Two volumes. Provides encyclopedic coverage of many aspects of environmental pollution, including air, water, noise, and soil. (Macmillan Reference USA imprint.).

HANDBOOKS AND MANUALS

Environmental Engineering. Joseph A. Salvato and others. John Wiley and Sons, Inc. • 2003. $240.00. Fifth edition. Written for environmental engineers, civil engineers, environmental scientists, public health professionals, and others concerned with the technical aspects of protecting the environment. Covers a wide range of topics, including sanitation management, groundwater contamination, incineration, wastewater treatment, communicable diseases, and noise control.

Handbook of Acoustics. Malcolm Crocker. John Wiley and Sons, Inc. • 1998. $225.00. Covers the fundamentals of acoustics, noise control, and vibration, for engineers, architects, and designers.

PERIODICALS AND NEWSLETTERS

Acoustical Society of America Journal. Acoustical Society of America. • Monthly. Institutions, $1,325.00 per year. Includes print and online editions.

Noise Control Engineering Journal. Institute of Noise Control Engineering. • Bimonthly. $70.00 per year.

Noise Regulation Report: The Nation's Only Noise Control Publication. Great Circle Communications LLC. • Monthly. $487.00 per year. Newsletter. Covers federal and state rules and regulations for the control of excessive noise.

Sound and Vibration (S/V). Acoustical Publications, Inc. • Monthly. Free to qualified personnel; others, $60.00 per year.

RESEARCH CENTERS AND INSTITUTES

Center for Acoustics and Vibration. Pennsylvania State University. 157 Hammond Bldg., University Park, PA 16802. Phone: (814)865-2761 Fax: (814)863-7222 E-mail: ghk@kirkof.psu.edu • URL: http://kirkof.psu.edu.

Joint Institute for Advancement of Flight Sciences. NASA Langley Research Center, MS 335, 227 Hunting Ave., Hampton, VA 23681-2199. Phone: (757)864-1982 Fax: (757)864-5894 E-mail: jiafs@seas.gwu.edu • URL: http://www.seas.gwu.edu/ • Conducts research in aeronautics, astronautics, and acoustics (flight-produced noise).

TRADE/PROFESSIONAL ASSOCIATIONS

Acoustical Society of America. Two Huntington Quadrangle, Ste. 1N01, Melville, NY 11797-4502. Phone: (516)576-2360 Fax: (516)576-2377 E-mail: asa@aip.org • URL: http://www.asa.aip.org.

Institute of Noise Control Engineering. P.O. Box 220, Saddle River, NJ 07458. Phone: (201)760-1101 Fax: (201)236-1210 E-mail: hq@ince.org.

NONFERROUS METAL INDUSTRY

See also: METAL INDUSTRY

ABSTRACTS AND INDEXES

Applied Science and Technology Index. H. W. Wilson Co. • 11 times a year. Quarterly and annual cumulations. Price varies. Indexes a wide variety of English language technical, industrial, and engineering periodicals.

F & S Index: United States. Gale Cengage Learning. • Monthly. $1,450.00 per year, including quarterly and annual cumulations. Provides annotated citations to marketing, business, financial, and industrial literature. Coverage of U. S. business activity includes trade journals, financial magazines, business newspapers, and special reports.

IMM Abstracts and Index: A Survey of World Literature on the Economic Geology and Mining of All Minerals (Except Coal), Mineral Processing, and Nonferrous Extraction Metallurgy. Institution of Mining and Metallurgy. • Bimonthly. $500.00 per year. Provides international coverage of the literature of mining and nonferrous metallurgy. Includes mineral economics, tunnelling, and rock mechanics.

CD-ROM DATABASES

WILSONDISC: Applied Science and Technology Abstracts. H. W. Wilson Co. • Monthly. Includes unlimited access to the online version of *Applied Science and Technology Abstracts* through WILSONLINE. Provides CD-ROM indexing and abstracting of 500 prominent scientific, technical, engineering, and industrial periodicals. Indexing coverage is provided from 1983 to date and abstracting from 1993 to date.

DIRECTORIES

North American Scrap Metals Directory. Recycling Today Media Group. • Covers: Suppliers of scrap metal materials in North America. Entries include: Contact information.

HANDBOOKS AND MANUALS

ASM Metals Reference Book. Michael L. Bauccio, editor. ASM International. • 1993. $155.00. Third edition. Includes glossary, tables, formulas, and diagrams. Covers a wide range of ferrous and nonferrous metals.

INTERNET DATABASES

Manufacturing Profiles. U. S. Bureau of the Census. Phone: (301)763-4636 E-mail: webmaster@census. gov • URL: http://www.census.gov/prod/www/abs/mfg-prof.html • The Census Bureau makes available free on PDF (Portable Document Format) an annual consolidation of the entire Current Industrial Report series, presenting "all the data compiled." Contains statistics on production, shipments, inventories, consumption, exports, imports, and orders for a wide variety of manufactured products.

ONLINE DATABASES

Applied Science and Technology Index Online. H. W. Wilson Co. • Provides online indexing of 500 major scientific, technical, industrial, and engineering periodicals. Time period is 1983 to date. Monthly updates. Inquire as to online cost and availability.

F & S Index. Gale Cengage Learning. • Contains about four million citations to worldwide business, financial, and industrial or consumer product literature appearing from 1972 to date. Weekly updates. Inquire as to online cost and availability.

Trade & Industry Database. Gale Cengage Learning. • Provides indexing of business periodicals, January 1981 to date. Daily updates. (Full text articles from some periodicals are available online, 1983 to date. Inquire as to online cost and availability).

PERIODICALS AND NEWSLETTERS

Foundry Management and Technology. Penton Media, Inc. • Monthly. Free to qualified personnel; others, $50.00 per year. Coverage includes nonferrous casting technology and production.

JOM: The Member Journal of the Minerals, Metals and Materials Society. Minerals, Metals, and Materials Society. • Four times a year. Membership. A scholarly journal covering all phases of metals and metallurgy.

Light Metal Age. Fellom Publishing Co. • Bimonthly. $40.00 per year. Edited for production and engineering executives of the aluminum industry and other nonferrous light metal industries.

Metal Bulletin. Metal Bulletin, Inc. • Semiweekly. $1,378 per year. Provides news of international trends, prices, and market conditions for both steel and non-ferrous metal industries. (Published in England.).

Metal Bulletin Monthly. Metal Bulletin, Inc. • Monthly. Price on application. Edited for international metal industry business executives and senior technical personnel. Covers business, economic, and technical developments. (Published in England.).

Modern Metals. Trend Publishing, Inc. • Monthly. $85.00 per year. Covers management and production for plants that fabricate and finish metals of various kinds.

33 Metalproducing: For Primary Producers of Steel, Aluminum, and Copper-Base Alloys. Penton Media, Inc. • Monthly. $65.00 per year. Covers metal production technology and methods and industry news. Includes a bimonthly *Nonferrous Supplement.*

RESEARCH CENTERS AND INSTITUTES

Cast Metals Laboratory. University of Wisconsin-Madison, Dept. of Materials Science and Engineering, 1509 University Ave., Madison, WI 53706-1595. Phone: (608)262-2562 Fax: (608)262-8353 • URL: http://www.engr.wisc.edu/mse.

Materials Processing Center. Massachusetts Institute of Technology, 77 Massachusetts Ave., Room 12-007, Cambridge, MA 02139-4307. Phone: (617)253-5179 Fax: (617)258-6900 E-mail: fmpage@.mit.edu • URL: http://www.web.mit.edu/mpc • Conducts processing, engineering, and economic research in ferrous and nonferrous metals, ceramics, polymers, photonic materials, superconductors, welding, composite materials, and other materials.

Metal Casting Laboratory. Pennsylvania State

University, 207 Hammond Bldg., University Park, PA 16802. Phone: (814)863-7290 Fax: (814)863-4745 E-mail: rvoight@psu.edu • URL: http://www.tntech.edu/it/metalcastlab.

STATISTICS SOURCES

Annual Survey of Manufactures. Available from U. S. Government Printing Office. • Annual. Prices vary. Issued by the U. S. Census Bureau as an interim update to the *Census of Manufactures.* Includes data on number of manufacturing establishments in various industries, employment, labor costs, value of shipments, capital expenditures, inventories, energy costs, and assets. (See also Census Bureau home page, http://www.census.gov/.).

Metal Statistics. Reed Business Information. • Annual. $250.00. Provides statistical data on a wide variety of metals, metal products, ores, alloys, and scrap metal. Includes data on prices, production, consumption, shipments, imports, and exports.

Non-Ferrous Metal Data Yearbook. American Bureau of Metal Statistics. • Annual. $405.00. Provides worldwide data on approximately about 200 statistical tables covering many nonferrous metals. Includes production, consumption, inventories, exports, imports, and other data.

Nonferrous Castings. U. S. Bureau of the Census. • Annual. (Current Industrial Reports MA-33E.).

TRADE/PROFESSIONAL ASSOCIATIONS

American Bureau of Metal Statistics. P.O. Box 805, Chatham, NJ 07928. Phone: (973)701-2299 Fax: (973)701-2152 E-mail: info@abms.com • URL: http://www.abms.com • Members are metal companies. Compiles and publishes detailed statistical data on a wide variety of nonferrous metals: aluminum, copper, gold, lead, nickel, platinum, silver, tin, titanium, uranium, zinc, and others.

Minerals, Metals and Materials Society. 184 Thorn Hill Dr., Warrendale, PA 15086-7514. Phone: (724)776-9000 Fax: (724)776-3770 E-mail: tmsgeneral@tms.org • URL: http://www.tms.org • Members are metallurgists, metallurgical engineers, and materials scientists. Divisions include Light Metals and Electronic, Magnetic, and Photonic Materials. Formerly The Metallurigical Society.

Non-Ferrous Founders' Society. 1480 Renaissance Dr., Ste. 310, Park Ridge, IL 60068. Phone: (847)299-0950 Fax: (847)299-3598 E-mail: nffstaff@nffs.org • URL: http://www.nffs.org • Manufacturers of brass, bronze, aluminum, and other nonferrous castings.

Non-Ferrous Metals Producers Committee. 2030 M St. NW, Ste. 800, 2030 M St. NW, Ste. 800, 2030 M. St., N.W., Suite 800, Washington, DC 20036. Phone: (202)466-7720 Fax: (202)466-2710 E-mail: nffstaff@nffs.org • URL: http://www.arcat.com/arcatcos/cos37/arc37679.cfm • Represents domestic copper, lead, and zinc producers. Promotes the interests of copper, lead, and zinc mining and metal industries in the U.S. with emphasis on tariffs, laws, regulations, and government policies affecting international trade and foreign imports.

NON-FOODS MERCHANDISERS

See: RACK JOBBERS

NONPRESCRIPTION DRUG INDUSTRY

See also: PHARMACEUTICAL INDUSTRY

GENERAL WORKS

Dietary Supplements: Current Issues. Donna V. Porter. Nova Science Publishers, Inc. • 2003. $29.

50. Covers the legislative and regulatory status of vitamin and mineral supplements.

CD-ROM DATABASES

Pharmacopeia of Herbs. CME, Inc. • $149.00. Frequently updated CD-ROM provides searchable data on a wide variety of herbal medicines, vitamins, and amino acids. Includes information on clinical studies, contraindications, side-effects, phytoactivity, and 534 therapeutic use categories. Contains a 1,000 word glossary.

World Marketing Forecasts on CD-ROM. Gale Cengage Learning. • Annual. $2,500.00. Produced by Euromonitor. Provides detailed forecast data for the years to 2012 on CD-ROM for 54 countries in all parts of the world. Covers a wide range of social, demographic, economic, and market factors. Includes specific forecasts for many kinds of consumer products.

DIRECTORIES

Drug Facts and Comparisons. Facts and Comparisons. • Annual. $359.95. Provides detailed information on more than 20,000 prescription drugs and 6000 over-the-counter products. Arrangement is according to 13 therapeutic categories. Includes charts and tables.

Drug Interaction Facts. Facts and Comparisons. • Annual. $179.95. Contains data on the interactions of some 20,000 prescription drugs. Interactions are rated according to magnitude and likelihood of effects, from one (most severe) to five (least severe). Includes drug/drug and drug/food interactions.

Major Pharmaceutical Companies of the World. Available from Gale Cengage Learning. • 2003. $880.00. Fifth edition. Published by Graham & Whiteside. Contains detailed information and trade names for more than 2,500 important pharmaceutical companies in various countries.

PDR for Nutritional Supplements. Medical Economics Co., Inc. • Annual. $59.95. Includes trade names, usage, adverse reactions, dosage, and other information about vitamins and minerals.

Physicians' Desk Reference for Nonprescription Drugs. Medical Economics Co. • Annual. $49.95. Contains detailed descriptions of "commonly used" over-the-counter drug products. Includes drug identification photographs. Indexing is by product category, product name, manufacturer, and active ingredient. Formerly *Physicians' Desk Reference for Nonprescription Drugs.*

Red Book. American Monument Association. • Covers: 7,000 retail monument dealers, suppliers of granite and marble, wholesalers, quarriers, funeral homes and cemeteries. Entries include: company; name, address, phone, fax; trade classification, names of owner or corporate officers and their titles. Available only to members of The American Monument Association.

ENCYCLOPEDIAS AND DICTIONARIES

Dictionary of Natural Products. George M. Hocking. Available from Information Today, Inc. • 1997. $139.50. Published by Plexus Publishing (http://www.plexuspublishing.com). Explains terms relating to the raw materials and products used in natural, folk, or alternative medicine.

HANDBOOKS AND MANUALS

Herbal Drugs and Phytopharmaceuticals. Max Wichtl and Norman G. Bisset, editors. CRC Press LLC. • 1994. $190.00. Provides a scientific approach to the medicinal use of herbs. (English translation of original German edition.).

ONLINE DATABASES

F-D-C Reports. FDC Reports, Inc. • An online version of "The Gray Sheet" (medical devices), "The Pink Sheet" (pharmaceuticals), "The Rose Sheet" (cosmetics), "The Blue Sheet" (biomedical), and "The Tan Sheet" (nonprescription). Contains full-

text information on legal, technical, corporate, financial, and marketing developments from 1987 to date, with weekly updates. Inquire as to online cost and availability.

PERIODICALS AND NEWSLETTERS

Chain Drug Review: The Reporter for the Chain Drug Store Industry. Racher Press, Inc. • 21 times a year. $136.00 per year. Covers news and trends of concern to the chain drug store industry. Includes special articles on OTC (over-the-counter) drugs.

HSR: Health Supplement Retailer. Virgo Publishing, Inc. • Monthly. $50.00 per year. Covers all aspects of the vitamin and health supplement market, including new products. Includes an annual buyer's guide, an annual compilation of industry statistics, and annual guides to vitamins and herbs.

Journal of Dietary Supplements. Haworth Press, Inc. • Quarterly. $175.00 per year to libraries; $50.00 per year to individuals. Edited with a view to both academic research and industry concerns. Sections of the journal are dedicated to health professionals, educators, dieticians, and an "Industry Spotlight." Includes book reviews and short reviews of research appearing elsewhere. Formerly *Journal of Nutraceuticals, Functional & Medical Foods.*

Nutrition Industry Executive. Vitamin Retailer Magazine, Inc. • 10 times a year. $50.00 per year. Edited for manufacturers of vitamins and other dietary supplements. Covers marketing, new products, industry trends, regulations, manufacturing procedures, and related topics. Includes a directory of suppliers to the industry.

The Tan Sheet: Nonprescription Pharmaceuticals and Nutritionals. F-D-C Reports, Inc. • Weekly. $1,220.00 per year. Newsletter covering over-the-counter drugs and vitamin supplements. Emphasis is on regulatory activities of the U. S. Food and Drug Administration (FDA).

Vitamin Retailer: The Dietary Supplement Industry's Leading Magazine. Vitamin Retailer Magazine, Inc. • Monthly. $60.00 per year. Edited for retailers of vitamins, herbal remedies, minerals, antioxidants, essential fatty acids, and other food supplements.

STATISTICS SOURCES

Consumer International. Available from Gale Cengage Learning. • Annual. $1,290.00. Published by Euromonitor. Contains extensive consumer market, economic, and demographic data for 25 major, non-European countries, including the U. S. and Canada. Includes consumer market size (volume and value) for 150 product types in 14 categories (food, clothing, automobiles, cosmetics, appliances, etc.).

European Marketing Forecasts. Available from Gale Cengage Learning. • Annual. $1,250.00. Published by Euromonitor. Contains demographic, economic, and market forecasts for the countries of Europe to the year 2010. Forecasts include market-size data for 15 consumer product sectors (food, clothing, automobiles, consumer electronics, etc.).

Industry Profile and Healthcare Factbook. Healthcare Distribution Management Association. • Annual. $349.00. Provides 266 statistical tables in three sections: "Industry Profile" (financial ratios related to drug distribution), "Pharmaceutical and Healthcare Distribution Trends and Facts," and "Healthcare Factbook" (expenditures, insurance utilization, company/product rankings, drug price inflation, generics, OTC, drug store data, hospital statistics, healthcare consumer summaries, etc.). Also known as *HDMA Factbook.* The Healthcare Distribution Management Association was formerly the National Wholesale Druggists' Association.

International Marketing Forecasts. Available from Gale Cengage Learning. • Annual. $1,250.00. Published by Euromonitor. Contains demographic, economic, and market forecasts to the year 2013 for major, non-European countries, including the U. S.

and Canada. Forecasts include market-size data for 15 consumer product sectors, such as food, clothing, and automobiles.

TRADE/PROFESSIONAL ASSOCIATIONS

Consumer Healthcare Products Association. 900 19th St. NW, Ste. 700, Washington, DC 20006. Phone: (202)429-9260 Fax: (202)223-6835 E-mail: lsuydam@chpa-info.org • URL: http://www.chpa-info.org • Marketers of nonprescription medicines and dietary supplements, which are packaged and available over-the-counter; associate members include suppliers, consultants, research and testing laboratories, advertising agencies, and media. Obtains and disseminates business, legislative, regulatory, and scientific information; conducts voluntary labeling review service to assist members in complying with laws and regulations.

OTHER SOURCES

The Market for Rx-to-OTC Switched Drugs. MarketResearch.com. • 2000. $3,250.00. Market research report. Covers the market for over-the-counter drugs that were formerly available only by prescription. Includes profiles of relevant pharmaceutical companies.

NONPROFIT CORPORATIONS

See also: ASSOCIATIONS; FOUNDATIONS

GENERAL WORKS

The Leader of the Future: New Essays by World-Class Leaders and Thinkers. Frances Hesselbein. John Wiley and Sons, Inc. • 2000. $16.50. Contains articles on leadership by "executives, consultants, and commentators." (Management Series).

Management Control in Nonprofit Organizations. Robert N. Anthony and David W. Young. McGraw-Hill. • 2002. $115.31. Seventh edition.

Managing the Non-Profit Organization: Practices and Principles. Peter F. Drucker. HarperInformation. • 1992. $16.00. General advice on strategy, leadership, marketing, and human relations for the non-profit manager.

ALMANACS AND YEARBOOKS

Nonprofit Almanac: A Publication Independent Sector. Virginia A. Hodgkinson and others. John Wiley and Sons, Inc. • 1996. $35.00. Provides trends and statistics for nonprofit wages, finances, employment, and giving patterns. Includes a glossary. (Jossey-Bass Nonprofit Sector Series).

BIBLIOGRAPHIES

Literature of the Nonprofit Sector: A Bibliography with Abstracts. The Foundation Center. • Dates vary. Six volumes. $45.00 per volume. Covers the literature of philanthropy, foundations, nonprofit organizations, fund-raising, and federal aid.

The Non-Profit Handbook: Everything You Need to Know to Start and Run Your Nonprofit Organization. Gary M. Grobman. Chronicle of Higher Education, Inc. • 2002. $29.95. Third edition.

Resource Center Product Catalog. Society for Nonprofit Organizations. • Included in subscription to *Non-profit World.*

BIOGRAPHICAL SOURCES

Who Knows Who: Networking Through Corporate Boards. Jeannette E. Glynn. Who Knows Who Publishing. • 1998. $165.00. Fifth edition. Shows the connections between the board members of major U. S. corporations and major foundations and nonprofit organizations.

CD-ROM DATABASES

Leadership Library on CD-ROM: Who's Who in the Leadership of the United States. Leadership Directories, Inc. • Quarterly. Including access to Internet version (weekly updates). Contains all 14 *Yellow Book* personnel directories on CD-ROM, providing contact and brief biographical information for about 400,000 individuals. Covers business, government, financial institutions, news media, law firms, associations, foreign representatives, and nonprofit organizations. Includes photographs.

DIRECTORIES

Charitable Organizations of the U. S.: A Descriptive and Financial Information Guide. Gale Cengage Learning. • 1991. $180.00. Second edition. Describes nearly 800 nonprofit groups active in soliciting funds from the American public. Includes nearly 800 data on sources of income, administrative expenses, and payout.

Cumulative List of Organizations Described in Section 170(c) of the Internal Revenue Code of 1986. Available from U. S. Government Printing Office. • Annual. $153.00 per year, including quarterly supplements. Lists about 300,000 organizations eligible for contributions deductible for federal income tax purposes. Provides name of each organization and city, but not complete address information. Arranged alphabetically by name of institution. (Office of Employee Plans and Exempt Organizations, Internal Revenue Service.).

Directory of Operating Grants. Richard M. Eckstein. Research Grant Guides. • Annual. $59.50. Contains profiles for approximately 800 foundations that award grants to nonprofit organizations for such operating expenses as salaries, rent, and utilities. Geographical arrangement, with indexes.

Gale's Guide to Nonprofits: A Gale Ready Reference Handbook. Gale Cengage Learning. • 2000. $135.00. Serves to provide a wide variety of information sources of interest to nonprofit organizations, including publications, online databases, and associations. Contains three indexes and a glossary.

Gale's Guide to the Arts: A Gale Ready Reference Handbook. Gale Cengage Learning. • 2000. $125.00. Contains descriptions of information sources of interest to nonprofit art groups, including publications, online databases, museums, government agencies, and associations. Three indexes and a glossary are provided.

Gale's Guide to the Media: A Gale Ready Reference Handbook. Gale Cengage Learning. • 2000. $125.00. Provides profiles of a wide variety of media-related organizations, publications, broadcasters, agencies, and databases, of interest to nonprofit groups. Contains three indexes and a glossary.

Guide to Federal Funding for Governments and Non-Profits. Government Information Services. • Quarterly. $339.00 per year. Looseleaf service. Contains detailed descriptions of federal grant programs in economic development, housing, transportation, social services, science, etc. Semimonthly *Supplement* available: *Federal Grant Deadline Calendar.*

National Directory of Nonprofit Organizations. Available from Gale Cengage Learning. • 2003. $590.00. 16th edition. Three volumes. Published by the TAFT Group. Contains over 250,000 listings of nonprofit organizations, indexed by 260 areas of activity. Indicates income range and IRS tax filing status for each organization.

Nonprofit Sector Yellow Book: Who's Who in the Management of the Leading Foundations, Universities, Museums, and Other Nonprofit Organizations. Leadership Directories, Inc. • Semiannual. $265.00 per year. Covers management personnel and board members of about 1,300 prominent, nonprofit organizations: foundations, colleges, museums, performing arts groups, medical institutions, librar-ies, private preparatory schools, and charitable service organizations.

ENCYCLOPEDIAS AND DICTIONARIES

International Encyclopedia of Public Policy and Administration. Jay M. Shafritz, editor. Westview Press. • 1997. $550.00. Four volumes. Covers 20 major areas, such as public administration, government budgeting, industrial policy, nonprofit management, organizational theory, public finance, labor relations, and taxation. Includes a brief bibliography for each major entry and a comprehensive index.

HANDBOOKS AND MANUALS

Accounting and Budgeting in Public and Non-profit Organizations: A Manager's Guide. C. William Garner. John Wiley and Sons, Inc. • 1991. $49.00. An accounting primer for non-profit executives with no formal training in accounting. Includes an explanation of Generally Accepted Accounting Principles (GAAP) as applied to non-profit organizations. (Public Administration-Non Profit Sector Series).

Accounting for Libraries and Other Not-for-Profit Organizations. G. Stevenson Smith. American Library Association. • 1999. $82.00. Second edition. Covers accounting fundamentals for nonprofit organizations. Includes a glossary.

Conducting a Successful Capital Campaign. Kent E. Dove. John Wiley and Sons, Inc. • 1999. $55.00. Second expanded revised edition. (Nonprofit and Public Management Series).

Financial and Accounting Guide for Not-for-Profit Organizations, Cumulative Supplement. Malvern J. Gross and Richard F. Larkin. John Wiley and Sons, Inc. • 2000. $170.00. Sixth edition. Covers key concepts, financial statement preparation, accounting guidelines, and financial control. Includes tax laws and forms. 2003 *Supplement* available. (Nonprofit Law, Finance and Management Series).

Guide to Preparing Nonprofit Financial Statements. Practitioners Publishing Co. • 2002. Three looseleaf volumes. Price on application.

How to Form a Nonprofit Corporation. Anthony Mancuso. Nolo. • 2002. $44.99. Fifth edition.

How to Write Proposals that Produce. Joel P. Bowman and Bernadine P. Branchaw. Greenwood Publishing Group, Inc. • 1992. $23.50. An extensive guide to effective proposal writing for both nonprofit organizations and businesses. Covers writing style, intended audience, format, use of graphs, charts, and tables, documentation, evaluation, oral presentation, and related topics.

Law of Tax-Exempt Organizations. Bruce R. Hopkins. John Wiley and Sons, Inc. • 2003. $210.00. Eighth edition.

The Management of Nonprofit Organizations. Sharon M. Oster, editor. Ashgate Publishing Co. • 1994. $275.00. Published by Dartmouth Publisher in England.

Managerial Accounting for Libraries and Other Not-for-Profit Organizations. G. Stevenson Smith. American Library Association. • 2002. $55.00. Coverage includes responsibility accounting, life cycle costing, and activity-based accounting, as opposed to traditional cost accounting for profit-based organizations.

The Nonprofit Entrepreneur: Creating Ventures to Earn Income. Edward Skloot, editor. The Foundation Center. • 1988. $19.95. Advice on earning income through fees and service charges.

Not-for-Profit GAAP 2001: Interpretation and Application of Generally Accepted Ating Principles for Not-for-Profit Organizations. Richard F. Larkin and Marie DiTommaso. John Wiley and Sons, Inc. • 2001. $65.00.

Parliamentary Law and Practice for Nonprofit Organizations. Howard L. Oleck and Cami Green. American Law Institute-American Bar Association

Committee on Continuing Professional Education. • 1991. $20.00. Second edition. Covers meeting procedures, motions, debate, voting, nominations, elections, committees, duties of officers, rights of members, and other topics.

Raise More Money for Your Nonprofit Organization: A Guide to Evaluating and Improving Your Fundraising. Anne L. New. The Foundation Center. • 1991. $14.95.

Starting and Running a Nonprofit Organization. Joan Hummel. University of Minnesota Press. • 1996. $14.95. Second revised edition.

Strategic Management in Non-Profit Organizations: An Administrator's Handbook. Robert D. Hay. Greenwood Publishing Group, Inc. • 1990. $84.95.

Tax Planning and Compliance for Tax-Exempt Organizations: Forms, Checklists, Procedures. Jody Blazek. John Wiley and Sons, Inc. • 1999. $165.00. Third edition. 2002 *Supplement,* $70.00. (Nonprofit, Law, Finance, and Management Series).

ONLINE DATABASES

Encyclopedia of Associations [Online]. Gale Cengage Learning. • Provides detailed information on about 170,000 U. S. and International non-profit organizations. Semiannual updates. Inquire as to online cost and availability.

PERIODICALS AND NEWSLETTERS

Board Member: The Periodical for Members of the National Center for Nonprofit Boards. BoardSource. • 10 times a year. Membership. Newsletter for trustees of nonprofit organizations.

Journal of Nonprofit and Public Sector Marketing. Haworth Press, Inc. • Semiannual. Institutions, $365.00 per year. Subject matter has to do with the promotion or marketing of the services of nonprofit organizations and governmental agencies.

Leader to Leader. Peter F. Drucker Foundation for Nonprofit Management. Jossey-Bass. • Quarterly. Institutions, $199.00 per year. Contains articles on "management, leadership, and strategy" written by "leading executives, thinkers, and consultants." Covers both business and nonprofit issues.

Non-Profit Legal and Tax Letter. Organization Management Inc. • 18 times a year. $235.00 per year. Newsletter. Covers fund raising, taxation, management, postal regulations, and other topics for nonprofit organizations.

Nonprofit Counsel. John Wiley and Sons, Inc., Journals Div. • Monthly. Institutions, $399.00 per year; with print edition, $419.00 per year. Newsletter.

Nonprofit Issues. Donald W. Kramer. • Description: Presents legal information for nonprofit executives and their professional advisors.

Nonprofit Management and Leadership. Jossey-Bass. • Quarterly. Institutions, $160.00 per year.

The Nonprofit Times: The Leading Publication for Nonprofit News and Management. Davis Information Group. • Monthly. $59.00 per year. Edited for executives of nonprofit organizations. Covers fund raising, personnel, management, and technology topics. Includes an annual nonprofit salary survey.

Nonprofit World: The National Bi-Monthly Nonprofit Leadership and Management Journal. Society for Nonprofit Organizations. • Bimonthly. Membership.

RESEARCH CENTERS AND INSTITUTES

Mandel Center for Nonprofit Organizations. Case Western Reserve University. 10900 Euclid Ave., Cleveland, OH 44106-7167. Phone: (216)368-2275 Fax: (216)368-8592 • URL: http://www.cwru.edu/mandelcenter • Engages in research relating to the management of nonprofit organizations.

STATISTICS SOURCES

By the Numbers: Electronic and Online Publishing. Gale Cengage Learning. • 1997-98. $305.00. Four

volumes. $85.00 per volume. Covers "high-interest" industries: 1. *By the Numbers: Electronic and Online Publishing*; 2. *By the Numbers: Emerging Industries*; 3. *By the Numbers: Nonprofits*; 4. *By the Numbers: Publishing.* Each volume provides about 600 tabulations of industry data on revenues, market share, employment, trends, financial ratios, profits, salaries, and so forth. Citations to data sources are included. (By the Numbers Series).

TRADE/PROFESSIONAL ASSOCIATIONS

Alliance for Nonprofit Management. 1899 L St., NW, 6th Fl., Washington, DC 20036. Phone: (202)955-8406 Fax: (202)721-0086 E-mail: alliance@allianceonline.org • URL: http://www.allianceonline.org • Members are devoted to building the capacity of nonprofit organizations in order to increase their effectiveness.

Alliance of Nonprofit Mailers. 1211 Connecticut Ave., No. 620, Washington, DC 20036. Phone: (202)462-5132 Fax: (202)462-0423 E-mail: alliance@nonprofitmailers.org • URL: http://www.nonprofitmailers.org.

Broadsource. 1828 L St., N. W., Suite 900, Washington, DC 20036. Phone: 800-883-6262 or (202)452-6262 Fax: (202)452-6299 • URL: http://www.boardsource.org • Seeks to improve the effectiveness of nonprofit boards of trustees. Formerly National Center for Nonprofit Boards.

Council of Institutional Investors. 1730 Rhode Island Ave., N. W., Suite 512, Washington, DC 20036. Phone: (202)822-0800 Fax: (202)822-0801 E-mail: info@cii.org • URL: http://www.cii.org • Members are nonprofit organization pension plans and other nonprofit institutional investors.

DMA Nonprofit Federation. 1615 L St. NW, Ste. 1100, Washington, DC 20036. Phone: (202)628-4380 Fax: (202)628-4383 E-mail: nonprofitfederation@the-dma.org • URL: http://www.the-dma.org/nonprofitfederation • Trade and lobbying group for non-profit organizations that use direct and online marketing to raise funds and communicate with members. Sponsors professional development conferences and seminars, lobbies on state and federal legislation, regulation, and standards related to direct marketing and related issues. Provides information about and participants in litigation affecting non-profits. Promotes the overall welfare of non-profits. Represents health care charities, social service agencies, religious groups, colleges and universities and fraternal organizations.

Society for Nonprofit Organizations. 5820 Canton Rd., No. 165, Canton, MI 48187. Phone: 800-424-7367 or (734)451-3582 Fax: (734)451-5935 E-mail: info@snpo.org • URL: http://www.snpo.org • The society is dedicated to bringing together those who serve in the nonprofit world in order to build a strong network of professionals throughout the country.

OTHER SOURCES

Charitable Giving and Solicitation. RIA. • $495.00 per year. Looseleaf service. Updates 13 times a year. Bulletin discusses federal tax rules pertaining to charitable contributions.

Managing Nonprofit Organizations in the 21st Century. James P. Gelatt. Greenwoood Publishing Group, Inc. • 1992. $32.95. The author "emphasizes successful ideas and working solutions." Includes charts and tables.

NON-WAGE PAYMENTS

See: EMPLOYEE BENEFIT PLANS; FRINGE BENEFITS

NONWOVEN FABRICS INDUSTRY

See also: INDUSTRIAL FABRICS INDUSTRY

ABSTRACTS AND INDEXES

Applied Science and Technology Index. H. W. Wilson Co. • 11 times a year. Quarterly and annual cumulations. Price varies. Indexes a wide variety of English language technical, industrial, and engineering periodicals.

Textile Technology Digest. Institute of Textile Technology. • Annual. $535.00. Provides indexing and abstracting of a wide variety of textile technology literature.

CD-ROM DATABASES

Textile Technology Digest [CD-ROM]. Textile Information Center, Institute of Textile Technology. • Quarterly. Provides CD-ROM indexing and abstracting of worldwide journals and monographs in various areas of textile technology, production, and management. Covers 1978 to date.

DIRECTORIES

International Directory of the Nonwoven Fabrics Industry. INDA, Association of the Nonwoven Fabrics Industry. • Biennial. Members, $195.00 per year; non-members, $275.00 per year. Lists more than 2,200 manufacturers of nonwoven fabrics and suppliers of raw material and equipment.

ENCYCLOPEDIAS AND DICTIONARIES

Textile Terms and Definitions. J.E. McIntyre and Paul N. Daniels, editors. Available from State Mutual Book and Periodical Service Ltd. • 1996. $180.00. 10th edition. Published by the Textile Insitute (UK). Includes more than 1,000 definitions of textile processes, fiber types, and end products. Illustrated.

HANDBOOKS AND MANUALS

Nonwoven Fabrics: Raw Materials, Manufacture, Applications, Characteristics. Wilhelm Albrecht and others. John Wiley and Sons, Inc. • 2003. $215.00. Covers nonwoven fabric design, production planning, manufacturing, testing, and related topics.

ONLINE DATABASES

Textile Technology Digest [online]. Institute of Textile Technology. • Contains indexing and abstracting of more than 300 worldwide journals and monographs in various areas of textile technology, production, and management. Time period is 1978 to date, with monthly updating. Inquire as to online cost and availability.

World Textiles. Elsevier Science, Inc. • Provides abstracting and indexing from 1970 of worldwide textile literature (periodicals, books, pamphlets, and reports). Includes U. S., European, and British patent information. Updating is monthly. Inquire as to online cost and availability.

PERIODICALS AND NEWSLETTERS

International Textile Bulletin: Nonwovens and Industrial Textiles Edition. ITS Publishing, International Textile Service. • Quarterly. $170.00 per year. Editions in Chinese, English, French, German, Italian and Spanish.

Nonwovens Industry: The International Magazine for the Nonwoven Fabrics and Disposable Soft Goods Industry. Rodman Publications. • Monthly. $48.00 per year.

RESEARCH CENTERS AND INSTITUTES

Fibrous Materials Research Center. Drexel University, Dept. of Materials Engineering, 31st and Market St., Philadelphia, PA 19104. Phone: (215)895-1640 Fax: (215)895-6684 E-mail: fko@coe.drexel.edu • URL: http://www.fmac.coe.drexel.edu • Research fields include computer-aided design of nonwoven fabrics and design curves for industrial fibers.

Textiles and Materials. Philadelphia University, Schoolhouse Lane and Henry Ave., Philadelphia, PA 19144-5497. Phone: (215)951-2751 Fax: (215)951-2651 E-mail: brooksteind@philau.edu • URL: http://www.philaau.edu/schools • Many research areas, including industrial and nonwoven textiles.

TRADE/PROFESSIONAL ASSOCIATIONS

INDA, Association of the Nonwoven Fabrics Industry. P.O. Box 1288, Cary, NC 27512-1288. Phone: (919)233-1210 Fax: (919)233-1282 E-mail: twritz@inda.org • URL: http://www.inda.org • Formerly International Nonwovens and Disposables Association.

Industrial Fabrics Association International. 1801 County Rd. B W, Roseville, MN 55113-4061. Phone: 800-225-4324 or (651)222-2508 Fax: (651)631-9334 E-mail: generalinfo@ifai.com • URL: http://www.ifai.com • Fiber producers, weavers, non-woven producers, coaters, laminators, finishers, and producers and manufacturers of canvas and specialty fabric end products in more than 36 countries. Provides technical, marketing, production, governmental and public relations services.

Institutional and Service Textile Distributors Association. 1609 Connecticut Ave., Washington, DC 20009. Phone: (202)986-0105 Fax: (202)986-0448 E-mail: istdatextiles@aol.com • URL: http://www.istda.org • Members are wholesalers of textile products to hospitals, hotels, airlines, etc.

Textile Institute. St. James's Buildings, 1st Fl., 79 Oxford St., Manchester M1 6FQ, United Kingdom. Phone: 44 161 2371188 Fax: 44 161 2361991 E-mail: tiihq@textileinst.org.uk • URL: http://www.texi.org • Companies and individuals in 100 countries involved in management, science, technology, design, information transfer, and marketing of textiles including clothing and footwear. Promotes interests of the textile industry worldwide; serves professional interests of members; confers qualifications and recognizes achievements in research, application of ideas, education, business, and public affairs. Maintains Information Service to collect information relating to textile industrial and economic conditions in different countries and economic sectors.

OTHER SOURCES

Nonwoven Disposables. Theta Reports. • 1999. $1,495.00. Provides market research data, including sales projections. Covers hospital disposable items, such as surgical drapes, masks, head covers, patient gowns, and incontinence products. (Theta Report No. 922.).

NORTH AMERICAN FREE TRADE AGREEMENT

See also: LATIN AMERICAN MARKETS

GENERAL WORKS

NAFTA Revisited. C. V. Anderson, editor. Nova Science Publishers, Inc. • 2002. $69.00. Provides articles by various authors on the status and economic effects of the North American Free Trade Agreement. Covers worker dislocation, environmental considerations, motor truck safety, Mexican trade policy, and other issues.

Study on the Operation and Effects of the North American Free Trade Agreement. Available from U. S. Government Printing Office. • 1997. $17.00. Produced by the Executive Office of the President (http://www.whitehouse.gov). Presents a generally favorable view of the effects of NAFTA on the U. S. and Mexican economies.

United States Agricultural Trade: Trends, Policy,

and Direction. Larry V. Fedorov, editor. Nova Science Publishers, Inc. • 2003. $59.00. Includes data on the impact of NAFTA on the import and export of farm products.

ABSTRACTS AND INDEXES

Business Periodicals Index. H. W. Wilson Co. • 11 times a year. Quarterly and annual cumulations. Price varies.

PAIS International in Print. Public Affairs Information Service, Inc. • Monthly. $850.00 per year; cumulations three times a year. Provides topical citations to the worldwide literature of public affairs, economics, demographics, sociology, and trade. Text in English; indexed materials in English, French, German, Italian, Portuguese and Spanish.

Readers' Guide to Periodical Literature. H. W. Wilson Co. • Monthly. $345.00 per year. Includes annual *Cumulation*. Indexes about 250 peridicals of general interest.

CD-ROM DATABASES

PAIS on CD-ROM. Public Affairs Information Service, Inc. • Quarterly. $1,995.00 per year. Provides a CD-ROM version of the online service, *PAIS International*. Contains over 500,000 citations to the literature of contemporary social, political, and economic issues.

WILSONDISC: Wilson Business Abstracts. H. W. Wilson Co. • Monthly. Includes unlimited online access to *Wilson Business Abstracts* through WILSONLINE. Provides CD-ROM "cover-to-cover" abstracting and indexing of over 600 prominent business periodicals. Indexing is from 1982, abstracting from 1990. (*Business Periodicals Index* without abstracts is available on CD-ROM at $1,495 per year.).

ENCYCLOPEDIAS AND DICTIONARIES

Encyclopedia of Business. Gale Cengage Learning. • 2000. $425.00. Second edition. Two volumes. Contains more than 700 signed articles covering major business disciplines and concepts. International in scope. (Encyclopedia of Business Series).

HANDBOOKS AND MANUALS

Mexico Business: The Portable Encyclopedia for Doing Business with Mexico. World Trade Press. • 1994. $24.95. Covers economic data, import/export possibilities, basic tax and trade laws, travel information, and other useful facts for doing business with Mexico. Includes a special section on NAFTA. (Country Business Guides Series).

ONLINE DATABASES

F & S Index. Gale Cengage Learning. • Contains about four million citations to worldwide business, financial, and industrial or consumer product literature appearing from 1972 to date. Weekly updates. Inquire as to online cost and availability.

PAIS International. Public Affairs Information Service, Inc. • Corresponds to the former printed publications, *PAIS Bulletin* (1976-90) and *PAIS Foreign Language Index* (1972-90), and to the current *PAIS International in Print* (1991 to date). Covers economic, political, and sociological material appearing in periodicals, books, government documents, and other publications. Updating is monthly. Inquire as to online cost and availability.

PROMT: Predicasts Overview of Markets and Technology. Gale Cengage Learning. • Companies, products, applied technologies and markets. U.S. and international literature coverage, 1972 to date. Inquire as to online cost and availability. Provides abstracts from more than 1,600 publications. Weekly updates.

Readers' Guide Abstracts Online. H. W. Wilson Co. • Indexes and abstracts general interest periodicals, 1983 to date. Weekly updates. Inquire as to online cost and availability.

Wilson Business Abstracts Online. H. W. Wilson Co. • Indexes and abstracts 600 major business periodicals, plus the *Wall Street Journal* and the business section of the *New York Times*. Indexing is from 1982, abstracting from 1990, with the two newspapers included from 1993. Updated weekly. Inquire as to online cost and availability. (*Business Periodicals Index* without abstracts is also available online.).

RESEARCH CENTERS AND INSTITUTES

Lowe Institute of Political Economy. Claremont McKenna College, 850 Columbia Ave., Claremont, CA 91711. Phone: (909)621-8012 Fax: (909)607-8008 E-mail: lowe@claremontmckenna.edu • URL: http://www.lowe.research.mckenna.edu/lowe • Research topics include NAFTA.

STATISTICS SOURCES

Handbook of North American Industry: NAFTA and the Economies of its Member Nations. John E. Cremeans. Bernan Press. • 1999. $115.00. Second revised edition. Provides detailed industry statistics for the U.S., Canada, and Mexico.

OTHER SOURCES

NAFTA Works for America: Administration Update on the North American Free Trade Agreement, 1993-1998. Available from U. S. Government Printing Office. • 1999. $7.00. Cover title: *Bridging into the 21st Century*. Issued by the Office of the U. S. Trade Representative, Executive Office of the President (http://www.ustr.gov). Summarizes the accomplishment of NAFTA over its first five years.

NOTARIES

ENCYCLOPEDIAS AND DICTIONARIES

Notary Public Practices and Glossary. Raymond C. Rothman. National Notary Association. • 1998. $22.00. Second edition.

HANDBOOKS AND MANUALS

Anderson's Manual for Notaries Public: A Complete Guide for Notaries Public and Commissioners. Anderson Publishing Co. • 1999. $25.00. Eighth edition.

PERIODICALS AND NEWSLETTERS

American Notary. American Society of Notaries. • Description: Articles of interest to notaries, educational and informative. Presents "new legislation and court decisions affecting the office of notary public, news about the American Society of Notaries," and related matters. Recurring features include Questions and Answers, and educational workshops.

The National Notary. National Notary Association. • Bimonthly. $36.00 per year.

Notary Bulletin. National Notary Association. • Bimonthly. Membership. Formerly *State Notary Bulletin*.

TRADE/PROFESSIONAL ASSOCIATIONS

American Society of Notaries. P.O. Box 5707, Tallahassee, FL 32314-5707. Phone: 800-522-3392 or (850)671-5164 Fax: (850)671-5165 E-mail: randi@notaries.org • URL: http://www.notaries.org.

National Notary Association. PO Box 2402, 9350 DeSoto Ave., Chatsworth, CA 91313-2402. Phone: 800-876-6827 or (818)739-4000 Fax: 800-833-1211 E-mail: services@nationalnotary.org • URL: http://www.nationalnotary.org • Notaries public (officers empowered to witness the signing of documents, identify the signers, take acknowledgments, and administer oaths). Works to teach notaries public in the U.S. their duties, powers, limitations, liabilities, and obligations. Keeps members informed of changes in notary law; offers various services, supplies, and insurance plans to members. Maintains speakers' bureau.

NOTEBOOK COMPUTERS

See: PORTABLE COMPUTERS

NOTIONS

See: GIFT BUSINESS

NUCLEAR ENERGY

See also: ENERGY SOURCES

ABSTRACTS AND INDEXES

Applied Science and Technology Index. H. W. Wilson Co. • 11 times a year. Quarterly and annual cumulations. Price varies. Indexes a wide variety of English language technical, industrial, and engineering periodicals.

Environmental Knowledge Base: An Electronic Bibliography Featuring Citations and Abstracts of Scientific and Popular Articles on Environmental Issues, Including Social Policy, Economics, Regulatory, and Legal Topics. Environmental Studies Institute. • Monthly. Price varies. An index to current environmental literature. Formerly *Environmental Periodicals Bibliography.*

NTIS Alerts: Energy. National Technical Information Service. • Semimonthly. $245.00 per year. Provides descriptions of government-sponsored research reports and software, with ordering information. Covers electric power, batteries, fuels, geothermal energy, heating/cooling systems, nuclear technology, solar energy, energy policy, and related subjects. Formerly *Abstract Newsletter.*

Science Citation Index. Thomson/ISI. • Bimonthly. $15,020.00 per year. Annual cumulation. Includes *Source Index, Citation Index, Permuterm Subject Index,* and *Corporate Index.*

ALMANACS AND YEARBOOKS

Annual Review of Nuclear and Particle Science. Annual Reviews. • Annual. Individuals, $84.00. Includes print and online edition. Institutions, $189.00; with online edition, $227.00.

BIBLIOGRAPHIES

Nuclear Power. Available from U. S. Government Printing Office. • Annual. Free. Lists government publications. GPO Subject Bibliography Number 200.

BIOGRAPHICAL SOURCES

Energy and Nuclear Sciences International Who's Who. Addison Wesley/Benjamin Cummings. • 1990. $310.00. Third edition.

CD-ROM DATABASES

Science Citation Index: Compact Disc Edition. Institute for Scientific Information. • Monthly. Provides CD-ROM indexing of the world's scientific and technical literature. Corresponds to online *Scisearch* and printed *Science Citation Index.*

DIRECTORIES

Companies Holding Nuclear Certificates. American Society of Mechanical Engineers. • Covers: about 170 manufacturers accredited by the society's subcommittee on Nuclear Accreditation Committee for production of one or more types of pressure vessels and other components for nuclear applications. Entries include: Company name, address, and limitations of items which it is authorized by its certificate to produce.

Nuclear News Buyers Guide. American Nuclear Society. • Annual. $91.00. Lists approximately 1,500 manufacturers and suppliers of nuclear components. Included with subscription to *Nuclear News.*

Nuclear News-World List of Nuclear Power Plants.

American Nuclear Society. • Annual. $19.00 per copy. List of over 100 U. S. and foreign nuclear power plants that are in operation, under construction, or on order.

Platt's Directory of Electric Power Producers and Distributors. Platts. • Annual. $410.00. Over 3,500 investor-owned, municipal, rural cooperative and government electric utility systems in the U.S. and Canada. Formerly *Directory of Electric Power Producers and Distributors.*

World Energy and Nuclear Directory. Specialist Journals. • Biennial. $385.00. Lists 5,000 public and private, international research and development organizations functioning in a wide variety of areas related to energy.

ENCYCLOPEDIAS AND DICTIONARIES

Encyclopedia of Energy. Cutler J. Cleveland, editor. Elsevier, Inc. • 2004. $1,560.00. Six volumes. Covers all aspects of energy sources and energy-related environmental issues.

Encyclopedia of Global Change: Environmental Change and Human Society. Andrew S. Goudie, editor. Oxford University Press. • 2001. $275.00. Two volumes. Contains 300 signed articles on a wide variety of topics relating to changes in the environment and the atmosphere. Includes bibliographies and illustrations.

Macmillan Encyclopedia of Energy. Available from Gale Cengage Learning. • 2001. $395.00. Three volumes. Published by Macmillan Reference USA. Covers the business, technology, and history of a wide variety of energy sources.

Wiley Encyclopedia of Energy and the Environment. Attilio Bisio and Sharon Boots. John Wiley and Sons, Inc. • 1996. $285.00. Abriged edition. Two volumes. Covers a wide variety of energy and environmental topics, including legal and policy issues. (Encyclopedia of Energy and the Environment Series: Vol. 2).

HANDBOOKS AND MANUALS

Moody's Public Utility Manual. Mergent, Inc. • Annual. $1,995.00. Updated weekly online. Contains financial and other information concerning publicly-held utility companies (electric, gas, telephone, water).

ONLINE DATABASES

Globalbase. Gale Cengage Learning. • Provides more than one million online summaries of business, industrial, and economic news reports from more than 1,000 publications worldwide. Covers a wide range of material appearing in international trade journals, professional magazines, and newspapers. Time period is 1984 to date, with weekly updates. Inquire as to online cost and availability.

PAIS International. Public Affairs Information Service, Inc. • Corresponds to the former printed publications, *PAIS Bulletin* (1976-90) and *PAIS Foreign Language Index* (1972-90), and to the current *PAIS International in Print* (1991 to date). Covers economic, political, and sociological material appearing in periodicals, books, government documents, and other publications. Updating is monthly. Inquire as to online cost and availability.

PROMT: Predicasts Overview of Markets and Technology. Gale Cengage Learning. • Companies, products, applied technologies and markets. U.S. and international literature coverage, 1972 to date. Inquire as to online cost and availability. Provides abstracts from more than 1,600 publications. Weekly updates.

Scisearch. Institute for Scientific Information. • Broad, multidisciplinary index to the literature of science and technology, 1974 to present. Inquire as to online cost and availability. Coverage of literature

is worldwide, with weekly updates.

PERIODICALS AND NEWSLETTERS

American Nuclear Society Transactions. American Nuclear Society. • Semiannual. Institutions, $800.00 per year. *Supplement* available.

Annals of Nuclear Energy. Elsevier. • 18 times a year. Qualified personnel, $98.00 per year; institutions, $3,304.00 per year. Text and summaries in English, French and German.

Atomic Energy. Russian Academy of Sciences, RU. Kluwer Academic Publishers. • Monthly. Institutions, $2,901.00 per year. Includes print and online editions. Formerly *Soviet Atomic Energy.*

Bulletin of the Atomic Scientists: The Magazine of Global Security News and Analysis. Educational Foundation for Nuclear Science. • Bimonthly. $28.00 per year.

DOE This Month. Available from U. S. Government Printing Office. • Monthly. $42.00 per year. Describes the U.S. Department of Energy's research and development activities and DOE publications. Includes information on nuclear energy, renewable energy sources, and synthetic fuels.

INIS Newsletter. International Atomic Energy Agency, Division of Publications. • Irregular. Free. Newsletter of the International Nuclear Information System (INIS).

Journal of Energy Engineering: The International Journal. American Society of Civil Engineers. • Three times a year. Members, $40.00 per year; with online edition, $46.00 per year; non-members, $60.00 per year; with online edition, $69.00 per year.

Journal of Nuclear Materials Management. Institute of Nuclear Materials Management, Inc. • Quarterly. $100.00 per year. Summaries in English and Japanese.

Nuclear Engineering International. Wilmington Publishers Ltd. • Monthly. $341.00 per year. Text in English; summaries in French and German.

Nuclear Fuel. Platts. • Biweekly. $1,870.00 per year. Newsletter.

Nuclear News. American Nuclear Society. • Monthly. $325.00 per year. Includes *Nuclear News Buyers Guide* and 3 Special Issues.

Nuclear Plant Journal. International Nuclear Power Industry. EQES, Inc. • Bimonthly. $120.00 per year.

Nuclear Science and Engineering: Research and Development Related to Peaceful Utilization of Nuclear Energy. American Nuclear Society. • Nine times per year. Institutions, $900.00 per year. Includes online edition.

Nuclear Standards News. American Nuclear Society. • Description: Provides current information on nuclear standards, U.S. Nuclear Regulatory Commission (NRC) regulations and licensing issues, and developments in the domestic and international nuclear standards field. Recurring features include a calendar of standards meetings and notices of pertinent publications.

Nuclear Technology: Applications for Nuclear Science, Nuclear Engineering and Related Arts. American Nuclear Society. • Institutions, $1,030.00 per year. Includes online edition.

Nucleonics Week. Energy and Business Newsletters. • Description: Provides an overview of all international developments relating to commercial nuclear power. Offers coverage of plant construction, low-level waste issues, government policies, plant performance, services, and decommissioning, as well as "comprehensive statistical coverage of plant production and the economics of nuclear power." Recurring features include a monthly listing of nuclear power electric generation worldwide. **Remarks:** Also available in electronic format.

Power. McGraw-Hill Inc. • Description: Covers

design, operation, construction, and maintenance of power plants for utilities, process industries, and manufacturers.

RESEARCH CENTERS AND INSTITUTES

Canadian Energy Research Institute. Canadian Energy Research Institute. 3512 33rd St. NW, No. 150, Calgary, AB, Canada T2L 2A6. Phone: (403)282-1231 Fax: (403)284-4181 E-mail: mmasri@ceri.ca • URL: http://www.ceri.ca • Economic issues relating to all forms of energy, including oil, natural gas, coal, nuclear and hydroelectric power, and alternative energy sources. Develops software such as the World Oil Market Model.

Center for Energy and Combustion Research. University of California, San Diego. 9500 Gillman Dr., EBU 11, La Jolla, CA 92093-0411. Phone: (858)534-4285 Fax: (858)534-5354 E-mail: faw@ames.ucsd.edu • URL: http://www.maeweb.ucsd.edu/.

Laboratory for Energy and the Environment. Massachusetts Institute of Technology. 77 Massachusetts Ave., Bldg. E40-455, Cambridge, MA 02139-4307. Phone: (617)258-8891 Fax: (617)253-8013 E-mail: jwilmson@mit.edu • URL: http://www.lfee.mit.edu • Formerly Energy Laboratory.

Laboratory for Nuclear Science. Massachusetts Institute of Technology, 77 Massachusetts Ave., Bldg. 26, Room 505, Cambridge, MA 02139. Phone: (617)253-2361 Fax: (617)253-0111 • URL: http://www.pierre.mit.edu.

Los Alamos National Laboratory. P.O. Box 1663, Los Alamos, NM 87545. Phone: (505)667-7000 • URL: http://www.lanl.gov.

Michigan Memorial-Phoenix Project. University of Michigan, Phoenix Memorial Laboratory, 2301 Bonisteel Blvd., Ann Arbor, MI 48109-2100. Phone: (734)764-1817 Fax: (734)936-1571 E-mail: pmlmail@engin.umich.edu • URL: http://www.umich.edu/~mmpp • Conducts research in peaceful uses of nuclear energy.

Oak Ridge National Laboratory. Bethel Valley Rd., Oak Ridge, TN 37831-6255. Phone: (865)576-2900 Fax: (865)241-2967 E-mail: madia@ornl.gov • URL: http://www.ornl.gov.

STATISTICS SOURCES

Annual Energy Outlook [year], with Projections to [year]. Available from U. S. Government Printing Office. • Annual. $42.00. Issued by the Energy Information Administration, U. S. Department of Energy (http://www.eia.doe.gov). Contains detailed statistics and 20-year projections for electricity, oil, natural gas, coal, and renewable energy. Text provides extensive discussion of energy issues and "Market Trends.".

Annual Energy Review. Available from U. S. Government Printing Office. • Annual. $51.00. Issued by the Energy Information Administration, Office of Energy Markets and End Use, U. S. Department of Energy. Presents long-term historical as well as recent data on production, consumption, stocks, imports, exports, and prices of the principal energy commodities in the U. S.

Budget of the United States Government. U.S. Office of Management and Budget. Available from U.S. Government Printing Office. • Annual. $52.00.

OECD Nuclear Energy Data. Organization for Economic Cooperation and Development. Available from OECD Publications and Information Center. • Annual. $32.00. Produced by the OECD Nuclear Energy Agency. Provides a yearly compilation of basic statistics on electricity generation and nuclear power in OECD member countries. Text in English and French.

Statistical Record of the Environment. Gale Cengage Learning. • 1996. $130.00. Third edition. Provides over 875 charts, tables, and graphs of major environmental statistics, arranged by subject. Covers population growth, hazardous waste, nuclear energy, acid rain, pesticides, and other subjects related to the environment. A keyword index is included. (Gale Environmental Library Series).

Uranium: Resources, Production, and Demand. Organization for Economic Cooperation and Development. • Annual. $77.00. Produced by the OECD Nuclear Energy Agency and the International Atomic Energy Agency. Provides detailed statistics and trend analysis for uranium based on official information from 49 countries.

TRADE/PROFESSIONAL ASSOCIATIONS

American Nuclear Insurers. 95 Glastonbury Blvd., Glastonbury, CT 06033-4438. Phone: (860)682-1301 Fax: (860)659-0002 E-mail: info@nuclearinsurance.com • URL: http://www.amnucins.com • Domestic property/casualty nuclear insurance companies. Strives to ensure safe and secure insurance capacity for customers. Audits financial performance of all member companies annually, ensures compliance with guidelines.

American Nuclear Society. 555 N Kensington Ave., La Grange Park, IL 60526. Phone: 800-323-3044 or (708)352-6611 Fax: (708)352-0499 E-mail: info@nuclearinsurance.com • URL: http://www.ans.org • Physicists, chemists, educators, mathematicians, life scientists, engineers, metallurgists, managers, and administrators with professional experience in nuclear science or nuclear engineering. Works to advance science and engineering in the nuclear industry. Disseminates information; promotes research; conducts meetings devoted to scientific and technical papers; works with government agencies, educational institutions, and other organizations dealing with nuclear issues.

Educational Foundation for Nuclear Science. 6042 S. Kimbark Ave., Chicago, IL 60637. Phone: (773)702-2555 Fax: (773)702-0725 E-mail: bulletin@thebulletin.org • URL: http://www.bullatomsci.org.

Environmental Coalition on Nuclear Power. 433 Orlando Ave., State College, PA 16803. Phone: (814)237-3900 Fax: (814)237-3900 E-mail: johnsrud@uplink.net • Seeks establishment of non-nuclear energy policy.

IEEE Nuclear and Plasma Sciences Society. c/o IEEE Corporate Office, 3 Park Ave., 17th Fl., New York, NY 10016-5997. Phone: 800-678-4333 or (212)419-7900 Fax: (212)752-4929 E-mail: ieeeusa@ieee.org • URL: http://www.ieee.org.

Institute of Nuclear Materials Management. 60 Revere Dr., Suite 500, Northbrook, IL 60062. Phone: (847)480-9573 Fax: (847)480-9282 E-mail: inmm@inmm.org • URL: http://www.inmm.org • Affiliated with American National Standards Institute.

Institute of Nuclear Power Operations. 700 Galleria Pky. SE, Ste. 100, Atlanta, GA 30339-5957. Phone: (770)644-8000 Fax: (770)644-8549 E-mail: grillma@inpo.org • An organization of electric utilities operating nuclear power plants.

Mutual Atomic Energy Liability Underwriters. 330 N. Wabash, Ste. 2611, Chicago, IL 60611. Phone: (312)467-0003 Fax: (312)467-0774 E-mail: geobev@consolidated.net • Underwriting syndicate of 4 mutual casualty insurance companies writing nuclear energy liability policies.

Nuclear Energy Institute. 1776 I St. NW, Ste. 400, Washington, DC 20006-3708. Phone: (202)739-8000 Fax: (202)785-4019 E-mail: webmasterp@nei.org • URL: http://www.nei.org • Represents Electric utilities, manufacturers, industrial firms, research and service organizations, educational institutions, labor groups, and governmental agencies engaged in development and utilization of nuclear energy, especially nuclear-produced electricity, and other energy matters. Maintains speakers' bureau; compiles statistics and public attitude data.

Nuclear Information and Records Management Association. 10 Almas Rd., Windham, NH 03087. Phone: (603)432-6476 Fax: (603)432-3024 E-mail: jnirma@nirma.mv.com • URL: http://www.nirma.org • Concerned with the maintenance of nuclear industry corporate records. Formerly Nuclear Records Management Association.

Nuclear Information and Resource Service. 1424 16th St., N.W., No. 404, Washington, DC 20036. Phone: (202)328-0002 Fax: (202)462-2183 E-mail: nirsnet@nirs.org • URL: http://www.nirs.org • Promotes alternatives to nuclear power. Affiliated with World Information Service on Energy.

Nuclear Suppliers Association. PO Box 2038, Springfield, VA 22152. Phone: (703)451-1912 Fax: (703)451-2334 E-mail: nsanews@aol.com • URL: http://www.nuclearsuppliers.org • Companies involved in the manufacture or distribution of products and services for the nuclear industry. Promotes nuclear power and the interests of the nuclear industry.

Oak Ridge Associated Universities. PO Box 117, PO Box 117, Oak Ridge, TN 37831-0117. Phone: (865)576-3146 Fax: (865)241-2923 E-mail: carla.phillips@orau.org • URL: http://www.orau.org • Represents private, not-for-profit corporations and a consortium of 91 doctoral-granting colleges and universities. Serves the government, academia, and the private sector in important areas of science and technology. Manages and operates the Oak Ridge Institute for Science and Education (ORISE) for the U.S. Department of Energy. ORISE undertakes national and international programs in education, training, health, and the environment.

Professional Reactor Operator Society. PO Box 484, Byron, IL 61010-0484. Phone: (815)234-8140 Fax: (815)234-8140 E-mail: info@pngdealers.com • URL: http://nucpros.com • Plenary members are licensed and certified nuclear reactor operators; associate members include equipment manufacturers and utility companies. Aims to develop a communication network between nuclear reactor operators and government agencies, Congress, and industry in order to promote safety and efficiency in nuclear facilities. Believes that the education, experience, and training of nuclear facility operators have not been fairly considered in the formation of regulations, guidelines, and decisions that affect their careers. Areas of concern include educational requirements and job stress. Plans to survey the views and concerns of members and other involved parties; also plans personal presentations of members' views, supported by scientific data, to persons in the decision-making process. Offers direct mailing service to members from advertisers and placement agencies. Compiles statistics.

Public Citizen's Critical Mass Energy Project. 1600 20th St. NW, Washington, DC 20009. Phone: (202)588-1000 Fax: (202)547-7392 E-mail: cmep@citizen.org • URL: http://www.citizen.org/cmep • Maintains national network of anti-nuclear groups. Affiliated with Public Citizen. Formerly Public Citizen's Critical Mass Energy and Environment Project.

OTHER SOURCES

Major Energy Companies of the World. Available from Gale Cengage Learning. • Annual. $880.00. Published by Graham & Whiteside. Contains detailed information on more than 3,300 important energy companies in various countries. Industries include electricity generation, coal, natural gas, nuclear energy, petroleum, fuel distribution, and equipment for energy production.

For publishers addresses, refer to SOURCES CITED section at the back of the book.

657

NUMERICAL CONTROL OF MACHINERY (NC))

See: COMPUTER-AIDED DESIGN AND MANUFACTURING (CAD/CAM)

NUMISMATICS

See: COINS AS AN INVESTMENT

NURSERIES (HORTICULTURAL)

See also: FLORIST SHOPS

ABSTRACTS AND INDEXES

Horticultural Abstracts: Compiled from World Literature on Temperate and Tropical Fruits, Vegetables, Ornaments, Plantation Crops. Available from CABI Publishing North America. • Monthly. $2,010.00 per year. Print and online edition, $2,030.00 per year. Published in England by CABI Publishing. Provides worldwide coverage of the literature of fruits, vegetables, flowers, plants, and all aspects of gardens and gardening.

NTIS Alerts: Agriculture & Food. National Technical Information Service. • Semimonthly. $195.00 per year. Provides descriptions of government-sponsored research reports and software, with ordering information. Covers agricultural economics, horticulture, fisheries, veterinary medicine, food technology, and related subjects. Formerly *Abstract Newsletter*.

DIRECTORIES

American Nursery and Landscape Association Membership Directory. American Nursery and Landscape Association. • Annual. Free to members; non-members, $250.00 per year. Lists 2,200 member firms. Formerly *American Association of Nurserymen Membership Directory*.

Nursery Stock and Supply Locator. American Nursery and Landscape Association. • Annual. $3.00.

ONLINE DATABASES

CAB Abstracts. CAB Publishing North America. • Contains 46 specialized abstract collections covering over 10,000 journals and monographs in the areas of agriculture, horticulture, forest products, farm products, nutrition, dairy science, poultry, grains, animal health, entomology, etc. Time period is 1972 to date, with monthly updates. Inquire as to online cost and availability. *CAB Abstracts on CD-ROM* also available, with annual updating.

PERIODICALS AND NEWSLETTERS

American Nurseryman. American Nurseryman Publishing Co. • Semimonthly. $48.00 per year.

Greenhouse Grower. Meister Media. • 14 times a year. $37.45 per year. Concerned with all crops grown under glass or plastic.

Horticulture: Gardening at its Best. Krause Publications Inc. • Bimonthly. $19.95 per year.

Nursery Business Retailer. Brantwood Publications, Inc. • Bimonthly. Price on application.

TRADE/PROFESSIONAL ASSOCIATIONS

American Nursery and Landscape Association. 1000 Vermont Ave. No. 300, Washington, DC 20005-4914. Phone: (202)789-2900 Fax: (202)789-1893 • URL: http://www.anla.org • Formerly Wholesale Nursery Growers of America.

NURSERY SCHOOLS

See: DAY CARE CENTERS

NURSING HOMES

See also: LONG-TERM CARE INSURANCE; RETIREMENT COMMUNITIES

GENERAL WORKS

Caring for Frail Elderly People: New Directions in Care. OECD Publications and Information Center. • 1994. $27.00. Discusses the problem in OECD countries of providing good quality care to the elderly at manageable cost. Includes trends in family care, housing policies, and private financing.

Continuing Care Retirement Communities. Sylvia Sherwood and others. Johns Hopkins University Press. • 1996. $44.00. Presents research based on a study of continuing care retirement communities and 2,000 residents of the communities.

Long-Term Care and Its Alternatives. Charles B. Inlander and others. People's Medical Society. • 1996. $16.95. Provides practical advice on the financing of long-term health care. The author is a consumer advocate and president of the People's Medical Society.

BIBLIOGRAPHIES

AAHSA Resource Catalog. American Association of Homes and Services for the Aging. • Annual. Free. Provides descriptions of material relating to managed care, senior housing, assisted living, continuing care retirement communities (CCRCs), nursing facilities, and home health care. Publishers are AAHSA and others.

Long-Term Care: An Annotated Bibliography. Theodore H. Koff. Greenwood Publishing Group, Inc. • 1995. $59.95. (Bibliographies and Indexes in Gerontology Series: No. 25).

CD-ROM DATABASES

Authority Health Care Law Library. LexisNexis/Matthew Bender. • Periodic updates. Price on request. Full text CD-ROM provides legal information, case law, and analysis relating to health care facilities, health insurance, longterm care, Medigap, and Medicare.

DIRECTORIES

AHA Integrated Delivery Network Directory: U.S. Health Care Systems, Networks, and Alliances. American Hospital Association. • Annual. $250.00. Provides information about a wide variety of U.S. health care groups and affiliations, including hospitals, nursing homes, rehabilitation centers, psychiatric facilities, home health care agencies, clinical laboratories, outpatient facilities, and diagnostic imaging centers. Includes names of more than 8,000 key executives.

Buyers' Guide for the Health Care Market: A Directory of Products and Services for Health Care Institutions. Health Forum. • Annual. $17.95. Lists 1,200 suppliers and manufacturers of health care products and services for hospitals, nursing homes, and related organizations.

The Consumers' Directory of Continuing Care Retirement Communities. American Association of Homes and Services for the Aging. • Irregular. $30.00. Contains information on fees, services, and accreditation of about 500 U. S. retirement facilities providing lifetime housing, meals, and health care. Introductory text discusses factors to be considered in selecting a continuing care community.

Contemporary Long-Term Care--Fax Directory. VNU Business Media. • Covers: Approximately 900 manufacturers and suppliers of products and services for long-term patient care in nursing homes and retirement communities. Entries include: Company name, address, phone, fax.

Directory of Nursing Homes. Solucient. • Biennial. $125.00. Provides information on more than 15,000 nursing homes, including admission requirements, facilities, number of beds, and name of owner.

McKnight's Long-Term Care News--Industry Directory. McKnight's Long-Term Care News. • Publication includes: List of suppliers of products and services for nursing homes, as well as general information about the long-term care industry. Entries include: Company, name, address, phone, fax, name and title of contact, e-mail, web site if available.

Provider: LTC Buyers' Guide. American Health Care Association. • Annual. $10.00. Lists several hundred manufacturers and suppliers of products and services for long term care (LTC) facilities.

FINANCIAL RATIOS

Annual Statement Studies. The Risk Management Association. • Annual. Median and quartile financial ratios are given for over 400 kinds of manufacturing, wholesale, retail, construction, and consumer finance establishments. Data is sorted by both asset size and sales volume. Includes a clearly written "Definition of Ratios" and an alphabetical industry index.

Annual Statement Studies: Industry Default Probabilities and Cash Flow Measures. The Risk Management Association. • Annual. $145.00. Serves as a companion volume to the original *Annual Statement Studies*. Gives probability of default estimates on a percentage scale for more than 450 industries. Includes changes in position year-by-year for eight financial statement line items and provides percentage measures of cash flow.

HANDBOOKS AND MANUALS

Healthcare Finance for the Non-Financial Manager: Basic Guide to Financial Analysis & Control. Louis Gapenski. McGraw-Hill. • 1994. $47.50.

How to Cover the Gaps in Medicare: Health Insurance and Long-Term Care Options for the Retired. Robert A. Gilmour. American Institute for Economic Research. • 2003. $10.00. Four parts: "The Medicare Quandry," "How to Protect Yourself Against the Medigap," "Long-Term Care Options", and "End-of-Life Decisions" (living wills). Includes discussions of long-term care insurance, retirement communities, and HMO Medicare insurance.

The Managed Care Contracting Handbook: Planning and Negotiating the Managed Care Relationship. Maria K. Todd. Available from McGraw Hill Higher Education. • 1996. $65.00. Co-published by McGraw-Hill Healthcare Education Group and the Healthcare Financial Management Association. Covers managed care planning, proposals, strategy, negotiation, and contract law. Written for healthcare providers.

Nursing Home Regulations Manual. Thompson Publishing Group, Inc. • $295.00 per year. Looseleaf service. Includes monthly updates, newsletters and internet access. Serves as a comprehensive guide to the Nursing Home Reform Act, federal regulations, resident assessment, deficiency findings, Medicare, Medicaid, Health Care Financing Administration (HCFA) policies, and related topics for nursing home and assisted living facility owners and managers.

INTERNET DATABASES

Medicare: The Official U. S. Government Site for Medicare Information. Centers for Medicare and Medicaid Services. Phone: (202)690-6726 • URL: http://www.medicare.gov • Web site provides extensive information on Medicare health plans, publications, fraud, nursing homes, top 20 questions and answers, etc. Includes access to the National Nursing Home Database, providing summary compliance information on "every Medicare and Medicaid certified nursing home in the country." Online searching is offered. Fees: Free.

PERIODICALS AND NEWSLETTERS

AHA News. American Hospital Association. HealthForum. • Description: Highlights major news affecting hospitals and the health care field. Reports on legislation and regulation, court cases, surveys, and federal programs. Carries information on individual hospitals and allied hospital associations.

American Health Care Association: Provider. American Health Care Association. • Monthly. $48.00 per year. Formerly *American Health Care Association Journal.*

Assisted Living Success. Virgo Publishing, Inc. • Monthly. $55.00 per year. Edited for owners, operators, and managers of assisted living facilities.

Assisted Living Today. Assisted Living Federation of America. • Nine times a year. $30.00 per year. Covers the management, marketing, and financing of assisted living residences.

Balance. American College of Health Care Administrators. • Eight times a year. Free to members; non-members, $80.00 per year. Includes research papers and articles on the administration of long term care facilities. Formerly*Continnum.*

Contemporary Longterm Care. Leisure Publications. • Monthly. Free to qualified personnel. Edited for the long term health care industry, including retirement centers with life care, continuing care communities, and nursing homes.

Continuing Care News: Supporting the Transition into Post Hospital Care. Stevenson Publishing Corp. • Monthly. $99.00 per year. Topics include insurance, legal issues, health business news, ethics, and case management. Includes annual *Buyer's Guide.*

Geriatric Care. Eymann Publications. • Monthly. $87.50 per year.

Health Facilities Management. American Hospital Association. American Hospital Publishing, Inc. • Monthly. $40.00 per year. Covers building maintenance and engineering for hospitals and nursing homes.

Health Forum Journal: Leadership Strategies for Healthcare Executives. Health Forum. • Biweekly. $65.00 per year. Covers the general management of hospitals, nursing homes, and managed care organizations. Formerly *HospitalsHealthNetworks.*

Housing the Elderly Report. Community Development Services, Inc. CD Publications. • Monthly. $249.00 per year. Newsletter. Edited for retirement communities, apartment projects, and nursing homes. Covers news relative to business and property management issues.

McKnight's Long Term Care News. Thomson Medical Economics. • 16 times a year. $47.95 per year. Edited for retirement housing directors and nursing home administrators.

Modern Healthcare: The Newsmagazine for Administrators and Managers in Hospitals and Other Healthcare Institutions. Crain Communications, Inc. • Weekly. $145.00 per year; students, $63.00 per year.

Nursing Homes: Long Term Care Management. Medquest Communications, LLC. • Monthly. $95.00 per year. Covers business, finance, and management topics for nursing home directors and administrators.

Older Americans Report. Business Publishers Inc. • Description: Features brief articles on legislative, judicial, and federal agency activities concerning older Americans. Covers news of developments in such areas as Social Security, social services, Medicare, programs for retirement and pension funds, research projects, and the Older Americans Act. Recurring features include book reviews and a calendar of events.

Provider: For Long Term Care Professionals. American Health Care Association. • Monthly. $48.00 per year. Free to qualified personnel; others, $48.00 per year. Edited for medical directors, administrators, owners, and others concerned with extended care facilities and nursing homes. Covers

business management, legal issues, financing, reimbursement, care planning, ethics, human resources, etc. Includes *Buyers' Guide.*

STATISTICS SOURCES

Health Care Costs. DRI/McGraw-Hill. • Quarterly. Price on application. Cost indexes for hospitals, nursing homes, and home healthcare agencies.

Health, United States, 1999: Health and Aging Chartbook. Available from U. S. Government Printing Office. • 1999. $43.00. Issued by the National Center for Health Statistics, U. S. Department of Health and Human Services. Contains 34 bar charts in color, with related statistical tables. Provides detailed data on persons over 65 years of age, including population, living arrangements, life expectancy, nursing home residence, poverty, health status, assistive devices, health insurance, and health care expenditures.

Standard & Poor's Industry Surveys. Standard & Poor's. • Semiannual. $1,800.00. Two looseleaf volumes. Includes monthly *Supplements.* Provides detailed, individual surveys of 52 major industry groups. Each survey is revised on a semiannual basis. Also includes "Monthly Investment Review" (industry group investment analysis) and monthly "Trends & Projections" (economic analysis).

TRADE/PROFESSIONAL ASSOCIATIONS

American Association for Continuity of Care. P.O. Box 532, Dunedin, FL 34697. Phone: (727)738-1030 Fax: (727)738-8099 • URL: http://www.continuityofcare.com • Members are professionals concerned with continuity of care, health care after hospital discharge, and home health care.

American Association of Homes and Services for the Aging. 2519 Conneticut Ave., N.W., Washington, DC 20008-1520. Phone: (202)783-2242 Fax: (202)783-2255 E-mail: info@aahsa.org • URL: http://www.aahsa.org • Committed to advancing the vision of healthy, affordable, ethical aging services for America. Formerly American Association of Homes of the Aging.

American College of Health Care Administrators. 300 N. Lee St., No. 301, Alexandria, VA 22314. Phone: 888-882-2422 or (703)739-7900 Fax: (703)739-7901 E-mail: mtn@achca.org • URL: http://www.achca.org • Formerly American College of Nursing Home Administrators.

American Health Care Association. 1201 L St. NW, Washington, DC 20005. Phone: (202)842-4444 Fax: (202)842-3860 E-mail: hr@ahca.org • URL: http://www.ahcancal.org/Pages/Default.aspx • Federation of state associations of long-term health care facilities. Promotes standards for professionals in long-term health care delivery and quality care for patients and residents in a safe environment. Focuses on issues of availability, quality, affordability, and fair payment. Operates as liaison with governmental agencies, Congress, and professional associations. Compiles statistics.

OTHER SOURCES

The Long-Term Care Market. MarketResearch.com. • 1999. $3,250.00. Market data with forecasts to the year 2005. Emphasis is on the over-85 age group. Covers health insurance, the nursing home industry, pharmaceuticals, healthcare supplies, etc.

The U. S. Market for Assisted-Living Facilities. MarketResearch.com. • 1997. $2,750.00. Market research report. Includes market demographics and estimates of future revenues. Facility operators such as Emeritus, Manor Care, and Marriott Senior Living are profiled.

NUT INDUSTRY

ABSTRACTS AND INDEXES

Food Science and Technology Abstracts. International Food Information Service Publishing.

• Monthly. $1,780.00 per year. Provides worldwide coverage of the literature of food technology and food production.

Foods Adlibra: Key to the World's Food Literature. General Mills, Inc. Foods Adlibra Publications. • Semimonthly. $240.00 per year. Provides journal citations and abstracts to the literature of food technology and packaging.

ALMANACS AND YEARBOOKS

Agricultural and Mineral Commodities Year Book. Available from Taylor & Francis Group. • Annual. $225.00. Published by Europa Publications. Contains descriptive product profiles, price data, export-import data, and production statistics for major commodities of the world. Includes commodity histories, uses, markets, demand trends, and information about trade agreements and key commodity organizations.

CD-ROM DATABASES

Food Science and Technology Abstracts [CD-ROM]. Available from SilverPlatter Information, Inc. • Quarterly. Produced by International Food Information Service (home page is http://www.ifis.org). Provides worldwide coverage on CD-ROM of the literature of food technology and production. Various types of publications are indexed, with abstracts, including about 1,800 periodicals. Time period is 1969 to date.

DIRECTORIES

Major Food and Drink Companies of the World. Available from Gale Cengage Learning. • Annual. $880.00. Two volumes. Published by Graham & Whiteside. Contains profiles and trade names for more than 9,800 important food and beverage companies in various countries. In addition to foods, includes both alcoholic and nonalcoholic drink products.

Thomas Food and Beverage Market Place. Grey House Publishing. • 2004. $495.00. Three volumes. Contains more than 40,000 entries covering food companies, beverages, food equipment, warehouse companies, food brokers, wholesalers, importers, and exporters. Formerly *Thomas Food Industry Register.*

INTERNET DATABASES

USDA. United States Department of Agriculture. Phone: (202)720-2791 E-mail: agsec@usda.gov • URL: http://www.usda.gov • The USDA home page has six sections: News and Information; What's New; About USDA; Agencies; Opportunities; Search and Help. Keyword searching is offered from the USDA home page and from various individual agency home pages. Agencies are the Economic Research Service, Agricultural Marketing Service, National Agricultural Statistics Service, National Agricultural Library, and about 12 others. Updating varies. Fees: Free.

ONLINE DATABASES

Food Science and Technology Abstracts [online]. IFIS North American Desk. • Produced by International Food Information Service. Provides about 500,000 online citations, with abstracts, to the international literature of food science, technology, commodities, engineering, and processing. Approximately 2,000 periodicals are covered. Time period is 1969 to date, with monthly updates. Inquire as to online cost and availability.

FOODS ADLIBRA. General Mills, Inc. • Contains online citations, with abstracts, to the technical and business literature of food processing and packaging. New products and new ingredients are featured. Covers about 250 trade journals and 500 research journals from 1974 to date, with monthly updates. Inquire as to online cost and availability.

PERIODICALS AND NEWSLETTERS

The Nutshell. Northern Nut Growers Association. • Description: Brings information to amateur and expert nut growers on cultural practices, new developments in propagation, and knowledge of new and better cultivars and where to get them. Contains supplements of reports on the latest practices, experiments in progress, and storage of nuts. Recurring features include letters to the editor, interviews, news of research, a calendar of events, reports of meetings, book reviews, and notices of publications available.

Peanut Journal and Nut World. Virginia-Carolina Peanut Association. Peanut Journal Publishing Co. • Monthly. $8.00 per year.

RESEARCH CENTERS AND INSTITUTES

College of Tropical Agriculture and Human Resources. University of Hawaii at Manoa, 2515 Campus Rd., Miller Hall 110, Honolulu, HI 96822. Phone: (808)956-8105 Fax: (808)956-8105 E-mail: fcs@ctahr.hawaii.edu • URL: http://www.ctahr. hawaii.edu/ • Concerned with the production and marketing of tropical food and ornamental plant products, including pineapples, bananas, coffee, and macadamia nuts.

STATISTICS SOURCES

Agricultural Statistics. Available from U. S. Government Printing Office. • Annual. $38.00. Produced by the National Agricultural Statistics Service, U. S. Department of Agriculture. Provides a wide variety of statistical data relating to agricultural production, supplies, consumption, prices/price-supports, foreign trade, costs, and returns, as well as farm labor, loans, income, and population. In many cases, historical data is shown annually for 10 years. In addition to farm data, includes detailed fishery statistics.

FAO Production Yearbook. Available from Bernan Associates. • Annual. $45.00. Published by the Food and Agriculture Organization (http://www.fao.org). Contains worldwide data on agriculture, land use, farm crops, livestock, and agricultural prices.

FAO Trade Yearbook. Available from Bernan Associates. • Annual. $45.00. Published by the Food and Agriculture Organization (http://www.fao.org). Provides extensive worldwide data on exports and imports of agricultural commodities, fertilizers, tractors, and pesticides. Includes more than 130 tables of detailed statistics.

World Food Data and Statistics. Euromonitor International. • 2004. $650.00. Provides five-year data for a wide variety of food products in 52 countries. Includes market size, consumer expenditures, price indicators, and retail distribution data for many kinds of meat, fish, fruits, vegetables, dairy products, baked goods, condiments, canned food, and frozen food.

TRADE/PROFESSIONAL ASSOCIATIONS

Northern Nut Growers Association, Inc. 648 Oak Hill School Rd., Townsend, DE 19734. Phone: (302)659-1731 Fax: (302)659-1732 E-mail: tuckerh@epix.net • URL: http://www. northernnutgrowers.com.

OTHER SOURCES

The Market for Salted Snacks. MarketResearch. com. • 2002. $3,000.00. Market research report. Covers potato chips, corn chips, popcorn, nuts, pretzels, and other salted snacks. Market projections are provided to the year 2004.

NUTRITION

See: DIET

NYLON

See: SYNTHETIC TEXTILE FIBER INDUSTRY

O

OATS INDUSTRY

See: FEED AND FEEDSTUFFS INDUSTRY; GRAIN INDUSTRY

OBSOLETE SECURITIES

DIRECTORIES
Directory of Obsolete Securities. Financial Information, Inc. • Annual. $655.00.

PERIODICALS AND NEWSLETTERS
Financial History: Chronicling the History of America's Capital Markets. Museum of American Financial History. • Quarterly. Membership. Contains articles on early stock and bond markets and trading in the U. S., with photographs and other illustrations. Current trading in rare and unusual, obsolete stock and bond certificates is featured. Formerly Friends or Financial History.

PRICE SOURCES
National Bond Summary. Pink Sheets LLC. • Monthly, with semiannual cumulations. $504.00 per year. Includes price quotes for both active and inactive issues, with transfer agents, market makers (brokers), capital changes, name changes, and other corporate information. Formerly published by the National Quotation Bureau.

National Stock Summary. Pink Sheets LLC. • Monthly, with semiannual cumulations. $576.00 per year. Includes price quotes for both active and inactive issues, with transfer agents, market makers (brokers), capital changes, name changes, and other corporate information. Pink Sheets LLC also provides daily and weekly stock price services. Formerly published by the National Quotation Bureau.

OTHER SOURCES
Capital Changes Reports. CCH, Inc. • Weekly. $1,395.00. Six looseleaf volumes. Arranged alphabetically by company. This service presents a chronological capital history that includes reorganizations, mergers and consolidations. Recent actions are found in Volume One - "New Matters.".

OCCUPATIONAL HEALTH

See: INDUSTRIAL HYGIENE

OCCUPATIONAL SAFETY

See: INDUSTRIAL SAFETY

OCCUPATIONAL THERAPY

ABSTRACTS AND INDEXES
Psychological Abstracts. American Psychological Association. • Monthly. Members, $815.00 per year; individuals and institutions, $1,207.00 per year. Covers the international literature of psychology and the behavioral sciences. Includes journals, technical reports, dissertations, and other sources.

HANDBOOKS AND MANUALS
Conditions in Occupational Therapy: Effect on Occupational Performance. Ruth Hansen and Ben Atchison. Lippincott Williams and Wilkins. • 1999. $45.95. Second edition. Each chapter "describes a major condition that occupational therapists frequently treat." Includes case studies.

ONLINE DATABASES
PsycINFO. American Psychological Association. • Provides indexing and abstracting of the worldwide literature of psychology and the behavioral sciences. Time period is 1967 to date, with monthly updates. Inquire as to online cost and availability.

PERIODICALS AND NEWSLETTERS
American Journal of Occupational Therapy. American Occupational Therapy Association, Inc. • Six times a year. Individuals, $50.00 per year; institutions, $120.00 per year.

Occupational Therapy in Health Care: A Journal of Contemporary Practice. Haworth Press, Inc. • Quarterly. $275.00 per year.

Occupational Therapy in Mental Health: A Journal of Psychosocial Practice and Research. Haworth Press, Inc. • Quarterly. Institutions, $385.00 per year.

TRADE/PROFESSIONAL ASSOCIATIONS
American Occupational Therapy Association. 4720 Montgomery Ln., PO Box 31220, Bethesda, MD 20824-1220. Phone: 800-377-8555 or (301)652-2682 or (301)652-6611 Fax: (301)652-7711 E-mail: execdept@aota.org • URL: http://www.aota.org • Occupational therapists and occupational therapy assistants. Provides services to people whose lives have been disrupted by physical injury or illness, developmental problems, the aging process, or social or psychological difficulties. Occupational therapy focuses on the active involvement of the patient in specially designed therapeutic tasks and activities to improve function, performance capacity, and the ability to cope with demands of daily living.

OCCUPATIONS

See also: EMPLOYMENT; JOB DESCRIPTIONS; JOB RESUMES; VOCATIONAL EDUCATION; VOCATIONAL GUIDANCE

GENERAL WORKS
Careers in Golf: An Insider's Guide to Careers in the Golf Industry. Nancy Berkley. National Golf Foundation. • 2001. $19.95. Information on careers in golf product manufacturing, retailing, tour management, public relations, event management, course design, and instruction. Includes CD-ROM.

Encyclopedia of Careers and Vocational Guidance. Holli Cosgrove. Fact on File Inc. • 2002. 12th edition. Price on application.

Full Disclosure: The New Lawyer's Must-Read Career Guide. Christen C. Carey. American Lawyer Media, Inc. • 2001. $19.95. "All the Things Lawyers Wish They Had Known at the Beginning of Their Careers, Rather Than at the End." Covers such topics as job hunting, job interviews, summer associate programs, law firm economics, life as a law firm associate, and gender in law firms.

Is It Too Late to Run Away and Join the Circus? Finding the Life You Really Want. Marti Smye. John Wiley. • 1998. $14.95. Provides philosophical and inspirational advice on leaving corporate life and becoming self-employed as a consultant or whatever. Central theme is dealing with major changes in life style and career objectives.

Opportunities in Government Careers. Neale J. Baxter. McGraw-Hill. • 2001. $15.95. Edited for students and job seekers. Includes education requirements and salary data. (VGM Career Books.).

Opportunities in Journalism Careers. Jim Patten and Donald L. Ferguson. McGraw-Hill. • 2001. $15.95. Edited for students and job seekers. Includes education requirements and salary data. (Opportunities in....Series).

Opportunities in Visual Arts Careers. Mark Salmon. McGraw-Hill. • 2001. $15.95. Edited for students and job seekers. Includes education requirements and salary data. (Opportunities in...Series).

Women of the Street: Making It on Wall Street-The World's Toughest Business. Sue Herera. John Wiley and Sons, Inc. • 1998. $16.95. The author is a CNBC business television anchorperson.

BIBLIOGRAPHIES
Job Hunter's Sourcebook: Where to Find Employment Leads and Other Job Search Resources. Gale Cengage Learning. • 2002. $125.00. Fifth edition. Covers 206 professions and occupations.

Jobs-Careers-Professions: A Bibliography with Indexes. Leon V. Werner. Nova Science Publishers,

Inc. • 2001. $59.00. Contains more than 1,500 citations to books and periodical articles on job hunting, compensation, career choice, education, mobility, supply-demand factors, and other job topics. Includes author, title, and subject indexes.

Professional Careers Sourcebook. Gale Cengage Learning. • 2002. $155.00. Seventh edition. Includes information sources for 129 professional and technical occupations.

Vocational Careers Sourcebook. Gale Cengage Learning. • 2002. $135.00. Fifth edition. A companion volume to *Professional Careers Sourcebook.* Includes information sources for 139 occupations that typically do not require a four-year college degree. Compiled in cooperation with InfoPLACE of the Cuyahoga County Public Library, Ohio.

CD-ROM DATABASES

Magazine Index Plus. Gale Cengage Learning. • Monthly. $4,000.00 per year (includes InfoTrac workstation). Provides full text on CD-ROM for about 100 popular, general interest magazines and indexing for 300 others. Includes special indexing of reviews and product evaluations. Time period is 1980 to date.

Sourcebooks America CD-ROM. CACI Marketing Systems. • Annual. $1,250.00. Provides the CD-ROM version of *The Sourcebook of ZIP Code Demographics: Census Edition* and *The Sourcebook of County Demographics: Census Edition.*

DIRECTORIES

NACE Directory: Who's Who in Career Services and HR/Staffing t. National Association of Colleges and Employers. • Annual. Free to members; non-members, $47.95. Lists over 2,200 college placement offices and about 2,000 companies interested in recruiting college graduates. Gives names of placement and recruitment personnel. Formerly *CPC National Dierctory.*

Peterson's Job Opportunities for Business Majors. Peterson's. • 1999. $18.95. Provides career information for the 2,000 largest U. S. employers in various industries.

Professional and Occupational Licensing Directory. Gale Cengage Learning. • 1996. $125.00. Second edition. Provides detailed national and state information on the requirements for obtaining a license in each of about 500 occupations. Information needed to contact the appropriate licensing agency or organization is included in each case.

HANDBOOKS AND MANUALS

Career Guide to Industries. Available from U. S. Government Printing Office. • 2002. $32.00. Issued by the Bureau of Labor Statistics, U. S. Department of Labor (http://www.bls.gov). Presents background career information (text) and statistics for the 40 industries that account for 70 percent of wage and salary jobs in the U. S. Includes nature of the industry, employment data, working conditions, training, earnings, rate of job growth, outlook, and other career factors. (BLS Bulletin 2541.).

Occupational Outlook Handbook. Bureau of Labor Statistics, U.S. Department of Labor. Available from U.S. Government Printing Office. • Biennial. $53.00. Issued as one of the Bureau's *Bulletin* series and kept up to date by *Occupational Outlook Quarterly.*

Specialty Occupational Outlook: Professions. Gale Cengage Learning. • 1994. $75.00. Provides information on 150 professional occupations. (Career Information Guide Series).

Specialty Occupational Outlook: Trade and Technical. Gale Cengage Learning. • 1995. $75.00. Provides information on 150 "high-interest" careers that do not require a bachelor's degree.

Standard Occupational Classification Manual. Available from Bernan Associates. • 2000. $38.00. Replaces the *Dictionary of Occupational Titles.*

Produced by the federal Office of Management and Budget, Executive Office of the President. "Occupations are classified based on the work performed, and on the required skills, education, training, and credentials for each one." Six-digit codes contain elements for 23 Major Groups, 96 Minor Groups, 451 Broad Occupations, and 820 Detailed Occupations. Designed to reflect the occupational structure currently existing in the U. S.

PERIODICALS AND NEWSLETTERS

Career World. Weekly Reader Corp. • Six times a year. $33.95. per year. Up-to-the-minute, important career and vocational news for students in grades 7 thru 12.

Journal of Career Planning and Employment: The International Magazine of Placement and Recruitment. National Association of Colleges and Employers. • Quarterly. Free to members; non-members, $72.00 per year. Includes *Spotlight* newsletter. Formerly *Journal of College Placement.*

Occupational Outlook Quarterly. U.S. Department of Labor. Available from U.S. Government Printing Office. • Quarterly. $15.00 per year.

ReCareering Newsletter: An Idea and Resource Guide to Second Career and Relocation Planning. Publications Plus, Inc. • Monthly. $59.00 per year. Edited for "downsized managers, early retirees, and others in career transition after leaving traditional employment." Offers advice on second careers, franchises, starting a business, finances, education, training, skills assessment, and other matters of interest to the newly unemployed.

TECHniques. Informix Software. • Eight times a year. Free to members; non-members, $45.00 per year. Formerly *Vocational Educational Journal.*

Work and Occupations: An International Sociological Journal. Sage Publications, Inc. • Quarterly. $499.00 per year. Includes print and online editions.

STATISTICS SOURCES

Employment Outlook, 1998-2008: A Summary of BLS Projections. Available from U. S. Government Printing Office. • 2000. $10.00. Issued by the Bureau of Labor Statistics, U. S. Department of Labor (http://www.bls.gov). Provides 1998 employment data and 2008 projections for a wide variety of managerial, professional, technical, marketing, clerical, service, agricultural, and production occupations. Includes factors affecting the employment growth of various industries. (Bureau of Labor Statistics Bulletin 2522.).

Handbook of U. S. Labor Statistics: Employment, Earnings, Prices, Productivity, and Other Labor Data. Eva E. Jacobs, editor. Bernan Associates. • 1999. $74.00. Based on *Handbook of Labor Statistics,* formerly issued by the Bureau of Labor Statistics, U. S. Department of Labor. Includes the Bureau's projections of employment in the U. S. by industry and occupation. Provides a wide variety of data on the work force, prices, fringe benefits, and consumer expenditures.

Key Indicators of the Labour Market. Available from Routledge. • Biennial. $125.00. Published by the International Labour Office (http://www.ilo.org). Provides data on 20 key indicators in 220 countries. Includes labor force statistics, employment, unemployment, part-time workers, wages, productivity, poverty indicators, and related topics.

National Compensation Survey. Available from U. S. Government Printing Office. • Irregular. $300.00 per year. Consists of bulletins reporting on earnings for jobs in clerical, professional, technical, and other fields in 70 major metropolitan areas. Formerly *Occupational Compensation Survey.*

Occupational Projections and Training Data. Available from U. S. Government Printing Office. • Biennial. $21.00. Issued by Bureau of Labor Statistics, U. S. Department of Labor. Contains

projections of employment change and job openings over the next 15 years for about 500 specific occupations. Also includes the number of associate, bachelor's, master's, doctoral, and professional degrees awarded in a recent year for about 900 specific fields of study.

Social Statistics of the United States. Mark S. Littman, editor. Bernan Press. • 2000. $65.00. Includes statistical data on population growth, labor force, occupations, environmental trends, leisure time use, income, poverty, taxes, and other economic or demographic topics.

Statistical Handbook of Working America. Gale Cengage Learning. • 1997. $130.00. Second edition. Provides statistics, rankings, and forecasts relating to a wide variety of careers, occupations, and working conditions.

Statistics on Occupational Wages and Hours of Work and on Food Prices. International Labour Organization. • Annual. $28.00. Provides international data on wages and hours for 159 occupations within 49 industries. Includes retail prices for 93 food items.

TRADE/PROFESSIONAL ASSOCIATIONS

Association for Career and Technical Education. 1410 King St., Alexandria, VA 22314. Phone: 800-826-9772 or (703)683-3111 Fax: (703)683-7424 E-mail: acte@acteonline.org • URL: http://www.acteonline.org.

OTHER SOURCES

Chronicle Occupational Briefs. Chronicle Guidance Publications, Inc. • Approximately 600 pamphlets about various occupations. $2.25 per pamphlet. CD-ROM edition, $149.00.

OCEAN LINERS

See: STEAMSHIP LINES

OCEANOGRAPHIC INDUSTRIES

See also: MARINE ENGINEERING

GENERAL WORKS

Recent Advances and Issues in Environmental Science. Joan R. Callahan, editor. Greenwood Publishing Group, Inc. • 1999. $49.95. Includes environmental economic problems, such as saving jobs vs. protecting the environment. (Oryx Frontiers of Science Series.).

ABSTRACTS AND INDEXES

Applied Science and Technology Index. H. W. Wilson Co. • 11 times a year. Quarterly and annual cumulations. Price varies. Indexes a wide variety of English language technical, industrial, and engineering periodicals.

Meteorological and Geoastrophysical Abstracts. American Meteorological Society. • Bimonthly. $1,685.00 per year.

NTIS Alerts: Ocean Sciences and Technology. National Technical Information Service. • Semimonthly. $210.00 per year. Provides descriptions of government-sponsored research reports and software, with ordering information. Formerly *Abstract Newsletter.*

Oceanic Abstracts. CSA. • 11 times a year. $1,645.00 per year. Includes print and online editions. Covers oceanography, marine biology, ocean shipping, and a wide range of other marine-related subject areas.

ALMANACS AND YEARBOOKS

Earth Almanac: An Annual Geophysical Review of the State of the Planet. Natalie Goldstein.

Greenwood Publishing Group, Inc. • Annual. $69.95. Provides background information, statistics, and a summary of major events relating to the atmosphere, oceans, land, and fresh water.

DIRECTORIES

Sea Technology Buyers Guide/Directory. Compass Publications Inc. • Covers: manufacturing, service, research and development, engineering, construction, drilling, equipment lease and rental firms, and testing organizations providing goods and services to the oceanographic, offshore, marine sciences, and undersea defense industries. Eight informational sections. Entries include: Company name, contact information, executives' names, list of products and/or services.

ENCYCLOPEDIAS AND DICTIONARIES

Encyclopedia of Global Change: Environmental Change and Human Society. Andrew S. Goudie, editor. Oxford University Press. • 2001. $275.00. Two volumes. Contains 300 signed articles on a wide variety of topics relating to changes in the environment and the atmosphere. Includes bibliographies and illustrations.

Water Encyclopedia. Frits Von Der Leeden and others, editors. Lewis Publishers. • 1990. $249.95. Second edition. Covers a wide variety of topics relating to water. (Geraghty and Miller Environmental Science and Engineering Series).

ONLINE DATABASES

Applied Science and Technology Index Online. H. W. Wilson Co. • Provides online indexing of 500 major scientific, technical, industrial, and engineering periodicals. Time period is 1983 to date. Monthly updates. Inquire as to online cost and availability.

Aqualine. Cambridge Scientific Abstracts. • Provides online citations and abstracts to a wide variety of literature relating to the aquatic environment, including 400 journals, from 1960 to date. Updating is monthly. Inquire as to online cost and availability.

GEOARCHIVE. Geosystems. • Citations to literature on geoscience and water. 1974 to present. Monthly updates. Inquire as to online cost and availability.

Oceanic Abstracts (Online). Cambridge Scientific Abstracts. • Oceanographic and other marine-related technical literature, 1981 to present. Monthly updates. Inquire as to online cost and availability.

PERIODICALS AND NEWSLETTERS

Marine Policy; The International Journal of Ocean Affairs. Elsevier. • Bimonthly. Institutions, $882.00 per year.

Ocean Development and International Law; The Journal of Marine Affairs. Taylor & Francis Group. • Quarterly. Individuals, $225.00 per year; institutions, $454.00 per year.

Ocean Engineering: An International Journal of Research and Development. Elsevier Science. • 18 times a year. Qualified personnel, $261.00 per year; institutions, $2,367.00 per year.

Progress in Oceanography. Elsevier. • 16 times a year. Qualified personnel, $175.00 per year; individuals, $168.00 per year; institutions, $2,392.00 per year.

Sea Technology: For Design Engineering and Application of Equipment and Services for the Marine Environment. Compass Publications, Inc. • Monthly. $40.00 per year.

TRADE/PROFESSIONAL ASSOCIATIONS

International Oceanographic Foundation. University of Miami, Rosentiel School of Marine and Atmospheric Science, Miami, FL 33149-1098. Phone: (305)361-4888 or (305)361-4697 Fax: (305)361-4711 E-mail: oceans@nbc.com • URL:

http://www.rsmas.miami.edu/iof/ • Individuals interested in the sea. Encourages the protection and exploration of oceans. Topics include: game and food fish; other creatures of sea and shore; ocean currents; geology, chemistry, and physics of the sea and sea floor; submarine detection; industrial applications of oceanography.

Marine Technology Society. 5565 Sterrett Pl., Ste. 108, Columbia, MD 21044. Phone: (410)884-5330 Fax: (410)884-9060 E-mail: membership@mtsociety.org • URL: http://www.mtsociety.org • Scientists, engineers, educators, and others with professional interest in the marine sciences or related fields; includes institutional and corporate members. Disseminates marine scientific and technical information, including institutional, environmental, physical, and biological aspects; fosters a deeper understanding of the world's seas and attendant technologies. Maintains 13 sections and 29 professional committees. Conducts tutorials.

National Ocean Industries Association. 1120 G St. NW, Ste. 900, Washington, DC 20005. Phone: (202)347-6900 Fax: (202)347-8650 E-mail: mkearns@noia.org • URL: http://www.noia.org • Corporations organized to promote the common business interests of the offshore and ocean-oriented industries by: increasing public understanding of the ocean's use and its relation to the economy; encouraging interest in industrial, scientific, recreational, research, and educational activities in the field of ocean enterprise; encouraging the development and use of the resources of the ocean consistent with environmental practices and safeguards; encouraging compatible use of ocean resources; improving communication between industry and the federal government. Supports legislation and other governmental action favorable to the offshore and ocean industry and counsels against such action when it is not favorable. Seeks to expand the role of the free enterprise system in the development of ocean resources.

OECD

See: ORGANIZATION FOR ECONOMIC COOPERATION AND DEVELOPMENT

OFF-PRICE RETAILERS

See: DISCOUNT HOUSES

OFFICE APPLIANCES

See: OFFICE EQUIPMENT AND SUPPLIES

OFFICE AUTOMATION

See also: DESKTOP PUBLISHING; FACSIMILE SYSTEMS; MICROCOMPUTERS AND MINICOMPUTERS; WORD PROCESSING

ABSTRACTS AND INDEXES

Business Periodicals Index. H. W. Wilson Co. • 11 times a year. Quarterly and annual cumulations. Price varies.

Computer and Control Abstracts. Available from INSPEC, Inc. • Monthly. $2,400.00 per year. Section C of *Science Abstracts*.

Computer and Information Systems Abstracts Journal: An Abstract Journal Pertaining to the Theory, Design, Fabrication and Application of Computer and Information Systems. CSA. • 11 times a year. $1,750 per year.

Computer Literature Index: A Subject/Author Index to Computer and Data Processing Literature. EB-

SCO Publishing. • Quarterly, with annual cumulation. $245.00 per year. Contains brief abstracts of book and periodical literature covering all phases of computing, including approximately 70 specific application areas.

Key Abstracts: Business Automation. Available from INSPEC, Inc. • Monthly. $250.00 per year. Provides international coverage of journal and proceedings literature. Published in England by the Institution of Electrical Engineers (IEE).

DIRECTORIES

The Software Encyclopedia: A Guide for Personal, Professional, and Business Users. Gale. • Annual. $335.00. Two volumes. Volume one lists software programs by title and producer. Volume two provides information on programs according to application and operating system. Includes prices and requirements for hardware and memory.

HANDBOOKS AND MANUALS

Electronic Office Machines. William R. Pasewark. South-Western. • 1995. $25.95. Seventh edition.

Procedures for the Automated Office. Sharon Burton and others. Prentice Hall PTR. • 2000. $60.00. Fifth edition.

ONLINE DATABASES

Internet and Personal Computing Abstracts. Information Today, Inc. • Contains abstracts covering a wide variety of personal and business microcomputer literature appearing in more than 100 journals and popular magazines. Time period is 1981 to date, with monthly updates. Formerly *Microcomputer Index*. Inquire as to online cost and availability.

PROMT: Predicasts Overview of Markets and Technology. Gale Cengage Learning. • Companies, products, applied technologies and markets. U.S. and international literature coverage, 1972 to date. Inquire as to online cost and availability. Provides abstracts from more than 1,600 publications. Weekly updates.

Wilson Business Abstracts Online. H. W. Wilson Co. • Indexes and abstracts 600 major business periodicals, plus the *Wall Street Journal* and the business section of the *New York Times*. Indexing is from 1982, abstracting from 1990, with the two newspapers included from 1993. Updated weekly. Inquire as to online cost and availability. (*Business Periodicals Index* without abstracts is also available online.).

PERIODICALS AND NEWSLETTERS

EDP Weekly: The Leading Weekly Computer News Summary. Computer Age and EDP News Services. • Weekly. $495.00 per year. Newsletter. Summarizes news from all areas of the computer and microcomputer industries.

Law Technology News: Products, Systems, and Services for Legal Professionals. American Lawyer Media, Inc. • Monthly. $69.00 per year. Features descriptions of new technology products and services of interest to the legal profession.

Office Products Analyst: A Monthly Report Devoted to the Analysis of Office Products. Industry Analysts, Inc. • Monthly. $195.00 per year. Newsletter. Includes user ratings of office automation equipment.

Wireless Review: Intelligence for Competitive Providers. Primedia Business Magazines and Media. • Semimonthly. $48.00 per year. Covers business and technology developments for wireless service providers. Includes special issues on a wide variety of wireless topics. Formed by merger of *Cellular Business* and *Wireless World*.

RESEARCH CENTERS AND INSTITUTES

Collaboratory for Research on Electronic Work. University of Michigan, 1075 Beal Ave., Ann Arbor, MI 48109-2112. Phone: (734)647-4948 Fax:

(734)647-8044 E-mail: finholt@umich.edu • URL: http://www.crew.umich.edu/ • Concerned with the design and use of computer-based tools for thinking and planning in the professional office.

TRADE/PROFESSIONAL ASSOCIATIONS

IEEE Computer Society. 1828 L St. NW, Ste. 1202, Washington, DC 20036. Phone: (202)371-0101 Fax: (202)728-9614 E-mail: help@computer.org • URL: http://www.computer.org • Computer professionals. Promotes the development of computer and information sciences and fosters communication within the information processing community. Sponsors conferences, symposia, workshops, tutorials, technical meetings, and seminars. Operates Computer Society Press. Presents scholarships; bestows technical achievement and service awards and certificates.

OFFICE BUILDINGS

HANDBOOKS AND MANUALS

Guide to Energy Efficient Commercial Equipment. Margaret Suozzo and others. American Council for an Energy Efficient Economy. • 1997. $25.00. Provides information on specifying and purchasing energy-saving systems for buildings (heating, air conditioning, lighting, and motors).

Managing the Office Building. Mark Ingerbretsen, editor. Institute of Real Estate Management. • 1985. $62.95. Revised edition.

Office Building Safety and Health. Charles D. Reese. CRC Press. • 2004. $89.95. Covers a wide variety of topics relating to office building safety, including management of emergencies, common hazards, accident prevention, environmental health issues, and security.

Office Interior Design Guide: An Introduction for Facility and Design. Julie K. Rayfield. John Wiley and Sons, Inc. • 1997. $70.00. (Professional Series).

Office Planning and Design Desk Reference: A Guide for Architects and Design Professionals. James Rappoport and others, editors. John Wiley and Sons, Inc. • 1991. $130.00. Covers the planning and designing of new or retrofitted office space.

PERIODICALS AND NEWSLETTERS

Building Operating Management: The National Magazine for Commercial and Institutional Buildings Construction, Renovation, Facility Management. Trade Press Publishing Corp. • Monthly. Free to qualified personnel.

Business Facilities: The Location Advisor. Group C Communications, Inc. • Monthly. Free to qualified personnel; others, $30.00 per year. Facility planning and site selection.

Commercial Building: Tranforming Plans into Buildings. Stamats Communications. • Bimonthly. $48.00 per year. Edited for building contractors, engineers, and architects. Includes special features on new products, climate control, plumbing, and vertical transportation.

Marketscore. CB Richard Ellis. • Quarterly. Price on application. Newsletter. Provides proprietary forecasts of commercial real estate performance in metropolitan areas.

National Real Estate Investor. Primedia Business Magazines and Media. • Monthly. $85.00 per year. Includes annual *Directory.* Market surveys by city.

Office Relocation Magazine. ORM Group. • Bimonthly. $39.00 per year. Provides articles on the relocation of office facilities.

Quarterly Market Report. Property and Portfolio Research. • Quarterly. $1,000.00 per year for one property type; 2,000 per year for six property types. Newsletter. Reviews current prices, rents, capitalization rates, and occupancy trends for commercial real estate.

Real Estate Economics: Journal of the American Real Estate and Urban Economics Association. MIT Press. • Quarterly. Institutions, $295.00 per year. Includes print and online editions.

PRICE SOURCES

National Real Estate Index. CB Richard Ellis. • Price and frequency on application. Provides reports on commercial real estate prices, rents, capitalization rates, and trends in more than 65 metropolitan areas. Time span is 12 years. Includes urban office buildings, suburban offices, warehouses, retail properties, and apartments.

STATISTICS SOURCES

ULI Market Profiles: North America. Urban Land Institute. • Annual. Members, $249.95; non-members, $299.95. Provides real estate marketing data for residential, retail, office, and industrial sectors. Covers 76 U. S. metropolitan areas and 13 major foreign metropolitan areas.

TRADE/PROFESSIONAL ASSOCIATIONS

American Real Estate and Urban Economics Association. PO Box 1148, Portage, MI 49081-1148. Phone: (866)273-8321 Fax: (313)731-0174 E-mail: areuea@areuea.org • URL: http://www.areuea.org • Members are real estate teachers, researchers, economists, and others concerned with urban real estate and investment.

Building Owners and Managers Association International. 1201 New York Ave., NW, Ste. 300, Washington, DC 20005. Phone: (202)408-2662 Fax: (202)371-0181 E-mail: info@boma.org • URL: http://www.boma.org • Formerly National Association of Building Owners and Managers.

National Association of Industrial and Office Properties. 2201 Cooperative Way, 3rd Fl., Herndon, VA 20171. Phone: 800-666-6780 or (703)904-7100 Fax: (703)904-7942 E-mail: naiop@naiop.org • URL: http://www.naiop.org • Members are owners and developers of business, industrial, office, and retail properties. Formerly NAIOP - The Association of Commercial Real Estate.

OFFICE DESIGN

GENERAL WORKS

Color in the Office: Design Trends from 1950 to 1990 and Beyond. Sara O. Marberry. John Wiley and Sons, Inc. • 1993. $90.00. Presents past, present, and future color trends in corporate office design. Features color photographs of traditional, postmodern, and neoclassical office designs. (Architecture Series).

DIRECTORIES

Interiors and Sources: Directory and Buyer's Guide. L. C. Clark Publishing Co., Inc. • Annual. $10.00. Lists sources of surface materials, furniture, lighting, etc., for interior designers.

ENCYCLOPEDIAS AND DICTIONARIES

Encyclopedia of Interior Design. Joanna Banham, editor. Fitzroy Dearborn Publishers, Inc. • 1997. $295.00. Two volumes. Contains more than 500 essays on interior design topics. Includes bibliographies.

HANDBOOKS AND MANUALS

Facilities and Workplace Design: An Illustrated Guide. Quarterman Lee and others. Engineering and Management Press. • 1996. $25.00. Written for both new and experienced designers. Features "25 illustrated tasks that can be applied to most projects. "(Engineers in Business Series).

Home Office Design: Everything You Need to Know about Planning, Organizing, and Furnishing Your Work Space. Neal Zimmerman. John Wiley and Sons, Inc. • 1996. $19.95. Covers furniture, seating, workstations, filing, storage, task lighting, etc.

Interior Design for Libraries: Drawing on Function and Appeal. Carol R. Brown. American Library Association. • 2002. $45.00. Covers furniture, lighting, signs, acoustics, and other items important to interior design. Contains many illustrations of library interiors, including color plates.

Interior Graphic Standards. Maryrose T. McGowan. John Wiley and Sons, Inc. • 2003. $175.00. Provides guidelines for the planning and detailing of commercial and residential interiors. Includes more than 3,000 architectural drawings.

PERIODICALS AND NEWSLETTERS

Interiors and Sources. L. C. Clark Publishing Co., Inc. • Bimonthly. $27.00 per year. Promotes professionalism for interior designers and design firms. Includes special features on office systems, work stations, and office furniture.

Today's Facility Manager: The Magazine of Facilities-Interior Planning Team. Group C Communications. • Monthly. $30.00 per year. Covers office design, furnishings, and furniture, including open plan systems. Formerly *Business Interiors.*

Tradeline Exclusive Reports. Tradeline, Inc. • Monthly. $120.00 per year. Newsletter. Covers the planning, design, construction, and renovation of of a variety of corporate facilities. Formerly *FM Data Monthly.*

RESEARCH CENTERS AND INSTITUTES

Organizational Systems Research Association. Morehead State University, Dept. of Information Systems, P.O. Box 2478, Morehead, KY 40351-1689. Phone: (606)783-2718 Fax: (606)783-5025 E-mail: d.everett@morehead-st.edu • URL: http://www.osra.org • Research areas include the analysis, design, and administration of office systems. Formerly Office Systems Research Association.

OFFICE EQUIPMENT AND SUPPLIES

See also: COMPUTERS; OFFICE FURNITURE INDUSTRY; WORD PROCESSING

DIRECTORIES

Better Buys for Business: The Independent Consumer Guide to Office Equipment. What to Buy for Business, Inc. • 10 times a year. $134.00 per year. Each issue is on a particular office product, with detailed evaluation of specific models: 1. Low-Volume Copier Guide, 2. Mid-Volume Copier Guide, 3. High-Volume Copier Guide, 4. Plain Paper Fax and Low-Volume Multifunctional Guide, 5. Mid/High-Volume Multifunctional Guide, 6. Laser Printer Guide, 7. Color Printer and Color Copier Guide, 8. Scan-to-File Guide, 9. Business Phone Systems Guide, 10. Postage Meter Guide, with a Short Guide to Shredders.

Business Products Industry Association Membership Directory and Buyer's Guide. Independent Office Products and Furniture Dealers Association. • Annual. Free to members; non-members, $80.00. 9,000 manufacturers, wholesalers, retailers and sales and marketing representatives in the office products industry.

Directory of Discount and General Merchandise Stores. Chain Store Guide. • Annual. $327.00. On-line edition, $747.00. Includes retailers and wholesalers of housewares, giftwares, novelties, toys, hobby materials, crafts, and stationery.

HANDBOOKS AND MANUALS

Guide to Energy Efficient Office Equipment. Loretta A. Smith and others. American Council for an Energy Efficient Economy. • 1996. $12.00. Second edition. Provides information on selecting, purchasing, and using energy-saving computers, monitors, printers, copiers, and other office devices.

Office Equipment Adviser: The Essential What-to-Buy and How-to-Buy Resource for Offices with One to 100 People. John Derrick. What to Buy for Business, Inc. • 1995. $24.95. Third revised edition.

ONLINE DATABASES

PROMT: Predicasts Overview of Markets and Technology. Gale Cengage Learning. • Companies, products, applied technologies and markets. U.S. and international literature coverage, 1972 to date. Inquire as to online cost and availability. Provides abstracts from more than 1,600 publications. Weekly updates.

PERIODICALS AND NEWSLETTERS

Business Consumer's Advisor. Buyers Laboratory Inc. • Description: Focuses on office equipment and supplies, offering purchasing advice and exploring methods of increasing office productivity through appropriate management of the equipment and its operators. Offers readers a chance to share their experiences, evaluate products and equipment, and gives results of Buyers Laboratory's testing.

Office Dealer: Updating the Office Products Industry. Quality Publishing, Inc. • Six times a year. $36.00 per year. Edited primarily for retailers of office products and office furniture. Formerly *Office Systems Dealer.*

Office Solutions: The Magazine for Office Professionals. Quality Publishing, Inc. • Monthly. $36.00 per year. Edited for office managers. Covers office technology, services, and new products. Formerly *Office Systems,* incorporating *Managing Office Technology.*

PRICE SOURCES

Copier. Orion Research Corp. • Annual. $39.00. Quotes retail and wholesale prices of used office equipment. Original list prices and years of manufacture are also shown. Formerly *Orion Office Equipment Blue Book.*

STATISTICS SOURCES

Computers and Office and Accounting Machines. U. S. Bureau of the Census. • Annual. Provides data on shipments: value, quantity, imports, and exports. (Current Industrial Reports, MA-35R.).

TRADE/PROFESSIONAL ASSOCIATIONS

Business Technology Association. 12411 Wornall Rd., Ste. 200, Kansas City, MO 64145-1212. Phone: 800-505-2821 or (816)941-3100 Fax: (816)941-4838 E-mail: info@bta.org • URL: http://www.bta.org • Dealers and resellers of office equipment and networking products and services. Offers 60 seminars on management, service, technology, and business systems. Conducts research, provides business-supporting services and benefits, including insurance, and legal counsel.

Independent Office Products and Furniture Dealers Association. 301 N Fairfax St., Alexandria, VA 22314. Phone: 800-542-6672 or (703)549-9040 Fax: (703)683-7552 E-mail: info@iopfda.org • URL: http://www.iopfda.org • Formerly Office Furniture Dealers Alliance.

Information Technology Industry Council. 1250 Eye St. NW, Ste. 200, Washington, DC 20005. Phone: (202)737-8888 Fax: (202)638-4922 E-mail: rdawson@itic.org • URL: http://www.itic.org • Represents manufacturers of information technology products. Serves as secretariat and technology for ANSI-accredited standards committee x3 information technology group. Conducts public policy programs; compiles industry statistics.

OTHER SOURCES

Business Automation Reference Service: Office Equipment. Alltech Publishing Co. • Monthly. $100.00 per year. Looseleaf service.

Business Consumers's Network. Buyers Laboratory

Inc. • Monthly. $795.00 per year. Looseleaf service. Tests office equipment and issues reports. Formerly *Buyers Laboratory Report on Office Products.*

Writing and Marking Instruments. Available from MarketResearch.com. • 2002. $3,950.00. Published by Global Industry Analysts. Provides worldwide market research data, including profiles of major companies in the field.

OFFICE FORMS

See: FORMS AND BLANKS

OFFICE FURNITURE INDUSTRY

DIRECTORIES

FDM--The Source--Woodworking Industry Directory. Reed Business Information. • Publication includes: List of over 1,800 suppliers to secondary woodworking industry; coverage includes Canada. Entries include: Company name, address, phone, fax, product lines.

FINANCIAL RATIOS

Annual Statement Studies. The Risk Management Association. • Annual. Median and quartile financial ratios are given for over 400 kinds of manufacturing, wholesale, retail, construction, and consumer finance establishments. Data is sorted by both asset size and sales volume. Includes a clearly written "Definition of Ratios" and an alphabetical industry index.

Annual Statement Studies: Industry Default Probabilities and Cash Flow Measures. The Risk Management Association. • Annual. $145.00. Serves as a companion volume to the original *Annual Statement Studies.* Gives probability of default estimates on a percentage scale for more than 450 industries. Includes changes in position year-by-year for eight financial statement line items and provides percentage measures of cash flow.

HANDBOOKS AND MANUALS

Office Interior Design Guide: An Introduction for Facility and Design. Julie K. Rayfield. John Wiley and Sons, Inc. • 1997. $70.00. (Professional Series).

PERIODICALS AND NEWSLETTERS

Contract: The Business Magazine of Commercial and Institutional Interior Design, and Architecture, Planning and Construction. VNU Business Media. • Monthly. $94.00 per year. Firms engaged in specifying furniture and furnishings for commercial installations. Formerly *Contract Design.*

FDM: For Builders of Cabinets, Fixtures, Furniture, Millwork Furniture Design a nd Manufacturing. Chartwell Communications, Inc. • Monthly. Free to qualified personnel. Edited for furniture executives, production managers, and designers. Covers the manufacturing of household, office, and institutional furniture, store fixtures, and kitchen and bathroom cabinets.

Office World News. BUS Publications. • Monthly. Free to qualified personnel; others, $50.00 per year. Formerly *Office Products News.*

STATISTICS SOURCES

Annual Survey of Manufactures. Available from U. S. Government Printing Office. • Annual. Prices vary. Issued by the U. S. Census Bureau as an interim update to the *Census of Manufactures.* Includes data on number of manufacturing establishments in various industries, employment, labor costs, value of shipments, capital expenditures, inventories, energy costs, and assets. (See also Census Bureau home page, http://www.census.gov/.).

TRADE/PROFESSIONAL ASSOCIATIONS

Business and Institutional Furniture Manufacturers Association. 2680 Horizon Dr., S.E., Suite A1,

Grand Rapids, MI 49546-7500. Phone: (616)285-3963 Fax: (616)285-3765 E-mail: email@bifma.com • URL: http://www.bifma.com.

OFFICE IN THE HOME

See: SELF-EMPLOYMENT

OFFICE MACHINES

See: OFFICE EQUIPMENT AND SUPPLIES

OFFICE MANAGEMENT

See also: ADMINISTRATION; SYSTEMS IN MANAGEMENT; WORD PROCESSING

GENERAL WORKS

Administrative Office Management: An Introduction. Zane B. Quible. Prentice Hall PTR. • 2000. $73.00. 7th edition. (KU-Office Procedures Series).

ABSTRACTS AND INDEXES

Business Periodicals Index. H. W. Wilson Co. • 11 times a year. Quarterly and annual cumulations. Price varies.

CD-ROM DATABASES

WILSONDISC: Wilson Business Abstracts. H. W. Wilson Co. • Monthly. Includes unlimited online access to *Wilson Business Abstracts* through WILSONLINE. Provides CD-ROM "cover-to-cover" abstracting and indexing of over 600 prominent business periodicals. Indexing is from 1982, abstracting from 1990. (*Business Periodicals Index* without abstracts is available on CD-ROM at $1,495 per year.).

HANDBOOKS AND MANUALS

AMA Management Handbook. John J. Hampton, editor. AMACOM. • 1994. $110.00. Third edition. Provides 200 chapters in 16 major subject areas. Covers a wide variety of business and industrial management topics.

ONLINE DATABASES

Management Contents. Gale Cengage Learning. • Covers a wide range of management, financial, marketing, personnel, and administrative topics. About 150 leading business journals are indexed and abstracted from 1974 to date, with monthly updating. Inquire as to online cost and availability.

Wilson Business Abstracts Online. H. W. Wilson Co. • Indexes and abstracts 600 major business periodicals, plus the *Wall Street Journal* and the business section of the *New York Times.* Indexing is from 1982, abstracting from 1990, with the two newspapers included from 1993. Updated weekly. Inquire as to online cost and availability. (*Business Periodicals Index* without abstracts is also available online.).

PERIODICALS AND NEWSLETTERS

Hard at Work. Professional Training Associates, Inc. • Monthly. $89.00 per year. Newsletter on common personnel problems of supervisors and office managers. Formerly *Practical Supervision.*

Nine to Five Newsletter. 9 to 5 National Association of Working Women. • Five times a year. Free to members; individuals, $25.00 per year. A newsletter dealing with the rights and concerns of women office workers.

TRADE/PROFESSIONAL ASSOCIATIONS

National Association of Professional Organizers. 4700 W Lake Ave., Glenview, IL 60025. Phone: (847)375-4746 Fax: (847)734-9236 E-mail: hq@napo.net • URL: http://www.napo.net • Members are concerned with time management, productivity, and the efficient organization of documents and activities. Formerly Association of Professional Organizers.

Nine to Five: National Association of Working Women. 1430 W Peachtree St., Ste. 610, Atlanta, GA 30309. Phone: 800-522-0925 or (414)274-0925 Fax: (414)272-2870 E-mail: hotline9to5@igc.org • URL: http://www.9to5.org • Members are women office workers. Strives for the improvement of office working conditions for women and the elimination of sex and race discrimination.

OFFICE PRACTICE

See also: WORD PROCESSING

ENCYCLOPEDIAS AND DICTIONARIES
Professional Secretary's Encyclopedic Dictionary. Mary A. DeVries. Prentice Hall PTR. • 2001. $33.00. Fifth revised edition.

HANDBOOKS AND MANUALS
Career Legal Secretary. National Association of Legal Secretaries. West Publishing Co. • 1997. $35.50. Fourth edition.

Complete Secretary's Handbook. Mary A. De Vries. Prentice Hall PTR. • 1993. $24.95. Seventh edition.

Gregg Reference Manual. William A. Sabin. McGraw-Hill. • 2004. $46.55. 10th edition. Covers grammar, usage, and style, including changes evolving from the use of computers and the Internet. (Imprint: Irwin Professional Publishing.).

Office Professional's Quick Reference Handbook. Sheryl Lindsell-Roberts. Peterson's. • 1995. $9.00. Fifth revised edition.

Secretarial/Word Processing Service. Entrepreneur Media, Inc. • Looseleaf. $59.50. A practical guide to starting a secretarial and word processing business. Covers profit potential, start-up costs, market size evaluation, owner's time required, site selection, pricing, accounting, advertising, promotion, etc. (Start-Up Business Guide No. E1136.).

PERIODICALS AND NEWSLETTERS
Administrative Assistant's Update. MPL Communications Inc. • Description: Offers useful news, information, and suggestions to administrative assistants. Features articles on aspects of secretarial work, including items on problem-solving, office automation, computerization, and grammar and vocabulary development.

OfficePro. Stratton Publishing and Marketing Inc. • Nine times a year. $25.00 per year. Provides statistics and other information about secretaries and office trends. Formerly *Secretary.*

The Take-Charge Assistant. American Management Association. • Description: Features career and professional guidance, tips, and problem solving.

TRADE/PROFESSIONAL ASSOCIATIONS
International Association of Administrative Professionals. 10502 NW Ambassador Dr., Kansas City, MO 64195-0404. Phone: (816)891-6600 Fax: (816)891-9118 E-mail: service@iaap-hq.org • URL: http://www.iaap-hq.org • Formerly Professional Secretaries International.

OFFICE SUPPLIES

See: OFFICE EQUIPMENT AND SUPPLIES

OFFICE SYSTEMS

See: SYSTEMS IN MANAGEMENT; WORD PROCESSING

OFFICIAL PUBLICATIONS

See: GOVERNMENT PUBLICATIONS

OFFICIALS AND EMPLOYEES

See: GOVERNMENT EMPLOYEES

OFFSET PRINTING

See: GRAPHIC ARTS INDUSTRY; PRINTING AND PRINTING EQUIPMENT INDUSTRIES

OFFSHORE PETROLEUM INDUSTRY

See also: PETROLEUM INDUSTRY

ABSTRACTS AND INDEXES
Applied Science and Technology Index. H. W. Wilson Co. • 11 times a year. Quarterly and annual cumulations. Price varies. Indexes a wide variety of English language technical, industrial, and engineering periodicals.

DIRECTORIES
Financial Times Business Global Oil & Gas Directory. Available from Gale Cengage Learning. • Annual. $355.00. Published by Financial Times Business. Provides detailed information on 800 leading oil and gas companies worldwide. Includes financial data for three years. Formerly *Financial Times Energy Yearbook: Oil & Gas.*

Lloyd's Marine Equipment Buyers' Guide. Available from Informa UK Ltd. • Annual. $270.00. Published in the UK by Lloyd's List (http://www.lloydslist.com). Lists more than 6,000 companies worldwide supplying over 2,000 types of marine products and services, including offshore equipment.

Worldwide Offshore Petroleum Directory. PennWell Corp., Petroleum Div. • Annual. $135.00. Lists about 5,800 companies.

HANDBOOKS AND MANUALS
Modern Petroleum Technology. Richard A. Dawe, editor. John Wiley and Sons, Inc. • 2000. $600.00. Sixth edition. Two volumes. Volume one, entitled *Upstream,* covers oil rigs and other means of obtaining raw petroleum. Volume two, *Downstream,* covers petroleum refining and end products. Edited for industry technicians, managers, and engineers.

PERIODICALS AND NEWSLETTERS
Journal of Offshore Technology. Institute of Marine Engineering, Science, and Technology. • Bimonthly. Free to members; non-members, $100.00 per year. Covers the latest technological developments and trends for senior offshore engineers.

Marine Engineers Review (MER). Institute of Marine Engineering, Science, and Technology (IMarEST). • Monthly. Free to members; non-members, $150.00 per year. Covers marine engineering, offshore industries, and ocean shipping.

Marine Management Holdings: Transactions. Available from Information Today, Inc. • Bimonthly. $220.00 per year. Published in London by Marine Management Holdings Ltd. Contains technical and regulatory material on a wide variety of marine and offshore topics. Formerly *Institute of Marine Engineers: Transactions.*

Maritime IT & Electronics. Institute of Marine Engineering, Science, and Technology. • Bimonthly. $65.00 per year. Covers modern electronic technology as applied to all areas of the maritime industry.

Includes navigation systems, communications, control systems, monitoring, diagnostics, and software.

Ocean Oil Weekly Report: News, Analysis, and Market Trends of the Worldwide Offshore Oil and Gas Industry. PennWell Corp., Petroleum Div. • Weekly. $495.00 per year. Newsletter with emphasis on the Gulf of Mexico offshore oil industry. Includes statistics.

Offshore: Incorporating The Oilman. PennWell Corp., Industrial Div. • Monthly. $75.00 per year.

The Oilman Weekly Newsletter. PennWell Corp., Petroleum Div. • Weekly. $1,990.00 per year. Newsletter. Provides news of developments concerning the North Sea and European oil and gas businesses. Each issue contains four pages of statistical data.

RESEARCH CENTERS AND INSTITUTES
Geotechnical Engineering Center. University of Texas at Austin, Dept. of Civil Engineering, Austin, TX 78712. Phone: (512)471-4929 Fax: (512)471-6548 E-mail: swright@mail.utexas.edu • Areas of research include offshore complexes.

Southwest Research Institute. Southwest Research Institute. PO Box 28510, 6220 Culebra Rd., San Antonio, TX 78228-0510. Phone: (210)684-5111 Fax: (210)522-3547 E-mail: bd@swri.org • URL: http://www.swri.org • Automation, robotics, intelligent systems, space sciences, environmental sciences and engineering, bioengineering, micro encapsulation, chemistry, plant machinery and piping dynamics, radiolocation sciences and development, communications, electromagnetic compatibility, electronic systems, geophysical instrumentation, nondestructive evaluation research, nuclear waste regulatory analysis, fluid dynamics and hydraulics, offshore systems, structural analysis and testing, terminal ballistics and blast effects, materials development, solid mechanics, nonmetallic materials, engine systems engineering, engine emissions analysis and control, fuels and lubricants evaluation, fluids and lubrication technology, alternate energy systems, alternate fuels, mining systems engineering, vehicle and highway safety, and fire research.

TRADE/PROFESSIONAL ASSOCIATIONS
American Petroleum Institute. 1220 L St. NW, Washington, DC 20005-4070. Phone: (202)682-8000 Fax: (202)682-8033 E-mail: mediacenter@api.org • URL: http://www.api.org • Corporations in the petroleum and allied industries, including producers, refiners, marketers, and transporters of crude oil, lubricating oil, gasoline and natural gas. Provides public policy development, advocacy, research, and technical services to enhance the ability of the petroleum industry to fulfill its mission: meeting the nation's energy needs; enhancing the environmental, health, and safety performance of the industry; conducting research to advance petroleum technology, equipment, and standards; Consensus policies and collective action on issues impacting its members; and works collaboratively with all industry oil and gas associations, and other organizations, to enhance industry unity and effectiveness in its advocacy. Also provides the opportunity for standards development, technical cooperation and other activities to improve the industry's competitiveness through sponsorship of self-supporting programs.

Institute of Marine Engineers, Science and Technology. 80 Coleman St., London EC2R 5BJ, United Kingdom. Phone: 44 207 3822600 Fax: 44 207 3822670 E-mail: keith.read@imarest.org • URL: http://www.imarest.org • An international organization of marine engineers, offshore engineers, and naval architects.

International Association of Drilling Contractors. 15810 Park Ten Place, No. 242, Houston, TX 77210-

4287. Phone: (281)578-7171 Fax: (281)578-0589 E-mail: info@iadc.org • URL: http://www.iadc.org • Includes an Offshore Committee. Formerly American Association of Oilwell Drilling Contractors.

Offshore Marine Service Association. 990 N Corporate Dr., Ste. 210, Harahan, LA 70123. Phone: (504)734-7622 Fax: (504)734-7134 E-mail: kenwalsh@offshoremarine.org • URL: http://www.offshoremarine.org • Owners, operators, suppliers and crews of vessels servicing offshore oil and mineral installations. Seeks to advance the industry worldwide; monitors legislation and governmental regulations affecting the construction of offshore oil marine equipment and the operation of these specialized vessels, used primarily to supply and service offshore oil and gas operations worldwide. Conducts educational and personnel development and training programs; disseminates information on insurance and legal issues affecting offshore vessel operations. Maintains numerous committees representing all types of vessels engaged in the support of offshore installations.

OIL

See: OIL AND FATS INDUSTRY;
PETROLEUM INDUSTRY

OIL AND FATS INDUSTRY

ABSTRACTS AND INDEXES

Food Science and Technology Abstracts. International Food Information Service Publishing. • Monthly. $1,780.00 per year. Provides worldwide coverage of the literature of food technology and food production.

Foods Adlibra: Key to the World's Food Literature. General Mills, Inc. Foods Adlibra Publications. • Semimonthly. $240.00 per year. Provides journal citations and abstracts to the literature of food technology and packaging.

ALMANACS AND YEARBOOKS

Agricultural and Mineral Commodities Year Book. Available from Taylor & Francis Group. • Annual. $225.00. Published by Europa Publications. Contains descriptive product profiles, price data, export-import data, and production statistics for major commodities of the world. Includes commodity histories, uses, markets, demand trends, and information about trade agreements and key commodity organizations.

CD-ROM DATABASES

Food Science and Technology Abstracts [CD-ROM]. Available from SilverPlatter Information, Inc. • Quarterly. Produced by International Food Information Service (home page is http://www.ifis.org). Provides worldwide coverage on CD-ROM of the literature of food technology and production. Various types of publications are indexed, with abstracts, including about 1,800 periodicals. Time period is 1969 to date.

OECD Statistical Compendium. Organization for Economic Cooperation and Development. • Semiannual. $1,905.00 per year for 1 to 10 users. CD-ROM contains more than 730,000 monthly, quarterly, and annual time series for OECD countries, 1960 to date. Includes fully searchable data on agriculture, food, economic indicators, national accounts, employment, energy, finance, industry, technology, and foreign trade. Results can be displayed in various forms.

DIRECTORIES

Major Food and Drink Companies of the World. Available from Gale Cengage Learning. • Annual. $880.00. Two volumes. Published by Graham &

Whiteside. Contains profiles and trade names for more than 9,800 important food and beverage companies in various countries. In addition to foods, includes both alcoholic and nonalcoholic drink products.

OPD Chemical Buyers Directory. Schnell Publishing Company Inc. • Covers: about 1,500 suppliers of chemical process materials and more than 300 companies that transport and store chemicals in the United States. Entries include: Company name, address, phone, list of products or services, telex, fax, e-mail address, internet address, branch offices.

Thomas Food and Beverage Market Place. Grey House Publishing. • 2004. $495.00. Three volumes. Contains more than 40,000 entries covering food companies, beverages, food equipment, warehouse companies, food brokers, wholesalers, importers, and exporters. Formerly *Thomas Food Industry Register.*

ENCYCLOPEDIAS AND DICTIONARIES

Wiley Encyclopedia of Food Science and Technology. Frederick J. Francis, editor. John Wiley and Sons, Inc. • 2000. $1,650.00. Second edition. Four volumes. Contains about 400 entries. Coverage includes biotechnology, genetic engineering, nutrition, regulatory matters, food safety, labeling, food substitutes (sugar, fat, dairy), and many other topics.

HANDBOOKS AND MANUALS

Bailey's Industrial Oil and Fat Products. Alton E. Bailey. John Wiley and Sons, Inc. • 1996. $1,050.00. Fifth edition. $238.00 per volume. Five volumes.

INTERNET DATABASES

Business 2.0 Web Guide to the Best Business Links. Business 2.0 Media Inc. Phone: (415)293-4800 E-mail: support@business2.com • URL: http://www.business2.com/webguide • Web site presents an extensive, searchable directory of links to "the best, most informative, and authoritative web pages." Twenty main categories cover business, finance, career, company information, people, and technology topics, with thousands of subtopics, all linking to Web sites recommended by experienced business researchers. Fees: Free.

Fedstats. Federal Interagency Council on Statistical Policy. Phone: (202)395-7254 • URL: http://www.fedstats.gov • Web site features an efficient search facility for full-text statistics produced by more than 100 federal agencies, including the Census Bureau, the Bureau of Economic Analysis, and the Bureau of Labor Statistics. Boolean searches can be made within one agency or for all agencies combined. Links are offered to international statistical bureaus, including the UN, IMF, OECD, UNESCO, Eurostat, and 20 individual countries. Fees: Free.

FreeLunch.com. Economy.com, Inc. Phone: (610)696-8700 Fax: (610)696-1678 • URL: http://www.freelunch.com • Web site provides free access to more than 1.5 million economic and financial data series, covering industry, demographics, labor markets, prices, retail sales, government spending, trade, interest rates, housing starts, the stock market, and many other topics. Data is available for various time periods in either chart or table form. Searching is offered. Fees: Free, but registration required. Economy.com, Inc. also offers fee-based economic analysis at *The Dismal Scientist* site (http://www.dismal.com).

Manufacturing Profiles. U. S. Bureau of the Census. Phone: (301)763-4636 E-mail: webmaster@census.gov • URL: http://www.census.gov/prod/www/abs/mfg-prof.html • The Census Bureau makes available free on PDF (Portable Document Format) an annual consolidation of the entire Current Industrial Report series, presenting "all the data compiled." Contains statistics on production, shipments, inventories, consumption, exports, imports, and orders for a wide variety of manufactured products.

USDA. United States Department of Agriculture. Phone: (202)720-2791 E-mail: agsec@usda.gov • URL: http://www.usda.gov • The USDA home page has six sections: News and Information; What's New; About USDA; Agencies; Opportunities; Search and Help. Keyword searching is offered from the USDA home page and from various individual agency home pages. Agencies are the Economic Research Service, Agricultural Marketing Service, National Agricultural Statistics Service, National Agricultural Library, and about 12 others. Updating varies. Fees: Free.

ONLINE DATABASES

CAB Abstracts. CAB Publishing North America. • Contains 46 specialized abstract collections covering over 10,000 journals and monographs in the areas of agriculture, horticulture, forest products, farm products, nutrition, dairy science, poultry, grains, animal health, entomology, etc. Time period is 1972 to date, with monthly updates. Inquire as to online cost and availability. *CAB Abstracts on CD-ROM* also available, with annual updating.

Food Science and Technology Abstracts [online]. IFIS North American Desk. • Produced by International Food Information Service. Provides about 500,000 online citations, with abstracts, to the international literature of food science, technology, commodities, engineering, and processing. Approximately 2,000 periodicals are covered. Time period is 1969 to date, with monthly updates. Inquire as to online cost and availability.

FOODS ADLIBRA. General Mills, Inc. • Contains online citations, with abstracts, to the technical and business literature of food processing and packaging. New products and new ingredients are featured. Covers about 250 trade journals and 500 research journals from 1974 to date, with monthly updates. Inquire as to online cost and availability.

PERIODICALS AND NEWSLETTERS

Inform: International News on Fats, Oils, and Related Materials. American Oil Chemists Society. AOCS Press. • Monthly. Individuals, $120.00 per year; institutions, $360.00 per year. Covers a wide range of technical and business topics relating to the processing and utilization of edible oils, essential oils, and oilseeds.

JOACS (Journal of the American Oil Chemists' Society). American Oil Chemists' Society. AOCS Press. • Monthly. Individuals, $120.00 per year; institutions, $278.00 per year. Includes *INFORM: International News on Fats, Oils and Related Materials.*

RESEARCH CENTERS AND INSTITUTES

Food Protein Research and Development Center. Texas A & M University. Cater-Mattil Hall, College Station, TX 77843-2476. Phone: (979)845-2741 Fax: (979)845-2744 E-mail: mrm1@tamu.edu • URL: http://www.tamu.edu/food-protein/ • Formerly Food Research Center.

STATISTICS SOURCES

Agricultural Statistics. Available from U. S. Government Printing Office. • Annual. $38.00. Produced by the National Agricultural Statistics Service, U. S. Department of Agriculture. Provides a wide variety of statistical data relating to agricultural production, supplies, consumption, prices/price-supports, foreign trade, costs, and returns, as well as farm labor, loans, income, and population. In many cases, historical data is shown annually for 10 years. In addition to farm data, includes detailed fishery statistics.

Annual Survey of Manufactures. Available from U. S. Government Printing Office. • Annual. Prices vary. Issued by the U. S. Census Bureau as an interim update to the *Census of Manufactures.* Includes data on number of manufacturing establishments in various industries, employment, labor costs, value of shipments, capital expenditures, inventories, energy costs, and assets. (See also Census Bureau home page, http://www.census.gov/.).

Business Statistics of the United States. Linz Audain and Cornelia J. Strawser. Bernan Associates. • Annual. $147.00. Based on *Business Statistics,* formerly issue by the Bureau of Economic Analysis, U. S. Department of Commerce. Provides basic data for a wide variety of U. S. industries, services, and economic indicators. Most statistics are shown annually for 30 years and monthly for the most recent four years.

FAO Production Yearbook. Available from Bernan Associates. • Annual. $45.00. Published by the Food and Agriculture Organization (http://www.fao.org). Contains worldwide data on agriculture, land use, farm crops, livestock, and agricultural prices.

FAO Trade Yearbook. Available from Bernan Associates. • Annual. $45.00. Published by the Food and Agriculture Organization (http://www.fao.org). Provides extensive worldwide data on exports and imports of agricultural commodities, fertilizers, tractors, and pesticides. Includes more than 130 tables of detailed statistics.

Fats and Oils: Oilseed Crushings. U. S. Bureau of the Census. • Monthly and annual. Provides data on shipments of cottonseed oil and soybean oil: value, quantity, imports, and exports. (Current Industrial Reports, M20J.).

Fats and Oils: Production, Consumption, and Stocks. U. S. Bureau of the Census. • Monthly and annual. Covers the supply and distribution of cottonseed, soybean, and palm oils, and selected inedible products. (Current Industrial Reports, M20K.).

Survey of Current Business. Available from U. S. Government Printing Office. • Monthly. $63.00 per year. Issued by Bureau of Economic Analysis, U. S. Department of Commerce. Presents a wide variety of business and economic data.

World Food Data and Statistics. Euromonitor International. • 2004. $650.00. Provides five-year data for a wide variety of food products in 52 countries. Includes market size, consumer expenditures, price indicators, and retail distribution data for many kinds of meat, fish, fruits, vegetables, dairy products, baked goods, condiments, canned food, and frozen food.

TRADE/PROFESSIONAL ASSOCIATIONS

American Oil Chemists' Society. PO Box 17190, 2211 W Bradley Ave., Urbana, IL 61803-7190. Phone: (217)359-2344 Fax: (217)351-8091 E-mail: general@aocs.org • URL: http://www.aocs.org • Chemists, biochemists, chemical engineers, research directors, plant personnel, and others in laboratories and chemical process industries concerned with animal, marine, and vegetable oils and fats, and their extraction, refining, safety, packaging, quality control, and use in consumer and industrial products such as foods, drugs, paints, waxes, lubricants, soaps, and cosmetics. Sponsors short courses; certifies referee chemists; distributes cooperative check samples; sells official reagents. Maintains 100 committees. Operates job placement service for members only.

Institute of Shortening and Edible Oils. 1750 New York Ave., NW, Ste. 120, Washington, DC 20006. Phone: (202)783-7960 Fax: (202)393-1367 E-mail: info@iseo.org • URL: http://www.iseo.org • Refiners of edible vegetable oils and animal fats. Formerly Institute of Shortening Manufacturers.

National Cottonseed Products Association. 104 Timber Creek Dr., Ste. 200, PO Box 172267, Cordova, TN 38018-4234. Phone: (901)682-0800 Fax: (901)682-2856 E-mail: info@cottonseed.com • URL: http://www.cottonseed.com • Oil mills, refiners, dealers, brokers, chemists, and others interested in margarine, cooking fats, soaps, lubricants, cattle feed, and fertilizer. Maintains uniform trading rules covering the buying, selling, weighing, sampling, and analysis of cottonseed and its products; supports extensive research program to increase processing efficiency and to improve the quality and usefulness of cottonseed products. Conducts research programs and market development activities.

National Institute of Oilseed Products. 1156 15th St. N.W., Suite 900, Washington, DC 20005. Phone: (202)785-3232 Fax: (202)223-9741 E-mail: niop@kellencompany.com • URL: http://www.oilseed.org/.

National Renderers Association. 801 N Fairfax St., Ste. 205, Alexandria, VA 22314-1776. Phone: (703)683-0155 Fax: (703)683-2626 E-mail: renderers@nationalrenderers.com • URL: http://nationalrenderers.org • Producers of tallow and grease products (for use in soap and lubricants), and meat meal (for use in animal feeds), obtained as by-products of the meat-packing industry. Conducts research and educational programs; provides international and domestic market development services and legislative representation.

OIL BURNER INDUSTRY

See: FUEL OIL INDUSTRY

OIL FIELD MACHINERY

See: PETROLEUM EQUIPMENT INDUSTRY

OIL FUEL INDUSTRY

See: FUEL OIL INDUSTRY

OIL INDUSTRY

See: PETROLEUM INDUSTRY

OIL MARKETING

See: PETROLEUM MARKETING

OIL TANKERS

See: TANK SHIPS

OILSEED INDUSTRY

See: OIL AND FATS INDUSTRY

OLD AGE

See: RETIREMENT

OLD AGE AND SURVIVORS INSURANCE

See: SOCIAL SECURITY

OLD AGE HOMES

See: NURSING HOMES

OLDER CONSUMERS

See: MATURE CONSUMER MARKET

OLDER WORKERS

See: EMPLOYMENT OF OLDER WORKERS

OLEOMARGARINE INDUSTRY

See: MARGARINE INDUSTRY

OLIVE OIL INDUSTRY

ALMANACS AND YEARBOOKS

Agricultural and Mineral Commodities Year Book. Available from Taylor & Francis Group. • Annual. $225.00. Published by Europa Publications. Contains descriptive product profiles, price data, export-import data, and production statistics for major commodities of the world. Includes commodity histories, uses, markets, demand trends, and information about trade agreements and key commodity organizations.

CD-ROM DATABASES

Food Science and Technology Abstracts [CD-ROM]. Available from SilverPlatter Information, Inc. • Quarterly. Produced by International Food Information Service (home page is http://www.ifis.org). Provides worldwide coverage on CD-ROM of the literature of food technology and production. Various types of publications are indexed, with abstracts, including about 1,800 periodicals. Time period is 1969 to date.

DIRECTORIES

Major Food and Drink Companies of the World. Available from Gale Cengage Learning. • Annual. $880.00. Two volumes. Published by Graham & Whiteside. Contains profiles and trade names for more than 9,800 important food and beverage companies in various countries. In addition to foods, includes both alcoholic and nonalcoholic drink products.

Thomas Food and Beverage Market Place. Grey House Publishing. • 2004. $495.00. Three volumes. Contains more than 40,000 entries covering food companies, beverages, food equipment, warehouse companies, food brokers, wholesalers, importers, and exporters. Formerly *Thomas Food Industry Register.*

INTERNET DATABASES

USDA. United States Department of Agriculture. Phone: (202)720-2791 E-mail: agsec@usda.gov • URL: http://www.usda.gov • The USDA home page has six sections: News and Information; What's New; About USDA; Agencies; Opportunities; Search and Help. Keyword searching is offered from the USDA home page and from various individual agency home pages. Agencies are the Economic Research Service, Agricultural Marketing Service, National Agricultural Statistics Service, National Agricultural Library, and about 12 others. Updating varies. Fees: Free.

ONLINE DATABASES

Food Science and Technology Abstracts [online]. IFIS North American Desk. • Produced by International Food Information Service. Provides about 500,000 online citations, with abstracts, to the international literature of food science, technology, commodities, engineering, and processing. Approximately 2,000 periodicals are covered. Time period is 1969 to date, with monthly updates. Inquire as to online cost and availability.

STATISTICS SOURCES

Agricultural Statistics. Available from U. S. Government Printing Office. • Annual. $38.00. Produced by the National Agricultural Statistics Service, U. S.

Department of Agriculture. Provides a wide variety of statistical data relating to agricultural production, supplies, consumption, prices/price-supports, foreign trade, costs, and returns, as well as farm labor, loans, income, and population. In many cases, historical data is shown annually for 10 years. In addition to farm data, includes detailed fishery statistics.

FAO Production Yearbook. Available from Bernan Associates. • Annual. $45.00. Published by the Food and Agriculture Organization (http://www.fao.org). Contains worldwide data on agriculture, land use, farm crops, livestock, and agricultural prices.

FAO Trade Yearbook. Available from Bernan Associates. • Annual. $45.00. Published by the Food and Agriculture Organization (http://www.fao.org). Provides extensive worldwide data on exports and imports of agricultural commodities, fertilizers, tractors, and pesticides. Includes more than 130 tables of detailed statistics.

World Food Data and Statistics. Euromonitor International. • 2004. $650.00. Provides five-year data for a wide variety of food products in 52 countries. Includes market size, consumer expenditures, price indicators, and retail distribution data for many kinds of meat, fish, fruits, vegetables, dairy products, baked goods, condiments, canned food, and frozen food.

TRADE/PROFESSIONAL ASSOCIATIONS

Association of Food Industries. 3301 Rte. 66, Bldg. C, No. 205, Neptune, NJ 07747. Phone: (732)922-3008 Fax: (732)922-3590 E-mail: info@afius.org • URL: http://www.afius.org.

OTHER SOURCES

International Agreement on Olive Oil and Table Olives. United Nations Publications. • 1986. Trade agreements.

ON-THE-JOB TRAINING

See: TRAINING OF EMPLOYEES

ONION INDUSTRY

ALMANACS AND YEARBOOKS

Agricultural and Mineral Commodities Year Book. Available from Taylor & Francis Group. • Annual. $225.00. Published by Europa Publications. Contains descriptive product profiles, price data, export-import data, and production statistics for major commodities of the world. Includes commodity histories, uses, markets, demand trends, and information about trade agreements and key commodity organizations.

INTERNET DATABASES

USDA. United States Department of Agriculture. Phone: (202)720-2791 E-mail: agsec@usda.gov • URL: http://www.usda.gov • The USDA home page has six sections: News and Information; What's New; About USDA; Agencies; Opportunities; Search and Help. Keyword searching is offered from the USDA home page and from various individual agency home pages. Agencies are the Economic Research Service, Agricultural Marketing Service, National Agricultural Statistics Service, National Agricultural Library, and about 12 others. Updating varies. Fees: Free.

PERIODICALS AND NEWSLETTERS

National Onion Association--Newsletter. National Onion Association. • Description: Provides information on the onion industry.

STATISTICS SOURCES

Agricultural Statistics. Available from U. S. Government Printing Office. • Annual. $38.00. Produced by the National Agricultural Statistics Service, U. S.

Department of Agriculture. Provides a wide variety of statistical data relating to agricultural production, supplies, consumption, prices/price-supports, foreign trade, costs, and returns, as well as farm labor, loans, income, and population. In many cases, historical data is shown annually for 10 years. In addition to farm data, includes detailed fishery statistics.

FAO Production Yearbook. Available from Bernan Associates. • Annual. $45.00. Published by the Food and Agriculture Organization (http://www.fao.org). Contains worldwide data on agriculture, land use, farm crops, livestock, and agricultural prices.

FAO Trade Yearbook. Available from Bernan Associates. • Annual. $45.00. Published by the Food and Agriculture Organization (http://www.fao.org). Provides extensive worldwide data on exports and imports of agricultural commodities, fertilizers, tractors, and pesticides. Includes more than 130 tables of detailed statistics.

TRADE/PROFESSIONAL ASSOCIATIONS

National Onion Association. 822 7th St., Ste. 510, Greeley, CO 80631-3941. Phone: (970)353-5895 Fax: (970)353-5897 E-mail: nopa@nopa.org • URL: http://www.onions-usa.org • Growers, brokers, grower-shippers, shippers, suppliers, and support professionals engaged in the onion industry. Promotes the onion industry. Compiles monthly statistical report of stocks-on-hand, acreage, yield, and production of onions in the U.S. Lobbies issues of importance to national onion industry.

ONLINE COMMERCE

See: ELECTRONIC COMMERCE

ONLINE INFORMATION SYSTEMS

See also: COMPUTER COMMUNICATIONS; INFORMATION INDUSTRY; INTERNET

GENERAL WORKS

Creating Web-Accessible Databases: Case Studies for Libraries, Museums, and Other Non-Profits. Julie M. Still, editor. Information Today, Inc. • 2001. $39.50. Presents case studies of successful Web projects in libraries and other institutions.

Current Trends in Information: Research and Theory. William Katz and Robin Kinder, editors. The Haworth Press, Inc. • 1987. $49.95. (Reference Librarian Series: No. 18).

Data Smog: Surviving the Information Glut. David Shenk. HarperSanFrancisco. • 1997. $14.00. A critical view of both the electronic and print information industries. Emphasis is on information overload.

The Evolving Virtual Library: Practical and Philosophical Perspectives. Laverna M. Saunders, editor. Information Today, Inc. • 1999. $39.50. Various authors cover trends in library and school use of the Internet, intranets, extranets, and electronic databases.

The Internet Initiative: Libraries Providing Internet Services and How They Plan, Pay, and Manage. Edward J. Valauskas and others. American Library Association. • 1995. $27.00. Provides 18 reports on Internet services in various kinds of libraries.

Introductory Concepts in Information Science. Melanie J. Norton, editor. Information Today, Inc. • 2000. $39.50. Covers the basic concepts of information science and retrieval, both practical and theoretical. Published in conjunction with the American Society for Information Science and Technology. (ASIS Monograph Series).

Law of the Super Searchers: The Online Secrets of Top Legal Researchers. T. R. Halvorson. Informa-

tion Today, Inc. • 1999. $24.95. Eight law researchers explain how to find useful legal information online. (Super Searchers Series).

Mastering Online Investing: How to Use the Internet to Become a More Successful Investor. Michael C. Thomsett. Dearborn Trading Publishing, A Kaplan Professional Co. • 2001. $19.95. Emphasis is on the Internet as an information source for intelligent investing, avoiding "speculation and fads.".

Online Retrieval: A Dialogue of Theory and Practice. Geraldene Walker and Joseph Janes. Libraries Unlimited, Inc. • 1999. $55.00. Second edition. Edited by Carol Tenopir. Covers a wide variety of online information topics, with emphasis on bibliographic databases. (Database Searching Series.).

The Quintessential Searcher: The Wit and Wisdom of Barbara Quint. Marylaine Block, editor. Information Today, Inc. • 2001. $19.95. Presents the sayings of Barbara Quint, editor of *Searcher* magazine, who is often critical of the online information industry. (CyberAge Books.).

Secrets of the Super Searchers: The Accumulated Wisdom of 23 of the World's Top Online Searchers. Reva Basch. Information Today, Inc. • 1993. $39.95. Contains interviews with experienced online searchers, covering such topics as pre-search interviewing, search strategy, full-text considerations, search limiting, and client relations. (Super Searchers Series).

Silicon Snake Oil: Second Thoughts on the Information Highway. Clifford Stoll. Doubleday Publishing. • 1996. $14.00. The author discusses the extravagant claims being made for online networks and multimedia.

Super Searcher, Author, Scribe: Successful Writers Share Their Internet Research Secrets. Loraine Page. Information Today, Inc. • 2002. $24.95. Presents the results of interviews with 14 leading journalists, book authors, writing teachers, and professional literary researchers. Tips, techniques, and sources for searching the Web are featured. (Super Searchers Series).

Super Searchers Cover the World: The Online Secrets of International Business Researchers. Mary E. Bates. Information Today, Inc. • 2001. $24.95. Presents interviews with 15 experts in the area of online searching for international business information. (Super Searchers Series).

Super Searchers Do Business: The Online Secrets of Top Business Researchers. Mary E.Bates. Information Today, Inc. • 1999. $24.95. Presents the results of interviews with "11 leading researchers who use the Internet and online services to find critical business information." (Super Searchers Series.).

Super Searchers Go to the Source: The Interviewing and Hands-On Information Strategies of Top Primary Researchers - Online, On the Phone, and In Person. Risa Sacks. Information Today, Inc. • 2001. $24.95. Explains how information-search experts use various print, electronic, and live sources for competitive intelligence and other purposes. (Super Searchers Series).

Super Searchers in the News: The Online Secrets of Journalists and News Researchers. Paula J. Hane. Information Today, Inc. • 2000. $24.95. Contains online searching advice from 10 professional news researchers and fact checkers. (Super Searchers Series).

Super Searchers on Health and Medicine: The Online Secrets of Top Health and Medical Researchers. Susan M. Detwiler. Information Today, Inc. • 2000. $24.95. Provides the results of interviews with 10 experts in online searching for medical research data and healthcare information. Discusses both traditional sources and Web sites. (Super Searchers Series).

Super Searchers on Madison Avenue: Top Advertis-

ing and Marketing Professionals Share Their Online Research Strategies. Grace A. Villamora. Information Today, Inc. • 2003. $24.95. Provides research "tips, techniques, and resources" from 13 information professionals working in advertising and marketing. (Super Searchers Series).

Super Searchers on Mergers & Acquisitions: The Online Secrets of Top Corporate Researchers and M & A Professionals. Jan Tudor. Information Today, Inc. • 2001. $24.95. Presents the results of interviews with 13 "top M & A information pros." Covers the finding, evaluating, and delivering of relevant data on companies and industries. (Super Searchers Series).

Super Searchers on Wall Street: Top Investment Professionals Share Their Online Research Secrets. Amelia Kassel. Information Today, Inc. • 2000. $24.95. Gives the results of interviews with "10 leading financial industry research experts." Explains how online information is used by stock brokers, investment bankers, and individual investors. Includes relevant Web sites and other sources. (Super Searchers Series).

Towards Electronic Journals: Realities for Scientists, Librarians, and Publishers. Carol Tenopir and Donald W. King. Special Libraries Association. • 2000. $59.00. Discusses journals in electronic form vs. traditional (paper) scholarly journals, including the impact of subscription prices.

The Ultimate Digital Library: Where the New Information Players Meet. Andrew K. Pace. American Library Association. • 2003. $35.00. Discusses how libraries can remain competitive within the new digital information world.

Web of Deception: Misinformation on the Internet. Anne P. Mintz, editor. Information Today, Inc. • 2002. $24.95. Barbara Quint, Susan M. Detwiler, and others discuss the spread of intentionally misleading or erroneous information by Web sites. Provides advice on the evaluation of Internet sources. (CyberAge Books.).

What Will Be: How the New World of Information Will Change Our Lives. Michael L. Dertouzos. DIANE Publishing Co. • 1997. $25.00. A discussion of the "information market place" of the future, including telecommuting, virtual reality, and computer recognition of speech. The author is director of the MIT Laboratory for Computer Science.

ABSTRACTS AND INDEXES

Computer and Information Systems Abstracts Journal: An Abstract Journal Pertaining to the Theory, Design, Fabrication and Application of Computer and Information Systems. CSA. • 11 times a year. $1,750 per year.

Computer Literature Index: A Subject/Author Index to Computer and Data Processing Literature. EBSCO Publishing. • Quarterly, with annual cumulation. $245.00 per year. Contains brief abstracts of book and periodical literature covering all phases of computing, including approximately 70 specific application areas.

Information Science Abstracts. American Society for Information Science. Information Today, Inc. • Nine times a year. $789.00 per year.

Internet and Personal Computing Abstracts [print edition]. EBSCO Publishing. • Quarterly. $269.00 per year, including cumulative index. Provides more than 10,000 abstracts annually from both trade and academic publications. Covers computer hardware, software, product reviews, Web topics, e-commerce, networks, corporate news, security, and related topics. Formerly *Microcomputer Abstracts.*

Library Literature and Information Science Index. H. W. Wilson Co. • Quarterly. Annual cumulation. Price varies.

LISA: Library and Information Science Abstracts. R, R. Bowker. • 13 times a year. $1,055.00 per year;

includes print and online editions.

ALMANACS AND YEARBOOKS

Annual Society for Information Science and Technology, Information and Business Div. Martha E. Williams, editor. Information Today, Inc. • Annual. Members, $79.95; non-members, $99.95. Published on behalf of the American Society for Information Science (ASIS). Covers trends in planning, basic techniques, applications, and the information profession in general.

Business-Professional Online Markets. SIMBA Information, Inc. • Annual. $1,995.00; with online edition, $3,390.00. Provides a review of current conditions in the online information industry. Profiles of major database producers and online services are included.

BIBLIOGRAPHIES

Computer Book Review. • Quarterly. $30.00 per year. Includes annual index. Reviews new computer books. Back issues available.

BIOGRAPHICAL SOURCES

Net.people: The Personalities and Passions Behind the Web Sites. Thomas E. Bleier and Eric C. Steinert. Information Today, Inc. • 2000. $19.95. Presents the personal stories of 36 Web "entrepreneurs and visionaries." (CyberAge Books.).

CD-ROM DATABASES

Computer Database. Gale Cengage Learning. • Provides one year of full-text on CD-ROM for 150 leading computer-related publications. Also includes 70,000 product specifications and brief profiles of 13,000 computer product vendors and manufacturers.

LISA Plus. Available from Cambridge Scientific Abstracts (CSA). • Quarterly. $2,000.00 per year. CD-ROM version of Library Information and Science Abstracts, providing abstracting and indexing of the world's library and information science literature, 1969 to date. Contains more than 180,000 citations.

WILSONDISC: Library Literature and Information Science Index. H. W. Wilson Co. • Quarterly. Includes unlimited access to the online version of *Library Literature.* Provides CD-ROM indexing of about 300 periodicals, covering a wide range of topics having to do with libraries, library management, and the information industry.

World Database of Business Information Sources on CD-ROM. Gale Cengage Learning. • Annual. Produced by Euromonitor. Presents Euromonitor's entire information source database on CD-ROM. Contains a worldwide total of about 35,000 publications, organizations, libraries, trade fairs, and online databases.

DIRECTORIES

Books and Periodicals Online: The Guide to Business and Legal Information on Databases and CD-ROM's. Nuchine Nobari, editor. Library Technology Alliance, Ltd. • Annual. $379.00. Two volumes. 119,000 periodicals available as part of online and CD-ROM databases; international coverage.

Data Sources: The Comprehensive Guide to the Data Processing Industry: Hardware, Data Communications Products, Software, Company Profiles. Gale Cengage Learning. • Semiannual. $455.00 per year. Two volumes. Describes hardware and software for all computer operating sysems, including prices and technical details. Lists about 75,000 products from 14,000 suppliers. Industry-specific software applications are described.

Fulltext Sources Online. Information Today Inc. • Covers: over 21,000 periodicals, newspapers, newsletters, newswires; and tv/radio transcripts available in full text online. Entries include: Name of file, online services through which available, dates of coverage, lag time if applicable. Separate

list gives online service address and phone; indicates degree of online coverage and selection policy. Internet url's listed where applicable.

Gale Directory of Databases. Gale Cengage Learning. • 2003. $490.00. Two volumes. Volume 1, $315.00; volume 2, $195.00. *Volume 1: Online Databases* and *Volume 2: CD-ROM, Diskette, Magnetic Tape, Handheld, and Batch Access Database Products.*

Information Industry Directory. Gale. • Covers: Approximately 11,000 organizations, systems, and services involved in the production and distribution of information in electronic form: database producers and their products online host services, transactional services, library and information networks, bibliographic utilities, library management systems, information retrieval software, mailing list services, fee-based information on demand services, document delivery sources, data collection and analysis centers and firms, and related consultants, service companies, professional and trade associations, publishers, and research activities. Entries include: Name of parent organization, name of system of service, address, phone, toll-free phone, fax, telex, email address, year founded name of unit head, size of staff, names of any affiliated organizations, financial information. Internet access information, general description of electronic product, system, or service, subjects covered or areas of service offered, sources of data for the system, type and quantity of stored information in all forms, publications and microform products and services, computer-based products and services, other services, clientele served, availability and restrictions, name of contact.

The Internet Compendium: Guide to Resources by Subject: Subject Guides to Health and Science Resources. Joseph Janes and others, editors. Neal-Schuman Publishers, Inc. • 1995. $82.50. Editors are with the University of Michigan Internet Clearinghouse. Provides direct location access to "thousands" of Internet addresses, in a detailed subject arrangement, with critical analysis of content. Contains information databases, text archives, library catalogs, bulletin boards, newsletters, forums, etc. Includes topics in medicine, agriculture, biology, chemistry, mathematics, physics, engineering, computers, and science in general.

The Internet Compendium: Guide to Resources by Subject: Subject Guides to Social Sciences, Business, and Law Resources. Joseph Janes and others, editors. Neal-Schuman Publishers, Inc. • 1995. $82.50. Editors are with the University of Michigan Internet Clearinghouse. Provides direct location access to "thousands" of Internet addresses, in a detailed subject arrangement, with critical analysis of content. Contains information databases, text archives, library catalogs, bulletin boards, newsletters, forums, etc. Includes topics in economics, finance, taxation, history, population, civil rights law, law careers, women's studies, and so forth.

The Internet Compendium: Guide to Resources by Subject: Subject Guides to the Humanities. Joseph Janes. Neal-Schuman Publishers, Inc. • 1995. $82.50. Editors are with the University of Michigan Internet Clearinghouse. Provides direct location access to "thousands" of Internet addresses, in a detailed subject arrangement, with critical analysis of content. Contains information databases, text archives, library catalogs, bulletin boards, newsletters, forums, etc. Includes topics in literature, art, religion, philosophy, music, education, library science, games, magic, and the humanities in general.

Internet Plus Directory of Express Library Services. Steve Coffman and others, editors. American Library Association. • 1998. $55.00. Covers fee-based services of various U. S., Canadian, and international libraries. Paid services include online searches, faxed documents, and specialized profes-

670

For publishers addresses, refer to SOURCES CITED section at the back of the book.

sional research. Price ranges are quoted. (A joint production of FISCAL, the ALA/ACRL Discussion Group of Fee-Based Information Service Centers in Academic Libraries, and FYI, the Professional Research and Rapid Information Delivery Service of the County of Los Angeles Public Library.) Formerly *FISCAL Directory of Fee-Based Information Services in Libraries.*

Internet Tools of the Profession: A Guide for Information Professionals. Hope N. Tillman, editor. Special Libraries Association. • 1997. $49.00. Second edition. Consists of 14 sections by various authors or compilers. After two introductory articles on searching the Internet, there are 12 annotated lists of useful Web sites, covering the SLA, business and finance, chemistry, education, food and agriculture, information technology, insurance and employee benefits, law, library management, metals and materials, pharmaceuticals, and telecommunications. An index is provided.

Library Journal: Reference [year]: Print, CD-ROM, Online. Reed Business Information. • Annual. Issued in November as a supplement to *Library Journal.* Lists new and updated reference material, including general and trade print titles, directories, annuals, CD-ROM titles, and online sources. Includes material from more than 200 publishers, arranged by company name, with an index by subject. Addresses include e-mail and Web information.

Library Journal Sourcebook. Reed Business Information. • Publication includes: List of over 600 suppliers of products and services used by libraries from abstracting to word processing equipment. Entries include: Company name, address, phone, list of products or services. Complete listings for more than 100 architectural firms; Disaster planning for librarians.

Major Information Technology Companies of the World 2001. Available from Gale Cengage Learning. • Annual. $880.00. Published by Graham & Whiteside. Contains profiles of more than 3,100 leading information technology companies in various countries.

Major Telecommunications Companies of the World. Available from Gale Cengage Learning. • 2003. $885.00. Sixth edition. Published by Graham & Whiteside. Contains detailed information and trade names for more than 3,500 important telecommunications companies in various countries.

The Online 100: Online Magazine's Field Guide to the 100 Most Important Online Databases. Mick O'Leary. Information Today, Inc. • 1996. $22.95. Provides detailed descriptions of 100 "important and useful" online databases in various subject areas.

A S I S Handbook and Directory. American Society for Information Science. • Annual. Members, $25.00; non-members, $100.00.

SRDS Interactive Advertising Source. SRDS. • Quarterly. $569.00 per year. Provides descriptive profiles, rates, audience, personnel, etc., for producers of various forms of interactive or multimedia advertising: online/Internet, CD-ROM, interactive TV, interactive cable, interactive telephone, interactive kiosk, and others.

World Directory of Marketing Information Sources. Available from Gale Cengage Learning. • 2003. $650.00. Fourth edition. Published by Euromonitor. Provides details on approximately 6,000 sources of marketing information, including publications, libraries, associations, market research companies, online databases, and governmental organizations. Coverage is worldwide.

ENCYCLOPEDIAS AND DICTIONARIES

Acronyms of Computer Science and Communications: A Comprehensive Acronym Dictionary and Illustrated Encyclopedia. Enjob Kajan and Ejub Kajan. Springer Verlag. • 2002. $49.95. Explains more than 4,000 "broadly used" computer, telecommunica-

tions, and information technology acronyms. Includes illustrations and Web addresses, where applicable.

Communicating with Legal Databases: Terms and Abbreviations for the Legal Researcher. Anne L. McDonald. Neal-Schuman Publishers, Inc. • 1987. $82.50.

CyberDictionary: Your Guide to the Wired World. Spurge ink!. • 1996. $17.95. Includes many illustrations.

Cyberspace Lexicon: An Illustrated Dictionary of Terms from Multimedia to Virtual Reality. Bob Cotton and Richard Oliver. Phaidon Press. • 1994. $29.95. Defines more than 800 terms, with manyillustrations. Includes a bibliography.

Encyclopedia of Communication and Information. Available from Gale Cengage Learning. • 2001. $395.00. Three volumes. Published by Macmillan Reference USA.

Encyclopedia of Emerging Industries. Gale Cengage Learning. • 2001. $320.00. Fourth edition. Provides detailed information on 115 "newly flourishing" industries. Includes historical background, organizational structure, significant individuals, current conditions, major companies, work force, technology trends, research developments, and other industry facts.

Encyclopedia of Information Systems. Hossein Bidgoli, editor. Elsevier. • 2002. $1,200.00. Four volumes. Contains a wide range of articles relating to computers, databases, communication, and information technology. The 200 topics include coverage of hardware, software, artificial intelligence, the Internet, networks, knowledge management, electronic commerce, search engines, and systems design.

Encyclopedia of New Media: An Essential Reference to Communication and Technology. Steve Jones, editor. Sage Publications, Inc. • 2003. $125.00. Contains more than 250 entries dealing with such areas as multimedia, broadband access, information communication technology (ICT), content filtering, wireless networks, and cyberethics.

Internet Encyclopedia. Hossein Bidgoli, editor. John Wiley and Sons, Inc. • 2003. $750.00. Four volumes. Covers various aspects of the Internet, including information technology, electronic business, and telecommunications.

World Encyclopedia of Library and Information Services. Robert Wedgeworth, editor. American Library Association. • 1993. $200.00. Third edition. Contains about 340 articles from various contributors.

HANDBOOKS AND MANUALS

Best Bet Internet: Reference and Research When You Don't Have Time to Mess Around. Shirley D. Kennedy. American Library Association. • 1997. $35.00. Provides advice for librarians and others on the effective use of World Wide Web information sources.

Beyond Book Indexing: How to Get Started in Web Indexing, Embedded Indexing, and Other Computer-Based Media. Information Today, Inc. • 1999. $31.25. Published for the American Society of Indexers. Contains 12 chapters written by professional indexers. Part one discusses making an index by marking items in an electronic document (embedded indexing); part two is on indexing to make Web pages more accessible; part three covers CD-ROM and multimedia indexing; part four provides career and promotional advice for professionals in the field. Includes an index by Janet Perlman and a glossary.

Columbia Guide to Online Style. Janice R. Walker and Todd W. Taylor. Columbia University Press. • 1998. $40.50. Includes rules for bibliographic citation of online sources, formatting guidelines for online documents, and information on the electronic

preparation of texts for print publication.

The Cybrarian's Manual. Pat Ensor, editor. American Library Association. • 2000. $45.00. Second edition. Provides information for librarians concerning the Internet, expert systems, computer networks, client/server architecture, Web pages, multimedia, information industry careers, and other "cyberspace" topics.

Electronic Styles: A Handbook of Citing Electronic Information. Xia Li and Nancy Crane. Information Today, Inc. • 1996. $19.99. Second edition. Covers the citing of text-based information, electronic journals, Web sites, CD-ROM items, multimedia products, and online documents.

The Essential Guide to Bulletin Board Systems. Patrick R. Dewey. Information Today, Inc. • 1998. $39.50. Provides details on the setup and operation of online bulletin board systems. Covers both hardware and software.

Find It Online: The Complete Guide to Online Research. Alan M. Schlein. Facts on Demand Press. • 2002. $19.95. Third edition. Presents the general principles of online searching for information about people, phone numbers, public records, news, business, investments, etc. Covers both free and fee-based sources. (On Line Ease Series).

Finding Statistics Online: How to Locate the Elusive Numbers You Need. Paula Berinstein. Information Today, Inc. • 1998. $29.95. Provides advice on efficient searching when looking for statistical data on the World Wide Web or from commercial online services and database producers. (CyberAge Books.).

Going Live: Starting and Running a Virtual Reference Service. Steve Coffman. American Library Association. • 2003. $42.00. Serves as a practical manual for libraries wishing to start a Web-based, always available reference service. Includes a bibliography by Bernie Sloan.

How to Find Market Research on the Web. MarketResearch.com. • 2001. $239.00. Analyzes and compares the online products of 80 market research publishers. Describes popular Internet search engines and provides information on useful World Wide Web sites.

Improving Online Public Access Catalogs. Martha M. Yee and Sara S. Layne. American Library Association. • 1998. $48.00. A practical guide to developing user-friendly online catalogs (OPACs).

The Information Professional's Guide to Career Development Online. Sarah L. Nesbeitt and Rachel S. Gordon. Information Today, Inc. • 2001. $29.50. Provides advice to librarians and other information professionals about using online sources for career advancement. The Career Development Online Web Page (http://www.lisjobs.com/careerdev/) contains links to relevant resources.

International Business Information on the Web: Searcher Magazine's Guide to Sites and Strategies for Global Business Research. Sheri R. Lanza. Information Today, Inc. • 2001. $29.95. (CyberAge Books.).

Internet Business Intelligence: How to Build a Big Company System on a Small Company Budget. David Vine. Information Today, Inc. • 2000. $29.95. Covers the obtaining of valuable business intelligence data through use of the Internet.

The Invisible Web: Uncovering Information Sources Search Engines Can't See. Chris Sherman and Gary Price. Information Today, Inc. • 2001. $29.95. A guide to Web sites from universities, libraries, associations, government agencies, and other sources that are inadequately covered by conventional search engines (see also http://www.invisible-web.net). (CyberAge Books.).

Journalism Online. Mike Ward and Andy Dickinson. Elsevier. • 2002. $39.95. Covers the basic journalism skills needed for identifying, collecting, selecting, and presenting news and information for the World Wide Web.

The Librarian's Internet Survival Guide: Strategies for the High-Tech Reference Desk. Irene E. McDermott. Information Today, Inc. • 2002. $29.50. Provides practical advice relating to Web reference sources, information management strategies, Internet training issues, library Web pages, and patron relations.

Managing Public-Access Computers: A How-To-Do-It Manual for Librarians. Donald A. Barclay. Neal-Schuman Publishers, Inc. • 2000. $59.95. Part one covers hardware, software, and other components. Part two discusses computers users. Part three is about systems management, library policy, and legal issues. (How-to-Do-It Manuals Series).

Mining for Gold on the Internet: How to Find Investment and Financial Information on the Internet. Mary Ellen Bates. McGraw-Hill. • 2000. $24.95. Tells how to effectively search the Internet for financial advice and information. Specific websites are discussed.

Naked in Cyberspace: How to Find Personal Information Online. Carole A. Lane. Information Today, Inc. • 2002. $29.95. Second edition. Covers the availability of personal records on the Internet, including competitive intelligence data, customer characteristics, employee information, backgrounds of experts, public records, criminal records, and genealogical data. From an opposite viewpoint, advice is offered relative to the maintenance of privacy. Includes a Web directory with about 1,000 sources of information. (CyberAge Books.).

The Official America Online Tour Guide. Jennifer Watson and Dave Marx. John Wiley and Sons, Inc. • 2000. $24.99. Fifth edition. Provides a detailed explanation of the various features of versio of America Online, including electronic mail procedures and "Using the Internet.".

Online Deskbook: Online Magazine's Essential Desk Reference for Online and Internet Searchers. Mary E. Bates. Information Today, Inc. • 1995. $29.95. Covers the World Wide Web, as well as America Online, CompuServe, Dialog, Lexis-Nexis, and all other major online services. (Pemberton Press Books.).

Software for Indexing. Sandi Schroeder, editor. Information Today, Inc. • 2003. $35.00. Published in conjunction with the American Society of Indexers (ASI). Material by professional indexers covers dedicated indexing programs, embedded software, online indexing, Web indexing, database software, customized software, automatic indexing, and other indexing software topics.

Virtual Reference Training: The Complete Guide to Providing Anytime, Anywhere Answers. Buff Hirko and Mary Bucher Ross. American Library Association. • 2004. $42.00. Serves as a guide to effective, online library reference service. Emphasis is on staff training and "14 core competencies.".

INTERNET DATABASES

InfoTech Trends. Data Analysis Group. Phone: (925)462-1202 Fax: (925)462-1225 E-mail: support@infotechtrends.com • URL: http://www.infotechtrends.com • Web site provides both free and fee-based market research data on the information technology industry, including computers, peripherals, telecommunications, the Internet, software, CD-ROM/DVD, e-commerce, and workstations. Fees: Free for current (most recent year) data; more extensive information has various fee structures. Formerly *Computer Industry Forecasts.*

Search Engine Watch. Internet.com Corp. Phone: (203)662-2800 Fax: (203)655-4686 • URL: http://www.searchenginewatch.com • Web site offers information on various aspects of search engines, including new developments, indexing systems, technology, ratings and reviews of major operators, specialty services, tutorials, news, history, "Search Engine EKGs," "Facts and Fun," etc. Online searching is provided. Formerly *A Webmaster's Guide to Search Engines.*

Wired News. Lycos, Inc. Phone: (415)276-8400 Fax: (415)276-8500 E-mail: newsfeedback@wired.com • URL: http://www.wired.com • Provides summaries and full-text of "Top Stories" relating to the Internet, computers, multimedia, telecommunications, and the electronic information industry in general. These news stories are placed in the broad categories of Politics, Business, Culture, and Technology. Affiliated with *Wired* magazine. Fees: Free.

ONLINE DATABASES

Gale Directory of Databases [online]. Gale Cengage Learning. • Presents the online version of the printed *Gale Directory of Databases, Volume 1: Online Databases* and *Gale Directory of Databases, Volume 2: CD-ROM, Diskette, Magnetic Tape, Handheld, and Batch Access Database Products.* Semiannual updates. Inquire as to online cost and availability.

Information Science Abstracts [online]. Information Today, Inc. • Provides indexing and abstracting of the international literature of information science, including library science, from 1966 to date. Monthly updates. Inquire as to online cost and availability.

LISA: Library and Information Science Abstracts. Available from Cambridge Scientific Abstracts (CSA). • Provides abstracting and indexing of the world's library and information science literature, 1969 to date. Covers more than 440 periodicals from 68 countries. Updating is biweekly. Inquire as to online cost and availability.

PERIODICALS AND NEWSLETTERS

American Society for Information Science and Technology Journal. American Society for Information Science and Technology. John Wiley and Sons, Inc., Journals. • 14 times a year. $1,600.00 per year; with online edition, $1,680.00 per year.

Aslib Proceedings: New Information Perspectives. Available from Information Today, Inc. • Ten times a year. $349.00 per year. Published in London by Aslib Covers a wide variety of information industry and library management topics.

Cyberspace Lawyer. Glasser Legalworks. • 11 times a year. $300.00 per year. Newsletter. Covers various legal topics pertaining to use of the Internet. Includes advice on legal research via the Web.

Electronic Information Report: Empowering Industry Decision Makers Since 1979. SIMBA Information. • 46 times a year. $649.00 per year. Newsletter. Provides business and financial news and trends for online services, electronic publishing, storage media, multimedia, and voice services. Includes information on relevant IPOs (initial public offerings) and mergers. Formerly *Electronic Information Week.*

InfoAlert: Your Expert Guide to Online Business Information. Economics Press, Inc. • Monthly. $129.00 per year. Newsletter. Provides information on recommended World Wide Web sites in various business, marketing, industrial, and financial areas.

Information Hotline. Science Associates/International Inc. • Description: "The oldest, most respected, continuously published newsletter." Devoted to objective coverage of trends, policy, analysis, and opinion in the information field.

Information Outlook: The Monthly Magazine of the Special Libraries Association. Special Libraries Association. • Monthly. $65.00 per year. Topics include information technology, the Internet, copyright, research techniques, library management, and professional development. Replaces *Special Libraries* and *SpeciaList.*

Information Processing and Management: An International Journal. Elsevier Science. • Bimonthly. Qualified personnel, $301.00 per year; institutions, $1,196.00 per year. Text in English, French, German and Italian.

Information Retrieval and Library Automation. Lomond Publications, Inc. • Monthly. $75.00 per year. Summarizes research events and literature worldwide.

Information Sciences; An International Journal. Elsevier Science. • 36 times a year. Individuals, $106.00 per year; institutions, $3,557.00 per year. Three sections, A: Informatics and Computer Science, B: Intelligent Systems, C: Applications.

Information Systems; Data Bases: Their Creation, Management and Utilization. Elsevier. • Eight times a year. Institutions, $1,554.00 per year.

Information Today: The Newspaper for Users and Producers of Electronic Information Services. Information Today, Inc. • 11 times a year. $68.95 per year.

Innovative Publisher: Publishing Strategies for New Markets. Emmelle Publishing Co., Inc. • Biweekly. $69.00 per year. Provides articles and news on electronic publishing (CD-ROM or online) and desktop publishing.

Internet Law Researcher. Glasser Legalworks. • 11 times a year. $200.00 per year. Newsletter for legal professionals on how to search the Web efficiently. Provides detailed information on individual Web sites.

Internet Reference Services Quarterly: A Journal of Innovative Information Practice, Technologies, and Resources. Haworth Press, Inc. • Quarterly. $110.00 per year. Covers both theoretical research and practical applications.

Journal of Electronic Resources in Law Libraries. Haworth Press, Inc. • Quarterly. $300.00 per year to libraries; $48.00 per year to individuals.

Journal of Electronic Resources in Medical Libraries. Haworth Press, Inc. • Quarterly. $240.00 per year to libraries; $75.00 per year to individuals.

Journal of Information Science: Principles and Practice. Institute of Information Scientists. Sage Publications, Inc. • Bimonthly. $241.00 per year. Includes print and online editions.

Journal of Internet Cataloging: The International Quarterly of Digital Organization, Classification, and Access. Haworth Press, Inc. • Quarterly. $165.00 per year.

Law Technology News: Products, Systems, and Services for Legal Professionals. American Lawyer Media, Inc. • Monthly. $69.00 per year. Features descriptions of new technology products and services of interest to the legal profession.

Library Hi Tech News. MCB University Press North America. • Description: Offers "timely and late-breaking news about all aspects of technology related to library operations." Includes "news of new products, database developments, cooperative networks, technology vendors." Recurring features include book reviews and a calendar of events.

Multimedia Schools: A Practical Journal of Technology for Education including Multimedia, CD-ROM, Online and Internet and Hardware in K-12. Information Today, Inc. • Six times a year. $39.95 per year. Edited for school librarians, media center directors, computer coordinators, and others concerned with educational multimedia. Coverage includes the use of CD-ROM sources, the Internet, online services, and library technology.

Online Investor: Personal Investing for the Digital Age. Stock Trends, Inc. • Monthly. $14.95 per year.

Provides advice and Web site reviews for online traders.

Online Libraries and Microcomputers. Information Intelligence, Inc. • Ten times a year. Individuals $43.75 per year; libraries. $62.50 per year. Newsletter. Covers library automation and electronic information (online, CD-ROM). Reviews or describes new computer hardware and software for library use.

Online Newsletter. Information Intelligence Inc. • Description: Tracks developments in the fields of CD-ROM and online services. Contains news of online/CD-ROM developments and events, mergers and acquisitions, personnel movements, telecommunications and networks, new equipment and developments, microcomputer hardware and software, new and forthcoming databases, forthcoming meetings, and publications and user aids.

Online: The Leading Magazine for Information Professionals. Information Today, Inc. • Bimonthly. $110.00 per year. Edited for librarians, Webmasters, site designers, content managers, and others concerned with knowledge/information management. Includes critical reviews of Web sites, software, search engines, and information services. (Formerly published by Online, Inc.).

Physicians & Computers. Moorhead Publications Inc. • Monthly. $40.00 per year. Includes material on computer diagnostics, online research, medical and non-medical software, computer equipment, and practice management.

Reference Services Review: Information on All Aspects of the Reference Function. Emerald (North America). • Quarterly. $319.00 per year. Covers automation of library reference services, user needs, reference source evaluation, service delivery models, and related topics.

Searcher: The Magazine for Database Professionals. Information Today, Inc. • 10 times per year. $79.95 per year. Covers a wide range of topics relating to online and CD-ROM database searching.

Upgrade. Software and Information Industry Association. • Monthly. $79.00 per year. Covers news and trends relating to the software, information, and Internet industries. Formerly *SPA News* from Software Publisers Association.

WebFinance. Thomson Media. • Semimonthly. $995.00 per year. Newsletter (also available online at www.webfinance.net). Covers the Internet-based provision of online financial services by banks, online brokers, mutual funds, and insurance companies. Provides news stories, analysis, and descriptions of useful resources.

Wired. Wired Ventures Ltd. • Monthly. $10.00 per year. Edited for creators and managers in various areas of electronic information and entertainment, including multimedia, the Internet, and video. Often considered to be the primary publication of the "digital generation.".

RESEARCH CENTERS AND INSTITUTES

Bibliographical Center for Research, Inc., Rocky Mountain Region. 14394 E. Evans Ave., Aurora, CO 80014-1478. Phone: 800-397-1552 or (303)751-6277 Fax: (303)751-9787 E-mail: dbrunell@bcr.org • URL: http://www.bcr.org • Fields of research include information retrieval systems, Internet technology, CD-ROM technology, document delivery, and library automation.

Computer and Information Science and Engineering Research Center. Ohio State University. 395 Dreese Laboratories, Columbus, OH 43210-1277. Phone: (614)292-5813 Fax: (614)292-2911 E-mail: webmaster@cis.ohio-state.edu • URL: http://www.cis.ohio.state.edu.

Information Sciences Institute. University of Southern California, 4676 Admiralty Way, Suite 1001, Marina del Rey, CA 90292-6695. Phone: (310)822-1511 Fax: (310)823-6714 E-mail: schorr@isis.edu • URL: http://www.isi.edu • Research fields include online information and computer science, with emphasis on the World Wide Web.

Laboratory for Computer Science. Massachusetts Institute of Technology, 200 Technology Square, Bldg. NE43, Cambridge, MA 02139. Phone: (617)253-5851 Fax: (617)258-8682 E-mail: zue@mit.edu • URL: http://www.lcs.mit.edu/ • Research is in four areas: Intelligent Systems; Parallel Systems; Systems, Languages, and Networks; and Theory. Emphasis is on the application of online computing.

Management Information Systems Research Center. University of Minnesota. Carlson School of Management, 321 19th Ave. S., Minneapolis, MN 55455-0430. Phone: (612)624-6565 Fax: (612)624-2056 E-mail: misrc@csom.umn.edu • URL: http://www.misrc.umn.edu.

NERAC, Inc. One Technology Dr., Tolland, CT 06084. Phone: (860)872-7000 Fax: (860)875-1749 • URL: http://www.nerac.com.

STATISTICS SOURCES

By the Numbers: Electronic and Online Publishing. Gale Cengage Learning. • 1997-98. $305.00. Four volumes. $85.00 per volume. Covers "high-interest" industries: 1. *By the Numbers: Electronic and Online Publishing*; 2. *By the Numbers: Emerging Industries*; 3. *By the Numbers: Nonprofits*; 4. *By the Numbers: Publishing.* Each volume provides about 600 tabulations of industry data on revenues, market share, employment, trends, financial ratios, profits, salaries, and so forth. Citations to data sources are included. (By the Numbers Series).

Information, Finance, and Services USA. Gale Cengage Learning. • 2001. $240.00. Replaces *Service Industries USA* and *Finance, Insurance, and Real Estate USA.* Presents statistics and projections relating to economic activity in a wide variety of non-manufacturing areas.

Inter-NOT: Online & Internet Statistics Reality Check. Bruce Kushnick. New Networks Institute. • Annual. $495.00. Compares, analyzes, and criticizes statistics issued by Nielsen Media, Forrester Research, FIND/SVP, Yankelovich Partners and many others relating to online and Internet activities. For example, estimates of the number of Internet users have ranged from about 40 million down to six million. Topics include "Adjusting for the Puffery" and "The Most Plausible Statistics.".

OECD Information Technology Outlook 2000: ICTs, E-Commerce and the Information Economy. Organization for Economic Cooperation and Development. • 2000. $72.00. Provides data on information and communications technology (ICT) and electronic commerce in 11 OECD nations (includes U. S.). Coverage includes network infrastructure, electronic payment systems, financial transaction technologies, intelligent agents, global navigation systems, and portable flat panel display technologies.

Statistical Handbook on Technology. Paula Bernstein. Greenwood Publishing Group, Inc. • 1999. $69.95. Provides statistical data on such items as the Internet, online services, computer technology, recycling, patents, prescription drug sales, telecommunications, and aerospace. Includes charts, tables, and graphs. Edited for the general reader. (Statistical Handbook Series).

TRADE/PROFESSIONAL ASSOCIATIONS

American Society for Information Science and Technology. 1320 Fenwick Lane, No. 510, Silver Spring, MD 20910. Phone: (301)495-0900 Fax: (301)495-0810 E-mail: asis@asis.org • URL: http://www.asis.org • Members are information managers, scientists, librarians, and others who are interested in the storage, retrieval, and use of information.

Association of Information and Dissemination Centers. P.O. Box 3212, Maple Glen, PA 19002-8212. Phone: (215)654-9129 Fax: (215)654-9129 E-mail: info@asidic.org • URL: http://www.asidic.org.

Electronic Frontier Foundation. 454 Shotwell St., San Francisco, CA 94110-1914. Phone: (415)436-9333 Fax: (415)436-9993 E-mail: information@eff.org • URL: http://www.eff.org • Promotes the creation of legal and structural approaches to help ease the assimilation of new technologies by society. Seeks to: help policymakers develop a better understanding of issues underlying telecommunications; increase public understanding of the opportunities and challenges posed by computing and telecommunications fields. Fosters awareness of civil liberties issues arising from the advancements in new computer-based communications media and supports litigation to preserve, protect, and extend First Amendment rights in computing and telecommunications technology. Maintains speakers' bureau; conducts educational programs. Encourages and supports the development of tools to endow non-technical users with access to computer-based telecommunications.

International Federation for Information and Documentation. Prins Willem- Alexaderhof 5, NL-2509 LK The Hague LK, Netherlands. Phone: 31 70 3140671 Fax: 31 70 3140677 E-mail: fid@fid.nl • URL: http://www.fid.nl.

International Federation for Information Processing. IFIP Secretariat, Hofstrasse 3, A-2361 Laxenburg, Switzerland. Phone: 43 2336 73616 Fax: 43 2336 736169 E-mail: ifip@ifip.or.at • URL: http://www.ifip.or.at.

Internet Alliance. 1111 19th St. NW, Ste. 1100, Washington, DC 20035-5782. Phone: (202)861-2476 Fax: (202)955-8081 E-mail: info@internetalliance.org • URL: http://www.internetalliance.org • Companies offering Internet services. Seeks to "build the confidence and trust necessary for the Internet to become the global mass market medium of the 21st century". Represents members' commercial and regulatory interests; conducts promotional activities; facilitates communication and cooperation among members.

Library and Information Technology Association. 50 E. Huron St., Chicago, IL 60611. Phone: 800-545-2433 or (312)280-4270 Fax: (312)280-3257 E-mail: lita@ala.org • URL: http://www.lita.org • Affiliated with the American Library Association. Formerly Information Science and Automation Division of ALA.

Reference and User Services Association of American Library Association: Machine Assisted Reference Section. c/o American Library Association, 50 E Huron St., Chicago, IL 60611. Phone: 800-545-2433 or (312)280-4398 Fax: (312)944-8085 E-mail: rusa@ala.org • URL: http://www.ala.org/rusa • Affiliated with American Library Association. Formerly Reference and Adult Services Division of American Library Association.

Software and Information Industry Association. 1090 Vermont Ave. NW, 6th Fl., Washington, DC 20005. Phone: (202)289-7442 Fax: (202)289-7097 • URL: http://www.siia.net • A trade association for the software and digital content industry. Affiliated with Massachusetts Software and Internet Council.

Special Interest Group on Hypertext, Hypermedia, and Web. c/o Association for Computing Machinery, 1515 Broadway, New York, NY 10036. Phone: 800-342-6626 or (212)869-7440 Fax: (212)944-1318 E-mail: acmhelp@acm.org • URL: http://www.acm.org/sigweb • Concerned with the design, use, and evaluation of hypertext and hypermedia systems. Provides a multi-disciplinary forum for the promotion, dissemination, and exchange of ideas relating to research technologies and applications. Publishes the *SIGWEB Newsletter* three times a year.

Special Interest Group on Information Retrieval. c/o Association for Computing Machinery, 1515 Broadway, New York, NY 10036-5701. Phone: 800-342-6626 or (212)869-7440 Fax: (212)944-1318 E-mail: sigs@acm.org • URL: http://www.acm.org/sigir/.

Special Libraries Association; Information Technology Division. 1700 18th St., N.W., Washington, DC 20009-2514. Phone: (202)234-4700 Fax: (202)265-9317 E-mail: sla@sla.org • URL: http://www.sla.org/.

OTHER SOURCES

Consumer Online Services Report. JupiterMedia. • Annual. $1,895.00. Market research report. Provides analysis of trends in the online information industry, with projections of growth in future years (five-year forecasts). Contains profiles of electronic media companies.

Creating the Corporate Digital Library. Primary Research Group, Inc. • 2003. $135.00. Provides a survey of the electronic data policies of specific corporate libraries. Covers electronic journals, e-books, user training, alert services, vendor negotiation, web site development, knowledge management, outsourcing, and other topics.

E-Business, Internet, and Online Transactions. Michael L. Taviss and others. Glasser Legalworks. • Looseleaf. $225.00, including CD-ROM version. Periodic Supplementation. Covers the legal aspects of online content, marketing, advertising, domain names, software licensing, and other Internet issues. Includes many sample forms. (Emerging Growth Companies Series.).

Home Banking Report. JupiterMedia. • Annual. $695.00. Market research report. Covers banking from home by phone or online, with projections of growth in future years.

On-the-Job Research: How Usable are Corporate Research Intranets?. Alison J. Head and Shannon Staley. Special Libraries Association. • 2002. Members, $100.00; non-members, $135.00. Presents the results of a survey of how employees at seven major corporations make use of company intranets for news and information research. Searching by individual employees generally had a success rate of less than 50 percent.

World Online Markets. JupiterMedia. • Annual. $1,895.00. Market research report. Provides broad coverage of worldwide Internet and online information business activities, including country-by-country data. Includes company profiles and five-year forecasts or trend projections.

OPERATING RATIOS

See: FINANCIAL RATIOS

OPERATIONS MANAGEMENT

GENERAL WORKS

Principles of Operation Management. Raturi. Cengage Learning. • 2000. $35.00. Sixth edition. (SWC-Management Series).

ENCYCLOPEDIAS AND DICTIONARIES

Blackwell Encyclopedic Dictionary of Operations Management. Nigel Slack, editor. Blackwell Publishing. • 1997. $130.95. The editor is associated with the University of Warwick, England. Contains definitions of key terms combined with longer articles written by various U. S. and foreign business educators. Includes bibliographies and index. (Blackwell Encyclopedia of Management Series.).

HANDBOOKS AND MANUALS

Banking and Finance on the Internet. Mary J. Cronin, editor. John Wiley and Sons, Inc. • 1997. $45.00. Contains articles on Internet services, written by bankers, money mangers, investment analysts, and stockbrokers. Emphasis is on operations management. (Communications Series).

Production and Operations Management. Richard B. Chase. McGraw-Hill. • 2002. $39.69. Ninth edition. Covers capacity planning, facility location, process design, inventory planning, personnel scheduling, etc.

PERIODICALS AND NEWSLETTERS

Fee Income Growth Strategies. Siefer Consultants Inc. • Description: Discusses the role of fees and service charges for money orders, cashier's checks, nonsufficient funds, loans, automatic teller machine cards, and other ancillary services in the profitability of financial institutions.

Operations Management. Institutional Investor, Inc., Journals Group. • Weekly. $2,105.00 per year. Includes print and online editions. Newsletter. Edited for managers of securities clearance and settlement at financial institutions. Covers new products, technology, legalities, management practices, and other topics related to securities processing.

Production and Operations Management. Production and Operations Management Society. • Quarterly. Individuals, $70.00 per year; libraries, $200.00 per year.

TRADE/PROFESSIONAL ASSOCIATIONS

AFCOM. 742 E Chapman Ave., Orange, CA 92866. Phone: (714)997-7966 Fax: (714)997-9743 E-mail: afcom@afcom.com • URL: http://www.afcom.com • Data center, networking and enterprise systems management professionals from medium and large scale mainframe, midrange and client/server data centers worldwide. Works to meet the professional needs of the enterprise system management community. Provides information and support through educational events, research and assistance hotlines, and surveys.

Production and Operations Management Society. Florida International University, College of Engineering, 10555 W. Flagle St., EAS 2460, Miami, FL 33174. Phone: (305)348-1413 Fax: (305)348-6890 E-mail: poms@eng.fiu.edu • URL: http://www.poms.org • Members are professionals and educators in fields related to operations management and production.

OPERATIONS RESEARCH

See also: AUTOMATION; SYSTEMS IN MANAGEMENT

GENERAL WORKS

Operations Research: A Practical Introduction. Michael W. Carter and Camille C. Price. CRC Press. • 2000. $99.95. Provides a basic guide to the use of operations research problem-solving techniques in business, industry, and engineering.

ABSTRACTS AND INDEXES

International Abstracts in Operations Research. International Federation of Operational Research Societies. Palgrave Macmillan Ltd. • Bimonthly. Institutions, $980.00 per year. Includes print and online editions.

HANDBOOKS AND MANUALS

Operations Research Calculations Handbook. Dennis Blumenfeld. CRC Press. • 2001. $69.95. Contains more than 300 mathematical results and formulas used in operations research applications.

Formulas are utilized in manufacturing, inventory control, and managememt science in general.

PERIODICALS AND NEWSLETTERS

Operational Research Society Journal. JSTOR. • Monthly. $1,096.00 per year. Includes print and online editions. Covers various applications of operations research, including forecasting, inventory, logistics, project management, and scheduling. Includes technical approaches (simulation, mathematical programming, expert systems, etc.).

Operations Research. INFORMS. • Bimonthly. Individuals, $164.00 per year; institutions, $339.00 per year.

Operations Research Letters. Elsevier. • 10 times a year. Institutions, $622.00 per year.

RESEARCH CENTERS AND INSTITUTES

Engineering Systems Research Center. University of California at Berkeley. 3115 Etcheverry Hall, MC 1750, Berkeley, CA 94720-1750. Phone: (510)643-9150 Fax: (510)643-0966 E-mail: esrc@esrc.berkeley.edu • URL: http://www.esrc.berkeley.edu/.

OTHER SOURCES

Recent Developments in Operational Research. Manju Lata Agrawal and Kanar Sen. CRC Press. • 2002. $89.95. Major topics include mathematical programming, queuing theory, production control, statistical methods, and information technology. Covers both theoretical and practical aspects of operations research.

OPHTHALMIC INDUSTRY

See also: CONTACT LENS AND INTRAOCU-LAR LENS INDUSTRIES

ABSTRACTS AND INDEXES

Index Medicus. National Library of Medicine. Available from U. S. Government Printing Office. • Monthly. $620.00 per year. Bibliographic listing of references to current articles from approximately 3,000 of the world's biomedical journals.

Science Citation Index. Thomson/ISI. • Bimonthly. $15,020.00 per year. Annual cumulation. Includes *Source Index, Citation Index, Permuterm Subject Index,* and *Corporate Index.*

BIBLIOGRAPHIES

Medical and Health Care Books and Serials in Print: An Index to Literature in Health Sciences. R. R. Bowker. • Annual. $359.00. Two volumes.

BIOGRAPHICAL SOURCES

Dictionary of American Medical Biography. Joseph Carvalho and others. Greenwood Publishing Group Inc. • 1984. $210.00. Two volumes. Vol. one, $110.00; vol. two, $110.00.

CD-ROM DATABASES

Physicians' Desk Reference Library on CD-ROM. Medical Economics. • Three times a year. Contains the CD-ROM equivalent of *Physicians' Desk Reference (PDR), Physicians' Desk Reference for Nonprescription Drugs, Physicians' Desk Reference for Opthalmology,* and other PDR publications.

DIRECTORIES

Encyclopedia of Medical Organizations and Agencies. Gale Cengage Learning. • 2001. $295.00. 11th edition. Information on over 18,000 public and private organizations in medicine and related fields.

Medical and Health Information Directory. Gale Cengage Learning. • 2002. $675.00. Three volumes. 14th edition. Three volumes. $285.00 per volume. Vol. one covers medical organizations, agencies, and institutions; vol. two includes bibliographic, library, and database information; vol. three is a guide to services available for various medical and health problems.

Opticians of Association America-Reference Directory. Opticians Association of America. • Annual. $60.00. Lists 250 member firms with a total of 350 retail locations.

Optometry and Vision Science-Geographical Directory, American Academy of Optometry. American Academy of Optometry. • Biennial. $25.00. List of 3,400 members; international coverage.

OSA/SPIE/OSJ Membership Directory (Optical Societies of America and Japan). Optical Society of America, Inc. • Annual. Only available online. List of over 20,000 persons interested in any branch of optics. Includes coverage of the Optical Society of America, the Optical Society of Japan, and the International Society for Optical Engineering. Formerly *Optical Society of American Membership Directory.*

The Photonics Directory. Laurin Publishing Company Inc. • Description: A four-book set concerning the international photonics industry, including a 'Corporate Guide' listing manufacturers and suppliers; a 'Buyers' Guide'; a technical 'Handbook' for design and applications engineers; and a 'Dictionary' of terms and abbreviations. Entries include: Company name, address, phone, fax, e-mail, description of products and services.

FINANCIAL RATIOS

Almanac of Business and Industrial Financial Ratios. Leo Troy. Aspen Publishers, Inc. • 2003. $125.95. Includes CD-Rom. Contains financial ratios derived from federal tax returns. Ratios for each of about 200 industries are arranged according to company asset size. (Almanac of Business and Industrial Financial Ratios Series).

Annual Statement Studies. The Risk Management Association. • Annual. Median and quartile financial ratios are given for over 400 kinds of manufacturing, wholesale, retail, construction, and consumer finance establishments. Data is sorted by both asset size and sales volume. Includes a clearly written "Definition of Ratios" and an alphabetical industry index.

Annual Statement Studies: Industry Default Probabilities and Cash Flow Measures. The Risk Management Association. • Annual. $145.00. Serves as a companion volume to the original *Annual Statement Studies.* Gives probability of default estimates on a percentage scale for more than 450 industries. Includes changes in position year-by-year for eight financial statement line items and provides percentage measures of cash flow.

HANDBOOKS AND MANUALS

The Consumer Health Information Source Book. Alan Rees, editor. Greenwood Publishing Group, Inc. • 2003. $65.00. Seventh edition. Bibliography of current literature and guide to organizations.

Physicians' Desk Reference for Ophthalmology. Medical Economics Co. • Annual. $49.95. Provides detailed descriptions of ophthalmological instrumentation, equipment, supplies, lenses, and prescription drugs. Indexed by manufacturer, product name, product category, active drug ingredient, and instrumentation. Editorial discussion is included.

ONLINE DATABASES

Embase. Elsevier Science, Inc. • Worldwide medical literature, 1974 to present. Weekly updates. Inquire as to online cost and availability.

Globalbase. Gale Cengage Learning. • Provides more than one million online summaries of business, industrial, and economic news reports from more than 1,000 publications worldwide. Covers a wide range of material appearing in international trade journals, professional magazines, and newspapers. Time period is 1984 to date, with weekly updates. Inquire as to online cost and availability.

Medline. Medlars Management Section. • Provides indexing and abstracting of worldwide medical literature, 1966 to date. Weekly updates. Inquire as to online cost and availability.

Scisearch. Institute for Scientific Information. • Broad, multidisciplinary index to the literature of science and technology, 1974 to present. Inquire as to online cost and availability. Coverage of literature is worldwide, with weekly updates.

PERIODICALS AND NEWSLETTERS

American Journal of Ophthalmology. Elsevier. • Monthly. Individuals, $107.00 per year; institutions, $508.00 per year; students, $145.00 per year.

American Optometric Association News. American Optometric Association. • Semimonthly. Free to members; non-members, $89.00 per year.

Eyecare Business: The Magazine for Progressive Dispensing. Boucher Communications, Inc. • Monthly. Individuals, $75.00 per year. Covers the business side of optometry and optical retailing. Each issue features "Frames and Fashion.".

Ophthalmology. American Academy of Opthalmology. Elsevier. • Monthly. Individuals, $239.00 per year; institutions, $415.00 per year.

Ophthalmology Times: All the Clinical News in Sight. Advanstar Communications. • Bimonthly. $190.00 per year.

Optometric Management: The Business and Marketing Magazine for Optometry. Boucher Communications, Inc. • Monthly. $37.00 per year. Provides information and advice for optometrists on practice management and marketing.

Optometry: Journal of the American Optometric Society. American Optometric Association. • Monthly. Free to members; non-members, $106.00 per year. Formerly *American Optometric Association Journal.*

RESEARCH CENTERS AND INSTITUTES

Francis I. Proctor Foundation for Research in Ophthalmology. University of California, San Francisco, 95 Kirkham St., San Francisco, CA 94143. Phone: (415)476-1442 Fax: (415)476-0527 E-mail: tpms@itsa.ucf.edu.

Howe Laboratory of Ophthalmology. Harvard University. Massachusetts Eye and Ear Infirmary, 243 Charles St., Boston, MA 02114. Phone: (617)573-3963 Fax: (617)573-4290 • URL: http://www.howelaboratory.harvard.edu • A research unit of Harvard Medical School.

Ophthalmic Research Institute. 6110 Executive Blvd., Suite 506, Rockville, MD 20852. Phone: (301)984-4735 Fax: (301)984-4737.

Vision Research Center in Ophthalmology. Mount Sinai School of Medicine of City University of New Yor, k, One Gustave L. Levy Place, New York, NY 10029. Phone: (212)241-6249 Fax: (212)289-5945 E-mail: oscar.candia@mssm.edu • URL: http://www.mssm.edu/ophth/.

Visual Sciences Center. University of Chicago, 939 E. 57th St., Chicago, IL 60637. Phone: (773)702-8888 Fax: (773)702-8094 E-mail: jernest@midway.uchicago.edu • URL: http://www.ophthalmology.bsd.uchicago.edu.

STATISTICS SOURCES

Annual Survey of Manufactures. Available from U. S. Government Printing Office. • Annual. Prices vary. Issued by the U. S. Census Bureau as an interim update to the *Census of Manufactures.* Includes data on number of manufacturing establishments in various industries, employment, labor costs, value of shipments, capital expenditures, inventories, energy costs, and assets. (See also Census Bureau home page, http://www.census.gov/.).

U. S. Industry and Trade Outlook. Available from National Technical Information Service. • Annual.

$69.95. Produced by the International Trade Administration, U. S. Department of Commerce, in a "public-private" partnership with DRI/McGraw-Hill and Standard & Poor's. Provides basic data, outlook for the current year, and "Long-Term Prospects" (five-year projections) for a wide variety of products and services. Includes high technology industries. Formerly *U. S. Industrial Outlook.*

TRADE/PROFESSIONAL ASSOCIATIONS

American Academy of Optometry. 6110 Executive Blvd., Suite 506, Bethesda, MD 20852. Phone: 800-368-6263 or (301)984-1441 Fax: (301)984-4737 E-mail: aaoptom@aol.com • URL: http://www.aaopt.org • Optometrists, educators and scientists interested in optometric education and standards of care in visual problems.

American Board of Ophthalmology. 111 Presidential Blvd., Suite 241, Bala Cynwyd, PA 19004-1075. Phone: (610)664-1175 Fax: (610)664-6503 E-mail: info@abop.org • URL: http://www.abop.org.

American Optometric Association. 243 N Lindbergh Blvd., St. Louis, MO 63141-7881. Phone: 800-365-2219 or (314)991-4100 Fax: (314)991-4101 E-mail: klalexander@aoa.org • URL: http://www.aoa.org • Professional association of optometrists, students of optometry, and paraoptometric assistants and technicians. Purposes are: to improve the quality, availability, and accessibility of eye and vision care; to represent the optometric profession; to help members conduct their practices; to promote the highest standards of patient care. Monitors and promotes legislation concerning the scope of optometric practice, alternate health care delivery systems, health care cost containment, Medicare, and other issues relevant to eye/vision care. Supports the International Library, Archives and Museum of Optometry which includes references on ophthalmic and related sciences with emphasis on the history and socioeconomic aspects of optometry. Operates Vision U.S.A. program, which provides free eye care to the working poor, and the InfantSEE program, which provides free vision assessments for infants between six and twelve months of age. Conducts specialized education programs; operates placement service; compiles statistics. Maintains museum. Conducts Seal of Acceptance Program.

Better Vision Institute. 1700 Diagonal Rd., Ste. 500, Alexandria, VA 22314. Phone: 877-642-3253 or (703)548-4560 Fax: (703)548-4580 E-mail: info@thevisioncouncil.org • URL: http://www.visionsite.org • Advisory council of the Vision Council of America. Carried out in consultation with a board of eye care professionals who inform the public of the need for more adequate vision care.

National Academy of Opticianry. 8401 Corporate Dr. No. 605, Landover, MD 20785. Phone: 800-229-4828 or (301)577-4828 Fax: (301)577-3880 E-mail: info@nao.org • URL: http://www.nao.org.

National Association of Optometrists and Opticians. P.O. Box 479, Marblehead, OH 43440. Phone: (419)798-4071 or (419)798-2031 Fax: (419)798-8548 E-mail: fdrozak@cros.net • Formerly National Optical Association.

National Optometric Association. PO Box F, PO Box F, East Chicago, IN 46312. Phone: 877-394-2020 or (219)398-4483 Fax: (219)398-1077 E-mail: ddodpc@verizon.net • URL: http://www.natoptassoc.org • Represents optometrists dedicated to increasing awareness of the status of eye/vision health in the minority community and the national community at-large. Strives to make known the impact of the eye/vision dysfunction on the effectiveness and productivity of citizens and the academic proficiency of students. Conducts national minority recruiting programs, job placement, assistance programs for graduates, practitioners, and optometric organizations, and the promotion of delivery of care. Maintains speakers' bureau. Offers specialized education program.

Optical Laboratories Association. 11096 Lee Hwy., Ste. A-101, Fairfax, VA 22030-5039. Phone: 800-477-5652 or (703)359-2830 Fax: (703)359-2834 E-mail: ola@ola-labs.org • URL: http://www.ola-labs.org • Represents independent, wholesale ophthalmic laboratories and suppliers serving the ophthalmic field.

Opticians Association of America. 12100 Sunset Hills Rd., Ste. 130, Reston, VA 20190. Phone: 800-443-8997 or (703)234-4072 Fax: (703)435-4390 E-mail: oaa@oaa.org • URL: http://www.oaa.org • Formerly Guild of Prescription Opticians of America.

OTHER SOURCES

The Market for Ophthalmic Pharmaceuticals. MarketResearch.com. • 1997. $2,500.00. Market research report. Covers topical and internal drugs for eye disorders, with market estimates. Includes pharmaceutical company profiles.

New Ophthalmology: Treatments and Technologies. Theta Reports. • 2000. $1,695. Provides market research data relating to eye surgery, including LASIK, cataract surgery, and associated technology. (Theta Report No. 911.).

OPIATES

See: NARCOTICS

OPINION POLLS

See: PUBLIC OPINION

OPTICAL DISK STORAGE DEVICES

See also: INFORMATION INDUSTRY; MICROCOMPUTERS AND MINICOMPUTERS; MULTIMEDIA

ABSTRACTS AND INDEXES

Applied Science and Technology Index. H. W. Wilson Co. • 11 times a year. Quarterly and annual cumulations. Price varies. Indexes a wide variety of English language technical, industrial, and engineering periodicals.

Business Periodicals Index. H. W. Wilson Co. • 11 times a year. Quarterly and annual cumulations. Price varies.

Computer and Control Abstracts. Available from INSPEC, Inc. • Monthly. $2,400.00 per year. Section C of *Science Abstracts.*

Computer and Information Systems Abstracts Journal: An Abstract Journal Pertaining to the Theory, Design, Fabrication and Application of Computer and Information Systems. CSA. • 11 times a year. $1,750 per year.

Current Contents: Engineering, Computing and Technology. Thomson/ISI. • Weekly. $730.00 per year. Reproductions of contents pages of technical journals. Includes *Author Index, Address Directory, Current Book Contents* and *Title Word Index.* Formerly *Current Contents: Engineering, Technology and Applied Sciences.*

Electronics and Communications Abstracts Journal: Comprehensive Coverage of Essential Scientific Literature. CSA. • Monthly. $1,665.00 per year. Includes print and online editions.

Key Abstracts: Computer Communications and Storage. Available from INSPEC, Inc. • Monthly. $250.00 per year. Provides international coverage of journal and proceedings literature, including material on optical disks and networks. Published in England by the Institution of Electrical Engineers (IEE).

Library Literature and Information Science Index. H. W. Wilson Co. • Quarterly. Annual cumulation. Price varies.

CD-ROM DATABASES

LISA Plus. Available from Cambridge Scientific Abstracts (CSA). • Quarterly. $2,000.00 per year. CD-ROM version of Library Information and Science Abstracts, providing abstracting and indexing of the world's library and information science literature, 1969 to date. Contains more than 180,000 citations.

WILSONDISC: Library Literature and Information Science Index. H. W. Wilson Co. • Quarterly. Includes unlimited access to the online version of *Library Literature.* Provides CD-ROM indexing of about 300 periodicals, covering a wide range of topics having to do with libraries, library management, and the information industry.

DIRECTORIES

Broadcast Engineering--Equipment Reference Manual. Penton Media Inc. • Publication includes: List of more than 1,400 manufacturers and distributors of communications equipment for radio, television, and recording applications. Entries include: For manufacturers--Company name, address. For distributors and dealers--Company name, address, phone, product or service provided, geographic area covered.

CD-ROMS in Print. Gale Cengage Learning. • 2003. $185.00. 17th edition. Describes more than 20,000 currrently available reference and multimedia CD-ROM titles and provides contact information for about 4,000 CD-ROM publishing and distribution companies. Includes several indexes.

Gale Directory of Databases. Gale Cengage Learning. • 2003. $490.00. Two volumes. Volume 1, $315.00; volume 2, $195.00. *Volume 1: Online Databases* and *Volume 2: CD-ROM, Diskette, Magnetic Tape, Handheld, and Batch Access Database Products.*

Library Journal: Reference [year]: Print, CD-ROM, Online. Reed Business Information. • Annual. Issued in November as a supplement to *Library Journal.* Lists new and updated reference material, including general and trade print titles, directories, annuals, CD-ROM titles, and online sources. Includes material from more than 200 publishers, arranged by company name, with an index by subject. Addresses include e-mail and Web information.

Library Journal Sourcebook. Reed Business Information. • Publication includes: List of over 600 suppliers of products and services used by libraries from abstracting to word processing equipment. Entries include: Company name, address, phone, list of products or services. Complete listings for more than 100 architectural firms; Disaster planning for librarians.

MicroLeads Vendor Directory on Disk (Personal Computer Industry). Chromatic Communications Enterprises, Inc. • Annual. $495.00. Includes computer hardware manufacturers, software producers, book-periodical publishers, and franchised or company-owned chains of personal computer equipment retailers, support services and accessory manufacturers. Formerly *MicroLeads U.S. Vender Directory.*

Recording Industry Sourcebook. Thomson Course Technology PTR. • Covers: 14,000 contacts in the music industry in over 65 categories, including record producers, publishers, promoters, attorneys, major and independent record labels, and music production facilities. Entries include: Name, address, phone, fax, name and title of contact, subsidiary and branch names and locations, background information, email, web address.

SRDS Interactive Advertising Source. SRDS. • Quarterly. $569.00 per year. Provides descriptive profiles, rates, audience, personnel, etc., for producers of various forms of interactive or multimedia advertising: online/Internet, CD-ROM, interactive TV, interactive cable, interactive telephone, interactive kiosk, and others.

ENCYCLOPEDIAS AND DICTIONARIES

Dictionary of Information Technology and Computer Science. Tony Gunton. Blackwell Publishing. • 1994. $62.95. Second edition. Covers key words, phrases, abbreviations, and acronyms used in computing and data communications.

Multimedia and the Web from A to Z. David C. Leonard and Patrick M. Dillon. Greenwood Publishing Group, Inc. • 1998. $42.95. Second enlarged revised edition. Defines more than 1,500 terms relating to software and hardware in the areas of computing, online technology, telecommunications, audio, video, motion pictures, CD-ROM, and the Internet. Includes acronyms and an annotated bibliography. Formerly *Multimedia Technology from A to Z* (1994).

HANDBOOKS AND MANUALS

CD-ROM Primer: The ABC's of CD-ROM. Cheryl LaGuardia. Neal-Schuman Publishers, Inc. • 1994. $49.95. Provides advice for librarians and others on CD-ROM equipment, selection, collecting, and maintenance. Includes a glossary, bibliography, and directory of suppliers.

Compact Disc Handbook. Kenneth C. Pohlmann. A-R Editions, Inc. • 1992. $34.95. Second edition. A guide to compact disc technology, including player design and disc manufacturing. (Computer Music and Digital Audio Series).

Digital Audio and Compact Disk Technology. Baert Theunisse and Luc Theunisse. Elsevier. • 1995. $57.95. Third edition.

Interactive Music Handbook: The Definitive Guide to Internet Music Strategies, Enhanced CD Production and Business Development. Jodi Summers. Allworth Press. • 1996. $19.95. Covers interactive or enhanced music CD-ROMs and online music for producers, audio technicians, and musicians. Includes case studies and interviews.

Introductory CD-ROM Searching: The Key to Effective Ondisc Searching. Joseph Meloche. Haworth Press, Inc. • 1994. $49.95. Covers basic search strategies, with specific suggestions for Dialog OnDisc, Silverplatter, Wilsondisc, UMI, and others.

Principles of Digital Audio. Ken C. Pohlmann. McGraw-Hill. • 2000. $54.95. Fourth edition. Includes the details of digital audio recording, reproduction, error correction, compact disc technology, DVD, minidiscs, Internet audio, and related topics. (Video/Audio Engineering Series).

Standard Handbook of Audio and Radio Engineering. Jerry C. Whitaker and K. Blair Benson. McGraw-Hill. • 2002. $125.00. Second edition. Emphasis is on audio. Covers such topics as DVD, MP3, sound reproduction, amplification, noise reduction, and Internet audio.

INTERNET DATABASES

InfoTech Trends. Data Analysis Group. Phone: (925)462-1202 Fax: (925)462-1225 E-mail: support@infotechtrends.com • URL: http://www.infotechtrends.com • Web site provides both free and fee-based market research data on the information technology industry, including computers, peripherals, telecommunications, the Internet, software, CD-ROM/DVD, e-commerce, and workstations. Fees: Free for current (most recent year) data; more extensive information has various fee structures. Formerly . *Computer Industry Forecasts.*

ONLINE DATABASES

Applied Science and Technology Index Online. H. W. Wilson Co. • Provides online indexing of 500 major scientific, technical, industrial, and engineering periodicals. Time period is 1983 to date. Monthly updates. Inquire as to online cost and availability.

Gale Directory of Databases [online]. Gale Cengage Learning. • Presents the online version of the printed *Gale Directory of Databases, Volume 1: Online Databases* and *Gale Directory of Databases, Volume 2: CD-ROM, Diskette, Magnetic Tape, Handheld, and Batch Access Database Products.* Semiannual updates. Inquire as to online cost and availability.

Information Science Abstracts [online]. Information Today, Inc. • Provides indexing and abstracting of the international literature of information science, including library science, from 1966 to date. Monthly updates. Inquire as to online cost and availability.

Internet and Personal Computing Abstracts. Information Today, Inc. • Contains abstracts covering a wide variety of personal and business microcomputer literature appearing in more than 100 journals and popular magazines. Time period is 1981 to date, with monthly updates. Formerly *Microcomputer Index.* Inquire as to online cost and availability.

LISA: Library and Information Science Abstracts. Available from Cambridge Scientific Abstracts (CSA). • Provides abstracting and indexing of the world's library and information science literature, 1969 to date. Covers more than 440 periodicals from 68 countries. Updating is biweekly. Inquire as to online cost and availability.

PROMT: Predicasts Overview of Markets and Technology. Gale Cengage Learning. • Companies, products, applied technologies and markets. U.S. and international literature coverage, 1972 to date. Inquire as to online cost and availability. Provides abstracts from more than 1,600 publications. Weekly updates.

Wilson Business Abstracts Online. H. W. Wilson Co. • Indexes and abstracts 600 major business periodicals, plus the *Wall Street Journal* and the business section of the *New York Times.* Indexing is from 1982, abstracting from 1990, with the two newspapers included from 1993. Updated weekly. Inquire as to online cost and availability. (*Business Periodicals Index* without abstracts is also available online.).

PERIODICALS AND NEWSLETTERS

CD-ROM Information Products: The Evaluative Guide. Ashgate Publishing Co. • Quarterly. $110.00 per year. Provides detailed evaluations of new CD-ROM information products.

Computer Music Journal. MIT Press. • Quarterly. Individuals, $77.00 per year; instutitions, $215.00 per year. Includes print and online editions. Covers digital soound and the musical applications of computers.

Digital Imaging: The Magazine for the Imaging Professional. Cygnus Business Media, Inc. • Bimonthly. $24.95 per year. Edited for business and professional users of electronic publishing products and services. Topics covered include document imaging, CD-ROM publishing, digital video, and multimedia services. Formerly *Micro Publishing News.*

EDP Weekly: The Leading Weekly Computer News Summary. Computer Age and EDP News Services. • Weekly. $495.00 per year. Newsletter. Summarizes news from all areas of the computer and microcomputer industries.

Innovative Publisher: Publishing Strategies for New Markets. Emmelle Publishing Co., Inc. • Biweekly. $69.00 per year. Provides articles and news on electronic publishing (CD-ROM or online) and desktop publishing.

Interactive Marketing and P R News: News and Practical Advice on Using Interactive Advertising and Marketing to Sell Your Products. PBI Media, LLC. • Biweekly. $495.00 per year. Newsletter. Provides information and guidance on merchandising via CD-ROM ("multimedia catalogs"), the Internet, and interactive TV. Topics include "cybermoney", addresses for e-mail marketing, "virtual malls," and other interactive subjects. Formerly *Interactive Marketing News.*

Mass Storage News: Opportunities and Trends in Data Storage and Retrieval. Corry Publishing, Inc. • Biweekly. $597.00 per year. Newsletter. Provides descriptions of products and systems using optical storage. Formerly *Optical Memory News.*

Maximum PC (Personal Computer). Imagine Media, Inc. • Quarterly. $29.95 per year. Provides articles and reviews relating to multimedia hardware and software. Each issue includes a CD-ROM sampler (emphasis is on games). Formed by the merger of *Home PC* and *Boot.*

Searcher: The Magazine for Database Professionals. Information Today, Inc. • 10 times per year. $79.95 per year. Covers a wide range of topics relating to online and CD-ROM database searching.

Sound & Vision: Home Theater- Audio- Video-MultimediaMovies- Music. Hachette Filipacchi Media U.S., Inc. • 10 times a year. $24.00 per year. Popular magazine providing explanatory articles and critical reviews of equipment and media (CD-ROM, DVD, videocassettes, etc.). Supplement available *Stero Review's Sound and Vision Buyers Guide.* Replaces *Stereo Review* and *Video Magazine.*

RESEARCH CENTERS AND INSTITUTES

Bibliographical Center for Research, Inc., Rocky Mountain Region. 14394 E. Evans Ave., Aurora, CO 80014-1478. Phone: 800-397-1552 or (303)751-6277 Fax: (303)751-9787 E-mail: dbrunell@bcr.org • URL: http://www.bcr.org • Fields of research include information retrieval systems, Internet technology, CD-ROM technology, document delivery, and library automation.

Communications and Information Processing Group. Rensselaer Polytechnic Institute, 7010 JEC, 110 Eighth St., Troy, NY 12180-3590. Phone: (518)276-6823 Fax: (518)276-6261 E-mail: modestin@ipl.rpi.edu • URL: http://www.ecse.rpi.edu • Includes Optical Signal Processing Laboratory and Speech Processing Laboratory.

Institute for Information Storage Technology. Santa Clara University, IIST Engineering Bldg., Santa Clara, CA 95053. Phone: (408)554-6853 Fax: (408)554-7841 E-mail: hoagland@siist.scu.edu • URL: http://www.iist.scu.edu.

TRADE/PROFESSIONAL ASSOCIATIONS

AIIM - The Enterprise Content Management Association. 1100 Wayne Ave., Ste. 1100, Silver Spring, MD 20910. Phone: 800-477-2446 or (301)587-8202 Fax: (301)587-2711 E-mail: aiim@aiim.org • URL: http://www.aiim.org • Manufacturers, vendors, and individual users of information and image management equipment, products, and services. Holds special meetings for trade members and companies. Maintains speakers' bureau. Operates resource center. Compiles statistics.

Entertainment Software Association. 575 7th St. NW, Ste. 300, Washington, DC 20004. Phone: (202)223-2400 E-mail: esa@theesa.com • URL: http://www.theesa.com • Represents the interactive entertainment software publishing industry. Established an autonomous rating board to rate

interactive entertainment software. Established a program to combat piracy in the United States and around the world. Represents members on industry issues at the federal and state level. Provides market research and information. **Publications:** none.

OTHER SOURCES

DVD Assessment, No. 3. Julie B. Schwerin and Theodore A. Pine. InfoTech, Inc. • 1998. $1,295.00. Third edition. Provides detailed market research data on Digital Video Discs (also known as Digital Versatile Discs). Includes history of DVD, technical specifications, DVD publishing outlook, "Industry Overview," "Market Context," "Infrastructure Analysis," "Long-Range Forecast to 2005," and emerging technologies.

Optical Publishing Industry Assessment. Julie B. Schwerin and Theodore A. Pine. InfoTech, Inc. • 1997. $1,295.00. Ninth edition. Provides market research data and forecasts to 2005 for DVD-ROM, "Hybrid ROM/Online Media," and other segments of the interactive entertainment, digital information, and consumer electronics industries. Covers both software (content) and hardware. Includes Video-CD, DVD- Video, CD-Audio, DVD-Audio, DVD-ROM, PC-Desktop, TV Set-Top, CD-R, CD-RW, DVD-R and DVD-RAM.

OPTICAL ENGINEERING

See: OPTICS INDUSTRY

OPTICAL FIBERS

See: FIBER OPTICS INDUSTRY

OPTICAL PUBLISHING SYSTEMS

See: OPTICAL DISK STORAGE DEVICES

OPTICS INDUSTRY

See also: FIBER OPTICS INDUSTRY

GENERAL WORKS

Introduction to Glass Science and Technology. Springer-Verlag. • 1997. $49.95. Covers the basics of glass manufacture, including the physical, optical, electrical, chemical, and mechanical properties of glass. (RCS Paperback Series).

CD-ROM DATABASES

Science Citation Index: Compact Disc Edition. Institute for Scientific Information. • Monthly. Provides CD-ROM indexing of the world's scientific and technical literature. Corresponds to online *Scisearch* and printed *Science Citation Index.*

DIRECTORIES

The Photonics Directory. Laurin Publishing Company Inc. • Description: A four-book set concerning the international photonics industry, including a 'Corporate Guide' listing manufacturers and suppliers; a 'Buyers' Guide'; a technical 'Handbook' for design and applications engineers; and a 'Dictionary' of terms and abbreviations. Entries include: Company name, address, phone, fax, e-mail, description of products and services.

HANDBOOKS AND MANUALS

Optics. Eugene Hecht. Addison-Wesley. • 2001. $106.95. Fourth edition. (Manchester Physics Series).

ONLINE DATABASES

PROMT: Predicasts Overview of Markets and Technology. Gale Cengage Learning. • Companies, products, applied technologies and markets. U.S. and international literature coverage, 1972 to date. Inquire as to online cost and availability. Provides abstracts from more than 1,600 publications. Weekly updates.

Scisearch. Institute for Scientific Information. • Broad, multidisciplinary index to the literature of science and technology, 1974 to present. Inquire as to online cost and availability. Coverage of literature is worldwide, with weekly updates.

PERIODICALS AND NEWSLETTERS

Applied Optics. Optical Society of America, Inc. • 36 times a year. $2,437.00 per year.

Fiber Optics News. PBI Media, LLC. • Weekly. $797.00 per year. Newsletter.

Optical Engineering. SPIE-International Society for Optical Engineering. • Monthly. Members $55.00 per year; institutions, $550.00 per year. Technical papers and letters.

Optical Society of America Journal. Optical Society of America, Inc. • Monthly. Part A, $1,371.00 per year; Part B, $1,371.00 per year.

Photonics Spectra. Laurin Publishing Co., Inc. • Monthly. $112.00 per year.

RESEARCH CENTERS AND INSTITUTES

Institute of Optics. University of Rochester, Rochester, NY 14627. Phone: (716)275-2322 Fax: (716)273-1072 E-mail: wknox@optics.rochester. edu • URL: http://www.optics.rochester.edu.

Optical Sciences Center. University of Arizona, 1630 E. University Blvd., Tucson, AZ 85721. Phone: (520)621-6997 Fax: (520)621-9613 E-mail: jcwyant@optics.arizona.edu • URL: http://www. optics.arizona.edu.

TRADE/PROFESSIONAL ASSOCIATIONS

Optical Laboratories Association. 11096 Lee Hwy., Ste. A-101, Fairfax, VA 22030-5039. Phone: 800-477-5652 or (703)359-2830 Fax: (703)359-2834 E-mail: ola@ola-labs.org • URL: http://www.ola-labs.org • Represents independent, wholesale ophthalmic laboratories and suppliers serving the ophthalmic field.

Optical Society of America. 2010 Massachusetts Ave., N.W., Washington, DC 20036-1023. Phone: (202)223-8130 Fax: (202)223-1096 E-mail: info@osa.org • URL: http://www.osa.org.

SPIE-The International Society for Optical Engineering. P.O. Box 10, Bellingham, WA 98227-0010. Phone: (360)676-3290 Fax: (360)647-1445 E-mail: spie@spie.org • URL: http://www.spie.org • Formerly Society of Photo-Optical Instrumentation Engineers.

OPTIONS (PUTS AND CALLS)

See: STOCK OPTION CONTRACTS

OPTOELECTRONICS

See also: ELECTRONICS INDUSTRY; OPTICS INDUSTRY; PHOTONICS

GENERAL WORKS

Fundamentals of Optoelectronics. Clifford R. Pollock. McGraw-Hill. • 1994. $107.19.

Introduction to Laser Technology. C. Breck Hitz and others. John Wiley and Sons, Inc. • 2001. $79.95. Third edition. Published by the Institute of Electrical and Electronics Engineers (IEEE) (http://www.ieee.org). Provides basic information about a wide variety of commercial lasers. Edited for "professionals, students, and non-engineer executives interested in the design, sales, or applications of the laser and electro-optics industry.".

Optoelectronics: An Introduction. John Wilson. Prentice Hall PTR. • 1998. $94.00. Third edition.

ABSTRACTS AND INDEXES

Applied Science and Technology Index. H. W. Wilson Co. • 11 times a year. Quarterly and annual cumulations. Price varies. Indexes a wide variety of English language technical, industrial, and engineering periodicals.

Key Abstracts: Optoelectronics. Available from INSPEC, Inc. • Monthly. $250.00 per year. Provides international coverage of journal and proceedings literature relating to fiber optics, lasers, and optoelectronics in general. Published in England by the Institution of Electrical Engineers (IEE).

NTIS Alerts: Electrotechnology. National Technical Information Service. • Semimonthly. $210.00 per year. Provides descriptions of government-sponsored research reports and software, with ordering information. Covers electronic components, semiconductors, antennas, circuits, optoelectronic devices, and related subjects. Formerly *Abstract Newsletter.*

Science Citation Index. Thomson/ISI. • Bimonthly. $15,020.00 per year. Annual cumulation. Includes *Source Index, Citation Index, Permuterm Subject Index,* and *Corporate Index.*

CD-ROM DATABASES

Science Citation Index: Compact Disc Edition. Institute for Scientific Information. • Monthly. Provides CD-ROM indexing of the world's scientific and technical literature. Corresponds to online *Scisearch* and printed *Science Citation Index.*

DIRECTORIES

Frontline Solutions Buyer's Guide. Advanstar Communications. • Publication includes: List of manufacturers, suppliers, consultants, value added resellers, and dealers/distributors of automatic identification and data capture software, technology, equipment, and products for bar code, biometric identification, electronic data interchange, machine vision, magnetic stripe, optical character recognition, radio frequency data communications, radio frequency identification, smart cards, and voice data entry; also includes related organizations, and sources for industry standards. Entries include: Company name, address, phone, e-mail, web address, products or services.

Laser Focus World Buyers Guide. Advanced Technology Group. • Covers: over 2,000 manufacturers, suppliers, and consultants in the laser, fiber optic, electro-optic, optic, and related industries, worldwide. Entries include: Company name, address, phone, fax, e-mail, principal executives, number of employees, list of products and services, brief description of company.

OSA/SPIE/OSJ Membership Directory (Optical Societites of America and Japan). Optical Society of America, Inc. • Annual. Only available online. List of over 20,000 persons interested in any branch of optics. Includes coverage of the Optical Society of America, the Optical Society of Japan, and the International Society for Optical Engineering. Formerly *Optical Society of American Membership Directory.*

The Photonics Directory. Laurin Publishing Company Inc. • Description: A four-book set concerning the international photonics industry, including a 'Corporate Guide' listing manufacturers and suppliers; a 'Buyers' Guide'; a technical 'Handbook' for design and applications engineers; and a 'Dictionary' of terms and abbreviations. Entries include: Company name, address, phone, fax, e-mail, description of products and services.

ENCYCLOPEDIAS AND DICTIONARIES

Wiley Encyclopedia of Electrical and Electronics Engineering. John G. Webster, editor. John Wiley

and Sons, Inc. • 1999. $9,630.00. 25 volumes. Includes *Supplement 1* and *Supplement II.* Contains about 1,400 articles, each with bibliography. Arrangement is according to 64 categories.

HANDBOOKS AND MANUALS

Optoelectronic Devices. Safa Kasap. Addison-Wesley. • 2001. $105.00.

ONLINE DATABASES

Globalbase. Gale Cengage Learning. • Provides more than one million online summaries of business, industrial, and economic news reports from more than 1,000 publications worldwide. Covers a wide range of material appearing in international trade journals, professional magazines, and newspapers. Time period is 1984 to date, with weekly updates. Inquire as to online cost and availability.

INSPEC. Institution of Electrical Engineers (IEE). • Provides online citations, with abstracts, to the world literature of electrical engineering, electronics, optoelectronics, telecommunications, industrial controls, instrumentation, computer technology, information technology, and physics. Coverage includes more than 4,000 technical and scientific journals from 1969 to date, with weekly updating. (INSPEC is Information Services in Physics, Electronics, and Computing.) Inquire as to online cost and availability.

Scisearch. Institute for Scientific Information. • Broad, multidisciplinary index to the literature of science and technology, 1974 to present. Inquire as to online cost and availability. Coverage of literature is worldwide, with weekly updates.

PERIODICALS AND NEWSLETTERS

FiberSystems International. Available from IOP Publishing, Inc. • Seven times a year. Free to qualified personnel. Published in the UK by the Institute of Physics. "Covering the optical communications marketplace within the Americas and Asia." *Fibre Systems Europe* is also available, covering the business and marketing aspects of fiber optics communications in Europe.

Laser Focus World: The World of Optoelectronics. PennWell Corp., Advanced Technology Div. • Monthly. $165.00 per year. Covers business and technical aspects of electro-optics, including lasers and fiberoptics. Includes *Buyer's Guide.*

Microwave and Optical Technology Letters. John Wiley and Sons, Inc., Journals. • 24 times a year. $1,690.00 per year; with online edition, $1,775.00 per year. Four volumes.

Optical Engineering. SPIE-International Society for Optical Engineering. • Monthly. Members $55.00 per year; institutions, $550.00 per year. Technical papers and letters.

Photonics Spectra. Laurin Publishing Co., Inc. • Monthly. $112.00 per year.

RESEARCH CENTERS AND INSTITUTES

Center for Research and Education in Optics and Lasers. University of Central Florida, School of Optics, 4000 Central Florida Blvd., Orlando, FL 32816-2700. Phone: (407)823-6800 Fax: (407)823-6880 E-mail: ewvs@creol.ucf.edu • URL: http://www.creol.ucf.edu.

Fiber and Electro Optics Research Center. Virginia Polytechnic Institute and State University, Dept. of Electrical Engineering, 106 Plantation Rd., Blacksburg, VA 24061. Phone: (540)231-7203 Fax: (540)231-4561 E-mail: roclaus@vt.edu.

Institute of Optics. University of Rochester, Rochester, NY 14627. Phone: (716)275-2322 Fax: (716)273-1072 E-mail: wknox@optics.rochester. edu • URL: http://www.optics.rochester.edu.

Photonics Research Laboratory. University of Florida, 339 Larsen Hall, Gainesville, FL 32611. Phone: (352)392-9265 Fax: (352)392-4963 E-mail:

ramu@ece.ufl.edu • URL: http://www.ece.ufl.edu/labs/mphoton.

TRADE/PROFESSIONAL ASSOCIATIONS

IEEE Lasers and Electro-Optics Society. c/o IEEE Corporate Center, Three Park Ave., 17th Fl., New York, NY 10016-5997. Phone: (212)419-7900 or (212)752-4929 E-mail: ieeeusa@ieee.org • URL: http://www.ieee.org • Fields of interest include lasers, fiber optics, optoelectronics, and photonics.

SPIE-The International Society for Optical Engineering. P.O. Box 10, Bellingham, WA 98227-0010. Phone: (360)676-3290 Fax: (360)647-1445 E-mail: spie@spie.org • URL: http://www.spie.org • Formerly Society of Photo-Optical Instrumentation Engineers.

OPTOMETRIC INDUSTRY

See: OPHTHALMIC INDUSTRY

ORANGE INDUSTRY

See: CITRUS FRUIT INDUSTRY

ORDNANCE MARKET

See: MILITARY MARKET

ORGANIZATION

See: INDUSTRIAL MANAGEMENT

ORGANIZATION FOR ECONOMIC COOPERATION AND DEVELOPMENT

See also: FOREIGN TRADE

BIBLIOGRAPHIES

OECD Catalogue of Publications. Organization for Economic Cooperation and Development. Available from OECD Publications and Information Center. • Online only. No print edition.

CD-ROM DATABASES

OECD Statistical Compendium. Organization for Economic Cooperation and Development. • Semiannual. $1,905.00 per year for 1 to 10 users. CD-ROM contains more than 730,000 monthly, quarterly, and annual time series for OECD countries, 1960 to date. Includes fully searchable data on agriculture, food, economic indicators, national accounts, employment, energy, finance, industry, technology, and foreign trade. Results can be displayed in various forms.

DIRECTORIES

Europa World Year Book. Routledge Reference. • Covers: Background and statistical information on recent history, government, economic affairs, geography and the current situation in every country of the world as well as providing an extensive listing of national key organizations and firms and about 1,650 international organization. Entries include: For international organizations--Name, address, principal officials, organization, function, activities, financial structure. For national organizations--Lists with names, addresses, officials, and key facts as appropriate, for the government, religious bodies, newspapers, radio and television stations, banks, trade associations, transport industry, tourism and cultural organizations,

universities, research institutes.

PERIODICALS AND NEWSLETTERS

Central Banking: Policy, Markets, Supervision. Available from European Business Publications, Inc. • Quarterly. $260.00 per year, including annual *Central Banking Directory.* Published in England by Central Banking Publications. Reports and comments on the activities of central banks around the world. Also provides discussions of the International Monetary Fund (IMF), the Organization for Economic Cooperation and Development (OECD), the Bank for International Settlements (BIS), and the World Bank.

News from OECD. Available from OECD Publications and Information Center. • Monthly. Free. Lists OECD's calender of activities.

OECD Observer. Available from OECD Publications and Information Center. • Bimonthly. $50.00 per year.

STATISTICS SOURCES

Main Economic Indicators. OECD Publication and Information Center. • Monthly. $450.00 per year. "The essential source of timely statistics for OECD member countries." Includes a wide variety of business, economic, and industrial data for the 29 OECD nations.

OECD in Figures. Organization for Economic Cooperation and Development. • Annual. $13.00. A "pocket data book" providing a summary of key statistics for OECD countries, including economic growth, employment, education, the environment, and transportation.

TRADE/PROFESSIONAL ASSOCIATIONS

Organisation for Economic Co-Operation and Development. 2, rue Andre Pascal, F-75775 Paris Cedex 16, France. Phone: 33 1 45248200 E-mail: webmaster@oecd.org • URL: http://www.oecd.org.

ORGANIZATION FOR EUROPEAN ECONOMIC COOPERATION

See: ORGANIZATION FOR ECONOMIC COOPERATION AND DEVELOPMENT

ORGANIZATION THEORY

See: MANAGEMENT THEORY

ORGANIZATIONS

See: ASSOCIATIONS

ORGANIZED LABOR

See: LABOR UNIONS

ORIENTAL RUG INDUSTRY

DIRECTORIES

Floor Covering Weekly--Annual Product Source Guide. FCW. • Publication includes: Lists of manufacturers and importers of carpet, rugs, carpet cushion, fiber, resilient wood, and ceramic floor coverings; separate listing of distributors by state, retail groups and associations. Entries include: For manufacturers--Company name, address, phone, regional sales offices, names and titles of key personnel, local distributors, products. For distributors--Company name, address, phone,

manufacturers represented.

PERIODICALS AND NEWSLETTERS

Oriental Rug Review. Oriental Rug Auction Review, Inc. • Bimonthly. $48.00 per year.

TRADE/PROFESSIONAL ASSOCIATIONS

Oriental Rug Importers Association. 100 Park Plaza Dr., Secaucus, NJ 07094. Phone: (201)866-5054 Fax: (201)866-6169 E-mail: oria@oria.org • URL: http://www.oria.org • Represents wholesalers and importers of Oriental rugs. Fosters ethical business practices and promotes the best interests of the Oriental Rug Trade in the United States and in countries that produce Oriental rugs.

OTHER SOURCES

Carpets and Rugs. Available from MarketResearch. com. • 2001. $4,000.00. Market research data. Published by the Freedonia Group. Provides both historical data and forecasts to 2007 for various kinds of carpeting.

ORTHOPEDIC APPLIANCE INDUSTRY

See: PROSTHETICS INDUSTRY

OUTDOOR ADVERTISING

See also: SIGNS AND SIGN BOARDS

DIRECTORIES

Buyers Guide to Outdoor Advertising. Competitive Media Reporting. • Semiannual. $475.00 per year. Lists more than 800 outdoor advertising companies and their market rates, etc.

SRDS Out-of-Home Advertising Source. SRDS. • Annual. $341.00. Provides detailed information on non-traditional or "out-of-home" advertising media: outdoor, aerial, airport, mass transit, bus benches, school, hotel, in-flight, in-store, theater, stadium, taxi, truckstop, kiosk, shopping malls, and others. Formerly *Advertising Options Plus.*

FINANCIAL RATIOS

Annual Statement Studies. The Risk Management Association. • Annual. Median and quartile financial ratios are given for over 400 kinds of manufacturing, wholesale, retail, construction, and consumer finance establishments. Data is sorted by both asset size and sales volume. Includes a clearly written "Definition of Ratios" and an alphabetical industry index.

Annual Statement Studies: Industry Default Probabilities and Cash Flow Measures. The Risk Management Association. • Annual. $145.00. Serves as a companion volume to the original *Annual Statement Studies.* Gives probability of default estimates on a percentage scale for more than 450 industries. Includes changes in position year-by-year for eight financial statement line items and provides percentage measures of cash flow.

PERIODICALS AND NEWSLETTERS

Signs of the Times: The Industry Journal Since 1906. ST Media Group International. • 13 times a year. $36.00 per year. For designers and manufacturers of all types of signs. Features how-to-tips. Includes *Sign Erection, Maintenance Directory* and annual *Buyer's Guide.*

TRADE/PROFESSIONAL ASSOCIATIONS

Outdoor Advertising Association of America. 1850 M St., NW, Ste. 1040, Washington, DC 20036. Phone: (202)833-5566 Fax: (202)833-1522 E-mail: info@oaaa.org • URL: http://www.oaaa.org • Firms owning, erecting and maintaining standardized poster panels and painted display advertising facilities. Absorbed Shelter Advertising Association.

OUTDOOR AMUSEMENTS

See: AMUSEMENT INDUSTRY

OUTPLACEMENT CONSULTANTS

See: EMPLOYMENT AGENCIES AND SERVICES

OVER-THE-COUNTER DRUGS

See: NONPRESCRIPTION DRUG INDUSTRY

OVER-THE-COUNTER SECURITIES INDUSTRY

See also: SECURITIES; STOCK BROKERS; STOCKS

GENERAL WORKS

Investing in Small-Cap Stocks. Christopher Graja and Elizabeth Ungar. Bloomberg. • 1999. $26.95. Second expanded revised edition. Provides a practical strategy for investing in small-capitalization stocks. (Bloomberg Personal Bookshelf Series.).

Investing in the Over-the-Counter Markets: Stocks, Bonds, IPOs. Alvin D. Hall. John Wiley and Sons, Inc. • 1995. $29.95. Provides advice and information on investing in "unlisted" or NASDAQ (National Association of Securities Dealers Automated Quotation System) stocks, bonds, and initial public offerings (IPOs).

DIRECTORIES

Institutional Buyers of Small-Cap Stocks. Investment Data Corp. • Annual. $295.00. Provides detailed profiles of more than 837 institutional buyers of small capitalization stocks. Includes names of financial analysts and portfolio managers.

Mergent's Handbook of NASDAQ Stocks. Mergent, Inc. • Quarterly. $350.00 per year ($100.00 per copy). Contains one-page profiles of more than 600 major companies traded on the NASDAQ National Exchange or the American Stock Exchange. Includes price performance scores, analysis, comment, and seven-year financial statistics. Formerly *Moody's Handbook of NASDAQ Stocks.*

Standard and Poor's Security Dealers of North America. Standard & Poor's. • Semiannual. $480.00 per year; with *Supplements* every six weeks. Geographical listing of over 12,000 stock, bond, and commodity dealers.

Walker's Manual of Unlisted Stocks. Walker's Manual, LLC. • Annual. $99.00. Provides information on 500 over-the-counter stocks, including many "penny stocks" trading at less than $5.00 per share.

ENCYCLOPEDIAS AND DICTIONARIES

Dictionary of Finance and Investment Terms. John Downes. Barron's Educational Series, Inc. • 2002. $14.95. Sixth edition. Provides clear explanations of more than 5,000 business, banking, financial, investment, and tax terms. Includes a separate list of financial abbreviations and acronyms. (Business Dictionaries Series).

HANDBOOKS AND MANUALS

Handbook of Derivative Instruments: Investment Research, Analysis, and Portfolio Applications. Arsuo Konishi and Ravi Dattatreya, editors. McGraw-Hill. • 1996. $80.00. Second revised edition. Contains 41 chapters by various authors on all aspects of derivative securities, including such esoterica as "Inverse Floaters," "Positive Convexity,"

"Exotic Options," and "How to Use the Holes in Black-Scholes.".

Handbook of Equity Derivatives. Jack C. Francis and others, editors. John Wiley and Sons, Inc. • 1999. $105.00. Revised edition. Contains 27 chapters by various authors. Covers options (puts and calls), stock index futures, warrants, convertibles, over-the-counter options, swaps, legal issues, taxation, etc. (Financial Engineering Series).

Handbook of NASDAQ Stocks. Mergent, Inc. • Quarterly. $225.00 per year. Over 600 corporations, whose stocks are among the most actively traded in dollar volume on the Nasdaq market. Formerly *Moody's Handbook of NASDAQ Stocks.*

Mergent OTC Unlisted Manual (Over the Counter). Mergent. • Annual, $1,995.00 per year. Includes supplement *Moody's OTC Unlisted News Report.*

Moody's OTC Industrial Manual. Mergent, Inc. • Annual, $1,995.00 per year. Includes biweekly *Moody's OTC Industrial News Report.*

N A S D Manual. National Association of Securities Dealers, Inc. CCH, Inc. • Quarterly. $452.00 per year. CD-Rom, $459.00.

Understanding Financial Derivatives: How to Protect Your Investments. Donald Strassheim. McGraw-Hill. • 1996. $40.00. Covers three basic risk management instruments: options, futures, and swaps. Includes advice on equity index options, financial futures contracts, and over-the-counter derivatives markets.

INTERNET DATABASES

Factiva. Dow Jones Reuters Business Interactive, LLC. Phone: 800-369-7466 or (609)452-1511 Fax: (609)520-5770 E-mail: solutions@factiva.com • URL: http://www.factiva.com • Fee-based Web site provides "global news and business information through Web sites and content integration solutions." Includes Dow Jones and Reuters newswires, The Wall Street Journal, and more than 7,000 other sources of current news, historical articles, market research reports, and investment analysis. Content includes 96 major U. S. newspapers, 900 non-English sources, trade publications, media transcripts, country profiles, news photos, etc.

Nexis.com. Lexis-Nexis Group. Phone: 800-227-4908 or (937)865-6800 Fax: (937)865-6909 E-mail: webmaster@prod.lexis-nexis.com • URL: http://www.nexis.com • Fee-based Web site offers searching of about 2.8 billion documents in some 30,000 news, business, and legal information sources. Features include a subject directory covering 1,200 topics in 34 categories and a Company Dossier containing information on more than 500,000 public and private companies. Boolean searching is offered.

TheStreet.com: Your Insider's Look at Wall Street. TheStreet.com, Inc. Phone: 800-562-9571 or (212)321-1500 Fax: (212)321-5016 • URL: http://www.thestreet.com • Web site offers "Free Sections" and "Premium Sections" ($24.95 per month). Both sections offer iconoclastic advice and comment on the stock market, but premium service displays a more comprehensive selection of news and analysis. There are many by-lined articles. "Search the Site" is included.

Wall Street Journal Interactive Edition. Dow Jones & Co., Inc. Phone: 800-369-2834 or (212)416-2000 Fax: (212)416-2658 E-mail: inquiries@interactive.wsj.com • URL: http://www.wsj.com • Fee-based Web site providing online searching of worldwide information from the *The Wall Street Journal.* Includes "Company Snapshots," "The Journal's Greatest Hits," "Index to Market Data," "Journal Links," etc. Financial price quotes are available.

Fees: $49.00 per year; $29.00 per year to print subscribers.

ONLINE DATABASES

Disclosure SEC Database. Thomson Financial. • Provides online information from records filed with the Securities and Exchange Commission by more than 12,000 publicly-owned companies in the U.S. Includes about 200 financial data items and information relating to executives. Time span is 1977 to date, with weekly updates. Inquire as to online cost and availability.

EdgarPlus: SEC Basic Filings. Thomson Financial. • Online service provides full text of about 60,000 documents that have been filed with the U.S. Securities and Exchange Commission, 1987 to date, with daily updates. Filings include 6-K, 8-K, 10-K, 10-C, 10-Q, 20-F, and proxy statements. Inquire as to online cost and availability.

PERIODICALS AND NEWSLETTERS

Barron's: The Dow Jones Business and Financial Weekly. • Weekly. $145.00 per year.

Equities: Investment News of Promising Public Companies. Equities Magazine LLC. • Bimonthly. $21.00 per year. Formerly *OTC Review.*

Financial Sentinel: Your Beacon to the World of Investing. Gulf Atlantic Publishing, Inc. • Monthly. $29.95 per year. Provides "The only complete listing of all OTC Bulletin Board stocks, with all issues listed on the Nasdaq SmallCap Market, the Toronto, and Vancouver Stock Exchanges." Also includes investment advice and recommendations of small capitalization stocks.

The Penny Fortune Newsletter. James M. Fortune, editor. Phoenix Communications Group Ltd. • Description: Instructs small investors on how to invest modest sums of money every two weeks to build a portfolio of stocks and mutual funds.

Special Situations Newsletter: In-Depth Survey of Under-Valued Stocks. Charles Howard Kaplan. • Monthly. $75.00 per year. Newsletter. Principal content is "This Month's Recommendation," a detailed analysis of one special situation stock.

Standard & Poor's SmallCap 600 Guide. McGraw-Hill. • Monthly. $24.95. Contains detailed profiles of the companies included in Standard & Poor's SmallCap 600 Index of stock prices. Includes income and balance sheet data for up to 10 years, with growth and stability rankings for 600 small capitalization corporations.

The Wall Street Journal. Dow Jones & Co., Inc. • Daily. $189.00 per year. Covers news and trends relating to business, industry, finance, the economy, and international commerce. Provides extensive price and other data for the securities, commodity, options, futures, foreign exchange, and money markets.

PRICE SOURCES

Bank and Quotation Record. William B. Dana Co. • Monthly. $130.00 per year.

National Bond Summary. Pink Sheets LLC. • Monthly, with semiannual cumulations. $504.00 per year. Includes price quotes for both active and inactive issues, with transfer agents, market makers (brokers), capital changes, name changes, and other corporate information. Formerly published by the National Quotation Bureau.

National Stock Summary. Pink Sheets LLC. • Monthly, with semiannual cumulations. $576.00 per year. Includes price quotes for both active and inactive issues, with transfer agents, market makers (brokers), capital changes, name changes, and other corporate information. Pink Sheets LLC also provides daily and weekly stock price services.

Formerly published by the National Quotation Bureau.

STATISTICS SOURCES

Nasdaq Fact Book and Company Directory. National Association of Security Dealers, Inc. Corporate Communications. • Annual. $20.00. Contains statistical data relating to the Nasdaq Stock Market. Also provides corporate address, phone, symbol, stock price, and trading volume information for more than 5,000 securities traded through the National Association of Securities Dealers Automated Quotation System (Nasdaq), including Small-Cap Issues. Includes indexing by Standard Industrial Classification (SIC) number.

TRADE/PROFESSIONAL ASSOCIATIONS

Association of Publicly Traded Companies. 1200 G St., N.W., Suite 800, Washington, DC 20005. Phone: (202)434-8983 Fax: (202)434-8707 E-mail: info@ aptc.org • URL: http://www.aptc.org.

National Association of Securities Dealers (NASD). 1735 K St., N.W., Washington, DC 20006-1506. Phone: (202)728-8000 Fax: (202)293-6260 E-mail: waltere@nasd.com • URL: http://www.nasd.com • Formerly National Association of Securities Dealers.

Security Traders Association. 420 Lexington Ave., Ste. 2334, New York, NY 10170. Phone: (212)867-7002 Fax: (212)867-7030 E-mail: traders@ securitytraders.org • URL: http://www. securitytraders.org • Brokers and dealers handling listed and OTC securities, stocks, and bonds, and all securities. Conducts educational programs.

Promotes the interests of members throughout the global financial markets. Provides representation of these interests in the legislative, regulatory and technological processes. Fosters goodwill and high standards of integrity in accord with the Association's founding principle.

OVERSEAS EMPLOYMENT

See: EMPLOYMENT IN FOREIGN COUNTRIES

OXYACETYLENE WELDING

See: WELDING

OYSTER INDUSTRY

See also: SEAFOOD INDUSTRY; SHELLFISH INDUSTRY

PERIODICALS AND NEWSLETTERS

Seafood Business. Diversified Business Communications. • Monthly. $69.00 per year. Edited for a wide range of seafood buyers, including distributors, restaurants, supermarkets, and institutions. Special issues feature information on specific products, such as salmon or lobster.

STATISTICS SOURCES

Fisheries of the United States. Available from U. S. Government Printing Office. • Annual. $20.00. Is-

sued by the National Marine Fisheries Service, National Oceanic and Atmospheric Administration, U. S. Department of Commerce.

TRADE/PROFESSIONAL ASSOCIATIONS

Molluscan Shellfish Institute. 7918 Jones Branch Dr., Ste. 700, McLean, VA 22102. Phone: (703)752-8880 Fax: (703)752-7583 E-mail: ccfma@ sbcglobal.net • URL: http://www.aboutseafood.com • A division of the National Fisheries Institute (see separate entry). Shellfish producers, processors, distributors, growers, and suppliers to the industry. Works to promote, protect, and advance the interests of the shellfish industry. Cooperates with federal, state, and municipal authorities in matters of legislation, sanitation standards, controls, and conservation.

National Shellfisheries Association. 14 Carter Ln., P.O. Box 350, East Quogue, NY 11942. Phone: (631)653-6327 Fax: (631)653-6327 E-mail: jdavis@bainbridge.net • URL: http://www.shellfish. org • Biologists, hydrographers, public health workers, shellfish producers, and fishery administrators. Encourages research on mollusks and crustaceans, with emphasis on those forms of economic importance known as shellfish.

Pacific Coast Shellfish Growers Association. 120 State Ave. NE, PMB No. 142, Olympia, WA 98501. Phone: (360)754-2744 Fax: (360)754-2743 E-mail: pcsga@pcsga.org • URL: http://www.pcsga.org • Oyster, clam, mussel, scallop, geoduck growers, openers, packers and shippers in Alaska, California, Oregon, Washington, Hawaii, and Mexico.

P

PACKAGING

See also: CONTAINER INDUSTRY; PAPER BOX AND PAPER CONTAINER INDUSTRIES; PAPERBOARD AND PAPERBOARD PACKAGING INDUSTRIES

ABSTRACTS AND INDEXES
Foods Adlibra: Key to the World's Food Literature. General Mills, Inc. Foods Adlibra Publications. • Semimonthly. $240.00 per year. Provides journal citations and abstracts to the literature of food technology and packaging.

BIOGRAPHICAL SOURCES
Who's Who in Packaging. Institute of Packaging Professionals. • Annual. Price on application. Formerly *Who's Who and What's What in Packaging.*

DIRECTORIES
Household and Personal Products Industry - Buyers Guide. Rodman Publications. • Annual. $12.00. Lists of suppliers to manufacturers of cosmetics, toiletries, soaps, detergents, and related household and personal products.

Household and Personal Products Industry Contract Packaging and Private Label Directory. Rodman Publications. • Annual. $12.00. Provides information for about 450 companies offering private label or contract packaged household and personal care products, such as detergents, cosmetics, polishes, insecticides, and various aerosol items.

Packaging Digest Machinery/Materials Guide. Reed Business Information. • Annual. $46.00. List of more than 3,100 manufacturers of machinery and materials for the packaging industry, and about 260 contract packagers.

Paperboard Packaging Resource Directory. Advanstar Communications. • Covers: about 3,000 manufacturers of corrugated and solid fiber containers, folding cartons, rigid boxes, fiber cans and tubes, and fiber drums. Entries include: For manufacturers--Company name, address, phone, equipment, names of executives, plants, and type of containers manufactured.

ENCYCLOPEDIAS AND DICTIONARIES
Wiley Encyclopedia of Food Science and Technology. Frederick J. Francis, editor. John Wiley and Sons, Inc. • 2000. $1,650.00. Second edition. Four volumes. Contains about 400 entries. Coverage includes biotechnology, genetic engineering, nutrition, regulatory matters, food safety, labeling, food substitutes (sugar, fat, dairy), and many other topics.

Wiley Encyclopedia of Packaging Technology.

Aaron Brody and Kenneth Marsh, editors. John Wiley and Sons, Inc. • 1997. $330.00. Second edition.

ONLINE DATABASES
FOODS ADLIBRA. General Mills, Inc. • Contains online citations, with abstracts, to the technical and business literature of food processing and packaging. New products and new ingredients are featured. Covers about 250 trade journals and 500 research journals from 1974 to date, with monthly updates. Inquire as to online cost and availability.

PIRA. PIRA International Information Centre. • Citations and abstracts pertaining to bookbinding and other pulp, paper, and packaging industries, 1975 to present. Weekly updates. Inquire as to online cost and availability.

PERIODICALS AND NEWSLETTERS
Household and Personal Products Industry: The Magazine for the Detergent, Soap, Cosmetic and Toiletry, Wax, Polish and Aerosol Industries. Rodman Publications. • Monthly. $48.00 per year. Covers marketing, packaging, production, technical innovations, private label developments, and aerosol packaging for soap, detergents, cosmetics, insecticides, and a variety of other household products.

Packaging Digest. Reed Business Information. • 13 times a year. $119.90 per year.

Packaging Technology and Science. John Wiley and Sons, Inc., Journals. • Bimonthly. Individuals, $650.00 per year; institutions, $1,295.00 per year. Provides international coverage of subject matter. Published in England by John Wiley & Sons Ltd.

RESEARCH CENTERS AND INSTITUTES
Institute for Food Laws and Regulations. Michigan State University, 165 National Food Safety and Toxicology Ctr., East Lansing, MI 48224. Phone: (517)355-8295 • URL: http://www.iflr.msu.edu/ • Conducts research on the food industry, including processing, packaging, marketing, and new products.

Institute of Food Science. Cornell University, 114 Stocking Hall, Ithaca, NY 14853-7201. Phone: (607)255-7900 E-mail: cifs@cornell.edu • URL: http://www.nysaes.cornell.edu/cifs/ • Research areas include the chemistry and processing of food commodities, food processing engineering, food packaging, and nutrition.

TRADE/PROFESSIONAL ASSOCIATIONS
Flexible Packaging Association. 971 Corporate Blvd., Ste. 403, Linthicum, MD 21090-2253. Phone: (410)694-0800 Fax: (410)694-0900 E-mail: fpa@flexpack.org • URL: http://www.flexpack.org • Converters of paper, foil, and plastic packaging

materials; associate members are industry suppliers. Promotes the welfare of the flexible packaging industry by: communicating with federal and state governments and the public on subjects of concern to the industry; promoting the use of flexible packaging; conducting technical, manufacturing, and statistical programs; establishing standards and specifications. Offers six lesson plans on packaging for grades 5-9. Sponsors children's services; compiles statistics.

Institute of Packaging Professionals. 1601 N Bond St., No. 101, Naperville, IL 60563. Phone: 800-432-4085 or (630)544-5050 Fax: (630)544-5055 E-mail: info@iopp.org • URL: http://www.iopp.org • Members are practicing professionals in the fields of packaging and handling.

International Beverage Packaging Association. Anheuser-Busch, Inc., One Ocean Spray Dr., Fort Collins, CO 80524. Phone: 888-662-3263 or (508)946-1000 Fax: (702)566-7166 E-mail: info@ibpa.org • URL: http://www.ibpa.org • Beverage industry personnel interested in the concerns of the beverage packaging industry, including soft drink, beer, bottled water, juice manufacturers and packagers, allied suppliers.

OTHER SOURCES
Converted Flexible Packaging. Available from MarketResearch.com. • 2001. $3,700.00. Published by the Freedonia Group. Market data with forecasts to the year 2006. Covers plastic, paper, and foil packaging for food and non-food products.

Food Law Reports. CCH, Inc. • Weekly. $1,459.00 per year. Six looseleaf volumes. Covers regulation of adulteration, packaging, labeling, and additives. Formerly *Food Drug Cosmetic Law Reports.*

PACKAGING LABELS

See: LABELS AND LABELING

PACKAGING MACHINERY

DIRECTORIES
Packaging Digest Machinery/Materials Guide. Reed Business Information. • Annual. $46.00. List of more than 3,100 manufacturers of machinery and materials for the packaging industry, and about 260 contract packagers.

PMMI Packaging Machinery Directory. PMMI. • Covers: 500 member companies that design, manufacture, sell, and service packaging and packaging-related converting machinery. Entries include: Company name, address, phone, names and titles of key personnel, products and services.

ENCYCLOPEDIAS AND DICTIONARIES

Wiley Encyclopedia of Packaging Technology. Aaron Brody and Kenneth Marsh, editors. John Wiley and Sons, Inc. • 1997. $330.00. Second edition.

PERIODICALS AND NEWSLETTERS

Packaging Digest. Reed Business Information. • 13 times a year. $119.90 per year.

STATISTICS SOURCES

U. S. Industry and Trade Outlook. Available from National Technical Information Service. • Annual. $69.95. Produced by the International Trade Administration, U. S. Department of Commerce, in a "public-private" partnership with DRI/McGraw-Hill and Standard & Poor's. Provides basic data, outlook for the current year, and "Long-Term Prospects" (five-year projections) for a wide variety of products and services. Includes high technology industries. Formerly *U. S. Industrial Outlook.*

TRADE/PROFESSIONAL ASSOCIATIONS

Packaging Machinery Manufacturers Institute. 4350 N Fairfax Dr., Ste. 600, Arlington, VA 22203-1632. Phone: 888-275-7664 or (703)243-8555 Fax: (703)243-8556 E-mail: pmmiwebhelp@pmmi.org • URL: http://www.pmmi.org • Represents manufacturers of machinery used for all packaging operations including filling, capping, labeling, wrapping, cartoning, case loading, blister packaging, aerosol, check weighing, coding, counting, form-fill-seal, and bagging.

PACKAGING, PRESSURE

See: PRESSURE PACKAGING

PACKING INDUSTRY

See: MEAT INDUSTRY

PAINT AND PAINTING

See also: INDUSTRIAL COATINGS; VARNISH AND VARNISHING

GENERAL WORKS

The Chemistry and Physics of Coatings. Alastair R. Marrion, editor. Springer-Verlag. • 1994. $46.95. Published by The Royal Society of Chemistry. Provides an overview of paint science and technology, including environmental considerations.

ABSTRACTS AND INDEXES

CPI Digest: Key to World Literature Serving the Coatings, Plastics, Fibers, Adhesives, and Related Industries (Chemical Process Industries). CPI Information Services. • Monthly. $397.00 per year. Abstracts of business and technical articles for polymer-based, chemical process industries. Includes a monthly list of relevant U. S. patents. International coverage.

World Surface Coatings Abstracts. Paint Research Association. • 13 times a year. Members, $1,230.00 per year; non-members, $1,695.00 per year.

CD-ROM DATABASES

OECD Statistical Compendium. Organization for Economic Cooperation and Development. • Semiannual. $1,905.00 per year for 1 to 10 users. CD-ROM contains more than 730,000 monthly, quarterly, and annual time series for OECD countries, 1960 to date. Includes fully searchable data on agriculture, food, economic indicators, national accounts, employment, energy, finance, industry, technology, and foreign trade. Results can be displayed in various forms.

DIRECTORIES

Directory of Home Center Operators and Hardware Chains. Chain Store Guide. • Annual. $327.00. Online edition, $747.00. Nearly 4,700 home center operators, paint and home decorating chains, and lumber and building materials companies. Covers United States and Canada.

FINANCIAL RATIOS

Almanac of Business and Industrial Financial Ratios. Leo Troy. Aspen Publishers, Inc. • 2003. $125.95. Includes CD-Rom. Contains financial ratios derived from federal tax returns. Ratios for each of about 200 industries are arranged according to company asset size. (Almanac of Business and Industrial Financial Ratios Series).

Annual Statement Studies. The Risk Management Association. • Annual. Median and quartile financial ratios are given for over 400 kinds of manufacturing, wholesale, retail, construction, and consumer finance establishments. Data is sorted by both asset size and sales volume. Includes a clearly written "Definition of Ratios" and an alphabetical industry index.

Annual Statement Studies: Industry Default Probabilities and Cash Flow Measures. The Risk Management Association. • Annual. $145.00. Serves as a companion volume to the original *Annual Statement Studies.* Gives probability of default estimates on a percentage scale for more than 450 industries. Includes changes in position year-by-year for eight financial statement line items and provides percentage measures of cash flow.

HANDBOOKS AND MANUALS

House Painting. Entrepreneur Media, Inc. • Looseleaf. $59.50. A practical guide to starting a house painting business. Covers profit potential, start-up costs, market size evaluation, owner's time required, pricing, accounting, advertising, promotion, etc. (Start-Up Business Guide No. E1249.).

Maintenance Engineering Handbook. Lindley R. Higgins and R. Keith Mobley. McGraw-Hill. • 2001. $150.00. Sixth edition. Contains about 60 chapters by various authors in 12 major sections covering all elements of industrial and plant maintenance.

Surface Coatings: Science and Technology. Swaraj Paul, editor. John Wiley and Sons, Inc. • 1996. $375.00. Second edition.

INTERNET DATABASES

Business 2.0 Web Guide to the Best Business Links. Business 2.0 Media Inc. Phone: (415)293-4800 E-mail: support@business2.com • URL: http://www.business2.com/webguide • Web site presents an extensive, searchable directory of links to "the best, most informative, and authoritative web pages." Twenty main categories cover business, finance, career, company information, people, and technology topics, with thousands of subtopics, all linking to Web sites recommended by experienced business researchers. Fees: Free.

Fedstats. Federal Interagency Council on Statistical Policy. Phone: (202)395-7254 • URL: http://www.fedstats.gov • Web site features an efficient search facility for full-text statistics produced by more than 100 federal agencies, including the Census Bureau, the Bureau of Economic Analysis, and the Bureau of Labor Statistics. Boolean searches can be made within one agency or for all agencies combined. Links are offered to international statistical bureaus, including the UN, IMF, OECD, UNESCO, Eurostat, and 20 individual countries. Fees: Free.

FreeLunch.com. Economy.com, Inc. Phone: (610)696-8700 Fax: (610)696-1678 • URL: http://www.freelunch.com • Web site provides free access to more than 1.5 million economic and financial data series, covering industry, demographics, labor markets, prices, retail sales, government spending, trade, interest rates, housing starts, the stock market, and many other topics. Data is available for various time periods in either chart or table form. Searching is offered. Fees: Free, but registration required. Economy.com, Inc. also offers fee-based economic analysis at *The Dismal Scientist* site (http://www.dismal.com).

Manufacturing Profiles. U. S. Bureau of the Census. Phone: (301)763-4636 E-mail: webmaster@census.gov • URL: http://www.census.gov/prod/www/abs/mfg-prof.html • The Census Bureau makes available free on PDF (Portable Document Format) an annual consolidation of the entire Current Industrial Report series, presenting "all the data compiled." Contains statistics on production, shipments, inventories, consumption, exports, imports, and orders for a wide variety of manufactured products.

ONLINE DATABASES

World Surface Coatings Abstracts [Online]. Paint Research Association of Great Britain. • Indexing and abstracting of the literature of paint and surface coatings, 1976 to present. Monthly updates. Inquire as to online cost and availability.

PERIODICALS AND NEWSLETTERS

American Painting Contractor. Douglas Publications, Inc. • Nine times a year. $35.00 per year.

Modern Paint and Coatings. Chemical Week Associates. • Monthly. $52.00 per year.

Paint and Coatings Industry. Business News Publishing Co. • Monthly. Free to members, non-members, $55.00 per year. Includes annual *Raw Material* and *Equipment Directory and Buyers Guide.*

Paint and Decorating Retailer. Paint and Decorating Retailers Association. • Monthly. $45.00 per year. Formerly *Decorating Retailer.*

RESEARCH CENTERS AND INSTITUTES

Emulsion Polymers Institute. Lehigh University, Iacocca Hall, 111 Research Dr., Bethlehem, PA 18015. Phone: (610)758-3590 Fax: (610)758-5880 E-mail: mse0@lehigh.edu • URL: http://www.lehigh.edu/ • Includes latex paint research.

STATISTICS SOURCES

Annual Survey of Manufactures. Available from U. S. Government Printing Office. • Annual. Prices vary. Issued by the U. S. Census Bureau as an interim update to the *Census of Manufactures.* Includes data on number of manufacturing establishments in various industries, employment, labor costs, value of shipments, capital expenditures, inventories, energy costs, and assets. (See also Census Bureau home page, http://www.census.gov/.).

Business Statistics of the United States. Linz Audain and Cornelia J. Strawser. Bernan Associates. • Annual. $147.00. Based on *Business Statistics,* formerly issue by the Bureau of Economic Analysis, U. S. Department of Commerce. Provides basic data for a wide variety of U. S. industries, services, and economic indicators. Most statistics are shown annually for 30 years and monthly for the most recent four years.

Paint, Varnish, and Lacquer. U. S. Bureau of the Census. • Quarterly and annual. Provides data on shipments: value, quantity, imports, and exports. Includes paint, varnish, lacquer, product finishes, and special purpose coatings. (Current Industrial Reports, MQ-28F.).

Survey of Current Business. Available from U. S. Government Printing Office. • Monthly. $63.00 per year. Issued by Bureau of Economic Analysis, U. S. Department of Commerce. Presents a wide variety of business and economic data.

TRADE/PROFESSIONAL ASSOCIATIONS

Federation of Societies for Coatings Technology. 492 Norristown Rd., Blue Bell, PA 19422-2350. Phone: (610)940-0777 Fax: (610)940-0292 E-mail: fsct@coatingstech.org • URL: http://ww. coatingstech.org • Formerly Federation of Societies for Paint Technology.

National Paint and Coatings Association. 1500 Rhode Island Ave., N.W., Washington, DC 20005-5597. Phone: (202)462-6272 Fax: (202)462-8549 E-mail: npca@paint.org • URL: http://www.paint. org • Formerly National Paint, Varnish and Lacquer Association.

Painting and Decorating Contractors of America. 11960 Westline Industrial Dr., Ste. 201, Saint Louis, MO 63146-2309. Phone: 800-332-7322 or (314)-514-7322 Fax: (314)-514-9417 E-mail: lwerle@ pdca.org • URL: http://www.pdca.org • Painting and wallcovering contractors.

OTHER SOURCES

Coatings. National Paint and Coatings Association. • 10 times a year. $62.00 per year.

PAMPHLETS

ABSTRACTS AND INDEXES

Vertical File Index: Guide to Pamphlets and References to Current Topics. H. W. Wilson Co. • 11 times a year. $115.00 per year. A subject and title index to selected pamphlet material.

HANDBOOKS AND MANUALS

How to Produce Creative Advertising: Traditional Techniques and Computer Applications. Thomas Bivins and Ann Keding. McGraw Hill. • 1993. $37.95. Covers copywriting, advertising design, and the use of desktop publishing techniques in advertising. (NTC Business Books Series).

How to Produce Creative Publications: Traditional Techniques and Computer Applications. Thomas Bivins and Ann Keding. McGraw-Hill. • 1993. $37.95. A practical guide to the writing, designing, and production of magazines, annual reports, brochures, and newsletters by traditional methods and by desktop publishing. (NTC Business Books Series).

The Perfect Sales Piece: A Complete Do-It-Yourself Guide to Creating Brochures, Catalogs, Fliers, and Pamphlets. Robert W. Bly. John Wiley and Sons, Inc. • 1994. $50.00. A guide to the use of various forms of printed literature for direct selling, sales promotion, and marketing. (Small Business Series).

RESEARCH CENTERS AND INSTITUTES

Design Research Unit. Massachusetts College of Art, 621 Huntington Ave., Boston, MA 02115. Phone: (617)879-7733 Fax: (617)566-4034 E-mail: rstreit@massart.edu • URL: http://www.babel. massart.edu/dru • Conducts research related to the design of printed matter, including annual reports, letterheads, posters, and brochures.

PAPER BAG INDUSTRY

DIRECTORIES

Sources of Supply/Buyers Guide. William O. Dannhausen Corp. • Annual. $90.00. About 2,200 mills and converters, 2,700 merchants and 500 manufacturers' representatives in paper, films, foils, and allied lines.

PERIODICALS AND NEWSLETTERS

Paper, Film and Foil Converter. Primedia Business Magazines and Media. • Monthly. $88.00 per year.

STATISTICS SOURCES

Annual Survey of Manufactures. Available from U. S. Government Printing Office. • Annual. Prices vary. Issued by the U. S. Census Bureau as an interim update to the *Census of Manufactures.* Includes data on number of manufacturing establishments in various industries, employment, labor costs, value of shipments, capital expenditures, inventories, energy costs, and assets. (See also Census Bureau home page, http://www.census. gov/.).

TRADE/PROFESSIONAL ASSOCIATIONS

Paper Shipping Sack Manufacturers' Association. 520 E Oxford St., Coopersburg, PA 18036. Phone: (610)282-6845 Fax: (610)282-6921 E-mail: admin@pssma.org • URL: http://www.pssma.com • Manufacturers of multi-wall (3-4-5-6 walls) paper shipping sacks designed for packaging and shipping products in domestic and export commerce.

PAPER BOARD INDUSTRY

See: PAPERBOARD AND PAPERBOARD PACKAGING INDUSTRIES

PAPER BOX AND PAPER CONTAINER INDUSTRIES

See also: BOX INDUSTRY; CONTAINER INDUSTRY; PAPERBOARD AND PAPERBOARD PACKAGING INDUSTRIES

DIRECTORIES

National Paperbox Association Membership Directory. National Paperbox Association. • Annual. $150.00.

Paperboard Packaging Resource Directory. Advanstar Communications. • Covers: about 3,000 manufacturers of corrugated and solid fiber containers, folding cartons, rigid boxes, fiber cans and tubes, and fiber drums. Entries include: For manufacturers--Company name, address, phone, equipment, names of executives, plants, and type of containers manufactured.

Sources of Supply/Buyers Guide. William O. Dannhausen Corp. • Annual. $90.00. About 2,200 mills and converters, 2,700 merchants and 500 manufacturers' representatives in paper, films, foils, and allied lines.

ONLINE DATABASES

PIRA. PIRA International Information Centre. • Citations and abstracts pertaining to bookbinding and other pulp, paper, and packaging industries, 1975 to present. Weekly updates. Inquire as to online cost and availability.

STATISTICS SOURCES

U. S. Industry and Trade Outlook. Available from National Technical Information Service. • Annual. $69.95. Produced by the International Trade Administration, U. S. Department of Commerce, in a "public-private" partnership with DRI/McGraw-Hill and Standard & Poor's. Provides basic data, outlook for the current year, and "Long-Term Prospects" (five-year projections) for a wide variety of products and services. Includes high technology industries. Formerly *U. S. Industrial Outlook.*

TRADE/PROFESSIONAL ASSOCIATIONS

Fibre Box Association. 25 NW Point Blvd., Ste. 510, Elk Grove Village, IL 60007. Phone: (847)364-9600 Fax: (847)364-9639 E-mail: fba@fibrebox.org • URL: http://www.fibrebox.org • Works to bring together North American manufacturers of corrugated paperboard products to provide comprehensive services for the industry. Compiles statistical reports and industry forecasts; disseminates information on labor negotiations and settlements; presents industry positions to government agencies; develops performance test methods, standards and requirements; monitors environmental issues and/or regulations.

North American Packaging Association. 113 S West St., 3rd Fl., Alexandria, VA 22314. Phone: (703)684-2212 Fax: (703)683-6920 E-mail: info@paperbox. org • URL: http://www.paperbox.org • Independent package converters, including manufacturers of rigid (set-up) and folding paper boxes; suppliers to the industry. Aims to further the development, use, and sale of members' products; to deal with common industry problems; to foster greater operating economies and efficiencies. Represents the industry before legislative and regulatory bodies. Conducts technical workshops and seminars on sales, marketing, costing, computers, and management methods. Compiles statistics.

PAPER CONTAINERS

See: PAPER BOX AND PAPER CONTAINER INDUSTRIES

PAPER INDUSTRY

See also: PAPERBOARD AND PAPERBOARD PACKAGING INDUSTRIES; WOODPULP INDUSTRY

ABSTRACTS AND INDEXES

Abstract Bulletin of Paper Science and Technology. Engineering Information, Inc. • Monthly. Institutions, $1,874.00 per year. Worldwide coverage of the scientific and technical literature of interest to the pulp and paper industry.

NTIS Alerts: Materials Sciences. National Technical Information Service. • Semimonthly. $220.00 per year. Provides descriptions of government-sponsored research reports and software, with ordering information. Covers ceramics, glass, coatings, composite materials, alloys, plastics, wood, paper, adhesives, fibers, lubricants, and related subjects. Formerly *Abstract Newsletter.*

CD-ROM DATABASES

OECD Statistical Compendium. Organization for Economic Cooperation and Development. • Semiannual. $1,905.00 per year for 1 to 10 users. CD-ROM contains more than 730,000 monthly, quarterly, and annual time series for OECD countries, 1960 to date. Includes fully searchable data on agriculture, food, economic indicators, national accounts, employment, energy, finance, industry, technology, and foreign trade. Results can be displayed in various forms.

World Marketing Forecasts on CD-ROM. Gale Cengage Learning. • Annual. $2,500.00. Produced by Euromonitor. Provides detailed forecast data for the years to 2012 on CD-ROM for 54 countries in all parts of the world. Covers a wide range of social, demographic, economic, and market factors. Includes specific forecasts for many kinds of consumer products.

DIRECTORIES

Lockwood-Post's Directory of the Pulp, Paper and Allied Trades. Paperloop. • Annual. $395.00. Formerly *Lockwood's Directory of the Paper and Allied Trades.*

Pulp and Paper Buyer's Guide. Paperloop. • Annual. $75.00. Supplies and equipment.

Sources of Supply/Buyers Guide. William O. Dannhausen Corp. • Annual. $90.00. About 2,200 mills and converters, 2,700 merchants and 500 manufacturers' representatives in paper, films, foils, and allied lines.

Walden's ABC Guide. Walden-Mott Corp. • Covers: about 7,662 firms which manufacture, convert, and sell paper products and their suppliers. Entries include: Company name, address, phone, names of executives, and products and services offered.

FINANCIAL RATIOS

Almanac of Business and Industrial Financial Ratios. Leo Troy. Aspen Publishers, Inc. • 2003. $125.95. Includes CD-Rom. Contains financial ratios derived from federal tax returns. Ratios for each of about 200 industries are arranged according to company asset size. (Almanac of Business and Industrial Financial Ratios Series).

IRS Corporate Financial Ratios. Available from MarketResearch.com. • 2002. $225.00. Published by Schonfeld & Associates, Inc. Presents 70 key financial ratios for 260 industries. Ratios are calculated from income statement and balance sheet data available from the Internal Revenue Service. Includes four asset size classes.

HANDBOOKS AND MANUALS

Paper Basics: Forestry, Manufacture, Selection, Purchasing, Mathematics and Metrics, Recycling. David Saltman. Krieger Publishing Co. • 1978. $29.50.

INTERNET DATABASES

Business 2.0 Web Guide to the Best Business Links. Business 2.0 Media Inc. Phone: (415)293-4800 E-mail: support@business2.com • URL: http://www.business2.com/webguide • Web site presents an extensive, searchable directory of links to "the best, most informative, and authoritative web pages." Twenty main categories cover business, finance, career, company information, people, and technology topics, with thousands of subtopics, all linking to Web sites recommended by experienced business researchers. Fees: Free.

Fedstats. Federal Interagency Council on Statistical Policy. Phone: (202)395-7254 • URL: http://www.fedstats.gov • Web site features an efficient search facility for full-text statistics produced by more than 100 federal agencies, including the Census Bureau, the Bureau of Economic Analysis, and the Bureau of Labor Statistics. Boolean searches can be made within one agency or for all agencies combined. Links are offered to international statistical bureaus, including the UN, IMF, OECD, UNESCO, Eurostat, and 20 individual countries. Fees: Free.

FreeLunch.com. Economy.com, Inc. Phone: (610)696-8700 Fax: (610)696-1678 • URL: http://www.freelunch.com • Web site provides free access to more than 1.5 million economic and financial data series, covering industry, demographics, labor markets, prices, retail sales, government spending, trade, interest rates, housing starts, the stock market, and many other topics. Data is available for various time periods in either chart or table form. Searching is offered. Fees: Free, but registration required. Economy.com, Inc. also offers fee-based economic analysis at _The Dismal Scientist_ site (http://www.dismal.com).

ONLINE DATABASES

Business and Industry. Gale Cengage Learning. • Contains online citations, abstracts, and selected fulltext from more than 1,000 trade journals, newspapers, and other publications. Provides general coverage of both manufacturing and service industries, including marketing, production, industry trends, key events, and information on specific companies. Time span is 1994 to date. Daily updates. Inquire as to online cost and availability. (Also available in a CD-ROM version.).

PaperChem Database. Information Services Div. • Worldwide coverage of the scientific and technical paper industry chemical literature, including patents, 1967 to present. Weekly updates. Inquire as to on-line cost and availability.

PIRA. PIRA International Information Centre. • Citations and abstracts pertaining to bookbinding and other pulp, paper, and packaging industries,

1975 to present. Weekly updates. Inquire as to on-line cost and availability.

Tablebase. Gale Cengage Learning. • Provides on-line numerical tabular data from a wide variety of business, organization, and government sources, including about 1,000 trade journals. Includes industry and individual company statistics relating to products, market share, sales forecasts, production, exports, market trends, etc. Time span is 1997 to date. Weekly updates. Inquire as to online cost and availability. (Also available in a CD-ROM version.).

PERIODICALS AND NEWSLETTERS

Paper Age. Global Publications. • 10 times a year. $20.00 per year.

Pulp and Paper. Paperloop. • 11 times a year. $135.00 per year.

Pulp and Paper Week. Paperloop. • 48 times a year. $867.00 per year; with online edition, $1,099.00 per year. Newsletter.

Solutions! The Official Publication of TAPPI and PIMA. Technical Association of the Pulp and Paper Industry. • Monthly. Membership. Formerly _TAPPI Journal_.

RESEARCH CENTERS AND INSTITUTES

Robertson Pulp and Paper Laboratory. North Carolina State University. Dept. of Wood and Paper Science, P.O. 8005, Raleigh, NC 27695-8005. Phone: (919)515-5812 Fax: (919)515-6302 E-mail: mike_kocurek@ncsu.edu • URL: http://www.cfr.ncsu.edu/wps/.

STATISTICS SOURCES

Annual Survey of Manufactures. Available from U. S. Government Printing Office. • Annual. Prices vary. Issued by the U. S. Census Bureau as an interim update to the _Census of Manufactures_. Includes data on number of manufacturing establishments in various industries, employment, labor costs, value of shipments, capital expenditures, inventories, energy costs, and assets. (See also Census Bureau home page, http://www.census.gov/.).

Business Statistics of the United States. Linz Audain and Cornelia J. Strawser. Bernan Associates. • Annual. $147.00. Based on _Business Statistics_, formerly issue by the Bureau of Economic Analysis, U. S. Department of Commerce. Provides basic data for a wide variety of U. S. industries, services, and economic indicators. Most statistics are shown annually for 30 years and monthly for the most recent four years.

Consumer International. Available from Gale Cengage Learning. • Annual. $1,290.00. Published by Euromonitor. Contains extensive consumer market, economic, and demographic data for 25 major, non-European countries, including the U. S. and Canada. Includes consumer market size (volume and value) for 150 product types in 14 categories (food, clothing, automobiles, cosmetics, appliances, etc.).

Encyclopedia of American Industries. Gale Cengage Learning. • 2000. $560.00. Third edition. Two volumes. $280.00 per volume. Volume one is _Manufacturing Industries_ and volume two is _Service and Non-Manufacturing Industries_. Provides the history, development, and recent status of approximately 1,000 industries. Includes statistical graphs, with industry and general indexes.

European Marketing Forecasts. Available from Gale Cengage Learning. • Annual. $1,250.00. Published by Euromonitor. Contains demographic, economic, and market forecasts for the countries of Europe to the year 2010. Forecasts include market-size data for 15 consumer product sectors (food, clothing, automobiles, consumer electronics, etc.).

International Marketing Forecasts. Available from Gale Cengage Learning. • Annual. $1,250.00. Published by Euromonitor. Contains demographic,

economic, and market forecasts to the year 2013 for major, non-European countries, including the U. S. and Canada. Forecasts include market-size data for 15 consumer product sectors, such as food, clothing, and automobiles.

The Pulp and Paper Industry in OECD Member Countries. Organization for Economic Cooperation and Development. Available from OECD Publications and Information Center. • Annual. $31.00. Presents annual data on production, consumption, capacity, utilization, and foreign trade. Covers 33 pulp and paper products in OECD countries. Text in English and French.

Standard & Poor's Industry Surveys. Standard & Poor's. • Semiannual. $1,800.00. Two looseleaf volumes. Includes monthly _Supplements_. Provides detailed, individual surveys of 52 major industry groups. Each survey is revised on a semiannual basis. Also includes "Monthly Investment Review" (industry group investment analysis) and monthly "Trends & Projections" (economic analysis).

Statistics of Paper, Paperboard and Wood Pulp. American Forest and Paper Association. • Annual. $395.00. Formerly _Statistics of Paper and Paperboard_.

Survey of Current Business. Available from U. S. Government Printing Office. • Monthly. $63.00 per year. Issued by Bureau of Economic Analysis, U. S. Department of Commerce. Presents a wide variety of business and economic data.

WEFA Industrial Monitor. John Wiley and Sons, Inc. • Annual. $65.00. Prepared by industry analysts at WEFA, an economic forecasting and consulting firm (originally Wharton Econometric Forecasting Associates). Contains discussions of the outlook for major U. S. industries, with many 10-year forecasts (WEFA Web site is http://www.wefa.com).

TRADE/PROFESSIONAL ASSOCIATIONS

American Forest and Paper Association. 1111 19th St., N.W., Ste. 800, Washington, DC 20036. Phone: (202)463-2700 Fax: (202)463-2471 E-mail: info@afandpa.org • URL: http://www.afandpa.org.

National Paper Trade Association. 500 Bi-County Blvd., Ste. 200E, Farmingdale, NY 11735. Phone: 800-355-6782 or (631)777-2223 Fax: (631)777-2224 E-mail: bill@gonpta.com • URL: http://www.gonpta.com • Wholesale distributors and suppliers of paper, plastics and allied products.

Paper Industry Management Association. 15 Technology Pkwy. S, Norcross, GA 30092. Phone: 877-527-5973 or (770)209-7230 Fax: (770)209-7359 E-mail: mcornell@pimaweb.org • URL: http://www.pimaweb.org • Professional organization of pulp, paper mill, and paper converting production executives.

TAPPI - Technical Association of the Pulp and Paper Industry. 15 Technology Pkwy. S, Norcross, GA 30092. Phone: 800-332-8686 or (770)446-1400 Fax: (770)446-6947 E-mail: memberconnection@tappi.org • URL: http://www.tappi.org.

OTHER SOURCES

Disposable Paper Products. Available from MarketResearch.com. • 2001. $5,900.00. Published by Euromonitor Publications Ltd. Provides consumer market data and forecasts to 2004 for the United States, the United Kingdom, Germany, France, and Italy.

PAPER MONEY

See also: MONEY

ALMANACS AND YEARBOOKS

World Currrency Yearbook. International Currency Analysis, Inc. • Annual. $250.00. Directory of more than 110 central banks worldwide.

HANDBOOKS AND MANUALS

Comprehensive Catalog of United States Paper Money. Gene Hessler. BNR Press. • 1992. $42.50. Fifth edtion.

Paper Money of the United States: A Complete Guide with Valuations. Arthur L. Friedberg. Coin and Currency Institute, Inc. • 2000. $38.75. 16th edition.

PERIODICALS AND NEWSLETTERS

Paper Money. Society of Paper Money Collectors, Inc. • Bimonthly. Membership.

TRADE/PROFESSIONAL ASSOCIATIONS

Society of Paper Money Collectors. P.O. Box 79341, Dallas, TX 75379-3941. E-mail: fred@spmc.org • URL: http://www.spmc.org.

PAPERBACK BOOKS

See: PAPERBOUND BOOK INDUSTRY

PAPERBOARD AND PAPERBOARD PACKAGING INDUSTRIES

See also: CONTAINER INDUSTRY; PAPER BOX AND PAPER CONTAINER INDUSTRIES; PAPER INDUSTRY

CD-ROM DATABASES

OECD Statistical Compendium. Organization for Economic Cooperation and Development. • Semiannual. $1,905.00 per year for 1 to 10 users. CD-ROM contains more than 730,000 monthly, quarterly, and annual time series for OECD countries, 1960 to date. Includes fully searchable data on agriculture, food, economic indicators, national accounts, employment, energy, finance, industry, technology, and foreign trade. Results can be displayed in various forms.

DIRECTORIES

Paperboard Packaging Resource Directory. Advanstar Communications. • Covers: about 3,000 manufacturers of corrugated and solid fiber containers, folding cartons, rigid boxes, fiber cans and tubes, and fiber drums. Entries include: For manufacturers--Company name, address, phone, equipment, names of executives, plants, and type of containers manufactured.

ENCYCLOPEDIAS AND DICTIONARIES

Wiley Encyclopedia of Packaging Technology. Aaron Brody and Kenneth Marsh, editors. John Wiley and Sons, Inc. • 1997. $330.00. Second edition.

FINANCIAL RATIOS

Annual Statement Studies. The Risk Management Association. • Annual. Median and quartile financial ratios are given for over 400 kinds of manufacturing, wholesale, retail, construction, and consumer finance establishments. Data is sorted by both asset size and sales volume. Includes a clearly written "Definition of Ratios" and an alphabetical industry index.

Annual Statement Studies: Industry Default Probabilities and Cash Flow Measures. The Risk Management Association. • Annual. $145.00. Serves as a companion volume to the original *Annual Statement Studies.* Gives probability of default estimates on a percentage scale for more than 450 industries. Includes changes in position year-by-year for eight financial statement line items and provides percentage measures of cash flow.

INTERNET DATABASES

Business 2.0 Web Guide to the Best Business Links. Business 2.0 Media Inc. Phone: (415)293-4800

E-mail: support@business2.com • URL: http://www.business2.com/webguide • Web site presents an extensive, searchable directory of links to "the best, most informative, and authoritative web pages." Twenty main categories cover business, finance, career, company information, people, and technology topics, with thousands of subtopics, all linking to Web sites recommended by experienced business researchers. Fees: Free.

Fedstats. Federal Interagency Council on Statistical Policy. Phone: (202)395-7254 • URL: http://www.fedstats.gov • Web site features an efficient search facility for full-text statistics produced by more than 100 federal agencies, including the Census Bureau, the Bureau of Economic Analysis, and the Bureau of Labor Statistics. Boolean searches can be made within one agency or for all agencies combined. Links are offered to international statistical bureaus, including the UN, IMF, OECD, UNESCO, Eurostat, and 20 individual countries. Fees: Free.

FreeLunch.com. Economy.com, Inc. Phone: (610)696-8700 Fax: (610)696-1678 • URL: http://www.freelunch.com • Web site provides free access to more than 1.5 million economic and financial data series, covering industry, demographics, labor markets, prices, retail sales, government spending, trade, interest rates, housing starts, the stock market, and many other topics. Data is available for various time periods in either chart or table form. Searching is offered. Fees: Free, but registration required. Economy.com, Inc. also offers fee-based economic analysis at *The Dismal Scientist* site (http://www.dismal.com).

ONLINE DATABASES

PIRA. PIRA International Information Centre. • Citations and abstracts pertaining to bookbinding and other pulp, paper, and packaging industries, 1975 to present. Weekly updates. Inquire as to online cost and availability.

PERIODICALS AND NEWSLETTERS

Paperboard Packaging Worldwide. Advanstar Communications. • Monthly. $39.00 per year.

PRICE SOURCES

Official Board Markets: "The Yellow Sheet". Mark Arzoumanian. Advanstar Communications. • Weekly. $160.00 per year. Covers the corrugated container, folding carton, rigid box and waste paper industries.

STATISTICS SOURCES

Annual Survey of Manufactures. Available from U. S. Government Printing Office. • Annual. Prices vary. Issued by the U. S. Census Bureau as an interim update to the *Census of Manufactures.* Includes data on number of manufacturing establishments in various industries, employment, labor costs, value of shipments, capital expenditures, inventories, energy costs, and assets. (See also Census Bureau home page, http://www.census.gov/.).

Business Statistics of the United States. Linz Audain and Cornelia J. Strawser. Bernan Associates. • Annual. $147.00. Based on *Business Statistics,* formerly issue by the Bureau of Economic Analysis, U. S. Department of Commerce. Provides basic data for a wide variety of U. S. industries, services, and economic indicators. Most statistics are shown annually for 30 years and monthly for the most recent four years.

Statistics of Paper, Paperboard and Wood Pulp. American Forest and Paper Association. • Annual. $395.00. Formerly *Statistics of Paper and Paperboard.*

Survey of Current Business. Available from U. S. Government Printing Office. • Monthly. $63.00 per year. Issued by Bureau of Economic Analysis, U. S. Department of Commerce. Presents a wide variety

of business and economic data.

TRADE/PROFESSIONAL ASSOCIATIONS

Paperboard Packaging Council. 700 Princess St., Ste. 202, Alexandria, VA 22314-2265. Phone: (703)836-3300 Fax: (703)836-3290 E-mail: paperboardpackaging@ppcnet.org • URL: http://www.ppcnet.org • Represents manufacturers of paperboard packaging. Sponsors public relations activities, safety programs, and biannual human resource seminars. Conducts overall industry statistical studies, marketing surveys, product reviews, and labor relations and bargaining agreement studies. Provides active technical and production service.

PAPERBOUND BOOK INDUSTRY

See also: BOOK INDUSTRY; PUBLISHING INDUSTRY

ALMANACS AND YEARBOOKS

The Bowker Annual: Library and Book Trade Almanac. Information Today, Inc. • Annual. $199.00. Reviews key trends and events and provides basic statistical information. Includes financial averages: library expenditures, salaries, and book prices. Contains lists of "best books, literary prizes, winners, and bestsellers." Formerly published by R. R. Bowker.

CD-ROM DATABASES

Books in Print On Disc: The Complete Books in Print System on Compact Laser Disc. Bowker Electronic Publishing. • Monthly. $550.00 per year. The CD-ROM version of *Books in Print, Forthcoming Books,* and other Bowker bibliographic publications: lists the books of over 50,000 U.S. publishers. Includes books recently declared out-of-print. Also available with full text book reviews.

DIRECTORIES

American Book Trade Directory. Information Today Inc. • Covers: Nearly 25,500 retail and antiquarian book dealers, plus 1,200 book and magazine wholesalers, distributors, and jobbers-in all 50 states and U.S. territories. Also included are sections of auctioneers of literary property, exporters/importers, booktrade associations, foreign language book dealers, book and literary appraisers, and rental library chains. Entries include: Bookstore name, address, phone, owner or manager, types and subjects of books stocked, specialty, sidelines, year established, SAN (Standard Address Number), number of volumes stocked, square footage.

International Literary Market Place: The Directory of the International Book Publishing Industry. Information Today, Inc. • Annual. $219.00. Covers more than 180 countries. Listings include publishers, literary agents, major booksellers, book clubs, literary prizes, distributors, trade associations, etc. Formerly published by R. R. Bowker.

Literary Market Place: The Directory of the American Book Publishing Industry. Information Today, Inc. • Annual. $299.00. Two volumes. Listings include publishers, agents, ad agencies, associations, distributors, events, key executives, services, and suppliers (50 directory sections in all). Formerly published by R. R. Bowker.

ONLINE DATABASES

Books in Print Online. Bowker Electronic Publishing. • The online version of *Books in Print, Forthcoming Books, Paperbound Books in Print,* and other Bowker bibliographic publications: lists the books of over 50,000 U. S. publishers. Includes books recently declared out-of-print. Updated monthly. Inquire as to online cost and availability.

PERIODICALS AND NEWSLETTERS

Publishers Weekly: The International News Magazine of Book Publishing. Reed Business

Information. • 51 times a year. $214.00 per year. The international news magazine of book publishing.

PAPERWORK MANAGEMENT

See: OFFICE MANAGEMENT; RECORDS MANAGEMENT

PARKING

BIBLIOGRAPHIES
Parking Publications for Planners. Dennis Jenks. Sage Publications, Inc. • 1993. $10.00.

HANDBOOKS AND MANUALS
Urban Parks and Open Space. Gayle L. Berens and others. Urban Land Institute. • 1997. $40.95. Covers financing, design, management, and public-private partnerships relative to the development of open space for new urban parks. Includes color illustrations and the history of urban parks.

PERIODICALS AND NEWSLETTERS
Downtown Idea Exchange: Essential Information for Downtown Research and Development Center. Downtown Research and Development Center. Alexander Communications Group, Inc. • Semimonthly. $187.00 per year. Newsletter for those concerned with central business districts. Provides news and other information on planning, development, parking, mass transit, traffic, funding, and other topics.

Parking: The Magazine of the Parking Industry. National Parking Association. • 10 times a year. $95.00 per year. Includes *Product and Services Directory.*

TRADE/PROFESSIONAL ASSOCIATIONS
National Parking Association. 1112 16th St. NW, Ste. 300, Washington, DC 20036. Phone: 800-647-PARK or (202)296-4336 Fax: (202)296-3102 E-mail: info@npapark.org • URL: http://www.npapark.org • Owners and operators of off-street parking facilities; architects, traffic engineers, equipment suppliers and manufacturers, colleges, universities, municipalities, airport authorities; others with an interest in downtown parking. Provides specialized education programs; offers scholarship program through the Parking Industry Institute.

PARKS

See also: AMUSEMENT INDUSTRY

GENERAL WORKS
Our National Parks and the Search for Sustainability. Bob R. O'Brien. University of Texas Press. • 1999. $40.00. Sustainability is defined as "a balance that allows as many people as possible to visit a park that is kept in as natural a state as possible.".

ABSTRACTS AND INDEXES
Environment Abstracts. Congressional Information Service, Inc. • Monthly. Price varies. Provides multidisciplinary coverage of the world's environmental literature. Incorporates *Acid Rain Abstracts.*

Environment Abstracts Annual: A Guide to the Key Environmental Literature of the Year. Congressional Information Service, Inc. • Annual. $495.00. A yearly cumulation of *Environment Abstracts.*

Environmental Knowledge Base: An Electronic Bibliography Featuring Citations and Abstracts of Scientific and Popular Articles on Environmental Issues, Including Social Policy, Economics, Regulatory, and Legal Topics. Environmental Studies Institute. • Monthly. Price varies. An index to current environmental literature. Formerly *Environmental Periodicals Bibliography.*

CD-ROM DATABASES
Environment Abstracts on CD-ROM. LEXIS-NEXIS. • Quarterly. $1,295.00 per year. Contains the following CD-ROM databases: *Environment Abstracts, Energy Abstracts,* and *Acid Rain Abstracts.* Length of coverage varies.

DIRECTORIES
Parks and Recreation Buyers' Guide. National Recreation and Park Association. • Annual. Price upon application. List of 800 companies supplying products and services to private and governmental park and recreation agencies.

Parks Directory of the United States: A Guide to 4,700 National and State Parks, Recreation Areas, Historic Sites, Battlefields, Monuments, Forests, Preserves, Memorials, Seashores...and Other Designated Recreation Areas in the United State. Darren L. Smith, editor. Omnigraphics, Inc. • 2001. $180.00. Third edition. Consists of three sections: National Parks, State Parks, and Park-Related Organizations and Agencies. Includes an alphabetical index and a park classification index.

Resorts and Parks Purchasing Guide. Klevens Publications, Inc. • Annual. $85.00. Lists suppliers of products and services for resorts and parks, including national parks, amusement parks, dude ranches, golf resorts, ski areas, and national monument areas.

TRADE/PROFESSIONAL ASSOCIATIONS
National Association of County Park and Recreation Officials. Genessee County Parks and Recreation Commission, 5045 Stanley Rd., Flint, MI 48506. Phone: (810)736-7100 Fax: (810)736-7220 • URL: http://www.nacpro.org.

National Recreation and Park Association. 22377 Belmont Ridge Rd., Ashburn, VA 20148-4501. Phone: (703)858-0784 Fax: (703)858-0794 E-mail: info@nrpa.org • URL: http://www.nrpa.org • Formerly National Conference on State Parks.

OTHER SOURCES
Atlas & Gazetteer Series. DeLorme Mapping Co. • Dates vary. $983.50 complete ($19.95 region). Consists of 50 volumes covering all areas of the U. S. Includes detailed maps, as well as descriptions of attractions, natural areas, and historic sites. (CD-ROM versions available.).

PARLIAMENTARY PROCEDURE

ABSTRACTS AND INDEXES
Current Law Index: Multiple Access to Legal Periodicals. Gale Cengage Learning. • Monthly. $725.00 per year. Produced in cooperation with the American Association of Law Libraries. Indexes more than 900 law journals, legal newspapers, and specialty publications from the U.S., Canada, U.K., Ireland, Australia, and New Zealand.

ENCYCLOPEDIAS AND DICTIONARIES
Encyclopedia of Corporate Meetings, Minutes and Resolutions. William Sardell, editor. Prentice Hall PTR. • 1985. $125.00. Third edition. Two volumes.

HANDBOOKS AND MANUALS
Mason's Manual of Legislative Procedure. American Society of Legislative Clerks and Secretaries. National Conference of State Legislatures. • 2000. $60.00. Contains parliamentary law and rules, rules of debate, rules governing motions, how to conduct business, etc.

Meeting Procedures: Parliamentary Law and Rules of Order for the 21st Century. James Lochrie. Scarecrow Press, Inc. • 2003. $29.95. A simplified guide to modern meeting procedures.

Modern Parliamentary Procedure. Ray E. Keesey. American Psychological Association. • 1994. $24.95. Revised edition. A modernization and simplification of traditional, complex rules of procedure. Written for associations, clubs, community groups, and other deliberative bodies.

Parliamentary Law and Practice for Nonprofit Organizations. Howard L. Oleck and Cami Green. American Law Institute-American Bar Association Committee on Continuing Professional Education. • 1991. $20.00. Second edition. Covers meeting procedures, motions, debate, voting, nominations, elections, committees, duties of officers, rights of members, and other topics.

Robert's Rules of Order. Henry M. Roberts, editors. Perseus Books Group. • 2000. $35.00. 10th revised edition.

INTERNET DATABASES
Lexis.com Research System. Lexis-Nexis Group. Phone: 800-227-4908 or (937)865-6800 Fax: (937)865-6909 E-mail: webmaster@prod.lexis-nexis.com • URL: http://www.lexis.com • Fee-based Web site offers extensive searching of a wide variety of legal sources. Additional features include Daily Opinion Service, lexis.com Bookstore, Career Center, CLE Center, Law Schools, and Practice Pages ("Pages specific to areas of specialty").

PERIODICALS AND NEWSLETTERS
National Parliamentarian. National Association of Parliamentarians. • Quarterly. $20.00 per year. Articles and questions with answers on parliamentary procedure.

Parliamentary Journal. American Institute of Parliamentarians. • Quarterly. $20.00 per year.

TRADE/PROFESSIONAL ASSOCIATIONS
American Institute of Parliamentarians. P.O. Box 2173, Wilmington, DE 19899-2173. Phone: 888-664-0428 or (302)762-1811 Fax: (302)762-2170 E-mail: aip@paliamentaryprocedure.org • URL: http://www.parliamentaryprocedure.org.

National Association of Parliamentarians. 213 S. Main St., Independence, MO 64050-3808. Phone: 888-627-2929 or (816)833-3892 Fax: (816)833-3893 E-mail: hq@nap2.org • URL: http://www.parliamentarians.org.

PARTICIPATIVE MANAGEMENT

GENERAL WORKS
The Art and Science of Leadership. Afsaneh Nahavandi. Prentice Hall PTR. • 2002. $73.33. Third edition. Includes a discussion of participative management. Emphasis is on strategic leadership.

Creating a Culture of Competence. Michael Zwell. John Wiley and Sons, Inc. • 2000. $35.95. Emphasizes employee participation to arrive at a desired change in organizational culture.

Participative Management: An Analysis of Its Affect on Productivity. Michael H. Swearingen. Garland Publishing, Inc. • 1997. $35.00. (Garland Studies on Industrial Productivity).

A Primer on Organizational Behavior. James L. Bowditch and Anthony F. Buono. John Wiley and Sons, Inc. • 2000. $50.95. Fifth edition. Includes a discussion of participative management. Emphasis is on research and the theory of organizations. (Management Series).

DIRECTORIES
Employee Involvement Association--Membership Directory. Employee Involvement Association. • Covers: About 400 companies, associations, and federal, state, county, and municipal government agencies operating or contemplating employee suggestion systems or other employee involvement

programs. Entries include: Company, association, or agency name; address; employee involvement administrator.

PERIODICALS AND NEWSLETTERS

IPA Magazine. Involvement and Participation Association. • Quarterly. $57.00 per year. Formerly *Involvement of Participation.*

Motivational Manager: Strategies to Increase Morale and Productivity in the Workplace. Lawrence Ragan Communications, Inc. • Monthly. $119.00 per year. Newsletter. Emphasis is on participative management.

New Horizons. Horticultural Research Institute. • Description: Explores research of the science and art of nursery, retail garden center, and landscape plant production, marketing, and care.

Team Leader. LRP Publications. • Description: Keeps business team leaders up to date on team-leading techniques and provides solutions to team-oriented issues.

RESEARCH CENTERS AND INSTITUTES

Institute of Management, Innovation and Organization. University of California, Berkeley, F402 Haas School of Business, Berkeley, CA 94720-1930. Phone: (510)642-4041 Fax: (510)642-2826 E-mail: teece@haas.berkeley.edu • URL: http://www.haas.berkeley.edu • Research areas include a wide range of business management functions.

STATISTICS SOURCES

Employee Involvement Association Statistical Report. Employee Involvement Association. • Annual. 150.00.

TRADE/PROFESSIONAL ASSOCIATIONS

Employee Involvement Association. PO Box 2307, Dayton, OH 45401-2307. Phone: (937)586-3724 Fax: (937)586-3699 E-mail: eia@meinet.com • URL: http://www.eianet.org • Represents finance, commerce, industry, and government professionals. Dedicated to the worth, contributions, and benefits of employee suggestion systems and other employee involvement processes. Supports communication between employees and employer for the purpose of exchanging ideas.

Involvement and Participation Association. 42 Colebrooke Row, London N1 8Af, England. Phone: 44 207 3548040 Fax: 44 207 3548041 E-mail: involve@ipa-involve.com • URL: http://www.ip-involve.com • Promotes employee participation in the workplace.

PART-TIME EMPLOYEES

See: TEMPORARY EMPLOYEES

PARTNERSHIP

ABSTRACTS AND INDEXES

Current Law Index: Multiple Access to Legal Periodicals. Gale Cengage Learning. • Monthly. $725.00 per year. Produced in cooperation with the American Association of Law Libraries. Indexes more than 900 law journals, legal newspapers, and specialty publications from the U.S., Canada, U.K., Ireland, Australia, and New Zealand.

HANDBOOKS AND MANUALS

Business Taxpayer Information Publications. Available from U. S. Government Printing Office. • Annual. $63.00. Two volumes, consisting of *Circular E, Employer's Tax Guide* and *Employer's Supplemental Tax Guide.* Issued by the Internal Revenue Service (http://www.irs.ustreas.gov). Includes a wide variety of business-related tax information, including withholding tables, tax calendars, self-employment issues, partnership mat-

ters, corporation topics, depreciation, and bankruptcy.

Corporate, Partnership, Estate, and Gift Taxation 1997. James W. Pratt and William Kulsrud, editors. McGraw-Hill. • 1996. $71.25. 10th edition.

Corporation and Partnership Tax Return Guide (1999 Taxes). Bill Massey and others. RIA. • 2000. $16.50. Revised edition.

Corporation-Partnership-Fiduciary Filled-in Tax Return Forms, 2002. CCH, Inc. • 2002. $34.00.

Federal Tax Course. Aspen Publishers, Inc. • Annual. $210.00. Provides basic reference and training for various forms of federal taxation: individual, business, corporate, partnership, estate, gift, etc.

Partnership Book: How to Write a Partnership Agreement. Ralph Warner and Dennis Clifford. Nolo. • 2001. $39.95. Sixth edition. Includes CD-Rom. (Partnership Book Series).

Professional's Guide to Successful Management: The Eight Essentials for Running Your Firm, Practice, or Partnership. Carol A. O'Connor. McGraw-Hill. • 1994. Price on application.

INTERNET DATABASES

Lexis.com Research System. Lexis-Nexis Group. Phone: 800-227-4908 or (937)865-6800 Fax: (937)865-6909 E-mail: webmaster@prod.lexis-nexis.com • URL: http://www.lexis.com • Fee-based Web site offers extensive searching of a wide variety of legal sources. Additional features include Daily Opinion Service, lexis.com Bookstore, Career Center, CLE Center, Law Schools, and Practice Pages ("Pages specific to areas of specialty").

PERIODICALS AND NEWSLETTERS

Business Strategies Bulletin. CCH Inc. • Description: Reports tax and business planning information for all sizes of business, with emphasis on small to mid-sized business advisors.

Law Firm Partnership and Benefits Report. American Lawyer Media, Inc. • Monthly. $215.00 per year. Newsletter. Covers personnel issues for law firms, including compensation, partnership agreements, malpractice, employment discrimination, training, health insurance, pension plans, and other matters relating to human resources management. (A Law Journal Newsletter, formerly published by Leader Publications).

Stanger Report: A Guide to Partnership Investing. Robert A. Stanger and Co. • Quarterly. $447.00 per year. Newsletter providing analysis of limited partnership investments.

OTHER SOURCES

Business Strategies. CCH, Inc. • Semimonthly. $795.00 per year. Four looseleaf volumes. Semimonthly updates. Legal, tax, and accounting aspects of business planning and decision-making. Provides information on start-ups, forms of ownership (partnerships, corporations), failing businesses, reorganizations, acquisitions, and so forth. Includes *Business Strategies Bulletin,* a monthly newsletter.

Partnerships and LLCs: Tax Practice and Analysis. Thomas G. Manolakas. CCH, Inc. • 2000. $95.00. Covers the taxation of partnerships and limited liability companies.

PARTY PLAN SELLING

See: DIRECT MARKETING

PASSPORTS

GENERAL WORKS

Safe Trip Abroad. Available from U. S. Government Printing Office. • 2002. $2.50. Issued by the Bureau of Consular Affairs, U. S. State Department (http://

www.state.gov). Provides practical advice for international travel.

PASTA INDUSTRY

ABSTRACTS AND INDEXES

Food Science and Technology Abstracts. International Food Information Service Publishing. • Monthly. $1,780.00 per year. Provides worldwide coverage of the literature of food technology and food production.

Foods Adlibra: Key to the World's Food Literature. General Mills, Inc. Foods Adlibra Publications. • Semimonthly. $240.00 per year. Provides journal citations and abstracts to the literature of food technology and packaging.

CD-ROM DATABASES

Food Science and Technology Abstracts [CD-ROM]. Available from SilverPlatter Information, Inc. • Quarterly. Produced by International Food Information Service (home page is http://www.ifis.org). Provides worldwide coverage on CD-ROM of the literature of food technology and production. Various types of publications are indexed, with abstracts, including about 1,800 periodicals. Time period is 1969 to date.

DIRECTORIES

Major Food and Drink Companies of the World. Available from Gale Cengage Learning. • Annual. $880.00. Two volumes. Published by Graham & Whiteside. Contains profiles and trade names for more than 9,800 important food and beverage companies in various countries. In addition to foods, includes both alcoholic and nonalcoholic drink products.

Pasta Industry Directory. National Pasta Association. • Covers: Pasta manufacturers and industry suppliers. Entries include: contact names.

Thomas Food and Beverage Market Place. Grey House Publishing. • 2004. $495.00. Three volumes. Contains more than 40,000 entries covering food companies, beverages, food equipment, warehouse companies, food brokers, wholesalers, importers, and exporters. Formerly *Thomas Food Industry Register.*

ENCYCLOPEDIAS AND DICTIONARIES

Foods and Nutrition Encyclopedia. Audrey H. Ensminger and others. CRC Press, Inc. • 1993. $309.95. Second edition. Two volumes.

INTERNET DATABASES

I Love Pasta. National Pasta Association. Phone: (202)637-5888 Fax: (202)223-9741 E-mail: npa@ilovepasta.org • URL: http://www.ilovepasta.org • Web site provides a wide variety of information about pasta and the pasta industry. Includes 300 pasta recipes, pasta FAQs, and nutritional data. Industry statistics can be displayed, including data on imports, production, and per capita use in various countries. Extensive durum wheat data is provided.

ONLINE DATABASES

Food Science and Technology Abstracts [online]. IFIS North American Desk. • Produced by International Food Information Service. Provides about 500,000 online citations, with abstracts, to the international literature of food science, technology, commodities, engineering, and processing. Approximately 2,000 periodicals are covered. Time period is 1969 to date, with monthly updates. Inquire as to online cost and availability.

FOODS ADLIBRA. General Mills, Inc. • Contains online citations, with abstracts, to the technical and business literature of food processing and packaging. New products and new ingredients are featured. Covers about 250 trade journals and 500 research journals from 1974 to date, with monthly updates. Inquire as to online cost and availability.

PROMT: Predicasts Overview of Markets and Technology. Gale Cengage Learning. • Companies, products, applied technologies and markets. U.S. and international literature coverage, 1972 to date. Inquire as to online cost and availability. Provides abstracts from more than 1,600 publications. Weekly updates.

PERIODICALS AND NEWSLETTERS

Fancy Food and Culinary Products. Talcott Communications Corp. • Monthly. $34.00 per year. Emphasizes new specialty food products and the business management aspects of the specialty food and confection industries. Includes special issues on wine, cheese, candy, "upscale" cookware, and gifts. Formerly (Fancy Foods).

National Pasta Association FYI Newsletter. National Pasta Association. • Weekly. Membership.

Pasta Journal. National Pasta Association. • Bimonthly. $35.00 per year.

STATISTICS SOURCES

World Food Data and Statistics. Euromonitor International. • 2004. $650.00. Provides five-year data for a wide variety of food products in 52 countries. Includes market size, consumer expenditures, price indicators, and retail distribution data for many kinds of meat, fish, fruits, vegetables, dairy products, baked goods, condiments, canned food, and frozen food.

TRADE/PROFESSIONAL ASSOCIATIONS

National Pasta Association. 1156 15th St. NW, Ste. 900, Washington, DC 20005. Phone: (202)637-5888 Fax: (202)223-9741 E-mail: info@ilovepasta.org • URL: http://www.ilovepasta.org • Manufacturers of pasta in the U.S. and suppliers to the industry. Seeks to improve manufacturer and supplier efficiency. Conducts agricultural and technical research programs. Sponsors U.S. pasta product public relations program and pasta/durum wheat technical course.

OTHER SOURCES

The Market for Pasta. MarketResearch.com. • 2000. $3,250.00. Provides market data on various kinds of pasta, with sales forecasts to 2004.

PATENTS

See also: INVENTIONS; NEW PRODUCTS; TECHNOLOGY TRANSFER

GENERAL WORKS

General Information Concerning Patents. Available from U. S. Government Printing Office. • 2001. $4.75. Issued by Patent and Trademark Office, U. S. Department of Commerce. Provides basic information on patent applications, fees, searches, specifications, and infringement. Includes "Answers to Questions Frequently Asked.".

ABSTRACTS AND INDEXES

CPI Digest: Key to World Literature Serving the Coatings, Plastics, Fibers, Adhesives, and Related Industries (Chemical Process Industries). CPI Information Services. • Monthly. $397.00 per year. Abstracts of business and technical articles for polymer-based, chemical process industries. Includes a monthly list of relevant U. S. patents. International coverage.

Index of Patents Issued from the United States Patent and Trademark Office, Part One: List of Patentees. Available from U. S. Government Printing Office. • Annual. $160.00. Lists patentees and reissue patentees for each year.

Index of Patents Issued from the United States Patent and Trademark Office, Part Two: Index to Subjects of Invention. Available from U. S. Government Printing Office. • Annual. $71.00. A subject index to patents issued each year, arranged by class

and subclass numbers. Includes a list of patent and tradmark depository libraries.

World Patent Information: International Journal for Patent Documentation, Clasification and Statistics. European Commission BEL. Elsevier. • Quarterly. $656.00 per year.

ALMANACS AND YEARBOOKS

Intellectual Property Law Review. West Group. • 1999. $299.00. Patent, trademark, and copyright practices.

CD-ROM DATABASES

Authority Intellectual Property Library. LexisNexis/Matthew Bender. • Quarterly. Price on request. CD-ROM contains updated full text of *Intellectual Property Counseling and Litigation, Computer Law, International Computer Law, Nimmer on Copyright, Milgrim on Trade Secrets, Patent Litigation, Patent Licensing Transactions, Trademark Protection and Practice*, and other Matthew Bender publications relating to the law of intellectual property.

CASSIS (Patents). U. S. Patent and Trademark Office, Office of Electronic Information Products. • A series of CD-ROM products, including *Patents ASSIGN* (assignment deeds, quarterly), *Patents ASSIST* (search tools, quarterly), *Patents BIB* (abstracts and search information, bimonthly), *Patents CLASS* (classifications, 1790 to date, bimonthly), *Patents SNAP* (serial number concordance, annual).

U. S. FullText. MicroPatent. • Monthly. Contains complete text on CD-ROM of all patents issued by the U. S. Patent and Trademark Office. Archival discs are available from 1975.

DIRECTORIES

Attorneys and Agents Registered to Practice Before United States Patent and Trademark Office. U.S. Patent and Trademark Office. Available from U.S. Government Printing Office. • Annual. $56.00.

Directory of Intellectual Property Attorneys, 1995. Aspen Publishers, Inc. • 1994. $195.00.

ENCYCLOPEDIAS AND DICTIONARIES

Attorney's Dictionary of Patent Claims: Legal Materials and Practice Commentaries. Irwin M. Aisenberg. LexisNexis Matthew Bender. • $607.00. Three looseleaf volumes. Periodic supplementation. Operational guidance for bank officers, with analysis of statutory law and agency regulations.

McCarthy's Desk Encyclopedia of Intellectual Property. J. Thomas McCarthy. BNA, Inc. • 1995. $75.00.Second edition. Defines legal terms relating to patents, trademarks, copyrights, trade secrets, entertainment, and the computer industry.

HANDBOOKS AND MANUALS

Antitrust-Intellectual Property Handbook. Alan J. Weinschel. Glasser Legalworks. • Looseleaf. $175.00. Periodic supplementation. Covers patent licensing, patent antitrust issues, innovation markets, intervention by government agencies, standard-setting activities, royalty arrangements, and related intellectual property/antitrust topics. Provides explanations, legal guidance, and historical background.

Copyrights, Patents, and Trademarks: Protect Your Rights Worldwide. Hoyt L. Barber. McGraw-Hill. • 1996. $32.95. Second edition.

Drafting Patent License Agreements. Brian G. Brunsvold and others. BNA, Inc. • 1998. $125.00. Fourth edition.

Intellectual Property Infringement Damages: A Litigation Support Handbook 2003 Cumulative Supplement. Russell L. Parr. John Wiley and Sons, Inc. • 2003. $78.00. Second edition. Describes how to calculate damages for patent, trademark, and copyright infringement. (Intellectual Property-General, Law, Accounting and Finance, Management, Licensing and Special Topics Series).

Intellectual Property Primary Law Soucebook. LexisNexis Matthew Bender. • Annual. $88.00. Provides federal copyright, patent, and trademark statutes and regulations.

Inventing and Patenting Sourcebook. Gale Cengage Learning. • 1992. $120.00. Second edition. A general guide for inventors. Contains how-to-do-it text, information sources, and sample forms.

Librarian's Guide to Intellectual Property in the Digital Age: Copyrights, Patents, and Trademarks. Timothy L. Wherry. American Library Association. • 2002. $38.00. Includes lists of patent and trademark depositories, relevant Web sites, and questions & answers.

Manual of Classification. U.S. Patent Office. Available from U.S. Government Printing Office. • Two volumes. Index and revised looseleaf pages for an indefinite period. Lists patent classes and subclasses.

Manual of Patent Examining Procedure. U.S. Patent Office. Available from U.S. Government Printing Office. • Looseleaf. $248.00. Periodic supplementation included. Information on the practices and procedures relative to the prosecution of patent applications before the Patent and Trademark Office.

Patent, Copyright, and Trademark: An Intellectual Property Desk Reference. Stephen Elias. Nolo. • 2003. $39.99. Sixth revised edition. Contains practical explanations of the legalities of patents, copyrights, trademarks, and trade secrets. Includes examples of relevant legal forms. A 1985 version was called *Nolo's Intellectual Property Law Dictionary.* (Nolo Press Self-Help Law Series).

Patent It Yourself. David R. Pressman. Nolo. • 2003. $49.99. Ninth edition. (Patent It Yourself Series).

Patent Law Basics. West Group. • $225.00. Looseleaf service. Annual updates. Covers Patent and Trademark Office applications, patent ownership, rights, protection, infringement, litigation, and other fundamentals of patent law.

Patent Law Handbook. West Group. • Annual. $321.00.

Patent, Trademark, and Copyright Laws, 2003. Jeffrey Samuels, editor. BNA, Inc. • 2003. $115.00. Contains text of "all pertinent intellectual property legislation to date.".

Protecting Trade Secrets, Patents, Copyrights, and Trademarks. Robert C. Dorr and Christopher H. Munch. Aspen Publishers, Inc. • $165.00. Looseleaf service.

INTERNET DATABASES

Delphion Research. Thomson Delphion. Phone: 800-411-4811 or (630)799-0600 Fax: (630)799-0688 E-mail: support@delphion.com • URL: http://www.delphion.com • Fee-based Web site provides more than 40 million records of full-text patent information from the U. S. Patent and Trademark Office and from about 70 foreign countries. Corporate and individual subscriptions are available.

United States Patent and Trademark Office. U. S. Department of Commerce. Phone: 800-786-9199 or (703)308-4357 Fax: (703)305-7786 • URL: http://www.uspto.gov • Web site provides extensive information about patents and trademarks, with advanced search facilities for specific documents or names. "Special Pages" are available for "How to Search," "Trademarks-Logos-Brands," "Inventor Resources," and other topics. A complete fee schedule is available for filing applications, appeals, copies, etc.

ONLINE DATABASES

CLAIMS. IFI/Plenum Data Corp. • Includes seven separate databases: *CLAIMS/Citation, CLAIMS/Compound Registry, CLAIMS/Comprehensive Data Base, CLAIMS/Reassignment & Reexamination, CLAIMS/Reference, CLAIMS/U. S. Patent Abstracts*, and *CLAIMS/Uniterm*. Provides extensive current and historical information on U. S.

Patents. Inquire as to online cost and availability.

Derwent U. S. Patents. Derwent, Inc. • Provides citations and abstracts for more then one million U. S. patents issued since 1971. Weekly updates. Inquire as to online cost and availability.

Derwent World Patents Index. Derwent, Inc. • Contains abstracts of more than 20 million patent documents from many countries. Time span varies. Weekly updates. Inquire as to online cost and availability.

U. S. Patents Fulltext. Available from DIALOG. • Contains complete text of patents issued by the U. S. Patent and Trademark Office since 1971. Weekly updates. Inquire as to online cost and availability.

PERIODICALS AND NEWSLETTERS

BNA's Patent, Trademark and Copyright Journal. BNA, Inc. • Weekly. $1,495.00 per year. Looseleaf service.

Intellectual Property Today. • Monthly. $96.00 per year. Covers legal developments in copyright, patents, trademarks, and licensing. Emphasizes the effect of new technology on intellectual property. Formerly *Law Works.*

Les Nouvelles. Licensing Executives Society International. • Description: Concerned with technological licensing and related subjects. Covers technology, patents, trademarks, and licensing "know-how" world-wide.

Official Gazette of the United States Patent and Trademark Office: Patents. Available from U. S. Government Printing Office. • Weekly. Contains the Patents, Patent Office Notices, and Designs issued each week (http://www.uspto.gov). Annual indexes are sold separately.

Patent and Trademark Office Society Journal. Patent and Trademark Office Society. • Individuals, $20.00 per year.

Patent Strategy and Management. American Lawyer Media, Inc. • Monthly. $225.00 per year. Newsletter. Provides news of recent legal and business trends in the area of patent issuance and litigation. (A Law Journal Newsletter, formerly published by Leader Publications).

STATISTICS SOURCES

Commissioner of Patents Annual Report. U.S. Patent Office. Available from U.S. Government Printing Office. • Annual.

Statistical Handbook on Technology. Paula Bernstein. Greenwood Publishing Group, Inc. • 1999. $69.95. Provides statistical data on such items as the Internet, online services, computer technology, recycling, patents, prescription drug sales, telecommunications, and aerospace. Includes charts, tables, and graphs. Edited for the general reader. (Statistical Handbook Series).

TRADE/PROFESSIONAL ASSOCIATIONS

American Intellectual Property Law Association. 241 18th St. S, Ste. 700, Arlington, VA 22202. Phone: (703)415-0780 Fax: (703)415-0786 E-mail: aipla@aipla.org • URL: http://www.aipla.org • Voluntary bar association of lawyers practicing in the fields of patents, trademarks, copyrights, and trade secrets. Aids in the operation and improvement of U.S. patent, trademark, and copyright systems, including the laws by which they are governed and rules and regulations under which federal agencies administer those laws. Sponsors moot court and legal writing competitions.

International Intellectual Property Association. 1255 23rd St. NW, Ste. 200, Washington, DC 20037. Phone: (202)466-2396 Fax: (202)466-2893 E-mail: herb@ipo.org • URL: http://www.ipo.org • Lawyers who have professional qualifications and interest in the international protection of patents, designs, trademarks, copyrights, and other intellectual property rights. American group of the International

Association for the Protection of Industrial Property. Monitors international developments that may affect industrial property and related rights. Studies, discusses, and reports on proposed national and foreign legislation treaties and conventions that are likely to affect national and international intellectual property interests.

OTHER SOURCES

Chisum on Patents. LexisNexis Matthew Bender. • Five times a year. 2,105.00. 16 looseleaf volumes. An analysis of patent law in the U. S. Includes bibliography and glossary.

Intellectual Property and Antitrust Law. William C. Holmes. West Group. • Semiannual. $389.00 per year. Two looseleaf volumes. Includes patent, trademark, and copyright practices.

PAY PLANNING

See: EXECUTIVE COMPENSATION; WAGES AND SALARIES

PAYROLL ADMINISTRATION

See: WAGES AND SALARIES

PEACH INDUSTRY

See also: FRUIT INDUSTRY

ALMANACS AND YEARBOOKS

Agricultural and Mineral Commodities Year Book. Available from Taylor & Francis Group. • Annual. $225.00. Published by Europa Publications. Contains descriptive product profiles, price data, export-import data, and production statistics for major commodities of the world. Includes commodity histories, uses, markets, demand trends, and information about trade agreements and key commodity organizations.

CD-ROM DATABASES

Food Science and Technology Abstracts [CD-ROM]. Available from SilverPlatter Information, Inc. • Quarterly. Produced by International Food Information Service (home page is http://www.ifis. org). Provides worldwide coverage on CD-ROM of the literature of food technology and production. Various types of publications are indexed, with abstracts, including about 1,800 periodicals. Time period is 1969 to date.

DIRECTORIES

Major Food and Drink Companies of the World. Available from Gale Cengage Learning. • Annual. $880.00. Two volumes. Published by Graham & Whiteside. Contains profiles and trade names for more than 9,800 important food and beverage companies in various countries. In addition to foods, includes both alcoholic and nonalcoholic drink products.

Thomas Food and Beverage Market Place. Grey House Publishing. • 2004. $495.00. Three volumes. Contains more than 40,000 entries covering food companies, beverages, food equipment, warehouse companies, food brokers, wholesalers, importers, and exporters. Formerly *Thomas Food Industry Register.*

INTERNET DATABASES

USDA. United States Department of Agriculture. Phone: (202)720-2791 E-mail: agsec@usda.gov • URL: http://www.usda.gov • The USDA home page has six sections: News and Information; What's New; About USDA; Agencies; Opportunities; Search and Help. Keyword searching is offered from the USDA home page and from various individual agency home pages. Agencies are the Economic

Research Service, Agricultural Marketing Service, National Agricultural Statistics Service, National Agricultural Library, and about 12 others. Updating varies. Fees: Free.

ONLINE DATABASES

Food Science and Technology Abstracts [online]. IFIS North American Desk. • Produced by International Food Information Service. Provides about 500,000 online citations, with abstracts, to the international literature of food science, technology, commodities, engineering, and processing. Approximately 2,000 periodicals are covered. Time period is 1969 to date, with monthly updates. Inquire as to online cost and availability.

PERIODICALS AND NEWSLETTERS

Journal of Tree Fruit Production. Haworth Press, Inc. • Semiannual. Institutions, $95.00 per year. A research journal for tree fruit growers.

Peach-Times. National Peach Council. • Quarterly. Membership.

STATISTICS SOURCES

Agricultural Statistics. Available from U. S. Government Printing Office. • Annual. $38.00. Produced by the National Agricultural Statistics Service, U. S. Department of Agriculture. Provides a wide variety of statistical data relating to agricultural production, supplies, consumption, prices/price-supports, foreign trade, costs, and returns, as well as farm labor, loans, income, and population. In many cases, historical data is shown annually for 10 years. In addition to farm data, includes detailed fishery statistics.

FAO Production Yearbook. Available from Bernan Associates. • Annual. $45.00. Published by the Food and Agriculture Organization (http://www.fao.org). Contains worldwide data on agriculture, land use, farm crops, livestock, and agricultural prices.

FAO Trade Yearbook. Available from Bernan Associates. • Annual. $45.00. Published by the Food and Agriculture Organization (http://www.fao.org). Provides extensive worldwide data on exports and imports of agricultural commodities, fertilizers, tractors, and pesticides. Includes more than 130 tables of detailed statistics.

World Food Data and Statistics. Euromonitor International. • 2004. $650.00. Provides five-year data for a wide variety of food products in 52 countries. Includes market size, consumer expenditures, price indicators, and retail distribution data for many kinds of meat, fish, fruits, vegetables, dairy products, baked goods, condiments, canned food, and frozen food.

TRADE/PROFESSIONAL ASSOCIATIONS

National Peach Council. 12 Nicklaus Ln., Ste. 101, Columbia, SC 29229. Phone: (803)788-7101 Fax: (803)865-8090 E-mail: peachcouncil@att.net • URL: http://www.nationalpeach.org • Represents peach growers, allied industries, and research and extension personnel. Lobbies the U.S. Congress on behalf of fresh market peach growers, compiles and publishes statistics on the peach industry and prepares annual preseason crop estimates.

PEANUT AND PEANUT OIL INDUSTRIES

See also: NUT INDUSTRY; OIL AND FATS INDUSTRY

ALMANACS AND YEARBOOKS

Agricultural and Mineral Commodities Year Book. Available from Taylor & Francis Group. • Annual. $225.00. Published by Europa Publications. Contains descriptive product profiles, price data, export-import data, and production statistics for major commodities of the world. Includes commodity histories, uses, markets, demand trends, and information about trade agreements and key commodity organizations.

CD-ROM DATABASES

Food Science and Technology Abstracts [CD-ROM]. Available from SilverPlatter Information, Inc. • Quarterly. Produced by International Food Information Service (home page is http://www.ifis. org). Provides worldwide coverage on CD-ROM of the literature of food technology and production. Various types of publications are indexed, with abstracts, including about 1,800 periodicals. Time period is 1969 to date.

DIRECTORIES

American Peanut Council--Membership Directory. American Peanut Council Inc. • Covers: about 250 growers, shellers, processors, manufacturers, brokers, and allied businesses providing goods and services to the peanut industry. Entries include: Company name, address, phone, fax, telex, e-mail, names of principal executives, subsidiary and branch names and locations, products.

Major Food and Drink Companies of the World. Available from Gale Cengage Learning. • Annual. $880.00. Two volumes. Published by Graham & Whiteside. Contains profiles and trade names for more than 9,800 important food and beverage companies in various countries. In addition to foods, includes both alcoholic and nonalcoholic drink products.

Thomas Food and Beverage Market Place. Grey House Publishing. • 2004. $495.00. Three volumes. Contains more than 40,000 entries covering food companies, beverages, food equipment, warehouse companies, food brokers, wholesalers, importers, and exporters. Formerly *Thomas Food Industry Register.*

INTERNET DATABASES

USDA. United States Department of Agriculture. Phone: (202)720-2791 E-mail: agsec@usda.gov • URL: http://www.usda.gov • The USDA home page has six sections: News and Information; What's New; About USDA; Agencies; Opportunities; Search and Help. Keyword searching is offered from the USDA home page and from various individual agency home pages. Agencies are the Economic Research Service, Agricultural Marketing Service, National Agricultural Statistics Service, National Agricultural Library, and about 12 others. Updating varies. Fees: Free.

ONLINE DATABASES

Food Science and Technology Abstracts [online]. IFIS North American Desk. • Produced by International Food Information Service. Provides about 500,000 online citations, with abstracts, to the international literature of food science, technology, commodities, engineering, and processing. Approximately 2,000 periodicals are covered. Time period is 1969 to date, with monthly updates. Inquire as to online cost and availability.

PERIODICALS AND NEWSLETTERS

The Peanut Farmer: For Commercial Growers of Peanuts and Related Agribusiness. SpecComm International, Inc. • Seven times a year. $15.00 per year.

Peanut Journal and Nut World. Virginia-Carolina Peanut Association. Peanut Journal Publishing Co. • Monthly. $8.00 per year.

Peanut Science. American Peanut Research and Education Association Society. • Semiannual. $40.00 per issue.

STATISTICS SOURCES

Agricultural Statistics. Available from U. S. Government Printing Office. • Annual. $38.00. Produced by the National Agricultural Statistics Service, U. S. Department of Agriculture. Provides a wide variety

of statistical data relating to agricultural production, supplies, consumption, prices/price-supports, foreign trade, costs, and returns, as well as farm labor, loans, income, and population. In many cases, historical data is shown annually for 10 years. In addition to farm data, includes detailed fishery statistics.

FAO Production Yearbook. Available from Bernan Associates. • Annual. $45.00. Published by the Food and Agriculture Organization (http://www.fao.org). Contains worldwide data on agriculture, land use, farm crops, livestock, and agricultural prices.

FAO Trade Yearbook. Available from Bernan Associates. • Annual. $45.00. Published by the Food and Agriculture Organization (http://www.fao.org). Provides extensive worldwide data on exports and imports of agricultural commodities, fertilizers, tractors, and pesticides. Includes more than 130 tables of detailed statistics.

World Food Data and Statistics. Euromonitor International. • 2004. $650.00. Provides five-year data for a wide variety of food products in 52 countries. Includes market size, consumer expenditures, price indicators, and retail distribution data for many kinds of meat, fish, fruits, vegetables, dairy products, baked goods, condiments, canned food, and frozen food.

TRADE/PROFESSIONAL ASSOCIATIONS

American Peanut Council. 1500 King St., Ste. 301, Alexandria, VA 22314. Phone: (703)838-9500 Fax: (703)838-9508 E-mail: info@peanutsusa.com • URL: http://www.peanutsusa.com • Growers, shellers, brokers, processors, and manufacturers; allied businesses providing goods and services to the peanut industry. Encourages research to improve quality of peanuts.

American Peanut Research and Education Society. Oklahoma State University, 376 AG Hall, Stillwater, OK 74078. Phone: (405)372-3052 Fax: (405)624-6718 • URL: http://www.apress.okstate.edu.

Peanut and Tree Nut Processors Association. PO Box 59811, Potomac, MD 20859-9811. Phone: (301)365-2521 Fax: (301)365-7705 E-mail: ptnpa@mindspring.com • URL: http://www.ptnpa.org • Formerly Peanut Butter Manufacturers and Nut-Salters Association.

PEAR INDUSTRY

See also: FRUIT INDUSTRY

ALMANACS AND YEARBOOKS

Agricultural and Mineral Commodities Year Book. Available from Taylor & Francis Group. • Annual. $225.00. Published by Europa Publications. Contains descriptive product profiles, price data, export-import data, and production statistics for major commodities of the world. Includes commodity histories, uses, markets, demand trends, and information about trade agreements and key commodity organizations.

CD-ROM DATABASES

Food Science and Technology Abstracts [CD-ROM]. Available from SilverPlatter Information, Inc. • Quarterly. Produced by International Food Information Service (home page is http://www.ifis. org). Provides worldwide coverage on CD-ROM of the literature of food technology and production. Various types of publications are indexed, with abstracts, including about 1,800 periodicals. Time period is 1969 to date.

DIRECTORIES

Major Food and Drink Companies of the World. Available from Gale Cengage Learning. • Annual. $880.00. Two volumes. Published by Graham & Whiteside. Contains profiles and trade names for more than 9,800 important food and beverage

companies in various countries. In addition to foods, includes both alcoholic and nonalcoholic drink products.

Thomas Food and Beverage Market Place. Grey House Publishing. • 2004. $495.00. Three volumes. Contains more than 40,000 entries covering food companies, beverages, food equipment, warehouse companies, food brokers, wholesalers, importers, and exporters. Formerly *Thomas Food Industry Register.*

INTERNET DATABASES

USDA. United States Department of Agriculture. Phone: (202)720-2791 E-mail: agsec@usda.gov • URL: http://www.usda.gov • The USDA home page has six sections: News and Information; What's New; About USDA; Agencies; Opportunities; Search and Help. Keyword searching is offered from the USDA home page and from various individual agency home pages. Agencies are the Economic Research Service, Agricultural Marketing Service, National Agricultural Statistics Service, National Agricultural Library, and about 12 others. Updating varies. Fees: Free.

ONLINE DATABASES

Food Science and Technology Abstracts [online]. IFIS North American Desk. • Produced by International Food Information Service. Provides about 500,000 online citations, with abstracts, to the international literature of food science, technology, commodities, engineering, and processing. Approximately 2,000 periodicals are covered. Time period is 1969 to date, with monthly updates. Inquire as to online cost and availability.

PERIODICALS AND NEWSLETTERS

Journal of Tree Fruit Production. Haworth Press, Inc. • Semiannual. Institutions, $95.00 per year. A research journal for tree fruit growers.

STATISTICS SOURCES

Agricultural Statistics. Available from U. S. Government Printing Office. • Annual. $38.00. Produced by the National Agricultural Statistics Service, U. S. Department of Agriculture. Provides a wide variety of statistical data relating to agricultural production, supplies, consumption, prices/price-supports, foreign trade, costs, and returns, as well as farm labor, loans, income, and population. In many cases, historical data is shown annually for 10 years. In addition to farm data, includes detailed fishery statistics.

FAO Production Yearbook. Available from Bernan Associates. • Annual. $45.00. Published by the Food and Agriculture Organization (http://www.fao.org). Contains worldwide data on agriculture, land use, farm crops, livestock, and agricultural prices.

FAO Trade Yearbook. Available from Bernan Associates. • Annual. $45.00. Published by the Food and Agriculture Organization (http://www.fao.org). Provides extensive worldwide data on exports and imports of agricultural commodities, fertilizers, tractors, and pesticides. Includes more than 130 tables of detailed statistics.

World Food Data and Statistics. Euromonitor International. • 2004. $650.00. Provides five-year data for a wide variety of food products in 52 countries. Includes market size, consumer expenditures, price indicators, and retail distribution data for many kinds of meat, fish, fruits, vegetables, dairy products, baked goods, condiments, canned food, and frozen food.

PECAN INDUSTRY

See also: NUT INDUSTRY

ALMANACS AND YEARBOOKS

Agricultural and Mineral Commodities Year Book. Available from Taylor & Francis Group. • Annual.

$225.00. Published by Europa Publications. Contains descriptive product profiles, price data, export-import data, and production statistics for major commodities of the world. Includes commodity histories, uses, markets, demand trends, and information about trade agreements and key commodity organizations.

CD-ROM DATABASES

Food Science and Technology Abstracts [CD-ROM]. Available from SilverPlatter Information, Inc. • Quarterly. Produced by International Food Information Service (home page is http://www.ifis.org). Provides worldwide coverage on CD-ROM of the literature of food technology and production. Various types of publications are indexed, with abstracts, including about 1,800 periodicals. Time period is 1969 to date.

DIRECTORIES

Major Food and Drink Companies of the World. Available from Gale Cengage Learning. • Annual. $880.00. Two volumes. Published by Graham & Whiteside. Contains profiles and trade names for more than 9,800 important food and beverage companies in various countries. In addition to foods, includes both alcoholic and nonalcoholic drink products.

Thomas Food and Beverage Market Place. Grey House Publishing. • 2004. $495.00. Three volumes. Contains more than 40,000 entries covering food companies, beverages, food equipment, warehouse companies, food brokers, wholesalers, importers, and exporters. Formerly *Thomas Food Industry Register.*

INTERNET DATABASES

USDA. United States Department of Agriculture. Phone: (202)720-2791 E-mail: agsec@usda.gov • URL: http://www.usda.gov • The USDA home page has six sections: News and Information; What's New; About USDA; Agencies; Opportunities; Search and Help. Keyword searching is offered from the USDA home page and from various individual agency home pages. Agencies are the Economic Research Service, Agricultural Marketing Service, National Agricultural Statistics Service, National Agricultural Library, and about 12 others. Updating varies. Fees: Free.

ONLINE DATABASES

Food Science and Technology Abstracts [online]. IFIS North American Desk. • Produced by International Food Information Service. Provides about 500,000 online citations, with abstracts, to the international literature of food science, technology, commodities, engineering, and processing. Approximately 2,000 periodicals are covered. Time period is 1969 to date, with monthly updates. Inquire as to online cost and availability.

PERIODICALS AND NEWSLETTERS

Pecan South. Texas Pecan Growers Association. • Monthly. $18.00 per year.

STATISTICS SOURCES

Agricultural Statistics. Available from U. S. Government Printing Office. • Annual. $38.00. Produced by the National Agricultural Statistics Service, U. S. Department of Agriculture. Provides a wide variety of statistical data relating to agricultural production, supplies, consumption, prices/price-supports, foreign trade, costs, and returns, as well as farm labor, loans, income, and population. In many cases, historical data is shown annually for 10 years. In addition to farm data, includes detailed fishery statistics.

FAQ Production Yearbook. Available from Bernan Associates. • Annual. $45.00. Published by the Food and Agriculture Organization (http://www.fao.org). Contains worldwide data on agriculture, land use, farm crops, livestock, and agricultural prices.

FAO Trade Yearbook. Available from Bernan Associates. • Annual. $45.00. Published by the Food and Agriculture Organization (http://www.fao.org). Provides extensive worldwide data on exports and imports of agricultural commodities, fertilizers, tractors, and pesticides. Includes more than 130 tables of detailed statistics.

World Food Data and Statistics. Euromonitor International. • 2004. $650.00. Provides five-year data for a wide variety of food products in 52 countries. Includes market size, consumer expenditures, price indicators, and retail distribution data for many kinds of meat, fish, fruits, vegetables, dairy products, baked goods, condiments, canned food, and frozen food.

TRADE/PROFESSIONAL ASSOCIATIONS

National Pecan Shellers Association. 1100 Johnson Ferry Rd., Ste. 300, Atlanta, GA 30342. Phone: (404)252-3663 Fax: (404)252-0774 E-mail: info@ilovepecans.org • URL: http://www.ilovepecans.org • Shellers and processors of pecans. Promotes the welfare and interests of the pecan shelling and processing industry.

PENCILS

See: WRITING INSTRUMENTS

PENNY STOCKS

See: OVER-THE-COUNTER SECURITIES INDUSTRY

PENS

See: WRITING INSTRUMENTS

PENSIONS

See also: EMPLOYEE BENEFIT PLANS; ESTATE PLANNING; 401(K) RETIREMENT PLANS; INDIVIDUAL RETIREMENT ACCOUNTS; RETIREMENT; TRUSTS AND TRUSTEES

GENERAL WORKS

Financial Institutions and Markets. Meir J. Kohn. Oxford University Press, Inc. • 2003. $115.00. Second edition.

Fundamentals of Employee Benefit Programs. Employee Benefit Research Institute. • 1996. $49.95. Fifth edition. Provides basic explanation of employee benefit programs in both the private and public sectors, including health insurance, pension plans, retirement planning, social security, and long-term care insurance.

Fundamentals of Private Pensions. Dan M. McGill and others. University of Pennsylvania Press. • 1996. $79.95. Seventh revised edition. (Pension Research Council Publications Series).

New Ideas About Old Age Security: Toward Sustainable Pension Systems in the 21st Century. Holzmann, editor. The World Bank Group. • 2001. $35.00. Discusses worldwide problems in dealing with the pension needs of aging populations.

Social Security, Medicare, and Government Pensions: Get the Most Out\of Your Retirement and Medical Benefits. Joseph Matthews and Dorothy M. Berman. Nolo. • 2002. $29.99. Eighth edition. In addition to the basic topics, includes practical information on Supplemental Security Income (SSI), disability benefits, veterans benefits, 401(k) plans, Medicare HMOs, medigap insurance, Medicaid, and how to appeal decisions. (Social Security, Medicare and Pensions Series).

Vanguard Retirement Investing Guide: Charting Your Course to a Secure Retirement. McGraw-Hill. • 1995. $24.95. Second edition. Covers saving and investing for future retirement. Topics include goal setting, investment fundamentals, mutual funds, asset allocation, defined contribution retirement savings plans, social security, and retirement savings strategies. Includes glossary and worksheet for retirement saving.

ABSTRACTS AND INDEXES

Insurance Periodicals Index. Specials Libraries Association, Insurance and Employees Benefits Div. NILS Publishing Co. • Annual. $250.00. Compiled by the Insurance and Employee Benefits Div., Special Libraries Association. A yearly index of over 15,000 articles from about 35 insurance periodicals. Arrangement is by subject, with an index to authors.

ALMANACS AND YEARBOOKS

Older Americans Information Directory. Grey House Publshing, Inc. • 2002. $165.00. Fourth edition. Presents articles (text) and sources of information on a wide variety of aging and retirement topics. Includes an index to personal names, organizations, and subjects.

BIBLIOGRAPHIES

Insurance and Employee Benefits Literature. Special Libraries Association, Insurance and Employee Benefits Div. • Bimonthly. $15.00 per year. Lists a wide variety of literature in all branches of the insurance industry. Includes annotations.

DIRECTORIES

America's Corporate Finance Directory. LexisNexis Group. • Covers: Financial personnel and outside financial services relationships of 5,000 leading United States corporations and their wholly-owned United States subsidiaries. Entries include: Company name, address, phone, fax, telex, e-mail addresses, stock exchange information, earnings, total assets, size of pension/profit-sharing fund portfolio, number of employees, description of business, wholly-owned U.S. Subsidiaries of parent company; name and title of key executives; outside suppliers of financial services.

Money Market Directory of Pension Funds and Their Investment Managers. Money Market Directories, Inc. • Annual. $1,150.00. Institutional funds and managers.

Nelson Information's Directory of Pension Fund Consultants. Nelson Information. • Annual. $610.00. Covers the pension plan sponsor industry. More than 325 worldwide consulting firms are described. Formerly *Nelson's Guide to Pension Fund Consultants.*

Nelson Information's Directory of Plan Sponsors. Nelson Information. • Annual. $610.00. Three volumes. Formerly *Nelson's Directory of Plan Sponsors and Tax-Exempt Funds.*

Pensions and Investments 1000 Largest Retirement Funds. Crain Communications, Inc. • Annual. $50.00. List of the largest retirement plans in terms of total assets. Formerly *Pensions and Investments Top 100 Retirement Funds.*

ENCYCLOPEDIAS AND DICTIONARIES

Dictionary of Finance and Investment Terms. John Downes. Barron's Educational Series, Inc. • 2002. $14.95. Sixth edition. Provides clear explanations of more than 5,000 business, banking, financial, investment, and tax terms. Includes a separate list of financial abbreviations and acronyms. (Business Dictionaries Series).

Encyclopedia of Aging. David J. Ekerdt, editor. Available from Gale Cengage Learning. • 2002. $450.00. Four volumes. Published by Macmillan Reference USA. Includes articles relating to the financial aspects of aging, such as housing, long-term care insurance, pensions, social security, individual retirement accounts, savings, and retirement planning.

Glossary of Insurance Policy Terms. Organization for Economic Cooperation and Development. • 1999. $30.00. "The selected topics range from insurance policy regulation/supervision to general trade issues and include technical terms related to issues such as claims, premiums, and provisions." Edited for government, academic, business, and insurance organizations.

FINANCIAL RATIOS

Financial Planning for Older Clients. James E. Pearman. CCH, Inc. • 2000. $49.00. Covers income sources, social security, Medicare, Medicaid, investment planning, estate planning, and other retirement-related topics. Edited for accountants, attorneys, and other financial advisors. (Solutions for Professional Advisors Series).

HANDBOOKS AND MANUALS

ERISA: The Law and the Code (Employee Retirement Income Security Act). Janet K. Song and Michael G. Kushner. BNA, Inc. • Annual. $105.00. The Employee Retirement Income Security Act, as amended, withrelevant provisions of the Internal Revenue Code.

Estate Plan Book 2000. William S. Moore. American Institute for Economic Research. • 2000. $10.00. Revision of 1997 edition. Part one: "Basic Estate Planning." Part two: "Reducing Taxes on the Disposition of Your Estate." Part three: "Putting it All Together: Examples of Estate Plans." Provides succinct information on wills, trusts, tax planning, and gifts. (Economic Education Bulletin.).

Guidebook to Pension Planning. CCH, Inc. • Annual.

How to Build Wealth with Tax-Sheltered Investments. Kerry Anne Lynch. American Institute for Economic Research. • 2000. $6.00. Provides practical information on conservative tax shelters, including defined-contribution pension plans, individual retirement accounts, Keogh plans, U. S. savings bonds, municipal bonds, and various kinds of annuities: deferred, variable-rate, immediate, and foreign-currency. (Economic Education Bulletin.).

The New Working Woman's Guide to Retirement Planning: Saving and Investing Now for a Secure Future. Martha P. Patterson. University of Pennsylvania Press. • 1999. $19.95. Second edition. Provides retirement advice for employed women, including information on various kinds of IRAs, cash balance and other pension plans, 401(k) plans, and social security. Four case studies are provided to illustrate retirement planning at specific life and career stages.

Pension and Employee Benefits: Code-ERISA and Regulations. CCH, Inc. • $123.00. Two volumes.

Pension and Profit Sharing Plans for Small or Medium Size Businesses. Aspen Publishers, Inc. • Monthly. $191.50 per year. Newsletter. Topics of interest and concern to professionals who serve small and medium size pension and profit sharing plans.

Pension Fund Investment Management: A Handbook for Sponsors and Their Advisors. Fran K. Fabozzi, editor. John Wiley and Sons, Inc. • 1997. $95.00. Second revised edition. (Frank K. Fabozzi Series: Vol. 25).

Pension Plan Fix-It Handbook. Thompson Publishing Group, Inc. • Two looseleaf volumes. $499.00 per year. Two looseleaf volumes. Monthly updates and newsletters. Serves as a comprehensive guide to pension plan administration, taxation, and federal regulation. Includes both defined benefit and defined contribution plans.

Pension Planning: Pensions, Profit Sharing, and Other Deferred Compensation Plans. Joseph T. Mel-

one and others. McGraw-Hill. • 2002. $104.38. Ninth edition.

Retirement Benefits Tax Guide. CCH, Inc. • $199.00. Looseleaf service.

U. S. Master Pension Guide. CCH, Inc. • Annual. $56.95. Explains IRS rules and regulations applying to 401(k) plans, 403(k) plans, ESOPs (employee stock ownership plans), IRAs, SEPs (simplified employee pension plans), Keogh plans, and non-qualified plans.

INTERNET DATABASES

EBSCO Information Services. Ebsco Publishing. Phone: 800-653-2726 or (978)356-6500 Fax: (978)356-6565 E-mail: ep@epnet.com • URL: http://www.epnet.com • Fee-based Web site providing Internet access to a wide variety of databases, including business-related material. Full text is available for many periodical titles, with daily updates. Fees: Apply.

InSite 2. Intelligence Data/Thomson Financial. Phone: 800-654-0393 or (617)856-1890 Fax: (617)737-3182 E-mail: intelligence.data@tfn.com • URL: http://www.insite2.gale.com/ • Fee-based Web site consolidates information in a "Base Pack" consisting of Business InSite, Market InSite, and Company InSite. Optional databases are Consumer InSite, Health and Wellness InSite, Newsletter InSite, and Computer InSite. Includes fulltext content from more than 2,500 trade publications, journals, newsletters, newspapers, analyst reports, and other sources. Continuous updating. Formerly produced by The Gale Group.

InsWeb. InsWeb Corp. Phone: (916)853-3300 E-mail: info@insweb.com • URL: http://www.insweb.com • Web site offers a wide variety of advice and information on automobile, life, health, and "other" insurance. Includes glossaries of insurance terms, Standard & Poor's ratings of individual insurance companies, and "Financial Needs Estimators." Searching is available. Fees: Free.

ProQuest Direct. ProQuest Inc. Phone: 800-889-3358 or (734)761-4700 Fax: (734)662-4554 • URL: http://proquest.com • Fee-based Web site providing Internet access to more than 3,000 periodicals, newspapers, and other publications. Many items are available full-text, with daily updates. Includes extensive corporate and financial information. Fees: Apply.

Small Business Retirement Savings Advisor. U. S. Department of Labor. Phone: (202)219-8921 • URL: http://www.dol.gov/elaws/pwbaplan.htm • Web site provides "answers to a variety of commonly asked questions about retirement saving options for small business employers." Includes a comparison chart and detailed descriptions of various plans: 401(k), SEP-IRA, SIMPLE-IRA, Payroll Deduction IRA, Keogh Profit-Sharing, Keogh Money Purchase, and Defined Benefit. Searching is offered. Fees: Free.

PERIODICALS AND NEWSLETTERS

Contingencies: The Magazine of the Actuarial Profession. American Academy of Actuaries. • Bimonthly. $30.00 per year. Provides non-technical articles on the actuarial aspects of insurance, employee benefits, and pensions.

Defined Contribution News. Aspen Publishers. • Description: Covers all aspects of the defined contribution pension plan market from the plan sponsor and vendor points of view. Discusses topics such as searches for investment managers; record keepers, administrators, and trustees; legislative and regulatory developments; plan profiles; sponsor forums; new vendor products; and personnel changes and DC Database.

Employee Benefit Plan Review. Charles D. Spencer and Associates, Inc. • Monthly. $302.00 per year. Provides a review of recent events affecting the administration of employee benefit programs.

Journal of Pension Planning and Compliance. Aspen Publishers. • Quarterly. $265.00 per year. Technical articles and regular columns on major issues confronting the pension community.

Journal of Retirement Planning. CCH, Inc. • Bimonthly. $179.00 per year. Emphasis is on retirement and estate planning advice provided by lawyers and accountants as part of their practices.

Money Management Letter: Bi-Weekly Newsletter Covering the Pensions and Money Maagement Industry. Institutional Investor, Inc., Journals Group. • Biweekly. $2,440.00 per year. Newsletter. Includes print and online editions. Edited for pension fund investment managers.

Older Americans Report. Business Publishers Inc. • Description: Features brief articles on legislative, judicial, and federal agency activities concerning older Americans. Covers news of developments in such areas as Social Security, social services, Medicare, programs for retirement and pension funds, research projects, and the Older Americans Act. Recurring features include book reviews and a calendar of events.

Pensions and Investments: The Newspaper of Corporate and Institutional Investing. Crain Communications, Inc. • Biweekly. $225.00 per year. Formerly *Pensions and Investment Age.*

Retirement Plans Bulletin: Practical Explanations for the IRA and Retirement Plan Professional. Universal Pensions, Inc. • Monthly. $99.00 per year. Newsletter. Provides information on the rules and regulations governing qualified (tax-deferred) retirement plans.

RESEARCH CENTERS AND INSTITUTES

Center for Pension and Retirement Research. Miami University, Department of Economics, 109E Laws Hall, Oxford, OH 45056. Phone: (513)529-2850 Fax: (513)529-3308 E-mail: swilliamson@eh.net • URL: http://www.eh.net/cprr • Research areas include pension economics, pension plans, and retirement decisions.

Employee Benefit Research Institute. Employee Benefit Research Institute. 1100 13 St. NW, Ste. 878, Washington, DC 20005. Phone: (202)659-0670 Fax: (202)775-6312 E-mail: salisbury@ebri.org • URL: http://www.ebri.org • Employee benefits in the public and private sectors, including studies on individual retirement accounts, retirement income, flexible benefits, financing health care for the elderly, health care costs, long-term care, employee benefits and federal tax policy, social security, changing benefits, and government regulation of employee benefit plans.

Pension Research Council. University of Pennsylvania, 304 CPC, 3641 Locust Walk, Philadelphia, PA 19104-6218. Phone: (215)898-7620 Fax: (215)898-0310 E-mail: prc@wharton.upenn.edu • URL: http://www.prc.wharton.upenn.edu/prc • Research areas include various types of private sector and public employee pension plans.

STATISTICS SOURCES

EBRI's Databook on Employee Benefits: What is the Promise?. Ken McDonnell and others. Employee Benefit Research Institute. • 1997 $99.00. Fourth edition. Contains more than 350 tables and charts presenting data on employee benefits in the U. S., including pensions, health insurance, social security, and medicare. Includes a glossary of employee benefit terms.

Employee Benefits in Medium and Large Private Establishments. Available from U. S. Government Printing Office. • Biennial. Issued by Bureau of Labor Statistics, U. S. Department of Labor. Provides data on benefits provided by companies with 100 or more employees. Covers benefits for both full-time and part-time workers, including health insurance, pensions, a wide variety of paid time-off policies (holidays, vacations, personal leave, maternity leave, etc.), and other fringe benefits.

Employee Benefits in Small Private Establishments. Available from U. S. Government Printing Office. • Biennial. $12.00. Issued by Bureau of Labor Statistics, U. S. Department of Labor. Supplies data on a wide variety of benefits provided by companies with fewer than 100 employees. Includes statistics for both full-time and part-time workers.

Handbook of U. S. Labor Statistics: Employment, Earnings, Prices, Productivity, and Other Labor Data. Eva E. Jacobs, editor. Bernan Associates. • 1999. $74.00. Based on *Handbook of Labor Statistics,* formerly issued by the Bureau of Labor Statistics, U. S. Department of Labor. Includes the Bureau's projections of employment in the U. S. by industry and occupation. Provides a wide variety of data on the work force, prices, fringe benefits, and consumer expenditures.

Key Indicators of the Labour Market. Available from Routledge. • Biennial. $125.00. Published by the International Labour Office (http://www.ilo.org). Provides data on 20 key indicators in 220 countries. Includes labor force statistics, employment, unemployment, part-time workers, wages, productivity, poverty indicators, and related topics.

Pension Facts. American Council of Life Insurance. • Biennial. Free.

Pension Investment Report. Employee Benefit Research Institute. • Irregualr. Membership.

Private Pensions in OECD Countries: The United States. OECD Publications and Information Center. • 1993. $22.00. Provides data relating to the characteristics of private pension arrangements in the U. S.

Statistical Handbook on Aging Americans. Renee Schick. Greenwood Publishing Group, Inc. • 1994. $69.95. Second edition. Provides data on demographics, social characteristics, health, employment, economic conditions, income, pensions, and social security. Includes bibliographic information and a glossary. (Statistical Handbook Series).

Statistical Record of Older Americans. Gale Cengage Learning. • 1996. $130.00. Second edition. Includes income and pension data.

TRADE/PROFESSIONAL ASSOCIATIONS

American Benefits Council. 1212 New York Ave. NW, Ste. 1250, Washington, DC 20005-3987. Phone: (202)289-6700 Fax: (202)289-4582 E-mail: info@abcstaff.org • URL: http://www.americanbenefitscouncil.org • Serves as national trade association for companies concerned about federal legislation and regulations affecting all aspects of the employee benefits system. Represents the entire spectrum of the private employee benefits community and sponsors or administers retirement and health plans covering more than one hundred million Americans.

American Society of Pension Actuaries. 4245 N. Fairfax Dr., Suite 750, Arlington, VA 22203. Phone: (703)516-9300 Fax: (703)516-9308 E-mail: aspa@aspa.org • URL: http://www.aspa.org • Members are involved in the pension and insurance aspects of employee benefits. Includes an Insurance and Risk Management Committee, and sponsors an annual 401(k) Workshop.

Council of Institutional Investors. 1730 Rhode Island Ave., N. W., Suite 512, Washington, DC 20036. Phone: (202)822-0800 Fax: (202)822-0801 E-mail: info@cii.org • URL: http://www.cii.org • Members are nonprofit organization pension plans and other nonprofit institutional investors.

OTHER SOURCES

BNA Pension and Benefits Reporter. BNA, Inc. • Weekly. $996.00 per year. Three looseleaf volumes.

Legal developments affecting pensions. Formerly *BNA Pension Reporter.*

Corporate Compliance Series. Joseph E. Murphy and Paul H. Dawes. West Group. • $1,210.00. 12 looseleaf volumes. Covers criminal and civil liability problems for corporations. Includes employee safety, product liability, pension requirements, securities violations, equal employment opportunity issues, intellectual property, employee hiring and firing, and other corporate compliance topics.

Employee Benefits Management. CCH, Inc. • Semimonthly. $839.00 per year. Looseleaf service. Emphasis on pension plans.

How to Plan for a Secure Retirement. Elias Zuckerman and others. Consumer Reports Books. • 2000. $29.95. Covers pension plans, health insurance, estate planning, retirement communities, and related topics. (Consumer Reports Money Guide.).

Individual Retirement Plans Guide. CCH, Inc. • $540.00 per year. Looseleaf service. Monthly updates. Covers IRA plans (Individual Retirement Accounts), SEP plans (Simplified Employee Pensions), and Keogh plans (self-employed retirement accounts).

Lieber on Pensions. William M. Lieber. Aspen Publishers, Inc. • $595.00. Five volumes. Looseleaf service. Periodic supplementation. Organizes, describes, and analyzes ERISA and IRS pension rules. Topical arrangement.

Pension Fund Litigation Reporter. Andrews Publications. • Semimonthly. $750.00 per year. Newsletter. Contains reports on legal cases involving pension fund fiduciaries (trustees).

PEPPER INDUSTRY

See: SPICE INDUSTRY

PERFORMANCE EVALUATION

See: RATING OF EMPLOYEES

PERFORMING ARTS

See: SHOW BUSINESS

PERFUME INDUSTRY

See also: COSMETICS INDUSTRY

DIRECTORIES

Fragrance Foundation Reference Guide. The Fragrance Foundation Inc. • Covers: Manufacturers of over 1100 fragrances available in the United States. Entries include: Company name, address, phone, listing of fragrances (with date of introduction and description).

Who's Who: The CTFA Membership Directory (Cosmetics Industry). Cosmetic, Toiletry, and Fragrance Association. • Annual. Free to members; non-members, $100.00. Lists 600 member companies, with key personnel, products, and services.

World Cosmetics and Toiletries Marketing Directory. Available from Gale Cengage Learning. • 2002. $1,190.00. Third edition. Three volumes. Published by Euromonitor. Provides detailed descriptions of the world's cosmetics and toiletries companies. Includes consumers market research data.

HANDBOOKS AND MANUALS

The Chemistry of Fragrances. D. Pybus and C. Sell. Springer-Verlag New York, Inc. • 1999. $39.00.

(RSC Paperback Series). Published by The Royal Society of Chemistry.

Formulary of Cosmetic Preparations. Anthony L. Hunting, editor. Micelle Press, Inc. • 1991. $135.00. Two volumes. Volume one, *Decorative Cosmetics* $60.00; volume two *Creams, Lotions and Milks* $105.00.

ONLINE DATABASES

F-D-C Reports. FDC Reports, Inc. • An online version of "The Gray Sheet" (medical devices), "The Pink Sheet" (pharmaceuticals), "The Rose Sheet" (cosmetics), "The Blue Sheet" (biomedical), and "The Tan Sheet" (nonprescription). Contains full-text information on legal, technical, corporate, financial, and marketing developments from 1987 to date, with weekly updates. Inquire as to online cost and availability.

PROMT: Predicasts Overview of Markets and Technology. Gale Cengage Learning. • Companies, products, applied technologies and markets. U.S. and international literature coverage, 1972 to date. Inquire as to online cost and availability. Provides abstracts from more than 1,600 publications. Weekly updates.

PERIODICALS AND NEWSLETTERS

CTFA News. Cosmetic, Toiletry, and Fragrance Association. • Bimonthly. Newsletter.

Perfumer and Flavorist. Allured Publishing. • Bimonthly. $135.00 per year. Provides information on the art and technology of flavors and fragrances, including essential oils, aroma chemicals, and spices.

The Rose Sheet: Toiletries, Fragrances and Skin Care. F-D-C Reports, Inc. • 51 times a year. $916.00 per year. Newsletter. Provides industry news, regulatory news, market data, and a "Weekly Trademark Review" for the cosmetics industry.

STATISTICS SOURCES

Synthetic Organic Chemicals: United States Production and Sales. International Trade Commission. Available from U.S. Government Printing Office. • Annual.

World Cosmetics and Toiletries Data and Statistics. Euromonitor International. • 2004. $650.00. Provides five-year data for a wide variety of cosmetics and toiletries in 52 countries. Includes market size, consumer expenditures, price indicators, and retail distribution data for such items as perfume, shampoo, sun products, soap, deodorants, toothpaste, hair care products, and skin care products.

TRADE/PROFESSIONAL ASSOCIATIONS

Cosmetic, Toiletry and Fragrance Association. 1101 17th St., N.W., Suite 300, Washington, DC 20036. Phone: (202)331-1770 Fax: (202)331-1969 E-mail: membership@ctfa.org • URL: http://www.ctfa.org/ • Formerly Associated Manufacturers of Toilet Articles.

Fragrance Foundation. 145 E 32nd St., New York, NY 10016-6002. Phone: (212)725-2755 Fax: (212)779-9058 E-mail: info@fragrance.org • URL: http://www.fragrance.org • Fragrance manufacturers, suppliers to the trade, publications, package designers, analysts, and advertising agencies. Seeks to educate consumers on the pleasures, use and care of fragrance and allied products. Initiates public relations programs.

OTHER SOURCES

Fragrances and Perfumes. Available from MarketResearch.com. • 2002. $3,950.00. Published by Global Industry Analysts. Provides worldwide market research data, including profiles of major perfume companies.

PERIODICAL CIRCULATION

See: CIRCULATION MANAGEMENT (PUBLISHING)

PERIODICALS

See also: CIRCULATION MANAGEMENT (PUBLISHING); HOUSE ORGANS; NEWSLETTERS; NEWSPAPERS; TRADE JOURNALS

GENERAL WORKS

Business Journals of the United States: Historical Guides to the World's Periodicals and Newspapers. William Fisher, editor. Greenwood Publishing Group, Inc. • 1991. $82.95. Contains historical and descriptive essays covering over 100 leading business publications.

Introduction to Serial Management. Marcia Tuttle. Elsevier. • 1983. $78.50. (Foundations in Library and Information Science Series, Vol. 11).

Towards Electronic Journals: Realities for Scientists, Librarians, and Publishers. Carol Tenopir and Donald W. King. Special Libraries Association. • 2000. $59.00. Discusses journals in electronic form vs. traditional (paper) scholarly journals, including the impact of subscription prices.

ABSTRACTS AND INDEXES

Applied Science and Technology Index. H. W. Wilson Co. • 11 times a year. Quarterly and annual cumulations. Price varies. Indexes a wide variety of English language technical, industrial, and engineering periodicals.

Business Periodicals Index. H. W. Wilson Co. • 11 times a year. Quarterly and annual cumulations. Price varies.

Canadian Periodical Index. Gale Cengage Learning. • Monthly. $595.00 per year. Annual cumulation. Indexes more than 400 English and French language periodicals.

Humanities Index. H. W. Wilson Co. • Quarterly. Annual cumulation. Price varies.

Readers' Guide to Periodical Literature. H. W. Wilson Co. • Monthly. $345.00 per year. Includes annual *Cumulation*. Indexes about 250 peridicals of general interest.

Social Sciences Index. H. W. Wilson Co. • Quarterly, with annual cumulation. Price varies. Indexes more than 400 periodicals covering economics, environmental policy, government, insurance, labor, health care policy, plannning, public administration, public welfare, urban studies, women's issues, criminology, and related topics.

U. S. Government Periodicals Index. Congressional Information Service, Inc. • Quarterly. $995.00 per year; with annual cumulation, $1,295.00 per year. An index to approximately 180 periodicals issued by various agencies of the federal government.

BIBLIOGRAPHIES

Guide to Special Issues and Indexes of Periodicals. Miriam Uhlan and Doris B. Katz, editors. Special Libraries Association. • 1994. $59.00. Fourth edition. A listing, with prices, of the special issues of over 1700 U. S. and Canadian periodicals in business, industry, technology, science, and the arts. Includes a comprehensive subject index.

Magazines for Libraries: Reviewing the Best Publications for All Serials Collections Since 1969. R. R. Bowker. • 2002. 12th edition. $225.00.

U.S. Government Subscriptions. U. S. Government Printing Office. • Quarterly. Free. Includes agency and subject indexes.

CD-ROM DATABASES

CPI.Q: The Canadian Periodical Index Full-Text on CD-ROM. Gale Cengage Learning. • Bimonthly.

Provides CD-ROM citations from 1988 to date for more than 400 English and French language periodicals. Contains full-text coverage from 1995 to date for 150 periodicals.

Leadership Library on CD-ROM: Who's Who in the Leadership of the United States. Leadership Directories, Inc. • Quarterly. Including access to Internet version (weekly updates). Contains all 14 *Yellow Book* personnel directories on CD-ROM, providing contact and brief biographical information for about 400,000 individuals. Covers business, government, financial institutions, news media, law firms, associations, foreign representatives, and nonprofit organizations. Includes photographs.

Magazine Index Plus. Gale Cengage Learning. • Monthly. $4,000.00 per year (includes InfoTrac workstation). Provides full text on CD-ROM for about 100 popular, general interest magazines and indexing for 300 others. Includes special indexing of reviews and product evaluations. Time period is 1980 to date.

MediaFinder CD-ROM: Oxbridge Directories of Print Media and Catalogs. Oxbridge Communications, Inc. • Quarterly. $1,995.00 per year. CD-ROM includes about 100,000 listings from *Standard Periodical Directory, National Directory of Catalogs, National Directory of British Mail Order Catalogs, National Directory of German Mail Order Catalogs, Oxbridge Directory of Newsletters, National Directory of Mailing Lists, College Media Directory,* and *National Directory of Magazines.*

Serials Directory: EBSCO CD-ROM. Ebsco Publishing. • Quarterly. The CD-ROM version of Ebsco's *The Serials Directory: An International Reference Book.*

Social Sciences Citation Index. ISI. • Monthly. Price on request. Provides CD-ROM indexing of articles appearing in 1700 leading social science journals worldwide, with additional selections from more than 5700 other journals. Time span is 1992 to date. Coverage includes economics, business, finance, management, communications, demographics, library and information science, political science, sociology, and many other subjects.

Social Sciences Citation Index: Compact Disc Edition with Abstracts. Institute for Scientific Information. • Monthly. Provides CD-ROM indexing and abstracting of "significant articles" from 1,700 social science journals worldwide, with additional selections from 3,200 other journals, 1986 to date. Includes economics, business, finance, management, communications, demographics, information and library science, political science, sociology, and many other subjects.

Ulrich's on Disc: The Complete International Serials Database on Compact Laser Disc. Bowker Electronic Publishing. • Quarterly. $950.00 per year. The CD-ROM version of *Ulrich's International Periodicals Directory* and *Magazines for Libraries.*

WILSONDISC: Wilson Social Sciences Abstracts. H. W. Wilson Co. • Monthly. Includes unlimited online access to *Social Sciences Index* through WILSONLINE. Provides CD-ROM indexing from 1983 and abstracting from 1994 of more than 500 periodicals covering economics, area studies, community health, public administration, public welfare, urban studies, and many other topics related to the social sciences.

DIRECTORIES

Books and Periodicals Online: The Guide to Business and Legal Information on Databases and CD-ROM's. Nuchine Nobari, editor. Library Technology Alliance, Ltd. • Annual. $379.00. Two volumes. 119,000 periodicals available as part of online and CD-ROM databases; international coverage.

Burrelle's Media Directory: Magazines and Newsletters. Burrelle's Information Services. • Annual. $550.00. Provides detailed descriptions of

more than 13,500 magazines and newsletters published in the U. S., Canada, and Mexico. Categories are professional, consumer, trade, and college. Semiannual *Updates.* Includes CD-ROM.

Cabell's Directory of Publishing Opportunities in Curriculum and Methods. Cabell Publishing Co. • 2002. $99.95. Over 350 journals in education which will consider manuscripts for publication. Formerly *Cabell's Directory of Publishing Opportunities in Education.*

Cabell's Directory of Publishing Opportunities in Management. Cabell Publishing Co. • 1997. $149.95. Seventh edition. Four volumes. Over 540 scholarly periodicals in management.

CARD The Media Information Network. Rogers Media Publishing. • Covers: Radio and television stations and networks; daily and weekend newspapers; consumer, farm, and business publications; advertising agencies and international media representatives; advertising, marketing, and media associations; and transportation and out-of-home advertising. Entries include: For publications--Title, company name, address, phone, frequency, names and titles of key personnel, advertising rates, discounts, mechanical requirements, copy regulations, circulation, closing and publication dates. For broadcasting stations--Call letters, name of owning company, address, phone, name of firm or individual representing station for advertising, special features, format, facilities, affiliations, rates, participation programs. For agencies and associations--Name, address, phone, personnel.

Cyberhound's Guide to Publications on the Internet. Gale Cengage Learning. • 1996. $79.00. Presents critical descriptions and ratings of more than 3,400 Internet databases of journals, newspapers, newsletters, and other publications. Includes a glossary of Internet terms, a bibliography, and three indexes. (Cyberhound's Series).

The Directory of Business Information Resources: Associations, Newsletters, Magazine Trade Shows. Grey House Publishing, Inc. • Annual. $250.00. Provides concise information on associations, newsletters, magazines, and trade shows for each of 90 major industry groups. An "Entry & Company Index" serves as a guide to titles, publishers, and organizations.

Fulltext Sources Online. Information Today Inc. • Covers: over 21,000 periodicals, newspapers, newsletters, newswires; and tv/radio transcripts available in full text online. Entries include: Name of file, online services through which available, dates of coverage, lag time if applicable. Separate list gives online service address and phone; indicates degree of online coverage and selection policy. Internet url's listed where applicable.

Gale Directory of Publications and Broadcast Media. Gale Cengage Learning. • Annual. $770.00. Five volumes. *Interedition Supplement,* Free. A guide to publications and broadcasting stations in the U. S. and Canada, including newspapers, magazines, journals, radio stations, television stations, and cable systems. Geographic arrangement. Volume three consists of statistical tables, maps, subject indexes, and title index.

International Directory of Little Magazines and Small Presses. Dustbooks. • Annual. $55.00. Over 5,000 small, independent magazines, presses, and papers.

Magazines Career Directory: A Practical One-Stop Guide to Getting a Job in Publ c Relations. Visible Ink Press. • 1993. $39.00. Fifth edition. Includes information on magazine publishing careers in art, editing, sales, and business management. Provides advice from "insiders," resume suggestions, a directory of companies that may offer entry-level positions, and a directory of career information sources. (Career Advisor Series).

News Media Yellow Book: Who's Who Among Reporters, Writers, Editors, and Producers in the Leading National News Media. Leadership Directories, Inc. • Quarterly. $360.00 per year. Lists the staffs of major newspapers and news magazines, TV and radio networks, news services and bureaus, and feature syndicates. Includes syndicated columnists and programs. Seven specialized indexes are provided.

Samir Husni's Guide to New Consumer Magazines. Samir Husni. R. R. Bowker. • Annual. $95.00. A directory of more than 540 consumer magazines that began publication during the previous year. Includes names of key personnel.

Serials Directory: An International Reference Book. EBSCO Publishing Inc. • Covers: Over 185,000 current and ceased periodicals and serials worldwide. Entries include: Serial title, publisher, address, phone, price, ISSN; Library of Congress, Dewey Decimal, National Library of Medicine, and Universal Decimal classification numbers; CODEN designations, description of editorial content; whether publication is peer reviewed; name of advertising manager; registration at the Copyright Clearance Center. Other format availabilities (CD-Rom), indexing and abstracting information.

SRDS Consumer Magazine Advertising Source. SRDS. • Annual. $699.00 per year. Contains advertising rates and other data for U. S. consumer magazines and agricultural publications. Also provides consumer market data for population, households, income, and retail sales. Formerly *Consumer Magazine and Advertising Source.*

SRDS International Media Guides. SRDS. • Covers: In five volumes (Newspapers worldwide, Consumer magazines worldwide, Business Publications: Asia-Pacific/Middle East/Africa, Business Publications: Europe, Business Publications: The Americas), advertising rates and data for 20,000 newspapers, consumer magazines and business publications worldwide. Entries include: contact names, addresses, phone and fax numbers, and e-mail.

SRDS Print Media Production Source. SRDS. • Quarterly. $808.00 per year. Contains details of printing and mechanical production requirements for advertising in specific trade journals, consumer magazines, and newspapers. Formerly *Print Media Production Source.*

Standard Periodical Directory. Oxbridge Communications Inc. • Covers: 58,000 magazines, journals, newsletters, directories, house organs, association publications, etc. , in the United States and Canada. Entries include: Publication current and former title; publisher name, address, phone; names and titles of key personnel; circulation and advertising rates; description of contents; ISSN, year founded, frequency; subscription rates, print method, page size, number of pages.

Ulrich's Periodicals Directory. R.R. Bowker L.L.C. • Covers: nearly 186,000 current periodicals and newspapers published worldwide. Entries include: In main list--Publication title; Dewey Decimal Classification number, Library of Congress Classification Number (where applicable), CODEN designation (for sci-tech serials), British Library Document Supply Centre shelfmark number, country code, ISSN; subtitle, language(s) of text, year first published, frequency, subscription prices, sponsoring organization, publishing company name, address, phone, fax, e-mail and website addresses, editor and publisher names; regular features (reviews, advertising, abstracts, bibliographies, trade literature, etc.), indexes, circulation, format, brief description of content; availability of microforms and reprints; whether refereed; CD-ROM availability with vendor name; online availability with service name; services that index or abstract the periodical, with years covered; advertising rates and

contact; right and permissions contact name and phone; availability through document deliver.

Working Press of the Nation. R. R. Bowker. • Annual. $530.00. $295.00 per volume. Three volumes: (1) *Newspaper Directory*; (2) *Magazine and Internal Publications Directory*; (3) *Radio and Television Directory*. Includes names of editors and other personnel.

ENCYCLOPEDIAS AND DICTIONARIES

Periodical Title Abbreviations. Gale Cengage Learning. • 2002. $520.00. 14th edition. Two volumes. $260.00 per volume Vol. 1 *By Abbreviation*; vol. 2 *By Title*. Lists more than 145,000 different abbreviations.

FINANCIAL RATIOS

Almanac of Business and Industrial Financial Ratios. Leo Troy. Aspen Publishers, Inc. • 2003. $125.95. Includes CD-Rom. Contains financial ratios derived from federal tax returns. Ratios for each of about 200 industries are arranged according to company asset size. (Almanac of Business and Industrial Financial Ratios Series).

Annual Statement Studies. The Risk Management Association. • Annual. Median and quartile financial ratios are given for over 400 kinds of manufacturing, wholesale, retail, construction, and consumer finance establishments. Data is sorted by both asset size and sales volume. Includes a clearly written "Definition of Ratios" and an alphabetical industry index.

Annual Statement Studies: Industry Default Probabilities and Cash Flow Measures. The Risk Management Association. • Annual. $145.00. Serves as a companion volume to the original *Annual Statement Studies*. Gives probability of default estimates on a percentage scale for more than 450 industries. Includes changes in position year-by-year for eight financial statement line items and provides percentage measures of cash flow.

HANDBOOKS AND MANUALS

Buying Serials: A How-To-Do-It Manual for Librarians. N. Bernard Basch and Judy McQueen. Neal-Schuman Publishers, Inc. • 1990. $49.95. (How-to-Do-It Manuals Series).

Developing and Managing Electronic Journal Collections: A How-To-DoIt Manual forLibrarians. Donnelyn Curtis and others. Neal-Schuman Publishers, Inc. • 2000. $55.00. Covers the acquisition, management, and integration of journals published in electronic form. (How-To-Do-It Manuals Series).

INTERNET DATABASES

EBSCO Information Services. Ebsco Publishing. Phone: 800-653-2726 or (978)356-6500 Fax: (978)356-6565 E-mail: ep@epnet.com • URL: http://www.epnet.com • Fee-based Web site providing Internet access to a wide variety of databases, including business-related material. Full text is available for many periodical titles, with daily updates. Fees: Apply.

ProQuest Direct. ProQuest Inc. Phone: 800-889-3358 or (734)761-4700 Fax: (734)662-4554 • URL: http://proquest.com • Fee-based Web site providing Internet access to more than 3,000 periodicals, newspapers, and other publications. Many items are available full-text, with daily updates. Includes extensive corporate and financial information. Fees: Apply.

PubList.com: The Internet Directory of Publications. Bowes & Associates, Inc. Phone: (781)792-0999 Fax: (781)792-0988 E-mail: info@publist.com • URL: http://www.publist.com • "The premier online global resource for information about print and electronic publications." Provides online searching for information on more than 150,000 magazines, journals, newsletters, e-journals, and monographs. Database entries generally include

title, publisher, format, address, editor, circulation, subject, and International Standard Serial Number (ISSN). Fees: Free.

Ulrichsweb.com. R. R. Bowker. Phone: 888-269-5372 or (908)464-6800 Fax: (908)464-3553 E-mail: info@bowker.com • URL: http://www.ulrichsweb.com • Web site provides fee-based access to about 250,000 serials records from the *Ulrich's International Periodicals Directory* database. Includes periodical evaluations from *Library Journal* and *Magazines for Libraries.* Monthly updates.

WilsonWeb Periodicals Databases. H. W. Wilson. Phone: 800-367-6770 or (718)588-8400 Fax: 800-590-1617 or (718)992-8003 E-mail: custserv@hwwilson.com • URL: http://www.hwwilson.com/ • Web sites provide fee-based access to *Wilson Business Full Text, Applied Science & Technology Full Text, Biological & Agricultural Index, Library Literature & Information Science Full Text,* and *Readers' Guide Full Text, Mega Edition.* Daily updates.

ONLINE DATABASES

Gale Database of Publications and Broadcast Media. Gale Cengage Learning. • An online directory containing detailed information on over 67,000 periodicals, newspapers, broadcast stations, cable systems, directories, and newsletters. Corresponds to the following print sources: *Gale Directory of Publications and Broadcast Media; Directories in Print; City and State Directories in Print; Newsletters in Print.* Semiannual updates. Inquire as to online cost and availability.

Magazine Index. Gale Cengage Learning. • General magazine indexing (popular literature), 1973 to present. Daily updates. Inquire as to online cost and availability.

Newspaper Abstracts Daily. ProQuest Inc. • Provides online coverage (citations and abstracts) of 25 major newspapers. Covers business, economics, current affairs, health, fitness, sports, education, technology, government, consumer affairs, psychology, the arts, and the social sciences. Time period is 1986 to date, with daily updates. Inquire as to online cost and availability.

Trade & Industry Database. Gale Cengage Learning. • Provides indexing of business periodicals, January 1981 to date. Daily updates. (Full text articles from some periodicals are available online, 1983 to date. Inquire as to online cost and availability).

Ulrich's International Periodicals Directory Online. Bowker Electronic Publishing. • Includes over 275,000 periodicals currently published worldwide and publications discontinued. Corresponds to *Ulrich's International Periodcals Directory, Irregular Serials and Annuals, Bowker International Serials Database Update,* and *Sources of Serials.* Inquire as to online cost and availability.

Wilson Social Sciences Abstracts Online. H. W. Wilson Co. • Provides online abstracting and indexing of more than 500 periodicals covering area studies, community health, public administration, public welfare, urban studies, and many other social science topics. Time period is 1994 to date for abstracts and 1983 to date for indexing, with updates weekly. Inquire as to online cost and availability.

PERIODICALS AND NEWSLETTERS

Circulation Management. Media Central. • Monthly. $39.00 per year. Edited for circulation professionals in the magazine and newsletter publishing industry. Covers marketing, planning, promotion, management, budgeting, and related topics.

Folio: The New Dynamics of Magazine Publishing. Primedia Business Magazines and Media. • Monthly. $96.00 per year.

Magazine and Bookseller: The Retailer's Guide to Magazines and Paperbacks. North American Publishing Co. • Bimonthly. Free to qualified personnel; others, $59.00 per year.

The Serials Librarian: The International Quarterly Journal of Theory, Research and Practice on Serial, Continuing, and Integrating Print and Electronic Resources. Haworth Press, Inc. • Quarterly. Institutions, $275.50 per year. Two volumes.

Serials Review. JAI Press. • Quarterly. Individuals, $101.00 per year; institutions, $274.00 per year.

STATISTICS SOURCES

Computer Publishing Market Forecast. SIMBA Information. • Biennial. $1,895.00. Provides market data on computer-related books, magazines, newsletters, and other publications. Includes profiles of major publishers of computer-related material.

U. S. Industry and Trade Outlook. Available from National Technical Information Service. • Annual. $69.95. Produced by the International Trade Administration, U. S. Department of Commerce, in a "public-private" partnership with DRI/McGraw-Hill and Standard & Poor's. Provides basic data, outlook for the current year, and "Long-Term Prospects" (five-year projections) for a wide variety of products and services. Includes high technology industries. Formerly *U. S. Industrial Outlook.*

TRADE/PROFESSIONAL ASSOCIATIONS

American Society of Magazine Editors. c/o Magazine Publishers of America, 810 Seventh Ave., 24th Fl., New York, NY 10019. Phone: (212)872-3737 E-mail: asme@magazine.org • URL: http://www.magazine.org.

Audit Bureau of Circulations. 900 N. Meacham Rd., Schaumburg, IL 60173-4968. Phone: (847)605-0909 Fax: (847)605-0483 E-mail: corpcomdebt@accessabc.com • URL: http://www.accessabc.com • Verifies newspaper and periodical circulation statements. Includes a Business Publications Industry Committee and a Magazine Directors Advisory Committee.

BPA International. 2 Corporate Dr., Ste. 900, Shelton, CT 06484. Phone: (203)447-2800 Fax: (203)447-2900 E-mail: info@bpai.com • URL: http://www.bpai.com • Verifies business and consumer periodical circulation statements. Includes a Circulation Managers Committee. Formerly Business Publications Audit of Circulation.

Magazine Publishers of America. 919 Third Ave., 22nd Fl., New York, NY 10022. Phone: (212)872-3700 Fax: (212)888-4217 E-mail: infocenter@magazine.org • URL: http://www.magazine.org • Members are publishers of consumer and other periodicals. Affiliated with American Society of Magazine Editors; Media Credit Association; Publishers Information Bureau. Formerly Magazine Publishers Association.

Publishers Information Bureau. 810 7th Ave., 24th Fl., New York, NY 10019. Phone: 888-567-3227 or (212)872-3722 Fax: (212)753-2768 E-mail: pib@magazine.org • URL: http://www.magazine.org • Measures the amount and type of advertising in magazines and reports this information monthly through printed and electronic formats; service prepared by TNSMI/Competitive Media Reporting (contracting agent).

OTHER SOURCES

Bacon's Newspaper and Magazine Directories. Bacon's Information Inc. • Annual. $325.00 per year. Two volumes: Magazines and Newspapers. Covers print media in the United States and Canada. Formerly *Bacon's Publicity Checker.*

PERIODICALS, BUSINESS

See: TRADE JOURNALS

PERSONAL CARE PRODUCTS

See: COSMETICS INDUSTRY

PERSONAL COMPUTERS

See: MICROCOMPUTERS AND MINICOMPUTERS; PORTABLE COMPUTERS

PERSONAL FINANCE

See also: ESTATE PLANNING; FINANCIAL PLANNING; HOME OWNERSHIP; INVESTMENTS; LIFE INSURANCE; PENSIONS; TAX SHELTERS

GENERAL WORKS

Consumer Reports Money Book: How to Get It, Save It, and Spend It Wisely. Janet Bamford and others. Consumers Union of the United States, Inc. • 2000. $19.95. Third edition. Covers budgeting, retirement planning, bank accounts, insurance, and other personal finance topics.

Don't Die Broke: How to Turn Your Retirement Savings into Lasting Income. Margaret A. Malaspina. Bloomberg. • 1999. $21.95. Provides advice on such matters as retirement portfolio asset allocation and retirement spending accounts. (Bloomberg Personal Bookshelf Series).

Everyone's Money Book: Everything You Need to Know About Investing Wisely, Buying a Home... Jordan E. Goodman. Dearborn Trade Publishing, A Kaplan Professional Co. • 2001. $30.00. Third edition. Covers investing, taxes, mortgages, retirement planning and other personal finance topics. Jordan E. Goodman is a writer for *Money* magazine.

Financial Planning for the Utterly Confused. Joel Lerner. McGraw-Hill. • 1998. $12.95. Fifth edition. Covers annuities, certificates of deposit, bonds, mutual funds, insurance, home ownership, retirement, social security, wills, etc.

The Fragile Middle Class: Americans in Debt. Teresa A. Sullivan and others. Yale University Press. • 2000. $40.00. Provides an analysis of a 1991 survey of personal bankruptcies in five states of the U. S. Serves as a sequel to the authors' *As We Forgive Our Debtors* (1989), an analysis of 1981 bankruptcies.

How to Avoid Financial Tangles. American Institute for Economic Research. • 2001. $8.00. Provides basic information and advice on such topics as property ownership, taxes, wills, trusts, insurance, record retention, and professional assistance. (Economic Education Bulletin.).

Never Call Your Broker on Monday: And 300 Other Financial Lessons You Can't Afford Not to Know. Nancy Dunnan. HarperInformation. • 1997. $8.50. Presents a wide range of personal finance advice, covering investments, insurance, wills, credit, real estate, etc.

New Century Family Money Book: Your Comprehensive Guide to a Lifetime of Financial Security. Jonathan D. Pond. Bantam Dell Publishing Group. • 1995. $11.00.

A Random Walk Down Wall Street: The Best Investment Advice for the New Century. Burton G. Malkiel. W. W. Norton & Co., Inc. • 1999. $29.95. Seventh revised edition.

Staying Wealthy: Strategies for Protecting Your Assets. Brian H. Breuel. Bloomberg. • 1998. $21.95. Presents ideas for estate planning and personal wealth preservation. Includes case studies. (Bloomberg Personal Bookshelf Series).

CD-ROM DATABASES

Magazine Index Plus. Gale Cengage Learning. • Monthly. $4,000.00 per year (includes InfoTrac

workstation). Provides full text on CD-ROM for about 100 popular, general interest magazines and indexing for 300 others. Includes special indexing of reviews and product evaluations. Time period is 1980 to date.

Newspaper Abstracts Ondisc. PROQUEST. • Monthly. $2,950.00 per year (covers 1989 to date; archival discs are available for 1985-88). Provides cover-to-cover CD-ROM indexing and abstracting of 19 major newspapers, including the *New York Times, Wall Street Journal, Washington Post, Chicago Tribune,* and *Los Angeles Times.*

WILSONDISC: Readers' Guide to Periodical Literature. H. W. Wilson Co. • Monthly. $1,095.00 per year, including unlimited online access to *Readers' Guide to Periodical Literature* through WILSONLINE. Provides CD-ROM indexing of about 270 general interest periodicals. Covers 1983 to date. (*Readers' Guide Abstracts* also available on CD-ROM at $1,995 per year.).

DIRECTORIES

How to Save on Prescription Drugs: The AIER Guide to Prescription Drug Assistance Programs for Seniors. Kerry A. Lynch. American Institute for Economic Research. • 2003. $5.00. Contains a state-by-state directory of 39 state assistance programs offering prescription drug coverage, usually for low-income residents age 65 or older. Provides phone numbers, websites, coverage, eligibility details, and "How it works" for each state. A separate section describes five drug company discount cards. (Economic Education Bulletin.).

Plunkett's On-Line Trading, Finance, and Investment Web Sites Almanac. Plunkett Research, Ltd. • Annual. $149.99. Provides profiles and usefulness rankings of financial Web sites. Sites are rated from 1 to 5 for specific uses. Includes CD-ROM.

FINANCIAL RATIOS

Financial Planning for Older Clients. James E. Pearman. CCH, Inc. • 2000. $49.00. Covers income sources, social security, Medicare, Medicaid, investment planning, estate planning, and other retirement-related topics. Edited for accountants, attorneys, and other financial advisors. (Solutions for Professional Advisors Series).

HANDBOOKS AND MANUALS

Barron's Finance & Investment Handbook. John Downes and Jordan Goodman. Barron's Educational Series, Inc. • 1998. $35.00. Fifth edition. Mainly concerned with personal finance, including advice on stocks, bonds, mutual funds, annuities, life insurance, real estate, futures, and collectibles. Includes a glossary of financial and investment terms.

Best Practices for Financial Advisors. Mary Rowland. Bloomberg. • 1997. $40.00. Provides advice for professional financial advisors on practice management, ethics, marketing, and legal concerns. (Bloomberg Professional Library.).

Complete Book of Personal Legal Forms. Daniel Sitarz. Nova Publishing Co. • 2001. $24.95. Third edition. Provides more than 100 forms, including contracts, bills of sale, promissory notes, leases, deeds, receipts, and wills. Forms are also available on IBM or MAC diskettes. (Legal Self-Help Series).

Credit Consulting. Entrepreneur Media, Inc. • Looseleaf. $59.50. A practical guide to starting a consumer credit and debt counseling and consulting service. Covers profit potential, start-up costs, market size evaluation, owner's time required, pricing, accounting, advertising, promotion, etc. (Start-Up Business Guide No. E1321.).

Ernst & Young's Personal Financial Planning Guide. John Wiley and Sons, Inc. • 2001. $19.95. Fourth edition.

Estate and Retirement Planning Answer Book. William D. Mitchell. Aspen Publishers, Inc. • 2000.

$145.00. Third edition. Basic questions and answers by a lawyer.

Getting Started in Investment Planning Services. James E. Grant. CCH, Inc. • 1999. $85.00. Second edition. Provides advice and information for lawyers and accountants who are planning to initiate fee-based investment services.

Homeowner or Tenant? How to Make a Wise Choice. Lawrence S. Pratt. American Institute for Economic Research. • 2002. $8.00. Provides detailed information for making rent or buy decisions. Includes "Mortgage Arithmetic," "Hints for Buyers, Sellers, and Renters," worksheets, mortgage loan interest tables, and other data. (Economic Education Bulletin.).

Mining for Gold on the Internet: How to Find Investment and Financial Information on the Internet. Mary Ellen Bates. McGraw-Hill. • 2000. $24.95. Tells how to effectively search the Internet for financial advice and information. Specific websites are discussed.

Personal Finance. Robert Rosefsky. John Wiley and Sons, Inc. • 2001. $96.95. Eighth edition.

Personal Financial Planning. G. Victor Hallman and Jerry S. Rosenbloom. McGraw-Hill. • 2003. $49.95. Seventh edition.

Personal Financial Planning: The Advisor's Guide. Rolf Austen. CCH, Inc. • 1998. $55.95. Third edition. Covers personal taxes, investments, credit, mortgages, insurance, pensions, social security, estate planning, etc.

Tools and Techniques of Financial Planning. Stephan Leimberg and others. National Underwriter Co. • 2004. $74.95.

Wall Street Journal Guide to Planning Your Financial Future: The Easy-to-Read Guide to Lifetime Planning for Retirement. Kenneth M. Morris and Virginia B. Morris. Simon & Schuster Trade. • 2002. $15.95. Third edition. (Wall Street Journal Guides Series).

INTERNET DATABASES

BanxQuote Banking, Mortgage, and Finance Center. BanxQuote, Inc. Phone: (914)722-1600 Fax: (914)722-6630 E-mail: info@banx.com • URL: http://www.banx.com • Web site quotes interest rates paid by banks around the country on various savings products, as well as rates paid by consumers for automobile loans, mortgages, credit cards, home equity loans, and personal loans. Also provided: stock quotes, indexes, stock options, futures trading data, economic indicators, and links to many other financial sites. Daily updates. Fees: Free.

ONLINE DATABASES

Banking Information Source. PROQUEST. • Provides indexing and abstracting of periodical and other literature from 1982 to date, with weekly updates. Covers the financial services industry: banks, savings institutions, investment houses, credit unions, insurance companies, and real estate organizations. Emphasis is on marketing and management. Inquire as to online cost and availability. (Formerly *FINIS: Financial Industry Information Service.*).

Information Bank Abstracts. New York Times Index Dept. • Provides indexing and abstracting of current affairs, primarily from the final late edition of *The New York Times* and the Eastern edition of *The Wall Street Journal.* Time period is 1969 to present, with daily updates. Inquire as to online cost and availability.

PAIS International. Public Affairs Information Service, Inc. • Corresponds to the former printed publications, *PAIS Bulletin* (1976-90) and *PAIS Foreign Language Index* (1972-90), and to the current *PAIS International in Print* (1991 to date). Covers economic, political, and sociological material appearing in periodicals, books, government documents, and other publications. Updating is monthly. Inquire as to online cost and availability.

Readers' Guide Abstracts Online. H. W. Wilson Co. • Indexes and abstracts general interest periodicals, 1983 to date. Weekly updates. Inquire as to online cost and availability.

PERIODICALS AND NEWSLETTERS

American Banker: The Financial Services Daily. Thomson Media. • Daily. $895.00 per year. Provides news of banking, investment products, mortgages, credit unions, finance, bank technology, and legal developments.

Barron's: The Dow Jones Business and Financial Weekly. • Weekly. $145.00 per year.

Bottom Line/Personal. Boardroom Inc. • Description: Publishes "expert advice on how to live longer, better, richer, and wiser." Covers topical issues with a personal slant aimed at helping those involved with careers handle their personal lives more successfully. Features articles on tax issues, money information, traveling, family, friends, and general health and happiness. Contains informational items throughout on various aspects of business/personal life.

Estate Planner's Alert. RIA. • Monthly. $140.00 per year. Newsletter. Covers the tax aspects of personal finance, including home ownership, investments, insurance, retirement planning, and charitable giving. Formerly *Estate and Financial Planners Alert.*

Family Economics and Nutrition Review. Available from U. S. Government Printing Office. • Semi-annual. $13.00 per year. Issued by the Consumer and Food Economics Institute, U. S. Department of Agriculture. Provides articles on consumer expenditures and budgeting for food, clothing, housing, energy, education, etc.

Financial Counseling and Planning. Association for Financial Counseling and Planning Education. • Semiannual. Members, $60. per year; institutional members, $100.00 per year; libraries, $60.00 per year. Disseminates scholarly research relating to financial planning and counseling .

Forbes. Forbes, Inc. • Biweekly. $59.95 per year. Includes supplements: *Forbes ASAP* and *Forbes FYI.*

Investment Advisor: The Advisor to Advisors. Wicks Business Information. • Monthly. $79.00 per year. Edited for professional investment advisors, financial planners, stock brokers, bankers, and others concerned with the management of assets.

Investment News: The Weekly Newspaper for Financial Advisers. Crain Communications, Inc. • Weekly. $29.00 per year. Edited for both personal and institutional investment advisers, planners, and managers.

The Investment Reporter. MPL Communications Inc. • Description: Profiles specific companies and market trends and developments, making recommendations to assist in formulating investment strategies. Includes short articles offering advice on investment decisions.

Journal of Wealth Management. Institutional Investor, Inc., Journals Group. • Quarterly. $410.00 per year. Includes print and online editions. Edited for managers of wealthy individuals' investment portfolios. Formerly *Journal of Private Portfolio Management.*

Kiplinger's Personal Finance Magazine. Kiplinger Washington Editors, Inc. • Monthly. $23.95 per year.

Money. • 13 times a year. $19.95 per year. Covers all aspects of family finance; investments, careers, shopping, taxes, insurance, consumerism, etc.

Personal Finance. KCI Communications Inc. • Description: Contains articles on subjects of interest to those investigating personal finance strategies.

Provides news, information, and suggestions on investment decisions. Covers stock and growth stock activity, individual retirement accounts, market trends and developments, and real estate. Recurring features include columns titled Capsule Advisory and Answers to Your Money Questions.

Predictions: Specific Investment Forecasts and Recommendations from the World's Top Financial Experts. Lee Euler, editor. Agora, Inc. • Monthly. $78.00 per year. Newsletter.

Private Asset Management. Institutional Investor, Inc., Journals Group. • Biweekly. $2,335.00 per year. Newsletter. Includes print and online editions. Edited for managers investing the private assets of wealthy ("high-net-worth") individuals. Includes marketing, taxation, regulation, and fee topics.

U. S. Banker. Thomson Media. • Monthly. $65.00 per year. Edited for bank executives and managers. Covers a wide variety of banking and financial topics.

RESEARCH CENTERS AND INSTITUTES

American Institute for Economic Research. P.O. Box 1000, Great Barrington, MA 01230. Phone: (413)528-1216 Fax: (413)528-0103 E-mail: info@aier.org • URL: http://www.aier.org.

Center for Financial Responsibility. College of Human Sciences, Box 41162, Texas Tech University, Lubbock, TX 79409-1162. Phone: (806)742-9781 Fax: (806)742-9784 E-mail: bill.gustafson@ttu.edu • URL: http://www.hs.ttu.edu/cfr/ • Research areas include financial preparation for retirement, financial education, determinants of financial satisfaction, risk tolerance, and the career preparation of retirement industry professionals.

C.V. Starr Center for Applied Economics. New York University, Dept. of Economics, 269 Mercer St., 3rd Fl., New York, NY 10003. Phone: (212)998-8936 Fax: (212)995-3932 • URL: http://www.econ.nyu.edu/.

STATISTICS SOURCES

Consumer Expenditure Survey. Available from U. S. Government Printing Office. • Biennial. Issued by the Bureau of Labor Statistics, U. S. Department of Labor (http://www.bls.gov). Contains data on various kinds of consumer spending, according to household income, education, etc. (Bureau of Labor Statistics Bulletin.).

Current Population Reports: Household Economic Studies, Series P-70. Available from U. S. Government Printing Office. • Irregular. $21.00 per year. Issued by the U.S. Bureau of the Census (http://www.census.gov). Each issue covers a special topic relating to household socioeconomic characteristics.

Statistical Information on the Financial Services Industry. American Bankers Association. • Annual. Members, $150.00; non-members, $275.00. Presents a wide variety of data relating to banking and financial services, including consumer economics, personal finance, credit, government loans, capital markets, and international banking.

Statistics of Income Bulletin. Available from U.S. Government Printing Office. • Quarterly. $44.00 per year. Current data compiled from tax returns relating to income, assets, and expenses of individuals and businesses. (U. S. Internal Revenue Service.).

Working Americans, 1880-1999, Volume One: The Working Class. Scott Derks, editor. Grey House Publishing. • 2000. $375.00. Provides detailed information on the lifestyles and economic life of working class families in the 12 decades from 1880 to 1999. Includes such items as selected consumer prices, income, family finances, budgets, life at home, jobs, and working conditions. (Universal Reference Publications.).

Working Americans, 1880-1999, Volume Two: The Middle Class. Scott Derks, editor. Grey House Publishing. • 2000. $135.00. Three volumes.

Furnishes details of the social and economic lives of middle class Americans during the years 1880 to 1999. Describes such items as selected consumer prices, income, family finances, budgets, life at home, jobs, and working conditions. (Universal Reference Publications.).

TRADE/PROFESSIONAL ASSOCIATIONS

Association for Financial Counseling and Planning Education. 2121 Arlington Ave., Ste. 5, Upper Arlington, OH 43221-4339. Phone: (614)485-9650 Fax: (614)485-9621 • URL: http://www.afcpe.org • Members are researchers, academics, financial counselors and financial planners.

Conference on Consumer Finance Law. Oklahoma City University School of Law, 2501 N Blackwelder, Oklahoma City, OK 73106-1493. Phone: 800-633-7242 or (405)521-5337 Fax: (405)521-5802 • URL: http://www.okcu.edu/law • Formerly Conference on Personal Finance Law.

Financial Planning Association. 4100 E Mississippi Ave., Ste. 400, Denver, CO 80246-3053. Phone: 800-322-4237 or (303)759-4910 Fax: (303)759-0749 E-mail: marv.tuttle@fpanet.org • URL: http://www.fpanet.org • Works to support the financial planning process in order to help people achieve their goals and dreams. Believes that everyone needs objective advice to make smart financial decisions and that when seeking the advice of a financial planner, the planner should be a CFP professional.

OTHER SOURCES

Divorce and Taxes. CCH, Inc. • 2000. $25.00. Second edition. In addition to tax problems, topics include alimony, division of property, and divorce decrees.

Family Law Tax Guide. CCH, Inc. • Monthly. $619.00 per year. Looseleaf service.

Financial Planning and Financial Planning Ideas. Prentice Hall PTR. • Two looseleaf volumes. Periodic supplementation. Price on application.

Individual Retirement Plans Guide. CCH, Inc. • $540.00 per year. Looseleaf service. Monthly updates. Covers IRA plans (Individual Retirement Accounts), SEP plans (Simplified Employee Pensions), and Keogh plans (self-employed retirement accounts).

PERSONAL FINANCE COMPANIES

See: FINANCE COMPANIES

PERSONNEL INTERVIEWING

See: INTERVIEWING

PERSONNEL MANAGEMENT

See also: HUMAN RELATIONS; INDUSTRIAL RELATIONS

GENERAL WORKS

Advancing Women in Business-The Catalyst Guide: Best Practices from the Corporate Leaders. Catalyst Staff. John Wiley and Sons, Inc. • 1998. $26.00. Explains the human resources practices of corporations providing a favorable climate for the advancement of female employees. (Jossey-Bass Business and Management Series).

EEO Law and Personnel Practices. Arthur Gutman. Sage Publications, Inc. • 2000. $93.95. Second edition. Discusses the practical effect of federal regulations dealing with race, color, religion, sex, national origin, age, and disability. Explains administrative procedures, litigation actions, and penalties. (Management Studies Series).

Human Resource Management. David A. DeCenzo and Stephen P. Robbins. John Wiley and Sons, Inc. • 2001. $89.95. Seventh edition.

Human Resource Management: A Strategic and Global Perspective. J.S. Black. Addison-Wesley. • 1997. Price on application.

Human Resource Management in the Knowledge Economy: New Challenges, New Roles, New Capabilities. Mark L. Lengnick-Hall and Cynthia A. Lengnick-Hall. Berrett-Koehler Publishers, Inc. • 2002. $24.95.

Human Resources. Richard B. Renckly. Barron's Educational Series, Inc. • 2004. $18.95. Second edition. Emphasis is on investigating, interviewing, hiring, and evaluating employees.

Human Resources and Personnel Management. William B. Werther and Keith Davis. McGraw-Hill. • 1995. $91.25. Fifth edition. (Management Series).

Managing Human Resources. Arthur W. Sherman and George Bohlander. Cengage Learning. • 2000. $50.50. 12th edition. (SWC-Management Series).

ABSTRACTS AND INDEXES

Business Periodicals Index. H. W. Wilson Co. • 11 times a year. Quarterly and annual cumulations. Price varies.

Human Resources Abstracts: An International Information Service. Sage Publications, Inc. • Quarterly. Institutions, $968.00 per year; includes print and online editions.

Personnel Management Abstracts. • Quarterly. $190.00 per year. Includes annual cumulation.

ALMANACS AND YEARBOOKS

Human Resources Yearbook. Craig T. Norback. Prentice Hall PTR. • 1997. $75.00.

Research in Personnel and Human Resources Management. Gerald D. Ferris, editor. Elsevier. • Dates vary. $78.50. 21 volumes.

CD-ROM DATABASES

WILSONDISC: Wilson Business Abstracts. H. W. Wilson Co. • Monthly. Includes unlimited online access to *Wilson Business Abstracts* through WILSONLINE. Provides CD-ROM "cover-to-cover" abstracting and indexing of over 600 prominent business periodicals. Indexing is from 1982, abstracting from 1990. (*Business Periodicals Index* without abstracts is available on CD-ROM at $1,495 per year.).

ENCYCLOPEDIAS AND DICTIONARIES

BLR Encyclopedia of Prewritten Job Descriptions. Stephen D. Bruce. Business and Legal Reports, Inc. • $159.95. Looseleaf service. Two volumes. Covers all levels "from president to mail clerk.".

Encyclopedia of Business. Gale Cengage Learning. • 2000. $425.00. Second edition. Two volumes. Contains more than 700 signed articles covering major business disciplines and concepts. International in scope. (Encyclopedia of Business Series).

Encyclopedia of Human Behavior. Vangipuram S. Ramachandran, editor. Elsevier. • 1994. $1,000.00. Four volumes. Contains signed articles on aptitude testing, arbitration, career development, consumer psychology, crisis management, decision making, economic behavior, group dynamics, leadership, motivation, negotiation, organizational behavior, planning, problem solving, stress, work efficiency, and other human behavior topics applicable to business situations.

HR Words You Gotta Know! Essential Human Resources, Terms, Laws, Acronyms and Abbreviations for Everyone in Business. William R. Tracey, editor. AMACOM. • 1994. $17.95. Explains important human relations management terms.

Human Resources Glossary: A Complete Desk Reference for HR Professionals. William R. Tracey.

Saint Lucie Press. • 1997. $79.95. Second edition.

HANDBOOKS AND MANUALS

AMA Management Handbook. John J. Hampton, editor. AMACOM. • 1994. $110.00. Third edition. Provides 200 chapters in 16 major subject areas. Covers a wide variety of business and industrial management topics.

Company Policy and Personnel Workbook. Ardella Ramey. PSI Research. • 1999. $29.95. Fourth edition. Contains about 50 model company personnel policies for use as examples in developing a personnel manual. Explains the basic laws governing employee-employer relationships. (Successful Business Library Series).

Fair, Square, and Legal: Safe Hiring, Managing, and Firing Practices to Keep You and Your Company Out of Court. Donald Weiss. AMACOM. • 1999. $29.95. Third edition. Covers recruiting, interviewing, sexual discrimination, evaluation of employees, disipline, defamation charges, and wrongful discharge.

Hiring Right: A Practical Guide. Susan J. Herman. Sage Publications, Inc. • 1994. $77.95. A practical manual covering job definition, recruitment, interviewing, testing, and checking of references.

How to Design and Install Management Incentive Compensation Plans: A Practical Guide to Installing Performance Bonus Plans. Dale Arahood. Dale Arahood and Associates. • 1996. $129.00. Revised edition. "This book focuses on how pay should be determined rather than how much should be paid.".

How to Develop a Personnel Policy Manual. Joseph Lawson. AMACOM. • 1998. $75.00. Sixth edition.

How to Develop an Employee Handbook. Joseph W. Lawson. AMACOM. • 1997. $75.00. Second edition. Includes sample handbooks, personnel policy statements, and forms.

Kennedy's Pocket Guide to Working with Executive Recruiters. James H. Kennedy, editor. Kennedy Information, Inc. • 2002. $17.95. Second revised editon. Consists of 30 chapters written by various experts. Includes a glossary: "Lexicon of Executive Recruiting.".

Library Personnel Administration. Lowell A. Martin. Scarecrow Press, Inc. • 1994. $35.00. (Library Administration Series: No. 11).

Personnel Management: Communications. Prentice Hall PTR. • Looseleaf. Periodic supplementation. Price on application. Includes how to write effectively and how to prepare employee publications.

Personnel Management: Compensation. Prentice Hall PTR. • Looseleaf. Periodic supplementation. Price on application.

Personnel Management: Labor Relations Guide. Prentice Hall PTR. • Three looseleaf volumes. Periodic supplementation. Price on application.

Personnel Management: Policies and Practices. Prentice Hall PTR. • Looseleaf. Periodic supplementation. Price on application.

Recruiting, Interviewing, Selecting, and Orienting New Employees. Diane Arthur. AMACOM. • 1998. $59.95. Third edition. A practical guide to the basics of hiring, including legal considerations and sample forms.

Sexual Orientation in the Workplace: Gays, Lesbians, Bisexuals and Heterosexuals Working Together. Amy J. Zuckerman and George F. Simons. Sage Publications, Inc. • 1994. $34.95. A workbook containing "a variety of simple tools and exercises" to provide skills for "working realistically and effectively with diverse colleagues.".

Studying Your Workforce: Applied Research Methods and Tools for the Training and Development Practitioner. Alan Clardy. Sage Publications, Inc. • 1997. $79.95. Describes how to apply specific research methods to common training problems.

Emphasis is on data collection methods: testing, observation, surveys, and interviews. Topics include performance problems and assessment.

Turning Your Human Resources Department into a Profit Center. Michael W. Mercer. AMACOM. • 1989. $59.95. Concerned with costs, employee efficiency, and productivity.

INTERNET DATABASES

Wageweb: Salary Survey Data On-Line. HRPDI: Human Resources Programs Development and Improvement. Phone: (804)363-1792 Fax: (804)594-3721 E-mail: salaries@wageweb.com • URL: http://www.wageweb.com • Web site provides salary information for more than 170 benchmark positions, including (for example) 29 information management jobs. Data shows average minimum, median, and average maximum compensation for each position, based on salary surveys. Fees: Free for national salary data; $169.00 per year for more detailed information (geographic, organization size, specific industries).

ONLINE DATABASES

Wilson Business Abstracts Online. H. W. Wilson Co. • Indexes and abstracts 600 major business periodicals, plus the *Wall Street Journal* and the business section of the *New York Times.* Indexing is from 1982, abstracting from 1990, with the two newspapers included from 1993. Updated weekly. Inquire as to online cost and availability. (*Business Periodicals Index* without abstracts is also available online.).

PERIODICALS AND NEWSLETTERS

Employment Law Strategist. Law Journal Newsletter. • Monthly. 279 individuals for print version per year. Covers employment law topics, including immigration laws, repetitive stress claims, workplace violence, liability of actions of intoxicated employees, record keeping, liability for fetal injury, independent contractor, and employee issues. Monthly. 229 individuals electronic edition. Description: Reports on legal strategy and substantive developments in the area of matrimonial law, including such topics as tax considerations, custody, visitation, division of property, and valuation. Recurring features include litigation roundup and a legislative update.

HR Focus: The Hands-On Tool for Human Resources Professionals. American Management Association. IOMA. • Monthly. $99.00 per year. Newsletter. Covers "all aspects of HR management," including corporate culture, the impact of technology, recruiting strategies, and training. Formerly *Personnel.*

HR Magazine (Human Resources): Strategies and Solutions for Human Resource Professionals. Society for Human Resource Management. • Monthly. Free to members; non-members, $70.00 per year. Formerly *Personnel Administrator.*

Human Resource Executive. LRP Publications. • 16 times a year. $89.95 per year. Edited for directors of corporate human resource departments. Special issues emphasize training, benefits, retirement planning, recruitment, outplacement, workers' compensation, legal pitfalls, and oes emphasize training, benefits, retirement planning, recruitment, outplacement, workers' compensation, legal pitfalls, and other personnel topics.

Human Resource Planning. Human Resource Planning Society. • Quarterly. $90.00 per year.

Law Firm Partnership and Benefits Report. American Lawyer Media, Inc. • Monthly. $215.00 per year. Newsletter. Covers personnel issues for law firms, including compensation, partnership agreements, malpractice, employment discrimination, training, health insurance, pension plans, and other matters relating to human resources management. (A Law Journal Newsletter, formerly published by Leader Publications).

People to People. American Public Power Association. • Description: Reports on public sector labor and personnel issues, especially those concerning the electric utility industry. Summarizes case studies in public labor relations.

Personnel Psychology. Personnel Psychology, Inc. • Quarterly. $70.00 per year. Publishes research articles and book reviews.

Perspective. Magna Publications Inc. • Description: Provides administrators with guidelines for keeping their schools out of court. Examines current trends in law related to higher education, as well as past and future legal issues affecting students, faculty, administrators and the public. Recurring features include columns titled Key Case Review, Follow-Up, Resources, Legislative Note, Outside the Courts, Cross-Examination, and Cases Noted.

Privacy and Information Law Report. Glasser Legalworks. • 10 times a year. $375.00 per year. Newsletter. Coverage includes the legal aspects of health record privacy, employee records, anti-spam, and privacy-enhancing technology. Provides reports on relevant court cases and consumer advocacy.

Public Personnel Management. International Personnel Management Association. • Quarterly. $50.00 per year.

Workforce: H R Trends and Tools for Business Results. Crain Communications, Inc. • Monthly. $59.00 per year. Edited for human resources managers. Covers employee benefits, compensation, relocation, recruitment, training, personnel legalities, and related subjects. Supplements include bimonthly "New Product News" and semiannual "Recruitment/Staffing Sourcebook." Formerly *Personnel Journal.*

RESEARCH CENTERS AND INSTITUTES

Center for Youth and Communities. Brandeis University, 60 Turner St., Waltham, MA 02453. Phone: (781)736-3770 Fax: (781)736-3773 E-mail: curran@brandeis.org • URL: http://www.heller. brandeis.edu/chr • Formerly Center for Human Resources.

Human Resources Research Organization. Human Resources Research Organization. 66 Canal Center Plz., Ste. 400, Alexandria, VA 22314-1591. Phone: (703)549-3611 Fax: (703)549-9025 E-mail: webmaster@humrro.orgg • URL: http://www. humrro.org • Training, training device requirements, instructional technology, recruitment and workforce analysis, personnel selection and classification, ability testing, simulation and modeling, system and job analysis, cognitive task analysis, performance appraisal, assessment centers, and program evaluation.

TRADE/PROFESSIONAL ASSOCIATIONS

Catalyst. 120 Wall St., 5th Fl., New York, NY 10005-3904. Phone: (212)514-7600 Fax: (212)514-8470 E-mail: info@catalyst.org • URL: http://www. catalystwomen.org • Works to advance women in Business and the professions. Serves as a source of information on women in business for past four decades. Helps companies and women maximize their potential. Holds current statistics, print media, and research materials on issues related to women in business.

Human Resource Planning Society. 401 N Michigan Ave., Ste. 2200, Chicago, IL 60611. Phone: (312)321-6805 Fax: (312)673-6944 E-mail: info@ hrps.org • URL: http://www.hrps.org • Human resource planning professionals representing 160 corporations and 3000 individual members, including strategic human resources planning and development specialists, staffing analysts, business planners, line managers, and others who function as business partners in the application of strategic human resource management practices. Seeks to increase the impact of human resource planning and management on business and organizational

performance. Sponsors program of professional development in human resource planning concepts, techniques, and practices. Offers networking opportunities.

International Personnel Management Association. 1617 Duke St., Alexandria, VA 22314. Phone: (703)549-7100 Fax: (703)684-0948 E-mail: ipma@ impa-hr.org • URL: http://www.ipma-hr.org.

National Human Resources Association. PO Box 7326, Nashua, NH 03060-7326. Phone: (866)523-4417 Fax: (603)891-5760 E-mail: info@ humanresources.org • URL: http://www. humanresources.org • Represents human resource executives in business, industry, education, and government. Established to expand and improve the professionalism of those in human resource management.

Society for Human Resource Management. 1800 Duke St., Alexandria, VA 22314. Phone: 800-283-7476 or (703)548-3440 Fax: (703)535-6490 • URL: http://www.shrm.org • Affiliated with Human Resource Certification Institute; Media Human Resources Association and SHRM Global Forum. Formerly American Society for Personnel Administration.

OTHER SOURCES

BNA Policy and Practice Series. BNA, Inc. • Weekly. $1,965.00 per year. Three looseleaf volumes. Includes personnel management, labor relations, fair employment practice, compensation, and wage-hour laws.

Employment Forms and Policies. LexisNexis Matthew Bender. • Looseleaf. $120.00, including CD-ROM. Periodic supplementation available. Contains more than 300 forms, policies, and checklists for use by small or medium-sized businesses. Covers such topics as employee selection, payroll issues, benefits, performance appraisal, dress codes, and employee termination.

Fundamentals of Human Resources. American Management Association Extension Institute. • Looseleaf. $139.00. Self-study course on a wide range of personnel topics. Emphasis is on practical explanations, examples, and problem solving. Quizzes and a case study are included.

Human Resources Management Whole. CCH, Inc. • Nine looseleaf volumes. $1,572 per year. Includes monthly updates. Components are *Ideas and Trends Newsletter, Employment Relations, Compensation, Equal Employment Opportunity, Personnel Practices/Communications* and *OSHA Compliance.* Components are available separately.

PERSONNEL MANUALS

See: PROCEDURE MANUALS

PERSONNEL RECRUITMENT

See: RECRUITMENT OF PERSONNEL

PERSONNEL TESTING

See: PSYCHOLOGICAL TESTING; RATING OF EMPLOYEES

PERT (PROGRAM EVALUATION AND REVIEW TECHNIQUE)

See: CRITICAL PATH METHOD/PERT (PROGRAM EVALUATION AND REVIEW TECHNIQUE)

PEST CONTROL INDUSTRY

See also: PESTICIDE INDUSTRY

ABSTRACTS AND INDEXES

Biological and Agricultural Index. H. W. Wilson Co. • 11 times a year. Annual and quarterly cumulations. Price varies.

Entomology Abstracts. CSA. • 11 times a year. $1,570.00 per year. Includes print and online editions.

CD-ROM DATABASES

WILSONDISC: Biological and Agricultural Index. H. W. Wilson Co. • Monthly. Includes unlimited online access to *Biological and Agricultural Index* through WILSONLINE. Provides CD-ROM indexing of over 250 periodicals covering agriculture, agricultural chemicals, biochemistry, biotechnology, entomology, horticulture, and related topics.

HANDBOOKS AND MANUALS

Handbook of Pest Management in Agriculture. David Pimentel, editor. CRC Press, Inc. • 1990. $1,229.85. Second edition. Three volumes. $409.95 per volume.

INTERNET DATABASES

PestWeb: The Pest Control Industry Website. Univar USA. Phone: 800-888-4897 or (425)889-3400 E-mail: webmaster@pestweb.com • URL: http://www.pestweb.com • Web site provides a wide variety of information on pest control products, manufacturers, associations, news, and education. Includes "Insects and Other Organisms," featuring details on 27 different kinds of pests, from ants to wasps. Online searching is offered. Fees: Free.

ONLINE DATABASES

CAB Abstracts. CAB Publishing North America. • Contains 46 specialized abstract collections covering over 10,000 journals and monographs in the areas of agriculture, horticulture, forest products, farm products, nutrition, dairy science, poultry, grains, animal health, entomology, etc. Time period is 1972 to date, with monthly updates. Inquire as to online cost and availability. *CAB Abstracts on CD-ROM* also available, with annual updating.

CSA Life Sciences Collection. Cambridge Scientific Abstracts. • Includes online versions of *Biotechnology Research Abstracts, Entomology Abstracts, Genetics Abstracts,* and about 20 other abstract collections. Time period is 1978 to date, with monthly updates. Inquire as to online cost and availability.

PERIODICALS AND NEWSLETTERS

Pest Control. Advanstar Communications. • Monthly. $44.00 per year.

Pest Control Technology. Group Interest Enterprises. GIE, Inc., Publishers. • Monthly. $32.00 per year. Provides technical and business management information for pest control personnel.

RESEARCH CENTERS AND INSTITUTES

Center for Urban and Industrial Pest Management. Purdue University, 1158 Smith Hall, West Lafayette, IN 47907. Phone: (765)494-4564 Fax: (765)494-0535 E-mail: gary_bennett@entm.purdue.edu • URL: http://www.purdue.edu/entomology/urban/home • Conducts research on the control of household and structural insect pests.

Laboratory for Pest Control Application Technology. Ohio State University, Ohio Agricultural Research and Development Center, 1680 Madison Ave., Wooster, OH 44691-4096. Phone: (330)263-3931 Fax: (330)263-3686 E-mail: downer.2@osu.edu • URL: http://www.oardc.ohio-state.edu/lpcat • Conducts pest control research in

cooperation with the U. S. Department of Agriculture.

TRADE/PROFESSIONAL ASSOCIATIONS

National Pest Management Association International. 10460 N St., Fairfax, VA 22030. Phone: 800-678-6722 or (703)352-6762 Fax: (703)352-3031 E-mail: info@pestworld.org • URL: http://www.pestworld.org • Represents firms engaged in control of insects, rodents, birds, and other pests, in or around structures, through use of insecticides, rodenticides, miticides, fumigants, and non-chemical methods. Provides advisory services on control procedures, new products, and safety and business administration practices. Promotes June as National Pest Control Month. Sponsors research, periodic technical and management seminars.

PESTICIDE INDUSTRY

See also: AGRICULTURAL CHEMICALS; PEST CONTROL INDUSTRY

ABSTRACTS AND INDEXES

NTIS Alerts: Environmental Pollution & Control. National Technical Information Service. • Semimonthly. $245.00 per year. Provides descriptions of government-sponsored research reports and software, with ordering information. Covers the following categories of environmental pollution: air, water, solid wastes, radiation, pesticides, and noise. Formerly *Abstract Newsletter.*

Review of Agricultural Entomology: Consisting of Abstracts of Reviews of Current Literature on Applied Entomology Throughout the World. Available from CABI Publishing, North America. • Monthly. Institutions, $1,505.00 per year. Print and online edition, $1,505.00 per year. Published in England by CABI Publishing. Provides worldwide coverage of the literature. (Formerly *Review of Applied Entomology, Series A: Agricultural*).

Review of Medical and Veterinary Entomology. Available from CABI Publishing, North America. • Monthly. Institutions, $855.00 per year. Print and online edition, $885.00 per year. Provides worldwide coverage of the literature. Formerly *Review of Applied Entomology, Series B: Medical and Veterinary.*

CD-ROM DATABASES

AGRICOLA on SilverPlatter. Available from SilverPlatter Information, Inc. • Quarterly. $825.00 per year. Produced by the National Agricultural Library. Provides about three million citations on CD-ROM to the literature of agriculture, agricultural economics, animal sciences, entomology, fertilizer, food, forestry, nutrition, pesticides, plant science, water resources, and other topics. Each quarterly disc covers the past ten years, with archival discs available from 1970.

DIRECTORIES

The Agrochemical Companies Fact File. PJB Publications Ltd. • Covers: 300 agrochemical manufacturers; formulators; biopesticide manufacturers, and agrochemical trading companies worldwide. Entries include: Details on key executives, financial data, operating locations, main markets, products, subsidiaries, joint ventures, and portfolios.

Household and Personal Products Industry - Buyers Guide. Rodman Publications. • Annual - $12.00. Lists of suppliers to manufacturers of cosmetics, toiletries, soaps, detergents, and related household and personal products.

Household and Personal Products Industry Contract Packaging and Private Label Directory. Rodman Publications. • Annual. $12.00. Provides information for about 450 companies offering private label or contract packaged household and

personal care products, such as detergents, cosmetics, polishes, insecticides, and various aerosol items.

Major Chemical and Petrochemical Companies of the World. Available from Gale Cengage Learning. • 2002. $880.00. Sixth edition. Published by Graham & Whiteside. Contains profiles of more than 7,000 important chemical and petrochemical companies in various countries. Subject areas include general chemicals, specialty chemicals, agricultural chemicals, petrochemicals, industrial gases, and fertilizers.

Spraying--Insect Control Directory. infoUSA Inc. • Number of listings: 1,287. Entries include: Name, address, phone, size of advertisement, name of owner or manager, number of employees, year first in "Yellow Pages." Compiled from telephone company "Yellow Pages," nationwide.

ENCYCLOPEDIAS AND DICTIONARIES

Encyclopedia of Agriculture Science. Charles J. Arntzen and Ellen M. Ritter, editors. Elsevier. • 1994. $900.00. Four volumes.

Encyclopedia of Agrochemicals. Jack R. Plimmer. John Wiley and Sons, Inc. • 2003. $945.00. Three volumes. Includes pesticides, animal food additives, veterinary drugs, and other compounds.

HANDBOOKS AND MANUALS

Agrochemicals: Composition, Production, Toxicology, Applications. Franz Muller, editor. John Wiley and Sons, Inc. • 2000. $375.00. Coverage includes fertilizers, herbicides, fungicides, insecticides, and biological control agents. Content is both theoretical and practical.

Crop Protection Chemicals Reference. Chemical and Pharmaceutical Press, Inc. • 1994. $130.00. 10th edition. Contains the complete text of product labels. Indexed by manufacturer, product category, pest use, crop use, chemical name, and brand name.

Defending Pesticides in Litigation. George W. Ware and Mark J. Carpenter. West Group. • Annual. $364.00. Discusses liability and other legal issues related to the manufacture and use of pesticides. Includes a guide to FIFRA (Federal Insecticide, Fungicide, and Rodenticide Act). (Environmental Law Series).

ONLINE DATABASES

Derwent Crop Protection File. Derwent, Inc. • Provides citations to the international journal literature of agricultural chemicals and pesticides from 1968 to date, with updating eight times per year. Formerly *PESTDOC.* Inquire as to online cost and availability.

PERIODICALS AND NEWSLETTERS

Dealer Progress: How Smart Agribusiness is Growing. Fertilizer Institute. • Bimonthly. Free to qualified personnel; others, $40.00 per year. Published in association with the Fertilizer Institute. Includes information on fertilizers and agricultural chemicals, including farm pesticides. Formerly *Progress.*

Household and Personal Products Industry: The Magazine for the Detergent, Soap, Cosmetic and Toiletry, Wax, Polish and Aerosol Industries. Rodman Publications. • Monthly. $48.00 per year. Covers marketing, packaging, production, technical innovations, private label developments, and aerosol packaging for soap, detergents, cosmetics, insecticides, and a variety of other household products.

Pest Control. Advanstar Communications. • Monthly. $44.00 per year.

Pest Control Technology. Group Interest Enterprises. GIE, Inc., Publishers. • Monthly. $32.00 per year. Provides technical and business management information for pest control personnel.

Pesticide Biochemistry and Physiology: An International Journal. Elsevier. • Nine times a year. Individuals, $487.00 per year; institutions,

$1,000.00 per year; students, $89.00 per year.

STATISTICS SOURCES

FAO Trade Yearbook. Available from Bernan Associates. • Annual. $45.00. Published by the Food and Agriculture Organization (http://www.fao.org). Provides extensive worldwide data on exports and imports of agricultural commodities, fertilizers, tractors, and pesticides. Includes more than 130 tables of detailed statistics.

Statistical Record of the Environment. Gale Cengage Learning. • 1996. $130.00. Third edition. Provides over 875 charts, tables, and graphs of major environmental statistics, arranged by subject. Covers population growth, hazardous waste, nuclear energy, acid rain, pesticides, and other subjects related to the environment. A keyword index is included. (Gale Environmental Library Series).

Synthetic Organic Chemicals: United States Production and Sales. International Trade Commission. Available from U.S. Government Printing Office. • Annual.

TRADE/PROFESSIONAL ASSOCIATIONS

American Entomological Society. 9301 Annapolis Rds., Ste. 300, Lanham, MD 20706. Phone: (301)731-4535 Fax: (301)731-4538 E-mail: esa@entsoc.org • URL: http://www.entsoc.org/ • Professional and amateur entomologists. Promotes the study of insects and publishes the results of research in the systematics and morphology of insects.

Association of American Pesticide Control Officials. Office of the Secretary, P.O. Box 1249, Hardwick, VT 05843. Phone: (802)472-6956 Fax: (802)472-6957 E-mail: aapco@vtlink.net • URL: http://www.aapco.ceris.purdue.edu.

National Pest Management Association International. 10460 N St., Fairfax, VA 22030. Phone: 800-678-6722 or (703)352-6762 Fax: (703)352-3031 E-mail: info@pestworld.org • URL: http://www.pestworld.org • Represents firms engaged in control of insects, rodents, birds, and other pests, in or around structures, through use of insecticides, rodenticides, miticides, fumigants, and non-chemical methods. Provides advisory services on control procedures, new products, and safety and business administration practices. Promotes June as National Pest Control Month. Sponsors research, periodic technical and management seminars.

National Pest Management International. 8100 Oak St., Dunn Loring, VA 22027. Phone: 800-678-6722 or (703)573-8330 Fax: (703)573-4116 E-mail: lederer@pestworld.com • URL: http://www.pestworld.org.

OTHER SOURCES

World Agrochemical Markets. Theta Reports. • 2000. $1,040.00. Market research data. Covers the demand for crop protection products in 11 countries having major markets and 20 countries having minor markets. (Theta Report No. DS196E.).

World Non-Agricultural Pesticide Markets. Theta Reports. • 2000. $1,670.00. Market research data. Includes home/garden pesticides, herbicides, professional pest-control products, and turf pesticides. (Theta Report No. DS191E.).

PET FOOD

See: PET INDUSTRY

PET INDUSTRY

See also: VETERINARY PRODUCTS

DIRECTORIES

Food Chemicals News Directory. Food Chemical News. CRC Press LLC. • Semiannual. $497.00.

Over 2,000 subsidiaries belonging to nearly 250 corporate parents plus an additional 3,000 independent processors. Formerly *Hereld's 1,500.*

Pet Dealer Purchasing Guide. Cygnus Business Media, Inc. • Annual. $75.00. Lists of manufacturers and importers of pet supplies; distributors and wholesalers of pet supples; wholesalers, breeders, and importers of pets (livestock); trade associations; publishers of pet books, records, and educational and training materials; pet care schools. Formerly *Pet Supplies Marketing Directory.*

HANDBOOKS AND MANUALS

Pet Shop. Entrepreneur Media, Inc. • Looseleaf. $59.50. A practical guide to starting a pet store. Covers profit potential, start-up costs, market size evaluation, owner's time required, site selection, lease negotiation, pricing, accounting, advertising, promotion, etc. (Start-Up Business Guide No. E1007.).

PERIODICALS AND NEWSLETTERS

Pet Age: The Magazine for the Professional Retailer. Karen Long MacLeod, editor. H.H. Backer Associates, Inc. • Monthly. Free to qualified personnel; others, $25.00 per year.

Pet Product News. Fancy Publications. • Monthly. Free to qualified personnel; others, $420.00 per year.

Pet Product News. Fancy Publications, Inc. • Free to qualified personnel; others, $118.00 per year. Supplement available *Pet Product News Buyer's Guide.*

Petfood Industry. Watt Publishing Co. • Bimonthly. $36.00 per year.

TRADE/PROFESSIONAL ASSOCIATIONS

American Pet Products Manufacturers Association, Inc. 255 Glenville Rd., Greenwich, CT 06831. Phone: 800-452-1225 or (203)532-0000 Fax: (203)532-0551 E-mail: info@appma.org • URL: http://www.appma.org.

Pet Food Institute. 2025 M St. NW, Ste. 800, Washington, DC 20036-2422. Phone: (202)367-1120 Fax: (202)367-2120 E-mail: info@petfoodinstitute.org • URL: http://www.petfoodinstitute.org • Represents the manufacturers of 97% of the commercial pet food produced in the United States. Serves as the voice of the industry before legislative and regulatory bodies at both the federal and state levels.

Pet Industry Distributors Association. 2105 Laurel Bush Rd., Ste. 200, Bel Air, MD 21015-5200. Phone: (443)640-1060 Fax: (443)640-1031 E-mail: pida@ksgroup.org • URL: http://www.pida.org • Strives to enhance the well-being of the pet product wholesaler-distributor. Promotes partnerships between suppliers and customers. Fosters the human-companion animal bond.

Pet Industry Joint Advisory Council. 1220 19th St. NW, Ste. 400, Washington, DC 20036-2438. Phone: 800-553-7387 or (202)452-1525 Fax: (202)293-4377 E-mail: info@pijac.org • URL: http://www.pijac.org • Pet retailers, manufacturers, and distributors; companion animal suppliers; pet industry trade associations. Works to monitor federal and state regulations and legislation affecting the industry. Sponsors research projects and industry-related educational programs.

World Wide Pet Industry Association. 135 W Lemon Ave., Monrovia, CA 91016-2809. Phone: 800-999-7295 or (626)447-2222 Fax: (626)447-8350 E-mail: info@wwpia.org • URL: http://www.wwpia.org • Manufacturers, retailers, and distributors of pet food and services and of avian, aquarium, and companion animal care products, equipment, and services. Seeks to advance the economic interests of members; promotes responsible pet ownership. Conducts trade shows, certificate training courses, and seminars for pet shop retailers, grooming

establishments, and veterinary clinics.

OTHER SOURCES

Pet Supplies Market. Available from MarketResearch.com. • 2001. $2,750.00. Published by Packaged Facts. Provides market data with projections to 2003 on products for dogs, cats, fish, birds, and other pets.

PETROCHEMICAL INDUSTRY

See also: CHEMICAL INDUSTRIES; PETROLEUM INDUSTRY

GENERAL WORKS

Petrochemicals: The Rise of an Industry. Peter H. Spitz. John Wiley and Sons, Inc. • 1988. $150.00.

ABSTRACTS AND INDEXES

Applied Science and Technology Index. H. W. Wilson Co. • 11 times a year. Quarterly and annual cumulations. Price varies. Indexes a wide variety of English language technical, industrial, and engineering periodicals.

ALMANACS AND YEARBOOKS

Worldwide Petrochemical Directory. PennWell Corp., Petroleum Div. • Annual. $165.00. Do more than 3,400 petrochemical plants; separate section on new construction; worldwide coverage. Formerly *Refining and Petrochemical Technology Yearbook.*

BIOGRAPHICAL SOURCES

Who's Who in World Petrochemicals and Plastics. Reed Business Information. • Annual. $175.00. Names, addresses, telephone numbers, and company affiliations of individuals active in the petrochemical business. Formerly *Who's Who in World Petrochemicals.*

DIRECTORIES

Chemcyclopedia. American Chemical Society. • Publication includes: List of over 900 chemical manufacturers and suppliers in the United States and Canada. Entries include: Company name, address, phone, fax, telex, trade name; chemical available grades, packaging, special shipping requirements, and potential applications. Principal content of publication is technical and commercial information on about 10,000 chemicals produced and sold arranged by product group.

Major Chemical and Petrochemical Companies of Europe. Available from Gale Cengage Learning. • 2003. $880.00. Fifth edition. Two volumes. Published by Graham & Whiteside Ltd., London. Includes financial, personnel, and product information for chemical companies in Western Europe.

Major Chemical and Petrochemical Companies of the World. Available from Gale Cengage Learning. • 2002. $880.00. Sixth edition. Published by Graham & Whiteside. Contains profiles of more than 7,000 important chemical and petrochemical companies in various countries. Subject areas include general chemicals, specialty chemicals, agricultural chemicals, petrochemicals, industrial gases, and fertilizers.

Petro Process Directory. Atlantic Communications L.L.C. • Covers: 9,000 companies in the United States engaged in petrochemical and refining industries; incorporating health, safety and environment; suppliers of products and services to the industry. Entries include: Company name, address, phone, fax, telex, E-mail, URL, WATS number, names and titles of key personnel, branch offices.

ENCYCLOPEDIAS AND DICTIONARIES

Kirk-Othmer Encyclopedia of Chemical Technology. Raymond E. Kirk and Donald F. Othmer. John Wiley and Sons, Inc. • 1991-97. $9,895.00, prepaid. 27 volumes. Fourth edition. Four volumes are scheduled to be published each year, with individual volumes available at $415.00. (Kirk-Othmer Encyclopedia of Chemical Technology Series).

FINANCIAL RATIOS

Industry Norms and Key Business Ratios. Desk Top Edition. Dun and Bradstreet Corp. • Annual. Five volumes. $475.00 per volume. $1,890.00 per set. Covers over 800 kinds of businesses, arranged by Standard Industrial Classification number. More detailed editions covering longer periods of time are also available.

HANDBOOKS AND MANUALS

Handbook of Petrochemicals and Processes. G. Margaret Wells. Ashgate Publishing Co. • 1999. $170.00. Second edition. Published by Gower in England.

Modern Petroleum Technology. Richard A. Dawe, editor. John Wiley and Sons, Inc. • 2000. $600.00. Sixth edition. Two volumes. Volume one, entitled *Upstream,* covers oil rigs and other means of obtaining raw petroleum. Volume two, *Downstream,* covers petroleum refining and end products. Edited for industry technicians, managers, and engineers.

ONLINE DATABASES

PROMT: Predicasts Overview of Markets and Technology. Gale Cengage Learning. • Companies, products, applied technologies and markets. U.S. and international literature coverage, 1972 to date. Inquire as to online cost and availability. Provides abstracts from more than 1,600 publications. Weekly updates.

PERIODICALS AND NEWSLETTERS

Hydrocarbon Processing. Gulf Publishing Co. • Monthly. $120.00 per year. International edition available.

Oil, Gas and Petrochem Equipment. PennWell Corp., Industrial Div. • Monthly. $35.00 per year.

PetroChemical News: A Weekly News Service in English Devoted to the Worldwide Petrochemical Industry. William F. Bland Co. • Weekly. $807.00 per year. Report of current and significant news about the petrochemical business worldwide.

TRADE/PROFESSIONAL ASSOCIATIONS

American Chemical Society. 1155 16th St. NW, Washington, DC 20036. Phone: 800-227-5558 or (202)872-4600 Fax: (202)872-4615 E-mail: help@ acs.org • URL: http://portal.chemistry.org/portal/ acs/corg/memberapp • Scientific and educational society of chemists and chemical engineers. Conducts: studies and surveys; special programs for disadvantaged persons; legislation monitoring, analysis, and reporting; courses for graduate chemists and chemical engineers; radio and television programming. Offers career guidance counseling; administers the Petroleum Research Fund and other grants and fellowship programs. Operates Employment Clearing Houses. Compiles statistics. Maintains Speaker's Bureau and 33 divisions.

Synthetic Organic Chemical Manufacturers Association. 1850 M St. NW, Ste. 700, Washington, DC 20036-5810. Phone: (202)721-4100 Fax: (202)296-8120 E-mail: info@socma.com • URL: http://www.socma.com • Represents manufacturers of synthetic organic chemicals, which are products manufactured from coal, natural gas, crude petroleum, and certain natural substances such as vegetable oils, fats, proteins, carbohydrates, rosin, grains, and their derivatives.

PETROLEUM EQUIPMENT INDUSTRY

DIRECTORIES

Composite Catalog of Oilfield Equipment and Services. Gulf Publishing Co. • Biennial. $750.00. Includes CD-Rom.

Financial Times Business Global Oil & Gas Directory. Available from Gale Cengage Learning. • Annual. $355.00. Published by Financial Times Business. Provides detailed information on 800 leading oil and gas companies worldwide. Includes financial data for three years. Formerly *Financial Times Energy Yearbook: Oil & Gas.*

Petroleum Equipment Directory. Petroleum Equipment Institute. • Covers: over 1,600 member manufacturers, distributors, and installers of petroleum marketing equipment worldwide. Entries include: Company name, address, phone, names of executives, list of products or services.

Supply, Distribution Manufacturing and Service: Supply and Service Companies and Equipment Manufacturers. Midwest Publishing Co. • Annual. $115.00. Two volumes. 8,000 oil well supply stores, service companies, and equipment manufacturers. Formerly *Directory of Oil Well Supply Companies.*

FINANCIAL RATIOS

Annual Statement Studies. The Risk Management Association. • Annual. Median and quartile financial ratios are given for over 400 kinds of manufacturing, wholesale, retail, construction, and consumer finance establishments. Data is sorted by both asset size and sales volume. Includes a clearly written "Definition of Ratios" and an alphabetical industry index.

Annual Statement Studies: Industry Default Probabilities and Cash Flow Measures. The Risk Management Association. • Annual. $145.00. Serves as a companion volume to the original *Annual Statement Studies.* Gives probability of default estimates on a percentage scale for more than 450 industries. Includes changes in position year-by-year for eight financial statement line items and provides percentage measures of cash flow.

HANDBOOKS AND MANUALS

Modern Petroleum Technology. Richard A. Dawe, editor. John Wiley and Sons, Inc. • 2000. $600.00. Sixth edition. Two volumes. Volume one, entitled *Upstream,* covers oil rigs and other means of obtaining raw petroleum. Volume two, *Downstream,* covers petroleum refining and end products. Edited for industry technicians, managers, and engineers.

PERIODICALS AND NEWSLETTERS

Hart's E and P (Exploration and Production). Hart Publications, Inc. • Monthly. Free to qualified personnel; others $149.00 per year. Edited for "decision makers" in petroleum exploration and production. Emphasis is on technology. Formerly *Petroleum Engineer International.*

Journal of Petroleum Technology. Society of Petroleum Engineers, Inc. • Monthly. Free to members; non-members, $45.00 per year. Covers oil and gas exploration, drilling and production, engineering management, resevoir engineering, geothermal energy sources and emerging technologies. Also includes society news, programs, events and activities. Supplement available *SPE Computer Applications.*

Oil, Gas and Petrochem Equipment. PennWell Corp., Industrial Div. • Monthly. $35.00 per year.

STATISTICS SOURCES

Annual Survey of Manufactures. Available from U. S. Government Printing Office. • Annual. Prices vary. Issued by the U. S. Census Bureau as an interim update to the *Census of Manufactures.* Includes data on number of manufacturing establishments in various industries, employment, labor costs, value of shipments, capital expenditures, inventories, energy costs, and assets. (See also Census Bureau home page, http://www.census. gov/.).

Standard & Poor's Industry Surveys. Standard & Poor's. • Semiannual. $1,800.00. Two looseleaf

volumes. Includes monthly *Supplements.* Provides detailed, individual surveys of 52 major industry groups. Each survey is revised on a semiannual basis. Also includes "Monthly Investment Review" (industry group investment analysis) and monthly "Trends & Projections" (economic analysis).

U. S. Industry and Trade Outlook. Available from National Technical Information Service. • Annual. $69.95. Produced by the International Trade Administration, U. S. Department of Commerce, in a "public-private" partnership with DRI/McGraw-Hill and Standard & Poor's. Provides basic data, outlook for the current year, and "Long-Term Prospects" (five-year projections) for a wide variety of products and services. Includes high technology industries. Formerly *U. S. Industrial Outlook.*

TRADE/PROFESSIONAL ASSOCIATIONS

Petroleum Equipment Institute. PO Box 2380, Tulsa, OK 74101-2380. Phone: (918)494-9696 Fax: (918)491-9895 E-mail: info@pei.org • URL: http:// www.pei.org • Distributors and manufacturers of equipment used in service stations, bulk plants, and other petroleum marketing operations.

Petroleum Equipment Suppliers Association. 9225 Katy Fwy., Ste. 310, Houston, TX 77024-1510. Phone: (713)932-0168 Fax: (713)932-0497 E-mail: webmaster@pesa.org • URL: http://www.pesa.org • Promotes improvement of the petroleum equipment, service, and supply industries. Represents members' interests; cooperates with the federal government in matters of national concern; gathers and disseminates information. Conducts educational programs.

Society of Petroleum Engineers. 222 Palisades Creek Dr., Richardson, TX 75080. Phone: 800-456-6863 or (972)952-9393 Fax: (972)952-9435 E-mail: spedal@spe.org • URL: http://www.spe.org • Formerly Petroleum Branch of AIME.

PETROLEUM INDUSTRY

See also: FUEL OIL INDUSTRY; GASOLINE INDUSTRY; OFFSHORE PETROLEUM INDUSTRY; PETROCHEMICAL INDUSTRY; PETROLEUM EQUIPMENT INDUSTRY; PETROLEUM MARKETING; PIPELINE INDUSTRY; PROPANE AND BUTANE GAS INDUSTRY

ABSTRACTS AND INDEXES

Fuel and Energy Abstracts: A Summary of World Literature on All Scientific, Technical, Commercial and Environmental Aspects of Fuel and Energy. Elsevier. • Bimonthly. Institutions, $1,931.00 per year.

NTIS Alerts: Energy. National Technical Information Service. • Semimonthly. $245.00 per year. Provides descriptions of government-sponsored research reports and software, with ordering information. Covers electric power, batteries, fuels, geothermal energy, heating/cooling systems, nuclear technology, solar energy, energy policy, and related subjects. Formerly *Abstract Newsletter.*

Petroleum Abstracts. University of Tulsa, Information Services Div. • 50 times a year. Service basis. Worldwide literature related to petroleum exploration and production.

Petroleum-Energy Business News Index Elsevier Engineering Information, Inc. Elsevier. • Monthly. Members, $475.00 per year; non-members, $950.00 per year.

ALMANACS AND YEARBOOKS

Agricultural and Mineral Commodities Year Book. Available from Taylor & Francis Group. • Annual. $225.00. Published by Europa Publications. Contains descriptive product profiles, price data, export-import data, and production statistics for major commodities of the world. Includes commodity histories, uses, markets, demand trends, and information about trade agreements and key commodity organizations.

CD-ROM DATABASES

OECD Statistical Compendium. Organization for Economic Cooperation and Development. • Semiannual. $1,905.00 per year for 1 to 10 users. CD-ROM contains more than 730,000 monthly, quarterly, and annual time series for OECD countries, 1960 to date. Includes fully searchable data on agriculture, food, economic indicators, national accounts, employment, energy, finance, industry, technology, and foreign trade. Results can be displayed in various forms.

DIRECTORIES

Energy Intelligence Top 100: Ranking the World's Top Oil Companies. Energy Intelligence Group, Inc. • Annual. $775.00. Provides detailed profiles of the world's 100 largest oil companies, with rankings by numerous key criteria. Includes both stockholder-owned and government-owned companies.

Financial Times Business Global Oil & Gas Directory. Available from Gale Cengage Learning. • Annual. $355.00. Published by Financial Times Business. Provides detailed information on 800 leading oil and gas companies worldwide. Includes financial data for three years. Formerly *Financial Times Energy Yearbook: Oil & Gas.*

The Geophysical Directory. Claudia LaCalli, editor. Geophysical Directory Inc. • Covers: about 4,000 companies that provide geophysical equipment, supplies, or services, and mining and petroleum companies that use geophysical techniques; international coverage. Entries include: Company name, address, phone, fax, names of principal executives, operations, and sales personnel; similar information for branch locations.

Institutional Buyers of Energy Stocks. Investment Data Corp. • Annual. $645.00. Provides detailed profiles 555 institutional buyers of petroleum-related and other energy stocks. Includes names of financial analysts and portfolio managers.

Plunkett's Energy Industry Almanac: Complete Profiles on the Energy Industry 500 Companies. Plunkett Research Ltd. • Annual. $199.99. Includes major oil companies, utilities, pipelines, alternative energy companies, etc. Provides information on industry trends.

Refining and Gas Processing Industry Worldwide. Midwest Publishing Co. • Annual. $145.00. Over 5,200 refineries, gas processing plants, engineering contractors, equipment manufacturers, supply companies and liquid terminals. Formerly *Refining and Gas Processing.*

ENCYCLOPEDIAS AND DICTIONARIES

Encyclopedia of Energy. Cutler J. Cleveland, editor. Elsevier, Inc. • 2004. $1,560.00. Six volumes. Covers all aspects of energy sources and energy-related environmental issues.

International Petroleum Encyclopedia. PennWell Corp., Industrial Div. • 2002. $160.00. A worldwide petroleum directory. Features statistics and a complete atlas of the international petroleum market.

Macmillan Encyclopedia of Energy. Available from Gale Cengage Learning. • 2001. $395.00. Three volumes. Published by Macmillan Reference USA. Covers the business, technology, and history of a wide variety of energy sources.

Manual of Oil and Gas Terms. LexisNexis Matthew Bender. • $109.00. 12th edition. Defines technical, legal, and tax terms relating to the oil and gas industry.

FINANCIAL RATIOS

Almanac of Business and Industrial Financial Ratios. Leo Troy. Aspen Publishers, Inc. • 2003.

$125.95. Includes CD-Rom. Contains financial ratios derived from federal tax returns. Ratios for each of about 200 industries are arranged according to company asset size. (Almanac of Business and Industrial Financial Ratios Series).

IRS Corporate Financial Ratios. Available from MarketResearch.com. • 2002. $225.00. Published by Schonfeld & Associates, Inc. Presents 70 key financial ratios for 260 industries. Ratios are calculated from income statement and balance sheet data available from the Internal Revenue Service. Includes four asset size classes.

HANDBOOKS AND MANUALS

Ernst and Young's Oil and Gas Federal Income Taxation. John R. Braden and others. CCH, Inc. • Annual. $92.95. Formerly *Miller's Oil and Gas Federal Income Taxation.*

Modern Petroleum Technology. Richard A. Dawe, editor. John Wiley and Sons, Inc. • 2000. $600.00. Sixth edition. Two volumes. Volume one, entitled *Upstream,* covers oil rigs and other means of obtaining raw petroleum. Volume two, *Downstream,* covers petroleum refining and end products. Edited for industry technicians, managers, and engineers.

Summers on Oil and Gas. West Group. • $625.00. Annual updates. Legal aspects of the petroleum industry.

INTERNET DATABASES

Business 2.0 Web Guide to the Best Business Links. Business 2.0 Media Inc. Phone: (415)293-4800 E-mail: support@business2.com • URL: http://www.business2.com/webguide • Web site presents an extensive, searchable directory of links to "the best, most informative, and authoritative web pages." Twenty main categories cover business, finance, career, company information, people, and technology topics, with thousands of subtopics, all linking to Web sites recommended by experienced business researchers. Fees: Free.

Fedstats. Federal Interagency Council on Statistical Policy. Phone: (202)395-7254 • URL: http://www.fedstats.gov • Web site features an efficient search facility for full-text statistics produced by more than 100 federal agencies, including the Census Bureau, the Bureau of Economic Analysis, and the Bureau of Labor Statistics. Boolean searches can be made within one agency or for all agencies combined. Links are offered to international statistical bureaus, including the UN, IMF, OECD, UNESCO, Eurostat, and 20 individual countries. Fees: Free.

FreeLunch.com. Economy.com, Inc. Phone: (610)696-8700 Fax: (610)696-1678 • URL: http://www.freelunch.com • Web site provides free access to more than 1.5 million economic and financial data series, covering industry, demographics, labor markets, prices, retail sales, government spending, trade, interest rates, housing starts, the stock market, and many other topics. Data is available for various time periods in either chart or table form. Searching is offered. Fees: Free, but registration required. Economy.com, Inc. also offers fee-based economic analysis at *The Dismal Scientist* site (http://www.dismal.com).

ONLINE DATABASES

Business and Industry. Gale Cengage Learning. • Contains online citations, abstracts, and selected fulltext from more than 1,000 trade journals, newspapers, and other publications. Provides general coverage of both manufacturing and service industries, including marketing, production, industry trends, key events, and information on specific companies. Time span is 1994 to date. Daily updates. Inquire as to online cost and availability. (Also available in a CD-ROM version.).

Tablebase. Gale Cengage Learning. • Provides online numerical tabular data from a wide variety of business, organization, and government sources,

including about 1,000 trade journals. Includes industry and individual company statistics relating to products, market share, sales forecasts, production, exports, market trends, etc. Time span is 1997 to date. Weekly updates. Inquire as to online cost and availability. (Also available in a CD-ROM version.).

Tulsa (Petroleum Abstracts). Information Services. • Worldwide literature in the petroleum and natural gas areas, 1965 to present. Inquire as to online cost and availability. Includes petroleum exploration patents. Updated weekly.

PERIODICALS AND NEWSLETTERS

Energy and Fuels. American Chemical Society. • Bimonthly. Institutions, $852.00 per year; others, price on application. An interdisciplinary technical journal covering non-nuclear energy sources: petroleum, gas, synthetic fuels, etc.

Energy Compass. Energy Intelligence Group. • Description: Focuses on worldwide geopolitical developments and their impact on the oil industry. Also includes marketing and trading information, political risk assessment, and current events and trends. **Remarks:** Available via fax, e-mail, or online.

Hart's E and P (Exploration and Production). Hart Publications, Inc. • Monthly. Free to qualified personnel; others $149.00 per year. Edited for "decision makers" in petroleum exploration and production. Emphasis is on technology. Formerly *Petroleum Engineer International.*

International Journal of Energy Research. John Wiley and Sons, Inc., Journals. • 15 times a year. Individuals, $2,685.00 per year; institutions, $3,500.00 per year. Published in England by John Wiley & Sons Ltd.

International Oil News. William F. Bland Co. • Description: Covers "timely and significant developments in the international oil business, including exploration, production, transportation, refining, and marketing.".

Lundberg Letter. Lundberg Survey, Incorporated. • Description: Provides statistics and analysis of U.S. oil marketing primary data. Includes an in-depth single-subject profile of a development in the petroleum market in each issue. Discusses such topics as retail/wholesale pricing, market shares, and station characteristics nationwide and regionally.

Oil and Gas Investor. Hart Publications, Inc. • Monthly. $259.00 per year.

Oil and Gas Journal. PennWell Corp., Industrial Div. • Weekly. $84.00 per year.

Oil Daily: Daily Newspaper of the Petroleum Industry. Energy Intelligence Group, Inc. • Daily. Email, $1,595.00 per year; fax, $2,395.00 per year, online, $1,495.00 per year. Newspaper for the petroleum industry.

Oil, Gas and Energy Quarterly. LexisNexis Matthew Bender. • Quarterly. $234.00 per year. Covers latest tax ideas, techniques, and practice pointers in oil and gas taxation and accounting features.

The Oilman Weekly Newsletter. PennWell Corp., Petroleum Div. • Weekly. $1,990.00 per year. Newsletter. Provides news of developments concerning the North Sea and European oil and gas businesses. Each issue contains four pages of statistical data.

PetroChemical News: A Weekly News Service in English Devoted to the Worldwide Petrochemical Industry. William F. Bland Co. • Weekly. $807.00 per year. Report of current and significant news about the petrochemical business worldwide.

Petroleum Intelligence Weekly. PIW Publications Inc. • Description: Provides a "concise weekly summary and analysis of key developments in world oil and natural gas markets." Supplies highlights in petroleum news on an international scale.

Concerned with OPEC (Organization of Petroleum Exporting Countries) and non-OPEC production levels, coverage of OPEC meetings and policy decisions, and quarterly demand and oil trade figures. Recurring features include analyses of emerging trends in oil and gas markets, notices of publications available, and columns titled Marketview (a weekly wrap-up of crude oil trading) and What's New Around the World (news briefs relating to the petroleum industry and market).

World Oil. Gulf Publishing Co. • Monthly. $130.00 per year. Covers worldwide oil and gas exploration, drilling and production.

PRICE SOURCES

Energy Prices and Taxes. International Energy Agency. OECD Publications and Information Center. • Quarterly. $385.00 per year. Includes print and online edition. Compiled by the International Energy Agency. Provides data on prices and taxation of petroleum products, natural gas, coal, and electricity. Diskette edition, $800.00. (Published in Paris).

Energy Prices and Taxes. Organization for Economic Cooperation and Development. • Quarterly. $355.00 per year. Includes both industrial and consumer prices for oil products, natural gas, coal, and electricity in various countries. (Also available on CD-ROM.).

Platt's Oilgram Price Report: an International Daily Oil-Gas Price and Marketing Letter. Platts. • Daily. Newsletter. Price on application. Prices and marketing intelligence for petroleum products. Includes weekly statistical summaries. Worldwide coverage.

RESEARCH CENTERS AND INSTITUTES

Canadian Energy Research Institute. Canadian Energy Research Institute. 3512 33rd St. NW, No. 150, Calgary, AB, Canada T2L 2A6. Phone: (403)282-1231 Fax: (403)284-4181 E-mail: mmasri@ceri.ca • URL: http://www.ceri.ca • Economic issues relating to all forms of energy, including oil, natural gas, coal, nuclear and hydroelectric power, and alternative energy sources. Develops software such as the World Oil Market Model.

STATISTICS SOURCES

Annual Energy Outlook [year], with Projections to [year]. Available from U. S. Government Printing Office. • Annual. $42.00. Issued by the Energy Information Administration, U. S. Department of Energy (http://www.eia.doe.gov). Contains detailed statistics and 20-year projections for electricity, oil, natural gas, coal, and renewable energy. Text provides extensive discussion of energy issues and "Market Trends.".

Annual Energy Review. Available from U. S. Government Printing Office. • Annual. $51.00. Issued by the Energy Information Administration, Office of Energy Markets and End Use, U. S. Department of Energy. Presents long-term historical as well as recent data on production, consumption, stocks, imports, exports, and prices of the principal energy commodities in the U. S.

Annual Survey of Manufactures. Available from U. S. Government Printing Office. • Annual. Prices vary. Issued by the U. S. Census Bureau as an interim update to the *Census of Manufactures.* Includes data on number of manufacturing establishments in various industries, employment, labor costs, value of shipments, capital expenditures, inventories, energy costs, and assets. (See also Census Bureau home page, http://www.census.gov/.).

Basic Petroleum Data Book. American Petroleum Institute. • Three times a year. $230.00 per year.

Business Statistics of the United States. Linz Audain and Cornelia J. Strawser. Bernan Associates. •

Annual. $147.00. Based on *Business Statistics,* formerly issue by the Bureau of Economic Analysis, U. S. Department of Commerce. Provides basic data for a wide variety of U. S. industries, services, and economic indicators. Most statistics are shown annually for 30 years and monthly for the most recent four years.

Encyclopedia of American Industries. Gale Cengage Learning. • 2000. $560.00. Third edition. Two volumes. $280.00 per volume. Volume one is *Manufacturing Industries* and volume two is *Service and Non-Manufacturing Industries.* Provides the history, development, and recent status of approximately 1,000 industries. Includes statistical graphs, with industry and general indexes.

Energy Balances of OECD Countries. Organization for Economic Cooperation and Development. Available from OECD Publications and Information Center. • Annual. $115.00. Presents two-year data on the supply and consumption of solid fuels, oil, gas, and electricity, expressed in oil equivalency terms. Historical tables are also provided. Relates to OECD member countries.

International Energy Annual. Available from U. S. Government Printing Office. • Annual. $34.00. Issued by the Energy Information Administration, U. S. Department of Energy. Provides production, consumption, import, and export data for primary energy commodities in more than 200 countries and areas. In addition to petroleum products and alcohol, renewable energy sources are covered (hydroelectric, geothermal, solar, and wind).

Metropolitan Life Insurance Co. Statistical Bulletin SB. Metropolitan Life Insurance Co. • Quarterly. Individuals, $50.00 per year. Covers a wide range of social, economic and demographic health concerns.

Monthly Energy Review. Available from U. S. Government Printing Office. • Monthly. $126.00 per year. Issued by the Energy Information Administration, Office of Energy Markets and End Use, U. S. Department of Energy. Contains current and historical statistics on U. S. production, storage, imports, and consumption of petroleum, natural gas, and coal.

OECD Oil and Gas Information. Available from OECD Publications and Information Center. • Annual. Price varies. Data on oil and gas balances, supplies, consumption by end use sector and trade of OECD countries. Text in English and French.

The Oil and Natural Gas Producing Industry in Your State. Independent Petroleum Association of America. Petroleum Independent Publishers, Inc. • Annual. Free to members; non-members, $50.00. Statistical issue of *Petroleum Independent.*

Oil/Energy Statistics Bulletin: And Canadian Oil Reports. Oil Statistics Co., Inc. • Biweekly. $185.00 per year.

Oil, Gas, Coal, and Electricity: Quarterly Statistics. Organization for Economic Cooperation and Development. • Quarterly. $355.00 per year. Provides detailed data for OECD countries. Covers crude oil, nine oil product groups, hard coal, brown coal (lignite), natural gas, and electric power.

Oil Information. Organization for Economic Cooperation and Development. • Annual. $150.00. Contains international data for major petroleum product groups. Includes statistics on supply, demand, trade, production, prices, and consumption for individual OECD countries and regions. Various time series cover about 30 years. (Also available on CD-ROM.).

Petroleum Supply Annual. Available from U. S. Government Printing Office. • Annual. $78.00. Two volumes. Produced by the Energy Information Administration, U. S. Department of Energy. Contains worldwide data on the petroleum industry and petroleum products.

Petroleum Supply Monthly. Available from U. S.

Government Printing Office. • Monthly. Produced by the Energy Information Administration, U. S. Department of Energy. Provides worldwide statistics on a wide variety of petroleum products. Covers production, supplies, exports and imports, transportation, refinery operations, and other aspects of the petroleum industry.

Reserves of Crude Oil, Natural Gas Liquids and Natural Gas in the United States and Canada and United States Productive Capacity. American Gas Association. • Annual. Price on application.

Short-Term Energy Outlook: Quarterly Projections. Available from U. S. Government Printing Office. • Semiannual. Issued by Energy Information Administration, U. S. Department of Energy. Contains forecasts of U. S. energy supply, demand, and prices.

Standard & Poor's Industry Surveys. Standard & Poor's. • Semiannual. $1,800.00. Two looseleaf volumes. Includes monthly *Supplements.* Provides detailed, individual surveys of 52 major industry groups. Each survey is revised on a semiannual basis. Also includes "Monthly Investment Review" (industry group investment analysis) and monthly "Trends & Projections" (economic analysis).

Survey of Current Business. Available from U. S. Government Printing Office. • Monthly. $63.00 per year. Issued by Bureau of Economic Analysis, U. S. Department of Commerce. Presents a wide variety of business and economic data.

Weekly Petroleum Status Report. Energy Information Administration. Available from U.S. Government Printing Office. • Weekly. Current statistics in the context of both historical information and selected prices and forecasts.

WEFA Industrial Monitor. John Wiley and Sons, Inc. • Annual. $65.00. Prepared by industry analysts at WEFA, an economic forecasting and consulting firm (originally Wharton Econometric Forecasting Associates). Contains discussions of the outlook for major U. S. industries, with many 10-year forecasts (WEFA Web site is http://www.wefa.com).

TRADE/PROFESSIONAL ASSOCIATIONS

American Petroleum Institute. 1220 L St. NW, Washington, DC 20005-4070. Phone: (202)682-8000 Fax: (202)682-8033 E-mail: mediacenter@api.org • URL: http://www.api.org • Corporations in the petroleum and allied industries, including producers, refiners, marketers, and transporters of crude oil, lubricating oil, gasoline and natural gas. Provides public policy development, advocacy, research, and technical services to enhance the ability of the petroleum industry to fulfill its mission: meeting the nation's energy needs; enhancing the environmental, health, and safety performance of the industry; conducting research to advance petroleum technology, equipment, and standards; Consensus policies and collective action on issues impacting its members; and works collaboratively with all industry oil and gas associations, and other organizations, to enhance industry unity and effectiveness in its advocacy. Also provides the opportunity for standards development, technical cooperation and other activities to improve the industry's competitiveness through sponsorship of self-supporting programs.

Independent Petroleum Association of America. 1201 15th St., N.W., No. 300, Washington, DC 20005. Phone: (202)857-4722 Fax: (202)857-4799 E-mail: rcarter@ipaa.org • URL: http://www.ipaa.org.

National Petrochemical and Refiners Association. 1899 L St., N.W., Suite 1000, Washington, DC 20036-3896. Phone: (202)457-0480 Fax: (202)457-0486 E-mail: info@npradc.org • URL: http://www.npradc.org.

National Petroleum Council. 1625 K St. NW, Ste. 600, Washington, DC 20006. Phone: (202)393-6100

Fax: (202)331-8539 E-mail: info@npc.org • URL: http://www.npc.org • Advisory council to the Secretary of Energy on matters relating to oil and gas.

OTHER SOURCES

Energy Management and Federal Energy Guidelines. CCH, Inc. • Biweekly. $1,827.00 per year. Seven looseleaf volumes. Periodic supplementation. Reports on petroleum allocation rules, conservation efforts, new technology, and other energy concerns.

Federal Taxation of Oil and Gas Transactions. LexisNexis Matthew Bender. • Semiannual. $414.00 per year. Two looseleaf volumes.

Major Energy Companies of the World. Available from Gale Cengage Learning. • Annual. $880.00. Published by Graham & Whiteside. Contains detailed information on more than 3,300 important energy companies in various countries. Industries include electricity generation, coal, natural gas, nuclear energy, petroleum, fuel distribution, and equipment for energy production.

Oil Price Information Service. United Comunications Group. • Weekly. $545.00 per year. Regional editions available at $150.00 per year. Quotes wholesale terminal prices for various petroleum products.

PETROLEUM INDUSTRY, OFFSHORE

See: OFFSHORE PETROLEUM INDUSTRY

PETROLEUM MARKETING

See also: PETROLEUM INDUSTRY

DIRECTORIES

The Geophysical Directory. Claudia LaCalli, editor. Geophysical Directory Inc. • Covers: about 4,000 companies that provide geophysical equipment, supplies, or services, and mining and petroleum companies that use geophysical techniques; international coverage. Entries include: Company name, address, phone, fax, names of principal executives, operations, and sales personnel; similar information for branch locations.

U.S.A. Oil Industry Directory. PennWell Publishing Co. • Covers: over 4,000 associations, brokers/dealers, drilling contractors, explorers, producers, gas processors/treaters, government agencies, marketing companies, refineries, and other companies related to the oil industry. Entries include: Name, address, phone, fax, e-mail, URL, key personnel, and brief company synopsis.

ENCYCLOPEDIAS AND DICTIONARIES

International Petroleum Encyclopedia. PennWell Corp., Industrial Div. • 2002. $160.00. A worldwide petroleum directory. Features statistics and a complete atlas of the international petroleum market.

FINANCIAL RATIOS

Industry Norms and Key Business Ratios. Desk Top Edition. Dun and Bradstreet Corp. • Annual. Five volumes. $475.00 per volume. $1,890.00 per set. Covers over 800 kinds of businesses, arranged by Standard Industrial Classification number. More detailed editions covering longer periods of time are also available.

HANDBOOKS AND MANUALS

International Crude Oil Market Handbook. Energy Intelligence Group, Inc. • Annual. $1,195.00. An overview covers "The Inner Workings of Crude Oil Markets," including a glossary of terms. Reference sections contain detailed profiles of 44 "key produc-

ing countries," legal terms, crude oil sales contracts, prices, and other information.

ONLINE DATABASES

PROMT: Predicasts Overview of Markets and Technology. Gale Cengage Learning. • Companies, products, applied technologies and markets. U.S. and international literature coverage, 1972 to date. Inquire as to online cost and availability. Provides abstracts from more than 1,600 publications. Weekly updates.

PERIODICALS AND NEWSLETTERS

The Marketer: Official Voice of Petroleum Marketers in Oklahoma. Oklahoma Petroleum Marketers Association. • Quarterly. $12.00 per year.

Oil and Gas Journal. PennWell Corp., Industrial Div. • Weekly. $84.00 per year.

Oil Daily: Daily Newspaper of the Petroleum Industry. Energy Intelligence Group, Inc. • Daily. Email, $1,595.00 per year; fax, $2,395.00 per year, online, $1,495.00 per year. Newspaper for the petroleum industry.

Oil Express: Inside Report on Trends in Petroleum Marketing Without the Influnce of Advertising. United Communications Group. • 50 times a year. $337.00 per year. Newsletter. Provides news of trends in petroleum marketing and convenience store operations. Includes *U. S. Oil Week's Price Monitor* (petroleum product prices) and *C-Store Digest* (news concerning convenience stores operated by the major oil companies) and *Fuel Oil Update.* Formerly *U.S. Oil Week.*

Oil Market Intelligence. PIW Publications Inc. • Description: Provides analysis and statistics on worldwide oil markets and leading regional markets, including both the Atlantic Basin (Europe and the Americas) and Pacific Basins (East of Suez and the Far East). Covers futures and options markets and furnishes a monthly scorecard of prices for key products and crudes.

The Oil Marketing Bulletin. United Communications Group. • Weekly. $695.00 per year. Newsletter. Marketing information service.

Platt's Oilgram News. McGraw-Hill Inc. • Description: Monitors the latest developments in the politics and economics of petroleum. Covers exploration, production, supply and transportation, refining, and marketing. Recurring features include interviews, news of research, and reports of meetings. Coverage is global in scope.

STATISTICS SOURCES

Petroleum Marketing Monthly. Available from U. S. Government Printing Office. • Monthly. Current information and statistics relating to a wide variety of petroleum products. (Office of Oil and Gas, Energy Information Administration, U. S. Department of Energy.).

Standard & Poor's Industry Surveys. Standard & Poor's. • Semiannual. $1,800.00. Two looseleaf volumes. Includes monthly *Supplements.* Provides detailed, individual surveys of 52 major industry groups. Each survey is revised on a semiannual basis. Also includes "Monthly Investment Review" (industry group investment analysis) and monthly "Trends & Projections" (economic analysis).

Standard & Poor's Statistical Service. Current Statistics. Standard & Poor's. • Monthly. $688.00 per year. Includes 10 *Basic Statistics* sections, *Current Statistics Supplements* and *Annual Security Price Index Record.*

TRADE/PROFESSIONAL ASSOCIATIONS

American Petroleum Institute. 1220 L St. NW, Washington, DC 20005-4070. Phone: (202)682-8000 Fax: (202)682-8033 E-mail: mediacenter@api.org • URL: http://www.api.org • Corporations in the petroleum and allied industries, including producers, refiners, marketers, and transporters of crude oil,

lubricating oil, gasoline and natural gas. Provides public policy development, advocacy, research, and technical services to enhance the ability of the petroleum industry to fulfill its mission: meeting the nation's energy needs; enhancing the environmental, health, and safety performance of the industry; conducting research to advance petroleum technology, equipment, and standards; Consensus policies and collective action on issues impacting its members; and works collaboratively with all industry oil and gas associations, and other organizations, to enhance industry unity and effectiveness in its advocacy. Also provides the opportunity for standards development, technical cooperation and other activities to improve the industry's competitiveness through sponsorship of self-supporting programs.

Petroleum Marketers Association of America. 1901 N Fort Meyer Dr., Ste. 1200, Arlington, VA 22209. Phone: (703)351-8000 Fax: (703)351-9160 E-mail: info@pmaa.org • URL: http://www.pmaa.org • Absorbed National Oil Fuel Institute and Oil Heat Institute of America. Formerly National Jobbers Council.

Society of Independent Gasoline Marketers of America. 11911 Freedom Dr., Ste. 590, Reston, VA 20190. Phone: (703)709-7000 Fax: (703)709-7007 E-mail: sigma@sigma.org • URL: http://www.sigma.org • Chain gasoline marketers, wholesale and retail.

PHARMACEUTICAL INDUSTRY

See also: DRUG STORES; GENERIC DRUG INDUSTRY; NONPRESCRIPTION DRUG INDUSTRY

GENERAL WORKS

The Chemistry of Mind-Altering Drugs: History, Pharmacology, and Cultural Context. Daniel M. Perrine. American Chemical Society. • 1996. $45.00. Contains detailed descriptions of the pharmacological and psychological effects of a wide variety of drugs, "from alcohol to zopiclone.".

Pharmaceutical Marketing in the 21st Century. Mickey C. Smith, editor. Haworth Press, Inc. • 1996. $49.95. Various authors discuss the marketing, pricing, distribution, and retailing of prescription drugs. (Pharmaceutical Marketing and Management Series, Vol. 10, Nos. 2,3&4).

Pharmacy: What It Is and How It Works. William N. Kelly. CRC Press. • 2002. $39.95. Serves as an introduction to the field of pharmacy, including a history of the profession and information on career opportunities. Chapters are included on drug development, uses of drugs, pricing, information technology for pharmacies, and career planning.

ABSTRACTS AND INDEXES

Applied Science and Technology Index. H. W. Wilson Co. • 11 times a year. Quarterly and annual cumulations. Price varies. Indexes a wide variety of English language technical, industrial, and engineering periodicals.

International Pharmaceutical Abstracts: Key to the World's Literature of Pharmacy. American Society of Health-System Pharmacists. • Semimonthly. $565.50 per year.

Science Citation Index. Thomson/ISI. • Bimonthly. $15,020.00 per year. Annual cumulation. Includes *Source Index, Citation Index, Permuterm Subject Index,* and *Corporate Index.*

ALMANACS AND YEARBOOKS

Annual Review of Pharmacology and Toxicology. Annual Reviews. • Annual. Individuals, $74.00. Includes print and online editions. Institutions, $173.

00; with online edition, $208.00.

BIBLIOGRAPHIES

Medical and Health Care Books and Serials in Print: An Index to Literature in Health Sciences. R. R. Bowker. • Annual. $359.00. Two volumes.

BIOGRAPHICAL SOURCES

Dictionary of American Medical Biography. Joseph Carvalho and others. Greenwood Publishing Group Inc. • 1984. $210.00. Two volumes: Vol. one, $110.00; vol. two, $110.00.

CD-ROM DATABASES

International Pharmaceutical Abstracts [CD-ROM]. American Society of Health-System Pharmacists. • Monthly. $1,795.00 per year. Contains CD-ROM indexing and abstracting of international pharmaceutical literature from 1970 to date.

Mosby's GenRx [year]. CME, Inc. • Quarterly. $250.00. CD-ROM contains detailed monographs for more than 45,000 generic and brand name prescription drugs. Includes color pill images and customizable patient education handouts.

Physicians' Desk Reference Library on CD-ROM. Medical Economics. • Three times a year. Contains the CD-ROM equivalent of *Physicians' Desk Reference (PDR), Physicians' Desk Reference for Nonprescription Drugs, Physicians' Desk Reference for Opthalmology,* and other PDR publications.

DIRECTORIES

BioScan: The Worldwide Biotech Industry Reporting Service. Greenwood Publishing Group, Inc. • Annual. $975.00 per year. Bimonthly updates. Provides detailed information on over 1,000 U.S. and foreign companies broadly classified as biotechnological. In addition to medical technology and advanced pharmaceutical firms, includes firms doing research in food processing, waste management, agriculture, and veterinary science.

Drug Facts and Comparisons. Facts and Comparisons. • Annual. $359.95. Provides detailed information on more than 20,000 prescription drugs and 6000 over-the-counter products. Arrangement is according to 13 therapeutic categories. Includes charts and tables.

Drug Interaction Facts. Facts and Comparisons. • Annual. $179.95. Contains data on the interactions of some 20,000 prescription drugs. Interactions are rated according to magnitude and likelihood of effects, from one (most severe) to five (least severe). Includes drug/drug and drug/food interactions.

Encyclopedia of Medical Organizations and Agencies. Gale Cengage Learning. • 2001. $295.00. 11th edition. Information on over 18,000 public and private organizations in medicine and related fields.

How to Save on Prescription Drugs: The AIER Guide to Prescription Drug Assistance Programs for Seniors. Kerry A. Lynch. American Institute for Economic Research. • 2003. $5.00. Contains a state-by-state directory of 39 state assistance programs offering prescription drug coverage, usually for low-income residents age 65 or older. Provides phone numbers, websites, coverage, eligibility details, and "How it works" for each state. A separate section describes five drug company discount cards. (Economic Education Bulletin.).

Internet Tools of the Profession: A Guide for Information Professionals. Hope N. Tillman, editor. Special Libraries Association. • 1997. $49.00. Second edition. Consists of 14 sections by various authors or compilers. After two introductory articles on searching the Internet, there are 12 annotated lists of useful Web sites, covering the SLA, business and finance, chemistry, education, food and agriculture, information technology, insurance and employee benefits, law, library management, metals and materials, pharmaceuticals, and telecommunications. An index is provided.

Major Pharmaceutical Companies of the World. Available from Gale Cengage Learning. • 2003. $880.00. Fifth edition. Published by Graham & Whiteside. Contains detailed information and trade names for more than 2,500 important pharmaceutical companies in various countries.

Medical and Health Information Directory. Gale Cengage Learning. • 2002. $675.00. Three volumes. 14th edition. Three volumes. $285.00 per volume. Vol. one covers medical organizations, agencies, and institutions; vol. two includes bibliographic, library, and database information; vol. three is a guide to services available for various medical and health problems.

Medical and Healthcare Marketplace Guide. IDD, Inc. • Annual. $595.00. Two volumes. Provides market survey summaries for about 500 specific product and service categories (volume one: "Research Reports"). Contains profiles of nearly 5,500 pharmaceutical, medical product, and healthcare service companies (volume two: "Company Profiles").

Mosby's GenRx: The Complete Reference for Generic and Brand Drugs. Mosby, Inc. • 2000. $72.95. 11th edition. Provides detailed information on a wide variety of generic and brand name prescription drugs. Includes color identification pictures, prescribing data, and price comparisons. (Mosby's Physicians GenRx Series).

NDA Pipeline(New Drug Approval). F-D-C Reports, Inc. • Annual. Available online only. Provides information on U. S. drugs in the development stage and products receiving new drug approval (NDA) from the Food and Drug Administration. Listings are company-by-company and by generic name, with orphan drug designations. Includes an industry directory.

Pharmaceutical Marketers Directory. CPS Communications Inc. • Covers: about 15,000 personnel of pharmaceutical, medical device and equipment manufacturers, and biotechnology companies; advertising agencies with clients in the healthcare field; health care publications; alternative media and healthcare industry suppliers. Entries include: Company name, address, list of personnel by job classification (with titles, phone, internet and e-mail addresses, direct dial and fax numbers).

Pharmaceutical Processing Annual Buyers Guide. Reed Business Information. • Annual. $69.95. Includes *Buyer's Guide.* Lists makers and distributors of supplies and equipment for the pharmaceutical manufacturing industry.

Red Book. American Monument Association. • Covers: 7,000 retail monument dealers, suppliers of granite and marble, wholesalers, quarriers, funeral homes and cemeteries. Entries include: company; name, address, phone, fax; trade classification, names of owner or corporate officers and their titles. Available only to members of The American Monument Association.

ENCYCLOPEDIAS AND DICTIONARIES

American Drug Index. Facts and Comparisons. • Annual. $69.95. Lists over 20,000 drug entries in dictionary style.

Drugs and Controlled Substances: Information for Students. Gale Cengage Learning. • 2002. $115.00. Arranged alphabetically by drug name. Provides detailed information on the psychological and physiological effects of addictive drugs and substances. Includes illegal drugs, addictive prescription drugs, and over-the-counter items.

Pharmacological and Chemical Synonyms: A Collection of Names of Drugs, Pesticides, and Other Compounds Drawn from the Medical Literature of the World. E. E. Marler. Elsevier. • 1994. $272.00. Tenth edition.

USAN and the USP Dictionary of Drug Names. United States Pharmacopeial Convention. • Annual. $279.00. Adopted names, brand names, compendial and other generic names, CAS Registry Numbers, molecular weights, and other information.

FINANCIAL RATIOS

Almanac of Business and Industrial Financial Ratios. Leo Troy. Aspen Publishers, Inc. • 2003. $125.95. Includes CD-Rom. Contains financial ratios derived from federal tax returns. Ratios for each of about 200 industries are arranged according to company asset size. (Almanac of Business and Industrial Financial Ratios Series).

Annual Statement Studies. The Risk Management Association. • Annual. Median and quartile financial ratios are given for over 400 kinds of manufacturing, wholesale, retail, construction, and consumer finance establishments. Data is sorted by both asset size and sales volume. Includes a clearly written "Definition of Ratios" and an alphabetical industry index.

Annual Statement Studies: Industry Default Probabilities and Cash Flow Measures. The Risk Management Association. • Annual. $145.00. Serves as a companion volume to the original *Annual Statement Studies.* Gives probability of default estimates on a percentage scale for more than 450 industries. Includes changes in position year-by-year for eight financial statement line items and provides percentage measures of cash flow.

Quarterly Financial Report for Manufacturing, Mining, and Trade Corporations. U.S. Federal Trade Commission and U.S. Securities and Exchange Commission. Available from U.S. Government Printing Office. • Quarterly. $49.00 per year.

HANDBOOKS AND MANUALS

AHFS Drug Information. American Hospital Formulary Service. American Society of Health-System Pharmacists. • 2003. $174.95. 44th edition. Detailed information about drugs and groups of drugs.

Approved Drug Products, with Therapeutic Equivalence Evaluations. Available from U. S. Government Printing Office. • $108.00 for basic manual and supplemental material for an indeterminate period. Issued by the Food and Drug Administration, U. S. Department of Health and Human Services. Lists prescription drugs that have been approved by the FDA. Includes therapeutic equivalents to aid in containment of health costs and to serve State drug selection laws.

Complete Guide to Prescription and Non-Prescription Drugs: Side Effects, Warnings, and Vital Data for Safe Use. H. Winter Griffith. Berkley Publishing Group. • Annual. $17.95. A guide for consumers.

The Consumer Health Information Source Book. Alan Rees, editor. Greenwood Publishing Group, Inc. • 2003. $65.00. Seventh edition. Bibliography of current literature and guide to organizations.

Dun & Bradstreet/Gale Group Industry Handbooks. Gale Cengage Learning. • 2000. $650.00. Five volumes. $130.00 per volume. Each volume covers two or more major industries: 1. *Entertainment and Hospitality;* 2. *Construction and Agriculture;* 3. *Chemicals and Pharmaceuticals;* 4. *Computers & Software and Broadcasting & Telecommunications;* 5. *Insurance and Health & Medical Services.* The following are included for each industry: overview, statistics, financial ratios, rankings, merger information, company directory, directory of associations, and consultants directory. (Dun and Bradstreet/Gale Industry Reference Handbook Series).

Financial Management for Pharmacists: A Decision-Making Approach. Norman V. Carroll. Lippincott Williams and Wilkins. • 1997. $39.00. Second edition.

Handbook of Nonprescription Drugs. Rosemary R. Berardi, editor. American Pharmacists Association. • 2002. $135.00. 13th edition. Contains comprehensive, technical information on over-the-counter drugs.

Managing Pharmacy Practice: Principles, Strategies, and Systems. Andrew M. Peterson. CRC Press. • 2004. $69.95. Covers basic management theory and systems as applied to pharmacies. Includes discussion of current trends in managed care systems, reimbursement, formularies, and drug benefit systems.

PDR Drug Guide for Mental Health Professionals. Thomson Medical Economics. • Annual. $39.95. Contains detailed profiles of more than 70 "common psychotropic drugs organized by brand name." Also contains information on the psychological side effects of about 1,000 other prescription drugs.

PDR Guide to Drug Interactions, Side Effects, Indications. American Medical Association. Medical Economics Co., Inc. • Annual. $48.95. Includes a list of prescription drugs by "precise clinical situation.".

Physicians' Desk Reference. Medical Economics Co. • Annual. $82.95. Generally known as "PDR". Provides detailed descriptions, effects, and adverse reactions for about 4,000 prescription drugs. Includes data on more than 250 drug manufacturers, with brand name and generic name indexes and drug identification photographs. Discontinued drugs are also listed.

Physicians' Desk Reference for Ophthalmology. Medical Economics Co. • Annual. $49.95. Provides detailed descriptions of ophthalmological instrumentation, equipment, supplies, lenses, and prescription drugs. Indexed by manufacturer, product name, product category, active drug ingredient, and instrumentation. Editorial discussion is included.

United States Pharmacopeia National Formulary. United States Pharmacopeial Convention. • Quinquennial.

INTERNET DATABASES

Manufacturing Profiles. U. S. Bureau of the Census. Phone: (301)763-4636 E-mail: webmaster@census.gov • URL: http://www.census.gov/prod/www/abs/mfg-prof.html • The Census Bureau makes available free on PDF (Portable Document Format) an annual consolidation of the entire Current Industrial Report series, presenting "all the data compiled". Contains statistics on production, shipments, inventories, consumption, exports, imports, and orders for a wide variety of manufactured products.

National Library of Medicine (NLM). National Institutes of Health (NIH). Phone: 888-346-3656 or (301)496-1131 Fax: (301)480-3537 E-mail: access@nlm.nih.gov • URL: http://www.nlm.nih.gov • NLM Web site offers free access through MEDLINE ("PubMed") to about nine million references to articles appearing in some 4,000 biomedical journals, with abstracts. Search interfaces range from "simple keywords to advanced Boolean expressions." The NLM site offers many links to other sources of biomedical and technical information (the National Center for Biotechnology Information, for example). Fees: Free.

RxList: The Internet Drug Index. Neil Sandow. Phone: (707)746-8754 E-mail: info@rxlist.com • URL: http://www.rxlist.com • Web site features detailed information (cost, usage, dosage, side effects, etc.) from Mosby, Inc. for about 300 major pharmaceutical products, representing two thirds of prescriptions filled in the U. S. (3,700 other products are listed). The "Top 200" drugs are ranked by number of prescriptions filled. Keyword searching is provided. Fees: Free.

ONLINE DATABASES

Derwent Drug File. Derwent, Inc. • Provides indexing and abstracting of the world's pharmaceutical journal literature since 1964, with weekly updates. Formerly *RINGDOC*. Inquire as to online cost and availability.

Drug Information Fulltext. American Society of Health-System Pharmacists. • Provides full text monographs from the *American Hospital Formulary Service* and the *Handbook On Injectable Drugs*. Inquire as to online cost and availability.

F-D-C Reports. FDC Reports, Inc. • An online version of "The Gray Sheet" (medical devices), "The Pink Sheet" (pharmaceuticals), "The Rose Sheet" (cosmetics), "The Blue Sheet" (biomedical), and "The Tan Sheet" (nonprescription). Contains full-text information on legal, technical, corporate, financial, and marketing developments from 1987 to date, with weekly updates. Inquire as to online cost and availability.

Globalbase. Gale Cengage Learning. • Provides more than one million online summaries of business, industrial, and economic news reports from more than 1,000 publications worldwide. Covers a wide range of material appearing in international trade journals, professional magazines, and newspapers. Time period is 1984 to date, with weekly updates. Inquire as to online cost and availability.

International Pharmaceutical Abstracts [online]. American Society of Health-System Pharmacists. • Provides online indexing and abstracting of the world's pharmaceutical literature from 1970 to date. Monthly updates. Inquire as to online cost and availability.

Pharmaceutical News Index. ProQuest Inc. • Indexes major pharmaceutical industry newsletters, 1974 to present. Weekly updates. Inquire as to online cost and availability.

PROMT: Predicasts Overview of Markets and Technology. Gale Cengage Learning. • Companies, products, applied technologies and markets. U.S. and international literature coverage, 1972 to date. Inquire as to online cost and availability. Provides abstracts from more than 1,600 publications. Weekly updates.

Scisearch. Institute for Scientific Information. • Broad, multidisciplinary index to the literature of science and technology, 1974 to present. Inquire as to online cost and availability. Coverage of literature is worldwide, with weekly updates.

PERIODICALS AND NEWSLETTERS

American Journal of Health-System Pharmacy. American Society of Health-System Pharmacists. • Semimonthly. $195.00 per year. Formerly *American Journal of Hospital Pharmacy*.

Clin-Alert. Rowman & Littlefield Education. • Description: Reports on adverse drug reactions, drug interactions, and related therapeutic hazards. Summarizes information from leading medical and pharmaceutical journals, reporting patient history, diagnosis, treatment, dosage, author's conclusion and warning, trade names of drugs, legal actions, if any, and dispositions.

Community Pharmacist: Meeting the Professional and Educational Needs of Today's Practitioner. ELF Publicatons, Inc. • Bimonthly. $25.00 per year. Edited for retail pharmacists in various settings, whether independent or chain-operated. Covers both pharmaceutical and business topics.

Drug Benefit Trends: For Pharmacy Managers and Managed HealthCare Professionals. Cliggott Publishing Co. • Monthly. Individuals, $95.00 per year; libraries, $120.00 per year; students, $40.00 per year. Covers the business of managed care drug benefits.

Drug Development Research. John Wiley and Sons, Inc. • Monthly. Institutions, $4,295.00 per year; with online edition, $4,510.00 per year.

Drug Topics. Thomson Medical Economics. • 23 times a year. $61.00 per year. Edited for retail pharmacists, hospital pharmacists, pharmacy chain store executives, wholesalers, buyers, and others concerned with drug dispensing and drug store management. Provides information on new products, including personal care items and cosmetics.

FDA Consumer. Available from U. S. Government Printing Office. • Bimonthly. $14.00 per year. Issued by the U. S. Food and Drug Administration. Provides consumer information about FDA regulations and product safety.

The Green Sheet. F-D-C Reports, Inc. • Weekly. $109.00 per year. Newsletter for retailers and wholesalers of pharmaceutical products. Includes pricing developments and new drug announcements.

Health News Daily. F-D-C Reports Inc. • Description: Tracks developments in health care policy, legislation and regulation, insurance, pharmaceuticals, delivery, manufacturing, technology and treatment, funding, and research.

Healthcare Distributor: The Industry's Multi-Market Information Resource. ELF Publications. • Bimonthly. $30.00 per year. Formerly *Wholesale Drugs Magazine*.

Hospital Pharmacist Report. Thomson Medical Economics. • Monthly. $39.00 per year. Covers both business and clinical topics for hospital pharmacists.

Journal of Pharmaceutical, Finance, Economics and Policy. FDC Reports. • Quarterly. Institutions, $365.00 per year. Formerly *Journal of Research in Pharmaceutical Economics*.

Journal of Pharmaceutical Marketing and Management. Haworth Press, Inc. • Quarterly. $365.00 per year.

Med Ad News. Engel Publishing Partners. • Monthly. $225.00 per year. Covers the field of pharmaceutical advertising and marketing.

The Medical Letter on Drugs and Therapeutics. The Medical Letter, Inc. • Biweekly. $55.00 per year. Newsletter. Provides critical evaluation of new drugs, including effectiveness, toxicity, cost, and possible alternatives.

Medical Marketing and Media. Haymarket Media, Inc. • Monthly. Individuals, $96.00 per year; institutions, $108.00 per person. Contains articles on marketing, direct marketing, advertising media, and sales personnel for the healthcare and pharmaceutical industries.

Pharma Business: The International Magazine of Pharmaceutical Business and Marketing. Engel Publishing Partners. • Six times a year. $235.00 per year. Circulated mainly in European countries. Coverage includes worldwide industry news, new drug products, regulations, and research developments.

Pharma Marketletter. Marketletter Publications Ltd. • Fifty times a year. $525.00 per year. Newsletter. Formerly *Marketletter*.

Pharmaceutical and Medical Device Law Bulletin. American Lawyer Media, Inc. • Monthly. $199.00 per year. Newsletter. Edited for lawyers concerned with drug product or medical device litigation. Contains industry news items of special interest, reports on new products, legal case summaries, Food and Drug Administration actions, patent issues, and related news reports. (A Law Journal Newsletter, formerly published by Leader Publications).

Pharmaceutical Engineering. International Society for Pharmaceutical Engineering, Inc. • Bimonthly. $60.00 per year. Feature articles provide practical application and specification information on the design, construction, supervision and maintenance of process equipment, plant systems, instrumentation and pharmaceutical facilities.

Pharmaceutical Executive: For Global Business and Marketing Leaders. Advanstar Communications. • Monthly. $64.00 per year.

Pharmaceutical Processing. Reed Business Information. • Monthly. $62.90 per year. Includes *Buyers' Guide.* Formerly *Pharmaceutical and Cosmetic Equipment.*

Pharmaceutical Representative. McKnight Medical Communications. • Monthly. $37.95 per year. Edited for drug company salespeople and sales managers.

Pharmaceutical Technology. Advanstar Communications. • Monthly. $64.00 per year. Practical hands on information about the manufacture of pharmaceutical products, focusing on applied technology.

Pharmacopeial Forum. United States Pharmacopeial Convention, Inc. • Bimonthly. $469.00 per year.

The Pink Sheet: Prescription Pharmaceuticals and Biotechnology. F-D-C Reports, Inc. • 51 times a year. Institutions, $1,431.00 per year. Newsletter covering business and regulatory developments affecting the pharmaceutical and biotechnology industries. Provides information on generic drug approvals and includes a drug sector stock index.

The Tan Sheet: Nonprescription Pharmaceuticals and Nutritionals. F-D-C Reports, Inc. • Weekly. $1,220.00 per year. Newsletter covering over-the-counter drugs and vitamin supplements. Emphasis is on regulatory activities of the U. S. Food and Drug Administration (FDA).

Worst Pills Best Pills News. Public Citizen. • Monthly. $20.00 per year. Newsletter. Provides pharmaceutical news and information for consumers, with an emphasis on harmful drug interactions.

PRICE SOURCES

First DataBank Blue Book. Hearst Corp. • Annual. $65.00. List of manufacturers of prescription and over-the-counter drugs, sold in retail drug stores. Formerly *American Druggist Blue Book.*

RESEARCH CENTERS AND INSTITUTES

Pharmaceutical Marketing and Management Research Program. University of Mississippi, Waller Lab Complex, Room 101, University, MS 38677. Phone: (662)915-5948 Fax: (662)915-5262 E-mail: mkolassa@olemiss.edu • URL: http://www.olemiss.edu/depts/rips.

Pharmacology Research Laboratory. Indiana University-Purdue University at Indianapolis, School of Medicine, 635 Barnhill Dr., Indianapolis, IN 46202-5120. Phone: (317)274-7844 Fax: (317)274-7714 E-mail: besch@iupui.edu • URL: http://www.iupui.edu/.

Upjohn Center for Clinical Pharmacology. University of Michigan. School of Medicine, 3709 Upjohn Center, Ann Arbor, MI 48109-0504. Phone: (734)764-9121 Fax: (734)763-3438 E-mail: plf@umich.edu.

STATISTICS SOURCES

Annual Survey of Manufactures. Available from U. S. Government Printing Office. • Annual. Prices vary. Issued by the U. S. Census Bureau as an interim update to the *Census of Manufactures.* Includes data on number of manufacturing establishments in various industries, employment, labor costs, value of shipments, capital expenditures, inventories, energy costs, and assets. (See also Census Bureau home page, http://www.census.gov/.)

Industry Profile and Healthcare Factbook. Healthcare Distribution Management Association. • Annual. $349.00. Provides 266 statistical tables in

three sections: "Industry Profile" (financial ratios related to drug distribution), "Pharmaceutical and Healthcare Distribution Trends and Facts," and "Healthcare Factbook" (expenditures, insurance utilization, company/product rankings, drug price inflation, generics, OTC, drug store data, hospital statistics, healthcare consumer summaries, etc.). Also known as *HDMA Factbook.* The Healthcare Distribution Management Association was formerly the National Wholesale Druggists' Association.

Narcotic Drugs: Estimated World Requirements. International Narcotics Control Board. United Nations Publications. • Annual. $38.00. Includes production and utilization data relating to legal narcotics. Text in French, English and Spanish.

Pharmaceutical Research Manufacturers Association Annual Fact Book. Pharmaceutical Research and Manufacturers Association. • Annual.

Standard & Poor's Industry Surveys. Standard & Poor's. • Semiannual. $1,800.00. Two looseleaf volumes. Includes monthly *Supplements.* Provides detailed, individual surveys of 52 major industry groups. Each survey is revised on a semiannual basis. Also includes "Monthly Investment Review" (industry group investment analysis) and monthly "Trends & Projections" (economic analysis).

Standard & Poor's Statistical Service. Current Statistics. Standard & Poor's. • Monthly. $688.00 per year. Includes 10 *Basic Statistics* sections, *Current Statistics Supplements* and *Annual Security Price Index Record.*

Statistical Handbook on Technology. Paula Bernstein. Greenwood Publishing Group, Inc. • 1999. $69.95. Provides statistical data on such items as the Internet, online services, computer technology, recycling, patents, prescription drug sales, telecommunications, and aerospace. Includes charts, tables, and graphs. Edited for the general reader. (Statistical Handbook Series).

U. S. Industry and Trade Outlook. Available from National Technical Information Service. • Annual. $69.95. Produced by the International Trade Administration, U. S. Department of Commerce, in a "public-private" partnership with DRI/McGraw-Hill and Standard & Poor's. Provides basic data, outlook for the current year, and "Long-Term Prospects" (five-year projections) for a wide variety of products and services. Includes high technology industries. Formerly *U. S. Industrial Outlook.*

TRADE/PROFESSIONAL ASSOCIATIONS

American College of Apothecaries. 2830 Summer Oaks Dr., Bartlett, TN 38134-3811. Phone: (901)383-8119 Fax: (901)383-8882 E-mail: acaninfo@caresourcecenter.org • A professional society of pharmacists.

American Pharmaceutical Association-Academy of Pharmacy Practice and Management. c/o Anne Burns, 2215 Constitution Ave., N.W., Washington, DC 20037-2895. Phone: 800-237-2742 or (202)628-4410 Fax: (202)783-2351 E-mail: apha-appm@mail.aphanet.org • URL: http://www.aphanet.org • Pharmacists concerned with rendering professional services directly to the public, without regard for status of employment or environment of practice. Formerly Academy of Pharmacy Practice and Management.

American Society of Health System Pharmacists. 7272 Wisconsin Ave., Bethesda, MD 20814. Phone: (301)657-3000 Fax: (301)664-8867 E-mail: ahfs@ashp.org • URL: http://www.ashp.org • Affiliated with American Hospital Association and American Nurses Association.

Council on Family Health. 1155 Connecticut Ave., Suite 1200B, Washington, DC 20036. Phone: (202)331-7373 Fax: (202)223-6835 E-mail: cfhinfo99@aol.com • URL: http://www.cfhinfo.org • Members are drug manufacturers. Concerned with proper use of medications.

Drug, Chemical and Allied Trades Association. 510 Route 130, Suite B1, East Windsor, NJ 08520. Phone: 800-640-3228 or (609)448-1000 Fax: (609)448-1944 E-mail: mtimony@dcat.org • URL: http://www.dcat.org • Formerly Drug, Chemical and Allied Trades Section of the New York Board of Trade.

Drug Information Association. 800 Enterprise Rd., Ste. 200, Horsham, PA 19044-3595. Phone: (215)442-6100 Fax: (215)442-6199 E-mail: dia@diahome.org • URL: http://www.diahome.org • Provides neutral, global forum promoting exchange of information critical to professional performance and achievement in the discovery, development, regulation, surveillance, or marketing of pharmaceuticals or related products.

Generic Pharmaceutical Association. 2300 Clarendon Blvd., Ste. 400, Arlington, VA 22201. Phone: (703)647-2480 Fax: (703)647-2481 E-mail: info@gphaonline.org • URL: http://www.gphaonline.org • Promotes the common interests of the members and the general welfare of the pharmaceutical industry; prepares and disseminates among members and others, accurate and reliable information concerning the industry, products, needs and requirements; participates in international, federal, state and municipal legislative, regulatory and administrative proceedings with respect to law, rules and orders affecting the pharmaceutical industry; participates in scientific research and product development with intent to increase consumer access to generic products; and raises awareness and visibility of the significant benefits and value of generic drugs to the consumers.

Healthcare Distribution Management Association. 901 N Glebe Rd., Ste. 1000, 1821 Michael Faraday Dr., Ste. 400, Arlington, VA 22203. Phone: (703)787-0000 Fax: (703)935-3200 E-mail: info@hdmanet.org • URL: http://www.healthcaredistribution.org • Wholesalers and manufacturers of drug and health care products and industry service providers. Seeks to secure safe and effective distribution of health care products, create and exchange industry knowledge affecting the future of distribution management, and influence standards and business processes that produce efficient health care commerce. Compiles statistics; sponsors research and specialized education programs.

ISPE, The Society for Life Science Professionals. 3109 W Dr. Martin Luther King, Jr. Blvd., Ste. 250, Tampa, FL 33607. Phone: (813)960-2105 Fax: (813)264-2816 E-mail: customerservice@ispe.org • URL: http://www.ispe.org • Formerly International Society of Pharmaceutical Engineers.

National Association of Boards of Pharmacy. 700 Busse Highway, Park Ridge, IL 60068. Phone: (847)698-6227 Fax: (847)698-0124 E-mail: info@nabp.net • URL: http://www.nabp.net.

National Association of Chain Drug Stores. 413 N Lee St., Alexandria, VA 22313. Phone: (703)549-3001 Fax: (703)836-4869 • URL: http://www.nacds.org.

National Council for Prescription Drug Programs. 9240 E Raintree Dr., Scottsdale, AZ 85260-7519. Phone: (480)477-1000 Fax: (480)767-1042 E-mail: ncpdp@ncpdp.org • URL: http://www.ncpdp.org • Concerned with standardization of third party prescription drug programs.

National Pharmaceutical Association. 107 Kilmayne Dr., Ste. C, Cary, NC 27511. Phone: 800-944-NPHA or (919)831-5368 Fax: (919)469-5870 E-mail: npha@npha.net • URL: http://www.npha.net • State and local associations of professional minority pharmacists. Provides a means whereby members may "contribute to their common improvement, share their experiences, and contribute to the public good".

For publishers addresses, refer to SOURCES CITED section at the back of the book.

National Pharmaceutical Council. 1894 Preston White Dr., Reston, VA 20191-5433. Phone: (703)620-6390 Fax: (703)476-0904 E-mail: info@npcnow.com • URL: http://www.npcnow.org • Pharmaceutical manufacturers producing high quality prescription medication and other pharmaceutical products. Generates research; conducts specialized educational programs, and forums.

Pharmaceutical Research and Manufacturers Association. 1100 15th St., N.W., Suite 900, Washington, DC 20005. Phone: (202)835-3400 Fax: (202)835-3429 • URL: http://www.phrma.org • Formerly Pharmaceutical Manufacturers Association.

United States Pharmacopeia. 12601 Twinbrook Pkwy., Rockville, MD 20852-1790. Phone: 800-822-8772 or (301)881-0666 Fax: (301)816-8299 E-mail: webmaster@usp.org • URL: http://www.usp.org • Promotes the public health by establishing and disseminating officially recognized standards of quality and authoritative information for the use of medicines and other health care technologies by health professionals, patients and consumers. Helps to monitor quality and prevent medication errors through national reporting programs. Achieves its goals through the contributions of volunteers representing pharmacy, medicine, and other health care professions, as well as science, academia, the U.S. government, the pharmaceutical industry, and consumer organizations.

OTHER SOURCES

Drug Product Liability. LexisNexis Matthew Bender. • $803.00. Four looseleaf volumes. Periodic supplementation. All aspects of drugs: manufacturing, marketing, distribution, quality control, multiple prescription problems, drug identification, FDA coverage, etc.

Food Law Reports. CCH, Inc. • Weekly. $1,459.00 per year. Six looseleaf volumes. Covers regulation of adulteration, packaging, labeling, and additives. Formerly *Food Drug Cosmetic Law Reports.*

Mail Service Pharmacy Market. MarketResearch.com. • 1999. $3,250.00. Provides detailed market data, with forecasts to the year 2003.

The Market for Generic Drugs. MarketResearch.com. • 2000. $3,250.00. Market research data. Includes a discussion of current trends in the use of generic prescription drugs to reduce healthcare costs, with forecasts to 2004.

The Market for Ophthalmic Pharmaceuticals. MarketResearch.com. • 1997. $2,500.00. Market research report. Covers topical and internal drugs for eye disorders, with market estimates. Includes pharmaceutical company profiles.

The Market for Rx-to-OTC Switched Drugs. MarketResearch.com. • 2000. $3,250.00. Market research report. Covers the market for over-the-counter drugs that were formerly available only by prescription. Includes profiles of relevant pharmaceutical companies.

The Market for Stress Management Products and Services. Available from MarketResearch.com. • 1996. $1,195.00. Market research report published by Marketdata Enterprises. Covers anti-anxiety drugs, stress management clinics, biofeedback centers, devices, seminars, workshops, spas, institutes, etc. Includes market size projections.

New and Breaking Technologies in the Pharmaceutical and Medical Device Industries. Theta Reports. • 1999. $1,695.00. Contains market research predictions of medical technology trends over the next 5 to 10 years (2004-2009), including developments in biotechnology, genetic engineering, medical device technology, therapeutic vaccines, non-invasive diagnostics, and minimally-invasive surgery. (Theta Report No. 931.).

Pharmaceutical Litigation Reporter: The National Journal of Record of Pharmaceutical Litigation. An-drews Publications. • Monthly. $775.00 per year. Newsletter. Reports on a wide variety of legal cases involving the pharmaceutical and medical device industries. Includes product liability lawsuits.

PHARMACIES

See: DRUG STORES

PHILANTHROPY

ABSTRACTS AND INDEXES

Index to Legal Periodicals and Books. H. W. Wilson Co. • Monthly. $490.00 per year. Quarterly and annual cumulations.

BIBLIOGRAPHIES

Literature of the Nonprofit Sector: A Bibliography with Abstracts. The Foundation Center. • Dates vary. Six volumes. $45.00 per volume. Covers the literature of philanthropy, foundations, nonprofit organizations, fund-raising, and federal aid.

The Non-Profit Handbook: Everything You Need to Know to Start and Run Your Nonprofit Organization. Gary M. Grobman. Chronicle of Higher Education, Inc. • 2002. $29.95. Third edition.

Philanthropy and Voluntarism: An Annotated Bibliography. Daphne N. Layton. The Foundation Center. • 1987. $18.50.

CD-ROM DATABASES

Leadership Library on CD-ROM: Who's Who in the Leadership of the United States. Leadership Directories, Inc. • Quarterly. Including access to Internet version (weekly updates). Contains all 14 *Yellow Book* personnel directories on CD-ROM, providing contact and brief biographical information for about 400,000 individuals. Covers business, government, financial institutions, news media, law firms, associations, foreign representatives, and nonprofit organizations. Includes photographs.

Prospector's Choice: The Electronic Product Profiling 10,000 Corporate and Foundation Grantmakers. Gale Cengage Learning. • Annual. Provides detailed CD-ROM information on foundations and corporate philanthropies. Also known as *Corporate and Foundation Givers on Disk.*

DIRECTORIES

Charitable Organizations of the U. S.: A Descriptive and Financial Information Guide. Gale Cengage Learning. • 1991. $180.00. Second edition. Describes nearly 800 nonprofit groups active in soliciting funds from the American public. Includes nearly 800 data on sources of income, administrative expenses, and payout.

Corporate Giving Directory: Comprehensive Profiles of America's Major Corporate Foundations and Corporate Charitable Giving Programs. Gale Cengage Learning. • Annual. $550.00. Contains detailed descriptions of the philanthropic foundations of over 1,000 major U. S. corporations. Includes grant types, priorities for giving, recent grants, and advice on approaching corporate givers.

Cumulative List of Organizations Described in Section 170(c) of the Internal Revenue Code of 1986. Available from U. S. Government Printing Office. • Annual. $153.00 per year, including quarterly supplements. Lists about 300,000 organizations eligible for contributions deductible for federal income tax purposes. Provides name of each organization and city, but not complete address information. Arranged alphabetically by name of institution. (Office of Employee Plans and Exempt Organizations, Internal Revenue Service.).

International Directory of Corporate Philanthropy. Available from Taylor & Francis Group. • Annual. $295.00. Published by Europa Publications (http://www.europapublications.com). Contains profiles of about 1,000 corporate foundations and "co-ordinating organizations" in various countries of the world. Provides details of charitable activities and philanthropic expenditures.

National Directory of Corporate Giving: A Guide to Corporate Giving Programs and Corporate Foundations. The Foundation Center. • Biennial. $195.00. Provides information on 2,895 corporations that maintain philanthropic programs (direct giving programs or company-sponsored foundations).

Nonprofit Sector Yellow Book: Who's Who in the Management of the Leading Foundations, Universities, Museums, and Other Nonprofit Organizations. Leadership Directories, Inc. • Semiannual. $265.00 per year. Covers management personnel and board members of about 1,300 prominent, nonprofit organizations: foundations, colleges, museums, performing arts groups, medical institutions, libraries, private preparatory schools, and charitable service organizations.

Wise Giving Guide. BBB Wise Giving Alliance. • Quarterly. Single copy free; individuals, $25.00 per year. Evaluates 400 national charities against a set of standards concerning management, government, and budget.

ENCYCLOPEDIAS AND DICTIONARIES

Encyclopedia of Social Welfare History in North America. John M. Herrick and Paul H. Stuart, editors. Sage Publications, Inc. • 2004. $150.00. Includes entries on the historical aspects of charity, economic conditions, tax policy, health policy, social welfare legislation, poverty, social security, and social problems.

HANDBOOKS AND MANUALS

Charitable Planning Primer. Ralph G. Miller and Adam Smalley. CCH, Inc. • 1999. $99.00. Covers the legal and tax aspects of charitable giving and planned gifts. Includes annuity documents, tax forms, tables, and examples.

Fundraising: Hands-On Tactics for Nonprofit Groups. L. Peter Edles. McGraw-Hill • 1992. $16.95. Covers fundamental premises, soliciting major gifts, small gift prospecting, canvassing, telephone appeals, creating publications, direct mail, and other fund-raising topics for nonprofit organizations.

The Law of Fundraising. Bruce R. Hopkins. John Wiley and Sons, Inc. • 2002. $170.00. Third edition. Annual supplements available. Covers all aspects of state and federal nonprofit fund-raising law. Includes summaries of the relevant laws and regulations of each state. (Nonprofit Law, Finance and Management Series).

INTERNET DATABASES

ACGA: Partners in Philanthropy. American Council on Gift Annuities. Phone: (317)269-6271 Fax: (317)269-6276 E-mail: acga@acga-web.org • URL: http://www.acga-web.org • Web site provides detailed information on gift annuities, including suggested charitable gift annuity rates for use by charities and their donors. Rates for immediate and deferred annuities are presented in the form of tables for ages 20 to 90 (and over), for both "Single Life" and "Two Lives - Joint and Survivor." Other items covered include the philosophy of gift annuities, state regulations, "What's New," and a search site. Fees: Free.

Welcome to the Foundation Center. The Foundation Center. Phone: (212)620-4230 or (212)807-3679 Fax: (212)807-3677 E-mail: mfn@fdncenter.org • URL: http://www.fdncenter.org • Web site provides a wide variety of information about foundations, grants, and philanthropy, with links to philanthropic organizations. "Grantmaker Information" link furnishes descriptions of available funding.

ONLINE DATABASES

Index to Legal Periodicals and Books (Online). H. W. Wilson Co. • Broad coverage of law journals and books 1981 to date. Monthly updates. Inquire as to online cost and availability.

Legal Resource Index. Gale Cengage Learning. • Broad coverage of law literature appearing in legal, business, and other periodicals, 1980 to date. Daily updates. Inquire as to online cost and availability.

LEXIS. LEXIS-NEXIS. • The various LEXIS databases provide full text and indexing for a wide variety of legal cases, statutes, orders, and opinions.

PERIODICALS AND NEWSLETTERS

Chronicle of Philanthropy:The Newspaper of the Non-Profit World. Chronicle of Higher Education, Inc. • Biweekly. $69.50 per year.

Corporate Philanthropy Report. Aspen Publishers Inc. • Description: Tracks charity donations by corporations.

Foundation News and Commentary: Philanthropy and the Nonprofit Sector. Council on Foundations, Inc. • Bimonthly. $48.00 per year. Formerly *Foundation News.*

Nonprofit Issues. Donald W. Kramer. • Description: Presents legal information for nonprofit executives and their professional advisors.

Trusts and Estates. Primedia Business Magazines and Media. • Monthly. $139.00 per year. Includes annual *Directory.*

RESEARCH CENTERS AND INSTITUTES

Center for Corporate Citizenship. Boston College, 55 Lee Rd., Chestnut Hill, MA 02467. Phone: (617)552-4545 Fax: (617)552-8499 E-mail: cccr@bc.edu • URL: http://www.bc.edu/cccbc • Areas of study include corporate images within local communities, corporate community relations, social vision, and philanthropy. Formerly Center for Corporate Community Relations.

Foundation Center. Foundation Center. 79 5th Ave./ 16th St., New York, NY 10003-3076. Phone: 800-424-9836 or (212)620-4230 Fax: (212)807-3677 E-mail: communications@foundationcenter.org • URL: http://foundationcenter.org • Strengthens the nonprofit sector by advancing knowledge about U.S. philanthropy, maintains a comprehensive database on U.S. grantmakers and their grants, and operates research, education and training programs designed to advance philanthropy.

STATISTICS SOURCES

The Corporate Contributions Plan: From Strategy to Budget. The Conference Board Inc. • Annual. Members, $30.00, non-members, $120.00.

Giving U.S.A: The Annual Report on Philanthropy. American Association of Fund-Raising Counsel. AAFRC Trust for Philanthropy. • Annual. $65.00.

TRADE/PROFESSIONAL ASSOCIATIONS

American Association of Fund-Raising Counsel. 10293 N. Meridian St., Suite 175, Indianapolis, IN 46290-1130. Phone: (317)816-1613 Fax: (317)816-1633 E-mail: info@aafrc.org • URL: http://www.aafrc.org.

Association of Fundraising Professionals. 1101 King St., Ste. 700, Alexandria, VA 22314-2967. Phone: 800-666-3863 or (703)684-0410 Fax: (703)684-0540 • URL: http://www.afpnet.org • Formerly National Society of Fundraising Executives.

BBB Wise Giving Alliance. 4200 Wilson Blvd., Ste. 800, Arlington, VA 22203-1838. Phone: (703)276-0100 Fax: (703)525-8277 E-mail: kbrannigan@cottoninc.com • URL: http://www.give.org • Supported by companies and local Better Business Bureaus operated autonomously in the United States and Puerto Rico, which are in turn supported by

270,000 local business members. Seeks to promote and foster the highest ethical relationship between businesses and the public through voluntary self-regulation, consumer and business education, and service excellence. Provides support to local Better Business Bureaus. Administers the advertising industry's self-regulatory program that monitors and investigates the truth and accuracy of national advertising claims; monitors and pre-screens advertising directed towards children. Develops information on national charitable organizations and whether they meet voluntary ethical standards for soliciting organizations. Provides information to help consumers and businesses make informed purchasing decisions and avoid costly scams and frauds; and settles consumer complaints through arbitration and other means. Operates BBB AUTO LINE, a national mediation and arbitration service providing an independent forum to resolve consumer complaints involving 32 participating auto manufacturers; Local Better Business Bureaus respond to more than 23 million requests for service annually, fielding 20 million pre-purchase inquiries and 3 million complaints.

BBB Wise Giving Council. 4200 Wilson Blvd., Ste. 800, Arlington, VA 22203-0100. Phone: (703)276-0100 Fax: (703)525-8277 E-mail: info@bbb.org • URL: http://www.give.org • Sets accountability standards and provides information for nonprofit organizations that solicit contributions from the public. Formerly National Charities Information Bureau.

Council on Foundations. 1828 L St. NW, Ste. 300, Washington, DC 20036. Phone: (202)466-6512 Fax: (202)785-3926 E-mail: webmaster@cof.org • URL: http://www.cof.org • Formerly National Council on Community Foundations.

Independent Sector. 1200 18th St. NW, Ste. 200, Washington, DC 20036. Phone: 888-860-8118 or (202)467-6100 Fax: (202)467-6101 E-mail: info@independentsector.org • URL: http://www.independentsector.org • Represents charities and foundations. Organizes corporate giving programs committed to advancement of the common good in America and around the world. Leads, strengthens, and mobilizes charitable community.

National Association of State Charity Officials. c/o Daniel Moore, Office of Attorney General, P.O. Drawer 1508, Santa Fe, NM 87504. Phone: (505)827-6693 • URL: http://www.nasconet.org • Members are state officials responsible for the administration of charitable solicitation laws.

National Committee for Responsive Philanthropy. 2001 S St., N.W., Suite 620, Washington, DC 20009. Phone: (202)387-9177 Fax: (202)332-5084 E-mail: info@ncrp.org • URL: http://www.ncrp.org • Promotes charitable giving to new organizations working for social change or controversial issues. Formerly Committee for Responsive Philanthropy.

Women and Philanthropy. 1015 18th St., N.W., Suite 202, Washington, DC 20036. Phone: (202)887-9660 Fax: (202)861-5483 E-mail: webmaster@womenphil.org • URL: http://www.womenphil.org • Purpose is to increase the amount of money given to programs benefiting women.

PHILATELY

See: STAMPS AS AN INVESTMENT

PHONOGRAPH AND PHONOGRAPH RECORD INDUSTRIES

See also: HIGH FIDELITY/STEREO; SOUND RECORDERS AND RECORDING

GENERAL WORKS

America on Record: A History of Recorded Sound. Andre Millard. Cambridge University Press. • 1995. $22.00.

ABSTRACTS AND INDEXES

Music Library Association Notes: Quarterly Journal of the Music Library Association. Music Library Association. • Quarterly. Individuals, $70.00 per year; institutions, $80.00 per year. Indexes record reviews (classical).

DIRECTORIES

Billboard's International Buyer's Guide. VNU Business Media. • Covers: record companies; music publishers; record and tape wholesalers; services and supplies for the music-record-tape-video industry; record and tape dealer accessories, fixtures, and merchandising products; includes United States and over 65 other countries. Entries include: Company name, address, phone, names of principal executives, trade and brand names and/or list of products and services.

Directory of Computer and Consumer Electronics Retailers. Chain Store Guide. • Annual. $335.00. Online edition, $775.00. Lists 4,500 United States and Canada companies operating almost 59,000 stores with at least $1,000,000 in sales.

Record Retailing Directory. VNU Business Media. • Covers: over 7,000 independent and chain store record retailers (including audiobooks and online) in the U.S., American Samoa, Guam, and Puerto Rico. Entries include: For independents--Name, address, phone, store owner. For chain stores--Name, address, phone, fax, corporate management staff, number of outlets, year founded, corporate headquarters address and phone.

HANDBOOKS AND MANUALS

Modern Recording Techniques. David M. Huber and Robert Runstein. Elsevier. • 2001. $36.99. Fifth edition.

Releasing an Independent Record: How to Successfully Start and Run Your Own Record Label in the 1990s. Gary Hustwit. Rockpress Publishing. • 1998. $24.95. Sixth edition.

PERIODICALS AND NEWSLETTERS

Billboard: The International Newsweekly of Music, Video, and Home Entertainment. VNU Business Media. • 51 times a year. $299.00 per year. Newsweekly for the music and home entertainment industries.

Cash Box: The International Music-Record Weekly. Cash Box Publishing Co., Inc. • Weekly. $185.00 per year.

Dealerscope: Product and Strategy for Consumer Technology Retailing. North American Publishing Co. • Monthly. Free to qualified personnel; others, $79.00 per year. Formerly *Dealerscope Consumer Electronics Marketplace.*

Radio & Records. Radio & Records, Inc. • Weekly. $325.00 per year. Provides news and information relating to the record industry and to regional and national radio broadcasting. Special features cover specific types of programming, such as "classic rock," "adult alternative," "oldies," "country," and "news/talk." Radio station business and management topics are included.

PRICE SOURCES

Audio. Orion Research Corp. • Annual. $179.00. Quotes retail and wholesale prices of used audio equipment. Original list prices and years of manufacture are also shown.

TRADE/PROFESSIONAL ASSOCIATIONS

National Academy of Recording Arts and Sciences. 3402 Pico Blvd., Santa Monica, CA 90405. Phone: (310)392-3777 Fax: (310)392-9262 E-mail: info@grammyfoundation.org • URL: http://www.grammy.com.

National Association of Recording Merchandisers. Nine Eves Dr., Suite 120, Marlton, NJ 08053. Phone: (856)596-2221 Fax: (856)596-3268 E-mail: rosum@narm.com • URL: http://www.narm.com.

Recording Industry Association of America. 1330 Connecticut Ave., Suite 300, Washington, DC 20036. Phone: (202)775-0101 Fax: (202)775-7253 E-mail: websmaster@riaa.com • URL: http://www.riaa.com • Formerly Record Industry Association of America.

OTHER SOURCES

Phonolog. Muze, Inc. • Annual. $550.00. 10 volumes. Provides detailed information on more than 370,000 titles of commercially available and out-of-print music recordings. Includes popular, jazz, and classical titles.

PHOTOCOPYING INDUSTRY

See: COPYING MACHINE INDUSTRY

PHOTOENGRAVING

See also: PRINTING AND PRINTING EQUIPMENT INDUSTRIES

PERIODICALS AND NEWSLETTERS

Prepress Bulletin. Bessie Halfacre, editor. International Prepress Association. • Bimonthly. $20.00 per year. Provides management and technical information on the graphic arts prepress industry.

TRADE/PROFESSIONAL ASSOCIATIONS

International Prepress Association. 7200 France Ave., S., Suite 223, Edina, MN 55435. Phone: 800-255-8141 or (612)896-1908 Fax: (612)896-0181 E-mail: info@ipa.org • URL: http://www.ipa.org • Formerly International Association of Photoplatemakers.

PHOTOGRAPHIC INDUSTRY

See also: CAMERA INDUSTRY; COMMERCIAL PHOTOGRAPHY; GRAPHIC ARTS INDUSTRY; MOTION PICTURE PHOTOGRAPHY

ABSTRACTS AND INDEXES

Art Index. H. W. Wilson Co. • Quarterly. Annual cumulations. Price varies. Subject and author index to periodicals in art, architecture, industrial design, city planning, photography, and various related topics.

Imaging Abstracts. Royal Photographic Society of Great Britain, Imaging Science and Technology Grou. Elsevier. • Bimonthly. $860.00 per year. Formerly *Photographic Abstracts.*

BIOGRAPHICAL SOURCES

Contemporary Photographers. Available from Gale Cengage Learning. • 1995. $190.00. Third edition. Provides biographical and critical information on more than 850 international photographers.

DIRECTORIES

Who's Who in Professional Imaging. Professional Photographers of America, Inc. • Annual. $110.00. Lists over 18,000 members. Formerly *Buyers Guide*

to Qualified Photographers.

ENCYCLOPEDIAS AND DICTIONARIES

Focal Encyclopedia of Photography. Leslie Stroebel and Richard D. Zakia, editors. Elsevier. • 1996. $69.95. Third edition.

FINANCIAL RATIOS

Cost of Doing Business Survey. Photo Marketing Association International. • Biennial. $225.00. Emphasis is on photographic retailing.

HANDBOOKS AND MANUALS

One-Hour Photo Processing Lab. Entrepreneur Media, Inc. • Looseleaf. $59.50. A practical guide to starting a film developing and printing business. Covers profit potential, start-up costs, market size evaluation, owner's time required, site selection, lease negotiation, pricing, accounting, advertising, promotion, etc. (Start-Up Business Guide No. E1209.).

ONLINE DATABASES

Art Index Online. H. W. Wilson Co. • Indexes a wide variety of art-related periodicals, 1984 to date. Monthly updates. Inquire as to online cost and availability.

F & S Index. Gale Cengage Learning. • Contains about four million citations to worldwide business, financial, and industrial or consumer product literature appearing from 1972 to date. Weekly updates. Inquire as to online cost and availability.

PERIODICALS AND NEWSLETTERS

The Journal of Imaging Science and Technology. Society for Imaging Science and Technolgy. • Bimonthly. Individuals, $135.00 per year; institutions, $155.00 per year. Incorporates *Journal of Imaging Technology.*

Photo Marketing. Photo Marketing Association International. • Monthly. Membership.

Shutterbug. PRIMEDIA Inc. • Monthly. $17.95 per year. Articles about new equipment, test reports on film accessories, how-to articles, etc. Annual *Buying Guide* available, $5.99.

PRICE SOURCES

Camera. Orion Research Corp. • Annual. $144.00. Quotes retail and wholesale prices of used cameras and equipment. Original list prices and years of manufacture are also shown.

STATISTICS SOURCES

Annual Survey of Manufactures. Available from U. S. Government Printing Office. • Annual. Prices vary. Issued by the U. S. Census Bureau as an interim update to the *Census of Manufactures.* Includes data on number of manufacturing establishments in various industries, employment, labor costs, value of shipments, capital expenditures, inventories, energy costs, and assets. (See also Census Bureau home page, http://www.census.gov/.).

U. S. Industry and Trade Outlook. Available from National Technical Information Service. • Annual. $69.95. Produced by the International Trade Administration, U. S. Department of Commerce, in a "public-private" partnership with DRI/McGraw-Hill and Standard & Poor's. Provides basic data, outlook for the current year, and "Long-Term Prospects" (five-year projections) for a wide variety of products and services. Includes high technology industries. Formerly *U. S. Industrial Outlook.*

TRADE/PROFESSIONAL ASSOCIATIONS

International Imaging Industry Association. 701 Westchester Ave., Ste. 317W, White Plains, NY 10604-3018. Phone: (914)285-4933 Fax: (914)285-4937 E-mail: i3ainfo@i3a.org • URL: http://www.i3a.org • Develops and promotes the adoption of open industry standards, addressing environmental issues and providing a voice for the industry that

will benefit all users. Promotes environment, health and safety concerns; works with various government agencies including the EPA, TSA, and WTO to ensure the best interests of the imaging industry are represented.

Photographic Society of America. 3000 United Founders Blvd., Suite 103, Oklahoma City, OK 73112. Phone: (405)843-1437 Fax: (405)843-1438 E-mail: hq@psa-photo.org • URL: http://www.psa-photo.org • Formerly Associated Camera Clubs of America.

Photoimaging Manufacturers and Distributors Association. 109 White Oak Lane, Suite 72F, Old Bridge, NJ 08857. Phone: (732)679-3460 Fax: (732)679-2294 E-mail: bclarkpmda@aol.com • Formerly Photographic Manufacturers and Distributors Association.

PMA - The Worldwide Community of Imaging Associations. 3000 Picture Pl., Jackson, MI 49201-8853. Phone: 800-762-9287 or (517)788-8100 Fax: (517)788-8371 E-mail: pma_membership@pmai.org • URL: http://www.pmai.org • Retailers of photo and video equipment, film, and supplies; firms developing and printing film. Maintains hall of fame. Compiles statistics; conducts research and educational programs.

Professional Photographers of America. 229 Peachtree St., N.E., Suite 2200, Atlanta, GA 30303. Phone: 800-786-6277 or (404)522-8600 Fax: (404)614-6404 E-mail: csc@ppa.com • URL: http://www.ppa.com • Formerly Photographer's Association of America.

Society for Imaging Science and Technology. 7003 Kilworth Lane, Springfield, VA 22151. Phone: (703)642-9090 Fax: (703)642-9094 E-mail: info@imaging.org • URL: http://www.imaging.org • Individuals apply photography and imaging to science, engineering and industry. Formerly Society of Photographic Scientists and Engineering.

PHOTOGRAPHY, COMMERCIAL

See: COMMERCIAL PHOTOGRAPHY

PHOTOGRAPHY, INDUSTRIAL

See: COMMERCIAL PHOTOGRAPHY

PHOTOMECHANICAL PROCESSES

See: GRAPHIC ARTS INDUSTRY

PHOTONICS

See also: OPTOELECTRONICS

GENERAL WORKS

Elements of Photonics. Keigo Iizuka. John Wiley and Sons, Inc. • 2002. $200.00. Two volumes. (Pure and Applied Optics Series, vol. 41).

Fundamentals of Photonics. Bahaa E. Seleh and Malvin C. Teich. John Wiley and Sons, Inc. • 1991. $120.00. (Pure and Applied Optics Series).

Photonics. Ralf Menzel. Springer-Verlag. • 2001. $89.95. "...covers the fundamental properties and the description of single photons and light beams, experimentally and theoretically." Provides basic information about modern lasers. Edited for graduate students and scientists.

ABSTRACTS AND INDEXES

Applied Science and Technology Index. H. W. Wilson Co. • 11 times a year. Quarterly and annual cumulations. Price varies. Indexes a wide variety of English language technical, industrial, and engineering periodicals.

DIRECTORIES

The Photonics Directory. Laurin Publishing Company Inc. • Description: A four-book set concerning the international photonics industry, including a 'Corporate Guide' listing manufacturers and suppliers; a 'Buyers' Guide'; a technical 'Handbook' for design and applications engineers; and a 'Dictionary' of terms and abbreviations. Entries include: Company name, address, phone, fax, e-mail, description of products and services.

ENCYCLOPEDIAS AND DICTIONARIES

Wiley Encyclopedia of Electrical and Electronics Engineering. John G. Webster, editor. John Wiley and Sons, Inc. • 1999. $9,630.00. 25 volumes. Includes *Supplement I* and *Supplement II.* Contains about 1,400 articles, each with bibliography. Arrangement is according to 64 categories.

ONLINE DATABASES

Applied Science and Technology Index Online. H. W. Wilson Co. • Provides online indexing of 500 major scientific, technical, industrial, and engineering periodicals. Time period is 1983 to date. Monthly updates. Inquire as to online cost and availability.

PROMT: Predicasts Overview of Markets and Technology. Gale Cengage Learning. • Companies, products, applied technologies and markets. U.S. and international literature coverage, 1972 to date. Inquire as to online cost and availability. Provides abstracts from more than 1,600 publications. Weekly updates.

PERIODICALS AND NEWSLETTERS

FiberSystems International. Available from IOP Publishing, Inc. • Seven times a year. Free to qualified personnel. Published in the UK by the Institute of Physics. "Covering the optical communications marketplace within the Americas and Asia." *Fibre Systems Europe* is also available, covering the business and marketing aspects of fiber optics communications in Europe.

Optics and Photonics News. Optical Society of America, Inc. • Monthly. $99.00 per year. Includes print and online editions.

Photonics Spectra. Laurin Publishing Co., Inc. • Monthly. $112.00 per year.

RESEARCH CENTERS AND INSTITUTES

Center for Advanced Phototonic and Electronic Materials. State University of New York at Buffalo, Fronczak Hall, Room 227-229, North Campus, P.O. Box 601500, Buffalo, NY 14260. Phone: (716)645-2422 Fax: (716)645-5964 E-mail: ub-capem@acsu. buffalo.edu • URL: http://www.grad.buffalo.edu/ • Does integrated optics research, including photonic circuitry.

Center for Advanced Technology in Telecommunications. Polytechnic University, Five Metrotech Center, Rm. LC208, Brooklyn, NY 11201. Phone: (718)260-3050 Fax: (718)260-3074 E-mail: panwar@catt.poly.edu • URL: http://www. catt.poly.edu • Research fields include active media for optical communication.

Communications and Information Processing Group. Rensselaer Polytechnic Institute, 7010 JEC, 110 Eighth St., Troy, NY 12180-3590. Phone: (518)276-6823 Fax: (518)276-6261 E-mail: modestin@ipl.rpi.edu • URL: http://www.ecse.rpi. edu • Includes Optical Signal Processing Laboratory and Speech Processing Laboratory.

Materials Processing Center. Massachusetts Institute of Technology, 77 Massachusetts Ave., Room 12-007, Cambridge, MA 02139-4307. Phone: (617)253-5179 Fax: (617)258-6900 E-mail: fmpage@.mit.edu • URL: http://www.web.mit.edu/mpc • Conducts processing, engineering, and economic research in ferrous and nonferrous metals, ceramics, polymers, photonic materials, superconductors, welding, composite materials, and other materials.

Mediphotonics Laboratory. City College of City University of New York, 138th and Convent Ave., New York, NY 10031. Phone: (212)650-5531 Fax: (212)650-5530.

Optoelectronic Computing Systems Center. University of Colorado at Boulder, Campus Box 525, Boulder, CO 80309-0525. Phone: (303)492-7135 Fax: (303)492-3674 E-mail: jneff@colorado. edu • URL: http://www.ocs.colorado.edu • Explores the advantages of optics over electronics for information processing.

Photonics Research Laboratory. University of Florida, 339 Larsen Hall, Gainesville, FL 32611. Phone: (352)392-9265 Fax: (352)392-4963 E-mail: ramu@ece.ufl.edu • URL: http://www.ece.ufl.edu/labs/mphoton.

TRADE/PROFESSIONAL ASSOCIATIONS

IEEE Lasers and Electro-Optics Society. c/o IEEE Corporate Center, Three Park Ave., 17th Fl., New York, NY 10016-5997. Phone: (212)419-7900 or (212)752-4929 E-mail: ieeeusa@ieee.org • URL: http://www.ieee.org • Fields of interest include lasers, fiber optics, optoelectronics, and photonics.

Minerals, Metals and Materials Society. 184 Thorn Hill Dr., Warrendale, PA 15086-7514. Phone: (724)776-9000 Fax: (724)776-3770 E-mail: tmsgeneral@tms.org • URL: http://www.tms.org • Members are metallurgists, metallurgical engineers, and materials scientists. Divisions include Light Metals and Electronic, Magnetic, and Photonic Materials. Formerly The Metallurigical Society.

Optical Society of America. 2010 Massachusetts Ave., N.W., Washington, DC 20036-1023. Phone: (202)223-8130 Fax: (202)223-1096 E-mail: info@osa.org • URL: http://www.osa.org.

SPIE-The International Society for Optical Engineering. P.O. Box 10, Bellingham, WA 98227-0010. Phone: (360)676-3290 Fax: (360)647-1445 E-mail: spie@spie.org • URL: http://www.spie.org • Formerly Society of Photo-Optical Instrumentation Engineers.

PHYSICAL DISTRIBUTION

See: DISTRIBUTION

PHYSICAL FITNESS INDUSTRY

See: FITNESS INDUSTRY

PICKETING

See: STRIKES AND LOCKOUTS

PIERS

See: PORTS

PIG INDUSTRY

See: SWINE INDUSTRY

PIGGYBACK TRANSPORT

See: TRUCK TRAILERS

PILOTS

See: AIR PILOTS

PINEAPPLE INDUSTRY

See also: FRUIT INDUSTRY

RESEARCH CENTERS AND INSTITUTES

College of Tropical Agriculture and Human Resources. University of Hawaii at Manoa, 2515 Campus Rd., Miller Hall 110, Honolulu, HI 96822. Phone: (808)956-8105 Fax: (808)956-8105 E-mail: fcs@ctahr.hawaii.edu • URL: http://www.ctahr. hawaii.edu/ • Concerned with the production and marketing of tropical food and ornamental plant products, including pineapples, bananas, coffee, and macadamia nuts.

STATISTICS SOURCES

FAO Production Yearbook. Available from Bernan Associates. • Annual. $45.00. Published by the Food and Agriculture Organization (http://www.fao.org). Contains worldwide data on agriculture, land use, farm crops, livestock, and agricultural prices.

FAO Trade Yearbook. Available from Bernan Associates. • Annual. $45.00. Published by the Food and Agriculture Organization (http://www.fao.org). Provides extensive worldwide data on exports and imports of agricultural commodities, fertilizers, tractors, and pesticides. Includes more than 130 tables of detailed statistics.

TRADE/PROFESSIONAL ASSOCIATIONS

Pineapple Growers Association of Hawaii. 1116 Whitmore Ave., Wahiawa, HI 96786. Phone: (808)621-1220 Fax: (808)621-1213 • Promotes the sale of fresh and canned pineapple products. Supersedes Pineapple Producers Cooperative Association.

PIPE

See also: PLUMBING INDUSTRY

CD-ROM DATABASES

OECD Statistical Compendium. Organization for Economic Cooperation and Development. • Semiannual. $1,905.00 per year for 1 to 10 users. CD-ROM contains more than 730,000 monthly, quarterly, and annual time series for OECD countries, 1960 to date. Includes fully searchable data on agriculture, food, economic indicators, national accounts, employment, energy, finance, industry, technology, and foreign trade. Results can be displayed in various forms.

DIRECTORIES

HPAC Engineering Info-Dex (Heating, Piping, Air Conditioning). Penton Media Inc. • Annual. $30.00. Industry directory of products, manufacturers, and trade names and a composite of catalog data for mechanical systems engineering professionals.

The Wholesaler "The Wholesaling 100". TMB Publishing, Inc. • Annual. $25.00. Provides information on the 100 leading wholesalers of plumbing, piping, heating, and air conditioning equipment.

Who's Who in Metal Forming and Fabricating. Fabricators and Manufacturers Association International. • Annual. Free to members; non-members, $200.00. Lists members of the Fabricators and Manufacturers Association (FMA), International; and members of the Tube and Pipe Association. Includes five indexes. Formerly *FMA Member Resource Directory.*

FINANCIAL RATIOS

Annual Statement Studies. The Risk Management Association. • Annual. Median and quartile financial

ratios are given for over 400 kinds of manufacturing, wholesale, retail, construction, and consumer finance establishments. Data is sorted by both asset size and sales volume. Includes a clearly written "Definition of Ratios" and an alphabetical industry index.

Annual Statement Studies: Industry Default Probabilities and Cash Flow Measures. The Risk Management Association. • Annual. $145.00. Serves as a companion volume to the original *Annual Statement Studies.* Gives probability of default estimates on a percentage scale for more than 450 industries. Includes changes in position year-by-year for eight financial statement line items and provides percentage measures of cash flow.

HANDBOOKS AND MANUALS

Piping Guide: A Compact Reference for the Design and Drafting of Piping Systems. David R. Sherwood and Dennis J. Whistance. SYNTEC, Inc. • 1991. $89.00. Second edition.

INTERNET DATABASES

Business 2.0 Web Guide to the Best Business Links. Business 2.0 Media Inc. Phone: (415)293-4800 E-mail: support@business2.com • URL: http://www.business2.com/webguide • Web site presents an extensive, searchable directory of links to "the best, most informative, and authoritative web pages." Twenty main categories cover business, finance, career, company information, people, and technology topics, with thousands of subtopics, all linking to Web sites recommended by experienced business researchers. Fees: Free.

Fedstats. Federal Interagency Council on Statistical Policy. Phone: (202)395-7254 • URL: http://www.fedstats.gov • Web site features an efficient search facility for full-text statistics produced by more than 100 federal agencies, including the Census Bureau, the Bureau of Economic Analysis, and the Bureau of Labor Statistics. Boolean searches can be made within one agency or for all agencies combined. Links are offered to international statistical bureaus, including the UN, IMF, OECD, UNESCO, Eurostat, and 20 individual countries. Fees: Free.

FreeLunch.com. Economy.com, Inc. Phone: (610)696-8700 Fax: (610)696-1678 • URL: http://www.freelunch.com • Web site provides free access to more than 1.5 million economic and financial data series, covering industry, demographics, labor markets, prices, retail sales, government spending, trade, interest rates, housing starts, the stock market, and many other topics. Data is available for various time periods in either chart or table form. Searching is offered. Fees: Free, but registration required. Economy.com, Inc. also offers fee-based economic analysis at *The Dismal Scientist* site (http://www.dismal.com).

PERIODICALS AND NEWSLETTERS

The Fabricator. Fabricators and Manufacturers Association International. • Monthly. $75.00 per year. Covers the manufacture of sheet, coil, tube, pipe, and structural metal shapes.

Heating/Piping/Air Conditioning Engineering: The Magazine of Mechanical Systems Engineering. Penton Media, Inc. • Monthly. $65.00 per year. Covers design, specification, installation, operation, and maintenance for systems in industrial, commercial, and institutional buildings. Formerly (Heating, Piping and Air Conditioning).

The Wholesaler. TMB Publishing, Inc. • Monthly. $75.00 per year. Edited for wholesalers and distributors of plumbing, piping, heating, and air conditioning equipment.

STATISTICS SOURCES

American Iron and Steel Annual Statistical Report. American Iron and Steel Institute. • Annual. $100.00 per year.

Business Statistics of the United States. Linz Audain and Cornelia J. Strawser. Bernan Associates. • Annual. $147.00. Based on *Business Statistics,* formerly issue by the Bureau of Economic Analysis, U. S. Department of Commerce. Provides basic data for a wide variety of U. S. industries, services, and economic indicators. Most statistics are shown annually for 30 years and monthly for the most recent four years.

Survey of Current Business. Available from U. S. Government Printing Office. • Monthly. $63.00 per year. Issued by Bureau of Economic Analysis, U. S. Department of Commerce. Presents a wide variety of business and economic data.

TRADE/PROFESSIONAL ASSOCIATIONS

Ductile Iron Pipe Research Association. 245 Riverchase Pkwy. E, Ste. O, Birmingham, AL 35244. Phone: (205)402-8700 Fax: (205)402-8730 E-mail: dia@diahome.org • URL: http://www.dipra.org • Provides engineering information about cast iron and ductile iron pipe to utility and construction engineers.

Fabricators and Manufacturers Association, International. 833 Featherstone Rd., Rockford, IL 61107-6302. Phone: (815)399-8700 Fax: (815)484-7701 E-mail: info@fmanet.org • URL: http://www.fmanet.org • Members are individuals concerned with metal forming, cutting, and fabricating. Includes a Sheet Metal Division and the Tube and Pipe Fabricators Association. Formerly Fabricating Manufacturers Association.

Manufacturers Standardization Society of the Valve and Fittings Industry. 127 Park St., N. E., Vienna, VA 22180-4602. Phone: (703)281-6613 Fax: (703)281-6671 E-mail: info@mss-hq.com • URL: http://www.mss-hq.com • Members are valve and fitting companies. Publishes standards and specifications.

National Certified Pipe Welding Bureau. 1385 Piccard Dr., 1385 Piccard Dr., Rockville, MD 20850. Phone: 800-556-3653 or (301)869-5800 Fax: (301)990-9690 E-mail: nnikpourfard@mcaa.org • URL: http://www.mcaa.org/ncpwb • Contractors in the piping field. Conducts research on development in the field of certified welding for the piping industry; establishes uniform welding procedures for pipe welding; provides for interchange of records of qualified welders.

National Clay Pipe Institute. PO Box 759, Lake Geneva, WI 53147. Phone: (262)248-9094 Fax: (262)248-1564 E-mail: info@ncpi.org • URL: http://www.ncpi.org • Manufacturers of vitrified clay sewer pipe and fittings. Promotes use of clay pipe for sanitary sewer systems. Provides engineering advisory services; conducts scientific research; acts as government liaison.

National Corrugated Steel Pipe Association. 14070 Proton Rd., Ste. 100, LB 9, 13140 Coit Rd., Ste. 320, Dallas, TX 75244. Phone: (972)850-1907 Fax: (972)490-4219 E-mail: info@ncspa.org • URL: http://www.ncspa.org • Represents firms fabricating corrugated steel drainage pipe and structures; steel mills; allied industries. Provides engineering service in design and installation of drainage products and systems. Conducts research programs.

Plastics Pipe Institute. 105 Decker Ct., Ste. 825, Irving, TX 75062. Phone: 888-314-6774 or (469)499-1044 Fax: (469)499-1063 E-mail: info@plasticpipe.org • URL: http://www.plasticpipe.org • Manufacturers of plastic pipe and fittings and suppliers of plastic pipe raw materials. Develops technical reports and promotes trade and user acceptance. Compiles statistics; offers research programs. Conducts periodic training seminar on plastic piping.

PIPELINE INDUSTRY

ABSTRACTS AND INDEXES

NTIS Alerts: Transportation. National Technical Information Service. • Semimonthly. $210.00 per year. Provides descriptions of government-sponsored research reports and software, with ordering information. Covers air, marine, highway, inland waterway, pipeline, and railroad transportation. Formerly *Abstract Newsletter.*

DIRECTORIES

Pipeline and Gas Journal Buyer's Guide. Oildom Publishing Co. of Texas Inc. • Annual. $75.00. Supplies and services. Lists over 700 companies supplying products and services used in construction and operation of cross-country pipeline and gas distribution systems.

Plunkett's Energy Industry Almanac: Complete Profiles on the Energy Industry 500 Companies. Plunkett Research Ltd. • Annual. $199.99. Includes major oil companies, utilities, pipelines, alternative energy companies, etc. Provides information on industry trends.

FINANCIAL RATIOS

Almanac of Business and Industrial Financial Ratios. Leo Troy. Aspen Publishers, Inc. • 2003. $125.95. Includes CD-Rom. Contains financial ratios derived from federal tax returns. Ratios for each of about 200 industries are arranged according to company asset size. (Almanac of Business and Industrial Financial Ratios Series).

PERIODICALS AND NEWSLETTERS

Pipe Line and Gas Industry: Crude Oil and Products Pipelines, Gas Transmission and Gas Distribution. Gulf Publishing Co. • Monthly. Free to qualified personnel; others, $29.00 per year. International edition available.

Pipeline and Gas Journal: Energy Construction, Transportation and Distribution. Oildom Publishing of Texas, Inc. • Monthly. $33.00 per year. Covers engineering and operating methods on cross-country pipelines that transport crude oil products and natural gas. Includes *Energy Management Report.* Incorporates *Pipeline.*

STATISTICS SOURCES

Infrastructure Industries USA. Gale Cengage Learning. • 2001. $260.00. Presents statistics and projections relating to economic activity in a wide variety of natural resource and construction industries.

TRADE/PROFESSIONAL ASSOCIATIONS

Association of Oil Pipe Lines. 1101 Vermont Ave., N.W., Suite 604, Washington, DC 20005. Phone: (202)408-7970 Fax: (202)408-7983 E-mail: aopl@aopl.org • URL: http://www.aopl.org.

Pipe Line Contractors Association. 1700 Pacific Ave., Ste. 4100, Dallas, TX 75201-4675. Phone: (214)969-2700 Fax: (214)969-2705 E-mail: plca@plca.org • URL: http://www.plca.org • Contractors of mainline cross-country pipeline. Associate members are equipment manufacturers, suppliers, and dealers. Represents the industry in labor negotiations.

PIPES (SMOKING)

See: TOBACCO AND TOBACCO INDUSTRY

PISTOLS

See: FIREARMS INDUSTRY

PLACEMENT BUREAUS

See: COLLEGE PLACEMENT BUREAUS

PLANNED ECONOMY

See: ECONOMIC POLICY

PLANNING

GENERAL WORKS

The Art of the Long View: Planning for the Future in an Uncertain World. Peter Schwartz. Doubleday. • 1996. $30.95. Covers strategic planning for corporations and smaller firms. Includes "The World in 2005: Three Scenarios.".

Strategic Planning Plus: An Organizational Guide. Roger Kaufman. Sage Publications, Inc. • 1992. $80.95.

ABSTRACTS AND INDEXES

Social Sciences Index. H. W. Wilson Co. • Quarterly, with annual cumulation. Price varies. Indexes more than 400 periodicals covering economics, environmental policy, government, insurance, labor, health care policy, planning, public administration, public welfare, urban studies, women's issues, criminology, and related topics.

CD-ROM DATABASES

Social Sciences Citation Index. ISI. • Monthly. Price on request. Provides CD-ROM indexing of articles appearing in 1700 leading social science journals worldwide, with additional selections from more than 5700 other journals. Time span is 1992 to date. Coverage includes economics, business, finance, management, communications, demographics, library and information science, political science, sociology, and many other subjects.

Social Sciences Citation Index: Compact Disc Edition with Abstracts. Institute for Scientific Information. • Monthly. Provides CD-ROM indexing and abstracting of "significant articles" from 1,700 social science journals worldwide, with additional selections from 3,200 other journals, 1986 to date. Includes economics, business, finance, management, communications, demographics, information and library science, political science, sociology, and many other subjects.

WILSONDISC: Wilson Business Abstracts. H. W. Wilson Co. • Monthly. Includes unlimited online access to *Wilson Business Abstracts* through WILSONLINE. Provides CD-ROM "cover-to-cover" abstracting and indexing of over 600 prominent business periodicals. Indexing is from 1982, abstracting from 1990. (*Business Periodicals Index* without abstracts is available on CD-ROM at $1,495 per year.).

WILSONDISC: Wilson Social Sciences Abstracts. H. W. Wilson Co. • Monthly. Includes unlimited online access to *Social Sciences Index* through WILSONLINE. Provides CD-ROM indexing from 1983 and abstracting from 1994 of more than 500 periodicals covering economics, area studies, community health, public administration, public welfare, urban studies, and many other topics related to the social sciences.

ENCYCLOPEDIAS AND DICTIONARIES

Blackwell Encyclopedic Dictionary of Strategic Management. Derek F. Channon, editor. Blackwell Publishing. • 1997. $128.95. The editor is associated with Imperial College, London. Contains definitions of key terms combined with longer articles written by various U. S. and foreign business educators. Includes bibliographies and index. (Blackwell Encyclopedia of Management Series.).

HANDBOOKS AND MANUALS

AMA Management Handbook. John J. Hampton, editor. AMACOM. • 1994. $110.00. Third edition. Provides 200 chapters in 16 major subject areas. Covers a wide variety of business and industrial management topics.

How to Write a Successful Marketing Plan: A Disciplined and Comprehensive Approach. Roman G. Hiebing. Prentice Hall PTR. • 1999. $79.95. Second edition. The four main sections cover marketing background, the marketing plan, plan execution, and evaluation. Includes worksheets and formats.

Marketing Planning Guide. Robert E. Stevens and others. Haworth Press, Inc. • 1997. $49.95. Second edition. Covers market segmentation, product positioning, and other marketing planning topics.

Marketing Plans: How to Prepare Them, How to Use Them. Malcolm H. McDonald. Elsevier. • 2002. $49.99. Fifth edition.

Strategic Planning: A Practical Guide. Peter J. Rea and Harold Kerzner. John Wiley and Sons, Inc. • 1997. $90.00. Covers strategic planning for manufacturing firms, small businesses, and large corporations. (Industrial Engineering Series).

Total Business Planning: A Step-by-Step Guide with Forms. E. James Burton. John Wiley and Sons, Inc. • 1999. $29.95. Second edition. How to construct and activate an internal business plan, whether short-term or long-term. Includes CD-ROM.

INTERNET DATABASES

Intelligence Data. Thomson Financial. Phone: 800-654-0393 Fax: (617)824-2477 • URL: http://www.intelligencedata.com • Fee-based Web site provides a wide variety of information relating to competitive intelligence, strategic planning, business development, mergers, acquisitions, sales, and marketing. "Intelliscope" feature offers searching of other Thomson units, such as Investext, MarkIntel, InSite 2, and Industry Insider. Weekly updating.

ONLINE DATABASES

Management Contents. Gale Cengage Learning. • Covers a wide range of management, financial, marketing, personnel, and administrative topics. About 150 leading business journals are indexed and abstracted from 1974 to date, with monthly updating. Inquire as to online cost and availability.

Wilson Business Abstracts Online. H. W. Wilson Co. • Indexes and abstracts 600 major business periodicals, plus the *Wall Street Journal* and the business section of the *New York Times.* Indexing is from 1982, abstracting from 1990, with the two newspapers included from 1993. Updated weekly. Inquire as to online cost and availability. (*Business Periodicals Index* without abstracts is also available online.).

Wilson Social Sciences Abstracts Online. H. W. Wilson Co. • Provides online abstracting and indexing of more than 500 periodicals covering area studies, community health, public administration, public welfare, urban studies, and many other social science topics. Time period is 1994 to date for abstracts and 1983 to date for indexing, with updates weekly. Inquire as to online cost and availability.

PERIODICALS AND NEWSLETTERS

Business Strategies Bulletin. CCH Inc. • Description: Reports tax and business planning information for all sizes of business, with emphasis on small to mid-sized business advisors.

Futures; The Journal of Forecasting, Planning and Policy. Elsevier. • 10 times a year. Qualified personnel, $233.00 per year; institutions, $932.00 per year.

Journal of Business Strategy. Thomson Media. • Bimonthly. $98.00 per year. Covers management planning techniques and corporate strategy for senior executives.

Long Range Planning. Strategic Planning Society. Elsevier. • Bimonthly. Qualified personnel, $197.00 per year; institutions, $1,346.00 per year.

Planning. American Planning Association. • Monthly. Free to members; non-members, $65.00 per year.

Strategy and Business. • Quarterly. $38.00 per year.

RESEARCH CENTERS AND INSTITUTES

Institute of State and Regional Affairs. Pennsylvania State University at Harrisburg, 777 W. Harrisburg Pike, Middletown, PA 17057-4898. Phone: (717)948-6336 Fax: (717)948-6754 E-mail: xvc@psu.edu • URL: http://www.psdc.hbg.psu.edu/isra • Conducts research in environmental, general, and socioeconomic planning. Zoning is included.

Program in International Studies in Planning. Cornell University, Dept. of City Regional Planning, 106 W. Sibley Hall, Ithaca, NY 14853-3901. Phone: (607)255-4331 Fax: (607)255-1971 E-mail: bdl5@cornell.edu • URL: http://www.inet.crp.cornell.edu/organizations/isp • Research activities are related to international urban and regional planning, with emphasis on developing areas.

TRADE/PROFESSIONAL ASSOCIATIONS

American Institute of Certified Planners. 1776 Massachusetts Ave., N.W., Suite 400, Washington, DC 20036-1904. Phone: 800-954-1669 or (202)872-0611 Fax: (202)872-0643 E-mail: aicp@planning.org • URL: http://www.planning.org/aicp.

American Planning Association. 122 S Michigan Ave., Ste. 1600, Chicago, IL 60603-6107. Phone: (312)431-9100 Fax: (312)431-9985 E-mail: customerservice@planning.org • URL: http://www.planning.org • Public and private planning agency officials, professional planners, planning educators, elected and appointed officials, and other persons involved in urban and rural development. Works to foster the best techniques and decisions for the planned development of communities and regions. Provides extensive professional services and publications to professionals and laypeople in planning and related fields; serves as a clearinghouse for information. Through Planning Advisory Service, a research and inquiry-answering service, provides, on an annual subscription basis, advice on specific inquiries and a series of research reports on planning, zoning, and environmental regulations. Supplies information on job openings and makes definitive studies on salaries and recruitment of professional planners. Conducts research; collaborates in joint projects with local, national, and international organizations.

National Policy Association. 3424 Porter St. NW, Washington, DC 20016-3126. Phone: (202)265-7685 Fax: (202)797-5516 E-mail: npa@npa1.org • URL: http://www.npa1.org • Research institution that helps private and public sector leaders from agriculture, business, labor, and academia to better understand national economic and social issues. Conducts research and analysis on national and international economic and social issues.

Strategic Leadership Forum. 230 E Ohio St., No. 400, PO Box 5329, Chicago, IL 60611-3265. Phone: (403)240-1245 Fax: (403)240-0776 E-mail: ssci_office@steelcontainers.com • URL: http://www.strategicleadershipforum.org • Professional society primarily comprised of executives involved in international strategic management and planning. Conducts education programs. Maintains numerous committees.

OTHER SOURCES

Business Strategies. CCH, Inc. • Semimonthly. $795.00 per year. Four looseleaf volumes. Semimonthly updates. Legal, tax, and accounting aspects of business planning and decision-making. Provides information on start-ups, forms of ownership (partnerships, corporations), failing businesses, reorganizations, acquisitions, and so forth. Includes *Business Strategies Bulletin,* a monthly newsletter.

How to Write a Business Plan. American Management Association Extension Institute. • Looseleaf. $159.00. Self-study course. Emphasis is on practical explanations, examples, and problem solving. Quizzes and a case study are included.

Macroeconomics and Company Planning. Continuing Professional Education Div. American Institute of Certified Public Accountants. • Looseleaf. Self-study course.

PLANS, BUSINESS

See: BUSINESS START-UP PLANS AND PROPOSALS; PLANNING

PLANT ENGINEERING

See: FACTORY MANAGEMENT

PLANT LOCATION

See: LOCATION OF INDUSTRY

PLANT MAINTENANCE

See: MAINTENANCE OF BUILDINGS

PLANT MANAGEMENT

See: FACTORY MANAGEMENT

PLANT PROTECTION

See: INDUSTRIAL SECURITY PROGRAMS

PLANT SITES

See: LOCATION OF INDUSTRY

PLASTER AND PLASTERING

DIRECTORIES
Who's Who in the Wall and Ceiling Industry. Association of the Wall and Ceiling Industries International. • Annual. $45.00. Contractors, manufacturers, suppliers, unions, organizations, and periodicals affiliated with the industry.

FINANCIAL RATIOS
Annual Statement Studies. The Risk Management Association. • Annual. Median and quartile financial ratios are given for over 400 kinds of manufacturing, wholesale, retail, construction, and consumer finance establishments. Data is sorted by both asset size and sales volume. Includes a clearly written "Definition of Ratios" and an alphabetical industry index.

Annual Statement Studies: Industry Default Probabilities and Cash Flow Measures. The Risk Management Association. • Annual. $145.00. Serves as a companion volume to the original *Annual Statement Studies.* Gives probability of default estimates on a percentage scale for more than 450 industries. Includes changes in position year-by-year for eight financial statement line items and provides percentage measures of cash flow.

PERIODICALS AND NEWSLETTERS
ENR: Connecting the Industry Worldwide (Engineering News-Record). McGraw-Hill. • Weekly. $74.00 per year.

TRADE/PROFESSIONAL ASSOCIATIONS
Association of the Wall and Ceiling Industries - International. 803 W. Broad St., Suite 600, Falls Church, VA 22046-3108. Phone: (703)534-8300 Fax: (703)534-8307 E-mail: info@awci.org • URL: http://www.awci.org.

International Institute for Lath and Plaster. PO Box 1663, Lafayette, CA 94549. Phone: (925)283-5160 Fax: (925)283-5161 E-mail: frank@fenunes.com • URL: http://www.iilp.org.

PLASTIC CONTAINERS

See: CONTAINER INDUSTRY

PLASTICS INDUSTRY

See also: COMPOSITE MATERIALS

GENERAL WORKS
The Development of Plastics. S. Mossman and P. Morris, editors. CRC Press LLC. • 1994. $68.00. Published by The Royal Society of Chemistry. Covers the history of plastics from the Victorian era to the present. Includes technical, scientific, and cultural perspectives.

ABSTRACTS AND INDEXES
Applied Science and Technology Index. H. W. Wilson Co. • 11 times a year. Quarterly and annual cumulations. Price varies. Indexes a wide variety of English language technical, industrial, and engineering periodicals.

CPI Digest: Key to World Literature Serving the Coatings, Plastics, Fibers, Adhesives, and Related Industries (Chemical Process Industries). CPI Information Services. • Monthly. $397.00 per year. Abstracts of business and technical articles for polymer-based, chemical process industries. Includes a monthly list of relevant U. S. patents. International coverage.

Engineered Materials Abstracts. Cambridge Information Group. • Monthly. $995.00 per year. Provides citations to the technical and engineering literature of plastic, ceramic, and composite materials.

NTIS Alerts: Materials Sciences. National Technical Information Service. • Semimonthly. $220.00 per year. Provides descriptions of government-sponsored research reports and software, with ordering information. Covers ceramics, glass, coatings, composite materials, alloys, plastics, wood, paper, adhesives, fibers, lubricants, and related subjects. Formerly *Abstract Newsletter.*

RAPRA Abstracts. Rubber and Plastics Research Association of Great Britian. RAPRA Technology Ltd. • Monthly. $2,700.00 per year. Up-to-date survey of current international information relevant to the rubber, plastics and associated industries.

CD-ROM DATABASES
METADEX Materials Collection: Metals-Polymers-Ceramics. Cambridge Scientific Abstracts. • Quarterly. Provides CD-ROM citations to the worldwide literature of materials science and metallurgy. Corresponds to *Metals Abstracts, Alloys Index, Steels Alert, Nonferrous Alert, Polymers/Ceramics/Composites Alert,* and *Engineered Materials Abstracts.* (Formerly produced by ASM International.).

OECD Statistical Compendium. Organization for Economic Cooperation and Development. • Semiannual. $1,905.00 per year for 1 to 10 users. CD-ROM contains more than 730,000 monthly, quarterly, and annual time series for OECD countries, 1960 to date. Includes fully searchable data on agriculture, food, economic indicators, national accounts, employment, energy, finance, industry, technology, and foreign trade. Results can be displayed in various forms.

Plastics Digest on CD-ROM. Global Engineering Documents. • Semiannual. CD-ROM index version (technical data only), $695.00 per year or $495.00 per disc. CD-ROM image version (technical data

and specification sheet images), $1,295.00 per year or $995.00 per disc. Provides detailed information on the properties of 20,000 types of plastic, both current and obsolete. Time period is 1977 to date. Includes trade names and supplier names and addresses.

DIRECTORIES
Engineering Plastics and Composites. William A. Woishnis and others, editors. ASM International. • 1993. $149.00. Second edition. In four sections: (1) Trade names of plastics, reinforced plastics, and resin composites; (2) Index to materials, with suppliers and other information; (3) Suppliers alphabetically, with trade names; (4) Supplier contact information. (Materials Data Series).

Materials Research Centres: A World Directory of Organizations and Programmes in Materials Science. Specialist Journals. • Biennial. $445.00. Profiles of research centers in 75 countries. Materials include plastics, metals, fibers, etc.

Plastics Technology Processing Handbook and Buyers' Guide. Gardner Publications Inc. • Annual. $89.00. Over 4,000 manufacturers of plastics processing equipment and materials. Included in subscription to *Plastics Technology.* Formerly *Plastcs Technology Manufacturing Handbook and Buyer's Guide.*

ENCYCLOPEDIAS AND DICTIONARIES
ASM Materials Engineering Dictionary. Joseph R. Davis, editor. ASM International. • 1992. $166.00. Contains 10,000 entries, 700 illustrations, and 150 tables relating to metals, plastics, ceramics, composites, and adhesives. Includes "Technical Briefs" on 64 key material groups.

Dictionary of Plastics Technology. H. D. Junge. John Wiley and Sons, Inc. • 1987. $150.00.

Encyclopedia of Advanced Materials. David Bloor and others. Elsevier. • 1994. $1,534.00. Four volumes.

Encyclopedia of Emerging Industries. Gale Cengage Learning. • 2001. $320.00. Fourth edition. Provides detailed information on 115 "newly flourishing" industries. Includes historical background, organizational structure, significant individuals, current conditions, major companies, work force, technology trends, research developments, and other industry facts.

Encyclopedia of Materials: Science and Technology. K.H.J. Buschow and others, editors. Elsevier. • 2001. $4,985.00. Eleven volumes. Provides extensive technical information on a wide variety of materials, including metals, ceramics, plastics, optical materials, and building materials. Includes more than 2,000 articles and 5,000 illustrations.

Encyclopedia of Polymer Science and Engineering. Herman F. Mark and others. John Wiley and Sons, Inc. • 1985. $8,536.00. 22 volumes. $388.00 per volume.

Encyclopedia of Polymer Science and Technology. Corinna Czekaj. John Wiley and Sons, Inc. • 2004. $3,600.00. Third edition. 12 volumes. Covers new techniques and methods, as well as "traditional topics of continuing interest.".

Kirk-Othmer Encyclopedia of Chemical Technology. Raymond E. Kirk and Donald F. Othmer. John Wiley and Sons, Inc. • 1991-97. $9,895.00, prepaid. 27 volumes. Fourth edition. Four volumes are scheduled to be published each year, with individual volumes available at $415.00. (Kirk-Othmer Encyclopedia of Chemical Technology Series).

Modern Plastics Encyclopedia. McGraw-Hill. • Annual. $85.00. List of about 5,000 suppliers of over 350 types of products and services to the plastic industry in the U.S. and Canada. Included with subscription to *Modern Plastics.*

Whittington's Dictionary of Plastics. James F. Carley, editor. CRC Press LLC. • 1993. $129.95. Third expanded revised edition.

FINANCIAL RATIOS

Annual Statement Studies. The Risk Management Association. • Annual. Median and quartile financial ratios are given for over 400 kinds of manufacturing, wholesale, retail, construction, and consumer finance establishments. Data is sorted by both asset size and sales volume. Includes a clearly written "Definition of Ratios" and an alphabetical industry index.

Annual Statement Studies: Industry Default Probabilities and Cash Flow Measures. The Risk Management Association. • Annual. $145.00. Serves as a companion volume to the original *Annual Statement Studies*. Gives probability of default estimates on a percentage scale for more than 450 industries. Includes changes in position year-by-year for eight financial statement line items and provides percentage measures of cash flow.

IRS Corporate Financial Ratios. Available from MarketResearch.com. • 2002. $225.00. Published by Schonfeld & Associates, Inc. Presents 70 key financial ratios for 260 industries. Ratios are calculated from income statement and balance sheet data available from the Internal Revenue Service. Includes four asset size classes.

HANDBOOKS AND MANUALS

ASM Engineered Materials Reference Book. Michael L. Bauccio, editor. ASM International. • 1994. $155.00. Third edition. Provides information on a wide range of materials, with special sections on ceramics, industrial glass products, and plastics.

Handbook of Materials Selection. Myer Kutz. John Wiley and Sons, Inc. • 2002. $225.00. First section of handbook covers materials relative to the type of engineering application. Second section deals with the specific properties of materials. Covers both traditional materials and high-tech composites.

Industrial Polymers Handbook: Products, Processes, Applications. Edward S. Wilks, editor. John Wiley and Sons, Inc. • 2001. $1,400.00. Four volumes. Covers both naturally occurring and synthetic polymers that have industrial uses.

Plastics Processing Technology. Edward A. Muccio. ASM International. • 1994. $99.00. Contains basic terminology and information on plastics for engineers, managers, technicians, purchasing agents, and students. Written to serve as a primer on plastics technology and processing.

Polymer Handbook. Johannes Brandup and others, editors. John Wiley and Sons, Inc. • 2003. $197.50. Fifth edition. Emphasis is on advances in polymer science since 1989 and descriptions of polymeric materials. (Polymer Handbook Series).

Polymer Processing: Principles and Design. Donald G. Baird and Dimitria I. Collias. John Wiley and Sons, Inc. • 1998. $105.95. A practical guide to thermoplastics.

INTERNET DATABASES

Business 2.0 Web Guide to the Best Business Links. Business 2.0 Media Inc. Phone: (415)293-4800 E-mail: support@business2.com • URL: http://www.business2.com/webguide • Web site presents an extensive, searchable directory of links to "the best, most informative, and authoritative web pages." Twenty main categories cover business, finance, career, company information, people, and technology topics, with thousands of subtopics, all linking to Web sites recommended by experienced business researchers. Fees: Free.

Fedstats. Federal Interagency Council on Statistical Policy. Phone: (202)395-7254 • URL: http://www.fedstats.gov • Web site features an efficient search facility for full-text statistics produced by more than 100 federal agencies, including the Census Bureau, the Bureau of Economic Analysis, and the Bureau of

Labor Statistics. Boolean searches can be made within one agency or for all agencies combined. Links are offered to international statistical bureaus, including the UN, IMF, OECD, UNESCO, Eurostat, and 20 individual countries. Fees: Free.

FreeLunch.com. Economy.com, Inc. Phone: (610)696-8700 Fax: (610)696-1678 • URL: http://www.freelunch.com • Web site provides free access to more than 1.5 million economic and financial data series, covering industry, demographics, labor markets, prices, retail sales, government spending, trade, interest rates, housing starts, the stock market, and many other topics. Data is available for various time periods in either chart or table form. Searching is offered. Fees: Free, but registration required. Economy.com, Inc. also offers fee-based economic analysis at *The Dismal Scientist* site (http://www.dismal.com).

ONLINE DATABASES

Applied Science and Technology Index Online. H. W. Wilson Co. • Provides online indexing of 500 major scientific, technical, industrial, and engineering periodicals. Time period is 1983 to date. Monthly updates. Inquire as to online cost and availability.

Business and Industry. Gale Cengage Learning. • Contains online citations, abstracts, and selected fulltext from more than 1,000 trade journals, newspapers, and other publications. Provides general coverage of both manufacturing and service industries, including marketing, production, industry trends, key events, and information on specific companies. Time span is 1994 to date. Daily updates. Inquire as to online cost and availability. (Also available in a CD-ROM version.).

Engineered Materials Abstracts [online]. Cambridge Scientific Abstracts. • Provides online citations to the technical and engineering literature of plastic, ceramic, and composite materials. Time period is 1986 to date, with monthly updates. (Formerly produced by ASM International.) Inquire as to online cost and availability.

Materials Business File. Cambridge Scientific Abstracts. • Provides online abstracts and citations to worldwide materials literature, covering the business and industrial aspects of metals, plastics, ceramics, and composites. Corresponds to *Steels Alert, Nonferrous Metals Alert,* and *Polymers/Ceramics/Composites Alert.* Time period is 1985 to date, with monthly updates. (Formerly produced by ASM International.) Inquire as to online cost and availability.

METADEX. Cambridge Scientific Abstracts. • Covers the worldwide literature of metals, metallurgy, and materials science, 1966 to date. Includes detailed alloys indexing from 1974. Biweekly updating. Inquire as to online cost and availability. (Formerly produced by ASM International.).

Tablebase. Gale Cengage Learning. • Provides online numerical tabular data from a wide variety of business, organization, and government sources, including about 1,000 trade journals. Includes industry and individual company statistics relating to products, market share, sales forecasts, production, exports, market trends, etc. Time span is 1997 to date. Weekly updates. Inquire as to online cost and availability. (Also available in a CD-ROM version.).

PERIODICALS AND NEWSLETTERS

Advances in Polymer Technology. Polymer Processing Institute. John Wiley and Sons, Inc. • Quarterly. Institutions, $950.00 per year; with online edition, $998.00 per year.

Journal of Applied Polymer Science. John Wiley and Sons, Inc., Journals. • 56 times a year. $14,495.00 per year; with online edition, $15,220.00, four volumes.

Journal of Elastomers and Plastics. Sage

Publications. • Quarterly. Institutions, $730.00 per year. Includes print and online editions.

Plastics Engineering. Society of Plastics Engineers, Inc. • Monthly. Free to members; non-members, $142.00 per year; corporations and libraries, $180.00 per year.

Plastics News. Crain Communications, Inc. • Weekly. $69.00 per year.

Plastics Technology: The Only Magazine for Plastics Processors. VNU Business Media. • 13 times a year. Free to qualified personnel; others, $89.00 per year.

Plastics Week: The Global Newsletter. McGraw-Hill. • Weekly. $530.00 per year. Newsletter. Covers international trends in plastics production, technology, research, and legislation.

Polymer Engineering and Science. Society of Plastics Engineers, Inc. • Monthly. Members, $330.00 per year; non-members, $470.00 per year; institutions, $915.00 per year. Includes six special issues.

Urethanes Technology. Crain Communications, Inc. • Bimonthly. $108.00 per year. Covers the international polyurethane industry.

RESEARCH CENTERS AND INSTITUTES

Materials Processing Center. Massachusetts Institute of Technology, 77 Massachusetts Ave., Room 12-007, Cambridge, MA 02139-4307. Phone: (617)253-5179 Fax: (617)258-6900 E-mail: fmpage@.mit.edu • URL: http://www.web.mit.edu/mpc • Conducts processing, engineering, and economic research in ferrous and nonferrous metals, ceramics, polymers, photonic materials, superconductors, welding, composite materials, and other materials.

Plastics Institute of America. 333 Aiken St., Lowell, MA 01854. Phone: (978)934-3130 Fax: (978)459-9420 E-mail: pia@uml.edu • URL: http://www.plasticsinstitute.org.

Polymer Research Center. University of Cincinnati. College of Engineering, P.O. Box 21002, Cincinnati, OH 45221-0012. Phone: (513)556-5430 Fax: (513)556-2569 E-mail: stephen.carlson@uc.edu.

Polymer Research Laboratory. University of Michigan. 2014 H.H. Dow Bldg., Ann Arbor, MI 48109. Phone: (734)763-9867 Fax: (734)763-4788 E-mail: rer@umich.edu.

STATISTICS SOURCES

Annual Survey of Manufactures. Available from U. S. Government Printing Office. • Annual. Prices vary. Issued by the U. S. Census Bureau as an interim update to the *Census of Manufactures.* Includes data on number of manufacturing establishments in various industries, employment, labor costs, value of shipments, capital expenditures, inventories, energy costs, and assets. (See also Census Bureau home page, http://www.census.gov/.).

Business Statistics of the United States. Linz Audain and Cornelia J. Strawser. Bernan Associates. • Annual. $147.00. Based on *Business Statistics,* formerly issue by the Bureau of Economic Analysis, U. S. Department of Commerce. Provides basic data for a wide variety of U. S. industries, services, and economic indicators. Most statistics are shown annually for 30 years and monthly for the most recent four years.

Encyclopedia of American Industries. Gale Cengage Learning. • 2000. $560.00. Third edition. Two volumes. $280.00 per volume. Volume one is *Manufacturing Industries* and volume two is *Service and Non-Manufacturing Industries.* Provides the history, development, and recent status of approximately 1,000 industries. Includes statistical graphs, with industry and general indexes.

Standard & Poor's Industry Surveys. Standard & Poor's. • Semiannual. $1,800.00. Two looseleaf volumes. Includes monthly *Supplements.* Provides detailed, individual surveys of 52 major industry groups. Each survey is revised on a semiannual basis. Also includes "Monthly Investment Review" (industry group investment analysis) and monthly "Trends & Projections" (economic analysis).

Survey of Current Business. Available from U. S. Government Printing Office. • Monthly. $63.00 per year. Issued by Bureau of Economic Analysis, U. S. Department of Commerce. Presents a wide variety of business and economic data.

TRADE/PROFESSIONAL ASSOCIATIONS

International Association of Plastic Distributors. 4707 College Blvd., Suite 105, Leawood, KS 66211. Phone: (913)345-1005 Fax: (913)345-1006 E-mail: iapd@iapd.org • URL: http://www.iapd.org • Formerly National Association of Plastics Distributors.

Society of Plastics Engineers. PO Box 403, Brookfield, CT 06804-0403. Phone: (203)775-0471 Fax: (203)775-8490 E-mail: info@4spe.org • URL: http://www.4spe.org.

Society of the Plastics Industry. 1801 K St., N.W., Suite 600K, Washington, DC 20006. Phone: (202)974-5200 Fax: (202)296-7005 E-mail: feedback@socplas.org • URL: http://www.socplas.org.

PLATING

See: METAL FINISHING

PLATINUM INDUSTRY

ALMANACS AND YEARBOOKS

Agricultural and Mineral Commodities Year Book. Available from Taylor & Francis Group. • Annual. $225.00. Published by Europa Publications. Contains descriptive product profiles, price data, export-import data, and production statistics for major commodities of the world. Includes commodity histories, uses, markets, demand trends, and information about trade agreements and key commodity organizations.

HANDBOOKS AND MANUALS

Jake Bernstein's New Guide to Investing in Metals. Jacob Bernstein. John Wiley and Sons, Inc. • 1991. $34.95. Covers bullion, coins, futures, options, mining stocks, and precious metal mutual funds. Includes the history of metals as an investment.

PERIODICALS AND NEWSLETTERS

Platinum Metals Review. Johnson Matthey PLC. • Quarterly. Free. Text in English and Japanese.

STATISTICS SOURCES

Mineral Commodity Summaries. Available from U. S. Government Printing Office. • Annual. $26.00. Published by the U. S. Geological Survey, Department of the Interior (http://www.usgs.gov). Contains detailed, five-year data for about 90 nonfuel minerals. Covers a wide range of statistics, including production, imports, exports, consumption, reserves, prices, tariff information, and industry employment. (Two pages are devoted to each mineral.).

Non-Ferrous Metal Data Yearbook. American Bureau of Metal Statistics. • Annual. $405.00. Provides worldwide data on approximately about 200 statistical tables covering many nonferrous metals. Includes production, consumption, inventories, exports, imports, and other data.

Standard & Poor's Industry Surveys. Standard & Poor's. • Semiannual. $1,800.00. Two looseleaf volumes. Includes monthly *Supplements.* Provides detailed, individual surveys of 52 major industry groups. Each survey is revised on a semiannual basis. Also includes "Monthly Investment Review"

(industry group investment analysis) and monthly "Trends & Projections" (economic analysis).

TRADE/PROFESSIONAL ASSOCIATIONS

American Bureau of Metal Statistics. P.O. Box 805, Chatham, NJ 07928. Phone: (973)701-2299 Fax: (973)701-2152 E-mail: info@abms.com • URL: http://www.abms.com • Members are metal companies. Compiles and publishes detailed statistical data on a wide variety of nonferrous metals: aluminum, copper, gold, lead, nickel, platinum, silver, tin, titanium, uranium, zinc, and others.

PLUMBING INDUSTRY

See also: HEATING AND VENTILATION

DIRECTORIES

The Wholesaler "The Wholesaling 100". TMB Publishing, Inc. • Annual. $25.00. Provides information on the 100 leading wholesalers of plumbing, piping, heating, and air conditioning equipment.

FINANCIAL RATIOS

Almanac of Business and Industrial Financial Ratios. Leo Troy. Aspen Publishers, Inc. • 2003. $125.95. Includes CD-Rom. Contains financial ratios derived from federal tax returns. Ratios for each of about 200 industries are arranged according to company asset size. (Almanac of Business and Industrial Financial Ratios Series).

American Supply Association Operating Performance Report. American Supply Association. • Annual. Members, $45.00; non-members, $150.00.

Annual Statement Studies. The Risk Management Association. • Annual. Median and quartile financial ratios are given for over 400 kinds of manufacturing, wholesale, retail, construction, and consumer finance establishments. Data is sorted by both asset size and sales volume. Includes a clearly written "Definition of Ratios" and an alphabetical industry index.

Annual Statement Studies: Industry Default Probabilities and Cash Flow Measures. The Risk Management Association. • Annual. $145.00. Serves as a companion volume to the original *Annual Statement Studies.* Gives probability of default estimates on a percentage scale for more than 450 industries. Includes changes in position year-by-year for eight financial statement line items and provides percentage measures of cash flow.

HANDBOOKS AND MANUALS

National Plumbing Codes Handbook. R. Dodge Woodson. McGraw-Hill. • 1997. $44.95. Second revised edition.

Plumbers Handbook. Howard C. Massey. Craftsman Book Co. • 1998. $32.00. Third revised edition.

INTERNET DATABASES

Manufacturing Profiles. U. S. Bureau of the Census. Phone: (301)763-4636 E-mail: webmaster@census.gov • URL: http://www.census.gov/prod/www/abs/mfg-prof.html • The Census Bureau makes available free on PDF (Portable Document Format) an annual consolidation of the entire Current Industrial Report series, presenting "all the data compiled." Contains statistics on production, shipments, inventories, consumption, exports, imports, and orders for a wide variety of manufactured products.

PERIODICALS AND NEWSLETTERS

Plumbing Engineer. American Society of Plumbing Engineers. • Monthly. $50.00 per year.

The Wholesaler. TMB Publishing, Inc. • Monthly. $75.00 per year. Edited for wholesalers and distributors of plumbing, piping, heating, and air conditioning equipment.

STATISTICS SOURCES

Annual Survey of Manufactures. Available from U. S. Government Printing Office. • Annual. Prices

vary. Issued by the U. S. Census Bureau as an interim update to the *Census of Manufactures.* Includes data on number of manufacturing establishments in various industries; employment, labor costs, value of shipments, capital expenditures, inventories, energy costs, and assets. (See also Census Bureau home page, http://www.census.gov/.).

Plumbing Fixtures. U. S. Bureau of the Census. • Quarterly and annual. Provides data on shipments: value, quantity, imports, and exports. Includes both metal and plastic fixtures. (Current Industrial Reports, MQ-34E.).

U. S. Industry and Trade Outlook. Available from National Technical Information Service. • Annual. $69.95. Produced by the International Trade Administration, U. S. Department of Commerce, in a "public-private" partnership with DRI/McGraw-Hill and Standard & Poor's. Provides basic data, outlook for the current year, and "Long-Term Prospects" (five-year projections) for a wide variety of products and services. Includes high technology industries. Formerly *U. S. Industrial Outlook.*

TRADE/PROFESSIONAL ASSOCIATIONS

American Society of Plumbing Engineers. 8614 W. Catalpa Ave., No. 1007, Chicago, IL 60656-1116. Phone: (773)693-2773 Fax: (773)693-9007 E-mail: aspehq@aol.com • URL: http://www.aspe.org.

American Supply Association. 222 Merchandise Mart Plz., Ste. 1400, Chicago, IL 60654. Phone: 800-464-0314 or (312)464-0090 Fax: (312)464-0091 E-mail: info@asa.net • URL: http://www.asa.net • Represents wholesale, distributors, and manufacturers of plumbing and heating, cooling, pipes, valves, and fittings. Compiles statistics on operating costs and makes occasional studies of compensation, fringe benefits, wages, and salaries. Conducts research studies and forecasting surveys. Offers group insurance. Maintains management institutes, home study courses under the ASA Education Foundation and Endowment program, provides technology and produces a CD-ROM and internet catalogue of manufacturers.

Plumbing and Drainage Institute. c/o W.C. Whitehead, 45 Bristol Dr., South Easton, MA 02375. Phone: 800-589-8956 Fax: (508)230-3529 E-mail: info@pdionline.org • URL: http://www.pdionline.org • Formerly Plumbing and Drainage Manufacturers Association.

Plumbing-Heating-Cooling Contractors Association. PO Box 6808, PO Box 6808, Falls Church, VA 22046. Phone: 800-533-7694 or (703)237-8100 Fax: (703)237-7442 E-mail: naphcc@naphcc.org • URL: http://www.phccweb.org • Federation of state and local associations of plumbing, heating, and cooling contractors. Seeks to advance sanitation, encourage sanitary laws, and generally improve the plumbing, heating, ventilating, and air conditioning industries. Conducts apprenticeship training programs, workshops, seminars, political action committee, educational and research programs.

OTHER SOURCES

Plumbing Fittings and Brass Goods. Available from MarketResearch.com. • 2002. $3,950.00. Published by Global Industry Analysts. Provides worldwide market research data, including profiles of major plumbing equipment companies.

PLYWOOD INDUSTRY

See also: LUMBER INDUSTRY

ABSTRACTS AND INDEXES

Forest Products Abstracts. CABI Publishing North America. • Bimonthly. $770.00 per year; with online edition, $805.00 per year. Published in England by CABI Publishing. Provides worldwide coverage of forest products literature.

DIRECTORIES

Panel World Directory and Buyers' Guide. Hatton-Brown Publisher, Inc. • Annual. $20.00. Included with subscription to *Paper, Film and Foil Converter.* Supersedes *Plywood and Panel World Directory and Buyer's Guide.*

Where to Buy Hardwood Plywood, Veneer, and Engineered Hardwood Flooring. Hardwood Plywood and Veneer Association. • Annual. Free. Lists about 190 member manufacturers, prefinishers, and suppliers of hardwood veneer and plywood.

ENCYCLOPEDIAS AND DICTIONARIES

Illustrated Dictionary of Building Materials and Techniques: An Invaluable Sourcebook to the Tools, Terms, Materials, and Techniques Used by Building Professionals. Paul Bianchina. John Wiley and Sons, Inc. • 1993. $19.95. Contains 4,000 definitions of building and building materials terms, with 500 illustrations. Includes materials grades, measurements, and specifications.

PERIODICALS AND NEWSLETTERS

ENR: Connecting the Industry Worldwide (Engineering News-Record). McGraw-Hill. • Weekly. $74.00 per year.

Panel World. Hatton-Brown Publishers, Inc. • Bimonthly. $28.00. Formerly *Plywood and Panel World.*

STATISTICS SOURCES

Annual Survey of Manufactures. Available from U. S. Government Printing Office. • Annual. Prices vary. Issued by the U. S. Census Bureau as an interim update to the *Census of Manufactures.* Includes data on number of manufacturing establishments in various industries, employment, labor costs, value of shipments, capital expenditures, inventories, energy costs, and assets. (See also Census Bureau home page, http://www.census.gov/.).

U. S. Industry and Trade Outlook. Available from National Technical Information Service. • Annual. $69.95. Produced by the International Trade Administration, U. S. Department of Commerce, in a "public-private" partnership with DRI/McGraw-Hill and Standard & Poor's. Provides basic data, outlook for the current year, and "Long-Term Prospects" (five-year projections) for a wide variety of products and services. Includes high technology industries. Formerly *U. S. Industrial Outlook.*

TRADE/PROFESSIONAL ASSOCIATIONS

APA: The Engineered Wood Association. 7011 S 19th, PO Box 11700, Tacoma, WA 98466. Phone: 888-773-2272 or (253)565-6600 Fax: (253)565-7265 E-mail: help@apawood.org • URL: http://www.apawood.org • Manufacturers of structural panel products, oriented strand board and composites. Conducts trade promotion through advertising, publicity, merchandising, and field promotion. Maintains quality supervision in accordance with U.S. product standards, APA performance standards, and APA trademarking. Conducts research to improve products, applications, and manufacturing techniques. Sponsors Engineered Wood Research Foundation; compiles statistics.

Engineered Wood Technology Association. 7011 S 19th St., PO Box 11700, Tacoma, WA 98466. Phone: (253)565-6600 Fax: (253)565-7265 E-mail: ema@enginemanufacturers.org • URL: http://www.apawood.org • Represents manufacturers of construction and industrial panels and related products; associate members. Sponsors research programs on improvement in panel production processes and techniques.

Hardwood Plywood and Veneer Association. 1825 Michael Faraday Dr., Reston, VA 20195-0789. Phone: (703)435-2900 Fax: (703)435-2537 E-mail: hpva@hpva.org • URL: http://www.hpva.org • Formerly Hardwood Plywood Manufactures Association.

POINT-OF-PURCHASE ADVERTISING

See also: DISPLAY OF MERCHANDISE

DIRECTORIES

Creative's Illustrated Guide to P-O-P Exhibits and Promotion. Magazines Creative, Inc. • Annual. $25.00. Lists sources of point-of-purchase displays, signs, and exhibits and sources of other promotional materials and equipment. Available online.

The PROMO 100 Promotion Agency Ranking. PROMO Magazine. • Covers: Ranking of the top 100 U.S. Promotion agencies. Entries include: Name, address, phone, financial data, client lists, rate of growth, name of CEO, and description of product/service.

SRDS Out-of-Home Advertising Source. SRDS. • Annual. $341.00. Provides detailed information on non-traditional or "out-of-home" advertising media: outdoor, aerial, airport, mass transit, bus benches, school, hotel, in-flight, in-store, theater, stadium, taxi, truckstop, kiosk, shopping malls, and others. Formerly *Advertising Options Plus.*

PERIODICALS AND NEWSLETTERS

P-O-P Design (Point-of-Purchase): Products and News for High-Volume Pro ducers and Designers of Displays, Signs and Fixtures. Hoyt Publishing Co. • Nine times a year. $59.00 per year.

PROMO: Promotion Marketing Worldwide. Primedia Business Magazines and Media. • Monthly. $65.00 per year. Edited for companies and agencies that utilize couponing, point-of-purchase advertising, special events, games, contests, premiums, product samples, and other unique promotional items.

TRADE/PROFESSIONAL ASSOCIATIONS

Point-of-Purchase Advertising International. 1600 Duke St., Ste. 400, Alexandria, VA 22314. Phone: (703)373-8800 Fax: (703)373-8801 E-mail: info@popai.com • URL: http://www.popai.com • Producers and suppliers of point-of-purchase advertising signs and displays and national and regional advertisers and retailers interested in use and effectiveness of signs, displays, and other point-of-purchase media. Conducts student education programs; maintains speakers' bureau.

POINT-OF-SALE SYSTEMS (POS)

See also: AUTOMATIC IDENTIFICATION SYSTEMS

GENERAL WORKS

Using Bar Code: Why It's Taking Over. David J. Collins and Nancy N. Whipple. Data Capture Press. • 1994. $34.95. Second edition.

DIRECTORIES

Frontline Solutions Buyer's Guide. Advanstar Communications. • Publication includes: List of manufacturers, suppliers, consultants, value added resellers, and dealers/distributors of automatic identification and data capture software, technology, equipment, and products for bar code, biometric identification, electronic data interchange, machine vision, magnetic stripe, optical character recognition, radio frequency data communications, radio frequency identification, smart cards, and voice data entry; also includes related organizations, and

sources for industry standards. Entries include: Company name, address, phone, e-mail, web address, products or services.

PERIODICALS AND NEWSLETTERS

Corporate EFT Report (Electronic Funds Tranfer). Phillips International, Inc. • Biweekly. $695.00 per year. Newsletter on subject of electronic funds transfer.

End Point Express: Exclusive Report for Bank Operations Professionals. United Communications Group. • Biweekly. $247.00 per year. Newsletter. Covers bank payment systems, including checks, electronic funds transfer (EFT), point-of-sale (POS), and automated teller machine (ATM) operations. Formerly *Bank Office Bulletin.*

STATISTICS SOURCES

Statistical Information on the Financial Services Industry. American Bankers Association. • Annual. Members, $150.00; non-members, $275.00. Presents a wide variety of data relating to banking and financial services, including consumer economics, personal finance, credit, government loans, capital markets, and international banking.

TRADE/PROFESSIONAL ASSOCIATIONS

Electronic Funds Transfer Association. 11350 Random Hills Rd., Ste. 800, Fairfax, VA 22030. Phone: (703)934-6052 Fax: (703)934-6058 E-mail: melanierenner@efta.org • URL: http://www.efta.org • Financial institutions, credit card companies, ATM owners, networks and processors, hardware and software manufacturers and e-commerce companies dedicated to the advancement of electronic payment systems and commerce.

GS1 US. Princeton Pike Corporate Center, 1009 Lenox Dr., Ste. 202, Lawrenceville, NJ 08648. Phone: (609)620-0200 Fax: (609)620-1200 E-mail: info@gs1us.org • URL: http://www.uc-council.org • Develops and implements standard-based, global supply chain solutions. Operates two wholly owned subsidiaries, UCCnet and RosettaNet, and co-manages the global EAN.UCC System with EAN International. Manages the United Nations Standard Products and Services Code (UNSPSC) for the United Nations Development Programme (UNDP). Evaluates the effects of brand and size demand, competitor actions, pricing policy, and shelf location of merchandise. Administers Universal Product Code and Symbol (UPC), Uniform Communications Standard (UCS), Warehouse Information Network Standard (WINS), and Voluntary Inter-Industry Communications Standard (VICSEDI).

POLICE EQUIPMENT

See: LAW ENFORCEMENT INDUSTRIES

POLICY MANUALS

See: PROCEDURE MANUALS

POLITICAL ACTION COMMITTEE

TRADE/PROFESSIONAL ASSOCIATIONS

National Association of Business Political Action Committees. 101 Constitution Ave. NW, Ste. 800-West, Washington, DC 20001. Phone: (202)341-3780 Fax: (202)478-0342 E-mail: nabpac@nabpac.org • URL: http://www.nabpac.org • Political action professionals and government affairs representatives interested in campaign finance reform issues and innovations in political action committee management.

OTHER SOURCES

AAP Political Action Committee. • Raises funds to help elect individuals to Congress who realize how vital the production of books, knowledge, and ideas is to the country, who want to see publishing prosper, and who will be alert to how federal laws and federal spending programs can help or harm the publishing industry.

American Medical Political Action Committee. • Represents physicians, their spouses, and others interested in political action and participation in public affairs. Seeks to further political knowledge of its members and to provide them with means for concerted political action.

Americans for the National Interest. • A political action committee that supports candidates for office who share the views of Governor Bruce Babbitt (D-Arizona). Endorses and provides funds for candidates running for state or national office. **Publications:** none.

Best Candidate Committee. • To improve the quality of Congress by encouraging the selection of the "best" candidates for election. Conducts research and evaluates the performance and potential of candidates.

Business-Industry Political Action Committee. • Works as independent, bipartisan organization that works to elect pro-business candidates to Congress; has group's Business Institute for Political Analysis that carries out extensive programs of political analysis, research, and communication on campaigns and elections, and fosters business participation in the political process.

Campaign for Space Political Action Committee. • Individuals dedicated to a renewal of U.S. space efforts through direct involvement in the political process. Solicits contributions from individuals and uses these funds to assist in the election of candidates who support a strong U.S. civil space program. Believes that the technology is currently available to tap the "limitless energy and abundant natural resources which space offers," but that there is a lack of long-range national commitment to utilize sophisticated space hardware. Goals are: to maintain the United States' position as the leader in mankind's exploration and use of space; to reap the economic benefits that result from an expanded space program; to use space technology to enrich life on earth; to provide an alternative to the "limits-to-growth, closed world concept" now suggested as the only possible future course for mankind. Plans to maintain continued pressure on the administration and Congress to enlarge the space effort; keeps supporters informed of the status of space-related legislation.

Citizens for a Competitive America. • A political action committee that raises funds for the election campaigns of candidates who support the committee's objective of U.S. economic competitiveness.

Citizens in Politics. • A project of National Committee for an Effective Congress (see separate entry). Artists, musicians, film and television personalities, and sports and literary figures. Acts as a referral service for celebrities who want to work on political action campaigns. Celebrities volunteer their time to attract money, attention, and votes through participation in such activities as congressional election campaigns or comedy and musical benefits that champion progressive positions on public policy issues. **Convention/Meeting:** none.

Congressional Agenda: Millennium. • Raises funds for congressional representatives working to alter current administration policy trends so that programs developed in the 1970s can be adapted to present needs. Areas of specific attention include the economy, nuclear arms, and environmental preservation. Seeks to reduce interest rates, defer some proposed tax cuts, eliminate unnecessary defense expenditures, and end cuts in domestic programs that are seen as investments in future growth, such as employment training, education, transport, housing, utilities, and water systems.

Works toward restoration of funding and governmental support for environmental preservation programs.

Conservative Democratic Political Action Committee. • Members of the Conservative Democratic Forum. Makes contributions to the campaigns of moderate/conservative congressional candidates.

Fund for a Republican Majority. • Political action committee that raises funds for Republican congressional candidates, particulary for the Senate.

Fund for the Future Committee. • Political action committee that supports the campaigns of Republican candidates for federal office from Missouri.

German American National Public Affairs. • Seeks to represent what the committee considers to be the interests of German-Americans. Aims to "unite all Americans of German descent, and those who have the same ethical and moral values, into one politically potent force." Works to inform the public of the contributions of German-Americans to American society; opposes the "constant defamation of all things German by the American news media.".

Hollywood Women's Political Committee. • Women working in the entertainment industry and related fields. Raises funds for federal political candidates, grass roots organizations, and statewide initiatives that pledge to represent the group's beliefs on nuclear disarmament, increased environmental protection, improved public education, and expanded civil rights for women. Seeks to heighten community involvement in national politics. **Publications:** none. **Convention/Meeting:** none.

House Leadership Fund. • Political action committee that raises funds for the election campaigns of Democratic congressional candidates.

Human Rights Political Action Committee. • Individuals concerned about the place of human rights in U.S. foreign policy. Is devoted solely to raising money to support candidacies of human rights activists running for Congress. **Publications:** none. **Convention/Meeting:** none.

Independent Action. • Seeks to build a political counterforce to the New Right and elect progressive Democrats to federal office. Plans to seek out progressive candidates and provide them with the financial and technical support they need at the early stages of the campaign process; make direct contributions to IA-endorsed candidates; make independent expenditures to counter the efforts of right-wing political action groups.

International Union, UAW - Community Action Program. • Serves as a program of the International Union, United Automobile, Aerospace and Agricultural Implement Workers of America (UAW) (see separate entry). Informs UAW members through political education programs on topics including lobbying, the relationship between collective bargaining and the ballot box, and voluntary fundraising for political contributions. Maintains speakers' bureau; compiles statistics.

JustLife. • Political action committee comprising Christian individuals. Supports candidates working for the establishment of what the group considers consistent, pro-life governmental policies. Advocates multilateral disarmament through negotiation; endorses governmental programs that encourage self-sufficiency of the poor (such as education and training projects to develop employable skills) and provide assistance in the areas of health care, food, and housing; opposes abortion, except when necessary to save the mother's life; believes the government should promote and offer social assistance and adoption programs as options to abortion or motherhood with inadequate economic support. Conducts educational activities. Also conducts grass roots campaign activities;

makes modest campaign contributions. Maintains educational fund.

Majority Congress Committee. • Democratic congressional political action committee.

National Conservative Congressional Committee. • Political action committee whose purpose is to produce a conservative majority in the Congress in 1988. Makes contributions and places advertisements supporting conservative incumbents and opponents of liberal candidates and incumbents targeted by the group for defeat. Address unknown since 21st edition.

National Security Political Action Committee. • No further information was available for this edition Presently inactive.

Parker-Coltrane Political Action Committee. • Political action organization supported by financial contributions of individuals. Organized by Congressman John Conyers and others to encourage and help blacks and progressive candidates to win election to public office in the southern U.S. through direct campaign contributions and technical assistance. Conducts training sessions on methods and techniques of running for office. Initial efforts have been concentrated in Georgia, although the committee now operates throughout the South. Plans to extend operations on a national level. Presently inactive.

Progressive Political Action Committee. • Contributors: 10,000. To support, by independent expenditure, the election of progressive candidates and the reelection of progressive incumbents. Actively works to defeat conservative politicians.

Ruff Political Action Committee. • Provides campaign advice and funding for selected conservative political candidates; conducts research; lobbies conservative issues. Committee is named after chairman Howard Ruff (1931-), financial adviser and editor. **Convention/Meeting:** none.

Senior PAC. • A political action committee dedicated to representing older and retired Americans. Works to strengthen and defend Social Security and Medicare programs. Supports congressional and presidential candidates who, through their statements and actions, advance the principle of "an adequate retirement income for all Americans.".

Zoological Action Committee. • Zoological institutions, animal suppliers and interested individuals. Lobbies in Washington, DC and state capitals on behalf of zoos, aquariums, oceanariums, private animal breeders and zoological suppliers. Presently inactive.

POLITICAL ACTION ORGANIZATION

RESEARCH CENTERS AND INSTITUTES

Free Congress Research and Education Foundation. 717 2nd St. NE, Washington, DC 20002. Phone: (202)546-3000 Fax: (202)543-5605 E-mail: jborda@freecongress.org • URL: http://www. freecongress.org • Brings messages of traditional values, conservative government, and institutional reform to America through publications and TV programs on America's Voice network. Includes projects such as: Judicial Selection Monitoring Project, "Taking Back Our Constitution" seminar services and the Center for Technology Policy's privacy papers.

TRADE/PROFESSIONAL ASSOCIATIONS

Better Government Association. 11 E Adams St., Ste. 608, Chicago, IL 60603. Phone: (312)427-8330 Fax: (312)386-9203 E-mail: info@bettergov.org • URL: http://bettergov.org • Individuals and corporations concerned with major public policy questions and dedicated to promoting efficient use of tax dollars and high standards of public service. Encourages a responsive and economical government by improving government institutions' performance and maintaining high ethical standards among public officials. Uses official documents, on-the-record interviews, undercover operations, and sophisticated techniques of investigative reporting to uncover corruption. Works closely with national and local media to expose waste, inefficiency, and corruption and to educate the public on the inner workings of the government. Sponsors intern programs for students in law and investigative research.

OTHER SOURCES

AIDS Action Council. • Serves as a representative in Washington, DC, of community-based AIDS service organizations. Advocates, at the federal level, for more effective AIDS policy, legislation, and funding. Works collaboratively with AIDS Action Foundation, a national public policy research organization.

Alliance for Acid Rain Control and Energy Policy. • Former and current U.S. governors, corporate executives, public interest leaders, and academicians who are concerned about conservation issues and national energy policy. Follows implementation of acid rain control legislation. Makes use of the findings of the Center for Clean Air Policy (see separate entry) to set specific emissions goals for states, industries, and utilities and suggest emissions-reducing tactics such as emiss ions trading among industries, use of clean coal by utilities, and more efficient use of energy by industrial and utility plants. Favors enactment of comprehensive national energy legislation, including increased energy efficiency, expanded domestic energy production, protection of the environment, and increased competition in energy markets.

American Renewal Foundation. • Explores opportunities for renewal; seeks to provide a voice in the national conversation as well as the vision of the nation's founders, through research and promotion of Christian, ethical solutions to national and global issues. Broadcasts a daily radio news show, The World from Washington, and a weekly radio show for teens called SpeakOut. Runs the web newspaper, Page One Daily. Maintains a large student program; new members are always invited to apply. Provides internship opportunities.

Americans for Common Sense. • Bipartisan coalition of politically progressive citizens who wish to develop an issue-oriented practical political agenda to counter the activities of New Right organizations such as the Moral Majority (see separate entry). Believes that the New Right is often politically successful because individuals do not have all of the facts necessary to make a completely informed decision on the issues; helps citizens understand the complexities of current political issues by presenting alternative points of view to those adopted by the New Right; encourages individuals to avoid adopting opinions without examining alternative positions. While not taking stands on particular issues, ACS encourages progressive alternatives to New Right positions. Staff members participate in radio and television interview shows to provide a forum for public discussion of issues. Plans to make field organizers available to assist chapters with local issues, forums and news releases; also plans to organize regional seminars, develop media and outreach programs and produce film presentations. Maintains library of news clippings, public and private reference files, and publications.

Americans for Constitutional Action. • Political action organization supported by financial contributions of individuals. Undertakes "to help elect to the Senate and House of Representatives of the United States individuals who, by their actions, have proved their allegiance to the original spirit and principles of the Constitution." Presents biennial distinguished

service award to selected members of Congress. Address unknown since 1992 edition.

Americans for the Environment. • Educational organization that encourages the public to influence the formation of environmental policy through effective use of elections. Sponsors political and electoral skills training programs for environmental and conservation activists at the national and local levels. Maintains data bank of environmental referenda; operates political trainers' bureau. **Convention/Meeting:** none.

Asian American Voters Coalition. • Coalition of organizations representing 6.5 million Asian-Americans. Seeks to enhance the political influence of Asian-Americans; promotes equal treatment of Asian-Americans in the U.S. political system. Lobbies the U.S. government on immigration legislation and other matters of interest to the Asian-American community; attempts to influence party platforms and presidential candidates on issues pertinent to Asian-Americans. Sponsors voter registration and education drives; encourages Asian-Americans to run for public office. Maintains speakers' bureau; bestows award for distinguished service.

Business Alliance for Commerce in Hemp. • Businesses, consumers, and other individuals and organizations with an interest in hemp and hemp products. Promotes "full and unrestricted restoration of hemp as a sustainable farm crop and industrial resource"; seeks to legalize therapeutic use of marijuana and regulate adult consumption. Conducts lobbying, community organization, and outreach activities supporting hemp producers and consumers; consulting services; disseminates information on the commercial and industrial uses of hemp and the therapeutic benefits of marijuana.

Campaign California. • State organization that attempts to introduce new issues into the political arena such as: rebuilding the Democratic party; controlling toxic wastes; developing affordable and better child care; stopping environmental cancer; achieving low-cost housing and tenants' rights. Works to elect progressive candidates to office in California.

Campaign for America. • Political fund organization.

Campaign for Working Families. • Represents the interests and values of America's traditional families in the political arena. Works on electing pro-family, pro-life and pro-free enterprise candidates to federal and state offices. Conducts extensive media campaigns and distribution of literature.

Catholics for Christian Political Action. • Catholic laymen interested in promoting the life of the family. Objectives are to voice the views of Catholics on social and political issues affecting the family, and to educate members as to where they can apply pressure to ensure that their views will be heeded. Issues of concern include war and peace, abortion, pornography, crime, drug abuse, sex education, and tax matters. Plans to conduct seminars and is in the process of organizing state and local groups. Presently inactive.

Citizen Action Fund. • Citizens working for economic democracy and social justice. Goal is to make the concerns of the majority of Americans felt in economic, environmental, and political decision-making. Seeks more jobs, safe and affordable energy, fair taxes, equal voting rights, and a safe and healthy community and workplace, free of toxic hazards. Conducts research, training, and educational programs.

Citizens for Bush. • Independent grass roots lobby organization supporting the legislative agenda and policies of President George Bush (1924-). Collaborates with several grass roots organizations to lobby Congress. Conducts seminars and legislative ratings. Maintains speakers' bureau.

Committee for a Progressive Congress. • Raises funds for Democratic Party candidates for the U.S. House of Representatives. **Convention/Meeting:** none. **Publications:** none.

Common Cause. • Nonpartisan citizens' lobby. Dedicated to fighting for open, honest, and accountable government at the national, state, and local levels. Gathers and disseminates information on the effects of money in politics; lobbies for political finance and other campaign reforms.

Conservative Leadership Political Action Committee. • Assists in the election of conservative candidates to congressional and statewide offices. Identifies, places, and supports youth coordinators; works to organize thousands of youth votes, volunteer hours, and special activities in targeted states and congressional districts. Offers placement service that matches trained youth coordinators who are available to work full-time in a fall election cycle with conservative campaigns desiring a full-time youth effort. **Convention/Meeting:** none. **Publications:** none.

Democracy International. • Seeks to build a movement of individuals dedicated to practical action on behalf of common commitments to human rights and pluralistic democracy including freedom of speech and press, religious liberty, free political parties, and the right to contest elections. Works to develop political and economic self-determination of citizens allowing them to control their resources, choose their social systems, and end discrimination. Aims to: revive democracy where it has been destroyed; encourage and sustain democrats trying to bring democracy to dictatorships. Calls upon democracies to: increase help for democratic leaders and politicians in the Third World; provide economic sustenance to relieve human suffering; strengthen democracy where it exists. Provides a forum for democrats to express solidarity and to help each other; encourages membership in an effort to build an international force of people working to make the cause of democracy an enduring ideal. Publicizes the efforts of democratic movements in dictatorships; attempts to increase the amount of uncensored information to closed societies. **Convention/Meeting:** none.

Dredging Industry Size Standard Committee. • Provides a legislative forum for the dredging industry. Represents the interests of the industry; lobbies for favorable federal legislation.

Earthcare Network. • Environmental groups united for the purpose of providing mutual assistance in the conducting of environmental campaigns. Compiles and exchanges information on these campaigns and communicates with relevant authorities. Maintains liaison with Sierra Club, which acts as secretariat for the network.

EMILY's List. • Political network for Democratic women. Seeks to raise campaign funds for the election of pro-choice Democratic women to political office. (EMILY stands for Early +Money is Like Yeast.) **Convention/Meeting:** none.

Environmental Action. • National political lobby organization. Prime focuses are: solid waste; toxic substances; recycling; global warming; utility policy; ozone and acid rain. Coordinated efforts on Clean Air Act, Clean Water Act, Occupational Safety and Health Act, Toxic Substances Control Act, Resource Conservation and Recovery Act in Congress, and Superfund. Engages in educational activities and community organizing. **Convention/Meeting:** none.

Federation for Progress. • National and Regional Groups: 100. Multi-issue, ongoing coalition of progressive organizations composed of single-issue groups and community and labor organizers who mobilize on the grass roots level for jobs, peace, and equality.

FreedomWorks. • Devoted to ensuring that government actions foster growth, economic well being and individual responsibility. Sponsors an internship program, introducing its participants to the Washington policy world, giving them a broader base of knowledge about the organization and its inner operations.

Fund for New Priorities in America. • Believes that the United States must reorder its national priorities. Works to inform the public, to build active networks and coalitions, and to enhance participatory democracy, in pursuit of a more just, peaceful, open, and humane society. Sponsors public forums.

Good Samaritan Coalition. • Organizations supporting passage of "Good Samaritan" legislation which would protect from liability volunteer third parties who render assistance at the scene of an emergency involving hazardous material. Entities such as chemical firms, petroleum companies, and liquid propane gas dealers are often called upon to assist police and fire departments in hazardous material emergencies such as train derailments and overturned trucks. Good Samaritan legislation would protect from lawsuit those providing assistance in the event that their actions aggravate rather than alleviate the hazardous condition, provided that assistance is not rendered in a grossly negligent manner.

Impac. • Raises funds for Democratic candidates for public office.

International Action Center. • Opposes U.S. militarism. Organizes opposition to U.S. intervention abroad and to racism and political repression at home. Sponsors educational activities and research.

League of Revolutionaries for a New America. • Works toward a vision of a cooperative world where the full potential of all can contribute to the good of everyone.

Military Toxics Project. • Promotes clean up of military pollution, safeguards transportation of hazardous materials, advances development of preventative solutions to toxic, radioactive pollution from military activities.

Movimiento Popular Peru. • Provides research, informational, and educational programs.

National Coalition for Science and Technology. • Scientists, engineers, and educators. Lobbies for responsible legislation that will enable the U.S. to make greater advances in science and technology. Encourages scientists and educators to become more active in the political process. Presents Congressional Friend of Science Award to ten members of Congress every two years. Maintains membership database. Sponsors public forums on public policy issues affecting science and technology.

National Toxics Campaign. • National labor, environmental, and citizens' groups. Purposes are to: obtain support for stronger laws against chemical contamination through canvassing and petition drives in 280 congressional districts; monitor government enforcement practices; provide legislative advocacy. Goal is to win legislation and enforcement that guarantees all Americans the right to be safe from harmful exposure to toxic substances. Maintains speakers' bureau; compiles statistics.

National Women's Coalition. • Professional and activist women drawn from business, the arts, academia, sports, and politics. Seeks to promote the rights, success, and independence of women. Believes "opportunity for all Americans can best be achieved through the policies of President Reagan, the current administration, and the Republican Party." Has initiated discussion on government policies that have benefited women.

Naval Sea Cadet Corps. • Youths aged 11-17 years interested in the Navy, Marine Corps, Coast Guard, and Merchant Marines. Works to instill good citizenship and patriotism in youth. Encourages qualities such as personal neatness, loyalty, obedience, dependability, and responsibility to others. Offers courses in physical fitness and military drill, first aid, water safety, basic seamanship, and naval history and traditions.

Paul Revere Society. • Seeks to have a strong voice to the political arena; strives for the reassertion of America's borders, language and culture. Opposes the viewpoint that English is only one of many languages in the new "Multicultural America" and that Americans share no common history or values; believes in the Sovereignty of America, that English is the national "glue", that all Americans do share in the pillars of the Bible, the U.S. Constitution, and the Bill of Rights, and that these documents stand for American's common cultural heritage.

Pay for Schools by Regulating Cannabis. • Concerned citizens who believe in hemp's environmental benefits. Seeks to regulate cannabis sales in state liquor stores to fund education and drug treatment programs. Promotes hemp manufacture for paper, fabrics, oil and pharmaceutical prescriptions. Conducts educational programs; compiles statistics; maintains speakers' bureau.

People's Anti-War Mobilization. • Local community and welfare rights organizations, workers, and students who seek to: mobilize a mass movement to prevent U.S. military intervention abroad; pressure the federal government to reorient national priorities so that money appropriated for military use is shifted to social welfare programs. Sponsors demonstrations.

Project '88: Americans for the Reagan Agenda. • U.S. citizens who support the economic and foreign policies of President Ronald Reagan (1911-) and his administration. Seeks a continuation of these policies beyond President Reagan's term in office by organizing grass roots support for his positions on various issues, most notably contra aid, the Strategic Defense Initiative (Star Wars), and the national budget. Plans to publish a newsletter and various briefs pertaining to current issues in foreign and domestic policy.

Project on Government Oversight. • Promotes accountability in government; monitors governmental agencies; exposes abuses of power, and waste and fraud committed by the government and its contractors. **Convention/Meeting:** none.

Refuse and Resist. • Participants seek to build mass resistance to the "entire agenda of repression in the U.S." Works to unite grassroots activists, prominent entertainers, teachers, plumbers, artists, student, etc. in opposition to the fundamentalist right-wing agenda. Opposes racism, restrictions on abortion rights, the escalation of the "war on women", censorship, homophobia, xenophobia, and the execution of Mumia Abu-Jamal. Has demonstrated to prevent the closing of abortion clinics and the incarceration of immigrants. Participates in debates; maintains speakers' bureau.

Social Democrats, U.S.A. • Serves as political action and education organization of young people, students, and trade unionists. Supports Independent and Democratic liberal-labor candidates for public office. Seeks realignment of the major political parties in the U.S. Maintains speakers' bureau. Supports "greater democratic decision-making over the social forces that control our everyday economic lives." Recommends democratic economic planning to ease pains of the economic crisis and to allocate resources in the public interest. Favors public aid to education and increased public investment in such areas as national health care, mass transit, low-cost housing, and new sources of energy. Supports trade unionism. Believes in foreign policy that supports democratic movements and governments.

Society of the 3rd Infantry Division. • Past and present members of the 3rd Infantry Division of the U.S. Army and attached and supporting units; families of veterans of the division. Fosters and strengthens associations and friendships formed during service with the Third Infantry Division. Honors the Third Infantry Division War Dead and perpetuates their memory. Encourages and achieves the mutual benefit and support resulting from a close and cooperative alliance between the Society and the Third Infantry Division, U.S. Army. Supports the government of the United States. Assists in the maintenance of monuments dedicated to the Third Infantry Division. Organizes and conducts wreath laying and memorial ceremonies.

Student Coalition for the Right to Drink. • A federation of state coalitions of students opposed to the establishment of a federal drinking age of 21, viewing it as contrary to the interest of college students (most of whom are under 21), and as an unnecessary form of government regulation. Works to have both the federal drinking age and voting age constitutionally mandated at age 18.

Twentieth Anniversary Mobilization. • Civil rights, labor, and peace organizations and others joined together in a national effort to concentrate on three key issues: jobs, peace, and freedom. Sponsored a March on Washington on Aug. 27, 1983 commemorating the 20th anniversary of Martin Luther King's "I Have a Dream" speech. Works for legislative passage designating January 15 as a national holiday honoring Martin Luther King's birthday. Promotes the work of the coalition on state and local levels.

20/20 Vision National Project. • Promotes citizen involvement in influencing public policies that endorse protection of the environment, an increase in national and global security, reduction of military spending, and the support of individual economic and social needs. Encourages individual political activism by providing convenient, simple, effective activities designed to take less than 20 minutes to complete. (Organization name is derived from the belief that an individual's contribution of 20 minutes a month and $20 a year can have a significant impact on public policy.) Maintains network of local lobbying groups; provides training and promotional materials to local organizers.

Urban Environment Conference. • National labor, minority, and environmental organizations. Lobbies in Washington, DC, and at a grass roots level for strong environmental and occupational health laws. Offers educational programs to enable minorities, workers, and others to participate more effectively in decisions affecting their health and interests.

U.S.English. • Aims to preserve the common bond by making English the official language of government in the U.S. Promotes opportunities for people living here to learn English.

Women Against Military Madness. • Advocates a "radical shift in our nations priorities away from militarism, military spending, arms trade, military intervention, and the militarization of schools".

Zoological Action Committee. • Zoological institutions, animal suppliers and interested individuals. Lobbies in Washington, DC and state capitals on behalf of zoos, aquariums, oceanariums, private animal breeders and zoological suppliers. Presently inactive.

POLITICAL ECONOMY
See: ECONOMICS

POLLS, OPINION
See: PUBLIC OPINION

POLLUTION OF AIR
See: AIR POLLUTION

POLLUTION OF WATER

See: WATER POLLUTION

POLYMERS

See: CHEMICAL INDUSTRIES; PLASTICS INDUSTRY

POPCORN INDUSTRY

See: SNACK FOOD INDUSTRY

POPULATION

See also: CENSUS REPORTS; VITAL STATISTICS

GENERAL WORKS

Global Economic Prospects 2004. The World Bank Group. • 2003. $38.00. "..offers an in-depth analysis of the economic prospects of developing countries.." Emphasis is on the impact of recessions and financial crises. Regional statistical data is included.

Moving Power and Money: The Politics of Census Taking. Barbara E. Bryant and William Dunn. New Strategist Publications, Inc. • 1995. $24.95. Barbara Everitt Bryant was Director of the U. S. Census Bureau from 1989 to 1993. She provides a plan for reducing the costs of census taking, improving accuracy, and overcoming public resistance to the census.

ABSTRACTS AND INDEXES

PAIS International in Print. Public Affairs Information Service, Inc. • Monthly. $850.00 per year; cumulations three times a year. Provides topical citations to the worldwide literature of public affairs, economics, demographics, sociology, and trade. Text in English; indexed materials in English, French, German, Italian, Portuguese and Spanish.

Social Sciences Citation Index. Thomson/ISI. • Three times a year. $6,900 per year. Annual cumulation. Includes *Source Index, Citation Index, Permuterm Subject Index,* and *Corporate Index.*

Social Sciences Index. H. W. Wilson Co. • Quarterly, with annual cumulation. Price varies. Indexes more than 400 periodicals covering economics, environmental policy, government, insurance, labor, health care policy, plannning, public administration, public welfare, urban studies, women's issues, criminology, and related topics.

ALMANACS AND YEARBOOKS

Research in Population Economics. Elsevier. • Irregular. $90.25. Volumes 4-9.

Vital Signs [year]: The Trends That Are Shaping Our Future. Worldwatch Institute. • Annual. $14.95. Provides access to selected indicators showing social, economic, and environmental trends throughout the world. Includes data relating to food, energy, transportation, finance, population, and other topics.

World Development Report 2004. The World Bank Group. • Annual. $26.00. Covers history, conditions, and trends relating to economic globalization and localization. Includes selected data from *World Development Indicators* for 132 countries or economies. Key indicators are provided for 78 additional countries or economies.

BIBLIOGRAPHIES

Census Catalog and Guide. U. S. Government Printing Office. • Annual. Lists publications and electronic media products currently available from the U. S. Bureau of the Census, along with some out of print items. Includes comprehensive title and subject indexes. Formerly *Bureau of the Census Catalog.*

Global Data Locator. George T. Kurian. Bernan Associates. • 1997. $89.00. Provides detailed descriptions of international statistical sourcebooks and electronic databases. Covers a wide variety of trade, economic, and demographic topics.

Monthly Product Announcement. U. S. Bureau of the Census. • Monthly. Lists Census Bureau publications and products that became available during the previous month.

CD-ROM DATABASES

OECD Statistical Compendium. Organization for Economic Cooperation and Development. • Semiannual. $1,905.00 per year for 1 to 10 users. CD-ROM contains more than 730,000 monthly, quarterly, and annual time series for OECD countries, 1960 to date. Includes fully searchable data on agriculture, food, economic indicators, national accounts, employment, energy, finance, industry, technology, and foreign trade. Results can be displayed in various forms.

PAIS on CD-ROM. Public Affairs Information Service, Inc. • Quarterly. $1,995.00 per year. Provides a CD-ROM version of the online service, *PAIS International.* Contains over 500,000 citations to the literature of contemporary social, political, and economic issues.

Social Sciences Citation Index. ISI. • Monthly. Price on request. Provides CD-ROM indexing of articles appearing in 1700 leading social science journals worldwide, with additional selections from more than 5700 other journals. Time span is 1992 to date. Coverage includes economics, business, finance, management, communications, demographics, library and information science, political science, sociology, and many other subjects.

Social Sciences Citation Index: Compact Disc Edition with Abstracts. Institute for Scientific Information. • Monthly. Provides CD-ROM indexing and abstracting of "significant articles" from 1,700 social science journals worldwide, with additional selections from 3,200 other journals, 1986 to date. Includes economics, business, finance, management, communications, demographics, information and library science, political science, sociology, and many other subjects.

Sourcebook America. Gale Cengage Learning. • Annual. $995.00. Produced by CACI Marketing Systems. A combination on CD-ROM of *The Sourcebook of ZIP Code Demographics* and *The Sourcebook of County Demographics.* Provides detailed population and socio-economic data (about 75 items) for each of 3,141 U. S. counties and approximately 30,000 ZIP codes, plus states, metropolitan areas, and media market areas. Includes forecasts to the year 2004.

Sourcebooks America CD-ROM. CACI Marketing Systems. • Annual. $1,250.00. Provides the CD-ROM version of *The Sourcebook of ZIP Code Demographics: Census Edition* and *The Sourcebook of County Demographics: Census Edition.*

Statistical Abstract of the United States on CD-ROM. Hoover's, Inc. • Annual. $49.95. Provides all statistics from official print version, plus expanded historical data, greater detail, and keyword searching features.

WILSONDISC: Wilson Social Sciences Abstracts. H. W. Wilson Co. • Monthly. Includes unlimited online access to *Social Sciences Index* through WILSONLINE. Provides CD-ROM indexing from 1983 and abstracting from 1994 of more than 500 periodicals covering economics, area studies, community health, public administration, public welfare, urban studies, and many other topics related to the social sciences.

World Development Report [CD-ROM]. The World Bank, Office of the Publisher. • Annual. CD-ROM includes the current edition of *World Development Report* and 21 previous editions.

World Marketing Data and Statistics on CD-ROM. Gale Cengage Learning. • Annual. $1,750.00. Published by Euromonitor. Provides demographic, marketing, socioeconomic, and political data on CD-ROM for each of 209 countries.

World Marketing Forecasts on CD-ROM. Gale Cengage Learning. • Annual. $2,500.00. Produced by Euromonitor. Provides detailed forecast data for the years to 2012 on CD-ROM for 54 countries in all parts of the world. Covers a wide range of social, demographic, economic, and market factors. Includes specific forecasts for many kinds of consumer products.

DIRECTORIES

Where to Write for Vital Records: Births, Deaths, Marriages, and Divorces. Available from U. S. Government Printing Office. • 2002. $3.00. Issued by the National Center for Health Statistics, U. S. Department of Health and Human Services. Arranged by state. Provides addresses, telephone numbers, and cost of copies for various kinds of vital records or certificates. (DHHS Publication No. PHS 93-1142.).

ENCYCLOPEDIAS AND DICTIONARIES

Encyclopedia of Population. Available from Gale Cengage Learning. • 2003. $265.00. Two volumes. Published by Macmillan Reference USA. Formerly *Macmillan's International Encyclopedia of Population.* Covers a broad range of topics in demography and neighboring disciplines. Emphasis is on developments in population research during the past 20 years.

INTERNET DATABASES

Business 2.0 Web Guide to the Best Business Links. Business 2.0 Media Inc. Phone: (415)293-4800 E-mail: support@business2.com • URL: http://www.business2.com/webguide • Web site presents an extensive, searchable directory of links to "the best, most informative, and authoritative web pages." Twenty main categories cover business, finance, career, company information, people, and technology topics, with thousands of subtopics, all linking to Web sites recommended by experienced business researchers. Fees: Free.

Fedstats. Federal Interagency Council on Statistical Policy. Phone: (202)395-7254 • URL: http://www.fedstats.gov • Web site features an efficient search facility for full-text statistics produced by more than 100 federal agencies, including the Census Bureau, the Bureau of Economic Analysis, and the Bureau of Labor Statistics. Boolean searches can be made within one agency or for all agencies combined. Links are offered to international statistical bureaus, including the UN, IMF, OECD, UNESCO, Eurostat, and 20 individual countries. Fees: Free.

FreeLunch.com. Economy.com, Inc. Phone: (610)696-8700 Fax: (610)696-1678 • URL: http://www.freelunch.com • Web site provides free access to more than 1.5 million economic and financial data series, covering industry, demographics, labor markets, prices, retail sales, government spending, trade, interest rates, housing starts, the stock market, and many other topics. Data is available for various time periods in either chart or table form. Searching is offered. Fees: Free, but registration required. Economy.com, Inc. also offers fee-based economic analysis at *The Dismal Scientist* site (http://www.dismal.com).

ONLINE DATABASES

PAIS International. Public Affairs Information Service, Inc. • Corresponds to the former printed publications, *PAIS Bulletin* (1976-90) and *PAIS Foreign Language Index* (1972-90), and to the current *PAIS International in Print* (1991 to date). Covers economic, political, and sociological material appearing in periodicals, books, government documents, and other publications. Updating is monthly. Inquire as to online cost and availability.

Social Scisearch. Institute for Scientific Information. • Broad, multidisciplinary index to the literature of the social sciences, 1972 to present. Weekly updates. Worldwide coverage. Inquire as to online cost and availability.

Wilson Social Sciences Abstracts Online. H. W. Wilson Co. • Provides online abstracting and indexing of more than 500 periodicals covering area studies, community health, public administration, public welfare, urban studies, and many other social science topics. Time period is 1994 to date for abstracts and 1983 to date for indexing, with updates weekly. Inquire as to online cost and availability.

PERIODICALS AND NEWSLETTERS

American Demographics: Consumer Trends for Business Leaders. Media Central. • Monthly. $58.00 per year.

Demography. Population Association of America. • Quarterly. $85.00 per year.

Population Bulletin. Population Reference Bureau, Inc. • Quarterly. $49.00 per year.

World Watch: Working for a Sustainable Future. Worldwatch Institute. • Bimonthly. $25.00 per year. Emphasis is on environmental trends, including developments in population growth, climate change, human behavior, the role of government, and other factors.

The ZPG Reporter. Population Connection. • Description: Reports on population growth and related social, environmental, and economic issues. Tracks legislative developments. Recurring features include interviews, news of research, book reviews, and regular columns.

RESEARCH CENTERS AND INSTITUTES

Center for Population and Development Studies. Harvard University. Nine Bow St., Cambridge, MA 02138. Phone: (617)495-2021 Fax: (617)495-5418 E-mail: cpds@hsph.harvard.edu • URL: http://www.hsph.harvard.edu/hcpds.

Population Research Center. University of Chicago. 1155 E. 60th St., Chicago, IL 60637. Phone: (773)256-6302 Fax: (773)256-6313 E-mail: pari@midway.uchicago.edu • URL: http://www.src.uchicago.edu/orgs/prc.

Population Studies Center. University of Michigan. 426 Thompson St., Ann Arbor, MI 48106. Phone: (734)998-7275 Fax: (734)998-7415 E-mail: david1@umich.edu • URL: http://www.psc.lsa.umich.edu.

Worldwatch Institute. Worldwatch Institute. 1776 Massachusetts Ave. NW, Washington, DC 20036-1904. Phone: (202)452-1999 or (202)452-1999 Fax: (202)296-7365 E-mail: worldwatch@worldwatch.org • URL: http://www.worldwatch.org • Global trends in the availability and management of both human and natural resources, including research in energy, food policy, population, development, technology, the environment, economics, toxics, and recycling.

STATISTICS SOURCES

American Business Climate and Economic Profiles. Priscilla C. Geahigan. Gale Cengage Learning. • 1993. $170.00. Provides business, industrial, demographic, and economic figures for all states and 300 metropolitan areas. Includes production, taxation, population, growth rates, labor force data, incomes, total sales, etc.

American Places Dictionary: A Guide to Populated Places, Natural Features , and Other United States Places. Frank R. Abate, editor. Omnigraphics, Inc. • 1994. $350.00. Four regional volumes: Northeast, South, Midwest, and West. Provides statistical data and other information on 45,000 U. S. cities, towns,

townships, boroughs, and villages. Includes detailed state profiles, county profiles, and more than 10,000 name origins. Arranged by state, then by county. (Individual regional volumes are available at $100.00.).

Comparative Guide to American Suburbs, 2003/2004. Grey House Publishing. • 2003. $130.00. Third edition. Contains detailed profiles of 1,800 suburban communities having a population of 10,000 or more and located within the 50 largest metropolitan areas. Includes ranking tables for income, unemployment, new housing permits, home prices, and crime, as well as information on school districts. (Universal Reference Publications.).

Consumer International. Available from Gale Cengage Learning. • Annual. $1,290.00. Published by Euromonitor. Contains extensive consumer market, economic, and demographic data for 25 major, non-European countries, including the U. S. and Canada. Includes consumer market size (volume and value) for 150 product types in 14 categories (food, clothing, automobiles, cosmetics, appliances, etc.).

Counties USA: A Directory of United States Counties. Omnigraphics, Inc. • 2003. $85.00. Second edition. Contains extensive economic and demographic data from the 2000 Census for about 3,100 counties of the U. S.

County and City Data Book 2000: A Statistical Abstract Supplement. Available from U. S. Government Printing Office. • 2002. $68.00. 13th edition. Issued by the U. S. Bureau of the Census (http://www.census.gov). Contains a wide variety of data on 3,141 U.S. counties, 1,078 cities, and 11,097 places of 2,500 or more inhabitants. Includes statistical information on retailing, manufacturing, banking, service industries, income, employment, housing, education, crime, and population. Updated metropolitan areas are included.

County and City Extra: Annual Metro, City and County Data Book. Deirdre A. Gaquin and Mark S. Littman. Bernan Press. • 2001. $120.00. Updates and augments data published irregularly in print form by the U. S. Census Bureau in *County and City Data Book.* Covers "every state, county, metropolitan area, and congressional district in the United States, as well as all U. S. cities with a 1990 population of 25,000 or more." Contains a wide range tic maps.

County and City Extra: Special Decennial Census Edition. Deidre A. Gaquin and Katherine A. De-Brandt, editors. Bernan Press. • 2002. $95.00. Presents conveniently arranged population, housing, and other data from the 2000 census, with many 1980 and 1990 comparisons. Includes maps and tables with rankings of about 20 items for various geographic locations. Complements the annual *County and City Extra.*

Current Population Reports: Household Economic Studies, Series P-70. Available from U. S. Government Printing Office. • Irregular. $21.00 per year. Issued by the U.S. Bureau of the Census (http://www.census.gov). Each issue covers a special topic relating to household socioeconomic characteristics.

Current Population Reports: Population Characteristics, Special Studies, and Consumer Income, Series P-20, P-23, and P-60. Available from U. S. Government Printing Office. • Irregular. $80.00 per year. Issued by the U.S. Bureau of the Census (http://www.census.gov). Each issue covers a special topic relating to population or income. Series P-20, *Population Characteristics,* provides statistical studies on such items as mobility, fertility, education, and marital status. Series P-23, *Special Studies,* consists of occasional reports on methodology. Series P-60, *Consumer Income,* publishes reports on income in relation to age, sex, education, occupation, family size, etc.

Datapedia of the United States: American History in

Numbers. George T. Kurian, editor. Bernan Press. • 2004. $125.00. Third edition. Based on the Census Bureau publication, *Historical Statistics of the United States.* Provides data from Colonial times to the present on agriculture, business, consumer income, energy, finance, labor, national income, population, and many other subjects. Includes "narrative highlights," maps, charts, and statistical projections.

Demographic Yearbook. United Nations, Dept. of Economic and Social Affairs. United Nations Publications. • Annual. $125.00. Text in English and French.

Demographics USA: County Edition. Trade Dimensions. • Annual. $435.00. Contains 200 statistical series for each of 3,000 counties. Includes population, household income, employment, retail sales, and consumer expenditures. Also provides Effective Buying Income, Buying Power Index, and data summaries by Metro Market, Media Market, and State. (CD-ROM version is available.).

Demographics USA: ZIP Edition. Trade Dimensions. • Annual. $435.00. Contains 50 statistical series for each of 40,000 ZIP codes. Includes population, household income, employment, retail sales, and consumer expenditures. Also provides Effective Buying Income, Business Characteristics, and data summaries by state, region, and the first three digits of ZIP codes. (CD-ROM version is available.).

European Marketing Forecasts. Available from Gale Cengage Learning. • Annual. $1,250.00. Published by Euromonitor. Contains demographic, economic, and market forecasts for the countries of Europe to the year 2010. Forecasts include market-size data for 15 consumer product sectors (food, clothing, automobiles, consumer electronics, etc.).

The Future Demographic: Global Population Trends and Forecasts to 2010 and Beyond. Euromonitor International. • 2003. $470.00. Presents detailed demographic statistics and forecasts for about 200 countries. Includes age group profiles and data on consumer spending potential.

Gale Country and World Rankings Reporter. Gale Cengage Learning. • 1997. $160.00. Second edition. Provides about 3,000 statistical ranking tables and charts covering more than 235 nations. Sources include the United Nations and various government publications.

Gale State Rankings Reporter. Gale Cengage Learning. • 1996. $130.00. Second edition Provides 3,000 ranked lists of states under 35 subject headings. Sources are newspapers, periodicals, books, research institute publications, and government publications.

Geographic Reference Report: Annual Report of Costs, Wages, Salaries, and Human Resource Statistics for the United States and Canada. ERI (Economic Research Institute). • Annual. $389.00. Provides demographic and other data for each of 298 North American metropolian areas, including local salaries, wage differentials, cost-of-living, housing costs, income taxation, employment, unemployment, population, major employers, crime rates, weather, etc.

Handbook of U. S. Labor Statistics: Employment, Earnings, Prices, Productivity, and Other Labor Data. Eva E. Jacobs, editor. Bernan Associates. • 1999. $74.00. Based on *Handbook of Labor Statistics,* formerly issued by the Bureau of Labor Statistics, U. S. Department of Labor. Includes the Bureau's projections of employment in the U. S. by industry and occupation. Provides a wide variety of data on the work force, prices, fringe benefits, and consumer expenditures.

International Marketing Forecasts. Available from Gale Cengage Learning. • Annual. $1,250.00. Published by Euromonitor. Contains demographic, economic, and market forecasts to the year 2013 for major, non-European countries, including the U. S. and Canada. Forecasts include market-size data for 15 consumer product sectors, such as food, clothing, and automobiles.

Key Indicators of the Labour Market. Available from Routledge. • Biennial. $125.00. Published by the International Labour Office (http://www.ilo.org). Provides data on 20 key indicators in 220 countries. Includes labor force statistics, employment, unemployment, part-time workers, wages, productivity, poverty indicators, and related topics.

Labour Force Statistics. Organization for Economic Cooperation and Development. Available from OECD Publications and Information Center. • Annual. $98.00. Provides 21 years of data for OECD member countries on population, employment, unemployment, civilian labor force, armed forces, and other labor factors.

Metropolitan Life Insurance Co. Statistical Bulletin SB. Metropolitan Life Insurance Co. • Quarterly. Individuals, $50.00 per year. Covers a wide range of social, economic and demographic health concerns.

Monthly Bulletin of Statistics. United Nations Publications. • Monthly. $295.00 per year. Provides current data for about 200 countries on a wide variety of economic, industrial, and demographic subjects. Compiled by United Nations Statistical Office.

Moving and Relocation Sourcebook and Directory: Reference Guide to the 120 Largest Metropolitan Areas in the United States. Omnigraphics, Inc. • Annual. $225.00 Provides extensive statistical and other descriptive data for the 120 largest metropolitan areas in the U. S. Includes maps and a discussion of factors to be considered when relocating.

Nations of the World: A Political, Economic, and Business Handbook. Grey House Publishing. • 2002. $135.00. Third edition. Includes descriptive data on economic characteristics, population, gross domestic product (GDP), banking, inflation, agriculture, tourism, and other factors. Covers "all the nations of the world.".

Places, Towns, and Townships, 1998. Deirdre A. Gaquin and Richard W. Dodge, editors. Bernan Press. • 1997. $89.00. Second edition. Presents demographic and economic statistics from the U. S. Census Bureau and other government sources for places, cities, towns, villages, census designated places, and minor civil divisions. Contains more than 60 data categories. (Places, Towns and Townships Series).

Population Abstract of the U. S. Gale Cengage Learning. • 1999. $190.00. Historical emphasis. Includes a "breakdown of urban and rural population from the earliest census to the present.".

Population and Vital Statistics Report. United Nations Publications. • Quarterly. $40.00 per year. Contains worldwide demographic statistics.

Population of States and Counties of the United States: 1790-1990. Available from National Technical Information Service. • 1996. $35.00. Issued by the U. S. Census Bureau (http://www.census.gov). Provides data on the number of inhabitants of the U. S., states, territories, and counties according to 21 decennial censuses from 1790 to 1990. Includes descriptions of county origins and lists prior county names, where applicable.

Quarterly Labour Force Statistics. Organization for Economic Cooperation and Development. Available from OECD Publications and Information Center. • Quarterly. $90.00 per year. Provides current data for OECD member countries on population, employment, unemployment, civilian labor force, armed forces, and other labor factors.

Social Statistics of the United States. Mark S. Littman, editor. Bernan Press. • 2000. $65.00. Includes

statistical data on population growth, labor force, occupations, environmental trends, leisure time use, income, poverty, taxes, and other economic or demographic topics.

Social Trends and Indicators USA. Monique D. Magee, editor. Gale Cengage Learning. • 2003. $450.00. Four volumes. Includes data on labor, economics, the health care industry, crime, leisure, population, education, social security, and many other topics. Sources include various government agencies and major publications.

The Sourcebook of ZIP Code Demographics. Available from Gale Cengage Learning. • Annual. $495.00. Published by ESRI Business Information Systems. Presents detailed statistical profiles of every ZIP code in America. Each profile contains data on more than 70 variables with 2003 updates and 2008 forecasts.

Sourcebook of Zip Code Demographics. ESRI Business Information Solutions. • 2002. $495.00. 16th edition. Provides data on 75 demographic and socioeconomic characteristics for each ZIP code in the U. S.

State and Metropolitan Area Data Book. Available from U. S. Government Printing Office. • 1998. Issued by the U. S. Bureau of the Census. Presents a wide variety of statistical data for U. S. regions, states, counties, metropolitan areas, and central cities, with ranking tables. Time period is 1970 to 1990.

State Profiles: The Population and Economy of Each U. S. State. Courtenay Slater and Others. Bernan Press. • 1999. $89.00. Presents charts, tables, and text in an eight-page profile for each state. Covers population, labor force, income, poverty, employment, wages, industry, trade, housing, education, health, taxes, and government finances. (The Population and Economy of Each United States Series).

Statistical Abstract of the United States. Available from U. S. Government Printing Office. • Annual. $51.00. Issued by the U. S. Bureau of the Census.

Statistical Abstract of the World. Gale Cengage Learning. • 1997. $85.00. Third edition. Provides data on a wide variety of economic, social, and political topics for about 200 countries. Arranged by country.

Statistical Forecasts of the United States. Gale Cengage Learning. • 1995. $115.00. Second edition. Provides both long-term and short-term statistical forecasts relating to basic items in the U. S.: population, employment, labor, crime, education, and health care. Data in the form of charts, graphs, and tables has been taken from a wide variety of government and private sources. Includes a subject index and an "Index of Forecast by Year.".

Statistical Handbook on the American Family. Bruce A. Chadwick and Tim B. Heaton. Greenwood Publishing Group, Inc. • 1998. $69.95. Second edition. Includes data on education, health, politics, employment, expenditures, social characteristics, the elderly, and women in the labor force. Historical statistics on marriage, birth, and divorce are shown from 1900 on. A list of sources and a subject index are provided. (Statistical Handbooks Series).

Statistical Record of the Environment. Gale Cengage Learning. • 1996. $130.00. Third edition. Provides over 875 charts, tables, and graphs of major environmental statistics, arranged by subject. Covers population growth, hazardous waste, nuclear energy, acid rain, pesticides, and other subjects related to the environment. A keyword index is included. (Gale Environmental Library Series).

Statistical Yearbook. United Nations Publications. • Annual. $125.00. Contains statistics for about 200 countries on a wide variety of economic, industrial, and demographic topics. Compiled by United Nations Statistical Office.

Trends in International Migration. Organization for Economic Cooperation and Development. • 2001. $59.00. Contains detailed data on population migration flows, channels of immigration, and migrant nationalities. Includes demographic analysis.

UNESCO Statistical Yearbook. Bernan Press. • 1998. $95.00. Co-published by Bernan Press and the United Nations Educational, Scientific, and Cultural Organization (http://www.unesco.org). Presents statistical data from more than 200 countries on education, technology, research, broadcasting, cinema, book publishing, newspapers, libraries, museums, and population. Includes charts, maps, and graphs.

United States Census of Population. Bureau of the Census, U.S. Department of Commerce. Available from U.S. Government Printing Office. • Quinquennial.

The World Bank Atlas. World Bank Group. • Annual. $10.00. Contains "color maps, charts, and graphs representing the main social, economic, and environmental indicators for 209 countries and territories" (publisher).

World Development Indicators. The World Bank Group. • Annual. $60.00. Provides data and information on the people, economy, environment, and markets of 148 countries. Emphasis is on statistics relating to major development issues.

The World Economy: A Millennial Perspective. Angus Maddison. Organization for Economic Cooperation and Development. • 2001. $63.00. "...covers the development of the entire world economy over the past 2000 years," including data on world population and gross domestic product (GDP) since the year 1000, and exports since 1820. Focuses primarily on the disparity in economic performance among nations over the very long term. More than 200 statistical tables and figures are provided.

World Factbook. U.S. National Technical Information Service. • Annual. $83.00. Prepared by the Central Intelligence Agency. For all countries of the world, provides current economic, demographic, geographic, communications, government, defense force, and illicit drug trade information (where applicable).

World Population Chart. United Nations Publications. • 1998. $5.95. Shows population, birth rate, death rate, etc., for all countries of the world, with forecasts to the year 2015 and to the year 2050.

World Population Data Sheet. Population Reference Bureau, Inc. • Annual. $4.50.

TRADE/PROFESSIONAL ASSOCIATIONS

Population Action International. 1300 19th St. NW, Ste. 200, Washington, DC 20036. Phone: (202)557-3400 Fax: (202)728-4177 E-mail: pai@popact.org • URL: http://www.populationaction.org • Seeks to advance policies and programs that slow population growth in order to enhance the quality of life for all ages. Advocates expansion of voluntary family planning, other reproductive health services, and educational and economic opportunities for girls and women.

Population Association of America. 8630 Fenton St., Ste. 722, Silver Spring, MD 20910. Phone: (301)565-6710 Fax: (301)565-7850 E-mail: info@popassoc.org • URL: http://www.popassoc.org • Individuals interested in demography and its scientific aspects.

Population Connection. 2120 L St. NW, Ste. 500, Washington, DC 20037. Phone: 800-POP-1956 or (202)332-2200 Fax: (202)332-2302 E-mail: info@populationconnection.org • URL: http://www.populationconnection.org • Works to educate and motivate Americans to help meet global population challenge, and to mobilize support for the adoption of policies and programs necessary to stop global population growth. Participates in coalitions, influences governmental policies on the international,

national, state, and local levels; works with the media; engages in teacher training and public education programs. Conducts research, interprets and applies the research of others. Maintains speakers' bureau; compiles statistics.

Population Council. 1 Dag Hammarskjold Plz., New York, NY 10017. Phone: (212)339-0500 Fax: (212)755-6052 E-mail: pubinfo@popcouncil.org • URL: http://www.popcouncil.org • Seeks to improve the well-being and reproductive health of current and future generations around the world. Helps achieve a humane, equitable, and sustainable balance between people and resources.

Population Reference Bureau. 1875 Connecticut Ave. NW, Ste. 520, Washington, DC 20009-5728. Phone: 800-877-9881 or (202)483-1100 Fax: (202)328-3937 E-mail: popref@prb.org • URL: http://www.prb.org • Gathers, interprets, and disseminates information on the facts and implications of national and world population trends.

OTHER SOURCES

Omni Gazetteer of the United States of America: A Guide to 1,500,000 Place Names in the United States and Territories. Frank R. Abate, editor. Omnigraphics, Inc. • 1991. $700.00. 11 volumes. Comprehensive listing of cities, towns, suburbs, villages, boroughs, structures, facilities, locales, historic places, and named geographic features. Population is shown where applicable. Individual regional volumes are available at $150.00.

World Population Projections to 2150. United Nations Publications. • 1998. $15.00. Presents very long-range population projections for eight major areas of the world: Africa, Asia, China, Europe, India, Latin America, North America, and Oceania.

Zip Code Mapbook of Metropolitan Areas. ESRI Business Information Solutions. • 1992. $195.00. Second edition. Contains Zip Code two-color maps of 326 metropolitan areas. Includes summary statistical profiles of each area: population characteristics, employment, housing, and income.

PORCELAIN INDUSTRY

See: POTTERY INDUSTRY

PORK

See: SWINE INDUSTRY

PORT AUTHORITIES

See: PORTS

PORTABLE COMPUTERS

ABSTRACTS AND INDEXES

Business Periodicals Index. H. W. Wilson Co. • 11 times a year. Quarterly and annual cumulations. Price varies.

CompuMath Citation Index. Institute for Scientific Information. • Three times a year. $1,090.00 per year. Provides citations to the worldwide literature of computer science and mathematics.

Computer and Information Systems Abstracts Journal: An Abstract Journal Pertaining to the Theory, Design, Fabrication and Application of Computer and Information Systems. CSA. • 11 times a year. $1,750 per year.

Computer Literature Index: A Subject/Author Index to Computer and Data Processing Literature. EBSCO Publishing. • Quarterly, with annual cumulation. $245.00 per year. Contains brief abstracts of book and periodical literature covering

all phases of computing, including approximately 70 specific application areas.

Internet and Personal Computing Abstracts [print edition]. EBSCO Publishing. • Quarterly. $269.00 per year, including cumulative index. Provides more than 10,000 abstracts annually from both trade and academic publications. Covers computer hardware, software, product reviews, Web topics, e-commerce, networks, corporate news, security, and related topics. Formerly *Microcomputer Abstracts.*

CD-ROM DATABASES

ABI/INFORM. PROQUEST. • Monthly. Provides CD-ROM indexing and abstracting of worldwide business literature. Archival discs are available from 1971. Formerly *ABI/INFORM OnDisc.*

Computer Database. Gale Cengage Learning. • Provides one year of full-text on CD-ROM for 150 leading computer-related publications. Also includes 70,000 product specifications and brief profiles of 13,000 computer product vendors and manufacturers.

WILSONDISC: Wilson Business Abstracts. H. W. Wilson Co. • Monthly. Includes unlimited online access to *Wilson Business Abstracts* through WILSONLINE. Provides CD-ROM "cover-to-cover" abstracting and indexing of over 600 prominent business periodicals. Indexing is from 1982, abstracting from 1990. (*Business Periodicals Index* without abstracts is available on CD-ROM at $1,495 per year.)

DIRECTORIES

Data Sources: The Comprehensive Guide to the Data Processing Industry: Hardware, Data Communications Products, Software, Company Profiles. Gale Cengage Learning. • Semiannual. $455.00 per year. Two volumes. Describes hardware and software for all computer operating sysems, including prices and technical details. Lists about 75,000 products from 14,000 suppliers. Industry-specific software applications are described.

Laptop: Mobile Solutions for Business and Life. Bedford Communications, Inc. • Monthly. $12.00 per year. Contains informative articles and critical reviews of laptop, notebook, subnotebook, and handheld computers. Includes portable peripheral equipment, such as printers and scanners. Directory information includes company profiles (major manufacturers), product comparison charts, street price guide, list of manufacturers, and list of dealers. Formerly *Laptop Buyer's Guide and Handbook.*

ENCYCLOPEDIAS AND DICTIONARIES

Acronyms of Computer Science and Communications: A Comprehensive Acronym Dictionary and Illustrated Encyclopedia. Enjob Kajan and Ejub Kajan. Springer Verlag. • 2002. $49.95. Explains more than 4,000 "broadly used" computer, telecommunications, and information technology acronyms. Includes illustrations and Web addresses, where applicable.

Encyclopedia of Information Systems. Hossein Bidgoli, editor. Elsevier. • 2002. $1,200.00. Four volumes. Contains a wide range of articles relating to computers, databases, communication, and information technology. The 200 topics include coverage of hardware, software, artificial intelligence, the Internet, networks, knowledge management, electronic commerce, search engines, and systems design.

HANDBOOKS AND MANUALS

Point, Click & Wow! A Quick Guide to Brilliant Laptop Presentations. Claudyne Wilder and David Fine. John Wiley and Sons, Inc. • 2002. $19.95. Second edition. Emphasis is on thorough preparation for effective presentations via a laptop computer. Provides general advice on color, graphics, animation, content, and relating to a specific audience or

customer. Includes checklists and CD-ROM.

INTERNET DATABASES

InfoTech Trends. Data Analysis Group. Phone: (925)462-1202 Fax: (925)462-1225 E-mail: support@infotechtrends.com • URL: http://www.infotechtrends.com • Web site provides both free and fee-based market research data on the information technology industry, including computers, peripherals, telecommunications, the Internet, software, CD-ROM/DVD, e-commerce, and workstations. Fees: Free for current (most recent year) data; more extensive information has various fee structures. Formerly *Computer Industry Forecasts.*

Wired News. Lycos, Inc. Phone: (415)276-8400 Fax: (415)276-8500 E-mail: newsfeedback@wired.com • URL: http://www.wired.com • Provides summaries and full-text of "Top Stories" relating to the Internet, computers, multimedia, telecommunications, and the electronic information industry in general. These news stories are placed in the broad categories of Politics, Business, Culture, and Technology. Affiliated with *Wired* magazine. Fees: Free.

ONLINE DATABASES

Internet and Personal Computing Abstracts. Information Today, Inc. • Contains abstracts covering a wide variety of personal and business microcomputer literature appearing in more than 100 journals and popular magazines. Time period is 1981 to date, with monthly updates. Formerly *Microcomputer Index.* Inquire as to online cost and availability.

PROMT: Predicasts Overview of Markets and Technology. Gale Cengage Learning. • Companies, products, applied technologies and markets. U.S. and international literature coverage, 1972 to date. Inquire as to online cost and availability. Provides abstracts from more than 1,600 publications. Weekly updates.

Trade & Industry Database. Gale Cengage Learning. • Provides indexing of business periodicals, January 1981 to date. Daily updates. (Full text articles from some periodicals are available online, 1983 to date. Inquire as to online cost and availability).

Wilson Business Abstracts Online. H. W. Wilson Co. • Indexes and abstracts 600 major business periodicals, plus the *Wall Street Journal* and the business section of the *New York Times.* Indexing is from 1982, abstracting from 1990, with the two newspapers included from 1993. Updated weekly. Inquire as to online cost and availability. (*Business Periodicals Index* without abstracts is also available online.).

PERIODICALS AND NEWSLETTERS

Handheld Computing: The Number One Guide to Handheld Devices. Mobile Media Group. • Nine times a year. $18.95 per year. Covers handheld devices for consumers, including PDAs, cell phones, digital cameras, MP3 players, tablet PCs, accessories, and software. Includes product reviews.

Laptop: Mobile Solutions for Business and Life. Bedford Communications. • Monthly. $18.00 per year. Consumer magazine containing articles and product reviews for notebook/laptop computers, handheld computers, tablet devices, cell phones, digital cameras, and other consumer electronic products.

Mobile PC. Future Network USA. • Monthly. $20.00 per year. Provides information and detailed product reviews for consumers. Covers notebook/laptop computers, personal digital assistants (PDAs), wireless network equipment, cell phones, digital cameras, and other electronic products.

Mobility: Handheld and Wireless Solutions for Today's Business. Mobile Media Group. • Quarterly.

$14.95 per year. Edited for business users of wireless handheld devices and notebook computers.

STATISTICS SOURCES

U. S. Industry and Trade Outlook. Available from National Technical Information Service. • Annual. $69.95. Produced by the International Trade Administration, U. S. Department of Commerce, in a "public-private" partnership with DRI/McGraw-Hill and Standard & Poor's. Provides basic data, outlook for the current year, and "Long-Term Prospects" (five-year projections) for a wide variety of products and services. Includes high technology industries. Formerly *U. S. Industrial Outlook.*

TRADE/PROFESSIONAL ASSOCIATIONS

Computing Technology Industry Association. 1815 S Meyers Rd., Ste. 300, Oakbrook Terrace, IL 60181-5228. Phone: (630)678-8300 Fax: (630)678-8384 E-mail: information@comptia.org • URL: http://www.comptia.org • Trade association of more than 19,000 companies and professional IT members in the rapidly converging computing and communications market. Has members in more than 89 countries and provides a unified voice for the industry in the areas of e-commerce standards, vendor-neutral certification, service metrics, public policy and workforce development. Serves as information clearinghouse and resource for the industry; sponsors educational programs.

Information Technology Industry Council. 1250 Eye St. NW, Ste. 200, Washington, DC 20005. Phone: (202)737-8888 Fax: (202)638-4922 E-mail: rdawson@itic.org • URL: http://www.itic.org • Represents manufacturers of information technology products. Serves as secretariat and technology for ANSI-accredited standards committee x3 information technology group. Conducts public policy programs; compiles industry statistics.

PORTABLE DATABASES

See: OPTICAL DISK STORAGE DEVICES

PORTFOLIO MANAGEMENT

See: INSTITUTIONAL INVESTMENTS

PORTLAND CEMENT

See: CEMENT INDUSTRY

PORTS

BIBLIOGRAPHIES

Waterfront Revitalization. Eric J. Fournier. Sage Publications, Inc. • 1994. $10.00. (CPL Bibliographies Series, No. 310).

DIRECTORIES

Fairplay Ports Directory. Fairplay Publications Ltd. • Covers: 6,500 ports and over 17,700 port authorities, port agents, towage companies, repairers, and bunkerers worldwide. Entries include: Port name, address, phone, fax, name of port authority or responsible agency, location; description of facilities for navigation and cargo handling, and port service firms, including agencies, repair firms, and towage, probable charges and fees, 3,500 port plans and color atlas.

Lloyd's List Ports of the World. Informa Group PLC. • 2002 $442.00. Provides detailed information on more than 2,700 ports worldwide.

Maritime Guide. Lloyd's Register--Fairplay Ltd. • Covers: international shipbuilders, marine engine builders, boilermakers, and shipbreakers; port and docking facilities; marine associations. Entries

include: For shipbuilders, marine engine builders, and boilermakers--Company name, address, phone, telex. For shipbreakers--Company name, address. For port and docking facilities--Name, location, name and title of contact, services.

U.S. Custom House Guide. Commonwealth Business Media Inc. • Publication includes: List of ports having customs facilities, customs officials, port authorities, chambers of commerce, embassies and consulates, foreign trade zones, and other organizations; related trade services. Entries include: For each principal port--Name of organization or agency, address, phone, fax, names and titles of key personnel; description and limitations of port facilities. For service firms--Company name, address, phone, fax. Principal content is U.S. tariff schedules and customs regulations, and a "How to Import" manual.

ENCYCLOPEDIAS AND DICTIONARIES

Exporters' Encyclopedia. Dun and Bradstreet Information Services. • 1995. $495.00. Lease basis.

PERIODICALS AND NEWSLETTERS

The Journal of Commerce. Commonwealth Business Media. • Weekly. $146.00 per year. Topics include transatlantic shipping, domestic shipping, customs brokers, freight forwarders, ports, air freight, containerization, and other aspects of transportation and shipping logistics. Formerly *Journal of Commerce.*

Lloyd's Port Management. Available from Informa Publishing Group Ltd. • Quarterly. $135.00 per year. Published in the UK by Lloyd's List (http://www.lloydslist.com). Covers port management issues for port operators and users.

RESEARCH CENTERS AND INSTITUTES

National Ports and Waterways Institute. University of New Orleans, 2300 Claredon Blvd., Suite 300, Arlington, VA 22201. Phone: (703)276-7101 Fax: (703)276-7102 E-mail: npwi@seas.gwu.edu • URL: http://www.members.tripod.com/npwi.

TRADE/PROFESSIONAL ASSOCIATIONS

American Association of Port Authorities. 1010 Duke St., Alexandria, VA 22314-3589. Phone: (703)684-5700 Fax: (703)684-6321 E-mail: info@aapa-ports.org • URL: http://www.aapa-ports.org.

International Association of Ports and Harbors. New Pier Takeshiba, N. Tower, 5th Fl., 1-11-1 Kaigan, Minato-ku, Tokyo 105-0022, Japan. Phone: 81 3 54032770 Fax: 81 3 54037651 E-mail: info@iaphworldports.org • URL: http://www.iaphworldports.org.

OTHER SOURCES

Lloyd's Maritime Atlas. Available from Informa UK Limited. • Biennial. $119.00. Contains more than 70 pages of world, ocean, regional, and port maps in color. Provides additional information for the planning of world shipping routes, including data on distances, port facilities, recurring weather hazards at sea, international load line zones, and sailing times.

POSITIONS

See: OCCUPATIONS

POST EXCHANGES

PERIODICALS AND NEWSLETTERS

Exchange and Commissary News. Executive Business Media, Inc. • Monthly. $95.00 per year.

Navy Supply Corps Newsletter. Available from U. S. Government Printing Office. • Bimonthly. $30.00 per year. Newsletter issued by U. S. Navy Supply Systems Command. Provides news of Navy supplies and stores activities.

POSTAL SERVICES

BIBLIOGRAPHIES

Postal Service. Available from U. S. Government Printing Office. • Annual. Free. Issued by the Superintendent of Documents. A list of government publications on mail services and the post office. (Subject Bibliography No. 169.).

DIRECTORIES

Better Buys for Business: The Independent Consumer Guide to Office Equipment. What to Buy for Business, Inc. • 10 times a year. $134.00 per year. Each issue is on a particular office product, with detailed evaluation of specific models: 1. Low-Volume Copier Guide, 2. Mid-Volume Copier Guide, 3. High-Volume Copier Guide, 4. Plain Paper Fax and Low-Volume Multifunctional Guide, 5. Mid/High-Volume Multifunctional Guide, 6. Laser Printer Guide, 7. Color Printer and Color Copier Guide, 8. Scan-to-File Guide, 9. Business Phone Systems Guide, 10. Postage Meter Guide, with a Short Guide to Shredders.

National Five Digit Zip Code and Post Office Directory. U.S. Postal Service. • Annual. Two volumes. Formerly *National Zip Code and Post Office Directory-.*

SRDS Direct Marketing List Source. SRDS. • Bimonthly. $561.00 per year. Provides detailed information and rates for business, farm, and consumer mailing lists (U. S., Canadian, and international). Includes current postal information and directories of list brokers, compilers, and managers. Formerly *Direct Mail List Source.*

HANDBOOKS AND MANUALS

Domestic Mail Manual. Available from U. S. Government Printing Office. • Looseleaf. $42.00 per year. Issued by U. S. Postal Service. Contains rates, regulations, classes of mail, special services, etc., for mail within the U. S.

International Mail Manual. Available from U. S. Government Printing Office. • Semiannual. $40.00 per year. Issued by U. S. Postal Service. Contains rates, regulations, classes of mail, special services, etc., for mail sent from the U. S. to foreign countries.

Mailing Services. Entrepreneur Media, Inc. • Looseleaf. $59.50. A practical guide to starting a mailing services business. Covers profit potential, start-up costs, market size evaluation, owner's time required, site selection, pricing, accounting, advertising, promotion, etc. (Start-Up Business Guide No. E1354.).

INTERNET DATABASES

United States Postal Service: Make Your Mark. U. S. Postal Service. Phone: (202)268-2000 E-mail: webmaster@email.usps.com • URL: http://www.usps.com • Web site contains detailed information on U. S. mail services and post offices, including ZIP codes, postage rates, stamps, addressing, Express Mail tracking, and consumer postal information in general. Links are provided to the State Department for passport procedures and to the IRS for tax forms.

PERIODICALS AND NEWSLETTERS

Postal Bulletin. Available from U. S. Government Printing Office. • Biweekly. $163.00 per year. Issued by the United States Postal Service. Contains orders, instructions, and information relating to U. S. mail service.

Postal World. United Communications Group. • Description: Disseminates information to help readers run a more efficient mail operation. "Discusses how to trim postage costs, speed delivery, improve mailroom productivity, and plan for rate increases." Recurring features include an annual salary survey and periodic special reports.

STATISTICS SOURCES

Annual Report of Postmaster General. U.S. Postal Service. • Annual.

U.S. Postal Service Revenue and Cost Analysis Report. U.S. Postal Service. • Annual.

TRADE/PROFESSIONAL ASSOCIATIONS

Association for Postal Commerce. 1901 N Fort Myer Dr., Ste. 401, Arlington, VA 22209-1609. Phone: (703)524-0096 Fax: (703)524-1871 E-mail: info@postcom.org • URL: http://www.postcom.org • Formerly Advertising Mail Marketing Association.

Parcel Shippers Association. 1420 King St., Ste. 620, Alexandria, VA 22314. Phone: (571)257-7617 Fax: (571)257-7613 E-mail: psa@parcelshippers. org • URL: http://www.parcelshippers.org • Wholesalers, retailers, mail order houses, and other firms using parcel post service for distribution of products. Promotes the efficient and economical distribution of small package shipments.

Periodical Publications Association. PO Box 10669, PO Box 10669, Rockville, MD 20849-0669. Phone: (301)260-0929 Fax: (301)260-1647 E-mail: periodicalpubs@yahoo.com • Business publications, magazines, and newspapers qualifying for periodical postage rates. Protects periodical mail rates by appropriate activity in Washington, DC. Endeavors to find solutions to postal problems of concern to members. Follows postal issues in Congress and regulation changes at United States Postal Service headquarters.

OTHER SOURCES

Bullinger's Postal and Shippers Guide for the United States and Canada. Alber Leland Publishing. • Annual. $375.00. Approximately 260,000 communities in the United States and Canada.

Zip Code Mapbook of Metropolitan Areas. ESRI Business Information Solutions. • 1992. $195.00. Second edition. Contains Zip Code two-color maps of 326 metropolitan areas. Includes summary statistical profiles of each area: population characteristics, employment, housing, and income.

POSTERS

See also: ART IN INDUSTRY; COMMERCIAL ART; SIGNS AND SIGN BOARDS

RESEARCH CENTERS AND INSTITUTES

Design Research Unit. Massachusetts College of Art, 621 Huntington Ave., Boston, MA 02115. Phone: (617)879-7733 Fax: (617)566-4034 E-mail: rstreit@massart.edu • URL: http://www.babel. massart.edu/dru • Conducts research related to the design of printed matter, including annual reports, letterheads, posters, and brochures.

POTASH INDUSTRY

See also: FERTILIZER INDUSTRY

DIRECTORIES

Major Chemical and Petrochemical Companies of the World. Available from Gale Cengage Learning. • 2002. $880.00. Sixth edition. Published by Graham & Whiteside. Contains profiles of more than 7,000 important chemical and petrochemical companies in various countries. Subject areas include general chemicals, specialty chemicals, agricultural chemicals, petrochemicals, industrial gases, and fertilizers.

HANDBOOKS AND MANUALS

Agrochemicals: Composition, Production, Toxicology, Applications. Franz Muller, editor. John Wiley and Sons, Inc. • 2000. $375.00. Coverage includes fertilizers, herbicides, fungicides, insecticides, and biological control agents. Content is both theoretical and practical.

PRICE SOURCES

Green Markets. Pike and Fischer, Inc. • Weekly. $915.00 per year. Newsletter including prices for

potash and other agricultural chemicals.

STATISTICS SOURCES

Mineral Commodity Summaries. Available from U. S. Government Printing Office. • Annual. $26.00. Published by the U. S. Geological Survey, Department of the Interior (http://www.usgs.gov). Contains detailed, five-year data for about 90 nonfuel minerals. Covers a wide range of statistics, including production, imports, exports, consumption, reserves, prices, tariff information, and industry employment. (Two pages are devoted to each mineral.).

TRADE/PROFESSIONAL ASSOCIATIONS

Potash and Phosphate Institute. 655 Engineering Dr., No. 110, Norcross, GA 30092-2837. Phone: (770)447-0335 Fax: (770)448-0439 E-mail: ppi@ ppi-ppic.org • URL: http://www.ppi-ppic.org • Formerly Potash Institute.

POTATO CHIP INDUSTRY

See: POTATO INDUSTRY; SNACK FOOD INDUSTRY

POTATO INDUSTRY

See also: SWEET POTATO INDUSTRY; VEGETABLE INDUSTRY

ABSTRACTS AND INDEXES

Field Crop Abstracts: Monthly Abstract Journal on World Annual Cereal, Legume, Root, Oilseed and Fibre Crops. Available from CABI Publishing North America. • Monthly. Institutions, $1,775.00 per year. Online edition available, $1,820.00 per year. Published in England by CABI Publishing, formerly Commonwealth Agricultural Bureaux. Provides worldwide coverage of the literature.

Potato Abstracts. Available from CABI Publishing, North America. • Bimonthly. Institutions, $610.00 per year. Online edition available, $640.00 per year. Includes single site internet access. Published in England by CABI Publishing. Provides worldwide coverage of the literature.

ALMANACS AND YEARBOOKS

Agricultural and Mineral Commodities Year Book. Available from Taylor & Francis Group. • Annual. $225.00. Published by Europa Publications. Contains descriptive product profiles, price data, export-import data, and production statistics for major commodities of the world. Includes commodity histories, uses, markets, demand trends, and information about trade agreements and key commodity organizations.

CD-ROM DATABASES

Food Science and Technology Abstracts [CD-ROM]. Available from SilverPlatter Information, Inc. • Quarterly. Produced by International Food Information Service (home page is http://www.ifis. org). Provides worldwide coverage on CD-ROM of the literature of food technology and production. Various types of publications are indexed, with abstracts, including about 1,800 periodicals. Time period is 1969 to date.

DIRECTORIES

Major Food and Drink Companies of the World. Available from Gale Cengage Learning. • Annual. $880.00. Two volumes. Published by Graham & Whiteside. Contains profiles and trade names for more than 9,800 important food and beverage companies in various countries. In addition to foods, includes both alcoholic and nonalcoholic drink products.

Thomas Food and Beverage Market Place. Grey House Publishing. • 2004. $495.00. Three volumes.

Contains more than 40,000 entries covering food companies, beverages, food equipment, warehouse companies, food brokers, wholesalers, importers, and exporters. Formerly *Thomas Food Industry Register.*

HANDBOOKS AND MANUALS

Knott's Handbook for Vegetable Growers. Donald N. Maynard and George J. Hochmuth. John Wiley and Sons, Inc. • 1997. $99.00. Fourth edition. Written for commercial vegetable growers, truck farmers, horticulturists, and other professionals. Covers such topics as spacing of plants, disease control, insect pests, seeds, weeds, water management, and irrigation.

INTERNET DATABASES

USDA. United States Department of Agriculture. Phone: (202)720-2791 E-mail: agsec@usda.gov • URL: http://www.usda.gov • The USDA home page has six sections: News and Information; What's New; About USDA; Agencies; Opportunities; Search and Help. Keyword searching is offered from the USDA home page and from various individual agency home pages. Agencies are the Economic Research Service, Agricultural Marketing Service, National Agricultural Statistics Service, National Agricultural Library, and about 12 others. Updating varies. Fees: Free.

ONLINE DATABASES

CAB Abstracts. CAB Publishing North America. • Contains 46 specialized abstract collections covering over 10,000 journals and monographs in the areas of agriculture, horticulture, forest products, farm products, nutrition, dairy science, poultry, grains, animal health, entomology, etc. Time period is 1972 to date, with monthly updates. Inquire as to online cost and availability. *CAB Abstracts on CD-ROM* also available, with annual updating.

Food Science and Technology Abstracts [online]. IFIS North American Desk. • Produced by International Food Information Service. Provides about 500,000 online citations, with abstracts, to the international literature of food science, technology, commodities, engineering, and processing. Approximately 2,000 periodicals are covered. Time period is 1969 to date, with monthly updates. Inquire as to online cost and availability.

PERIODICALS AND NEWSLETTERS

American Journal of Potato Research. Potato Association of America. • Bimonthly. Individuals, $75.00 per year; students, $15.00 per year. Information relating to production, marketing, processing, storage, disease control, insect control and new variety releases. Formerly *American Potato Journal.*

Potato Grower of Idaho. Harris Publishing, Inc. • Monthly. $15.95 per year.

STATISTICS SOURCES

Agricultural Statistics. Available from U. S. Government Printing Office. • Annual. $38.00. Produced by the National Agricultural Statistics Service, U. S. Department of Agriculture. Provides a wide variety of statistical data relating to agricultural production, supplies, consumption, prices/price-supports, foreign trade, costs, and returns, as well as farm labor, loans, income, and population. In many cases, historical data is shown annually for 10 years. In addition to farm data, includes detailed fishery statistics.

FAO Production Yearbook. Available from Bernan Associates. • Annual. $45.00. Published by the Food and Agriculture Organization (http://www.fao.org). Contains worldwide data on agriculture, land use, farm crops, livestock, and agricultural prices.

FAO Trade Yearbook. Available from Bernan Associates. • Annual. $45.00. Published by the Food and Agriculture Organization (http://www.fao.org).

Provides extensive worldwide data on exports and imports of agricultural commodities, fertilizers, tractors, and pesticides. Includes more than 130 tables of detailed statistics.

Vegetables and Specialties Situation and Outlook. Available from U. S. Government Printing Office. • Three times a year. Issued by the Economic Research Service of the U. S. Department of Agriculture. Provides current statistical information on supply, demand, and prices.

World Food Data and Statistics. Euromonitor International. • 2004. $650.00. Provides five-year data for a wide variety of food products in 52 countries. Includes market size, consumer expenditures, price indicators, and retail distribution data for many kinds of meat, fish, fruits, vegetables, dairy products, baked goods, condiments, canned food, and frozen food.

TRADE/PROFESSIONAL ASSOCIATIONS

National Potato Council. 1300 L St. NW, No. 910, Washington, DC 20005-4107. Phone: (202)682-9456 Fax: (202)682-0333 E-mail: spudinfo@nationalpotatocouncil.org • URL: http://www.nationalpotatocouncil.org • Commercial potato growers. Takes action on national potato legislative, regulatory, and environmental issues.

Potato Association of America. University of Maine, 575 Coburn Hall, Rm. 6, Orono, ME 04469-5715. Phone: (207)581-3042 Fax: (207)581-3015 E-mail: umpotato@mail.maine.edu • URL: http://www.ume.maine.edu/paa.

Snack Food Association. 1600 Wilson Blvd., Ste. 650, Arlington, VA 22209. Phone: 800-628-1334 or (703)836-4500 Fax: (703)836-8262 E-mail: sfa@sfa.org • URL: http://www.sfa.org • Manufacturers of potato chips, pretzels, corn chips, tortilla chips, popcorn, cheese snacks, pork rinds, cookies, crackers, nuts, meat snacks, fruit snacks, and grain-based snacks; associate members are suppliers and distributors of fats and oils, packaging supplies, machinery, seasonings, and potato and corn growers.

OTHER SOURCES

The Market for Salted Snacks. MarketResearch.com. • 2002. $3,000.00. Market research report. Covers potato chips, corn chips, popcorn, nuts, pretzels, and other salted snacks. Market projections are provided to the year 2004.

POTATOES, SWEET

See: SWEET POTATO INDUSTRY

POTTERY INDUSTRY

See also: CERAMICS INDUSTRY; GLASSWARE INDUSTRY

ENCYCLOPEDIAS AND DICTIONARIES

Potter's Dictionary of Materials and Techniques. Frank Hamer and Janet Hamer. Gordon and Breach Publishing Group. • 1997. $85.00. Fourth edition.

HANDBOOKS AND MANUALS

Ceramics: A Potter's Handbook. Glenn C. Nelson. Wadsworth Publishing Co. • 2001. $63.95. Sixth edition.

PERIODICALS AND NEWSLETTERS

Giftware News: The International Magazine for Gifts, China and Glass, Stationery and Home Accessories. Talcott Communications Corp. • Monthly. $36.00 per year. Includes annual *Directory.*

TRADE/PROFESSIONAL ASSOCIATIONS

Associated Glass and Pottery Manufacturers. 912 Country Club Dr., Greensburg, PA 15601. Phone:

(724)837-9451 Fax: (724)523-2022 E-mail: robrupp@helicon.net.

POULTRY INDUSTRY

See also: TURKEY INDUSTRY

ABSTRACTS AND INDEXES

Food Science and Technology Abstracts. International Food Information Service Publishing. • Monthly. $1,780.00 per year. Provides worldwide coverage of the literature of food technology and food production.

Foods Adlibra: Key to the World's Food Literature. General Mills, Inc. Foods Adlibra Publications. • Semimonthly. $240.00 per year. Provides journal citations and abstracts to the literature of food technology and packaging.

Poultry Abstracts. Available from CABI Publishing, North America. • Monthly. Institutions, $760.00 per year. Online edition available. Single site internet access, $735.00 per year. Published in England by CABI Publishing. Provides worldwide coverage of the literature.

ALMANACS AND YEARBOOKS

Agricultural and Mineral Commodities Year Book. Available from Taylor & Francis Group. • Annual. $225.00. Published by Europa Publications. Contains descriptive product profiles, price data, export-import data, and production statistics for major commodities of the world. Includes commodity histories, uses, markets, demand trends, and information about trade agreements and key commodity organizations.

CD-ROM DATABASES

Food Science and Technology Abstracts [CD-ROM]. Available from SilverPlatter Information, Inc. • Quarterly. Produced by International Food Information Service (home page is http://www.ifis.org). Provides worldwide coverage on CD-ROM of the literature of food technology and production. Various types of publications are indexed, with abstracts, including about 1,800 periodicals. Time period is 1969 to date.

OECD Statistical Compendium. Organization for Economic Cooperation and Development. • Semiannual. $1,905.00 per year for 1 to 10 users. CD-ROM contains more than 730,000 monthly, quarterly, and annual time series for OECD countries, 1960 to date. Includes fully searchable data on agriculture, food, economic indicators, national accounts, employment, energy, finance, industry, technology, and foreign trade. Results can be displayed in various forms.

DIRECTORIES

Major Food and Drink Companies of the World. Available from Gale Cengage Learning. • Annual. $880.00. Two volumes. Published by Graham & Whiteside. Contains profiles and trade names for more than 9,800 important food and beverage companies in various countries. In addition to foods, includes both alcoholic and nonalcoholic drink products.

Meat and Poultry Inspection Directory. U.S. Department of Agriculture. Available from U.S. Government Printing Office. • Semiannual. $49.00 per year.

Thomas Food and Beverage Market Place. Grey House Publishing. • 2004. $495.00. Three volumes. Contains more than 40,000 entries covering food companies, beverages, food equipment, warehouse companies, food brokers, wholesalers, importers, and exporters. Formerly *Thomas Food Industry Register.*

Who's Who in the Egg and Poultry Industries. Watt Publishing Co. • Annual. $100.00. Producers, processors, and distributors of poultry meat and eggs

in the United States; manufacturers of supplies and equipment for the poultry industry; breeders and hatcheries; refrigerated public warehouses;. food chain buyers of poultry meat and eggs; related government agencies; poultry associations.

FINANCIAL RATIOS

Annual Statement Studies. The Risk Management Association. • Annual. Median and quartile financial ratios are given for over 400 kinds of manufacturing, wholesale, retail, construction, and consumer finance establishments. Data is sorted by both asset size and sales volume. Includes a clearly written "Definition of Ratios" and an alphabetical industry index.

Annual Statement Studies: Industry Default Probabilities and Cash Flow Measures. The Risk Management Association. • Annual. $145.00. Serves as a companion volume to the original *Annual Statement Studies.* Gives probability of default estimates on a percentage scale for more than 450 industries. Includes changes in position year-by-year for eight financial statement line items and provides percentage measures of cash flow.

HANDBOOKS AND MANUALS

Commercial Chicken Meat and Egg Production. Donald D. Bell and others. Kluwer Academic Publishers. • 2001.$399.95. 5th edition.

Meat and Poultry Inspection Regulations. U.S. Department of Agriculture. Available from U.S. Government Printing Office. • Looseleaf. Regulations for slaughter and processing of livestock and poultry as well as for certain voluntary services and humane slaughter.

Poultry Science. Colin G. Scanes and others. Prentice Hall PTR. • 2003. $100.00. Fourth edition.

INTERNET DATABASES

Business 2.0 Web Guide to the Best Business Links. Business 2.0 Media Inc. Phone: (415)293-4800 E-mail: support@business2.com • URL: http://www.business2.com/webguide • Web site presents an extensive, searchable directory of links to "the best, most informative, and authoritative web pages." Twenty main categories cover business, finance, career, company information, people, and technology topics, with thousands of subtopics, all linking to Web sites recommended by experienced business researchers. Fees: Free.

Fedstats. Federal Interagency Council on Statistical Policy. Phone: (202)395-7254 • URL: http://www.fedstats.gov • Web site features an efficient search facility for full-text statistics produced by more than 100 federal agencies, including the Census Bureau, the Bureau of Economic Analysis, and the Bureau of Labor Statistics. Boolean searches can be made within one agency or for all agencies combined. Links are offered to international statistical bureaus, including the UN, IMF, OECD, UNESCO, Eurostat, and 20 individual countries. Fees: Free.

FreeLunch.com. Economy.com, Inc. Phone: (610)696-8700 Fax: (610)696-1678 • URL: http://www.freelunch.com • Web site provides free access to more than 1.5 million economic and financial data series, covering industry, demographics, labor markets, prices, retail sales, government spending, trade, interest rates, housing starts, the stock market, and many other topics. Data is available for various time periods in either chart or table form. Searching is offered. Fees: Free, but registration required. Economy.com, Inc. also offers fee-based economic analysis at *The Dismal Scientist* site (http://www.dismal.com).

USDA. United States Department of Agriculture. Phone: (202)720-2791 E-mail: agsec@usda.gov • URL: http://www.usda.gov • The USDA home page has six sections: News and Information; What's New; About USDA; Agencies; Opportunities; Search and Help. Keyword searching is offered from the USDA home page and from various individual agency home pages. Agencies are the Economic Research Service, Agricultural Marketing Service, National Agricultural Statistics Service, National Agricultural Library, and about 12 others. Updating varies. Fees: Free.

ONLINE DATABASES

CAB Abstracts. CAB Publishing North America. • Contains 46 specialized abstract collections covering over 10,000 journals and monographs in the areas of agriculture, horticulture, forest products, farm products, nutrition, dairy science, poultry, grains, animal health, entomology, etc. Time period is 1972 to date, with monthly updates. Inquire as to online cost and availability. *CAB Abstracts on CD-ROM* also available, with annual updating.

Food Science and Technology Abstracts [online]. IFIS North American Desk. • Produced by International Food Information Service. Provides about 500,000 online citations, with abstracts, to the international literature of food science, technology, commodities, engineering, and processing. Approximately 2,000 periodicals are covered. Time period is 1969 to date, with monthly updates. Inquire as to online cost and availability.

FOODS ADLIBRA. General Mills, Inc. • Contains online citations, with abstracts, to the technical and business literature of food processing and packaging. New products and new ingredients are featured. Covers about 250 trade journals and 500 research journals from 1974 to date, with monthly updates. Inquire as to online cost and availability.

PERIODICALS AND NEWSLETTERS

Egg Industry: Covering Egg Production, Processing and Marketing. Watt Publishing Co. • Monthly. Free to qualified personnel; others, $36.00 per year. Newsletter. Formerly *Poultry Tribune.*

Poultry and Egg Marketing: The Bi-Monthly News Magazine of the Poultry Marketing Industry. Poultry and Egg News. • Bimonthly. Free to qualified personnel; others, $6.00 per year. Processing and marketing of eggs and poultry products.

Poultry Science. Poultry Science Association, Inc. • Monthly. Members, $95.00 per year; institutions, $400.00 per year. Includes print and online editions.

Poultry Times. Poultry and Egg News. • Biweekly. $9.00 per year. Directed to grow-out operations for the egg and poultry business.

Poultry USA. Watt Publishing Co. • Bionthly. $28.00 per year. Incorporate *Broiler Industry.*

STATISTICS SOURCES

Agricultural Statistics. Available from U. S. Government Printing Office. • Annual. $38.00. Produced by the National Agricultural Statistics Service, U. S. Department of Agriculture. Provides a wide variety of statistical data relating to agricultural production, supplies, consumption, prices/price-supports, foreign trade, costs, and returns, as well as farm labor, loans, income, and population. In many cases, historical data is shown annually for 10 years. In addition to farm data, includes detailed fishery statistics.

Annual Survey of Manufactures. Available from U. S. Government Printing Office. • Annual. Prices vary. Issued by the U. S. Census Bureau as an interim update to the *Census of Manufactures.* Includes data on number of manufacturing establishments in various industries, employment, labor costs, value of shipments, capital expenditures, inventories, energy costs, and assets. (See also Census Bureau home page, http://www.census. gov/.).

Business Statistics of the United States. Linz Audain and Cornelia J. Strawser. Bernan Associates. • Annual. $147.00. Based on *Business Statistics,* formerly issue by the Bureau of Economic Analysis, U. S. Department of Commerce. Provides basic data

for a wide variety of U. S. industries, services, and economic indicators. Most statistics are shown annually for 30 years and monthly for the most recent four years.

FAO Production Yearbook. Available from Bernan Associates. • Annual. $45.00. Published by the Food and Agriculture Organization (http://www.fao.org). Contains worldwide data on agriculture, land use, farm crops, livestock, and agricultural prices.

FAO Trade Yearbook. Available from Bernan Associates. • Annual. $45.00. Published by the Food and Agriculture Organization (http://www.fao.org). Provides extensive worldwide data on exports and imports of agricultural commodities, fertilizers, tractors, and pesticides. Includes more than 130 tables of detailed statistics.

Survey of Current Business. Available from U. S. Government Printing Office. • Monthly. $63.00 per year. Issued by Bureau of Economic Analysis, U. S. Department of Commerce. Presents a wide variety of business and economic data.

World Food Data and Statistics. Euromonitor International. • 2004. $650.00. Provides five-year data for a wide variety of food products in 52 countries. Includes market size, consumer expenditures, price indicators, and retail distribution data for many kinds of meat, fish, fruits, vegetables, dairy products, baked goods, condiments, canned food, and frozen food.

TRADE/PROFESSIONAL ASSOCIATIONS

American Egg Board. 1460 Renaissance Dr., Ste. 301, Park Ridge, IL 60068. Phone: (847)296-7043 Fax: (847)296-7007 E-mail: aeb@aeb.org • URL: http://www.aeb.org • Board of American egg producers appointed by the Secretary of Agriculture. Offers advertising, educational, research, and promotional programs designed to increase consumption of eggs and egg products. Conducts consumer educators and food-service seminars, and food safety education programs.

American Poultry Association. 947 Grand Ave., Fillmore, CA 93015. Phone: (805)524-4046 Fax: (508)473-8769 E-mail: danderson@keygroupinc. com • URL: http://www.amerpoultryassn.com • Poultry industry. Strives to protect and promote the standard-bred poultry industry in all of its phases.

National Chicken Council. 1015 15th St. NW, Ste. 930, Washington, DC 20005-2622. Phone: (202)296-2622 Fax: (202)293-4005 E-mail: ncc@ chickenusa.org • URL: http://www. nationalchickencouncil.com • Membership includes producers/processors of broiler chickens; distributors and allied industry. Sponsors National Chicken Cooking Contest and National Chicken Month. Compiles statistics; conducts generic promotion program for chicken; provides government relations services for member companies and the broiler industry.

Poultry Science Association. 1111 N Dunlap Ave., Savoy, IL 61874. Phone: (217)356-5285 Fax: (217)398-4119 E-mail: jcarey@poultry.tamu.edu • URL: http://www.poultryscience.org • Members are from academia, industry, and government, with many involved in the research, teaching, or extension of poultry science and related fields.

POVERTY

See: PUBLIC WELFARE

POWDER METALLURGY INDUSTRY

ABSTRACTS AND INDEXES

Metal Powder Report. Elsevier. • 11 times a year. Institutions, $438.00 per year. Technical articles,

company reports, up-to-date news and book reviews cover powder metallurgy worldwide.

Metalforming Digest. CSA. • Monthly. Price on application. Provides abstracts of the international literature of metal forming, including powder metallurgy, stamping, extrusion, forging, etc.

ONLINE DATABASES

METADEX. Cambridge Scientific Abstracts. • Covers the worldwide literature of metals, metallurgy, and materials science, 1966 to date. Includes detailed alloys indexing from 1974. Biweekly updating. Inquire as to online cost and availability. (Formerly produced by ASM International.).

PERIODICALS AND NEWSLETTERS

International Journal of Powder Metallurgy. American Powder Metallurgy Institute. APMI International. • Eight times a year. Individuals, $85.00 per year; institutions, $180.00 per year.

Powder Metallurgy. Institute of Materials, Minerals and Mining. • Quarterly. Institutions, $557.00 per Year.

STATISTICS SOURCES

Metal Statistics. Reed Business Information. • Annual. $250.00. Provides statistical data on a wide variety of metals, metal products, ores, alloys, and scrap metal. Includes data on prices, production, consumption, shipments, imports, and exports.

TRADE/PROFESSIONAL ASSOCIATIONS

Metal Powder Industries Federation. 105 College Rd. E, Princeton, NJ 08540-6692. Phone: (609)452-7700 Fax: (609)987-8523 E-mail: info@mpif.org • URL: http://www.mpif.org • Manufacturers of metal powders, powder metallurgy processing equipment and tools, powder metallurgy products, and refractory and reactive metals. Member associations are: Metal Injection Molding Association; Metal Powder Producers Association; Advanced Particulate Materials Association; Powder Metallurgy Equipment Association; Powder Metallurgy Parts Association; Refractory Metals Association. Promotes the science and industry of powder metallurgy and metal powder application through: sponsorship of technical meetings, seminars, and exhibits; establishment of standards; compilation of statistics; public relations; publications. Maintains speakers' bureau and placement service; conducts research.

POWER COMPANIES

See: ELECTRIC UTILITIES

POWER (MECHANICAL)

See also: FUEL; MECHANICAL ENGINEERING

DIRECTORIES

Design News OEM Directory. Reed Business Information. • Covers: about 5,000 manufacturers and suppliers of power transmission products, fluid power products, and electrical/electronic components to the OEM (original equipment manufacturer) market in SIC groups 34-39. Entries include: Company name, address, phone, fax, url, e-mail.

HANDBOOKS AND MANUALS

Mechanical Engineer's Reference Book. E. H. Smith, editor. Society of Automotive Engineers. • 1994. $135.00. 12th edition. Covers mechanical engineering principles, computer integrated engineering systems, design standards, materials, power transmission, and many other engineering topics. (Authored Series).

Motion Systems Handbook. Penton Media Inc. • Annual. $30.00.

PERIODICALS AND NEWSLETTERS

IEEE Industry Applications Magazine. Institute of Electrical and Electronics Engineers. • Bimonthly.

$190.00 per year. Covers new industrial applications of power conversion, drives, lighting, and control. Emphasis is on the petroleum, chemical, rubber, plastics, textile, and mining industries.

Journal of Turbomachinery. ASME International. • Quarterly. Members, $50.00 per year; includes print and online editions. Non-members, $250.00 per year; includes print and online editions.

Power Engineering International. PennWell Corp., Industrial Div. • Monthly. $170.00 per year.

TRADE/PROFESSIONAL ASSOCIATIONS

Mechanical Power Transmission Association. 6724 Lone Oak Blvd., Naples, FL 34109. Phone: (239)514-3441 Fax: (239)514-3470 E-mail: bob@mpta.org • URL: http://www.mpta.org • Manufacturers of multiple V-belt drive sheaves and elastomeric couplings for mechanical power transmission machinery.

National Association of Power Engineers. One Springfield St., Chicopee, MA 01013. Phone: (413)592-6273 Fax: (413)592-1998 E-mail: napenatl@aol.com • URL: http://www.powerengineers.com.

Power-Motion Technology Representatives Association. 1 Spectrum Pointe, Ste. 150, Lake Forest, CA 92630. Phone: 888-817-7872 or (949)859-2885 Fax: (949)855-2973 E-mail: info@ptra.org • URL: http://www.ptra.org • Manufacturers and independent manufacturers representatives in the power transmission industry. Seeks to provide a channel of communication between manufacturers' independent representatives and their principals, and other manufacturers within the industry by allowing interchange of sound business management ideas and by offering consultation on solving operational problems. Provides information and referral; compiles surveys. Offers training programs that include panels, table talk discussions, and seminars on special topics.

Power Transmission Distributors Association. 230 W Monroe, Ste. 1410, Chicago, IL 60606-4703. Phone: (312)516-2100 Fax: (312)516-2101 E-mail: ptda@ptda.org • URL: http://www.ptda.org • Distributors and manufacturers of power transmission/motion and position control equipment. Maintains business management and continuing education resources; conducts educational programs; compiles statistics; sponsors industry summit; conducts research; cosponsors industry tradeshows.

POWER PLANTS, ELECTRIC

See: ELECTRIC POWER PLANTS

POWER TOOL INDUSTRY

See also: TOOL INDUSTRY

GENERAL WORKS

Portable Power Tools. Time-Life, Inc. • 1992. $14.95. Contains popular descriptions of power tools for woodworking. (Art of Woodworking Series).

ABSTRACTS AND INDEXES

Engineering Index Monthly: Abstracting and Indexing Services Covering Sources of the World's Engineering Literature. Engineering Information Inc. • Monthly. Institutions, $5,279.00 per year. Provides indexing and abstracting of the world's engineering and technical literature.

Mechanical Engineering Abstracts. CSA. • Bimonthly. $1,620.00 per year. Includes print and online editions. Formerly *ISMEC - Mechanical Engineering Abstracts.*

NTIS Alerts: Manufacturing Technology. National Technical Information Service. • Semimonthly.

$265.00 per year. Provides descriptions of government-sponsored research reports and software, with ordering information. Covers computer-aided design and manufacturing (CAD/CAM), engineering materials, quality control, machine tools, robots, lasers, productivity, and related subjects. Formerly *Abstract Newsletter.*

DIRECTORIES

Assembly Buyers Guide. Reed Business Information. • Annual. $68.00. Lists manufacturers and suppliers of equipment relating to assembly automation, fasteners, adhesives, robotics, and power tools.

ProSales Buyer's Guide. Hanley-Wood, LLC. • Annual. Price on application. A directory of equipment for professional builders.

Tools of the Trade Annual Buyers Guide. Hanley-Wood, LLC. • Annual. Price on application. A directory of tools for the construction industry.

ONLINE DATABASES

PROMT: Predicasts Overview of Markets and Technology. Gale Cengage Learning. • Companies, products, applied technologies and markets. U.S. and international literature coverage, 1972 to date. Inquire as to online cost and availability. Provides abstracts from more than 1,600 publications. Weekly updates.

PERIODICALS AND NEWSLETTERS

Assembly: Design and Manufacturing Technology for Better Assembled Products. Business News Publishing Co. • Monthly. $68.00 per year. Covers assembly, fastening, and joining systems. Includes information on automation and robotics.

Building Material Dealer. National Lumber and Building Material Dealers Association. • Monthly. $48.00 per year. Includes special feature issues on hand and power tools, lumber, roofing, kitchens, flooring, windows and doors, and insulation. Formerly *Builder Material Retailer.*

Building Products. Hanley-Wood, LLC. • Quarterly. $36.00 per year. Covers building products and materials for the construction industry, including new products.

Hardware Age. Reed Business Information. • Monthly. $75.00 per year.

Journal of Light Construction. Hanley-Wood, LLC. • Monthly. $35.95 per year. Provides jobsite tips, techniques, and product advice for builders and contractors.

National Home Center News: News and Analysis for the Home Improvement, Building Material Industry. Lebhar-Friedman, Inc. • 22 times a year. $99.00 per year. Includes special feature issues on hardware and tools, building materials, millwork, electrical supplies, lighting, and kitchens.

ProSales: For Dealers and Distributors Serving the Professional Contractor. Hanley-Wood LLC. • Monthly. $36.00 per year. Includes special feature issues on selling, credit, financing, and the marketing of power tools.

Tools of the Trade. Hanley-Wood, LLC. • Five times a year. $19.80 per year. Provides advice and information on tools for the construction industry. Includes product tests and evaluations.

STATISTICS SOURCES

Annual Survey of Manufactures. Available from U.S. Government Printing Office. • Annual. Prices vary. Issued by the U.S. Census Bureau as an interim update to the *Census of Manufactures.* Includes data on number of manufacturing establishments in various industries, employment, labor costs, value of shipments, capital expenditures, inventories, energy costs, and assets. (See also Census Bureau home page, http://www.census.gov/.).

U. S. Industry and Trade Outlook. Available from

National Technical Information Service. • Annual. $69.95. Produced by the International Trade Administration, U. S. Department of Commerce, in a "public-private" partnership with DRI/McGraw-Hill and Standard & Poor's. Provides basic data, outlook for the current year, and "Long-Term Prospects" (five-year projections) for a wide variety of products and services. Includes high technology industries. Formerly *U. S. Industrial Outlook.*

TRADE/PROFESSIONAL ASSOCIATIONS

Portable Power Equipment Manufacturers Association. 4330 East-West Hwy., Ste. 310, Bethesda, MD 20814. Phone: (301)652-0774 Fax: (301)654-6138 E-mail: popref@prb.org • URL: http://www.ppema.org • Manufacturers of gasoline and electric powered chain saws, monofilament trimmers, brush cutters, hand-held blowers, backpack blowers, hedge trimmers, cut-off saws, and portable gasoline-powered generators. Encourages research and development of standards.

Power Tool Institute. 1300 Sumner Ave., 1300 Sumner Ave., Cleveland, OH 44115-2851. Phone: (216)241-7333 Fax: (216)241-0105 E-mail: pti@powertoolinstitute.com • URL: http://www.powertoolinstitute.com • Represents manufacturers of portable and stationary tools, both electric and battery operated. Distributes publications and videos on power tool safety. Offers educational programs.

OTHER SOURCES

Outdoor Appliances and Power Tools. Available from MarketResearch.com. • 2002. $3,950.00. Published by Global Industry Analysts. Provides worldwide market research data, including profiles of major companies in the field.

POWER TRANSMISSION (MECHANICAL)

See: POWER (MECHANICAL)

PRACTICE MANAGEMENT

See: MEDICAL ECONOMICS (PRACTICE MANAGEMENT)

PRECIOUS METALS

See: GOLD; METAL INDUSTRY; PLATINUM INDUSTRY; SILVER INDUSTRY

PRECIOUS STONES

See: GEMS AND GEMSTONES

PREFABRICATED HOUSE INDUSTRY

See also: BUILDING INDUSTRY; MOBILE HOME INDUSTRY

GENERAL WORKS

Manufactured Homes; Making Sense of a Housing Opportunity. Thomas E. Nutt-Powell. Greenwood Publishing Group, Inc. • 1982. $69.95.

DIRECTORIES

Automated Builder Annual Buyers' Guide. • Annual. $12.00. Over 250 manufacturers and suppliers to the manufactured and pre-fabricated housing industry.

PERIODICALS AND NEWSLETTERS

Automated Builder: The No. 1 International Housing Technology Transfer Magazine for Manufacturing and Marketing. • Monthly. $50.00 per year. Annual *Buyers' Guide* available.

Journal of Light Construction. Hanley-Wood, LLC. • Monthly. $35.95 per year. Provides jobsite tips, techniques, and product advice for builders and contractors.

STATISTICS SOURCES

U. S. Industry and Trade Outlook. Available from National Technical Information Service. • Annual. $69.95. Produced by the International Trade Administration, U. S. Department of Commerce, in a "public-private" partnership with DRI/McGraw-Hill and Standard & Poor's. Provides basic data, outlook for the current year, and "Long-Term Prospects" (five-year projections) for a wide variety of products and services. Includes high technology industries. Formerly *U. S. Industrial Outlook.*

TRADE/PROFESSIONAL ASSOCIATIONS

Building Systems Councils of NAHB. 1201 15th St., N.W., Washington, DC 20005. Phone: 800-368-5242 or (202)822-0576 Fax: (202)861-2141 E-mail: bsc@nahb.com • URL: http://www.buildingsystems.org • Formerly Home Manufacturers Councils of NAHB.

Manufactured Housing Institute. 2101 Wilson Blvd., Ste. 610, Arlington, VA 22201-3062. Phone: 800-505-5500 or (703)558-0400 Fax: (703)558-0401 E-mail: info@mfghome.org • URL: http://www.manufacturedhousing.org • Manufacturers of manufactured homes; suppliers of equipment, components, furnishings and services, financial services companies, state association organizations, retailers and community owners. Promotes sales of manufactured homes through programs and services in six key areas: government relations, technical activities, financing, public relations, site development, and community operations. Conducts research and educational programs; provides statistics.

PREMIUMS

See also: ADVERTISING SPECIALTIES

DIRECTORIES

Creative's Illustrated Guide to P-O-P Exhibits and Promotion. Magazines Creative, Inc. • Annual. $25.00. Lists sources of point-of-purchase displays, signs, and exhibits and sources of other promotional materials and equipment. Available online.

Incentive's Buyer's Guide. VNU Business Media. • Publication includes: List of 1,500 merchandise suppliers, hotels, cruise lines, airlines, and other companies that provide services to companies offering incentive travel and merchandise programs. Entries include: Company name, address, phone, name of sales contact, description of facilities (for hotels).

Premium, Incentive, and Travel Buyers Directory. Douglas Publications, Inc. • Annual. $275.00. Lists more than 12,000 firms who purchase premiums and incentives. Provides information on about 20,000 buyers of premiums, incentive programs, and travel programs for motivation of sales personnel.

PROMO Annual SourceBook: The Only Guide to the $70 Billion Promotion Industry. Primedia Business Magazines and Media. • Annual. $49.95. Lists service and supply companies for the promotion industry. Includes annual salary survey and award winning campaigns.

The PROMO 100 Promotion Agency Ranking. PROMO Magazine. • Covers: Ranking of the top 100 U.S. Promotion agencies. Entries include: Name, address, phone, financial data, client lists, rate of growth, name of CEO, and description of product/service.

HANDBOOKS AND MANUALS

Specialty Advertising. Entrepreneur Media, Inc. • Looseleaf. $59.50. A practical guide to starting a

business dealing in advertising specialties. Covers profit potential, market size evaluation, start-up costs, pricing, accounting, advertising, promotion, etc. (Start-Up Business Guide No. E1292.).

PERIODICALS AND NEWSLETTERS

Incentive: Managing and Marketing Through Motivation. VNU Business Media. • Monthly. $59.00 per year.

Potentials: Ideas and Products that Motivate. VNU Business Media. • Monthly. $59.00 per year. Covers incentives, premiums, awards, and gifts as related to promotional activities. Formerly *Potentials in Marketing.*

PROMO: Promotion Marketing Worldwide. Primedia Business Magazines and Media. • Monthly. $65.00 per year. Edited for companies and agencies that utilize couponing, point-of-purchase advertising, special events, games, contests, premiums, product samples, and other unique promotional items.

STATISTICS SOURCES

Incentive-State of the Industry and Annual Facts Review. VNU Business Media. • Annual. $5.00. A special issue of *Incentive* magazine.

TRADE/PROFESSIONAL ASSOCIATIONS

Incentive Manufacturers Representatives Association. 1801 N. Mill St., Suite R, Naerville, IL 60563. Phone: 888-285-4672 or (630)369-7786 Fax: (630)369-3773 E-mail: info@imra1.org • URL: http://www.imral.org • Formerly National Premium Manufacturers Representatives.

OTHER SOURCES

Idea Source Guide; A Monthly Report to Executives in Advertising, Merchandising and Sales Promotion. Bramlee, Inc. • Monthly. $150.00 per year. Lists new premiums and novelty products.

PREPAID MEDICAL CARE

See: HEALTH INSURANCE; HEALTH MAINTENANCE ORGANIZATIONS

PREPARED FOODS

See: PROCESSED FOOD INDUSTRY

PRESIDENTS OF COMPANIES

See: EXECUTIVES

PRESS CLIPPINGS

See: CLIPPING SERVICES

PRESSURE GROUPS

ALMANACS AND YEARBOOKS

Congressional Quarterly Almanac. CQ Press. • Annual. $215.00.

CD-ROM DATABASES

Leadership Library on CD-ROM: Who's Who in the Leadership of the United States. Leadership Directories, Inc. • Quarterly. Including access to Internet version (weekly updates). Contains all 14 *Yellow Book* personnel directories on CD-ROM, providing contact and brief biographical information for about 400,000 individuals. Covers business, government, financial institutions, news media, law firms, associations, foreign representatives, and

nonprofit organizations. Includes photographs.

DIRECTORIES

Government Affairs Yellow Book: Who's Who in Government Affairs. Leadership Directories, Inc. • Semiannual. $265.00 per year. Includes in-house lobbyists of corporations and organizations, Political Action Committees (PACs), congressional liaisons, and independent lobbying firms.

Public Interest Profiles, 2001-2002. CQ Press. • 2002. $215.00. Provides detailed information on more than 250 influential public interest and public policy organizations (lobbyists) in the U.S. Includes e-mail addresses and Web sites where available. (Public Interest Profile Series).

Special Interest Group Profiles for Students. Gale Cengage Learning. • 1999. $115.00. Provides detailed descriptions for more than 175 lobbies, political action committees, civic action groups, and political parties. Includes a glossary, chronology, and index.

Washington Representatives: Lobbyists, Foreign Agents, Consultants, Legal Advisors, Public Affairs, and Government Relations... Columbia Books, Inc. • Annual. $149.00. Over 17,000 individuals and law or public relations firms registered as lobbyists, foreign agents, or otherwise acting as representatives in Washington, DC, for companies, associations, labor unions, and special interest groups; legislative affairs personnel of federal government agencies and departments and the White House.

PERIODICALS AND NEWSLETTERS

Congressional Record. U.S. Congress. Available from U.S. Government Printing Office. • Daily. Indexes give names, subjects, and history of bills. Texts of bills not included.

Influence: Clients' Guide to the Business of Lobbying. American Lawyer Media, Inc. • Monthly. $349.00 per year. Newsletter. Provides influence-related news about "lobby shops," companies, associations, and the government. Covers grass-roots campaigns, public relations strategies, new client signings, and fresh registrations. Edited for government relations personnel, public affairs professionals, and lawyers. (Legal Times).

Legal Times: Law and Lobbying in the Nation's Capital. American Lawyer Media, Inc. • Weekly. $318.00 per year. Published in Washington, DC. Provides news relating to lawyers and the federal government. Special features cover a variety of topics relating to law firm administration.

TRADE/PROFESSIONAL ASSOCIATIONS

American League of Lobbyists. P.O. Box 30005, Alexandria, VA 22310. Phone: (703)960-3011 Fax: (703)960-4070 E-mail: alldc.org@erols.com • URL: http://www.alldc.org • Registered lobbyists and other professionals interested in the lobbying profession.

OTHER SOURCES

CQ Weekly. CQ Press. • 48 times a year. $1,696.00 per year. Includes annual *Almanac.* Formerly *Congressional Quarterly Weekly Report.*

PRESSURE PACKAGING

See also: PACKAGING

DIRECTORIES

Spray Equipment Directory. infoUSA. • Annual. Price on application.

ONLINE DATABASES

PIRA. PIRA International Information Centre. • Citations and abstracts pertaining to bookbinding and other pulp, paper, and packaging industries, 1975 to present. Weekly updates. Inquire as to online cost and availability.

PERIODICALS AND NEWSLETTERS

Spray Technology and Marketing: The Magazine of Spray Pressure Packaging. Industry Publications,

Inc. • Monthly. $30.00 per year. Formerly *Aerosol Age*.

PRESSURE SENSITIVE TAPE INDUSTRY

See: ADHESIVES

PRETZEL INDUSTRY

See: SNACK FOOD INDUSTRY

PRICE CODING, ELECTRONIC

See: POINT-OF-SALE SYSTEMS (POS)

PRICES AND PRICING

See also: CONSUMER PRICE INDEXES; INFLATION

ALMANACS AND YEARBOOKS

Agricultural and Mineral Commodities Year Book. Available from Taylor & Francis Group. • Annual. $225.00. Published by Europa Publications. Contains descriptive product profiles, price data, export-import data, and production statistics for major commodities of the world. Includes commodity histories, uses, markets, demand trends, and information about trade agreements and key commodity organizations.

CD-ROM DATABASES

OECD Statistical Compendium. Organization for Economic Cooperation and Development. • Semiannual. $1,905.00 per year for 1 to 10 users. CD-ROM contains more than 730,000 monthly, quarterly, and annual time series for OECD countries, 1960 to date. Includes fully searchable data on agriculture, food, economic indicators, national accounts, employment, energy, finance, industry, technology, and foreign trade. Results can be displayed in various forms.

HANDBOOKS AND MANUALS

Marketing Manager's Handbook. Sidney J. Levy and others. Prentice Hall PTR. • 2000. Price on application. Contains 71 chapters by various authors on a wide variety of marketing topics, including market segmentation, market research, international marketing, industrial marketing, survey methods, customer service, advertising, pricing, planning, strategy, and ethics.

Power Pricing: How Managing Price Transforms the Bottom Line. Robert J. Dolan and Hermann Simon. The Free Press. • 1997. $40.00. Among topics included are pricing strategy, price customization, international pricing, nonlinear pricing, product-line pricing, and price bundling.

INTERNET DATABASES

Bureau of Economic Analysis (BEA). U. S. Department of Commerce, Bureau of Economic Analysis. Phone: (202)606-9900 Fax: (202)606-5310 E-mail: webmaster@bea.doc.gov • URL: http://www.bea.doc.gov • Web site includes "News Release Information" covering national, regional, and international economic estimates from the BEA. Highlights of releases appear online the same day, complete text and tables appear the next day. "Recent News Releases" section provides titles for past nine months, with links. "BEA Data and Methodology" includes "Frequently Requested NIPA Data" (national income and product accounts, such as gross domestic product and personal income). Other statistics are available. Fees: Free.

Business 2.0 Web Guide to the Best Business Links. Business 2.0 Media Inc. Phone: (415)293-4800 E-mail: support@business2.com • URL: http://www.business2.com/webguide • Web site presents an extensive, searchable directory of links to "the best, most informative, and authoritative web pages." Twenty main categories cover business, finance, career, company information, people, and technology topics, with thousands of subtopics, all linking to Web sites recommended by experienced business researchers. Fees: Free.

CRB Markets Overview. Commodity Research Bureau. Phone: 800-621-5271 or (312)554-8456 Fax: (312)939-4135 E-mail: info@crbtrader.com • URL: http://www.crbtrader.com/data/ • Web site provides free, detailed, current price quotes for about 100 futures contracts, covering Currencies, Energies, Financials, Grains, Meats, Metals, "Softs" (orange juice, coffee, etc.) and stock price indexes. Includes contract specifications and detailed prices of options on futures.

Fedstats. Federal Interagency Council on Statistical Policy. Phone: (202)395-7254 • URL: http://www.fedstats.gov • Web site features an efficient search facility for full-text statistics produced by more than 100 federal agencies, including the Census Bureau, the Bureau of Economic Analysis, and the Bureau of Labor Statistics. Boolean searches can be made within one agency or for all agencies combined. Links are offered to international statistical bureaus, including the UN, IMF, OECD, UNESCO, Eurostat, and 20 individual countries. Fees: Free.

FreeLunch.com. Economy.com, Inc. Phone: (610)696-8700 Fax: (610)696-1678 • URL: http://www.freelunch.com • Web site provides free access to more than 1.5 million economic and financial data series, covering industry, demographics, labor markets, prices, retail sales, government spending, trade, interest rates, housing starts, the stock market, and many other topics. Data is available for various time periods in either chart or table form. Searching is offered. Fees: Free, but registration required. Economy.com, Inc. also offers fee-based economic analysis at *The Dismal Scientist* site (http://www.dismal.com).

Summary of Commentary on Current Economic Conditions by Federal Reserve District [the Beige Book]. Board of Governors of the Federal Reserve System. Phone: (202)452-3000 Fax: (202)452-3819 • URL: http://www.federalreserve.gov/fomc/beigebook/2004/ • Free Web site provides current "anecdotal information" eight times a year on economic conditions within each of the 12 Federal Reserve Districts, plus an extensive national *Summary.* Text is based on the opinions of bank officials, business executives, economists, financial market experts, and others. Typically contains views of consumer spending, manufacturing, services, credit, employment, prices, wages, and the economy in general. Usually referred to as the Beige Book.

PRICE SOURCES

CPI Detailed Report: Consumer Price Index. Available from U.S. Government Printing Office. • Monthly. $45.00 per year. Cost of living data.

Monthly Commodity Price Bulletin. United Nations Publications. • Monthly. $125.00 per year. Provides monthly average prices for the previous 12 months for a wide variety of commodities traded internationally.

PPI Detailed Report. Bureau of Labor Statistics, U.S. Department of Labor. Available from U.S. Government Printing Office. • Monthly. $55.00 per year. Formerly *Producer Price Indexes.*

The Value of a Dollar: Millennium Edition, 1860-1999. Grey House Publishing. • 1999. $135.00. Second edition. Shows the actual prices of thousands of items available to consumers from the Civil War era to recent years. Includes selected data

on consumer expenditures, investments, income, and jobs. (Universal Reference Publications.).

STATISTICS SOURCES

American Cost of Living Survey. Gale Cengage Learning. • 2001. $245.00. Third edition. Cost of living data is provided for 455 U.S. cities and metroploitan areas.

Bulletin of Labour Statistics: Supplementing the Annual Data Presented in the Year Book of Labour Statistics. International Labour Ofice. • Quarterly. $84.00 per year. Includes five *Supplements.* A supplement to *Yearbook of Labour Statistics.* Provides current labor and price index statistics for over 130 countries. Generally includes data for the most recent four years. Text in English, French and Spanish.

Business Statistics of the United States. Linz Audain and Cornelia J. Strawser. Bernan Associates. • Annual. $147.00. Based on *Business Statistics,* formerly issue by the Bureau of Economic Analysis, U. S. Department of Commerce. Provides basic data for a wide variety of U. S. industries, services, and economic indicators. Most statistics are shown annually for 30 years and monthly for the most recent four years.

Economic Report of the President: Together with the Annual Report of the Council of Economic Advisors. Available from U. S. Government Printing Office. • Annual. $32.00. Includes about 130 pages of "Statistical Tables Relating to Income, Employment, and Production." Tables cover national income, employment, wages, productivity, manufacturing, prices, credit, finance (public and private), corporate profits, and foreign trade.

FAO Production Yearbook. Available from Bernan Associates. • Annual..$45.00. Published by the Food and Agriculture Organization (http://www.fao.org). Contains worldwide data on agriculture, land use, farm crops, livestock, and agricultural prices.

Handbook of U. S. Labor Statistics: Employment, Earnings, Prices, Productivity, and Other Labor Data. Eva E. Jacobs, editor. Bernan Associates. • 1999. $74.00. Based on *Handbook of Labor Statistics,* formerly issued by the Bureau of Labor Statistics, U. S. Department of Labor. Includes the Bureau's projections of employment in the U. S. by industry and occupation. Provides a wide variety of data on the work force, prices, fringe benefits, and consumer expenditures.

Key Indicators of the Labour Market. Available from Routledge. • Biennial. $125.00. Published by the International Labour Office (http://www.ilo.org). Provides data on 20 key indicators in 220 countries. Includes labor force statistics, employment, unemployment, part-time workers, wages, productivity, poverty indicators, and related topics.

Monthly Bulletin of Statistics. United Nations Publications. • Monthly. $295.00 per year. Provides current data for about 200 countries on a wide variety of economic, industrial, and demographic subjects. Compiled by United Nations Statistical Office.

Monthly Labor Review. Available from U. S. Government Printing Office. • Monthly. $49.00 per year. Issued by the Bureau of Labor Statistics, U. S. Department of Labor. Contains data on the labor force, wages, work stoppages, price indexes, productivity, economic growth, and occupational injuries and illnesses.

Prices and Earnings Around the Globe. Union Bank of Switzerland. • Triennial. Free. Published in Zurich. Compares prices and purchasing power in 48 major cities of the world. Wages and hours are also compared.

Statistical Yearbook. United Nations Publications. • Annual. $125.00. Contains statistics for about 200 countries on a wide variety of economic, industrial, and demographic topics. Compiled by United Nations Statistical Office.

Statistics on Occupational Wages and Hours of Work and on Food Prices. International Labour Organization. • Annual. $28.00. Provides international data on wages and hours for 159 occupations within 49 industries. Includes retail prices for 93 food items.

Survey of Current Business. Available from U. S. Government Printing Office. • Monthly. $63.00 per year. Issued by Bureau of Economic Analysis, U. S. Department of Commerce. Presents a wide variety of business and economic data.

The Value of a Dollar: Millenium Edition. Scott Derks, editor. Grey House Publishing, Inc. • 1999. $135.00. Second edition.

World Cost of Living Survey. Gale Cengage Learning. • 1999. $275.00. Second edition. Arranged by country and then by city within each country. Provides cost of living data for many products and services. Includes indexes and an annotated bibliography.

Yearbook of Labour Statistics. Available from Bernan Associates. • Annual. $168.00. Published by the International Labour Organizaton (http://www.ilo.org). Provides data for more than 180 countries on employment, unemployment, wages, hours of work, cost of labor, strikes, industrial accidents, and consumer prices.

PRIME RATE

See: INTEREST

PRINTING AND PRINTING EQUIPMENT INDUSTRIES

See also: COPYING MACHINE INDUSTRY; GRAPHIC ARTS INDUSTRY; PHOTOENGRAVING; TYPESETTING

CD-ROM DATABASES

OECD Statistical Compendium. Organization for Economic Cooperation and Development. • Semiannual. $1,905.00 per year for 1 to 10 users. CD-ROM contains more than 730,000 monthly, quarterly, and annual time series for OECD countries, 1960 to date. Includes fully searchable data on agriculture, food, economic indicators, national accounts, employment, energy, finance, industry, technology, and foreign trade. Results can be displayed in various forms.

DIRECTORIES

Graphic Arts Monthly Sourcebook. Cahners Publishing Co. • Covers: About 1,400 manufacturers and distributors of graphic arts equipment, supplies, and services, and 700 graphic arts dealers. Entries include: Company name, address, phone, name and title of contact.

In-Plant Printer Buyer's Guide. Innes Publishing Co. • Annual. $10.00. Manufacturers of equipment for the in-plant and grahic arts industry. Formerly *In-Plant Printer and Electronic Publisher Buyer's Guide.*

SRDS Print Media Production Source. SRDS. • Quarterly. $808.00 per year. Contains details of printing and mechanical production requirements for advertising in specific trade journals, consumer magazines, and newspapers. Formerly *Print Media Production Source.*

ENCYCLOPEDIAS AND DICTIONARIES

Graphically Speaking: An Illustrated Guide to the Working Language of Design and Publishing. Mark Beach. Coast to Coast Books. • 1992. $29.50. Provides practical definitions of 2,800 terms used in

printing, graphic design, publishing, and desktop publishing. Over 300 illustrations are included, about 40 in color.

FINANCIAL RATIOS

Almanac of Business and Industrial Financial Ratios. Leo Troy. Aspen Publishers, Inc. • 2003. $125.95. Includes CD-Rom. Contains financial ratios derived from federal tax returns. Ratios for each of about 200 industries are arranged according to company asset size. (Almanac of Business and Industrial Financial Ratios Series).

PIA Financial Ratio Studies. Printing Industries of America, Inc. • Annual. $3,582.00. 18 volumes. $199.00 per volume.

HANDBOOKS AND MANUALS

Getting It Printed: How to Work with Printers and Graphic Arts Services to Assure Quality, Stay on Schedule, and Control Costs. Mark Beach and Eric Kenly. F and W. Publications, Inc. • 1999. $32.99. Third edition.

Instant Print/Copy Shop. Entrepreneur Media, Inc. • Looseleaf. $59.50. A practical guide to starting a quick printing and copying business. Covers profit potential, start-up costs, market size evaluation, owner's time required, site selection, lease negotiation, pricing, accounting, advertising, promotion, etc. (Start-Up Business Guide No. E1298.).

INTERNET DATABASES

Business 2.0 Web Guide to the Best Business Links. Business 2.0 Media Inc. Phone: (415)293-4800 E-mail: support@business2.com • URL: http://www.business2.com/webguide • Web site presents an extensive, searchable directory of links to "the best, most informative, and authoritative web pages." Twenty main categories cover business, finance, career, company information, people, and technology topics, with thousands of subtopics, all linking to Web sites recommended by experienced business researchers. Fees: Free.

Fedstats. Federal Interagency Council on Statistical Policy. Phone: (202)395-7254 • URL: http://www.fedstats.gov • Web site features an efficient search facility for full-text statistics produced by more than 100 federal agencies, including the Census Bureau, the Bureau of Economic Analysis, and the Bureau of Labor Statistics. Boolean searches can be made within one agency or for all agencies combined. Links are offered to international statistical bureaus, including the UN, IMF, OECD, UNESCO, Eurostat, and 20 individual countries. Fees: Free.

FreeLunch.com. Economy.com, Inc. Phone: (610)696-8700 Fax: (610)696-1678 • URL: http://www.freelunch.com • Web site provides free access to more than 1.5 million economic and financial data series, covering industry, demographics, labor markets, prices, retail sales, government spending, trade, interest rates, housing starts, the stock market, and many other topics. Data is available for various time periods in either chart or table form. Searching is offered. Fees: Free, but registration required. Economy.com, Inc. also offers fee-based economic analysis at *The Dismal Scientist* site (http://www.dismal.com).

PERIODICALS AND NEWSLETTERS

American Printer: The Graphic Arts Manager Magazine. Primedia Business Magazines and Media. • Monthly. Free to qualified personnel; others, $73.00 per year. Serves the printing and lithographic industries and allied manufacturing and service segments.

Color Publishing. PennWell Corp., Advanced Technology Div. • Bimonthly. $29.70 per year.

Graphic Arts Monthly: The Magazine of the Printing Industry. Reed Business Information. • Monthly. Free to qualified personnel; others, $142.99 per year.

In-Plant Printer: The In-Plant Management

Magazine. Innes Publishing Co. • Bimonthly. $75.00 per year. Formerly *In-Plant Printer and Electronic Publisher.*

Printing Impressions. North American Publishing Co. • Monthly. Free to qualified personnel; others, $90.00 per year. Annual buyer's guide *Master Specifier.*

Quick Printing: The Information Source for Commercial Copyshops and Printshops. Cygnus Business Media. • Monthly. $66.00 per year.

RESEARCH CENTERS AND INSTITUTES

Chester F. Carlson Center for Imaging Science. Rochester Institute of Technology, 54 Lomb Memorial Dr., Rochester, NY 14623. Phone: 800-724-2536 or (716)475-5944 Fax: (716)475-5988 E-mail: garley@cis.rit.edu • URL: http://www.cis.rit.edu/.

STATISTICS SOURCES

Annual Survey of Manufactures. Available from U. S. Government Printing Office. • Annual. Prices vary. Issued by the U. S. Census Bureau as an interim update to the *Census of Manufactures.* Includes data on number of manufacturing establishments in various industries, employment, labor costs, value of shipments, capital expenditures, inventories, energy costs, and assets. (See also Census Bureau home page, http://www.census.gov/.).

Business Statistics of the United States. Linz Audain and Cornelia J. Strawser. Bernan Associates. • Annual. $147.00. Based on *Business Statistics,* formerly issue by the Bureau of Economic Analysis, U. S. Department of Commerce. Provides basic data for a wide variety of U. S. industries, services, and economic indicators. Most statistics are shown annually for 30 years and monthly for the most recent four years.

Survey of Current Business. Available from U. S. Government Printing Office. • Monthly. $63.00 per year. Issued by Bureau of Economic Analysis, U. S. Department of Commerce. Presents a wide variety of business and economic data.

TRADE/PROFESSIONAL ASSOCIATIONS

International Association of Printing House Craftsmen. 7042 Brooklyn Blvd., Minneapolis, MN 55429-1370. Phone: 800-466-4274 or (763)560-1620 Fax: (763)560-1350 E-mail: headquarters@iaphc.org • URL: http://www.iaphc.org.

National Association for Printing Leadership. 75 W. Century Rd., Paramus, NJ 07652-1408. Phone: 800-642-6275 or (201)634-9600 Fax: (201)634-0325 E-mail: info@napl.org • URL: http://www.napl.org • Text: Formerly National Association of Printers and Lithographers.

National Association of Quick Printers. 2250 E Devon Ave., Ste. 302, Des Plaines, IL 60018. Phone: 800-234-0040 or (847)298-8680 Fax: (847)298-8705 E-mail: info@naqp.com • URL: http://www.naqp.com • Independent printers and printing franchise businesses; industry suppliers. Seeks to bring recognition, improved quality, and increased profits to the entire quick printing field. Provides services to members; works to advance the collective interests of the printing industries at the national and international levels.

NPES-The Association for Suppliers of Printing and Publishing and Converting Technologies. 1899 Preston White Dr., Reston, VA 22091-4367. Phone: (703)264-7200 Fax: (703)620-0994 E-mail: npes@npes.org • URL: http://www.npes.org • Formerly Association for Suppliers of Printing and Publishing and Converting Technologies.

Printing Industries of America. 100 Daingerfield Rd., Alexandria, VA 22314-2888. Phone: 800-742-2666 or (703)519-8100 Fax: (703)548-3227 E-mail: gain@printing.org • URL: http://www.printing.org • Commercial printing firms (lithography, letterpress, gravure, platemakers, typographic houses)

---

and allied firms in the graphic arts. Formerly Printing Industry of America.

PRINTING INK INDUSTRY

ABSTRACTS AND INDEXES

CPI Digest: Key to World Literature Serving the Coatings, Plastics, Fibers, Adhesives, and Related Industries (Chemical Process Industries). CPI Information Services. • Monthly. $397.00 per year. Abstracts of business and technical articles for polymer-based, chemical process industries. Includes a monthly list of relevant U. S. patents. International coverage.

DIRECTORIES

American Inkmaker Buyers' Guide. Cygnus Business Media, Inc. • Annual. $20.00. Guide to suppliers of raw materials, equipment, and services for manufacturers of printing ink, pigments, varnishes, graphic chemicals, and similar products.

Rauch Guide to the U. S. Ink Industry. Impact Marketing Consultants. • 2002. $495.00. 237 leading ink manufacturers with over $1 million in annual sales; and lists of activities, organizations, and sources of information in the ink industry. Formerly *Kline Guide to the U.S. Ink Industry*.

PERIODICALS AND NEWSLETTERS

Ink Maker: For Manufacturers of Printing Inks and Related Graphic Arts Specialty Colors. Cygnus Business Media. • Monthly. $60.00 per year. Formerly *American Inkmaker*.

RESEARCH CENTERS AND INSTITUTES

Chester F. Carlson Center for Imaging Science. Rochester Institute of Technology, 54 Lomb Memorial Dr., Rochester, NY 14623. Phone: 800-724-2536 or (716)475-5944 Fax: (716)475-5988 E-mail: garley@cis.rit.edu • URL: http://www.cis.rit.edu/.

STATISTICS SOURCES

Annual Survey of Manufactures. Available from U. S. Government Printing Office. • Annual. Prices vary. Issued by the U. S. Census Bureau as an interim update to the *Census of Manufactures*. Includes data on number of manufacturing establishments in various industries, employment, labor costs, value of shipments, capital expenditures, inventories, energy costs, and assets. (See also Census Bureau home page, http://www.census. gov/.).

TRADE/PROFESSIONAL ASSOCIATIONS

National Association of Printing Ink Manufacturers. 581 Main St., Woodbridge, NJ 07095-1104. Phone: (732)855-1525 Fax: (732)855-1838 E-mail: napim@napim.org • URL: http://www.napim.org • Formerly National Association of Printing Ink Makers.

PRINTING STYLE MANUALS

GENERAL WORKS

Style: Toward Clarity and Grace. Joseph M. Williams. The University of Chicago Press. • 1990. $17.95.

HANDBOOKS AND MANUALS

ACS Style Guide: A Manual for Authors and Editors. Janet S. Dodd, editor. American Chemical Society. • 1997. $35.00. Second edition. A style manual for scientific and technical writers. Includes the use of illustrations, tables, lists, numbers, and units of measure.

Associated Press Stylebook and Libel Manual. Addison-Wesley. • 1996. $14.00. Sixth edition.

Banishing Bureaucratese: Using Plain English in Government Writing. Judith G. Myers. Management Concepts, Inc. • 2001. $39.00. Covers plain writing style for government memos, letters, e-mail, agency communications, budget justification statements, and other bureaucratic documents.

The Chicago Manual of Style: The Essential Guide for Authors, Editors, and Publishers. The University of Chicago Press. • 1993. $40.00. 14th edition.

Columbia Guide to Online Style. Janice R. Walker and Todd W. Taylor. Columbia University Press. • 1998. $40.50. Includes rules for bibliographic citation of online sources, formatting guidelines for online documents, and information on the electronic preparation of texts for print publication.

Easy Access: The Reference Handbook for Writers. Michael Keene and Katherine Adams. McGraw-Hill. • 2001. $35.31. Third edition. Covers documentation styles and "Common Writing Problems" (punctuation, grammar, and sentence construction).

Electronic Styles: A Handbook of Citing Electronic Information. Xia Li and Nancy Crane. Information Today, Inc. • 1996. $19.99. Second edition. Covers the citing of text-based information, electronic journals, Web sites, CD-ROM items, multimedia products, and online documents.

Gregg Reference Manual. William A. Sabin. McGraw-Hill. • 2004. $46.55. 10th edition. Covers grammar, usage, and style, including changes evolving from the use of computers and the Internet. (Imprint: Irwin Professional Publishing.).

Guide for Authors: Manuscript, Proof, and Illustration. Payne E. Thomas. Charles C. Thomas Publishers, Ltd. • 1993. $21.95. Fourth edition.

Handbook for Proofreading. Laura K. Anderson. McGraw-Hill. • 1993. $24.95. (NTC Business Book Series).

Hot Text: Web Writing That Works. Jonathan Price and Lisa Price. New Riders Publishing. • 2002. $40. 00. Provides practical advice on writing text for Web sites, including such details as headlines and menu design. As the attention span of many Web surfers is limited, clarity and brevity become of great importance.

MLA Handbook for Writers of Research Papers. Joseph Gibaldi. Modern Language Association of America. • 2003. $25.00. Fifth edition. Includes style guidelines for both print and online citations. (MLA Handbook for Writers of Research Papers).

MLA Style Manual and Guide to Scholarly Publishing. Joseph Gibaldi. Modern Language Association of America. • 1998. $25.00. Second edition. Covers preparation of manuscripts for publication, legal issues, basic writing principles, documentation, and use of abbreviations.

The New York Public Library Writer's Guide to Style and Usage. Andrea Sutcliffe, editor. HarperInformation. • 1994. $40.00.

The New York Times Manual of Style and Usage: The Official Style Guide Used by the Writers and Editors of the World's Most Authoriatative Newspaper. Allan M. Siegal and William G. Connolly, editors. Harmony Books. • 2002. $15.00. Revised edition.

United States Government Printing Office Style Manual. U. S. Government Printing Office. • 2000. $41.00. 29th edition. Supersedes the 1984 edition (28th). Designed to achieve uniformity in the style and form of government printing.

Wall Street Journal Guide to Business Style and Usage. Paul R. Martin, editor. The Free Press. • 2002. $30.00. Contains definitions and explanations relating to grammar, spelling, punctuation, and the use of specialized business terms. (Wall Street Journal Book Series).

PERIODICALS AND NEWSLETTERS

Copy Editor: Language News for the Publishing Profession. McMurry Newsletters. • Bimonthly. $69.00 per year. Newsletter for professional copy editors and proofreaders. Includes such items as "Top Ten Resources for Copy Editors.".

PRISONS

See: LAW ENFORCEMENT INDUSTRIES

PRIVATE COMPANIES

See also: CLOSELY HELD CORPORATIONS

ABSTRACTS AND INDEXES

Business Periodicals Index. H. W. Wilson Co. • 11 times a year. Quarterly and annual cumulations. Price varies.

CD-ROM DATABASES

Corporate Affiliations Plus. National Register Publishing, Reed Reference Publishing. • Quarterly. $1,995.00 per year. Provides CD-ROM discs corresponding to *Directory of Corporate Affiliations* and *Corporate Finance Bluebook*. Contains corporate financial services information and worldwide data on subsidiaries and affiliates.

D & B Business Locator. Dun & Bradstreet, Inc. • Quarterly. $2,495.00 per year. CD-ROM provides concise information on more than 10 million U. S. companies or businesses. Includes data on number of employees.

Hoover's Company Capsules on CD-ROM. Hoover's, Inc. • Quarterly. $399.95 per year (single-user). Provides the CD-ROM version of *Hoover's Handbook of American Business*, *Hoover's Handbook of Emerging Companies*, *Hoover's Handbook of World Business*, *Hoover's Guide to Computer Companies*, *Hoover's Guide to Media Companies*, *Hoover's Handbook of Private Companies*, and various regional guides. Includes more than 11,000 profiles of companies.

16 Million Businesses Phone Directory. Info USA. • Annual. $29.95. Provides more than 16 million yellow pages telephone directory listings on CD-ROM for all ZIP Code areas of the U. S.

Standard & Poor's Corporations. Available from Dialog OnDisc. • Monthly. Price on application. Produced by Standard & Poor's. Contains three CD-ROM files: Executives, Private Companies, and Public Companies, providing detailed information on more than 70,000 business executives, 55,000 private companies, and 12,000 publicly-traded corporations.

DIRECTORIES

American Big Businesses Directory. infoUSA Inc. • Covers: 218,000 U.S. businesses with more than 100 employees, and 500,000 key executives and directors. CD-ROM version contains 160,000 top firms and 431,000 key executives. Entries include: Name, address, phone, names and titles of key personnel, number of employees, sales volume, Standard Industrial Classification (SIC) codes, subsidiaries and parent company names, stock exchanges on which traded.

American Manufacturers Directory. infoUSA Inc. • Covers: more than 150,000 manufacturing companies with 20 or more employees. CD-ROM version lists all 531,000 U.S. manufacturers, in all employee size ranges. Entries include: Company name, address, phone, contact name, Standard Industrial Classification (SIC) codes, number of employees, sales volume code, credit rating scores.

Business Organizations, Agencies, and Publications Directory. Gale Cengage Learning. • 2003. $480.00. 15th edition. Over 40,000 entries describing 39 types of business information sources. Classified by type of organization, publication, or serviceIncludes state, national, and international agencies and organizations. Master index to names and keywords. Also includes e-mail addresses and web site URL's.

Hoover's Handbook of American Business: Profiles of Major U. S. Companies. Hoover's, Inc. • Annual. $195.95. Two volumes. Provides detailed profiles of more than 750 large public and private companies, including history, executives, brand names, key competitors, and up to 10 years of financial data. Includes indexes by industry, location, executive name, company name, and brand name.

Hoover's Handbook of Private Companies: Profiles of Major U. S. Private Enterprises. Hoover's, Inc. • Annual. $155.00. Contains profiles of 900 private companies and organizations. Includes indexes by industry, location, executive name, and product.

Hoover's Masterlist of Major U. S. Companies. Hoover's, Inc. • 2003. $275.00. Provides brief information, including annual sales, number of employees, and chief executive, for about 5,000 U. S. companies, both public and private.

Inc.-The Inc. 500. • Annual. $3.50. Information on each of the 500 fastest-growing privately held companies in the U. S. Based on percentage increase in sales over the five year period prior to compilation of current year's list.

Job Seeker's Guide to Private and Public Companies. Gale Cengage Learning. • 1993. $390.00. Second edition. $99.00 per volume. Four regional volumes: *The West, The Midwest, The Northeast,* and *The South.* Covers about 15,000 companies, providing information on personnel department contacts, corporate officials, company benefits, application procedures, etc.

Ward's Business Directory of U. S. Private and Public Companies. Gale Cengeage Learning. • 2002. $2,765.00. 45th edition. Eight volumes. *Ward's* contains basic information on about 120,000 business firms, of which 90 percent are private companies. Includes mid-year *Supplement.* Volumes available individually. Prices vary.

Ward's Private Company Profiles: Excerpts and Articles on 150 Privately Held U. S. Companies. Gale Cengage Learning. • 1994. $139.00. Second edition. A collection of detailed information on 150 private companies.

HANDBOOKS AND MANUALS

Researching Private Companies. Washington Researchers Ltd. • 2002. $59.00.

INTERNET DATABASES

EBSCO Information Services. Ebsco Publishing. Phone: 800-653-2726 or (978)356-6500 Fax: (978)356-6565 E-mail: ep@epnet.com • URL: http://www.epnet.com • Fee-based Web site providing Internet access to a wide variety of databases, including business-related material. Full text is available for many periodical titles, with daily updates. Fees: Apply.

Factiva. Dow Jones Reuters Business Interactive, LLC. Phone: 800-369-7466 or (609)452-1511 Fax: (609)520-5770 E-mail: solutions@factiva.com • URL: http://www.factiva.com • Fee-based Web site provides "global news and business information through Web sites and content integration solutions." Includes Dow Jones and Reuters newswires, The Wall Street Journal, and more than 7,000 other sources of current news, historical articles, market research reports, and investment analysis. Content includes 96 major U. S. newspapers, 900 non-English sources, trade publications, media transcripts, country profiles, news photos, etc.

Hoover's Online. Hoover's, Inc. Phone: 800-486-8666 or (512)374-4500 Fax: (512)374-4501 • URL: http://www.hoovers.com • Web site provides stock quotes, lists of companies, and a variety of business information at no charge. In-depth company profiles are available.

InSite 2. Intelligence Data/Thomson Financial. Phone: 800-654-0393 or (617)856-1890 Fax: (617)737-3182 E-mail: intelligence.data@tfn.com •

URL: http://www.insite2.gale.com/ • Fee-based Web site consolidates information in a "Base Pack" consisting of Business InSite, Market InSite, and Company InSite. Optional databases are Consumer InSite, Health and Wellness InSite, Newsletter In-Site, and Computer InSite. Includes fulltext content from more than 2,500 trade publications, journals, newsletters, newspapers, analyst reports, and other sources. Continuous updating. Formerly produced by The Gale Group.

Nexis.com. Lexis-Nexis Group. Phone: 800-227-4908 or (937)865-6800 Fax: (937)865-6909 E-mail: webmaster@prod.lexis-nexis.com • URL: http://www.nexis.com • Fee-based Web site offers searching of about 2.8 billion documents in some 30,000 news, business, and legal information sources. Features include a subject directory covering 1,200 topics in 34 categories and a Company Dossier containing information on more than 500,000 public and private companies. Boolean searching is offered.

ProQuest Direct. ProQuest Inc. Phone: 800-889-3358 or (734)761-4700 Fax: (734)662-4554 • URL: http://proquest.com • Fee-based Web site providing Internet access to more than 3,000 periodicals, newspapers, and other publications. Many items are available full-text, with daily updates. Includes extensive corporate and financial information. Fees: Apply.

Switchboard. Switchboard, Inc. Phone: (508)898-8000 Fax: (508)898-1755 E-mail: webmaster@switchboard.com • URL: http://www.switchboard.com • Web site provides telephone numbers and street addresses for more than 100 million business locations and residences in the U. S. Broad industry categories are available. Fees: Free.

ONLINE DATABASES

American Business Directory. InfoUSA, Inc. • Provides brief online information on more than 10 million U. S. companies, including individual plants and branches. Entries typically include address, phone number, industry classification code, and contact name. Updating is quarterly. Inquire as to online cost and availability.

TRW Business Credit Profiles. Experian. • Provides credit history (trade payments, payment trends, payment totals, payment history, etc.) for public and private U. S. companies. Key facts and banking information are also given. Updates are weekly. Inquire as to online cost and availability.

Wilson Business Abstracts Online. H. W. Wilson Co. • Indexes and abstracts 600 major business periodicals, plus the *Wall Street Journal* and the business section of the *New York Times.* Indexing is from 1982, abstracting from 1990, with the two newspapers included from 1993. Updated weekly. Inquire as to online cost and availability. (*Business Periodicals Index* without abstracts is also available online.).

PERIODICALS AND NEWSLETTERS

Inc.: The Magazine for Growing Companies. INC. • 18 times a year. $14.00 per year. Edited for small office and office-in-the-home businesses with from one to 25 employees. Covers management, office technology, and lifestyle. Incorporates *Self-Employed Professional.*

RESEARCH CENTERS AND INSTITUTES

Center for Private Enterprise. Baylor University, Hankamer School of Business, P.O. Box 98003, Waco, TX 76798-8003. Phone: (254)710-2263 Fax: (254)710-1092 E-mail: jim_truitt@baylor.edu • URL: http://129.62.162.136/enterprise/ • Includes studies of entrepreneurship and women entrepreneurs.

TRADE/PROFESSIONAL ASSOCIATIONS

Center for Family Business. PO Box 24219, Cleveland, OH 44124. Phone: (440)442-0800 Fax: (440)460-5407 E-mail: grummi@aol.com •

Members are family-owned, independent, private, and closely-held businesses. Formerly University Services Institute.

Center for International Private Enterprise. 1155 15th St., N.W. Ste. 700, Washington, DC 20005. Phone: (202)721-9200 Fax: (202)721-9250 E-mail: cipe@cipe.org • URL: http://www.cipe.org • Members are people involved in small businesses.

OTHER SOURCES

Going Private. American Lawyer Media, Inc. • Looseleaf. $169.00. Updated as needed. Discusses the legal ramifications of a publicly-owned company "going private" by way of a sale, leveraged buyout, reverse stock split, or merger. (Law Journal Press).

PRIVATE LABEL PRODUCTS

ABSTRACTS AND INDEXES

Business Periodicals Index. H. W. Wilson Co. • 11 times a year. Quarterly and annual cumulations. Price varies.

CD-ROM DATABASES

ABI/INFORM. PROQUEST. • Monthly. Provides CD-ROM indexing and abstracting of worldwide business literature. Archival discs are available from 1971. Formerly *ABI/INFORM OnDisc.*

WILSONDISC: Wilson Business Abstracts. H. W. Wilson Co. • Monthly. Includes unlimited online access to *Wilson Business Abstracts* through WILSONLINE. Provides CD-ROM "cover-to-cover" abstracting and indexing of over 600 prominent business periodicals. Indexing is from 1982, abstracting from 1990. (*Business Periodicals Index* without abstracts is available on CD-ROM at $1,495 per year.).

DIRECTORIES

Household and Personal Products Industry - Buyers Guide. Rodman Publications. • Annual. $12.00. Lists of suppliers to manufacturers of cosmetics, toiletries, soaps, detergents, and related household and personal products.

Household and Personal Products Industry Contract Packaging and Private Label Directory. Rodman Publications. • Annual. $12.00. Provides information for about 450 companies offering private label or contract packaged household and personal care products, such as detergents, cosmetics, polishes, insecticides, and various aerosol items.

International Private Label Directory. E. W. Williams Publications Co. • Annual. $75.00. Provides information on over 2,000 suppliers of a wide variety of private label and generic products: food, over-the-counter health products, personal care items, and general merchandise. Formerly *Private Label Directory.*

ONLINE DATABASES

F & S Index. Gale Cengage Learning. • Contains about four million citations to worldwide business, financial, and industrial or consumer product literature appearing from 1972 to date. Weekly updates. Inquire as to online cost and availability.

PROMT: Predicasts Overview of Markets and Technology. Gale Cengage Learning. • Companies, products, applied technologies and markets. U.S. and international literature coverage, 1972 to date. Inquire as to online cost and availability. Provides abstracts from more than 1,600 publications. Weekly updates.

Trade & Industry Database. Gale Cengage Learning. • Provides indexing of business periodicals, January 1981 to date. Daily updates. (Full text articles from some periodicals are available online, 1983 to date. Inquire as to online cost and availability).

Wilson Business Abstracts Online. H. W. Wilson Co. • Indexes and abstracts 600 major business periodicals, plus the *Wall Street Journal* and the business section of the *New York Times*. Indexing is from 1982, abstracting from 1990, with the two newspapers included from 1993. Updated weekly. Inquire as to online cost and availability. (*Business Periodicals Index* without abstracts is also available online.).

PERIODICALS AND NEWSLETTERS

Household and Personal Products Industry: The Magazine for the Detergent, Soap, Cosmetic and Toiletry, Wax, Polish and Aerosol Industries. Rodman Publications. • Monthly. $48.00 per year. Covers marketing, packaging, production, technical innovations, private label developments, and aerosol packaging for soap, detergents, cosmetics, insecticides, and a variety of other household products.

Private Label Buyer. Stagnito Communcitions, Inc. • Eight times a year. $85.08 per year. Covers new private label product developments for chain stores. Formerly *Private Label News.*

Private Label International: The Magazine for Store Labels (Own Brands) and Generics. E. W. Williams Publications Co. • Semiannual. $20.00 per year. Edited for large chain store buyers and for manufacturers of private label products. Text in English; summaries in French and German.

Private Label: The Magazine for House Brands and Generics. E. W. Williams Publications Co. • Bimonthly. $36.00 per year. Edited for buyers of private label, controlled packer, and generic-labeled products. Concentrates on food, health and beauty aids, and general merchandise.

TRADE/PROFESSIONAL ASSOCIATIONS

Private Label Manufacturers Association. 630 3rd Ave., 4th Fl., New York, NY 10017. Phone: (212)972-3131 Fax: (212)983-1382 E-mail: info@plma.com • URL: http://www.plma.com • Membership consists of manufacturers, brokers, suppliers, and consultants. Educates consumers on the quality and value of private label or store brand products; promotes private label industry. Compiles statistics; conducts research programs for members.

PRIVATE SCHOOLS

See also: SCHOOLS

CD-ROM DATABASES

ERIC on SilverPlatter. Available from SilverPlatter Information, Inc. • Quarterly. $700.00 per year. Produced by the Office of Educational Research and Improvement, U. S. Dept. of Education. Provides CD-ROM indexing and abstracting of a wide variety of literature relating to education. Archival discs are available from 1966.

Leadership Library on CD-ROM: Who's Who in the Leadership of the United States. Leadership Directories, Inc. • Quarterly. Including access to Internet version (weekly updates). Contains all 14 *Yellow Book* personnel directories on CD-ROM, providing contact and brief biographical information for about 400,000 individuals. Covers business, government, financial institutions, news media, law firms, associations, foreign representatives, and nonprofit organizations. Includes photographs.

DIRECTORIES

Handbook of Private Schools: An Annual Descriptive Survey of Independent Education. Porter Sargent Publishers, Inc. • 2001. $99.00. Lists more than 1,600 elementary and secondary boarding and day schools in the United States.

Nonprofit Sector Yellow Book: Who's Who in the Management of the Leading Foundations, Universities, Museums, and Other Nonprofit Organizations. Leadership Directories, Inc. • Semiannual. $265.00 per year. Covers management personnel and board

members of about 1,300 prominent, nonprofit organizations: foundations, colleges, museums, performing arts groups, medical institutions, libraries, private preparatory schools, and charitable service organizations.

Patterson's American Education. Educational Directories Inc. • Covers: Over 11,400 school districts in the United States; more than 34,000 public, private, and Catholic high schools, middle schools, and junior high schools; Approximately 300 parochial superintendents; 400 state department of education personnel. Entries include: For school districts and schools--District and superintendent Name, address, phone, fax, grade ranges, enrollment, school names, addresses, phone numbers, grade ranges, enrollment, names of principals. For postsecondary schools--School name, address, phone number, URL, e-mail, names of administrator or director of admissions. For private and Catholic high schools--name, address, phone, fax, enrollment, grades offered, name of principal. Postsecondary institutions are covered in 'Patterson's Schools Classified' (see separate entry).

Peterson's Private Secondary Schools. Peterson's. • Annual. $29.95. Provides information on more than 1,400 accredited private secondary schools in the U. S. (Peterson's Private Secondary School Series). Formerly *Peterson's Guide to Private Secondary Schools.*

Private Independent Schools. Bunting and Lyon Inc. • Covers: 1,200 English-speaking elementary and secondary private schools and summer programs in North America and abroad. Entries include: School name, address, phone, fax, e-mail, website, enrollment, tuition and other fees, financial aid information, administrator's name and educational background, director of admission, regional accreditation, description of programs, curriculum, activities, learning differences grid.

ONLINE DATABASES

ERIC. Educational Resources Information Center. • Funded by the U. S. Department of Education, Institute of Education Sciences (formerly Office of Educational Research and Improvement). Provides access to more than one million online records covering education-related journal and report literature, 1966 to date. Updating is monthly. Inquire as to online cost and availability.

PERIODICALS AND NEWSLETTERS

Independent School. National Association of Independent Schools. • Three times a year. $17.50 per year. An open forum for exchange of information about elementary and secondary education in general, and independent education in particular.

STATISTICS SOURCES

Digest of Education Statistics. Available from U. S. Government Printing Office. • Annual. $51.00. Covers all areas of education from kindergarten through graduate school. Includes data from both government and private sources. Compiled by National Center for Education Statistics, U. S. Department of Education.

TRADE/PROFESSIONAL ASSOCIATIONS

National Association of Independent Schools. 1620 L St. NW, Ste. 1100, Washington, DC 20036-5695. Phone: (202)973-9700 Fax: (202)973-9790 E-mail: info@nais.org • URL: http://www.nais.org.

PRIVATIZATION

GENERAL WORKS

Does Privatization Deliver?: Highlights from a World Bank Conference. Mary M. Shirley and Ahmed Galal. The World Bank Group. • 1994. $22.00. Includes 12 international case studies on airlines, telecommunications, electric utilities, and other industries. Presents a favorable view of

privatization. (EDI Development Studies Series).

Innovation and Entrepreneurship: Practice and Principles. Peter F. Drucker. HarperInformation. • 1993. $16.95.

Privatising State-Owned Enterprises: An Overview of Policies and Practices in OECD Countries. Organization for Economic Cooperation and Development. • 2003. $35.00. Provides information on the methods, techniques, and implementation of privatization in OECD countries. Includes case examples.

ABSTRACTS AND INDEXES

Index to Legal Periodicals and Books. H. W. Wilson Co. • Monthly. $490.00 per year. Quarterly and annual cumulations.

ONLINE DATABASES

Index to Legal Periodicals and Books (Online). H. W. Wilson Co. • Broad coverage of law journals and books 1981 to date. Monthly updates. Inquire as to online cost and availability.

Legal Resource Index. Gale Cengage Learning. • Broad coverage of law literature appearing in legal, business, and other periodicals, 1980 to date. Daily updates. Inquire as to online cost and availability.

LEXIS. LEXIS-NEXIS. • The various LEXIS databases provide full text and indexing for a wide variety of legal cases, statutes, orders, and opinions.

TRADE/PROFESSIONAL ASSOCIATIONS

Citizens for a Sound Economy. 1250 H St., NW, Ste. 700, Washington, DC 20005-3908. Phone: 888-564-6273 or (202)783-3870 Fax: (202)783-4687 E-mail: cse@cse.org • URL: http://www.cse.org • Absorbed Council for a Competitive Economy and Tax Foundation.

National Council for Public-Private Partnerships. 1660 L. St., N.W., Washington, DC 20036. Phone: (202)467-6800 Fax: (202)467-6312 E-mail: ncppp@ncppp.org • URL: http://www.ncppp.org • Promotes private ownership of public services. Formerly Privitization Council, Inc.

PRIZES

See: CONTESTS, PRIZES, AND AWARDS

PROCEDURE MANUALS

See also: TECHNICAL WRITING

GENERAL WORKS

Designing the User Interface: Strategies for Effective Human-Computer Interaction. Ben Shneiderman. Addison-Wesley. • 2002. $70.00. Third edition. Provides an introduction to computer user-interface design. Covers usability testing, dialog boxes, menus, command languages, interaction devices, tutorials, printed user manuals, and related subjects.

ENCYCLOPEDIAS AND DICTIONARIES

BLR Encyclopedia of Prewritten Job Descriptions. Stephen D. Bruce. Business and Legal Reports, Inc. • $159.95. Looseleaf service. Two volumes. Covers all levels "from president to mail clerk.".

HANDBOOKS AND MANUALS

Company Policy and Personnel Workbook. Ardella Ramey. PSI Research. • 1999. $29.95. Fourth edition. Contains about 50 model company personnel policies for use as examples in developing a personnel manual. Explains the basic laws governing employee-employer relationships. (Successful Business Library Series).

How to Develop an Employee Handbook. Joseph W. Lawson. AMACOM. • 1997. $75.00. Second edition. Includes sample handbooks, personnel policy statements, and forms.

How to Research, Write, and Package Administrative Manuals. Leo R. Lunine. AMACOM. • 1985. $75.00.

How to Write Usable User Documentation. Edmond H. Weiss. Greenwood Publishing Group, Inc. • 1991. $24.95. Second edition. Shows how to explain a product, system, or procedure. Includes a glossary and a list of books and periodicals.

Writing and Designing Manuals: Operator Manuals, Service Manuals, Manuals for International Markets. Patricia A. Robinson and Ryn Etter. Lewis Publishers. • 2000. $69.95. Third edition. Includes planning, organization, format, visuals, writing strategies, and other topics.

PERIODICALS AND NEWSLETTERS

Technical Communication. Society for Technical Communication. • Quarterly. $60.00 per year. Production of technical literature.

TRADE/PROFESSIONAL ASSOCIATIONS

Society for Technical Communication. 901 N. Stuart St., Suite 904, Arlington, VA 22203-1822. Phone: (703)522-4114 Fax: (703)522-2075 E-mail: stc@stc.org • URL: http://www.stc.org • Formerly Society of Technical Writers and Publishers.

PROCESS CONTROL EQUIPMENT

See: CONTROL EQUIPMENT INDUSTRY

PROCESSED FOOD INDUSTRY

See also: FOOD INDUSTRY

ABSTRACTS AND INDEXES

Food Science and Technology Abstracts. International Food Information Service Publishing. • Monthly. $1,780.00 per year. Provides worldwide coverage of the literature of food technology and food production.

Foods Adlibra: Key to the World's Food Literature. General Mills, Inc. Foods Adlibra Publications. • Semimonthly. $240.00 per year. Provides journal citations and abstracts to the literature of food technology and packaging.

NTIS Alerts: Agriculture & Food. National Technical Information Service. • Semimonthly. $195.00 per year. Provides descriptions of government-sponsored research reports and software, with ordering information. Covers agricultural economics, horticulture, fisheries, veterinary medicine, food technology, and related subjects. Formerly *Abstract Newsletter.*

ALMANACS AND YEARBOOKS

Almanac of the Canning, Freezing, Preserving Industries, Vol. Two. Edward E. Judge and Sons, Inc. • Annual. $73.00. Contains U. S. food laws and regulations and detailed production statistics.

CD-ROM DATABASES

Food Science and Technology Abstracts [CD-ROM]. Available from SilverPlatter Information, Inc. • Quarterly. Produced by International Food Information Service (home page is http://www.ifis.org). Provides worldwide coverage on CD-ROM of the literature of food technology and production. Various types of publications are indexed, with abstracts, including about 1,800 periodicals. Time period is 1969 to date.

DIRECTORIES

BioScan: The Worldwide Biotech Industry Reporting Service. Greenwood Publishing Group, Inc. •

Annual. $975.00 per year. Bimonthly updates. Provides detailed information on over 1,000 U.S. and foreign companies broadly classified as biotechnological. In addition to medical technology and advanced pharmaceutical firms, includes firms doing research in food processing, waste management, agriculture, and veterinary science.

Food Processing Guide and Directory. Putman Media Inc. • Annual. $90.00. Lists over 5,390 food ingredient and equipment manufacturers.

Judge's Peerless Food Processors. Edward E. Judge & Sons Inc. • Covers: over 4,000 North American plants producing frozen, refrigerated, and shelf-stable foods, fruits, vegetables, juices, preserves, jams and jellies (SIC 2033); canned specialties (SIC 2032); frozen fruits and vegetables (SIC 2037); frozen specialties (SIC 2038); pickles, sauces and salad dressings (SIC 2035); canned and cured seafood (SIC 2091); fresh or frozen packaged fish (SIC 2092); refrigerated canned and frozen meat and poultry (SIC's 2013 and 2015); meat slaughtering (SIC 2011); butler (SIC 2021); cheese (SIC 2022); ice cream (SIC 2024); fluid milk and dry milk (SIC 2026, 2023). Entries include: Company name, address, phone, divisions, subsidiaries, factories, pack volume, names and titles of key personnel, container sizes, association affiliation, brands, products by factory and process. Plant SIC codes, number of employees for each plant.

Major Food and Drink Companies of the World. Available from Gale Cengage Learning. • Annual. $880.00. Two volumes. Published by Graham & Whiteside. Contains profiles and trade names for more than 9,800 important food and beverage companies in various countries. In addition to foods, includes both alcoholic and nonalcoholic drink products.

Plunkett's Food Industry Almanac. Plunkett Research Ltd. • Covers: 340 leading companies in the global food industry. Entries include: Name, address, phone, fax, and key executives. Also includes analysis and information on trends, technology, and statistics in the field.

Prepared Foods Sourcebook. Reed Business Information. • Annual. $75.00. Lists approximately 600 food and veverage companies.

Thomas Food and Beverage Market Place. Grey House Publishing. • 2004. $495.00. Three volumes. Contains more than 40,000 entries covering food companies, beverages, food equipment, warehouse companies, food brokers, wholesalers, importers, and exporters. Formerly *Thomas Food Industry Register.*

World Food Marketing Directory. Euromonitor International. • Covers: Over 2,000 retailers and wholesalers, 1,600 manufacturers, over 2,000 international and European organizations, statistical agencies, trade journals and associations, databases, and trade fairs in the grocery and food industries worldwide. Entries include: Company name, address, phone, telex, names of parent company and subsidiaries, number of employees, financial data, products and brand names handled; retailers and wholesalers include type of outlet, names and titles of key personnel.

ENCYCLOPEDIAS AND DICTIONARIES

Encyclopedia of Food Science, Food Technology, and Nutrition. Robert Macrae and others, editors. Elsevier. • 1993. Eight volumes. $3,056.00. $382.00 per volume.

Foods and Nutrition Encyclopedia. Audrey H. Ensminger and others. CRC Press, Inc. • 1993. $309.95. Second edition. Two volumes.

Wiley Encyclopedia of Food Science and Technology. Frederick J. Francis, editor. John Wiley and Sons, Inc. • 2000. $1,650.00. Second edition. Four volumes. Contains about 400 entries. Coverage includes biotechnology, genetic engineering,

nutrition, regulatory matters, food safety, labeling, food substitutes (sugar, fat, dairy), and many other topics.

ONLINE DATABASES

F & S Index. Gale Cengage Learning. • Contains about four million citations to worldwide business, financial, and industrial or consumer product literature appearing from 1972 to date. Weekly updates. Inquire as to online cost and availability.

Food Science and Technology Abstracts [online]. IFIS North American Desk. • Produced by International Food Information Service. Provides about 500,000 online citations, with abstracts, to the international literature of food science, technology, commodities, engineering, and processing. Approximately 2,000 periodicals are covered. Time period is 1969 to date, with monthly updates. Inquire as to online cost and availability.

FOODS ADLIBRA. General Mills, Inc. • Contains online citations, with abstracts, to the technical and business literature of food processing and packaging. New products and new ingredients are featured. Covers about 250 trade journals and 500 research journals from 1974 to date, with monthly updates. Inquire as to online cost and availability.

PROMT: Predicasts Overview of Markets and Technology. Gale Cengage Learning. • Companies, products, applied technologies and markets. U.S. and international literature coverage, 1972 to date. Inquire as to online cost and availability. Provides abstracts from more than 1,600 publications. Weekly updates.

PERIODICALS AND NEWSLETTERS

Food Manufacturing. Reed Business Information. • Monthly. $86.99 per year. Edited for food processing operations managers and food engineering managers. Includes end-of-year *Food Products and Equipment Literature Review.* Formerly *Food Products and Equipment.*

Food Processing. Putman Media. • Monthly. Free to qualified personnel; others, $89.00 per year. Edited for executive and operating personnel in the food processing industry.

Food Processing Newsletter. Putman Publishing Co. • Weekly. $100.00 per year. Covers food processing industry news and trends.

Journal of Food Products Marketing: Innovations in Food Advertising, Food Promotion, Food Publicity, Food Sales Promotion. Haworth Press, Inc. • Semiannual. $300.00 per year.

National Packing News. National Packing News. • Description: Discusses topics that affect the food processing industry in the nation, including production, marketing, new developments and products, new plants and plant expansions, and professional appointments. Recurring features include news of research, statistics, book reviews, and obituaries. **Remarks:** Incorporates the former Eastern Packing News and Western Packing News.

Prepared Foods. Business News Publishing Co. • Monthly. $99.90 per year. Edited for food manufacturing management, marketing, and operations personnel.

RESEARCH CENTERS AND INSTITUTES

Food Industries Center. Ohio State University, Howlett Hall, 2001 Fyffe Court, Columbus, OH 43210-1007. Phone: (614)292-7004 Fax: (614)292-4233 E-mail: bash1@osu.edu • URL: http://www.fst.ohio-state.edu.

Institute for Food Laws and Regulations. Michigan State University, 165 National Food Safety and Toxicology Ctr., East Lansing, MI 48224. Phone: (517)355-8295 • URL: http://www.iflr.msu.edu/ • Conducts research on the food industry, including processing, packaging, marketing, and new products.

Institute of Food Science. Cornell University, 114

Stocking Hall, Ithaca, NY 14853-7201. Phone: (607)255-7900 E-mail: cifs@cornell.edu • URL: http://www.nysaes.cornell.edu/cifs/ • Research areas include the chemistry and processing of food commodities, food processing engineering, food packaging, and nutrition.

National Food Processors Association Research Foundation. 1350 Eye St., N.W., Suite 300, Washington, DC 20005. Phone: (202)639-5900 Fax: (202)639-5932 E-mail: nfpa@nfpa.org • URL: http://www.nfpa-food.org • Conducts research on food processing engineering, chemistry, microbiology, sanitation, preservation aspects, and public health factors.

STATISTICS SOURCES

World Food Data and Statistics. Euromonitor International. • 2004. $650.00. Provides five-year data for a wide variety of food products in 52 countries. Includes market size, consumer expenditures, price indicators, and retail distribution data for many kinds of meat, fish, fruits, vegetables, dairy products, baked goods, condiments, canned food, and frozen food.

TRADE/PROFESSIONAL ASSOCIATIONS

Food Processors Institute. 1350 I St. NW, Washington, DC 20005-3305. Phone: 800-355-0983 or (202)639-5945 or (202)639-5945 Fax: (202)639-5932 E-mail: fpi@fpa-food.org • URL: http://www.fpi-food.org • The education provider for the National Food Processors Association, its members, and affiliates. Presents seminars and courses that support the food processing industry, and develops publications, videos, software, and other educational materials for the continuing education of food industry and related personnel. Provides custom design workshops for specific company training needs.

Food Products Association. 1350 I St. NW, Ste. 300, Washington, DC 20005. Phone: 800-355-0983 or (202)639-5900 Fax: (202)639-5932 E-mail: membership@fpa-food.org • URL: http://www.fpa-food.org • Leading authority on food science and food safety for the food industry. Members produce processed and packaged fruits and vegetables, meat and poultry, seafood, cereals, dairy products, drinks, juices, and other specialty items or provides supplies and services to food manufacturers.

PROCUREMENT, GOVERNMENT

See: GOVERNMENT PURCHASING

PRODUCE INDUSTRY

See: VEGETABLE INDUSTRY

PRODUCT CODING

See: POINT-OF-SALE SYSTEMS (POS)

PRODUCT DESIGN

See: DESIGN IN INDUSTRY

PRODUCT DEVELOPMENT

See: NEW PRODUCTS

PRODUCT LIABILITY

See: PRODUCT SAFETY AND LIABILITY

PRODUCT MANAGEMENT

See: MARKETING

PRODUCT QUALITY

See: QUALITY OF PRODUCTS

PRODUCT RATING RESEARCH

See: QUALITY OF PRODUCTS

PRODUCT SAFETY AND LIABILITY

GENERAL WORKS

Crisis Response: Inside Stories on Managing Image Under Siege. Gale Cengage Learning. • 1993. $80.00. Presents first-hand accounts by media relations professionals of major business crises and how they were handled. Topics include the following kinds of crises: environmental, governmental, corporate image, communications, and product.

Food Safety: Is Anyone Watching?. V. L. Smyth, editor. Nova Science Publishers, Inc. • 2002. $59.00. Provides material by several authors on governmental oversight of the American food industry. Includes a food safety chronology of selected events, 1992-1999.

ABSTRACTS AND INDEXES

Applied Science and Technology Index. H. W. Wilson Co. • 11 times a year. Quarterly and annual cumulations. Price varies. Indexes a wide variety of English language technical, industrial, and engineering periodicals.

Index to Legal Periodicals and Books. H. W. Wilson Co. • Monthly. $490.00 per year. Quarterly and annual cumulations.

CD-ROM DATABASES

Consumers Reference Disc. National Information Services Corp. • Quarterly. Provides the CD-ROM version of *Consumer Health and Nutrition Index* from Oryx Press and *Consumers Index to Product Evaluations and Information Sources* from Pierian Press. Contains citations to consumer health articles and consumer product evaluations, tests, warnings, and recalls.

DIRECTORIES

Directory of Certified Product Safety Managers. Board of Certified Product Safety Management. • Biennial. $15.00. Available only online. Membership directory.

HANDBOOKS AND MANUALS

Fundamentals of Product Liability Law for Engineers. Linda K. Enghagen. Industrial Press, Inc. • 1992. $39.95. Covers theories of liability, strategies for protection, defenses, and proving a case. Includes case histories.

ONLINE DATABASES

I.I.I. Data Base Search. Insurance Information Institute. • Provides online citations and abstracts of insurance-related literature in magazines, newspapers, trade journals, and books. Emphasis is on property and casualty insurance issues, including highway safety, product safety, and environmental liability. Inquire as to online cost and availability.

Index to Legal Periodicals and Books (Online). H. W. Wilson Co. • Broad coverage of law journals and books 1981 to date. Monthly updates. Inquire as to online cost and availability.

Legal Resource Index. Gale Cengage Learning. •

Broad coverage of law literature appearing in legal, business, and other periodicals, 1980 to date. Daily updates. Inquire as to online cost and availability.

LEXIS. LEXIS-NEXIS. • The various LEXIS databases provide full text and indexing for a wide variety of legal cases, statutes, orders, and opinions.

PERIODICALS AND NEWSLETTERS

Consumer Product Safety Review. Available from U. S. Government Printing Office. • Quarterly. $18.00 per year. Issued by the U. S. Consumer Product Safety Commission.

FDA Consumer. Available from U. S. Government Printing Office. • Bimonthly. $14.00 per year. Issued by the U. S. Food and Drug Administration. Provides consumer information about FDA regulations and product safety.

Pharmaceutical and Medical Device Law Bulletin. American Lawyer Media, Inc. • Monthly. $199.00 per year. Newsletter. Edited for lawyers concerned with drug product or medical device litigation. Contains industry news items of special interest, reports on new products, legal case summaries, Food and Drug Administration actions, patent issues, and related news reports. (A Law Journal Newsletter, formerly published by Leader Publications).

Product Liability Law and Strategy. American Lawyer Media, Inc. • Monthly. $189.00 per year. Newsletter. Contains product liability verdict and settlement reports, legislative proposal analysis, and strategies for both the plaintiff's counsel and the defendant's counsel. (A Law Journal Newsletter, formerly published by Leader Publications).

Product Safety Letter. Washington Business Information Inc. • Description: Follows the actions of the Consumer Product Safety Commission and other regulatory agencies and monitors developments and trends in the manufacturing industry. Offers "inside information about major regulatory trends, actions, opinions, and ideas." Spotlights stringent new rules which affect the production and sale of many common items. Recurring features include news of research and reports of meetings.

RESEARCH CENTERS AND INSTITUTES

Institute for Advanced Safety Studies. 5950 W. Touhy Ave., Niles, IL 60714. Phone: (847)647-1101 Fax: (847)647-2047 E-mail: iass@tridyne.com.

Keystone Center. Keystone Center. 1628 St. John Rd., Keystone, CO 80435. Phone: (970)513-5800 Fax: (970)262-0152 E-mail: marketing@irrc.com • URL: http://www.keystone.org • Promotes the development of effective policy and the resolution of environmental and natural resource disputes through active facilitation of policy dialogues and information exchange between individuals in the private sector, environmental community, academia, and government. Activities focus on negotiations for policies in the fields of energy, environment, and science/technology, including energy futures, international pesticides use, superfund, biotechnology regulation, toxic waste, public utilities, food safety, science and technology policy, and expanded access to therapeutic drugs.

Law and Economics Center. George Mason University, School of Law, 3401 N. Fairfax Dr., Arlington, VA 22201-4498. Phone: (703)993-8028 Fax: (703)993-8088 E-mail: fbuckley@gmu.edu • URL: http://www.lawecon.org • Research fields include product liability law.

TRADE/PROFESSIONAL ASSOCIATIONS

Board of Certified Product Safety Management. 8009 Carita Court, Bethesda, MD 20817. Phone: (301)469-0648 E-mail: info@chcm-chsp.org • URL: http://www.chcm.chsp.org • Evaluates qualifications of product safety managers. Formerly International Product Safety Management Certification Board.

National Safety Council. 1121 Spring Lake Dr.,

Itasca, IL 60143-3201. Phone: 800-621-7619 or (630)285-1121 Fax: (630)285-1613 E-mail: nrhc@nrhcweb.org • URL: http://www.nsc.org • Individuals whose professional activities are related to the safety of employees and college or university students.

The Product Liability Alliance. 1325 G St. NW, Ste. 1000, 1725 K St., NW, Ste. 300, Washington, DC 20005. Phone: (202)872-0885 Fax: (202)785-0586 E-mail: naw@naw.org • URL: http://www.naw.org • Coalition of trade associations, manufacturers, and nonmanufacturing product sellers. Seeks enactment of federal product liability tort reform legislation. Supports and coordinates members' efforts in gaining passage of a product liability law. Works with the business community to develop suggestions and guidelines for such a law.

OTHER SOURCES

Consumer Product Litigation Reporter. Andrews Publications. • Monthly. $725.00 per year. Newsletter. Provides reports on legislation and litigation relating to product liability.

Corporate Compliance Series. Joseph E. Murphy and Paul H. Dawes. West Group. • $1,210.00. 12 looseleaf volumes. Covers criminal and civil liability problems for corporations. Includes employee safety, product liability, pension requirements, securities violations, equal employment opportunity issues, intellectual property, employee hiring and firing, and other corporate compliance topics.

Pharmaceutical Litigation Reporter: The National Journal of Record of Pharmaceutical Litigation. Andrews Publications. • Monthly. $775.00 per year. Newsletter. Reports on a wide variety of legal cases involving the pharmaceutical and medical device industries. Includes product liability lawsuits.

Product Liability. American Lawyer Media, Inc. • Looseleaf. $169.00. Updated as needed. Covers product liability litigation as viewed by both the plaintiff and the defendant. Provides detailed discussion of pre-trial and trial procedures. (Law Journal Press).

PRODUCT TESTING

See: QUALITY OF PRODUCTS

PRODUCTION CONTROL

See also: INVENTORY CONTROL; QUALITY CONTROL

ENCYCLOPEDIAS AND DICTIONARIES

Blackwell Encyclopedic Dictionary of Operations Management. Nigel Slack, editor. Blackwell Publishing. • 1997. $130.95. The editor is associated with the University of Warwick, England. Contains definitions of key terms combined with longer articles written by various U. S. and foreign business educators. Includes bibliographies and index. (Blackwell Encyclopedia of Management Series.).

HANDBOOKS AND MANUALS

Production and Inventory Control Handbook. James H. Greene. McGraw-Hill. • 1997. $95.00. Third edition.

Production and Operations Management: Total Quality and Responsiveness. Hamid Noori and Russell Radford. McGraw-Hill. • 1994. $70.25.

PERIODICALS AND NEWSLETTERS

Production. Gardner Publications, Inc. • Monthly. $48.00 per year. Covers the latest manufacturing management issues. Discusses the strategic and financial implications of various tecnologies as they impact factory management, quality and competitiveness.

Production and Inventory Management Journal. A P I C S: The Educational Society for Resource Management. • Quarterly. Members, $64.00 per year; non-members, $80.00 per year.

TRADE/PROFESSIONAL ASSOCIATIONS

APICS-The Educational Society for Resource Management. 5301 Shawnee Rd., Alexandria, VA 22312-2317. Phone: 800-444-2742 or (703)354-8851 Fax: (703)354-8106 E-mail: webmaster@apicshq.org • URL: http://www.apics.org • Members are professional resource managers.

OTHER SOURCES

Federal Income Taxation of Inventories. LexisNexis Matthew Bender. • Semiannual. $838.00 per year. Three looseleaf volumes.

PRODUCTION ENGINEERING

See: INDUSTRIAL ENGINEERING

PRODUCTION MANAGEMENT

See: OPERATIONS MANAGEMENT

PRODUCTIVITY

GENERAL WORKS

Chaos on the Shop Floor: A Worker's View of Quality, Productivity, and Management. Tom Juravich. Temple University Press. • 1988. $19.95. (Labor and Social Change Series).

Participative Management: An Analysis of Its Affect on Productivity. Michael H. Swearingen. Garland Publishing, Inc. • 1997. $35.00. (Garland Studies on Industrial Productivity).

Profit Sharing: Does It Make a Difference? The Productivity and Stability Effects of Profit Sharing Plans. Douglas L. Kruse. W. E. Upjohn Institute for Employment Research. • 1993. $37.00.

Reengineering Management: The Mandate for New Leadership. James Champy. DIANE Publishing Co. • 1998. $25.00.

Reengineering the Corporation: A Manifesto for Business Revolution. Michael Hammer and James Champy. HarperInformation. • 2001. $16.00. Revised edition.

ABSTRACTS AND INDEXES

NTIS Alerts: Manufacturing Technology. National Technical Information Service. • Semimonthly. $265.00 per year. Provides descriptions of government-sponsored research reports and software, with ordering information. Covers computer-aided design and manufacturing (CAD/CAM), engineering materials, quality control, machine tools, robots, lasers, productivity, and related subjects. Formerly *Abstract Newsletter.*

ENCYCLOPEDIAS AND DICTIONARIES

Blackwell Encyclopedic Dictionary of Organizational Behavior. Nigel Nicholson, editor. Blackwell Publishing. • 1997. $130.95. The editor is associated with the London Business School. Contains definitions of key terms combined with longer articles written by various U. S. and foreign business educators. Includes bibliographies and index. *Blackwell Encyclopedia of Management Series.*

HANDBOOKS AND MANUALS

AMA Management Handbook. John J. Hampton, editor. AMACOM. • 1994. $110.00. Third edition.

Provides 200 chapters in 16 major subject areas. Covers a wide variety of business and industrial management topics.

Reengineering Revolution: A Handbook. Michael Hammer and Steven Stanton. HarperInformation. • 1995. $17.95.

INTERNET DATABASES

Summary of Commentary on Current Economic Conditions by Federal Reserve District [the Beige Book]. Board of Governors of the Federal Reserve System. Phone: (202)452-3000 Fax: (202)452-3819 • URL: http://www.federalreserve.gov/fomc/beigebook/2004/ • Free Web site provides current "anecdotal information" eight times a year on economic conditions within each of the 12 Federal Reserve Districts, plus an extensive national *Summary.* Text is based on the opinions of bank officials, business executives, economists, financial market experts, and others. Typically contains views of consumer spending, manufacturing, services, credit, employment, prices, wages, and the economy in general. Usually referred to as the Beige Book.

ONLINE DATABASES

Business and Industry. Gale Cengage Learning. • Contains online citations, abstracts, and selected fulltext from more than 1,000 trade journals, newspapers, and other publications. Provides general coverage of both manufacturing and service industries, including marketing, production, industry trends, key events, and information on specific companies. Time span is 1994 to date. Daily updates. Inquire as to online cost and availability. (Also available in a CD-ROM version.).

Management Contents. Gale Cengage Learning. • Covers a wide range of management, financial, marketing, personnel, and administrative topics. About 150 leading business journals are indexed and abstracted from 1974 to date, with monthly updating. Inquire as to online cost and availability.

Tablebase. Gale Cengage Learning. • Provides online numerical tabular data from a wide variety of business, organization, and government sources, including about 1,000 trade journals. Includes industry and individual company statistics relating to products, market share, sales forecasts, production, exports, market trends, etc. Time span is 1997 to date. Weekly updates. Inquire as to online cost and availability. (Also available in a CD-ROM version.).

PERIODICALS AND NEWSLETTERS

Lean Manufacturing Advisor: Techniques and Technologies Supporting Lean Manufacturing and TPM. Productivity, Inc. • Monthly. $167.00 per year. Formerly Productivity.

Motivational Manager: Strategies to Increase Morale and Productivity in the Workplace. Lawrence Ragan Communications, Inc. • Monthly. $119.00 per year. Newsletter. Emphasis is on participative management.

RESEARCH CENTERS AND INSTITUTES

Center for Quality and Productivity. University of North Texas, College of Business Administration, P.P. Box 305249, Denton, TX 76203-3677. Phone: (940)565-4767 E-mail: prybutok@unt.edu • URL: http://www.coba.unt.edu • Fields of research include the management of quality systems and statistical methodology.

Center for Quality and Productivity Improvement. University of Wisconsin-Madison, 610 N. Walnut St., 575 WARF Bldg., Madison, WI 53705. Phone: (608)263-2520 Fax: (608)263-1425 E-mail: quality@engr.wisc.edu • URL: http://www.engr.wisc.edu/centers/cqpi • Research areas include quality management and industrial engineering.

W. E. Upjohn Institute for Employment Research. 300 S. Westnedge Ave., Kalamazoo, MI 49007-

4686. Phone: (616)343-5541 Fax: (616)343-3308
E-mail: eberts@we.upjohninst.org • URL: http://
www.upjohninst.org • Research fields include
unemployment, unemployment insurance, worker's
compensation, labor productivity, profit sharing, the
labor market, economic development, earnings,
training, and other areas related to employment.

STATISTICS SOURCES

*Economic Report of the President: Together with the
Annual Report of the Council of Economic Advisors.*
Available from U. S. Government Printing Office. •
Annual. $32.00. Includes about 130 pages of
"Statistical Tables Relating to Income, Employment,
and Production." Tables cover national income,
employment, wages, productivity, manufacturing,
prices, credit, finance (public and private), corporate
profits, and foreign trade.

*Handbook of U. S. Labor Statistics: Employment,
Earnings, Prices, Productivity, and Other Labor
Data.* Eva E. Jacobs, editor. Bernan Associates. •
1999. $74.00. Based on *Handbook of Labor
Statistics,* formerly issued by the Bureau of Labor
Statistics, U. S. Department of Labor. Includes the
Bureau's projections of employment in the U. S. by
industry and occupation. Provides a wide variety of
data on the work force, prices, fringe benefits, and
consumer expenditures.

Key Indicators of the Labour Market. Available
from Routledge. • Biennial. $125.00. Published by
the International Labour Office (http://www.ilo.org).
Provides data on 20 key indicators in 220 countries.
Includes labor force statistics, employment,
unemployment, part-time workers, wages,
productivity, poverty indicators, and related topics.

Report on the American Workforce. Available from
U. S. Government Printing Office. • Annual. Issued
by the U. S. Department of Labor (http://www.dol.
gov). Appendix contains tabular statistics, including
employment, unemployment, price indexes,
consumer expenditures, employee benefits (retirement, insurance, vacation, etc.), wages, productivity, hours of work, and occupational injuries. Annual
figures are shown for up to 50 years.

*Services: Statistics on Value Added and
Employment.* Organization for Economic Cooperation and Development. • 2000. $69.00. Provides 10-
year data on service industry employment and
output (value added) for all OECD countries. Covers such industries as telecommunications, business
services, and information technology services.

TRADE/PROFESSIONAL ASSOCIATIONS

National Association of Professional Organizers.
4700 W Lake Ave., Glenview, IL 60025. Phone:
(847)375-4746 Fax: (847)734-9236 E-mail: hq@
napo.net • URL: http://www.napo.net • Members
are concerned with time management, productivity,
and the efficient organization of documents and
activities. Formerly Association of Professional
Organizers.

PRODUCTS, NEW

See: NEW PRODUCTS

PRODUCTS, QUALITY OF

See: QUALITY OF PRODUCTS

PROFESSIONAL
ASSOCIATIONS

See: ASSOCIATIONS

PROFESSIONAL
CORPORATIONS

See also: CORPORATIONS

ABSTRACTS AND INDEXES

Index to Legal Periodicals and Books. H. W. Wilson
Co. • Monthly. $490.00 per year. Quarterly and an-
nual cumulations.

HANDBOOKS AND MANUALS

*How to Incorporate: A Handbook for Entrepreneurs
and Professionals.* Michael Diamond and Julia L.
Williams. John Wiley and Sons, Inc. • 2000. $24.95.
Fourth edition.

Professional Corporations and Associations. Berrien C. Eaton. LexisNexis Matthew Bender. •
Semiannual. $1,432.00 per year. Six looseleaf
volumes. Detailed information on forming, operating and changing a professional corporation or
association.

*Valuing Professional Practices: A Practitioner's
Guide.* Robert Reilly and Robert Schweihs. CCH,
Inc. • 1997. $99.00. Provides a basic introduction to
estimating the dollar value of practices in various
professional fields.

ONLINE DATABASES

Legal Resource Index. Gale Cengage Learning. •
Broad coverage of law literature appearing in legal,
business, and other periodicals, 1980 to date. Daily
updates. Inquire as to online cost and availability.

PERIODICALS AND NEWSLETTERS

Business Strategies Bulletin. CCH Inc. • Description: Reports tax and business planning information
for all sizes of business, with emphasis on small to
mid-sized business advisors.

OTHER SOURCES

Business Strategies. CCH, Inc. • Semimonthly.
$795.00 per year. Four looseleaf volumes.
Semimonthly updates. Legal, tax, and accounting
aspects of business planning and decision-making.
Provides information on start-ups, forms of ownership (partnerships, corporations), failing businesses,
reorganizations, acquisitions, and so forth. Includes
Business Strategies Bulletin, a monthly newsletter.

PROFESSIONAL LIABILITY

GENERAL WORKS

Professional Liability: An Economic Analysis.
Roger Bowles and Philip Jones. Macmillan Publish-
ing Co., Inc. • 1989. $14.00. (David Hume Papers:
No. 11).

ABSTRACTS AND INDEXES

*Current Law Index: Multiple Access to Legal
Periodicals.* Gale Cengage Learning. • Monthly.
$725.00 per year. Produced in cooperation with the
American Association of Law Libraries. Indexes
more than 900 law journals, legal newspapers, and
specialty publications from the U.S., Canada, U.K.,
Ireland, Australia, and New Zealand.

Index to Legal Periodicals and Books. H. W. Wilson
Co. • Monthly. $490.00 per year. Quarterly and an-
nual cumulations.

BIBLIOGRAPHIES

Encyclopedia of Legal Information Sources. Gale
Cengage Learning. • 1992. $180.00. Second edition.
Lists more than 23,000 law-related information
sources, including print, nonprint, and
organizational.

CD-ROM DATABASES

Authority Health Care Law Library. LexisNexis/
Matthew Bender. • Periodic updates. Price on
request. Full text CD-ROM provides legal information, case law, and analysis relating to health care

facilities, health insurance, longterm care, Medigap,
and Medicare.

LegalTrac. Gale Cengage Learning. • Monthly.
$5,000.00 per year. Price includes workstation.
Provides CD-ROM indexing of periodical literature
relating to legal matters from 1980 to date. Corresponds to online *Legal Resource Index.*

*WILSONDISC: Index to Legal Periodicals and
Books.* H. W. Wilson Co. • Monthly. Includes
unlimited online access to *Index to Legal
Periodicals* through WILSONLINE. Contains CD-
ROM indexing of more than 1,400 English language
legal periodicals from 1981 to date and 2,500 books.

DIRECTORIES

*Insurance Marketplace: The Agents and Brokers
Guide to Non-Standard and Special ty Lines, Aviation, Marine and International Insurance.* The
Rough Notes Co., Inc. • Annual. Included in
subscription to*Rough Notes Magazine*; others, $15.
95. Lists specialty, excess, and surplus insurance
lines.

Law and Legal Information Directory. Gale Cengage Learning. • Annual. $440.00. Contains a wide
range of sources of legal information, such as associations, law schools, courts, federal agencies,
referral services, libraries, publishers, and research
centers. There is a separate chapter for each of 23
types of information source or service.

*Physician Insurers Association of America:
Membership Directory.* Physician Insurers Association of America. • Annual. $25.00. Lists 60 coopera-
tive physicians' professional liability insurers affiliated with state medical societies.

HANDBOOKS AND MANUALS

Accountants' Liability. Practising Law Institute. •
$160.00. Covers all aspects of accountants' profes-
sional liability issues, including depositions and
court cases.

*Codes of Professional Responsibility: Ethic
Standards in Business, Health and Law.* Rena Gorlin, editor. BNA, Inc. • 1999. $95.00. Fourth edition.
Contains full text or substantial excerpts of the official codes of ethics of major professional groups in
the fields of law, business, and health care.

*How to Avoid Liability: The Information Profession-
als' Guide to Negligence and Warrant Risks.* T. R.
Halvorson. Burwell Enterprises. • 1998. $24.50.
Second edition. Provides legal advice, cases, and
decisions relating to information brokers and others
in the information business.

*Legal Liability Problems in Cyberspace: Craters in
the Information Highway.* T. R. Halvorson. Burwell
Enterprises. • 1998. $24.50. Covers the legal risks
and liabilities involved in doing online research as a
paid professional. Includes a table of cases.

Medical Malpractice. David W. Louisell and Harold
Williams. LexisNexis Matthew Bender. • $1,063.
00. Five looseleaf volumes. Periodic
supplementation.

INTERNET DATABASES

Lexis.com Research System. Lexis-Nexis Group.
Phone: 800-227-4908 or (937)865-6800 Fax:
(937)865-6909 E-mail: webmaster@prod.lexis-
nexis.com • URL: http://www.lexis.com • Fee-
based Web site offers extensive searching of a wide
variety of legal sources. Additional features include
Daily Opinion Service, lexis.com Bookstore, Career
Center, CLE Center, Law Schools, and Practice
Pages ("Pages specific to areas of specialty").

ONLINE DATABASES

Index to Legal Periodicals and Books (Online). H.
W. Wilson Co. • Broad coverage of law journals and
books 1981 to date. Monthly updates. Inquire as to
online cost and availability.

Legal Resource Index. Gale Cengage Learning. •
Broad coverage of law literature appearing in legal,

business, and other periodicals, 1980 to date. Daily updates. Inquire as to online cost and availability.

PERIODICALS AND NEWSLETTERS

Healthcare Risk Management. American Health Consultants Inc. • Description: Analyzes specific legal cases and trends relevant to healthcare liability. Discusses malpractice, liability for patients, staff and visitor injury, injury prevention, biomedical engineering, and medical staff credentials. Also covers high-risk areas of hospitals, hospital-owned home health and physician practices, accreditation, Medicare reimbursement, physician liability, medical records, and claims management. Recurring features include interviews, statistics, news of research, guest columns, legal briefs, and commentaries.

Medical Economics. Advanstar Medical. • Semimonthly. $109.00 per year. Covers the financial, economic, insurance, administrative, and other non-clinical aspects of private medical practice. Provides investment and estate planning advice.

Medical Economics General Surgery-Orthopedic Surgery. Thomson Medical Economics. • Monthly. $65.00 per year. Provides information and advice on practice management (non-clinical) for surgeons. Formerly *Medical Economics for Surgeons.*

Medical Malpractice Law and Strategy. American Lawyer Media, Inc. • Monthly. $189.00 per year. Newsletter. Covers malpractice legal issues for lawyers representing physicians and for lawyers representing patients. Includes news of judicial, legislative, and medical developments affecting malpractice strategies. (A Law Journal Newsletter, formerly published by Leader Publications).

Professional Negligence Law Reporter. American Association for Justice. • Description: Covers professional negligence cases, including verdicts, settlements, and court opinions. Coverage focuses on health care providers, accountants, lawyers, engineers, insurance brokers and nursing homes, among other areas. Recurring features include by-lined articles, bibliographies, and indexes.

TRADE/PROFESSIONAL ASSOCIATIONS

American Board of Professional Liability Attorneys. 5712 244th St., Douglaston, NY 11362. Phone: (718)631-1400 Fax: (717)631-1456 E-mail: abpla03@aol.com • URL: http://www.abpla.org • Members are liability litigation lawyers who meet specific requirements as to experience and who pass written and oral Board examinations.

Defense Research Institute. 150 N Michigan Ave., Ste. 300, Chicago, IL 60601. Phone: 800-667-8108 or (312)795-1101 Fax: (312)795-0747 E-mail: dri@dri.org • URL: http://www.dri.org • Lawyers, claims people, adjusters, insurance companies, trade associations, corporations, and "target" defendants in civil litigation, such as doctors, pharmacists, engineers, manufacturers, and other professional and skilled personnel. Seeks to increase the knowledge and improve the skills of defense lawyers and to improve the adversary system of justice. Maintains research facilities, including files of speeches, briefs, and names of expert witnesses in various fields. Maintains Expert Witness Index.

Insurance Services Office (ISO). 545 Washington Blvd., Jersey City, NJ 07310-1686. Phone: 800-888-4476 or (201)469-2000 Fax: (201)748-1472 E-mail: info@iso.com • URL: http://www.iso.com • Provides statistical, actuarial, underwriting, and claims information to property and casualty insurance companies.

Physician Insurers Association of America. 2275 Research Blvd., Ste. 250, Rockville, MD 20850. Phone: (301)947-9000 Fax: (301)947-9090 E-mail: ahorwich@thepiaa.org • URL: http://www.thepiaa.org • Members are cooperative physicians' professional liability insurers affiliated with state medical societies.

OTHER SOURCES

Andrews' Professional Liability Litigation Reporter. Andrews Publications. • Monthly. $550.00 per year. Provides reports on lawsuits against attorneys, accountants, and investment professionals.

Avoiding Tax Malpractice. CCH, Inc. • 2000. $75.00. Covers malpractice considerations for professional tax practitioners.

Citation: Current Legal Developments Relating to Medicine and Allied Professions. American Medical Association, Health Law Div. Citation Publishing Corp. • Semimonthly. $130.00 per year. Newsletter. Contains summaries of lawsuits affecting medical personnel or hospitals.

Corporate Officers and Directors Liability Litigation Reporter: The Twice Monthly National Journal of Record of Litigation Based on Fiduciary Responsibility. Andrews Publications. • Semimonthly. $890.00 per year. Newsletter. Provides reports on lawsuits in the area of corporate officers' fiduciary responsibility.

Directors and Officers Liability: Prevention, Insurance, and Indemnification. American Lawyer Media, Inc. • Looseleaf. $179.00. Updated as needed. Covers the legal risks faced by corporate directors and officers. (Law Journal Press).

Hospital Liability. American Lawyer Media, Inc. • Looseleaf. $189.00. Updated as needed. Written for attorneys representing either hospitals or patients of hospitals. Covers a wide variety of legal topics relating to hospital/physician malpractice, including the expansion of HMO liability. (Law Journal Press).

PROFESSIONAL PRACTICE MANAGEMENT, MEDICAL

See: MEDICAL ECONOMICS (PRACTICE MANAGEMENT)

PROFESSIONS

See: OCCUPATIONS

PROFESSORS AND INSTRUCTORS

See: COLLEGE FACULTIES

PROFIT SHARING

See also: EMPLOYEE BENEFIT PLANS

GENERAL WORKS

Profit Sharing: Does It Make a Difference? The Productivity and Stability Effects of Profit Sharing Plans. Douglas L. Kruse. W. E. Upjohn Institute for Employment Research. • 1993. $37.00.

ENCYCLOPEDIAS AND DICTIONARIES

Dictionary of Finance and Investment Terms. John Downes. Barron's Educational Series, Inc. • 2002. $14.95. Sixth edition. Provides clear explanations of more than 5,000 business, banking, financial, investment, and tax terms. Includes a separate list of financial abbreviations and acronyms. (Business Dictionaries Series).

HANDBOOKS AND MANUALS

Pension and Profit Sharing Plans for Small or Medium Size Businesses. Aspen Publishers, Inc. • Monthly. $191.50 per year. Newsletter. Topics of interest and concern to professionals who serve small and medium size pension and profit sharing plans.

PERIODICALS AND NEWSLETTERS

Profit Sharing. Profit Sharing-401(K) Council of America. • Bimonthly. Membership.

RESEARCH CENTERS AND INSTITUTES

W. E. Upjohn Institute for Employment Research. 300 S. Westnedge Ave., Kalamazoo, MI 49007-4686. Phone: (616)343-5541 Fax: (616)343-3308 E-mail: eberts@we.upjohninst.org • URL: http://www.upjohninst.org • Research fields include unemployment, unemployment insurance, worker's compensation, labor productivity, profit sharing, the labor market, economic development, earnings, training, and other areas related to employment.

TRADE/PROFESSIONAL ASSOCIATIONS

Profit Sharing/401(K) Council of America. 10 S. Riverside Plaza, No. 1610, Chicago, IL 60606-3802. Phone: (312)441-8550 Fax: (312)441-8559 E-mail: psca@psca.org • URL: http://www.psca.org • Members are business firms with profit sharing and/or 401(K) plans. Affiliated with the Profit Sharing/401(K) Education Foundation. Formerly Profit Sharing Council of America.

Profit Sharing/401(K) Education Foundation. 10 S. Riverside Plaza, Chicago, IL 60606-3802. Phone: (312)441-8550 Fax: (312)441-8559 E-mail: psca@psca.org • URL: http://www.psca.org • Affiliated with Profit Sharing/401(k) Council of America. Formerly Profit Sharing Research Foundation.

PROGRAM EVALUATION AND REVIEW TECHNIQUE

See: CRITICAL PATH METHOD/PERT (PROGRAM EVALUATION AND REVIEW TECHNIQUE)

PROGRAMMED LEARNING

PERIODICALS AND NEWSLETTERS

Educational Technology: The Magazine for Managers of Change in Education. Educational Technology Publications, Inc. • Bimonthly. $139.00 per year.

Innovations in Education and Training International. Association for Education and Training Technology. Routledge. • Quarterly. Individuals, $81.00 per year; libraries and other institutions, $290.00 per year. Provides up-to-date coverage of educational and training technologies. Formerly *Educational and Training Technology International.*

TRADE/PROFESSIONAL ASSOCIATIONS

International Society for Performance Improvement. 1400 Spring St., Suite 260, Silver Spring, MD 20910. Phone: (310)587-8570 Fax: (310)587-8573 E-mail: info@ispi.org • URL: http://www.ispi.org • Formerly National Society for Performance and Instruction.

PROGRAMMING, COMPUTER

See: COMPUTER SOFTWARE INDUSTRY

PROGRAMMING, LINEAR

See: LINEAR PROGRAMMING

PROGRAMS, TELEVISION

See: TELEVISION PROGRAMS

PROJECT MANAGEMENT

See also: INDUSTRIAL MANAGEMENT

GENERAL WORKS

Essentials of Project Management. Dennis Lock. Ashgate Publishing Co. • 2000. $29.95. Second edition. Published by Gower in England.

Fundamentals of Project Management. James P. Lewis. AMACOM. • 2001. Second edition. Price on application.

Project Leadership. James P. Lewis. McGraw-Hill. • 2002. $29.95. Provides detailed advice for project managers in a leadership role. (Teach Yourself Series).

Project Management. Dennis Lock. John Wiley and Sons, Inc. • 2000. $87.95. Seventh edition.

Project Management Casebook. David I. Cleland and others, editors. Project Management Institute. • 1998. $69.95. Provides 50 case studies in various areas of project management.

CD-ROM DATABASES

Annotated Bibliography of Project and Team Management. Project Management Institute. • Provides citations and annotations on CD-ROM for selected project management literature since 1956.

WILSONDISC: Business Periodicals Index. H. W. Wilson Co. • Monthly. Provides CD-ROM indexing of business periodicals from 1982 to date. Price includes online service.

HANDBOOKS AND MANUALS

AMA Management Handbook. John J. Hampton, editor. AMACOM. • 1994. $110.00. Third edition. Provides 200 chapters in 16 major subject areas. Covers a wide variety of business and industrial management topics.

Effective Project Management: How to Plan, Manage, and Deliver a Project on Time and Within Budget. Robert K. Wysocki and others. John Wiley and Sons, Inc. • 2000. $60.00. Second edition. Selected by the Project Management Institute (PMI) as a reference for the Project Management Professional Certification Examination. Includes CD-ROM.

Field Guide to Project Management. David I. Cleland. John Wiley and Sons, Inc. • 1998. $39.95. Provides 38 articles by various authors on the major aspects of project management.

Gower Handbook of Project Management. J. Rodney Turner and Stephen J. Simister. Ashgate Publishing Co. • 2000. $144.95. Third edition. Consists of chapters written by various authors, with bibliographical references and index. Published by Gower in England.

Guide to the Project Management Body of Knowledge. Project Management Institute Staff. Project Management Institute. • 2004. Price on application. Presents the fundamental tenets of project management. Covers the management of integration, scope, time, cost, quality, human resources, communications, risk, and procurement. Includes an extensive glossary. (Trial Lawyer's Series: Vol. 2).

Human Resource Skills for the Project Manager: The Human Aspects of Project Management, Volume Two. Vijay K. Verma. Project Management Institute. • 1996. $32.95. (Human Aspects of Project Management Series).

Little Black Book of Project Management. Michael C. Thomsett. AMACOM. • 2002 $15.00. Second Edition. Gives practical advice on the day-to-day management of new projects, including budgeting and scheduling. (Little Black Book Series).

Managing High-Technology Programs and Projects. Russell D. Archibald. John Wiley and Sons, Inc. • 2003. $100.00. Third edition. Written

for senior executives, professional project managers, engineers, and information systems managers.

Managing the Project Team: The Human Aspects of Project Management, Volume Three. Vijay K. Verma. Project Management Institute. • 1997. $32.95. (Human Aspects of Project Management Series: Vol. 3).

Organizing Projects for Success: The Human Aspects of Project Management, Volume One. Vijay K. Verma. Project Management Institute. • 1995. $32.95. (Human Aspects of Project Management Series: Vol. 1).

PMI Book of Project Management Forms. Project Management Institute. • 1997. $49.95. Contains more than 100 sample forms for use in project management. Includes checklists, reports, charts, agreements, schedules, requisitions, order forms, and other documents.

Principles of Project Management: Collected Handbooks from the Project Management Institute. John R. Adams and others. Project Management Institute. • 1997. $59.95. Consists of reprints of eight "handbooks" by various authors, previously published by the Project Management Institute. Includes such topics as contract administration, conflict management, team building, and coping with stress.

Project Management: A Managerial Approach. Jack R. Meredith and Samuel J. Mantel. John Wiley and Sons, Inc. • 2002. $109.95. Fifth edition. (Productions-Operations Management Series).

Project Management: A Systems Approach to Planning, Scheduling, and Controlling. Harold Kerzner. John Wiley & Sons, Inc. • 2003. $80.00. Eighth edition. Includes chapters on time management, risk management, quality management, and program evaluation and review techniques (PERT). (Industrial Engineering Series).

Project Management Essential Library. Management Concepts, Inc. • 2002. $190.00. Consists of 11 separate books by various authors, covering many project management topics, including leadership, value determination, risk management, estimating, scheduling, results measurement, and quality control. (Books are available individually at $24.95.).

Project Management: How to Plan and Manage Successful Projects. Joan Knutson and Others. AMACOM. • 1991. $55.00. Covers both technical and organizational skills.

Project Management: Strategic Design and Implementation. David I. Cleland and Lewis R. Ireland. McGraw-Hill. • 2002. $64.95. Fourth edition.

Project Manager's Desk Reference: A Comprehensive Guide to Project Planning, Evaluation and Control. James P. Lewis. McGraw-Hill. • 1999. $70.00. Second edition. Includes scheduling with PERT (Program Evaluation and Review Technique), CPM (Critical Path Method), and Gantt schedules. Covers the steps for "planning, monitoring, and controlling any project.".

ONLINE DATABASES

Management Contents. Gale Cengage Learning. • Covers a wide range of management, financial, marketing, personnel, and administrative topics. About 150 leading business journals are indexed and abstracted from 1974 to date, with monthly updating. Inquire as to online cost and availability.

Wilson Business Abstracts Online. H. W. Wilson Co. • Indexes and abstracts 600 major business periodicals, plus the *Wall Street Journal* and the business section of the *New York Times.* Indexing is from 1982, abstracting from 1990, with the two newspapers included from 1993. Updated weekly. Inquire as to online cost and availability. (*Business*

Periodicals Index without abstracts is also available online.).

PERIODICALS AND NEWSLETTERS

Journal of Structured and Project Finance. Institutional Investor, Inc., Journals Group. • Quarterly. $365.00 per year. Includes print and online editions. Covers the financing of large-scale construction projects, such as power plants and convention centers. Formerly *Journal of Project Finance.*

Project Management Journal. Project Management Institute. • Four times a year. Membership. Contains technical articles dealing with the interests of the field of project management.

STATISTICS SOURCES

Project Management Salary Survey. Project Management Institute. • Annual. $129.00. Gives compensation data for key project management positions in North America, according to job title, level of responsibility, number of employees supervised, and various other factors. Includes data on retirement plans and benefits.

TRADE/PROFESSIONAL ASSOCIATIONS

Project Management Institute. 14 Campus Blvd., Newtown Square, PA 19073-3299. (610)356-4600 Fax: (610)356-4647 E-mail: customercare@pmi.org • URL: http://www.pmi.org • Corporations and individuals engaged in the practice of project management; project management students and educators. Seeks to advance the study, teaching, and practice of project management. Establishes project management standards; conducts educational and professional certification courses; bestows Project Management Professional credential upon qualified individuals. Offers educational seminars and global congresses.

PROMOTION

See: SALES PROMOTION

PROMOTIONAL MERCHANDISE

See: PREMIUMS

PROOFREADING

See: PRINTING STYLE MANUALS

PROPANE AND BUTANE GAS INDUSTRY

See also: NATURAL GAS; PETROLEUM INDUSTRY

CD-ROM DATABASES

Environment Abstracts on CD-ROM. LEXIS-NEXIS. • Quarterly. $1,295.00 per year. Contains the following CD-ROM databases: *Environment Abstracts, Energy Abstracts,* and *Acid Rain Abstracts.* Length of coverage varies.

FINANCIAL RATIOS

Annual Statement Studies. The Risk Management Association. • Annual. Median and quartile financial ratios are given for over 400 kinds of manufacturing, wholesale, retail, construction, and consumer finance establishments. Data is sorted by both asset size and sales volume. Includes a clearly written "Definition of Ratios" and an alphabetical industry index.

Annual Statement Studies: Industry Default Probabilities and Cash Flow Measures. The Risk

Management Association. • Annual. $145.00. Serves as a companion volume to the original *Annual Statement Studies*. Gives probability of default estimates on a percentage scale for more than 450 industries. Includes changes in position year-by-year for eight financial statement line items and provides percentage measures of cash flow.

HANDBOOKS AND MANUALS

Modern Petroleum Technology. Richard A. Dawe, editor. John Wiley and Sons, Inc. • 2000. $600.00. Sixth edition. Two volumes. Volume one, entitled *Upstream,* covers oil rigs and other means of obtaining raw petroleum. Volume two, *Downstream,* covers petroleum refining and end products. Edited for industry technicians, managers, and engineers.

PERIODICALS AND NEWSLETTERS

Butane-Propane News. Butane-Propane News, Inc. • Monthly. Qualified personnel, $30.00 per year.

LP-GAS. Elsevier. • Monthly. $33.00 per year. Covers the production, storage, utilization, and marketing of liquefied petroleum gas (propane). Gas appliances are included. Includes *Annual Supplement.*

Oil Daily: Daily Newspaper of the Petroleum Industry. Energy Intelligence Group, Inc. • Daily. Email, $1,595.00 per year; fax, $2,395.00 per year, online, $1,495.00 per year. Newspaper for the petroleum industry.

STATISTICS SOURCES

Gas Facts: A Statistical Record of the Gas Utility Industry. American Gas Association, Dept. of Statistics. • Annual. Members, $40.00; non-members, $80.00.

Petroleum Supply Annual. Available from U. S. Government Printing Office. • Annual. $78.00. Two volumes. Produced by the Energy Information Administration, U. S. Department of Energy. Contains worldwide data on the petroleum industry and petroleum products.

Petroleum Supply Monthly. Available from U. S. Government Printing Office. • Monthly. Produced by the Energy Information Administration, U. S. Department of Energy. Provides worldwide statistics on a wide variety of petroleum products. Covers production, supplies, exports and imports, transportation, refinery operations, and other aspects of the petroleum industry.

TRADE/PROFESSIONAL ASSOCIATIONS

Gas Technology Institute. 1700 S Mt. Prospect Rd., Des Plaines, IL 60018-1804. Phone: (847)768-0500 Fax: (847)768-0501 E-mail: businessdevelopmentinfo@gastechnology.org • URL: http://www.gastechnology.org • Educational and research facility sponsored by companies engaged in the production, processing, transmission, and distribution of natural gas and related fuels; engineering firms; large energy consumers. Conducts contract research for government and industry in the field of non-nuclear energy technology. Offers short courses in gas production, transmission, distribution, economics, and marketing. Sponsors symposia on current topics in non-nuclear energy.

National Propane Gas Association. 1150 17th St. NW, Ste. 310, Washington, DC 20036-4623. Phone: (202)466-7200 Fax: (202)466-7205 E-mail: info@npga.org • URL: http://www.npga.org • Represents the propane industry, including small businesses and large corporations engaged in the retail marketing of propane gas and appliances, producers and wholesalers of propane gas and equipment, manufacturers and fabricators of propane gas cylinders and tanks, propane transporters, and manufacturer's representatives. Works to promote the safe and increased use of propane; advocates in Congress and federal regulatory agencies for favorable environment for production, distributing, and marketing of propane gas. Develops safety standards

and training materials for the safe use and distribution of propane gas.

PROPERTY AND LIABILITY INSURANCE

See also: CASUALTY INSURANCE; FIRE INSURANCE; INSURANCE; MARINE INSURANCE; PROFESSIONAL LIABILITY; RISK MANAGEMENT

GENERAL WORKS

Property and Liability Insurance. Solomon S. Huebner and Kenneth Black. Prentice Hall PTR. • 2000. $72.00. Fourth edition.

Smarter Insurance Solutions. Janet Bamford. Bloomberg. • 1996. $19.95. Provides practical advice to consumers, with separate chapters on the following kinds of insurance: automobile, homeowners, health, disability, and life. (Bloomberg Personal Bookshelf Series).

ABSTRACTS AND INDEXES

Insurance Periodicals Index. Specials Libraries Association, Insurance and Employees Benefits Div. NILS Publishing Co. • Annual. $250.00. Compiled by the Insurance and Employee Benefits Div., Special Libraries Association. A yearly index of over 15,000 articles from about 35 insurance periodicals. Arrangement is by subject, with an index to authors.

BIBLIOGRAPHIES

Insurance and Employee Benefits Literature. Special Libraries Association, Insurance and Employee Benefits Div. • Bimonthly. $15.00 per year. Lists a wide variety of literature in all branches of the insurance industry. Includes annotations.

CD-ROM DATABASES

U. S. Insurance: Property and Casualty. Sheshunoff Information Services, Inc. • Monthly. Price on application. CD-ROM provides detailed, current financial information on more than 3,200 property and casualty insurance companies.

DIRECTORIES

Best's Directory of Recommended Insurance Attorneys and Adjusters. A.M. Best Co. • Annual. $1,175.00. More than 5,000 American, Canadian, and foreign insurance defense law firms; lists 1,200 national and international insurance adjusting firms. Formerly *Best's Recommended Insurance Adjusters.*

S & P's Insurance Book. Standard & Poor's Ratings Group, Insurance Rating Services. • Quarterly. Price on application. Contains detailed financial analyses and ratings of various kinds of insurance companies.

S & P's Insurance Digest: Property-Casualty and Reinsurance Edition. Standard & Poor's Ratings Group, Insurance Rating Services. • Quarterly. Contains concise financial analyses and ratings of property-casualty insurance companies.

ENCYCLOPEDIAS AND DICTIONARIES

Dictionary of Insurance Terms. Harvey W. Rubin. Barron's Educational Series, Inc. • 2000. $14.95. Fourth edition. Defines terms in a wide variety of insurance fields. (Business Dictionaries Series).

Glossary of Insurance Policy Terms. Organization for Economic Cooperation and Development. • 1999. $30.00. "The selected topics range from insurance policy regulation/supervision to general trade issues and include technical terms related to issues such as claims, premiums, and provisions." Edited for government, academic, business, and insurance organizations.

Insurance Words and Their Meanings: A Glossary of Insurance Terms. The Rough Notes Co., Inc. • 2001. 17th edition. Price on application.

HANDBOOKS AND MANUALS

The Complete Book of Insurance: Protecting Your Life, Health Property, and Income. Ben G. Baldwin.

McGraw-Hill. • 1991. $24.95. Provides basic information and advice on various kinds of insurance: life, health, property (fire), disability, long-term care, automobile, liability, and annuities.

ONLINE DATABASES

I.I.I. Data Base Search. Insurance Information Institute. • Provides online citations and abstracts of insurance-related literature in magazines, newspapers, trade journals, and books. Emphasis is on property and casualty insurance issues, including highway safety, product safety, and environmental liability. Inquire as to online cost and availability.

PERIODICALS AND NEWSLETTERS

Best's Review: Inurance Issues and Analysis. A.M. Best Co. • Monthly. $25.00 per year. Editorial coverage of significant industry trends, developments, and important events. Formerly *Best's Review: Property-Casualty Insurance.*

Chartered Property and Casualty Underwriters Society Journal. Chartered Property and Casualty Underwriters Society. • Quarterly. $30.00 per year. Published by the Chartered Property and Casualty Underwriters Society (CPCU). Edited for professional insurance underwriters and agents.

Fire, Casualty and Surety Bulletin. The National Underwriter Co. • Monthly. $420.00 per year. Five looseleaf volumes.

Insurance and Technology. CMP Media LLC. • Monthly. $65.00 per year. Covers information technology and systems management as applied to the operation of life, health, casualty, and property insurance companies.

Insurance Coverage Law Bulletin. American Lawyer Media, Inc. • Monthly. $199.00 per year. Newsletter. Provides news of property insurance claims management and coverage disputes. Edited for both legal and non-legal insurance professionals. (A Law Journal Newsletter, formerly published by Leader Publications).

Insurance Day. Available from Informa Publishing Group Ltd. • Three times a week. $440.00 per year. Published in the UK by Lloyd's List (http://www.lloydslist.com). A newspaper providing international coverage of property/casualty/liability insurance, reinsurance, and risk, with an emphasis on marine insurance.

The John Liner Letter. Standard Publishing Corp. • Description: Provides risk management and technical insurance advice for business firms, such as broadening coverage, cutting costs, and anticipating special insurance problems.

National Underwriter, Property and Casualty Edition. The National Underwriter Co. • Weekly. $92.00 per year.

Risk Management. Risk and Insurance Management Society. Risk Management Society Publishing, Inc. • Monthly. $59.00 per year.

Rough Notes: Property, Casualty, Surety. The Rough Notes Co., Inc. • Monthly. $27.50 per year.

RESEARCH CENTERS AND INSTITUTES

S. S. Huebner Foundation. University of Pennsylvania, 3733 Spruce St., Vance Hall, Suite 430, Philadelphia, PA 19104-6301. Phone: (215)898-9631 Fax: (215)573-2218 E-mail: cummins@wharton.upenn.edu • URL: http://www.rider.wharton.upenn.edu/ • Awards grants for research in various areas of insurance.

STATISTICS SOURCES

Property-Casualty Insurance Facts. Insurance Information Institute. • Annual. $22.50. Formerly *Insurance Facts.*

Standard & Poor's Industry Surveys. Standard & Poor's. • Semiannual. $1,800.00. Two looseleaf volumes. Includes monthly *Supplements.* Provides detailed, individual surveys of 52 major industry groups. Each survey is revised on a semiannual basis. Also includes "Monthly Investment Review" (industry group investment analysis) and monthly "Trends & Projections" (economic analysis).

U. S. Industry and Trade Outlook. Available from National Technical Information Service. • Annual. $69.95. Produced by the International Trade Administration, U. S. Department of Commerce, in a "public-private" partnership with DRI/McGraw-Hill and Standard & Poor's. Provides basic data, outlook for the current year, and "Long-Term Prospects" (five-year projections) for a wide variety of products and services. Includes high technology industries. Formerly *U. S. Industrial Outlook.*

TRADE/PROFESSIONAL ASSOCIATIONS

American Institute for CPCU. 720 Providence Rd., Malvern, PA 19355-0716. Phone: 800-644-2101 or (610)644-2100 Fax: (610)640-9576 E-mail: cserv@cpuiia.org • URL: http://www.aicpcu.com.

American Insurance Association. 1130 Connecticut Ave. NW, Ste. 1000, Washington, DC 20036. Phone: 800-242-2302 or (202)828-7100 or (202)828-7183 Fax: (202)293-1219 E-mail: info@aiadc.org • URL: http://www.aiadc.org/aiadotnet • Represents companies providing property and casualty insurance and suretyship. Monitors and reports on economic, political, and social trends; serves as a clearinghouse for ideas, advice, and technical information. Represents members' interests before state and federal legislative and regulatory bodies; coordinates members' litigation.

Insurance Information Institute. 110 William St., New York, NY 10038. Phone: 800-331-9146 or (212)346-5500 Fax: (212)791-1807 E-mail: members@iii.org • URL: http://www.iii.org • Property and casualty insurance companies. Provides information and educational services to mass media, educational institutions, trade associations, businesses, government agencies, and the public.

Insurance Services Office (ISO). 545 Washington Blvd., Jersey City, NJ 07310-1686. Phone: 800-888-4476 or (201)469-2000 Fax: (201)748-1472 E-mail: info@iso.com • URL: http://www.iso.com • Provides statistical, actuarial, underwriting, and claims information to property and casualty insurance companies.

National Association of Professional Insurance Agents. 400 N. Washington St., Alexandria, VA 22314. Phone: (703)836-9340 Fax: (703)836-1279 E-mail: piaweb@pianet.org • URL: http://www.pianet.com • Members are independent agents in various fields of insurance. Formerly National Association of Mutual Insurance Agents.

Risk and Insurance Management Society. 655 Third Ave., 2nd Fl., New York, NY 10017. Phone: (212)286-9292 Fax: (212)986-9716 E-mail: jwaldman@rims.org • URL: http://www.rims.org • Formerly American Society of Insurance Management.

OTHER SOURCES

Best's Insurance Reports: Property-Casualty. A.M. Best Co. • Annual. $750.00. Guide to over 3,200 major property/casualty companies.

Fire and Casualty Insurance Law Reports. CCH, Inc. • $870.00 per year. Looseleaf service. Semimonthly updates.

The Law of Liability Insurance. LexisNexis Matthew Bender. • $1,451.00. Five looseleaf volumes. Periodic supplementation. Explains the terms and phases essential for a general understanding of liability insurance, and discusses injuries to both persons and property.

PROPERTY MANAGEMENT

See also: REAL ESTATE BUSINESS

ABSTRACTS AND INDEXES

Real Estate Index. National Association of Realtors. • 1987. $169.00 Two volumes. Vol. one, Author-Title, $99.00; vol. two, Subject, $99.00; vol. 3, 1998 *Supplement,* $49.50.

DIRECTORIES

CRS Referral Directory. Council of Residential Specialists. • Covers: 35,000 Certified Residential Specialists (CRS). Entries include: Member name, firm name, address, phone, fax; designations held, areas of specialization, e-mail; web page address; years of experience, voicemail; 2nd business phone.

U.S. Real Estate Register. Barry Inc. • Covers: real estate departments of large national companies, industrial economic/development organizations, utilities, real estate brokers, and railroads involved in commercial and industrial real estate development. Entries include: Company or organization name, address; many listings include name of contact.

ENCYCLOPEDIAS AND DICTIONARIES

Dictionary of Real Estate. Jae K. Shim and others. John Wiley and Sons, Inc. • 1995. $145.00. Contains 3,000 definitions of commercial and residential real estate terms. Covers appraisal, escrow, investment, finance, mortgages, property management, construction, legal aspects, etc. Includes illustrations and formulas. (Business Dictionary Series).

HANDBOOKS AND MANUALS

Every Landlord's Legal Guide. Marcia Stewart and others. Nolo. • 2003. $44.99. Sixth edition.

Every Tenant's Legal Guide. Janet Portman and Marcia Stewart. Nolo. • 2002. $29.99. Third edition.

The Landlord's Handbook: A Complete Guide to Managing Small Residential and Commercial Properties. Daniel Goodwin and Richard Rusdorf. Dearborn Trade Publishing, A Kaplan Professional Co. • 2003. $29.95. Third edition. Covers such topics as finding good tenants, rent collection, insurance, taxes, environmental issues, leases, security deposits, and evictions.

PERIODICALS AND NEWSLETTERS

Building Operating Management: The National Magazine for Commercial and Institutional Buildings Construction, Renovation, Facility Management. Trade Press Publishing Corp. • Monthly. Free to qualified personnel.

Buildings: The Source for Facilities Decision-Makers. Stamats Communications, Inc. • Monthly. $70.00 per year. Serves professional building ownership/management organizations.

Housing the Elderly Report. Community Development Services, Inc. CD Publications. • Monthly. $249.00 per year. Newsletter. Edited for retirement communities, apartment projects, and nursing homes. Covers news relative to business and property management issues.

Journal of Property Management: The Official Publication of the Institute of Real Estate Management. Institute of Real Estate Management. • Bimonthly. $43.95 per year.

Ledger Quarterly: A Financial Review for Community Association Practitioners. Community Associations Institute. • Quarterly. $67.00 per year. Newsletter. Provides current information on issues affecting the finances of condominium, cooperative, homeowner, apartment, and other community housing associations.

Managing Housing Letter. Community Development Services, Inc. CD Publications. • Description: Provides news and advice for owners and managers of rental housing--public, private, and subsidized--

including news from Washington and practical management tips. Recurring features include news of research.

Properties. Properties Magazine, Inc. • Monthly. $17.95 per year. News and features of interest to income property owners managers and related industries in Northeastern Ohio.

Real Estate New York. • Ten times a year. $35.00 per year. Formerly *Better Bulidings.*

RESEARCH CENTERS AND INSTITUTES

Center for Finance and Real Estate. University of California, Los Angeles, John E. Anderson Graduate School of Management, 110 Westwood Plaza, Los Angeles, CA 90095-1481. Phone: (310)206-5455 Fax: (310)206-5455 E-mail: wtorous@anderson.ucla.edu • URL: http://www.agsm.ucla.edu.

TRADE/PROFESSIONAL ASSOCIATIONS

Building Owners and Managers Association International. 1201 New York Ave., NW, Ste. 300, Washington, DC 20005. Phone: (202)408-2662 Fax: (202)371-0181 E-mail: info@boma.org • URL: http://www.boma.org • Formerly National Association of Building Owners and Managers.

Community Associations Institute. 225 Reinekers Ln., Ste. 300, Alexandria, VA 22314. Phone: 888-CAI-4321 or (703)548-8600 Fax: (703)684-1581 E-mail: caidirect@caionline.org • URL: http://www.caionline.org • Condominium and homeowner associations, cooperatives, and association-governed planned communities of all sizes and architectural types; community or property managers and management firms; individual homeowners; community association managers and management firms; public officials; and lawyers, accountants, engineers, reserve specialists, builder/developers and other providers of professional services and products for CAs. Seeks to educate and represent America's 250,000 residential condominium, cooperative and homeowner associations and related professionals and service providers. Aims to foster vibrant, responsive, competent community associations that promote harmony, community and responsible leadership.

Institute of Real Estate Management. 430 N. Michigan Ave., Chicago, IL 60611-4090. Phone: 800-837-0706 or (312)329-6000 Fax: 800-837-4736 E-mail: custserv@irem.org • URL: http://www.irem.org.

National Apartment Association. 4300 Wilson Blvd., Ste. 400, Arlington, VA 22203-4168. Phone: (703)518-6141 Fax: (703)248-9440 E-mail: webmaster@naahq.com • URL: http://www.naahq.org • Federation of 155 state and local associations of industry professionals engaged in all aspects of the multifamily housing industry, including owners, builders, investors, developers, managers, and allied service representatives. Provides education and certification for property management executives, on-site property managers, maintenance personnel, property supervisors, and leasing agents. Offers a nationwide legislative network concerned with governmental decisions at the federal, state, and local levels.

National Property Management Association. 28100 U.S. Hwy. 19 N, Ste. 400, Clearwater, FL 33761. Phone: (727)736-3788 Fax: (727)736-6707 E-mail: hq@npma.org • URL: http://www.npma.org • Aims to build leadership by educating, training and promoting standards of competency and ethical behavior in the asset management of personal property. Serves property professionals throughout the United States; members represent companies and organizations in both the public and private sectors, including scientific laboratories, universities, hospitals, public school systems, and local, state and federal government agencies.

Property Management Association. 7900 Wisconsin Ave., Ste. 305, Bethesda, MD 20814. Phone:

(301)657-9200 Fax: (301)907-9326 E-mail: info@pma-dc.org • URL: http://www.pma-dc.org • Property management professionals who own and operate multifamily residential, commercial, retail, industrial and other income-producing properties and firms that provide goods and services used in real property management. Works to enhance the interests and welfare of property owners, managers, supervisory employees, and contractors involved in the management of multifamily residential and commercial property. Provides education and a forum for exchange of ideas on efficient methods of operation and progressive policies of management.

PROPERTY TAX

See also: INDUSTRIAL REAL ESTATE; TAX SHELTERS

GENERAL WORKS

How to Avoid Financial Tangles. American Institute for Economic Research. • 2001. $8.00. Provides basic information and advice on such topics as property ownership, taxes, wills, trusts, insurance, record retention, and professional assistance. (Economic Education Bulletin.).

Tips and Traps for Saving on All Your Real Estate Taxes. Robert Irwin and Norman Lane. McGraw-Hill. • 1992. $12.95.

ABSTRACTS AND INDEXES

Index to Legal Periodicals and Books. H. W. Wilson Co. • Monthly. $490.00 per year. Quarterly and annual cumulations.

BIBLIOGRAPHIES

The Tax Reform Act of 1986 and Its Impact on the Real Estate Industry. Marilyn Hankel. Sage Publications, Inc. • 1993. $10.00.

DIRECTORIES

International Association of Assessing Officers: Membership Directory. International Association of Assessing Officers. • Annual. $400.00. Lists about 8,500 state and local officials concerned with valuation of property tax.

HANDBOOKS AND MANUALS

Real Estate Taxation: A Practitioner's Guide. David F. Windish. CCH, Inc. • Date not set. $125.00. Second edition. Serves as a guide to the federal tax consequences of real estate ownership and operation. Covers mortgages, rental agreements, interest, landlord income, forms of ownership, and other tax-oriented topics.

U. S. Master Property Tax Guide. CCH, Inc. • Annual. $72.00. Provides state-by-state coverage of "key property tax issues and concepts," including exemptions, assessments, taxpayer remedies, and property tax calendars.

ONLINE DATABASES

Index to Legal Periodicals and Books (Online). H. W. Wilson Co. • Broad coverage of law journals and books 1981 to date. Monthly updates. Inquire as to online cost and availability.

Legal Resource Index. Gale Cengage Learning. • Broad coverage of law literature appearing in legal, business, and other periodicals, 1980 to date. Daily updates. Inquire as to online cost and availability.

LEXIS. LEXIS-NEXIS. • The various LEXIS databases provide full text and indexing for a wide variety of legal cases, statutes, orders, and opinions.

PERIODICALS AND NEWSLETTERS

Assessment Journal. International Association of Assessing Officers. • Bimonthly. Free to members; non-members, $200.00 per year. Formed by merger of *Assessment* and *Valuation Legal Reporter and IAAO Update.*

*The Journal of Taxation: A National Journal of Cur-*rent Developments, Analysis and Commentary for Tax Professionals.* RIA. • Monthly. $305.00 per year. Analysis of current tax developments for tax specialists.

Property Tax Alert. State Taxation Institute. • Description: Features updates on property tax issues. Recurring features include a calendar of events and notices of publications available.

Real Estate Finance. Institutional Investor, Inc., Journals Group. • Bimonthly. $350.00 per year. Covers real estate for professional investors. Provides information on complex financing, legalities, and industry trends.

RESEARCH CENTERS AND INSTITUTES

Center for Real Estate Studies. Indiana University Bloomington, Kelley School of Business, 1300 E. 10th St., Bloomington, IN 47405. Phone: (812)855-7794 Fax: (812)855-9472 • URL: http://www.indiana.edu/~cres/.

Office of Real Estate Research. University of Illinois at Urbana-Chamapign, 1407 W. Gregory Dr., 304 David Kinley Hall, Urbana, IL 61801. Phone: (217)333-1185 Fax: (217)244-9867 E-mail: orer@uiuc.edu • URL: http://www.cba.uiuc.edu/orer.

Office of Tax Policy Research. University of Michigan, 701 Tappan St., Ann Arbor, MI 48109-1234. Phone: (734)763-3068 Fax: (734)763-4032 E-mail: otpr@umich.edu • URL: http://www.taxpolicyresearch.umich.edu/.

Tax Foundation. Tax Foundation. 2001 L St. NW, Ste. 1050, Washington, DC 20036. Phone: (202)464-6200 Fax: (202)464-6201 E-mail: hodge@taxfoundation.org • URL: http://www.taxfoundation.org • Fiscal and management aspects of federal, state, and local government, including studies on government expenditures, the federal budget, taxation, and international competitiveness. Serves as a national information agency for individuals and organizations concerned with problems of government expenditures, taxation, and debt.

Urban Land Institute. Urban Land Institute. 1025 Thomas Jefferson St. NW, Ste. 500 W, Washington, DC 20007. Phone: (202)624-7000 Fax: (202)624-7140 E-mail: customerservice@uli.org • URL: http://www.uli.org • Urban land use policy, planning, and development issues, including studies on central city problems, industrial development, new community development, residential developments of all types, taxation, smart growth, shopping center development and economics, metropolitan and urbanized area growth and development, mixed use development, and environmental factors affecting development.

TRADE/PROFESSIONAL ASSOCIATIONS

Institute for Professionsals in Taxation. 3350 Peachtree Rd., N.E., Suite 280, Atlanta, GA 30326. Phone: (404)240-2300 Fax: (404)240-2315 E-mail: ipt@ipt.org • URL: http://www.ipt.org • Promotes education in the area of property taxation. Formerly Institute of Property Taxation.

International Association of Assessing Officers. 130 E Randolph St., Chicago, IL 60601. Phone: (312)819-6100 Fax: (312)819-6149 E-mail: membership@iaaa.org • URL: http://www.iaao.org • Formerly National Association of Assessing Officers.

OTHER SOURCES

Manufacturers' Tax Alert. CCH, Inc. • Monthly $297.00 per year. Newsletter. Covers the major tax issues affecting manufacturing companies. Includes current developments in various kind of federal, state, and international taxes: sales, use, franchise, property, and corporate income.

PROPOSALS, BUSINESS

See: BUSINESS START-UP PLANS AND PROPOSALS

PROSTHETICS INDUSTRY

ABSTRACTS AND INDEXES

NTIS Alerts: Biomedical Technology & Human Factors Engineering. National Technical Information Service. • Semimonthly. $210.00 per year. Provides descriptions of government-sponsored research reports and software, with ordering information. Covers biotechnology, ergonomics, bionics, artificial intelligence, prosthetics, and related subjects. Formerly *Abstract Newsletter.*

FINANCIAL RATIOS

Annual Statement Studies. The Risk Management Association. • Annual. Median and quartile financial ratios are given for over 400 kinds of manufacturing, wholesale, retail, construction, and consumer finance establishments. Data is sorted by both asset size and sales volume. Includes a clearly written "Definition of Ratios" and an alphabetical industry index.

Annual Statement Studies: Industry Default Probabilities and Cash Flow Measures. The Risk Management Association. • Annual. $145.00. Serves as a companion volume to the original *Annual Statement Studies.* Gives probability of default estimates on a percentage scale for more than 450 industries. Includes changes in position year-by-year for eight financial statement line items and provides percentage measures of cash flow.

TRADE/PROFESSIONAL ASSOCIATIONS

American Orthotic and Prosthetic Association. 303 John Carlyle St., Suite 200, Alexandria, VA 22314. Phone: (571)431-0876 Fax: (571)431-0899 E-mail: info@aopanet.org • URL: http://www.aopanet.org.

PROTECTIVE SERVICES

See: INDUSTRIAL SECURITY PROGRAMS

PSYCHOLOGICAL TESTING

See also: INDUSTRIAL PSYCHOLOGY; RATING OF EMPLOYEES

GENERAL WORKS

Essentials of Psychological Testing. Lee J. Cronbach. Addison-Wesley. • 1997. $125.00. Fifth edition.

Psychological Testing: A Practical Introduction. Thomas P. Hogan. John Wiley and Sons, Inc. • 2002. $111.95.

ABSTRACTS AND INDEXES

Psychological Abstracts. American Psychological Association. • Monthly. Members, $815.00 per year; individuals and institutions, $1,207.00 per year. Covers the international literature of psychology and the behavioral sciences. Includes journals, technical reports, dissertations, and other sources.

ALMANACS AND YEARBOOKS

Mental Measurements Yearbook. University of Nebraska-Lincoln Buros Institute of Mental Measurements. • Biennial. $195.00 per year.

BIBLIOGRAPHIES

Tests in Print. Linda L. Murphy and others. University of Nebraska-Lincoln Buros Institute of Mental Measurements. • Quinquennial. Price varies. Two volumes. Lists over 4,000 testing instruments.

DIRECTORIES

Tests: A Comprehensive Reference for Assessments in Psychology, Education and Business. Available from Gale Cengage Learning. • 2003. $96.00. Fifth edition. List nearly 200 publishers for over 2,000 tests. Published by Pro-Ed Inc.

ENCYCLOPEDIAS AND DICTIONARIES

Encyclopedia of Psychological Assessment. Rocio Fernandez-Ballesteros, editor. Sage Publications, Inc. • 2003. $525.00. Two volumes. Contains about 235 alphabetically arranged entries covering various areas of applied psychology and testing.

The Gale Encyclopedia of Psychology. Gale Cengage Learning. • 2001. $155.00. Second edition. Includes bibliographies arranged by topic and a glossary. More than 650 topics are covered.

HANDBOOKS AND MANUALS

Comprehensive Handbook of Psychological Assessment. Michel Hersen, editor. John Wiley and Sons, Inc. • 2003. $500.00. Four volumes. Covers psychological testing and evaluation. Volume one: *Intellectual and Neuropsychological Assessment.* Volume two: *Personality Assessment.* Volume three: *Behavioral Assessment.* Volume four: *Industrial/Organizational Assessment.* (Individual volumes are available at $150.00.).

Handbook of Psychological Assessment. Gary Groth-Marnat. John Wiley and Sons, Inc. • 2003. $95.00. Fourth edition. Provides information on widely used intelligence and personality tests. Covers assessment, evaluation, writing of reports, and referral.

ONLINE DATABASES

Mental Health Abstracts. IFI/Plenum Data Corp. • Provides indexing and abstracting of mental health and mental illness literature appearing in more than 1,200 journals and other sources from 1969 to date. Monthly updates. Inquire as to online cost and availability.

PsycINFO. American Psychological Association. • Provides indexing and abstracting of the worldwide literature of psychology and the behavioral sciences. Time period is 1967 to date, with monthly updates. Inquire as to online cost and availability.

PERIODICALS AND NEWSLETTERS

Educational and Psychological Measurement: Devoted to the Development and Application of Measures of Individual Differences. Sage Publications, Inc. • Bimonthly. Institutions, $599.00 per year.

Journal of Business and Psychology. Business Psychology Research Institute. Kluwer Academic Publishers. • Quarterly. Institutions, $614.00 per year; with online edition, $736.80 per year.

Measurement and Evaluation in Counseling and Development. Association for Measurement and Evaluation in Counseling. American Counseling Association. • Quarterly. Free to members; nonmembers, $60.00 per year.

TRADE/PROFESSIONAL ASSOCIATIONS

American Counseling Association. 5999 Stevenson Ave., Alexandria, VA 22304. Phone: 800-347-6647 or (703)823-9800 Fax: (703)823-0252 E-mail: ryep@counseling.org • URL: http://www. counseling.org • Counseling professionals in elementary and secondary schools, higher education, community agencies and organizations, rehabilitation programs, government, industry, business, private practice, career counseling, and mental health counseling. Conducts professional development institutes and provides liability insurance. Maintains Counseling and Human Development Foundation to fund counseling projects.

PSYCHOLOGY

See: HUMAN RELATIONS; MENTAL HEALTH; MOTIVATION (PSYCHOLOGY)

PSYCHOLOGY, INDUSTRIAL

See: INDUSTRIAL PSYCHOLOGY

PUBLIC ACCOUNTANTS

See: CERTIFIED PUBLIC ACCOUNTANTS

PUBLIC ADMINISTRATION

See also: CIVIL SERVICE; COMPUTERS IN GOVERNMENT; MUNICIPAL GOVERNMENT; STATE GOVERNMENT

GENERAL WORKS

From Red Tape to Smart Tape: Administrative Simplification in OECD Countries. Organization for Economic Cooperation and Development. • 2003. $58.00. "This report looks at a set of tools and practices commonly used by governments to make administrative regulations simpler and less burdensome to comply with." Includes information on one-stop facilitation, license/permit simplification, decision-making time limits, small business assistance, and the use of information technology (IT) for administrative simplification.

The Leader of the Future: New Essays by World-Class Leaders and Thinkers. Frances Hesselbein. John Wiley and Sons, Inc. • 2000. $16.50. Contains articles on leadership by "executives, consultants, and commentators." (Management Series).

Performance Budgeting for State and Local Government. Janet M. Kelly and William C. Rivenbark. M. E. Sharpe, Inc. • 2003. $69.95. Covers performance-based management as applied to local government budgeting.

Performance Management in Government: Contemporary Illustrations. David Shand. OECD Publications and Information Center. • 1996. (Public Management Occasional Papers: No. 9).

Public Administration and Public Affairs. Nicholas L. Henry. Prentice Hall PTR. • 2003. $59.00. Ninth edition.

Public Administration: Design and Problem Solving. Jong S. Jun. Chatelaine Press. • 1986. $41.95.

Public Personnel Administration: Problems and Prospects. Steven W. Hays and Richard C. Kearney, editors. Prentice Hall PTR. • 2002. $44.00.

Unmasking Administrative Evil. Guy B. Adams and Danny L. Balfour. M. E. Sharpe, Inc. • 2004. $59.95. Revised edition. Discusses bureaucratic mismanagement and the resulting evil or even tragedy.

ABSTRACTS AND INDEXES

PAIS International in Print. Public Affairs Information Service, Inc. • Monthly. $850.00 per year; cumulations three times a year. Provides topical citations to the worldwide literature of public affairs, economics, demographics, sociology, and trade. Text in English; indexed materials in English, French, German, Italian, Portuguese and Spanish.

Sage Public Administration Abstracts. Sage Publications, Inc. • Quarterly. Institutions, $785.00 per year.

Social Sciences Citation Index. Thomson/ISI. • Three times a year. $6,900 per year. Annual cumulation. Includes *Source Index, Citation Index, Permuterm Subject Index,* and *Corporate Index.*

Social Sciences Index. H. W. Wilson Co. • Quarterly, with annual cumulation. Price varies. Indexes more than 400 periodicals covering economics, environmental policy, government, insurance, labor, health care policy, planning, public administration, public welfare, urban studies, women's issues, criminology, and related topics.

CD-ROM DATABASES

PAIS on CD-ROM. Public Affairs Information Service, Inc. • Quarterly. $1,995.00 per year.

Provides a CD-ROM version of the online service, *PAIS International.* Contains over 500,000 citations to the literature of contemporary social, political, and economic issues.

Social Sciences Citation Index. ISI. • Monthly. Price on request. Provides CD-ROM indexing of articles appearing in 1700 leading social science journals worldwide, with additional selections from more than 5700 other journals. Time span is 1992 to date. Coverage includes economics, business, finance, management, communications, demographics, library and information science, political science, sociology, and many other subjects.

Social Sciences Citation Index: Compact Disc Edition with Abstracts. Institute for Scientific Information. • Monthly. Provides CD-ROM indexing and abstracting of "significant articles" from 1,700 social science journals worldwide, with additional selections from 3,200 other journals, 1986 to date. Includes economics, business, finance, management, communications, demographics, information and library science, political science, sociology, and many other subjects.

WILSONDISC: Wilson Social Sciences Abstracts. H. W. Wilson Co. • Monthly. Includes unlimited online access to *Social Sciences Index* through WILSONLINE. Provides CD-ROM indexing from 1983 and abstracting from 1994 of more than 500 periodicals covering economics, area studies, community health, public administration, public welfare, urban studies, and many other topics related to the social sciences.

DIRECTORIES

CSG State Directories II: Legislative, Leadership, Committees and Staff by Function. Council of State Governments. • Annual. $49.99. Legislative leaders, committee members and staff, personnel of principal legislative staff offices. Formerly *Book of the States, Supplement Two: State Legislative Leadership, Committees, and Staff.*

ENCYCLOPEDIAS AND DICTIONARIES

International Encyclopedia of Public Policy and Administration. Jay M. Shafritz, editor. Westview Press. • 1997. $550.00. Four volumes. Covers 20 major areas, such as public administration, government budgeting, industrial policy, nonprofit management, organizational theory, public finance, labor relations, and taxation. Includes a brief bibliography for each major entry and a comprehensive index.

HANDBOOKS AND MANUALS

The Federal Manager's Handbook: A Guide to Rehabilitating or Removing the Problem Employee. G. Jerry Shaw and William L. Bransford. FPMI Communications, Inc. • 1997. $29.95. Third revised edition.

Handbook of Public Administration. B. Guy Peters and Jon Pierre, editors. Sage Publications, Inc. • 2003. $125.00. Emphasis is on academic studies and public administration theory.

ONLINE DATABASES

PAIS International. Public Affairs Information Service, Inc. • Corresponds to the former printed publications, *PAIS Bulletin* (1976-90) and *PAIS Foreign Language Index* (1972-90), and to the current *PAIS International in Print* (1991 to date). Covers economic, political, and sociological material appearing in periodicals, books, government documents, and other publications. Updating is monthly. Inquire as to online cost and availability.

Social Scisearch. Institute for Scientific Information. • Broad, multidisciplinary index to the literature of the social sciences, 1972 to present. Weekly updates. Worldwide coverage. Inquire as to online cost and availability.

Wilson Social Sciences Abstracts Online. H. W. Wilson Co. • Provides online abstracting and indexing of more than 500 periodicals covering area studies, community health, public administration, public welfare, urban studies, and many other social science topics. Time period is 1994 to date for abstracts and 1983 to date for indexing, with updates weekly. Inquire as to online cost and availability.

PERIODICALS AND NEWSLETTERS

Administration and Society. Sage Publications, Inc. • Bimonthly. Institutions, $612.00 per year. Scholarly journal concerned with public administration and the effects of bureaucracy.

Administrative Science Quarterly. Cornell University, Johnson Graduate School of Management. • Individuals: $65.00 per year; institutions, $130.00 per year.

Governing: The States and Localities. • Monthly. $39.95 per year. Edited for state and local government officials. Covers finance, office management, computers, telecommunications, environmental concerns, etc.

Journal of Nonprofit and Public Sector Marketing. Haworth Press, Inc. • Semiannual. Institutions, $365.00 per year. Subject matter has to do with the promotion or marketing of the services of nonprofit organizations and governmental agencies.

Leader to Leader. Peter F. Drucker Foundation for Nonprofit Management. Jossey-Bass. • Quarterly. Institutions, $199.00 per year. Contains articles on "management, leadership, and strategy" written by "leading executives, thinkers, and consultants." Covers both business and nonprofit issues.

Public Administration and Development: An International Journal of Training, Research and Practice. John Wiley and Sons, Inc., Journals. • Five times a year. Individuals, $485.00 per year; institutions, $970.00 per year. Focuses on administrative practice at the local, regional and national levels. International coverage. Published in England by John Wiley and Sons Ltd.

Public Administration Review. American Society for Public Administration. • Bimonthly. Institutions, $209.00 per year. Includes online edition.

Public Risk. Public Risk Management Association. • 10 times a year. $125.00 per year. Covers risk management for state and local governments, including various kinds of liabilities.

TRADE/PROFESSIONAL ASSOCIATIONS

American Society for Public Administration. 1120 G St., N.W., Suite 700, Washington, DC 20005-3885. Phone: (202)393-7878 Fax: (202)638-4952 E-mail: mhamilton@aspanet.org • URL: http://www.aspanet.org.

Institute of Public Administration. 411 Lafayette St., 3rd Fl., New York, NY 1003-7032. Phone: (212)992-9899 Fax: (212)995-4876 E-mail: info@theipa.org • URL: http://www.theipa.org • Formerly National Institute of Public Administration.

Public Administration Service. 7927 Jones Branch Dr. S, No. 100, McLean, VA 22102. Phone: (703)734-8970 Fax: (703)734-4965 E-mail: info@pma-dc.org • URL: http://www.pashq.org • Promotes improvement of public administration through research and provision of consultation services covering a full range of governmental operations in local, state, and federal units. Provides consultancy services on an international level to governments and international agencies in support of national development projects and programs. Convention/Meeting: none.

Public Risk Management Association. 500 Montgomery St., Ste. 750, Alexandria, VA 22314. Phone: (703)528-7701 Fax: (703)739-0200 E-mail: info@primacentral.org • URL: http://www.primacentral.org • Public agency risk, insurance, human resources, attorneys, and/or safety managers from cities, counties, villages, towns, school boards, and other related areas. Provides an information

clearinghouse and communications network for public risk managers to share resources, ideas, and experiences. Offers information on risk, insurance, and safety management. Monitors state and federal legislative actions and court decisions that deal with immunity, tort liability, and intergovernmental risk pools. Maintains library containing current reports from governmental units on their insurance procedures, self-insurance plans, and loss control and safety programs; and copies of policy statements, job descriptions, contractual arrangements, and indemnification clauses.

Section for Women in Public Administration. 1120 G St., NW, Ste. 700, Washington, DC 20005-3885. Phone: (202)393-7878 Fax: (202)638-4952 E-mail: mhamilton@aspanet.org • URL: http://www.aspanet.org • Initiates action programs appropriate to the needs and concerns of women in public administration. Formerly National Committee for Women in Public Administration.

PUBLIC ASSISTANCE

See: PUBLIC WELFARE

PUBLIC DOCUMENTS

See: GOVERNMENT PUBLICATIONS

PUBLIC FINANCE

See also: COUNTY FINANCE; FEDERAL BUDGET; MUNICIPAL FINANCE; TAXATION

ABSTRACTS AND INDEXES

PAIS International in Print. Public Affairs Information Service, Inc. • Monthly. $850.00 per year; cumulations three times a year. Provides topical citations to the worldwide literature of public affairs, economics, demographics, sociology, and trade. Text in English; indexed materials in English, French, German, Italian, Portuguese and Spanish.

Social Sciences Index. H. W. Wilson Co. • Quarterly, with annual cumulation. Price varies. Indexes more than 400 periodicals covering economics, environmental policy, government, insurance, labor, health care policy, plannning, public administration, public welfare, urban studies, women's issues, criminology, and related topics.

ALMANACS AND YEARBOOKS

State Budget Actions, 2000. Corina Eckl and Arturo Perez. National Conference of State Legislatures. • 2000. $35.00. Presents yearly summaries of state spending priorities and fiscal climates. Includes end-of-year general fund balances and other information on state funds.

CD-ROM DATABASES

OECD Statistical Compendium. Organization for Economic Cooperation and Development. • Semiannual. $1,905.00 per year for 1 to 10 users. CD-ROM contains more than 730,000 monthly, quarterly, and annual time series for OECD countries, 1960 to date. Includes fully searchable data on agriculture, food, economic indicators, national accounts, employment, energy, finance, industry, technology, and foreign trade. Results can be displayed in various forms.

PAIS on CD-ROM. Public Affairs Information Service, Inc. • Quarterly. $1,995.00 per year. Provides a CD-ROM version of the online service, *PAIS International.* Contains over 500,000 citations to the literature of contemporary social, political, and economic issues.

Social Sciences Citation Index. ISI. • Monthly. Price

on request. Provides CD-ROM indexing of articles appearing in 1700 leading social science journals worldwide, with additional selections from more than 5700 other journals. Time span is 1992 to date. Coverage includes economics, business, finance, management, communications, demographics, library and information science, political science, sociology, and many other subjects.

Social Sciences Citation Index: Compact Disc Edition with Abstracts. Institute for Scientific Information. • Monthly. Provides CD-ROM indexing and abstracting of "significant articles" from 1,700 social science journals worldwide, with additional selections from 3,200 other journals, 1986 to date. Includes economics, business, finance, management, communications, demographics, information and library science, political science, sociology, and many other subjects.

WILSONDISC: Wilson Social Sciences Abstracts. H. W. Wilson Co. • Monthly. Includes unlimited online access to *Social Sciences Index* through WILSONLINE. Provides CD-ROM indexing from 1983 and abstracting from 1994 of more than 500 periodicals covering economics, area studies, community health, public administration, public welfare, urban studies, and many other topics related to the social sciences.

DIRECTORIES

Book of the States. Council of State Governments. • Biennial. $99.00. Includes information on state constitutions, state-by-state voting in recent elections, data on state finances, and federal-state survey articles.

ENCYCLOPEDIAS AND DICTIONARIES

International Encyclopedia of Public Policy and Administration. Jay M. Shafritz, editor. Westview Press. • 1997. $550.00. Four volumes. Covers 20 major areas, such as public administration, government budgeting, industrial policy, nonprofit management, organizational theory, public finance, labor relations, and taxation. Includes a brief bibliography for each major entry and a comprehensive index.

FINANCIAL RATIOS

Financial Report of the United States Government. Available from U. S. Government Printing Office. • Annual. $21.00. Issued by the U. S. Treasury Department (http://www.treas.gov). Presents information about the financial condition and operations of the federal government. Program accounting systems of various government agencies provide data for the report.

HANDBOOKS AND MANUALS

Government Auditing Standards. Available from U. S. Government Printing Office. • 1994. $6.50. Revised edition. Issued by the U. S. General Accounting Office (http://www.gao.gov). Contains standards for CPA firms to follow in financial and performance audits of federal government agencies and programs. Also known as the "Yellow Book.".

Handbook for Muni Bond Issuers. Joe Mysak. Bloomberg. • 1998. $40.00. Written primarily for the officers and attorneys of municipalities. Provides a practical explanation of the municipal bond market. (Bloomberg Professional Library.).

INTERNET DATABASES

Business 2.0 Web Guide to the Best Business Links. Business 2.0 Media Inc. Phone: (415)293-4800 E-mail: support@business2.com • URL: http://www.business2.com/webguide • Web site presents an extensive, searchable directory of links to "the best, most informative, and authoritative web pages." Twenty main categories cover business, finance, career, company information, people, and technology topics, with thousands of subtopics, all linking to Web sites recommended by experienced business researchers. Fees: Free.

Fedstats. Federal Interagency Council on Statistical Policy. Phone: (202)395-7254 • URL: http://www.fedstats.gov • Web site features an efficient search facility for full-text statistics produced by more than 100 federal agencies, including the Census Bureau, the Bureau of Economic Analysis, and the Bureau of Labor Statistics. Boolean searches can be made within one agency or for all agencies combined. Links are offered to international statistical bureaus, including the UN, IMF, OECD, UNESCO, Eurostat, and 20 individual countries. Fees: Free.

FreeLunch.com. Economy.com, Inc. Phone: (610)696-8700 Fax: (610)696-1678 • URL: http://www.freelunch.com • Web site provides free access to more than 1.5 million economic and financial data series, covering industry, demographics, labor markets, prices, retail sales, government spending, trade, interest rates, housing starts, the stock market, and many other topics. Data is available for various time periods in either chart or table form. Searching is offered. Fees: Free, but registration required. Economy.com, Inc. also offers fee-based economic analysis at *The Dismal Scientist* site (http://www.dismal.com).

ONLINE DATABASES

EconLit. American Economic Association. • Covers the worldwide literature of economics as contained in selected monographs and about 550 journals. Subjects include microeconomics, macroeconomics, economic history, inflation, money, credit, finance, accounting theory, trade, natural resource economics, and regional economics. Time period is 1969 to present, with monthly updates. Inquire as to online cost and availability.

PAIS International. Public Affairs Information Service, Inc. • Corresponds to the former printed publications, *PAIS Bulletin* (1976-90) and *PAIS Foreign Language Index* (1972-90), and to the current *PAIS International in Print* (1991 to date). Covers economic, political, and sociological material appearing in periodicals, books, government documents, and other publications. Updating is monthly. Inquire as to online cost and availability.

Social Scisearch. Institute for Scientific Information. • Broad, multidisciplinary index to the literature of the social sciences, 1972 to present. Weekly updates. Worldwide coverage. Inquire as to online cost and availability.

Wilson Social Sciences Abstracts Online. H. W. Wilson Co. • Provides online abstracting and indexing of more than 500 periodicals covering area studies, community health, public administration, public welfare, urban studies, and many other social science topics. Time period is 1994 to date for abstracts and 1983 to date for indexing, with updates weekly. Inquire as to online cost and availability.

PERIODICALS AND NEWSLETTERS

American Banker: The Financial Services Daily. Thomson Media. • Daily. $895.00 per year. Provides news of banking, investment products, mortgages, credit unions, finance, bank technology, and legal developments.

The Journal of Government Financial Management. Association of Government Accountants. • Quarterly. $90.00 per year. Formerly*Government Accountants Journal.*

Journal of Structured and Project Finance. Institutional Investor, Inc., Journals Group. • Quarterly. $365.00 per year. Includes print and online editions. Covers the financing of large-scale construction projects, such as power plants and convention centers. Formerly *Journal of Project Finance.*

Project Finance: The Magazine for Global Development. American Educational Systems. • 11 times a year. $740.00 per year. Includes print and online editions. Provides articles on the financing of the infrastructure (transportation, utilities, com-

munications, the environment, etc). Coverage is international. Supplements available *World Export Credit Guide* and *Project Finance Book of Lists.* Formed by the merger of *Infrastructure Finance* and *Project and Trade Finance.*

Public Finance Review. Sage Publications, Inc. • Bimonthly. Institutions, $599.00 per year; includes print and online editions. Formerly *Public Finance Quarterly.*

U. S. Banker. Thomson Media. • Monthly. $65.00 per year. Edited for bank executives and managers. Covers a wide variety of banking and financial topics.

RESEARCH CENTERS AND INSTITUTES

Government Finance Officers Association. Government Finance Officers Association. 203 N LaSalle St., Ste. 2700, Chicago, IL 60601-1210. Phone: (312)977-9700 Fax: (312)977-4806 E-mail: communications@foundationcenter.org • URL: http://www.gfoa.org • Provides consulting and research services in state and local government finance and management. Areas of expertise include: accounting, budgeting, cash management, debt management, pension/benefits, revenue and expenditure forecasting, technology procurement, reengineering/privatization, and state/local fiscal relations.

STATISTICS SOURCES

Business Statistics of the United States. Linz Audain and Cornelia J. Strawser. Bernan Associates. • Annual. $147.00. Based on *Business Statistics,* formerly issue by the Bureau of Economic Analysis, U. S. Department of Commerce. Provides basic data for a wide variety of U. S. industries, services, and economic indicators. Most statistics are shown annually for 30 years and monthly for the most recent four years.

Combined Statement of Receipts, Outlays, and Balances of the United States Government. Available from U. S. Government Printing Office. • Annual. $54.00. Issued by the Financial Mangement Service, U. S. Treasury Department (http://www.fms.treas.gov). In three parts: "Fiscal Year Summary," "Details of Receipts," and "Details of Appropriations, Outlays, and Balances.".

Daily Treasury Statement: Cash and Debt Operations of the United States Treasury. Available from U. S. Government Printing Office. • Daily, except Saturdays, Sundays, and holidays. (Financial Management Service, U. S. Treasury Department.).

Economic Report of the President: Together with the Annual Report of the Council of Economic Advisors. Available from U. S. Government Printing Office. • Annual. $32.00. Includes about 130 pages of "Statistical Tables Relating to Income, Employment, and Production." Tables cover national income, employment, wages, productivity, manufacturing, prices, credit, finance (public and private), corporate profits, and foreign trade.

Facts and Figures on Government Finance. Tax Foundation. • Annual. $45.00.

Monthly Statement of the Public Debt of the United States. U. S. Dept. of the Treasury, Public Debt Bureau. Available from U. S. Government Printing Office. • Monthly. $42.00 per year.

Monthly Treasury Statement of Receipts and Outlays of the United States Government. Available from U. S. Government Printing Office. • Monthly. $58.00 per year. Issued by the Financial Management Service, U. S. Treasury Department.

Revenue Statistics. OECD Publications and Information Center. • Annual. $65.00. Presents data on government revenues in OECD countries, classified by type of tax and level of government. Text in English and French.

State Profiles: The Population and Economy of Each U. S. State. Courtenay Slater and Others. Bernan

Press. • 1999. $89.00. Presents charts, tables, and text in an eight-page profile for each state. Covers population, labor force, income, poverty, employment, wages, industry, trade, housing, education, health, taxes, and government finances. (The Population and Economy of Each United States Series).

Statistical Information on the Financial Services Industry. American Bankers Association. • Annual. Members, $150.00; non-members, $275.00. Presents a wide variety of data relating to banking and financial services, including consumer economics, personal finance, credit, government loans, capital markets, and international banking.

Survey of Current Business. Available from U. S. Government Printing Office. • Monthly. $63.00 per year. Issued by Bureau of Economic Analysis, U. S. Department of Commerce. Presents a wide variety of business and economic data.

Treasury Bulletin. Available from U. S. Government Printing Office. • Quarterly. $45.00 per year. Issued by the Financial Management Service, U. S. Treasury Department. Provides data on the federal budget, government securities and yields, the national debt, and the financing of the federal government in general.

TRADE/PROFESSIONAL ASSOCIATIONS

Association of Government Accountants. 2208 Mount Vernon Ave., Alexandria, VA 22301-1314. Phone: 800-242-7211 or (703)684-6931 Fax: (703)548-9367 E-mail: agamembers@agacgfm.org • URL: http://www.agacgfm.org • Members are employed by federal, state, county, and city government agencies. Includes accountants, auditors, budget officers, and other government finance administrators and officials.

Bond Market Association. 360 Madison Ave., New York, NY 10017-7111. Phone: (646)637-9200 Fax: (646)637-9126 E-mail: membership@bondmarkets.com • URL: http://www.bondmarkets.com • Represents securities firms and banks that underwrite, trade and sell debt securities, both domestically and internationally.

Citizens for a Sound Economy. 1250 H St., NW, Ste. 700, Washington, DC 20005-3908. Phone: 888-564-6273 or (202)783-3870 Fax: (202)783-4687 E-mail: cse@cse.org • URL: http://www.cse.org • Absorbed Council for a Competitive Economy and Tax Foundation.

PUBLIC HOUSING

See: HOUSING

PUBLIC LIBRARIES

See: LIBRARIES

PUBLIC OPINION

GENERAL WORKS

Public Opinion: Politics, Communication and Social Process. Carroll J. Glyn and others. Westview Press. • 1998. $75.00.

ABSTRACTS AND INDEXES

Business Periodicals Index. H. W. Wilson Co. • 11 times a year. Quarterly and annual cumulations. Price varies.

PAIS International in Print. Public Affairs Information Service, Inc. • Monthly. $850.00 per year; cumulations three times a year. Provides topical citations to the worldwide literature of public affairs, economics, demographics, sociology, and trade. Text in English; indexed materials in English, French, German, Italian, Portuguese and Spanish.

Social Sciences Index. H. W. Wilson Co. • Quarterly, with annual cumulation. Price varies. Indexes more than 400 periodicals covering economics, environmental policy, government, insurance, labor, health care policy, plannning, public administration, public welfare, urban studies, women's issues, criminology, and related topics.

BIBLIOGRAPHIES

Public Opinion: A Bibliography with Indexes. William A. Blade, editor. Nova Science Publishers, Inc. • 2002. $59.00. Covers public opinion "in its many forms," including polls. Author, title, and subject indexes are provided.

Public Opinion Polls and Survey Research: A Selected Annotated Bibliography of U.S. Guides and Studies from the 1980s. Graham R. Waldon. Garland Publishing, Inc. • 1990. $15.00. (Public Affairs and Administration Series: vol. 24).

CD-ROM DATABASES

PAIS on CD-ROM. Public Affairs Information Service, Inc. • Quarterly. $1,995.00 per year. Provides a CD-ROM version of the online service, *PAIS International.* Contains over 500,000 citations to the literature of contemporary social, political, and economic issues.

Social Sciences Citation Index. ISI. • Monthly. Price on request. Provides CD-ROM indexing of articles appearing in 1700 leading social science journals worldwide, with additional selections from more than 5700 other journals. Time span is 1992 to date. Coverage includes economics, business, finance, management, communications, demographics, library and information science, political science, sociology, and many other subjects.

Social Sciences Citation Index: Compact Disc Edition with Abstracts. Institute for Scientific Information. • Monthly. Provides CD-ROM indexing and abstracting of "significant articles" from 1,700 social science journals worldwide, with additional selections from 3,200 other journals, 1986 to date. Includes economics, business, finance, management, communications, demographics, information and library science, political science, sociology, and many other subjects.

WILSONDISC: Wilson Social Sciences Abstracts. H. W. Wilson Co. • Monthly. Includes unlimited online access to *Social Sciences Index* through WILSONLINE. Provides CD-ROM indexing from 1983 and abstracting from 1994 of more than 500 periodicals covering economics, area studies, community health, public administration, public welfare, urban studies, and many other topics related to the social sciences.

DIRECTORIES

Agencies and Organizations Represented in AAPOR/WAPOR Membership. American Association for Public Opinion Research. • Annual. Free. Lists over 220 firms engaged in public opinion research.

Business Organizations, Agencies, and Publications Directory. Gale Cengage Learning. • 2003. $480.00. 15th edition. Over 40,000 entries describing 39 types of business information sources. Classified by type of organization, publication, or serviceIncludes state, national, and international agencies and organizations. Master index to names and keywords. Also includes e-mail addresses and web site URL's.

HANDBOOKS AND MANUALS

An American Profile: Attitudes and Behaviors of the American People, 1972-1989. Gale Cengage Learning. • 1990. $89.50. A summary of responses to about 300 questions in the General Social Survey conducted annually by the National Opinion Research Center, covering family characteristics, social behavior, religion, political opinions, etc. Includes a chronology of significant world events

from 1972 to 1989 and a subject-keyword index.

INTERNET DATABASES

Pew Research Center for the People and the Press. Pew Charitable Trusts. Phone: (202)293-3126 Fax: (202)293-2569 E-mail: mailprc@people-press.org • URL: http://www.people-press.org • Free Web site includes public opinion poll "Reports by Topic." Five broad subject areas cover business, social issues, foreign policy, news media, and politics. Searching is offered within each of these broad areas, and there are links to other major sources of public opinion poll results ("FYI Other Polls").

ONLINE DATABASES

PAIS International. Public Affairs Information Service, Inc. • Corresponds to the former printed publications, *PAIS Bulletin* (1976-90) and *PAIS Foreign Language Index* (1972-90), and to the current *PAIS International in Print* (1991 to date). Covers economic, political, and sociological material appearing in periodicals, books, government documents, and other publications. Updating is monthly. Inquire as to online cost and availability.

Wilson Business Abstracts Online. H. W. Wilson Co. • Indexes and abstracts 600 major business periodicals, plus the *Wall Street Journal* and the business section of the *New York Times.* Indexing is from 1982, abstracting from 1990, with the two newspapers included from 1993. Updated weekly. Inquire as to online cost and availability. (*Business Periodicals Index* without abstracts is also available online.).

Wilson Social Sciences Abstracts Online. H. W. Wilson Co. • Provides online abstracting and indexing of more than 500 periodicals covering area studies, community health, public administration, public welfare, urban studies, and many other social science topics. Time period is 1994 to date for abstracts and 1983 to date for indexing, with updates weekly. Inquire as to online cost and availability.

PERIODICALS AND NEWSLETTERS

AAPOR Newsletter. American Association for Public Opinion Research. • Description: Publishes news of the Association. Recurring features include a president's column, new member list, and personal notes.

Polling Report: An Independent Survey of Trends Affecting Elections, Government, and Business. Polling Report, Inc. • Biweekly. Individuals, $195.00 per year; students, $78.00 per year. Newsletter. Reports on the results of a wide variety of public opinion polls.

Public Opinion Quarterly. American Association for Public Opinion Research. The University of Chicago Press, Journals Div. • Quarterly. Institutions, $120.00 per year.

Public Pulse: Roper's Authoritative Report on What Americans are Thinking, D oing, and Buying. Roper Starch Worldwide. • Monthly. $297.00. Newsletter. Contains news of surveys of American attitudes, values, and behavior. Each issue includes a research supplement giving "complete facts and figures behind each survey question.".

World Opinion Update. Survey Research Consultants International, Inc. Survey Research Consultants International Inc. • Description: Gives tabular results of recent public opinion polls conducted in many countries on international public affairs subjects: sociological, political, economic, military, and religious. Recurring features include statistics.

RESEARCH CENTERS AND INSTITUTES

Center for Public Interest Polling. Rutgers University, 185 Ryders Ln., New Brunswick, NJ 08901. Phone: (732)932-9384 Fax: (732)932-1551 E-mail: zukin@rci.rutgers.edu • URL: http://www.rci.rutgers.edu/ • Provides survey research and program evaluation services.

Institute for Social Research. University of Michigan, 426 Thompson St., Ann Arbor, MI 48104-2321. Phone: (734)764-8354 Fax: (734)647-4575 E-mail: isr-info@isr.umich.edu • URL: http://www.isr.umich.edu.

Institute for Survey Research. Temple University Center for Public Policy, 1601 N. Broad St., Philadelphia, PA 19122. Phone: 800-827-5477 or (215)204-8355 Fax: (215)204-3797 E-mail: lenlo@temss2.isr.temple.edu • URL: http://www.temple.edu/isr • Conducts large scale in-person surveys that represent the United States househould population.

TRADE/PROFESSIONAL ASSOCIATIONS

American Association for Public Opinion Research. P.O. Box 14263, Lenexa, KS 66285-4263. Phone: (913)310-0118 Fax: (913)310-5340 E-mail: aapor-info@goamp.com • URL: http://www.aapor.org • Members are individuals interested in methods and applications of opinion research.

National Council on Public Polls. c/o Edward J. Efchak, 150 River St., Hackensack, NJ 07601. Phone: (201)646-4379 E-mail: info@ncpp.org • URL: http://www.ncpp.org • Members are public opinion polling organizations.

World Association for Public Opinion Research. University of Texas Pan American, 1405 Driftwood 1, Mission, TX 78572. Phone: (956)618-4048 Fax: (956)618-4943 E-mail: ghanem@panam.edu • URL: http://www.unl.edu/wapor • Members are opinion survey research experts, both academic and commercial. Promotes the use of objective, scientific, public opinion methodology and research. International emphasis.

PUBLIC RELATIONS AND PUBLICITY

See also: ADVERTISING

GENERAL WORKS

How to Promote, Publicize, and Advertise Your Growing Business: Getting the Word Out Without Spending a Fortune. Kim Baker and Sunny Baker. John Wiley and Sons, Inc. • 1992. $12.95.

PR News Casebook. Gale Cengage Learning. • 1993. $110.00. A collection of about 1,000 case studies covering major public relations campaigns and events, taken from the pages of *PR News.* Covers such issues as boycotts, new products, anniversaries, plant closings, downsizing, and stockholder relations.

Public Relations Practices: Managerial Case Studies and Problems. Allen H. Center. Prentice Hall PTR. • 2002. $84.00. Sixth edition.

DIRECTORIES

Gale's Guide to the Media: A Gale Ready Reference Handbook. Gale Cengage Learning. • 2000. $125.00. Provides profiles of a wide variety of media-related organizations, publications, broadcasters, agencies, and databases, of interest to nonprofit groups. Contains three indexes and a glossary.

IEG Sponsorship Sourcebook. IEG Inc. • Covers: about 5,000 corporate sponsors and 1,600 major sports, events, and organizations worldwide available for commercial sponsorship; companies serving special events and sponsors (sports marketing agencies, fireworks suppliers, public relations firms, etc.). Entries include: For events--Event title, site, dates, name, and address of contact (including year-round phone number), attendance figures, event budget, and major present and past sponsors. For service firms--Company name, address, phone, contact, speciality/services. New sponsorship events are reported in "IEG Sponsorship Report", published every two weeks, which also includes a frequent "In Depth" directory of corporations and their special events contact, budget, priorities, events sponsored, etc.; $445 per year; $370 for nonprofit organizations.

National Directory of Corporate Public Affairs. Columbia Books, Inc. • Annual. $109.00. Lists about 1,900 corporations that have foundations or other public affairs activities.

O'Dwyer's Directory of Corporate Communications. J. R. O'Dwyer Co., Inc. • Annual. $130.00. Public relations departments of major corporations.

O'Dwyer's Directory of Public Relations Firms. J. R. O'Dwyer Co., Inc. • Triennial. $120.00. Over 9,300 corporation and public relations firms.

Public Relations Tactics Member Services Directory: The Blue Book. Public Relations Society of America. • Annual. Free to members; nonmembers, $250.00; universities, educational institutions, libraries, $375.00. About 17,000 public relations practioners in business, government, education, etc. who are members. Formerly *Public Relations Journal-Register.*

ENCYCLOPEDIAS AND DICTIONARIES

Dictionary of Marketing Communications. Norman A. P. Govoni. Sage Publications, Inc. • 2003. $69.95. Contains more than 4,000 concise definitions of terms relating to advertising, sales promotion, public relations, direct marketing, and selling.

Encyclopedia of Public Relations. Robert L. Heath, editor. Sage Publications, Inc. • 2004. $295.00. Two volumes. Contains about 450 entries on such topics as crisis management, ethics, public relations research, theories, jargon, mass media, public relations education, and the history of public relations.

HANDBOOKS AND MANUALS

Complete Guide to Special Event Management: Business Insights, Financial Advice and Successful Strategies from Ernst and Young, Consultants to the Olympics. John Wiley and Sons, Inc. • 1992. $39.95. Covers the marketing, financing, and general management of special events in the fields of art, entertainment, and sports.

Dartnell's Public Relations Handbook. Robert L. Dilenschneider, editor. Dartnell Corp. • 1996. $69.95. Fourth revised edition. Covers press releases, media kits, media contacts, crisis management, and other topics.

Handbook for Public Relations Writing. Thomas Bivins. McGraw-Hill. • 1992. $17.95. Second edition. (NTC Business Books Series).

Handbook of Public Relations. Robert L. Heath, editor. Sage Publications, Inc. • 2000. $117.00. Covers best practices, academic research, and theory. Contains articles by various advertising specialists.

Lesly's Handbook of Public Relations and Communications. Philip Lesly. McGraw-Hill. • 1997. $100.00. Fifth edition.

Managing a Public Relations Firm for Growth and Profit. A. C. Croft, editor. The Haworth Press, Inc. • 1995. $39.95.

The New Publicity Kit. Jeanette Smith. John Wiley and Sons, Inc. • 1995. $19.95. Multi-media campaigns, and other forms of publicity.

Powerful Public Relations: A How-To Guide for Libraries. Rashelle S. Karp, editor. American Library Association. • 2002. $32.00. Provides concise coverage of library press releases, public service announcements, brochures, special events, exhibits, and use of multimedia.

Public Relations Writer's Handbook. Merry Aronson and Donald E. Spetner. John Wiley and Sons, Inc. • 1998. $24.95.

The Publicity Handbook: How to Maximize Publicity for Products, Services, and Organizations. David

Yale. McGraw-Hill. • 1994. $19.95. (NTC Business Books Series).

INTERNET DATABASES

EBSCO Information Services. Ebsco Publishing. Phone: 800-653-2726 or (978)356-6500 Fax: (978)356-6565 E-mail: ep@epnet.com • URL: http://www.epnet.com • Fee-based Web site providing Internet access to a wide variety of databases, including business-related material. Full text is available for many periodical titles, with daily updates. Fees: Apply.

InSite 2. Intelligence Data/Thomson Financial. Phone: 800-654-0393 or (617)856-1890 Fax: (617)737-3182 E-mail: intelligence.data@tfn.com • URL: http://www.insite2.gale.com/ • Fee-based Web site consolidates information in a "Base Pack" consisting of Business InSite, Market InSite, and Company InSite. Optional databases are Consumer InSite, Health and Wellness InSite, Newsletter InSite, and Computer InSite. Includes fulltext content from more than 2,500 trade publications, journals, newsletters, newspapers, analyst reports, and other sources. Continuous updating. Formerly produced by The Gale Group.

ProQuest Direct. ProQuest Inc. Phone: 800-889-3358 or (734)761-4700 Fax: (734)662-4554 • URL: http://proquest.com • Fee-based Web site providing Internet access to more than 3,000 periodicals, newspapers, and other publications. Many items are available full-text, with daily updates. Includes extensive corporate and financial information. Fees: Apply.

PERIODICALS AND NEWSLETTERS

Communication Briefings: A Monthly Idea Source for Decision Makers. Briefings Publishing Group. • Monthly. $139.00 per year. Newsletter. Presents useful ideas for communication, public relations, customer service, human resources, and employee training.

Communication World: The Magazine for Communication Professionals. International Association of Business Communicators. • Seven times a year. Free to members; libraries, $95.00 per year. Emphasis is on public relations, media relations, corporate communication, and writing.

The Customer Communicator. The Customer Service Group. • Description: Serves as a guideline for customer relations skills while it "boosts morale." Covers customer representative skills and provides tips on customer contact, handling complaints, checklists, and promotional contests. **Remarks:** a monthly training module.

Journal of Promotion Management: Innovations in Planning and Applied Research. Haworth Press, Inc. • Semiannual. Institutions, $200.00 per year.

Marketing Magazine: Canada's Weekly Newspaper for Marketing, Advertising and Sales Executives. Rogers Media Publishing. • Weekly. $95.00 per year. "Canada's national weekly publication dedicated to the businesses of marketing, advertising, and media." Includes annual Marketing Awards, quarterly Digital Marketing (emerging technology), Promo Marketing, and PR Quarterly (special issues on public relations).

PR Reporter: The Newsletter of Behavioral Public Relations, Public Affairs, and Communication Strategies. Lawrence Ragan Communications, Inc. • Weekly. $250.00 per year. Newsletter. Presents a "digest of theories, research, public opinion, case studies, and successful public relations techniques.".

Public Relations. PBI Media, LLC. • Biweekly. $397.00 per year. Newsletter on public relations and client communications for the healthcare industry. Incorporates (Healthcare PR and Marketing News).

Public Relations News. PBI Media, LLC. • Weekly. $597.00 per year. Newsletter on public relations for business, government, and nonprofit organizations.

Public Relations Quarterly. Hudson Associates. • Quarterly. $65.00 per year. Opinion articles and case studies on the theory and practice of public relations for and by leading practitioners and academicians.

Public Relations Review: Journal of Research and Comment. Elsevier. • Five times a year. Individuals, $137.00 per year; institutions, $366.00 per year. Includes annual *Bibliography.*

Public Relations Strategist: Issues and Trends That Affect Management. Public Relations Society of America. • Quarterly. $48.00 per year. Provides public relations advice for corporate and government executives.

TRADE/PROFESSIONAL ASSOCIATIONS

Public Relations Society of America. 33 Irving Pl., 3rd Fl., New York, NY 10003-2376. Phone: (212)995-2230 Fax: (212)995-0757 E-mail: hq@prsa.org • URL: http://www.prsa.org • Absorbed American Public Relations Association and National Communication Council for Human Services.

PUBLIC SERVICE CORPORATIONS

See: PUBLIC UTILITIES

PUBLIC SPEAKING

See also: DEBATES AND DEBATING; TOASTS

ABSTRACTS AND INDEXES

Speech Index: An Index to Collections of World Famous Orations and Speeches for Various Occasions, 1966-1980. Charity Mitchell. Scarecrow Press, Inc. • 1982. $82.50. Fourth edition.

HANDBOOKS AND MANUALS

American Speaker: Your Guide to Successful Speaking. Briefings Publishing Group. • Bimonthly. $399.00. Newsletter. Provides practical advice on public speaking.

Complete Speaker's and Toastmaster's Library. Jacob M. Braude. Prentice Hall PTR. • 1992. $69.95. Second edition.

The Manager's Book of Quotations. Lewis D. and Jonathan P. Siegel Eigen. AMACOM. • 1991. $24.95. Reprint edition. Provides 5,000 modern and traditional quotations arranged by topics useful to business people for speeches and writing.

Persuasive Business Speaking. Elayne Snyder. AMACOM. • 1990. $17.95. Includes ready-to-use openers, sample speeches, anecdotes, and quotes.

Public Speaking. Michael Osborn and Suzanne Osborn. Houghton Mifflin Co. • 2000. $34.17. Fifth edition.

PERIODICALS AND NEWSLETTERS

Vital Speeches of the Day. City News Publishing Co., Inc. • Bimonthly. $45.00 per year.

TRADE/PROFESSIONAL ASSOCIATIONS

International Training in Communication. 2519 Woodland Dr., Anaheim, CA 92801-2637. Phone: (714)995-3660 Fax: (714)995-6974 E-mail: itcintl@mediamatters.co.nz • URL: http://www.itcintl.com • Members are interested in speech improvement, communication, lexicology, leadership training and skill in organizational techniques and self-development.

National Speakers Association. 1500 S Priest Dr., Tempe, AZ 85281. Phone: (480)968-2552 Fax: (480)968-0911 E-mail: information@nsaspeaker.org • URL: http://www.nsaspeaker.org • Professional speakers. Works to increase public awareness of the speaking profession, advance the integrity and visibility of professional speakers, and provide a learning and communication vehicle to professional speakers. Sponsors workshops, conventions, and labs.

Toastmasters International. PO Box 9052, PO Box 9052, Mission Viejo, CA 92690-9052. Phone: 800-993-7732 or (949)858-8255 Fax: (949)858-1207 E-mail: tminfo@toastmasters.org • URL: http://www.toastmasters.org • Men and women who wish to improve their communication and leadership skills. Sponsors clubs in corporate, government, and military facilities, as well as local communities in over 90 countries. Sponsors annual World Championship of Public Speaking. Special activities include: advanced communication and leadership program; youth leadership programs for junior and senior high school students; Gavel Clubs in schools, prisons, and other institutions.

PUBLIC TRANSPORTATION

See also: MOTOR BUSES; RAILROADS; TRANSPORTATION INDUSTRY

ABSTRACTS AND INDEXES

NTIS Alerts: Transportation. National Technical Information Service. • Semimonthly. $210.00 per year. Provides descriptions of government-sponsored research reports and software, with ordering information. Covers air, marine, highway, inland waterway, pipeline, and railroad transportation. Formerly *Abstract Newsletter.*

Readers' Guide to Periodical Literature. H. W. Wilson Co. • Monthly. $345.00 per year. Includes annual *Cumulation.* Indexes about 250 periodicals of general interest.

CD-ROM DATABASES

OECD Statistical Compendium. Organization for Economic Cooperation and Development. • Semiannual. $1,905.00 per year for 1 to 10 users. CD-ROM contains more than 730,000 monthly, quarterly, and annual time series for OECD countries, 1960 to date. Includes fully searchable data on agriculture, food, economic indicators, national accounts, employment, energy, finance, industry, technology, and foreign trade. Results can be displayed in various forms.

DIRECTORIES

Mass Transit: Consultants. Cygnus Business Media, Inc. • Annual. $64.00. Listings for over 300 urban transportation architects, designers, engineers, planners, consultants and other specialists serving the urban transportation industry.

Mass Transit: Supplier's Guide. Mass Transit. • Eight times a year. $48.00 per year. Directory of over 800 manufacturers and distributors serving the urban transportation industry.

ENCYCLOPEDIAS AND DICTIONARIES

Macmillan Encyclopedia of Transportation. Available from Gale Cengage Learning. • 1999. $450.00. Six volumes. Published by Macmillan Reference USA. Covers the business, technology, and history of transportation on land, on water, in the air, and in space. Includes definitions, cross-references, and 200 color illustrations.

FINANCIAL RATIOS

Almanac of Business and Industrial Financial Ratios. Leo Troy. Aspen Publishers, Inc. • 2003. $125.95. Includes CD-Rom. Contains financial ratios derived from federal tax returns. Ratios for each of about 200 industries are arranged according to company asset size. (Almanac of Business and Industrial Financial Ratios Series).

HANDBOOKS AND MANUALS

Transportation Planning Handbook. John D. Edwards. Institute of Transportation Engineers. •

1999. $100.00. Second edition.

INTERNET DATABASES

Business 2.0 Web Guide to the Best Business Links. Business 2.0 Media Inc. Phone: (415)293-4800 E-mail: support@business2.com • URL: http://www.business2.com/webguide • Web site presents an extensive, searchable directory of links to "the best, most informative, and authoritative web pages." Twenty main categories cover business, finance, career, company information, people, and technology topics, with thousands of subtopics, all linking to Web sites recommended by experienced business researchers. Fees: Free.

Fedstats. Federal Interagency Council on Statistical Policy. Phone: (202)395-7254 • URL: http://www.fedstats.gov • Web site features an efficient search facility for full-text statistics produced by more than 100 federal agencies, including the Census Bureau, the Bureau of Economic Analysis, and the Bureau of Labor Statistics. Boolean searches can be made within one agency or for all agencies combined. Links are offered to international statistical bureaus, including the UN, IMF, OECD, UNESCO, Eurostat, and 20 individual countries. Fees: Free.

FreeLunch.com. Economy.com, Inc. Phone: (610)696-8700 Fax: (610)696-1678 • URL: http://www.freelunch.com • Web site provides free access to more than 1.5 million economic and financial data series, covering industry, demographics, labor markets, prices, retail sales, government spending, trade, interest rates, housing starts, the stock market, and many other topics. Data is available for various time periods in either chart or table form. Searching is offered. Fees: Free, but registration required. Economy.com, Inc. also offers fee-based economic analysis at *The Dismal Scientist* site (http://www.dismal.com).

ONLINE DATABASES

Readers' Guide Abstracts Online. H. W. Wilson Co. • Indexes and abstracts general interest periodicals, 1983 to date. Weekly updates. Inquire as to online cost and availability.

TRIS: Transportation Research Information Service. National Research Council. • Contains abstracts and citations to a wide range of transportation literature, 1968 to present, with monthly updates. Includes references to the literature of air transportation, highways, ships and shipping, railroads, trucking, and urban mass transportation. Formerly *TRIS-ONLINE.* Inquire as to online cost and availability.

PERIODICALS AND NEWSLETTERS

Downtown Idea Exchange: Essential Information for Downtown Research and Development Center. Downtown Research and Development Center. Alexander Communications Group, Inc. • Semimonthly. $187.00 per year. Newsletter for those concerned with central business districts. Provides news and other information on planning, development, parking, mass transit, traffic, funding, and other topics.

Mass Transit: Better Transit Through Better Management. Cygnus Publishing. • Bimonthly. 48.00 per year.

Metro. Bobit Publishing Co. • Nine times a year. $40.00 per year. Subject matter is the management of public transportation systems. Includes *Factbook.*

Nation's Cities Weekly. National League of Cities. • Description: Presents news on the latest developments in Congress, the White House, federal agencies, and other public interest groups which may affect the nation's cities.

Passenger Transport. American Public Transportation Association. • Weekly. $65.00 per year. Covers current events and trends in mass transportation.

Urban Transport News: Management-Funding Terrorism-Ridership-Technology. Business Publishers, Inc. • 25 times a year. $437.00 per year.

Newsletter. Provides current news from Capitol Hill, the White House, the Dept. of Transportation, as well as transit operations and industries across the country.

RESEARCH CENTERS AND INSTITUTES

Battelle Memorial Institute. Battelle Memorial Institute. 505 King Ave., Columbus, OH 43201. Phone: 800-201-2011 or (614)424-5853 Fax: (614)424-5263 E-mail: solutions@battelle.org • URL: http://www.battelle.org/ • Environment and energy; national security; transportation; health and life sciences; medical, pharmaceutical, agrochemical, and consumer product development. Conducts marine research at three coastal locations: Florida Marine Research Facility (Daytona Beach), Northwest Marine Research Laboratory (Sequim, Washington), and the Ocean Sciences Laboratory (Duxbury, Massachusetts). Specialized facilities and units include: Aviation Safety Reporting System Office; the Breakthrough Center for Strategic Product Development; the Human Engineering, Ergonomics, and Organizational Research Center; and the William R. Wiley Environmental Molecular Sciences Laboratory.

Carnegie Mellon Research Institute-Computer Automation and Robotics. Carnegie Mellon University, 700 Technology Dr., Pittsburgh, PA 15219. Phone: (412)268-3363 Fax: (412)368-7759 • URL: http://www.cmu.edu/cmri • Multidisciplinary research activities include expert systems applications, minicomputer and microcomputer systems design, genetic engineering, and transportation systems analysis.

Center for Business and Industrial Studies. University of Missouri-St. Louis, School of Business Administration, 8001 Natural Bridge Rd., St. Louis, MO 63121. Phone: (314)516-5000 • URL: http://www.umsl.edu/ • Research fields include inventory and management control. Specific projects also include development of computer software for operations in public transit systems.

Center for Transportation Studies. Massachusetts Institute of Technology. 77 Massachusetts Ave. Room 1-235, Cambridge, MA 02139. Phone: (617)253-5320 Fax: (617)253-4560 E-mail: sheffi@mit.edu • URL: http://www.web.mit.edu/cts/www/.

Center for Urban Transportation Studies. University of Wisconsin at Milwaukee, P.O. Box 784, Milwaukee, WI 53201-0784. Phone: (414)229-5787 Fax: (414)229-6958 E-mail: beimborn@uwm.edu • URL: http://www.uwm.edu/dept/cuts.

MPC Corporation. MPC Corporation. 5000 Forbes Ave., Pittsburgh, PA 15213. Phone: (412)268-2091 Fax: (412)268-5841 E-mail: rkloss@andrew.cmu.edu • Engineering and technology, including cooperative studies with local industry on mass rapid transit for metropolitan areas, systems planning, and systems evaluation. Serve as administrative and coordinating agency for joint research activities of staff members of affiliated institutions.

Texas Transportation Institute. Texas A & M University System, CE/TTI, Room 801 B, College Station, TX 77843-3135. Phone: (979)845-1713 Fax: (979)845-9356 E-mail: herbert-richardson@tamu.edu • URL: http://www.tii.tamu.edu • Concerned with all forms and modes of transportation. Research areas include transportation economics, highway construction, traffic safety, public transportation, and highway engineering.

Transportation Research Center. University of Florida. 512 Weil Hall, Gainesville, FL 32611. Phone: 800-226-1013 or (352)392-7575 Fax: (352)392-3224 E-mail: uftrc@ce.ufl.edu • URL: http://www.uftrc.ce.ufl.edu.

Transportation Systems Institute. University of Central Florida, Dept. of Civil and Environmental Engineering, P.O. Box 162450, Orlando, FL 32816-2450. Phone: (407)823-2988 Fax: (407)823-3315

E-mail: haldeek@pegasus.cc.ucf.edu • URL: http://www.catss.ucf.edu/tsi • Research areas include mass transportation systems.

STATISTICS SOURCES

Business Statistics of the United States. Linz Audain and Cornelia J. Strawser. Bernan Associates. • Annual. $147.00. Based on *Business Statistics*, formerly issue by the Bureau of Economic Analysis, U. S. Department of Commerce. Provides basic data for a wide variety of U. S. industries, services, and economic indicators. Most statistics are shown annually for 30 years and monthly for the most recent four years.

Gale Country and World Rankings Reporter. Gale Cengage Learning. • 1997. $160.00. Second edition. Provides about 3,000 statistical ranking tables and charts covering more than 235 nations. Sources include the United Nations and various government publications.

Gale State Rankings Reporter. Gale Cengage Learning. • 1996. $130.00. Second edition Provides 3,000 ranked lists of states under 35 subject headings. Sources are newspapers, periodicals, books, research institute publications, and government publications.

Infrastructure Industries USA. Gale Cengage Learning. • 2001. $260.00. Presents statistics and projections relating to economic activity in a wide variety of natural resource and construction industries.

Survey of Current Business. Available from U. S. Government Printing Office. • Monthly. $63.00 per year. Issued by Bureau of Economic Analysis, U. S. Department of Commerce. Presents a wide variety of business and economic data.

Transportation Statistics Annual Report. Available from U. S. Government Printing Office. • Annual. $43.00. Issued by the U. S. Bureau of Transportation Statistics, Transportation Department (http://www.bts.gov). Summarizes national data for various forms of transportation, including airlines, railroads, and motor vehicles. Information on the use of roads and highways is included.

TRADE/PROFESSIONAL ASSOCIATIONS

American Disabled for Attendant Program Today. 201 S. Cherokee St., Denver, CO 80223-1836. Phone: (303)733-9324 Fax: (303)733-6211 E-mail: adapt@adapt.org • URL: http://www.adapt.org • Members are disabled individuals promoting wheelchair accessibility in all forms of public transportation.

American Public Transportation Association. 1666 K St. NW, Ste. 1100, Washington, DC 20006. Phone: (202)496-4800 Fax: (202)496-4321 E-mail: info@apta.com • URL: http://www.apta.com • Motor bus and rapid transit systems; organizations responsible for planning, designing, constructing, financing, and operating transit systems; business organizations which supply products and services to transit, academic institutions, and state associations and departments of transportation. Represents the public interest in improving transit. Encourages cooperation among its members, their employees, the general public and compliance with the letter and spirit of equal opportunity principles. Seeks to: collect information relative to public transit; assist in the training, education, and professional development of all persons involved in public transit; and engage in activities which promote public transit. Provides a medium for exchange of experiences, discussion, and a comparative study of public transit affairs; Promotes research.

Institute of Transportation Engineers. 1099 14th St., N.W., Suite 300 W, Washington, DC 20005-3438. Phone: (202)289-0222 Fax: (202)289-7722 E-mail: ite_staff@site.org • URL: http://www.ite.org • Members are professionals in surface transportation, mass transit, and traffic engineering. Formerly

Institute of Traffic Engineers.

PUBLIC UTILITIES

See also: ELECTRIC UTILITIES; ENERGY SOURCES; GAS INDUSTRY; TELEPHONE INDUSTRY; WATER SUPPLY

CD-ROM DATABASES

Environment Abstracts on CD-ROM. LEXIS-NEXIS. • Quarterly. $1,295.00 per year. Contains the following CD-ROM databases: *Environment Abstracts*, *Energy Abstracts*, and *Acid Rain Abstracts*. Length of coverage varies.

OECD Statistical Compendium. Organization for Economic Cooperation and Development. • Semiannual. $1,905.00 per year for 1 to 10 users. CD-ROM contains more than 730,000 monthly, quarterly, and annual time series for OECD countries, 1960 to date. Includes fully searchable data on agriculture, food, economic indicators, national accounts, employment, energy, finance, industry, technology, and foreign trade. Results can be displayed in various forms.

DIRECTORIES

Plunkett's Energy Industry Almanac: Complete Profiles on the Energy Industry 500 Companies. Plunkett Research Ltd. • Annual. $199.99. Includes major oil companies, utilities, pipelines, alternative energy companies, etc. Provides information on industry trends.

FINANCIAL RATIOS

Almanac of Business and Industrial Financial Ratios. Leo Troy. Aspen Publishers, Inc. • 2003. $125.95. Includes CD-Rom. Contains financial ratios derived from federal tax returns. Ratios for each of about 200 industries are arranged according to company asset size. (Almanac of Business and Industrial Financial Ratios Series).

HANDBOOKS AND MANUALS

Moody's Public Utility Manual. Mergent, Inc. • Annual. $1,995.00. Updated weekly online. Contains financial and other information concerning publicly-held utility companies (electric, gas, telephone, water).

INTERNET DATABASES

Bureau of Economic Analysis (BEA). U. S. Department of Commerce, Bureau of Economic Analysis. Phone: (202)606-9900 Fax: (202)606-5310 E-mail: webmaster@bea.doc.gov • URL: http://www.bea.doc.gov • Web site includes "News Release Information" covering national, regional, and international economic estimates from the BEA. Highlights of releases appear online the same day, complete text and tables appear the next day. "Recent News Releases" section provides titles for past nine months, with links. "BEA Data and Methodology" includes "Frequently Requested NIPA Data" (national income and product accounts, such as gross domestic product and personal income). Other statistics are available. Fees: Free.

Business 2.0 Web Guide to the Best Business Links. Business 2.0 Media Inc. Phone: (415)293-4800 E-mail: support@business2.com • URL: http://www.business2.com/webguide • Web site presents an extensive, searchable directory of links to "the best, most informative, and authoritative web pages." Twenty main categories cover business, finance, career, company information, people, and technology topics, with thousands of subtopics, all linking to Web sites recommended by experienced business researchers. Fees: Free.

Fedstats. Federal Interagency Council on Statistical Policy. Phone: (202)395-7254 • URL: http://www.fedstats.gov • Web site features an efficient search facility for full-text statistics produced by more than 100 federal agencies, including the Census Bureau,

the Bureau of Economic Analysis, and the Bureau of Labor Statistics. Boolean searches can be made within one agency or for all agencies combined. Links are offered to international statistical bureaus, including the UN, IMF, OECD, UNESCO, Eurostat, and 20 individual countries. Fees: Free.

FreeLunch.com. Economy.com, Inc. Phone: (610)696-8700 Fax: (610)696-1678 • URL: http://www.freelunch.com • Web site provides free access to more than 1.5 million economic and financial data series, covering industry, demographics, labor markets, prices, retail sales, government spending, trade, interest rates, housing starts, the stock market, and many other topics. Data is available for various time periods in either chart or table form. Searching is offered. Fees: Free, but registration required. Economy.com, Inc. also offers fee-based economic analysis at *The Dismal Scientist* site (http://www.dismal.com).

PERIODICALS AND NEWSLETTERS

Public Utilities Fortnightly. Public Utilities Reports, Inc. • 22 times a year. $139.00 per year. Management magazine for utility executives in electric, gas, telecommunications and water industries.

RESEARCH CENTERS AND INSTITUTES

Public Utility Research Center. University of Florida. College of Business Administration, 205 Matherly, Gainesville, FL 32611. Phone: (352)392-6148 Fax: (352)392-7796 E-mail: purcecon@dale.cba.ufl.edu • URL: http://www.bear.cba.ufl.edu/centers/purc.

STATISTICS SOURCES

American Housing Survey for the United States in [year]. Available from U. S. Government Printing Office. • Biennial. $51.00. Issued by the U. S. Census Bureau (http://www.census.gov). Covers both owner-occupied and renter-occupied housing. Includes data on such factors as condition of building, type of mortgage, utility costs, and housing occupied by minorities. (Current Housing Reports, H150.).

Business Statistics of the United States. Linz Audain and Cornelia J. Strawser. Bernan Associates. • Annual. $147.00. Based on *Business Statistics*, formerly issue by the Bureau of Economic Analysis, U. S. Department of Commerce. Provides basic data for a wide variety of U. S. industries, services, and economic indicators. Most statistics are shown annually for 30 years and monthly for the most recent four years.

Energy Balances of OECD Countries. Organization for Economic Cooperation and Development. Available from OECD Publications and Information Center. • Annual. $115.00. Presents two-year data on the supply and consumption of solid fuels, oil, gas, and electricity, expressed in oil equivalency terms. Historical tables are also provided. Relates to OECD member countries.

Housing Statistics of the United States. Patrick A. Simmons. Bernan Press. • 2000. $89.00. Third edition. (Housing Statistics of the United States Series).

Infrastructure Industries USA. Gale Cengage Learning. • 2001. $260.00. Presents statistics and projections relating to economic activity in a wide variety of natural resource and construction industries.

Structural Statistics for Industry and Services: Core Data. Organization for Economic Cooperation and Development. • Annual. $63.00. Provides annual data for eight years for both industrial and service sectors. Industries include mining, manufacturing, utilities, and construction. Statistics for OECD countries cover production, value added, investment, employment, wages, hours worked, and number of establishments.

Survey of Current Business. Available from U. S.

Government Printing Office. • Monthly. $63.00 per year. Issued by Bureau of Economic Analysis, U. S. Department of Commerce. Presents a wide variety of business and economic data.

WEFA Industrial Monitor. John Wiley and Sons, Inc. • Annual. $65.00. Prepared by industry analysts at WEFA, an economic forecasting and consulting firm (originally Wharton Econometric Forecasting Associates). Contains discussions of the outlook for major U. S. industries, with many 10-year forecasts (WEFA Web site is http://www.wefa.com).

TRADE/PROFESSIONAL ASSOCIATIONS

National Association of Regulatory Utility Commissioners. 1101 Vermont Ave., N.W., Ste. 200, Washington, DC 20005. Phone: (202)898-2200 Fax: (202)898-2213 E-mail: cgray@naruc.com • URL: http://www.naruc.com • Formerly National Association of Railway and Utility Commissioners.

Utility Communicators International. 1818 Country Creek Ct., 5525 E Grandview Dr., Magnolia, TX 77354. Phone: (936)271-5005 Fax: (936)271-5060 E-mail: eboardman@att.net • URL: http://www.uci-online.com • Advertising and public relations directors of electric, gas, water, telephone, and other utility companies and allied industries. Sponsors utility advertising/communications contest.

OTHER SOURCES

Utilities Industry Litigation Reporter: National Coverage of the Many Types of Litigation Stemming From the Transmission and Distribution of Energy By Publicly and Privately Owned Utilities. Andrews Publications. • Monthly. $775.00 per year. Newsletter. Reports on legal cases involving the generation or distribution of energy.

PUBLIC WELFARE

GENERAL WORKS

From Poor Law to Welfare State: A History of Social Welfare in America. Walter I. Trattner. Simon and Schuster Trade. • 1998. $17.95. Sixth edition.

Housing the Poor: An Overview. Morton J. Schussheim. Nova Science Publishers, Inc. • 2003. $29.50. Discusses current and emerging housing problems affecting the poor. Covers housing rehabilitation programs, community development block grants, and other programs for low-income households.

Improving Poor People: The Welfare State, the "Underclass," and Urban Schools as History. Michael B. Katz. Princeton University Press. • 1995. $42.50.

Nickel and Dimed: On Not Getting By in America. Barbara Ehrenreich. Gale Cengage Learning. • 2001. $29.95. The author temporarily became a low-wage worker to experience American life at the bottom. Dramatizes the inadequacy of the minimum wage. (Metropolitan Books.).

Welfare, the Working Poor, and Labor. Louise Simmons, editor. M. E. Sharpe, Inc. • 2004. $66.95. Presents material by various authors on poverty, welfare reform, and the market for low-wage labor.

ABSTRACTS AND INDEXES

PAIS International in Print. Public Affairs Information Service, Inc. • Monthly. $850.00 per year; cumulations three times a year. Provides topical citations to the worldwide literature of public affairs, economics, demographics, sociology, and trade. Text in English; indexed materials in English, French, German, Italian, Portuguese and Spanish.

Social Sciences Citation Index. Thomson/ISI. • Three times a year. $6,900 per year. Annual cumulation. Includes *Source Index*, *Citation Index*, *Permuterm Subject Index*, and *Corporate Index*.

Social Sciences Index. H. W. Wilson Co. • Quarterly, with annual cumulation. Price varies. Indexes more than 400 periodicals covering economics,

environmental policy, government, insurance, labor, health care policy, plannning, public administration, public welfare, urban studies, women's issues, criminology, and related topics.

CD-ROM DATABASES

Newspaper Abstracts Ondisc. PROQUEST. • Monthly. $2,950.00 per year (covers 1989 to date; archival discs are available for 1985-88). Provides cover-to-cover CD-ROM indexing and abstracting of 19 major newspapers, including the *New York Times, Wall Street Journal, Washington Post, Chicago Tribune,* and *Los Angeles Times.*

PAIS on CD-ROM. Public Affairs Information Service, Inc. • Quarterly. $1,995.00 per year. Provides a CD-ROM version of the online service, *PAIS International.* Contains over 500,000 citations to the literature of contemporary social, political, and economic issues.

Social Sciences Citation Index. ISI. • Monthly. Price on request. Provides CD-ROM indexing of articles appearing in 1700 leading social science journals worldwide, with additional selections from more than 5700 other journals. Time span is 1992 to date. Coverage includes economics, business, finance, management, communications, demographics, library and information science, political science, sociology, and many other subjects.

Social Sciences Citation Index: Compact Disc Edition with Abstracts. Institute for Scientific Information. • Monthly. Provides CD-ROM indexing and abstracting of "significant articles" from 1,700 social science journals worldwide, with additional selections from 3,200 other journals, 1986 to date. Includes economics, business, finance, management, communications, demographics, information and library science, political science, sociology, and many other subjects.

WILSONDISC: Readers' Guide to Periodical Literature. H. W. Wilson Co. • Monthly. $1,095.00 per year, including unlimited online access to *Readers' Guide to Periodical Literature* through WILSONLINE. Provides CD-ROM indexing of about 270 general interest periodicals. Covers 1983 to date. (*Readers' Guide Abstracts* also available on CD-ROM at $1,995 per year.).

WILSONDISC: Wilson Social Sciences Abstracts. H. W. Wilson Co. • Monthly. Includes unlimited online access to *Social Sciences Index* through WILSONLINE. Provides CD-ROM indexing from 1983 and abstracting from 1994 of more than 500 periodicals covering economics, area studies, community health, public administration, public welfare, urban studies, and many other topics related to the social sciences.

DIRECTORIES

Catalog of Federal Domestic Assistance. U.S. Office of Management and Budget. Available from U.S. Government Printing Office. • Annual. $87.00. Looseleaf service. Includes up-dating service for indeterminate period. Summary of financial and nonfinanacial Federal programs, projects, services and activities that provide assistance or benefits to the American public.

Government Assistance Almanac: The Guide to Federal, Domestic, Financial and Other Programs Covering Grants, Loans, Insurance, Personal Payments and Benefits. J. Robert Dumouchel, editor. Omnigraphics, Inc. • Annual. $235.00. Describes more than 1,400 federal assistance programs available from about 50 agencies. Includes statistics, a directory of 3,000 field offices, and comprehensive indexing.

How to Save on Prescription Drugs: The AIER Guide to Prescription Drug Assistance Programs for Seniors. Kerry A. Lynch. American Institute for Economic Research. • 2003. $5.00. Contains a state-by-state directory of 39 state assistance programs offering prescription drug coverage, usually for low-

income residents age 65 or older. Provides phone numbers, websites, coverage, eligibility details, and "How it works" for each state. A separate section describes five drug company discount cards. (Economic Education Bulletin.).

Public Human Services Directory. American Public Human Services Association. • Covers: Federal, state, territorial, county, and major municipal public human service agencies. Entries include: Agency name, address, phone, fax, e-mail address, web site address, names of key personnel, program area.

ENCYCLOPEDIAS AND DICTIONARIES

Encyclopedia of Homelessness. David Levinson, editor. Sage Publications, Inc. • 2004. $295.00. Two volumes. Topics relating to homelessness include Causes, Health Issues, History in the United States, Legal Issues, and Organizations. Contains about 150 entries, arranged alphabetically, by various contributors. Appendices provide additional features, such as examples of homelessness in film and literaure. Includes extensive bibliographic information.

Encyclopedia of Social Welfare History in North America. John M. Herrick and Paul H. Stuart, editors. Sage Publications, Inc. • 2004. $150.00. Includes entries on the historical aspects of charity, economic conditions, tax policy, health policy, social welfare legislation, poverty, social security, and social problems.

Work in America: An Encyclopedia of History, Policy, and Society. Carl E. Van Horn and Herbert A. Schaffner. ABC-CLIO, Inc. • 2003. $185.00. Two volumes. Contains 265 A-Z entries covering work in the U. S. from the Industrial Revolution to modern times. Covers labor-related topics in economics, history, law, welfare, employment policy, and other areas.

HANDBOOKS AND MANUALS

Social Security Handbook. Available from U. S. Government Printing Office. • Annual. $53.00. Issued by the Social Security Administration (http://www.ssa.gov). Provides detailed information about social security programs, including Medicare, with brief descriptions of related programs administered by agencies other than the Social Security Administration.

INTERNET DATABASES

FedWorld: A Program of the United States Department of Commerce. National Technical Information Service. Phone: (703)605-6000 Fax: (703)605-6900 E-mail: webmaster@fedworld.gov • URL: http://www.fedworld.gov • Web site offers "a comprehensive central access point for searching, locating, ordering, and acquiring government and business information." Emphasis is on searching the Web pages, databases, and government reports of a wide variety of federal agencies. Fees: Free.

FirstGov: Your First Click to the U. S. Government. General Services Administration. Phone: 800-333-4636 or (202)501-0705 E-mail: public.affairs@gsa.gov • URL: http://www.firstgov.gov • Free Web site provides extensive links to federal agencies covering a wide variety of topics, such as agriculture, business, consumer safety, education, the environment, government jobs, grants, health, social security, statistics sources, taxes, technology, travel, and world affairs. Also provides links to federal forms, including IRS tax forms. Searching is offered, both keyword and advanced.

Social Security Online: The Official Web Site of the Social Security Administration. U. S. Social Security Administration. Phone: 800-772-1213 or (410)965-7700 • URL: http://www.ssa.gov • Web site provides a wide variety of online information relating to social security and Medicare. Topics include benefits, disability, employer wage reporting, personal earnings statements, statistics, government financing, social security law, and public welfare reform legislation.

U. S. Census Bureau: The Official Statistics. U. S. Bureau of the Census. Phone: (301)763-4100 Fax: (301)763-4794 • URL: http://www.census.gov • Web site is "Your Source for Social, Demographic, and Economic Information." Contains "Current U. S. Population Count," "Current Economic Indicators," and a wide variety of data under "Other Official Statistics." Keyword searching is provided. Fees: Free.

ONLINE DATABASES

Information Bank Abstracts. New York Times Index Dept. • Provides indexing and abstracting of current affairs, primarily from the final late edition of *The New York Times* and the Eastern edition of *The Wall Street Journal*. Time period is 1969 to present, with daily updates. Inquire as to online cost and availability.

Newspaper Abstracts Daily. ProQuest Inc. • Provides online coverage (citations and abstracts) of 25 major newspapers. Covers business, economics, current affairs, health, fitness, sports, education, technology, government, consumer affairs, psychology, the arts, and the social sciences. Time period is 1986 to date, with daily updates. Inquire as to online cost and availability.

PAIS International. Public Affairs Information Service, Inc. • Corresponds to the former printed publications, *PAIS Bulletin* (1976-90) and *PAIS Foreign Language Index* (1972-90), and to the current *PAIS International in Print* (1991 to date). Covers economic, political, and sociological material appearing in periodicals, books, government documents, and other publications. Updating is monthly. Inquire as to online cost and availability.

Readers' Guide Abstracts Online. H. W. Wilson Co. • Indexes and abstracts general interest periodicals, 1983 to date. Weekly updates. Inquire as to online cost and availability.

Social Scisearch. Institute for Scientific Information. • Broad, multidisciplinary index to the literature of the social sciences, 1972 to present. Weekly updates. Worldwide coverage. Inquire as to online cost and availability.

Wilson Social Sciences Abstracts Online. H. W. Wilson Co. • Provides online abstracting and indexing of more than 500 periodicals covering area studies, community health, public administration, public welfare, urban studies, and many other social science topics. Time period is 1994 to date for abstracts and 1983 to date for indexing, with updates weekly. Inquire as to online cost and availability.

PERIODICALS AND NEWSLETTERS

Journal of Human Resources: Education, Manpower and Welfare Economics. University of Wisconsin at Madison, Industrial Relations Research Institute. University of Wisconsin Press. • Quarterly. Individuals, $60.00 per year; institutions, $150.00 per year. Articles on manpower, health and welfare policies as they relate to the labor market and to economic and social development.

Journal of Poverty: Innovations on Social, Political, and Economic Inequalities. Haworth Press, Inc. • Quarterly. $180.00 per year to libraries; $50.00 per year to individuals. Covers the social, emotional, and economic consequences of public assistance. Topics include welfare policy, immigrants' rights, hiring practices, managed healthcare, child support, disabilities, food programs, and affirmative action. (See also http://www.journalofpoverty.org).

Journal of Social Welfare and Family Law. Taylor & Francis Group. • Quarterly. Individuals, $99.00 per year; institutions, $385.00 per year.

Policy and Practice of Public Human Services. American Public Human Services Association. • Quarterly. $75.00 per year. Formerly*Public Welfare*.

Public Assistance and Welfare Trends: State Capitals. Wakeman-Walworth, Inc. • 50 times a year. $245.00 per year; print and online editions, $350.00 per year. Newsletter. Formerly *From the State Capitals: Public Assistance and Welfare Trends*.

Review of Social Economy. Association for Social Economics. Taylor and Francis Group. • Quarterly. Individuals, $78.00 per year; institutions, $211.00 per year. Subject matter is concerned with the relationships between social values and economics. Includes articles on income distribution, poverty, labor, and class.

RESEARCH CENTERS AND INSTITUTES

Social Welfare Research Institute. Boston College. 140 Commonwealth Ave., McGuinn Hall, Room 515, Chestnut Hill, MA 02167. Phone: (617)552-4070 Fax: (617)552-3903 E-mail: swri508@bc.edu • URL: http://www.bc.edu/swri.

STATISTICS SOURCES

Benefits and Wages: OECD Indicators. Organization for Economic Cooperation and Development. • Biennial. $19.00. Provides data for 28 countries on unemployment benefits and related welfare benefits. Includes a cross-country comparison of family incomes, in work and out of work. Formerly *Benefit Systems and Work Incentives*.

County and City Data Book 2000: A Statistical Abstract Supplement. Available from U. S. Government Printing Office. • 2002. $68.00. 13th edition. Issued by the U. S. Bureau of the Census (http://www.census.gov). Contains a wide variety of data on 3,141 U.S. counties, 1,078 cities, and 11,097 places of 2,500 or more inhabitants. Includes statistical information on retailing, manufacturing, banking, service industries, income, employment, housing, education, crime, and population. Updated metropolitan areas are included.

County and City Extra: Annual Metro, City and County Data Book. Deirdre A. Gaquin and Mark S. Littman. Bernan Press. • 2001. $120.00. Updates and augments data published irregularly in print form by the U. S. Census Bureau in *County and City Data Book*. Covers "every state, county, metropolitan area, and congressional district in the United States, as well as all U. S. cities with a 1990 population of 25,000 or more." Contains a wide range tic maps.

County and City Extra: Special Decennial Census Edition. Deidre A. Gaquin and Katherine A. De-Brandt, editors. Bernan Press. • 2002. $95.00. Presents conveniently arranged population, housing, and other data from the 2000 census, with many 1980 and 1990 comparisons. Includes maps and tables with rankings of about 20 items for various geographic locations. Complements the annual *County and City Extra*.

Datapedia of the United States: American History in Numbers. George T. Kurian, editor. Bernan Press. • 2004. $125.00. Third edition. Based on the Census Bureau publication, *Historical Statistics of the United States*. Provides data from Colonial times to the present on agriculture, business, consumer income, energy, finance, labor, national income, population, and many other subjects. Includes "narrative highlights," maps, charts, and statistical projections.

Social Security Bulletin. Social Security Administration. Available from U.S. Government Printing Office. • Quarterly. $27.00 per year. Annual statistical supplement.

Social Statistics of the United States. Mark S. Littman, editor. Bernan Press. • 2000. $65.00. Includes statistical data on population growth, labor force, occupations, environmental trends, leisure time use, income, poverty, taxes, and other economic or demographic topics.

Social Trends and Indicators USA. Monique D. Ma-gee, editor. Gale Cengage Learning. • 2003. $450.00. Four volumes. Includes data on labor, economics, the health care industry, crime, leisure, population, education, social security, and many other topics. Sources include various government agencies and major publications.

State Profiles: The Population and Economy of Each U. S. State. Courtenay Slater and Others. Bernan Press. • 1999. $89.00. Presents charts, tables, and text in an eight-page profile for each state. Covers population, labor force, income, poverty, employment, wages, industry, trade, housing, education, health, taxes, and government finances. (The Population and Economy of Each United States Series).

Statistical Abstract of the United States. Available from U. S. Government Printing Office. • Annual. $51.00. Issued by the U. S. Bureau of the Census.

Statistical Handbook on Poverty in the Developing World. Chandrika Kaul. Greenwood Publishing Group, Inc. • 1999. $69.95. Provides international coverage, including special sections on women and children, and on selected cities. (Statistical Handbooks Series).

A Statistical Portrait of the United States: Social Conditions and Trends. Mark S. Littman, editor. Bernan Press. • 1998. $89.00. Covers "social, economic, and environmental trends in the United States over the past 25 years." Includes statistical tables, graphs, and analysis relating to such topics as population, income, poverty, wealth, labor, housing, education, healthcare, air/water quality, and government. (Statistical Portrait of the United States: Social Conditions and Trends Series).

Taxing Wages. Organization for Economic Cooperation and Development. • Annual. $52.00. Contains data on income tax and social security levies collected from employees and employers in OECD countries. Includes marginal and effective tax burden figures for various family income levels and statistics on cash transfers paid as family benefits.

TRADE/PROFESSIONAL ASSOCIATIONS

American Public Human Services Association. 810 1st St. NE, Ste. 500, Washington, DC 20002. Phone: (202)682-0100 Fax: (202)289-6555 E-mail: jerry.friedman@aphsa.org • URL: http://www.aphsa.org • Public human service agencies, their professional staff members, and others interested in public human services. Works to develop, promote and implement human service policies that improve the health and well-being of families, children and adults.

OTHER SOURCES

Resist. • Provides grants to small progressive groups in all parts of the country; has aided groups that have organized for reproductive rights for women, gay rights, nuclear disarmament, the rights of Third World people, and work for social and economic justice.

PUBLIC WORKS

See also: BUILDING CONTRACTS; BUILDING INDUSTRY

ABSTRACTS AND INDEXES

PAIS International in Print. Public Affairs Information Service, Inc. • Monthly. $850.00 per year; cumulations three times a year. Provides topical citations to the worldwide literature of public affairs, economics, demographics, sociology, and trade. Text in English; indexed materials in English, French, German, Italian, Portuguese and Spanish.

CD-ROM DATABASES

PAIS on CD-ROM. Public Affairs Information Service, Inc. • Quarterly. $1,995.00 per year. Provides a CD-ROM version of the online service, *PAIS International*. Contains over 500,000 citations to the literature of contemporary social, political, and economic issues.

DIRECTORIES

Public Works Manual. Public Works Journal Corp. • Publication includes: List of about 3,500 manufacturers and distributors of equipment, materials, services, computers, and software used in the design, construction, maintenance, and operation of streets and highways, water systems, wastewater and solid wastes processing, and recreation areas. Entries include: Company name, address, products. Principal content is technical articles on public works topics.

ENCYCLOPEDIAS AND DICTIONARIES

Wiley Dictionary of Civil Engineering and Construction. Len F. Webster, editor. John Wiley and Sons, Inc. • 1997. $85.00. Provides more than 30,000 definitions in the fields of civil engineering, construction, architecture, forestry, mining, and public works. (Professional Series).

ONLINE DATABASES

PAIS International. Public Affairs Information Service, Inc. • Corresponds to the former printed publications, *PAIS Bulletin* (1976-90) and *PAIS Foreign Language Index* (1972-90), and to the current *PAIS International in Print* (1991 to date). Covers economic, political, and sociological material appearing in periodicals, books, government documents, and other publications. Updating is monthly. Inquire as to online cost and availability.

PERIODICALS AND NEWSLETTERS

APWA Reporter. American Public Works Association. • Monthly. Membership.

ENR: Connecting the Industry Worldwide (Engineering News-Record). McGraw-Hill. • Weekly. $74.00 per year.

Project Finance: The Magazine for Global Development. American Educational Systems. • 11 times a year. $740.00 per year. Includes print and online editions. Provides articles on the financing of the infrastructure (transportation, utilities, communications, the environment, etc). Coverage is international. Supplements available *World Export Credit Guide* and *Project Finance Book of Lists.* Formed by the merger of *Infrastructure Finance* and *Project and Trade Finance.*

Public Works: City, County and State. Public Works Journal Corp. • 13 times a year. Free to qualified personnel. Includes *Public Works Manual.*

RESEARCH CENTERS AND INSTITUTES

Municipal Technical Advisory Service Library. University of Tennessee, Knoxville, Conference Center Bldg.,, 600 Henley St., Ste. 120, Knoxville, TN 37996-4105. Phone: (865)974-0411 Fax: (865)974-0423 E-mail: schwartzr@tennessee.edu • URL: http://www.mtas.utk.edu/library • Research areas include municipal finance, police administration, and public works.

STATISTICS SOURCES

United States Census of Construction Industries. U.S. Bureau of the Census. • Quinquennial. Results presented in reports, tape, and CD-ROM files.

TRADE/PROFESSIONAL ASSOCIATIONS

American Public Works Association. 2345 Grand Blvd., Ste. 700, Kansas City, MO 64108-2625. Phone: 800-848-APWA or (816)472-6100 Fax: (816)472-1610 E-mail: pking@apwa.net • URL: http://www.apwa.net • Chief administrators, commissioners, and directors of public works, city engineers, superintendents, and department heads of transportation, water, waste water, solid waste, equipment services, and buildings and grounds; federal, provincial, and state administrators and engineers; consultants and educators; associate members are equipment manufacturers' representa-

tives, utility company officials, and contractors; student members are engineering and public administration students interested in the theory and practice of the design, construction, maintenance, administration, and operation of public works facilities and services. Conducts historical research on public works subjects and demonstrates applicability of history to current public works problems and issues through Public Works Historical Society (see separate entry). Sponsors research and education foundations.

OTHER SOURCES

Dodge Construction News. McGraw-Hill. • Daily. Los Angeles, $1,392.00 per year; Chicago, $1,245.00 per year.

PUBLICITY

See: PUBLIC RELATIONS AND PUBLICITY

PUBLISHERS, COLLEGE

See: UNIVERSITY PRESSES

PUBLISHING, DESKTOP

See: DESKTOP PUBLISHING

PUBLISHING, ELECTRONIC

See: ELECTRONIC PUBLISHING

PUBLISHING INDUSTRY

See also: BIBLIOGRAPHY; BOOK CATALOGS; BOOK INDUSTRY; BOOKSELLING; ELECTRONIC PUBLISHING; PAPERBOUND BOOK INDUSTRY; PERIODICALS; UNIVERSITY PRESSES

GENERAL WORKS

The Business of Publishing: How to Survive and Prosper in the Publishing and Bookselling Industry. Leonard Shatzkin. McGraw-Hill. • 1995. $24.95.

How to Get Happily Published: A Complete and Candid Guide. Judith Appelbaum. HarperInformation. • 1998. $14.00. Fifth edition. Provides advice for writers on dealing with book and magazine publishers.

Towards Electronic Journals: Realities for Scientists, Librarians, and Publishers. Carol Tenopir and Donald W. King. Special Libraries Association. • 2000. $59.00. Discusses journals in electronic form vs. traditional (paper) scholarly journals, including the impact of subscription prices.

ABSTRACTS AND INDEXES

Book Review Digest: An Index to Reviews of Current Books. H. W. Wilson Co. • 10 times a year. Quarterly and annual cumulation. Price varies.

ALMANACS AND YEARBOOKS

Trade Book Publishing: Analysis by Category. Kathleen Martucci and others. SIMBA Information, Inc. • 1998. $1,495.00. 6th revised edition. Reviews current conditions in the book publishing industry, including analysis of market segments, retailing aspects, and profiles of major publishers.

BIBLIOGRAPHIES

American Book Publishing Record: Arranged by Dewey Decimal Classification and Indexed by Author, Title, and Subject. R. R. Bowker. • Monthly. $395.00 per year. Includes annual cumulation.

Booklist. American Library Association. • 22 times

a year. $79.95. Reviews library materials for school and public libraries. Incorporates *Reference Books Bulletin.*

Books in Print. R. R. Bowker. • Annual. $769.00. Eight volumes.

Forthcoming Books. R. R. Bowker. • Bimonthly. $299.95 per year. Supplement to *Books in Print.*

Managing the Publishing Process: An Annotated Bibliography. Bruce W. Speck. Greenwood Publishing Group, Inc. • 1995. $82.95. (Bibliographies and Indexes in Mass Media and Communications Series: No. 9).

CD-ROM DATABASES

Books in Print On Disc: The Complete Books in Print System on Compact Laser Disc. Bowker Electronic Publishing. • Monthly. $550.00 per year. The CD-ROM version of *Books in Print, Forthcoming Books,* and other Bowker bibliographic publications: lists the books of over 50,000 U.S. publishers. Includes books recently declared out-of-print. Also available with full text book reviews.

Books in Print with Book Reviews On Disc. Bowker Electronic Publishing. • Monthly. $2,075 per year. The CD-ROM version of *Books in Print, Forthcoming Books,* and other Bowker bibliographic publications, with the addition of full text book reviews from *Publishers Weekly, Library Journal, Booklist, Choice,* and other periodicals.

Bowker/Whitaker Global Books in Print On Disc. R. R. Bowker. • Monthly. $2,055.00 per year. Provides CD-ROM listing of English language books published throughout the world, including U. S., U. K., Canada, and Australia. Combines data from R. R. Bowker's *Books in Print Plus* and J. Whitaker & Sons Ltd.'s *Bookbank.* Includes more than two million titles.

Hoover's Company Capsules on CD-ROM. Hoover's, Inc. • Quarterly. $399.95 per year (single-user). Provides the CD-ROM version of *Hoover's Handbook of American Business, Hoover's Handbook of Emerging Companies, Hoover's Handbook of World Business, Hoover's Guide to Computer Companies, Hoover's Guide to Media Companies, Hoover's Handbook of Private Companies,* and various regional guides. Includes more than 11,000 profiles of companies.

LISA Plus. Available from Cambridge Scientific Abstracts (CSA). • Quarterly. $2,000.00 per year. CD-ROM version of Library Information and Science Abstracts, providing abstracting and indexing of the world's library and information science literature, 1969 to date. Contains more than 180,000 citations.

DIRECTORIES

Continnum and the Publishers Association Directory of Publishing. Continnum. • Annual. $175.00. Published in London. Provides detailed profiles of United Kingdom and British Commonwealth publishers and agencies. Includes "publishers' turnover figures.".

International Literary Market Place: The Directory of the International Book Publishing Industry. Information Today, Inc. • Annual. $219.00. Covers more than 180 countries. Listings include publishers, literary agents, major booksellers, book clubs, literary prizes, distributors, trade associations, etc. Formerly published by R. R. Bowker.

Library Journal: Reference [year]: Print, CD-ROM, Online. Reed Business Information. • Annual. Issued in November as a supplement to *Library Journal.* Lists new and updated reference material, including general and trade print titles, directories, annuals, CD-ROM titles, and online sources. Includes material from more than 200 publishers, arranged by company name, with an index by subject. Addresses include e-mail and Web information.

Library Journal Sourcebook. Reed Business

Information. • Publication includes: List of over 600 suppliers of products and services used by libraries from abstracting to word processing equipment. Entries include: Company name, address, phone, list of products or services. Complete listings for more than 100 architectural firms; Disaster planning for librarians.

Literary Market Place: The Directory of the American Book Publishing Industry. Information Today, Inc. • Annual. $299.00. Two volumes. Listings include publishers, agents, ad agencies, associations, distributors, events, key executives, services, and suppliers (50 directory sections in all). Formerly published by R. R. Bowker.

Publishers Directory: A Guide to New and Established Private and Special-Interest, Avant-Garde and Alternative, Organizational Association, Government and Institution Presses. Gale Cengage Learning. • 2003. $450.00. 26th edition. Contains detailed information on more than 20,000 U.S. and Canadian publishers as well as small, independent presses.

Publishers, Distributors, and Wholesalers of the United States: A Directory of Publishers, Distributors, Associations, Wholesalers, Software Producers and Manufactureres Listing Editorial and Ordering Addresses, and and ISBN Publisher Prefi. Gale. • Annual. $349.00. Two volumes. Lists more than 101,000 publishers, book distributors, and wholesalers. Includes museum and association imprints, inactive publishers, and publishers' fields of activity.

Publishers' International ISBN Directory. International ISBN Agency. • Covers: About 620,000 publishers in the United States and 218 other countries, of which about 555,000 have been assigned International Standard Book Numbers (ISBNs) by one of 140 ISBN Group Agencies. Entries include: For publishers--Name, address, phone, fax, telex, e-mail, ISBN, group, and prefix numbers. For agencies--Name, address, phone, fax, e-mail, group number, names and titles of key personnel in charge of ISBN matters. Publication is a merger of "International ISBN Publishers' Directory" and "Publishers' International Directory.".

VNU Business Media. ADWEEK Directories. • Annual. $100.00. Presents cost, circulation, and audience statistics for various mass media segments, including television, radio, magazines, newspapers, telephone yellow pages, and cinema.

Writer's Guide to Book Editors, Publishers, and Literary Agents, Who They Are, What They Want, and How to Win Them Over. Prima Publishing. • Annual. $27.95; with CD-ROM, $49.95. Directory for authors includes information on publishers' response times and pay rates.

ENCYCLOPEDIAS AND DICTIONARIES

Dictionary of Bibliometrics. Virgil Diodato. Haworth Press, Inc. • 1994. $39.95. Contains detailed explanations of 225 terms, with references. (Bibliometrics is "the application of mathematical and statistical techniques to the study of publishing and professional communication.").

Graphically Speaking: An Illustrated Guide to the Working Language of Design and Publishing. Mark Beach. Coast to Coast Books. • 1992. $29.50. Provides practical definitions of 2,800 terms used in printing, graphic design, publishing, and desktop publishing. Over 300 illustrations are included, about 40 in color.

FINANCIAL RATIOS

Annual Statement Studies. The Risk Management Association. • Annual. Median and quartile financial ratios are given for over 400 kinds of manufacturing, wholesale, retail, construction, and consumer finance establishments. Data is sorted by both asset size and sales volume. Includes a clearly written

"Definition of Ratios" and an alphabetical industry index.

Annual Statement Studies: Industry Default Probabilities and Cash Flow Measures. The Risk Management Association. • Annual. $145.00. Serves as a companion volume to the original *Annual Statement Studies.* Gives probability of default estimates on a percentage scale for more than 450 industries. Includes changes in position year-by-year for eight financial statement line items and provides percentage measures of cash flow.

HANDBOOKS AND MANUALS

Columbia Guide to Digital Publishing: In Print and On the Web. William E. Kasdorf, editor. Columbia University Press. • 2002. $65.00. Covers the practical production of both written and graphic material in digital format, including archives, new technology, "information architecture," and copyright.

Getting Your Book Published. Christine S. Smedley and Mitchell Allen. Sage Publications, Inc. • 1993. $59.95. A practical guide for academic and professional authors. Covers the initial book prospectus, contract negotiation, production procedures, and marketing. (Survival Skills for Scholars, vol. 10).

Handbook of Digital Publishing. Michael L. Kleper. Prentice Hall PTR. • 2001. $129.99. Two volumes. Edited for the digital publishing industry. Covers print publishing, electronic documents, and Internet (Web) publishing, including basic desktop procedures. Provides information on typography, design, layout, image creation, and page creation.

MLA Style Manual and Guide to Scholarly Publishing. Joseph Gibaldi. Modern Language Association of America. • 1998. $25.00. Second edition. Covers preparation of manuscripts for publication, legal issues, basic writing principles, documentation, and use of abbreviations.

INTERNET DATABASES

Publishers' Catalogues Home Page. EBSCO Publishing. Phone: (306)931-0020 Fax: (306)931-7667 E-mail: info@lights.com • URL: http://www.lights.com/publisher • Provides links to the Web home pages of about 1,700 U. S. publishers (including about 80 University presses) and publishers in 48 foreign countries. "International/Multinational Publishers" are included, such as the International Monetary Fund, the World Bank, and the World Trade Organization. Publishers are arranged in convenient alphabetical lists. Searching is offered. Fees: Free.

ONLINE DATABASES

Book Review Index [Online]. Gale Cengage Learning. • Cites reviews of books and periodicals in journals, 1969 to present. Inquire as to online cost and availability.

Books in Print Online. Bowker Electronic Publishing. • The online version of *Books in Print, Forthcoming Books, Paperbound Books in Print,* and other Bowker bibliographic publications: lists the books of over 50,000 U. S. publishers. Includes books recently declared out-of-print. Updated monthly. Inquire as to online cost and availability.

LISA: Library and Information Science Abstracts. Available from Cambridge Scientific Abstracts (CSA). • Provides abstracting and indexing of the world's library and information science literature, 1969 to date. Covers more than 440 periodicals from 68 countries. Updating is biweekly. Inquire as to online cost and availability.

PERIODICALS AND NEWSLETTERS

Book Publishing Report: Weekly News and Analysis of Events Shaping the Book Industry. SIMBA Information. • 50 times a year. $549.00 per year. Newsletter. Covers book publishing mergers, marketing, finance, personnel, and trends in general. Formerly *BP Report on the Business of Book Publishing.*

Choice Magazine: Current Reviews for Academic Libraries. Association of College Research Libraries. American Library Association. • 11 times a year. $237.00 per year. A publication of the Association of College and Research Libraries. Contains book reviews, primarily for college and university libraries.

Color Publishing. PennWell Corp., Advanced Technology Div. • Bimonthly. $29.70 per year.

Copy Editor: Language News for the Publishing Profession. McMurry Newsletters. • Bimonthly. $69.00 per year. Newsletter for professional copy editors and proofreaders. Includes such items as "Top Ten Resources for Copy Editors.".

Educational Marketer: The Educational Publishing Industry's Voice of Authority Since 1968. SIMBA Information. • Three times a month. $599.00 per year. Newsletter. Edited for suppliers of educational materials to schools and colleges at all levels. Covers print and electronic publishing, software, audiovisual items, and multimedia. Includes corporate news and educational statistics.

Independent Publisher: Leading the World of Book Selling in New Directions. Jenkins Group, Inc. • Bimonthly. Free. Covers business, finance, production, marketing, and other management topics for small publishers, including college presses. Emphasis is on book publishing.

Innovative Publisher: Publishing Strategies for New Markets. Emmelle Publishing Co., Inc. • Biweekly. $69.00 per year. Provides articles and news on electronic publishing (CD-ROM or online) and desktop publishing.

Learned Publishing. Association of Learned and Professional Society Publishers. • Quarterly. Members, $60.00 per year; non-members, $80.00 per year; institutions, $170.00 per year. Articles and news of interest to publishers of academic and learned society material. Formerly *ALPSP Bulletin.*

Publishers Weekly: The International News Magazine of Book Publishing. Reed Business Information. • 51 times a year. $214.00 per year. The international news magazine of book publishing.

The SIMBA Report on Directory Publishing. SIMBA Information. • Monthly. $359.00 per year. Newsletter.

STATISTICS SOURCES

By the Numbers: Electronic and Online Publishing. Gale Cengage Learning. • 1997-98. $305.00. Four volumes. $85.00 per volume. Covers "high-interest" industries: 1. *By the Numbers: Electronic and Online Publishing*; 2. *By the Numbers: Emerging Industries*; 3. *By the Numbers: Nonprofits*; 4. *By the Numbers: Publishing.* Each volume provides about 600 tabulations of industry data on revenues, market share, employment, trends, financial ratios, profits, salaries, and so forth. Citations to data sources are included. (By the Numbers Series).

Computer Publishing Market Forecast. SIMBA Information. • Biennial. $1,895.00. Provides market data on computer-related books, magazines, newsletters, and other publications. Includes profiles of major publishers of computer-related material.

Librarian's Companion: A Handbook of Thousands of Facts on Libraries, Librarians, Books, Newspapers, Publishers, Booksellers. Vladimir F. Wertsman. Greenwood Publishing Group, Inc. • 1996. $69.95. Provides international statistics on libraries and publishing. Includes directory and biographical information.

Media Market Guide. Media Market Resources. • Quarterly. $675.00 per year. Presents circulation and cost data for television, radio, magazines, newspapers and outdoor markets.

Standard & Poor's Industry Surveys. Standard & Poor's. • Semiannual. $1,800.00. Two looseleaf volumes. Includes monthly *Supplements.* Provides detailed, individual surveys of 52 major industry groups. Each survey is revised on a semiannual basis. Also includes "Monthly Investment Review" (industry group investment analysis) and monthly "Trends & Projections" (economic analysis).

U. S. Industry and Trade Outlook. Available from National Technical Information Service. • Annual. $69.95. Produced by the International Trade Administration, U. S. Department of Commerce, in a "public-private" partnership with DRI/McGraw-Hill and Standard & Poor's. Provides basic data, outlook for the current year, and "Long-Term Prospects" (five-year projections) for a wide variety of products and services. Includes high technology industries. Formerly *U. S. Industrial Outlook.*

UNESCO Statistical Yearbook. Bernan Press. • 1998. $95.00. Co-published by Bernan Press and the United Nations Educational, Scientific, and Cultural Organization (http://www.unesco.org). Presents statistical data from more than 200 countries on education, technology, research, broadcasting, cinema, book publishing, newspapers, libraries, museums, and population. Includes charts, maps, and graphs.

TRADE/PROFESSIONAL ASSOCIATIONS

Association of American Publishers. 71 Fifth Ave., New York, NY 10003-3004. Phone: (212)255-0200 Fax: (212)255-7007 E-mail: amyg@publishers.org • URL: http://www.publishers.org.

Association of American University Presses. 71 W. 23rd St., Suite 901, New York, NY 10010-4102. Phone: (212)989-1010 Fax: (212)989-0275 E-mail: info@aaupnet.org • URL: http://www.aaupnet.org.

Association of Learned and Professional Society Publishers. South House, The Street, Clapham, Worthing, W. Sussex BN13 3UU, United Kingdom. Phone: 44 1903 871686 Fax: 44 1903 871457 E-mail: chief-exec@alpsp.org • URL: http://www.alpsp.org.

Book Industry Study Group. 370 Lexington Ave., Ste. 900, New York, NY 10017. Phone: (646)336-7141 Fax: (646)336-6214 E-mail: info@bisg.org • URL: http://www.bisg.org • Represents publishers, manufacturers, suppliers, wholesalers, retailers, librarians, and other engaged in the business of print and electronic media.

Women's National Book Association. PO Box 237, 26 W 17th St., No. 504, New York, NY 10150. Phone: (212)208-4629 Fax: (212)208-4629 E-mail: publicity@bookbuzz.com • URL: http://www.wnba-books.org • Women and men who work with and value books. Exists to promote reading and to support the role of women in the book community.

OTHER SOURCES

Huenefeld Report: For Managers and Planners in Modest-Sized Book Publishing Houses. John Huenefeld, editor. Huenefeld Co., Inc. • Biweekly. $88.00 per year.

Lindey on Entertainment, Publishing and the Arts: Agreements and the Law. Alexander Lindey, editor. West Group. • $935.00 per year. Six looseleaf volumes. Periodic supplementation. Provides basic forms, applicable law, and guidance.

PULPWOOD INDUSTRY

See: WOODPULP INDUSTRY

PUMPS AND COMPRESSORS

ABSTRACTS AND INDEXES

Applied Science and Technology Index. H. W. Wilson Co. • 11 times a year. Quarterly and annual cumulations. Price varies. Indexes a wide variety of English language technical, industrial, and engineering periodicals.

Current Contents: Engineering, Computing and Technology. Thomson/ISI. • Weekly. $730.00 per year. Reproductions of contents pages of technical journals. Includes *Author Index, Address Directory, Current Book Contents* and *Title Word Index.* Formerly *Current Contents: Engineering, Technology and Applied Sciences.*

Fluid Abstracts: Process Engineering. Elsevier. • Monthly. Institutions, $1,709.00 per year. Includes annual cumulation. Formerly *Pumps and Other Fluids Machinery: Abstracts.*

DIRECTORIES

Fluid Power Handbook and Directory. Penton Media, Inc. • Biennial. $95.00 per year. Over 1,500 manufacturers and 3,000 distributors of fluid power products in the United States and Canada.

Thomas Register of American Manufacturers. Thomas Publishing Co., Inc. • Annual. $149.00. 34 volumes. A three-part system offering information on a wide variety of industrial equipment and supplies. Lists more than 151,000 industrial product and services companies.

HANDBOOKS AND MANUALS

Pump Application Desk Book. Paul N. Garay. Fairmont Press Inc. • 1996. $88.00. Third edition.

INTERNET DATABASES

Manufacturing Profiles. U. S. Bureau of the Census. Phone: (301)763-4636 E-mail: webmaster@census.gov • URL: http://www.census.gov/prod/www/abs/mfg-prof.html • The Census Bureau makes available free on PDF (Portable Document Format) an annual consolidation of the entire Current Industrial Report series, presenting "all the data compiled." Contains statistics on production, shipments, inventories, consumption, exports, imports, and orders for a wide variety of manufactured products.

ONLINE DATABASES

Applied Science and Technology Index Online. H. W. Wilson Co. • Provides online indexing of 500 major scientific, technical, industrial, and engineering periodicals. Time period is 1983 to date. Monthly updates. Inquire as to online cost and availability.

FLUIDEX. Elsevier Science, Inc. • Produced in the Netherlands by Elsevier Science B.V. Provides indexing and abstracting of the international literature of fluid engineering and technology, 1973 to date, with monthly updates. Also known as *Fluid Engineering Abstracts.* Inquire as to online cost and availability.

PROMT: Predicasts Overview of Markets and Technology. Gale Cengage Learning. • Companies, products, applied technologies and markets. U.S. and international literature coverage, 1972 to date. Inquire as to online cost and availability. Provides abstracts from more than 1,600 publications. Weekly updates.

Thomas Register Online. Thomas Publishing Co., Inc. • Provides concise information on approximately 194,000 U. S. companies, mainly manufacturers, with over 50,000 product classifications. Indexes over 115,000 trade names. Information is updated semiannually. Inquire as to online cost and availability.

PERIODICALS AND NEWSLETTERS

Hydraulics and Pneumatics: The Magazine of Fluid Power and Motion Control Systems. Penton Media, Inc. • Monthly. $65.00 per year.

Industrial Equipment News. Thomas Publishing Co., LLC. • Monthly. $65.00 per year. What's new in equipment, parts and materials.

New Equipment Digest. Penton Media, Inc. • Monthly. Free to qualified personnel; others, $60.00 per year. Formerly *Material Handling Engineering.*

New Equipment Reporter: New Products Industrial News. De Roche Publications. • Monthly. Controlled circulation.

Plant Engineering. Reed Business Information. • 13 times a year. $131.99. per year. Includes *Plant Engineering Product Supplier Guide.*

Processing. Putman Media. • 14 times a year. $54.00 per year. Emphasis is on descriptions of new products for all areas of industrial processing, including valves, controls, filters, pumps, compressors, fluidics, and instrumentation.

World Pumps. Elsevier. • Monthly. Institutions, $307.00 per year. Text in English, French and German.

RESEARCH CENTERS AND INSTITUTES

Ray W. Herrick Laboratories. Purdue University, 1077 Ray W. Herrick Laboratories, West Lafayette, IN 47907-1077. Phone: (765)494-2132 Fax: (765)494-0787 E-mail: rhlab@ecn.purdue.edu • URL: http://www.herrick.ecn.purdue.edu.

STATISTICS SOURCES

Annual Survey of Manufactures. Available from U. S. Government Printing Office. • Annual. Prices vary. Issued by the U. S. Census Bureau as an interim update to the *Census of Manufactures.* Includes data on number of manufacturing establishments in various industries, employment, labor costs, value of shipments, capital expenditures, inventories, energy costs, and assets. (See also Census Bureau home page, http://www.census.gov/.).

Pumps and Compressors. U. S. Bureau of the Census. • Annual. Provides data on value of manufacturers' shipments, quantity, exports, imports, etc. (Current Industrial Reports, MA-35P.).

TRADE/PROFESSIONAL ASSOCIATIONS

Contractors Pump Bureau. 6737 W Washington St., Ste. 2400, Milwaukee, WI 53214-5647. Phone: (866)236-0442 or (414)272-0943 Fax: (414)272-1170 E-mail: info@aem.org • URL: http://www.aem.org/CBC/ProdSpec/CPB • A bureau of the Association of Equipment Manufacturers. Manufacturers of pumping machinery and engines for the construction industry; suppliers to the manufacturers. Works toward the standardization of sizes and capacities of contractors' pumps.

Submersible Wastewater Pump Association. 1866 Sheridan Rd., Ste. 201, Highland Park, IL 60035-2545. Phone: (847)681-1868 Fax: (847)681-1869 E-mail: swpaexdir@sbcglobal.net • URL: http://www.swpa.org • Represents manufacturers of submersible wastewater pumps and pumping systems for municipal and industrial applications; manufacturers of component parts and accessory items for those pumps and systems, and companies who provide services to users of those products, including consulting engineers, distributors, rep organizations, service shops, systems packagers and publishers.

Sump and Sewage Pump Manufacturers Association. PO Box 647, Northbrook, IL 60065-0647. Phone: (847)559-9233 Fax: (847)559-9235 • URL: http://www.sspma.org • Formerly Sump Pump Manufacturers Association.

Water Systems Council. 1101 30th St. NW, Ste. 500, 1101 30th St. NW, Ste. 500, Washington, DC 20007. Phone: 888-395-1033 or (202)625-4387 Fax: (202)625-4363 E-mail: wsc@watersystemcouncil.org • URL: http://www.watersystemscouncil.org • Manufacturers of pitless adapters and units for water wells. Promotes sound principles of pitless equipment construction and installation; maintains standards. Seeks to educate customers and users of pitless adapters. Conducts workshops for local health officials. Maintains speakers' bureau and library of state water well regulations.

OTHER SOURCES

Industrial Pumps and Pumping Equipment. Available from MarketResearch.com. • 1997. $1,195.00. Market research report published by Specialists in Business Information. Covers centrifugal, rotary, turbine, reciprocating, and other types of pumps. Presents market data relative to sales growth, shipments, exports, imports, and end-use. Includes company profiles.

PURCHASING

GENERAL WORKS

Management of Retail Buying. R. Patrick Cash and others. John Wiley and Sons, Inc. • 1995. $180.00. Third edition. (National Retail Federation Series, vol. 25).

Purchasing and Materials Management. Michael R. Leenders and Harold E. Fearon. McGraw-Hill. • 1996. $93.75. 11th edition.

Purchasing and Supply Management. Michael R. Leenders. McGraw-Hill. • 2001. $112.50. 12th edition.

ABSTRACTS AND INDEXES

Business Periodicals Index. H. W. Wilson Co. • 11 times a year. Quarterly and annual cumulations. Price varies.

CD-ROM DATABASES

WILSONDISC: Wilson Business Abstracts. H. W. Wilson Co. • Monthly. Includes unlimited online access to *Wilson Business Abstracts* through WILSONLINE. Provides CD-ROM "cover-to-cover" abstracting and indexing of over 600 prominent business periodicals. Indexing is from 1982, abstracting from 1990. (*Business Periodicals Index* without abstracts is available on CD-ROM at $1,495 per year.).

DIRECTORIES

Directory of Sporting Goods and Activewear Buyers Directory. Douglas Publications, Inc. • Annual. $329.00. About 10,700 retail stores selling athletic and recreational equipment, footwear, apparel. *Salesman's Guide Directories.*

Gift, Housewares and Home Textiles Buyers Directory. Douglas Publications, Inc. • Annual. $259.00. Lists more than 7,300 companies with names of over 15,200 buyers.

Mass Merchandisers and Off-Price Apparel Buyers Directory. Douglas Publications, Inc. • Annual. $229.00. Lists buyers of clothing for major retailers. (Does not include the metropolitan New York City area.) *Salesman's Guide Directories.*

Men's and Boys' Wear Buyers Directory. Douglas Publications, Inc. • Annual. $329.00. About 6,800 retail stores selling men's and boys' clothing, sportswear, furnishings, and accessories; coverage does not include New York metropolitan area. *Salesman's Guide Directories.*

Thomas Register of American Manufacturers. Thomas Publishing Co., Inc. • Annual. $149.00. 34 volumes. A three-part system offering information on a wide variety of industrial equipment and supplies. Lists more than 151,000 industrial product and services companies.

Women's and Children's Wear Buyers Directory. Douglas Publications, Inc. • Annual. $329.00. About 10,500 retail stores selling women's dresses, coats, sportswear, intimate apparel, and women's accessories, infants' to teens wear, and accessories; coverage does not include New York metropolitan area. *Salesman's Guide Directories.*

ENCYCLOPEDIAS AND DICTIONARIES

Blackwell Encyclopedic Dictionary of Operations Management. Nigel Slack, editor. Blackwell

Publishing. • 1997. $130.95. The editor is associated with the University of Warwick, England. Contains definitions of key terms combined with longer articles written by various U. S. and foreign business educators. Includes bibliographies and index. (Blackwell Encyclopedia of Management Series.).

Encyclopedia of Business. Gale Cengage Learning. • 2000. $425.00. Second edition. Two volumes. Contains more than 700 signed articles covering major business disciplines and concepts. International in scope. (Encyclopedia of Business Series).

HANDBOOKS AND MANUALS

Managing Purchasing: Making the Supply Team Work. John W. Kamuff and Kenneth H. Killen. McGraw-Hill. • 1995. $45.00. (NAPM Professional Development Series: Vol. 2).

ONLINE DATABASES

Thomas Register Online. Thomas Publishing Co., Inc. • Provides concise information on approximately 194,000 U. S. companies, mainly manufacturers, with over 50,000 product classifications. Indexes over 115,000 trade names. Information is updated semiannually. Inquire as to online cost and availability.

Wilson Business Abstracts Online. H. W. Wilson Co. • Indexes and abstracts 600 major business periodicals, plus the *Wall Street Journal* and the business section of the *New York Times.* Indexing is from 1982, abstracting from 1990, with the two newspapers included from 1993. Updated weekly. Inquire as to online cost and availability. (*Business Periodicals Index* without abstracts is also available online.).

PERIODICALS AND NEWSLETTERS

Business Consumer's Advisor. Buyers Laboratory Inc. • Description: Focuses on office equipment and supplies, offering purchasing advice and exploring methods of increasing office productivity through appropriate management of the equipment and its operators. Offers readers a chance to share their experiences, evaluate products and equipment, and gives results of Buyers Laboratory's testing.

Healthcare Purchasing News: A Magazine for Hospital Materials Management Central Service, Infection Control Practitioners. Thomson/Medical Economics. • Monthly. $47.95 per year. Edited for personnel responsible for the purchase of medical, surgical, and hospital equipment and supplies. Features new purchasing techniques and new products. Includes news of the activities of two major purchasing associations, Health Care Material Management Society and International Association of Healthcare Central Service Materiel Management.

Industrial Purchasing Agent. Publications for Industry. • Description: Covers new product releases pertaining to the industrial manufacturing industry. Recurring features include by-line spreads, news of research, and new literature releases.

Journal of Supply Chain Management: A Global Review of Purchasing and Supply. Institute for Supply Management. • Quarterly. $59.00 per year. Text in English. Summaries in French, German and Spanish. Formerly *International Journal of Purchasing and Materials Management.*

Purchasing: The Magazine of Total Supply Chain Management. Reed Business Information. • 24 times a year. $109.90 per year. Includes *Guide and Directory.*

Purchasing Today: For the Purchasing and Supply Professional. Institute for Supply Management. • Monthly. Membership. Includes special issues on

logistics, transportation, cost management, and supply chain management.

TRADE/PROFESSIONAL ASSOCIATIONS

Association for Healthcare Resource and Materials Management. c/o American Hospital Association, One N Franklin St., Chicago, IL 60606-3420. Phone: (312)422-3840 Fax: (312)422-4573 E-mail: ahrmm@aha.org • URL: http://www.ahrmm.org • Members are involved with the purchasing and distribution of supplies and equipment for hospitals and other healthcare establishments. Formerly American Society for Healthcare Materials Management.

Institute for Supply Management. P.O. Box 22160, Tempe, AZ 85285-2160. Phone: 800-888-6276 or (480)752-6276 Fax: (480)752-7890 • URL: http://www.ism.ws.

International Association of Healthcare Central Service Materiel Management. 213 W. Institute Place, Suite 307, Chicago, IL 60610. Phone: 800-962-8274 or (312)440-0078 Fax: (312)440-9474 E-mail: mailbox@iahcsmm.com • URL: http://www.iahcsmm.com • Members are professional personnel responsible for management and distribution of supplies from a central service material management (purchasing) department of a hospital. Formerly International Association of Hospital Central Service Management.

PURCHASING AGENTS

See: PURCHASING

PURCHASING POWER

See also: CONSUMER ECONOMICS; INCOME; MARKET STATISTICS

CD-ROM DATABASES

Sourcebook America. Gale Cengage Learning. • Annual. $995.00. Produced by CACI Marketing Systems. A combination on CD-ROM of *The Sourcebook of ZIP Code Demographics* and *The Sourcebook of County Demographics.* Provides detailed population and socio-economic data (about 75 items) for each of 3,141 U. S. counties and approximately 30,000 ZIP codes, plus states, metropolitan areas, and media market areas. Includes forecasts to the year 2004.

World Marketing Forecasts on CD-ROM. Gale Cengage Learning. • Annual. $2,500.00. Produced by Euromonitor. Provides detailed forecast data for the years to 2012 on CD-ROM for 54 countries in all parts of the world. Covers a wide range of social, demographic, economic, and market factors. Includes specific forecasts for many kinds of consumer products.

DIRECTORIES

Editor and Publisher Market Guide. Editor and Publisher Co., Inc. • Annual. $150.00. More than 1,700 newspaper markets in the United States and Canada.

STATISTICS SOURCES

The AIER Chart Book. AIER Research Staff. American Institute for Economic Research. • Annual. $4.00. A compact compilation of long-range charts ("Purchasing Power of the Dollar," for example, goes back to 1780) covering various aspects of the U. S. economy. Includes inflation, interest rates, debt, gold, taxation, stock prices, etc. (Economic Education Bulletin.).

Consumer Expenditure Survey. Available from U. S. Government Printing Office. • Biennial. Issued by the Bureau of Labor Statistics, U. S. Department of Labor (http://www.bls.gov). Contains data on various kinds of consumer spending, according to household income, education, etc. (Bureau of Labor Statistics Bulletin.).

Consumer International. Available from Gale Cengage Learning. • Annual. $1,290.00. Published by Euromonitor. Contains extensive consumer market, economic, and demographic data for 25 major, non-European countries, including the U. S. and Canada. Includes consumer market size (volume and value) for 150 product types in 14 categories (food, clothing, automobiles, cosmetics, appliances, etc.).

Consumer Power: How Americans Spend. Margaret Ambry. McGraw-Hill. • 1992. $27.50. Contains detailed statistics on consumer income and spending. Nine major categories of products and services are covered, with spending data and dollar size of market for each item.

Consumer USA. Available from Gale Cengage Learning. • Annual. $1,090.00. Fifth edition. Published by Euromonitor. Provides demographic and consumer market data for the United States. Forecasts to the year 2005.

Current Population Reports: Household Economic Studies, Series P-70. Available from U. S. Government Printing Office. • Irregular. $21.00 per year. Issued by the U.S. Bureau of the Census (http://www.census.gov). Each issue covers a special topic relating to household socioeconomic characteristics.

Demographics USA: County Edition. Trade Dimensions. • Annual. $435.00. Contains 200 statistical series for each of 3,000 counties. Includes population, household income, employment, retail sales, and consumer expenditures. Also provides Effective Buying Income, Buying Power Index, and data summaries by Metro Market, Media Market, and State. (CD-ROM version is available.).

Demographics USA: ZIP Edition. Trade Dimensions. • Annual. $435.00. Contains 50 statistical series for each of 40,000 ZIP codes. Includes population, household income, employment, retail sales, and consumer expenditures. Also provides Effective Buying Income, Business Characteristics, and data summaries by state, region, and the first three digits of ZIP codes. (CD-ROM version is available.).

European Marketing Forecasts. Available from Gale Cengage Learning. • Annual. $1,250.00. Published by Euromonitor. Contains demographic, economic, and market forecasts for the countries of Europe to the year 2010. Forecasts include market-size data for 15 consumer product sectors (food, clothing,

automobiles, consumer electronics, etc.).

The Future Demographic: Global Population Trends and Forecasts to 2010 and Beyond. Euromonitor International. • 2003. $470.00. Presents detailed demographic statistics and forecasts for about 200 countries. Includes age group profiles and data on consumer spending potential.

Handbook of U. S. Labor Statistics: Employment, Earnings, Prices, Productivity, and Other Labor Data. Eva E. Jacobs, editor. Bernan Associates. • 1999. $74.00. Based on *Handbook of Labor Statistics*, formerly issued by the Bureau of Labor Statistics, U. S. Department of Labor. Includes the Bureau's projections of employment in the U. S. by industry and occupation. Provides a wide variety of data on the work force, prices, fringe benefits, and consumer expenditures.

Household Spending: Who Spends How Much On What. New Strategist Publications, Inc. • 1999. $94.95. Fifth edition. Gives facts about the buying habits of U. S. consumers according to income, age, household type, and household size. Includes spending data for about 1,000 products and services.

International Marketing Forecasts. Available from Gale Cengage Learning. • Annual. $1,250.00. Published by Euromonitor. Contains demographic, economic, and market forecasts to the year 2013 for major, non-European countries, including the U. S. and Canada. Forecasts include market-size data for 15 consumer product sectors, such as food, clothing, and automobiles.

Key Indicators of the Labour Market. Available from Routledge. • Biennial. $125.00. Published by the International Labour Office (http://www.ilo.org). Provides data on 20 key indicators in 220 countries. Includes labor force statistics, employment, unemployment, part-time workers, wages, productivity, poverty indicators, and related topics.

Money Income in the United States. Available from U. S. Government Printing Office. • Annual. $5.50. Issued by the U. S. Bureau of the Census. Presents data on consumer income in current and constant dollars, both totals and averages (means, medians, distributions). Includes figures for a wide variety of demographic and occupational characteristics. (Current Population Reports.).

Prices and Earnings Around the Globe. Union Bank of Switzerland. • Triennial. Free. Published in Zurich. Compares prices and purchasing power in

48 major cities of the world. Wages and hours are also compared.

Sales and Marketing Management Survey of Buying Power. VNU Business Media. • Annual. $150.00.

Sourcebook of Zip Code Demographics. ESRI Business Information Solutions. • 2002. $495.00. 16th edition. Provides data on 75 demographic and socio-economic characteristics for each ZIP code in the U. S.

Statistical Handbook on Consumption and Wealth in the United States. Greenwood Publishing Group, Inc. • 1999. $69.95. Provides more than 400 graphs, tables, and charts dealing with basic income levels, income inequalities, spending patterns, taxation, subsidies, etc. (Statistical Handbook Series).

World Consumer Expenditure Patterns. Euromonitor International. • 2003. $1,190.00. Contains detailed consumer expenditure data for 71 countries. Covers 70 specific categories within the areas of food, beverages, tobacco, clothing, housing, appliances, health, transportation, leisure, etc. Provides 10 years of data and includes consumer price indexes.

World Consumer Income and Expenditure Patterns. Available from Gale Cengage Learning. • Annual. $1,090.00. Two volumes. Published by Euromonitor. Provides data for countries worldwide on consumer income, earning power, spending patterns, and savings. Expenditures are detailed for product or service categories.

World Consumer Income Patterns. Euromonitor International. • 2003. $1,190.00. Provides detailed data on household income in 71 countries (10-year statistics). Covers income by age, sex, and level of education, with further data on savings, earnings, and average taxes.

World Consumer Lifestyles Databook: Key Trends. Euromonitor International. • 2003. $1,190.00. Second edition. Covers 71 countries. Presents statistical data relating to such consumer lifestyle characteristics as family size, household income, family expenditures, home ownership, shopping habits, eating habits, drinking habits, savings, transportation, travel, health characteristics, and education.

PUTS AND CALLS

See: STOCK OPTION CONTRACTS

Q

QUALITY CONTROL

See also: PRODUCTION CONTROL; STANDARDIZATION; TOTAL QUALITY MANAGEMENT (TQM)

GENERAL WORKS

Chaos on the Shop Floor: A Worker's View of Quality, Productivity, and Management. Tom Juravich. Temple University Press. • 1988. $19.95. (Labor and Social Change Series).

Principles of Total Quality. Vincent K. Omachonu. CRC Press. • 2004. $54.95. Third edition. Covers the general management of quality control, including leadership, human resources, information analysis, strategic planning, and customer satisfaction.

Process Quality Control. Ellis R. Ott and others. McGraw-Hill. • 2000. $74.95. Third edition. (Professional Engineering Series).

Quality Control. Dale H. Besterfield. Prentice Hall PTR. • 2000. $99.00. Sixth edition. Includes CD-ROM. Covers basic quality control concepts and procedures, including statistical process control (SPC). Includes disk.

Quality Planning and Analysis: From Product Development Through Use. Frank M. Gryna. McGraw-Hill. • 2000. $122.50. Fourth edition. (Industrial Engineering and Management Science Series).

ABSTRACTS AND INDEXES

NTIS Alerts: Manufacturing Technology. National Technical Information Service. • Semimonthly. $265.00 per year. Provides descriptions of government-sponsored research reports and software, with ordering information. Covers computer-aided design and manufacturing (CAD/CAM), engineering materials, quality control, machine tools, robots, lasers, productivity, and related subjects. Formerly *Abstract Newsletter.*

DIRECTORIES

Quality-Buyers Guide for QA/QC Equipment, Software, and Services. Reed Business Information. • Annual. $15.00. List of manufacturers and distributors of quality control equipment for measurement, inspection, data analysis evaluation and destructive and nondestructive testing; also lists testing laboratories, consultants, software and training organizations. Formerly *Quality Buyers Guide for Test, Inspection, Measurement and Evaluation.*

ENCYCLOPEDIAS AND DICTIONARIES

Blackwell Encyclopedic Dictionary of Operations Management. Nigel Slack, editor. Blackwell Publishing. • 1997. $130.95. The editor is associ-

ated with the University of Warwick, England. Contains definitions of key terms combined with longer articles written by various U. S. and foreign business educators. Includes bibliographies and index. (Blackwell Encyclopedia of Management Series.).

HANDBOOKS AND MANUALS

Gower Handbook of Quality Management. Dennis Lock, editor. Ashgate Publishing Co. • 1994. Second edition. Price on application. Consists of 41 chapters written by various authors. Published by Gower in England.

Juran's Quality Control Handbook. Joseph M. Juran and A. Blandford Godfrey, editors. McGraw-Hill. • 1998. $150.00. Fifth edition.

Modern Methods for Quality Control and Improvement. Harrison M. Wadsworth and others. John Wiley and Sons, Inc. • 2001. $104.95. Second edition.

Statistical Quality Control: Strategies and Tools for Continual Improvement. Johannes Ledolter and Claude W. Burrill. John Wiley and Sons, Inc. • 1998. $104.95.

World Class Quality: Using Design of Experiments to Make It Happen. Keki R. Bhote and Adi K. Bhote. AMACOM. • 1999. $45.00. Second revised expanded edition. An explanation of seven Shainin techniques for quality control. Exercises and case studies are included.

PERIODICALS AND NEWSLETTERS

Journal of Quality Technology: A Quarterly Journal of Methods, Applications, and Related Topics. American Society for Quality. • Quarterly. Members, $26.00 per year; non-members, $37.00 per year; institutions, $100.00 per year.

Quality and Reliability Engineering International. Available from John Wiley and Sons, Inc., Journals Div. • Bimonthly. $1,500.00 per year. Designed to bridge the gap between existing theoretical methods and scientific research on the one hand, and current industrial practices on the other. Published in England by John Wiley and Sons Ltd.

Quality Management Journal. American Society for Quality. • Quarterly. Members, $50.00 per year; non-members, $60.00 per year. Emphasizes research in quality control and management.

Quality Progress. American Society for Quality. • Monthly. Individuals, $60.00 per year; institutions, $120.00 per year. Covers developments in quality improvement throughout the world.

RESEARCH CENTERS AND INSTITUTES

Institute of Advanced Manufacturing Sciences. 1111 Edison Dr., Cincinnati, OH 45230. Phone: (513)948-2000 Fax: 800-345-4482 • Fields of

research include quality improvement, computer-aided design, artificial intelligence, and employee training.

National Center for Manufacturing Sciences. 3025 Boardwalk St., Ann Arbor, MI 48108. Phone: (734)995-0300 Fax: (734)995-4004 E-mail: johnd@ncms.org • URL: http://www.ncms.org • Research areas include process technology and control, machine mechanics, sensors, testing methods, and quality assurance.

TRADE/PROFESSIONAL ASSOCIATIONS

American Society for Quality. 600 N. Plankinton Ave., Milwaukee, WI 53201-3005. Phone: 800-248-1946 or (414)272-8575 Fax: (414)272-1734 E-mail: cs@asq.org • URL: http://www.asq.org.

Association for Quality and Participation. PO Box 2005, Milwaukee, WI 53201-2005. Phone: 800-733-3310 or (414)765-7219 Fax: (414)272-2145 E-mail: aqp@aqp.org • URL: http://www.aqp.org.

QUALITY OF PRODUCTS

See also: CONSUMER EDUCATION; STANDARDIZATION

CD-ROM DATABASES

Consumers Reference Disc. National Information Services Corp. • Quarterly. Provides the CD-ROM version of *Consumer Health and Nutrition Index* from Oryx Press and *Consumers Index to Product Evaluations and Information Sources* from Pierian Press. Contains citations to consumer health articles and consumer product evaluations, tests, warnings, and recalls.

ENCYCLOPEDIAS AND DICTIONARIES

Consumers' Guide to Product Grades and Terms: From Grade A to VSOP-Definitions of 8,000 Terms Describing Food Housewares and Other Everyday Terms. Gale Cengage Learning. • 1992. $95.00. Includes product grades and classifications defined by government agencies, such as the Food and Drug Administration (FDA), and by voluntary standards organizations, such as the American National Standards Institute (ANSI).

PERIODICALS AND NEWSLETTERS

Consumer Reports. Consumers Union of the United States, Inc. • Monthly. $26.00 per year. Includes *Annual Buying Guide.*

Consumer's Research Magazine: Analyzing Consumer Issues. Consumers' Research Inc. • Monthly. $24.00 per year.

NDT and E International; The Independent Journal of Non-Destructive Testing. Elsevier. • Eight times a year. Institutions, $727.00 per year. Formerly *NDT International*.

TRADE/PROFESSIONAL ASSOCIATIONS

American National Standards Institute. 1819 L St. NW, 6th Fl., Washington, DC 20036. Phone: (202)293-8020 Fax: (202)293-9287 E-mail: info@ansi.org • URL: http://www.ansi.org • Industrial firms, trade associations, technical societies, labor organizations, consumer organizations, and government agencies. Serves as clearinghouse for nationally coordinated voluntary standards for fields ranging from information technology to building construction. Gives status as American National Standards to standards developed by agreement from all groups concerned, in such areas as: definitions, terminology, symbols, and abbreviations; materials, performance characteristics, procedure, and methods of rating; methods of testing and analysis; size, weight, volume, and rating; practice, safety, health, and building construction. Provides information on foreign standards and represents United States interests in international standardization work.

Consumers Union of United States. 101 Truman Ave., Yonkers, NY 10703-1057. Phone: (914)378-2000 Fax: (914)378-2900 • URL: http://www.consumerreports.org.

QUARRYING

See also: CLAY INDUSTRY; LIMESTONE INDUSTRY; MARBLE

ABSTRACTS AND INDEXES

IMM Abstracts and Index: A Survey of World Literature on the Economic Geology and Mining of All Minerals (Except Coal), Mineral Processing, and Nonferrous Extraction Metallurgy. Institution of Mining and Metallurgy. • Bimonthly. $500.00 per year. Provides international coverage of the literature of mining and nonferrous metallurgy. Includes mineral economics, tunnelling, and rock mechanics.

DIRECTORIES

Pit and Quarry Reference Manual and Buyers' Guide. Advanstar Communications. • Annual. $25.00. Lists approximately 1,000 manufacturers and other suppliers of equipment products and services to the nonmetallic mining and quarrying industry.

Absorbed: *Ready-Mix-Reference Manual.*

FINANCIAL RATIOS

Almanac of Business and Industrial Financial Ratios. Leo Troy. Aspen Publishers, Inc. • 2003. $125.95. Includes CD-Rom. Contains financial ratios derived from federal tax returns. Ratios for each of about 200 industries are arranged according to company asset size. (Almanac of Business and Industrial Financial Ratios Series).

Annual Statement Studies. The Risk Management Association. • Annual. Median and quartile financial ratios are given for over 400 kinds of manufacturing, wholesale, retail, construction, and consumer finance establishments. Data is sorted by both asset size and sales volume. Includes a clearly written "Definition of Ratios" and an alphabetical industry index.

Annual Statement Studies: Industry Default Probabilities and Cash Flow Measures. The Risk Management Association. • Annual. $145.00. Serves as a companion volume to the original *Annual Statement Studies.* Gives probability of default estimates on a percentage scale for more than 450 industries. Includes changes in position year-by-year for eight financial statement line items and provides percentage measures of cash flow.

ONLINE DATABASES

GEOARCHIVE. Geosystems. • Citations to literature on geoscience and water. 1974 to present. Monthly updates. Inquire as to online cost and availability.

GEOREF. American Geological Institute. • Bibliography and index of geology and geosciences literature, 1785 to present. Inquire as to online cost and availability.

PERIODICALS AND NEWSLETTERS

Building Stone Magazine. Building Stone Institute. • Bimonthly. $65.00 per year.

Pit and Quarry. Advanstar Communications. • Monthly. $45.00 per year. Covers crushed stone, sand and gravel, etc.

Rock Products: The Aggregate Industry's Journal of Applied Technology. Primedia Business Magazines and Media. • Monthly. $56.00 per year.

STATISTICS SOURCES

Annual Survey of Manufactures. Available from U. S. Government Printing Office. • Annual. Prices vary. Issued by the U. S. Census Bureau as an interim update to the *Census of Manufactures.*

Includes data on number of manufacturing establishments in various industries, employment, labor costs, value of shipments, capital expenditures, inventories, energy costs, and assets. (See also Census Bureau home page, http://www.census.gov/.).

Mineral Commodity Summaries. Available from U. S. Government Printing Office. • Annual. $26.00. Published by the U. S. Geological Survey, Department of the Interior (http://www.usgs.gov). Contains detailed, five-year data for about 90 nonfuel minerals. Covers a wide range of statistics, including production, imports, exports, consumption, reserves, prices, tariff information, and industry employment. (Two pages are devoted to each mineral.).

United States Census of Mineral Industries. Bureau of the Census, U.S. Department of Commerce. Available from U.S. Government Printing Office. • Quinquennial.

WEFA Industrial Monitor. John Wiley and Sons, Inc. • Annual. $65.00. Prepared by industry analysts at WEFA, an economic forecasting and consulting firm (originally Wharton Econometric Forecasting Associates). Contains discussions of the outlook for major U. S. industries, with many 10-year forecasts (WEFA Web site is http://www.wefa.com).

TRADE/PROFESSIONAL ASSOCIATIONS

Building Stone Institute. 551 Tollgate Rd., Ste. C, Elgin, IL 60123-9357. Phone: (866)786-6313 or (847)695-0170 Fax: (847)695-0174 E-mail: margie@buildingstoneinstitute.org • URL: http://www.buildingstoneinstitute.org • Represents Natural Stone quarriers, fabricators, installers, dealers, importers, expo and restorers. Serves as a clearinghouse of information for architects, contractors, decorstors, and masons. Promotes the use of Natural Stone.

National Building Granite Quarries Association. 1220 L St. NW, Ste. 100-167, Washington, DC 20005. Phone: 800-557-2848 Fax: (603)225-4801 E-mail: ncc@chickenusa.org • URL: http://www.nbgqa.com • Represents quarriers and manufacturers of building granites. Provides specifications for designers.

National Stone, Sand and Gravel Association. 2101 Wilson Blvd., Ste. 100, Arlington, VA 22201. Phone: 800-342-1415 or (703)525-8788 Fax: (703)525-7782 E-mail: info@nssga.org • URL: http://www.aggregates.org • Formerly National Stone Association.

R

RACK JOBBERS

HANDBOOKS AND MANUALS

Progressive Grocer Guidebook. Trade Dimensions. • Annual. $375.00. Over 800 major chain and independent food retailers and wholesalers in the United States and Canada; also includes food brokers, rack jobbers, candy and tobacco distributors, and magazine distributors.

PERIODICALS AND NEWSLETTERS

Non-Foods Management: The Annual Supermarket State of the Industry Report. Millennium Media Corp. • Annual. $45.00. Written for top management and non-foods decision makers and executives at supermarkets.

TRADE/PROFESSIONAL ASSOCIATIONS

National Association of Recording Merchandisers. Nine Eves Dr., Suite 120, Marlton, NJ 08053. Phone: (856)596-2221 Fax: (856)596-3268 E-mail: rosum@narm.com • URL: http://www.narm.com.

RADIO AND TELEVISION ADVERTISING

See also: ADVERTISING; ADVERTISING MEDIA; RADIO BROADCASTING INDUSTRY; TELEVISION BROADCASTING INDUSTRY

GENERAL WORKS

Electronic Media Ratings. Karen Buzzard. Elsevier. • 1992. $22.95. Provides basic information about TV and radio audience-rating techniques. Includes glossary and bibliography. (Electronic Media Guide Series).

BIBLIOGRAPHIES

Topicator: Classified Guide to Articles in the Advertising/Communications/Marketing Periodical Press. • Bimonthly. $110.00 per year. An index of major articles appearing in 20 leading magazines in the advertising, communications, and marketing fields.

DIRECTORIES

Advertising Age-Leading National Advertisers. Crain Communications, Inc. • Annual. $5.00. List of the 100 leading advertisers in terms of the amount spent in national advertising and below-the-line forms of spending.

CARD The Media Information Network. Rogers Media Publishing. • Covers: Radio and television stations and networks; daily and weekend newspapers; consumer, farm, and business publications; advertising agencies and international media representatives; advertising, marketing, and media associations; and transportation and out-of-home advertising. Entries include: For publications--Title, company name, address, phone, frequency, names and titles of key personnel, advertising rates, discounts, mechanical requirements, copy regulations, circulation, closing and publication dates. For broadcasting stations--Call letters, name of owning company, address, phone, name of firm or individual representing station for advertising, special features, format, facilities, affiliations, rates, participation programs. For agencies and associations--Name, address, phone, personnel.

International Television and Video Almanac: Reference Tool of the Television and Home Video Industries. Quigley Publishing Co., Inc. • Annual. $130.00.

Radio Co-op Directory. Radio Advertising Bureau. • Database covers: Over 5,000 manufacturers that provide cooperative allowances for radio advertising. Database includes: Company name, address, name of contact, phone, fax, allowance, accrual rate, whether plan is administered by distributor, expiration dates.

The SHOOT Directory for Commercial Production and Postproduction. SHOOT. • Annual. $79.00. Lists production companies, advertising agencies, and sources of professional television, motion picture, and audio equipment.

VNU Business Media. ADWEEK Directories. • Annual. $100.00. Presents cost, circulation, and audience statistics for various mass media segments, including television, radio, magazines, newspapers, telephone yellow pages, and cinema.

ENCYCLOPEDIAS AND DICTIONARIES

Advertising Age Encyclopedia of Advertising. John McDonough and others, editors. Fitzroy Dearborn Publishers. • 2002. $385.00. Three volumes. Contains 600 entries in alphabetical order covering a wide variety of advertising and market research topics. Includes bibliographies.

HANDBOOKS AND MANUALS

Do-It-Yourself Advertising and Promotion: How to Produce Great Ads, Brochures, Catalogs, Direct Mail, Web Sites and more. Fred E. Hahn. John Wiley and Sons, Inc. • 2003. $19.95. Third edition. Covers magazines, newspapers, flyers, brochures, catalogs, direct mail, telemarketing, trade shows, and radio/TV promotions. Includes checklists. (Small Business Series).

Radio Advertising: The Authoritative Handbook. Pete Schulberg and Bob Schulberg. McGraw Hill. • 1994. $27.95. Second edition. (NTC Business Books Series).

Radio and Television Commercial. Albert C. Book and others. McGraw Hill. • 1995. $19.95. Third revised edition. How to guide showing how to create effective radio and television advertisements. (NTC Business Books Series).

ONLINE DATABASES

Arbitron Radio County Coverage. Arbitron Co. • Ratings of radio and TV stations plus audience measurement data, updated frequently. Inquire as to online cost and availability.

Nielsen Station Index. Nielsen Media Research. • Measures local television station audiences in about 220 U. S. geographic areas. Includes current and some historical data. Inquire as to online cost and availability.

Nielsen Television Index. Nielsen Media Research. • Measures national television program audiences by sampling approximately 4,000 U. S. households. Time period is 1970 to date, with weekly updates.

PERIODICALS AND NEWSLETTERS

Broadcasting and Cable. Reed Business Information. • 51 times a year. $179.00 per year; includes print and online editions. Formerly *Broadcasting.*

The Marketing Pulse: The Exclusive Insight Provider to the Entertainment, Marketing, Advertising and Media Industries. Unlimited Positive Communications, Inc. • Bimonthly. $300.00 per year. Newsletter concerned with advertising media forecasts and analyses. Emphasis is on TV and radio.

Radio Business Report: The Voice of the Radio Broadcasting Industry. Radio Business Report, Inc. • Weekly. $89.00 per year. Covers radio advertising, FCC regulations, audience ratings, market research, station management, business conditions, and related topics.

SHOOT: The Leading Newsweekly for Commercial Production and Postproduction. VNU Business Media. • Weekly. $125.00 per year. Covers animation, music, sound design, computer graphics, visual effects, cinematography, and other aspects of television and motion picture production, with emphasis on TV commercials.

STATISTICS SOURCES

Cable TV Facts. Cabletelevision Advertising Bureau. • Annual. $12.00. Provides statistics on cable TV and cable TV advertising in the U. S.

Media Market Guide. Media Market Resources. • Quarterly. $675.00 per year. Presents circulation and cost data for television, radio, magazines, newspapers and outdoor markets.

Radio Facts: The Voice of Urban Culture. RadioMan Publishing Inc. • Annual. $50.00.

Television and Cable Factbook. Warren Publishing,

For publishers addresses, refer to SOURCES CITED section at the back of the book.

765

Encyclopedia of Business Information Sources • 24th Edition

Inc. • Annual. $595.00. Three volumes. Weekly updates. Commercial and noncommercial television stations and networks.

TRADE/PROFESSIONAL ASSOCIATIONS

Radio Advertising Bureau. 1320 Greenway Dr., Ste. 500, 261 Madison Ave., 23rd Fl., Irving, TX 75038-2587. Phone: 800-232-3131 or (212)681-7214 Fax: (212)681-7217 E-mail: jhaley@rab.com • URL: http://www.rab.com • Includes radio stations, radio networks, station sales representatives, and allied industry services, such as producers, research firms, schools, and consultants. Calls on advertisers and agencies to promote the sale of radio time as an advertising medium. Sponsors program to increase professionalism of radio salespeople, awarding Certified Radio Marketing Consultant designation to those who pass examination. Sponsors regional marketing conferences. Conducts extensive research program into all phases of radio sales. Issues reports on use of radio by national, regional, and local advertisers. Speaks before conventions and groups to explain benefits of radio advertising. Sponsors Radio Creative Fund. Compiles statistics.

Television Bureau of Advertising. Three E. 54th St., New York, NY 10022. Phone: (212)486-1111 Fax: (212)935-5631 E-mail: info@tvb.org • URL: http://www.tvb.org.

RADIO AND TELEVISION REPAIR INDUSTRY

HANDBOOKS AND MANUALS

Troubleshooting and Repairing Color Television Systems. Robert Goodman. McGraw-Hill. • 1997. $24.95.

Troubleshooting and Repairing Solid-State TVs. Homer Davidson. McGraw-Hill. • 1996. $44.95. Third editionl. (Tab Electronics Technician Library).

PERIODICALS AND NEWSLETTERS

Electronic Servicing & Technology: The How-To Magazine of Electronics. CQ Communications, Inc. • Monthly. Free to qualified personnel; others, $26.95 per year. Provides how-to technical information to technicians who service consumer electronics equipment.

Poptronics. Gernsback Publications, Inc. • Monthly. $19.99 per year. Incorporates *Electronics Now.*

STATISTICS SOURCES

United States Census of Service Industries. U.S. Bureau of the Census. • Quinquennial. Various reports available.

TRADE/PROFESSIONAL ASSOCIATIONS

National Electronics Service Dealers Association. 3608 Pershing Ave., Fort Worth, TX 76107-4527. Phone: 800-797-9197 or (817)921-9061 Fax: (817)921-3741 E-mail: info@nesda.com • URL: http://www.nesda.com • Local and state electronic service associations and companies. Supplies technical service information on business management training to electronic service dealers. Offers certification and training programs through International Society of Certified Electronics Technicians. Conducts technical service and business management seminars.

RADIO BROADCASTING INDUSTRY

See also: RADIO AND TELEVISION ADVERTISING; RADIO EQUIPMENT INDUSTRY; TELEVISION BROADCASTING INDUSTRY

GENERAL WORKS

Minority Broadcast Ownership. Gregory L. Rohde. Nova Science Publishers, Inc. • 2002. $29.50.

Provides discussion and statistical data relating to minority ownership of radio and television stations in the U.S.

Perspectives on Radio and Television: Telecommunication in the United States. F. Leslie Smith and others. Lawrence Erlbaum Associates, Inc. • 1998. Fourth edition. Price on application. (Communication Series).

ABSTRACTS AND INDEXES

Communication Abstracts: An International Information Service. Sage Publications, Inc. • Bimonthly. Institutions, $1,150.00 per year. Provides broad coverage of the literature of communications, including broadcasting and advertising.

BIBLIOGRAPHIES

Topicator: Classified Guide to Articles in the Advertising/Communications/Marketing Periodical Press. • Bimonthly. $110.00 per year. An index of major articles appearing in 20 leading magazines in the advertising, communications, and marketing fields.

BIOGRAPHICAL SOURCES

Biographical Dictionary of American Journalism. Joseph P. McKerns, editor. Greenwood Publishing Group Inc. • 1989. $92.95. Covers major mass media: newspapers, radio, television, and magazines. Includes reporters, editors, columnists, cartoonists, commentators, etc.

CD-ROM DATABASES

Hoover's Company Capsules on CD-ROM. Hoover's, Inc. • Quarterly. $399.95 per year (single-user). Provides the CD-ROM version of *Hoover's Handbook of American Business, Hoover's Handbook of Emerging Companies, Hoover's Handbook of World Business, Hoover's Guide to Computer Companies, Hoover's Guide to Media Companies, Hoover's Handbook of Private Companies,* and various regional guides. Includes more than 11,000 profiles of companies.

DIRECTORIES

Bacon's Radio/TV/Cable Directory. Bacon's Information, Inc. • Annual. $325.00. Includes educational and public broadcasters. Covers all United States broadcast media.

Broadcasting and Cable Yearbook. Gale. • Annual. $179.95. Provides information on U. S. and Canadian TV stations, radio stations, cable TV companies, and radio-TV services of various kinds.

Burrelle's Media Directory: Broadcast Media. Burrelle's Information Services. • Annual. $550.00. Approximately 48,000 print and electronic media in North America. Provides detailed descriptions, including programming and key personnel.

Gale Directory of Publications and Broadcast Media. Gale Cengage Learning. • Annual. $770.00. Five volumes. *Interedition Supplement,* Free. A guide to publications and broadcasting stations in the U. S. and Canada, including newspapers, magazines, journals, radio stations, television stations, and cable systems. Geographic arrangement. Volume three consists of statistical tables, maps, subject indexes, and title index.

SRDS Radio Advertising Source. SRDS. • Quarterly. $535.00 per year. Contains detailed information on U. S. radio stations, networks, and corporate owners, with maps of market areas. Includes key personnel. Formerly *Radio Advertising Rates and Data.*

Working Press of the Nation. R. R. Bowker. • Annual. $530.00. $295.00 per volume. Three volumes: (1) *Newspaper Directory;* (2) *Magazine and Internal Publications Directory;* (3) *Radio and*

Television Directory. Includes names of editors and other personnel.

ENCYCLOPEDIAS AND DICTIONARIES

Broadcast Communications Dictionary. Lincoln Diamant, editor. Greenwood Publishing Group Inc. • 1989. $57.95. Third revised edition.

FINANCIAL RATIOS

Almanac of Business and Industrial Financial Ratios. Leo Troy. Aspen Publishers, Inc. • 2003. $125.95. Includes CD-Rom. Contains financial ratios derived from federal tax returns. Ratios for each of about 200 industries are arranged according to company asset size. (Almanac of Business and Industrial Financial Ratios Series).

Annual Statement Studies. The Risk Management Association. • Annual. Median and quartile financial ratios are given for over 400 kinds of manufacturing, wholesale, retail, construction, and consumer finance establishments. Data is sorted by both asset size and sales volume. Includes a clearly written "Definition of Ratios" and an alphabetical industry index.

Annual Statement Studies: Industry Default Probabilities and Cash Flow Measures. The Risk Management Association. • Annual. $145.00. Serves as a companion volume to the original *Annual Statement Studies.* Gives probability of default estimates on a percentage scale for more than 450 industries. Includes changes in position year-by-year for eight financial statement line items and provides percentage measures of cash flow.

HANDBOOKS AND MANUALS

Dun & Bradstreet/Gale Group Industry Handbooks. Gale Cengage Learning. • 2000. $650.00. Five volumes. $130.00 per volume. Each volume covers two or more major industries: 1. *Entertainment and Hospitality;* 2. *Construction and Agriculture;* 3. *Chemicals and Pharmaceuticals;* 4. *Computers & Software and Broadcasting & Telecommunications;* 5. *Insurance and Health & Medical Services.* The following are included for each industry: overview, statistics, financial ratios, rankings, merger information, company directory, directory of associations, and consultants directory. (Dun and Bradstreet/Gale Industry Reference Handbook Series).

ONLINE DATABASES

Gale Database of Publications and Broadcast Media. Gale Cengage Learning. • An online directory containing detailed information on over 67,000 periodicals, newspapers, broadcast stations, cable systems, directories, and newsletters. Corresponds to the following print sources: *Gale Directory of Publications and Broadcast Media; Directories in Print; City and State Directories in Print; Newsletters in Print.* Semiannual updates. Inquire as to online cost and availability.

PERIODICALS AND NEWSLETTERS

Broadcast Engineering: Journal of Broadcast Technology. Primedia Business Magazines and Media. • 10 times a year. Free to qualified personnel; others, $65.00 per year. Technical magazine for the broadcast industry.

Broadcast Investor: Newsletter on Radio-TV Station Finance. Paul Kagan Associates, Inc. • Monthly. $925.00 per year. Newsletter for investors in publicly held radio and television broadcasting companies.

Broadcasting and Cable. Reed Business Information. • 51 times a year. $179.00 per year; includes print and online editions. Formerly *Broadcasting.*

Entertainment Law and Finance. American Lawyer Media, Inc. • Monthly. $229.00 per year. Newsletter. Covers contracts, royalties, litigation, copyright, taxation, etc., for the music industry, motion pictures, broadcasting, publishing, video, and related media. (A Law Journal Newsletter, formerly published by Leader Publications.).

Entertainment Marketing Letter. EPM Communications Inc. • Description: Reports on techniques used in the marketing of films, music, videos, television, radio, and cable features. Covers tie-in campaigns, sponsorship, in-theatre advertising, and interactive telephone promotions.

Journal of Broadcasting and Electronic Media. Broadcast Education Association. • Quarterly. $86.50 per year. Scholarly articles about developments, trends and research.

Radio & Records. Radio & Records, Inc. • Weekly. $325.00 per year. Provides news and information relating to the record industry and to regional and national radio broadcasting. Special features cover specific types of programming, such as "classic rock," "adult alternative," "oldies," "country," and "news/talk." Radio station business and management topics are included.

Radio Business Report: The Voice of the Radio Broadcasting Industry. Radio Business Report, Inc. • Weekly. $89.00 per year. Covers radio advertising, FCC regulations, audience ratings, market research, station management, business conditions, and related topics.

Radio World. IMAS Publishing Group. • Biweekly. Free. Emphasis is on radio broadcast engineeri and equipment. Text in English, Portuguese and Spanish.

STATISTICS SOURCES

Infrastructure Industries USA. Gale Cengage Learning. • 2001. $260.00. Presents statistics and projections relating to economic activity in a wide variety of natural resource and construction industries.

Standard & Poor's Industry Surveys. Standard & Poor's. • Semiannual. $1,800.00. Two looseleaf volumes. Includes monthly *Supplements.* Provides detailed, individual surveys of 52 major industry groups. Each survey is revised on a semiannual basis. Also includes "Monthly Investment Review" (industry group investment analysis) and monthly "Trends & Projections" (economic analysis).

TRADE/PROFESSIONAL ASSOCIATIONS

American Sportscasters Association. 225 Broadway, Ste. 2030, New York, NY 10007. Phone: (212)227-8080 Fax: (212)571-0556 E-mail: lschwa8918@aol.com • URL: http://www.americansportscastersonline.com • Radio and television sportscasters. Sponsors seminars, clinics, and symposia for aspiring announcers and sportscasters. Compiles statistics. Operates Speaker's Bureau, placement service, hall of fame, and biographical archives. Maintains American Sportscaster Hall of Fame Trust. Is currently implementing Hall of Fame Museum, Community Programs.

Broadcast Education Association. 1771 N St. NW, Washington, DC 20036-2800. Phone: 888-380-7222 or (202)429-3935 Fax: (202)775-2981 E-mail: beainfo@beaweb.org • URL: http://www.beaweb.org • Universities and colleges; faculty and students; promotes improvement of curriculum and teaching methods, broadcasting research, television and radio production, and programming teaching on the college level.

International Radio and Television Society Foundation. 420 Lexington Ave., Suite 1714, New York, NY 10170. Phone: (212)867-6650 Fax: (212)867-6653 • URL: http://www.irts.org • Affiliated with National Broadcasting Society-Alpha Epsilon Pho. Formerly International Radio and Television Society.

National Association of Broadcasters. 1771 N St., NW, Washington, DC 20036. Phone: (202)429-5300 Fax: (202)429-4199 E-mail: sdelanghe@nab.org • URL: http://www.nab.org • Formerly National As-

sociation of Radio and Television Broadcasters.

OTHER SOURCES

FCC Record. Available from U. S. Government Printing Office. • Biweekly. $678.00 per year. Produced by the Federal Communications Commission (http://www.fcc.gov). An inclusive compilation of decisions, reports, public notices, and other documents of the FCC.

RADIO EQUIPMENT INDUSTRY

See also: COMMUNICATION SYSTEMS; HIGH FIDELITY/STEREO; TELEVISION APPARATUS INDUSTRY

ABSTRACTS AND INDEXES

NTIS Alerts: Communication. National Technical Information Service. • Semimonthly. $210.00 per year. . Provides descriptions of government-sponsored research reports and software, with ordering information. Covers common carriers, satellites, radio/TV equipment, telecommunication regulations, and related subjects.

DIRECTORIES

Broadcast Engineering--Equipment Reference Manual. Penton Media Inc. • Publication includes: List of more than 1,400 manufacturers and distributors of communications equipment for radio, television, and recording applications. Entries include: For manufacturers--Company name, address. For distributors and dealers--Company name, address, phone, product or service provided, geographic area covered.

Directory of Computer and Consumer Electronics Retailers. Chain Store Guide. • Annual. $335.00. Online edition, $775.00. Lists 4,500 United States and Canada companies operating almost 59,000 stores with at least $1,000,000 in sales.

FINANCIAL RATIOS

Annual Statement Studies. The Risk Management Association. • Annual. Median and quartile financial ratios are given for over 400 kinds of manufacturing, wholesale, retail, construction, and consumer finance establishments. Data is sorted by both asset size and sales volume. Includes a clearly written "Definition of Ratios" and an alphabetical industry index.

Annual Statement Studies: Industry Default Probabilities and Cash Flow Measures. The Risk Management Association. • Annual. $145.00. Serves as a companion volume to the original *Annual Statement Studies.* Gives probability of default estimates on a percentage scale for more than 450 industries. Includes changes in position year-by-year for eight financial statement line items and provides percentage measures of cash flow.

HANDBOOKS AND MANUALS

Principles of Digital Audio. Ken C. Pohlmann. McGraw-Hill. • 2000. $54.95. Fourth edition. Includes the details of digital audio recording, reproduction, error correction, compact disc technology, DVD, minidiscs, Internet audio, and related topics. (Video/Audio Engineering Series).

Standard Handbook of Audio and Radio Engineering. Jerry C. Whitaker and K. Blair Benson. McGraw-Hill. • 2002. $125.00. Second edition. Emphasis is on audio. Covers such topics as DVD, MP3, sound reproduction, amplification, noise reduction, and Internet audio.

PERIODICALS AND NEWSLETTERS

Broadcast Engineering: Journal of Broadcast Technology. Primedia Business Magazines and Media. • 10 times a year. Free to qualified personnel; others, $65.00 per year. Technical magazine for the broadcast industry.

Poptronics. Gernsback Publications, Inc. • Monthly. $19.99 per year. Incorporates *Electronics Now.*

RCR Wireless News: The Newspaper for the Wireless Communications Industry. Crain Communications. • Weekly. $64.00 per year. Covers news of the wireless communications industry, including business and financial developments. Formerly *RCR.*

Sound and Communications. Testa Communications, Inc. • Monthly. $15.00 per year. A business, news and technical journal for contractors, consultants, engineers and system managers who design, install and purchase sound and communications equipment.

Wireless Week. Reed Business Information. • 50 times a year. $99.00 per year. Covers news of cellular telephones, mobile radios, communications satellites, microwave transmission, and the wireless industry in general. Includes annual *Directory.*

TRADE/PROFESSIONAL ASSOCIATIONS

Electronic Industries Alliance. 2500 Wilson Blvd., Arlington, VA 22201. Phone: (703)907-7500 Fax: (703)907-7501 E-mail: mflanigan@eia.org • URL: http://www.eia.org • Seeks for the competitiveness of the American producer, represents all companies involved in the design and manufacture of electronic components, parts, systems and equipment for communications, industrial, government and consumer uses.

North American Retail Dealers Association. 4700 W Lake Ave., Glenview, IL 60025. Phone: 800-621-0298 or (847)375-4713 Fax: (866)879-7505 E-mail: nardasvc@narda.com • URL: http://www.narda.com • Firms engaged in the retailing of electronic and electrical devices and components. Promotes and represents members' interests. Makes available services to members including: legal and technical consulting; employee screening; bank card processing; long-distance phone discounts; financial statements analysis; in-store promotion kits; customer check authorization. Advocates for members' interests before federal regulatory bodies; disseminates information on new regulations affecting members. Conducts educational programs.

RADIO STATIONS

See: RADIO BROADCASTING INDUSTRY

RADIOISOTOPES

See: ISOTOPES

RADIOLOGICAL EQUIPMENT

See: X-RAY EQUIPMENT INDUSTRY

RADIOS

See: RADIO EQUIPMENT INDUSTRY

RAILROAD EQUIPMENT INDUSTRY

CD-ROM DATABASES

OECD Statistical Compendium. Organization for Economic Cooperation and Development. • Semiannual. $1,905.00 per year for 1 to 10 users. CD-ROM contains more than 730,000 monthly, quarterly, and annual time series for OECD countries, 1960 to date. Includes fully searchable data on agriculture, food, economic indicators, national accounts, employment, energy, finance, industry, technology, and foreign trade. Results can be displayed in various forms.

DIRECTORIES

Thomas Register of American Manufacturers. Thomas Publishing Co., Inc. • Annual. $149.00. 34 volumes. A three-part system offering information on a wide variety of industrial equipment and supplies. Lists more than 151,000 industrial product and services companies.

INTERNET DATABASES

Business 2.0 Web Guide to the Best Business Links. Business 2.0 Media Inc. Phone: (415)293-4800 E-mail: support@business2.com • URL: http://www.business2.com/webguide • Web site presents an extensive, searchable directory of links to "the best, most informative, and authoritative web pages." Twenty main categories cover business, finance, career, company information, people, and technology topics, with thousands of subtopics, all linking to Web sites recommended by experienced business researchers. Fees: Free.

Fedstats. Federal Interagency Council on Statistical Policy. Phone: (202)395-7254 • URL: http://www.fedstats.gov • Web site features an efficient search facility for full-text statistics produced by more than 100 federal agencies, including the Census Bureau, the Bureau of Economic Analysis, and the Bureau of Labor Statistics. Boolean searches can be made within one agency or for all agencies combined. Links are offered to international statistical bureaus, including the UN, IMF, OECD, UNESCO, Eurostat, and 20 individual countries. Fees: Free.

FreeLunch.com. Economy.com, Inc. Phone: (610)696-8700 Fax: (610)696-1678 • URL: http://www.freelunch.com • Web site provides free access to more than 1.5 million economic and financial data series, covering industry, demographics, labor markets, prices, retail sales, government spending, trade, interest rates, housing starts, the stock market, and many other topics. Data is available for various time periods in either chart or table form. Searching is offered. Fees: Free, but registration required. Economy.com, Inc. also offers fee-based economic analysis at *The Dismal Scientist* site (http://www.dismal.com).

ONLINE DATABASES

Thomas Register Online. Thomas Publishing Co., Inc. • Provides concise information on approximately 194,000 U. S. companies, mainly manufacturers, with over 50,000 product classifications. Indexes over 115,000 trade names. Information is updated semiannually. Inquire as to online cost and availability.

PERIODICALS AND NEWSLETTERS

Railway Track and Structures. Simmons-Boardman Publishing Corp. • Monthly. $30.00 per year.

STATISTICS SOURCES

Annual Survey of Manufactures. Available from U. S. Government Printing Office. • Annual. Prices vary. Issued by the U. S. Census Bureau as an interim update to the *Census of Manufactures.* Includes data on number of manufacturing establishments in various industries, employment, labor costs, value of shipments, capital expenditures, inventories, energy costs, and assets. (See also Census Bureau home page, http://www.census.gov/.).

Business Statistics of the United States. Linz Audain and Cornelia J. Strawser. Bernan Associates. • Annual. $147.00. Based on *Business Statistics,* formerly issue by the Bureau of Economic Analysis, U. S. Department of Commerce. Provides basic data for a wide variety of U. S. industries, services, and economic indicators. Most statistics are shown annually for 30 years and monthly for the most recent four years.

Railroad Facts. Association of American Railroads. • Annual.

Survey of Current Business. Available from U. S. Government Printing Office. • Monthly. $63.00 per year. Issued by Bureau of Economic Analysis, U. S. Department of Commerce. Presents a wide variety of business and economic data.

WEFA Industrial Monitor. John Wiley and Sons, Inc. • Annual. $65.00. Prepared by industry analysts at WEFA, an economic forecasting and consulting firm (originally Wharton Econometric Forecasting Associates). Contains discussions of the outlook for major U. S. industries, with many 10-year forecasts (WEFA Web site is http://www.wefa.com).

TRADE/PROFESSIONAL ASSOCIATIONS

Air Brake Association. 2098 E 10140 S, 2009 Oriole Trail, L.B., Sandy, UT 84092. Phone: (801)944-5270 Fax: (801)944-2916 E-mail: joefaust@comcast.net • Railway air brake engineers, suppliers, supervisors, and air brake manufacturing engineers.

American Railway Car Institute. 29W 140 Butterfield Rd., Ste. 103-A, Warrenville, IL 60555. Phone: 888-393-0107 or (630)393-0106 Fax: (630)393-0108 E-mail: rpi@rpi.org • URL: http://www.rsiweb.org/committees/com_arci.aspx • Independent manufacturers of railroad and freight cars. Conducts research and standardization activities, particularly in freight car design and container standards. Provides for exchange of data on new devices used in freight cars. Compiles statistics on orders, deliveries, and backlogs of railroad cars with Association of American Railroads (see separate entry). Maintains historical files.

American Railway Engineering and Maintenance of Way Association. 8201 Corporate Dr., Suite 1125, Andover, MD 20785-2230. Phone: (301)459-3200 Fax: (301)459-8077 E-mail: chemely@arema.org • URL: http://www.arema.org.

Railway Engineering-Maintenance Suppliers Association. 417 W Broad St., Ste. 203, Falls Church, VA 22046. Phone: 888-33-REMSA or (703)241-8514 Fax: (703)241-8589 E-mail: contact@remsa.org • URL: http://www.remsa.org • Provides global business development opportunities to members. Works to transfer knowledge about markets, products and the industry to members and their customers. Supports government initiatives that advance the North American railroad industry.

Railway Supply Association. 29 W. 140 Butterfield Rd., Ste. 103A, Warrenville, IL 60555. Phone: (630)393-0106 Fax: (630)393-0108 E-mail: contact@remsa.org • Companies that produce railroad rolling stock equipment and components or supply rolling stock maintenance services. Seeks to improve the efficiency, safety, maintenance, and operation of railroads. Provides means for cooperation among railroads and members by enabling members to exchange information as a unified body. Encourages interest by railroads in the railway supply industry. Cooperates with Air Brake Association, Car Department Officers Association, Locomotive Maintenance Officers' Association, and International Association of Railway Operating Officers.

Railway Systems Suppliers, Inc. 9304 New LaGrange Rd., Ste. 200, Louisville, KY 40242-3671. Phone: (502)327-7774 Fax: (502)327-0541 E-mail: rssi@rssi.org • URL: http://www.rssi.org • Corporations, partnerships, and individuals engaged in the manufacture, sale, and service of products, appliances, apparatus, and devices used in railway signals, controls, and communications; engineers and contractors engaged in construction or maintenance of any such product. Collects and disseminates information of interest to members.

RAILROAD TIME TABLES

See: TIMETABLES

RAILROADS

See also: TRANSPORTATION INDUSTRY

ABSTRACTS AND INDEXES

NTIS Alerts: Transportation. National Technical Information Service. • Semimonthly. $210.00 per year. Provides descriptions of government-sponsored research reports and software, with ordering information. Covers air, marine, highway, inland waterway, pipeline, and railroad transportation. Formerly *Abstract Newsletter.*

BIOGRAPHICAL SOURCES

Pocket List of Railroad Officials. Commonwealth Business Media. • Quarterly. $207.00 per year. Guide to over 30,000 officials in the freight railroad, rail transit and rail supply industries. Includes *Buyers' Guide.*

CD-ROM DATABASES

OECD Statistical Compendium. Organization for Economic Cooperation and Development. • Semiannual. $1,905.00 per year for 1 to 10 users. CD-ROM contains more than 730,000 monthly, quarterly, and annual time series for OECD countries, 1960 to date. Includes fully searchable data on agriculture, food, economic indicators, national accounts, employment, energy, finance, industry, technology, and foreign trade. Results can be displayed in various forms.

DIRECTORIES

Jane's World Railways. Jane's Information Group Ltd. • Covers: Global railway industry manufacturers, railway systems, and rapid transit systems throughout various countries; freight car leasing companies; international railway associations, agencies, and consultants. Entries include: For railway systems--Governmental or private authority responsible for operation, address, names and titles of key personnel, gauges, route length, description and history, equipment, statistics. For manufacturers--Company name, address, phone, fax, telex, clients and products; names and titles of key personnel. For leasing companies--Name, address, phone, fax, names and titles of key personnel, operations and equipment. For associations--Name, address, phone, fax, telex, key officers, objectives. For consultants--Firm name, address, phone, contact name, capabilities, projects. All sections except consultants and associations include numerous drawings and photographs. Jane's World Railways continues to be the foremost information source on the railway industry, giving you a truly global perspective on the development of more than 450 railway systems in over 140 countries worldwide.

Official Railway Guide--Freight Service Edition. Commonwealth Business Media Inc. • Covers: Railways in North America offering freight service. Includes lists of railroad associations, state railroad commissions, federal regulatory agencies. Entries include: Railroad name, general office, address, phone, names of executives, list of services, schedules, maps, local sales offices and their phone numbers and executives.

Railway Directory: A Railway Gazette Yearbook. Reed Business Information. • Annual. $230.00. Lists approximately 14,000 senior personnel from railroads worldwide and over 1,800 manufacturers, suppliers and consultants in the railroad industry.

Thomas Cook Overseas Timetable: Railway, Road and Shipping Services Outside Europe. Thomas Cook Publishing Co. • Bimonthly. $76.20. per year. International railroad passenger schedules. Text in

English; summaries in French, German, Italian and Spanish.

ENCYCLOPEDIAS AND DICTIONARIES
Macmillan Encyclopedia of Transportation. Available from Gale Cengage Learning. • 1999. $450.00. Six volumes. Published by Macmillan Reference USA. Covers the business, technology, and history of transportation on land, on water, in the air, and in space. Includes definitions, cross-references, and 200 color illustrations.

FINANCIAL RATIOS
Almanac of Business and Industrial Financial Ratios. Leo Troy. Aspen Publishers, Inc. • 2003. $125.95. Includes CD-Rom. Contains financial ratios derived from federal tax returns. Ratios for each of about 200 industries are arranged according to company asset size. (Almanac of Business and Industrial Financial Ratios Series).

INTERNET DATABASES
Business 2.0 Web Guide to the Best Business Links. Business 2.0 Media Inc. Phone: (415)293-4800 E-mail: support@business2.com • URL: http://www.business2.com/webguide • Web site presents an extensive, searchable directory of links to "the best, most informative, and authoritative web pages." Twenty main categories cover business, finance, career, company information, people, and technology topics, with thousands of subtopics, all linking to Web sites recommended by experienced business researchers. Fees: Free.

Fedstats. Federal Interagency Council on Statistical Policy. Phone: (202)395-7254 • URL: http://www.fedstats.gov • Web site features an efficient search facility for full-text statistics produced by more than 100 federal agencies, including the Census Bureau, the Bureau of Economic Analysis, and the Bureau of Labor Statistics. Boolean searches can be made within one agency or for all agencies combined. Links are offered to international statistical bureaus, including the UN, IMF, OECD, UNESCO, Eurostat, and 20 individual countries. Fees: Free.

FreeLunch.com. Economy.com, Inc. Phone: (610)696-8700 Fax: (610)696-1678 • URL: http://www.freelunch.com • Web site provides free access to more than 1.5 million economic and financial data series, covering industry, demographics, labor markets, prices, retail sales, government spending, trade, interest rates, housing starts, the stock market, and many other topics. Data is available for various time periods in either chart or table form. Searching is offered. Fees: Free, but registration required. Economy.com, Inc. also offers fee-based economic analysis at *The Dismal Scientist* site (http://www.dismal.com).

ONLINE DATABASES
TRIS: Transportation Research Information Service. National Research Council. • Contains abstracts and citations to a wide range of transportation literature, 1968 to present, with monthly updates. Includes references to the literature of air transportation, highways; ships and shipping, railroads, trucking, and urban mass transportation. Formerly *TRIS-ONLINE.* Inquire as to online cost and availability.

PERIODICALS AND NEWSLETTERS
International Railway Journal: The First International Railway and Rapid Transit Journal. Simmons-Boardman Publishing Corp. • Monthly. $72.00 per year. Formerly *International Railway Journal and Rapid Transit Review.* Text in English; summaries in French, German and Spanish.

Progressive Railroading. Trade Press Publishing Corp. • Monthly. Free to qualified personnel. Provides feature articles, news, new product information, etc. Relative to the railroad and rail transit industry.

Railway Age. Simmons-Boardman Publishing Corp.

• Monthly. $56.00 per year.

Trains; The Magazine of Railroading. Kalmbach Publishing Co. • Monthly. $39.95 per year.

U.S. Rail News. Business Publishers Inc. • Description: Reports developments in all aspects of the rail transportation industry. Covers topics such as deregulation, mergers and acquisitions, labor relations, and financial management. Recurring features include news briefs and a calendar of related conferences and meetings.

STATISTICS SOURCES
Business Statistics of the United States. Linz Audain and Cornelia J. Strawser. Bernan Associates. • Annual. $147.00. Based on *Business Statistics,* formerly issue by the Bureau of Economic Analysis, U. S. Department of Commerce. Provides basic data for a wide variety of U. S. industries, services, and economic indicators. Most statistics are shown annually for 30 years and monthly for the most recent four years.

Cars of Revenue Freight Loaded. Association of American Railroads. • Weekly.

Infrastructure Industries USA. Gale Cengage Learning. • 2001. $260.00. Presents statistics and projections relating to economic activity in a wide variety of natural resource and construction industries.

Railroad Facts. Association of American Railroads. • Annual.

Survey of Current Business. Available from U. S. Government Printing Office. • Monthly. $63.00 per year. Issued by Bureau of Economic Analysis, U. S. Department of Commerce. Presents a wide variety of business and economic data.

Transportation Statistics Annual Report. Available from U. S. Government Printing Office. • Annual. $43.00. Issued by the U. S. Bureau of Transportation Statistics, Transportation Department (http://www.bts.gov). Summarizes national data for various forms of transportation, including airlines, railroads, and motor vehicles. Information on the use of roads and highways is included.

WEFA Industrial Monitor. John Wiley and Sons, Inc. • Annual. $65.00. Prepared by industry analysts at WEFA, an economic forecasting and consulting firm (originally Wharton Econometric Forecasting Associates). Contains discussions of the outlook for major U. S. industries, with many 10-year forecasts (WEFA Web site is http://www.wefa.com).

TRADE/PROFESSIONAL ASSOCIATIONS
Association of American Railroads. 50 F St., N.W., Washington, DC 20001. Phone: (202)639-2100 Fax: (202)639-2986 E-mail: information@aar.org • URL: http://www.aar.org.

National Association of Railroad Passengers. 900 Second St., N.E., Suite 308, Washington, DC 20002. Phone: (202)408-8362 Fax: (202)408-8287 E-mail: narp@narprail.org • URL: http://www.narprail.org.

National Association of Railway Business Women. 757 Aldro Rd., Hudson, WI 54016-7826. E-mail: narbwinfo@narbw.org • URL: http://www.narbw.org • Formerly Railway Business Women's Association.

Railway Progress Institute. 700 N Fairfax St., No. 601, Alexandria, VA 22314. Phone: (703)836-2332 Fax: (703)548-0058 E-mail: rpi@rpi.org • URL: http://www.rpi.org • Formerly Railway Progress Institute.

OTHER SOURCES
Consumers United for Rail Equity. • Coalition of railroad shippers that are captive to a single railroad for their transportation needs.

RAISIN INDUSTRY

See also: FRUIT INDUSTRY

STATISTICS SOURCES
FAO Production Yearbook. Available from Bernan Associates. • Annual. $45.00. Published by the Food and Agriculture Organization (http://www.fao.org). Contains worldwide data on agriculture, land use, farm crops, livestock, and agricultural prices.

FAO Trade Yearbook. Available from Bernan Associates. • Annual. $45.00. Published by the Food and Agriculture Organization (http://www.fao.org). Provides extensive worldwide data on exports and imports of agricultural commodities, fertilizers, tractors, and pesticides. Includes more than 130 tables of detailed statistics.

TRADE/PROFESSIONAL ASSOCIATIONS
Diamond Walnut Growers. 1050 S Diamond St., PO Box 1727, Stockton, CA 95205. Phone: (209)467-6000 Fax: (209)467-6714 E-mail: mhochbaum@ddcny.com • URL: http://www.diamondnuts.com • Walnut processing and marketing organization.

RARE BOOKS

See: BOOK COLLECTING

RARE EARTH METALS

ONLINE DATABASES
METADEX. Cambridge Scientific Abstracts. • Covers the worldwide literature of metals, metallurgy, and materials science, 1966 to date. Includes detailed alloys indexing from 1974. Biweekly updating. Inquire as to online cost and availability. (Formerly produced by ASM International.).

PERIODICALS AND NEWSLETTERS
Rare Earth Bulletin. Multi-Science Publishing Co. Ltd. • Bimonthly. $318.00 per year.

RIC News (Rare-Earth Information Center). Rare-Earth Information Center, Institute for Physical Research and Technology. • Quarterly. Free. Newsletter. Containing items of current interest concerning the science and technology of the rare earth.

RESEARCH CENTERS AND INSTITUTES
Rare Earth Information Center. Iowa State University of Science and Technology, Institute for Physical Research and Technology, Ames, IA 50011-3020. Phone: (515)294-2272 Fax: (515)294-3709 E-mail: ric@ameslab.gov • URL: http://www.external.ameslab.gov/ric • Collects, stores, evaluates, and makes available information on the rare earth elements, alloys, and compounds.

STATISTICS SOURCES
Mineral Commodity Summaries. Available from U. S. Government Printing Office. • Annual. $26.00. Published by the U. S. Geological Survey, Department of the Interior (http://www.usgs.gov). Contains detailed, five-year data for about 90 nonfuel minerals. Covers a wide range of statistics, including production, imports, exports, consumption, reserves, prices, tariff information, and industry employment. (Two pages are devoted to each mineral.).

TRADE/PROFESSIONAL ASSOCIATIONS
Rare Earth Research Conference. c/o Professor Larry Thomson. University of California/Davis, 1 Shields Ave., Davis, CA 95616. Phone: (630)252-4364 Fax: (630)252-9289 E-mail: rssi@rssi.org • Researchers in chemistry, physics, metallurgy, biology, and other disciplines whose interests include the rare earth and actinide elements and/or their compounds. (The rare earth elements are those

whose atomic numbers range from 58 through 71; actinide elements range from 89-103.) Purposes are to develop and disseminate information related to the science, technology, and production of the rare earth elements, alloys, and compounds; bring together persons in science, business, and government throughout the world; to study and discuss policies related to worldwide use of elements; to assist in long-range industrial and government planning involving the use of these materials.

RATING OF EMPLOYEES

See also: INDUSTRIAL PSYCHOLOGY; PERSONNEL MANAGEMENT; PSYCHOLOGICAL TESTING

GENERAL WORKS

Abolishing Performance Appraisals: Why They Backfire and What to Do Instead. Tom Coens and Mary Jenkins. Berrett-Koehler Publishers, Inc. • 2002. $27.95. The authors recommend alternative methods of evaluating employees.

Human Resources. Richard B. Renckly. Barron's Educational Series, Inc. • 2004. $18.95. Second edition. Emphasis is on investigating, interviewing, hiring, and evaluating employees.

ENCYCLOPEDIAS AND DICTIONARIES

Encyclopedia of Psychological Assessment. Rocio Fernandez-Ballesteros, editor. Sage Publications, Inc. • 2003. $525.00. Two volumes. Contains about 235 alphabetically arranged entries covering various areas of applied psychology and testing.

HANDBOOKS AND MANUALS

Complete Guide to Performance Standards for Library Personnel. Carol F. Goodson. Neal-Schuman Publishers, Inc. • 1997. $55.00. Provides specific job descriptions and performance standards for both professional and paraprofessional library personnel. Includes a bibliography of performance evaluation literature, with annotations.

Evaluating Library Staff: A Performance Appraisal System. Patricia Belcastro. American Library Association. • 1998. $35.00. Provides information on an appraisal system applicable to a wide variety of jobs in all types of libraries. Includes guidelines, performance appraisal forms, sample employee profiles, and a "Code of Service.".

Fair, Square, and Legal: Safe Hiring, Managing, and Firing Practices to Keep You and Your Company Out of Court. Donald Weiss. AMACOM. • 1999. $29.95. Third edition. Covers recruiting, interviewing, sexual discrimination, evaluation of employees, disipline, defamation charges, and wrongful discharge.

How to Design and Install Management Incentive Compensation Plans: A Practical Guide to Installing Performance Bonus Plans. Dale Arahood. Dale Arahood and Associates. • 1996. $129.00. Revised edition. "This book focuses on how pay should be determined rather than how much should be paid.".

How to Do a Performance Appraisal: A Guide for Managers and Professionals. William S. Swan. John Wiley and Sons, Inc. • 1991. $34.95. Contains advice on face-to-face discussions and offers guidelines on legal aspects.

Studying Your Workforce: Applied Research Methods and Tools for the Training and Development Practitioner. Alan Clardy. Sage Publications, Inc. • 1997. $79.95. Describes how to apply specific research methods to common training problems. Emphasis is on data collection methods: testing, observation, surveys, and interviews. Topics include performance problems and assessment.

RATIO ANALYSIS

See: FINANCIAL RATIOS

REAL ESTATE APPRAISAL

See: REAL PROPERTY VALUATION

REAL ESTATE BUSINESS

See also: APARTMENT HOUSES; BUILDING INDUSTRY; CONDOMINIUMS; HOUSING; MORTGAGES; OFFICE BUILDINGS; REAL ESTATE INVESTMENTS; REAL PROPERTY VALUATION; TAX SHELTERS

GENERAL WORKS

Modern Real Estate. Charles H. Wurtzebach and Mike E. Miles. John Wiley and Sons, Inc. • 1994. $97.95. Fifth edition.

Questions and Answers on Real Estate. Robert W. Semenow. Prentice Hall PTR. • 1993. $24.95. Tenth edition.

Real Estate. Charles J. Jacobus. South-Western. • 2002. $41.95. Ninth edition.

ABSTRACTS AND INDEXES

Real Estate Index. National Association of Realtors. • 1987. $169.00 Two volumes. Vol. one, Author-Title, $99.00; vol. two, Subject, $99.00; vol. 3, 1998 *Supplement*, $49.50.

BIBLIOGRAPHIES

The Tax Reform Act of 1986 and Its Impact on the Real Estate Industry. Marilyn Hankel. Sage Publications, Inc. • 1993. $10.00.

DIRECTORIES

CRE Member Directory. Association of European Universities. • Covers: more 1,100 Counselors of Real Estate (CREs), including many Counselors in Canada, Great Britain, Japan, Australia, Israel, Austria, France, Switzerland, New Zealand, Italy, Mexico, Puerto Rico.. Entries include: Name, title, office address and phone, home address and phone, fax, areas of counseling specialty, and e-mail, where provided.

National Mortgage Directory: Lenders, Brokers & Servicers. Thomson Media. • Annual. $479.00. Covers both residential and commercial sectors. Includes the top 400 lenders, 300 servicers, 150 mortgage brokers, commercial lenders, subprime lenders and other listings, with rankings and statistical tables.

National Referral Roster: The Nation's Directory of Residential Real Estate Firms. Stamats Communications, Inc. • Annual. Realtors, $95.00; non-realtors, $175.00. Formerly *National Roster of Realtors*.

Plunkett's Real Estate and Construction Industry Almanac. Plunkett Research, Ltd. • 2004. $249.99. Contains profiles of 300 leading firms concerned with real estate or construction. Specialties include architecture, development, mortgages, building engineering, real estate sales, etc. Also covers industry trends and statistical data.

ENCYCLOPEDIAS AND DICTIONARIES

Dictionary of Real Estate. Jae K. Shim and others. John Wiley and Sons, Inc. • 1995. $145.00. Contains 3,000 definitions of commercial and residential real estate terms. Covers appraisal, escrow, investment, finance, mortgages, property management, construction, legal aspects, etc. Includes illustrations and formulas. (Business Dictionary Series).

Dictionary of Real Estate Terms. Jack P. Friedman and others. Barron's Educational Series, Inc. • 2004. $13.95. Sixth edition. Defines more than 2,500 terms relating to real estate business, including mortgages, financing, leasing, insurance, and home buying.

Encyclopedia of Business. Gale Cengage Learning. • 2000. $425.00. Second edition. Two volumes. Contains more than 700 signed articles covering major business disciplines and concepts.

International in scope. (Encyclopedia of Business Series).

Language of Real Estate. John Reilly. Dearborn Trade Publishing, A Kaplan Professional Co. • 2000. $34.65. Fifth edition. Encyclopedia of real estate terms.

Real Estate Dictionary. Barbara Cox and others. South-Western. • 2002. $33.95.

FINANCIAL RATIOS

Almanac of Business and Industrial Financial Ratios. Leo Troy. Aspen Publishers, Inc. • 2003. $125.95. Includes CD-Rom. Contains financial ratios derived from federal tax returns. Ratios for each of about 200 industries are arranged according to company asset size. (Almanac of Business and Industrial Financial Ratios Series).

Annual Statement Studies. The Risk Management Association. • Annual. Median and quartile financial ratios are given for over 400 kinds of manufacturing, wholesale, retail, construction, and consumer finance establishments. Data is sorted by both asset size and sales volume. Includes a clearly written "Definition of Ratios" and an alphabetical industry index.

Annual Statement Studies: Industry Default Probabilities and Cash Flow Measures. The Risk Management Association. • Annual. $145.00. Serves as a companion volume to the original *Annual Statement Studies*. Gives probability of default estimates on a percentage scale for more than 450 industries. Includes changes in position year-by-year for eight financial statement line items and provides percentage measures of cash flow.

HANDBOOKS AND MANUALS

Complete Guide to Your Real Estate Closing: Answers to All Your Questions from Opening Escrow to Negotiating Fees to Signing Closing Papers. Sandy Gadow. McGraw-Hill. • Date not set. $19.95. Includes sample forms and work sheets, with specific real estate closing information for all 50 states. (Teach Yourself Series).

Essentials of Real Estate Investment. David Sirota. Dearborn Trade Publishing, A Kaplan Professional Co. • 2001. $45.95. Sixth edition. Tax law revisions.

Every Landlord's Legal Guide. Marcia Stewart and others. Nolo. • 2003. $44.99. Sixth edition.

Every Tenant's Legal Guide. Janet Portman and Marcia Stewart. Nolo. • 2002. $29.99. Third edition.

Mastering Real Estate Mathematics. William L. Ventolo and others. Dearborn Trade Publishing, Kaplan Professional Co. • 2001. $31.35. Seventh edition. Step-by-step workbook written to help sharpen real estate math skills.

Modern Real Estate Practice. Fillmore W. Galaty. Dearborn Trade Publishing, Kaplan Professional Co. • 2002. $45.60. 16th edition. Provides essential up-to-date information to students preparing for a state licensing exam.

Real Estate Brokerage: A Management Guide. John E. Cyr and others. Dearborn Trade Publishing, A Kaplan Professional Co. • 1999. $46.50. Fifth edition. Covers the industry standard on opening and operation a real brokerage office.

Real Estate Handbook. Jack C. Harris and Jack P. Friedman. Barron's Educational Series, Inc. • 2001. $35.00. Fifth edition.

Real Estate Marketing and Sales. Paddy Amyett. Prentice Hall PTR. • 2001. $33.33.

Real Estate Taxation: A Practitioner's Guide. David F. Windish. CCH, Inc. • Date not set. $125.00. Second edition. Serves as a guide to the federal tax consequences of real estate ownership and operation. Covers mortgages, rental agreements, interest, landlord income, forms of ownership, and other tax-oriented topics.

Real Estate Transactions, Tax Planning and

Consequences. Mark L. Levine. West Group. • 1997. Periodic supplementation.

ONLINE DATABASES

Banking Information Source. PROQUEST. • Provides indexing and abstracting of periodical and other literature from 1982 to date, with weekly updates. Covers the financial services industry: banks, savings institutions, investment houses, credit unions, insurance companies, and real estate organizations. Emphasis is on marketing and management. Inquire as to online cost and availability. (Formerly *FINIS: Financial Industry Information Service.*).

PERIODICALS AND NEWSLETTERS

American Banker: The Financial Services Daily. Thomson Media. • Daily. $895.00 per year. Provides news of banking, investment products, mortgages, credit unions, finance, bank technology, and legal developments.

Commercial Leasing Law and Strategy. American Lawyer Media, Inc. • Monthly. $215.00 per year. Newsletter. Covers commercial real estate leasing developments relating to large retailers, tenant inducements, tax consequences, unbilled rent obligations, and other matters. (A Law Journal Newsletter, formerly published by Leader Publications).

Journal of Property Management: The Official Publication of the Institute of Real Estate Management. Institute of Real Estate Management. • Bimonthly. $43.95 per year.

National Real Estate Investor. Primedia Business Magazines and Media. • Monthly. $85.00 per year. Includes annual *Directory.* Market surveys by city.

The Practical Real Estate Lawyer. Committee on Continuing Professional Education. American Law Institute-American Bar Association Committee on Continuing Professional Education. • Bimonthly. $49.00 per year. Frequently includes legal forms for use in real estate practice.

Real Estate Forum: America's Premier Real Estate Business Magazine. Real Estate Media, Inc. • Monthly. $59.95 per year. Emphasis on corporate and industrial real estate.

Real Estate Issues. The Counselors of Real Estate. • Quarterly. $48.00 per year.

Real Estate Review. West Group. • Quarterly. $200.00 per year. Gives inside information on the latest ideas in real estate. Provides advice from the leaders of the real estate field.

Real Estate Taxation. RIA. • Quarterly. $225.00 per year. Looseleaf service. Continuing coverage of the latest tax developments. Formerly *Journal of Real Estate Taxation.*

Realtor Magazine. National Association of Realtors. • Monthly. Free to members; non-members, $54.00 per year. Provides industry news and trends for realtors. Special features include Annual Compensation Survey, Annual Technology Survey, Annual All Stars, and The Year in Real Estate.

Realty and Building. Realty and Building, Inc. • Biweekly. $54.00 per year.

Relocation Journal and Real Estate News. Mobility Services International. • Monthly. Free. Newsletter for real estate, building, financing and investing. Formed by the merger of *Real Estate News* and *Relocation Journal.*

U. S. Banker. Thomson Media. • Monthly. $65.00 per year. Edited for bank executives and managers. Covers a wide variety of banking and financial topics.

RESEARCH CENTERS AND INSTITUTES

Bureau of Economic and Business Research. University of Illinois at Urbana-Champaign, 1206 S. Sixth St., 403 Wohlers Hall, Champaign, IL 61820. Phone: (217)333-2330 Fax: (217)244-7410 E-mail:

g-oldman@uiuc.edu • URL: http://www.business. uiuc.edu/research.

Center for Finance and Real Estate. University of California, Los Angeles, John E. Anderson Graduate School of Management, 110 Westwood Plaza, Los Angeles, CA 90095-1481. Phone: (310)206-5455 Fax: (310)206-5455 E-mail: wtorous@anderson. ucla.edu • URL: http://www.agsm.ucla.edu.

Center for Real Estate Studies. University of Florida. College of Business Administration, P.O. Box 117168, Gainesville, FL 32611-7168. Phone: (352)392-9307 Fax: (352)392-0381 E-mail: archer@notes.cba.ufl.edu • URL: http://www. ufrealestate.com • Formerly Real Estate Research Center.

Guthrie Center for Real Estate Research. J. L. Kellogg Graduate School of Management, Northwestern University, Evanston, IL 60208. Phone: (847)491-2673 Fax: (847)491-6459 E-mail: tlys@nwu.edu • URL: http://www.kellogg.nwu.edu/research.

Samuel Zell and Robert Lurie Real Estate Center at Wharton. University of Pennsylvania, Lauder-Fischer Hall, 3rd Fl., 256 S. 37th St., Philadelphia, PA 19104-6330. Phone: (215)898-9687 Fax: (215)573-2220 E-mail: frostr@wharton.upenn.edu • URL: http://www.realestate.wharton.upenn.edu.

STATISTICS SOURCES

Information, Finance, and Services USA. Gale Cengage Learning. • 2001. $240.00. Replaces *Service Industries USA* and *Finance, Insurance, and Real Estate USA.* Presents statistics and projections relating to economic activity in a wide variety of non-manufacturing areas.

New One-Family Houses Sold. Available from U. S. Government Printing Office. • Monthly. $45.00 per year. Bureau of the Census Construction Report, C25. Provides data on new, privately-owned, one-family homes sold during the month and for sale at the end of the month.

U. S. Housing Markets. Hanley-Wood, LLC. • Monthly. $345.00 per year. Includes eight interim reports. Provides data on residential building permits, apartment building completions, rental vacancy rates, sales of existing homes, average home prices, housing affordability, etc. All major U. S. cities and areas are covered.

ULI Market Profiles: North America. Urban Land Institute. • Annual. Members, $249.95; non-members, $299.95. Provides real estate marketing data for residential, retail, office, and industrial sectors. Covers 76 U. S. metropolitan areas and 13 major foreign metropolitan areas.

TRADE/PROFESSIONAL ASSOCIATIONS

Counselors of Real Estate. 430 N. Michigan Ave., Chicago, IL 60611-4089. Phone: (312)329-8427 Fax: (312)329-8881 E-mail: cre@interaccess.com • URL: http://www.cre.org • Formerly American Society of Real Estate Counselors.

Institute of Real Estate Management. 430 N. Michigan Ave., Chicago, IL 60611-4090. Phone: 800-837-0706 or (312)329-6000 Fax: 800-837-4736 E-mail: custserv@irem.org • URL: http://www.irem.org.

National Association of Real Estate Brokers. 9831 Greenbelt Rd., Ste. 309, Lanham, MD 20706. Phone: (301)552-9340 Fax: (301)552-9216 E-mail: info@nareb.com • URL: http://www.nareb.com.

National Association of Realtors. 430 N. Michigan Ave., Chicago, IL 60611. Phone: 800-874-6500 or (312)329-8313 Fax: (312)329-5962 E-mail: infocentral@realtors.org • URL: http://www.realtor.org.

Society of Industrial and Office Realtors. 700 11th St., N.W., Suite 510, Washington, DC 20001-4507. Phone: (202)737-1150 Fax: (202)737-8796 E-mail: admin@sior.com • URL: http://www.sior.com.

Women's Council of Realtors. 430 N Michigan Ave., Chicago, IL 60611. Phone: 800-245-8512 or (312)329-8483 Fax: (312)329-3290 E-mail: wcr@wcr.org • URL: http://www.wcr.org • Formerly Women's Council of Realtors of the National Association of Realtors.

OTHER SOURCES

The Law of Distressed Real Estate: Foreclosure, Workouts, and Procedures. West Group. • $956.00. Five looseleaf volumes. Periodic supplementation. (Real Property LawSeries).

Real Estate Financing, with Forms on Disk. American Lawyer Media, Inc. • Looseleaf. $179.00. Updated as needed. Includes forms on two diskettes. Covers loan modifications, wraparound mortgage loans, loans for condos, co-ops, and time shares, sale-leasebacks, installment sales, sales of mortgage loans, and various related topics. (Law Journal Press).

REAL ESTATE, INDUSTRIAL

See: INDUSTRIAL REAL ESTATE

REAL ESTATE INVESTMENT TRUSTS

See also: REAL ESTATE INVESTMENTS

GENERAL WORKS

Investing in REITs: Real Estate Investment Trusts. Ralph L. Block. Bloomberg. • 2002. $26.95. Revised and updated edition. A basic guide to real estate investment trusts. (Bloomberg Personal Bookshelf Series).

DIRECTORIES

Institutional Buyers of REIT Securities. Investment Data Corp. • Semiannual. $995.00 per year. Provides detailed profiles of about 500 institutional buyers of REIT securities. Includes names of financial analysts and portfolio managers.

FINANCIAL RATIOS

Almanac of Business and Industrial Financial Ratios. Leo Troy. Aspen Publishers, Inc. • 2003. $125.95. Includes CD-Rom. Contains financial ratios derived from federal tax returns. Ratios for each of about 200 industries are arranged according to company asset size. (Almanac of Business and Industrial Financial Ratios Series).

HANDBOOKS AND MANUALS

Real Estate Investment Trusts Handbook: 1997. Peter M. Fass and others. West Group. • 2004. $295.00. Covers the legal and tax aspects of REITs. (Securities Law Series).

Real Estate Investment Trusts: Structure, Performance, and Investment Opportunities. Su Han Chan. Oxford University Press. • 2002. $45.00. Covers the history of REITs, organizational structure, institutional investing, dividends, debt, and "existing scholarly research." An appendix provides "Monthly Stock Returns and Performance Index of All Publicly Traded REITs (1962-2000 and 2001-2002)." (Financial Management Association Survey and Synthesis Series).

PERIODICALS AND NEWSLETTERS

Journal of Alternative Investments. Institutional Investor, Inc., Journals Group. • Quarterly. $540.00 per year. Includes print and online editions. Covers such items as hedge funds, private equity financing, funds of funds, real estate investment trusts, natural resource investments, foreign exchange, and emerging markets.

National Real Estate Investor. Primedia Business Magazines and Media. • Monthly. $85.00 per year.

Includes annual *Directory*. Market surveys by city.

STATISTICS SOURCES

Realty Stock Review: Market Analysis of Securities of REITS and Real Estate Companies. • Semimonthly. $325.00 per year. Looseleaf service.

TRADE/PROFESSIONAL ASSOCIATIONS

National Association of Real Estate Investment Trusts. 1875 Eye St., N.W., Washington, DC 20006. Phone: 800-362-7348 or (202)739-9400 Fax: (202)739-9401 E-mail: info@nareit.org • URL: http://www.nareit.com • Formerly National Association of Real Estste Investment Funds.

REAL ESTATE INVESTMENTS

See also: REAL ESTATE BUSINESS; REAL ESTATE INVESTMENT TRUSTS

GENERAL WORKS

Fundamentals of Real Estate Investment. Austin J. Jaffe. South-Western. • 2001. $77.95. Third edition.

Getting Started in Real Estate Investing. Michael C. Thomsett and others. John Wiley and Sons, Inc. • 1998. $19.95. Second edition. (Getting Started in... Series.).

How to Get Started in Real Estate Investing. Robert Irwin. McGraw-Hill. • 2002. $14.95. Presents basic information on real estate investing for beginners.

How to Invest in Real Estate Using Free Money. Laurie Blum. John Wiley and Sons, Inc. • 1991. $160.00.

Real Estate Finance and Investments. William B. Brueggeman and Jeffrey Fisher. McGraw-Hill. • 2001. 11th edition. Price on application. Covers mortgage loans, financing, risk analysis, income properties, land development, real estate investment trusts, and related topics. (Finance, Insurance and Real Estate Series).

ABSTRACTS AND INDEXES

Real Estate Index. National Association of Realtors. • 1987. $169.00 Two volumes. Vol. one, Author-Title, $99.00; vol. two, Subject, $99.00; vol. 3, 1998 *Supplement*, $49.50.

DIRECTORIES

Crittenden Directory of Real Estate Financing. Crittenden Research, Inc. • Semiannual. $399.00 per year. Includes weekly *Newsletter*. Provides information on major U. S. real estate lenders.

Nelson Information's Directory of Institutional Real Estate. Nelson Information. • Annual. $400.00. Includes real estate investment managers, service firms, consultants, real estate investment trusts (RE-ITs), and various institutional investors in real estate. Formerly *Nelson's Directory of Real Estate Investments.*

ENCYCLOPEDIAS AND DICTIONARIES

Dictionary of Finance and Investment Terms. John Downes. Barron's Educational Series, Inc. • 2002. $14.95. Sixth edition. Provides clear explanations of more than 5,000 business, banking, financial, investment, and tax terms. Includes a separate list of financial abbreviations and acronyms. (Business Dictionaries Series).

Dictionary of Real Estate. Jae K. Shim and others. John Wiley and Sons, Inc. • 1995. $145.00. Contains 3,000 definitions of commercial and residential real estate terms. Covers appraisal, escrow, investment, finance, mortgages, property management, construction, legal aspects, etc. Includes illustrations and formulas. (Business Dictionary Series).

HANDBOOKS AND MANUALS

Profiting from Real Estate Rehab. Sandra M. Brassfield. John Wiley and Sons, Inc. • 1992. $42.

95. How to fix up old houses and sell them at a profit.

Real Estate Finance and Investment Manual: A Guide to Money Making Strategies. Jack Cummings. Prentice Hall PTR. • 1997. $34.95. Second edition.

Real Estate Investor's Answer Book. Jack Cummings. McGraw-Hill. • 1994. $19.95. Answers key questions relating to both residential and commercial real estate investments.

ONLINE DATABASES

Trade & Industry Database. Gale Cengage Learning. • Provides indexing of business periodicals, January 1981 to date. Daily updates. (Full text articles from some periodicals are available online, 1983 to date. Inquire as to online cost and availability).

PERIODICALS AND NEWSLETTERS

Crittenden Report Real Estate Financing: The Nation's Leading Weekly Newslett er on Real Estate Finance. Crittenden Research, Inc. • Weekly. $395.00 per year. Newsletter on real estate lending and mortgages. Includes semiannual *Crittenden Directory of Real Estate Financing.*

Marketscore. CB Richard Ellis. • Quarterly. Price on application. Newsletter. Provides proprietary forecasts of commercial real estate performance in metropolitan areas.

National Real Estate Investor. Primedia Business Magazines and Media. • Monthly. $85.00 per year. Includes annual *Directory*. Market surveys by city.

Quarterly Market Report. Property and Portfolio Research. • Quarterly. $1,000.00 per year for one property type; 2,000 per year for six property types. Newsletter. Reviews current prices, rents, capitalization rates, and occupancy trends for commercial real estate.

Real Estate Economics: Journal of the American Real Estate and Urban Economics Association. MIT Press. • Quarterly. Institutions, $295.00 per year. Includes print and online editions.

Real Estate Finance. Institutional Investor, Inc., Journals Group. • Bimonthly. $350.00 per year. Covers real estate for professional investors. Provides information on complex financing, legalities, and industry trends.

Real Estate Finance and Investment. Institutional Investor, Inc., Journals Group. • Weekly. $2,275.00 per year. Includes print and online editions. Newsletter for professional investors in commercial real estate. Includes information on financing, restructuring, strategy, and regulation.

Real Estate Tax Digest. Matthew Bender & Co. • Description: Features articles on and analyses of legislation, Treasury regulations, federal court and Tax Court decisions, Revenue Rulings, Revenue Procedures, and selected Letter Rulings of the Internal Revenue Service pertaining to federal taxation affecting real estate activities. Includes columns titled Special Topic, New Developments, Practitioner's Corner, and Inside Washington.

Stanger Report: A Guide to Partnership Investing. Robert A. Stanger and Co. • Quarterly. $447.00 per year. Newsletter providing analysis of limited partnership investments.

PRICE SOURCES

National Real Estate Index. CB Richard Ellis. • Price and frequency on application. Provides reports on commercial real estate prices, rents, capitalization rates, and trends in more than 65 metropolitan areas. Time span is 12 years. Includes urban office buildings, suburban offices, warehouses, retail properties, and apartments.

RESEARCH CENTERS AND INSTITUTES

Rodney L. White Center for Financial Research. University of Pennsylvania, 3254 Steinberg Hall-

Dietrich Hall, Philadelphia, PA 19104. Phone: (215)898-7616 Fax: (215)573-8084 E-mail: rlwtcr@finance.wharton.upenn.edu • URL: http://www.finance.wharton.upenn.edu • Research areas include financial management, money markets, real estate finance, and international finance.

TRADE/PROFESSIONAL ASSOCIATIONS

American Real Estate and Urban Economics Association. PO Box 1148, Portage, MI 49081-1148. Phone: (866)273-8321 Fax: (313)731-0174 E-mail: areuea@areuea.org • URL: http://www.areuea.org • Members are real estate teachers, researchers, economists, and others concerned with urban real estate and investment.

Building Owners and Managers Association International. 1201 New York Ave., NW, Ste. 300, Washington, DC 20005. Phone: (202)408-2662 Fax: (202)371-0181 E-mail: info@boma.org • URL: http://www.boma.org • Formerly National Association of Building Owners and Managers.

OTHER SOURCES

Federal Taxes Affecting Real Estate. LexisNexis Matthew Bender. • Semiannual. $261.00 per year. Two looseleaf volumes. Explains and illustrates the most important federal tax principles applying to daily real estate transactions.

REAL ESTATE MANAGEMENT

See: PROPERTY MANAGEMENT

REAL ESTATE TAXES

See: PROPERTY TAX; TAX SHELTERS; TAXATION

REAL PROPERTY VALUATION

See also: REAL ESTATE BUSINESS; VALUATION

ALMANACS AND YEARBOOKS

Institute on Planning, Zoning and Eminent Domain. LexisNexis. • 1971. $199.00.

HANDBOOKS AND MANUALS

Appraisal of Real Estate. The Appraisal Institute. • 2001. 12th edition. Price on application. Provides an in-depth discussion of the driving concept of market value; guildelines for market analysis projections and updated information throughout that addresses developments affecting the movement of investment capital.

Fundamentals of Real Estate Appraisal. William L. Ventolo and Martha R. Williams. Dearborn Trade Publishing, A Kaplan Professional Co. • 2001. $51. 40. Eighth edition. Explanation of real estate appraisal.

Real Estate Appraisal. Walter R. Huber and William H. Pivar. Educational Textbook Co. Inc. • 2001. Price on application.

PERIODICALS AND NEWSLETTERS

Appraisal Journal. Appraisal Institute. • Quarterly. Free to members; non-members, $48.00 per year; libraries, $100.00 per year; students, $30.00 per year. Offers a broad variety of researched, documented articles.

Assessment Journal. International Association of Assessing Officers. • Bimonthly. Free to members; non-members, $200.00 per year. Formed by merger of *Assessment* and *Valuation Legal Reporter and IAAO Update.*

TRADE/PROFESSIONAL ASSOCIATIONS

American Society of Appraisers. 555 Herndon Parkway, Suite 125, Herndon, VA 20170. Phone:

800-272-8258 or (703)478-2228 Fax: (703)742-8471 E-mail: asainfo@appraisers.org • URL: http://www.appraisers.org.

Appraisal Institute. Headquarters Office, 550 W Van Buren St., Ste. 1000, Chicago, IL 60607. Phone: (312)335-4110 Fax: (312)335-4101 E-mail: information@appraisalinstitute.org • URL: http://www.appraisalinstitute.org • General appraisers who hold the MAI designation, and residential members who hold the SRA designation. Enforces Code of Professional Ethics and Standards of Professional Appraisal Practice. Confers one general designation, the MAI, and one residential designation, the SRA. Provides training in valuation of residential and income properties, market analysis, and standards of professional appraisal practice. Sponsors courses in preparation for state certification and licensing; offers continuing education programs for designated members.

International Association of Assessing Officers. 130 E Randolph St., Chicago, IL 60601. Phone: (312)819-6100 Fax: (312)819-6149 E-mail: membership@iaaa.org • URL: http://www.iaao.org • Formerly National Association of Assessing Officers.

National Association of Real Estate Appraisers. 1224 N. Nokomis Ave., N.E., Alexandria, MN 56308-5072. Phone: (320)763-7626 Fax: (320)763-9290 E-mail: narea@iami.org • URL: http://www.iami.org/narea.

RECESSIONS

See: BUSINESS CYCLES

RECORDING INDUSTRY

See: SOUND RECORDERS AND RECORDING; VIDEO RECORDING INDUSTRY

RECORDS MANAGEMENT

See also: FILES AND FILING (DOCUMENTS)

GENERAL WORKS

How to Avoid Financial Tangles. American Institute for Economic Research. • 2001. $8.00. Provides basic information and advice on such topics as property ownership, taxes, wills, trusts, insurance, record retention, and professional assistance. (Economic Education Bulletin.).

HANDBOOKS AND MANUALS

Business Records Control. Joseph S. Fosegan and Mary L. Ginn. South-Western. • 1999. $49.95. Eighth edition.

CCH Guide to Record Retention Requirements. CCH, Inc. • 1999. $49.95. Covers the record-keeping provisions of the Code of Federal Regulations. Explains which records must be kept and how long to keep them.

Guide to Record Retention Requirements in the Code of Federal Regulations. National Archives and Records Administration Office of the Federal Register. Bernan Associates. • 1992. Price on application. Explains federal recordkeeping regulations for individuals and businesses.

Records Management: A Practical Guide. Judy Read Smith and others. South-Western. • 2001. $54.95. Seventh edition. Includes audio compact disk.

PERIODICALS AND NEWSLETTERS

The Information Management Journal: The Journal for the Information Management Professionals. A R M A International. • Quarterly. Free to members; non-members, $95.00 per year; institutions and libraries, $53.00 per year. Formerly *Records management Quarterly.*

InForm. Victor O. Schinnerer & Company Inc. • Description: Reports national and state developments affecting architects and engineers.

TRADE/PROFESSIONAL ASSOCIATIONS

American Society of Corporate Secretaries. 521 Fifth Ave., New York, NY 10175-0003. Phone: (212)681-2000 Fax: (212)681-2005 E-mail: dsmith@ascs.org • URL: http://www.ascs.org.

ARMA International-The Association of Information Management Professionals. 13725 W 109th St., Ste. 101, Lenexa, KS 66215. Phone: 800-422-2762 or (913)341-3808 Fax: (913)341-3742 • URL: http://www.arma.org • Formerly ARMA International-The Information Management Professionals.

OTHER SOURCES

Information and Image Management: The State of the Industry. AIIM-The Enterprise Content Management Association. • Annual. $130.00. Market data with five-year forecasts. Covers electronic imaging, micrographics supplies and equipment, software, and records management services.

Keeping the Books: Basic Recordkeeping and Accounting for the Successful Small Business. Linda Pinson. Dearborn Trade Publishing, A Kaplan Professional Co. • 2001. $22.95. Fifth edition. Covers bookkeeping systems, financial statements, and IRS tax record requirements. Includes illustrations, worksheets, and forms.

RECORDS, PHONOGRAPH

See: PHONOGRAPH AND PHONOGRAPH RECORD INDUSTRIES

RECREATION, INDUSTRIAL

See: INDUSTRIAL RECREATION

RECREATION INDUSTRY

See also: AMUSEMENT INDUSTRY; INDUSTRIAL RECREATION; PARKS; SPORTING GOODS INDUSTRY; SPORTS BUSINESS

ABSTRACTS AND INDEXES

Leisure, Recreation, and Tourism Abstracts. Available from CABI Publishing North America. • Quarterly. Members, $280.00 per year; Institutions, $610.00 per year. Includes single site internet access. Published in England by CABI Publishing. Provides coverage of the worldwide literature of travel, recreation, sports, and the hospitality industry. Emphasis is on research.

DIRECTORIES

Camp Directors Purchasing Guide. Klevens Publications Inc. • Covers: suppliers of products and services used in the operation of children's summer camps. Publication includes: sporting goods, arts and crafts materials, food, food service equipment, and building and maintenance equipment. Entries include: Company name, address, phone, fax, brief description of product or service.

Camping Magazine Buyer's Guide. American Camping Association. • Annual. $4.50. Over 200 firms listing camp supplies.

Guide to ACA Accredited Camps. American Camping Association. • Annual. $14.95. Lists over 2,000 summer camps. Included with subscription to *Camping Magazine.* Formerly *Guide to Accredited Camps.*

Guide to Summer Camps and Summer Schools: An Objective, Comprehensive Reference Source. Porter Sargent Publishers, Inc. • 2002. $35.00. Over 1,300 summer camping, recreational, pioneering, and academic programs in the United States and Canada, as well as travel programs worldwide.

Resorts and Parks Purchasing Guide. Klevens Publications, Inc. • Annual. $85.00. Lists suppliers of products and services for resorts and parks, including national parks, amusement parks, dude ranches, golf resorts, ski areas, and national monument areas.

Tenting Directory. Woodall Publications Corp. • Covers: campgrounds in the U.S. and Canada that have tent sites and tent rentals. Entries include: Name of campground, driving directions, facilities, base rate, recreational activities, season, phone.

Tourist Attractions and Parks Magazine Buyers Guide. Kane Communications, Inc. • Annual. $10.00. Lists companies making products or services for leisure facilities.

Trailer Life Campground and RV Services Directory. Trailer Life Publishing Co., Inc. • Annual. $19.95. Describes and rates over 18,000 RV campgrounds, service centers and tourist attractions.

HANDBOOKS AND MANUALS

Resort Development Handbook. Urban Land Institute. • 1997. $89.95. Covers a wide range of resort settings and amenities, with details of development, market analysis, financing, design, and operations. Includes color photographs and case studies. (ULI Development Handbook Series).

Sports, Convention, and Entertainment Facilities. David C. Petersen. Urban Land Institute. • 1996. $61.95. Provides advice and information on developing, financing, and operating amphitheaters, arenas, convention centers, and stadiums. Includes case studies of 70 projects.

PERIODICALS AND NEWSLETTERS

Aquatics International: The Source for Facility Products, Services and Management. Hanley-Wood, LLC. • Monthly. $10.50 per year. Edited for managers of commercial and public swimming pools, including pools in hotels, schools, theme parks, health clubs, and community centers.

Campground Management: Business Publication for Profitable Outdoor Recreation. Woodall Publications Corp. • Monthly. $24.95 per year.

Camping Magazine. American Camping Association. • Monthly. $31.00 per year.

Employee Services Management: The Journal of Employee Services Recreation, Heal th and Education. Employee Services Management. • Bimonthly. Free to members; non-members, $52.00 per year.

Journal of Hospitality and Leisure Marketing: The International Forum for Research, Theory and Practice. Haworth Press, Inc. • Quarterly. $315.00 per year. An academic and practical journal covering various aspects of hotel, restaurant, and recreational marketing.

World Leisure Journal: Official Publication of the World Leisure and Recreation Association. World Leisure and Recreation Association. • Quarterly. Libraries $80.00 per year. Formerly *World Leisure and Recreation.*

STATISTICS SOURCES

Outlook for Travel and Tourism. Travel Industry Association of America. • Annual. Members, $100.00; non-members, $175.00. Contains forecasts of the performance of the U. S. travel industry, including air travel, business travel, recreation (attractions), and accomodations.

Social Statistics of the United States. Mark S. Littman, editor. Bernan Press. • 2000. $65.00. Includes statistical data on population growth, labor force, oc-

---

cupations, environmental trends, leisure time use, income, poverty, taxes, and other economic or demographic topics.

Social Trends and Indicators USA. Monique D. Magee, editor. Gale Cengage Learning. • 2003. $450.00. Four volumes. Includes data on labor, economics, the health care industry, crime, leisure, population, education, social security, and many other topics. Sources include various government agencies and major publications.

Statistical Abstract of the United States. Available from U. S. Government Printing Office. • Annual. $51.00. Issued by the U. S. Bureau of the Census.

TRADE/PROFESSIONAL ASSOCIATIONS

American Alliance for Health, Physical Education, Recreation, and Dance. 1900 Association Dr., Reston, VA 20191-1598. Phone: 800-213-7193 or (703)476-3400 Fax: (703)476-9527 • URL: http://www.aahperd.org.

American Camp Association. 5000 State Rd., 67 N, Martinsville, IN 46151-7902. Phone: 800-428-CAMP or (765)342-8456 Fax: (765)342-2065 E-mail: psmith@acacamps.org • URL: http://www.acacamps.org • Camp owners, directors, program directors, businesses, and students interested in resident and day camp programming for youth and adults. Conducts camp standards. Offers educational programs in areas of administration, staffing, child development, promotion, and programming.

Amusement Industry Manufacturers and Suppliers International. 1250 S.E. Port St., Lucie Blvd., Suite C, Port Lucie, FL 34952. Phone: (772)398-6701 Fax: (772)398-6702 E-mail: info@aimsintl.org • URL: http://www.aimsintl.org.

Employee Services Management Association. 568 Spring Rd., Ste. D, Elmhurst, IL 60126-3896. Phone: (630)559-0020 Fax: (630)559-0025 E-mail: esmahq@esmassn.org • URL: http://www.esmassn.org • Corporations and governmental agencies that sponsor recreation, fitness, and service programs for their employees; associate members are manufacturers and suppliers in the employee recreation market and distributors of consumer products and services. Serves as an information resource network for members nationwide. Implements and maintains a diverse range of employee services; believes that employee services, as practical solutions to work/life issues, are essential to sound business management. Conducts programs that improves relations between employees and management, increases overall productivity, boosts morale, and reduces absenteeism and turnover. Covers the 10 Components of a Well-Rounded Employee Services Program such as employee stores, convenience services, recognition programs, recreation programs, travel services, and special events.

National Association of RV Parks and Campgrounds. 113 Park Ave., Falls Church, VA 22046. Phone: (703)241-8801 Fax: (703)241-1004 E-mail: lprofaizer@arvc.org • URL: http://www.arvc.org • Formerly National Campground Owners Association.

Society of Recreation Executives. PO Box 520, Gonzalez, FL 35260-0520. Phone: 800-281-9186 or (850)937-8354 Fax: (850)937-8356 E-mail: rltresource@spydee.net • Members are corporate executives employed in the recreation, leisure and travel industries.

OTHER SOURCES

Superstudy of Sports Participation. Available from MarketResearch.com. • 2002. $700.00. Three volumes. Published by American Sports Data, Inc. Provides market research data on 102 sports and activities, Vol. 1: *Physical Fitness Activities.* Vol. 2: *Recreational Sports.* Vol. 3: *Outdoor Activities.* (Volumes are available separately at $295.00.).

RECREATIONAL VEHICLE INDUSTRY

See also: MOBILE HOME INDUSTRY

ABSTRACTS AND INDEXES

Trailer Life: RVing At Its Best. Good Sam Club. Affinity Group Inc., T L Enterprises. • Monthly. $22.00 per year.

DIRECTORIES

RV Buyer's Guide (Recreational Vehicle). Affinity Group, Inc.,T L Enterprises. • Annual. $7.95.

The RVDA Membership Directory and Resource Guide. Recreation Vehicle Dealers Association of North America. • Covers: Over 900 retail sales firms handling travel trailers, camping trailers, truck campers, and motor homes in the United States and Canada that are open for business twelve months of the year. Entries include: Company name, address, phone, and owner's or manager's name.

PERIODICALS AND NEWSLETTERS

Highways. Good Sam club. Affinity Group, Inc., T L Enterprises. • 11 times a year. Membership. Five regional editions. Formerly *Good Sam's Hi-Way Herald.*

MH/RV Builders News: The Magazine for Builders of Manufactured-Mobile-Modular-Marine Homes and Recreational Vehicles. Patrick Finn, editor. Dan Kamrow and Associates, Inc. • Bimonthly. Controlled circulation.

RV Business (Recreational Vehicle). T L Enterprises Inc. • Monthly. $48.00 per year. Includes annual *Directory.* News about the entire recreational vehicle industry in the U.S.

PRICE SOURCES

NADA Appraisal Guides. National Automobile Dealers Association. • Prices and frequencies vary. Guides to prices of used cars, old used cars, motorcycles, mobile homes, recreational vehicles, and mopeds.

STATISTICS SOURCES

Annual Survey of Manufactures. Available from U. S. Government Printing Office. • Annual. Prices vary. Issued by the U. S. Census Bureau as an interim update to the *Census of Manufactures.* Includes data on number of manufacturing establishments in various industries, employment, labor costs, value of shipments, capital expenditures, inventories, energy costs, and assets. (See also Census Bureau home page, http://www.census.gov/.).

TRADE/PROFESSIONAL ASSOCIATIONS

Good Sam Recreational Vehicle Club. PO Box 6888, Englewood, CO 80155-6888. Phone: 800-234-3450 or (805)667-4100 Fax: (805)667-4454 E-mail: info@goodsamclub.com • URL: http://www.goodsamclub.com • Recreational vehicle enthusiasts who act as "Good Samaritans" on the road by aiding members in distress. Offers free benefits to members, including credit card loss protection, trip routing service, and mail forwarding. Provides comprehensive discount programs on camping fees, RV financing and insurance, tour programs, emergency road service and magazine subscriptions for members. Conducts charitable program.

Recreation Vehicle Dealers Association of North America. 3930 University Dr., No. 100, Fairfax, VA 22030-2515. Phone: (703)591-7130 Fax: (703)591-0734 E-mail: info@rvda.com • URL: http://www.rvda.org.

Recreation Vehicle Industry Association. 1896 Preston White Dr., PO Box 2999, Reston, VA 20191. Phone: (703)620-6003 Fax: (703)620-5071 E-mail: rparsons@rvia.org • URL: http://www.rvia.org •

Recreation vehicle manufacturers, manufacturers' representatives, and suppliers of accessories and equipment used by manufacturers. Seeks to provide a unified recreation vehicle organization for manufacturers and component parts suppliers of motor homes, travel trailers, truck campers, folding camping trailers, and conversion vehicles. Promotes and represents the growth and concerns of the industry to federal and state government departments, the media, and the public. Collects shipment statistics, technical data, and consumer and media information. Monitors industry compliance with safety standards and the activities of federal and state governments that affect the RV industry. Provides legal and public relations services. Sponsors market research.

RECRUITMENT OF PERSONNEL

See also: COLLEGE PLACEMENT BUREAUS; PERSONNEL MANAGEMENT

BIBLIOGRAPHIES

Executive Search Books. Kennedy Information, Inc. • Annual. Free. Contains descriptions of selected books from various publishers on executive recruitment.

DIRECTORIES

Directory of Executive Recruiters. Kennedy Information, Inc. • Annual. $49.95. Contains profiles of more than 5,500 executive search firms in the U. S., Canada, and Mexico.

HANDBOOKS AND MANUALS

Executive Recruiting Service. Entrepreneur Media, Inc. • Looseleaf. $59.50. A practical guide to starting an executive recruitment service. Covers profit potential, start-up costs, market size evaluation, owner's time required, pricing, accounting, advertising, promotion, etc. (Start-Up Business Guide No. E1228.).

Fair, Square, and Legal: Safe Hiring, Managing, and Firing Practices to Keep You and Your Company Out of Court. Donald Weiss. AMACOM. • 1999. $29.95. Third edition. Covers recruiting, interviewing, sexual discrimination, evaluation of employees, disipline, defamation charges, and wrongful discharge.

Hiring Right: A Practical Guide. Susan J. Herman. Sage Publications, Inc. • 1994. $77.95. A practical manual covering job definition, recruitment, interviewing, testing, and checking of references.

Kennedy's Pocket Guide to Working with Executive Recruiters. James H. Kennedy, editor. Kennedy Information, Inc. • 2002. $17.95. Second revised editon. Consists of 30 chapters written by various experts. Includes a glossary: "Lexicon of Executive Recruiting.".

Recruiter's Research Blue Book: A How-To Guide for Researchers, Consultants, Corporate Recruiters, Small Business Owners, Venture Capitalists, and Line Executives. Andrea A. Jupina. Kennedy Information, Inc. • 2000. $179.00. Second edition. Provides detailed coverage of the role that research plays in executive recruiting. Includes such practical items as "Telephone Interview Guide," "Legal Issues in Executive Search," and "How to Create an Execuive Search Library." Covers both person-to-person research and research using printed and on-line business information sources. Includes an extensive directory of recommended sources. Formerly *Handbook of Executive Search Research.*

Recruiting, Interviewing, Selecting, and Orienting New Employees. Diane Arthur. AMACOM. • 1998. $59.95. Third edition. A practical guide to the basics of hiring, including legal considerations and sample forms.

Recruiting Library Staff: A How-To-Do-It Manual for Librarians. Kathleen Low. Neal-Schuman Publishers, Inc. • 1999. $45.00. Includes position description forms, sample announcements, and checklists. Discusses job fairs and other career events. (How-To-Do-It Manual for Librarians Series).

Smart Hiring: The Complete Guide for Recruiting Employees. Robert W. Wendover. Leadership Resources, Inc. • 1989. $17.95.

PERIODICALS AND NEWSLETTERS

Affirmative Action Register: The E E O Recruitment Publication. Affirmative Action, Inc. • Monthly. Free to qualified personnel; others, $15.00 per year. "The *Affirmative Action Register* is the only nationwide publication that provides for systematic distribution to mandated minorities, females, handicapped, veterans, and Native Americans." Each issue consists of recruitment advertisements placed by equal opportunity employers (institutions and companies).

Executive Recruiter News. Kennedy Information Inc. • Description: The authoritative voice of the recruiting industry, covering news, analysis, practice advice, proprietary data and opinion.

Human Resource Executive. LRP Publications. • 16 times a year. $89.95 per year. Edited for directors of corporate human resource departments. Special issues emphasize training, benefits, retirement planning, recruitment, outplacement, workers' compensation, legal pitfalls, and oes emphasize training, benefits, retirement planning, recruitment, outplacement, workers' compensation, legal pitfalls, and other personnel topics.

Human Resource Planning. Human Resource Planning Society. • Quarterly. $90.00 per year.

Recruiting Trends: The Monthly Newsletter for the Recruiting Executive. Kennedy Information, Inc. • Monthly. $179.00 per year.

Workforce: H R Trends and Tools for Business Results. Crain Communications, Inc. • Monthly. $59.00 per year. Edited for human resources managers. Covers employee benefits, compensation, relocation, recruitment, training, personnel legalities, and related subjects. Supplements include bimonthly "New Product News" and semiannual "Recruitment/Staffing Sourcebook." Formerly *Personnel Journal.*

TRADE/PROFESSIONAL ASSOCIATIONS

Association of Executive Search Consultants. 500 Fifth Ave., Suite 930, New York, NY 10110-0999. Phone: 877-843-2372 or (212)398-9556 Fax: (212)398-9560 E-mail: aesc@aesc.org • URL: http://www.aesc.org.

Human Resource Planning Society. 401 N Michigan Ave., Ste. 2200, Chicago, IL 60611. Phone: (312)321-6805 Fax: (312)673-6944 E-mail: info@hrps.org • URL: http://www.hrps.org • Human resource planning professionals representing 160 corporations and 3000 individual members, including strategic human resources planning and development specialists, staffing analysts, business planners, line managers, and others who function as business partners in the application of strategic human resource management practices. Seeks to increase the impact of human resource planning and management on business and organizational performance. Sponsors program of professional development in human resource planning concepts, techniques, and practices. Offers networking opportunities.

RECYCLING

See also: NATURAL RESOURCES; SURPLUS PRODUCTS; WASTE PRODUCTS

ABSTRACTS AND INDEXES

Environment Abstracts. Congressional Information Service, Inc. • Monthly. Price varies. Provides multidisciplinary coverage of the world's environmental literature. Incorporates *Acid Rain Abstracts.*

Environment Abstracts Annual: A Guide to the Key Environmental Literature of the Year. Congressional Information Service, Inc. • Annual. $495.00. A yearly cumulation of *Environment Abstracts.*

ALMANACS AND YEARBOOKS

Environmental Viewpoints. Gale Cengage Learning. • 1993. $195.00. Three volumes. $65.00 per volume. A compendium of excerpts of about 200 articles on a wide variety of environmental topics, selected from both popular and professional periodicals. Arranged alphabetically by topic, with a subject/keyword index.

Gale Environmental Almanac. Gale Cengage Learning. • 1993. $115.00. Contains 15 chapters, each on a broad topic related to the environment, such as "Waste and Recycling." Each chapter has a topical overview, charts, statistics, and illustrations. Includes a glossary of environmental terms and a bibliography.

CD-ROM DATABASES

Environment Abstracts on CD-ROM. LEXIS-NEXIS. • Quarterly. $1,295.00 per year. Contains the following CD-ROM databases: *Environment Abstracts, Energy Abstracts,* and *Acid Rain Abstracts.* Length of coverage varies.

DIRECTORIES

North American Scrap Metals Directory. Recycling Today Media Group. • Covers: Suppliers of scrap metal materials in North America. Entries include: Contact information.

Recycling Sourcebook. Gale. • Covers: Organizations concerned with policies, programs, and implications of recycling in the U.S.; companies performing recycling services. An appendix lists products made with recycled or recyclable materials and their manufacturers. Entries include: Organization name, address, phone, description of activities and purpose.

ENCYCLOPEDIAS AND DICTIONARIES

Encyclopedia of Global Change: Environmental Change and Human Society. Andrew S. Goudie, editor. Oxford University Press. • 2001. $275.00. Two volumes. Contains 300 signed articles on a wide variety of topics relating to changes in the environment and the atmosphere. Includes bibliographies and illustrations.

Environmental Encyclopedia. Gale Cengage Learning. • 2003. $275.00. Third edition. Provides over 1,300 articles on all aspects of the environment. Written in non-technical style.

PERIODICALS AND NEWSLETTERS

Biocycle; Journal of Composting and Recycling. JG Press, Inc. • Monthly. $69.00 per year. Authoritative reports on the management of municipal sludge and solid wastes via recycling and composting.

EM: A&WMA's Environmental Solutions That Make Good Business Sense. Air and Waste Management Association. • Monthly. Institutions, $299.00 per year; nonprofit and government agencies, $199.00 per year. Newsletter. Provides news of regulations, legislation, and technology relating to the environment, recycling, and waste control. Formerly *Environmental Manager.*

Environmental Business Journal: Strategic Information for a Changing Industry. Environmental Business International, Inc. • Monthly. $495.00 per year.

Newsletter. Includes both industrial and financial information relating to individual companies and to the environmental industry in general. Covers air pollution, wat es, U. S. Department of Health and Human Services. Provides conference, workshop, and symposium proceedings, as well as extensive reviews of environmental prospects.

Recycling Today. Group Interest Enterprises. G.I.E. Publishers Inc. • Monthly. $30.00 per year. Serves the recycling industry in all areas.

Resources, Conservation and Recycling. Elsevier. • Monthly. $1,547.00 per year.

Reuse/Recycle. Rowman & Littlefield Education. • Description: Contains information on "new processes, machinery, and uses for both industrial and municipal recycling." Publishes news of waste-to-energy and waste-to-materials processes, markets for recycled materials, recycling processing, plants, equipment and case history of successful projects and programs in the U.S. and Europe. Focuses on large-scale post-consumer, post-commercial and post-industrial waste recycling. Recurring features include a calendar of events.

Scrap. Institute of Scrap Recycling Industries, Inc. • Bimonthly. Free to members; non-members, $32.95 per year. Formerly *Scrap Processing and Recycling.*

Solid Waste Report: Resource Recovery-Recycling-Collection-Disposal. Business Publishers, Inc. • Weekly. $627.00 per year. Newsletter. Covers regulation, business news, technology, and international events relating to solid waste management.

STATISTICS SOURCES

Health and Environment in America's Top-Rated Cities: A Statistical Profile. Grey House Publishing. • Biennial. $125.00. Covers 75 U. S. cities. Includes statistical and other data on a wide variety of topics, such as air quality, water quality, recycling, hospitals, physicians, health care costs, death rates, infant mortality, accidents, and suicides.

Statistical Handbook on Technology. Paula Bernstein. Greenwood Publishing Group, Inc. • 1999. $69.95. Provides statistical data on such items as the Internet, online services, computer technology, recycling, patents, prescription drug sales, telecommunications, and aerospace. Includes charts, tables, and graphs. Edited for the general reader. (Statistical Handbook Series).

U. S. Industry and Trade Outlook. Available from National Technical Information Service. • Annual. $69.95. Produced by the International Trade Administration, U. S. Department of Commerce, in a "public-private" partnership with DRI/McGraw-Hill and Standard & Poor's. Provides basic data, outlook for the current year, and "Long-Term Prospects" (five-year projections) for a wide variety of products and services. Includes high technology industries. Formerly *U. S. Industrial Outlook.*

TRADE/PROFESSIONAL ASSOCIATIONS

Institute of Scrap Recycling Industries. 1325 G St., NW, Ste. 1000, Washington, DC 20005-3104. Phone: (202)737-1770 Fax: (202)626-0900 E-mail: isri@isri.org • URL: http://www.isri.org.

REDEVELOPMENT, URBAN

See: URBAN DEVELOPMENT

REFERENCE SOURCES

See: INFORMATION SOURCES

REFINERIES

See: PETROLEUM INDUSTRY

REFRACTORIES

See also: CERAMICS INDUSTRY; CLAY INDUSTRY

DIRECTORIES

Directory of the Refractories Industry. The Refractories Institute. • Quadrennial. Members, $30.00; non-members, $45.00. Lists approximately 120 manufactures and suppliers of heat-resistant materials and equipment called refractories, refractory installation companies, furnace design and engineering firms, furnance builders, refractory contractors and services.

INTERNET DATABASES

Manufacturing Profiles. U. S. Bureau of the Census. Phone: (301)763-4636 E-mail: webmaster@census.gov • URL: http://www.census.gov/prod/www/abs/mfg-prof.html • The Census Bureau makes available free on PDF (Portable Document Format) an annual consolidation of the entire Current Industrial Report series, presenting "all the data compiled." Contains statistics on production, shipments, inventories, consumption, exports, imports, and orders for a wide variety of manufactured products.

STATISTICS SOURCES

Annual Survey of Manufactures. Available from U. S. Government Printing Office. • Annual. Prices vary. Issued by the U. S. Census Bureau as an interim update to the *Census of Manufactures.* Includes data on number of manufacturing establishments in various industries, employment, labor costs, value of shipments, capital expenditures, inventories, energy costs, and assets. (See also Census Bureau home page, http://www.census.gov/.).

Refractories. U. S. Bureau of the Census. • Annual. Provides data on value of manufacturers' shipments, quantity, exports, imports, etc. (Current Industrial Reports, MA-32C.).

TRADE/PROFESSIONAL ASSOCIATIONS

Refractories Institute (TRI). 650 Smithfield St., Ste. 1160, Pittsburgh, PA 15222-3907. Phone: (412)281-6787 Fax: (412)281-6881 E-mail: triassn@aol.com • URL: http://www.refractoriesinstitute.org • Members are producers of fire brick and other refractory materials.

REFRIGERATION INDUSTRY

See also: AIR CONDITIONING INDUSTRY

GENERAL WORKS

Refrigeration and Air Conditioning. A.R. Trott and T. Welch. Elsevier. • 2000. $64.99. Third edition.

DIRECTORIES

Air Conditioning, Heating, and Refrigeration News-Directory. Business News Publishing Co. • Annual. $35.00.

Grocery Headquarters: The Newspaper for the Food Industry. Trend Publishing. • Monthly. $80.00 per year. Covers the sale and distribution of food products and other items sold in supermarkets and grocery stores. Edited mainly for retailers and wholesalers. Incorporates (Grocery Distribution).

INTERNET DATABASES

Manufacturing Profiles. U. S. Bureau of the Census. Phone: (301)763-4636 E-mail: webmaster@census.gov • URL: http://www.census.gov/prod/www/abs/mfg-prof.html • The Census Bureau makes available free on PDF (Portable Document Format) an annual consolidation of the entire Current Industrial Report series, presenting "all the data compiled." Contains statistics on production, shipments, inventories, consumption, exports, imports, and orders for a wide variety of manufactured products.

PERIODICALS AND NEWSLETTERS

Air Conditioning, Heating, and Refrigeration News: The HVACR Contractor's Weekly Newsmagazine. Business News Publishing Co. • Weekly. $87.00 per year. Includes *Supplement.*

ASHRAE Journal: The Magazine of the American Society of Heating, Refrigeration, Air-Conditioning, Ventilation. American Society of Heating, Refrigerating and Air Conditioning Engineers, Inc. • Monthly. Free to members; non-members, $59.00 per year.

International Journal of Refrigeration. Elsevier. • Eight times a year. Qualified personnel, $99.00 per year; institutions, $1,131.00 per year. Text in English and French.

Refrigeration. John W. Yopp Publications, Inc. • Monthly. $30.00 per year.

RESEARCH CENTERS AND INSTITUTES

Ray W. Herrick Laboratories. Purdue University, 1077 Ray W. Herrick Laboratories, West Lafayette, IN 47907-1077. Phone: (765)494-2132 Fax: (765)494-0787 E-mail: rhlab@ecn.purdue.edu URL: http://www.herrick.ecn.purdue.edu.

World Food Logistics Organization. World Food Logistics Organization. 1500 King St., Ste. 201, Alexandria, VA 22314. Phone: (703)373-4300 Fax: (703)373-4301 E-mail: bhudson@iarw.org • URL: http://www.wflo.org • Food storage.

STATISTICS SOURCES

AHAM Major Home Appliance Industry Fact Book: A Comprehensive Reference on the U States Major Home Appliance Industry. Association of Home Appliance Manufacturers. • Biennial. $75.00. Includes statistical data on manufacturing, industry shipments, distribution, and ownership.

Annual Survey of Manufactures. Available from U. S. Government Printing Office. • Annual. Prices vary. Issued by the U. S. Census Bureau as an interim update to the *Census of Manufactures.* Includes data on number of manufacturing establishments in various industries, employment, labor costs, value of shipments, capital expenditures, inventories, energy costs, and assets. (See also Census Bureau home page, http://www.census.gov/.).

Refrigeration, Air Conditioning, and Warm Air Heating Equipment. U. S. Bureau of the Census. • Annual. Provides data on quantity and value of shipments by manufacturers. Formerly *Air Conditioning and Refrigeration Equipment.* (Current Industrial Reports, MA-35M.).

U. S. Industry and Trade Outlook. Available from National Technical Information Service. • Annual. $69.95. Produced by the International Trade Administration, U. S. Department of Commerce, in a "public-private" partnership with DRI/McGraw-Hill and Standard & Poor's. Provides basic data, outlook for the current year, and "Long-Term Prospects" (five-year projections) for a wide variety of products and services. Includes high technology industries. Formerly *U. S. Industrial Outlook.*

TRADE/PROFESSIONAL ASSOCIATIONS

Air-Conditioning and Refrigeration Institute. 4301 N. Fairfax Dr., Suite 425, Arlington, VA 22203. Phone: (703)524-8800 Fax: (703)528-3816 E-mail: ari@ari.org • URL: http://www.ari.org.

American Society of Heating, Refrigerating and Air Conditioning Engineers. c/o Frank Coda, 1791 Tullie Circle, N.E., Atlanta, GA 30329. Phone: 800-527-4723 or (404)636-8400 Fax: (404)321-5478 E-mail: ashrae@ashrae.org • URL: http://www.ashrae.org.

Commercial Refrigerator Manufacturers Division. 4100 N Fairfax Dr., Ste. 200, Arlington, VA 22203. Phone: (703)524-8800 Fax: (703)524-9011 E-mail: crm@ari.org • URL: http://ariadman.tempdomainname.com/crm • Manufacturers of refrigerated display cases and cabinets, food service refrigerators, and sectional cooling rooms. Seeks to provide a voice for manufacturers and suppliers to address industry developments and problems with companies who share common interests. Maintains a continuing presence within Congress and government agencies to monitor and respond to policies and regulations affecting the industry and represent the collective interests of members. Acts as a clearinghouse on information including foreign sales opportunities, technological developments, domestic markets, and other data of importance to the refrigeration industry. Provides technical information concerning regulations to governmental agencies. Conducts research to eliminate waste and increase efficiency of the production, distribution, and marketing of merchandise, products, or equipment related to the industry. Develops health and sanitation standard for retail food store refrigerators. Compiles statistics.

International Association of Refrigerated Warehouses. 7315 Wisconsin Ave., 1200N, Bethesda, MD 20814-3202. Phone: (301)652-5674 Fax: (301)652-7269 E-mail: email@iarw.org • URL: http://www.iarw.org.

Refrigerating Engineers and Technicians Association. 4700 W. Lake Ave., Glenview, IL 60625-1485. Phone: (847)375-4738 Fax: 877-218-8369 or (847)375-6338 E-mail: info@reta.com • URL: http://www.reta.com/ • Formerly National Association Practical Refrigerating Engineers.

REFUSE DISPOSAL

See: SANITATION INDUSTRY

REGIONAL AIRLINES

See: AIRLINE INDUSTRY

REGIONAL PLANNING

See also: CITY PLANNING; PLANNING; ZONING

ABSTRACTS AND INDEXES

Journal of Planning Literature. Ohio State University, Dept. of City and Regional Planning. Sage Publications, Inc. • Quarterly. Institutions, $682.00 per year; includes print and online editions. Provides reviews and abstracts of city and regional planning lierature.

PAIS International in Print. Public Affairs Information Service, Inc. • Monthly. $850.00 per year; cumulations three times a year. Provides topical citations to the worldwide literature of public affairs, economics, demographics, sociology, and trade. Text in English; indexed materials in English, French, German, Italian, Portuguese and Spanish.

Social Sciences Citation Index. Thomson/ISI. • Three times a year. $6,900 per year. Annual cumulation. Includes *Source Index, Citation Index, Permuterm Subject Index,* and *Corporate Index.*

Social Sciences Index. H. W. Wilson Co. • Quarterly, with annual cumulation. Price varies. Indexes more than 400 periodicals covering economics, environmental policy, government, insurance, labor, health care policy, plannning, public administration, public welfare, urban studies, women's issues, criminology, and related topics.

CD-ROM DATABASES

PAIS on CD-ROM. Public Affairs Information Service, Inc. • Quarterly. $1,995.00 per year. Provides a CD-ROM version of the online service,

PAIS International. Contains over 500,000 citations to the literature of contemporary social, political, and economic issues.

Social Sciences Citation Index. ISI. • Monthly. Price on request. Provides CD-ROM indexing of articles appearing in 1700 leading social science journals worldwide, with additional selections from more than 5700 other journals. Time span is 1992 to date. Coverage includes economics, business, finance, management, communications, demographics, library and information science, political science, sociology, and many other subjects.

Social Sciences Citation Index: Compact Disc Edition with Abstracts. Institute for Scientific Information. • Monthly. Provides CD-ROM indexing and abstracting of "significant articles" from 1,700 social science journals worldwide, with additional selections from 3,200 other journals, 1986 to date. Includes economics, business, finance, management, communications, demographics, information and library science, political science, sociology, and many other subjects.

WILSONDISC: Wilson Social Sciences Abstracts. H. W. Wilson Co. • Monthly. Includes unlimited online access to *Social Sciences Index* through WILSONLINE. Provides CD-ROM indexing from 1983 and abstracting from 1994 of more than 500 periodicals covering economics, area studies, community health, public administration, public welfare, urban studies, and many other topics related to the social sciences.

DIRECTORIES

AICP Membership Directory. Association of Independent Commercial Producers. • Covers: General member companies that specialize in producing commercials on various media, including film, video, and computer, for advertisers and agencies. Associate member companies listed serve the industry, such as post-production and editorial houses, equipment and prop suppliers, casting agencies and others. AMP members are music production shops; press members are those in the press who cover the industry. Entries include: Company name, address, phone, fax, e-mail, URL, contact names, and names of people represented.

HANDBOOKS AND MANUALS

Zoning and Planning Deskbook, 2d. Douglas W. Kmiec. West Group. • $220.00. Two looseleaf volumes. Annual supplementation. Emphasis is on legal issues.

ONLINE DATABASES

PAIS International. Public Affairs Information Service, Inc. • Corresponds to the former printed publications, *PAIS Bulletin* (1976-90) and *PAIS Foreign Language Index* (1972-90), and to the current *PAIS International in Print* (1991 to date). Covers economic, political, and sociological material appearing in periodicals, books, government documents, and other publications. Updating is monthly. Inquire as to online cost and availability.

Social Scisearch. Institute for Scientific Information. • Broad, multidisciplinary index to the literature of the social sciences, 1972 to present. Weekly updates. Worldwide coverage. Inquire as to online cost and availability.

Wilson Social Sciences Abstracts Online. H. W. Wilson Co. • Provides online abstracting and indexing of more than 500 periodicals covering area studies, community health, public administration, public welfare, urban studies, and many other social science topics. Time period is 1994 to date for abstracts and 1983 to date for indexing, with updates weekly. Inquire as to online cost and availability.

PERIODICALS AND NEWSLETTERS

American Planning Association Journal. American Planning Association. • Quarterly. Members, $33.00 per year; non-members $75.00 per year.

Planning. American Planning Association. • Monthly. Free to members; non-members, $65.00 per year.

Planning and Zoning News. Planning and Zoning Center, Inc. • Monthly. $175.00 per year. Newsletter on planning and zoning issues in the United States.

Regional Economics and Markets: A Quarterly Analysis from the Conference Board. The Conference Board. • Quarterly. Members, $145.00 per year; non-members, $295.00 per year. Summarizes economic trends and prospects for nine geographic regions of the U. S. Provides data on key predictive indexes, including employment, housing permits, retail sales, consumer confidence, and help-wanted advertising. Charts and graphs are included.

TRADE/PROFESSIONAL ASSOCIATIONS

American Institute of Certified Planners. 1776 Massachusetts Ave., N.W., Suite 400, Washington, DC 20036-1904. Phone: 800-954-1669 or (202)872-0611 Fax: (202)872-0643 E-mail: aicp@planning.org • URL: http://www.planning.org/aicp.

American Planning Association. 122 S Michigan Ave., Ste. 1600, Chicago, IL 60603-6107. Phone: (312)431-9100 Fax: (312)431-9985 E-mail: customerservice@planning.org • URL: http://www.planning.org • Public and private planning agency officials, professional planners, planning educators, elected and appointed officials, and other persons involved in urban and rural development. Works to foster the best techniques and decisions for the planned development of communities and regions. Provides extensive professional services and publications to professionals and laypeople in planning and related fields; serves as a clearinghouse for information. Through Planning Advisory Service, a research and inquiry-answering service, provides, on an annual subscription basis, advice on specific inquiries and a series of research reports on planning, zoning, and environmental regulations. Supplies information on job openings and makes definitive studies on salaries and recruitment of professional planners. Conducts research; collaborates in joint projects with local, national, and international organizations.

American Society of Consulting Planners. 1776 Massachusetts Ave. NW, No. 400, Washington, DC 20036. Phone: (202)872-0611 Fax: (202)872-0643.

Regional Science Association International. 2149 Grey Ave., Bevier Hall, Rm. 83, 905 S Goodwin Ave., Evanston, IL 60201. Phone: (217)333-8904 Fax: (217)333-3065 E-mail: rsai@uiuc.edu • URL: http://www.regionalscience.org • Represents academic and professional individuals concerned with the practice and advancement of urban and regional analysis and related studies.

REGISTRATION OF TRADEMARKS

See: TRADEMARKS AND TRADE NAMES

REGULATION OF INDUSTRY

See also: LAWS

GENERAL WORKS

Business, Government, and Society: A Managerial Perspective: Text and Cases. George A. Steiner and John F. Steiner. McGraw-Hill. • 1999. $88.75. Ninth edition. (Management Series).

Businesses' Views on Red Tape: Administrative and Regulatory Burdens on Small and Medium-Sized Enterprises. Organization for Economic Cooperation and Development. • 2001. $22.00. Based on a survey of about 8,000 firms in 11 OECD countries. Provides opinions on the costs of complying with

governmental rules, regulations, and formalities.

Food Safety: Is Anyone Watching?. V. L. Smyth, editor. Nova Science Publishers, Inc. • 2002. $59.00. Provides material by several authors on governmental oversight of the American food industry. Includes a food safety chronology of selected events, 1992-1999.

From Red Tape to Smart Tape: Administrative Simplification in OECD Countries. Organization for Economic Cooperation and Development. • 2003. $58.00. "This report looks at a set of tools and practices commonly used by governments to make administrative regulations simpler and less burdensome to comply with." Includes information on one-stop facilitation, license/permit simplification, decision-making time limits, small business assistance, and the use of information technology (IT) for administrative simplification.

Regulatory Policy and Practices: Regulating Better and Regulating Less. Fred Thompson. Greenwood Publishing Group, Inc. • 1982. $68.00.

ABSTRACTS AND INDEXES

Current Law Index: Multiple Access to Legal Periodicals. Gale Cengage Learning. • Monthly. $725.00 per year. Produced in cooperation with the American Association of Law Libraries. Indexes more than 900 law journals, legal newspapers, and specialty publications from the U.S., Canada, U.K., Ireland, Australia, and New Zealand.

Index to Legal Periodicals and Books. H. W. Wilson Co. • Monthly. $490.00 per year. Quarterly and annual cumulations.

PAIS International in Print. Public Affairs Information Service, Inc. • Monthly. $850.00 per year; cumulations three times a year. Provides topical citations to the worldwide literature of public affairs, economics, demographics, sociology, and trade. Text in English; indexed materials in English, French, German, Italian, Portuguese and Spanish.

Social Sciences Index. H. W. Wilson Co. • Quarterly, with annual cumulation. Price varies. Indexes more than 400 periodicals covering economics, environmental policy, government, insurance, labor, health care policy, plannning, public administration, public welfare, urban studies, women's issues, criminology, and related topics.

ALMANACS AND YEARBOOKS

Advertising Law: Year in Review. CCH, Inc. • Annual. $85.00. Summarizes the year's significant legal and regulatory developments.

American Law Yearbook. Gale Cengage Learning. • Annual. $165.00. Serves as a yearly supplement to *West's Encyclopedia of American Law.* Describes new legal developments in many subject areas.

Securities, Commodities, and Federal Banking: 1999 in Review. CCH, Inc. • Irregular. $57.00. Summarizes the year's significant legal and regulatory developments.

CD-ROM DATABASES

Newspaper Abstracts Ondisc. PROQUEST. • Monthly. $2,950.00 per year (covers 1989 to date; archival discs are available for 1985-88). Provides cover-to-cover CD-ROM indexing and abstracting of 19 major newspapers, including the *New York Times, Wall Street Journal, Washington Post, Chicago Tribune,* and *Los Angeles Times.*

PAIS on CD-ROM. Public Affairs Information Service, Inc. • Quarterly. $1,995.00 per year. Provides a CD-ROM version of the online service, *PAIS International.* Contains over 500,000 citations to the literature of contemporary social, political, and economic issues.

Social Sciences Citation Index. ISI. • Monthly. Price on request. Provides CD-ROM indexing of articles appearing in 1700 leading social science journals worldwide, with additional selections from more than 5700 other journals. Time span is 1992 to date. Coverage includes economics, business, finance, management, communications, demographics, library and information science, political science, sociology, and many other subjects.

Social Sciences Citation Index: Compact Disc Edition with Abstracts. Institute for Scientific Information. • Monthly. Provides CD-ROM indexing and abstracting of "significant articles" from 1,700 social science journals worldwide, with additional selections from 3,200 other journals, 1986 to date. Includes economics, business, finance, management, communications, demographics, information and library science, political science, sociology, and many other subjects.

WILSONDISC: Index to Legal Periodicals and Books. H. W. Wilson Co. • Monthly. Includes unlimited online access to *Index to Legal Periodicals* through WILSONLINE. Contains CD-ROM indexing of more than 1,400 English language legal periodicals from 1981 to date and 2,500 books.

WILSONDISC: Wilson Business Abstracts. H. W. Wilson Co. • Monthly. Includes unlimited online access to *Wilson Business Abstracts* through WILSONLINE. Provides CD-ROM "cover-to-cover" abstracting and indexing of over 600 prominent business periodicals. Indexing is from 1982, abstracting from 1990. (*Business Periodicals Index* without abstracts is available on CD-ROM at $1,495 per year.).

WILSONDISC: Wilson Social Sciences Abstracts. H. W. Wilson Co. • Monthly. Includes unlimited online access to *Social Sciences Index* through WILSONLINE. Provides CD-ROM indexing from 1983 and abstracting from 1994 of more than 500 periodicals covering economics, area studies, community health, public administration, public welfare, urban studies, and many other topics related to the social sciences.

DIRECTORIES

Federal Agency Profiles for Students. Gale Cengage Learning. • 1999. $115.00. Provides detailed descriptions of more than 175 prominent U.S. government agencies, including major activities, organizational structure, political issues, budget, and history. Includes a glossary, chronology, and index.

Federal Regional Yellow Book: Who's Who in the Federal Government's Departments, Agencies, Military Installations, and Service Academies Outside of Washington, DC. Leadership Directories, Inc. • Semiannual. $265.00 per year. Lists over 35,000 federal officials and support staff at 8,000 regional offices.

Federal Regulatory Directory. CQ Press. • Covers: Over 100 federal regulatory agencies including about 15 major agencies, about 15 smaller independent agencies, and agencies within federal departments. Entries include: For major agencies-- Agency name, address, jurisdiction, description of responsibilities, list of key contacts and phone numbers, breakdown of divisions and offices with names of key officials and their phone numbers, organization chart, information sources within the agency, regional offices, analytical essays on history, recent developments, power, and outlook for agency. For other agencies--Same general information but less detail.

Public Interest Profiles, 2001-2002. CQ Press. • 2002. $215.00. Provides detailed information on more than 250 influential public interest and public policy organizations (lobbyists) in the U.S. Includes e-mail addresses and Web sites where available. (Public Interest Profile Series).

United States Government Manual. National Archives and Records Administration. Office of the Federal Register. • Description: Provides information on the agencies of the executive, judicial, and legislative branches of the Federal government.

Contains a section on terminated or transferred agencies.

ENCYCLOPEDIAS AND DICTIONARIES

Encyclopedia of Governmental Advisory Organizations. Gale Cengage Learning. • 2003. $685.00. 18th edition. Contains more than 7,300 entries describing activities and personnel. Complete contact information.

West's Encyclopedia of American Law. Available from Gale Cengage Learning. • 2003. $1,195.00. Second edition. 12 volumes. Published by West Group. Covers a wide variety of legal topics for the general reader.

HANDBOOKS AND MANUALS

ADA Compliance Guide. Thompson Publishing Group, Inc. • Two looseleaf volumes. $329.00 per year, including monthly updates and newslettrs. Provides detailed information for employers and others on complying with the Americans With Disabilities Act (ADA). Includes material on employment discrimination, transportation accessibility, accessibility in public accommodations, and state disability laws.

CCH Guide to Record Retention Requirements. CCH, Inc. • 1999. $49.95. Covers the record-keeping provisions of the Code of Federal Regulations. Explains which records must be kept and how long to keep them.

Code of Federal Regulations. Office of the Federal Register, U.S. General Services Administration. Available from U.S. Government Printing Office. • $1,094.00 per year. Complete service.

United States Export Administration Regulations. Available from U. S. Government Printing Office. • $132.00. Looseleaf. Includes basic manual and supplementary bulletins for one year. Issued by the Bureau of Export Administration, U. S. Department of Commerce (http://www.doc.gov). Consists of export licensing rules and regulations.

INTERNET DATABASES

Factiva. Dow Jones Reuters Business Interactive, LLC. Phone: 800-369-7466 or (609)452-1511 Fax: (609)520-5770 E-mail: solutions@factiva.com • URL: http://www.factiva.com • Fee-based Web site provides "global news and business information through Web sites and content integration solutions." Includes Dow Jones and Reuters newswires, The Wall Street Journal, and more than 7,000 other sources of current news, historical articles, market research reports, and investment analysis. Content includes 96 major U. S. newspapers, 900 non-English sources, trade publications, media transcripts, country profiles, news photos, etc.

FedWorld: A Program of the United States Department of Commerce. National Technical Information Service. Phone: (703)605-6000 Fax: (703)605-6900 E-mail: webmaster@fedworld.gov • URL: http://www.fedworld.gov • Web site offers "a comprehensive central access point for searching, locating, ordering, and acquiring government and business information." Emphasis is on searching the Web pages, databases, and government reports of a wide variety of federal agencies. Fees: Free.

FirstGov: Your First Click to the U. S. Government. General Services Administration. Phone: 800-333-4636 or (202)501-0705 E-mail: public.affairs@gsa.gov • URL: http://www.firstgov.gov • Free Web site provides extensive links to federal agencies covering a wide variety of topics, such as agriculture, business, consumer safety, education, the environment, government jobs, grants, health, social security, statistics sources, taxes, technology, travel, and world affairs. Also provides links to federal forms, including IRS tax forms. Searching is offered, both keyword and advanced.

GPO Access. U. S. Government Printing Office Sales Program, Bibliographic Systems Branch.

Phone: 888-293-6498 or (202)512-1530 Fax: (202)512-1262 E-mail: gpoaccess@gpo.gov • URL: http://www.access.gpo.gov • Web site provides searching of the GPO's Sales Product Catalog (SPC), also known as Publications Reference File (PRF). Covers all "Government information products currently offered for sale by the Superintendent of Documents." There are also specialized search pages for individual databases, such as the *Code of Federal Regulations*, the *Federal Register*, and *Commerce Business Daily*. Updated daily. Fees: Free.

Lexis.com Research System. Lexis-Nexis Group. Phone: 800-227-4908 or (937)865-6800 Fax: (937)865-6909 E-mail: webmaster@prod.lexis-nexis.com • URL: http://www.lexis.com • Fee-based Web site offers extensive searching of a wide variety of legal sources. Additional features include Daily Opinion Service, lexis.com Bookstore, Career Center, CLE Center, Law Schools, and Practice Pages ("Pages specific to areas of specialty").

Nexis.com. Lexis-Nexis Group. Phone: 800-227-4908 or (937)865-6800 Fax: (937)865-6909 E-mail: webmaster@prod.lexis-nexis.com • URL: http://www.nexis.com • Fee-based Web site offers searching of about 2.8 billion documents in some 30,000 news, business, and legal information sources. Features include a subject directory covering 1,200 topics in 34 categories and a Company Dossier containing information on more than 500,000 public and private companies. Boolean searching is offered.

U. S. Business Advisor. Small Business Administration. Phone: (202)205-6600 Fax: (202)205-7064 • URL: http://www.business.gov • Web site provides "a one-stop electronic link to all the information and services government provides for the business community." Covers about 60 federal agencies that exist to assist or regulate business. Detailed information is provided on financial assistance, workplace issues, taxes, regulations, international trade, and other business topics. Searching is offered. Fees: Free.

ONLINE DATABASES

Index to Legal Periodicals and Books (Online). H. W. Wilson Co. • Broad coverage of law journals and books 1981 to date. Monthly updates. Inquire as to online cost and availability.

Information Bank Abstracts. New York Times Index Dept. • Provides indexing and abstracting of current affairs, primarily from the final late edition of *The New York Times* and the Eastern edition of *The Wall Street Journal*. Time period is 1969 to present, with daily updates. Inquire as to online cost and availability.

PAIS International. Public Affairs Information Service, Inc. • Corresponds to the former printed publications, *PAIS Bulletin* (1976-90) and *PAIS Foreign Language Index* (1972-90), and to the current *PAIS International in Print* (1991 to date). Covers economic, political, and sociological material appearing in periodicals, books, government documents, and other publications. Updating is monthly. Inquire as to online cost and availability.

Wilson Business Abstracts Online. H. W. Wilson Co. • Indexes and abstracts 600 major business periodicals, plus the *Wall Street Journal* and the business section of the *New York Times*. Indexing is from 1982, abstracting from 1990, with the two newspapers included from 1993. Updated weekly. Inquire as to online cost and availability. (*Business Periodicals Index* without abstracts is also available online.).

Wilson Social Sciences Abstracts Online. H. W. Wilson Co. • Provides online abstracting and indexing of more than 500 periodicals covering area studies, community health, public administration, public welfare, urban studies, and many other social science topics. Time period is 1994 to date for abstracts

For publishers addresses, refer to SOURCES CITED section at the back of the book.

and 1983 to date for indexing, with updates weekly. Inquire as to online cost and availability.

PERIODICALS AND NEWSLETTERS

FCC Report: An Exclusive Report on Domestic and International Telecommunications Policy and Regulation. Warren Publishing, Inc. • 26 times a year. $670.00 per year. Newsletter concerned principally with Federal Communications Commission reglations and policy.

Federal Register. Office of the Federal Register. Available from U.S. Government Printing Office. • Daily except Saturday and Sunday. $764.00 per year. Publishes regulations and legal notices issued by federal agencies, including executive orders and presidential proclamations. Issued by the National Archives and Records Administration (http://www.nara.gov).

Warren's Cable Regulation Monitor: The Authoritative Weekly News Service Covering Federal, State, and Local Cable Activities and Trends. Warren Publishing, Inc. • Weekly. $594.00 per year. Newsletter. Emphasis is on Federal Communications Commission regulations affecting cable television systems. Covers rate increases made by local systems and cable subscriber complaints filed with the FCC.

STATISTICS SOURCES

Property-Casualty Insurance Facts. Insurance Information Institute. • Annual. $22.50. Formerly *Insurance Facts.*

OTHER SOURCES

ADA Compliance Manual for Employers. LexisNexis Matthew Bender. • Looseleaf. $95.00. Periodic supplementation available. "Every business with more than 15 employees must comply with the Americans with Disabilities Act." This guide provides practical advice on job requirements, accessibility, employee selection, reasonable accomodations, termination issues, and other matters.

Chemical Regulation Reporter: A Weekly Review of Activity Affecting Chemical Users and Manufacturers. BNA, Inc. • Weekly. $2,226 per year. Looseleaf service.

Corporate Compliance Series. Joseph E. Murphy and Paul H. Dawes. West Group. • $1,210.00. 12 looseleaf volumes. Covers criminal and civil liability problems for corporations. Includes employee safety, product liability, pension requirements, securities violations, equal employment opportunity issues, intellectual property, employee hiring and firing, and other corporate compliance topics.

FCC Record. Available from U. S. Government Printing Office. • Biweekly. $678.00 per year. Produced by the Federal Communications Commission (http://www.fcc.gov). An inclusive compilation of decisions, reports, public notices, and other documents of the FCC.

Occupational Safety and Health Handbook: An Employer's Guide to OSHA Laws. LexisNexis Matthew Bender. • Looseleaf. $115.00. Periodic supplementation available. Covers inspections, violations, the citation process, ergonomics, hazards, equipment, and other topics relating to the law enforced by the federal Occupational Safety and Health Administration (OSHA).

Practical Guide to the Occupational Safety and Health Act. American Lawyer Media, Inc. • Looseleaf. $149.00. Updated as needed. Covers the practical aspects of doing business while complying with OSHA regulations. Covers inspections, enforcement, rights of employees, the possibility of criminal prosecution, and related issues. (Law Journal Press).

REGULATION OF SECURITIES

See: SECURITIES LAW AND REGULATION

REGULATIONS

See: LAWS; REGULATION OF INDUSTRY

REHABILITATION, VOCATIONAL

See: VOCATIONAL REHABILITATION

REIT'S

See: REAL ESTATE INVESTMENT TRUSTS

RELOCATION OF EMPLOYEES

ABSTRACTS AND INDEXES

Business Periodicals Index. H. W. Wilson Co. • 11 times a year. Quarterly and annual cumulations. Price varies.

Personnel Management Abstracts. • Quarterly. $190.00 per year. Includes annual cumulation.

HANDBOOKS AND MANUALS

Company Relocation Handbook: Making the Right Move. Sharon K. Ward and William Ward. Entrepreneur Media Inc. • 1998. $19.95. A comprehensive guide to moving a business. (Successful Business Library Series).

A Guide to Employee Relocation and Relocation Policy Development. Employee Relocation Council. • 1987. $25.00. Second edition.

ONLINE DATABASES

Wilson Business Abstracts Online. H. W. Wilson Co. • Indexes and abstracts 600 major business periodicals, plus the *Wall Street Journal* and the business section of the *New York Times.* Indexing is from 1982, abstracting from 1990, with the two newspapers included from 1993. Updated weekly. Inquire as to online cost and availability. (*Business Periodicals Index* without abstracts is also available online.).

PERIODICALS AND NEWSLETTERS

Direction: For the Moving and Storage Industry. American Moving and Storage Association. • Monthly. $35.00 per year. Newsletter on developments affecting the household goods movingindustry. Formerly *American Mover.*

Insulation Outlook: Business Solutions for Expanding or Relocating Companies. National Insulation Association. • $45.00 per year. Covers site selection and related topics.

Mobility. Employee Relocation Council. • 12 times a year. $48.00 per year. Covers various aspects of the moving of corporate employees.

Office Relocation Magazine. ORM Group. • Bimonthly. $39.00 per year. Provides articles on the relocation of office facilities.

Runzheimer Reports on Relocation. Runzheimer International. • Monthly. $354.00 per year. Newsletter.

STATISTICS SOURCES

Moving and Relocation Sourcebook and Directory: Reference Guide to the 120 Largest Metropolitan Areas in the United States. Omnigraphics, Inc. • Annual. $225.00 Provides extensive statistical and other descriptive data for the 120 largest

metropolitan areas in the U. S. Includes maps and a discussion of factors to be considered when relocating.

Survey and Analysis of Employee Relocation Policies and Costs. Runzheimer International. • Annual. Based on surveys of relocation administrators.

TRADE/PROFESSIONAL ASSOCIATIONS

American Moving and Storage Association. c/o John Brewer. 1611 Duke St., Alexandria, VA 22314. Phone: (703)683-7410 Fax: (703)683-7527 E-mail: amconf@amconf.org • URL: http://www.amconf.org • Members are household goods movers, storage companies, and trucking firms.

Employee Relocation Council. 1717 Pennsylvania Ave. NW, Washington, DC 20006. Phone: 888-801-0005 or (202)857-0857 Fax: (202)659-8631 E-mail: sselleck@njrealestate.com • URL: http://ads4homes.com/erc • Members are major corporations seeking efficiency and minimum disruption when employee transfers take place. Formerly Employee Relocation Real Estate Advisory Council.

REMODELING

See: HOME IMPROVEMENT INDUSTRY

RENTAL, EQUIPMENT

See: EQUIPMENT LEASING

RENTAL HOUSING

See: APARTMENT HOUSES; REAL ESTATE INVESTMENTS

RENTAL SERVICES

See also: AUTOMOBILE LEASE AND RENTAL SERVICES; EQUIPMENT LEASING

DIRECTORIES

Leasing Sourcebook: The Directory of the U. S. Capital Equipment Leasing Industry. Bibliotechnology Systems and Publishing Co. • Every 12-18 months. $135.00. Lists approximately 5,200 capital equipment leasing companies.

Rental Equipment Register Buyer's Guide. Primedia Business Magazines and Media. • Annual. $43.95. Formerly *Rental Equipment Register Product Directory and Buyer's Guide.*

FINANCIAL RATIOS

Annual Statement Studies. The Risk Management Association. • Annual. Median and quartile financial ratios are given for over 400 kinds of manufacturing, wholesale, retail, construction, and consumer finance establishments. Data is sorted by both asset size and sales volume. Includes a clearly written "Definition of Ratios" and an alphabetical industry index.

Annual Statement Studies: Industry Default Probabilities and Cash Flow Measures. The Risk Management Association. • Annual. $145.00. Serves as a companion volume to the original *Annual Statement Studies.* Gives probability of default estimates on a percentage scale for more than 450 industries. Includes changes in position year-by-year for eight financial statement line items and provides percentage measures of cash flow.

NARDA's Cost of Doing Business Survey. North American Retail Dealers Association. • Annual. $295.00.

PERIODICALS AND NEWSLETTERS

Equipment Leasing Today. Equipment Leasing Association. • 10 times a year. $100.00 per year.

Edited for equipment leasing companies. Covers management, funding, marketing, etc.

Rental Equipment Register. Primedia Business Magazines and Media'. • Monthly. $75.00 per year.

Rental Management. American Rental Association. • Monthly. Free to qualified personnel; others, $24.00 per year.

Rental Product News. Cygnus Business Media. • Bimonthly. $48.00 per year. Includes annual *Product* issue.

STATISTICS SOURCES

Survey of Industry Activity. Equipment Leasing Association of America. • Annual. Provides financial and statistical data on the equipment leasing industry. Price on application.

U. S. Industry and Trade Outlook. Available from National Technical Information Service. • Annual. $69.95. Produced by the International Trade Administration, U. S. Department of Commerce, in a "public-private" partnership with DRI/McGraw-Hill and Standard & Poor's. Provides basic data, outlook for the current year, and "Long-Term Prospects" (five-year projections) for a wide variety of products and services. Includes high technology industries. Formerly *U. S. Industrial Outlook.*

TRADE/PROFESSIONAL ASSOCIATIONS

American Rental Association. 1900 19th St., Moline, IL 61265. Phone: 800-334-2177 or (309)764-2475 Fax: (309)764-1533 E-mail: chris.wehrman@ararental.org • URL: http://www.ararental.org • Firms engaged in the rental of event and party equipment, tools, machinery, and other products; includes independent, franchised, and chain store operators. Associates are suppliers of equipment, merchandise, and other items. Seeks to foster better business methods; promote study of economic trends in the rental industry.

Equipment Leasing Association of America. 4301 N. Fairfax Dr., Suite 550, Arlington, VA 22203-1627. Phone: (703)527-8655 Fax: (703)527-2649 E-mail: ela@elamail.com • URL: http://www.elaonline.com • Formerly Equipment Leasing Association.

RENTAL SERVICES, AUTOMOBILE

See: AUTOMOBILE LEASE AND RENTAL SERVICES

REPORT WRITING

See also: TECHNICAL WRITING

GENERAL WORKS

Business English. Mary E. Guffey. South-Western. • 2001. $78.95. Seventh edition. (South-Western College Busines Communications Series).

HANDBOOKS AND MANUALS

Banishing Bureaucratese: Using Plain English in Government Writing. Judith G. Myers. Management Concepts, Inc. • 2001. $39.00. Covers plain writing style for government memos, letters, e-mail, agency communications, budget justification statements, and other bureaucratic documents.

Business English: A Complete Guide to Developing an Effective Business Writing Style. Andrea B. Geffner. Barron's Educational Series, Inc. • 2004. $16.95. Fourth edition. Covers both traditional and electronic business communication.

Business Writing at Its Best. Minerva H. Neiditz. McGraw-Hill. • 1993. $22.50.

Handbook for Business Writing. L. Sue Baug and others. McGraw-Hill. • 1993. $24.95. Second

edition. Covers reports, letters, memos, and proposals. (Handbook for... Series).

Little Black Book of Business Reports. Michael C. Thomsett. AMACOM. • 1988. $14.95. How to write effective business reports. (Little Black Book Series).

Report Writing for Business. Raymond V. Lesikar and John Pettit. McGraw-Hill. • 1997. $83.75. 10th edition.

Wall Street Journal Guide to Business Style and Usage. Paul R. Martin, editor. The Free Press. • 2002. $30.00. Contains definitions and explanations relating to grammar, spelling, punctuation, and the use of specialized business terms. (Wall Street Journal Book Series).

PERIODICALS AND NEWSLETTERS

Harvard Management Communication Letter. Harvard Business School Publishing. • Description: Provides information and techniques for managers on effective communication.

REPORTS

See: CORPORATION REPORTS; REPORT WRITING

RESEARCH, ADVERTISING

See: ADVERTISING RESEARCH

RESEARCH AND DEVELOPMENT

See also: BUSINESS RESEARCH; ECONOMIC RESEARCH; INDUSTRIAL RESEARCH; LABORATORIES; MARKET RESEARCH; SCIENTIFIC APPARATUS AND INSTRUMENT INDUSTRIES; TECHNOLOGY

GENERAL WORKS

The Innovator's Dilemma: When New Technologies Cause Great Firms to Fail. Clayton M. Christensen. Harvard Business School Publishing. • 1997. $27.50. Discusses management myths relating to innovation, change, and research and development. (Mangement of Innovation and Change Series).

Probable Tomorrows: How Science and Technology Will Transform Our Lives in the Next Twenty Years. Marvin J. Cetron and Owen L. Davies. Saint Martin's Press. • 1997. $24.95. Predicts the developments in technological products, services, and "everyday conveniences" by the year 2017. Covers such items as personal computers, artificial intelligence, telecommunications, highspeed railroads, and healthcare.

Probable Tomorrows: How Science and Technology Will Transform Our Lives in the Next Twenty Years. Marvin J. Cetron and Owen L. Davies. Saint Martin's Press. • 1997. $24.95. Predicts the developments in technological products, services, and "everyday conveniences" by the year 2017. Covers such items as personal computers, artificial intelligence, telecommunications, highspeed railroads, and healthcare.

ABSTRACTS AND INDEXES

Applied Science and Technology Index. H. W. Wilson Co. • 11 times a year. Quarterly and annual cumulations. Price varies. Indexes a wide variety of English language technical, industrial, and engineering periodicals.

ALMANACS AND YEARBOOKS

Science and Technology Almanac. Greenwood Publishing Group, Inc. • Annual. $79.95. Covers

technological news, research, and statistics.

BIOGRAPHICAL SOURCES

American Men and Women of Science A Biographical Directory of Today's Leaders in Physical, Biological and Related Sciences. Gale. • 2002. $950.00. 21st edition. Eight volumes. Over 119,600 United States and Canadian scientists active in the physical, biological, mathematical, computer science and engineering fields.

Who's Who in Science and Engineering. Marquis Who's Who. • Biennial. $269.00. Provides concise biographical information on 35,000 prominent engineers and scientists. International coverage, with geographical and professional indexes.

CD-ROM DATABASES

NTIS on SilverPlatter. Available from SilverPlatter Information, Inc. • Quarterly. $2,850.00 per year. Produced by the National Technical Information Service. Provides a CD-ROM guide to over 500,000 government reports on a wide variety of technical, industrial, and business topics.

Science Citation Index: Compact Disc Edition. Institute for Scientific Information. • Monthly. Provides CD-ROM indexing of the world's scientific and technical literature. Corresponds to online *Scisearch* and printed *Science Citation Index.*

WILSONDISC: Applied Science and Technology Abstracts. H. W. Wilson Co. • Monthly. Includes unlimited access to the online version of *Applied Science and Technology Abstracts* through WILSONLINE. Provides CD-ROM indexing and abstracting of 500 prominent scientific, technical, engineering, and industrial periodicals. Indexing coverage is provided from 1983 to date and abstracting from 1993 to date.

DIRECTORIES

Directory of American Research and Technology: Organizations Active in Product Development for Business. Information Today. • Annual. $359.95. Lists over 13,000 publicly and privately owned research facilities. Formerly *Industrial Research Laboratories of the U.S.*

Government Research Directory. Gale. • Covers: About 6,000 research and development facilities operated or sponsored by the United States or Canadian governments, including research centers, bureaus, and institutes; testing and experiment stations; data collection and analysis centers; government-supported user facilities; cooperative research programs; and major research-supporting service units. Entries include: Unit name, address, phone, fax, mail address, e-mail addresses, name of director, staff, year founded, parent agencies, description of activities and fields of research, special research facilities, publications, public services, and library collections.

International Research Centers Directory. Gale. • Covers: Over 9,500 research and development facilities maintained outside the United States by governments, universities, or independent organizations, and concerned with all areas of physical, social, and life sciences, technology, business, military science, public policy, and the humanities. Entries include: Facility name, address, phone, fax, telex, e-mail, URLs, name of parent agency or other affiliation, date established, number of staff, type of activity and fields of research, special research facilities, publications, educational activities, services, and library holdings.

Materials Research Centres: A World Directory of Organizations and Programmes in Materials Science. Specialist Journals. • Biennial. $445.00. Profiles of research centers in 75 countries. Materials include plastics, metals, fibers, etc.

Medical Research Centres: A World Directory of Organizations and Programmes. FT Healthcare. • Biennial. $470.00. Two volumes. Contains profiles of more than 7,000 medical research facilities around the world. Includes medical, dental, nursing, pharmaceutical, psychiatric, and surgical research centers.

New Research Centers. Gale Cengage Learning. • 2002. $420.00. 29th edition. A supplement to *Research Centers Directory.*

Plunkett's Engineering and Research Industry Almanac. Plunkett Research, Ltd. • Annual. $179.99. Contains detailed profiles of major engineering and technology corporations. Includes CD-ROM.

Research Centers Directory. Gale. • Covers: About 13,600 university, government, and other nonprofit research organizations established on a permanent basis to carry on continuing research programs in all areas of study; includes research institutes, laboratories, experiment stations, research parks, technology transfer centers, and other facilities and activities; coverage includes Canada. Entries include: Unit name, name of parent institution, address, phone, fax, name of director, e-mail addresses, URLs, year founded, governance, staff, educational activities, public services, sources of support, annual volume of research, principal fields of research, publications, special library facilities, special research facilities.

Research Services Directory: Commercial & Corporate Research Centers. Grey House Publishing. • 2003. $495.00. Ninth edition. Lists more than 8,000 independent commercial research centers and laboratories offering contract or fee-based services. Includes corporate research departments, market research companies, and information brokers.

Unique 3-in-1 Research and Development Directory. Government Data Publications, Inc. • Annual. $15.00. Government contractors in the research and development fields. Included with subscription to *R and D Contracts Monthly.* Formerly *Research and Development Directory.*

World Energy and Nuclear Directory. Specialist Journals. • Biennial. $385.00. Lists 5,000 public and private, international research and development organizations functioning in a wide variety of areas related to energy.

ENCYCLOPEDIAS AND DICTIONARIES

Encyclopedia of Emerging Industries. Gale Cengage Learning. • 2001. $320.00. Fourth edition. Provides detailed information on 115 "newly flourishing" industries. Includes historical background, organizational structure, significant individuals, current conditions, major companies, work force, technology trends, research developments, and other industry facts.

FINANCIAL RATIOS

Annual Statement Studies. The Risk Management Association. • Annual. Median and quartile financial ratios are given for over 400 kinds of manufacturing, wholesale, retail, construction, and consumer finance establishments. Data is sorted by both asset size and sales volume. Includes a clearly written "Definition of Ratios" and an alphabetical industry index.

Annual Statement Studies: Industry Default Probabilities and Cash Flow Measures. The Risk Management Association. • Annual. $145.00. Serves as a companion volume to the original *Annual Statement Studies.* Gives probability of default estimates on a percentage scale for more than 450 industries. Includes changes in position year-by-year for eight financial statement line items and provides percentage measures of cash flow.

HANDBOOKS AND MANUALS

Managing High-Technology Programs and Projects. Russell D. Archibald. John Wiley and Sons, Inc. • 2003. $100.00. Third edition. Written for senior executives, professional project manag-

ers, engineers, and information systems managers.

INTERNET DATABASES

FedWorld: A Program of the United States Department of Commerce. National Technical Information Service. Phone: (703)605-6000 Fax: (703)605-6900 E-mail: webmaster@fedworld.gov • URL: http://www.fedworld.gov • Web site offers "a comprehensive central access point for searching, locating, ordering, and acquiring government and business information." Emphasis is on searching the Web pages, databases, and government reports of a wide variety of federal agencies. Fees: Free.

ONLINE DATABASES

Applied Science and Technology Index Online. H. W. Wilson Co. • Provides online indexing of 500 major scientific, technical, industrial, and engineering periodicals. Time period is 1983 to date. Monthly updates. Inquire as to online cost and availability.

Current Contents Connect. Institute for Scientific Information. • Provides online abstracts of articles listed in the tables of contents of about 7,500 journals. Coverage is very broad, including science, social science, life science, technology, engineering, industry, agriculture, the environment, economics, and arts and humanities. Time period is two years, with weekly updates. Inquire as to online cost and availability.

New Product Announcements Plus. Gale Cengage Learning. • Contains the full text of new product and corporate activity press releases, with special emphasis on high technology and emerging industries. Covers 1985 to date. Weekly updates. Inquire as to online cost and availability.

NTIS Database. National Technical Information Service. • Contains citations and abstracts to unrestricted reports of government-sponsored research; 1964 to date. Covers a wide range of technical, engineering, business, and social science topics. Monthly updates. Inquire as to online cost and availability.

Research Centers and Services Directories. Gale Cengage Learning. • Contains profiles of about 30,000 research centers, organizations, laboratories, and agencies in 147 countries. Corresponds to the printed *Research Centers Directory, International Research Centers Directory, Government Research Directory,* and *Research Services Directory.* Updating is semiannual. Inquire as to online cost and availability.

Scisearch. Institute for Scientific Information. • Broad, multidisciplinary index to the literature of science and technology, 1974 to present. Inquire as to online cost and availability. Coverage of literature is worldwide, with weekly updates.

Who's Who in Technology [Online]. Gale Cengage Learning. • Provides online biographical profiles of over 25,000 American scientists, engineers, and others in technology-related occupations. Inquire as to online cost and availability.

PERIODICALS AND NEWSLETTERS

DOE This Month. Available from U. S. Government Printing Office. • Monthly. $42.00 per year. Describes the U.S. Department of Energy's research and development activities and DOE publications. Includes information on nuclear energy, renewable energy sources, and synthetic fuels.

Inside R and D: A Weekly Report on Technical Innovation. Technical Insights. • Weekly. Institutions, $840.00 per year. Concentrates on new and significant developments. Formerly *Technolog Transfer Week.*

Research and Development: The Voice of the Research and Development Community. Reed Business Information. • 13 times a year. $81.90 per year.

Research-Technology Management: International Journal of Research Management. Industrial

Research Institute. • Bimonthly. Individuals, $65.00 per year; institutions, $150.00 per year. Covers both theoretical and practical aspects of the management of industrial research and development.

The Scientist. • Biweekly. Individuals, $29.00 per year; institutions, $58.00 per year. Contains news for scientific, research, and technical personnel.

RESEARCH CENTERS AND INSTITUTES

SRI International. SRI International. 333 Ravenswood Ave., Menlo Park, CA 94025-3493. Phone: (650)859-2000 Fax: (650)859-4111 E-mail: inquiry.line@sri.com • URL: http://www.sri.com • Physical and life sciences, engineering, industrial management, business, social sciences, and public policy. Areas of research include biosciences, economics, energy, engineering systems and development, environment, health, industry consulting, information and communications, public policy, national security, and physical, life, and social sciences.

STATISTICS SOURCES

Basic Science and Technology Statistics. Organization for Economic Cooperation and Development. • Biennial. $84.00. Contains eight years of data on resources devoted to research and development in OECD countries. Includes both financial and personnel information.

Main Science and Technology Indicators. OECD Publications and Information Center. • Semiannual. $80.00 per year. Includes online edition. Provides latest available data on research and development expenditures in OECD countries. A bilingual publication.

Research and Development Expenditure in Industry. Organization for Economic Cooperation and Development. • Annual. $51.00. Provides data for more than 10 years. Covers R&D expenditures in each of more than 50 industrial sectors in various OECD countries. Regional total for the European Union is also provided.

Research and Development Expenditures in Industry. Organization for Economic Cooperation and Development. • Annual. $51.00. Presents research and development expenditures for OECD countries and the European Union zone. Includes about 60 industrial sectors.

UNESCO Statistical Yearbook. Bernan Press. • 1998. $95.00. Co-published by Bernan Press and the United Nations Educational, Scientific, and Cultural Organization (http://www.unesco.org). Presents statistical data from more than 200 countries on education, technology, research, broadcasting, cinema, book publishing, newspapers, libraries, museums, and population. Includes charts, maps, and graphs.

TRADE/PROFESSIONAL ASSOCIATIONS

Industrial Research Institute. 2200 Clarendon Blvd., Ste. 1102, Arlington, VA 22201. Phone: (703)647-2580 Fax: (703)647-2581 E-mail: bernstein@iriinc.org • URL: http://www.iriinc.org • Manufacturers and industrial firms maintaining industrial research laboratories. Identifies and promotes effective techniques for the organization and management of research, development, and engineering in support of technological innovation.

National Research Council. 500 5th St. NW, Washington, DC 20001. Phone: 800-424-5156 or (202)334-2000 Fax: (202)334-2290 E-mail: news@nas.edu • URL: http://www.nationalacademies.org/nrc • Scientists, engineers, and other professionals serving pro bono on approximately 900 study committees. Serves as an independent adviser to the federal government on scientific and technical questions of national importance; is jointly administered by the National Academy of Sciences, National Academy of Engineering, and Institute of Medicine. Carries out objectives through conferences, technical committees, surveys, collection and analysis of scientific and technical data, and administration of public and private funds for research projects and fellowships.

Society of Research Administrators International. 1901 N Moore St., Ste. 1004, Arlington, VA 22209. Phone: (703)741-0140 Fax: (703)741-0142 E-mail: info@srainternational.org • URL: http://www. srainternational.org • Dedicated to advancing the profession and improving the efficiency and effectiveness of research administration.

OTHER SOURCES

Army AL&T: Acquisitions, Logistics, and Technology Bulletin. Available from U. S. Government Printing Office. • Bimonthly. $20.00 per year. Produced by the U. S. Army Materiel Command (http://www.amc.army.mil). Reports on Army research, development, and acquisition. Formerly *Army RD&A.*

RESEARCH, BUSINESS

See: BUSINESS RESEARCH

RESEARCH, ECONOMIC

See: ECONOMIC RESEARCH

RESEARCH, INDUSTRIAL

See: INDUSTRIAL RESEARCH

RESEARCH, LIBRARY

See: LIBRARY RESEARCH

RESEARCH, MARKETING

See: MARKET RESEARCH

RESELLERS, COMPUTER

See: COMPUTER RETAILING

RESINS

See: NAVAL STORES; PLASTICS INDUSTRY

RESOURCES

See: NATURAL RESOURCES

RESTAURANTS, LUNCHROOMS, ETC.

See also: CATERERS AND CATERING; DRIVE-IN AND CURB SERVICES; EMPLOYEE LUNCHROOMS AND CAFETERIAS; FOOD SERVICE INDUSTRY

GENERAL WORKS

Fundamentals of Professional Food Preparation: A Laboratory Text-Workbook. Donald V. Laconi. John Wiley and Sons, Inc. • 1995. $60.00.

CD-ROM DATABASES

OECD Statistical Compendium. Organization for Economic Cooperation and Development. • Semiannual. $1,905.00 per year for 1 to 10 users. CD-ROM contains more than 730,000 monthly, quarterly, and annual time series for OECD

countries, 1960 to date. Includes fully searchable data on agriculture, food, economic indicators, national accounts, employment, energy, finance, industry, technology, and foreign trade. Results can be displayed in various forms.

DIRECTORIES

Directory of Chain Restaurant Operators. Chain Store Guide. • Annual. $335.00. Includes fast food establishments, and leading chain hotel copanies operating foodservice unit.

Directory of Foodservice Distributors. Chain Store Guide. • Annual. $335.00. Available online. Covers distributors of food and equipment to restaurants and institutions.

Directory of High Volume Independent Restaurants. Chain Store Guide. • Annual. $327.00. Online edition, $775.00. Approximately 5,900 independently owned restaurants with minimum sales of at least $1 million.

FINANCIAL RATIOS

Almanac of Business and Industrial Financial Ratios. Leo Troy. Aspen Publishers, Inc. • 2003. $125.95. Includes CD-Rom. Contains financial ratios derived from federal tax returns. Ratios for each of about 200 industries are arranged according to company asset size. (Almanac of Business and Industrial Financial Ratios Series).

Annual Statement Studies. The Risk Management Association. • Annual. Median and quartile financial ratios are given for over 400 kinds of manufacturing, wholesale, retail, construction, and consumer finance establishments. Data is sorted by both asset size and sales volume. Includes a clearly written "Definition of Ratios" and an alphabetical industry index.

Annual Statement Studies: Industry Default Probabilities and Cash Flow Measures. The Risk Management Association. • Annual. $145.00. Serves as a companion volume to the original *Annual Statement Studies.* Gives probability of default estimates on a percentage scale for more than 450 industries. Includes changes in position year-by-year for eight financial statement line items and provides percentage measures of cash flow.

Restaurant Industry Operations Report. National Restaurant Association. • Annual. Members, $44.95 per year; non-members, $89.95 per year.

HANDBOOKS AND MANUALS

Donut Shop. Entrepreneur Media, Inc. • Looseleaf. $59.50. A practical guide to starting a doughnut shop. Covers profit potential, start-up costs, market size evaluation, owner's time required, site selection, lease negotiation, pricing, accounting, advertising, promotion, etc. (Start-Up Business Guide No. E1126.).

Hotel and Restaurant Business. Donald E. Lundberg. John Wiley and Sons, Inc. • 1994. $65.00. Sixth edition. (Hospitality, Travel and Tourism Series).

Pizzeria. Entrepreneur Media, Inc. • Looseleaf. $59.50. A practical guide to starting a pizza shop. Covers profit potential, start-up costs, market size evaluation, owner's time required, site selection, lease negotiation, pricing, accounting, advertising, promotion, etc. (Start-Up Business Guide No. E1006.).

Profitable Restaurant Management. Drysdale. Prentice Hall PTR. • 2000. Price on application.

Restaurant Start-Up. Entrepreneur Media, Inc. • Looseleaf. $59.50. A practical guide to starting a restaurant. Covers profit potential, start-up costs, market size evaluation, owner's time required, site selection, lease negotiation, pricing, accounting, advertising, promotion, etc. (Start-Up Business Guide No. E1279.).

Restaurant Start-Up Guide: A 12-Month Plan for

Successfully Starting a Restaurant. Peter Rainsford and David H. Bangs. Dearborn Trade Publishing, A Kaplan Professional Co. • 2000. $22.95. Second edition. Emphasizes the importance of advance planning for restaurant startups.

Sandwich Shop/Deli. Entrepreneur Media, Inc. • Looseleaf. $59.50. A practical guide to starting a sandwich shop and delicatessen. Covers profit potential, start-up costs, market size evaluation, owner's time required, site selection, lease negotiation, pricing, accounting, advertising, promotion, etc. (Start-Up Business Guide No. E1156.).

INTERNET DATABASES

Advance Monthly Sales for Retail Trade and Food Services. U. S. Census Bureau. Phone: 800-541-8345 or (301)763-4636 Fax: (301)457-3842 E-mail: rcb@census.gov • URL: http://www.census.gov/svsd/www/fullpub.html • Web pages provide monthly sales figures for a wide range of retail businesses. Advance, preliminary, and final statistics are provided for the latest month available in each case, with a previous-year comparison. Updates are monthly.

Business 2.0 Web Guide to the Best Business Links. Business 2.0 Media Inc. Phone: (415)293-4800 E-mail: support@business2.com • URL: http://www.business2.com/webguide • Web site presents an extensive, searchable directory of links to "the best, most informative, and authoritative web pages." Twenty main categories cover business, finance, career, company information, people, and technology topics, with thousands of subtopics, all linking to Web sites recommended by experienced business researchers. Fees: Free.

Fedstats. Federal Interagency Council on Statistical Policy. Phone: (202)395-7254 • URL: http://www.fedstats.gov • Web site features an efficient search facility for full-text statistics produced by more than 100 federal agencies, including the Census Bureau, the Bureau of Economic Analysis, and the Bureau of Labor Statistics. Boolean searches can be made within one agency or for all agencies combined. Links are offered to international statistical bureaus, including the UN, IMF, OECD, UNESCO, Eurostat, and 20 individual countries. Fees: Free.

FreeLunch.com. Economy.com, Inc. Phone: (610)696-8700 Fax: (610)696-1678 • URL: http://www.freelunch.com • Web site provides free access to more than 1.5 million economic and financial data series, covering industry, demographics, labor markets, prices, retail sales, government spending, trade, interest rates, housing starts, the stock market, and many other topics. Data is available for various time periods in either chart or table form. Searching is offered. Fees: Free, but registration required. Economy.com, Inc. also offers fee-based economic analysis at *The Dismal Scientist* site (http://www.dismal.com).

PERIODICALS AND NEWSLETTERS

Bottomline. Hospitality Financial and Technology Professionals. • Bimonthly. Free to members, educational institutions and libraries; non-members, $50.00 per year. Contains articles on accounting, finance, information technology, and management for hotels, resorts, casinos, clubs, and other hospitality businesses.

Chef. Talcott Communications Corp. • Monthly. $24.00 per year. Edited for executive chefs, food and beverage directors, caterers, banquet and club managers, and others responsible for food buying and food service. Special coverage of regional foods is provided.

Cooking for Profit. CP Publishing, Inc. • Monthly. $25.00 per year. The challenge of operations management in the food service industry.

The Cornell Hotel and Restaurant Administration Quarterly. Cornell University School of Hotel Administration. Sage Publications, Inc. •

Bimonthly. Individuals, \$113.00 per year; institutions, \$319.00 per year.

Foodservice Equipment and Supplies. Reed Business Information. • 13 times a year. \$106.90 per year.

Hospitality Technology: Guiding High-Growth Businesses to Best-Choice IT Solutions. Edgell Communications, Inc. • 10 times a year. Price on application. Covers information technology, computer communications, and software for foodservice and lodging enterprises.

International Journal of Hospitality and Tourism Administration: A Multinationaland Cross-Cultural Journal of Applied Research. Haworth Press, Inc. • Quarterly. \$200.00 per year. Includes print and online editions. An academic journal with articles relating to lodging, food service, travel, tourism, and the hospitality/leisure industries in general. Formerly *Journal of International Hospitality, Leisure, and Tourism Management.*

Journal of Foodservice Business Research. Haworth Press, Inc. • Quarterly. \$225.00 per year. Includes print and online editions. Formerly *Journal of Restaurant and Foodservice Marketing.*

Journal of Hospitality and Leisure Marketing: The International Forum for Research, Theory and Practice. Haworth Press, Inc. • Quarterly. \$315.00 per year. An academic and practical journal covering various aspects of hotel, restaurant, and recreational marketing.

Nation's Restaurant News: The Newspaper of the Food Service Industry. Lebhar-Friedman, Inc. • 50 times a year. \$39.95 per year.

Nightclub & Bar Magazine: The Magazine for Nightclub and Bar Management. Oxford Publishing. • Monthly. Free for qualified personnel; others, \$30.00 per year. Provides news and business advice for owners and managers of bars, nightclubs, and themed restaurants. Includes special issues on seasonal drinks, bar technology, beer trends, appetizers, food service, etc.

QSR: The Magazine of Quick Service Restaurant Success. Journalistic, Inc. • Ten times a year. \$30.00 per year. Provides news and management advice for quick-service restaurants, including franchisors and franchisees.

Restaurant Business. VNU Business Media. • Biweekly. \$119.00 per year. Formerly *Fast Food.*

Restaurant Hospitality. Penton Media, Inc. • Monthly. \$70.00 per year.

Restaurants and Institutions. Reed Business Information. • Semimonthly. \$149.00 per year. Features news, new products, recipes, menu concepts and merchandising ideas from the most successful foodservice operations around the U.S.

STATISTICS SOURCES

Annual Benchmark Report for Retail Trade and Food Services...A Detailed Summary of Retail Sales, Purchases, Accounts Receivable, Inventories, and Food Service Sales. Available from U. S. Government Printing Office. • Annual. \$13.00. Issued by the U.S. Census Bureau. Provides detailed annual and monthly retail statistics for the most recent 10 years. Includes data for various kinds of retail outlets, including automobiles, furniture, appliances, building supplies, grocery stores, drug stores, gasoline stations, clothing, sporting goods, department stores, and restaurants.

Business Statistics of the United States. Linz Audain and Cornelia J. Strawser. Bernan Associates. • Annual. \$147.00. Based on *Business Statistics*, formerly issue by the Bureau of Economic Analysis, U. S. Department of Commerce. Provides basic data for a wide variety of U. S. industries, services, and economic indicators. Most statistics are shown annually for 30 years and monthly for the most recent four years.

Standard & Poor's Industry Surveys. Standard & Poor's. • Semiannual. \$1,800.00. Two looseleaf volumes. Includes monthly *Supplements*. Provides detailed, individual surveys of 52 major industry groups. Each survey is revised on a semiannual basis. Also includes "Monthly Investment Review" (industry group investment analysis) and monthly "Trends & Projections" (economic analysis).

Survey of Current Business. Available from U. S. Government Printing Office. • Monthly. \$63.00 per year. Issued by Bureau of Economic Analysis, U. S. Department of Commerce. Presents a wide variety of business and economic data.

WEFA Industrial Monitor. John Wiley and Sons, Inc. • Annual. \$65.00. Prepared by industry analysts at WEFA, an economic forecasting and consulting firm (originally Wharton Econometric Forecasting Associates). Contains discussions of the outlook for major U. S. industries, with many 10-year forecasts (WEFA Web site is http://www.wefa.com).

TRADE/PROFESSIONAL ASSOCIATIONS

Hospitality Financial and Technology Professionals. 11709 Boulder Lane, Suite 110, Austin, TX 78726. Phone: 800-646-4387 or (512)249-5333 Fax: (512)249-1533 E-mail: frank.wolfe@hftp.org • URL: http://www.hftp.org • Members are accounting and finance officers in the hotel, motel, casino, club, and other areas of the hospitality industry. Formerly International Association of Hospitality Accountants.

National Restaurant Association. 1200 17th St. NW, Washington, DC 20036. Phone: 800-424-5156 or (202)331-5900 Fax: (202)331-2429 E-mail: info@dineout.org • URL: http://www.restaurant.org • Represents restaurants, cafeterias, clubs, contract foodservice management, drive-ins, caterers, institutional food services, and other members of the foodservice industry; also represents establishments belonging to non-affiliated state and local restaurant associations in governmental affairs. Supports foodservice education and research in several educational institutions. Is affiliated with the Educational Foundation of the National Restaurant Association to provide training and education for operators, food and equipment manufacturers, distributors, and educators. Has 300,000 member locations.

RESTRAINT OF TRADE

See: ANTITRUST ACTIONS

RESUMES

See: JOB RESUMES

RETAIL AUTOMATION

See: POINT-OF-SALE SYSTEMS (POS)

RETAIL SELLING

See: SALESMEN AND SALESMANSHIP

RETAIL TRADE

See also: CHAIN STORES; DEPARTMENT STORES; DISCOUNT HOUSES

GENERAL WORKS

Management of Retail Buying. R. Patrick Cash and others. John Wiley and Sons, Inc. • 1995. \$180.00. Third edition. (National Retail Federation Series, vol. 25).

Modern Retailing: Theory and Practice. Joseph B. Mason and others. McGraw-Hill. • 1992. \$69.95. Sixth edition.

Retailing Managment. Michael Levy and Barton A. Weitz. McGraw-Hill Higher Education. • 2003. \$110.63. Fifth edition.

CD-ROM DATABASES

OECD Statistical Compendium. Organization for Economic Cooperation and Development. • Semiannual. \$1,905.00 per year for 1 to 10 users. CD-ROM contains more than 730,000 monthly, quarterly, and annual time series for OECD countries, 1960 to date. Includes fully searchable data on agriculture, food, economic indicators, national accounts, employment, energy, finance, industry, technology, and foreign trade. Results can be displayed in various forms.

16 Million Businesses Phone Directory. Info USA. • Annual. \$29.95. Provides more than 16 million yellow pages telephone directory listings on CD-ROM for all ZIP Code areas of the U. S.

DIRECTORIES

American Big Businesses Directory. infoUSA Inc. • Covers: 218,000 U.S. businesses with more than 100 employees, and 500,000 key executives and directors. CD-ROM version contains 160,000 top firms and 431,000 key executives. Entries include: Name, address, phone, names and titles of key personnel, number of employees, sales volume, Standard Industrial Classification (SIC) codes, subsidiaries and parent company names, stock exchanges on which traded.

American Manufacturers Directory. infoUSA Inc. • Covers: more than 150,000 manufacturing companies with 20 or more employees. CD-ROM version lists all 531,000 U.S. manufacturers, in all employee size ranges. Entries include: Company name, address, phone, contact name, Standard Industrial Classification (SIC) codes, number of employees, sales volume code, credit rating scores.

Directory of Discount and General Merchandise Stores. Chain Store Guide. • Annual. \$327.00. Online edition, \$747.00. Includes retailers and wholesalers of housewares, giftwares, novelties, toys, hobby materials, crafts, and stationery.

Mass Merchandisers and Off-Price Apparel Buyers Directory. Douglas Publications, Inc. • Annual. \$229.00. Lists buyers of clothing for major retailers. (Does not include the metropolitan New York City area.) *Salesman's Guide Directories.*

Plunkett's Retail Industry Almanac: Complete Profiles on the Retail 500-The Leading Firms in Retail Stores, Services, Catalogs, and On-Line Sales. Plunkett Research, Ltd. • 2001. \$229.99. Includes CD-ROM. Provides detailed profiles of 500 major U. S. retailers. Industry trends are discussed.

Sheldon's Major Stores and Chains. Phelon Sheldon and Marsar, Inc. • Annual. \$200.00. Lists department stores and chains in, women's specialty and chains, home furnishing chains and resident buying offices in the U.S. and Canada. Formerly *Sheldon's Retail Stores.*

World Retail Directory and Sourcebook. Available from Gale Cengage Learning. • 2003. \$1,250.00. Fifth edition. Published by Euromonitor. Provides information on more than 2,400 retailers around the world. Information sources, conferences, trade fairs, and special libraries are also listed.

FINANCIAL RATIOS

Almanac of Business and Industrial Financial Ratios. Leo Troy. Aspen Publishers, Inc. • 2003. \$125.95. Includes CD-Rom. Contains financial ratios derived from federal tax returns. Ratios for each of about 200 industries are arranged according to company asset size. (Almanac of Business and Industrial Financial Ratios Series).

Cost of Doing Business for Retail Sporting Goods

Stores. National Sporting Goods Association. • Biennial. $125.00. Includes income statements, balance sheets, sales per employee, sales per square foot, inventory turnover, etc.

Financial and Operating Results of Department and Specialty Stores. National Retail Federation. John Wiley and Sons, Inc. • Annual. Members, $80.00; non-members, $100.00.

IRS Corporate Financial Ratios. Available from MarketResearch.com. • 2002. $225.00. Published by Schonfeld & Associates, Inc. Presents 70 key financial ratios for 260 industries. Ratios are calculated from income statement and balance sheet data available from the Internal Revenue Service. Includes four asset size classes.

INTERNET DATABASES

Advance Monthly Sales for Retail Trade and Food Services. U. S. Census Bureau. Phone: 800-541-8345 or (301)763-4636 Fax: (301)457-3842 E-mail: rcb@census.gov • URL: http://www.census.gov/svsd/www/fullpub.html • Web pages provide monthly sales figures for a wide range of retail businesses. Advance, preliminary, and final statistics are provided for the latest month available in each case, with a previous-year comparison. Updates are monthly.

Bureau of Economic Analysis (BEA). U. S. Department of Commerce, Bureau of Economic Analysis. Phone: (202)606-9900 Fax: (202)606-5310 E-mail: webmaster@bea.doc.gov • URL: http://www.bea.doc.gov • Web site includes "News Release Information" covering national, regional, and international economic estimates from the BEA. Highlights of releases appear online the same day, complete text and tables appear the next day. "Recent News Releases" section provides titles for past nine months, with links. "BEA Data and Methodology" includes "Frequently Requested NIPA Data" (national income and product accounts, such as gross domestic product and personal income). Other statistics are available. Fees: Free.

Business 2.0 Web Guide to the Best Business Links. Business 2.0 Media Inc. Phone: (415)293-4800 E-mail: support@business2.com • URL: http://www.business2.com/webguide • Web site presents an extensive, searchable directory of links to "the best, most informative, and authoritative web pages." Twenty main categories cover business, finance, career, company information, people, and technology topics, with thousands of subtopics, all linking to Web sites recommended by experienced business researchers. Fees: Free.

Fedstats. Federal Interagency Council on Statistical Policy. Phone: (202)395-7254 • URL: http://www.fedstats.gov • Web site features an efficient search facility for full-text statistics produced by more than 100 federal agencies, including the Census Bureau, the Bureau of Economic Analysis, and the Bureau of Labor Statistics. Boolean searches can be made within one agency or for all agencies combined. Links are offered to international statistical bureaus, including the UN, IMF, OECD, UNESCO, Eurostat, and 20 individual countries. Fees: Free.

FreeLunch.com. Economy.com, Inc. Phone: (610)696-8700 Fax: (610)696-1678 • URL: http://www.freelunch.com • Web site provides free access to more than 1.5 million economic and financial data series, covering industry, demographics, labor markets, prices, retail sales, government spending, trade, interest rates, housing starts, the stock market, and many other topics. Data is available for various time periods in either chart or table form. Searching is offered. Fees: Free, but registration required. Economy.com, Inc. also offers fee-based economic

analysis at *The Dismal Scientist* site (http://www.dismal.com).

ONLINE DATABASES

American Business Directory. InfoUSA, Inc. • Provides brief online information on more than 10 million U. S. companies, including individual plants and branches. Entries typically include address, phone number, industry classification code, and contact name. Updating is quarterly. Inquire as to online cost and availability.

Business and Industry. Gale Cengage Learning. • Contains online citations, abstracts, and selected fulltext from more than 1,000 trade journals, newspapers, and other publications. Provides general coverage of both manufacturing and service industries, including marketing, production, industry trends, key events, and information on specific companies. Time span is 1994 to date. Daily updates. Inquire as to online cost and availability. (Also available in a CD-ROM version.).

Market Research Monitor. Euromonitor International. • Contains full-text reports online from *Market Research Europe, Market Research Great Britain, Market Research International,* and *Retail Monitor International.* Time period is 1995 to date, with monthly updates. Inquire as to online cost and availability.

Tablebase. Gale Cengage Learning. • Provides online numerical tabular data from a wide variety of business, organization, and government sources, including about 1,000 trade journals. Includes industry and individual company statistics relating to products, market share, sales forecasts, production, exports, market trends, etc. Time span is 1997 to date. Weekly updates. Inquire as to online cost and availability. (Also available in a CD-ROM version.).

PERIODICALS AND NEWSLETTERS

DSN Retailing Today. Lebhar-Friedman Inc. • 23 times a year. $257.00 per year. Newsletter.

E-Retailing World. VNU Business Media. • Bimonthly. Controlled circulation. Covers various kinds of online retailing, including store-based, catalog-based, pure play, and "click-and-mortar." Includes both technology and management issues.

eShopper: Where Style Meets the Net. Element K Journals. • Bimonthly. $9.97 per year. A consumer magazine providing advice and information for "shopping on the Web.".

Internet Retailer: E-Business Strategies. Thomson Financial. • 10 times a year. $98.00 per year. Trade journal on the selling of retail merchandise through the Internet. Provides information on pricing, payment systems, order management, fraud, digital imaging, advertising, Web trends, and other topics.

Journal of Retailing. New York University, Leonard N. Stern School of Business. Elsevier. • Quarterly. Individuals, $131.00 per year; institutions, $350.00 per year.

NSGA Retail Focus. National Sporting Goods Association. • Bimonthly. Membership. Covers news and marketing trends for sporting goods retailers. Formerly *NSGA Sports Retailer.*

Regional Economics and Markets: A Quarterly Analysis from the Conference Board. The Conference Board. • Quarterly. Members, $145.00 per year; non-members, $295.00 per year. Summarizes economic trends and prospects for nine geographic regions of the U. S. Provides data on key predictive indexes, including employment, housing permits, retail sales, consumer confidence, and help-wanted advertising. Charts and graphs are included.

Retailing Today. Robert Kahn and Associates. • Description: Focuses on general merchandise, apparel, furniture, hardware, automotive, and food retailing. Offers "original research, comments on current trends and conditions, recommendations for

company policy, and emphasis on ethical conduct in business.".

Stores. National Retail Federation. NRF Enterprises, Inc. • Monthly. Individuals $49.00 per year; institutions, $120.00 per year.

Value Retail News: 'The Journal of Outlet and Off-Price Retail and Development. Off-Price Specialists, Inc. Value Retail News. • Monthly. Members, $144.00 per year; non-members, $175.00 per year. Provides news of the off-price and outlet store industry. Emphasis is on real estate for outlet store centers.

PRICE SOURCES

CPI Detailed Report: Consumer Price Index. Available from U.S. Government Printing Office. • Monthly. $45.00 per year. Cost of living data.

RESEARCH CENTERS AND INSTITUTES

Center for Retail Management. Kellogg School of Management, Northwestern University, 2001 Sheridan Rd., Evanston, IL 60208. Phone: (847)467-3600 Fax: (847)467-3620 E-mail: r-blattberg@kellogg.northwestern.edu • URL: http://www.kellogg.northwestern.edu • Conducts research related to retail marketing and management.

Center for Retailing Studies. Texas A & M University, Department of Marketing, 4112 TAMU, College Station, TX 77843-4112. Phone: (979)845-0325 Fax: (979)845-5230 E-mail: d-szymanski@tamu.edu • URL: http://www.crstamu.org • Research areas include retailing issues and consumer economics.

STATISTICS SOURCES

Annual Benchmark Report for Retail Trade and Food Services...A Detailed Summary of Retail Sales, Purchases, Accounts Receivable, Inventories, and Food Service Sales. Available from U. S. Government Printing Office. • Annual. $13.00. Issued by the U.S. Census Bureau. Provides detailed annual and monthly retail statistics for the most recent 10 years. Includes data for various kinds of retail outlets, including automobiles, furniture, appliances, building supplies, grocery stores, drug stores, gasoline stations, clothing, sporting goods, department stores, and restaurants.

Business Statistics of the United States. Linz Audain and Cornelia J. Strawser. Bernan Associates. • Annual. $147.00. Based on *Business Statistics,* formerly issue by the Bureau of Economic Analysis, U. S. Department of Commerce. Provides basic data for a wide variety of U. S. industries, services, and economic indicators. Most statistics are shown annually for 30 years and monthly for the most recent four years.

Demographics USA: County Edition. Trade Dimensions. • Annual. $435.00. Contains 200 statistical series for each of 3,000 counties. Includes population, household income, employment, retail sales, and consumer expenditures. Also provides Effective Buying Income, Buying Power Index, and data summaries by Metro Market, Media Market, and State. (CD-ROM version is available.).

Demographics USA: ZIP Edition. Trade Dimensions. • Annual. $435.00. Contains 50 statistical series for each of 40,000 ZIP codes. Includes population, household income, employment, retail sales, and consumer expenditures. Also provides Effective Buying Income, Business Characteristics, and data summaries by state, region, and the first three digits of ZIP codes. (CD-ROM version is available.).

Encyclopedia of American Industries. Gale Cengage Learning. • 2000. $560.00. Third edition. Two volumes. $280.00 per volume. Volume one is *Manufacturing Industries* and volume two is *Service and Non-Manufacturing Industries.* Provides the history, development, and recent status of approximately 1,000 industries. Includes statistical graphs, with industry and general indexes.

Manufacturing and Distribution USA. Gale Cengage Learning. • 2002. $395.00. Second edition. Three volumes. Presents statistics and projections relating to economic activity in more than 500 business classifications.

Retail Trade International. Gale Cengage Learning. • 2002. $1,990.00. 11th edition. Eight volumes. Published by Euromonitor. Presents comprehensive data on retail trends in 52 countries. Includes textual analysis and profiles of major retailers. Covers Europe, Asia, the Middle East, Africa and the Americas.

Standard & Poor's Industry Surveys. Standard & Poor's. • Semiannual. $1,800.00. Two looseleaf volumes. Includes monthly *Supplements.* Provides detailed, individual surveys of 52 major industry groups. Each survey is revised on a semiannual basis. Also includes "Monthly Investment Review" (industry group investment analysis) and monthly "Trends & Projections" (economic analysis).

Survey of Current Business. Available from U. S. Government Printing Office. • Monthly. $63.00 per year. Issued by Bureau of Economic Analysis, U. S. Department of Commerce. Presents a wide variety of business and economic data.

U. S. Industry Profiles: The Leading 100. Gale Cengage Learning. • 1998. $130.00. Second edition. Contains detailed profiles, with statistics, of 100 industries in the areas of manufacturing, construction, transportation, wholesale trade, retail trade, and entertainment.

ULI Market Profiles: North America. Urban Land Institute. • Annual. Members, $249.95; non-members, $299.95. Provides real estate marketing data for residential, retail, office, and industrial sectors. Covers 76 U. S. metropolitan areas and 13 major foreign metropolitan areas.

United States Census of Retail Trade. U.S. Bureau of the Census. • Quinquennial.

WEFA Industrial Monitor. John Wiley and Sons, Inc. • Annual. $65.00. Prepared by industry analysts at WEFA, an economic forecasting and consulting firm (originally Wharton Econometric Forecasting Associates). Contains discussions of the outlook for major U. S. industries, with many 10-year forecasts (WEFA Web site is http://www.wefa.com).

TRADE/PROFESSIONAL ASSOCIATIONS

International Mass Retail Association. 1700 N. Moore St., Suite 2250, Arlington, VA 22209. Phone: (703)841-2300 Fax: (703)841-1184 E-mail: klasu@imra.org • URL: http://www.imra.org • Formerly National Mass Retailing Institute.

National Retail Federation. 325 7th St. NW, Ste. 1100, Washington, DC 20004. Phone: 800-673-4692 or (202)783-7971 Fax: (202)737-2849 E-mail: mullint@nrf.com • URL: http://www.nrf.com • Represents state retail associations, several dozen national retail associations, as well as large and small corporate members representing the breadth and diversity of the retail industry's establishment and employees. Conducts informational and educational conferences related to all phases of retailing including financial planning and cash management, taxation, economic forecasting, expense planning, shortage control, credit, electronic data processing, telecommunications, merchandise management, buying, traffic, security, supply, materials handling, store planning and construction, personnel administration, recruitment and training, and advertising and display.

OTHER SOURCES

Key Note Market Report: Home Shopping. Jupitermedia. • 2001. $400.00. Market research report. Covers "interactive retailing," mainly through the Internet and television, with predictions of future trends. Formerly *Key Note Report: Home Shopping.*

Shopping Center and Store Leases. American Lawyer Media, Inc. • Looseleaf. $195.00. Two volumes. Updated as needed. Provides analysis of retail leases, financing, construction issues, insurance, taxation, bankruptcy, and condemnation of property. Includes detailed information about the shopping-center business and fast-food restaurants, with many examples of lease clauses. (Law Journal Press).

RETAILERS, COMPUTER

See: COMPUTER RETAILING

RETAILERS, OFF-PRICE

See: DISCOUNT HOUSES

RETIREE MARKET

See: MATURE CONSUMER MARKET

RETIREMENT

See also: EMPLOYMENT OF OLDER WORKERS; MATURE CONSUMER MARKET; PENSIONS; RETIREMENT COMMUNITIES; SOCIAL SECURITY

GENERAL WORKS

Consumer Reports Money Book: How to Get It, Save It, and Spend It Wisely. Janet Bamford and others. Consumers Union of the United States, Inc. • 2000. $19.95. Third edition. Covers budgeting, retirement planning, bank accounts, insurance, and other personal finance topics.

Don't Die Broke: How to Turn Your Retirement Savings into Lasting Income. Margaret A. Malaspina. Bloomberg. • 1999. $21.95. Provides advice on such matters as retirement portfolio asset allocation and retirement spending accounts. (Bloomberg Personal Bookshelf Series).

Financial Planning for the Utterly Confused. Joel Lerner. McGraw-Hill. • 1998. $12.95. Fifth edition. Covers annuities, certificates of deposit, bonds, mutual funds, insurance, home ownership, retirement, social security, wills, etc.

Fundamentals of Employee Benefit Programs. Employee Benefit Research Institute. • 1996. $49.95. Fifth edition. Provides basic explanation of employee benefit programs in both the private and public sectors, including health insurance, pension plans, retirement planning, social security, and long-term care insurance.

Smart Money Guide to Long-Term Investing: How to Build Real Wealth for Retirement and Other Future Goals. Nellie S. Huang and Peter Finch. John Wiley and Sons, Inc. • 2002. $24.95. The authors are associated with *Smart Money* magazine. Their book emphsizes the importance of effective asset allocation through the years and recommends specific stock and bond mutual funds for retirement, including "The Best and Worst Funds for Your 401(k).".

Smart Questions to Ask Your Financial Advisers. Lynn Brenner. Bloomberg. • 1997. $19.95. Provides practical advice on how to deal with financial planners, stockbrokers, insurance agents, and lawyers. Some of the areas covered are investments, estate planning, tax planning, house buying, prenuptial agreements, divorce arrangements, loss of a job, and retirement. (Bloomberg Personal Bookshelf Series).

Vanguard Retirement Investing Guide: Charting Your Course to a Secure Retirement. McGraw-Hill. • 1995. $24.95. Second edition. Covers saving and investing for future retirement. Topics include goal

setting, investment fundamentals, mutual funds, asset allocation, defined contribution retirement savings plans, social security, and retirement savings strategies. Includes glossary and worksheet for retirement saving.

ABSTRACTS AND INDEXES

Abstracts in Social Gerentology: Current Literature on Aging. National Council on the Aging. Sage Publications, Inc. • Quarterly. Individuals, $542.00 per year. Formerly *Current Literature on Aging.*

ALMANACS AND YEARBOOKS

Older Americans Information Directory. Grey House Publshing, Inc. • 2002. $165.00. Fourth edition. Presents articles (text) and sources of information on a wide variety of aging and retirement topics. Includes an index to personal names, organizations, and subjects.

CD-ROM DATABASES

Authority Tax and Estate Planning Library. LexisNexis/Matthew Bender. • Periodic revisions. Price on request. CD-ROM contains updated full text of *Bender's Payroll Tax Guide, Depreciation Handbook, Federal Income Taxation of Corporations, Tax Planning for Corporations, Modern Estate Planning, Planning for Large Estates, Murphy's Will Clauses, Tax & Estate Planning for the Elderly,* and 12 other Matthew Bender publications. The Internal Revenue Code is also included.

Magazine Index Plus. Gale Cengage Learning. • Monthly. $4,000.00 per year (includes InfoTrac workstation). Provides full text on CD-ROM for about 100 popular, general interest magazines and indexing for 300 others. Includes special indexing of reviews and product evaluations. Time period is 1980 to date.

DIRECTORIES

How to Save on Prescription Drugs: The AIER Guide to Prescription Drug Assistance Programs for Seniors. Kerry A. Lynch. American Institute for Economic Research. • 2003. $5.00. Contains a state-by-state directory of 39 state assistance programs offering prescription drug coverage, usually for low-income residents age 65 or older. Provides phone numbers, websites, coverage, eligibility details, and "How it works" for each state. A separate section describes five drug company discount cards. (Economic Education Bulletin.).

Older Americans Information Directory. Grey House Publishing. • Covers: Information on national and state organizations, government agencies, health, research centers, libraries and information Centers, print and electronic media, disability aids and assistive devices, assisted living centers and independent living facilities, legal resources, continuing education programs, and travel information; for and about older Americans.

ENCYCLOPEDIAS AND DICTIONARIES

Encyclopedia of Aging. David J. Ekerdt, editor. Available from Gale Cengage Learning. • 2002. $450.00. Four volumes. Published by Macmillan Reference USA. Includes articles relating to the financial aspects of aging, such as housing, long-term care insurance, pensions, social security, individual retirement accounts, savings, and retirement planning.

FINANCIAL RATIOS

Financial Planning for Older Clients. James E. Pearman. CCH, Inc. • 2000. $49.00. Covers income sources, social security, Medicare, Medicaid, investment planning, estate planning, and other retirement-related topics. Edited for accountants, attorneys, and other financial advisors. (Solutions for Professional Advisors Series).

HANDBOOKS AND MANUALS

ERISA: The Law and the Code (Employee Retirement Income Security Act). Janet K. Song and

Michael G. Kushner. BNA, Inc. • Annual. $105.00. The Employee Retirement Income Security Act, as amended, withrelevant provisions of the Internal Revenue Code.

Estate and Retirement Planning Answer Book. William D. Mitchell. Aspen Publishers, Inc. • 2000. $145.00. Third edition. Basic questions and answers by a lawyer.

How to Build Wealth with Tax-Sheltered Investments. Kerry Anne Lynch. American Institute for Economic Research. • 2000. $6.00. Provides practical information on conservative tax shelters, including defined-contribution pension plans, individual retirement accounts, Keogh plans, U. S. savings bonds, municipal bonds, and various kinds of annuities: deferred, variable-rate, immediate, and foreign-currency. (Economic Education Bulletin.).

Individual Retirement Account Answer Book. Donald R. Levy and others. Aspen Publishers, Inc. • 2002. $195.00. Ninth edition. Periodic supplementation available. Questions and answers include information about contributions, distributions, rollovers, Roth IRAs, SIMPLE IRAs (Savings Incentive Match Plans for Employees), Education IRAs, and SEPs (Simplified Employee Pension plans). Chapters are provided on retirement planning, estate planning, and tax planning.

The New Working Woman's Guide to Retirement Planning: Saving and Investing Now for a Secure Future. Martha P. Patterson. University of Pennsylvania Press. • 1999. $19.95. Second edition. Provides retirement advice for employed women, including information on various kinds of IRAs, cash balance and other pension plans, 401(k) plans, and social security. Four case studies are provided to illustrate retirement planning at specific life and career stages.

Planning for Your Retirement: IRA and Keogh Plans. CCH, Inc. • Annual.

Retirement Benefits Tax Guide. CCH, Inc. • $199.00. Looseleaf service.

Retirement Planning Guide. Sidney Kess and Barbara Weltman. CCH, Inc. • 2000. $49.00. Second edition. Presents an overview for attorneys, accountants, and other professionals of the various concepts involved in retirement planning. Includes checklists, tables, forms, and study questions.

INTERNET DATABASES

InsWeb. InsWeb Corp. Phone: (916)853-3300 E-mail: info@insweb.com • URL: http://www.insweb.com • Web site offers a wide variety of advice and information on automobile, life, health, and "other" insurance. Includes glossaries of insurance terms, Standard & Poor's ratings of individual insurance companies, and "Financial Needs Estimators." Searching is available. Fees: Free.

Small Business Retirement Savings Advisor. U. S. Department of Labor. Phone: (202)219-8921 • URL: http://www.dol.gov/elaws/pwbaplan.htm • Web site provides "answers to a variety of commonly asked questions about retirement saving options for small business employers." Includes a comparison chart and detailed descriptions of various plans: 401(k), SEP-IRA, SIMPLE-IRA, Payroll Deduction IRA, Keogh Profit-Sharing, Keogh Money Purchase, and Defined Benefit. Searching is offered. Fees: Free.

ONLINE DATABASES

Ageline. American Association of Retired Persons. • Provides indexing and abstracting of the literature of social gerontology, including consumer aspects, financial planning, employment, housing, health care services, mental health, social security, and retirement. Time period is 1978 to date. Inquire as to online cost and availability.

PERIODICALS AND NEWSLETTERS

AARP Bulletin. American Association of Retired Persons. • Description: Monitors issues and events

affecting Americans aged 50 and over. Covers medical benefits and other services of interest. Recurring features include Association news, editorials, and columns titled As We See It, Bulletin Board, Washingtonwatch, Statewatch, and Reader Forum.

AARP: The Magazine. American Association of Retired Persons. • Bimonthly. Membership. FormerlyModern Maturity.

Estate Planner's Alert. RIA. • Monthly. $140.00 per year. Newsletter. Covers the tax aspects of personal finance, including home ownership, investments, insurance, retirement planning, and charitable giving. Formerly *Estate and Financial Planners Alert.*

Financial Planning: The Magazine for Financial Service Professionals. Thomson Media. • Monthly. $79.00 per year. Edited for independent financial planners and insurance agents. Covers retirement planning, estate planning, tax planning, and insurance, including long-term healthcare considerations. Special features include a Retirement Planning Issue, Mutual Fund Performance Survey, and Variable Life and Annuity Survey.

Jounal of Finacial Services Professionals. Society of Financial Services Professional. • Bimonthly. $95.00 per year. Provides information on life insurance and financial planning, including estate planning, retirement, tax planning, trusts, business insurance, long-term care insurance, disability insurance, and employee benefits. Formerly (American Society of CLU and Ch F C Journal).

Journal of Aging and Social Policy: A Journal Devoted to Aging and Social Policy. Haworth Press, Inc. • Quarterly. $415.00 per year.

Journal of Retirement Planning. CCH, Inc. • Bimonthly. $179.00 per year. Emphasis is on retirement and estate planning advice provided by lawyers and accountants as part of their practices.

Kiplinger's Retirement Report. Kiplinger Washington Editors Inc. • Description: Offers information for the retired and soon-to-be-retired. Discusses such topics as money management, estate planning, health, travel and what's going on in Washington DC.

Older Americans Report. Business Publishers Inc. • Description: Features brief articles on legislative, judicial, and federal agency activities concerning older Americans. Covers news of developments in such areas as Social Security, social services, Medicare, programs for retirement and pension funds, research projects, and the Older Americans Act. Recurring features include book reviews and a calendar of events.

ReCareering Newsletter: An Idea and Resource Guide to Second Career and Relocation Planning. Publications Plus, Inc. • Monthly. $59.00 per year. Edited for "downsized managers, early retirees, and others in career transition after leaving traditional employment." Offers advice on second careers, franchises, starting a business, finances, education, training, skills assessment, and other matters of interest to the newly unemployed.

Retirement Letter: The Money Newsletter for Mature People. Peter A. Dickinson, editor. PBI Media, LLC. • Monthly. $49.00 per year.

Retirement Life. National Association of Retired Federal Employees. • Monthly. Free to members; non-members, $25.00 per year.

Retirement Plans Bulletin: Practical Explanations for the IRA and Retirement Plan Professional. Universal Pensions, Inc. • Monthly. $99.00 per year. Newsletter. Provides information on the rules and regulations governing qualified (tax-deferred) retirement plans.

RESEARCH CENTERS AND INSTITUTES

Center for Financial Responsibility. College of Human Sciences, Box 41162, Texas Tech University,

Lubbock, TX 79409-1162. Phone: (806)742-9781 Fax: (806)742-9784 E-mail: bill.gustafson@ttu.edu • URL: http://www.hs.ttu.edu/cfr/ • Research areas include financial preparation for retirement, financial education, determinants of financial satisfaction, risk tolerance, and the career preparation of retirement industry professionals.

Center for Pension and Retirement Research. Miami University, Department of Economics, 109E Laws Hall, Oxford, OH 45056. Phone: (513)529-2850 Fax: (513)529-3308 E-mail: swilliamson@eh.net • URL: http://www.eh.net/cprr • Research areas include pension economics, pension plans, and retirement decisions.

Employee Benefit Research Institute. Employee Benefit Research Institute. 1100 13 St. NW, Ste. 878, Washington, DC 20005. Phone: (202)659-0670 Fax: (202)775-6312 E-mail: salisbury@ebri.org • URL: http://www.ebri.org • Employee benefits in the public and private sectors, including studies on individual retirement accounts, retirement income, flexible benefits, financing health care for the elderly, health care costs, long-term care, employee benefits and federal tax policy, social security, changing benefits, and government regulation of employee benefit plans.

Retirement Research Foundation. 8765 W. Higgins Rd., Suite 430, Chicago, IL 60631-4170. Phone: (773)714-8080 Fax: (773)714-8089 E-mail: info@rrf.org • URL: http://www.rrf.org.

STATISTICS SOURCES

EBRI's Databook on Employee Benefits: What is the Promise?. Ken McDonnell and others. Employee Benefit Research Institute. • 1997 $99.00. Fourth edition. Contains more than 350 tables and charts presenting data on employee benefits in the U. S., including pensions, health insurance, social security, and medicare. Includes a glossary of employee benefit terms.

Income of the Population 55 and Older. Available from U. S. Government Printing Office. • Biennial. $23.00. Issued by the Social Security Administration (http://www.ssa.gov). Covers major sources and amounts of income for the 55 and older population in the U. S., "with special emphasis on some aspects of the income of the population 65 and older.".

Social Security Bulletin. Social Security Administration. Available from U.S. Government Printing Office. • Quarterly. $27.00 per year. Annual statistical supplement.

Statistical Handbook on Aging Americans. Renee Schick. Greenwood Publishing Group, Inc. • 1994. $69.95. Second edition. Provides data on demographics, social characteristics, health, employment, economic conditions, income, pensions, and social security. Includes bibliographic information and a glossary. (Statistical Handbook Series).

Statistical Handbook on the American Family. Bruce A. Chadwick and Tim B. Heaton. Greenwood Publishing Group, Inc. • 1998. $69.95. Second edition. Includes data on education, health, politics, employment, expenditures, social characteristics, the elderly, and women in the labor force. Historical statistics on marriage, birth, and divorce are shown from 1900 on. A list of sources and a subject index are provided. (Statistical Handbooks Series).

Statistical Record of Older Americans. Gale Cengage Learning. • 1996. $130.00. Second edition. Includes income and pension data.

TRADE/PROFESSIONAL ASSOCIATIONS

American Association of Retired Persons. 601 E St., N.W., Washington, DC 20049. Phone: 800-424-3410 Fax: (202)434-2320 E-mail: member@aarp.org • URL: http://www.aarp.org.

Institute for Retired Professionals. PO Box 248276, Coral Gables, FL 33124-2422. Phone: (305)284-

5072 Fax: (305)284-5851 E-mail: nfrye@miami. edu • URL: http://www.education.miami.edu/irp.

National Association of Retired Federal Employees. 606 N. Washington St., Alexandria, VA 22314-1914. Phone: 800-627-3394 or (703)838-7760 Fax: (703)838-7785 E-mail: hq@narfe.org • URL: http:// www.narfe.org • Formerly National Association of Retired Civil Employees.

National Interfaith Coalition on Aging. c/o National Council on the Aging, 300 D St. SW, Ste. 801, Washington, DC 20024. Phone: 800-424-9046 or (202)479-1200 Fax: (202)479-0735 E-mail: info@ ncoa.org • URL: http://www.ncoa.org • Affiliated with National Council on Aging.

Score Association-Service Corps of Retired Executives. c/o Service Corps of Retired Executives Association, 409 Third St., S.W. 6th Fl., Washington, DC 20024. Phone: 800-634-0245 or (202)205-6762 Fax: (202)205-7636 • URL: http:// www.score.org • Formerly Service Corps of Retired Executives.

OTHER SOURCES

How to Plan for a Secure Retirement. Elias Zuckerman and others. Consumer Reports Books. • 2000. $29.95. Covers pension plans, health insurance, estate planning, retirement communities, and related topics. (Consumer Reports Money Guide.).

Individual Retirement Plans Guide. CCH, Inc. • $540.00 per year. Looseleaf service. Monthly updates. Covers IRA plans (Individual Retirement Accounts), SEP plans (Simplified Employee Pensions), and Keogh plans (self-employed retirement accounts).

RETIREMENT AGE

See: EMPLOYMENT OF OLDER WORKERS

RETIREMENT COMMUNITIES

See also: NURSING HOMES

GENERAL WORKS

Continuing Care Retirement Communities. Sylvia Sherwood and others. Johns Hopkins University Press. • 1996. $44.00. Presents research based on a study of continuing care retirement communities and 2,000 residents of the communities.

Long-Term Care and Its Alternatives. Charles B. Inlander and others. People's Medical Society. • 1996. $16.95. Provides practical advice on the financing of long-term health care. The author is a consumer advocate and president of the People's Medical Society.

ABSTRACTS AND INDEXES

PAIS International in Print. Public Affairs Information Service, Inc. • Monthly. $850.00 per year; cumulations three times a year. Provides topical citations to the worldwide literature of public affairs, economics, demographics, sociology, and trade. Text in English; indexed materials in English, French, German, Italian, Portuguese and Spanish.

Readers' Guide to Periodical Literature. H. W. Wilson Co. • Monthly. $345.00 per year. Includes annual *Cumulation.* Indexes about 250 periodicals of general interest.

BIBLIOGRAPHIES

AAHSA Resource Catalog. American Association of Homes and Services for the Aging. • Annual. Free. Provides descriptions of material relating to managed care, senior housing, assisted living, continuing care retirement communities (CCRCs), nursing facilities, and home health care. Publishers are AAHSA and others.

CD-ROM DATABASES

PAIS on CD-ROM. Public Affairs Information Service, Inc. • Quarterly. $1,995.00 per year.

Provides a CD-ROM version of the online service, *PAIS International.* Contains over 500,000 citations to the literature of contemporary social, political, and economic issues.

WILSONDISC: Readers' Guide to Periodical Literature. H. W. Wilson Co. • Monthly. $1,095.00 per year, including unlimited online access to *Readers' Guide to Periodical Literature* through WILSONLINE. Provides CD-ROM indexing of about 270 general interest periodicals. Covers 1983 to date. (*Readers' Guide Abstracts* also available on CD-ROM at $1,995 per year.).

DIRECTORIES

The Consumers' Directory of Continuing Care Retirement Communities. American Association of Homes and Services for the Aging. • Irregular. $30. 00. Contains information on fees, services, and accreditation of about 500 U. S. retirement facilities providing lifetime housing, meals, and health care. Introductory text discusses factors to be considered in selecting a continuing care community.

Contemporary Long-Term Care--Fax Directory. VNU Business Media. • Covers: Approximately 900 manufacturers and suppliers of products and services for long-term patient care in nursing homes and retirement communities. Entries include: Company name, address, phone, fax.

Directory of Retirement Facilities. Solucient. • Biennial. $125.00. Provides information on more than 14,000 "senior citizen residential alternative facilities," including both assisted living settings and independent living communities.

McKnight's Long-Term Care News--Industry Directory. McKnight's Long-Term Care News. • Publication includes: List of suppliers of products and services for nursing homes, as well as general information about the long-term care industry. Entries include: Company, name, address, phone, fax, name and title of contact, e-mail, web site if available.

Provider: LTC Buyers' Guide. American Health Care Association. • Annual. $10.00. Lists several hundred manufacturers and suppliers of products and services for long term care (LTC) facilities.

HANDBOOKS AND MANUALS

How to Cover the Gaps in Medicare: Health Insurance and Long-Term Care Options for the Retired. Robert A. Gilmour. American Institute for Economic Research. • 2003. $10.00. Four parts: "The Medicare Quandry," "How to Protect Yourself Against the Medigap," "Long-Term Care Options", and "End-of-Life Decisions" (living wills). Includes discussions of long-term care insurance, retirement communities, and HMO Medicare insurance.

ONLINE DATABASES

Newspaper Abstracts Daily. ProQuest Inc. • Provides online coverage (citations and abstracts) of 25 major newspapers. Covers business, economics, current affairs, health, fitness, sports, education, technology, government, consumer affairs, psychology, the arts, and the social sciences. Time period is 1986 to date, with daily updates. Inquire as to online cost and availability.

PAIS International. Public Affairs Information Service, Inc. • Corresponds to the former printed publications, *PAIS Bulletin* (1976-90) and *PAIS Foreign Language Index* (1972-90), and to the current *PAIS International in Print* (1991 to date). Covers economic, political, and sociological material appearing in periodicals, books, government documents, and other publications. Updating is monthly. Inquire as to online cost and availability.

Readers' Guide Abstracts Online. H. W. Wilson Co. • Indexes and abstracts general interest periodicals,

1983 to date. Weekly updates. Inquire as to online cost and availability.

PERIODICALS AND NEWSLETTERS

American Health Care Association: Provider. American Health Care Association. • Monthly. $48.00 per year. Formerly *American Health Care Association Journal.*

Assisted Living Success. Virgo Publishing, Inc. • Monthly. $55.00 per year. Edited for owners, operators, and managers of assisted living facilities.

Assisted Living Today. Assisted Living Federation of America. • Nine times a year. $30.00 per year. Covers the management, marketing, and financing of assisted living residences.

Balance. American College of Health Care Administrators. • Eight times a year. Free to members; non-members, $80.00 per year. Includes research papers and articles on the administration of long term care facilities. Formerly*Continuum.*

Contemporary Longterm Care. Leisure Publications. • Monthly. Free to qualified personnel. Edited for the long term health care industry, including retirement centers with life care, continuing care communities, and nursing homes.

Housing the Elderly Report. Community Development Services, Inc. CD Publications. • Monthly. $249.00 per year. Newsletter. Edited for retirement communities, apartment projects, and nursing homes. Covers news relative to business and property management issues.

Housing the Elderly Report. Community Development Services, Inc. C D Publications. • Monthly. $249.00 per year. Newsletter. Contains practical information on designing, developing, financing, managing, and marketing residential facilities for the elderly.

Journal of Housing for the Elderly. Haworth Press, Inc. • Semiannual. $400.00 per year. Covers a wide variety of topics related to retirement communities and housing conditions for the elderly.

Ledger Quarterly: A Financial Review for Community Association Practitioners. Community Associations Institute. • Quarterly. $67.00 per year. Newsletter. Provides current information on issues affecting the finances of condominium, cooperative, homeowner, apartment, and other community housing associations.

McKnight's Long Term Care News. Thomson Medical Economics. • 16 times a year. $47.95 per year. Edited for retirement housing directors and nursing home administrators.

Retirement Community Business. Great River Publishing, Inc. • Quarterly. $15.00 per year. Contains articles on management, marketing, legal concerns, development, construction, and other business-related topics.

RESEARCH CENTERS AND INSTITUTES

Urban Land Institute. Urban Land Institute. 1025 Thomas Jefferson St. NW, Ste. 500 W, Washington, DC 20007. Phone: (202)624-7000 Fax: (202)624-7140 E-mail: customerservice@uli.org • URL: http://www.uli.org • Urban land use policy, planning, and development issues, including studies on central city problems, industrial development, new community development, residential developments of all types, taxation, smart growth, shopping center development and economics, metropolitan and urbanized area growth and development, mixed use development, and environmental factors affecting development.

TRADE/PROFESSIONAL ASSOCIATIONS

American Association of Homes and Services for the Aging. 2519 Connecticut Ave., N.W., Washington, DC 20008-1520. Phone: (202)783-2242 Fax: (202)783-2255 E-mail: info@aahsa.org • URL: http://www.aahsa.org • Committed to advancing the vision of healthy, affordable, ethical aging services for America. Formerly American Association of Homes of the Aging.

American College of Health Care Administrators. 300 N. Lee St., No. 301, Alexandria, VA 22314. Phone: 888-882-2422 or (703)739-7900 Fax: (703)739-7901 E-mail: mtn@achca.org • URL: http://www.achca.org • Formerly American College of Nursing Home Administrators.

Community Associations Institute. 225 Reinekers Ln., Ste. 300, Alexandria, VA 22314. Phone: 888-CAI-4321 or (703)548-8600 Fax: (703)684-1581 E-mail: caidirect@caionline.org • URL: http://www.caionline.org • Condominium and homeowner associations, cooperatives, and association-governed planned communities of all sizes and architectural types; community or property managers and management firms; individual homeowners; community association managers and management firms; public officials; and lawyers, accountants, engineers, reserve specialists, builder/developers and other providers of professional services and products for CAs. Seeks to educate and represent America's 250,000 residential condominium, cooperative and homeowner associations and related professionals and service providers. Aims to foster vibrant, responsive, competent community associations that promote harmony, community and responsible leadership.

National Institute of Senior Housing. c/o National Council on the Aging, 409 3rd St., S.W., Washington, DC 20024. Phone: 800-424-9046 or (202)479-1200 Fax: (202)479-0735 E-mail: info@ncoa.org • URL: http://www.ncoa.org • Members are organizations and individuals concerned with the housing needs of older persons. Provides information on the development and management of housing suitable for the elderly. Affiliated with National Council on Aging.

OTHER SOURCES

The U. S. Market for Assisted-Living Facilities. MarketResearch.com. • 1997. $2,750.00. Market research report. Includes market demographics and estimates of future revenues. Facility operators such as Emeritus, Manor Care, and Marriott Senior Living are profiled.

RETIREMENT INCOME PLANS

See: 401(K) RETIREMENT PLANS; INDIVIDUAL RETIREMENT ACCOUNTS

REVIEWS

See: BOOK REVIEWS

RICE INDUSTRY

GENERAL WORKS

Rice: Origin, History, Technology, and Production. C. Wayne Smith and Robert Dilday, editors. John Wiley and Sons, Inc. • 2002. $275.00. (Crop Science Series).

ABSTRACTS AND INDEXES

Biological and Agricultural Index. H. W. Wilson Co. • 11 times a year. Annual and quarterly cumulations. Price varies.

Rice Abstracts. Available from CABI Publishing, North America. • Quarterly. Published in England by CABI Publishing. Provides worldwide coverage of the literature.

ALMANACS AND YEARBOOKS

Agricultural and Mineral Commodities Year Book. Available from Taylor & Francis Group. • Annual.

$225.00. Published by Europa Publications. Contains descriptive product profiles, price data, export-import data, and production statistics for major commodities of the world. Includes commodity histories, uses, markets, demand trends, and information about trade agreements and key commodity organizations.

CD-ROM DATABASES

Food Science and Technology Abstracts [CD-ROM]. Available from SilverPlatter Information, Inc. • Quarterly. Produced by International Food Information Service (home page is http://www.ifis.org). Provides worldwide coverage on CD-ROM of the literature of food technology and production. Various types of publications are indexed, with abstracts, including about 1,800 periodicals. Time period is 1969 to date.

OECD Statistical Compendium. Organization for Economic Cooperation and Development. • Semiannual. $1,905.00 per year for 1 to 10 users. CD-ROM contains more than 730,000 monthly, quarterly, and annual time series for OECD countries, 1960 to date. Includes fully searchable data on agriculture, food, economic indicators, national accounts, employment, energy, finance, industry, technology, and foreign trade. Results can be displayed in various forms.

DIRECTORIES

Major Food and Drink Companies of the World. Available from Gale Cengage Learning. • Annual. $880.00. Two volumes. Published by Graham & Whiteside. Contains profiles and trade names for more than 9,800 important food and beverage companies in various countries. In addition to foods, includes both alcoholic and nonalcoholic drink products.

Thomas Food and Beverage Market Place. Grey House Publishing. • 2004. $495.00. Three volumes. Contains more than 40,000 entries covering food companies, beverages, food equipment, warehouse companies, food brokers, wholesalers, importers, and exporters. Formerly *Thomas Food Industry Register.*

INTERNET DATABASES

Business 2.0 Web Guide to the Best Business Links. Business 2.0 Media Inc. Phone: (415)293-4800 E-mail: support@business2.com • URL: http://www.business2.com/webguide • Web site presents an extensive, searchable directory of links to "the best, most informative, and authoritative web pages." Twenty main categories cover business, finance, career, company information, people, and technology topics, with thousands of subtopics, all linking to Web sites recommended by experienced business researchers. Fees: Free.

Fedstats. Federal Interagency Council on Statistical Policy. Phone: (202)395-7254 • URL: http://www.fedstats.gov • Web site features an efficient search facility for full-text statistics produced by more than 100 federal agencies, including the Census Bureau, the Bureau of Economic Analysis, and the Bureau of Labor Statistics. Boolean searches can be made within one agency or for all agencies combined. Links are offered to international statistical bureaus, including the UN, IMF, OECD, UNESCO, Eurostat, and 20 individual countries. Fees: Free.

FreeLunch.com. Economy.com, Inc. Phone: (610)696-8700 Fax: (610)696-1678 • URL: http://www.freelunch.com • Web site provides free access to more than 1.5 million economic and financial data series, covering industry, demographics, labor markets, prices, retail sales, government spending, trade, interest rates, housing starts, the stock market, and many other topics. Data is available for various time periods in either chart or table form. Searching is offered. Fees: Free, but registration required. Economy.com, Inc. also offers fee-based economic

analysis at *The Dismal Scientist* site (http://www.dismal.com).

USDA. United States Department of Agriculture. Phone: (202)720-2791 E-mail: agsec@usda.gov • URL: http://www.usda.gov • The USDA home page has six sections: News and Information; What's New; About USDA; Agencies; Opportunities; Search and Help. Keyword searching is offered from the USDA home page and from various individual agency home pages. Agencies are the Economic Research Service, Agricultural Marketing Service, National Agricultural Statistics Service, National Agricultural Library, and about 12 others. Updating varies. Fees: Free.

ONLINE DATABASES

CAB Abstracts. CAB Publishing North America. • Contains 46 specialized abstract collections covering over 10,000 journals and monographs in the areas of agriculture, horticulture, forest products, farm products, nutrition, dairy science, poultry, grains, animal health, entomology, etc. Time period is 1972 to date, with monthly updates. Inquire as to online cost and availability. *CAB Abstracts on CD-ROM* also available, with annual updating.

Food Science and Technology Abstracts [online]. IFIS North American Desk. • Produced by International Food Information Service. Provides about 500,000 online citations, with abstracts, to the international literature of food science, technology, commodities, engineering, and processing. Approximately 2,000 periodicals are covered. Time period is 1969 to date, with monthly updates. Inquire as to online cost and availability.

PERIODICALS AND NEWSLETTERS

Rice Farming. Vance Publishing Corp. • Six times a year. $30.00 per year.

Rice Journal: For Commerical Growers of Rice and Related Agribusiness. SpecComm International, Inc. • Seven times a year. $15.00 per year.

STATISTICS SOURCES

Agricultural Statistics. Available from U. S. Government Printing Office. • Annual. $38.00. Produced by the National Agricultural Statistics Service, U. S. Department of Agriculture. Provides a wide variety of statistical data relating to agricultural production, supplies, consumption, prices/price-supports, foreign trade, costs, and returns, as well as farm labor, loans, income, and population. In many cases, historical data is shown annually for 10 years. In addition to farm data, includes detailed fishery statistics.

Business Statistics of the United States. Linz Audain and Cornelia J. Strawser. Bernan Associates. • Annual. $147.00. Based on *Business Statistics,* formerly issue by the Bureau of Economic Analysis, U. S. Department of Commerce. Provides basic data for a wide variety of U. S. industries, services, and economic indicators. Most statistics are shown annually for 30 years and monthly for the most recent four years.

FAO Production Yearbook. Available from Bernan Associates. • Annual. $45.00. Published by the Food and Agriculture Organization (http://www.fao.org). Contains worldwide data on agriculture, land use, farm crops, livestock, and agricultural prices.

FAO Quarterly Bulletin of Statistics. Food and Agriculture Organization of the United Nations. Available from UNIPUB. • Quarterly. $20.00 per year. Provides international data on agricultural production, trade, and prices, covering the major commodities of many countries. Text in English, French, and Spanish. Formerly *FAO Monthly Bulletin of Statistics.*

FAO Trade Yearbook. Available from Bernan Associates. • Annual. $45.00. Published by the Food and Agriculture Organization (http://www.fao.org). Provides extensive worldwide data on exports and imports of agricultural commodities, fertilizers, tractors, and pesticides. Includes more than 130 tables of detailed statistics.

Survey of Current Business. Available from U. S. Government Printing Office. • Monthly. $63.00 per year. Issued by Bureau of Economic Analysis, U. S. Department of Commerce. Presents a wide variety of business and economic data.

WEFA Industrial Monitor. John Wiley and Sons, Inc. • Annual. $65.00. Prepared by industry analysts at WEFA, an economic forecasting and consulting firm (originally Wharton Econometric Forecasting Associates). Contains discussions of the outlook for major U. S. industries, with many 10-year forecasts (WEFA Web site is http://www.wefa.com).

World Food Data and Statistics. Euromonitor International. • 2004. $650.00. Provides five-year data for a wide variety of food products in 52 countries. Includes market size, consumer expenditures, price indicators, and retail distribution data for many kinds of meat, fish, fruits, vegetables, dairy products, baked goods, condiments, canned food, and frozen food.

World Trade Annual. United Nations Statistical Office. Walker and Co. • Annual. Prices vary.

TRADE/PROFESSIONAL ASSOCIATIONS

Rice Millers' Association. 4301 N Fairfax Dr., Ste. 425, 4301 N Fairfax Dr., Ste. 425, Arlington, VA 22203. Phone: (703)236-2300 Fax: (703)236-2301 E-mail: riceinfo@usarice.com • URL: http://www.usarice.com • Represents Independent and farmer-cooperative rice milling operators. Provides economic and statistical information on production, milling, and distribution of rice. Promotes research aimed at new uses for rice products and improvements in processing, packaging, storing, and distributing rice. Maintains liaison with U.S. and foreign government agencies, congress, and foreign buyers of U.S. rice.

RIFLES

See: FIREARMS INDUSTRY

RISK MANAGEMENT

See also: INSURANCE

GENERAL WORKS

Asset Allocation: Balancing Financial Risk. Roger C. Gibson. McGraw-Hill. • 2000. $55.00. Third edition. Provides a scholarly discussion of the fine points of investment asset allocation and financial risk management.

Fundamentals of Risk and Insurance. Emmett J. Vaughan and Therese J. Vaughan. John Wiley and Sons, Inc. • 2002. $115.95. Ninth edition.

The New Financial Order: Risk in the 21st Century. Robert J. Shiller. Princeton University Press. • 2003. $29.95. By the author of *Irrational Exuberance* (2000). Recommends that risk management schemes be developed for application to the risks of everyday life, as in such chapters as "Insurance for Livelihoods and Home Values," "Inequality Insurance: Protecting the Distribution of Income," and "Intergenerational Social Security: Sharing Risks Between Young and Old.".

ABSTRACTS AND INDEXES

Insurance Periodicals Index. Specials Libraries Association, Insurance and Employees Benefits Div. NILS Publishing Co. • Annual. $250.00. Compiled by the Insurance and Employee Benefits Div., Special Libraries Association. A yearly index of over 15,000 articles from about 35 insurance periodicals. Arrangement is by subject, with an index to authors.

BIBLIOGRAPHIES

Insurance and Employee Benefits Literature. Special Libraries Association, Insurance and Employee

Benefits Div. • Bimonthly. $15.00 per year. Lists a wide variety of literature in all branches of the insurance industry. Includes annotations.

CD-ROM DATABASES

OECD Statistical Compendium. Organization for Economic Cooperation and Development. • Semiannual. $1,905.00 per year for 1 to 10 users. CD-ROM contains more than 730,000 monthly, quarterly, and annual time series for OECD countries, 1960 to date. Includes fully searchable data on agriculture, food, economic indicators, national accounts, employment, energy, finance, industry, technology, and foreign trade. Results can be displayed in various forms.

DIRECTORIES

Thomson Derivatives and Risk Management Directory. Cengage Learning. • 1998. $247.00. Lists "over 9,000 contacts at more than 4,000 institutions." (Thomson Derivatives and Risk Management Directory 1999 Series: Vol. 1).

Who's Who in Risk Management. Underwriter Printing and Publishing Co. • Annual. $95.00. Contains specialized biographies of insurance buyers for large business and industrial firms throughout the U.S.

ENCYCLOPEDIAS AND DICTIONARIES

Rupp's Insurance and Risk Management Glossary. Richard V. Rupp. NILS Publishing Co. • 2001. $35.00. Second edition. Provides definitions of 6,400 insurance words and phrases. Includes a guide to acronyms and abbreviations.

HANDBOOKS AND MANUALS

Advanced Strategies in Financial Risk Management. Robert J. Schwartz and Clifford W. Smith. Prentice Hall PTR. • 1993. $65.00. Includes technical discussions of financial swaps and derivatives. (New York Institute of Finance Series).

Analyzing and Managing Banking Risk: A Framework for Assessing Corporate Governacial Risk Management. Hennie van Greuning and Sonja Brajovic Bratanovic. The World Bank Group. • 2003. $100.00. Provides a guide to the analysis of banking risk for bank executives, bank supervisors, and risk analysts. Includes a CD-ROM with spreadsheet-based tables to assist in the interpretation and analysis of a bank's financial risk.

Credit Risk Management: A Guide to Sound Business Decisions. H. A. Schaeffer. John Wiley and Sons, Inc. • 2000. $95.00. Covers corporate credit policies, credit authorization procedures, and analysis of business credit applications. Includes 12 "real-life" case studies.

Derivatives Handbook: Risk Management and Control. Robert J. Schwartz and Clifford W. Smith. John Wiley and Sons, Inc. • 1997. $90.00. Some chapter topics are legal risk, risk measurement, and risk oversight. Includes "Derivatives Debacles: Case Studies of Losses in DerivativesMarkets." A glossary of derivatives terminology is provided. (Financial Engineering Series, vol. 6).

Elements of Financial Risk Management. Peter F. Christoffersen. Elsevier Butterworth Heinemann. • 2003. $79.95. Includes material on the various kinds of financial market risk, simulation methods, hedging, options, and evaluation of risk models.

Handbook of Derivative Instruments: Investment Research, Analysis, and Portfolio Applications. Arsuo Konishi and Ravi Dattatreya, editors. McGraw-Hill. • 1996. $80.00. Second revised edition. Contains 41 chapters by various authors on all aspects of derivative securities, including such esoterica as "Inverse Floaters," "Positive Convexity," "Exotic Options," and "How to Use the Holes in Black-Scholes.".

Handbook of Equity Derivatives. Jack C. Francis and others, editors. John Wiley and Sons, Inc. • 1999. $105.00. Revised edition. Contains 27

chapters by various authors. Covers options (puts and calls), stock index futures, warrants, convertibles, over-the-counter options, swaps, legal issues, taxation, etc. (Financial Engineering Series).

Interest Rate Risk Measurement and Management. Sanjay K. Nawalkha and Donald R. Chambers, editors. Institutional Investor, Inc. • 1999. $95.00. Provides interest rate risk models for fixed-income derivatives and for investments by various kinds of financial institutions.

International Guide to Foreign Currency Management. Gary Shoup, editor. Glenlake Publishing Co., Ltd. • 1999. $65.00. Written for corporate financial managers. Covers the market for currencies, price forecasting, exposure of various kinds, and risk management.

McGill's Life Insurance. Edward E. Graves, editor. The American College. • 2002. $80.00. Fourth edition. Contains chapters by various authors on diverse kinds of life insurance, as well as annuities, disability insurance, long-term care insurance, risk management, reinsurance, and other insurance topics. (Huebner School Series).

Risk Management, Speculation, and Derivative Securities. Geoffrey Poitras. Elsevier Butterworth Heinemann. • 2002. $99.95. In addition to "Risk Management Concepts" and "Speculative Concepts," topics include financial futures, forward contracts, arbitrage, spread trading, hedging, and diversification. Three appendices are devoted to mathematical concepts and calculations.

Understanding Financial Derivatives: How to Protect Your Investments. Donald Strassheim. McGraw-Hill. • 1996. $40.00. Covers three basic risk management instruments: options, futures, and swaps. Includes advice on equity index options, financial futures contracts, and over-the-counter derivatives markets.

INTERNET DATABASES

Business 2.0 Web Guide to the Best Business Links. Business 2.0 Media Inc. Phone: (415)293-4800 E-mail: support@business2.com • URL: http://www.business2.com/webguide • Web site presents an extensive, searchable directory of links to "the best, most informative, and authoritative web pages." Twenty main categories cover business, finance, career, company information, people, and technology topics, with thousands of subtopics, all linking to Web sites recommended by experienced business researchers. Fees: Free.

Derivatives. Imagine Software Inc. Phone: (212)317-7600 Fax: (212)317-7601 • URL: http://www.derivatives.com • Web site mainly promotes proprietary software for the use of derivatives in risk management, but also provides free access to articles on a variety of derivatives-related topics.

ONLINE DATABASES

I.I.I. Data Base Search. Insurance Information Institute. • Provides online citations and abstracts of insurance-related literature in magazines, newspapers, trade journals, and books. Emphasis is on property and casualty insurance issues, including highway safety, product safety, and environmental liability. Inquire as to online cost and availability.

PERIODICALS AND NEWSLETTERS

Business Insurance: News Magazine for Corporate Risk, Employee Benefit and Financial Executives. Crain Communications, Inc. • Weekly. $95.00 per year. Covers a wide variety of business insurance topics, including risk management, employee benefits, workers compensation, marine insurance, and casualty insurance.

Claims. National Underwriter Co. • Monthly. $46.00 per year. Edited for insurance adjusters, risk managers, and claims professionals. Covers investigation, fraud, insurance law, and other claims-related topics.

For publishers addresses, refer to SOURCES CITED section at the back of the book.

Collections and Credit Risk: The Authority for Commercial and Consumer Credit Professionals. Thomson Media. • Monthly. $95.00 per year. Contains articles on the technology and business management of credit and collection functions. Includes coverage of bad debts, bankruptcy, and credit risk management.

CSO: The Resource for Security Executives. CXO Media, Inc. • Monthly. $64.95 per year. Edited for corporate chief security officers (CSOs). Covers a wide variety of business security issues, including computer security, identity theft, spam, physical security, loss prevention, risk management, privacy, and investigations.

D & O Advisor: Risk Management for Directors and Officers. American Lawyer Media, Inc. • Quarterly. $125.00 per year. Covers a wide range of legal topics of concern to corporate boards and key executives.

Futures and Derivatives Law Report: The Journal on the Law of Investment and Risk Management Products. Glasser Legalworks. • Monthly. $305.00 per year. Newsletter. Covers developments in regulation, legislation, and litigation concerning financial derivatives, futures trading, and options trading.

Healthcare Risk Management. American Health Consultants Inc. • Description: Analyzes specific legal cases and trends relevant to healthcare liability. Discusses malpractice, liability for patients, staff and visitor injury, injury prevention, biomedical engineering, and medical staff credentials. Also covers high-risk areas of hospitals, hospital-owned home health and physician practices, accreditation, Medicare reimbursement, physician liability, medical records, and claims management. Recurring features include interviews, statistics, news of research, guest columns, legal briefs, and commentaries.

Insurance Day. Available from Informa Publishing Group Ltd. • Three times a week. $440.00 per year. Published in the UK by Lloyd's List (http://www.lloydslist.com). A newspaper providing international coverage of property/casualty/liability insurance, re-insurance, and risk, with an emphasis on marine insurance.

Journal of Risk Finance: The Convergence of Financial Products and Insurance. Institutional Investor, Inc., Journals Group. • Quarterly. $500.00 per year. Includes print and online editions. Covers the field of customized risk management, including securitization, insurance, hedging, derivatives, and credit arbitrage.

Public Risk. Public Risk Management Association. • 10 times a year. $125.00 per year. Covers risk management for state and local governments, including various kinds of liabilities.

Quantitative Finance. Available from American Institute of Physics. • Bimonthly. $340.00 per year. Print and online edition, $765.00 per year. Published in the UK by the Institute of Physics. A technical journal on the use of quantitative tools and applications in financial analysis and financial engineering. Covers such topics as portfolio theory, derivatives, asset allocation, return on assets, risk management, price volatility, financial econometrics, market anomalies, and trading systems.

Risk and Insurance. LRP Publications. • 15 times a year. Price on application. Topics include risk management, workers' compensation, reinsurance, employee benefits, and managed care.

Risk Management. Risk and Insurance Management Society. Risk Management Society Publishing, Inc. • Monthly. $59.00 per year.

Treasury and Risk Management. Wicks Business Information. • 10 times a year. $64.00 per year. Cov-ers risk management tools and techniques. Incorporates *Treasury.*

RESEARCH CENTERS AND INSTITUTES

Center for Risk Management and Insurance Research. Georgia State University, P.O. Box 4036, Atlanta, GA 30302-4036. Phone: (404)651-4250 Fax: (404)651-4219 E-mail: rwklein@gsu.edu • URL: http://www.rmi.gsu.edu.

TRADE/PROFESSIONAL ASSOCIATIONS

American Risk and Insurance Association. 716 Providence Rd., Malvern, PA 19355-0728. Phone: (610)640-1997 or (610)644-2100 Fax: (610)725-1007 E-mail: aria@cpcuiia.org • URL: http://www.aria.org • Promotes education and research in the science of risk and insurance.

American Society of Pension Actuaries. 4245 N. Fairfax Dr., Suite 750, Arlington, VA 22203. Phone: (703)516-9300 Fax: (703)516-9308 E-mail: aspa@aspa.org • URL: http://www.aspa.org • Members are involved in the pension and insurance aspects of employee benefits. Includes an Insurance and Risk Management Committee, and sponsors an annual 401(k) Workshop.

Public Risk Management Association. 500 Montgomery St., Ste. 750, Alexandria, VA 22314. Phone: (703)528-7701 Fax: (703)739-0200 E-mail: info@primacentral.org • URL: http://www.primacentral.org • Public agency risk, insurance, human resources, attorneys, and/or safety managers from cities, counties, villages, towns, school boards, and other related areas. Provides an information clearinghouse and communications network for public risk managers to share resources, ideas, and experiences. Offers information on risk, insurance, and safety management. Monitors state and federal legislative actions and court decisions that deal with immunity, tort liability, and intergovernmental risk pools. Maintains library containing current reports from governmental units on their insurance procedures, self-insurance plans, and loss control and safety programs; and copies of policy statements, job descriptions, contractual arrangements, and indemnification clauses.

Risk and Insurance Management Society. 655 Third Ave., 2nd Fl., New York, NY 10017. Phone: (212)286-9292 Fax: (212)986-9716 E-mail: jwaldman@rims.org • URL: http://www.rims.org • Formerly American Society of Insurance Management.

OTHER SOURCES

Managing Financial Risk with Forwards, Futures, Options, and Swaps. American Management Association Extension Institute. • Looseleaf. $159.00. Self-study course. Emphasis is on practical explanations, examples, and problem solving. Quizzes and a case study are included.

ROAD MAPS

See: MAPS

ROAD MATERIALS

See: ASPHALT INDUSTRY; CONCRETE INDUSTRY

ROAD SIGNS

See: SIGNS AND SIGN BOARDS

ROADS AND HIGHWAYS

See also: TOLL ROADS

GENERAL WORKS

Principles of Highway Engineering and Traffic Analysis. Fred L. Mannering and Walter P. Kilareski. John Wiley and Sons, Inc. • 1997. $68.95. Second edition.

Safety in Tunnels: Transport of Dangerous Goods Through Road Tunnels. Organization for Economic Cooperation and Development. • 2001. $19.00. Discusses risks in road tunnels and the consequences of incidents.

Safety on Roads: What's the Vision?. Organization for Economic Cooperation and Development. • 2002. $22.00. Contains information on road safety programs in OECD countries. Describes the criteria that influence success or failure.

ABSTRACTS AND INDEXES

NTIS Alerts: Transportation. National Technical Information Service. • Semimonthly. $210.00 per year. Provides descriptions of government-sponsored research reports and software, with ordering information. Covers air, marine, highway, inland waterway, pipeline, and railroad transportation. Formerly *Abstract Newsletter.*

BIBLIOGRAPHIES

Road Construction and Safety. Available from U. S. Government Printing Office. • Annual. Free. Issued by the Superintendent of Documents. A list of government publications on highway construction and traffic safety. Formerly *Highway Construction, Safety and Traffic.* (Subject Bibliography No. 3.).

CD-ROM DATABASES

OECD Statistical Compendium. Organization for Economic Cooperation and Development. • Semiannual. $1,905.00 per year for 1 to 10 users. CD-ROM contains more than 730,000 monthly, quarterly, and annual time series for OECD countries, 1960 to date. Includes fully searchable data on agriculture, food, economic indicators, national accounts, employment, energy, finance, industry, technology, and foreign trade. Results can be displayed in various forms.

DIRECTORIES

American Road and Transportation Association Transportation Officials and Engineers Directory. American Road and Transportation Builders Association. • Annual. Members, $90.00; non-members, $120.00. Lists over 5,000 administrative engineers and officials in federal, state, and county transportation agencies.

Constructor-AGC Directory of Membership and Services. Associated General Contractors of America. AGC Information, Inc. • Annual. $250.00. Membership is made up of contractors and suppliers for general construction. Formerly *Associated General Contractors of America National Directory.*

Public Works Manual. Public Works Journal Corp. • Publication includes: List of about 3,500 manufacturers and distributors of equipment, materials, services, computers, and software used in the design, construction, maintenance, and operation of streets and highways, water systems, wastewater and solid wastes processing, and recreation areas. Entries include: Company name, address, products. Principal content is technical articles on public works topics.

ENCYCLOPEDIAS AND DICTIONARIES

Macmillan Encyclopedia of Transportation. Available from Gale Cengage Learning. • 1999. $450.00. Six volumes. Published by Macmillan Reference USA. Covers the business, technology, and history of transportation on land, on water, in the air, and in space. Includes definitions, cross-references, and 200 color illustrations.

Wiley Dictionary of Civil Engineering and Construction. Len F. Webster, editor. John Wiley and Sons, Inc. • 1997. $85.00. Provides more than 30,000 definitions in the fields of civil engineering, construction, architecture, forestry, mining, and public works. (Professional Series).

HANDBOOKS AND MANUALS

Standard Highway Signs, as Specified in the Manual on Uniform Traffic Control Devices. Available from U. S. Government Printing Office. • Looseleaf. $153.00. Issued by the U. S. Department of Transportation (http://www.dot.gov). Includes basic manual, with updates for an indeterminate period. Contains illustrations of typical standard signs approved for use on streets and highways, and provides information on dimensions and placement of symbols.

INTERNET DATABASES

Business 2.0 Web Guide to the Best Business Links. Business 2.0 Media Inc. Phone: (415)293-4800 E-mail: support@business2.com • URL: http://www.business2.com/webguide • Web site presents an extensive, searchable directory of links to "the best, most informative, and authoritative web pages." Twenty main categories cover business, finance, career, company information, people, and technology topics, with thousands of subtopics, all linking to Web sites recommended by experienced business researchers. Fees: Free.

Fedstats. Federal Interagency Council on Statistical Policy. Phone: (202)395-7254 • URL: http://www.fedstats.gov • Web site features an efficient search facility for full-text statistics produced by more than 100 federal agencies, including the Census Bureau, the Bureau of Economic Analysis, and the Bureau of Labor Statistics. Boolean searches can be made within one agency or for all agencies combined. Links are offered to international statistical bureaus, including the UN, IMF, OECD, UNESCO, Eurostat, and 20 individual countries. Fees: Free.

FreeLunch.com. Economy.com, Inc. Phone: (610)696-8700 Fax: (610)696-1678 • URL: http://www.freelunch.com • Web site provides free access to more than 1.5 million economic and financial data series, covering industry, demographics, labor markets, prices, retail sales, government spending, trade, interest rates, housing starts, the stock market, and many other topics. Data is available for various time periods in either chart or table form. Searching is offered. Fees: Free, but registration required. Economy.com, Inc. also offers fee-based economic analysis at *The Dismal Scientist* site (http://www.dismal.com).

ONLINE DATABASES

PAIS International. Public Affairs Information Service, Inc. • Corresponds to the former printed publications, *PAIS Bulletin* (1976-90) and *PAIS Foreign Language Index* (1972-90), and to the current *PAIS International in Print* (1991 to date). Covers economic, political, and sociological material appearing in periodicals, books, government documents, and other publications. Updating is monthly. Inquire as to online cost and availability.

TRIS: Transportation Research Information Service. National Research Council. • Contains abstracts and citations to a wide range of transportation literature, 1968 to present, with monthly updates. Includes references to the literature of air transportation, highways, ships and shipping, railroads, trucking, and urban mass transportation. Formerly *TRIS-ONLINE.* Inquire as to online cost and availability.

PERIODICALS AND NEWSLETTERS

Better Roads. James Informational Media, Inc. • Monthly. Free to qualified personnel.

ENR: Connecting the Industry Worldwide (Engineering News-Record). McGraw-Hill. • Weekly. $74.00 per year.

Highway Financing and Construction: State Capitals. Wakeman-Walworth, Inc. • 50 times a year. $345.00 per year.; print and online editions, $490.00 per year. Newsletter. Formerly *From the State Capitals: Highway Financing and Construction.*

Public Roads: A Journal of Highway Research and Development. Available from U.S. Government Printing Office. • Bimonthly. $26.00 per year.

Roads and Bridges. Scranton Gillette Communications, Inc. • Monthly. $35.00 per year. Provides information on the planning/design, administration/management, engineering and contract execution for the road and bridge industry.

Transportation Builder. American Road and Transportation Builders Association. Heartland Custom Publishers Group. • Monthly. $50.00 per year.

RESEARCH CENTERS AND INSTITUTES

Center for Transportation Research. University of Texas at Austin, 3208 Red River St., Suite 200, Austin, TX 78705-2650. Phone: (512)232-3100 Fax: (512)232-3153 E-mail: rbm@mail.utexas.edu • URL: http://www.utexas.edu/research/ctr/.

Center for Transportation Studies. Massachusetts Institute of Technology. 77 Massachusetts Ave. Room 1-235, Cambridge, MA 02139. Phone: (617)253-5320 Fax: (617)253-4560 E-mail: sheffi@mit.edu • URL: http://www.web.mit.edu/cts/www/.

Texas Transportation Institute. Texas A & M University System, CE/TTI, Room 801 B, College Station, TX 77843-3135. Phone: (979)845-1713 Fax: (979)845-9356 E-mail: herbert-richardson@tamu.edu • URL: http://www.tii.tamu.edu • Concerned with all forms and modes of transportation. Research areas include transportation economics, highway construction, traffic safety, public transportation, and highway engineering.

Transportation Center. Northwestern University, 600 Foster St., Evanston, IL 60208-4055. Phone: (847)491-7287 Fax: (847)491-3090 E-mail: tc-info@northwestern.edu • URL: http://www.nutc.northwestern.edu/public.

Transportation Research Institute. University of Michigan, 2901 Baxter Rd., Ann Arbor, MI 48109-2150. Phone: (734)764-6504 Fax: (734)936-1081 E-mail: umtri@umich.edu • URL: http://www.umtri.umich.edu • Research areas include highway safety, transportation systems, and shipbuilding.

STATISTICS SOURCES

Business Statistics of the United States. Linz Audain and Cornelia J. Strawser. Bernan Associates. • Annual. $147.00. Based on *Business Statistics,* formerly issue by the Bureau of Economic Analysis, U. S. Department of Commerce. Provides basic data for a wide variety of U. S. industries, services, and economic indicators. Most statistics are shown annually for 30 years and monthly for the most recent four years.

Highway Statistics. Federal Highway Administration, U.S. Department of Transportation. Available from U.S. Government Printing Office. • Annual. $26.00.

Statistical Report on Road Accidents. Organization for Economic Cooperation and Development. • Annual. $20.00. Provides data from various countries on road accidents resulting in injuries or fatalities. Includes 12-year statistical trends.

Survey of Current Business. Available from U. S. Government Printing Office. • Monthly. $63.00 per year. Issued by Bureau of Economic Analysis, U. S. Department of Commerce. Presents a wide variety of business and economic data.

Transportation Statistics Annual Report. Available from U. S. Government Printing Office. • Annual. $43.00. Issued by the U. S. Bureau of Transportation Statistics, Transportation Department (http://www.bts.gov). Summarizes national data for various forms of transportation, including airlines, railroads, and motor vehicles. Information on the use

of roads and highways is included.

TRADE/PROFESSIONAL ASSOCIATIONS

American Association of State Highway and Transportation Officials. 444 N. Capitol St., N.W., Suite 249, Washington, DC 20001. Phone: (202)624-5800 Fax: (202)624-5806 E-mail: jhorsley@aashto.org • URL: http://www.aashto.org.

American Concrete Pavement Association. 500 New Jersey Ave. NW, 7th Fl., Washington, DC 20001. Phone: (202)638-2272 Fax: (202)638-2688 E-mail: acpa@pavement.com • URL: http://www.pavement.com • Contractors, cement companies, equipment manufacturers, material service suppliers, ready mixed concrete producers, consultants, trucking companies/material haulers and others allied with the concrete pavement industry. Advocates the use of concrete pavement for highways, airports, streets, and roads.

American Highway Users Alliance. 1101 14th St. NW, Ste. 750, Washington, DC 20005. Phone: 800-483-4544 or (202)857-1200 or (202)857-1200 Fax: (202)857-1220 E-mail: info@highways.org • URL: http://www.highways.org • Broad-based consumers group for American motorists, truckers and businesses. Employs lobbying, media, communications and grassroots advocacy, promotes public policy that devotes highway use taxes to investments in safe and uncongested national highway systems.

American Road and Transportation Builders Association. The ARTBA Bldg., 1010 Massachusetts Ave., N.W., Washington, DC 20001-5402. Phone: (202)289-4434 Fax: (202)289-4435 E-mail: pruane@artba.org • URL: http://www.artba.org • Promotes on-the-job training programs.

Associated General Contractors of America: Highway Division. 333 John Carlyle St., Suite 200, Alexandria, VA 22314. Phone: (703)548-3118 Fax: (703)548-3119 E-mail: info@aednet.org • URL: http://www.agc.org.

International Road Federation. 500 Montgomery St., 5th Fl., Madison Pl., Alexandria, VA 22314-1565. Phone: (703)535-1001 Fax: (703)535-1007 E-mail: info@irfnews.org • URL: http://www.irfnet.org • Road associations, private sector firms, and public sector firms in 70 countries. Encourages the development and improvement of highways and highway transportation and the exchange of technologies. Provides educational grants to select countries for graduate training through the International Road Educational Foundation.

National Asphalt Pavement Association. 5100 Forbes Blvd., 5100 Forbes Blvd., Lanham, MD 20706. Phone: 888-468-6499 or (301)731-4748 or (301)731-4748 Fax: (301)731-4621 E-mail: mcervarich@hotmix.org • URL: http://www.hotmix.org • Manufacturers and producers of scientifically proportioned Hot Mix Asphalt for use in all paving, including highways, airfields, and environmental usages. Membership includes hot mix producers, paving contractors, equipment manufacturers, engineering consultants, and others. Supports research and publishes information on: producing, stockpiling, and feeding of the aggregate to the manufacturing facility; drying; methods of screening, storing, and proportioning in the manufacturing facility; production of the hot mix asphalt; transporting mix to paver; lay down procedure and rolling; general workmanship; and related construction practices and materials. Commits to product quality, environmental control, safety and health, and energy conservation. Conducts training programs on a variety of technical and managerial topics for industry personnel. Maintains speakers' bureau and Hot Mix Asphalt Hall of Fame.

The Road Information Program. 1726 M St. NW, Ste. 401, Washington, DC 20036-4521. Phone:

(202)466-6706 Fax: (202)785-4722 E-mail: trip@ tripnet.org • URL: http://www.tripnet.org • Conducts public education programs for the highway industry. Promotes transportation policies that relieve traffic congestion, improve air quality, make highway travel safer and enhance economic productivity.

ROADS, TOLL

See: TOLL ROADS

ROBOTS

See also: ARTIFICIAL INTELLIGENCE; AUTOMATION; MACHINE VISION

GENERAL WORKS

Foundations of Robotics: Analysis and Control. Tsuneo Yoshikawa. MIT Press. • 1990. $52.95.

Fundamentals of Robotics. David D. Ardayfio. Marcel Dekker, Inc. • 1987. $75.00. (Mechanical Engineering Series: Vol. 57).

ABSTRACTS AND INDEXES

Applied Science and Technology Index. H. W. Wilson Co. • 11 times a year. Quarterly and annual cumulations. Price varies. Indexes a wide variety of English language technical, industrial, and engineering periodicals.

Current Contents: Engineering, Computing and Technology. Thomson/ISI. • Weekly. $730.00 per year. Reproductions of contents pages of technical journals. Includes *Author Index, Address Directory, Current Book Contents* and *Title Word Index.* Formerly *Current Contents: Engineering, Technology and Applied Sciences.*

Engineering Index Monthly: Abstracting and Indexing Services Covering Sources of the World's Engineering Literature. Engineering Information Inc. • Monthly. Institutions, $5,279.00 per year. Provides indexing and abstracting of the world's engineering and technical literature.

Key Abstracts: Factory Automation. Available from INSPEC, Inc. • Monthly. $250.00 per year. Provides international coverage of journal and proceedings literature, including publications on CAD/CAM, materials handling, robotics, and factory management. Published in England by the Institution of Electrical Engineers (IEE).

Key Abstracts: Machine Vision. Available from INSPEC, Inc. • Monthly. $250.00 per year. Provides international coverage of journal and proceedings literature on optical noncontact sensing. Published in England by the Institution of Electrical Engineers (IEE).

Key Abstracts: Robotics and Control. Available from INSPEC, Inc. • Monthly. $250.00 per year. Provides international coverage of journal and proceedings literature. Published in England by the Institution of Electrical Engineers (IEE).

NTIS Alerts: Manufacturing Technology. National Technical Information Service. • Semimonthly. $265.00 per year. Provides descriptions of government-sponsored research reports and software, with ordering information. Covers computer-aided design and manufacturing (CAD/CAM), engineering materials, quality control, machine tools, robots, lasers, productivity, and related subjects. Formerly *Abstract Newsletter.*

Science Citation Index. Thomson/ISI. • Bimonthly. $15,020.00 per year. Annual cumulation. Includes *Source Index, Citation Index, Permuterm Subject Index,* and *Corporate Index.*

BIBLIOGRAPHIES

Automation. Available from U. S. Government Printing Office. • Annual. Free. Issued by the Superintendent of Documents. A list of government publications on automation, computers, and related topics. Formerly *Computers and Data Processing.* (Subject Bibliography No. 51.).

Robotics: A Bibliography with Indexes. Peter J. Benne, editor. Nova Science Publishers, Inc. • 2002. $59.00. Provides citations to books on robots in manufacturing, medical research, and other fields. Includes author, title, and subject indexes.

DIRECTORIES

Assembly Buyers Guide. Reed Business Information. • Annual. $68.00. Lists manufacturers and suppliers of equipment relating to assembly automation, fasteners, adhesives, robotics, and power tools.

ENCYCLOPEDIAS AND DICTIONARIES

Concise International Encyclopedia of Robotics: Applications and Automation. Richard C. Dorf and Shimon V. Nof, editors. John Wiley and Sons, Inc. • 1990. $375.00.

HANDBOOKS AND MANUALS

Robot Technology and Applications. Ulrich Rembold, editor. Marcel Dekker, Inc. • 1990. $230.00. (Manufacturing Engineering Material Processing Series: Vol. 34).

ONLINE DATABASES

Applied Science and Technology Index Online. H. W. Wilson Co. • Provides online indexing of 500 major scientific, technical, industrial, and engineering periodicals. Time period is 1983 to date. Monthly updates. Inquire as to online cost and availability.

Globalbase. Gale Cengage Learning. • Provides more than one million online summaries of business, industrial, and economic news reports from more than 1,000 publications worldwide. Covers a wide range of material appearing in international trade journals, professional magazines, and newspapers. Time period is 1984 to date, with weekly updates. Inquire as to online cost and availability.

PROMT: Predicasts Overview of Markets and Technology. Gale Cengage Learning. • Companies, products, applied technologies and markets. U.S. and international literature coverage, 1972 to date. Inquire as to online cost and availability. Provides abstracts from more than 1,600 publications. Weekly updates.

Scisearch. Institute for Scientific Information. • Broad, multidisciplinary index to the literature of science and technology, 1974 to present. Inquire as to online cost and availability. Coverage of literature is worldwide, with weekly updates.

PERIODICALS AND NEWSLETTERS

Advanced Manufacturing Technology: Monthly Report. Technical Insights. • Monthly. Institutions, $695.00 per year. Newsletter. Covers technological developments relating to robotics, computer graphics, automation, computer-integrated manufacturing, and machining.

Assembly: Design and Manufacturing Technology for Better Assembled Products. Business News Publishing Co. • Monthly. $68.00 per year. Covers assembly, fastening, and joining systems. Includes information on automation and robotics.

International Journal of Robotics Research. Sage Publications, Inc. • Monthly. Institutions, $1,144.00 per year; includes print and online editions.

Journal of Robotic Systems. John Wiley and Sons, Inc., Journals. • Monthly. $2,075.00 per year; with online edition, $2,179.00 per year. An international journal presenting high-level, scholarly discussions and case studies on automation, taskware design and implementation of robot systems. Text in English and Japanese; summaries in English and Japanese.

Robotics and Computer-Integrated Manufacturing: An International Journal. Elsevier. • Bimonthly. Institutions, $1,098.00 per year.

RESEARCH CENTERS AND INSTITUTES

Alliance for Innovative Manufacturing. Stanford University, Bldg.02-530, Rm. 225, Stanford, CA 94305-3036. Phone: (650)723-9038 Fax: (650)723-5034 E-mail: cborn@stanford.edu • URL: http://www.stanford.edu/group/aim • Development of new products and processing. Formerly Stanford Integrated Manufacturing Association.

Center for Automation and Robotics Research. University of Rhode Island, Kirk Bldg., Kingston, RI 02881. Phone: (401)874-2514 Fax: (401)874-2355 • URL: http://www.egr.uri.edu/centers.

Center for Automation Research. University of Maryland, College Park, MD 20742-3275. Phone: (301)405-4526 Fax: (301)314-9115 E-mail: janice@cfar.umd.edu • URL: http://www.cfar.umd.edu/.

Center for Intelligent Machines and Robotics. University of Florida, Dept. of Mechanical Engineering, P.O. Box 116300, Gainesville, FL 32611. Phone: (352)392-9461 Fax: (352)392-1071 E-mail: cimar@cimar.me.ufl.edu • URL: http://www.me.ufl.edu/cimar/.

General Robotics, Automation, Sensing and Perception (GRASP). University of Pennsylvania, 3401 Walnut St., GRASP Lab., Room 301C, Philadelphia, PA 19104-6228. Phone: (215)898-5814 Fax: (215)573-2048 E-mail: betsy@central.cis.upenn.edu • URL: http://www.cis.upenn.edu/~grasp/.

Imaging and Computer Vision Center. Drexel University, 32nd and Market Sts., Room 110-7, Philadelphia, PA 19104. Phone: (215)895-2279 Fax: (215)895-4987 E-mail: icvc-support@cbis.ece.drexel.edu • URL: http://www.cbis.ece.drexel.edu/icvc • Fields of research include computer vision, robot vision, and expert systems.

Robot Vision Laboratory. Purdue University, School of Electrical and Computer Engineering, 1285 EE Bldg., West Lafayette, IN 47907-1285. Phone: (765)494-3456 Fax: (765)494-6440 E-mail: kak@ecn.purdue.edu • URL: http://www.ecn.purdue.edu.

Robotics and Automation Laboratory. University of Toronto, Department of Mechanical Engineering, Five King's College Rd., Toronto, ON, Canada M5S 3G8. Phone: (416)978-5745 Fax: (416)978-5745 E-mail: golden@mie.utoronto.ca • URL: http://www.webmail.mie.utotonto.ca/labs/ral.

Robotics Institute. Carnegie Mellon University, 500 Forbes Ave., 4121 Newell Simon Hall, Pittsburgh, PA 15213. Phone: (412)268-3016 Fax: (412)268-6436 E-mail: cet@postbox.ius.cs.cmu.edu • URL: http://www.ri.cmu.edu.

STATISTICS SOURCES

U. S. Industry and Trade Outlook. Available from National Technical Information Service. • Annual. $69.95. Produced by the International Trade Administration, U. S. Department of Commerce, in a "public-private" partnership with DRI/McGraw-Hill and Standard & Poor's. Provides basic data, outlook for the current year, and "Long-Term Prospects" (five-year projections) for a wide variety of products and services. Includes high technology industries. Formerly *U. S. Industrial Outlook.*

World Robotics: Statistics, Market Analysis, Forecasts, Case Studies, and Profitability of Robot Investment. United Nations Publications. • Annual. $120.00. Presents international data on industrial robots and service robots. Statistical tables allow uniform comparison of numbers for 20 countries, broken down by type of application, type of robot, and other variables.

TRADE/PROFESSIONAL ASSOCIATIONS

American Automatic Control Council. Northwestern University, 2145 Sheridan Rd., 3640 Col Glenn Highway, Evanston, IL 60208-3118. Phone:

(937)775-5062 Fax: (937)775-3936 E-mail: ahaddad@eec.nwv.edu • URL: http://www.a2c2.org • Control engineering divisions of: American Institute of Aeronautics and Astronautics, American Institute of Chemical Engineers, American Society of Mechanical Engineers, Association of Iron and Steel Engineers, Institute of Electrical and Electronics Engineers, Instrument Society of America, and Society for Computer Simulation International (see separate entries). Covers the field of automatic control including control of manufacturing processes, computer control, process control, navigation, and guidance.

Association for Unmanned Vehicle Systems International. 3401 Columbia Pke., Suite 400, Arlington, VA 22204. Phone: (703)920-2720 Fax: (703)920-2889 E-mail: info@auvsi.org • URL: http://www.auvsi.org • Concerned with the development of unmanned systems and robotics technologies.

IEEE Computer Society. 1828 L St. NW, Ste. 1202, Washington, DC 20036. Phone: (202)371-0101 Fax: (202)728-9614 E-mail: help@computer.org • URL: http://www.computer.org • Computer professionals. Promotes the development of computer and information sciences and fosters communication within the information processing community. Sponsors conferences, symposia, workshops, tutorials, technical meetings, and seminars. Operates Computer Society Press. Presents scholarships; bestows technical achievement and service awards and certificates.

Robotic Industries Association. PO Box 3724, PO Box 3724, Ann Arbor, MI 48106. Phone: (734)994-6088 Fax: (734)994-3338 E-mail: ria@robotics.org • URL: http://www.roboticsonline.com • Only trade group in North America organized specifically to serve the robotics industry. Member companies include robot manufacturers, users, system integrators, component suppliers, research groups, and consulting firms. Sponsors the biennial International Robots and Vision Show, develops the ANSI/RIA national robot safety standard, collects and reports robotics industry statistics.

Robotics International of the Society of Manufacturing Engineers. 1 SME Dr., Dearborn, MI 48121. Phone: 800-733-4763 or (313)271-1500 Fax: (313)271-2861 E-mail: service@sme.org • URL: http://www.sme.org/ri • Engineers, managers, educators and government officials in 50 countries working or interested in the field of robotics. Affiliated with the Society of Manufacturing Engineers.

ROCK PRODUCTS

See: QUARRYING

ROCKET INDUSTRY

See also: AEROSPACE INDUSTRY
GENERAL WORKS
History of Rocketry and Astronautics. American Astronautical Society. Available from Univelt, Inc. • Various volumes and prices. Covers the history of rocketry and astronautics since 1880. Prices vary. (AAS History Series).

Space Sciences. Patricia Dasch, editor. Gale Cengage Learning. • 2002. $395.00. Four volumes. Includes business and economic aspects of aerospace technology. (Macmillan Reference USA imprint, Macmillan Science Library,).

ABSTRACTS AND INDEXES
International Aerospace Abstracts. American Institute of Aeronautics and Astronautics, Inc. CSA. • 11 times a year. $2,260.00 per year. Includes print and online editions.

ALMANACS AND YEARBOOKS
Progress in Aerospace Sciences: An International Journal. Elsevier. • Eight times a year. Institutions,

$1,533.00 per year. Text in English, French and German.

ENCYCLOPEDIAS AND DICTIONARIES
Encyclopedia of Space Science and Technology. Hans Mark, editor. John Wiley and Sons, Inc. • 2003. $475.00. Two volumes. Covers astronomical background, physical principles, launch technology, control systems, rockets, space vehicles, space stations, satellites, space environment, and related topics.

HANDBOOKS AND MANUALS
Rocket Propulsion Elements: An Introduction to the Engineering of Rockets. George P. Sutton and Oscar Biblarz. John Wiley and Sons, Inc. • 2000. $110.00. Seventh edition.

PERIODICALS AND NEWSLETTERS
Aerospace Daily. The McGraw-Hill Cos. • Description: Reports on developments in the aerospace industry in the U.S. and overseas. Covers related political decisions. **Remarks:** Available in print, e-mail, and URL format.

Aviation Week and Space Technology. McGraw-Hill Aviation Week Group. • Monthly. $92.00 per year.

Journal of Astronautical Sciences. American Astronautical Society. • Quarterly. $155.00 per year.

Journal of Spacecraft and Rockets: Devoted to Astronautical Science and Technology. American Institute of Aeronautics and Astronautics, Inc. • Bimonthly. Members, $45.00 per year; nonmembers, $165.00 per year; institutions, $330.00 per year.

Space Times. American Astronautical Society. • Description: Discusses current topics in astronautics, Society events, national and international space programs, and related items of interest to those in the field. Recurring features include a calendar of events, book reviews, editorials, and feature articles on space exploration: past, present, and future.

RESEARCH CENTERS AND INSTITUTES
California Institute of Technology. Jet Propulsion Laboratory, 4800 Oak Grove Dr., Bldg. 180, Rm. 904, Pasadena, CA 91109. Phone: (818)354-4321 Fax: (818)393-4218 E-mail: feefback@jpl.nasa.gov • URL: http://www.jpl.nasa.gov.

Joint Institute for Advancement of Flight Sciences. NASA Langley Research Center, MS 335, 227 Hunting Ave., Hampton, VA 23681-2199. Phone: (757)864-1982 Fax: (757)864-5894 E-mail: jiafs@seas.gwu.edu • URL: http://www.seas.gwu.edu/ • Conducts research in aeronautics, astronautics, and acoustics (flight-produced noise).

STATISTICS SOURCES
Aerospace Facts and Figures. Aerospace Industries Association of America. • Annual. $35.00. Includes financial data for the aerospace industries.

U. S. Industry and Trade Outlook. Available from National Technical Information Service. • Annual. $69.95. Produced by the International Trade Administration, U. S. Department of Commerce, in a "public-private" partnership with DRI/McGraw-Hill and Standard & Poor's. Provides basic data, outlook for the current year, and "Long-Term Prospects" (five-year projections) for a wide variety of products and services. Includes high technology industries. Formerly *U. S. Industrial Outlook.*

TRADE/PROFESSIONAL ASSOCIATIONS
Aerospace Education Foundation. 1501 Lee Hwy., Arlington, VA 22209-1198. Phone: 800-291-8480 or (703)247-5839 Fax: (703)247-5853 E-mail: aefstaff@aef.org • URL: http://www.aef.org • Provides America's youth with the tools needed to educate the public and the youth in math and the sciences to help keep America's edge in aerospace technology.

Aerospace Industries Association of America. 1250 Eye St., N.W., Ste. 1200, Washington, DC 20005-3924. Phone: (202)371-8400 Fax: (202)371-8470 E-mail: neale@aia-aerospace.org • URL: http://www.aia-aerospace.org.

American Astronautical Society. 6352 Rolling Mill Pl., Ste. 102, Springfield, VA 22152-2354. Phone: (703)866-0020 Fax: (703)866-3526 E-mail: aas@astronautical.org • URL: http://www.astronautical.org • Network of space professionals, technical and non-technical. Researchers, scientists, executives, educators, and other professionals in the field of astronautics and related areas. Promotes and supports research related to the development of astronautical sciences. Offers scholarships. Participates in student science fairs.

National Association of Rocketry. P.O. Box 177, Altoona, WI 54720. Phone: 800-262-4872 or (715)832-1946 Fax: (715)832-6432 E-mail: narhq@nar.org • URL: http://www.nar.org • Model rockets. Formerly Model Missile Association.

OTHER SOURCES
Advances in the Astronautical Sciences. American Astronautical Society. Available from Univelt, Inc. • Price varies. Volumes in this series cover the proceedings of various astronautical conferences and symposia.

ROLLER BEARINGS

See: BEARINGS AND BALL BEARINGS

ROOFING INDUSTRY

See also: BUILDING INDUSTRY; BUILDING MATERIALS INDUSTRY
FINANCIAL RATIOS
Annual Statement Studies. The Risk Management Association. • Annual. Median and quartile financial ratios are given for over 400 kinds of manufacturing, wholesale, retail, construction, and consumer finance establishments. Data is sorted by both asset size and sales volume. Includes a clearly written "Definition of Ratios" and an alphabetical industry index.

Annual Statement Studies: Industry Default Probabilities and Cash Flow Measures. The Risk Management Association. • Annual. $145.00. Serves as a companion volume to the original *Annual Statement Studies.* Gives probability of default estimates on a percentage scale for more than 450 industries. Includes changes in position year-by-year for eight financial statement line items and provides percentage measures of cash flow.

HANDBOOKS AND MANUALS
Roof Framing. Marshall Gross. Craftsman Book Co. • 1989. $22.00. Revised edition. (Home Craftsman Books).

PERIODICALS AND NEWSLETTERS
Building Material Dealer. National Lumber and Building Material Dealers Association. • Monthly. $48.00 per year. Includes special feature issues on hand and power tools, lumber, roofing, kitchens, flooring, windows and doors, and insulation. Formerly *Builder Material Retailer.*

RSI (Roofing, Siding, Insulation). Advanstar Communications. • Monthly. $44.00 per year.

STATISTICS SOURCES
Census of Construction Industries: Roofing Siding and Sheet Metal Work Special Trade Contractors. U.S. Bureau of the Census. • Quinquennial.

TRADE/PROFESSIONAL ASSOCIATIONS
Asphalt Roofing Manufacturers Association. 1156 15th St. NW, Ste. 900, Washington, DC 20005.

Phone: (202)207-0917 Fax: (202)223-9741 E-mail: info@asphaltinstitute.org • URL: http://asphaltroofing.org • Manufacturers of asphalt shingles, rollgoods, built-up roofing systems (BUR) and modified bitumen roofing systems. Compiles statistics.

National Roofing Contractors Association. 10255 W Higgins Rd., Ste. 600, Rosemont, IL 60018-5607. Phone: 800-323-9545 or (847)299-9070 Fax: (847)299-1183 E-mail: nrca@nrca.net • URL: http://www.nrca.net • Roofing, roof deck, and waterproofing contractors and industry-related associate members. Assists members to successfully satisfy their customers through technical support, testing and research, education, marketing, government relations, and consultation.

ROPE AND TWINE INDUSTRY

DIRECTORIES

Davison's Textile Blue Book. Davison Publishing Company L.L.C. • Covers: Over 8,400 companies in the textile industry in the United States, Canada, and Mexico including about 4,400 textile plants. Covers mills, manufacturers, dyers, bleachers, finishers, dealers, importers, exporters, brokers, shippers, and agents for various textiles, fibers, yarns, and cordage. Also includes supplies of equipment, materials and services. Entries include: Company name, address, phone, fax, e-mail, website addresses, names of executives, description of product/service, and trade names. Mill and other production facility listings include data on equipment and capacity.

TRADE/PROFESSIONAL ASSOCIATIONS

Cordage Institute. 994 Old Eagle School Rd., Ste. 1019, Wayne, PA 19087. Phone: (610)971-4854 Fax: (610)971-4859 E-mail: info@ropecord.com • URL: http://www.ropecord.com • Represents manufacturers of natural and synthetic fiber cordage, in constructions, industry suppliers, consultants, and machinery manufacturers. Offers standard technical information and educational programs. Operates speakers' bureau. Compiles statistics.

RUBBER AND RUBBER GOODS INDUSTRIES

See also: PLASTICS INDUSTRY; TIRE INDUSTRY

GENERAL WORKS

Rubber Technology. C. Hepburn, editor. Elsevier. • 2002. $160.00. Third edition.

ABSTRACTS AND INDEXES

CPI Digest: Key to World Literature Serving the Coatings, Plastics, Fibers, Adhesives, and Related Industries (Chemical Process Industries). CPI Information Services. • Monthly. $397.00 per year. Abstracts of business and technical articles for polymer-based, chemical process industries. Includes a monthly list of relevant U. S. patents. International coverage.

RAPRA Abstracts. Rubber and Plastics Research Association of Great Britian. RAPRA Technology Ltd. • Monthly. $2,700.00 per year. Up-to-date survey of current international information relevant to the rubber, plastics and associated industries.

ALMANACS AND YEARBOOKS

Agricultural and Mineral Commodities Year Book. Available from Taylor & Francis Group. • Annual. $225.00. Published by Europa Publications. Contains descriptive product profiles, price data, export-import data, and production statistics for major commodities of the world. Includes commod-

ity histories, uses, markets, demand trends, and information about trade agreements and key commodity organizations.

CD-ROM DATABASES

OECD Statistical Compendium. Organization for Economic Cooperation and Development. • Semiannual. $1,905.00 per year for 1 to 10 users. CD-ROM contains more than 730,000 monthly, quarterly, and annual time series for OECD countries, 1960 to date. Includes fully searchable data on agriculture, food, economic indicators, national accounts, employment, energy, finance, industry, technology, and foreign trade. Results can be displayed in various forms.

DIRECTORIES

Rubber Red Book: Directory of the Rubber Industry. Lippincott. • Annual. $106.00. Lists manufacturers and suppliers of rubber goods in U.S., Puerto Rico and Canada.

Rubber World Blue Book: Materials, Compounding Ingredients and Machinery for Rubber. Don R. Smith, editor. Lippincott. • Annual. $111.00. Lists 700 suppliers for more than 8,000 rubber chemicals, materials and compounding ingredients.

Urethanes Technology. Crain Communications Ltd. • Bimonthly. $108.00 per year.

FINANCIAL RATIOS

IRS Corporate Financial Ratios. Available from MarketResearch.com. • 2002. $225.00. Published by Schonfeld & Associates, Inc. Presents 70 key financial ratios for 260 industries. Ratios are calculated from income statement and balance sheet data available from the Internal Revenue Service. Includes four asset size classes.

INTERNET DATABASES

Business 2.0 Web Guide to the Best Business Links. Business 2.0 Media Inc. Phone: (415)293-4800 E-mail: support@business2.com • URL: http://www.business2.com/webguide • Web site presents an extensive, searchable directory of links to "the best, most informative, and authoritative web pages." Twenty main categories cover business, finance, career, company information, people, and technology topics, with thousands of subtopics, all linking to Web sites recommended by experienced business researchers. Fees: Free.

Fedstats. Federal Interagency Council on Statistical Policy. Phone: (202)395-7254 • URL: http://www.fedstats.gov • Web site features an efficient search facility for full-text statistics produced by more than 100 federal agencies, including the Census Bureau, the Bureau of Economic Analysis, and the Bureau of Labor Statistics. Boolean searches can be made within one agency or for all agencies combined. Links are offered to international statistical bureaus, including the UN, IMF, OECD, UNESCO, Eurostat, and 20 individual countries. Fees: Free.

FreeLunch.com. Economy.com, Inc. Phone: (610)696-8700 Fax: (610)696-1678 • URL: http://www.freelunch.com • Web site provides free access to more than 1.5 million economic and financial data series, covering industry, demographics, labor markets, prices, retail sales, government spending, trade, interest rates, housing starts, the stock market, and many other topics. Data is available for various time periods in either chart or table form. Searching is offered. Fees: Free, but registration required. Economy.com, Inc. also offers fee-based economic analysis at *The Dismal Scientist* site (http://www.dismal.com).

ONLINE DATABASES

Business and Industry. Gale Cengage Learning. • Contains online citations, abstracts, and selected fulltext from more than 1,000 trade journals, newspapers, and other publications. Provides general coverage of both manufacturing and service

industries, including marketing, production, industry trends, key events, and information on specific companies. Time span is 1994 to date. Daily updates. Inquire as to online cost and availability. (Also available in a CD-ROM version.).

Tablebase. Gale Cengage Learning. • Provides online numerical tabular data from a wide variety of business, organization, and government sources, including about 1,000 trade journals. Includes industry and individual company statistics relating to products, market share, sales forecasts, production, exports, market trends, etc. Time span is 1997 to date. Weekly updates. Inquire as to online cost and availability. (Also available in a CD-ROM version.).

PERIODICALS AND NEWSLETTERS

Rubber and Plastics News: The Rubber Industry's International Newspaper. Crain Communications, Inc. • Biweekly. $99.00 per year. Written for rubber product manufacturers.

Rubber Chemistry and Technology. American Chemical Society, Rubber Div. • Five times a year. $300.00 per year.

Rubber World. Lippincott. • 16 times a year. $34.00 per year.

RESEARCH CENTERS AND INSTITUTES

Tlargi Rubber Technology Foundation. University of Southern California. Los Angeles, CA 90089-1211. Phone: (213)740-2225 Fax: (213)740-8053 E-mail: salove@almaak.usc.edu.

STATISTICS SOURCES

Annual Survey of Manufactures. Available from U. S. Government Printing Office. • Annual. Prices vary. Issued by the U. S. Census Bureau as an interim update to the *Census of Manufactures.* Includes data on number of manufacturing establishments in various industries, employment, labor costs, value of shipments, capital expenditures, inventories, energy costs, and assets. (See also Census Bureau home page, http://www.census.gov/.).

Business Statistics of the United States. Linz Audain and Cornelia J. Strawser. Bernan Associates. • Annual. $147.00. Based on *Business Statistics,* formerly issue by the Bureau of Economic Analysis, U. S. Department of Commerce. Provides basic data for a wide variety of U. S. industries, services, and economic indicators. Most statistics are shown annually for 30 years and monthly for the most recent four years.

Encyclopedia of American Industries. Gale Cengage Learning. • 2000. $560.00. Third edition. Two volumes. $280.00 per volume. Volume one is *Manufacturing Industries* and volume two is *Service and Non-Manufacturing Industries.* Provides the history, development, and recent status of approximately 1,000 industries. Includes statistical graphs, with industry and general indexes.

Rubber Statistical Bulletin. International Rubber Study Group. • 10 times a year. $1,800.00 per year. $250.00 per issue.

Survey of Current Business. Available from U. S. Government Printing Office. • Monthly. $63.00 per year. Issued by Bureau of Economic Analysis, U. S. Department of Commerce. Presents a wide variety of business and economic data.

TRADE/PROFESSIONAL ASSOCIATIONS

International Institute of Synthetic Rubber Producers. 2077 S. Gessner Rd., Suite 133, Houston, TX 77063-1123. Phone: (713)783-7511 Fax: (713)783-7253 E-mail: info@iisrp.com • URL: http://www.iisrp.com • Formerly IISRP.

Rubber Manufacturers Association. 1400 K St. NW, Ste. 900, Washington, DC 20005. Phone: (202)682-4800 Fax: (202)682-4854 E-mail: info@rma.org • URL: http://www.rma.org • Manufacturers of tires, tubes, mechanical and industrial products, roofing, sporting goods, and other rubber products.

RUG INDUSTRY

See: FLOOR COVERINGS

RUGS, ORIENTAL

See: ORIENTAL RUG INDUSTRY

RULES OF ORDER

See: PARLIAMENTARY PROCEDURE

RUM INDUSTRY

See: DISTILLING INDUSTRY

RURAL COMMUNITY DEVELOPMENT

See: COMMUNITY DEVELOPMENT

RURAL CREDIT

See: AGRICULTURAL CREDIT

RURAL ELECTRIFICATION

CD-ROM DATABASES
Environment Abstracts on CD-ROM. LEXIS-NEXIS. • Quarterly. $1,295.00 per year. Contains the following CD-ROM databases: *Environment Abstracts, Energy Abstracts,* and *Acid Rain Abstracts.* Length of coverage varies.

PERIODICALS AND NEWSLETTERS
R E Magazine (Rural Electrification). National Rural Electric Cooperative Association. • Monthly. Free to members; non-members, $50.00 per year. News and information about the rural electric utility industry. Formerly *Rural Electrification.*

TRADE/PROFESSIONAL ASSOCIATIONS
National Rural Electric Cooperative Association. 4301 Wilson Blvd., Arlington, VA 22203. Phone: (703)907-5500 Fax: (703)907-5511 E-mail: nreca@nreca.coop • URL: http://www.nreca.org • Rural electric cooperative systems, public power districts, and public utility districts in 46 states. Conducts activities such as: legislative representation; energy and regulatory; management institutes; professional conferences; training and consulting services; insurance and safety programs; international program; wage and salary surveys.

RYE INDUSTRY

See also: GRAIN INDUSTRY

ABSTRACTS AND INDEXES
Biological and Agricultural Index. H. W. Wilson Co. • 11 times a year. Annual and quarterly cumulations. Price varies.

Wheat, Barley, and Triticale Abstracts. Available from CABI Publishing, North America. • Bimonthly. Institutions, $1,235.00 per year. Print and online editions, $1,250.00 per year. Published in England by CABI Publishing. Provides worldwide coverage of the literature of wheat, barley, and rye.

ALMANACS AND YEARBOOKS
Agricultural and Mineral Commodities Year Book. Available from Taylor & Francis Group. • Annual. $225.00. Published by Europa Publications. Contains descriptive product profiles, price data, export-import data, and production statistics for major commodities of the world. Includes commodity histories, uses, markets, demand trends, and information about trade agreements and key commodity organizations.

CD-ROM DATABASES
OECD Statistical Compendium. Organization for Economic Cooperation and Development. • Semiannual. $1,905.00 per year for 1 to 10 users. CD-ROM contains more than 730,000 monthly, quarterly, and annual time series for OECD countries, 1960 to date. Includes fully searchable data on agriculture, food, economic indicators, national accounts, employment, energy, finance, industry, technology, and foreign trade. Results can be displayed in various forms.

INTERNET DATABASES
Business 2.0 Web Guide to the Best Business Links. Business 2.0 Media Inc. Phone: (415)293-4800 E-mail: support@business2.com • URL: http://www.business2.com/webguide • Web site presents an extensive, searchable directory of links to "the best, most informative, and authoritative web pages." Twenty main categories cover business, finance, career, company information, people, and technology topics, with thousands of subtopics, all linking to Web sites recommended by experienced business researchers. Fees: Free.

Fedstats. Federal Interagency Council on Statistical Policy. Phone: (202)395-7254 • URL: http://www.fedstats.gov • Web site features an efficient search facility for full-text statistics produced by more than 100 federal agencies, including the Census Bureau, the Bureau of Economic Analysis, and the Bureau of Labor Statistics. Boolean searches can be made within one agency or for all agencies combined. Links are offered to international statistical bureaus, including the UN, IMF, OECD, UNESCO, Eurostat, and 20 individual countries. Fees: Free.

FreeLunch.com. Economy.com, Inc. Phone: (610)696-8700 Fax: (610)696-1678 • URL: http://www.freelunch.com • Web site provides free access to more than 1.5 million economic and financial data series, covering industry, demographics, labor markets, prices, retail sales, government spending, trade, interest rates, housing starts, the stock market, and many other topics. Data is available for various time periods in either chart or table form. Searching is offered. Fees: Free, but registration required. Economy.com, Inc. also offers fee-based economic analysis at *The Dismal Scientist* site (http://www.dismal.com).

USDA. United States Department of Agriculture. Phone: (202)720-2791 E-mail: agsec@usda.gov •

URL: http://www.usda.gov • The USDA home page has six sections: News and Information; What's New; About USDA; Agencies; Opportunities; Search and Help. Keyword searching is offered from the USDA home page and from various individual agency home pages. Agencies are the Economic Research Service, Agricultural Marketing Service, National Agricultural Statistics Service, National Agricultural Library, and about 12 others. Updating varies. Fees: Free.

ONLINE DATABASES
CAB Abstracts. CAB Publishing North America. • Contains 46 specialized abstract collections covering over 10,000 journals and monographs in the areas of agriculture, horticulture, forest products, farm products, nutrition, dairy science, poultry, grains, animal health, entomology, etc. Time period is 1972 to date, with monthly updates. Inquire as to online cost and availability. *CAB Abstracts on CD-ROM* also available, with annual updating.

STATISTICS SOURCES
Agricultural Statistics. Available from U. S. Government Printing Office. • Annual. $38.00. Produced by the National Agricultural Statistics Service, U. S. Department of Agriculture. Provides a wide variety of statistical data relating to agricultural production, supplies, consumption, prices/price-supports, foreign trade, costs, and returns, as well as farm labor, loans, income, and population. In many cases, historical data is shown annually for 10 years. In addition to farm data, includes detailed fishery statistics.

Business Statistics of the United States. Linz Audain and Cornelia J. Strawser. Bernan Associates. • Annual. $147.00. Based on *Business Statistics,* formerly issue by the Bureau of Economic Analysis, U. S. Department of Commerce. Provides basic data for a wide variety of U. S. industries, services, and economic indicators. Most statistics are shown annually for 30 years and monthly for the most recent four years.

FAO Production Yearbook. Available from Bernan Associates. • Annual. $45.00. Published by the Food and Agriculture Organization (http://www.fao.org). Contains worldwide data on agriculture, land use, farm crops, livestock, and agricultural prices.

FAO Trade Yearbook. Available from Bernan Associates. • Annual. $45.00. Published by the Food and Agriculture Organization (http://www.fao.org). Provides extensive worldwide data on exports and imports of agricultural commodities, fertilizers, tractors, and pesticides. Includes more than 130 tables of detailed statistics.

Flour Milling Products. U. S. Bureau of the Census. • Monthly and annual. Covers production, mill stocks, exports, and imports of wheat and rye flour. (Current Industrial Reports, M20A.).

Survey of Current Business. Available from U. S. Government Printing Office. • Monthly. $63.00 per year. Issued by Bureau of Economic Analysis, U. S. Department of Commerce. Presents a wide variety of business and economic data.

S

SAFE DEPOSITS (BANKING)

See also: BANKS AND BANKING

PERIODICALS AND NEWSLETTERS

Bank Systems and Technology: For Senior-Level Executives in Operations and Technology Management. CMP Media LLC. • 13 times a year. $65.00 per year. Focuses on strategic planning for banking executives. Formerly *Bank Systems and Equipment.*

The Safe Deposit Bulletin. New York State Safe Deposit Association. • Description: Discusses topics on safe and sound business practice for safe deposit organizations. Recurring features include news of research, notices of publications available, a calendar of events, news of educational opportunities, Association news, current legal and regulatory changes, current practices and procedures and Q&A section.

TRADE/PROFESSIONAL ASSOCIATIONS

The American Safe Deposit Association. PO Box 519, 140 E Jefferson St., Franklin, IN 46131. Phone: 800-768-8678 or (317)738-4432 Fax: (317)738-5267 E-mail: tasda1@aol.com • URL: http://www.tasda.com • Federation of state and local associations of banks, trust companies, and other firms engaged in the safe deposit business.

SAFETY

See also: ACCIDENTS; FIRE PROTECTION; INDUSTRIAL HYGIENE; INDUSTRIAL SAFETY

GENERAL WORKS

Safety in Tunnels: Transport of Dangerous Goods Through Road Tunnels. Organization for Economic Cooperation and Development. • 2001. $19.00. Discusses risks in road tunnels and the consequences of incidents.

Safety on Roads: What's the Vision?. Organization for Economic Cooperation and Development. • 2002. $22.00. Contains information on road safety programs in OECD countries. Describes the criteria that influence success or failure.

ABSTRACTS AND INDEXES

Health and Safety Science Abstracts. Institute of Safety and Systems Management. Cambridge Information Group. • Monthly. Online edition, $850.00 year. Formerly *Safety Science Abstracts Journal.*

CD-ROM DATABASES

OSH-ROM: Occupational Safety and Health Information on CD-ROM. Available from Silver-Platter Information, Inc. • Price and frequency on application. Produced in Geneva by the International Occupational Safety and Health Information Centre, International Labour Organization (http://www.ilo.org). Provides about two million citations and abstracts to the worldwide literature of industrial safety, industrial hygiene, hazardous materials, and accident prevention. Material is included from journals, technical reports, books, government publications, and other sources. Time span varies.

DIRECTORIES

Best's Safety and Security Directory. A.M. Best Co. • Annual. Free to members; non-members, $295.00. A manual of current industrial safety practices with a directory of manufacturers and distributors of plant safety, security and industrial hygiene products and services listed by hazard. Formerly *Best's Safety Directory.*

Safety and Health-Safety Equipment Buyers' Guide. National Safety Council. • Annual. $5.00. Directory of manufacturers and distributors of occupational health, safety and environment products and services.

ENCYCLOPEDIAS AND DICTIONARIES

Unabridged Dictionary of Occupational and Environmental Safety and Health with CD-ROM. Jeffrey W. Vincoli and Kathryn L. Bazan. Lewis Publishers. • 1999. $89.95.

HANDBOOKS AND MANUALS

Office Building Safety and Health. Charles D. Reese. CRC Press. • 2004. $89.95. Covers a wide variety of topics relating to office building safety, including management of emergencies, common hazards, accident prevention, environmental health issues, and security.

ONLINE DATABASES

NIOSHTIC: National Institute for Occupational Safety and Health Technical Information Center Database. National Institute for Occupational Safety and Health, Technical Information Bra. • Provides citations and abstracts of technical literature in the areas of industrial safety, industrial hygiene, and toxicology. Covers 1890 to date, but mostly 1973 to date. Monthly updates. (Database is also known as *Occupational Safety and Health.*) Inquire as to online cost and availability.

PERIODICALS AND NEWSLETTERS

Occupational Hazards: Magazine of Health and Environment. Penton Media, Inc. • Monthly. $55.00 per year. Industrial safety and security management.

Professional Safety. American Society of Safety Engineers. • Monthly. Free to members; non-members, $60.00 per year. Emphasis is on research and technology in the field of accident prevention.

Safety and Health: The International Safety, Health and Environment Magazine. National Safety Council,. • Monthly. Members, $45.00 per year; non-members, $58.50 per year. Formerly *National Safety and Health News.*

RESEARCH CENTERS AND INSTITUTES

Center for Health and Safety Studies. Indiana University Bloomington, Bloomington, IN 47405. Phone: (812)855-3627 Fax: (812)855-3936 E-mail: crowe@indiana.edu • URL: http://www.hyper.indian.edu/ahs.

STATISTICS SOURCES

Accident Facts. National Safety Council. • Annual. $37.95.

Metropolitan Life Insurance Co. Statistical Bulletin SB. Metropolitan Life Insurance Co. • Quarterly. Individuals, $50.00 per year. Covers a wide range of social, economic and demographic health concerns.

TRADE/PROFESSIONAL ASSOCIATIONS

American Society of Safety Engineers. 1800 E. Oakton St., Des Plaines, IL 60018. Phone: (847)699-2929 Fax: (847)768-3434 E-mail: customerservice@asse.org • URL: http://www.asse.org.

National Child Safety Council. PO Box 1368, PO Box 1368, Jackson, MI 49204. Phone: (517)764-6070 Fax: (517)764-3068 E-mail: info@nationalchildlabor.org • Furnishes complete child safety education programs through local law enforcement agencies and schools.

National Safety Council. 1121 Spring Lake Dr., Itasca, IL 60143-3201. Phone: 800-621-7619 or (630)285-1121 Fax: (630)285-1613 E-mail: nrhc@nrhcweb.org • URL: http://www.nsc.org • Individuals whose professional activities are related to the safety of employees and college or university students.

OTHER SOURCES

Consumer Product Safety Guide. CCH, Inc. • Weekly. $1,166.00 per year. Looseleaf service. Three volumes. Periodic suplementation.

Employment Safety and Health Guide. CCH, Inc. • Weekly. $1,139.00 per year. Four looseleaf volumes.

SAFETY APPLIANCES

See: INDUSTRIAL SAFETY

SAFETY EDUCATION

See: SAFETY

SAFETY, INDUSTRIAL

See: INDUSTRIAL SAFETY

SAFETY, PRODUCT

See: PRODUCT SAFETY AND LIABILITY

SALAD OIL INDUSTRY

See: OIL AND FATS INDUSTRY

SALARIES

See: EXECUTIVE COMPENSATION; WAGES AND SALARIES

SALE OF BUSINESS ENTERPRISES

See: BUSINESS ENTERPRISES, SALE OF

SALES AUCTION

See: AUCTIONS

SALES CONTESTS

See: SALES PROMOTION

SALES CONVENTIONS

See also: CONFERENCES, WORKSHOPS, AND SEMINARS; CONVENTIONS; SALES MANAGEMENT

DIRECTORIES

Corporate Meeting and Event Planners. Douglas Publications L.L.C. • Covers: Approximately 11,200 corporations that hold regular, off-site meetings arranged by nearly 14,300 corporate meeting planners. Includes companies in the United States, Puerto Rico, the Virgin Islands, and Canada. Entries include: Company name, address, phone, fax; e-mail; URL; names and titles of key personnel; geographical area served; branch/subsidiary office name and address; products and/or services provided; type of business; number of meetings; months when meetings are held; number of attendees; type of facility used; whether company utilizes services of professional speakers or entertainers.

Directory of Conventions Regional Editions. VNU Business Media. • Annual. $155.00 per volume. Four volumes. Set, $285.00. Over 14,000 meetings of North American national, regional, and state and local organizations.

Trade Shows Worldwide: An International Directory of Events, Facilities and Suppliers. Gale Cengage Learning. • 2003. $355.00. 19th edition. Provides detailed information from over 75 countries on more than 10,800 trade shows and exhibitions. Separate sections are provided for trade shows/exhibitions, for sponsors/organizers, and for services, facilities, and information sources. Indexing is by date, location, subject, name, and keyword.

HANDBOOKS AND MANUALS

Guerilla Trade Show Selling: New Unconventional Weapons and Tactics to Meet More People, Get More Leads, and Close More Sales. Jay C. Levinson and others. John Wiley and Sons, Inc. • 1997. $21.

95. (More People, Get More Leads and Close More Sales Series).

INTERNET DATABASES

Trade Show Center. Global Sources/Trade Media Holdings Ltd. [Singapore]. Phone: (656)574-2800 E-mail: service@globalsources.com • URL: http://www.globalsources.com/TRADESHW/TRDSHFRM.HTM • Free Web site provides current, detailed information on more than 1,000 major trade shows worldwide, including events in the U.S., but with an emphasis on "Asia and Greater China." Searching is offered by product, supplier, country, and month of year. Includes links to "Trade Information.".

PERIODICALS AND NEWSLETTERS

Successful Meetings: The Authority on Meetings and Incentive Travel Management. VNU Business Media. • Monthly. $79.00 per year.

SALES FINANCE COMPANIES

See: FINANCE COMPANIES

SALES MANAGEMENT

See also: MARKETING; SALESMEN AND SALESMANSHIP

GENERAL WORKS

Contemporary Sales Force Management. Tony Carter. Haworth Press, Inc. • 1997. $49.95. Emphasis is on motivation of sales personnel. Includes case studies.

Management of a Sales Force. William J. Stanton and Rosann Spiro. McGraw-Hill Higher Education. • 1998. $113.75. 10th edition.

Managing Sales Professionals: The Reality of Profitability. Joseph P. Vaccaro. The Haworth Press, Inc. • 1995. $49.95.

Sales and Sales Management. Elsevier. • 1998. $34.95.

Sales Management. William C. Moncrief and Shannon Shipp. Addison-Wesley. • 1997. $130.00. Includes chapters on personal selling, organization, training, motivation, compensation, evaluation, sales forecasting, and strategy. A glossary and case histories are provided.

Sales Management: Concepts and Cases. Douglas J. Dalyrmple. John Wiley and Sons, Inc. • 2000. $101.95 Seventh edition.

ENCYCLOPEDIAS AND DICTIONARIES

Blackwell Encyclopedic Dictionary of Marketing. Dale Littler and Barbara R. Lewis, editors. Blackwell Publishers. • 1997. $38.95. The editors are associated with the Manchester School of Management. Contains definitions of key terms combined with longer articles written by various U.S. and foreign business educators. Includes bibliographies and index. (Blackwell Encyclopedia of Management Series.).

HANDBOOKS AND MANUALS

AMA Management Handbook. John J. Hampton, editor. AMACOM. • 1994. $110.00. Third edition. Provides 200 chapters in 16 major subject areas. Covers a wide variety of business and industrial management topics.

The First-Time Sales Manager: A Survival Guide. Theodore Tyssen. Self-Counsel Press, Inc. • 1994. $8.95. Provides basic information and advice for beginning sales managers. (Self Counsel Business Series).

From Selling to Managing: Guidelines for the First-Time Sales Manager. Ronald Brown. AMACOM. •

1990. $17.95. Revised edition. A practical guide to the transformation of salesperson to sales manager.

Sales Compensation Handbook. Stockton Colt, editor. AMACOM. • 1998. $75.00. Second edition. Topics include salespeople compensation plans based on salary, commission, bonuses, and contests.

Sales Manager's Desk Book. Gene Garofalo. Prentice Hall PTR. • 1996. $69.95. Second edition. A handbook covering many aspects of selling and sales management. Includes information on telemarketing, communications technology, voice mail, and teleconferencing.

Sales Manager's Handbook. John P. Steinbrink. Dartnell Corp. • 1989. $93.50. 14th edition.

What America's Small Companies Pay Their Sales Forces and How They Make It Pay Off. Christen P. Heide. Dartnell Corp. • 1997. $29.95. Provides advice on attracting, motivating, and retaining productive sales personnel. Includes sales position descriptions and "latest sales compensation figures for companies under $5 million in sales.".

ONLINE DATABASES

Management Contents. Gale Cengage Learning. • Covers a wide range of management, financial, marketing, personnel, and administrative topics. About 150 leading business journals are indexed and abstracted from 1974 to date, with monthly updating. Inquire as to online cost and availability.

PERIODICALS AND NEWSLETTERS

Journal of Personal Selling and Sales Management. M. E. Sharpe, Inc. • Quarterly. $169.00 per year. An academic journal containing peer-reviewed articles. Includes "Selling and Sales Management Abstracts" (summaries of relevant articles appearing in various publications).

Marketing Management: Shaping the Profession of Marketing. American Marketing Association. • Quarterly. Members, $45.00 per year; non-members, $70.00 per year; institutions, $90.00 per year. Covers trends in the management of marketing, sales, and distribution.

Sales and Marketing Management. VNU Business Media. • Monthly. $48.00 per year.

Sales & Marketing Report: Practical Ideas for Successful Selling. Lawrence Ragan Communications, Inc. • Monthly. $119.00 per year. Newsletter. Emphasis is on sales training, staff morale, and marketing productivity.

TRADE/PROFESSIONAL ASSOCIATIONS

Sales and Marketing Executives International. PO Box 1390, Sumas, WA 98295-1390. Phone: 800-999-1414 or (312)893-0751 Fax: (604)855-0165 E-mail: smei@smei.org • URL: http://www.smei.org • Formerly Sales and Marketing Executives.

SALES MEETINGS

See: MEETING MANAGEMENT; SALES CONVENTIONS

SALES PROMOTION

See also: ADVERTISING; MARKETING; PREMIUMS; PUBLIC RELATIONS AND PUBLICITY; SALES MANAGEMENT

GENERAL WORKS

How to Promote, Publicize, and Advertise Your Growing Business: Getting the Word Out Without Spending a Fortune. Kim Baker and Sunny Baker. John Wiley and Sons, Inc. • 1992. $12.95.

Introduction to Advertising and Promotion: An Integrated Marketing Communications Perspective. George E. Belch and Michael A. Belch. McGraw-Hill. • 1994. $69.95. Third edition.

Sales Promotion. David Horchover. John Wiley and Sons, Inc. • 2002. $14.00. (Express Executive Series).

ALMANACS AND YEARBOOKS

Major Marketing Campaigns Annual. Gale Cengage Learning. • 1999. $160.00. Describes in detail "100 major marketing initiatives of the previous calendar year." Includes illustrations.

DIRECTORIES

AMA International Member and Marketing Services Guide. American Marketing Association. • Annual. $150.00. Lists professional members of the American Marketing Association. Also contains information on providers of marketing support services and products, including software, communications, direct marketing, promotion, research, and consulting companies. Includes geographical and alphabetical indexes. Formerly *Marketing Yellow Pages and AMA International Membership Directory.*

Creative's Illustrated Guide to P-O-P Exhibits and Promotion. Magazines Creative, Inc. • Annual. $25.00. Lists sources of point-of-purchase displays, signs, and exhibits and sources of other promotional materials and equipment. Available online.

Incentive's Buyer's Guide. VNU Business Media. • Publication includes: List of 1,500 merchandise suppliers, hotels, cruise lines, airlines, and other companies that provide services to companies offering incentive travel and merchandise programs. Entries include: Company name, address, phone, name of sales contact, description of facilities (for hotels).

Premium, Incentive, and Travel Buyers Directory. Douglas Publications, Inc. • Annual. $275.00. Lists more than 12,000 firms who purchase premiums and incentives. Provides information on about 20,000 buyers of premiums, incentive programs, and travel programs for motivation of sales personnel.

PROMO Annual SourceBook: The Only Guide to the $70 Billion Promotion Industry. Primedia Business Magazines and Media. • Annual. $49.95. Lists service and supply companies for the promotion industry. Includes annual salary survey and award winning campaigns.

The PROMO 100 Promotion Agency Ranking. PROMO Magazine. • Covers: Ranking of the top 100 U.S. Promotion agencies. Entries include: Name, address, phone, financial data, client lists, rate of growth, name of CEO, and description of product/service.

ENCYCLOPEDIAS AND DICTIONARIES

Dictionary of Marketing Communications. Norman A. P. Govoni. Sage Publications, Inc. • 2003. $69.95. Contains more than 4,000 concise definitions of terms relating to advertising, sales promotion, public relations, direct marketing, and selling.

Encyclopedia of Major Marketing Campaigns. Gale Cengage Learning. • 2000. $285.00. Covers 500 major marketing and advertising campaigns "of the 20th century." Examines historical context, target market, expectations, competition, strategy, development, and outcomes. Includes illustrations.

HANDBOOKS AND MANUALS

Coupon Mailer Service. Entrepreneur Media, Inc. • Looseleaf. $59.50. A practical guide to starting a service for mailing business promotion discount coupons to consumers. Covers profit potential, start-up costs, market size evaluation, owner's time required, pricing, accounting, advertising, promotion, etc. (Start-Up Business Guide No. E1232.).

Online Marketing Handbook: How to Promote, Advertise and Sell, Your Products and Services on the Internet. Daniel S. Janal. John Wiley and Sons, Inc. • 1999. $29.95. Revised edition. Provides step-by-step instructions for utilizing online publicity,

advertising, and sales promotion. Contains chapters on interactive marketing, online crisis communication, and Web home page promotion, with numerous examples and checklists. (Business Technology Series).

The Only Sales Promotion Techniques You'll Ever Need: Proven Tactics and Expert Insights. Tamara Block, editor. Dartnell Corp. • 1996. $39.95. Covers sampling, sweepstakes, co-op advertising, event marketing, database management, and other topics.

The Perfect Sales Piece: A Complete Do-It-Yourself Guide to Creating Brochures, Catalogs, Fliers, and Pamphlets. Robert W. Bly. John Wiley and Sons, Inc. • 1994. $50.00. A guide to the use of various forms of printed literature for direct selling, sales promotion, and marketing. (Small Business Series).

Promotional Marketing. Entrepreneur Media, Inc. • Looseleaf. $59.50. A practical guide to sales promotion and marketing for small businesses. (Start-Up Business Guide No. E1111.).

Sales Promotion Handbook. Tamara Brezen-Blocks and William Robinson, editors. Dartnell Corp. • 1994. $69.95. Eighth edition. Covers licensing, tie-ins, legal aspects, event marketing, database marketing, and other topics.

PERIODICALS AND NEWSLETTERS

Database Marketer. SIMBA Information. • Monthly. $329.00 per year.

Incentive: Managing and Marketing Through Motivation. VNU Business Media. • Monthly. $59.00 per year.

Journal of Promotion Management: Innovations in Planning and Applied Research. Haworth Press, Inc. • Semiannual. Institutions, $200.00 per year.

The Licensing Letter. EPM Communications Inc. • Description: Concerned with all aspects of licensed merchandising, "the business of associating someone's name, likeness or creation with someone else's product or service, for a consideration." Recurring features include statistics, research, events, mechanics, available properties, and identification of licensors, licensing agents, and licensees.

The Marketing Report: The Best Time-Saving Information Source for Marketing Executives. Progressive Business Publications. • Semimonthly. $264.00 per year. Newsletter. Covers marketing ideas, problem solving, and new product development. Includes case histories.

PROMO: Promotion Marketing Worldwide. Primedia Business Magazines and Media. • Monthly. $65.00 per year. Edited for companies and agencies that utilize couponing, point-of-purchase advertising, special events, games, contests, premiums, product samples, and other unique promotional items.

TRADE/PROFESSIONAL ASSOCIATIONS

Association of Promotion Marketing Agencies Worldwide. 750 Summer St., Stamford, CT 06901. Phone: (203)325-3911 Fax: (203)969-1499 E-mail: apmaw@aol.com • URL: http://www.apmaw.org.

OTHER SOURCES

Idea Source Guide; A Monthly Report to Executives in Advertising, Merchandising and Sales Promotion. Bramlee, Inc. • Monthly. $150.00 per year. Lists new premiums and novelty products.

SALES REPRESENTATIVES

See: MANUFACTURERS' AGENTS

SALES TAX

See also: STATE LAW

GENERAL WORKS

Internet Taxation. Albert Tokin, editor. Nova Science Publishers, Inc. • 2003. $29.50. Several authors

discuss the controversial issue of local taxation of e-commerce transactions.

HANDBOOKS AND MANUALS

Cybertaxation: The Taxation of E-Commerce. Karl A. Frieden. CCH, Inc. • 2000. $75.00. Includes state sales and use tax issues and corporate income tax rules, as related to doing business over the Internet.

Sales and Use Taxation of E-Commerce: State Tax Administrators' Current Thinking, with CCH Commentary. CCH, Inc. • 2000. $129.00. Provides advice and information on the impact of state sales taxes on e-commerce activity.

U. S. Master Sales and Use Tax Guide. CCH, Inc. • Annual. $69.00. Contains concise information on sales and use taxes in all states and the District of Columbia.

PERIODICALS AND NEWSLETTERS

E-Commerce Tax Alert. CCH Inc. • Description: Print and online newsletter covering e-commerce taxation issues, including compliance and sourcing, e-cash implications, the Internet tax debate, and other topics.

The Journal of Taxation: A National Journal of Current Developments, Analysis and Commentary for Tax Professionals. RIA. • Monthly. $305.00 per year. Analysis of current tax developments for tax specialists.

Sales and Use Tax Alert. CCH, Inc. • Monthly. $197.00 per year. Newsletter. Provides nationwide coverage of new developments in sales tax laws and regulations.

RESEARCH CENTERS AND INSTITUTES

Office of Tax Policy Research. University of Michigan, 701 Tappan St., Ann Arbor, MI 48109-1234. Phone: (734)763-3068 Fax: (734)763-4032 E-mail: otpr@umich.edu • URL: http://www.taxpolicyresearch.umich.edu/.

Tax Foundation. Tax Foundation. 2001 L St. NW, Ste. 1050, Washington, DC 20036. Phone: (202)464-6200 Fax: (202)464-6201 E-mail: hodge@taxfoundation.org • URL: http://www.taxfoundation.org • Fiscal and management aspects of federal, state, and local government, including studies on government expenditures, the federal budget, taxation, and international competitiveness. Serves as a national information agency for individuals and organizations concerned with problems of government expenditures, taxation, and debt.

OTHER SOURCES

Manufacturers' Tax Alert. CCH, Inc. • Monthly $297.00 per year. Newsletter. Covers the major tax issues affecting manufacturing companies. Includes current developments in various kind of federal, state, and international taxes: sales, use, franchise, property, and corporate income.

Multi-State Sales Tax Guide. CCH, Inc. • $1,349.00 per year. Looseleaf service. Nine volumes. Periodic supplementation. Formerly *All State Sales Tax Reports.*

SALESMEN AND SALESMANSHIP

See also: SALES MANAGEMENT

GENERAL WORKS

Be a Sales Superstar: 21 Great Ways to Sell More, Faster, Easier in Today's Tough Markets. Brian Tracy. Berrett-Koehler Publishers, Inc. • 2003. $19.95.

Consultative Selling: The Hanan Formula for High-Margin Sales at High Levels. Mack Hanan. AMACOM. • 1999. $27.95. Sixth revised edition. How to treat customers as friends to be helped and not as foes to be overcome.

Fundamentals of Selling: Customers for Life Through Service. Charles Futrell. McGraw-Hill. • 2003. Eighth edition. Price on application. (Marketing Series).

Personal Selling: Function, Theory and Practice. R. Wayne Mondy and others. Cengage Learning Custom Publishing. • 1999. $78.95. Fourth edition. Covers buying behavior, prospecting, presentation, objections, closing, selling as a career, and related topics. Includes a glossary.

Sales and Sales Management. Elsevier. • 1998. $34.95.

Sales Negotiation Skills That Sell. Robert E. Kellar. AMACOM. • 1996. $17.95. Covers negotiating objectives, risk assessment, planning, strategy, tactics, and face-to-face skills.

Secrets of Closing Sales. Charles B. Roth and Roy Alexander. Prentice Hall PTR. • 1997. $16.95. Sixth edition. (Business Classics Series).

Selling Today: Building Quality Partnerships. Gerald L. Manning and Barry L. Reece. Prentice Hall PTR. • 2000. $115.00. Eighth edition.

CD-ROM DATABASES

WILSONDISC: Wilson Business Abstracts. H. W. Wilson Co. • Monthly. Includes unlimited online access to *Wilson Business Abstracts* through WILSONLINE. Provides CD-ROM "cover-to-cover" abstracting and indexing of over 600 prominent business periodicals. Indexing is from 1982, abstracting from 1990. (*Business Periodicals Index* without abstracts is available on CD-ROM at $1,495 per year.).

HANDBOOKS AND MANUALS

ABCs of Relationship Selling: With Act! Express CD-ROM. Charles Futrell. McGraw-Hill. • 2002. $78.00. Seventh edition. Includes CD-ROM.

Electronic Selling: Twenty-Three Steps to E-Selling Profits. Brian Jamison and others. McGraw-Hill. • 1997. $24.95. Covers selling on the World Wide Web, including security and payment issues. Provides a glossary and directory information. The authors are consultants specializing in Web site production.

Guerilla Trade Show Selling: New Unconventional Weapons and Tactics to Meet More People, Get More Leads, and Close More Sales. Jay C. Levinson and others. John Wiley and Sons, Inc. • 1997. $21.95. (More People, Get More Leads and Close More Sales Series).

How to Recruit and Select Successful Salesmen. Ashgate Publishing Co. • 1983. $99.95. Revised edition. Published by Gower in England.

Selling Through Independent Reps. Harold J. Novick. AMACOM. • 1999. $75.00. Third edition. Tells how to make good use of independent sales representatives.

Selling Through Negotiation: The Handbook of Sales Negotiation. Homer B. Smith. Marketing Education Associates. • 1988. $14.95.

Selling to the Affluent: The Professional's Guide to Closing the Sales That Count. Thomas Stanley. McGraw-Hill. • 1990. $19.95.

Successful Cold Call Selling. Lee Boyan. AMACOM. • 1989. $16.95. Second edition.

ONLINE DATABASES

Wilson Business Abstracts Online. H. W. Wilson Co. • Indexes and abstracts 600 major business periodicals, plus the *Wall Street Journal* and the business section of the *New York Times.* Indexing is from 1982, abstracting from 1990, with the two newspapers included from 1993. Updated weekly. Inquire as to online cost and availability. (*Business*

Periodicals Index without abstracts is also available online.).

PERIODICALS AND NEWSLETTERS

Journal of Personal Selling and Sales Management. M. E. Sharpe, Inc. • Quarterly. $169.00 per year. An academic journal containing peer-reviewed articles. Includes "Selling and Sales Management Abstracts" (summaries of relevant articles appearing in various publications).

Pharmaceutical Representative. McKnight Medical Communications. • Monthly. $37.95 per year. Edited for drug company salespeople and sales managers.

Sales & Marketing Report: Practical Ideas for Successful Selling. Lawrence Ragan Communications, Inc. • Monthly. $119.00 per year. Newsletter. Emphasis is on sales training, staff morale, and marketing productivity.

STATISTICS SOURCES

Dartnell's 30th Sales Force Compensation Survey 1997-1998. Christen P .Heide. Dartnell Corp. • 1999. $159.00. 30th edition.

SALMON INDUSTRY

See also: FISH INDUSTRY; SEAFOOD INDUSTRY

ABSTRACTS AND INDEXES

Oceanic Abstracts. CSA. • 11 times a year. $1,645.00 per year. Includes print and online editions. Covers oceanography, marine biology, ocean shipping, and a wide range of other marine-related subject areas.

ONLINE DATABASES

Oceanic Abstracts (Online). Cambridge Scientific Abstracts. • Oceanographic and other marine-related technical literature, 1981 to present.Monthly updates. Inquire as to online cost and availability.

PERIODICALS AND NEWSLETTERS

Seafood Business. Diversified Business Communications. • Monthly. $69.00 per year. Edited for a wide range of seafood buyers, including distributors, restaurants, supermarkets, and institutions. Special issues feature information on specific products, such as salmon or lobster.

STATISTICS SOURCES

Fisheries of the United States. Available from U. S. Government Printing Office. • Annual. $20.00. Issued by the National Marine Fisheries Service, National Oceanic and Atmospheric Administration, U. S. Department of Commerce.

TRADE/PROFESSIONAL ASSOCIATIONS

Pacific Salmon Commission. 1155 Robson St., Ste. 600, Vancouver, BC, Canada V6E 1B5. Phone: (604)684-8081 Fax: (604)666-8707 E-mail: paperboardpackaging@ppcnet.org • URL: http://www.psc.org • Formed by treaty between Canada and the United States for the Conservation, management and optimum production of pacific salmon.

SALT INDUSTRY

STATISTICS SOURCES

Mineral Commodity Summaries. Available from U. S. Government Printing Office. • Annual. $26.00. Published by the U. S. Geological Survey, Department of the Interior (http://www.usgs.gov). Contains detailed, five-year data for about 90 nonfuel minerals. Covers a wide range of statistics, including production, imports, exports, consumption, reserves, prices, tariff information, and industry employment. (Two pages are devoted to each mineral.).

TRADE/PROFESSIONAL ASSOCIATIONS

Salt Institute. Fairfax Plz., Ste. 600, 700 N Fairfax St., Alexandria, VA 22314-2040. Phone: (703)549-

4648 Fax: (703)548-2194 E-mail: dick@saltinstitute.org • URL: http://www.saltinstitute.org • Works to increase public awareness of the benefits of salt and salt products. Promotes participation in public policy as it relates to salt production, salt distribution and salt products. Fosters research in ice and snow control, agricultural feeding practices, water treatment, and salt in nutrition. Conducts public information program. Maintains Tech Data Center on salt-related materials. Sponsors industry safety contest. Compiles sales statistics.

OTHER SOURCES

Spices and Seasonings. Available from MarketResearch.com. • 1999. $2,250.00. Market research data. Published by Specialists in Business Information. Covers salt, pepper, garlic, salt substitutes, seasoning mixes, etc.

SAND AND GRAVEL INDUSTRY

See: QUARRYING

SANITATION INDUSTRY

See also: AIR POLLUTION; PUBLIC WORKS; RECYCLING; WASTE MANAGEMENT; WATER POLLUTION; WATER SUPPLY

ABSTRACTS AND INDEXES

Environment Abstracts. Congressional Information Service, Inc. • Monthly. Price varies. Provides multidisciplinary coverage of the world's environmental literature. Incorporates *Acid Rain Abstracts.*

Environment Abstracts Annual: A Guide to the Key Environmental Literature of the Year. Congressional Information Service, Inc. • Annual. $495.00. A yearly cumulation of *Environment Abstracts.*

Environmental Knowledge Base: An Electronic Bibliography Featuring Citations and Abstracts of Scientific and Popular Articles on Environmental Issues, Including Social Policy, Economics, Regulatory, and Legal Topics. Environmental Studies Institute. • Monthly. Price varies. An index to current environmental literature. Formerly *Environmental Periodicals Bibliography.*

NTIS Alerts: Environmental Pollution & Control. National Technical Information Service. • Semimonthly. $245.00 per year. Provides descriptions of government-sponsored research reports and software, with ordering information. Covers the following categories of environmental pollution: air, water, solid wastes, radiation, pesticides, and noise. Formerly *Abstract Newsletter.*

Pollution Abstracts. Cambridge Information Group. • Monthly. $1,390.00 per year. Includes print and online editions; with index, $1,515.00 per year.

CD-ROM DATABASES

Environment Abstracts on CD-ROM. LEXIS-NEXIS. • Quarterly. $1,295.00 per year. Contains the following CD-ROM databases: *Environment Abstracts, Energy Abstracts,* and *Acid Rain Abstracts.* Length of coverage varies.

DIRECTORIES

Public Works Manual. Public Works Journal Corp. • Publication includes: List of about 3,500 manufacturers and distributors of equipment, materials, services, computers, and software used in the design, construction, maintenance, and operation of streets and highways, water systems, wastewater and solid wastes processing, and recreation areas. Entries include: Company name, address, products. Principal content is technical articles on public works topics.

Sanitary Maintenance Buyers' Guide. Trade Press Publishing Corp. • Annual. $20.00. For distributors and wholesalers of sanitary supplies.

ENCYCLOPEDIAS AND DICTIONARIES

Encyclopedia of Global Change: Environmental Change and Human Society. Andrew S. Goudie, editor. Oxford University Press. • 2001. $275.00. Two volumes. Contains 300 signed articles on a wide variety of topics relating to changes in the environment and the atmosphere. Includes bibliographies and illustrations.

HANDBOOKS AND MANUALS

Environmental Engineering. Joseph A. Salvato and others. John Wiley and Sons, Inc. • 2003. $240.00. Fifth edition. Written for environmental engineers, civil engineers, environmental scientists, public health professionals, and others concerned with the technical aspects of protecting the environment. Covers a wide range of topics, including sanitation management, groundwater contamination, incineration, wastewater treatment, communicable diseases, and noise control.

Solid Waste Handbook: A Practical Guide. William D. Robinson, editor. John Wiley and Sons, Inc. • 1986. $275.00.

Waste Treatment and Disposal. Paul T. Williams. John Wiley and Sons, Inc. • 1998. $200.00.

PERIODICALS AND NEWSLETTERS

Environmental Regulation: State Capitals. Wakeman-Walworth, Inc. • 50 times a year. $245.00 per year; print and online editions, $350.00 per year. Newsletter. Formerly *From the State Capitals: Environmental Regulation.*

OSHA Required Safety Training for Supervisors. Occupational Safety and Health Administration. Business and Legal Reports, Inc. • Monthly. $99.00 per year. Newsletter. Formerly *Safetyworks for Supervisors.*

Public Works: City, County and State. Public Works Journal Corp. • 13 times a year. Free to qualified personnel. Includes *Public Works Manual.*

Sanitary Maintenance: The Journal of the Sanitary Supply Industry. Trade Press Publishing Corp. • Monthly. Free to qualified personnel.

Sludge Newsletter: The Newsletter on Municipal Wastewater and Biosolids. Business Publishers, Inc. • Biweekly. $409.00 per year. per year. Newsletter. Monitors sludge management developments in Washington and around the country.

Solid Waste Report: Resource Recovery-Recycling-Collection-Disposal. Business Publishers, Inc. • Weekly. $627.00 per year. Newsletter. Covers regulation, business news, technology, and international events relating to solid waste management.

Water and Wastes Digest. Scranton Gillette Communications, Inc. • 12 times a year. Free to qualified personnel; others, $40.00 per year. Exclusively designed to serve engineers, consultants, superintendents, managers and operators who are involved in water supply, waste water treatment and control.

RESEARCH CENTERS AND INSTITUTES

Environmental Engineering Laboratory. Pennsylvania State University. 212 Sackett Bldg., University Park, PA 16802. Phone: (814)863-7908 Fax: (814)863-7304 E-mail: blogan@psu.edu • URL: http://www.engr.psu.edu/enve.

STATISTICS SOURCES

Infrastructure Industries USA. Gale Cengage Learning. • 2001. $260.00. Presents statistics and projections relating to economic activity in a wide

variety of natural resource and construction industries.

TRADE/PROFESSIONAL ASSOCIATIONS

American Public Works Association. 2345 Grand Blvd., Ste. 700, Kansas City, MO 64108-2625. Phone: 800-848-APWA or (816)472-6100 Fax: (816)472-1610 E-mail: pking@apwa.net • URL: http://www.apwa.net • Chief administrators, commissioners, and directors of public works, city engineers, superintendents, and department heads of transportation, water, waste water, solid waste, equipment services, and buildings and grounds; federal, provincial, and state administrators and engineers; consultants and educators; associate members are equipment manufacturers' representatives, utility company officials, and contractors; student members are engineering and public administration students interested in the theory and practice of the design, construction, maintenance, administration, and operation of public works facilities and services. Conducts historical research on public works subjects and demonstrates applicability of history to current public works problems and issues through Public Works Historical Society (see separate entry). Sponsors research and education foundations.

American Society of Sanitary Engineering. 901 Canterbury, Suite A, Westlake, OH 44145-1166. Phone: (440)835-3040 Fax: (440)835-3488 E-mail: info@asse-plumbing.org • URL: http://www.asse-plumbing.org.

International Sanitary Supply Association. 7373 N Lincoln Ave., Lincolnwood, IL 60712-1799. Phone: 800-225-4772 or (847)982-0800 Fax: (847)982-1012 E-mail: info@issa.com • URL: http://www.issa.com • Manufacturers, distributors, wholesalers, manufacturer representatives, publishers, and associate members of cleaning and maintenance supplies, chemicals, and equipment used by janitors, custodians, and maintenance workers in all types of industrial, commercial, and institutional buildings. Represents members in 83 countries. Produces videos and other educational materials. Offers specialized education seminars.

NSF International. 789 N Dixboro Rd., PO Box 130140, Ann Arbor, MI 48113-0140. Phone: 800-NSF-MARK or (734)769-8010 Fax: (734)769-0109 E-mail: info@nsf.org • URL: http://www.nsf.org • Specializes in the areas of public health and environmental quality focusing on water quality, food safety, indoor air health and the environment. Develops standards, operates product certification and listings programs for products that meet or exceed public health safety standards. Maintains a worldwide network of auditors who conduct unannounced inspections of manufacturer facilities to ensure compliance and to protect the integrity of the NSF Certification Mark. Provides special research and testing services to industry, government, and foundations.

OTHER SOURCES

Environment Reporter. BNA, Inc. • Weekly. $3,166.00 per year. 18 looseleaf volumes. Covers legal aspects of wide variety of environmental concerns.

SATELLITE COMMUNICATIONS

See: COMMUNICATIONS SATELLITES

SAVINGS AND LOAN ASSOCIATIONS

See also: SAVINGS BANKS

BIBLIOGRAPHIES

Financial Institutions. Available from U. S. Government Printing Office. • Annual. Free. Lists govern-

ment publications. Formerly *Banks and Banking.* GPO Subject Bibliography No. 128.

The Savings and Loan Crisis: An Annotated Bibliography. Pat L. Talley, compiler. Greenwood Publishing Group, Inc. • 1993. $65.00. Includes 360 scholarly and popular titles (books and research papers). (Bibliographies and Indexes in Economic History, No. 14).

CD-ROM DATABASES

OECD Statistical Compendium. Organization for Economic Cooperation and Development. • Semiannual. $1,905.00 per year for 1 to 10 users. CD-ROM contains more than 730,000 monthly, quarterly, and annual time series for OECD countries, 1960 to date. Includes fully searchable data on agriculture, food, economic indicators, national accounts, employment, energy, finance, industry, technology, and foreign trade. Results can be displayed in various forms.

DIRECTORIES

American Financial Directory. Accuity. • Covers: Approximately 23,000 banks, bank holding companies, credit unions, savings and loans, and other financial institutions and their approximately 56,000 branch offices. Entries include: Institution name, address, phone, fax, holding company affiliation, names and titles of key personnel, correspondent banks, FEDWIRE data and ABA number, balance sheet highlights, branches.

Institutional Buyers of Bank and Thrift Stocks: A Targeted Directory. Investment Data Corp. • Annual. $645.00. Provides detailed profiles of about 600 institutional buyers of bank and savings and loan stocks. Includes names of financial analysts and portfolio managers.

Thomson Savings Directory. Accuity. • Covers: nearly 2,000 savings institutions and their 13,000 branch offices. Entries include: Institution name, address, phone, fax, type, identification of mutual or stock ownership, type of insurance, routing number, number of employees, names and titles of key personnel, branch office locations, financial and operational data.

FINANCIAL RATIOS

Almanac of Business and Industrial Financial Ratios. Leo Troy. Aspen Publishers, Inc. • 2003. $125.95. Includes CD-Rom. Contains financial ratios derived from federal tax returns. Ratios for each of about 200 industries are arranged according to company asset size. (Almanac of Business and Industrial Financial Ratios Series).

INTERNET DATABASES

BanxQuote Banking, Mortgage, and Finance Center. BanxQuote, Inc. Phone: (914)722-1600 Fax: (914)722-6630 E-mail: info@banx.com • URL: http://www.banx.com • Web site quotes interest rates paid by banks around the country on various savings products, as well as rates paid by consumers for automobile loans, mortgages, credit cards, home equity loans, and personal loans. Also provided: stock quotes, indexes, stock options, futures trading data, economic indicators, and links to many other financial sites. Daily updates. Fees: Free.

The Bauer Group: Reporting On and Analyzing the Performance of U. S. Banks, Thrifts, and Credit Unions. Bauer Financial Reports, Inc. Phone: 800-388-6686 or (305)445-9500 Fax: 800-230-9569 or (305)445-6775 • URL: http://www.bauerfinancial.com • Web site provides ratings (0 to 5 stars) of individual banks and credit unions, based on capital ratios and other financial criteria. Online searching for bank or credit union names is offered. Fees: Free.

Business 2.0 Web Guide to the Best Business Links. Business 2.0 Media Inc. Phone: (415)293-4800 E-mail: support@business2.com • URL: http://www.business2.com/webguide • Web site presents an extensive, searchable directory of links to "the best, most informative, and authoritative web pages." Twenty main categories cover business, finance, career, company information, people, and technology topics, with thousands of subtopics, all linking to Web sites recommended by experienced business researchers. Fees: Free.

Fedstats. Federal Interagency Council on Statistical Policy. Phone: (202)395-7254 • URL: http://www.fedstats.gov • Web site features an efficient search facility for full-text statistics produced by more than 100 federal agencies, including the Census Bureau, the Bureau of Economic Analysis, and the Bureau of Labor Statistics. Boolean searches can be made within one agency or for all agencies combined. Links are offered to international statistical bureaus, including the UN, IMF, OECD, UNESCO, Eurostat, and 20 individual countries. Fees: Free.

FreeLunch.com. Economy.com, Inc. Phone: (610)696-8700 Fax: (610)696-1678 • URL: http://www.freelunch.com • Web site provides free access to more than 1.5 million economic and financial data series, covering industry, demographics, labor markets, prices, retail sales, government spending, trade, interest rates, housing starts, the stock market, and many other topics. Data is available for various time periods in either chart or table form. Searching is offered. Fees: Free, but registration required. Economy.com, Inc. also offers fee-based economic analysis at *The Dismal Scientist* site (http://www.dismal.com).

ONLINE DATABASES

Banking Information Source. PROQUEST. • Provides indexing and abstracting of periodical and other literature from 1982 to date, with weekly updates. Covers the financial services industry: banks, savings institutions, investment houses, credit unions, insurance companies, and real estate organizations. Emphasis is on marketing and management. Inquire as to online cost and availability. (Formerly *FINIS: Financial Industry Information Service.*).

PERIODICALS AND NEWSLETTERS

American Banker: The Financial Services Daily. Thomson Media. • Daily. $895.00 per year. Provides news of banking, investment products, mortgages, credit unions, finance, bank technology, and legal developments.

Bank Rate Monitor: The Weekly Financial Rate Reporter. Advertising News Service, Inc. • Weekly. $895.00 per year. Newsletter. Includes online addition and monthly supplement. Provides detailed information on interest rates currently paid by U. S. banks and savings institutions.

Community Banker. America's Community Bankers. • Monthly. Price on application. Covers community banking operations and management. Formerly *America's Community Banker.*

Fee Income Growth Strategies. Siefer Consultants Inc. • Description: Discusses the role of fees and service charges for money orders, cashier's checks, nonsufficient funds, loans, automatic teller machine cards, and other ancillary services in the profitability of financial institutions.

Guide to Banks and Thrifts: A Quarterly Compilation of Financial Institutions Ratings and Analysis. Weiss Ratings, Inc. • Quarterly. $438.00 per year. Emphasis is on rating of financial safety and relative risk. Includes annual summary.

Jumbo Rate News. BauerFinancial, Inc. • Description: Reports on high-yielding, insured Jumbo CD (Certificate of Deposit) rates nationwide. Analyzes each institution by current credit-worthiness, and lists current assets and capital ratios. Provides phone numbers, contacts, methods of computation, and information on how interest is paid. Also contains financial news, insights, and commentary of interest to Jumbo CD investors. Recurring features include editorials and news of interest.

Martin Weiss' Safe Money Report. Weiss Ratings, Inc. • Monthly. $189.00 per year. Newsletter. Provides financial advice and current safety ratings of various banks, savings and loan companies, insurance companies, and securities dealers. Formerly (The Safe Money Report).

One Hundred Highest Yields. Advertising News Service, Inc. • Weekly. $124.00 per year. Newsletter. List CD's and money markets offered by federally insured banks. National coverage.

Recommended Bank and Thrift Report. BauerFinancial, Inc. • Quarterly. $585.00 per year. Newsletter provides information on "safe, financially sound" commercial banks, savings banks, and savings and loan institutions. Various factors are considered, including tangible capital ratios and total risk-based capital ratios. (Six regional editions are also available at $150.00 per edition per year.).

Treasury Manager's Report: Strategic Information for the Financial Executive. PBI Media, LLC. • Biweekly. $630.00. Newsletter reporting on legal developments affecting the operations of banks, savings institutions, and other financial service organizations. Formerly *Financial Services Law Report.*

Troubled and Problematic Bank and Thrift Report. BauerFinancial, Inc. • Quarterly. $225.00 per year. Newsletter provides information on seriously undercapitalized ("Troubled") banks and savings institutions, as defined by a federal Prompt Corrective Action Rule. "Problematic" banks and thrifts are those meeting regulatory capital levels, but showing negative trends.

U. S. Banker. Thomson Media. • Monthly. $65.00 per year. Edited for bank executives and managers. Covers a wide variety of banking and financial topics.

STATISTICS SOURCES

Business Statistics of the United States. Linz Audain and Cornelia J. Strawser. Bernan Associates. • Annual. $147.00. Based on *Business Statistics,* formerly issue by the Bureau of Economic Analysis, U. S. Department of Commerce. Provides basic data for a wide variety of U. S. industries, services, and economic indicators. Most statistics are shown annually for 30 years and monthly for the most recent four years.

Economic Outlook: A Newsletter on Economic Issues for Financial Institutions. America's Community Bankers. • Monthly. Members, $106.00; non-members, $212.00 per year. Statistical profiles of the savings industry. Formerly *Economic Insight.*

Standard & Poor's Industry Surveys. Standard & Poor's. • Semiannual. $1,800.00. Two looseleaf volumes. Includes monthly *Supplements.* Provides detailed, individual surveys of 52 major industry groups. Each survey is revised on a semiannual basis. Also includes "Monthly Investment Review" (industry group investment analysis) and monthly "Trends & Projections" (economic analysis).

Statistical Information on the Financial Services Industry. American Bankers Association. • Annual. Members, $150.00; non-members, $275.00. Presents a wide variety of data relating to banking and financial services, including consumer economics, personal finance, credit, government loans, capital markets, and international banking.

Survey of Current Business. Available from U. S. Government Printing Office. • Monthly. $63.00 per year. Issued by Bureau of Economic Analysis, U. S. Department of Commerce. Presents a wide variety of business and economic data.

OTHER SOURCES

Savings Institutions: Mergers, Acquisitions, and Conversions. American Lawyer Media, Inc. • Looseleaf. $169.00. Updated as needed. Provides detailed information on the legal complexities of

mergers and acquisitions involving savings institutions. (Law Journal Press).

SAVINGS BANKS

See also: SAVINGS AND LOAN ASSOCIATIONS

BIBLIOGRAPHIES

Financial Institutions. Available from U. S. Government Printing Office. • Annual. Free. Lists government publications. Formerly *Banks and Banking.* GPO Subject Bibliography No. 128.

DIRECTORIES

Thomson Savings Directory. Accuity. • Covers: nearly 2,000 savings institutions and their 13,000 branch offices. Entries include: Institution name, address, phone, fax, type, identification of mutual or stock ownership, type of insurance, routing number, number of employees, names and titles of key personnel, branch office locations, financial and operational data.

FINANCIAL RATIOS

Almanac of Business and Industrial Financial Ratios. Leo Troy. Aspen Publishers, Inc. • 2003. $125.95. Includes CD-Rom. Contains financial ratios derived from federal tax returns. Ratios for each of about 200 industries are arranged according to company asset size. (Almanac of Business and Industrial Financial Ratios Series).

HANDBOOKS AND MANUALS

Bank Tax Guide. CCH, Inc. • Annual. $199.00. Summarizes and explains federal tax rules affecting financial institutions.

INTERNET DATABASES

BanxQuote Banking, Mortgage, and Finance Center. BanxQuote, Inc. Phone: (914)722-1600 Fax: (914)722-6630 E-mail: info@banx.com • URL: http://www.banx.com • Web site quotes interest rates paid by banks around the country on various savings products, as well as rates paid by consumers for automobile loans, mortgages, credit cards, home equity loans, and personal loans. Also provided: stock quotes, indexes, stock options, futures trading data, economic indicators, and links to many other financial sites. Daily updates. Fees: Free.

PERIODICALS AND NEWSLETTERS

Community Banker. America's Community Bankers. • Monthly. Price on application. Covers community banking operations and management. Formerly *America's Community Banker.*

Operations Alert. America's Community Bankers. • Description: Reviews recent regulatory and product developments that affect community bank operations.

Recommended Bank and Thrift Report. BauerFinancial, Inc. • Quarterly. $585.00 per year. Newsletter provides information on "safe, financially sound" commercial banks, savings banks, and savings and loan institutions. Various factors are considered, including tangible capital ratios and total risk-based capital ratios. (Six regional editions are also available at $150.00 per edition per year.).

STATISTICS SOURCES

Economic Outlook: A Newsletter on Economic Issues for Financial Institutions. America's Community Bankers. • Monthly. Members, $106.00; non-members, $212.00 per year. Statistical profiles of the savings industry. Formerly *Economic Insight.*

Federal Deposit Insurance Corporation; Annual Report. Federal Deposit Insurance Corp. • Annual. Price on application.

OTHER SOURCES

Savings Institutions: Mergers, Acquisitions, and Conversions. American Lawyer Media, Inc. •

Looseleaf. $169.00. Updated as needed. Provides detailed information on the legal complexities of mergers and acquisitions involving savings institutions. (Law Journal Press).

SAVINGS BONDS

See: GOVERNMENT BONDS

SAW INDUSTRY

See also: HARDWARE INDUSTRY; TOOL INDUSTRY; WOODWORKING INDUSTRIES

DIRECTORIES

ProSales Buyer's Guide. Hanley-Wood, LLC. • Annual. Price on application. A directory of equipment for professional builders.

Tools of the Trade Annual Buyers Guide. Hanley-Wood, LLC. • Annual. Price on application. A directory of tools for the construction industry.

PERIODICALS AND NEWSLETTERS

Building Products. Hanley-Wood, LLC. • Quarterly. $36.00 per year. Covers building products and materials for the construction industry, including new products.

Hardware Age. Reed Business Information. • Monthly. $75.00 per year.

Journal of Light Construction. Hanley-Wood, LLC. • Monthly. $35.95 per year. Provides jobsite tips, techniques, and product advice for builders and contractors.

Power Equipment Trade. Hatton-Brown Publishers, Inc. • 10 times a year. $40.00 per year. Formerly *Chain Saw Age and Power Equipment Trade.*

Tools of the Trade. Hanley-Wood, LLC. • Five times a year. $19.80 per year. Provides advice and information on tools for the construction industry. Includes product tests and evaluations.

TRADE/PROFESSIONAL ASSOCIATIONS

North American Saving Association. 1300 Sumner Ave., Cleveland, OH 44115-2851. Phone: (216)241-7333 Fax: (216)241-0105 E-mail: nasa@sewingassociation.com • URL: http://www.sawingassociation.com • Formerly Hack and Band Saw Manufactuers Association of America.

Portable Power Equipment Manufacturers Association. 4330 East-West Hwy., Ste. 310, Bethesda, MD 20814. Phone: (301)652-0774 Fax: (301)654-6138 E-mail: popref@prb.org • URL: http://www.ppema.org • Manufacturers of gasoline and electric powered chain saws, monofilament trimmers, brush cutters, hand-held blowers, backpack blowers, hedge trimmers, cut-off saws, and portable gasoline-powered generators. Encourages research and development of standards.

SAWMILLS

See: LUMBER INDUSTRY

SCHEDULES, TRANSPORTATION

See: TIMETABLES

SCHOLARSHIPS AND STUDENT AID

See also: STUDY ABROAD

ABSTRACTS AND INDEXES

Readers' Guide to Periodical Literature. H. W. Wilson Co. • Monthly. $345.00 per year. Includes

annual *Cumulation.* Indexes about 250 pericals of general interest.

BIBLIOGRAPHIES

How to Find Out About Financial Aid: 2002-2004. Gail A. Schlachter. Reference Service Press. • 2002. $37.50. Annotated bibliography of student aid directories. Author, title, subject, and geographical indexes.

CD-ROM DATABASES

College Blue Book CD-ROM. Available from Gale Cengage Learning. • Annual. $250.00. Produced by Macmillan Reference USA. Serves as electronic version of printed *College Blue Book.* Provides detailed information on programs, degrees, and financial aid sources in the U.S. and Canada.

DIRECTORIES

Chronicle Financial Aid Guide. Chronicle Guidance Publications Inc. • Covers: Over 1,770 financial aid programs offered primarily by private organizations, independent and AFL-CIO affiliated labor unions, and federal and state governments for high school students, undergraduate and graduate students, and adult learners. Entries include: Name of sponsoring organization, address, amount of aid, eligibility requirements, application, selection procedure.

Government Assistance Almanac: The Guide to Federal, Domestic, Financial and Other Programs Covering Grants, Loans, Insurance, Personal Payments and Benefits. J. Robert Dumouchel, editor. Omnigraphics, Inc. • Annual. $235.00. Describes more than 1,400 federal assistance programs available from about 50 agencies. Includes statistics, a directory of 3,000 field offices, and comprehensive indexing.

Peterson's College Money Handbook: The Only Complete Guide to Scholarships, College Costs, and Financial Aid at U. S. Colleges. Peterson's. • 2002. $29.95. Provides information on more than 1,600 scholarships, loans, and financial aid programs.

Peterson's Scholarships, Grants, and Prizes: Your Complete Guide to College Aid from Private Sources. Peterson's. • 1998. $26.95. Third edition.

The Scholarship Book: The Complete Guide to Private Scholarships, Grants, and Loans for Undergraduates. Daniel J. Cassidy. Prentice Hall PTR. • 2000. $48.00. Ninth edition. Includes CD-ROM. (Scholarship Books Series).

Scholarships, Fellowships, and Loans. Gale Cengage Learning. • 2002. $215.00. 19th edition. Describes more than 4,200 scholarships, fellowships, loans, and other educational funding sources available to U. S. and Canadian undergraduate and graduate students.

HANDBOOKS AND MANUALS

Financing Graduate School: How to Get Money for Your Master's or Ph.D. Patricia McWade. Peterson's. • 1996. $16.95. Second revised edition. Discusses the practical aspects of various types of financial aid for graduate students. Includes bibliographic and directory information.

The Student Guide: Financial Aid. U.S. Dept. of Education, Federal Student Aid Information Center. • Annual. Describes financial aid for college and vocational school students. Available online.

ONLINE DATABASES

ERIC. Educational Resources Information Center. • Funded by the U. S. Department of Education, Institute of Education Sciences (formerly Office of Educational Research and Improvement). Provides access to more than one million online records covering education-related journal and report literature, 1966 to date. Updating is monthly. Inquire as to online cost and availability.

Readers' Guide Abstracts Online. H. W. Wilson Co. • Indexes and abstracts general interest periodicals,

1983 to date. Weekly updates. Inquire as to online cost and availability.

PERIODICALS AND NEWSLETTERS

Student Aid News: The Independent Biweekly News Service on Student Financial Assistance Programs. Aspen Publishers, Inc. • Biweekly. $383.00 per year. Newsletter on federal student aid programs.

TRADE/PROFESSIONAL ASSOCIATIONS

Coalition of Higher Education Assistance Organizations. 1101 Vermont Ave., N.W., Suite 400, Washington, DC 20005. Phone: (202)289-3910 Fax: (202)371-0197 • URL: http://www.coheao.com • Purpose is to support student loan programs and monitor regulations.

National Association of Student Financial Aid Administrators. 1129 20th St., N.W., Suite 400, Washington, DC 20036-5020. Phone: (202)785-0453 Fax: (202)785-1487 E-mail: ask@nasfaa.org • URL: http://www.nsfaa.org • Serves as a national forum for matters related to student aid.

National Council of Higher Education Loan Programs. 1100 Connecticut Ave. N.W., 12th Fl., Washington, DC 20036. Phone: (202)822-2106 Fax: (202)822-2142 E-mail: info@nchelp.org • URL: http://www.nchelp.org • Attempts to coordinate federal, state, and private functions in the student loan program.

USA Funds. 555 Fairmount Ave., Ste. 310, Towson, MD 21286. Phone: 800-824-7044 or (317)849-6510 Fax: (317)951-5072 E-mail: contact@usafunds.org • URL: http://www.usafunds.org • USA Funds is a nonprofit corporation guaranteeing low-cost loans from about 10,000 lenders. Approximately 1,000 colleges participate.

SCHOOL COMPUTERS

See: COMPUTERS IN EDUCATION

SCHOOL JOURNALISM

See: COLLEGE AND SCHOOL NEWSPAPERS

SCHOOLS

See also: BUSINESS EDUCATION; COLLEGES AND UNIVERSITIES; PRIVATE SCHOOLS; STUDY ABROAD; VOCATIONAL EDUCATION

GENERAL WORKS

NetSavvy: Building Information Literacy in the Classroom. Ian Jukes and others. Corwin Press, Inc. • 2000. $69.95. Second edition. Provides practical advice on the teaching of computer, Internet, and technological literacy. Includes sample lesson plans and grade-level objectives. (One-Off Series).

Using Technology to Increase Student Learning. Linda E. Reksten. Corwin Press, Inc. • 2000. $74.95. Emphasis is on the use of computer technology in schools. (Technology Series).

ABSTRACTS AND INDEXES

Education Index. H. W. Wilson Co. • 10 times a year. Quarterly and annual cumulations. Price varies.

Educational Administration Abstracts. Sage Publication, Inc. • Quarterly. Institutions, $722.00 per year.

ALMANACS AND YEARBOOKS

Educational Media and Technology Yearbook. Libraries Unlimited, Inc. • Annual. $75.00.

National Society for the Study of Education Yearbook. National Society for the Study of

Education. The University of Chicago Press. • Annual. Membership. Two volumes per year.

BIOGRAPHICAL SOURCES

Who's Who in American Education. Marquis Who's Who. • Biennial. $159.95. Contains over 27,000 concise biographies of teachers, administrators, and other individuals involved in all levels of American education.

CD-ROM DATABASES

ERIC on SilverPlatter. Available from SilverPlatter Information, Inc. • Quarterly. $700.00 per year. Produced by the Office of Educational Research and Improvement, U. S. Dept. of Education. Provides CD-ROM indexing and abstracting of a wide variety of literature relating to education. Archival discs are available from 1966.

Magazine Index Plus. Gale Cengage Learning. • Monthly. $4,000.00 per year (includes InfoTrac workstation). Provides full text on CD-ROM for about 100 popular, general interest magazines and indexing for 300 others. Includes special indexing of reviews and product evaluations. Time period is 1980 to date.

Newspaper Abstracts Ondisc. PROQUEST. • Monthly. $2,950.00 per year (covers 1989 to date; archival discs are available for 1985-88). Provides cover-to-cover CD-ROM indexing and abstracting of 19 major newspapers, including the *New York Times, Wall Street Journal, Washington Post, Chicago Tribune,* and *Los Angeles Times.*

WILSONDISC: Education Index. H. W. Wilson Co. • Monthly. Provides CD-ROM indexing of education-related literature from 1983 to date. Price includes online service.

DIRECTORIES

American School and University-Who's Who Directory and Buyers' Guide. Primedia Business Magazines and Media. • Annual. $10.00. List of companies supplying products and service for physical plants and business offices of schools, colleges and universities.

Educators Resource Directory. Grey House Publishing. • Covers: Publishing opportunities, state by state information on enrollment, funding and grant resources, associations and conferences, teaching jobs abroad all geared toward elementary and secondary school professionals. Also covers online databases, textbook publishers, school suppliers, plus state and federal agencies. Entries include: Contact name, address, phone, fax, description, publications. A unique compilation of over 6,500 educational resources and over 130 tables and charts of education statistics and rankings.

Internet Tools of the Profession: A Guide for Information Professionals. Hope N. Tillman, editor. Special Libraries Association. • 1997. $49.00. Second edition. Consists of 14 sections by various authors or compilers. After two introductory articles on searching the Internet, there are 12 annotated lists of useful Web sites, covering the SLA, business and finance, chemistry, education, food and agriculture, information technology, insurance and employee benefits, law, library management, metals and materials, pharmaceuticals, and telecommunications. An index is provided.

Patterson's American Education. Educational Directories Inc. • Covers: Over 11,400 school districts in the United States; more than 34,000 public, private, and Catholic high schools, middle schools, and junior high schools; Approximately 300 parochial superintendents; 400 state department of education personnel. Entries include: For school districts and schools--District and superintendent Name, address, phone, fax, grade ranges, enrollment, school names, addresses, phone numbers, grade ranges, enrollment, names of principals. For postsecondary schools--School name, address, phone

number, URL, e-mail, names of administrator or director of admissions. For private and Catholic high schools--name, address, phone, fax, enrollment, grades offered, name of principal. Postsecondary institutions are covered in 'Patterson's Schools Classified' (see separate entry).

Patterson's Schools Classified. Educational Directories Inc. • Covers: Over 7,000 accredited colleges, universities, community colleges, junior colleges, career schools and teaching hospitals. Entries include: School name, address, phone, URL, e-mail, name of administrator or admissions officer, description, professional accreditation (where applicable). Updated from previous year's edition of 'Patterson's American Education' (see separate entry).

Peterson's Vocational and Technical Schools and Programs: East and West. Peterson's. • Annual. $69.90. Two volumes. $34.95 per volume. Provides information on vocational schools in the eastern part of the U. S. Covers more than 370 career fields.

HANDBOOKS AND MANUALS

School Administrator's Complete Letter Book. Gerald Tomlinson. John Wiley and Sons Inc. • 2003. $44.95. Includes CD-Rom.

INTERNET DATABASES

FedWorld: A Program of the United States Department of Commerce. National Technical Information Service. Phone: (703)605-6000 Fax: (703)605-6900 E-mail: webmaster@fedworld.gov • URL: http://www.fedworld.gov • Web site offers "a comprehensive central access point for searching, locating, ordering, and acquiring government and business information." Emphasis is on searching the Web pages, databases, and government reports of a wide variety of federal agencies. Fees: Free.

FirstGov: Your First Click to the U. S. Government. General Services Administration. Phone: 800-333-4636 or (202)501-0705 E-mail: public.affairs@gsa.gov • URL: http://www.firstgov.gov • Free Web site provides extensive links to federal agencies covering a wide variety of topics, such as agriculture, business, consumer safety, education, the environment, government jobs, grants, health, social security, statistics sources, taxes, technology, travel, and world affairs. Also provides links to federal forms, including IRS tax forms. Searching is offered, both keyword and advanced.

U. S. Census Bureau: The Official Statistics. U. S. Bureau of the Census. Phone: (301)763-4100 Fax: (301)763-4794 • URL: http://www.census.gov • Web site is "Your Source for Social, Demographic, and Economic Information." Contains "Current U. S. Population Count," "Current Economic Indicators," and a wide variety of data under "Other Official Statistics." Keyword searching is provided. Fees: Free.

ONLINE DATABASES

Education Index Online. H. W. Wilson Co. • Indexes a wide variety of periodicals related to schools, colleges, and education, 1984 to date. Monthly updates. Inquire as to online cost and availability.

ERIC. Educational Resources Information Center. • Funded by the U. S. Department of Education, Institute of Education Sciences (formerly Office of Educational Research and Improvement). Provides access to more than one million online records covering education-related journal and report literature, 1966 to date. Updating is monthly. Inquire as to online cost and availability.

Newspaper Abstracts Daily. ProQuest Inc. • Provides online coverage (citations and abstracts) of 25 major newspapers. Covers business, economics, current affairs, health, fitness, sports, education, technology, government, consumer affairs, psychology, the arts, and the social sciences. Time period is

1986 to date, with daily updates. Inquire as to online cost and availability.

PERIODICALS AND NEWSLETTERS

American School and University: Facilities, Purchasing, and Business Administration. Primedia Business Magazines and Media. • Monthly. Free to qualified personnel; others, $50.00 per year.

American School Board Journal. National School Boards Association. • Monthly. $54.00 per year. How to advice for community leaders who want to improve their schools.

Education Week: American Education's Newspaper of Record. Editorial Projects in Education, Inc. • 43 times a year. $79.94 per year.

Educational Administration Quarterly. University Council for Educational Administratiotion. Sage Publications, Inc. • Five times a year. Institutions, $489.00 per year.

Educational Marketer: The Educational Publishing Industry's Voice of Authority Since 1968. SIMBA Information. • Three times a month. $599.00 per year. Newsletter. Edited for suppliers of educational materials to schools and colleges at all levels. Covers print and electronic publishing, software, audiovisual items, and multimedia. Includes corporate news and educational statistics.

School Business Affairs. Association of School Business Officials. ASBO International. • Monthly. Membership.

School Planning and Management. Peter Li, Inc. • Monthly. $23.95 per year. Formerly *School and College.*

Taxes-Property: State Capitals. Wakeman-Walworth, Inc. • 50 times a year. $345.00 per year; print and online edition, $490.00. Formerly *From the State Capitals: Taxes-Property.*

STATISTICS SOURCES

Comparative Guide to American Elementary & Secondary Schools, 2002/03. Grey House Publishing. • 2002. $125.00. Second edition. Provides a "snapshot profile" of every public school district in the U. S. serving 2,500 or more students. Includes student-teacher ratios, expenditures per student, number of librarians, and socioeconomic indicators.

Datapedia of the United States: American History in Numbers. George T. Kurian, editor. Bernan Press. • 2004. $125.00. Third edition. Based on the Census Bureau publication, *Historical Statistics of the United States.* Provides data from Colonial times to the present on agriculture, business, consumer income, energy, finance, labor, national income, population, and many other subjects. Includes "narrative highlights," maps, charts, and statistical projections.

Digest of Education Statistics. Available from U. S. Government Printing Office. • Annual. $51.00. Covers all areas of education from kindergarten through graduate school. Includes data from both government and private sources. Compiled by National Center for Education Statistics, U. S. Department of Education.

Education at a Glance: OECD Indicators. Organization for Economic Cooperation and Development. • Annual. $49.00. Provides comparative education statistics and indicators for OECD countries.

Education Statistics of the United States. Deirdre A. Gaquin and Katherine A. Debrandt. Bernan Press. • 2001. $147.00. Third edition. Provides detailed county and state data, includes enrollment, educational attainment, per pupil expenditure, teacher pay and class size.

Investing in Education: Analysis of the 1999 World Education Indicators. Organization for Economic Cooperation and Development. • 2000. $31.00. Compares educational performance data in various countries of the world, including the U. S., other OECD countries, and selected non-OECD nations. (Education and Skills Series).

OECD in Figures. Organization for Economic Cooperation and Development. • Annual. $13.00. A "pocket data book" providing a summary of key statistics for OECD countries, including economic growth, employment, education, the environment, and transportation.

Projections of Education Statistics. Available from U. S. Government Printing Office. • Annual. $26.00. Issued by the U. S. Department of Education, National Center for Education Statistics (http://www.ed.gov). Provides 10-year projections of data relating to elementary schools, secondary schools, and institutions of higher learning. Includes projections of enrollment, graduates, classroom teachers, and expenditures.

School Enrollment, Social and Economic Characteristics of Students. Available from U. S. Government Printing Office. • Annual. $2.25. Issued by the U. S. Bureau of the Census. Presents detailed tabulations of data on school enrollment of the civilian noninstitutional population three years old and over. Covers nursery school, kindergarten, elementary school, high school, college, and graduate school. Information is provided on age, race, sex, family income, marital status, employment, and other characteristics.

Social Statistics of the United States. Mark S. Littman, editor. Bernan Press. • 2000. $65.00. Includes statistical data on population growth, labor force, occupations, environmental trends, leisure time use, income, poverty, taxes, and other economic or demographic topics.

Social Trends and Indicators USA. Monique D. Magee, editor. Gale Cengage Learning. • 2003. $450.00. Four volumes. Includes data on labor, economics, the health care industry, crime, leisure, population, education, social security, and many other topics. Sources include various government agencies and major publications.

State Profiles: The Population and Economy of Each U. S. State. Courtenay Slater and Others. Bernan Press. • 1999. $89.00. Presents charts, tables, and text in an eight-page profile for each state. Covers population, labor force, income, poverty, employment, wages, industry, trade, housing, education, health, taxes, and government finances. (The Population and Economy of Each United States Series).

Statistical Abstract of the United States. Available from U. S. Government Printing Office. • Annual. $51.00. Issued by the U. S. Bureau of the Census.

A Statistical Portrait of the United States: Social Conditions and Trends. Mark S. Littman, editor. Bernan Press. • 1998. $89.00. Covers "social, economic, and environmental trends in the United States over the past 25 years." Includes statistical tables, graphs, and analysis relating to such topics as population, income, poverty, wealth, labor, housing, education, healthcare, air/water quality, and government. (Statistical Portrait of the United States: Social Conditions and Trends Series).

UNESCO Statistical Yearbook. Bernan Press. • 1998. $95.00. Co-published by Bernan Press and the United Nations Educational, Scientific, and Cultural Organization (http://www.unesco.org). Presents statistical data from more than 200 countries on education, technology, research, broadcasting, cinema, book publishing, newspapers, libraries, museums, and population. Includes charts, maps, and graphs.

TRADE/PROFESSIONAL ASSOCIATIONS

American Association of School Administrators. 801 N. Quincy St., Suite 700, Arlington, VA 22203-1730. Phone: (703)528-0700 Fax: (703)841-1543 E-mail: info@aasa.org • URL: http://www.aasa.org.

Association of School Business Officials International. 11401 N Shore Dr., Reston, VA 20190-4200. Phone: (703)478-0405 Fax: (703)478-7060 E-mail: asboreg@asbointl.org • URL: http://www.asbointl.org.

National Education Association. 1201 16th St. NW, Washington, DC 20036-3290. Phone: (202)833-4000 Fax: (202)822-7974 E-mail: bobchase@nea.org • URL: http://www.nea.org • Professional organization and union of elementary and secondary school teachers, college and university professors, administrators, principals, counselors, and others concerned with education.

National School Boards Association. 1680 Duke St., Alexandria, VA 22314-3493. Phone: (703)838-6722 Fax: (703)683-7590 E-mail: info@nsba.org • URL: http://www.nsba.org • Federation of state school boards associations, the Board of Education of the District of Columbia and the Virgin Islands Board of Education. Advocates equity and quality education for primary and secondary public school children through legal counsel, research studies, legislative advocacy programs, and services for members, conferences, and magazines. Provides information on topics affecting K-12 public education and school policy. Maintains library and specialized clearinghouses.

National School Supply and Equipment Association. 8300 Colesville Rd., Suite 250, Silver Spring, MD 20910. Phone: 800-395-5550 or (301)495-0240 Fax: (301)495-3330 E-mail: nssea@nssea.org • URL: http://www.nssea.org • Absorbed Education Industries Association. Formerly National School Service Institute.

OTHER SOURCES

Education Law. LexisNexis Matthew Bender. • $874.00. Seven looseleaf volumes. Periodic supplementation. A reference for attorneys who represent persons having a grievance against educational institutions, and attorney representing such institutions, as well as school board members and administrators.

Educational Rankings Annual: A Compilation of Approximately 3,500 Published Rankings and Lists on Every Aspect of Education. Gale Cengage Learning. • Annual. $265.00. Provides national, regional, local, and international rankings of a wide variety of educational institutions, including business and professional schools.

SCHOOLS, PRIVATE

See: PRIVATE SCHOOLS

SCIENTIFIC APPARATUS AND INSTRUMENT INDUSTRIES

See also: LABORATORIES; RESEARCH AND DEVELOPMENT

ABSTRACTS AND INDEXES

Applied Science and Technology Index. H. W. Wilson Co. • 11 times a year. Quarterly and annual cumulations. Price varies. Indexes a wide variety of English language technical, industrial, and engineering periodicals.

Key Abstracts: Electronic Instrumentation. Available from INSPEC, Inc. • Monthly. $250.00 per year. Provides international coverage of journal and proceedings literature. Published in England by the Institution of Electrical Engineers (IEE).

BIOGRAPHICAL SOURCES

Who's Who in Science and Engineering. Marquis Who's Who. • Biennial. $269.00. Provides concise biographical information on 35,000 prominent engineers and scientists. International coverage, with geographical and professional indexes.

CD-ROM DATABASES

Science Citation Index: Compact Disc Edition. Institute for Scientific Information. • Monthly. Provides CD-ROM indexing of the world's scientific and technical literature. Corresponds to online *Scisearch* and printed *Science Citation Index.*

DIRECTORIES

ISA Directory of Instrumentation. ISA - The Instrumentation Systems and Automation Society. • Annual. $100.00. Over 2,400 manufacturers of control and instrumentation equipment, over 1,000 manufacturers' representatives, and several hundred service companies; coverage includes Canada.

ENCYCLOPEDIAS AND DICTIONARIES

Kirk-Othmer Encyclopedia of Chemical Technology. Raymond E. Kirk and Donald F. Othmer. John Wiley and Sons, Inc. • 1991-97. $9,895.00, prepaid. 27 volumes. Fourth edition. Four volumes are scheduled to be published each year, with individual volumes available at $415.00. (Kirk-Othmer Encyclopedia of Chemical Technology Series).

FINANCIAL RATIOS

Almanac of Business and Industrial Financial Ratios. Leo Troy. Aspen Publishers, Inc. • 2003. $125.95. Includes CD-Rom. Contains financial ratios derived from federal tax returns. Ratios for each of about 200 industries are arranged according to company asset size. (Almanac of Business and Industrial Financial Ratios Series).

HANDBOOKS AND MANUALS

Electronic Instrument Handbook. Clyde F. Coombs. McGraw-Hill. • 2001. $125.00. Fifth edition. (Engineering Handbook Series).

ONLINE DATABASES

Applied Science and Technology Index Online. H. W. Wilson Co. • Provides online indexing of 500 major scientific, technical, industrial, and engineering periodicals. Time period is 1983 to date. Monthly updates. Inquire as to online cost and availability.

INSPEC. Institution of Electrical Engineers (IEE). • Provides online citations, with abstracts, to the world literature of electrical engineering, electronics, optoelectronics, telecommunications, industrial controls, instrumentation, computer technology, information technology, and physics. Coverage includes more than 4,000 technical and scientific journals from 1969 to date, with weekly updating. (INSPEC is Information Services in Physics, Electronics, and Computing.) Inquire as to online cost and availability.

Scisearch. Institute for Scientific Information. • Broad, multidisciplinary index to the literature of science and technology, 1974 to present. Inquire as to online cost and availability. Coverage of literature is worldwide, with weekly updates.

PERIODICALS AND NEWSLETTERS

Control Engineering: Covering Control, Instrumentation and Automation Systems Worldwide. Reed Business Information. • Monthly. $109.90 per year.

Instrumentation and Automation News: Instruments, Controls, Manufacturing Software, Electronic and Mechanical Components. Reed Business Information. • Monthly. $61.90 per year.

INTECH: The International Journal of Instrumentation and Control. ISA Services, Inc. • Monthly. $72.00 per year.

ISA Transactions. ISA-The Instrumentation, Systems and Automation Society. American Institute of Physics. • Quarterly. $310.00 per year.

Measurements and Control. Measurements and Data Corp. • Bimonthly. $24.00 per year. Supplement available: *M & C: Measurement and Control News.*

Review of Scientific Instruments. American Institute of Physics. • Monthly. Institutions, $1,690.00 per year. Includes print and online editions.

Today's Chemist at Work. American Chemical Society. • Monthly. Institutions, $200.00 per year; others, price on application. Provide pracrtical information for chemists on day-to-day operations. Product coverage includes chemicals, equipment, apparatus, instruments, and supplies.

RESEARCH CENTERS AND INSTITUTES
Instrumentation and Control Laboratory. Princeton University. Dept. of Mechanical and Aerospace Engineering, Engineering Quadrangle, Princeton, NJ 08544. Phone: (609)452-5154 Fax: (609)452-6109 E-mail: enoch@princeton.edu.

STATISTICS SOURCES
Annual Survey of Manufactures. Available from U. S. Government Printing Office. • Annual. Prices vary. Issued by the U. S. Census Bureau as an interim update to the *Census of Manufactures.* Includes data on number of manufacturing establishments in various industries, employment, labor costs, value of shipments, capital expenditures, inventories, energy costs, and assets. (See also Census Bureau home page, http://www.census.gov/.).

Selected Instruments and Related Products. U.S. Bureau of the Census. • Annual. (Current Industrial Reports, MA-38B.).

U. S. Industry and Trade Outlook. Available from National Technical Information Service. • Annual. $69.95. Produced by the International Trade Administration, U. S. Department of Commerce, in a "public-private" partnership with DRI/McGraw-Hill and Standard & Poor's. Provides basic data, outlook for the current year, and "Long-Term Prospects" (five-year projections) for a wide variety of products and services. Includes high technology industries. Formerly *U. S. Industrial Outlook.*

TRADE/PROFESSIONAL ASSOCIATIONS
SAMA Group of Associations. 225 Reinekers Lane, Ste. 625, Alexandria, VA 23314. Phone: (703)836-1360 Fax: (703)836-6644 • Formerly Apparatus Makers Association of America.

OTHER SOURCES
Biotechnology Instrumentation. Available from MarketResearch.com. • 2002. $3,950.00. Published by Global Industry Analysts. Provides worldwide market research data, including profiles of major biotech instrument companies.

SCIENTIFIC LABORATORIES
See: LABORATORIES

SCIENTIFIC RESEARCH
See: RESEARCH AND DEVELOPMENT

SCRAP
See: WASTE PRODUCTS

SCRAP METAL
See: IRON AND STEEL SCRAP METAL INDUSTRY

SCREW MACHINE INDUSTRY
See: MACHINE TOOL INDUSTRY

SEAFOOD INDUSTRY

See also: FISH INDUSTRY; OYSTER INDUSTRY; SHELLFISH INDUSTRY

ABSTRACTS AND INDEXES
Food Science and Technology Abstracts. International Food Information Service Publishing. • Monthly. $1,780.00 per year. Provides worldwide coverage of the literature of food technology and food production.

Foods Adlibra: Key to the World's Food Literature. General Mills, Inc. Foods Adlibra Publications. • Semimonthly. $240.00 per year. Provides journal citations and abstracts to the literature of food technology and packaging.

NTIS Alerts: Agriculture & Food. National Technical Information Service. • Semimonthly. $195.00 per year. Provides descriptions of government-sponsored research reports and software, with ordering information. Covers agricultural economics, horticulture, fisheries, veterinary medicine, food technology, and related subjects. Formerly *Abstract Newsletter.*

Oceanic Abstracts. CSA. • 11 times a year. $1,645.00 per year. Includes print and online editions. Covers oceanography, marine biology, ocean shipping, and a wide range of other marine-related subject areas.

CD-ROM DATABASES
Food Science and Technology Abstracts [CD-ROM]. Available from SilverPlatter Information, Inc. • Quarterly. Produced by International Food Information Service (home page is http://www.ifis.org). Provides worldwide coverage on CD-ROM of the literature of food technology and production. Various types of publications are indexed, with abstracts, including about 1,800 periodicals. Time period is 1969 to date.

DIRECTORIES
Major Food and Drink Companies of the World. Available from Gale Cengage Learning. • Annual. $880.00. Two volumes. Published by Graham & Whiteside. Contains profiles and trade names for more than 9,800 important food and beverage companies in various countries. In addition to foods, includes both alcoholic and nonalcoholic drink products.

Thomas Food and Beverage Market Place. Grey House Publishing. • 2004. $495.00. Three volumes. Contains more than 40,000 entries covering food companies, beverages, food equipment, warehouse companies, food brokers, wholesalers, importers, and exporters. Formerly *Thomas Food Industry Register.*

ONLINE DATABASES
ASFA Aquaculture Abstracts [Online]. Cambridge Scientific Abstracts. • Indexing and abstracting of the literature of marine life, 1984 to present. Inquire as to online cost and availability.

Food Science and Technology Abstracts [online]. IFIS North American Desk. • Produced by International Food Information Service. Provides about 500,000 online citations, with abstracts, to the international literature of food science, technology, commodities, engineering, and processing. Approximately 2,000 periodicals are covered. Time period is 1969 to date, with monthly updates. Inquire as to online cost and availability.

FOODS ADLIBRA. General Mills, Inc. • Contains online citations, with abstracts, to the technical and business literature of food processing and packaging. New products and new ingredients are featured. Covers about 250 trade journals and 500 research journals from 1974 to date, with monthly updates. Inquire as to online cost and availability.

Oceanic Abstracts (Online). Cambridge Scientific

Abstracts. • Oceanographic and other marine-related technical literature, 1981 to present. Monthly updates. Inquire as to online cost and availability.

PERIODICALS AND NEWSLETTERS
Fishermen's News. Fishermen's News, Inc. • Monthly. $15.00 per year.

National Fisherman. Diversified Business Communications. • Monthly. $17.95 per year. American fishing industry and boat building trade.

Seafood Business. Diversified Business Communications. • Monthly. $69.00 per year. Edited for a wide range of seafood buyers, including distributors, restaurants, supermarkets, and institutions. Special issues feature information on specific products, such as salmon or lobster.

STATISTICS SOURCES
FAO Fishery Series. Food and Agriculture Organization of the United States. Available from Bernan Associates. • Irregular. Price varies. Text in English, French, and Spanish. Incorporates *Yearbook of Fishery Statistics.*

Fisheries of the United States. Available from U. S. Government Printing Office. • Annual. $20.00. Issued by the National Marine Fisheries Service, National Oceanic and Atmospheric Administration, U. S. Department of Commerce.

U. S. Industry and Trade Outlook. Available from National Technical Information Service. • Annual. $69.95. Produced by the International Trade Administration, U. S. Department of Commerce, in a "public-private" partnership with DRI/McGraw-Hill and Standard & Poor's. Provides basic data, outlook for the current year, and "Long-Term Prospects" (five-year projections) for a wide variety of products and services. Includes high technology industries. Formerly *U. S. Industrial Outlook.*

World Food Data and Statistics. Euromonitor International. • 2004. $650.00. Provides five-year data for a wide variety of food products in 52 countries. Includes market size, consumer expenditures, price indicators, and retail distribution data for many kinds of meat, fish, fruits, vegetables, dairy products, baked goods, condiments, canned food, and frozen food.

TRADE/PROFESSIONAL ASSOCIATIONS
Board of Trade of the Wholesale Seafood Merchants. Seven Dey St., Suite 801, New York, NY 10007. Phone: (212)732-4340 Fax: (212)732-6644.

OTHER SOURCES
Seafood: Frozen, Canned, and Fresh. Available from MarketResearch.com. • 2002. $3,850.00. Published by Global Industry Analysts. Provides worldwide market research data, including profiles of major seafood companies.

The Seafood Market. MarketResearch.com. • 1997. $1,625.00. Market research report. Covers fresh, frozen, and canned seafood. Market projections are provided.

SEALANTS
See: ADHESIVES

SEAPORTS
See: PORTS

SECRETARIAL PRACTICE
See: OFFICE PRACTICE

SECRETARIES
See: OFFICE PRACTICE

SECURITIES

See also: BONDS; CONVERTIBLE SECURI-
TIES; DERIVATIVE SECURITIES;
DIVIDENDS; FINANCIAL ANALYSIS;
GOVERNMENT BONDS; INVESTMENT
COMPANIES; CLOSED-END FUNDS;
INVESTMENTS; MUNICIPAL BONDS;
OBSOLETE SECURITIES; OVER-THE-
COUNTER SECURITIES INDUSTRY; REAL
ESTATE INVESTMENT TRUSTS; SECURI-
TIES LAW AND REGULATION

GENERAL WORKS

Financial History of the United States. Jerry W.
Markham. M. E. Sharpe, Inc. • 2002. $349.00. Three
volumes. Vol. 1: *From Christopher Columbus to the
Robber Barons (1492-1900).* Vol. 2: *From J. P.
Morgan to the Institutional Investor (1900-1970).*
Vol. 3: *From the Age of Derivatives to the Internet
(1970-2000).* Each volume contains name and
subject indexes, with cumulative indexes in volume
three.

Financial Markets and Institutions. Frederic S.
Mishkin and Stanley G. Eakins. Addison-Wesley. •
2002. $118.00. Fourth edition.

*Investing in the Over-the-Counter Markets: Stocks,
Bonds, IPOs.* Alvin D. Hall. John Wiley and Sons,
Inc. • 1995. $29.95. Provides advice and informa-
tion on investing in "unlisted" or NASDAQ
(National Association of Securities Dealers
Automated Quotation System) stocks, bonds, and
initial public offerings (IPOs).

ABSTRACTS AND INDEXES

Investment Statistics Locator. Linda H. Bentley and
Jennifer J. Kiesl, editors. Greenwood Publishing
Group, Inc. • 1994. $69.95. Expanded revised
edition. Provides detailed subject indexing of more
than 50 of the most-used sources of financial and
investment data. Includes an annotated bibliography.

BIOGRAPHICAL SOURCES

Who's Who in the Securities Industry. Economist
Publishing Co. • Annual. $15.00. Lists about 1,000
investment bankers.

CD-ROM DATABASES

OECD Statistical Compendium. Organization for
Economic Cooperation and Development. •
Semiannual. $1,905.00 per year for 1 to 10 users.
CD-ROM contains more than 730,000 monthly,
quarterly, and annual time series for OECD
countries, 1960 to date. Includes fully searchable
data on agriculture, food, economic indicators,
national accounts, employment, energy, finance,
industry, technology, and foreign trade. Results can
be displayed in various forms.

DIRECTORIES

*Association for Investment Management and
Research-Membership Directory.* Association for
Investment Management and Research. • Annual.
$150.00. Lists 38,000 professional investment
managers and securities analysts.

*Directory of Companies Required to File Annual
Reports with the Securities and Exchange
Commission.* Securities and Exchange Commission.
Available from U.S. Government Printing Office. •
Annual. $46.00.

*HedgeWorld Annual Compendium: The Hedge Fund
Industry's Definitive Reference Guide.* HedgeWorld
USA. • Annual. $499.00. Contains profiles of 500
domestic and offshore hedge funds with more than
$50 million in assets under management. Includes
articles on "The Basics of Investing in Hedge
Funds," "Beyond the Basics," and other information.

*HedgeWorld Service Provider League Tables &
Analyses.* HedgeWorld USA. • Annual. $595.00.
Provides quantitative and qualitative information on
firms providing services to hedge funds:

accountants/auditors, administrators, custodians,
legal counsel, and prime brokers. Detailed
categories cover banks, clearing services, consultants, derivatives business, investment companies,
wealth management services, etc.

Mergent International Manual and News Reports.
Mergent, Inc. • Annual. Price on application.
Financial and other information about 3,000
publicly-owned corporations in 100 countries.
Formerly *Moody's International Manual and News
Reports.*

Morningstar American Depositary Receipts. Morningstar, Inc. • Biweekly. $195.00 per year.
Looseleaf. Provides detailed profiles of 700 foreign
companies having shares traded in the U. S. through
American Depositary Receipts (ADRs).

*Mortgage & Asset-Based Desk Reference: U. S.
Buyside and Sellside Profiles.* Capital Access
International. • Annual. $395.00. Provides "detailed
buyside and sellside profiles and contacts" for the
mortgage and asset-based securities market.

Securities Industry Yearbook. Securities Industry
and Financial Markets Association. • Covers: over
600 member securities firms, with about 480 of them
covered in detail. Entries include: For firms covered
in detail--Company name, name of parent company,
address, phone, capital position and rank, number of
offices and type, number of employees, area of
specialization, names and titles of key personnel,
number of registered representatives, departments
with name of department head, dollar volume of
underwriting and syndication by type, other
financial data. For other firms--Company name, address, name of delegated liaison to the association.

*Standard and Poor's Security Dealers of North
America.* Standard & Poor's. • Semiannual. $480.00
per year; with *Supplements* every six weeks.
Geographical listing of over 12,000 stock, bond, and
commodity dealers.

ENCYCLOPEDIAS AND DICTIONARIES

The A-Z Vocabulary for Investors. American
Institute for Economic Research. • 1997. $7.00.
Second half of book is a "General Glossary" of about
400 financial terms "most-commonly used" in
investing. First half contains lengthier descriptions
of types of banking institutions (commercial banks,
thrift institutions, credit unions), followed by suc-
cinct explanations of various forms of investment:
stocks, bonds, options, futures, commodities, and
"Other Investments" (collectibles, currencies,
mortgages, precious metals, real estate, charitable
trusts). (Economic Education Bulletin.).

Blackwell Encyclopedic Dictionary of Finance.
Dean Paxson and Douglas Wood, editors. Blackwell
Publishing. • 1997. $110.00. The editors are associ-
ated with the University of Manchester. Contains
definitions of key terms combined with longer
articles written by various U. S. and foreign business educators. Includes bibliographies and index.
(Blackwell Encyclopedia of Management Series).

Dictionary of Finance and Investment Terms. John
Downes. Barron's Educational Series, Inc. • 2002.
$14.95. Sixth edition. Provides clear explanations of
more than 5,000 business, banking, financial, investment, and tax terms. Includes a separate list of
financial abbreviations and acronyms. (Business
Dictionaries Series).

Encyclopedia of Banking and Finance. Charles J.
Woelfel. McGraw-Hill. • 1996. $150.00. 10th
revised edition. Includes CD-ROM.

*Knowledge Exchange Business Encyclopedia: Your
Complete Business Advisor.* Lorraine Spurge.
Knowledge Exchange LLC. • 1998. $45.00.
Provides definitions of business terms and financial
expressions, profiles of leading industries, tables of
economic statistics, biographies of business leaders,
and other business information. Includes "A
Chronology of Business from 3000 B.C. Through

1995." Contains illustrations and three indexes.

HANDBOOKS AND MANUALS

Econometrics of Financial Markets. John Y. Campbell and others. Princeton University Press. • 1996.
$70.00. Written for advanced students and industry
professionals. Includes chapters on "The Predict-
ability of Asset Returns," "Derivative Pricing
Models," and "Fixed-Income Securities." Provides a
discussion of the random walk theory of investing
and tests of the theory.

Handbook of Fixed Income Securities. Frank J.
Fabozzi. McGraw-Hill. • 2000. $99.95. Sixth
edition. Topics include risk measurement, valuation
techniques, and portfolio strategy.

Handbook of Mortgage-Backed Securities. Frank J.
Fabozzi. McGraw-Hill. • 2001. $95.00. Fifth
edition.

Library of Investment Banking. Robert L. Kuhn,
editor. McGraw-Hill. • 1990. $475.00. Seven
volumes: 1. Investing and Risk Management; 2.
Capital Raising and Financial Structure; 3.
Corporate and Municipal Securities; 4. Mergers,
Acquisitions, and Leveraged Buyouts; 5. Mortgage
and Asset Securitization; 6. International Finance
and Investing; 7. Index.

Mergent OTC Unlisted Manual (Over the Counter).
Mergent. • Annual, $1,995.00 per year. Includes
supplement *Moody's OTC Unlisted News Report.*

*Moody's Manuals. Bank and Finance Manual,
Industrial Manual, Municipal and Government
Manual, OTC Industrial Manual, Public Utility
Manual, Transportation Manual.* Mergent Inc. •
Annual. Looseleaf supplements. Prices on
application.

*Mortgage-Backed Securities: Developments and
Trends in the Secondary Mortgage Market.* Cameron L. Cowan and Kenneth G. Lore. West Group. •
2003. $275.00. (Securities Handbook Series).

Options, Futures, and Other Derivatives. John C.
Hull. Prentice Hall PTR. • 2002. $135.00. Fifth
edition.

Securities: Public and Private Offerings, 2d. Wil-
liam W. Prifti. West Group. • Semiannual. $389.00.
Three looseleaf volumes. How to issue securities.
(Securities Law Series).

INTERNET DATABASES

Business 2.0 Web Guide to the Best Business Links.
Business 2.0 Media Inc. Phone: (415)293-4800
E-mail: support@business2.com • URL: http://
www.business2.com/webguide • Web site presents
an extensive, searchable directory of links to "the
best, most informative, and authoritative web
pages." Twenty main categories cover business,
finance, career, company information, people, and
technology topics, with thousands of subtopics, all
linking to Web sites recommended by experienced
business researchers. Fees: Free.

Business Week Online. McGraw-Hill. Phone:
(212)512-2511 Fax: (684)842-6101 • URL: http://
www.businessweek.com • Web site provides
complete contents of current issue of *Business Week*
plus "BW Daily" with additonal business news,
financial market quotes, and corporate information
from Standard & Poor's. Includes various features,
such as "Banking Center" with mortgage and interest data, and "Interactive Computer Buying Guide."
The "Business Week Archive" is fully searchable
back to 1996.

Factiva. Dow Jones Reuters Business Interactive,
LLC. Phone: 800-369-7466 or (609)452-1511 Fax:
(609)520-5770 E-mail: solutions@factiva.com •
URL: http://www.factiva.com • Fee-based Web site
provides "global news and business information
through Web sites and content integration solutions."
Includes Dow Jones and Reuters newswires, The
Wall Street Journal, and more than 7,000 other
sources of current news, historical articles, market

research reports, and investment analysis. Content includes 96 major U. S. newspapers, 900 non-English sources, trade publications, media transcripts, country profiles, news photos, etc.

Fedstats. Federal Interagency Council on Statistical Policy. Phone: (202)395-7254 • URL: http://www.fedstats.gov • Web site features an efficient search facility for full-text statistics produced by more than 100 federal agencies, including the Census Bureau, the Bureau of Economic Analysis, and the Bureau of Labor Statistics. Boolean searches can be made within one agency or for all agencies combined. Links are offered to international statistical bureaus, including the UN, IMF, OECD, UNESCO, Eurostat, and 20 individual countries. Fees: Free.

FreeLunch.com. Economy.com, Inc. Phone: (610)696-8700 Fax: (610)696-1678 • URL: http://www.freelunch.com • Web site provides free access to more than 1.5 million economic and financial data series, covering industry, demographics, labor markets, prices, retail sales, government spending, trade, interest rates, housing starts, the stock market, and many other topics. Data is available for various time periods in either chart or table form. Searching is offered. Fees: Free, but registration required. Economy.com, Inc. also offers fee-based economic analysis at *The Dismal Scientist* site (http://www.dismal.com).

Nexis.com. Lexis-Nexis Group. Phone: 800-227-4908 or (937)865-6800 Fax: (937)865-6909 E-mail: webmaster@prod.lexis-nexis.com • URL: http://www.nexis.com • Fee-based Web site offers searching of about 2.8 billion documents in some 30,000 news, business, and legal information sources. Features include a subject directory covering 1,200 topics in 34 categories and a Company Dossier containing information on more than 500,000 public and private companies. Boolean searching is offered.

Wall Street Journal Interactive Edition. Dow Jones & Co., Inc. Phone: 800-369-2834 or (212)416-2000 Fax: (212)416-2658 E-mail: inquiries@interactive.wsj.com • URL: http://www.wsj.com • Fee-based Web site providing online searching of worldwide information from the *The Wall Street Journal*. Includes "Company Snapshots," "The Journal's Greatest Hits," "Index to Market Data," "Journal Links," etc. Financial price quotes are available. Fees: $49.00 per year; $29.00 per year to print subscribers.

ONLINE DATABASES

F & S Index. Gale Cengage Learning. • Contains about four million citations to worldwide business, financial, and industrial or consumer product literature appearing from 1972 to date. Weekly updates. Inquire as to online cost and availability.

Fitch Ratings Delivery Service. Fitch Inc. • Provides online delivery of Fitch financial ratings in three sectors: "Corporate Finance" (corporate bonds, insurance companies), "Structured Finance" (asset-backed securities), and "U.S. Public Finance" (municipal bonds). Daily updates. Inquire as to online cost and availability.

Standard and Poor's Daily News Online. Standard and Poor's Corp. • Full text of business news and other information, 1984 to present. Inquire as to online cost and availability.

Value Line Convertible Data Base. Value Line Publishing, Inc. • Provides online data for about 600 convertible bonds and other convertible securities: price, yield, premium, issue size, liquidity, and maturity. Information is current, with weekly updates. Inquire as to online cost and availability.

Vickers On-Line. Vickers Stock Research Corp. • Provides detailed online information relating to insider trading and the securities holdings of institutional investors. Daily updates. Inquire as to

online cost and availability.

PERIODICALS AND NEWSLETTERS

Bank Credit Analyst. BCA Publications Ltd. • Monthly. $695.00 per year. "The independent monthly forecast and analysis of trends in business conditions and major investment markets based on a continuous appraisal of money and credit flows." Includes many charts and graphs relating to money, credit, and securities in the U. S.

Barron's: The Dow Jones Business and Financial Weekly. • Weekly. $145.00 per year.

Bloomberg Markets. Bloomberg. • Monthly. Free to qualified personnel. Edited for securities dealers and investment managers.

Financial Analysts Journal. Association for Investment Management and Research. • Bimonthly. $220.00 per year.

Financial Markets, Institutions, and Instruments. New York University, Salomon Center. Blackwell Publishing. • Five times a year. Institutions, $338.00 per year. Includes online edition. Edited to "bridge the gap between the academic and professional finance communities." Special fifth issue each year provides surveys of developments in four areas: money and banking, derivative securities, corporate finance, and fixed-income securities.

Financial Times [London]. The Financial Times, Inc. • Daily, except Sunday. $572.88 per year. An international business and financial newspaper, featuring news from London, Paris, Frankfurt, New York, and Tokyo. Includes worldwide stock and bond market data, commodity market data, and monetary/currency exchange information.

Institutional Investor: The Premier of Professional Magazine Finance. Institutional Investor, Inc., Journals Group. • Monthly. $445.00 per year. Includes print and online editions. Edited for portfolio managers and other investment professionals. Special feature issues include "Country Credit Ratings," "Fixed Income Trading Ranking," "All-America Research Team," and "Global Banking Ranking.".

International Bank Credit Analyst. BCA Publications Ltd. • Monthly. $795.00 per year. "A monthly forecast and analysis of currency movements, interest rates, and stock market developments in the principal countries, based on a continuous appraisal of money and credit trends worldwide." Includes many charts and graphs providing international coverage of money, credit, and securities.

Investment Dealers' Digest. Thomson Media. • Weekly. $750.00 per year. Covers financial news, trends, new products, people, private placements, new issues of securities, and other aspects of the investment business. Includes feature stories.

Investor's Business Daily. Investor's Business Daily, Inc. • Daily. $295.00 per year. Newspaper.

Mortgage-Backed Securities Letter. Securities Data Publishing. • Description: Covers developments in the structured finance markets. Analyzes transactions and their collateral; follows litigation, refinancing opportunities, and market conditions.

Operations Management. Institutional Investor, Inc., Journals Group. • Weekly. $2,105.00 per year. Includes print and online editions. Newsletter. Edited for managers of securities clearance and settlement at financial institutions. Covers new products, technology, legalities, management practices, and other topics related to securities processing.

Private Equity Week. Thomson Financial. • Weekly. $1,495.00 per year. Provides detailed information on both prospective and completed private equity transactions. Includes news, data, commentary, trends, developments, and analysis.

Private Placement Letter: The Weekly for Privately Placed Fixed-Income Securities. Thomson Media. •

Weekly. $895.00 per year. Newsletter. Provides information on private financing of debt and convertible securities.

SEC News Digest. U.S. Securities and Exchange Commission, Public Reference Room. • Daily.

Securities Industry News. Thomson Financial Corporate Communications. • Weekly. $275.00 per year. Newsletter covers securities dealing and processing, including regulatory compliance, shareholder services, human resources, transaction clearing, and technology.

Securities Week. McGraw-Hill Financial Services Co. • Description: Acts as a trade publication for Wall Street executives, publishing news stories on pertinent events and developments within the industry including those related to legislative and regulatory activity, major stock exchanges, investment banking and retail firms, institutional trading, and new products. Recurring features include reports on research departments and a column titled Financial Futures/Commodities Report.

The Wall Street Journal. Dow Jones & Co., Inc. • Daily. $189.00 per year. Covers news and trends relating to business, industry, finance, the economy, and international commerce. Provides extensive price and other data for the securities, commodity, options, futures, foreign exchange, and money markets.

Wall Street Transcript: A Professional Publication for the Business and Financial Community. Wall Street Transcript Corp. • Weekly. $1,890.00. per year. Provides reprints of investment research reports.

PRICE SOURCES

Bank and Quotation Record. William B. Dana Co. • Monthly. $130.00 per year.

National Bond Summary. Pink Sheets LLC. • Monthly, with semiannual cumulations. $504.00 per year. Includes price quotes for both active and inactive issues, with transfer agents, market makers (brokers), capital changes, name changes, and other corporate information. Formerly published by the National Quotation Bureau.

National Stock Summary. Pink Sheets LLC. • Monthly, with semiannual cumulations. $576.00 per year. Includes price quotes for both active and inactive issues, with transfer agents, market makers (brokers), capital changes, name changes, and other corporate information. Pink Sheets LLC also provides daily and weekly stock price services. Formerly published by the National Quotation Bureau.

RESEARCH CENTERS AND INSTITUTES

Bendheim Center for Finance. Princeton University, 26 Prospect Ave., Princeton, NJ 08540-5296. Phone: (609)258-0770 Fax: (609)258-0771 E-mail: yacine@princeton.edu • URL: http://www.princeton.edu/~bcf/ • Research areas include securities markets, portfolio analysis, credit markets, and corporate finance. Emphasis is on quantitative and mathematical perspectives.

Center for Research in Security Prices. University of Chicago, 725 S. Wells St., Suite 800, Chicago, IL 60607. Phone: (773)834-4610 Fax: (773)702-3036 E-mail: custom@crsp.uchicago.edu • URL: http://gsbwww.uchicago.edu/research/crsp.

Institute for Quantitative Research in Finance. Church Street Station, P.O. Box 6194, New York, NY 10249-6194. Phone: (212)744-6825 Fax: (212)517-2259 E-mail: daleberman@compuserve • Financial research areas include quantitative methods, securities analysis, and the financial structure of industries. Also known as the "Q Group.".

STATISTICS SOURCES

Business Statistics of the United States. Linz Audain and Cornelia J. Strawser. Bernan Associates. •

Annual. $147.00. Based on *Business Statistics*, formerly issue by the Bureau of Economic Analysis, U. S. Department of Commerce. Provides basic data for a wide variety of U. S. industries, services, and economic indicators. Most statistics are shown annually for 30 years and monthly for the most recent four years.

International Guide to Securities Market Indices. Henry Shilling, editor. Fitzroy Dearborn Publishers, Inc. • 1996. $150.00. Describes 400 stock market, bond market, and other financial price indexes maintained in various countries of the world (300 of the indexes are described in detail, including graphs and 10-year data).

Standard & Poor's Stock and Bond Guide. McGraw-Hill. • Annual. $24.95. Contains concise data on 6,000 stocks, 7,000 bonds, and 700 mutual funds. Includes year-end prices, earnings estimates for stocks, and debt ratings for bonds.

Standard & Poor's Stock Reports: NASDAQ and Regional Exchanges. Standard & Poor's. • Irregular. $1,100.00 per year. Looseleaf service. Provides two pages of financial details and other information for each corporation included.

Standard & Poor's Stock Reports: New York Stock Exchange. Standard & Poor's. • Irregular. $1,295.00 per year. Looseleaf service. Provides two pages of financial details and other information for each corporation with stock listed on the N. Y. Stock Exchange.

Statistical Information on the Financial Services Industry. American Bankers Association. • Annual. Members, $150.00; non-members, $275.00. Presents a wide variety of data relating to banking and financial services, including consumer economics, personal finance, credit, government loans, capital markets, and international banking.

Stocks, Bonds, Bills, and Inflation Yearbook. Ibbotson Associates. • Annual. $92.00. Provides detailed data from 1926 to the present on inflation and the returns from various kinds of financial investments, such as small-cap stocks and long-term government bonds.

Survey of Current Business. Available from U. S. Government Printing Office. • Monthly. $63.00 per year. Issued by Bureau of Economic Analysis, U. S. Department of Commerce. Presents a wide variety of business and economic data.

United States Securities and Exchange Commission Annual Report. U.S. Government Printing Office. • Annual. The Commission maintains a Web site at http://www.sec.gov.

TRADE/PROFESSIONAL ASSOCIATIONS

Association for Investment Management and Research. 560 Ray C. Hunt Dr., Charlottesville, VA 22903. Phone: 800-247-8132 or (434)951-5499 Fax: (434)951-5262 E-mail: info@aimr.org • URL: http://www.aimr.org • Members are practicing investment analysts.

National Association of Securities Dealers (NASD). 1735 K St., N.W., Washington, DC 20006-1506. Phone: (202)728-8000 Fax: (202)293-6260 E-mail: waltere@nasd.com • URL: http://www.nasd.com • Formerly National Association of Securities Dealers.

Securities Industry and Financial Markets Association. 120 Broadway, 35th Fl., New York, NY 10271-0080. Phone: (212)313-1200 Fax: (212)313-1301 E-mail: rbrockhaus@sifma.org • URL: http://www.sifma.org • Represents more than 650 member firms of all sizes, in all financial markets in the U.S. and around the world. Enhances the public's trust and confidence in the markets, delivering an efficient, enhanced member network of access and forward-looking services, as well as premiere educational resources for the professionals in the industry and the investors whom they serve.

Maintains offices in New York City and Washington, DC.

Security Traders Association. 420 Lexington Ave., Ste. 2334, New York, NY 10170. Phone: (212)867-7002 Fax: (212)867-7030 E-mail: traders@securitytraders.org • URL: http://www.securitytraders.org • Brokers and dealers handling listed and OTC securities, stocks, and bonds, and all securities. Conducts educational programs. Promotes the interests of members throughout the global financial markets. Provides representation of these interests in the legislative, regulatory and technological processes. Fosters goodwill and high standards of integrity in accord with the Association's founding principle.

OTHER SOURCES

Capital Changes Reports. CCH, Inc. • Weekly. $1,395.00. Six looseleaf volumes. Arranged alphabetically by company. This service presents a chronological capital history that includes reorganizations, mergers and consolidations. Recent actions are found in Volume One - "New Matters.".

Fitch Insights. Fitch Investors Service, Inc. • Biweekly. $1,040.00 per year. Includes bond rating actions and explanation of actions. Provides commentary and Fitch's view of the financial markets.

SECURITIES AND EXCHANGE COMMISSION

See: SECURITIES LAW AND REGULATION

SECURITIES, CONVERTIBLE

See: CONVERTIBLE SECURITIES

SECURITIES, DERIVATIVE

See: DERIVATIVE SECURITIES

SECURITIES LAW AND REGULATION

GENERAL WORKS

Corporate Finance and the Securities Laws. Charles J. Johnson and Joseph McLaughlin. Aspen Publishers, Inc. • 1997. $175.00. Second edition.

Securities Regulation. Joel Seligman and Louis Loss. Aspen Publishers, Inc. • 1995. $1,520.00. Third edition. 12 volumes. Includes 1969 supplement. Covers the fundamentals of government regulation of securities.

ABSTRACTS AND INDEXES

Current Law Index: Multiple Access to Legal Periodicals. Gale Cengage Learning. • Monthly. $725.00 per year. Produced in cooperation with the American Association of Law Libraries. Indexes more than 900 law journals, legal newspapers, and specialty publications from the U.S., Canada, U.K., Ireland, Australia, and New Zealand.

Index to Legal Periodicals and Books. H. W. Wilson Co. • Monthly. $490.00 per year. Quarterly and annual cumulations.

ALMANACS AND YEARBOOKS

American Law Yearbook. Gale Cengage Learning. • Annual. $165.00. Serves as a yearly supplement to *West's Encyclopedia of American Law.* Describes new legal developments in many subject areas.

Emerging Trends in Securities Law. West Group. • Annual. $295.00. Presents a detailed chronicle of events and analysis of evolving trends.(Securities Handbook Series).

Securities, Commodities, and Federal Banking: 1999 in Review. CCH, Inc. • Irregular. $57.00. Summarizes the year's significant legal and regulatory developments.

Securities Law Review. West Group. • Annual. $326.00. Current thinking in securities law.

CD-ROM DATABASES

Compact D/SEC. Thomson Financial. • Monthly. Provides 200 financial data items for 12,000 U. S. publicly-held corporations filing reports with the Securities and Exchange Commission. Includes company profiles.

WILSONDISC: Index to Legal Periodicals and Books. H. W. Wilson Co. • Monthly. Includes unlimited online access to *Index to Legal Periodicals* through WILSONLINE. Contains CD-ROM indexing of more than 1,400 English language legal periodicals from 1981 to date and 2,500 books.

ENCYCLOPEDIAS AND DICTIONARIES

West's Encyclopedia of American Law. Available from Gale Cengage Learning. • 2003. $1,195.00. Second edition. 12 volumes. Published by West Group. Covers a wide variety of legal topics for the general reader.

HANDBOOKS AND MANUALS

Financing the Corporation. Richard A. Booth. West Group. • Annual. $160.00. Looseleaf service. Covers a wide variety of corporate finance legal topics, from initial capital structure to public sale of securities.

Going Public in Good Times and Bad: A Legal and Business Guide. Robert G. Heim. American Lawyer Media, Inc. • 2002. $29.95. Provides practical advice for corporate officers and attorneys. Covers such items as underwriter selection, registration statements, relevant securities laws, and liability concerns. Contains examples of forms needed at various stages of taking a company public.

Guide to Federal Regulation of Derivatives. James Hamilton and others. CCH, Inc. • 1998. $85.00. Explains the complex derivatives regulations of the Securities and Exchange Commission. Covers swap agreements, third-party derivatives, credit derivatives, mutual fund liquidity, and other topics.

Money Manager's Compliance Guide. Thompson Publishing Group, Inc. • $649.00 per year. Two looseleaf volumes. Monthly updates and newletters. Edited for investment advisers and investment companies to help them be in compliance with governmental regulations, including SEC rules, restrictions based on the Employee Retirement Income Security Act (ERISA), and regulations issued by the Commodity Futures Trading Commission (CFTC).

Responsibilities of Corporate Officers and Directors Under Federal Securities Law. CCH, Inc. • Annual. $79.00. Includes discussions of indemnification, "D & O" insurance, corporate governance, and insider liability.

SEC Accounting Rules. CCH, Inc. • $448.00. Looseleaf service.

SEC Financial Reporting: Annual Reports to Shareholders, Form 10-K, and Quarterly Financial Reporting. LexisNexis Matthew Bender. • Annual. $254.00. Looseleaf service. Coverage of aspects of financial reporting with GAAP disclosure and Regulation S-X preparation Step-by-step procedures for preparing information for Form 10-K and annual shareholders reports.

SEC Handbook: Rules and Forms for Financial Statements and Related Disclosures. CCH, Inc. • Annual. $59.00. Contains full text of rules and requirements set by the Securities and Exchange Commisssion for preparation of corporate financial statements.

Securities Crimes. West Group. • Annual. $225.00.

Two looseleaf volumes. Analyzes the enfo of federal securities laws from the viewpoint of the defendant. Discusses Securities and Exchange Commission (SEC) investigations and federal sentencing guidelines. (Securities Law Series).

Securities Law Handbook. West Group. • Annual. $326.00. In-depth coverage of security issues. (Securities Handbook Series).

Securities: Public and Private Offerings, 2d. William W. Prifti. West Group. • Semiannual. $389.00. Three looseleaf volumes. How to issue securities. (Securities Law Series).

INTERNET DATABASES

Factiva. Dow Jones Reuters Business Interactive, LLC. Phone: 800-369-7466 or (609)452-1511 Fax: (609)520-5770 E-mail: solutions@factiva.com • URL: http://www.factiva.com • Fee-based Web site provides "global news and business information through Web sites and content integration solutions." Includes Dow Jones and Reuters newswires, The Wall Street Journal, and more than 7,000 other sources of current news, historical articles, market research reports, and investment analysis. Content includes 96 major U. S. newspapers, 900 non-English sources, trade publications, media transcripts, country profiles, news photos, etc.

Lexis.com Research System. Lexis-Nexis Group. Phone: 800-227-4908 or (937)865-6800 Fax: (937)865-6909 E-mail: webmaster@prod.lexis-nexis.com • URL: http://www.lexis.com • Fee-based Web site offers extensive searching of a wide variety of legal sources. Additional features include Daily Opinion Service, lexis.com Bookstore, Career Center, CLE Center, Law Schools, and Practice Pages ("Pages specific to areas of specialty").

Nexis.com. Lexis-Nexis Group. Phone: 800-227-4908 or (937)865-6800 Fax: (937)865-6909 E-mail: webmaster@prod.lexis-nexis.com • URL: http://www.nexis.com • Fee-based Web site offers searching of about 2.8 billion documents in some 30,000 news, business, and legal information sources. Features include a subject directory covering 1,200 topics in 34 categories and a Company Dossier containing information on more than 500,000 public and private companies. Boolean searching is offered.

Rutgers Accounting Web (RAW). Rutgers University Accounting Research Center. Phone: (973)353-5172 Fax: (973)353-1283 • URL: http://www.rutgers.edu/accounting • RAW Web site provides extensive links to sources of national and international accounting information, such as the Big Six accounting firms, the Financial Accounting Standards Board (FASB), SEC filings (EDGAR), journals, publishers, software, the International Accounting Network, and "Internet's largest list of accounting firms in USA." Searching is offered. Fees: Free.

U. S. Securities and Exchange Commission. Phone: 800-732-0330 or (202)942-7040 Fax: (202)942-9634 E-mail: webmaster@sec.gov • URL: http://www.sec.gov • SEC Web site offers free access through EDGAR to text of official corporate filings, such as annual reports (10-K), quarterly reports (10-Q), and proxies. (EDGAR is "Electronic Data Gathering, Analysis, and Retrieval System.") An example is given of how to obtain executive compensation data from proxies. Text of the daily *SEC News Digest* is offered, as are links to other government sites, non-government market regulators, and U. S. stock exchanges. Search facilities are extensive. Fees: Free.

ONLINE DATABASES

Disclosure SEC Database. Thomson Financial. • Provides online information from records filed with the Securities and Exchange Commission by more than 12,000 publicly-owned companies in the U.S. Includes about 200 financial data items and information relating to executives. Time span is 1977 to

date, with weekly updates. Inquire as to online cost and availability.

EdgarPlus: SEC Basic Filings. Thomson Financial. • Online service provides full text of about 60,000 documents that have been filed with the U.S. Securities and Exchange Commission, 1987 to date, with daily updates. Filings include 6-K, 8-K, 10-K, 10-C, 10-Q, 20-F, and proxy statements. Inquire as to online cost and availability.

Index to Legal Periodicals and Books (Online). H. W. Wilson Co. • Broad coverage of law journals and books 1981 to date. Monthly updates. Inquire as to online cost and availability.

PERIODICALS AND NEWSLETTERS

Compliance Reporter. Institutional Investor, Inc., Journals Group. • Biweekly. $2,330.00 per year. Includes print and online editions. Newsletter for investment dealers and others on complying with securities laws and regulations.

Futures and Derivatives Law Report: The Journal on the Law of Investment and Risk Management Products. Glasser Legalworks. • Monthly. $305.00 per year. Newsletter. Covers developments in regulation, legislation, and litigation concerning financial derivatives, futures trading, and options trading.

Journal of Taxation of Financial Products. CCH, Inc. • Bimonthly. $249.00 per year.

Legal Times. American Lawyer Media, L.P. • Weekly. Individuals, $249.00 per year; institutions, $635.00 per year.

The Review of Securities and Commodities Regulations: An Analysis of Current Laws, Regulations Affecting the Securities and Futures Industries. Standard and Poor's. • 22 times a year. $350.00 per year.

SEC News Digest. U.S. Securities and Exchange Commission, Public Reference Room. • Daily.

SEC Today (Securities Exchange Commission). Washington Service Bureau, Inc. • Daily. $760.00 per year. Newsletter. Includes the official *SEC News Digest* from the Securities and Exchange Commission and reports on public company filing activity.

Securities and Federal Corporate Law Report. West Group. • $526.00 per year. Newsletter. Periodic supplementation.

Securities Arbitration Commentator: Covering Significant Issues and Events in Securities-Commodities Arbitration. Richard P. Ryder. • Monthly. $348.00 per year. Newsletter. Edited for attorneys and other professionals concerned with securities arbitration.

Securities Week. McGraw-Hill Financial Services Co. • Description: Acts as a trade publication for Wall Street executives, publishing news stories on pertinent events and developments within the industry including those related to legislative and regulatory activity, major stock exchanges, investment banking and retail firms, institutional trading, and new products. Recurring features include reports on research departments and a column titled Financial Futures/Commodities Report.

Wall Street Letter: Newsweekly for Investment Banking and Brokerage Community. Institutional Investor, Inc., Journals Group. • Weekly. $2,665.00 per year. Includes print and online editions. Newsletter for stock brokers and companies providing services for stock brokers. Emphasis is on regulatory matters.

Wallstreetlawyer.com: Securities in the Electronic Age. Glasser Legalworks. • Monthly. $345.00 per year. Newsletter. Covers the latest regulatory developments in capital raising, disclosure, and enforcement.

TRADE/PROFESSIONAL ASSOCIATIONS

North American Securities Administrators Association. 750 1st St. NE, Ste. 1140, Washington, DC 20002-8034. Phone: 800-84-NASAA or

(202)737-0900 Fax: (202)783-3571 E-mail: info@nasaa.org • URL: http://www.nasaa.org • Represents the interests of the state, provincial and territorial securities administrators in the U.S., Canada, Mexico and Puerto Rico. Provides support to its members in government relations and with federal regulators, industry SROs and other groups.

OTHER SOURCES

Blue Sky Law Reports. Joseph C. Long. CCH Inc. • Loosleaf service. $1,130.00 per year. Periodic supplementation. Semimonthly updates.

Blue Sky Regulation. LexisNexis Matthew Bender. • $1,089.00. Four looseleaf volumes. Periodic supplementation. Covers state securities laws and regulations.

BNA's Banking Report: Legal and Regulatory Developments in the Financial Services Industry. BNA, Inc. • Weekly. $1,221.00 per year. Two looseleaf volumes. Emphasis on federal regulations.

Commodity Futures Law Reports. CCH, Inc. • Semimonthly. $948.00 per year. Looseleaf service. Periodic supplementation. Includes legal aspects of financial futures and stock options trading.

Corporate Compliance Series. Joseph E. Murphy and Paul H. Dawes. West Group. • $1,210.00. 12 looseleaf volumes. Covers criminal and civil liability problems for corporations. Includes employee safety, product liability, pension requirements, securities violations, equal employment opportunity issues, intellectual property, employee hiring and firing, and other corporate compliance topics.

Federal Securities Act of 1933-Treatise and Primary Source Material. A. A. Sommer. LexisNexis Matthew Bender. • $688.00. Two looseleaf volumes. Periodic supplementation. Covers application of the Federal Securities Act of 1933 and amendments.

Federal Securities Exchange Act of 1934. A. A. Sommer. LexisNexis Matthew Bender. • $688.00. Two looseleaf volumes. Periodic supplementation. Covers application of the Federal Securities Exchange Act of 1934 and amendments.

Federal Securities Law Reports. CCH, Inc. • Weekly. $1,764.00 per year. Looseleaf service. Seven volumes.

Formation and Financing of Emerging Companies. Daniel E. O'Connor and others. Glasser Legalworks. • Looseleaf. $225.00, including CD-ROM version. Periodic Supplementation. Covers incorporation, bylaws, indemnification, intellectual property, financing sources, venture capital, due diligence, bridge loans, investor rights, compliance, and other legal issues associated with company formation. (Emerging Growth Companies Series.).

Fund Governance: Legal Duties of Investment Company Directors. American Lawyer Media, Inc. • Looseleaf. $159.00. Updated as needed. Covers the legal obligations of directors of mutual funds and closed-end funds. (Law Journal Press).

Going Private. American Lawyer Media, Inc. • Looseleaf. $169.00. Updated as needed. Discusses the legal ramifications of a publicly-owned company "going private" by way of a sale, leveraged buyout, reverse stock split, or merger. (Law Journal Press).

International Capital Markets and Securities Regulation. Harold S. Bloomenthal. West Group. • $1,083.00. Nine looseleaf volumes. Periodic supplementation. Securities regulation in industrialized nations. (Securities Law Series).

Taxation of Securities Transactions. LexisNexis Matthew Bender. • Semiannual. $307.00. Looseleaf service. Covers taxation of a wide variety of securities transactions, including those involving stocks, bonds, options, short sales, new issues, mutual funds, dividend distributions, foreign securities, and annuities.

White Collar Crime: Business and Regulatory

Offenses. American Lawyer Media, Inc. • Looseleaf. $249.00. Updated as needed. Covers such legal matters as criminal tax cases, securities fraud, computer crime, mail fraud, bank embezzlement, criminal antitrust activities, extortion, perjury, the criminal liability of corporations, and RICO (Racketeer Influenced and Corrupt Organization Act). (Law Journal Press).

SECURITIES, OBSOLETE

See: OBSOLETE SECURITIES

SECURITIES, TAX EXEMPT

See: MUNICIPAL BONDS

SECURITY ANALYSIS

See: FINANCIAL ANALYSIS

SECURITY, COMPUTER

See: COMPUTER CRIME AND SECURITY

SECURITY DEALERS

See: STOCK BROKERS

SECURITY, INDUSTRIAL

See: INDUSTRIAL SECURITY PROGRAMS

SECURITY SYSTEMS, ELECTRONIC

See: ELECTRONIC SECURITY SYSTEMS

SEED INDUSTRY

ABSTRACTS AND INDEXES
Biological and Agricultural Index. H. W. Wilson Co. • 11 times a year. Annual and quarterly cumulations. Price varies.

Seed Abstracts. Available from CABI Publishing, North America. • Monthly. Institutions, $680.00 per year. Print and online edition, $700.00 per year. Published in England by CABI Publishing. Provides worldwide coverage of the literature.

DIRECTORIES
Global Seed Guide: World Reference Source for the Commercial Seed Industry. Ball Publishing. • Annual. $40.00. Includes company listings, type of business, type of seed, research centers, industry data, events calendar, and associations.

FINANCIAL RATIOS
Annual Statement Studies. The Risk Management Association. • Annual. Median and quartile financial ratios are given for over 400 kinds of manufacturing, wholesale, retail, construction, and consumer finance establishments. Data is sorted by both asset size and sales volume. Includes a clearly written "Definition of Ratios" and an alphabetical industry index.

Annual Statement Studies: Industry Default Probabilities and Cash Flow Measures. The Risk Management Association. • Annual. $145.00. Serves as a companion volume to the original *Annual Statement Studies.* Gives probability of default estimates on a percentage scale for more than 450

industries. Includes changes in position year-by-year for eight financial statement line items and provides percentage measures of cash flow.

HANDBOOKS AND MANUALS
Knott's Handbook for Vegetable Growers. Donald N. Maynard and George J. Hochmuth. John Wiley and Sons, Inc. • 1997. $99.00. Fourth edition. Written for commercial vegetable growers, truck farmers, horticulturists, and other professionals. Covers such topics as spacing of plants, disease control, insect pests, seeds, weeds, water management, and irrigation.

ONLINE DATABASES
CAB Abstracts. CAB Publishing North America. • Contains 46 specialized abstract collections covering over 10,000 journals and monographs in the areas of agriculture, horticulture, forest products, farm products, nutrition, dairy science, poultry, grains, animal health, entomology, etc. Time period is 1972 to date, with monthly updates. Inquire as to online cost and availability. *CAB Abstracts on CD-ROM* also available, with annual updating.

PERIODICALS AND NEWSLETTERS
Journal of New Seeds: Innovations in Production, Biotechnology, Quality, and Marketing. Haworth Press, Inc. • Quarterly. $240.00 per year to libraries; $65.00 per year to individuals. Covers research and development for a new generation of seeds having a high degree of quality and productivity. Topics relating to global seed production include marketing, economics, and intellectual property rights.

The Seed Technologist Newsletter. Society of Commercial Seed Technologists. • Three times a year. $35.00 per year. Includes annual *Proceedings.*

Seed Trade News. Ball Publishing. • Monthly. $48.00 per year. Includes *International Seed Directory.*

Seed World. Scranton Gillette Communications, Inc. • Monthly. $30.00 per year. Provides information on the seed industry for buyers and sellers. Supplement available *Seed Trade Buyer's Guide.*

TRADE/PROFESSIONAL ASSOCIATIONS
American Seed Research Foundation. 225 Reinekers Ln., Ste. 650, Alexandria, VA 22314-2875. Phone: (703)837-8140 Fax: (703)837-9365 E-mail: natl-office@asgs-glass.org • URL: http://www.amseed.com/asrf • Breeders, producers, and distributors of seeds. Seeks to advance seed technology by supporting research on seeds.

American Seed Trade Association. 225 Reinekers Ln., Ste. 650, Alexandria, VA 22314-2875. Phone: 888-890-SEED or (703)837-8140 or (703)837-8140 Fax: (703)837-9365 E-mail: alozanom@sakata.com.mx • URL: http://www.amseed.com • Breeders, growers, assemblers, conditioners, wholesalers, and retailers of grain, grass, vegetable, flower, and other seed for planting purposes.

Association of American Seed Control Officials. PO Box 9013, Springfield, IL 62794. Phone: (217)785-1082 Fax: (217)524-7801 • URL: http://www.seedcontrol.org.

National Council of Commercial Plant Breeders. 225 Reinkers Lane, Suite 650, Alexandria, VA 22314. Phone: (703)837-8140 Fax: (703)837-9365 • URL: http://www.amseed.org.

Society of Commercial Seed Technologists. 101 E State St., No. 214, c/o Anita Hall, Ithaca, NY 14850. Phone: (607)256-3313 Fax: (607)256-3313 E-mail: scst@twcny.rr.com • URL: http://www.seedtechnology.net • Affiliated with Association of Official Seed Analysts.

OTHER SOURCES
Global Seed Markets. Theta Reports. • 2000. $1,040.00. Market research data. Covers the major seed sectors, including cereal crops, legumes, oilseed crops, fibre crops, and beet crops. Provides

analysis of biotechnology developments. (Theta Report No. DS208E.).

SELENIUM INDUSTRY

ABSTRACTS AND INDEXES
CA Selects: Selenium and Tellurium Chemistry. American Chemical Society. Chemical Abstracts Service. • Semiweekly. Members, $92.00 per year; non-members, $305.00 per year. Looseleaf service. Incorporates *Selenium and Tellurium Abstracts.*

DIRECTORIES
OPD Chemical Buyers Directory. Schnell Publishing Company Inc. • Covers: about 1,500 suppliers of chemical process materials and more than 300 companies that transport and store chemicals in the United States. Entries include: Company name, address, phone, list of products or services, telex, fax, e-mail address, internet address, branch offices.

ONLINE DATABASES
Globalbase. Gale Cengage Learning. • Provides more than one million online summaries of business, industrial, and economic news reports from more than 1,000 publications worldwide. Covers a wide range of material appearing in international trade journals, professional magazines, and newspapers. Time period is 1984 to date, with weekly updates. Inquire as to online cost and availability.

PRICE SOURCES
Chemical Market Reporter. Schnell Publishing Co., Inc. • Weekly. $169.00 per year. Quotes current prices for a wide range of chemicals. Formerly *Chemical Marketing Reporter.*

STATISTICS SOURCES
Mineral Commodity Summaries. Available from U. S. Government Printing Office. • Annual. $26.00. Published by the U. S. Geological Survey, Department of the Interior (http://www.usgs.gov). Contains detailed, five-year data for about 90 nonfuel minerals. Covers a wide range of statistics, including production, imports, exports, consumption, reserves, prices, tariff information, and industry employment. (Two pages are devoted to each mineral.).

Non-Ferrous Metal Data Yearbook. American Bureau of Metal Statistics. • Annual. $405.00. Provides worldwide data on approximately about 200 statistical tables covering many nonferrous metals. Includes production, consumption, inventories, exports, imports, and other data.

TRADE/PROFESSIONAL ASSOCIATIONS
American Bureau of Metal Statistics. P.O. Box 805, Chatham, NJ 07928. Phone: (973)701-2299 Fax: (973)701-2152 E-mail: info@abms.com • URL: http://www.abms.com • Members are metal companies. Compiles and publishes detailed statistical data on a wide variety of nonferrous metals: aluminum, copper, gold, lead, nickel, platinum, silver, tin, titanium, uranium, zinc, and others.

SELF-EMPLOYMENT

See also: ENTREPRENEURS AND INTRA-PRENEURS; KEOGH PLANS; SMALL BUSINESS

GENERAL WORKS
Is It Too Late to Run Away and Join the Circus? Finding the Life You Really Want. Marti Smye. John Wiley. • 1998. $14.95. Provides philosophical and inspirational advice on leaving corporate life and becoming self-employed as a consultant or whatever. Central theme is dealing with major changes in life style and career objectives.

Working from Home: Everything You Need to Know

About Living and Working Under the Same Roof. Paul Edwards and Sarah Edwards. The Putnam Publishing Group. • 1999. $18.95. Fifth revised expanded edition.

ENCYCLOPEDIAS AND DICTIONARIES

Encyclopedia of Small Business. Gale Cengage Learning. • 2002. $450.00. Second edition. Two volumes. Contains about 600 informative entries on a wide variety of topics affecting small business. Arrangement is alphabetical.

HANDBOOKS AND MANUALS

Accounting and Recordkeeping for the Self-Employed. Jack Fox. John Wiley and Sons, Inc. • 1994. $19.95.

Business Taxpayer Information Publications. Available from U. S. Government Printing Office. • Annual. $63.00. Two volumes, consisting of *Circular E, Employer's Tax Guide* and *Employer's Supplemental Tax Guide.* Issued by the Internal Revenue Service (http://www.irs.ustreas.gov). Includes a wide variety of business-related tax information, including withholding tables, tax calendars, self-employment issues, partnership matters, corporation topics, depreciation, and bankruptcy.

CCH Guide to Car, Travel, Entertainment, and Home Office Deductions. CCH, Inc. • Annual. $45. 00. Explains how to claim maximum tax deductions for common business expenses. Includes automobile depreciation tables, lease value tables, worksheets, and examples of filled-in tax forms.

Home Business Bible: Everything You Need to Know to Start and Run Your Home-Based Business. David R. Eyler. John Wiley and Sons, Inc. • 1994. $60.00. Includes CD-ROM.

Home Office Design: Everything You Need to Know about Planning, Organizing, and Furnishing Your Work Space. Neal Zimmerman. John Wiley and Sons, Inc. • 1996. $19.95. Covers furniture, seating, workstations, filing, storage, task lighting, etc.

Homemade Money: How to Turn Your Talents, Experience, and Know-How into a Profitable Home-based Business That's Perfect for You!. Barbara Brabec. Evans, M and Co., Inc. • 2003. $19.95. Second edition. Covers sales, advertising, publicity, pricing, financing, legal issues, and other topics relating to businesses operated from home.

How to Start a Home-Based Web Design Business. Jim Smith. Globe Pequot Press. • 2004. $17.95. Second edition. Covers planning, marketing, subcontracting, setting fees, customer presentations, and other topics related to starting a freelance, web design business at home. Includes a sample customer contract. (Home-Based Business Series).

Legal Guide to Independent Contractor Status. Robert W. Wood. Aspen Publishers, Inc. • 2003. Price on application. A guide to the legal and tax-related differences between employers and independent contractors. Includes examples of both "safe" and "troublesome" independent contractor designations. Penalties and fines are discussed.

Start, Run, and Profit From Your Own Home-Based Business. Gregory Kishel and Patricia Kishel. John Wiley and Sons, Inc. • 1991. $16.95.

Telecom Made Easy: Money-Saving, Profit-Building Solutions for Home Businesses, Telecommuters. June Langhoff. Aegis Publishing Group, Ltd. • 2001. $19.95. Fouth revised edition.

INTERNET DATABASES

Small Business Retirement Savings Advisor. U. S. Department of Labor. Phone: (202)219-8921 • URL: http://www.dol.gov/elaws/pwbaplan.htm • Web site provides "answers to a variety of commonly asked questions about retirement saving options for small business employers." Includes a comparison chart and detailed descriptions of various plans: 401(k), SEP-IRA, SIMPLE-IRA, Payroll Deduction IRA,

Keogh Profit-Sharing, Keogh Money Purchase, and Defined Benefit. Searching is offered. Fees: Free.

PERIODICALS AND NEWSLETTERS

Home Business Magazine: The Home-Based Entrepreneur's Magazine. United Marketing and Research Co., Inc. • Bimonthly. $15.00 per year. Provides practical advice and ideas relating to the operation of a business in the home. Sections include "Marketing & Sales," "Money Corner" (financing), "Businesses & Opportunities," and "Home Office" (equipment, etc.). Includes an annual directory of more than 250 non-franchised home business opportunities, including start-up costs and information about providers.

Home Office Connections: A Monthly Journal of News, Ideas, Opportunities, and Savings for Those Who Work at Home. Home Office Association of America. • Monthly. Free to members; non-members, $49.00 per year.

HomeOffice: The Homebased Office Authority. Entrepreneur Media, Inc. • Bimonthly. $11.97 per year. Contains advice for operating a business in the home.

Inc.: The Magazine for Growing Companies. INC. • 18 times a year. $14.00 per year. Edited for small office and office-in-the-home businesses with from one to 25 employees. Covers management, office technology, and lifestyle. Incorporates *Self-Employed Professional.*

ReCareering Newsletter: An Idea and Resource Guide to Second Career and Relocation Planning. Publications Plus, Inc. • Monthly. $59.00 per year. Edited for "downsized managers, early retirees, and others in career transition after leaving traditional employment." Offers advice on second careers, franchises, starting a business, finances, education, training, skills assessment, and other matters of interest to the newly unemployed.

Self-Employed America. National Association for the Self-Employed. • Bimonthly. Members, $2.00 per year; non-members, $12.00 per year. Provides articles on marketing, management, motivation, accounting, taxes, and other topics for businesses having fewer than 15 employees.

Small Business Tax News. Inside Mortgage Finance Publications. • Monthly. $175.00 per year. Newsletter. Formerly *Small Business Tax Control.*

The Small Business Tax Review. A/N Group Inc. • Description: Reports tax news on such topics as new laws, court cases, IRS rulings, fringe benefits, and business and individual taxes, with emphasis on smaller businesses. Advises on financial planning and technical aspects of small business management.

SOHO Journal (Small Office Home Office). National Association for the Cottage Industry. • Members, $25.00 per year; libraries, $35.00 per year. Newsletter on business in thehome. Formerly *Mind Your Own Business at Home.*

TRADE/PROFESSIONAL ASSOCIATIONS

Home Office Association of America. PO Box 51, Sagaponack, NY 11962-0051. Phone: 800-809-4622 E-mail: hoaa@aol.com • URL: http://www.hoaa. com • A for-profit organization providing advice and information to home office workers and business owners.

National Association for the Self-Employed. DFW Airport, P.O. Box 612067, Dallas, TX 75261-2067. Phone: 800-232-6273 Fax: 800-551-4446 • URL: http://www.nase.org • Members are very small businesses and the self-employed. Acts as an advocacy group at the state and federal levels.

National Association of Home Based Businesses. 10451 Mill Run Cir., Ste. 400, Owing Mills, MD 21117. Phone: (410)363-3698 E-mail: nahbb@msn. com • URL: http://www.usahomebusiness.com • Affiliated with International Association for Busi-

ness Organizations and the Small Business Network. National Family Business Council. 1640 W Kennedy Rd., Lake Forest, IL 60045. Phone: (847)295-1040 Fax: (847)295-1898 E-mail: jmnfbc@msn.com • Serves as a consulting group and resource center on family-owned businesses. Offers consultation, speakers' bureau, and other communications with other family businesses; sponsors regional seminars on problems unique to family businesses. Conducts surveys.

National Federation of Independent Business. 53 Century Blvd., Ste. 250, Nashville, TN 37214. Phone: 800-634-2669 or (615)872-5800 Fax: (615)872-5353 • URL: http://www.nfib.com • Members are independent business and professional people.

OTHER SOURCES

Tax Strategies for the Self-Employed. Alan D. Campbell and others. CCH, Inc. • 2000. $95.00. Covers accounting methods, start-up expenses, transportation deductions, depreciation, pension deductions, tax penalties, and other topics related to tax planning for the self-employed.

SELLING

See: SALESMEN AND SALESMANSHIP

SELLING A BUSINESS

See: BUSINESS ENTERPRISES, SALE OF

SELLING BY TELEPHONE

See: TELEPHONE SELLING

SEMICONDUCTOR INDUSTRY

See also: MICROCOMPUTERS AND MINICOMPUTERS; SUPERCONDUCTORS

GENERAL WORKS

Crystal Fire: The Birth of the Information Age. Michael Riordan and Lillian Hoddeson. W. W. Norton & Co., Inc. • 1997. $27.50. A history of the transistor, from early electronic experiments to practical development at the former Bell Telephone Laboratories. (Sloan Technology Series).

ABSTRACTS AND INDEXES

Applied Science and Technology Index. H. W. Wilson Co. • 11 times a year. Quarterly and annual cumulations. Price varies. Indexes a wide variety of English language technical, industrial, and engineering periodicals.

Business Periodicals Index. H. W. Wilson Co. • 11 times a year. Quarterly and annual cumulations. Price varies.

Current Contents: Engineering, Computing and Technology. Thomson/ISI. • Weekly. $730.00 per year. Reproductions of contents pages of technical journals. Includes *Author Index, Address Directory, Current Book Contents* and *Title Word Index.* Formerly *Current Contents: Engineering, Technology and Applied Sciences.*

Key Abstracts: Semiconductor Devices. Available from INSPEC, Inc. • Monthly. $250.00 per year. Provides international coverage of journal and proceedings literature. Published in England by the Institution of Electrical Engineers (IEE).

NTIS Alerts: Electrotechnology. National Technical Information Service. • Semimonthly. $210.00 per year. Provides descriptions of government-sponsored research reports and software, with ordering information. Covers electronic components, semiconductors, antennas, circuits, optoelectronic devices, and related subjects. Formerly *Abstract Newsletter*.

Solid State and Superconductivity Abstracts. CSA. • Bimonthly. $1,695.00 per year. Includes print and online editions. Formerly *Solid State Abstracts Journal*.

DIRECTORIES

IC Master (Integrated circuits): The Electronics Industry's Leading Source of ICInformation. IC Master. • Annual. $195.00. Semiannual supplements. Product information on 120,000 commercially available integrated circuits.

Semiconductor International--Semi Source. Reed Business Information. • Publication includes: Lists of companies associated with the design, processing, assembly, packaging, and testing of semiconductor devices, integrated circuits, and hybrid circuits. Entries include: Company name, address, phone, fax, products.

SIA Annual Report and Directory. Semiconductor Industry Association. • Annual. Members, $105.00; non-members, $150.00. Provides information on key semiconductor issues. Formerly *SIA Status Report and Industry Directory*.

ENCYCLOPEDIAS AND DICTIONARIES

Wiley Encyclopedia of Electrical and Electronics Engineering. John G. Webster, editor. John Wiley and Sons, Inc. • 1999. $9,630.00. 25 volumes. Includes *Supplement I* and *Supplement II*. Contains about 1,400 articles, each with bibliography. Arrangement is according to 64 categories.

FINANCIAL RATIOS

Industry Norms and Key Business Ratios. Desk Top Edition. Dun and Bradstreet Corp. • Annual. Five volumes. $475.00 per volume. $1,890.00 per set. Covers over 800 kinds of businesses, arranged by Standard Industrial Classification number. More detailed editions covering longer periods of time are also available.

HANDBOOKS AND MANUALS

Handbook of Semiconductor Technology. Kenneth A. Jackson and Wolfgang Schroter, editors. John Wiley and Sons, Inc. • 2000. $625.00. Two volumes. Vol. one, $365.00; vol. two, $260.00. Volume one covers the electronic properties of semiconductors; volume two is on relevant materials technology.

Solid State Electronic Devices. Prentice Hall PTR. • 1999. $107.00. Fifth edition. (Solid State Physical Electronics Series).

INTERNET DATABASES

Manufacturing Profiles. U. S. Bureau of the Census. Phone: (301)763-4636 E-mail: webmaster@census. gov • URL: http://www.census.gov/prod/www/abs/mfg-prof.html • The Census Bureau makes available free on PDF (Portable Document Format) an annual consolidation of the entire Current Industrial Report series, presenting "all the data compiled." Contains statistics on production, shipments, inventories, consumption, exports, imports, and orders for a wide variety of manufactured products.

ONLINE DATABASES

Applied Science and Technology Index Online. H. W. Wilson Co. • Provides online indexing of 500 major scientific, technical, industrial, and engineering periodicals. Time period is 1983 to date. Monthly updates. Inquire as to online cost and availability.

INSPEC. Institution of Electrical Engineers (IEE). • Provides online citations, with abstracts, to the world literature of electrical engineering, electronics, optoelectronics, telecommunications, industrial controls, instrumentation, computer technology,

information technology, and physics. Coverage includes more than 4,000 technical and scientific journals from 1969 to date, with weekly updating. (INSPEC is Information Services in Physics, Electronics, and Computing.) Inquire as to online cost and availability.

PROMT: Predicasts Overview of Markets and Technology. Gale Cengage Learning. • Companies, products, applied technologies and markets. U.S. and international literature coverage, 1972 to date. Inquire as to online cost and availability. Provides abstracts from more than 1,600 publications. Weekly updates.

Scisearch. Institute for Scientific Information. • Broad, multidisciplinary index to the literature of science and technology, 1974 to present. Inquire as to online cost and availability. Coverage of literature is worldwide, with weekly updates.

Wilson Business Abstracts Online. H. W. Wilson Co. • Indexes and abstracts 600 major business periodicals, plus the *Wall Street Journal* and the business section of the *New York Times*. Indexing is from 1982, abstracting from 1990, with the two newspapers included from 1993. Updated weekly. Inquire as to online cost and availability. (*Business Periodicals Index* without abstracts is also available online.).

PERIODICALS AND NEWSLETTERS

Computer. Institute of Electrical and Electronic Engineers, Inc. • Monthly. $1,060.00 per year. Edited for computer technology professionals.

ECN Literature News (Electronic Component News). Reed Business Information. • Bimonthly. Price on application.

IEEE Micro. Institute of Electrical and Electronics Engineers, Inc. • Bimonthly. $650.00 per year.

Inside Chips Ventures: The Global Report with Executive Perspective. HTE Research, Inc. • Monthly. $595.00 per year. Tracks the activities of semiconductor firms worldwide. Formerly *Semiconductor Industry and Business Survey Newsletter*.

Integrated Circuits International: An International Bulletin for Suppliers and Users of Integrated Circuits. Elsevier. • Monthly. $541.00 per year. For suppliers and users of integrated circuits.

Microprocessor Report: The Insiders' Guide to Microprocessor Hardware. Reed Business Information. • 12 times a year. $695.00 per year. Newsletter. Covers the technical aspects of microprocessors from Intel, IBM, Cyrix, Motorola, and others.

Semiconductor International: The Industry Sourcebook for Processing, Assembly and Testing. Reed Electronics Group. • Monthly. $131.99 per year. Devoted to processing, assembly and testing techniques.

Solid State Technology. PennWell Corp., Advanced Technology Div. • Monthly. $217.00 per year. Covers the technical and business aspects of semiconductor and integrated circuit production. Includes *Buyers Guide*.

WaferNews Confidential. PennWell Corp., Advanced Technology Div. • 50 times a year. $799.00 per year. Newsletter. Covers developments and trends in the semiconductor equipment industry.

RESEARCH CENTERS AND INSTITUTES

Center for Integrated Systems. Stanford University, 420 Via Palou Mall, Stanford, CA 94305-4070. Phone: (650)725-3621 Fax: (650)725-0991 E-mail: rdasher@stanford.edu • URL: http://www.cis. stanford.edu • Research programs include manufacturing science, design science, computer architecture, semiconductor technology, and telecommunications.

Center for Solid State Electronics Research. Arizona State University. P.O. Box 876206, Tempe, AZ

85287-6206. Phone: (480)965-3708 Fax: (480)965-8118 E-mail: cssermail@asu.edu • URL: http://www.ceaspub.eas.asu.edu/csser.

Lincoln Laboratory. Massachusetts Institute of Technology, 244 Wood St., Lexington, MA 02420-9108. Phone: (781)981-5500 Fax: (781)981-7086 • URL: http://www.ll.mit.edu • Multidisciplinary off-campus research unit. Research fields include solid state devices.

Microelectronics Laboratory. Dept. of Electrical Engineering, Ohio State University, 2015 Neil Ave., Columbus, OH 43210-1272. Phone: (614)292-5110 Fax: (614)292-7596 E-mail: valco.1@osu.edu.

Nanofabrication Facility. Pennsylvania State University. 187 Materials Research Institute, University Park, PA 16802-7003. Phone: (814)863-0627 Fax: (814)865-7173 E-mail: nanofab.psu.edu • URL: http://www.nonafab.psu.edu • Formerly Electronic Materials and Processing Research Laboratory.

Semiconductor Device Laboratory. University of Virginia-Applied Electropysics Laboratories, Thornton Hall, Dept. of Electrical and Computing Engineering, Charlottesville, VA 22903. Phone: (424)924-7693 Fax: (424)924-8818 E-mail: twc8u@virginia.edu • URL: http://www.ece.virginia.edu.

Semiconductor Research Laboratory. Duke University, Dept. of Electrical and Computer Engineering, P.O. Box 90291, Durham, NC 27708. Phone: (919)660-5252 Fax: (919)660-5293 E-mail: abrown@ee.duke.edu • URL: http://www.ee.duke.edu.

Solid-State Device and Materials Research Laboratory. School of Electrical and Computer Engineering, Purdue University, 1285 Electrical Engineering, West Lafayette, IN 47907-1285. Phone: (765)494-3461 Fax: (765)494-6441 E-mail: miller@ecn.purdue.edu • URL: http://www.ece.purdue.edu.

STATISTICS SOURCES

Annual Survey of Manufactures. Available from U. S. Government Printing Office. • Annual. Prices vary. Issued by the U. S. Census Bureau as an interim update to the *Census of Manufactures*. Includes data on number of manufacturing establishments in various industries, employment, labor costs, value of shipments, capital expenditures, inventories, energy costs, and assets. (See also Census Bureau home page, http://www.census.gov/.).

Semiconductors, Printed Circuit Boards, and Other Electronic Components. U. S. Bureau of the Census. • Annual. Provides data on shipments: value, quantity, imports, and exports. (Current Industrial Reports, MA-36Q.).

Standard & Poor's Industry Surveys. Standard & Poor's. • Semiannual. $1,800.00. Two looseleaf volumes. Includes monthly *Supplements*. Provides detailed, individual surveys of 52 major industry groups. Each survey is revised on a semiannual basis. Also includes "Monthly Investment Review" (industry group investment analysis) and monthly "Trends & Projections" (economic analysis).

U. S. Industry and Trade Outlook. Available from National Technical Information Service. • Annual. $69.95. Produced by the International Trade Administration, U. S. Department of Commerce, in a "public-private" partnership with DRI/McGraw-Hill and Standard & Poor's. Provides basic data, outlook for the current year, and "Long-Term Prospects" (five-year projections) for a wide variety of products and services. Includes high technology industries. Formerly *U. S. Industrial Outlook*.

World Semiconductor Trade Statistics. Semiconductor Industry Association. • Monthly. $2,200.00 per year. Provides data on all world semiconductor markets including industry forecasts.

TRADE/PROFESSIONAL ASSOCIATIONS

Electronic Industries Alliance. 2500 Wilson Blvd., Arlington, VA 22201. Phone: (703)907-7500 Fax: (703)907-7501 E-mail: mflanigan@eia.org • URL: http://www.eia.org • Seeks for the competitiveness of the American producer, represents all companies involved in the design and manufacture of electronic components, parts, systems and equipment for communications, industrial, government and consumer uses.

IEEE Electron Devices Society. 445 Hoes Ln., PO Box 6804, Piscataway, NJ 08854. Phone: 800-678-4333 or (732)562-3926 Fax: (732)235-1626 E-mail: w.vandervort@ieee.org • URL: http://www.ieee.org/portal/pages/society/eds • A society of the Institute of Electrical and Electronics Engineers. Concerned with the theory, design, and performance of electron devices, including electron tubes, solid-state devices, integrated electron devices, energy sources, power devices, displays, and device reliability.

IEEE Solid State Circuits Council. c/o IEEE Corporate Office, 3 Park Ave., 17th Fl., New York, NY 10016-5997. Phone: 800-678-4333 or (212)419-7900 Fax: (212)752-4929 E-mail: ieeeusa@ieee.org • URL: http://www.ieee.org.

Joint Electron Device Engineering Council (JEDC). 2500 Wilson Blvd., Arlington, VA 22201-3834. Phone: (703)907-7534 Fax: (703)907-7583 E-mail: arlenec@jedec.org • URL: http://www.jedec.org • Affiliated with Electronic Industries Alliance. Formerly Joint Electron Device Engineering Council.

Semiconductor Industry Association. 181 Metro Dr., Ste. 450, San Jose, CA 95110-1344. Phone: (408)436-6600 Fax: (408)436-6646 E-mail: mailbox@sia-online.org • URL: http://www.sia-online.org/home.cfm • Companies that produce semiconductor products such as discrete components, integrated circuits, and microprocessors. Compiles industry trade statistics. Affiliate: Semiconductor Research Corporation and SEMATECH.

SEMINARS

See: CONFERENCES, WORKSHOPS, AND SEMINARS

SENATE

See: UNITED STATES CONGRESS

SENIOR CITIZENS

See: EMPLOYMENT OF OLDER WORKERS; MATURE CONSUMER MARKET; RETIREMENT

SENSORS, INDUSTRIAL

See: CONTROL EQUIPMENT INDUSTRY

SERIAL PUBLICATIONS

See: PERIODICALS

SERVICE, CUSTOMER

See: CUSTOMER SERVICE

SERVICE INDUSTRIES

GENERAL WORKS

Service Management: Strategy and Leadership in the Service Business. Richard Normann. John Wiley and Sons, Inc. • 2001. $60.00. Third edition. Discusses the characteristics of successful service management.

Smart Services: Competitive Information Strategies, Solutions, and Success Stories for Service Businesses. Deborah C. Sawyer. Information Today, Inc. • 2002. $29.95. Covers the use of competitive information by service-oriented firms. (CyberAge Books.).

CD-ROM DATABASES

OECD Statistical Compendium. Organization for Economic Cooperation and Development. • Semiannual. $1,905.00 per year for 1 to 10 users. CD-ROM contains more than 730,000 monthly, quarterly, and annual time series for OECD countries, 1960 to date. Includes fully searchable data on agriculture, food, economic indicators, national accounts, employment, energy, finance, industry, technology, and foreign trade. Results can be displayed in various forms.

16 Million Businesses Phone Directory. Info USA. • Annual. $29.95. Provides more than 16 million yellow pages telephone directory listings on CD-ROM for all ZIP Code areas of the U. S.

WILSONDISC: Wilson Business Abstracts. H. W. Wilson Co. • Monthly. Includes unlimited online access to *Wilson Business Abstracts* through WILSONLINE. Provides CD-ROM "cover-to-cover" abstracting and indexing of over 600 prominent business periodicals. Indexing is from 1982, abstracting from 1990. (*Business Periodicals Index* without abstracts is available on CD-ROM at $1,495 per year.).

DIRECTORIES

American Big Businesses Directory. infoUSA Inc. • Covers: 218,000 U.S. businesses with more than 100 employees, and 500,000 key executives and directors. CD-ROM version contains 160,000 top firms and 431,000 key executives. Entries include: Name, address, phone, names and titles of key personnel, number of employees, sales volume, Standard Industrial Classification (SIC) codes, subsidiaries and parent company names, stock exchanges on which traded.

American Manufacturers Directory. infoUSA Inc. • Covers: more than 150,000 manufacturing companies with 20 or more employees. CD-ROM version lists all 531,000 U.S. manufacturers, in all employee size ranges. Entries include: Company name, address, phone, contact name, Standard Industrial Classification (SIC) codes, number of employees, sales volume code, credit rating scores.

FINANCIAL RATIOS

Almanac of Business and Industrial Financial Ratios. Leo Troy. Aspen Publishers, Inc. • 2003. $125.95. Includes CD-Rom. Contains financial ratios derived from federal tax returns. Ratios for each of about 200 industries are arranged according to company asset size. (Almanac of Business and Industrial Financial Ratios Series).

IRS Corporate Financial Ratios. Available from MarketResearch.com. • 2002. $225.00. Published by Schonfeld & Associates, Inc. Presents 70 key financial ratios for 260 industries. Ratios are calculated from income statement and balance sheet data available from the Internal Revenue Service. Includes four asset size classes.

HANDBOOKS AND MANUALS

Service Quality Handbook. Eberhard E. Scheuing and William F. Christopher, editors. AMACOM. • 1993. $75.00. Contains articles by various authors on the management of service to customers.

INTERNET DATABASES

Business 2.0 Web Guide to the Best Business Links. Business 2.0 Media Inc. Phone: (415)293-4800 E-mail: support@business2.com • URL: http://www.business2.com/webguide • Web site presents an extensive, searchable directory of links to "the best, most informative, and authoritative web pages." Twenty main categories cover business, finance, career, company information, people, and technology topics, with thousands of subtopics, all linking to Web sites recommended by experienced business researchers. Fees: Free.

Fedstats. Federal Interagency Council on Statistical Policy. Phone: (202)395-7254 • URL: http://www.fedstats.gov • Web site features an efficient search facility for full-text statistics produced by more than 100 federal agencies, including the Census Bureau, the Bureau of Economic Analysis, and the Bureau of Labor Statistics. Boolean searches can be made within one agency or for all agencies combined. Links are offered to international statistical bureaus, including the UN, IMF, OECD, UNESCO, Eurostat, and 20 individual countries. Fees: Free.

FreeLunch.com. Economy.com, Inc. Phone: (610)696-8700 Fax: (610)696-1678 • URL: http://www.freelunch.com • Web site provides free access to more than 1.5 million economic and financial data series, covering industry, demographics, labor markets, prices, retail sales, government spending, trade, interest rates, housing starts, the stock market, and many other topics. Data is available for various time periods in either chart or table form. Searching is offered. Fees: Free, but registration required. Economy.com, Inc. also offers fee-based economic analysis at *The Dismal Scientist* site (http://www.dismal.com).

Summary of Commentary on Current Economic Conditions by Federal Reserve District [the Beige Book]. Board of Governors of the Federal Reserve System. Phone: (202)452-3000 Fax: (202)452-3819 • URL: http://www.federalreserve.gov/fomc/beigebook/2004/ • Free Web site provides current "anecdotal information" eight times a year on economic conditions within each of the 12 Federal Reserve Districts, plus an extensive national *Summary.* Text is based on the opinions of bank officials, business executives, economists, financial market experts, and others. Typically contains views of consumer spending, manufacturing, services, credit, employment, prices, wages, and the economy in general. Usually referred to as the Beige Book.

ONLINE DATABASES

American Business Directory. InfoUSA, Inc. • Provides brief online information on more than 10 million U. S. companies, including individual plants and branches. Entries typically include address, phone number, industry classification code, and contact name. Updating is quarterly. Inquire as to online cost and availability.

Business and Industry. Gale Cengage Learning. • Contains online citations, abstracts, and selected fulltext from more than 1,000 trade journals, newspapers, and other publications. Provides general coverage of both manufacturing and service industries, including marketing, production, industry trends, key events, and information on specific companies. Time span is 1994 to date. Daily updates. Inquire as to online cost and availability. (Also available in a CD-ROM version.).

Tablebase. Gale Cengage Learning. • Provides online numerical tabular data from a wide variety of business, organization, and government sources, including about 1,000 trade journals. Includes industry and individual company statistics relating to products, market share, sales forecasts, production, exports, market trends, etc. Time span is 1997 to date. Weekly updates. Inquire as to online cost and availability. (Also available in a CD-ROM version.).

Wilson Business Abstracts Online. H. W. Wilson Co. • Indexes and abstracts 600 major business periodicals, plus the *Wall Street Journal* and the business section of the *New York Times.* Indexing is from 1982, abstracting from 1990, with the two newspapers included from 1993. Updated weekly. Inquire as to online cost and availability. (*Business Periodicals Index* without abstracts is also available online.).

PERIODICALS AND NEWSLETTERS

Cleaning Business: Published Monthly for the Self-Employed Cleaning and Maintenance Professionals. William R. Griffin, Publisher. • Monthly. $20.00 per year. Formerly *Service Business.*

Hotels: The Magazine of the Worldwide Hotel Industry. International Hotel Association. Reed Business Information. • Monthly. $99.90 per year.

STATISTICS SOURCES

Business Statistics of the United States. Linz Audain and Cornelia J. Strawser. Bernan Associates. • Annual. $147.00. Based on *Business Statistics,* formerly issue by the Bureau of Economic Analysis, U. S. Department of Commerce. Provides basic data for a wide variety of U. S. industries, services, and economic indicators. Most statistics are shown annually for 30 years and monthly for the most recent four years.

Encyclopedia of American Industries. Gale Cengage Learning. • 2000. Third edition. Two volumes. $280.00 per volume. Volume one is *Manufacturing Industries* and volume two is *Service and Non-Manufacturing Industries.* Provides the history, development, and recent status of approximately 1,000 industries. Includes statistical graphs, with industry and general indexes.

Information, Finance, and Services USA. Gale Cengage Learning. • 2001. $240.00. Replaces *Service Industries USA* and *Finance, Insurance, and Real Estate USA.* Presents statistics and projections relating to economic activity in a wide variety of non-manufacturing areas.

Services: Statistics on International Transactions. Organization for Economic Cooperation and Development. Available from OECD Publications and Information Center. • Annual. $71.00. Presents a compilation and assessment of data on OECD member countries' international trade in services. Covers four major categories for 20 years: travel, transportation, government services, and other services.

Services: Statistics on Value Added and Employment. Organization for Economic Cooperation and Development. • 2000. $69.00. Provides 10-year data on service industry employment and output (value added) for all OECD countries. Covers such industries as telecommunications, business services, and information technology services.

Structural Statistics for Industry and Services: Core Data. Organization for Economic Cooperation and Development. • Annual. $63.00. Provides annual data for eight years for both industrial and service sectors. Industries include mining, manufacturing, utilities, and construction. Statistics for OECD countries cover production, value added, investment, employment, wages, hours worked, and number of establishments.

Survey of Current Business. Available from U. S. Government Printing Office. • Monthly. $63.00 per year. Issued by Bureau of Economic Analysis, U. S. Department of Commerce. Presents a wide variety of business and economic data.

United States Census of Service Industries. U.S. Bureau of the Census. • Quinquennial. Various reports available.

TRADE/PROFESSIONAL ASSOCIATIONS

National Association of Service Managers. 12603 224th Ave., P.M.B., No. 17, Bristol, WI 53104. Phone: (262)857-7227 Fax: (262)857-1127 E-mail: vince@nasm.com • URL: http://www.nasm.com • Absorbed Service Managers of America.

National Technical Services Association. 2121 Eisenhower Ave., Ste. 604, Alexandria, VA 22314-3501. Phone: (703)684-4722 Fax: (703)684-7627 E-mail: vjohnson@ntsa.com • URL: http://www.ntsa.com • Contract technical services firms that provide a variety of technical services including engineering, designing, and drafting to both industry and government. Goals are to increase understanding of the technical services industry and the role it plays in supplying engineers, draftsmen, and other contract personnel to American industry. Encourages programs in such areas as public relations, ethics, informing potential users of services provided by members, personnel classification and recruitment, technical personnel training and development, and effective utilization of technical manpower. Maintains speakers' bureau and hall of fame; conducts research programs; compiles statistics.

SERVICE INDUSTRY, FOOD

See: FOOD SERVICE INDUSTRY

SERVICE MEN, DISCHARGED

See: VETERANS

SERVICE MERCHANDISERS

See: RACK JOBBERS

SERVICE STATIONS

See: GASOLINE SERVICE STATIONS

SEVERANCE PAY

See: WAGES AND SALARIES

SEWAGE DISPOSAL

See: SANITATION INDUSTRY

SEWING MACHINE INDUSTRY

See also: TEXTILE MACHINERY

TRADE/PROFESSIONAL ASSOCIATIONS

American Apparel Machinery Trade Association. Sussman Automatic Products Corp., 43-20 34th St., 43-20 34th St., Long Island City, NY 11101. Phone: (718)937-4500 Fax: (718)786-4051 E-mail: sdale@sussmancorp.com • Firms engaged in the industrial sewing machine industry, including manufacturers of sewing machines, tables, motors, accessories, parts, and related items.

Home Sewing Association. PO Box 369, Monroeville, PA 15146. Phone: (412)372-5950 Fax: (412)372-5953 E-mail: info@sewing.org • URL: http://www.sewing.org • Manufacturers and retailers of home sewing merchandise, including fabrics, patterns, sewing machines, sewing notions, needlework, and crafts.

OTHER SOURCES

Sewing Machines. Available from MarketResearch. com. • 2002. $4,450.00. Published by Global Industry Analysts. Provides worldwide market research data, including profiles of major sewing machine companies.

SEXUAL HARASSMENT IN THE WORKPLACE

GENERAL WORKS

The 9 to 5 Guide to Combating Sexual Harassment: Candid Advice from 9 to 5, the National Association of Working Women. Ellen Bravo and Ellen Cassedy. John Wiley and Sons, Inc. • 1992. $14.95.

Sexual Harassment in the Workplace: How to Prevent, Investigate, and Resolve Problems in Your Organization. Ellen J. Wagner. AMACOM. • 1992. $17.95.

Sexual Harassment in the Workplace: Perspectives, Frontiers, and Response Strategies. Margaret S. Stockdale, editor. Sage Publications, Inc. • 1996. $103.00. Contains articles by various authors. (Women and Work Series: Vol. 5).

Sexual Harassment: Issues and Analyses. Janet V. Lewis, editor. Nova Science Publishers, Inc. • 2001. $59.00. Provides articles by various authors on sexual harassment and discrimination in the workplace, in education, and in the military. Includes an index.

Sexual Harassment on the Job: What It Is and How to Stop It. William Petrocelli and Barbara K. Repa. Nolo. • 1999. $24.95. Fourth edition. (Sexual Harassment on the Job: What It is and How to Stop It Series).

Violence at Work. Duncan Chappell and Vittorio Di Martino. International Labour Organization. • 2000. $23.00. Second edition. Discusses guidelines, practices, and international legislation aimed at establishing violence-free workplace environments. Problems covered include aggression, assault, physical abuse, and sexual harassment.

Women, Gender, and Work: What is Equality and How Do We Get There?. Martha F. Loutfi, editor. International Labour Organization. • 2001. $26.95. A collection of articles from the *International Labour Review* covering such topics as equal opportunity for women, family concerns, legal issues, the glass ceiling, wage inequality, and sexual harassment in the workplace. Includes statistical data.

ABSTRACTS AND INDEXES

Business Periodicals Index. H. W. Wilson Co. • 11 times a year. Quarterly and annual cumulations. Price varies.

Index to Legal Periodicals and Books. H. W. Wilson Co. • Monthly. $490.00 per year. Quarterly and annual cumulations.

PAIS International in Print. Public Affairs Information Service, Inc. • Monthly. $850.00 per year; cumulations three times a year. Provides topical citations to the worldwide literature of public affairs, economics, demographics, sociology, and trade. Text in English; indexed materials in English, French, German, Italian, Portuguese and Spanish.

Readers' Guide to Periodical Literature. H. W. Wilson Co. • Monthly. $345.00 per year. Includes annual *Cumulation.* Indexes about 250 peridicals of general interest.

Social Sciences Index. H. W. Wilson Co. • Quarterly, with annual cumulation. Price varies. Indexes more than 400 periodicals covering economics, environmental policy, government, insurance, labor, health care policy, plannning, public administration, public welfare, urban studies, women's issues, criminology, and related topics.

BIBLIOGRAPHIES

Sexual Harassment: A Selected, Annotated Bibliography. Lynda J. Hartell and Helena M. VonVille. Greenwood Publishing Group, Inc. • 1995. $64.95. Includes articles and books on workplace sexual harassment. (Bibliographies and

Indexes in Women's Studies, No. 23.).

CD-ROM DATABASES

ABI/INFORM. PROQUEST. • Monthly. Provides CD-ROM indexing and abstracting of worldwide business literature. Archival discs are available from 1971. Formerly *ABI/INFORM OnDisc.*

LegalTrac. Gale Cengage Learning. • Monthly. $5,000.00 per year. Price includes workstation. Provides CD-ROM indexing of periodical literature relating to legal matters from 1980 to date. Corresponds to online *Legal Resource Index.*

Newspaper Abstracts Ondisc. PROQUEST. • Monthly. $2,950.00 per year (covers 1989 to date; archival discs are available for 1985-88). Provides cover-to-cover CD-ROM indexing and abstracting of 19 major newspapers, including the *New York Times, Wall Street Journal, Washington Post, Chicago Tribune,* and *Los Angeles Times.*

PAIS on CD-ROM. Public Affairs Information Service, Inc. • Quarterly. $1,995.00 per year. Provides a CD-ROM version of the online service, *PAIS International.* Contains over 500,000 citations to the literature of contemporary social, political, and economic issues.

Social Sciences Citation Index. ISI. • Monthly. Price on request. Provides CD-ROM indexing of articles appearing in 1700 leading social science journals worldwide, with additional selections from more than 5700 other journals. Time span is 1992 to date. Coverage includes economics, business, finance, management, communications, demographics, library and information science, political science, sociology, and many other subjects.

Social Sciences Citation Index: Compact Disc Edition with Abstracts. Institute for Scientific Information. • Monthly. Provides CD-ROM indexing and abstracting of "significant articles" from 1,700 social science journals worldwide, with additional selections from 3,200 other journals, 1986 to date. Includes economics, business, finance, management, communications, demographics, information and library science, political science, sociology, and many other subjects.

WILSONDISC: Index to Legal Periodicals and Books. H. W. Wilson Co. • Monthly. Includes unlimited online access to *Index to Legal Periodicals* through WILSONLINE. Contains CD-ROM indexing of more than 1,400 English language legal periodicals from 1981 to date and 2,500 books.

WILSONDISC: Readers' Guide to Periodical Literature. H. W. Wilson Co. • Monthly. $1,095.00 per year, including unlimited online access to *Readers' Guide to Periodical Literature* through WILSONLINE. Provides CD-ROM indexing of about 270 general interest periodicals. Covers 1983 to date. (*Readers' Guide Abstracts* also available on CD-ROM at $1,995 per year.).

WILSONDISC: Wilson Business Abstracts. H. W. Wilson Co. • Monthly. Includes unlimited online access to *Wilson Business Abstracts* through WILSONLINE. Provides CD-ROM "cover-to-cover" abstracting and indexing of over 600 prominent business periodicals. Indexing is from 1982, abstracting from 1990. (*Business Periodicals Index* without abstracts is available on CD-ROM at $1,495 per year.).

WILSONDISC: Wilson Social Sciences Abstracts. H. W. Wilson Co. • Monthly. Includes unlimited online access to *Social Sciences Index* through WILSONLINE. Provides CD-ROM indexing from 1983 and abstracting from 1994 of more than 500 periodicals covering economics, area studies, community health, public administration, public welfare,

urban studies, and many other topics related to the social sciences.

DIRECTORIES

Women's Information Directory. Gale. • Covers: Nearly 10,800 sources of information for and about women in the U.S., including national, state, and local organizations; publishers and booksellers of women's materials; newspapers, magazines, newsletters, other directories, and videos; museums; awards, honors, and prizes; government agencies and assistance programs; research centers; women's studies programs at colleges and universities; consultants; scholarships and other financial aids; electronic resources; and library collections. Entries include: Organization or publication name, address, phone, name and title of contact, description of services, activities, etc.

HANDBOOKS AND MANUALS

Investigating Sexual Harassment: A Practical Guide to Resolving Complaints. Angela Bradbery and Rosemarie Lally. Thompson Publishing Group, Inc. • 1998. $79.00. Provides information for employers on sexual harassment liability, investigation of complaints, basics of interviewing, and related topics.

Investigations in the Workplace. Eugene F. Ferraro. CRC Press. • 2004. $79.95. Written for security professionals, lawyers, and human resource directors. Explains how to properly conduct internal investigations in the private sector and avoid litigation. Such investigations may relate to loss prevention, asset protection, or employee rights issues. (Imprint: Auerbach Publications.).

Sexual Harassment in Employment Law. Barbara Lindemann and David D. Kadue. BNA, Inc. • 1999. $140.00.

Sexual Harassment in the Workplace: A Guide to the Law and A Research Overview for Employers and Employees. Titus Aaron and Judith A. Isaksen. McFarland & Co., Inc., Publishers. • 1993. $32.50.

Sexual Orientation in the Workplace: Gays, Lesbians, Bisexuals and Heterosexuals Working Together. Amy J. Zuckerman and George F. Simons. Sage Publications, Inc. • 1994. $34.95. A workbook containing "a variety of simple tools and exercises" to provide skills for "working realistically and effectively with diverse colleagues.".

Women and Sexual Harassment: A Guide to the Legal Protections of Title VII and the Hostile Environment Claim. Anja A. Chan. Haworth Press, Inc. • 1994. $29.95. Emphasis is on hostile environment claims under Title VII of the Civil Rights Act of 1964. Discusses employer liability, the statute of limitations, remedies, discovery and evidence, and related claims. Includes a research guide and lists of primary and secondary sources.

Women and the Law. Carol H. Lefcourt, editor. West Group. • Annual. $302.00. Looseleaf service. Covers such topics as employment discrimination, pay equity (comparable worth), sexual harassment in the workplace, property rights, and child custody issues.

Workplace Sexual Harassment. Anne Levy and Michele A. Paludi. Prentice Hall PTR. • 2001. $38. 20. Second edition. A management guide to confronting and preventing sexual harassment in organizations. Includes case studies and training materials.

ONLINE DATABASES

Contemporary Women's Issues. Gale Cengage Learning. • Provides fulltext articles online from 150 periodicals and a wide variety of additional sources relating to economic, legal, social, political, education, health, and other women's issues. Time span is 1992 to date. Weekly updates. Inquire as to online cost and availability. (Also available in a CD-ROM version.).

Index to Legal Periodicals and Books (Online). H.

W. Wilson Co. • Broad coverage of law journals and books 1981 to date. Monthly updates. Inquire as to online cost and availability.

Legal Resource Index. Gale Cengage Learning. • Broad coverage of law literature appearing in legal, business, and other periodicals, 1980 to date. Daily updates. Inquire as to online cost and availability.

Newspaper Abstracts Daily. ProQuest Inc. • Provides online coverage (citations and abstracts) of 25 major newspapers. Covers business, economics, current affairs, health, fitness, sports, education, technology, government, consumer affairs, psychology, the arts, and the social sciences. Time period is 1986 to date, with daily updates. Inquire as to online cost and availability.

PAIS International. Public Affairs Information Service, Inc. • Corresponds to the former printed publications, *PAIS Bulletin* (1976-90) and *PAIS Foreign Language Index* (1972-90), and to the current *PAIS International in Print* (1991 to date). Covers economic, political, and sociological material appearing in periodicals, books, government documents, and other publications. Updating is monthly. Inquire as to online cost and availability.

Readers' Guide Abstracts Online. H. W. Wilson Co. • Indexes and abstracts general interest periodicals, 1983 to date. Weekly updates. Inquire as to online cost and availability.

Trade & Industry Database. Gale Cengage Learning. • Provides indexing of business periodicals, January 1981 to date. Daily updates. (Full text articles from some periodicals are available online, 1983 to date. Inquire as to online cost and availability).

Wilson Business Abstracts Online. H. W. Wilson Co. • Indexes and abstracts 600 major business periodicals, plus the *Wall Street Journal* and the business section of the *New York Times.* Indexing is from 1982, abstracting from 1990, with the two newspapers included from 1993. Updated weekly. Inquire as to online cost and availability. (*Business Periodicals Index* without abstracts is also available online.).

Wilson Social Sciences Abstracts Online. H. W. Wilson Co. • Provides online abstracting and indexing of more than 500 periodicals covering area studies, community health, public administration, public welfare, urban studies, and many other social science topics. Time period is 1994 to date for abstracts and 1983 to date for indexing, with updates weekly. Inquire as to online cost and availability.

PERIODICALS AND NEWSLETTERS

Nine to Five Newsletter. 9 to 5 National Association of Working Women. • Five times a year. Free to members; individuals, $25.00 per year. A newsletter dealing with the rights and concerns of women office workers.

The Webb Report: A Newsletter on Sexual Harassment. Susan L. Webb, editor. Pacific Resource Development Group, Inc. • Monthly. $120.00 per year. Contains news and information on sexual harassment issues and court cases. Provides guidelines for supervisors and employees as to what constitutes harassment.

Women's Rights Law Reporter. Rutgers University School of Law. • Three times a year. Individuals $20.00 per year; institutions, $40.00 per year; students, $15.00 per year. Provides analysis and commentary on legal issues affecting women, including gender-based discrimination.

RESEARCH CENTERS AND INSTITUTES

Center for Women Policy Studies. 1211 Connecticut Ave., N.W. Suite 312, Washington, DC 20036. Phone: (202)872-1770 Fax: (202)296-8962 E-mail: cwps@centerwomenpolicy.org • URL: http://www.centerwomenpolicy.org • Conducts research on the policy issues that affect the legal, economic, educational, and social status of women, including sexual harassment in the workplace, and women and AIDS.

Women Employed Institute. Women Employed Institute. 111 N Wabash, 13th Fl., Chicago, IL 60602. Phone: (312)782-3902 Fax: (312)782-5249 E-mail: info@womenemployed.org • URL: http://www.womenemployed.org • Economic status of working women, working women and the law, sexual harassment in the workplace, equal employment opportunity, women's access to vocational education and job training, comparable worth, working mothers, and career development.

TRADE/PROFESSIONAL ASSOCIATIONS

National Partnership for Women and Families. 1875 Connecticut Ave., N. W., Suite 710, Washington, DC 20009. Phone: (202)986-2600 Fax: (202)986-2539 E-mail: info@nationalpartnership.org • URL: http://www.nationalpartnership.org • Formerly Women's Legal Defense Fund.

National Women's Law Center. 11 Dupont Cir. NW, Ste. 800, Washington, DC 20036. Phone: (202)588-5180 Fax: (202)588-5185 E-mail: info@nwlc.org • URL: http://www.nwlc.org • Has "expanded the possibilities for women and girls in our country". Uses the law in all its forms: getting new laws on the books; litigating ground-breaking lawsuits all the way to the Supreme Court; and educating the public about how to make the law and public policies work for women and their families. "Takes on the issues that cut to the core of women's and girls' lives" in health, education, employment, and family economic security, with special priority given to the needs of low-income women and their families.

Nine to Five: National Association of Working Women. 1430 W Peachtree St., Ste. 610, Atlanta, GA 30309. Phone: 800-522-0925 or (414)274-0925 Fax: (414)272-2870 E-mail: hotline9to5@igc.org • URL: http://www.9to5.org • Members are women office workers. Strives for the improvement of office working conditions for women and the elimination of sex and race discrimination.

NOW Legal Defense and Education Fund. 395 Hudson St., 5th Fl., New York, NY 10014-3684. Phone: (212)925-6635 Fax: (212)226-1066 E-mail: peo@nowldef.org • URL: http://www.nowldef.org • Supersedes NOW Legal Committee.

Women's Law Project. 125 S 9th St., No. 300, Philadelphia, PA 19107. Phone: (215)928-9801 Fax: (215)928-9848 E-mail: info@womenslawproject.org • URL: http://www.womenslawproject.org/pages/contact_us.htm • Serves as feminist law firm working to challenge sex discrimination in the law and in legal and social institutions through litigation, public education, research and writing, representation of women's groups, and individual counseling. Specializes in the areas of family law, education, employment, reproductive rights, violence against women, and sex-based insurance rates.

OTHER SOURCES

Sex Discrimination and Sexual Harassment in the Work Place. American Lawyer Media, Inc. • Looseleaf. $169.00. Updated as needed. Considers both sides: the point of view of employers and the point of view of employees filing complaints. Coverage includes sexual harassment statutes, the Family Medical Leave Act, the Equal Pay Act, "glass ceiling" issues, pregnancy discrimination, childcare issues, reinstatement after a leave, and other legal matters. (Law Journal Press).

SHAREHOLDERS

See: STOCKHOLDERS

SHARES OF STOCK

See: STOCKS

SHEEP INDUSTRY

See also: LIVESTOCK INDUSTRY; WOOL AND WORSTED INDUSTRY

GENERAL WORKS

Sheep and Goat Science. M. E. Ensminger and Ronald B. Parker. Prentice Hall. • 2001. $69.00. Sixth edition.

INTERNET DATABASES

USDA. United States Department of Agriculture. Phone: (202)720-2791 E-mail: agsec@usda.gov • URL: http://www.usda.gov • The USDA home page has six sections: News and Information; What's New; About USDA; Agencies; Opportunities; Search and Help. Keyword searching is offered from the USDA home page and from various individual agency home pages. Agencies are the Economic Research Service, Agricultural Marketing Service, National Agricultural Statistics Service, National Agricultural Library, and about 12 others. Updating varies. Fees: Free.

PERIODICALS AND NEWSLETTERS

Sheep Breeder and Sheepman. Mead Livestock Services. • Monthly. $18.00 per year.

PRICE SOURCES

The National Provisioner: Serving Meat, Poultry, and Seafood Processors. Stagnito Communications, Inc. • Monthly. Free to qualified personnel; others, $85.04 per year. Annual *Buyer's Guide* available. Meat, poultry and seafood newsletter.

STATISTICS SOURCES

Agricultural Statistics. Available from U. S. Government Printing Office. • Annual. $38.00. Produced by the National Agricultural Statistics Service, U. S. Department of Agriculture. Provides a wide variety of statistical data relating to agricultural production, supplies, consumption, prices/price-supports, foreign trade, costs, and returns, as well as farm labor, loans, income, and population. In many cases, historical data is shown annually for 10 years. In addition to farm data, includes detailed fishery statistics.

FAO Production Yearbook. Available from Bernan Associates. • Annual. $45.00. Published by the Food and Agriculture Organization (http://www.fao.org). Contains worldwide data on agriculture, land use, farm crops, livestock, and agricultural prices.

FAO Trade Yearbook. Available from Bernan Associates. • Annual. $45.00. Published by the Food and Agriculture Organization (http://www.fao.org). Provides extensive worldwide data on exports and imports of agricultural commodities, fertilizers, tractors, and pesticides. Includes more than 130 tables of detailed statistics.

Livestock, Meat, Wool, Market News. U.S. Department of Agriculture. • Weekly.

TRADE/PROFESSIONAL ASSOCIATIONS

American Sheep Industry Association. 9785 Maroon Cir., Ste. 360, Centennial, CO 80112. Phone: (303)771-3500 Fax: (303)771-8200 E-mail: info@sheepusa.org • URL: http://www.sheepusa.org • Producers of sheep and wool. Goal is to advance the standards and profitability of the sheep industry. Conducts lobbying activities to promote legislation beneficial to the industry.

SHEET METAL INDUSTRY

See also: AIR CONDITIONING INDUSTRY; HEATING AND VENTILATION; ROOFING INDUSTRY

DIRECTORIES

HPAC Engineering Info-Dex (Heating, Piping, Air Conditioning). Penton Media Inc. • Annual. $30.00. Industry directory of products, manufacturers, and trade names and a composite of catalog data for mechanical systems engineering professionals.

Who's Who in Metal Forming and Fabricating. Fabricators and Manufacturers Association International. • Annual. Free to members; non-members, $200.00. Lists members of the Fabricators and Manufacturers Association (FMA), International; and members of the Tube and Pipe Association. Includes five indexes. Formerly *FMA Member Resource Directory*.

FINANCIAL RATIOS

Annual Statement Studies. The Risk Management Association. • Annual. Median and quartile financial ratios are given for over 400 kinds of manufacturing, wholesale, retail, construction, and consumer finance establishments. Data is sorted by both asset size and sales volume. Includes a clearly written "Definition of Ratios" and an alphabetical industry index.

Annual Statement Studies: Industry Default Probabilities and Cash Flow Measures. The Risk Management Association. • Annual. $145.00. Serves as a companion volume to the original *Annual Statement Studies.* Gives probability of default estimates on a percentage scale for more than 450 industries. Includes changes in position year-by-year for eight financial statement line items and provides percentage measures of cash flow.

HANDBOOKS AND MANUALS

Sheet Metal Cutting: Collected Articles and Technical Papers. Amy Nickel, editor. Croyden Group, Ltd. • 1994. $33.00.

PERIODICALS AND NEWSLETTERS

The Fabricator. Fabricators and Manufacturers Association International. • Monthly. $75.00 per year. Covers the manufacture of sheet, coil, tube, pipe, and structural metal shapes.

Heating/Piping/Air Conditioning Engineering: The Magazine of Mechanical Systems Engineering. Penton Media, Inc. • Monthly. $65.00 per year. Covers design, specification, installation, operation, and maintenance for systems in industrial, commercial, and institutional buildings. Formerly (Heating, Piping and Air Conditioning).

Snips. Business News Publishing Co. • Monthly. $18.00 per year. Provides information for heating, air conditioning, sheet metal and ventilating contractors, wholesalers, manufacturers representatives and manufacturers.

TRADE/PROFESSIONAL ASSOCIATIONS

Fabricators and Manufacturers Association, International. 833 Featherstone Rd., Rockford, IL 61107-6302. Phone: (815)399-8700 Fax: (815)484-7701 E-mail: info@fmanet.org • URL: http://www.fmanet.org • Members are individuals concerned with metal forming, cutting, and fabricating. Includes a Sheet Metal Division and the Tube and Pipe Fabricators Association. Formerly Fabricating Manufacturers Association.

Sheet Metal and Air Conditioning Contractors' National Association. 4201 Lafayette Center Dr., Chantilly, VA 20151-1209. Phone: (703)803-2980 Fax: (703)803-3732 E-mail: info@smacna.org • URL: http://www.smacna.org • Formerly Sheet Metal Contractors National Association.

Sheet Metal Industry Promotion Plan. 6058 Royalton Rd., North Royalton, OH 44133-5104. Phone: (216)398-5600 Fax: (216)398-5576 E-mail: smacnacle@aol.com • Heating, air conditioning, ventilating, roofing, and sheet metal contractors in Cuyahoga, Ashtabula, Geauga, and Lake counties of Ohio. Promotes quality sheet metal installations and pride in workmanship. Disseminates information on fabrication and erection of sheet metal construction. Has drawn up standards for mechanical sheet metal work; standards are to be adhered to by union members and participating contractors in fabrication and erection on residential, commercial, and industrial work involving sheet metal. Sponsors training classes for journeymen on sheet metal layout, heliarc welding, mechanical drawing, electric welding, balancing, and blueprint reading. **Publications:** none.

SHELLFISH INDUSTRY

See also: FISH INDUSTRY; LOBSTER INDUSTRY; OYSTER INDUSTRY; SEAFOOD INDUSTRY

CD-ROM DATABASES

Food Science and Technology Abstracts [CD-ROM]. Available from SilverPlatter Information, Inc. • Quarterly. Produced by International Food Information Service (home page is http://www.ifis.org). Provides worldwide coverage on CD-ROM of the literature of food technology and production. Various types of publications are indexed, with abstracts, including about 1,800 periodicals. Time period is 1969 to date.

DIRECTORIES

Major Food and Drink Companies of the World. Available from Gale Cengage Learning. • Annual. $880.00. Two volumes. Published by Graham & Whiteside. Contains profiles and trade names for more than 9,800 important food and beverage companies in various countries. In addition to foods, includes both alcoholic and nonalcoholic drink products.

Thomas Food and Beverage Market Place. Grey House Publishing. • 2004. $495.00. Three volumes. Contains more than 40,000 entries covering food companies, beverages, food equipment, warehouse companies, food brokers, wholesalers, importers, and exporters. Formerly *Thomas Food Industry Register.*

ONLINE DATABASES

Food Science and Technology Abstracts [online]. IFIS North American Desk. • Produced by International Food Information Service. Provides about 500,000 online citations, with abstracts, to the international literature of food science, technology, commodities, engineering, and processing. Approximately 2,000 periodicals are covered. Time period is 1969 to date, with monthly updates. Inquire as to online cost and availability.

PERIODICALS AND NEWSLETTERS

Commercial Fisheries News. Compass Publications, Fisheries Division. • Monthly. $21.95 per year. Covers the commercial fishing industry in New England. Includes news of marine technology, boatbuilding, fish and lobster prices, business trends, government regulation, and other topics.

Seafood Business. Diversified Business Communications. • Monthly. $69.00 per year. Edited for a wide range of seafood buyers, including distributors, restaurants, supermarkets, and institutions. Special issues feature information on specific products, such as salmon or lobster.

STATISTICS SOURCES

Fisheries of the United States. Available from U. S. Government Printing Office. • Annual. $20.00. Issued by the National Marine Fisheries Service, National Oceanic and Atmospheric Administration, U. S. Department of Commerce.

World Food Data and Statistics. Euromonitor International. • 2004. $650.00. Provides five-year data for a wide variety of food products in 52 countries. Includes market size, consumer expenditures, price indicators, and retail distribution data for many kinds of meat, fish, fruits, vegetables,

dairy products, baked goods, condiments, canned food, and frozen food.

TRADE/PROFESSIONAL ASSOCIATIONS

Molluscan Shellfish Institute. 7918 Jones Branch Dr., Ste. 700, McLean, VA 22102. Phone: (703)752-8880 Fax: (703)752-7583 E-mail: ccfma@sbcglobal.net • URL: http://www.aboutseafood.com • A division of the National Fisheries Institute (see separate entry). Shellfish producers, processors, distributors, growers, and suppliers to the industry. Works to promote, protect, and advance the interests of the shellfish industry. Cooperates with federal, state, and municipal authorities in matters of legislation, sanitation standards, controls, and conservation.

National Shellfisheries Association. 14 Carter Ln., P.O. Box 350, East Quogue, NY 11942. Phone: (631)653-6327 Fax: (631)653-6327 E-mail: jdavis@bainbridge.net • URL: http://www.shellfish.org • Biologists, hydrographers, public health workers, shellfish producers, and fishery administrators. Encourages research on mollusks and crustaceans, with emphasis on those forms of economic importance known as shellfish.

SHELTERS, TAX

See: TAX SHELTERS

SHIPBUILDING

See: SHIPS, SHIPPING AND SHIPBUILDING

SHIPMENT OF GOODS

See: FREIGHT TRANSPORT; PACKAGING; POSTAL SERVICES; TRAFFIC MANAGEMENT (INDUSTRIAL); TRUCKING INDUSTRY

SHIPPING

See: SHIPS, SHIPPING AND SHIPBUILDING

SHIPS, SHIPPING AND SHIPBUILDING

See also: BOAT INDUSTRY; EXPORT-IMPORT TRADE; FREIGHT TRANSPORT; MARINE ENGINEERING; OCEANOGRAPHIC INDUSTRIES; PORTS; STEAMSHIP LINES; TANK SHIPS; TRANSPORTATION INDUSTRY

ABSTRACTS AND INDEXES

NTIS Alerts: Ocean Sciences and Technology. National Technical Information Service. • Semimonthly. $210.00 per year. Provides descriptions of government-sponsored research reports and software, with ordering information. Formerly *Abstract Newsletter.*

NTIS Alerts: Transportation. National Technical Information Service. • Semimonthly. $210.00 per year. Provides descriptions of government-sponsored research reports and software, with ordering information. Covers air, marine, highway, inland waterway, pipeline, and railroad transportation. Formerly *Abstract Newsletter.*

Oceanic Abstracts. CSA. • 11 times a year. $1,645.00 per year. Includes print and online editions. Covers oceanography, marine biology, ocean shipping, and a wide range of other marine-related subject areas.

ALMANACS AND YEARBOOKS

American Bureau of Shipping-ABS International Directory of Offices. American Bureau of Shipping.

• Annual. $520.00 per year. Quarterly supplements.

DIRECTORIES

Capital for Shipping. Available from Informa Publishing Group Ltd. • Annual. $128.00. Published in the UK by Lloyd's List (http://www.lloydslist.com). Consists of a "Financial Directory" and a "Legal Directory," listing international ship finance providers and international law firms specializing in shipping. (Included with subscription to *Lloyd's Shipping Economist.*).

Fairplay World Shipping Directory. Fairplay Publications Ltd. • Covers: more than 76,000 companies worldwide engaged in some aspect of shipping, including over 10,000 shipowners with fleets totalling over 45,000 vessels, shipbuilders and repairers, marine insurance shipping finance, protection and indemnity associations, marine equipment suppliers, and towing, salvage, and dredging; also lists marine organizations, shipbrokers, and consulting engineers and surveyors. Entries include: Company name, address, phone, fax, e-mail, URL, names of directors and executives, brief description of business; listings may also include associated and subsidiary companies and financial data.

Guide to Shipbuilding, Repair, and Maintenance. Informa Marine and Transport. • Annual. Price on application. Provides worldwide coverage of shipbuilding, repair, and maintenance facilities and marine equipment suppliers for the maritime industry. (Included with subscription to *Lloyd's Ship Manager.*).

List of Shipowners, Managers, and Managing Agents. Lloyd's Register of Shipping. • Annual. $350.00, including 10 updates per year. Published in the UK by Lloyd's Register-Fairplay Ltd. Lists 40,000 shipowners, managers, and agents worldwide. Cross-referenced with *Lloyd's Register of Ships.*

Lloyd's Marine Equipment Buyers' Guide. Available from Informa UK Ltd. • Annual. $270.00. Published in the UK by Lloyd's List (http://www.lloydslist.com). Lists more than 6,000 companies worldwide supplying over 2,000 types of marine products and services, including offshore equipment.

Lloyd's Maritime Directory. Informa PLC. • Covers: Over 40,000 shipowners, managers, and operators with 75,000 vessels. Also includes Marine consultants; towing, salvage, solicitors, P&I clubs; ship building and repair firms; general maritime organizations, banking and finance and more. Entries include: Firm name, address, phone, fax, e-mail, internet; branch offices; names of principal executives; agents; parent and associated companies; and, for shipowners and lines, detailed information on ships owned, type, or capacity, etc. The former second volume of 'International Shipping and Shipbuilding Directory' is now published separately with the title 'Lloyd's List Marine Equipment Buyers' Guide' (see separate entry).

Maritime Guide. Lloyd's Register--Fairplay Ltd. • Covers: international shipbuilders, marine engine builders, boilermakers, and shipbreakers; port and docking facilities; marine associations. Entries include: For shipbuilders, marine engine builders, and boilermakers--Company name, address, phone, telex. For shipbreakers--Company name, address. For port and docking facilities--Name, location, name and title of contact, services.

ENCYCLOPEDIAS AND DICTIONARIES

Dictionary of Shipping Terms. Peter Brodie. LLP, Inc. • 1997. Third edition. Price on application. Published in the UK by Lloyd's List (http://www.lloydslist.com). Defines more than 2,000 words, phrases, and abbreviations related to the shipping and maritime industries.

Exporters' Encyclopedia. Dun and Bradstreet Information Services. • 1995. $495.00. Lease basis.

Illustrated Dictionary of Cargo Handling. Peter Brodie. LLP, Inc. • 1991. $90.00. Second edition. Published in the UK by Lloyd's List (http://www.lloydslist.com). Provides definitions of about 600 terms relating to "the vessels and equipment used in modern cargo handling and shipping," including containerization.

Macmillan Encyclopedia of Transportation. Available from Gale Cengage Learning. • 1999. $450.00. Six volumes. Published by Macmillan Reference USA. Covers the business, technology, and history of transportation on land, on water, in the air, and in space. Includes definitions, cross-references, and 200 color illustrations.

HANDBOOKS AND MANUALS

The Business of Shipping. James J. Buckley and Lane C. Kendall. Cornell Maritime Press, Inc. • 2001. $50.00. Seventh edition.

Importers Manual U. S. A.: The Single Source Reference Encyclopedia for Importated States. Edward G. Hinkelman. World Trade Press. • 1998. $87.00. Third edition. Published by World Trade Press. Covers U. S. customs regulations, letters of credit, contracts, shipping, insurance, and other items relating to importing. Includes 60 essays on practical aspects of importing.

Ship Management. John Spruyt. LLP, Inc. • 1994. $105.00. Second edition. Published in the UK by Lloyd's List (http://www.lloydslist.com). Covers recruitment of personnel, training, quality control, liability, safety, responsibilities of ship managers, and other topics.

INTERNET DATABASES

CDC Vessel Sanitation Program (VSP): Charting a Healthier Course. U. S. Centers for Disease Control and Prevention. Phone: (770)488-7070 Fax: 888-232-6789 E-mail: vsp@cdc.gov • URL: http://www.cdc.gov/nceh/vsp/ • Web site provides details of unannounced sanitation inspections of individual cruise ships arriving at U. S. ports. Includes detailed results of the most recent inspection of each ship and results of inspections taking place in years past. There are lists of "Ships Inspected Past 2 Months" and "Ships with Not Satisfactory Scores" (passing grade is 85). CDC standards cover drinking water, food, and general cleanliness. Online searching is possible by ship name, inspection date, and numerical scores. Fees: Free.

ONLINE DATABASES

Globalbase. Gale Cengage Learning. • Provides more than one million online summaries of business, industrial, and economic news reports from more than 1,000 publications worldwide. Covers a wide range of material appearing in international trade journals, professional magazines, and newspapers. Time period is 1984 to date, with weekly updates. Inquire as to online cost and availability.

Oceanic Abstracts (Online). Cambridge Scientific Abstracts. • Oceanographic and other marine-related technical literature, 1981 to present. Monthly updates. Inquire as to online cost and availability.

TRIS: Transportation Research Information Service. National Research Council. • Contains abstracts and citations to a wide range of transportation literature, 1968 to present, with monthly updates. Includes references to the literature of air transportation, highways, ships and shipping, railroads, trucking, and urban mass transportation. Formerly *TRIS-ONLINE.* Inquire as to online cost and availability.

PERIODICALS AND NEWSLETTERS

American Shipper: Ports, Transportation and Industry. Howard Publications, Inc. • Monthly. $120.00 per year.

Fairplay: The International Shipping Weekly. Fairplay Publications, Ltd. • Weekly. $465.00 per year.

Provides international shipping news, commentary, market reports, reports on shipbuilding activity, advice on operational problems, and other information.

International Trade Reporter Export Reference Manual. BNA, Inc. • Biweekly. $874.00 per year. Looseleaf service.

JOC Shipping Digest: For Export and Transportation Executives. Shipper Group. • Weekly. $57.00 per year. Formerly *Shipping Digest.*

The Journal of Commerce. Commonwealth Business Media. • Weekly. $146.00 per year. Topics include transatlantic shipping, domestic shipping, customs brokers, freight forwarders, ports, air freight, containerization, and other aspects of transportation and shipping logistics. Formerly *Journal of Commerce.*

Lloyd's List. Available from Informa UK Ltd. • Daily. $1,698.00 per year. Published in the UK by Lloyd's List (http://www.lloydslist.com). Marine industry newspaper. Covers a wide variety of maritime topics, including global news, business/insurance, regulation, shipping markets, financial markets, shipping movements, freight logistics, and marine technology. (Also available weekly at $385.00 per year.).

Lloyd's Ship Manager. LLP Inc. • 10 times a year. $478.00 per year, including annual supplementary guides and directories. Published in the UK by Lloyd's List (http://www.lloydslist.com). Covers all management, technical, and operational aspects of ocean-going shipping.

Lloyd's Shipping Economist. LLP Inc. • Monthly. $1,446.00 per year. Published in the UK by Lloyd's List (http://www.lloydslist.com). Provides current analysis of world shipping markets, including coverage of the economics and costs of various kinds of ship operations. Statistical data and financial/legal directory listings are included.

Marine Digest. Newman-Burrows Publishing. • Monthly. $28.00 per year. Formerly *Marine Digest.*

Marine Engineers Review (MER). Institute of Marine Engineering, Science, and Technology (IMarEST). • Monthly. Free to members; non-members, $150.00 per year. Covers marine engineering, offshore industries, and ocean shipping.

Marine Log. Simmons-Boardman Publishing Corp. • Monthly. $35.00 per year. Formerly *Marine Engineering-Log.*

Marine Management Holdings: Transactions. Available from Information Today, Inc. • Bimonthly. $220.00 per year. Published in London by Marine Management Holdings Ltd. Contains technical and regulatory material on a wide variety of marine and offshore topics. Formerly *Institute of Marine Engineers: Transactions.*

Maritime IT & Electronics. Institute of Marine Engineering, Science, and Technology. • Bimonthly. $65.00 per year. Covers modern electronic technology as applied to all areas of the maritime industry. Includes navigation systems, communications, control systems, monitoring, diagnostics, and software.

Maritime Reporter and Engineering News. Maritime Activity Reports, Inc. • Monthly. $44.00 per year.

Ocean Navigator: Marine Navigation and Ocean Voyaging. Navigator Publishing LLC. • Bimonthly. $26.00 per year.

Register of International Shipowning Groups. Available from Fairplay Publications, Inc. • Three times a year. $744.00 per year. Published in the UK by Lloyd's Register-Fairplay Ltd. "Provides intelligence on shipowners and managers, their subsidiary and associate companies, and owners' representatives." Includes detailed information on individual ships.

Shipcare. Available from Informa Publishing Group

Ltd. • Quarterly. $206.00 per year. Published in the UK by Lloyd's List (http://www.lloydslist.com). Edited for the global ship repair, conversion, and maintenance industry. Provides news, market information, and technical analysis, including contract and pricing data.

RESEARCH CENTERS AND INSTITUTES

Transportation Research Institute. University of Michigan, 2901 Baxter Rd., Ann Arbor, MI 48109-2150. Phone: (734)764-6504 Fax: (734)936-1081 E-mail: umtri@umich.edu • URL: http://www.umtri.umich.edu • Research areas include highway safety, transportation systems, and shipbuilding.

STATISTICS SOURCES

Annual Survey of Manufactures. Available from U. S. Government Printing Office. • Annual. Prices vary. Issued by the U. S. Census Bureau as an interim update to the *Census of Manufactures.* Includes data on number of manufacturing establishments in various industries, employment, labor costs, value of shipments, capital expenditures, inventories, energy costs, and assets. (See also Census Bureau home page, http://www.census.gov/.).

Infrastructure Industries USA. Gale Cengage Learning. • 2001. $260.00. Presents statistics and projections relating to economic activity in a wide variety of natural resource and construction industries.

Review of Maritime Transport. United Nations Conference on Trade and Development. United Nations Publications. • Annual. $55.00.

U. S. Industry and Trade Outlook. Available from National Technical Information Service. • Annual. $69.95. Produced by the International Trade Administration, U. S. Department of Commerce, in a "public-private" partnership with DRI/McGraw-Hill and Standard & Poor's. Provides basic data, outlook for the current year, and "Long-Term Prospects" (five-year projections) for a wide variety of products and services. Includes high technology industries. Formerly *U. S. Industrial Outlook.*

World Fleet Statistics. Available from Fairplay Publications, Inc. • Annual. $215.00. Published in the UK by Lloyd's Register-Fairplay Ltd. Provides data on the "world fleet of propelled seagoing merchant ships of 100 gross tonnage and above." Includes five-year summaries.

World Shipbuilding Statistics. Available from Fairplay Publications, Inc. • Quarterly. $215.00 per year. Published in the UK by Lloyd's Register-Fairplay Ltd. Contains detailed, current data on shipbuilding orders placed and completions.

TRADE/PROFESSIONAL ASSOCIATIONS

American Bureau of Shipping. 16855 Northchase Dr., Houston, TX 77060. Phone: (281)877-6000 Fax: (281)877-6001 E-mail: abs-amer@eagle.org • URL: http://www.eagle.org.

American Maritime Association. 485 Madison Ave., 15th Fl., New York, NY 10022. Phone: (646)840-0428 Fax: (212)753-8101 E-mail: membership@amanet.org • U.S. flag steamship companies, which operate vessels in foreign and domestic trades. Conducts collective bargaining with the various offshore maritime unions and promotes a strong American Merchant Marine. **Publications:** none. **Convention/Meeting:** none.

Chamber of Shipping of America. 1730 M. St., N.W., Suite 407, Washington, DC 20036. Phone: (202)775-4399 Fax: (202)659-3795 • United States based companies that own and operate tankers, dry bulk carriers, container ships and other oceangoing vessels in United States foreign and domestic commerce. Formerly United States Chamber of Shipping.

Institute of Marine Engineers, Science and Technology. 80 Coleman St., London EC2R 5BJ,

---

United Kingdom. Phone: 44 207 3822600 Fax: 44 207 3822670 E-mail: keith.read@imarest.org • URL: http://www.imarest.org • An international organization of marine engineers, offshore engineers, and naval architects.

National Association of Marine Services. 5458 Wagon Master Dr., Colorado Springs, CO 80917. Phone: (719)573-5946 Fax: (719)573-5952 E-mail: nams@namsshipchandler.com • URL: http://www.namsshipchandler.com • Affiliated with International Ship Suppliers Association. Formerly National Associated Marine Suppliers.

National Association of Waterfront Employers. 2011 Pennsylvania Ave., N.W., Suite 301, Washington, DC 20006. Phone: (202)296-2810 Fax: (202)331-7479 • Formerly National Association of Stevedoves.

Shipbuilders Council of America. 1455 F St., No. 225, Washington, DC 20005. Phone: (202)347-5462 Fax: (202)347-5464 E-mail: jmccluer@dc.bjllp.com • URL: http://www.shipbuilders.org • Absorbed Atlantic and Gulf Coasts Dry Dock Association. Formerly National Shipyard Association.

OTHER SOURCES

Federal Carriers Reports. CCH, Inc. • Biweekly. $1,484.00 per year. Four looseleaf volumes. Federal rules and regulations for motor carriers, water carriers, and freight forwarders.

Lloyd's Maritime Atlas. Available from Informa UK Limited. • Biennial. $119.00. Contains more than 70 pages of world, ocean, regional, and port maps in color. Provides additional information for the planning of world shipping routes, including data on distances, port facilities, recurring weather hazards at sea, international load line zones, and sailing times.

SHOE INDUSTRY

See also: LEATHER INDUSTRY

CD-ROM DATABASES

OECD Statistical Compendium. Organization for Economic Cooperation and Development. • Semiannual. $1,905.00 per year for 1 to 10 users. CD-ROM contains more than 730,000 monthly, quarterly, and annual time series for OECD countries, 1960 to date. Includes fully searchable data on agriculture, food, economic indicators, national accounts, employment, energy, finance, industry, technology, and foreign trade. Results can be displayed in various forms.

DIRECTORIES

American Shoemaking Directory. Shoe Trades Publishing Co. • Covers: Shoe manufacturers in the United States, Puerto Rico, and Canada. Entries include: Company name, address, phone, fax, names of executives, product information brand names. Also key personnel; Plant output, trade sold, and sales offices included.

Contemporary Fashion. St. James Press. • Publication includes: Contact information for designers featured. Entries include: name, address, phone, and Web site. Principal content of publication is essays evaluating contemporary clothing and accessories designers worldwide.

Directory of Apparel Specialty Stores. Chain Store Guide. • Annual. $335.00. 4,700 apparel and sporting goods specialty stores in the United States and Canada, operating more than 80,000 stores. Include company name, phone and fax numbers, company e-mail and web addresses and other information.

Shoe Factory Buyer's Guide: Directory of Suppliers to the Shoe Manufacturing Industry. Shoe Trades Publishing Co. • Annual. $59.00. Lists over 750 suppliers and their representatives to the North American footwear industry.

FINANCIAL RATIOS

Almanac of Business and Industrial Financial Ratios. Leo Troy. Aspen Publishers, Inc. • 2003. $125.95. Includes CD-Rom. Contains financial ratios derived from federal tax returns. Ratios for each of about 200 industries are arranged according to company asset size. (Almanac of Business and Industrial Financial Ratios Series).

Annual Statement Studies. The Risk Management Association. • Annual. Median and quartile financial ratios are given for over 400 kinds of manufacturing, wholesale, retail, construction, and consumer finance establishments. Data is sorted by both asset size and sales volume. Includes a clearly written "Definition of Ratios" and an alphabetical industry index.

Annual Statement Studies: Industry Default Probabilities and Cash Flow Measures. The Risk Management Association. • Annual. $145.00. Serves as a companion volume to the original *Annual Statement Studies*. Gives probability of default estimates on a percentage scale for more than 450 industries. Includes changes in position year-by-year for eight financial statement line items and provides percentage measures of cash flow.

HANDBOOKS AND MANUALS

Shoe Stats. Footwear Distributors and Retailers. • Annual. Free to members; non-members, $350.00; libraries, $225.00. Includes *Statistical Reporter*.

INTERNET DATABASES

Advance Monthly Sales for Retail Trade and Food Services. U. S. Census Bureau. Phone: 800-541-8345 or (301)763-4636 Fax: (301)457-3842 E-mail: rcb@census.gov • URL: http://www.census.gov/svsd/www/fullpub.html • Web pages provide monthly sales figures for a wide range of retail businesses. Advance, preliminary, and final statistics are provided for the latest month available in each case, with a previous-year comparison. Updates are monthly.

Business 2.0 Web Guide to the Best Business Links. Business 2.0 Media Inc. Phone: (415)293-4800 E-mail: support@business2.com • URL: http://www.business2.com/webguide • Web site presents an extensive, searchable directory of links to "the best, most informative, and authoritative web pages." Twenty main categories cover business, finance, career, company information, people, and technology topics, with thousands of subtopics, all linking to Web sites recommended by experienced business researchers. Fees: Free.

Fedstats. Federal Interagency Council on Statistical Policy. Phone: (202)395-7254 • URL: http://www.fedstats.gov • Web site features an efficient search facility for full-text statistics produced by more than 100 federal agencies, including the Census Bureau, the Bureau of Economic Analysis, and the Bureau of Labor Statistics. Boolean searches can be made within one agency or for all agencies combined. Links are offered to international statistical bureaus, including the UN, IMF, OECD, UNESCO, Eurostat, and 20 individual countries. Fees: Free.

FreeLunch.com. Economy.com, Inc. Phone: (610)696-8700 Fax: (610)696-1678 • URL: http://www.freelunch.com • Web site provides free access to more than 1.5 million economic and financial data series, covering industry, demographics, labor markets, prices, retail sales, government spending, trade, interest rates, housing starts, the stock market, and many other topics. Data is available for various time periods in either chart or table form. Searching is offered. Fees: Free, but registration required. Economy.com, Inc. also offers fee-based economic analysis at *The Dismal Scientist* site (http://www.dismal.com).

Manufacturing Profiles. U. S. Bureau of the Census.

Phone: (301)763-4636 E-mail: webmaster@census.gov • URL: http://www.census.gov/prod/www/abs/mfg-prof.html • The Census Bureau makes available free on PDF (Portable Document Format) an annual consolidation of the entire Current Industrial Report series, presenting "all the data compiled." Contains statistics on production, shipments, inventories, consumption, exports, imports, and orders for a wide variety of manufactured products.

PERIODICALS AND NEWSLETTERS

American Shoemaking. James Sutton. Shoe Trades Publishing Co. • Monthly. $55.00 per year.

Footwear News. Fairchild Publications. • Weekly. Individuals, $72.00 per year; domestic retailer, $59.00 per year.

STATISTICS SOURCES

Annual Benchmark Report for Retail Trade and Food Services...A Detailed Summary of Retail Sales, Purchases, Accounts Receivable, Inventories, and Food Service Sales. Available from U. S. Government Printing Office. • Annual. $13.00. Issued by the U.S. Census Bureau. Provides detailed annual and monthly retail statistics for the most recent 10 years. Includes data for various kinds of retail outlets, including automobiles, furniture, appliances, building supplies, grocery stores, drug stores, gasoline stations, clothing, sporting goods, department stores, and restaurants.

Annual Survey of Manufactures. Available from U. S. Government Printing Office. • Annual. Prices vary. Issued by the U. S. Census Bureau as an interim update to the *Census of Manufactures*. Includes data on number of manufacturing establishments in various industries, employment, labor costs, value of shipments, capital expenditures, inventories, energy costs, and assets. (See also Census Bureau home page, http://www.census.gov/.).

Business Statistics of the United States. Linz Audain and Cornelia J. Strawser. Bernan Associates. • Annual. $147.00. Based on *Business Statistics*, formerly issue by the Bureau of Economic Analysis, U. S. Department of Commerce. Provides basic data for a wide variety of U. S. industries, services, and economic indicators. Most statistics are shown annually for 30 years and monthly for the most recent four years.

Footwear. U. S. Bureau of the Census. • Quarterly. Covers production and value of shipments of leather and rubber footwear. (Current Industrial Reports, MQ-31A.).

Standard & Poor's Industry Surveys. Standard & Poor's. • Semiannual. $1,800.00. Two looseleaf volumes. Includes monthly *Supplements*. Provides detailed, individual surveys of 52 major industry groups. Each survey is revised on a semiannual basis. Also includes "Monthly Investment Review" (industry group investment analysis) and monthly "Trends & Projections" (economic analysis).

Survey of Current Business. Available from U. S. Government Printing Office. • Monthly. $63.00 per year. Issued by Bureau of Economic Analysis, U. S. Department of Commerce. Presents a wide variety of business and economic data.

TRADE/PROFESSIONAL ASSOCIATIONS

Footwear Distributors and Retailers of America. 1319 F St., N.W., Suite 700, Washington, DC 20004. Phone: (202)737-5660 Fax: (202)638-2615 E-mail: ptmangione@fdra.org • URL: http://www.fdra.org • Formerly Volume Footwear Retailers of America.

National Shoe Retailers Association. 7150 Columbia Gateway Dr., Ste. G, Columbia, MD 21046-1151. Phone: 800-673-8446 or (410)381-8282 Fax: (410)381-1167 E-mail: info@nsra.org • URL: http://www.nsra.org • Proprietors of independent shoe stores, and stores with major shoe departments. Provides business services and professional development programs including bankcard processing, shipping, freight discounts, free website listing, employee training; conducts research; monitors legislation.

OTHER SOURCES

Footware. Available from MarketResearch.com. • 2002. $3,950.00. Published by Global Industry Analysts. Provides worldwide market research data, including profiles of major shoe companies.

Footwear Market. Available from MarketResearch. com. • 2002. $1,695.00. Published by Business Trend Analysts. Provides market data on shoes for walking, running, and specific sports.

SHOP PRACTICE

See: MACHINE SHOPS

SHOPPING

See: CONSUMER ECONOMICS; CONSUMER EDUCATION

SHOPPING CENTERS

See also: RETAIL TRADE

DIRECTORIES

Canadian Directory of Shopping Centres. Rogers Media Publishing. • Annual. $400.00. Two volumes (Eastern Canada and Western Canada). Describes about 2,200 shopping centers and malls, including those under development.

Shopping Center Directory. National Research Bureau. • Covers: More than 40,000 shopping centers, in four regional volumes; East--Connecticut, Delaware, District of Columbia, Maine, Maryland, Massachusetts, New Hampshire, New Jersey, New York, Pennsylvania, Rhode Island, Vermont, Virginia, and West Virginia; Midwest--Illinois, Indiana, Iowa, Kansas, Kentucky, Michigan, Minnesota, Missouri, Nebraska, North Dakota, Ohio, South Dakota, and Wisconsin; South--Alabama, Arkansas, Florida, Georgia, Louisiana, Mississippi, North Carolina, Oklahoma, South Carolina, Tennessee, Texas; West--Alaska, Arizona, California, Colorado, Hawaii, Idaho, Montana, Nevada, New Mexico, Oregon, Utah, Washington, Wyoming. Entries include: Center name, address, mailing address, phone; owner, leasing agent, manager, developer, architect; year opened; physical description of center; square footage; number of stores; type of center (super-regional, regional, community, neighborhood); anchor/tenant list.

Top Contacts: Major Owners, Leasing Agents, and Managers. National Research Bureau, Inc. • Annual. $305.00. Contains information on more than 1,300 owners, agents, and managers, each with control of three or more shopping centers.

HANDBOOKS AND MANUALS

Shopping Center and Store Leases. Emanuel B. Halper. American Lawyer Media. • $195.00. Two looseleaf volumes. Periodic supplementation.

Shopping Center Development Handbook. Michael D. Beyard and W. Paul O'Mara. Urban Land Institute. • 1998. $89.95. Third edition. (Development Handbook Series).

PERIODICALS AND NEWSLETTERS

Chain Store Age: The NewsMagazine for Retail Executives. Lebhar-Friedman, Inc. • Monthly. $105.00 per year. Formerly *Chain Store Age Executive with Shopping Center Age.*

Retail Traffic. Primedia Business Magazines and Media. • Monthly. $74.00 per year. Provides cover-

age of all phases of the shopping center industry. Formerly *Shopping Center World.*

Value Retail News: The Journal of Outlet and Off-Price Retail and Development. Off-Price Specialists, Inc. Value Retail News. • Monthly. Members, $144.00 per year; non-members, $175.00 per year. Provides news of the off-price and outlet store industry. Emphasis is on real estate for outlet store centers.

RESEARCH CENTERS AND INSTITUTES

Urban Land Institute. Urban Land Institute. 1025 Thomas Jefferson St. NW, Ste. 500 W, Washington, DC 20007. Phone: (202)624-7000 Fax: (202)624-7140 E-mail: customerservice@uli.org • URL: http://www.uli.org • Urban land use policy, planning, and development issues, including studies on central city problems, industrial development, new community development, residential developments of all types, taxation, smart growth, shopping center development and economics, metropolitan and urbanized area growth and development, mixed use development, and environmental factors affecting development.

STATISTICS SOURCES

Dollars and Cents of Shopping Centers. Urban Land Institute. • Triennial. Members, $219.95; non-members, $239.95. Supplemental *Special Report* available.

TRADE/PROFESSIONAL ASSOCIATIONS

International Council of Shopping Centers. 1221 Ave. of the Americas, New York, NY 10020. Phone: (646)728-3800 Fax: (212)589-5555 E-mail: icsc@icsc.org • URL: http://www.icsc.org.

OTHER SOURCES

Shopping Center and Store Leases. American Lawyer Media, Inc. • Looseleaf. $195.00. Two volumes. Updated as needed. Provides analysis of retail leases, financing, construction issues, insurance, taxation, bankruptcy, and condemnation of property. Includes detailed information about the shopping-center business and fast-food restaurants, with many examples of lease clauses. (Law Journal Press).

SHORTHAND REPORTING

PERIODICALS AND NEWSLETTERS

Journal of Court Reporting. National Court Reporters Association. • 10 times a year. $49.00 per year. News and features about court reporting, reporter technology. Computer-aided transcription, real time translation captioning for the hearing-impaired, etc. Formerly *National Shorthand Reporter.*

TRADE/PROFESSIONAL ASSOCIATIONS

National Court Reporters Association. 8224 Old Courthouse Rd., Vienna, VA 22182-3808. Phone: 800-272-6272 or (703)556-6272 Fax: (703)556-6291 E-mail: msic@ncrahq.org • URL: http://www.ncraonline.org • Represents Independent state, regional, and local associations. Verbatim court reporters who work as official reporters for courts and government agencies, as freelance reporters for independent contractors, and as captioners for television programming; retired reporters, teachers of court reporting, and school officials; student court reporters. Conducts research; compiles statistics; offers several certification programs; and publishes journal.

SHOW BUSINESS

See also: AMUSEMENT INDUSTRY

ABSTRACTS AND INDEXES

Communication Abstracts: An International Information Service. Sage Publications, Inc. •

Bimonthly. Institutions, $1,150.00 per year. Provides broad coverage of the literature of communications, including broadcasting and advertising.

Readers' Guide to Periodical Literature. H. W. Wilson Co. • Monthly. $345.00 per year. Includes annual *Cumulation.* Indexes about 250 peridicals of general interest.

BIBLIOGRAPHIES

Performing Arts: A Guide to the Reference Literature. Linda K. Simons. Libraries Unlimited, Inc. • 1994. $42.00. (Reference Sources in the Humanities Series).

BIOGRAPHICAL SOURCES

Celebrity Register. Gale Cengage Learning. • 1990. $115.00. 90th edition. Compiled by Celebrity Services International (Earl Blackwell). Contains profiles of 1,300 famous individuals in the performing arts, sports, politics, business, and other fields.

Contemporary Theatre, Film, and Television. Gale Cengage Learning. • 2003. Three volumes. $185.00 per volume. Previous volumes available. Provides detailed biographical and career information on more than 11,000 currently popular performers, directors, writers, producers, designers, managers, choreographers, technicians, composers, executives, dancers, and critics.

CD-ROM DATABASES

Magazine Index Plus. Gale Cengage Learning. • Monthly. $4,000.00 per year (includes InfoTrac workstation). Provides full text on CD-ROM for about 100 popular, general interest magazines and indexing for 300 others. Includes special indexing of reviews and product evaluations. Time period is 1980 to date.

WILSONDISC: Readers' Guide to Periodical Literature. H. W. Wilson Co. • Monthly. $1,095.00 per year, including unlimited online access to *Readers' Guide to Periodical Literature* through WILSONLINE. Provides CD-ROM indexing of about 270 general interest periodicals. Covers 1983 to date. (*Readers' Guide Abstracts* also available on CD-ROM at $1,995 per year.).

DIRECTORIES

Billboard's International Talent and Touring Directory: The Music Industry's Worldwide Reference Source: Talent, Talent Management, Booking Agencies, Promoters, Venue Facilities, Venue Services and Products. Billboard Books. • Annual. $139.00. Lists entertainers, managers, booking agents, and others in the worldwide entertainment industry.

Cavalcade of Acts and Attractions. Amusement Business. • Annual. $85.00. Directory of personal appearance artists, touring shows and other specialized entertainment. Lists promoters, producers, managers and booking agents.

Celebrity Locator: How to Reach Over 6,000 Movie, TV Stars and Other Famous Ce lebrities. Axiom Information Resources. • Biennial. $39.95. Stars, agents, networks, studios, and other celebrities. Gives names and addresses.

Cyberhound's Guide to People on the Internet. Gale Cengage Learning. • 1996. $79.00. Second edition. Provides descriptions of about 5,500 Internet databases maintained by or for prominent individuals in business, the professions, entertainment, and sports. Indexed by name, subject, and keyword (master index). (Cyberhound's Series).

Entertainment Sourcebook: An Insider's Guide on Where to Find Everything. Applause Theatre & Cinema Books. • Annual. $45.00. Compiled by the Association of Theatrical Artists and Craftspeople (http://www.entertainmentsourcebook.com/ATAC. htm). Lists more than 5,000 sources of theatrical and entertainment supplies and services, such as props, costumes, publicity agencies, scenic shops, amusement park equipment, audio/video products, balloons, wigs, make-up, magic supplies, etc.

The Grey House Performing Arts Directory. Grey House Publishing. • Covers: More than 9,000 dance companies, instrumental music programs, opera companies, choral groups, theatre companies, performing arts series, and performing arts facilities. Entries include: Mailing address, telephone and fax numbers, e-mail addresses, Web sites, mission statement, key management contacts, and facility information such as capacity, season, and attendance.

Peterson's Professional Degree Programs in the Visual and Performing Arts. Peterson's. • Annual. $21.95. A directory of more than 900 degree programs in art, music, theater, and dance at 600 colleges and professional schools.

Protocol (Corporate Meetings, Entertainment, and Special Events). Protocol Directory, Inc. • Annual. $48.00. Provides information for about 4,000 suppliers of products and services for special events, shows (entertainment), and business meetings. Geographic arrangement.

Theatrical Index. Theatrical Index Ltd. • Covers: theatrical presentations in pre-production stage which are seeking investors; also covers producers, agents, and theaters. Entries include: For productions--Production name, brief details, contact. For agents and producers--Name, address, phone. For theaters--Name, address, box office and backstage phone numbers.

ENCYCLOPEDIAS AND DICTIONARIES

Encyclopedia of Popular Music. Colin Larkin, editor. Available from Groves Dictionaries, Inc. • 1998. $500.00. Third edition. Eight volumes. Covers a wide variety of music forms and pop culture. Includes bibliography and index.

HANDBOOKS AND MANUALS

Dun & Bradstreet/Gale Group Industry Handbooks. Gale Cengage Learning. • 2000. $650.00. Five volumes. $130.00 per volume. Each volume covers two or more major industries: 1. *Entertainment and Hospitality*; 2. *Construction and Agriculture*; 3. *Chemicals and Pharmaceuticals*; 4. *Computers & Software and Broadcasting & Telecommunications*; 5. *Insurance and Health & Medical Services*. The following are included for each industry: overview, statistics, financial ratios, rankings, merger information, company directory, directory of associations, and consultants directory. (Dun and Bradstreet/Gale Industry Reference Handbook Series).

Entertainment Industry Economics: A Guide for Financial Analysis. Harold Vogel. Cambridge University Press. • 2001. $45.00. Fifth revised edition.

Entertainment Law. Jeffrey A. Helewitz and Leah K. Edwards. Delmar Learning. • 2003. $52.95. (West Legal Studies).

Entertainment Law and Business, 1989-1993: A Guide to the Law and Business Prac Entertainment Industry. Harold Orenstein and David Sinacore-Guinn. LEXIS Publishing. • $180.00. Two volumes. Looseleaf Service. Periodic supplementation, $55.00.

Show Business Law: Motion Pictures, Television, Videos. Peter Muller. Greenwood Publishing Group, Inc. • 1990. $69.95.

ONLINE DATABASES

Readers' Guide Abstracts Online. H. W. Wilson Co. • Indexes and abstracts general interest periodicals, 1983 to date. Weekly updates. Inquire as to online cost and availability.

PERIODICALS AND NEWSLETTERS

Back Stage: The Performing Arts Weekly. VNU Business Media. • Weekly. $95.00 per year. A theatre trade newspaper for show business professionals.

Daily Variety: News of the Entertainment Industry. Reed Business Information. • Daily. $297.00 per year. Covers entire scope of the entertainment business on the East and West coast.

Entertainment Design: The Art and Technology of Show Business. Primedia Business Magazines. • Monthly. $34.97 per year. Contains material on performing arts management, staging, scenery, costuming, etc. Supersedes *TCI - Theatre Crafts International*.

Entertainment Law and Finance. American Lawyer Media, Inc. • Monthly. $229.00 per year. Newsletter. Covers contracts, royalties, litigation, copyright, taxation, etc., for the music industry, motion pictures, broadcasting, publishing, video, and related media. (A Law Journal Newsletter, formerly published by Leader Publications.).

Entertainment Marketing Letter. EPM Communications Inc. • Description: Reports on techniques used in the marketing of films, music, videos, television, radio, and cable features. Covers tie-in campaigns, sponsorship, in-theatre advertising, and interactive telephone promotions.

The Hollywood Reporter. • Daily. $219.00 per year. Covers the latest news in film, TV, cable, multimedia, music, and theatre. Includes box office grosses and entertainment industry financial data.

Performing Arts Forum. International Society for the Performing Arts Foundation. • Description: Directed toward producers, managers, promoters, and representatives of artists and performing arts events in the U.S. and other countries. Discusses techniques and problems involved with the development and administration of the performing arts. Recurring features include items from readers, news of research, Society reports, and notes on members.

Theatre Journal. Association for Theatre in Higher Education. Johns Hopkins University Press, Journals Publishing Div. • Quarterly. Individuals, $35.00 per year; institutions, $108.00 per year. Contains material on theatre history, theatre news, and reviews of books and plays.

Variety: The International Entertainment Weekly. Reed Business Information. • 50 times a year. $259.00 per year. Contains national and international news of show business, with emphasis on motion pictures and television. Includes *Market* and *Special Focus* issues.

RESEARCH CENTERS AND INSTITUTES

Wisconsin Center for Film and Theater Research. University of Wisconsin-Madison, 816 State St., Madison, WI 53706. Phone: (608)264-6466 Fax: (608)264-6472 • URL: http://www.shsw.wisc.edu/archives/wcftr • Studies the performing arts in America, including theater, cinema, radio, and television.

STATISTICS SOURCES

United States Census of Service Industries. U.S. Bureau of the Census. • Quinquennial. Various reports available.

TRADE/PROFESSIONAL ASSOCIATIONS

Association of Theatrical Artists and Craftspeople (ATAC). 604 Riverside Dr., New York, NY 10031. Phone: (212)234-9001 • Members are artists and craftspeople working in theatre, film, TV, and advertising. Areas of expertise include props, costumes, millinery, puppetry, display, and special effects.

International Society for the Performing Arts. 17 Prudy Ave., Rye, NY 10580. Phone: (914)921-1550 Fax: (914)921-1593 E-mail: info@ispa.org • URL: http://www.ispa.org • Formerly International Society of Performing Arts Administrators.

OTHER SOURCES

Sports and Entertainment Litigation Reporter. Andrews Publications. • Monthly. $899.00 per year.

Newsletter. Provides reports on lawsuits involving films, TV, cable broadcasting, stage productions, radio, and other areas of the entertainment business. Formerly *Sports and Entertainment Litigation Reporter*.

SHOW WINDOWS

See: DISPLAY OF MERCHANDISE

SICKNESS INSURANCE

See: HEALTH INSURANCE

SIGNS AND SIGN BOARDS

See also: COMMERCIAL ART; DISPLAY OF MERCHANDISE; OUTDOOR ADVERTISING; POSTERS

FINANCIAL RATIOS

Annual Statement Studies. The Risk Management Association. • Annual. Median and quartile financial ratios are given for over 400 kinds of manufacturing, wholesale, retail, construction, and consumer finance establishments. Data is sorted by both asset size and sales volume. Includes a clearly written "Definition of Ratios" and an alphabetical industry index.

Annual Statement Studies: Industry Default Probabilities and Cash Flow Measures. The Risk Management Association. • Annual. $145.00. Serves as a companion volume to the original *Annual Statement Studies*. Gives probability of default estimates on a percentage scale for more than 450 industries. Includes changes in position year-by-year for eight financial statement line items and provides percentage measures of cash flow.

HANDBOOKS AND MANUALS

Instant Sign Store. Entrepreneur Media, Inc. • Looseleaf. $59.50. A practical guide to starting an instant sign store. Covers profit potential, start-up costs, market size evaluation, owner's time required, site selection, lease negotiation, pricing, accounting, advertising, promotion, etc. (Start-Up Business Guide No. E1336.).

Practical Sign Shop Operation. Bob Fitzgerald. ST Publications, Inc. • 1992. $19.95. Seventh revised edition.

Standard Highway Signs, as Specified in the Manual on Uniform Traffic Control Devices. Available from U. S. Government Printing Office. • Looseleaf. $153.00. Issued by the U. S. Department of Transportation (http://www.dot.gov). Includes basic manual, with updates for an indeterminate period. Contains illustrations of typical standard signs approved for use on streets and highways, and provides information on dimensions and placement of symbols.

PERIODICALS AND NEWSLETTERS

Signs of the Times: The Industry Journal Since 1906. ST Media Group International. • 13 times a year. $36.00 per year. For designers and manufacturers of all types of signs. Features how-to-tips. Includes *Sign Erection, Maintenance Directory* and annual *Buyer's Guide*.

TRADE/PROFESSIONAL ASSOCIATIONS

International Sign Association. 707 N St. Asaph St., Alexandria, VA 22314. Phone: (703)836-4012 Fax: (703)836-8353 E-mail: lori.anderson@signs.org • URL: http://www.signs.org • Manufacturers, users, and suppliers of on-premise signs and sign products produced by more than 400,000 employees in all 50 states and 69 countries. Exists to support, promote and improve the $30 billion-a-year sign industry, which sustains the nation's nearly $3 trillion-a-year retail industry.

SILK INDUSTRY

See also: TEXTILE INDUSTRY

ABSTRACTS AND INDEXES
Textile Technology Digest. Institute of Textile Technology. • Annual. $535.00. Provides indexing and abstracting of a wide variety of textile technology literature.

CD-ROM DATABASES
Textile Technology Digest [CD-ROM]. Textile Information Center, Institute of Textile Technology. • Quarterly. Provides CD-ROM indexing and abstracting of worldwide journals and monographs in various areas of textile technology, production, and management. Covers 1978 to date.

DIRECTORIES
Davison's Textile Blue Book. Davison Publishing Company L.L.C. • Covers: Over 8,400 companies in the textile industry in the United States, Canada, and Mexico including about 4,400 textile plants. Covers mills, manufacturers, dyers, bleachers, finishers, dealers, importers, exporters, brokers, shippers, and agents for various textiles, fibers, yarns, and cordage. Also includes supplies of equipment, materials and services. Entries include: Company name, address, phone, fax, e-mail, website addresses, names of executives, description of product/service, and trade names. Mill and other production facility listings include data on equipment and capacity.

ENCYCLOPEDIAS AND DICTIONARIES
Textile Terms and Definitions. J.E. McIntyre and Paul N. Daniels, editors. Available from State Mutual Book and Periodical Service Ltd. • 1996. $180.00. 10th edition. Published by the Textile Insitute (UK). Includes more than 1,000 definitions of textile processes, fiber types, and end products. Illustrated.

ONLINE DATABASES
Globalbase. Gale Cengage Learning. • Provides more than one million online summaries of business, industrial, and economic news reports from more than 1,000 publications worldwide. Covers a wide range of material appearing in international trade journals, professional magazines, and newspapers. Time period is 1984 to date, with weekly updates. Inquire as to online cost and availability.

Textile Technology Digest [online]. Institute of Textile Technology. • Contains indexing and abstracting of more than 300 worldwide journals and monographs in various areas of textile technology, production, and management. Time period is 1978 to date, with monthly updating. Inquire as to online cost and availability.

World Textiles. Elsevier Science, Inc. • Provides abstracting and indexing from 1970 of worldwide textile literature (periodicals, books, pamphlets, and reports). Includes U. S., European, and British patent information. Updating is monthly. Inquire as to online cost and availability.

PERIODICALS AND NEWSLETTERS
Journal of Natural Fibers. Haworth Press, Inc. • Quarterly. $400.00 per year to libraries; $45.00 per year to individuals. Covers applications, technology, research, and world markets relating to fibers from silk, wool, cotton, flax, hemp, jute, etc. Previously *Natural Fibres,* published annually.

STATISTICS SOURCES
FAO Production Yearbook. Available from Bernan Associates. • Annual. $45.00. Published by the Food

and Agriculture Organization (http://www.fao.org). Contains worldwide data on agriculture, land use, farm crops, livestock, and agricultural prices.

FAO Trade Yearbook. Available from Bernan Associates. • Annual. $45.00. Published by the Food and Agriculture Organization (http://www.fao.org). Provides extensive worldwide data on exports and imports of agricultural commodities, fertilizers, tractors, and pesticides. Includes more than 130 tables of detailed statistics.

TRADE/PROFESSIONAL ASSOCIATIONS
International Silk Association - U.S.A. One Madison St., One Madison St., East Rutherford, NJ 07073. Phone: (973)472-4200 Fax: (973)472-0222 E-mail: lori.anderson@signs.org • Firms engaged in various phases of the silk industry. Promotes the use of silk in all its forms.

Textile Institute. St. James's Buildings, 1st Fl., 79 Oxford St., Manchester M1 6FQ, United Kingdom. Phone: 44 161 2371188 Fax: 44 161 2361991 E-mail: tiihq@textileinst.org.uk • URL: http://www. texi.org • Companies and individuals in 100 countries involved in management, science, technology, design, information transfer, and marketing of textiles including clothing and footwear. Promotes interests of the textile industry worldwide; serves professional interests of members; confers qualifications and recognizes achievements in research, application of ideas, education, business, and public affairs. Maintains Information Service to collect information relating to textile industrial and economic conditions in different countries and economic sectors.

SILVER INDUSTRY

See also: COINS AS AN INVESTMENT; METAL INDUSTRY; MONEY

ALMANACS AND YEARBOOKS
Agricultural and Mineral Commodities Year Book. Available from Taylor & Francis Group. • Annual. $225.00. Published by Europa Publications. Contains descriptive product profiles, price data, export-import data, and production statistics for major commodities of the world. Includes commodity histories, uses, markets, demand trends, and information about trade agreements and key commodity organizations.

CD-ROM DATABASES
METADEX Materials Collection: Metals-Polymers-Ceramics. Cambridge Scientific Abstracts. • Quarterly. Provides CD-ROM citations to the worldwide literature of materials science and metallurgy. Corresponds to *Metals Abstracts, Alloys Index, Steels Alert, Nonferrous Alert, Polymers/Ceramics/Composites Alert,* and *Engineered Materials Abstracts.* (Formerly produced by ASM International.).

DIRECTORIES
Financial Times Business Global Mining Directory. Available from Gale Cengage Learning. • Annual. $355.00. Published by Financial Times Business. Provides detailed information on 1,000 leading mining companies worldwide. Includes financial data for three years. Formerly *Financial Times Energy Yearbook: Mining.*

ENCYCLOPEDIAS AND DICTIONARIES
Encyclopedia of American Silver Manufacturers. Dorothy T. Rainwater and others. Schiffer Publishing, Ltd. • 2003. $29.95. Fifth revised edition.

HANDBOOKS AND MANUALS
Jake Bernstein's New Guide to Investing in Metals. Jacob Bernstein. John Wiley and Sons, Inc. • 1991. $34.95. Covers bullion, coins, futures, options, mining stocks, and precious metal mutual funds.

Includes the history of metals as an investment.

Silversmithing. Rupert Finegold and William Seitz. DIANE Publishing Co. • 1997. $39.95.

ONLINE DATABASES
Materials Business File. Cambridge Scientific Abstracts. • Provides online abstracts and citations to worldwide materials literature, covering the business and industrial aspects of metals, plastics, ceramics, and composites. Corresponds to *Steels Alert, Nonferrous Metals Alert,* and *Polymers/Ceramics/Composites Alert.* Time period is 1985 to date, with monthly updates. (Formerly produced by ASM International.) Inquire as to online cost and availability.

METADEX. Cambridge Scientific Abstracts. • Covers the worldwide literature of metals, metallurgy, and materials science, 1966 to date. Includes detailed alloys indexing from 1974. Biweekly updating. Inquire as to online cost and availability. (Formerly produced by ASM International.).

STATISTICS SOURCES
London Currency Report. World Reports Ltd. • 10 times a year. $950.00 per year. Formerly *Gold and Silver Survey.*

Mineral Commodity Summaries. Available from U. S. Government Printing Office. • Annual. $26.00. Published by the U. S. Geological Survey, Department of the Interior (http://www.usgs.gov). Contains detailed, five-year data for about 90 nonfuel minerals. Covers a wide range of statistics, including production, imports, exports, consumption, reserves, prices, tariff information, and industry employment. (Two pages are devoted to each mineral.).

Minerals Yearbook. Available from U.S. Government Printing Office. • Annual. Three volumes.

Non-Ferrous Metal Data Yearbook. American Bureau of Metal Statistics. • Annual. $405.00. Provides worldwide data on approximately about 200 statistical tables covering many nonferrous metals. Includes production, consumption, inventories, exports, imports, and other data.

Standard & Poor's Industry Surveys. Standard & Poor's. • Semiannual. $1,800.00. Two looseleaf volumes. Includes monthly *Supplements.* Provides detailed, individual surveys of 52 major industry groups. Each survey is revised on a semiannual basis. Also includes "Monthly Investment Review" (industry group investment analysis) and monthly "Trends & Projections" (economic analysis).

Statistical Annual: Interest Rates, Metals, Stock Indices, Options on Financial Futures, Options on Metals Futures. Chicago Board of Trade. • Annual. Includes historical data on GNMA CDR Futures, Cash-Settled GNMA Futures, U. S. Treasury Bond Futures, U. S. Treasury Note Futures, Options on Treasury Note Futures, NASDAQ-100 Futures, Major Market Index Futures, Major Market Index MAXI Futures, Municipal Bond Index Futures, 1,000-Ounce Silver Futures, Options on Silver Futures, and Kilo Gold Futures.

United States Census of Mineral Industries. Bureau of the Census, U.S. Department of Commerce. Available from U.S. Government Printing Office. • Quinquennial.

TRADE/PROFESSIONAL ASSOCIATIONS
American Bureau of Metal Statistics. P.O. Box 805, Chatham, NJ 07928. Phone: (973)701-2299 Fax: (973)701-2152 E-mail: info@abms.com • URL: http://www.abms.com • Members are metal companies. Compiles and publishes detailed statistical data on a wide variety of nonferrous metals: aluminum, copper, gold, lead, nickel, platinum, silver, tin, titanium, uranium, zinc, and others.

Silver Institute. 1200 G St. NW, Ste. 800, Washington, DC 20005. Phone: (202)835-0185 Fax: (202)835-0155 E-mail: info@silverinstitute.org •

URL: http://www.silverinstitute.org • Companies that mine, refine, and manufacture silver-containing products; silver bullion suppliers. Seeks to encourage the development and use of silver and silver products. Helps develop markets. Fosters research on present and prospective uses of silver. Collects and publishes statistics and other information regarding production, distribution, marketing consumption, and uses of silver and silver products.

Silver Users Association. 11240 Waples Mill Rd., No. 200, Fairfax, VA 22030. Phone: 800-245-6999 or (703)930-7790 Fax: (703)359-7562 E-mail: pmiller@mwcapitol.com • URL: http://www.silverusersassociation.org • Represents companies that make, sell and distribute products and services in which silver is an essential component. Informs members, government and the public on all the facets of the silver market in a timely manner.

SILVERWARE

See: TABLEWARE

SKIP TRACERS

See: COLLECTING OF ACCOUNTS

SLOT MACHINES

See: VENDING MACHINES

SMALL ARMS

See: FIREARMS INDUSTRY

SMALL BUSINESS

See also: BUSINESS; BUSINESS ENTERPRISES, SALE OF; BUSINESS START-UP PLANS AND PROPOSALS; FRANCHISES; SELF-EMPLOYMENT; SMALL BUSINESS INVESTMENT COMPANIES; VENTURE CAPITAL

GENERAL WORKS

Businesses' Views on Red Tape: Administrative and Regulatory Burdens on Small and Medium-Sized Enterprises. Organization for Economic Cooperation and Development. • 2001. $22.00. Based on a survey of about 8,000 firms in 11 OECD countries. Provides opinions on the costs of complying with governmental rules, regulations, and formalities.

Managing the Small to Mid-Sized Company: Concepts and Cases. James C. Collins and William C. Lazier. McGraw-Hill. • 1994. $92.50.

Net Income: Cut Costs, Boost Profits, and Enhance Operations Online. Wally Bock and Jeff Senne. John Wiley and Sons, Inc. • 1997. $29.95. "Net Income" in this case is hoped-for Internet income. Promotes the use of the Internet, intranet, and extranet to improve business operations or start new businesses. The authors take a nontechnical, business strategy approach.

Women Entrepreneurs: Moving Beyond the Glass Ceiling. Dorothy P. Moore and E. Holly Buttner. Sage Publications, Inc. • 1997. $79.95. Contains profiles of "129 successful female entrepreneurs who previously worked in corporate environments.".

BIBLIOGRAPHIES

Small Business Sourcebook. Gale Cengage Learning. • 2003. $380.00. 17th edtion. Two volumes. Information sources for about 100 kinds of small businesses.

CD-ROM DATABASES

OECD Statistical Compendium. Organization for Economic Cooperation and Development. •

Semiannual. $1,905.00 per year for 1 to 10 users. CD-ROM contains more than 730,000 monthly, quarterly, and annual time series for OECD countries, 1960 to date. Includes fully searchable data on agriculture, food, economic indicators, national accounts, employment, energy, finance, industry, technology, and foreign trade. Results can be displayed in various forms.

16 Million Businesses Phone Directory. Info USA. • Annual. $29.95. Provides more than 16 million yellow pages telephone directory listings on CD-ROM for all ZIP Code areas of the U. S.

DIRECTORIES

Business Capital Sources. Tyler G. Hicks. IWS Inc. • Covers: about 1,500 banks, insurance and mortgage companies, commercial finance, leasing, and venture capital firms that lend money for business investment. Entries include: Company or institution name, address, phone.

ENCYCLOPEDIAS AND DICTIONARIES

Encyclopedia of Small Business. Gale Cengage Learning. • 2002. $450.00. Second edition. Two volumes. Contains about 600 informative entries on a wide variety of topics affecting small business. Arrangement is alphabetical.

HANDBOOKS AND MANUALS

Business Brokerage. Entrepreneur Media, Inc. • Looseleaf. $59.50. A practical guide to starting a brokerage service for the sale and purchase of small businesses. Covers profit potential, start-up costs, market size evaluation, owner's time required, pricing, accounting, advertising, promotion, etc. (Start-Up Business Guide No. E1317.).

Business Plans that Work for Your Small Business. Alice H. Magos and Steve Crow, editors. CCH, Inc. • 2003. $19.95. Second edition. Part one is "Creating a Business Plan that Works" and part two is "Five Sample Business Plans.".

Complete Book of Small Business Legal Forms. Daniel Sitarz. Nova Publishing Co. • 2002. $24.95. Third edition. Includes CD-Rom and basic forms and instructions for use by small businesses in routine legal situations. Forms are also available on IBM or MAC diskettes. (Small Business Library Series).

Entrepreneur's Guide to Finance and Business: Wealth Creation Techniques for Growing a Business. Steven Rogers. McGraw-Hill. • 2003. $49.95. Coverage includes entrepreneurial financing, business plan development, and structuring a deal.

Financial Management Techniques for Small Business. Art R. DeThomas. PSI Research. • 1991. $19.95. (Successful Business Library Series).

Financing Your Small Business. Robert Walter. Barron's Educational Series, Inc. • 2004. $18.95. Explains various sources of capital for small businesses, including bank loans, venture capital, and initial public offerings of stock.

How to Run a Small Business. McGraw-Hill. • 1994. $27.95. Seventh edition.

Incorporate Your Business: The National Corporation Kit. Daniel Sitarz. Nova Publishing Co. • 2001. $29.95. Third edition. IncludesCD-ROM and basic forms and instructions for incorporating a small business in any state. Forms are also available on IBM or MAC diskettes. (Small Business Library Series).

Incorporation Kit. Entrepreneur Media, Inc. • Looseleaf. $59.50. A practical guide to incorporating a small business. Includes sample forms and information on how to construct bylaws and articles of incorporation. (Start-Up Business Guide No. E7100.).

Insuring Your Business: What You Need to Know to Get the Best Insurance Coverage for Your Business.

Sean Mooney. Insurance Information Institute. • 1992. $22.50.

The Law in (Plain English) for Small Businesses. Leonard D. DuBoff. Allworth Press. • 1998. $19.95. Third revised edition. Discusses and explains legal issues relating to the organization, financing, and operation of a small business.

Legal Forms for Starting and Running a Small Business. Fred Steingold. Nolo Press. • 2004. $29.99. Third edition.

Marketing Without Advertising. Michael Phillips and Salli Rasberry. Nolo. • 2001. $24.00. Fourth edition. How to market a small business economically.

SBA Loan Guide. Entrepreneur Meida, Inc. • Looseleaf. $59.50. A practical guide to obtaining loans through the Small Business Administration. (Start-Up Business Guide No. E1315.).

Small Business Accounting Simplefied. Daniel Sitarz. Nova Publishing Co. • 2002. $22.95. Third edition. Includes basic forms and instructions for small business accounting and bookkeeping. (Small Business Library Series).

Small Business IPOs: From Concept to Closing. Robert.W. Walter. CCH, Inc. • 2004. $85.00. Edited mainly for lawyers. Provides a step-by-step guide to taking a relatively small firm public. Covers use of investment bankers, valuation, letter of intent, due diligence, dealing with the SEC, and other topics. Appendices include samples of various forms, letters, and agreements.

Small Business Legal Smarts. Deborah L. Jacobs. Bloomberg. • 1998. $16.95. Discusses common legal problems encountered by small business owners. (Small Business Series).

Small Business Management: An Entrepreneurial Emphasis. Justin Longenecker. Cengage Learning. • 1999. $94.95. 11th edition. (Small Business Management Series).

Small Business Management Fundamentals. John Burgess. McGraw-Hill. • 1993. $45.93. Sixth edition.

Small Business Survival Guide: How to Manage Your Cash, Profits and Taxes. Robert E. Fleury. Sourcebooks, Inc. • 1995. $17.95. Third revised edition. (Small Business Series).

Small Time Operator: How to Start Your Own Small Business, Keep Your Books, Pay Your Taxes, and Stay Out of Trouble. Bernard Kamoroff. Bell Springs Publishing. • 2001. $16.95. 26th edition. Concise, practical advice. Includes bookkeeping forms.

Standard Business Forms for the Entrepreneur. Entrepreneur Media, Inc. • Looseleaf. $59.50. A practical collection of forms useful to entrepreneurial small businesses. (Start-Up Business Guide No. E1319.).

Start-Up Business Guides. Entrepreneur Media, Inc. • Looseleaf. $59.50 each. Practical guides to starting a wide variety of small businesses.

Startup: An Entrepreneur's Guide to Launching and Managing a New Venture. William J. Stolze. Rock Beach Press. • 1989. $24.95.

Steps to Small Business Start-Up: Everything You Need to Know to Turn Your Idea into a Successful Business. Linda Pinson and Jerry Jinnett. Dearborn Trade Publishing, A Kaplan Professional Co. • 2003. $22.95. Fifth edition. Covers such topics as location, legal structure, cash flow, financing, appropriateness, taxes, and insurance. Includes charts, sample calculations, spreadsheets, and forms.

Telecom Made Easy: Money-Saving, Profit-Building Solutions for Home Businesses, Telecommuters. June Langhoff. Aegis Publishing Group, Ltd. • 2001. $19.95. Fouth revised edition.

Ultimate Guide to Raising Money for Growing Companies. Michael C. Thomsett. McGraw-Hill. •

1990. $45.00. Discusses the preparation of a practical business plan, how to manage cash flow, and debt vs. equity decisions.

Where to Go When the Bank Says No: Alternatives to Financing Your Business. David R. Evanson. Bloomberg. • 1998. $24.95. Emphasis is on obtaining business financing in the $250,000 to $15,000,000 range. Business plans are discussed. (Bloomberg Small Business Series).

Win Government Contracts for Your Small Business. John DiGiacomo and James Kleckner. CCH, Inc. • 2003. $24.95. Second edition. Provides 10 "easy-to-understand steps" to obtain government contracts. Appendices include a glossary, sample forms, and other information.

INTERNET DATABASES

Business 2.0 Web Guide to the Best Business Links. Business 2.0 Media Inc. Phone: (415)293-4800 E-mail: support@business2.com • URL: http://www.business2.com/webguide • Web site presents an extensive, searchable directory of links to "the best, most informative, and authoritative web pages." Twenty main categories cover business, finance, career, company information, people, and technology topics, with thousands of subtopics, all linking to Web sites recommended by experienced business researchers. Fees: Free.

MBEMAG. Minority Business Entrepreneur Magazine. Phone: (310)540-9398 Fax: (310)792-8263 E-mail: webmaster@mbemag.com • URL: http://www.mbemag.com • Web site's main feature is the "MBE Business Resources Directory." This provides complete mailing addresses, phone, fax, and Web site addresses (URL) for more than 40 organizations and government agencies having information or assistance for ethnic minority and women business owners. Some other links are "Current Events," "Calendar of Events," and "Business Opportunities." Updating is bimonthly. Fees: Free.

Small Business Retirement Savings Advisor. U. S. Department of Labor. Phone: (202)219-8921 • URL: http://www.dol.gov/elaws/pwbaplan.htm • Web site provides "answers to a variety of commonly asked questions about retirement saving options for small business employers." Includes a comparison chart and detailed descriptions of various plans: 401(k), SEP-IRA, SIMPLE-IRA, Payroll Deduction IRA, Keogh Profit-Sharing, Keogh Money Purchase, and Defined Benefit. Searching is offered. Fees: Free.

Switchboard. Switchboard, Inc. Phone: (508)898-8000 Fax: (508)898-1755 E-mail: webmaster@switchboard.com • URL: http://www.switchboard.com • Web site provides telephone numbers and street addresses for more than 100 million business locations and residences in the U. S. Broad industry categories are available. Fees: Free.

U. S. Business Advisor. Small Business Administration. Phone: (202)205-6600 Fax: (202)205-7064 • URL: http://www.business.gov • Web site provides "a one-stop electronic link to all the information and services government provides for the business community." Covers about 60 federal agencies that exist to assist or regulate business. Detailed information is provided on financial assistance, workplace issues, taxes, regulations, international trade, and other business topics. Searching is offered. Fees: Free.

ONLINE DATABASES

American Business Directory. InfoUSA, Inc. • Provides brief online information on more than 10 million U. S. companies, including individual plants and branches. Entries typically include address, phone number, industry classification code, and contact name. Updating is quarterly. Inquire as to online cost and availability.

PERIODICALS AND NEWSLETTERS

Business Start-Ups: Smart Ideas for Your Small Business. Entrepreneur Media, Inc. • Monthly.

$14.97 per year. Provides advice for starting a small business. Includes business trends, new technology, E-commerce, and case histories ("real-life stories").

Entrepreneur: The Small Business Authority. Entrepreneur Media, Inc. • Monthly. $19.97 per year. Contains advice for small business owners and prospective owners. Includes numerous franchise advertisements.

Entrepreneurship: Theory and Practice. Baylor University, Hankamer School of Business Available from Blackwell Publishing, Inc. • Quarterly. Institutions, $280.00 per year. Includes online edition. Formerly *American Journal of Small Business.*

Home Office Connections: A Monthly Journal of News, Ideas, Opportunities, and Savings for Those Who Work at Home. Home Office Association of America. • Monthly. Free to members; non-members, $49.00 per year.

HomeOffice: The Homebased Office Authority. Entrepreneur Media, Inc. • Bimonthly. $11.97 per year. Contains advice for operating a business in the home.

In Business: The Magazine for Environmental Entrepreneuring. JG Press, Inc. • Bimonthly. $33.00 per year. Magazine for environmental entrepreneuring.

Inc.: The Magazine for Growing Companies. INC. • 18 times a year. $14.00 per year. Edited for small office and office-in-the-home businesses with from one to 25 employees. Covers management, office technology, and lifestyle. Incorporates *Self-Employed Professional.*

International Wealth Success Newsletter: The Monthly Newsletter of Worldwide Wealth Opportunities. Tyler G. Hicks, editor. International Wealth Success, Inc. • Monthly. $24.00 per year. Newsletter. Provides information on a variety of small business topics, including financing, mail order, foreign opportunities, licensing, and franchises.

Journal of Small Business Management. West Virginia University Bureau of Business Research. Blackwell Publishing, Inc. • Quarterly. $166.00 per year. Includes print and online editions. Articles and features on small business and entrepreneurship.

Minority Business Entrepreneur. • Bimonthly. $16.00 per year. Reports on issues "critical to the growth and development of minority and women-owned firms." Provides information on relevant legislation and profiles successful women and minority entrepreneurs.

Smart Business for the New Economy. Element K Journals. • Monthly. $12.00 per year. Provides practical advice for doing business in an economy dominated by technology and electronic commerce.

RESEARCH CENTERS AND INSTITUTES

Arthur M. Bank Center for Entrepreneurship. Babson College, Babson Park, MA 02459-0310. Phone: (781)239-4623 Fax: (781)239-4178 E-mail: spinelli@babson.edu • URL: http://www.babson.edu/entrep • Sponsors annual Babson College Entrepreneurship Research Conference.

The Darla Moore School of Business - Division of Research. University of South Carolina at Columbia, Columbia, SC 29208. Phone: (803)777-2510 Fax: (803)777-9344 E-mail: woodward@darla.badm.sa.edu • URL: http://www.mooreschool.sc.edu.

Small Business Development Center. Lehigh University, Rauch Business Center, 621 Taylor St., Bethlehem, PA 18015-3117. Phone: (610)758-3980 Fax: (610)758-5205 E-mail: insbdc@lehigh.edu • URL: http://www.lehigh.edu/~insbdc/.

STATISTICS SOURCES

New Business Incorporations. Dun & Bradstreet Corp. • Monthly. $25.00 per year. Gives the number of new business incorporations in each of the 50 states. Includes commentary.

TRADE/PROFESSIONAL ASSOCIATIONS

Home Office Association of America. PO Box 51, Sagaponack, NY 11962-0051. Phone: 800-809-4622 E-mail: hoaa@aol.com • URL: http://www.hoaa.com • A for-profit organization providing advice and information to home office workers and business owners.

International Council for Small Business. c/o Jefferson Smurfit Center for Entrepreneurial Studies, St. Louis University, 3674 Lindell Blvd., St. Louis, MO 63108. Phone: (314)977-3628 Fax: (314)977-3627 E-mail: icsb@slu.edu • URL: http://www.icsb.org • Formerly National Committee for Small Business Management Development.

National Business Incubation Association. 20 E Circle Dr., No. 37198, Athens, OH 45701-3571. Phone: (740)593-4331 Fax: (740)593-1996 E-mail: info@nbia.org • URL: http://www.NBIA.org • Incubator developers and managers; corporate joint venture partners, venture capital investors; economic development professionals. (Incubators are business assistance programs providing business consulting services and financing assistance to start-up and fledgling companies.) Helps newly formed businesses to succeed. Educates businesses and investors on incubator benefits; offers specialized training in incubator formation and management. Conducts research and referral services; compiles statistics; maintains speakers' bureau; publishes information relevant to business incubation and growing companies.

National Federation of Independent Business. 53 Century Blvd., Ste. 250, Nashville, TN 37214. Phone: 800-634-2669 or (615)872-5800 Fax: (615)872-5353 • URL: http://www.nfib.com • Members are independent business and professional people.

National Small Business United. 1156 15th St., N.W., Suite 1100, Washington, DC 20005. Phone: 800-345-6728 or (202)293-8830 Fax: (202)872-8543 E-mail: nsbu@nsbu.org • URL: http://www.nsbu.org.

OTHER SOURCES

Keeping the Books: Basic Recordkeeping and Accounting for the Successful Small Business. Linda Pinson. Dearborn Trade Publishing, A Kaplan Professional Co. • 2001. $22.95. Fifth edition. Covers bookkeeping systems, financial statements, and IRS tax record requirements. Includes illustrations, worksheets, and forms.

Start-Up and Emerging Companies: Planning, Financing, and Operating the Successful Business, with Forms on Disk. American Lawyer Media, Inc. • Looseleaf. $289.00. Two volumes. Updated as needed. Covers a wide variety of business and legal topics relating to new enterprises. Provides information on venture financing, formation of corporations, tax laws, limited liability companies, employee benefits, contracts, and accounting. Includes a CD-ROM containing more than 75 sample legal forms, clauses, agreements, organizational resolutions, and checklists. (Law Journal Press).

Tax Planning for Individuals and Small Businesses. Sidney Kess. CCH, Inc. • 2002. $52.00. Second edition. Includes illustrations, charts, and sample client letters. Edited primarily for accountants and lawyers.

SMALL BUSINESS INVESTMENT COMPANIES

FINANCIAL RATIOS

Almanac of Business and Industrial Financial Ratios. Leo Troy. Aspen Publishers, Inc. • 2003. $125.95. Includes CD-Rom. Contains financial ratios derived from federal tax returns. Ratios for each of about 200 industries are arranged according to company asset size. (Almanac of Business and Industrial Financial Ratios Series).

HANDBOOKS AND MANUALS

Moody's Bank and Finance Manual. Mergent. • Annual. $1,750.00 per year. Four volumes. Includes biweekly supplements in *Moody's Bank and Finance News Report.*

SBIC Directory and Handbook of Small Business Finance. International Wealth Success, Inc. • Annual. $15.00 per year. Includes small business investment companies.

STATISTICS SOURCES

Small Business Administration. Annual Report. U.S. Government Printing Office. • Annual. Two volumes.

TRADE/PROFESSIONAL ASSOCIATIONS

National Association of Small Business Investment Companies. 666 11th St., N.W., No. 750, Washington, DC 20001. Phone: (202)628-5055 Fax: (202)628-5080 E-mail: nasbic@nasbic.org • URL: http://www.nasbic.org • Affiliated with Small Business Legislative Council.

SMALL LOAN COMPANIES

See: FINANCE COMPANIES

SMOKING POLICY

See also: TOBACCO AND TOBACCO INDUSTRY

GENERAL WORKS

Cigarettes: Anatomy of an Industry from Seed to Smoke. Tara Parker-Pope. The New Press. • 2001. $24.95. Covers the history, economic ramifications, marketing strategies, and legal problems of the cigarette industry. Popularly written.

Drugs, Alcohol, and Tobacco: Learning About Addictive Behavior. Gale Cengage Learning. • 2002. $295.00. Three volumes. Contains 200 articles on various aspects of addiction. Includes color illustrations, a glossary, and comprehensive indexing. (Macmillan Reference USA imprint.).

Rise and Fall of the Cigarette: A Social and Cultural History of Smoking in the U. S. Allan Brandt. Basic Books. • 2000. $25.00. Second edition.

Smoking and Politics: Policy Making and the Federal Bureaucracy. A. Lee Fritschler and James M. Hoepler. Prentice Hall PTR. • 1995. $44.00. Fifth edition.

ABSTRACTS AND INDEXES

Readers' Guide to Periodical Literature. H. W. Wilson Co. • Monthly. $345.00 per year. Includes annual *Cumulation.* Indexes about 250 peridicals of general interest.

BIBLIOGRAPHIES

Smoking: The Health Consequences of Tobacco Use. Richard A. Gray and Cecilia M. Schmitz. Pierian Press. • 1995. $30.00. (Science and Social Responsibility Series: No.2).

ONLINE DATABASES

Readers' Guide Abstracts Online. H. W. Wilson Co. • Indexes and abstracts general interest periodicals, 1983 to date. Weekly updates. Inquire as to online cost and availability.

RESEARCH CENTERS AND INSTITUTES

Tobacco and Health Research Institute. University of Kentucky. Cooper and University Drives, Lexington, KY 40546-0236. Phone: (859)257-5798 Fax: (859)323-1077 E-mail: mdavies@pop.uky.edu

• URL: http://www.uky.edu/~rgs/thri.

STATISTICS SOURCES

Statistics on Alcohol, Drug, and Tobacco Use: A Selection of Statistical Charts, Graphs and Tables about Alcohol, Drug and Tobacco Use from a Variety of Published Sources with Explanatory Comments. Gale Cengage Learning. • 1995. $85.00. Includes graphs, charts, and tables arranged within subject chapters. Citations to data sources are provided. (Statistics on...Series: vol. 1).

TRADE/PROFESSIONAL ASSOCIATIONS

Action on Smoking and Health. 2013 H St., N. W., Washington, DC 20006. Phone: (202)659-4310 Fax: (202)833-3921 E-mail: webmaster@ash.org • URL: http://www.ash.org • Promotes national legal action against smoking.

Group Against Smokers' Pollution. PO Box 632, College Park, MD 20741-0632. E-mail: gaspamerica@aol.com • Nonsmokers who are adversely affected by tobacco smoke united to promote the rights of nonsmokers, educate the public about the problems of second-hand smoke, and regulate smoking in places where nonsmokers are exposed. Supports the establishment and enforcement of laws and other public policy measures which reduce environmental tobacco smoke. Provides information and referral services; distributes educational literature, buttons, posters, and bumper stickers. Helps members find local GASP chapters or establish a chapter.

SNACK FOOD INDUSTRY

See also: BAKING INDUSTRY; FOOD INDUSTRY

CD-ROM DATABASES

Food Science and Technology Abstracts [CD-ROM]. Available from SilverPlatter Information, Inc. • Quarterly. Produced by International Food Information Service (home page is http://www.ifis.org). Provides worldwide coverage on CD-ROM of the literature of food technology and production. Various types of publications are indexed, with abstracts, including about 1,800 periodicals. Time period is 1969 to date.

DIRECTORIES

Major Food and Drink Companies of the World. Available from Gale Cengage Learning. • Annual. $880.00. Two volumes. Published by Graham & Whiteside. Contains profiles and trade names for more than 9,800 important food and beverage companies in various countries. In addition to foods, includes both alcoholic and nonalcoholic drink products.

Snack Food and Wholesale Baker's Buyer's Guide. Stagnito Publishing Co. • Annual. $55.00. Lists approximately 900 companies that provide supplies and services to the snack food industry. Formerly *Snack Food Buyer's Guide.*

Specialty Food Industry Directory. Phoenix Media Network, Inc. • Annual. Included in subscription to Food Distribution Magazine. Lists manufacturers and suppliers of specialty foods, and services and equipment for the specialty food industry. Featured food products include legumes, sauces, spices, upscale cheese, specialty beverages, snack foods, baked goods, ethnic foods, and specialty meats.

Thomas Food and Beverage Market Place. Grey House Publishing. • 2004. $495.00. Three volumes. Contains more than 40,000 entries covering food companies, beverages, food equipment, warehouse companies, food brokers, wholesalers, importers, and exporters. Formerly *Thomas Food Industry Register.*

Who's Who in the Snack Food Industry. Snack Food Association. • Annual. $150.00. A directory of more

than 800 snack food manufacturers and suppliers to the industry.

HANDBOOKS AND MANUALS

Donut Shop. Entrepreneur Media, Inc. • Looseleaf. $59.50. A practical guide to starting a doughnut shop. Covers profit potential, start-up costs, market size evaluation, owner's time required, site selection, lease negotiation, pricing, accounting, advertising, promotion, etc. (Start-Up Business Guide No. E1126.).

Ice Cream Store. Entrepreneur Media, Inc. • Looseleaf. $59.50. A practical guide to starting an ice cream shop. Covers profit potential, start-up costs, market size evaluation, owner's time required, site selection, lease negotiation, pricing, accounting, advertising, promotion, etc. (Start-Up Business Guide No. E1187.).

ONLINE DATABASES

F & S Index. Gale Cengage Learning. • Contains about four million citations to worldwide business, financial, and industrial or consumer product literature appearing from 1972 to date. Weekly updates. Inquire as to online cost and availability.

Food Science and Technology Abstracts [online]. IFIS North American Desk. • Produced by International Food Information Service. Provides about 500,000 online citations, with abstracts, to the international literature of food science, technology, commodities, engineering, and processing. Approximately 2,000 periodicals are covered. Time period is 1969 to date, with monthly updates. Inquire as to online cost and availability.

Globalbase. Gale Cengage Learning. • Provides more than one million online summaries of business, industrial, and economic news reports from more than 1,000 publications worldwide. Covers a wide range of material appearing in international trade journals, professional magazines, and newspapers. Time period is 1984 to date, with weekly updates. Inquire as to online cost and availability.

PROMT: Predicasts Overview of Markets and Technology. Gale Cengage Learning. • Companies, products, applied technologies and markets. U.S. and international literature coverage, 1972 to date. Inquire as to online cost and availability. Provides abstracts from more than 1,600 publications. Weekly updates.

PERIODICALS AND NEWSLETTERS

Baking and Snack. Sosland Publishing Co. • Monthly. Free to qualified personnel; others, $30.00 per year. Covers manufacturing systems and ingredients for baked goods and snack foods.

Confectioner: The Magazine. Stagnito Communcations, Inc. • Bimonthly. $70.17 per year. Covers a wide variety of topics relating to the distribution and retailing of candy and snacks.

Food Distribution Magazine. Phoenix Media Network, Inc. • Monthly. $49.00 per year. Edited for marketers and buyers of domestic and imported, specialty or gourmet food products, including ethnic foods, seasonings, and bakery items.

Snack Food and Wholesale Bakery: The Magazine That Defines the Snack Food Industry. Stagnito Publishing Co. • Monthly. Free to qualified personnel; others, $85.06 per year. Provides news and information for producers of pretzels, potato chips, cookies, crackers, nuts, and other snack foods. Includes *Annual Buyers Guide* and *State of Industry Report.*

STATISTICS SOURCES

World Food Data and Statistics. Euromonitor International. • 2004. $650.00. Provides five-year data for a wide variety of food products in 52 countries. Includes market size, consumer expenditures, price indicators, and retail distribution data for many kinds of meat, fish, fruits, vegetables, dairy products, baked goods, condiments, canned food, and frozen food.

TRADE/PROFESSIONAL ASSOCIATIONS

Biscuit and Cracker Distributors Association. 5024 Campbell Blvd., Ste. R, Baltimore, MD 21236. Phone: (312)644-6610 • Members are distributors and manufacturers of cookies, crackers, and related products.

Biscuit and Cracker Manufacturers Association. 8484 Georgia Ave., Suite 700, Silver Spring, MD 20910. Phone: (301)608-1552 Fax: (301)608-1557 E-mail: frooney@thebcma.org • URL: http://www. thebcma.org • Members are bakers of crackers and cookies. Formerly Biscuit Bakers Institute.

Cookie and Snack Bakers Association. P.O. Box 37320, Cleveland, TN 37320. Phone: (423)472-1561 • Members are bakers of snacks and cookies.

Peanut and Tree Nut Processors Association. PO Box 59811, Potomac, MD 20859-9811. Phone: (301)365-2521 Fax: (301)365-7705 E-mail: ptnpa@ mindspring.com • URL: http://www.ptnpa.org • Formerly Peanut Butter Manufacturers and Nut-Salters Association.

Popcorn Institute. 401 N Michigan Ave., Ste. 2200, Chicago, IL 60611-4267. Phone: 877-POP-ALOT or (312)644-6610 Fax: 877-767-2568 or (312)527-6783 E-mail: gbertalmio@smithbucklin.com • URL: http://www.popcorn.org • Represents companies engaged in popcorn processing and trade management activities as well as government relations. Provides a platform for discussion on the popcorn industry. Maintains hall of fame for retired members who have made contributions to the industry.

Snack Food Association. 1600 Wilson Blvd., Ste. 650, Arlington, VA 22209. Phone: 800-628-1334 or (703)836-4500 Fax: (703)836-8262 E-mail: sfa@ sfa.org • URL: http://www.sfa.org • Manufacturers of potato chips, pretzels, corn chips, tortilla chips, popcorn, cheese snacks, pork rinds, cookies, crackers, nuts, meat snacks, fruit snacks, and grain-based snacks; associate members are suppliers and distributors of fats and oils, packaging supplies, machinery, seasonings, and potato and corn growers.

OTHER SOURCES

Market for Healthy Snacks. MarketResearch.com. • 1996. $3,250.00. Provides market data on granola bars, dried fruit, trail mix, rice cakes, etc.

The Market for Salted Snacks. MarketResearch. com. • 2002. $3,000.00. Market research report. Covers potato chips, corn chips, popcorn, nuts, pretzels, and other salted snacks. Market projections are provided to the year 2004.

SNUFF

See: TOBACCO AND TOBACCO INDUSTRY

SOAPS AND DETERGENTS

See: CLEANING PRODUCTS INDUSTRY

SOCIAL ACCOUNTING

See: NATIONAL ACCOUNTING

SOCIAL CLUB

OTHER SOURCES

Arnold Air Society. • Honorary professional fraternity within AFROTC. Organizes community service projects. Sponsors Silver Wings, a nonmilitary campus service organization.

The Creative Coalition. • Actors, writers, directors and other arts and entertainment professionals. Aims to educate members about social and political issues, particularly in the areas of the First Amendment, arts advocacy and public education.

Hollywood Women's Political Committee. • Women working in the entertainment industry and related fields. Raises funds for federal political candidates, grass roots organizations, and statewide initiatives that pledge to represent the group's beliefs on nuclear disarmament, increased environmental protection, improved public education, and expanded civil rights for women. Seeks to heighten community involvement in national politics. **Publications:** none. **Convention/Meeting:** none.

National Society of Pershing Rifles. • Members range from military to civilian, male to female. Seeks to foster a spirit of friendship and cooperation among men and women in the military department and to maintain a highly efficient drill company.

National Society of Scabbard and Blade. • Honorary and recognition fraternity - men and women, military; advanced ROTC; junior ROTC, and all-Service. Maintains speakers' bureau.

Navy Club of the United States of America. • Persons who are, or have been, in the active service of the U.S. Navy, Naval Reserve, Marine Corps, Marine Corps Reserve, and Coast Guard. Promotes and encourages further public interest in the U.S. Navy and its history and to uphold the spirit and ideals of the U.S. Navy. Acts as public forum for members' views on national defense. Assists Navy Recruiting Command. Conducts charitable activities.

Navy Club of the United States of America Auxiliary. • Women relatives of men who have served in the United States Navy, Marine Corps, Coast Guard, and component reserve services; women who are eligible in their own right for membership in the Navy Club of the United States of America. Provides assistance to the Navy Club; promotes fraternal love and sociability; encourages interest in the U.S. Navy and its history. Activities include veterans' service, rehabilitation programs, child welfare assistance, handicapped services, and overseas relief, memorials, and community service. Supports U.S. Navy special services. Maintains museum.

Silver Wings. • Works as a national, co-ed, professional organization dedicated to creating proactive, knowledgeable, and effective civic leaders through community service and education about national defense. Its mission includes the following interrelated objectives; a. Personal Development b. Professional Development and c. Civic Awareness.

Vatel Club. • Social club for chefs, cooks, and other members of the culinary profession.

SOCIAL RESPONSIBILITY

See also: BUSINESS ETHICS; COMMUNITY RELATIONS

GENERAL WORKS

Business and Society: A Managerial Approach. Heidi Vernon. McGraw-Hill. • 1997. $110.31. Sixth edition. Emphasizes ethics and social accountability.

Business, Government, and Society: A Managerial Perspective: Text and Cases. George A. Steiner and John F. Steiner. McGraw-Hill. • 1999. $88.75. Ninth edition. (Management Series).

Corporate Social Challenge: Cases and Commentaries. James E. Stacey and Frederick D. Sturdivant, editors. McGraw-Hill. • 1994. $41.95. Fifth edition.

Corporate Social Responsibility: Partners for Progress. Organization for Economic Cooperation and Development. • 2001. $25.00. Reviews the

function of corporate social responsibility at the local level and its influence on economic development.

Value Shift: Merging Social and Financial Imperatives to Achive Superior Performance. Lynn S. Paine. McGraw-Hill. • 2002. $27.95. Emphasizes the financial merits of corporate social responsibility. (Teach Yourself Series).

Wired Neighborhood. Stephen Doheny-Farina. Yale University Press. • 1996. $40.00. The author examines both the hazards and the advantages of "making the computer the center of our public and private lives," as exemplified by the Internet and telecommuting.

ABSTRACTS AND INDEXES

PAIS International in Print. Public Affairs Information Service, Inc. • Monthly. $850.00 per year; cumulations three times a year. Provides topical citations to the worldwide literature of public affairs, economics, demographics, sociology, and trade. Text in English; indexed materials in English, French, German, Italian, Portuguese and Spanish.

Social Sciences Citation Index. Thomson/ISI. • Three times a year. $6,900 per year. Annual cumulation. Includes *Source Index, Citation Index, Permuterm Subject Index,* and *Corporate Index.*

Social Sciences Index. H. W. Wilson Co. • Quarterly, with annual cumulation. Price varies. Indexes more than 400 periodicals covering economics, environmental policy, government, insurance, labor, health care policy, plannning, public administration, public welfare, urban studies, women's issues, criminology, and related topics.

ALMANACS AND YEARBOOKS

Research in Corporate Social Performance and Policy: An Annual Compilation of Research. Elsevier. • Dates vary. $78.50. 15 volumes.

CD-ROM DATABASES

Newspaper Abstracts Ondisc. PROQUEST. • Monthly. $2,950.00 per year (covers 1989 to date; archival discs are available for 1985-88). Provides cover-to-cover CD-ROM indexing and abstracting of 19 major newspapers, including the *New York Times, Wall Street Journal, Washington Post, Chicago Tribune,* and *Los Angeles Times.*

PAIS on CD-ROM. Public Affairs Information Service, Inc. • Quarterly. $1,995.00 per year. Provides a CD-ROM version of the online service, *PAIS International.* Contains over 500,000 citations to the literature of contemporary social, political, and economic issues.

Social Sciences Citation Index. ISI. • Monthly. Price on request. Provides CD-ROM indexing of articles appearing in 1700 leading social science journals worldwide, with additional selections from more than 5700 other journals. Time span is 1992 to date. Coverage includes economics, business, finance, management, communications, demographics, library and information science, political science, sociology, and many other subjects.

Social Sciences Citation Index: Compact Disc Edition with Abstracts. Institute for Scientific Information. • Monthly. Provides CD-ROM indexing and abstracting of "significant articles" from 1,700 social science journals worldwide, with additional selections from 3,200 other journals, 1986 to date. Includes economics, business, finance, management, communications, demographics, information and library science, political science, sociology, and many other subjects.

WILSONDISC: Wilson Social Sciences Abstracts. H. W. Wilson Co. • Monthly. Includes unlimited online access to *Social Sciences Index* through WILSONLINE. Provides CD-ROM indexing from 1983 and abstracting from 1994 of more than 500 periodicals covering economics, area studies, community health, public administration, public welfare, urban studies, and many other topics related to the social sciences.

DIRECTORIES

National Directory of Corporate Public Affairs. Columbia Books, Inc. • Annual. $109.00. Lists about 1,900 corporations that have foundations or other public affairs activities.

Shopping for a Better World: A Quick and Easy Guide to Socially Responsible Supermarket Shopping. Council on Economic Priorities. • Annual. $14.00. Rates 186 major corporations according to 10 social criteria: advancement of minorities, advancement of women, environmental concerns, South African investments, charity, community outreach, nuclear power, animal testing, military contracts, and social disclosure. Includes American, Japanese and British firms.

ENCYCLOPEDIAS AND DICTIONARIES

Blackwell Encyclopedic Dictionary of Business Ethics. Patricia H. Werhane and R. Edward Freeman. Blackwell Publishing. • 1997. $38.95. The editors are associated with the University of Virginia. Contains definitions of key terms combined with longer articles written by various U. S. and foreign business educators. Includes bibliographies and index. (Blackwell Encyclopedia of Management Series).

HANDBOOKS AND MANUALS

Codes of Professional Responsibility: Ethic Standards in Business, Health and Law. Rena Gorlin, editor. BNA, Inc. • 1999. $95.00. Fourth edition. Contains full text or substantial excerpts of the official codes of ethics of major professional groups in the fields of law, business, and health care.

ONLINE DATABASES

Information Bank Abstracts. New York Times Index Dept. • Provides indexing and abstracting of current affairs, primarily from the final late edition of *The New York Times* and the Eastern edition of *The Wall Street Journal*. Time period is 1969 to present, with daily updates. Inquire as to online cost and availability.

Newspaper Abstracts Daily. ProQuest Inc. • Provides online coverage (citations and abstracts) of 25 major newspapers. Covers business, economics, current affairs, health, fitness, sports, education, technology, government, consumer affairs, psychology, the arts, and the social sciences. Time period is 1986 to date, with daily updates. Inquire as to online cost and availability.

PAIS International. Public Affairs Information Service, Inc. • Corresponds to the former printed publications, *PAIS Bulletin* (1976-90) and *PAIS Foreign Language Index* (1972-90), and to the current *PAIS International in Print* (1991 to date). Covers economic, political, and sociological material appearing in periodicals, books, government documents, and other publications. Updating is monthly. Inquire as to online cost and availability.

Social Scisearch. Institute for Scientific Information. • Broad, multidisciplinary index to the literature of the social sciences, 1972 to present. Weekly updates. Worldwide coverage. Inquire as to online cost and availability.

Wilson Social Sciences Abstracts Online. H. W. Wilson Co. • Provides online abstracting and indexing of more than 500 periodicals covering area studies, community health, public administration, public welfare, urban studies, and many other social science topics. Time period is 1994 to date for abstracts and 1983 to date for indexing, with updates weekly. Inquire as to online cost and availability.

PERIODICALS AND NEWSLETTERS

Business and Society: A Journal of Interdisciplinary Exploration. International Association for Business and Society Research Committee. Sage Publica-

tions, Inc. • Quarterly. $402.00 per year.

Business and Society Review: Journal of the Center for Business Ethics at Bentley College. Blackwell Publishing. • Quarterly. Institutions, $179.00 per year. Includes online edition.

Journal of Public Policy and Marketing. American Marketing Association. • Semiannual. Members, $45.00 per year; non-members, $70.00 per year; institutions, $100.00 per year. Devoted to the social and cultural impact of marketing activities.

Positive Leadership: Improving Performance Through Value-Centered Management. Lawrence Ragan Communications, Inc. • Monthly. $99.00 per year. Newsletter. Emphasis is on employee motivation, family issues, ethics, and community relations.

Review of Social Economy. Association for Social Economics. Taylor and Francis Group. • Quarterly. Individuals, $78.00 per year; institutions, $211.00 per year. Subject matter is concerned with the relationships between social values and economics. Includes articles on income distribution, poverty, labor, and class.

RESEARCH CENTERS AND INSTITUTES

Business, Government, and Society Research Institute. University of Pittsburgh. School of Business, Mervis Hall, Pittsburgh, PA 15260. Phone: (412)648-1555 Fax: (412)648-1693 E-mail: mitnick@pitt.edu.

Center for Corporate Citizenship. Boston College, 55 Lee Rd., Chestnut Hill, MA 02467. Phone: (617)552-4545 Fax: (617)552-8499 E-mail: cccr@bc.edu • URL: http://www.bc.edu/cccbc • Areas of study include corporate images within local communities, corporate community relations, social vision, and philanthropy. Formerly Center for Corporate Community Relations.

TRADE/PROFESSIONAL ASSOCIATIONS

Special Interest Group on Computers and Society. c/o Association for Computing Machinery, 1515 Broadway, New York, NY 10036. Phone: 800-342-6626 or (212)869-7440 Fax: (212)944-1318 E-mail: acmhelp@acm.org • URL: http://www.acm.org/sigcas.

SOCIAL SECURITY

See also: MEDICARE

GENERAL WORKS

Fundamentals of Employee Benefit Programs. Employee Benefit Research Institute. • 1996. $49.95. Fifth edition. Provides basic explanation of employee benefit programs in both the private and public sectors, including health insurance, pension plans, retirement planning, social security, and long-term care insurance.

Social Security, Medicare, and Government Pensions: Get the Most Out of Your Retirement and Medical Benefits. Joseph Matthews and Dorothy M. Berman. Nolo. • 2002. $29.99. Eighth edition. In addition to the basic topics, includes practical information on Supplemental Security Income (SSI), disability benefits, veterans benefits, 401(k) plans, Medicare HMOs, medigap insurance, Medicaid, and how to appeal decisions. (Social Security, Medicare and Pensions Series).

ABSTRACTS AND INDEXES

Social Sciences Index. H. W. Wilson Co. • Quarterly, with annual cumulation. Price varies. Indexes more than 400 periodicals covering economics, environmental policy, government, insurance, labor, health care policy, plannning, public administration, public welfare, urban studies, women's issues, criminology, and related topics.

ALMANACS AND YEARBOOKS

Older Americans Information Directory. Grey House Publshing, Inc. • 2002. $165.00. Fourth

edition. Presents articles (text) and sources of information on a wide variety of aging and retirement topics. Includes an index to personal names, organizations, and subjects.

CD-ROM DATABASES

Magazine Index Plus. Gale Cengage Learning. • Monthly. $4,000.00 per year (includes InfoTrac workstation). Provides full text on CD-ROM for about 100 popular, general interest magazines and indexing for 300 others. Includes special indexing of reviews and product evaluations. Time period is 1980 to date.

Social Sciences Citation Index. ISI. • Monthly. Price on request. Provides CD-ROM indexing of articles appearing in 1700 leading social science journals worldwide, with additional selections from more than 5700 other journals. Time span is 1992 to date. Coverage includes economics, business, finance, management, communications, demographics, library and information science, political science, sociology, and many other subjects.

Social Sciences Citation Index: Compact Disc Edition with Abstracts. Institute for Scientific Information. • Monthly. Provides CD-ROM indexing and abstracting of "significant articles" from 1,700 social science journals worldwide, with additional selections from 3,200 other journals, 1986 to date. Includes economics, business, finance, management, communications, demographics, information and library science, political science, sociology, and many other subjects.

SSA Publications on CD-ROM. Available from U. S. Government Printing Office. • Monthly. $238.00 per year. Provides updated text of three Social Security Administration publications: *Program Operations Manual; Social Security Handbook; Social Security Rulings.*

WILSONDISC: Readers' Guide to Periodical Literature. H. W. Wilson Co. • Monthly. $1,095.00 per year, including unlimited online access to *Readers' Guide to Periodical Literature* through WILSONLINE. Provides CD-ROM indexing of about 270 general interest periodicals. Covers 1983 to date. (*Readers' Guide Abstracts* also available on CD-ROM at $1,995 per year.).

WILSONDISC: Wilson Social Sciences Abstracts. H. W. Wilson Co. • Monthly. Includes unlimited online access to *Social Sciences Index* through WILSONLINE. Provides CD-ROM indexing from 1983 and abstracting from 1994 of more than 500 periodicals covering economics, area studies, community health, public administration, public welfare, urban studies, and many other topics related to the social sciences.

DIRECTORIES

Government Assistance Almanac: The Guide to Federal, Domestic, Financial and Other Programs Covering Grants, Loans, Insurance, Personal Payments and Benefits. J. Robert Dumouchel, editor. Omnigraphics, Inc. • Annual. $235.00. Describes more than 1,400 federal assistance programs available from about 50 agencies. Includes statistics, a directory of 3,000 field offices, and comprehensive indexing.

ENCYCLOPEDIAS AND DICTIONARIES

Encyclopedia of Social Welfare History in North America. John M. Herrick and Paul H. Stuart, editors. Sage Publications, Inc. • 2004. $150.00. Includes entries on the historical aspects of charity, economic conditions, tax policy, health policy, social welfare legislation, poverty, social security, and social problems.

FINANCIAL RATIOS

Financial Planning for Older Clients. James E. Pearman. CCH, Inc. • 2000. $49.00. Covers income sources, social security, Medicare, Medicaid, investment planning, estate planning, and other retirement-related topics. Edited for accountants, attorneys, and other financial advisors. (Solutions for Professional Advisors Series).

HANDBOOKS AND MANUALS

Complete and Easy Guide to Social Security, Healthcare Rights and Government Benefits. Faustin Jehle. Emerson-Adams Press, Inc. • 2000. $18.95. 16th unabridged edition.

Medicare Explained. CCH, Inc. • Annual. $37.50.

The New Working Woman's Guide to Retirement Planning: Saving and Investing Now for a Secure Future. Martha P. Patterson. University of Pennsylvania Press. • 1999. $19.95. Second edition. Provides retirement advice for employed women, including information on various kinds of IRAs, cash balance and other pension plans, 401(k) plans, and social security. Four case studies are provided to illustrate retirement planning at specific life and career stages.

Social Security Benefits, Including Medicare. CCH, Inc. • Annual. $11.00.

Social Security Claims and Procedures. Harvey L. McCormick. West Group. • 1991. Two volumes. Fourth edition. Price on application.

Social Security Explained. CCH, Inc. • Annual. $37.00.

Social Security Handbook. Available from U. S. Government Printing Office. • Annual. $53.00. Issued by the Social Security Administration (http://www.ssa.gov). Provides detailed information about social security programs, including Medicare, with brief descriptions of related programs administered by agencies other than the Social Security Administration.

Social Security Manual. The National Underwriter Co. • Annual. $22.95.

Social Security Practice Guide. LexisNexis Matthew Bender. • Irregular. $1,027.00. Four looseleaf volumes. Periodic supplementation. Complete, practical guide on all substantive and procedural aspects of social security practice. Prepared under the supervision of the National Organization of Social Security Claimants' Representatives (NOSSCR).

Social Security Programs Throughout the World. Available from U. S. Government Printing Office. • Annual. Issued by the Social Security Administration (http://www.ssa.gov). Presents basic information on more than 170 social security systems around the world.

INTERNET DATABASES

Social Security Online: The Official Web Site of the Social Security Administration. U. S. Social Security Administration. Phone: 800-772-1213 or (410)965-7700 • URL: http://www.ssa.gov • Web site provides a wide variety of online information relating to social security and Medicare. Topics include benefits, disability, employer wage reporting, personal earnings statements, statistics, government financing, social security law, and public welfare reform legislation.

ONLINE DATABASES

Ageline. American Association of Retired Persons. • Provides indexing and abstracting of the literature of social gerontology, including consumer aspects, financial planning, employment, housing, health care services, mental health, social security, and retirement. Time period is 1978 to date. Inquire as to online cost and availability.

Newspaper Abstracts Daily. ProQuest Inc. • Provides online coverage (citations and abstracts) of 25 major newspapers. Covers business, economics, current affairs, health, fitness, sports, education, technology, government, consumer affairs, psychology, the arts, and the social sciences. Time period is 1986 to date, with daily updates. Inquire as to online cost and availability.

Readers' Guide Abstracts Online. H. W. Wilson Co. • Indexes and abstracts general interest periodicals, 1983 to date. Weekly updates. Inquire as to online cost and availability.

Wilson Social Sciences Abstracts Online. H. W. Wilson Co. • Provides online abstracting and indexing of more than 500 periodicals covering area studies, community health, public administration, public welfare, urban studies, and many other social science topics. Time period is 1994 to date for abstracts and 1983 to date for indexing, with updates weekly. Inquire as to online cost and availability.

PERIODICALS AND NEWSLETTERS

Journal of Aging and Social Policy: A Journal Devoted to Aging and Social Policy. Haworth Press, Inc. • Quarterly. $415.00 per year.

Older Americans Report. Business Publishers Inc. • Description: Features brief articles on legislative, judicial, and federal agency activities concerning older Americans. Covers news of developments in such areas as Social Security, social services, Medicare, programs for retirement and pension funds, research projects, and the Older Americans Act. Recurring features include book reviews and a calendar of events.

RESEARCH CENTERS AND INSTITUTES

Employee Benefit Research Institute. Employee Benefit Research Institute. 1100 13 St. NW, Ste. 878, Washington, DC 20005. Phone: (202)659-0670 Fax: (202)775-6312 E-mail: salisbury@ebri.org • URL: http://www.ebri.org • Employee benefits in the public and private sectors, including studies on individual retirement accounts, retirement income, flexible benefits, financing health care for the elderly, health care costs, long-term care, employee benefits and federal tax policy, social security, changing benefits, and government regulation of employee benefit plans.

STATISTICS SOURCES

EBRI's Databook on Employee Benefits: What is the Promise?. Ken McDonnell and others. Employee Benefit Research Institute. • 1997 $99.00. Fourth edition. Contains more than 350 tables and charts presenting data on employee benefits in the U. S., including pensions, health insurance, social security, and medicare. Includes a glossary of employee benefit terms.

Fast Facts About Social Security. Available from U. S. Government Printing Office. • Annual. $5.50. Issued by the Social Security Administration (http://www.ssa.gov). Provides concise data and charts relating to social security benefits, beneficiaries, disability payments, supplemental security income, and income of the aged.

Income of the Population 55 and Older. Available from U. S. Government Printing Office. • Biennial. $23.00. Issued by the Social Security Administration (http://www.ssa.gov). Covers major sources and amounts of income for the 55 and older population in the U. S., "with special emphasis on some aspects of the income of the population 65 and older.".

Social Security Bulletin. Social Security Administration. Available from U.S. Government Printing Office. • Quarterly. $27.00 per year. Annual statistical supplement.

Social Trends and Indicators USA. Monique D. Magee, editor. Gale Cengage Learning. • 2003. $450.00. Four volumes. Includes data on labor, economics, the health care industry, crime, leisure, population, education, social security, and many other topics. Sources include various government agencies and major publications.

Statistical Abstract of the United States. Available from U. S. Government Printing Office. • Annual. $51.00. Issued by the U. S. Bureau of the Census.

Statistical Handbook on Aging Americans. Renee Schick. Greenwood Publishing Group, Inc. • 1994.

$69.95. Second edition. Provides data on demographics, social characteristics, health, employment, economic conditions, income, pensions, and social security. Includes bibliographic information and a glossary. (Statistical Handbook Series).

Taxing Wages. Organization for Economic Cooperation and Development. • Annual. $52.00. Contains data on income tax and social security levies collected from employees and employers in OECD countries. Includes marginal and effective tax burden figures for various family income levels and statistics on cash transfers paid as family benefits.

TRADE/PROFESSIONAL ASSOCIATIONS

National Conference of State Social Security Administrators. Social Security Div. Two Northside 75, Suite 300, Atlanta, GA 30318. Phone: (404)352-6414 Fax: (404)352-6431 E-mail: bijenkin@ers.state.ga.us • URL: http://www.ncssa.org • Formerly Conference of State Social Security Administrators.

SOCIAL WELFARE

See: PUBLIC WELFARE

SOCIETY AND BUSINESS

See: SOCIAL RESPONSIBILITY

SODIUM CHLORIDE INDUSTRY

See: SALT INDUSTRY

SOFT DRINK INDUSTRY

DIRECTORIES

Beverage Industry - Annual Manual. Stagnito Communications, Inc. • Annual. $55.00. Provides statistical information on multiple beverage markets. Includes an industry directory. Supplement to *Beverage Industry*.

Beverage Marketing Directory. Beverage Marketing Corp. • Covers: About 11,000 beer wholesalers, wine and spirits wholesalers, soft drink bottlers and franchisors, breweries, wineries, distilleries, alcoholic beverage importers, bottled water companies; and trade associations, government agencies, micro breweries, juice, coffee, tea, milk companies, and others concerned with the beverage and bottling industries; coverage includes Canada. Entries include: Beverage and bottling company listings contain company name, address, phone, names of key executives, number of employees, brand names, and other information, including number of franchisees, number of delivery trucks, sales volume. Suppliers and related companies and organizations listings include similar but less detailed information.

Beverage World Buyers Guide. VNU Business Media. • Annual. $7.00. Lists suppliers to the beverage industry.

Major Food and Drink Companies of the World. Available from Gale Cengage Learning. • Annual. $880.00. Two volumes. Published by Graham & Whiteside. Contains profiles and trade names for more than 9,800 important food and beverage companies in various countries. In addition to foods, includes both alcoholic and nonalcoholic drink products.

Thomas Food and Beverage Market Place. Grey House Publishing. • 2004. $495.00. Three volumes. Contains more than 40,000 entries covering food companies, beverages, food equipment, warehouse companies, food brokers, wholesalers, importers, and exporters. Formerly *Thomas Food Industry Register*.

World Drinks Marketing Directory. Euromonitor International. • Covers: 500 retailers and wholesalers, 1,000 manufacturers, over 2,000 international and European organizations, statistical agencies, market research companies, trade journals and associations, databases, and trade fairs in the beverage industry worldwide. Entries include: Company name, address, phone, telex, number of employees, parent company and subsidiary names, financial data, products and brand names handled; retailers and wholesalers include type of outlets, names and titles of key personnel.

FINANCIAL RATIOS

Almanac of Business and Industrial Financial Ratios. Leo Troy. Aspen Publishers, Inc. • 2003. $125.95. Includes CD-Rom. Contains financial ratios derived from federal tax returns. Ratios for each of about 200 industries are arranged according to company asset size. (Almanac of Business and Industrial Financial Ratios Series).

Annual Statement Studies. The Risk Management Association. • Annual. Median and quartile financial ratios are given for over 400 kinds of manufacturing, wholesale, retail, construction, and consumer finance establishments. Data is sorted by both asset size and sales volume. Includes a clearly written "Definition of Ratios" and an alphabetical industry index.

Annual Statement Studies: Industry Default Probabilities and Cash Flow Measures. The Risk Management Association. • Annual. $145.00. Serves as a companion volume to the original *Annual Statement Studies*. Gives probability of default estimates on a percentage scale for more than 450 industries. Includes changes in position year-by-year for eight financial statement line items and provides percentage measures of cash flow.

Industry Norms and Key Business Ratios. Desk Top Edition. Dun and Bradstreet Corp. • Annual. Five volumes. $475.00 per volume. $1,890.00 per set. Covers over 800 kinds of businesses, arranged by Standard Industrial Classification number. More detailed editions covering longer periods of time are also available.

PERIODICALS AND NEWSLETTERS

Beverage Digest. John Sicher. • Description: Focuses primarily on non-alcoholic drinks. Reports on industry news in relation to pricing, marketing, competition, mergers and acquisitions, and new products.

Beverage Industry. Stagnito Communications, Inc. • Monthly. Free to qualified personnel; others, $85.05 per year. Supplement available *Beverage Industry-Annual Manual*.

Beverage World: Magazine of the Beverage Industry. VNU Business Media. • Monthly. $79.00 per year.

Soft Drink Letter. Whitaker Newsletters Inc. • Description: Covers news pertaining to the beverage industry with emphasis on soft drinks, mixers, and bottled water. Includes reports on new products and federal/state regulations, interviews with leading industry executives, marketing trends, and advertising and marketing research.

STATISTICS SOURCES

The Global Drinks Market Impact Databank. M. Shanken Communications, Inc. • Annual. $2,975.00. Detailed compilations of data for various segments of the liquor, beer, and soft drink industries.

U. S. Industry and Trade Outlook. Available from National Technical Information Service. • Annual. $69.95. Produced by the International Trade Administration, U. S. Department of Commerce, in a "public-private" partnership with DRI/McGraw-

Hill and Standard & Poor's. Provides basic data, outlook for the current year, and "Long-Term Prospects" (five-year projections) for a wide variety of products and services. Includes high technology industries. Formerly *U. S. Industrial Outlook*.

World Drinks Data and Statistics. Euromonitor International. • 2004. $650.00. Provides five-year data for both alcoholic and non-alcoholic beverages in 52 countries. Includes market size, consumer expenditures, price indicators, and retail distribution data for beer, wine, spirits, tea, coffee, soft drinks, fruit juices, bottled water, and other drinks.

TRADE/PROFESSIONAL ASSOCIATIONS

American Beverage Association. 1101 16th St. NW, Washington, DC 20036-4803. Phone: (202)463-6732 Fax: (202)659-5349 E-mail: info@ameribev.org • URL: http://www.ameribev.org • Active members are bottlers and distributors of soft drinks and franchise companies; associate members are suppliers of materials and services. Conducts government affairs activities on the national and state levels, discussion of industry problems, and general improvement of operating procedures. Conducts research on beverage laws.

International Society of Beverage Technologists. 8110 S. Suncoast Blvd., Homosassa, FL 34446. Phone: (352)382-2008 Fax: (352)382-2018 E-mail: isbt@bevetch.org • URL: http://www.bevtech.org • Members are professionals engaged in the technical areas of soft drink production. Formerly Society of Soft Drink Technologies.

OTHER SOURCES

Soft Drinks (Excluding Juices). Available from MarketResearch.com. • 2002. $3,950.00. Published by Global Industry Analysts. Provides worldwide market research data, including profiles of major soft drink companies.

SOFTWARE INDUSTRY, COMPUTER

See: COMPUTER SOFTWARE INDUSTRY

SOFTWOOD INDUSTRY

See: FOREST PRODUCTS; LUMBER INDUSTRY

SOLAR ENERGY

GENERAL WORKS

Renewables for Power Generation: Status and Prospect. Organization for Economic Cooperation and Development. • 2003. $75.00. Presents the global outlook for electrical power generation from renewable sources, including water power, wind power, solar power, and geothermal power.

ABSTRACTS AND INDEXES

Applied Science and Technology Index. H. W. Wilson Co. • 11 times a year. Quarterly and annual cumulations. Price varies. Indexes a wide variety of English language technical, industrial, and engineering periodicals.

NTIS Alerts: Energy. National Technical Information Service. • Semimonthly. $245.00 per year. Provides descriptions of government-sponsored research reports and software, with ordering information. Covers electric power, batteries, fuels, geothermal energy, heating/cooling systems, nuclear technology, solar energy, energy policy, and related subjects. Formerly *Abstract Newsletter*.

Science Citation Index. Thomson/ISI. • Bimonthly. $15,020.00 per year. Annual cumulation. Includes *Source Index, Citation Index, Permuterm Subject*

Index, and *Corporate Index*.

BIBLIOGRAPHIES

Solar Energy. Available from U. S. Government Printing Office. • Annual. Free. Lists government publications. GPO Subject Bibliography Number 9.

BIOGRAPHICAL SOURCES

Energy and Nuclear Sciences International Who's Who. Addison Wesley/Benjamin Cummings. • 1990. $310.00. Third edition.

CD-ROM DATABASES

Science Citation Index: Compact Disc Edition. Institute for Scientific Information. • Monthly. Provides CD-ROM indexing of the world's scientific and technical literature. Corresponds to online *Scisearch* and printed *Science Citation Index*.

DIRECTORIES

Directory of SRCC Certified Collectors and Solar Water Heating Systems Ratings. Solar Rating and Certification Corp. • Irregular. Free. About 20 manufacturers of solar collectors and systems certified by the Organization. Includes technical information.

Energy User News: Energy Technology Buyers Guide. Business News Publishing Co. • Annual. $10.00. List of about 400 manufacturers, manufacturers' representatives, dealers, and distributors of energy management equipment. *Annual Review* and *Forecast* issue.

The International Competitive Power Industry Directory. PennWell Corp. • Publication includes: List of 1,400 companies active in the global power industry, providing information on developers, financial firms, law firms, engineering and construction firms, fuel suppliers, consultants, manufacturers and other suppliers of products, equipment ot the hydro, geothermal, solar and wind industries. Entries include: Company name, address, phone, fax; contact name; business area or tyope; technology used; region covered; products.

SYNERJY: A Directory of Renewable Energy. Synerjy. • Semiannual. Individuals, $30.00 per year; others, $62.00 per year. Includes organizations, publishers, and other resources. Lists articles, patents, government publications, research groups and facilities.

ENCYCLOPEDIAS AND DICTIONARIES

Encyclopedia of Energy. Cutler J. Cleveland, editor. Elsevier, Inc. • 2004. $1,560.00. Six volumes. Covers all aspects of energy sources and energy-related environmental issues.

Macmillan Encyclopedia of Energy. Available from Gale Cengage Learning. • 2001. $395.00. Three volumes. Published by Macmillan Reference USA. Covers the business, technology, and history of a wide variety of energy sources.

Wiley Encyclopedia of Energy and the Environment. Attilio Bisio and Sharon Boots. John Wiley and Sons, Inc. • 1996. $285.00. Abriged edition. Two volumes. Covers a wide variety of energy and environmental topics, including legal and policy issues. (Encyclopedia of Energy and the Environment Series: Vol. 2).

HANDBOOKS AND MANUALS

The Solar Home: How to Design and Build a House You Heat with the Sun. Mark Freeman. Stackpole Books. • 1994. $14.95. (How-To Guides).

ONLINE DATABASES

Globalbase. Gale Cengage Learning. • Provides more than one million online summaries of business, industrial, and economic news reports from more than 1,000 publications worldwide. Covers a wide range of material appearing in international trade journals, professional magazines, and newspapers. Time period is 1984 to date, with weekly updates. Inquire as to online cost and availability.

PAIS International. Public Affairs Information Service, Inc. • Corresponds to the former printed publications, *PAIS Bulletin* (1976-90) and *PAIS Foreign Language Index* (1972-90), and to the current *PAIS International in Print* (1991 to date). Covers economic, political, and sociological material appearing in periodicals, books, government documents, and other publications. Updating is monthly. Inquire as to online cost and availability.

Scisearch. Institute for Scientific Information. • Broad, multidisciplinary index to the literature of science and technology, 1974 to present. Inquire as to online cost and availability. Coverage of literature is worldwide, with weekly updates.

PERIODICALS AND NEWSLETTERS

Alternative Energy Retailer. Zackin Publications, Inc. • Monthly. $32.00 per year.

Energy Conversion and Management. Elsevier. • 20 times a year. Institutions, $3,457.00 per year. Presents a scholarly approach to alternative or renewable energy sources. Text in English, French and German.

Independent Energy: The Power Industry's Business Magazine. PennWell Corp., Industrial Div. • 10 times a year. $127.00 per year. Covers non-utility electric power plants (cogeneration) and other alternative sources of electric energy.

Journal of Energy Engineering: The International Journal. American Society of Civil Engineers. • Three times a year. Members, $40.00 per year; with online edition, $46.00 per year; non-members, $60.00 per year; with online edition, $69.00 per year.

Renewable Energy: An International Journal. Elsevier. • 15 times a year. $1,835.00 per year. Incorporates *Solar and Wind Technology.*

Solar Energy: International Journal for Scientists, Engineers and Technologists Energy and Its Application. International Solar Energy Society. Elsevier. • 18 times a year. $2,304.00 per year.

RESEARCH CENTERS AND INSTITUTES

Hawaii Natural Energy Institute. University of Hawaii at Manoa, 2540 Dole St., Holmes Hall 246, Honolulu, HI 96822. Phone: (808)956-8890 Fax: (808)956-2336 E-mail: hnei@hawaii.edu • URL: http://www.soest.hawaii.edu • Research areas include geothermal, wind, solar, hydroelectric, and other energy sources.

Laboratory for Energy and the Environment. Massachusetts Institute of Technology. 77 Massachusetts Ave., Bldg. E40-455, Cambridge, MA 02139-4307. Phone: (617)258-8891 Fax: (617)253-8013 E-mail: jwilmson@mit.edu • URL: http://www.lfee.mit.edu • Formerly Energy Laboratory.

Solar Energy and Energy Conversion Laboratory. University of Florida, Dept. of Mechanical Engineering, P.O. Box 116300, Gainesville, FL 32611-6300. Phone: (352)392-0812 Fax: (352)392-1071 E-mail: solar@cimar.me.ufl.edu • URL: http://www.me.ufl.edu/solar.

Solar Energy Center. University of Oregon, Dept. of Physics, Eugene, OR 97403. Phone: (541)346-3656 Fax: (541)346-5861 E-mail: fev@oregon.uoregon.edu.

STATISTICS SOURCES

Annual Energy Outlook [year], with Projections to [year]. Available from U. S. Government Printing Office. • Annual. $42.00. Issued by the Energy Information Administration, U. S. Department of Energy (http://www.eia.doe.gov). Contains detailed statistics and 20-year projections for electricity, oil, natural gas, coal, and renewable energy. Text provides extensive discussion of energy issues and "Market Trends.".

International Energy Annual. Available from U. S. Government Printing Office. • Annual. $34.00. Issued by the Energy Information Administration, U. S. Department of Energy. Provides production, consumption, import, and export data for primary energy commodities in more than 200 countries and areas. In addition to petroleum products and alcohol, renewable energy sources are covered (hydroelectric, geothermal, solar, and wind).

U. S. Industry and Trade Outlook. Available from National Technical Information Service. • Annual. $69.95. Produced by the International Trade Administration, U. S. Department of Commerce, in a "public-private" partnership with DRI/McGraw-Hill and Standard & Poor's. Provides basic data, outlook for the current year, and "Long-Term Prospects" (five-year projections) for a wide variety of products and services. Includes high technology industries. Formerly *U. S. Industrial Outlook.*

TRADE/PROFESSIONAL ASSOCIATIONS

Alternative Energy Resources Organization. 432 N Last Chance Gulch, Helena, MT 59601-5014. Phone: (406)443-7272 Fax: (406)442-9120 E-mail: aero@aeromt.org • URL: http://www.aeromt.org • Promotes sustainable agriculture, resource conservation and transportation choices through community education and citizen representation. Provides current programs that focus on sustainable agriculture, farm improvement clubs, beginning and retiring farmers, smart growth, and a more localized food system for greater community self-reliance.

American Solar Energy Society. 2400 Central Ave., Ste. G-1, Boulder, CO 80301. Phone: (303)443-3130 Fax: (303)443-3212 E-mail: ases@ases.org • URL: http://www.ases.org • Advises industry members on financing of construction projects and represents their interests before Congress, federal agencies, and state bodies.

Solar Energy Industries Association. 805 15th St. NW, Ste. 510, Washington, DC 20005. Phone: (202)682-0556 Fax: (202)682-0559 E-mail: info@seia.org • URL: http://www.seia.org • Manufacturers, installers, distributors, contractors, and engineers of solar energy systems and components. Aims to accelerate and foster commercialization of solar energy conversion for economic purposes. Maintains Solar +Energy +Research and +Education Foundation. Compiles statistics; offers computerized services.

Sustainable Buildings Industry Council. 1112 16th St. NW, Ste. 240, Washington, DC 20036. Phone: (202)628-7400 Fax: (202)393-5043 E-mail: sbic@sbicouncil.org • URL: http://www.sbicouncil.org • Works to advance the design, affordability, energy performance, and environmental soundness of commercial, institutional, and residential buildings nationwide. Offers professional training, consumer education, and energy analysis tools. Provides accurate, easy-to-use guidelines, software, and general information about energy conservation measures, energy efficient equipment and appliances, daylighting, and sustainable architecture. Active in presenting workshops and seminars geared toward improving building energy performance in cities and towns throughout the nation.

OTHER SOURCES

Major Energy Companies of the World. Available from Gale Cengage Learning. • Annual. $880.00. Published by Graham & Whiteside. Contains detailed information on more than 3,300 important energy companies in various countries. Industries include electricity generation, coal, natural gas, nuclear energy, petroleum, fuel distribution, and equipment for energy production.

SOLE PROPRIETORSHIP

See: SELF-EMPLOYMENT

SOLID STATE DEVICES

See: SEMICONDUCTOR INDUSTRY

SOLID WASTE TREATMENT

See: SANITATION INDUSTRY

SOUND RECORDERS AND RECORDING

See also: HIGH FIDELITY/STEREO; PHONOGRAPH AND PHONOGRAPH RECORD INDUSTRIES

GENERAL WORKS

Sound and Recording: An Introduction. Francis Rumsey and Tim McCormick. Elsevier. • 2002. $42.99. Fourth edition. Covers the theory and principles of sound recording and reproduction, with chapters on amplifiers, microphones, mixers, and other components. (Music Technology Series).

Sound Check: The Basics of Sound and Sound Systems. Tony Moscal. Hal Leonard Corp. • 1994. $14.95. Explains the fundamentals of sound and related electronics.

DIRECTORIES

Directory of Computer and Consumer Electronics Retailers. Chain Store Guide. • Annual. $335.00. Online edition, $775.00. Lists 4,500 United States and Canada companies operating almost 59,000 stores with at least $1,000,000 in sales.

Music Technology Buyer's Guide. United Entertainment Media. • $6.95. Annual. Lists more than 4,000 hardware and software music production products from 350 manufacturers. Includes synthesizers, MIDI hardware and software, mixers, microphones, music notation software, etc. Produced by the editorial staffs of *Keyboard* and *EQ* magazines.

Pro Audio Review Gear Guide. IMAS Publishing, Inc. • Annual. Issued as February issue of *Pro Audio Review.* Contains detailed product listings of professional audio equipment and recording gear. Includes prices, specifications, and addresses of manufacturers.

Recording Industry Sourcebook. Thomson Course Technology PTR. • Covers: 14,000 contacts in the music industry in over 65 categories, including record producers, publishers, promoters, attorneys, major and independent record labels, and music production facilities. Entries include: Name, address, phone, fax, name and title of contact, subsidiary and branch names and locations, background information, email, web address.

The SHOOT Directory for Commercial Production and Postproduction. SHOOT. • Annual. $79.00. Lists production companies, advertising agencies, and sources of professional television, motion picture, and audio equipment.

HANDBOOKS AND MANUALS

The Art of Recording: Understanding and Crafting the Mix. William Moylan. Elsevier. • 2002. $29.99. Emphasizes the ways in which recorded sound is different from live sound. Covers the recording of audio as a creative process.

Audio Recording and Reproduction: Practical Measures for Audio Enthusiasts. Michael Talbot-Smith. Elsevier. • 1994. $29.95.

Compact Disc Handbook. Kenneth C. Pohlmann. A-R Editions, Inc. • 1992. $34.95. Second edition. A guide to compact disc technology, including player design and disc manufacturing. (Computer Music and Digital Audio Series).

Digital Audio and Compact Disk Technology. Baert

Theunisse and Luc Theunisse. Elsevier. • 1995. $57.95. Third edition.

Handbook for Sound Engineers. Glen M. Ballou, editor. Elsevier. • 2002. $120.00. Third edition. Covers fundamentals of sound, sound-system design, loudspeaker building, sound recording, audio circuits, and computer-generated music.

Master Handbook of Acoustics. F. Alton Everest. McGraw-Hill. • 2001. $39.95. Fourth edition. Covers the theory of acoustics and practical applications of acoustics, as in the design of audio control rooms, recording studios, and listening rooms for the home. (Tab Electronics Series).

Principles of Digital Audio. Ken C. Pohlmann. McGraw-Hill. • 2000. $54.95. Fourth edition. Includes the details of digital audio recording, reproduction, error correction, compact disc technology, DVD, minidiscs, Internet audio, and related topics. (Video/Audio Engineering Series).

Standard Handbook of Audio and Radio Engineering. Jerry C. Whitaker and K. Blair Benson. McGraw-Hill. • 2002. $125.00. Second edition. Emphasis is on audio. Covers such topics as DVD, MP3, sound reproduction, amplification, noise reduction, and Internet audio.

Studio Business Book: A Guide to Professional Recording Studio Business and Management. Jim Mandell. artistpro.com, LLC. • 1995. $34.95. Second expanded edition. Includes information on business plans, studio equipment, financing, expenses, rate setting, and personnel.

PERIODICALS AND NEWSLETTERS

Computer Music Journal. MIT Press. • Quarterly. Individuals, $77.00 per year; institutions, $215.00 per year. Includes print and online editions. Covers digital soound and the musical applications of computers.

EQ: The Project Recording and Sound Magazine. United Entertainment Media, Inc. • Monthly. $24.95 per year. Provides advice on professional music recording equipment and technique.

Mix Magazine: Professional Recording, Sound, and Music Production. Primedia Business Magazine and Media. • Monthly. $34.97 per year.

Music and Sound Retailer: The Newsmagazine for Musical Instrument and Sound Product Merchandisers. Testa Communications, Inc. • Monthly. Free to qualified personnel; others, $18.00 per year. Provides news and advice on the retailing of a wide range of music and sound products, including musical instruments, electronic keyboards, sound amplification systems, music software, and recording equipment.

Pro Audio Review: The Industry's Equipment Authority. IMAS Publishing, Inc. • Monthly. $35.00 per year. Provides critical product reviews of professional audio equipment and recording gear, including bench tests and user reports.

ProSound News: The International Newsmagazine for the Professional Recording an d Sound Production Industry. United Entertainment Media. • Monthly. $30.00 per year. Provides industry news for recording studios, audio contractors, sound engineers, and sound reinforcement specialists.

SHOOT: The Leading Newsweekly for Commercial Production and Postproduction. VNU Business Media. • Weekly. $125.00 per year. Covers animation, music, sound design, computer graphics, visual effects, cinematography, and other aspects of television and motion picture production, with emphasis on TV commercials.

Sound & Vision: Home Theater- Audio- Video- MultimediaMovies- Music. Hachette Filipacchi Media U.S., Inc. • 10 times a year. $24.00 per year. Popular magazine providing explanatory articles and critical reviews of equipment and media (CD-ROM, DVD, videocassettes, etc.). Supplement

available *Stero Review's Sound and Vision Buyers Guide.* Replaces *Stereo Review* and *Video Magazine.*

PRICE SOURCES

Audio. Orion Research Corp. • Annual. $179.00. Quotes retail and wholesale prices of used audio equipment. Original list prices and years of manufacture are also shown.

Guitars and Musical Instruments. Orion Research Corp. • Annual. $179.00. List of manufacturers of guitars and musical instruments. Original list prices and years of manufacture are also shown.

RESEARCH CENTERS AND INSTITUTES

Computer Graphics Laboratory. New York Institute of Technology, Fine Arts, Old Westbury, NY 11568. Phone: (516)686-7542 Fax: (516)686-7428 E-mail: pvoci@nyit.edu • Research areas include computer graphics, computer animation, and digital sound.

Inter-Arts Center. San Francisco State University, School of Creative Arts, 1600 Holloway Ave., San Francisco, CA 94132. Phone: (415)338-1478 Fax: (415)338-6159 E-mail: jimdavis@sfsu.edu • URL: http://www.sfsu.edu/~iac • Research areas include multimedia, computerized experimental arts processes, and digital sound.

TRADE/PROFESSIONAL ASSOCIATIONS

Special Interest Group on Electronic Sound Technology. c/o Association for Computing Machinery, 1515 Broadway, New York, NY 10036. Phone: 800-342-6626 or (212)626-0603 Fax: (212)944-1318 E-mail: barish@acm.org • URL: http://www.acm.org/sigsound • Concerned with software, algorithms, hardware, and applications relating to digitally generated audio.

OTHER SOURCES

Keyboard: The World's Leading Music Technology Magazine. United Entertainment Media, Inc. • Monthly. $25.95 per year. Emphasis is on recording systems, keyboard technique, and computer-assisted music (MIDI) systems.

SOUTH AMERICA

See: LATIN AMERICAN MARKETS

SOYBEAN INDUSTRY

See also: COMMODITY FUTURES TRADING; OIL AND FATS INDUSTRY

ABSTRACTS AND INDEXES

Field Crop Abstracts: Monthly Abstract Journal on World Annual Cereal, Legume, Root, Oilseed and Fibre Crops. Available from CABI Publishing North America. • Monthly. Institutions, $1,775.00 per year. Online edition available, $1,820.00 per year. Published in England by CABI Publishing, formerly Commonwealth Agricultural Bureaux. Provides worldwide coverage of the literature.

Soyabean Abstracts. Available from CABI Publishing, North America. • Bimonthly. $450.00 per year. Internet access only. Published in England by CABI Publishing. Provides worldwide coverage of the literature.

ALMANACS AND YEARBOOKS

Agricultural and Mineral Commodities Year Book. Available from Taylor & Francis Group. • Annual. $225.00. Published by Europa Publications. Contains descriptive product profiles, price data, export-import data, and production statistics for major commodities of the world. Includes commodity histories, uses, markets, demand trends, and information about trade agreements and key commodity organizations.

CD-ROM DATABASES

Food Science and Technology Abstracts [CD-ROM]. Available from SilverPlatter Information,

Inc. • Quarterly. Produced by International Food Information Service (home page is http://www.ifis.org). Provides worldwide coverage on CD-ROM of the literature of food technology and production. Various types of publications are indexed, with abstracts, including about 1,800 periodicals. Time period is 1969 to date.

DIRECTORIES

Major Food and Drink Companies of the World. Available from Gale Cengage Learning. • Annual. $880.00. Two volumes. Published by Graham & Whiteside. Contains profiles and trade names for more than 9,800 important food and beverage companies in various countries. In addition to foods, includes both alcoholic and nonalcoholic drink products.

Thomas Food and Beverage Market Place. Grey House Publishing. • 2004. $495.00. Three volumes. Contains more than 40,000 entries covering food companies, beverages, food equipment, warehouse companies, food brokers, wholesalers, importers, and exporters. Formerly *Thomas Food Industry Register.*

INTERNET DATABASES

USDA. United States Department of Agriculture. Phone: (202)720-2791 E-mail: agsec@usda.gov • URL: http://www.usda.gov • The USDA home page has six sections: News and Information; What's New; About USDA; Agencies; Opportunities; Search and Help. Keyword searching is offered from the USDA home page and from various individual agency home pages. Agencies are the Economic Research Service, Agricultural Marketing Service, National Agricultural Statistics Service, National Agricultural Library, and about 12 others. Updating varies. Fees: Free.

ONLINE DATABASES

CAB Abstracts. CAB Publishing North America. • Contains 46 specialized abstract collections covering over 10,000 journals and monographs in the areas of agriculture, horticulture, forest products, farm products, nutrition, dairy science, poultry, grains, animal health, entomology, etc. Time period is 1972 to date, with monthly updates. Inquire as to online cost and availability. *CAB Abstracts on CD-ROM* also available, with annual updating.

Food Science and Technology Abstracts [online]. IFIS North American Desk. • Produced by International Food Information Service. Provides about 500,000 online citations, with abstracts, to the international literature of food science, technology, commodities, engineering, and processing. Approximately 2,000 periodicals are covered. Time period is 1969 to date, with monthly updates. Inquire as to online cost and availability.

PERIODICALS AND NEWSLETTERS

Barron's: The Dow Jones Business and Financial Weekly. • Weekly. $145.00 per year.

Consensus: National Futures and Financial Weekly. Consensus, Inc. • Weekly. $365.00 per year. Newspaper. Contains news, statistics, and special reports relating to agricultural, industrial, and financial futures markets. Features daily basis price charts, reprints of market advice, and "The Consensus Index of Bullish Market Opinion" (charts show percent bullish of advisors for various futures).

Corn and Soybean Digest. American Soybean Association. Primedia Business Magazines and Media. • 11 times a year. $25.00 per year. Provides high acreage farmers who grow soy beans in rotation with other crops timely production, marketing and management information.

Soya and Oilseed Bluebook. Soyatech, Inc. • Annual. $70.00. Includes quarterly *Bluebook*

832

For publishers addresses, refer to SOURCES CITED section at the back of the book.

Update. Formerly *Soya Bluebook Plus.*

STATISTICS SOURCES

Agricultural Statistics. Available from U. S. Government Printing Office. • Annual. $38.00. Produced by the National Agricultural Statistics Service, U. S. Department of Agriculture. Provides a wide variety of statistical data relating to agricultural production, supplies, consumption, prices/price-supports, foreign trade, costs, and returns, as well as farm labor, loans, income, and population. In many cases, historical data is shown annually for 10 years. In addition to farm data, includes detailed fishery statistics.

FAO Production Yearbook. Available from Bernan Associates. • Annual. $45.00. Published by the Food and Agriculture Organization (http://www.fao.org). Contains worldwide data on agriculture, land use, farm crops, livestock, and agricultural prices.

FAO Trade Yearbook. Available from Bernan Associates. • Annual. $45.00. Published by the Food and Agriculture Organization (http://www.fao.org). Provides extensive worldwide data on exports and imports of agricultural commodities, fertilizers, tractors, and pesticides. Includes more than 130 tables of detailed statistics.

Fats and Oils: Oilseed Crushings. U. S. Bureau of the Census. • Monthly and annual. Provides data on shipments of cottonseed oil and soybean oil: value, quantity, imports, and exports. (Current Industrial Reports, M20J.).

Fats and Oils: Production, Consumption, and Stocks. U. S. Bureau of the Census. • Monthly and annual. Covers the supply and distribution of cottonseed, soybean, and palm oils, and selected inedible products. (Current Industrial Reports, M20K.).

Statistical Annual: Grains, Options on Agricultural Futures. Chicago Board of Trade. • Annual. Includes historical data on Wheat Futures, Options on Wheat Futures, Corn Futures, Options on Corn Futures, Oats Futures, Soybean Futures, Options on Soybean Futures, Soybean Oil Futures, Soybean Meal Futures.

WEFA Industrial Monitor. John Wiley and Sons, Inc. • Annual. $65.00. Prepared by industry analysts at WEFA, an economic forecasting and consulting firm (originally Wharton Econometric Forecasting Associates). Contains discussions of the outlook for major U. S. industries, with many 10-year forecasts (WEFA Web site is http://www.wefa.com).

TRADE/PROFESSIONAL ASSOCIATIONS

American Soybean Association. 12125 Woodcrest Executive Dr., Ste. 100, St. Louis, MO 63141-5009. Phone: 800-688-7692 or (314)576-1770 Fax: (314)576-2786 E-mail: scensky@asaim.soy.org • URL: http://www.soygrowers.com • Develops and implements policies to increase the profitability of its members and the entire soybean industry.

National Oilseed Processors Association. 1300 L St. NW, Ste. 1020, Washington, DC 20005-4168. Phone: (202)842-0463 Fax: (202)842-9126 E-mail: nopa@nopa.org • URL: http://www.nopa.org • Represents processors of oilseeds.

SPACE INDUSTRY

See: AEROSPACE INDUSTRY; ROCKET INDUSTRY

SPECIAL DAYS AND WEEKS

See: ANNIVERSARIES AND HOLIDAYS

SPECIAL EVENT PLANNING

GENERAL WORKS

PR News Casebook. Gale Cengage Learning. • 1993. $110.00. A collection of about 1,000 case studies covering major public relations campaigns and events, taken from the pages of *PR News.* Covers such issues as boycotts, new products, anniversaries, plant closings, downsizing, and stockholder relations.

DIRECTORIES

Chase's Calendar of Events: The Day-by-Day Directory. McGraw-Hill. • Annual. $52.95. Provides information for over 12,000 special days and special events throughout the world. Chronological arrangement with an alphabetical index. Formerly *Chase's Annual Events.*

IEG Sponsorship Sourcebook. IEG Inc. • Covers: about 5,000 corporate sponsors and 1,600 major sports, events, and organizations worldwide available for commercial sponsorship; companies serving special events and sponsors (sports marketing agencies, fireworks suppliers, public relations firms, etc.). Entries include: For events--Event title, site, dates, name, and address of contact (including year-round phone number), attendance figures, event budget, and major present and past sponsors. For service firms--Company name, address, phone, contact, speciality/services. New sponsorship events are reported in "IEG Sponsorship Report", published every two weeks, which also includes a frequent "In Depth" directory of corporations and their special events contact, budget, priorities, events sponsored, etc.; $445 per year; $370 for nonprofit organizations.

The PROMO 100 Promotion Agency Ranking. PROMO Magazine. • Covers: Ranking of the top 100 U.S. Promotion agencies. Entries include: Name, address, phone, financial data, client lists, rate of growth, name of CEO, and description of product/service.

Protocol (Corporate Meetings, Entertainment, and Special Events). Protocol Directory, Inc. • Annual. $48.00. Provides information for about 4,000 suppliers of products and services for special events, shows (entertainment), and business meetings. Geographic arrangement.

HANDBOOKS AND MANUALS

Black Tie Optional: The Ultimate Guide to Planning and Producing Successful Special Events. Harry A. Freedman and Karen F. Smith. Fund Raising Institute. • 1994. $35.00. Includes checklists, flow charts, and worksheets.

The Business of Special Events: Fundraising Strategies for Changing Times. Harry A. Freedman and Karen Feldman. Pineapple Press, Inc. • 1998. $21.95.

Complete Guide to Special Event Management: Business Insights, Financial Advice and Successful Strategies from Ernst and Young, Consultants to the Olympics. John Wiley and Sons, Inc. • 1992. $39.95. Covers the marketing, financing, and general management of special events in the fields of art, entertainment, and sports.

Event Planning Service. Entrepreneur Media, Inc. • Looseleaf. $59.50. A practical guide to starting a social or corporate event planning service. Covers profit potential, start-up costs, market size evaluation, pricing, accounting, advertising, promotion, etc. (Start-Up Business Guide No. E1313.).

ONLINE DATABASES

Management Contents. Gale Cengage Learning. • Covers a wide range of management, financial, marketing, personnel, and administrative topics. About 150 leading business journals are indexed and abstracted from 1974 to date, with monthly updating. Inquire as to online cost and availability.

PERIODICALS AND NEWSLETTERS

IEG's Sponsorship Report: The International Newsletter of Event Sponsorship and Lifestyle Marketing. International Events Group, Inc. • Biweekly. $445.00 per year. Includes print and on-line editions. Newsletter reporting on corporate sponsorship of special events: sports, music, festivals, and the arts. Edited for event producers, directors, and marketing personnel.

PROMO: Promotion Marketing Worldwide. Primedia Business Magazines and Media. • Monthly. $65.00 per year. Edited for companies and agencies that utilize couponing, point-of-purchase advertising, special events, games, contests, premiums, product samples, and other unique promotional items.

The Special Event Magazine. Primedia Business Magazines and Media. • Monthly. $48.00 per year. Edited for professionals concerned with parties, meetings, galas, and special events of all kinds and sizes. Provides practical ideas for the planning of special events. Formerly *Special Events.*

TRADE/PROFESSIONAL ASSOCIATIONS

International Special Events Society. 401 N Michigan Ave., Chicago, IL 60611-4267. Phone: 800-688-4737 or (312)321-6853 Fax: (312)673-6953 E-mail: info@ises.com • URL: http://www.ises.com • Special events planners, caterers, designers, event marketers, technical experts, transportation and destination professionals. Seeks to educate, advance, and promote special events.

SPECIAL LIBRARIES

See also: LIBRARIES

GENERAL WORKS

The Best of OPL, II: Selected Readings from the One-Person Library: 1990-1994. Andrew Berner and Guy St. Clair. Special Libraries Association. • 1996. $36.00. Contains reprints of useful material from *The One-Person Library: A Newsletter for Librarians and Management.*

Corporate Library Excellence. James M. Matarazzo. Special Libraries Association. • 1990. $28.00.

Expanding Technologies, Expanding Careers: Librarianship in Transition. Ellis Mount, editor. Special Libraries Association. • 1997. $45.00. Contains articles on alternative, non-traditional career paths for librarians, whether as entrepreneurs or employees. All the careers are related to computer-based, information retrieval and technology.

Extending the Librarian's Domain: A Survey of Emerging Occupational Opportunities for Librarians and Information Professionals. Forest W. Horton. Special Libraries Association. • 1994. $38.00. An examination of non-traditional career possibilities for special librarians. (Occasional Papers: No. 4).

Opening New Doors: Alternative Careers for Librarians. Ellis Mount, editor. Special Libraries Association. • 1992. $39.00. Information professionals in careers outside the library field discuss the nature of their work, qualifications, rewards, finding a job, etc.

Special Libraries: A Guide for Management. Cathy A. Porter and Elin B. Christianson. Special Libraries Association. • 1997. $42.00. Fourth edition. Provides basic information for the managers of business and other organizations on starting, staffing, and maintaining a special library.

Special Libraries and Information Centers: An Introductory Text. Ellis Mount and Renee Massoud. Special Libraries Association. • 1999. $49.00. Fourth edition. Descriptions of 13 outstanding libraries and information centers. Includes audio cassette.

Valuating Information Intangibles: Measuring the Bottom Line Contribution of Librarians and Information Professionals. Frank H. Portugal. Special Libraries Association. • 2000. $79.00.

Focuses on the importance of the intangible aspects of appraising information resources and services.

ABSTRACTS AND INDEXES

Library Literature and Information Science Index. H. W. Wilson Co. • Quarterly. Annual cumulation. Price varies.

Social Sciences Citation Index. Thomson/ISI. • Three times a year. $6,900 per year. Annual cumulation. Includes *Source Index, Citation Index, Permuterm Subject Index,* and *Corporate Index.*

ALMANACS AND YEARBOOKS

The Bowker Annual: Library and Book Trade Almanac. Information Today, Inc. • Annual. $199.00. Reviews key trends and events and provides basic statistical information. Includes financial averages: library expenditures, salaries, and book prices. Contains lists of "best books, literary prizes, winners, and bestsellers." Formerly published by R. R. Bowker.

BIBLIOGRAPHIES

The Basic Business Library: Core Resources. Rashells S. Karp and Bernard S. Schlessinger. Greenwood Publishing Group, Inc. • 2002. $64.95. Fourth edition. Consists of three parts: (1) "Core List of Printed Business Reference Sources," (2) "The Literature of Business Reference and Business Libraries: 1976-1994," and (3) "Business Reference Sources and Services: Essays." Part one lists 200 basic titles, with annotations and evaluations.

CD-ROM DATABASES

LISA Plus. Available from Cambridge Scientific Abstracts (CSA). • Quarterly. $2,000.00 per year. CD-ROM version of Library Information and Science Abstracts, providing abstracting and indexing of the world's library and information science literature, 1969 to date. Contains more than 180,000 citations.

Social Sciences Citation Index. ISI. • Monthly. Price on request. Provides CD-ROM indexing of articles appearing in 1700 leading social science journals worldwide, with additional selections from more than 5700 other journals. Time span is 1992 to date. Coverage includes economics, business, finance, management, communications, demographics, library and information science, political science, sociology, and many other subjects.

Social Sciences Citation Index: Compact Disc Edition with Abstracts. Institute for Scientific Information. • Monthly. Provides CD-ROM indexing and abstracting of "significant articles" from 1,700 social science journals worldwide, with additional selections from 3,200 other journals, 1986 to date. Includes economics, business, finance, management, communications, demographics, information and library science, political science, sociology, and many other subjects.

WILSONDISC: Library Literature and Information Science Index. H. W. Wilson Co. • Quarterly. Includes unlimited access to the online version of *Library Literature.* Provides CD-ROM indexing of about 300 periodicals, covering a wide range of topics having to do with libraries, library management, and the information industry.

World Database of Business Information Sources on CD-ROM. Gale Cengage Learning. • Annual. Produced by Euromonitor. Presents Euromonitor's entire information source database on CD-ROM. Contains a worldwide total of about 35,000 publications, organizations, libraries, trade fairs, and online databases.

DIRECTORIES

American Library Directory. Information Today Inc. • Covers: Over 37,000 U.S. and Canadian academic, public, county, provincial, and regional libraries; library systems; medical, law, and other special libraries; and libraries for the blind and physically handicapped. Separate section lists over 350 library networks and consortia and 220 accredited and unaccredited library school programs. Entries include: For libraries--Name, supporting or affiliated institution or firm name, address, phone, fax, electronic mail address, Standard Address Number (SANs), names of librarian and department heads, income, collection size, special collections, computer hardware, automated functions, and type of catalog. For library systems--Name, location. For library schools--Name, address, phone, fax, electronic mail address, director, type of training and degrees, admission requirements, tuition, faculty size. For networks and consortia--Name, address, phone, names of affiliates, name of director, function.

Directory of Federal Libraries. William R. Evinger, editor. Greenwood Publishing Group, Inc. • 1997. $99.50. Third edition. (Directory of Federal Library Series).

Directory of Special Libraries and Information Centers. Gale Cengage Learning. • 2003. $975.00. 28th edition. Three volumes. Two available separately: volume one,*Directory of Special Libraries and Information Centers,* $740.00; volume two *Geographic and Personnel Indexes,* $560.00. Contains 34,000 entries from the U.S., Canada, and 80 other countries. A detailed subject index is included in volume one.

Internet Tools of the Profession: A Guide for Information Professionals. Hope N. Tillman, editor. Special Libraries Association. • 1997. $49.00. Second edition. Consists of 14 sections by various authors or compilers. After two introductory articles on searching the Internet, there are 12 annotated lists of useful Web sites, covering the SLA, business and finance, chemistry, education, food and agriculture, information technology, insurance and employee benefits, law, library management, metals and materials, pharmaceuticals, and telecommunications. An index is provided.

Subject Collections: A Guide to Special Book Collections and Subject Emphasis in Libraries. Lee Ash and William G. Miller, editors. R. R. Bowker. • Irregular. $275.00. Two volumes. A guide to special book collections and subject emphases as reported by university, college, public and special libraries in th United States and Canada.

Subject Directory of Special Libraries and Information Centers. Gale Cengage Learning. • Annual. $960.00. Three volumes, available separately: volume one, *Business, Government, and Law Libraries,* $375.00; volume two, *Computer, Engineering, and Law Libraries,* $375.00; volume three, *Health Sciences Libraries,* $375.00. Altogether, 14,000 entries from the *Directory of Special Libraries and Information Centers* are arranged in 14 subject chapters.

Who's Who in Special Libraries. Special Libraries Association. • Annual. $125.00. Available only online. About 14,000 librarians of libraries and special collections having a specific subject focus.

The World Directory of Business Information Libraries. Available from Gale Cengage Learning. • 2003. $650.00. Fifth edition. Published by Euromonitor. Provides detailed information on 2,000 major business libraries in 180 countries. Emphasis is on collections relevant to consumer goods and services markets.

World Directory of Marketing Information Sources. Available from Gale Cengage Learning. • 2003. $650.00. Fourth edition. Published by Euromonitor. Provides details on approximately 6,000 sources of marketing information, including publications, libraries, associations, market research companies, online databases, and governmental organizations. Coverage is worldwide.

World Guide to Special Libraries. Available from Gale Cengage Learning. • 2001. $400.00. Fifth edition. Two volumes. Published by K. G. Saur. Classifies more than 38,000 libraries in 183 countries under 750 subject headings.

ENCYCLOPEDIAS AND DICTIONARIES

Encyclopedic Guide to Searching and Finding Health Information on the Web. P. F. Anderson and Nancy J. Allee, editors. Neal-Schuman Publishers. • 2004. $395.00. Three volumes. Comprehensive guide to searching the Web for reliable information on hundreds of specific diseases, disorders, and health issues. Volume three covers Search Strategies and provides a Cumulative Index. (Published in conjunction with the Medical Library Association.).

World Encyclopedia of Library and Information Services. Robert Wedgeworth, editor. American Library Association. • 1993. $200.00. Third edition. Contains about 340 articles from various contributors.

HANDBOOKS AND MANUALS

The Business Library and How to Use It: A Guide to Sources and Research Strategies for Information on Business and Management. Elizabeth Wood and others, editors. Omnigraphics, Inc. • 1996. $28.00. Sixth edition. Explains library research methods and describes specific sources of business information. A revision of *How to Use the Business Library,* by H. Webster Johnson and others.

The Information Professional's Guide to Career Development Online. Sarah L. Nesbeitt and Rachel S. Gordon. Information Today, Inc. • 2001. $29.50. Provides advice to librarians and other information professionals about using online sources for career advancement. The Career Development Online Web Page (http://www.lisjobs.com/careerdev/) contains links to relevant resources.

The Map Library in the New Millennium. R. B. Parry and others, editors. American Library Association. • 2001. $75.00. Coverage includes new technologies, standards, geographical information systems, conservation, and intellectual property rights.

The OPL Sourcebook: A Guide for Solo and Small Libraries. Judith A. Siess. Information Today, Inc. • 2001. $39.50. The editor of *The One-Person Library* newsletter covers a wide variety of practical topics for improving the management and efficiency of OPLs.

Position Descriptions in Special Libraries. Del Sweeney and Karin Zilla, editors. Special Libraries Association. • 1996. $41.00. Third revised edition. Provides 87 descriptions of library and information management positions.

The SOLO Librarian's Sourcebook. Judith A. Siess. Information Today, Inc. • 1997. $39.50. Covers management and other aspects of one-librarian libraries.

Space Planning in the Special Library. Caryl Masyr and Roberta Freifield. Special Libraries Association. • 1991. $23.00. Provides practical advice for planners of new libraries, renovations, and relocations.

University Science and Engineering Libraries. Ellis Mount. Greenwood Publishing Group, Inc. • 1985. $67.00. Second edition. (Contributions in Librarianship and Information Science Series: No. 49).

ONLINE DATABASES

American Library Directory Online. Information Today, Inc. • Provides information on more than 30,000 public, college, and special libraries in the U.S. and Canada, with annual updates. Includes library networks, consortia, organizations, and schools. Inquire as to online cost and availability.

Information Science Abstracts [online]. Information Today, Inc. • Provides indexing and abstracting of the international literature of information science, including library science, from 1966 to date. Monthly updates. Inquire as to online cost and availability.

LISA: Library and Information Science Abstracts. Available from Cambridge Scientific Abstracts (CSA). • Provides abstracting and indexing of the world's library and information science literature, 1969 to date. Covers more than 440 periodicals from 68 countries. Updating is biweekly. Inquire as to on-line cost and availability.

Social Scisearch. Institute for Scientific Information. • Broad, multidisciplinary index to the literature of the social sciences, 1972 to present. Weekly updates. Worldwide coverage. Inquire as to online cost and availability.

PERIODICALS AND NEWSLETTERS

Art Reference Services Quarterly. Haworth Press, Inc. • Quarterly. Institutions, $110.00 per year. A journal for art librarians.

Aslib Proceedings: New Information Perspectives. Available from Information Today, Inc. • Ten times a year. $349.00 per year. Published in London by Aslib Covers a wide variety of information industry and library management topics.

Behavioral and Social Sciences Librarian. Haworth Press, Inc. • Semiannual. Individuals, $48.00 per year; institutions, $175.00 per year; libraries, $175.00 per year.

Business and Finance Division Bulletin. Special Libraries Association, Business and Finance Div. • Quarterly. $12.00 per year.

Information Outlook: The Monthly Magazine of the Special Libraries Association. Special Libraries Association. • Monthly. $65.00 per year. Topics include information technology, the Internet, copyright, research techniques, library management, and professional development. Replaces *Special Libraries* and *SpeciaList.*

Journal of Agricultural and Food Information. Haworth Press, Inc. • Quarterly. Institutions, $95.00 per year. A journal for librarians and others concerned with the acquisition of information on food and agriculture.

Journal of Business and Finance Librarianship. Haworth Press, Inc. • Quarterly. $165.00 per year.

Journal of Electronic Resources in Law Libraries. Haworth Press, Inc. • Quarterly. $300.00 per year to libraries; $48.00 per year to individuals.

Journal of Electronic Resources in Medical Libraries. Haworth Press, Inc. • Quarterly. $240.00 per year to libraries; $75.00 per year to individuals.

Legal Reference Services Quarterly. Haworth Press, Inc. • Quarterly. Institutions, $225.00 per year.

Medical Reference Services Quarterly. Haworth Press, Inc. • Quarterly. Institutions, $275.00 per year. An academic and practical journal for medical reference librarians.

Music Reference Services Quarterly. Haworth Press, Inc. • Quarterly. Institutions, $95.00 per year. An academic journal for music librarians.

The One-Person Library: A Newsletter for Librarians and Management. Information Bridges International, Inc. • Monthly. $85.00 per year. Newsletter for librarians working alone or with minimal assistance. Contains reports on library literature, management advice, case studies, book reviews, and general information.

Science and Technology Libraries. Haworth Press, Inc. • Quarterly. Institutions, $275.00 per year.

STATISTICS SOURCES

Report on Corporate Library Spending. Primary Research. • 1995. $75.00. Provides market research data on corporate library expenditures for books, periodicals, and online/CD-ROM sources.

SLA Annual Salary Survey. Special Libraries Association. • Annual. Members, $45.00; non-members, $125.00. Provides data on salaries for special librarians in the U. S. and Canada, according to location, job title, industry, budget, and years of experience.

TRADE/PROFESSIONAL ASSOCIATIONS

Special Libraries Association. 331 S Patrick St., Alexandria, VA 22314-3501. Phone: (703)647-4900 Fax: (703)647-4901 E-mail: sla@sla.org • URL: http://www.sla.org • International association of information professionals who work in special libraries serving business, research, government, universities, newspapers, museums, and institutions that use or produce specialized information. Seeks to advance the leadership role of special librarians. Offers consulting services to organizations that wish to establish or expand a library or information services. Conducts strategic learning and development courses, public relations, and government relations programs. Provides employment services. Operates knowledge exchange on topics pertaining to the development and management of special libraries. Maintains Hall of Fame.

OTHER SOURCES

Creating the Corporate Digital Library. Primary Research Group, Inc. • 2003. $135.00. Provides a survey of the electronic data policies of specific corporate libraries. Covers electronic journals, e-books, user training, alert services, vendor negotiation, web site development, knowledge management, outsourcing, and other topics.

Legal Research and Law Library Management. American Lawyer Media, Inc. • Looseleaf. $169.00. Updated as needed. Covers the planning and operation of libraries for law firms, including personnel selection and selection of books, periodicals, online services, microforms, and other materials. (Law Journal Press).

SPECIALISTS

See: CONSULTANTS

SPECIALTY FOOD INDUSTRY

See also: FOOD INDUSTRY

ABSTRACTS AND INDEXES

Food Science and Technology Abstracts. International Food Information Service Publishing. • Monthly. $1,780.00 per year. Provides worldwide coverage of the literature of food technology and food production.

Foods Adlibra: Key to the World's Food Literature. General Mills, Inc. Foods Adlibra Publications. • Semimonthly. $240.00 per year. Provides journal citations and abstracts to the literature of food technology and packaging.

CD-ROM DATABASES

Food Science and Technology Abstracts [CD-ROM]. Available from SilverPlatter Information, Inc. • Quarterly. Produced by International Food Information Service (home page is http://www.ifis.org). Provides worldwide coverage on CD-ROM of the literature of food technology and production. Various types of publications are indexed, with abstracts, including about 1,800 periodicals. Time period is 1969 to date.

DIRECTORIES

Directory of Delicatessen Products. Pacific Rim Publishing Co. • Annual. Included with February issue of *Deli News*. Lists suppliers of cheeses, lunch meats, packaged fresh meats, kosher foods, gourmet-specialty items, and bakery products.

Major Food and Drink Companies of the World. Available from Gale Cengage Learning. • Annual. $880.00. Two volumes. Published by Graham & Whiteside. Contains profiles and trade names for more than 9,800 important food and beverage companies in various countries. In addition to foods, includes both alcoholic and nonalcoholic drink products.

Specialty Food Industry Directory. Phoenix Media Network, Inc. • Annual. Included in subscription to Food Distribution Magazine. Lists manufacturers and suppliers of specialty foods, and services and equipment for the specialty food industry. Featured food products include legumes, sauces, spices, upscale cheese, specialty beverages, snack foods, baked goods, ethnic foods, and specialty meats.

Thomas Food and Beverage Market Place. Grey House Publishing. • 2004. $495.00. Three volumes. Contains more than 40,000 entries covering food companies, beverages, food equipment, warehouse companies, food brokers, wholesalers, importers, and exporters. Formerly *Thomas Food Industry Register.*

ONLINE DATABASES

F & S Index. Gale Cengage Learning. • Contains about four million citations to worldwide business, financial, and industrial or consumer product literature appearing from 1972 to date. Weekly updates. Inquire as to online cost and availability.

Food Science and Technology Abstracts [online]. IFIS North American Desk. • Produced by International Food Information Service. Provides about 500,000 online citations, with abstracts, to the international literature of food science, technology, commodities, engineering, and processing. Approximately 2,000 periodicals are covered. Time period is 1969 to date, with monthly updates. Inquire as to online cost and availability.

FOODS ADLIBRA. General Mills, Inc. • Contains online citations, with abstracts, to the technical and business literature of food processing and packaging. New products and new ingredients are featured. Covers about 250 trade journals and 500 research journals from 1974 to date, with monthly updates. Inquire as to online cost and availability.

PROMT: Predicasts Overview of Markets and Technology. Gale Cengage Learning. • Companies, products, applied technologies and markets. U.S. and international literature coverage, 1972 to date. Inquire as to online cost and availability. Provides abstracts from more than 1,600 publications. Weekly updates.

PERIODICALS AND NEWSLETTERS

Deli News. Delicatessen Council of Southern California, Inc. Pacific Rim Publishing Co. • Monthly. $25.00 per year. Includes product news and comment related to cheeses, lunch meats, packaged fresh meats, kosher foods, gourmet-specialty items, and bakery products.

Fancy Food and Culinary Products. Talcott Communications Corp. • Monthly. $34.00 per year. Emphasizes new specialty food products and the business management aspects of the specialty food and confection industries. Includes special issues on wine, cheese, candy, "upscale" cookware, and gifts. Formerly (Fancy Foods).

Food Distribution Magazine. Phoenix Media Network, Inc. • Monthly. $49.00 per year. Edited for marketers and buyers of domestic and imported, specialty or gourmet food products, including ethnic foods, seasonings, and bakery items.

Gourmet News: The Business Newspaper for the Gourmet Industry. United Publications, Inc. • Monthly. $60.00 per year. Provides news of the gourmet food industry, including specialty food stores, upscale cookware shops, and gift shops.

Gourmet Retailer. VNU Business Media. • Monthly. Free to qualified personnel; others, $75.00 per year. Covers upscale food and housewares, including confectionery items, bakery operations, and coffee.

Pizza Today. National Association of Pizza Operators. Pete Lachapelle. • Monthly. $29.95 per year. Covers both practical business topics and food topics for pizza establishments.

STATISTICS SOURCES

World Food Data and Statistics. Euromonitor International. • 2004. $650.00. Provides five-year data for a wide variety of food products in 52 countries. Includes market size, consumer expenditures, price indicators, and retail distribution data for many kinds of meat, fish, fruits, vegetables, dairy products, baked goods, condiments, canned food, and frozen food.

TRADE/PROFESSIONAL ASSOCIATIONS

National Association for the Specialty Food Trade. 120 Wall St., 27th Fl., New York, NY 10005-4001. Phone: (212)482-6440 Fax: (212)482-6459 E-mail: catalog@fancyfoodshows.com • URL: http://www.fancyfoodshows.com • Members are manufacturers, processors, importers, retailers, and brokers of specialty and gourmet food items.

National Association of Pizzaria Operators. PO Box 2132, New Albany, NY 47151. Phone: 800-489-8324 or (216)766-5710 E-mail: webmaster@napa.com • URL: http://www.napo.com • Members are pizza establishment operators, food suppliers, and equipment manufacturers. Affiliated with American Society of Association Executives, Meeting Professionals International and National Restaurant Association.

OTHER SOURCES

From Kitchen to Market: Selling Your Gourmet Food Specialty. Stephen F. Hall, Dearborn Trade Publishing, A Kaplan Professional Co. • 2000. $28.95. Third edition. Covers packaging, labeling, marketing, and distribution of specialty and gourmet food products. Includes charts, graphs, tables, guidelines, checklists, and industry examples.

The Gourmet/Specialty Foods Market. Available from MarketResearch.com. • 2001. $3,299.00. Market research data. Published by Packaged Facts. Discusses current trends, with projections to 2005.

The Market for Sweet Baked Goods. MarketResearch.com • 2000. $2,750.00. Market research data. Covers both fresh and frozen, bakery products.

SPECULATION

See also: TECHNICAL ANALYSIS
(FINANCE)

GENERAL WORKS

Devil Take the Hindmost: A History of Financial Speculation. Edward Chancellor. Dutton/Plume. • 2000. $15.00. Covers such events as the Dutch tulip mania of 1637, the South Sea bubble of 1720, and the Japanese real estate and stock market boom of the 1980's.

Dumb Money: Adventures of a Day Trader. Gary Wolf and Joey Anuff. Random House, Inc. • 2000. $9.95. An account of the day trading ordeals of one of the authors, Joey Anuff.

Education of a Speculator. Victor Niederhoffer. John Wiley and Sons, Inc. • 1998. $18.95. An autobiography providing basic advice on speculation, investment, and the commodity futures market.

Extraordinary Popular Delusions and the Madness of Crowds. Charles Mackay. Prometheus Books. • 2001. $19.00. A classic work on speculation and crowd psychology, originally published in 1841. (Great Minds Series).

Famous First Bubbles: The Fundamentals of Early Manias. Peter M. Garber. MIT Press. • 2000. $15.95. Provides scholarly explanations of three historic price bubbles: the Dutch Tulipmania, the Missis-sippi Bubble, and the South Sea Bubble.

Futures Markets. A. G. Malliaris, editor. Edward Elgar Publishing, Inc. • 1997. $550.00. Three volumes. Consists of reprints of 70 articles dating from 1959 to 1993, on futures market volatility, speculation, hedging, stock indexes, portfolio insurance, interest rates, and foreign currencies. (International Library of Critical Writings in Financial Economics Series: No. 2).

Manias, Panics, and Crashes: A History of Financial Crises. Charles P. Kindleberger. John Wiley and Sons, Inc. • 2000. $19.95. Fourth edition. Provides a history of financial troubles from 1618 to modern times, with greed as a central theme. (Investment Classic Series).

Money Madness: Strange Manias and Extraordinary Schemes On and Off Wall Street. John M. Waggoner. McGraw-Hill. • 1990. $26.00.

A Short History of Financial Euphoria. John Kenneth Galbraith. Penguin Group. • 1994. $13.00. An analysis of speculative euphoria and subsequent crashes, from the Holland tulip mania in 1637 to the 1987 unpleasantness in the U. S. stock market. (Whittle Series).

Stock Market Crashes and Speculative Manias. Eugene N. White, editor. Edward Elgar Publishing, Inc. • 1996. $255.00. Contains reprints of 23 articles dating from 1905 to 1994. (International Library of Macroeconomic and Financial History Series: No. 13).

Trading to Win: The Psychology of Mastering the Markets. Ari Kiev. John Wiley and Sons, Inc. • 1998. $39.95. A mental health guide for stock, bond, and commodity traders. Tells how to keep speculative emotions in check, overcome self-doubt, and focus on a winning strategy. (Trading Series).

Wheels of Fortune: The History of Speculation from Scandal to Respectability. Charles R. Geisst. John Wiley and Sons, Inc. • 2002. $29.95. Provides a colorful history of speculation in the U. S. commodity futures markets from 1850 to about 2000.

ALMANACS AND YEARBOOKS

Supertrader's Almanac-Reference Manual: Reference Guide and Analytical Techniques for Investors. Frank A. Taucher. • 1991. $55.00. Explains technical methods for the trading of commodity futures, and includes data on seasonality, cycles, trends, contract characteristics, highs and lows, etc.

DIRECTORIES

Futures Magazine SourceBook: The Most Complete List of Exchanges, Companies, Regulators, Organizations, etc., Offering Products and Services to the Futures and Options Industry. Futures Magazine, Inc. • Annual. $19.50. Provides information on commodity futures brokers, trading method services, publications, and other items of interest to futures traders and money managers.

Standard and Poor's Security Dealers of North America. Standard & Poor's. • Semiannual. $480.00 per year; with *Supplements* every six weeks. Geographical listing of over 12,000 stock, bond, and commodity dealers.

Walker's Manual of Unlisted Stocks. Walker's Manual, LLC. • Annual. $99.00. Provides information on 500 over-the-counter stocks, including many "penny stocks" trading at less than $5.00 per share.

HANDBOOKS AND MANUALS

Day-Trader's Manual: Theory, Art, and Science of Profitable Short-Term Investing. William F. Eng. John Wiley and Sons, Inc. • 1992. $79.95. Covers short-term trading in stocks, futures, and options. Various technical trading systems are considered. (Finance Series, vol. 5).

Derivatives: A Comprehensive Resource for Options, Futures, Interest Rate Swaps, and Mortgage Securities. Fred D. Arditti. Harvard Business School Publishing. • 1996. $60.00. Published by Harvard Business School Press. Provides detailed explanations of various kinds of financial derivatives (options, futures, swaps, etc.) and their trading tactics, uses, and risks. (Financial Management Association Survey and Synthesis Series).

Money Management Strategies for Futures Traders. Nauzer J. Balsara. John Wiley and Sons, Inc. • 1992. $75.00. How to limit risk and avoid catastrophic losses. (Finance Series).

101 Rules of Trading Discipline. Pejman Hamidi. McGraw-Hill. • 2002. $39.95. Trading rules for investors or speculators are presented in three categories: "Trading Disciplines," "Market Disciplines," and "Personal Disciplines." (Teach Yourself Series).

The Prudent Speculator: Al Frank on Investing. Al Frank. McGraw-Hill. • 1989. $30.00. How to be a sensible investor or speculator. Includes advice on the use of margin accounts and stock market timing.

Risk Management, Speculation, and Derivative Securities. Geoffrey Poitras. Elsevier Butterworth Heinemann. • 2002. $99.95. In addition to "Risk Management Concepts" and "Speculative Concepts," topics include financial futures, forward contracts, arbitrage, spread trading, hedging, and diversification. Three appendices are devoted to mathematical concepts and calculations.

Streetsmart Guide to Short Selling: Techniques the Pros Use to Profit in Any Market. Tom Taulli. McGraw-Hill. • 2002. $29.95. Provides the details of short sale procedures and offers practical advice for individual investors or traders. (Teach Yourself Series).

Swap Literacy. Elizabeth Ungar. Bloomberg. • 1996. $40.00. Written for corporate finance officers. Provides basic information on arbitrage, hedging, and speculation, involving interest rate, currency, and other types of financial swaps. (Bloomberg Professional Library.).

Trader Vic: Methods of a Wall Street Master. Victor Sperandeo and T. Sullivan Brown. John Wiley and Sons, Inc. • 1993. $22.95.

Trading and Exchanges: Market Microstructure for Practitioners. Larry Harris. Oxford University Press. • 2002. $95.00. Explains the function and workings of modern stock markets. Covers such topics as liquidity, volatility, speculation, market efficiency, stock indexes, and the structure of trading. (Financial Management Association Survey and Synthesis Series).

Trading for a Living: Psychology, Trading Tactics, Money Management. Alexander Elder. John Wiley and Sons, Inc. • 1993. $70.00. Covers technical and chart methods of trading in commodity and financial futures, options, and stocks. Includes Elliott Wave Theory, oscillators, moving averages, point-and-figure, and other technical approaches. (Finance Series).

INTERNET DATABASES

Futures Online. Futures Magazine Inc. Phone: (312)846-4600 Fax: (312)846-4638 • URL: http://www.futuresmag.com • Web site presents updates of *Futures* magazine and links to other futures-related sites.

TheStreet.com: Your Insider's Look at Wall Street. TheStreet.com, Inc. Phone: 800-562-9571 or (212)321-5000 Fax: (212)321-5016 • URL: http://www.thestreet.com • Web site offers "Free Sections" and "Premium Sections" ($24.95 per month). Both sections offer iconoclastic advice and comment on the stock market, but premium service displays a more comprehensive selection of news and analysis.

There are many by-lined articles. "Search the Site" is included.

PERIODICALS AND NEWSLETTERS

The Cheap Investor: The Investor's Guide to Micro-cap and Turn Around Stocks Under $5 Per Share. Mathews and Associates, Inc. • Monthly. $125.00 per year. Newsletter. Gives three to six buy recommendations, updates on precious recommendations and investment tips on quality stock under $5.00. Free issue available upon request.

Financial Sentinel: Your Beacon to the World of Investing. Gulf Atlantic Publishing, Inc. • Monthly. $29.95 per year. Provides "The only complete listing of all OTC Bulletin Board stocks traded, with all issues listed on the Nasdaq SmallCap Market, the Toronto, and Vancouver Stock Exchanges." Also includes investment advice and recommendations of small capitalization stocks.

Futures: News, Analysis, and Strategies for Futures, Options, and Derivatives Traders. Futures Magazine. • Monthly. $39.00 per year. Edited for institutional money managers and traders, brokers, risk managers, and individual investors or speculators. Includes special feature issues on interest rates, technical indicators, currencies, charts, precious metals, hedge funds, and derivatives. Supplements available.

The Low Priced Stock Survey. Horizon Publishing Company L.L.C. • Description: Reviews and analyzes stocks offered at a price of $20 or less. Analysis is divided into sections: Emerging Growth Opportunities, The Fundamentalist, Bargain Spotlight, Stock of the Month, and Master List Highlights. Includes weekly closes of the Dow Jones Industrials and NASDAQ, and statistics.

Managed Account Reports: The Clearing House for Commodity Money Management. Managed Account Reports, Inc. • Monthly. $425.00 per year. Newsletter. Reviews the performance and other characteristics of commodity trading advisors and their commodity futures funds or managed accounts. Includes tables and graphs.

The Penny Fortune Newsletter. James M. Fortune, editor. Phoenix Communications Group Ltd. • Description: Instructs small investors on how to invest modest sums of money every two weeks to build a portfolio of stocks and mutual funds.

The Prudent Speculator. Al Frank Asset Management Inc. • Description: Presents a fundamental approach to stock selection and buying strategies for long-term capital gains appreciation. Provides technical analysis to aid market timing for both speculators and conservative investors. Reviews editor's personal common stock portfolio in comparison with the Dow Jones Industrials and New York Stock Exchange Composite Index. Recurring features include a column titled Currently Recommended Stocks with follow-up reviews.

SFO: Stocks, Futures & Options. Wasendorf & Associates, Inc. • Monthly. $49.95 per year. Subtitle: *Official Journal for Personal Investing in Stocks, Futures, and Options.* Covers mainly speculative techniques for stocks, commodity futures, financial futures, stock index futures, foreign exchange, short selling, and various kinds of options.

Special Situations Newsletter: In-Depth Survey of Under-Valued Stocks. Charles Howard Kaplan. • Monthly. $75.00 per year. Newsletter. Principal content is "This Month's Recommendation," a detailed analysis of one special situation stock.

RESEARCH CENTERS AND INSTITUTES

Center for Research in Security Prices. University of Chicago, 725 S. Wells St., Suite 800, Chicago, IL 60607. Phone: (773)834-4610 Fax: (773)702-3036 E-mail: custom@crsp.uchicago.edu • URL: http://gsbwww.uchicago.edu/research/crsp.

Glucksman Institute. New York University. Salomon

Center, Stern School of Business, 44 W. Fourth St., Room 9-65, New York, NY 10012-0267. Phone: (212)998-0714 Fax: (212)995-4220 E-mail: wsilber@stern.nyu.edu.

Rodney L. White Center for Financial Research. University of Pennsylvania, 3254 Steinberg Hall-Dietrich Hall, Philadelphia, PA 19104. Phone: (215)898-7616 Fax: (215)573-8084 E-mail: rlwtcr@finance.wharton.upenn.edu • URL: http://www.finance.wharton.upenn.edu • Research areas include financial management, money markets, real estate finance, and international finance.

OTHER SOURCES

The Options Workbook: Proven Strategies from a Market Wizard. Anthony J. Saliba. Dearborn Trade Publishing, A Kaplan Professional Co. • 2001. $40.00. Emphasis is on computerized trading on the Chicago Board Options Exchange. Includes information on specific trading strategies.

SPEECH RECOGNITION

See: VOICE RECOGNITION

SPEECHES

See: PUBLIC SPEAKING

SPICE INDUSTRY

CD-ROM DATABASES

Food Science and Technology Abstracts [CD-ROM]. Available from SilverPlatter Information, Inc. • Quarterly. Produced by International Food Information Service (home page is http://www.ifis.org). Provides worldwide coverage on CD-ROM of the literature of food technology and production. Various types of publications are indexed, with abstracts, including about 1,800 periodicals. Time period is 1969 to date.

DIRECTORIES

Major Food and Drink Companies of the World. Available from Gale Cengage Learning. • Annual. $880.00. Two volumes. Published by Graham & Whiteside. Contains profiles and trade names for more than 9,800 important food and beverage companies in various countries. In addition to foods, includes both alcoholic and nonalcoholic drink products.

Thomas Food and Beverage Market Place. Grey House Publishing. • 2004. $495.00. Three volumes. Contains more than 40,000 entries covering food companies, beverages, food equipment, warehouse companies, food brokers, wholesalers, importers, and exporters. Formerly *Thomas Food Industry Register.*

ONLINE DATABASES

Food Science and Technology Abstracts [online]. IFIS North American Desk. • Produced by International Food Information Service. Provides about 500,000 online citations, with abstracts, to the international literature of food science, technology, commodities, engineering, and processing. Approximately 2,000 periodicals are covered. Time period is 1969 to date, with monthly updates. Inquire as to online cost and availability.

PERIODICALS AND NEWSLETTERS

Journal of Herbs, Spices and Medicinal Plants. Haworth Press, Inc. • Quarterly. $285.00 per year. An academic and practical journal on production, marketing, and other aspects of herbs and spices.

Perfumer and Flavorist. Allured Publishing. • Bimonthly. $135.00 per year. Provides information on the art and technology of flavors and fragrances,

including essential oils, aroma chemicals, and spices.

STATISTICS SOURCES

World Food Data and Statistics. Euromonitor International. • 2004. $650.00. Provides five-year data for a wide variety of food products in 52 countries. Includes market size, consumer expenditures, price indicators, and retail distribution data for many kinds of meat, fish, fruits, vegetables, dairy products, baked goods, condiments, canned food, and frozen food.

TRADE/PROFESSIONAL ASSOCIATIONS

American Spice Trade Association. 2025 M St. NW, Ste. 800, Washington, DC 20036. Phone: (202)367-1127 Fax: (202)367-2127 E-mail: info@astaspice.org • URL: http://www.astaspice.org • Works to foment the export of American spices. Promotes the interests of the American spice industry.

OTHER SOURCES

Spices and Seasonings. Available from MarketResearch.com. • 1999. $2,250.00. Market research data. Published by Specialists in Business Information. Covers salt, pepper, garlic, salt substitutes, seasoning mixes, etc.

SPORTING GOODS INDUSTRY

See also: RECREATION INDUSTRY

DIRECTORIES

Directory of Sporting Goods and Activewear Buyers Directory. Douglas Publications, Inc. • Annual. $329.00. About 10,700 retail stores selling athletic and recreational equipment, footwear, apparel. *Salesman's Guide Directories.*

FINANCIAL RATIOS

Annual Statement Studies. The Risk Management Association. • Annual. Median and quartile financial ratios are given for over 400 kinds of manufacturing, wholesale, retail, construction, and consumer finance establishments. Data is sorted by both asset size and sales volume. Includes a clearly written "Definition of Ratios" and an alphabetical industry index.

Annual Statement Studies: Industry Default Probabilities and Cash Flow Measures. The Risk Management Association. • Annual. $145.00. Serves as a companion volume to the original *Annual Statement Studies.* Gives probability of default estimates on a percentage scale for more than 450 industries. Includes changes in position year-by-year for eight financial statement line items and provides percentage measures of cash flow.

Cost of Doing Business for Retail Sporting Goods Stores. National Sporting Goods Association. • Biennial. $125.00. Includes income statements, balance sheets, sales per employee, sales per square foot, inventory turnover, etc.

HANDBOOKS AND MANUALS

Sporting Goods Store. Entrepreneur Media, Inc. • Looseleaf. $59.50. A practical guide to starting a retail sporting goods business. Covers profit potential, start-up costs, market size evaluation, owner's time required, site selection, lease negotiation, pricing, accounting, advertising, promotion, etc. (Start-Up Business Guide No. E1286.).

INTERNET DATABASES

Advance Monthly Sales for Retail Trade and Food Services. U. S. Census Bureau. Phone: 800-541-8345 or (301)763-4636 Fax: (301)457-3842 E-mail: rcb@census.gov • URL: http://www.census.gov/svsd/www/fullpub.html • Web pages provide monthly sales figures for a wide range of retail businesses. Advance, preliminary, and final statistics are provided for the latest month available in each case, with a previous-year comparison. Updates are monthly.

PERIODICALS AND NEWSLETTERS

NSGA Retail Focus. National Sporting Goods Association. • Bimonthly. Membership. Covers news and marketing trends for sporting goods retailers. Formerly *NSGA Sports Retailer.*

Sporting Goods Business: The National Newsmagazine of the Sporting Goods Industry. VNU Business Media. • 16 times a year. Free to qualified personnel; others, $65.00 per year. The national news magazine of the sporting goods industry.

Sporting Goods Dealer: The Voice of Team Dealers Since 1899. VNU Business Media. • Quarterly. $38.00 per year. Covers the merchandising of sports products to consumers, as well as to schools, colleges, and professional teams.

Sports Trend. Shore-Verrone, Inc. • Monthly. $75.00 per year. Formerly *Sports Merchandiser.*

STATISTICS SOURCES

Annual Benchmark Report for Retail Trade and Food Services...A Detailed Summary of Retail Sales, Purchases, Accounts Receivable, Inventories, and Food Service Sales. Available from U. S. Government Printing Office. • Annual. $13.00. Issued by the U.S. Census Bureau. Provides detailed annual and monthly retail statistics for the most recent 10 years. Includes data for various kinds of retail outlets, including automobiles, furniture, appliances, building supplies, grocery stores, drug stores, gasoline stations, clothing, sporting goods, department stores, and restaurants.

Annual Survey of Manufactures. Available from U. S. Government Printing Office. • Annual. Prices vary. Issued by the U. S. Census Bureau as an interim update to the *Census of Manufactures.* Includes data on number of manufacturing establishments in various industries, employment, labor costs, value of shipments, capital expenditures, inventories, energy costs, and assets. (See also Census Bureau home page, http://www.census.gov/.).

U. S. Industry and Trade Outlook. Available from National Technical Information Service. • Annual. $69.95. Produced by the International Trade Administration, U. S. Department of Commerce, in a "public-private" partnership with DRI/McGraw-Hill and Standard & Poor's. Provides basic data, outlook for the current year, and "Long-Term Prospects" (five-year projections) for a wide variety of products and services. Includes high technology industries. Formerly *U. S. Industrial Outlook.*

TRADE/PROFESSIONAL ASSOCIATIONS

National Association of Sporting Goods Wholesalers. 400 E. Randolph St., Suite 700, Chicago, IL 60601-7329. Phone: (312)565-0233 Fax: (312)565-2654 E-mail: nasgw@nasgw.org • URL: http://www.nasgw.org.

National Sporting Goods Association. 1601 Feehanville Dr., Ste. 300, Mount Prospect, IL 60056. Phone: 800-815-5422 or (847)296-6742 Fax: (847)391-9827 E-mail: info@nsga.org • URL: http://www.nsga.org • Provides services, education and information to assist member to profit in a competitive marketplace.

Sporting Goods Manufacturers Association. 1150 17th St. NW, Ste. 850, Washington, DC 20036. Phone: (202)775-1762 Fax: (202)296-7462 E-mail: info@sgma.com • URL: http://www.sgma.com • Manufacturers of athletic clothing, footwear, and sporting goods. Seeks to increase sports participation and create growth in the sporting goods industry. Owns and operates the largest sports

products trade show in the world.

OTHER SOURCES

American Sports Analysis. Available from MarketResearch.com. • 2001. $375.00. Published by American Sports Data, Inc. Consumer market data. A study of participation in sports activities (golf, tennis, swimming, running, etc.) by American consumers.

Footwear Market. Available from MarketResearch.com. • 2002. $1,695.00. Published by Business Trend Analysts. Provides market data on shoes for walking, running, and specific sports.

SPORTS BUSINESS

See also: GOLF INDUSTRY; RECREATION INDUSTRY

GENERAL WORKS

Market Structure of Sports. Gerald W. Scully. The University of Chicago Press. • 1995. $39.95.

Winning is the Only Thing: Sports in America Since 1945. Randy Roberts and James Olson. Johns Hopkins University Press. • 1989. $16.95. (American Moments Series).

ABSTRACTS AND INDEXES

Leisure, Recreation, and Tourism Abstracts. Available from CABI Publishing North America. • Quarterly. Members, $280.00 per year; Institutions, $610.00 per year. Includes single site internet access. Published in England by CABI Publishing. Provides coverage of the worldwide literature of travel, recreation, sports, and the hospitality industry. Emphasis is on research.

Readers' Guide to Periodical Literature. H. W. Wilson Co. • Monthly. $345.00 per year. Includes annual *Cumulation.* Indexes about 250 periodicals of general interest.

ALMANACS AND YEARBOOKS

Sportbil. International Sport Summit. • Annual. Price on application. A yearly review of the business of sport.

BIOGRAPHICAL SOURCES

Celebrity Register. Gale Cengage Learning. • 1990. $115.00. 90th edition. Compiled by Celebrity Services International (Earl Blackwell). Contains profiles of 1,300 famous individuals in the performing arts, sports, politics, business, and other fields.

CD-ROM DATABASES

WILSONDISC: Readers' Guide to Periodical Literature. H. W. Wilson Co. • Monthly. $1,095.00 per year, including unlimited online access to *Readers' Guide to Periodical Literature* through WILSONLINE. Provides CD-ROM indexing of about 270 general interest periodicals. Covers 1983 to date. (*Readers' Guide Abstracts* also available on CD-ROM at $1,995 per year.).

DIRECTORIES

Athletic Business Professional Directory. Athletic Business Publications, Inc. • Monthly. $72.00 per year. $8.00 per issue. Lists consultants in athletic facility planning, with architects, engineers, and contractors. Appears in each issue of *Athletic Business.*.

Resorts and Parks Purchasing Guide. Klevens Publications, Inc. • Annual. $85.00. Lists suppliers of products and services for resorts and parks, including national parks, amusement parks, dude ranches, golf resorts, ski areas, and national monument areas.

Sports Market Place. Sports Careers. • Covers: manufacturers, organizations, professional sports teams, broadcasting networks, sports arenas, syndicators, publications, trade shows, marketing services, corporate sports sponsors, and other groups

concerned with the business and promotional aspects of sports generally and with air sports, arm wrestling, auto sports, badminton, baseball, basketball, biathlon, bowling, boxing, curling, equestrian, exercise, fencing, field hockey, football, golf, gymnastics, ice hockey, lacrosse, martial arts, paddleball, paddle tennis, platform tennis, pentathlon, racquetball, rowing, rugby, running/jogging, skiing, soccer, softball, squash, swimming, table tennis, tennis, track and field, volleyball, water sports, weightlifting, and wrestling. Entries include: Name of company or organization, address, fax, e-mail, URL, name of key personnel with titles, and description of products or services.

HANDBOOKS AND MANUALS

Complete Guide to Special Event Management: Business Insights, Financial Advice and Successful Strategies from Ernst and Young, Consultants to the Olympics. John Wiley and Sons, Inc. • 1992. $39.95. Covers the marketing, financing, and general management of special events in the fields of art, entertainment, and sports.

Financial Management of Sport-Related Organizations. Terry Haggerty and Garth Paton. Stipes Publishing L.L.C. • 1984. $4.80. (Sport and Physical Education Management Series).

Sports, Convention, and Entertainment Facilities. David C. Petersen. Urban Land Institute. • 1996. $61.95. Provides advice and information on developing, financing, and operating amphitheaters, arenas, convention centers, and stadiums. Includes case studies of 70 projects.

ONLINE DATABASES

Globalbase. Gale Cengage Learning. • Provides more than one million online summaries of business, industrial, and economic news reports from more than 1,000 publications worldwide. Covers a wide range of material appearing in international trade journals, professional magazines, and newspapers. Time period is 1984 to date, with weekly updates. Inquire as to online cost and availability.

Newspaper Abstracts Daily. ProQuest Inc. • Provides online coverage (citations and abstracts) of 25 major newspapers. Covers business, economics, current affairs, health, fitness, sports, education, technology, government, consumer affairs, psychology, the arts, and the social sciences. Time period is 1986 to date, with daily updates. Inquire as to online cost and availability.

PROMT: Predicasts Overview of Markets and Technology. Gale Cengage Learning. • Companies, products, applied technologies and markets. U.S. and international literature coverage, 1972 to date. Inquire as to online cost and availability. Provides abstracts from more than 1,600 publications. Weekly updates.

Readers' Guide Abstracts Online. H. W. Wilson Co. • Indexes and abstracts general interest periodicals, 1983 to date. Weekly updates. Inquire as to online cost and availability.

PERIODICALS AND NEWSLETTERS

Athletic Business. Athletic Business Publications, Inc. • Monthly. $55.00 per year. Published for those whose responsibility is the business of planning, financing and operating athletic/recreation/fitness programs and facilities.

Athletic Management. MomentumMedia. • Bimonthly. $24.00 per year. Formerly *College Athletic Management.*

Media Sports Business. Kagan World Media. • Description: Discusses the economics of national and regional cable and pay TV sports. Includes semiannual census of cable and pay sports channels, coverage of values of sports media rights, and news of other developments in the field. **Remarks:** Also available via e-mail and fax.

Sports Industry News: Management and Finance, Regulation and Litigation, Media and Marketing. Game Point Publishing. • Weekly. $244.00 per year. Newsletter. Covers ticket promotions, TV rights, player contracts, concessions, endorsements, etc.

RESEARCH CENTERS AND INSTITUTES

Center for the Study of Sport in Society. Northeastern University, 360 Huntington Ave., Ste. 161CP, Boston, MA 02115-5000. Phone: (617)373-4025 Fax: (617)373-4566 E-mail: sportinsociety@hotmail.com • URL: http://www.sportinsociety.org • Research fields include sport sociology, sport journalism, and sport business.

National Sports Law Institute. Marquette University Law School, 1103 W. Wisconsin Ave., Milwaukee, WI 53201-1881. Phone: (414)288-7494 Fax: (414)288-5818 E-mail: matt.mitten@mu.edu • URL: http://www.marquette.edu/law/sports • Promotes ethical practices in amateur and professional sports activities.

STATISTICS SOURCES

United States Census of Service Industries. U.S. Bureau of the Census. • Quinquennial. Various reports available.

TRADE/PROFESSIONAL ASSOCIATIONS

American Sportscasters Association. 225 Broadway, Ste. 2030, New York, NY 10007. Phone: (212)227-8080 Fax: (212)571-0556 E-mail: lschwa8918@aol.com • URL: http://www.americansportscastersonline.com • Radio and television sportscasters. Sponsors seminars, clinics, and symposia for aspiring announcers and sportscasters. Compiles statistics. Operates Speaker's Bureau, placement service, hall of fame, and biographical archives. Maintains American Sportscaster Hall of Fame Trust. Is currently implementing Hall of Fame Museum, Community Programs.

National Sportscasters and Sportswriters Association. 322 E Innes St., Salisbury, NC 28144. Phone: (704)633-4275 Fax: (704)633-2027 • Members are sportswriters and radio/TV sportscasters.

Society of Recreation Executives. PO Box 520, Gonzalez, FL 35260-0520. Phone: 800-281-9186 or (850)937-8354 Fax: (850)937-8356 E-mail: rltresource@spydee.net • Members are corporate executives employed in the recreation, leisure and travel industries.

OTHER SOURCES

Law of Professional and Amateur Sports. West Group. • Annual. $345.00 per year. Three looseleaf volumes. Covers agent-player agreements, collective bargaining, negotiation of player contracts, taxation, and other topics.

Superstudy of Sports Participation. Available from MarketResearch.com. • 2002. $700.00. Three volumes. Published by American Sports Data, Inc. Provides market research data on 102 sports and activities. Vol. 1: *Physical Fitness Activities.* Vol. 2: *Recreational Sports.* Vol. 3: *Outdoor Activities.* (Volumes are available separately at $295.00.).

SPORTSWEAR

See: CLOTHING INDUSTRY; WOMEN'S APPAREL

SPOT RADIO ADVERTISING

See: RADIO AND TELEVISION ADVERTISING

SPOT WELDING

See: WELDING

STAFF MAGAZINES

See: HOUSE ORGANS

STAINLESS STEEL

See: IRON AND STEEL INDUSTRY

STAMPS AS AN INVESTMENT

DIRECTORIES

Stamp Exchangers Directory. Levine Publications. • Covers: over 1000 people who are interested in exchanging stamps, coins, and other collectibles with Americans; international coverage. Entries include: Name, address, item collected.

PERIODICALS AND NEWSLETTERS

Linn's Stamp News. Amos Press, Inc. • Weekly. $39.90 per year.

Scott Stamp Monthly. Scott Publishing Co. • Monthly. $17.95 per year.

Stamp Collector. Krause Publications, Inc. • Biweekly. $32.98 per year. Newspaper.

Stamps: The Weekly Magazine of Philately. American Publishing Co. of New York. • Weekly. $23.50 per year.

TRADE/PROFESSIONAL ASSOCIATIONS

American Philatelic Society. 100 Match Factory Pl., Bellefonte, PA 16823. Phone: (814)933-3803 Fax: (814)933-6128 E-mail: dngc@stamps.org • URL: http://www.stamps.org • Collectors of postage and revenue stamps, first day covers, postal history, and related philatelic items. Helps members buy and sell stamps; operates expertise service; offers stamp insurance program; circulates slide programs. Maintains hall of fame; offers correspondence courses; accredits judges for philatelic competitions. Conducts philatelic seminars.

American Stamp Dealers Association. 3 School St., Ste. 205, Glen Cove, NY 11542-2548. Phone: (516)759-7000 Fax: (516)759-7014 E-mail: asda@asdaonline.com • URL: http://www.asdaonline.com • Dealers and wholesalers of stamps, albums, and other philatelic materials. Sponsors National Stamp Collecting Week in November.

Philatelic Foundation. 70 W 40th St., 15th Fl., New York, NY 10018. Phone: (212)221-6555 Fax: (212)221-6208 E-mail: philatelicfoundation@verizon.net • URL: http://www.philatelicfoundation.org • Educational institution chartered by New York State Department of Education for philatelic study and research. Offers philatelic slide programs as an educational aid for schools, organized youth groups, and stamp clubs. Renders opinions on stamps and other philatelic material. Prepares exhibitions for stamp shows.

STANDARD INDUSTRIAL CLASSIFICATION

See: INDUSTRY

STANDARD METROPOLITAN STATISTICAL AREAS

See: CITIES AND TOWNS; CITY PLANNING; URBAN DEVELOPMENT

STANDARDIZATION

See also: MATERIALS; QUALITY CONTROL

ABSTRACTS AND INDEXES

Index and Directory of Industry Standards. IHS Energy. • Annual. $395.00 Seven volumes. Covers approximately 20,000 international and 35,000 U.S. industrial standards as well as 362 industrial organizations.

BIBLIOGRAPHIES

Publications of the National Institute of Standards and Technology. U.S. Government Printing Office. • Annual. Keyword and author indexes.

DIRECTORIES

Catalog of American National Standards. American National Standards Institute. • Annual. Free to members; non-members, $20.00.

Directory of Standards Laboratories. NCSL International. • Biennial. Available only online. Lists about 1,500 measurement standards laboratories.

Standards Activities of Organizations in the United States. Available from U. S. Government Printing Office. • 1996. Prepared by the Office of Standards Code and Information, National Institute of Standards and Technology, U. S. Dept. of Commerce. Describes the activities of over 750 U. S. organizations that develop and publish standards. Formerly *Directory of United States Standardization Activities.*

ENCYCLOPEDIAS AND DICTIONARIES

Consumers' Guide to Product Grades and Terms: From Grade A to VSOP-Definitions of 8,000 Terms Describing Food Housewares and Other Everyday Terms. Gale Cengage Learning. • 1992. $95.00. Includes product grades and classifications defined by government agencies, such as the Food and Drug Administration (FDA), and by voluntary standards organizations, such as the American National Standards Institute (ANSI).

HANDBOOKS AND MANUALS

Book of ASTM Standards. ASTM. • Annual. Price on application.

Industry's Guide to ISO 9000. Adedeji B. Badiru. John Wiley and Sons, Inc. • 1995. $120.00. (Engineering and Technology Management Series).

International Standards Desk Reference: Your Passport to World Markets. Amy Zuckerman. AMACOM. • 1996. $35.00. Provides information on standards important in export-import trade, such as ISO 9000.

ISO 9000 and the Service Sector: A Critical Interpretation of the 1994 Revisions. James L. Lamprecht. ASQ Quality Press. • 1994. $38.00. A review of the ISO 9000 quality standards as they relate to service organizations. Includes examples of applications.

ISO 9000 Auditor's Companion. Kent A. Keeney. ASQ Quality Press. • 1995. $30.00. Designed to help companies prepare for ISO 9000 quality management audits.

ISO 9000 Book: A Global Competitor's Guide to Compliance and Certification. John T. Rabbitt and Peter Bergh. AMACOM. • 1994. $29.95. Second edition.

ISO 9000 Handbook. Robert W. Peach. QSU Publishing Co. • 2003. $99.95. Fourth edition. Includes detailed information for the ISO 9000 registration process.

ISO 9000 Made Easy: A Cost-Saving Guide to Documentation and Registration. Amy Zuckerman. AMACOM. • 1994. $75.00.

ONLINE DATABASES

Scisearch. Institute for Scientific Information. • Broad, multidisciplinary index to the literature of science and technology, 1974 to present. Inquire as to online cost and availability. Coverage of literature is worldwide, with weekly updates.

PERIODICALS AND NEWSLETTERS

ASTM Standardization News. American Society for Testing and Materials. • Monthly. $18.00 per year.

ISO Management Systems. Available from American National Standards Institute. • Bimonthly. Price on application. Newsletter on quality standards. Published by the International Organization for Standardization (ISO). Text in English. Formerly *ISO 9000 and ISO 14000 News.*

Journal of Research of the National Institute of Standards and Technology. Available from U. S. Government Printing Office. • Bimonthly. $47.00 per year. Formerly *Journal of Research of the National Bureau of Standards.*

Standards Action. American National Standards Institute Inc. • Description: Lists new and proposed American National Standards and draft international standards of the International Organization for Standardization (ISO), International Electrotechnical Commission (IEC), European Committee for Standardization (CEN), and European Committee for Electrotechnical Standardization (CENELEC). Lists proposed foreign government regulations from countries that signed the General Agreement on Tariffs and Trade (GATT) Standards Code. Provides listing for registration of organization names in the United States. **Remarks:** Subscription includes ANSI Reporter (see separate listing).

Standards Engineering. Standards Engineering Society. • Bimonthly. $45.00 per year.

TRADE/PROFESSIONAL ASSOCIATIONS

American National Standards Institute. 1819 L St. NW, 6th Fl., Washington, DC 20036. Phone: (202)293-8020 Fax: (202)293-9287 E-mail: info@ansi.org • URL: http://www.ansi.org • Industrial firms, trade associations, technical societies, labor organizations, consumer organizations, and government agencies. Serves as clearinghouse for nationally coordinated voluntary standards for fields ranging from information technology to building construction. Gives status as American National Standards to standards developed by agreement from all groups concerned, in such areas as: definitions, terminology, symbols, and abbreviations; materials, performance characteristics, procedure, and methods of rating; methods of testing and analysis; size, weight, volume, and rating; practice, safety, health, and building construction. Provides information on foreign standards and represents United States interests in international standardization work.

International Organization for Standardization. 1 rue de Varembe-CP56, CH-1211 Geneva 20, Switzerland. Phone: 41 22 7490111 Fax: 41 22 7490948 E-mail: rh@iso.org • URL: http://www.iso.ch/ • Members are national standards organizations. Develops and publishes international standards, including ISO 9000 quality management standards. Affiliated with American National Standards Institute.

NCSL International. 2995 Wilderness Pl., Ste. 107, Boulder, CO 80301-5404. Phone: (303)440-3339 Fax: (303)440-3384 E-mail: info@ncsli.org • URL: http://www.ncsli.org • Representatives of measurements standards and calibration laboratories; organizations with related interests. Seeks cost reduction or solution of problems, both technical and administrative, that besiege all measurement activities in the physical sciences, engineering, and technology. Conducts conferences and meetings for presentation of papers and discussions pertaining to technical and managerial problems, operating practices, and policies for measurement standards laboratories. Works with educational organizations to develop programs for training technical personnel and professional metrologists.

Standards Engineering Society. 13340 SW 96th Ave., Miami, FL 33176. Phone: (305)971-4798 Fax: (305)971-4799 E-mail: admin@ses-standards.org • URL: http://www.ses-standards.org • Engineers, teachers, executives, and scholars interested in practicing standardization. Seeks to further

standardization as a means of enhancing general welfare and to promote knowledge and use of approved standards issued by regularly constituted standardizing bodies.

START-UP PLANS

See: BUSINESS START-UP PLANS AND PROPOSALS

STATE EMPLOYEES

See: GOVERNMENT EMPLOYEES

STATE FINANCE

See: PUBLIC FINANCE

STATE GOVERNMENT

See also: PUBLIC ADMINISTRATION

GENERAL WORKS

Lawmaking and the Legislative Process: Committees, Connections, and Compromises. Greenwood Publishing Group, Inc. • 1996. $29.95. Explains how bills are enacted into laws through the state legislative process. Provides step-by-step examples, using fictitious bills.

Performance Budgeting for State and Local Government. Janet M. Kelly and William C. Rivenbark. M. E. Sharpe, Inc. • 2003. $69.95. Covers performance-based management as applied to local government budgeting.

ABSTRACTS AND INDEXES

Current Law Index: Multiple Access to Legal Periodicals. Gale Cengage Learning. • Monthly. $725.00 per year. Produced in cooperation with the American Association of Law Libraries. Indexes more than 900 law journals, legal newspapers, and specialty publications from the U.S., Canada, U.K., Ireland, Australia, and New Zealand.

ALMANACS AND YEARBOOKS

State Budget Actions, 2000. Corina Eckl and Arturo Perez. National Conference of State Legislatures. • 2000. $35.00. Presents yearly summaries of state spending priorities and fiscal climates. Includes end-of-year general fund balances and other information on state funds.

Suggested State Legislation. Council of State Governments. • Annual. $59.00. A source of legislative ideas and drafting assistance for state government officials.

BIOGRAPHICAL SOURCES

Who's Who in American Politics. Marquis Who's Who. • Biennial. $275.00. Two volumes. Contains about 27,000 biographical sketches of local, state, and national elected or appointed individuals.

CD-ROM DATABASES

Leadership Library on CD-ROM: Who's Who in the Leadership of the United States. Leadership Directories, Inc. • Quarterly. Including access to Internet version (weekly updates). Contains all 14 *Yellow Book* personnel directories on CD-ROM, providing contact and brief biographical information for about 400,000 individuals. Covers business, government, financial institutions, news media, law firms, associations, foreign representatives, and nonprofit organizations. Includes photographs.

Newspaper Abstracts Ondisc. PROQUEST. • Monthly. $2,950.00 per year (covers 1989 to date; archival discs are available for 1985-88). Provides cover-to-cover CD-ROM indexing and abstracting

of 19 major newspapers, including the *New York Times, Wall Street Journal, Washington Post, Chicago Tribune,* and *Los Angeles Times.*

OECD Statistical Compendium. Organization for Economic Cooperation and Development. • Semiannual. $1,905.00 per year for 1 to 10 users. CD-ROM contains more than 730,000 monthly, quarterly, and annual time series for OECD countries, 1960 to date. Includes fully searchable data on agriculture, food, economic indicators, national accounts, employment, energy, finance, industry, technology, and foreign trade. Results can be displayed in various forms.

DIRECTORIES

Book of the States. Council of State Governments. • Biennial. $99.00. Includes information on state constitutions, state-by-state voting in recent elections, data on state finances, and federal-state survey articles.

Business Organizations, Agencies, and Publications Directory. Gale Cengage Learning. • 2003. $480.00. 15th edition. Over 40,000 entries describing 39 types of business information sources. Classified by type of organization, publication, or serviceIncludes state, national, and international agencies and organizations. Master index to names and keywords. Also includes e-mail addresses and web site URL's.

Carroll's State Directory. Carroll Publishing. • Covers: about 73,000 state government officials in all branches of government; officers, committees and members of state legislatures; managers of boards and authorities. Entries include: Name, address, phone, fax, title.

Carroll's State Directory: CD-ROM Edition. Carroll Publishing. • Three times a year. $325.00 per year. Provides CD-ROM listings of about 43,000 state officials, plus the text of all state constitutions and biographies of all governors. Also available online.

CSG State Directories I. Council of State Governments. • Covers: About 8,000 state legislators, elected state executive branch officials, and state supreme court judges. Entries include: Name, title, address, district, party affiliation, fax and facts about each state-motto, flower, bird, nickname, capitol address, bill status phone, land area, population, D. C. Liaison, term limits, election and session dates.

CSG State Directories II: Legislative, Leadership, Committees and Staff by Function. Council of State Governments. • Annual. $49.99. Legislative leaders, committee members and staff, personnel of principal legislative staff offices. Formerly *Book of the States, Supplement Two: State Legislative Leadership, Committees, and Staff.*

Directory of Legislative Leaders. National Conference of State Legislatures. • Annual. $20.00. Lists state presiding officers, majority and minority leaders, and key staff members. Preferred addresses, telephone numbers, and fax numbers are included.

Directory of State Legislatures. National Conference of State Legislatures. • Annual. $85.00. Provides names, addresses, telephone numbers, and e-mail addresses of state legislators and executive officials. Available only online. Formerly *Election Results Directory.*

Government Phone Book USA: Your Comprehensive Guide to Federal, State, County, and Local Government Offices in the United States. Omnigraphics, Inc. • Annual. $265.00. Contains more than 270,000 listings of federal, state, county, and local government offices and personnel, including legislatures. Formerly *Government Directory of Addresses and Phone Numbers.*

Governors' Staff Directory. National Governor's Association. National Governors' Association. • Publication includes: List of more than 1,000 key staff members and their titles in each of the 55 governor's offices. Entries include: Name of governor; addresses, phone numbers and fax numbers of governor's main, district, and Washington offices; names and titles of key staff members; separate listing of addresses and phone numbers of governors' chiefs of staff and media contacts; list of contacts in each office by issue area; list of NGA staff members, their titles, phone numbers, issue areas, and description of the resources NGA provides.

Judicial Yellow Book: Who's Who in Federal and State Courts. Leadership Directories, Inc. • Semiannual. $245.00 per year. Lists more than 3,200 judges and staffs in various federal courts and 1,200 judges and staffs in state courts. Includes biographical profiles of judges.

State Yellow Book: Who's Who in the Executive and Legislative Branches of the 50 Governments. Leadership Directories, Inc. • Quarterly. $360.00 per year. Lists more than 37,000 elected and administrative officials by state, District of Columbia, and U. S. Territory. Includes state profiles, with historical and statistical data. County population and per capita income is also included.

HANDBOOKS AND MANUALS

Mason's Manual of Legislative Procedure. American Society of Legislative Clerks and Secretaries. National Conference of State Legislatures. • 2000. $60.00. Contains parliamentary law and rules, rules of debate, rules governing motions, how to conduct business, etc.

INTERNET DATABASES

Business 2.0 Web Guide to the Best Business Links. Business 2.0 Media Inc. Phone: (415)293-4800 E-mail: support@business2.com • URL: http://www.business2.com/webguide • Web site presents an extensive, searchable directory of links to "the best, most informative, and authoritative web pages." Twenty main categories cover business, finance, career, company information, people, and technology topics, with thousands of subtopics, all linking to Web sites recommended by experienced business researchers. Fees: Free.

Fedstats. Federal Interagency Council on Statistical Policy. Phone: (202)395-7254 • URL: http://www.fedstats.gov • Web site features an efficient search facility for full-text statistics produced by more than 100 federal agencies, including the Census Bureau, the Bureau of Economic Analysis, and the Bureau of Labor Statistics. Boolean searches can be made within one agency or for all agencies combined. Links are offered to international statistical bureaus, including the UN, IMF, OECD, UNESCO, Eurostat, and 20 individual countries. Fees: Free.

FreeLunch.com. Economy.com, Inc. Phone: (610)696-8700 Fax: (610)696-1678 • URL: http://www.freelunch.com • Web site provides free access to more than 1.5 million economic and financial data series, covering industry, demographics, labor markets, prices, retail sales, government spending, trade, interest rates, housing starts, the stock market, and many other topics. Data is available for various time periods in either chart or table form. Searching is offered. Fees: Free, but registration required. Economy.com, Inc. also offers fee-based economic analysis at *The Dismal Scientist* site (http://www.dismal.com).

Lexis.com Research System. Lexis-Nexis Group. Phone: 800-227-4908 or (937)865-6800 Fax: (937)865-6909 E-mail: webmaster@prod.lexis-nexis.com • URL: http://www.lexis.com • Fee-based Web site offers extensive searching of a wide variety of legal sources. Additional features include Daily Opinion Service, lexis.com Bookstore, Career Center, CLE Center, Law Schools, and Practice

Pages ("Pages specific to areas of specialty").

ONLINE DATABASES

Information Bank Abstracts. New York Times Index Dept. • Provides indexing and abstracting of current affairs, primarily from the final late edition of *The New York Times* and the Eastern edition of *The Wall Street Journal.* Time period is 1969 to present, with daily updates. Inquire as to online cost and availability.

PAIS International. Public Affairs Information Service, Inc. • Corresponds to the former printed publications, *PAIS Bulletin* (1976-90) and *PAIS Foreign Language Index* (1972-90), and to the current *PAIS International in Print* (1991 to date). Covers economic, political, and sociological material appearing in periodicals, books, government documents, and other publications. Updating is monthly. Inquire as to online cost and availability.

PERIODICALS AND NEWSLETTERS

Governing: The States and Localities. • Monthly. $39.95 per year. Edited for state and local government officials. Covers finance, office management, computers, telecommunications, environmental concerns, etc.

Government Technology: Solutions for State and Local Government in the Information Age. E. Republic Inc. • Monthly. Free to qualified personnel.

Public Risk. Public Risk Management Association. • 10 times a year. $125.00 per year. Covers risk management for state and local governments, including various kinds of liabilities.

Spectrum: Journal of State Government. Council of State Governments. • Quarterly. $49.99 per year. Formerly *Journal of State Government.*

State Capitals. Wakeman-Walworth, Inc. • Irregular. Prices may vary. A group of 39 newsletters, with each publication having its own subtitle and topic of relevance to state government.

State Government News: The Monthly Magazine Covering All Facets of State Government. Council of State Governments. • Monthly. $39.00 per year.

State Legislative Report. National Conference of State Legislatures. • Description: Contains briefings on topics of state legislative concerns covering a broad range of policy issues.

State Legislatures. National Conference of State Legislatures. • Description: Provides a national perspective on government and policy in the each state. Features articles on public policy issues.

RESEARCH CENTERS AND INSTITUTES

Academy for State and Local Government. 444 N. Capitol St., N.W., Suite 345, Washington, DC 20001. Phone: (202)434-4850 Fax: (202)434-4851 E-mail: aelsbree@sso.org.

STATISTICS SOURCES

Almanac of the Fifty States: Basic Data Profiles with Comparative Tables. Information Publications. • Annual. $65.00.

Business Statistics of the United States. Linz Audain and Cornelia J. Strawser. Bernan Associates. • Annual. $147.00. Based on *Business Statistics,* formerly issue by the Bureau of Economic Analysis, U. S. Department of Commerce. Provides basic data for a wide variety of U. S. industries, services, and economic indicators. Most statistics are shown annually for 30 years and monthly for the most recent four years.

Gale State Rankings Reporter. Gale Cengage Learning. • 1996. $130.00. Second edition Provides 3,000 ranked lists of states under 35 subject headings. Sources are newspapers, periodicals, books, research institute publications, and government publications.

State Profiles: The Population and Economy of Each U. S. State. Courtenay Slater and Others. Bernan Press. • 1999. $89.00. Presents charts, tables, and text in an eight-page profile for each state. Covers population, labor force, income, poverty, employment, wages, industry, trade, housing, education, health, taxes, and government finances. (The Population and Economy of Each United States Series).

Survey of Current Business. Available from U. S. Government Printing Office. • Monthly. $63.00 per year. Issued by Bureau of Economic Analysis, U. S. Department of Commerce. Presents a wide variety of business and economic data.

TRADE/PROFESSIONAL ASSOCIATIONS

Council of State Governments. 2760 Research Park Dr., Lexington, KY 40578-1910. Phone: 800-800-1910 or (859)244-8000 Fax: (859)244-8001 E-mail: web_editor@csg.org • URL: http://www.csg.org • Supersedes American Legislator Association.

National Association of State Budget Officers. Hall of States, 444 N Capitol St. NW, Ste. 642, Washington, DC 20001-1511. Phone: (202)624-5382 Fax: (202)624-7745 E-mail: nasbo-direct@nasbo.org • URL: http://www.nasbo.org.

National Association of State Procurement Officials. c/o Association Management Resources, 167 W. Main St., Suite 600, Lexington, KY 40507. Phone: (859)231-1877 or (606)231-1963 Fax: (859)514-9188 E-mail: msisler@amrinc.net • URL: http://www.naspo.org • Purchasing officials of the states and territories. Formerly National Association of State Purchasing Officials.

National Conference of State Legislatures. 1560 Broadway, Ste. 700, 7700 E First Pl., Denver, CO 80230. Phone: (303)364-7700 Fax: (303)364-7800 E-mail: info@ncsl.org • URL: http://www.ncsl.org • Affiliated with Council of State Governments.

National Governors Association. Hall of States, 444 N Capitol St., Ste. 267, Washington, DC 20001-1512. Phone: (202)624-5300 Fax: (202)624-5313 E-mail: webmaster@nga.org • URL: http://www.nga.org • Governors of the 50 states, Guam, American Samoa, the Virgin Islands, the Northern Mariana Islands, and Puerto Rico. Serves as vehicle through which governors influence the development and implementation of national policy and apply creative leadership to state problems. Keeps the federal establishment informed of the needs and perceptions of states. Through its Center for Best Practices, it provides a vehicle for sharing information on innovative programs among the states and providing technical assistance to governors on a wide range of issues.

Public Risk Management Association. 500 Montgomery St., Ste. 750, Alexandria, VA 22314. Phone: (703)528-7701 Fax: (703)739-0200 E-mail: info@primacentral.org • URL: http://www.primacentral.org • Public agency risk, insurance, human resources, attorneys, and/or safety managers from cities, counties, villages, towns, school boards, and other related areas. Provides an information clearinghouse and communications network for public risk managers to share resources, ideas, and experiences. Offers information on risk, insurance, and safety management. Monitors state and federal legislative actions and court decisions that deal with immunity, tort liability, and intergovernmental risk pools. Maintains library containing current reports from governmental units on their insurance procedures, self-insurance plans, and loss control and safety programs; and copies of policy statements, job descriptions, contractual arrangements, and indemnification clauses.

State Government Affairs Council. 515 King St., Ste. 325, Alexandria, VA 22314. Phone: (703)684-0967 Fax: (703)684-0968 E-mail: stategov@sgac.org • URL: http://www.sgac.org • Businesses and organizations of businesses operating in multiple states. Each member has an established officer, employee or department who represents the company or organization in state legislative, regulatory or public affairs matters. Seeks to improve the state legislative process through interaction with major state governmental conferences. Acts as liaison with National Conference of State Legislatures, Council of State Governments (see separate entries) and governors' associations. Through State +Government +Affairs Council Foundation program, conducts educational programs on issues of public policy concern in order to further understanding between private sector business and state legislatures and agencies.

OTHER SOURCES

Government Discrimination: Equal Protection Law and Litigation. James A. Kushner. West Group. • Semiannual. $244.00 per year. Looseleaf service. Covers discrimination in employment, housing, and other areas by local, state, and federal offices or agencies. (Civil Rights Series).

STATE INCOME TAX

See: STATE TAXES

STATE LAW

See also: SALES TAX

ABSTRACTS AND INDEXES
Index to Legal Periodicals and Books. H. W. Wilson Co. • Monthly. $490.00 per year. Quarterly and annual cumulations.

ALMANACS AND YEARBOOKS
Suggested State Legislation. Council of State Governments. • Annual. $59.00. A source of legislative ideas and drafting assistance for state government officials.

BIBLIOGRAPHIES
Encyclopedia of Legal Information Sources. Gale Cengage Learning. • 1992. $180.00. Second edition. Lists more than 23,000 law-related information sources, including print, nonprint, and organizational.

DIRECTORIES
Book of the States. Council of State Governments. • Biennial. $99.00. Includes information on state constitutions, state-by-state voting in recent elections, data on state finances, and federal-state survey articles.

Directory of Building Codes and Regulations. National Conference of States on Building Codes and Standards. • Annual. Optional quarterly updates. Two volumes. Members, $115.00; non-members, $150.00. In addition to information about residential and commerical building codes,includes a directory of state and majority administrators concerned with enforcement of the codes.

Law and Legal Information Directory. Gale Cengage Learning. • Annual. $440.00. Contains a wide range of sources of legal information, such as associations, law schools, courts, federal agencies, referral services, libraries, publishers, and research centers. There is a separate chapter for each of 23 types of information source or service.

Martindale-Hubbell Law Directory. Martindale-Hubbell Inc. • Covers: lawyers and law firms in the United States, its possessions, and Canada, plus leading law firms worldwide; includes a biographical section by firm, and a separate list of patent lawyers, attorneys in government service, in-house counsel, and services, suppliers, and consultants to the legal profession. Entries include: For nonsubscribing lawyers--Name, year of birth and of first admission to bar, code indicating college and law school attended and first degree, firm name (or other affiliation, if any) and relationship to firm, whether practicing other than as individual or in partnership. For subscribing lawyers--Above information plus complete address, phone, fax, e-mail and URL, type of practice, clients, plus additional personal details (education, certifications, etc.). A general law list. See separate listing, 'Law Lists'.

HANDBOOKS AND MANUALS
National Survey of State Laws. Gale Cengage Learning. • 2002. $105.00. Fourth edition. Provides concise state-by-state comparisons of current state laws on a wide variety of topics. Includes references to specific codes or statutes.

ONLINE DATABASES
Index to Legal Periodicals and Books (Online). H. W. Wilson Co. • Broad coverage of law journals and books 1981 to date. Monthly updates. Inquire as to online cost and availability.

Legal Resource Index. Gale Cengage Learning. • Broad coverage of law literature appearing in legal, business, and other periodicals, 1980 to date. Daily updates. Inquire as to online cost and availability.

LEXIS. LEXIS-NEXIS. • The various LEXIS databases provide full text and indexing for a wide variety of legal cases, statutes, orders, and opinions.

PERIODICALS AND NEWSLETTERS
Land Use Law and Zoning Digest. American Planning Association. • Monthly. $275.00 per year. Covers judicial decisions and state laws affecting zoning and land use. Edited for city planners and lawyers. Monthly supplement available *Zoning News.*

State Legislative Report. National Conference of State Legislatures. • Description: Contains briefings on topics of state legislative concerns covering a broad range of policy issues.

TRADE/PROFESSIONAL ASSOCIATIONS
Council of State Governments. 2760 Research Park Dr., Lexington, KY 40578-1910. Phone: 800-800-1910 or (859)244-8000 Fax: (859)244-8001 E-mail: web_editor@csg.org • URL: http://www.csg.org • Supersedes American Legislator Association.

National Association of Attorneys General. 750 First St., N.E., Suite 1100, Washington, DC 20002. Phone: (202)326-6000 Fax: (202)408-7014 • URL: http://www.naag.org.

National Conference of Commissioners on Uniform State Laws. 211 E. Ontario St., Ste. 1300, Chicago, IL 60611. Phone: (312)915-0195 Fax: (312)915-0187 E-mail: nccusl@nccusl.org • URL: http://www.nccusl.org.

National Conference of State Legislatures. 1560 Broadway, Ste. 700, 7700 E First Pl., Denver, CO 80230. Phone: (303)364-7700 Fax: (303)364-7800 E-mail: info@ncsl.org • URL: http://www.ncsl.org • Affiliated with Council of State Governments.

North American Securities Administrators Association. 750 1st St. NE, Ste. 1140, Washington, DC 20002-8034. Phone: 800-84-NASAA or (202)737-0900 Fax: (202)783-3571 E-mail: info@nasaa.org • URL: http://www.nasaa.org • Represents the interests of the state, provincial and territorial securities administrators in the U.S., Canada, Mexico and Puerto Rico. Provides support to its members in government relations and with federal regulators, industry SROs and other groups.

OTHER SOURCES
Labor Relations. CCH, Inc. • $2,589.00 per year. Seven looseleaf volumes. Weekly updates. Covers labor relations, wages and hours, state labor laws, and employment practices. Supplement available. *Labor Law Reports.* Summary Newsletter.

STATE LEGISLATURES

See: LEGISLATURES; STATE GOVERNMENT

STATE TAXES

See also: TAXATION

CD-ROM DATABASES
The Tax Directory [CD-ROM]. Tax Analysts. • Quarterly. Provides *The Tax Directory* listings on CD-ROM, covering federal, state, and international tax officials, tax practitioners, and corporate tax executives.

DIRECTORIES
The Tax Directory. Tax Analysts. • Covers: Volume One--Approximately 15,000 federal and state government tax legislators, policymakers, administrators, and employees; tax regulation attorneys; over 500 international tax officials with central banks, ministries of finance, foreign embassies and consulate, and chambers of commerce; over 300 tax and business journalists and editors working for magazines, journals, newspapers, television, and radio; tax sections of over 100 trade and professional associations; state CPA, bar, and enrolled agent associations. Volume Two--Over 5,000 corporate tax managers of large U.S. and international firms. Entries include: For government and international officials--Name, title, address, phone, fax, email and website. For corporate tax managers--Name, address, phone, fax, email, website, and company name. For journalists--Name, address, phone, fax, email, website, and name of publication/network. For organizations and associations--Name, address, phone, fax, email, website, budget, membership, background information, and description of purpose.

HANDBOOKS AND MANUALS
All States Tax Handbook. RIA. • Annual. $53.50. Tax structures for fifty states.

Cybertaxation: The Taxation of E-Commerce. Karl A. Frieden. CCH, Inc. • 2000. $75.00. Includes state sales and use tax issues and corporate income tax rules, as related to doing business over the Internet.

Sales and Use Taxation of E-Commerce: State Tax Administrators' Current Thinking, with CCH Commentary. CCH, Inc. • 2000. $129.00. Provides advice and information on the impact of state sales taxes on e-commerce activity.

State Tax Actions. National Conference of State Legislatures. • Annual. $35.00. Summarizes yearly tax changes by type and by state.

U. S. Master Multistate Corporate Tax Guide. CCH, Inc. • Annual. $72.00. Provides corporate income tax information for 47 states, New York City, and the District of Columbia.

U. S. Master Property Tax Guide. CCH, Inc. • Annual. $72.00. Provides state-by-state coverage of "key property tax issues and concepts," including exemptions, assessments, taxpayer remedies, and property tax calendars.

U. S. Master Sales and Use Tax Guide. CCH, Inc. • Annual. $69.00. Contains concise information on sales and use taxes in all states and the District of Columbia.

INTERNET DATABASES
Rutgers Accounting Web (RAW). Rutgers University Accounting Research Center. Phone: (973)353-5172 Fax: (973)353-1283 • URL: http://www.rutgers.edu/accounting • RAW Web site provides extensive links to sources of national and international accounting information, such as the Big Six accounting firms, the Financial Accounting Standards Board (FASB), SEC filings (EDGAR), journals, publishers, software, the International Accounting Network, and "Internet's largest list of accounting firms in USA." Searching is offered. Fees: Free.

ONLINE DATABASES
Accounting and Tax Database. PROQUEST. • Provides indexing and abstracting of the literature of

accounting, taxation, and financial management, 1971 to date. Updating is weekly. Especially covers accounting, auditing, banking, bankruptcy, employee compensation and benefits, cash management, financial planning, and credit. Inquire as to online cost and availability.

PERIODICALS AND NEWSLETTERS

E-Commerce Tax Alert. CCH Inc. • Description: Print and online newsletter covering e-commerce taxation issues, including compliance and sourcing, e-cash implications, the Internet tax debate, and other topics.

Highlights and Documents. Tax Analysts. • Daily. $2,249.00 per year, including monthly indexes. Newsletter. Provides daily coverage of IRS, congressional, judicial, state, and international tax developments. Includes abstracts and citations for "all tax documents released within the previous 24 to 48 hours." Annual compilation available *Highlights and Documents on Microfiche*.

Interstate Tax Insights. Interstate Tax Corp. • Monthly. $195.00 per year. Looseleaf service. Formerly *Interstate Tax Report*.

State Income Tax Alert. State Taxation Institute. • Description: Features updates on state income tax issues. Recurring features include a calendar of events, book reviews, and news of educational opportunities.

State Tax Notes. Tax Analysts. • Weekly. $949.00 per year, including annual CD-ROM. Newsletter. Covers tax developments in all states. Provides state tax document summaries and citations.

RESEARCH CENTERS AND INSTITUTES

Office of Tax Policy Research. University of Michigan, 701 Tappan St., Ann Arbor, MI 48109-1234. Phone: (734)763-3068 Fax: (734)763-4032 E-mail: otpr@umich.edu • URL: http://www.taxpolicyresearch.umich.edu/.

Tax Foundation. Tax Foundation. 2001 L St. NW, Ste. 1050, Washington, DC 20036. Phone: (202)464-6200 Fax: (202)464-6201 E-mail: hodge@taxfoundation.org • URL: http://www.taxfoundation.org • Fiscal and management aspects of federal, state, and local government, including studies on government expenditures, the federal budget, taxation, and international competitiveness. Serves as a national information agency for individuals and organizations concerned with problems of government expenditures, taxation, and debt.

STATISTICS SOURCES

Gale State Rankings Reporter. Gale Cengage Learning. • 1996. $130.00. Second edition Provides 3,000 ranked lists of states under 35 subject headings. Sources are newspapers, periodicals, books, research institute publications, and government publications.

State Profiles: The Population and Economy of Each U. S. State. Courtenay Slater and Others. Bernan Press. • 1999. $89.00. Presents charts, tables, and text in an eight-page profile for each state. Covers population, labor force, income, poverty, employment, wages, industry, trade, housing, education, health, taxes, and government finances. (The Population and Economy of Each United States Series).

Statistical Abstract of the United States. Available from U. S. Government Printing Office. • Annual. $51.00. Issued by the U. S. Bureau of the Census.

TRADE/PROFESSIONAL ASSOCIATIONS

Federation of Tax Administrators. 444 N. Capitol St., Suite 348, Washington, DC 20001. Phone: (202)624-5890 Fax: (202)624-7888 E-mail: fta@taxadmin.org • URL: http://www.taxadmin.org.

OTHER SOURCES

All States Tax Guide. Prentice Hall PTR. • Looseleaf. Periodic supplementation. Price on

application. One volume summary of taxes for all states.

Manufacturers' Tax Alert. CCH, Inc. • Monthly $297.00 per year. Newsletter. Covers the major tax issues affecting manufacturing companies. Includes current developments in various kind of federal, state, and international taxes: sales, use, franchise, property, and corporate income.

Multi-State Sales Tax Guide. CCH, Inc. • $1,349.00 per year. Looseleaf service. Nine volumes. Periodic supplementation. Formerly *All State Sales Tax Reports*.

STATIONERY INDUSTRY

See: OFFICE EQUIPMENT AND SUPPLIES

STATISTICAL METHODS

See also: BUSINESS MATHEMATICS; BUSINESS STATISTICS; ECONOMIC STATISTICS; MARKET STATISTICS

GENERAL WORKS

Business Statistics: Contemporary Decision Making. Ken Black. South-Western. • 2000. $107.95. Third edition.

Business Statistics for Management and Economics. Wayne W. Daniel and James C. Terrell. Houghton Mifflin Co. • 1995. $23.96. Seventh edition.

Business Statistics for Quality and Productivity. John M. Levine. Prentice Hall PTR. • 1994. $94.07. (Prentice Hall College Title Series).

Business Statistics Practice. Bruce L. Bowerman and others. McGraw-Hill. • 2001. $68.00. Second edition.

How to Lie with Statistics. Darrell Huff. W. W. Norton and Co., Inc. • 1993. $11.00.

Statistics for People Who Think They Hate Statistics. Neil J. Salkind. Sage Publications, Inc. • 2004. $84.95. Second edition. Serves as a clearly-written introduction to a wide variety of statistical procedures. Includes a glossary.

The Visual Display of Quantitative Information. Edward R. Tufte. Graphics Press. • 2001. $40.00. Second edition. A classic work on the graphic display of numerical data, including many illustrations. The two parts are "Graphical Practice," and "Theory of Data Graphics.".

ABSTRACTS AND INDEXES

Current Index to Statistics: Applications, Methods, and Theory. American Statistical Association. • Annual. Price on application. An index to journal articles on statistical applications and methodology.

Institute of Mathematical Statistics Bulletin. Institute of Mathematical Statistics. • Bimonthly. $60.00 per year.

Statistical Theory and Method Abstracts. International Statistical Institute. • Quarterly. Members, $100.00 per year; non-members, $140.00 per year. Worldwide coverage of published papers on mathematical statistics and probability.

CD-ROM DATABASES

MathSci Disc. American Mathematical Society. • Semiannual. Price on application. Provides CD-ROM citations, with abstracts, to the literature of mathematics, statistics, and computer science, 1940 to date.

Science Citation Index: Compact Disc Edition. Institute for Scientific Information. • Monthly. Provides CD-ROM indexing of the world's scientific and technical literature. Corresponds to online *Scisearch* and printed *Science Citation Index*.

ENCYCLOPEDIAS AND DICTIONARIES

A Dictionary of Statistical Terms. F.H. Marriott. Addison-Wesley. • 1996. $76.67. Fifth edition.

Encyclopedia of Statistical Sciences. Samuel I. Kotz and others, editors. John Wiley and Sons, Inc. • 2003. $3,725.00. 13 volumes. Includes *Supplements* and *Updates*. Price varies for each individual volume.

HANDBOOKS AND MANUALS

Basic Statistics for Business and Economics. Douglas A. Lind and others. McGraw-Hill. • 2002. Fourth edition. Price on application. (Operations and Decision Sciences Series).

Descriptive Statistical Techniques for Librarians. Arthur W. Hafner. American Library Association. • 1997. $55.00 Second edition.

General Statistics. Warren Chase and Fred Brown. John Wiley and Sons, Inc. • 1999. $98.95 Fourth edition. Includes CD-ROM.

The Numbers You Need. Gale Cengage Learning. • 1993. $75.00. Contains mathematical equations, formulas, charts, and graphs, including many that are related to business or finance. Explanations, step-by-step directions, and examples of use are provided.

Practical Business Statistics: StatPad Manual. Andrew F. Siegel. McGraw-Hill. • 1996. Third edition. $20.63.

Statistical Methods for the Information Professional: A Practical, Painless Approach to Understanding, Using, and Interpreting Statistics. Liwen Vaughan. Information Today, Inc. • 2001. $39.50. Published in conjunction with the American Society for Information Science and Technology (ASIST).

Statistical Techniques in Business and Economics. Douglas A. Lind and others. McGraw-Hill. • 2001. 11th edition. Price on application.

Statistics for the Environment: Statistical Aspects of Health and the Environment. Vic Barnett and others. John Wiley and Sons, Inc. • 1999. $180.00. Two volumes. Vol. 3, $205.00; vol. 4, $225.00. Contains articles on the statistical analysis and interpretation of environmental monitoring and sampling data. Areas covered include meteorology, pollution of the environment, and forest resources. (Statistics for the Environment Series).

ONLINE DATABASES

MathSci. American Mathematical Society. • Provides online citations, with abstracts, to the literature of mathematics, statistics, and computer science. Time period is 1940 to date, with monthly updates. Inquire as to online cost and availability.

Scisearch. Institute for Scientific Information. • Broad, multidisciplinary index to the literature of science and technology, 1974 to present. Inquire as to online cost and availability. Coverage of literature is worldwide, with weekly updates.

PERIODICALS AND NEWSLETTERS

American Statistician. American Statistical Association. • Quarterly. Individuals, $15.00 per year; libraries, $75.00 per year; students, $15.00 per year.

Annals of Probability. Institute of Mathematical Statistics. • Quarterly. $200.00 per year.

Annals of Statistics. Institute of Mathematical Statistics. • Bimonthly. $220.00 per year.

JASA (Journal of the American Statistical Association). American Statistical Association. • Quarterly. Members, $39.00 per year; non-members, $310.00 per year; students, $10.00 per year.

Journal of Business and Economic Statistics. American Statistical Association. • Quarterly. Libraries, $90.00 per year. Emphasis is on statistical measurement and applications for business and economics.

Mathematical Finance: An International Journal of Mathematics, Statistics, and Financial Economics.

Blackwell Publishing. • Quarterly. Institutions, $683.00 per year. Includes online edition. Covers the use of sophisticated mathematical tools in financial research and practice.

The Review of Economics and Statistics. Harvard University, Economics Dept. MIT Press. • Quarterly. Individuals, $53.00 per year; institutions, $275.00 per year; students and retired persons, $28.00 per year.

RESEARCH CENTERS AND INSTITUTES

Center for Mathematical Studies in Economics and Management Sciences. Northwestern University, Weinberg College of Arts and Sciences, Dept. of Economics, 2001 Sheridan Rd., 302 Arthur Andersen Hall, Evanston, IL 60208-2600. Phone: (847)491-5140 Fax: (847)491-7001 • URL: http://www.kellogg.nwu.edu/research/math.

Center for Quality and Productivity. University of North Texas, College of Business Administration, P.P. Box 305249, Denton, TX 76203-3677. Phone: (940)565-4767 E-mail: prybutok@unt.edu • URL: http://www.coba.unt.edu • Fields of research include the management of quality systems and statistical methodology.

Center for Statistical Consultation and Research. University of Michigan. 3550 Rockham, 915 E. Washington St., Ann Arbor, MI 48109-1070. Phone: (734)764-7828 Fax: (734)647-2440 E-mail: cscar@umich.edu • URL: http://www.umich.edu/.

Cowles Foundation for Research in Economics. Yale University. 30 Hillhouse Ave., New Haven, CT 06520-8281. Phone: (203)432-3704 Fax: (203)432-6167 E-mail: john.geanakoplos@yale.edu • URL: http://www.cowles.econ.yale.edu.

TRADE/PROFESSIONAL ASSOCIATIONS

American Statistical Association. 732 N Washington St., Alexandria, VA 22314-1943. Phone: 888-231-3473 or (703)684-1221 Fax: (703)684-2037 E-mail: asainfo@amstat.org • URL: http://www.amstat.org • Professional society of persons interested in the theory, methodology, and application of statistics to all fields of human endeavor.

Institute of Mathematical Statistics. PO Box 22718, Beachwood, OH 44122. Phone: (216)295-2340 Fax: (216)921-6703 E-mail: ims@stat.org • URL: http://www.imstat.org • Professional society of mathematicians and others interested in mathematical statistics and probability theory.

STATISTICS, BUSINESS

See: BUSINESS STATISTICS

STATISTICS, MATHEMATICAL

See: STATISTICAL METHODS

STATISTICS SOURCES

See also: BUSINESS STATISTICS; ECONOMIC STATISTICS; MARKET STATISTICS

GENERAL WORKS

Global Economic Prospects 2004. The World Bank Group. • 2003. $38.00. "..offers an in-depth analysis of the economic prospects of developing countries.." Emphasis is on the impact of recessions and financial crises. Regional statistical data is included.

ABSTRACTS AND INDEXES

American Statistics Index: A Comprehensive Guide and Index to the Statistical Publications of the United States Government. Congressional Informa-

tion Service, Inc. • Monthly. Price varies. Quarterly and annual cumulations.

Investment Statistics Locator. Linda H. Bentley and Jennifer J. Kiesl, editors. Greenwood Publishing Group, Inc. • 1994. $69.95. Expanded revised edition. Provides detailed subject indexing of more than 50 of the most-used sources of financial and investment data. Includes an annotated bibliography.

Statistical Reference Index: A Selective Guide to American Statistical Publications from Sources Other than the United States Government. Congressional Information Service, Inc. • Monthly. Price varies. Quarterly and annual cumulations. Service basis.

ALMANACS AND YEARBOOKS

Irwin Business and Investment Almanac, 1994: Dow Jones and Company Edition. Summer N. Levine and Caroline Levine. McGraw-Hill. • 1994. $75.00. 18th edition. A review of last year's business activity. Covers a wide variety of business and economic data: stock market statistics, industrial information, commodity futures information, art market trends, comparative living costs for U. S. metropolitan areas, foreign stock market data, etc. Formerly *Business One Irwin Business and Investment Almanac.*

The Statesman's Yearbook: Statistical and Historical Annual of the States of the World. Saint Martin's Press. • Annual. $120.00.

The World Almanac and Book of Facts. World Almanac Books. • Annual. $11.95.

World Development Report 2004. The World Bank Group. • Annual. $26.00. Covers history, conditions, and trends relating to economic globalization and localization. Includes selected data from *World Development Indicators* for 132 countries or economies. Key indicators are provided for 78 additional countries or economies.

BIBLIOGRAPHIES

Data Sources for Business and Market Analysis. John Ganly. Scarecrow Press, Inc. • 1994. $60.00. Fourth edition. Emphasis is on sources of statistics for market research, especially government sources. Relevant directories, periodicals, and research aids are included.

Global Data Locator. George T. Kurian. Bernan Associates. • 1997. $89.00. Provides detailed descriptions of international statistical sourcebooks and electronic databases. Covers a wide variety of trade, economic, and demographic topics.

Guide to Special Issues and Indexes of Periodicals. Miriam Uhlan and Doris B. Katz, editors. Special Libraries Association. • 1994. $59.00. Fourth edition. A listing, with prices, of the special issues of over 1700 U. S. and Canadian periodicals in business, industry, technology, science, and the arts. Includes a comprehensive subject index.

Statistics Sources: A Subject Guide to Data on Industrial, Business, Social, Educational, Financial and Other Topics for the U. S. and Selected Foreign Countries. Gale Cengage Learning. • 2003. $515.00. 27th edition. Two volumes. Lists sources of statistical information for more than 20,000 topics.

World Directory of Non-Official Statistical Sources. Gale Group, Inc. • 2002. $650.00. Fourth edition. Provides detailed descriptions of more than 4,000 regularly published, non-governmental statistics sources. Includes surveys, studies, market research reports, trade journals, databank compilations, and other print sources. Coverage is international, with four indexes.

CD-ROM DATABASES

OECD Statistical Compendium. Organization for Economic Cooperation and Development. • Semiannual. $1,905.00 per year for 1 to 10 users. CD-ROM contains more than 730,000 monthly, quarterly, and annual time series for OECD countries, 1960 to date. Includes fully searchable

data on agriculture, food, economic indicators, national accounts, employment, energy, finance, industry, technology, and foreign trade. Results can be displayed in various forms.

Sourcebook America. Gale Cengage Learning. • Annual. $995.00. Produced by CACI Marketing Systems. A combination on CD-ROM of *The Sourcebook of ZIP Code Demographics* and *The Sourcebook of County Demographics.* Provides detailed population and socio-economic data (about 75 items) for each of 3,141 U. S. counties and approximately 30,000 ZIP codes, plus states, metropolitan areas, and media market areas. Includes forecasts to the year 2004.

Statistical Abstract of the United States on CD-ROM. Hoover's, Inc. • Annual. $49.95. Provides all statistics from official print version, plus expanded historical data, greater detail, and keyword searching features.

World Development Report [CD-ROM]. The World Bank, Office of the Publisher. • Annual. CD-ROM includes the current edition of *World Development Report* and 21 previous editions.

DIRECTORIES

The Internet Blue Pages: The Guide to Federal Government Web Sites. Information Today, Inc. • Annual. $34.95. Provides information on more than 1,800 Web sites used by various agencies of the federal government. Includes indexes to agencies and topics. Links to all Web sites listed are available at http://www.fedweb.com. (CyberAge Books.).

Marketing Know-How: Your Guide to the Best Marketing Tools and Sources. Primedia Business Magazines and Media. • 1996. $49.95. Describes more than 700 public and private sources of consumer marketing data. Also discusses market trends and provides information on such marketing techniques as cluster analysis, focus groups, and geodemographic analysis.

HANDBOOKS AND MANUALS

Dun & Bradstreet/Gale Group Industry Handbooks. Gale Cengage Learning. • 2000. $650.00. Five volumes. $130.00 per volume. Each volume covers two or more major industries: 1. *Entertainment and Hospitality*; 2. *Construction and Agriculture*; 3. *Chemicals and Pharmaceuticals*; 4. *Computers & Software and Broadcasting & Telecommunications*; 5. *Insurance and Health & Medical Services.* The following are included for each industry: overview, statistics, financial ratios, rankings, merger information, company directory, directory of associations, and consultants directory. (Dun and Bradstreet/Gale Industry Reference Handbook Series).

Finding Statistics Online: How to Locate the Elusive Numbers You Need. Paula Berinstein. Information Today, Inc. • 1998. $29.95. Provides advice on efficient searching when looking for statistical data on the World Wide Web or from commercial online services and database producers. (CyberAge Books.).

The Skeptical Business Searcher: The Information Advisor's Guide to Evaluating Web Data, Sites, and Sources. Robert Berkman. Information Today, Inc. • 2003. $29.95. Covers free Internet sources of company backgrounds, sales data, earnings, SEC documents, competitive intelligence information, poll data, business news, economic statistics, etc. The author is editor of *The Information Advisor* newsletter. (CyberAge Books).

Tracking America's Economy. Norman Frumkin. M. E. Sharpe, Inc. • 2004. $72.95. Fourth edition. Provides detailed explanations of the meaning and methodology of the leading U. S. economic indicators. Covers such topics as employment data, financial indicators, productivity, housing, government spending, balance of payments, and taxation.

Understanding the Census: A Guide for Marketers, Planners, Grant Writers, and Other Data Users.

Michael R. Lavin. Epoch Books, Inc. • 1996. $49.95. Contains basic explanations of U. S. Census "concepts, methods, terminology, and data sources." Includes practical advice for locating and using Census data.

Using Government Information Sources, Electronic and Print. Marilyn K. Moody and Jean L. Sears. Greenwood Publishing Group, Inc. • 2001. $125.00. Third edition. Contains detailed information in four sections on subject searches, agency searches, statistical searches, and special techniques for searching. Appendixes give selected agency and publisher addresses, telephone numbers, and computer communications numbers.

INTERNET DATABASES

Business 2.0 Web Guide to the Best Business Links. Business 2.0 Media Inc. Phone: (415)293-4800 E-mail: support@business2.com • URL: http://www.business2.com/webguide • Web site presents an extensive, searchable directory of links to "the best, most informative, and authoritative web pages." Twenty main categories cover business, finance, career, company information, people, and technology topics, with thousands of subtopics, all linking to Web sites recommended by experienced business researchers. Fees: Free.

Fedstats. Federal Interagency Council on Statistical Policy. Phone: (202)395-7254 • URL: http://www.fedstats.gov • Web site features an efficient search facility for full-text statistics produced by more than 100 federal agencies, including the Census Bureau, the Bureau of Economic Analysis, and the Bureau of Labor Statistics. Boolean searches can be made within one agency or for all agencies combined. Links are offered to international statistical bureaus, including the UN, IMF, OECD, UNESCO, Eurostat, and 20 individual countries. Fees: Free.

FedWorld: A Program of the United States Department of Commerce. National Technical Information Service. Phone: (703)605-6000 Fax: (703)605-6900 E-mail: webmaster@fedworld.gov • URL: http://www.fedworld.gov • Web site offers "a comprehensive central access point for searching, locating, ordering, and acquiring government and business information." Emphasis is on searching the Web pages, databases, and government reports of a wide variety of federal agencies. Fees: Free.

FirstGov: Your First Click to the U. S. Government. General Services Administration. Phone: 800-333-4636 or (202)501-0705 E-mail: public.affairs@gsa.gov • URL: http://www.firstgov.gov • Free Web site provides extensive links to federal agencies covering a wide variety of topics, such as agriculture, business, consumer safety, education, the environment, government jobs, grants, health, social security, statistics sources, taxes, technology, travel, and world affairs. Also provides links to federal forms, including IRS tax forms. Searching is offered, both keyword and advanced.

FreeLunch.com. Economy.com, Inc. Phone: (610)696-8700 Fax: (610)696-1678 • URL: http://www.freelunch.com • Web site provides free access to more than 1.5 million economic and financial data series, covering industry, demographics, labor markets, prices, retail sales, government spending, trade, interest rates, housing starts, the stock market, and many other topics. Data is available for various time periods in either chart or table form. Searching is offered. Fees: Free, but registration required. Economy.com, Inc. also offers fee-based economic analysis at *The Dismal Scientist* site (http://www.dismal.com).

InSite 2. Intelligence Data/Thomson Financial. Phone: 800-654-0393 or (617)856-1890 Fax: (617)737-3182 E-mail: intelligence.data@tfn.com. • URL: http://www.insite2.gale.com/ • Fee-based Web site consolidates information in a "Base Pack" consisting of Business InSite, Market InSite, and Company InSite. Optional databases are Consumer InSite, Health and Wellness InSite, Newsletter InSite, and Computer InSite. Includes fulltext content from more than 2,500 trade publications, journals, newsletters, newspapers, analyst reports, and other sources. Continuous updating. Formerly produced by The Gale Group.

U. S. Census Bureau: The Official Statistics. U. S. Bureau of the Census. Phone: (301)763-4100 Fax: (301)763-4794 • URL: http://www.census.gov • Web site is "Your Source for Social, Demographic, and Economic Information." Contains "Current U. S. Population Count," "Current Economic Indicators," and a wide variety of data under "Other Official Statistics." Keyword searching is provided. Fees: Free.

ONLINE DATABASES

Catalog of U.S. Government Publications. U. S. Government Printing Office. • Contains over 375,000 online citations to U. S. government publications, 1976 to date, with monthly updates. Corresponds to the printed *Monthly Catalog of United States Government Publications.* Inquire as to online cost and availability.

Globalbase. Gale Cengage Learning. • Provides more than one million online summaries of business, industrial, and economic news reports from more than 1,000 publications worldwide. Covers a wide range of material appearing in international trade journals, professional magazines, and newspapers. Time period is 1984 to date, with weekly updates. Inquire as to online cost and availability.

GPO Sales Product Catalog. U. S. Government Printing Office. • An online guide to federal government publications in print (currently for sale), forthcoming, and recently out-of-print. Daily updates. Inquire as to online cost and availability.

Market Share Reporter (MSR) [online]. Gale Cengage Learning. • Provides online market share data for individual companies, products, and services, covering all industries. Sources include various publications, trade journals, associations, government agencies, corporate reports, investment research reports, etc. Time period is 1991 to date, with annual updates. Inquire as to online cost and availability.

Tablebase. Gale Cengage Learning. • Provides online numerical tabular data from a wide variety of business, organization, and government sources, including about 1,000 trade journals. Includes industry and individual company statistics relating to products, market share, sales forecasts, production, exports, market trends, etc. Time span is 1997 to date. Weekly updates. Inquire as to online cost and availability. (Also available in a CD-ROM version.).

PERIODICALS AND NEWSLETTERS

Internet Connection: Your Guide to Government Resources. Glasser Legalworks. • 10 times a year. $89.00 per year. Newsletter (print) devoted to finding free or low-cost U. S. Government information on the Internet. Provides detailed descriptions of government Web sites.

STATISTICS SOURCES

Business Statistics of the United States. Linz Audain and Cornelia J. Strawser. Bernan Associates. • Annual. $147.00. Based on *Business Statistics,* formerly issue by the Bureau of Economic Analysis, U. S. Department of Commerce. Provides basic data for a wide variety of U. S. industries, services, and economic indicators. Most statistics are shown annually for 30 years and monthly for the most recent four years.

Counties USA: A Directory of United States Counties. Omnigraphics, Inc. • 2003. $85.00. Second edition. Contains extensive economic and demographic data from the 2000 Census for about 3,100 counties of the U. S.

County and City Data Book, a Statistical Abstract Supplement. U.S. Bureau of the Census. Available from U.S. Government Printing Office. • 1994. $60.00.

County and City Data Book 2000: A Statistical Abstract Supplement. Available from U. S. Government Printing Office. • 2002. $68.00. 13th edition. Issued by the U. S. Bureau of the Census (http://www.census.gov). Contains a wide variety of data on 3,141 U.S. counties, 1,078 cities, and 11,097 places of 2,500 or more inhabitants. Includes statistical information on retailing, manufacturing, banking, service industries, income, employment, housing, education, crime, and population. Updated metropolitan areas are included.

County and City Extra: Annual Metro, City and County Data Book. Deirdre A. Gaquin and Mark S. Littman. Bernan Press. • 2001. $120.00. Updates and augments data published irregularly in print form by the U. S. Census Bureau in *County and City Data Book.* Covers "every state, county, metropolitan area, and congressional district in the United States, as well as all U. S. cities with a 1990 population of 25,000 or more." Contains a wide range tic maps.

County and City Extra: Special Decennial Census Edition. Deidre A. Gaquin and Katherine A. DeBrandt, editors. Bernan Press. • 2002. $95.00. Presents conveniently arranged population, housing, and other data from the 2000 census, with many 1980 and 1990 comparisons. Includes maps and tables with rankings of about 20 items for various geographic locations. Complements the annual *County and City Extra.*

County Business Patterns. Available from U. S. Government Printing Office. • Irregular. 52 issues containing annual data for each state, the District of Columbia, and a U. S. Summary. Produced by U.S. Bureau of the Census (http://www.census.gov). Provides local establishment and employment statistics by industry.

Eurostat Yearbook: A Statistical View on Europe. Available from Bernan Associates. • Annual. $65.00. Published by European Communities (http://www.europa.eu.int/comm/eurostat/). Statistical topics include economics, national income, population, land, agriculture, environment, government, housing, and crime. Covers "every country in Europe and the European Union.".

Gale Book of Averages. Gale Cengage Learning. • 1994. $75.00. Contains 1,100-1,200 statistical averages on a variety of topics, with references to published sources. Subjects include business, labor, consumption, crime, and other areas of contemporary society.

Historical Statistics of the United States, Colonial Times to 1970: A Statistical Abstract Supplement. U.S. Bureau of the Census. Available from U.S. Government Printing Office. • 1975. $109.00. Two volumes.

International Financial Statistics. International Monetary Fund, Publications Services. • Monthly. Individuals, $495.00 per year; students, $247.00 per year. Includes a wide variety of current data for individual countries in Europe and elsewhere. Includes *Annual* issue.

The Little Data Book. The World Bank. • 2003. $15.00. Contains "key development data for 208 countries," including country profiles and 54 statistical indicators relating to such factors as population, economics, trade, technology, finance, and environment.

Main Economic Indicators. OECD Publication and Information Center. • Monthly. $450.00 per year. "The essential source of timely statistics for OECD member countries." Includes a wide variety of business, economic, and industrial data for the 29 OECD nations.

Main Economic Indicators: Historical Statistics. OECD Publications and Information Center. • Annual. $475.00. Includes online edition.

Manufacturers' Shipments, Inventories, and Orders. Available from U. S. Government Printing Office. • Monthly. $79.00 per year. Issued by Bureau of the Census, U. S. Department of Commerce. Includes monthly *Advance Report on Durable Goods.* Provides data on production, value, shipments, and consumption for a wide variety of manufactured products. (Current Industrial Reports, M3-1.).

Metropolitan Life Insurance Co. Statistical Bulletin SB. Metropolitan Life Insurance Co. • Quarterly. Individuals, $50.00 per year. Covers a wide range of social, economic and demographic health concerns.

Monthly Bulletin of Statistics. United Nations Publications. • Monthly. $295.00 per year. Provides current data for about 200 countries on a wide variety of economic, industrial, and demographic subjects. Compiled by United Nations Statistical Office.

Panorama of European Business. Available from Bernan Associates. • Annual. $65.00. Presents statistical data for manufacturing and service industries in major European countries. Text in English, French and Spanish.

Places, Towns, and Townships, 1998. Deirdre A. Gaquin and Richard W. Dodge, editors. Bernan Press. • 1997. $89.00. Second edition. Presents demographic and economic statistics from the U. S. Census Bureau and other government sources for places, cities, towns, villages, census designated places, and minor civil divisions. Contains more than 60 data categories. (Places, Towns and Townships Series).

Social Statistics of the United States. Mark S. Littman, editor. Bernan Press. • 2000. $65.00. Includes statistical data on population growth, labor force, occupations, environmental trends, leisure time use, income, poverty, taxes, and other economic or demographic topics.

The Sourcebook of ZIP Code Demographics. Available from Gale Cengage Learning. • Annual. $495.00. Published by ESRI Business Information Systems. Presents detailed statistical profiles of every ZIP code in America. Each profile contains data on more than 70 variables with 2003 updates and 2008 forecasts.

State and Metropolitan Area Data Book. Available from U. S. Government Printing Office. • 1998. Issued by the U. S. Bureau of the Census. Presents a wide variety of statistical data for U. S. regions, states, counties, metropolitan areas, and central cities, with ranking tables. Time period is 1970 to 1990.

Statistical Abstract of the United States. Available from U. S. Government Printing Office. • Annual. $51.00. Issued by the U. S. Bureau of the Census.

Statistical Abstract of the World. Gale Cengage Learning. • 1997. $85.00. Third edition. Provides data on a wide variety of economic, social, and political topics for about 200 countries. Arranged by country.

Statistical Forecasts of the United States. Gale Cengage Learning. • 1995. $115.00. Second edition. Provides both long-term and short-term statistical forecasts relating to basic items in the U. S.: population, employment, labor, crime, education, and health care. Data in the form of charts, graphs, and tables has been taken from a wide variety of government and private sources. Includes a subject index and an "Index of Forecast by Year.".

Statistical Handbook on Women in America. Cynthia M. Taeuber, editor. Greenwood Publishing Group, Inc. • 1996. $69.95. Second edition. Includes

data on demographics, employment, earnings, economic status, educational status, marriage, divorce, household units, health, and other topics. (Statistical Handbook Series).

A Statistical Portrait of the United States: Social Conditions and Trends. Mark S. Littman, editor. Bernan Press. • 1998. $89.00. Covers "social, economic, and environmental trends in the United States over the past 25 years." Includes statistical tables, graphs, and analysis relating to such topics as population, income, poverty, wealth, labor, housing, education, healthcare, air/water quality, and government. (Statistical Portrait of the United States: Social Conditions and Trends Series).

Statistical Yearbook. United Nations Publications. • Annual. $125.00. Contains statistics for about 200 countries on a wide variety of economic, industrial, and demographic topics. Compiled by United Nations Statistical Office.

Survey of Current Business. Available from U. S. Government Printing Office. • Monthly. $63.00 per year. Issued by Bureau of Economic Analysis, U. S. Department of Commerce. Presents a wide variety of business and economic data.

The World Bank Atlas. World Bank Group. • Annual. $10.00. Contains "color maps, charts, and graphs representing the main social, economic, and environmental indicators for 209 countries and territories" (publisher).

World Development Indicators. The World Bank Group. • Annual. $60.00. Provides data and information on the people, economy, environment, and markets of 148 countries. Emphasis is on statistics relating to major development issues.

World Statistics Pocketbook. United Nations Publications. • Annual $10.00.

OTHER SOURCES

Business Rankings Annual. Gale Cengage Learning. • Annual. $325.00. Two volumes. Compiled by the Business Library Staff of the Brooklyn Public Library. This is a guide to lists and rankings appearing in major business publications. The top ten names are listed in each case.

Commercial Atlas and Marketing Guide. Rand McNally. • Annual. $395.00. Includes maps and marketing data: population, transportation, communication, and local area business statistics. Provides information on more than 128,000 U.S. locations. (Commercial Atlas and Marketing Guide series).

STATISTICS, VITAL

See: VITAL STATISTICS

STATUTES

See: LAWS

STEAM HEATING

See: HEATING AND VENTILATION

STEAMSHIP LINES

See also: SHIPS, SHIPPING AND SHIPBUILDING

DIRECTORIES

Ford's Freighter Travel Guide. Ford's Travel Guides. • Covers: steamship lines which operate cargo vessels with accommodations for passengers; travel agencies which have chosen to advertise as freighter travel specialists; foreign government tour-

ist offices in the United States, and sports and casual cruises, some on yachts, barges, and sailboats. Entries include: For steamship lines--Company name, address, phone; ships names, facilities, itineraries, fares, etc. For travel agents--Name, address, phone. For tourist bureaus--Name, address, phone, branches.

List of Shipowners, Managers, and Managing Agents. Lloyd's Register of Shipping. • Annual. $350.00, including 10 updates per year. Published in the UK by Lloyd's Register-Fairplay Ltd. Lists 40,000 shipowners, managers, and agents worldwide. Cross-referenced with *Lloyd's Register of Ships.*

Plunkett's Airline, Hotel, and Travel Industry Almanac. Plunkett Research, Ltd. • Annual. $249.95. Contains profiles of 300 leading companies, including airlines, hotels, travel agencies, theme parks, cruise lines, casinos, and car rental companies.

Star Service: The Critical Guide to Hotels and Cruise Ships. New Concepts Canada. • $210.00. Looseleaf. Quarterly updates. Provides "honest and unbiased descriptions of accommodations, facilities, amenities, ambience, appearance, and service" for more than 10,000 hotels worldwide and 150 cruise ships. Ship information includes history, passenger profiles, crew profiles, and other data.

ENCYCLOPEDIAS AND DICTIONARIES

Dictionary of Shipping Terms. Peter Brodie. LLP, Inc. • 1997. Third edition. Price on application. Published in the UK by Lloyd's List (http://www.lloydslist.com). Defines more than 2,000 words, phrases, and abbreviations related to the shipping and maritime industries.

Macmillan Encyclopedia of Transportation. Available from Gale Cengage Learning. • 1999. $450.00. Six volumes. Published by Macmillan Reference USA. Covers the business, technology, and history of transportation on land, on water, in the air, and in space. Includes definitions, cross-references, and 200 color illustrations.

HANDBOOKS AND MANUALS

Cruise Ship Law. LexisNexis Matthew Bender. • 2003. $198.00. Provides analysis of federal cruise ship law, relevant international treaties, and court forms. Covers the law relating to passengers, crew members, stowaways, concessionaires, shipboard medical care, cruise line bankruptcies, and other items.

Ship Management. John Spruyt. LLP, Inc. • 1994. $105.00. Second edition. Published in the UK by Lloyd's List (http://www.lloydslist.com). Covers recruitment of personnel, training, quality control, liability, safety, responsibilities of ship managers, and other topics.

INTERNET DATABASES

CDC Vessel Sanitation Program (VSP): Charting a Healthier Course. U. S. Centers for Disease Control and Prevention. Phone: (770)488-7070 Fax: 888-232-6789 E-mail: vsp@cdc.gov • URL: http://www.cdc.gov/nceh/vsp/ • Web site provides details of unannounced sanitation inspections of individual cruise ships arriving at U. S. ports. Includes detailed results of the most recent inspection of each ship and results of inspections taking place in years past. There are lists of "Ships Inspected Past 2 Months" and "Ships with Not Satisfactory Scores" (passing grade is 85). CDC standards cover drinking water, food, and general cleanliness. Online searching is possible by ship name, inspection date, and numerical scores. Fees: Free.

PERIODICALS AND NEWSLETTERS

Cruise Travel: Ships, Ports, Schedules, Prices. World Publishing Co. • Bimonthly. $23.94 per year.

Lloyd's Cruise International. Available from Informa Publishing Group Ltd. • Bimonthly. $217.00 per year. Published in the UK by Lloyd's List (http://www.lloydslist.com). Edited for management professionals in the cruise ship industry. Covers industry trends, technical/equipment developments, regulatory issues, new cruise ships, ship management, cruise marketing, and related topics.

Lloyd's Ship Manager. LLP Inc. • 10 times a year. $478.00 per year, including annual supplementary guides and directories. Published in the UK by Lloyd's List (http://www.lloydslist.com). Covers all management, technical, and operational aspects of ocean-going shipping.

Register of International Shipowning Groups. Available from Fairplay Publications, Inc. • Three times a year. $744.00 per year. Published in the UK by Lloyd's Register-Fairplay Ltd. "Provides intelligence on shipowners and managers, their subsidiary and associate companies, and owners' representatives." Includes detailed information on individual ships.

Summary of Sanitation Inspections of International Cruise Ships. Centers for Disease Control and Prevention (CDC). • Biweekly. Apply. "All passenger cruise ships arriving at U. S. ports are subject to unannounced inspection..to achieve levels of sanitation that will minimize the potential for gastrointestinal disease outbreaks on these ships." Individual ships are listed, with sanitation rating and date of inspection. (CDC Document No. 510051.).

Travel Weekly. Northstar Travel Media, LLC. • Weekly. $266.00 per year. Includes cruise guides, a weekly "Business Travel Update," and special issues devoted to particular destinations and areas. Edited mainly for travel agents and tour operators.

TRADE/PROFESSIONAL ASSOCIATIONS

Chamber of Shipping of America. 1730 M. St., N.W., Suite 407, Washington, DC 20036. Phone: (202)775-4399 Fax: (202)659-3795 • United States based companies that own and operate tankers, dry bulk carriers, container ships and other oceangoing vessels in United States foreign and domestic commerce. Formerly United States Chamber of Shipping.

STEEL FOUNDRIES

See: FOUNDRIES

STEEL INDUSTRY

See: IRON AND STEEL INDUSTRY

STENOGRAPHERS

See: OFFICE PRACTICE

STEREOPHONIC SOUND

See: HIGH FIDELITY/STEREO

STOCK AND STOCK BREEDING

See: LIVESTOCK INDUSTRY

STOCK BROKERS

GENERAL WORKS

In the Black: A History of African Americans on Wall Street. Gregory S. Bell. John Wiley and Sons, Inc. • 2001. $24.95. Written by the son of Travers Bell, co-founder of Daniels Bell stockbrokers, the first black-owned New York Stock Exchange member firm.

License to Steal: The Secret World of Wall Street Brokers and the Systematic Pluof the American Investor. Timothy Harper. DIANE Publishing Co. •` 2001. $26.00. A former stockbroker explains how brokers use persuavive and sometimes shady techniques to keep effective control of customers' accounts, regardless of losses. (HarperBusiness.).

Never Call Your Broker on Monday: And 300 Other Financial Lessons You Can't Afford Not to Know. Nancy Dunnan. HarperInformation. • 1997. $8.50. Presents a wide range of personal finance advice, covering investments, insurance, wills, credit, real estate, etc.

Smart Questions to Ask Your Financial Advisers. Lynn Brenner. Bloomberg. • 1997. $19.95. Provides practical advice on how to deal with financial planners, stockbrokers, insurance agents, and lawyers. Some of the areas covered are investments, estate planning, tax planning, house buying, prenuptial agreements, divorce arrangements, loss of a job, and retirement. (Bloomberg Personal Bookshelf Series).

Thriving as a Broker in the 21st Century. Thomas J. Dorsey. Bloomberg. • 1999. $39.95. Provides advice for stockbrokers operating in today's rapidly changing financial environment. (Bloomberg Professional Library).

Women of the Street: Making It on Wall Street-The World's Toughest Business. Sue Herera. John Wiley and Sons, Inc. • 1998. $16.95. The author is a CNBC business television anchorperson.

BIOGRAPHICAL SOURCES

Who's Who in Finance and Industry. Marquis Who's Who. • Biennial. $259.95. Provides over 21,000 concise biographies of business leaders in all fields.

DIRECTORIES

Major Financial Institutions of the World 2001. Available from Gale Cengage Learning. • 2003. $880.00. Sixth edition. Two volumes. Published by Graham & Whiteside. Contains detailed information on more than 7,500 important financial institutions in various countries. Includes banks, investment companies, and insurance companies.

Plunkett's Financial Services Industry Almanac: The Only Comprehensive Overview of the Banking, Insurance, Credit and Investment Sectors. Plunkett Research, Ltd. • Annual. $229.99. Includes CD-ROM. Discusses important trends in various sectors of the financial industry. Five hundred major banking, credit card, investment, and financial services companies are profiled. (Business, Careers and Internet Reference Tools Series).

Plunkett's On-Line Trading, Finance, and Investment Web Sites Almanac. Plunkett Research, Ltd. • Annual. $149.99. Provides profiles and usefulness rankings of financial Web sites. Sites are rated from 1 to 5 for specific uses. Includes CD-ROM.

Retail Broker-Dealer Directory. Securities Data Publishing. • Covers: 1,300 retail brokerages serving the marketplace through the warehouse, regional, independent, bank, discount, and insurance distribution channels. Entries include: Company snapshot, key contacts, number of employees, products, specialization, financial data, assets, and other details.

Standard and Poor's Security Dealers of North America. Standard & Poor's. • Semiannual. $480.00 per year; with *Supplements* every six weeks. Geographical listing of over 12,000 stock, bond, and commodity dealers.

Zacks Analyst Directory: Listed by Broker. Zacks Investment Research. • Quarterly. $395.00 per year. Lists stockbroker investment analysts and gives the names of major U. S. corporations covered by those analysts.

FINANCIAL RATIOS

Almanac of Business and Industrial Financial Ratios. Leo Troy. Aspen Publishers, Inc. • 2003. $125.95. Includes CD-Rom. Contains financial ratios derived from federal tax returns. Ratios for each of about 200 industries are arranged according to company asset size. (Almanac of Business and Industrial Financial Ratios Series).

HANDBOOKS AND MANUALS

Audits of Brokers and Dealers in Securities With Conforming Changes as of May 1, 1999. American Institute of Certified Public Accountants. • 1999. $42.00. Fifth edition. (Audit and Accounting Guide Series).

Best Practices for Financial Advisors. Mary Rowland. Bloomberg. • 1997. $40.00. Provides advice for professional financial advisors on practice management, ethics, marketing, and legal concerns. (Bloomberg Professional Library.).

N A S D Manual. National Association of Securities Dealers, Inc. CCH, Inc. • Quarterly. $452.00 per year. CD-Rom, $459.00.

Securities Crimes. West Group. • Annual. $225.00. Two looseleaf volumes. Analyzes the enfo of federal securities laws from the viewpoint of the defendant. Discusses Securities and Exchange Commission (SEC) investigations and federal sentencing guidelines. (Securities Law Series).

Successful Cold Call Selling. Lee Boyan. AMACOM. • 1989. $16.95. Second edition.

PERIODICALS AND NEWSLETTERS

Bank Investment Product News. Institutional Investor, Inc., Journals Group. • Weekly. $1,195.00 per year. Newsletter. Edited for bank executives. Covers the marketing and regulation of financial products sold through banks, such as mutual funds, stock brokerage services, and insurance.

Bloomberg Markets. Bloomberg. • Monthly. Free to qualified personnel. Edited for securities dealers and investment managers.

Investment Advisor: The Advisor to Advisors. Wicks Business Information. • Monthly. $79.00 per year. Edited for professional investment advisors, financial planners, stock brokers, bankers, and others concerned with the management of assets.

Investment Dealers' Digest. Thomson Media. • Weekly. $750.00 per year. Covers financial news, trends, new products, people, private placements, new issues of securities, and other aspects of the investment business. Includes feature stories.

Investment Management Weekly. Thomson Media. • Weekly. $1,370.00 per year. Newsletter. Edited for money managers and other investment professionals. Covers personnel news, investment strategies, and industry trends.

Investment News: The Weekly Newspaper for Financial Advisers. Crain Communications, Inc. • Weekly. $29.00 per year. Edited for both personal and institutional investment advisers, planners, and managers.

Journal of Wealth Management. Institutional Investor, Inc., Journals Group. • Quarterly. $410.00 per year. Includes print and online editions. Edited for managers of wealthy individuals' investment portfolios. Formerly *Journal of Private Portfolio Management.*

Martin Weiss' Safe Money Report. Weiss Ratings, Inc. • Monthly. $189.00 per year. Newsletter. Provides financial advice and current safety ratings of various banks, savings and loan companies, insurance companies, and securities dealers. Formerly (The Safe Money Report).

On Wall Street. Thomson Media. • Monthly. $96.00 per year. Edited for securities dealers. Includes articles on financial planning, retirement planning, variable annuities, and money management, with special coverage of 401(k) plans and IRAs.

Operations Management. Institutional Investor, Inc., Journals Group. • Weekly. $2,105.00 per year. Includes print and online editions. Newsletter. Edited for managers of securities clearance and settlement at financial institutions. Covers new products, technology, legalities, management practices, and other topics related to securities processing.

Registered Representative. Primedia Business Magazines and Media. • Monthly. $48.00 per year.

Securities Arbitration Commentator: Covering Significant Issues and Events in Securities-Commodities Arbitration. Richard P. Ryder. • Monthly. $348.00 per year. Newsletter. Edited for attorneys and other professionals concerned with securities arbitration.

Securities Industry News. Thomson Financial Corporate Communications. • Weekly. $275.00 per year. Newsletter covers securities dealing and processing, including regulatory compliance, shareholder services, human resources, transaction clearing, and technology.

Traders Magazine. Thomson Media. • Monthly. $60.00 per year. Edited for institutional buy side and sell side equity traders. Covers industry news, market trends, regulatory developments, and personnel news. Serves as the official publication of the Security Traders Association.

Wall Street and Technology: For Senior-Level Executives in Technology and Information Management in Securities and Invesment Firms. CMP Media LLC. • Monthly. $85.00 per year. Includes material on the use of computers in technical investment strategies. Formerly *Wall Computer Review.*

Wall Street Letter: Newsweekly for Investment Banking and Brokerage Community. Institutional Investor, Inc., Journals Group. • Weekly. $2,665.00 per year. Includes print and online editions. Newsletter for stock brokers and companies providing services for stock brokers. Emphasis is on regulatory matters.

STATISTICS SOURCES

Information, Finance, and Services USA. Gale Cengage Learning. • 2001. $240.00. Replaces *Service Industries USA* and *Finance, Insurance, and Real Estate USA.* Presents statistics and projections relating to economic activity in a wide variety of non-manufacturing areas.

Standard & Poor's Industry Surveys. Standard & Poor's. • Semiannual. $1,800.00. Two looseleaf volumes. Includes monthly *Supplements.* Provides detailed, individual surveys of 52 major industry groups. Each survey is revised on a semiannual basis. Also includes "Monthly Investment Review" (industry group investment analysis) and monthly "Trends & Projections" (economic analysis).

U. S. Industry and Trade Outlook. Available from National Technical Information Service. • Annual. $69.95. Produced by the International Trade Administration, U. S. Department of Commerce, in a "public-private" partnership with DRI/McGraw-Hill and Standard & Poor's. Provides basic data, outlook for the current year, and "Long-Term Prospects" (five-year projections) for a wide variety of products and services. Includes high technology industries. Formerly *U. S. Industrial Outlook.*

United States Securities and Exchange Commission Annual Report. U.S. Government Printing Office. • Annual. The Commission maintains a Web site at http://www.sec.gov.

TRADE/PROFESSIONAL ASSOCIATIONS

National Association of Securities Dealers (NASD). 1735 K St., N.W., Washington, DC 20006-1506. Phone: (202)728-8000 Fax: (202)293-6260 E-mail: waltere@nasd.com • URL: http://www.nasd.com •

Formerly National Association of Securities Dealers.

Securities Industry and Financial Markets Association. 120 Broadway, 35th Fl., New York, NY 10271-0080. Phone: (212)313-1200 Fax: (212)313-1301 E-mail: rbrockhaus@sifma.org • URL: http://www.sifma.org • Represents more than 650 member firms of all sizes, in all financial markets in the U.S. and around the world. Enhances the public's trust and confidence in the markets, delivering an efficient, enhanced member network of access and forward-looking services, as well as premiere educational resources for the professionals in the industry and the investors whom they serve. Maintains offices in New York City and Washington, DC.

Security Traders Association. 420 Lexington Ave., Ste. 2334, New York, NY 10170. Phone: (212)867-7002 Fax: (212)867-7030 E-mail: traders@securitytraders.org • URL: http://www.securitytraders.org • Brokers and dealers handling listed and OTC securities, stocks, and bonds, and all securities. Conducts educational programs. Promotes the interests of members throughout the global financial markets. Provides representation of these interests in the legislative, regulatory and technological processes. Fosters goodwill and high standards of integrity in accord with the Association's founding principle.

OTHER SOURCES

Andrews' Professional Liability Litigation Reporter. Andrews Publications. • Monthly. $550.00 per year. Provides reports on lawsuits against attorneys, accountants, and investment professionals.

Broker-Dealer Regulation. David A. Lipton. West Group. • Semiannual. $429.00 per year. Looseleaf service. Focuses on the basics of stockbroker license application procedure, registration, regulation, and responsibilities. (Securities Law Series).

STOCK DIVIDENDS

See: DIVIDENDS

STOCK EXCHANGES

See also: STOCKS

GENERAL WORKS

Deal Engines: The Science of Auctions, Stock markets, and e-Markets. Robert E. Hall. W. W. Norton & Co., Inc. • 2003. $14.95. A practical, economic analysis of how auction markets work, whether simple (eBay) or complex (stock exchanges). Covers both theory and application. (Originally published as *Digital Dealing.*).

Financial Markets and Institutions. Frederic S. Mishkin and Stanley G. Eakins. Addison-Wesley. • 2002. $118.00. Fourth edition.

The Great Game: The Emergence of Wall Street as a World Power, 1653-2000. John S. Gordon. Gale Cengage Learning. • 1999. $25.00. Provides a history of U. S. financial markets, featuring such key figures as Alexander Hamilton, Commodore Vanderbilt, J. P. Morgan, Charles Merrill, and Michael Milken.

It Was a Very Good Year: Extraordinary Moments in Stock Market History. Martin S. Fridson. John Wiley and Sons, Inc. • 1997. $29.95. Provides details on what happened during each of the ten best years for the stock market since 1900. (Investment Series).

100 Years of Wall Street. Charles R. Geisst. McGraw-Hill. • 1999. $29.95. A popularly written, illustrated history of the American stock market. About 200 photographs, charts, cartoons, and reproductions of stock certificates are included.

Wall Street: A History. Charles R. Geisst. Oxford University Press. • 1997. $18.95. Presents the history of the U. S. stock market according to four distinct eras: 1790 to the Civil War, the Civil War to 1929, 1929 to 1954, and from 1954 to recent years.

ALMANACS AND YEARBOOKS

Emerging Markets Analyst. • Monthly. $895.00 per year. Provides an annual overview of the emerging financial markets in 24 countries of Latin America, Asia, and Europe. Includes data on international mutual funds and closed-end funds.

BIBLIOGRAPHIES

The American Stock Exchange: A Guide to Information Resources. Carol Z. Womack and Alice C. Littlejohn. Garland Publishing, Inc. • 1995. $15.00. (Research and Information Guides in Business, Industry, and Economic Institutions Series: Vol. 7).

DIRECTORIES

American Stock Exchange Directory. CCH, Inc. • 2000. $30.00.

Asia Pacific Securities Handbook. Hoover's Inc. • Covers: stock exchanges and brokers in Australia, Bangladesh, China, Hong Kong, India, Indonesia, Japan, Malaysia, Nepal, New Zealand, Pakistan, Philippines, Singapore, South Korea, Sri Lanka, Taiwan, and Thailand. Entries include: Name, address, phone, fax; exchanges also list market practices, most active and highest capitalized stocks.

Brazil Company Handbook: Data on Major Listed Companies. Hoovers, Inc. • Annual. $59.95. Contains profiles of approximately 54 publicly traded companies in Brazil. Includes information on local stock exchanges and the nation's economic situation.

Business Organizations, Agencies, and Publications Directory. Gale Cengage Learning. • 2003. $480.00. 15th edition. Over 40,000 entries describing 39 types of business information sources. Classified by type of organization, publication, or serviceIncludes state, national, and international agencies and organizations. Master index to names and keywords. Also includes e-mail addresses and web site URL's.

FP Survey Industrials (Canada). Globe Information Services. • Annual. $49.95. Provides information on more than 3,000 Canadian manufacturing and service companies.

Handbook of World Stock and Commodity Exchanges. Blackwell Publishing. • Annual. $265.00. Provides detailed information on over 200 stock and commodity exchanges in more than 50 countries.

Trade Directory of Mexico. Available from Hoovers, Inc. • Annual. $99.95. Published by IMF Editora. Contains profiles of 6,000 Mexican companies involved in foreign trade. Includes profile of Mexico and of the individual states.

Trade Directory of Mexico. Mexican Foreign Trade Bank. • Annual. $100.00. Provides information on more than 6,000 Mexican companies involved in foreign trade. Lists forwarding agencies, customs brokers, consulting groups, transportation companies, and other trade-related Mexican organizations.

Venezuela Company Handbook: Data on Major Listed Companies. Hoovers, Inc. • Annual. $29.95. Published by IMF Editora. Contains profiles of publicly traded companies in Venezuela. Includes information on local stock exchanges and the nation's economic situation. Text in English.

ENCYCLOPEDIAS AND DICTIONARIES

Common Stock Newspaper Abbreviations and Trading Symbols. Howard R. Jarrell. Scarecrow Press, Inc. • 1989. $60.00. Gives the meanings of financial page company name abbreviations and stock symbols.

Common Stock Newspaper Abbreviations and Trad-

ing Symbols: Supplement One. Howard R. Jarrell. Scarecrow Press, Inc. • 1991. $40.00. Provides changes and new listings occurring since the publication of Jarrell's original volume in 1989.

International Encyclopedia of the Stock Market. Michael Sheimo and Andreas Loizou, editors. Fitzroy Dearborn Publishers, Inc. • 1999. $290.00. Two volumes. Covers the terminology of stock exchanges around the world. Individual country entries provide details of stock exchange conditions, practices, regulation, and brokers.

HANDBOOKS AND MANUALS

N A S D Manual. National Association of Securities Dealers, Inc. CCH, Inc. • Quarterly. $452.00 per year. CD-Rom, $459.00.

Trading and Exchanges: Market, Microstructure for Practitioners. Larry Harris. Oxford University Press. • 2002. $95.00. Explains the function and workings of modern stock markets. Covers such topics as liquidity, volatility, speculation, market efficiency, stock indexes, and the structure of trading. (Financial Management Association Survey and Synthesis Series).

INTERNET DATABASES

Factiva. Dow Jones Reuters Business Interactive, LLC. Phone: 800-369-7466 or (609)452-1511 Fax: (609)520-5770 E-mail: solutions@factiva.com • URL: http://www.factiva.com • Fee-based Web site provides "global news and business information through Web sites and content integration solutions." Includes Dow Jones and Reuters newswires, The Wall Street Journal, and more than 7,000 other sources of current news, historical articles, market research reports, and investment analysis. Content includes 96 major U. S. newspapers, 900 non-English sources, trade publications, media transcripts, country profiles, news photos, etc.

Nexis.com. Lexis-Nexis Group. Phone: 800-227-4908 or (937)865-6800 Fax: (937)865-6909 E-mail: webmaster@prod.lexis-nexis.com • URL: http://www.nexis.com • Fee-based Web site offers searching of about 2.8 billion documents in some 30,000 news, business, and legal information sources. Features include a subject directory covering 1,200 topics in 34 categories and a Company Dossier containing information on more than 500,000 public and private companies. Boolean searching is offered.

U. S. Securities and Exchange Commission. Phone: 800-732-0330 or (202)942-7040 Fax: (202)942-9634 E-mail: webmaster@sec.gov • URL: http://www.sec.gov • SEC Web site offers free access through EDGAR to text of official corporate filings, such as annual reports (10-K), quarterly reports (10-Q), and proxies. (EDGAR is "Electronic Data Gathering, Analysis, and Retrieval System.") An example is given of how to obtain executive compensation data from proxies. Text of the daily *SEC News Digest* is offered, as are links to other government sites, non-government market regulators, and U. S. stock exchanges. Search facilities are extensive. Fees: Free.

Wall Street Journal Interactive Edition. Dow Jones & Co., Inc. Phone: 800-369-2834 or (212)416-2000 Fax: (212)416-2658 E-mail: inquiries@interactive. wsj.com • URL: http://www.wsj.com • Fee-based Web site providing online searching of worldwide information from the *The Wall Street Journal.* Includes "Company Snapshots," "The Journal's Greatest Hits," "Index to Market Data," "Journal Links," etc. Financial price quotes are available. Fees: $49.00 per year; $29.00 per year to print subscribers.

PERIODICALS AND NEWSLETTERS

Financial History: Chronicling the History of America's Capital Markets. Museum of American Financial History. • Quarterly. Membership. Contains articles on early stock and bond markets and trading in the U. S., with photographs and other illustrations. Current trading in rare and unusual, obsolete stock and bond certificates is featured. Formerly *Friends or Financial History.*

Financial Sentinel: Your Beacon to the World of Investing. Gulf Atlantic Publishing, Inc. • Monthly. $29.95 per year. Provides "The only complete listing of all OTC Bulletin Board stocks traded, with all issues listed on the Nasdaq SmallCap Market, the Toronto, and Vancouver Stock Exchanges." Also includes investment advice and recommendations of small capitalization stocks.

The Wall Street Journal. Dow Jones & Co., Inc. • Daily. $189.00 per year. Covers news and trends relating to business, industry, finance, the economy, and international commerce. Provides extensive price and other data for the securities, commodity, options, futures, foreign exchange, and money markets.

STATISTICS SOURCES

American Stock Exchange Weekly Bulletin. Nasdaq-AMEX Market Group. • Weekly. $20.00 per year. Looseleaf service.

Emerging Stock Markets Factbook 1999. International Finance Corp. • 1998. $150.00. Provides statistical profiles for emerging stock markets in various countries of the world. Includes regional, composite, and industry indexes.

Financial Market Trends. Organization for Economic Cooperation and Development. • Quarterly. $80.00 per year. Provides analysis of developments and trends in international and national capital markets. Includes charts and graphs on interest rates, exchange rates, stock market indexes, bank stock indexes, trading volumes, and loans outstanding. Data from OECD countries includes international direct investment, bank profitability, institutional investment, and privatization.

International Guide to Securities Market Indices. Henry Shilling, editor. Fitzroy Dearborn Publishers, Inc. • 1996. $150.00. Describes 400 stock market, bond market, and other financial price indexes maintained in various countries of the world (300 of the indexes are described in detail, including graphs and 10-year data).

NASDAQ-AMEX Market Group Fact Book. NASD MediaSource. • Annual. $20.00. Published by the American Stock Exchange, Inc. Contains statistical data relating to the American Stock Exchange. Also provides the address and phone number for each company listed on the Exchange. Formerly *American Stock Exchange Fact Book.*

Nasdaq Fact Book and Company Directory. National Association of Security Dealers, Inc. Corporate Communications. • Annual. $20.00. Contains statistical data relating to the Nasdaq Stock Market. Also provides corporate address, phone, symbol, stock price, and trading volume information for more than 5,000 securities traded through the National Association of Securities Dealers Automated Quotation System (Nasdaq), including Small-Cap Issues. Includes indexing by Standard Industrial Classification (SIC) number.

New York Stock Exchange Fact Book. Available from Hoover's, Inc. • Annual. $9.95. Published by the New York Stock Exchange, Inc. Contains statistical data relating to the New York Stock Exchange. Includes information on new listings and name changes.

SRC Green Book of 5 Trend 35-Year Charts. Securities Research Co. • Annual. $150.00. Chart book presents statistical information on the stocks of 400 leading companies over a 35-year period. Each full page chart is in semi-log format to avoid visual distortion. Also includes charts of 12 leading market averages or indexes and 39 major industry groups.

TRADE/PROFESSIONAL ASSOCIATIONS

Securities Industry and Financial Markets Association. 120 Broadway, 35th Fl., New York, NY 10271-0080. Phone: (212)313-1200 Fax: (212)313-1301 E-mail: rbrockhaus@sifma.org • URL: http://www.sifma.org • Represents more than 650 member firms of all sizes, in all financial markets in the U.S. and around the world. Enhances the public's trust and confidence in the markets, delivering an efficient, enhanced member network of access and forward-looking services, as well as premiere educational resources for the professionals in the industry and the investors whom they serve. Maintains offices in New York City and Washington, DC.

OTHER SOURCES

American Stock Exchange Guide. CCH, Inc. • Annual. $490.00 per year. Monthly updates. Contains exchange rules and regulations, constitution, and a directory.

New York Stock Exchange Guide. CCH, Inc. • Monthly. $692.00 per year.

STOCK INDEX TRADING

See also: FINANCIAL FUTURES TRADING

GENERAL WORKS

Futures Markets. A. G. Malliaris, editor. Edward Elgar Publishing, Inc. • 1997. $550.00. Three volumes. Consists of reprints of 70 articles dating from 1959 to 1993, on futures market volatility, speculation, hedging, stock indexes, portfolio insurance, interest rates, and foreign currencies. (International Library of Critical Writings in Financial Economics Series: No. 2).

Stock Index Options: How to Use and Profit from Indexed Options in Volatile and Uncertain Markets. Scot G. Barenblat and Donald T. Mesler. McGraw-Hill. • 1991. $29.95. Revised editon.

ABSTRACTS AND INDEXES

Business Periodicals Index. H. W. Wilson Co. • 11 times a year. Quarterly and annual cumulations. Price varies.

DIRECTORIES

Futures Magazine SourceBook: The Most Complete List of Exchanges, Companies, Regulators, Organizations, etc., Offering Products and Services to the Futures and Options Industry. Futures Magazine, Inc. • Annual. $19.50. Provides information on commodity futures brokers, trading method services, publications, and other items of interest to futures traders and money managers.

HANDBOOKS AND MANUALS

Derivatives: A Comprehensive Resource for Options, Futures, Interest Rate Swaps, and Mortgage Securities. Fred D. Arditti. Harvard Business School Publishing. • 1996. $60.00. Published by Harvard Business School Press. Provides detailed explanations of various kinds of financial derivatives (options, futures, swaps, etc.) and their trading tactics, uses, and risks. (Financial Management Association Survey and Synthesis Series).

Handbook of Derivative Instruments: Investment Research, Analysis, and Portfolio Applications. Arsuo Konishi and Ravi Dattatreya, editors. McGraw-Hill. • 1996. $80.00. Second revised edition. Contains 41 chapters by various authors on all aspects of derivative securities, including such esoterica as "Inverse Floaters," "Positive Convexity," "Exotic Options," and "How to Use the Holes in Black-Scholes.".

Handbook of Equity Derivatives. Jack C. Francis and others, editors. John Wiley and Sons, Inc. • 1999. $105.00. Revised edition. Contains 27 chapters by various authors. Covers options (puts and calls), stock index futures, warrants, convertibles, over-the-counter options, swaps, legal issues, taxation, etc. (Financial Engineering Series).

Options: The International Guide to Valuation and Trading Strategies. Gordon Gemmill. McGraw-Hill. • 1992. $37.95. Covers valuation techniques for American, European, and Asian options. Trading strategies are discussed for options on currencies, stock indexes, interest rates, and commodities.

Stock Index Futures: Buying and Selling the Market Averages. Charles Sutcliffe. Cengage Learning. • 1998. $37.95. Third edition.

Understanding Financial Derivatives: How to Protect Your Investments. Donald Strassheim. McGraw-Hill. • 1996. $40.00. Covers three basic risk management instruments: options, futures, and swaps. Includes advice on equity index options, financial futures contracts, and over-the-counter derivatives markets.

INTERNET DATABASES

BanxQuote Banking, Mortgage, and Finance Center. BanxQuote, Inc. Phone: (914)722-1600 Fax: (914)722-6630 E-mail: info@banx.com • URL: http://www.banx.com • Web site quotes interest rates paid by banks around the country on various savings products, as well as rates paid by consumers for automobile loans, mortgages, credit cards, home equity loans, and personal loans. Also provided: stock quotes, indexes, stock options, futures trading data, economic indicators, and links to many other financial sites. Daily updates. Fees: Free.

CRB Markets Overview. Commodity Research Bureau. Phone: 800-621-5271 or (312)554-8456 Fax: (312)939-4135 E-mail: info@crbtrader.com • URL: http://www.crbtrader.com/data/ • Web site provides free, detailed, current price quotes for about 100 futures contracts, covering Currencies, Energies, Financials, Grains, Meats, Metals, "Softs" (orange juice, coffee, etc.) and stock price indexes. Includes contract specifications and detailed prices of options on futures.

ETF Connect. Nuveen Investments. Phone: 800-257-8787 • URL: http://www.etfconnect.com • Free Web site makes available extensive, searchable information on individual closed-end investment funds, preferred share funds, and exchange-traded index funds. Information on a particular fund is available by name or as part of a classification (high yield, investment grade, municipal, emerging markets, global equity, etc.). Fund charts are available for various time periods, as is data concerning premiums or discounts, dividends, annualized total return, credit quality, "Top 10 Holdings," and so forth.

Futures Online. Futures Magazine Inc. Phone: (312)846-4600 Fax: (312)846-4638 • URL: http://www.futuresmag.com • Web site presents updates of *Futures* magazine and links to other futures-related sites.

ONLINE DATABASES

Wilson Business Abstracts Online. H. W. Wilson Co. • Indexes and abstracts 600 major business periodicals, plus the *Wall Street Journal* and the business section of the *New York Times.* Indexing is from 1982, abstracting from 1990, with the two newspapers included from 1993. Updated weekly. Inquire as to online cost and availability. (*Business Periodicals Index* without abstracts is also available online.).

PERIODICALS AND NEWSLETTERS

Barron's: The Dow Jones Business and Financial Weekly. • Weekly. $145.00 per year.

Futures: News, Analysis, and Strategies for Futures, Options, and Derivatives Traders. Futures Magazine. • Monthly. $39.00 per year. Edited for institutional money managers and traders, brokers,

risk managers, and individual investors or speculators. Includes special feature issues on interest rates, technical indicators, currencies, charts, precious metals, hedge funds, and derivatives. Supplements available.

SFO: Stocks, Futures & Options. Wasendorf & Associates, Inc. • Monthly. $49.95 per year. Subtitle: *Official Journal for Personal Investing in Stocks, Futures, and Options.* Covers mainly speculative techniques for stocks, commodity futures, financial futures, stock index futures, foreign exchange, short selling, and various kinds of options.

Technical Analysis of Stocks & Commodities: The Traders Magazine. Technical Analysis, Inc. • 13 times a year. $64.95 per year. Covers use of personal computers for stock trading, price movement analysis by means of charts, and other technical trading methods.

RESEARCH CENTERS AND INSTITUTES

Center for Research in Security Prices. University of Chicago, 725 S. Wells St., Suite 800, Chicago, IL 60607. Phone: (773)834-4610 Fax: (773)702-3036 E-mail: custom@crsp.uchicago.edu • URL: http://gsbwww.uchicago.edu/research/crsp.

STATISTICS SOURCES

Statistical Annual: Interest Rates, Metals, Stock Indices, Options on Financial Futures, Options on Metals Futures. Chicago Board of Trade. • Annual. Includes historical data on GNMA CDR Futures, Cash-Settled GNMA Futures, U. S. Treasury Bond Futures, U. S. Treasury Note Futures, Options on Treasury Note Futures, NASDAQ-100 Futures, Major Market Index Futures, Major Market Index MAXI Futures, Municipal Bond Index Futures, 1,000-Ounce Silver Futures, Options on Silver Futures, and Kilo Gold Futures.

TRADE/PROFESSIONAL ASSOCIATIONS

National Association of Securities Dealers (NASD). 1735 K St., N.W., Washington, DC 20006-1506. Phone: (202)728-8000 Fax: (202)293-6260 E-mail: waltere@nasd.com • URL: http://www.nasd.com • Formerly National Association of Securities Dealers.

STOCK MARKET

See: STOCK EXCHANGES

STOCK MARKET CHARTS

See: TECHNICAL ANALYSIS (FINANCE)

STOCK OFFERINGS, INITIAL

See: NEW ISSUES (FINANCE)

STOCK OPTION CONTRACTS

GENERAL WORKS

Introduction to Futures and Options Markets. John C. Hull. Prentice Hall PTR. • 1997. $110.00. Third edition.

DIRECTORIES

Futures Magazine SourceBook: The Most Complete List of Exchanges, Companies, Regulators, Organizations, etc., Offering Products and Services to the Futures and Options Industry. Futures Magazine, Inc. • Annual. $19.50. Provides information on commodity futures brokers, trading method services, publications, and other items of interest to

futures traders and money managers.

ENCYCLOPEDIAS AND DICTIONARIES

International Encyclopedia of Futures and Options. Fitzroy Dearborn Publishers, Inc. • 2000. $285.00. Two volumes. Covers terminology, concepts, events, individuals, and markets.

HANDBOOKS AND MANUALS

Day-Trader's Manual: Theory, Art, and Science of Profitable Short-Term Investing. William F. Eng. John Wiley and Sons, Inc. • 1992. $79.95. Covers short-term trading in stocks, futures, and options. Various technical trading systems are considered. (Finance Series, vol. 5).

Derivatives: A Comprehensive Resource for Options, Futures, Interest Rate Swaps, and Mortgage Securities. Fred D. Arditti. Harvard Business School Publishing. • 1996. $60.00. Published by Harvard Business School Press. Provides detailed explanations of various kinds of financial derivatives (options, futures, swaps, etc.) and their trading tactics, uses, and risks. (Financial Management Association Survey and Synthesis Series).

Handbook of Derivative Instruments: Investment Research, Analysis, and Portfolio Applications. Arsuo Konishi and Ravi Dattatreya, editors. McGraw-Hill. • 1996. $80.00. Second revised edition. Contains 41 chapters by various authors on all aspects of derivative securities, including such esoterica as "Inverse Floaters," "Positive Convexity," "Exotic Options," and "How to Use the Holes in Black-Scholes.".

Handbook of Equity Derivatives. Jack C. Francis and others, editors. John Wiley and Sons, Inc. • 1999. $105.00. Revised edition. Contains 27 chapters by various authors. Covers options (puts and calls), stock index futures, warrants, convertibles, over-the-counter options, swaps, legal issues, taxation, etc. (Financial Engineering Series).

Investing in Call Options; An Alternative to Common Stock and Real Estate. James A. Willson. Greenwood Publishing Group, Inc. • 1982. $59.95.

Money Management Strategies for Futures Traders. Nauzer J. Balsara. John Wiley and Sons, Inc. • 1992. $75.00. How to limit risk and avoid catastrophic losses. (Finance Series).

Options: Essential Concepts and Trading Strategies. McGraw-Hill. • 1999. $55.00. Third edition.

Portfolio Management Formulas: Mathematical Trading Methods for the Futures, Options, and Stock Markets. Ralph Vince. John Wiley and Sons, Inc. • 1990. $90.00. Discusses optimization of trading systems by exploiting the rules of probability and making use of the principles of modern portfolio management theory. Computer programs are included. (Finance Series).

Understanding Financial Derivatives: How to Protect Your Investments. Donald Strassheim. McGraw-Hill. • 1996. $40.00. Covers three basic risk management instruments: options, futures, and swaps. Includes advice on equity index options, financial futures contracts, and over-the-counter derivatives markets.

INTERNET DATABASES

BanxQuote Banking, Mortgage, and Finance Center. BanxQuote, Inc. Phone: (914)722-1600 Fax: (914)722-6630 E-mail: info@banx.com • URL: http://www.banx.com • Web site quotes interest rates paid by banks around the country on various savings products, as well as rates paid by consumers for automobile loans, mortgages, credit cards, home equity loans, and personal loans. Also provided: stock quotes, indexes, stock options, futures trading data, economic indicators, and links to many other financial sites. Daily updates. Fees: Free.

Futures Online. Futures Magazine Inc. Phone: (312)846-4600 Fax: (312)846-4638 • URL: http://

www.futuresmag.com • Web site presents updates of *Futures* magazine and links to other futures-related sites.

PERIODICALS AND NEWSLETTERS

Barron's: The Dow Jones Business and Financial Weekly. • Weekly. $145.00 per year.

Futures and Derivatives Law Report: The Journal on the Law of Investment and Risk Management Products. Glasser Legalworks. • Monthly. $305.00 per year. Newsletter. Covers developments in regulation, legislation, and litigation concerning financial derivatives, futures trading, and options trading.

Futures: News, Analysis, and Strategies for Futures, Options, and Derivatives Traders. Futures Magazine. • Monthly. $39.00 per year. Edited for institutional money managers and traders, brokers, risk managers, and individual investors or speculators. Includes special feature issues on interest rates, technical indicators, currencies, charts, precious metals, hedge funds, and derivatives. Supplements available.

Option Advisor. Investment Research Institute Inc. • Monthly. $200.00 per year. Newsletter. Provides specific advice and recommendations for trading in stock option contracts (puts and calls).

SFO: Stocks, Futures & Options. Wasendorf & Associates, Inc. • Monthly. $49.95 per year. Subtitle: *Official Journal for Personal Investing in Stocks, Futures, and Options.* Covers mainly speculative techniques for stocks, commodity futures, financial futures, stock index futures, foreign exchange, short selling, and various kinds of options.

Wall Street Transcript: A Professional Publication for the Business and Financial Community. Wall Street Transcript Corp. • Weekly. $1,890.00. per year. Provides reprints of investment research reports.

TRADE/PROFESSIONAL ASSOCIATIONS

Chicago Board Options Exchange. 400 S LaSalle St., Chicago, IL 60605. Phone: 877-THE-CBOE or (312)786-5600 Fax: (312)786-7409 E-mail: calvinj@cboe.com • URL: http://www.cboe.com • Individuals, institutions and firms engaged in the buying and selling of various products including stock options, cash-settled index options, options on HOLDRs, options on Exchange Traded Funds and Structured Products.

OTHER SOURCES

Chicago Board Options Exchange. CCH, Inc. • Monthly. $561.00 per year. Looseleaf service. Periodic supplementation. Rules, regulations and legal aspects for the trading of puts and calls.

Commodity Futures Law Reports. CCH, Inc. • Semimonthly. $948.00 per year. Looseleaf service. Periodic supplementation. Includes legal aspects of financial futures and stock options trading.

Daily Graphs. Option Guide. Daily Graphs, Inc. • Weekly. $300.00 per year.

Managing Financial Risk with Forwards, Futures, Options, and Swaps. American Management Association Extension Institute. • Looseleaf. $159.00. Self-study course. Emphasis is on practical explanations, examples, and problem solving. Quizzes and a case study are included.

The Options Workbook: Proven Strategies from a Market Wizard. Anthony J. Saliba. Dearborn Trade Publishing, A Kaplan Professional Co. • 2001. $40.00. Emphasis is on computerized trading on the Chicago Board Options Exchange. Includes information on specific trading strategies.

STOCK OWNERSHIP PLANS

See: EMPLOYEE BENEFIT PLANS; EMPLOYEE STOCK OWNERSHIP PLANS; EXECUTIVE COMPENSATION

STOCKBROKERS

See: STOCK BROKERS

STOCKHOLDERS

See also: INSIDER TRADING

ABSTRACTS AND INDEXES

Business Periodicals Index. H. W. Wilson Co. • 11 times a year. Quarterly and annual cumulations. Price varies.

INTERNET DATABASES

U. S. Securities and Exchange Commission. Phone: 800-732-0330 or (202)942-7040 Fax: (202)942-9634 E-mail: webmaster@sec.gov • URL: http://www.sec.gov • SEC Web site offers free access through EDGAR to text of official corporate filings, such as annual reports (10-K), quarterly reports (10-Q), and proxies. (EDGAR is "Electronic Data Gathering, Analysis, and Retrieval System.") An example is given of how to obtain executive compensation data from proxies. Text of the daily *SEC News Digest* is offered, as are links to other government sites, non-government market regulators, and U. S. stock exchanges. Search facilities are extensive. Fees: Free.

ONLINE DATABASES

Wilson Business Abstracts Online. H. W. Wilson Co. • Indexes and abstracts 600 major business periodicals, plus the *Wall Street Journal* and the business section of the *New York Times.* Indexing is from 1982, abstracting from 1990, with the two newspapers included from 1993. Updated weekly. Inquire as to online cost and availability. (*Business Periodicals Index* without abstracts is also available online.)

PERIODICALS AND NEWSLETTERS

Barron's: The Dow Jones Business and Financial Weekly. • Weekly. $145.00 per year.

Investor Relations Business. Thomson Media. • Semimonthly. $495.00 per year. Covers the issues affecting stockholder relations, corporate public relations, and institutional investor relations.

Pensions and Investments: The Newspaper of Corporate and Institutional Investing. Crain Communications, Inc. • Biweekly. $225.00 per year. Formerly *Pensions and Investment Age.*

Securities Industry News. Thomson Financial Corporate Communications. • Weekly. $275.00 per year. Newsletter covers securities dealing and processing, including regulatory compliance, shareholder services, human resources, transaction clearing, and technology.

Trusts and Estates. Primedia Business Magazines and Media. • Monthly. $139.00 per year. Includes annual *Directory.*

TRADE/PROFESSIONAL ASSOCIATIONS

Fund for Stockowners Rights. P.O. 65563, Washington, DC 20035. Phone: (703)241-3700 Fax: (818)223-8080 • Seeks to improve methods of electing corporate boards of directors and encourages the holding of annual meetings for stockholders.

STOCKINGS

See: HOSIERY INDUSTRY

STOCKS

See also: DIVIDENDS; INVESTMENT ADVISORY SERVICES; INVESTMENTS; OVER-THE-COUNTER SECURITIES INDUSTRY; SECURITIES; STOCK EXCHANGES

GENERAL WORKS

All About Stock Market Strategies. David Brown and Kassandra Bentley. McGraw-Hill. • 2002. $16.

95. Describes various, conservative ways of trying to obtain better than average stock investment results. (All About Series).

The Bear Book: Survive and Profit in Ferocious Markets. John Rothchild. John Wiley and Sons, Inc. • 1998. $24.95. Tells how to invest when the stock market is sinking.

Beating the Street: The Best-Selling Author of "One Up on Wall Street" Shows You How to Pick Winning Stocks and Mutual Funds. Peter Lynch and John Rothchild. Simon & Schuster Trade. • 1993. $23.00.

Dow 40,000 Portfolio: The Stock to Own to Out Perform Today's Leading Benchmark. David Elias. McGraw Hill. • 2000. $24.95.

Dow 40,000: Strategies for Profiting from the Greatest Bull Market in History. David Elias. Soaring Eagle Communications. • 1999. $15.95. Predicts continuing strong growth in the U. S. economy, low interest rates, and low inflation, resulting in a level of 40,000 for the Dow Jones Industrial Average in the year 2016.

Dow 100,000: Fact or Fiction. Charles W. Kadlec. Prentice Hall PTR. • 1999. $25.00. Predicts a level of 100,000 for the Dow Jones Industrial Average in the year 2020, based mainly on a technological revolution.

Dumb Money: Adventures of a Day Trader. Gary Wolf and Joey Anuff. Random House, Inc. • 2000. $9.95. An account of the day trading ordeals of one of the authors, Joey Anuff.

Financial Institutions and Markets. Meir J. Kohn. Oxford University Press, Inc. • 2003. $115.00. Second edition.

The Five Rules for Successful Stock Investing: Morningstar's Guide to Building Wealth and Winning in the Market. Pat Dorsey. John Wiley and Sons, Inc. • 2004. $24.95. Provides conservative investment advice from Morningstar's Director of Stock Analysis.

Getting Started in Stocks, Bonds, Online Investing. Alvin D. Hall. John Wiley and Sons, Inc. • 1999. $56.85. (Getting Started in... Series).

How to Buy Stocks. Louis Engel and Henry L. Hecht. Little Brown and Co. • 1994. $15.95. Eighth edition.

How to Invest Wisely. Lawrence S. Pratt. American Institute for Economic Research. • 2002. $12.00. Presents a conservative policy of investing, with emphasis on dividend-paying common stocks. Gold and other inflation hedges are compared. Includes a reprint of *Toward an Optimal Stock Selection Strategy* (1997). (Economic Education Bulletin.).

How to Make Money in Stocks: A Winning System in Good Times or Bad. William J. O'Neil. McGraw-Hill. • 2002. $12.95. Third edition. The author is the founder of *Investor's Business Daily.*

The Individual Investor's Revolution: Unlock the Secrets of Wall Street and Invest Like a Pro. Charles B. Carlson. McGraw-Hill. • 2000. $15.95. Emphasizes the growing importance of the individual investor, especially with regard to online trading (e-trading). Includes the author's favorite websites for investors and traders.

The Intelligent Asset Allocator: How to Build Your Portfolio to Maximize Returns and Minimize Risk. William J. Bernstein. McGraw-Hill. • 2000. $29.95. Contains popularly written, conservative advice for the average investor. Explains such items as portfolio theory, market efficiency, stock valuation models, and index investing.

Intelligent Investor: A Book of Practical Counsel. Benjamin Graham. HarperInformation. • 1997. $30.00. Fourth revised edition.

The Internet Bubble: Inside the Overvalued World of High-Tech Stocks, and What You Should Know to Avoid the Coming Catastrophe. Anthony Perkins and Michael C. Perkins. HarperInformation. • 2001.

$28.00. Revised edition. The authors predict a shakeout in e-commerce stocks and other Internet-related investments. (HarperBusiness.).

Investing in Small-Cap Stocks. Christopher Graja and Elizabeth Ungar. Bloomberg. • 1999. $26.95. Second expanded revised edition. Provides a practical strategy for investing in small-capitalization stocks. (Bloomberg Personal Bookshelf Series.).

Investing in the Over-the-Counter Markets: Stocks, Bonds, IPOs. Alvin D. Hall. John Wiley and Sons, Inc. • 1995. $29.95. Provides advice and information on investing in "unlisted" or NASDAQ (National Association of Securities Dealers Automated Quotation System) stocks, bonds, and initial public offerings (IPOs).

Irrational Exuberance. Robert J. Shiller. Princeton University Press. • 2000. $35.00. States that below-average stock market returns occur in the years following very high price-earnings ratios and very low dividend yields. 1901, 1929, 1966, and 2000 are cited as portentous years.

It Was a Very Good Year: Extraordinary Moments in Stock Market History. Martin S. Fridson. John Wiley and Sons, Inc. • 1997. $29.95. Provides details on what happened during each of the ten best years for the stock market since 1900. (Investment Series).

Keys to Investing in Common Stocks. Barbara Apostolou and Nicholas Apostolou. Barron's Educational Series, Inc. • 2004. $7.95. Fourth edition. Provides basic information for the average small investor. Covers investing in both individual stocks and mutual funds.

Learn to Earn: An Introduction to the Basics of Investing and Business. Peter Lynch and John Rothchild. Simon & Schuster Trade. • 1996. $14.00.

Market Efficiency: Stock Market Behavior in Theory and Practice. Andrew W. Lo, editor. Edward Elgar Publishing, Inc. • 1997. $465.00. Two volumes. Consists of reprints of 49 articles dating from 1937 to 1993, in five sections: "Theoretical Foundations," "The Random Walk Hypothesis," "Variance Bounds Tests," "Overreaction and Underreaction," and "Anomalies." (International Library of Critical Writings in Financial Economics Series: No. 3).

One Up on Wall Street: How to Use What You Already Know to Make Money in the Market. Peter Lynch and John Rothchild. Simon and Schuster. • 2000. $14.00.

A Random Walk Down Wall Street: The Best Investment Advice for the New Century. Burton G. Malkiel. W. W. Norton & Co., Inc. • 1999. $29.95. Seventh revised edition.

Security Analysis. S. Cottle and Others. McGraw-Hill. • 1988. $59.95. Fifth edition.

Stock Market Crashes and Speculative Manias. Eugene N. White, editor. Edward Elgar Publishing, Inc. • 1996. $255.00. Contains reprints of 23 articles dating from 1905 to 1994. (International Library of Macroeconomic and Financial History Series: No. 13).

Stocks for the Long Run: The Definitive Guide to Financial Market Returns and Long-Term Investment Strategies. Jeremy J. Siegel. McGraw-Hill. • 2002. $29.95. Third revised edition. A favorable view of a buy-and-hold strategy for stock market investors. (Teach Yourself Series).

Trading to Win: The Psychology of Mastering the Markets. Ari Kiev. John Wiley and Sons, Inc. • 1998. $39.95. A mental health guide for stock, bond, and commodity traders. Tells how to keep speculative emotions in check, overcome self-doubt, and focus on a winning strategy. (Trading Series).

What Works on Wall Street: A Guide to the Best Performing Investment Strategies of All Time. James P. O'Shaughnessy. McGraw-Hill. • 1998. $49.95. Second revised edition. Examines investment strategies over a 43-year period and concludes that large

capitalization, high-dividend-yield stocks produce the best results. Includes digital audio.

Yes, You Can Time the Market!. Ben Stein and Phil DeMuth. John Wiley and Sons, Inc. • 2003. $24.95. Despite the title, provides generally conservative advice for investors. Timing, in this case, relates to longterm trends and valuations.

ABSTRACTS AND INDEXES

Investment Statistics Locator. Linda H. Bentley and Jennifer J. Kiesl, editors. Greenwood Publishing Group, Inc. • 1994. $69.95. Expanded revised edition. Provides detailed subject indexing of more than 50 of the most-used sources of financial and investment data. Includes an annotated bibliography.

CD-ROM DATABASES

OECD Statistical Compendium. Organization for Economic Cooperation and Development. • Semiannual. $1,905.00 per year for 1 to 10 users. CD-ROM contains more than 730,000 monthly, quarterly, and annual time series for OECD countries, 1960 to date. Includes fully searchable data on agriculture, food, economic indicators, national accounts, employment, energy, finance, industry, technology, and foreign trade. Results can be displayed in various forms.

DIRECTORIES

FII Annual Guide to Stocks. Financial Information, Inc. • Annual. $2,250.00. Two volumes. Formerly *Financial Stock Guide Service: Directory of Active Stocks.*

Institutional Buyers of Small-Cap Stocks. Investment Data Corp. • Annual. $295.00. Provides detailed profiles of more than 837 institutional buyers of small capitalization stocks. Includes names of financial analysts and portfolio managers.

Mergent's Handbook of Common Stocks. Mergent, Inc. • Quarterly. $350.00 per year ($100.00 per copy). Contains one-page profiles of about 1,000 major corporations listed on the New York Stock Exchange. Includes analysis, comment, stock price performance data, and 10-year financial statistics. Formerly *Moody's Handbook of Common Stocks.*

Mergent's Handbook of Dividend Achievers. Mergent, Inc. • Quarterly. $160.00 per year ($45.00 per copy). Provides information on about 300 companies that have increased cash dividends for the past 10 or more consecutive years. Formerly *Moody's Handbook of Dividend Achievers.*

Mergent's Handbook of NASDAQ Stocks. Mergent, Inc. • Quarterly. $350.00 per year ($100.00 per copy). Contains one-page profiles of more than 600 major companies traded on the NASDAQ National Exchange or the American Stock Exchange. Includes price performance scores, analysis, comment, and seven-year financial statistics. Formerly *Moody's Handbook of NASDAQ Stocks.*

Morningstar American Depositary Receipts. Morningstar, Inc. • Biweekly. $195.00 per year. Looseleaf. Provides detailed profiles of 700 foreign companies having shares traded in the U. S. through American Depositary Receipts (ADRs).

S & P MidCap 400 Directory. Standard and Poors Corp. • Annual. $66.00. Contains detailed profiles of the companies included in Standard & Poor's MidCap 400 Index of stock prices. Includes income and balance sheet data for up to 10 years, with growth and stability rankings for 400 midsized corporations.

Standard & Poor's 500 Guide. McGraw-Hill. • Annual. $27.95. Contains detailed profiles of the companies included in Standard & Poor's 500 Index of stock prices. Includes income and balance sheet data for up to 10 years, with growth and stability rankings for 500 major corporations.

Standard and Poor's Security Dealers of North America. Standard & Poor's. • Semiannual. $480.00 per year; with *Supplements* every six weeks.

Geographical listing of over 12,000 stock, bond, and commodity dealers.

Walker's Manual of Unlisted Stocks. Walker's Manual, LLC. • Annual. $99.00. Provides information on 500 over-the-counter stocks,including many "penny stocks" trading at less than $5.00 per share.

Zacks Analyst Directory: Listed by Broker. Zacks Investment Research. • Quarterly. $395.00 per year. Lists stockbroker investment analysts and gives the names of major U. S. corporations covered by those analysts.

Zacks Analyst Directory: Listed by Company. Zacks Investment Research. • Quarterly. $395.00 per year. Lists major U. S. corporations and gives the names of stockbroker investment analysts covering those companies.

Zacks EPS Calendar. Zacks Investment Research. • Biweekly. $1,250.00 per year. (Also available monthly at $895.00 per year.) Lists anticipated reporting dates of earnings per share for major U. S. corporations.

ENCYCLOPEDIAS AND DICTIONARIES

The A-Z Vocabulary for Investors. American Institute for Economic Research. • 1997. $7.00. Second half of book is a "General Glossary" of about 400 financial terms "most-commonly used" in investing. First half contains lengthier descriptions of types of banking institutions (commercial banks, thrift institutions, credit unions), followed by succinct explanations of various forms of investment: stocks, bonds, options, futures, commodities, and "Other Investments" (collectibles, currencies, mortgages, precious metals, real estate, charitable trusts). (Economic Education Bulletin.).

Common Stock Newspaper Abbreviations and Trading Symbols. Howard R. Jarrell. Scarecrow Press, Inc. • 1989. $60.00. Gives the meanings of financial page company name abbreviations and stock symbols.

Common Stock Newspaper Abbreviations and Trading Symbols: Supplement One. Howard R. Jarrell. Scarecrow Press, Inc. • 1991. $40.00. Provides changes and new listings occurring since the publication of Jarrell's original volume in 1989.

Dictionary of Finance and Investment Terms. John Downes. Barron's Educational Series, Inc. • 2002. $14.95. Sixth edition. Provides clear explanations of more than 5,000 business, banking, financial, investment, and tax terms. Includes a separate list of financial abbreviations and acronyms. (Business Dictionaries Series).

Encyclopedia of Chart Patterns. Thomas N. Bulkowski. John Wiley and Sons, Inc. • 2000. $79.95. Provides explanations of the predictive value of various chart patterns formed by stock and commodity price movements. (Trading Series).

HANDBOOKS AND MANUALS

Indexing for Maximum Investment Results. Albert S. Neuberg. Fitzroy Dearborn Publishers, Inc. • 1998. $65.00. Covers the Standard & Poor's 500 and other indexing strategies for both individual and institutional investors.

Mergent Handbook of Common Stocks. Mergent, Inc. • Annual. Price on application. Facts, performance trends and financial summaries on nearly 1,000 New York Stock Exchange companies. Formerly *Moody's Handbook of Common Stocks.*

101 Rules of Trading Discipline. Pejman Hamidi. McGraw-Hill. • 2002. $39.95. Trading rules for investors or speculators are presented in three categories: "Trading Disciplines," "Market Disciplines," and "Personal Disciplines." (Teach Yourself Series).

Streetsmart Guide to Short Selling: Techniques the Pros Use to Profit in Any Market. Tom Taulli. McGraw-Hill. • 2002. $29.95. Provides the details of short sale procedures and offers practical advice

STOCK OPTION CONTRACTS

Technical Analysis of Stock Trends. John Magee and others. Saint Lucie Press. • 2001. $99.95. Eighth edition. Standard manual of technical analysis.

Trading for a Living: Psychology, Trading Tactics, Money Management. Alexander Elder. John Wiley and Sons, Inc. • 1993. $70.00. Covers technical and chart methods of trading in commodity and financial futures, options, and stocks. Includes Elliott Wave Theory, oscillators, moving averages, point-and-figure, and other technical approaches. (Finance Series).

INTERNET DATABASES

BanxQuote Banking, Mortgage, and Finance Center. BanxQuote, Inc. Phone: (914)722-1600 Fax: (914)722-6630 E-mail: info@banx.com • URL: http://www.banx.com • Web site quotes interest rates paid by banks around the country on various savings products, as well as rates paid by consumers for automobile loans, mortgages, credit cards, home equity loans, and personal loans. Also provided: stock quotes, indexes, stock options, futures trading data, economic indicators, and links to many other financial sites. Daily updates. Fees: Free.

Business 2.0 Web Guide to the Best Business Links. Business 2.0 Media Inc. Phone: (415)293-4800 E-mail: support@business2.com • URL: http://www.business2.com/webguide • Web site presents an extensive, searchable directory of links to "the best, most informative, and authoritative web pages." Twenty main categories cover business, finance, career, company information, people, and technology topics, with thousands of subtopics, all linking to Web sites recommended by experienced business researchers. Fees: Free.

Business Week Online. McGraw-Hill. Phone: (212)512-2511 Fax: (684)842-6101 • URL: http://www.businessweek.com • Web site provides complete contents of current issue of *Business Week* plus "BW Daily" with additonal business news, financial market quotes, and corporate information from Standard & Poor's. Includes various features, such as "Banking Center" with mortgage and interest data, and "Interactive Computer Buying Guide." The "Business Week Archive" is fully searchable back to 1996.

CANOE: Canadian Online Explorer. Canoe Limited Partnership. Phone: (416)947-2154 Fax: (416)947-2209 • URL: http://www.canoe.ca • Web site provides a wide variety of Canadian news and information, including business and financial data. Includes "Money," "Your Investment," "Technology," and "Stock Quotes." Allows keyword searching, with links to many other sites. Daily updating. Fees: Free.

Factiva. Dow Jones Reuters Business Interactive, LLC. Phone: 800-369-7466 or (609)452-1511 Fax: (609)520-5770 E-mail: solutions@factiva.com • URL: http://www.factiva.com • Fee-based Web site provides "global news and business information through Web sites and content integration solutions." Includes Dow Jones and Reuters newswires, The Wall Street Journal, and more than 7,000 other sources of current news, historical articles, market research reports, and investment analysis. Content includes 96 major U. S. newspapers, 900 non-English sources, trade publications, media transcripts, country profiles, news photos, etc.

Fedstats. Federal Interagency Council on Statistical Policy. Phone: (202)395-7254 • URL: http://www.fedstats.gov • Web site features an efficient search facility for full-text statistics produced by more than 100 federal agencies, including the Census Bureau, the Bureau of Economic Analysis, and the Bureau of Labor Statistics. Boolean searches can be made within one agency or for all agencies combined. Links are offered to international statistical bureaus,

including the UN, IMF, OECD, UNESCO, Eurostat, and 20 individual countries. Fees: Free.

The Financial Post (Web site). National Post Online. Phone: 800-805-1184 or (244)383-2300 Fax: (416)383-2443 • URL: http://www.nationalpost.com/financialpost/ • Provides a broad range of Canadian business news online, with daily updates. Includes news, opinion, and special reports, as well as "Investing," "Money Rates," "Market Watch," and "Daily Mutual Funds." Allows advanced searching (Boolean operators), with links to various other sites. Fees: Free.

FreeLunch.com. Economy.com, Inc. Phone: (610)696-8700 Fax: (610)696-1678 • URL: http://www.freelunch.com • Web site provides free access to more than 1.5 million economic and financial data series, covering industry, demographics, labor markets, prices, retail sales, government spending, trade, interest rates, housing starts, the stock market, and many other topics. Data is available for various time periods in either chart or table form. Searching is offered. Fees: Free, but registration required. Economy.com, Inc. also offers fee-based economic analysis at *The Dismal Scientist* site (http://www.dismal.com).

Hoover's Online. Hoover's, Inc. Phone: 800-486-8666 or (512)374-4500 Fax: (512)374-4501 • URL: http://www.hoovers.com • Web site provides stock quotes, lists of companies, and a variety of business information at no charge. In-depth company profiles are available.

Mergent Online. Mergent, Inc. Phone: 800-342-5647 or (704)559-7601 Fax: (704)559-6945 E-mail: customerservice@mergent.com • URL: http://www.mergentonline.com • Fee-based Web site provides detailed information on 20,000 publicly-owned companies in 100 foreign countries, as well as more than 10,000 corporations listed on the New York Stock Exchange, American Stock Exchange, NASDAQ, and U. S. regional exchanges. Searching is offered on many financial variables and text fields. Weekly updating. Formerly *FIS Online.*

Morningstar.com: Your First Second Opinion. Morningstar, Inc. Phone: 800-735-0700 or (312)696-6000 Fax: (312)696-6001 E-mail: productsupport@morningstar.com • URL: http://www.morningstar.com • Web site provides a broad selection of information and advice on both mutual funds and individual stocks, including financial news and articles on investment fundamentals. Basic service is free, with "Premium Membership" available at $109.00 per year. Annual fee provides personal portfolio analysis, screening tools, and more extensive profiles of funds and stocks.

Nexis.com. Lexis-Nexis Group. Phone: 800-227-4908 or (937)865-6800 Fax: (937)865-6909 E-mail: webmaster@prod.lexis-nexis.com • URL: http://www.nexis.com • Fee-based Web site offers searching of about 2.8 billion documents in some 30,000 news, business, and legal information sources. Features include a subject directory covering 1,200 topics in 34 categories and a Company Dossier containing information on more than 500,000 public and private companies. Boolean searching is offered.

TheStreet.com: Your Insider's Look at Wall Street. TheStreet.com, Inc. Phone: 800-562-9571 or (212)321-5000 Fax: (212)321-5016 • URL: http://www.thestreet.com • Web site offers "Free Sections" and "Premium Sections" ($24.95 per month). Both sections offer iconoclastic advice and comment on the stock market, but premium service displays a more comprehensive selection of news and analysis. There are many by-lined articles. "Search the Site" is included.

ONLINE DATABASES

Disclosure SEC Database. Thomson Financial. • Provides online information from records filed with the Securities and Exchange Commission by more

than 12,000 publicly-owned companies in the U.S. Includes about 200 financial data items and information relating to executives. Time span is 1977 to date, with weekly updates. Inquire as to online cost and availability.

EdgarPlus: SEC Basic Filings. Thomson Financial. • Online service provides full text of about 60,000 documents that have been filed with the U.S. Securities and Exchange Commission, 1987 to date, with daily updates. Filings include 6-K, 8-K, 10-K, 10-C, 10-Q, 20-F, and proxy statements. Inquire as to online cost and availability.

F & S Index. Gale Cengage Learning. • Contains about four million citations to worldwide business, financial, and industrial or consumer product literature appearing from 1972 to date. Weekly updates. Inquire as to online cost and availability.

First Call Consensus Earnings Estimates. Thomson Financial. • Online service provides corporate earnings estimates for more than 2,500 U. S. companies, based on data from leading brokerage firms. Weekly updates. Inquire as to online cost and availability.

Standard and Poor's Daily News Online. Standard and Poor's Corp. • Full text of business news and other information, 1984 to present. Inquire as to online cost and availability.

Zacks Earnings Estimates. Zacks Investment Research. • Provides online earnings projections for about 6,000 U. S. corporations, based on investment analysts' reports. Data is mainly from 200 major brokerage firms. Time span varies according to online provider, with daily or weekly updates. Inquire as to online cost and availability.

PERIODICALS AND NEWSLETTERS

The Asian Wall Street Journal. Dow Jones & Co., Inc. • Daily. $970.00 per year (air mail). Published in Hong Kong. Also available in a weekly edition at $259.00 per year: *Asian Wall Street Journal Weekly.*

Barron's: The Dow Jones Business and Financial Weekly. • Weekly. $145.00 per year.

BI Research. Thomas Bishop, editor. BI Research, Inc. • Every six weeks. $110.00 per year. Newsletter. Five to eight in-depth investment recommendations per year.

The Cabot Market Letter. Cabot Heritage Corp. • Description: Analyzes and recommends stock investments. Emphasizes that "optimum profits depend upon good market timing and good stock selection." Each issue follows a model portfolio made up of 12 stocks from lesser known companies chosen for their high potential for rapid, long-term growth.

Canadian Resources and PennyMines Analyst: The Canadian Newsletter for Penny-Mines Investors Who Insist on Geological Value. MPL Communications, Inc. • Weekly. $145.00 per year. Newsletter. Mainly on Canadian gold mine stocks. Formerly *Canadian PennyMines Analyst.*

Dick Davis Digest. Dick Davis Publishing. • Description: Carries excerpts from over 400 stock market letters and stock, bond, and mutual fund recommendations from leading analysts on Wall Street. Provides overview of general market trends and news of specific industries and companies. Recurring features include columns titled Personal Note, Spotlight Stock, Where's the Market Going, and The Last Word.

Dow Theory Forecasts: Business and Stock Market. Dow Theory Forecasts, Inc. • Weekly. $233.00 per year. Provides information and advice on blue chip and income stocks.

Dow Theory Letters. Dow Theory Letters, Inc. • 17 times a year. $250.00 per year. Newsletter on stock market trends, investing, and economic conditions.

DRIP Investor: Your Guide to Buying Stocks Without a Broker. Horizon Publishing, Co., LLC. • Monthly. $89.00 per year. Newsletter covering the dividend

For publishers addresses, refer to SOURCES CITED section at the back of the book.

853

reinvestment plans (DRIPs) of various publicly-owned corporations. Includes model portfolios and *Directory of Dividend Reinvestment Plans.*

The Financial Post: Canadian's Business Voice. Financial Post Datagroup. • Daily. $200.00 per year. Provides Canadian business, economic, financial, and investment news. Features extensive price quotes from all major Canadian markets: stocks, bonds, mutual funds, commodities, and currencies. Supplement available: *Financial Post 500.* Includes annual supplement.

Financial Sentinel: Your Beacon to the World of Investing. Gulf Atlantic Publishing, Inc. • Monthly. $29.95 per year. Provides "The only complete listing of all OTC Bulletin Board stocks traded, with all issues listed on the Nasdaq SmallCap Market, the Toronto, and Vancouver Stock Exchanges." Also includes investment advice and recommendations of small capitalization stocks.

Financial Times [London]. The Financial Times, Inc. • Daily, except Sunday. $572.88 per year. An international business and financial newspaper, featuring news from London, Paris, Frankfurt, New York, and Tokyo. Includes worldwide stock and bond market data, commodity market data, and monetary/currency exchange information.

Forbes. Forbes, Inc. • Biweekly. $59.95 per year. Includes supplements: *Forbes ASAP* and *Forbes FYI.*

Gilder Technology Report. George Gilder, editor. Gilder Publishing. • Monthly. $295.00 per year. Newsletter. Makes specific recommendations for investing in technology stocks. (A joint publication of Forbes Magazine and the Gilder Technology Group.).

Growth Stock Outlook. Charles Allmon, editor. Growth Stock Outlook Inc. • Description: Provides data on stock earnings, sales, price-earnings ratios, dividends, book values, returns on shareholder equity, and institutional holdings. Recommends specific companies for long-term investment. Recurring features include a stock selection guide, and a $10,000 supervised portfolio. **Remarks:** Subscription includes the supplements Junior Growth Stocks, New Issue Digest, and (see separate listings); also includes access to a telephone hotline.

InvesTech Market Analyst: Technical and Monetary Investment Analysis. InvesTech Research. • Every three weeks. $190.00 per year. Newsletter. Provides interpretation of monetary statistics and Federal Reserve actions, especially as related to technical analysis of stock market price trends.

Investment Guide. American Investment Services Inc. • Description: Contains analyses of stock market activity and strategies for investment. Recurring features include market statistics, Dow high-yield stock investing.

The Investment Reporter. MPL Communications Inc. • Description: Profiles specific companies and market trends and developments, making recommendations to assist in formulating investment strategies. Includes short articles offering advice on investment decisions.

Investor's Business Daily. Investor's Business Daily, Inc. • Daily. $295.00 per year. Newspaper.

Investors Intelligence. Michael Burke, editor. Chartcraft Inc. • Description: Serves as a "comprehensive and authoritative Stock Market Advisory Service dedicated to bringing the investor facts, original projections, and a cross section of the recommendations of other leading Services.".

The Low Priced Stock Survey. Horizon Publishing Company L.L.C. • Description: Reviews and analyzes stocks offered at a price of $20 or less. Analysis is divided into sections: Emerging Growth Opportunities, The Fundamentalist, Bargain Spotlight, Stock of the Month, and Master List Highlights. Includes weekly closes of the Dow Jones

Industrials and NASDAQ, and statistics.

Medical Technology Stock Letter. Medical Technology Stock Letter. • Description: Specializes in investments in biotechnology companies. Offers news of the industry and recommendations for buying, selling, and holding stocks. Recurring features include news of research, a model portfolio reflecting the editors' investment strategy, and columns titled Pulse of the Market and Industry Scan. **Remarks:** Also available through e-mail.

The Moneypaper. Temper of the Times Communications, Inc. Temper of the Times Communications Inc. • Description: Contains strategies to minimize stock sales costs and articles on investing and market trends. Includes a summary of monthly financial news drawn from over 70 financial publications and advisory services. Recurring features include columns titled Summing Up, Market Outlook, and Stocktrack.

Morningstar StockInvestor. Morningstar, Inc. • Monthly. $89.00 per year. Newsletter. Features about a dozen stocks in an aggressive "Hare Portfolio" and a dozen in a conservative "Tortoise Portfolio." Includes general advice on investing in stocks.

MPT Review; Specializing in Modern Portfolio Theory. Navellier and Associates, Inc. • Monthly. $275.00 per year. Newsletter. Provides specific stock selection and model portfolio advice (conservative, moderately aggressive, and aggressive) based on quantitative analysis and modern portfolio theory.

Richard C. Young's Intelligence Report. Access Intelligence L.L.C. • Description: Provides information for "serious, conservative investors (buy and hold as opposed to active traders)." Features investing advice and recommendations for best funds, stocks, and bonds for current or retirement income.

SFO: Stocks, Futures & Options. Wasendorf & Associates, Inc. • Monthly. $49.95 per year. Subtitle: *Official Journal for Personal Investing in Stocks, Futures, and Options.* Covers mainly speculative techniques for stocks, commodity futures, financial futures, stock index futures, foreign exchange, short selling, and various kinds of options.

Special Situations Newsletter: In-Depth Survey of Under-Valued Stocks. Charles Howard Kaplan. • Monthly. $75.00 per year. Newsletter. Principal content is "This Month's Recommendation," a detailed analysis of one special situation stock.

Standard & Poor's SmallCap 600 Guide. McGraw-Hill. • Monthly. $24.95. Contains detailed profiles of the companies included in Standard & Poor's SmallCap 600 Index of stock prices. Includes income and balance sheet data for up to 10 years, with growth and stability rankings for 600 small capitalization corporations.

Technology Investing. Michael Murphy, editor. PBI Media, Inc. • Monthly. $195.00 per year. Newsletter. Provides specific recommendations for investing in high technology companies.

The Wall Street Digest. Donald H. Rowe. • Description: Covers major investment areas, including stocks and bonds; foreign currencies; gold, silver, and other precious metals; real estate; tax shelters; and estate planning. Recurring features include "a digest of the month's best" investment and financial seminars, newsletter reviews, and statistics.

The Wall Street Journal. Dow Jones & Co., Inc. • Daily. $189.00 per year. Covers news and trends relating to business, industry, finance, the economy, and international commerce. Provides extensive price and other data for the securities, commodity, options, futures, foreign exchange, and money markets.

Wall Street Journal/Europe. Dow Jones & Co., Inc. • Daily. $300.00 per year (air mail). Published in Europe. Text in English.

Wall Street Transcript: A Professional Publication for the Business and Financial Community. Wall Street Transcript Corp. • Weekly. $1,890.00. per year. Provides reprints of investment research reports.

Zacks Analyst Watch. Zacks Investment Research. • Biweekly. $250.00 per year. Provides the results of research by stockbroker investment analysts on major U. S. corporations.

Zacks Earnings Forecaster. Zacks Investment Research. • Biweekly. $495.00 per year. (Also available monthly at $375.00 per year.) Provides estimates by stockbroker investment analysts of earnings per share of individual U. S. companies.

Zacks Profit Guide. Zacks Investment Research. • Quarterly. $375.00 per year. Provides analysis of total return and stock price performance of major U. S. companies.

PRICE SOURCES

National Stock Summary. Pink Sheets LLC. • Monthly, with semiannual cumulations. $576.00 per year. Includes price quotes for both active and inactive issues, with transfer agents, market makers (brokers), capital changes, name changes, and other corporate information. Pink Sheets LLC also provides daily and weekly stock price services. Formerly published by the National Quotation Bureau.

Standard and Poor's Daily Stock Price Records. Standard and Poor's. • Quarterly. New York Stock Exchange, $420.00 per year; American Stock Exchange, $441.00 per year; NASDAQ, $530.00 per year.

Stock Market Values and Yields 2000. RIA. • 2000. $22.00. Revised edition. Gives year-end prices and dividends for tax purposes.

RESEARCH CENTERS AND INSTITUTES

Center for Research in Security Prices. University of Chicago, 725 S. Wells St., Suite 800, Chicago, IL 60607. Phone: (773)834-4610 Fax: (773)702-3036 E-mail: custom@crsp.uchicago.edu • URL: http://gsbwww.uchicago.edu/research/crsp.

STATISTICS SOURCES

Advance-Decline Album. Dow Theory Letters, Inc. • Annual. Contains one page for each year since 1931. Includes charts of the New York Stock Exchange advance-decline ratio and the Dow Jones industrial average.

The AIER Chart Book. AIER Research Staff. American Institute for Economic Research. • Annual. $4.00. A compact compilation of long-range charts ("Purchasing Power of the Dollar," for example, goes back to 1780) covering various aspects of the U. S. economy. Includes inflation, interest rates, debt, gold, taxation, stock prices, etc. (Economic Education Bulletin.).

Business Statistics of the United States. Linz Audain and Cornelia J. Strawser. Bernan Associates. • Annual. $147.00. Based on *Business Statistics,* formerly issue by the Bureau of Economic Analysis, U. S. Department of Commerce. Provides basic data for a wide variety of U. S. industries, services, and economic indicators. Most statistics are shown annually for 30 years and monthly for the most recent four years.

Dow Jones Averages Chart Album. Dow Theory Letters, Inc. • Annual. $140.00. Contains one page for each year since 1885. Includes line charts of the Dow Jones industrial, transportation, utilities, and bond averages. Important historical and economic dates are shown.

Security Owner's Stock Guide. Standard and Poor's. • Monthly. $125.00 per year.

SRC Green Book of 5 Trend 35-Year Charts. Securities Research Co. • Annual. $150.00. Chart book presents statistical information on the stocks of 400

leading companies over a 35-year period. Each full page chart is in semi-log format to avoid visual distortion. Also includes charts of 12 leading market averages or indexes and 39 major industry groups.

Standard & Poor's Stock and Bond Guide. McGraw-Hill. • Annual. $24.95. Contains concise data on 6,000 stocks, 7,000 bonds, and 700 mutual funds. Includes year-end prices, earnings estimates for stocks, and debt ratings for bonds.

Standard & Poor's Stock Reports: NASDAQ and Regional Exchanges. Standard & Poor's. • Irregular. $1,100.00 per year. Looseleaf service. Provides two pages of financial details and other information for each corporation included.

Standard & Poor's Stock Reports: New York Stock Exchange. Standard & Poor's. • Irregular. $1,295.00 per year. Looseleaf service. Provides two pages of financial details and other information for each corporation with stock listed on the N. Y. Stock Exchange.

Stocks, Bonds, Bills, and Inflation Yearbook. Ibbotson Associates. • Annual. $92.00. Provides detailed data from 1926 to the present on inflation and the returns from various kinds of financial investments, such as small-cap stocks and long-term government bonds.

Survey of Current Business. Available from U. S. Government Printing Office. • Monthly. $63.00 per year. Issued by Bureau of Economic Analysis, U. S. Department of Commerce. Presents a wide variety of business and economic data.

TRADE/PROFESSIONAL ASSOCIATIONS

National Association of Securities Dealers (NASD). 1735 K St., N.W., Washington, DC 20006-1506. Phone: (202)728-8000 Fax: (202)293-6260 E-mail: waltere@nasd.com • URL: http://www.nasd.com • Formerly National Association of Securities Dealers.

Securities Industry and Financial Markets Association. 120 Broadway, 35th Fl., New York, NY 10271-0080. Phone: (212)313-1200 Fax: (212)313-1301 E-mail: rbrockhaus@sifma.org • URL: http://www.sifma.org • Represents more than 650 member firms of all sizes, in all financial markets in the U.S. and around the world. Enhances the public's trust and confidence in the markets, delivering an efficient, enhanced member network of access and forward-looking services, as well as premiere educational resources for the professionals in the industry and the investors whom they serve. Maintains offices in New York City and Washington, DC.

OTHER SOURCES

Blue Book of Stock Reports. MPL Communications Inc. • Biweekly. $260.00 per year. Canadian Business Service reports on over 250 Canadian companies.

Chartcraft Monthly NYSE and ASE Chartbook. Chartcraft, Inc. • Monthly. $402.00 per year. Includes all common stocks on New York and American Stock Exchanges.

Chartcraft Over-the-Counter Chartbook. Chartcraft, Inc. • Quarterly. $114.00 per year. Includes more than 1,000 unlisted stocks. Long term charts.

Daily Graphs. Daily Graphs, Inc. • New York Stock Exchange edition, $363.00 per year. NASDAQ O.T.C.-American Stock Exchange edition, $363.00 per year. Both editions include the 200 leading over-the-counter stocks.

Elliott Wave Theorist. Robert Prechter, editor. Elliott Wave International. • Monthly. $233.00 per year. Newsletter Formerly *Elliott Wave Commodity Forecasts.*

Granville Market Letter. Joseph Granville, editor. • 46 times a year. $250.00 per year.

Mansfield Stock Chart Service. R.W. Mansfield Co., Inc. • Weekly. Price varies. Newsletter. Covers New York Stock Exchange, American Stock Exchange, OTC exchange, international stocks and industry groups. Partial subscriptions available.

Mergent's Annual Dividend Record. Mergent, Inc. • Annual. $49.00. Provides detailed dividend data, including tax information, for 12,000 stocks and 18,000 mutual funds. Covers the most recent year. Formerly *Moody's Annual Dividend Record.*

The Value Line Investment Survey. Value Line Publishing, Inc. • Weekly. $570.00 per year. Newsletter. Provides detailed information and ratings for 1,700 stocks actively-traded in the U. S.

STOCKYARDS

See: LIVESTOCK INDUSTRY; MEAT INDUSTRY

STONE INDUSTRY

See: QUARRYING

STORAGE

See: WAREHOUSES

STORE DISPLAYS

See: DISPLAY OF MERCHANDISE

STORES, CONVENIENCE

See: CONVENIENCE STORES

STORES, DEPARTMENT

See: DEPARTMENT STORES

STORES (RETAIL TRADE)

See: RETAIL TRADE

STRATEGIC PLANNING

See: PLANNING

STRATEGY, BUSINESS

See: BUSINESS STRATEGY

STREET LIGHTING

See: LIGHTING

STREET MAPS

See: MAPS

STRESS (ANXIETY)

See also: INDUSTRIAL PSYCHOLOGY; MENTAL HEALTH

GENERAL WORKS

Managing Stress: Subjectivity and Power in the Workplace. Tim Newton. Sage Publications, Inc. • 1995. $74.50.

Managing Workplace Stress. Cary L. Cooper and Susan Cartwright. Sage Publications, Inc. • 1996. $70.95. Includes references and indexes. *Advanced Topics in Organizational Behavior Series, vol. 1.*

Psychological Symptoms. Frank J. Bruno. John Wiley and Sons, Inc. • 1994. $29.95. Explains the meaning of common mental symptoms, what may cause them, and how to deal with them.

Stress and Burnout in Library Service. Janette S. Caputo. Greenwood Publishing Group, Inc. • 1991. $24.95. Discusses symptoms of stress in library staff members and ways of dealing with stress. Includes self-help checklists and a list of references for further information.

Surviving Job Stress: How to Overcome Workday Pressures. John B. Arden. Career Press, Inc. • 2002. $14.99. Includes information on stress-related medical problems, nutrition issues, and the side effects of medication for stress.

ABSTRACTS AND INDEXES

Psychological Abstracts. American Psychological Association. • Monthly. Members, $815.00 per year; individuals and institutions, $1,207.00 per year. Covers the international literature of psychology and the behavioral sciences. Includes journals, technical reports, dissertations, and other sources.

BIBLIOGRAPHIES

Stress: A Bibliography with Indexes. Clarke M. Ivanich, editor. Nova Science Publishers, Inc. • 2002. $59.00. Provides book and journal citations to the literature of emotional stress. Includes author, title, and subject indexes.

CD-ROM DATABASES

Consumers Reference Disc. National Information Services Corp. • Quarterly. Provides the CD-ROM version of *Consumer Health and Nutrition Index* from Oryx Press and *Consumers Index to Product Evaluations and Information Sources* from Pierian Press. Contains citations to consumer health articles and consumer product evaluations, tests, warnings, and recalls.

Magazine Index Plus. Gale Cengage Learning. • Monthly. $4,000.00 per year (includes InfoTrac workstation). Provides full text on CD-ROM for about 100 popular, general interest magazines and indexing for 300 others. Includes special indexing of reviews and product evaluations. Time period is 1980 to date.

ENCYCLOPEDIAS AND DICTIONARIES

The Gale Encyclopedia of Psychology. Gale Cengage Learning. • 2001. $155.00. Second edition. Includes bibliographies arranged by topic and a glossary. More than 650 topics are covered.

HANDBOOKS AND MANUALS

Personal Health Reporter. Gale Cengage Learning. • 1992. $150.00. Two volumes. Volume one, $115.00; volume two, $115.00. Presents a collection of professional and popular articles on 150 topics relating to physical and mental health conditions and treatments.

Stress and Well-Being at Work: Assessments and Interventions for Occupational Mental Health. James C. Quick and others, editors. American Psychological Association. • 1992. $19.95.

ONLINE DATABASES

Mental Health Abstracts. IFI/Plenum Data Corp. • Provides indexing and abstracting of mental health and mental illness literature appearing in more than 1,200 journals and other sources from 1969 to date. Monthly updates. Inquire as to online cost and availability.

PsycINFO. American Psychological Association. • Provides indexing and abstracting of the worldwide literature of psychology and the behavioral sciences. Time period is 1967 to date, with monthly updates.

Inquire as to online cost and availability.

PERIODICALS AND NEWSLETTERS

Behavioral Medicine: An Interdisciplinary Journal of Research and Practice. Helen Dwight Reid Educational Foundation. Heldref Publications. • Quarterly. Individuals, $69.00 per year; institutions, $129.00 per year. An interdisciplinary journal of particular interest to physicians, psychologists, nurses, educators and all who are interested in behavorial and social influences on mental and physical health. Formerly *Journal of Human Stress.*

Journal of Business and Psychology. Business Psychology Research Institute. Kluwer Academic Publishers. • Quarterly. Institutions, $614.00 per year; with online edition, $736.80 per year.

Stress and Health. John Wiley and Sons, Inc., Journals. • Five times a year. Individuals, $310.00 per year; institutions, $620.00 per year. A forum for discussion of all aspects of stress which affect the individual in both health and disease. Provides international coverage. Formerly *Stress Medicine.*

RESEARCH CENTERS AND INSTITUTES

American Institute of Stress. 124 Park Ave., Yonkers, NY 10703. Phone: (914)963-1200 Fax: (914)965-6267 E-mail: stress124@earthlink.net • URL: http://www.stress.org • Explores personal and social consequences of stress. Compiles research data on occupational stress and executive stress or "burn out.".

OTHER SOURCES

The Market for Stress Management Products and Services. Available from MarketResearch.com. • 1996. $1,195.00. Market research report published by Marketdata Enterprises. Covers anti-anxiety drugs, stress management clinics, biofeedback centers, devices, seminars, workshops, spas, institutes, etc. Includes market size projections.

Personal Strategies for Managing Stress. American Management Association Extension Institute. • Looseleaf. $139.00. Self-study course. Emphasis is on practical explanations, examples, and problem solving. Quizzes and a case study are included.

STRIKES AND LOCKOUTS

See also: ARBITRATION; COLLECTIVE BARGAINING; LABOR; LABOR LAW AND REGULATION; LABOR UNIONS

GENERAL WORKS

Strike!. Jeremy Brecher. South End Press. • 1997. $40.00. Fourth revised edition. (Classics Series: Vol. 1.).

CD-ROM DATABASES

OECD Statistical Compendium. Organization for Economic Cooperation and Development. • Semiannual. $1,905.00 per year for 1 to 10 users. CD-ROM contains more than 730,000 monthly, quarterly, and annual time series for OECD countries, 1960 to date. Includes fully searchable data on agriculture, food, economic indicators, national accounts, employment, energy, finance, industry, technology, and foreign trade. Results can be displayed in various forms.

ENCYCLOPEDIAS AND DICTIONARIES

Encyclopedia of Labor History Worldwide. Gale Cengage Learning. • 2003. $295.00. Two volumes. Cover 300 key events, national and international, that took place in labor history over the past 200 years. Includes illustrations, maps, a glossary, a bibliography, and indexes. (St. James Press imprint.).

HANDBOOKS AND MANUALS

Labor Management Relations: Strikes, Lockouts, and Boycotts. West Group. • Annual. $165.00.

Looseleaf service. Covers legal issues involved in labor-management confrontations. Includes recent decisions of the National Labor Relations Board (NLRB).

Operating During Strikes: Company Experience, NLRB Policies, and Governmental Regulations. Charles R. Perry and others. Univ. of Pennsylvania, Center for Human Resources, The Wharton School. • 1982. $20.00. (Labor Relations and Public Policy Series: No. 23).

INTERNET DATABASES

Business 2.0 Web Guide to the Best Business Links. Business 2.0 Media Inc. Phone: (415)293-4800 E-mail: support@business2.com • URL: http://www.business2.com/webguide • Web site presents an extensive, searchable directory of links to "the best, most informative, and authoritative web pages." Twenty main categories cover business, finance, career, company information, people, and technology topics, with thousands of subtopics, all linking to Web sites recommended by experienced business researchers. Fees: Free.

Fedstats. Federal Interagency Council on Statistical Policy. Phone: (202)395-7254 • URL: http://www.fedstats.gov • Web site features an efficient search facility for full-text statistics produced by more than 100 federal agencies, including the Census Bureau, the Bureau of Economic Analysis, and the Bureau of Labor Statistics. Boolean searches can be made within one agency or for all agencies combined. Links are offered to international statistical bureaus, including the UN, IMF, OECD, UNESCO, Eurostat, and 20 individual countries. Fees: Free.

FreeLunch.com. Economy.com, Inc. Phone: (610)696-8700 Fax: (610)696-1678 • URL: http://www.freelunch.com • Web site provides free access to more than 1.5 million economic and financial data series, covering industry, demographics, labor markets, prices, retail sales, government spending, trade, interest rates, housing starts, the stock market, and many other topics. Data is available for various time periods in either chart or table form. Searching is offered. Fees: Free, but registration required. Economy.com, Inc. also offers fee-based economic analysis at *The Dismal Scientist* site (http://www.dismal.com).

PERIODICALS AND NEWSLETTERS

Union Labor Report. Bureau of National Affairs Inc. • Description: Covers legal, legislative, and regulatory developments and trends affecting management and labor in the workplace.

STATISTICS SOURCES

Business Statistics of the United States. Linz Audain and Cornelia J. Strawser. Bernan Associates. • Annual. $147.00. Based on *Business Statistics*, formerly issue by the Bureau of Economic Analysis, U. S. Department of Commerce. Provides basic data for a wide variety of U. S. industries, services, and economic indicators. Most statistics are shown annually for 30 years and monthly for the most recent four years.

Monthly Labor Review. Available from U. S. Government Printing Office. • Monthly. $49.00 per year. Issued by the Bureau of Labor Statistics, U. S. Department of Labor. Contains data on the labor force, wages, work stoppages, price indexes, productivity, economic growth, and occupational injuries and illnesses.

Survey of Current Business. Available from U. S. Government Printing Office. • Monthly. $63.00 per year. Issued by Bureau of Economic Analysis, U. S. Department of Commerce. Presents a wide variety of business and economic data.

Yearbook of Labour Statistics. Available from Bernan Associates. • Annual. $168.00. Published by the International Labour Organizaton (http://www.ilo.org). Provides data for more than 180 countries on

employment, unemployment, wages, hours of work, cost of labor, strikes, industrial accidents, and consumer prices.

STRUCTURAL MATERIALS

See: BUILDING MATERIALS INDUSTRY

STUDENT AID

See: SCHOLARSHIPS AND STUDENT AID

STUDY ABROAD

GENERAL WORKS

Study Abroad, 2003. Jerry S. Carlson and others. Peterson's. • 2002. $29.95. 10th edition.

ABSTRACTS AND INDEXES

Education Index. H. W. Wilson Co. • 10 times a year. Quarterly and annual cumulations. Price varies.

Readers' Guide to Periodical Literature. H. W. Wilson Co. • Monthly. $345.00 per year. Includes annual *Cumulation.* Indexes about 250 peridicals of general interest.

CD-ROM DATABASES

ERIC on SilverPlatter. Available from SilverPlatter Information, Inc. • Quarterly. $700.00 per year. Produced by the Office of Educational Research and Improvement, U. S. Dept. of Education. Provides CD-ROM indexing and abstracting of a wide variety of literature relating to education. Archival discs are available from 1966.

WILSONDISC: Education Index. H. W. Wilson Co. • Monthly. Provides CD-ROM indexing of education-related literature from 1983 to date. Price includes online service.

WILSONDISC: Readers' Guide to Periodical Literature. H. W. Wilson Co. • Monthly. $1,095.00 per year, including unlimited online access to *Readers' Guide to Periodical Literature* through WILSONLINE. Provides CD-ROM indexing of about 270 general interest periodicals. Covers 1983 to date. (*Readers' Guide Abstracts* also available on CD-ROM at $1,995 per year.).

DIRECTORIES

Academic Year Abroad. Institute of International Education Inc. • Covers: almost 6,000 undergraduate and graduate study-abroad programs conducted worldwide during the academic year by United States and foreign colleges and universities and other organizations in 80 countries. Entries include: Program name, sponsoring institution, contact person, address, phone, e-mail, website, pertinent dates, orientation, subjects offered, credits, housing, scholarships, language of instruction, related travel, teaching methods, tuition and other costs, prerequisites, work-study or internship opportunities, etc. Not to be confused with 'Academic Year and Summer Programs Abroad,' described separately.

Academic Year, Semester and Summer Programs Abroad. American Institute for Foreign Study. • Annual. Free. Formerly *Academic Year and Summer Programs Abroad.*

Bricker's International Directory: Long-Term University- Based Executive Programs. Peterson's. • Annual. $395.00. Presents detailed information about executive education programs offered by 85 universities and nonprofit organizations in the U. S. and around the world. Includes general management and function-specific programs.

Peterson's Guide to MBA Programs: The Most Comprehensive Guide to U. S., Canadian, and

International Business Schools. Peterson's. • 2002. $29.95. Provides detailed information on about 850 graduate programs in business at 700 colleges and universities in the U. S., Canada, and other countries.

Peterson's Study Abroad. Peterson's. • Covers: More than 1,800 academic year and semester Study Abroad programs. Entries include: Sponsor name, address, description of programs, course offerings, host institutions, admission requirements, costs, availability of college credit.

Study Abroad: Scholarships and Higher Education Courses Worldwide. Available from Bernan Associates. • Biennial. $34.95 provides information on a wide variety of scholarships, fellowships, and educational exchange programs in over 100 countries. Text in English, French, and Spanish. Published by the United Nations Educational, Scientific, and Cultural Organization (UNESCO).

Vacation Study Abroad. Institute of International Education Inc. • Covers: more than 2,200 college-level and adult education summer and short-term courses sponsored by United States and foreign colleges, language schools, and private and public organizations. Courses run from as briefly as two weeks to three months. Entries include: Name of institution or other sponsor, inclusive dates, subjects offered, orientation information, language of instruction, whether United States college credit is offered and how much, related travel, housing, costs, scholarships, work-study or internship opportunities, deadline, phone, fax, e-mail, website and address for application.

ONLINE DATABASES

Education Index Online. H. W. Wilson Co. • Indexes a wide variety of periodicals related to schools, colleges, and education, 1984 to date. Monthly updates. Inquire as to online cost and availability.

ERIC. Educational Resources Information Center. • Funded by the U. S. Department of Education, Institute of Education Sciences (formerly Office of Educational Research and Improvement). Provides access to more than one million online records covering education-related journal and report literature, 1966 to date. Updating is monthly. Inquire as to online cost and availability.

Readers' Guide Abstracts Online. H. W. Wilson Co. • Indexes and abstracts general interest periodicals, 1983 to date. Weekly updates. Inquire as to online cost and availability.

PERIODICALS AND NEWSLETTERS

NAFSA Newsletter. NAFSA: Association of International Educators. • Description: Concerned with international educational interchange. Reports on English as a second language, foreign admissions, study abroad, foreign student advising, community programming, and other subjects. Recurring features include government news, book reviews, news of members, Association news, and columns titled News and Briefs and From the Front Lines of Advocacy.

Transitions Abroad: The Guide to Learning, Living, and Working Overseas. Transitions Abroad Publishing, Inc. • Bimonthly. $28.00 per year, including annual directory of information sources. Provides practical information and advice on foreign education and employment. Supplement available *Overseas Travel Planner.*

STATISTICS SOURCES

Digest of Education Statistics. Available from U. S. Government Printing Office. • Annual. $51.00. Covers all areas of education from kindergarten through graduate school. Includes data from both government and private sources. Compiled by National

Center for Education Statistics, U. S. Department of Education.

TRADE/PROFESSIONAL ASSOCIATIONS

The College Board. 45 Columbus Ave., 45 Columbus Ave., New York, NY 10023-6992. Phone: (866)392-3017 or (212)713-8000 Fax: (212)649-8442 E-mail: publicaffairs@collegeboard.org • URL: http://www.collegeboard.com • Represents the schools, colleges, universities, and other educational organizations that seeks to connect members to success and opportunity. Serves students, parents, high schools, and colleges through major programs and services in college admission, guidance, assessment, financial aid, enrollment, and teaching and learning.

Council on International Educational Exchange - USA. Seven Custom House St., 3rd Fl., Portland, OR 04101. Phone: 800-407-8839 or (207)553-7600 Fax: (207)553-7699 • URL: http://www.ciee.org • Members are educational institutions and agencies that promote and sponsor international education exchange. Formerly Council on Student Travel.

EF Foundation for Foreign Study. EF Center Boston, One Education St., Cambridge, MA 02141. Phone: 800-447-4273 E-mail: foundation@ef.com • URL: http://www.effoundation.org • Seeks to further international understanding through cultural and academic exchange. Sponsors academic homestay programs, such as High School Year in Europe. Formerly EF Educational Foundation for Foreign Study.

Institute of International Education. 809 United Nations Plaza, New York, NY 10017-3580. Phone: (212)984-5200 Fax: (212)984-5452 E-mail: info@iie.org • URL: http://www.iie.org • Promotes international educational exchange programs. Administers scholarships, fellowships, and other grants provided by over 120 sponsors.

NAFSA: Association of International Educators. 1307 New York Ave., NW, 8th Fl., Washington, DC 20005-4701. Phone: (202)737-3699 Fax: (202)737-3657 E-mail: inbox@nafsa.org • URL: http://www.nafsa.org • Members are individuals, organizations, and institutions involved with international educational interchange, including foreign student advisors, overseas educational advisers, foreign student admission officers, and U. S. students abroad. Formerly National Association for Foreign Student Affairs.

National Registration Center for Study Abroad. P.O. Box 1393, Milwaukee, WI 53201. Phone: (414)278-7410 Fax: (414)271-8884 E-mail: inquire@nrcsa.com • URL: http://www.nrcsa.com • Members are foreign universities, foreign language institutions, and other institutions or organizations offering foreign study programs designed for North Americans.

Youth for Understanding International Exchange. 6400 Goldboro Rd. Ste. 100, Bethesda, MD 20817. Phone: (866)493-8872 or (240)235-2100 Fax: (240)235-2104 E-mail: admissions@yfo.org • URL: http://www.youthforunderstanding.org • Provides educational opportunities for young people and adults through international student exchange. Administers study abroad scholarship programs in cooperation with other governments, the U. S. Senate, the U. S. Information Agency, and various educational organizations.

STYLE MANUALS

See: PRINTING STYLE MANUALS

SUBCHAPTER "S" CORPORATIONS

See: CORPORATIONS; PROFESSIONAL CORPORATIONS

SUBJECT HEADINGS

See: INDEXING

SUBLIMINAL ADVERTISING

See: ADVERTISING

SUBSTANCE ABUSE

See: ALCOHOLISM; DRUG ABUSE AND TRAFFIC

SUBURBAN SHOPPING CENTERS

See: SHOPPING CENTERS

SUGAR INDUSTRY

ALMANACS AND YEARBOOKS

Agricultural and Mineral Commodities Year Book. Available from Taylor & Francis Group. • Annual. $225.00. Published by Europa Publications. Contains descriptive product profiles, price data, export-import data, and production statistics for major commodities of the world. Includes commodity histories, uses, markets, demand trends, and information about trade agreements and key commodity organizations.

CD-ROM DATABASES

Food Science and Technology Abstracts [CD-ROM]. Available from SilverPlatter Information, Inc. • Quarterly. Produced by International Food Information Service (home page is http://www.ifis.org). Provides worldwide coverage on CD-ROM of the literature of food technology and production. Various types of publications are indexed, with abstracts, including about 1,800 periodicals. Time period is 1969 to date.

OECD Statistical Compendium. Organization for Economic Cooperation and Development. • Semiannual. $1,905.00 per year for 1 to 10 users. CD-ROM contains more than 730,000 monthly, quarterly, and annual time series for OECD countries, 1960 to date. Includes fully searchable data on agriculture, food, economic indicators, national accounts, employment, energy, finance, industry, technology, and foreign trade. Results can be displayed in various forms.

DIRECTORIES

Major Food and Drink Companies of the World. Available from Gale Cengage Learning. • Annual. $880.00. Two volumes. Published by Graham & Whiteside. Contains profiles and trade names for more than 9,800 important food and beverage companies in various countries. In addition to foods, includes both alcoholic and nonalcoholic drink products.

Sugar y Azucar Yearbook. RUSPAM Communications, Inc. • Annual. $75.00. List of over 1,700 cane sugar mills and refineries-international coverage.

Thomas Food and Beverage Market Place. Grey House Publishing. • 2004. $495.00. Three volumes. Contains more than 40,000 entries covering food companies, beverages, food equipment, warehouse companies, food brokers, wholesalers, importers, and exporters. Formerly *Thomas Food Industry Register.*

HANDBOOKS AND MANUALS

Cane Sugar Handbook: A Manual for Cane Sugar Manufacturers and Their Chemists. James C. Chen and Chung-Chi Chou. John Wiley and Sons, Inc. •

1993. $400.00. 12th edition.

INTERNET DATABASES

Business 2.0 Web Guide to the Best Business Links. Business 2.0 Media Inc. Phone: (415)293-4800 E-mail: support@business2.com • URL: http://www.business2.com/webguide • Web site presents an extensive, searchable directory of links to "the best, most informative, and authoritative web pages." Twenty main categories cover business, finance, career, company information, people, and technology topics, with thousands of subtopics, all linking to Web sites recommended by experienced business researchers. Fees: Free.

Fedstats. Federal Interagency Council on Statistical Policy. Phone: (202)395-7254 • URL: http://www.fedstats.gov • Web site features an efficient search facility for full-text statistics produced by more than 100 federal agencies, including the Census Bureau, the Bureau of Economic Analysis, and the Bureau of Labor Statistics. Boolean searches can be made within one agency or for all agencies combined. Links are offered to international statistical bureaus, including the UN, IMF, OECD, UNESCO, Eurostat, and 20 individual countries. Fees: Free.

FreeLunch.com. Economy.com, Inc. Phone: (610)696-8700 Fax: (610)696-1678 • URL: http://www.freelunch.com • Web site provides free access to more than 1.5 million economic and financial data series, covering industry, demographics, labor markets, prices, retail sales, government spending, trade, interest rates, housing starts, the stock market, and many other topics. Data is available for various time periods in either chart or table form. Searching is offered. Fees: Free, but registration required. Economy.com, Inc. also offers fee-based economic analysis at *The Dismal Scientist* site (http://www.dismal.com).

USDA. United States Department of Agriculture. Phone: (202)720-2791 E-mail: agsec@usda.gov • URL: http://www.usda.gov • The USDA home page has six sections: News and Information; What's New; About USDA; Agencies; Opportunities; Search and Help. Keyword searching is offered from the USDA home page and from various individual agency home pages. Agencies are the Economic Research Service, Agricultural Marketing Service, National Agricultural Statistics Service, National Agricultural Library, and about 12 others. Updating varies. Fees: Free.

ONLINE DATABASES

CAB Abstracts. CAB Publishing North America. • Contains 46 specialized abstract collections covering over 10,000 journals and monographs in the areas of agriculture, horticulture, forest products, farm products, nutrition, dairy science, poultry, grains, animal health, entomology, etc. Time period is 1972 to date, with monthly updates. Inquire as to online cost and availability. *CAB Abstracts on CD-ROM* also available, with annual updating.

Food Science and Technology Abstracts [online]. IFIS North American Desk. • Produced by International Food Information Service. Provides about 500,000 online citations, with abstracts, to the international literature of food science, technology, commodities, engineering, and processing. Approximately 2,000 periodicals are covered. Time period is 1969 to date, with monthly updates. Inquire as to online cost and availability.

PERIODICALS AND NEWSLETTERS

Sugar Bulletin. American Sugar Cane League of the U.S.A. • Monthly. Free to members; non-members, $15.00 per year.

Sugar Journal: Covering the World's Sugar Industry. Kriedt Enterprises Ltd. • Monthly. $45.00 per year. A monthly technical publication designed to inform sugar beet and cane farms, factories, and refineries throughout the world about the latest developments in the sugar industry.

Sugar Producer: Representing the Sugar Beet Industry in the United States. Harris Publishing, Inc. • Seven times a year. $10.95 per year. Supplies sugar beet growers with information to assist them in production of quality sugar beet crops.

Sugar y Azucar. RUSPAM Communications, Inc. • Monthly. $75.00 per year. Text in English and Spanish.

STATISTICS SOURCES

Agricultural Statistics. Available from U. S. Government Printing Office. • Annual. $38.00. Produced by the National Agricultural Statistics Service, U. S. Department of Agriculture. Provides a wide variety of statistical data relating to agricultural production, supplies, consumption, prices/price-supports, foreign trade, costs, and returns, as well as farm labor, loans, income, and population. In many cases, historical data is shown annually for 10 years. In addition to farm data, includes detailed fishery statistics.

Business Statistics of the United States. Linz Audain and Cornelia J. Strawser. Bernan Associates. • Annual. $147.00. Based on *Business Statistics,* formerly issue by the Bureau of Economic Analysis, U. S. Department of Commerce. Provides basic data for a wide variety of U. S. industries, services, and economic indicators. Most statistics are shown annually for 30 years and monthly for the most recent four years.

FAO Production Yearbook. Available from Bernan Associates. • Annual. $45.00. Published by the Food and Agriculture Organization (http://www.fao.org). Contains worldwide data on agriculture, land use, farm crops, livestock, and agricultural prices.

FAO Trade Yearbook. Available from Bernan Associates. • Annual. $45.00. Published by the Food and Agriculture Organization (http://www.fao.org). Provides extensive worldwide data on exports and imports of agricultural commodities, fertilizers, tractors, and pesticides. Includes more than 130 tables of detailed statistics.

Sugar and Sweetener Situation and Outlook. Available from U. S. Government Printing Office. • Three times per year. $18.00 per year. Issued by Economic Research Service, U. S. Department of Agriculture. Provides current statistical information on supply, demand, and prices.

Survey of Current Business. Available from U. S. Government Printing Office. • Monthly. $63.00 per year. Issued by Bureau of Economic Analysis, U. S. Department of Commerce. Presents a wide variety of business and economic data.

TRADE/PROFESSIONAL ASSOCIATIONS

American Sugar Alliance. 2111 Wilson Blvd., Ste. 600, Arlington, VA 22201. Phone: (703)351-5055 Fax: (703)351-6698 E-mail: info@sugaralliance.org • URL: http://www.sugaralliance.org • Domestic producers, processors, and refiners of sugar beets, and sugarcane; labor organizations; allied organizations that supply goods and services to the domestic sweetener producing industry. Works to increase public awareness of the international economic and political factors influencing sweetener production; seeks increased support from consumers and the government for a U.S. sugar policy that is favorable to domestic sugar and sweetener producers; strives to maintain among domestic producers the ability to meet the sweetener needs of the U.S.

American Sugar Cane League of the U.S.A. 206 E Bayou Rd., Thibodaux, LA 70301. Phone: (985)448-3707 Fax: (985)448-3722 E-mail: lasugar@amscl.org • URL: http://www.amscl.org • Louisiana sugar cane growers and processors.

Coffee, Sugar and Cocoa Exchange. 1 N End Ave., New York, NY 10282-1101. Phone: (212)748-4000 E-mail: webmaster@nybot.com • URL: http://www.csce.com • Members are commodity traders.

Sugar Association. 1300 L St. NW, Ste. 1001, Washington, DC 20005. Phone: (202)785-1122 Fax: (202)785-5019 E-mail: sugar@sugar.org • URL: http://www.sugar.org • Represents processors, refiners, and growers of beet sugar and cane sugar. Disseminates scientifically based information on the nutritional and health aspects of sucrose. Promotes research. Sponsors educational programs on sugar and its role in a balanced diet.

Sweetener Users Association. 3231 Valley Ln., Falls Church, VA 22044. Phone: (703)532-2683 Fax: (703)532-9361 E-mail: info@acmanet.org • Industrial users of sugar and other sweeteners; companies and associations in the sweetener industry. Seeks legislative or administrative actions which will result in more market-oriented sweetener prices and an adequate and reliable supply of domestic and imported sugar. **Publications:** none.

United States Beet Sugar Association. 1156 15th St. NW, Ste. 1019, Washington, DC 20005. Phone: (202)296-4820 Fax: (202)331-2065 E-mail: hguerra@upi.com • URL: http://www.beetsugar.org • Represents beet sugar processing companies.

SUGGESTION SYSTEMS

DIRECTORIES

Employee Involvement Association--Membership Directory. Employee Involvement Association. • Covers: About 400 companies, associations, and federal, state, county, and municipal government agencies operating or contemplating employee suggestion systems or other employee involvement programs. Entries include: Company, association, or agency name; address; employee involvement administrator.

PERIODICALS AND NEWSLETTERS

New Horizons. Horticultural Research Institute. • Description: Explores research of the science and art of nursery, retail garden center, and landscape plant production, marketing, and care.

STATISTICS SOURCES

Employee Involvement Association Statistical Report. Employee Involvement Association. • Annual. 150.00.

TRADE/PROFESSIONAL ASSOCIATIONS

Employee Involvement Association. PO Box 2307, Dayton, OH 45401-2307. Phone: (937)586-3724 Fax: (937)586-3699 E-mail: eia@meinet.com • URL: http://www.eianet.org • Represents finance, commerce, industry, and government professionals. Dedicated to the worth, contributions, and benefits of employee suggestion systems and other employee involvement processes. Supports communication between employees and employer for the purpose of exchanging ideas.

SULPHUR INDUSTRY

See also: CHEMICAL INDUSTRIES

CD-ROM DATABASES

OECD Statistical Compendium. Organization for Economic Cooperation and Development. • Semiannual. $1,905.00 per year for 1 to 10 users. CD-ROM contains more than 730,000 monthly, quarterly, and annual time series for OECD countries, 1960 to date. Includes fully searchable data on agriculture, food, economic indicators, national accounts, employment, energy, finance, industry, technology, and foreign trade. Results can be displayed in various forms.

DIRECTORIES

Major Chemical and Petrochemical Companies of the World. Available from Gale Cengage Learning. • 2002. $880.00. Sixth edition. Published by Graham

& Whiteside. Contains profiles of more than 7,000 important chemical and petrochemical companies in various countries. Subject areas include general chemicals, specialty chemicals, agricultural chemicals, petrochemicals, industrial gases, and fertilizers.

OPD Chemical Buyers Directory. Schnell Publishing Company Inc. • Covers: about 1,500 suppliers of chemical process materials and more than 300 companies that transport and store chemicals in the United States. Entries include: Company name, address, phone, list of products or services, telex, fax, e-mail address, internet address, branch offices.

INTERNET DATABASES

Business 2.0 Web Guide to the Best Business Links. Business 2.0 Media Inc. Phone: (415)293-4800 E-mail: support@business2.com • URL: http://www.business2.com/webguide • Web site presents an extensive, searchable directory of links to "the best, most informative, and authoritative web pages." Twenty main categories cover business, finance, career, company information, people, and technology topics, with thousands of subtopics, all linking to Web sites recommended by experienced business researchers. Fees: Free.

Fedstats. Federal Interagency Council on Statistical Policy. Phone: (202)395-7254 • URL: http://www.fedstats.gov • Web site features an efficient search facility for full-text statistics produced by more than 100 federal agencies, including the Census Bureau, the Bureau of Economic Analysis, and the Bureau of Labor Statistics. Boolean searches can be made within one agency or for all agencies combined. Links are offered to international statistical bureaus, including the UN, IMF, OECD, UNESCO, Eurostat, and 20 individual countries. Fees: Free.

FreeLunch.com. Economy.com, Inc. Phone: (610)696-8700 Fax: (610)696-1678 • URL: http://www.freelunch.com • Web site provides free access to more than 1.5 million economic and financial data series, covering industry, demographics, labor markets, prices, retail sales, government spending, trade, interest rates, housing starts, the stock market, and many other topics. Data is available for various time periods in either chart or table form. Searching is offered. Fees: Free, but registration required. Economy.com, Inc. also offers fee-based economic analysis at *The Dismal Scientist* site (http://www.dismal.com).

ONLINE DATABASES

Globalbase. Gale Cengage Learning. • Provides more than one million online summaries of business, industrial, and economic news reports from more than 1,000 publications worldwide. Covers a wide range of material appearing in international trade journals, professional magazines, and newspapers. Time period is 1984 to date, with weekly updates. Inquire as to online cost and availability.

PERIODICALS AND NEWSLETTERS

Sulphur: Covers All Aspects of World Sulphur and Sulphuric Acid Industry. British Sulphur Publishing. • Bimonthly. $520.00 per year.

STATISTICS SOURCES

Annual Survey of Manufactures. Available from U. S. Government Printing Office. • Annual. Prices vary. Issued by the U. S. Census Bureau as an interim update to the *Census of Manufactures.* Includes data on number of manufacturing establishments in various industries, employment, labor costs, value of shipments, capital expenditures, inventories, energy costs, and assets. (See also Census Bureau home page, http://www.census.gov/.).

Business Statistics of the United States. Linz Audain and Cornelia J. Strawser. Bernan Associates. • Annual. $147.00. Based on *Business Statistics,*

formerly issue by the Bureau of Economic Analysis, U. S. Department of Commerce. Provides basic data for a wide variety of U. S. industries, services, and economic indicators. Most statistics are shown annually for 30 years and monthly for the most recent four years.

Mineral Commodity Summaries. Available from U. S. Government Printing Office. • Annual. $26.00. Published by the U. S. Geological Survey, Department of the Interior (http://www.usgs.gov). Contains detailed, five-year data for about 90 nonfuel minerals. Covers a wide range of statistics, including production, imports, exports, consumption, reserves, prices, tariff information, and industry employment. (Two pages are devoted to each mineral.).

Survey of Current Business. Available from U. S. Government Printing Office. • Monthly. $63.00 per year. Issued by Bureau of Economic Analysis, U. S. Department of Commerce. Presents a wide variety of business and economic data.

TRADE/PROFESSIONAL ASSOCIATIONS

The Sulphur Institute. 1140 Connecticut Ave. NW, Ste. 612, Washington, DC 20036. Phone: (202)331-9660 Fax: (202)293-2940 E-mail: sulphur@sulphurinstitute.org • URL: http://www.sulphurinstitute.org • International organization supported by the sulphur industry to promote and expand the use of sulphur in all forms worldwide.

SULPHURIC ACID

See: SULPHUR INDUSTRY

SUN, ENERGY FROM

See: SOLAR ENERGY

SUPERCONDUCTORS

See also: SEMICONDUCTOR INDUSTRY

GENERAL WORKS

Superconductivity. John B. Ketterson and Shengnian Song. Cambridge University Press. • 1999. $140.00.

Superconductivity: The Next Revolution?. Gianfranco Vidali. Cambridge University Press. • 1993. $20.00.

ABSTRACTS AND INDEXES

Applied Science and Technology Index. H. W. Wilson Co. • 11 times a year. Quarterly and annual cumulations. Price varies. Indexes a wide variety of English language technical, industrial, and engineering periodicals.

Key Abstracts: High Temperature Superconductors. Available from INSPEC, Inc. • Monthly. $250.00 per year. Provides international coverage of journal and proceedings literature. Published in England by the Institution of Electrical Engineers (IEE).

Solid State and Superconductivity Abstracts. CSA. • Bimonthly. $1,695.00 per year. Includes print and online editions. Formerly *Solid State Abstracts Journal.*

BIBLIOGRAPHIES

Guide to Superconductivity Books. Arnold Spinks, editor. Nova Science Publishers, Inc. • 2002. $79.00. Covers books on superconductivity and its applications. Includes author, title, and subject indexes.

Superconductivity: An Annotated Bibliography with Abstracts. A. Bisarsh, editor. Nova Science Publishers, Inc. • 1998. $115.00.

ONLINE DATABASES

Applied Science and Technology Index Online. H. W. Wilson Co. • Provides online indexing of 500

major scientific, technical, industrial, and engineering periodicals. Time period is 1983 to date. Monthly updates. Inquire as to online cost and availability.

PROMT: Predicasts Overview of Markets and Technology. Gale Cengage Learning. • Companies, products, applied technologies and markets. U.S. and international literature coverage, 1972 to date. Inquire as to online cost and availability. Provides abstracts from more than 1,600 publications. Weekly updates.

PERIODICALS AND NEWSLETTERS

Superconductor and Cyroelectronics. WestTech. • Quarterly. $22.00 per year.

RESEARCH CENTERS AND INSTITUTES

Edward L. Ginzton Laboratory. Stanford University, 450 Via Palou, Stanford, CA 94305-4085. Phone: (650)723-0111 Fax: (650)725-9355 E-mail: dabm@ee.stanford.edu • URL: http://www.stanford.edu/group/ginzton • Research fields include low-temperature physics and superconducting electronics.

Institute for Pure and Applied Physical Sciences. University of California, San Diego, 9500 Gilman Dr., Ste. 0360, La Jolla, CA 92093-0360. Phone: (858)534-3560 Fax: (858)534-7649 E-mail: mbmaple@uscd.edu • URL: http://www.ipaps.uscd.edu/ • Areas of study include superconductivity.

Materials Processing Center. Massachusetts Institute of Technology, 77 Massachusetts Ave., Room 12-007, Cambridge, MA 02139-4307. Phone: (617)253-5179 Fax: (617)258-6900 E-mail: fmpage@.mit.edu • URL: http://www.web.mit.edu/mpc • Conducts processing, engineering, and economic research in ferrous and nonferrous metals, ceramics, polymers, photonic materials, superconductors, welding, composite materials, and other materials.

STATISTICS SOURCES

U. S. Industry and Trade Outlook. Available from National Technical Information Service. • Annual. $69.95. Produced by the International Trade Administration, U. S. Department of Commerce, in a "public-private" partnership with DRI/McGraw-Hill and Standard & Poor's. Provides basic data, outlook for the current year, and "Long-Term Prospects" (five-year projections) for a wide variety of products and services. Includes high technology industries. Formerly *U. S. Industrial Outlook.*

OTHER SOURCES

Superconductor Week: The Newsletter of Record in the Field of Superconductivity. WestTech. • 30 times a year. $437.00 per year. Newsletter. Covers applications of superconductivity and cryogenics, including new markets and products.

SUPERMARKETS

See also: CHAIN STORES; GROCERY BUSINESS

DIRECTORIES

Directory of Single Unit Supermarket Operators. Chain Store Guide. • Annual. $327.00. Online edition, $747.00. Covers more than 7,900 one-store supermarket establishments with annual sales of at least $1,000,000. Includes names of primary wholesalers.

Directory of Supermarket, Grocery, and Convenience Store Chains. Chain Store Guide. • Annual. $327.00. Online edition, $747.00. Provides information on about 3,300 food store chains operating 120,000 individual stores. Store locations are given.

Grocery Headquarters: The Newspaper for the Food Industry. Trend Publishing. • Monthly. $80.00 per year. Covers the sale and distribution of food products and other items sold in supermarkets and grocery stores. Edited mainly for retailers and wholesalers. Incorporates (Grocery Distribution).

Plunkett's Food Industry Almanac. Plunkett Research Ltd. • Covers: 340 leading companies in the global food industry. Entries include: Name, address, phone, fax, and key executives. Also includes analysis and information on trends, technology, and statistics in the field.

Trade Dimensions' Market Scope. Trade Dimensions. • Covers: Market share for over 1,400 supermarket chains and wholesalers. Entries include: Company name, location, number of stores in the area, market share. Syndicated market areas include 52 AC Nielsen Scantrack markets, all 64 IRI InfoScan markets, all 205 DMAs (Designated Market Areas) and 100 MSAs (government-defined), plus 48 Trad Dimensions markets.

FINANCIAL RATIOS

FMI Annual Financial Review. Food Marketing Institute. • Annual. Members, $30.00; non-members, $75.00. Provides financial data on the supermarket industry.

Food Marketing Industry Speaks. Food Marketing Institute. • Annual. Members, $30.00; non-members, $75.00. Provides data on overall food industry marketing performance, including retail distribution and store operations.

Operating Results of Independent Supermarkets. Food Marketing Institute. • Annual. Members, $30.00; non-members, $75.00. Includes data on gross margins, inventory turnover, expenses, etc.

Operations Review. Food Marketing Institute. • Quarterly. $50.00 per year. Includes operating ratios for food retailing companies.

HANDBOOKS AND MANUALS

Progressive Grocer Guidebook. Trade Dimensions. • Annual. $375.00. Over 800 major chain and independent food retailers and wholesalers in the United States and Canada; also includes food brokers, rack jobbers, candy and tobacco distributors, and magazine distributors.

ONLINE DATABASES

PROMT: Predicasts Overview of Markets and Technology. Gale Cengage Learning. • Companies, products, applied technologies and markets. U.S. and international literature coverage, 1972 to date. Inquire as to online cost and availability. Provides abstracts from more than 1,600 publications. Weekly updates.

PERIODICALS AND NEWSLETTERS

Military Grocer. Downey Communications, Inc. • Five times a year. $30.00 per year. Edited for managers and employees of supermarkets on military bases. (These are supermarkets administered by the Defense Commissary Agency.).

Progressive Grocer. VNU Business Media. • 18 times a year. $129.00 per year. Formerly *Supermarket Business.*

Progressive Grocer: The Magazine of Supermarketing. VNU Business Media. • 18 times a year. $129.00 per year.

PRICE SOURCES

Supermarket News: The Industry's Weekly Newspaper. Fairchild Publications. • Weekly. Individuals, $196.00 per year; retailers, $45.00 per year; manufacturers, $89.00 per year.

STATISTICS SOURCES

Standard & Poor's Industry Surveys. Standard & Poor's. • Semiannual. $1,800.00. Two looseleaf volumes. Includes monthly *Supplements.* Provides detailed, individual surveys of 52 major industry groups. Each survey is revised on a semiannual basis. Also includes "Monthly Investment Review" (industry group investment analysis) and monthly

"Trends & Projections" (economic analysis).

TRADE/PROFESSIONAL ASSOCIATIONS

Food Marketing Institute. 2345 Crystal Dr., Ste. 800, Arlington, VA 22202-4801. Phone: (202)452-8444 Fax: (202)429-4519 E-mail: info@ifps.org • URL: http://www.fmi.org • Grocery retailers and wholesalers. Maintains liaison with government and consumers. Conducts 30 educational conferences and seminars per year. Conducts research programs; compiles statistics.

National Grocers Association. 1005 N Glebe Rd., Ste. 250, Arlington, VA 22201-5758. Phone: (703)516-0700 Fax: (703)516-0115 E-mail: info@ nationalgrocers.org • URL: http://www. nationalgrocers.org • Independent food retailers; wholesale food distributors servicing 29,000 food stores. Promotes industry interests and works to advance understanding, trade, and cooperation among all sectors of the food industry. Represents members' interests before the government. Aids in the development of programs designed to improve the productivity and efficiency of the food distribution industry. Offers services in areas such as store planning and engineering, personnel selection and training, operations, and advertising. Sponsors seminars and in-house training. Maintains liaison with Women Grocers of America (see separate entry), which serves as an advisory arm.

SUPERVISION

See: ADMINISTRATION; FACTORY MANAGEMENT; INDUSTRIAL MANAGEMENT

SUPPLY MANAGEMENT

See: INVENTORY CONTROL; PURCHASING

SURGICAL INSTRUMENTS INDUSTRY

See also: DENTAL SUPPLY INDUSTRY; HOSPITAL EQUIPMENT; MEDICAL TECHNOLOGY

ABSTRACTS AND INDEXES

Excerpta Medica: Biophysics, Bioengineering, and Medical Instrumentation. Elsevier. • 16 times a year. Institutions, $2,859 per year. Section 27 of *Excerpta Medica.*

CD-ROM DATABASES

Health Devices Alerts [CD-ROM]. ECRI. • Weekly. $2,450.00 per year. Provides CD-ROM reports of medical equipment defects, problems, failures, misuses, and recalls.

DIRECTORIES

Health Devices Sourcebook. ECRI. • Covers: Over 6,800 suppliers of patient care equipment, medical and surgical instruments, implants, clinical laboratory equipment and supplies, medical and hospital disposable supplies, and testing instruments; also lists companies that service, recondition, lease, or buy and sell used equipment; coverage includes U.S. and Canada. Entries include: Company name, address, phone, toll-free phone, fax, toll-free fax, URL, e-mail, total sales, names of key executives and contacts, product categories handled, trade names, methods of distribution, typical pricing, annual volume. Price of directory includes custom updates upon request.

Health Industry Buyers Guide. Lippincott Williams & Wilkins. • Covers: 4,000 manufacturers of hospital and physician's supplies and equipment, including medical laboratory, oxygen therapy, and

X-ray supplies, home health care products, and orthopedic appliances. Entries include: Manufacturer name, address, phone, fax, full product line.

Medical Device Register. Canon Communications L.L.C. • Covers: More than 65,000 U.S. Manufacturers of medical devices and clinical laboratory products; includes OEM manufacturers. Entries include: For manufacturers--Company name, address, phone, fax, telex, names and titles of key personnel, ownership, medical product sales volume, number of employees, method of distribution, medical product subsidiaries; public company listings include annual revenues and net income.

FINANCIAL RATIOS

Annual Statement Studies. The Risk Management Association. • Annual. Median and quartile financial ratios are given for over 400 kinds of manufacturing, wholesale, retail, construction, and consumer finance establishments. Data is sorted by both asset size and sales volume. Includes a clearly written "Definition of Ratios" and an alphabetical industry index.

Annual Statement Studies: Industry Default Probabilities and Cash Flow Measures. The Risk Management Association. • Annual. $145.00. Serves as a companion volume to the original *Annual Statement Studies.* Gives probability of default estimates on a percentage scale for more than 450 industries. Includes changes in position year-by-year for eight financial statement line items and provides percentage measures of cash flow.

INTERNET DATABASES

National Library of Medicine (NLM). National Institutes of Health (NIH). Phone: 888-346-3656 or (301)496-1131 Fax: (301)480-3537 E-mail: access@nlm.nih.gov • URL: http://www.nlm.nih. gov • NLM Web site offers free access through MEDLINE ("PubMed") to about nine million references to articles appearing in some 4,000 biomedical journals, with abstracts. Search interfaces range from "simple keywords to advanced Boolean expressions." The NLM site offers many links to other sources of biomedical and technical information (the National Center for Biotechnology Information, for example). Fees: Free.

ONLINE DATABASES

Embase. Elsevier Science, Inc. • Worldwide medical literature, 1974 to present. Weekly updates. Inquire as to online cost and availability.

F-D-C Reports. FDC Reports, Inc. • An online version of "The Gray Sheet" (medical devices), "The Pink Sheet" (pharmaceuticals), "The Rose Sheet" (cosmetics), "The Blue Sheet" (biomedical), and "The Tan Sheet" (nonprescription). Contains full-text information on legal, technical, corporate, financial, and marketing developments from 1987 to date, with weekly updates. Inquire as to online cost and availability.

Health Devices Alerts [online]. ECRI. • Provides online reports of medical equipment defects, problems, failures, misuses, and recalls. Time period is 1977 to date, with weekly updates. Inquire as to online cost and availability.

PERIODICALS AND NEWSLETTERS

The Gray Sheet Reports: Medical Devices, Diagnostics and Instrumentation. F-D-C Reports, Inc. • Weekly. Institutions, $1,172.00 per year. Newsletter. Provides industry and financial news, including a medical sector stock index. Monitors regulatory developments at the Center for Devices and Radiological Health of the U. S. Food and Drug Administration.

Health Devices Alerts: A Summary of Reported Problems, Hazards, Recalls, and Updates. ECRI (Emergency Care Research Institute). • Weekly. $3,649.40 per year. Looseleaf service. Contains reviews of health equipment problems. Includes *Health Devices Alerts Action Items, Health Devices Alerts Abstracts, Health Devices Alerts FDA Data, Health Devices Alerts Implants, Health Devices Alerts Hazards Bulletin.*

Health Industry Today: The Market Letter for Health Care Industry Vendors. Business Word, Inc. • Monthly. $360.00 per year; online edition, $420.00 per year.

Healthcare Products Today Magazine. Health Industry Distribution Association. Douglas Publications, Inc. • 10 times a year. $49.95 per year. Formerly*Medical Product Sales.*

Healthcare Purchasing News: A Magazine for Hospital Materials Management Central Service, Infection Control Practitioners. Thomson/Medical Economics. • Monthly. $47.95 per year. Edited for personnel responsible for the purchase of medical, surgical, and hospital equipment and supplies. Features new purchasing techniques and new products. Includes news of the activities of two major purchasing associations, Health Care Material Management Society and International Association of Healthcare Central Service Materiel Management.

Medical Product Manufacturing News. Canon Communications LLC. • 10 times a year. Free to qualified personnel; others, $150.00 per year. Directed at manufacturers of medical devices and medical electronic equipment. Covers industry news, service news, and new products.

MEEN Imaging Technology News. Reilly Publishing Co. • Bimonthly. Free to qualified personnel. Provides medical electronics industry news and new product information. Formerly*Medical Electronics and Equipment News.*

Pharmaceutical and Medical Device Law Bulletin. American Lawyer Media, Inc. • Monthly. $199.00 per year. Newsletter. Edited for lawyers concerned with drug product or medical device litigation. Contains industry news items of special interest, reports on new products, legal case summaries, Food and Drug Administration actions, patent issues, and related news reports. (A Law Journal Newsletter, formerly published by Leader Publications).

Surgical Products. Reed Business Information. • Monthly. $41.90 per year. Covers new Technology and products for surgeons and operation rooms.

STATISTICS SOURCES

Annual Survey of Manufactures. Available from U. S. Government Printing Office. • Annual. Prices vary. Issued by the U. S. Census Bureau as an interim update to the *Census of Manufactures.* Includes data on number of manufacturing establishments in various industries, employment, labor costs, value of shipments, capital expenditures, inventories, energy costs, and assets. (See also Census Bureau home page, http://www.census. gov/.).

Standard & Poor's Industry Surveys. Standard & Poor's. • Semiannual. $1,800.00. Two looseleaf volumes. Includes monthly *Supplements.* Provides detailed, individual surveys of 52 major industry groups. Each survey is revised on a semiannual basis. Also includes "Monthly Investment Review" (industry group investment analysis) and monthly "Trends & Projections" (economic analysis).

U. S. Industry and Trade Outlook. Available from National Technical Information Service. • Annual. $69.95. Produced by the International Trade Administration, U. S. Department of Commerce, in a "public-private" partnership with DRI/McGraw-Hill and Standard & Poor's. Provides basic data, outlook for the current year, and "Long-Term Prospects" (five-year projections) for a wide variety of products and services. Includes high technology

industries. Formerly *U. S. Industrial Outlook.*

TRADE/PROFESSIONAL ASSOCIATIONS

Advanced Medical Technology Association. 701 Pennsylvania Ave. NW, Ste. 800, Washington, DC 20004-2654. Phone: (202)783-8700 Fax: (202)783-8750 E-mail: info@advamed.org • URL: http://www.advamed.org • Represents domestic (including U.S. territories and possessions) manufacturers of medical devices, diagnostic products, and healthcare information systems. Develops programs and activities on economic, technical, medical, and scientific matters affecting the industry. Gathers and disseminates information concerning the United States and international developments in legislative, regulatory, scientific or standards-making areas. Conducts scientific and educational seminars and programs.

Association for Healthcare Resource and Materials Management. c/o American Hospital Association, One N Franklin St., Chicago, IL 60606-3420. Phone: (312)422-3840 Fax: (312)422-4573 E-mail: ahrmm@aha.org • URL: http://www.ahrmm.org • Members are involved with the purchasing and distribution of supplies and equipment for hospitals and other healthcare establishments. Formerly American Society for Healthcare Materials Management.

Association for the Advancement of Medical Instrumentation. 1110 N. Glebe Rd., No. 220, Arlington, VA 22201-4795. Phone: 800-332-2264 or (703)525-4890 Fax: (703)525-1424 • URL: http://www.aami.org • Members are engineers, technicians, physicians, manufacturers, and others with an interest in medical instrumentation.

Health Industry Distributors Association. 310 Montgomery St., Alexandria, VA 22314-1516. Phone: 800-549-4432 or (703)549-4432 Fax: (703)549-6495 E-mail: rowan@hida.org • URL: http://www.hida.org • Represents distributors of medical, laboratory, surgical, and other health care equipment and supplies to hospitals, physicians, nursing homes, and industrial medical departments. Conducts sales training, management seminars, and research through the HIDA Educational Foundation.

International Association of Healthcare Central Service Materiel Management. 213 W. Institute Place, Suite 307, Chicago, IL 60610. Phone: 800-962-8274 or (312)440-0078 Fax: (312)440-9474 E-mail: mailbox@iahcsmm.com • URL: http://www.iahcsmm.com • Members are professional personnel responsible for management and distribution of supplies from a central service material management (purchasing) department of a hospital. Formerly International Association of Hospital Central Service Management.

OTHER SOURCES

Computer Assisted Surgery: Automation, Virtual Reality, Robotics, and Radiosurgery. Theta Reports/PJB Medical Publications, Inc. • 2000. $2,295.00. Contains market research data relating to surgical systems technology. (Theta Report No. 1105.).

New and Breaking Technologies in the Pharmaceutical and Medical Device Industries. Theta Reports. • 1999. $1,695.00. Contains market research predictions of medical technology trends over the next 5 to 10 years (2004-2009), including developments in biotechnology, genetic engineering, medical device technology, therapeutic vaccines, non-invasive diagnostics, and minimally-invasive surgery. (Theta Report No. 931.).

New Ophthalmology: Treatments and Technologies. Theta Reports. • 2000. $1,695. Provides market research data relating to eye surgery, including LASIK, cataract surgery, and associated technology. (Theta Report No. 911.).

SURPLUS FARM PRODUCE

See: FARM PRODUCE

SURPLUS PRODUCTS

See also: RECYCLING; WASTE PRODUCTS

DIRECTORIES

Used Equipment Directory. Penton Technology and Lifestyle Media Inc. • Publication includes: List of 800 dealers in used metalworking, electrical, power, process, and material handling equipment, woodworking and machine tools. Entries include: Company name, address, phone; principal executive; types of equipment handled; description of machinery offered. Principal content is approximately 30,000 paid listings of used equipment for sale, classified by type.

PERIODICALS AND NEWSLETTERS

Commerce Business Daily. Industry and Trade Administration, U.S. Department of Commerce. U.S. Department of Commerce. • Description: Lists notices of proposed government procurement actions, contract awards, sales of government property, and other procurement information. Includes 500-1,000 notices in each edition; notices appear in the publication only once.

Surplus Record: Machinery and Equipment Directory. Surplus Record, Inc. • Monthly. $33.00 per year. Lists over 46,000 items of used and surplus machine tools, chemical processing and electrical equipment.

TRADE/PROFESSIONAL ASSOCIATIONS

Associated Surplus Dealers. 11835 W Olympic Blvd., Ste. 550E, Los Angeles, CA 90064-5810. Phone: 800-421-4511 or (310)481-7300 Fax: (310)481-1900 E-mail: dgw@necanet.org • URL: http://www.merchandisegroup.com • Represents surplus, general merchandise, and close-out dealers, manufacturers, manufacturers' representatives, and others. Promotes trade shows; provides liaison with government agencies; offers group life insurance coverage.

Machinery Dealers National Association. 315 S Patrick St., Alexandria, VA 22314. Phone: 800-872-7807 or (703)836-9300 Fax: (703)836-9303 E-mail: office@mdna.org • URL: http://www.mdna.org • Dealers in used, rebuilt, and reconditioned industrial machinery.

SURVEY METHODS

See also: MARKET RESEARCH

ABSTRACTS AND INDEXES

Current Index to Statistics: Applications, Methods, and Theory. American Statistical Association. • Annual. Price on application. An index to journal articles on statistical applications and methodology.

DIRECTORIES

GreenBook. New York AMA. • Annual. $100.00. Contains information on companies offering focus group facilities, including recruiting, moderating, and transcription services.

GreenBook Worldwide Directory of Marketing Research Companies and Services. New York AMA-Green Book. • Annual. $250.00. Contains information in 300 categories on more than 2,500 market research companies, consultants, field services, computer services, survey research companies, etc. Indexed by specialty, industry, company, computer program, and personnel. Available online. Formerly *Greenbook Worldwide International Directory of Marketing Research Companies and Services.*

Marketing Know-How: Your Guide to the Best Marketing Tools and Sources. Primedia Business Magazines and Media. • 1996. $49.95. Describes more than 700 public and private sources of consumer marketing data. Also discusses market trends and provides information on such marketing techniques as cluster analysis, focus groups, and geodemographic analysis.

MRA Blue Book Research Services Directory. Marketing Research Association. • Covers: over 1,200 marketing research companies and field interviewing services. Entries include: Company name, address, phone, names of executives, services, facilities, special interviewing capabilities.

ENCYCLOPEDIAS AND DICTIONARIES

The Sage Encyclopedia of Social Science Research Methods. Michael S. Lewis-Beck and others, editors. Sage Publications, Inc. • 2004. $550.00. Three volumes. Includes more than 800 signed entries on such topics as basic statistics, econometrics, evaluation, linear models, data analysis, sampling, and survey design.

HANDBOOKS AND MANUALS

Assessing Service Quality: Satisfying the Expectations of Library Customers. Peter Hernon and Ellen Altman. American Library Association. • 1998. $40.00. Discusses surveys, focus groups, and other data collection methods for measuring the quality of library service. Includes sample forms and an annotated bibliography.

Constructing Effective Questionnaires. Robert A. Peterson. Sage Publications, Inc. • 1999. $86.95. Covers the construction and wording of questionnaires for survey research.

Focus Group Kit. David L. Morgan and Richard A. Krueger. Sage Publications, Inc. • 1997. $150.00. Six volumes. Various authors cover the basics of focus group research, including planning, developing questions, moderating, and analyzing results. (Focus Group Kit Series).

Focus Groups: A Practical Guide for Applied Research. Richard A. Krueger and Mary Anne Casey. Sage Publications, Inc. • 2000. $81.95. Third edition. A step-by-step guide to obtaining useful research data from a focus group.

Gower Handbook of Customer Service. Peter Murley, editor. Ashgate Publishing Co. • 1996. $129.95. Consists of 40 articles (chapters) written by various authors. Among the topics covered are benchmarking, customer surveys, focus groups, control groups, employee selection, incentives, training, teamwork, and telephone techniques. Published by Gower in England.

Handbook for Focus Group Research. Thomas L. Greenbaum. Sage Publications, Inc. • 1998. $97.95. Second edition. Includes glossary and index.

Marketing Manager's Handbook. Sidney J. Levy and others. Prentice Hall PTR. • 2000. Price on application. Contains 71 chapters by various authors on a wide variety of marketing topics, including market segmentation, market research, international marketing, industrial marketing, survey methods, customer service, advertising, pricing, planning, strategy, and ethics.

Marketing Research Project Manual. Glen R. Jarboe. South-Western. • 1998. $32.95. Fourth edition. Covers the methodology of market research surveys. (Marketing Series).

Moderating Focus Groups: A Practical Guide for Group Facilitation. Thomas L. Greenbaum. Sage Publications, Inc. • 1999. $92.95. Covers participant recruitment, characteristics of successful moderators, moderating fundamentals, and related topics.

Studying Your Workforce: Applied Research Methods and Tools for the Training and Development Practitioner. Alan Clardy. Sage Publications, Inc. • 1997. $79.95. Describes how to apply specific

research methods to common training problems. Emphasis is on data collection methods: testing, observation, surveys, and interviews. Topics include performance problems and assessment.

The Survey Kit. Arlene Fink, editor. Sage Publications, Inc. • 2003. $130.00. Second edition. Ten volumes. Covers various survey research topics, such as in-person interviews, telephone interviewing, focus groups, content analysis, sampling, database management, and Internet surveys. Each volume contains a glossary.

Survey Research Handbook: Guidelines and Strategies for Conducting a Survey. Pamela L. Alreck and Robert B. Settle. McGraw-Hill. • 1994. $50.00. Second edition. Consists of four major parts: 1. Planning and Designing the Survey, 2. Developing Survey Instruments, 3. Collecting and Processing Data, 4. Interpreting and Reporting Results. Includes a glossary and index. (Marketing Series).

Workshops: Designing and Facilitating Experiential Learning. Jeff E. Brooks-Harris and Susan R. Stock-Ward. Sage Publications, Inc. • 1999. $80.95. Presents a practical approach to designing, running, and evaluating workshops in business, adult education, and other areas. Includes references.

PERIODICALS AND NEWSLETTERS

Journal of Business and Economic Statistics. American Statistical Association. • Quarterly. Libraries, $90.00 per year. Emphasis is on statistical measurement and applications for business and economics.

Survey Research. Survey Research Laboratory. • Description: Contains "descriptions of current survey research projects by academic and not-for-profit survey research organizations; news from survey research centers; descriptions of recent methodological publications on survey research." Recurring features include news of research and columns titled Current Research, Personnel Notes, and New Methodological Publications.

RESEARCH CENTERS AND INSTITUTES

Survey Research Center. University of California at Berkeley, 2538 Channing Way, Berkeley, CA 94720-5100. Phone: (510)642-6578 Fax: (510)643-8292 E-mail: hbrady@bravo.berkeley.edu • URL: http://www.grad.berkeley.edu • Research areas include the utilization and development of survey methods.

Survey Research Laboratory. University of Illinois at Chicago, 412 S. Peoria St., Chicago, IL 60607. Phone: (312)996-5300 Fax: (312)996-3358 E-mail: info@srl.uic.edu • URL: http://www.srl.uic.edu • Research areas include survey methodology and sampling techniques.

TRADE/PROFESSIONAL ASSOCIATIONS

American Association for Public Opinion Research. P.O. Box 14263, Lenexa, KS 66285-4263. Phone: (913)310-0118 Fax: (913)310-5340 E-mail: aapor-info@goamp.com • URL: http://www.aapor.org • Members are individuals interested in methods and applications of opinion research.

American Statistical Association. 732 N Washington St., Alexandria, VA 22314-1943. Phone: 888-231-3473 or (703)684-1221 Fax: (703)684-2037 E-mail: asainfo@amstat.org • URL: http://www.amstat.org • Professional society of persons interested in the theory, methodology, and application of statistics to all fields of human endeavor.

Council of American Survey Research Organizations. 170 N Country Rd., Ste. 4, Port Jefferson, NY 11777. Phone: (631)928-6954 Fax: (631)928-6041 E-mail: casro@casro.org • URL: http://www.casro.org • Members are survey research companies. Various committees are concerned with standards, survey research quality, and technology.

World Association for Public Opinion Research. University of Texas Pan American, 1405 Driftwood 1, Mission, TX 78572. Phone: (956)618-4048 Fax:

(956)618-4943 E-mail: ghanem@panam.edu • URL: http://www.unl.edu/wapor • Members are opinion survey research experts, both academic and commercial. Promotes the use of objective, scientific, public opinion methodology and research. International emphasis.

SURVEYS, CONSUMER

See: CONSUMER SURVEYS

SWEET POTATO INDUSTRY

See also: POTATO INDUSTRY

ALMANACS AND YEARBOOKS

Agricultural and Mineral Commodities Year Book. Available from Taylor & Francis Group. • Annual. $225.00. Published by Europa Publications. Contains descriptive product profiles, price data, export-import data, and production statistics for major commodities of the world. Includes commodity histories, uses, markets, demand trends, and information about trade agreements and key commodity organizations.

HANDBOOKS AND MANUALS

Knott's Handbook for Vegetable Growers. Donald N. Maynard and George J. Hochmuth. John Wiley and Sons, Inc. • 1997. $99.00. Fourth edition. Written for commercial vegetable growers, truck farmers, horticulturists, and other professionals. Covers such topics as spacing of plants, disease control, insect pests, seeds, weeds, water management, and irrigation.

INTERNET DATABASES

USDA. United States Department of Agriculture. Phone: (202)720-2791 E-mail: agsec@usda.gov • URL: http://www.usda.gov • The USDA home page has six sections: News and Information; What's New; About USDA; Agencies; Opportunities; Search and Help. Keyword searching is offered from the USDA home page and from various individual agency home pages. Agencies are the Economic Research Service, Agricultural Marketing Service, National Agricultural Statistics Service, National Agricultural Library, and about 12 others. Updating varies. Fees: Free.

STATISTICS SOURCES

Agricultural Statistics. Available from U. S. Government Printing Office. • Annual. $38.00. Produced by the National Agricultural Statistics Service, U. S. Department of Agriculture. Provides a wide variety of statistical data relating to agricultural production, supplies, consumption, prices/price-supports, foreign trade, costs, and returns, as well as farm labor, loans, income, and population. In many cases, historical data is shown annually for 10 years. In addition to farm data, includes detailed fishery statistics.

FAO Production Yearbook. Available from Bernan Associates. • Annual. $45.00. Published by the Food and Agriculture Organization (http://www.fao.org). Contains worldwide data on agriculture, land use, farm crops, livestock, and agricultural prices.

FAO Trade Yearbook. Available from Bernan Associates. • Annual. $45.00. Published by the Food and Agriculture Organization (http://www.fao.org). Provides extensive worldwide data on exports and imports of agricultural commodities, fertilizers, tractors, and pesticides. Includes more than 130 tables of detailed statistics.

Vegetables and Specialties Situation and Outlook. Available from U. S. Government Printing Office. • Three times a year. Issued by the Economic Research Service of the U. S. Department of Agriculture. Provides current statistical information on supply, demand, and prices.

SWEETENER INDUSTRY

See: SUGAR INDUSTRY

SWIMMING POOL INDUSTRY

DIRECTORIES

Pool and Spa News Source Book Directory. Leisure Publications. • Annual. $49.50. List of 1,500 manufacturers and distributors of pool, spa, and hot water equipment and supplies.

Swimming Pool/Spa Age--Product Directory. Primedia Business. • Covers: about 2,000 manufacturers of swimming pool and spa equipment and supplies, and suppliers of services for the industry; manufacturers of spas and hot tubs; distributors and manufacturers' representatives; and pool industry associations. Entries include: Company or association name, address, phone, name and title of contact, branch offices.

FINANCIAL RATIOS

Annual Statement Studies. The Risk Management Association. • Annual. Median and quartile financial ratios are given for over 400 kinds of manufacturing, wholesale, retail, construction, and consumer finance establishments. Data is sorted by both asset size and sales volume. Includes a clearly written "Definition of Ratios" and an alphabetical industry index.

Annual Statement Studies: Industry Default Probabilities and Cash Flow Measures. The Risk Management Association. • Annual. $145.00. Serves as a companion volume to the original *Annual Statement Studies.* Gives probability of default estimates on a percentage scale for more than 450 industries. Includes changes in position year-by-year for eight financial statement line items and provides percentage measures of cash flow.

PERIODICALS AND NEWSLETTERS

Aquatics International: The Source for Facility Products, Services and Management. Hanley-Wood, LLC. • Monthly. $10.50 per year. Edited for managers of commercial and public swimming pools, including pools in hotels, schools, theme parks, health clubs, and community centers.

Pool and Spa News: The National Trade Magazine for the Swimming Poool & Spa Industry. Hanley-Wood, LLc. • Semimonthly. $19.97 per year.

TRADE/PROFESSIONAL ASSOCIATIONS

National Spa and Pool Institute. 2111 Eisenhower Ave., Alexandria, VA 22314. Phone: (703)838-0083 Fax: (703)549-0493 E-mail: memberservices@nspi. org • URL: http://www.nspi.org • Members include a wide variety of business firms and individuals involved in some way with health spas, swimming pools, or hot tubs. Formerly National Swimming Pool Institute.

SWINDLERS AND SWINDLING

See: CRIME AND CRIMINALS; FRAUD AND EMBEZZLEMENT

SWINE INDUSTRY

See also: LIVESTOCK INDUSTRY; MEAT INDUSTRY

ALMANACS AND YEARBOOKS

Agricultural and Mineral Commodities Year Book. Available from Taylor & Francis Group. • Annual.

$225.00. Published by Europa Publications. Contains descriptive product profiles, price data, export-import data, and production statistics for major commodities of the world. Includes commodity histories, uses, markets, demand trends, and information about trade agreements and key commodity organizations.

INTERNET DATABASES

USDA. United States Department of Agriculture. Phone: (202)720-2791 E-mail: agsec@usda.gov • URL: http://www.usda.gov • The USDA home page has six sections: News and Information; What's New; About USDA; Agencies; Opportunities; Search and Help. Keyword searching is offered from the USDA home page and from various individual agency home pages. Agencies are the Economic Research Service, Agricultural Marketing Service, National Agricultural Statistics Service, National Agricultural Library, and about 12 others. Updating varies. Fees: Free.

ONLINE DATABASES

CAB Abstracts. CAB Publishing North America. • Contains 46 specialized abstract collections covering over 10,000 journals and monographs in the areas of agriculture, horticulture, forest products, farm products, nutrition, dairy science, poultry, grains, animal health, entomology, etc. Time period is 1972 to date, with monthly updates. Inquire as to online cost and availability. *CAB Abstracts on CD-ROM* also available, with annual updating.

PERIODICALS AND NEWSLETTERS

National Hog Farmer. Primedia Business Magazines and Media. • Monthly. $115.00 per year.

STATISTICS SOURCES

Agricultural Statistics. Available from U. S. Government Printing Office. • Annual. $38.00. Produced by the National Agricultural Statistics Service, U. S. Department of Agriculture. Provides a wide variety of statistical data relating to agricultural production, supplies, consumption, prices/price-supports, foreign trade, costs, and returns, as well as farm labor, loans, income, and population. In many cases, historical data is shown annually for 10 years. In addition to farm data, includes detailed fishery statistics.

FAO Production Yearbook. Available from Bernan Associates. • Annual. $45.00. Published by the Food and Agriculture Organization (http://www.fao.org). Contains worldwide data on agriculture, land use, farm crops, livestock, and agricultural prices.

FAO Trade Yearbook. Available from Bernan Associates. • Annual. $45.00. Published by the Food and Agriculture Organization (http://www.fao.org). Provides extensive worldwide data on exports and imports of agricultural commodities, fertilizers, tractors, and pesticides. Includes more than 130 tables of detailed statistics.

TRADE/PROFESSIONAL ASSOCIATIONS

National Association of Swine Records. P.O. Box 2417, West Lafayette, IN 47996. Phone: (765)463-3594 Fax: (765)497-2959.

National Pork Producers Council. 10664 Justin Dr., Urbandale, IA 50322. Phone: (515)278-8012 Fax: (515)278-8011 E-mail: flynnk@nppc.org • URL: http://www.nppc.org • Federation of state pork producer associations. Promotes the pork industry through research programs, consumer education, and lobbying activities. Compiles statistics; maintains speakers' bureau and hall of fame.

SYNTHETIC FUELS

See also: FUEL

ABSTRACTS AND INDEXES

Applied Science and Technology Index. H. W. Wilson Co. • 11 times a year. Quarterly and annual

cumulations. Price varies. Indexes a wide variety of English language technical, industrial, and engineering periodicals.

NTIS Alerts: Energy. National Technical Information Service. • Semimonthly. $245.00 per year. Provides descriptions of government-sponsored research reports and software, with ordering information. Covers electric power, batteries, fuels, geothermal energy, heating/cooling systems, nuclear technology, solar energy, energy policy, and related subjects. Formerly *Abstract Newsletter.*

CD-ROM DATABASES

Environment Abstracts on CD-ROM. LEXIS-NEXIS. • Quarterly. $1,295.00 per year. Contains the following CD-ROM databases: *Environment Abstracts, Energy Abstracts,* and *Acid Rain Abstracts.* Length of coverage varies.

DIRECTORIES

SYNERJY: A Directory of Renewable Energy. Synerjy. • Semiannual. Individuals, $30.00 per year; others, $62.00 per year. Includes organizations, publishers, and other resources. Lists articles, patents, government publications, research groups and facilities.

ENCYCLOPEDIAS AND DICTIONARIES

Encyclopedia of Energy. Cutler J. Cleveland, editor. Elsevier, Inc. • 2004. $1,560.00. Six volumes. Covers all aspects of energy sources and energy-related environmental issues.

Macmillan Encyclopedia of Energy. Available from Gale Cengage Learning. • 2001. $395.00. Three volumes. Published by Macmillan Reference USA. Covers the business, technology, and history of a wide variety of energy sources.

ONLINE DATABASES

PAIS International. Public Affairs Information Service, Inc. • Corresponds to the former printed publications, *PAIS Bulletin* (1976-90) and *PAIS Foreign Language Index* (1972-90), and to the current *PAIS International in Print* (1991 to date). Covers economic, political, and sociological material appearing in periodicals, books, government documents, and other publications. Updating is monthly. Inquire as to online cost and availability.

PROMT: Predicasts Overview of Markets and Technology. Gale Cengage Learning. • Companies, products, applied technologies and markets. U.S. and international literature coverage, 1972 to date. Inquire as to online cost and availability. Provides abstracts from more than 1,600 publications. Weekly updates.

PERIODICALS AND NEWSLETTERS

DOE This Month. Available from U. S. Government Printing Office. • Monthly. $42.00 per year. Describes the U.S. Department of Energy's research and development activities and DOE publications. Includes information on nuclear energy, renewable energy sources, and synthetic fuels.

Energy and Fuels. American Chemical Society. • Bimonthly. Institutions, $852.00 per year; others, price on application. An interdisciplinary technical journal covering non-nuclear energy sources: petroleum, gas, synthetic fuels, etc.

Journal of Energy Engineering: The International Journal. American Society of Civil Engineers. • Three times a year. Members, $40.00 per year; with online edition, $46.00 per year; non-members, $60.00 per year; with online edition, $69.00 per year.

Power Generation Technology and Markets. Pasha Publishing Inc. • Weekly. $790.00 per year. Newsletter. Formerly *Coal and Synfuels Technology.*

RESEARCH CENTERS AND INSTITUTES

Energy Institute of the Americas. University of Oklahoma, Sarkeys Energy Center, 100 E. Boyd,

Suite 510, Norman, OK 73019-1006. Phone: (405)325-3821 Fax: (405)325-3180 E-mail: ggertsch@ou.edu • URL: http://www.ou.edu/sec/institutes-programs.

Laboratory for Energy and the Environment. Massachusetts Institute of Technology. 77 Massachusetts Ave., Bldg. E40-455, Cambridge, MA 02139-4307. Phone: (617)258-8891 Fax: (617)253-8013 E-mail: jwilmson@mit.edu • URL: http://www.lfee.mit.edu • Formerly Energy Laboratory.

TRADE/PROFESSIONAL ASSOCIATIONS

Gas Technology Institute. 1700 S Mt. Prospect Rd., Des Plaines, IL 60018-1804. Phone: (847)768-0500 Fax: (847)768-0501 E-mail: businessdevelopmentinfo@gastechnology.org • URL: http://www.gastechnology.org • Educational and research facility sponsored by companies engaged in the production, processing, transmission, and distribution of natural gas and related fuels; engineering firms; large energy consumers. Conducts contract research for government and industry in the field of non-nuclear energy technology. Offers short courses in gas production, transmission, distribution, economics, and marketing. Sponsors symposia on current topics in non-nuclear energy.

U.S. Energy Association; Research and Development Committee. 1300 Pennsylvania Ave., N.W., Suite 550, Washington, DC 20004-3022. Phone: (202)312-1230 Fax: (202)682-1682 • URL: http://www.usea.org.

OTHER SOURCES

Major Energy Companies of the World. Available from Gale Cengage Learning. • Annual. $880.00. Published by Graham & Whiteside. Contains detailed information on more than 3,300 important energy companies in various countries. Industries include electricity generation, coal, natural gas, nuclear energy, petroleum, fuel distribution, and equipment for energy production.

SYNTHETIC TEXTILE FIBER INDUSTRY

See also: FIBER INDUSTRY; TEXTILE INDUSTRY

GENERAL WORKS

Manufactured Fiber Fact Book. Fiber Economics Bureau, Inc. • Biennial. $5.00. Provides a general review of the history and development of the synthetic fiber industry. (Fiber Economics Bureau is a subsidiary of the American Fiber Manufacturers Association.).

ABSTRACTS AND INDEXES

CPI Digest: Key to World Literature Serving the Coatings, Plastics, Fibers, Adhesives, and Related Industries (Chemical Process Industries). CPI Information Services. • Monthly. $397.00 per year. Abstracts of business and technical articles for polymer-based, chemical process industries. Includes a monthly list of relevant U. S. patents. International coverage.

Textile Technology Digest. Institute of Textile Technology. • Annual. $535.00. Provides indexing and abstracting of a wide variety of textile technology literature.

World Textile Abstracts. Elsevier. • Monthly. Institutions $1,696.00 per year. Digests of articles published in the world's textile literature. Includes subscription to *World Textile Digest.*

CD-ROM DATABASES

OECD Statistical Compendium. Organization for Economic Cooperation and Development. • Semiannual. $1,905.00 per year for 1 to 10 users. CD-ROM contains more than 730,000 monthly,

quarterly, and annual time series for OECD countries, 1960 to date. Includes fully searchable data on agriculture, food, economic indicators, national accounts, employment, energy, finance, industry, technology, and foreign trade. Results can be displayed in various forms.

Textile Technology Digest [CD-ROM]. Textile Information Center, Institute of Textile Technology. • Quarterly. Provides CD-ROM indexing and abstracting of worldwide journals and monographs in various areas of textile technology, production, and management. Covers 1978 to date.

DIRECTORIES

Davison's Textile Blue Book. Davison Publishing Company L.L.C. • Covers: Over 8,400 companies in the textile industry in the United States, Canada, and Mexico including about 4,400 textile plants. Covers mills, manufacturers, dyers, bleachers, finishers, dealers, importers, exporters, brokers, shippers, and agents for various textiles, fibers, yarns, and cordage. Also includes supplies of equipment, materials and services. Entries include: Company name, address, phone, fax, e-mail, web-site addresses, names of executives, description of product/service, and trade names. Mill and other production facility listings include data on equipment and capacity.

World Directory of Manufactured Fiber Producers. Fiber Economics Bureau, Inc. • Annual. Print edition, $135.00. Print edition with CD-ROM, $195.00. Provides information on 2,000 fiber producers in 75 countries. (Fiber Economics Bureau is a subsidiary of the American Fiber Manufacturers Association.).

ENCYCLOPEDIAS AND DICTIONARIES

Textile Terms and Definitions. J.E. McIntyre and Paul N. Daniels, editors. Available from State Mutual Book and Periodical Service Ltd. • 1996. $180.00. 10th edition. Published by the Textile Insitute (UK). Includes more than 1,000 definitions of textile processes, fiber types, and end products. Illustrated.

HANDBOOKS AND MANUALS

Industrial Polymers Handbook: Products, Processes, Applications. Edward S. Wilks, editor. John Wiley and Sons, Inc. • 2001. $1,400.00. Four volumes. Covers both naturally occurring and synthetic polymers that have industrial uses.

Polymer Handbook. Johannes Brandup and others, editors. John Wiley and Sons, Inc. • 2003. $197.50. Fifth edition. Emphasis is on advances in polymer science since 1989 and descriptions of polymeric materials. (Polymer Handbook Series).

INTERNET DATABASES

Business 2.0 Web Guide to the Best Business Links. Business 2.0 Media Inc. Phone: (415)293-4800 E-mail: support@business2.com • URL: http://www.business2.com/webguide • Web site presents an extensive, searchable directory of links to "the best, most informative, and authoritative web pages." Twenty main categories cover business, finance, career, company information, people, and technology topics, with thousands of subtopics, all linking to Web sites recommended by experienced business researchers. Fees: Free.

Fedstats. Federal Interagency Council on Statistical Policy. Phone: (202)395-7254 • URL: http://www.fedstats.gov • Web site features an efficient search facility for full-text statistics produced by more than 100 federal agencies, including the Census Bureau, the Bureau of Economic Analysis, and the Bureau of Labor Statistics. Boolean searches can be made within one agency or for all agencies combined. Links are offered to international statistical bureaus, including the UN, IMF, OECD, UNESCO, Eurostat, and 20 individual countries. Fees: Free.

FreeLunch.com. Economy.com, Inc. Phone:

(610)696-8700 Fax: (610)696-1678 • URL: http://www.freelunch.com • Web site provides free access to more than 1.5 million economic and financial data series, covering industry, demographics, labor markets, prices, retail sales, government spending, trade, interest rates, housing starts, the stock market, and many other topics. Data is available for various time periods in either chart or table form. Searching is offered. Fees: Free, but registration required. Economy.com, Inc. also offers fee-based economic analysis at *The Dismal Scientist* site (http://www.dismal.com).

ONLINE DATABASES

Textile Technology Digest [online]. Institute of Textile Technology. • Contains indexing and abstracting of more than 300 worldwide journals and monographs in various areas of textile technology, production, and management. Time period is 1978 to date, with monthly updating. Inquire as to online cost and availability.

World Textiles. Elsevier Science, Inc. • Provides abstracting and indexing from 1970 of worldwide textile literature (periodicals, books, pamphlets, and reports). Includes U. S., European, and British patent information. Updating is monthly. Inquire as to online cost and availability.

PERIODICALS AND NEWSLETTERS

DNR: The Men's Fashion Retail Textile Authority. Fairchild Publications. • Daily. $85.00 per year. Formerly *Daily News Record.*

Fiber Organon: Featuring Manufactured Fibers. Fiber Economics Bureau, Inc. • Monthly. $300.00 per year. Summarizes "confidential producer information on the U.S. manufactured fiber market." Provides detailed statistics on production, shipments, exports, and capacity. Special issues cover worldwide data and specific end use products. (Fiber Economics Bureau is a subsidiary of the American Fiber Manufacturers Association.).

International Fiber Journal. International Media Group, Inc. • Bimonthly. $36.00 per year. Covers manmade fiber technology and manufacturing.

Manufactured Fiber Review. Fiber Economics Bureau, Inc. • Monthly. $350.00 per year. Provides a "quick-release four-page monthly review of the latest U.S. data on manufactured fiber." Coverage includes production, shipments, exports, and utilization rates. (Fiber Economics Bureau is a subsidiary of the American Fiber Manufacturers Association.).

STATISTICS SOURCES

Business Statistics of the United States. Linz Audain and Cornelia J. Strawser. Bernan Associates. • Annual. $147.00. Based on *Business Statistics,* formerly issue by the Bureau of Economic Analysis, U. S. Department of Commerce. Provides basic data for a wide variety of U. S. industries, services, and economic indicators. Most statistics are shown annually for 30 years and monthly for the most recent four years.

Manufactured Fiber Handbook. Fiber Economics Bureau, Inc. • $6,000.00 per year. Looseleaf service. Provides comprehensive data, both current and historical, on all aspects of the U.S. manufactured fiber industry. (Fiber Economics Bureau is a subsidiary of the American Fiber Manufacturers Association.).

Survey of Current Business. Available from U. S. Government Printing Office. • Monthly. $63.00 per year. Issued by Bureau of Economic Analysis, U. S. Department of Commerce. Presents a wide variety of business and economic data.

TRADE/PROFESSIONAL ASSOCIATIONS

American Fiber Manufacturers Association. 1530 Wilson Blvd., Ste. 690, Arlington, VA 22209-2418. Phone: (703)875-0432 Fax: (703)875-0907 E-mail: afma@afma.org • URL: http://www.fibersource.

com • Producers of manufactured fibers used in apparel, household goods, industrial materials, and other types of products. Represents the industry in educational, governmental, and foreign trade matters. Distributes a video depicting production and end uses of manufactured fibers.

Textile Institute. St. James's Buildings, 1st Fl., 79 Oxford St., Manchester M1 6FQ, United Kingdom. Phone: 44 161 2371188 Fax: 44 161 2361991 E-mail: tiihq@textileinst.org.uk • URL: http://www.texi.org • Companies and individuals in 100 countries involved in management, science, technology, design, information transfer, and marketing of textiles including clothing and footwear. Promotes interests of the textile industry worldwide; serves professional interests of members; confers qualifications and recognizes achievements in research, application of ideas, education, business, and public affairs. Maintains Information Service to collect information relating to textile industrial and economic conditions in different countries and economic sectors.

SYRUP INDUSTRY

See: MOLASSES INDUSTRY; SUGAR INDUSTRY

SYSTEMS ENGINEERING

See: INDUSTRIAL ENGINEERING

SYSTEMS IN MANAGEMENT

See also: COMPUTERS; MANAGEMENT INFORMATION SYSTEMS; OFFICE MANAGEMENT; WORD PROCESSING

GENERAL WORKS

Information Systems Concept Management. Henry C. Lucas. McGraw-Hill. • 1994. $25.00. Fifth edition.

Information Technology and Management. William Cats-Baril and Ronald L. Thompson. McGraw-Hill. • 2002. $96.25. Second edition. Covers information systems, networks, telecommunication, and database management.

Systems Analysis and Design. Kenneth E. Kendall and Julie E. Kendall. Prentice Hall PTR. • 2002. $75.00. Fifth edition.

ABSTRACTS AND INDEXES

Key Abstracts: Software Engineering. Available from INSPEC, Inc. • Monthly. $250.00 per year. Provides international coverage of journal and proceedings literature. Published in England by the Institution of Electrical Engineers (IEE).

ENCYCLOPEDIAS AND DICTIONARIES

Blackwell Encyclopedic Dictionary of Operations Management. Nigel Slack, editor. Blackwell Publishing. • 1997. $130.95. The editor is associated with the University of Warwick, England. Contains definitions of key terms combined with longer articles written by various U. S. and foreign business educators. Includes bibliographies and index. (Blackwell Encyclopedia of Management Series.).

HANDBOOKS AND MANUALS

Handbook of Systems Engineering and Management. Andrew P. Sage and William B. Rouse, editors. John Wiley and Sons, Inc. • 1999. $200.00. Emphasis is on information technology and systems software.

ONLINE DATABASES

Management Contents. Gale Cengage Learning. • Covers a wide range of management, financial,

marketing, personnel, and administrative topics. About 150 leading business journals are indexed and abstracted from 1974 to date, with monthly updating. Inquire as to online cost and availability.

PERIODICALS AND NEWSLETTERS

Computertalk: For Contemporary Pharmacy Management. Computertalk Associates, Inc. • Bimonthly. $50.00 per year. Provides detailed advice and information on computer systems for pharmacies, including a buyers' guide issue.

Insurance and Technology. CMP Media LLC. • Monthly. $65.00 per year. Covers information technology and systems management as applied to the operation of life, health, casualty, and property insurance companies.

Office Solutions: The Magazine for Office Professionals. Quality Publishing, Inc. • Monthly. $36.00 per year. Edited for office managers. Covers office technology, services, and new products. Formerly *Office Systems,* incorporating *Managing Office Technology.*

PlugIn Datamation: Profit and Value from Information Technology. EarthWeb. • Monthly. Price on application. Technical, semi-technical and general news covering EDP topics.

Software Economics Letter: Maximizing Your Return on Corporate Software. Computer Economics, Inc. • Monthly. $395.00 per year. Newsletter for information systems managers. Contains data on business software trends, vendor licensing policies, and other corporate software management issues.

TRADE/PROFESSIONAL ASSOCIATIONS

Special Interest Group on Management of Data. c/o Association for Computing Machinery, 1515 Broadway, New York, NY 10036. Phone: 800-342-6626 or (212)869-7440 Fax: (212)944-1318 E-mail: acmhelp@acm.org • URL: http://www.acm.org/sigmod • Focuses on network architecture, protocols, and distributed systems. Publishes a quarterly newsletter *Computer Communication Review.* Formerly Special Interest Group on Data Communication.

SYSTEMS INTEGRATION

ABSTRACTS AND INDEXES

Applied Science and Technology Index. H. W. Wilson Co. • 11 times a year. Quarterly and annual cumulations. Price varies. Indexes a wide variety of English language technical, industrial, and engineering periodicals.

Business Periodicals Index. H. W. Wilson Co. • 11 times a year. Quarterly and annual cumulations. Price varies.

CompuMath Citation Index. Institute for Scientific Information. • Three times a year. $1,090.00 per year. Provides citations to the worldwide literature of computer science and mathematics.

Computer and Information Systems Abstracts Journal: An Abstract Journal Pertaining to the Theory, Design, Fabrication and Application of Computer and Information Systems. CSA. • 11 times a year. $1,750 per year.

Computer Literature Index: A Subject/Author Index to Computer and Data Processing Literature. EBSCO Publishing. • Quarterly, with annual cumulation. $245.00 per year. Contains brief abstracts of book and periodical literature covering all phases of computing, including approximately 70 specific application areas.

Internet and Personal Computing Abstracts [print edition]. EBSCO Publishing. • Quarterly. $269.00 per year, including cumulative index. Provides more than 10,000 abstracts annually from both trade and academic publications. Covers computer hardware, software, product reviews, Web topics, e-commerce,

networks, corporate news, security, and related topics. Formerly *Microcomputer Abstracts.*

CD-ROM DATABASES

ABI/INFORM. PROQUEST. • Monthly. Provides CD-ROM indexing and abstracting of worldwide business literature. Archival discs are available from 1971. Formerly *ABI/INFORM OnDisc.*

Computer Database. Gale Cengage Learning. • Provides one year of full-text on CD-ROM for 150 leading computer-related publications. Also includes 70,000 product specifications and brief profiles of 13,000 computer product vendors and manufacturers.

WILSONDISC: Applied Science and Technology Abstracts. H. W. Wilson Co. • Monthly. Includes unlimited access to the online version of *Applied Science and Technology Abstracts* through WILSONLINE. Provides CD-ROM indexing and abstracting of 500 prominent scientific, technical, engineering, and industrial periodicals. Indexing coverage is provided from 1983 to date and abstracting from 1993 to date.

WILSONDISC: Wilson Business Abstracts. H. W. Wilson Co. • Monthly. Includes unlimited online access to *Wilson Business Abstracts* through WILSONLINE. Provides CD-ROM "cover-to-cover" abstracting and indexing of over 600 prominent business periodicals. Indexing is from 1982, abstracting from 1990. (*Business Periodicals Index* without abstracts is available on CD-ROM at $1,495 per year.).

DIRECTORIES

Computing and Software Career Directory. Gale Cengage Learning. • 1993. $39.00. Includes career information relating to programmers, software engineers, technical writers, systems experts, and other computer specialists. Provides advice from "insiders," resume suggestions, a directory of companies that may offer entry-level positions, and a directory of career information sources. (Career Advisor Series.).

Data Sources: The Comprehensive Guide to the Data Processing Industry: Hardware, Data Communications Products, Software, Company Profiles. Gale Cengage Learning. • Semiannual. $455.00 per year. Two volumes. Describes hardware and software for all computer operating sysems, including prices and technical details. Lists about 75,000 products from 14,000 suppliers. Industry-specific software applications are described.

Manufacturing Systems: Buyers Guide. Reed Business Information. • Annual. Price on application. Contains information on companies manufacturing or supplying materials handling systems, CAD/CAM systems, specialized software for manufacturing, programmable controllers, machine vision systems, and automatic identification systems.

ENCYCLOPEDIAS AND DICTIONARIES

Acronyms of Computer Science and Communications: A Comprehensive Acronym Dictionary and Illustrated Encylopedia. Enjob Kajan and Ejub Kajan. Springer Verlag. • 2002. $49.95. Explains more than 4,000 "broadly used" computer, telecommunications, and information technology acronyms. Includes illustrations and Web addresses, where applicable.

Encyclopedia of Emerging Industries. Gale Cengage Learning. • 2001. $320.00. Fourth edition. Provides detailed information on 115 "newly flourishing" industries. Includes historical background, organizational structure, significant individuals, current conditions, major companies, work force, technology trends, research developments, and other industry facts.

Encyclopedia of Information Systems. Hossein Bidgoli, editor. Elsevier. • 2002. $1,200.00. Four volumes. Contains a wide range of articles relating to computers, databases, communication, and information technology. The 200 topics include coverage of hardware, software, artificial intelligence, the Internet, networks, knowledge management, electronic commerce, search engines, and systems design.

HANDBOOKS AND MANUALS

The Business of Systems Integration. Andrea Prencipe and Andrew Davies, editors. Oxford University Press. • 2004. $74.50.

Enterprise Integration: An Architecture for Enterprise Application and Systems Integration. Fred A. Cummins. John Wiley and Sons, Inc. • 2002. $44.99. Covers "Establishing the Enterprise Infrastructure," "Creating a Business System Domain," "Integrating with XML" (Extensible Markup Language), and related topics. Includes information on Web-based user access, system security, and enterprise intelligence support.

System Integration. Jeffrey O. Grady. CRC Press LLC. • 1994. $139.95. (Systems Engineering Series).

INTERNET DATABASES

InfoTech Trends. Data Analysis Group. Phone: (925)462-1202 Fax: (925)462-1225 E-mail: support@infotechtrends.com • URL: http://www.infotechtrends.com • Web site provides both free and fee-based market research data on the information technology industry, including computers, peripherals, telecommunications, the Internet, software, CD-ROM/DVD, e-commerce, and workstations. Fees: Free for current (most recent year) data; more extensive information has various fee structures. Formerly *Computer Industry Forecasts.*

ONLINE DATABASES

Applied Science and Technology Index Online. H. W. Wilson Co. • Provides online indexing of 500 major scientific, technical, industrial, and engineering periodicals. Time period is 1983 to date. Monthly updates. Inquire as to online cost and availability.

Internet and Personal Computing Abstracts. Information Today, Inc. • Contains abstracts covering a wide variety of personal and business microcomputer literature appearing in more than 100 journals and popular magazines. Time period is 1981 to date, with monthly updates. Formerly *Microcomputer Index.* Inquire as to online cost and availability.

Management Contents. Gale Cengage Learning. • Covers a wide range of management, financial, marketing, personnel, and administrative topics. About 150 leading business journals are indexed and abstracted from 1974 to date, with monthly updating. Inquire as to online cost and availability.

Trade & Industry Database. Gale Cengage Learning. • Provides indexing of business periodicals, January 1981 to date. Daily updates. (Full text articles from some periodicals are available online, 1983 to date. Inquire as to online cost and availability).

Wilson Business Abstracts Online. H. W. Wilson Co. • Indexes and abstracts 600 major business periodicals, plus the *Wall Street Journal* and the business section of the *New York Times.* Indexing is from 1982, abstracting from 1990, with the two newspapers included from 1993. Updated weekly. Inquire as to online cost and availability. (*Business Periodicals Index* without abstracts is also available online.).

PERIODICALS AND NEWSLETTERS

Advanced Manufacturing Technology: Monthly Report. Technical Insights. • Monthly. Institutions, $695.00 per year. Newsletter. Covers technological developments relating to robotics, computer graphics, automation, computer-integrated manufacturing, and machining.

Industrial Computing. Industrial Computing Society. ISA Services, Inc. • Monthly. Members $100.00 per year; non-members, $80.00 per year. Published by the Instrument Society of America. Edited for engineering managers and systems integrators. Subject matter includes industrial software, programmable controllers, artificial intelligence systems, and industrial computer networking systems.

Managing Automation. Thomas Publishing Co., LLC. • Monthly. Free to qualified personnel; others, $60.00 per year. Coverage includes software for manufacturing, systems planning, integration in process industry automation, computer integrated manufacturing (CIM), computer networks for manufacturing, management problems, industry news, and new products.

Manufacturing Computer Solutions. • Monthly. $88.00 per year. Edited for managers of factory automation, emphasizing the integration of systems in manufacturing. Subjects include materials handling, CAD/CAM, specialized software for manufacturing, programmable controllers, machine vision, and automatic identification systems. Formerly *Manufacturing Systems.*

RESEARCH CENTERS AND INSTITUTES

Alliance for Innovative Manufacturing. Stanford University, Bldg.02-530, Rm. 225, Stanford, CA 94305-3036. Phone: (650)723-9038 Fax: (650)723-5034 E-mail: cborn@stanford.edu • URL: http://www.stanford.edu/group/aim • Development of new products and processing. Formerly Stanford Integrated Manufacturing Association.

Center for Integrated Systems. Stanford University, 420 Via Palou Mall, Stanford, CA 94305-4070. Phone: (650)725-3621 Fax: (650)725-0991 E-mail: rdasher@stanford.edu • URL: http://www.cis.

stanford.edu • Research programs include manufacturing science, design science, computer architecture, semiconductor technology, and telecommunications.

Institute for Systems Research. University of Maryland at College Park, A. V. Williams Bldg., 2nd Fl., No. 115, College Park, MD 20742-3311. Phone: (301)405-6615 Fax: (301)314-9220 E-mail: isr@isr.umd.edu • URL: http://www.isr.umd.edu/ • A National Science Foundation Engineering Research Center. Areas of research include communication systems, manufacturing systems, chemical process systems, artificial intelligence, and systems integration.

TRADE/PROFESSIONAL ASSOCIATIONS

AIM Global. 125 Warrendale-Bayne Rd., Ste. 100, Warrendale, PA 15086. Phone: (724)934-4470 Fax: (724)934-4495 E-mail: dan@aimglobal.org • URL: http://www.aimglobal.org • Serves as a trade association for the automatic identification data captures technology industry.

AIM, Inc. 125 Warrendale Bayne Rd., Warrendale, PA 15086. Phone: 800-338-0206 or (724)934-4470 Fax: (724)934-4495 E-mail: info@aimglobal.org • URL: http://www.aimglobal.org • Members are companies concerned with automatic identification and data capture, including bar code systems, magnetic stripes, machine vision, voice technology, optical character recognition, and systems integration technology.

Information Technology Association of America. 1401 Wilson Blvd., Suite 1100, Arlington, VA 22209. Phone: (703)522-5055 Fax: (703)525-2279 E-mail: hmiller@itaa.org • URL: http://www.itaa.org • Members are computer software and services companies. Maintains an Information Systems Integration Services Section. Formerly Software Industry Division of ADAPSO.

Instrumentation Systems and Automation Society. 67 Alexander Dr., Research Triangle Park, NC 27709. Phone: (919)549-8411 Fax: (919)549-8288 E-mail: info@isa.org • URL: http://www.isa.org • Members are engineers and others concerned with industrial instrumentation, systems, computers, and automation. Formerly Instrument Society of America.

Network and Systems Professionals Association. 7044 S. 13th St., Milwaukee, WI 53154. Phone: (414)768-8000 Fax: (414)768-8001 E-mail: sherer@naspa.com • URL: http://www.naspa.com • Members are systems programmers, communications analysts, database administrators, and other technical management personnel.

Special Interest Group on Operating Systems. c/o Association for Computing Machinery, 1515 Broadway, New York, NY 10036. Phone: 800-342-6626 or (212)626-0500 Fax: (212)302-5826 E-mail: sigs@acm.org • URL: http://www.acm.org/sigops.

T

TABLEWARE

DIRECTORIES
Jewelers' Circular/Keystone-Jewelers' Directory. Reed Business Information. • Annual. $33.95. About 8,500 manufacturers, importers and wholesale jewelers providing merchandise and supplies to the jewelry retailing industry; and related trade organizations. Included with subscription to *Jewelers' Circular Keystone.*

PERIODICALS AND NEWSLETTERS
Gifts and Decorative Accessories: The International Business Magazine of Gifts, Tabletop, Gourmet, Home Accessories, Greeting Card and Social Stationery. Reed Business Information. • Monthly. $53.95 per year. Includes *Annual Directory.*

Giftware News: The International Magazine for Gifts, China and Glass, Stationery and Home Accessories. Talcott Communications Corp. • Monthly. $36.00 per year. Includes annual *Directory.*

JCK (Jewelers' Circular Keystone). Reed Business Information. • Monthly. $90.00 per year.

TRADE/PROFESSIONAL ASSOCIATIONS
Associated Glass and Pottery Manufacturers. 912 Country Club Dr., Greensburg, PA 15601. Phone: (724)837-9451 Fax: (724)523-2022 E-mail: robrupp@helicon.net.

OTHER SOURCES
Silverware, Plateware & Cutlery. Available from MarketResearch.com. • 2002. $3,950.00. Published by Global Industry Analysts. Provides worldwide market research data, including profiles of major tableware companies.

The Tabletop Market. Available from MarketResearch.com. • 2000. $2,750.00. Published by Packaged Facts. Provides market data on dinnerware, glassware, and flatware, with projections to 2002.

TAILORING

See also: CLOTHING INDUSTRY; FASHION INDUSTRY; MEN'S CLOTHING INDUSTRY

PERIODICALS AND NEWSLETTERS
Custom Tailor. Custom Tailors and Designers Association of America. • Three times a year. $50.00 per year. Controlled circulation.

TRADE/PROFESSIONAL ASSOCIATIONS
Custom Tailors and Designers Association of America. P.O. Box 53052, Washington, DC 20009-9052. Phone: (202)387-7220 Fax: (202)387-7713

E-mail: info@ctda.com • URL: http://www.ctda.com • Formerly Merchant Tailors and Designers Association of America.

TALL OIL INDUSTRY

See also: OIL AND FATS INDUSTRY

ALMANACS AND YEARBOOKS
CRB Commodity Yearbook. Commodity Research Bureau. CRB. • Annual. $99.95.

TRADE/PROFESSIONAL ASSOCIATIONS
Pine Chemicals Association. 3350 Riverwood Pkwy. SE, Ste. 1900, Atlanta, GA 30339. Phone: (770)984-5340 Fax: (770)984-5341 E-mail: wjones@pinechemicals.org • URL: http://www.pinechemicals.org • Represents manufacturers of chemical products (other than pulp, paper, and paper products) produced by, or from, wood pulp industry products. Sponsors educational and management meetings. Collects statistical data.

TANK SHIPS

See also: SHIPS, SHIPPING AND SHIPBUILDING

DIRECTORIES
Fairplay World Shipping Directory. Fairplay Publications Ltd. • Covers: more than 76,000 companies worldwide engaged in some aspect of shipping, including over 10,000 shipowners with fleets totalling over 45,000 vessels, shipbuilders and repairers, marine insurance shipping finance, protection and indemnity associations, marine equipment suppliers, and towing, salvage, and dredging; also lists marine organizations, shipbrokers, and consulting engineers and surveyors. Entries include: Company name, address, phone, fax, e-mail, URL, names of directors and executives, brief description of business; listings may also include associated and subsidiary companies and financial data.

List of Shipowners, Managers, and Managing Agents. Lloyd's Register of Shipping. • Annual. $350.00, including 10 updates per year. Published in the UK by Lloyd's Register-Fairplay Ltd. Lists 40,000 shipowners, managers, and agents worldwide. Cross-referenced with *Lloyd's Register of Ships.*

Lloyd's Maritime Directory. Informa PLC. • Covers: Over 40,000 shipowners, managers, and operators with 75,000 vessels. Also includes Marine consultants; towing, salvage, solicitors, P&I clubs; ship building and repair firms; general maritime organizations, banking and finance and more.

Entries include: Firm name, address, phone, fax, e-mail, internet; branch offices; names of principal executives; agents; parent and associated companies; and, for shipowners and lines, detailed information on ships owned, type, or capacity, etc. The former second volume of 'International Shipping and Shipbuilding Directory' is now published separately with the title 'Lloyd's List Marine Equipment Buyers' Guide' (see separate entry).

Tanker Register. Clarkson Research Studies. • Covers: More than 4,282 tankers and combined carriers throughout the world having deadweight tonnage exceeding 10,000, and their owners and managers. Entries include: Ship name, owner or manager, where registered, when and where built, tonnage, draft, capacity, engines, etc.

ENCYCLOPEDIAS AND DICTIONARIES
Dictionary of Shipping Terms. Peter Brodie. LLP, Inc. • 1997. Third edition. Price on application. Published in the UK by Lloyd's List (http://www.lloydslist.com). Defines more than 2,000 words, phrases, and abbreviations related to the shipping and maritime industries.

Macmillan Encyclopedia of Transportation. Available from Gale Cengage Learning. • 1999. $450.00. Six volumes. Published by Macmillan Reference USA. Covers the business, technology, and history of transportation on land, on water, in the air, and in space. Includes definitions, cross-references, and 200 color illustrations.

HANDBOOKS AND MANUALS
Tanker Operations: A Handbook for the Person-in-Charge. Mark Huber and G.S Marton. Cornell Maritime Press, Inc. • 2001. $50.00. Fourth edition.

PERIODICALS AND NEWSLETTERS
Lloyd's List. Available from Informa UK Ltd. • Daily. $1,698.00 per year. Published in the UK by Lloyd's List (http://www.lloydslist.com). Marine industry newspaper. Covers a wide variety of maritime topics, including global news, business/insurance, regulation, shipping markets, financial markets, shipping movements, freight logistics, and marine technology. (Also available weekly at $385.00 per year.).

Lloyd's Ship Manager. LLP Inc. • 10 times a year. $478.00 per year, including annual supplementary guides and directories. Published in the UK by Lloyd's List (http://www.lloydslist.com). Covers all management, technical, and operational aspects of ocean-going shipping.

Register of International Shipowning Groups. Available from Fairplay Publications, Inc. • Three times a year. $744.00 per year. Published in the UK by Lloyd's Register-Fairplay Ltd. "Provides intelligence on shipowners and managers, their subsidiary and associate companies, and owners' representatives." Includes detailed information on individual ships.

Tanker Market Quarterly. Available from Informa Publishing Group Ltd. • Quarterly. $495.00 per year. Published in the UK by Lloyd's List (http://www. lloydslist.com). Provides supply and demand information "required to make accurate market decisions." Includes detailed graphs and analytical commentary.

PRICE SOURCES

American Tanker Rate Schedule. Association of Ship Brokers and Agents-USA. • Annual. $1,500.00. Contains tanker freight rates.

STATISTICS SOURCES

World Oil Tanker Trends. Jacobs and Partners Ltd. • Semiannual. $520.00 per year.

TRADE/PROFESSIONAL ASSOCIATIONS

Association of Ship Brokers and Agents-U.S.A. 510 Sylvan Ave., Ste. 201, Englewood Cliffs, NJ 07632-3039. Phone: (201)569-2882 Fax: (201)569-9082 E-mail: asba@asba.org • URL: http://www.asba.org • Includes a Tanker Committee.

TANK TRUCKS

See: TRUCKING INDUSTRY

TANKERS

See: TANK SHIPS

TANNING INDUSTRY

See also: LEATHER INDUSTRY

DIRECTORIES

American Leather Chemists Association-- Membership Directory. American Leather Chemists Association. • Covers: about 500 chemists, leather technologists, and educators concerned with the tanning and leather industry. Entries include: Personal name, address; company name, address, phone, fax.

Leather Manufacturer Directory. Shoe Trades Publishing Co. • Covers: Tanneries, leather finishers, and hide processors and their suppliers in the United States and Canada. Entries include: Company name, address, phone, names of executives, list of products or services and over 300 companies classified by their goods and services.

PERIODICALS AND NEWSLETTERS

American Leather Chemists Association Journal. American Leather Chemists Association. • Monthly. Members, $8.50 per year; non-members, $115.00 per year.

Leather Manufacturer. Shoe Trades Publishing Co. • Monthly. $40.00 per year. Edited for hide processors, tanners and leather finishers in the U.S. and Canada.

Newsbreak. Leather Industries of America. • Free to members and other qualified personnel. Reports on issues and events in the luggage industry.

Society of Leather Technologists and Chemists Journal. Society of Leather Technologies and Chemists. • Bimonthly. $75.00 per year. Scientific, technical, historical and commercial papers on leather and allied industries.

TRADE/PROFESSIONAL ASSOCIATIONS

American Leather Chemists Association. 1314 50th St., Ste. 103, P.O. Box 45300, Lubbock, TX 79412-2940. Phone: (806)744-1798 Fax: (806)744-1785 E-mail: alca@leatherchemists.org • URL: http://

www.leatherchemists.org • Chemists, leather technologists, and educators concerned with the tanning and leather industry. Works to devise and perfect methods for the analysis and testing of leathers and materials used in leather manufacture. Promotes advancement of chemistry and other sciences, especially their application to problems confronting the leather industry.

Leather Industries of America. 1900 L St., NW, Ste 710, Washington, DC 20036. Phone: (202)296-4806 Fax: (202)296-7882 E-mail: info@leatherusa.com • URL: http://www.leatherusa.com • Formerly Tanners' Council of America.

TAPE RECORDING

See: SOUND RECORDERS AND RECORD-ING; VIDEO RECORDING INDUSTRY

TARIFF

DIRECTORIES

U.S. Custom House Guide. Commonwealth Business Media Inc. • Publication includes: List of ports having customs facilities, customs officials, port authorities, chambers of commerce, embassies and consulates, foreign trade zones, and other organizations; related trade services. Entries include: For each principal port--Name of organization or agency, address, phone, fax, names and titles of key personnel; description and limitations of port facilities. For service firms--Company name, address, phone, fax. Principal content is U.S. tariff schedules and customs regulations, and a "How to Import" manual.

HANDBOOKS AND MANUALS

Harmonized Tariff Schedule of the United States, Annotated, Basic Manual. Available from U.S. Government Printing Office. • $84.00, including basic volumes and supplementary service for an indefinite period.

PERIODICALS AND NEWSLETTERS

Customs Bulletin and Decisions. Available from U. S. Government Printing Office. • Weekly. $247.00 per year. Issued by U. S. Customs Service, Department of the Treasury. Contains regulations, rulings, decisions, and notices relating to customs laws.

TRADE/PROFESSIONAL ASSOCIATIONS

International Customs Tariffs Bureau. rue des Petits Carmes, 15, B-1000 Brussels, Belgium. Phone: 32 2 5018774 or 32 2 5018779 Fax: 32 2 5013147 E-mail: dir@bitd.org • URL: http://www.bitd.org • Executive instrument of the International Union for the Publication of Customs Tariffs. Translates and publishes the customs tariffs of all countries into 5 languages: English, French, German, Italian, and Spanish.

OTHER SOURCES

Customs Regulations of the United States. Available from U. S. Government Printing Office. • Looseleaf. $175.00. Issued by U. S. Customs Service, Department of the Treasury. Reprint of regulations published to carry out customs laws of the U. S. Includes supplementary material for an indeterminate period.

Worldtariff Guidebook on Customs Tariff Schedules of Import Duties. Worldtariff Division, Morse Agri-Energy Associates. • Looseleaf. Over 60 volumes. Prices vary. Consists generally of volumes for individual countries and volumes for broad classes of products, such as clothing. (Country volumes are typically $500.00 each.).

TAX ADMINISTRATION

See also: TAXATION
HANDBOOKS AND MANUALS
Federal Taxation Practice and Procedure Problem Supplement. Robert E. Meldman and Richard J.

Sideman. CCH, Inc. • 1998. $40.00. Provides information on the administrative structure of the Internal Revenue Service. Includes discussions of penalties, ethical duties, statute of limitations, litigation, and IRS collection procedures. Contains IRS standardized letters and notices.

ONLINE DATABASES

Accounting and Tax Database. PROQUEST. • Provides indexing and abstracting of the literature of accounting, taxation, and financial management, 1971 to date. Updating is weekly. Especially covers accounting, auditing, banking, bankruptcy, employee compensation and benefits, cash management, financial planning, and credit. Inquire as to online cost and availability.

PERIODICALS AND NEWSLETTERS

Accounting Today: The Business Newspaper for the Tax & Accounting Community. Thomson Media. • Biweekly. $99.00 per year. Covers news affecting tax and accounting professionals.

The Journal of Taxation: A National Journal of Current Developments, Analysis and Commentary for Tax Professionals. RIA. • Monthly. $305.00 per year. Analysis of current tax developments for tax specialists.

Tax Administrators News. Federation of Tax Administrators. • Description: Focuses on state tax legislation and administration. Covers research results and federal legislation that affects state taxation. Recurring features include state-by-state news of tax changes and innovations in administration, announcements of conferences and meetings, profiles of state revenue commissioners, and special sections on motor fuel taxes and technology in tax administration.

The Tax Executive. Tax Executives Institute. • Bimonthly. $120.00 per year. Professional journal for corporate tax executives.

RESEARCH CENTERS AND INSTITUTES

International Tax Program. Harvard University, 1563 Massachusetts Ave., Pound Hall, Room 400, Cambridge, MA 02138. Phone: (617)495-4406 Fax: (617)495-0423 E-mail: itp@law.harvard.edu • URL: http://www.law.harvard.edu/programs/itp • Studies the worldwide problems of taxation, including tax law and tax administration.

TRADE/PROFESSIONAL ASSOCIATIONS

Federation of Tax Administrators. 444 N. Capitol St., Suite 348, Washington, DC 20001. Phone: (202)624-5890 Fax: (202)624-7888 E-mail: fta@taxadmin.org • URL: http://www.taxadmin.org.

Tax Executives Institute. 1200 G St. NW, Ste. 300, Washington, DC 20005-3814. Phone: (202)638-5601 Fax: (202)638-5607 E-mail: administration@tei.org • URL: http://www.tei.org • Professional society of executives administering and directing tax affairs for corporations and businesses. Maintains TEI +Education Fund.

OTHER SOURCES

Internal Revenue Manual: Audit and Administration. CCH, Inc. • Irregular. $1,254.00. Six looseleaf volumes. Reproduces IRS tax administration provisions and procedures.

Partnerships and LLCs: Tax Practice and Analysis. Thomas G. Manolakas. CCH, Inc. • 2000. $95.00. Covers the taxation of partnerships and limited liability companies.

TAX, ESTATE

See: INHERITANCE TAX

TAX, EXCISE

See: EXCISE TAX

TAX EXEMPT SECURITIES

See: MUNICIPAL BONDS

TAX, GIFT

See: GIFT TAX

TAX, INCOME

See: INCOME TAX

TAX, INHERITANCE

See: INHERITANCE TAX

TAX LAW AND REGULATION

See also: INCOME TAX; STATE TAXES; TAXATION

GENERAL WORKS

Tax Policy and the Economy. MIT Press. • Annual. $58.00. Reviews "issues in the current tax debate." Produced by the National Bureau of Economic Research. (NBER Tax Policy and the Economy Series).

ABSTRACTS AND INDEXES

Current Law Index: Multiple Access to Legal Periodicals. Gale Cengage Learning. • Monthly. $725.00 per year. Produced in cooperation with the American Association of Law Libraries. Indexes more than 900 law journals, legal newspapers, and specialty publications from the U.S., Canada, U.K., Ireland, Australia, and New Zealand.

Index to Legal Periodicals and Books. H. W. Wilson Co. • Monthly. $490.00 per year. Quarterly and annual cumulations.

ALMANACS AND YEARBOOKS

Tax Year in Review. CCH, Inc. • Annual. Covers the year's "major new legislative and regulatory changes.".

CD-ROM DATABASES

Authority Tax and Estate Planning Library. LexisNexis/Matthew Bender. • Periodic revisions. Price on request. CD-ROM contains updated full text of *Bender's Payroll Tax Guide, Depreciation Handbook, Federal Income Taxation of Corporations, Tax Planning for Corporations, Modern Estate Planning, Planning for Large Estates, Murphy's Will Clauses, Tax & Estate Planning for the Elderly,* and 12 other Matthew Bender publications. The Internal Revenue Code is also included.

Federal Tax Products. Available from U. S. Government Printing Office. • Annual. $27.00. CD-ROM issued by the Internal Revenue Service (http://www.irs.treas.gov/forms_pubs/). Provides current tax forms, instructions, and publications. Also includes older tax forms beginning with 1991.

WILSONDISC: Index to Legal Periodicals and Books. H. W. Wilson Co. • Monthly. Includes unlimited online access to *Index to Legal Periodicals* through WILSONLINE. Contains CD-ROM indexing of more than 1,400 English language legal periodicals from 1981 to date and 2,500 books.

HANDBOOKS AND MANUALS

Bank Tax Guide. CCH, Inc. • Annual. $199.00. Summarizes and explains federal tax rules affecting financial institutions.

How to Practice Before the New IRS. Robert S. Schriebman. CCH, Inc. • 1999. $115.00. Reflects changes made by the IRS Restructuring and Reform Act of 1998. Covers audits, appeals, tax court basics,

refunds, penalties, etc., for tax professionals.

Income Tax Regulations. CCH, Inc. • Annual. $119.00. Six volumes. Contains full text of official Internal Revenue Code regulations.

Internal Revenue Code. RIA. • Annual. $86.50. Provides full text of the Internal Revenue Code (5,000 pages), including procedural and administrative provisions.

IRS Tax Collection Procedures. CCH, Inc. • $195.00. Looseleaf service. Periodic supplementation. Covers IRS collection personnel, payment arrangements, penalties, abatements, summons, liens, etc.

Law of Federal Estate and Gift Taxation-Code Commentary. West Group. • Annual. $177.00. Looseleaf service.

Practical Guide to Tax Issues in Employment. Julia K. Brazelton. CCH, Inc. • 1999. $95.00. Covers income taxation as related to labor law and tax law, including settlements and awards. Written for tax professionals.

INTERNET DATABASES

CCH Essentials: An Internet Tax Research and Primary Source Library. CCH, Inc. Phone: 800-248-3248 or (773)866-6000 Fax: 800-224-8299 or (773)866-3608 E-mail: cust_serv@cch.com • URL: http://tax.cch.com/essentials • Fee-based Web site provides full-text coverage of federal tax law and regulations, including rulings, procedures, tax court decisions, and IRS publications, announcements, notices, and penalties. Includes explanation, analysis, tax planning guides, and a daily tax news service. Searching is offered, including citation search.

Factiva. Dow Jones Reuters Business Interactive, LLC. Phone: 800-369-7466 or (609)452-1511 Fax: (609)520-5770 E-mail: solutions@factiva.com • URL: http://www.factiva.com • Fee-based Web site provides "global news and business information through Web sites and content integration solutions." Includes Dow Jones and Reuters newswires, The Wall Street Journal, and more than 7,000 other sources of current news, historical articles, market research reports, and investment analysis. Content includes 96 major U. S. newspapers, 900 non-English sources, trade publications, media transcripts, country profiles, news photos, etc.

Internal Revenue Service IRS.gov. Internal Revenue Service. Phone: 800-829-1040 or (202)622-5000 Fax: (202)622-5844 • URL: http://www.irs.gov • Web site provides a wide variety of tax information, including IRS forms and publications. Searching is available. Fees: Free.

Lexis.com Research System. Lexis-Nexis Group. Phone: 800-227-4908 or (937)865-6800 Fax: (937)865-6909 E-mail: webmaster@prod.lexis-nexis.com • URL: http://www.lexis.com • Fee-based Web site offers extensive searching of a wide variety of legal sources. Additional features include Daily Opinion Service, lexis.com Bookstore, Career Center, CLE Center, Law Schools, and Practice Pages ("Pages specific to areas of specialty").

Nexis.com. Lexis-Nexis Group. Phone: 800-227-4908 or (937)865-6800 Fax: (937)865-6909 E-mail: webmaster@prod.lexis-nexis.com • URL: http://www.nexis.com • Fee-based Web site offers searching of about 2.8 billion documents in some 30,000 news, business, and legal information sources. Features include a subject directory covering 1,200 topics in 34 categories and a Company Dossier containing information on more than 500,000 public and private companies. Boolean searching is offered.

Rutgers Accounting Web (RAW). Rutgers University Accounting Research Center. Phone: (973)353-5172 Fax: (973)353-1283 • URL: http://www.rutgers.edu/accounting • RAW Web site provides extensive links to sources of national and international accounting information, such as the Big Six accounting firms, the Financial Accounting Standards Board (FASB),

SEC filings (EDGAR), journals, publishers, software, the International Accounting Network, and "Internet's largest list of accounting firms in USA." Searching is offered. Fees: Free.

Tax Analysts [Web site]. Tax Analysts. Phone: 800-955-3444 or (703)533-4400 Fax: (703)533-4444 • URL: http://www.tax.org • The three main sections of Tax Analysts home page are "Tax News" (Today's Tax News, Feature of the Week, Tax Snapshots, Tax Calendar); "Products & Services" (Product Catalog, Press Releases); and "Public Interest" (Discussion Groups, Tax Clinic, Tax History Project). Fees: Free for coverage of current tax events; fee-based for comprehensive information. Daily updating.

ONLINE DATABASES

Index to Legal Periodicals and Books (Online). H. W. Wilson Co. • Broad coverage of law journals and books 1981 to date. Monthly updates. Inquire as to online cost and availability.

PERIODICALS AND NEWSLETTERS

Daily Tax Report: From Today's Daily Report for Executives. BNA, Inc. • Daily. $2,595.00 per year. Looseleaf service. Monitors tax legislation, hearings, rulings, and court decisions.

E-Commerce Tax Alert. CCH Inc. • Description: Print and online newsletter covering e-commerce taxation issues, including compliance and sourcing, e-cash implications, the Internet tax debate, and other topics.

Highlights and Documents. Tax Analysts. • Daily. $2,249.00 per year, including monthly indexes. Newsletter. Provides daily coverage of IRS, congressional, judicial, state, and international tax developments. Includes abstracts and citations for "all tax documents released within the previous 24 to 48 hours." Annual compilation available *Highlights and Documents on Microfiche.*

Internal Revenue Bulletin. Research Institute of America. • Description: Presents new treasury and IRS releases in full official text. Contains rulings and decisions, releases on treaties, tax legislation, administrative and procedural releases, disbarment and suspensions.

Internal Revenue Cumulative Bulletin. Available from U. S. Government Printing Office. • Semiannual. Issued by the Internal Revenue Service. Cumulates all items of a "permanent nature" appearing in the weekly *Internal Revenue Bulletin.*

Journal of Tax Practice and Procedure. CCH, Inc. • Bimonthly. $215.00 per year. Covers the representation of taxpayers before the IRS, "from initial contact through litigation.".

The Kiplinger Tax Letter. Kiplinger Washington Editors Inc. • Description: Reports new tax regulations, changes, decisions, and pending legislation. Includes coverage of the House Ways and Means and Senate Committees, federal monetary and fiscal policy, securities, finance, and social security.

The Practical Tax Lawyer. Committee on Continuing Professional Education. American Law Institute-American Bar Association Committee on Continuing Professional Education. • Quarterly. Members, $38.50 per year; non-members, $49.00 per year.

Tax Notes: The Weekly Tax Service. Tax Analysts. • Weekly. $1,699.00 per year. Includes an *Annual* and 1985-1996 compliations on CD-ROM. Newsletter. Covers "tax news from all federal sources," including congressional committees, tax courts, and the Internal Revenue Service. Each issue contains "summaries of every document that pertains to federal tax law," with citations. Commentary is provided.

Tax Practice. Tax Analysts. • Weekly. $199.00 per year. Newsletter. Covers news affecting tax practitioners and litigators, with emphasis on federal court decisions, rules and regulations, and tax petitions. Provides a guide to Internal Revenue Service audit issues.

Taxation and Revenue Policies: State Capitals. Wakeman-Walworth, Inc. • 50 times a year. $345.00 per year; print and online edition, $490.00 per year. Formerly *From the State Capitals: Taxation and Revenue Policies.*

Taxes-Property: State Capitals. Wakeman-Walworth, Inc. • 50 times a year. $345.00 per year; print and online edition, $490.00. Formerly *From the State Capitals: Taxes-Property.*

Taxes: The Tax Magazine. CCH, Inc. • Monthly. $215.00. per year. Mainly for accountants and lawyers.

RESEARCH CENTERS AND INSTITUTES

International Tax Program. Harvard University, 1563 Massachusetts Ave., Pound Hall, Room 400, Cambridge, MA 02138. Phone: (617)495-4406 Fax: (617)495-0423 E-mail: itp@law.harvard.edu • URL: http://www.law.harvard.edu/programs/itp • Studies the worldwide problems of taxation, including tax law and tax administration.

Office of Tax Policy Research. University of Michigan, 701 Tappan St., Ann Arbor, MI 48109-1234. Phone: (734)763-3068 Fax: (734)763-4032 E-mail: otpr@umich.edu • URL: http://www.taxpolicyresearch.umich.edu/.

Tax Foundation. Tax Foundation. 2001 L St. NW, Ste. 1050, Washington, DC 20036. Phone: (202)464-6200 Fax: (202)464-6201 E-mail: hodge@taxfoundation.org • URL: http://www.taxfoundation.org • Fiscal and management aspects of federal, state, and local government, including studies on government expenditures, the federal budget, taxation, and international competitiveness. Serves as a national information agency for individuals and organizations concerned with problems of government expenditures, taxation, and debt.

TRADE/PROFESSIONAL ASSOCIATIONS

International Bureau of Fiscal Documentation. P.O. Box 20237, NL-1000 HE Amsterdam, Netherlands. Phone: 31 20 5540100 Fax: 31 20 6228658 E-mail: info@ibfd.nl • URL: http://www.ibfd.nl.

Tax Analysts. 400 S Maple Ave., Ste. 400, Falls Church, VA 22046. Phone: 800-955-2444 or (703)533-4400 Fax: (703)533-4444 E-mail: cservice@tax.org • URL: http://www.tax.org • Reviews all tax law developments, federal, state, international comprehensively; compiles statistics. **Convention/Meeting:** none.

OTHER SOURCES

Avoiding Tax Malpractice. CCH, Inc. • 2000. $75.00. Covers malpractice considerations for professional tax practitioners.

Estate Planning Strategies After Estate Tax Reform: Insights and Analysis. Charles D. Fox and Thomas W. Aberdroth. CCH, Inc. • 2001. $45.00. Produced by the Estate Planning Department of Schiff, Hardin & Waite. Covers estate planning techniques and opportunities resulting from tax legislation of 2001.

Estate Planning Under the New Law: What You Need to Know. CCH, Inc. • 2001. $7.00. Booklet summarizes significant changes in estate planning brought about by tax legislation of 2001.

Federal Tax Coordinator Library. RIA. • $2,125.00 per year. Available only online.

Foreign Tax and Trade Briefs. LexisNexis Matthew Bender. • Quarterly. $550.00 per year. Two looseleaf volumes. The latest tax and trade information for over 100 foreign countries.

Tax Legislation 2001: Law, Explanation, and Analysis. CCH, Inc. • 2001. $42.50. Provides explanation and interpretation of federal tax legislation enacted in 2001.

Tax Legislation 2002: Highlights. CCH, Inc. • 2002. $7.00. Booklet summarizes significant changes in U.S. tax law resulting from the legislation of 2001.

White Collar Crime: Business and Regulatory Offenses. American Lawyer Media, Inc. • Looseleaf. $249.00. Updated as needed. Covers such legal matters as criminal tax cases, securities fraud, computer crime, mail fraud, bank embezzlement, criminal antitrust activities, extortion, perjury, the criminal liability of corporations, and RICO (Racketeer Influenced and Corrupt Organization Act). (Law Journal Press).

TAX MANAGEMENT

See: TAXATION

TAX PLANNING

See also: ESTATE PLANNING; FINANCIAL PLANNING; INCOME TAX

GENERAL WORKS

How to Avoid Financial Tangles. American Institute for Economic Research. • 2001. $8.00. Provides basic information and advice on such topics as property ownership, taxes, wills, trusts, insurance, record retention, and professional assistance. (Economic Education Bulletin.).

Smart Questions to Ask Your Financial Advisers. Lynn Brenner. Bloomberg. • 1997. $19.95. Provides practical advice on how to deal with financial planners, stockbrokers, insurance agents, and lawyers. Some of the areas covered are investments, estate planning, tax planning, house buying, prenuptial agreements, divorce arrangements, loss of a job, and retirement. (Bloomberg Personal Bookshelf Series).

ABSTRACTS AND INDEXES

Business Periodicals Index. H. W. Wilson Co. • 11 times a year. Quarterly and annual cumulations. Price varies.

CD-ROM DATABASES

Authority Tax and Estate Planning Library. LexisNexis/Matthew Bender. • Periodic revisions. Price on request. CD-ROM contains updated full text of *Bender's Payroll Tax Guide, Depreciation Handbook, Federal Income Taxation of Corporations, Tax Planning for Corporations, Modern Estate Planning, Planning for Large Estates, Murphy's Will Clauses, Tax & Estate Planning for the Elderly,* and 12 other Matthew Bender publications. The Internal Revenue Code is also included.

DIRECTORIES

Business Organizations, Agencies, and Publications Directory. Gale Cengage Learning. • 2003. $480.00. 15th edition. Over 40,000 entries describing 39 types of business information sources. Classified by type of organization, publication, or serviceIncludes state, national, and international agencies and organizations. Master index to names and keywords. Also includes e-mail addresses and web site URL's.

HANDBOOKS AND MANUALS

Asset Protection Planning Guide: A State-of-the-Art Approach to Integrated Estate Planning. Barry S. Engel and others. CCH, Inc. • 2001. $99.00. Provides advice for attorneys, trust officers, accountants, and others engaged in financial planning for protection of assets.

CCH Analysis of Top Tax Issues. CCH, Inc. • Annual. $49.00. Covers yearly tax changes affecting business and personal transactions, planning, and returns.

CCH Financial and Estate Planning Guide. CCH, Inc. • Annual. $63.00. Contains four main parts: General Principles and Techniques, Special Situations, Building the Estate, and Planning Aids.

CCH Guide to Car, Travel, Entertainment, and Home Office Deductions. CCH, Inc. • Annual. $45.

00. Explains how to claim maximum tax deductions for common business expenses. Includes automobile depreciation tables, lease value tables, worksheets, and examples of filled-in tax forms.

Charitable Planning Primer. Ralph G. Miller and Adam Smalley. CCH, Inc. • 1999. $99.00. Covers the legal and tax aspects of charitable giving and planned gifts. Includes annuity documents, tax forms, tables, and examples.

Ernst & Young's Personal Financial Planning Guide. John Wiley and Sons, Inc. • 2001. $19.95. Fourth edition.

Essentials of Federal Income Taxation for Individuals and Business. CCH, Inc. • Annual. $72.00. Covers basic tax planning and tax reduction strategies as affected by tax law changes and IRS interpretations. Includes sample filled-in forms.

Estate Plan Book 2000. William S. Moore. American Institute for Economic Research. • 2000. $10.00. Revision of 1997 edition. Part one: "Basic Estate Planning." Part two: "Reducing Taxes on the Disposition of Your Estate." Part three: "Putting it All Together: Examples of Estate Plans." Provides succinct information on wills, trusts, tax planning, and gifts. (Economic Education Bulletin.).

Family Tax Guide. Executive Reports Corp. • 1985. $44.95.

Federal Tax Course. Aspen Publishers, Inc. • Annual. $210.00. Provides basic reference and training for various forms of federal taxation: individual, business, corporate, partnership, estate, gift, etc.

Individual Retirement Account Answer Book. Donald R. Levy and others. Aspen Publishers, Inc. • 2002. $195.00. Ninth edition. Periodic supplementation available. Questions and answers include information about contributions, distributions, rollovers, Roth IRAs, SIMPLE IRAs (Savings Incentive Match Plans for Employees), Education IRAs, and SEPs (Simplified Employee Pension plans). Chapters are provided on retirement planning, estate planning, and tax planning.

Retirement Benefits Tax Guide. CCH, Inc. • $199.00. Looseleaf service.

Tax Planning and Compliance for Tax-Exempt Organizations: Forms, Checklists, Procedures. Jody Blazek. John Wiley and Sons, Inc. • 1999. $165.00. Third edition. 2002 *Supplement*, $70.00. (Nonprofit, Law, Finance, and Management Series).

Tax Planning for Highly Compensated Individuals. RIA Group. • $235.00. Looseleaf service. Biennial supplementation.

INTERNET DATABASES

CCH Essentials: An Internet Tax Research and Primary Source Library. CCH, Inc. Phone: 800-248-3248 or (773)866-6000 Fax: 800-224-8299 or (773)866-3608 E-mail: cust_serv@cch.com • URL: http://tax.cch.com/essentials • Fee-based Web site provides full-text coverage of federal tax law and regulations, including rulings, procedures, tax court decisions, and IRS publications, announcements, notices, and penalties. Includes explanation, analysis, tax planning guides, and a daily tax news service. Searching is offered, including citation search.

ONLINE DATABASES

Wilson Business Abstracts Online. H. W. Wilson Co. • Indexes and abstracts 600 major business periodicals, plus the *Wall Street Journal* and the business section of the *New York Times.* Indexing is from 1982, abstracting from 1990, with the two newspapers included from 1993. Updated weekly. Inquire as to online cost and availability. (*Business Periodicals Index* without abstracts is also available online.).

PERIODICALS AND NEWSLETTERS

Financial Planning: The Magazine for Financial Service Professionals. Thomson Media. • Monthly.

$79.00 per year. Edited for independent financial planners and insurance agents. Covers retirement planning, estate planning, tax planning, and insurance, including long-term healthcare considerations. Special features include a Retirement Planning Issue, Mutual Fund Performance Survey, and Variable Life and Annuity Survey.

Jounal of Finacial Services Professionals. Society of Financial Services Professional. • Bimonthly. $95.00 per year. Provides information on life insurance and financial planning, including estate planning, retirement, tax planning, trusts, business insurance, long-term care insurance, disability insurance, and employee benefits. Formerly (American Society of CLU and Ch F C Journal).

The Journal of Taxation: A National Journal of Current Developments, Analysis and Commentary for Tax Professionals. RIA. • Monthly. $305.00 per year. Analysis of current tax developments for tax specialists.

Journal of Taxation of Corporate Transactions. CCH, Inc. • Bimonthly. $225.00 per year. Covers the planning and compliance issues faced by corporate taxpayers.

Money. • 13 times a year. $19.95 per year. Covers all aspects of family finance; investments, careers, shopping, taxes, insurance, consumerism, etc.

Practical Tax Strategies. RIA. • Monthly. $275.00 per year. Emphasis is on current tax developments as they affect accountants and their clients. Includes advice on tax software and computers. Formerly *Taxation for Accountants.*

Retirement Plans Bulletin: Practical Explanations for the IRA and Retirement Plan Professional. Universal Pensions, Inc. • Monthly. $99.00 per year. Newsletter. Provides information on the rules and regulations governing qualified (tax-deferred) retirement plans.

The Tax Adviser: A Magazine of Tax Planning, Trends and Techniques. American Institute of Certified Public Accountants. • Monthly. Members, $71.00 per year; non-members, $98.00 per year. Newsletter.

Tax Management Weekly Report. Tax Management Inc. • Description: Covers developments affecting taxation and the tax aspects of accounting. Includes summaries of federal cases including the U.S. Tax Court, synopses of IRS general counsel and technical advice memoranda, analysis of selected IRS revenue rulings, procedures and private letter rulings, and status reports of Treasury Department actions on pending regulations. Covers topics in financial planning, including memoranda on current financial and tax planning strategies.

Taxes: The Tax Magazine. CCH, Inc. • Monthly. $215.00 per year. Mainly for accountants and lawyers.

RESEARCH CENTERS AND INSTITUTES

American Institute for Economic Research. P.O. Box 1000, Great Barrington, MA 01230. Phone: (413)528-1216 Fax: (413)528-0103 E-mail: info@aier.org • URL: http://www.aier.org.

TRADE/PROFESSIONAL ASSOCIATIONS

Institute of Tax Consultants. 7500 212th St., S.W., No. 205, Edmonds, WA 98026. Phone: (425)774-3521 Fax: (425)672-0461 E-mail: kraemerc@juno.com • URL: http://www.taxprofessionals.homestead.com.

National Association of Tax Professionals. 720 Association Dr., Appleton, WI 54914. Phone: 800-558-3402 or (920)749-1040 Fax: 800-747-0001 E-mail: natp@natptax.com • URL: http://www.natptax.com • Promotes high professional standards for tax practitioners. Formerly National Association for Tax Practitioners.

Tax Executives Institute. 1200 G St. NW, Ste. 300, Washington, DC 20005-3814. Phone: (202)638-

5601 Fax: (202)638-5607 E-mail: administration@tei.org • URL: http://www.tei.org • Professional society of executives administering and directing tax affairs for corporations and businesses. Maintains TEI +Education Fund.

OTHER SOURCES

Divorce and Taxes. CCH, Inc. • 2000. $25.00. Second edition. In addition to tax problems, topics include alimony, division of property, and divorce decrees.

Tax Planning for Individuals and Small Businesses. Sidney Kess. CCH, Inc. • 2002. $52.00. Second edition. Includes illustrations, charts, and sample client letters. Edited primarily for accountants and lawyers.

Tax Strategies for the Self-Employed. Alan D. Campbell and others. CCH, Inc. • 2000. $95.00. Covers accounting methods, start-up expenses, transportation deductions, depreciation, pension deductions, tax penalties, and other topics related to tax planning for the self-employed.

TAX, PROPERTY

See: PROPERTY TAX

TAX, SALES

See: SALES TAX; STATE TAXES; TAXATION

TAX SHELTERS

See also: INCOME TAX; INDUSTRIAL REAL ESTATE; INTERNATIONAL TAXATION; KEOGH PLANS; PROPERTY TAX; REAL ESTATE INVESTMENTS; TAXATION

GENERAL WORKS

What the IRS Doesn't Want You to Know: A CPA Reveals the Tricks of the Trade. Martin Kaplan. John Wiley and Sons, Inc. • 2003. $18.95. Ninth edition. Explains how to legally pay as little income tax as possible.

ABSTRACTS AND INDEXES

Business Periodicals Index. H. W. Wilson Co. • 11 times a year. Quarterly and annual cumulations. Price varies.

Index to Legal Periodicals and Books. H. W. Wilson Co. • Monthly. $490.00 per year. Quarterly and annual cumulations.

HANDBOOKS AND MANUALS

How to Build Wealth with Tax-Sheltered Investments. Kerry Anne Lynch. American Institute for Economic Research. • 2000. $6.00. Provides practical information on conservative tax shelters, including defined-contribution pension plans, individual retirement accounts, Keogh plans, U.S. savings bonds, municipal bonds, and various kinds of annuities: deferred, variable-rate, immediate, and foreign-currency. (Economic Education Bulletin.).

Practical Guide to Handling IRS Income Tax Audits. Ralph L. Guyette. Prentice Hall PTR. • 1986. $39.95.

Real Estate Transactions, Tax Planning and Consequences. Mark L. Levine. West Group. • 1997. Periodic supplementation.

Tax Planning for Highly Compensated Individuals. RIA Group. • $235.00. Looseleaf service. Biennial supplementation.

Working with Tax-Sheltered Annuities: 403(b) Plans Explained. Steven Leventhal. CCH, Inc. • 2001. $75.95. Fourth edition. Emphasis is on legal aspects of tax-deferred annuities.

ONLINE DATABASES

Index to Legal Periodicals and Books (Online). H. W. Wilson Co. • Broad coverage of law journals and

books 1981 to date. Monthly updates. Inquire as to online cost and availability.

Legal Resource Index. Gale Cengage Learning. • Broad coverage of law literature appearing in legal, business, and other periodicals, 1980 to date. Daily updates. Inquire as to online cost and availability.

LEXIS. LEXIS-NEXIS. • The various LEXIS databases provide full text and indexing for a wide variety of legal cases, statutes, orders, and opinions.

Wilson Business Abstracts Online. H. W. Wilson Co. • Indexes and abstracts 600 major business periodicals, plus the *Wall Street Journal* and the business section of the *New York Times.* Indexing is from 1982, abstracting from 1990, with the two newspapers included from 1993. Updated weekly. Inquire as to online cost and availability. (*Business Periodicals Index* without abstracts is also available online.).

PERIODICALS AND NEWSLETTERS

Bottom Line/Personal. Boardroom Inc. • Description: Publishes "expert advice on how to live longer, better, richer, and wiser." Covers topical issues with a personal slant aimed at helping those involved with careers handle their personal lives more successfully. Features articles on tax issues, money information, traveling, family, friends, and general health and happiness. Contains informational items throughout on various aspects of business/personal life.

The Journal of Taxation: A National Journal of Current Developments, Analysis and Commentary for Tax Professionals. RIA. • Monthly. $305.00 per year. Analysis of current tax developments for tax specialists.

Journal of Taxation of Financial Products. CCH, Inc. • Bimonthly. $249.00 per year.

Limited Partnership Investment Review. Limited Partnership Investment Review, Inc. • Monthly. $197.00 per year. Newsletter. Formerly *Tax Shelter Investment Review.*

Money. • 13 times a year. $19.95 per year. Covers all aspects of family finance; investments, careers, shopping, taxes, insurance, consumerism, etc.

Personal Finance. KCI Communications Inc. • Description: Contains articles on subjects of interest to those investigating personal finance strategies. Provides news, information, and suggestions on investment decisions. Covers stock and growth stock activity, individual retirement accounts, market trends and developments, and real estate. Recurring features include columns titled Capsule Advisory and Answers to Your Money Questions.

Real Estate Tax Digest. Matthew Bender & Co. • Description: Features articles on and analyses of legislation, Treasury regulations, federal court and Tax Court decisions, Revenue Rulings, Revenue Procedures, and selected Letter Rulings of the Internal Revenue Service pertaining to federal taxation affecting real estate activities. Includes columns titled Special Topic, New Developments, Practitioner's Corner, and Inside Washington.

Stanger Report: A Guide to Partnership Investing. Robert A. Stanger and Co. • Quarterly. $447.00 per year. Newsletter providing analysis of limited partnership investments.

Tax-Advantaged Securities Law Report. Robert J. Haft. West Group. • Description: Devotes each issue to one or two articles on federal or major state law concerning tax-advantaged securities. Presents explanation and analysis of new decisions, laws, rulings, and regulations. Gives practical advice and cautions for selected tax investments.

RESEARCH CENTERS AND INSTITUTES

Office of Tax Policy Research. University of Michigan, 701 Tappan St., Ann Arbor, MI 48109-1234. Phone: (734)763-3068 Fax: (734)763-4032 E-mail: otpr@umich.edu • URL: http://www.

taxpolicyresearch.umich.edu/.

Tax Foundation. Tax Foundation. 2001 L St. NW, Ste. 1050, Washington, DC 20036. Phone: (202)464-6200 Fax: (202)464-6201 E-mail: hodge@taxfoundation.org • URL: http://www.taxfoundation.org • Fiscal and management aspects of federal, state, and local government, including studies on government expenditures, the federal budget, taxation, and international competitiveness. Serves as a national information agency for individuals and organizations concerned with problems of government expenditures, taxation, and debt.

TRADE/PROFESSIONAL ASSOCIATIONS

Institute of Tax Consultants. 7500 212th St., S.W., No. 205, Edmonds, WA 98026. Phone: (425)774-3521 Fax: (425)672-0461 E-mail: kraemerc@juno.com • URL: http://www.taxprofessionals.homestead.com.

OTHER SOURCES

Federal Taxes Affecting Real Estate. LexisNexis Matthew Bender. • Semiannual. $261.00 per year. Two looseleaf volumes. Explains and illustrates the most important federal tax principles applying to daily real estate transactions.

TAXATION

GENERAL WORKS

The Decline (and Fall?) of the Income Tax: How to Make Sense of the American Tax Mess and the Flat-Tax Cures That Are Supposed to Fix It. Michael J. Graetz. W. W. Norton & Co., Inc. • 1997. $27.50. The author, a former U. S. Treasury official, proposes a value-added tax (VAT) to augment federal income tax. He reviews recent tax history and provides entertaining tax anecdotes.

The Flat Tax. Robert E. Hall and Alvin Rabushka. Hoover Institution Press. • 1995. $14.95. Second edition. A favorable view of a flat tax as a replacement for the graduated federal income tax. (Publication Series: No. 423).

Internet Taxation. Albert Tokin, editor. Nova Science Publishers, Inc. • 2003. $29.50. Several authors discuss the controversial issue of local taxation of e-commerce transactions.

Politics of Taxation: Revenue Without Representation. Susan B. Hansen. Greenwood Publishing Group, Inc. • 1983. $70.00.

Tax Policy and the Economy. MIT Press. • Annual. $58.00. Reviews "issues in the current tax debate." Produced by the National Bureau of Economic Research. (NBER Tax Policy and the Economy Series).

ABSTRACTS AND INDEXES

Accounting and Tax Index. UMI. • Quarterly. Price on application. Annual cumulation. Indexes accounting, auditing, and taxation literature appearing in journals, books, pamphlets, conference proceedings, and newsletters.

Index to Federal Tax Articles. RIA. • $695.00 per year. Looseleaf service. Quarterly supplementation. Bibliographic listing of every significant article on federal income, estate and gift taxation since 1913. Lists over 36,000 articles.

Monthly Digest of Tax Articles. Newkirk Products Inc. • Monthly. $60.00 per year.

ALMANACS AND YEARBOOKS

National Tax Association Proceedings of the Annual Conference on Taxation. National Tax Association-Tax Institute of America. • Annual. Members, $85.00; individuals, $70.00; libraries, $90.00; corporations, $130.00.

New York University Annual Institute on Federal Taxation. Melvin Cornfield. LexisNexis Matthew Bender. • Annual. $366.00. Two looseleaf volumes.

CD-ROM DATABASES

Authority Tax and Estate Planning Library. LexisNexis/Matthew Bender. • Periodic revisions. Price on request. CD-ROM contains updated full text of *Bender's Payroll Tax Guide, Depreciation Handbook, Federal Income Taxation of Corporations, Tax Planning for Corporations, Modern Estate Planning, Planning for Large Estates, Murphy's Will Clauses, Tax & Estate Planning for the Elderly,* and 12 other Matthew Bender publications. The Internal Revenue Code is also included.

EconLit. Available from SilverPlatter Information, Inc. • Monthly. Single-user, $1,600.00 per year. Provides CD-ROM citations, with abstracts, to articles from more than 500 economics journals. Time period is 1969 to date. Produced by the American Economic Association.

Newspaper Abstracts Ondisc. PROQUEST. • Monthly. $2,950.00 per year (covers 1989 to date; archival discs are available for 1985-88). Provides cover-to-cover CD-ROM indexing and abstracting of 19 major newspapers, including the *New York Times, Wall Street Journal, Washington Post, Chicago Tribune,* and *Los Angeles Times.*

OECD Statistical Compendium. Organization for Economic Cooperation and Development. • Semiannual. $1,905.00 per year for 1 to 10 users. CD-ROM contains more than 730,000 monthly, quarterly, and annual time series for OECD countries, 1960 to date. Includes fully searchable data on agriculture, food, economic indicators, national accounts, employment, energy, finance, industry, technology, and foreign trade. Results can be displayed in various forms.

The Tax Directory [CD-ROM]. Tax Analysts. • Quarterly. Provides *The Tax Directory* listings on CD-ROM, covering federal, state, and international tax officials, tax practitioners, and corporate tax executives.

U. S. Master Tax Guide on CD-ROM. CCH, Inc. • Annual. CD-ROM version of the printed *U. S. Master Tax Guide.* Includes search commands, link commands, and on-screen prompts.

WILSONDISC: Wilson Business Abstracts. H. W. Wilson Co. • Monthly. Includes unlimited online access to *Wilson Business Abstracts* through WILSONLINE. Provides CD-ROM "cover-to-cover" abstracting and indexing of over 600 prominent business periodicals. Indexing is from 1982, abstracting from 1990. (*Business Periodicals Index* without abstracts is available on CD-ROM at $1,495 per year.).

DIRECTORIES

Property Tax Manual. Vertex, Inc. • Price on application. Lists tax rates, assessment ratios, assessors, filing requirements, depreciation schedules, etc.

Sales Tax Rate Directory. Vertex, Inc. • Annual. Price on application. U.S. and Canadian sales/use tax rates in standardized format.

The Tax Directory. Tax Analysts. • Covers: Volume One--Approximately 15,000 federal and state government tax legislators, policymakers, administrators, and employees; tax regulation attorneys; over 500 international tax officials with central banks, ministries of finance, foreign embassies and consulate, and chambers of commerce; over 300 tax and business journalists and editors working for magazines, journals, newspapers, television, and radio; tax sections of over 100 trade and professional associations; state CPA, bar, and enrolled agent associations. Volume Two--Over 5,000 corporate tax managers of large U.S. and international firms. Entries include: For government and international officials--Name, title, address, phone, fax, email and website. For corporate tax managers--Name, address, phone, fax, email, web-site, and company name. For journalists--Name, address, phone, fax, email, website, and name of publication/network. For organizations and associations--Name, address, phone, fax, email, website, budget, membership, background information, and description of purpose.

ENCYCLOPEDIAS AND DICTIONARIES

Dictionary of Finance and Investment Terms. John Downes. Barron's Educational Series, Inc. • 2002. $14.95. Sixth edition. Provides clear explanations of more than 5,000 business, banking, financial, investment, and tax terms. Includes a separate list of financial abbreviations and acronyms. (Business Dictionaries Series).

Dictionary of Taxation. Simon James. Edward Elgar Publishing, Inc. • 1998. $65.00. Provides detailed definitions of terms relating to "various aspects of taxes and tax systems throughout the world.".

International Encyclopedia of Public Policy and Administration. Jay M. Shafritz, editor. Westview Press. • 1997. $550.00. Four volumes. Covers 20 major areas, such as public administration, government budgeting, industrial policy, nonprofit management, organizational theory, public finance, labor relations, and taxation. Includes a brief bibliography for each major entry and a comprehensive index.

HANDBOOKS AND MANUALS

Bender's Tax Return Manual. Ernest D. Fiore and others. LexisNexis Matthew Bender. • Annual. $91.00. One looseleaf volume. Periodic supplementation. Includes all major federal tax forms and schedules.

CCH Analysis of Top Tax Issues. CCH, Inc. • Annual. $49.00. Covers yearly tax changes affecting business and personal transactions, planning, and returns.

Corporate, Partnership, Estate, and Gift Taxation 1997. James W. Pratt and William Kulsrud, editors. McGraw-Hill. • 1996. $71.25. 10th edition.

Cybertaxation: The Taxation of E-Commerce. Karl A. Frieden. CCH, Inc. • 2000. $75.00. Includes state sales and use tax issues and corporate income tax rules, as related to doing business over the Internet.

Federal Tax Course. Aspen Publishers, Inc. • Annual. $210.00. Provides basic reference and training for various forms of federal taxation: individual, business, corporate, partnership, estate, gift, etc.

Federal Tax Handbook. RIA. • 2004. $57.00. Revised edition.

Federal Tax Manual. CCH, Inc. • Monthly. $342.00 per year. Looseleaf service. Covers "basic federal tax rules and forms affecting individuals and businesses." Includes a copy of *Annuity, Depreciation, and Withholding Tables.*

Individual Taxation. James W. Pratt and William N. Kulsrud. McGraw-Hill. • 1996. $69.95. Tenth edition. Focuses on the federal income tax.

RIA Federal Tax Handbook. RIA. • Annual. $57.00.

Tax Guide for Small Business. U.S. Department of the Treasury, Internal Revenue Service. Available from U.S. Government Printing Office. • Annual. $8.00.

U. S. Master Estate and Gift Tax Guide. CCH, Inc. • Annual. $55.00. Covers federal estate and gift taxes, including generation-skipping transfer tax plans. Includes tax tables and sample filled-in tax return forms.

U. S. Master Tax Guide. CCH, Inc. • $184.00. Looseleaf service. Periodic supplementation. Provides concise information on personal and business income tax, with cross-references to the Internal Revenue Code and Income Tax Regulations.

INTERNET DATABASES

Business 2.0 Web Guide to the Best Business Links. Business 2.0 Media Inc. Phone: (415)293-4800

E-mail: support@business2.com • URL: http://www.business2.com/webguide • Web site presents an extensive, searchable directory of links to "the best, most informative, and authoritative web pages." Twenty main categories cover business, finance, career, company information, people, and technology topics, with thousands of subtopics, all linking to Web sites recommended by experienced business researchers. Fees: Free.

CCH Essentials: An Internet Tax Research and Primary Source Library. CCH, Inc. Phone: 800-248-3248 or (773)866-6000 Fax: 800-224-8299 or (773)866-3608 E-mail: cust_serv@cch.com • URL: http://tax.cch.com/essentials • Fee-based Web site provides full-text coverage of federal tax law and regulations, including rulings, procedures, tax court decisions, and IRS publications, announcements, notices, and penalties. Includes explanation, analysis, tax planning guides, and a daily tax news service. Searching is offered, including citation search.

Factiva. Dow Jones Reuters Business Interactive, LLC. Phone: 800-369-7466 or (609)452-1511 Fax: (609)520-5770 E-mail: solutions@factiva.com • URL: http://www.factiva.com • Fee-based Web site provides "global news and business information through Web sites and content integration solutions." Includes Dow Jones and Reuters newswires, The Wall Street Journal, and more than 7,000 other sources of current news, historical articles, market research reports, and investment analysis. Content includes 96 major U. S. newspapers, 900 non-English sources, trade publications, media transcripts, country profiles, news photos, etc.

Fedstats. Federal Interagency Council on Statistical Policy. Phone: (202)395-7254 • URL: http://www.fedstats.gov • Web site features an efficient search facility for full-text statistics produced by more than 100 federal agencies, including the Census Bureau, the Bureau of Economic Analysis, and the Bureau of Labor Statistics. Boolean searches can be made within one agency or for all agencies combined. Links are offered to international statistical bureaus, including the UN, IMF, OECD, UNESCO, Eurostat, and 20 individual countries. Fees: Free.

FedWorld: A Program of the United States Department of Commerce. National Technical Information Service. Phone: (703)605-6000 Fax: (703)605-6900 E-mail: webmaster@fedworld.gov • URL: http://www.fedworld.gov • Web site offers "a comprehensive central access point for searching, locating, ordering, and acquiring government and business information." Emphasis is on searching the Web pages, databases, and government reports of a wide variety of federal agencies. Fees: Free.

FirstGov: Your First Click to the U. S. Government. General Services Administration. Phone: 800-333-4636 or (202)501-0705 E-mail: public.affairs@gsa.gov • URL: http://www.firstgov.gov • Free Web site provides extensive links to federal agencies covering a wide variety of topics, such as agriculture, business, consumer safety, education, the environment, government jobs, grants, health, social security, statistics sources, taxes, technology, travel, and world affairs. Also provides links to federal forms, including IRS tax forms. Searching is offered, both keyword and advanced.

FreeLunch.com. Economy.com, Inc. Phone: (610)696-8700 Fax: (610)696-1678 • URL: http://www.freelunch.com • Web site provides free access to more than 1.5 million economic and financial data series, covering industry, demographics, labor markets, prices, retail sales, government spending, trade, interest rates, housing starts, the stock market, and many other topics. Data is available for various time periods in either chart or table form. Searching is offered. Fees: Free, but registration required. Economy.com, Inc. also offers fee-based economic

analysis at *The Dismal Scientist* site (http://www.dismal.com).

Nexis.com. Lexis-Nexis Group. Phone: 800-227-4908 or (937)865-6800 Fax: (937)865-6909 E-mail: webmaster@prod.lexis-nexis.com • URL: http://www.nexis.com • Fee-based Web site offers searching of about 2.8 billion documents in some 30,000 news, business, and legal information sources. Features include a subject directory covering 1,200 topics in 34 categories and a Company Dossier containing information on more than 500,000 public and private companies. Boolean searching is offered.

Tax Analysts [Web site]. Tax Analysts. Phone: 800-955-3444 or (703)533-4400 Fax: (703)533-4444 • URL: http://www.tax.org • The three main sections of Tax Analysts home page are "Tax News" (Today's Tax News, Feature of the Week, Tax Snapshots, Tax Calendar); "Products & Services" (Product Catalog, Press Releases); and "Public Interest" (Discussion Groups, Tax Clinic, Tax History Project). Fees: Free for coverage of current tax events; fee-based for comprehensive information. Daily updating.

TAXNET.PRO. Carswell. Phone: 800-387-5164 or (416)609-3800 Fax: (416)298-5082 E-mail: orders@carswell.com • URL: http://www.carswell.com/taxnetpro.asp • Fee-based Web site provides complete coverage of Canadian tax law and regulation, including income tax, provincial taxes, accounting, and payrolls. Daily updates. Base price varies according to product.

ONLINE DATABASES

Accounting and Tax Database. PROQUEST. • Provides indexing and abstracting of the literature of accounting, taxation, and financial management, 1971 to date. Updating is weekly. Especially covers accounting, auditing, banking, bankruptcy, employee compensation and benefits, cash management, financial planning, and credit. Inquire as to online cost and availability.

EconLit. American Economic Association. • Covers the worldwide literature of economics as contained in selected monographs and about 550 journals. Subjects include microeconomics, macroeconomics, economic history, inflation, money, credit, finance, accounting theory, trade, natural resource economics, and regional economics. Time period is 1969 to present, with monthly updates. Inquire as to online cost and availability.

Information Bank Abstracts. New York Times Index Dept. • Provides indexing and abstracting of current affairs, primarily from the final late edition of *The New York Times* and the Eastern edition of *The Wall Street Journal*. Time period is 1969 to present, with daily updates. Inquire as to online cost and availability.

Wilson Business Abstracts Online. H. W. Wilson Co. • Indexes and abstracts 600 major business periodicals, plus the *Wall Street Journal* and the business section of the *New York Times*. Indexing is from 1982, abstracting from 1990, with the two newspapers included from 1993. Updated weekly. Inquire as to online cost and availability. (*Business Periodicals Index* without abstracts is also available online.).

PERIODICALS AND NEWSLETTERS

The Canadian Taxpayer. Thomson Carswell. • Description: Provides "analyses of Canadian tax trends, political appointments, tax policies and landmark cases.".

Corporate Taxation. RIA. • Bimonthly. $400.00 per year. Analysis and guidance for practitioners. Provides ongoing coverage of currently proposed tax reform bills. Formerly (Journal of Corporate Taxation).

Daily Tax Report: From Today's Daily Report for Executives. BNA, Inc. • Daily. $2,595.00 per year. Looseleaf service. Monitors tax legislation, hearings, rulings, and court decisions.

E-Commerce Tax Alert. CCH Inc. • Description: Print and online newsletter covering e-commerce taxation issues, including compliance and sourcing, e-cash implications, the Internet tax debate, and other topics.

Highlights and Documents. Tax Analysts. • Daily. $2,249.00 per year, including monthly indexes. Newsletter. Provides daily coverage of IRS, congressional, judicial, state, and international tax developments. Includes abstracts and citations for "all tax documents released within the previous 24 to 48 hours." Annual compilation available *Highlights and Documents on Microfiche.*

International Tax Report: Maximizing Tax Opportunities Worldwide. Informa Group PLC. • Monthly. $1,100.00 per year.

The Journal of Taxation: A National Journal of Current Developments, Analysis and Commentary for Tax Professionals. RIA. • Monthly. $305.00 per year. Analysis of current tax developments for tax specialists.

The Kiplinger Tax Letter. Kiplinger Washington Editors Inc. • Description: Reports new tax regulations, changes, decisions, and pending legislation. Includes coverage of the House Ways and Means and Senate Committees, federal monetary and fiscal policy, securities, finance, and social security.

National Tax Journal. National Tax Association - Tax Institute of America. • Quarterly. Membership. Topics of current interest in the field of taxation and public finance in the U.S. and foreign countries.

The Practical Accountant: Providing the Competitive Edge. Thomson Media. • Monthly. $65.00 per year. Covers tax planning, financial planning, practice management, client relationships, and related topics.

Practical Tax Strategies. RIA. • Monthly. $275.00. per year. Emphasis is on current tax developments as they affect accountants and their clients. Includes advice on tax software and computers. Formerly *Taxation for Accountants.*

The Tax Adviser: A Magazine of Tax Planning, Trends and Techniques. American Institute of Certified Public Accountants. • Monthly. Members, $71.00 per year; non-members, $98.00 per year. Newsletter.

Tax Notes: The Weekly Tax Service. Tax Analysts. • Weekly. $1,699.00 per year. Includes an *Annual* and 1985-1996 compliations on CD-ROM. Newsletter. Covers "tax news from all federal sources," including congressional committees, tax courts, and the Internal Revenue Service. Each issue contains "summaries of every document that pertains to federal tax law," with citations. Commentary is provided.

Tax Practice. Tax Analysts. • Weekly. $199.00 per year. Newsletter. Covers news affecting tax practitioners and litigators, with emphasis on federal court decisions, rules and regulations, and tax petitions. Provides a guide to Internal Revenue Service audit issues.

Taxes on Parade. CCH, Inc. • Weekly. $129.00 per year. Newsletter.

Taxes: The Tax Magazine. CCH, Inc. • Monthly. $215.00. per year. Mainly for accountants and lawyers.

RESEARCH CENTERS AND INSTITUTES

International Tax Program. Harvard University, 1563 Massachusetts Ave., Pound Hall, Room 400, Cambridge, MA 02138. Phone: (617)495-4406 Fax: (617)495-0423 E-mail: itp@law.harvard.edu • URL: http://www.law.harvard.edu/programs/itp • Studies the worldwide problems of taxation, including tax law and tax administration.

Office of Tax Policy Research. University of Michigan, 701 Tappan St., Ann Arbor, MI 48109-1234. Phone: (734)763-3068 Fax: (734)763-4032 E-mail: otpr@umich.edu • URL: http://www.

taxpolicyresearch.umich.edu/.

Tax Foundation. Tax Foundation. 2001 L St. NW, Ste. 1050, Washington, DC 20036. Phone: (202)464-6200 Fax: (202)464-6201 E-mail: hodge@taxfoundation.org • URL: http://www. taxfoundation.org • Fiscal and management aspects of federal, state, and local government, including studies on government expenditures, the federal budget, taxation, and international competitiveness. Serves as a national information agency for individuals and organizations concerned with problems of government expenditures, taxation, and debt.

STATISTICS SOURCES

The AIER Chart Book. AIER Research Staff. American Institute for Economic Research. • Annual. $4.00. A compact compilation of long-range charts ("Purchasing Power of the Dollar," for example, goes back to 1780) covering various aspects of the U. S. economy. Includes inflation, interest rates, debt, gold, taxation, stock prices, etc. (Economic Education Bulletin.).

Budget of the United States Government. U.S. Office of Management and Budget. Available from U.S. Government Printing Office. • Annual. $52.00.

Business Statistics of the United States. Linz Audain and Cornelia J. Strawser. Bernan Associates. • Annual. $147.00. Based on *Business Statistics,* formerly issue by the Bureau of Economic Analysis, U. S. Department of Commerce. Provides basic data for a wide variety of U. S. industries, services, and economic indicators. Most statistics are shown annually for 30 years and monthly for the most recent four years.

Revenue Statistics. OECD Publications and Information Center. • Annual. $65.00. Presents data on government revenues in OECD countries, classified by type of tax and level of government. Text in English and French.

Social Statistics of the United States. Mark S. Littman, editor. Bernan Press. • 2000. $65.00. Includes statistical data on population growth, labor force, occupations, environmental trends, leisure time use, income, poverty, taxes, and other economic or demographic topics.

Statistical Handbook on Consumption and Wealth in the United States. Greenwood Publishing Group, Inc. • 1999. $69.95. Provides more than 400 graphs, tables, and charts dealing with basic income levels, income inequalities, spending patterns, taxation, subsidies, etc. (Statistical Handbook Series).

Statistics of Income Bulletin. Available from U.S. Government Printing Office. • Quarterly. $44.00 per year. Current data compiled from tax returns relating to income, assets, and expenses of individuals and businesses. (U. S. Internal Revenue Service.).

Survey of Current Business. Available from U. S. Government Printing Office. • Monthly. $63.00 per year. Issued by Bureau of Economic Analysis, U. S. Department of Commerce. Presents a wide variety of business and economic data.

Taxing Wages. Organization for Economic Cooperation and Development. • Annual. $52.00. Contains data on income tax and social security levies collected from employees and employers in OECD countries. Includes marginal and effective tax burden figures for various family income levels and statistics on cash transfers paid as family benefits.

TRADE/PROFESSIONAL ASSOCIATIONS

Citizens for a Sound Economy. 1250 H St., NW, Ste. 700, Washington, DC 20005-3908. Phone: 888-564-6273 or (202)783-3870 Fax: (202)783-4687 E-mail: cse@cse.org • URL: http://www.cse.org • Absorbed Council for a Competitive Economy and Tax Foundation.

National Tax Association-Tax Institute of America. 725 15th St., N.W., No. 600, Washington, DC 20005-2109. Phone: (202)737-3325 Fax: (202)737-7308 E-mail: natltax@aol.com • URL: http://www. ntanet.org.

National Taxpayers Union. 108 N Alfred St., Alexandria, VA 22314. Phone: 800-829-4258 or (703)683-5700 Fax: (703)683-5722 E-mail: ntu@ ntu.org • URL: http://www.ntu.org • Seeks to: reduce government spending; cut taxes; protect the rights of taxpayers. Claims to have helped generate federal budget cuts of over 120 billion dollars. Activities include research programs and an intense lobbying campaign in Washington, DC; has been a leader in the fights against government ventures such as: social security tax; guaranteed income; congressional and bureaucratic pay raises; federal subsidies; foreign aid; national health insurance. Works for a balanced federal budget/tax limitation constitutional amendment; federal pension reform; reduction of capital gains and personal income tax; social security reform. Has worked for airline deregulation; indexing of federal income tax, California's Proposition 13, Massachusetts Proposition 2 1/2, and other state tax cutting initiatives. Conducts annual voting study of congressmen and senators, rating their votes on spending and tax issues and presenting awards for best and worst records.

OTHER SOURCES

All States Tax Guide. Prentice Hall PTR. • Looseleaf. Periodic supplementation. Price on application. One volume summary of taxes for all states.

Federal Income, Gift and Estate Taxation. LexisNexis Matthew Bender. • $1,220.00. Seven looseleaf volumes. Periodic supplementation.

Federal Tax Coordinator Library. RIA. • $2,125.00 per year. Available only online.

Federal Taxation of Income, Estates and Gifts. Warren, Gorham and Lamont/RIA. • $1,165.00. Five looseleaf volumes. Updates three times a year. Covers aspects of income taxation of individuals, corporations, partnerships, estates, and gifts. Clear analysis to exact answers to tax questions.

Federal Taxes Citator. MacMillan Publishing Co. • $550.00 per year. Two looseleaf volumes. Monthly supplements.

Taxation of Securities Transactions. LexisNexis Matthew Bender. • Semiannual. $307.00. Looseleaf service. Covers taxation of a wide variety of securities transactions, including those involving stocks, bonds, options, short sales, new issues, mutual funds, dividend distributions, foreign securities, and annuities.

TAXATION, INTERNATIONAL

See: INTERNATIONAL TAXATION

TAXES, STATE

See: STATE TAXES

TAXICABS

GENERAL WORKS

Economic Aspects of Taxi Accessibility. Organization for Economic Cooperation and Development. • 2001. $19.00. Contains information on taxi use in 14 countries, including use by disabled and older people. Emphasis is on affordability.

DIRECTORIES

Taxicab and Transportation Service Directory. infoUSA. • Annual. Price on application. Provides a geographical list for over 9,065 taxicab companies.

Compiled from telephone company yellow pages. Formerly *Taxicab Directory.*

HANDBOOKS AND MANUALS

Limousine Service. Entrepreneur Media, Inc. • Looseleaf. $59.50. A practical guide to starting a limousine service. Covers profit potential, start-up costs, market size evaluation, owner's time required, site selection, lease negotiation, pricing, accounting, advertising, promotion, etc. (Start-Up Business Guide No. E1224.).

PERIODICALS AND NEWSLETTERS

Taxi and Livery Management. International Taxicab and Livery Association. • Quarterly. $16.00 per year.

TRADE/PROFESSIONAL ASSOCIATIONS

Taxicab, Limousine and Paratransit Association. 3849 Farragut Ave., Kensington, MD 20895. Phone: (301)946-5701 Fax: (301)946-4641 E-mail: info@ tlpa.org • URL: http://www.tlpa.org • Formerly International Taxicab and Livery Association.

TAYLOR SYSTEM OF SHOP MANAGEMENT

See: TIME AND MOTION STUDY

TEA INDUSTRY

See also: COFFEE INDUSTRY

ALMANACS AND YEARBOOKS

Agricultural and Mineral Commodities Year Book. Available from Taylor & Francis Group. • Annual. $225.00. Published by Europa Publications. Contains descriptive product profiles, price data, export-import data, and production statistics for major commodities of the world. Includes commodity histories, uses, markets, demand trends, and information about trade agreements and key commodity organizations.

CRB Commodity Yearbook. Commodity Research Bureau. CRB. • Annual. $99.95.

DIRECTORIES

Uker's International Tea and Coffee Directory and Buyers' Guide. Lockwood Trade Publications, Inc. • Annual. $40.00. Lists firms which export and import tea and coffee.

HANDBOOKS AND MANUALS

Coffee and Tea Store. Entrepreneur Media, Inc. • Looseleaf. $59.50. A practical guide to starting a coffee and tea store. Covers profit potential, start-up costs, market size evaluation, owner's time required, site selection, lease negotiation, pricing, accounting, advertising, promotion, etc. (Start-Up Business Guide No. E1202.).

INTERNET DATABASES

USDA. United States Department of Agriculture. Phone: (202)720-2791 E-mail: agsec@usda.gov • URL: http://www.usda.gov • The USDA home page has six sections: News and Information; What's New; About USDA; Agencies; Opportunities; Search and Help. Keyword searching is offered from the USDA home page and from various individual agency home pages. Agencies are the Economic Research Service, Agricultural Marketing Service, National Agricultural Statistics Service, National Agricultural Library, and about 12 others. Updating varies. Fees: Free.

ONLINE DATABASES

Globalbase. Gale Cengage Learning. • Provides more than one million online summaries of business, industrial, and economic news reports from more than 1,000 publications worldwide. Covers a wide range of material appearing in international trade journals, professional magazines, and newspapers. Time period is 1984 to date, with weekly updates. Inquire as to online cost and availability.

PERIODICALS AND NEWSLETTERS

Fancy Food and Culinary Products. Talcott Communications Corp. • Monthly. $34.00 per year. Emphasizes new specialty food products and the business management aspects of the specialty food and confection industries. Includes special issues on wine, cheese, candy, "upscale" cookware, and gifts. Formerly (Fancy Foods).

Sri Lanka Journal of Tea Science. Tea Research Institute of Sri Lanka. • Semiannual. $20.00 per year. Text in English. Formerly *Tea Quarterly.*

Tea and Coffee Trade Journal. Lockwood Publications. • Monthly. $30.00 per year. Current trends in coffee roasting and tea packing industry.

STATISTICS SOURCES

Agricultural Statistics. Available from U. S. Government Printing Office. • Annual. $38.00. Produced by the National Agricultural Statistics Service, U. S. Department of Agriculture. Provides a wide variety of statistical data relating to agricultural production, supplies, consumption, prices/price-supports, foreign trade, costs, and returns, as well as farm labor, loans, income, and population. In many cases, historical data is shown annually for 10 years. In addition to farm data, includes detailed fishery statistics.

FAO Production Yearbook. Available from Bernan Associates. • Annual. $45.00. Published by the Food and Agriculture Organization (http://www.fao.org). Contains worldwide data on agriculture, land use, farm crops, livestock, and agricultural prices.

FAO Trade Yearbook. Available from Bernan Associates. • Annual. $45.00. Published by the Food and Agriculture Organization (http://www.fao.org). Provides extensive worldwide data on exports and imports of agricultural commodities, fertilizers, tractors, and pesticides. Includes more than 130 tables of detailed statistics.

World Drinks Data and Statistics. Euromonitor International. • 2004. $650.00. Provides five-year data for both alcoholic and non-alcoholic beverages in 52 countries. Includes market size, consumer expenditures, price indicators, and retail distribution data for beer, wine, spirits, tea, coffee, soft drinks, fruit juices, bottled water, and other drinks.

TRADE/PROFESSIONAL ASSOCIATIONS

Tea Council of the United States of America. 420 Lexington Ave., Suite 825, New York, NY 10170. Phone: (212)986-6998 Fax: (212)697-8658 E-mail: simrany@teausa.com • URL: http://www.teausa.com • Affiliated with Tea Association of the U.S.A. Companies and countries trading tea in the United States.

OTHER SOURCES

Coffee and Tea Market. MarketResearch.com. • 1999. $2,750.00. Market data with forecasts to 2004. Covers many types of coffee and tea.

TEA ROOMS

See: RESTAURANTS, LUNCHROOMS, ETC.

TECHNICAL ANALYSIS (FINANCE)

See also: COMPUTERS IN FINANCE; DOW THEORY; FINANCIAL ANALYSIS

GENERAL WORKS

All About Technical Analysis. Constance Brown. McGraw-Hill. • 2002. $16.95. Provides basic

information on the use of stock price charts for trend analysis and market forecasts.

Forecasting Financial Markets: Exchange Rates Interest Rates and Asset Management. Christian Dunis, editor. John Wiley and Sons, Inc. • 1996. $150.00. Examines what are said to be the more reliable or "classic" theories of continuously recurring price patterns. Practical investment applications are discussed. (Financial Economics and Quantitative Analysis Series).

Introduction to the Magee System of Technical Analysis. W.H.C. Bassetti. CRC Press. • 2002. $59.95. Serves as a basic guide to the technical analysis of stock trends promulgated by John Magee.

The New Science of Technical Analysis. Thomas R. DeMark. John Wiley and Sons, Inc. • 1994. $65.00. (Finance Series).

ALMANACS AND YEARBOOKS

Supertrader's Almanac-Reference Manual: Reference Guide and Analytical Techniques for Investors. Frank A. Taucher. • 1991. $55.00. Explains technical methods for the trading of commodity futures, and includes data on seasonality, cycles, trends, contract characteristics, highs and lows, etc.

DIRECTORIES

Association for Investment Management and Research-Membership Directory. Association for Investment Management and Research. • Annual. $150.00. Lists 38,000 professional investment managers and securities analysts.

Futures Magazine SourceBook: The Most Complete List of Exchanges, Companies, Regulators, Organizations, etc., Offering Products and Services to the Futures and Options Industry. Futures Magazine, Inc. • Annual. $19.50. Provides information on commodity futures brokers, trading method services, publications, and other items of interest to futures traders and money managers.

ENCYCLOPEDIAS AND DICTIONARIES

Encyclopedia of Chart Patterns. Thomas N. Bulkowski. John Wiley and Sons, Inc. • 2000. $79.95. Provides explanations of the predictive value of various chart patterns formed by stock and commodity price movements. (Trading Series).

Encyclopedia of Technical Market Indicators. Robert W. Colby. McGraw-Hill. • 2002. $70.00. Second edition.

Technical Analysis from A to Z: Covers Every Trading Tool from the Absolute Breadth Index to Zig Zag. Steven B. Achelis. McGraw-Hill. • 2000. $39.95. Second edition. Provides definitions and explanations of more than 100 technical indicators used in attempts to predict stock and commodity price trends. Includes a general introduction to technical analysis.

HANDBOOKS AND MANUALS

Day-Trader's Manual: Theory, Art, and Science of Profitable Short-Term Investing. William F. Eng. John Wiley and Sons, Inc. • 1992. $79.95. Covers short-term trading in stocks, futures, and options. Various technical trading systems are considered. (Finance Series, vol. 5).

Derivatives: A Comprehensive Resource for Options, Futures, Interest Rate Swaps, and Mortgage Securities. Fred D. Arditti. Harvard Business School Publishing. • 1996. $60.00. Published by Harvard Business School Press. Provides detailed explanations of various kinds of financial derivatives (options, futures, swaps, etc.) and their trading tactics, uses, and risks. (Financial Management Association Survey and Synthesis Series).

Fibonacci Applications and Strategies for Traders. Robert Fischer. John Wiley and Sons, Inc. • 1993. $60.00. Provides a new look at the Elliott Wave Theory and Fibonacci numbers as applied to commodity prices, business cycles, and interest rate

movements. (Traders Advantage Series).

Portfolio Management Formulas: Mathematical Trading Methods for the Futures, Options, and Stock Markets. Ralph Vince. John Wiley and Sons, Inc. • 1990. $90.00. Discusses optimization of trading systems by exploiting the rules of probability and making use of the principles of modern portfolio management theory. Computer programs are included. (Finance Series).

Technical Analysis Explained: The Successful Investor's Guide to Spotting Investment Trends and Turning Points. Martin J. Pring. McGraw-Hill. • 2002. $55.00. Fourth edition.

Technical Analysis of Stock Trends. John Magee and others. Saint Lucie Press. • 2001. $99.95. Eighth edition. Standard manual of technical analysis.

Trading for a Living: Psychology, Trading Tactics, Money Management. Alexander Elder. John Wiley and Sons, Inc. • 1993. $70.00. Covers technical and chart methods of trading in commodity and financial futures, options, and stocks. Includes Elliott Wave Theory, oscillators, moving averages, point-and-figure, and other technical approaches. (Finance Series).

Using Technical Analysis: A Step-by-Step Guide to Understanding and Applying Stock Market. Clifford Pistolese. McGraw-Hill. • 1994. $32.95. Revised edition.

INTERNET DATABASES

Futures Online. Futures Magazine Inc. Phone: (312)846-4600 Fax: (312)846-4638 • URL: http://www.futuresmag.com • Web site presents updates of *Futures* magazine and links to other futures-related sites.

PERIODICALS AND NEWSLETTERS

Computerized Investing. American Association of Individual Investors. • Description: Furnishes articles on computer-aided investment analysis and investment-related software programs and database. Contains information on hardware and software, new product announcements, and editorial commentary. Recurring features include columns titled Product Reviews, New Products, Product Comparisons, BBS Update, Bookshelf, and Member Software Services.

Dow Theory Letters. Dow Theory Letters, Inc. • 17 times a year. $250.00 per year. Newsletter on stock market trends, investing, and economic conditions.

Futures: News, Analysis, and Strategies for Futures, Options, and Derivatives Traders. Futures Magazine. • Monthly. $39.00 per year. Edited for institutional money managers and traders, brokers, risk managers, and individual investors or speculators. Includes special feature issues on interest rates, technical indicators, currencies, charts, precious metals, hedge funds, and derivatives. Supplements available.

InvesTech Market Analyst: Technical and Monetary Investment Analysis. InvesTech Research. • Every three weeks. $190.00 per year. Newsletter. Provides interpretation of monetary statistics and Federal Reserve actions, especially as related to technical analysis of stock market price trends.

SFO: Stocks, Futures & Options. Wasendorf & Associates, Inc. • Monthly. $49.95 per year. Subtitle: *Official Journal for Personal Investing in Stocks, Futures, and Options.* Covers mainly speculative techniques for stocks, commodity futures, financial futures, stock index futures, foreign exchange, short selling, and various kinds of options.

Technical Analysis of Stocks & Commodities: The Traders Magazine. Technical Analysis, Inc. • 13 times a year. $64.95 per year. Covers use of personal computers for stock trading, price movement analysis by means of charts, and other technical trading methods.

Technical Trends: The Indicator Accuracy Service.

Technical Trends Inc. • 40 times a year. $147.00 per year. Technical investment newsletter.

Wall Street and Technology: For Senior-Level Executives in Technology and Information Management in Securities and Invesment Firms. CMP Media LLC. • Monthly. $85.00 per year. Includes material on the use of computers in technical investment strategies. Formerly *Wall Computer Review.*

PRICE SOURCES

CRB Futures Perspective: Agricultural Edition. Commodity Research Bureau. • Weekly. $230.00 per year. Service provides comprehensive price charts for more than 20 agricultural commodity futures, from cocoa to wheat (includes lumber). Also provides technical analysis of price movements and market commentary. Formerly part of *CRB Futures Chart Service.*

CRB Futures Perspective: Financial Edition. Commodity Research Bureau. • Weekly. $275.00 per year. Service provides comprehensive price charts for more than 50 financial futures, from Australian Bills to Swiss Francs (includes precious metals and oil). Also provides technical analysis of price movements and market commentary. Formerly part of *CRB Futures Chart Service.*

RESEARCH CENTERS AND INSTITUTES

Center for Research in Security Prices. University of Chicago, 725 S. Wells St., Suite 800, Chicago, IL 60607. Phone: (773)834-4610 Fax: (773)702-3036 E-mail: custom@crsp.uchicago.edu • URL: http://gsbwww.uchicago.edu/research/crsp.

Glucksman Institute. New York University. Salomon Center, Stern School of Business, 44 W. Fourth St., Room 9-65, New York, NY 10012-0267. Phone: (212)998-0714 Fax: (212)995-4220 E-mail: wsilber@stern.nyu.edu.

Institute for Quantitative Research in Finance. Church Street Station, P.O. Box 6194, New York, NY 10249-6194. Phone: (212)744-6825 Fax: (212)517-2259 E-mail: daleberman@compuserve • Financial research areas include quantitative methods, securities analysis, and the financial structure of industries. Also known as the "Q Group.".

Research Foundation of Association for Investment Management and Research. 560 Ray C. Hunt Dr., Charlottesville, VA 22903-0668. Phone: 800-247-8132 or (434)951-5499 Fax: (434)951-5262 E-mail: info@aimr.com • URL: http://www.aimr.org • Affiliated with Financial Analysts Federation.

Rodney L. White Center for Financial Research. University of Pennsylvania, 3254 Steinberg Hall-Dietrich Hall, Philadelphia, PA 19104. Phone: (215)898-7616 Fax: (215)573-8084 E-mail: rlwtcr@finance.wharton.upenn.edu • URL: http://www.finance.wharton.upenn.edu • Research areas include financial management, money markets, real estate finance, and international finance.

STATISTICS SOURCES

Advance-Decline Album. Dow Theory Letters, Inc. • Annual. Contains one page for each year since 1931. Includes charts of the New York Stock Exchange advance-decline ratio and the Dow Jones industrial average.

Dow Jones Averages Chart Album. Dow Theory Letters, Inc. • Annual. $140.00. Contains one page for each year since 1885. Includes line charts of the Dow Jones industrial, transportation, utilities, and bond averages. Important historical and economic dates are shown.

SRC Green Book of 5 Trend 35-Year Charts. Securities Research Co. • Annual. $150.00. Chart book presents statistical information on the stocks of 400 leading companies over a 35-year period. Each full page chart is in semi-log format to avoid visual distortion. Also includes charts of 12 leading market averages or indexes and 39 major industry groups.

TRADE/PROFESSIONAL ASSOCIATIONS

Association for Investment Management and Research. 560 Ray C. Hunt Dr., Charlottesville, VA 22903. Phone: 800-247-8132 or (434)951-5499 Fax: (434)951-5262 E-mail: info@aimr.org • URL: http://www.aimr.org • Members are practicing investment analysts.

OTHER SOURCES

Daily Graphs. Daily Graphs, Inc. • New York Stock Exchange edition, $363.00 per year. NASDAQ O.T.C.-American Stock Exchange edition, $363.00 per year. Both editions include the 200 leading over-the-counter stocks.

Mansfield Stock Chart Service. R.W. Mansfield Co., Inc. • Weekly. Price varies. Newsletter. Covers New York Stock Exchange, American Stock Exchange, OTC exchange, international stocks and industry groups. Partial subscriptions available.

The Options Workbook: Proven Strategies from a Market Wizard. Anthony J. Saliba. Dearborn Trade Publishing, A Kaplan Professional Co. • 2001. $40.00. Emphasis is on computerized trading on the Chicago Board Options Exchange. Includes information on specific trading strategies.

TECHNICAL ASSISTANCE

See also: DEVELOPING AREAS

PERIODICALS AND NEWSLETTERS

Peace Corps Times. U. S. Peace Corps. • Quarterly. Free to qualified personnel. Presents news of the programs and activities of the Peace Corps.

TRADE/PROFESSIONAL ASSOCIATIONS

Volunteers in Technical Assistance. 1600 Wilson Blvd., Suite 710, Arlington, VA 22209. Phone: (703)276-1800 Fax: (703)243-1865 E-mail: vita@vita.org • URL: http://www.vita.org • Formerly Volunteers for International Technical Assistance.

TECHNICAL BOOKS

See: TECHNOLOGY

TECHNICAL EDUCATION

See also: VOCATIONAL EDUCATION

ABSTRACTS AND INDEXES

Education Index. H. W. Wilson Co. • 10 times a year. Quarterly and annual cumulations. Price varies.

Technical Education and Training Abstracts. Taylor and Francis Group. • Quarterly. Individuals, $283.00 per year; institutions, $920.00 per year. Published in England. Formerly *Technical Education Abstracts.*

CD-ROM DATABASES

ERIC on SilverPlatter. Available from SilverPlatter Information, Inc. • Quarterly. $700.00 per year. Produced by the Office of Educational Research and Improvement, U. S. Dept. of Education. Provides CD-ROM indexing and abstracting of a wide variety of literature relating to education. Archival discs are available from 1966.

DIRECTORIES

American Association of Community Colleges Directory. American Association of Community Colleges. • Annual. $35.00. Formerly *Community, Junior and Technical College Directory.*

American Trade Schools Directory. Croner Publications Inc. • Covers: over 12,000 private and public trade, technical, and vocational schools. Entries include: School name, address, phone, contact person, year school founded, private or public, accrediting agencies, whether approved by state or Veterans Administration, home study courses offered.

Peterson's Vocational and Technical Schools and Programs: East and West. Peterson's. • Annual. $69.90. Two volumes. $34.95 per volume. Provides information on vocational schools in the eastern part of the U. S. Covers more than 370 career fields.

HANDBOOKS AND MANUALS

Specialty Occupational Outlook: Trade and Technical. Gale Cengage Learning. • 1995. $75.00. Provides information on 150 "high-interest" careers that do not require a bachelor's degree.

ONLINE DATABASES

Education Index Online. H. W. Wilson Co. • Indexes a wide variety of periodicals related to schools, colleges, and education, 1984 to date. Monthly updates. Inquire as to online cost and availability.

ERIC. Educational Resources Information Center. • Funded by the U. S. Department of Education, Institute of Education Sciences (formerly Office of Educational Research and Improvement). Provides access to more than one million online records covering education-related journal and report literature, 1966 to date. Updating is monthly. Inquire as to online cost and availability.

PERIODICALS AND NEWSLETTERS

ATEA Journal. American Technical Education Association. • Description: Reports on meetings, conferences, and conventions; equipment and teaching aids; news of members in the field of technical education; and reviews of books, pamphlets, and magazine articles. Recurring features include news from industry, and book reviews.

Technical Education News. Glencoe-McGraw Hill. • Semiannual. Free to qualified personnel.

TRADE/PROFESSIONAL ASSOCIATIONS

American Technical Education Association. c/o North Dakota State College of Science. 800 N 6th St., Wahpeton, ND 58076-0002. Phone: (701)671-2240 or (701)671-2240 Fax: (701)671-2260 E-mail: betty.krump@ndscs.edu • URL: http://www.ateaonline.org • Dedicated to excellence in the quality of post-secondary technical education with emphasis on professional development.

Career College Association. 1101 Connecticut Ave. NW, Ste. 900, Washington, DC 20036. Phone: (202)336-6700 Fax: (202)336-6828 E-mail: cca@career.org • URL: http://www.career.org • Represents private post-secondary schools, institutes, colleges and universities that provide career-specific educational programs.

Special Interest Group for Computer Science Education. c/o Association for Computing Machinery, 1515 Broadway, New York, NY 10036-5701. Phone: 800-342-6626 or (212)626-0500 E-mail: acmhelp@acm.org • URL: http://www.acm.org • Concerned with education relating to computer science and technology on various levels, ranging from secondary school to graduate degree programs.

TECHNICAL LITERATURE

See: TECHNOLOGY

TECHNICAL SOCIETIES

See: ASSOCIATIONS

TECHNICAL WRITING

See also: PROCEDURE MANUALS

HANDBOOKS AND MANUALS

ACS Style Guide: A Manual for Authors and Editors. Janet S. Dodd, editor. American Chemical

Society. • 1997. $35.00. Second edition. A style manual for scientific and technical writers. Includes the use of illustrations, tables, lists, numbers, and units of measure.

Effective Writing for Engineers, Managers, Scientists. H. J. Tichy and Sylvia Fourdrinier. John Wiley and Sons, Inc. • 1988. $125.00. Second edition.

Freelance Writing. Entrepreneur Media, Inc. • Looseleaf. $59.50. A practical guide to starting a freelance writing service. Covers profit potential, start-up costs, market size evaluation, pricing, accounting, advertising, promotion, etc. (Start-Up Business Guide No. E1258.).

How to Write and Present Technical Information. Charles H. Sides. Greenwood Publishing Group, Inc. • 1998. $29.95. Third edition.

Technical Report Writing Today. Steven E. Pauley and Daniel Riordan. Houghton Mifflin Co. • 1999. Seventh edition. Price on application.

Writing and Designing Manuals: Operator Manuals, Service Manuals, Manuals for International Markets. Patricia A. Robinson and Ryn Etter. Lewis Publishers. • 2000. $69.95. Third edition. Includes planning, organization, format, visuals, writing strategies, and other topics.

PERIODICALS AND NEWSLETTERS

ACM Journal of Computer Documentation. Special Interest Group for Docuemntation. Association for Computing Machinery. • Quarterly. Members, $36.00 per year; $99.00 per year; Students, $42.00 per year. Formerly *Journal of Computer Documentation.*

Journal of Business and Technical Communication. Sage Publications, Inc. • Institutions, $445.00 per year; includes print and online editions.

Journal of Technical Writing and Communication. Baywood Publishing Co., Inc. • Quarterly. Individuals, $60.00 per year; institutions, $237.00 per year.

Technical Communication. Society for Technical Communication. • Quarterly. $60.00 per year. Production of technical literature.

TRADE/PROFESSIONAL ASSOCIATIONS

Society for Technical Communication. 901 N. Stuart St., Suite 904, Arlington, VA 22203-1822. Phone: (703)522-4114 Fax: (703)522-2075 E-mail: stc@stc.org • URL: http://www.stc.org • Formerly Society of Technical Writers and Publishers.

TECHNOLOGICAL UNEMPLOYMENT

See: UNEMPLOYMENT

TECHNOLOGY

See also: RESEARCH AND DEVELOPMENT

GENERAL WORKS

Forecasting and Management of Technology. Alan L. Porter and others. John Wiley and Sons, Inc. • 1991. $190.00. Includes business aspects of technology. (Engineering and Management Technology Series).

How Products Are Made. Gale Cengage Learning. • 2002. Three volumes. $115.00. Previous volumes available. Provides easy-to-read, step-by-step descriptions of how approximately 100 different products are manufactured. Items are of all kinds, both mechanical and non-mechanical.

The Innovator's Dilemma: When New Technologies Cause Great Firms to Fail. Clayton M. Christensen. Harvard Business School Publishing. • 1997. $27.50. Discusses management myths relating to innovation, change, and research and development.

(Mangement of Innovation and Change Series).

The Intentional Entrepreneur: Bringing Technology and Engineering to the Real New Economy. David L. Bodde. M. E. Sharpe, Inc. • 2004. $69.95. Covers the "art of entrepreneurship" for engineering and technology professionals. Includes material on marketing, business models, venture capital, and intellectual property.

Interface Culture: How New Technology Transforms the Way We Create and Communicate. Steven Johnson. HarperSanFrancisco. • 1997. $24.00. A discussion of how computer interfaces and online technology ("cyberspace") affect society in general.

Probable Tomorrows: How Science and Technology Will Transform Our Lives in the Next Twenty Years. Marvin J. Cetron and Owen L. Davies. Saint Martin's Press. • 1997. $24.95. Predicts the developments in technological products, services, and "everyday conveniences" by the year 2017. Covers such items as personal computers, artificial intelligence, telecommunications, highspeed railroads, and healthcare.

Science and Technology Desk Reference: Answers to Frequently Asked and Difficult to Answer Reference Questions in Science and Technology. Carnegie Library of Pittsburgh, Science and Technology Department Staff, editors. Gale Cengage Learning. • 1997. $90.00. Second edition. *The Handy Science Answer Book.* Covers a wide variety of subject areas, including biology, astronomy, chemistry, geology, the environment, and health.

When Technology Fails. Gale Cengage Learning. • 1994. $85.00. The stories of about 100 important technological disasters, accidents, and failures in the 20th century, caused by faults in design, construction, planning, and testing. Arranged in broad subject categories, with a keyword index.

ABSTRACTS AND INDEXES

Applied Science and Technology Index. H. W. Wilson Co. • 11 times a year. Quarterly and annual cumulations. Price varies. Indexes a wide variety of English language technical, industrial, and engineering periodicals.

Current Contents: Engineering, Computing and Technology. Thomson/ISI. • Weekly. $730.00 per year. Reproductions of contents pages of technical journals. Includes *Author Index*, *Address Directory*, *Current Book Contents* and *Title Word Index*. Formerly *Current Contents: Engineering, Technology and Applied Sciences.*

Engineering Index Monthly: Abstracting and Indexing Services Covering Sources of the World's Engineering Literature. Engineering Information Inc. • Monthly. Institutions, $5,279.00 per year. Provides indexing and abstracting of the world's engineering and technical literature.

NTIS Alerts: Manufacturing Technology. National Technical Information Service. • Semimonthly. $265.00 per year. Provides descriptions of government-sponsored research reports and software, with ordering information. Covers computer-aided design and manufacturing (CAD/CAM), engineering materials, quality control, machine tools, robots, lasers, productivity, and related subjects. Formerly *Abstract Newsletter.*

ALMANACS AND YEARBOOKS

McGraw-Hill Yearbook of Science and Technology. McGraw-Hill. • Annual. $145.00.

Research in Philosophy and Technology. Elsevier. • Dates vary. Price varies. 21 volumes.

Research on Technological Innovation, Management and Policy. Richard S. Rosenbloom and Robert A. Burgelman, editors. Elsevier. • Dates vary. Prices vary. Seven volumes.

Science and Technology Almanac. Greenwood Publishing Group, Inc. • Annual. $79.95. Covers

technological news, research, and statistics.

BIBLIOGRAPHIES

Bibliographic Guide to Technology. Available from Gale Cengage Learning. • Annual. $575.00. Two volumes. Published by G. K. Hall & Co. Lists technology publications cataloged by the New York Public Library and the Library of Congress.

Encyclopedia of Physical Science and Engineering Information. Gale Cengage Learning. • 1996. $160.00. Second edition. Includes print, electronic, and other information sources for a wide range of scientific, technical, and engineering topics.

New Technical Books: A Selective List With Descriptive Annotations. New York Public Library, Science and Technology Research Center. • Bimonthly. $30.00 per year.

Reference Reviews. Available from Information Today, Inc. • Eight times a year. Price on application. Published in London by Aslib: The Association for Information Management. Incorporates *Aslib Book Guide.*

BIOGRAPHICAL SOURCES

American Men and Women of Science A Biographical Directory of Today's Leaders in Physical, Biological and Related Sciences. Gale. • 2002. $950.00. 21st edition. Eight volumes. Over 119,600 United States and Canadian scientists active in the physical, biological, mathematical, computer science and engineering fields.

Who's Who in Science and Engineering. Marquis Who's Who. • Biennial. $269.00. Provides concise biographical information on 35,000 prominent engineers and scientists. International coverage, with geographical and professional indexes.

CD-ROM DATABASES

NTIS on SilverPlatter. Available from SilverPlatter Information, Inc. • Quarterly. $2,850.00 per year. Produced by the National Technical Information Service. Provides a CD-ROM guide to over 500,000 government reports on a wide variety of technical, industrial, and business topics.

OECD Statistical Compendium. Organization for Economic Cooperation and Development. • Semiannual. $1,905.00 per year for 1 to 10 users. CD-ROM contains more than 730,000 monthly, quarterly, and annual time series for OECD countries, 1960 to date. Includes fully searchable data on agriculture, food, economic indicators, national accounts, employment, energy, finance, industry, technology, and foreign trade. Results can be displayed in various forms.

WILSONDISC: Applied Science and Technology Abstracts. H. W. Wilson Co. • Monthly. Includes unlimited access to the online version of *Applied Science and Technology Abstracts* through WILSONLINE. Provides CD-ROM indexing and abstracting of 500 prominent scientific, technical, engineering, and industrial periodicals. Indexing coverage is provided from 1983 to date and abstracting from 1993 to date.

DIRECTORIES

Emerson's Directory of Leading U.S. Technology Consulting Firms. Emerson Co. • 2000. $195.00. Provides information on major consulting firms specializing in technology.

Peterson's Graduate and Professional Programs in Engineering and Applied Sciences. Peterson's. • Annual. $49.95. Provides details of more than 3,400 graduate and professional programs in engineering and related fields at colleges and universities. (Peterson's Graduate in Professional Programs Series). Formerly *Peterson's Guide to Graduate Programs in Engineering and Professional Sciences.*

Plunkett's Engineering and Research Industry Almanac. Plunkett Research, Ltd. • Annual. $179.99. Contains detailed profiles of major engineering and technology corporations. Includes CD-ROM.

SRDS Technology Media Source. SRDS. • Annual. $312.00. Contains detailed information on business publications, consumer magazines, and direct mail lists that may be of interest to "technology marketers." Emphasis is on aviation and telecommunications. Formerly*Technology Media Source.*

ENCYCLOPEDIAS AND DICTIONARIES

Concise Chemical and Technical Dictionary. Harry Bennett. Chemical Publishing Co., Inc. • 1986. $170.00. Fourth edition.

Encyclopedia of Emerging Industries. Gale Cengage Learning. • 2001. $320.00. Fourth edition. Provides detailed information on 115 "newly flourishing" industries. Includes historical background, organizational structure, significant individuals, current conditions, major companies, work force, technology trends, research developments, and other industry facts.

Every Manager's Guide to Information Technology: A Glossary of Key Terms and Concepts for Today's Business Leader. Peter G. W. Keen. Harvard Business School Publishing. • 1994. $18.95. Second edition. Provides definitions of terms related to computers, data communications, and information network systems. (Harvard Business Reference Series).

Gale Five Language Dictionary of Technology: Simultaneous Translations of English, French, Spanish, German, and Italian. Gale Cengage Learning. • 1993. $75.00. Contains translations of frequently-used technological words and phrases.

Kirk-Othmer Concise Encyclopedia of Chemical Technology. John Wiley and Sons, Inc. • 2001. $295.00. Fourth edition. Contains abstracts of articles from the multivolume *Kirk-Othmer Encyclopedia of Chemical Technology*.

McGraw-Hill Encyclopedia of Science & Technology. McGraw-Hill. • 2002. $2,495.00. Ninth edition. 20 volumes.

Scientific and Technical Acronyms, Symbols, and Abbreviations. Uwe Erb and Harald Keller. John Wiley and Sons, Inc. • 2001. $250.00. Contains more than 200,000 entries covering a wide variety of scientific and technical fields.

World of Computer Science. Gale Cengage Learning. • 2002. $160.00. Alphabetical arrangement. Contains 650 entries covering discoveries, theories, concepts, issues, ethics, and people in the broad area of computer science and technology.

FINANCIAL RATIOS

IRS Corporate Financial Ratios. Available from MarketResearch.com. • 2002. $225.00. Published by Schonfeld & Associates, Inc. Presents 70 key financial ratios for 260 industries. Ratios are calculated from income statement and balance sheet data available from the Internal Revenue Service. Includes four asset size classes.

HANDBOOKS AND MANUALS

Dun & Bradstreet/Gale Group Industry Handbooks. Gale Cengage Learning. • 2000. $650.00. Five volumes. $130.00 per volume. Each volume covers two or more major industries: 1. *Entertainment and Hospitality*; 2. *Construction and Agriculture*; 3. *Chemicals and Pharmaceuticals*; 4. *Computers & Software and Broadcasting & Telecommunications*; 5. *Insurance and Health & Medical Services.* The following are included for each industry: overview, statistics, financial ratios, rankings, merger information, company directory, directory of associations, and consultants directory. (Dun and Bradstreet/Gale Industry Reference Handbook Series).

Managing High-Technology Programs and Projects. Russell D. Archibald. John Wiley and Sons, Inc. • 2003. $100.00. Third edition. Written for senior executives, professional project managers, engineers, and information systems managers.

INTERNET DATABASES

FedWorld: A Program of the United States Department of Commerce. National Technical Information Service. Phone: (703)605-6000 Fax: (703)605-6900 E-mail: webmaster@fedworld.gov • URL: http://www.fedworld.gov • Web site offers "a comprehensive central access point for searching, locating, ordering, and acquiring government and business information." Emphasis is on searching the Web pages, databases, and government reports of a wide variety of federal agencies. Fees: Free.

InSite 2. Intelligence Data/Thomson Financial. Phone: 800-654-0393 or (617)856-1890 Fax: (617)737-3182 E-mail: intelligence.data@tfn.com • URL: http://www.insite2.gale.com/ • Fee-based Web site consolidates information in a "Base Pack" consisting of Business InSite, Market InSite, and Company InSite. Optional databases are Consumer InSite, Health and Wellness InSite, Newsletter InSite, and Computer InSite. Includes fulltext content from more than 2,500 trade publications, journals, newsletters, newspapers, analyst reports, and other sources. Continuous updating. Formerly produced by The Gale Group.

WilsonWeb Periodicals Databases. H. W. Wilson. Phone: 800-367-6770 or (718)588-8400 Fax: 800-590-1617 or (718)992-8003 E-mail: custserv@hwwilson.com • URL: http://www.hwwilson.com/ • Web sites provide fee-based access to *Wilson Business Full Text, Applied Science & Technology Full Text, Biological & Agricultural Index, Library Literature & Information Science Full Text,* and *Readers' Guide Full Text, Mega Edition.* Daily updates.

ONLINE DATABASES

Aerospace America [online]. American Institute of Aeronautics and Astronautics. • Provides complete text of the periodical, *Aerospace America*, 1984 to date, with monthly updates. Also includes news from the *AIAA Bulletin*. Inquire as to online cost and availability.

Aerospace Database. American Institute of Aeronautics and Astronautics. • Contains abstracts of literature covering all aspects of the aerospace and aircraft industry 1983 to date. Monthly updates. Inquire as to online cost and availability.

Aerospace/Defense Markets and Technology. Gale Cengage Learning. • Abstracts of commerical aerospace/defense related literature, 1982 to date. Also includes information about major defense contracts awarded by the U. S. Department of Defense. International coverage. Inquire as to online cost and availability.

Applied Science and Technology Index Online. H. W. Wilson Co. • Provides online indexing of 500 major scientific, technical, industrial, and engineering periodicals. Time period is 1983 to date. Monthly updates. Inquire as to online cost and availability.

Business and Industry. Gale Cengage Learning. • Contains online citations, abstracts, and selected fulltext from more than 1,000 trade journals, newspapers, and other publications. Provides general coverage of both manufacturing and service industries, including marketing, production, industry trends, key events, and information on specific companies. Time span is 1994 to date. Daily updates. Inquire as to online cost and availability. (Also available in a CD-ROM version.).

Current Contents Connect. Institute for Scientific Information. • Provides online abstracts of articles listed in the tables of contents of about 7,500 journals. Coverage is very broad, including science, social science, life science, technology, engineering, industry, agriculture, the environment, economics, and arts and humanities. Time period is two years,

with weekly updates. Inquire as to online cost and availability.

INSPEC. Institution of Electrical Engineers (IEE). • Provides online citations, with abstracts, to the world literature of electrical engineering, electronics, optoelectronics, telecommunications, industrial controls, instrumentation, computer technology, information technology, and physics. Coverage includes more than 4,000 technical and scientific journals from 1969 to date, with weekly updating. (INSPEC is Information Services in Physics, Electronics, and Computing.) Inquire as to online cost and availability.

New Product Announcements Plus. Gale Cengage Learning. • Contains the full text of new product and corporate activity press releases, with special emphasis on high technology and emerging industries. Covers 1985 to date. Weekly updates. Inquire as to online cost and availability.

Newspaper Abstracts Daily. ProQuest Inc. • Provides online coverage (citations and abstracts) of 25 major newspapers. Covers business, economics, current affairs, health, fitness, sports, education, technology, government, consumer affairs, psychology, the arts, and the social sciences. Time period is 1986 to date, with daily updates. Inquire as to online cost and availability.

NTIS Database. National Technical Information Service. • Contains citations and abstracts to unrestricted reports of government-sponsored research, 1964 to date. Covers a wide range of technical, engineering, business, and social science topics. Monthly updates. Inquire as to online cost and availability.

Research Centers and Services Directories. Gale Cengage Learning. • Contains profiles of about 30,000 research centers, organizations, laboratories, and agencies in 147 countries. Corresponds to the printed *Research Centers Directory, International Research Centers Directory, Government Research Directory,* and *Research Services Directory.* Updating is semiannual. Inquire as to online cost and availability.

Tablebase. Gale Cengage Learning. • Provides online numerical tabular data from a wide variety of business, organization, and government sources, including about 1,000 trade journals. Includes industry and individual company statistics relating to products, market share, sales forecasts, production, exports, market trends, etc. Time span is 1997 to date. Weekly updates. Inquire as to online cost and availability. (Also available in a CD-ROM version.).

Who's Who in Technology [Online]. Gale Cengage Learning. • Provides online biographical profiles of over 25,000 American scientists, engineers, and others in technology-related occupations. Inquire as to online cost and availability.

PERIODICALS AND NEWSLETTERS

Adweek Magazines' Technology Marketing. VNU Business Media. • Monthly. $55.00 per year. Edited for marketing executives in high technology industries. Covers both advertising and marketing. Formerly *MC Technology Marketing Intelligence.*

Futuretech. Technical Insights/John Wiley & Sons Inc. • Description: Contains briefings on newly emerging technologies and the markets that they will create. Each issue focuses on one technology, analyzes its market impact, and provides access to developers looking for partners, licenses, or marketing agreements.

Gilder Technology Report. George Gilder, editor. Gilder Publishing. • Monthly. $295.00 per year. Newsletter. Makes specific recommendations for investing in technology stocks. (A joint publication of Forbes Magazine and the Gilder Technology Group.).

Internet Marketing and Technology Report: Advis-

ing Marketing, Sales, and Corporate Executives on Online Opportunities. Computer Economics, Inc. • Monthly. $387.00 per year. Newsletter. Covers strategic marketing, sales, advertising, public relations, and corporate communications, all in relation to the Internet. Includes information on "cutting-edge technology" for the Internet.

Journal of Research of the National Institute of Standards and Technology. Available from U. S. Government Printing Office. • Bimonthly. $47.00 per year. Formerly *Journal of Research of the National Bureau of Standards.*

Research-Technology Management: International Journal of Research Management. Industrial Research Institute. • Bimonthly. Individuals, $65.00 per year; institutions, $150.00 per year. Covers both theoretical and practical aspects of the management of industrial research and development.

Technological Forecasting and Social Change: An International Journal of the Dragon Project. Elsevier. • Nine times a year. Individuals, $131.00 per year; institutions, $839.00 per year.

Technology Forecasts and Technology Surveys. Technology Forecasts. • Monthly. $192.00 per year. Newsletter. Information on major breakthroughs in advanced technologies along with forecasts of effects on future applications and markets.

Technology in Society: An International Journal. Elsevier. • Quarterly. Individuals, $233.00 per year; institutions, $981.00 per year.

Technology Investing. Michael Murphy, editor. PBI Media, Inc. • Monthly. $195.00 per year. Newsletter. Provides specific recommendations for investing in high technology companies.

Technology Review: MITs National Magazine of Technology and Policy. Massachusetts Institute of Technology. • Ten times a year. $30.00 per year. Examines current technological issues facing society.

21.C: Scanning the Future: A Magazine of Culture, Technology, and Science. International Publishers Distributors. • Quarterly. $24.00 per year. Contains multidisciplinary articles relating to the 21st century.

RESEARCH CENTERS AND INSTITUTES

Center for the Study of Law, Science, and Technology. Arizona State University, College of Law, P.O. Box 877906, Tempe, AZ 85287-7906. Phone: (480)965-2554 Fax: (480)965-2427 E-mail: gary.marchant@asu.edu • URL: http://www.law. asu.edu • Studies the legal problems created by technological advances.

SRI International. SRI International. 333 Ravenswood Ave., Menlo Park, CA 94025-3493. Phone: (650)859-2000 Fax: (650)859-4111 E-mail: inquiry. line@sri.com • URL: http://www.sri.com • Physical and life sciences, engineering, industrial management, business, social sciences, and public policy. Areas of research include biosciences, economics, energy, engineering systems and development, environment, health, industry consulting, information and communications, public policy, national security, and physical, life, and social sciences.

STATISTICS SOURCES

Basic Science and Technology Statistics. Organization for Economic Cooperation and Development. • Biennial. $84.00. Contains eight years of data on resources devoted to research and development in OECD countries. Includes both financial and personnel information.

Encyclopedia of American Industries. Gale Cengage Learning. • 2000. $560.00. Third edition. Two volumes. $280.00 per volume. Volume one is *Manufacturing Industries* and volume two is *Service and Non-Manufacturing Industries.* Provides the history, development, and recent status of approximately 1,000 industries. Includes statistical graphs, with industry and general indexes.

OECD Science, Technology, and Industry: Scoreboard 2003. Organization for Economic Cooperation and Development. • 2003. $56.00. Presents data on technology trends in OECD countries. Includes more than 200 graphs relating to the performance of various countries in areas of science and technology. Issued biennially.

Standard & Poor's Industry Surveys. Standard & Poor's. • Semiannual. $1,800.00. Two looseleaf volumes. Includes monthly *Supplements.* Provides detailed, individual surveys of 52 major industry groups. Each survey is revised on a semiannual basis. Also includes "Monthly Investment Review" (industry group investment analysis) and monthly "Trends & Projections" (economic analysis).

Statistical Handbook on Technology. Paula Bernstein. Greenwood Publishing Group, Inc. • 1999. $69.95. Provides statistical data on such items as the Internet, online services, computer technology, recycling, patents, prescription drug sales, telecommunications, and aerospace. Includes charts, tables, and graphs. Edited for the general reader. (Statistical Handbook Series).

U. S. Industry and Trade Outlook. Available from National Technical Information Service. • Annual. $69.95. Produced by the International Trade Administration, U. S. Department of Commerce, in a "public-private" partnership with DRI/McGraw-Hill and Standard & Poor's. Provides basic data, outlook for the current year, and "Long-Term Prospects" (five-year projections) for a wide variety of products and services. Includes high technology industries. Formerly *U. S. Industrial Outlook.*

UNESCO Statistical Yearbook. Bernan Press. • 1998. $95.00. Co-published by Bernan Press and the United Nations Educational, Scientific, and Cultural Organization (http://www.unesco.org). Presents statistical data from more than 200 countries on education, technology, research, broadcasting, cinema, book publishing, newspapers, libraries, museums, and population. Includes charts, maps, and graphs.

TRADE/PROFESSIONAL ASSOCIATIONS

Society for the History of Technology. John Hopkins University, Department of History, Science, Medicine and Technology, 216B Ames Hall, Baltimore, MD 21218. Phone: (410)516-8349 Fax: (410)516-7502 E-mail: shot@jhu.edu • URL: http://www.shot.jhu.edu.

Technology Transfer Society. 2005 Arthur Ln., Austin, TX 78704. Phone: (512)447-4409 Fax: (512)447-1814 E-mail: t2s@t2s.org • URL: http://www.t2society.org • Individuals, institutions, and other professional societies involved in the process of technology transfer. Encourages development of technology assessment, transfer, utilization, and forecasting techniques; disseminates information on these new techniques. Seeks to develop an environment for and promote the enhancement of professional competence in the field. Establishes standards and ethics; defines terms. Acts as a liaison among disciplines within the technological community such as scientific, management, engineering, and other professional societies. Provides a nonprofit capability to accept charitable contributions, contracts, and grants for the performance of pilot technological transfer programs that will aid the nation.

OTHER SOURCES

Survey of Advanced Technology: A Strategic Analysis of Today's Leading-edge Information Technologies. I.T. Works, Innovation Center. • Annual. $795.00. Surveys the corporate use (or neglect) of advanced computer technology. Topics include major technology trends and emerging technologies.

TECHNOLOGY TRANSFER

ABSTRACTS AND INDEXES

Business Periodicals Index. H. W. Wilson Co. • 11 times a year. Quarterly and annual cumulations. Price varies.

DIRECTORIES

Business Organizations, Agencies, and Publications Directory. Gale Cengage Learning. • 2003. $480.00. 15th edition. Over 40,000 entries describing 39 types of business information sources. Classified by type of organization, publication, or serviceIncludes state, national, and international agencies and organizations. Master index to names and keywords. Also includes e-mail addresses and web site URL's.

ONLINE DATABASES

Wilson Business Abstracts Online. H. W. Wilson Co. • Indexes and abstracts 600 major business periodicals, plus the *Wall Street Journal* and the business section of the *New York Times.* Indexing is from 1982, abstracting from 1990, with the two newspapers included from 1993. Updated weekly. Inquire as to online cost and availability. (*Business Periodicals Index* without abstracts is also available online.).

PERIODICALS AND NEWSLETTERS

Journal of Technology Transfer. Technology Transfer Society. Kluwer Academic Publishers. • Quarterly. Institutions, $371.00 per year; with online edition, $445.20 per year. Topics include technology transfer ventures, models, mechanisms, and case studies.

Technology Forecasts and Technology Surveys. Technology Forecasts. • Monthly. $192.00 per year. Newsletter. Information on major breakthroughs in advanced technologies along with forecasts of effects on future applications and markets.

Technology Transfer Highlights. Argonne National Laboratory Industrial Technology Development Div. • Description: Provides information on federally-developed technology available for transfer and commercialization.

RESEARCH CENTERS AND INSTITUTES

Argonne National Laboratory Industrial - Office of Technology Transfer. 9700 S Cass Ave., Argonne, IL 60439. Phone: 800-627-2596 or (630)252-7694 Fax: (630)252-5230 E-mail: weso@anl.gov • URL: http://www.itd.anl.gov • Formerly Industrial Technology Development Center.

Battelle Memorial Institute. Battelle Memorial Institute. 505 King Ave., Columbus, OH 43201. Phone: 800-201-2011 or (614)424-5853 Fax: (614)424-5263 E-mail: solutions@battelle.org • URL: http://www.battelle.org/ • Environment and energy; national security; transportation; health and life sciences; medical, pharmaceutical, agrochemical, and consumer product development. Conducts marine research at three coastal locations: Florida Marine Research Facility (Daytona Beach), Northwest Marine Research Laboratory (Sequim, Washington), and the Ocean Sciences Laboratory (Duxbury, Massachusetts). Specialized facilities and units include: Aviation Safety Reporting System Office; the Breakthrough Center for Strategic Product Development; the Human Engineering, Ergonomics, and Organizational Research Center; and the William R. Wiley Environmental Molecular Sciences Laboratory.

Center for International Science and Technology Policy. George Washington University, 2013 G St., N. W., Stuart Hall, Suite 201, Washington, DC 20052. Phone: (202)994-7292 Fax: (202)994-1639 E-mail: cistp@gwu.edu • URL: http://www.gwu. edu/ • Research areas include technology transfer.

Office for Sponsored Research. Harvard University, Holyoke Center, Room 620, 1350 Massachusetts Ave., Cambridge, MA 02138. Phone: (617)495-

---

2522 Fax: (617)495-2900 E-mail: elizabeth_mora@ harvard.edu • URL: http://www.vpf-web.harvard. edu/osr.

Office of Research Services. University of Pennsylvania, 3451 Walnut St., Rm. P-221, Philadelphia, PA 19104-6205. Phone: (215)898-7293 Fax: (215)898-9708 E-mail: abrud@pobox. upenn.edu • URL: http://www.upenn.edu/ researchservices.

Office of Sponsored Programs. Massachusetts Institute of Technology, Bldg. E19-750, Cambridge, MA 02139. Phone: (617)253-2492 Fax: (617)253-4734 E-mail: jnorris@mit.edu • URL: http://www. web.mit.edu/org/osp.

Office of Sponsored Research. California Institute of Technology, 1200 E. Califorina Blvd., MC 201-15, Pasadena, CA 91125. Phone: (626)395-6357 Fax: (626)795-4571 E-mail: richard.seligman@caltech. edu • URL: http://www.atc.caltech.edu/osr.

Princeton Forrestal Center. Princeton University, 105 College Rd., E., Princeton, NJ 08540. Phone: (609)452-7720 Fax: (609)452-7485 E-mail: picus@ picusassociates.com • Designed to create an interdependent mix of academia and business enterprise.

Rensselaer Polytechnic Institute. Rensselaer Technology Park, 100 Jordan Rd., Troy, NY 12180. Phone: (518)283-7102 Fax: (518)283-0695 E-mail: wachom@rpi.edu • URL: http://www.rpi.edu/dept/ rtp • Serves as a conduit for research interactions between Rensselaer Polytechnic Institute and private companies.

Research Corporation Technologies. Research Corporation Technologies. 5210 E Williams Cir., Ste. 240, Tucson, AZ 85711-4410. Phone: (520)748-4400 Fax: (520)748-0025 E-mail: csouvignier@ rctech.com • URL: http://www.rctech.com • Appraises, protects, develops, and commercializes inventions from colleges, universities, medical research organizations, and other research laboratories. Among the variety of inventions that have been developed and marketed are agricultural and other chemicals, chemical processes, biotechnologies, bioprocessing, diagnostics, foods and additives, pharmaceuticals, plants, vaccines, veterinary products, agricultural equipment, analytical instruments, chemicals, electronics, materials, industrial processes, machines, medical/surgical diagnostics, and optics/optical instruments. Provides incentives for invention disclosure, funds selected applied research, new business formation.

RTI International. RTI International. 3040 Cornwallis Rd., PO Box 12194, Research Triangle Park, NC 27709-2194. Phone: (919)485-2666 Fax: (919)541-5985 E-mail: listen@rti.org • URL: http://www.rti. org • Public health, medicine, environmental protection, electronic technology, and public policy.

Stanford Research Park. Stanford University, 2770 Sand Hill Rd., Menlo Park, CA 94025. Phone: (650)926-0200 • Links research resources of Stanford University with private enterprise.

TRADE/PROFESSIONAL ASSOCIATIONS

Industry Coalition on Technolgy Transfer. 1400 L St., N.W., Washington, DC 20005-3502. Phone: (202)371-5994 Fax: (202)371-5950 • Members are computer industry associations concerned with federal regulations on technology transfer in the computer industry.

Technology Transfer Society. 2005 Arthur Ln., Austin, TX 78704. Phone: (512)447-4409 Fax: (512)447-1814 E-mail: t2s@t2s.org • URL: http:// www.t2society.org • Individuals, institutions, and other professional societies involved in the process of technology transfer. Encourages development of technology assessment, transfer, utilization, and forecasting techniques; disseminates information on these new techniques. Seeks to develop an environment for and promote the enhancement of profes-

sional competence in the field. Establishes standards and ethics; defines terms. Acts as a liaison among disciplines within the technological community such as scientific, management, engineering, and other professional societies. Provides a nonprofit capability to accept charitable contributions, contracts, and grants for the performance of pilot technological transfer programs that will aid the nation.

TEENAGE MARKET

See: YOUTH MARKET

TELECOMMUNICATIONS

See also: CABLE ADDRESSES; COMMUNICATION SYSTEMS; COMPUTER COMMUNICATIONS; TELEGRAPH; TELEPHONE INDUSTRY

GENERAL WORKS

Analog and Digital Communications. Hwei P. Hsu. McGraw-Hill. • 2003. $16.95. Second edition. (Schaum's Outlines Series).

Applying Telecommunications and Technology from a Global Business Perspective. Jay J. Zajas and Olive D. Church. Haworth Press, Inc. • 1997. $29. 95. Provides an international, multicultural perspective.

Telecommunications. Warren Hioki. Prentice Hall PTR. • 2000. $120.00. Fourth edition.

Telecommunications: Issues in Focus. Agnes S. Corwall, editor. Nova Science Publishers, Inc. • 2002. $69.00. Provides reviews of many aspects of telecommunications, including broadband, wireless, access fees, encryption, telemarketing, telephone bills, remote sensing, and regulation. Includes an index.

Worldwide History of Telecommunications. Anton Huurdeman. John Wiley and Sons, Inc. • 2003. $125.00. Covers the evolution and history of telecommunications from before 1800 to 2000. Topics include telegraph, telephone, radio, satellite tramsmission, optical fiber transmission, electronic switching, telefax, multimedia, and many other subjects. Includes a two-century chronology, worldwide statistics, a glossary, and an index.

ABSTRACTS AND INDEXES

Communication Abstracts: An International Information Service. Sage Publications, Inc. • Bimonthly. Institutions, $1,150.00 per year. Provides broad coverage of the literature of communications, including broadcasting and advertising.

Electronics and Communications Abstracts Journal: Comprehensive Coverage of Essential Scientific Literature. CSA. • Monthly. $1,665.00 per year. Includes print and online editions.

Key Abstracts: Telecommunications. Available from INSPEC, Inc. • Monthly. $250.00 per year. Provides international coverage of journal and proceedings literature. Published in England by the Institution of Electrical Engineers (IEE).

NTIS Alerts: Communication. National Technical Information Service. • Semimonthly. $210.00 per year. . Provides descriptions of government-sponsored research reports and software, with ordering information. Covers common carriers, satellites, radio/TV equipment, telecommunication regulations, and related subjects.

ALMANACS AND YEARBOOKS

Communication Technology Update. Elsevier. • 2000. $36.95. 7th edition. A yearly review of developments in electronic media, telecommunications, and the Internet.

OECD Communications Outlook. OECD Publica-

tions and Information Center. • Annual. $104.00. Provides international coverage of yearly telecommunications activity. Includes charts, graphs, and maps.

BIOGRAPHICAL SOURCES

The Highwaymen: Warriors on the Information Superhighway. Ken Auletta. Harcourt Trade Publications. • 1998. $13.00. Revised expanded edition. Contains critical articles about Ted Turner, Rupert Murdoch, Barry Diller, Michael Eisner, and other key figures in electronic communications, entertainment, and information. (Harvest Book Series).

CD-ROM DATABASES

Authority Computer and Telecommunications Law Library. LexisNexis/Matthew Bender. • Quarterly. Price on request. Full text CD-ROM provides cases, analysis, sample agreements, and other information relating to computer law, telecommunications regulation (cable, broadcasting, satellite, Internet), international computer law, and computer contracts.

Datapro on CD-ROM: Communications Analyst. Gartner Group, Inc. • Monthly. Price on application. Provides detailed information on products and services for communications systems, including local area networks and voice systems.

Hoover's Company Capsules on CD-ROM. Hoover's, Inc. • Quarterly. $399.95 per year (single-user). Provides the CD-ROM version of *Hoover's Handbook of American Business, Hoover's Handbook of Emerging Companies, Hoover's Handbook of World Business, Hoover's Guide to Computer Companies, Hoover's Guide to Media Companies, Hoover's Handbook of Private Companies,* and various regional guides. Includes more than 11,000 profiles of companies.

OECD Statistical Compendium. Organization for Economic Cooperation and Development. • Semiannual. $1,905.00 per year for 1 to 10 users. CD-ROM contains more than 730,000 monthly, quarterly, and annual time series for OECD countries, 1960 to date. Includes fully searchable data on agriculture, food, economic indicators, national accounts, employment, energy, finance, industry, technology, and foreign trade. Results can be displayed in various forms.

DIRECTORIES

Internet Tools of the Profession: A Guide for Information Professionals. Hope N. Tillman, editor. Special Libraries Association. • 1997. $49.00. Second edition. Consists of 14 sections by various authors or compilers. After two introductory articles on searching the Internet, there are 12 annotated lists of useful Web sites, covering the SLA, business and finance, chemistry, education, food and agriculture, information technology, insurance and employee benefits, law, library management, metals and materials, pharmaceuticals, and telecommunications. An index is provided.

Major Telecommunications Companies of the World. Available from Gale Cengage Learning. • 2003. $885.00. Sixth edition. Published by Graham & Whiteside. Contains detailed information and trade names for more than 3,500 important telecommunications companies in various countries.

Plunkett's E-Commerce and Internet Business Almanac. Plunkett Research, Ltd. • Annual. $249. 99. Contains detailed profiles of 250 large companies engaged in various areas of Internet commerce, including e-business Web sites, communications equipment manufacturers, and Internet service providers. Includes CD-ROM.

Plunkett's InfoTech Industry Almanac: Complete Profiles on the InfoTech 500-the Leading Firms in the Movement and Management of Voice, Data, and Video. Plunkett Research, Ltd. • Biennial. $229.99. Includes CD-ROM. Five hundred major information companies are profiled, with corporate culture aspects. Discusses major trends in various sectors of the computer and information industry, including data on careers and job growth. Includes several indexes.

Plunkett's Telecommunications Industry Almanac. Plunkett Research Ltd. • Covers: 500 of the largest companies involved in telecommunications. Entries include: Name, address, phone, fax, names and titles of key personnel, subsidiary and branch names and locations, financial data, salaries and benefits, description of products/services, overview of company culture/activities.

Telecommunications Directory. Gale. • Covers: Two volumes-North America and International, Cover approximately 6,000 national and international voice and data communications networks, electronic mail services, teleconferencing facilities and services, facsimile services, Internet access providers, videotex and teletext operations, transactional services, local area networks, audiotex services, microwave systems/networkers, satellite facilities, and others involved in telecommunications, including related consultants, advertisers/marketers; associations, regulatory bodies, and publishers. Entries include: Company or organization name, address, phone, fax, year established, name and title of contact, executive officers and board of directors, function or type of service; geographical area served; NAICS and SIC codes; number of employees; general description, including telecommunications-related activities; product/service; specific applications; means of access and equipment required; publications; intended market and availability; pricing; stock exchanges traded and ticker symbols; financial figures.

Telehealth Buyer's Guide. Miller Freeman. • Annual. $10.00. Lists sources of telecommunications and information technology products and services for the health care industry.

TIA Directory and Desk Reference. Telecommunications Industry Association. • Annual. Members, $50.00; non-members, $100.00. Lists manufacturers and suppliers of interconnect telephone equipment. Formerly *Multimedia Telecommunications Sourcebook.*

ENCYCLOPEDIAS AND DICTIONARIES

Acronyms of Computer Science and Communications: A Comprehensive Acronym Dictionary and Illustrated Encyclopedia. Enjob Kajan and Ejub Kajan. Springer Verlag. • 2002. $49.95. Explains more than 4,000 "broadly used" computer, telecommunications, and information technology acronyms. Includes illustrations and Web addresses, where applicable.

CyberDictionary: Your Guide to the Wired World. Spurge ink!. • 1996. $17.95. Includes many illustrations.

Encyclopedia of Communication and Information. Available from Gale Cengage Learning. • 2001. $395.00. Three volumes. Published by Macmillan Reference USA.

Encyclopedia of Emerging Industries. Gale Cengage Learning. • 2001. $320.00. Fourth edition. Provides detailed information on 115 "newly flourishing" industries. Includes historical background, organizational structure, significant individuals, current conditions, major companies, work force, technology trends, research developments, and other industry facts.

Encyclopedia of New Media: An Essential Reference to Communication and Technology. Steve Jones, editor. Sage Publications, Inc. • 2003. $125.00. Contains more than 250 entries dealing with such areas as multimedia, broadband access, information communication technology (ICT), content filtering, wireless networks, and cyberethics.

The Froehlich-Kent Encyclopedia of

Telecommunications. Fritz E. Froehlich and Allen Kent, editors. Marcel Dekker, Inc. • 18 volumes. $3,510.00. $195.00 per volume. Dates vary. Contains scholarly articles written by telecommunications experts. Includes bibliographies.

Hargrave's Communications Dictionary. Frank Hargrave. Available from John Wiley and Sons, Inc. • 2001. $140.00. Published by IEEE. Contains more than 10,000 definitions relating to voice and data communications, plus definitions in the areas of computer science, optics, networks, and the Internet. Includes acronyms, charts, equations, and drawings.

Internet Encyclopedia. Hossein Bidgoli, editor. John Wiley and Sons, Inc. • 2003. $750.00. Four volumes. Covers various aspects of the Internet, including information technology, electronic business, and telecommunications.

Multimedia and the Web from A to Z. David C. Leonard and Patrick M. Dillon. Greenwood Publishing Group, Inc. • 1998. $42.95. Second enlarged revised edition. Defines more than 1,500 terms relating to software and hardware in the areas of computing, online technology, telecommunications, audio, video, motion pictures, CD-ROM, and the Internet. Includes acronyms and an annotated bibliography. Formerly *Multimedia Technology from A to Z* (1994).

Wiley Encyclopedia of Electrical and Electronics Engineering. John G. Webster, editor. John Wiley and Sons, Inc. • 1999. $9,630.00. 25 volumes. Includes *Supplement I* and *Supplement II*. Contains about 1,400 articles, each with bibliography. Arrangement is according to 64 categories.

Wiley Encyclopedia of Telecommunications and Signal Processing. John G. Proakis, editor. John Wiley and Sons, Inc. • 2002. $1,250.00. Five volumes. Contains about 300 articles covering both fundamentals and recent advances in telecommunications and signal processing. Emphasis is on material for electrical engineers.

HANDBOOKS AND MANUALS

Dun & Bradstreet/Gale Group Industry Handbooks. Gale Cengage Learning. • 2000. $650.00. Five volumes. $130.00 per volume. Each volume covers two or more major industries: 1. *Entertainment and Hospitality*; 2. *Construction and Agriculture*; 3. *Chemicals and Pharmaceuticals*; 4. *Computers & Software and Broadcasting & Telecommunications*; 5. *Insurance and Health & Medical Services*. The following are included for each industry: overview, statistics, financial ratios, rankings, merger information, company directory, directory of associations, and consultants directory. (Dun and Bradstreet/Gale Industry Reference Handbook Series).

Fiber Optic Reference Guide. David R. Goff. Elsevier. • 2002. $44.99. Third edition. A basic guide to fiber optics as utilized in telecommunications. Coverage includes fiber optic cables, light emitters, detectors, optical amplifiers, fiber for video, fiber for data transmission, interconnections, system design, testing, and future trends.

Irwin Handbook of Telecommunications. James H. Green. McGraw-Hill • 2000. $95.00. Fourth edition. Formerly *Dow Jones-Irwin Handbook of Telecommunications.*

Reference Manual for Telecommunications Engineering. Roger L. Freeman. John Wiley and Sons, Inc. • 2001. $695.00. Third edition. Two volumes. Presents detailed information and specific data on the most commonly used telecommunications standards.

Telecommunication Transmission Handbook. Roger L. Freeman. John Wiley and Sons, Inc. • 1998. $198.00. Fourth edition. (Telecommunications and Signal Processing Series).

Telecommunications Engineer's Reference Book.

Fraidoon Mazda. Elsevier. • 1998. $170.00. Second edition.

INTERNET DATABASES

Business 2.0 Web Guide to the Best Business Links. Business 2.0 Media Inc. Phone: (415)293-4800 E-mail: support@business2.com • URL: http://www.business2.com/webguide • Web site presents an extensive, searchable directory of links to "the best, most informative, and authoritative web-pages." Twenty main categories cover business, finance, career, company information, people, and technology topics, with thousands of subtopics, all linking to Web sites recommended by experienced business researchers. Fees: Free.

InfoTech Trends. Data Analysis Group. Phone: (925)462-1202 Fax: (925)462-1225 E-mail: support@infotechtrends.com • URL: http://www.infotechtrends.com • Web site provides both free and fee-based market research data on the information technology industry, including computers, peripherals, telecommunications, the Internet, software, CD-ROM/DVD, e-commerce, and workstations. Fees: Free for current (most recent year) data; more extensive information has various fee structures. Formerly *Computer Industry Forecasts.*

Wired News. Lycos, Inc. Phone: (415)276-8400 Fax: (415)276-8500 E-mail: newsfeedback@wired.com • URL: http://www.wired.com • Provides summaries and full-text of "Top Stories" relating to the Internet, computers, multimedia, telecommunications, and the electronic information industry in general. These news stories are placed in the broad categories of Politics, Business, Culture, and Technology. Affiliated with *Wired* magazine. Fees: Free.

ONLINE DATABASES

INSPEC. Institution of Electrical Engineers (IEE). • Provides online citations, with abstracts, to the world literature of electrical engineering, electronics, optoelectronics, telecommunications, industrial controls, instrumentation, computer technology, information technology, and physics. Coverage includes more than 4,000 technical and scientific journals from 1969 to date, with weekly updating. (INSPEC is Information Services in Physics, Electronics, and Computing.) Inquire as to online cost and availability.

PERIODICALS AND NEWSLETTERS

Broadband Solutions. North American Publishing Co. • Monthly. Controlled circulation. Covers the high-bandwidth telecommunications industry, including new products and emerging technologies.

Broadband Week. Reed Business Information. • 51 times a year. $139.00 per year. Provides news and trends for all parts of the evolving broadband industry, including operations, marketing, finance, and technology. Incorporates *Broadband.*

Business Communications Review. Key3Media Group, Inc. • Monthly. $45.00 per year. Edited for communications managers in large end-user companies and institutions. Includes special feature issues on intranets and network management.

Communications Daily: The Authoritative News Service of Electronic Communications. Warren Publishing, Inc. • Daily. $3,006.00 per year. Newsletter. Covers telecommunications, including the telephone industry, broadcasting, cable TV, satellites, data communications, and electronic publishing. Features corporate and industry news.

Communications News. Nelson Publishing Co. • Monthly. Free to qualified personnel; others, $84.00 per year.

Communications News: Solutions for Today's Networking Decision Managers. Nelson Publishing, Inc. • Monthly. Free to qualified personnel; others, $84.00 per year. Includes coverage of "Internetworking" and "Intranetworking." Emphasis is on emerging telecommunications technologies.

Convergence: The Journal of Research Into New Media Technologies. Reed Business Information. • Monthly. Individuals, $40.00 per year; institutions, $160.00 per year. Covers the merging of communications technologies. Includes telecommunications networks, interactive TV, multimedia, wireless phone service, and electronic information services.

Electronic Information Report: Empowering Industry Decision Makers Since 1979. SIMBA Information. • 46 times a year. $649.00 per year. Newsletter. Provides business and financial news and trends for online services, electronic publishing, storage media, multimedia, and voice services. Includes information on relevant IPOs (initial public offerings) and mergers. Formerly *Electronic Information Week.*

Fat Pipe: The Business of Marketing Broadband Services. Dagda Mor Media, Inc. • Monthly. Controlled circulation. Edited for those who plan, develop, and market broadband Internet and telecommunications services.

FCC Report: An Exclusive Report on Domestic and International Telecommunications Policy and Regulation. Warren Publishing, Inc. • 26 times a year. $670.00 per year. Newsletter concerned principally with Federal Communications Commission reglations and policy.

Fiber Optics and Communications. Information Gatekeepers, Inc. • Monthly. $695.00. Emphasis on the use of fiber optics in telecommunications.

FiberSystems International. Available from IOP Publishing, Inc. • Seven times a year. Free to qualified personnel. Published in the UK by the Institute of Physics. "Covering the optical communications marketplace within the Americas and Asia." *Fibre Systems Europe* is also available, covering the business and marketing aspects of fiber optics communications in Europe.

Harvard Management Communication Letter. Harvard Business School Publishing. • Description: Provides information and techniques for managers on effective communication.

Healthcare Informatics: The Business of Healthcare Information Technology. McGraw-Hill. • Monthly. $39.95 per year. Covers various aspects of information and computer technology for the health care industry.

Interactive Home: Consumer Technology Monthly. Jupiter Communications. • Monthly. $625.00 per year; with online edition, $725.00 per year. Newsletter on devices to bring the Internet into the average American home. Covers TV set-top boxes, game devices, telephones with display screens, handheld computer communication devices, the usual PCs, etc.

International Journal of Communication Systems. John Wiley and Sons, Inc., Journals. • Bimonthly. Individuals, $1,055.00 per year; institutions, $1,405.00 per year. Published in England by John Wiley and Sons Ltd. Formerly *International Journal of Digital and Analog Communication Systems.*

RCR Wireless News: The Newspaper for the Wireless Communications Industry. Crain Communications. • Weekly. $64.00 per year. Covers news of the wireless communications industry, including business and financial developments. Formerly *RCR.*

State and Local Communications Report. Aspen Publishers. • Biweekly. $645.00 per year. Newsletter. Formerly *Telecommunications Week.*

Telecommunications. • Monthly. Free to qualified personnel; others, $145.00 per year. International coverage.

Telecommunications Policy. Elsevier. • 11 times a year. Individuals, $267.00 per year; institutions, $1,077.00 per year.

Telecommunications Reports. • Weekly. Institutions, $1,695.00 per year. Includes *TR Daily.* Regulatory newsletter.

Wireless Review: Intelligence for Competitive Providers. Primedia Business Magazines and Media. • Semimonthly. $48.00 per year. Covers business and technology developments for wireless service providers. Includes special issues on a wide variety of wireless topics. Formed by merger of *Cellular Business* and *Wireless World.*

X-Change. Virgo Publishing, Inc. • 18 times per year. $70.00 per year. Edited for local telecommunications exchange services, both wireline and wireless.

RESEARCH CENTERS AND INSTITUTES

Center for Integrated Systems. Stanford University, 420 Via Palou Mall, Stanford, CA 94305-4070. Phone: (650)725-3621 Fax: (650)725-0991 E-mail: rdasher@stanford.edu • URL: http://www.cis. stanford.edu • Research programs include manufacturing science, design science, computer architecture, semiconductor technology, and telecommunications.

International Data Corp. (IDC). Five Speen St., Framingham, MA 01701. Phone: (508)872-8200 Fax: (508)935-4015 E-mail: leads@idc.com • URL: http://www.idc.com • Private research firm specializing in market research related to computers, multimedia, and telecommunications.

Studio for Creative Inquiry. Carnegie Mellon University, College of Fine Arts, Pittsburgh, PA 15213-3890. Phone: (412)268-3454 Fax: (412)268-2829 E-mail: mmbm@andrew.cmu.edu/. • URL: http://www.cmu.edu/studio/ • Research areas include artificial intelligence, virtual reality, hypermedia, multimedia, and telecommunications, in relation to the arts.

STATISTICS SOURCES

Communication Equipment, and Other Electronic Systems and Equipment. U. S. Bureau of the Census. • Annual. Provides data on shipments: value, quantity, imports, and exports. (Current Industrial Reports, MA-36P.).

OECD Information Technology Outlook 2000: ICTs, E-Commerce and the Information Economy. Organization for Economic Cooperation and Development. • 2000. $72.00. Provides data on information and communications technology (ICT) and electronic commerce in 11 OECD nations (includes U. S.). Coverage includes network infrastructure, electronic payment systems, financial transaction technologies, intelligent agents, global navigation systems, and portable flat panel display technologies.

Standard & Poor's Industry Surveys. Standard & Poor's. • Semiannual. $1,800.00. Two looseleaf volumes. Includes monthly *Supplements.* Provides detailed, individual surveys of 52 major industry groups. Each survey is revised on a semiannual basis. Also includes "Monthly Investment Review" (industry group investment analysis) and monthly "Trends & Projections" (economic analysis).

Statistical Handbook on Technology. Paula Bernstein. Greenwood Publishing Group, Inc. • 1999. $69.95. Provides statistical data on such items as the Internet, online services, computer technology, recycling, patents, prescription drug sales, telecommunications, and aerospace. Includes charts, tables, and graphs. Edited for the general reader. (Statistical Handbook Series).

U. S. Industry and Trade Outlook. Available from National Technical Information Service. • Annual. $69.95. Produced by the International Trade Administration, U. S. Department of Commerce, in a "public-private" partnership with DRI/McGraw-Hill and Standard & Poor's. Provides basic data, outlook for the current year, and "Long-Term Prospects" (five-year projections) for a wide variety of products and services. Includes high technology industries. Formerly *U. S. Industrial Outlook.*

WEFA Industrial Monitor. John Wiley and Sons, Inc. • Annual. $65.00. Prepared by industry analysts at WEFA, an economic forecasting and consulting firm (originally Wharton Econometric Forecasting Associates). Contains discussions of the outlook for major U. S. industries, with many 10-year forecasts (WEFA Web site is http://www.wefa.com).

TRADE/PROFESSIONAL ASSOCIATIONS

Competitive Telecommunications Association. 1900 M. St., N.W.. Suite 800, Washington, DC 20036. Phone: (202)296-6650 Fax: (202)296-7585 E-mail: tmonroe@comptel.org • URL: http://www.comptel. org • Formerly Association of Long Distance Telephone Companies.

TCA - The Information Technology and Telecommunications Association-Sacramento Valley. PO Box 278076, Sacramento, CA 95827-8076. Phone: (916)845-3140 Fax: (916)845-3140 E-mail: shirley. helfand@ftb.ca.gov • URL: http://www.tca.org.

OTHER SOURCES

Cellular Telephones and Communication Equipment. Available from MarketResearch.com. • 2002. $4,450.00. Published by Global Industry Analysts. Provides worldwide market research data, including profiles of major cell phone manufacturers and service providers.

Telecommunications Regulation: Cable, Broadcasting, Satellite, and the Internet. LexisNexis Matthew Bender. • Semiannual. $826.00. Four looseleaf volumes. Covers local, state, and federal regulation, with emphasis on the Telecommunications Act of 1996. Includes regulation of television, telephone, cable, satellite, computer communication, and online services. Formerly *Cable Television Law.*

Wireless Data Networks. Gupta. Prentice Hall PTR. • 2000. Price on application. Presents market research information relating to cellular data networks, paging networks, packet radio networks, satellite systems, and other areas of wireless communication. Contains "summaries of recent developments and trends in wireless markets.".

TELECOMMUTING

See also: COMPUTER COMMUNICATIONS

GENERAL WORKS

Data Smog: Surviving the Information Glut. David Shenk. HarperSanFrancisco. • 1997. $14.00. A critical view of both the electronic and print information industries. Emphasis is on information overload.

Making Telecommuting Happen: A Guide for Telemangers and Telecommuters. Jack M. Nilles. John Wiley and Sons, Inc. • 1994. $25.95. Includes tips for working productively in a home environment while maintaining good relationships with workers in the corporate office.

101 Tips for Telecommuters: Successfully Manage Your Work, Team, Technology, and Family. Debra A. Dinnocenzo. Berrett-Koehler Publishers, Inc. • 1999. $15.95.

Telecommute! Go to Work Without Leaving Home. Lisa Shaw. John Wiley and Sons, Inc. • 1996. $14.95. Includes "Are You Right for Telecommuting?" and "How to Negotiate with Your Boss.".

What Will Be: How the New World of Information Will Change Our Lives. Michael L. Dertouzos. DIANE Publishing Co. • 1997. $25.00. A discussion of the "information market place" of the future, including telecommuting, virtual reality, and computer recognition of speech. The author is director of the MIT Laboratory for Computer Science.

Wired Neighborhood. Stephen Doheny-Farina. Yale University Press. • 1996. $40.00. The author examines both the hazards and the advantages of "making the computer the center of our public and private lives," as exemplified by the Internet and telecommuting.

BIBLIOGRAPHIES

Telecommuters, the Workforce of the Twenty-First Century: An Annotated Bibliography. Teri R. Switzer. Scarecrow Press, Inc. • 1996. $34.00. Covers material published since 1970.

CD-ROM DATABASES

OECD Statistical Compendium. Organization for Economic Cooperation and Development. • Semiannual. $1,905.00 per year for 1 to 10 users. CD-ROM contains more than 730,000 monthly, quarterly, and annual time series for OECD countries, 1960 to date. Includes fully searchable data on agriculture, food, economic indicators, national accounts, employment, energy, finance, industry, technology, and foreign trade. Results can be displayed in various forms.

HANDBOOKS AND MANUALS

Manual of Remote Working. Kevin Curran and Geoff Williams. Ashgate Publishing Co. • 1997. Price on application. A British approach to telecommuting or "remote working." Among the chapters are "Planning a Remote Working Operation," "Human Resources," "Communication Systems," and "Project Management." Includes bibliographical references, glossary, and index. Published by Gower in England.

Telecom Made Easy: Money-Saving, Profit-Building Solutions for Home Businesses, Telecommuters. June Langhoff. Aegis Publishing Group, Ltd. • 2001. $19.95. Fouth revised edition.

Virtual Office Survival Handbook: What Telecommuters and Entrepreneurs Need to Succeed in Today's Nontraditional Workplace. Alice Bredin. John Wiley and Sons, Inc. • 1996. $16.95. Presents broad coverage of telecommuting considerations, including workplace customizing and the evaluation of electronic office equipment. Coping with distractions and psychological issues are discussed.

INTERNET DATABASES

Business 2.0 Web Guide to the Best Business Links. Business 2.0 Media Inc. Phone: (415)293-4800 E-mail: support@business2.com • URL: http://www.business2.com/webguide • Web site presents an extensive, searchable directory of links to "the best, most informative, and authoritative web pages." Twenty main categories cover business, finance, career, company information, people, and technology topics, with thousands of subtopics, all linking to Web sites recommended by experienced business researchers. Fees: Free.

Telecommuting, Teleworking, and Alternative Officing. Gil Gordon Associates. Phone: (732)329-2266 Fax: (732)329-2703 • URL: http://www.gilgordon.com • Web site includes "About Telecommuting" (questions and answers), "Worldwide Resources" (news groups, publications, conferences), and "Technology" (virtual office, intranets, groupware). Other features include monthly updates and an extensive list of telecommuting/telework related books. Fees: Free.

PERIODICALS AND NEWSLETTERS

Desktop Video Communications. BCR Enterprises, Inc,. • Bimonthly. Free per year. Covers multimedia technologies, with emphasis on video conferencing and the "virtual office.".

Home Office Connections: A Monthly Journal of News, Ideas, Opportunities, and Savings for Those Who Work at Home. Home Office Association of America. • Monthly. Free to members; non-members, $49.00 per year.

InterActive Consumers. MarketResearch.com. • Monthly. $395.00 per year. Newsletter. Covers the emerging markets for digital content, products, and services. Includes market information on telecommuting, online services, the Internet, online investing, and other areas of electronic commerce.

Telecons. Applied Business Telecommunications. • Bimonthly. $30.00 per year. Topics include teleconferencing, videoconferencing, distance learning, telemedicine, and telecommuting.

TeleTrends. International Telework Association Council. • Quarterly. Newsletter. Price on application.

RESEARCH CENTERS AND INSTITUTES

Computerized Conferencing and Communications Center. New Jersey Institute of Technology, University Heights, Newark, NJ 07102-1982. Phone: (973)596-3000 • URL: http://www.njit.edu • Research areas include computer conferencing software and computer-mediated communication systems.

TRADE/PROFESSIONAL ASSOCIATIONS

Home Office Association of America. PO Box 51, Sagaponack, NY 11962-0051. Phone: 800-809-4622 E-mail: hoaa@aol.com • URL: http://www.hoaa.com • A for-profit organization providing advice and information to home office workers and business owners.

Interactive Multimedia and Collaborative Commuincations Alliance. PO Box 756, Syosset, NY 11791-0756. Phone: (516)818-8184 Fax: (516)922-2170 E-mail: staff@imcca.org • URL: http://www.imcca.org • Members are vendors and users of teleconferencing equipment. Formerly International Teleconferencing Association.

International Telework Association and Council. 8403 Colesville Rd., Ste. 865, Silver Spring, MD 20910. Phone: (301)650-2322 E-mail: info@workingfromanywhere.com • URL: http://www.telecommute.org • Members are individuals and organizations promoting the benefits of telecommuting and the "virtual office." Formerly Telecommuting Advisory Council/International Telework Association.

TELEGRAPH

See also: CABLE ADDRESSES; TELECOMMUNICATIONS

STATISTICS SOURCES

Communication Equipment, and Other Electronic Systems and Equipment. U. S. Bureau of the Census. • Annual. Provides data on shipments: value, quantity, imports, and exports. (Current Industrial Reports, MA-36P.).

TELEMARKETING

See also: TELEPHONE SELLING

GENERAL WORKS

Applying Telecommunications and Technology from a Global Business Perspective. Jay J. Zajas and Olive D. Church. Haworth Press, Inc. • 1997. $29.95. Provides an international, multicultural perspective.

ABSTRACTS AND INDEXES

Business Periodicals Index. H. W. Wilson Co. • 11 times a year. Quarterly and annual cumulations. Price varies.

DIRECTORIES

Customer Inter@actions Buyer's Guide and Directory. Technology Marketing Corp. • Annual. $25.00. Over 1,100 domestic and foreign suppliers of equipment, products, and services to the telecommunications/telemarketing industry. Formerly *Call Center Solutions Buyer's Guide and Directory.*

HANDBOOKS AND MANUALS

Successful Telemarketing: Opportunities and Techniques for Increasing Sales and Profits. Bob Stone. McGraw-Hill. • 1995. $39.95. Second edition. Includes case histories and examples of effective telemarketing. (NTC Business Books Series).

Total Telemarketing: Complete Guide to Increasing Sales and Profits. Robert J. McHatton. John Wiley and Sons, Inc. • 1988. $16.95.

ONLINE DATABASES

PROMT: Predicasts Overview of Markets and Technology. Gale Cengage Learning. • Companies, products, applied technologies and markets. U.S. and international literature coverage, 1972 to date. Inquire as to online cost and availability. Provides abstracts from more than 1,600 publications. Weekly updates.

Wilson Business Abstracts Online. H. W. Wilson Co. • Indexes and abstracts 600 major business periodicals, plus the *Wall Street Journal* and the business section of the *New York Times.* Indexing is from 1982, abstracting from 1990, with the two newspapers included from 1993. Updated weekly. Inquire as to online cost and availability. (*Business Periodicals Index* without abstracts is also available online.).

PERIODICALS AND NEWSLETTERS

Call Center. CMP Media LLC. • Monthly. Free to qualified personnel. Emphasis is on telemarketing, selling, and customer service. Includes articles on communication technology. Formerly *Call Center Solutions.*

CC News: The Business Newspaper for Call Center and Customer Care Professionals. United Publications, Inc. • Monthly. Free to qualified personnel; others, $60.00 per year. Includes news of call center technical developments.

DM News: The Newspaper of Direct Marketing. Courtenay Communications Corp. • 48 times a year. $49.00 per year. Includes special feature issues on catalog marketing, telephone marketing, database marketing, and fundraising. Includes monthly supplements, *DM News International, DRTV News,* and *TeleServices.*

Target Marketing: The Leading Magazine for Integrated Database Marketing. North American Publishing Co. • Monthly. $65.00 per year. Dedicated to direct marketing excellence. Formerly *Zip Target Marketing.*

Telemarketer. Actel Marketing. • Semimonthly. $285.00 per year. Newsletter.

Telephone Selling Report: Providing Proven Sales Ideas You Can Use. Art Sobczak, editor. Business By Phone, Inc. • Bimonthly. $69.00 per year. Newsletter. How-to newsletter providing proven ideas, tips, and techniques for telephone prospecting and selling.

TRADE/PROFESSIONAL ASSOCIATIONS

American Teleservices Association. 3815 River Crossing Pkwy., Ste. 20, Indianapolis, IN 46240. Phone: 877-779-3974 or (317)816-9336 Fax: (317)218-0323 E-mail: contact@ataconnect.org • URL: http://www.ataconnect.org • Businesses involved in teleservices, telephone marketing sales, including suppliers, distributors, users, and hardware and software manufacturers; educators and teleservice businesses. Provides for the specific needs of the total telephone services community; assists in understanding and using telephone communications for marketing purposes; sponsors educational programs.

OTHER SOURCES

Telemarketing Law Guide. CCH, Inc. • Looseleaf. $700.00. Quarterly updates available. Contains detailed information on federal do-not-call legislation, various state laws, court decisions, and penalties.

TELEMETERING

PERIODICALS AND NEWSLETTERS

Wireless Review: Intelligence for Competitive Providers. Primedia Business Magazines and Media. • Semimonthly. $48.00 per year. Covers business and technology developments for wireless service providers. Includes special issues on a wide variety of wireless topics. Formed by merger of *Cellular Business* and *Wireless World.*

TRADE/PROFESSIONAL ASSOCIATIONS

International Foundation for Telemetering. 5959 Topanga Canyon Blvd., Suite 150, Woodland Hills, CA 91367. Phone: (818)884-9568 Fax: (818)884-9671 E-mail: webmaster@telemetry.org • URL: http://www.telemetry.org.

TELEPHONE ANSWERING SERVICE

HANDBOOKS AND MANUALS

Telephone Answering Service. Entrepreneur Media, Inc. • Looseleaf. $59.50. A practical guide to starting a telephone answering service. Covers profit potential, start-up costs, market size evaluation, owner's time required, pricing, accounting, advertising, promotion, etc. (Start-Up Business Guide No. E1148).

PERIODICALS AND NEWSLETTERS

Answer. Association of Teleservices International. • Bimonthly. Members, $30.00 per year; nonmembers, $50.00 per year.

TeleCommunicator. Association of Teleservices International. • Description: Contains news concerning telephone company, legislative and governmental actions, and Association activities.

STATISTICS SOURCES

United States Census of Service Industries. U.S. Bureau of the Census. • Quinquennial. Various reports available.

TRADE/PROFESSIONAL ASSOCIATIONS

Association of Telephone Answering Services. c/o Monte Engler, Phillips, Nizer, Benjamin Krim and Ballon LLP, 666 Fifth Ave., New York, NY 10103-0084. Phone: (212)977-9700 Fax: (212)262-5152 • URL: http://www.phillipsnizer.com.

Association of Teleservices International. 12 Academy Ave., Atkinson, NH 03811. Phone: (866)892-2874 or (603)362-9489 Fax: (603)362-9486 E-mail: help@atsi.org • URL: http://www.atsi.org • An organization of telephone answering and voice message services.

TELEPHONE EQUIPMENT INDUSTRY

ABSTRACTS AND INDEXES

Applied Science and Technology Index. H. W. Wilson Co. • 11 times a year. Quarterly and annual cumulations. Price varies. Indexes a wide variety of English language technical, industrial, and engineering periodicals.

Science Citation Index. Thomson/ISI. • Bimonthly. $15,020.00 per year. Annual cumulation. Includes *Source Index, Citation Index, Permuterm Subject Index,* and *Corporate Index.*

DIRECTORIES

Better Buys for Business: The Independent Consumer Guide to Office Equipment. What to Buy for Business, Inc. • 10 times a year. $134.00 per year. Each issue is on a particular office product, with detailed evaluation of specific models: 1. Low-Volume Copier Guide, 2. Mid-Volume Copier Guide, 3. High-Volume Copier Guide, 4. Plain Paper Fax and Low-Volume Multifunctional Guide, 5. Mid/High-Volume Multifunctional Guide, 6. Laser Printer Guide, 7. Color Printer and Color Copier Guide, 8. Scan-to-File Guide, 9. Business Phone Systems Guide, 10. Postage Meter Guide, with a Short Guide to Shredders.

Directory of Computer and Consumer Electronics Retailers. Chain Store Guide. • Annual. $335.00. Online edition, $775.00. Lists 4,500 United States and Canada companies operating almost 59,000 stores with at least $1,000,000 in sales.

Major Telecommunications Companies of the World. Available from Gale Cengage Learning. • 2003. $885.00. Sixth edition. Published by Graham & Whiteside. Contains detailed information and trade names for more than 3,500 important telecommunications companies in various countries.

Plunkett's Telecommunications Industry Almanac. Plunkett Research Ltd. • Covers: 500 of the largest companies involved in telecommunications. Entries include: Name, address, phone, fax, names and titles of key personnel, subsidiary and branch names and locations, financial data, salaries and benefits, description of products/services, overview of company culture/activities.

Sound and Communications: The Blue Book. Testa Communications Inc. • Annual. $15.00. Included with subscription. Approximately 1,000 suppliers of sound and communications equipment; including audio/video products in the United States and Canada.

Telecommunications Directory. Gale. • Covers: Two volumes-North America and International, Cover approximately 6,000 national and international voice and data communications networks, electronic mail services, teleconferencing facilities and services, facsimile services, Internet access providers, videotex and teletext operations, transactional services, local area networks, audiotex services, microwave systems/networkers, satellite facilities, and others involved in telecommunications, including related consultants, advertisers/marketers; associations, regulatory bodies, and publishers. Entries include: Company or organization name, address, phone, fax, year established, name and title of contact, executive officers and board of directors, function or type of service; geographical area served; NAICS and SIC codes; number of employees; general description, including telecommunications-related activities; product/service; specific applications; means of access and equipment required; publications; intended market and availability; pricing; stock exchanges traded and ticker symbols; financial figures.

TIA Directory and Desk Reference. Telecommunications Industry Association. • Annual. Members, $50.00; non-members, $100.00. Lists manufacturers and suppliers of interconnect telephone equipment. Formerly *Multimedia Telecommunications Sourcebook.*

FINANCIAL RATIOS

Annual Statement Studies. The Risk Management Association. • Annual. Median and quartile financial ratios are given for over 400 kinds of manufacturing, wholesale, retail, construction, and consumer finance establishments. Data is sorted by both asset size and sales volume. Includes a clearly written "Definition of Ratios" and an alphabetical industry index.

Annual Statement Studies: Industry Default Probabilities and Cash Flow Measures. The Risk Management Association. • Annual. $145.00. Serves as a companion volume to the original *Annual Statement Studies.* Gives probability of default estimates on a percentage scale for more than 450 industries. Includes changes in position year-by-year for eight financial statement line items and provides percentage measures of cash flow.

INTERNET DATABASES

Manufacturing Profiles. U. S. Bureau of the Census. Phone: (301)763-4636 E-mail: webmaster@census.gov • URL: http://www.census.gov/prod/www/abs/mfg-prof.html • The Census Bureau makes available free on PDF (Portable Document Format) an annual consolidation of the entire Current Industrial Report series, presenting "all the data compiled." Contains statistics on production, shipments, inventories, consumption, exports, imports, and orders for a wide variety of manufactured products.

ONLINE DATABASES

Globalbase. Gale Cengage Learning. • Provides more than one million online summaries of business, industrial, and economic news reports from more than 1,000 publications worldwide. Covers a wide range of material appearing in international trade journals, professional magazines, and newspapers. Time period is 1984 to date, with weekly updates. Inquire as to online cost and availability.

PROMT: Predicasts Overview of Markets and Technology. Gale Cengage Learning. • Companies, products, applied technologies and markets. U.S. and international literature coverage, 1972 to date. Inquire as to online cost and availability. Provides abstracts from more than 1,600 publications. Weekly updates.

Scisearch. Institute for Scientific Information. • Broad, multidisciplinary index to the literature of science and technology, 1974 to present. Inquire as to online cost and availability. Coverage of literature is worldwide, with weekly updates.

PERIODICALS AND NEWSLETTERS

America's Network: A Telecommunications Magazine. Advanstar Communications. • 18 times a year. $100.00 per year. Formerly *Telephone Engineer and Management.*

Communications News. Nelson Publishing Co. • Monthly. Free to qualified personnel; others, $84.00 per year.

Communications News: Solutions for Today's Networking Decision Managers. Nelson Publishing, Inc. • Monthly. Free to qualified personnel; others, $84.00 per year. Includes coverage of "Internetworking" and "Intrenetworking." Emphasis is on emerging telecommunications technologies.

IEEE Communications Magazine. Institute of Electrical and Electronics Engineers, Inc. • Monthly. $270.00 per year.

T W I C E: This Week in Consumer Electronics. Reed Business Information. • 29 times a year. $129.90 per year. Contains marketing and manufacturing news relating to a wide variety of consumer electronic products, including video, audio, telephone, and home office equipment.

Telephony: Intelligence for the Broadband Economy. Primedia Business Magazines and Media. • Biweekly. $114.00 per year.

STATISTICS SOURCES

Annual Survey of Manufactures. Available from U. S. Government Printing Office. • Annual. Prices vary. Issued by the U. S. Census Bureau as an interim update to the *Census of Manufactures.* Includes data on number of manufacturing establishments in various industries, employment, labor costs, value of shipments, capital expenditures, inventories, energy costs, and assets. (See also Census Bureau home page, http://www.census.gov/.).

Communication Equipment, and Other Electronic Systems and Equipment. U. S. Bureau of the Census. • Annual. Provides data on shipments: value, quantity, imports, and exports. (Current Industrial Reports, MA-36P.).

Standard & Poor's Industry Surveys. Standard & Poor's. • Semiannual. $1,800.00. Two looseleaf volumes. Includes monthly *Supplements.* Provides detailed, individual surveys of 52 major industry groups. Each survey is revised on a semiannual basis. Also includes "Monthly Investment Review" (industry group investment analysis) and monthly "Trends & Projections" (economic analysis).

TRADE/PROFESSIONAL ASSOCIATIONS

Telecommunications Industry Association. 2500 Wilson Blvd., Ste. 300, Arlington, VA 22201-3834. Phone: 800-799-6682 or (703)907-7700 Fax: (703)907-7727 E-mail: gseiffert@tiaonline.org • URL: http://www.tiaonline.org • Serves the communications and IT industry, with proven strengths in standards development, domestic and international public policy, and trade shows. Facilitates business development and opportunities and a competitive market environment; provides a forum for member companies, the manufacturers and suppliers of products and services used in global communications. Represents the communications sector of the Electronic Industries Alliance.

TELEPHONE INDUSTRY

See also: TELECOMMUNICATIONS

GENERAL WORKS

Telecommunications: Issues in Focus. Agnes S. Corwall, editor. Nova Science Publishers, Inc. • 2002. $69.00. Provides reviews of many aspects of telecommunications, including broadband, wireless, access fees, encryption, telemarketing, telephone bills, remote sensing, and regulation. Includes an index.

DIRECTORIES

Association of Teleservices International-Membership Directory. Association of Teleservices International, Inc. • Annual. $100.00. Lists 825 telephone answering services.

AT & T National Toll-Free Directories. • Annual. Business edition, $24.99 per year; consumer edition, $14.99 per year.

Telecommunications Directory. Gale. • Covers: Two volumes-North America and International, Cover approximately 6,000 national and international voice and data communications networks, electronic mail services, teleconferencing facilities and services, facsimile services, Internet access providers, videotex and teletext operations, transactional services, local area networks, audiotex services, microwave systems/networkers, satellite facilities, and others involved in telecommunications, including related consultants, advertisers/marketers; associations, regulatory bodies, and publishers. Entries include: Company or organization name, address, phone, fax, year established, name and title of contact, executive officers and board of directors, function or type of service; geographical area served; NAICS and SIC codes; number of employees; general description, including telecommunications-related activities; product/service; specific applications; means of access and equipment required; publications; intended market and availability; pricing; stock exchanges traded and ticker symbols; financial figures.

The Telephone Industry Directory. Access Intelligence L.L.C. • Covers: 7,000 companies and 14,000 contacts in the telephone industry.

ENCYCLOPEDIAS AND DICTIONARIES

Hargrave's Communications Dictionary. Frank Hargrave. Available from John Wiley and Sons, Inc. • 2001. $140.00. Published by IEEE. Contains more than 10,000 definitions relating to voice and data communications, plus definitions in the areas of computer science, optics, networks, and the Internet. Includes acronyms, charts, equations, and drawings.

FINANCIAL RATIOS

Almanac of Business and Industrial Financial Ratios. Leo Troy. Aspen Publishers, Inc. • 2003. $125.95. Includes CD-Rom. Contains financial ratios derived from federal tax returns. Ratios for each of about 200 industries are arranged according to company asset size. (Almanac of Business and Industrial Financial Ratios Series).

Annual Statement Studies. The Risk Management Association. • Annual. Median and quartile financial ratios are given for over 400 kinds of manufacturing, wholesale, retail, construction, and consumer finance establishments. Data is sorted by both asset size and sales volume. Includes a clearly written "Definition of Ratios" and an alphabetical industry index.

Annual Statement Studies: Industry Default Probabilities and Cash Flow Measures. The Risk Management Association. • Annual. $145.00. Serves as a companion volume to the original *Annual Statement Studies.* Gives probability of default estimates on a percentage scale for more than 450 industries. Includes changes in position year-by-year for eight financial statement line items and provides percentage measures of cash flow.

Industry Norms and Key Business Ratios. Desk Top Edition. Dun and Bradstreet Corp. • Annual. Five volumes. $475.00 per volume. $1,890.00 per set. Covers over 800 kinds of businesses, arranged by Standard Industrial Classification number. More detailed editions covering longer periods of time are also available.

HANDBOOKS AND MANUALS

Moody's Public Utility Manual. Mergent, Inc. • Annual. $1,995.00. Updated weekly online. Contains financial and other information concerning publicly-held utility companies (electric, gas, telephone, water).

Reference Manual for Telecommunications Engineering. Roger L. Freeman. John Wiley and Sons, Inc. • 2001. $695.00. Third edition. Two volumes. Presents detailed information and specific data on the most commonly used telecommunications standards.

INTERNET DATABASES

Switchboard. Switchboard, Inc. Phone: (508)898-8000 Fax: (508)898-1755 E-mail: webmaster@switchboard.com • URL: http://www.switchboard.com • Web site provides telephone numbers and street addresses for more than 100 million business locations and residences in the U. S. Broad industry categories are available. Fees: Free.

PERIODICALS AND NEWSLETTERS

America's Network: A Telecommunications Magazine. Advantar Communications. • 18 times a year. $100.00 per year. Formerly *Telephone Engineer and Management.*

Communications News. Nelson Publishing Co. • Monthly. Free to qualified personnel; others, $84.00 per year.

Communications News: Solutions for Today's Networking Decision Managers. Nelson Publishing, Inc. • Monthly. Free to qualified personnel; others, $84.00 per year. Includes coverage of "Internetworking" and "Intranetworking." Emphasis is on emerging telecommunications technologies.

FCC Report: An Exclusive Report on Domestic and

International Telecommunications Policy and Regulation. Warren Publishing, Inc. • 26 times a year. $670.00 per year. Newsletter concerned principally with Federal Communications Commission regulations and policy.

Telco Business Report: Executive Briefings on the Bell Operating Companies, Regional Holding Companies and Independent Telcos. Briefings Publishing Group. • 26 times a year. $759.00 per year. Newsletter. Covers long-distance markets, emerging technologies, strategies of Bell operating companies, and other telephone business topics.

Telecommunications. • Monthly. Free to qualified personnel; others, $145.00 per year. International coverage.

Telecommunications Reports. • Weekly. Institutions, $1,695.00 per year. Includes *TR Daily.* Regulatory newsletter.

Telephone Management Strategist. Buyers Laboratory, Inc. • Monthly. $125.00 per year. Newsletter. Information on business telecommunications.

Telephony: Intelligence for the Broadband Economy. Primedia Business Magazines and Media. • Biweekly. $114.00 per year.

X-Change. Virgo Publishing, Inc. • 18 times per year. $70.00 per year. Edited for local telecommunications exchange services, both wireline and wireless.

Yellow Pages and Directory Report: The Newsletter for the Yellow Page and Directory Publishing Industry. SIMBA Information. • 22 times a year. $689.00 per year. Newsletter. Covers the yellow pages publishing industry, including electronic directory publishing, directory advertising, and special interest directories.

Your Telephone Personality. Economics Press, Inc. • Biweekly. $33.00 per year. Telephone skills for office employees.

RESEARCH CENTERS AND INSTITUTES

National Regulatory Research Institute. Ohio State University, 1080 Carmack Rd., Columbus, OH 43210. Phone: (614)292-9404 Fax: (614)292-7196 E-mail: lawton.1@osu.edu • URL: http://www.nrri.ohio-state.edu.

STATISTICS SOURCES

Annual Statistical Reports of Independent Telephone Companies. Federal Communications Commission. • Annual.

Infrastructure Industries USA. Gale Cengage Learning. • 2001. $260.00. Presents statistics and projections relating to economic activity in a wide variety of natural resource and construction industries.

Phonefacts. United States Telephone Association. • Annual. Members, $5.00; non-members, $10.00. Presents basic statistics on the independent telephone industry in the U. S.

Quarterly Operating Data of 68 Telephone Carriers. Federal Communications Commission. • Quarterly.

Standard & Poor's Statistical Service. Current Statistics. Standard & Poor's. • Monthly. $688.00 per year. Includes 10 *Basic Statistics* sections, *Current Statistics Supplements* and *Annual Security Price Index Record.*

TPG Briefing on Local Exchange Statistics. Warren Communication News. • Annual. $325.00. Contains statistics on local telephone companies: revenues, expenses, debt, income, advertising, access lines, network usage, etc. Provides "Current Information on Major Competitors.".

U. S. Industry and Trade Outlook. Available from National Technical Information Service. • Annual. $69.95. Produced by the International Trade Administration, U. S. Department of Commerce, in a "public-private" partnership with DRI/McGraw-

Hill and Standard & Poor's. Provides basic data, outlook for the current year, and "Long-Term Prospects" (five-year projections) for a wide variety of products and services. Includes high technology industries. Formerly *U. S. Industrial Outlook.*

TRADE/PROFESSIONAL ASSOCIATIONS

Competitive Telecommunications Association. 1900 M. St., N.W., Suite 800, Washington, DC 20036. Phone: (202)296-6650 Fax: (202)296-7585 E-mail: tmonroe@comptel.org • URL: http://www.comptel.org • Formerly Association of Long Distance Telephone Companies.

National Telephone Cooperative Association. 4121 Wilson Blvd., 10th Fl., Arlington, VA 22203. Phone: (703)351-2000 Fax: (703)351-2000 E-mail: frs@ntca.com • URL: http://www.ntca.org • Members are telephone cooperatives and statewide associations.

Organization for the Promotion and Advancement of Small Telecommunications Companies. 21 Dupont Circle, N.W., Suite 700, Washington, DC 20036. Phone: (202)659-5990 Fax: (202)659-4619 E-mail: tnb@opastco.org • URL: http://www.opastco.org • Members are small telephone companies serving rural areas. Formerly Organization for the Protection and Advancement of Small Telephone Companies.

Power and Communication Contractors Association. 103 Oronoco St., Ste. 200, Alexandria, VA 22314. Phone: 800-542-7222 or (703)212-7734 Fax: (703)548-3733 E-mail: info@pccaweb.org • URL: http://www.pccaweb.org • Contractors engaged in electrical power and communication line construction.

Telecommunications Industry Association. 2500 Wilson Blvd., Ste. 300, Arlington, VA 22201-3834. Phone: 800-799-6682 or (703)907-7700 Fax: (703)907-7727 E-mail: gseiffert@tiaonline.org • URL: http://www.tiaonline.org • Serves the communications and IT industry, with proven strengths in standards development, domestic and international public policy, and trade shows. Facilitates business development and opportunities and a competitive market environment; provides a forum for member companies, the manufacturers and suppliers of products and services used in global communications. Represents the communications sector of the Electronic Industries Alliance.

United States Telecom Association. 607 14th St. NW, Ste. 400, Washington, DC 20005. Phone: (202)326-7300 Fax: (202)315-3603 E-mail: membership@ustelecom.org • URL: http://www.usta.org • Local operating telephone companies or telephone holding companies. Members represent a total of 114 million access lines. Conducts educational and training programs. Maintains 21 committees.

OTHER SOURCES

Cellular Telephones and Communication Equipment. Available from MarketResearch.com. • 2002. $4,450.00. Published by Global Industry Analysts. Provides worldwide market research data, including profiles of major cell phone manufacturers and service providers.

TELEPHONE SELLING

See also: TELEMARKETING

GENERAL WORKS

Selling by Phone: How to Reach and Sell to Customers. Linda Richardson. McGraw-Hill. • 1995. $14.95.
Teleselling Techniques That Close the Sale. Flyn L. Penoyer. AMACOM. • 1997. $19.95.

HANDBOOKS AND MANUALS

Teleselling: A Self-Teaching Guide. James D. Porterfield. John Wiley and Sons, Inc. • 1996. $24.

95. Second revised edition. Provides practical information and advice on selling by telephone, including strategy, prospecting, script development, and performance evaluation. (Self-Teaching Guides Series, vol. 135).

PERIODICALS AND NEWSLETTERS

Call Center. CMP Media LLC. • Monthly. Free to qualified personnel. Emphasis is on telemarketing, selling, and customer service. Includes articles on communication technology. Formerly *Call Center Solutions.*

TELEPHONES

See: TELEPHONE EQUIPMENT INDUSTRY

TELEPHONES, MOBILE

See: MOBILE TELEPHONE INDUSTRY

TELESCOPES

See also: OPTICS INDUSTRY

HANDBOOKS AND MANUALS

How to Buy and Understand Refracting Telescopes. Jordan Levenson. Levenson Press. • 1991. $43.50. Third edition.

PERIODICALS AND NEWSLETTERS

Astronomy. Kalmbach Publishing Co. • Monthly. $39.95 per year.
Sky and Telescope: The Essential Magazine of Astronomy. Sky Publishing Co. • Monthly. $39.95 per year. Reports astronomy and space science for amateurs and professionals. Many "how to" features.

TELETEXT

See: VIDEOTEX/TELETEXT

TELEVISION ADVERTISING

See: RADIO AND TELEVISION ADVERTISING

TELEVISION APPARATUS INDUSTRY

See also: TELEVISION ENGINEERING; VIDEO RECORDING INDUSTRY

DIRECTORIES

Broadcast Engineering--Equipment Reference Manual. Penton Media Inc. • Publication includes: List of more than 1,400 manufacturers and distributors of communications equipment for radio, television, and recording applications. Entries include: For manufacturers--Company name, address. For distributors and dealers--Company name, address, phone, product or service provided, geographic area covered.
Directory of Computer and Consumer Electronics Retailers. Chain Store Guide. • Annual. $335.00. Online edition, $775.00. Lists 4,500 United States and Canada companies operating almost 59,000 stores with at least $1,000,000 in sales.
DV Buyer's Guide. CMP Media LLC. • Annual. $10.00. A directory of professional video products, including digital cameras, monitors, editing systems, and software.
EIA Publications Index/EIA Trade Directory. Electronic Industries Alliance. • Annual. Free.

Interactive TV Investor Buyer's Guide and Directory. Paul Kagan Associates Inc. • Annual. Price on application. (A special issue of the periodical *Convergence.*).
The SHOOT Directory for Commercial Production and Postproduction. SHOOT. • Annual. $79.00. Lists production companies, advertising agencies, and sources of professional television, motion picture, and audio equipment.
Video Systems: Equipment Buyer's Guide. Primedia Business Magazines and Media. • Annual. $10.00. Lists approximately 1,000 manufacturers and suppliers of professional video equipment.

ENCYCLOPEDIAS AND DICTIONARIES

Encyclopedia of Emerging Industries. Gale Cengage Learning. • 2001. $320.00. Fourth edition. Provides detailed information on 115 "newly flourishing" industries. Includes historical background, organizational structure, significant individuals, current conditions, major companies, work force, technology trends, research developments, and other industry facts.

FINANCIAL RATIOS

Annual Statement Studies. The Risk Management Association. • Annual. Median and quartile financial ratios are given for over 400 kinds of manufacturing, wholesale, retail, construction, and consumer finance establishments. Data is sorted by both asset size and sales volume. Includes a clearly written "Definition of Ratios" and an alphabetical industry index.
Annual Statement Studies: Industry Default Probabilities and Cash Flow Measures. The Risk Management Association. • Annual. $145.00. Serves as a companion volume to the original *Annual Statement Studies.* Gives probability of default estimates on a percentage scale for more than 450 industries. Includes changes in position year-by-year for eight financial statement line items and provides percentage measures of cash flow.
NARDA's Cost of Doing Business Survey. North American Retail Dealers Association. • Annual. $295.00.

HANDBOOKS AND MANUALS

Home Entertainment Installation. Entrepreneur Media, Inc. • Looseleaf. $59.50. A practical guide to starting a home entertainment installation service. Covers profit potential, start-up costs, market size evaluation, owner's time required, pricing, accounting, advertising, promotion, etc. (Start-Up Business Guide No. E1349.).

INTERNET DATABASES

Manufacturing Profiles. U. S. Bureau of the Census. Phone: (301)763-4636 E-mail: webmaster@census.gov • URL: http://www.census.gov/prod/www/abs/mfg-prof.html • The Census Bureau makes available free on PDF (Portable Document Format) an annual consolidation of the entire Current Industrial Report series, presenting "all the data compiled." Contains statistics on production, shipments, inventories, consumption, exports, imports, and orders for a wide variety of manufactured products.

PERIODICALS AND NEWSLETTERS

Convergence: The Journal of Research Into New Media Technologies. Reed Business Information. • Monthly. Individuals, $40.00 per year; institutions, $160.00 per year. Covers the merging of communications technologies. Includes telecommunications networks, interactive TV, multimedia, wireless phone service, and electronic information services.
Dealerscope: Product and Strategy for Consumer Technology Retailing. North American Publishing Co. • Monthly. Free to qualified personnel; others, $79.00 per year. Formerly *Dealerscope Consumer Electronics Marketplace.*
Digital Video. CMP Media LLC. • Monthly. $60.00

per year. Edited for professionals in the field of digital video production. Covers such topics as operating systems, videography, digital video cameras, audio, workstations, web video, software development, and interactive television.

NARDA Independent Retailer. North American Retail Dealers Association. • Monthly. $78.00. Formerly *NARDA News.*

Robb Report Home Entertaining & Design. CurtCo Robb Media. • Nine times a year. $21.95 per year. Covers "high end" home theaters, audio, video, wireless home networks, and custom installations.

Smart TV and Sound: Interactive Television and DVD-MP3-Internet Audio and Video-Satellite Television. York Publishing. • Semiannual. $14.97 per year. Consumer magazine covering WebTV, PC/TV appliances, DVD players, "Smart TV," advanced VCRs, and other topics relating to interactive television, the Internet, and multimedia. Formerly *Smart TV.*

Video Technology News. Access Intelligence L.L.C. • Description: Reports on video technologies from a business point of view. Provides industry analyses and forecasts, reports on new products and emerging media trends. Covers legal and regulatory developments. **Remarks:** Incorporates the former FutureHome Technology News, merged December 1992.

Videography. United Entertainment Media. • Monthly. $72.00 per year. Edited for the professional video production industry. Covers trends in technique and technology.

PRICE SOURCES

Video and Television. Orion Research Corp. • Annual. $144.00. Quotes retail and wholesale prices of used video and TV equipment. Original list prices and years of manufacture are also shown.

STATISTICS SOURCES

Annual Survey of Manufactures. Available from U. S. Government Printing Office. • Annual. Prices vary. Issued by the U. S. Census Bureau as an interim update to the *Census of Manufactures.* Includes data on number of manufacturing establishments in various industries, employment, labor costs, value of shipments, capital expenditures, inventories, energy costs, and assets. (See also Census Bureau home page, http://www.census.gov/.).

Electronic Market Data Book. Consumer Electronics Association. • Annual. Price on application.

Standard & Poor's Industry Surveys. Standard & Poor's. • Semiannual. $1,800.00. Two looseleaf volumes. Includes monthly *Supplements.* Provides detailed, individual surveys of 52 major industry groups. Each survey is revised on a semiannual basis. Also includes "Monthly Investment Review" (industry group investment analysis) and monthly "Trends & Projections" (economic analysis).

TRADE/PROFESSIONAL ASSOCIATIONS

Electronic Industries Alliance. 2500 Wilson Blvd., Arlington, VA 22201. Phone: (703)907-7500 Fax: (703)907-7501 E-mail: mflanigan@eia.org • URL: http://www.eia.org • Seeks for the competitiveness of the American producer, represents all companies involved in the design and manufacture of electronic components, parts, systems and equipment for communications, industrial, government and consumer uses.

North American Retail Dealers Association. 4700 W Lake Ave., Glenview, IL 60025. Phone: 800-621-0298 or (847)375-4713 Fax: (866)879-7505 E-mail: nardasvc@narda.com • URL: http://www.narda.com • Firms engaged in the retailing of electronic and electrical devices and components. Promotes and represents members' interests. Makes available services to members including: legal and technical consulting; employee screening; bank card process-

ing; long-distance phone discounts; financial statements analysis; in-store promotion kits; customer check authorization. Advocates for members' interests before federal regulatory bodies; disseminates information on new regulations affecting members. Conducts educational programs.

OTHER SOURCES

New-Format Digital Television. Available from MarketResearch.com. • 1999. $3,995.00. Market research data. Published by Fuji- Keizai USA. Covers the developing U. S. market for digital TV.

U. S. Home Theater Market. Available from MarketResearch.com. • 1997. $1,3750.00. Market research report published by Packaged Facts. Covers big-screen TV, high definition TV, audio equipment, and video sources. Market projections are provided.

TELEVISION BROADCASTING INDUSTRY

See also: CABLE TELEVISION INDUSTRY; TELEVISION APPARATUS INDUSTRY; TELEVISION ENGINEERING

GENERAL WORKS

Minority Broadcast Ownership. Gregory L. Rohde. Nova Science Publishers, Inc. • 2002. $29.50. Provides discussion and statistical data relating to minority ownership of radio and television stations in the U.S.

Perspectives on Radio and Television: Telecommunication in the United States. F. Leslie Smith and others. Lawrence Erlbaum Associates, Inc. • 1998. Fourth edition. Price on application. (Communication Series).

ABSTRACTS AND INDEXES

Communication Abstracts: An International Information Service. Sage Publications, Inc. • Bimonthly. Institutions, $1,150.00 per year. Provides broad coverage of the literature of communications, including broadcasting and advertising.

BIOGRAPHICAL SOURCES

Biographical Dictionary of American Journalism. Joseph P. McKerns, editor. Greenwood Publishing Group Inc. • 1989. $92.95. Covers major mass media: newspapers, radio, television, and magazines. Includes reporters, editors, columnists, cartoonists, commentators, etc.

Celebrity Register. Gale Cengage Learning. • 1990. $115.00. 90th edition. Compiled by Celebrity Services International (Earl Blackwell). Contains profiles of 1,300 famous individuals in the performing arts, sports, politics, business, and other fields.

Contemporary Theatre, Film, and Television. Gale Cengage Learning. • 2003. Three volumes. $185.00 per volume. Previous volumes available. Provides detailed biographical and career information on more than 11,000 currently popular performers, directors, writers, producers, designers, managers, choreographers, technicians, composers, executives, dancers, and critics.

The Highwaymen: Warriors on the Information Superhighway. Ken Auletta. Harcourt Trade Publications. • 1998. $13.00. Revised expanded edition. Contains critical articles about Ted Turner, Rupert Murdoch, Barry Diller, Michael Eisner, and other key figures in electronic communications, entertainment, and information. (Harvest Book Series).

CD-ROM DATABASES

Hoover's Company Capsules on CD-ROM. Hoover's, Inc. • Quarterly. $399.95 per year (single-user). Provides the CD-ROM version of *Hoover's Handbook of American Business, Hoover's*

Handbook of Emerging Companies, Hoover's Handbook of World Business, Hoover's Guide to Computer Companies, Hoover's Guide to Media Companies, Hoover's Handbook of Private Companies, and various regional guides. Includes more than 11,000 profiles of companies.

Magazine Index Plus. Gale Cengage Learning. • Monthly. $4,000.00 per year (includes InfoTrac workstation). Provides full text on CD-ROM for about 100 popular, general interest magazines and indexing for 300 others. Includes special indexing of reviews and product evaluations. Time period is 1980 to date.

DIRECTORIES

Bacon's Radio/TV/Cable Directory. Bacon's Information, Inc. • Annual. $325.00. Includes educational and public broadcasters. Covers all United States broadcast media.

Broadcasting and Cable Yearbook. Gale. • Annual. $179.95. Provides information on U. S. and Canadian TV stations, radio stations, cable TV companies, and radio-TV services of various kinds.

Burrelle's Media Directory: Broadcast Media. Burrelle's Information Services. • Annual. $550.00. Approximately 48,000 print and electronic media in North America. Provides detailed descriptions, including programming and key personnel.

Gale Directory of Publications and Broadcast Media. Gale Cengage Learning. • Annual. $770.00. Five volumes. *Interedition Supplement,* Free. A guide to publications and broadcasting stations in the U. S. and Canada, including newspapers, magazines, journals, radio stations, television stations, and cable systems. Geographic arrangement. Volume three consists of statistical tables, maps, subject indexes, and title index.

Hollywood Creative Directory: International Film Buyers. • Annual. $59.95. Lists more than 1,750 film and television buyers. Worldwide coverage.

International Television and Video Almanac: Reference Tool of the Television and Home Video Industries. Quigley Publishing Co., Inc. • Annual. $130.00.

NATPE International--Media Content Directory. National Association of Television Program Executives Inc. • Covers: distributors of television programs. Entries include: Company name, address, phone, telex, fax, names and titles of key personnel, description of company, list of programs available.

NATPE: Pocket Guides Reps Groups Distributors. National Association of Television Program Executives. • Semiannual. Free to members; nonmembers, $75.00 per year. Includes station representatives, group owners (with stations owned), and program distributors.

News Media Yellow Book: Who's Who Among Reporters, Writers, Editors, and Producers in the Leading National News Media. Leadership Directories, Inc. • Quarterly. $360.00 per year. Lists the staffs of major newspapers and news magazines, TV and radio networks, news services and bureaus, and feature syndicates. Includes syndicated columnists and programs. Seven specialized indexes are provided.

Pocket Station Listing Guide. Publications Dept. • Covers: 1,500 network-affiliated, independent, and public television stations in the U.S., Canada, and Latin America. Entries include: Station name, address, phone, fax, names and titles of key personnel, geographical area served, call letters, channel station numbers, owner, sales representative.

Producers Directory. IFILM Publishing. • Covers: over 1,700 film and TV production companies, studios, networks, and TV shows, and over 7,700 creative executives within those companies. Majority of listings are located in Los Angeles and New York. Entries include: Company name, staff names and titles, address, phone, fax, e-mail address, web site address, company type, studio deals, and select credits.

Producer's Masterguide: The International Film Production Guide and Directory for Motion Picture, Television, Industries in the United States, the United Kingdom, Europe, the Caribbean Islands, Mexico, Israel, Morocco and Australia. • Annual. $140.00. A standard reference guide of the professional film, television, commercial and video tape industry throughout the U.S. and Canada, Europe, the Caribbean Islands, Mexico, Israel, Morocco, Australia, etc.

SRDS TV and Cable Source. SRDS. • Quarterly. $525.00 per year. Provides detailed information on U. S. television stations, cable systems, networks, and group owners, with maps and market data. Includes key personnel.

Working Press of the Nation. R. R. Bowker. • Annual. $530.00. $295.00 per volume. Three volumes: (1) *Newspaper Directory*; (2) *Magazine and Internal Publications Directory*; (3) *Radio and Television Directory*. Includes names of editors and other personnel.

World Radio TV Handbook. World Radio TV Handbook. • Covers: 25,000 radio and television stations worldwide; national regulatory bodies. Entries include: For stations--Name, frequency, address, phone, telex, name and title of contact and key personnel, description of programming. For agencies--Name, address, phone.

ENCYCLOPEDIAS AND DICTIONARIES

Broadcast Communications Dictionary. Lincoln Diamant, editor. Greenwood Publishing Group Inc. • 1989. $57.95. Third revised edition.

Encyclopedia of Television. Horace Newcomb, editor. Fitzroy Dearborn Publishers, Inc. • 1997. $350.00. Three volumes. Contains about 1,000 entries on TV performers, programs, organizations, social issues, technical aspects, and historical details.

International Film, Television, and Video Acronyms. Matthew Stevens, editor. Greenwood Publishing Group, Inc. • 1993. $85.00. A guide to 3,400 acronyms and 1,400 technical terms.

Multimedia and the Web from A to Z. David C. Leonard and Patrick M. Dillon. Greenwood Publishing Group, Inc. • 1998. $42.95. Second enlarged revised edition. Defines more than 1,500 terms relating to software and hardware in the areas of computing, online technology, telecommunications, audio, video, motion pictures, CD-ROM, and the Internet. Includes acronyms and an annotated bibliography. Formerly *Multimedia Technology from A to Z* (1994).

FINANCIAL RATIOS

Almanac of Business and Industrial Financial Ratios. Leo Troy. Aspen Publishers, Inc. • 2003. $125.95. Includes CD-Rom. Contains financial ratios derived from federal tax returns. Ratios for each of about 200 industries are arranged according to company asset size. (Almanac of Business and Industrial Financial Ratios Series).

Annual Statement Studies. The Risk Management Association. • Annual. Median and quartile financial ratios are given for over 400 kinds of manufacturing, wholesale, retail, construction, and consumer finance establishments. Data is sorted by both asset size and sales volume. Includes a clearly written "Definition of Ratios" and an alphabetical industry index.

Annual Statement Studies: Industry Default Probabilities and Cash Flow Measures. The Risk Management Association. • Annual. $145.00. Serves as a companion volume to the original *Annual Statement Studies*. Gives probability of default estimates on a percentage scale for more than 450

industries. Includes changes in position year-by-year for eight financial statement line items and provides percentage measures of cash flow.

Industry Norms and Key Business Ratios. Desk Top Edition. Dun and Bradstreet Corp. • Annual. Five volumes. $475.00 per volume. $1,890.00 per set. Covers over 800 kinds of businesses, arranged by Standard Industrial Classification number. More detailed editions covering longer periods of time are also available.

HANDBOOKS AND MANUALS

Contracts for the Film and Television Industry. Mark Litwak. Silman-James Press. • 1999. $35.95. Second expanded edition. Contains a wide variety of sample entertainment contracts. Includes material on rights, employment, joint ventures, music, financing, production, distribution, merchandising, and the retaining of attorneys.

Dun & Bradstreet/Gale Group Industry Handbooks. Gale Cengage Learning. • 2000. $650.00. Five volumes. $130.00 per volume. Each volume covers two or more major industries: 1. *Entertainment and Hospitality*; 2. *Construction and Agriculture*; 3. *Chemicals and Pharmaceuticals*; 4. *Computers & Software and Broadcasting & Telecommunications*; 5. *Insurance and Health & Medical Services*. The following are included for each industry: overview, statistics, financial ratios, rankings, merger information, company directory, directory of associations, and consultants directory. (Dun and Bradstreet/Gale Industry Reference Handbook Series).

Entertainment Law: Legal Concepts and Business Practices. West Group. • Annual. $560.00. Five looseleaf volumes.

Television Production Handbook. Herbert Zettl. Wadsworth Publishing Co. • 2000. $95.95. Seventh edition. (Radio/TV/Film Series).

ONLINE DATABASES

Gale Database of Publications and Broadcast Media. Gale Cengage Learning. • An online directory containing detailed information on over 67,000 periodicals, newspapers, broadcast stations, cable systems, directories, and newsletters. Corresponds to the following print sources: *Gale Directory of Publications and Broadcast Media; Directories in Print; City and State Directories in Print; Newsletters in Print*. Semiannual updates. Inquire as to online cost and availability.

Newspaper Abstracts Daily. ProQuest Inc. • Provides online coverage (citations and abstracts) of 25 major newspapers. Covers business, economics, current affairs, health, fitness, sports, education, technology, government, consumer affairs, psychology, the arts, and the social sciences. Time period is 1986 to date, with daily updates. Inquire as to online cost and availability.

PROMT: Predicasts Overview of Markets and Technology. Gale Cengage Learning. • Companies, products, applied technologies and markets. U.S. and international literature coverage, 1972 to date. Inquire as to online cost and availability. Provides abstracts from more than 1,600 publications. Weekly updates.

PERIODICALS AND NEWSLETTERS

Broadcast Investor: Newsletter on Radio-TV Station Finance. Paul Kagan Associates, Inc. • Monthly. $925.00 per year. Newsletter for investors in publicly held radio and television broadcasting companies.

Broadcasting and Cable. Reed Business Information. • 51 times a year. $179.00 per year; includes print and online editions. Formerly *Broadcasting*.

Digital TV Television Broadcast. United Entertainment Media. • Monthly. $52.00 per year. Contains articles on management, production, and technology for TV stations. Formerly *Digital TV*.

Entertainment Law and Finance. American Lawyer Media, Inc. • Monthly. $229.00 per year. Newsletter. Covers contracts, royalties, litigation, copyright, taxation, etc., for the music industry, motion pictures, broadcasting, publishing, video, and related media. (A Law Journal Newsletter, formerly published by Leader Publications.).

Entertainment Marketing Letter. EPM Communications Inc. • Description: Reports on techniques used in the marketing of films, music, videos, television, radio, and cable features. Covers tie-in campaigns, sponsorship, in-theatre advertising, and interactive telephone promotions.

The Hollywood Reporter. • Daily. $219.00 per year. Covers the latest news in film, TV, cable, multimedia, music, and theatre. Includes box office grosses and entertainment industry financial data.

International Radio and Television Society Newsletter. International Radio and Television Society. • Quarterly.

Ross Reports Television and Film: Casting, Production, Scripts. VNU Business Media. • 10 times a year. $59.00. per year. Directory, production and casting guide, designed for actors and writers. Formerly *Ross Reports Television*.

Television Digest with Consumer Electronics. Warren Publishing, Inc. • Weekly. $944.00 per year. Newsletter featuring new consumer entertainment products utilizing electronics. Also covers the television broadcasting and cable TV industries, with corporate and industry news.

Television Quarterly. National Academy of Television Arts and Sciences. • Quarterly. Individuals, $30.00 per year; students, $22.00 per year.

Television Week. Crain Communications, Inc. • Weekly. $119.00 per year. Formerly *Electronic Media*.

TV Technology. IMAS Publishing Group. • Biweekly. $75.00 per year. International coverage available.

Variety: The International Entertainment Weekly. Reed Business Information. • 50 times a year. $259.00 per year. Contains national and international news of show business, with emphasis on motion pictures and television. Includes *Market* and *Special Focus* issues.

Video Week: Devoted to the Business of Program Sales and Distribution for Videocassettes, Disc, Pay TV and Allied News Media. Warren Publishing Inc. • Weekly. $907.00 per year. Newsletter. Covers video industry news and corporate developments.

RESEARCH CENTERS AND INSTITUTES

Center for Mass Media Research. Marquette University, 1131 W. Wisconsin Ave., Milwaukee, WI 53233. Phone: (414)288-3453 E-mail: robert. griffin@marquette.edu.

Institute for Telecommunications Studies. Ohio University, Nine S. College St., Athens, OH 45701. Phone: (740)593-4870 Fax: (740)593-9184 E-mail: don.flournoy@ohiou.edu • URL: http://www.ou. edu.

STATISTICS SOURCES

Infrastructure Industries USA. Gale Cengage Learning. • 2001. $260.00. Presents statistics and projections relating to economic activity in a wide variety of natural resource and construction industries.

SRDS Circulation [year]. SRDS. • Annual. $297. 00. Contains detailed statistical analysis of newspaper circulation by metropolitan area or county and data on television viewing by area. Includes maps. Formerly*Circulation Year*.

Standard & Poor's Industry Surveys. Standard & Poor's. • Semiannual. $1,800.00. Two looseleaf volumes. Includes monthly *Supplements*. Provides detailed, individual surveys of 52 major industry groups. Each survey is revised on a semiannual basis. Also includes "Monthly Investment Review" (industry group investment analysis) and monthly "Trends & Projections" (economic analysis).

Television and Cable Factbook. Warren Publishing, Inc. • Annual. $595.00. Three volumes. Weekly updates. Commercial and noncommercial television stations and networks.

U. S. Industry Profiles: The Leading 100. Gale Cengage Learning. • 1998. $130.00. Second edition. Contains detailed profiles, with statistics, of 100 industries in the areas of manufacturing, construction, transportation, wholesale trade, retail trade, and entertainment.

United States Census of Service Industries. U.S. Bureau of the Census. • Quinquennial. Various reports available.

TRADE/PROFESSIONAL ASSOCIATIONS

Academy of Television Arts and Sciences. 5220 Lankershim Blvd., North Hollywood, CA 91601. Phone: (818)754-2800 Fax: (818)761-2827 E-mail: bryce@emmys.org • URL: http://www.emmys.org.

Alliance of Motion Picture and Television Producers. 15503 Ventura Blvd., Encino, CA 91436-3140. Phone: (818)995-3600 Fax: (818)382-1793 E-mail: info@tw.amptp.org • URL: http://www.amptp.org.

American Federation of Television and Radio Artists. 260 Madison Ave., New York, NY 10016-2402. Phone: (212)532-0800 Fax: (212)532-2242 E-mail: aftra@aftra.com • URL: http://www.aftra.com • Formerly American Federation of Radio Artist.

American Sportscasters Association. 225 Broadway, Ste. 2030, New York, NY 10007. Phone: (212)227-8080 Fax: (212)571-0556 E-mail: lschwa8918@aol.com • URL: http://www.americansportscastersonline.com • Radio and television sportscasters. Sponsors seminars, clinics, and symposia for aspiring announcers and sportscasters. Compiles statistics. Operates Speaker's Bureau, placement service, hall of fame, and biographical archives. Maintains American Sportscaster Hall of Fame Trust. Is currently implementing Hall of Fame Museum, Community Programs.

American Women in Radio and Television. 8405 Greensboro Dr., Ste. 800, McLean, VA 22102. Phone: (703)506-3290 Fax: (703)506-3266 E-mail: info@awrt.org • URL: http://www.awrt.org.

Association of America's Public Television Stations. 666 11th St. NW, Washington, DC 20001. Phone: (202)654-4200 Fax: (202)654-4236 E-mail: john@apts.org • URL: http://www.apts.org.

Association of Local Television Stations. 1320 19th St., N.W., Suite 300, Washington, DC 20036. Phone: (202)887-1970 Fax: (202)887-0950 E-mail: altv@aol.com • URL: http://www.altv.com • Members are TV stations not affiliated with a major network.

Broadcast Cable Financial Management Association, Inc. 929 Lee St., Ste. 204, Des Plaines, IL 60016. Phone: (847)296-0200 Fax: (847)296-7510 E-mail: mcollins@bcfm.com • URL: http://www.bcfm.com • Members are accountants and other financial personnel in the radio and television broadcasting industries. Formerly Broadcast Financial Management Association.

Corporation for Public Broadcasting. 401 E St., N.W., Washington, DC 20004-2149. Phone: (202)879-9600 Fax: (202)879-9700 E-mail: comments@cpb.org • URL: http://www.cpb.org.

International Radio and Television Society Foundation. 420 Lexington Ave., Suite 1714, New York, NY 10170. Phone: (212)867-6650 Fax: (212)867-6653 • URL: http://www.irts.org • Affiliated with National Broadcasting Society-Alpha Epsilon Pho. Formerly International Radio and Television Society.

Media Rating Council. 370 Lexington Ave., Ste. 902, New York, NY 10017. Phone: (212)972-0300 Fax: (212)972-2786 E-mail: staff@mediaratingcouncil.org • URL: http://www.mediaratingcouncil.org • Broadcast and cable trade associations, media owners, advertising agencies, cable networks, and national networks including National Association of Broadcasters, Television Bureau of Advertising, Radio Advertising Bureau, Cable Advertising Bureau (see separate entries). Establishes minimum standards for electronic media ratings surveys. Commissions audits by CPA firms of the collection and processing of data gathered by audience measurement services, including A.C. Nielsen, Arbitron, Statistical Research Inc., and Mediafax. **Convention/Meeting:** none.

National Academy of Television Arts and Sciences. 111 W. 57th St., Suite 1020, New York, NY 10019. Phone: (212)586-8424 Fax: (212)246-8129 E-mail: natashq@aol.com • URL: http://www.emmyonline.com.

National Association of Black Owned Broadcasters. 1155 Connecticut, NW, Ste. 600, Washington, DC 20036. Phone: (202)463-8970 Fax: (202)429-0657 E-mail: info@nabob.org • URL: http://www.nabob.org.

National Association of Broadcasters. 1771 N St., NW, Washington, DC 20036. Phone: (202)429-5300 Fax: (202)429-4199 E-mail: sdelanghe@nab.org • URL: http://www.nab.org • Formerly National Association of Radio and Television Broadcasters.

National Association of Television Program Executives. 2425 Olympic Blvd., Suite 600E, Santa Monica, CA 90404. Phone: 800-628-7346 or (310)453-4440 Fax: (310)453-5258 E-mail: info@natpe.org • URL: http://www.natpe.org • Formerly National Association of Television Program Executives.

National Sportscasters and Sportswriters Association. 322 E Innes St., Salisbury, NC 28144. Phone: (704)633-4275 Fax: (704)633-2027 • Members are sportswriters and radio/TV sportscasters.

PROMAX. 9000 W Sunset Blvd., Ste. 900, Los Angeles, CA 90069. Phone: (310)788-7600 Fax: (310)788-7616 E-mail: michael.d.benson@abc.com • URL: http://www.promax.tv • Advertising, public relations, and promotion managers of cable, radio, and television stations, systems and networks; syndicators. Seeks to: advance the role and increase the effectiveness of promotion and marketing within the industry, related industries, and educational communities. Conducts workshops and weekly fax service for members. Operates employment service. Maintains speakers' bureau, hall of fame, and resource center with print, audio, and visual materials.

Society for the Eradication of Television. PO Box 10491, Oakland, CA 94610-0491. Phone: (510)763-8712 E-mail: set.info@webwm.com • URL: http://www.webwm.com/set • Encourages the removal of television sets from homes.

Society of Broadcast Engineers. 9247 N Meridian St., Ste. 305, Indianapolis, IN 46260. Phone: (317)846-9000 Fax: (317)846-9120 E-mail: jporay@sbe.org • URL: http://www.sbe.org • Broadcast engineers, students and broadcast professionals in closely allied fields. Formerly Institute of Braodcast Engineers.

Society of Motion Picture and Television Engineers. 595 W Hartsdale Ave., White Plains, NY 10607. Phone: (914)761-1100 Fax: (914)761-3115 E-mail: smpte@smpte.org • URL: http://www.smpte.org • Professional engineers and technicians in motion poctures, television, motion imaging and allied arts and sciences.

Station Representatives Association. 16 W. 77th St. No. 9-E, New York, NY 10024-5126. Phone:

(212)362-8868 Fax: (212)362-4999 E-mail: srajerry@aol.com • Sales representatives for television stations concerned with the sale of "spot" advertising. **Publications:** none.

Television Bureau of Advertising. Three E. 54th St., New York, NY 10022. Phone: (212)486-1111 Fax: (212)935-5631 E-mail: info@tvb.org • URL: http://www.tvb.org.

OTHER SOURCES

FCC Record. Available from U. S. Government Printing Office. • Biweekly. $678.00 per year. Produced by the Federal Communications Commission (http://www.fcc.gov). An inclusive compilation of decisions, reports, public notices, and other documents of the FCC.

The Market for Interactive Television. MarketResearch.com. • 2000. $995.00. Market research data.

North American Interactive Television Markets. Available from MarketResearch.com. • 1999. $3,450.00. Published by Frost & Sullivan. Contains market research data on growth, end-user trends, and market strategies. Company profiles are included.

Sports and Entertainment Litigation Reporter. Andrews Publications. • Monthly. $899.00 per year. Newsletter. Provides reports on lawsuits involving films, TV, cable broadcasting, stage productions, radio, and other areas of the entertainment business. Formerly *Sports and Entertainment Litigation Reporter.*

Telecommunications Regulation: Cable, Broadcasting, Satellite, and the Internet. LexisNexis Matthew Bender. • Semiannual. $826.00. Four looseleaf volumes. Covers local, state, and federal regulation, with emphasis on the Telecommunications Act of 1996. Includes regulation of television, telephone, cable, satellite, computer communication, and online services. Formerly *Cable Television Law.*

TELEVISION, CABLE

See: CABLE TELEVISION INDUSTRY

TELEVISION ENGINEERING

See also: TELEVISION APPARATUS INDUSTRY

DIRECTORIES

Broadcast Engineering--Equipment Reference Manual. Penton Media Inc. • Publication includes: List of more than 1,400 manufacturers and distributors of communications equipment for radio, television, and recording applications. Entries include: For manufacturers--Company name, address. For distributors and dealers--Company name, address, phone, product or service provided, geographic area covered.

Video Systems: Equipment Buyer's Guide. Primedia Business Magazines and Media. • Annual. $10.00. Lists approximately 1,000 manufacturers and suppliers of professional video equipment.

HANDBOOKS AND MANUALS

Creating Digital Content: A Video Production for Web, Broadcast, and Cinema. John Rice and Brian McKernan. McGraw-Hill. • 2001. $49.95. Discusses the technicalities of digital content with a light touch, as in "Throw Another Analog on the Digital Fire." Other chapter titles are "Digital Recording," "Datacasting," "Coming to a Theatre Near You: Digital Cinema," and "The Promise of Digital Interactive Television.".

Master Handbook of Video Production. Jerry Whitaker. McGraw-Hill. • 2002. $39.95. Covers such technical topics as facility design, sound isolation, production standards, video signal processing, lighting, and equipment.

Standard Handbook of Video and Television Engineering. Jerry C. Whitaker. McGraw-Hill. • 2000. $150.00. Fourth edition. Covers the design, production, installation, operation, and maintenance of video recording or TV broadcasting facilities.

Video Engineering. Arch Luther and Andrew Inglis. McGraw-Hill. • 2000. $65.00. Third edition. Covers such topics as digital postproduction technology, streaming video on the Internet, digital HDTV, digital cameras, and satellite TV systems.

PERIODICALS AND NEWSLETTERS

Broadcast Engineering: Journal of Broadcast Technology. Primedia Business Magazines and Media. • 10 times a year. Free to qualified personnel; others, $65.00 per year. Technical magazine for the broadcast industry.

SHOOT: The Leading Newsweekly for Commercial Production and Postproduction. VNU Business Media. • Weekly. $125.00 per year. Covers animation, music, sound design, computer graphics, visual effects, cinematography, and other aspects of television and motion picture production, with emphasis on TV commercials.

SMPTE Motion Imaging Journal. Society of Motion Picture and Television Engineers. • Monthly. Membership. Formerly *SMPTE Journal.*

Video Systems: The Magazine for Video Professionals. Primedia Business Magazines and Media. • Monthly. $70.00 per year.

Video Technology News. Access Intelligence L.L.C. • Description: Reports on video technologies from a business point of view. Provides industry analyses and forecasts, reports on new products and emerging media trends. Covers legal and regulatory developments. **Remarks:** Incorporates the former FutureHome Technology News, merged December 1992.

Videography. United Entertainment Media. • Monthly. $72.00 per year. Edited for the professional video production industry. Covers trends in technique and technology.

TRADE/PROFESSIONAL ASSOCIATIONS

Society of Motion Picture and Television Engineers. 595 W Hartsdale Ave., White Plains, NY 10607. Phone: (914)761-1100 Fax: (914)761-3115 E-mail: smpte@smpte.org • URL: http://www.smpte.org • Professional engineers and technicians in motion pictures, television, motion imaging and allied arts and sciences.

TELEVISION, FOREIGN

See: FOREIGN RADIO AND TELEVISION

TELEVISION PROGRAMS

DIRECTORIES

NATPE International--Media Content Directory. National Association of Television Program Executives Inc. • Covers: distributors of television programs. Entries include: Company name, address, phone, telex, fax, names and titles of key personnel, description of company, list of programs available.

HANDBOOKS AND MANUALS

Creativity Rules! A Writer's Workbook. John Vorhaus. Silman-James Press. • 1999. $15.95. Covers the practical process of conceiving, outlining, and developing a story, especially for TV or film scripts. Includes "tactics and exercises.".

PERIODICALS AND NEWSLETTERS

Better Radio and Television. National Association for Better Broadcasting. • Quarterly. $6.00 per year.

Digital TV Television Broadcast. United Entertainment Media. • Monthly. $52.00 per year. Contains articles on management, production, and technology for TV stations. Formerly *Digital TV.*

Multichannel News. Reed Business Information. • 51 times a year. $139.00 per year. Covers the business, programming, market and technology concerns of cable television operators and their suppliers:

The TV Guide. Gemstar-TV Guide International. • Weekly. $46.28 per year.

STATISTICS SOURCES

Nielsen Report on Television. Nielsen Media Research. • Annual. $25.00. General statistics on television programming, plus ranking of the year's most popular shows. Pamphlet.

TRADE/PROFESSIONAL ASSOCIATIONS

National Association of Television Program Executives. 2425 Olympic Blvd., Suite 600E, Santa Monica, CA 90404. Phone: 800-628-7346 or (310)453-4440 Fax: (310)453-5258 E-mail: info@natpe.org • URL: http://www.natpe.org • Formerly National Association of Television Program Executives.

TELEVISION RECORDING

See: VIDEO RECORDING INDUSTRY

TELEVISION REPAIR INDUSTRY

See: RADIO AND TELEVISION REPAIR INDUSTRY

TELEVISION, SATELLITE

See: COMMUNICATIONS SATELLITES

TELEVISION STATIONS

See: TELEVISION BROADCASTING INDUSTRY

TELLER MACHINES

See: BANK AUTOMATION

TEMPERATURE (CLIMATE)

See: CLIMATE; WEATHER AND WEATHER FORECASTING

TEMPORARY EMPLOYEES

GENERAL WORKS

Flesh Peddlers and Warm Bodies: The Temporary Help Industry and Its Workers. Robert E. Parker. Rutgers University Press. • 1994. $40.00. A critical view of temporary work. (Arnold and Caroline Rose Monograph Series of the American Sociological Association).

Managing Contingent Workers: How to Reap the Benefits and Reduce the Risk. Helen Axel and Stanley Nollen. AMACOM. • 1995. $55.00.

ABSTRACTS AND INDEXES

Business Periodicals Index. H. W. Wilson Co. • 11 times a year. Quarterly and annual cumulations. Price varies.

Personnel Management Abstracts. • Quarterly.

$190.00 per year. Includes annual cumulation.

FINANCIAL RATIOS

Annual Statement Studies. The Risk Management Association. • Annual. Median and quartile financial ratios are given for over 400 kinds of manufacturing, wholesale, retail, construction, and consumer finance establishments. Data is sorted by both asset size and sales volume. Includes a clearly written "Definition of Ratios" and an alphabetical industry index.

Annual Statement Studies: Industry Default Probabilities and Cash Flow Measures. The Risk Management Association. • Annual. $145.00. Serves as a companion volume to the original *Annual Statement Studies.* Gives probability of default estimates on a percentage scale for more than 450 industries. Includes changes in position year-by-year for eight financial statement line items and provides percentage measures of cash flow.

HANDBOOKS AND MANUALS

Legal Guide to Independent Contractor Status. Robert W. Wood. Aspen Publishers, Inc. • 2003. Price on application. A guide to the legal and tax-related differences between employers and independent contractors. Includes examples of both "safe" and "troublesome" independent contractor designations. Penalties and fines are discussed.

Temporary Help Service. Entrepreneur Media, Inc. • Looseleaf. $59.50. A practical guide to starting an employment agency for temporary workers. Covers profit potential, start-up costs, market size evaluation, owner's time required, site selection, lease negotiation, pricing, accounting, advertising, promotion, etc. (Start-Up Business Guide No. E1189.).

ONLINE DATABASES

PROMT: Predicasts Overview of Markets and Technology. Gale Cengage Learning. • Companies, products, applied technologies and markets. U.S. and international literature coverage, 1972 to date. Inquire as to online cost and availability. Provides abstracts from more than 1,600 publications. Weekly updates.

Wilson Business Abstracts Online. H. W. Wilson Co. • Indexes and abstracts 600 major business periodicals, plus the *Wall Street Journal* and the business section of the *New York Times.* Indexing is from 1982, abstracting from 1990, with the two newspapers included from 1993. Updated weekly. Inquire as to online cost and availability. (*Business Periodicals Index* without abstracts is also available online.).

PERIODICALS AND NEWSLETTERS

Working Options. Association of Part-Time Professionals. • Description: Advocates alternative work schedules, particularly part-time employment for professionals. Topics include job sharing, older workers, personnel policies, employee benefits, insurance, chapter news, and legislative news. Also provides how-to information on part-time employment and profiles employees and employers who have used flexible work schedules and part-time employment to their advantage. Recurring features include news about the Association and a column titled Point of View, the Executive Director's Corner and Members' Mail Box.

TRADE/PROFESSIONAL ASSOCIATIONS

American Staffing Association. 277 S Washington St., Ste. 200, Alexandria, VA 22314-3675. Phone: (703)253-2020 Fax: (703)253-2053 E-mail: asa@americanstaffing.net • URL: http://www.americanstaffing.net • Promotes and represents the staffing industry through legal and legislative advocacy, public relations, education, and the establishment of high standards of ethical conduct.

OTHER SOURCES

Contingent Workforce: Business and Legal Strategies. American Lawyer Media, Inc. • Looseleaf. $169.00. Updated as needed. Covers the legal, employee benefit, and taxation aspects of alternative work arrangements (temporary employees, independent contractors, outsourcing). (Law Journal Press).

TENNIS INDUSTRY

PERIODICALS AND NEWSLETTERS

Tennis Industry. Tennis Industry Inc. • Bimonthly. $22.00 per year. Edited for retailers serving the "serious tennis enthusiast." Provides news of apparel, rackets, equipment, and court construction.

TRADE/PROFESSIONAL ASSOCIATIONS

United States Professional Tennis Association. 3535 Briarpark Dr., Ste. 1, 3535 Briarpark Dr., Suite 1, Houston, TX 77042. Phone: 800-USPTA-4U or (713)978-7782 Fax: (713)978-7780 E-mail: uspta@uspta.org • URL: http://www.uspta.com • Professional tennis instructors, tennis-teaching professionals and college coaches. Seeks to improve tennis instruction in the United States; maintains placement bureau and library. Offers specialized education; sponsors competitions; administrates an adult tennis league and a nationwide program to introduce children ages 3-10 to tennis. Sponsors annual "Tennis Across America" program each spring.

United States Tennis Association. 70 W Red Oak Ln., White Plains, NY 10604. Phone: 800-990-8782 or (914)696-7000 Fax: (914)696-7167 E-mail: eliezer@usta.com • URL: http://www.usta.com • Federation of local tennis clubs, educational institutions, recreation departments, and other groups and individuals interested in the promotion of tennis. Works to develop tennis as a means of healthful recreation and physical fitness and maintain high standards of fair play and sportsmanship. Sanctions thousands of tennis tournaments for all age groups throughout the U.S. each year. Sponsors Junior Program for boys and girls under 18 years of age; U.S. national tennis team; national championships for various age groups; National Circuit tournament for pro and amateur players; Davis Cup, Fed Cup, Olympics international matches; and adult recreational leagues. Compiles statistics on leading professional and amateur players.

OTHER SOURCES

Superstudy of Sports Participation. Available from MarketResearch.com. • 2002. $700.00. Three volumes. Published by American Sports Data, Inc. Provides market research data on 102 sports and activities. Vol. 1: *Physical Fitness Activities.* Vol. 2: *Recreational Sports.* Vol. 3: *Outdoor Activities.* (Volumes are available separately at $295.00.).

TERMINATION OF EMPLOYMENT

See: DISMISSAL OF EMPLOYEES

TESTING OF MATERIALS

See: MATERIALS; STANDARDIZATION

TESTING OF PERSONNEL

See: PSYCHOLOGICAL TESTING; RATING OF EMPLOYEES

TESTING OF PRODUCTS

See: QUALITY OF PRODUCTS

TEXTBOOKS

See: BOOK INDUSTRY; PUBLISHING INDUSTRY

TEXTILE DESIGN

See also: TEXTILE INDUSTRY

ABSTRACTS AND INDEXES

Textile Technology Digest. Institute of Textile Technology. • Annual. $535.00. Provides indexing and abstracting of a wide variety of textile technology literature.

CD-ROM DATABASES

Textile Technology Digest [CD-ROM]. Textile Information Center, Institute of Textile Technology. • Quarterly. Provides CD-ROM indexing and abstracting of worldwide journals and monographs in various areas of textile technology, production, and management. Covers 1978 to date.

DIRECTORIES

Plunkett's Apparel and Textiles Industry Almanac. Plunkett Research, Ltd. • 2004. $249.99. Includes detailed profiles of 300 leading companies in such industries as clothing, footware, textile design, textile manufacturing, and apparel retailing. Also covers industry trends and statistical data.

ENCYCLOPEDIAS AND DICTIONARIES

Textile Terms and Definitions. J.E. McIntyre and Paul N. Daniels, editors. Available from State Mutual Book and Periodical Service Ltd. • 1996. $180.00. 10th edition. Published by the Textile Institute (UK). Includes more than 1,000 definitions of textile processes, fiber types, and end products. Illustrated.

ONLINE DATABASES

Textile Technology Digest [online]. Institute of Textile Technology. • Contains indexing and abstracting of more than 300 worldwide journals and monographs in various areas of textile technology, production, and management. Time period is 1978 to date, with monthly updating. Inquire as to online cost and availability.

World Textiles. Elsevier Science, Inc. • Provides abstracting and indexing from 1970 of worldwide textile literature (periodicals, books, pamphlets, and reports). Includes U. S., European, and British patent information. Updating is monthly. Inquire as to online cost and availability.

TRADE/PROFESSIONAL ASSOCIATIONS

Textile Institute. St. James's Buildings, 1st Fl., 79 Oxford St., Manchester M1 6FQ, United Kingdom. Phone: 44 161 2371188 Fax: 44 161 2361991 E-mail: tiihq@textileinst.org.uk • URL: http://www.texi.org • Companies and individuals in 100 countries involved in management, science, technology, design, information transfer, and marketing of textiles including clothing and footwear. Promotes interests of the textile industry worldwide; serves professional interests of members; confers qualifications and recognizes achievements in research, application of ideas, education, business, and public affairs. Maintains Information Service to collect information relating to textile industrial and economic conditions in different countries and economic sectors.

TEXTILE FIBERS

See: FIBER INDUSTRY; SYNTHETIC TEXTILE FIBER INDUSTRY

TEXTILE FIBERS, SYNTHETIC

See: SYNTHETIC TEXTILE FIBER INDUSTRY

TEXTILE INDUSTRY

ABSTRACTS AND INDEXES

AATC Review. American Association of Textile Chemists and Colorists. • Monthly. Free to members; non-members, $60.00 per year. Annual *Buyer's Guide* available. Formerly *Textile Chemist and Colorist and American Dyestuff Reporter.*

Textile Technology Digest. Institute of Textile Technology. • Annual. $535.00. Provides indexing and abstracting of a wide variety of textile technology literature.

World Textile Abstracts. Elsevier. • Monthly. Institutions $1,696.00 per year. Digests of articles published in the world's textile literature. Includes subscription to *World Textile Digest.*

CD-ROM DATABASES

OECD Statistical Compendium. Organization for Economic Cooperation and Development. • Semiannual. $1,905.00 per year for 1 to 10 users. CD-ROM contains more than 730,000 monthly, quarterly, and annual time series for OECD countries, 1960 to date. Includes fully searchable data on agriculture, food, economic indicators, national accounts, employment, energy, finance, industry, technology, and foreign trade. Results can be displayed in various forms.

Textile Technology Digest [CD-ROM]. Textile Information Center, Institute of Textile Technology. • Quarterly. Provides CD-ROM indexing and abstracting of worldwide journals and monographs in various areas of textile technology, production, and management. Covers 1978 to date.

DIRECTORIES

America's Textiles International-The Textile Redbook. Billian/Transworld Publishing Inc. • Annual. $155.00. Lists more than 6,000 textile mills and suppliers to the textile industry in North America.

Davison's Textile Blue Book. Davison Publishing Company L.L.C. • Covers: Over 8,400 companies in the textile industry in the United States, Canada, and Mexico including about 4,400 textile plants. Covers mills, manufacturers, dyers, bleachers, finishers, dealers, importers, exporters, brokers, shippers, and agents for various textiles, fibers, yarns, and cordage. Also includes supplies of equipment, materials and services. Entries include: Company name, address, phone, fax, e-mail, web-site addresses, names of executives, description of product/service, and trade names. Mill and other production facility listings include data on equipment and capacity.

Garment Manufacturers Index. Klevens Publications Inc. • Covers: about 8,000 manufacturers and suppliers of products and services such as fabrics, trimmings, factory equipment, and sewing contractors used in the manufacture of apparel. Publication includes: fabrics, trimmings, supplies, services, equipment, and contractors. Entries include: Company name, address, phone, fax, list of products or services, brief description of product.

LDB Interior Textiles Annual Buyers' Guide. E.W. Williams Publications Co. • Covers: Over 3,000 manufacturers, importers, and suppliers of home fashions products and services, decorative fabric converters, and alternative window coverings; fabricators; manufacturer's representatives; and others allied to the home fashions trade. Entries include: For manufacturers, importers, converters, fabricators, and suppliers--Company name, address, phone, fax, contact, product line. For manufacturer's representatives--Name, address, phone, contact, lines carried. For others--Name, address, phone, fax.

Plunkett's Apparel and Textiles Industry Almanac. Plunkett Research, Ltd. • 2004. $249.99. Includes detailed profiles of 300 leading companies in such industries as clothing, footware, textile design, textile manufacturing, and apparel retailing. Also covers industry trends and statistical data.

Textile World Blue Book. Primedia Business Magazines and Media. • Annual. $160.00. Provides information on more than 5,200 textile mills in the U. S., Canada, and Mexico, including number of employees and names of about 17,000 key personnel. Also provides data on 2,500 suppliers of equipment and products for textile mills. Also known as *Official North American Textile World Blue Book*, formerly *Textile Red Book*.

ENCYCLOPEDIAS AND DICTIONARIES

Fairchild's Dictionary of Textiles. Phyllis B. Tortora, editor. Fairchild Books. • 1996. $75.00. Seventh edition.

Textile Terms and Definitions. J.E. McIntyre and Paul N. Daniels, editors. Available from State Mutual Book and Periodical Service Ltd. • 1996. $180.00. 10th edition. Published by the Textile Institute (UK). Includes more than 1,000 definitions of textile processes, fiber types, and end products. Illustrated.

FINANCIAL RATIOS

Almanac of Business and Industrial Financial Ratios. Leo Troy. Aspen Publishers, Inc. • 2003. $125.95. Includes CD-Rom. Contains financial ratios derived from federal tax returns. Ratios for each of about 200 industries are arranged according to company asset size. (Almanac of Business and Industrial Financial Ratios Series).

IRS Corporate Financial Ratios. Available from MarketResearch.com. • 2002. $225.00. Published by Schonfeld & Associates, Inc. Presents 70 key financial ratios for 260 industries. Ratios are calculated from income statement and balance sheet data available from the Internal Revenue Service. Includes four asset size classes.

Quarterly Financial Report for Manufacturing, Mining, and Trade Corporations. U.S. Federal Trade Commission and U.S. Securities and Exchange Commission. Available from U.S. Government Printing Office. • Quarterly. $49.00 per year.

HANDBOOKS AND MANUALS

Fabric Science Swatch Kit, Gray. J.J. Pizzuto and others. Fairchild Books. • 1998. $32.00. Seventh revised edition. Looseleaf service.

INTERNET DATABASES

Business 2.0 Web Guide to the Best Business Links. Business 2.0 Media, Inc. Phone: (415)293-4800 E-mail: support@business2.com • URL: http://www.business2.com/webguide • Web site presents an extensive, searchable directory of links to "the best, most informative, and authoritative web pages." Twenty main categories cover business, finance, career, company information, people, and technology topics, with thousands of subtopics, all linking to Web sites recommended by experienced business researchers. Fees: Free.

Fedstats. Federal Interagency Council on Statistical Policy. Phone: (202)395-7254 • URL: http://www.fedstats.gov • Web site features an efficient search facility for full-text statistics produced by more than 100 federal agencies, including the Census Bureau, the Bureau of Economic Analysis, and the Bureau of Labor Statistics. Boolean searches can be made within one agency or for all agencies combined. Links are offered to international statistical bureaus, including the UN, IMF, OECD, UNESCO, Eurostat, and 20 individual countries. Fees: Free.

FreeLunch.com. Economy.com, Inc. Phone: (610)696-8700 Fax: (610)696-1678 • URL: http://www.freelunch.com • Web site provides free access to more than 1.5 million economic and financial data series, covering industry, demographics, labor markets, prices, retail sales, government spending,

trade, interest rates, housing starts, the stock market, and many other topics. Data is available for various time periods in either chart or table form. Searching is offered. Fees: Free, but registration required. Economy.com, Inc. also offers fee-based economic analysis at *The Dismal Scientist* site (http://www.dismal.com).

Manufacturing Profiles. U. S. Bureau of the Census. Phone: (301)763-4636 E-mail: webmaster@census.gov • URL: http://www.census.gov/prod/www/abs/mfg-prof.html • The Census Bureau makes available free on PDF (Portable Document Format) an annual consolidation of the entire Current Industrial Report series, presenting "all the data compiled." Contains statistics on production, shipments, inventories, consumption, exports, imports, and orders for a wide variety of manufactured products.

ONLINE DATABASES

Business and Industry. Gale Cengage Learning. • Contains online citations, abstracts, and selected fulltext from more than 1,000 trade journals, newspapers, and other publications. Provides general coverage of both manufacturing and service industries, including marketing, production, industry trends, key events, and information on specific companies. Time span is 1994 to date. Daily updates. Inquire as to online cost and availability. (Also available in a CD-ROM version.).

Tablebase. Gale Cengage Learning. • Provides online numerical tabular data from a wide variety of business, organization, and government sources, including about 1,000 trade journals. Includes industry and individual company statistics relating to products, market share, sales forecasts, production, exports, market trends, etc. Time span is 1997 to date. Weekly updates. Inquire as to online cost and availability. (Also available in a CD-ROM version.).

Textile Technology Digest [online]. Institute of Textile Technology. • Contains indexing and abstracting of more than 300 worldwide journals and monographs in various areas of textile technology, production, and management. Time period is 1978 to date, with monthly updating. Inquire as to online cost and availability.

World Textiles. Elsevier Science, Inc. • Provides abstracting and indexing from 1970 of worldwide textile literature (periodicals, books, pamphlets, and reports). Includes U. S., European, and British patent information. Updating is monthly. Inquire as to online cost and availability.

PERIODICALS AND NEWSLETTERS

DNR: The Men's Fashion Retail Textile Authority. Fairchild Publications. • Daily. $85.00 per year. Formerly *Daily News Record.*

International Dyer. World Textile Publications Ltd. • Monthly. $90.00 per year.

International Textile Bulletin: Dyeing-Printing-Finishing Edition. ITS Publishing, International Textile Service. • Quarterly. $170.00 per year. Editions in Chinese, English, French, German, Italian and Spanish.

International Textile Bulletin: Nonwovens and Industrial Textiles Edition. ITS Publishing, International Textile Service. • Quarterly. $170.00 per year. Editions in Chinese, English, French, German, Italian and Spanish.

International Textile Bulletin: Yarn and Fabric Forming Edition. ITS Publishing, International Textile Service. • Quarterly. $170.00 per year. Editions in Chinese, English, French, German, Italian and Spanish.

International Textiles: Information and Inspiration. Textile Institute. Benjamin Dent and Co., Ltd. • 10 times a year. $220.00 per year. Text in English, French and German; supplement in Japanese.

Journal of Natural Fibers. Haworth Press, Inc. •

Quarterly. $400.00 per year to libraries; $45.00 per year to individuals. Covers applications, technology, research, and world markets relating to fibers from silk, wool, cotton, flax, hemp, jute, etc. Previously *Natural Fibres*, published annually.

LDB Interior Textiles. EW Williams Publications Co. • Monthly. $66.00 per year. Supplement available *Linens, Domestics and Baths-Interior Textile Annual Buyer's Guide.* Formerly *Interior Textiles.*

Textile Horizons: Providing Essential Reading for All Present and Future Decision Makers in Textiles and Fashion Worldwide. World Textile Publications Ltd. • Bimonthly. $115.00 per year.

Textile Industries. Billian Publishing Inc. • Monthly. $43.00 per year. Formerly *America's Textiles International.*

Textile Research Journal. TRI/Princeton (Textile Research Institute). • Monthly. Individuals, $325.00 per year; college and university libraries, $500.00 per year.

Textile World. Biilian Publishing Inc. • Monthly. Free to qualified personnel.

RESEARCH CENTERS AND INSTITUTES

Institute of Textile Technology. 2551 Ivy Rd., Charlottesville, VA 22903-4614. Phone: (434)296-5511 Fax: (434)296-2957 E-mail: library@itt.edu • URL: http://www.itt.edu.

Textiles and Materials. Philadelphia University, Schoolhouse Lane and Henry Ave., Philadelphia, PA 19144-5497. Phone: (215)951-2751 Fax: (215)951-2651 E-mail: brooksteind@philau.edu • URL: http://www.philau.edu/schools • Many research areas, including industrial and nonwoven textiles.

TRI/Princeton. 601 Prospect Ave., PO Box 625, Princeton, NJ 08542. Phone: (609)430-4820 Fax: (609)683-7149 E-mail: info@triprinceton.org • URL: http://www.triprinceton.org • Physics, chemistry, and engineering as related to raw materials, processes, and products of polymer, fiber, and textile systems with special strengths in: surface physics and chemistry; micro and nano structure characterization; fluid flow in porous materials; resins and composites; process-structure-property relationships; human hair chemistry, physics, and mechanics; on-line monitoring of spin finish; dye transport; fabric wear and soiling; modeling of sorption and transport phenomena; and instrument design and development.

STATISTICS SOURCES

Annual Survey of Manufactures. Available from U. S. Government Printing Office. • Annual. Prices vary. Issued by the U. S. Census Bureau as an interim update to the *Census of Manufactures.* Includes data on number of manufacturing establishments in various industries, employment, labor costs, value of shipments, capital expenditures, inventories, energy costs, and assets. (See also Census Bureau home page, http://www.census.gov/.).

Broadwoven Fabrics (Gray). U.S. Bureau of the Census. • Quarterly. Provides statistical data on production, value, shipments, and consumption. Includes woolen and worsted fabrics, tire fabrics, cotton broadwoven fabrics, etc. (Current Industrial Reports, MQ-22T.).

Business Statistics of the United States. Linz Audain and Cornelia J. Strawser. Bernan Associates. • Annual. $147.00. Based on *Business Statistics*, formerly issue by the Bureau of Economic Analysis, U. S. Department of Commerce. Provides basic data for a wide variety of U. S. industries, services, and economic indicators. Most statistics are shown annually for 30 years and monthly for the most recent four years.

Consumption on the Woolen System and Worsted Combing. U. S. Bureau of the Census. • Quarterly and annual. Provides data on consumption of fibers in woolen and worsted spinning mills, by class of fibers and end use. (Current Industrial Reports, MQ-22D.).

Encyclopedia of American Industries. Gale Cengage Learning. • 2000. $560.00. Third edition. Two volumes. $280.00 per volume. Volume one is *Manufacturing Industries* and volume two is *Service and Non-Manufacturing Industries*. Provides the history, development, and recent status of approximately 1,000 industries. Includes statistical graphs, with industry and general indexes.

Survey of Current Business. Available from U. S. Government Printing Office. • Monthly. $63.00 per year. Issued by Bureau of Economic Analysis, U. S. Department of Commerce. Presents a wide variety of business and economic data.

WEFA Industrial Monitor. John Wiley and Sons, Inc. • Annual. $65.00. Prepared by industry analysts at WEFA, an economic forecasting and consulting firm (originally Wharton Econometric Forecasting Associates). Contains discussions of the outlook for major U. S. industries, with many 10-year forecasts (WEFA Web site is http://www.wefa.com).

TRADE/PROFESSIONAL ASSOCIATIONS

American Association of Textile Chemists and Colorists. P.O. Box 12215, Research Triangle Park, NC 27709-2215. Phone: (919)549-8141 Fax: (919)549-8933 E-mail: hammona@aatcc.org • URL: http://www.aatcc.org.

American Textile Manufacturers Institute. 1130 Connecticut Ave. NW, Washington, DC 20036-3954. Phone: (202)862-0500 Fax: (202)862-0570 E-mail: info@atmanet.org • URL: http://www.textileweb.com/storefronts/amertextile.html • Textile mill firms operating machinery for manufacturing and processing cotton, man-made, wool, and silk textile products; includes spinning, weaving, bleaching, finishing, knitting, and allied plants; does not include manufacturers of hosiery or firms that produce man-made fibers and yarn by a chemical process. Operates public relations program for the industry, government relations program, textile market program, and statistical and economic information service. Holds seminars and meetings. Sponsors safety contest among textile mills.

Textile Distributors Association. 980 Ave. of the Americas, New York, NY 10018-3617. Phone: (212)868-2210 Fax: (212)868-2214 E-mail: tda104@msn.com • Distributors or converters of fabrics made predominantly of man-made and natural fibers and blends for all end uses. Member services include routing assistance and Trademark and +Copyright Bureau.

Textile Institute. St. James's Buildings, 1st Fl., 79 Oxford St., Manchester M1 6FQ, United Kingdom. Phone: 44 161 2371188 Fax: 44 161 2361991 E-mail: tiihq@textileinst.org.uk • URL: http://www.texi.org • Companies and individuals in 100 countries involved in management, science, technology, design, information transfer, and marketing of textiles including clothing and footwear. Promotes interests of the textile industry worldwide; serves professional interests of members; confers qualifications and recognizes achievements in research, application of ideas, education, business, and public affairs. Maintains Information Service to collect information relating to textile industrial and economic conditions in different countries and economic sectors.

TEXTILE MACHINERY

See also: MACHINERY; TEXTILE INDUSTRY

RESEARCH CENTERS AND INSTITUTES

Institute of Textile Technology. 2551 Ivy Rd., Charlottesville, VA 22903-4614. Phone: (434)296-5511 Fax: (434)296-2957 E-mail: library@itt.edu • URL: http://www.itt.edu.

STATISTICS SOURCES

U. S. Industry and Trade Outlook. Available from National Technical Information Service. • Annual. $69.95. Produced by the International Trade Administration, U. S. Department of Commerce, in a "public-private" partnership with DRI/McGraw-Hill and Standard & Poor's. Provides basic data, outlook for the current year, and "Long-Term Prospects" (five-year projections) for a wide variety of products and services. Includes high technology industries. Formerly *U. S. Industrial Outlook.*

TRADE/PROFESSIONAL ASSOCIATIONS

American Textile Machinery Association. 201 Park Washington Ct., Falls Church, VA 22046. Phone: (703)538-1789 Fax: (703)241-5603 E-mail: info@atmanet.org • URL: http://www.atmanet.org • Manufacturers of capital equipment for textile manufacture and interested individuals from academia, industry, banking, transportation, insurance, engineering, textiles, and other industries.

TEXTILE MILLS

See: TEXTILE INDUSTRY

TEXTILES, HOME

See: LINEN INDUSTRY

TEXTILES, INDUSTRIAL

See: INDUSTRIAL FABRICS INDUSTRY

TEXTILES, NONWOVEN

See: NONWOVEN FABRICS INDUSTRY

THEATER MANAGEMENT

DIRECTORIES

Entertainment Sourcebook: An Insider's Guide on Where to Find Everything. Applause Theatre & Cinema Books. • Annual. $45.00. Compiled by the Association of Theatrical Artists and Craftspeople (http://www.entertainmentsourcebook.com/ATAC.htm). Lists more than 5,000 sources of theatrical and entertainment supplies and services, such as props, costumes, publicity agencies, scenic shops, amusement park equipment, audio/video products, balloons, wigs, make-up, magic supplies, etc.

The Grey House Performing Arts Directory. Grey House Publishing. • Covers: More than 9,000 dance companies, instrumental music programs, opera companies, choral groups, theatre companies, performing arts series, and performing arts facilities. Entries include: Mailing address, telephone and fax numbers, e-mail addresses, Web sites, mission statement, key management contacts, and facility information such as capacity, season, and attendance.

Peterson's Professional Degree Programs in the Visual and Performing Arts. Peterson's. • Annual. $21.95. A directory of more than 900 degree programs in art, music, theater, and dance at 600 colleges and professional schools.

Theatrical Index. Theatrical Index Ltd. • Covers: theatrical presentations in pre-production stage which are seeking investors; also covers producers, agents, and theaters. Entries include: For productions--Production name, brief details, contact. For agents and producers--Name, address, phone. For theaters--Name, address, box office and backstage phone numbers.

HANDBOOKS AND MANUALS

Handbook for Theatrical Production Managers. Robert S. Telford. Samuel French, Inc. • 1983. $8.95.

Illustrated Theatre Production Guide. John Holloway. Elsevier. • 2002. $34.99. Covers the details of the construction of wooden, fabric, plastic, and metal scenery for stage productions.

PERIODICALS AND NEWSLETTERS

Entertainment Design: The Art and Technology of Show Business. Primedia Business Magazines. • Monthly. $34.97 per year. Contains material on performing arts management, staging, scenery, costuming, etc. Supersedes *TCI - Theatre Crafts International.*

Facility Manager. International Association of Assembly Managers, Inc. • Quarterly. Free to members; non-members, $55.00 per year.

In Focus. National Association for Visually Handicapped. • Description: Reaches visually handicapped children through stories, poems, and drawings contributed by young readers. Covers subjects of interest to youngsters, especially those related to their experiences and hopes for the future. Also includes puzzles, contests, and items of interest to parents and educators, such as new book and symposium announcements.

Theatre Design and Technology. U. S. Institute for Theatre Technology. • Quarterly. $48.00 per year. Covers developments in theatre lighting, sound, scenic design, costuming, and safety.

RESEARCH CENTERS AND INSTITUTES

International Theatre Studies Center. University of Kansas, 339 Murphy Hall, 1530 Naismith Dr., Rm. 356, Lawrence, KS 66045. Phone: (785)864-3511.

Jerome Lawrence and Robert E. Lee Theatre Research Institute. Ohio State University, 1430 Lincoln Tower, 1800 Cannon Dr., Columbus, OH 43210-1230. Phone: (614)292-6614 Fax: (614)688-8417 E-mail: theatreinst@osu.edu • URL: http://www.lib.ohio-state.edu/triweb.

Martin E. Segal Theatre Center. City University of New York, 365 Fifth Ave., New York, NY 10016. Phone: (212)817-1862 Fax: (212)817-1562 E-mail: mestc@gc.cuny.edu • URL: http://www.gc.cuny.edu/mestc.

Wisconsin Center for Film and Theater Research. University of Wisconsin-Madison, 816 State St., Madison, WI 53706. Phone: (608)264-6466 Fax: (608)264-6472 • URL: http://www.shsw.wisc.edu/archives/wcftr • Studies the performing arts in America, including theater, cinema, radio, and television.

TRADE/PROFESSIONAL ASSOCIATIONS

Association of Theatrical Artists and Craftspeople (ATAC). 604 Riverside Dr., New York, NY 10031. Phone: (212)234-9001 • Members are artists and craftspeople working in theatre, film, TV, and advertising. Areas of expertise include props, costumes, millinery, puppetry, display, and special effects.

Association of Theatrical Press Agents and Managers. 1560 Broadway, Ste. 700, New York, NY 10036-2501. Phone: (212)719-3666 Fax: (212)302-1585 E-mail: info@atpam.com • URL: http://www.atpam.com • A labor union for theater managers and press agents. Affiliated with AFL-CIO.

International Association of Assembly Managers. 635 Fritz Dr., Ste. 100, Coppell, TX 75019-4442. Phone: 800-935-4226 or (972)255-8020 Fax: (972)255-9582 E-mail: dexter.king@iaam.org • URL: http://www.iaam.org • Members are auditorium, theater, exhibit hall, and other facility managers. Formerly International Association of Auditorium Managers.

International Ticketing Association. 330 W 38th St., No. 605, New York, NY 10018. Phone: (212)629-4036 Fax: (212)629-8532 E-mail: info@intix.org • URL: http://www.intix.org • Ticket managers and directors, treasurers, financial and marketing and systems directors, and others involved in the marketing, selling, and manufacture of tickets in the performing arts and sports fields. Promotes growth and development in the ticket management industry. Works to: advance and upgrade management techniques and systems; maintain high standards of professionalism in box office management; monitor and analyze technological advances in ticket selling and accounting. Acts as an information exchange and resource center for addressing control and service issues. Provides advisory, consulting, and reference services, and job opportunity information and referral services. Compiles statistics.

League of American Theatres and Producers. 226 W. 47th St., New York, NY 10036. Phone: (212)764-1122 or (212)703-0200 Fax: (212)719-4389 E-mail: league@broadway.org • URL: http://www.broadway.org • Members are legitimate theater producers and owners and operators of legitimate theaters. Formerly League of New York Theatres and Producers.

National Association of Theatre Owners. 4605 Lankershim Blvd., Suite 340, North Hollywood, CA 91602. Phone: (818)506-1778 Fax: (818)506-0269 E-mail: nato@mindspring.com • URL: http://www.natoonline.org.

United States Institute for Theatre Technology. 6443 Ridings Rd., Syracuse, NY 13206-1111. Phone: 800-938-7488 or (315)463-6463 Fax: (315)463-6525 E-mail: info@office.usitt.org • URL: http://www.usitt.org • Members include acousticians, architects, costumers, educators, engineers, lighting designers, and others.

THEATERS, MOTION PICTURE

See: MOTION PICTURE THEATERS

THEFT

See: CRIME AND CRIMINALS

THESES

See: DISSERTATIONS

THIRD WORLD NATIONS

See: DEVELOPING AREAS

TILE INDUSTRY

DIRECTORIES
Tile and Decorative Surfaces: Directory and Purchasing Guide. Ashlee Publishing Co. Inc. • Annual. $6.00. Lists more than 2,000 manufacturers and distributors of the products and tile setting materials.

FINANCIAL RATIOS
Industry Norms and Key Business Ratios. Desk Top Edition. Dun and Bradstreet Corp. • Annual. Five volumes. $475.00 per volume. $1,890.00 per set. Covers over 800 kinds of businesses, arranged by Standard Industrial Classification number. More detailed editions covering longer periods of time are also available.

PERIODICALS AND NEWSLETTERS
Tile and Decorative Surfaces: The Voice of America's Tile Market. Ashlee Publishing Co., Inc. •

Monthly. $50.00 per year.

Tile Design and Installation. Business News Publishing Co. • Quarterly. $55.00 per year. Formerly *Tile World.*

STATISTICS SOURCES
U. S. Industry and Trade Outlook. Available from National Technical Information Service. • Annual. $69.95. Produced by the International Trade Administration, U. S. Department of Commerce, in a "public-private" partnership with DRI/McGraw-Hill and Standard & Poor's. Provides basic data, outlook for the current year, and "Long-Term Prospects" (five-year projections) for a wide variety of products and services. Includes high technology industries. Formerly *U. S. Industrial Outlook.*

TRADE/PROFESSIONAL ASSOCIATIONS
Ceramic Tile Distributors Association. 800 Roosevelt Rd., Bldg. C, Ste. 312, Bldg. C, Ste. 312, Glen Ellyn, IL 60137. Phone: 800-938-CTDA or (630)545-9415 Fax: (630)790-3095 E-mail: info@ctdahome.org • URL: http://www.ctdahome.org • Wholesale distributors and manufacturers of ceramic tile and related products. Promotes the increase of sales volumes in the ceramic tile industry through educational programs and networking. Promotes independent ceramic tile distributors and represents their interests. Provides technical information; compiles statistics. Sponsors competitions. Maintains insurance program for members and speakers' bureau.

Italian Trade Commission. 33 E 67th St., New York, NY 10021-5949. Phone: (212)980-1500 Fax: (212)758-1050 E-mail: newyork@newyork.ice.it • URL: http://www.italtrade.com • Promotes Italian exports to the United States. Assists Italian firms wishing to enter the US market as well as US firms wishing to source product in Italy. Provides assistance to Italian firms wishing to invest in the US and US firms wishing to invest in Italy. Publishes promotional material on the benefits of Italian Products such as Wine, Cheese, & Ceramic Tile. Organizes trade missions, tradeshow pavillions, seminars and special events.

Resilient Floor Covering Institute. 115 Broad St., Ste. 201, LaGrange, GA 30240. Phone: (706)882-3833 Fax: (706)882-3880 E-mail: info@rfci.com • URL: http://www.rfci.com • Supports the manufacturers of vinyl composition tile, solid vinyl tile, or sheet vinyl and rubber tile and people who use its products. Provides technical information and data regarding the resilient flooring industry.

Roof Tile Institute. 230 E Ohio St., Ste. 400, Chicago, IL 60611-3265. Phone: 888-321-9236 or (312)670-4177 Fax: (312)644-8557 E-mail: info@rooftile.com • URL: http://www.ntrma.org • Members are producers of clay and concrete tile roofing. Formerly National Tile Roofing Manufacturers Association.

OTHER SOURCES
Ceramic Tile. Available from MarketResearch.com. • 1998. $1295.00. Market research report published by Specialists in Business Information. Presents market data relative to demographics, sales growth, shipments, exports, imports, price trends, and end-use. Includes company profiles.

U. S. Floor Coverings Industry. Available from MarketResearch.com. • 2000. $1,795.00. Market research report published by Specialists in Business Information. Covers carpets, hardwood flooring, and tile. Presents market data relative to demographics, sales growth, shipments, exports, imports, price trends, and end-use. Includes company profiles.

Vinyl Sheet and Floor Tile. Available from MarketResearch.com. • 1997. $495.00. Market research report published by Specialists in Business Information. Presents vinyl flooring market data relative to demographics, sales growth, shipments,

exports, imports, price trends, and end-use. Includes company profiles.

TIMBER INDUSTRY

See: LUMBER INDUSTRY

TIME AND MOTION STUDY

ENCYCLOPEDIAS AND DICTIONARIES
Blackwell Encyclopedic Dictionary of Operations Management. Nigel Slack, editor. Blackwell Publishing. • 1997. $130.95. The editor is associated with the University of Warwick, England. Contains definitions of key terms combined with longer articles written by various U. S. and foreign business educators. Includes bibliographies and index. (Blackwell Encyclopedia of Management Series.).

HANDBOOKS AND MANUALS
Work Simplification: An Analyst's Handbook. Pierre Theriault. Engineering and Management Press. • 1996. $25.00. A basic guide to work simplification as an industrial management technique.

PERIODICALS AND NEWSLETTERS
International Journal of Productivity and Performance Management. Emerald. • Eight times a year. $6,069.00 per year. Provides information on management services and industrial engineering. Formerly *Work Study.*

TRADE/PROFESSIONAL ASSOCIATIONS
The MTM Association for Standards and Research. 1111 E. Touhy Ave., Des Plaines, IL 60018. Phone: (847)299-1111 Fax: (847)299-3509 E-mail: webmaster@mtm.org • URL: http://www.mtm.org.

TIMETABLES

DIRECTORIES
OAG Desktop Flight Guide, North American Edition. OAG Worldwide. • Biweekly. $285.00 per year. Provides detailed airline travel schedules for the U. S., Canada, Mexico, and the Caribbean. Includes aircraft seat charts and airport diagrams. Formerly *Official Airline Guide, North American Edition.*

OAG Flight Guide: Worldwide. OAG Worldwide. • Monthly. $469.00 per year. Provides detailed airline schedules for international travel. Travel within North America not included.

OAG Pocket Flight Guide. OAG Worldwide. • Monthly. Price varies. Regional editions available for international areas.

Official Bus Guide. Russells Guides Inc. • Publication includes: List of about 475 intercity bus companies in the U.S., Canada, and Mexico. Entries include: Company name, address, phone, executives' names and titles, list of terminals and stations with terminal managers' names. Principal content of publication is intercity operating timetables.

Official Railway Guide--Freight Service Edition. Commonwealth Business Media Inc. • Covers: Railways in North America offering freight service. Includes lists of railroad associations, state railroad commissions, federal regulatory agencies. Entries include: Railroad name, general office, address, phone, names of executives, list of services, schedules, maps, local sales offices and their phone numbers and executives.

Thomas Cook Overseas Timetable: Railway, Road and Shipping Services Outside Europe. Thomas Cook Publishing Co. • Bimonthly. $76.20. per year. International railroad passenger schedules. Text in English; summaries in French, German, Italian and Spanish.

TRADE/PROFESSIONAL ASSOCIATIONS
Forum Train Europe. c/o Swiss Federal Railways. Schanzenstrasse 5, CH-3000 Bern, Switzerland.

Phone: 41 512 202715 Fax: 41 512 201242 E-mail: mailbox@forumtraineurope.org • URL: http://www.forumtraineurope.org • Serves as a forum of railway undertakings and service companies for international production planning and timetable coordination of European rail traffic.

TIN INDUSTRY

GENERAL WORKS

Tin: Its Production and Marketing. William Robertson. Greenwood Publishing Group, Inc. • 1982. $60.00. (Contributions in Economics and Economic History Series: No. 51).

ABSTRACTS AND INDEXES

IMM Abstracts and Index: A Survey of World Literature on the Economic Geology and Mining of All Minerals (Except Coal), Mineral Processing, and Nonferrous Extraction Metallurgy. Institution of Mining and Metallurgy. • Bimonthly. $500.00 per year. Provides international coverage of the literature of mining and nonferrous metallurgy. Includes mineral economics, tunnelling, and rock mechanics.

ALMANACS AND YEARBOOKS

CRB Commodity Yearbook. Commodity Research Bureau. CRB. • Annual. $99.95.

CD-ROM DATABASES

OECD Statistical Compendium. Organization for Economic Cooperation and Development. • Semiannual. $1,905.00 per year for 1 to 10 users. CD-ROM contains more than 730,000 monthly, quarterly, and annual time series for OECD countries, 1960 to date. Includes fully searchable data on agriculture, food, economic indicators, national accounts, employment, energy, finance, industry, technology, and foreign trade. Results can be displayed in various forms.

DIRECTORIES

Dun's Industrial Guide: The Metalworking Directory. Dun and Bradstreet Corp. • Annual. Libraries, $485; commercial institutions, $795.00. Lease basis. Three volumes. Lists about 65,000 U. S. manufacturing plants using metal and suppliers of metalworking equipment and materials. Includes names and titles of key personnel. Products, purchases, and processes are indicated.

HANDBOOKS AND MANUALS

Tin: Its Production and Marketing. William Robertson. Greenwood Publishing. • 1982. $60.00. (Contributions in Economics and Economic istory Series: No. 51).

INTERNET DATABASES

Business 2.0 Web Guide to the Best Business Links. Business 2.0 Media Inc. Phone: (415)293-4800 E-mail: support@business2.com • URL: http://www.business2.com/webguide • Web site presents an extensive, searchable directory of links to "the best, most informative, and authoritative web pages." Twenty main categories cover business, finance, career, company information, people, and technology topics, with thousands of subtopics, all linking to Web sites recommended by experienced business researchers. Fees: Free.

Fedstats. Federal Interagency Council on Statistical Policy. Phone: (202)395-7254 • URL: http://www.fedstats.gov • Web site features an efficient search facility for full-text statistics produced by more than 100 federal agencies, including the Census Bureau, the Bureau of Economic Analysis, and the Bureau of Labor Statistics. Boolean searches can be made within one agency or for all agencies combined. Links are offered to international statistical bureaus, including the UN, IMF, OECD, UNESCO, Eurostat, and 20 individual countries. Fees: Free.

FreeLunch.com. Economy.com, Inc. Phone: (610)696-8700 Fax: (610)696-1678 • URL: http://www.freelunch.com • Web site provides free access to more than 1.5 million economic and financial data series, covering industry, demographics, labor markets, prices, retail sales, government spending, trade, interest rates, housing starts, the stock market, and many other topics. Data is available for various time periods in either chart or table form. Searching is offered. Fees: Free, but registration required. Economy.com, Inc. also offers fee-based economic analysis at *The Dismal Scientist* site (http://www.dismal.com).

ONLINE DATABASES

Globalbase. Gale Cengage Learning. • Provides more than one million online summaries of business, industrial, and economic news reports from more than 1,000 publications worldwide. Covers a wide range of material appearing in international trade journals, professional magazines, and newspapers. Time period is 1984 to date, with weekly updates. Inquire as to online cost and availability.

METADEX. Cambridge Scientific Abstracts. • Covers the worldwide literature of metals, metallurgy, and materials science, 1966 to date. Includes detailed alloys indexing from 1974. Biweekly updating. Inquire as to online cost and availability. (Formerly produced by ASM International.).

PERIODICALS AND NEWSLETTERS

The Northern Miner: Devoted to the Mineral Resources Industry of Canada. Business Information Group. • Monthly. $91.50 per year.

Tin International. Tin Magazines Ltd. • Monthly. $215.00 per year. News and analysis for the international tin industry.

PRICE SOURCES

Platt's Metals Week. Platt's. • Weekly. $770.00 per year.

STATISTICS SOURCES

Business Statistics of the United States. Linz Audain and Cornelia J. Strawser. Bernan Associates. • Annual. $147.00. Based on *Business Statistics*, formerly issue by the Bureau of Economic Analysis, U. S. Department of Commerce. Provides basic data for a wide variety of U. S. industries, services, and economic indicators. Most statistics are shown annually for 30 years and monthly for the most recent four years.

International Tin Council. Quarterly Statistical Bulletin. International Tin Council. • Quarterly. $100.00 per year. Includes eight monthly statistical summaries.

Mineral Commodity Summaries. Available from U. S. Government Printing Office. • Annual. $26.00. Published by the U. S. Geological Survey, Department of the Interior (http://www.usgs.gov). Contains detailed, five-year data for about 90 nonfuel minerals. Covers a wide range of statistics, including production, imports, exports, consumption, reserves, prices, tariff information, and industry employment. (Two pages are devoted to each mineral.).

Non-Ferrous Metal Data Yearbook. American Bureau of Metal Statistics. • Annual. $405.00. Provides worldwide data on approximately about 200 statistical tables covering many nonferrous metals. Includes production, consumption, inventories, exports, imports, and other data.

Survey of Current Business. Available from U. S. Government Printing Office. • Monthly. $63.00 per year. Issued by Bureau of Economic Analysis, U. S. Department of Commerce. Presents a wide variety of business and economic data.

TRADE/PROFESSIONAL ASSOCIATIONS

American Bureau of Metal Statistics. P.O. Box 805, Chatham, NJ 07928. Phone: (973)701-2299 Fax: (973)701-2152 E-mail: info@abms.com • URL: http://www.abms.com • Members are metal companies. Compiles and publishes detailed statistical data on a wide variety of nonferrous metals: aluminum, copper, gold, lead, nickel, platinum, silver, tin, titanium, uranium, zinc, and others.

TIRE INDUSTRY

See also: RUBBER AND RUBBER GOODS INDUSTRIES

ABSTRACTS AND INDEXES

RAPRA Abstracts. Rubber and Plastics Research Association of Great Britian. RAPRA Technology Ltd. • Monthly. $2,700.00 per year. Up-to-date survey of current international information relevant to the rubber, plastics and associated industries.

ALMANACS AND YEARBOOKS

Tire and Rim Association Year Book. Tire and Rim Association, Inc. • Annual. $55.00.

CD-ROM DATABASES

OECD Statistical Compendium. Organization for Economic Cooperation and Development. • Semiannual. $1,905.00 per year for 1 to 10 users. CD-ROM contains more than 730,000 monthly, quarterly, and annual time series for OECD countries, 1960 to date. Includes fully searchable data on agriculture, food, economic indicators, national accounts, employment, energy, finance, industry, technology, and foreign trade. Results can be displayed in various forms.

DIRECTORIES

Modern Tire Dealer: Facts/Directory. VNU Business Media. • Annual. $30.00. Directories of tire and car service suppliers, tire shop jobbers, and national state associations.

INTERNET DATABASES

Business 2.0 Web Guide to the Best Business Links. Business 2.0 Media Inc. Phone: (415)293-4800 E-mail: support@business2.com • URL: http://www.business2.com/webguide • Web site presents an extensive, searchable directory of links to "the best, most informative, and authoritative web pages." Twenty main categories cover business, finance, career, company information, people, and technology topics, with thousands of subtopics, all linking to Web sites recommended by experienced business researchers. Fees: Free.

Fedstats. Federal Interagency Council on Statistical Policy. Phone: (202)395-7254 • URL: http://www.fedstats.gov • Web site features an efficient search facility for full-text statistics produced by more than 100 federal agencies, including the Census Bureau, the Bureau of Economic Analysis, and the Bureau of Labor Statistics. Boolean searches can be made within one agency or for all agencies combined. Links are offered to international statistical bureaus, including the UN, IMF, OECD, UNESCO, Eurostat, and 20 individual countries. Fees: Free.

FreeLunch.com. Economy.com, Inc. Phone: (610)696-8700 Fax: (610)696-1678 • URL: http://www.freelunch.com • Web site provides free access to more than 1.5 million economic and financial data series, covering industry, demographics, labor markets, prices, retail sales, government spending, trade, interest rates, housing starts, the stock market, and many other topics. Data is available for various time periods in either chart or table form. Searching is offered. Fees: Free, but registration required. Economy.com, Inc. also offers fee-based economic analysis at *The Dismal Scientist* site (http://www.dismal.com).

PERIODICALS AND NEWSLETTERS

Dealernews: The Voice of the Powersports Vehicle Industry. Advanstar Communications. • 13 times a year. $40.00 per year. News concerning the power sports motor vehicle industry.

Modern Tire Dealer: Covering Tire Sales and Car Service. • Monthly. $65.00 per year. Serves independent tire dealers. Cover automotive service and dealership management topics.

Tire Business. Crain Communications, Inc. • Semimonthly. $71.00 per year. Edited for independent tire retailers and wholesalers.

Tire Review: The Authority on Tire Dealer Profitability. Babcox Publications, Inc. • Monthly. $64.00. Includes *LiftGuide, Custom Wheel and Tire Style Guide, Sourcebook and Directory and NTDRA Show.*

STATISTICS SOURCES

Annual Survey of Manufactures. Available from U. S. Government Printing Office. • Annual. Prices vary. Issued by the U. S. Census Bureau as an interim update to the *Census of Manufactures.* Includes data on number of manufacturing establishments in various industries, employment, labor costs, value of shipments, capital expenditures, inventories, energy costs, and assets. (See also Census Bureau home page, http://www.census.gov/.).

Business Statistics of the United States. Linz Audain and Cornelia J. Strawser. Bernan Associates. • Annual. $147.00. Based on *Business Statistics,* formerly issue by the Bureau of Economic Analysis, U. S. Department of Commerce. Provides basic data for a wide variety of U. S. industries, services, and economic indicators. Most statistics are shown annually for 30 years and monthly for the most recent four years.

Survey of Current Business. Available from U. S. Government Printing Office. • Monthly. $63.00 per year. Issued by Bureau of Economic Analysis, U. S. Department of Commerce. Presents a wide variety of business and economic data.

TRADE/PROFESSIONAL ASSOCIATIONS

Tire and Rim Association. 175 Montrose Ave., W., Copley, OH 44321. Phone: (330)666-8121 Fax: (330)666-8340 E-mail: tireandrim@aol.com.

Tire Industry Association. 1532 Pointer Ridge Pl., Ste. G, Bowie, MD 20716-1874. Phone: 800-876-8372 or (301)430-7280 Fax: (301)430-7283 E-mail: info@tireindustry.org • URL: http://www.tireindustry.org • Corporations engaged in all sectors of the replacement tire industry. Seeks to advance members' interests. Serves as a clearinghouse on economic and regulatory issues affecting the replacement tire industry; conducts educational programs; sponsors lobbying activities.

Tire Industry Safety Council. 1400 K St. NW, Ste. 900, Washington, DC 20005. Phone: (202)682-4800 Fax: (202)682-4854 E-mail: info@rma.org • URL: http://www.rma.org • Represents companies and organizations in the rubber industry producing rubber or rubber-related products.

OTHER SOURCES

Tires. Available from MarketResearch.com. • 2002. $3,950.00. Published by Global Industry Analysts. Provides worldwide market research data, including profiles of major tire companies.

TITANIUM INDUSTRY

See also: METAL INDUSTRY; MINES AND MINERAL RESOURCES

GENERAL WORKS

Titanium Technology: Present Status and Future Trends. F. H. Froes and others. International Titanium Association. • 1985. $19.95.

ABSTRACTS AND INDEXES

IMM Abstracts and Index: A Survey of World Literature on the Economic Geology and Mining of

All Minerals (Except Coal), Mineral Processing, and Nonferrous Extraction Metallurgy. Institution of Mining and Metallurgy. • Bimonthly. $500.00 per year. Provides international coverage of the literature of mining and nonferrous metallurgy. Includes mineral economics, tunnelling, and rock mechanics.

ALMANACS AND YEARBOOKS

CRB Commodity Yearbook. Commodity Research Bureau. CRB. • Annual. $99.95.

DIRECTORIES

International Titanium Association Buyers Guide. International Titanium Association. • Annual. Members, $5.00; non-members, $20.00.

International Titanium Association Guide to Products and Services of Member Comp. • Annual. Free. Lists about 130 titanium metal industry companies.

HANDBOOKS AND MANUALS

Materials Properties Handbook: Titanium Alloys. R. Boyer and others, editors. ASM International. • 1994. $299.00. Covers titanium alloy applications, fabrication, properties, specifications, effects of processing, corrosion, etc.

Titanium: A Technical Guide. Matthew J. Donachie, editor. ASM International. • 2000. $160.00. Second edition. Provides coverage of all major, technical aspects of titanium and titanium alloys.

ONLINE DATABASES

CA Search. Chemical Abstracts Service. • Guide to chemical literature, 1967 to present. Inquire as to online cost and availability.

Globalbase. Gale Cengage Learning. • Provides more than one million online summaries of business, industrial, and economic news reports from more than 1,000 publications worldwide. Covers a wide range of material appearing in international trade journals, professional magazines, and newspapers. Time period is 1984 to date, with weekly updates. Inquire as to online cost and availability.

PERIODICALS AND NEWSLETTERS

Light Metal Age. Fellom Publishing Co. • Bimonthly. $40.00 per year. Edited for production and engineering executives of the aluminum industry and other nonferrous light metal industries.

33 Metalproducing: For Primary Producers of Steel, Aluminum, and Copper-Base Alloys. Penton Media, Inc. • Monthly. $65.00 per year. Covers metal production technology and methods and industry news. Includes a bimonthly *Nonferrous Supplement.*

Titanium Newsletter. Titanium Development Association. • Description: Presents news on the titanium industry. Covers corporate and Association activities, personnel changes, and legislative news. Recurring features include news of research, news of members, a calendar of events, product information, and columns titled Ti News Pipeline and Ti Reference Library.

PRICE SOURCES

Platt's Metals Week. Platt's. • Weekly. $770.00 per year.

STATISTICS SOURCES

Mineral Commodity Summaries. Available from U. S. Government Printing Office. • Annual. $26.00. Published by the U. S. Geological Survey, Department of the Interior (http://www.usgs.gov). Contains detailed, five-year data for about 90 nonfuel minerals. Covers a wide range of statistics, including production, imports, exports, consumption, reserves, prices, tariff information, and industry employment. (Two pages are devoted to each mineral.).

Non-Ferrous Metal Data Yearbook. American Bureau of Metal Statistics. • Annual. $405.00. Provides worldwide data on approximately about 200 statistical tables covering many nonferrous metals. Includes production, consumption, inventories, exports, imports, and other data.

Titanium: A Statistical Review. International Titanium Association. • Annual. Free to members; non-members, $100.00.

U. S. Industry and Trade Outlook. Available from National Technical Information Service. • Annual. $69.95. Produced by the International Trade Administration, U. S. Department of Commerce, in a "public-private" partnership with DRI/McGraw-Hill and Standard & Poor's. Provides basic data, outlook for the current year, and "Long-Term Prospects" (five-year projections) for a wide variety of products and services. Includes high technology industries. Formerly *U. S. Industrial Outlook.*

TRADE/PROFESSIONAL ASSOCIATIONS

American Bureau of Metal Statistics. P.O. Box 805, Chatham, NJ 07928. Phone: (973)701-2299 Fax: (973)701-2152 E-mail: info@abms.com • URL: http://www.abms.com • Members are metal companies. Compiles and publishes detailed statistical data on a wide variety of nonferrous metals: aluminum, copper, gold, lead, nickel, platinum, silver, tin, titanium, uranium, zinc, and others.

International Titanium Association. 2655 W Midway Blvd., Ste. 300, 350 Interlocken Blvd., Ste. 390, Broomfield, CO 80020-7187. Phone: (303)404-2221 Fax: (303)404-9111 E-mail: ita@titanium.org • URL: http://www.titanium.org • Represents producers, fabricators, extruders, and users of titanium (a metallic element used especially in alloys); companies performing some value-added function to titanium. Works to expand existing market, increase awareness and understanding of titanium in engineering and academic communities, and maintain an appropriate and meaningful statistics program. Maintains speakers' bureau; answers technical questions; provides application committees; sponsors educational programs.

TITLE INSURANCE

PERIODICALS AND NEWSLETTERS

Title News. American Land Title Association. • Description: Provides information for title companies and property investors.

TRADE/PROFESSIONAL ASSOCIATIONS

American Land Title Association - Sections: Abstractors and Title Insurance AgenTitle Insurance and Underwriters. 1828 L St., N.W., Suite 705, Washington, DC 20036. Phone: 800-787-2582 or (202)296-3671 Fax: (202)223-5843 E-mail: service@alta.org • URL: http://www.alta.org.

TITLES OF DEGREES

See: ACADEMIC DEGREES

TOASTS

See also: PUBLIC SPEAKING

GENERAL WORKS

Great Toasts: From Births to Weddings to Retirement Parties and Everything in Between. Andrew Frothingham. Career Press, Inc. • 2002. $13.99. Includes samples of toasts for business events.

DIRECTORIES

Roster of Clubs. International Training in Communication. • Annual. Price on application.

Toastmasters International Club Directory.

Toastmasters International. • Annual. Price on application. Lists toastmasters clubs across the world.

PERIODICALS AND NEWSLETTERS

The Toastmaster: For Better Listening, Thinking, Speaking. Suzanne Frey, editor. Toastmasters International. • Monthly. Membership. Provides information and "how-to" articles on communication and leadership.

TRADE/PROFESSIONAL ASSOCIATIONS

International Training in Communication. 2519 Woodland Dr., Anaheim, CA 92801-2637. Phone: (714)995-3660 Fax: (714)995-6974 E-mail: itcintl@ mediamatters.co.nz • URL: http://www.itcintl.com • Members are interested in speech improvement, communication, lexicology, leadership training and skill in organizational techniques and self-development.

Toastmasters International. PO Box 9052, PO Box 9052, Mission Viejo, CA 92690-9052. Phone: 800-993-7732 or (949)858-8255 Fax: (949)858-1207 E-mail: tminfo@toastmasters.org • URL: http:// www.toastmasters.org • Men and women who wish to improve their communication and leadership skills. Sponsors clubs in corporate, government, and military facilities, as well as local communities in over 90 countries. Sponsors annual World Championship of Public Speaking. Special activities include: advanced communication and leadership program; youth leadership programs for junior and senior high school students; Gavel Clubs in schools, prisons, and other institutions.

TOBACCO AND TOBACCO INDUSTRY

See also: CIGAR AND CIGARETTE INDUSTRY; SMOKING POLICY

GENERAL WORKS

Drugs, Alcohol, and Tobacco: Learning About Addictive Behavior. Gale Cengage Learning. • 2002. $295.00. Three volumes. Contains 200 articles on various aspects of addiction. Includes color illustrations, a glossary, and comprehensive indexing. (Macmillan Reference USA imprint.).

ABSTRACTS AND INDEXES

Tobacco Abstracts: World Literature on Nicotiana. Tobacco Literature Service. • Bimonthly. $120.00 per year.

ALMANACS AND YEARBOOKS

Agricultural and Mineral Commodities Year Book. Available from Taylor & Francis Group. • Annual. $225.00. Published by Europa Publications. Contains descriptive product profiles, price data, export-import data, and production statistics for major commodities of the world. Includes commodity histories, uses, markets, demand trends, and information about trade agreements and key commodity organizations.

Tobacco Retailers Almanac. Retail Tobacco Dealers of America Inc. • Annual. Price on application. Lists virtually every tobacco related product available (including cigars, cigarettes, pipes, tobacco, lighters and gift items).

BIBLIOGRAPHIES

Smoking: The Health Consequences of Tobacco Use. Richard A. Gray and Cecilia M. Schmitz. Pierian Press. • 1995. $30.00. (Science and Social Responsibility Series: No.2).

CD-ROM DATABASES

OECD Statistical Compendium. Organization for Economic Cooperation and Development. • Semiannual. $1,905.00 per year for 1 to 10 users. CD-ROM contains more than 730,000 monthly,

quarterly, and annual time series for OECD countries, 1960 to date. Includes fully searchable data on agriculture, food, economic indicators, national accounts, employment, energy, finance, industry, technology, and foreign trade. Results can be displayed in various forms.

World Marketing Forecasts on CD-ROM. Gale Cengage Learning. • Annual. $2,500.00. Produced by Euromonitor. Provides detailed forecast data for the years to 2012 on CD-ROM for 54 countries in all parts of the world. Covers a wide range of social, demographic, economic, and market factors. Includes specific forecasts for many kinds of consumer products.

DIRECTORIES

Tobacco International Buyers' Guide and Directory. Lockwood Publications, Inc. • Annual. $40.00. Formerly *Tobacco Internatonal Directory and Buyers' Guide.*

ENCYCLOPEDIAS AND DICTIONARIES

Encyclopedia of Smoking and Tobacco. Arlene B. Hirschfelder. Greenwood Publishing Group, Inc. • 1999. $69.95. Includes information on the economics of the tobacco industry, health issues, tobacco history, advertising, legal issues, government subsidies, etc. Provides illustrations, charts, and statistical data.

FINANCIAL RATIOS

Almanac of Business and Industrial Financial Ratios. Leo Troy. Aspen Publishers, Inc. • 2003. $125.95. Includes CD-Rom. Contains financial ratios derived from federal tax returns. Ratios for each of about 200 industries are arranged according to company asset size. (Almanac of Business and Industrial Financial Ratios Series).

Quarterly Financial Report for Manufacturing, Mining, and Trade Corporations. U.S. Federal Trade Commission and U.S. Securities and Exchange Commission. Available from U.S. Government Printing Office. • Quarterly. $49.00 per year.

INTERNET DATABASES

Business 2.0 Web Guide to the Best Business Links. Business 2.0 Media Inc. Phone: (415)293-4800 E-mail: support@business2.com • URL: http:// www.business2.com/webguide • Web site presents an extensive, searchable directory of links to "the best, most informative, and authoritative web pages." Twenty main categories cover business, finance, career, company information, people, and technology topics, with thousands of subtopics, all linking to Web sites recommended by experienced business researchers. Fees: Free.

Fedstats. Federal Interagency Council on Statistical Policy. Phone: (202)395-7254 • URL: http://www. fedstats.gov • Web site features an efficient search facility for full-text statistics produced by more than 100 federal agencies, including the Census Bureau, the Bureau of Economic Analysis, and the Bureau of Labor Statistics. Boolean searches can be made within one agency or for all agencies combined. Links are offered to international statistical bureaus, including the UN, IMF, OECD, UNESCO, Eurostat, and 20 individual countries. Fees: Free.

FreeLunch.com. Economy.com, Inc. Phone: (610)696-8700 Fax: (610)696-1678 • URL: http:// www.freelunch.com • Web site provides free access to more than 1.5 million economic and financial data series, covering industry, demographics, labor markets, prices, retail sales, government spending, trade, interest rates, housing starts, the stock market, and many other topics. Data is available for various time periods in either chart or table form. Searching is offered. Fees: Free, but registration required. Economy.com, Inc. also offers fee-based economic analysis at *The Dismal Scientist* site (http://www. dismal.com).

USDA. United States Department of Agriculture. Phone: (202)720-2791 E-mail: agsec@usda.gov • URL: http://www.usda.gov • The USDA home page has six sections: News and Information; What's New; About USDA; Agencies; Opportunities; Search and Help. Keyword searching is offered from the USDA home page and from various individual agency home pages. Agencies are the Economic Research Service, Agricultural Marketing Service, National Agricultural Statistics Service, National Agricultural Library, and about 12 others. Updating varies. Fees: Free.

PERIODICALS AND NEWSLETTERS

Bureau of Alcohol, Tobacco, and Firearms Quarterly Bulletin. Bureau of Alcohol, Tobacco, and Firearms, U.S. Department of the Treasury. Available from U.S. Government Printing Office. • Quarterly. $25.00 per year. Laws and regulations.

Smokeshop. • Bimonthly. $32.00 per year.

Tobacco International. Lockwood Publications, Inc. • Weekly. $32.00 per year.

Tobacco Reporter: Devoted to All Segments of the International Tobacco Trade Processing, Trading, Manufacturing. SpecComm International, Inc. • Monthly. $36.00 per year.

World Tobacco. DMG World Media Ltd. • Six times a year. $132.00 per year.

RESEARCH CENTERS AND INSTITUTES

Tobacco and Health Research Institute. University of Kentucky. Cooper and University Drives, Lexington, KY 40546-0236. Phone: (859)257-5798 Fax: (859)323-1077 E-mail: mdavies@pop.uky.edu • URL: http://www.uky.edu/~rgs/thri.

STATISTICS SOURCES

Agricultural Statistics. Available from U. S. Government Printing Office. • Annual. $38.00. Produced by the National Agricultural Statistics Service, U. S. Department of Agriculture. Provides a wide variety of statistical data relating to agricultural production, supplies, consumption, prices/price-supports, foreign trade, costs, and returns, as well as farm labor, loans, income, and population. In many cases, historical data is shown annually for 10 years. In addition to farm data, includes detailed fishery statistics.

Annual Survey of Manufactures. Available from U. S. Government Printing Office. • Annual. Prices vary. Issued by the U. S. Census Bureau as an interim update to the *Census of Manufactures.* Includes data on number of manufacturing establishments in various industries, employment, labor costs, value of shipments, capital expenditures, inventories, energy costs, and assets. (See also Census Bureau home page, http://www.census. gov/.).

Business Statistics of the United States. Linz Audain and Cornelia J. Strawser. Bernan Associates. • Annual. $147.00. Based on *Business Statistics,* formerly issue by the Bureau of Economic Analysis, U. S. Department of Commerce. Provides basic data for a wide variety of U. S. industries, services, and economic indicators. Most statistics are shown annually for 30 years and monthly for the most recent four years.

Consumer International. Available from Gale Cengage Learning. • Annual. $1,290.00. Published by Euromonitor. Contains extensive consumer market, economic, and demographic data for 25 major, non-European countries, including the U. S. and Canada. Includes consumer market size (volume and value) for 150 product types in 14 categories (food, clothing, automobiles, cosmetics, appliances, etc.).

European Marketing Forecasts. Available from Gale Cengage Learning. • Annual. $1,250.00. Published by Euromonitor. Contains demographic, economic, and market forecasts for the countries of Europe to the year 2010. Forecasts include market-size data for

15 consumer product sectors (food, clothing, automobiles, consumer electronics, etc.).

FAO Production Yearbook. Available from Bernan Associates. • Annual. $45.00. Published by the Food and Agriculture Organization (http://www.fao.org). Contains worldwide data on agriculture, land use, farm crops, livestock, and agricultural prices.

FAO Trade Yearbook. Available from Bernan Associates. • Annual. $45.00. Published by the Food and Agriculture Organization (http://www.fao.org). Provides extensive worldwide data on exports and imports of agricultural commodities, fertilizers, tractors, and pesticides. Includes more than 130 tables of detailed statistics.

International Marketing Forecasts. Available from Gale Cengage Learning. • Annual. $1,250.00. Published by Euromonitor. Contains demographic, economic, and market forecasts to the year 2013 for major, non-European countries, including the U. S. and Canada. Forecasts include market-size data for 15 consumer product sectors, such as food, clothing, and automobiles.

Monthly Statistical Release: Tobacco Products. U.S. Bureau of Alcohol, Tobacco, and Firearms. • Monthly.

Standard & Poor's Industry Surveys. Standard & Poor's. • Semiannual. $1,800.00. Two looseleaf volumes. Includes monthly *Supplements.* Provides detailed, individual surveys of 52 major industry groups. Each survey is revised on a semiannual basis. Also includes "Monthly Investment Review" (industry group investment analysis) and monthly "Trends & Projections" (economic analysis).

Statistics on Alcohol, Drug, and Tobacco Use: A Selection of Statistical Charts, Graphs and Tables about Alcohol, Drug and Tobacco Use from a Variety of Published Sources with Explanatory Comments. Gale Cengage Learning. • 1995. $85.00. Includes graphs, charts, and tables arranged within subject chapters. Citations to data sources are provided. (Statistics on...Series: vol. 1).

Survey of Current Business. Available from U. S. Government Printing Office. • Monthly. $63.00 per year. Issued by Bureau of Economic Analysis, U. S. Department of Commerce. Presents a wide variety of business and economic data.

WEFA Industrial Monitor. John Wiley and Sons, Inc. • Annual. $65.00. Prepared by industry analysts at WEFA, an economic forecasting and consulting firm (originally Wharton Econometric Forecasting Associates). Contains discussions of the outlook for major U. S. industries, with many 10-year forecasts (WEFA Web site is http://www.wefa.com).

TRADE/PROFESSIONAL ASSOCIATIONS

American Wholesale Marketers Association. 2750 Prosperity Ave., Ste. 530, Fairfax, VA 22031. Phone: 800-482-2962 or (703)208-3358 Fax: (703)573-5738 E-mail: info@awmanet.org • URL: http://www.awmanet.org • Represents the interests of distributors of convenience products. Its members include wholesalers, retailers, manufacturers, brokers and allied organizations from across the U.S. and abroad. Programs include strong legislative representation in Washington and a broad spectrum of targeted education, business and information services. Sponsors the country's largest show for candy and convenience related products in conjunction with its semi-annual convention.

Retail Tobacco Dealers of America. 12 Galloway Ave., Suite 1B, Cockeysville, MD 21030. Phone: (410)628-1674 Fax: (410)628-1679 E-mail: info@rtda.org • URL: http://www.rtda.org.

Tobacco Associates. 8452 Holly Leaf Dr., McLean, VA 22102. Phone: (703)821-1255 Fax: (703)821-1511 E-mail: taw@tobaccoassociatesinc.org • URL: http://www.tobaccoassociatesinc.org • Represents U.S. flue-cured producers in export promotion and market development.

Tobacco Association of the U.S. 3716 National Dr., Suite 114, Raleigh, NC 27612. Phone: (919)782-5151 Fax: (919)781-0915 • Buyers, packers, and distributors of American leaf tobacco and manufacturers of tobacco products.

Tobacco Merchants Association. PO Box 8019, Princeton, NJ 08543-8019. Phone: (609)275-4900 Fax: (609)275-8379 E-mail: tma@tma.org • URL: http://www.tma.org • Manufacturers of tobacco products, leaf dealers, suppliers, distributors, and others related to the tobacco industry. Maintains records of trademarks.

OTHER SOURCES

Tobacco Industry Litigation Reporter: The National Journal of Record of Litigation Affecting the Tobacco Industry. Andrews Publications. • Monthly. $725.00 per year. Newsletter. Reports on major lawsuits brought against tobacco companies.

TOILETRIES

See: COSMETICS INDUSTRY; PERFUME INDUSTRY

TOLL ROADS

See also: ROADS AND HIGHWAYS

BIBLIOGRAPHIES

Road Construction and Safety. Available from U. S. Government Printing Office. • Annual. Free. Issued by the Superintendent of Documents. A list of government publications on highway construction and traffic safety. Formerly *Highway Construction, Safety and Traffic.* (Subject Bibliography No. 3.).

ENCYCLOPEDIAS AND DICTIONARIES

Macmillan Encyclopedia of Transportation. Available from Gale Cengage Learning. • 1999. $450.00. Six volumes. Published by Macmillan Reference USA. Covers the business, technology, and history of transportation on land, on water, in the air, and in space. Includes definitions, cross-references, and 200 color illustrations.

ONLINE DATABASES

TRIS: Transportation Research Information Service. National Research Council. • Contains abstracts and citations to a wide range of transportation literature, 1968 to present, with monthly updates. Includes references to the literature of air transportation, highways, ships and shipping, railroads, trucking, and urban mass transportation. Formerly *TRIS-ONLINE.* Inquire as to online cost and availability.

PERIODICALS AND NEWSLETTERS

Tollways. International Bridge, Tunnel and Turnpike Association. • Description: Focuses on trends, developments, and news about the worldwide toll industry for members.

STATISTICS SOURCES

Highway Statistics. Federal Highway Administration, U.S. Department of Transportation. Available from U.S. Government Printing Office. • Annual. $26.00.

Transportation Statistics Annual Report. Available from U. S. Government Printing Office. • Annual. $43.00. Issued by the U. S. Bureau of Transportation Statistics, Transportation Department (http://www.bts.gov). Summarizes national data for various forms of transportation, including airlines, railroads, and motor vehicles. Information on the use of roads and highways is included.

TRADE/PROFESSIONAL ASSOCIATIONS

International Bridge, Tunnel and Turnpike Association. 1146 19th St., N.W., No. 800, Washington, DC 20036. Phone: (202)659-4620 Fax:

(202)659-0500 E-mail: pjones@ibbta.org • URL: http://www.ibtta.org • Formerly American Bridge, Tunnel and Turnpike Association.

TOMATO INDUSTRY

See also: VEGETABLE INDUSTRY

CD-ROM DATABASES

Food Science and Technology Abstracts [CD-ROM]. Available from SilverPlatter Information, Inc. • Quarterly. Produced by International Food Information Service (home page is http://www.ifis.org). Provides worldwide coverage on CD-ROM of the literature of food technology and production. Various types of publications are indexed, with abstracts, including about 1,800 periodicals. Time period is 1969 to date.

DIRECTORIES

Major Food and Drink Companies of the World. Available from Gale Cengage Learning. • Annual. $880.00. Two volumes. Published by Graham & Whiteside. Contains profiles and trade names for more than 9,800 important food and beverage companies in various countries. In addition to foods, includes both alcoholic and nonalcoholic drink products.

Thomas Food and Beverage Market Place. Grey House Publishing. • 2004. $495.00. Three volumes. Contains more than 40,000 entries covering food companies, beverages, food equipment, warehouse companies, food brokers, wholesalers, importers, and exporters. Formerly *Thomas Food Industry Register.*

HANDBOOKS AND MANUALS

Knott's Handbook for Vegetable Growers. Donald N. Maynard and George J. Hochmuth. John Wiley and Sons, Inc. • 1997. $99.00. Fourth edition. Written for commercial vegetable growers, truck farmers, horticulturists, and other professionals. Covers such topics as spacing of plants, disease control, insect pests, seeds, weeds, water management, and irrigation.

INTERNET DATABASES

USDA. United States Department of Agriculture. Phone: (202)720-2791 E-mail: agsec@usda.gov • URL: http://www.usda.gov • The USDA home page has six sections: News and Information; What's New; About USDA; Agencies; Opportunities; Search and Help. Keyword searching is offered from the USDA home page and from various individual agency home pages. Agencies are the Economic Research Service, Agricultural Marketing Service, National Agricultural Statistics Service, National Agricultural Library, and about 12 others. Updating varies. Fees: Free.

ONLINE DATABASES

Food Science and Technology Abstracts [online]. IFIS North American Desk. • Produced by International Food Information Service. Provides about 500,000 online citations, with abstracts, to the international literature of food science, technology, commodities, engineering, and processing. Approximately 2,000 periodicals are covered. Time period is 1969 to date, with monthly updates. Inquire as to online cost and availability.

STATISTICS SOURCES

Agricultural Statistics. Available from U. S. Government Printing Office. • Annual. $38.00. Produced by the National Agricultural Statistics Service, U. S. Department of Agriculture. Provides a wide variety of statistical data relating to agricultural production, supplies, consumption, prices/price-supports, foreign trade, costs, and returns, as well as farm labor, loans, income, and population. In many cases, historical data is shown annually for 10 years. In addition to farm data, includes detailed fishery statistics.

FAO Production Yearbook. Available from Bernan Associates. • Annual. $45.00. Published by the Food and Agriculture Organization (http://www.fao.org). Contains worldwide data on agriculture, land use, farm crops, livestock, and agricultural prices.

FAO Trade Yearbook. Available from Bernan Associates. • Annual. $45.00. Published by the Food and Agriculture Organization (http://www.fao.org). Provides extensive worldwide data on exports and imports of agricultural commodities, fertilizers, tractors, and pesticides. Includes more than 130 tables of detailed statistics.

Vegetables and Specialties Situation and Outlook. Available from U. S. Government Printing Office. • Three times a year. Issued by the Economic Research Service of the U. S. Department of Agriculture. Provides current statistical information on supply, demand, and prices.

World Food Data and Statistics. Euromonitor International. • 2004. $650.00. Provides five-year data for a wide variety of food products in 52 countries. Includes market size, consumer expenditures, price indicators, and retail distribution data for many kinds of meat, fish, fruits, vegetables, dairy products, baked goods, condiments, canned food, and frozen food.

TOOL INDUSTRY

See also: HARDWARE INDUSTRY; MACHINE TOOL INDUSTRY; POWER TOOL INDUSTRY

ABSTRACTS AND INDEXES

Engineering Index Monthly: Abstracting and Indexing Services Covering Sources of the World's Engineering Literature. Engineering Information Inc. • Monthly. Institutions, $5,279.00 per year. Provides indexing and abstracting of the world's engineering and technical literature.

Mechanical Engineering Abstracts. CSA. • Bimonthly. $1,620.00 per year. Includes print and online editions. Formerly *ISMEC - Mechanical Engineering Abstracts.*

DIRECTORIES

Dun's Industrial Guide: The Metalworking Directory. Dun and Bradstreet Corp. • Annual. Libraries, $485; commercial institutions, $795.00. Lease basis. Three volumes. Lists about 65,000 U. S. manufacturing plants using metal and suppliers of metalworking equipment and materials. Includes names and titles of key personnel. Products, purchases, and processes are indicated.

Thomas Register of American Manufacturers. Thomas Publishing Co., Inc. • Annual. $149.00. 34 volumes. A three-part system offering information on a wide variety of industrial equipment and supplies. Lists more than 151,000 industrial product and services companies.

ONLINE DATABASES

Thomas Register Online. Thomas Publishing Co., Inc. • Provides concise information on approximately 194,000 U. S. companies, mainly manufacturers, with over 50,000 product classifications. Indexes over 115,000 trade names. Information is updated semiannually. Inquire as to online cost and availability.

PERIODICALS AND NEWSLETTERS

American Tool, Die and Stamping News. Eagle Publications, Inc. • Bimonthly. Free.

Cutting Tool Engineering. CTE Publications, Inc. • Nine times a year. $30.00 per year.

Die Casting Engineer. North American Die Casting Association. • Bimonthly. Free to members; non-

members, $55.00 per year.

STATISTICS SOURCES

U. S. Industry and Trade Outlook. Available from National Technical Information Service. • Annual. $69.95. Produced by the International Trade Administration, U. S. Department of Commerce, in a "public-private" partnership with DRI/McGraw-Hill and Standard & Poor's. Provides basic data, outlook for the current year, and "Long-Term Prospects" (five-year projections) for a wide variety of products and services. Includes high technology industries. Formerly *U. S. Industrial Outlook.*

TRADE/PROFESSIONAL ASSOCIATIONS

National Tooling and Machining Association. 9300 Livingston Rd., Fort Washington, MD 20744-4998. Phone: 800-248-6862 Fax: (301)248-7104 • URL: http://www.ntma.org.

North American Die Casting Association. 241 Holbrook Dr., Wheeling, IL 60090-5809. Phone: (847)279-0001 Fax: (847)279-0002 E-mail: nadca@diecasting.org • URL: http://www.diecasting.org • Represents producers of die castings and suppliers to the industry, product and die designers, metallurgists, and students. Develops product standards; compiles trade statistics on metal consumption trends; conducts promotional activities; provides information on chemistry, mechanics, engineering, and other arts and sciences related to die casting. Provides training materials and short, intensive courses in die casting. Maintains speakers' bureau.

TOOLS, POWER

See: POWER TOOL INDUSTRY

TOTAL QUALITY MANAGEMENT (TQM)

See also: QUALITY CONTROL

GENERAL WORKS

Cases in Total Quality Management: Manufacturing and Services. Jay H. Heizer. Course Technology, Inc. • 1997. $48.95. (GC Principles in Management Series.).

Managing Quality in America's Most Admired Companies. Jay W. Spechler. Engineering and Management Press. • 1993. $49.95. Part one provides "Guidelines for Implementing Quality Management," including detailed information on the Malcolm Baldrige National Quality Award. Part two contains 30 "Case Studies of Quality Management in Leading Companies.".

Principles and Practices of TQM. Thomas J. Cartin. ASQ Quality Press. • 1993. $28.00.

Principles of Total Quality. Vincent K. Omachonu. CRC Press. • 2004. $54.95. Third edition. Covers the general management of quality control, including leadership, human resources, information analysis, strategic planning, and customer satisfaction.

Putting Total Quality Management to Work: What TQM Means, How to Use It, and How to Sustain It Over the Long Run. Marshall Sashkin and Kenneth J. Kiser. Berrett-Koehler Publishers, Inc. • 1993. $19.95. Includes control charts, flow charts, scatter diagrams, and criteria for the Baldridge Quality Award.

ABSTRACTS AND INDEXES

Business Periodicals Index. H. W. Wilson Co. • 11 times a year. Quarterly and annual cumulations. Price varies.

CD-ROM DATABASES

ABI/INFORM. PROQUEST. • Monthly. Provides CD-ROM indexing and abstracting of worldwide

business literature. Archival discs are available from 1971. Formerly *ABI/INFORM OnDisc.*

WILSONDISC: Wilson Business Abstracts. H. W. Wilson Co. • Monthly. Includes unlimited online access to *Wilson Business Abstracts* through WILSONLINE. Provides CD-ROM "cover-to-cover" abstracting and indexing of over 600 prominent business periodicals. Indexing is from 1982, abstracting from 1990. (*Business Periodicals Index* without abstracts is available on CD-ROM at $1,495 per year.).

DIRECTORIES

Quality Progress: QA/QC Services Directory. American Society for Quality. • Annual. $12.00. Provides information on companies offering services related to quality management, such as consulting, inspection, auditing, calibrating, and training.

Quality Progress: Quality Assurance and Quality Control Software Directory. American Society for Quality. • Annual. Available only online. Price on application. Covers computer software application packages related to quality management. Includes information about software companies and descriptions of programs offered. Formerly *Quality Progress Directory of Software for Quality Assurance and Quality Contol.*

HANDBOOKS AND MANUALS

Industry's Guide to ISO 9000. Adedeji B. Badiru. John Wiley and Sons, Inc. • 1995. $120.00. (Engineering and Technology Management Series).

International Standards Desk Reference: Your Passport to World Markets. Amy Zuckerman. AMACOM. • 1996. $35.00. Provides information on standards important in export-import trade, such as ISO 9000.

ISO 9000 and the Service Sector: A Critical Interpretation of the 1994 Revisions. James L. Lamprecht. ASQ Quality Press. • 1994. $38.00. A review of the ISO 9000 quality standards as they relate to service organizations. Includes examples of applications.

ISO 9000 Auditor's Companion. Kent A. Keeney. ASQ Quality Press. • 1995. $30.00. Designed to help companies prepare for ISO 9000 quality management audits.

ISO 9000 Book: A Global Competitor's Guide to Compliance and Certification. John T. Rabbitt and Peter Bergh. AMACOM. • 1994. $29.95. Second edition.

ISO 9000 Handbook. Robert W. Peach. QSU Publishing Co. • 2003. $99.95. Fourth edition. Includes detailed information for the ISO 9000 registration process.

ISO 9000 Made Easy: A Cost-Saving Guide to Documentation and Registration. Amy Zuckerman. AMACOM. • 1994. $75.00.

Production and Operations Management: Total Quality and Responsiveness. Hamid Noori and Russell Radford. McGraw-Hill. • 1994. $70.25.

Quality Manager's Complete Guide to ISO 9000. Richard B. Clements. Prentice Hall PTR. • 2000. $79.95. (Quality Manager's Complete Guide to ISO 9000).

Quality Manager's Complete Guide to ISO 9000: 2000 Edition. Richard B. Clements. Prentice Hall PTR. • 2000. $39.95. Supplement to *Quality Manager's Complete Guide to ISO 9000.*

Teambuilding and Total Quality: A Guidebook to TQM Success. Gene Milas. Engineering and Management Press. • 1997. $29.95. A practical, how-to-do-it guide to total quality management in industry. The importance of employee involvement is stressed.

Total Quality Management Handbook. John L.

Hradesky. McGraw-Hill. • 1994. $74.50.

ONLINE DATABASES

Management Contents. Gale Cengage Learning. • Covers a wide range of management, financial, marketing, personnel, and administrative topics. About 150 leading business journals are indexed and abstracted from 1974 to date, with monthly updating. Inquire as to online cost and availability.

Trade & Industry Database. Gale Cengage Learning. • Provides indexing of business periodicals, January 1981 to date. Daily updates. (Full text articles from some periodicals are available online, 1983 to date. Inquire as to online cost and availability).

Wilson Business Abstracts Online. H. W. Wilson Co. • Indexes and abstracts 600 major business periodicals, plus the *Wall Street Journal* and the business section of the *New York Times.* Indexing is from 1982, abstracting from 1990, with the two newspapers included from 1993. Updated weekly. Inquire as to online cost and availability. (*Business Periodicals Index* without abstracts is also available online.).

PERIODICALS AND NEWSLETTERS

ISO Management Systems. Available from American National Standards Institute. • Bimonthly. Price on application. Newsletter on quality standards. Published by the International Organization for Standardization (ISO). Text in English. Formerly *ISO 9000 and ISO 14000 News.*

Lakewood Report on Positive Employee Practices. Lakewood Publications, Inc. • Monthly. $128.00 per year. Newsletter. Provides news for quality improvement managers. Includes columns entitled "Eye on Quality" and "Quality Movement News." Formerly *Total Quality.*

Quality Management Journal. American Society for Quality. • Quarterly. Members, $50.00 per year; non-members, $60.00 per year. Emphasizes research in quality control and management.

Quality Progress. American Society for Quality. • Monthly. Individuals, $60.00 per year; institutions, $120.00 per year. Covers developments in quality improvement throughout the world.

RESEARCH CENTERS AND INSTITUTES

Center for Quality and Productivity. University of North Texas, College of Business Administration, P.P. Box 305249, Denton, TX 76203-3677. Phone: (940)565-4767 E-mail: prybutok@unt.edu • URL: http://www.coba.unt.edu • Fields of research include the management of quality systems and statistical methodology.

Center for Quality and Productivity Improvement. University of Wisconsin-Madison, 610 N. Walnut St., 575 WARF Bldg., Madison, WI 53705. Phone: (608)263-2520 Fax: (608)263-1425 E-mail: quality@engr.wisc.edu • URL: http://www.engr.wisc.edu/centers/cqpi • Research areas include quality management and industrial engineering.

TRADE/PROFESSIONAL ASSOCIATIONS

American Society for Quality. 600 N. Plankinton Ave., Milwaukee, WI 53201-3005. Phone: 800-248-1946 or (414)272-8575 Fax: (414)272-1734 E-mail: cs@asq.org • URL: http://www.asq.org.

International Organization for Standardization. 1 rue de Varembe-CP56, CH-1211 Geneva 20, Switzerland. Phone: 41 22 7490111 Fax: 41 22 7490948 E-mail: rh@iso.org • URL: http://www.iso.ch/ • Members are national standards organizations. Develops and publishes international standards, including ISO 9000 quality management standards. Affiliated with American National Standards Institute.

TOURIST INDUSTRY

See: TRAVEL INDUSTRY

TOWN GOVERNMENT

See: MUNICIPAL GOVERNMENT

TOWN PLANNING

See: CITY PLANNING

TOWNS AND CITIES

See: CITIES AND TOWNS

TOXIC SUBSTANCES

See: HAZARDOUS MATERIALS

TOXICOLOGY, INDUSTRIAL

See: INDUSTRIAL HYGIENE

TOY INDUSTRY

CD-ROM DATABASES

World Marketing Forecasts on CD-ROM. Gale Cengage Learning. • Annual. $2,500.00. Produced by Euromonitor. Provides detailed forecast data for the years to 2012 on CD-ROM for 54 countries in all parts of the world. Covers a wide range of social, demographic, economic, and market factors. Includes specific forecasts for many kinds of consumer products.

DIRECTORIES

Directory of Discount and General Merchandise Stores. Chain Store Guide. • Annual. $327.00. Online edition, $747.00. Includes retailers and wholesalers of housewares, giftwares, novelties, toys, hobby materials, crafts, and stationery.

Playthings--Buyers Guide. Reed Elsevier. • Publication includes: Lists of toy manufacturers and their suppliers, designers and inventors, manufacturers' representatives, licensor, importers. Entries include: Company name, address, phone, description of products manufactured or lines carried.

FINANCIAL RATIOS

Annual Statement Studies. The Risk Management Association. • Annual. Median and quartile financial ratios are given for over 400 kinds of manufacturing, wholesale, retail, construction, and consumer finance establishments. Data is sorted by both asset size and sales volume. Includes a clearly written "Definition of Ratios" and an alphabetical industry index.

Annual Statement Studies: Industry Default Probabilities and Cash Flow Measures. The Risk Management Association. • Annual. $145.00. Serves as a companion volume to the original *Annual Statement Studies.* Gives probability of default estimates on a percentage scale for more than 450 industries. Includes changes in position year-by-year for eight financial statement line items and provides percentage measures of cash flow.

PERIODICALS AND NEWSLETTERS

Playthings: For Today's Merchandiser of Toys, Hobbies and Crafts. Reed Business Information. • Monthly. $39.95 per year. Includes annual *Directory.* Covers the major toy and hobby categories, industry news and news products.

STATISTICS SOURCES

Annual Survey of Manufactures. Available from U. S. Government Printing Office. • Annual. Prices vary. Issued by the U. S. Census Bureau as an interim update to the *Census of Manufactures.*

Includes data on number of manufacturing establishments in various industries, employment, labor costs, value of shipments, capital expenditures, inventories, energy costs, and assets. (See also Census Bureau home page, http://www.census.gov/.).

Consumer International. Available from Gale Cengage Learning. • Annual. $1,290.00. Published by Euromonitor. Contains extensive consumer market, economic, and demographic data for 25 major, non-European countries, including the U. S. and Canada. Includes consumer market size (volume and value) for 150 product types in 14 categories (food, clothing, automobiles, cosmetics, appliances, etc.).

European Marketing Forecasts. Available from Gale Cengage Learning. • Annual. $1,250.00. Published by Euromonitor. Contains demographic, economic, and market forecasts for the countries of Europe to the year 2010. Forecasts include market-size data for 15 consumer product sectors (food, clothing, automobiles, consumer electronics, etc.).

International Marketing Forecasts. Available from Gale Cengage Learning. • Annual. $1,250.00. Published by Euromonitor. Contains demographic, economic, and market forecasts to the year 2013 for major, non-European countries, including the U. S. and Canada. Forecasts include market-size data for 15 consumer product sectors, such as food, clothing, and automobiles.

TRADE/PROFESSIONAL ASSOCIATIONS

Official International Toy Center Directory. PO Box 173, 177 Sound Beach Ave., Old Greenwich, CT 06870-0173. Fax: (203)637-8549 E-mail: tcdnyc@aol.com • Toy manufacturers and toy sales representatives who maintain permanent sales offices and showrooms at 200 5th Ave. and 1107 Broadway in New York City. "To promote the Greater Toy Center as the toy center of the world, thereby making toy buying and selling more convenient and economical.".

Toy Industry Association. 1115 Broadway, Ste. 400, New York, NY 10010. Phone: (212)675-1141 Fax: (212)633-1429 E-mail: info@toyassociation.org • URL: http://www.toy-tia.org • Provides business services to U.S. manufacturers and importers of toys. Manages American International Toy Fair; represents the industry before Federal, State and Local government on issues of importance; provides legal and legislative counsel; conducts educational programs; compiles industry statistics.

TRACTORS

See: AGRICULTURAL MACHINERY

TRADE

See: BUSINESS; FOREIGN TRADE

TRADE ASSOCIATIONS

See: ASSOCIATIONS

TRADE, BOARDS OF

See: CHAMBERS OF COMMERCE

TRADE CATALOGS

See: CATALOGS AND DIRECTORIES

TRADE DIRECTORIES

See: CATALOGS AND DIRECTORIES

TRADE EXHIBITS

See: CONVENTIONS; FAIRS; TRADE SHOWS

TRADE FAIRS

See: CONVENTIONS; FAIRS; TRADE SHOWS

TRADE JOURNALS

See also: PERIODICALS

GENERAL WORKS

Business Journals of the United States: Historical Guides to the World's Periodicals and Newspapers. William Fisher, editor. Greenwood Publishing Group, Inc. • 1991. $82.95. Contains historical and descriptive essays covering over 100 leading business publications.

ABSTRACTS AND INDEXES

Business Periodicals Index. H. W. Wilson Co. • 11 times a year. Quarterly and annual cumulations. Price varies.

Canadian Periodical Index. Gale Cengage Learning. • Monthly. $595.00 per year. Annual cumulation. Indexes more than 400 English and French language periodicals.

BIBLIOGRAPHIES

Guide to Special Issues and Indexes of Periodicals. Miriam Uhlan and Doris B. Katz, editors. Special Libraries Association. • 1994. $59.00. Fourth edition. A listing, with prices, of the special issues of over 1700 U. S. and Canadian periodicals in business, industry, technology, science, and the arts. Includes a comprehensive subject index.

CD-ROM DATABASES

CPI.Q: The Canadian Periodical Index Full-Text on CD-ROM. Gale Cengage Learning. • Bimonthly. Provides CD-ROM citations from 1988 to date for more than 400 English and French language periodicals. Contains full-text coverage from 1995 to date for 150 periodicals.

MediaFinder CD-ROM: Oxbridge Directories of Print Media and Catalogs. Oxbridge Communications, Inc. • Quarterly. $1,995.00 per year. CD-ROM includes about 100,000 listings from *Standard Periodical Directory, National Directory of Catalogs, National Directory of British Mail Order Catalogs, National Directory of German Mail Order Catalogs, Oxbridge Directory of Newsletters, National Directory of Mailing Lists, College Media Directory,* and *National Directory of Magazines.*

DIRECTORIES

Books and Periodicals Online: The Guide to Business and Legal Information on Databases and CD-ROM's. Nuchine Nobari, editor. Library Technology Alliance, Ltd. • Annual. $379.00. Two volumes. 119,000 periodicals available as part of online and CD-ROM databases; international coverage.

Burrelle's Media Directory: Magazines and Newsletters. Burrelle's Information Services. • Annual. $550.00. Provides detailed descriptions of more than 13,500 magazines and newsletters published in the U. S., Canada, and Mexico. Categories are professional, consumer, trade, and college. Semiannual *Updates.* Includes CD-ROM.

Cabell's Directory of Publishing Opportunities in Management. Cabell Publishing Co. • 1997. $149.95. Seventh edition. Four volumes. Over 540 scholarly periodicals in management.

CARD The Media Information Network. Rogers Media Publishing. • Covers: Radio and television stations and networks; daily and weekend newspapers; consumer, farm, and business publications; advertising agencies and international media representatives; advertising, marketing, and media associations; and transportation and out-of-home advertising. Entries include: For publications--Title, company name, address, phone, frequency, names and titles of key personnel, advertising rates, discounts, mechanical requirements, copy regulations, circulation, closing and publication dates. For broadcasting stations--Call letters, name of owning company, address, phone, name of firm or individual representing station for advertising, special features, format, facilities, affiliations, rates, participation programs. For agencies and associations--Name, address, phone, personnel.

Cyberhound's Guide to Publications on the Internet. Gale Cengage Learning. • 1996. $79.00. Presents critical descriptions and ratings of more than 3,400 Internet databases of journals, newspapers, newsletters, and other publications. Includes a glossary of Internet terms, a bibliography, and three indexes. (Cyberhound's Series).

Fulltext Sources Online. Information Today Inc. • Covers: over 21,000 periodicals, newspapers, newsletters, newswires; and tv/radio transcripts available in full text online. Entries include: Name of file, online services through which available, dates of coverage, lag time if applicable. Separate list gives online service address and phone; indicates degree of online coverage and selection policy. Internet url's listed where applicable.

Gale Directory of Publications and Broadcast Media. Gale Cengage Learning. • Annual. $770.00. Five volumes. *Interedition Supplement,* Free. A guide to publications and broadcasting stations in the U. S. and Canada, including newspapers, magazines, journals, radio stations, television stations, and cable systems. Geographic arrangement. Volume three consists of statistical tables, maps, subject indexes, and title index.

Grey House Directory of Special Issues: A Guide to Business Magazines' Buyer's Guides & Directory Issues. Grey House Publishing. • 2001. $175.00. Second edition. Provides information on more than 2,500 specialized directories issued by business and trade journals, arranged according to 90 industry groups.

International Media Guide: Business-Professional: Asia/Pacific, Middle East, Africa. SRDS. • Annual. $300.00. Provides information on 14,000 trade journals "from Africa to the Pacific Rim," including advertising rates and circulation data.

International Media Guide Business-Professional Publications: Europe. SRDS. • Annual. $300.00. Describes 6,000 trade journals from Eastern and Western Europe, with advertising rates and circulation data.

International Media Guide: Business/Professional Publications: The Americas. SRDS. • Annual. $300.00. Describes trade journals from North, South, and Central America, with advertising rates and circulation data.

Magazines Career Directory: A Practical One-Stop Guide to Getting a Job in Publc Relations. Visible Ink Press. • 1993. $39.00. Fifth edition. Includes information on magazine publishing careers in art, editing, sales, and business management. Provides advice from "insiders," resume suggestions, a directory of companies that may offer entry-level positions, and a directory of career information sources. (Career Advisor Series).

SRDS Business Publication Advertising Source. SRDS. • Monthly. $714.00 per year. Issued in three parts: (1) U. S. Business Publications, (2) U. S. Healthcare Publications, and (3) International Publications. Provides detailed advertising rates, profiles of editorial content, management names, "Multiple Publications Publishers," circulation data, and other trade journal information. Formerly *Business Publication Advertising Source.*

SRDS Print Media Production Source. SRDS. • Quarterly. $808.00 per year. Contains details of printing and mechanical production requirements for advertising in specific trade journals, consumer magazines, and newspapers. Formerly *Print Media Production Source.*

SRDS Technology Media Source. SRDS. • Annual. $312.00. Contains detailed information on business publications, consumer magazines, and direct mail lists that may be of interest to "technology marketers." Emphasis is on aviation and telecommunications. Formerly*Technology Media Source.*

World Directory of Trade and Business Journals. Euromonitor International. • 2003. $650.00. Second edition. Contains descriptions of more than 2,300 trade and business journals published in various countries of the world.

INTERNET DATABASES

EBSCO Information Services. Ebsco Publishing. Phone: 800-653-2726 or (978)356-6500 Fax: (978)356-6565 E-mail: ep@epnet.com • URL: http://www.epnet.com • Fee-based Web site providing Internet access to a wide variety of databases, including business-related material. Full text is available for many periodical titles, with daily updates. Fees: Apply.

InSite 2. Intelligence Data/Thomson Financial. Phone: 800-654-0393 or (617)856-1890 Fax: (617)737-3182 E-mail: intelligence.data@tfn.com • URL: http://www.insite2.gale.com/ • Fee-based Web site consolidates information in a "Base Pack" consisting of Business InSite, Market InSite, and Company InSite. Optional databases are Consumer InSite, Health and Wellness InSite, Newsletter In-Site, and Computer InSite. Includes fulltext content from more than 2,500 trade publications, journals, newsletters, newspapers, analyst reports, and other sources. Continuous updating. Formerly produced by The Gale Group.

ProQuest Direct. ProQuest Inc. Phone: 800-889-3358 or (734)761-4700 Fax: (734)662-4554 • URL: http://proquest.com • Fee-based Web site providing Internet access to more than 3,000 periodicals, newspapers, and other publications. Many items are available full-text, with daily updates. Includes extensive corporate and financial information. Fees: Apply.

PubList.com: The Internet Directory of Publications. Bowes & Associates, Inc. Phone: (781)792-0999 Fax: (781)792-0988 E-mail: info@publist.com • URL: http://www.publist.com • "The premier online global resource for information about print and electronic publications." Provides online searching for information on more than 150,000 magazines, journals, newsletters, e-journals, and monographs. Database entries generally include title, publisher, format, address, editor, circulation, subject, and International Standard Serial Number (ISSN). Fees: Free.

Ulrichsweb.com. R. R. Bowker. Phone: 888-269-5372 or (908)464-6800 Fax: (908)464-3553 E-mail: info@bowker.com • URL: http://www.ulrichsweb.com • Web site provides fee-based access to about 250,000 serials records from the *Ulrich's International Periodicals Directory* database. Includes periodical evaluations from *Library Journal* and *Magazines for Libraries.* Monthly updates.

WilsonWeb Periodicals Databases. H. W. Wilson. Phone: 800-367-6770 or (718)588-8400 Fax: 800-590-1617 or (718)992-8003 E-mail: custserv@hwwilson.com • URL: http://www.hwwilson.com/ • Web sites provide fee-based access to *Wilson Business Full Text, Applied Science & Technology Full*

Text, Biological & Agricultural Index, Library Literature & Information Science Full Text, and *Readers' Guide Full Text, Mega Edition.* Daily updates.

ONLINE DATABASES

Gale Database of Publications and Broadcast Media. Gale Cengage Learning. • An online directory containing detailed information on over 67,000 periodicals, newspapers, broadcast stations, cable systems, directories, and newsletters. Corresponds to the following print sources: *Gale Directory of Publications and Broadcast Media; Directories in Print; City and State Directories in Print; Newsletters in Print.* Semiannual updates. Inquire as to online cost and availability.

Trade & Industry Database. Gale Cengage Learning. • Provides indexing of business periodicals, January 1981 to date. Daily updates. (Full text articles from some periodicals are available online, 1983 to date. Inquire as to online cost and availability).

PERIODICALS AND NEWSLETTERS

Folio: The New Dynamics of Magazine Publishing. Primedia Business Magazines and Media. • Monthly. $96.00 per year.

SI: Special Issues. Trip Wyckoff, editor. Hoover's, Inc. • Bimonthly. $149.95 per year. Newsletter. Serves as a supplement to *Directory of Business Periodical Special Issues.* Provides current information on trade journal special issues and editorial calendars.

RESEARCH CENTERS AND INSTITUTES

Knight Center for Specialized Journalism. University of Maryland, 1117 Cole Field House, College Park, MD 20742-1024. Phone: (301)405-4817 E-mail: knight@umail.umd.edu • URL: http://www.knightcenter.umd.edu/ • Research area is media coverage of complex subjects, such as economics, law, science, and medicine.

STATISTICS SOURCES

Computer Publishing Market Forecast. SIMBA Information. • Biennial. $1,895.00. Provides market data on computer-related books, magazines, newsletters, and other publications. Includes profiles of major publishers of computer-related material.

TRADE/PROFESSIONAL ASSOCIATIONS

American Society of Business Publications Editors. 710 E Ogden Ave., Ste. 600, Naperville, IL 60563-8603. Phone: (603)579-3288 Fax: (603)369-2488 E-mail: info@asbpe.org • URL: http://www.asbpe.com.

BPA International. 2 Corporate Dr., Ste. 900, Shelton, CT 06484. Phone: (203)447-2800 Fax: (203)447-2900 E-mail: info@bpai.com • URL: http://www.bpai.com • Verifies business and consumer periodical circulation statements. Includes a Circulation Managers Committee. Formerly Business Publications Audit of Circulation.

TRADE NAMES

See: TRADEMARKS AND TRADE NAMES

TRADE SECRETS

See also: INTELLECTUAL PROPERTY

ABSTRACTS AND INDEXES

Business Periodicals Index. H. W. Wilson Co. • 11 times a year. Quarterly and annual cumulations. Price varies.

Index to Legal Periodicals and Books. H. W. Wilson Co. • Monthly. $490.00 per year. Quarterly and annual cumulations.

HANDBOOKS AND MANUALS

Protecting Trade Secrets, Patents, Copyrights, and Trademarks. Robert C. Dorr and Christopher H.

Munch. Aspen Publishers, Inc. • $165.00. Looseleaf service.

Trade Secret Protection in an Information Age. Gale R. Peterson. Glasser LegalWorks. • Looseleaf. $149.00, including sample forms on disk. Periodic supplementation available. Covers trade secret law relating to computer software, online databases, and multimedia products. Explanations are based on more than 1,000 legal cases. Sample forms on disk include work-for-hire examples and covenants not to compete.

Worldwide Trade Secrets Law. Terrence F. MaLaren, editor. West Group. • $440.00. Three looseleaf volume. Annual supplementation.

ONLINE DATABASES

Index to Legal Periodicals and Books (Online). H. W. Wilson Co. • Broad coverage of law journals and books 1981 to date. Monthly updates. Inquire as to online cost and availability.

Legal Resource Index. Gale Cengage Learning. • Broad coverage of law literature appearing in legal, business, and other periodicals, 1980 to date. Daily updates. Inquire as to online cost and availability.

LEXIS. LEXIS-NEXIS. • The various LEXIS databases provide full text and indexing for a wide variety of legal cases, statutes, orders, and opinions.

Wilson Business Abstracts Online. H. W. Wilson Co. • Indexes and abstracts 600 major business periodicals, plus the *Wall Street Journal* and the business section of the *New York Times.* Indexing is from 1982, abstracting from 1990, with the two newspapers included from 1993. Updated weekly. Inquire as to online cost and availability. (*Business Periodicals Index* without abstracts is also available online.).

PERIODICALS AND NEWSLETTERS

Security Management. American Society for Industrial Security. • Monthly. Members, $38.00 per year; non-members, $48.00 per year. Articles cover the protection of corporate assets, including personnel property and information security.

TRADE/PROFESSIONAL ASSOCIATIONS

American Society for Industrial Security. 1625 Prince St., Alexandria, VA 22314-2818. Phone: (703)519-6200 Fax: (703)519-6299 E-mail: asis@asisonline • URL: http://www.asisonline.org.

OTHER SOURCES

Trade Secrets. American Lawyer Media, Inc. • Looseleaf. $169.00. Updated as needed. Covers the legal protection of trade secrets, including information on the Economic Espionage Act of 1996. Includes a CD-ROM with samples of applicable legal forms. (Law Journal Press).

TRADE SHOWS

See also: CONVENTIONS

ABSTRACTS AND INDEXES

Business Periodicals Index. H. W. Wilson Co. • 11 times a year. Quarterly and annual cumulations. Price varies.

CD-ROM DATABASES

World Database of Business Information Sources on CD-ROM. Gale Cengage Learning. • Annual. Produced by Euromonitor. Presents Euromonitor's entire information source database on CD-ROM. Contains a worldwide total of about 35,000 publications, organizations, libraries, trade fairs, and online databases.

DIRECTORIES

Business Organizations, Agencies, and Publications Directory. Gale Cengage Learning. • 2003. $480.00. 15th edition. Over 40,000 entries describing 39 types of business information sources. Classified by

type of organization, publication, or serviceIncludes state, national, and international agencies and organizations. Master index to names and keywords. Also includes e-mail addresses and web site URL's.

The Directory of Business Information Resources: Associations, Newsletters, Magazine Trade Shows. Grey House Publishing, Inc. • Annual. $250.00. Provides concise information on associations, newsletters, magazines, and trade shows for each of 90 major industry groups. An "Entry & Company Index" serves as a guide to titles, publishers, and organizations.

Directory of Conventions Regional Editions. VNU Business Media. • Annual. $155.00 per volume. Four volumes. Set, $285.00. Over 14,000 meetings of North American national, regional, and state and local organizations.

Encyclopedia of Associations. Gale Cengage Learning. • Annual. $1,530.00. Three volumes. Volume 1, National Organizations, $585.00; Volume 2, Geographic and Executive Indexes, $460.00; Volume 3, supplement, $485.00.

Exhibitor Magazine Buyer's Guide to Trade Show Exhibits. Exhibitor Magazine Group, Inc. • Annual. $35.00. Covers about 200 manufacturers of trade show exhibit equipment. Formerly *Buyer's Guide to Trade Show Displays.*

International Tradeshow Directory: The Annual Statistical Directory of U.S. and Canadian Tradeshows and Public Shows. Tradeshow Week. • Semiannual. Free to qualified personnel. Provides detailed information for more than 9,000 U. S. and Canadian trade shows of 5,000 square feet or more scheduled for the next four years.

Trade Show Exhibitors Association Membership Directory and Industry Buyer's Guide. Trade Show Exhibitors Association. • Annual. Free to members; non-members, $99.00. Provides listings and details for approximately 2,300 exhibit professionals.

Trade Shows Worldwide: An International Directory of Events, Facilities and Suppliers. Gale Cengage Learning. • 2003. $355.00. 19th edition. Provides detailed information from over 75 countries on more than 10,800 trade shows and exhibitions. Separate sections are provided for trade shows/exhibitions, for sponsors/organizers, and for services, facilities, and information sources. Indexing is by date, location, subject, name, and keyword.

Tradeshow and Exhibit Manager Buyer's Guide. Goldstein and Associates. • Annual. $10.00. Lists about 1,000 suppliers providing products and services for exhibits and tradeshows.

HANDBOOKS AND MANUALS

Guerilla Trade Show Selling: New Unconventional Weapons and Tactics to Meet More People, Get More Leads, and Close More Sales. Jay C. Levinson and others. John Wiley and Sons, Inc. • 1997. $21.95. (More People, Get More Leads and Close More Sales Series).

How to Get the Most Out of Trade Shows. Steve Miller. McGraw-Hill. • 1999. $29.95. Third revised edition. (NTC Business Books Series).

Show and Sell: 133 Business Building Ways to Promote Your Trade Show Exhibit. Margit B. Weisgal. AMACOM. • 1996. $55.00. Contains information and advice on pre-show advertising and promotion, booth management, literature distribution, customer dialogue, "damage control," follow-up, evaluation, and other exhibit topics. Includes bibliography, checklists, worksheets, and index.

INTERNET DATABASES

Trade Show Center. Global Sources/Trade Media Holdings Ltd. [Singapore]. Phone: (656)574-2800 E-mail: service@globalsources.com • URL: http://www.globalsources.com/TRADESHW/TRDSHFRM.HTM • Free Web site provides current, detailed information on more than 1,000 major trade shows worldwide, including events in the U. S., but with an emphasis on "Asia and Greater China." Searching is offered by product, supplier, country, and month of year. Includes links to "Trade Information.".

ONLINE DATABASES

Wilson Business Abstracts Online. H. W. Wilson Co. • Indexes and abstracts 600 major business periodicals, plus the *Wall Street Journal* and the business section of the *New York Times.* Indexing is from 1982, abstracting from 1990, with the two newspapers included from 1993. Updated weekly. Inquire as to online cost and availability. (*Business Periodicals Index* without abstracts is also available online.).

PERIODICALS AND NEWSLETTERS

Exhibit Builder. Exhibit Builder, Inc. • Seven timees a year. $40.00 per year. For designers and builders of trade show exhibits.

Facility Manager. International Association of Assembly Managers, Inc. • Quarterly. Free to members; non-members, $55.00 per year.

Journal of Convention and Event Tourism. Haworth Press, Inc. • Quarterly. $165.00 per year. Formerly *Journal of Convention and Exhibition Management.*

Successful Meetings: The Authority on Meetings and Incentive Travel Management. VNU Business Media. • Monthly. $79.00 per year.

Tradeshow and Exhibit Manager. Goldstein and Associates. • Bimonthly. $80.00 per year. Edited for exhibit, tradeshow, and exposition managers. Covers design trends, site selection, shipping problems, industry news, etc. Supplement available *Tradeshow Directory.*

Tradeshow Week: Since 1971, the Only Weekly Source of News and Statistics on the Tradeshow Industry. Reed Business Information. • 50 times a year. $419.00 per year; includes 18 *Supplements and 7 Websites.* Edited for corporate and association trade show and exhibit managers. Includes show calendars and labor rates.

TRADE/PROFESSIONAL ASSOCIATIONS

Center for Exhibition Industry Research. 2301 S. Lake Shore Dr., Suite E1002, Chicago, IL 60616. Phone: (312)808-2347 Fax: (312)949-3472 E-mail: ceir@mpea.com • URL: http://www.ceir.org • Promotes the trade show as a marketing device. Formerly Trade Show Bureau.

Exhibit Designers and Producers Association. 5775G Peachtree-Dunwoody Rd., N.E., Suite 500, Atlanta, GA 30342. Phone: (404)303-7310 Fax: (404)252-0774 E-mail: lhoward@kellencompany.com • URL: http://www.edpa.com • Members are firms that design and build displays for trade shows.

Exposition Service Contractors Association. 22 Corporate Cir., No. 400, Henderson, NV 89074-7701. Phone: 877-792-3722 or (702)319-9561 or (702)450-7662 Fax: (702)450-7732 E-mail: askus@esca.org • URL: http://www.esca.org • Members are companies providing supplies and services for trade shows and conventions.

International Association for Exhibition Management. 8111 LBJ.Fwy., Ste. 750, Dallas, TX 75251-1313. Phone: (972)458-8002 Fax: (972)458-8119 E-mail: iaem@iaem.org • URL: http://www.iaem.org • Formerly International Association of Exposition Management.

International Association of Assembly Managers. 635 Fritz Dr., Ste. 100, Coppell, TX 75019-4442. Phone: 800-935-4226 or (972)255-8020 Fax: (972)255-9582 E-mail: dexter.king@iaam.org • URL: http://www.iaam.org • Members are auditorium, theater, exhibit hall, and other facility managers. Formerly International Association of Auditorium Managers.

Trade Show Exhibitors Association. 2301 S Lake Shore Dr., Ste. 1005, 2301 S Lakeshore Dr., No. 1005, Chicago, IL 60616. Phone: (312)842-8732 Fax: (312)842-8744 E-mail: tsea@tsea.org • URL: http://www.tsea.org • Exhibitors working to improve the effectiveness of trade shows as a marketing tool. Purposes are to promote the progress and development of trade show exhibiting; to collect and disseminate trade show information; conduct studies, surveys, and stated projects designed to improve trade shows; to foster good relations and communications with organizations representing others in the industry; to undertake other activities necessary to promote the welfare of member companies. Sponsors Exhibit +Industry +Education Foundation and professional exhibiting seminars; the forum series of educational programs on key issues affecting the industry. Maintains placement services; compiles statistics.

TRADE UNIONS

See: LABOR UNIONS

TRADEMARKS AND TRADE NAMES

See also: COPYRIGHT; PATENTS

GENERAL WORKS

Advertising Media Planning: A Brand Management Approach. Larry D. Kelley and Donald W. Jugenheimer. M. E. Sharpe, Inc. • 2003. $69.95. Emphasizes the importance of brand recognition in media planning.

Basic Facts About Trademarks. Available from U. S. Government Printing Office. • 2001. $4.25. Issued by the Patent and Trademark Office, U. S. Department of Commerce. Includes filing requirements and sample applications.

Living Logos: How U. S. Corporations Revitalize Their Trademarks. David E. Carter, editor. Art Direction Book Co., Inc. • 1993. $22.95. Traces the history and evolution of 70 famous U. S. company logos.

The 22 Immutable Laws of Branding: How to Build a Product or Service Into a World-Class Brand. Al Ries and Laura Ries. HarperInformation. • 1998. $25.00. Provides advice on attaining positive brand recognition.

What's in a Name? Advertising and the Concept of Brands. John P. Jones and Jan S. Slater. M. E. Sharpe, Inc. • 2003. $79.95. Second edition. Covers brand identity and loyalty from the viewpoint of modern marketing theory.

ABSTRACTS AND INDEXES

Index of Trademarks Issued from the United States Patent and Trademark Office. Available from U. S. Government Printing Office. • Annual. $98.00. Arranged alphabetically by name of registrant. The caption title is "List of Trademark Registrants.".

ALMANACS AND YEARBOOKS

Intellectual Property Law Review. West Group. • 1999. $299.00. Patent, trademark, and copyright practices.

CD-ROM DATABASES

Authority Intellectual Property Library. LexisNexis/Matthew Bender. • Quarterly. Price on request. CD-ROM contains updated full text of *Intellectual Property Counseling and Litigation, Computer Law, International Computer Law, Nimmer on Copyright, Milgrim on Trade Secrets, Patent Litigation, Patent Licensing Transactions, Trademark Protection and Practice,* and other Matthew Bender publications relating to the law of intellectual property.

CASSIS (Trademarks). U. S. Patent and Trademark Office, Office of Electronic Information Products. • CD-ROM products include *Trademarks ASSIGN* (assignment deeds, bimonthly), *Trademarks ASSIST* (search tools, single- disc), *Trademarks PENDING* (applications on file, bimonthly), *Trademarks REGISTERED* (active trademarks, 1884 to date).

TRADEMARKSCAN: U. S. Federal [CD-ROM]. Thomson & Thomson. • Monthly. $7,500.00 per year. Contains information on CD-ROM for more than two million trademarks from the U. S. Patent and Trademark Office. For active trademarks, time period is 1884 to date. Graphic images are shown for many of the records.

TRADEMARKSCAN: U. S. State [CD-ROM]. Thomson & Thomson. • Monthly. $3,500.00 per year. Provides information on CD-ROM for more than one million trademarks registered with the Office of the Secretary of State in all 50 states and in Puerto Rico. For active trademarks, time period is 1900 to date.

World Database of Consumer Brands and Their Owners on CD-ROM. Gale Cengage Learning. • Annual. $3,190.00. Produced by Euromonitor. Provides detailed information on CD-ROM for about 10,000 companies and 80,000 brands around the world. Covers 1,000 product sectors.

DIRECTORIES

Brands and Their Companies. Gale Cengage Learning. • 2003. $895.00. 24th edition. Three volumes. Includes mid-year *Supplement.* Provides over 365,000 entries ontrade names, trademarks, and brand names of consumer-oriented products and their 80,000 manufacturers, importers, marketers, or distributors. Formerly *Trade Names Dictionary.*

Companies and Their Brands. Gale Cengage Learning. • 2003. $595.00. 24th edition. Two volumes. Lists companies alphabetically, with their names. (A rearrangment of the data in *Brands and Their Companies.*).

Directory of Canadian Trademarks. Thomson & Thomson. • Annual. Price on application. Provides owner, registration, and classification information for Canadian trademarks registered with the Canadian Intellectual Property Office (CIPO).

Directory of Consumer Brands and Their Owners: Asia Pacific. Euromonitor International, Business Reference Div. • 1998. $990.00. Provides information about brands available from major Asia Pacific companies. Descriptions of companies are also included.

Directory of Consumer Brands and Their Owners: Eastern Europe. Euromonitor International, Business Reference Div. • 1998. $990.00. Provides information about brands available from major Eastern European companies. Descriptions of companies are also included.

Directory of Consumer Brands and Their Owners: Latin America. Euromonitor International, Business Reference Div. • 1999. $990.00. Provides information about brands available from major Latin American companies. Descriptions of companies are also included.

Official Gazette of the United States Patent and Trademark Office. Superintendent of Documents. • Weekly. $110.00. Lists all trademarks currently registered and renewed trademarks in the U.S. Patent and Trademark Office.

Plunkett's Advertising and Branding Industry Almanac. Plunkett Research, Ltd. • 2004. $249.99. Provides profiles of 300 leading firms in the areas of advertising, brand promotion, and corporate image, including marketing media, online advertising, and direct mail. Also covers industry trends and statistical data.

Plunkett's Food Industry Almanac. Plunkett Research Ltd. • Covers: 340 leading companies in the global food industry. Entries include: Name, address, phone, fax, and key executives. Also includes analysis and information on trends, technology, and statistics in the field.

Thomas Register of American Manufacturers. Thomas Publishing Co., Inc. • Annual. $149.00. 34 volumes. A three-part system offering information on a wide variety of industrial equipment and supplies. Lists more than 151,000 industrial product and services companies.

World Drinks Marketing Directory. Euromonitor International. • Covers: 500 retailers and wholesalers, 1,000 manufacturers, over 2,000 international and European organizations, statistical agencies, market research companies, trade journals and associations, databases, and trade fairs in the beverage industry worldwide. Entries include: Company name, address, phone, telex, number of employees, parent company and subsidiary names, financial data, products and brand names handled; retailers and wholesalers include type of outlets, names and titles of key personnel.

World Food Marketing Directory. Euromonitor International. • Covers: Over 2,000 retailers and wholesalers, 1,600 manufacturers, over 2,000 international and European organizations, statistical agencies, trade journals and associations, databases, and trade fairs in the grocery and food industries worldwide. Entries include: Company name, address, phone, telex, names of parent company and subsidiaries, number of employees, financial data, products and brand names handled; retailers and wholesalers include type of outlet, names and titles of key personnel.

World Leading Global Brand Owners. Euromonitor International. • 2003. $1,190.00. Second edition. Contains detailed profiles of multinational consumer product companies. Includes sales, market share, brand names, and financial information. (*Global Market Share Planner*, vol. 3.).

World's Greatest Brands: An International Review by Interbrand. John Wiley and Sons, Inc. • 1992. $49.95. Compiled by Interbrand. Provides details on 330 of the most successful international brand names and trademarks. Includes color illustrations.

ENCYCLOPEDIAS AND DICTIONARIES

Dictionary of Trade Name Origins. Adrian Room. McGraw-Hill. • 1990. $39.95.

McCarthy's Desk Encyclopedia of Intellectual Property. J. Thomas McCarthy. BNA, Inc. • 1995. $75.00.Second edition. Defines legal terms relating to patents, trademarks, copyrights, trade secrets, entertainment, and the computer industry.

HANDBOOKS AND MANUALS

Copyrights, Patents, and Trademarks: Protect Your Rights Worldwide. Hoyt L. Barber. McGraw-Hill. • 1996. $32.95. Second edition.

Gilson Trademark Protection and Practice. Jerome Gilson. LexisNexis Matthew Bender. • $1,279.00. 13 looseleaf volumes. Periodic supplementation. Covers U. S. trademark practice.

Intellectual Property Infringement Damages: A Litigation Support Handbook 2003 Cumulative Supplement. Russell L. Parr. John Wiley and Sons, Inc. • 2003. $78.00. Second edition. Describes how to calculate damages for patent, trademark, and copyright infringement. (Intellectual Property-General, Law, Accounting and Finance, Management, Licensing and Special Topics Series).

Intellectual Property Primary Law Soucebook. LexisNexis Matthew Bender. • Annual. $88.00. Provides federal copyright, patent, and trademark statutes and regulations.

Librarian's Guide to Intellectual Property in the Digital Age: Copyrights, Patents, and Trademarks. Timothy L. Wherry. American Library Association. • 2002. $38.00. Includes lists of patent and trademark depositories, relevant Web sites, and questions & answers.

Patent, Copyright, and Trademark: An Intellectual Property Desk Reference. Stephen Elias. Nolo. • 2003. $39.99. Sixth revised edition. Contains practical explanations of the legalities of patents, copyrights, trademarks, and trade secrets. Includes examples of relevant legal forms. A 1985 version was called *Nolo's Intellectual Property Law Dictionary*. (Nolo Press Self-Help Law Series).

Patent, Trademark, and Copyright Laws, 2003. Jeffrey Samuels, editor. BNA, Inc. • 2003. $115.00. Contains text of "all pertinent intellectual property legislation to date.".

Trademark Manual of Examining Procedure. Available from U. S. Government Printing Office. • $168.00 for basic manual and semiannual changes for an indeterminate period. Covers "practices and procedures" relating to the processing of applications to register trademarks in the U. S. Patent and Trademark Office.

World Trademark Law and Practice. LexisNexis Matthew Bender. • $849.00. Five looseleaf volumes. Periodic supplementation. A guide to international trademark practice with detailed coverage of 35 major jurisdictions and summary coverage for over 100.

INTERNET DATABASES

SAEGIS Internet Search. Thomson & Thomson. Phone: 800-692-8833 or (617)479-1600 Fax: (617)786-8273 E-mail: support@thomson-thomson.com • URL: http://www.thomson-thomson.com • Fee-based Web site provides extensive, common law screening of the World Wide Web for trademarks. Searches are performed offline, with final report delivered to user's "SAEGIS Inbox." Context of trademark within each relevant Web site is indicated, and links are provided.

United States Patent and Trademark Office. U. S. Department of Commerce. Phone: 800-786-9199 or (703)308-4357 Fax: (703)305-7786 • URL: http://www.uspto.gov • Web site provides extensive information about patents and trademarks, with advanced search facilities for specific documents or names. "Special Pages" are available for "How to Search," "Trademarks-Logos-Brands," "Inventor Resources," and other topics. A complete fee schedule is available for filing applications, appeals, copies, etc.

ONLINE DATABASES

Brands and Their Companies Database. Gale Cengage Learning. • An online directory of about 400,000 domestic and international trade names, with a primary focus on consumer goods. Semiannual updates. Inquire as to online cost and availability.

Thomas Register Online. Thomas Publishing Co., Inc. • Provides concise information on approximately 194,000 U. S. companies, mainly manufacturers, with over 50,000 product classifications. Indexes over 115,000 trade names. Information is updated semiannually. Inquire as to online cost and availability.

TRADEMARKSCAN: International Register. Thomson & Thomson. • Supplies current information on more than 400,000 trademarks registered with the World Intellectual Property Organization. Updates are monthly. Inquire as to online cost and availability. (TRADEMARKSCAN also maintains extensive databases for individual countries: Canada, U. K., Germany, Italy, France, and others.).

TRADEMARKSCAN: U. S. Federal. Thomson & Thomson. • Provides information on more than two million trademarks registered and pending at the U. S. Patent and Trademark Office. Time period is 1884 to date for active trademarks, with updates twice a week. Graphic images are show. Inquire as to online cost and availability.

TRADEMARKSCAN: U. S. State. Thomson & Thomson. • Contains information on more than 970,000 trademarks registered with the Office of the Secretary of State in all 50 states and in Puerto Rico. Time period is 1900 to date for active trademarks, with weekly updates. Inquire as to online cost and availability.

PERIODICALS AND NEWSLETTERS

BNA's Patent, Trademark and Copyright Journal. BNA, Inc. • Weekly. $1,495.00 per year. Looseleaf service.

Intellectual Property Today. • Monthly. $96.00 per year. Covers legal developments in copyright, patents, trademarks, and licensing. Emphasizes the effect of new technology on intellectual property. Formerly *Law Works*.

Les Nouvelles. Licensing Executives Society International. • Description: Concerned with technological licensing and related subjects. Covers technology, patents, trademarks, and licensing "know-how" world-wide.

Official Gazette of the United States Patent and Trademark Office: Trademarks. Available from U. S. Government Printing Office. • Weekly. $1,229.00 per year by first class mail. Contains Trademarks, Trademark Notices, Marks Published for Opposition, Trademark Registrations Issued, and Index of Registrants (http://www.uspto.gov).

The Trademark Reporter. International Trademark Association. • Bimonthly. Free to members; libraries, $60.00 per year. Contains articles on trademark developments, trademark law, and the use of trademarks.

The Trademarker Reporter. International Trademark Association. • Bimonthly. Free to members; others, $50.00 per year. Newsletter.

TRADE/PROFESSIONAL ASSOCIATIONS

International Intellectual Property Association. 1255 23rd St. NW, Ste. 200, Washington, DC 20037. Phone: (202)466-2396 Fax: (202)466-2893 E-mail: herb@ipo.org • URL: http://www.ipo.org • Lawyers who have professional qualifications and interest in the international protection of patents, designs, trademarks, copyrights, and other intellectual property rights. American group of the International Association for the Protection of Industrial Property. Monitors international developments that may affect industrial property and related rights. Studies, discusses, and reports on proposed national and foreign legislation treaties and conventions that are likely to affect national and international intellectual property interests.

International Trademark Association. 655 3rd Ave., 10th Fl., New York, NY 10017-5617. Phone: (212)642-1700 Fax: (212)768-7796 E-mail: info@inta.org • URL: http://www.inta.org • Trademark owners; associate members are lawyers, law firms, advertising agencies, designers, market researchers, and others in the trademark industries. Seeks to: protect the interests of the public in the use of trademarks and trade names; promote the interests of members and of trademark owners generally in the use of their trademarks and trade names; disseminate information concerning the use, registration, and protection of trademarks in the United States, its territories, and in foreign countries. Maintains job bank and speakers' bureau.

OTHER SOURCES

Callmann on Unfair Competition, Trademarks and Monopolies. Louis Altman and Rudolf Callmann. West Group. • Semiannual. $1,270.00 per year. 10 looseleaf volumes. Covers various aspects of anti-competitive behavior.

Intellectual Property and Antitrust Law. William C. Holmes. West Group. • Semiannual. $389.00 per year. Two looseleaf volumes. Includes patent, trademark, and copyright practices.

TRADES

See: OCCUPATIONS

TRADING

See: BARTER AND COUNTERTRADE

TRAFFIC ACCIDENTS AND TRAFFIC SAFETY

See also: ACCIDENTS

GENERAL WORKS

Highway and Traffic Safety and Accident Research, Management, and Issues. Norman Solomon, editor. Transportation Research Board. • 1993. $28.00. (Record Series).

Safety in Tunnels: Transport of Dangerous Goods Through Road Tunnels. Organization for Economic Cooperation and Development. • 2001. $19.00. Discusses risks in road tunnels and the consequences of incidents.

Safety on Roads: What's the Vision?. Organization for Economic Cooperation and Development. • 2002. $22.00. Contains information on road safety programs in OECD countries. Describes the criteria that influence success or failure.

ABSTRACTS AND INDEXES

Highway Safety Literature. • Annual. $80.00.

Transportation Research Information Services (TRIS). Transportation Research Board, Highway Research Information. • Monthly. Price on application.

BIBLIOGRAPHIES

Road Construction and Safety. Available from U. S. Government Printing Office. • Annual. Free. Issued by the Superintendent of Documents. A list of government publications on highway construction and traffic safety. Formerly *Highway Construction, Safety and Traffic.* (Subject Bibliography No. 3.).

ONLINE DATABASES

I.I.I. Data Base Search. Insurance Information Institute. • Provides online citations and abstracts of insurance-related literature in magazines, newspapers, trade journals, and books. Emphasis is on property and casualty insurance issues, including highway safety, product safety, and environmental liability. Inquire as to online cost and availability.

TRIS: Transportation Research Information Service. National Research Council. • Contains abstracts and citations to a wide range of transportation literature, 1968 to present, with monthly updates. Includes references to the literature of air transportation, highways, ships and shipping, railroads, trucking, and urban mass transportation. Formerly *TRIS-ON-LINE.* Inquire as to online cost and availability.

PERIODICALS AND NEWSLETTERS

Insurance Institute for Highway Safety, Status Report. Insurance Institute for Highway Safety. • 10 times a year. Free.

Journal of Safety Research. National Safety Council. Elsevier. • Quarterly. Institutions, $800.00 per year. Published in United Kingdom.

Journal of Traffic Safety Education. California Association for Safety Education. • Quarterly. $8.00 per year.

Traffic Safety: The Magazine for Traffic Safety Professionals. National Safety Council, Periodicals Dept. • Bimonthly. Members, $24.00 per year; non-members, $31.20 per year.

RESEARCH CENTERS AND INSTITUTES

Insurance Institute for Highway Safety. 1005 N. Glebe Rd., Ste. 800, Arlington, VA 22201-4751.

Phone: (703)247-1500 Fax: (703)247-1678 E-mail: iihs@highwaysafety.org • URL: http://www. hwysafety.org • Studies highway safety, including seat belt use, air bags, property damage, vehicle recalls, and the role of alcohol and drugs.

Texas Transportation Institute. Texas A & M University System, CE/TTI, Room 801 B, College Station, TX 77843-3135. Phone: (979)845-1713 Fax: (979)845-9356 E-mail: herbert-richardson@ tamu.edu • URL: http://www.tii.tamu.edu • Concerned with all forms and modes of transportation. Research areas include transportation economics, highway construction, traffic safety, public transportation, and highway engineering.

Transportation Research Institute. University of Michigan, 2901 Baxter Rd., Ann Arbor, MI 48109-2150. Phone: (734)764-6504 Fax: (734)936-1081 E-mail: umtri@umich.edu • URL: http://www. umtri.umich.edu • Research areas include highway safety, transportation systems, and shipbuilding.

STATISTICS SOURCES

Accident Facts. National Safety Council. • Annual. $37.95.

Statistical Report on Road Accidents. Organization for Economic Cooperation and Development. • Annual. $20.00. Provides data from various countries on road accidents resulting in injuries or fatalities. Includes 12-year statistical trends.

TRADE/PROFESSIONAL ASSOCIATIONS

American Driver and Traffic Safety Education Association. Highway Safety Center, Indiana University of Pennsylvania, Indiana, PA 15705. Phone: 800-896-7703 or (724)357-4051 Fax: (724)357-7595 E-mail: bbradsha@ivp.edu • URL: http://www.adtsea.iup.edu.

American Highway Users Alliance. 1101 14th St. NW, Ste. 750, Washington, DC 20005. Phone: 800-483-4544 or (202)857-1200 or (202)857-1200 Fax: (202)857-1220 E-mail: info@highways.org • URL: http://www.highways.org • Broad-based consumers group for American motorists, truckers and businesses. Employs lobbying, media, communications and grassroots advocacy, promotes public policy that devotes highway use taxes to investments in safe and uncongested national highway systems.

Center for Auto Safety. 1825 Connecticut Ave., Ste. 330, Washington, DC 20009-5708. Phone: (202)328-7700 E-mail: mbarclift@autosafety.org • URL: http://www.autosafety.org.

National Safety Council. 1121 Spring Lake Dr., Itasca, IL 60143-3201. Phone: 800-621-7619 or (630)285-1121 Fax: (630)285-1613 E-mail: nrhc@ nrhcweb.org • URL: http://www.nsc.org • Individuals whose professional activities are related to the safety of employees and college or university students.

TRAFFIC ENGINEERING

See also: TOLL ROADS; TRAFFIC MANAGEMENT (STREETS AND HIGHWAYS); TRANSPORTATION INDUSTRY

GENERAL WORKS

Principles of Highway Engineering and Traffic Analysis. Fred L. Mannering and Walter P. Kilareski. John Wiley and Sons, Inc. • 1997. $68.95. Second edition.

ABSTRACTS AND INDEXES

Transportation Research Information Services (TRIS). Transportation Research Board, Highway Research Information. • Monthly. Price on application.

ENCYCLOPEDIAS AND DICTIONARIES

Macmillan Encyclopedia of Transportation. Available from Gale Cengage Learning. • 1999. $450.00.

Six volumes. Published by Macmillan Reference USA. Covers the business, technology, and history of transportation on land, on water, in the air, and in space. Includes definitions, cross-references, and 200 color illustrations.

HANDBOOKS AND MANUALS

Transportation Engineering and Planning. C. S. Papacostas and Panos D. Prevedouros. Prentice Hall PTR. • 2000. $115.00. Third edition.

Transportation Planning Handbook. John D. Edwards. Institute of Transportation Engineers. • 1999. $100.00. Second edition.

PERIODICALS AND NEWSLETTERS

ITE Journal. Institute of Transportation Engineers. • Monthly. $60.00 per year. Formerly *Transportation Engineering.*

Traffic Engineering and Control: The International Journal of Traffic Management and Transportation Planning. Printerhall Ltd. • Monthly. $120.00 per year. Provides authoritative articles on planning, engineering and management of highways for safe and efficient operation.

Traffic World: The Logistics News Weekly n. Journal of Commerce, Inc. • Weekly. $174.00 per year.

Transportation Quarterly: An Independent Journal for Better Transportation Policy. Eno Transportation Foundation. • Quarterly. $55.00 per year. To qualify a written request must be submitted.

TRADE/PROFESSIONAL ASSOCIATIONS

American Road and Transportation Builders Association. The ARTBA Bldg., 1010 Massachusetts Ave., N.W., Washington, DC 20001-5402. Phone: (202)289-4434 Fax: (202)289-4435 E-mail: pruane@artba.org • URL: http://www.artba. org • Promotes on-the-job training programs.

Eno Transportation Foundation. 1250 I St. NW, Ste. 750, Washington, DC 20005-3910. Phone: (202)879-4700 Fax: (202)879-4719 E-mail: svanbeek@enotrans.com • URL: http://www. enotrans.com • Seeks to educate the public and disseminate information about transportation in the U.S. Fosters careers in the field. Conducts research, educational programs, and policy forums; maintains museum; compiles statistics. Financed by an endowment made by William Phelps Eno.

Institute of Transportation Engineers. 1099 14th St., N.W., Suite 300 W, Washington, DC 20005-3438. Phone: (202)289-0222 Fax: (202)289-7722 E-mail: ite_staff@site.org • URL: http://www.ite.org • Members are professionals in surface transportation, mass transit, and traffic engineering. Formerly Institute of Traffic Engineers.

TRAFFIC MANAGEMENT (INDUSTRIAL)

See also: DISTRIBUTION; TRANSPORTATION INDUSTRY

DIRECTORIES

Plunkett's Transportation and Logistics Industry Almanac. Plunkett Research, Ltd. • 2004. $249.99. Contains profiles of 300 leading companies in the fields of transportation, logistics, supply chain management, warehousing, distribution, and intermodal shipment systems. Includes industry trends and statistics.

ENCYCLOPEDIAS AND DICTIONARIES

Blackwell Encyclopedic Dictionary of Operations Management. Nigel Slack, editor. Blackwell Publishing. • 1997. $130.95. The editor is associated with the University of Warwick, England. Contains definitions of key terms combined with longer articles written by various U. S. and foreign business educators. Includes bibliographies and index. (Blackwell Encyclopedia of Management Series.).

PERIODICALS AND NEWSLETTERS

Chilton's Distribution: The Transportation and Business Logistics Magazine. Reed Business Information. • Monthly. $65.00 per year.

Logistics Management. Reed Business Information. • Monthly. $99.000 per year. Includes *International Shipping* and *Warehousing and Distribution.* Formerly *Logistics Management and Distribution Report.*

Traffic World: The Logistics News Weekly n. Journal of Commerce, Inc. • Weekly. $174.00 per year.

Transportation and Distribution: Integrating Logistics in Supply Chain Management. Penton Media, Inc. • Monthly. Free to qualified personnel; others, $50.00 per year. Essential information on transportation and distribution practices in domestic and international trade.

Transportation Journal. American Society of Transportation and Logistics, Inc. • Quarterly. $61.95 per year.

TRADE/PROFESSIONAL ASSOCIATIONS

American Society of Transportation and Logistics. 1700 N Moore St., Ste. 1900, Arlington, VA 22209. Phone: (703)524-5011 Fax: (703)524-5017 E-mail: info@astl.org; ast1@astl.org.

National Industrial Transportation League. 1700 N Moore St., Ste. 1900, Arlington, VA 22209. Phone: (703)524-5011 Fax: (703)524-5017 E-mail: info@nitl.org • URL: http://www.nitl.org • Seeks to promote adequate national and international transportation; encourages the exchange of ideas and information concerning traffic and transportation; and cooperates with regulatory agencies and other transportation companies in developing an understanding of legislation.

TRAFFIC MANAGEMENT (STREETS AND HIGHWAYS)

See also: TRAFFIC ENGINEERING; TRANSPORTATION INDUSTRY

GENERAL WORKS

Moving Beyond Gridlock: Traffic and Development. Robert T. Dunphy. Urban Land Institute. • 1996. $49.95. Describes how various regions have dealt with traffic growth. Includes case studies from seven cities.

ABSTRACTS AND INDEXES

Transportation Research Information Services (TRIS). Transportation Research Board, Highway Research Information. • Monthly. Price on application.

BIBLIOGRAPHIES

Road Construction and Safety. Available from U. S. Government Printing Office. • Annual. Free. Issued by the Superintendent of Documents. A list of government publications on highway construction and traffic safety. Formerly *Highway Construction, Safety and Traffic.* (Subject Bibliography No. 3.).

DIRECTORIES

Jane's Road Traffic Management and ITS (Intelligent Transport Systems). Jane's Information Group, Inc. • Annual. $470.00. A directory of traffic control equipment and services. Includes detailed product descriptions.

HANDBOOKS AND MANUALS

Standard Highway Signs, as Specified in the Manual on Uniform Traffic Control Devices. Available from U. S. Government Printing Office. • Looseleaf. $153.00. Issued by the U. S. Department of Transportation (http://www.dot.gov). Includes basic

manual, with updates for an indeterminate period. Contains illustrations of typical standard signs approved for use on streets and highways, and provides information on dimensions and placement of symbols.

ONLINE DATABASES

TRIS: Transportation Research Information Service. National Research Council. • Contains abstracts and citations to a wide range of transportation literature, 1968 to present, with monthly updates. Includes references to the literature of air transportation, highways, ships and shipping, railroads, trucking, and urban mass transportation. Formerly *TRIS-ONLINE.* Inquire as to online cost and availability.

PERIODICALS AND NEWSLETTERS

Downtown Idea Exchange: Essential Information for Downtown Research and Development Center. Downtown Research and Development Center. Alexander Communications Group, Inc. • Semimonthly. $187.00 per year. Newsletter for those concerned with central business districts. Provides news and other information on planning, development, parking, mass transit, traffic, funding, and other topics.

Public Roads: A Journal of Highway Research and Development. Available from U.S. Government Printing Office. • Bimonthly. $26.00 per year.

Transportation Journal. American Society of Transportation and Logistics, Inc. • Quarterly. $61.95 per year.

World Highways. International Road Federation. • Eight times a year. $165.00 per year. Text in English, French, German and Spanish.

RESEARCH CENTERS AND INSTITUTES

Center for Public Safety. Northwestern University. 405 Church St., Evanston, IL 60204. Phone: 800-323-4011 or (847)491-5476 Fax: (847)491-5270 E-mail: alweiss@northwestern.edu • URL: http://www.northwestern.edu/nucps.

STATISTICS SOURCES

Highway Statistics. Federal Highway Administration, U.S. Department of Transportation. Available from U.S. Government Printing Office. • Annual. $26.00.

TRADE/PROFESSIONAL ASSOCIATIONS

American Association of Motor Vehicle Administrators. 4301 Wilson Blvd., Suite 400, Arlington, VA 22203-1800. Phone: 888-226-8280 or (703)522-4200 Fax: (703)522-1553 E-mail: llewis@aamva.org • URL: http://www.aamva.org.

American Society of Transportation and Logistics. 1700 N Moore St., Ste. 1900, Arlington, VA 22209. Phone: (703)524-5011 Fax: (703)524-5017 E-mail: info@astl.org; ast1@astl.org.

TRAILERS

See: MOBILE HOME INDUSTRY; RECREATIONAL VEHICLE INDUSTRY; TRUCK TRAILERS

TRAINING OF EMPLOYEES

See also: EXECUTIVE TRAINING AND DEVELOPMENT

GENERAL WORKS

Breaking Out of the Pink-Collar Ghetto: Policy Solutions for Non-College Women. Sharon H. Mastracci. M. E. Sharpe, Inc. • 2004. $65.95. Emphasis is on innovative education and training programs for women in low-paying service jobs.

ALMANACS AND YEARBOOKS

Training and Development Yearbook. Carolyn Nilson. Prentice Hall PTR. • 2002. $130.00.

Includes reprints of journal articles on employee training and development. (Training and Development Yearbook Series).

DIRECTORIES

Training and Development Organizations Directory. Gale Cengage Learning. • 1994. $415.00. Sixth edition.

HANDBOOKS AND MANUALS

Career Guide to Industries. Available from U. S. Government Printing Office. • 2002. $32.00. Issued by the Bureau of Labor Statistics, U. S. Department of Labor (http://www.bls.gov). Presents background career information (text) and statistics for the 40 industries that account for 70 percent of wage and salary jobs in the U. S. Includes nature of the industry, employment data, working conditions, training, earnings, rate of job growth, outlook, and other career factors. (BLS Bulletin 2541.).

Equality in the Workplace: An Equal Opportunities Handbook for Trainers. Helen Collins. Blackwell Publishing. • 1995. $55.95. (Human Resource Management in Action Series).

Gower Handbook of Training and Development. John Prior, editor. Ashgate Publishing Co. • 1999. $144.95. Third edition. Consists of 40 chapters written by various authors. Includes glossary and index. Published by Gower in England.

Handbook of Training Evaluation and Measurement Methods. Jack J. Phillips. • 1997. $55.00. Third edition. (Improving Human Performance Series).

How to Develop a Personnel Policy Manual. Joseph Lawson. AMACOM. • 1998. $75.00. Sixth edition.

How to Manage Training: A Guide to Administration, Design and Delivery. Carolyn Nilson. AMACOM. • 1991. $69.95. Looseleaf service. Presents ideas and techniques for cost-effective training.

Studying Your Workforce: Applied Research Methods and Tools for the Training and Development Practitioner. Alan Clardy. Sage Publications, Inc. • 1997. $79.95. Describes how to apply specific research methods to common training problems. Emphasis is on data collection methods: testing, observation, surveys, and interviews. Topics include performance problems and assessment.

Training for Non-Trainers: A Do-It-Yourself Guide for Managers. Carolyn Nilson. AMACOM. • 1990. $16.95.

PERIODICALS AND NEWSLETTERS

Human Resource Executive. LRP Publications. • 16 times a year. $89.95 per year. Edited for directors of corporate human resource departments. Special issues emphasize training, benefits, retirement planning, recruitment, outplacement, workers' compensation, legal pitfalls, and oes emphasize training, benefits, retirement planning, recruitment, outplacement, workers' compensation, legal pitfalls, and other personnel topics.

T and D Magazine. American Society for Training and Development. • Monthly. Free to members; non-members, $85.00 per year.

Team Leader. LRP Publications. • Description: Keeps business team leaders up to date on team-leading techniques and provides solutions to team-oriented issues.

Training: The Magazine of Covering the Human Side of Business. VNU Business Media. • Monthly. $78.00 per year.

Vocational Training News: The Independent Weekly Report on Employment, Training, and Vocational Education. Aspen Publishers, Inc. • Biweekly. $377.00 per year. Newsletter. Emphasis is on federal job training and vocational education programs. Formerly *Manpower and Vocational Education Weekly.*

Workforce: H R Trends and Tools for Business

Results. Crain Communications, Inc. • Monthly. $59.00 per year. Edited for human resources managers. Covers employee benefits, compensation, relocation, recruitment, training, personnel legalities, and related subjects. Supplements include bimonthly "New Product News" and semiannual "Recruitment/Staffing Sourcebook." Formerly *Personnel Journal.*

RESEARCH CENTERS AND INSTITUTES

Industrial Relations Section. Princeton University, Firestone Library, Pinceton, NJ 08544. Phone: (609)258-4040 Fax: (609)258-2907 • URL: http://www.irs.princeton.edu/ • Fields of research include labor supply, manpower training, unemployment, and equal employment opportunity.

Institute of Advanced Manufacturing Sciences. 1111 Edison Dr., Cincinnati, OH 45230. Phone: (513)948-2000 Fax: 800-345-4482 • Fields of research include quality improvement, computer-aided design, artificial intelligence, and employee training.

National Institute for Work and Learning. Academy for Educational Development, 1875 Connecticut Ave., N.W., Washington, DC 20009-5721. Phone: (202)884-8186 Fax: (202)884-8422 E-mail: niwl@aed.org • URL: http://www.niwl.org • Research areas include adult education, training, unemployment insurance, and career development.

W. E. Upjohn Institute for Employment Research. 300 S. Westnedge Ave., Kalamazoo, MI 49007-4686. Phone: (616)343-5541 Fax: (616)343-3308 E-mail: eberts@we.upjohninst.org • URL: http://www.upjohninst.org • Research fields include unemployment, unemployment insurance, worker's compensation, labor productivity, profit sharing, the labor market, economic development, earnings, training, and other areas related to employment.

STATISTICS SOURCES

Occupational Projections and Training Data. Available from U. S. Government Printing Office. • Biennial. $21.00. Issued by Bureau of Labor Statistics, U. S. Department of Labor. Contains projections of employment change and job openings over the next 15 years for about 500 specific occupations. Also includes the number of associate, bachelor's, master's, doctoral, and professional degrees awarded in a recent year for about 900 specific fields of study.

TRADE/PROFESSIONAL ASSOCIATIONS

American Society for Training and Development. 1640 King St., Alexandria, VA 22313-2043. Phone: 800-628-2783 or (703)683-8100 Fax: (703)683-1523 • URL: http://www.astd.org.

American Technical Education Association. c/o North Dakota State College of Science. 800 N 6th St., Wahpeton, ND 58076-0002. Phone: (701)671-2240 or (701)671-2240 Fax: (701)671-2260 E-mail: betty.krump@ndscs.edu • URL: http://www.ateaonline.org • Dedicated to excellence in the quality of post-secondary technical education with emphasis on professional development.

Center on Education and Training for Employment. The Ohio State University College of Education. 1900 Kenny Rd., Columbus, OH 43210-1090. Phone: 800-848-4815 or (614)292-4353 Fax: (614)292-1260 E-mail: chambers.2@osu.edu • URL: http://www.cete.org/products/ • Formerly National Center for Research in Vocational Education.

Manpower Education Institute. 715 Ladd Rd., Bronx, NY 10471-1203. Phone: (718)548-4200 Fax: (718)548-4202 E-mail: info@meipublishing.com • URL: http://www.manpower-education.org • Individuals from the fields of business, labor, and education who develop educational film series for the U.S. labor force. Series includes: Ready or Not (pre-retirement planning), Your Future Is Now (high

school equivalency programs), Read Your Way Up (reading skills improvement), Out of Work (for the unemployed), If You Don't Come In Sunday, Don't Come In Monday (history of the American labor movement), Plug Us In (to assist workers reentering the labor market), and Where Do I Fit In (new worker orientation).

National Association for Industry-Education Cooperation. 235 Hendricks Blvd., Buffalo, NY 14226-3304. Phone: (716)834-7047 Fax: (716)834-7047 E-mail: naiec@pcom.net • URL: http://www.2.pcom.net/naiec.

National Association of State Supervisors of Trade and Industrial Education. c/o Ralph Green, Division of Technical and Adult Education, Capital Complex Bldg. 6, 1900 Kanawha Blvd., E., Room 243, Charleston, WV 25305. Phone: (304)558-6314 or (304)558-6313 Fax: (304)558-1149 E-mail: rgreen@access.k12.wv.us • URL: http://www.itednt.ited.uidaho.edu/nasstie.

OTHER SOURCES

Employment and Training Reporter. MII Publications, Inc. • Weekly. $897.00 per year. Looseleaf service. Two volumes. Online edition, $747.00 per year.

TRAINS

See: RAILROADS

TRANSDUCERS, INDUSTRIAL

See: CONTROL EQUIPMENT INDUSTRY

TRANSISTORS

See: SEMICONDUCTOR INDUSTRY

TRANSLATING MACHINES

See: MACHINE TRANSLATING

TRANSLATIONS AND TRANSLATORS

See also: MACHINE TRANSLATING

ABSTRACTS AND INDEXES

Transdex Index. UMI. • Monthly. Price on application.

DIRECTORIES

ATA Directory of Translaters and Interpreters. American Translators Association. • Only avalible online. Over 5,000 member translators and interpreters. Formerly *ATA Translation Services Directory.*

ENCYCLOPEDIAS AND DICTIONARIES

Lexique General; A General Lexicon of Terms-United Nations as Well as General-Used by Translators, Interpreters, etc. United Nations Publications. • 1991. Fourth edition.

HANDBOOKS AND MANUALS

Language Translation Service. Entrepreneur Media, Inc. • Looseleaf. $59.50. A practical guide to starting a language translation service. Covers profit potential, start-up costs, market size evaluation, pricing, accounting, advertising, promotion, etc. (Start-Up Business Guide No. E1353.).

PERIODICALS AND NEWSLETTERS

ATA Chronicle. American Translators Association. • Monthly. $50.00.

TRADE/PROFESSIONAL ASSOCIATIONS

American Translators Association. 225 Reinekers Ln., Ste. 590, Alexandria, VA 22314-2875. Phone:

(703)683-6100 Fax: (703)683-6122 E-mail: ata@atanet.org • URL: http://www.atanet.org • Fosters the professional development of translators and interpreters and promotes the translation and interpretation professions.

International Association of Conference Translators. 15, route des Morillons, CH-1218 Grand-Saconnex, Geneva, Switzerland. Phone: 41 22 7910666 Fax: 41 22 7885644 E-mail: webmaster@aitc.ch • URL: http://www.aitc.ch.

TRANSPORTATION EQUIPMENT INDUSTRY

FINANCIAL RATIOS

Almanac of Business and Industrial Financial Ratios. Leo Troy. Aspen Publishers, Inc. • 2003. $125.95. Includes CD-Rom. Contains financial ratios derived from federal tax returns. Ratios for each of about 200 industries are arranged according to company asset size. (Almanac of Business and Industrial Financial Ratios Series).

Industry Norms and Key Business Ratios. Desk Top Edition. Dun and Bradstreet Corp. • Annual. Five volumes. $475.00 per volume. $1,890.00 per set. Covers over 800 kinds of businesses, arranged by Standard Industrial Classification number. More detailed editions covering longer periods of time are also available.

Quarterly Financial Report for Manufacturing, Mining, and Trade Corporations. U.S. Federal Trade Commission and U.S. Securities and Exchange Commission. Available from U.S. Government Printing Office. • Quarterly. $49.00 per year.

ONLINE DATABASES

TRIS: Transportation Research Information Service. National Research Council. • Contains abstracts and citations to a wide range of transportation literature, 1968 to present, with monthly updates. Includes references to the literature of air transportation, highways, ships and shipping, railroads, trucking, and urban mass transportation. Formerly *TRIS-ON-LINE.* Inquire as to online cost and availability.

PERIODICALS AND NEWSLETTERS

ITE Journal. Institute of Transportation Engineers. • Monthly. $60.00 per year. Formerly *Transportation Engineering.*

STATISTICS SOURCES

Annual Survey of Manufactures. Available from U. S. Government Printing Office. • Annual. Prices vary. Issued by the U. S. Census Bureau as an interim update to the *Census of Manufactures.* Includes data on number of manufacturing establishments in various industries, employment, labor costs, value of shipments, capital expenditures, inventories, energy costs, and assets. (See also Census Bureau home page, http://www.census.gov/.).

WEFA Industrial Monitor. John Wiley and Sons, Inc. • Annual. $65.00. Prepared by industry analysts at WEFA, an economic forecasting and consulting firm (originally Wharton Econometric Forecasting Associates). Contains discussions of the outlook for major U. S. industries, with many 10-year forecasts (WEFA Web site is http://www.wefa.com).

TRANSPORTATION INDUSTRY

GENERAL WORKS

Transportation. Rob Bowden. Gale. • 2004.

ABSTRACTS AND INDEXES

NTIS Alerts: Transportation. National Technical Information Service. • Semimonthly. $210.00 per

For publishers addresses, refer to SOURCES CITED section at the back of the book.

907

year. Provides descriptions of government-sponsored research reports and software, with ordering information. Covers air, marine, highway, inland waterway, pipeline, and railroad transportation. Formerly *Abstract Newsletter*.

ALMANACS AND YEARBOOKS

Research in Transportation Economics. Elsevier. • Dates vary. Price varies. Six volumes.

CD-ROM DATABASES

OECD Statistical Compendium. Organization for Economic Cooperation and Development. • Semiannual. $1,905.00 per year for 1 to 10 users. CD-ROM contains more than 730,000 monthly, quarterly, and annual time series for OECD countries, 1960 to date. Includes fully searchable data on agriculture, food, economic indicators, national accounts, employment, energy, finance, industry, technology, and foreign trade. Results can be displayed in various forms.

WILSONDISC: Wilson Business Abstracts. H. W. Wilson Co. • Monthly. Includes unlimited online access to *Wilson Business Abstracts* through WILSONLINE. Provides CD-ROM "cover-to-cover" abstracting and indexing of over 600 prominent business periodicals. Indexing is from 1982, abstracting from 1990. (*Business Periodicals Index* without abstracts is available on CD-ROM at $1,495 per year.).

DIRECTORIES

Jane's Urban Transport Systems. Jane's Information Group Ltd. • Covers: Operating bus, metro, light rail, tram, ferry, and trolley bus transport systems; manufacturers of equipment for urban systems; experimental systems, and manufacturers of support equipment; consultants; worldwide coverage. Entries include: For systems--Name of operating company or authority, address, phone, fax, telex, names and titles of key personnel, services, equipment, finances, developments. For manufacturers--Name, address, phone, fax, telex, names and titles of key personnel, products, current contracts, new developments in equipment. For consultants--Firm name, address, phone, fax, telex, names and titles of key personnel, description of firm capabilities, past projects.

Plunkett's Transportation and Logistics Industry Almanac. Plunkett Research, Ltd. • 2004. $249.99. Contains profiles of 300 leading companies in the fields of transportation, logistics, supply chain management, warehousing, distribution, and inter-modal shipment systems. Includes industry trends and statistics.

Transportation Telephone Tickler. Journal of Commerce. • Covers: 24,000 companies and agents in North American port districts which provide transportation services ranging from air freight forwarding to warehousing. Published in a four-volume national edition and 7 regional editions. Entries include: Company name, headquarters and branch addresses, phone and fax numbers, names of key personnel, e-mail and web addresses.

ENCYCLOPEDIAS AND DICTIONARIES

Dictionary of Shipping Terms. Peter Brodie. LLP, Inc. • 1997. Third edition. Price on application. Published in the UK by Lloyd's List (http://www.lloydslist.com). Defines more than 2,000 words, phrases, and abbreviations related to the shipping and maritime industries.

Macmillan Encyclopedia of Transportation. Available from Gale Cengage Learning. • 1999. $450.00. Six volumes. Published by Macmillan Reference USA. Covers the business, technology, and history of transportation on land, on water, in the air, and in

space. Includes definitions, cross-references, and 200 color illustrations.

FINANCIAL RATIOS

Almanac of Business and Industrial Financial Ratios. Leo Troy. Aspen Publishers, Inc. • 2003. $125.95. Includes CD-Rom. Contains financial ratios derived from federal tax returns. Ratios for each of about 200 industries are arranged according to company asset size. (Almanac of Business and Industrial Financial Ratios Series).

IRS Corporate Financial Ratios. Available from MarketResearch.com. • 2002. $225.00. Published by Schonfeld & Associates, Inc. Presents 70 key financial ratios for 260 industries. Ratios are calculated from income statement and balance sheet data available from the Internal Revenue Service. Includes four asset size classes.

HANDBOOKS AND MANUALS

Recommendations on the Transport of Dangerous Goods. United Nations Publications. • 1999. $120.00. 11th edition. Covers regulations imposed by various governments and international organizations.

Transportation Engineering and Planning. C. S. Papacostas and Panos D. Prevedouros. Prentice Hall PTR. • 2000. $115.00. Third edition.

Transportation Planning Handbook. John D. Edwards. Institute of Transportation Engineers. • 1999. $100.00. Second edition.

INTERNET DATABASES

Bureau of Economic Analysis (BEA). U. S. Department of Commerce, Bureau of Economic Analysis. Phone: (202)606-9900 Fax: (202)606-5310 E-mail: webmaster@bea.doc.gov • URL: http://www.bea.doc.gov • Web site includes "News Release Information" covering national, regional, and international economic estimates from the BEA. Highlights of releases appear online the same day, complete text and tables appear the next day. "Recent News Releases" section provides titles for past nine months, with links. "BEA Data and Methodology" includes "Frequently Requested NIPA Data" (national income and product accounts, such as gross domestic product and personal income). Other statistics are available. Fees: Free.

Business 2.0 Web Guide to the Best Business Links. Business 2.0 Media Inc. Phone: (415)293-4800 E-mail: support@business2.com • URL: http://www.business2.com/webguide • Web site presents an extensive, searchable directory of links to "the best, most informative, and authoritative web pages." Twenty main categories cover business, finance, career, company information, people, and technology topics, with thousands of subtopics, all linking to Web sites recommended by experienced business researchers. Fees: Free.

Fedstats. Federal Interagency Council on Statistical Policy. Phone: (202)395-7254 • URL: http://www.fedstats.gov • Web site features an efficient search facility for full-text statistics produced by more than 100 federal agencies, including the Census Bureau, the Bureau of Economic Analysis, and the Bureau of Labor Statistics. Boolean searches can be made within one agency or for all agencies combined. Links are offered to international statistical bureaus, including the UN, IMF, OECD, UNESCO, Eurostat, and 20 individual countries. Fees: Free.

FreeLunch.com. Economy.com, Inc. Phone: (610)696-8700 Fax: (610)696-1678 • URL: http://www.freelunch.com • Web site provides free access to more than 1.5 million economic and financial data series, covering industry, demographics, labor markets, prices, retail sales, government spending, trade, interest rates, housing starts, the stock market, and many other topics. Data is available for various time periods in either chart or table form. Searching is offered. Fees: Free, but registration required.

Economy.com, Inc. also offers fee-based economic analysis at *The Dismal Scientist* site (http://www.dismal.com).

ONLINE DATABASES

Business and Industry. Gale Cengage Learning. • Contains online citations, abstracts, and selected fulltext from more than 1,000 trade journals, newspapers, and other publications. Provides general coverage of both manufacturing and service industries, including marketing, production, industry trends, key events, and information on specific companies. Time span is 1994 to date. Daily updates. Inquire as to online cost and availability. (Also available in a CD-ROM version.)

Tablebase. Gale Cengage Learning. • Provides online numerical tabular data from a wide variety of business, organization, and government sources, including about 1,000 trade journals. Includes industry and individual company statistics relating to products, market share, sales forecasts, production, exports, market trends, etc. Time span is 1997 to date. Weekly updates. Inquire as to online cost and availability. (Also available in a CD-ROM version.).

TRIS: Transportation Research Information Service. National Research Council. • Contains abstracts and citations to a wide range of transportation literature, 1968 to present, with monthly updates. Includes references to the literature of air transportation, highways, ships and shipping, railroads, trucking, and urban mass transportation. Formerly *TRIS-ONLINE*. Inquire as to online cost and availability.

Wilson Business Abstracts Online. H. W. Wilson Co. • Indexes and abstracts 600 major business periodicals, plus the *Wall Street Journal* and the business section of the *New York Times*. Indexing is from 1982, abstracting from 1990, with the two newspapers included from 1993. Updated weekly. Inquire as to online cost and availability. (*Business Periodicals Index* without abstracts is also available online.).

PERIODICALS AND NEWSLETTERS

Defense Transportation Journal: Magazine of International Defense Transportation and Logistics. National Defense Transportation Association. • Bimonthly. Free to members; non-members, $35.00 per year.

ITE Journal. Institute of Transportation Engineers. • Monthly. $60.00 per year. Formerly *Transportation Engineering*.

The Journal of Commerce. Commonwealth Business Media. • Weekly. $146.00 per year. Topics include transatlantic shipping, domestic shipping, customs brokers, freight forwarders, ports, air freight, containerization, and other aspects of transportation and shipping logistics. Formerly *Journal of Commerce*.

Journal of Transport Economics and Policy. University of Bath. • Three times a year. Individuals, $55.00 per year; institutions, $165.00 per year; students, $20.00 per year. Text in English, French, German and Spanish.

Modern Bulk Transporter. Primedia Business Magazines and Media. • Monthly. $50.00 per year.

Passenger Transport. American Public Transportation Association. • Weekly. $65.00 per year. Covers current events and trends in mass transportation.

Research on Transport Economics. OECD Publications and Information Center. • Annual. Quarterly $138.00. Text in French.

Transportation Journal. American Society of Transportation and Logistics, Inc. • Quarterly. $61.95 per year.

Transportation Review Part E: Logistics and Transportation Review. University of British Columbia Centre for Transportation Studies. Elsevier. • Bimonthly. Individuals, $213.00 per year; institutions, $897.00 per year.

Transportation Science. INFORMS. • Quarterly. Individuals, $155.00 per year. Includes print and on-line editions. Institutions, $221.00 per year. Includes print and online editions.

Urban Transport News: Management-Funding Terrorism-Ridership-Technology. Business Publishers, Inc. • 25 times a year. $437.00 per year. Newsletter. Provides current news from Capitol Hill, the White House, the Dept. of Transportation, as well as transit operations and industries across the country.

RESEARCH CENTERS AND INSTITUTES

Center for Transportation Studies. Massachusetts Institute of Technology. 77 Massachusetts Ave. Room 1-235, Cambridge, MA 02139. Phone: (617)253-5320 Fax: (617)253-4560 E-mail: sheffi@mit.edu • URL: http://www.web.mit.edu/cts/www/.

Institute of Transportation Studies. University of California at Berkeley. 109 McLaughlin Hall, Berkeley, CA 94720. Phone: (510)642-3585 Fax: (510)642-1246 E-mail: its@its.berkeley.edu • URL: http://www.its.berkeley.edu.

Texas Transportation Institute. Texas A & M University System, CE/TTI, Room 801 B, College Station, TX 77843-3135. Phone: (979)845-1713 Fax: (979)845-9356 E-mail: herbert-richardson@tamu.edu • URL: http://www.tii.tamu.edu • Concerned with all forms and modes of transportation. Research areas include transportation economics, highway construction, traffic safety, public transportation, and highway engineering.

Transportation Center. Northwestern University, 600 Foster St., Evanston, IL 60208-4055. Phone: (847)491-7287 Fax: (847)491-3090 E-mail: tc-info@northwestern.edu • URL: http://www.nutc.northwestern.edu/public.

Transportation Research Center. University of Florida. 512 Weil Hall, Gainesville, FL 32611. Phone: 800-226-1013 or (352)392-7575 Fax: (352)392-3224 E-mail: uftrc@ce.ufl.edu • URL: http://www.uftrc.ce.ufl.edu.

Transportation Research Institute. University of Michigan, 2901 Baxter Rd., Ann Arbor, MI 48109-2150. Phone: (734)764-6504 Fax: (734)936-1081 E-mail: umtri@umich.edu • URL: http://www.umtri.umich.edu • Research areas include highway safety, transportation systems, and shipbuilding.

STATISTICS SOURCES

Annual Bulletin of Transport Statistics for Europe and North America. United Nations Publications. • Annual. $60.00. Presents detailed transportation statistics for European countries, Canada, and the U. S. Includes data on energy consumption for transport.

Business Statistics of the United States. Linz Audain and Cornelia J. Strawser. Bernan Associates. • Annual. $147.00. Based on *Business Statistics,* formerly issue by the Bureau of Economic Analysis, U. S. Department of Commerce. Provides basic data for a wide variety of U. S. industries, services, and economic indicators. Most statistics are shown annually for 30 years and monthly for the most recent four years.

Datapedia of the United States: American History in Numbers. George T. Kurian, editor. Bernan Press. • 2004. $125.00. Third edition. Based on the Census Bureau publication, *Historical Statistics of the United States.* Provides data from Colonial times to the present on agriculture, business, consumer income, energy, finance, labor, national income, population, and many other subjects. Includes "narrative highlights," maps, charts, and statistical projections.

Encyclopedia of American Industries. Gale Cengage Learning. • 2000. $560.00. Third edition. Two volumes. $280.00 per volume. Volume one is *Manufacturing Industries* and volume two is *Service and Non-Manufacturing Industries.* Provides the history, development, and recent status of approximately 1,000 industries. Includes statistical graphs, with industry and general indexes.

Infrastructure Industries USA. Gale Cengage Learning. • 2001. $260.00. Presents statistics and projections relating to economic activity in a wide variety of natural resource and construction industries.

Monthly Bulletin of Statistics. United Nations Publications. • Monthly. $295.00 per year. Provides current data for about 200 countries on a wide variety of economic, industrial, and demographic subjects. Compiled by United Nations Statistical Office.

OECD in Figures. Organization for Economic Cooperation and Development. • Annual. $13.00. A "pocket data book" providing a summary of key statistics for OECD countries, including economic growth, employment, education, the environment, and transportation.

Standard & Poor's Industry Surveys. Standard & Poor's. • Semiannual. $1,800.00. Two looseleaf volumes. Includes monthly *Supplements.* Provides detailed; individual surveys of 52 major industry groups. Each survey is revised on a semiannual basis. Also includes "Monthly Investment Review" (industry group investment analysis) and monthly "Trends & Projections" (economic analysis).

Statistical Yearbook. United Nations Publications. • Annual. $125.00. Contains statistics for about 200 countries on a wide variety of economic, industrial, and demographic topics. Compiled by United Nations Statistical Office.

Survey of Current Business. Available from U. S. Government Printing Office. • Monthly. $63.00 per year. Issued by Bureau of Economic Analysis, U. S. Department of Commerce. Presents a wide variety of business and economic data.

Transportation Statistics Annual Report. Available from U. S. Government Printing Office. • Annual. $43.00. Issued by the U. S. Bureau of Transportation Statistics, Transportation Department (http://www.bts.gov). Summarizes national data for various forms of transportation, including airlines, railroads, and motor vehicles. Information on the use of roads and highways is included.

U. S. Industry and Trade Outlook. Available from National Technical Information Service. • Annual. $69.95. Produced by the International Trade Administration, U. S. Department of Commerce, in a "public-private" partnership with DRI/McGraw-Hill and Standard & Poor's. Provides basic data, outlook for the current year, and "Long-Term Prospects" (five-year projections) for a wide variety of products and services. Includes high technology industries. Formerly *U. S. Industrial Outlook.*

U. S. Industry Profiles: The Leading 100. Gale Cengage Learning. • 1998. $130.00. Second edition. Contains detailed profiles, with statistics, of 100 industries in the areas of manufacturing, construction, transportation, wholesale trade, retail trade, and entertainment.

United States Census of Transportation. Bureau of the Census, U.S. Department of Commerce. Available from U.S. Government Printing Office. • Quinquennial.

TRADE/PROFESSIONAL ASSOCIATIONS

American Public Transportation Association. 1666 K St. NW, Ste. 1100, Washington, DC 20006. Phone: (202)496-4800 Fax: (202)496-4321 E-mail: info@apta.com • URL: http://www.apta.com • Motor bus and rapid transit systems; organizations responsible for planning, designing, constructing, financing, and operating transit systems; business organizations which supply products and services to transit, academic institutions, and state associations and departments of transportation. Represents the public interest in improving transit. Encourages cooperation among its members, their employees, the general public and compliance with the letter and spirit of equal opportunity principles. Seeks to collect information relative to public transit; assist in the training, education, and professional development of all persons involved in public transit; and engage in activities which promote public transit. Provides a medium for exchange of experiences, discussion, and a comparative study of public transit affairs; Promotes research.

American Society of Transportation and Logistics. 1700 N Moore St., Ste. 1900, Arlington, VA 22209. Phone: (703)524-5011 Fax: (703)524-5017 E-mail: info@astl.org; ast1@astl.org.

Institute of Transportation Engineers. 1099 14th St., N.W., Suite 300 W, Washington, DC 20005-3438. Phone: (202)289-0222 Fax: (202)289-7722 E-mail: ite_staff@site.org • URL: http://www.ite.org • Members are professionals in surface transportation, mass transit, and traffic engineering. Formerly Institute of Traffic Engineers.

National Defense Transportation Association. 50 S Pickett St., Ste. 220, Alexandria, VA 22304-7296. Phone: (703)751-5011 Fax: (703)823-8761 E-mail: info@ndtahq.com • URL: http://www.ndtahq.com • Men and women in the field of transportation, travel logistics and related areas in the Armed Forces, federal government, private industry and the academic sector. Strives to foster a strong and efficient transportation system in support of national defense. Serves as link between government and industry on transportation matters. Operates a job placement service for members.

Transportation Clubs International. PO Box 2223, Ocean Shores, WA 98569. Phone: 877-858-8627 Fax: (360)289-3188 E-mail: info@transportationclubsinternational.com • URL: http://www.transportationclubsinternational.com • Men and women in the traffic and transportation fields, including railroads, bus lines, trucking firms, and traffic managers of industrial firms. Sponsors National Transportation Week.

OTHER SOURCES

Federal Carriers Reports. CCH, Inc. • Biweekly. $1,484.00 per year. Four looseleaf volumes. Federal rules and regulations for motor carriers, water carriers, and freight forwarders.

TRANSPORTATION, PUBLIC

See: PUBLIC TRANSPORTATION

TRANSPORTATION TIME TABLES

See: TIMETABLES

TRAVEL AGENCIES

See also: TRAVEL INDUSTRY

BIBLIOGRAPHIES

Travel and Tourism. Available from U. S. Government Printing Office. • Annual. Free. Issued by the Superintendent of Documents. A list of government publications on the travel industry and tourism. Formerly *Mass Transit, Travel and Tourism.* (Subject Bibliography No. 302.).

DIRECTORIES

American Society of Travel Agents-Membership Directory. American Society of Travel Agents. • Annual. $195.00. Listings of over 13,500 worldwide members of ASTA.

Plunkett's Airline, Hotel, and Travel Industry Almanac. Plunkett Research, Ltd. • Annual. $249.95. Contains profiles of 300 leading companies, including airlines, hotels, travel agencies, theme parks, cruise lines, casinos, and car rental companies.

FINANCIAL RATIOS

Annual Statement Studies. The Risk Management Association. • Annual. Median and quartile financial ratios are given for over 400 kinds of manufacturing, wholesale, retail, construction, and consumer finance establishments. Data is sorted by both asset size and sales volume. Includes a clearly written "Definition of Ratios" and an alphabetical industry index.

Annual Statement Studies: Industry Default Probabilities and Cash Flow Measures. The Risk Management Association. • Annual. $145.00. Serves as a companion volume to the original *Annual Statement Studies.* Gives probability of default estimates on a percentage scale for more than 450 industries. Includes changes in position year-by-year for eight financial statement line items and provides percentage measures of cash flow.

HANDBOOKS AND MANUALS

Travel Agency. Entrepreneur Media, Inc. • Looseleaf. $59.50. A practical guide to starting a travel agency. Covers profit potential, start-up costs, market size evaluation, owner's time required, site selection, lease negotiation, pricing, accounting, advertising, promotion, etc. (Start-Up Business Guide No. E1154.).

PERIODICALS AND NEWSLETTERS

ASTA Agency Management. American Society of Travel Agents. Pohly and Partners Inc. • Monthly. $36.00 per year.

Travel Agent: The National Newsweekly Magazine of the Travel Industry. Advanstar Communications. • 51 times a year. 250.00 per. year.

TRADE/PROFESSIONAL ASSOCIATIONS

American Society of Travel Agents. 1101 King St., Suite 200, Alexandria, VA 22314. Phone: 800-440-2782 or (703)739-2782 Fax: (703)684-8319 E-mail: askasta@astahq.com • URL: http://www.astanet.com.

Association of Retail Travel Agents. 3161 Custer Dr., Ste. 8, Lexington, KY 40517-4067. Phone: (859)269-9739 Fax: (859)266-9396 • URL: http://www.artaonline.com.

Institute of Certified Travel Agents. 148 Linden St., Wellesley, MA 02482. Phone: 800-542-4282 or (781)237-0280 Fax: (781)237-3860 E-mail: info@icta.com • URL: http://www.icta.com.

OTHER SOURCES

ICTA Travel Management Text Series. Institute of Certified Travel Agents. • Four volumes. Volume one, *Business Management for Travel Agents*; volume two, *Personnel Management for Travel Agents*; volume three, *Marketing for Travel Agents*; volume four, *Domestic Leisure and International Tourism.*

TRAVEL, AIR

See: AIR TRAVEL

TRAVEL, BUSINESS

See: BUSINESS TRAVEL

TRAVEL INDUSTRY

See also: AIR TRAVEL; BUSINESS TRAVEL; HOTEL AND MOTEL INDUSTRY; TIMETABLES; TRAVEL AGENCIES

GENERAL WORKS

International Travel and Tourism. H. Sorensen. Delmar Learning. • 1997. $86.95. (Hospitality, Travel and Tourism Series).

Tourism: Principles, Practices, Philosophies. Charles R. Goeldner. John Wiley and Sons, Inc. • 2002. $70.00. Ninth edition. General review of the travel industry.

ABSTRACTS AND INDEXES

Leisure, Recreation, and Tourism Abstracts. Available from CABI Publishing North America. • Quarterly. Members, $280.00 per year; Institutions, $610.00 per year. Includes single site internet access. Published in England by CABI Publishing. Provides coverage of the worldwide literature of travel, recreation, sports, and the hospitality industry. Emphasis is on research.

BIBLIOGRAPHIES

Tourism Planning. David Marcouiller. Sage Publications, Inc. • 1995. $10.00. (Bibliographies Series No. 316).

Travel and Tourism. Available from U. S. Government Printing Office. • Annual. Free. Issued by the Superintendent of Documents. A list of government publications on the travel industry and tourism. Formerly *Mass Transit, Travel and Tourism.* (Subject Bibliography No. 302.).

CD-ROM DATABASES

OECD Statistical Compendium. Organization for Economic Cooperation and Development. • Semiannual. $1,905.00 per year for 1 to 10 users. CD-ROM contains more than 730,000 monthly, quarterly, and annual time series for OECD countries, 1960 to date. Includes fully searchable data on agriculture, food, economic indicators, national accounts, employment, energy, finance, industry, technology, and foreign trade. Results can be displayed in various forms.

DIRECTORIES

Golf Index. Ingledue Travel Publications. • Semiannual. $40.00 per year. Provides directory listings of golf courses and resorts around the world. Contains information on golf travel packages, tour operators, and tournaments.

Resorts and Parks Purchasing Guide. Klevens Publications, Inc. • Annual. $85.00. Lists suppliers of products and services for resorts and parks, including national parks, amusement parks, dude ranches, golf resorts, ski areas, and national monument areas.

HANDBOOKS AND MANUALS

Health Information for International Travel. U.S. Dept. of Health and Human Services, Centers for Disease Control and Prefabricated. • Annual. $20.00. Produced by the Centers for Disease Control and Prevention (CDC). Primarily edited for "healthcare providers who administer pre- and post-travel counseling and care." Also serves as a reference for airlines, cruise lines, and the travel industry in general. Covers such items as injuries during travel, motion sickness, disabilities, vaccines, insect repellents, and travel with children. Sometimes known as "The Yellow Book.".

Health Information for International Travel. Available from U. S. Government Printing Office. • Annual. Issued by Centers for Disease Control, U. S. Department of Health and Human Services. Discusses potential health risks of international travel and specifies vaccinations required by different countries.

Marketing in Travel and Tourism. Victor Middleton. Elsevier. • 2001. $37.95. Third edition. Explains, with examples, the application of marketing concepts and principles to the travel industry.

Resort Development Handbook. Urban Land Institute. • 1997. $89.95. Covers a wide range of resort settings and amenities, with details of development, market analysis, financing, design, and operations. Includes color photographs and case studies. (ULI Development Handbook Series).

INTERNET DATABASES

Business 2.0 Web Guide to the Best Business Links. Business 2.0 Media Inc. Phone: (415)293-4800 E-mail: support@business2.com • URL: http://www.business2.com/webguide • Web site presents an extensive, searchable directory of links to "the best, most informative, and authoritative web pages." Twenty main categories cover business, finance, career, company information, people, and technology topics, with thousands of subtopics, all linking to Web sites recommended by experienced business researchers. Fees: Free.

Fedstats. Federal Interagency Council on Statistical Policy. Phone: (202)395-7254 • URL: http://www.fedstats.gov • Web site features an efficient search facility for full-text statistics produced by more than 100 federal agencies, including the Census Bureau, the Bureau of Economic Analysis, and the Bureau of Labor Statistics. Boolean searches can be made within one agency or for all agencies combined. Links are offered to international statistical bureaus, including the UN, IMF, OECD, UNESCO, Eurostat, and 20 individual countries. Fees: Free.

FreeLunch.com. Economy.com, Inc. Phone: (610)696-8700 Fax: (610)696-1678 • URL: http://www.freelunch.com • Web site provides free access to more than 1.5 million economic and financial data series, covering industry, demographics, labor markets, prices, retail sales, government spending, trade, interest rates, housing starts, the stock market, and many other topics. Data is available for various time periods in either chart or table form. Searching is offered. Fees: Free, but registration required. Economy.com, Inc. also offers fee-based economic analysis at *The Dismal Scientist* site (http://www.dismal.com).

ONLINE DATABASES

United States International Air Travel Statistics. U. S. Department of Transportation, Center for Transportation Information. • Provides detailed statistics on air passenger travel between the U. S. and foreign countries for both scheduled and charter flights. Time period is 1975 to date, with monthly updates. Inquire as to online cost and availability.

PERIODICALS AND NEWSLETTERS

ASTA Agency Management. American Society of Travel Agents. Pohly and Partners Inc. • Monthly. $36.00 per year.

Consumer Reports Travel Letter. Consumers Union of U.S. Inc. • Description: Provides travelers with information and advice on travel goods and services. Discusses such topics as air and rail passes, air fare, hotel rates, car rental fees, and techniques for optimizing foreign exchange rates.

Cruise Travel: Ships, Ports, Schedules, Prices. World Publishing Co. • Bimonthly. $23.94 per year.

International Journal of Hospitality and Tourism Administration: A Multinationaland Cross-Cultural Journal of Applied Research. Haworth Press, Inc. • Quarterly. $200.00 per year. Includes print and online editions. An academic journal with articles relating to lodging, food service, travel, tourism, and the hospitality/leisure industries in general. Formerly *Journal of International Hospitality, Leisure, and Tourism Management.*

Journal of Quality Assurance in Hospitality and Tourism: Improvements in Marketing, Management, and Development. Haworth Press, Inc. • Quarterly. $240.00 per year to libraries; $50.00 per year to individuals. Includes research papers, case studies, abstracts of dissertations, book reviews, conference reviews, and Web site reviews.

Journal of Travel and Tourism Marketing. Haworth Press, Inc. • Quarterly. $310.00 per year.

Journal of Travel Research. University of Colorado, Business Research Div. Sage Publications, Inc. • Quarterly. Institutions, $350.00 per year. Includes print and online editions.

Lloyd's Cruise International. Available from Informa Publishing Group Ltd. • Bimonthly. $217.00 per year. Published in the UK by Lloyd's List (http://www.lloydslist.com). Edited for management professionals in the cruise ship industry. Covers industry trends, technical/equipment developments, regulatory issues, new cruise ships, ship management, cruise marketing, and related topics.

Newsline: Research News from the U. S. Travel Data Center. U.S. National Research Council. • Monthly. $55.00 per year. Newsletter. Covers trends in the U. S. travel industry.

Passport Newsletter. Remy Publishing Co. • Monthly. $89.00 per year. Formerly *Passport.*

Resort Management and Operations: The Resort Resource. Finan Publishing Co., Inc. • Bimonthly. Price on application. Edited for hospitality professionals at both large and small resort facilities.

Summary of Health Information for International Travel. U. S. Department of Health and Human Services. • Biweekly. Formerly *Weekly Summary of Health Information for International Travel.*

Travel and Leisure. American Express Publishing Corp. • Monthly. $39.00 per year. In three regional editions and one demographic edition.

Travel Management Daily. Cahners Business Information. • Description: E-mail and internet publication which offers news and advice for those who work in the travel industry.

Travel Smart: Pay Less, Enjoy More. Dunan Communications, Inc. • Monthly. $39.00 per year. Newsletter. Provides information and recommendations for travelers. Emphasis is on travel value and opportunities for bargains. Incorporates*Joy of Travel.*

Travel Trade News Edition: The Business Paper of the Travel Industry. Travel Trade Publications. • Weekly. $10.00 per year. Formerly *Travel Trade.*

Travel Weekly. Northstar Travel Media, LLC. • Weekly. $266.00 per year. Includes cruise guides, a weekly "Business Travel Update," and special issues devoted to particular destinations and areas. Edited mainly for travel agents and tour operators.

STATISTICS SOURCES

Business Statistics of the United States. Linz Audain and Cornelia J. Strawser. Bernan Associates. • Annual. $147.00. Based on *Business Statistics,* formerly issue by the Bureau of Economic Analysis, U. S. Department of Commerce. Provides basic data for a wide variety of U. S. industries, services, and economic indicators. Most statistics are shown annually for 30 years and monthly for the most recent four years.

Economic Review of Travel in America. Travel Industry Association of America. • Annual. Members, $75.00; non-members, $125.00. Presents a statistical summary of travel in the U.S., including travel expenditures, travel industry employment, tax data, international visitors, etc.

Outlook for Travel and Tourism. Travel Industry Association of America. • Annual. Members, $100.00; non-members, $175.00. Contains forecasts of the performance of the U. S. travel industry, including air travel, business travel, recreation (attractions), and accomodations.

Services: Statistics on International Transactions. Organization for Economic Cooperation and Development. Available from OECD Publications and Information Center. • Annual. $71.00. Presents a compilation and assessment of data on OECD member countries' international trade in services. Covers four major categories for 20 years: travel, transportation, government services, and other services.

Summary of International Travel to the United States. International Trade Administration, Tourism Industries. U.S. Dept. of Commerce. • Monthly. Quarterly and annual versions available. Provides statistics on air travel to the U.S. from each of 90 countries. Formerly *Summary and Analysis of International Travel to the United States.*

Survey of Current Business. Available from U. S. Government Printing Office. • Monthly. $63.00 per year. Issued by Bureau of Economic Analysis, U. S. Department of Commerce. Presents a wide variety of business and economic data.

Tourism Policy and International Tourism in OECD Member Countries. Available from OECD Publications and Information Center. • Annual. $50.00. Reviews developments in the international tourism industry in OECD member countries. Includes statistical information.

TRADE/PROFESSIONAL ASSOCIATIONS

National Tour Association. 546 E Main St., Lexington, KY 40508-2300. Phone: 800-682-8886 or (859)226-4444 Fax: (606)226-4414 E-mail: questions@ntastaff.com • URL: http://www.ntaonline.com • Formerly National Tour Brokers Association.

Travel and Tourism Research Association. P.O. Box 2133, Boise, ID 83701. Phone: (208)429-9511 Fax: (208)429-9512 E-mail: ttra@worldnet.att.net • URL: http://www.ttra.com • Members are travel directors, airline officials, hotels, government agencies, and others interested in the travel field.

Travel Industry Association of America. 1100 New York Ave., N.W., Suite 450, Washington, DC 20005. Phone: (202)408-8422 Fax: (202)408-1255 E-mail: membership@tia.org • URL: http://www.tia.org • Corporations engaged in the hospitality and travel industry.

OTHER SOURCES

Travel Law. American Lawyer Media, Inc. • Looseleaf. $149.00. Updated as needed. Emphasis is on the legal rights of travelers, including a consideration of class action suits. Includes such matters as tour operator liability, hotel responsibilities, overbooking by airlines, and frequent-flyer issues. (Law Journal Press).

TRAVEL TRAILERS

See: RECREATIONAL VEHICLE INDUSTRY

TREASURERS

See: CORPORATE DIRECTORS AND OFFICERS

TREASURY BONDS

See: GOVERNMENT BONDS

TREES

See: FOREST PRODUCTS; LUMBER INDUSTRY

TRENDS, BUSINESS

See: BUSINESS CYCLES; BUSINESS FORECASTING

TRIALS AND JURIES

See also: STATE LAW

GENERAL WORKS

Great American Trials. Gale Cengage Learning. • 2002. $170.00. Second edition. Two volumes. Contains discussions and details of momentous American trials from 1637 to 1993.

Inside the Juror: The Psychology of Juror Decision Making. Reid Hastie, editor. Cambridge University Press. • 1994. $29.00. (Judgement and Decision Making Series).

Jury Persuasion: Psychological Strategies & Trial Techniques. Donald E. Vinson and David S. Davis. Glasser Legalworks. • 1996. $55.00. Third revised edition. Covers voir dire (questioning prospective jurors), juror selection, opening statements, visual support of oral evidence, witness likeability, and "special tactics.".

ABSTRACTS AND INDEXES

Index to Legal Periodicals and Books. H. W. Wilson Co. • Monthly. $490.00 per year. Quarterly and annual cumulations.

DIRECTORIES

International Academy of Trial Lawyers Roster. International Academy of Trial Lawyers. • Biennial. Free. More than 2,400 trial lawyers board certified in civil and criminal trial advocacy; members of the board.

HANDBOOKS AND MANUALS

Jury Manual: A Guide for Prospective Jurors. William R. Pabst. Metro Publishing. • 1985. $19.95.

ONLINE DATABASES

Index to Legal Periodicals and Books (Online). H. W. Wilson Co. • Broad coverage of law journals and books 1981 to date. Monthly updates. Inquire as to online cost and availability.

Legal Resource Index. Gale Cengage Learning. • Broad coverage of law literature appearing in legal, business, and other periodicals, 1980 to date. Daily updates. Inquire as to online cost and availability.

LEXIS. LEXIS-NEXIS. • The various LEXIS databases provide full text and indexing for a wide variety of legal cases, statutes, orders, and opinions.

PERIODICALS AND NEWSLETTERS

Champion. National Association of Criminal Defense Lawyers. • 10 times a year. $25.00 per year.

Judges' Journal. American Bar Association, Judicial Administration Div., Section of Environment, Energy and Resources. • Quarterly. Free to members; non-members, $25.00 per year. Focuses on the court.

Judicature. American Judicature Society. • Bimonthly. Free to members; institutions, $48.00 per year.

Trial. Association of Trial Lawyers of America. • Monthly. $79.00 per year.

Trial Lawyers Quarterly. New York State Trial Lawyers Association. • Quarterly. $50.00 per year.

TRADE/PROFESSIONAL ASSOCIATIONS

American Judges Association. 300 Newport Ave., Williamsburg, VA 23185-4147. Phone: 800-616-6165 or (757)259-1841 Fax: (757)259-1520 E-mail: aja@ncsc.dni.us • URL: http://aja.ncsc.dni.us • Seeks to improve the administration of justice at all levels of the courts.

American Judicature Society. Drake University, The Opperman Ctr., 2700 University Ave., Des Moines, IA 50311. Phone: 800-626-4089 or (515)271-2281 Fax: (515)279-3090 E-mail: dperrault@ajs.org • URL: http://www.ajs.org • Lawyers, judges, law teachers, government officials, and citizens interested in the effective administration of justice.

Conducts research; presents educational programs; offers a consultation service; sponsors and organizes citizens' conferences on judicial improvement. Coordinates the work of states in judicial discipline and removal through its Center for +Judicial Conduct Organizations.

Association of Trial Lawyers of America. 1050 31st. NW, Washington, DC 20007. Phone: 800-424-2725 or (202)965-3500 or (202)944-2800 Fax: (202)625-7312 E-mail: info@atlahq.org • URL: http://www.atlanet.org • Concerned with the behavioral aspects of litigation.

Council for Court Excellence. 1717 K St. NW, Ste. 510, Washington, DC 20036. Phone: (202)785-5917 Fax: (202)785-5922 E-mail: office@courtexcellence.org • URL: http://www.courtexcellence.org.

Institute of Judicial Administration. New York School of Law, Vanderbilt Hall, 40 Washington Square S, New York, NY 10012. Phone: (212)998-6100 or (212)998-6149 Fax: (212)995-4036 E-mail: alison.kinney@nyu.edu.

National Association for Court Management. c/o Association Management National Center for State Courts, 300 Newport Ave., Williamsburg, VA 23185-4147. Phone: 800-616-6165 or (757)259-1841 Fax: (757)259-1520 E-mail: nacm@ncsc.dni.us • URL: http://www.nacmnet.org.

National Association of Criminal Defense Lawyers. 1150 18th St., N.W., Suite 950, Washington, DC 20036. Phone: (202)872-8600 Fax: (202)872-8690 E-mail: assist@nacdl.com • URL: http://www.criminaljustice.org • Formerly National Association of Defense Lawyers in Criminal Cases.

National Center for State Courts. 300 Newport Ave., Williamsburg, VA 23185. Phone: 800-616-6164 or (757)253-2000 Fax: (757)220-0449 E-mail: webmaster@ncse.dni.us • URL: http://www.ncsconline.org.

OTHER SOURCES

The Law of Juries. Nancy Gertner and Judith Mizner. Glasser Legalworks. • Looseleaf. $124.00. Periodic supplementation. Topics include voir dire & juror selection, peremptory challenges, trial location (venue), jury structure, jury deliberation, and jury conduct or misconduct.

TRUCK TRAILERS

See also: AUTOMOTIVE INDUSTRY; TRUCKING INDUSTRY

CD-ROM DATABASES

OECD Statistical Compendium. Organization for Economic Cooperation and Development. • Semiannual. $1,905.00 per year for 1 to 10 users. CD-ROM contains more than 730,000 monthly, quarterly, and annual time series for OECD countries, 1960 to date. Includes fully searchable data on agriculture, food, economic indicators, national accounts, employment, energy, finance, industry, technology, and foreign trade. Results can be displayed in various forms.

DIRECTORIES

Truck Trailer Manufacturers Association Membership Directory. Truck Trailer Manufacturers Association. • Annual. $135.00. About 100 trucks and tank trailer manufacturers and 120 suppliers to the industry.

FINANCIAL RATIOS

Annual Statement Studies. The Risk Management Association. • Annual. Median and quartile financial ratios are given for over 400 kinds of manufacturing, wholesale, retail, construction, and consumer finance establishments. Data is sorted by both asset size and sales volume. Includes a clearly written

"Definition of Ratios" and an alphabetical industry index.

Annual Statement Studies: Industry Default Probabilities and Cash Flow Measures. The Risk Management Association. • Annual. $145.00. Serves as a companion volume to the original *Annual Statement Studies.* Gives probability of default estimates on a percentage scale for more than 450 industries. Includes changes in position year-by-year for eight financial statement line items and provides percentage measures of cash flow.

INTERNET DATABASES

Business 2.0 Web Guide to the Best Business Links. Business 2.0 Media Inc. Phone: (415)293-4800 E-mail: support@business2.com • URL: http://www.business2.com/webguide • Web site presents an extensive, searchable directory of links to "the best, most informative, and authoritative web pages." Twenty main categories cover business, finance, career, company information, people, and technology topics, with thousands of subtopics, all linking to Web sites recommended by experienced business researchers. Fees: Free.

Fedstats. Federal Interagency Council on Statistical Policy. Phone: (202)395-7254 • URL: http://www.fedstats.gov • Web site features an efficient search facility for full-text statistics produced by more than 100 federal agencies, including the Census Bureau, the Bureau of Economic Analysis, and the Bureau of Labor Statistics. Boolean searches can be made within one agency or for all agencies combined. Links are offered to international statistical bureaus, including the UN, IMF, OECD, UNESCO, Eurostat, and 20 individual countries. Fees: Free.

FreeLunch.com. Economy.com, Inc. Phone: (610)696-8700 Fax: (610)696-1678 • URL: http://www.freelunch.com • Web site provides free access to more than 1.5 million economic and financial data series, covering industry, demographics, labor markets, prices, retail sales, government spending, trade, interest rates, housing starts, the stock market, and many other topics. Data is available for various time periods in either chart or table form. Searching is offered. Fees: Free, but registration required. Economy.com, Inc. also offers fee-based economic analysis at *The Dismal Scientist* site (http://www.dismal.com).

Manufacturing Profiles. U. S. Bureau of the Census. Phone: (301)763-4636 E-mail: webmaster@census.gov • URL: http://www.census.gov/prod/www/abs/mfg-prof.html • The Census Bureau makes available free on PDF (Portable Document Format) an annual consolidation of the entire Current Industrial Report series, presenting "all the data compiled." Contains statistics on production, shipments, inventories, consumption, exports, imports, and orders for a wide variety of manufactured products.

PERIODICALS AND NEWSLETTERS

Trailer Body Builders Buyers Guide. Primedia Business Magazines and Media. • Annual. Controlled circulation. List of 8,000 products used by original equipment manufacturers of truck trailers and truck bodies.

STATISTICS SOURCES

Annual Survey of Manufactures. Available from U. S. Government Printing Office. • Annual. Prices vary. Issued by the U. S. Census Bureau as an interim update to the *Census of Manufactures.* Includes data on number of manufacturing establishments in various industries, employment, labor costs, value of shipments, capital expenditures, inventories, energy costs, and assets. (See also Census Bureau home page, http://www.census.gov/.).

Business Statistics of the United States. Linz Audain and Cornelia J. Strawser. Bernan Associates. • Annual. $147.00. Based on *Business Statistics,* formerly issue by the Bureau of Economic Analysis,

U. S. Department of Commerce. Provides basic data for a wide variety of U. S. industries, services, and economic indicators. Most statistics are shown annually for 30 years and monthly for the most recent four years.

Survey of Current Business. Available from U. S. Government Printing Office. • Monthly. $63.00 per year. Issued by Bureau of Economic Analysis, U. S. Department of Commerce. Presents a wide variety of business and economic data.

Truck Trailers. U. S. Bureau of the Census. • Monthly and annual. Provides data on shipments of truck trailers and truck trailer vans: value, quantity, imports, and exports. (Current Industrial Reports, M37L.).

TRADE/PROFESSIONAL ASSOCIATIONS

Truck Trailer Manufacturers Association. 1020 Princess St., Alexandria, VA 22314-2247. Phone: (703)549-3010 Fax: (703)549-3014 E-mail: ttma@erols.com • URL: http://www.ttmanet.org • Manufacturers of commercial trailers; manufacturers of supplies for the truck trailer industry.

TRUCKING INDUSTRY

ALMANACS AND YEARBOOKS

Ward's Automotive Yearbook. Ward's Communications. • Annual. $425.00. Comprehensive statistical information on automotive production, sales, truck data and suppliers. Included with subscription to *Ward's Automotive Reports.*

DIRECTORIES

American Motor Carrier Directory. Commonwealth Business Media Inc. • Publication includes: Lists of all licensed Less Than Truckload (LTL) general commodity carriers in the United States; includes specialized motor carriers and related services; includes refrigerated carriers, heavy haulers, bulk haulers, riggers, and specified commodity carriers; state and federal regulatory bodies governing the trucking industry; tariff publishing bureaus; freight claim councils; industry associations; etc. Entries include: For carriers and services--Company name, address of headquarters and terminals, phones, tariffs followed, names of executives, insurance, and equipment information, services or commodities handled. Principal content of publication is listing of direct point-to-point services of LTL general commodity carriers throughout the United States and to Canada and Mexico.

Modern Bulk Transporter Buyers Guide. Primedia Business Magazines and Media. • Annual. Controlled circulation. Suppliers of products or services for companies operating tank trucks.

Motor Carrier Permit and Tax Bulletin. J.J. Keller and Associates, Inc. • Monthly. $125.00 per year. Looseleaf service. Formerly *Trucking Permit and Tax Bulletin.*

My Little Salesman Truck and Trailer Catalog. My Little Salesman. • Monthly. $24.95 per year. Products serving the trucking industry. Central and Western editions.

National Tank Truck Carrier Directory. National Tank Truck Carriers, Inc. • Covers: For-hire tank truck carriers serving petroleum, chemical, and other industries in the United States, Canada, Australia, England, Europe, Japan, Mexico, and South Africa. Also lists major shippers who use tank trucks, intermodal bulk facilities, industry suppliers, and state related associations affiliated with the American Trucking Associations. Entries include: Company name, address, phone, names of executives, list of products or services.

Official Motor Shippers Guide. Official Motor Freight Guide, Inc. • Annual. $60.50. 17 regional editions. Includes one update. Formerly *Offical Mo-*

tor Freight-Shippers Guide.

ENCYCLOPEDIAS AND DICTIONARIES

Macmillan Encyclopedia of Transportation. Available from Gale Cengage Learning. • 1999. $450.00. Six volumes. Published by Macmillan Reference USA. Covers the business, technology, and history of transportation on land, on water, in the air, and in space. Includes definitions, cross-references, and 200 color illustrations.

FINANCIAL RATIOS

Almanac of Business and Industrial Financial Ratios. Leo Troy. Aspen Publishers, Inc. • 2003. $125.95. Includes CD-Rom. Contains financial ratios derived from federal tax returns. Ratios for each of about 200 industries are arranged according to company asset size. (Almanac of Business and Industrial Financial Ratios Series).

Annual Statement Studies. The Risk Management Association. • Annual. Median and quartile financial ratios are given for over 400 kinds of manufacturing, wholesale, retail, construction, and consumer finance establishments. Data is sorted by both asset size and sales volume. Includes a clearly written "Definition of Ratios" and an alphabetical industry index.

Annual Statement Studies: Industry Default Probabilities and Cash Flow Measures. The Risk Management Association. • Annual. $145.00. Serves as a companion volume to the original *Annual Statement Studies.* Gives probability of default estimates on a percentage scale for more than 450 industries. Includes changes in position year-by-year for eight financial statement line items and provides percentage measures of cash flow.

ONLINE DATABASES

TRIS: Transportation Research Information Service. National Research Council. • Contains abstracts and citations to a wide range of transportation literature, 1968 to present, with monthly updates. Includes references to the literature of air transportation, highways, ships and shipping, railroads, trucking, and urban mass transportation. Formerly *TRIS-ONLINE.* Inquire as to online cost and availability.

PERIODICALS AND NEWSLETTERS

Commercial Carrier Journal. Randall Publishing Co. • Monthly. $45.00 per year.

Fleet Owner. Primedia Business Magazines and Media. • Monthly. $45.00 per year.

Heavy Duty Trucking: The Business Magazine of Trucking. Newport Communications. • Monthly. $65.00 per year.

Lifting and Transportation International. Specialized Carriers and Rigging Association. Douglas Publications, Inc. • Nine times a year.$65.00 per year. Covers specialized trucking, including oversized loads, cranes, hauling steel, heavy rigging, etc. Serves as the official publication of the Specialized Carriers and Rigging Association.

Modern Bulk Transporter. Primedia Business Magazines and Media. • Monthly. $50.00 per year.

Transport Topics. American Trucking Associations Inc. • Description: Covers news of the trucking transportation industry.

STATISTICS SOURCES

American Trucking Trends. American Trucking Associations. Trucking Information Services, Inc. • Annual. $45.00.

F and OS Motor Carrier Annual Report: Results of Operations Class I & II Motor Carriers of Property: Regulated by the Interstate Commerce Commission. American Trucking Associations. Trucking Information Services, Inc. • Annual. $400.00.

F and OS Motor Carrier Quarterly Report (Financial and Operating Statistics). American Trucking Associations. Trucking Information

Services, Inc. • Quarterly. $150.00 per number. Includes *Motor Carrier Annual Report.*

Infrastructure Industries USA. Gale Cengage Learning. • 2001. $260.00. Presents statistics and projections relating to economic activity in a wide variety of natural resource and construction industries.

Monthly Truck Tonnage Report. American Trucking Associations. Trucking Information Services, Inc. • Monthly. $50.00 per year.

Transportation Statistics Annual Report. Available from U. S. Government Printing Office. • Annual. $43.00. Issued by the U. S. Bureau of Transportation Statistics, Transportation Department (http://www.bts.gov). Summarizes national data for various forms of transportation, including airlines, railroads, and motor vehicles. Information on the use of roads and highways is included.

U. S. Industry and Trade Outlook. Available from National Technical Information Service. • Annual. $69.95. Produced by the International Trade Administration, U. S. Department of Commerce, in a "public-private" partnership with DRI/McGraw-Hill and Standard & Poor's. Provides basic data, outlook for the current year, and "Long-Term Prospects" (five-year projections) for a wide variety of products and services. Includes high technology industries. Formerly *U. S. Industrial Outlook.*

WEFA Industrial Monitor. John Wiley and Sons, Inc. • Annual. $65.00. Prepared by industry analysts at WEFA, an economic forecasting and consulting firm (originally Wharton Econometric Forecasting Associates). Contains discussions of the outlook for major U. S. industries, with many 10-year forecasts (WEFA Web site is http://www.wefa.com).

TRADE/PROFESSIONAL ASSOCIATIONS

American Moving and Storage Association. c/o John Brewer. 1611 Duke St., Alexandria, VA 22314. Phone: (703)683-7410 Fax: (703)683-7527 E-mail: amconf@amconf.org • URL: http://www.amconf. org • Members are household goods movers, storage companies, and trucking firms.

American Trucking Associations. 950 N Glebe Rd., Ste. 210, Arlington, VA 22203-4181. Phone: 888-333-1759 or (703)838-1700 Fax: (703)838-1852 E-mail: atamembership@trucking.org • URL: http://www.truckline.com • Motor carriers, suppliers, state trucking associations, and national conferences of trucking companies. Works to influence the decisions of federal, state, and local government bodies; promotes increased efficiency, productivity, and competitiveness in the trucking industries; sponsors American +Trucking Associations Foundation. Provides quarterly financial and operating statistics service. Offers comprehensive accounting service for all sizes of carriers. Promotes highway and driver safety; supports highway research projects; and studies technical and regulatory problems of the trucking industry. Sponsors competitions; compiles statistics. Maintains numerous programs and services including: Management Information Systems Directory; Compensation Survey; Electronic Data Interchange Standards.

Distribution and LTL Carriers Association. 2200 Mill Rd., Alexandria, VA 22314. Phone: (703)838-1806 Fax: (703)684-8143 E-mail: dltlca@aol.com • URL: http://www.dltlca.org • Formerly Regular Common Carrier Conference.

National Motor Freight Traffic Association. 1001 N Fairfax St., Ste. 600, Alexandria, VA 22314. Phone: (866)411-6632 or (703)838-1810 or (703)838-1811 Fax: (703)683-6296 E-mail: membership@nmfta. org • URL: http://www.nmfta.org • Motor common carriers of general commodities. Represents interests of membership before the Surface Transportation Board, the Congress, the courts and state regulatory agencies.

National Private Truck Council. 950 N Gelebe Rd.,

Ste. 530, Arlington, VA 22203-4183. Phone: (703)683-1300 Fax: (703)683-1217 E-mail: info@ nptc.org • URL: http://www.nptc.org • Represents private motor carrier truck fleets and their suppliers.

National Tank Truck Carriers. 950 N Glebe Rd., Ste. 520, Arlington, VA 22203. Phone: (703)838-1960 Fax: (703)838-8860 E-mail: jconley@tanktruck.org • URL: http://www.tanktruck.org • Common or contract "for-hire" tank truck carriers transporting liquid and dry bulk commodities, chemicals, food processing commodities, petroleum, and related products; allied industry suppliers. Promotes federal standards of construction, design, operation, and use of tank trucks and equipment. Coordinates truck transportation system for shippers of bulk commodities. Secures improvements in tank specifications. Sponsors annual schools; conducts research.

OTHER SOURCES

Federal Carriers Reports. CCH, Inc. • Biweekly. $1,484.00 per year. Four looseleaf volumes. Federal rules and regulations for motor carriers, water carriers, and freight forwarders.

TRUCKS (MANUFACTURING)

See also: AUTOMOTIVE INDUSTRY; TRANSPORTATION INDUSTRY; TRUCK TRAILERS; TRUCKING INDUSTRY

CD-ROM DATABASES

OECD Statistical Compendium. Organization for Economic Cooperation and Development. • Semiannual. $1,905.00 per year for 1 to 10 users. CD-ROM contains more than 730,000 monthly, quarterly, and annual time series for OECD countries, 1960 to date. Includes fully searchable data on agriculture, food, economic indicators, national accounts, employment, energy, finance, industry, technology, and foreign trade. Results can be displayed in various forms.

DIRECTORIES

National Truck Equipment Association Membership Roster and Product Directory. National Truck Equipment Association. • Annual. $50.00. Provides company information and products for over 850 of the nation's commercial truck body and equipment manufacturers and distributors.

Plunkett's Automobile Industry Almanac. Plunkett Research Ltd. • Covers: 300 leading companies in the automotive industry. Entries include: Name, address, phone, fax, and key executives. Also includes analysis and information on trends, technology, and statistics in the field.

Truck Trailer Manufacturers Association Membership Directory. Truck Trailer Manufacturers Association. • Annual. $135.00. About 100 trucks and tank trailer manufacturers and 120 suppliers to the industry.

INTERNET DATABASES

Business 2.0 Web Guide to the Best Business Links. Business 2.0 Media Inc. Phone: (415)293-4800 E-mail: support@business2.com • URL: http://www.business2.com/webguide • Web site presents an extensive, searchable directory of links to "the best, most informative, and authoritative web pages." Twenty main categories cover business, finance, career, company information, people, and technology topics, with thousands of subtopics, all linking to Web sites recommended by experienced business researchers. Fees: Free.

Fedstats. Federal Interagency Council on Statistical Policy. Phone: (202)395-7254 • URL: http://www.fedstats.gov • Web site features an efficient search facility for full-text statistics produced by more than 100 federal agencies, including the Census Bureau, the Bureau of Economic Analysis, and the Bureau of

Labor Statistics. Boolean searches can be made within one agency or for all agencies combined. Links are offered to international statistical bureaus, including the UN, IMF, OECD, UNESCO, Eurostat, and 20 individual countries. Fees: Free.

FreeLunch.com. Economy.com, Inc. Phone: (610)696-8700 Fax: (610)696-1678 • URL: http://www.freelunch.com • Web site provides free access to more than 1.5 million economic and financial data series, covering industry, demographics, labor markets, prices, retail sales, government spending, trade, interest rates, housing starts, the stock market, and many other topics. Data is available for various time periods in either chart or table form. Searching is offered. Fees: Free, but registration required. Economy.com, Inc. also offers fee-based economic analysis at *The Dismal Scientist* site (http://www.dismal.com).

ONLINE DATABASES

Ward's AutoInfoBank. Ward's Communications, Inc. • Provides weekly, monthly, quarterly, and annual statistical data from 1980 to date for U. S. and imported cars and trucks. Covers production, shipments, sales, inventories, optional equipment, etc. Updating varies by series. Inquire as to online cost and availability.

PERIODICALS AND NEWSLETTERS

Successful Dealer. Kona Communications, Inc. • Bimonthly. $50.00 per year. For truck and heavy duty equipment dealers.

STATISTICS SOURCES

Business Statistics of the United States. Linz Audain and Cornelia J. Strawser. Bernan Associates. • Annual. $147.00. Based on *Business Statistics*, formerly issue by the Bureau of Economic Analysis, U. S. Department of Commerce. Provides basic data for a wide variety of U. S. industries, services, and economic indicators. Most statistics are shown annually for 30 years and monthly for the most recent four years.

Survey of Current Business. Available from U. S. Government Printing Office. • Monthly. $63.00 per year. Issued by Bureau of Economic Analysis, U. S. Department of Commerce. Presents a wide variety of business and economic data.

TRADE/PROFESSIONAL ASSOCIATIONS

National Truck Equipment Association. 37400 Hills Tech Dr., Farmington Hills, MI 48331-3414. Phone: 800-441-NTEA or (248)489-7090 Fax: (248)489-8590 E-mail: info@ntea.com • URL: http://www.ntea.com • Serves as a trade group for commercial truck, truck body, truck equipment, trailer and accessory manufacturers and distributors. Advises members of current federal regulations affecting the manufacturing and installation of truck bodies and equipment; works to enhance the professionalism of management and improve profitability in the truck equipment business.

TRUST COMPANIES

See: BANKS AND BANKING; TRUSTS AND TRUSTEES

TRUSTS AND TRUSTEES

See also: ESTATE PLANNING; FOUNDATIONS; INSTITUTIONAL INVESTMENTS; INVESTMENT COMPANIES

GENERAL WORKS

How to Avoid Financial Tangles. American Institute for Economic Research. • 2001. $8.00. Provides basic information and advice on such topics as property ownership, taxes, wills, trusts, insurance, record retention, and professional assistance.

(Economic Education Bulletin.).

Staying Wealthy: Strategies for Protecting Your Assets. Brian H. Breuel. Bloomberg. • 1998. $21.95. Presents ideas for estate planning and personal wealth preservation. Includes case studies. (Bloomberg Personal Bookshelf Series).

ABSTRACTS AND INDEXES

Accounting and Tax Index. UMI. • Quarterly. Price on application. Annual cumulation. Indexes accounting, auditing, and taxation literature appearing in journals, books, pamphlets, conference proceedings, and newsletters.

Current Law Index: Multiple Access to Legal Periodicals. Gale Cengage Learning. • Monthly. $725.00 per year. Produced in cooperation with the American Association of Law Libraries. Indexes more than 900 law journals, legal newspapers, and specialty publications from the U.S., Canada, U.K., Ireland, Australia, and New Zealand.

Index to Legal Periodicals and Books. H. W. Wilson Co. • Monthly. $490.00 per year. Quarterly and annual cumulations.

ALMANACS AND YEARBOOKS

American Law Yearbook. Gale Cengage Learning. • Annual. $165.00. Serves as a yearly supplement to *West's Encyclopedia of American Law.* Describes new legal developments in many subject areas.

CD-ROM DATABASES

WILSONDISC: Index to Legal Periodicals and Books. H. W. Wilson Co. • Monthly. Includes unlimited online access to *Index to Legal Periodicals* through WILSONLINE. Contains CD-ROM indexing of more than 1,400 English language legal periodicals from 1981 to date and 2,500 books.

DIRECTORIES

Directory of Trust Banking. Thomson Financial Publishing. • Annual. $344.00. Contains profiles of bank affiliated trust companies, independent trust companies, trust investment advisors, and trust fund managers. Provides contact information for professional personnel at more than 3,000 banking and other financial institutions.

Money Market Directory of Pension Funds and Their Investment Managers. Money Market Directories, Inc. • Annual. $1,150.00. Institutional funds and managers.

Plunkett's Financial Services Industry Almanac: The Only Comprehensive Overview of the Banking, Insurance, Credit and Investment Sectors. Plunkett Research, Ltd. • Annual. $229.99. Includes CD-ROM. Discusses important trends in various sectors of the financial industry. Five hundred major banking, credit card, investment, and financial services companies are profiled. (Business, Careers and Internet Reference Tools Series).

Trusts and Estates - Directory of Trust Institutions. Primedia Business Magazines and Media. • Annual. $79.95. Lists approximately 5,000 trust departments in U.S. and Canadian banks.

Vickers Directory of Institutional Investors. Vickers Stock Research Corp. • Semiannual. $195.00 per year. Detailed alphabetical listing of more than 4,000 U. S., Canadian, and foreign institutional investors. Includes insurance companies, banks, endowment funds, and investment companies. Formerly *Directory of Institutional Investors.*

ENCYCLOPEDIAS AND DICTIONARIES

Dictionary of Finance and Investment Terms. John Downes. Barron's Educational Series, Inc. • 2002. $14.95. Sixth edition. Provides clear explanations of more than 5,000 business, banking, financial, investment, and tax terms. Includes a separate list of financial abbreviations and acronyms. (Business Dictionaries Series).

West's Encyclopedia of American Law. Available

from Gale Cengage Learning. • 2003. $1,195.00. Second edition. 12 volumes. Published by West Group. Covers a wide variety of legal topics for the general reader.

HANDBOOKS AND MANUALS

Best Practices for Financial Advisors. Mary Rowland. Bloomberg. • 1997. $40.00. Provides advice for professional financial advisors on practice management, ethics, marketing, and legal concerns. (Bloomberg Professional Library.).

Corporation-Partnership-Fiduciary Filled-in Tax Return Forms, 2002. CCH, Inc. • 2002. $34.00.

Federal Income Taxes of Decedents, Estates, and Trusts. CCH, Inc. • 2001. $48.00. 20th revised edition. Provides rules for preparing a decedent's final income tax return. Includes discussions of fiduciary duties, grantor trusts, and bankruptcy estates.

Federal Taxation of Trusts, Grantors, and Beneficiaries. John L. Peschel and Edward D. Spurgeon. RIA. • Semiannual. $235.00 per year. Looseleaf service.

Fiduciary Tax Return Guide 2000. RIA. • 2000. $17.25. Revised edition.

How to Save Time and Taxes Preparing Fiduciary Income Tax Returns. LexisNexis Matthew Bender. • Biennial. $272.00 per year. Looseleaf service. Comprehensive coverage of the federal income taxation of trusts and estates.

Inheritor's Handbook: A Definitive Guide for Beneficiaries. Dan Rottenberg. Bloomberg. • 1998. $23.95. Covers both financial and emotional issues faced by beneficiaries. (Bloomberg Personal Bookshelf Series.).

The Living Trust: The Failproof Way to Pass Along Your Estate to Your Heirs Without Lawyers, Courts, or the Probate System. Henry W. Abts. McGraw-Hill. • 2002. $24.95. Third edition.

Trust Administration and Taxation. LexisNexis Matthew Bender. • Semiannual. $1,007.00. Four looseleaf volumes. Text on establishment, administration, and taxation of trusts.

Trust Department Administration and Operations. LexisNexis Matthew Bender. • Biennial. $360.00 per year. Two looseleaf volumes. A procedural manual, training guide and idea source.

INTERNET DATABASES

Lexis.com Research System. Lexis-Nexis Group. Phone: 800-227-4908 or (937)865-6800 Fax: (937)865-6909 E-mail: webmaster@prod.lexis-nexis.com • URL: http://www.lexis.com • Fee-based Web site offers extensive searching of a wide variety of legal sources. Additional features include Daily Opinion Service, lexis.com Bookstore, Career Center, CLE Center, Law Schools, and Practice Pages ("Pages specific to areas of specialty").

ONLINE DATABASES

Banking Information Source. PROQUEST. • Provides indexing and abstracting of periodical and other literature from 1982 to date, with weekly updates. Covers the financial services industry: banks, savings institutions, investment houses, credit unions, insurance companies, and real estate organizations. Emphasis is on marketing and management. Inquire as to online cost and availability. (Formerly *FINIS: Financial Industry Information Service.*).

Index to Legal Periodicals and Books (Online). H. W. Wilson Co. • Broad coverage of law journals and books 1981 to date. Monthly updates. Inquire as to online cost and availability.

PERIODICALS AND NEWSLETTERS

American Banker: The Financial Services Daily. Thomson Media. • Daily. $895.00 per year. Provides news of banking, investment products, mortgages, credit unions, finance, bank technology, and legal developments.

Bank Investment Consultant: Sales Strategies for the Financial Adviser. Thomson Media. • Monthly. Controlled circulation. Covers sales and marketing techniques for bank investment and asset management divisions. Formerly *Bank Investment Marketing.*

Investment Advisor: The Advisor to Advisors. Wicks Business Information. • Monthly. $79.00 per year. Edited for professional investment advisors, financial planners, stock brokers, bankers, and others concerned with the management of assets.

Investment Management Weekly. Thomson Media. • Weekly. $1,370.00 per year. Newsletter. Edited for money managers and other investment professionals. Covers personnel news, investment strategies, and industry trends.

Investment News: The Weekly Newspaper for Financial Advisers. Crain Communications, Inc. • Weekly. $29.00 per year. Edited for both personal and institutional investment advisers, planners, and managers.

Jounal of Finacial Services Professionals. Society of Financial Services Professional. • Bimonthly. $95.00 per year. Provides information on life insurance and financial planning, including estate planning, retirement, tax planning, trusts, business insurance, long-term care insurance, disability insurance, and employee benefits. Formerly (*American Society of CLU and Ch F C Journal*).

Journal of Wealth Management. Institutional Investor, Inc., Journals Group. • Quarterly. $410.00 per year. Includes print and online editions. Edited for managers of wealthy individuals' investment portfolios. Formerly *Journal of Private Portfolio Management.*

Private Asset Management. Institutional Investor, Inc., Journals Group. • Biweekly. $2,335.00 per year. Newsletter. Includes print and online editions. Edited for managers investing the private assets of wealthy ("high-net-worth") individuals. Includes marketing, taxation, regulation, and fee topics.

Robb Report Worth: Wealth in Perspective. CurtCo Robb Media. • Monthly. $54.95 per year. Glossy magazine featuring articles for the affluent on personal financial management, investments, estate planning, trusts, private bankers, taxes, travel, yachts, and lifestyle. Formerly *Worth: Financial Intelligence.*

Trust Letter. American Bankers Association. • Description: Contains updates of national legislation and regulation that impacts the trust and investment businesses. Reports on significant industry happenings, important research, and provides coverage of ABA legislative/regulatory testimony and committee activities, especially in the areas of taxation, securities, and employee benefits.

Trust Management Update. American Bankers Association. • Bimonthly. $95.00 per year.

Trusts and Estates. Primedia Business Magazines and Media. • Monthly. $139.00 per year. Includes annual *Directory.*

U. S. Banker. Thomson Media. • Monthly. $65.00 per year. Edited for bank executives and managers. Covers a wide variety of banking and financial topics.

STATISTICS SOURCES

Pension Investment Report. Employee Benefit Research Institute. • Irregualr. Membership.

TRADE/PROFESSIONAL ASSOCIATIONS

American Bankers Association. 1120 Connecticut Ave. NW, Washington, DC 20036. Phone: 800-BAN-KERS or (202)663-5000 Fax: (202)663-7543 E-mail: custserv@aba.com • URL: http://www.aba. com • Members are principally commercial banks and trust companies; combined assets of members represent approximately 90% of the U.S. banking industry; approximately 94% of members are community banks with less than $500 million in assets. Seeks to enhance the role of commercial bankers as preeminent providers of financial services through communications, research, legal action, lobbying of federal legislative and regulatory bodies, and education and training programs. Serves as spokesperson for the banking industry; facilitates exchange of information among members. Maintains the American Institute of +Banking, an industry-sponsored adult education program. Conducts educational and training programs for bank employees and officers through a wide range of banking schools and national conferences. Maintains liaison with federal bank regulators; lobbies Congress on issues affecting commercial banks; testifies before congressional committees; represents members in U.S. postal rate proceedings. Serves as secretariat of the International Monetary Conference and the Financial Institutions Committee for the American National Standards Institute. Files briefs and lawsuits in major court cases affecting the industry. Conducts teleconferences with state banking associations on such issues as regulatory compliance; works to build consensus and coordinate activities of leading bank and financial service trade groups. Provides services to members including: public advocacy; news media contact; insurance program providing directors and officers with liability coverage, financial institution bond, and trust errors and omissions coverage; research service operated through ABA Center for Banking Information; fingerprint set processing in conjunction with the Federal Bureau of Investigation; discounts on operational and income-producing projects through the Corporation for American Banking. Conducts conferences, forums, and workshops covering subjects such as small business, consumer credit, agricultural and community banking, trust management, bank operations, and automation. Sponsors ABA Educational Foundation and the Personal +Economics Program, which educates schoolchildren and the community on banking, economics, and personal finance.

OTHER SOURCES

Estate Planning: Wills, Trusts and Forms. RIA. • Looseleaf service. Includes bimonthly updates.

Fiduciary Tax Guide. CCH, Inc. • Monthly. $478.00 per year. Looseleaf service. Covers federal income taxation of estates, trusts, and beneficiaries. Provides information on gift and generation-skipping taxation.

Pension Fund Litigation Reporter. Andrews Publications. • Semimonthly. $750.00 per year. Newsletter. Contains reports on legal cases involving pension fund fiduciaries (trustees).

TRUSTS, INVESTMENT

See: INVESTMENT COMPANIES

TUNA FISH INDUSTRY

See also: FISH INDUSTRY

ABSTRACTS AND INDEXES

Oceanic Abstracts. CSA. • 11 times a year. $1,645.00 per year. Includes print and online editions. Covers oceanography, marine biology, ocean shipping, and a wide range of other marine-related subject areas.

ALMANACS AND YEARBOOKS

Inter-American Tropical Tuna Commission Annual Report. William H. Bayliff, editor. Inter-American Tropical Tuna Commission. • Annual. Price varies. Summary of scientific research carried on during the year. Includes financial statements. Text in English and Spanish.

ONLINE DATABASES

Oceanic Abstracts (Online). Cambridge Scientific Abstracts. • Oceanographic and other marine-related technical literature, 1981 to present.Monthly updates. Inquire as to online cost and availability.

PERIODICALS AND NEWSLETTERS

Inter-American Tropical Tuna Commission Bulletin. Inter-American Tropical Tuna Commission. • Irregular. Price varies. Description of results of scientific studies. Text in English and Spanish.

Seafood Business. Diversified Business Communications. • Monthly. $69.00 per year. Edited for a wide range of seafood buyers, including distributors, restaurants, supermarkets, and institutions. Special issues feature information on specific products, such as salmon or lobster.

STATISTICS SOURCES

Fisheries of the United States. Available from U. S. Government Printing Office. • Annual. $20.00. Issued by the National Marine Fisheries Service, National Oceanic and Atmospheric Administration, U. S. Department of Commerce.

TRADE/PROFESSIONAL ASSOCIATIONS

Inter-American Tropical Tuna Commission. 8604 La Jolla Shores Dr., 8604 La Jolla Shores Dr., La Jolla, CA 92037-1508. Phone: (858)546-7100 Fax: (858)546-7133 E-mail: info@iattc.org • URL: http://www.iattc.org • Appointed commissioners representing Japan, France, Nicaragua, Guatemala, Peru, Mexico, Ecuador, El Salvador, Costa Rica, Panama, Vanuatu, Venezuela and the United States. Conducts studies on Pacific Ocean tunas and dolphins associated with tunas. Recommends conservation measures to member governments in order to maintain optimum levels of tuna stock and maximum level of dolphin stock. (Dolphins are frequently caught and inadvertently killed in tuna nets.) Monitors population and mortality levels; conducts research. Provides the secretariat for the International Dolphin Conservation Program. Responsibility are met with its two programs, the Tuna-Billfish Program and the Tuna-Dolphin program. The principal responsibilities of the Tuna-Billfish program are: to study the biology of tunas and related species of the eastern Pacific Ocean to estimate the effects that fishing and natural factors have on their abundance; to recommend appropriate conservation measures so that the stocks of fish can be maintained at levels which will afford maximum sustainable catches; to collect information on compliance with Commission resolutions. The principal responsibilities of the Tuna-Dolphin program are: to monitor the abundance of dolphins and their mortality incidental to purse-seine fishing in the eastern Pacific Ocean; to study the causes of mortality of dolphins during fishing operations and promote the use of fishing techniques and equipment that minimize these mortalities; to study the effects of different modes of fishing on the various fish and other animals of the pelagic ecosystem; and to provide a secretariat for the International Dolphin Conservation Program.

United States Tuna Foundation. 7918 Jones Branch Dr., Ste. 700, McLean, VA 22102. Phone: (703)752-8880 Fax: (202)331-9686 E-mail: eliezer@usta.com • URL: http://www.tunafacts.com • Represents tuna boat owners, fishermen, processors, fishermen's unions, and cannery workers' unions. Analyzes all matters related to or affecting the industry as a whole.

TURKEY INDUSTRY

See also: POULTRY INDUSTRY

ALMANACS AND YEARBOOKS

CRB Commodity Yearbook. Commodity Research Bureau. CRB. • Annual. $99.95.

INTERNET DATABASES

USDA. United States Department of Agriculture. Phone: (202)720-2791 E-mail: agsec@usda.gov • URL: http://www.usda.gov • The USDA home page has six sections: News and Information; What's New; About USDA; Agencies; Opportunities; Search and Help. Keyword searching is offered from the USDA home page and from various individual agency home pages. Agencies are the Economic Research Service, Agricultural Marketing Service, National Agricultural Statistics Service, National Agricultural Library, and about 12 others. Updating varies. Fees: Free.

PRICE SOURCES

PPI Detailed Report. Bureau of Labor Statistics, U.S. Department of Labor. Available from U.S. Government Printing Office. • Monthly. $55.00 per year. Formerly *Producer Price Indexes.*

STATISTICS SOURCES

Agricultural Statistics. Available from U. S. Government Printing Office. • Annual. $38.00. Produced by the National Agricultural Statistics Service, U. S. Department of Agriculture. Provides a wide variety of statistical data relating to agricultural production, supplies, consumption, prices/price-supports, foreign trade, costs, and returns, as well as farm labor, loans, income, and population. In many cases, historical data is shown annually for 10 years. In addition to farm data, includes detailed fishery statistics.

FAO Production Yearbook. Available from Bernan Associates. • Annual. $45.00. Published by the Food and Agriculture Organization (http://www.fao.org). Contains worldwide data on agriculture, land use, farm crops, livestock, and agricultural prices.

FAO Trade Yearbook. Available from Bernan Associates. • Annual. $45.00. Published by the Food and Agriculture Organization (http://www.fao.org).

Provides extensive worldwide data on exports and imports of agricultural commodities, fertilizers, tractors, and pesticides. Includes more than 130 tables of detailed statistics.

TRADE/PROFESSIONAL ASSOCIATIONS

National Turkey Federation. 1225 New York Ave., Ste., 400, Washington, DC 20005. Phone: (202)898-0100 Fax: (202)898-0203 E-mail: info@turkeyfed.org • URL: http://www.eatturkey.com • Serves as the national advocate for all segments of the turkey industry. Provides services and conducts activities that increase demand for its members' products by protecting and enhancing their ability to profitably provide wholesome, high-quality, and nutritious products.

TURNOVER, LABOR

See: LABOR TURNOVER

TURNPIKES

See: TOLL ROADS

TURPENTINES AND RESINS

See: NAVAL STORES

TWINE INDUSTRY

See: ROPE AND TWINE INDUSTRY

TWO-INCOME FAMILIES

See: EMPLOYMENT OF WOMEN; WOMEN IN THE WORK FORCE

TYPE AND TYPE FOUNDING

See also: PRINTING AND PRINTING EQUIPMENT INDUSTRIES; TYPESETTING

TRADE/PROFESSIONAL ASSOCIATIONS

Type Directors Club. 347 W 36 St., Ste. 603, New York, NY 10018. Phone: (212)633-8943 Fax:

(212)633-8944 E-mail: director@tdc.org • URL: http://www.tdc.org • Serves as a professional society of typographic designers, type directors, and teachers of typography; sustaining members are individuals with interests in typographic education. Seeks to stimulate research and disseminate information. Provides speakers, classes and offers presentations on history and new developments in typography.

TYPESETTING

FINANCIAL RATIOS

Annual Statement Studies. The Risk Management Association. • Annual. Median and quartile financial ratios are given for over 400 kinds of manufacturing, wholesale, retail, construction, and consumer finance establishments. Data is sorted by both asset size and sales volume. Includes a clearly written "Definition of Ratios" and an alphabetical industry index.

Annual Statement Studies: Industry Default Probabilities and Cash Flow Measures. The Risk Management Association. • Annual. $145.00. Serves as a companion volume to the original *Annual Statement Studies.* Gives probability of default estimates on a percentage scale for more than 450 industries. Includes changes in position year-by-year for eight financial statement line items and provides percentage measures of cash flow.

TRADE/PROFESSIONAL ASSOCIATIONS

International Digital Imaging Association. PO Box 81261, PO Box 81261, Chamblee, GA 30366. Phone: (770)452-8119 Fax: (770)234-9058 E-mail: idia@bellsouth.net • Represents members' interest.

TYPEWRITER INDUSTRY

See: OFFICE EQUIPMENT AND SUPPLIES; WORD PROCESSING

TYPOGRAPHY

See: PRINTING AND PRINTING EQUIPMENT INDUSTRIES; TYPESETTING

　　　　　For publishers addresses, refer to SOURCES CITED section at the back of the book.

U

ULTRASONICS

ABSTRACTS AND INDEXES
Acoustics Abstracts. Multi-Science Publishing Co., Ltd. • Monthly. $600.00. per year. Parts A and B.

DIRECTORIES
Sensors Buyers Guide. Advanstar Communications. • Covers: Lists manufacturers and vendors of sensors and transducers for use in high-technology applications engineering. Also covers related products and services. Entries include: Company name, address, phone, fax, e-mail, URL, contact person, type of sensors manufactured and/or physical, chemical, or biological characteristics utilized in sensing.

PERIODICALS AND NEWSLETTERS
Journal of Clinical Ultrasound. John Wiley and Sons, Inc., Journals. • Nine times a year. Institutions, $895.00 per year; with online editions, $940.00 per year. Devoted exclusively to the clinical application of ultrasound in medicine.

Seminars in Ultrasound, CT, and MR (Computerized Tomography and Magnetic Resonance. W.B. Saunders Co. • Bimonthly. Individuals, $212.00 per year; institutions, $316.00 per year.

Sensors: Your Resource for Sensing, Communications, and Control. Advanstar Communications. • Monthly. $70.00 per year. Edited for design, production, and manufacturing engineers involved with sensing systems. Emphasis is on emerging technology.

Ultrasonic Imaging, An International Journal. Dynamedia, Inc. • Quarterly. $325.00 per year.

Ultrasonics: The World's Leading Journal Covering the Science and Technology of Ultrasound. Elsevier. • 10 times a year. Institutions, $131.00 per year; institutions, $1,461.00 per year.

Ultrasound in Medicine and Biology. Elsevier. • Monthly. Institutions, $1,305.00 per year.

TRADE/PROFESSIONAL ASSOCIATIONS
Ultrasonic Industry Association. PO Box 2307, Dayton, OH 45401-2307. Phone: (937)586-3725 Fax: (937)586-3699 E-mail: uia@ultrasonics.org • URL: http://www.ultrasonics.org • Manufacturers and users of ultrasonic equipment and component parts for ultrasonic equipment. Promotes the ultrasonic industry; cooperation with government on legislation and relations affecting ultrasonic equipment; collection and dissemination of information; research into use and safety of ultrasonic products; establishment of liaison with other organizations in the field.

UNDERDEVELOPED AREAS AND COUNTRIES

See: DEVELOPING AREAS; ECONOMIC DEVELOPMENT; TECHNICAL ASSISTANCE

UNDERTAKERS AND UNDERTAKING

See: FUNERAL HOMES AND DIRECTORS

UNDERWEAR INDUSTRY

See also: KNIT GOODS INDUSTRY

DIRECTORIES
Body Fashions/Intimate Apparel Buyer's Guide. Advanstar Communications. • Publication includes: List of suppliers and manufacturers within the intimate apparel and hosiery industry. Entries include: Company name, address, phone.

HANDBOOKS AND MANUALS
Lingerie Shop. Entrepreneur Media, Inc. • Looseleaf. $59.50. A practical guide to starting a lingerie store. Covers profit potential, start-up costs, market size evaluation, owner's time required, site selection, lease negotiation, pricing, accounting, advertising, promotion, etc. (Start-Up Business Guide No. E1152.).

PERIODICALS AND NEWSLETTERS
WWD: The Retailer's Daily Newspaper (Women's Wear Daily). Fairchild Publications. • Daily. Individuals, $195.00 per year; retailers, $99.00 per year; manufacturers, $135.00 per year.

TRADE/PROFESSIONAL ASSOCIATIONS
Associated Corset and Brassiere Manufacturers. 1430 Broadway, Suite 1603, New York, NY 10018. Phone: (212)354-0707 Fax: (212)221-3540.

Intimate Apparel Council. c/o American Apparel and Footwear Association, 1601 N Kent St., Ste. 1200, Arlington, VA 22209. Phone: 800-520-2262 or (212)807-0870 Fax: (703)522-6761 • URL: http://www.americanapparel.org.

OTHER SOURCES
Women's Undergarments. Available from MarketResearch.com. • 1997. $995.00. Published by Specialists in Business Information, Inc. Provides market data with forecasts of sales to the year 2005 for various kinds of women's underwear.

UNDERWRITERS

See: INSURANCE UNDERWRITERS

UNEMPLOYMENT

See also: DISMISSAL OF EMPLOYEES; EMPLOYMENT; UNEMPLOYMENT INSURANCE

ABSTRACTS AND INDEXES
Human Resources Abstracts: An International Information Service. Sage Publications, Inc. • Quarterly. Institutions, $968.00 per year; includes print and online editions.

CD-ROM DATABASES
OECD Statistical Compendium. Organization for Economic Cooperation and Development. • Semiannual. $1,905.00 per year for 1 to 10 users. CD-ROM contains more than 730,000 monthly, quarterly, and annual time series for OECD countries, 1960 to date. Includes fully searchable data on agriculture, food, economic indicators, national accounts, employment, energy, finance, industry, technology, and foreign trade. Results can be displayed in various forms.

Sourcebooks America CD-ROM. CACI Marketing Systems. • Annual. $1,250.00. Provides the CD-ROM version of *The Sourcebook of ZIP Code Demographics: Census Edition* and *The Sourcebook of County Demographics: Census Edition.*

ENCYCLOPEDIAS AND DICTIONARIES
Encyclopedia of Social Welfare History in North America. John M. Herrick and Paul H. Stuart, editors. Sage Publications, Inc. • 2004. $150.00. Includes entries on the historical aspects of charity, economic conditions, tax policy, health policy, social welfare legislation, poverty, social security, and social problems.

INTERNET DATABASES
Bureau of Economic Analysis (BEA). U. S. Department of Commerce, Bureau of Economic Analysis. Phone: (202)606-9900 Fax: (202)606-5310 E-mail: webmaster@bea.doc.gov • URL: http://www.bea.doc.gov • Web site includes "News Release Information" covering national, regional, and international economic estimates from the BEA. Highlights of releases appear online the same day, complete text and tables appear the next day. "Recent News Releases" section provides titles for past nine months, with links. "BEA Data and Methodology" includes "Frequently Requested NIPA Data" (national income and product accounts, such as gross domestic product and personal income). Other

statistics are available. Fees: Free.

Business 2.0 Web Guide to the Best Business Links. Business 2.0 Media Inc. Phone: (415)293-4800 E-mail: support@business2.com • URL: http://www.business2.com/webguide • Web site presents an extensive, searchable directory of links to "the best, most informative, and authoritative web pages." Twenty main categories cover business, finance, career, company information, people, and technology topics, with thousands of subtopics, all linking to Web sites recommended by experienced business researchers. Fees: Free.

Fedstats. Federal Interagency Council on Statistical Policy. Phone: (202)395-7254 • URL: http://www.fedstats.gov • Web site features an efficient search facility for full-text statistics produced by more than 100 federal agencies, including the Census Bureau, the Bureau of Economic Analysis, and the Bureau of Labor Statistics. Boolean searches can be made within one agency or for all agencies combined. Links are offered to international statistical bureaus, including the UN, IMF, OECD, UNESCO, Eurostat, and 20 individual countries. Fees: Free.

FreeLunch.com. Economy.com, Inc. Phone: (610)696-8700 Fax: (610)696-1678 • URL: http://www.freelunch.com • Web site provides free access to more than 1.5 million economic and financial data series, covering industry, demographics, labor markets, prices, retail sales, government spending, trade, interest rates, housing starts, the stock market, and many other topics. Data is available for various time periods in either chart or table form. Searching is offered. Fees: Free, but registration required. Economy.com, Inc. also offers fee-based economic analysis at *The Dismal Scientist* site (http://www.dismal.com).

RESEARCH CENTERS AND INSTITUTES

Industrial Relations Section. Princeton University, Firestone Library, Pineeton, NJ 08544. Phone: (609)258-4040 Fax: (609)258-2907 • URL: http://www.irs.princeton.edu/ • Fields of research include labor supply, manpower training, unemployment, and equal employment opportunity.

W. E. Upjohn Institute for Employment Research. 300 S. Westnedge Ave., Kalamazoo, MI 49007-4686. Phone: (616)343-5541 Fax: (616)343-3308 E-mail: eberts@we.upjohninst.org • URL: http://www.upjohninst.org • Research fields include unemployment, unemployment insurance, worker's compensation, labor productivity, profit sharing, the labor market, economic development, earnings, training, and other areas related to employment.

STATISTICS SOURCES

Benefits and Wages: OECD Indicators. Organization for Economic Cooperation and Development. • Biennial. $19.00. Provides data for 28 countries on unemployment benefits and related welfare benefits. Includes a cross-country comparison of family incomes, in work and out of work. Formerly *Benefit Systems and Work Incentives.*

Bulletin of Labour Statistics: Supplementing the Annual Data Presented in the Year Book of Labour Statistics. International Labour Ofice. • Quarterly. $84.00 per year. Includes five *Supplements.* A supplement to *Yearbook of Labour Statistics.* Provides current labor and price index statistics for over 130 countries. Generally includes data for the most recent four years. Text in English, French and Spanish.

Business Statistics of the United States. Linz Audain and Cornelia J. Strawser. Bernan Associates. • Annual. $147.00. Based on *Business Statistics,* formerly issue by the Bureau of Economic Analysis, U. S. Department of Commerce. Provides basic data for a wide variety of U. S. industries, services, and economic indicators. Most statistics are shown annually for 30 years and monthly for the most recent four years.

County and City Data Book 2000: A Statistical Abstract Supplement. Available from U. S. Government Printing Office. • 2002. $68.00. 13th edition. Issued by the U. S. Bureau of the Census (http://www.census.gov). Contains a wide variety of data on 3,141 U.S. counties, 1,078 cities, and 11,097 places of 2,500 or more inhabitants. Includes statistical information on retailing, manufacturing, banking, service industries, income, employment, housing, education, crime, and population. Updated metropolitan areas are included.

County and City Extra: Annual Metro, City and County Data Book. Deirdre A. Gaquin and Mark S. Littman. Bernan Press. • 2001. $120.00. Updates and augments data published irregularly in print form by the U. S. Census Bureau in *County and City Data Book.* Covers "every state, county, metropolitan area, and congressional district in the United States, as well as all U. S. cities with a 1990 population of 25,000 or more." Contains a wide range tic maps.

County and City Extra: Special Decennial Census Edition. Deidre A. Gaquin and Katherine A. De-Brandt, editors. Bernan Press. • 2002. $95.00. Presents conveniently arranged population, housing, and other data from the 2000 census, with many 1980 and 1990 comparisons. Includes maps and tables with rankings of about 20 items for various geographic locations. Complements the annual *County and City Extra.*

Economic Report of the President: Together with the Annual Report of the Council of Economic Advisors. Available from U. S. Government Printing Office. • Annual. $32.00. Includes about 130 pages of "Statistical Tables Relating to Income, Employment, and Production." Tables cover national income, employment, wages, productivity, manufacturing, prices, credit, finance (public and private), corporate profits, and foreign trade.

Employment and Earnings. Available from U. S. Government Printing Office. • Monthly. $50.00 per year, including annual supplement. Produced by the Bureau of Labor Statistics, U. S. Department of Labor. Provides current data on employment, hours, and earnings for the U. S. as a whole, for states, and for more than 200 local areas.

Geographic Profile of Employment and Unemployment. Available from U. S. Government Printing Office. • Annual. $23.00. Issued by Bureau of Labor Statistics, U. S. Department of Labor. Presents detailed, annual average employment, unemployment, and labor force data for regions, states, and metropolitan areas. Characteristics include sex, age, race, Hispanic origin, marital status, occupation, and type of industry.

Geographic Reference Report: Annual Report of Costs, Wages, Salaries, and Human Resource Statistics for the United States and Canada. ERI (Economic Research Institute). • Annual. $389.00. Provides demographic and other data for each of 298 North American metropolian areas, including local salaries, wage differentials, cost-of-living, housing costs, income taxation, employment, unemployment, population, major employers, crime rates, weather, etc.

Handbook of U. S. Labor Statistics: Employment, Earnings, Prices, Productivity, and Other Labor Data. Eva E. Jacobs, editor. Bernan Associates. • 1999. $74.00. Based on *Handbook of Labor Statistics,* formerly issued by the Bureau of Labor Statistics, U. S. Department of Labor. Includes the Bureau's projections of employment in the U. S. by industry and occupation. Provides a wide variety of data on the work force, prices, fringe benefits, and consumer expenditures.

Key Indicators of the Labour Market. Available from Routledge. • Biennial. $125.00. Published by the International Labour Office (http://www.ilo.org). Provides data on 20 key indicators in 220 countries.

Includes labor force statistics, employment, unemployment, part-time workers, wages, productivity, poverty indicators, and related topics.

Labour Force Statistics. Organization for Economic Cooperation and Development. Available from OECD Publications and Information Center. • Annual. $98.00. Provides 21 years of data for OECD member countries on population, employment, unemployment, civilian labor force, armed forces, and other labor factors.

Monthly Labor Review. Available from U. S. Government Printing Office. • Monthly. $49.00 per year. Issued by the Bureau of Labor Statistics, U. S. Department of Labor. Contains data on the labor force, wages, work stoppages, price indexes, productivity, economic growth, and occupational injuries and illnesses.

Quarterly Labour Force Statistics. Organization for Economic Cooperation and Development. Available from OECD Publications and Information Center. • Quarterly. $90.00 per year. Provides current data for OECD member countries on population, employment, unemployment, civilian labor force, armed forces, and other labor factors.

Report on the American Workforce. Available from U. S. Government Printing Office. • Annual. Issued by the U. S. Department of Labor (http://www.dol.gov). Appendix contains tabular statistics, including employment, unemployment, price indexes, consumer expenditures, employee benefits (retirement, insurance, vacation, etc.), wages, productivity, hours of work, and occupational injuries. Annual figures are shown for up to 50 years.

Survey of Current Business. Available from U. S. Government Printing Office. • Monthly. $63.00 per year. Issued by Bureau of Economic Analysis, U. S. Department of Commerce. Presents a wide variety of business and economic data.

Yearbook of Labour Statistics. Available from Bernan Associates. • Annual. $168.00. Published by the International Labour Organizaton (http://www.ilo.org). Provides data for more than 180 countries on employment, unemployment, wages, hours of work, cost of labor, strikes, industrial accidents, and consumer prices.

OTHER SOURCES

Foreign Labor Trends. Available from U. S. Government Printing Office. • Irregular (50 to 60 issues per year, each on an individual country). $95.00 per year. Prepared by various American Embassies. Issued by the Bureau of International Labor Affairs, U. S. Department of Labor. Covers labor developments in important foreign countries, including trends in wages, working conditions, labor supply, employment, and unemployment.

UNEMPLOYMENT INSURANCE

BIBLIOGRAPHIES

Insurance and Employee Benefits Literature. Special Libraries Association, Insurance and Employee Benefits Div. • Bimonthly. $15.00 per year. Lists a wide variety of literature in all branches of the insurance industry. Includes annotations.

CD-ROM DATABASES

OECD Statistical Compendium. Organization for Economic Cooperation and Development. • Semiannual. $1,905.00 per year for 1 to 10 users. CD-ROM contains more than 730,000 monthly, quarterly, and annual time series for OECD countries, 1960 to date. Includes fully searchable data on agriculture, food, economic indicators, national accounts, employment, energy, finance, industry, technology, and foreign trade. Results can

be displayed in various forms.

ENCYCLOPEDIAS AND DICTIONARIES
Glossary of Insurance Policy Terms. Organization for Economic Cooperation and Development. • 1999. $30.00. "The selected topics range from insurance policy regulation/supervision to general trade issues and include technical terms related to issues such as claims, premiums, and provisions." Edited for government, academic, business, and insurance organizations.

HANDBOOKS AND MANUALS
Payroll Management Guide. CCH, Inc. • Weekly. $599.00. Eight looseleaf volumes. Covers the basics of payroll management, including employer obligations, recordkeeping, taxation, unemployment insurance, processing of new employees, and government penalties.

INTERNET DATABASES
Business 2.0 Web Guide to the Best Business Links. Business 2.0 Media Inc. Phone: (415)293-4800 E-mail: support@business2.com • URL: http://www.business2.com/webguide • Web site presents an extensive, searchable directory of links to "the best, most informative, and authoritative web pages." Twenty main categories cover business, finance, career, company information, people, and technology topics, with thousands of subtopics, all linking to Web sites recommended by experienced business researchers. Fees: Free.

Fedstats. Federal Interagency Council on Statistical Policy. Phone: (202)395-7254 • URL: http://www.fedstats.gov • Web site features an efficient search facility for full-text statistics produced by more than 100 federal agencies, including the Census Bureau, the Bureau of Economic Analysis, and the Bureau of Labor Statistics. Boolean searches can be made within one agency or for all agencies combined. Links are offered to international statistical bureaus, including the UN, IMF, OECD, UNESCO, Eurostat, and 20 individual countries. Fees: Free.

FreeLunch.com. Economy.com, Inc. Phone: (610)696-8700 Fax: (610)696-1678 • URL: http://www.freelunch.com • Web site provides free access to more than 1.5 million economic and financial data series, covering industry, demographics, labor markets, prices, retail sales, government spending, trade, interest rates, housing starts, the stock market, and many other topics. Data is available for various time periods in either chart or table form. Searching is offered. Fees: Free, but registration required. Economy.com, Inc. also offers fee-based economic analysis at *The Dismal Scientist* site (http://www.dismal.com).

ONLINE DATABASES
I.I.I. Data Base Search. Insurance Information Institute. • Provides online citations and abstracts of insurance-related literature in magazines, newspapers, trade journals, and books. Emphasis is on property and casualty insurance issues, including highway safety, product safety, and environmental liability. Inquire as to online cost and availability.

RESEARCH CENTERS AND INSTITUTES
National Institute for Work and Learning. Academy for Educational Development, 1875 Connecticut Ave., N.W., Washington, DC 20009-5721. Phone: (202)884-8186 Fax: (202)884-8422 E-mail: niwl@aed.org • URL: http://www.niwl.org • Research areas include adult education, training, unemployment insurance, and career development.

STATISTICS SOURCES
Business Statistics of the United States. Linz Audain and Cornelia J. Strawser. Bernan Associates. • Annual. $147.00. Based on *Business Statistics,* formerly issue by the Bureau of Economic Analysis, U. S. Department of Commerce. Provides basic data for a wide variety of U. S. industries, services, and economic indicators. Most statistics are shown annually for 30 years and monthly for the most recent four years.

Survey of Current Business. Available from U. S. Government Printing Office. • Monthly. $63.00 per year. Issued by Bureau of Economic Analysis, U. S. Department of Commerce. Presents a wide variety of business and economic data.

Unemployment Insurance Claims Weekly Report. U.S. Department of Labor, Employment and Training Administration. • Weekly.

UNIFORM COMMERCIAL CODE

See: BUSINESS LAW

UNIFORMS

GENERAL WORKS
Uniforms: Why We Are What We Wear. Paul Fussell. Houghton Mifflin Co. • 2002. $22.00. Provides an informal discussion of the cultural, social, and historical significance of uniforms. Popularly written.

DIRECTORIES
Law and Order Magazine Police Equipment Buyer's Guide. Hendon, Inc. • Annual. $15.00. Lists manufacturers, dealers, and distributors of equipment and services for police departments.

Law Enforcement Technology Directory. Cygnus Business Media, Inc. • Annual. $60.00 per year. $6.00 per issue; a directory of products, equipment, services, and technology for police professionals. Includes weapons, uniforms, communications equipment, and software.

PERIODICALS AND NEWSLETTERS
Law and Order Magazine: The Magazine for Police Management. Hendon Publishing Co. • Monthly. $24.95 per year. Edited for law enforcement officials. Includes special issues on communications, technology, weapons, and uniforms and equipment.

Law Enforcement Technology. Cygnus Business Media. • Monthly. $60.00 per year. Covers new products and technologies for police professionals. Includes special issues on weapons, uniforms, communications equipment, computers (hardware-software), vehicles, and enforcement of drug laws.

Made to Measure. Halper Publishing Co. • Semiannual. Controlled circulation.

NAUMD News. National Association of Uniform Manufacturers and Distributors. • Description: Reports news that affects the uniform manufacturing and distributing industry. Also discusses Association programs and seminars, committee activities, and governmental trends and regulations.

TRADE/PROFESSIONAL ASSOCIATIONS
National Association of Uniform Manufacturers and Distributors. 1156 Ave. of the Americas, Room 700, New York, NY 10036. Phone: (212)869-0670 Fax: (212)575-2847 E-mail: nyoffice@naumd.com • URL: http://www.naumd.com • Formerly Uniform Manufacturers Exchange.

UNIONS

See: LABOR UNIONS

UNITED FUNDS

See: COMMUNITY FUNDS

UNITED NATIONS

See also: INTERNATIONAL AGENCIES

GENERAL WORKS
Building Parterships: Cooperarion Between the United Nations System and the Private Sector. United Nations Publications. • 2002. $27.50. Describes "the main types of cooperation between the UN and business." (A joint initiative of the UN Global Compact and the UN Department of Public Information in cooperation with the Prince of Wales International Business Leaders Forum).

ABSTRACTS AND INDEXES
Index to Proceedings of the Economic and Social Council. United Nations Publications. • Irregular.

UNDOC: Current Index (United Nations Documents). United Nations Publications. • Quarterly. $150.00. Annual cumulation on microfiche. Text in English.

ALMANACS AND YEARBOOKS
Annual Review of United Nations Affairs. Oceana Publications, Inc. • 1999. $270.00. Three volumes.

National Accounts Statistics: Main Aggregates and Detailed Tables. United Nations Publications. • Annual. $160.00.

BIBLIOGRAPHIES
Monthly Bibliography. United Nations Publications. • Monthly. $125.00 per year. Text in English and French.

DIRECTORIES
Directory of United Nations Databases and Information Systems. United Nations Publications. • Annual. $35.00. Nearly 38 United Nations organizations maintaining over 615 databases and information systems.

ENCYCLOPEDIAS AND DICTIONARIES
Lexique General; A General Lexicon of Terms-United Nations as Well as General-Used by Translators, Interpreters, etc. United Nations Publications. • 1991. Fourth edition.

HANDBOOKS AND MANUALS
Basic Facts About the United Nations. United Nations Publications. • 2000. $12.50.

PERIODICALS AND NEWSLETTERS
UN Chronicle. United Nations Pulications. • 11 times a year. $25.00 per year. Editions in English, French and Spanish.

STATISTICS SOURCES
Demographic Yearbook. United Nations, Dept. of Economic and Social Affairs. United Nations Publications. • Annual. $125.00. Text in English and French.

Industrial Commodity Statistics Yearbook. United Nations Dept. of Economic and Social Affairs. United Nations Publications. • Annual.

International Trade Statistics Yearbook. United Nations Statistical Office. United Nations Publications. • Annual. $135.00. Two volumes.

Monthly Bulletin of Statistics. United Nations Publications. • Monthly. $295.00 per year. Provides current data for about 200 countries on a wide variety of economic, industrial, and demographic subjects. Compiled by United Nations Statistical Office.

Statistical Yearbook. United Nations Publications. • Annual. $125.00. Contains statistics for about 200 countries on a wide variety of economic, industrial, and demographic topics. Compiled by United Nations Statistical Office.

World Statistics Pocketbook. United Nations Publications. • Annual $10.00.

TRADE/PROFESSIONAL ASSOCIATIONS
United Nations Association of the United States of America. 801 Second Ave., 2nd Fl., New York, NY

10017. Phone: (212)907-1300 Fax: (212)682-9185 E-mail: unahq@unausa.org • URL: http://www. unausa.org • Absorbed Conference Group of U.S. National Organizations on the United Nations.

OTHER SOURCES

International Standard Industrial Classification of All Economic Activities. United Nations Publications. • 1992. Third revised edition.

UNITED STATES CONGRESS

See also: LAWS

GENERAL WORKS

Congressional Investigations: Law and Practice. John C. Grabow. Aspen Publishers, Inc. • $95.00. Looseleaf service. Periodic supplementation.

Guide to Congress; Origins, History and Procedure. CQ Press. • 2000. Fifth edition. Price on application.

ABSTRACTS AND INDEXES

Congressional Index. CCH, Inc. • Weekly when Congress is in session. $1,283.00 per year. Index to action on Public Bills from introduction to final disposition. Subject, author, and bill number indexes.

Current Law Index: Multiple Access to Legal Periodicals. Gale Cengage Learning. • Monthly. $725.00 per year. Produced in cooperation with the American Association of Law Libraries. Indexes more than 900 law journals, legal newspapers, and specialty publications from the U.S., Canada, U.K., Ireland, Australia, and New Zealand.

ALMANACS AND YEARBOOKS

Congressional Quarterly Almanac. CQ Press. • Annual. $215.00.

BIBLIOGRAPHIES

Congress in Print: The Weekly Catalog of Congressional Documents. Congressional Quarterly, Inc. • 48 times a year. $198.00 per year. Newsletter.

BIOGRAPHICAL SOURCES

Almanac of American Politics. National Journal Group, Inc. • Biennial. $54.95. Includes biographies of U.S. senators and representatives, with group ratings, key votes, and election results.

Biographical Directory of the American Congress, 1774-1996. Joel Treese. CQ Staff Directories, Inc. • 1996. $295.00. Provides detailed biographies of members of the Continental Congress (1774-1789) and the U. S. Congress (1789-1996). Includes presidential Cabinet members.

Who's Who in American Politics. Marquis Who's Who. • Biennial. $275.00. Two volumes. Contains about 27,000 biographical sketches of local, state, and national elected or appointed individuals.

CD-ROM DATABASES

Newspaper Abstracts Ondisc. PROQUEST. • Monthly. $2,950.00 per year (covers 1989 to date; archival discs are available for 1985-88). Provides cover-to-cover CD-ROM indexing and abstracting of 19 major newspapers, including the *New York Times, Wall Street Journal, Washington Post, Chicago Tribune,* and *Los Angeles Times.*

DIRECTORIES

Almanac of the Unelected: Staff of the U. S. Congress. Bernan Associates. • Annual. $275.00. Provides detailed information on key staff members of the legislative branch of the federal government. Includes educational background, previous employment, job responsibilities, etc.

Carroll's Federal & Federal Regional Directory. Carroll Publishing. • Semiannual. $325.00 per year; with online edition, $1,200 per year. Lists more than 23,000 U. S. government officials throughout the country, including military installations.

Carroll's Federal Directory. Carroll Publishing. • Covers: About 38,000 executive managers in federal government offices in Washington, DC, including executive, congressional and judicial branches; members of Congress and Congressional committees and staff. Entries include: Agency names, titles, office address (including room numbers), e-mail addresses, and telephone and fax numbers. Also available as part of a "library edition" titled "Federal Directory Annual".

Congressional Directory. Office of Membership Grassroots Management. • Covers: Members of Congress. Entries include: List of members of Congress by state includes member party and home city; alphabetical list by member name includes addresses, phone, fax, e-mail, committee/subcommittee assignments, names of key staff members, and photos.

Congressional Staff Directory: With Biographical Information on Members and Key Congressional Staff. CQ Press. • Three times a year. $225.00 per year. Contains more than 3,200 detailed biographies of members of Congress and their staffs. Includes committees and subcommittees. Keyword and name indexes are provided.

Congressional Yellow Book: Who's Who in Congress, Including Committees and Key Staff. Leadership Directories, Inc. • Quarterly. $360.00 per year. Looseleaf. A directory of members of congress, including their committees and their key aides.

Washington Information Directory. CQ Press. • Covers: 5,000 governmental agencies, congressional committees, and non-governmental associations considered competent sources of specialized information. Entries include: Name of agency, committee, or association; address, phone, fax, and Internet; annotation concerning function or activities of the office; and name of contact.

HANDBOOKS AND MANUALS

Constitution, Jefferson's Manual and Rules of the House of Representatives. U.S. Government Printing Office. • Biennial. $58.00.

Senate Manual. U.S. Government Printing Office. • Biennial. $57.00.

INTERNET DATABASES

FedWorld: A Program of the United States Department of Commerce. National Technical Information Service. Phone: (703)605-6000 Fax: (703)605-6900 E-mail: webmaster@fedworld.gov • URL: http:// www.fedworld.gov • Web site offers "a comprehensive central access point for searching, locating, ordering, and acquiring government and business information." Emphasis is on searching the Web pages, databases, and government reports of a wide variety of federal agencies. Fees: Free.

FirstGov: Your First Click to the U. S. Government. General Services Administration. Phone: 800-333-4636 or (202)501-0705 E-mail: public.affairs@gsa. gov • URL: http://www.firstgov.gov • Free Web site provides extensive links to federal agencies covering a wide variety of topics, such as agriculture, business, consumer safety, education, the environment, government jobs, grants, health, social security, statistics sources, taxes, technology, travel, and world affairs. Also provides links to federal forms, including IRS tax forms. Searching is offered, both keyword and advanced.

Lexis.com Research System. Lexis-Nexis Group. Phone: 800-227-4908 or (937)865-6800 Fax: (937)865-6909 E-mail: webmaster@prod.lexis-nexis.com • URL: http://www.lexis.com • Fee-based Web site offers extensive searching of a wide variety of legal sources. Additional features include Daily Opinion Service, lexis.com Bookstore, Career Center, CLE Center, Law Schools, and Practice

Pages ("Pages specific to areas of specialty").

ONLINE DATABASES

Information Bank Abstracts. New York Times Index Dept. • Provides indexing and abstracting of current affairs, primarily from the final late edition of *The New York Times* and the Eastern edition of *The Wall Street Journal.* Time period is 1969 to present, with daily updates. Inquire as to online cost and availability.

Newspaper Abstracts Daily. ProQuest Inc. • Provides online coverage (citations and abstracts) of 25 major newspapers. Covers business, economics, current affairs, health, fitness, sports, education, technology, government, consumer affairs, psychology, the arts, and the social sciences. Time period is 1986 to date, with daily updates. Inquire as to online cost and availability.

PERIODICALS AND NEWSLETTERS

Congressional Monitor: Daily Listing of All Scheduled Congressional Committee Hearings with Witnesses. Congressional Quarterly. Inc. • Daily. $1,349.00 per year. Weekly *Supplements.*

Congressional Record. U.S. Congress. Available from U.S. Government Printing Office. • Daily. Indexes give names, subjects, and history of bills. Texts of bills not included.

Congressional Record Scanner. Congressional Quarterly. • Description: Contains abstracts of the Congressional Record.

National Journal: The Weekly on Politics and Government. National Journal Group, Inc. • Weekly $1,499.00 per year. Includes semiannual supplement *Capital Source.* A non-partisan weekly magazine on politics and government.

TRADE/PROFESSIONAL ASSOCIATIONS

National Committee for an Effective Congress. 122 C St., NW, Ste. 650, Washington, DC 20001. Phone: 800-547-5911 or (202)639-8300 • URL: http:// www.ncec.org • Raises funds from private citizens and distributes them to its endorsed candidates for the United States Senate and House of Representatives.

United States Association of Former Members of Congress. 233 Pennsylvania Ave., S.E., Suite 200, Washington, DC 20003-1107. Phone: (202)543-8676 Fax: (202)543-7145 E-mail: usafmcl@ mindspring.com • URL: http://www.usafmc.org • Formerly Former Members of Congress.

OTHER SOURCES

CQ Weekly. CQ Press. • 48 times a year. $1,696.00 per year. Includes annual *Almanac.* Formerly *Congressional Quarterly Weekly Report.*

UNITED STATES CUSTOMS SERVICE

See: CUSTOMS HOUSE, U.S. CUSTOMS SERVICE

UNITED STATES GOVERNMENT BONDS

See: GOVERNMENT BONDS

UNITED STATES GOVERNMENT PUBLICATIONS

See: GOVERNMENT PUBLICATIONS

UNIVERSAL PRODUCT CODE (UPC)

See: POINT-OF-SALE SYSTEMS (POS)

UNIVERSITIES

See: COLLEGES AND UNIVERSITIES

UNIVERSITY DEGREES

See: ACADEMIC DEGREES

UNIVERSITY LIBRARIES

See: COLLEGE AND UNIVERSITY LIBRAR-IES

UNIVERSITY PRESSES

See also: PUBLISHING INDUSTRY

CD-ROM DATABASES

ERIC on SilverPlatter. Available from SilverPlatter Information, Inc. • Quarterly. $700.00 per year. Produced by the Office of Educational Research and Improvement, U. S. Dept. of Education. Provides CD-ROM indexing and abstracting of a wide variety of literature relating to education. Archival discs are available from 1966.

INTERNET DATABASES

Publishers' Catalogues Home Page. EBSCO Publishing. Phone: (306)931-0020 Fax: (306)931-7667 E-mail: info@lights.com • URL: http://www.lights.com/publisher • Provides links to the Web home pages of about 1,700 U. S. publishers (including about 80 University presses) and publishers in 48 foreign countries. "International/Multinational Publishers" are included, such as the International Monetary Fund, the World Bank, and the World Trade Organization. Publishers are arranged in convenient alphabetical lists. Searching is offered. Fees: Free.

ONLINE DATABASES

ERIC. Educational Resources Information Center. • Funded by the U. S. Department of Education, Institute of Education Sciences (formerly Office of Educational Research and Improvement). Provides access to more than one million online records covering education-related journal and report literature, 1966 to date. Updating is monthly. Inquire as to online cost and availability.

PERIODICALS AND NEWSLETTERS

Independent Publisher: Leading the World of Book Selling in New Directions. Jenkins Group, Inc. • Bimonthly. Free. Covers business, finance, production, marketing, and other management topics for small publishers, including college presses. Emphasis is on book publishing.

Learned Publishing. Association of Learned and Professional Society Publishers. • Quarterly. Members, $60.00 per year; non-members, $80.00 per year; institutions, $170.00 per year. Articles and news of interest to publishers of academic and learned society material. Formerly *ALPSP Bulletin.*

TRADE/PROFESSIONAL ASSOCIATIONS

Association of American University Presses. 71 W. 23rd St., Suite 901, New York, NY 10010-4102. Phone: (212)989-1010 Fax: (212)989-0275 E-mail: info@aaupnet.org • URL: http://www.aaupnet.org.

Association of Learned and Professional Society Publishers. South House, The Street, Clapham, Worthing, W. Sussex BN13 3UU, United Kingdom. Phone: 44 1903 871686 Fax: 44 1903 871457 E-mail: chief-exec@alpsp.org • URL: http://www.alpsp.org.

UNIX

See also: COMPUTER SOFTWARE INDUSTRY

ABSTRACTS AND INDEXES

Computer Literature Index: A Subject/Author Index to Computer and Data Processing Literature. EB-SCO Publishing. • Quarterly, with annual cumulation. $245.00 per year. Contains brief abstracts of book and periodical literature covering all phases of computing, including approximately 70 specific application areas.

Internet and Personal Computing Abstracts [print edition]. EBSCO Publishing. • Quarterly. $269.00 per year, including cumulative index. Provides more than 10,000 abstracts annually from both trade and academic publications. Covers computer hardware, software, product reviews, Web topics, e-commerce, networks, corporate news, security, and related topics. Formerly *Microcomputer Abstracts.*

Key Abstracts: Software Engineering. Available from INSPEC, Inc. • Monthly. $250.00 per year. Provides international coverage of journal and proceedings literature. Published in England by the Institution of Electrical Engineers (IEE).

CD-ROM DATABASES

Computer Database. Gale Cengage Learning. • Provides one year of full-text on CD-ROM for 150 leading computer-related publications. Also includes 70,000 product specifications and brief profiles of 13,000 computer product vendors and manufacturers.

Datapro on CD-ROM: Computer Systems Analyst. Gartner Group, Inc. • Monthly. Price on application. Includes detailed information on specific computer hardware and software products, such as peripherals, security systems, document imaging systems, and UNIX-related products.

DIRECTORIES

Data Sources: The Comprehensive Guide to the Data Processing Industry: Hardware, Data Communications Products, Software, Company Profiles. Gale Cengage Learning. • Semiannual. $455.00 per year. Two volumes. Describes hardware and software for all computer operating sysems, including prices and technical details. Lists about 75,000 products from 14,000 suppliers. Industry-specific software applications are described.

The Software Encyclopedia: A Guide for Personal, Professional, and Business Users. Gale. • Annual. $335.00. Two volumes. Volume one lists software programs by title and producer. Volume two provides information on programs according to application and operating system. Includes prices and requirements for hardware and memory.

ENCYCLOPEDIAS AND DICTIONARIES

Acronyms of Computer Science and Communications: A Comprehensive Acronym Dictionary and Illustrated Encyclopedia. Enjob Kajan and Ejub Kajan. Springer Verlag. • 2002. $49.95. Explains more than 4,000 "broadly used" computer, telecommunications, and information technology acronyms. Includes illustrations and Web addresses, where applicable.

Encyclopedia of Information Systems. Hossein Bidgoli, editor. Elsevier. • 2002. $1,200.00. Four volumes. Contains a wide range of articles relating to computers, databases, communication, and information technology. The 200 topics include coverage of hardware, software, artificial intelligence, the Internet, networks, knowledge management, electronic commerce, search engines, and systems design.

Every Manager's Guide to Information Technology: A Glossary of Key Terms and Concepts for Today's Business Leader. Peter G. W. Keen. Harvard Business School Publishing. • 1994. $18.95. Second edition. Provides definitions of terms related to computers, data communications, and information network systems. (Harvard Business Reference Series).

HANDBOOKS AND MANUALS

Halting the Hacker: A Practical Guide to Computer Security. Donald L. Pipkin. Prentice Hall PTR. • 2002. $44.99. Second edition. (Hewlett-Packard Professional Book Series).

Schaum's Outline of Unix. Harley Hahn. McGraw-Hill. • 1995. $7.38. (Schaum's Outline Series).

UNIX and Windows 2000 Integration Toolkit: A Complete Guide for System Administrators and Developers. Rawn Shah. John Wiley and Sons, Inc. • 2000. $49.99. Includes CD-ROM.

UNIX and Windows 2000: Interoperability Guide. Alan Roberts. Prentice Hall PTR. • 2001. $34.99. (Hewlett-Packard Professional Books).

UNIX System Administration Handbook. Evi Nemeth and others. Prentice Hall PTR. • 1995. $110.00. Second edition. Includes CD-ROM.

UNIX Unbounded: A Beginning Approach. Amir Afzal. Prentice Hall PTR. • 2002. $96.00. Fourth edition.

UNIX Weekend Crash Course. Arthur Griffith. John Wiley and Sons, Inc. • 2002. $24.99. Covers UNIX in 30 "easy lessons" (15 hours). Topics range from "The Many Flavors of UNIX" to "Archiving and Compressing Files." Includes CD-ROM with general UNIX utilities and resources, security utilities, code examples, and an assessment test to gauge progress. (Weekend Crash Course Series).

INTERNET DATABASES

InfoTech Trends. Data Analysis Group. Phone: (925)462-1202 Fax: (925)462-1225 E-mail: support@infotechtrends.com • URL: http://www.infotechtrends.com • Web site provides both free and fee-based market research data on the information technology industry, including computers, peripherals, telecommunications, the Internet, software, CD-ROM/DVD, e-commerce, and workstations. Fees: Free for current (most recent year) data; more extensive information has various fee structures. Formerly *Computer Industry Forecasts.*

ONLINE DATABASES

Globalbase. Gale Cengage Learning. • Provides more than one million online summaries of business, industrial, and economic news reports from more than 1,000 publications worldwide. Covers a wide range of material appearing in international trade journals, professional magazines, and newspapers. Time period is 1984 to date, with weekly updates. Inquire as to online cost and availability.

Internet and Personal Computing Abstracts. Information Today, Inc. • Contains abstracts covering a wide variety of personal and business microcomputer literature appearing in more than 100 journals and popular magazines. Time period is 1981 to date, with monthly updates. Formerly *Microcomputer Index.* Inquire as to online cost and availability.

PROMT: Predicasts Overview of Markets and Technology. Gale Cengage Learning. • Companies, products, applied technologies and markets. U.S. and international literature coverage, 1972 to date. Inquire as to online cost and availability. Provides abstracts from more than 1,600 publications. Weekly updates.

PERIODICALS AND NEWSLETTERS

Dr. Dobb's Journal: Software Tools for the Professional Programmer. CMP Media LLC. • Monthly. $34.95 per year. A technical publication covering software development, languages, operating systems, and applications.

Information Week: Business Innovation Powered by Technology. CMP Publications, Inc. • Weekly. $199.00 per year. The magazine for information systems management.

Sys Admin: The Journal for Unix System Administrators. CMP Media LLC. • Monthly. $39.00 per year. Provides technical information for managers of Unix systems.

TRADE/PROFESSIONAL ASSOCIATIONS

USENIX Association. 2560 9th St., Ste. 215, 2560 Ninth St., Ste. 215, Berkeley, CA 94710. Phone: (510)528-8649 Fax: (510)548-5738 E-mail: office@usenix.org • URL: http://www.usenix.org • Individuals with an interest in Advanced Computing Systems in a professional or technical capacity; and (commercial computer firms) institutions, colleges and universities, and research institutes. Promotes innovation in advanced computing systems; fosters the development of research and technological information pertaining to advanced computer systems.

UNLISTED SECURITIES

See: OVER-THE-COUNTER SECURITIES INDUSTRY

UPHOLSTERY

HANDBOOKS AND MANUALS

Practical Upholstering: And the Cutting of Slip Covers. Frederick Palmer. Madison Books, Inc., USA. • 1982. $11.95.

Upholstering Fundamentals. Clois E. Kicklighter and Joan C. Klicklighter. Goodheart-Willcox Publishers. • 2000. $33.28. *Answer Key?*, $4.00.

TRADE/PROFESSIONAL ASSOCIATIONS

National Association of Decorative Fabric Distributors. 3008 Millwood Ave., Columbia, SC 29205. Phone: 800-445-8629 Fax: (803)765-0860 E-mail: info@nadfd.com • URL: http://www.nadfd.com • Formerly National Association of Upholstery Fabric Distributors.

Upholstered Furniture Action Council. Box 2436, High Point, NC 27261. Phone: (336)885-5065 Fax: (336)885-5072 E-mail: info@ufac.org • URL: http://www.ufac.org • Conducts research and disseminates information regarding the development and adoption of voluntary guidelines for production of more cigarette-resistant upholstered furniture; educates the public in the safe use of smoking materials. Maintains speakers' bureau; compiles statistics.

URANIUM INDUSTRY

See also: MINES AND MINERAL RESOURCES

ALMANACS AND YEARBOOKS

CRB Commodity Yearbook. Commodity Research Bureau. CRB. • Annual. $99.95.

CD-ROM DATABASES

Environment Abstracts on CD-ROM. LEXIS-NEXIS. • Quarterly. $1,295.00 per year. Contains the following CD-ROM databases: *Environment Abstracts, Energy Abstracts*, and *Acid Rain Abstracts.* Length of coverage varies.

ONLINE DATABASES

GEOARCHIVE. Geosystems. • Citations to literature on geoscience and water. 1974 to present. Monthly updates. Inquire as to online cost and availability.

GEOREF. American Geological Institute. • Bibliography and index of geology and geosciences literature, 1785 to present. Inquire as to online cost and availability.

PERIODICALS AND NEWSLETTERS

Nuclear Fuel. Platts. • Biweekly. $1,870.00 per year. Newsletter.

STATISTICS SOURCES

Non-Ferrous Metal Data Yearbook. American Bureau of Metal Statistics. • Annual. $405.00.

Provides worldwide data on approximately about 200 statistical tables covering many nonferrous metals. Includes production, consumption, inventories, exports, imports, and other data.

Uranium: Resources, Production, and Demand. Organization for Economic Cooperation and Development. • Annual. $77.00. Produced by the OECD Nuclear Energy Agency and the International Atomic Energy Agency. Provides detailed statistics and trend analysis for uranium based on official information from 49 countries.

TRADE/PROFESSIONAL ASSOCIATIONS

American Bureau of Metal Statistics. P.O. Box 805, Chatham, NJ 07928. Phone: (973)701-2299 Fax: (973)701-2152 E-mail: info@abms.com • URL: http://www.abms.com • Members are metal companies. Compiles and publishes detailed statistical data on a wide variety of nonferrous metals: aluminum, copper, gold, lead, nickel, platinum, silver, tin, titanium, uranium, zinc, and others.

URBAN AREAS

See: CITIES AND TOWNS

URBAN DEVELOPMENT

See also: CITY PLANNING; COMMUNITY DEVELOPMENT; HOUSING

GENERAL WORKS

Cities for the 21st Century. OECD Publications and Information Center. • 1994. $39.00. Contains discussions of the economic, social, and environmental problems of today's cities.

Moving Beyond Gridlock: Traffic and Development. Robert T. Dunphy. Urban Land Institute. • 1996. $49.95. Describes how various regions have dealt with traffic growth. Includes case studies from seven cities.

Urban Economics and Land Use in America: The Transformation of Cities in the Twentieth Century. Alan Rabinowitz. M. E. Sharpe, Inc. • 2004. $72.95. Covers suburbanization and its problems from 1900 to modern times.

Urban Revitalization: Policies and Prgrams. Timothy E. Joder. Sage Publications, Inc. • 1995. $76.95.

ABSTRACTS AND INDEXES

Index to Current Urban Documents. Greenwood Publishing Group, Inc. • Quarterly. $500.00 per year. Includes annual *cumulation.*

Sage Urban Studies Abstracts. Sage Publications, Inc. • Quarterly. Institutions, $797.00 per year.

Social Sciences Index. H. W. Wilson Co. • Quarterly, with annual cumulation. Price varies. Indexes more than 400 periodicals covering economics, environmental policy, government, insurance, labor, health care policy, plannning, public administration, public welfare, urban studies, women's issues, criminology, and related topics.

ALMANACS AND YEARBOOKS

Institute on Planning, Zoning and Eminent Domain. LexisNexis. • 1971. $199.00.

BIBLIOGRAPHIES

Waterfront Revitalization. Eric J. Fournier. Sage Publications, Inc. • 1994. $10.00. (CPL Bibliographies Series, No. 310).

CD-ROM DATABASES

Newspaper Abstracts Ondisc. PROQUEST. • Monthly. $2,950.00 per year (covers 1989 to date; archival discs are available for 1985-88). Provides cover-to-cover CD-ROM indexing and abstracting of 19 major newspapers, including the *New York*

Times, Wall Street Journal, Washington Post, Chicago Tribune, and *Los Angeles Times.*

Social Sciences Citation Index. ISI. • Monthly. Price on request. Provides CD-ROM indexing of articles appearing in 1700 leading social science journals worldwide, with additional selections from more than 5700 other journals. Time span is 1992 to date. Coverage includes economics, business, finance, management, communications, demographics, library and information science, political science, sociology, and many other subjects.

Social Sciences Citation Index: Compact Disc Edition with Abstracts. Institute for Scientific Information. • Monthly. Provides CD-ROM indexing and abstracting of "significant articles" from 1,700 social science journals worldwide, with additional selections from 3,200 other journals, 1986 to date. Includes economics, business, finance, management, communications, demographics, information and library science, political science, sociology, and many other subjects.

WILSONDISC: Wilson Social Sciences Abstracts. H. W. Wilson Co. • Monthly. Includes unlimited online access to *Social Sciences Index* through WILSONLINE. Provides CD-ROM indexing from 1983 and abstracting from 1994 of more than 500 periodicals covering economics, area studies, community health, public administration, public welfare, urban studies, and many other topics related to the social sciences.

DIRECTORIES

Funding Sources for Community and Economic Development 2003-2004: A Guide to Current Sources for Local Programs and Projects. Greenwood Publishing Group, Inc. • 2003. $64.95. Sixth edition. Provides information on 2,600 funding sources. Includes "A Guide to Proposal Planning." (Funding Sources for Community and Economic Development Series).

HANDBOOKS AND MANUALS

Hotel Development. Urban Land Institute. • 1996. $39.95. Provides practical information on developing, acquiring, and renovating hotels in urban areas. Covers market analysis, financing, construction, and management. Includes case studies.

New Uses for Obsolete Buildings. Urban Land Institute. • 1996. $65.95. Covers various aspects of redevelopment: zoning, building codes, environment, economics, financing, and marketing. Includes eight case studies and 75 descriptions of completed "adaptive use projects.".

Resort Development Handbook. Urban Land Institute. • 1997. $89.95. Covers a wide range of resort settings and amenities, with details of development, market analysis, financing, design, and operations. Includes color photographs and case studies. (ULI Development Handbook Series).

Sports, Convention, and Entertainment Facilities. David C. Petersen. Urban Land Institute. • 1996. $61.95. Provides advice and information on developing, financing, and operating amphitheaters, arenas, convention centers, and stadiums. Includes case studies of 70 projects.

Urban Parks and Open Space. Gayle L. Berens and others. Urban Land Institute. • 1997. $40.95. Covers financing, design, management, and public-private partnerships relative to the development of open space for new urban parks. Includes color illustrations and the history of urban parks.

Zoning and Planning Law Handbook. West Group. • $264.50.

ONLINE DATABASES

Information Bank Abstracts. New York Times Index Dept. • Provides indexing and abstracting of current affairs, primarily from the final late edition of *The New York Times* and the Eastern edition of *The Wall Street Journal.* Time period is 1969 to present, with daily updates. Inquire as to online cost and availability.

Wilson Social Sciences Abstracts Online. H. W. Wilson Co. • Provides online abstracting and indexing of more than 500 periodicals covering area studies, community health, public administration, public welfare, urban studies, and many other social science topics. Time period is 1994 to date for abstracts and 1983 to date for indexing, with updates weekly. Inquire as to online cost and availability.

PERIODICALS AND NEWSLETTERS

Downtown Idea Exchange: Essential Information for Downtown Research and Development Center. Downtown Research and Development Center. Alexander Communications Group, Inc. • Semimonthly. $187.00 per year. Newsletter for those concerned with central business districts. Provides news and other information on planning, development, parking, mass transit, traffic, funding, and other topics.

Downtown Promotion Reporter. Downtown Research and Development Center. Alexander Communications Group Inc. • Description: Focuses primarily on helping downtown areas be as competitive and successful as possible on a day-to-day basis. Reports on market research, retailing, advertising approaches, public relations techniques, budgeting, and organization. Provides news of promotional strategies used in cities throughout the nation. Recurring features include case studies.

Journal of Housing and Community Development. National Association of Housing and Redevelopment Officials (NAHRO). • Bimonthly. $33.00 per year. Formerly *Journal of Housing.*

Land Use Law and Zoning Digest. American Planning Association. • Monthly. $275.00 per year. Covers judicial decisions and state laws affecting zoning and land use. Edited for city planners and lawyers. Monthly supplement available *Zoning News.*

Real Estate Economics: Journal of the American Real Estate and Urban Economics Association. MIT Press. • Quarterly. Institutions. $295.00 per year. Includes print and online editions.

Urban Affairs Review. Sage Publications, Inc. • Bimonthly. Institutions, $601.00 per year; includes print and online editions. Formerly *Urban Affairs Quarterly.*

Urban Land: News and Trends in Land Development. Urban Land Institute. • Monthly. Membership.

Zoning and Planning Law Report. West Group. • Monthly. $483.00 per year. Newsletter.

RESEARCH CENTERS AND INSTITUTES

Institute of Urban and Regional Development. University of California at Berkeley, 316 Wurster Hall, Berkeley, CA 94720-1870. Phone: (510)642-4874 Fax: (510)643-9576 E-mail: iurd@uclink. berkeley.edu • URL: http://www.ced.berkeley.edu/iurd • Research topics include the effects of changing economic trends in urban areas.

Urban Institute. Urban Institute. 2100 M St. NW, Washington, DC 20037. Phone: (202)833-7200 Fax: (202)728-0232 E-mail: paffairs@ui.urban.org • URL: http://www.urban.org • Domestic, social, and economic affairs, including multidisciplinary studies and government program evaluations in the areas of tax and budget reform, education policy, health policy, crime and justice, housing and community development, labor and human services, income security and retirement, welfare reform, international activities, nonprofit sector and philanthropy, public finance, productivity and economic development, social services, and immigration. Also conducts research programs on employment and training, children's issues and family policy, minorities and social policy, poverty, state

and local governments, and community impact and demography.

Urban Land Institute. Urban Land Institute. 1025 Thomas Jefferson St. NW, Ste. 500 W, Washington, DC 20007. Phone: (202)624-7000 Fax: (202)624-7140 E-mail: customerservice@uli.org • URL: http://www.uli.org • Urban land use policy, planning, and development issues, including studies on central city problems, industrial development, new community development, residential developments of all types, taxation, smart growth, shopping center development and economics, metropolitan and urbanized area growth and development, mixed use development, and environmental factors affecting development.

STATISTICS SOURCES

Budget of the United States Government. U.S. Office of Management and Budget. Available from U.S. Government Printing Office. • Annual. $52.00.

Facts About the Cities. Allan Carpenter and Carl Provorse. H. W. Wilson Co. • 1996. $100.00. Second edition. Contains a wide variety of information on 300 American cities, including cities in Puerto Rico, Guam, and the U. S. Virgin Islands. Data is provided on the workplace, taxes, revenues, cost of living, population, climate, housing, transportation, etc.

Housing and Urban Development Trends: Annual Summary. U.S. Department of Housing and Urban Development. • Annual.

TRADE/PROFESSIONAL ASSOCIATIONS

American Planning Association. 122 S Michigan Ave., Ste. 1600, Chicago, IL 60603-6107. Phone: (312)431-9100 Fax: (312)431-9985 E-mail: customerservice@planning.org • URL: http://www.planning.org • Public and private planning agency officials, professional planners, planning educators, elected and appointed officials, and other persons involved in urban and rural development. Works to foster the best techniques and decisions for the planned development of communities and regions. Provides extensive professional services and publications to professionals and laypeople in planning and related fields; serves as a clearinghouse for information. Through Planning Advisory Service, a research and inquiry-answering service, provides, on an annual subscription basis, advice on specific inquiries and a series of research reports on planning, zoning, and environmental regulations. Supplies information on job openings and makes definitive studies on salaries and recruitment of professional planners. Conducts research; collaborates in joint projects with local, national, and international organizations.

American Real Estate and Urban Economics Association. PO Box 1148, Portage, MI 49081-1148. Phone: (866)273-8321 Fax: (313)731-0174 E-mail: areuea@areuea.org • URL: http://www.areuea.org • Members are real estate teachers, researchers, economists, and others concerned with urban real estate and investment.

National Association of Housing and Redevelopment Officials. 630 Eye St., N.W., Washington, DC 20001. Phone: 877-866-2476 or (202)289-3500 Fax: (202)289-8181 E-mail: nahro@nahro.org • URL: http://www.nahro.org • Formerly National Association of Housing Officials.

OTHER SOURCES

American Land Planning Law. John Taylor and Norma Williams. West Group. • $780.00. Eight volumes. Annual cumulative updates. (Real Property and Zoning Series.)

URBAN MANAGEMENT

See: MUNICIPAL GOVERNMENT

URBAN PLANNING

See: CITY PLANNING

URBAN TRANSPORTATION

See: PUBLIC TRANSPORTATION; TRANSPORTATION INDUSTRY

USED CAR INDUSTRY

See also: AUTOMOBILE DEALERS

GENERAL WORKS

What Your Car Really Costs: How to Keep a Financially Safe Driving Record. American Institute for Economic Research. • 2002. $6.00. Contains "Should You Buy or Lease?," "Should You Buy New or Used?," "Dealer Trade-in or Private Sale?," "Lemon Laws," and other car buying information. Includes rankings of specific models for resale value, 1995 to 2001. (Economic Education Bulletin.).

HANDBOOKS AND MANUALS

Used-Car Rental Agency. Entrepreneur Media, Inc. • Looseleaf. $59.50. A practical guide to starting a used-car rental business. Covers profit potential, start-up costs, market size evaluation, owner's time required, site selection, lease negotiation pricing, accounting, advertising, promotion, etc. (Start-Up Business Guide No. E1108.).

Used Car Sales. Entrepreneur Media, Inc. • Looseleaf. $59.50. A practical guide to getting started in the business of selling used cars. Covers profit potential, start-up costs, market size evaluation, owner's time required, site selection, lease negotiation, pricing, accounting, advertising, etc. (Start-Up Business Guide No. E2330.).

INTERNET DATABASES

Advance Monthly Sales for Retail Trade and Food Services. U. S. Census Bureau. Phone: 800-541-8345 or (301)763-4636 Fax: (301)457-3842 E-mail: rcb@census.gov • URL: http://www.census.gov/svsd/www/fullpub.html • Web pages provide monthly sales figures for a wide range of retail businesses. Advance, preliminary, and final statistics are provided for the latest month available in each case, with a previous-year comparison. Updates are monthly.

PERIODICALS AND NEWSLETTERS

Used Car Dealer. National Independent Automobile Dealers Association. • Monthly. Free to members; non-members, $60.00 per year.

PRICE SOURCES

Automotive Market Report. Automotive Auction Publishing, Inc. • Biweekly. $130.00 Per Year. Current wholesale values of used vehicles.

Edmund's Used Cars and Trucks, Prices and Ratings. Edmund Publications Corp. • Four times a year. Individuals, $39.96 per year; libraries, $26.80 per year. Lists American and foreign used car prices for the past 10 years.

NADA Appraisal Guides. National Automobile Dealers Association. • Prices and frequencies vary. Guides to prices of used cars, old used cars, motorcycles, mobile homes, recreational vehicles, and mopeds.

STATISTICS SOURCES

Annual Benchmark Report for Retail Trade and Food Services...A Detailed Summary of Retail Sales, Purchases, Accounts Receivable, Inventories, and Food Service Sales. Available from U. S. Government Printing Office. • Annual. $13.00. Issued by the U.S. Census Bureau. Provides detailed annual and monthly retail statistics for the most recent 10 years. Includes data for various kinds of retail outlets, including automobiles, furniture, appliances, building supplies, grocery stores, drug stores, gasoline stations, clothing, sporting goods; department stores, and restaurants.

TRADE/PROFESSIONAL ASSOCIATIONS

National Auto Auction Association. 5320 Spectrum Dr., Ste. D, Frederick, MD 21703. Phone: (301)696-0400 Fax: (301)631-1359 E-mail: naaa@naaa.com • URL: http://www.naaa.com • Owners/operators of wholesale automobile and truck auctions; associate members are car and truck manufacturers, insurers of checks and titles, car and truck rental companies, publishers of auto price guide books, and others connected with the industry. Maintains hall of fame.

National Independent Automobile Dealers Association. 2521 Brown Blvd., Arlington, TX 76006. Phone: 800-682-3837 or (817)640-3838 Fax: (817)649-5866 E-mail: mike@niada.com • URL: http://www.niada.com • Individuals, companies, or corporations licensed by their states as dealers to buy and sell used motor vehicles; associate members are businesses related to or associated with the buying or selling of motor vehicles. Gathers and disseminates information relative to the used car industry; represents used car dealers before regulatory and legislative bodies; provides educational and other programs to help used car dealers understand their responsibilities; works for the betterment of the automobile industry. Works closely with local and state independent automobile dealers' associations and others concerning dealers and the public. Maintains code of fair dealing for members. Conducts seminars, meetings, and professional training programs. Maintains speakers' bureau, services for children, and charitable programs. Sponsors competitions; compiles statistics.

USED PRODUCTS

See: SURPLUS PRODUCTS

UTENSILS, COOKING

See: HOUSEWARES INDUSTRY

UTILITIES, PUBLIC

See: PUBLIC UTILITIES

V

VACUUM CLEANERS

CD-ROM DATABASES

OECD Statistical Compendium. Organization for Economic Cooperation and Development. • Semiannual. $1,905.00 per year for 1 to 10 users. CD-ROM contains more than 730,000 monthly, quarterly, and annual time series for OECD countries, 1960 to date. Includes fully searchable data on agriculture, food, economic indicators, national accounts, employment, energy, finance, industry, technology, and foreign trade. Results can be displayed in various forms.

INTERNET DATABASES

Business 2.0 Web Guide to the Best Business Links. Business 2.0 Media Inc. Phone: (415)293-4800 E-mail: support@business2.com • URL: http://www.business2.com/webguide • Web site presents an extensive, searchable directory of links to "the best, most informative, and authoritative web pages." Twenty main categories cover business, finance, career, company information, people, and technology topics, with thousands of subtopics, all linking to Web sites recommended by experienced business researchers. Fees: Free.

Fedstats. Federal Interagency Council on Statistical Policy. Phone: (202)395-7254 • URL: http://www.fedstats.gov • Web site features an efficient search facility for full-text statistics produced by more than 100 federal agencies, including the Census Bureau, the Bureau of Economic Analysis, and the Bureau of Labor Statistics. Boolean searches can be made within one agency or for all agencies combined. Links are offered to international statistical bureaus, including the UN, IMF, OECD, UNESCO, Eurostat, and 20 individual countries. Fees: Free.

FreeLunch.com. Economy.com, Inc. Phone: (610)696-8700 Fax: (610)696-1678 • URL: http://www.freelunch.com • Web site provides free access to more than 1.5 million economic and financial data series, covering industry, demographics, labor markets, prices, retail sales, government spending, trade, interest rates, housing starts, the stock market, and many other topics. Data is available for various time periods in either chart or table form. Searching is offered. Fees: Free, but registration required. Economy.com, Inc. also offers fee-based economic analysis at *The Dismal Scientist* site (http://www.dismal.com).

STATISTICS SOURCES

Business Statistics of the United States. Linz Audain and Cornelia J. Strawser. Bernan Associates. • Annual. $147.00. Based on *Business Statistics,* formerly issue by the Bureau of Economic Analysis, U. S. Department of Commerce. Provides basic data for a wide variety of U. S. industries, services, and economic indicators. Most statistics are shown annually for 30 years and monthly for the most recent four years.

Survey of Current Business. Available from U. S. Government Printing Office. • Monthly. $63.00 per year. Issued by Bureau of Economic Analysis, U. S. Department of Commerce. Presents a wide variety of business and economic data.

TRADE/PROFESSIONAL ASSOCIATIONS

Vacuum Cleaner Manufacturers Association. 1300 Sumner Ave., Cleveland, OH 44115. Phone: (216)241-7333 Fax: (216)241-0105 E-mail: eboardman@att.net • URL: http://www.vacuumcleaners.org • Manufacturers of household electric floor-care products, including vacuum cleaners and soil extractors. Publications: none.

VALUATION

See also: REAL PROPERTY VALUATION

HANDBOOKS AND MANUALS

CCH Guide to Business Valuation. CCH, Inc. • Looseleaf. $295.00 per year, including quarterly newsletter. Covers latest developments and trends in the evaluation of businesses.

Corporate Valuation: Tools for Effective Appraisal and Decision Making. Stephen A. Ross and others. McGraw-Hill. • 1994. $76.95. Discusses the four most widely-used corporate appraisal methods.

Handbook of Business Valuation. Thomas L. West and Jeffrey D. Jones, editors. John Wiley and Sons, Inc. • 1999. $145.00. Second edition. A collection of articles, worksheets, and appraisal techniques.

Manager's Guide to Financial Statement Analysis. Stephen F. Jablonsky and Noah P. Barsky. John Wiley and Sons, Inc. • 2001. $49.95. Second edition. The two main sections are "Financial Statements and Business Strategy" and "Market Valuation and Business Strategy.".

Valuation: Measuring and Managing the Value of Companies. Tom Copeland and others. John Wiley and Sons, Inc. • 2000. $115.00. Third edition. A practical guide to economic value analysis for bankers, accountants, financial analysts, and others concerned with company valuation. Includes CD-ROM. (Frontiers in Finance Series).

Valuing a Business: Analysis and Appraisal of Closely Held Companies. Shannon P. Pratt and others. McGraw-Hill. • 2000. $95.00. Fourth edition. Includes information on how to appraise partial interests and how to write a valuation report.

Valuing Professional Practices: A Practitioner's Guide. Robert Reilly and Robert Schweihs. CCH, Inc. • 1997. $99.00. Provides a basic introduction to estimating the dollar value of practices in various professional fields.

PERIODICALS AND NEWSLETTERS

ASA Newsletter. American Society of Anesthesiologists. • Description: Reports on the educational and scientific work of the organization, which represents anesthesiologists in the U.S. Recurring features include legislative updates, reports of meetings, news of research, historical items, editorials, letters to the editor and news of members.

Journal of Corporate Accounting and Finance. John Wiley and Sons, Inc., Journals. • Bimonthly. $495.00 per year; with online edition, $520.00 per year. Topics include government regulation, corporate taxation, financial risk, business valuation, and strategic planning.

TRADE/PROFESSIONAL ASSOCIATIONS

American Society of Appraisers. 555 Herndon Parkway, Suite 125, Herndon, VA 20170. Phone: 800-272-8258 or (703)478-2228 Fax: (703)742-8471 E-mail: asainfo@appraisers.org • URL: http://www.appraisers.org.

Appraisers Association of America. 386 Park Ave., S., Suite 2000, New York, NY 10016. Phone: (212)889-5404 Fax: (212)889-5503 E-mail: aaa1@rcn.com • URL: http://www.appraiserassoc.org.

VALVES

FINANCIAL RATIOS

Annual Statement Studies. The Risk Management Association. • Annual. Median and quartile financial ratios are given for over 400 kinds of manufacturing, wholesale, retail, construction, and consumer finance establishments. Data is sorted by both asset size and sales volume. Includes a clearly written "Definition of Ratios" and an alphabetical industry index.

Annual Statement Studies: Industry Default Probabilities and Cash Flow Measures. The Risk Management Association. • Annual. $145.00. Serves as a companion volume to the original *Annual Statement Studies.* Gives probability of default estimates on a percentage scale for more than 450 industries. Includes changes in position year-by-year for eight financial statement line items and provides percentage measures of cash flow.

INTERNET DATABASES

Manufacturing Profiles. U. S. Bureau of the Census. Phone: (301)763-4636 E-mail: webmaster@census.gov • URL: http://www.census.gov/prod/www/abs/mfg-prof.html • The Census Bureau makes available free on PDF (Portable Document Format) an annual consolidation of the entire Current Industrial Report series, presenting "all the data compiled." Contains statistics on production, shipments, inventories, consumption, exports, imports, and orders for a wide variety of manufactured products.

PERIODICALS AND NEWSLETTERS

Processing. Putman Media. • 14 times a year. $54.00 per year. Emphasis is on descriptions of new products for all areas of industrial processing, including valves, controls, filters, pumps, compressors, fluidics, and instrumentation.

STATISTICS SOURCES

Annual Survey of Manufactures. Available from U. S. Government Printing Office. • Annual. Prices vary. Issued by the U. S. Census Bureau as an interim update to the *Census of Manufactures.* Includes data on number of manufacturing establishments in various industries, employment, labor costs, value of shipments, capital expenditures, inventories, energy costs, and assets. (See also Census Bureau home page, http://www.census. gov/.).

U. S. Industry and Trade Outlook. Available from National Technical Information Service. • Annual. $69.95. Produced by the International Trade Administration, U. S. Department of Commerce, in a "public-private" partnership with DRI/McGraw-Hill and Standard & Poor's. Provides basic data, outlook for the current year, and "Long-Term Prospects" (five-year projections) for a wide variety of products and services. Includes high technology industries. Formerly *U. S. Industrial Outlook.*

TRADE/PROFESSIONAL ASSOCIATIONS

Manufacturers Standardization Society of the Valve and Fittings Industry. 127 Park St., N. E., Vienna, VA 22180-4602. Phone: (703)281-6613 Fax: (703)281-6671 E-mail: info@mss-hq.com • URL: http://www.mss-hq.com • Members are valve and fitting companies. Publishes standards and specifications.

Valve Manufacturers Association of America. 1050 17th St., N.W., Suite 280, Washington, DC 20036. Phone: (202)331-8105 Fax: (202)296-0378 E-mail: vma@vma.org • URL: http://www.vma.org • Formerly Valve Manufacturers Association.

VARIABLE ANNUITIES

See: ANNUITIES

VARIETY STORES

See also: RETAIL TRADE

CD-ROM DATABASES

OECD Statistical Compendium. Organization for Economic Cooperation and Development. • Semiannual. $1,905.00 per year for 1 to 10 users. CD-ROM contains more than 730,000 monthly, quarterly, and annual time series for OECD countries, 1960 to date. Includes fully searchable data on agriculture, food, economic indicators, national accounts, employment, energy, finance, industry, technology, and foreign trade. Results can be displayed in various forms.

DIRECTORIES

Directory of Discount and General Merchandise Stores. Chain Store Guide. • Annual. $327.00. Online edition, $747.00. Includes retailers and wholesalers of housewares, giftwares, novelties, toys, hobby materials, crafts, and stationery.

FINANCIAL RATIOS

Annual Statement Studies. The Risk Management Association. • Annual. Median and quartile financial ratios are given for over 400 kinds of manufacturing, wholesale, retail, construction, and consumer finance establishments. Data is sorted by both asset size and sales volume. Includes a clearly written "Definition of Ratios" and an alphabetical industry index.

Annual Statement Studies: Industry Default Probabilities and Cash Flow Measures. The Risk Management Association. • Annual. $145.00. Serves as a companion volume to the original *Annual Statement Studies.* Gives probability of default estimates on a percentage scale for more than 450 industries. Includes changes in position year-by-year for eight financial statement line items and provides percentage measures of cash flow.

INTERNET DATABASES

Business 2.0 Web Guide to the Best Business Links. Business 2.0 Media Inc. Phone: (415)293-4800 E-mail: support@business2.com • URL: http:// www.business2.com/webguide • Web site presents an extensive, searchable directory of links to "the best, most informative, and authoritative web pages." Twenty main categories cover business, finance, career, company information, people, and technology topics, with thousands of subtopics, all linking to Web sites recommended by experienced business researchers. Fees: Free.

Fedstats. Federal Interagency Council on Statistical Policy. Phone: (202)395-7254 • URL: http://www. fedstats.gov • Web site features an efficient search facility for full-text statistics produced by more than 100 federal agencies, including the Census Bureau, the Bureau of Economic Analysis, and the Bureau of Labor Statistics. Boolean searches can be made within one agency or for all agencies combined. Links are offered to international statistical bureaus, including the UN, IMF, OECD, UNESCO, Eurostat, and 20 individual countries. Fees: Free.

FreeLunch.com. Economy.com, Inc. Phone: (610)696-8700 Fax: (610)696-1678 • URL: http:// www.freelunch.com • Web site provides free access to more than 1.5 million economic and financial data series, covering industry, demographics, labor markets, prices, retail sales, government spending, trade, interest rates, housing starts, the stock market, and many other topics. Data is available for various time periods in either chart or table form. Searching is offered. Fees: Free, but registration required. Economy.com, Inc. also offers fee-based economic analysis at *The Dismal Scientist* site (http://www. dismal.com).

STATISTICS SOURCES

Business Statistics of the United States. Linz Audain and Cornelia J. Strawser. Bernan Associates. • Annual. $147.00. Based on *Business Statistics,* formerly issue by the Bureau of Economic Analysis, U. S. Department of Commerce. Provides basic data for a wide variety of U. S. industries, services, and economic indicators. Most statistics are shown annually for 30 years and monthly for the most recent four years.

Survey of Current Business. Available from U. S. Government Printing Office. • Monthly. $63.00 per year. Issued by Bureau of Economic Analysis, U. S. Department of Commerce. Presents a wide variety of business and economic data.

TRADE/PROFESSIONAL ASSOCIATIONS

International Mass Retail Association. 1700 N. Moore St., Suite 2250, Arlington, VA 22209. Phone: (703)841-2300 Fax: (703)841-1184 E-mail: klasu@ imra.org • URL: http://www.imra.org • Formerly National Mass Retailing Institute.

VARNISH AND VARNISHING

See also: PAINT AND PAINTING

INTERNET DATABASES

Manufacturing Profiles. U. S. Bureau of the Census. Phone: (301)763-4636 E-mail: webmaster@census. gov • URL: http://www.census.gov/prod/www/abs/ mfg-prof.html • The Census Bureau makes available free on PDF (Portable Document Format) an annual consolidation of the entire Current Industrial Report series, presenting "all the data compiled." Contains statistics on production, shipments, inventories, consumption, exports, imports, and orders for a wide variety of manufactured products.

ONLINE DATABASES

World Surface Coatings Abstracts [Online]. Paint Research Association of Great Britain. • Indexing and abstracting of the literature of paint and surface coatings, 1976 to present. Monthly updates. Inquire as to online cost and availability.

PERIODICALS AND NEWSLETTERS

Modern Paint and Coatings. Chemical Week Associates. • Monthly. $52.00 per year.

STATISTICS SOURCES

Annual Survey of Manufactures. Available from U. S. Government Printing Office. • Annual. Prices vary. Issued by the U. S. Census Bureau as an interim update to the *Census of Manufactures.* Includes data on number of manufacturing establishments in various industries, employment, labor costs, value of shipments, capital expenditures, inventories, energy costs, and assets. (See also Census Bureau home page, http://www.census. gov/.).

Paint, Varnish, and Lacquer. U. S. Bureau of the Census. • Quarterly and annual. Provides data on shipments: value, quantity, imports, and exports. Includes paint, varnish, lacquer, product finishes, and special purpose coatings. (Current Industrial Reports, MQ-28F.).

TRADE/PROFESSIONAL ASSOCIATIONS

National Paint and Coatings Association. 1500 Rhode Island Ave., N.W., Washington, DC 20005-5597. Phone: (202)462-6272 Fax: (202)462-8549 E-mail: npca@paint.org • URL: http://www.paint: org • Formerly National Paint, Varnish and Lacquer Association.

VCR

See: VIDEO RECORDING INDUSTRY

VEGETABLE INDUSTRY

ABSTRACTS AND INDEXES

Field Crop Abstracts: Monthly Abstract Journal on World Annual Cereal, Legume, Root, Oilseed and Fibre Crops. Available from CABI Publishing North America. • Monthly. Institutions, $1775.00 per year. Online edition available, $1,820.00 per year. Published in England by CABI Publishing, formerly Commonwealth Agricultural Bureaux. Provides worldwide coverage of the literature.

Food Science and Technology Abstracts. International Food Information Service Publishing. • Monthly. $1,780.00 per year. Provides worldwide coverage of the literature of food technology and food production.

Foods Adlibra: Key to the World's Food Literature. General Mills, Inc. Foods Adlibra Publications. • Semimonthly. $240.00 per year. Provides journal citations and abstracts to the literature of food technology and packaging.

Horticultural Abstracts: Compiled from World

Literature on Temperate and Tropical Fruits, Vegetables, Ornaments, Plantation Crops. Available from CABI Publishing North America. • Monthly. $2,010.00 per year. Print and online edition, $2,030.00 per year. Published in England by CABI Publishing. Provides worldwide coverage of the literature of fruits, vegetables, flowers, plants, and all aspects of gardens and gardening.

ALMANACS AND YEARBOOKS

Agricultural and Mineral Commodities Year Book. Available from Taylor & Francis Group. • Annual. $225.00. Published by Europa Publications. Contains descriptive product profiles, price data, export-import data, and production statistics for major commodities of the world. Includes commodity histories, uses, markets, demand trends, and information about trade agreements and key commodity organizations.

CD-ROM DATABASES

AGRICOLA on SilverPlatter. Available from Silver-Platter Information, Inc. • Quarterly. $825.00 per year. Produced by the National Agricultural Library. Provides about three million citations on CD-ROM to the literature of agriculture, agricultural economics, animal sciences, entomology, fertilizer, food, forestry, nutrition, pesticides, plant science, water resources, and other topics. Each quarterly disc covers the past ten years, with archival discs available from 1970.

Food Science and Technology Abstracts [CD-ROM]. Available from SilverPlatter Information, Inc. • Quarterly. Produced by International Food Information Service (home page is http://www.ifis.org). Provides worldwide coverage on CD-ROM of the literature of food technology and production. Various types of publications are indexed, with abstracts, including about 1,800 periodicals. Time period is 1969 to date.

DIRECTORIES

Agriculture: Websites and Glossary. Carol Canada. Nova Science Publishers, Inc. • 2003. $29.50. Lists agricultural Web sites according to 24 main categories and 16 subcategories. Includes a glossary and an index.

American Vegetable Grower--Source Book. Meister Media Worldwide. • Publication includes: Lists of suppliers of agricultural chemicals and manufacturers and suppliers of other agricultural products, equipment, and services including packaging equipment, transportation services, direct marketing suppliers, plants and seeds, etc. Entries include: Company name, address, phone, fax, e-mail.

Major Food and Drink Companies of the World. Available from Gale Cengage Learning. • Annual. $880.00. Two volumes. Published by Graham & Whiteside. Contains profiles and trade names for more than 9,800 important food and beverage companies in various countries. In addition to foods, includes both alcoholic and nonalcoholic drink products.

Packer Produce Availability and Merchandising Guide. Vance Publishing Corp., Produce Div. • Annual. $35.00. A buyer's directory giving sources of fresh fruits and vegetables. Shippers are listed by location for each commodity.

Specialty Food Industry Directory. Phoenix Media Network, Inc. • Annual. Included in subscription to Food Distribution Magazine. Lists manufacturers and suppliers of specialty foods, and services and equipment for the specialty food industry. Featured food products include legumes, sauces, spices, upscale cheese, specialty beverages, snack foods, baked goods, ethnic foods, and specialty meats.

Thomas Food and Beverage Market Place. Grey House Publishing. • 2004. $495.00. Three volumes. Contains more than 40,000 entries covering food companies, beverages, food equipment, warehouse companies, food brokers, wholesalers, importers, and exporters. Formerly *Thomas Food Industry Register.*

Western Growers Association--Membership Directory. Western Growers Association. • Covers: 2,700 growers, shippers, packers, brokers, and distributors of fruits, vegetables, nuts, and allied industries in California and Arizona. Entries include: Company name, address, phone and fax, names of executives, list of commodities.

ENCYCLOPEDIAS AND DICTIONARIES

Encyclopedia of Agriculture Science. Charles J. Arntzen and Ellen M. Ritter, editors. Elsevier • 1994. $900.00. Four volumes.

Encyclopedia of Food and Culture. Gale Cengage Learning. • 2002. $395.00. Three volumes. Contains 600 articles covering various aspects of food and its place in society, from agronomy to zucchini. Includes illustrations and a detailed index.

Foods and Nutrition Encyclopedia. Audrey H. Ensminger and others. CRC Press, Inc. • 1993. $309.95. Second edition. Two volumes.

Wiley Encyclopedia of Food Science and Technology. Frederick J. Francis, editor. John Wiley and Sons, Inc. • 2000. $1,650.00. Second edition. Four volumes. Contains about 400 entries. Coverage includes biotechnology, genetic engineering, nutrition, regulatory matters, food safety, labeling, food substitutes (sugar, fat, dairy), and many other topics.

HANDBOOKS AND MANUALS

Knott's Handbook for Vegetable Growers. Donald N. Maynard and George J. Hochmuth. John Wiley and Sons, Inc. • 1997. $99.00. Fourth edition. Written for commercial vegetable growers, truck farmers, horticulturists, and other professionals. Covers such topics as spacing of plants, disease control, insect pests, seeds, weeds, water management, and irrigation.

Vegetable Growing: Traditional Methods. Arthur Billitt. Trans-Atlantic Publications, Inc. • 1988. $55.00. Third edition.

INTERNET DATABASES

USDA. United States Department of Agriculture. Phone: (202)720-2791 E-mail: agsec@usda.gov • URL: http://www.usda.gov • The USDA home page has six sections: News and Information; What's New; About USDA; Agencies; Opportunities; Search and Help. Keyword searching is offered from the USDA home page and from various individual agency home pages. Agencies are the Economic Research Service, Agricultural Marketing Service, National Agricultural Statistics Service, National Agricultural Library, and about 12 others. Updating varies. Fees: Free.

ONLINE DATABASES

Agricola. U.S. National Agricultural Library. • Covers worldwide agricultural literature. Over 3.3 million citations, 1970 to present, with monthly updates. Inquire as to online cost and availability.

Food Science and Technology Abstracts [online]. IFIS North American Desk. • Produced by International Food Information Service. Provides about 500,000 online citations, with abstracts, to the international literature of food science, technology, commodities, engineering, and processing. Approximately 2,000 periodicals are covered. Time period is 1969 to date, with monthly updates. Inquire as to online cost and availability.

FOODS ADLIBRA. General Mills, Inc. • Contains online citations, with abstracts, to the technical and business literature of food processing and packaging. New products and new ingredients are featured. Covers about 250 trade journals and 500 research journals from 1974 to date, with monthly updates. Inquire as to online cost and availability.

PERIODICALS AND NEWSLETTERS

American Vegetable Grower. Meister Media. • Monthly. $27.47 per year.

Food Distribution Magazine. Phoenix Media Network, Inc. • Monthly. $49.00 per year. Edited for marketers and buyers of domestic and imported, specialty or gourmet food products, including ethnic foods, seasonings, and bakery items.

Journal of Vegetable Crop Production. Haworth Press, Inc. • Semiannual. Institutions, $225.00 per year. Covers the production and marketing of vegetables.

The Packer: Devoted to the Interest of Commericial Growers, Packers, Shippers, Receivers and Retailers of Fruits, Vegetables and Other Products. Vance Publishing Corp., Produce Div. • Weekly. $65.00 per year. *Supplments* available: *Brand Directory* and *Fresh Trends, Packer's Produce Availability and Merchandising Guide* and *Produce Services Sourcebooks.*

Produce Merchandising: The Packer's Retailing and Merchandising Magazine. Vance Publishing Corp. • Monthly. $35.00 per year. Provides information and advice on the retail marketing and promotion of fresh fruits and vegetalbe.

Produce News. Zim-Mer Trade Publications, Inc. • Weekly. $35.00 per year.

Western Grower and Shipper: The Business Magazine of the Western Product Industry. Western Growers Association. • Monthly. $18.00 per year.

STATISTICS SOURCES

Agricultural Statistics. Available from U. S. Government Printing Office. • Annual. $38.00. Produced by the National Agricultural Statistics Service, U. S. Department of Agriculture. Provides a wide variety of statistical data relating to agricultural production, supplies, consumption, prices/price-supports, foreign trade, costs, and returns, as well as farm labor, loans, income, and population. In many cases, historical data is shown annually for 10 years. In addition to farm data, includes detailed fishery statistics.

FAO Production Yearbook. Available from Bernan Associates. • Annual. $45.00. Published by the Food and Agriculture Organization (http://www.fao.org). Contains worldwide data on agriculture, land use, farm crops, livestock, and agricultural prices.

FAO Quarterly Bulletin of Statistics. Food and Agriculture Organization of the United Nations. Available from UNIPUB. • Quarterly. $20.00 per year. Provides international data on agricultural production, trade, and prices, covering the major commodities of many countries. Text in English, French, and Spanish. Formerly *FAO Monthly Bulletin of Statistics.*

FAO Trade Yearbook. Available from Bernan Associates. • Annual. $45.00. Published by the Food and Agriculture Organization (http://www.fao.org). Provides extensive worldwide data on exports and imports of agricultural commodities, fertilizers, tractors, and pesticides. Includes more than 130 tables of detailed statistics.

Vegetables and Specialties Situation and Outlook. Available from U. S. Government Printing Office. • Three times a year. Issued by the Economic Research Service of the U. S. Department of Agriculture. Provides current statistical information on supply, demand, and prices.

World Agricultural Supply and Demand Estimates. Available from U. S. Government Printing Office. • Monthly. $52.00 per year. Issued by the Economics and Statistics Service and the Foreign Agricultural Service of the U. S. Department of Agriculture. Consists mainly of statistical data and tables.

World Food Data and Statistics. Euromonitor International. • 2004. $650.00. Provides five-year data for a wide variety of food products in 52 countries. Includes market size, consumer expenditures, price indicators, and retail distribution data for many kinds of meat, fish, fruits, vegetables, dairy products, baked goods, condiments, canned food, and frozen food.

TRADE/PROFESSIONAL ASSOCIATIONS

United Fresh Fruit and Vegetable Association. 1901 Pennsylvania Ave. NW, Ste. 1100, Washington, DC 20006. Phone: (202)303-3400 Fax: (202)303-3433 E-mail: united@uffva.org • URL: http://www.uffva.org.

OTHER SOURCES

The Market for Value-Added Fresh Produce. MarketResearch.com. • 1999. $2,750.00. Market research report. Covers packaged salad mixes, bulk salad mixes, pre-cut fruits, and pre-cut vegetables. Market projections are provided to the year 2003.

VEGETABLE OIL INDUSTRY

See: OIL AND FATS INDUSTRY

VENDING MACHINES

DIRECTORIES

Automatic Merchandiser Blue Book Buyer's Guide. Cygnus Business Media. • Annual. $35.00. Suppliers of products, services, and equipment to the merchandise vending, contract food services, and office coffee service industries.

National Automatic Merchandising Association-Directory of Members. National Automatic Merchandising Association. • Annual. $150.00. Lists 2,300 vending and food service management firms, along with vending machine manufacturers and distributors and producers of other equipment and food items.

Vending Times Buyers Guide and Directory. Vending Times Inc. • Annual. $35.00. Formerly *Vending Times International Buyers Guide and Directory.*

FINANCIAL RATIOS

Annual Statement Studies. The Risk Management Association. • Annual. Median and quartile financial ratios are given for over 400 kinds of manufacturing, wholesale, retail, construction, and consumer finance establishments. Data is sorted by both asset size and sales volume. Includes a clearly written "Definition of Ratios" and an alphabetical industry index.

Annual Statement Studies: Industry Default Probabilities and Cash Flow Measures. The Risk Management Association. • Annual. $145.00. Serves as a companion volume to the original *Annual Statement Studies.* Gives probability of default estimates on a percentage scale for more than 450 industries. Includes changes in position year-by-year for eight financial statement line items and provides percentage measures of cash flow.

HANDBOOKS AND MANUALS

Making Money with Vending Machines. Billy Mason. Kelso Manufacturing Co. • 1995. $7.00.

INTERNET DATABASES

Manufacturing Profiles. U. S. Bureau of the Census. Phone: (301)763-4636 E-mail: webmaster@census.gov • URL: http://www.census.gov/prod/www/abs/mfg-prof.html • The Census Bureau makes available free on PDF (Portable Document Format) an annual consolidation of the entire Current Industrial Report series, presenting "all the data compiled." Contains statistics on production, shipments, inventories, consumption, exports, imports, and orders for a wide variety of manufactured products.

PERIODICALS AND NEWSLETTERS

Automatic Merchandiser. Cygnus Business Media. • 11 times a year. $66.00 per year. Includes annual

Product issue. Formerly *American Automatic Merchandiser.*

Cash Box: The International Music-Record Weekly. Cash Box Publishing Co., Inc. • Weekly. $185.00 per year.

Vending Times: Vending-Feeding-Coffee Service-Music and Games. Vending Times, Inc. • Monthly. $35.00 per year. Incorporates *V-T Music and Games.*

STATISTICS SOURCES

Annual Survey of Manufactures. Available from U. S. Government Printing Office. • Annual. Prices vary. Issued by the U. S. Census Bureau as an interim update to the *Census of Manufactures.* Includes data on number of manufacturing establishments in various industries, employment, labor costs, value of shipments, capital expenditures, inventories, energy costs, and assets. (See also Census Bureau home page, http://www.census.gov/.).

Vending Machines. U. S. Bureau of the Census. • Annual. Provides data on value of manufacturers' shipments, quantity, exports, imports, etc. (Current Industrial Reports, MA-35U.).

Vending Times Census of the Industry. Vending Times, Inc. • Annual. $25.00.

TRADE/PROFESSIONAL ASSOCIATIONS

National Automatic Merchandising Association. 20 N Wacker Dr., Ste. 3500, Chicago, IL 60606-3102. Phone: 888-337-VEND or (312)346-0370 Fax: (312)704-4140 E-mail: rgeerdes@vending.org • URL: http://www.vending.org • Manufacturing and operating companies in the automatic vending machine industry; food service management firms; office coffee machine operators; suppliers of products and services. Compiles industry statistics.

National Bulk Vendors Association. 191 N Wacker Dr., Ste. 1800, Chicago, IL 60606-1615. Phone: (312)521-2400 Fax: (312)521-2300 E-mail: nbva@muchshelist.com • URL: http://www.nbva.org • Manufacturers, distributors, and operators of bulk vending merchandise and equipment.

VENEERS AND VENEERING

See also: LUMBER INDUSTRY; PLYWOOD INDUSTRY

DIRECTORIES

Where to Buy Hardwood Plywood, Veneer, and Engineered Hardwood Flooring. Hardwood Plywood and Veneer Association. • Annual. Free. Lists about 190 member manufacturers, prefinishers, and suppliers of hardwood veneer and plywood.

PERIODICALS AND NEWSLETTERS

Wood and Wood Products: Furniture, Cabinets, Woodworking and Allied Products Management and Operations. Vance Publishing Corp. • 13 times a year. $55.00 per year.

TRADE/PROFESSIONAL ASSOCIATIONS

American Walnut Manufacturers Association. 6516 Linchmere Ln., Dublin, OH 43017. Phone: (614)923-4421 Fax: (614)923-4421 E-mail: bshardwoods1@yahoo.com • URL: http://www.walnutassociation.org • Manufacturers of hardwood veneer and lumber, especially American black walnut. Seeks to improve the sale of products made from hardwoods through advertising, promotion, sales education, and product improvement; also promotes good forest management.

VENTURE CAPITAL

GENERAL WORKS

The Leap: A Memoir of Love and Madness in the Internet Gold Rush. Tom Ashbrook. Houghton Mifflin

Co. • 2000. $25.00. The author relates his personal and family tribulations while attempting to obtain financing for an eventually successful e-business startup, HomePortfolio.com.

ALMANACS AND YEARBOOKS

National Venture Capital Association Yearbook. Thomson Financial. • Annual. $195.00. Provides a yearly review of the U.S. venture capital industry, including statistical data.

DIRECTORIES

Business Capital Sources. Tyler G. Hicks. IWS Inc. • Covers: about 1,500 banks, insurance and mortgage companies, commercial finance, leasing, and venture capital firms that lend money for business investment. Entries include: Company or institution name, address, phone.

Directory of Venture Capital and Private Equity Firms. Grey House Publishing. • 2003. $450.00. Eighth edition. Provides detailed information on more than 3,000 U. S. and foreign sources of venture capital.

Pratt's Guide to Venture Capital Sources. Thomson Financial. • Annual. $625.00. Describes about 1,400 venture capital firms, including key personnel, capital under management, and recent investments. Company, personnel, and industry indexes are provided.

Venture Capital Directory (Small Business Administration). Forum Publishing Co. • Annual. $12.95. Over 500 members of the Small Business Administration and the Small Business Investment. Companies that provide funding for small and minority businesses.

HANDBOOKS AND MANUALS

Cyberfinance: Raising Capital for the E-Business. Martin B. Robins. CCH, Inc. • 2001. $79.00. Covers the taxation, financial, and legal aspects of raising money for new Internet-based ("dot.com") companies, including the three stages of startup, growth, and initial public offering. (Solutions for Professional Advisers Series).

Financing Your Small Business. Robert Walter. Barron's Educational Series, Inc. • 2004. $18.95. Explains various sources of capital for small businesses, including bank loans, venture capital, and initial public offerings of stock.

Handbook of Alternative Investment Strategies. Thomas Schneeweis and Joseph F. Pescatore, editors. Institutional Investor, Inc., Journals Group. • 1999. $95.00. Covers various forms of alternative investment, including hedge funds, managed futures, derivatives, venture capital, and natural resource financing.

New Venture Creation: Entrepreneurship for the 21st Century. Jeffrey A. Timmons and Stephen Spinelli. McGraw-Hill. • 2003. Sixth edition. Price on application.

SBIC Directory and Handbook of Small Business Finance. International Wealth Success, Inc. • Annual. $15.00 per year. Includes small business investment companies.

Starting on a Shoestring: Building a Business Without a Bankroll. Arnold S. Goldstein. John Wiley and Sons, Inc. • 2002. $19.95. Fourth edition. Includes chapters on venture capital and Small Business Administration (SBA) loans.

Venture Capital: An Authoritative Guide for Investors, Entrepreneurs, and Managers. Douglas A. Lindgren. McGraw-Hill. • 1998. $65.00.

Where to Go When the Bank Says No: Alternatives to Financing Your Business. David R. Evanson. Bloomberg. • 1998. $24.95. Emphasis is on obtaining business financing in the $250,000 to $15,000,000 range. Business plans are discussed.

(Bloomberg Small Business Series).

PERIODICALS AND NEWSLETTERS

Black Enterprise. Earl G. Graves Publishing Co. • Monthly. $17.95 per year. Covers careers, personal finances and leisure.

Corporate Financing Week: The Newsweekly of Corporate Finance, Investment Banking and M and A. Institutional Investor, Inc., Journals Group. • Weekly. $2,550.00 per year. Includes print and online editions. Newsletter for corporate finance officers. Emphasis is on debt and equity financing, mergers, leveraged buyouts, investment banking, and venture capital.

Inc.: The Magazine for Growing Companies. INC. • 18 times a year. $14.00 per year. Edited for small office and office-in-the-home businesses with from one to 25 employees. Covers management, office technology, and lifestyle. Incorporates *Self-Employed Professional.*

The Journal of Business Venturing. Elsevier. • Bimonthly. Individuals, $148.00 per year; institutions, $768.00 per year.

Journal of Private Equity: Strategies and Techniques for Venture Investing. Institutional Investor, Inc., Journals Group. • Quarterly. $450.00 per year. Includes print and online editions. Includes venture capital case histories, financial applications, foreign opportunities, industry analysis, management methods, etc.

Venture Capital Journal. Venture Economics Inc. • Description: Hard news, analysis and data on the North American private equity market.

STATISTICS SOURCES

U. S. Industry and Trade Outlook. Available from National Technical Information Service. • Annual. $69.95. Produced by the International Trade Administration, U. S. Department of Commerce, in a "public-private" partnership with DRI/McGraw-Hill and Standard & Poor's. Provides basic data, outlook for the current year, and "Long-Term Prospects" (five-year projections) for a wide variety of products and services. Includes high technology industries. Formerly *U. S. Industrial Outlook.*

TRADE/PROFESSIONAL ASSOCIATIONS

American Council for Capital Formation. 1750 K St., N.W., Suite 400, Washington, DC 20006. Phone: (202)293-5811 Fax: (202)785-8165 E-mail: info@accf.org • URL: http://www.accf.org • Supports capital formation as a general concept. Formerly American Council on Capitol Gain and Estate Taxation.

Chief Executive Officers Club. 4 W 22nd St., 10th Fl., New York, NY 10010. Phone: (212)925-7911 Fax: (212)925-7463 E-mail: main@ceoclubs.org • URL: http://ceoclubs.org • Serves as a management resource for entrepreneurial managers and their professional advisers. Selects and makes available publications on developing business plans, organizing an entrepreneurial team, attracting venture capital, and obtaining patents, trademarks, and copyrights. Develops, collects, and disseminates information on business trends, new laws and regulations, and tax guidance. Conducts intensive-study courses and seminars. Has identified stages of the entrepreneurial process and, through essays and audiocassettes, addresses problems pertinent to each stage.

Interracial Council for Business Opportunity. 350 5th Ave., Ste. 2202, New York, NY 10118. URL: http://www.mbda.gov • Provides technical and financial assistance to minority business people.

National Association of Investment Companies. 1300 Pennsylvania Ave., N.W., Suite 700, Washington, DC 20004. Phone: (202)289-4336 Fax: (202)289-4329 • Formerly American Association of Minority Enterprise Small Business Investment Companies.

National Association of Small Business Investment Companies. 666 11th St., N.W., No. 750, Washington, DC 20001. Phone: (202)628-5055 Fax: (202)628-5080 E-mail: nasbic@nasbic.org • URL: http://www.nasbic.org • Affiliated with Small Business Legislative Council.

National Business Incubation Association. 20 E Circle Dr., No. 37198, Athens, OH 45701-3571. Phone: (740)593-4331 Fax: (740)593-1996 E-mail: info@nbia.org • URL: http://www.NBIA.org • Incubator developers and managers; corporate joint venture partners, venture capital investors; economic development professionals. (Incubators are business assistance programs providing business consulting services and financing assistance to start-up and fledgling companies.) Helps newly formed businesses to succeed. Educates businesses and investors on incubator benefits; offers specialized training in incubator formation and management. Conducts research and referral services; compiles statistics; maintains speakers' bureau; publishes information relevant to business incubation and growing companies.

National Development Council. 708 Third Ave., Ste. 710, New York, NY 10017. Phone: (212)682-1106 Fax: (212)573-6118 E-mail: training@nationaldevelopmentcouncil.org • URL: http://www.nationaldevelopmentcouncil.org • Brings innovative economic development financing programs to urban and rural communities interested in local business and industrial growth, commercial revitalization, and permanent job creation. Finances professionals' work with cities, counties, and states to: build permanent systems for developing financing; train local staff; structure and negotiate financing for development projects, local business development, and industrial expansion. Conducts intensive training program for economic development professionals with courses in business credit analysis, real estate financing, loan packaging, federal financing, and program management and implementation; has provided advice to congress and federal agencies that has helped create lending programs for job creation and small business investment; has initiated and managed presidential programs for Presidents Nixon, Ford, Carter, and Reagan.

National Venture Capital Association. 1655 N Ft. Myer Dr., Ste. 850, Arlington, VA 22209. Phone: (703)524-2549 Fax: (703)524-3940 E-mail: mheesen@nvca.org • URL: http://www.nvca.org • Venture capital organizations, corporate financiers, and individual venture capitalists who are responsible for investing private capital in young companies on a professional basis. Fosters a broader understanding of the importance of venture capital to the vitality of the U.S. economy and to stimulate the free flow of capital to young companies. Seeks to improve communications among venture capitalists throughout the country and to improve the general level of knowledge of the venturing process in government, universities, and the business community.

OTHER SOURCES

Formation and Financing of Emerging Companies. Daniel E. O'Connor and others. Glasser Legalworks. • Looseleaf. $225.00, including CD-ROM version. Periodic Supplementation. Covers incorporation, bylaws, indemnification, intellectual property, financing sources, venture capital, due diligence, bridge loans, investor rights, compliance, and other legal issues associated with company formation. (Emerging Growth Companies Series.).

Start-Up and Emerging Companies: Planning, Financing, and Operating the Successful Business, with Forms on Disk. American Lawyer Media, Inc. • Looseleaf. $289.00. Two volumes. Updated as needed. Covers a wide variety of business and legal topics relating to new enterprises. Provides informa-

tion on venture financing, formation of corporations, tax laws, limited liability companies, employee benefits, contracts, and accounting. Includes a CD-ROM containing more than 75 sample legal forms, clauses, agreements, organizational resolutions, and checklists. (Law Journal Press).

VETERANS

GENERAL WORKS

Social Security, Medicare, and Government Pensions: Get the Most Out of Your Retirement and Medical Benefits. Joseph Matthews and Dorothy M. Berman. Nolo. • 2002. $29.99. Eighth edition. In addition to the basic topics, includes practical information on Supplemental Security Income (SSI), disability benefits, veterans benefits, 401(k) plans, Medicare HMOs, medigap insurance, Medicaid, and how to appeal decisions. (Social Security, Medicare and Pensions Series).

HANDBOOKS AND MANUALS

Federal Benefits for Veterans and Dependents (Veterans Administration). U.S. Government Printing Office. • Annual. $5.00.

Veterans Benefits Manual. LexisNexis Matthew Bender. • 2003. $125.00. Compiled by the National Veterans Legal Service Program. Explains a wide range of benefits available from the U. S. Department of Veterans Affairs.

INTERNET DATABASES

U. S. Census Bureau: The Official Statistics. U. S. Bureau of the Census. Phone: (301)763-4100 Fax: (301)763-4794 • URL: http://www.census.gov • Web site is "Your Source for Social, Demographic, and Economic Information." Contains "Current U. S. Population Count," "Current Economic Indicators," and a wide variety of data under "Other Official Statistics." Keyword searching is provided. Fees: Free.

PERIODICALS AND NEWSLETTERS

The American Legion Magazine. • Monthly. Free to members; non-members, $15.00 per year.

Military Officer. The Military Officers Association. • Monthly. $20.00 per year. Formerly *The Retired Officer.*

VFW Magazine: Ensuring Rights, Recognition, and Remembrance. Veterans of Foreign Wars of the United States: Ensuring Rights Recognition and Remembrance. • 11 times a year. Free to members; non-members, $10.00 per year. Events and general features.

STATISTICS SOURCES

Annual Report of the Secretary of Veterans Affairs. U.S. Department of Veterans Affairs. • Annual. Shows monies distributed and received by the Dept. of Veterans Affairs. Describes the activities of the Department during the fiscal year.

Budget of the United States Government. U.S. Office of Management and Budget. Available from U.S. Government Printing Office. • Annual. $52.00.

Datapedia of the United States: American History in Numbers. George T. Kurian, editor. Bernan Press. • 2004. $125.00. Third edition. Based on the Census Bureau publication, *Historical Statistics of the United States.* Provides data from Colonial times to the present on agriculture, business, consumer income, energy, finance, labor, national income, population, and many other subjects. Includes "narrative highlights," maps, charts, and statistical projections.

Social Statistics of the United States. Mark S. Littman, editor. Bernan Press. • 2000. $65.00. Includes statistical data on population growth, labor force, occupations, environmental trends, leisure time use, income, poverty, taxes, and other economic or demographic topics.

Statistical Abstract of the United States. Available from U. S. Government Printing Office. • Annual. $51.00. Issued by the U. S. Bureau of the Census.

A Statistical Portrait of the United States: Social Conditions and Trends. Mark S. Littman, editor. Bernan Press. • 1998. $89.00. Covers "social, economic, and environmental trends in the United States over the past 25 years." Includes statistical tables, graphs, and analysis relating to such topics as population, income, poverty, wealth, labor, housing, education, healthcare, air/water quality, and government. (Statistical Portrait of the United States: Social Conditions and Trends Series).

TRADE/PROFESSIONAL ASSOCIATIONS

American Legion. PO Box 1055, PO Box 1055, Indianapolis, IN 46206. Phone: 800-433-3318 or (317)630-1200 Fax: (317)630-1223 E-mail: natlcmdr@legion.org • URL: http://www.legion.org • Consists of honorably discharged wartime veterans of the U.S. armed forces. Provides a unified voice for veterans in Washington, DC. Offers free assistance with Veterans Administration claims and benefits. Sponsors American Legion baseball competition, national high school oratorical contest, and children's services; cosponsors National Education Week. Maintains museum.

Military Officers Association of America. 201 N Washington St., Alexandria, VA 22314-2539. Phone: 800-245-6622 or (703)549-2311 Fax: (703)838-8173 E-mail: msc@moaa.org • URL: http://www.moaa.org • Formerly The Retired Oficers Association.

National Association of State Directors of Veterans Affairs. c/o Joey Strickland Soldiers and Sailors War Memorial Bldg., 1885 Woodale Blvd., 10th Fl., Baton Rouge, LA 70804. Phone: (225)922-0500 Fax: (225)922-0511 E-mail: dperkins@vetaffairs.com • URL: http://www.nasdva.com.

Veterans of Foreign Wars of the United States. 406 W. 34th St., Kansas, MO 64111. Phone: (816)756-3390 Fax: (816)968-1157 E-mail: info@vfw.org • URL: http://www.vfw.org • Affiliated with Ladies Auxiliary to the Veterans of Foreign Wars of the United States.

Women's Army Corps Veterans' Association. PO Box 5577, Fort McClellan, AL 36205-0577. Phone: (256)820-6824 E-mail: info@armywomen.org • URL: http://www.armywomen.org • Veterans of the United States Women's Army Corps and Women's Army Auxiliary Corps, women soldiers and officers of the line who are on a tour of active duty with, or have been honorably discharged from, the United States Army, and women who have served honorably or are serving in the United States Reserve or Army National Guard. Seeks "to be of service to all veterans and the communities in which we live and promote justice, tolerance, peace and goodwill". Conducts hospital and community service programs. Supports the U.S. Army Women's Museum at Ft. Lee, VA. Has assisted in the establishment of Women's Army Corps Veterans Redwood Memorial Grove in Big Basin Redwoods State Park, CA. Conducts charitable projects and educational programs.

VETERINARY PRODUCTS

See also: PET INDUSTRY

ABSTRACTS AND INDEXES

Index Veterinarius: Comprehensive Monthly Subject and Author Index to the World's Veterinary Literature. Availabe in Print and on the Internet. Available from CABI Publishing North America. • Monthly. Institutions, $1,660.00 per year. Annual cumulation. Includes single site internet access.

Published in England by CABI Publishing. Provides worldwide coverage of the literature.

NTIS Alerts: Agriculture & Food. National Technical Information Service. • Semimonthly. $195.00 per year. Provides descriptions of government-sponsored research reports and software, with ordering information. Covers agricultural economics, horticulture, fisheries, veterinary medicine, food technology, and related subjects. Formerly *Abstract Newsletter.*

Review of Medical and Veterinary Entomology. Available from CABI Publishing, North America. • Monthly. Institutions, $855.00 per year. Print and online edition, $885.00 per year. Provides worldwide coverage of the literature. Formerly *Review of Applied Entomology, Series B: Medical and Veterinary.*

ALMANACS AND YEARBOOKS

Advances in Veterinary Medicine. Elsevier. • Irregular. $174.95.

BIOGRAPHICAL SOURCES

AVMA Directory. American Veterinary Medical Association. • Annual. $100.00. 62,500 veterinarians; not limited to AVMA members. Formerly *American Veterinary Medical Association Directory.*

CD-ROM DATABASES

AGRICOLA on SilverPlatter. Available from Silver-Platter Information, Inc. • Quarterly. $825.00 per year. Produced by the National Agricultural Library. Provides about three million citations on CD-ROM to the literature of agriculture, agricultural economics, animal sciences, entomology, fertilizer, food, forestry, nutrition, pesticides, plant science, water resources, and other topics. Each quarterly disc covers the past ten years, with archival discs available from 1970.

DIRECTORIES

BioScan: The Worldwide Biotech Industry Reporting Service. Greenwood Publishing Group, Inc. • Annual. $975.00 per year. Bimonthly updates. Provides detailed information on over 1,000 U.S. and foreign companies broadly classified as biotechnological. In addition to medical technology and advanced pharmaceutical firms, includes firms doing research in food processing, waste management, agriculture, and veterinary science.

ENCYCLOPEDIAS AND DICTIONARIES

Encyclopedia of Agriculture Science. Charles J. Arntzen and Ellen M. Ritter, editors. Elsevier. • 1994. $900.00. Four volumes.

Encyclopedia of Agrochemicals. Jack R. Plimmer. John Wiley and Sons, Inc. • 2003. $945.00. Three volumes. Includes pesticides, animal food additives, veterinary drugs, and other compounds.

HANDBOOKS AND MANUALS

Merck Veterinary Manual: A Handbook of Diagnosis and Therapy for the Veterinarian. Merck and Company, Inc. • 1998. $32.00. 8th revised edition.

ONLINE DATABASES

CAB Abstracts. CAB Publishing North America. • Contains 46 specialized abstract collections covering over 10,000 journals and monographs in the areas of agriculture, horticulture, forest products, farm products, nutrition, dairy science, poultry, grains, animal health, entomology, etc. Time period is 1972 to date, with monthly updates. Inquire as to online cost and availability. *CAB Abstracts on CD-ROM* also available, with annual updating.

Derwent Veterinary Drug File. Derwent, Inc. • Provides indexing and abstracting of the world's veterinary drug literature since 1968, with monthly

updates. Formerly *VETDOC.* Inquire as to online cost and availability.

PERIODICALS AND NEWSLETTERS

American Veterinary Medical Association Journal. American Veterinary Medical Association. • Semimonthly. $120.00 per year.

DVM: The Newsmagazine of Veterinary Medicine. Advanstar Communications, Healthcare Group. • Monthly. $39.00 per year. Includes new drugs and new products.

Veterinary Economics: Business Solutions for Practicing Veterinarians. Thomson Veterinary Healthcare Communications. • Monthly. Free to qualified personnel; others, $42.00 per year. Provides business management and financial articles for veterinarians.

TRADE/PROFESSIONAL ASSOCIATIONS

American Veterinary Exhibitors Association. 712 N Broadway, Menomonie, WI 54751. Phone: 877-990-1836 or (480)990-1887 Fax: (715)232-9936 E-mail: avea@wwt.net • Manufacturers and dealers of products for the veterinary profession. To give firms exhibiting at veterinary conventions a voice in planning the time, place, program, and facilities of such meetings; to cooperate and consult with veterinary associations in matters of mutual interest.

American Veterinary Medical Association. 1931 N Meacham Rd., Ste. 100, Schaumburg, IL 60173. Phone: 800-248-2862 or (847)925-8070 Fax: (847)925-1329 E-mail: avmainfo@avma.org • URL: http://www.avma.org • Professional society of veterinarians. Conducts educational and research programs. Provides placement service. Sponsors American +Veterinary +Medical Association Foundation (also known as AVMF Foundation) and Educational +Commission for +Foreign +Veterinary Graduates. Compiles statistics. Accredits veterinary medical education programs and veterinary technician education programs.

OTHER SOURCES

World Animal Health Markets. Theta Reports. • 2000. $830.00. Market research data. Covers the market for animal health products in 15 major countries, including the U.S. (Theta Report No. SR198E.).

VICE

See: CRIME AND CRIMINALS

VIDEO CAMERAS

See: VIDEO RECORDING INDUSTRY

VIDEO RECORDING INDUSTRY

ABSTRACTS AND INDEXES

Applied Science and Technology Index. H. W. Wilson Co. • 11 times a year. Quarterly and annual cumulations. Price varies. Indexes a wide variety of English language technical, industrial, and engineering periodicals.

Business Periodicals Index. H. W. Wilson Co. • 11 times a year. Quarterly and annual cumulations. Price varies.

Communication Abstracts: An International Information Service. Sage Publications, Inc. • Bimonthly. Institutions, $1,150.00 per year. Provides broad coverage of the literature of communications, including broadcasting and advertising.

Current Contents: Engineering, Computing and Technology. Thomson/ISI. • Weekly. $730.00 per year. Reproductions of contents pages of technical journals. Includes *Author Index, Address Directory, Current Book Contents* and *Title Word Index*. Formerly *Current Contents: Engineering, Technology and Applied Sciences*.

Electronics and Communications Abstracts Journal: Comprehensive Coverage of Essential Scientific Literature. CSA. • Monthly. $1,665.00 per year. Includes print and online editions.

BIBLIOGRAPHIES

Films and Audiovisual Information. Available from U. S. Government Printing Office. • Annual. Free. Issued by the Superintendent of Documents. A list of government publications on motion picture and audiovisual topics. Formerly *Motion Pictures, Films and Audiovisual Information*. (Subject Bibliography No. 73.).

CD-ROM DATABASES

Bowker's Complete Video Directory on Disc. Bowker Electronic Publishing. • Quarterly. $520.00 per year. An extensive CD-ROM directory of video tapes and laserdisks. Includes film reviews from *Variety*.

DIRECTORIES

AV Market Place: The Complete Business Directory of Audio, Audio Visual, Computer Systems, Film, Video, and Programming, with Industry Yellow Pages. Information Today, Inc. • Annual. $195.00. Provides information on "more than 7,500 companies that create, apply, or distribute AV equipment and services for business, education, science, and government." Multimedia, virtual reality, presentation software, and interactive video are among the categories. Formerly published by R. R. Bowker.

Broadcast Engineering--Equipment Reference Manual. Penton Media Inc. • Publication includes: List of more than 1,400 manufacturers and distributors of communications equipment for radio, television, and recording applications. Entries include: For manufacturers--Company name, address. For distributors and dealers--Company name, address, phone, product or service provided, geographic area covered.

Directory of Computer and Consumer Electronics Retailers. Chain Store Guide. • Annual. $335.00. Online edition, $775.00. Lists 4,500 United States and Canada companies operating almost 59,000 stores with at least $1,000,000 in sales.

DV Buyer's Guide. CMP Media LLC. • Annual. $10.00. A directory of professional video products, including digital cameras, monitors, editing systems, and software.

Film and Video Finder. National Information Center for Educational Media. c/o Plexus Publishing, Inc. • Biennial. $295.00. Contains 92,000 listings of film and video educational, technical and vocational children's programs and literary materials.

International Television and Video Almanac: Reference Tool of the Television and Home Video Industries. Quigley Publishing Co., Inc. • Annual. $130.00.

Plunkett's InfoTech Industry Almanac: Complete Profiles on the InfoTech 500-the Leading Firms in the Movement and Management of Voice, Data, and Video. Plunkett Research, Ltd. • Biennial. $229.99. Includes CD-ROM. Five hundred major information companies are profiled, with corporate culture aspects. Discusses major trends in various sectors of the computer and information industry, including data on careers and job growth. Includes several indexes.

Producer's Masterguide: The International Film Production Guide and Directory for Motion Picture, Television, Industries in the United States, the United Kingdom, Europe, the Caribbean Islands, Mexico, Israel, Morocco and Australia. • Annual.

$140.00. A standard reference guide of the professional film, television, commercial and video tape industry throughout the U.S. and Canada, Europe, the Caribbean Islands, Mexico, Israel, Morocco, Australia, etc.

The SHOOT Directory for Commercial Production and Postproduction. SHOOT. • Annual. $79.00. Lists production companies, advertising agencies, and sources of professional television, motion picture, and audio equipment.

Telecommunications Directory. Gale. • Covers: Two volumes-North America and International, Cover approximately 6,000 national and international voice and data communications networks, electronic mail services, teleconferencing facilities and services, facsimile services, Internet access providers, videotex and teletext operations, transactional services, local area networks, audiotex services, microwave systems/networkers, satellite facilities, and others involved in telecommunications, including related consultants, advertisers/marketers; associations, regulatory bodies, and publishers. Entries include: Company or organization name, address, phone, fax, year established, name and title of contact, executive officers and board of directors, function or type of service; geographical area served; NAICS and SIC codes; number of employees; general description, including telecommunications-related activities; product/service; specific applications; means of access and equipment required; publications; intended market and availability; pricing; stock exchanges traded and ticker symbols; financial figures.

Video Recorder Dealers Directory. infoUSA. • Annual. Price on application. Lists over 1,106 dealers. Compiled from U.S. yellow pages.

Video Source Book. Gale. • Covers: Approximately 160,000 videos covering more than 120,000 complete programs available from more than 2,100 distributors. Entries include: Video title, release year, description, run time, format, audience, MPAA rating, credits, producer, awards, distributor, price. Distributor's address and phone are given in a separate list.

Video Systems: Guide to Production Services. Primedia Business Magazines and Media. • Annual. $10.00. Lists about 1,000 firms offering services to videotape production companies. Price on application.

ENCYCLOPEDIAS AND DICTIONARIES

International Film, Television, and Video Acronyms. Matthew Stevens, editor. Greenwood Publishing Group, Inc. • 1993. $85.00. A guide to 3,400 acronyms and 1,400 technical terms.

Multimedia and the Web from A to Z. David C. Leonard and Patrick M. Dillon. Greenwood Publishing Group, Inc. • 1998. $42.95. Second enlarged revised edition. Defines more than 1,500 terms relating to software and hardware in the areas of computing, online technology, telecommunications, audio, video, motion pictures, CD-ROM, and the Internet. Includes acronyms and an annotated bibliography. Formerly *Multimedia Technology from A to Z* (1994).

HANDBOOKS AND MANUALS

Creating Digital Content: A Video Production for Web, Broadcast, and Cinema. John Rice and Brian McKernan. McGraw-Hill. • 2001. $49.95. Discusses the technicalities of digital content with a light touch, as in "Throw Another Analog on the Digital Fire." Other chapter titles are "Digital Recording," "Datacasting," "Coming to a Theatre Near You: Digital Cinema," and "The Promise of Digital Interactive Television.".

Digital Filmmaking 101: An Essential Guide to Producing Low-Budget Movies. Dale Newton and John Gaspard. Michael Wiese Productions. • 2001. $24.95. Using a light touch, covers the essentials of

making a low-budget film, including scripting, budgeting, funding, equipping, casting, and recruiting a crew.

Master Handbook of Video Production. Jerry Whitaker. McGraw-Hill. • 2002. $39.95. Covers such technical topics as facility design, sound isolation, production standards, video signal processing, lighting, and equipment.

Standard Handbook of Video and Television Engineering. Jerry C. Whitaker. McGraw-Hill. • 2000. $150.00. Fourth edition. Covers the design, production, installation, operation, and maintenance of video recording or TV broadcasting facilities.

Video Engineering. Arch Luther and Andrew Inglis. McGraw-Hill. • 2000. $65.00. Third edition. Covers such topics as digital postproduction technology, streaming video on the Internet, digital HDTV, digital cameras, and satellite TV systems.

Videocassette Rental Store. Entrepreneur Media, Inc. • Looseleaf. $59.50. A practical guide to starting a videocassette rental store. Covers profit potential, start-up costs, market size evaluation, owner's time required, site selection, lease negotiation, pricing, accounting, advertising, promotion, etc. (Start-Up Business Guide No. E1192.).

ONLINE DATABASES

Applied Science and Technology Index Online. H. W. Wilson Co. • Provides online indexing of 500 major scientific, technical, industrial, and engineering periodicals. Time period is 1983 to date. Monthly updates. Inquire as to online cost and availability.

Marketing and Advertising Reference Service (MARS). Gale Cengage Learning. • Provides abstracts of literature relating to consumer marketing and advertising, including all forms of advertising media. Time period is 1984 to date. Daily updates. Inquire as to online cost and availability.

PROMT: Predicasts Overview of Markets and Technology. Gale Cengage Learning. • Companies, products, applied technologies and markets. U.S. and international literature coverage, 1972 to date. Inquire as to online cost and availability. Provides abstracts from more than 1,600 publications. Weekly updates.

Wilson Business Abstracts Online. H. W. Wilson Co. • Indexes and abstracts 600 major business periodicals, plus the *Wall Street Journal* and the business section of the *New York Times*. Indexing is from 1982, abstracting from 1990, with the two newspapers included from 1993. Updated weekly. Inquire as to online cost and availability. (*Business Periodicals Index* without abstracts is also available online.).

PERIODICALS AND NEWSLETTERS

Digital Video. CMP Media LLC. • Monthly. $60.00 per year. Edited for professionals in the field of digital video production. Covers such topics as operating systems, videography, digital video cameras, audio, workstations, web video, software development, and interactive television.

Digital Video Magazine. CMP Media LLC. • Monthly. $29.97 per year. Edited for producers and creators of digital media. Includes topics relating to video, audio, animation, multimedia, interactive design, and special effects. Covers both hardware and software, with product reviews. Formerly *Digital Video Magazine*.

EContent: Digital Content Strategies and Resources. Online, Inc. • Monthly. $110.00 per year. Emphasis is on the business management and financial aspects of the digital content industry. (Formerly published by Online, Inc.)

eMedia: The Digital Studio Magazine. Online, Inc. • Monthly. $98.00 per year. Covers video production equipment, digital video editing, electronic publishing, digital content streaming, encoding, and other topics related to digital content creation and multimedia. (Formerly published by Online, Inc.).

Entertainment Law and Finance. American Lawyer Media, Inc. • Monthly. $229.00 per year. Newsletter. Covers contracts, royalties, litigation, copyright, taxation, etc., for the music industry, motion pictures, broadcasting, publishing, video, and related media. (A Law Journal Newsletter, formerly published by Leader Publications.).

Entertainment Marketing Letter. EPM Communications Inc. • Description: Reports on techniques used in the marketing of films, music, videos, television, radio, and cable features. Covers tie-in campaigns, sponsorship, in-theatre advertising, and interactive telephone promotions.

Presentations: Technology and Techniques for Effective Communication. VNU Business Media. • Monthly. Free to qualified personnel; others, $69.00 per year. Covers the use of presentation hardware and software, including audiovisual equipment and computerized display systems. Includes an annual *"Buyers Guide to Presentation Products."*.

SHOOT: The Leading Newsweekly for Commercial Production and Postproduction. VNU Business Media. • Weekly. $125.00 per year. Covers animation, music, sound design, computer graphics, visual effects, cinematography, and other aspects of television and motion picture production, with emphasis on TV commercials.

Smart TV and Sound: Interactive Television and DVD-MP3-Internet Audio and Video-Satellite Television. York Publishing. • Semiannual. $14.97 per year. Consumer magazine covering WebTV, PC/TV appliances, DVD players, "Smart TV," advanced VCRs, and other topics relating to interactive television, the Internet, and multimedia. Formerly *Smart TV.*

Sound & Vision: Home Theater- Audio- Video-MultimediaMovies- Music. Hachette Filipacchi Media U.S., Inc. • 10 times a year. $24.00 per year. Popular magazine providing explanatory articles and critical reviews of equipment and media (CD-ROM, DVD, videocassettes, etc.). Supplement available *Stero Review's Sound and Vision Buyers Guide.* Replaces *Stereo Review* and *Video Magazine.*

T W I C E: This Week in Consumer Electronics. Reed Business Information. • 29 times a year. $129.90 per year. Contains marketing and manufacturing news relating to a wide variety of consumer electronic products, including video, audio, telephone, and home office equipment.

Television Digest with Consumer Electronics. Warren Publishing, Inc. • Weekly. $944.00 per year. Newsletter featuring new consumer entertainment products utilizing electronics. Also covers the television broadcasting and cable TV industries, with corporate and industry news.

Television Week. Crain Communications, Inc. • Weekly. $119.00 per year. Formerly *Electronic Media.*

Video Investor. Kagan World Media. • Description: Reports videocassette industry developments, including sales statistics and forecasts. Provides news of related conventions and events and focuses on sales and rentals of film product, performance of retail outlets, market shares of suppliers and distributors, the sale of chains and outlets, hardware revenues and sales, and laser disk technologies. **Remarks:** Also available via e-mail and fax.

Video Librarian: The Video Review Magazine. Video Librarian. • Bimonthly. $64.00 per year. $99.00 per year with online access to archives (15,000 reviews). Edited for public and school libraries. Each issue includes reviews of hundreds of video DVDs or cassettes, in various subject areas.

Video Store Magazine. Advantar Communications. • Weekly. $105.99 per year.

Video Systems: The Magazine for Video Professionals. Primedia Business Magazines and Media. • Monthly. $70.00 per year.

Video Week: Devoted to the Business of Program Sales and Distribution for Videocassettes, Disc, Pay TV and Allied News Media. Warren Publishing Inc. • Weekly. $907.00 per year. Newsletter. Covers video industry news and corporate developments.

Videography. United Entertainment Media. • Monthly. $72.00 per year. Edited for the professional video production industry. Covers trends in technique and technology.

PRICE SOURCES

Video and Television. Orion Research Corp. • Annual. $144.00. Quotes retail and wholesale prices of used video and TV equipment. Original list prices and years of manufacture are also shown.

STATISTICS SOURCES

Standard & Poor's Industry Surveys. Standard & Poor's. • Semiannual. $1,800.00. Two looseleaf volumes. Includes monthly *Supplements.* Provides detailed, individual surveys of 52 major industry groups. Each survey is revised on a semiannual basis. Also includes "Monthly Investment Review" (industry group investment analysis) and monthly "Trends & Projections" (economic analysis).

U. S. Industry and Trade Outlook. Available from National Technical Information Service. • Annual. $69.95. Produced by the International Trade Administration, U. S. Department of Commerce, in a "public-private" partnership with DRI/McGraw-Hill and Standard & Poor's. Provides basic data, outlook for the current year, and "Long-Term Prospects" (five-year projections) for a wide variety of products and services. Includes high technology industries. Formerly *U. S. Industrial Outlook.*

TRADE/PROFESSIONAL ASSOCIATIONS

Association of Cinema and Video Laboratories. c/o Rob Monaco, Monaco Labs and Video, 234 Ninth St., San Francisco, CA 15205. Phone: (415)864-5350 Fax: (415)864-5682 E-mail: usc7153@email. msn.com • URL: http://www.acvl.org.

Association of Imaging Technology and Sound. 1899 L St., NW, Ste. 600, Washington, DC 20036-3849. E-mail: katy@itsnet.org • Members are individuals interested in various aspects of prerecorded videotape production. Acts as a source of general information about videotape.

Content Delivery and Storage Association. 182 Nassau St., Ste. 204, Princeton, NJ 08542-7005. Phone: (609)279-1700 Fax: (609)279-1999 E-mail: info@contentdeliveryandstorage.org • URL: http://www.recordingmedia.org • Serves as the advocate for the growth and development of all recording media and as a forum for the exchange of information regarding global trends and innovations. Provides members an opportunity to join forces and be a strong industry voice allowing them to grow and expand their business. Encompasses all facets of the recording media.

Entertainment Software Association. 575 7th St. NW, Ste. 300, Washington, DC 20004. Phone: (202)223-2400 E-mail: esa@theesa.com • URL: http://www.theesa.com • Represents the interactive entertainment software publishing industry. Established an autonomous rating board to rate interactive entertainment software. Established a program to combat piracy in the United States and around the world. Represents members on industry issues at the federal and state level. Provides market research and information. **Publications:** none.

Home Recording Rights Coalition. PO Box 14267, Washington, DC 20044-4267. Phone: 800-282-8273 or (202)628-9212 Fax: (202)628-9227 E-mail: info@hrrc.org • URL: http://www.hrrc.org • Consumers, retailers, and manufacturers of audio and video electronics products. Advocates the

consumer's right to use consumer electronics equipment for private, noncommercial purposes; current issues range from new audio and video technologies to the digital information superhighway and multimedia.

InfoComm International. 11242 Waples Mill Rd., Ste. 200, Fairfax, VA 22030-6079. Phone: 800-659-7469 or (703)273-7200 Fax: (703)278-8082 E-mail: customerservice@infocomm.org • URL: http://www.infocomm.org • Represents for-profit individuals and organizations that derive revenue from the commercialization or utilization of communications technology. Ensures the credibility and desirability of its members' products and services by representing the communications industry to the public, business, education, and governments.

Media Communications Association International. 2810 Crossroads Dr., Ste. 3800, Madison, WI 53718. Phone: (608)443-2464 Fax: (608)443-2474 E-mail: info@mca-i.org • URL: http://www.mca-i.org • Individuals engaged in multimedia communications needs analysis, scriptwriting, producing, directing, consulting, and operations management in the video, multimedia, and film fields. Seeks to advance the benefits and image of media communications professionals.

National Association of Video Distributors. 700 Frederica St., Suite 205, Owensboro, KY 42301. Phone: (270)926-6002 Fax: (270)685-6080 • Members are wholesalers of home video software, both tapes and discs.

Professional Audiovideo Retailers Association. 2500 Wilson Blvd., Arlington, VA 22201-3834. Phone: (630)268-1500 Fax: (630)953-8957 E-mail: para@ce.org • URL: http://www.paralink.org • Retailers of specialty high end audio/video equipment. To educate the public on the value, desirability, and quality of audio equipment; to unite manufacturers for the exchange of information on the latest equipment and technological advancements in the industry. Provides computer seminar, service managers seminar, sales training course, and retail financial management course. Offers correspondence course leading to certification as professional audio specialist.

Semiconductor Industry Association. 181 Metro Dr., Ste. 450, San Jose, CA 95110-1344. Phone: (408)436-6600 Fax: (408)436-6646 E-mail: mailbox@sia-online.org • URL: http://www.sia-online.org/home.cfm • Companies that produce semiconductor products such as discrete components, integrated circuits, and microprocessors. Compiles industry trade statistics. Affiliate: Semiconductor Research Corporation and SEMATECH.

Video Software Dealers Association. 16530 Ventura Blvd., Ste. 400, Encino, CA 91436-4551. Phone: 800-955-8732 or (818)385-1500 Fax: (818)385-0567 E-mail: vsdaoffice@vsda.org • URL: http://www.vsda.org • Retailers and distributors of videocassettes and videodiscs; associate members are major studios or independent companies that produce video programming and manufacturers of video games, accessories, and other goods and services for the video software industry. Represents and acts as spokesperson for the video software merchandising industry. Conducts statistical survey of video retailing; offers legal counsel representing members' interests in Washington, DC. Offers seminars on management and inventory control.

OTHER SOURCES

DVD Assessment, No. 3. Julie B. Schwerin and Theodore A. Pine. InfoTech, Inc. • 1998. $1,295.00. Third edition. Provides detailed market research data on Digital Video Discs (also known as Digital Versatile Discs). Includes history of DVD, technical specifications, DVD publishing outlook, "Industry Overview," "Market Context," "Infrastructure

Analysis," "Long-Range Forecast to 2005," and emerging technologies.

Optical Publishing Industry Assessment. Julie B. Schwerin and Theodore A. Pine. InfoTech, Inc. • 1997. $1,295.00. Ninth edition. Provides market research data and forecasts to 2005 for DVD-ROM, "Hybrid ROM/Online Media," and other segments of the interactive, entertainment, digital information, and consumer electronics industries. Covers both software (content) and hardware. Includes Video-CD, DVD- Video, CD-Audio, DVD-Audio, DVD-ROM, PC-Desktop, TV Set-Top, CD-R, CD-RW, DVD-R and DVD-RAM.

U. S. Home Theater Market. Available from MarketResearch.com. • 1997. $3750.00. Market research report published by Packaged Facts. Covers big-screen TV, high definition TV, audio equipment, and video sources. Market projections are provided.

Videolog. Muze, Inc. • Annual. $250.00. Five volumes. Provides detailed information on more than 170,000 VHS and DVD video titles. Includes a "Directory of Stars and Directors" and 13 category sections.

VIDEOCASSETTES

See: VIDEO RECORDING INDUSTRY

VIDEODISCS

See: VIDEO RECORDING INDUSTRY

VIDEOTAPE

See: VIDEO RECORDING INDUSTRY

VIDEOTEX/TELETEXT

GENERAL WORKS

Interactive Television Demystified. Jerry C. Whitaker. McGraw-Hill. • 2001. $49.95. Discusses the current applications and future possibilities of interactive TV, including business models. Case histories are provided. (Demystified Series).

ALMANACS AND YEARBOOKS

Interactive TV Investor. Paul Kagan Associates, Inc. • Semimonthly. $895.00. Provides current information on interactive-TV applications and technical developments. Includes forecasts. Formerly *Interactive Television.*

CD-ROM DATABASES

LISA Plus. Available from Cambridge Scientific Abstracts (CSA). • Quarterly. $2,000.00 per year. CD-ROM version of Library Information and Science Abstracts, providing abstracting and indexing of the world's library and information science literature, 1969 to date. Contains more than 180,000 citations.

DIRECTORIES

DV Buyer's Guide. CMP Media LLC. • Annual. $10.00. A directory of professional video products, including digital cameras, monitors, editing systems, and software.

Interactive TV Investor Buyer's Guide and Directory. Paul Kagan Associates Inc. • Annual. Price on application. (A special issue of the periodical *Convergence.*).

SRDS Interactive Advertising Source. SRDS. • Quarterly. $569.00 per year. Provides descriptive profiles, rates, audience, personnel, etc., for producers of various forms of interactive or multimedia advertising: online/Internet, CD-ROM, interactive

TV, interactive cable, interactive telephone, interactive kiosk, and others.

Telecommunications Directory. Gale. • Covers: Two volumes-North America and International, Cover approximately 6,000 national and international voice and data communications networks, electronic mail services, teleconferencing facilities and services, facsimile services, Internet access providers, videotex and teletext operations, transactional services, local area networks, audiotex services, microwave systems/networkers, satellite facilities, and others involved in telecommunications, including related consultants, advertisers/marketers; associations, regulatory bodies, and publishers. Entries include: Company or organization name, address, phone, fax, year established, name and title of contact, executive officers and board of directors, function or type of service; geographical area served; NAICS and SIC codes; number of employees; general description, including telecommunications-related activities; product/service; specific applications; means of access and equipment required; publications; intended market and availability; pricing; stock exchanges traded and ticker symbols; financial figures.

ENCYCLOPEDIAS AND DICTIONARIES

Multimedia and the Web from A to Z. David C. Leonard and Patrick M. Dillon. Greenwood Publishing Group, Inc. • 1998. $42.95. Second enlarged revised edition. Defines more than 1,500 terms relating to software and hardware in the areas of computing, online technology, telecommunications, audio, video, motion pictures, CD-ROM, and the Internet. Includes acronyms and an annotated bibliography. Formerly *Multimedia Technology from A to Z* (1994).

HANDBOOKS AND MANUALS

Creating Digital Content: A Video Production for Web, Broadcast, and Cinema. John Rice and Brian McKernan. McGraw-Hill. • 2001. $49.95. Discusses the technicalities of digital content with a light touch, as in "Throw Another Analog on the Digital Fire." Other chapter titles are "Digital Recording," "Datacasting," "Coming to a Theatre Near You: Digital Cinema," and "The Promise of Digital Interactive Television.".

Interactive Computer Systems: Videotex and Multimedia. Antone F. Alber. Perseus Publishing. • 1993. $79.50.

ONLINE DATABASES

LISA: Library and Information Science Abstracts. Available from Cambridge Scientific Abstracts (CSA). • Provides abstracting and indexing of the world's library and information science literature, 1969 to date. Covers more than 440 periodicals from 68 countries. Updating is biweekly. Inquire as to online cost and availability.

PROMT: Predicasts Overview of Markets and Technology. Gale Cengage Learning. • Companies, products, applied technologies and markets. U.S. and international literature coverage, 1972 to date. Inquire as to online cost and availability. Provides abstracts from more than 1,600 publications. Weekly updates.

PERIODICALS AND NEWSLETTERS

Computer Video. IMAS Publishing, Inc. • Bimonthly. $35.00 per year.

Convergence: The Journal of Research Into New Media Technologies. Reed Business Information. • Monthly. Individuals, $40.00 per year; institutions, $160.00 per year. Covers the merging of communications technologies. Includes telecommunications networks, interactive TV, multimedia, wireless phone service, and electronic information services.

Digital Imaging: The Magazine for the Imaging Professional. Cygnus Business Media, Inc. • Bimonthly. $24.95 per year. Edited for business and

professional users of electronic publishing products and services. Topics covered include document imaging, CD-ROM publishing, digital video, and multimedia services. Formerly *Micro Publishing News.*

Digital Video. CMP Media LLC. • Monthly. $60.00 per year. Edited for professionals in the field of digital video production. Covers such topics as operating systems, videography, digital video cameras, audio, workstations, web video, software development, and interactive television.

Interactive Home: Consumer Technology Monthly. Jupiter Communications. • Monthly. $625.00 per year; with online edition, $725.00 per year. Newsletter on devices to bring the Internet into the average American home. Covers TV set-top boxes, game devices, telephones with display screens, handheld computer communication devices, the usual PCs, etc.

Report on Electronic Commerce: Online Business, Financial and Consumer Strategies and Trends. Aspen Publishers. • Biweekly. $1,789.00 per year. Newsletter. Includes *Daily Multimedia News Service.* Incorporates *Interactive Services Report.*

Smart TV and Sound: Interactive Television and DVD-MP3-Internet Audio and Video-Satellite Television. York Publishing. • Semiannual. $14.97 per year. Consumer magazine covering WebTV, PC/TV appliances, DVD players, "Smart TV," advanced VCRs, and other topics relating to interactive television, the Internet, and multimedia. Formerly *Smart TV.*

Telecons. Applied Business Telecommunications. • Bimonthly. $30.00 per year. Topics include teleconferencing, videoconferencing, distance learning, telemedicine, and telecommuting.

Telematics and Informatics: An International Journal on Telecommunications and Internet Technology. Elsevier. • Four times a year. Institutions, $938.00 per year.

Television Week. Crain Communications, Inc. • Weekly. $119.00 per year. Formerly *Electronic Media.*

Video Systems: The Magazine for Video Professionals. Primedia Business Magazines and Media. • Monthly. $70.00 per year.

Videography. United Entertainment Media. • Monthly. $72.00 per year. Edited for the professional video production industry. Covers trends in technique and technology.

Wired. Wired Ventures Ltd. • Monthly. $10.00 per year. Edited for creators and managers in various areas of electronic information and entertainment, including multimedia, the Internet, and video. Often considered to be the primary publication of the "digital generation.".

PRICE SOURCES

Opportunities in Interactive TV Applications & Services: An Analysis of Market Interest & Price Sensitivity. Available from MarketResearch.com. • 2001. $1,395. Published by TechTrends, Inc. Market research data. Includes an analysis of how much consumers are willing to pay per month for each application.

RESEARCH CENTERS AND INSTITUTES

Media Laboratory. Massachusetts Institute of Technology, 20 Ames St., Room E-15, Cambridge, MA 02139-4307. Phone: (617)253-0300 Fax: (617)258-6264 E-mail: casr@media.mit.edu • URL: http://www.media.mit.edu • Research areas include electronic publishing, spatial imaging, human-machine interface, computer vision, and advanced television.

TRADE/PROFESSIONAL ASSOCIATIONS

Association for Interactex Marketing. 1430 Broadway, 8th Fl., New York, NY 10018. Phone:

888-337-0008 or (212)790-1408 Fax: (212)391-9233 • URL: http://www.interactivehq.org • Members are companies engaged in various interactive enterprises, utilizing the internet, interactive television, computer communications and multimedia. Formerly Association for Interactive Media.

Association of Internet Professionals. 2929 Main St., No. 136, Santa Monica, CA 90405. Phone: (866)247-9700 or (501)423-2248 Fax: (501)423-2248 E-mail: info@association.org • URL: http://www.iproa.org • Members are interactive media professionals concerned with intetractive arts and technologies. Formerly International Interactive Communications Society.

OTHER SOURCES

Key Note Market Report: Home Shopping. Jupitermedia. • 2001. $400.00. Market research report. Covers "interactive retailing," mainly through the Internet and television, with predictions of future trends. Formerly *Key Note Report: Home Shopping.*

The Market for Interactive Television. MarketResearch.com. • 2000. $995.00. Market research data.

North American Interactive Television Markets. Available from MarketResearch.com. • 1999. $3,450.00. Published by Frost & Sullivan. Contains market research data on growth, end-user trends, and market strategies. Company profiles are included.

World Interactive Television and Video Transmission Overview. Primary Research. • 1994. Contains market research data. Price on application.

VIEWTEXT

See: VIDEOTEX/TELETEXT

VIRTUAL REALITY

See also: COMPUTER ANIMATION

GENERAL WORKS

Data Smog: Surviving the Information Glut. David Shenk. HarperSanFrancisco. • 1997. $14.00. A critical view of both the electronic and print information industries. Emphasis is on information overload.

Virtual Realism. Michael Heim. Oxford University Press. • 1998. $21.00. Discusses computer simulation and human/computer interaction.

Virtual Reality: Computers Mimic the Physical World. Sean M. Grady. Facts on File, Inc. • 1998. $25.00. (Science Sourcebooks Series.).

What Will Be: How the New World of Information Will Change Our Lives. Michael L. Dertouzos. DIANE Publishing Co. • 1997. $25.00. A discussion of the "information market place" of the future, including telecommuting, virtual reality, and computer recognition of speech. The author is director of the MIT Laboratory for Computer Science.

ABSTRACTS AND INDEXES

Internet and Personal Computing Abstracts [print edition]. EBSCO Publishing. • Quarterly. $269.00 per year, including cumulative index. Provides more than 10,000 abstracts annually from both trade and academic publications. Covers computer hardware, software, product reviews, Web topics, e-commerce, networks, corporate news, security, and related topics. Formerly *Microcomputer Abstracts.*

ALMANACS AND YEARBOOKS

Virtual Reality Annual International Symposium. IEEE Computer Society. • Annual. $70.00.

CD-ROM DATABASES

Computer Database. Gale Cengage Learning. • Provides one year of full-text on CD-ROM for 150

leading computer-related publications. Also includes 70,000 product specifications and brief profiles of 13,000 computer product vendors and manufacturers.

DIRECTORIES

AV Market Place: The Complete Business Directory of Audio, Audio Visual, Computer Systems, Film, Video, and Programming, with Industry Yellow Pages. Information Today, Inc. • Annual. $195.00. Provides information on "more than 7,500 companies that create, apply, or distribute AV equipment and services for business, education, science, and government." Multimedia, virtual reality, presentation software, and interactive video are among the categories. Formerly published by R. R. Bowker.

Data Sources: The Comprehensive Guide to the Data Processing Industry: Hardware, Data Communications Products, Software, Company Profiles. Gale Cengage Learning. • Semiannual. $455.00 per year. Two volumes. Describes hardware and software for all computer operating sysems, including prices and technical details. Lists about 75,000 products from 14,000 suppliers. Industry-specific software applications are described.

ENCYCLOPEDIAS AND DICTIONARIES

Acronyms of Computer Science and Communications: A Comprehensive Acronym Dictionary and Illustrated Encyclopedia. Enjob Kajan and Ejub Kajan. Springer Verlag. • 2002. $49.95. Explains more than 4,000 "broadly used" computer, telecommunications, and information technology acronyms. Includes illustrations and Web addresses, where applicable.

Encyclopedia of Emerging Industries. Gale Cengage Learning. • 2001. $320.00. Fourth edition. Provides detailed information on 115 "newly flourishing" industries. Includes historical background, organizational structure, significant individuals, current conditions, major companies, work force, technology trends, research developments, and other industry facts.

Encyclopedia of Information Systems. Hossein Bidgoli, editor. Elsevier. • 2002. $1,200.00. Four volumes. Contains a wide range of articles relating to computers, databases, communication, and information technology. The 200 topics include coverage of hardware, software, artificial intelligence, the Internet, networks, knowledge management, electronic commerce, search engines, and systems design.

New Hacker's Dictionary. Eric S. Raymond. MIT Press. • 1996. $65.00. Third edition. Includes three classifications of hacker communication: slang, jargon, and "techspeak.".

HANDBOOKS AND MANUALS

PC Graphics Handbook. Julio Sanchez and Maria P. Canton. CRC Press. • 2003. $129.95. Covers both the hardware and software specifics of PC graphics programming. Includes such practical and theoretical topics as graphics algorithms, relevant mathematics, artificial life, virtual reality, device drivers, antimation techniques, and video games.

INTERNET DATABASES

InfoTech Trends. Data Analysis Group. Phone: (925)462-1202 Fax: (925)462-1225 E-mail: support@infotechtrends.com • URL: http://www.infotechtrends.com • Web site provides both free and fee-based market research data on the information technology industry, including computers, peripherals, telecommunications, the Internet, software, CD-ROM/DVD, e-commerce, and workstations. Fees: Free for current (most recent year) data; more extensive information has various fee structures. Formerly *Computer Industry Forecasts.*

Wired News. Lycos, Inc. Phone: (415)276-8400 Fax:

(415)276-8500 E-mail: newsfeedback@wired.com • URL: http://www.wired.com • Provides summaries and full-text of "Top Stories" relating to the Internet, computers, multimedia, telecommunications, and the electronic information industry in general. These news stories are placed in the broad categories of Politics, Business, Culture, and Technology. Affiliated with *Wired* magazine. Fees: Free.

PERIODICALS AND NEWSLETTERS

IMAGES. IMAGE Society. • Semiannual. $25.00 per year. Newsletter Provides news of virtual reality developments and the IMAGE Society.

RESEARCH CENTERS AND INSTITUTES

Electronic Visualization Laboratory. University of Illinois at Chicago, Engineering Research Facility, 842 W. Taylor St., Room 2032, Chicago, IL 60607-7053. Phone: (312)996-3002 Fax: (312)413-7585 E-mail: tom@uic.edu • URL: http://www.evl.uic.edu • Research areas include computer graphics, virtual reality, multimedia, and interactive techniques.

Graphics, Visualization, and Usability Center. Georgia Institute of Technology. GVU Center, 801 Atlantic Dr., Atlanta, GA 30332-0280. Phone: (404)894-4488 Fax: (404)894-0673 E-mail: afb@cc.gatech.edu • URL: http://www.cc.gatech.edu/gvu/ • Research areas include computer graphics, multimedia, image recognition, interactive graphics systems, animation, and virtual realities.

Studio for Creative Inquiry. Carnegie Mellon University, College of Fine Arts, Pittsburgh, PA 15213-3890. Phone: (412)268-3454 Fax: (412)268-2829 E-mail: mmbm@andrew.cmu.edu/ • URL: http://www.cmu.edu/studio/ • Research areas include artificial intelligence, virtual reality, hypermedia, multimedia, and telecommunications, in relation to the arts.

TRADE/PROFESSIONAL ASSOCIATIONS

IMAGE Society. PO Box 6221, Chandler, AZ 85246-6221. Phone: (602)839-8709 E-mail: image@asu.edu • URL: http://image-society.org • Individuals and organizations interested in the technological advancement and application of realtime visual simulation (medical, virtual reality, telepresence, aeronautical, and automotive) and other related virtual reality technologies.

VIRUSES, COMPUTER

See: COMPUTER CRIME AND SECURITY

VISUAL EDUCATION

See: AUDIOVISUAL AIDS IN EDUCATION

VITAL STATISTICS

See also: CENSUS REPORTS; POPULATION

ALMANACS AND YEARBOOKS

Vital Signs [year]: The Trends That Are Shaping Our Future. Worldwatch Institute. • Annual. $14.95. Provides access to selected indicators showing social, economic, and environmental trends throughout the world. Includes data relating to food, energy, transportation, finance, population, and other topics.

BIBLIOGRAPHIES

Vital and Health Statistics. Available from U. S. Government Printing Office. • Annual. Free. Lists government publications. (GPO Subject Bibliography Number 121).

CD-ROM DATABASES

OECD Statistical Compendium. Organization for Economic Cooperation and Development. •

Semiannual. $1,905.00 per year for 1 to 10 users. CD-ROM contains more than 730,000 monthly, quarterly, and annual time series for OECD countries, 1960 to date. Includes fully searchable data on agriculture, food, economic indicators, national accounts, employment, energy, finance, industry, technology, and foreign trade. Results can be displayed in various forms.

Statistical Abstract of the United States on CD-ROM. Hoover's, Inc. • Annual. $49.95. Provides all statistics from official print version, plus expanded historical data, greater detail, and keyword searching features.

DIRECTORIES

Where to Write for Vital Records: Births, Deaths, Marriages, and Divorces. Available from U. S. Government Printing Office. • 2002. $3.00. Issued by the National Center for Health Statistics, U. S. Department of Health and Human Services. Arranged by state. Provides addresses, telephone numbers, and cost of copies for various kinds of vital records or certificates. (DHHS Publication No. PHS 93-1142.).

HANDBOOKS AND MANUALS

International Vital Records Handbook: Births, Marriages, Deaths. Thomas J. Kemp. Genealogical Publishing Co., Inc. • 2000. $34.95. Fourth edition. Provides procedures and copies of forms for obtaining birth, marriage, divorce, and death records from 67 countries and territories in North America, the British Isles and other English-speaking countries and Europe.

INTERNET DATABASES

Business 2.0 Web Guide to the Best Business Links. Business 2.0 Media Inc. Phone: (415)293-4800 E-mail: support@business2.com • URL: http://www.business2.com/webguide • Web site presents an extensive, searchable directory of links to "the best, most informative, and authoritative web pages." Twenty main categories cover business, finance, career, company information, people, and technology topics, with thousands of subtopics, all linking to Web sites recommended by experienced business researchers. Fees: Free.

Fedstats. Federal Interagency Council on Statistical Policy. Phone: (202)395-7254 • URL: http://www.fedstats.gov • Web site features an efficient search facility for full-text statistics produced by more than 100 federal agencies, including the Census Bureau, the Bureau of Economic Analysis, and the Bureau of Labor Statistics. Boolean searches can be made within one agency or for all agencies combined. Links are offered to international statistical bureaus, including the UN, IMF, OECD, UNESCO, Eurostat, and 20 individual countries. Fees: Free.

FreeLunch.com. Economy.com, Inc. Phone: (610)696-8700 Fax: (610)696-1678 • URL: http://www.freelunch.com • Web site provides free access to more than 1.5 million economic and financial data series, covering industry, demographics, labor markets, prices, retail sales, government spending, trade, interest rates, housing starts, the stock market, and many other topics. Data is available for various time periods in either chart or table form. Searching is offered. Fees: Free, but registration required. Economy.com, Inc. also offers fee-based economic analysis at *The Dismal Scientist* site (http://www.dismal.com).

National Center for Health Statistics: Monitoring the Nation's Health. National Center for Health Statistics, Centers for Disease Control and Preventio. Phone: (301)458-4000 E-mail: nchsquery@cdc.gov • URL: http://www.cdc.gov/nchswww • Web site provides detailed data on diseases, vital statistics, and health care in the U. S. Includes a search facility and links to many other health-related Web sites. "Fastats A to Z" offers quick data on hundreds of topics from Accidents to

Work-Loss Days, with links to Comprehensive Data and related sources. Frequent updates. Fees: Free.

U. S. Census Bureau: The Official Statistics. U. S. Bureau of the Census. Phone: (301)763-4100 Fax: (301)763-4794 • URL: http://www.census.gov • Web site is "Your Source for Social, Demographic, and Economic Information." Contains "Current U. S. Population Count," "Current Economic Indicators," and a wide variety of data under "Other Official Statistics." Keyword searching is provided. Fees: Free.

PERIODICALS AND NEWSLETTERS

World Watch: Working for a Sustainable Future. Worldwatch Institute. • Bimonthly. $25.00 per year. Emphasis is on environmental trends, including developments in population growth, climate change, human behavior, the role of government, and other factors.

RESEARCH CENTERS AND INSTITUTES

Worldwatch Institute. Worldwatch Institute. 1776 Massachusetts Ave. NW, Washington, DC 20036-1904. Phone: (202)452-1999 or (202)452-1999 Fax: (202)296-7365 E-mail: worldwatch@worldwatch.org • URL: http://www.worldwatch.org • Global trends in the availability and management of both human and natural resources, including research in energy, food policy, population, development, technology, the environment, economics, toxics, and recycling.

STATISTICS SOURCES

County and City Data Book 2000: A Statistical Abstract Supplement. Available from U. S. Government Printing Office. • 2002. $68.00. 13th edition. Issued by the U. S. Bureau of the Census (http://www.census.gov). Contains a wide variety of data on 3,141 U.S. counties, 1,078 cities, and 11,097 places of 2,500 or more inhabitants. Includes statistical information on retailing, manufacturing, banking, service industries, income, employment, housing, education, crime, and population. Updated metropolitan areas are included.

County and City Extra: Annual Metro, City and County Data Book. Deirdre A. Gaquin and Mark S. Littman. Bernan Press. • 2001. $120.00. Updates and augments data published irregularly in print form by the U. S. Census Bureau in *County and City Data Book.* Covers "every state, county, metropolitan area, and congressional district in the United States, as well as all U. S. cities with a 1990 population of 25,000 or more." Contains a wide range tic maps.

County and City Extra: Special Decennial Census Edition. Deirdre A. Gaquin and Katherine A. DeBrandt, editors. Bernan Press. • 2002. $95.00. Presents conveniently arranged population, housing, and other data from the 2000 census, with many 1980 and 1990 comparisons. Includes maps and tables with rankings of about 20 items for various geographic locations. Complements the annual *County and City Extra.*

Current Population Reports: Population Characteristics, Special Studies, and Consumer Income, Series P-20, P-23, and P-60. Available from U. S. Government Printing Office. • Irregular. $80.00 per year. Issued by the U.S. Bureau of the Census (http://www.census.gov). Each issue covers a special topic relating to population or income. Series P-20, *Population Characteristics*, provides statistical studies on such items as mobility, fertility, education, and marital status. Series P-23, *Special Studies*, consists of occasional reports on methodology. Series P-60, *Consumer Income*, publishes reports on income in relation to age, sex, education, occupation, family size, etc.

Datapedia of the United States: American History in Numbers. George T. Kurian, editor. Bernan Press. • 2004. $125.00. Third edition. Based on the Census Bureau publication, *Historical Statistics of the*

United States. Provides data from Colonial times to the present on agriculture, business, consumer income, energy, finance, labor, national income, population, and many other subjects. Includes "narrative highlights," maps, charts, and statistical projections.

Gale Country and World Rankings Reporter. Gale Cengage Learning. • 1997. $160.00. Second edition. Provides about 3,000 statistical ranking tables and charts covering more than 235 nations. Sources include the United Nations and various government publications.

Gale State Rankings Reporter. Gale Cengage Learning. • 1996. $130.00. Second edition Provides 3,000 ranked lists of states under 35 subject headings. Sources are newspapers, periodicals, books, research institute publications, and government publications.

Health and Environment in America's Top-Rated Cities: A Statistical Profile. Grey House Publishing. • Biennial. $125.00. Covers 75 U. S. cities. Includes statistical and other data on a wide variety of topics, such as air quality, water quality, recycling, hospitals, physicians, health care costs, death rates, infant mortality, accidents, and suicides.

Health, United States, 1999: Health and Aging Chartbook. Available from U. S. Government Printing Office. • 1999. $43.00. Issued by the National Center for Health Statistics, U. S. Department of Health and Human Services. Contains 34 bar charts in color, with related statistical tables. Provides detailed data on persons over 65 years of age, including population, living arrangements, life expectancy, nursing home residence, poverty, health status, assistive devices, health insurance, and health care expenditures.

Monthly Bulletin of Statistics. United Nations Publications. • Monthly. $295.00 per year. Provides current data for about 200 countries on a wide variety of economic, industrial, and demographic subjects. Compiled by United Nations Statistical Office.

Monthly Vital Statistics Report. U. S. Department of Health and Human Services. • Monthly. Provides data on births, deaths, cause of death, marriage, and divorce.

Morbidity and Mortality Weekly Report. Available from U. S. Government Printing Office. • Weekly. $450.00 per year (priority mail). Issued by the Centers for Disease Control (Atlanta), U. S. Department of Health and Human Services. Provides analysis and statistics on the occurrence of disease and death from all causes in the U. S.

Population and Vital Statistics Report. United Nations Publications. • Quarterly. $40.00 per year. Contains worldwide demographic statistics.

Social Statistics of the United States. Mark S. Littman, editor. Bernan Press. • 2000. $65.00. Includes statistical data on population growth, labor force, occupations, environmental trends, leisure time use, income, poverty, taxes, and other economic or demographic topics.

Social Trends and Indicators USA. Monique D. Magee, editor. Gale Cengage Learning. • 2003. $450.00. Four volumes. Includes data on labor, economics, the health care industry, crime, leisure, population, education, social security, and many other topics. Sources include various government agencies and major publications.

Statistical Abstract of the United States. Available from U. S. Government Printing Office. • Annual. $51.00. Issued by the U. S. Bureau of the Census.

Statistical Abstract of the World. Gale Cengage Learning. • 1997. $85.00. Third edition. Provides data on a wide variety of economic, social, and political topics for about 200 countries. Arranged by country.

For publishers addresses, refer to SOURCES CITED section at the back of the book.

Statistical Handbook on the American Family. Bruce A. Chadwick and Tim B. Heaton. Greenwood Publishing Group, Inc. • 1998. $69.95. Second edition. Includes data on education, health, politics, employment, expenditures, social characteristics, the elderly, and women in the labor force. Historical statistics on marriage, birth, and divorce are shown from 1900 on. A list of sources and a subject index are provided. (Statistical Handbooks Series).

A Statistical Portrait of the United States: Social Conditions and Trends. Mark S. Littman, editor. Bernan Press. • 1998. $89.00. Covers "social, economic, and environmental trends in the United States over the past 25 years." Includes statistical tables, graphs, and analysis relating to such topics as population, income, poverty, wealth, labor, housing, education, healthcare, air/water quality, and government. (Statistical Portrait of the United States: Social Conditions and Trends Series).

Statistical Yearbook. United Nations Publications. • Annual. $125.00. Contains statistics for about 200 countries on a wide variety of economic, industrial, and demographic topics. Compiled by United Nations Statistical Office.

The Universal Healthcare Almanac: A Complete Guide for the Healthcare Professional - Facts, Figures, Analysis. Silver & Cherner, Ltd. • $195.00 per year. Looseleaf service. Quarterly updates. Includes a wide variety of health care statistics: national expenditures, hospital data, health insurance, health professionals, vital statistics, demographics, etc. Years of coverage vary, with long range forecasts provided in some cases.

Vital Statistics of the United States. Public Health Service, U.S. Dept. of Health and Human Services. Available from U.S. Government Printing Office. • Annual.

Vital Statistics of the United States: Births, Life Expectancy, Deaths, and Selected Health Data. Helmut F. Wendel and Christopher S. Wendel, editors. Bernan Press. • 2004. $95.00. Serves as "the successor to the National Center for Health Statistics' discontinued compendia, *Vital Statistics of the United States.*" Contains both recent and historical data.

Vital Statistics of the United States: Life Tables. Available from U. S. Government Printing Office. • Annual. $64.00. Produced by the National Center for Health Statistics, Public Health Service, U. S. Department of Health and Human Services. Provides detailed data on expectation of life by age, race, and sex. Historical data is shown annually from the year 1900. (Vital Statistics, volume 2.).

TRADE/PROFESSIONAL ASSOCIATIONS

National Association for Public Health Statistics and Information Systems. 801 Roeder Rd., Ste. 650, Silver Spring, MD 20910. Phone: (301)563-6001 Fax: (301)563-6012 E-mail: hq@napshsis.org • URL: http://www.naphsis.org • Members are officials of state and local health agencies.

VITAMINS

See also: DIET; HEALTH FOOD INDUSTRY

GENERAL WORKS

Dietary Supplements: Current Issues. Donna V. Porter. Nova Science Publishers, Inc. • 2003. $29.50. Covers the legislative and regulatory status of vitamin and mineral supplements.

ABSTRACTS AND INDEXES

Nutrition Abstracts and Reviews, Series A: Human and Experimental. Available from CABI Publishing, North America. • Monthly. Institutions, $1,835.00 per year. Includes single site internet access. Published in England by CABI Publishing. Provides worldwide coverage of the literature.

CD-ROM DATABASES

International Pharmaceutical Abstracts [CD-ROM]. American Society of Health-System Pharmacists. • Monthly. $1,795.00 per year. Contains CD-ROM indexing and abstracting of international pharmaceutical literature from 1970 to date.

Pharmacopeia of Herbs. CME, Inc. • $149.00. Frequently updated CD-ROM provides searchable data on a wide variety of herbal medicines, vitamins, and amino acids. Includes information on clinical studies, contraindications, side-effects, phytoactivity, and 534 therapeutic use categories. Contains a 1,000 word glossary.

DIRECTORIES

PDR for Nutritional Supplements. Medical Economics Co., Inc. • Annual. $59.95. Includes trade names, usage, adverse reactions, dosage, and other information about vitamins and minerals.

ENCYCLOPEDIAS AND DICTIONARIES

CRC Desk Reference for Nutrition. Carolyn D. Berdanier. CRC Press LLC. • 1997. $79.95. Encyclopedic, alphabetical arrangement of topics. (Desk Reference Series).

Dictionary of Natural Products. George M. Hocking. Available from Information Today, Inc. • 1997. $139.50. Published by Plexus Publishing (http://www.plexuspublishing.com). Explains terms relating to the raw materials and products used in natural, folk, or alternative medicine.

Encyclopedia of Food Science, Food Technology, and Nutrition. Robert Macrae and others, editors. Elsevier. • 1993. Eight volumes. $3,056.00. $382.00 per volume.

Foods and Nutrition Encyclopedia. Audrey H. Ensminger and others. CRC Press, Inc. • 1993. $309.95. Second edition. Two volumes.

HANDBOOKS AND MANUALS

Advanced Nutrition: Micronutrients. Carolyn D. Berdanier. CRC Press LLC. • 2000. $119.95. Provides detailed coverage of essential vitamins and minerals. Written for professional dietitions and nutritionists. (Modern Nutrition Series).

Health Food/Vitamin Store. Entrepreneur Media, Inc. • Looseleaf. $59.50. A practical guide to starting a health food store. Covers profit potential, start-up costs, market size evaluation, owner's time required, site selection, lease negotiation, pricing, accounting, advertising, promotion, etc. (Start-Up Business Guide No. E1296.).

Vitamin Book. Simon and Schuster Trade Bantam. • 1999. $6.99. Revised edition.

INTERNET DATABASES

National Library of Medicine (NLM). National Institutes of Health (NIH). Phone: 888-346-3656 or (301)496-1131 Fax: (301)480-3537 E-mail: access@nlm.nih.gov • URL: http://www.nlm.nih.gov • NLM Web site offers free access through MEDLINE ("PubMed") to about nine million references to articles appearing in some 4,000 biomedical journals, with abstracts. Search interfaces range from "simple keywords to advanced Boolean expressions." The NLM site offers many links to other sources of biomedical and technical information (the National Center for Biotechnology Information, for example). Fees: Free.

ONLINE DATABASES

Embase. Elsevier Science, Inc. • Worldwide medical literature, 1974 to present. Weekly updates. Inquire as to online cost and availability.

International Pharmaceutical Abstracts [online]. American Society of Health-System Pharmacists. • Provides online indexing and abstracting of the world's pharmaceutical literature from 1970 to date. Monthly updates. Inquire as to online cost and availability.

PERIODICALS AND NEWSLETTERS

HSR: Health Supplement Retailer. Virgo Publishing, Inc. • Monthly. $50.00 per year. Covers all aspects of the vitamin and health supplement market, including new products. Includes an annual buyer's guide, an annual compilation of industry statistics, and annual guides to vitamins and herbs.

International Journal for Vitamin and Nutrition Research. Hogrefe & Huber Publishers. • Quarterly. $202.00 per year.

Journal of Dietary Supplements. Haworth Press, Inc. • Quarterly. $175.00 per year to libraries; $50.00 per year to individuals. Edited with a view to both academic research and industry concerns. Sections of the journal are dedicated to health professionals, educators, dieticians, and an "Industry Spotlight." Includes book reviews and short reviews of research appearing elsewhere. Formerly *Journal of Nutraceuticals, Functional & Medical Foods.*

Journal of Nutritional Science and Vitaminology. Japanese Society of Nutrition and Food Science. Center for Academic Publications. • Bimonthly. $145.00 per year. Formal *Journal of Vitaminology.*

Natural Business: The Journal of Business and Financial News for the Natural Products Industry. Natural Business Communications. • Monthly. $279.00 per year. Covers the business aspects of natural and organic products and dietary supplements, including information about private and public companies in the industry.

Nutrition Industry Executive. Vitamin Retailer Magazine, Inc. • 10 times a year. $50.00 per year. Edited for manufacturers of vitamins and other dietary supplements. Covers marketing, new products, industry trends, regulations, manufacturing procedures, and related topics. Includes a directory of suppliers to the industry.

Prevention: The Magazine for Better Health. Rodale. • Monthly $15.94. per year.

The Tan Sheet: Nonprescription Pharmaceuticals and Nutritionals. F-D-C Reports, Inc. • Weekly. $1,220.00 per year. Newsletter covering over-the-counter drugs and vitamin supplements. Emphasis is on regulatory activities of the U. S. Food and Drug Administration (FDA).

Vitamin Retailer: The Dietary Supplement Industry's Leading Magazine. Vitamin Retailer Magazine, Inc. • Monthly. $60.00 per year. Edited for retailers of vitamins, herbal remedies, minerals, antioxidants, essential fatty acids, and other food supplements.

TRADE/PROFESSIONAL ASSOCIATIONS

Natural Products Association. 2112 E 4th St., Ste. 200, Santa Ana, CA 92705. Phone: 800-966-6632 or (714)460-7732 Fax: (714)460-7444 E-mail: natural@naturalproductsassoc.org • URL: http://www.naturalproductsassoc.org • Represents retailers, wholesalers, brokers, distributors and manufacturers of natural, nutritional, dietetic foods, supplements, and natural body care products.

OTHER SOURCES

The U. S. Market for Vitamins, Supplements, and Minerals. Available from MarketResearch.com. • 2002. $3,000.00. Market research report published by Packaged Facts. Includes company profiles and sales forecasts to the year 2005.

VOCABULARY

ENCYCLOPEDIAS AND DICTIONARIES

Oxford English Dictionary. John Simpson. Oxford University Press. • 2002. $1,195.00. Second edition. 20 volumes. Includes CD-Rom.

Roget's International Thesaurus. Barbara A. Kipfer,

editor. • 2001. $20.95. Sixth edition.

HANDBOOKS AND MANUALS
Gaining Word Power. Dorothy Rubin. Longman Publishing Group. • 2002. $52.00. Sixth edition. Purpose of book is to help students and others build a "college-level" vocabulary, including information-age words.

VOCATIONAL EDUCATION

See also: TECHNICAL EDUCATION; TRAINING OF EMPLOYEES

GENERAL WORKS
Breaking Out of the Pink-Collar Ghetto: Policy Solutions for Non-College Women. Sharon H. Mastracci. M. E. Sharpe, Inc. • 2004. $65.95. Emphasis is on innovative education and training programs for women in low-paying service jobs.

ABSTRACTS AND INDEXES
Education Index. H. W. Wilson Co. • 10 times a year. Quarterly and annual cumulations. Price varies.

BIBLIOGRAPHIES
Materials for Occupational Education: An Annotated Source Guide. Patricia Glass Schuman, editor'. Neal-Schuman Publishers, Inc. • 1983. $39.95. Second edition. (Neal-Schuman Sourcebook Series).

CD-ROM DATABASES
ERIC on SilverPlatter. Available from SilverPlatter Information, Inc. • Quarterly. $700.00 per year. Produced by the Office of Educational Research and Improvement, U. S. Dept. of Education. Provides CD-ROM indexing and abstracting of a wide variety of literature relating to education. Archival discs are available from 1966.

DIRECTORIES
American Trade Schools Directory. Croner Publications Inc. • Covers: over 12,000 private and public trade, technical, and vocational schools. Entries include: School name, address, phone, contact person, year school founded, private or public, accrediting agencies, whether approved by state or Veterans Administration, home study courses offered.

Patterson's Schools Classified. Educational Directories Inc. • Covers: Over 7,000 accredited colleges, universities, community colleges, junior colleges, career schools and teaching hospitals. Entries include: School name, address, phone, URL, e-mail, name of administrator or admissions officer, description, professional accreditation (where applicable). Updated from previous year's edition of 'Patterson's American Education' (see separate entry).

Peterson's Vocational and Technical Schools and Programs: East and West. Peterson's. • Annual. $69.90. Two volumes. $34.95 per volume. Provides information on vocational schools in the eastern part of the U. S. Covers more than 370 career fields.

HANDBOOKS AND MANUALS
Resume Writing and Career Counseling. Entrepreneur Media, Inc. • Looseleaf. $59.50. A practical guide to starting a resume writing and career counseling service. Covers profit potential, start-up costs, market size evaluation, owner's time required, site selection, pricing, accounting, advertising, promotion, etc. (Start-Up Business Guide No. E1260.).

ONLINE DATABASES
Education Index Online. H. W. Wilson Co. • Indexes a wide variety of periodicals related to schools, colleges, and education, 1984 to date. Monthly updates. Inquire as to online cost and availability.

ERIC. Educational Resources Information Center. • Funded by the U. S. Department of Education, Institute of Education Sciences (formerly Office of Educational Research and Improvement). Provides access to more than one million online records covering education-related journal and report literature, 1966 to date. Updating is monthly. Inquire as to online cost and availability.

PERIODICALS AND NEWSLETTERS
TECHniques. Informix Software. • Eight times a year. Free to members; non-members, $45.00 per year. Formerly *Vocational Educational Journal.*

Vocational Training News: The Independent Weekly Report on Employment, Training, and Vocational Education. Aspen Publishers, Inc. • Biweekly. $377.00 per year. Newsletter. Emphasis is on federal job training and vocational education programs. Formerly *Manpower and Vocational Education Weekly.*

TRADE/PROFESSIONAL ASSOCIATIONS
American Vocational Educational Research Association. c/o Dr. Kirk A. Swortzel, Auburn University, Agrisciene Education, 5084 Haley Center, Auburn, FL 36849. c/o Dr. Kirk A. Swortzel, Auburn University, Agrisciene Education, 5084 Haley Center,.

Association for Career and Technical Education. 1410 King St., Alexandria, VA 22314. Phone: 800-826-9772 or (703)683-3111 Fax: (703)683-7424 E-mail: acte@acteonline.org • URL: http://www.acteonline.org.

Center on Education and Training for Employment. The Ohio State University College of Education. 1900 Kenny Rd., Columbus, OH 43210-1090. Phone: 800-848-4815 or (614)292-4353 Fax: (614)292-1260 E-mail: chambers.2@osu.edu • URL: http://www.cete.org/products/ • Formerly National Center for Research in Vocational Education.

VOCATIONAL GUIDANCE

See also: COUNSELING; JOB HUNTING; OCCUPATIONS

GENERAL WORKS
Encyclopedia of Careers and Vocational Guidance. Holli Cosgrove. Fact on File Inc. • 2002. 12th edition. Price on application.

Is It Too Late to Run Away and Join the Circus? Finding the Life You Really Want. Marti Smye. John Wiley. • 1998. $14.95. Provides philosophical and inspirational advice on leaving corporate life and becoming self-employed as a consultant or whatever. Central theme is dealing with major changes in life style and career objectives.

BIBLIOGRAPHIES
Educators Guide to Free Guidance Materials. Educators Progress Service, Inc. • Annual. $34.95. Lists free-loan films, filmstrips, audiotapes, videotapes and free printed materials on guidance.

Job & Career Books. Kennedy Information. • Annual. Free. Contains descriptions of selected books from various publishers on job searching and choice of career.

Professional Careers Sourcebook. Gale Cengage Learning. • 2002. $155.00. Seventh edition. Includes information sources for 129 professional and technical occupations.

Vocational Careers Sourcebook. Gale Cengage Learning. • 2002. $135.00. Fifth edition. A companion volume to *Professional Careers Sourcebook.* Includes information sources for 139 occupations that typically do not require a four-year college degree. Compiled in cooperation with In-

foPLACE of the Cuyahoga County Public Library, Ohio.

DIRECTORIES
Computing and Software Career Directory. Gale Cengage Learning. • 1993. $39.00. Includes career information relating to programmers, software engineers, technical writers, systems experts, and other computer specialists. Provides advice from "insiders," resume suggestions, a directory of companies that may offer entry-level positions, and a directory of career information sources. (Career Advisor Series.).

Directory of Counseling Services. International Association of Counseling Services. • Annual. $50.00. About 200 accredited services in the United States and Canada concerned with psychological educational, and vocational counseling, including those at colleges and universities and public and private agencies.

Magazines Career Directory: A Practical One-Stop Guide to Getting a Job in Publc Relations. Visible Ink Press. • 1993. $39.00. Fifth edition. Includes information on magazine publishing careers in art, editing, sales, and business management. Provides advice from "insiders," resume suggestions, a directory of companies that may offer entry-level positions, and a directory of career information sources. (Career Advisor Series).

HANDBOOKS AND MANUALS
Career Guide to Industries. Available from U. S. Government Printing Office. • 2002. $32.00. Issued by the Bureau of Labor Statistics, U. S. Department of Labor (http://www.bls.gov). Presents background career information (text) and statistics for the 40 industries that account for 70 percent of wage and salary jobs in the U. S. Includes nature of the industry, employment data, working conditions, training, earnings, rate of job growth, outlook, and other career factors. (BLS Bulletin 2541.).

The Information Professional's Guide to Career Development Online. Sarah L. Nesbeitt and Rachel S. Gordon. Information Today, Inc. • 2001. $29,50. Provides advice to librarians and other information professionals about using online sources for career advancement. The Career Development Online Web Page (http://www.lisjobs.com/careerdev/) contains links to relevant resources.

Occupational Outlook Handbook. Bureau of Labor Statistics, U.S. Department of Labor. Available from U.S. Government Printing Office. • Biennial. $53.00. Issued as one of the Bureau's *Bulletin* series and kept up to date by *Occupational Outlook Quarterly.*

Specialty Occupational Outlook: Professions. Gale Cengage Learning. • 1994. $75.00. Provides information on 150 professional occupations. (Career Information Guide Series).

Specialty Occupational Outlook: Trade and Technical. Gale Cengage Learning. • 1995. $75.00. Provides information on 150 "high-interest" careers that do not require a bachelor's degree.

Standard Occupational Classification Manual. Available from Bernan Associates. • 2000. $38.00. Replaces the *Dictionary of Occupational Titles.* Produced by the federal Office of Management and Budget, Executive Office of the President. "Occupations are classified based on the work performed, and on the required skills, education, training, and credentials for each one." Six-digit codes contain elements for 23 Major Groups, 96 Minor Groups, 451 Broad Occupations, and 820 Detailed Occupations. Designed to reflect the occupational structure currently existing in the U. S.

PERIODICALS AND NEWSLETTERS
The Career Development Quarterly. National Career Development Association. American Counseling Association. • Quarterly. Individuals, $45.00 per year; institutions, $80.00 per year.

Counseling and Values. Association for Spiritual, Ethical and Religious Values in Counseling. American Counseling Association. • Three times a year. Institutions, $35.00 per year.

Counseling Today. American Counseling Association. • Description: Covers news and issues relevant to the counseling profession.

Journal of Counseling and Development. American Counseling Association. • Quarterly. Free to members; non-members, $140.00 per year; institutions, $175.00 per year. Contains authoritative in-depth articles on professional and scientific issues. Formerly *Personnel and Guidance Journal.*

Journal of Employment Counseling. National Employment Counsel Association. American Counseling Association. • Quarterly. Free to members; non-members, $40.00 per year.

Occupational Outlook Quarterly. U.S. Department of Labor. Available from U.S. Government Printing Office. • Quarterly. $15.00 per year.

RESEARCH CENTERS AND INSTITUTES

National Institute for Work and Learning. Academy for Educational Development, 1875 Connecticut Ave., N.W., Washington, DC 20009-5721. Phone: (202)884-8186 Fax: (202)884-8422 E-mail: niwl@aed.org • URL: http://www.niwl.org • Research areas include adult education, training, unemployment insurance, and career development.

STATISTICS SOURCES

Statistical Handbook of Working America. Gale Cengage Learning. • 1997. $130.00. Second edition. Provides statistics, rankings, and forecasts relating to a wide variety of careers, occupations, and working conditions.

TRADE/PROFESSIONAL ASSOCIATIONS

American Counseling Association. 5999 Stevenson Ave., Alexandria, VA 22304. Phone: 800-347-6647 or (703)823-9800 Fax: (703)823-0252 E-mail: ryep@counseling.org • URL: http://www.counseling.org • Counseling professionals in elementary and secondary schools, higher education, community agencies and organizations, rehabilitation programs, government, industry, business, private practice, career counseling, and mental health counseling. Conducts professional development institutes and provides liability insurance. Maintains Counseling and Human Development Foundation to fund counseling projects.

National Career Development Association. 305 N Beech Cir., 10820 E 45th St., Ste. 210, Broken Arrow, OK 74012. Phone: (866)367-6232 or (918)663-7060 Fax: (918)663-7058 E-mail: dpennington@ncda.org • URL: http://www.ncda.org • Represents professionals and others interested in career development or counseling in various work environments. Supports counselors, education and training personnel, and allied professionals working in schools, colleges, business/industry, community and government agencies, and in private practice. Provides publications, support for state and local activities, human equity programs, and continuing education and training for these professionals. Provides networking opportunities for career professionals in business, education, and government.

VOCATIONAL REHABILITATION

DIRECTORIES

Complete Directory for People with Disabilities. Grey House Publishing. • Annual. $195.00. Provides information on a wide variety of products, goods, services, and facilities, including job training programs, rehabilitation services, and funding sources. Indexed by organization name, disability/need, and location.

Encyclopedia of Medical Organizations and Agencies. Gale Cengage Learning. • 2001. $295.00. 11th edition. Information on over 18,000 public and private organizations in medicine and related fields.

Medical and Health Information Directory. Gale Cengage Learning. • 2002. $675.00. Three volumes. 14th edition. Three volumes. $285.00 per volume. Vol. one covers medical organizations, agencies, and institutions; vol. two includes bibliographic, library, and database information; vol. three is a guide to services available for various medical and health problems.

PERIODICALS AND NEWSLETTERS

American Rehabilitation: AR. U. S. Dept. of Health, Education, and Welfare; Rehabilitation Services Administr. Available from U. S. Government Printing Office. • Quarterly. $15.00 per year. Official publication of the Rehabilitation Services Administration. Comments on all aspects of life affecting handicapped people.

International Rehabilitation Review. Rehabilitation International. • Description: Contains news and articles on international, national, and local developments in the fields of disability prevention and rehabilitation. Provides regular coverage of United Nations agencies, discusses the elimination of architectural and attitudinal barriers to disabled persons, and examines new trends in service delivery. Recurring features include news of research, book reviews, and a calendar of events.

RESEARCH CENTERS AND INSTITUTES

Vocational and Rehabilitation Research Institute. 3304 33rd St., N.W., Calgary, AB, Canada T2L 2A6. Phone: (403)284-1121 Fax: (403)284-1146 E-mail: vrri@cadvision.com • URL: http://www.vrri.org • Associated with University of Calgary.

TRADE/PROFESSIONAL ASSOCIATIONS

American Medical Rehabilitation Providers Association. 206 S 6th St., Springfield, IL 62701. Phone: 888-346-4624 or (217)753-1190 Fax: (217)525-1271 E-mail: czollar@13x.com • URL: http://www.amrpa.org • Rehabilitation facilities in the U.S. and Canada; agencies operating established medical, residential and vocational rehabilitation facilities. Promotes expansion and improvement of rehabilitation services to disabled persons as provided in rehabilitation facilities. Represents the concerns of rehabilitation providers before Congress and government agencies. Is concerned with quality operation of rehabilitation centers and facilities. Conducts research and development programs in national rehabilitation policy. Sponsors seminars and provides specialized education programs.

CARF, The Rehabilitation Accreditation Commission. 4891 E. Grant Rd., Tucson, AZ 85712. Phone: (520)325-1044 Fax: (520)318-1129 E-mail: info@carf.org • URL: http://www.carf.org • Formerly Commission on Accreditation of Rehabilitation.

Council of State Administrators of Vocational Rehabilitation. 4733 Bethesda Ave., Ste. 330, Bethesda, MD 20814. Phone: (301)654-8414 Fax: (301)654-5542.

International Association of Jewish Vocational Services. 1845 Walnut St., No. 640, Philadelphia, PA 19103. Phone: (215)854-0233 Fax: (215)854-0212 E-mail: coheng@iajvs.org • URL: http://www.iajvs.org • Formerly National Association of Jewish Vocational Services.

National Rehabilitation Information Center. 8201 Corporate Dr., Ste. 600, Landover, MD 20785. Phone: 800-346-2742 or (301)459-5900 Fax: (301)459-4263 E-mail: naricinfo@heitechservices.com • URL: http://www.naric.com • Aims to improve delivery of information to the rehabilitation community. Disseminates the findings of programs funded by the National Institute on Disability and

Rehabilitation Research; prepares custom bibliographies; helps locate answers to reference questions; searches for relevant materials in other commercially available databases.

Rehabilitation International; Vocational Commission. 25 E. 21st St., New York, NY 10010. Phone: (212)420-1500 Fax: (212)505-0871 E-mail: rehabintl@rehab-international.org • URL: http://www.rehab-international.org • Formerly International Society for Rehabilitation of the Disabled.

Vocational Evaluation and Work Adjustment Association. PO Box 26273, Colorado Spings, CO 80936. Phone: (719)638-4787 Fax: (719)638-6153 E-mail: info@vewaa.org • URL: http://www.vewaa.org.

OTHER SOURCES

Disability and Rehabilitation Products Markets. Theta Reports/PJB Medical Publications, Inc. • 1999. $1,295.00. Market research data. Covers the market for products designed to help differently-abled people lead more active lives. Includes such items as adaptive computers, augmentative communication devices, lifts/vans, and bath/home products. Profiles of leading suppliers are included. (Theta Report No. 800.).

VOCATIONS

See: OCCUPATIONS

VOICE RECOGNITION

See also: COMPUTER COMMUNICATIONS; MICROCOMPUTERS AND MINICOMPUTERS

GENERAL WORKS

Data Smog: Surviving the Information Glut. David Shenk. HarperSanFrancisco. • 1997. $14.00. A critical view of both the electronic and print information industries. Emphasis is on information overload.

What Will Be: How the New World of Information Will Change Our Lives. Michael L. Dertouzos. DIANE Publishing Co. • 1997. $25.00. A discussion of the "information market place" of the future, including telecommuting, virtual reality, and computer recognition of speech. The author is director of the MIT Laboratory for Computer Science.

ABSTRACTS AND INDEXES

Applied Science and Technology Index. H. W. Wilson Co. • 11 times a year. Quarterly and annual cumulations. Price varies. Indexes a wide variety of English language technical, industrial, and engineering periodicals.

Business Periodicals Index. H. W. Wilson Co. • 11 times a year. Quarterly and annual cumulations. Price varies.

Communication Abstracts: An International Information Service. Sage Publications, Inc. • Bimonthly. Institutions, $1,150.00 per year. Provides broad coverage of the literature of communications, including broadcasting and advertising.

Computer and Control Abstracts. Available from INSPEC, Inc. • Monthly. $2,400.00 per year. Section C of *Science Abstracts.*

Computer and Information Systems Abstracts Journal: An Abstract Journal Pertaining to the Theory, Design, Fabrication and Application of Computer and Information Systems. CSA. • 11 times a year. $1,750 per year.

Computer Literature Index: A Subject/Author Index to Computer and Data Processing Literature. EBSCO Publishing. • Quarterly, with annual cumulation. $245.00 per year. Contains brief abstracts of book and periodical literature covering all phases of computing, including approximately 70 specific application areas.

Current Contents: Engineering, Computing and Technology. Thomson/ISI. • Weekly. $730.00 per year. Reproductions of contents pages of technical journals. Includes *Author Index, Address Directory, Current Book Contents* and *Title Word Index.* Formerly *Current Contents: Engineering, Technology and Applied Sciences.*

Electronics and Communications Abstracts Journal: Comprehensive Coverage of Essential Scientific Literature. CSA. • Monthly. $1,665.00 per year. Includes print and online editions.

DIRECTORIES

Audiotex Directory and Buyer's Guide. ADBG Publishing. • Annual. $55.00. Lists more than 1,200 voice processing product and service companies. Includes speech synthesis and recognition products.

Frontline Solutions Buyer's Guide. Advanstar Communications. • Publication includes: List of manufacturers, suppliers, consultants, value added resellers, and dealers/distributors of automatic identification and data capture software, technology, equipment, and products for bar code, biometric identification, electronic data interchange, machine vision, magnetic stripe, optical character recognition, radio frequency data communications, radio frequency identification, smart cards, and voice data entry; also includes related organizations, and sources for industry standards. Entries include: Company name, address, phone, e-mail, web address, products or services.

Telecommunications Directory. Gale. • Covers: Two volumes-North America and International, Cover approximately 6,000 national and international voice and data communications networks, electronic mail services, teleconferencing facilities and services, facsimile services, Internet access providers, videotex and teletext operations, transactional services, local area networks, audiotex services, microwave systems/networkers, satellite facilities, and others involved in telecommunications, including related consultants, advertisers/marketers; associations, regulatory bodies, and publishers. Entries include: Company or organization name, address, phone, fax, year established, name and title of contact, executive officers and board of directors, function or type of service; geographical area served; NAICS and SIC codes; number of employees; general description, including telecommunications-related activities; product/service; specific applications; means of access and equipment required; publications; intended market and availability; pricing; stock exchanges traded and ticker symbols; financial figures.

ENCYCLOPEDIAS AND DICTIONARIES

Dictionary of Computing. Valerie Illingworth, editor. Oxford University Press. • 1997. $18.00. Fourth edition.

Dictionary of Information Technology and Computer Science. Tony Gunton. Blackwell Publishing. • 1994. $62.95. Second edition. Covers

key words, phrases, abbreviations, and acronyms used in computing and data communications.

HANDBOOKS AND MANUALS

Speech Synthesis and Recognition. John Holmes and Wendy Holmes. Routledge. • 2001. $72.00.

ONLINE DATABASES

Applied Science and Technology Index Online. H. W. Wilson Co. • Provides online indexing of 500 major scientific, technical, industrial, and engineering periodicals. Time period is 1983 to date. Monthly updates. Inquire as to online cost and availability.

Internet and Personal Computing Abstracts. Information Today, Inc. • Contains abstracts covering a wide variety of personal and business microcomputer literature appearing in more than 100 journals and popular magazines. Time period is 1981 to date, with monthly updates. Formerly *Microcomputer Index.* Inquire as to online cost and availability.

PROMT: Predicasts Overview of Markets and Technology. Gale Cengage Learning. • Companies, products, applied technologies and markets. U.S. and international literature coverage, 1972 to date. Inquire as to online cost and availability. Provides abstracts from more than 1,600 publications. Weekly updates.

Wilson Business Abstracts Online. H. W. Wilson Co. • Indexes and abstracts 600 major business periodicals, plus the *Wall Street Journal* and the business section of the *New York Times.* Indexing is from 1982, abstracting from 1990, with the two newspapers included from 1993. Updated weekly. Inquire as to online cost and availability. (*Business Periodicals Index* without abstracts is also available online.).

PERIODICALS AND NEWSLETTERS

EDP Weekly: The Leading Weekly Computer News Summary. Computer Age and EDP News Services. • Weekly. $495.00 per year. Newsletter. Summarizes news from all areas of the computer and microcomputer industries.

Frontline Solutions. Advanstar Communications. • Thirteen times per year. $41.00 per year. Provides news and information about the applications and technology of automated data capture systems. Formerly (*Automatic I.D. News*).

The Gray Sheet. F-D-C Reports Inc. • Description: Monitors the complex regulatory environment for devices, instrumentation, and diagnostics. Topics include device-related Congressional activity, Medicare reimbursement policies, international regulatory intiatives, enforcement and premarket approval programs at FDA's Center for Devices and Radiological Health. Recurring features include device approvals, 510(k) clearances, FDA recalls and seizures, mergers and acquisitions, and sales and earnings.

RESEARCH CENTERS AND INSTITUTES

Artificial Language Laboratory. Michigan State University, 405 Computer Center, East Lansing, MI 48824-1042. Phone: (517)353-0870 Fax: (517)353-

4766 E-mail: artlang@msu.edu • URL: http://www.msu.edu/unit/artlang/ • Research areas include speech analysis and synthesis by computer.

Center for Intelligent Systems, Controls, and Signal Processing. Marquette University, Haggerty Hall, Milwaukee, WI 53201. Phone: (414)288-3501 Fax: (414)288-5579 E-mail: ronald.brown@marquette.edu • URL: http://www.fourier.eeece.mu.edu/.

Communications and Information Processing Group. Rensselaer Polytechnic Institute, 7010 JEC, 110 Eighth St., Troy, NY 12180-3590. Phone: (518)276-6823 Fax: (518)276-6261 E-mail: modestin@ipl.rpi.edu • URL: http://www.ecse.rpi.edu • Includes Optical Signal Processing Laboratory and Speech Processing Laboratory.

Computer Vision Laboratory. University of Arizona, Department of Electrical and Computer Engineering, ECE Bldg. 104, Room 230, Tucson, AZ 85721. Phone: (520)621-6191 Fax: (520)621-8076 E-mail: strickland@ece.arizona.edu • URL: http://www.ece.arizona.edu • Research areas include computer vision and speech synthesis.

Information Systems Laboratory. Stanford University, Packard 267, Stanford, CA 94305-9510. Phone: (650)723-4731 Fax: (650)723-8473 E-mail: denise@ee.stanford.edu • URL: http://www.isl.stanford.edu • Research fields include speech coding and recognition.

Laboratory for Computer Science. Massachusetts Institute of Technology, 200 Technology Square, Bldg. NE43, Cambridge, MA 02139. Phone: (617)253-5851 Fax: (617)258-8682 E-mail: zue@mit.edu • URL: http://www.lcs.mit.edu/ • Research is in four areas: Intelligent Systems; Parallel Systems; Systems, Languages, and Networks; and Theory. Emphasis is on the application of online computing.

Mind-Machine Interaction Research Center. University of Florida, Electrical and Computer Engineering Dept., P.O. Box 116200, Gainesville, FL 32611-6200. Phone: (352)392-0912 Fax: (352)392-8671 E-mail: childers@ece.ufl.edu.

TRADE/PROFESSIONAL ASSOCIATIONS

AIM, Inc. 125 Warrendale Bayne Rd., Warrendale, PA 15086. Phone: 800-338-0206 or (724)934-4470 Fax: (724)934-4495 E-mail: info@aimglobal.org • URL: http://www.aimglobal.org • Members are companies concerned with automatic identification and data capture, including bar code systems, magnetic stripes, machine vision, voice technology, optical character recognition, and systems integration technology.

The Association for Work Process Improvement. 185 Devonshire St., Suite 770, Boston, MA 02110-9555. Phone: 800-998-2974 or (617)426-1167 Fax: (617)521-8675 E-mail: info@tawpi.org • URL: http://www.tawpi.org • Members are companies that use or supply various recognition technologies equipment.

VOLUME FEEDING

See: FOOD SERVICE INDUSTRY

W

WAGE DIFFERENTIALS

See: WAGES AND SALARIES

WAGE INCENTIVES

See: WAGES AND SALARIES

WAGE NEGOTIATIONS

See: COLLECTIVE BARGAINING

WAGES AND SALARIES

See also: EXECUTIVE COMPENSATION;
INCOME

GENERAL WORKS

Compensation. George T. Milkovich. McGraw-Hill. • 2001. $114.38. Seventh edition.

Compensation. Robert E. Sibson. AMACOM. • 1990. $75.00. Fifth edition. Discusses planning, implementing, and managing employee compensation.

Nickel and Dimed: On Not Getting By in America. Barbara Ehrenreich. Gale Cengage Learning. • 2001. $29.95. The author temporarily became a low-wage worker to experience American life at the bottom. Dramatizes the inadequacy of the minimum wage. (Metropolitan Books.).

Welfare, the Working Poor, and Labor. Louise Simmons, editor. M. E. Sharpe, Inc. • 2004. $66.95. Presents material by various authors on poverty, welfare reform, and the market for low-wage labor.

BIBLIOGRAPHIES

Available Pay Survey Reports: An Annotated Bibliography. Abbott, Langer and Associates. • 1995. $610.00. Fourth edition. Two volumes. Vol. 1, $450.00; Vol. 2, $160.00.

CD-ROM DATABASES

Authority Tax and Estate Planning Library. LexisNexis/Matthew Bender. • Periodic revisions. Price on request. CD-ROM contains updated full text of *Bender's Payroll Tax Guide, Depreciation Handbook, Federal Income Taxation of Corporations, Tax Planning for Corporations, Modern Estate Planning, Planning for Large Estates, Murphy's Will Clauses, Tax & Estate Planning for the Elderly*, and 12 other Matthew Bender publications. The Internal Revenue Code is also included.

OECD Statistical Compendium. Organization for Economic Cooperation and Development. •

Semiannual. $1,905.00 per year for 1 to 10 users. CD-ROM contains more than 730,000 monthly, quarterly, and annual time series for OECD countries, 1960 to date. Includes fully searchable data on agriculture, food, economic indicators, national accounts, employment, energy, finance, industry, technology, and foreign trade. Results can be displayed in various forms.

Sourcebooks America CD-ROM. CACI Marketing Systems. • Annual. $1,250.00. Provides the CD-ROM version of *The Sourcebook of ZIP Code Demographics: Census Edition* and *The Sourcebook of County Demographics: Census Edition.*

WILSONDISC: Wilson Business Abstracts. H. W. Wilson Co. • Monthly. Includes unlimited online access to *Wilson Business Abstracts* through WILSONLINE. Provides CD-ROM "cover-to-cover" abstracting and indexing of over 600 prominent business periodicals. Indexing is from 1982, abstracting from 1990. (*Business Periodicals Index* without abstracts is available on CD-ROM at $1,495 per year.).

DIRECTORIES

World at Work Membership Directory. American Compensation Association. • Annual. Free to members; non-members, $150.00. Covers 20,000 member benefits and compensation professionals in Canada and United States.

HANDBOOKS AND MANUALS

Bender's Payroll Tax Guide. LexisNexis Matthew Bender. • Annual. $149.00. Guide to payroll tax planning. Includes procedures, forms, and examples.

Career Guide to Industries. Available from U. S. Government Printing Office. • 2002. $32.00. Issued by the Bureau of Labor Statistics, U. S. Department of Labor (http://www.bls.gov). Presents background career information (text) and statistics for the 40 industries that account for 70 percent of wage and salary jobs in the U. S. Includes nature of the industry, employment data, working conditions, training, earnings, rate of job growth, outlook, and other career factors. (BLS Bulletin 2541.).

Payroll Management Guide. CCH, Inc. • Weekly. $599.00. Eight looseleaf volumes. Covers the basics of payroll management, including employer obligations, recordkeeping, taxation, unemployment insurance, processing of new employees, and government penalties.

Personnel Management: Compensation. Prentice Hall PTR. • Looseleaf. Periodic supplementation. Price on application.

Practical Guide to Tax Issues in Employment. Julia K. Brazelton. CCH, Inc. • 1999. $95.00. Covers income taxation as related to labor law and tax law,

including settlements and awards. Written for tax professionals.

Sales Compensation Handbook. Stockton Colt, editor. AMACOM. • 1998. $75.00. Second edition. Topics include salespeople compensation plans based on salary, commission, bonuses, and contests.

U. S. Master Compensation Tax Guide. Dennis R. Lassila and Bob G. Kilpatrick. CCH, Inc. • 2001. $57.00. Third edition. Provides concise coverage of taxes on salaries, bonuses, fringe benefits, other current compensation, and deferred compensation (qualified and nonqualified).

INTERNET DATABASES

Bureau of Economic Analysis (BEA). U. S. Department of Commerce, Bureau of Economic Analysis. Phone: (202)606-9900 Fax: (202)606-5310 E-mail: webmaster@bea.doc.gov • URL: http://www.bea.doc.gov • Web site includes "News Release Information" covering national, regional, and international economic estimates from the BEA. Highlights of releases appear online the same day, complete text and tables appear the next day. "Recent News Releases" section provides titles for past nine months, with links. "BEA Data and Methodology" includes "Frequently Requested NIPA Data" (national income and product accounts, such as gross domestic product and personal income). Other statistics are available. Fees: Free.

Business 2.0 Web Guide to the Best Business Links. Business 2.0 Media Inc. Phone: (415)293-4800 E-mail: support@business2.com • URL: http://www.business2.com/webguide • Web site presents an extensive, searchable directory of links to "the best, most informative, and authoritative web pages." Twenty main categories cover business, finance, career, company information, people, and technology topics, with thousands of subtopics, all linking to Web sites recommended by experienced business researchers. Fees: Free.

EBSCO Information Services. Ebsco Publishing. Phone: 800-653-2726 or (978)356-6500 Fax: (978)356-6565 E-mail: ep@epnet.com • URL: http://www.epnet.com • Fee-based Web site providing Internet access to a wide variety of databases, including business-related material. Full text is available for many periodical titles, with daily updates. Fees: Apply.

Fedstats. Federal Interagency Council on Statistical Policy. Phone: (202)395-7254 • URL: http://www.fedstats.gov • Web site features an efficient search facility for full-text statistics produced by more than 100 federal agencies, including the Census Bureau, the Bureau of Economic Analysis, and the Bureau of Labor Statistics. Boolean searches can be made within one agency or for all agencies combined. Links are offered to international statistical bureaus,

---

including the UN, IMF, OECD, UNESCO, Eurostat, and 20 individual countries. Fees: Free.

FreeLunch.com. Economy.com, Inc. Phone: (610)696-8700 Fax: (610)696-1678 • URL: http://www.freelunch.com • Web site provides free access to more than 1.5 million economic and financial data series, covering industry, demographics, labor markets, prices, retail sales, government spending, trade, interest rates, housing starts, the stock market, and many other topics. Data is available for various time periods in either chart or table form. Searching is offered. Fees: Free, but registration required. Ecohomy.com, Inc. also offers fee-based economic analysis at *The Dismal Scientist* site (http://www.dismal.com).

InSite 2. Intelligence Data/Thomson Financial. Phone: 800-654-0393 or (617)856-1890 Fax: (617)737-3182 E-mail: intelligence.data@tfn.com • URL: http://www.insite2.gale.com/ • Fee-based Web site consolidates information in a "Base Pack" consisting of Business InSite, Market InSite, and Company InSite. Optional databases are Consumer InSite, Health and Wellness InSite, Newsletter InSite, and Computer InSite. Includes fulltext content from more than 2,500 trade publications, journals, newsletters, newspapers, analyst reports, and other sources. Continuous updating. Formerly produced by The Gale Group.

ProQuest Direct. ProQuest Inc. Phone: 800-889-3358 or (734)761-4700 Fax: (734)662-4554 • URL: http://proquest.com • Fee-based Web site providing Internet access to more than 3,000 periodicals, newspapers, and other publications. Many items are available full-text, with daily updates. Includes extensive corporate and financial information. Fees: Apply.

Summary of Commentary on Current Economic Conditions by Federal Reserve District [the Beige Book]. Board of Governors of the Federal Reserve System. Phone: (202)452-3000 Fax: (202)452-3819 • URL: http://www.federalreserve.gov/fomc/beigebook/2004/ • Free Web site provides current "anecdotal information" eight times a year on economic conditions within each of the 12 Federal Reserve Districts, plus an extensive national *Summary.* Text is based on the opinions of bank of- ficials, business executives, economists, financial market experts, and others. Typically contains views of consumer spending, manufacturing, services, credit, employment, prices, wages, and the economy in general. Usually referred to as the Beige Book.

Wageweb: Salary Survey Data On-Line. HRPDI: Human Resources Programs Development and Improvement. Phone: (804)363-1792 Fax: (804)594-3721 E-mail: salaries@wageweb.com • URL: http://www.wageweb.com • Web site provides salary information for more than 170 benchmark positions, including (for example) 29 information management jobs. Data shows average minimum, median, and average maximum compensation for each position, based on salary surveys. Fees: Free for national salary data; $169.00 per year for more detailed information (geographic, organization size, specific industries).

ONLINE DATABASES

Accounting and Tax Database. PROQUEST. • Provides indexing and abstracting of the literature of accounting, taxation, and financial management, 1971 to date. Updating is weekly. Especially covers accounting, auditing, banking, bankruptcy, employee compensation and benefits, cash manage- ment, financial planning, and credit. Inquire as to online cost and availability.

Wilson Business Abstracts Online. H. W. Wilson Co. • Indexes and abstracts 600 major business periodicals, plus the *Wall Street Journal* and the business section of the *New York Times.* Indexing is from 1982, abstracting from 1990, with the two newspapers included from 1993. Updated weekly.

Inquire as to online cost and availability. (*Business Periodicals Index* without abstracts is also available online.).

PERIODICALS AND NEWSLETTERS

Compensation and Benefits Review: The Journal of Total Compensation Strategies. Sage Publications, Inc. • Institutions, $358.00 per year; includes print and online editions.

Paytech. American Payroll Association. • Monthly. Membership. Covers the details and technology of payroll administration.

RESEARCH CENTERS AND INSTITUTES

W. E. Upjohn Institute for Employment Research. 300 S. Westnedge Ave., Kalamazoo, MI 49007-4686. Phone: (616)343-5541 Fax: (616)343-3308 E-mail: eberts@we.upjohninst.org • URL: http://www.upjohninst.org • Research fields include unemployment, unemployment insurance, worker's compensation, labor productivity, profit sharing, the labor market, economic development, earnings, training, and other areas related to employment.

STATISTICS SOURCES

ALA Survey of Librarian Salaries. American Library Association. • Annual. $55.00. Provides data on salaries paid to librarians in academic and public libraries. Position categories range from beginning librarian to director.

American Salaries and Wages Survey. Gale Cen- gage Learning. • 2003. $195.00. Seventh edition. Arranged alphabetically by 4,402 occupational classifications. Provides salary data for different experience levels and in specific areas of the U.S. Includes cost of living data for metropolitan areas.

Bulletin of Labour Statistics: Supplementing the An- nual Data Presented in the Year Book of Labour Statistics. International Labour Ofice. • Quarterly. $84.00 per year. Includes five *Supplements.* A supplement to *Yearbook of Labour Statistics.* Provides current labor and price index statistics for over 130 countries. Generally includes data for the most recent four years. Text in English, French and Spanish.

Business Statistics of the United States. Linz Audain and Cornelia J. Strawser. Bernan Associates. • Annual. $147.00. Based on *Business Statistics,* formerly issue by the Bureau of Economic Analysis, U. S. Department of Commerce. Provides basic data for a wide variety of U. S. industries, services, and economic indicators. Most statistics are shown an- nually for 30 years and monthly for the most recent four years.

Compensation and Working Conditions. Available from U. S. Government Printing Office. • Quarterly. Issued by the Bureau of Labor Statistics, U. S. Department of Labor. Presents wage and benefit changes that result from collective bargaining settle- ments and unilateral management decisions. Includes statistical summaries and special reports on wage trends. Formerly *Current Wage Developments.*

Compensation Systems in Private Law Firms. Alt- man Weil Publications, Inc. • Annual. $325.00. Provides legal-office compensation standards ar- ranged by region, firm size, legal specialty, and vari- ous other factors. Covers attorneys, paralegals, and other personnel.

Dartnell's 30th Sales Force Compensation Survey 1997-1998. Christen P .Heide. Dartnell Corp. • 1999. $159.00. 30th edition.

Economic Report of the President: Together with the Annual Report of the Council of Economic Advisors. Available from U. S. Government Printing Office. • Annual. $32.00. Includes about 130 pages of "Statistical Tables Relating to Income, Employment, and Production." Tables cover national income, employment, wages, productivity, manufacturing, prices, credit, finance (public and private), corporate profits, and foreign trade.

Employment and Earnings. Available from U. S. Government Printing Office. • Monthly. $50.00 per year, including annual supplement. Produced by the Bureau of Labor Statistics, U. S. Department of Labor. Provides current data on employment, hours, and earnings for the U. S. as a whole, for states, and for more than 200 local areas.

Employment and Wages: Annual Averages. Avail- able from U. S. Government Printing Office. • Annual. $53.00. Issued by the Bureau of Labor Statistics, U. S. Department of Labor. Presents a wide variety of data arranged by state and industry.

Executive Compensation Survey Report. MidAtlan- tic Employees' Association. • Annual. $400.00. Looseleaf service.

Geographic Reference Report: Annual Report of Costs, Wages, Salaries, and Human Resource Statistics for the United States and Canada. ERI (Economic Research Institute). • Annual. $389.00. Provides demographic and other data for each of 298 North American metropolian areas, including local salaries, wage differentials, cost-of-living, housing costs, income taxation, employment, unemploy- ment, population, major employers, crime rates, weather, etc.

Handbook of U. S. Labor Statistics: Employment, Earnings, Prices, Productivity, and Other Labor Data. Eva E. Jacobs, editor. Bernan Associates. • 1999. $74.00. Based on *Handbook of Labor Statistics,* formerly issued by the Bureau of Labor Statistics, U. S. Department of Labor. Includes the Bureau's projections of employment in the U. S. by industry and occupation. Provides a wide variety of data on the work force, prices, fringe benefits, and consumer expenditures.

Key Indicators of the Labour Market. Available from Routledge. • Biennial. $125.00. Published by the International Labour Office (http://www.ilo.org). Provides data on 20 key indicators in 220 countries. Includes labor force statistics, employment, unemployment, part-time workers, wages, productivity, poverty indicators, and related topics.

Monthly Labor Review. Available from U. S. Government Printing Office. • Monthly. $49.00 per year. Issued by the Bureau of Labor Statistics, U. S. Department of Labor. Contains data on the labor force, wages, work stoppages, price indexes, productivity, economic growth, and occupational injuries and illnesses.

National Compensation Survey. Available from U. S. Government Printing Office. • Irregular. $300.00 per year. Consists of bulletins reporting on earnings for jobs in clerical, professional, technical, and other fields in 70 major metropolitan areas. Formerly *Oc- cupational Compensation Survey.*

Occupational Earnings and Wage Trends in Metropolitan Areas. U.S. Bureau of Labor Statistics. • Three times a year.

Prices and Earnings Around the Globe. Union Bank of Switzerland. • Triennial. Free. Published in Zurich. Compares prices and purchasing power in 48 major cities of the world. Wages and hours are also compared.

Project Management Salary Survey. Project Management Institute. • Annual. $129.00. Gives compensation data for key project management positions in North America, according to job title, level of responsibility, number of employees supervised, and various other factors. Includes data on retirement plans and benefits.

Report on the American Workforce. Available from U. S. Government Printing Office. • Annual. Issued by the U. S. Department of Labor (http://www.dol.gov). Appendix contains tabular statistics, including employment, unemployment, price indexes, consumer expenditures, employee benefits (retire- ment, insurance, vacation, etc.), wages, productiv- ity, hours of work, and occupational injuries. Annual figures are shown for up to 50 years.

State Profiles: The Population and Economy of Each U. S. State. Courtenay Slater and Others. Bernan Press. • 1999. $89.00. Presents charts, tables, and text in an eight-page profile for each state. Covers population, labor force, income, poverty, employment, wages, industry, trade, housing, education, health, taxes, and government finances. (The Population and Economy of Each United States Series).

Statistics on Occupational Wages and Hours of Work and on Food Prices. International Labour Organization. • Annual. $28.00. Provides international data on wages and hours for 159 occupations within 49 industries. Includes retail prices for 93 food items.

Survey of Current Business. Available from U. S. Government Printing Office. • Monthly. $63.00 per year. Issued by Bureau of Economic Analysis, U. S. Department of Commerce. Presents a wide variety of business and economic data.

The Value of a Dollar: Millenium Edition. Scott Derks, editor. Grey House Publishing, Inc. • 1999. $135.00. Second edition.

Yearbook of Labour Statistics. Available from Bernan Associates. • Annual. $168.00. Published by the International Labour Organizaton (http://www.ilo. org). Provides data for more than 180 countries on employment, unemployment, wages, hours of work, cost of labor, strikes, industrial accidents, and consumer prices.

TRADE/PROFESSIONAL ASSOCIATIONS

American Payroll Association. 660 N Main Ave., Ste. 100, San Antonio, TX 78205-1217. Phone: 800-398-8681 or (210)226-4600 Fax: (210)226-4027 E-mail: apa@americanpayroll.org • URL: http:// www.americanpayroll.org • Payroll employees. Works to increase members' skills and professionalism through education and mutual support. Represents the interest of members before legislative bodies. Conducts training courses. Operates speakers' bureau; conducts educational programs. Administers the certified payroll professional program of recognition.

WorldatWork. 14040 N Northsight Blvd., Scottsdale, AZ 85260. Phone: 877-951-9191 or (480)951-9191 Fax: (480)483-8352 E-mail: customerrelations@worldatwork.org • URL: http:// www.worldatwork.org • Dedicated to knowledge leadership in compensation, benefits and total rewards, focusing on disciplines associated with attracting, retaining and motivating employees. Offers CCP, CBP, and GRP certification and education programs, conducts surveys, research and provides networking opportunities.

OTHER SOURCES

BNA Policy and Practice Series: Compensation. BNA, Inc. • Weekly. $938.00 per year.

BNA Policy and Practice Series: Wages and Hours. BNA, Inc. • Weekly. $938.00 per year. Looseleaf service.

Business Rankings Annual. Gale Cengage Learning. • Annual. $325.00. Two volumes. Compiled by the Business Library Staff of the Brooklyn Public Library. This is a guide to lists and rankings appearing in major business publications. The top ten names are listed in each case.

Foreign Labor Trends. Available from U. S. Government Printing Office. • Irregular (50 to 60 issues per year, each on an individual country). $95.00 per year. Prepared by various American Embassies. Issued by the Bureau of International Labor Affairs, U. S. Department of Labor. Covers labor developments in important foreign countries, including trends in wages, working conditions, labor supply, employment, and unemployment.

Labor Relations. CCH, Inc. • $2,589.00 per year.

Seven looseleaf volumes. Weekly updates. Covers labor relations, wages and hours, state labor laws, and employment practices. Supplement available, *Labor Law Reports.* Summary Newsletter.

WALLPAPER INDUSTRY

DIRECTORIES

Directory of Home Center Operators and Hardware Chains. Chain Store Guide. • Annual. $327.00. On-line edition, $747.00. Nearly 4,700 home center operators, paint and home decorating chains, and lumber and building materials companies. Covers United States and Canada.

Paint and Decorating Retailer's Directory of the Wallcoverings Industry: The Gold Book. Paint and Decorating Retailers Association. • Annual. Membership.

PERIODICALS AND NEWSLETTERS

Paint and Decorating Retailer. Paint and Decorating Retailers Association. • Monthly. $45.00 per year. Formerly *Decorating Retailer.*

Waland Window Trends. Cygnus Business Media, Inc. • Monthly $36.00 per year. Edited for retailers of interior decoration products, with an emphasis on wallcoverings. Formerly *Wallcoverings, Windows and Interior Fashion.*

The Wall Fashions. Grace McNamara, Inc. • Monthly. $39.00 per year. News, events, trends, marketing, and merchandising covering the wallcovering industry. Formerly *The Wall Paper.*

TRADE/PROFESSIONAL ASSOCIATIONS

Painting and Decorating Contractors of America. 11960 Westline Industrial Dr., Ste. 201, Saint Louis, MO 63146-2309. Phone: 800-332-7322 or (314)-514-7322 Fax: (314)-514-9417 E-mail: lwerle@ pdca.org • URL: http://www.pdca.org • Painting and wallcovering contractors.

Wallcoverings Association. 401 N Michigan Ave., Ste. 2200, Chicago, IL 60611. Phone: (312)644-6610 Fax: (312)527-6705 E-mail: rpietrzak@ smithbucklin.com • URL: http://www. wallcoverings.org • Manufacturers, converters, distributors, and suppliers in the wallcoverings industry.

WAREHOUSES

DIRECTORIES

American Chain of Warehouses-Membership Directory. American Chain of Warehouses. • Annual. Free. Controlled circulation. About 45 member public warehouses in the United States.

Grocery Headquarters: The Newspaper for the Food Industry. Trend Publishing. • Monthly. $80.00 per year. Covers the sale and distribution of food products and other items sold in supermarkets and grocery stores. Edited mainly for retailers and wholesalers. Incorporates (Grocery Distribution).

International Directory of Refrigerated Warehouses and Distribution Cente rs. International Association of Refrigerated Warehouses. • Annual. Free to qualified personnel; others, $150.00 per year. Lists locations/services of 1,000 public refrigerated warehouses in 30 countries. Formerly *International Directory of Public Refrigerated Warehouses.*

International Warehouse Logistics Association Membership Directory and Resource Guide. International Warehouse Logistics Association. • Annual. Free to members, manufacturers, and distributors. Detailed listing of 500 public merchandise warehousing firms located throughout the U.S., Canada, Mexico, Costa Rica, Dominacan Republic, Panama, Venezuela, and Russia. Formerly *American Warehouse Association and Canadian Association of Warehousing and Distribution Services*

Membership Directory and Resource Guide.

Plunkett's Transportation and Logistics Industry Almanac. Plunkett Research, Ltd. • 2004. $249.99. Contains profiles of 300 leading companies in the fields of transportation, logistics, supply chain management, warehousing, distribution, and intermodal shipment systems. Includes industry trends and statistics.

Warehouse Management's Guide to Public Warehousing. Reed Business Information. • Annual. $55.00. List of general merchandise,contract and refrigerated warehouses.

Warehousing Distribution Directory. Commonwealth Business Media Inc. • Publication includes: List of about 800 warehousing and consolidation companies and firms offering trucking, trailer on flatcar, container on flatcar, and piggyback carrier services. Entries include: Name of firm, address, phone, name and title of contact, services, insurance provided, bank references, territory covered, restrictions, number of staff, and branches or subsidiaries with their locations.

FINANCIAL RATIOS

Annual Statement Studies. The Risk Management Association. • Annual. Median and quartile financial ratios are given for over 400 kinds of manufacturing, wholesale, retail, construction, and consumer finance establishments. Data is sorted by both asset size and sales volume. Includes a clearly written "Definition of Ratios" and an alphabetical industry index.

Annual Statement Studies: Industry Default Probabilities and Cash Flow Measures. The Risk Management Association. • Annual. $145.00. Serves as a companion volume to the original *Annual Statement Studies.* Gives probability of default estimates on a percentage scale for more than 450 industries. Includes changes in position year-by-year for eight financial statement line items and provides percentage measures of cash flow.

HANDBOOKS AND MANUALS

Warehouse Management Handbook. James A. Tompkins. McGraw-Hill. • 1997. $89.95. Second edition. Covers site selection, order fulfillment, inventory control systems, storage space determination, equipment maintenance programs, and other warehousing topics.

World Class Warehousing and Material Handling. Edward Frazelle. McGraw-Hill. • 2001. $49.95. (Logistics Management Library).

PERIODICALS AND NEWSLETTERS

Chilton's Distribution: The Transportation and Business Logistics Magazine. Reed Business Information. • Monthly. $65.00 per year.

Distribution Center Management. Alexander Research & Communications Inc. • Description: The monthly newsletter for distribution centers and warehouse managers with ideas and information on how to run their facilities more productively.

Transportation and Distribution: Integrating Logistics in Supply Chain Management. Penton Media, Inc. • Monthly. Free to qualified personnel; others, $50.00 per year. Essential information on transportation and distribution practices in domestic and international trade.

RESEARCH CENTERS AND INSTITUTES

World Food Logistics Organization. World Food Logistics Organization. 1500 King St., Ste. 201, Alexandria, VA 22314. Phone: (703)373-4300 Fax: (703)373-4301 E-mail: bhudson@iarw.org • URL:

http://www.wflo.org • Food storage.

STATISTICS SOURCES

Capacity of Refrigerated Warehouses. U.S. Department of Agriculture. • Annual.

TRADE/PROFESSIONAL ASSOCIATIONS

American Chain of Warehouses. 156 Flamingo Dr., Beecher, IL 60401-9725. Phone: (708)946-9792 Fax: (708)946-9793 E-mail: bjurus@acwi.org • URL: http://www.acwi.org.

American Moving and Storage Association. c/o John Brewer. 1611 Duke St., Alexandria, VA 22314. Phone: (703)683-7410 Fax: (703)683-7527 E-mail: amconf@amconf.org • URL: http://www.amconf.org • Members are household goods movers, storage companies, and trucking firms.

International Association of Refrigerated Warehouses. 7315 Wisconsin Ave., 1200N, Bethesda, MD 20814-3202. Phone: (301)652-5674 Fax: (301)652-7269 E-mail: email@iarw.org • URL: http://www.iarw.org.

International Warehouse Logistics Association. 2800 S River Rd., Ste. 260, Des Plaines, IL 60018-6003. Phone: 800-525-0165 or (847)813-4699 Fax: (847)813-0115 E-mail: email@iwla.com • URL: http://www.iwla.com • Fosters and promotes the growth and success of public and contract warehousing and related logistics services. Serves as the unified voice of the global outsourced warehouse logistics industry, representing 3PLs (third party logistics providers), 4PLs (fourth party logistics providers), public and contract warehouse logistics companies and their suppliers, setting standards, legal frameworks and best practices for the warehousing logistics industry for 110 years. Members of the Association receive services including legal assistance, marketing assistance and group buying programs. Owns its own insurance company (passing cost savings to members), holds an annual convention each year, and produces educational programs.

OTHER SOURCES

How to Plan and Manage Warehouse Operations. American Management Association Extension Institute. • Looseleaf. $159.00. Self-study course. Emphasis is on practical explanations, examples, and problem solving. Quizzes and a case study are included.

WARM AIR HEATING

See: HEATING AND VENTILATION

WASHING MACHINE INDUSTRY

See: ELECTRIC APPLIANCE INDUSTRY

WASTE DISPOSAL

See: SANITATION INDUSTRY

WASTE MANAGEMENT

See also: HAZARDOUS MATERIALS

GENERAL WORKS

Hazardous Waste Management. Michael D. La Gregor and others. McGraw-Hill. • 2000. $113.75. Second edition. (Environmental Engineering and Water Resources Series).

ABSTRACTS AND INDEXES

Applied Science and Technology Index. H. W. Wilson Co. • 11 times a year. Quarterly and annual cumulations. Price varies. Indexes a wide variety of English language technical, industrial, and engineering periodicals.

DIRECTORIES

BioScan: The Worldwide Biotech Industry Reporting Service. Greenwood Publishing Group, Inc. • Annual. $975.00 per year. Bimonthly updates. Provides detailed information on over 1,000 U.S. and foreign companies broadly classified as biotechnological. In addition to medical technology and advanced pharmaceutical firms, includes firms doing research in food processing, waste management, agriculture, and veterinary science.

EI Environmental Services Directory. Environmental Information Ltd. • Covers: Over 8,000 environmental services businesses, including waste-handling facilities, transportation firms, spill response firms, consultants, laboratories, soil boring/well drilling firms; also includes incineration services, polychlorinated biphenyl (PCB) detoxification and mobile solvent-recovery services, asbestos services and underground tank services, summaries of states' regulatory programs. Entries include: Company name, address, phone, description of services, regulatory status, on and off site processes used, type of waste handled.

Hazardous Waste Consultant Directory of Commercial Hazardous Waste Management Facilities. Elsevier. • Annual. $115.00. List of 170 facilities that process, store, and dispose of hazardous waste materials.

National Solid Waste Management Association Directory of Professional Services. National Solid Wastes Management Association. • Annual. Lists waste management consulting firms.

Waste Age Buyers' Guide. Primedia Business Magazines and Media. • Annual. $64.95. Manufacturers of equipment and supplies for the waste management industry.

ENCYCLOPEDIAS AND DICTIONARIES

Encyclopedia of Global Change: Environmental Change and Human Society. Andrew S. Goudie, editor. Oxford University Press. • 2001. $275.00. Two volumes. Contains 300 signed articles on a wide variety of topics relating to changes in the environment and the atmosphere. Includes bibliographies and illustrations.

Wiley Encyclopedia of Environmental Pollution and Cleanup. Robert A. Meyers, editor. John Wiley and Sons, Inc. • 1999. $350.00. Two volumes. Presents generally nontechnical, basic coverage of environmental hazards and methods of detection and cleanup, with consideration of risk assessment, regulatory policy, and economic factors.

HANDBOOKS AND MANUALS

Hazardous Waste Management in Small Businesses: Regulating and Assisting the Smaller Generator. Robert E. Deyle. Greenwood Publishing Group, Inc. • 1989. $59.95. Emphasis on legal aspects.

Waste Treatment and Disposal. Paul T. Williams. John Wiley and Sons, Inc. • 1998. $200.00.

PERIODICALS AND NEWSLETTERS

Air and Waste Management Association Journal. • Monthly. Individuals, $150.00 per year; institutions, $329.00 per year: nonprofit institutions, $229.00 per year. Includes annual *Directory of Governmental Air Pollution Agencies.*

EM: A&WMA's Environmental Solutions That Make Good Business Sense. Air and Waste Management Association. • Monthly. Institutions, $299.00 per year; nonprofit and government agencies, $199.00 per year. Newsletter. Provides news of regulations, legislation, and technology relating to the environment, recycling, and waste control. Formerly *Environmental Manager.*

Environmental Regulation: State Capitals. Wakeman-Walworth, Inc. • 50 times a year. $245.00 per year; print and online editions, $350.00 per year. Newsletter. Formerly *From the State Capitals: Environmental Regulation.*

Sludge Newsletter: The Newsletter on Municipal Wastewater and Biosolids. Business Publishers, Inc. • Biweekly. $409.00 per year. per year. Newsletter. Monitors sludge management developments in Washington and around the country.

Solid Waste Report: Resource Recovery-Recycling-Collection-Disposal. Business Publishers, Inc. • Weekly. $627.00 per year. Newsletter. Covers regulation, business news, technology, and international events relating to solid waste management.

Waste Age. Environmental Industry Association. Primedia Business Magazines and Media. • Monthly. Price on application.

Waste Management: Industrial-Radioactive-Hazardous. Elsevier. • 10 times a year. Individuals, $120.00 per year; institutions, $1,646.00 per year. Formerly *Nuclear and Chemical Waste Management.*

Waste Treatment Technology News. BCC Research. • Description: Profiles existing and developing industrial waste treatment techniques. Follows governmental action such as Superfund legislation and EPA (Environmental Protection Agency) activities. Focuses on the research and development of waste treatment technologies, listing recent patents in the field. Recurring features include news of research.

RESEARCH CENTERS AND INSTITUTES

Battelle Memorial Institute. Battelle Memorial Institute. 505 King Ave., Columbus, OH 43201. Phone: 800-201-2011 or (614)424-5853 Fax: (614)424-5263 E-mail: solutions@battelle.org • URL: http://www.battelle.org/ • Environment and energy; national security; transportation; health and life sciences; medical, pharmaceutical, agrochemical, and consumer product development. Conducts marine research at three coastal locations: Florida Marine Research Facility (Daytona Beach), Northwest Marine Research Laboratory (Sequim, Washington), and the Ocean Sciences Laboratory (Duxbury, Massachusetts). Specialized facilities and units include: Aviation Safety Reporting System Office; the Breakthrough Center for Strategic Product Development; the Human Engineering, Ergonomics, and Organizational Research Center; and the William R. Wiley Environmental Molecular Sciences Laboratory.

Center for the Environment. Cornell University, 200 Rice Hall, Ithaca, NY 14853-5601. Phone: (607)255-7535 Fax: (607)255-0238 E-mail: cucfe@cornell.edu • URL: http://www.cfe.cornell.edu • Includes Waste Management Institute and New York State Solid Waste Combustion Institute.

Environmental Engineering Center. Michigan Technological University, 1400 Townsend Dr., Houghton, MI 49931. Phone: (906)487-2520 Fax: (906)487-3167 E-mail: biology@mtu.edu • URL: http://www.bio.mtu.edu/research • Applies biotechnological research to waste management and resource recovery.

Waste Management Research and Education Institute. University of Tennessee, Knoxville, Conference Center Bldg., Suite 311, Knoxville, TN 37996-4134. Phone: (865)974-4251 Fax: (865)974-1838 E-mail: kdavis17@utk.edu • URL: http://www.eerc.ra.utk.edu/divisions/wmrei • Research fields include chemical, nuclear, and solid waste management, especially waste policy and environmental biotechnology studies.

STATISTICS SOURCES

OECD Environmental Indicators. Organization for Economic Cooperation and Development. • Annual. $27.00. Provides statistical information relating to climate change, air pollution, biodiversity, waste management, water resources, and other environmental topics.

TRADE/PROFESSIONAL ASSOCIATIONS

Air and Waste Management Association. One Gateway Center, 3rd Fl., 420 Duquesne Blvd., Pittsburgh, PA 15222. Phone: 800-270-3444 or (412)232-3444 Fax: (412)232-3450 E-mail: info@awma.org • URL: http://www.awma.org.

Solid Waste Association of North America. 1100 Wayne Ave., Silver Spring, MD 20907. Phone: 800-467-9262 or (301)585-2898 Fax: (301)589-7068 E-mail: info@swana.org • URL: http://www.swana.org • Members are officials from both public agencies and private companies. Attempts to improve waste management services to the public and industry. Formerly Governmental Refuse Collection and Disposal Association.

OTHER SOURCES

Hazardous Waste Litigation Reporter: The National Journal of Record of Hazardous Waste-Related Litigation. Andrews Publications. • Semimonthly. $875.00 per year. Newsletter. Reports on hazardous waste legal cases.

WASTE PRODUCTS

See also: IRON AND STEEL SCRAP METAL INDUSTRY; RECYCLING; SANITATION INDUSTRY

ABSTRACTS AND INDEXES

Environment Abstracts. Congressional Information Service, Inc. • Monthly. Price varies. Provides multidisciplinary coverage of the world's environmental literature. Incorporates *Acid Rain Abstracts.*

Environment Abstracts Annual: A Guide to the Key Environmental Literature of the Year. Congressional Information Service, Inc. • Annual. $495.00. A yearly cumulation of *Environment Abstracts.*

Environmental Knowledge Base: An Electronic Bibliography Featuring Citations and Abstracts of Scientific and Popular Articles on Environmental Issues, Including Social Policy, Economics, Regulatory, and Legal Topics. Environmental Studies Institute. • Monthly. Price varies. An index to current environmental literature. Formerly *Environmental Periodicals Bibliography.*

Pollution Abstracts. Cambridge Information Group. • Monthly. $1,390.00 per year. Includes print and online editions; with index, $1,515.00 per year.

CD-ROM DATABASES

Environment Abstracts on CD-ROM. LEXIS-NEXIS. • Quarterly. $1,295.00 per year. Contains the following CD-ROM databases: *Environment Abstracts, Energy Abstracts,* and *Acid Rain Abstracts.* Length of coverage varies.

PERIODICALS AND NEWSLETTERS

Scrap. Institute of Scrap Recycling Industries, Inc. • Bimonthly. Free to members; non-members, $32.95 per year. Formerly *Scrap Processing and Recycling.*

Waste Age. Environmental Industry Association. Primedia Business Magazines and Media. • Monthly. Price on application.

Waste Treatment Technology News. BCC Research. • Description: Profiles existing and developing industrial waste treatment techniques. Follows governmental action such as Superfund legislation and EPA (Environmental Protection Agency) activities. Focuses on the research and development of waste treatment technologies, listing recent patents in the field. Recurring features include news of research.

TRADE/PROFESSIONAL ASSOCIATIONS

Institute of Scrap Recycling Industries. 1325 G St., NW, Ste. 1000, Washington, DC 20005-3104.

Phone: (202)737-1770 Fax: (202)626-0900 E-mail: isri@isri.org • URL: http://www.isri.org.

WATCH INDUSTRY

See: CLOCK AND WATCH INDUSTRY

WATER POLLUTION

See also: SANITATION INDUSTRY; WATER SUPPLY

GENERAL WORKS

Pollution: Causes, Effects, and Control. R. M. Harrison. Springer-Verlag. • 2001. $62.00. Fourth edition. Published by The Royal Society of Chemistry. A basic introduction to pollution of air, water, and land. Includes discussions of pollution control technologies.

ABSTRACTS AND INDEXES

Environment Abstracts. Congressional Information Service, Inc. • Monthly. Price varies. Provides multidisciplinary coverage of the world's environmental literature. Incorporates *Acid Rain Abstracts.*

Environment Abstracts Annual: A Guide to the Key Environmental Literature of the Year. Congressional Information Service, Inc. • Annual. $495.00. A yearly cumulation of *Environment Abstracts.*

Environmental Knowledge Base: An Electronic Bibliography Featuring Citations and Abstracts of Scientific and Popular Articles on Environmental Issues, Including Social Policy, Economics, Regulatory, and Legal Topics. Environmental Studies Institute. • Monthly. Price varies. An index to current environmental literature. Formerly *Environmental Periodicals Bibliography.*

Excerpta Medica: Environmental Health and Pollution Control. Elsevier. • 16 times a year. Institutions, $3,246.00 per year. Section 46 of *Excerpta Medica.* Covers air, water, and land pollution and noise control.

NTIS Alerts: Environmental Pollution & Control. National Technical Information Service. • Semimonthly. $245.00 per year. Provides descriptions of government-sponsored research reports and software, with ordering information. Covers the following categories of environmental pollution: air, water, solid wastes, radiation, pesticides, and noise. Formerly *Abstract Newsletter.*

Pollution Abstracts. Cambridge Information Group. • Monthly. $1,390.00 per year. Includes print and online editions; with index, $1,515.00 per year.

ALMANACS AND YEARBOOKS

Environmental Viewpoints. Gale Cengage Learning. • 1993. $195.00. Three volumes. $65.00 per volume. A compendium of excerpts of about 200 articles on a wide variety of environmental topics, selected from both popular and professional periodicals. Arranged alphabetically by topic, with a subject/keyword index.

Gale Environmental Almanac. Gale Cengage Learning. • 1993. $115.00. Contains 15 chapters, each on a broad topic related to the environment, such as "Waste and Recycling." Each chapter has a topical overview, charts, statistics, and illustrations. Includes a glossary of environmental terms and a bibliography.

BIBLIOGRAPHIES

Literature Review. Water Environment Federation. • Annual. Price on application.

CD-ROM DATABASES

Environment Abstracts on CD-ROM. LEXIS-NEXIS. • Quarterly. $1,295.00 per year. Contains the following CD-ROM databases: *Environment Abstracts, Energy Abstracts,* and *Acid Rain*

Abstracts. Length of coverage varies.

DIRECTORIES

Gale Environmental Sourcebook: A Guide to Organizations, Agencies, and Publications. Gale Cengage Learning. • 1993. $115.00. Second edition. A directory of print and non-print information sources on a wide variety of environmental topics.

Pollution Equipment News Buyer's Guide. Rimbach Publishing, Inc. • Annual. $100.00. Over 3,000 manufacturers of pollution control equipment and products.

ENCYCLOPEDIAS AND DICTIONARIES

Encyclopedia of Environmental Science. John Mongillo and Linda Zierdt-Warshaw, editors. Greenwood Publishing Group, Inc. • 2000. $99.95. Provides information on more than 1,000 topics relating to the environment. Includes graphs, tables, maps, illustrations, and 400 Web site addresses.

Environmental Encyclopedia. Gale Cengage Learning. • 2003. $275.00. Third edition. Provides over 1,300 articles on all aspects of the environment. Written in non-technical style.

Pollution A to Z. Gale Cengage Learning. • 2003. $195.00. Two volumes. Provides encyclopedic coverage of many aspects of environmental pollution, including air, water, noise, and soil. (Macmillan Reference USA imprint.).

Wiley Encyclopedia of Environmental Pollution and Cleanup. Robert A. Meyers, editor. John Wiley and Sons, Inc. • 1999. $350.00. Two volumes. Presents generally nontechnical, basic coverage of environmental hazards and methods of detection and cleanup, with consideration of risk assessment, regulatory policy, and economic factors.

HANDBOOKS AND MANUALS

Environmental Engineering. Joseph A. Salvato and others. John Wiley and Sons, Inc. • 2003. $240.00. Fifth edition. Written for environmental engineers, civil engineers, environmental scientists, public health professionals, and others concerned with the technical aspects of protecting the environment. Covers a wide range of topics, including sanitation management, groundwater contamination, incineration, wastewater treatment, communicable diseases, and noise control.

Industrial Pollution Prevention Handbook. Harry M. Freeman. McGraw-Hill. • 1994. $115.00.

Statistics for the Environment: Statistical Aspects of Health and the Environment. Vic Barnett and others. John Wiley and Sons, Inc. • 1999. $180.00. Two volumes. Vol. 3, $205.00; vol. 4, $225.00. Contains articles on the statistical analysis and interpretation of environmental monitoring and sampling data. Areas covered include meteorology, pollution of the environment, and forest resources. (Statistics for the Environment Series).

ONLINE DATABASES

Aqualine. Cambridge Scientific Abstracts. • Provides online citations and abstracts to a wide variety of literature relating to the aquatic environment, including 400 journals, from 1960 to date. Updating is monthly. Inquire as to online cost and availability.

Pollution Abstracts [online]. Cambridge Scientific Abstracts. • Provides indexing and abstracting of international, environmentally related literature, 1970 to date. Monthly updates. Inquire as to online cost and availability.

PERIODICALS AND NEWSLETTERS

Environmental Business Journal: Strategic Information for a Changing Industry. Environmental Business International, Inc. • Monthly. $495.00 per year. Newsletter. Includes both industrial and financial information relating to individual companies and to the environmental industry in general. Covers air pollution, wat es, U. S. Department of Health and

Human Services. Provides conference, workshop, and symposium proceedings, as well as extensive reviews of environmental prospects.

Environmental Regulation: State Capitals. Wakeman-Walworth, Inc. • 50 times a year. $245.00 per year; print and online editions, $350.00 per year. Newsletter. Formerly *From the State Capitals: Environmental Regulation.*

Marine Pollution Bulletin: The International Journal for Marine Environmentalists, Scientists, Engineers, Administrators, Politicians, and Lawyers. Elsevier. • Semimonthly. Qualified personnel, $227.00 per year; institutions, $1,149.00 per year.

Pollution Engineering: Magazine of Environmental Control. Business News Publishing Co. • 13 times a year. $85.90 per year.

Water, Air and Soil Pollution: An International Journal of Environmental Pollution. Kluwer Academic Publishers. • 32 times a year. Institutions, $3,985.00. Includes print and online editions.

Water and Environment Manager. Chartered Institution of Water and Environmental Management. Terence Dalton Ltd. • 10 times a year. $90.00 per year. Formerly *Chartered Institution of Water and Environmental Management Newsletter.*

Water and Wastes Digest. Scranton Gillette Communications, Inc. • 12 times a year. Free to qualified personnel; others, $40.00 per year. Exclusively designed to serve engineers, consultants, superintendents, managers and operators who are involved in water supply, waste water treatment and control.

Water Engineering and Management. Scranton Gillette Communications, Inc. • Monthly. $40.00 per year.

Water Environment Research. Water Environment Federation. • Bimonthly. Members, $158.00 per year; non-members, $404.00 per year. Formerly *Water Pollution Control Federation. Research Journal.*

Water Research. International Association on Water Quality. Elsevier. • 20 times a year. Institutions, $4,537.00 per year.

Water Science and Technology. International Association on Water Quality. Elsevier. • 24 times a year. $4,495.00 per year. Includes print and online editions.

STATISTICS SOURCES

Health and Environment in America's Top-Rated Cities: A Statistical Profile. Grey House Publishing. • Biennial. $125.00. Covers 75 U. S. cities. Includes statistical and other data on a wide variety of topics, such as air quality, water quality, recycling, hospitals, physicians, health care costs, death rates, infant mortality, accidents, and suicides.

Standard & Poor's Industry Surveys. Standard & Poor's. • Semiannual. $1,800.00. Two looseleaf volumes. Includes monthly *Supplements.* Provides detailed, individual surveys of 52 major industry groups. Each survey is revised on a semiannual basis. Also includes "Monthly Investment Review" (industry group investment analysis) and monthly "Trends & Projections" (economic analysis).

Statistical Record of the Environment. Gale Cengage Learning. • 1996. $130.00. Third edition. Provides over 875 charts, tables, and graphs of major environmental statistics, arranged by subject. Covers population growth, hazardous waste, nuclear energy, acid rain, pesticides, and other subjects related to the environment. A keyword index is included. (Gale Environmental Library Series).

U. S. Industry and Trade Outlook. Available from National Technical Information Service. • Annual. $69.95. Produced by the International Trade Administration, U. S. Department of Commerce, in a "public-private" partnership with DRI/McGraw-

Hill and Standard & Poor's. Provides basic data, outlook for the current year, and "Long-Term Prospects" (five-year projections) for a wide variety of products and services. Includes high technology industries. Formerly *U. S. Industrial Outlook.*

TRADE/PROFESSIONAL ASSOCIATIONS

Association of State and Interstate Water Pollution Control Administrators. 750 1st St., NE, Ste. 1010, Washington, DC 20002. Phone: (202)898-0905 Fax: (202)898-0929 E-mail: c.fortier@asiwpca.org • URL: http://www.asiwpca.org.

United Kingdom Committee of International Association. c/o R.G. Ainsworth, Lower Common House, The Avenue, Bucklebury RG7 6NS, United Kingdom. Phone: 44 118 9712489 E-mail: r.ainsworth@btinternet.com • Formerly United Kingdom National Committee of the International Association on Water Pollution Research and Control.

Water Environment Federation. 601 Wythe St., Alexandria, VA 22314-1994. Phone: 800-666-0206 or (703)684-2400 Fax: (703)684-2492 E-mail: wbertera@wef.org • URL: http://www.wef.org • Technical societies representing chemists, biologists, ecologists, geologists, operators, educational and research personnel, industrial wastewater engineers, consultant engineers, municipal officials, equipment manufacturers, and university professors and students dedicated to the enhancement and preservation of water quality and resources. Seeks to advance fundamental and practical knowledge concerning the nature, collection, treatment, and disposal of domestic and industrial wastewaters, and the design, construction, operation, and management of facilities for these purposes. Disseminates technical information; and promotes good public relations and regulations that improve water quality and the status of individuals working in this field. Conducts educational and research programs.

Water Quality Association. 4151 Naperville Rd., Lisle, IL 60532-1088. Phone: (630)505-0160 Fax: (630)505-9637 E-mail: info@wqa.org • URL: http://www.wqa.org • Individuals or firms engaged in the manufacture and/or assembly and distribution and/or retail selling of water treatment equipment, supplies, and services. Promotes the acceptance and use of industry equipment, products, and services. Provides activities, programs, and services designed to improve economy and efficiency within the industry. Conducts expositions and certification and equipment validation programs. Compiles statistics.

OTHER SOURCES

Environment Reporter. BNA, Inc. • Weekly. $3,166.00 per year. 18 looseleaf volumes. Covers legal aspects of wide variety of environmental concerns.

WATER POWER

See: HYDROELECTRIC INDUSTRY

WATER SUPPLY

See also: DESALINATION INDUSTRY; SANITATION INDUSTRY; WATER POLLUTION

GENERAL WORKS

Recent Advances and Issues in Environmental Science. Joan R. Callahan, editor. Greenwood Publishing Group, Inc. • 1999. $49.95. Includes environmental economic problems, such as saving jobs vs. protecting the environment. (Oryx Frontiers of Science Series.).

ABSTRACTS AND INDEXES

Environmental Knowledge Base: An Electronic Bibliography Featuring Citations and Abstracts of

Scientific and Popular Articles on Environmental Issues, Including Social Policy, Economics, Regulatory, and Legal Topics. Environmental Studies Institute. • Monthly. Price varies. An index to current environmental literature. Formerly *Environmental Periodicals Bibliography.*

Pollution Abstracts. Cambridge Information Group. • Monthly. $1,390.00 per year. Includes print and online editions; with index, $1,515.00 per year.

ALMANACS AND YEARBOOKS

Earth Almanac: An Annual Geophysical Review of the State of the Planet. Natalie Goldstein. Greenwood Publishing Group, Inc. • Annual. $69.95. Provides background information, statistics, and a summary of major events relating to the atmosphere, oceans, land, and fresh water.

BIBLIOGRAPHIES

Planning for Water Source Protection. Philip M. Kappen. Sage Publications, Inc. • 1993. $10.00.

Protecting Stream Corridors. Lee Nellis. Sage Publications, Inc. • 1993. $10.00.

CD-ROM DATABASES

AGRICOLA on SilverPlatter. Available from SilverPlatter Information, Inc. • Quarterly. $825.00 per year. Produced by the National Agricultural Library. Provides about three million citations on CD-ROM to the literature of agriculture, agricultural economics, animal sciences, entomology, fertilizer, food, forestry, nutrition, pesticides, plant science, water resources, and other topics. Each quarterly disc covers the past ten years, with archival discs available from 1970.

DIRECTORIES

American Water Works Association--Sourcebook. American Water Works Association. • Covers: member suppliers and distributors of water supply products and services, contractors for water supply projects, and engineering consultants. Entries include: Company name, address, names of executives, trade and brand names, products and services offered.

National Ground Water Association--Membership Directory. National Ground Water Association. • Covers: About 16,500 water well drilling contractors, manufacturers and suppliers of equipment, and related technical professionals such as geologists and engineers in the United States, Canada, Mexico, and foreign countries. Entries include: Name, office address, phone, fax.

ENCYCLOPEDIAS AND DICTIONARIES

Encyclopedia of Agriculture Science. Charles J. Arntzen and Ellen M. Ritter, editors. Elsevier. • 1994. $900.00. Four volumes.

Encyclopedia of Global Change: Environmental Change and Human Society. Andrew S. Goudie, editor. Oxford University Press. • 2001. $275.00. Two volumes. Contains 300 signed articles on a wide variety of topics relating to changes in the environment and the atmosphere. Includes bibliographies and illustrations.

Water Encyclopedia. Frits Von Der Leeden and others, editors. Lewis Publishers. • 1990. $249.95. Second edition. Covers a wide variety of topics relating to water. (Geraghty and Miller Environmental Science and Engineering Series).

FINANCIAL RATIOS

Almanac of Business and Industrial Financial Ratios. Leo Troy. Aspen Publishers, Inc. • 2003. $125.95. Includes CD-Rom. Contains financial ratios derived from federal tax returns. Ratios for each of about 200 industries are arranged according to company asset size. (Almanac of Business and Industrial Financial Ratios Series).

HANDBOOKS AND MANUALS

Water Resources: Distribution, Use and Management. John R. Mather. John Wiley and Sons,

Inc. • 1983. $199.00. (Environmental Science and Technology Series).

ONLINE DATABASES

Aqualine. Cambridge Scientific Abstracts. • Provides online citations and abstracts to a wide variety of literature relating to the aquatic environment, including 400 journals, from 1960 to date. Updating is monthly. Inquire as to online cost and availability.

GEOARCHIVE. Geosystems. • Citations to literature on geoscience and water. 1974 to present. Monthly updates. Inquire as to online cost and availability.

PERIODICALS AND NEWSLETTERS

American Water Works Association Journal. American Water Works Association. • Monthly. Free to members; libraries and governmental agencies only, $85.00 per year.

Environmental Regulation: State Capitals. Wakeman-Walworth, Inc. • 50 times a year. $245.00 per year; print and online editions, $350.00 per year. Newsletter. Formerly *From the State Capitals: Environmental Regulation.*

Ground Water. National Ground Water Association. Ground Water Publishing Co. • Bimonthly. Members, $19.00 per year; non-members, $260.00 per year.

National Water Conditions. Water Resources Div. • Description: Describes the month's water conditions in the U.S. and Canada, compiling data on streamflow, ground water conditions, surface water, reservoirs, the flow of large rivers, water temperatures, and dissolved solids.

Water Engineering and Management. Scranton Gillette Communications, Inc. • Monthly. $40.00 per year.

Water Operation and Maintenance Bulletin. • Quarterly.

Water Well Journal. National Ground Water Association. • Monthly. Free to qualified personnel; others, $65.00 per year.

RESEARCH CENTERS AND INSTITUTES

Water Resources Center. University of Delaware. Dept. of Plant and Soil Sciences, 163 Townsend Hall, Newark, DE 19717-1303. Phone: (302)831-1392 Fax: (302)831-0605 E-mail: jtsims@udel.edu • URL: http://www.ag.udel.edu/dewrc.

STATISTICS SOURCES

Infrastructure Industries USA. Gale Cengage Learning. • 2001. $260.00. Presents statistics and projections relating to economic activity in a wide variety of natural resource and construction industries.

OECD Environmental Indicators. Organization for Economic Cooperation and Development. • Annual. $27.00. Provides statistical information relating to climate change, air pollution, biodiversity, waste management, water resources, and other environmental topics.

TRADE/PROFESSIONAL ASSOCIATIONS

American Water Resources Association. PO Box 1626, PO Box 1626, Middleburg, VA 20118-1626. Phone: (540)687-8390 Fax: (540)687-8395 E-mail: info@awra.org • URL: http://www.awra.org • Engineers; natural, physical, and social scientists; other persons engaged in any aspect of the field of water resources; business concerns and other organizations; students in water resources. Includes members from 62 nations. Seeks to advance water resources research, planning, development, and management. Endeavors to collect and disseminate ideas and information relative to water resources science and technology via scientific journal, newsletter, conferences and symposia and published proceedings.

American Water Works Association. 6666 W Quincy Ave., 6666 W. Quincy Ave., Denver, CO 80235-3098. Phone: 800-926-7337 or (303)794-7711 Fax: (303)347-0804 E-mail: custsvc@awwa.org • URL: http://www.awwa.org • Water utility managers, superintendents, engineers, chemists, bacteriologists, and other individuals interested in public water supply; municipal- and investor-owned water departments; boards of health; manufacturers of waterworks equipment; government officials and consultants interested in water supply. Develops standards and supports research programs in waterworks design, construction, operation, and management. Conducts in-service training schools and prepares manuals for waterworks personnel. Maintains hall of fame. Offers placement service via member newsletter; compiles statistics. Offers training; children's services; and information center on the water utilities industry, potable water, and water reuse.

International Association of Theoretical and Applied Limnology. c/o Gene Likens, Institute of Ecosystems Studies, PO Box AB, Millbrook, NY 12545. Phone: (205)348-1793 or (205)348-1787 Fax: (205)348-1403 E-mail: likensg@ecostudies. org • URL: http://www.limnology.org/sil.

National Ground Water Association. 601 Dempsey Rd., Westerville, OH 43081-8978. Phone: 800-551-7379 or (614)898-7791 Fax: (614)898-7786 E-mail: ngwa@ngwa.org • URL: http://www.ngwa.org • Ground water drilling contractors; manufacturers and suppliers of drilling equipment; ground water scientists such as geologists, engineers, public health officials, and others interested in the problems of locating, developing, preserving, and using ground water supplies. Conducts seminars, and continuing education programs. Encourages scientific education, research, and the development of standards; offers placement services; compiles market statistics. Offers charitable program. Maintains speakers' bureau.

Water and Wastewater Equipment Manufacturers Association. P.O. Box 17402, Washington, DC 20041. Phone: (703)444-1777 Fax: (703)444-1779 E-mail: info@wwema.org • URL: http://www. wwema.org • Formerly Water and Sewage Works Manufacturers Association.

OTHER SOURCES

Water Treatment Equipment and Supplies. Available from MarketResearch.com. • 2002. $3,850.00. Published by Global Industry Analysts. Provides worldwide market research data, including profiles of major water treatment supply companies.

WATERFRONTS

See: PORTS

WATERWAYS

ABSTRACTS AND INDEXES

NTIS Alerts: Transportation. National Technical Information Service. • Semimonthly. $210.00 per year. Provides descriptions of government-sponsored research reports and software, with ordering information. Covers air, marine, highway, inland waterway, pipeline, and railroad transportation. Formerly *Abstract Newsletter.*

Oceanic Abstracts. CSA. • 11 times a year. $1,645.00 per year. Includes print and online editions. Covers oceanography, marine biology, ocean shipping, and a wide range of other marine-related subject areas.

DIRECTORIES

Inland River Guide Record. Waterways Journal, Inc. • Annual. $35.00. Covers barge and towing companies operating on Mississippi River System,

Warrior-Tom Bigbee System, and Gulf Intracoastal Waterwa: all inland and Gulf Coast shipyards; public and private terminals on waterway:; contracting and dredging firms; government agencies dealing with waterways.

Waterway Guide--The Yachtman's Bible. Primedia Business. • Covers: inland and coastal waterways in the eastern half of the United States; published in three editions. Northern edition covers coastal waterways from the Delaware Bay to the U.S.-Canadian border; plus New York canals, Champlain Waterways, and St. Lawrence River; Middle Atlantic edition covers waterways from the Chesapeake Bay to the Florida-Georgia line; Southern edition covers intracoastal waterways from the Florida-Georgia line to the Texas-Mexico border and the Bahamas. Entries include: Name of marine facility, location, navigation information and courses, points of interest, anchorages.

ENCYCLOPEDIAS AND DICTIONARIES

Macmillan Encyclopedia of Transportation. Available from Gale Cengage Learning. • 1999. $450.00. Six volumes. Published by Macmillan Reference USA. Covers the business, technology, and history of transportation on land, on water, in the air, and in space. Includes definitions, cross-references, and 200 color illustrations.

ONLINE DATABASES

Oceanic Abstracts (Online). Cambridge Scientific Abstracts. • Oceanographic and other marine-related technical literature, 1981 to present. Monthly updates. Inquire as to online cost and availability.

PERIODICALS AND NEWSLETTERS

AWO Letter. American Waterways Operators. • Description: Discusses national and local legislative, regulatory, and economic issues affecting the inland and coastal barge and towing industry.

Waterways Journal: Devoted to the Marine Profession and Commercial Interest of All Inland Waterways. Waterways Journal, Inc. • Weekly. $32.00 per year. Weekly business journal serving nation's inland marine industry. Supplement available *Annual Review Number.*

TRADE/PROFESSIONAL ASSOCIATIONS

National Waterways Conference. 4650 Washington Blvd., No. 608, Arlington, VA 22201. Phone: (703)243-4090 Fax: (866)371-1390 E-mail: amy@ waterways.org • URL: http://www.waterways.org • Petroleum, coal, chemical, electric power, building materials, iron and steel, and grain companies; industrial development agencies, port authorities, and other governmental bodies; water carriers; companies which build, repair, service, or insure vessels; water resource development associations, banks, chambers of commerce, and individuals. Seeks to promote a better understanding of the public value of the American waterways system. Conducts research on the economics of water transportation; sponsors an educational program to point up the diverse benefits of efficient water transport; keeps members and other waterway proponents posted on developments affecting national waterways policy.

WATERWORKS

See: WATER SUPPLY

WEALTHY CONSUMERS

See: AFFLUENT MARKET

WEAPONS MARKET

See: DEFENSE INDUSTRIES; MILITARY MARKET

WEATHER AND WEATHER FORECASTING

See also: CLIMATE

ABSTRACTS AND INDEXES

Meteorological and Geoastrophysical Abstracts. American Meteorological Society. • Bimonthly. $1,685.00 per year.

ALMANACS AND YEARBOOKS

AMS Conference Proceedings. American Meteorological Society. • Annual.

The Weather Almanac: A Reference Guide to Weather, Climate, and Air Quality in the United States and Its Key Cities, Comprising Statistics, Principles, and Terminology. Gale Cengage Learning. • 2001. $165.00. 10th edition. Weather reports for 108 major U.S. cities and a climatic overview of the country.

ENCYCLOPEDIAS AND DICTIONARIES

Encyclopedia of Climate and Weather. Stephen H. Schneider, editor. Oxford University Press. • 1996. $275.00. Two volumes. Contains more than 300 multidisciplinary entries, with photographs, line drawings, and charts.

Macmillan Encyclopedia of Weather. Available from Gale Cengage Learning. • 2001. $140.00. Published by Macmillan Reference USA. Contains 150 entries covering the basics of weather and weather forecasting. Includes illustrations in color.

HANDBOOKS AND MANUALS

Climates of the States. Gale Cengage Learning. • 2002. $275.00. Fourth edition. Two volumes. State-by-state summaries of climatebased on first order weather reporting stations.

Handbook of Weather, Climate, and Water: Atmospheric Chemistry, Hydrology, and Societal Impacts. Thomas D. Potter and Bradley R. Coleman. John Wiley and Sons, Inc. • 2003. $275.00. Two volumes. $150.00 per volume. Provides a detailed weather and climate reference for "both professionals and laypersons.".

USA Today Weather Book. Jack Williams. Random House, Inc. • 1997. $20.00. Contains a state-by-state guide to U.S. climate, with color illustrations. Author (weather editor of *USA Today*) includes discussions of weather patterns and computerized forecasting.

Weather of U.S. Cities. Gale Cengage Learning. • 1996. $235.00. Fifth edition.

ONLINE DATABASES

Accu-Data. Accu-Weather, Inc. • Provides detailed, current weather conditions and weather forecasts for many U.S. and foreign cities and regions. Updating is continuous. Inquire as to online cost and availability.

PERIODICALS AND NEWSLETTERS

Daily Weather Maps (Weekly Series). U.S. Dept. of Commerce.

Hourly Precipitation Data. U.S. National Climatic Data Center. • Monthly. Published separately for 41 states.

Journal of Applied Meteorology. American Meteorological Society. • Monthly. Members, $55.00 per year; individuals, $365.00 per year.

Journal of the Atmospheric Sciences. American Meteorological Society. • Semimonthly. Members, $80.00 per year; institutions, $545.00 per year.

Monthly Climatic Data for the World. U.S. National Climatic Data Center. • Monthly.

Monthly Weather Review. American Meteorological Society. • Monthly. Members, $65.00 per year; institutions, $500.00 per year.

Storm Data. U.S. National Climatic Data Center. • Monthly.

Weather and Climate Report. Nautilus Press, Inc. • Monthly. $95.00 per year. Newsletter.

Weatherwise: The Magazine About the Weather. Helen Dwight Reid Educational Foundation. Heldref Publications. • Bimonthly. Individuals, $38.00 per year; institutions, $80.00 per year. Popular magazine devoted to weather.

STATISTICS SOURCES

Weather America: A Thirty-Year Summary of Statistical Data and Weather Trends. David Garoogian, editor. Grey House Publishing. • 2000. $175.00. Second edition. Contains detailed climatological data for 4,000 national and cooperative weather stations in the U.S. Organized by state, with an index to cities. (Universal Reference Publications.).

TRADE/PROFESSIONAL ASSOCIATIONS

American Meteorological Society. 45 Beacon St., Boston, MA 02108-3693. Phone: (617)227-2425 Fax: (617)742-8718 E-mail: amsinfo@ametsoc.org • URL: http://www.ametsoc.org • Professional meteorologists, oceanographers, and hydrologists; interested students and nonprofessionals. Develops and disseminates information on the atmospheric and related oceanic and hydrospheric sciences; seeks to advance professional applications. Activities include guidance service, scholarship programs, career information, certification of consulting meteorologists, and a seal of approval program to recognize competence in radio and television weathercasting. Issues statements of policy to assist public understanding on subjects such as weather modification, forecasting, tornadoes, hurricanes, flash floods, and meteorological satellites. Provides abstracting services. Prepares educational films, filmstrips, and slides for a new curriculum in meteorology at the ninth grade level. Issues monthly announcements of job openings for meteorologists.

Weather Modification Association. PO Box 26926, Fresno, CA 93729-6926. Phone: (559)434-3486 Fax: (559)434-3486 E-mail: wxmod@comcast.net • URL: http://www.weathermodification.org • Individuals and organizations interested in weather modification problems; universities and non-profit research institutes; public utilities, power and water companies, and districts; private meteorological firms, government agencies, and foreign organizations; and other groups and firms. Encourages scientific research; coordinates efforts of different weather modification projects and encourages standardization of weather modification recording procedures. Renders technical assistance in developing legislation pertaining to weather modification.

OTHER SOURCES

Lloyd's Maritime Atlas. Available from Informa UK Limited. • Biennial. $119.00. Contains more than 70 pages of world, ocean, regional, and port maps in color. Provides additional information for the planning of world shipping routes, including data on distances, port facilities, recurring weather hazards at sea, international load line zones, and sailing times.

WEAVING

See also: TEXTILE INDUSTRY

ABSTRACTS AND INDEXES

Textile Technology Digest. Institute of Textile Technology. • Annual. $535.00. Provides indexing and abstracting of a wide variety of textile technology literature.

CD-ROM DATABASES

Textile Technology Digest [CD-ROM]. Textile Information Center, Institute of Textile Technology. • Quarterly. Provides CD-ROM indexing and abstracting of worldwide journals and monographs in various areas of textile technology, production,

and management. Covers 1978 to date.

ENCYCLOPEDIAS AND DICTIONARIES

Textile Terms and Definitions. J.E. McIntyre and Paul N. Daniels, editors. Available from State Mutual Book and Periodical Service Ltd. • 1996. $180.00. 10th edition. Published by the Textile Insitute (UK). Includes more than 1,000 definitions of textile processes, fiber types, and end products. Illustrated.

HANDBOOKS AND MANUALS

The Art of Weaving. Else Regensteiner. Schiffer Publishing, Ltd. • 1986. $29.95.

ONLINE DATABASES

Textile Technology Digest [online]. Institute of Textile Technology. • Contains indexing and abstracting of more than 300 worldwide journals and monographs in various areas of textile technology, production, and management. Time period is 1978 to date, with monthly updating. Inquire as to online cost and availability.

World Textiles. Elsevier Science, Inc. • Provides abstracting and indexing from 1970 of worldwide textile literature (periodicals, books, pamphlets, and reports). Includes U.S., European, and British patent information. Updating is monthly. Inquire as to online cost and availability.

PERIODICALS AND NEWSLETTERS

International Textile Bulletin: Yarn and Fabric Forming Edition. ITS Publishing, International Textile Service. • Quarterly. $170.00 per year. Editions in Chinese, English, French, German, Italian and Spanish.

Shuttle, Spindle, and Dyepot. Handweavers Guild of America, Inc. • Quarterly. $25.00 per year.

STATISTICS SOURCES

Consumption on the Woolen System and Worsted Combing. U.S. Bureau of the Census. • Quarterly and annual. Provides data on consumption of fibers in woolen and worsted spinning mills, by class of fibers and end use. (Current Industrial Reports, MQ-22D.).

TRADE/PROFESSIONAL ASSOCIATIONS

Handweavers Guild of America. 1255 Buford Hwy., Ste. 211, Suwanee, GA 30024. Phone: (678)730-0010 E-mail: hga@weavespindye.org • URL: http://www.weavesypindye.org

Textile Institute. St. James's Buildings, 1st Fl., 79 Oxford St., Manchester M1 6FQ, United Kingdom. Phone: 44 161 2371188 Fax: 44 161 2361991 E-mail: tiihq@textileinst.org.uk • URL: http://www.texi.org • Companies and individuals in 100 countries involved in management, science, technology, design, information transfer, and marketing of textiles including clothing and footwear. Promotes interests of the textile industry worldwide; serves professional interests of members; confers qualifications and recognizes achievements in research, application of ideas, education, business, and public affairs. Maintains Information Service to collect information relating to textile industrial and economic conditions in different countries and economic sectors.

WEEKLY NEWSPAPERS

See: NEWSPAPERS

WEIGHT CONTROL

See: DIET

WEIGHTS AND MEASURES

ALMANACS AND YEARBOOKS

International Society of Weighing and Measurement Membership Directory and Product Guide.

    For publishers addresses, refer to SOURCES CITED section at the back of the book.

International Society of Weighing and Measurement. • Annual. Free to members; non-members, $50.00.

ONLINE DATABASES

Scisearch. Institute for Scientific Information. • Broad, multidisciplinary index to the literature of science and technology, 1974 to present. Inquire as to online cost and availability. Coverage of literature is worldwide, with weekly updates.

PERIODICALS AND NEWSLETTERS

ISWM News. International Society of Weighing and Measurement. • Description: Contains calendar of events, new product information, industry updates, technical articles, and association news.

Metric Today. U.S. Metric Association Inc. • Description: Provides news on metric system conversion in the U.S., Canada, and abroad. Covers metrication updates in industry, government, education, and consumer areas. Recurring features include news of members, metric book reviews, editorials, data on metric standards, and letters to the editor.

Weighing and Measurement. Key Markets Publishing Co. • Bimonthly. $30.00 per year. Provides information relating to industrial weighing methods.

TRADE/PROFESSIONAL ASSOCIATIONS

American National Metric Council. 900 Mix Ave., Ste. 1, Hamden, CT 06514-5106. Phone: (203)287-9849 E-mail: anmcmetric@pi-c.com • URL: http://lamar.colostate.edu/~hillger/anmc.htm • Companies, organizations, and individuals interested in keeping up-to-date on all the latest information on the status of metric transition in the U.S. Aims to coordinate metric transition planning activities for all affected segments in the private sector of American society.

International Bureau of Weights and Measures. 2 bis Grande Rue, 1-92310 Sevres, France. Phone: 33 1 45077070 Fax: 33 1 45342021 E-mail: webmaster@bipm.org • URL: http://www.bipm.org • Works for the establishment of international weights and measures standards, including international time standards. Absorbed International Time Bureau-Time Section.

International Society of Weighing and Measurement. 10 W. Kimball St., Windsor, GA 30680. Phone: (770)868-5300 Fax: (770)868-5301 E-mail: staff@iswm.org • URL: http://www.iswm.org • Formerly National Scale Men's Association.

National Conference on Weights and Measures. 15245 Shady Grove Rd., Suite 130, Rockville, MD 20850-3222. Phone: (301)258-9210 Fax: (301)990-9771 E-mail: ncwm@mgmtsol.com • URL: http://www.ncwm.net.

Scale Manufacturers Association. 6724 Lone Oak Blvd., Naples, FL 34109. Phone: (239)514-3441 Fax: (239)514-3470 E-mail: phil@scalemanufacturers.org • URL: http://www.scalemanufacturers.org • Manufacturers of commercial weighing equipment.

U.S. Metric Association. 10245 Andasol Ave., Northridge, CA 91325-1504. Phone: (818)363-5606 Fax: (818)363-5606 E-mail: valerie.antoine@verizon.net • URL: http://lamar.colostate.edu/~hillger • Scientists, engineers, teachers, government and industry personnel, students, and laymen interested in promoting greater use of the metric system of measurement; appointed by the U.S. Department of Commerce to represent the private sector on government metric committees. Aids teachers, consumers, government, and industry in implementing the metric system. Maintains a Certified Metrication Specialist Board which is responsible for screening qualified applicants to work with metric system units. Distributes educational fliers on the metric system. Compiles statistics.

United Weighers Association. PO Box 1027, Floral Park, NY 11002. Phone: (516)352-2673 Fax: (516)352-3569 E-mail: info@uswheat.org • Weighers and supervisors of raw commodities (sugar, coffee, cocoa, rubber, tin, and wool) imported to U.S. by ship.

WELDING

GENERAL WORKS

Fundamentals. William A. Bowditch and Kevin E. Bowditch. Goodheart-Wilcox Publishers. • 1997. $44.80.

Science and Practice of Welding: The Practice of Welding. A. C. Davies. Cambridge University Press. • 1993. $110.00. 10th edition.

ABSTRACTS AND INDEXES

Applied Science and Technology Index. H. W. Wilson Co. • 11 times a year. Quarterly and annual cumulations. Price varies. Indexes a wide variety of English language technical, industrial, and engineering periodicals.

ALMANACS AND YEARBOOKS

Welding Research Council Yearbook. Welding Research Council. • Annual. Membership.

FINANCIAL RATIOS

Annual Statement Studies. The Risk Management Association. • Annual. Median and quartile financial ratios are given for over 400 kinds of manufacturing, wholesale, retail, construction, and consumer finance establishments. Data is sorted by both asset size and sales volume. Includes a clearly written "Definition of Ratios" and an alphabetical industry index.

Annual Statement Studies: Industry Default Probabilities and Cash Flow Measures. The Risk Management Association. • Annual. $145.00. Serves as a companion volume to the original *Annual Statement Studies.* Gives probability of default estimates on a percentage scale for more than 450 industries. Includes changes in position year-by-year for eight financial statement line items and provides percentage measures of cash flow.

ONLINE DATABASES

Applied Science and Technology Index Online. H. W. Wilson Co. • Provides online indexing of 500 major scientific, technical, industrial, and engineering periodicals. Time period is 1983 to date. Monthly updates. Inquire as to online cost and availability.

METADEX. Cambridge Scientific Abstracts. • Covers the worldwide literature of metals, metallurgy, and materials science, 1966 to date. Includes detailed alloys indexing from 1974. Biweekly updating. Inquire as to online cost and availability. (Formerly produced by ASM International.).

Weldasearch. The Welding Institute. • Contains abstracts of international welding literature, 1967 to date. Inquire as to online cost and availability.

PERIODICALS AND NEWSLETTERS

The Gases and Welding Distributor. Penton Media Inc. • Bimonthly. Free to qualified personnel; others, $55.00 Per year. Formerly *Welding Distributor.*

Welding and Metal Fabrication. Media Scores Ltd. • 10 times a year. $168.00 per year.

Welding Design and Fabrication. Penton Media, Inc. • Monthly. Free to qualified personnel; others, $75.00 per year.

Welding in the World. International Institute of Welding. Elsevier. • Semimonthly. $449.00 per year. Text in English and French.

Welding Journal. American Welding Society. • Monthly. Membership.

Welding Research Abroad. Welding Research Council. • 10 times a year. $1,100.00. Includes *Progress Reports, WRC Bulletins, WRC News* and *Welding Journal.*

WRC Progress Reports. Welding Research Council. • Bimonthly. $1,100 per year. Includes *Welding Research Abroad; WRC Bulletins, WRC News* and *Welding Journal.*

RESEARCH CENTERS AND INSTITUTES

Materials Processing Center. Massachusetts Institute of Technology, 77 Massachusetts Ave., Room 12-007, Cambridge, MA 02139-4307. Phone: (617)253-5179 Fax: (617)258-6900 E-mail: fmpage@.mit.edu • URL: http://www.web.mit.edu/mpc • Conducts processing, engineering, and economic research in ferrous and nonferrous metals, ceramics, polymers, photonic materials, superconductors, welding, composite materials, and other materials.

STATISTICS SOURCES

U. S. Industry and Trade Outlook. Available from National Technical Information Service. • Annual. $69.95. Produced by the International Trade Administration, U. S. Department of Commerce, in a "public-private" partnership with DRI/McGraw-Hill and Standard & Poor's. Provides basic data, outlook for the current year, and "Long-Term Prospects" (five-year projections) for a wide variety of products and services. Includes high technology industries. Formerly *U. S. Industrial Outlook.*

United States Census of Service Industries. U.S. Bureau of the Census. • Quinquennial. Various reports available.

TRADE/PROFESSIONAL ASSOCIATIONS

American Council of the International Institute of Welding. 13340 S.W. Sixth Ave., Miami, FL 33176. Phone: 800-443-9353 or (305)971-4798 Fax: (305)971-4799 E-mail: hgziggy@worldnet.att.net • URL: http://www.iiw-iis.org.

American Welding Society. 550 NW Le Jeune Rd., Miami, FL 33126. Phone: 800-443-9353 or (305)443-9353 Fax: (305)443-5647 E-mail: info@aws.org • URL: http://www.aws.org • One of several sponsors of the Welding Research Council and the Materials Properties Council. Professional engineering society in the field of welding. Sponsors seminars. Maintains over 130 technical and handbook committees, 171 sections, educational committees, and task forces.

Gas Welding and Distributors Association. 1900 Arch St., Philadelphia, PA 19103. Phone: (215)564-3484 Fax: (215)963-9784 E-mail: gawda@gawda.org • URL: http://www.nwsa.com • Formerly *National Welding Supply Assoication.*

Resistance Welding Manufacturing Alliance. 550 NW Lejeune Rd., Miami, FL 33126. Phone: (305)443-9353 Fax: (305)442-7451 E-mail: rwma@aws.org • URL: http://www.aws.org/rwma • Manufacturers, suppliers, and users of resistance welding equipment and supplies. Conducts Resistance Welding School, an annual educational program. Compiles statistics. Offers VHS tape program on basics of resistance welding.

Welding Research Council. PO Box 1942, New York, NY 10156. Phone: (216)658-3847 Fax: (216)658-3854 E-mail: mprager@forengineers.org • URL: http://foreng1.securesites.net/wrc • Established by the Engineering Foundation under the sponsorship of the major engineering societies to conduct needed cooperative research in welding and closely allied fields, to disseminate research information, to promote welding research in the universities, and to provide a means for cooperation with similar agencies abroad. Activities include administration of large projects by specific committees, as well as sponsorship of small grants-in-aid by the University +Research Committee to foster interest in welding research in universities. The council is guided by 24 corporation executives who establish broad policies and prepare overall budgets for its projects. In itself, or through its committees, the Council is considered the welding research arm of eight engineering societies and six trade associations. In addition, it acts in an advisory capacity to the public utility industry, aerospace industry, and the Atomic Energy Commission. Financed by subscriptions from corporations, associations, and government departments; it has more than 900 scientists affiliated with its work, which is carried out in some 45 laboratories. Acts as one of the two sponsor body representatives of the American Council of the International Institute of Welding.

WELFARE, PUBLIC

See: PUBLIC WELFARE

WELLNESS PROGRAMS

See: EMPLOYEE WELLNESS PROGRAMS

WHARVES

See: PORTS

WHEAT INDUSTRY

See also: COMMODITY FUTURES TRADING; FLOUR INDUSTRY; GRAIN INDUSTRY

ABSTRACTS AND INDEXES

Wheat, Barley, and Triticale Abstracts. Available from CABI Publishing, North America. • Bimonthly. Institutions, $1,235.00 per year. Print and online editions, $1,250.00 per year. Published in England by CABI Publishing. Provides worldwide coverage of the literature of wheat, barley, and rye.

ALMANACS AND YEARBOOKS

Agricultural and Mineral Commodities Year Book. Available from Taylor & Francis Group. • Annual. $225.00. Published by Europa Publications. Contains descriptive product profiles, price data, export-import data, and production statistics for major commodities of the world. Includes commodity histories, uses, markets, demand trends, and information about trade agreements and key commodity organizations.

CRB Commodity Yearbook. Commodity Research Bureau. CRB. • Annual. $99.95.

CD-ROM DATABASES

OECD Statistical Compendium. Organization for Economic Cooperation and Development. • Semiannual. $1,905.00 per year for 1 to 10 users. CD-ROM contains more than 730,000 monthly, quarterly, and annual time series for OECD countries, 1960 to date. Includes fully searchable data on agriculture, food, economic indicators, national accounts, employment, energy, finance, industry, technology, and foreign trade. Results can be displayed in various forms.

INTERNET DATABASES

Business 2.0 Web Guide to the Best Business Links. Business 2.0 Media Inc. Phone: (415)293-4800 E-mail: support@business2.com • URL: http://www.business2.com/webguide • Web site presents an extensive, searchable directory of links to "the best, most informative, and authoritative web pages." Twenty main categories cover business, finance, career, company information, people, and technology topics, with thousands of subtopics, all linking to Web sites recommended by experienced business researchers. Fees: Free.

Fedstats. Federal Interagency Council on Statistical Policy. Phone: (202)395-7254 • URL: http://www.fedstats.gov • Web site features an efficient search facility for full-text statistics produced by more than 100 federal agencies, including the Census Bureau, the Bureau of Economic Analysis, and the Bureau of Labor Statistics. Boolean searches can be made within one agency or for all agencies combined. Links are offered to international statistical bureaus, including the UN, IMF, OECD, UNESCO, Eurostat, and 20 individual countries. Fees: Free.

FreeLunch.com. Economy.com, Inc. Phone: (610)696-8700 Fax: (610)696-1678 • URL: http://www.freelunch.com • Web site provides free access to more than 1.5 million economic and financial data series, covering industry, demographics, labor markets, prices, retail sales, government spending, trade, interest rates, housing starts, the stock market, and many other topics. Data is available for various time periods in either chart or table form. Searching is offered. Fees: Free, but registration required. Economy.com, Inc. also offers fee-based economic analysis at *The Dismal Scientist* site (http://www.dismal.com).

USDA. United States Department of Agriculture. Phone: (202)720-2791 E-mail: agsec@usda.gov • URL: http://www.usda.gov • The USDA home page has six sections: News and Information; What's New; About USDA; Agencies; Opportunities; Search and Help. Keyword searching is offered from the USDA home page and from various individual agency home pages. Agencies are the Economic Research Service, Agricultural Marketing Service, National Agricultural Statistics Service, National Agricultural Library, and about 12 others. Updating varies. Fees: Free.

ONLINE DATABASES

CAB Abstracts. CAB Publishing North America. • Contains 46 specialized abstract collections covering over 10,000 journals and monographs in the areas of agriculture, horticulture, forest products, farm products, nutrition, dairy science, poultry, grains, animal health, entomology, etc. Time period is 1972 to date, with monthly updates. Inquire as to online cost and availability. *CAB Abstracts on CD-ROM* also available, with annual updating.

PERIODICALS AND NEWSLETTERS

Amber Waves. Available from U. S. Government Printing Office. • Quarterly. $38.00 per year. Replaces *Agricultural Outlook; Food Review*; and *Rural America.* Provides research and analysis from the U.S. Department of Agriculture's Economic Research Service. Includes economic data on agriculture, food, trade, and environmental factors.

Kansas Farmer. Farm Progress Companies. • 15 times a year. $23.95 per year.

The Montana Farmer-Stockman. Farm Progress Companies. • 14 times a year. $23.95 per year. Formerly *Montana Farmer.*

Oregon Wheat. Oregon Wheat Growers League. • Monthly. Free to members; non-members, $15.00 per year. Deals with planting, weeds, and disease warnings, storage and marketing of wheat and barley. Specifically for Oregon growers.

Wheat Life. Washington Association of Wheat Growers. • 11 times a year. $12.00 per year. Covers research, marketing information, and legislative and regulatory news pertinent to the wheat and barley industries of the Pacific Northwest.

PRICE SOURCES

Nebraska Farmer. Farm Progress Companies. • 15 times a year. $23.95 per year.

STATISTICS SOURCES

Agricultural Statistics. Available from U. S. Government Printing Office. • Annual. $38.00. Produced by the National Agricultural Statistics Service, U. S.

Department of Agriculture. Provides a wide variety of statistical data relating to agricultural production, supplies, consumption, prices/price-supports, foreign trade, costs, and returns, as well as farm labor, loans, income, and population. In many cases, historical data is shown annually for 10 years. In addition to farm data, includes detailed fishery statistics.

Business Statistics of the United States. Linz Audain and Cornelia J. Strawser. Bernan Associates. • Annual. $147.00. Based on *Business Statistics*, formerly issue by the Bureau of Economic Analysis, U. S. Department of Commerce. Provides basic data for a wide variety of U. S. industries, services, and economic indicators. Most statistics are shown annually for 30 years and monthly for the most recent four years.

Chicago Board of Trade Statistical Annual. Board of Trade of the City of Chicago. • Annual.

FAO Production Yearbook. Available from Bernan Associates. • Annual. $45.00. Published by the Food and Agriculture Organization (http://www.fao.org). Contains worldwide data on agriculture, land use, farm crops, livestock, and agricultural prices.

FAO Quarterly Bulletin of Statistics. Food and Agriculture Organization of the United Nations. Available from UNIPUB. • Quarterly. $20.00 per year. Provides international data on agricultural production, trade, and prices, covering the major commodities of many countries. Text in English, French, and Spanish. Formerly *FAO Monthly Bulletin of Statistics.*.

FAO Trade Yearbook. Available from Bernan Associates. • Annual. $45.00. Published by the Food and Agriculture Organization (http://www.fao.org). Provides extensive worldwide data on exports and imports of agricultural commodities, fertilizers, tractors, and pesticides. Includes more than 130 tables of detailed statistics.

Flour Milling Products. U. S. Bureau of the Census. • Monthly and annual. Covers production, mill stocks, exports, and imports of wheat and rye flour. (Current Industrial Reports, M20A.).

International Grains Council. World Grain Statistics. International Grains Council. • Annual. $160.00. Text in English, French, Russian and Spanish. Formerly *International Wheat Council. World Grain Statistics.*

Statistical Annual: Grains, Options on Agricultural Futures. Chicago Board of Trade. • Annual. Includes historical data on Wheat Futures, Options on Wheat Futures, Corn Futures, Options on Corn Futures, Oats Futures, Soybean Futures, Options on Soybean Futures, Soybean Oil Futures, Soybean Meal Futures.

Survey of Current Business. Available from U. S. Government Printing Office. • Monthly. $63.00 per year. Issued by Bureau of Economic Analysis, U. S. Department of Commerce. Presents a wide variety of business and economic data.

WEFA Industrial Monitor. John Wiley and Sons, Inc. • Annual. $65.00. Prepared by industry analysts at WEFA, an economic forecasting and consulting firm (originally Wharton Econometric Forecasting Associates). Contains discussions of the outlook for major U. S. industries, with many 10-year forecasts (WEFA Web site is http://www.wefa.com).

Wheat Facts. National Association of Wheat Growers. • Annual. Price on application.

World Trade Annual. United Nations Statistical Office. Walker and Co. • Annual. Prices vary.

TRADE/PROFESSIONAL ASSOCIATIONS

National Association of Wheat Growers. 415 Second St., N.E., Suite 300, Washington, DC 20002-4993. Phone: (202)547-7800 Fax: (202)546-2638 E-mail: wheatworld@wheatworld.org • URL: http://www.wheatworld.org.

For publishers addresses, refer to SOURCES CITED section at the back of the book.

North American Millers' Association. 600 Maryland Ave. SW, Ste. 825 W, Washington, DC 20024. Phone: (202)484-2200 Fax: (202)488-7416 E-mail: generalinfo@namamillers.org • URL: http://www. namamillers.org • Millers of wheat, corn, oats, durum, and rye flour; members mill 95 percent of total U.S. capacity.

United States Durum Growers Association. 2409 Jackson Ave., Bismarck, ND 58501. Phone: 800-463-8786 or (701)214-3203 Fax: (701)250-1730 E-mail: dawn@durumgrowers.com • URL: http:// www.durumgrowers.com • Durum wheat growers. Cooperates with other organizations to promote favorable conditions for the production and marketing of durum wheat.

U.S. Wheat Associates. 3103 10th St. N, Ste. 300, Arlington, VA 22201. Phone: (202)463-0999 Fax: (703)524-4399 E-mail: info@uswheat.org • URL: http://www.uswheat.org • Works as the industry export market development organization.

OTHER SOURCES

Grains: Production, Processing, Marketing. Chicago Board of Trade. • 1992. $12.00. Revised edition.

WHISKEY INDUSTRY

See: DISTILLING INDUSTRY

WHITE COLLAR CRIME

See: CRIME AND CRIMINALS; FRAUD AND EMBEZZLEMENT

WHOLESALE TRADE

See also: DISTRIBUTION; RACK JOBBERS

CD-ROM DATABASES

OECD Statistical Compendium. Organization for Economic Cooperation and Development. • Semiannual. $1,905.00 per year for 1 to 10 users. CD-ROM contains more than 730,000 monthly, quarterly, and annual time series for OECD countries, 1960 to date. Includes fully searchable data on agriculture, food, economic indicators, national accounts, employment, energy, finance, industry, technology, and foreign trade. Results can be displayed in various forms.

16 Million Businesses Phone Directory. Info USA. • Annual. $29.95. Provides more than 16 million yellow pages telephone directory listings on CD-ROM for all ZIP Code areas of the U. S.

DIRECTORIES

American Big Businesses Directory. infoUSA Inc. • Covers: 218,000 U.S. businesses with more than 100 employees, and 500,000 key executives and directors. CD-ROM version contains 160,000 top firms and 431,000 key executives. Entries include: Name, address, phone, names and titles of key personnel, number of employees, sales volume, Standard Industrial Classification (SIC) codes, subsidiaries and parent company names; stock exchanges on which traded.

American Book Trade Directory. Information Today Inc. • Covers: Nearly 25,500 retail and antiquarian book dealers, plus 1,200 book and magazine wholesalers, distributors, and jobbers-in all 50 states and U.S. territories. Also included are sections of auctioneers of literary property, exporters/importers, booktrade associations, foreign language book dealers, book and literary appraisers, and rental library chains. Entries include: Bookstore name, address, phone, owner or manager, types and subjects of books stocked, specialty, sidelines, year established,

SAN (Standard Address Number), number of volumes stocked, square footage.

American Manufacturers Directory. infoUSA Inc. • Covers: more than 150,000 manufacturing companies with 20 or more employees. CD-ROM version lists all 531,000 U.S. manufacturers, in all employee size ranges. Entries include: Company name; address, phone, contact name, Standard Industrial Classification (SIC) codes, number of employees, sales volume code, credit rating scores.

American Wholesalers and Distributors Directory. Gale Cengage Learning. • 2003. $250.00. 12th edition. Lists more than 30,000 national, regional, state, and local wholesalesrs.

Directory of Automotive Aftermarket Suppliers. Chain Store Guide. • Annual. $327.00. Covers auto supply store chains. Includes distributors.

Directory of Computer and Consumer Electronics Retailers. Chain Store Guide. • Annual. $335.00. Online edition, $775.00. Lists 4,500 United States and Canada companies operating almost 59,000 stores with at least $1,000,000 in sales.

Directory of Discount and General Merchandise Stores. Chain Store Guide. • Annual. $327.00. Online edition, $747.00. Includes retailers and wholesalers of housewares, giftwares, novelties, toys, hobby materials, crafts, and stationery.

Directory of Foodservice Distributors. Chain Store Guide. • Annual. $335.00. Available online. Covers distributors of food and equipment to restaurants and institutions.

Directory of Home Furnishings Retailers. Chain Store Guide. • Annual. $335.00. Online edition, $775.00. Includes more than 5,500 furniture retailers and wholesalers. Covers United States and Canada.

Directory of Single Unit Supermarket Operators. Chain Store Guide. • Annual. $327.00. Online edition, $747.00. Covers more than 7,900 one-store supermarket establishments with annual sales of at least $1,000,000. Includes names of primary wholesalers.

Directory of Wholesale Grocers. Chain Store Guide. • Annual. $327.00. Online edition, $747.00. Profiles over 1,100 cooperatives, voluntaries, non-sponsoring wholesalers, cash and carry warehouses, and nearly 220 service merchandisers. Covers United States and Canada.

Grocery Headquarters: The Newspaper for the Food Industry. Trend Publishing. • Monthly. $80.00 per year. Covers the sale and distribution of food products and other items sold in supermarkets and grocery stores. Edited mainly for retailers and wholesalers. Incorporates (Grocery Distribution).

The Wholesaler "The Wholesaling 100". TMB Publishing, Inc. • Annual. $25.00. Provides information on the 100 leading wholesalers of plumbing, piping, heating, and air conditioning equipment.

FINANCIAL RATIOS

Almanac of Business and Industrial Financial Ratios. Leo Troy. Aspen Publishers, Inc. • 2003. $125.95. Includes CD-Rom. Contains financial ratios derived from federal tax returns. Ratios for each of about 200 industries are arranged according to company asset size. (Almanac of Business and Industrial Financial Ratios Series).

IRS Corporate Financial Ratios. Available from MarketResearch.com. • 2002. $225.00. Published by Schonfeld & Associates, Inc. Presents 70 key financial ratios for 260 industries. Ratios are calculated from income statement and balance sheet data available from the Internal Revenue Service. Includes four asset size classes.

INTERNET DATABASES

Bureau of Economic Analysis (BEA). U. S. Department of Commerce, Bureau of Economic Analysis. Phone: (202)606-9900 Fax: (202)606-5310 E-mail:

webmaster@bea.doc.gov • URL: http://www.bea. doc.gov • Web site includes "News Release Information" covering national, regional, and international economic estimates from the BEA. Highlights of releases appear online the same day, complete text and tables appear the next day. "Recent News Releases" section provides titles for past nine months, with links. "BEA Data and Methodology" includes "Frequently Requested NIPA Data" (national income and product accounts, such as gross domestic product and personal income). Other statistics are available. Fees: Free.

Business 2.0 Web Guide to the Best Business Links. Business 2.0 Media Inc. Phone: (415)293-4800 E-mail: support@business2.com • URL: http:// www.business2.com/webguide • Web site presents an extensive, searchable directory of links to "the best, most informative, and authoritative web pages." Twenty main categories cover business, finance, career, company information, people, and technology topics, with thousands of subtopics, all linking to Web sites recommended by experienced business researchers. Fees: Free.

Fedstats. Federal Interagency Council on Statistical Policy. Phone: (202)395-7254 • URL: http://www. fedstats.gov • Web site features an efficient search facility for full-text statistics produced by more than 100 federal agencies, including the Census Bureau, the Bureau of Economic Analysis, and the Bureau of Labor Statistics. Boolean searches can be made within one agency or for all agencies combined. Links are offered to international statistical bureaus, including the UN, IMF, OECD, UNESCO, Eurostat, and 20 individual countries. Fees: Free.

FreeLunch.com. Economy.com, Inc. Phone: (610)696-8700 Fax: (610)696-1678 • URL: http:// www.freelunch.com • Web site provides free access to more than 1.5 million economic and financial data series, covering industry, demographics, labor markets, prices, retail sales, government spending, trade, interest rates, housing starts, the stock market, and many other topics. Data is available for various time periods in either chart or table form. Searching is offered. Fees: Free, but registration required. Economy.com, Inc. also offers fee-based economic analysis at *The Dismal Scientist* site (http://www. dismal.com).

ONLINE DATABASES

American Business Directory. InfoUSA, Inc. • Provides brief online information on more than 10 million U. S. companies, including individual plants and branches. Entries typically include address, phone number, industry classification code, and contact name. Updating is quarterly. Inquire as to online cost and availability.

Business and Industry. Gale Cengage Learning. • Contains online citations, abstracts, and selected fulltext from more than 1,000 trade journals, newspapers, and other publications. Provides general coverage of both manufacturing and service industries, including marketing, production, industry trends, key events, and information on specific companies. Time span is 1994 to date. Daily updates. Inquire as to online cost and availability. (Also available in a CD-ROM version.).

Tablebase. Gale Cengage Learning. • Provides online numerical tabular data from a wide variety of business, organization, and government sources, including about 1,000 trade journals. Includes industry and individual company statistics relating to products, market share, sales forecasts, production, exports, market trends, etc. Time span is 1997 to date. Weekly updates. Inquire as to online cost and availability. (Also available in a CD-ROM version.).

PERIODICALS AND NEWSLETTERS

The Wholesaler. TMB Publishing, Inc. • Monthly. $75.00 per year. Edited for wholesalers and distributors of plumbing, piping, heating, and air conditioning equipment.

PRICE SOURCES

PPI Detailed Report. Bureau of Labor Statistics, U.S. Department of Labor. Available from U.S. Government Printing Office. • Monthly. $55.00 per year. Formerly *Producer Price Indexes.*

STATISTICS SOURCES

Business Statistics of the United States. Linz Audain and Cornelia J. Strawser. Bernan Associates. • Annual. $147.00. Based on *Business Statistics,* formerly issue by the Bureau of Economic Analysis, U. S. Department of Commerce. Provides basic data for a wide variety of U. S. industries, services, and economic indicators. Most statistics are shown annually for 30 years and monthly for the most recent four years.

Encyclopedia of American Industries. Gale Cengage Learning. • 2000. $560.00. Third edition. Two volumes. $280.00 per volume. Volume one is *Manufacturing Industries* and volume two is *Service and Non-Manufacturing Industries.* Provides the history, development, and recent status of approximately 1,000 industries. Includes statistical graphs, with industry and general indexes.

Industry Profile and Healthcare Factbook. Healthcare Distribution Management Association. • Annual. $349.00. Provides 266 statistical tables in three sections: "Industry Profile" (financial ratios related to drug distribution), "Pharmaceutical and Healthcare Distribution Trends and Facts," and "Healthcare Factbook" (expenditures, insurance utilization, company/product rankings, drug price inflation, generics, OTC, drug store data, hospital statistics, healthcare consumer summaries, etc.). Also known as *HDMA Factbook.* The Healthcare Distribution Management Association was formerly the National Wholesale Druggists' Association.

Manufacturing and Distribution USA. Gale Cengage Learning. • 2002. $395.00. Second edition. Three volumes. Presents statistics and projections relating to economic activity in more than 500 business classifications.

Survey of Current Business. Available from U. S. Government Printing Office. • Monthly. $63.00 per year. Issued by Bureau of Economic Analysis, U. S. Department of Commerce. Presents a wide variety of business and economic data.

U. S. Industry Profiles: The Leading 100. Gale Cengage Learning. • 1998. $130.00. Second edition. Contains detailed profiles, with statistics, of 100 industries in the areas of manufacturing, construction, transportation, wholesale trade, retail trade, and entertainment.

United States Census of Wholesale Trade. Bureau of the Census, U.S. Department of Commerce. Available from U.S. Government Printing Office. • Quinquennial.

WEFA Industrial Monitor. John Wiley and Sons, Inc. • Annual. $65.00. Prepared by industry analysts at WEFA, an economic forecasting and consulting firm (originally Wharton Econometric Forecasting Associates). Contains discussions of the outlook for major U. S. industries, with many 10-year forecasts (WEFA Web site is http://www.wefa.com).

TRADE/PROFESSIONAL ASSOCIATIONS

National Association of Wholesaler-Distributors. 1725 K St., N.W., Ste. 00, Washington, DC 20006. Phone: (202)872-0885 Fax: (202)785-0586 E-mail: naw@nawd.org • URL: http://www.naw.org • Formerly National Association of Wholesalers.

OTHER SOURCES

Product Distribution Law Guide. CCH, Inc. • $199.00. Looseleaf service. Annual updates available. Covers the legal aspects of various methods of product distribution, including franchising.

WILLS

See also: ESTATE PLANNING

GENERAL WORKS

How to Avoid Financial Tangles. American Institute for Economic Research. • 2001. $8.00. Provides basic information and advice on such topics as property ownership, taxes, wills, trusts, insurance, record retention, and professional assistance. (Economic Education Bulletin.).

CD-ROM DATABASES

Authority Tax and Estate Planning Library. LexisNexis/Matthew Bender. • Periodic revisions. Price on request. CD-ROM contains updated full text of *Bender's Payroll Tax Guide, Depreciation Handbook, Federal Income Taxation of Corporations, Tax Planning for Corporations, Modern Estate Planning, Planning for Large Estates, Murphy's Will Clauses, Tax & Estate Planning for the Elderly,* and 12 other Matthew Bender publications. The Internal Revenue Code is also included.

HANDBOOKS AND MANUALS

The Complete Probate Kit. Jens C. Appel and others. John Wiley and Sons, Inc. • 1991. $35.00. A practical guide to settling estates. Provides summaries of the applicable state laws and definitions of relevant terms.

Inheritor's Handbook: A Definitive Guide for Beneficiaries. Dan Rottenberg. Bloomberg. • 1998. $23.95. Covers both financial and emotional issues faced by beneficiaries. (Bloomberg Personal Bookshelf Series.).

Murphy's Will Clauses: Annotations and Forms with Tax Effects. LexisNexis Matthew Bender. • Biennial. $1,157.00 per year. Four looseleaf volumes. Over 1,400 framed will and trust clauses.

TRADE/PROFESSIONAL ASSOCIATIONS

American College of Trust and Estate Counsel. 3415 S. Sepulveda Blvd., Suite 330, Los Angeles, CA 90034. Phone: (310)398-1888 Fax: (310)572-7280 E-mail: info@actec.org • URL: http://www.actec.org.

OTHER SOURCES

Estate Planning: Wills, Trusts and Forms. RIA. • Looseleaf service. Includes bimonthly updates.

WIND ENERGY

See: COGENERATION OF ENERGY

WINDOW COVERING INDUSTRY

See also: INTERIOR DECORATION

GENERAL WORKS

Curtains, Blinds and Valances. Rightfield Business Publications. • 1998. $18.99. (Sew in a Weekend Series).

Window Treatments. Karla J. Nielson. John Wiley and Sons, Inc. • 1989. $85.00.

ABSTRACTS AND INDEXES

Art Index. H. W. Wilson Co. • Quarterly. Annual cumulations. Price varies. Subject and author index to periodicals in art, architecture, industrial design, city planning, photography, and various related topics.

CD-ROM DATABASES

WILSONDISC: Art Index. H. W. Wilson Co. • Monthly. Provides CD-ROM indexing of art-related literature from 1982 to date. Price includes online service.

DIRECTORIES

Decorating Registry. Paint and Decorating Retailers Association. • Publication includes: List of about

1,500 manufacturers, manufacturers' representatives, distributors, and suppliers of decorating merchandise; a comprehensive trademark and brand name directory; associations, societies, and trade shows related to the home decorating industry. Entries include: For companies and manufacturer representatives--Firm name, address, phone, fax, name and title of contact, trademark, brand names. For associations--Name, address, phone, statement of purpose or description of service, key personnel, trade shows sponsored with dates and locations. Principal content of publication is decorative products (coatings, wallcoverings, window treatments, flooring, sundries).

Draperies and Window Coverings: Directory and Buyer's Guide. L. C. Clark Publishing Co., Inc. • Annual. $15.00. Includes about 2,000 manufacturers and distributors of window coverings and related products.

Home Fashions: Buyer's Guide. Fairchild Publications. • Annual. $10.00. Lists manufacturers, importers, and regional sales representatives supplying bed, bath, kitchen, and table linens; window treatments; wall coverings; and fibers and fabrics.

LDB Interior Textiles Annual Buyers' Guide. E.W. Williams Publications Co. • Covers: Over 3,000 manufacturers, importers, and suppliers of home fashions products and services, decorative fabric converters, and alternative window coverings; fabricators; manufacturer's representatives; and others allied to the home fashions trade. Entries include: For manufacturers, importers, converters, fabricators, and suppliers--Company name, address, phone, fax, contact, product line. For manufacturer's representatives--Name, address, phone, contact, lines carried. For others--Name, address, phone, fax.

Window Fashions Magazine: Design and Education Magazine. Grace McNamara Publishing, Inc. • Monthly. $39.00 per year. A directory of suppliers, manufacturers, and fabricators of vertical blinds, soft shades, curtains, draperies, and other window treatment items. Appears as a regular feature of *Window Fashions Magazine* and covers a different product category each month.

FINANCIAL RATIOS

Annual Statement Studies. The Risk Management Association. • Annual. Median and quartile financial ratios are given for over 400 kinds of manufacturing, wholesale, retail, construction, and consumer finance establishments. Data is sorted by both asset size and sales volume. Includes a clearly written "Definition of Ratios" and an alphabetical industry index.

Annual Statement Studies: Industry Default Probabilities and Cash Flow Measures. The Risk Management Association. • Annual. $145.00. Serves as a companion volume to the original *Annual Statement Studies.* Gives probability of default estimates on a percentage scale for more than 450 industries. Includes changes in position year-by-year for eight financial statement line items and provides percentage measures of cash flow.

HANDBOOKS AND MANUALS

Custom Draperies in Interior Design. M. Neal. Prentice Hall PTR. • 1982. $40.25.

ONLINE DATABASES

Art Index Online. H. W. Wilson Co. • Indexes a wide variety of art-related periodicals, 1984 to date. Monthly updates. Inquire as to online cost and availability.

Avery Architectural Periodicals Index. Avery Architectural and Fine Arts Library. • Indexes a wide range of periodicals related to architecture and design. Subjects include building design, building materials, interior design, housing, land use, and city planning. Time span: 1977 to date. *bul* URL: http://www.rlg.stanford.edu/cit-ave.html.

Globalbase. Gale Cengage Learning. • Provides more than one million online summaries of business, industrial, and economic news reports from more than 1,000 publications worldwide. Covers a wide range of material appearing in international trade journals, professional magazines, and newspapers. Time period is 1984 to date, with weekly updates. Inquire as to online cost and availability.

PROMT: Predicasts Overview of Markets and Technology. Gale Cengage Learning. • Companies, products, applied technologies and markets. U.S. and international literature coverage, 1972 to date. Inquire as to online cost and availability. Provides abstracts from more than 1,600 publications. Weekly updates.

PERIODICALS AND NEWSLETTERS

Draperies and Window Coverings. L. C. Clark Publishing Co., Inc. • 13 times a year. $33.00 per year. Published for retailers, designers, manufacturers, and distributors of window coverings.

LDB Interior Textiles. EW Williams Publications Co. • Monthly. $66.00 per year. Supplement available *Linens, Domestics and Baths-Interior Textile Annual Buyer's Guide.* Formerly *Interior Textiles.*

Waland Window Trends. Cygnus Business Media, Inc. • Monthly $36.00 per year. Edited for retailers of interior decoration products, with an emphasis on wallcoverings. Formerly *Wallcoverings, Windows and Interior Fashion.*

Window Fashions. Grace McNamara Publishing, Inc. • Monthly. $39.00 per year. Published for designers and retailers of draperies, blinds, and shades.

RESEARCH CENTERS AND INSTITUTES

Interior Design Laboratory. Lambuth University, 7051 Lambuth Blvd., Jackson, TN 38301. Phone: 800-526-2884.

TRADE/PROFESSIONAL ASSOCIATIONS

Contractors Co-Op Council. 164 N Main St., Porterville, CA 93257. Phone: (559)784-5394 Fax: (714)891-5616 E-mail: clmassociation@aol.com • Custom drapery merchants. Organizes cooperative advertising, warehousing, and purchasing. Sponsors workshops on computers, bookkeeping, sales, and manufacturing. Compiles statistics.

Home Fashions Products Association. 355 Lexington Ave., 17th Fl., New York, NY 10017-6603. Phone: (212)297-2122 Fax: (212)370-9047 • Members are manufacturers of curtains and draperies.

Window Coverings Association of America. 3550 McKelvey Rd., No. 202 C, Bridgeton, MO 63044-2535. Phone: 888-298-9222 or (314)770-0229 Fax: (314)770-0263 E-mail: info@wcaa.org • URL: http://www.wcaa.org • Members are manufacturers of venetian blinds, vertical blinds, and pleated shades.

WINDOW DISPLAYS

See: DISPLAY OF MERCHANDISE

WINDOWS (SOFTWARE)

See also: COMPUTER SOFTWARE INDUSTRY

GENERAL WORKS

The Mother of All Windows 98 Books. Woody Leonhard and Barry Simon. Addison-Wesley. • 1993. Price on application.

Windows ME Annoyances. David Karp. O'Reilly & Associates, Inc. • 2001. $29.95. A critical but helpful view of Windows Millennium Edition.

Windows 98 in a Nutshell. Tim O'Reilly. O'Reilly & Associates, Inc. • 1999. $24.95. (In a Nutshell Series).

Windows 95 is Driving Me Crazy! A Practical Guide to Windows 95 Headaches, Hassles, Bugs, Potholes, and Installation Problems. Kay Y. Nelson. Peachpit Press. • 1996. $24.95. Includes many illustrations.

Windows 2000: A Beginner's Guide. Martin S. Matthews. McGraw-Hill. • 2000. $39.99. (Network Professional's Library).

Windows XP in a Nutshell. David A. Karp and others. O'Reilly & Associates, Inc. • 2002. $29.95.

ABSTRACTS AND INDEXES

CompuMath Citation Index. Institute for Scientific Information. • Three times a year. $1,090.00 per year. Provides citations to the worldwide literature of computer science and mathematics.

Computer and Information Systems Abstracts Journal: An Abstract Journal Pertaining to the Theory, Design, Fabrication and Application of Computer and Information Systems. CSA. • 11 times a year. $1,750 per year.

Computer Literature Index: A Subject/Author Index to Computer and Data Processing Literature. EBSCO Publishing. • Quarterly, with annual cumulation. $245.00 per year. Contains brief abstracts of book and periodical literature covering all phases of computing, including approximately 70 specific application areas.

Internet and Personal Computing Abstracts [print edition]. EBSCO Publishing. • Quarterly. $269.00 per year, including cumulative index. Provides more than 10,000 abstracts annually from both trade and academic publications. Covers computer hardware, software, product reviews, Web topics, e-commerce, networks, corporate news, security, and related topics. Formerly *Microcomputer Abstracts.*

CD-ROM DATABASES

Computer Database. Gale Cengage Learning. • Provides one year of full-text on CD-ROM for 150 leading computer-related publications. Also includes 70,000 product specifications and brief profiles of 13,000 computer product vendors and manufacturers.

DIRECTORIES

Data Sources: The Comprehensive Guide to the Data Processing Industry: Hardware, Data Communications Products, Software, Company Profiles. Gale Cengage Learning. • Semiannual. $455.00 per year. Two volumes. Describes hardware and software for all computer operating sysems, including prices and technical details. Lists about 75,000 products from 14,000 suppliers. Industry-specific software applications are described.

The Software Encyclopedia: A Guide for Personal, Professional, and Business Users. Gale. • Annual. $335.00. Two volumes. Volume one lists software programs by title and producer. Volume two provides information on programs according to application and operating system. Includes prices and requirements for hardware and memory.

ENCYCLOPEDIAS AND DICTIONARIES

Acronyms of Computer Science and Communications: A Comprehensive Acronym Dictionary and Illustrated Encyclopedia. Enjob Kajan and Ejub Kajan. Springer Verlag. • 2002. $49.95. Explains more than 4,000 "broadly used" computer, telecommunications, and information technology acronyms. Includes illustrations and Web addresses, where applicable.

Encyclopedia of Information Systems. Hossein Bidgoli, editor. Elsevier. • 2002. $1,200.00. Four volumes. Contains a wide range of articles relating to computers, databases, communication, and information technology. The 200 topics include coverage of hardware, software, artificial intel-ligence, the Internet, networks, knowledge management, electronic commerce, search engines, and systems design.

HANDBOOKS AND MANUALS

Microsoft Windows XP Inside Out. Ed Bott. Microsoft Press. • 2001. $44.99. Provides detailed coverage of both Professional and Home versions of Windows XP.

UNIX and Windows 2000 Integration Toolkit: A Complete Guide for System Administrators and Developers. Rawn Shah. John Wiley and Sons, Inc. • 2000. $49.99. Includes CD-ROM.

UNIX and Windows 2000: Interoperability Guide. Alan Roberts. Prentice Hall PTR. • 2001. $34.99. (Hewlett-Packard Professional Books).

Unix Secrets. James Armstrong. • 1999. $39.99. Second edition. (UNIX Secrets Series).

Windows ME: The Missing Manual - The Book That Should Have Been in the Box. David Pogue. O'Reilly & Associates, Inc. • 2000. $19.95. Popularly written explanation of Windows ME features. (Pogue Press.).

Windows Millennium Edition: The Complete Reference. John R. Levine and Margaret L. Young. McGraw-Hill. • 2000. $39.99. (Complete Reference Series).

Windows 98 Bible. Alan Simpton and others. John Wiley and Sons, Inc. • 1998. $39.99.

Windows 98 for Busy People. Ron Mansfield and Peter Weverka. Macmillian Inc. • 1999. $19.99. Second edition.

Windows NT Administration and Security. Richard O. Hudson. Prentice Hall PTR. • 2001. $95.00.

Windows NT Server Concise. Jerry Dixon and J. Scott Reeves. New Riders Publishing. • Date not set. $19.99.

Windows 2000 Commands Pocket Reference. Aeleen Frisch. O'Reilly & Associates, Inc. • 2001. $9.95. (Pocket Reference Series).

Windows 2000 Performance Guide: Help for Windows 2000 Administrators. Mark Friedman. O'Reilly & Associates, Inc. • 2002. $44.95.

Windows 2000 Professional Reference. Karanjit Siyan. Gale Group. • 2000. $75.00. Third edition.

Windows 2000 Quick Fixes. Jim Boyce. O'Reilly & Associates, Inc. • 2000. $29.95. Covers troubleshooting for Windows 2000, both Professional Edition and Server Edition.

Windows 2000 System Administration Handbook. David Watts and others. Prentice Hall PTR. • 2000. $59.99. (Microsoft Technologies Series).

Windows XP Home Edition: The Missing Manual - The Book That Should Have Been in the Box. David Pogue. O'Reilly & Associates, Inc. • 2002. $24.95. The title says it all. David Pogue is a computer and technology columnist for *The New York Times.*

Windows XP in 10 Steps or Less. Bill Hatfield and Bradley L. Jones. John Wiley and Sons, Inc. • 2003. $24.99. Explains more than 250 Windows XP procedures that require no more than 10 steps each. Includes tips, warnings, and cross-references.

Windows XP Professional Network Administration. Toby J. Velte. McGraw-Hill. • 2002. $49.99. Covers design, implementation, administration, configuration, networking, functionality, remote desktop assistance, and other matters. (Networking Series).

INTERNET DATABASES

InfoTech Trends. Data Analysis Group. Phone: (925)462-1202 Fax: (925)462-1225 E-mail: support@infotechtrends.com • URL: http://www.infotechtrends.com • Web site provides both free and fee-based market research data on the information technology industry, including computers, peripherals, telecommunications, the Internet, software, CD-ROM/DVD, e-commerce, and workstations. Fees: Free for current (most recent year) data; more extensive information has various fee structures. Formerly *Computer Industry Forecasts.*

ONLINE DATABASES

Internet and Personal Computing Abstracts. Information Today, Inc. • Contains abstracts covering a wide variety of personal and business microcomputer literature appearing in more than 100 journals and popular magazines. Time period is 1981 to date, with monthly updates. Formerly *Microcomputer Index.* Inquire as to online cost and availability.

PERIODICALS AND NEWSLETTERS

Exploring Windows NT for Professionals. Element K Journals. • Monthly. $139.00 per year. Newsletter on the Windows operating system for networks. Formerly *Exploring Windows NT.*

MSDN Magazine (Microsoft Systems for Developers). CMP Media LLC. • Monthly. $84.95 per year. Produced for professional software developers using Windows, MS-DOS, Visual Basic, and other Microsoft Corporation products. Incorporates *Microsoft Internet Developer.*

Windows and .Net Magazine. Penton Media, Inc. • 14 times a year. $49.95 per year. Edited for information systems personnel developing business applications for Windows NT software. Formerly *Windows2000Magazine.*

Windows Developer's Network: Application Development from Windows to Web. CMP Media LLC. • Monthly. $34.99 per year. Edited for advanced programming developers. Formerly *Windows Developer's Journal.*

Windows in Financial Services. • Quarterly. $39.00 per year. Covers information technology applications and products for Microsoft Windows users in the financial sector.

WINE INDUSTRY

See also: DISTILLING INDUSTRY

GENERAL WORKS

Red and White: Wine Made Simple. Max Allen. Wine Appreciation Guild. • 2001. $24.95. Revised edition. A sophisticated wine primer for consumers. Includes information and advice on wine selection, grape varieties, and the matching of food and wine.

Wine: Nutritional and Therapeutic Benefits. Thomas R. Watkins, editor. American Chemical Society. • 1997. $95.00. A review of wine chemistry, agronomic practice at vineyards, and the potential health benefits of wine drinking. (ACS Symposium Series, No. 661.).

ALMANACS AND YEARBOOKS

The U.S. Wine Market: Impact Databank Review and Forecast. M. Shanken Communications, Inc. • Annual. $845.00. Includes industry commentary and statistics.

CD-ROM DATABASES

OECD Statistical Compendium. Organization for Economic Cooperation and Development. • Semiannual. $1,905.00 per year for 1 to 10 users. CD-ROM contains more than 730,000 monthly, quarterly, and annual time series for OECD countries, 1960 to date. Includes fully searchable data on agriculture, food, economic indicators, national accounts, employment, energy, finance, industry, technology, and foreign trade. Results can be displayed in various forms.

DIRECTORIES

Beverage Marketing Directory. Beverage Marketing Corp. • Covers: About 11,000 beer wholesalers, wine and spirits wholesalers, soft drink bottlers and franchisors, breweries, wineries, distilleries,

alcoholic beverage importers, bottled water companies; and trade associations, government agencies, micro breweries, juice, coffee, tea, milk companies, and others concerned with the beverage and bottling industries; coverage includes Canada. Entries include: Beverage and bottling company listings contain company name, address, phone, names of key executives, number of employees, brand names, and other information, including number of franchisees, number of delivery trucks, sales volume. Suppliers and related companies and organizations listings include similar but less detailed information.

Major Food and Drink Companies of the World. Available from Gale Cengage Learning. • Annual. $880.00. Two volumes. Published by Graham & Whiteside. Contains profiles and trade names for more than 9,800 important food and beverage companies in various countries. In addition to foods, includes both alcoholic and nonalcoholic drink products.

Thomas Food and Beverage Market Place. Grey House Publishing. • 2004. $495.00. Three volumes. Contains more than 40,000 entries covering food companies, beverages, food equipment, warehouse companies, food brokers, wholesalers, importers, and exporters. Formerly *Thomas Food Industry Register.*

Wines and Vines: Annual Directory/Buyer's Guide. The Hiaring Co. • Annual. $95.00. List of wineries and wine bottlers in the United States, Canada, and Mexico; also lists industry suppliers.

ENCYCLOPEDIAS AND DICTIONARIES

Global Encyclopedia of Wine. Peter Forrestal, editor. Wine Appreciation Guild. • 2001. $75.00. Includes CD-ROM. Thirty-six "leading wine experts" discuss wines from all regions of the world. Includes a wine reference table with concise descriptions, price ranges, and food compatibility of 5,000 wines. Definitions of wine terms and a detailed index are included.

Larousse Encyclopedia of Wine. Christopher Foulkes. Larousse Kingfisher Chambers, Inc. Houghton Mifflin. • 2001. $45.00. Provides information on major wine producers of the world, with emphasis on French vineyards. Includes statistics and a glossary.

Oxford Companion to the Wines of North America. Bruce Cass. Oxford University Press. • 2000. $49.95. Second edition. Contains approximately 3,000 entries explaining the making of wine, varieties of wine, and characteristics of vineyards.

FINANCIAL RATIOS

Annual Statement Studies. The Risk Management Association. • Annual. Median and quartile financial ratios are given for over 400 kinds of manufacturing, wholesale, retail, construction, and consumer finance establishments. Data is sorted by both asset size and sales volume. Includes a clearly written "Definition of Ratios" and an alphabetical industry index.

Annual Statement Studies: Industry Default Probabilities and Cash Flow Measures. The Risk Management Association. • Annual. $145.00. Serves as a companion volume to the original *Annual Statement Studies.* Gives probability of default estimates on a percentage scale for more than 450 industries. Includes changes in position year-by-year for eight financial statement line items and provides percentage measures of cash flow.

HANDBOOKS AND MANUALS

Concepts in Wine Chemistry. Yair Margalit. Wine Appreciation Guild. • 1997. $79.95. Explains wine chemical changes in fermentation, aging, cellaring, and shipping.

Handbook of Enology. Pascal Ribereau-Gayon and others. John Wiley and Sons, Inc. • 2001. $220.00.

Two volumes. Vol. one, $330.00; vol. two, $180.00. Volume one is *The Microbiology of Wine and Vinifications.* Volume two is *The Chemistry of Wine Stabilization and Treatments.* Discusses the science of winemaking and associated technical problems.

Understanding Wine Technology: The Science of Wine Explained. David Bird. Wine Appreciation Guild. • 2001. $30.00. Provides basic information on vineyards, grape processing, fermentation, stabilization, wine quality control, and bottling. Includes color illustrations, diagrams, graphs, index, and glossary.

Winemaking Basics. Cornelius S. Ough. Haworth Press, Inc. • 1992. $59.95. Covers all practical aspects of commercial winemaking from harvesting grapes to bottling and storage.

Winery Technology and Operations: A Handbook for Small Wineries. Yair Margalit. Wine Appreciation Guild. • 1990. $29.95. Covers a wide variety of topics from grape harvest to wine bottling, including aging and quality control.

INTERNET DATABASES

Business 2.0 Web Guide to the Best Business Links. Business 2.0 Media Inc. Phone: (415)293-4800 E-mail: support@business2.com • URL: http://www.business2.com/webguide • Web site presents an extensive, searchable directory of links to "the best, most informative, and authoritative web pages." Twenty main categories cover business, finance, career, company information, people, and technology topics, with thousands of subtopics, all linking to Web sites recommended by experienced business researchers. Fees: Free.

Fedstats. Federal Interagency Council on Statistical Policy. Phone: (202)395-7254 • URL: http://www.fedstats.gov • Web site features an efficient search facility for full-text statistics produced by more than 100 federal agencies, including the Census Bureau, the Bureau of Economic Analysis, and the Bureau of Labor Statistics. Boolean searches can be made within one agency or for all agencies combined. Links are offered to international statistical bureaus, including the UN, IMF, OECD, UNESCO, Eurostat, and 20 individual countries. Fees: Free.

FreeLunch.com. Economy.com, Inc. Phone: (610)696-8700 Fax: (610)696-1678 • URL: http://www.freelunch.com • Web site provides free access to more than 1.5 million economic and financial data series, covering industry, demographics, labor markets, prices, retail sales, government spending, trade, interest rates, housing starts, the stock market, and many other topics. Data is available for various time periods in either chart or table form. Searching is offered. Fees: Free, but registration required. Economy.com, Inc. also offers fee-based economic analysis at *The Dismal Scientist* site (http://www.dismal.com).

PERIODICALS AND NEWSLETTERS

American Journal of Enology and Viticulture. American Society for Enology and Viticulture. • Quarterly. $155.00 per year.

Fancy Food and Culinary Products. Talcott Communications Corp. • Monthly. $34.00 per year. Emphasizes new specialty food products and the business management aspects of the specialty food and confection industries. Includes special issues on wine, cheese, candy, "upscale" cookware, and gifts. Formerly (Fancy Foods).

Impact: U.S. News and Research for the Wine, Spirits, and Beer Industries. M. Shanken Communications, Inc. • Semimonthly. $375.00 per year. Newsletter covering the marketing, economic, and financial aspects of alcoholic beverages.

Kane's Beverage Week: The Newsletter of Beverage Marketing. Whitaker Newsletters, Inc. • Weekly. $469.00 per year. Newsletter. Covers news relating to the alcoholic beverage industries, including social, health, and legal issues.

Wine Business Monthly: Grower and Seller News. Wine Business Communications, Inc. • Monthly. $39.00 per year; students, $24.00 per year. Edited for executives in the North American wine making industry. Covers marketing, finance, export-import, management, new technology, etc.

Wine Enthusiast. • 13 times a year. $32.95 per year. Covers domestic and world wine. Formerly *Wine Times.*

The Wine Spectator. M. Shanken Communications, Inc. • 18 times a year. $45.00 per year. Wine ratings.

Wines and Vines: The Authoritative Voice of the Grape and Wine Industry. Hiaring Co. • Monthly. $32.50 per year.

PRICE SOURCES

Beverage Media. Beverage Network. Beverage Media, Ltd. • Monthly. $78.00 per year. Wholesale prices.

Consumers Guide to Varietal Wines. Wine Appreciation Guild. • Annual. $45.00.

STATISTICS SOURCES

Business Statistics of the United States. Linz Audain and Cornelia J. Strawser. Bernan Associates. • Annual. $147.00. Based on *Business Statistics*, formerly issue by the Bureau of Economic Analysis, U. S. Department of Commerce. Provides basic data for a wide variety of U. S. industries, services, and economic indicators. Most statistics are shown annually for 30 years and monthly for the most recent four years.

The Global Drinks Market Impact Databank. M. Shanken Communications, Inc. • Annual. $2,975. 00. Detailed compilations of data for various segments of the liquor, beer, and soft drink industries.

Monthly Statistical Release: Wines. U.S. Bureau of Alcohol, Tobacco, and Firearms. • Monthly.

Survey of Current Business. Available from U. S. Government Printing Office. • Monthly. $63.00 per year. Issued by Bureau of Economic Analysis, U. S. Department of Commerce. Presents a wide variety of business and economic data.

World Drinks Data and Statistics. Euromonitor International. • 2004. $650.00. Provides five-year data for both alcoholic and non-alcoholic beverages in 52 countries. Includes market size, consumer expenditures, price indicators, and retail distribution data for beer, wine, spirits, tea, coffee, soft drinks, fruit juices, bottled water, and other drinks.

TRADE/PROFESSIONAL ASSOCIATIONS

American Society for Enology and Viticulture. P.O. Box 1855, Davis, CA 95617. Phone: (530)753-3142 Fax: (530)753-3318 E-mail: society@asev.org • URL: http://www.asev.org.

American Wine Society. 113 S Perry St., Lawrenceville, GA 30045. Phone: (678)377-7070 Fax: (678)377-7005 E-mail: coskery@americanwinesociety.org • URL: http://www.americanwinesociety.org • Amateur and professional winegrowers, winemakers, wine connoisseurs, wine merchants, and other interested persons. Seeks to further the knowledge, appreciation and enjoyment of wines produced on the American continent without bias toward European or other wines. Encourages legislation requiring honest labeling of both American and imported wines; fosters production of home wine-makers; seeks to further the use of American terms for American wines. Sponsors educational programs at national and local levels. Conducts wine tastings and trips to vineyards and wineries; arranges gourmet wine dinners; provides speakers on grape growing, wine-making, and wine appreciation.

Society of Wine Educators. 1200 G St., N.W., Suite 360, Washington, DC 20005. Phone: (202)347-5677 Fax: (202)347-5667 E-mail: vintage@erols.com • URL: http://www.wine.gurus.com.

Wine and Spirits Guild of America. 1766 Dupont Ave. S, Minneapolis, MN 55403. Phone: (612)377-6211 Fax: (612)377-6459.

Wine and Spirits Wholesalers of America. 805 15th St., N.W., Suite 430, Washington, DC 20005. Phone: (202)371-9792 Fax: (202)789-2405 E-mail: juanita. duggan@wswa.org • URL: http://www.wswa.org • Wholesale distributors of domestic and imported wine and distilled spirits. Affiliated with Wine and Spirits Shippers Association.

Wine Institute. 425 Market St., Ste. 1000, 425 Market St., Suite 1000, San Francisco, CA 94105. Phone: (415)512-0151 Fax: (415)442-0742 E-mail: tcoreywg@aol.com • URL: http://www.wineinstitute.org • Initiates and advocates state, federal, and international public policy to enhance the environment for the responsible consumption and enjoyment of wine.

OTHER SOURCES

Liquor Control Law Reporter: Federal and All States. CCH, Inc. • Biweekly. $3,649.00 per year. Nine looseleaf volumes. Federal and state regulation and taxation of alcoholic beverages.

WIRE INDUSTRY

CD-ROM DATABASES

OECD Statistical Compendium. Organization for Economic Cooperation and Development. • Semiannual. $1,905.00 per year for 1 to 10 users. CD-ROM contains more than 730,000 monthly, quarterly, and annual time series for OECD countries, 1960 to date. Includes fully searchable data on agriculture, food, economic indicators, national accounts, employment, energy, finance, industry, technology, and foreign trade. Results can be displayed in various forms.

DIRECTORIES

Directory of Wire Companies of North America. CRU International. • Annual. $179.00. Profiles approximately 1,050 companies in the wire industry in North America. Also profiles fiber optic companies having to do with fiber optic cables and a supplier section profiling supplier companies.

Dun's Industrial Guide: The Metalworking Directory. Dun and Bradstreet Corp. • Annual. Libraries, $485; commercial institutions, $795.00. Lease basis. Three volumes. Lists about 65,000 U. S. manufacturing plants using metal and suppliers of metalworking equipment and materials. Includes names and titles of key personnel. Products, purchases, and processes are indicated.

Wire and Cable Technology International Buyers' Guide. Initial Publications, Inc. • Annual. $40.00. About 2,000 companies listed by product categories. Formerly *Wire Tech Buyers' Guide.*

Wire Journal International Reference Guide. Wire Association International. Wire Journal Inc. • Covers: Manufacturers and suppliers of steel and nonferrous rods, strip, wire, wire products, electrical wire and cable, fiber optics, and machinery and equipment to the industry (SIC 33). Entries include: Company name, address, phone, fax, e-mail and website addresses, year established, number of employees, names of executives, trade and brand names, product indices and geographical cross reference.

FINANCIAL RATIOS

Annual Statement Studies. The Risk Management Association. • Annual. Median and quartile financial ratios are given for over 400 kinds of manufacturing, wholesale, retail, construction, and consumer finance establishments. Data is sorted by both asset size and sales volume. Includes a clearly written "Definition of Ratios" and an alphabetical industry index.

Annual Statement Studies: Industry Default Probabilities and Cash Flow Measures. The Risk Management Association. • Annual. $145.00. Serves as a companion volume to the original *Annual Statement Studies.* Gives probability of default estimates on a percentage scale for more than 450 industries. Includes changes in position year-by-year for eight financial statement line items and provides percentage measures of cash flow.

Annual Statement Studies: Industry Default Probabilities and Cash Flow Measures. The Risk Management Association. • Annual. $145.00. Serves as a companion volume to the original *Annual Statement Studies.* Gives probability of default estimates on a percentage scale for more than 450 industries. Includes changes in position year-by-year for eight financial statement line items and provides percentage measures of cash flow.

INTERNET DATABASES

Business 2.0 Web Guide to the Best Business Links. Business 2.0 Media Inc. Phone: (415)293-4800 E-mail: support@business2.com • URL: http://www.business2.com/webguide • Web site presents an extensive, searchable directory of links to "the best, most informative, and authoritative web pages." Twenty main categories cover business, finance, career, company information, people, and technology topics, with thousands of subtopics, all linking to Web sites recommended by experienced business researchers. Fees: Free.

Fedstats. Federal Interagency Council on Statistical Policy. Phone: (202)395-7254 • URL: http://www.fedstats.gov • Web site features an efficient search facility for full-text statistics produced by more than 100 federal agencies, including the Census Bureau, the Bureau of Economic Analysis, and the Bureau of Labor Statistics. Boolean searches can be made within one agency or for all agencies combined. Links are offered to international statistical bureaus, including the UN, IMF, OECD, UNESCO, Eurostat, and 20 individual countries. Fees: Free.

FreeLunch.com. Economy.com, Inc. Phone: (610)696-8700 Fax: (610)696-1678 • URL: http://www.freelunch.com • Web site provides free access to more than 1.5 million economic and financial data series, covering industry, demographics, labor markets, prices, retail sales, government spending, trade, interest rates, housing starts, the stock market, and many other topics. Data is available for various time periods in either chart or table form. Searching is offered. Fees: Free, but registration required. Economy.com, Inc. also offers fee-based economic analysis at *The Dismal Scientist* site (http://www.dismal.com).

Manufacturing Profiles. U. S. Bureau of the Census. Phone: (301)763-4636 E-mail: webmaster@census.gov • URL: http://www.census.gov/prod/www/abs/mfg-prof.html • The Census Bureau makes available free on PDF (Portable Document Format) an annual consolidation of the entire Current Industrial Report series, presenting "all the data compiled." Contains statistics on production, shipments, inventories, consumption, exports, imports, and orders for a wide variety of manufactured products.

PERIODICALS AND NEWSLETTERS

Wire Industry: International Monthly Journal. Publex International Ltd. • Monthly. $151.00 per year. News, information and technical articles on manufacture of wire, wire products and cable. International coverage.

Wire: International Technical Journal for the Wire and Cable Industries and All Areas of Wire Processing. Meisenbach GMBH. • Bimonthly. $118.00 per year. (English edition of *Draht-Welt.*).

Wire Journal International. Wire Association

International. Wire Journal, Inc. • Monthly. $75.00 per year.

STATISTICS SOURCES

Annual Survey of Manufactures. Available from U. S. Government Printing Office. • Annual. Prices vary. Issued by the U. S. Census Bureau as an interim update to the *Census of Manufactures.* Includes data on number of manufacturing establishments in various industries, employment, labor costs, value of shipments, capital expenditures, inventories, energy costs, and assets. (See also Census Bureau home page, http://www.census. gov/.).

Business Statistics of the United States. Linz Audain and Cornelia J. Strawser. Bernan Associates. • Annual. $147.00. Based on *Business Statistics,* formerly issue by the Bureau of Economic Analysis, U. S. Department of Commerce. Provides basic data for a wide variety of U. S. industries, services, and economic indicators. Most statistics are shown annually for 30 years and monthly for the most recent four years.

Survey of Current Business. Available from U. S. Government Printing Office. • Monthly. $63.00 per year. Issued by Bureau of Economic Analysis, U. S. Department of Commerce. Presents a wide variety of business and economic data.

TRADE/PROFESSIONAL ASSOCIATIONS

American Wire Producers Association. 801 N Fairfax St., Ste. 211, Alexandria, VA 22314-1757. Phone: (703)299-4434 Fax: (703)299-9233 E-mail: info@awpa.org • URL: http://www.awpa.org • Represents manufacturers of steel wire and wire products; suppliers of wire rods, dies, machinery, and related equipment. Assures free and fair access to a global supply of wire rod and to encourage an adequate domestic supply.

Wire Association International. 1570 Boston Post Rd., PO Box 578, Guilford, CT 06437. Phone: (203)453-2777 Fax: (203)453-8384 E-mail: tcoreywg@aol.com • URL: http://www.wirenet.org • Finances educational and research activities that will enhance the scientific endeavors of the wire industry.

Wire Industry Suppliers Association. 201 Park Washington Ct., Falls Church, VA 22046. Phone: (703)538-1797 Fax: (703)241-5603 E-mail: atmahq@aol.com • Firms engaged in the designing, building, and selling of machinery and equipment for use in plants producing wire or wire products. Includes wire and rod drawing machinery and accessories, shaping and flattening mills, stranding, cabling cutting off, pointing straightening, armoring, bending, forming, and cold heading equipment.

Wire Reinforcement Institute. 942 Main St., Ste. 300, Hartford, CT 06103. Phone: 800-552-4974 or 800-552-4974 Fax: (860)808-3009 E-mail: wwrinfo@wirereinforcementinstitute.org • URL: http://www.wirereinforcementinstitute.org • Manufacturers of steel welded wire reinforcement (WWR), sometimes referred to as fabric, mesh or WWF and wire products for concrete construction. Works to disseminate technical information and extend the use of welded wire reinforcement through scientific and market research, consumer education, engineering, product development, and general construction technology. Provides technical service to users and specifiers of welded wire reinforcement such as architects, consulting engineers, contractors, and governmental department engineers. Conducts research programs on properties and performance of welded wire reinforcement.

WIRING, ELECTRIC

See: ELECTRICAL CONSTRUCTION INDUSTRY

WOMEN ACCOUNTANTS

ABSTRACTS AND INDEXES

Accounting and Tax Index. UMI. • Quarterly. Price on application. Annual cumulation. Indexes accounting, auditing, and taxation literature appearing in journals, books, pamphlets, conference proceedings, and newsletters.

BIOGRAPHICAL SOURCES

Who's Who of American Women. Marquis Who's Who. • Biennial. $275.00. Provides over 25,000 biographical profiles of important women, including individuals prominent in business, finance, and industry.

INTERNET DATABASES

Rutgers Accounting Web (RAW). Rutgers University Accounting Research Center. Phone: (973)353-5172 Fax: (973)353-1283 • URL: http://www.rutgers.edu/ accounting • RAW Web site provides extensive links to sources of national and international accounting information, such as the Big Six accounting firms, the Financial Accounting Standards Board (FASB), SEC filings (EDGAR), journals, publishers, software, the International Accounting Network, and "Internet's largest list of accounting firms in USA." Searching is offered. Fees: Free.

TRADE/PROFESSIONAL ASSOCIATIONS

American Society of Women Accountants. 8405 Greensboro Dr., Ste. 800, McLean, VA 22102. Phone: 800-326-2163 or (703)506-3265 Fax: (703)506-3266 E-mail: aswa@aswa.org • URL: http://www.aswa.org.

American Woman's Society of Certified Public Accountants. 136 S Keowee St., Dayton, OH 45402. Phone: 800-297-2721 or (973)222-1872 Fax: (973)222-5794 E-mail: info@awscpa.org • URL: http://www.awscpa.org.

WOMEN ENGINEERS

BIOGRAPHICAL SOURCES

Who's Who of American Women. Marquis Who's Who. • Biennial. $275.00. Provides over 25,000 biographical profiles of important women, including individuals prominent in business, finance, and industry.

PERIODICALS AND NEWSLETTERS

SWE. Anne Perusek, editor. Society of Women Engineers. • Bimonthly. Members, $10.00 per year; non-members, $20.00 per year. Covers technical articles, continuing development, career guidance and recruitment and product advertising. Formerly *U.S. Woman Engineer.*

TRADE/PROFESSIONAL ASSOCIATIONS

Society of Women Engineers. 230 E Ohio St., Ste. 400, Chicago, IL 60611-3265. Phone: (312)596-5223 Fax: (312)596-5252 E-mail: hq@swe.org • URL: http://www.swe.org • Educational and service organization representing both students and professional women in engineering and technical fields. Affiliated with American Association of Engineering Societies.

WOMEN EXECUTIVES

See also: ENTREPRENEURS AND INTRAPRENEURS

GENERAL WORKS

Advancing Women in Business-The Catalyst Guide: Best Practices from the Corporate Leaders. Catalyst Staff. John Wiley and Sons, Inc. • 1998. $26.00. Explains the human resources practices of corporations providing a favorable climate for the advancement of female employees. (Jossey-Bass Business and Management Series).

Breaking Through the Glass Ceiling: Women in Management. Linda Wirth. International Labour Organization. • 2001. $16.95. Portrays "national and international efforts to improve equal opportunities amd promote gender equality in management." Includes statistical information and discussion of earnings gaps, recruitment of women, education, training, and career-building strategies for women.

Secrets of Six-Figure Women: Seven Surprising Strategies of Successful High Earners. Barbara Stanny. HarperCollins Publishers, Inc. • 2002. $23. 95. Provides results of interviews with 150 women in high-paying jobs ($100,000 and over).

Women Breaking Through: Overcoming the Final 10 Obstacles at Work. Deborah J. Swiss. Peterson's. • 1996. $24.95. Discusses specific strategies for women to use to advance beyond the middle management level. Based on a survey of 300 women "on the leading edge of change.".

Women Entrepreneurs: Moving Beyond the Glass Ceiling. Dorothy P. Moore and E. Holly Buttner. Sage Publications, Inc. • 1997. $79.95. Contains profiles of "129 successful female entrepreneurs who previously worked in corporate environments.".

Women in Management: Trends, Issues, and Challenges in Managerial Diversity. Ellen A. Fagenson, editor. Sage Publications, Inc. • 1993. $46.95. Includes material from 22 contributors on topics related to the experiences of women managers. (Women and Work Series: Vol. 4).

Women of the Street: Making It on Wall Street-The World's Toughest Business. Sue Herera. John Wiley and Sons, Inc. • 1998. $16.95. The author is a CNBC business television anchorperson.

ABSTRACTS AND INDEXES

Women Studies Abstracts. Transaction Publishers. • Quarterly. Individuals, $102.00 per year; institutions, $240.00 per year.

BIOGRAPHICAL SOURCES

Who's Who of American Women. Marquis Who's Who. • Biennial. $275.00. Provides over 25,000 biographical profiles of important women, including individuals prominent in business, finance, and industry.

DIRECTORIES

American Women Managers and Administrators: A Selective Biographical Dictionary of Twentieth Century Leaders in Business, Education, and Government. Judith A. Leavitt. Greenwood Publishing Group Inc. • 1985. $78.50. A directory of 20th-century women who hold or have held administrative, managerial, or leadership positions in business, education, or government.

D & B Women-Owned Business Directory. Dun & Bradstreet. • 2000. Price on application.

National Directory of Women-Owned Business Firms. Gale Cengage Learning. • 2003. $295.00. 12th edition. Published by Business Research Services. Includes more than 28,000 businesses owned by women.

INTERNET DATABASES

MBEMAG. Minority Business Entrepreneur Magazine. Phone: (310)540-9398 Fax: (310)792-8263 E-mail: webmaster@mbemag.com • URL: http://www.mbemag.com • Web site's main feature is the "MBE Business Resources Directory." This provides complete mailing addresses, phone, fax, and Web site addresses (URL) for more than 40 organizations and government agencies having information or assistance for ethnic minority and women business owners. Some other links are "Current Events," "Calendar of Events," and "Business Opportunities." Updating is bimonthly. Fees: Free.

ONLINE DATABASES

Management Contents. Gale Cengage Learning. • Covers a wide range of management, financial, marketing, personnel, and administrative topics. About 150 leading business journals are indexed and abstracted from 1974 to date, with monthly updating. Inquire as to online cost and availability.

PERIODICALS AND NEWSLETTERS

Minority Business Entrepreneur. • Bimonthly. $16.00 per year. Reports on issues "critical to the growth and development of minority and women-owned firms." Provides information on relevant legislation and profiles successful women and minority entrepreneurs.

Perspective. Magna Publications Inc. • Description: Provides administrators with guidelines for keeping their schools out of court. Examines current trends in law related to higher education, as well as past and future legal issues affecting students, faculty, administrators and the public. Recurring features include columns titled Key Case Review, Follow-Up, Resources, Legislative Note, Outside the Courts, Cross-Examination, and Cases Noted.

Self. Conde Nast Publications, Inc. • Monthly. $12.00 per year. Written for business women.

Today's Insurance Professionals. National Association of Insurance Women. • Quarterly. Free to members; non-members, $15.00 per year. Provides advice on professional and personal development in the insurance business. Formerly *Today's Insurance Woman.*

WIN News: All the News that is Fit to Print By, For and About Women. Women's International Network. • Quarterly. Individuals $35.00 per year; institutions, $48.00 per year. World-wide communication system by, for and about women of all backgrounds, beliefs, nationalities and age-groups.

Women as Managers: Strategies for Success. Economics Press, Inc. • Biweekly. $69.00 per year. Newsletter. Covers management skills and techniques leading to higher career levels. Discusses problems women face on the job.

Working Mother. Working Mother Media. • 10 times a year. $19.97 per year.

RESEARCH CENTERS AND INSTITUTES

Business and Professional Women's Foundation. 2012 Massachusetts Ave., N.W., Washington, DC 20036. Phone: (202)293-1200 Fax: (202)861-0298 E-mail: jsmith@bpwusa.org • URL: http://www. bpwusa.org.

Center for Private Enterprise. Baylor University, Hankamer School of Business, P.O. Box 98003, Waco, TX 76798-8003. Phone: (254)710-2263 Fax: (254)710-1092 E-mail: jim_truitt@baylor.edu • URL: http://129.62.162.136/enterprise/ • Includes studies of entrepreneurship and women entrepreneurs.

Center for Women's Business Research. 1411 K St. N.W., Ste. 1350, Washington, DC 20005-3407. Phone: (202)638-3060 Fax: (202)638-3064 E-mail: info@womensbusinessresearch.org • URL: http:// www.nfwbo.org • Provides research reports and statistical studies relating to various aspects of women-owned business enterprises. Affiliated with the National Association of Women Business Owners.

Institute for Case Development and Research. Simmons College, Graduate School of Management, 409 Commonwealth Ave., Boston, MA 02215. Phone: (617)521-3840 Fax: (617)521-3880 E-mail: somadm@simmons.edu • URL: http://www. simmons.edu • Studies issues and problems confronting women in management.

National Council for Research on Women. 11 Hanover Square, 20th Fl., New York, NY 10005. Phone: (212)785-7335 Fax: (212)785-7350 E-mail: ncrw@ncrw.org • URL: http://www.ncrw.org.

Women Employed Institute. Women Employed Institute. 111 N Wabash, 13th Fl., Chicago, IL 60602. Phone: (312)782-3902 Fax: (312)782-5249

E-mail: info@womenemployed.org • URL: http:// www.womenemployed.org • Economic status of working women, working women and the law, sexual harassment in the workplace, equal employment opportunity, women's access to vocational education and job training, comparable worth, working mothers, and career development.

TRADE/PROFESSIONAL ASSOCIATIONS

American Business Women's Association. PO Box 8728, PO Box 8728, Kansas City, MO 64114-0728. Phone: 800-228-0007 or (816)361-6621 Fax: (816)361-4991 E-mail: abwa@abwa.org • URL: http://www.abwa.org • Women in business, including women owning or operating their own businesses, women in professions, and women employed in any level of government, education, or retailing, manufacturing, and service companies. Provides opportunities for businesswomen to help themselves and others grow personally and professionally through leadership, education, networking support, and national recognition. Offers leadership training, business skills training and business education; special membership options for retired businesswomen and the Company Connection for business owners, a resume service, credit card and programs, various travel and insurance benefits. Sponsors American Business Women's Day and National Convention and regional conferences held annually.

Association of African-American Women Business Owners. 3363 Alden Place, N.E., Washington, DC 20019. Phone: (202)399-3645 Fax: (202)399-3645 E-mail: aaawbo@aol.com • URL: http://www. blackpgs.com/aawboa.

Catalyst. 120 Wall St., 5th Fl., New York, NY 10005-3904. Phone: (212)514-7600 Fax: (212)514-8470 E-mail: info@catalyst.org • URL: http://www. catalystwomen.org • Works to advance women in Business and the professions. Serves as a source of information on women in business for past four decades. Helps companies and women maximize their potential. Holds current statistics, print media, and research materials on issues related to women in business.

Cosmetic Executive Women. 286 Madison Ave., 19th Fl., New York, NY 10017. Phone: (212)685-5955 Fax: (212)685-3334 E-mail: cew@cew.org • URL: http://cew.org • Women in the cosmetic and allied industries. Unites women executives in the cosmetic field for industry awareness and business advancement. Promotes products, people, professional development and philanthropy.

Executive Women International. 515 S 700 E, Ste. 2A, Salt Lake City, UT 84102. Phone: 877-4EWI-NOW or (801)355-2800 Fax: (801)355-2852 E-mail: ewi@executivewomen.org • URL: http:// www.executivewomen.org • Individuals holding key positions in business professions. Conducts networking educational and charitable programs.

Financial Women's Association of New York. 215 Park Ave. S., Suite 1713, New York, NY 10003. Phone: (212)533-2141 Fax: (212)982-3008 E-mail: fwaoffice@fwa.org • URL: http://www.fwa.org • Members are professional women in finance. Formerly Young Women's Financial Association of New York.

The International Alliance of Executive and Professional Women. 8405 Grennsboro Dr., Ste. 800, McLean, VA 22102. Phone: (703)506-3284 E-mail: info@tiaw.org • URL: http://www.tiaw.org • Facilitates communication (networking) among women executives. Formerly The International Alliance, An Association of Executive and Professional Women.

National Association for Female Executives. P.O. Box 156, Congers, NY 10920-0156. Phone: 800-634-6233 Fax: (212)351-6486 E-mail: nafe@nafe. com • URL: http://www.nafe.com.

National Association of Women Business Owners. 8405 Greensboro Dr., Ste. 800, McLean, VA 22102. Phone: 800-556-2926 or (703)506-3268 Fax: (703)506-3266 E-mail: national@nawbo.org • URL: http://www.nawbo.org • Formerly Association of Women Business Owners.

Women Executives in Public Relations. FDR Station, PO Box 7657, New York, NY 10150-7657. Phone: (212)289-7375 Fax: (212)289-7375 • URL: http://www.wepr.org • Formerly Committee on Women in Public Relations.

WOMEN IN INDUSTRY

See: EMPLOYMENT OF WOMEN; WOMEN IN THE WORK FORCE

WOMEN IN THE WORK FORCE

See also: EMPLOYMENT OF WOMEN

GENERAL WORKS

Breaking Out of the Pink-Collar Ghetto: Policy Solutions for Non-College Women. Sharon H. Mastracci. M. E. Sharpe, Inc. • 2004. $65.95. Emphasis is on innovative education and training programs for women in low-paying service jobs.

When Work Doesn't Work Anymore: Women, Work, and Identity. Elizabeth P. McKenna. Doubleday Publishing. • 1998. $12.95. A popularly written discussion of the conflict between corporate culture and the traditional, family roles of women.

Women and Careers: Issues and Challenges. Carol W. Konek and Sally L. Kitch. Sage Publications, Inc. • 1993. $77.95. Based on a major survey assessing women's experiences in the workplace.

Women and the Economy: A Reader. Ellen Mutari and Deborah M. Figart, editors. M. E. Sharpe, Inc. • 2003. $69.95. A collection of essays presenting a feminist approach to economic issues.

Women and Work: Exploring Race, Ethnicity, and Class. Mary Romero. Sage Publications, Inc. • 1997. $103.00. Contains articles by various authors, including material on the historical and economic background of women in the workplace. (Women and Work: Vol. 6.).

Women, Gender, and Work: What is Equality and How Do We Get There?. Martha F. Loutfi, editor. International Labour Organization. • 2001. $26.95. A collection of articles from the *International Labour Review* covering such topics as equal opportunity for women, family concerns, legal issues, the glass ceiling, wage inequality, and sexual harassment in the workplace. Includes statistical data.

ABSTRACTS AND INDEXES

Social Sciences Index. H. W. Wilson Co. • Quarterly, with annual cumulation. Price varies. Indexes more than 400 periodicals covering economics, environmental policy, government, insurance, labor, health care policy, plannning, public administration, public welfare, urban studies, women's issues, criminology, and related topics.

Sociological Abstracts. Cambridge Information Group. • Bimonthly. $720.00 per year; with cumulative index, $860.00 per year. Includes print and on-line editions. A compendium of non-evaluative abstracts covering the field of sociology and related disciplines.

CD-ROM DATABASES

Magazine Index Plus. Gale Cengage Learning. • Monthly. $4,000.00 per year (includes InfoTrac workstation). Provides full text on CD-ROM for about 100 popular, general interest magazines and indexing for 300 others. Includes special indexing of reviews and product evaluations. Time period is 1980 to date.

Social Sciences Citation Index. ISI. • Monthly. Price on request. Provides CD-ROM indexing of articles appearing in 1700 leading social science journals worldwide, with additional selections from more than 5700 other journals. Time span is 1992 to date. Coverage includes economics, business, finance, management, communications, demographics, library and information science, political science, sociology, and many other subjects.

Social Sciences Citation Index: Compact Disc Edition with Abstracts. Institute for Scientific Information. • Monthly. Provides CD-ROM indexing and abstracting of "significant articles" from 1,700 social science journals worldwide, with additional selections from 3,200 other journals, 1986 to date. Includes economics, business, finance, management, communications, demographics, information and library science, political science, sociology, and many other subjects.

WILSONDISC: Wilson Social Sciences Abstracts. H. W. Wilson Co. • Monthly. Includes unlimited online access to *Social Sciences Index* through WILSONLINE. Provides CD-ROM indexing from 1983 and abstracting from 1994 of more than 500 periodicals covering economics, area studies, community health, public administration, public welfare, urban studies, and many other topics related to the social sciences.

DIRECTORIES

Women's Information Directory. Gale. • Covers: Nearly 10,800 sources of information for and about women in the U.S., including national, state, and local organizations; publishers and booksellers of women's materials; newspapers, magazines, newsletters, other directories, and videos; museums; awards, honors, and prizes; government agencies and assistance programs; research centers; women's studies programs at colleges and universities; consultants; scholarships and other financial aids; electronic resources; and library collections. Entries include: Organization or publication name, address, phone, name and title of contact, description of services, activities, etc.

HANDBOOKS AND MANUALS

ABC of Women Workers' Rights and Gender Equality. International Labour Organization. • 2000. $12.95. Second edition. Provides a concise guide to international laws and agreements relating to the rights of women workers.

The New Working Woman's Guide to Retirement Planning: Saving and Investing Now for a Secure Future. Martha P. Patterson. University of Pennsylvania Press. • 1999. $19.95. Second edition. Provides retirement advice for employed women, including information on various kinds of IRAs, cash balance and other pension plans, 401(k) plans, and social security. Four case studies are provided to illustrate retirement planning at specific life and career stages.

Women and the Law. Carol H. Lefcourt, editor. West Group. • Annual. $302.00. Looseleaf service. Covers such topics as employment discrimination, pay equity (comparable worth), sexual harassment in the workplace, property rights, and child custody issues.

INTERNET DATABASES

U. S. Census Bureau: The Official Statistics. U. S. Bureau of the Census. Phone: (301)763-4100 Fax: (301)763-4794 • URL: http://www.census.gov • Web site is "Your Source for Social, Demographic, and Economic Information." Contains "Current U. S. Population Count," "Current Economic Indicators," and a wide variety of data under "Other Official

Statistics." Keyword searching is provided. Fees: Free.

ONLINE DATABASES

Contemporary Women's Issues. Gale Cengage Learning. • Provides fulltext articles online from 150 periodicals and a wide variety of additional sources relating to economic, legal, social, political, education, health, and other women's issues. Time span is 1992 to date. Weekly updates. Inquire as to online cost and availability. (Also available in a CD-ROM version.).

Wilson Social Sciences Abstracts Online. H. W. Wilson Co. • Provides online abstracting and indexing of more than 500 periodicals covering area studies, community health, public administration, public welfare, urban studies, and many other social science topics. Time period is 1994 to date for abstracts and 1983 to date for indexing, with updates weekly. Inquire as to online cost and availability.

PERIODICALS AND NEWSLETTERS

Feminist Economics. International Association for Feminist Economics. Taylor and Francis Group. • Three times a year. Individuals, $68.00 per year; institutions, $184.00 per year. Includes articles on issues relating to the employment and economic opportunities of women.

Nine to Five Newsletter. 9 to 5 National Association of Working Women. • Five times a year. Free to members; individuals, $25.00 per year. A newsletter dealing with the rights and concerns of women office workers.

Perspective. Magna Publications Inc. • Description: Provides administrators with guidelines for keeping their schools out of court. Examines current trends in law related to higher education, as well as past and future legal issues affecting students, faculty, administrators and the public. Recurring features include columns titled Key Case Review, Follow-Up, Resources, Legislative Note, Outside the Courts, Cross-Examination, and Cases Noted.

RESEARCH CENTERS AND INSTITUTES

Consumer Research Center. Conference Board, Inc., 845 Third Ave., New York, NY 10022. Phone: (212)339-0304 Fax: (212)836-9714 E-mail: crc@conference-board.org • URL: http://www.crc-conquest.org • Conducts research on the consumer market, including elderly and working women segments.

Women Employed Institute. Women Employed Institute. 111 N Wabash, 13th Fl., Chicago, IL 60602. Phone: (312)782-3902 Fax: (312)782-5249 E-mail: info@womenemployed.org • URL: http://www.womenemployed.org • Economic status of working women, working women and the law, sexual harassment in the workplace, equal employment opportunity, women's access to vocational education and job training, comparable worth, working mothers, and career development.

STATISTICS SOURCES

Datapedia of the United States: American History in Numbers. George T. Kurian, editor. Bernan Press. • 2004. $125.00. Third edition. Based on the Census Bureau publication, *Historical Statistics of the United States.* Provides data from Colonial times to the present on agriculture, business, consumer income, energy, finance, labor, national income, population, and many other subjects. Includes "narrative highlights," maps, charts, and statistical projections.

Handbook of U. S. Labor Statistics: Employment, Earnings, Prices, Productivity, and Other Labor Data. Eva E. Jacobs, editor. Bernan Associates. • 1999. $74.00. Based on *Handbook of Labor Statistics,* formerly issued by the Bureau of Labor Statistics, U. S. Department of Labor. Includes the Bureau's projections of employment in the U. S. by industry and occupation. Provides a wide variety of

data on the work force, prices, fringe benefits, and consumer expenditures.

Job Patterns for Minorities and Women in Private Industry. Available from U. S. Government Printing Office. • Annual. $61.00. Issued by the Equal Employment Opportunity Commission (http://www.eeoc.gov). "Provides statistical information on the composition of the United States workforce in private industry by sex, race, and ethnic category.".

Key Indicators of the Labour Market. Available from Routledge. • Biennial. $125.00. Published by the International Labour Office (http://www.ilo.org). Provides data on 20 key indicators in 220 countries. Includes labor force statistics, employment, unemployment, part-time workers, wages, productivity, poverty indicators, and related topics.

Social Statistics of the United States. Mark S. Littman, editor. Bernan Press. • 2000. $65.00. Includes statistical data on population growth, labor force, occupations, environmental trends, leisure time use, income, poverty, taxes, and other economic or demographic topics.

Statistical Abstract of the United States. Available from U. S. Government Printing Office. • Annual. $51.00. Issued by the U. S. Bureau of the Census.

Statistical Handbook on the American Family. Bruce A. Chadwick and Tim B. Heaton. Greenwood Publishing Group, Inc. • 1998. $69.95. Second edition. Includes data on education, health, politics, employment, expenditures, social characteristics, the elderly, and women in the labor force. Historical statistics on marriage, birth, and divorce are shown from 1900 on. A list of sources and a subject index are provided. (Statistical Handbooks Series).

Statistical Handbook on Women in America. Cynthia M. Taeuber, editor. Greenwood Publishing Group, Inc. • 1996. $69.95. Second edition. Includes data on demographics, employment, earnings, economic status, educational status, marriage, divorce, household units, health, and other topics. (Statistical Handbook Series).

A Statistical Portrait of the United States: Social Conditions and Trends. Mark S. Littman, editor. Bernan Press. • 1998. $89.00. Covers "social, economic, and environmental trends in the United States over the past 25 years." Includes statistical tables, graphs, and analysis relating to such topics as population, income, poverty, wealth, labor, housing, education, healthcare, air/water quality, and government. (Statistical Portrait of the United States: Social Conditions and Trends Series).

Statistical Record of Women Worldwide. Gale Cengage Learning. • 1995. $130.00. Second edition. Includes employment data and other economic statistics relating to women in the U. S. and internationally.

Women in the World of Work: Statistical Analysis and Projections to the Year 2000. Shirley Nuss and others. International Labour Office. • 1989. $18.00. (Women, Work, and Development Series, No. 18).

TRADE/PROFESSIONAL ASSOCIATIONS

Catalyst. 120 Wall St., 5th Fl., New York, NY 10005-3904. Phone: (212)514-7600 Fax: (212)514-8470 E-mail: info@catalyst.org • URL: http://www.catalystwomen.org • Works to advance women in Business and the professions. Serves as a source of information on women in business for past four decades. Helps companies and women maximize their potential. Holds current statistics, print media, and research materials on issues related to women in business.

International Association for Feminist Economics. c/o Barbara Krohn, 100D Roberts Hall, Bucknell University, Lewisburg, PA 17837. Phone: (570)577-3637 Fax: (570)577-3451 E-mail: iaffe@bucknell.edu • URL: http://www.iaffe.org • Members are economists having a feminist viewpoint. Promotes greater economic opportunities for women.

Nine to Five: National Association of Working Women. 1430 W Peachtree St., Ste. 610, Atlanta, GA 30309. Phone: 800-522-0925 or (414)274-0925 Fax: (414)272-2870 E-mail: hotline9to5@igc.org • URL: http://www.9to5.org • Members are women office workers. Strives for the improvement of office working conditions for women and the elimination of sex and race discrimination.

OTHER SOURCES

Sex Discrimination and Sexual Harassment in the Work Place. American Lawyer Media, Inc. • Looseleaf. $169.00. Updated as needed. Considers both sides: the point of view of employers and the point of view of employees filing complaints. Coverage includes sexual harassment statutes, the Family Medical Leave Act, the Equal Pay Act, "glass ceiling" issues, pregnancy discrimination, childcare issues, reinstatement after a leave, and other legal matters. (Law Journal Press).

Working Women: A World Survey. Available from MarketResearch.com. • 2001. $3,500.00. Published by Euromonitor International. Worldwide market research data on consumer spending patterns of women in the work force, with forecasts to 2005.

WOMEN LAWYERS

See also: LAWYERS

GENERAL WORKS

Full Disclosure: The New Lawyer's Must-Read Career Guide. Christen C. Carey. American Lawyer Media, Inc. • 2001. $19.95. "All the Things Lawyers Wish They Had Known at the Beginning of Their Careers, Rather Than at the End." Covers such topics as job hunting, job interviews, summer associate programs, law firm economics, life as a law firm associate, and gender in law firms.

Gender on Trial: Sexual Stereotypes and Work/Life Balance in the Legal Workplace. Holly English. American Lawyer Media, Inc. • 2003. $44.95. Provides an "oral history" of legal profession employment practices, based on interviews with lawyers from around the U.S., psychologists, consultants, and recruiters. Contains recommendations for "new models to help firms and individuals achieve a workplace free of gender bias for both men and women." (ALM Publishing).

Getting Down to Business: Marketing and Women Lawyers. Deborah Graham. Glasser Legalworks. • 1996. $49.00. Provides advice to women lawyers concerning law firm marketing and business development. Five parts cover "The Internal Glass Ceiling", "Gender Gaps," "Clients' Attitudes," "Institutional Strategies," and "The Rules of the Game.".

BIOGRAPHICAL SOURCES

Who's Who in American Law. Marquis Who's Who. • Biennial. $295.00. Contains over 23,000 concise biographies of American lawyers, judges, and others in the legal field.

Who's Who of American Women. Marquis Who's Who. • Biennial. $275.00. Provides over 25,000 biographical profiles of important women, including individuals prominent in business, finance, and industry.

PERIODICALS AND NEWSLETTERS

National Association of Women Lawyers. President's Newsletter. National Association of Women Lawyers. • Quarterly. Newsletter. Price on application.

Women Lawyers Journal. National Association of Women Lawyers. • Quarterly. $16.00 per year.

TRADE/PROFESSIONAL ASSOCIATIONS

National Association of Women Lawyers. 750 N. Lake Shore Dr., Chicago, IL 60611. Phone: (312)988-6186 Fax: (312)988-6281 E-mail: nawl@staff.abanet.org • URL: http://www.abanet.org/nawl.

WOMEN MANAGERS

See: WOMEN EXECUTIVES

WOMEN PHYSICIANS

BIOGRAPHICAL SOURCES

Who's Who of American Women. Marquis Who's Who. • Biennial. $275.00. Provides over 25,000 biographical profiles of important women, including individuals prominent in business, finance, and industry.

ONLINE DATABASES

Embase. Elsevier Science, Inc. • Worldwide medical literature, 1974 to present. Weekly updates. Inquire as to online cost and availability.

Medline. Medlars Management Section. • Provides indexing and abstracting of worldwide medical literature, 1966 to date. Weekly updates. Inquire as to online cost and availability.

PERIODICALS AND NEWSLETTERS

AMWA Journal. American Medical Writers Association. • Quarterly. $35.00 per year.

TRADE/PROFESSIONAL ASSOCIATIONS

American Medical Women's Association. 211 N. Union St., Ste. 100, Alexandria, VA 22314. Phone: 800-995-AMWA or (703)838-0500 Fax: (703)549-3864 E-mail: info@amwa-doc.org • URL: http://www.amwa-doc.org • Women holding a MD or DO degree from approved medical colleges; women interns, residents, and medical students. Promotes women's health issues in medical education and public policy. Seeks to find solutions to problems common to women studying or practicing medicine, such as career advancement and the integration of professional and family responsibilities. Provides student members with educational loans and personal counseling. Sponsors continuing medical education programs.

WOMEN'S APPAREL

See also: CLOTHING INDUSTRY; FASHION INDUSTRY; MILLINERY INDUSTRY; UNDERWEAR INDUSTRY

ABSTRACTS AND INDEXES

Textile Technology Digest. Institute of Textile Technology. • Annual. $535.00. Provides indexing and abstracting of a wide variety of textile technology literature.

CD-ROM DATABASES

OECD Statistical Compendium. Organization for Economic Cooperation and Development. • Semiannual. $1,905.00 per year for 1 to 10 users. CD-ROM contains more than 730,000 monthly, quarterly, and annual time series for OECD countries, 1960 to date. Includes fully searchable data on agriculture, food, economic indicators, national accounts, employment, energy, finance, industry, technology, and foreign trade. Results can be displayed in various forms.

Textile Technology Digest [CD-ROM]. Textile Information Center, Institute of Textile Technology. • Quarterly. Provides CD-ROM indexing and abstracting of worldwide journals and monographs in various areas of textile technology, production, and management. Covers 1978 to date.

DIRECTORIES

Contemporary Fashion. St. James Press. • Publication includes: Contact information for designers featured. Entries include: name, address, phone, and Web site. Principal content of publication is essays evaluating contemporary clothing and accessories designers worldwide.

Directory of Apparel Specialty Stores. Chain Store Guide. • Annual. $335.00. 4,700 apparel and sporting goods specialty stores in the United States and Canada, operating more than 80,000 stores. Include company name, phone and fax numbers, company e-mail and web addresses and other information.

Garment Manufacturers Index. Klevens Publications Inc. • Covers: about 8,000 manufacturers and suppliers of products and services such as fabrics, trimmings, factory equipment, and sewing contractors used in the manufacture of apparel. Publication includes: fabrics, trimmings, supplies, services, equipment, and contractors. Entries include: Company name, address, phone, fax, list of products or services, brief description of product.

Women's and Children's Wear Buyers Directory. Douglas Publications, Inc. • Annual. $329.00. About 10,500 retail stores selling women's dresses, coats, sportswear, intimate apparel, and women's accessories, infants' to teens wear, and accessories; coverage does not include New York metropolitan area. *Salesman's Guide Directories.*

ENCYCLOPEDIAS AND DICTIONARIES

Textile Terms and Definitions. J.E. McIntyre and Paul N. Daniels, editors. Available from State Mutual Book and Periodical Service Ltd. • 1996. $180.00. 10th edition. Published by the Textile Insitute (UK). Includes more than 1,000 definitions of textile processes, fiber types, and end products. Illustrated.

FINANCIAL RATIOS

Annual Statement Studies. The Risk Management Association. • Annual. Median and quartile financial ratios are given for over 400 kinds of manufacturing, wholesale, retail, construction, and consumer finance establishments. Data is sorted by both asset size and sales volume. Includes a clearly written "Definition of Ratios" and an alphabetical industry index.

Annual Statement Studies: Industry Default Probabilities and Cash Flow Measures. The Risk Management Association. • Annual. $145.00. Serves as a companion volume to the original *Annual Statement Studies.* Gives probability of default estimates on a percentage scale for more than 450 industries. Includes changes in position year-by-year for eight financial statement line items and provides percentage measures of cash flow.

HANDBOOKS AND MANUALS

Lingerie Shop. Entrepreneur Media, Inc. • Looseleaf. $59.50. A practical guide to starting a lingerie store. Covers profit potential, start-up costs, market size evaluation, owner's time required, site selection, lease negotiation, pricing, accounting, advertising, promotion, etc. (Start-Up Business Guide No. E1152.).

Women's Accessories Store. Entrepreneur Media, Inc. • Looseleaf. $59.50. A practical guide to starting a women's clothing accessories shop. Covers profit potential, start-up costs, market size evaluation, owner's time required, site selection, lease negotiation, pricing, accounting, advertising, promotion, etc. (Start-Up Business Guide No. E1333.).

Women's Apparel Shop. Entrepreneur Media, Inc. • Looseleaf. $59.50. A practical guide to starting a women's clothing store. Covers profit potential, start-up costs, market size evaluation, owner's time required, site selection, lease negotiation, pricing, accounting, advertising, promotion, etc. (Start-Up

Business Guide No. E1107.).

INTERNET DATABASES

Advance Monthly Sales for Retail Trade and Food Services. U. S. Census Bureau. Phone: 800-541-8345 or (301)763-4636 Fax: (301)457-3842 E-mail: rcb@census.gov • URL: http://www.census.gov/svsd/www/fullpub.html • Web pages provide monthly sales figures for a wide range of retail businesses. Advance, preliminary, and final statistics are provided for the latest month available in each case, with a previous-year comparison. Updates are monthly.

Business 2.0 Web Guide to the Best Business Links. Business 2.0 Media Inc. Phone: (415)293-4800 E-mail: support@business2.com • URL: http://www.business2.com/webguide • Web site presents an extensive, searchable directory of links to "the best, most informative, and authoritative web pages." Twenty main categories cover business, finance, career, company information, people, and technology topics, with thousands of subtopics, all linking to Web sites recommended by experienced business researchers. Fees: Free.

Fedstats. Federal Interagency Council on Statistical Policy. Phone: (202)395-7254 • URL: http://www.fedstats.gov • Web site features an efficient search facility for full-text statistics produced by more than 100 federal agencies, including the Census Bureau, the Bureau of Economic Analysis, and the Bureau of Labor Statistics. Boolean searches can be made within one agency or for all agencies combined. Links are offered to international statistical bureaus, including the UN, IMF, OECD, UNESCO, Eurostat, and 20 individual countries. Fees: Free.

FreeLunch.com. Economy.com, Inc. Phone: (610)696-8700 Fax: (610)696-1678 • URL: http://www.freelunch.com • Web site provides free access to more than 1.5 million economic and financial data series, covering industry, demographics, labor markets, prices, retail sales, government spending, trade, interest rates, housing starts, the stock market, and many other topics. Data is available for various time periods in either chart or table form. Searching is offered. Fees: Free, but registration required. Economy.com, Inc. also offers fee-based economic analysis at *The Dismal Scientist* site (http://www.dismal.com).

Manufacturing Profiles. U. S. Bureau of the Census. Phone: (301)763-4636 E-mail: webmaster@census.gov • URL: http://www.census.gov/prod/www/abs/mfg-prof.html • The Census Bureau makes available free on PDF (Portable Document Format) an annual consolidation of the entire Current Industrial Report series, presenting "all the data compiled." Contains statistics on production, shipments, inventories, consumption, exports, imports, and orders for a wide variety of manufactured products.

ONLINE DATABASES

F & S Index. Gale Cengage Learning. • Contains about four million citations to worldwide business, financial, and industrial or consumer product literature appearing from 1972 to date. Weekly updates. Inquire as to online cost and availability.

PROMT: Predicasts Overview of Markets and Technology. Gale Cengage Learning. • Companies, products, applied technologies and markets. U.S. and international literature coverage, 1972 to date. Inquire as to online cost and availability. Provides abstracts from more than 1,600 publications. Weekly updates.

Textile Technology Digest [online]. Institute of Textile Technology. • Contains indexing and abstracting of more than 300 worldwide journals and monographs in various areas of textile technology, production, and management. Time period is 1978 to date, with monthly updating. Inquire as to online cost and availability.

World Textiles. Elsevier Science, Inc. • Provides abstracting and indexing from 1970 of worldwide textile literature (periodicals, books, pamphlets, and reports). Includes U. S., European, and British patent information. Updating is monthly. Inquire as to online cost and availability.

PERIODICALS AND NEWSLETTERS

Accessories. Business Journals, Inc. • 11 times a year. $35.00 per year. Covers the merchandising of women's fashion accessories, including handbags, belts, jewelry, gloves, hats, and umbrellas.

Apparel. VNU Business Media. • Monthly. $69.00 per year. Written for executives and top managers. Formerly *Bobbin*.

Apparel Merchandising. Lebhar-Friedman, Inc. • Eight times a year. $24.00 per year. Reports on fashion trends in women's, men's, and children's clothing. Supplement to (DSN Retailing Today).

Fashion Market Magazine. Fashion Market Magazine Group, Inc. • Monthly. $59.00 per year. Covers the women's apparel industry, including photographs of "current collections of apparel available on the wholesale market." Includes news of all categories of women's clothing.

Femme-Lines. Earl Barron Publications, Inc. • Bimonthly. $8.00 per year.

Harper's Bazaar. Hearst Corp. • Monthly. $18.00 per year.

Tobe Report. Tobe. • 38 times a year. Price on application. Edited for fashion retailers. Provides detailed information and analysis relating to current trends in the women's, children's, and men's apparel and accessories markets.

Vogue. Conde Nast Publications, Inc. • Monthly. $18.00 per year.

WWD: The Retailer's Daily Newspaper (Women's Wear Daily). Fairchild Publications. • Daily. Individuals, $195.00 per year; retailers, $99.00 per year; manufacturers, $135.00 per year.

STATISTICS SOURCES

Annual Benchmark Report for Retail Trade and Food Services...A Detailed Summary of Retail Sales, Purchases, Accounts Receivable, Inventories, and Food Service Sales. Available from U. S. Government Printing Office. • Annual. $13.00. Issued by the U.S. Census Bureau. Provides detailed annual and monthly retail statistics for the most recent 10 years. Includes data for various kinds of retail outlets, including automobiles, furniture, appliances, building supplies, grocery stores, drug stores, gasoline stations, clothing, sporting goods, department stores, and restaurants.

Annual Survey of Manufactures. Available from U. S. Government Printing Office. • Annual. Prices vary. Issued by the U. S. Census Bureau as an interim update to the *Census of Manufactures.* Includes data on number of manufacturing establishments in various industries, employment, labor costs, value of shipments, capital expenditures, inventories, energy costs, and assets. (See also Census Bureau home page, http://www.census.gov/.).

Business Statistics of the United States. Linz Audain and Cornelia J. Strawser. Bernan Associates. • Annual. $147.00. Based on *Business Statistics,* formerly issue by the Bureau of Economic Analysis, U. S. Department of Commerce. Provides basic data for a wide variety of U. S. industries, services, and economic indicators. Most statistics are shown annually for 30 years and monthly for the most recent four years.

Survey of Current Business. Available from U. S. Government Printing Office. • Monthly. $63.00 per year. Issued by Bureau of Economic Analysis, U. S. Department of Commerce. Presents a wide variety of business and economic data.

TRADE/PROFESSIONAL ASSOCIATIONS

American Cloak and Suit Manufacturers Association. 450 Seventh Ave., New York, NY 10123. Phone: (212)244-7300.

Textile Institute. St. James's Buildings, 1st Fl., 79 Oxford St., Manchester M1 6FQ, United Kingdom. Phone: 44 161 2371188 Fax: 44 161 2361991 E-mail: tiihq@textileinst.org.uk • URL: http://www.texi.org • Companies and individuals in 100 countries involved in management, science, technology, design, information transfer, and marketing of textiles including clothing and footwear. Promotes interests of the textile industry worldwide; serves professional interests of members; confers qualifications and recognizes achievements in research, application of ideas, education, business, and public affairs. Maintains Information Service to collect information relating to textile industrial and economic conditions in different countries and economic sectors.

WOMEN'S CLUBS

PERIODICALS AND NEWSLETTERS

GFWC Clubwoman: Magazine of the General Federation of Women's Club. General Federation of Women's Clubs. • Bimonthly. $6.00 per year.

TRADE/PROFESSIONAL ASSOCIATIONS

Business and Professional Women USA. 1900 M St., NW, Ste. 310, Washington, DC 20036. Phone: (202)293-1100 Fax: (202)861-0298 E-mail: memberservices@bpwusa.org • URL: http://www.bpwusa.org • Formerly National Federation of Business and Professional Women's Clubs.

General Federation of Women's Clubs. 1734 N St., N.W., Washington, DC 20036-2990. Phone: 800-443-4392 or (202)347-3168 Fax: (202)835-0246 E-mail: gfwc@gfwc.org • URL: http://www.gfwc.org.

National Council of Women of the United States. 777 United Nations Plaza, New York, NY 10017. Phone: (212)697-1278 Fax: (212)972-0164 • Works for the education, participation and advancement of women in all areas of society. Affiliated with International Council of Women.

WOOD

See: FOREST PRODUCTS; LUMBER INDUSTRY

WOOD FINISHING

See: WOODWORKING INDUSTRIES

WOODPULP INDUSTRY

See also: PAPER INDUSTRY; TALL OIL INDUSTRY

CD-ROM DATABASES

OECD Statistical Compendium. Organization for Economic Cooperation and Development. • Semiannual. $1,905.00 per year for 1 to 10 users. CD-ROM contains more than 730,000 monthly, quarterly, and annual time series for OECD countries, 1960 to date. Includes fully searchable data on agriculture, food, economic indicators, national accounts, employment, energy, finance, industry, technology, and foreign trade. Results can be displayed in various forms.

DIRECTORIES

International Pulp and Paper Directory. CMP Media LLC. • Annual. $287.00. Lists over 6,000 pulp and papermills. International coverage.

Lockwood-Post's Directory of the Pulp, Paper and Allied Trades. Paperloop. • Annual. $395.00. Formerly *Lockwood's Directory of the Paper and Allied Trades*.

PIMA Directory. Paper Industry Management Association. • Covers: 5,000 pulp, paper mill, and paper converting production executives; affiliated supplier firms and their representatives. Entries include: Executive name, title, office address and phone, home address, and name of spouse.

Pulp and Paper Buyer's Guide. Paperloop. • Annual. $75.00. Supplies and equipment.

INTERNET DATABASES

Business 2.0 Web Guide to the Best Business Links. Business 2.0 Media Inc. Phone: (415)293-4800 E-mail: support@business2.com • URL: http://www.business2.com/webguide • Web site presents an extensive, searchable directory of links to "the best, most informative, and authoritative web pages." Twenty main categories cover business, finance, career, company information, people, and technology topics, with thousands of subtopics, all linking to Web sites recommended by experienced business researchers. Fees: Free.

Fedstats. Federal Interagency Council on Statistical Policy. Phone: (202)395-7254 • URL: http://www.fedstats.gov • Web site features an efficient search facility for full-text statistics produced by more than 100 federal agencies, including the Census Bureau, the Bureau of Economic Analysis, and the Bureau of Labor Statistics. Boolean searches can be made within one agency or for all agencies combined. Links are offered to international statistical bureaus, including the UN, IMF, OECD, UNESCO, Eurostat, and 20 individual countries. Fees: Free.

FreeLunch.com. Economy.com, Inc. Phone: (610)696-8700 Fax: (610)696-1678 • URL: http://www.freelunch.com • Web site provides free access to more than 1.5 million economic and financial data series, covering industry, demographics, labor markets, prices, retail sales, government spending, trade, interest rates, housing starts, the stock market, and many other topics. Data is available for various time periods in either chart or table form. Searching is offered. Fees: Free, but registration required. Economy.com, Inc. also offers fee-based economic analysis at *The Dismal Scientist* site (http://www.dismal.com).

ONLINE DATABASES

PaperChem Database. Information Services Div. • Worldwide coverage of the scientific and technical paper industry chemical literature, including patents, 1967 to present. Weekly updates. Inquire as to on-line cost and availability.

PERIODICALS AND NEWSLETTERS

Pulp and Paper. Paperloop. • 11 times a year. $135.00 per year.

Pulp and Paper Canada. Pulp and Paper Technical Association of Canada. Business Information Group. • Monthly. $80.00 per year.

Pulp and Paper International. Paperloop. • Monthly. Free to qualified personnel; others, $130.00 per year.

Solutions! The Official Publication of TAPPI and PIMA. Technical Association of the Pulp and Paper Industry. • Monthly. Membership. Formerly *TAPPI Journal*.

PRICE SOURCES

Official Board Markets: "The Yellow Sheet". Mark Arzoumanian. Advanstar Communications. • Weekly. $160.00 per year. Covers the corrugated

container, folding carton, rigid box and waste paper industries.

RESEARCH CENTERS AND INSTITUTES

Robertson Pulp and Paper Laboratory. North Carolina State University. Dept. of Wood and Paper Science, P.O. 8005, Raleigh, NC 27695-8005. Phone: (919)515-5812 Fax: (919)515-6302 E-mail: mike_kocurek@ncsu.edu • URL: http://www.cfr.ncsu.edu/wps/.

STATISTICS SOURCES

Business Statistics of the United States. Linz Audain and Cornelia J. Strawser. Bernan Associates. • Annual. $147.00. Based on *Business Statistics*, formerly issue by the Bureau of Economic Analysis, U. S. Department of Commerce. Provides basic data for a wide variety of U. S. industries, services, and economic indicators. Most statistics are shown annually for 30 years and monthly for the most recent four years.

The Pulp and Paper Industry in OECD Member Countries. Organization for Economic Cooperation and Development. Available from OECD Publications and Information Center. • Annual. $31.00. Presents annual data on production, consumption, capacity, utilization, and foreign trade. Covers 33 pulp and paper products in OECD countries. Text in English and French.

Survey of Current Business. Available from U. S. Government Printing Office. • Monthly. $63.00 per year. Issued by Bureau of Economic Analysis, U. S. Department of Commerce. Presents a wide variety of business and economic data.

TRADE/PROFESSIONAL ASSOCIATIONS

Forest Resources Association, Inc. 600 E Jefferson St., Ste. 350, Rockville, MD 20852-1157. Phone: (301)838-9385 Fax: (301)838-9481 E-mail: rlewis@forestresources.org • URL: http://www.forestresources.org.

TAPPI - Technical Association of the Pulp and Paper Industry. 15 Technology Pkwy. S, Norcross, GA 30092. Phone: 800-332-8686 or (770)446-1400 Fax: (770)446-6947 E-mail: memberconnection@tappi.org • URL: http://www.tappi.org.

WOODWORKING INDUSTRIES

See also: CARPENTRY; FOREST PRODUCTS; FURNITURE INDUSTRY; VENEERS AND VENEERING

DIRECTORIES

FDM--The Source--Woodworking Industry Directory. Reed Business Information. • Publication includes: List of over 1,800 suppliers to secondary woodworking industry; coverage includes Canada. Entries include: Company name, address, phone, fax, product lines.

Wood Digest-Showcase. Cygnus Business Media. • Publication includes: List of suppliers of materials, machinery, tools, and services for woodworking, cabinetry, casegoods, and furniture manufacturing processes (SIC 24, 25, 37, and 39). Entries include: Company name, phone number, photograph of product, services.

ENCYCLOPEDIAS AND DICTIONARIES

Illustrated Dictionary of Building Materials and Techniques: An Invaluable Sourcebook to the Tools, Terms, Materials, and Techniques Used by Building Professionals. Paul Bianchina. John Wiley and Sons, Inc. • 1993. $19.95. Contains 4,000 definitions of building and building materials terms, with 500 illustrations. Includes materials grades, measurements, and specifications.

FINANCIAL RATIOS

Annual Statement Studies. The Risk Management Association. • Annual. Median and quartile financial

ratios are given for over 400 kinds of manufacturing, wholesale, retail, construction, and consumer finance establishments. Data is sorted by both asset size and sales volume. Includes a clearly written "Definition of Ratios" and an alphabetical industry index.

Annual Statement Studies: Industry Default Probabilities and Cash Flow Measures. The Risk Management Association. • Annual. $145.00. Serves as a companion volume to the original *Annual Statement Studies*. Gives probability of default estimates on a percentage scale for more than 450 industries. Includes changes in position year-by-year for eight financial statement line items and provides percentage measures of cash flow.

HANDBOOKS AND MANUALS

Advanced Woodwork and Furniture Making. John L. Feirer and Gilbert R. Hutchings. Glencoe/McGraw-Hill. • 1982. $43.56. Fourth revised edition.

Woodturner's Bible. Percy Blandford. McGraw-Hill. • 1990. $26.95. Third edition.

PERIODICALS AND NEWSLETTERS

FDM: For Builders of Cabinets, Fixtures, Furniture, Millwork Furniture Design a nd Manufacturing. Chartwell Communications, Inc. • Monthly. Free to qualified personnel. Edited for furniture executives, production managers, and designers. Covers the manufacturing of household, office, and institutional furniture, store fixtures, and kitchen and bathroom cabinets.

Forest Products Journal. Forest Products Society. • 10 times a year. $145.00 per year.

National Home Center News: News and Analysis for the Home Improvement, Building Material Industry. Lebhar-Friedman, Inc. • 22 times a year. $99.00 per year. Includes special feature issues on hardware and tools, building materials, millwork, electrical supplies, lighting, and kitchens.

Wood and Wood Products: Furniture, Cabinets, Woodworking and Allied Products Management and Operations. Vance Publishing Corp. • 13 times a year. $55.00 per year.

Wood Digest. Cygnus Business Media. • Monthly. $60.00 per year. Formerly *Furniture Wood Digest*.

RESEARCH CENTERS AND INSTITUTES

Wood and Paper Science. North Carolina State University, P.O. Box 8005, Raleigh, NC 27695. Phone: (919)515-5807 Fax: (919)515-6302 E-mail: mike_kocurek@ncsu.edu • URL: http://www.cfr.ncsu.edu/wps/ • Studies the mechanical and engineering properties of wood, wood finishing, wood anatomy, wood chemistry, etc.

Wood Research Laboratory. Purdue University, Department of Forestry and Natural Resources, West Lafayette, IN 47907-1200. Phone: (765)494-3615 Fax: (765)496-1344 E-mail: mhunt@fnr.purdue.edu • URL: http://www.fnr.purdue.edu.

STATISTICS SOURCES

Annual Survey of Manufactures. Available from U. S. Government Printing Office. • Annual. Prices vary. Issued by the U. S. Census Bureau as an interim update to the *Census of Manufactures*. Includes data on number of manufacturing establishments in various industries, employment, labor costs, value of shipments, capital expenditures, inventories, energy costs, and assets. (See also Census Bureau home page, http://www.census.gov/.).

U. S. Industry and Trade Outlook. Available from National Technical Information Service. • Annual. $69.95. Produced by the International Trade Administration, U. S. Department of Commerce, in a "public-private" partnership with DRI/McGraw-Hill and Standard & Poor's. Provides basic data, outlook for the current year, and "Long-Term Prospects" (five-year projections) for a wide variety of products and services. Includes high technology industries. Formerly *U. S. Industrial Outlook*.

TRADE/PROFESSIONAL ASSOCIATIONS

Architectural Woodwork Institute. 46179 Westlake Dr., Ste. 120, Potomac Falls, VA 20165. Phone: (571)323-3636 Fax: (571)323-3630 E-mail: pduvic@awinet.org • URL: http://www.awinet.org • Manufacturers of architectural woodwork products (casework, fixtures, and paneling) and associated suppliers of equipment and materials. Works to: raise industry standards; research new and improved materials and methods; publish technical data helpful in the design and use of architectural woodwork. Conducts seminars and training course.

Wood Machinery Manufacturers of America. 1900 Arch St., Philadelphia, PA 19103-1498. Phone: 800-289-9662 or (215)564-3484 Fax: (215)963-9785 E-mail: wmma@fernley.com • URL: http://www.wmma.org • Formerly Woodworking Machinery Manufacturers of America.

OTHER SOURCES

Kitchen Cabinets and Countertops. Available from MarketResearch.com. • 2002. $2,250.00. Market research report published by Catalina Research. Covers both custom and stock cabinets. Presents market data relative to demographics, sales growth, shipments, exports, imports, price trends, and end-use. Includes company profiles.

WOOL AND WORSTED INDUSTRY

See also: SHEEP INDUSTRY; TEXTILE INDUSTRY; YARN

ABSTRACTS AND INDEXES

Textile Technology Digest. Institute of Textile Technology. • Annual. $535.00. Provides indexing and abstracting of a wide variety of textile technology literature.

ALMANACS AND YEARBOOKS

Agricultural and Mineral Commodities Year Book. Available from Taylor & Francis Group. • Annual. $225.00. Published by Europa Publications. Contains descriptive product profiles, price data, export-import data, and production statistics for major commodities of the world. Includes commodity histories, uses, markets, demand trends, and information about trade agreements and key commodity organizations.

CRB Commodity Yearbook. Commodity Research Bureau. CRB. • Annual. $99.95.

CD-ROM DATABASES

OECD Statistical Compendium. Organization for Economic Cooperation and Development. • Semiannual. $1,905.00 per year for 1 to 10 users. CD-ROM contains more than 730,000 monthly, quarterly, and annual time series for OECD countries, 1960 to date. Includes fully searchable data on agriculture, food, economic indicators, national accounts, employment, energy, finance, industry, technology, and foreign trade. Results can be displayed in various forms.

Textile Technology Digest [CD-ROM]. Textile Information Center, Institute of Textile Technology. • Quarterly. Provides CD-ROM indexing and abstracting of worldwide journals and monographs in various areas of textile technology, production, and management. Covers 1978 to date.

ENCYCLOPEDIAS AND DICTIONARIES

Textile Terms and Definitions. J.E. McIntyre and Paul N. Daniels, editors. Available from State Mutual Book and Periodical Service Ltd. • 1996. $180.00. 10th edition. Published by the Textile Institute (UK). Includes more than 1,000 definitions of textile processes, fiber types, and end products. Illustrated.

INTERNET DATABASES

Business 2.0 Web Guide to the Best Business Links. Business 2.0 Media Inc. Phone: (415)293-4800 E-mail: support@business2.com • URL: http://www.business2.com/webguide • Web site presents an extensive, searchable directory of links to "the best, most informative, and authoritative web pages." Twenty main categories cover business, finance, career, company information, people, and technology topics, with thousands of subtopics, all linking to Web sites recommended by experienced business researchers. Fees: Free.

Fedstats. Federal Interagency Council on Statistical Policy. Phone: (202)395-7254 • URL: http://www.fedstats.gov • Web site features an efficient search facility for full-text statistics produced by more than 100 federal agencies, including the Census Bureau, the Bureau of Economic Analysis, and the Bureau of Labor Statistics. Boolean searches can be made within one agency or for all agencies combined. Links are offered to international statistical bureaus, including the UN, IMF, OECD, UNESCO, Eurostat, and 20 individual countries. Fees: Free.

FreeLunch.com. Economy.com, Inc. Phone: (610)696-8700 Fax: (610)696-1678 • URL: http://www.freelunch.com • Web site provides free access to more than 1.5 million economic and financial data series, covering industry, demographics, labor markets, prices, retail sales, government spending, trade, interest rates, housing starts, the stock market, and many other topics. Data is available for various time periods in either chart or table form. Searching is offered. Fees: Free, but registration required. Economy.com, Inc. also offers fee-based economic analysis at *The Dismal Scientist* site (http://www.dismal.com).

Manufacturing Profiles. U. S. Bureau of the Census. Phone: (301)763-4636 E-mail: webmaster@census.gov • URL: http://www.census.gov/prod/www/abs/mfg-prof.html • The Census Bureau makes available free on PDF (Portable Document Format) an annual consolidation of the entire Current Industrial Report series, presenting "all the data compiled." Contains statistics on production, shipments, inventories, consumption, exports, imports, and orders for a wide variety of manufactured products.

USDA. United States Department of Agriculture. Phone: (202)720-2791 E-mail: agsec@usda.gov • URL: http://www.usda.gov • The USDA home page has six sections: News and Information; What's New; About USDA; Agencies; Opportunities; Search and Help. Keyword searching is offered from the USDA home page and from various individual agency home pages. Agencies are the Economic Research Service, Agricultural Marketing Service, National Agricultural Statistics Service, National Agricultural Library, and about 12 others. Updating varies. Fees: Free.

ONLINE DATABASES

Globalbase. Gale Cengage Learning. • Provides more than one million online summaries of business, industrial, and economic news reports from more than 1,000 publications worldwide. Covers a wide range of material appearing in international trade journals, professional magazines, and newspapers. Time period is 1984 to date, with weekly updates. Inquire as to online cost and availability.

Textile Technology Digest [online]. Institute of Textile Technology. • Contains indexing and abstracting of more than 300 worldwide journals and monographs in various areas of textile technology, production, and management. Time period is 1978 to date, with monthly updating. Inquire as to online cost and availability.

World Textiles. Elsevier Science, Inc. • Provides abstracting and indexing from 1970 of worldwide textile literature (periodicals, books, pamphlets, and reports). Includes U. S., European, and British patent information. Updating is monthly. Inquire as to online cost and availability.

PERIODICALS AND NEWSLETTERS

Canadian Co-Operative Wool Growers Magazine. Canadian Cooperative Wool Growers, Ltd. • Annual. Free to members; non-members, $3.00.

Journal of Natural Fibers. Haworth Press, Inc. • Quarterly. $400.00 per year to libraries; $45.00 per year to individuals. Covers applications, technology, research, and world markets relating to fibers from silk, wool, cotton, flax, hemp, jute, etc. Previously *Natural Fibres*, published annually.

Wool Record. World Textile Publications Ltd. • Monthly. $115.00 per year.

The Wool Sack. Mid-States Wool Growers Cooperative. • Semiannual. Free. Newsletter. Information on lamb production and the wool industry.

RESEARCH CENTERS AND INSTITUTES

Montana Wool Laboratory. Montana State University-Bozeman. Bozeman, MT 59717. Phone: (406)994-2100 Fax: (406)994-5589 E-mail: woollab@myavista.com.

STATISTICS SOURCES

Agricultural Statistics. Available from U. S. Government Printing Office. • Annual. $38.00. Produced by the National Agricultural Statistics Service, U. S. Department of Agriculture. Provides a wide variety of statistical data relating to agricultural production, supplies, consumption, prices/price-supports, foreign trade, costs, and returns, as well as farm labor, loans, income, and population. In many cases, historical data is shown annually for 10 years. In addition to farm data, includes detailed fishery statistics.

Annual Survey of Manufactures. Available from U. S. Government Printing Office. • Annual. Prices vary. Issued by the U. S. Census Bureau as an interim update to the *Census of Manufactures*. Includes data on number of manufacturing establishments in various industries, employment, labor costs, value of shipments, capital expenditures, inventories, energy costs, and assets. (See also Census Bureau home page, http://www.census.gov/.).

Broadwoven Fabrics (Gray). U.S. Bureau of the Census. • Quarterly. Provides statistical data on production, value, shipments, and consumption. Includes woolen and worsted fabrics, tire fabrics, cotton broadwoven fabrics, etc. (Current Industrial Reports, MQ-22T.).

Business Statistics of the United States. Linz Audain and Cornelia J. Strawser. Bernan Associates. • Annual. $147.00. Based on *Business Statistics*, formerly issue by the Bureau of Economic Analysis, U. S. Department of Commerce. Provides basic data for a wide variety of U. S. industries, services, and economic indicators. Most statistics are shown annually for 30 years and monthly for the most recent four years.

Consumption on the Woolen System and Worsted Combing. U. S. Bureau of the Census. • Quarterly and annual. Provides data on consumption of fibers in woolen and worsted spinning mills, by class of fibers and end use. (Current Industrial Reports, MQ-22D.).

FAO Production Yearbook. Available from Bernan Associates. • Annual. $45.00. Published by the Food and Agriculture Organization (http://www.fao.org). Contains worldwide data on agriculture, land use, farm crops, livestock, and agricultural prices.

FAO Trade Yearbook. Available from Bernan Associates. • Annual. $45.00. Published by the Food and Agriculture Organization (http://www.fao.org).

Provides extensive worldwide data on exports and imports of agricultural commodities, fertilizers, tractors, and pesticides. Includes more than 130 tables of detailed statistics.

Livestock, Meat, Wool, Market News. U.S. Department of Agriculture. • Weekly.

Survey of Current Business. Available from U. S. Government Printing Office. • Monthly. $63.00 per year. Issued by Bureau of Economic Analysis, U. S. Department of Commerce. Presents a wide variety of business and economic data.

World Trade Annual. United Nations Statistical Office. Walker and Co. • Annual. Prices vary.

TRADE/PROFESSIONAL ASSOCIATIONS

American Sheep Industry Association. 9785 Maroon Cir., Ste. 360, Centennial, CO 80112. Phone: (303)771-3500 Fax: (303)771-8200 E-mail: info@sheepusa.org • URL: http://www.sheepusa.org • Producers of sheep and wool. Goal is to advance the standards and profitability of the sheep industry. Conducts lobbying activities to promote legislation beneficial to the industry.

Textile Institute. St. James's Buildings, 1st Fl., 79 Oxford St., Manchester M1 6FQ, United Kingdom. Phone: 44 161 2371188 Fax: 44 161 2361991 E-mail: tiihq@textileinst.org.uk • URL: http://www.texi.org • Companies and individuals in 100 countries involved in management, science, technology, design, information transfer, and marketing of textiles including clothing and footwear. Promotes interests of the textile industry worldwide; serves professional interests of members; confers qualifications and recognizes achievements in research, application of ideas, education, business, and public affairs. Maintains Information Service to collect information relating to textile industrial and economic conditions in different countries and economic sectors.

Woolmark Company. 1156 Ave. of the Americas, Ste. 701, New York, NY 10036. Phone: 800-986-WOOL or (212)221-8161 Fax: (212)221-8152 E-mail: stuart.mccullough@wool.com • URL: http://www.woolmark.com • Sponsored by the wool growers of Australia to carry out global promotional and research programs. Works with American mills, apparel, upholstery fabric, carpet, and other end-product manufacturers and retailers at promotional and technical levels; conducts programs of product and market development; provides wool industry with marketing and statistical information; offers technical advice to increase manufacturing efficiency and assist in the introduction at the commercial level of new processes and products. Maintains Technical Services Center that tests and evaluates chemical and finishing processes developed to add new performance characteristics to wool products and to create new market outlets. **Convention/Meeting:** none.

WORD PROCESSING

See also: COMPUTERS; DESKTOP PUBLISHING; MICROCOMPUTERS AND MINICOMPUTERS; OFFICE AUTOMATION; OFFICE EQUIPMENT AND SUPPLIES; OFFICE MANAGEMENT

ABSTRACTS AND INDEXES

Computer and Information Systems Abstracts Journal: An Abstract Journal Pertaining to the Theory, Design, Fabrication and Application of Computer and Information Systems. CSA. • 11 times a year. $1,750 per year.

Computer Literature Index: A Subject/Author Index to Computer and Data Processing Literature. EBSCO Publishing. • Quarterly, with annual cumulation. $245.00 per year. Contains brief abstracts of book and periodical literature covering all phases of computing, including approximately 70 specific application areas.

Internet and Personal Computing Abstracts [print edition]. EBSCO Publishing. • Quarterly. $269.00 per year, including cumulative index. Provides more than 10,000 abstracts annually from both trade and academic publications. Covers computer hardware, software, product reviews, Web topics, e-commerce, networks, corporate news, security, and related topics. Formerly *Microcomputer Abstracts.*

LAMP (Literature Analysis of Microcomputer Publications). Soft Images. • Bimonthly. $89.95 per year. Annual cumulation.

BIBLIOGRAPHIES

Computer Book Review. • Quarterly. $30.00 per year. Includes annual index. Reviews new computer books. Back issues available.

CD-ROM DATABASES

Computer Database. Gale Cengage Learning. • Provides one year of full-text on CD-ROM for 150 leading computer-related publications. Also includes 70,000 product specifications and brief profiles of 13,000 computer product vendors and manufacturers.

DIRECTORIES

Data Sources: The Comprehensive Guide to the Data Processing Industry: Hardware, Data Communications Products, Software, Company Profiles. Gale Cengage Learning. • Semiannual. $455.00 per year. Two volumes. Describes hardware and software for all computer operating sysems, including prices and technical details. Lists about 75,000 products from 14,000 suppliers. Industry-specific software applications are described.

MicroLeads Vendor Directory on Disk (Personal Computer Industry). Chromatic Communications Enterprises, Inc. • Annual. $495.00. Includes computer hardware manufacturers, software producers, book-periodical publishers, and franchised or company-owned chains of personal computer equipment retailers, support services and accessory manufacturers. Formerly *MicroLeads U.S. Vender Directory.*

ENCYCLOPEDIAS AND DICTIONARIES

Acronyms of Computer Science and Communications: A Comprehensive Acronym Dictionary and Illustrated Encyclopedia. Enjob Kajan and Ejub Kajan. Springer Verlag. • 2002. $49.95. Explains more than 4,000 "broadly used" computer, telecommunications, and information technology acronyms. Includes illustrations and Web addresses, where applicable.

Dictionary of Computing. Valerie Illingworth, editor. Oxford University Press. • 1997. $18.00. Fourth edition.

Dictionary of Information Technology and Computer Seience. Tony Gunton. Blackwell Publishing. • 1994. $62.95. Second edition. Covers key words, phrases, abbreviations, and acronyms used in computing and data communications.

Encyclopedia of Information Systems. Hossein Bidgoli, editor. Elsevier. • 2002. $1,200.00. Four volumes. Contains a wide range of articles relating to computers, databases, communication, and information technology. The 200 topics include coverage of hardware, software, artificial intelligence, the Internet, networks, knowledge management, electronic commerce, search engines, and systems design.

HANDBOOKS AND MANUALS

Effective Executive's Guide to Microsoft Word 2002: The Seven Core Skills Required to Turn Word into a Business Power Tool. Pat Coleman. Redmond Technology Press. • 2001. $24.95. Written to provide basic word processing skills to nontechnical business managers and executives.

Microsoft Word Version 2002 Plain and Simple. Jerry Joyce and Marianne Moon. Microsoft Press. • 2001. $19.99. A standard manual providing detailed, step-by-step instructions for the many functions of Word 2002.

Secretarial/Word Processing Service. Entrepreneur Media, Inc. • Looseleaf. $59.50. A practical guide to starting a secretarial and word processing business. Covers profit potential, start-up costs, market size evaluation, owner's time required, site selection, pricing, accounting, advertising, promotion, etc. (Start-Up Business Guide No. E1136.).

ONLINE DATABASES

Internet and Personal Computing Abstracts. Information Today, Inc. • Contains abstracts covering a wide variety of personal and business microcomputer literature appearing in more than 100 journals and popular magazines. Time period is 1981 to date, with monthly updates. Formerly *Microcomputer Index.* Inquire as to online cost and availability.

PROMT: Predicasts Overview of Markets and Technology. Gale Cengage Learning. • Companies, products, applied technologies and markets. U.S. and international literature coverage, 1972 to date. Inquire as to online cost and availability. Provides abstracts from more than 1,600 publications. Weekly updates.

PERIODICALS AND NEWSLETTERS

Distributed Computing Monitor. Patricia Seybold Group. • Description: Covers trends and applications within distributed network computing.

The Gray Sheet. F-D-C Reports Inc. • Description: Monitors the complex regulatory environment for devices, instrumentation, and diagnostics. Topics include device-related Congressional activity, Medicare reimbursement policies, international regulatory intiatives, enforcement and premarket approval programs at FDA's Center for Devices and Radiological Health. Recurring features include device approvals, 510(k) clearances, FDA recalls and seizures, mergers and acquisitions, and sales and earnings.

In Command! A Series of Messages About Getting the Most From Your Word Processor. Economics Press, Inc. • Weekly. $146.00 per year. Quantity prices available. A newsletter for word processing operators.

Inside Microsoft Word: Tips and Techniques for Microsoft Windows. Element K Journals. • Monthly. $87.00 per year. Newsletter on word processing with Microsoft Word for Windows. Covers applications and problem-solving.

Inside Wordperfect for Windows. Element K Journals. • Monthly. $59.00 per year. Newsletter on word processing with Wordperfect software. Includes tips and techniques for both beginners and experts.

The Page. The Cobb Group. • Description: Acts as a visual guide to McIntosh computer desktop publishing.

Prompt. Pasadena IBM User Group. • Monthly. Membership. Helps users of IBM compatibles understand their system.

WORDS

See: VOCABULARY

WORK CLOTHES

See: UNIFORMS

WORK FORCE

See: LABOR SUPPLY

WORK MEASUREMENT

See: TIME AND MOTION STUDY

WORK SCHEDULES

See: FACTORY MANAGEMENT; INDUSTRIAL MANAGEMENT

WORK SIMPLIFICATION

See: TIME AND MOTION STUDY

WORK STOPPAGES

See: STRIKES AND LOCKOUTS

WORK STUDY

See: TIME AND MOTION STUDY

WORKERS' COMPENSATION

ABSTRACTS AND INDEXES

Current Law Index: Multiple Access to Legal Periodicals. Gale Cengage Learning. • Monthly. $725.00 per year. Produced in cooperation with the American Association of Law Libraries. Indexes more than 900 law journals, legal newspapers, and specialty publications from the U.S., Canada, U.K., Ireland, Australia, and New Zealand.

Index to Legal Periodicals and Books. H. W. Wilson Co. • Monthly. $490.00 per year. Quarterly and annual cumulations.

Insurance Periodicals Index. Specials Libraries Association, Insurance and Employees Benefits Div. NILS Publishing Co. • Annual. $250.00. Compiled by the Insurance and Employee Benefits Div., Special Libraries Association. A yearly index of over 15,000 articles from about 35 insurance periodicals. Arrangement is by subject, with an index to authors.

Personnel Management Abstracts. • Quarterly. $190.00 per year. Includes annual cumulation.

BIBLIOGRAPHIES

Insurance and Employee Benefits Literature. Special Libraries Association, Insurance and Employee Benefits Div. • Bimonthly. $15.00 per year. Lists a wide variety of literature in all branches of the insurance industry. Includes annotations.

CD-ROM DATABASES

Authority Worker's Compensation Library. LexisNexis/Matthew Bender. • Periodic revisions. Price on request. CD-ROM contains updated full text of *Larson's Workmen's Compensation, Occupational Injuries and Illnesses*, and other Matthew Bender publications relating to the law of worker's compensation.

ENCYCLOPEDIAS AND DICTIONARIES

Glossary of Insurance Policy Terms. Organization for Economic Cooperation and Development. • 1999. $30.00. "The selected topics range from insurance policy regulation/supervision to general trade issues and include technical terms related to issues such as claims, premiums, and provisions." Edited for government, academic, business, and insurance organizations.

HANDBOOKS AND MANUALS

Managing Worker's Compensation: A Guide to Injury Reduction and Effective Claim Management. Keith Wertz and others. Lewis Publishers. • 2000. $69.95. (Occupation Safety and Health Guide Series).

Modern Workers Compensation. West Group. • Quarterly. $511.00 per year. Three looseleaf volumes. Provides detailed coverage of workers' compensation law and procedure, including medical benefits, rehabilitation benefits, compensation costs, noncompensable injuries, etc.

U. S. Master Employee Benefits Guide. CCH, Inc. • $56.95. Seventh edition. Explains federal tax and labor laws relating to health care benefits, disability benefits, workers' compensation, employee assistance plans, etc.

INTERNET DATABASES

Lexis.com Research System. Lexis-Nexis Group. Phone: 800-227-4908 or (937)865-6800 Fax: (937)865-6909 E-mail: webmaster@prod.lexisnexis.com • URL: http://www.lexis.com • Fee-based Web site offers extensive searching of a wide variety of legal sources. Additional features include Daily Opinion Service, lexis.com Bookstore, Career Center, CLE Center, Law Schools, and Practice Pages ("Pages specific to areas of specialty").

National Center for Health Statistics: Monitoring the Nation's Health. National Center for Health Statistics, Centers for Disease Control and Preventio. Phone: (301)458-4000 E-mail: nchsquery@cdc.gov • URL: http://www.cdc.gov/nchswww • Web site provides detailed data on diseases, vital statistics, and health care in the U. S. Includes a search facility and links to many other health-related Web sites. "Fastats A to Z" offers quick data on hundreds of topics from Accidents to Work-Loss Days, with links to Comprehensive Data and related sources. Frequent updates. Fees: Free.

ONLINE DATABASES

I.I.I. Data Base Search. Insurance Information Institute. • Provides online citations and abstracts of insurance-related literature in magazines, newspapers, trade journals, and books. Emphasis is on property and casualty insurance issues, including highway safety, product safety, and environmental liability. Inquire as to online cost and availability.

Index to Legal Periodicals and Books (Online). H. W. Wilson Co. • Broad coverage of law journals and books 1981 to date. Monthly updates. Inquire as to online cost and availability.

Legal Resource Index. Gale Cengage Learning. • Broad coverage of law literature appearing in legal, business, and other periodicals, 1980 to date. Daily updates. Inquire as to online cost and availability.

LEXIS. LEXIS-NEXIS. • The various LEXIS databases provide full text and indexing for a wide variety of legal cases, statutes, orders, and opinions.

PERIODICALS AND NEWSLETTERS

Business Insurance: News Magazine for Corporate Risk, Employee Benefit and Financial Executives. Crain Communications, Inc. • Weekly. $95.00 per year. Covers a wide variety of business insurance topics, including risk management, employee benefits, workers compensation, marine insurance, and casualty insurance.

Human Resource Executive. LRP Publications. • 16 times a year. $89.95 per year. Edited for directors of corporate human resource departments. Special issues emphasize training, benefits, retirement planning, recruitment, outplacement, workers' compensation, legal pitfalls, and oes emphasize training, benefits, retirement planning, recruitment, outplacement, workers' compensation, legal pitfalls, and other personnel topics.

Journal of Workers Compensation. John Liner Organization. Standard Publishing Corp. • Quarterly. $138.00 per year. Compensation topics include legal considerations, cost control, worker coverage, appropriate medical treatment, and managed care.

Risk and Insurance. LRP Publications. • 15 times a year. Price on application. Topics include risk

management, workers' compensation, reinsurance, employee benefits, and managed care.

Workers' Compensation Law Bulletin. Quinlan Publishing Co. • Description: Summarizes in layman's terms recent court cases deriving from the worker compensation law, with specific identification of cases and brief explanations of the court decisions.

Workers' Compensation Monitor. LRP Publications. • Description: Suggests ways to reduce workers' compensation costs and improve your return-to-work programs. Provides proven solutions your colleagues have implemented to resolve their challenges. Keeps readers up-to-date on the latest developments in national workers' compensation issues including benefits, insurance coverage, legislative reform and costs.

RESEARCH CENTERS AND INSTITUTES

Center for Youth and Communities. Brandeis University, 60 Turner St., Waltham, MA 02453. Phone: (781)736-3770 Fax: (781)736-3773 E-mail: curnan@brandeis.org • URL: http://www.heller.brandeis.edu/chr • Formerly Center for Human Resources.

W. E. Upjohn Institute for Employment Research. 300 S. Westnedge Ave., Kalamazoo, MI 49007-4686. Phone: (616)343-5541 Fax: (616)343-3308 E-mail: eberts@we.upjohninst.org • URL: http://www.upjohninst.org • Research fields include unemployment, unemployment insurance, worker's compensation, labor productivity, profit sharing, the labor market, economic development, earnings, training, and other areas related to employment.

TRADE/PROFESSIONAL ASSOCIATIONS

International Association of Industrial Accident Boards and Commissions. 5610 Medical Ctr, Ste. 24, Madison, WI 53719. Phone: (608)663-6355 Fax: (608)663-1546 E-mail: fhowe@iaiabc.org • URL: http://www.iaiabc.org • Members are government agencies, insurance companies, lawyers, unions, self-insurers, and others with an interest in industrial safety and the administration of workers' compensation laws.

National Council on Compensation Insurance. 901 Peninsula Corporate Circle, Boca Raton, FL 33487. Phone: 800-622-4123 or (561)893-1000 Fax: (561)893-1191 • URL: http://www.ncci.com • Members are insurance companies. Formerly National Council on Workmen's Compensation Insurance.

National Foundation for Unemployment Compensation and Workers Compensation. 1331 Pennsylvania Ave, N.W., Ste. 600, Washington, DC 20004-1790. Phone: (202)637-3464 Fax: (202)783-1616 E-mail: info@uwcstrategy.org • URL: http://www.uwcstrategy.org.

OTHER SOURCES

BNA's Workers' Compensation Report. BNA, Inc. • Biweekly. $604.00 per year. Looseleaf business and legal service.

Worker's Compensation: The Survival Guide for Business. LexisNexis Matthew Bender. • Looseleaf. $100.00. Periodic supplementation available. Edited for business managers and executives. Covers the basics of worker's compensation, including accident prevention, post-accident activities, accident investigation, medical management, insurance issues, and recent legislation. Includes a glossary, checklists, sample letters, a sample employers liability insurance policy, and statistics.

WORKING CLASS

See: LABOR

WORKING MOTHERS

See: EMPLOYMENT OF WOMEN; WOMEN IN THE WORK FORCE

WORKING WOMEN

See: EMPLOYMENT OF WOMEN; WOMEN IN THE WORK FORCE

WORKMEN'S COMPENSATION

See: WORKERS' COMPENSATION

WORKSHOPS

See: CONFERENCES, WORKSHOPS, AND SEMINARS

WORLD BANKING

See: INTERNATIONAL FINANCE

WORLD LAW

See: INTERNATIONAL LAW AND REGULATION

• WORLD TRADE

See: FOREIGN TRADE

WORLD WIDE WEB

See: INTERNET

WORSTED INDUSTRY

See: WOOL AND WORSTED INDUSTRY

WORTHLESS SECURITIES

See: OBSOLETE SECURITIES

WRITERS AND WRITING

See also: REPORT WRITING; TECHNICAL WRITING

GENERAL WORKS

Business English. Mary E. Guffey. South-Western. • 2001. $78.95. Seventh edition. (South-Western College Busines Communications Series).

First Have Something to Say: Writing for the Library Profession. Walt Crawford. American Library Association. • 2003. $29.00. Provides practical advice for librarian-writers on such matters as copyright, contracts, and getting published.

How to Get Happily Published: A Complete and Candid Guide. Judith Appelbaum. HarperInformation. • 1998. $14.00. Fifth edition. Provides advice for writers on dealing with book and magazine publishers.

How to Take the Fog Out of Business Writing. Robert Gunning and Richard A. Kallan. Dartnell Corp. • 1994. $12.95. Includes "The 10 Principles of Clear Statement.".

Super Searcher, Author, Scribe: Successful Writers

Share Their Internet Research Secrets. Loraine Page. Information Today, Inc. • 2002. $24.95. Presents the results of interviews with 14 leading journalists, book authors, writing teachers, and professional literary researchers. Tips, techniques, and sources for searching the Web are featured. (Super Searchers Series).

Thinking Like Your Editor: How to Write Great Serious Nonfiction and Get It Published. Susan Rabiner and Alfred Fortunato. W. W. Norton & Co., Inc. • 2003. $14.95. Emphasizes the importance of submitting an effective proposal. The authors operate the Susan Rabiner Literary Agency in New York.

ABSTRACTS AND INDEXES

Author Biographies Master Index. Gale Cengage Learning. • 1997. $299.00. Fifth edition. Two volumes. Contains over 1,140,000 references to biographies of 550,000 different authors.

BIOGRAPHICAL SOURCES

Contemporary Authors. Gale Cengage Learning. • Annual. $180.00. Provides biographical information on over 112,000 modern authors, including novelists, nonfiction writers, poets, play wrights, journalists, and scriptwriters.

International Authors and Writers Who's Who. Available from Taylor & Francis, Inc. • Biennial. $180.00. About 8,000 authors, writers, and poets, primarily American and British but including writers from nearly 40 countries in the English-speaking world. Published by Melrose Press Ltd.

Major 20th-Century Writers: A Selection of Sketches from Contemporary Authors. Gale Cengage Learning. • 1998. $355.00. Second edition. Five volumes. Includes important nonfiction writers and journalists.

CD-ROM DATABASES

Contemporary Authors on CD-ROM. Gale Cengage Learning. • Semiannual. $795.00 per year. Provides CD-ROM biographical and bibliographical information on about 100,000 modern authors. Includes novelists, nonfiction writers, poets, playwrights, screenwriters, editors, and journalists.

Leadership Library on CD-ROM: Who's Who in the Leadership of the United States. Leadership Directories, Inc. • Quarterly. Including access to Internet version (weekly updates). Contains all 14 *Yellow Book* personnel directories on CD-ROM, providing contact and brief biographical information for about 400,000 individuals. Covers business, government, financial institutions, news media, law firms, associations, foreign representatives, and nonprofit organizations. Includes photographs.

DIRECTORIES

American Society of Journalists and Authors-Directory. American Society of Journalists and Authors. • Annual. $98.00. Lists 1,050 freelance nonfiction writers. Formerly *American Society of Journalists and Authors Directory of Professional Writers.*

Cabell's Directory of Publishing Opportunities in Curriculum and Methods. Cabell Publishing Co. • 2002. $99.95. Over 350 journals in education which will consider manuscripts for publication. Formerly *Cabell's Directory of Publishing Opportunities in Education.*

Cabell's Directory of Publishing Opportunities in Management. Cabell Publishing Co. • 1997. $149.95. Seventh edition. Four volumes. Over 540 scholarly periodicals in management.

Editor and Publisher Syndicate Directory: Annual Directory of Syndicate Services. Editor and Publisher Co., Inc. • Annual. $28.00. Directory of several hundred syndicates serving newspapers in the United States and abroad with news, columns, features, comic strips, editorial cartoons, etc.

Hollywood Creative Directory: Film Writers.

IFILMpro. • Annual. $85.00. Lists more than 8,000 screenwriters and their associated 35,000 film titles. Includes projects in development and unsold screenplays.

International Literary Market Place: The Directory of the International Book Publishing Industry. Information Today, Inc. • Annual. $219.00. Covers more than 180 countries. Listings include publishers, literary agents, major booksellers, book clubs, literary prizes, distributors, trade associations, etc. Formerly published by R. R. Bowker.

Literary Market Place: The Directory of the American Book Publishing Industry. Information Today, Inc. • Annual. $299.00. Two volumes. Listings include publishers, agents, ad agencies, associations, distributors, events, key executives, services, and suppliers (50 directory sections in all). Formerly published by R. R. Bowker.

News Media Yellow Book: Who's Who Among Reporters, Writers, Editors, and Producers in the Leading National News Media. Leadership Directories, Inc. • Quarterly. $360.00 per year. Lists the staffs of major newspapers and news magazines, TV and radio networks, news services and bureaus, and feature syndicates. Includes syndicated columnists and programs. Seven specialized indexes are provided.

Novel and Short Story Writer's Market. F&W Publications, Inc. • Annual. $24.99. List of 2,000 literary magazines, general periodicals, small presses, book publishers, and authors' agents; contests awards; and writers' organizations.

Working Press of the Nation. R. R. Bowker. • Annual. $530.00. $295.00 per volume. Three volumes: (1) *Newspaper Directory*; (2) *Magazine and Internal Publications Directory*; (3) *Radio and Television Directory*. Includes names of editors and other personnel.

Writers' and Artists' Yearbook: A Directory for Writers, Artists, Playwrights, Writers for Film, Radio and Television, Photographers and Composers. Mid Point Trade Books. • Annual. $25.00. A worldwide guide to markets for various kinds of writing and artwork. Published in England by A O C Black. Formerly *International Writers' and Artists' Yearbook.*

Writers Directory. infoUSA Inc. • Number of listings: 2,400. Entries include: Name, address, phone, size of advertisement, name of owner or manager, number of employees, year first in "Yellow Pages." Compiled from telephone company "Yellow Pages," nationwide.

Writer's Guide to Book Editors, Publishers, and Literary Agents, Who They Are, What They Want, and How to Win Them Over. Prima Publishing. • Annual. $27.95; with CD-ROM, $49.95. Directory for authors includes information on publishers' response times and pay rates.

The Writer's Handbook. Kalmbach Publishing Co. • Publication includes: compilation of 50-plus articles for publication, many by recognized authors and editors. Features list of 3,000-plus markets for the sale of manuscripts (fiction, nonfiction, poetry, drama, greeting card), plus lists of American literary agents, writers' organizations, literary contests, and writing conferences. Entries include: Markets--name of firm or publication, contact information, editorial preferences, payment rate. Agents--agency name, contact information, submission guidelines, commission rates. Organizations--name, contact information, description of purpose and activities. Contests--name, contact information, prize or award, deadline. Conferences--name, contact information, date/place, description of workshops/activities.

Writer's Market. Writer's Digest Books. • Covers: Over 8,000 buyers of books, articles, short stories, plays, gags, verse, fillers, and other original written material. Includes book and periodical publishers, greeting card publishers, play producers and publishers, audiovisual material producers, syndicates, and contests and awards. Entries include: Name and address of buyer, phone, payment rates, editorial requirements, reporting time, how to break in.

HANDBOOKS AND MANUALS

Banishing Bureaucratese: Using Plain English in Government Writing. Judith G. Myers. Management Concepts, Inc. • 2001. $39.00. Covers plain writing style for government memos, letters, e-mail, agency communications, budget justification statements, and other bureaucratic documents.

Business English: A Complete Guide to Developing an Effective Business Writing Style. Andrea B. Geffner. Barron's Educational Series, Inc. • 2004. $16.95. Fourth edition. Covers both traditional and electronic business communication.

Business Writing at Its Best. Minerva H. Neiditz. McGraw-Hill. • 1993. $22.50.

Creativity Rules! A Writer's Workbook. John Vorhaus. Silman-James Press. • 1999. $15.95. Covers the practical process of conceiving, outlining, and developing a story, especially for TV or film scripts. Includes "tactics and exercises.".

Easy Access: The Reference Handbook for Writers. Michael Keene and Katherine Adams. McGraw-Hill. • 2001. $35.31. Third edition. Covers documentation styles and "Common Writing Problems" (punctuation, grammar, and sentence construction).

Effective Writing for Engineers, Managers, Scientists. H. J. Tichy and Sylvia Fourdrinier. John Wiley and Sons, Inc. • 1988. $125.00. Second edition.

Freelance Writing. Entrepreneur Media, Inc. • Looseleaf. $59.50. A practical guide to starting a freelance writing service. Covers profit potential, start-up costs, market size evaluation, pricing, accounting, advertising, promotion, etc. (Start-Up Business Guide No. E1258.).

Getting Your Book Published. Christine S. Smedley and Mitchell Allen. Sage Publications, Inc. • 1993. $59.95. A practical guide for academic and professional authors. Covers the initial book prospectus, contract negotiation, production procedures, and marketing. (Survival Skills for Scholars, vol. 10).

Handbook for Business Writing. L. Sue Baug and others. McGraw-Hill. • 1993. $24.95. Second edition. Covers reports, letters, memos, and proposals. (Handbook for... Series).

Handbook for Memo Writing. L. Sue Baugh. McGraw-Hill. • 1995. $32.95. (NTC Business Book Series).

Handbook for Practical Letter Writing. L. Sue Baugh. McGraw-Hill. • 1993. $12.95.

Handbook for Proofreading. Laura K. Anderson. McGraw-Hill. • 1993. $24.95. (NTC Business Book Series).

Handbook for Public Relations Writing. Thomas Bivins. McGraw-Hill. • 1992. $17.95. Second edition. (NTC Business Books Series).

Hot Text: Web Writing That Works. Jonathan Price and Lisa Price. New Riders Publishing. • 2002. $40.00. Provides practical advice on writing text for Web sites, including such details as headlines and menu design. As the attention span of many Web surfers is limited, clarity and brevity become of great importance.

How to Produce Creative Advertising: Traditional Techniques and Computer Applications. Thomas Bivins and Ann Keding. McGraw Hill. • 1993. $37.95. Covers copywriting, advertising design, and the use of desktop publishing techniques in advertising. (NTC Business Books Series).

How to Produce Creative Publications: Traditional Techniques and Computer Applications. Thomas Bivins and Ann Keding. McGraw-Hill. • 1993. $37.95. A practical guide to the writing, designing, and production of magazines, annual reports, brochures, and newsletters by traditional methods and by desktop publishing. (NTC Business Books Series).

Librarian-Author: A Practical Guide on How to Get Published. Betty Carol Sellen, editor. Neal-Schuman Publishers, Inc. • 1985. $38.50.

The Manager's Book of Quotations. Lewis D. and Jonathan P. Siegel Eigen. AMACOM. • 1991. $24.95. Reprint edition. Provides 5,000 modern and traditional quotations arranged by topics useful to business people for speeches and writing.

MLA Handbook for Writers of Research Papers. Joseph Gibaldi. Modern Language Association of America. • 2003. $25.00. Fifth edition. Includes style guidelines for both print and online citations. (MLA Handbook for Writers of Research Papers).

NTC's Business Writer's Handbook. Arthur H. Bell. McGraw-Hill. • 1995. $35.00. (NTC Business Books Series).

Personnel Management: Communications. Prentice Hall PTR. • Looseleaf. Periodic supplementation. Price on application. Includes how to write effectively and how to prepare employee publications.

Public Relations Writer's Handbook. Merry Aronson and Donald E. Spetner. John Wiley and Sons, Inc. • 1998. $24.95.

Screenwriting 101: The Essential Craft of Feature Film Writing. Neill D. Hicks. Michael Wiese Productions. • 1999. $16.95. Covers both the mechanics of screenwriting and the "practicalities of the business.".

Wall Street Journal Guide to Business Style and Usage. Paul R. Martin, editor. The Free Press. • 2002. $30.00. Contains definitions and explanations relating to grammar, spelling, punctuation, and the use of specialized business terms. (Wall Street Journal Book Series).

PERIODICALS AND NEWSLETTERS

Copy Editor: Language News for the Publishing Profession. McMurry Newsletters. • Bimonthly. $69.00 per year. Newsletter for professional copy editors and proofreaders. Includes such items as "Top Ten Resources for Copy Editors.".

Freelance Writer's Report. Dana K. Cassell, editor. CNW Publishing, Editing & Promotion Inc. • Description: Offers up-to-date news and information concerning effective marketing/production techniques, writing tips, self-promotion, and other topics of interest "to freelance writers who intend to earn a good income from their work and improve the quality of their work." Recurring features include interviews, book reviews, news of writing seminars, conferences, and market news. **Remarks:** Members of the Florida Freelance Writers Association receive an extra association section (4 pages).

Publishers Weekly: The International News Magazine of Book Publishing. Reed Business Information. • 51 times a year. $214.00 per year. The international news magazine of book publishing.

Quill: The Magazine for Journalists. Society of Professional Journalists, Eugene S. Pullman Nationalo Journalism Center. • Monthly. $35.00 per year.

The Writer. Kalmbach Publishing Co. • Monthly. $29.00 per year. Freelance writers.

Writer's Digest. F&W Publications, Inc. • Monthly. $19.96 per year.

Written Communication: A Quarterly Journal of Research, Theory, and Application. Sage Publications, Inc. • Quarterly. Institutions, $499.00 per year; includes print and online editions.

TRADE/PROFESSIONAL ASSOCIATIONS

American Society of Business Publications Editors. 710 E Ogden Ave., Ste. 600, Naperville, IL 60563-8603. Phone: (603)579-3288 Fax: (603)369-2488 E-mail: info@asbpe.org • URL: http://www.asbpe.com.

American Society of Journalists and Authors. 1501 Broadway, Suite 302, New York, NY 10036. Phone: (212)997-0947 Fax: (212)768-7414 E-mail: staff@asja.org • URL: http://www.asja.org.

Associated Writing Programs The Association of Writers and Writing Programs. George Mason University, Carty House, Mail Stop 1E3, Fairfax, VA 22030. Phone: (703)933-4301 Fax: (703)933-4302 E-mail: awp@gmu.edu • URL: http://www.awpwriter.org • Supports writers and writing programs worldwide.

Association for Business Communication. Baruch College, Communications Studies, One Bernard Baruch Way, New York, NY 10010. Phone: (646)312-3726 Fax: (646)349-5297 E-mail: abcrjm@cs.com • URL: http://www.theabc.org.

Association of Authors' Representatives. Ansonia Station, P.O. Box 237201, New York, NY 10023. Phone: (212)252-3695 E-mail: aarinc@mindspring.com • URL: http://www.aar-online.org.

Authors Guild. 31 E 32nd St., 7th Fl., New York, NY 10016-7923. Phone: (212)563-5904 Fax: (212)564-5363 E-mail: staff@authorsguild.org • URL: http://www.authorsguild.org • Professional book and magazine writers. Maintains legal staff to provide book and magazine contract reviews for members. Group health insurance available. Members of the guild are also members of the Authors League of America.

Authors League of America. 31 E 28th St., 10th Fl., New York, NY 10016-7923. Phone: (212)564-8350 Fax: (212)564-8363 E-mail: staff@authorsguild.org.

Council of Writers Organizations. 12724 Sagamore Rd., Leawood, KS 66209. Phone: (913)451-9023 Fax: (913)451-4866 E-mail: hurleypr@sound.net • URL: http://www.councilofwriters.com.

Editorial Freelancers Association. 71 W 23rd St., 4th Fl., New York, NY 10010-4181. Phone: (866)929-5400 or (212)929-5400 Fax: (212)929-5439 E-mail: office@the-efa.org • URL: http://www.the-efa.org • Represents persons who work full or part-time as freelance writers or editorial freelancers. Promotes professionalism and facilitates the exchange of information and support. Conducts professional training seminars; and offers job listings.

International Black Writers and Artists. PO Box 43576, Los Angeles, CA 90043. Phone: (213)964-3721 E-mail: ibwa_la@yahoo.com • URL: http://members.tripod.com/~ibwa/home.htm • Seeks to discover and support new black writers. Conducts research and monthly seminars in poetry, fiction, nonfiction, music, and jazz. Provides writing services and children's services. Maintains speakers' bureau. Offers referral service. Plans to establish hall of fame, biographical archives, and museum.

International Women's Writing Guild. PO Box 810, Gracie Sta., New York, NY 10028-0082. Phone: (212)737-7536 Fax: (212)737-9469 E-mail: dirhahn@iwwg.org • URL: http://www.iwwg.org • Women writers in 24 countries interested in expressing themselves through the written word professionally and for personal growth regardless of portfolio. Seeks to empower women personally and professionally through writing. Facilitates manuscript submissions to literary agents and independent presses. Participates in international network. Maintains dental and vision program at group rates.

National Sportscasters and Sportswriters Association. 322 E Innes St., Salisbury, NC 28144. Phone: (704)633-4275 Fax: (704)633-2027 •

Members are sportswriters and radio/TV sportscasters.

National Writers Association. 10940 S Parker Rd., No. 508, Parker, CO 80134. Phone: (303)841-0246 Fax: (303)841-2607 E-mail: natlwritersassn@hotmail.com • URL: http://www.nationalwriters.com • Professional full- or part-time freelance writers who specialize in business writing. Aims to serve as a marketplace whereby business editors can easily locate competent writing talent. Establishes communication among editors and writers.

Society of American Business Editors and Writers, Inc. c/o University of Missouri,, School of Journalism, 134 Neff Annex, Columbia, MO 65211-1200. Phone: (573)882-7862 or (573)882-8985 Fax: (573)884-1372 E-mail: sabew@missouri.edu • URL: http://www.sabew.org • Affiliated with Association for Education in Journalism and Mass Communication. Formerly Society of American Business and Economic Writers.

Society of Professional Journalists. 3909 N. Meridian St., Indianapolis, IN 46208-4011. Phone: (317)927-8000 Fax: (317)920-4789 E-mail: questions@spj.org • URL: http://www.spj.org • Affiliated with Sigma Delta Chi Foundation. Absorbed Economics News Broadcaster Association.

OTHER SOURCES

Lindey on Entertainment, Publishing and the Arts: Agreements and the Law. Alexander Lindey, editor. West Group. • $935.00 per year. Six looseleaf volumes. Periodic supplementation. Provides basic forms, applicable law, and guidance.

WRITING, BUSINESS

See: BUSINESS CORRESPONDENCE; REPORT WRITING; WRITERS AND WRITING

WRITING INSTRUMENTS

See also: OFFICE EQUIPMENT AND SUPPLIES

CD-ROM DATABASES

World Marketing Forecasts on CD-ROM. Gale Cengage Learning. • Annual. $2,500.00. Produced by Euromonitor. Provides detailed forecast data for the years to 2012 on CD-ROM for 54 countries in all parts of the world. Covers a wide range of social, demographic, economic, and market factors. Includes specific forecasts for many kinds of consumer products.

DIRECTORIES

Directory of Manufacturers Supporting the Writing and Marking Instrument Industry. Writing Instrument Manufacturers Association. • Biennial. Available only online. About 200 manufacturers; includes non-members. Formerly *Directory of Manufacturers and Products of the Handwriting and Marking Instrument Manufacturing Industry.*

PERIODICALS AND NEWSLETTERS

WIMA Bulletin. Writing Instrument Manufacturers Association. • 50 times a year. Price on application.

WIMA Directory. Writing Instrument Manufacturers Association. • Semiannual. $50.00. Lists manufacturers, suppliers and products of the writing industry.

STATISTICS SOURCES

Annual Survey of Manufactures. Available from U. S. Government Printing Office. • Annual. Prices vary. Issued by the U. S. Census Bureau as an interim update to the *Census of Manufactures.* Includes data on number of manufacturing establishments in various industries, employment, labor costs, value of shipments, capital expenditures, inventories, energy costs, and assets. (See also Census Bureau home page, http://www.census.gov/.).

Consumer International. Available from Gale Cengage Learning. • Annual. $1,290.00. Published by Euromonitor. Contains extensive consumer market, economic, and demographic data for 25 major, non-European countries, including the U. S. and Canada. Includes consumer market size (volume and value) for 150 product types in 14 categories (food, clothing, automobiles, cosmetics, appliances, etc.).

European Marketing Forecasts. Available from Gale Cengage Learning. • Annual. $1,250.00. Published by Euromonitor. Contains demographic, economic, and market forecasts for the countries of Europe to the year 2010. Forecasts include market-size data for 15 consumer product sectors (food, clothing, automobiles, consumer electronics, etc.).

International Marketing Forecasts. Available from Gale Cengage Learning. • Annual. $1,250.00. Published by Euromonitor. Contains demographic, economic, and market forecasts to the year 2013 for major, non-European countries, including the U. S. and Canada. Forecasts include market-size data for 15 consumer product sectors, such as food, clothing, and automobiles.

TRADE/PROFESSIONAL ASSOCIATIONS

Writing Instrument Manufacturers Association. 15000 Commerce Pkwy., Ste. C, Mount Laurel, NJ 08054-2212. Phone: (856)638-0426 Fax: (856)439-0525 E-mail: wima@ahint.com • URL: http://www.wima.org • Manufacturers of handwriting and marking instruments and parts; industry suppliers. Conducts activities in government and public relations; offers product certification program. Compiles import and export statistics, annual total industry sales, and quarterly industry product sales with detailed breakdowns. Collects information on trademarks.

OTHER SOURCES

Writing and Marking Instruments. Available from MarketResearch.com. • 2002. $3,950.00. Published by Global Industry Analysts. Provides worldwide market research data, including profiles of major companies in the field.

WRITING, TECHNICAL

See: TECHNICAL WRITING

X

X-RAY EQUIPMENT INDUSTRY

See also: HOSPITAL EQUIPMENT; MEDI-CAL TECHNOLOGY

ABSTRACTS AND INDEXES

Applied Science and Technology Index. H. W. Wilson Co. • 11 times a year. Quarterly and annual cumulations. Price varies. Indexes a wide variety of English language technical, industrial, and engineering periodicals.

CD-ROM DATABASES

WILSONDISC: Applied Science and Technology Abstracts. H. W. Wilson Co. • Monthly. Includes unlimited access to the online version of *Applied Science and Technology Abstracts* through WILSONLINE. Provides CD-ROM indexing and abstracting of 500 prominent scientific, technical, engineering, and industrial periodicals. Indexing coverage is provided from 1983 to date and abstracting from 1993 to date.

DIRECTORIES

Health Industry Buyers Guide. Lippincott Williams & Wilkins. • Covers: 4,000 manufacturers of hospital and physician's supplies and equipment, including medical laboratory, oxygen therapy, and X-ray supplies, home health care products, and orthopedic appliances. Entries include: Manufacturer name, address, phone, fax, full product line.

INTERNET DATABASES

Manufacturing Profiles. U. S. Bureau of the Census. Phone: (301)763-4636 E-mail: webmaster@census. gov • URL: http://www.census.gov/prod/www/abs/ mfg-prof.html • The Census Bureau makes available free on PDF (Portable Document Format) an annual consolidation of the entire Current Industrial Report series, presenting "all the data compiled." Contains statistics on production, shipments, inventories, consumption, exports, imports, and orders for a wide variety of manufactured products.

ONLINE DATABASES

Applied Science and Technology Index Online. H. W. Wilson Co. • Provides online indexing of 500 major scientific, technical, industrial, and engineering periodicals. Time period is 1983 to date. Monthly updates. Inquire as to online cost and availability.

Globalbase. Gale Cengage Learning. • Provides more than one million online summaries of business, industrial, and economic news reports from more than 1,000 publications worldwide. Covers a wide range of material appearing in international

trade journals, professional magazines, and newspapers. Time period is 1984 to date, with weekly updates. Inquire as to online cost and availability.

Health Devices Alerts [online]. ECRI. • Provides online reports of medical equipment defects, problems, failures, misuses, and recalls. Time period is 1977 to date, with weekly updates. Inquire as to online cost and availability.

PROMT: Predicasts Overview of Markets and Technology. Gale Cengage Learning. • Companies, products, applied technologies and markets. U.S. and international literature coverage, 1972 to date. Inquire as to online cost and availability. Provides abstracts from more than 1,600 publications. Weekly updates.

Trade & Industry Database. Gale Cengage Learning. • Provides indexing of business periodicals, January 1981 to date. Daily updates. (Full text articles from some periodicals are available online, 1983 to date. Inquire as to online cost and availability).

PERIODICALS AND NEWSLETTERS

Decisions in Imaging Economics: The Journal of Imaging Technology Management. Curant Communications, Inc. • Bimonthly. Controlled circulation. Edited for health care executives and radiologists concerned with the purchase and management of imaging technology.

The Gray Sheet Reports: Medical Devices, Diagnostics and Instrumentation. F-D-C Reports, Inc. • Weekly. Institutions, $1,172.00 per year. Newsletter. Provides industry and financial news, including a medical sector stock index. Monitors regulatory developments at the Center for Devices and Radiological Health of the U. S. Food and Drug Administration.

Healthcare Purchasing News: A Magazine for Hospital Materials Management Central Service, Infection Control Practitioners. Thomson/Medical Economics. • Monthly. $47.95 per year. Edited for personnel responsible for the purchase of medical, surgical, and hospital equipment and supplies. Features new purchasing techniques and new products. Includes news of the activities of two major purchasing associations, Health Care Material Management Society and International Association of Healthcare Central Service Materiel Management.

RESEARCH CENTERS AND INSTITUTES

Mallinckrodt Institute of Radiology - Hyperthermia Service. Washington University in Saint Louis, Radiation Oncology Center, Euclid and Forest Park Aves., St. Louis, MO 63110. Phone: (314)362-8503 Fax: (314)362-8521 • URL: http://www.mir.wustl.

edu/ • Maintains laboratories for research pertaining to various kinds of radiological equipment.

STATISTICS SOURCES

Annual Survey of Manufactures. Available from U. S. Government Printing Office. • Annual. Prices vary. Issued by the U. S. Census Bureau as an interim update to the *Census of Manufactures.* Includes data on number of manufacturing establishments in various industries, employment, labor costs, value of shipments, capital expenditures, inventories, energy costs, and assets. (See also Census Bureau home page, http://www.census. gov/.).

Electromedical Equipment and Irradiation Equipment, Including X-Ray. U. S. Bureau of the Census. • Annual. Contains shipment quantity, value of shipment, export, and import data. (Current Industrial Report No. MA-38R.).

TRADE/PROFESSIONAL ASSOCIATIONS

American College of Radiology. 1891 Preston White Dr., Reston, VA 20191-4397. Phone: 800-227-5463 or (703)648-8900 Fax: (703)295-6773 E-mail: info@acr.org • URL: http://www.acr.org • A professional society of physicians. Affiliated with International Society of Radiology.

Association for Healthcare Resource and Materials Management. c/o American Hospital Association, One N Franklin St., Chicago, IL 60606-3420. Phone: (312)422-3840 Fax: (312)422-4573 E-mail: ahrmm@aha.org • URL: http://www.ahrmm.org • Members are involved with the purchasing and distribution of supplies and equipment for hospitals and other healthcare establishments. Formerly American Society for Healthcare Materials Management.

International Association of Healthcare Central Service Materiel Management. 213 W. Institute Place, Suite 307, Chicago, IL 60610. Phone: 800-962-8274 or (312)440-0078 Fax: (312)440-9474 E-mail: mailbox@iahcsmm.com • URL: http:// www.iahcsmm.com • Members are professional personnel responsible for management and distribution of supplies from a central service material management (purchasing) department of a hospital. Formerly International Association of Hospital Central Service Management.

Radiological Society of North America. 820 Jorie Blvd., Oak Brook, IL 60523-2251. Phone: (630)571-2670 Fax: (630)571-7837 E-mail: informat@rsna. org • URL: http://www.rsna.org • Members are radiologists and scientists. Includes a Technical Exhibits Committee and a Scientific Exhibits Committee. Formerly Western Roentgen Society.

Radiology Business Management Association. 10300 Eaton Pl., Ste. 460, Fairfax, VA 22030.

Phone: 888-224-7262 or (703)621-3355 Fax: (703)621-3356 E-mail: info@rbma.org • URL: http://www.rbma.org • Provides education, resources and solutions to manage the business of

radiology. Offers an online course in radiology coding.

OTHER SOURCES

Digital X-Ray Markets: Imaging in the 21st Century. Theta Reports/PJB Medical Publications, Inc. • 2000. $1,995.00. Market research data. Covers digital filmless radiography as a replacement for

traditional x-ray technology. (Theta Report No. 1027.).

X-Ray Films and Chemicals. Available from MarketResearch.com. • 2002. $3,450.00. Published by Global Industry Analysts. Provides worldwide market research data, including profiles of major x-ray supply companies.

Y

YACHTS

See: BOAT INDUSTRY

YARN

See also: COTTON INDUSTRY; SILK INDUSTRY; TEXTILE INDUSTRY; WEAVING; WOOL AND WORSTED INDUSTRY

ABSTRACTS AND INDEXES

Textile Technology Digest. Institute of Textile Technology. • Annual. $535.00. Provides indexing and abstracting of a wide variety of textile technology literature.

CD-ROM DATABASES

OECD Statistical Compendium. Organization for Economic Cooperation and Development. • Semiannual. $1,905.00 per year for 1 to 10 users. CD-ROM contains more than 730,000 monthly, quarterly, and annual time series for OECD countries, 1960 to date. Includes fully searchable data on agriculture, food, economic indicators, national accounts, employment, energy, finance, industry, technology, and foreign trade. Results can be displayed in various forms.

Textile Technology Digest [CD-ROM]. Textile Information Center, Institute of Textile Technology. • Quarterly. Provides CD-ROM indexing and abstracting of worldwide journals and monographs in various areas of textile technology, production, and management. Covers 1978 to date.

ENCYCLOPEDIAS AND DICTIONARIES

Textile Terms and Definitions. J.E. McIntyre and Paul N. Daniels, editors. Available from State Mutual Book and Periodical Service Ltd. • 1996. $180.00. 10th edition. Published by the Textile Insitute (UK). Includes more than 1,000 definitions of textile processes, fiber types, and end products. Illustrated.

FINANCIAL RATIOS

Annual Statement Studies. The Risk Management Association. • Annual. Median and quartile financial ratios are given for over 400 kinds of manufacturing, wholesale, retail, construction, and consumer finance establishments. Data is sorted by both asset size and sales volume. Includes a clearly written "Definition of Ratios" and an alphabetical industry index.

Annual Statement Studies: Industry Default Probabilities and Cash Flow Measures. The Risk Management Association. • Annual. $145.00. Serves as a companion volume to the original *Annual Statement Studies.* Gives probability of default estimates on a percentage scale for more than 450 industries. Includes changes in position year-by-year for eight financial statement line items and provides percentage measures of cash flow.

INTERNET DATABASES

Business 2.0 Web Guide to the Best Business Links. Business 2.0 Media Inc. Phone: (415)293-4800 E-mail: support@business2.com • URL: http://www.business2.com/webguide • Web site presents an extensive, searchable directory of links to "the best, most informative, and authoritative web pages." Twenty main categories cover business, finance, career, company information, people, and technology topics, with thousands of subtopics, all linking to Web sites recommended by experienced business researchers. Fees: Free.

Fedstats. Federal Interagency Council on Statistical Policy. Phone: (202)395-7254 • URL: http://www.fedstats.gov • Web site features an efficient search facility for full-text statistics produced by more than 100 federal agencies, including the Census Bureau, the Bureau of Economic Analysis, and the Bureau of Labor Statistics. Boolean searches can be made within one agency or for all agencies combined. Links are offered to international statistical bureaus, including the UN, IMF, OECD, UNESCO, Eurostat, and 20 individual countries. Fees: Free.

FreeLunch.com. Economy.com, Inc. Phone: (610)696-8700 Fax: (610)696-1678 • URL: http://www.freelunch.com • Web site provides free access to more than 1.5 million economic and financial data series, covering industry, demographics, labor markets, prices, retail sales, government spending, trade, interest rates, housing starts, the stock market, and many other topics. Data is available for various time periods in either chart or table form. Searching is offered. Fees: Free, but registration required. Economy.com, Inc. also offers fee-based economic analysis at *The Dismal Scientist* site (http://www.dismal.com).

Manufacturing Profiles. U. S. Bureau of the Census. Phone: (301)763-4636 E-mail: webmaster@census.gov • URL: http://www.census.gov/prod/www/abs/mfg-prof.html • The Census Bureau makes available free on PDF (Portable Document Format) an annual consolidation of the entire Current Industrial Report series, presenting "all the data compiled." Contains statistics on production, shipments, inventories, consumption, exports, imports, and orders for a wide variety of manufactured products.

ONLINE DATABASES

Textile Technology Digest [online]. Institute of Textile Technology. • Contains indexing and abstracting of more than 300 worldwide journals and monographs in various areas of textile technology, production, and management. Time period is 1978 to date, with monthly updating. Inquire as to online cost and availability.

World Textiles. Elsevier Science, Inc. • Provides abstracting and indexing from 1970 of worldwide textile literature (periodicals, books, pamphlets, and reports). Includes U. S., European, and British patent information. Updating is monthly. Inquire as to online cost and availability.

PERIODICALS AND NEWSLETTERS

American Sportswear and Knitting Times. National Knitwear and Sportswear Association. • Monthly. $40.00 per year. Includes *American Sportswear and Knitting Times Buyer's Guide.* Formerly *Knitting Times.*

DNR: The Men's Fashion Retail Textile Authority. Fairchild Publications. • Daily. $85.00 per year. Formerly *Daily News Record.*

International Textile Bulletin: Yarn and Fabric Forming Edition. ITS Publishing, International Textile Service. • Quarterly. $170.00 per year. Editions in Chinese, English, French, German, Italian and Spanish.

STATISTICS SOURCES

Annual Survey of Manufactures. Available from U. S. Government Printing Office. • Annual. Prices vary. Issued by the U. S. Census Bureau as an interim update to the *Census of Manufactures.* Includes data on number of manufacturing establishments in various industries, employment, labor costs, value of shipments, capital expenditures, inventories, energy costs, and assets. (See also Census Bureau home page, http://www.census.gov/.).

Business Statistics of the United States. Linz Audain and Cornelia J. Strawser. Bernan Associates. • Annual. $147.00. Based on *Business Statistics,* formerly issue by the Bureau of Economic Analysis, U. S. Department of Commerce. Provides basic data for a wide variety of U. S. industries, services, and economic indicators. Most statistics are shown annually for 30 years and monthly for the most recent four years.

Consumption on the Woolen System and Worsted Combing. U. S. Bureau of the Census. • Quarterly and annual. Provides data on consumption of fibers in woolen and worsted spinning mills, by class of fibers and end use. (Current Industrial Reports, MQ-22D.).

Survey of Current Business. Available from U. S. Government Printing Office. • Monthly. $63.00 per year. Issued by Bureau of Economic Analysis, U. S. Department of Commerce. Presents a wide variety of business and economic data.

TRADE/PROFESSIONAL ASSOCIATIONS

American Yarn Spinners Association. 2500 Lowell Rd., Gastonia, NC 28053. Phone: (704)824-3522 Fax: (704)824-0630 E-mail: info@awpa.org • URL: http://www.textileweb.com/storefronts/aysa.html • Manufacturers of combed cotton sales yarn and carded yarns spun from cotton, wool, and/or synthetics. Provides full service to the sales yarn industry.

Textile Institute. St. James's Buildings, 1st Fl., 79 Oxford St., Manchester M1 6FQ, United Kingdom. Phone: 44 161 2371188 Fax: 44 161 2361991 E-mail: tiihq@textileinst.org.uk • URL: http://www. texi.org • Companies and individuals in 100 countries involved in management, science, technology, design, information transfer, and marketing of textiles including clothing and footwear. Promotes interests of the textile industry worldwide; serves professional interests of members; confers qualifications and recognizes achievements in research, application of ideas, education, business, and public affairs. Maintains Information Service to collect information relating to textile industrial and economic conditions in different countries and economic sectors.

YOUTH MARKET

See also: CHILDREN'S APPAREL INDUSTRY

ALMANACS AND YEARBOOKS

Research Alert Yearbook: Vital Facts on Consumer Behavior and Attitudes. EPM Communications, Inc. • Annual. $295.00. Provides summaries of consumer market research from the newsletters *Research Alert, Youth Markets Alert,* and *Minority Markets Alert.* Includes tables, charts, graphs, and textual summaries for 41 subject categories. Sources include reports, studies, polls, and focus groups.

CD-ROM DATABASES

Magazine Index Plus. Gale Cengage Learning. • Monthly. $4,000.00 per year (includes InfoTrac workstation). Provides full text on CD-ROM for about 100 popular, general interest magazines and indexing for 300 others. Includes special indexing of reviews and product evaluations. Time period is 1980 to date.

PERIODICALS AND NEWSLETTERS

Selling to Kids: News and Practical Advice on Successfully Marketing to Kids and Teens. EPM Communications. • Biweekly. $495.00 per year.

Newsletter. Includes market research information, news items, and case studies.

Youth Markets Alert. EPM Communications Inc. • Description: Features information and research results related to young consumers from elementary school through high school.

OTHER SOURCES

Teenage Economic Power. Available from MarketResearch.com. • 2001. $1,200.00. Published by Rand Youth Poll. Provides consumer market data on the 13-year to 19-year age group. Gives results of an extensive survey of teenage attitudes toward shopping and spending.

The U. S. College Market. Available from MarketResearch.com. • 2001. $2,799.00. Published by Packaged Facts. Market research report on college students as consumers.

The U. S. Kids Market. Available from MarketResearch.com. • 2002. $3,000.00. Published by Packaged Facts. Provides market research data on American consumers aged 5 to 14.

The U. S. Tweens Market. Available from MarketResearch.com. • 2001. $2,750.00. Published by Packaged Facts. Market research report on American consumers aged 8 to 14.

Z

ZERO-BASE BUDGETING

See: BUDGETING, BUSINESS

ZERO DEFECTS

See: QUALITY CONTROL

ZINC INDUSTRY

See also: METAL INDUSTRY; MINES AND
MINERAL RESOURCES

ABSTRACTS AND INDEXES

*IMM Abstracts and Index: A Survey of World
Literature on the Economic Geology and Mining of
All Minerals (Except Coal), Mineral Processing,
and Nonferrous Extraction Metallurgy.* Institution of
Mining and Metallurgy. • Bimonthly. $500.00 per
year. Provides international coverage of the
literature of mining and nonferrous metallurgy.
Includes mineral economics, tunnelling, and rock
mechanics.

*Zincscan: A Review of Recent Technical Literature
On the Use of Zinc and Its Products.* C & C
Associates. • Quarterly. $125.00. per year. Provides
technical articles and abstracts of recent technical
and market related literature on zinc. Formerly *Zinc
Abstracts.*

ALMANACS AND YEARBOOKS

Agricultural and Mineral Commodities Year Book.
Available from Taylor & Francis Group. • Annual.
$225.00. Published by Europa Publications.
Contains descriptive product profiles, price data,
export-import data, and production statistics for
major commodities of the world. Includes commodity histories, uses, markets, demand trends, and
information about trade agreements and key commodity organizations.

CRB Commodity Yearbook. Commodity Research
Bureau. CRB. • Annual. $99.95.

CD-ROM DATABASES

*METADEX Materials Collection: Metals-Polymers-
Ceramics.* Cambridge Scientific Abstracts. •
Quarterly. Provides CD-ROM citations to the
worldwide literature of materials science and
metallurgy. Corresponds to *Metals Abstracts, Alloys
Index, Steels Alert, Nonferrous Alert, Polymers/
Ceramics/Composites Alert,* and *Engineered Materi-
als Abstracts.* (Formerly produced by ASM
International.).

OECD Statistical Compendium. Organization for
Economic Cooperation and Development. •

Semiannual. $1,905.00 per year for 1 to 10 users.
CD-ROM contains more than 730,000 monthly,
quarterly, and annual time series for OECD
countries, 1960 to date. Includes fully searchable
data on agriculture, food, economic indicators,
national accounts, employment, energy, finance,
industry, technology, and foreign trade. Results can
be displayed in various forms.

INTERNET DATABASES

Business 2.0 Web Guide to the Best Business Links.
Business 2.0 Media Inc. Phone: (415)293-4800
E-mail: support@business2.com • URL: http://
www.business2.com/webguide • Web site presents
an extensive, searchable directory of links to "the
best, most informative, and authoritative web
pages." Twenty main categories cover business,
finance, career, company information, people, and
technology topics, with thousands of subtopics, all
linking to Web sites recommended by experienced
business researchers. Fees: Free.

Fedstats. Federal Interagency Council on Statistical
Policy. Phone: (202)395-7254 • URL: http://www.
fedstats.gov • Web site features an efficient search
facility for full-text statistics produced by more than
100 federal agencies, including the Census Bureau,
the Bureau of Economic Analysis, and the Bureau of
Labor Statistics. Boolean searches can be made
within one agency or for all agencies combined.
Links are offered to international statistical bureaus,
including the UN, IMF, OECD, UNESCO, Eurostat,
and 20 individual countries. Fees: Free.

FreeLunch.com. Economy.com, Inc. Phone:
(610)696-8700 Fax: (610)696-1678 • URL: http://
www.freelunch.com • Web site provides free access
to more than 1.5 million economic and financial data
series, covering industry, demographics, labor
markets, prices, retail sales, government spending,
trade, interest rates, housing starts, the stock market,
and many other topics. Data is available for various
time periods in either chart or table form. Searching
is offered. Fees: Free, but registration required.
Economy.com, Inc. also offers fee-based economic
analysis at *The Dismal Scientist* site (http://www.
dismal.com).

ONLINE DATABASES

GEOARCHIVE. Geosystems. • Citations to
literature on geoscience and water. 1974 to present.
Monthly updates. Inquire as to online cost and
availability.

GEOREF. American Geological Institute. •
Bibliography and index of geology and geosciences
literature, 1785 to present. Inquire as to online cost
and availability.

Materials Business File. Cambridge Scientific
Abstracts. • Provides online abstracts and citations

to worldwide materials literature, covering the business and industrial aspects of metals, plastics,
ceramics, and composites. Corresponds to *Steels
Alert, Nonferrous Metals Alert,* and *Polymers/
Ceramics/Composites Alert.* Time period is 1985 to
date, with monthly updates. (Formerly produced by
ASM International.) Inquire as to online cost and
availability.

METADEX. Cambridge Scientific Abstracts. • Covers the worldwide literature of metals, metallurgy,
and materials science, 1966 to date. Includes
detailed alloys indexing from 1974. Biweekly
updating. Inquire as to online cost and availability.
(Formerly produced by ASM International.).

PERIODICALS AND NEWSLETTERS

The Mining Record. The Mining Record. • Description: Discusses a myriad of issues within the mining
industry, particularly exploration, development,
production, and milling.

PRICE SOURCES

Platt's Metals Week. Platt's. • Weekly. $770.00 per
year.

STATISTICS SOURCES

Business Statistics of the United States. Linz Audain
and Cornelia J. Strawser. Bernan Associates. •
Annual. $147.00. Based on *Business Statistics,*
formerly issue by the Bureau of Economic Analysis,
U. S. Department of Commerce. Provides basic data
for a wide variety of U. S. industries, services, and
economic indicators. Most statistics are shown annually for 30 years and monthly for the most recent
four years.

Lead and Zinc Statistics. International Lead and
Zinc Study Group. • Monthly. $390.00 per year.
Supplement available *Advance Data Service.* Text in
English and French.

Mineral Commodity Summaries. Available from U.
S. Government Printing Office. • Annual. $26.00.
Published by the U. S. Geological Survey, Department of the Interior (http://www.usgs.gov). Contains
detailed, five-year data for about 90 nonfuel
minerals. Covers a wide range of statistics, including production, imports, exports, consumption,
reserves, prices, tariff information, and industry
employment. (Two pages are devoted to each
mineral.).

Non-Ferrous Metal Data Yearbook. American
Bureau of Metal Statistics. • Annual. $405.00.
Provides worldwide data on approximately about
200 statistical tables covering many nonferrous
metals. Includes production, consumption,
inventories, exports, imports, and other data.

Survey of Current Business. Available from U. S.
Government Printing Office. • Monthly. $63.00 per

year. Issued by Bureau of Economic Analysis, U. S. Department of Commerce. Presents a wide variety of business and economic data.

WEFA Industrial Monitor. John Wiley and Sons, Inc. • Annual. $65.00. Prepared by industry analysts at WEFA, an economic forecasting and consulting firm (originally Wharton Econometric Forecasting Associates). Contains discussions of the outlook for major U. S. industries, with many 10-year forecasts (WEFA Web site is http://www.wefa.com).

World Trade Annual. United Nations Statistical Office. Walker and Co. • Annual. Prices vary.

TRADE/PROFESSIONAL ASSOCIATIONS

American Bureau of Metal Statistics. P.O. Box 805, Chatham, NJ 07928. Phone: (973)701-2299 Fax: (973)701-2152 E-mail: info@abms.com • URL: http://www.abms.com • Members are metal companies. Compiles and publishes detailed statistical data on a wide variety of nonferrous metals: aluminum, copper, gold, lead, nickel, platinum, silver, tin, titanium, uranium, zinc, and others.

International Lead Zinc Research Organization. 2525 Meridian Pkwy., Ste. 100, Durham, NC 27713. Phone: (919)361-4647 Fax: (919)361-1957 E-mail: rputnam@ilzro.org • URL: http://www.ilzro.org • Seeks to develop new applications for lead and zinc. Improves current uses of lead and zinc; compiles technical information on these metals. Directs approximately 150 research programs through its contracts with universities, governments, independent laboratories, industrial companies, and member companies. Research and development projects deal with die castings, wrought zinc, alloys, galvanized steel, plating, welding, lead and zinc chemistry, environmental studies, batteries, lead for architectural uses, and other subjects. Acts as a Research organization sponsored by major producers, smelters, and refiners of lead and/or zinc from 15 countries.

Non-Ferrous Metals Producers Committee. 2030 M St. NW, Ste. 800, 2030 M St. NW, Ste. 800, 2030 M. St., N.W., Suite 800, Washington, DC 20036. Phone: (202)466-7720 Fax: (202)466-2710 E-mail: nffstaff@nffs.org • URL: http://www.arcat.com/ arcatcos/cos37/arc37679.cfm • Represents domestic copper, lead, and zinc producers. Promotes the interests of copper, lead, and zinc mining and metal industries in the U.S. with emphasis on tariffs, laws, regulations, and government policies affecting international trade and foreign imports.

ZIP CODE

See: POSTAL SERVICES

ZONING

See also: CITY PLANNING; REGIONAL PLANNING

ABSTRACTS AND INDEXES

Current Law Index: Multiple Access to Legal Periodicals. Gale Cengage Learning. • Monthly. $725.00 per year. Produced in cooperation with the American Association of Law Libraries. Indexes more than 900 law journals, legal newspapers, and specialty publications from the U.S., Canada, U.K., Ireland, Australia, and New Zealand.

Index to Legal Periodicals and Books. H. W. Wilson Co. • Monthly. $490.00 per year. Quarterly and annual cumulations.

PAIS International in Print. Public Affairs Information Service, Inc. • Monthly. $850.00 per year; cumulations three times a year. Provides topical citations to the worldwide literature of public affairs, economics, demographics, sociology, and trade. Text in English; indexed materials in English, French, German, Italian, Portuguese and Spanish.

ALMANACS AND YEARBOOKS

American Law Yearbook. Gale Cengage Learning. • Annual. $165.00. Serves as a yearly supplement to *West's Encyclopedia of American Law.* Describes new legal developments in many subject areas.

BIBLIOGRAPHIES

NIMBYS and LULUs (Not-in-My-Back-Yard and Locally-Unwanted-Land-Uses). Jan Horah and Heather Scott. Sage Publications, Inc. • 1993. $10.00.

CD-ROM DATABASES

PAIS on CD-ROM. Public Affairs Information Service, Inc. • Quarterly. $1,995.00 per year. Provides a CD-ROM version of the online service, *PAIS International.* Contains over 500,000 citations to the literature of contemporary social, political, and economic issues.

WILSONDISC: Index to Legal Periodicals and Books. H. W. Wilson Co. • Monthly. Includes unlimited online access to *Index to Legal Periodicals* through WILSONLINE. Contains CD-ROM indexing of more than 1,400 English language legal periodicals from 1981 to date and 2,500 books.

ENCYCLOPEDIAS AND DICTIONARIES

Encyclopedia of Housing. Willem van Vliet, editor. Sage Publications, Inc. • 1998. $216.00. Contains 500 entries covering all aspects of housing. Includes index of names and subjects.

West's Encyclopedia of American Law. Available from Gale Cengage Learning. • 2003. $1,195.00. Second edition. 12 volumes. Published by West Group. Covers a wide variety of legal topics for the general reader.

HANDBOOKS AND MANUALS

New Uses for Obsolete Buildings. Urban Land Institute. • 1996. $65.95. Covers various aspects of

redevelopment: zoning, building codes, environment, economics, financing, and marketing. Includes eight case studies and 75 descriptions of completed "adaptive use projects.".

Zoning and Planning Deskbook, 2d. Douglas W. Kmiec. West Group. • $220.00. Two looseleaf volumes. Annual supplementation. Emphasis is on legal issues.

Zoning and Planning Law Handbook. West Group. • $264.50.

INTERNET DATABASES

Lexis.com Research System. Lexis-Nexis Group. Phone: 800-227-4908 or (937)865-6800 Fax: (937)865-6909 E-mail: webmaster@prod.lexis-nexis.com • URL: http://www.lexis.com • Fee-based Web site offers extensive searching of a wide variety of legal sources. Additional features include Daily Opinion Service, lexis.com Bookstore, Career Center, CLE Center, Law Schools, and Practice Pages ("Pages specific to areas of specialty").

ONLINE DATABASES

Index to Legal Periodicals and Books (Online). H. W. Wilson Co. • Broad coverage of law journals and books 1981 to date. Monthly updates. Inquire as to online cost and availability.

PAIS International. Public Affairs Information Service, Inc. • Corresponds to the former printed publications, *PAIS Bulletin* (1976-90) and *PAIS Foreign Language Index* (1972-90), and to the current *PAIS International in Print* (1991 to date). Covers economic, political, and sociological material appearing in periodicals, books, government documents, and other publications. Updating is monthly. Inquire as to online cost and availability.

PERIODICALS AND NEWSLETTERS

Land Use Law and Zoning Digest. American Planning Association. • Monthly. $275.00 per year. Covers judicial decisions and state laws affecting zoning and land use. Edited for city planners and lawyers. Monthly supplement available *Zoning News.*

Planning and Zoning News. Planning and Zoning Center, Inc. • Monthly. $175.00 per year. Newsletter on planning and zoning issues in the United States.

Zoning and Planning Law Report. West Group. • Monthly. $483.00 per year. Newsletter.

Zoning Bulletin. Quinlan Publishing Co., Inc. • Semimonthly. $89.00 per year. Newsletter dealing with zoning legal issues.

Zoning News. American Planning Association. • Monthly. $60.00 per year. Newsletter on local community zoning.

RESEARCH CENTERS AND INSTITUTES

Institute of State and Regional Affairs. Pennsylvania State University at Harrisburg, 777 W. Harrisburg Pike, Middletown, PA 17057-4898. Phone: (717)948-6336 Fax: (717)948-6754 E-mail: xvc@psu.edu • URL: http://www.psdc.hbg.psu.edu/isra • Conducts research in environmental, general, and socioeconomic planning. Zoning is included.

974

For publishers addresses, refer to SOURCES CITED section at the back of the book.

SOURCES CITED

A/C Flyer: Best Read Resale Magazine Worldwide (Aircraft). McGraw-Hill, 1221 Ave. of the Americas New York, NY 10020. Phone: 800-722-4726 or (212)512-2000 Fax: (212)512-4502 E-mail: customer.service@mcgraw-hill.com • URL: http://www.mcgraw-hill.com • Monthly. Individuals $49.00 per year; students, $28.00 per year. Lists used airplanes for sale by dealers, brokers, and private owners. Provides news and trends relating to the aircraft resale industry. Special issues include "Product & Service Buyer's Guide" and "Dealer/Broker Directory."

A-V Online. Access Innovations, Inc., National Information Center for Educational Media, P. O. Box 8640 Albuquerque, NM 87198. Phone: 800-926-8328 or (505)265-3591 Fax: (505)256-1080 Provides online descriptions of non-print educational materials for all levels, kindergarten to graduate school. Includes all types of audio, film, and video media. Updated quarterly. Inquire as to online cost and availability.

A-V Online (CD-ROM). Access Innovations, Inc., National Information Center for Educational Media, P. O. Box 8640 Albuquerque, NM 87198. Phone: 800-926-8328 or (505)998-0800 Fax: (505)998-3372 Annual. $795.00 per year. Provides CD-ROM descriptions of all types of non-print educational materials, covering all learning levels.

The A-Z Vocabulary for Investors. American Institute for Economic Research, PO Box 1000 Great Barrington, MA 01230-1000. Phone: (413)528-1216 Fax: (413)528-0103 E-mail: info@aier.org • URL: http://www.aier.org • 1997. $7.00. Second half of book is a "General Glossary" of about 400 financial terms "most-commonly used" in investing. First half contains lengthier descriptions of types of banking institutions (commercial banks, thrift institutions, credit unions), followed by succinct explanations of various forms of investment: stocks, bonds, options, futures, commodities, and "Other Investments" (collectibles, currencies, mortgages, precious metals, real estate, charitable trusts). (Economic Education Bulletin.)

AACE International-Directory of Members. AACE International, 209 Prairie Ave., Suite 100 Morgantown, WV 26501. Phone: 800-858-2678 or (304)296-8444 Fax: (304)291-5728 E-mail: info@aacei.org • URL: http://www.aacei.com • Annual. $20.00 per year. 6,000 cost engineers, estimators, and cost management professionals worldwide.

AACE International. Transactions of the Annual Meetings. American Assoiciation of Cost Engineers. AACE International, 209 Prarier Ave., Ste. 100 Morgantown, WV 26501. Phone: 800-858-2678 or (304)296-8444 Fax: (304)291-5728 E-mail: info@aacei.org • URL: http://www.aacei.org • Annual. Price varies. Contains texts of papers presented at AACE meetings.

AACSB International - The Association to Advance Collegiate Schools of Business., 600 Emerson Rd., Suite 300 St. Louis, MO 63141-6762. Phone: (314)872-8481 Fax: (314)872-8495 E-mail: webmaster@aacsb.edu • URL: http://www.aacsb.edu • Formerly AACSB - International Association for Management Education.

AACSB Newsline. AACSB—American Assembly of Collegiate Schools of Business, 777 South Harbour Island Boulevard, Ste. 750 Tampa, FL 33602-5730. Phone: (813)769-6500 Fax: (813)769-6559 • URL: http://www.aacsb.edu • Description: Covers issues and events affecting management education, and Association projects and activities. Recurring features include notices of publications available and news of educational opportunities.

AACSB: The International Association for Management Education Membership Directory. AACSB-The Association to Advance Collegiate Schools of Business, 600 Emerson Rd., Suite 300 Saint Louis, MO 63141-6762. Phone: (314)872-8481 Fax: (314)872-8495 • URL: http://www.aacsb.edu •

Annual. $15.00. Lists over 800 member institutions offering instructional programs in business administration at the college level.

AAHSA Resource Catalog. American Association of Homes and Services for the Aging, 901 E St., N. W., Suite 500 Washington, DC 20004-2011. Phone: 800-508-9442 or (202)783-2242 Fax: (202)783-2255 E-mail: info@aahsa.org • URL: http://www.aahsa.org • Annual. Free. Provides descriptions of material relating to managed care, senior housing, assisted living, continuing care retirement communities (CCRCs), nursing facilities, and home health care. Publishers are AAHSA and others.

AAII Journal. American Association of Individual Investors, 625 N. Michigan Ave., Suite No. 1900 Chicago, IL 60611. Phone: (312)280-0170 Fax: (312)280-1625 E-mail: members@aaii.com • URL: http://www.aii.org • 10 times a year. $49.00 per year. Covers strategy and investment techniques.

AAMVA Bulletin. American Association of Motor Vehicle Administrators, 4301 Wilson Blvd., Ste. 400 Arlington, VA 22203. Phone: (703)522-4200 Fax: (703)522-1905 Description: Provides news and legislative information for motor vehicle administrators. Recurring features include news of research, announcements, and legislative information.

AAP Political Action Committee., 1718 Connecticut Ave. NW, Ste. 700 Washington, DC 20009. Phone: (202)232-3335 Fax: (202)745-0694 E-mail: info@democracyinternational.us Raises funds to help elect individuals to Congress who realize how vital the production of books, knowledge, and ideas is to the country, who want to see publishing prosper, and who will be alert to how federal laws and federal spending programs can help or harm the publishing industry.

AAPOR Newsletter. American Association for Public Opinion Research, 8310 Nieman Rd., PO Box 14263 Lenexa, KS 66285-4263. Phone: (913)895-4601 Fax: (913)895-4652 E-mail: aapor-info@goamp.com • URL: http://www.aapor.org • Description: Publishes news of the Association. Recurring features include a president's column, new member list, and personal notes.

AARP Bulletin. American Association of Retired Persons, 601 East St. NW Washington, DC 20049. Phone: 888-687-2277 or (202)434-2277 Fax: (202)434-6451 E-mail: aarp1@aol.com • URL: http://www.aarp.org • Description: Monitors issues and events affecting Americans aged 50 and over. Covers medical benefits and other services of interest. Recurring features include Association news, editorials, and columns titled As We See It, Bulletin Board, Washingtonwatch, Stateswatch, and Reader Forum.

AARP: The Magazine. American Association of Retired Persons, 601 E. St., N.W. Washington, DC 20049. Phone: 800-424-3410 or (202)434-2277 Fax: (202)434-6408 • URL: http://www.aarp.org • Bimonthly. Membership. Formerly *Modern Maturity*.

AATC Review. American Association of Textile Chemists and Colorists, P.O. Box 12215 Research Triangle Park, NC 27709-2215. Phone: (919)549-8141 Fax: (919)549-8933 E-mail: orders@aatc.org • URL: http://www.aatcc.org • Monthly. Free to members; non-members, $60.00 per year. Annual *Buyer's Guide* available. Formerly *Textile Chemist and Colorist and American Dyestuff Reporter*.

AAUW Outlook. American Association of University Women, 1111 16th St., N.W. Washington, DC 20036. Phone: 800-326-2289 Fax: (202)872-1425 E-mail: info@aauw.org • URL: http://www.aauw.org • Quarterly. Free to members; non-members, $15.00 per year. Formerly *Graduate Woman*.

ABA Bank Marketing. Bank Marketing Association, 1120 Connecticut Ave., N.W. Washington, DC 20036-7971. Phone: 800-338-0626 or (202)663-5278 Fax: (202)663-7543 E-mail: custserv@aba.com • URL: http://www.bmanet.org • 10 times a year. Members, $80.00 per year; non-members, $120.00 per year. Includes a *Buyer's Guide*. Formerly *Bank Marketing*.

ABA Bankers News. American Bankers Association, Member Communications, 1120 Connecticut Ave., N.W. Washington, DC 20036-3971. Phone: 800-226-5377 or (202)663-5000 Fax: (202)296-9258 E-mail: custserv@aba.com • URL: http://www.aba.com • Biweekly. Members, $48.00 per year; non-members, $96.00 per year. Formerly *Banker News*.

ABA Banking Journal. American Bankers Association, Member Communications. Simmons-Boardman Books, 1809 Capitol Ave. Omaha, NE 68102-4972. Phone: 800-228-9670 or (402)346-4300 Fax: (402)346-1783 E-mail: customer_service@transalert.com • URL: http://www.transalert.com • Monthly. Free to qualified personnel; others, $25.00 per year.

ABA/BNA Lawyer's Manual on Professional Conduct. American Bar Association. BNA, Inc., 1231 25th St., NW Washington, DC 20037. Phone: 800-372-1033 E-mail: customercare@bna.com • URL: http://www.bna.com • Bimonthly. $595.00 per year. Looseleaf service. Covers American Bar Association's model rules governing ethical practice of law.

ABA Book Buyer's Handbook. American Booksellers Association, 828 S. Broadway Tarrytown, NY 10591. Phone: 800-637-0037 or (914)591-2665 Fax: (914)591-2720 E-mail: info@bookweb.org • URL: http://www.bookweb.org • Annual. Membership. Trade policies. Formerly *Book Buyer's Handbook*.

ABA Journal: The Lawyer's Magazine. American Bar Association, 750 N Lake Shore Dr. Chicago, IL 60611. Phone: 800-285-2221 or (312)988-5000 Fax: orders@abanet.org • URL: http://www.abanet.org • Monthly. Individuals, $75.00 per year; institutions, $120.00 per year. Includes five regular sections: news affecting lawyers, practical applications of court decisions, pratice management advice, feature articles, and lifestyle stories.

ABA Marketing Network., 1120 Connecticut Ave. NW Washington, DC 20036. Phone: 800-BAN-KERS or (202)663-5360 Fax: (202)828-4540 E-mail: webmaster@aba.com • URL: http://www.aba.com/MarketingNetwork/default.htm • Marketing and public relations executives for commercial and savings banks, credit unions, and savings and loans associations, and related groups such as advertising agencies and research firms. Provides marketing education, information, and services to the financial services industry. Conducts research; cosponsors summer sessions of fundamentals and advanced courses in marketing at the University of Colorado at Boulder; compiles statistics.

Abbreviations Dictionary. Dean A. Stahl and Karen Kerchelich. CRC Press, LLC, 2000 NW Corporate Blvd. Boca Raton, FL 33431. Phone: 800-272-7737 or (561)994-0555 Fax: 800-374-3401 or (561)989-9732 E-mail: orders@crcpress.com • URL: http://www.crcpress.com • 2001. $79.95. 10th edition. Contains about 270,000 abbreviations, acronyms, initialisms, and nicknames. Covers most areas of knowledge, including business, science, and technology.

ABC of Women Workers' Rights and Gender Equality. International Labour Organization, 1828 L St., N.W., Suite 600 Washington, DC 20036-5121. Phone: (202)653-7652 Fax: (202)653-7687 E-mail: washington@ilo.org • URL: http://www.ilo.org • 2000. $12.95. Second edition. Provides a concise guide to international laws and agreements relating to the rights of women workers.

ABC Today-Associated Builders and Contractors National Membership Directory. Associated Builders and Contractors, Inc.., 1300 N. 17th St. Arlington, VA 22209. Phone: (703)812-2000 Fax: (703)812-8203 E-mail: info@abc.org Annual. $150.00. List of approximately 19,000 member construction contractors and suppliers. Formerly *Builder and Contractor-Associated Builders and Contractors Membership Directory*.

ABCs of Relationship Selling: With Act! Express CD-ROM. Charles Futrell. McGraw-Hill, 1221 Ave. of the Americas New York, NY 10020. Phone: 800-722-4726 or (212)512-

2000 Fax: (212)512-4502 E-mail: customer.service@mcgraw-hill.com • URL: http://www.mcgraw-hill.com • 2002. $78.00. Seventh edition. Includes CD-ROM.

ABD—Aviation Buyer's Directory. Air Service Directory Inc., 116 Radio Circle Dr. Mount Kisco, NY 10549. Phone: (914)242-8700 Fax: (914)242-5422 E-mail: abd@abdonline.com • URL: http://www.aviationbuyers.com • Covers: aircraft, parts, and equipment manufacturers and dealers, and service firms in the aviation industry. Entries include: Company name, address, phone.

ABI/INFORM. PROQUEST, 300 N. Zeeb Rd. Ann Arbor, MI 48103. Phone: (734)761-4700 or 800-521-0600 Fax: 800-864-0019 • URL: http://www.umi.com • Monthly. Provides CD-ROM indexing and abstracting of worldwide business literature. Archival discs are available from 1971. Formerly *ABI/INFORM OnDisc*.

Abolishing Performance Appraisals: Why They Backfire and What to Do Instead. Tom Coens and Mary Jenkins. Berrett-Koehler Publishers, Inc., 235 Montgomery St., Suite 650 San Francisco, CA 94104-2916. Phone: 800-929-2929 or (415)288-0260 Fax: (802)864-7626 E-mail: bkpub@bkpub.com • URL: http://www.bkconnection.com • 2002. $27.95. The authors recommend alternative methods of evaluating employees.

Abrasive Engineering Society., 144 Moore Rd. Butler, PA 16001. Phone: (724)282-6210 Fax: (724)234-2376 E-mail: aes@abrasiveengineering.com • URL: http://www.abrasiveengineering.com • Promotes knowledge and understanding of abrasives (abrasive wheels, coated abrasives, media, diamonds and diamond products, dressers, dressing devices and abrasive grains) and their application in metalworking. Sponsors courses.

Abrasive Engineering Society Conference Proceedings. Abrasive Engineering Society, 144 Moore Rd. Butler, PA 16001. Phone: (724)282-6210 Fax: (724)282-6210 Irregular. Price on application.

Abridged Biography and Genealogy Master Index. Gale Cengage Learning, 27500 Drake Rd. Farmington Hills, MI 48331-3535. Phone: 800-877-GALE or (248)699-GALE Fax: 800-414-5043 or (248)699-8069 E-mail: gale.galeord@cengage.com • URL: http://gale.cengage.com • 1994. $475.00. Second edition. Three volumes. Indexes 266 widely held biographical reference sources, with approximately 2.2 million citations. Based on the larger *Biography and Genealogy Master Index*.

The Absolute Sound: The High End Journal of Audio and Music. Harry Pearson, editor. Absolute Multimedia Inc., 8121 Bee Caves Rd., Ste. 100 Austin, TX 78746. Phone: 888-475-5991 or (512)479-4661 Fax: (512)328-7528 E-mail: editor@theabsolute.com • URL: http://www.theabsolutesound.com • Six times a year. $36.00 per year.

Abstract Bulletin of Paper Science and Technology. Engineering Information, Inc., One Castle Point Terrace Hoboken, NJ 07030-5996. Phone: 800-221-1044 or (201)356-6801 Fax: (404)894-9596 • URL: http://www.eicustomersupport.org • Monthly. Institutions, $1,874.00 per year. Worldwide coverage of the scientific and technical literature of interest to the pulp and paper industry.

Abstracts in Social Gerentology: Current Literature on Aging. National Council on the Aging. Sage Publications, Inc., 2455 Teller Rd. Thousand Oaks, CA 91320. Phone: 800-818-7243 or (805)499-9774 Fax: 800-583-2665 or (805)499-0871 E-mail: webmaster@ssagepub.com • URL: http://www.sagepub.com • Quarterly. Individuals, $542.00 per year. Formerly *Current Literature on Aging*.

ACA-The International Association of Credit and Collections Professionals., ACA International, PO Box 390106 Minneapolis, MN 55439. Phone: (959)926-6547 Fax: (959)926-1624 • URL: http://www.acainternational.org • Formerly American Collectors Association.

ACADEME. American Association of University Professors, 1012 14th St., N.W., Suite 500 Washington, DC 20005-3465. Phone: (202)737-5900 Fax: (202)737-5526 E-mail: aaup@aaup.org • URL: http://www.aaup.org • Bimonthly. $64.00 per year.

The Academic Library in Transition: Planning for the 1990s. Beverly P. Lynch, editor. Neal-Schuman Publishers, Inc., 100 William St., Ste. 2004 New York, NY 10038. Phone: (866)672-6657 or (212)925-8650 Fax: (866)209-7932 or (212)219-8916 E-mail: info@neal-schuman.com • URL: http://www.neal-schuman.com • 1989. $49.95.

Academic Year Abroad. Institute of International Education Inc., 809 United Nations Plz. New York, NY 10017-3580. Phone: 800-445-0443 or (212)883-8200 Fax: (212)984-5452 E-mail: iiebooks@iie.org • URL: http://www.iie.org • Covers: almost 6,000 undergraduate and graduate study-abroad programs conducted worldwide during the academic year by United States and foreign colleges and universities and other organizations in 80 countries. Entries include: Program name, sponsoring institution, contact person, address, phone, e-mail, website, pertinent dates, orientation, subjects offered, credits, housing, scholarships, language of instruction, related travel, teaching methods, tuition and other costs, prerequisites, work-study or internship opportunities, etc. Not to be confused with 'Academic Year and Summer Programs Abroad,' described separately.

Academic Year, Semester and Summer Programs Abroad. American Institute for Foreign Study, College Div., River Plaza, Nine W. Broad St. Stamford, CT 06902-3788. Phone: 800-727-2437 or (203)399-5000 Fax: (203)399-5597 E-mail: college.info@aifs.com • URL: http://www.aifsabroad.com • Annual. Free. Formerly *Academic Year and Summer Programs Abroad*.

Academy for Educational Development.

Academy for State and Local Government.

Academy of Arts and Sciences of the Americas., 9450 Old Cutler Rd. Miami, FL 33156. Phone: (305)663-9897 Fax: (305)667-5600 E-mail: atsworld@bellsouth.net Seeks an interdisciplinary approach to the 21st century.

Academy of Food Marketing. Saint Joseph's University

Academy of Legal Studies in Business.

Academy of Management., P.O. Box 3020 Briarcliff Manor, NY 10510-3020. Phone: (914)923-2607 Fax: (914)923-2615 E-mail: academy@pace.edu • URL: http://www.aomonline.edu • Members are university professors of management and selected business executives.

Academy of Management Executive. Academy of Management, 235 Elm Rd. Briarcliff Manor, NY 10510. E-mail: academy@pace.com • URL: http://www.aom.pace.edu • Bimonthly. $125.00 per year. Contains articles relating to the practical application of management principles and theory.

Academy of Management Journal. Academy of Management, 235 Elm Rd. Briarcliff Manor, NY 10510. Phone: (914)923-2607 Fax: (914)923-2615 E-mail: academy@pace.edu • URL: http://www.aom.pace.edu • Bimonthly. $125.00 per year. Presents research papers on management-related topics.

Academy of Management Review. Academy of Management, 255 Elm Rd. Briar Cliff, NY 10510. Phone: (914)923-2607 Fax: (914)923-2615 E-mail: academy@pace.edu • URL: http://www.aom.pace.edu • Quarterly. $105.00 per year. A scholarly journal concerned with the theory of management and organizations.

Academy of Motion Picture Arts and Sciences.

Academy of Television Arts and Sciences.

Access Reports: Freedom of Information. Access Reports, Inc., 1624 Dogwood Lane Lynchburg, VA 24503. Phone: (804)384-5334 Fax: (804)384-8272 Biweekly. $350.00 per year. Newsletter.

Access to European Union: Law, Economics, Policies. Euroconfidentiel S. A., Rue de Rixensart 18 1332 Genval, Belgium. Phone: 32 2 6520284 Fax: 32 2 6530180 E-mail: nigel.hunt@skynet.be 2001. $62.00. Covers EU legislation and policy in major industrial and commercial sectors. Includes customs policy, the common market, monetary union, taxation, competition, "The EU in the World," and related topics. Contains more than 300 bibliographical references.

Accessories. Business Journals, Inc., 50 Day St. Norwalk, CT 06856. Phone: 800-521-0227 or (203)853-6015 Fax: (203)852-8175 E-mail: lorrief@busjour.com • URL: http://www.busjour.com • 11 times a year. $35.00 per year. Covers the merchandising of women's fashion accessories, including handbags, belts, jewelry, gloves, hats, and umbrellas.

Accessories Resources Directory. Business Journals Inc., 50 Day St. Norwalk, CT 06854. Phone: 800-521-0227 or (203)853-6015 Fax: (203)852-8175 E-mail: stunifoo@busjour.com • URL: http://www.busjour.com • Covers: 1,600 manufacturers, importers, and sales representatives producing or handling belts, gloves, handbags, scarves, hosiery, jewelry, sunglasses, and umbrellas. Entries include: Company, name, address, phone, fax.

Accident Analysis and Prevention. Elsevier, 655 Ave. of the Americas New York, NY 10010-5107. Phone: 800-366-2665 or (212)989-5800 Fax: 800-535-9935 or (212)633-3680 E-mail: custserv@elsevier.com • URL: http://www.elsevier.com • Bimonthly. Qualified personnel, $339.00 per year; institutions, $1,370.00 per year.

Accident Facts. National Safety Council, Statistics Dept., 1121 Spring Lake Dr. Itasca, IL 60143-3201. Phone: 800-621-7619 or (630)285-1121 Fax: (630)285-1315 E-mail: customerservice@nsc.org • URL: http://www.nsc.org • Annual. $37.95.

Accident Prevention. Flight Safety Foundation Inc., 601 Madison St., Ste. 300 Alexandria, VA 22314-1756. Phone: (703)739-6700 Fax: (703)739-6708 E-mail: aarp1@aol.com Description: Carries items of particular value to professional pilots: general air safety material and reports of dangerous situations, incidents, near misses by professional pilots, ground crew, or other persons involved.

Accidental Systems Librarian. Rachel S. Gordon. Information Today, Inc., 143 Old Marlton Pike Medford, NJ 08055-8750. Phone: 800-300-9868 or (609)654-6266 Fax: (609)654-4309 E-mail: custserv@infotoday.com • URL: http://www.infotoday.com • 2003. $29.50. Provides practical advice for librarians with newly-assigned, computer systems technology responsibilities.

Accidental Webmaster. Julie M. Still. Information Today, Inc., 143 Old Marlton Pike Medford, NJ 08055-8750. Phone: 800-300-9868 or (609)654-6266 Fax: (609)654-4309 E-mail: custserv@infotoday.com • URL: http://www.infotoday.com • 2003. $29.50. Covers the practical aspects of designing and maintaining a successful Web site. Written for librarians and others without previous Webmaster experience.

Accountant's Business Manual. American Institute of Certified Public Accountants, 1211 Ave. of the Americas New York, NY 10036-8775. Phone: 800-862-4272 or (212)596-6200 Fax: (212)596-6213 E-mail: lmorales@aicpa.org • URL: http://www.aicpa.org • $189.75. Looseleaf. Two volumes. Semiannual updates. Covers a wide variety of topics relating to financial and accounting management, including types of ownership, business planning, financing, cash management, valuation, retirement plans, estate planning, workers' compensation, unemployment insurance, social security, and employee benefits management.

Accountants' Handbook. Douglas R. Carmichael and Paul Rosenfeld. John Wiley and Sons, Inc., 111 River St. Hoboken, NJ 07030. Phone: 800-225-5945 or (201)748-6000 Fax: (201)748-6088 E-mail: info@wiley.com • URL: http://www.wiley.com • 2003. $160.00. 10th edition. Two volumes. Vol. one, $95.00; vol. two, $95.00. Chapters are written by various accounting and auditing specialists.

Accountant's Handbook of Fraud and Commercial Crime. G. Jack Bologna and others. John Wiley and Sons, Inc., 111 River St. Hoboken, NJ 07030. Phone: 800-225-5945 or (201)748-6000 Fax: (201)748-6088 E-mail: info@wiley.com • URL: http://www.wiley.com • 1992. $225.00.

Accountants' Liability. Practising Law Institute, 810 7th Ave. New York, NY 10019-5818. Phone: 800-260-4754 or (212)824-5710 E-mail: info@pli.edu • URL: http://www.pli.edu • $160.00. Covers all aspects of accountants' professional liability issues, including depositions and court cases.

Accounting and Budgeting in Public and Non-profit Organizations: A Manager's Guide. C. William Garner. John Wiley and Sons, Inc., 111 River St. Hoboken, NJ 07030. Phone: 800-225-5945 or (201)748-6000 Fax: (201)748-6088 E-mail: info@wiley.com • URL: http://www.wiley.com • 1991. $49.00. An accounting primer for non-profit executives with no formal training in accounting. Includes an explanation of Generally Accepted Accounting Principles (GAAP) as applied to non-profit organizations. (Public Administration-Non Profit Sector Series).

Accounting and Finance for Non-Specialists. Peter Atrill and Eddie McLaney. Pearson Education, 1 Lake St. Upper Saddle River, NJ 07458. Phone: 800-428-5331 or (201)236-7000 Fax: 800-922-0579 or (201)236-6549 • URL: http://www.pearsoned.com • 2003. $77.00. Fourth edition. Includes the measurement and reporting of financial performance and cash flow.

Accounting and Financial Planning for Law Firms. American Lawyer Media, Inc., 105 Madison Ave. New York, NY 10016. Phone: 800-888-8300 or (212)779-9200 Fax: (212)481-8110 E-mail: lawcatalog@amlaw.com • URL: http://www.lawcatalog.com/ • Monthly. $225.00 per year. Newsletter. Covers budgeting, liability issues, billing systems, benefits management, and other topics relating to law firm administration. (A Law Journal Newsletter, formerly published by Leader Publications).

Accounting and Recordkeeping for the Self-Employed. Jack Fox. John Wiley and Sons, Inc., 111 River St. Hoboken, NJ 07030. Phone: 800-225-5945 or (201)748-6000 Fax: (201)748-6088 E-mail: info@wiley.com • URL: http://www.wiley.com • 1994. $19.95.

Accounting and Tax Database. PROQUEST, 300 N. Zeeb Rd. Ann Arbor, MI 48103. Phone: 800-521-0600 or (734)761-4700 Fax: 800-864-0019 • URL: http://www.umi.com • Provides indexing and abstracting of the literature of accounting, taxation, and financial management, 1971 to date. Updating is weekly. Especially covers accounting, auditing, banking, bankruptcy, employee compensation and benefits, cash management, financial planning, and credit. Inquire as to online cost and availability.

Accounting and Tax Index. UMI, 300 N. Zeeb Rd. Ann Arbor, MI 48106. Phone: 800-521-0600 or (734)761-4700 Fax: 800-864-0019 E-mail: info@il.proquest.com • URL: http://www.umi.com • Quarterly. Price on application. Annual cumulation. Indexes accounting, auditing, and taxation literature appearing in journals, books, pamphlets, conference proceedings, and newsletters.

Accounting Articles. CCH, Inc., 2700 Lake Cook Rd. Riverwoods, IL 60015. Phone: 800-525-3335 or (847)267-7000 E-mail: cust_serv@cch.com • URL: http://www.cch.com • Monthly. $624.00 per year. Looseleaf service.

Accounting Desk Book: The Accountant's Everyday Instant Answer Book. Tom M. Plank and Lois R. Plank. Prentice Hall PTR, 240 Frisch Ct. Paramus, NJ 07652. Phone: 800-282-0693 Fax: 800-445-6991 • URL: http://www.phptr.com • 2000. $100.00. 11th edition. Covers more than 230 accounting topics with examples, checklists, worksheets and tables. (Accounting Desk Book Series).

Accounting for Governmental and Non-Profit Entities. Earl R. Wilson and Susan C. Kattleus. McGraw-Hill, 1221 Ave. of the Americas New York, NY 10020. Phone: 800-722-4726 or (212)512-2000 Fax: (212)512-4502 E-mail: customer.service@mcgraw-hill.com • URL: http://www.mcgraw-hill.com • 2003. 13th edition. Price on application.

Accounting for Libraries and Other Not-for-Profit Organizations. G. Stevenson Smith. American Library Association, 50 E. Huron St. Chicago, IL 60611. Phone: 800-545-2433 or (312)944-6780 Fax: (312)440-9374 E-mail: ala@ala.org • URL: http://www.ala.org • 1999. $82.00. Second edition. Covers accounting fundamentals for nonprofit organizations. Includes a glossary.

Accounting Research Directory: Database of Accounting Literature. Lawrence D. Brown and others. Markus Wiener Publishing, Inc., 231 Nassau St. Princeton, NJ 08542. Phone: (609)921-1141 Fax: (908)921-1141 E-mail: wiener95@aol.com 1994. $69.95. Third edition. Contains lists and evaluations of all publications in seven leading accounting, journals.

Accounting Research Program.

Accounting Research Studies. American Institute of Certified Public Accountants, 1211 Ave. of the Americas New York, NY 10036-8775. Phone: 800-862-4272 or (212)596-6200 Fax: (212)596-6213 E-mail: lmorales@aicpa.org • URL: http://www.aicpa.org • Irregular.

Accounting Review. University of Georgia, J.M. Tull School of Accounting. American Accounting Association, 5717 Bessie Dr. Sarasota, FL 34233. Phone: (914)921-7747 Fax: (914)923-4093 E-mail: accounting-review@terry.uga.edu • URL: http://www.rutgers.edu/ • Quarterly. Members, $85.00 per year; non-members, $110.00 per year.

Accounting Technology: Turning Technology into Business Know How. Thomson Media, 1 State St. Plz., 27th Fl. New York, NY 10004. Phone: 800-221-1809 or (212)803-8200 Fax: (212)292-5216 E-mail: cust.serv@thomsonmedia.com • URL: http://www.thomsonmedia.com • 11 times a year. $61.00 per year. Provides advice and information on computers and software for the accounting profession. Formerly *Computers in Accounting*.

Accounting: The Basis for Business Decisions. Robert Meigs and others. McGraw-Hill, 1221 Ave. of the Americas New York, NY 10020. Phone: 800-722-4726 or (212)512-2000 Fax: (212)512-4502 E-mail: customer.service@mcgraw-hill.com • URL: http://www.mcgraw-hill.com • 2000. $95.63. 11th edition.

Accounting Theory. Ahmed Riahi-Belkaoui. The Thomson Corporation, Metro Ctr., 1 Station Pl. Stamford, CT 06902. Phone: 800-347-7707 or (203)969-8700 Fax: 800-487-8488 or (203)977-8354 E-mail: generalinfo@cengage.com • URL: http://www.thomson.com • 2000. $77.99. Fourth edition. (ITBP Textbook Series.)

Accounting Today: The Business Newspaper for the Tax & Accounting Community. Thomson Media, 1 State St. Plz., 27th Fl. New York, NY 10004. Phone: 800-221-1809 or (212)803-8200 Fax: (212)292-5216 E-mail: cust.serv@thomsonmedia.com • URL: http://www.thomsonmedia.com • Biweekly. $99.00 per year. Covers news affecting tax and accounting professionals.

Accounting Trends and Techniques in Published Corporate Annual Reports. American Institute of Certified Public Accountants, 1211 Ave. of the Americas New York, NY 10036-8775. Phone: 800-862-4272 or (212)596-6200 Fax: (212)596-6213 E-mail: lmorales@aicpa.org • URL: http://www.aicpa.org • Annual. Price on application.

ACCRA Cost of Living Index (Association for Applied Community Reseach). ACCRA, 3401 N. Fairfax Dr., 3B1 Arlington, VA 22210. Phone: (703)522-4980 Fax: (703)522-4985 E-mail: san@acura.org • URL: http://www.accra.org • Quarterly. $130.00 per year. Compares price levels for 280-310 U.S. cities.

Accredited Institutions of Postsecondary Education, Programs, Candidates. Greenwood Publishing Group, Inc., 88 Post Rd., W Westport, CT 06881. Phone: 800-225-5800 or (203)226-3571 Fax: (203)431-2214 E-mail: customer-service@greenwood.com • URL: http://www.greenwood.com • Annual. $80.00. Lists more than 6,600 public and private accredited institutions and programs.

Accredited Journalism and Mass Communication Education. School of Journalism. Accrediting Council on Education for Journalism and Mass Communications, University of Kansas, School of Journalism, Stauffer-Flint Hall, 1435 Jayhawk Blvd. Lawrence, KS 66045-7575. Phone: (913)864-3973 Fax: (913)864-5225 • URL: http://www.ukans.edu • Annual. Free. Lists about 109 accredited schools.

Accredited Programs in Architecture. National Architectural Accrediting Board, 1735 New York Ave., N.W. Washington, DC 20006. Phone: (202)783-2007 Fax: (202)783-2822 E-mail: info@naab.org • URL: http://www.naab.org • Annual. Free.

Accrediting Council on Education in Journalism and Mass Communications. University of Kansas

Accu-Data. Accu-Weather, Inc., 385 Science Park Rd. State College, PA 16803. Phone: 800-566-6606 or (814)234-9601 Fax: (814)238-1339 • URL: http://www.accuweather.com • Provides detailed, current weather conditions and weather forecasts for many U. S. and foreign cities and regions. Updating is continuous. Inquire as to online cost and availability.

Accuracy in Media., 4455 Connecticut Ave., N.W.,, Suite 330 Washington, DC 20008. Phone: 800-787-0044 or (202)364-4401 Fax: (202)364-4098 E-mail: ar1@aim.org • URL: http://www.aim.org • A nonpartisan organization that receives and researches complaints from the public relating to factual errors made by the news media. Affiliated with Accuracy in Academia.

ACGA: Partners in Philanthropy. American Council on Gift AnnuitiesPhone: (317)269-6271 Fax: (317)269-6276 E-mail: acga@acga-web.org • URL: http://www.acga-web.org • Web site provides detailed information on gift annuities, including suggested charitable gift annuity rates for use by charities and their donors. Rates for immediate and deferred annuities are presented in the form of tables for ages 20 to 90 (and over), for both "Single Life" and "Two Lives - Joint and Survivor." Other items covered include the philosophy of gift annuities, state regulations, "What's New," and a search site. Fees: Free.

ACI Manual of Concrete Practice. American Concrete Institute, 38800 Country Club Dr. Farmington Hills, MI 48331. Phone: (248)848-3700 Fax: (248)848-3701 E-mail: bkstore@concrete.org • URL: http://www.aci-int.org • Annual. Free to members; non-members, $595.00. Five volumes.

ACM Computing Surveys: The Survey and Tutorial Journal of the ACM. Association for Computing Machinery, 1515 Broadway New York, NY 10036. Phone: (212)869-7440 Fax: (212)944-1318 E-mail: acmhelp@acm.org • URL: http://www.acm.org • Quarterly. Members, $26.00 per year; non-members, $160.00 per year; students, $21.00 per year.

ACM Journal of Computer Documentation. Special Interest Group for Docuemntation. Association for Computing Machinery, 1515 Broadway New York, NY 10036-5701. Phone: (212)869-7440 Fax: (212)869-0481 E-mail: acmhelp@acm.org • URL: http://www.acm.org • Quarterly. Members, $36.00 per year; $99.00 per year; Students, $42.00 per year. Formerly *Journal of Computer Documentation*.

ACM Transactions on Graphics. Association for Computing Machinery, 1515 Broadway New York, NY 10036. Phone: (212)869-7440 Fax: (212)869-0481 E-mail: acmhelp@acm.org • URL: http://www.acm.org • Quarterly. Members, $41.00 per year; non-members, $170.00 per year; students, $36.00 per year.

Acoustic and Ultrasonic Laboratory. Argonne National Laboratory, Bldg. 308, Rm. D135, 9700 S Cass Ave. Argonne, IL 60439. Phone: (630)252-2000 Fax: (630)252-3250 E-mail: raptis@anl.gov • URL: http://www.anl.gov • Acoustic and ultrasonic technology, developing sensors and instrumentation and solving difficult applications problems. Also develops NDE techniques for material characterizations.

Acoustical Society of America.

Acoustical Society of America Journal. Acoustical Society of America., One Physics Ellipse, Two Huntington Quadrangle, Ste. 1NO1 College Park, MD 20740-3843. Phone: (301)209-3100 Fax: (301)209-0843 E-mail: aip@aip.org • URL: http://www.aip.org • Monthly. Institutions, $1,325.00 per year. Includes print and online editions.

Acoustics Abstracts. Multi-Science Publishing Co., Ltd, Five Wates Way Brentwood CM15 9TB, United Kingdom. Phone: 44 1277 244632 Fax: 44 1277 223453 E-mail: mscience@globalnet.co.uk • URL: http://www.multi-science.co.uk • Monthly. $600.00. per year. Parts A and B.

Acquisitions and Mergers: Negotiated and Contested Transactions. Joy M. Bryan and Simone M. Lorne. West Group, 610 Opperman Dr. Eagan, MN 55123. Phone: 800-328-4880 or (651)687-7000 Fax: 800-340-9378 E-mail: bookstore@westgroup.com • URL: http://www.westgroup.com • Three times a year. $1,172.00 per year. Five looseleaf volumes. Includes legal forms and documents. (Securities Law Series).

Acquisitions Monthly. Thomson Financial, 195 Broadway New York, NY 10007. Phone: 800-262-6000 or (646)822-2000 Fax: (646)822-6270 E-mail: custserv@tfn.com • URL: http://www.tfn.com • Monthly. $790.00 per year. Published in London. Provides detailed information, commentary, and statistics on merger, acquisition, and buyout activity in Europe, the U.S., and Asia.

Acronym Finder: The Web's Most Comprehensive Database of Acronyms, Abbreviations, and Initialisms. Mountain Data SystemsPhone: (970)586-5556 E-mail: acronyms@mtnds.com • URL: http://www.acronymfinder.com • Web site provides more than 345,000 definitions. Searching offers a choice of "exact acronym," "acronym begins with," "acronym (wildcard)," or "reverse lookup (keywords)." Fees: Free.

Acronyms, Initialisms, and Abbreviations Dictionary. Gale Cengage Learning, 27500 Drake Rd. Farmington Hills, MI 48331-3535. Phone: 800-877-GALE or (248)699-GALE Fax: 800-414-5043 or (248)699-8069 E-mail: gale.galeord@cengage.com • URL: http://gale.cengage.com • Annual. $865.00. Four parts. Provides more than 780,000 definitions in all subject areas.

Acronyms of Computer Science and Communications: A Comprehensive Acronym Dictionary and Illustrated Encylopedia. Enjob Kajan and Ejub Kajan. Springer Verlag, 175 Fifth Ave. New York, NY 10010. Phone: 800-777-4643 or (212)460-1500 Fax: (201)348-4505 E-mail: service@springer-ny.com • URL: http://www.springer-ny.com • 2002. $49.95. Explains more than 4,000 "broadly used" computer, telecommunications, and information technology acronyms. Includes illustrations and Web addresses, where applicable.

ACS Style Guide: A Manual for Authors and Editors. Janet S. Dodd, editor. American Chemical Society, 1155 16th St., N.W. Washington, DC 20036. Phone: 800-227-5558 or (202)872-4600 Fax: (202)776-8258 E-mail: help@acs.org • URL: http://www.chemistry.org • 1997. $35.00. Second edition. A style manual for scientific and technical writers. Includes the use of illustrations, tables, lists, numbers, and units of measure.

ACT., PO Box 168, PO Box 168 Iowa City, IA 52244-0168. Phone: (319)337-1000 Fax: (319)339-3020 E-mail: mediarelations@act.org • URL: http://www.act.org • Provides guidance-oriented assessment and research programs for students, schools, colleges, universities, vocational-technical institutes, and scholarship agencies. ACT Assessment Program, which consists of a profile questionnaire, interest inventory, and four 35-60 minute tests in English, mathematics, reading, and scientific reasoning, is completed by more than 1,700,000 students annually. Provides colleges and universities with information used in admission, placement, and advising. ASSET and COMPASS, placement programs for two-year colleges, are completed by more than 1,600,000 students annually. Also offers eighth grade and tenth grade assessments; Work Keys, the nation's leading work skills testing system; and DISCOVER, an interactive educational and career planning program. Conducts more than 90 other assessment programs on behalf of organizations, and agencies. Conducts research, compiles statistics, and processes federal financial aid applications.

ACTA Materalia: An International Journal for the Science of Materials. Elsevier, 655 Ave. of the Americas New York, NY 10010-5107. Phone: 800-366-2665 or (212)989-5800 Fax: 800-535-9935 or (212)633-3680 E-mail: custserv@elsevier.com • URL: http://www.elsevier.com • 20 times a year. $2,475.00 per year. Text in English, French and German. Formerly *ACTA Metallutgical et Materalia*.

Action on Smoking and Health., 2013 H St., N. W. Washington, DC 20006. Phone: (202)659-4310 Fax: (202)833-3921 E-mail: webmaster@ash.org • URL: http://www.ash.org • Promotes national legal action against smoking.

Active Portfolio Management: Quantitative Theory and Applications. Richard C. Grinold and Ronald N. Kahn. McGraw-Hill, 1221 Ave. of the Americas New York, NY 10020. Phone: 800-722-4726 or (212)512-2000 Fax: (212)512-4502 E-mail: customer.service@mcgraw-hill.com • URL: http://www.mcgraw-hill.com • 1999. $75.00. Second edition.

Active Seniors Market. MarketResearch.com, 641 Ave. of the Americas, 4th Fl. New York, NY 10011. Phone: 800-298-5699 or (212)807-2629 Fax: (212)807-2676 E-mail: customerservice@marketresearch.com • URL: http://www.marketresearch.com • 2002. $2,100.00. Published by Packaged Facts. Provides market research data contrasting the consumer-oriented interests of age groups defined as conventionally working (under 55), young mature (55-64), active seniors (65-74), and elderly (75 and over). Covers finances, computer use, cars, housing, leisure activities, sports, and other items.

Actuaries' Survival Guide: How to Succeed in One of the Most Desirable Professions. Fred Szabo. Elsevier Butterworth Heinemann, 200 Wheeler Rd., Sixth Floor Burlington, MA 01803. Phone: 800-545-2522 or (781)221-2212 Fax: 800-568-5136 or (781)313-4880 E-mail: usbkinfo@elsevier.com • URL: http://www.books.elsevier.com/finance • 2004. $39.95. Serves as a guide for students and graduates of "number-based disciplines" who are considering a career in actuarial science. Covers careers, education, and jobs. (Imprint: Academic Press.)

The Actuary. Society of Actuaries, 475 N Martingale Rd., Ste. 600 Schaumburg, IL 60173-2226. Phone: (847)706-3500 Fax: (847)706-3599 E-mail: bhaynes@soa.org • URL: http://www.soa.org • Description: Features information about actuaries practicing in life and health insurance, pensions, and investments in the U.S. and Canada. Recurring features include letters to the editor, news of research and education, a calendar of events, reports of meetings, notices of publications available, and puzzles.

The Ad Men and Women: A Biographical Dictionary of Advertising. Edd Applegate, editor. Greenwood Publishing Group, Inc., 88 Post Rd., W Westport, CT 06881. Phone: 800-225-5800 or (203)226-3571 Fax: (203)431-2214 E-mail: customer-service@greenwood.com • URL: http://www.greenwood.com • 1994. $94.95. Provides extended biographical profiles of "54 men and women who have shaped advertising from the nineteenth century to the present." Includes bibliographies.

ADA Compliance Guide. Thompson Publishing Group, Inc., 1725 K St., N.W., Suite 700 Washington, DC 20006. Phone: 800-444-8741 or (202)872-4000 • URL: http://www.thompson.com • Two looseleaf volumes. $329.00 per year, including monthly updates and newslettrs. Provides detailed information for employers and others on complying with the Americans With Disabilities Act (ADA). Includes material on employment discrimination, transportation accessibility, accessibility in public accommodations, and state disability laws.

ADA Compliance Manual for Employers. LexisNexis Matthew Bender, 1275 Broadway Albany, NY 12204-4026. Phone: 800-424-4200 or (518)487-3000 Fax: 800-828-8341 or (518)487-3584 E-mail: customer.support@lexisnexis.com • URL: http://www.lexisnexis.com/matthewbender/ • Looseleaf. $95.00. Periodic supplementation available. "Every business with more than 15 employees must comply with the Amricans with Disabilities Act." This guide provides practical advice on job requirements, accessibility, employee selection, reasonable accomodations, termination issues, and other matters.

Addiction Research Foundation Journal: Addiction News for Professionals. Addiction Research Foundation of Ontario, Subscription-Marketing Dept., 33 Russell St. Toronto, ON, Canada M5S 2S1. Phone: 800-661-1111 or (416)595-6059 Six times a year. $19.00 per year. News and opinions from the drug and alcohol field around th world. Formerly *Alcoholism and Drug Addiction Research Foundation Journal*.

Adhesion Science. J. Comyn. Springer-Verlag, 175 5th Ave. New York, NY 10010. Phone: 800-777-4643 or (212)460-1500 Fax: (201)348-4505 E-mail: service@springer-ny.com • URL: http://www.springer-ny.com • 1997. $52.95. Published by The Royal Society of Chemistry. Provides basic scientific and technical information on "common adhesives." (RSC Paperback Series).

Adhesive and Sealant Council.

Adhesives Age. Chemical Week Associates, 110 Williams St. New York, NY 10038. Phone: (212)621-4900 Fax: (212)621-4800 E-mail: acortessr@chemweek.com • URL: http://www.chemweek.com • Monthly. $60.00 per year. Includes annual *Directory*.

Adhesives Age Buyers Guide. Chemical Week Associates, 110 William St. New York, NY 10038. Phone: (212)621-4900 Fax: (212)621-4949 E-mail: acortessr@chemweek.com • URL: http://www.chemweek.com • Annual. $60.00. Lists manufacturers and suppliers of raw materials, chemicals, equipment, and machinery for the adhesives industry.

Adhesives and Sealants. ASM International, 9639 Kinsman Rd. Materials Park, OH 44073-0002. Phone: 800-336-5152 or (440)338-5151 Fax: (440)338-4634 E-mail: cust-srv@asminternational.org • URL: http://www.asminternational.org • 1990. $198.00. Volume three. (Engineered Materials Handbook Series).

Adhesives Technology Handbook. Arthur H. Landrock. Noyes Data Corp., 169 Kinderkamack Rd., Suite 5 Park Ridge, NJ 07676-1338. Phone: (201)505-4965 1986. $64.00.

Adjutants General Association of the United States., Delaware National Guard, 1st Regiment Rd. Wilmington, DE 19808. Phone: 888-226-6427 or (302)326-7008 Fax: (302)326-7196 E-mail: kirsten.fitzgerald@us.army.mil • URL: http://www.ngaus.org • Adjutants General (National Guard) of the states and territories.

Administering Successful Programs for Adults: Promoting Excellence in Adult, Community, and Continuing Education. Michael W. Galbraith and others. Krieger Publishing Co., P.O. Box 9542 Melbourne, FL 32902-9542. Phone: 800-724-0025 or (321)724-9542 Fax: (321)951-3671 E-mail: info@krieger-publishing.com • URL: http://www.krieger-publishing.com • 1996. $24.50. Provides practical advice on the "day-to-day duties and responsibilities of organizing and administering successful programs in adult, community, and continuing education settings." (Professional Practices in Adult Education and Human Resource Development Series).

Administration and Society. Sage Publications, Inc., 2455 Teller Rd. Thousand Oaks, CA 91320. Phone: 800-818-7243 or (805)499-9774 Fax: 800-583-2665 or (805)499-0871 E-mail: webmaster@sagepub.com • URL: http://www.sagepub.com • Bimonthly. Institutions, $612.00 per year. Scholarly journal concerned with public administration and the effects of bureaucracy.

Administration of the Small Public Library. Darlene E. Weingand. American Library Association, 50 E Huron St. Chicago, IL 60611. Phone: 800-545-2433 or (301)280-2425 E-mail: library@ala.org • URL: http://www.scarecrowpress.com • 2001. $45.00. Fourth edition.

Administrative Assistant's Update. MPL Communications Inc., 133 Richmond St. W, Ste. 700, 2075 Kennedy Rd. Toronto, ON, Canada M5H 3M8. Phone: 800-804-8846 or (416)869-1177 Fax: (416)869-0616 E-mail: customers@mplcomm.com • URL: http://www.carswell.com • Description: Offers useful news, information, and suggestions to administrative assistants. Features articles on aspects of secretarial work, including items on problem-solving, office automation, computerization, and grammar and vocabulary development.

Administrative Law. LexisNexis Matthew Bender, 1275 Broadway Albany, NY 12204. Phone: 800-424-4200 or (518)487-3000 Fax: (518)487-3584 E-mail: bookstore.support@lexisnexis.com Three times a year. $1,416.00. Six looseleaf volumes. Covers investigations, adjudications, hearings, licenses, judicial review, and so forth.

Administrative Law. Steven J. Cann. Sage Publications, Inc., 2455 Teller Rd. Thousand Oaks, CA 91320. Phone: 800-818-7243 or (805)499-9774 Fax: 800-583-2665 or (805)499-0871 E-mail: webmaster@sagepub.com • URL: http://www.sagepub.com • 2001. $89.95. Third edition.

Administrative Law Desk Manual for Lawyers. John H. Reese. LexisNexis Matthew Bender, 1275 Broadway Albany, NY 12204-4026. Phone: 800-424-4200 or (518)487-3000 Fax: 800-828-8341 or (518)487-3584 E-mail: customer.support@lexisnexis.com • URL: http://www.lexisnexis.com/matthewbender/ • 2003. $90.00. Provides detailed coverage of the federal Administrative Procedure Act and summarizes relevant state law in 17 of the largest states.

Administrative Law Review. American University, Washington College of Law, 4801 Massachusetts Ave., NW Washington, DC 20016. Phone: (202)274-4000 • URL: http://www.wcl.american.edu • Quarterly. Members; $35.00 per year; nonmembers, $40.00 per year. Scholarly legal journal on developments in the field of administrative law.

Administrative Office Management: An Introduction. Zane B. Quible. Prentice Hall PTR, 240 Frisch Ct. Paramus, NJ 07652. Phone: 800-282-0693 Fax: 800-445-6991 • URL: http://www.phptr.com • 2000. $73.00. 7th edition. (KU-Office Procedures Series).

Administrative Science Quarterly. Cornell University, Johnson Graduate School of Management, 20 Thornwood Dr., Suite 100 Ithaca, NY 14850-1265. Phone: 800-666-2211 or (607)254-7143 Fax: (607)254-7100 E-mail: asq_journal@cornell.edu • URL: http://www.johnson.cornell.edu • Individuals: $65.00 per year; institutions, $130.00 per year.

Administrator's Handbook for Community Health and Home Care Services. Anne S. Smith. National League for Nursing Press, 61 Broadway New York, NY 10006-2701. Phone: 800-

669-1656 or (212)363-5555 Fax: (212)812-0391 E-mail: rcorcor@nln.org • URL: http://www.nln.org • 1988. $175.00.

Adult and Continuing Education Today. Learning Resources Network, PO Box 9 Falls, WI 54022-0009. Phone: (913)539-5376 BiWeekly. $95.00 per year. Newsletter.

Adult Education Quarterly: A Journal of Research and Theory. American Association for Adult and Continuing Education. Sage Publications, 2455 Teller Rd. Thousand Oaks, CA 91320. Phone: 800-818-7243 or (805)499-9774 Fax: 800-583-2665 or (805)499-0871 E-mail: webmaster@sagepub.com • URL: http://www.sagepub.com • Quarterly. Institutions, $206.00 per year.

Adult Learning. American Association for Adult and Continuing Education, 4380 Forbes Blvd. Lanham, MD 20706. Phone: (301)918-1913 Fax: (301)918-1846 E-mail: aaace10@aol.com • URL: http://www.aaace.org • Quarterly. $45.00 per year.

Adults as Learners: Increasing Participation and Facilities Learning. Kathryn P. Cross. John Wiley and Sons, Inc., 111 River St. Hoboken, NJ 07030. Phone: 800-225-5945 or (201)748-6000 Fax: (201)748-6088 E-mail: info@wiley.com • URL: http://www.wiley.com • 1981. $35.00. (Classic Series).

Advance-Decline Album. Dow Theory Letters, Inc., P.O. Box 1759 La Jolla, CA 92038-1759. Phone: (858)454-0481 E-mail: staff@dowtheoryletters.com • URL: http://www.dowtheoryletters.com • Annual. Contains one page for each year since 1931. Includes charts of the New York Stock Exchange advance-decline ratio and the Dow Jones industrial average.

Advance Monthly Sales for Retail Trade and Food Services. U. S. Census BureauPhone: 800-541-8345 or (301)763-4636 Fax: (301)457-3842 E-mail: rcb@census.gov • URL: http://www.census.gov/svsd/www/fullpub.html • Web pages provide monthly sales figures for a wide range of retail businesses. Advance, preliminary, and final statistics are provided for the latest month available in each case, with a previous-year comparison. Updates are monthly.

Advanced Accounting. Joe B. Hoyle and others. McGraw-Hill, 1221 Ave. of the Americas New York, NY 10020. Phone: 800-722-4726 or (212)512-2000 Fax: (212)512-4502 E-mail: customer.service@mcgraw-hill.com • URL: http://www.mcgrawhill.com • 2003. $112.50. Seventh edition.

Advanced Battery Technology. Seven Mountains Scientific, Inc., 913 Tressler St. Boalsburg, PA 16827. Phone: (814)466-6559 Fax: (814)466-2777 E-mail: sevmtnsci@srlink.net • URL: http://www.7ms.com • Monthly. $165.00 per year. Newsletter. Provides technical and marketing information for the international battery industry.

Advanced Coatings and Surface Technology. Technical Insights, 605 Third Ave. New York, NY 10158-0012. Phone: 800-825-7550 or (212)850-8600 Fax: (212)850-8800 E-mail: insights@wiley.com • URL: http://www.wiley.com • Institutions. Monthly. $650.00 per year. Newsletter on technical developments relating to industrial coatings.

Advanced Composites Monthly. Composite Market Reports Inc., 7670 Opportunity Rd., Ste. 250 San Diego, CA 92111. Phone: (619)560-1085 Fax: (619)560-0234 E-mail: customers@mplcomm.com Description: Covers advanced composite materials processes and markets in the aerospace industry worldwide. "Prepared for engineering, program, and manufacturing management at primes and their subcontractors where aerospace components made of high-performance composite materials are designed, fabricated, or assembled." Discusses subcontract opportunities of interest to U.S., Canadian, and overseas aerospace companies. Recurring features include a calendar of events, reports of meetings, interviews, news of research, and application case histories.

Advanced Fixed Income Analysis. Moorad Choudhry. Elsevier Butterworth Heinemann, 200 Wheeler Rd., Sixth Floor Burlington, MA 01803. Phone: 800-545-2522 or (781)221-2212 Fax: 800-568-5136 or (781)313-4880 E-mail: usbkinfo@elsevier.com • URL: http://www.books.elsevier.com/finance • 2004. $60.00. Edited for "experienced practitioners in the corporate bond markets." Covers trading, hedging, interest rate models, corporate bond default risk, the yield curve, long bond yields, and other topics.

Advanced Imaging Buyers Guide: The Most Comprehensive Worldwide Directory of Imaging Product and Equipment Vendors. Cygnus Business Media, 445 Broad Hollow Rd. Melville, NY 11747. Phone: 800-308-6397 or (631)845-2700 Fax: (631)845-2798 E-mail: rich.reiff@cygnuspub.com • URL: http://www.cygnusbzb.com • Annual. $19.95. Lists 800 electronic imaging companies and their products.

Advanced Imaging: Solutions for the Electronic Imaging Professional. Cygnus Business Media, 445 Broad Hollow Rd. Melville, NY 11747. Phone: 800-308-6397 or (631)845-2700 Fax: (631)845-2798 E-mail: rich.reiff@cygnuspub.com • URL: http://www.cygnusbzb.com • Monthly. $60.00 per year Covers document-based imaging technologies, products, systems, and services. Coverage is also devoted to multimedia and electronic printing and publishing.

Advanced Manufacturing Engineering Institute.

Advanced Manufacturing Technology: Monthly Report. Technical Insights, 605 Third Ave. New York, NY 10158-0012. Phone: 800-825-7550 or (212)850-8600 Fax: (212)850-8800 E-mail: insights@wiley.com • URL: http://www.wiley.com • Monthly. Institutions, $695.00 per year. Newsletter. Covers technological developments relating to robotics, computer

graphics, automation, computer-integrated manufacturing, and machining.

Advanced Materials and Processes. ASM International, 9639 Kinsman Rd. Materials Park, OH 44073-0002. Phone: 800-336-5152 or (440)338-5151 Fax: (440)338-4634 E-mail: asminternational.org • URL: http://www.asminternational.org • Monthly. Free to members; institutions, $325.00 per year. Incorporates *Metal Progress*.Technical information and reports on new developments in the technology of engineered materials and manufacturing processes.

Advanced Medical Technology Association., 701 Pennsylvania Ave. NW, Ste. 800 Washington, DC 20004-2654. Phone: (202)783-8700 Fax: (202)783-8750 E-mail: info@advamed.org • URL: http://www.advamed.org • Represents domestic (including U.S. territories and possessions) manufacturers of medical devices, diagnostic products, and healthcare information systems. Develops programs and activities on economic, technical, medical, and scientific matters affecting the industry. Gathers and disseminates information concerning the United States and international developments in legislative, regulatory, scientific or standards-making areas. Conducts scientific and educational seminars and programs.

Advanced Networking Research Group., Washington University, One Brookings Dr. St. Louis, MO 63130-4899. Phone: (314)935-6160 Fax: (314)935-7302 E-mail: jst@cs.wustl.edu Research fields include the design of high speed internetworks and the design of host interfaces.

Advanced Nutrition: Micronutrients. Carolyn D. Berdanier. CRC Press LLC, 2000 NW Corporate Blvd. Boca Raton, FL 33431. Phone: 800-272-7737 or (561)994-0555 Fax: 800-374-3401 or (561)898-9732 E-mail: orders@crcpress.com • URL: http://www.crcpress.com • 2000. $119.95. Provides detailed coverage of essential vitamins and minerals. Written for professional dietitions and nutritionists. (Modern Nutrition Series).

Advanced Strategies in Financial Risk Management. Robert J. Schwartz and Clifford W. Smith. Prentice Hall PTR, 240 Frisch Ct. Paramus, NJ 07652. Phone: 800-282-0693 Fax: 800-445-6991 • URL: http://www.prenhall.com • 1993. $65.00. Includes technical discussions of financial swaps and derivatives. (New York Institute of Finance Series).

Advanced Woodwork and Furniture Making. John L. Feirer and Gilbert R. Hutchings. Glencoe/McGraw-Hill, PO Box 543 Blacklick, OH 43004-0544. Phone: 800-334-7344 Fax: (614)755-5682 E-mail: customer.service@mcgraw-hill.com • URL: http://www.glencoe.com • 1982. $43.56. Fourth revised edition.

Advances and Innovations in the Bond and Mortgage Markets. Frank J. Fabozzi, editor. McGraw-Hill, 1221 Ave. of the Americas New York, NY 10020. Phone: 800-722-4726 or (212)512-2000 Fax: (212)512-4502 E-mail: customer.service@mcgraw-hill.com • URL: http://www.mcgraw-hill.com • 1989. $65.00.

Advances in Agronomy. American Society for Agronomy, Inc. Elsevier, 655 Avenue of the Americas New York, NY 10010-5107. Phone: 800-366-2665 or (212)989-5800 Fax: 800-535-9935 or (212)633-3680 E-mail: custserv@elsevier.com • URL: http://www.elsevier.com • Annual. Prices vary.

Advances in Chemical Engineering. Elsevier, 655 Avenue of the Americas New York, NY 10010-5107. Phone: 800-366-2665 or (212)989-5800 Fax: 800-535-9935 or (212)633-3680 E-mail: custserv@elsevier.com • URL: http://www.elsevier.com • Irregular. Prices vary.

Advances in Computers. Elsevier, 655 Avenue of the Americas New York, NY 10010-5107. Phone: 800-366-2665 or (212)989-5800 Fax: 800-535-9935 or (212)633-3680 E-mail: custserv@elsevier.com • URL: http://www.elsevier.com • Irregular. Price on application.

Advances in Cryogenic Engineering. Perseus Publishing, 11 Cambridge Ctr. Cambridge, MA 02142. Phone: 800-225-2514 or (617)252-5200 Fax: (617)252-5285 E-mail: info@perseuspublishing.com • URL: http://www.perseusbooks.com • Irregular. Price varies. Represents *Cryogenic Engineering Conference Proceedings*.

Advances in Econometrics and Quantitative Economics. Morris H. DeGroot and others. Blackwell Publishing, 350 Main St. Malden, MA 02148. Phone: 800-216-2522 or (781)388-8200 Fax: 800-864-7626 or (781)388-8210 E-mail: books@blackwellpub.com • URL: http://www.blackwellpub.com • 1995. $122.95.

Advances in Industrial and Labor Relations. David B. Lipsky and David Levin, editors. Elsevier, 360 Park Ave., S New York, NY 10010-1710. Phone: 888-437-4636 or (212)989-5800 Fax: (212)633-3990 E-mail: usinfo-f@elsevier.com • URL: http://www.elsevier.com • Dates vary. 12 volumes. Prices vary.

Advances in Investment Analysis and Portfolio Management. Chung-Few Lee, editor. Elsevier, 360 Park Ave., S New York, NY 10010-1710. Phone: 888-437-4636 or (212)989-5800 Fax: (212)633-3990 E-mail: usinfo-f@elsevier.com • URL: http://www.elsevier.com • Dates vary. Six volumes. Price varies.

Advances in Librarianship. Elsevier, 655 Avenue of the Americas New York, NY 10010-5107. Phone: 800-366-2665 or (212)989-5800 Fax: 800-535-9935 or (212)633-3680 E-mail: custserv@elsevier.com • URL: http://www.elsevier.com • Irregular. Prices vary.

Advances in Library Administration and Organization. JAI Press, Inc., 100 Prospect St. Stamford, CT 06904. Phone:

SOURCES CITED

(203)323-9606 Fax: (203)357-8446 E-mail: order@jaipress.com • URL: http://www.jaipress.com • Annual. Price varies. 20 volumes.

Advances in Polymer Technology. Polymer Processing Institute. John Wiley and Sons, Inc., 111 River St. Hoboken, NJ 07030. Phone: 800-225-5945 or (201)748-6000 Fax: (201)748-6088 E-mail: customer@wiley.com • URL: http://www.wiley.com • Quarterly. Institutions, $950.00 per year; with online edition, $998.00 per year.

Advances in the Astronautical Sciences. American Astronautical Society. Available from Univelt, Inc., 740 Metcalf St., Nos. 13+15 Escondido, CA 92025. Phone: (760)746-4005 Fax: (760)746-3139 E-mail: 76121.1532@compuserve.com • URL: http://www.univelt.com • Price varies. Volumes in this series cover the proceedings of various astronautical conferences and symposia.

Advances in Veterinary Medicine. Elsevier, 655 Avenue of the Americas New York, NY 10010-5107. Phone: 800-366-2665 or (212)989-5800 Fax: 800-535-9935 or (212)633-3680 E-mail: custserv@elsevier.com • URL: http://www.elsevier.com • Irregular. $174.95.

Advancing Women in Business-The Catalyst Guide: Best Practices from the Corporate Leaders. Catalyst Staff. John Wiley and Sons, Inc., 111 River St. Hoboken, NJ 07030. Phone: 800-225-5945 or (201)748-6000 Fax: (201)748-6088 E-mail: info@wiley.com • URL: http://www.wiley.com • 1998. $26.00. Explains the human resources practices of corporations providing a favorable climate for the advancement of female employees. (Jossey-Bass Business and Management Series).

Advertiser and Agency Red Books Plus. National Register Publishing, 121 Chanlon Rd. New Providence, NJ 07974. Phone: 800-323-3288 or (908)464-6800 Fax: (908)508-7671 Quarterly. $1,295.00 per year. The CD-ROM version of *Standard Directory of Advertisers, Standard Directory of Advertising Agencies*, and *Standard Directory of International Advertisers and Agencies*.

Advertisers Annual. Hollis Directories Ltd., Harlequin House, Seven High St. Teddington TW11 8EL, United Kingdom. Phone: 44 20 8977 7711 Fax: 44 20 8977 1133 E-mail: hollis@hollis-pr.co.uk • URL: http://www.hollis-pr.co.uk • Annual. $325.00. About 2,000 advertising and media agencies in the United Kingdom, Ireland and abroad, relevant to all forms of advertising.

Advertising. Ray Wright. Trans-Atlantic Publications, Inc., 311 Bainbridge St. Philadelphia, PA 19147. Phone: (215)925-5083 Fax: (215)925-1912 E-mail: order@transatlanticpub.com • URL: http://www.transatlanticpub.com • 2000. $49.50.

Advertising Age Encyclopedia of Advertising. John McDonough and others, editors. Fitzroy Dearborn Publishers, 919 N Michigan Ave. Chicago, IL 60611. Phone: 800-850-8102 or (312)587-0131 Fax: (312)587-1049 E-mail: fitzroyd@aol.com • URL: http://www.fitzroydearborn.com • 2002. $385.00. Three volumes. Contains 600 entries in alphabetical order covering a wide variety of advertising and market research topics. Includes bibliographies.

Advertising Age-Leading National Advertisers. Crain Communications, Inc., 711 Third Ave. New York, NY 10017-4036. Phone: 800-678-9595 or (212)210-0100 E-mail: info@crain.com • URL: http://www.crain.com • Annual. $5.00. List of the 100 leading advertisers in terms of the amount spent in national advertising and below-the-line forms of spending.

Advertising Age: National Expenditures in Newspapers. Crain Communications, Inc., 711 Third Ave. New York, NY 10017-4036. Phone: 800-678-9595 or (212)210-0100 E-mail: info@crain.com • URL: http://www.crain.com • Annual.

Advertising Age: The International Newspaper of Marketing. Crain Communications, Inc., 711 Third Ave. New York, NY 10017-4036. Phone: 800-678-9595 or (212)210-0100 E-mail: info@crain.com • URL: http://www.crain.com • Weekly. $178.50 per year. Includes supplement *Creativity*.

Advertising Agency. Entrepreneur Media, Inc., 2445 McCabe Way Irvine, CA 92614. Phone: 800-421-2300 or (949)261-2325 Fax: (949)261-0234 E-mail: entmag@entrepreneur.com • URL: http://www.entrepreneur.com • Looseleaf. $59.50. A practical guide to starting a small advertising agency. Covers profit potential, start-up costs, market size evaluation, pricing, accounting, advertising, promotion, etc. (Start-Up Business Guide No. E1223.)

Advertising Age's Euromarketing. Crain Communications, Inc., 711 Third Ave. New York, NY 10017-4036. Phone: 800-678-9595 or (212)210-0100 E-mail: info@crain.com • URL: http://www.crain.com • Weekly. $295.00 per year. Newsletter on European advertising and marketing.

Advertising and Marketing International Network.

The Advertising Business: Operations, Creativity, Media Planning, Integrated Communications. John P. Jones, editor. Sage Publications, Inc., 2455 Teller Rd. Thousand Oaks, CA 91320. Phone: 800-818-7243 or (805)499-9774 Fax: 800-583-2665 or (805)499-0871 E-mail: webmaster@sagepub.com • URL: http://www.sagepub.com • 1999. $91.95. Contains articles by professionals in various fields of advertising.

Advertising Compliance Service Newsletter. John Lichtenberger, 26 Hawthorn Dr. Roxbury, NJ 07876-2112. Phone: (973)252-7552 Fax: (973)252-7552 E-mail: lawpublish@aol.com Bimonthly. $495.00 per year.

Advertising Copywriting. Philip W. Burton. McGraw Hill, 1221 Ave. of the Americas New York, NY 10020. Phone: 800-722-4726 or (212)512-2000 Fax: (212)512-4502 E-mail: customerservice@mcgrawhill.com • URL: http://www.mcgrawhill.com • 1996. $44.95. Seventh edition. (NTC Business Book Series).

Advertising Council., 815 2nd Ave., 9th Fl. New York, NY 10017. Phone: 800-933-7727 or (212)922-1500 Fax: (212)922-1676 E-mail: info@adcouncil.org • URL: http://www.adcouncil.org • Founded and supported by American business, media, and advertising sectors to conduct public service advertising campaigns. Encourages advertising media to contribute time and space and advertising agencies to supply creative talent and facilities to further timely national causes. Specific campaigns include: Drug Abuse Prevention; AIDS Prevention; Teen-Alcoholism; Child Abuse; Crime Prevention; Forest Fire Prevention.

Advertising Handbook for Health Care Services. William J. Winston, editor. The Haworth Press, Inc., 10 Alice St. Binghamton, NY 13904-1580. Phone: 800-429-6784 or (607)722-5857 Fax: 800-895-0582 or (607)722-1424 E-mail: getinfo@haworthpressinc.com • URL: http://www.haworthpressinc.com • 1986. $8.95. (Health Marketing Quarterly Series: Supplement No. 1).

Advertising Law: Year in Review. CCH, Inc., 2700 Lake Cook Rd. Riverwoods, IL 60015. Phone: 800-835-5224 or (847)267-7000 E-mail: custserv@cch.com • URL: http://www.cch.com • Annual. $85.00. Summarizes the year's significant legal and regulatory developments.

Advertising Manager's Handbook. Robert W. Bly. Prentice Hall PTR, 240 Frisch Ct. Paramus, NJ 07652. Phone: 800-282-0693 Fax: 800-445-6991 • URL: http://www.phptr.com • 1998. $79.95. Second edition.

Advertising Media Planning. Roger B. Baron and Jack Z. Sissors. McGraw-Hill, 1221 Ave. of the Americas New York, NY 10020. Phone: 800-722-4726 or (212)512-2000 Fax: (212)512-4502 E-mail: customer.service@mcgraw-hill.com • URL: http://www.mcgraw-hill.com • 2002. $64.95. Sixth edition. Introduction to media planning.

Advertising Media Planning: A Brand Management Approach. Larry D. Kelley and Donald W. Jugenheimer. M. E. Sharpe, Inc., 80 Business Park Drive Armonk, NY 10504. Phone: 800-541-6563 or (914)273-1800 Fax: (914)273-2106 E-mail: custserv@mesharpe.com • URL: http://www.mesharpe.com • 2003. $69.95. Emphasizes the importance of brand recognition in media planning.

Advertising Organizations and Publications: A Resource Guide. John P. Jones. Sage Publications, Inc., 2455 Teller Rd. Thousand Oaks, CA 91320-2218. Phone: 800-818-7243 or (805)499-9774 Fax: 800-583-2665 or (805)499-0871 E-mail: webmaster@sagepub.com • URL: http://www.sagepub.com • 2000. $86.95. Describes advertising associations, books, periodicals, etc.

Advertising: Principles and Practice. William Wells and others. Prentice Hall PTR, 240 Frisch Ct. Paramus, NJ 07652. Phone: 800-282-0693 Fax: 800-445-6991 • URL: http://www.phptr.com • 2000. $120.00. Sixth edition.

Advertising: What It Is and How to Do It. Roderick White. McGraw-Hill, 1221 Ave. of the Americas New York, NY 10020. Phone: 800-722-4726 or (212)512-2000 Fax: (212)512-4502 E-mail: customer.service@mcgraw-hill.com • URL: http://www.mcgraw-hill.com • 1993. $16.95. Third edition.

Advisor Today. National Association of Insurance and Finacial Advisors, 2901 Telestar Court Falls Church, VA 22042. Phone: 877-866-2432 or (703)770-8100 Fax: (703)770-8142 • URL: http://www.naifa.org • Monthly. Free to members; non-members, $7.00 per year. Edited for individual life and health insurance agents. Among the topics included are disability insurance and long-term care insurance. Formerly Life Association News.

ADWEEK. VNU Business Media, 770 Broadway New York, NY 10003. Phone: 800-722-6658 or (646)654-4500 Fax: (646)654-7372 • URL: http://www.vnubusinessmedia.com • Weekly. $149.00 per year. Covers local, national, and international advertising news and trends. Includes critiques of advertising campaigns.

The ADWEEK Directory. ADWEEK Magazines, 770 Broadway, 7th Fl. New York, NY 10003-9595. Phone: 800-641-2030 or (646)654-5105 Fax: (646)654-5350 E-mail: stunifoo@busjour.com • URL: http://www.adweek.com/directories • Covers: over 6,400 U.S. Advertising agencies, public relations firms, media buying services, direct marketing and related organizations. Entries include: Agency name, address, phone, fax/e-mail, URL; names and titles of key personnel; major accounts; Ultimate parent company; headquarters location; major subsidiaries and other operating units; year founded; number of employees; fee income; billings; percentage of billings by medium. Individual listings for each agency branch.

Adweek Magazines' Technology Marketing. VNU Business Media, 770 Broadway, 7th Fl. New York, NY 10003. Phone: 800-344-7119 or (646)654-5500 • URL: http://www.vnubusinessmedia.com • Monthly. $55.00 per year. Edited for marketing executives in high technology industries. Covers both advertising and marketing. Formerly *MC Technology Marketing Intelligence*.

AEA - Advancing the Business of Technology., 601 Pennsylvania Ave., North Bldg., Ste. 1600 Washington, DC 20004. Phone: 800-284-4232 or (202)682-9110 Fax: (202)682-9111 E-mail: rhonda_starr@aeanet.org • URL: http://www.aeanet.org • Formerly American Electronics Association.

AEM Marketing Council., 6737 W Washington St., Ste. 2400 Milwaukee, WI 53214-5647. Phone: (866)AEM-0442 or (414)272-0943 Fax: (414)272-1170 E-mail: us.office@ciesnet.com • URL: http://www.aem.org • Advertising and marketing executives of equipment manufacturers and their advertising agencies directly interested in the marketing, advertising and sales promotion of construction equipment.

Aerobics and Fitness Association of America., 15250 Ventura Blvd., Suite 200 Sherman Oaks, CA 91403. Phone: 877-968-7263 or 800-446-2322 Fax: (818)788-6301 E-mail: contactafaa@afaa.com • URL: http://www.afaa.com • Members are fitness professionals and aerobic exercise instructors.

Aeronautical Repair Station Association., 121 N Henry St. Alexandria, VA 22314-2903. Phone: (703)739-9543 Fax: (703)739-9488 E-mail: arsa@arsa.org • URL: http://www.arsa.org • Represents FAA-certified repair stations, suppliers and distributors. Assists members on regulatory and legislative issues before the FAA and other governmental agencies.

Aerospace America. American Institute of Aeronautics and Astronautics, Inc., 1801 Alexander Bell Dr., Ste. 500 Reston, VA 20191. Phone: 800-639-2422 or (703)264-7567 Fax: (703)264-7551 E-mail: custserv@aiaa.org • URL: http://www.aiaa.org • Monthly. Free to members; non-members, $140.00 per year. Provides coverage of key issues affecting the aerospace field.

Aerospace America [online]. American Institute of Aeronautics and Astronautics, 1801 Alexander Bell Drive, Suite 500 Reston, VA 20191-4344. Phone: 800-639-2422 or (703)264-7500 Fax: (703)264-7551 E-mail: access@aiaa.org • URL: http://www.aiaa.org • Provides complete text of the periodical, *Aerospace America*, 1984 to date, with monthly updates. Also includes news from the *AIAA Bulletin*. Inquire as to online cost and availability.

Aerospace Daily. The McGraw-Hill Cos., 1221 Ave. of the Americas New York, NY 10020. Phone: 800-752-4959 or (212)512-2000 Fax: (202)383-2438 E-mail: awgnews@mcgraw-hill.com • URL: http://www.mcgraw-hill.com • Description: Reports on developments in the aerospace industry in the U.S. and overseas. Covers related political decisions. **Remarks:** Available in print, e-mail, and URL format.

Aerospace Database. American Institute of Aeronautics and Astronautics, 1801 Alexander Bell Drive, Suite 500 Reston, VA 20191-4344. Phone: 800-639-2422 or (703)264-7500 Fax: (703)264-7551 E-mail: access@aiaa.org • URL: http://www.aiaa.org • Contains abstracts of literature covering all aspects of the aerospace and aircraft industry 1983 to date. Monthly updates. Inquire as to online cost and availability.

Aerospace/Defense Markets and Technology. Gale Cengage Learning, 27500 Drake Rd. Farmington Hills, MI 48331-3535. Phone: 800-877-GALE or (248)699-GALE Fax: 800-414-5043 or (248)699-8069 E-mail: galeord@gale.com • URL: http://gale.cengage.com • Abstracts of commerical aerospace/defense related literature, 1982 to date. Also includes information about major defense contracts awarded by the U. S. Department of Defense. International coverage. Inquire as to online cost and availability.

Aerospace Education Foundation., 1501 Lee Hwy. Arlington, VA 22209-1198. Phone: 800-291-8480 or (703)247-5839 Fax: (703)247-5853 E-mail: aefstaff@aef.org • URL: http://www.aef.org • Provides America's youth with the tools needed to educate the public and the youth in math and the sciences to help keep America's edge in aerospace technology.

Aerospace Electrical Society., 18231 Fernando Cir. Villa Park, CA 92861. Phone: (714)538-1002 Fax: (714)538-1002 E-mail: aefstaff@aef.org Technicians, engineers, and management personnel engaged in the development and use of electrical and electronic equipment and systems for air and space craft.

Aerospace Engineering Magazine. Society of Automotive Engineers, 400 Commonwealth Dr. Warrendale, PA 15096-0001. Phone: 877-606-7323 or (724)776-4841 Fax: (724)776-5760 E-mail: customerservice@sae.org • URL: http://www.sae.org • Monthly. $66.00 per year. Provides technical information that can be used in the design of new and improved aerospace systems.

Aerospace Facts and Figures. Aerospace Industries Association of America, 1250 Eye St., NW, Ste. 1200 Washington, DC 20005. Phone: (202)371-8561 Fax: (202)371-8470 • URL: http://www.aia-aerospace.org • Annual. $35.00. Includes financial data for the aerospace industries.

Aerospace Industries Association of America.

AESF Shop Guide-A Directory of Surface Finishing Shops. American Electroplaters' and Surface Finishers Society, Inc., 12644 Research Parkway Orlando, FL 32826-3298. Phone: 800-334-2052 or (407)281-6441 Fax: (407)281-6446 E-mail: asef@aesf.org • URL: http://www.aesf.org • Annual. Price on application. List of over 1,200 electroplating, coating, and other surface finishing firms.

AF and PA Statistical Roundup. American Forest and Paper Association, 1119 19th St., N. W., Suite 200 Washington, DC 20036. Phone: (202)463-2700 Fax: (202)463-2785 Monthly. Members, $57.00 per year; non-members, $157.00 per year. Contains monthly statistical data for hardwood and softwood products. Formerly *NFPA Statistical Roundup*.

AFCOM., 742 E Chapman Ave. Orange, CA 92866. Phone: (714)997-7966 Fax: (714)997-9743 E-mail: afcom@afcom.com • URL: http://www.afcom.com • Data center, networking and enterprise systems management professionals from medium and large scale mainframe, midrange and client/server data centers worldwide. Works to meet the professional needs of the enterprise system management community. Provides information and support through educational events, research and assistance hotlines, and surveys.

AFE Newsline elsewhere. Association for Facilities Engineering, 12100 Sunset Hills Rd., Ste. 130 Reston, VA 20190. Phone: (703)234-4066 Fax: (703)234-4066 E-mail: info@afe.org Description: Internal newsletter of the association.

Affirmative Action. Lynne Eisaguirre. ABC-CLIO, Inc., 130 Cremona Dr. Santa Barbara, CA 93117. Phone: 800-368-6868 or (805)968-1911 Fax: (805)685-9685 E-mail: customerservice@abc-clio.com • URL: http://www.abc-clio.com • 1999. $45.00. Provides an impartial survey and analysis of affirmative action controversies, including historical background and statistical data. (Contemporary World Issues.)

Affirmative Action: An Annotated Bibliography. A. M. Babkina, editor. Nova Science Publishers, Inc., 400 Oser Ave., Suite 1600 Hauppauge, NY 11788-3619. Phone: (631)231-7269 Fax: (631)231-8175 E-mail: novascience@earthlink.net • URL: http://www.novapublishers.com • 2003. $49.00. Second edition. Covers books, reports, and articles on all aspects of affirmative action. Includes author, title, and subject indexes.

Affirmative Action Compliance Manual for Federal Contractors. BNA, Inc., 1231 25th St., NW Washington, DC 20037. Phone: 800-372-1033 E-mail: customercare@bna.com • URL: http://www.bna.com • Monthly. $410.00 per year. Two looseleaf volumes.

Affirmative Action Register: The E E O Recruitment Publication. Affirmative Action, Inc., 8356 Olive Blvd. St. Louis, MO 63132. Phone: (314)991-1335 Fax: (314)997-1788 E-mail: aareeo@concentric.net • URL: http://www.aar-eeo.com • Monthly. Free to qualified personnel; others, $15.00 per year. "The *Affirmative Action Register* is the only nationwide publication that provides for systematic distribution to mandated minorities, females, handicapped, veterans, and Native Americans." Each issue consists of recruitment advertisements placed by equal opportunity employers (institutions and companies).

Affirmative Action Revisited. Charles V. Dale. Nova Science Publishers, Inc., 400 Oser Ave., Suite 1600 Hauppauge, NY 11788-3619. Phone: (631)231-7269 Fax: (631)231-8175 E-mail: novascience@earthlink.net • URL: http://www.novapublishers.com • 2001. $59.00. Provides an assessment of the history, current status, and future of affirmative action.

The Affluent Market. MarketResearch.com, 641 Ave. of the Americas, 4th Fl. New York, NY 10011. Phone: 800-298-5699 or (212)807-2629 Fax: (212)807-2676 E-mail: customerservice@marketresearch.com • URL: http://www.marketresearch.com • 2002. $2,750.00 Consumer market data. Includes demographics of affluent house holds and the expenditures of the affluent on 250 types of products.

Affordable Housing Finance. Alexander & Edwards Publishing, 220 Samsone St., 11th Fl. San Francisco, CA 94104. Phone: (415)546-7255 Fax: (415)249-1595 E-mail: ahf@housingfinance.com • URL: http://www.housingfinance.com • Ten times a year. $119.00 per year. Provides advice and information on obtaining financing for lower-cost housing. Covers both government and private sources.

AFL-CIO., 815 16th St. NW Washington, DC 20006. Phone: (202)637-5137 Fax: (202)637-5058 E-mail: info@workingamerica.org • URL: http://www.aflcio.org • Federation of national unions, state federations, city central bodies, and directly affiliated local unions.

AFP Exchange. Association for Financial Professionals, 7315 Wisconsin Ave., Suite 600 W. Bethesda, MD 20814-3211. Phone: (301)907-2862 Fax: (301)907-2864 E-mail: afp@afponline.org • URL: http://www.afponline.org • Monthly. Membership. Newsletter.

African-American Business Leaders and Entrepreneurs. Rachel Kranz. Facts on File, Inc., 132 W 31st St., 17th Fl. New York, NY 10001. Phone: 800-322-8755 Fax: 800-678-3633 E-mail: custserv@factsonfile.com • URL: http://www.factsonfile.com • 2004. $44.00. (A to Z of African Americans Series).

The African American Market. Available from MarketResearch.com, 641 Ave. of the Americas, 3rd Fl. New York, NY 10011. Phone: 800-298-5699 or (212)807-2629 Fax: (212)807-2716 E-mail: order@marketresearch.com • URL: http://www.marketresearch.com • 2002. $3,000.00. Published by Packaged Facts. Provides consumer market data and demographics, with projections to 2006.

AFSCME Public Employee. American Federation of State, County, and Municipal Employees, AFL-CIO, 1625 L St., N.W. Washington, DC 20036-5687. Phone: (202)429-1144 Fax: (202)429-1120 • URL: http://www.afscme.org • Bimonthly. Membership. Newsletter. Formerly *Public Employee Magazine*.

Aftermarket Business. Advanstar Communications, 545 Boylston St. Boston, MA 02116. Phone: 888-527-7008 or (617)267-6500 Fax: (617)267-6900 E-mail: info@advanstar.com • URL: http://www.advanstar.com • Monthly. $48.00 per year. Automobile aftermarket, including batteries.

Ag Executive. Ag Executive Inc., 115 E Twyman St. Bushnell, IL 61422. Phone: (309)772-2168 Fax: (309)772-2167 E-mail: agexecutive@earthlink.net • URL: http://www.agexecutive.com • Description: Focuses on financial, personnel, and risk management issues for commercial agriculture. Covers business analysis and practical management ideas for improving profitability. Includes such topics as accounting, farm business organization, financing, economic forecasting, resource/risk control, and taxes.

Ag Lender. Doane Agricultural Services Co., 11701 Borman Dr. St. Louis, MO 63146-4199. Phone: 800-535-2342 or (314)569-2700 Fax: (314)569-1083 • URL: http://www.edoane.com • Monthly. $139.00 per year. Formerly *Agri Finance*.

Ag Professional. Doane Agricultural Services, 11701 Borman Dr., Suite 300 St. Louis, MO 63146-4199. Phone: 800-535-2342 or (314)569-2700 Fax: (314)569-1083 • URL: http://www.edoane.com • 10 times a year. Free to qualified personnel. Published to meet the business needs of the retail fertilizer and agrichemical dealer industry. Formerly *Ag Retailer Magazine*.

AGA Rate Service. American Gas Association, 400 N Capitol St., NW Washington, DC 20001. Phone: (202)824-7000 Fax: (202)824-7115 • URL: http://www.aga.org • Semiannual. Members, $175.00 per year; non-members, $300.00 per year. Looseleaf service.

Age of Diminished Expectations: U. S. Economic Policy in the 1990s. Paul Krugman. MIT Press, Five Cambridge Ctr. Cambridge, MA 02142-1493. Phone: 800-356-0343 or (617)253-2864 Fax: (617)253-6779 • URL: http://www.mitpress.mit.edu • 1997. $50.00. Third edition. States that the big problem is slow growth in productivity.

Age of Giant Corporations: A Microeconomic History of American Business, 1914-1992. Robert Sobel. Greenwood Publishing Group Inc., 88 Post Rd. W. Westport, CT 06881-5007. Phone: 800-225-5800 or (203)226-3571 Fax: 800-678-3633 or (203)431-2214 E-mail: customer-service@greenwood.com • URL: http://www.greenwood.com • 1993. $57.95. Third edition. (Contributions in Economics and Economic History Series, No. 146).

The Age of Spiritual Machines: When Computers Exceed Human Intelligence. Ray Kurzweil. Penguin Group, 375 Hudson St. New York, NY 10014-3657. Phone: 800-331-4624 or (212)366-2000 Fax: 800-227-9604 or (212)366-2952 • URL: http://www.penguingroup.com • 1998. $25.95. Provides speculation on the future of artificial intelligence and "computer consciousness."

Ageless Marketing: Strategies for Reaching the Hearts and Minds of the New Customer Majority. David Wolfe and Robert Snyder. Dearborn Trade Publishing, 30 S Wacker Dr., Ste. 2500 Chicago, IL 60606. Phone: 800-621-9621 or (312)836-4400 Fax: (312)836-1021 E-mail: trade@dearborn.com • URL: http://www.dearborntrade.com • 2003. $25.00. Explains how to create marketing campaigns that will attract older comsumers.

Ageline. American Association of Retired Persons, Research Information Center, 601 E. St., N. W. Washington, DC 20049. Phone: 800-424-3410 or (202)434-6231 Fax: (202)434-6408 Provides indexing and abstracting of the literature of social gerontology, including consumer aspects, financial planning, employment, housing, health care services, mental health, social security, and retirement. Time period is 1978 to date. Inquire as to online cost and availability.

Agencies and Organizations Represented in AAPOR/WAPOR Membership. American Association for Public Opinion Research, PO Box 14263 Lenexa, KS 66285-4263. Phone: (913)310-0118 Fax: (913)599-5340 E-mail: aapor-info@goamp.com • URL: http://www.aapor.org • Annual. Free. Lists over 220 firms engaged in public opinion research.

Agency Sales: The Marketing Magazine for Manufacturers' Agencies and Their Principals. Manufacturers' Agents National Association, 1 Spectrum Pointe, Ste. 150 Lake Forest, CA 92654. Phone: 877-626-2776 or (949)859-4040 Fax: (949)855-2973 E-mail: mana@manaonline.org • URL: http://www.manaonline.org • Monthly. $49.00 per year.

AgExporter. Available from U. S. Government Printing Office, Washington, DC 20402. Phone: (202)512-1800 Fax: (202)512-2250 E-mail: gpoaccess@gpo.gov • URL: http://www.access.gpo.gov • Monthly. $44.00 per year. Issued by the Foreign Agricultural Service, U. S. Department of Agriculture. Edited for U. S. exporters of farm products. Provides practical information on exporting, including overseas trade opportunities.

Aggregate Reserves of Depository Institutions and the Monetary Base. U.S. Federal Reserve System, Publications Servicesm Room MS-138 Washington, DC 20551. Phone: (202)452-3244 Fax: (202)728-5886 Weekly. $20.00 per year.

Agri Marketing: Marketing Services Guide. Doane Agricultural Services, 11701 Borman Dr., Ste. 300 St. Louis, MO 63146-4199. Phone: 800-535-2342 or (314)569-2700 Fax: (314)569-1083 • URL: http://www.edoane.com • Annual. $30.00. Wide range of listings related to agricultural marketing.

Agri Marketing: The Magazine for Professionals Selling to the Farm Market. Doane Agricultural Services, 11701 Borman Dr., Suite 300 St. Louis, MO 63146-4199. Phone: 800-535-2342 or (314)569-2700 Fax: (314)564-1083 • URL: http://www.edoane.com • Monthly. $30.00 per year.

Agribusiness Council., 1312 18th St. NW, Ste. 300 Washington, DC 20036. Phone: (202)296-4563 or (202)887-0238 Fax: (202)887-9178 E-mail: info@agribusinesscouncil.org • URL: http://www.agribusinesscouncil.org • Business organizations, universities and foundations, and individuals interested in stimulating and encouraging agribusiness in cooperation with the public sector, both domestic and international. Seeks to aid in relieving the problems of world food supply. Supports coordinated agribusiness in the developing nations by identifying opportunities for investment of U.S. private-sector technology management and financial resources. Advises agribusiness leaders about selected developing countries with good investment climates; brings potential investment opportunities to the attention of U.S. agribusiness firms; coordinates informal network of state agribusiness councils and grassroots organization; encourages companies to make investment feasibility studies in agribusiness; provides liaison and information exchange between agribusiness firms, governments, international organizations, universities, foundations, and other groups with the objective of identifying areas of cooperation and mutual interest; encourages projects geared to the conversion of subsistence farming to intensive, higher income agriculture in order to bring the world's rural populations, wherever feasible, into the market economy.

Agribusiness Fieldman. Western Agricultural Publishing Co., Inc., 4969 E. Clinton Way, Suite 104 Fresno, CA 93727-1549. Phone: (559)252-7000 Fax: (559)252-7387 Monthly. $19.95 per year.

Agribusiness Management. Steven P. Erickson and others. McGraw-Hill, 1221 Ave. of the Americas New York, NY 10020. Phone: 800-722-4276 or (212)512-2000 Fax: (212)512-4502 E-mail: customer.service@mcgraw-hill.com • URL: http://www.mcgraw-hill.com • 2001. $111.56. Third edition.

Agricola. U.S. National Agricultural Library, Beltsville, MD 20705. Phone: (301)504-5755 Fax: (301)504-7473 • URL: http://www.NALUSDA.gov • Covers worldwide agricultural literature. Over 3.3 million citations, 1970 to present, with monthly updates. Inquire as to online cost and availability.

AGRICOLA on SilverPlatter. Available from SilverPlatter Information, Inc., 100 River Ridge Rd. Norwood, MA 02062-5026. Phone: 800-343-0064 or (781)769-2599 Fax: (781)769-8763 Quarterly. $825.00 per year. Produced by the National Agricultural Library. Provides about three million citations on CD-ROM to the literature of agriculture, agricultural economics, animal sciences, entomology, fertilizer, food, forestry, nutrition, pesticides, plant science, water resources, and other topics. Each quarterly disc covers the past ten years, with archival discs available from 1970.

Agricultural and Environmental Biotechnology Abstracts. CSA, 7200 Wisconsin Ave. Bethesda, MD 20814. Phone: 800-843-7751 or (301)961-6700 Fax: (301)961-6720 E-mail: service@csa.com • URL: http://www.csa.com • Online edition, $390.00 per year. Formerly *Biotechnology Research Abstracts*.

Agricultural and Mineral Commodities Year Book. Available from Taylor & Francis Group, 325 Chestnut St. Philadelphia, PA 19106. Phone: 800-821-8312 or (215)625-8900 Fax: 800-248-4724 or (215)625-2940 E-mail: info@taylorandfrancis.com • URL: http://www.taylorandfrancis.com • Annual. $225.00. Published by Europa Publications. Contains descriptive product profiles, price data, export-import data, and production statistics for major commodities of the world. Includes commodity histories, uses, markets, demand trends, and information about trade agreements and key commodity organizations.

Agricultural Biotechnology: An Economic Perspective. Margriet F. Caswell and others. Nova Science Publishers, Inc., 400 Oser Ave., Suite 1600 Hauppauge, NY 11788-3619. Phone: (631)231-7269 Fax: (631)231-8175 E-mail: novascience@earthlink.net • URL: http://www.novapublishers.com • 2003. $30.00. Considers such factors as consumer demand, producer demand, public policies, regulation, food safety, and research funding.

Agricultural Communicators in Education.

Agricultural Credit and Related Data. American Bankers Association, 1120 Connecticut Ave., N.W. Washington, DC 20036-3971. Phone: 800-338-0626 or (202)663-5000 Fax: (202)663-7543 E-mail: custserv@aba.com • URL: http://www.aba.com • Annual.

Agricultural Economics and Agribusiness. Gail L. Cramer and others. John Wiley and Sons, Inc., 111 River St. Hoboken, NJ 07030. Phone: 800-225-5945 or (201)748-6000 Fax: (201)748-6088 E-mail: info@wiley.com • URL: http://www.wiley.com • 2000. $104.95. Eighth edition.

Agricultural Engineering Abstracts. Available from CABI Publishing North America, 875 Massachusetts Ave., 7th Fl. Cambridge, MA 02139. Phone: 800-528-4841 or (617)395-4056 Fax: (617)354-6875 E-mail: cabi-nao@cabi.org • URL: http://www.cabi-publishing.org • Bimonthly. Institutions, $1,030.00 per year. Online edition available, $1,050.00 per year. Published in England by CABI Publishing.

Agricultural Experiment Station. Cornell University

Agricultural Experiment Station. New Mexico State University

Agricultural Finance. Warren F. Lee and others. Blackwell Publishing, 350 Main St. Malden, MA 02148. Phone: (781)388-8200 Fax: (781)388-8210 E-mail: subscrip@blackwellpub.com • URL: http://www.blackwellpublishing.com • 1988. $44.95. Eighth revised edition.

Agricultural Finance Databook. U. S. Federal Reserve System, 20th and Constitutions Ave., NW, Publications Services, MS-138, Board of Governors Washington, DC 20551. Phone: (202)452-3244 Fax: (202)728-5886 • URL: http://www.federalreserve.gov • Quarterly. $5.00 per year. (Federal Reserve Statistical Release, E.15.)

Agricultural Guide to Washington: Whom to Contact and Where. Dow Elunco, 9002 Purdue Rd., Quad IV Indianapolis, IN 46268. Biennial. Free. Heads of congressional committees and subcommittees in Washington, D.C. that deal with agricultural matters, and members of federal agencies and trade associations concerned with agribusiness.

Agricultural Law. LexisNexis Matthew Bender, 1275 Broadway Albany, NY 12204. Phone: 800-424-4200 or (518)487-3000 Fax: (518)487-3584 E-mail: bookstore.support@lexisnexis.com Semiannual. $2,501.00. 15 looseleaf volumes. Covers all aspects of state and federal law relating to farms, ranches and other agricultural interests. Includes five volumes dealing with agricultural estate, tax and business planning.

Agricultural Letter. Federal Reserve Bank of Chicago, Public Information Center, P.O. Box 834 Chicago, IL 60690. Phone: 888-372-2446 or (312)322-5111 Fax: (312)322-5515 Quarterly. Free. Looseleaf service.

Agricultural Options: Trading, Risk Management, and Hedging. Christopher A. Bobin. John Wiley and Sons, Inc., 111 River St. Hoboken, NJ 07030. Phone: 800-225-5945 or (201)748-6000 Fax: (201)748-6088 E-mail: info@wiley.com • URL: http://www.wiley.com • 1990. $49.95. Practical advice on trading commodity futures options (puts and calls).

Agricultural Policies, Markets, and Trade: Monitoring and Evaluation. Organization for Economic Cooperation and Development. Available from OECD Publications and Information Center, 2001 L St., N. W., Suite 650 Washington, DC 20036-4922. Phone: 800-456-6323 or (202)785-6323 Fax: (202)785-0350 E-mail: washington.contact@oecd.org • URL: http://www.oecdwash.org • Annual. $62.00. A yearly report on agricultural and trade policy developments in OECD member countries.

Agricultural Product Prices. William G. Tomek and Kenneth L. Robinson. Cornell University Press, Sage House, 512 E. State St. Ithaca, NY 14851. Phone: 800-666-2211 or (607)277-2211 Fax: 800-688-2877 E-mail: cupress-sales@cornell.edu • URL: http://www.cornellpress.cornell.edu • 1990. $37.50. Third edition.

Agricultural Research. Available from U. S. Government Printing Office, Washington, DC 20402. Phone: (202)512-1800 Fax: (202)512-2250 E-mail: gpoaccess@gpo.gov • URL: http://www.access.gpo.gov • Monthly. $50.00 per year. Issued by the Agricultural Research Service of the U. S. Department of Agriculture. Presents results of research projects related to a wide variety of farm crops and products.

Agricultural Research and Extension Center at Uvalde. Overeas Development Institute, Portland House, Stag Pl. London SWIE 5DP, England. Phone: 44 1713 931600 Fax: 44 1713 931699 • URL: http://www.oneworld.org • Semiannual. Price on application. Newsletter.

Agricultural Research Center. Washington State University, PO Box 646240, P.O. Box 646240 Pullman, WA 99164-6240. Phone: (509)335-4563 Fax: (509)335-6751 E-mail: agresearch@wsu.edu • URL: http://arc.wsu.edu • Agriculture and food safety, including economics; biological systems engineering; agronomy and soils; animal sciences; human development; food science and human nutrition; apparel; merchandising; interior design; rural sociology; entomology; natural resource management; horticulture and landscape architecture; plant pathology; veterinary science; plant and animal biotechnology; wood materials; and low-input sustainable agriculture. Performs forage, seed, and minor pesticide testing.

Agricultural Research Division. University of Nebraska - Lincoln

Agricultural Research Institute., 9650 Rockville Pike Bethesda, MD 20814-3998. Phone: (301)530-7122 Fax: (301)530-7007 E-mail: info@agribusinesscouncil.org Originally an integral part of the National Academy of Sciences (see separate entry), incorporated separately in 1973. Analyzes agricultural problems and promotes research by its members to solve them. (ARI does not engage in research activities itself.)

Agricultural Retailers Association., 1156 15th St. NW, Ste. 302 Washington, DC 20005. Phone: 800-535-6272 or (202)457-0825 Fax: (202)457-0864 E-mail: ara@aradc.org • URL: http://www.aradc.org • Retailers, manufacturers, and suppliers of fertilizers and agrochemicals; equipment manufacturers; retail affiliations; and state association affiliates.

Agricultural Statistics. Available from U. S. Government Printing Office, Washington, DC 20402. Phone: (202)512-1800 Fax: (202)512-2250 E-mail: gpoaccess@gpo.gov • URL: http://www.access.gpo.gov • Annual. $38.00. Produced by the National Agricultural Statistics Service, U. S. Department of Agriculture. Provides a wide variety of statistical data relating to agricultural production, supplies, consumption, prices/price-supports, foreign trade, costs, and returns, as well as farm labor, loans, income, and population. In many cases, historical data is shown annually for 10 years. In addition to farm data, includes detailed fishery statistics.

Agriculture Fact Book. Available from U. S. Government Printing Office, Washington, DC 20402. Phone: (202)512-1800 Fax: (202)512-2250 E-mail: gpoaccess@gpo.gov • URL: http://www.access.gpo.gov • Annual. $26.00. Issued by the Office of Communications, U. S. Department of Agriculture. Includes data on U. S. agriculture, farmers, food, nutrition, and rural America. Programs of the Department of Agriculture in six areas are described: rural economic development, foreign trade, nutrition, the environment, inspection, and education.

Agriculture: Websites and Glossary. Carol Canada. Nova Science Publishers, Inc., 400 Oser Ave., Suite 1600 Hauppauge, NY 11788-3619. Phone: (631)231-7269 Fax: (631)231-8175 E-mail: novascience@earthlink.net • URL: http://www.novapublishers.com • 2003. $29.50. Lists agricultural Web sites according to 24 main categories and 16 subcategories. Includes a glossary and an index.

Agrindex: International Information System for the Agricultural Sciences and Technology. Food and Agriculture Organization of the United Nations. Bernan Press, 4611-F Assembly Dr. Lanham, MD 20706. Phone: 800-274-4888 or (301)459-2255 Fax: 800-865-3450 or (301)459-0056 E-mail: order@bernan.com • URL: http://www.bernan.com • Monthly. $500.00 per year. Text in English, French, and Spanish.

The Agrochemical Companies Fact File. PJB Publications Ltd., Telephone House, 69-77 Paul St. London EC2A 4LQ, United Kingdom. Phone: (44)20 70175000 Fax: (44)20 70176792 E-mail: pjb.enquiries@informa.com Covers: 300 agrochemical manufacturers; formulators; biopesticide manufacturers, and agrochemical trading companies worldwide. Entries include: Details on key executives, financial data, operating locations, main markets, products, subsidiaries, joint ventures, and portfolios.

Agrochemicals: Composition, Production, Toxicology, Applications. Franz Muller, editor. John Wiley and Sons, Inc., 111 River St. Hoboken, NJ 07030. Phone: 800-225-5945 or (201)748-6000 Fax: (201)748-6088 E-mail: info@wiley.com • URL: http://www.wiley.com • 2000. $375.00. Coverage includes fertilizers, herbicides, fungicides, insecticides, and biological control agents. Content is both theoretical and practical.

Agronomy Journal: An International Journal. American Society of Agronomy, Inc., 677 S. Segoe Rd. Madison, WI 53711. Phone: (608)273-8080 Fax: (608)273-2021 E-mail: journal@agronomy.org • URL: http://www.agronomy.org • Bimonthly. Free to members; non-members, $216.00 per year.

AGS Quarterly. The Association for Gravestone Studies, 278 Main St., Ste. 207 Greenfield, MA 01301-3230. Phone: (413)772-0836 Fax: (904)273-5726 E-mail: info@gravestonestudies.org Description: Concerned with the study and preservation of national and international gravestones: folk art carvings, lettering, epitaphs, shapes, materials used, and symbolism. Recurring features include articles on conservation procedures, Association news, book reviews, news of research, and regional news.

AHA Guide to the Health Care Field. American Hospital Association., One N Franklin, Ste. 27 Chicago, IL 60606. Phone: 800-242-2626 or (312)422-3000 Fax: (312)422-4796 E-mail: kjackson@healthforumcom • URL: http://www.aha.org • Annual. $295.00. A directory of hospitals and health care systems.

AHA Hospital Statistics. American Hospital Association. American Hospital Publishing, Inc., One N Franklin St., 27th Fl. Chicago, IL 60606. Phone: 800-242-2626 or (312)422-3000 Fax: (312)422-4796 • URL: http://www.aha.org • Annual. Members, $59.00 per year; non-members $139.00 per year. Provides detailed statistical data on the nation's hospitals, including revenues, expenses, utilization, and personnel. Formerly *Hospital Statistics*.

AHA Integrated Delivery Network Directory: U.S. Health Care Systems, Networks, and Alliances. American Hospital Association, One N Franklin St. Chicago, IL 60606. Phone: 800-242-2626 or (312)422-3000 Fax: (312)422-4505 • URL: http://www.aha.org • Annual. $250.00. Provides information about a wide variety of U.S. health care groups and affiliations, including hospitals, nursing homes, rehabilitation centers, psychiatric facilities, home health care agencies, clinical laboratories, outpatient facilities, and diagnostic imaging centers. Includes names of more than 8,000 key executives.

AHA News. American Hospital Association. HealthForum, 1 North Franklin St., 29th Fl. Chicago, IL 60606. Phone: 800-821-2039 or (312)422-2100 Fax: (312)433-4506 E-mail: hfcustsvc@healthforum.com • URL: http://www.aha.org • Description: Highlights major news affecting hospitals and the health care field. Reports on legislation and regulation, court cases, surveys, and federal programs. Carries information on individual hospitals and allied hospital associations.

AHAM Major Home Appliance Industry Fact Book: A Comprehensive Reference on the U States Major Home Appliance Industry. Association of Home Appliance Manufacturers, 1111 19th St., N.W., Suite 402 Washington, DC 20036. Phone: (202)872-5955 Fax: (202)872-9354 E-mail: aham@aham.org • URL: http://www.aham.org • Biennial. $75.00. Includes statistical data on manufacturing, industry shipments, distribution, and ownership.

AHFS Drug Information. American Hospital Formulary Service. American Society of Health-System Pharmacists, 7272 Wisconsin Ave. Bethesda, MD 20814. Phone: (301)657-3000 Fax: 800-665-2747 or (301)657-1641 E-mail: custserv@ashp.org • URL: http://www.ashp.org • 2003. $174.95. 44th edition. Detailed information about drugs and groups of drugs.

AHS International - The Vertical Flight Society.

AI Magazine (Artificial Intelligence). American Association for Artificial Intelligence. AAAI Press, 445 Burgess Dr. Menlo Park, CA 94025. Phone: (650)328-3123 Fax: (650)321-4457 E-mail: aimagazine@aaai.org • URL: http://www.aaai.org • Quarterly. Individuals, $95.00 per year; institutions, $190.00 per year. Information on artificial intelligence research and innovative applications of the science.

AIAA Journal: Devoted to Aerospace Research and Development. American Institute of Aeronautics and Astronautics, Inc., 1801 Alexander Bell Dr., Suite 500 Reston, VA 20191-4344. Phone: 800-639-2422 or (703)264-7500 Fax: (703)264-7551 E-mail: custserv@aiaa.org • URL: http://www.aiaa.org • Monthly. Members, $68.00 per year. Includes print and online editions. Non-members, $890.00 per year; with online edition, $1,025.00 per year.

AIChe Journal. American Institute of Chemical Engineers, Three Park Ave. New York, NY 10016-5901. Phone: 800-242-4363 or (212)591-7338 Fax: (212)591-8887 E-mail: journaledit@aiche.org • URL: http://www.aiche.org • Monthly. Members, $105.00 per year; non-members, $950.00 per year. Devoted to research and technological developments in chemical engineering and allied fields. Available online.

AICP Membership Directory. Association of Independent Commercial Producers, 3 W 18th St., 5th Fl. New York, NY 10011. Phone: 800-954-1669 or (212)929-3000 Fax: (212)929-3359 E-mail: info@aicp.com • URL: http://www.planning.org • Covers: General member companies that specialize in producing commercials on various media, including film, video, and computer, for advertisers and agencies. Associate member companies listed serve the industry, such as post-production and editorial houses, equipment and prop suppliers, casting agencies and others. AMP members are music production shops; press members are those in the press who cover the industry. Entries include: Company name, address, phone, fax, e-mail, URL, contact names, and names of people represented.

AICPA Audit and Accounting Manual. American Institute of Certified Public Accountants, 1211 Ave. of the Americas New York, NY 10036-8775. Phone: 800-862-4272 or (212)596-6200 Fax: (212)596-6213 E-mail: lmorales@aicpa.org • URL: http://www.aicpa.org • 1999. $90.50. Covers working papers, internal control, audit approach, etc.

AICPA Codification of Statements on Auditing Standards. American Institute of Certified Public Accountants, 1211 Ave. of the Americas New York, NY 10036-8775. Phone: 800-862-4272 or (212)596-6200 Fax: (212)596-6213 E-mail: lmorales@aicpa.org • URL: http://www.aicpa.org • 1999. $81.25. Includes *Auditing Interpretations* and *International Auditing Guidelines*.

AICPA Professional Standards, U. S. Auditing Standards, Accounting and Review Services, Ethics, Bylaws, International Accounting, International Auditing, Management Advisory Services, Quality Control, and Tax Practice. American Institute of Certified Public Accountants, 1211 Ave. of the Americas New York, NY 10036-8775. Phone: 800-862-4272 or (212)569-6200 Fax: (212)569-6213 E-mail: lmorales@aicpa.org • URL: http://www.aicpa.org • 1999. $123.50. Two volumes.

AICPA Technical Practice Aids. American Institute of Certified Public Accountants, 1211 Ave. of the Americas New York, NY 10036-8775. Phone: 800-862-4272 or (212)596-6200 Fax: (212)596-6213 E-mail: lmorales@aicpa.org • URL: http://www.aicpa.org • 1998. $119.00 per year. Two volumes. Advisory opinions, statements of position, and other material.

AIDS: Abstracts of the Psychological and Behavioral Literature, 1983-1991. John Anderson and others, editors. American Psychological Association, 750 1st St. NE Washington, DC 20002-4242. Phone: 800-374-2721 or (202)366-5500 Fax: (202)336-6069 • URL: http://www.apa.org • 1991. $19.95. Third edition. (Bibliographies in Psychology Series: No.1).

AIDS Action Council., 1730 M St. NW, Ste. 611 Washington, DC 20036. Phone: (202)530-8030 Fax: (202)530-8031 E-mail: members@aidsaction.org • URL: http://www.aidsaction.org • Serves as a representative in Washington, DC, of community-based AIDS service organizations. Advocates, at the federal level, for more effective AIDS policy, legislation, and funding. Works collaboratively with AIDS Action Foundation, a national public policy research organization.

AIDS and Public Policy Journal. University Publishing Group, Inc., 138 W Washington St., Ste. 403-405 Hagerstown, MD 21740. Phone: 800-654-8188 or (240)420-0036 Fax: (240)420-0037 E-mail: sales@upgbooks.com • URL: http://www.upgbooks.com • Quarterly. Individuals, $59.00 per year; institutions, $115.00 per year.

AIDS and the Law. Margaret C. Jasper. Oceana Publications, 75 Main St. Dobbs Ferry, NY 10522. Phone: (914)693-8100 Fax: (914)693-0402 E-mail: info@oceanalaw.com • URL: http://www.oceanalaw.com • 2000. $27.50. Second edition. (Legal Almanac Series).

AIDS Benefits Handbook: Everything You Need to Know to Get Social Security, Welfare, Medicaid, Medicare, Food Stamps, Housing, Drugs, and Other Benefits. Thomas P. McCormack. Yale University Press, 302 Temple St. New Haven, CT 06511. Phone: 800-987-7323 or (203)432-0960 Fax: (203)432-0948 E-mail: customer.care@triliteral.org • URL: http://www.yale.edu/yup/ • 1990. $37.50.

AIDS Issues in the Workplace: A Response Model for Human Resource Management. Dale A. Masi. Greenwood Publishing Group, Inc., 88 Post Rd., W Westport, CT 06881. Phone: 800-225-5800 or (203)226-3571 Fax: (203)431-2214 E-mail: custserv@factsonfile.com • URL: http://www.greenwood.com • 1990. $64.95.

AIDS Law Today: A New Guide for the Public. Yale AIDS Law Project Staff and others. Yale University Press, 302 Temple St. New Haven, CT 06511. Phone: 800-987-7323 or (203)432-0960 Fax: (203)432-0948 E-mail: customer.care@triliteral.org • URL: http://www.yale.edu/yup/ • 1993. $20.00. Second edition.

AIDS Literature and Law Review. University Publishing Group, Inc., 138 W Washington St., Ste. 403-405 Hagerstown, MD 231740. Phone: 800-654-8188 or (240)420-0036 Fax: (240)420-0037 E-mail: sales@upgbooks.com • URL: http://www.upgbooks.com • Monthly. $225.00 per year. Contains abstracts of journal and newspaper articles. Formerly *AIDS Literature and News Review*.

AIDS Litigation Reporter (Acquired Immune Deficiency Syndrome): The National Journal of Record of AIDS-Related Litigation. Andrews Publications, 175 Strafford Ave., Bldg. 4, Suite 140 Wayne, PA 19087. Phone: 800-345-1101 or (610)622-0510 Fax: (610)622-0501 E-mail: customer@andrewspub.com • URL: http://www.andrewspub.com • Semimonthly. $951.00 per year. Newsletter. Provides reports on a wide variety of legal cases in which AIDS is a factor.

AIDS Policy and Law: The Biweekly Newsletter on Legislation, Regulation, and Litigation Concerning AIDS. LRP Publications, 747 Dresher Rd., Suite 500 Horsham, PA 19044. Phone: 800-341-7874 or (215)784-0860 Fax: (215)784-9639 E-mail: custserv@lrp.com • URL: http://www.lrp.com • 22 times a year. $514.00 per year. Newsletter for personnel managers, lawyers, and others.

AIDS Reference Guide: A Sourcebook for Planners and Decision Makers. Frances Fernald, editor. Atlantic Information Services, Inc., 1100 17th St., N. W., Suite 300 Washington, DC 20036-4601. Phone: 800-521-4323 or (202)775-9008 Fax: (202)331-9542 E-mail: customerserv@aispub.com • URL: http://www.aishealth.com • $448.00 Looseleaf Service. Two volumes. Includes twelve updates and twelve newsletters. Covers a wide range of AIDS topics, including "Employment Policies and Issues," "Legal Issues," "Financing Issues," "Impact on Healthcare Providers," "Global Issues," and "Legislative, Regulatory, and Governance Issues."

The AIER Chart Book. AIER Research Staff. American Institute for Economic Research, PO Box 1000 Great Barrington, MA 01230-1000. Phone: (413)528-1216 Fax: (413)528-0103 E-mail: info@aier.org • URL: http://www.aier.org • Annual. $4.00. A compact compilation of long-range charts ("Purchasing Power of the Dollar," for example, goes back to 1780) covering various aspects of the U. S. economy. Includes inflation, interest rates, debt, gold, taxation, stock prices, etc. (Economic Education Bulletin.)

AIHA Journal: Journal for the Science of Occupational and Environmental Health. American Industrial Hygiene Association, 2700 Prosperity Ave., Suite 250 Fairfax, VA 22031-4307. Phone: (703)849-8888 Fax: (703)207-3561 E-mail: infonet@aiha.org • URL: http://www.aiha.org • Bimonthly. Institutions, $185.00 per year.

AIIM Buying Guide. Association for Information and Image Management International Headquarters, 1100 Wayne Ave., Ste. 1100 Silver Spring, MD 20910. Phone: 800-477-2446 or (301)587-8202 Fax: (301)587-2711 E-mail: aiim@aiim.org • URL: http://www.aiim.org • Publication includes: List of approximately 460 manufacturers, software developers, suppliers, service companies, consultants, and systems integrators in the document management industry. Entries include: Company name, address, phone, product/service provided, product or sales contact, business descriptions, number of employees. Organization was formerly called National Micrographics Association.

AIIM - The Enterprise Content Management Association., 1100 Wayne Ave., Ste. 1100 Silver Spring, MD 20910. Phone: 800-477-2446 or (301)587-8202 Fax: (301)587-2711 E-mail: aiim@aiim.org • URL: http://www.aiim.org • Manufacturers, vendors, and individual users of information and image management equipment, products, and services. Holds special meetings for trade members and companies. Maintains speakers' bureau. Operates resource center. Compiles statistics.

AIM Global., 125 Warrendale-Bayne Rd., Ste. 100 Warrendale, PA 15086. Phone: (724)934-4470 Fax: (724)934-4495 E-mail: dan@aimglobal.org • URL: http://www.aimglobal.org • Serves as a trade association for the automatic identification data captures technology industry.

AIM, Inc., 125 Warrendale Bayne Rd. Warrendale, PA 15086. Phone: 800-338-0206 or (724)934-4470 Fax: (724)934-4495 E-mail: info@aimglobal.org • URL: http://www.aimglobal.org • Members are companies concerned with automatic identification and data capture, including bar code systems, magnetic stripes, machine vision, voice technology, optical character recognition, and systems integration technology.

Air and Expedited Motor Carriers Association.

Air and Waste Management Association.

Air and Waste Management Association Journal., One Gateway Center, 3rd Fl. Pittsburgh, PA 15222. Phone: 800-270-3444 or (412)232-3444 Fax: (412)232-3450 • URL: http://www.awma.org • Monthly. Individuals, $150.00 per year; institutions, $329.00 per year: nonprofit institutions, $229.00 per year. Includes annual *Directory of Governmental Air Pollution Agencies*.

Air Brake Association., 2098 E 10140 S, 2009 Oriole Trail, L.B. Sandy, UT 84092. Phone: (801)944-5270 Fax: (801)944-2916 E-mail: joefaust@comcast.net Railway air brake engineers, suppliers, supervisors, and air brake manufacturing engineers.

Air Cargo News. Air Cargo News, Inc., Borough Hall Station, PO Box 98 Portage, MI 49081. Phone: (718)651-3591 Monthly. $39.95 per year.

Air Cargo World: International Trends and Analysis., 980 Canton St., Bldg. 1, Ste. D Roswell, GA 30075. Phone: (770)642-9170 Fax: (770)642-9982 E-mail: customerservice@bizmedia.com • URL: http://www.aircargoworld.com • Monthly. $58.00 per year. Provides news and information concerning air freight carriers, freight forwarding, and cargo operations at airports.

Air Carrier Financial Statistics. U. S. Department of Transportation, Bureau of Transportation Statistics, 400 7th St., SW, Rm. 3103 Washington, DC 20590. Phone: 800-853-1351 E-mail: answers@bts.gov • URL: http://www.bts.gov • Quarterly. Contains profit and loss and asset information for specific airlines.

Air Carrier Industry Scheduled Service Traffic Statistics. U. S. Department of Transportation, 400 7th St., SW Washington, DC 20590. Phone: (202)366-4000 E-mail: dot.comments@ost.dot.gov • URL: http://www.dot.gov • Quarterly. Includes data for commuter airlines.

Air Carrier Traffic Statistics Monthly. U. S. Department of Transportation, 400 7th St., SW Washington, DC 20590. Phone: (202)366-4000 E-mail: dot.comments@ost.dot.gov • URL: http://www.dot.gov • Monthly. Provides passenger traffic data for large airlines.

Air-Conditioning and Refrigeration Institute.

Air Conditioning Contractors of America.

Air Conditioning, Heating, and Refrigeration News-Directory. Business News Publishing Co., 755 W. Big Beaver Rd., Suite 1000 Troy, MI 48084. Phone: 800-837-7370 or (248)362-3700 Fax: (248)362-0317 E-mail: tuttlea@bnp.com • URL: http://www.achrnews.com • Annual. $35.00.

Air Conditioning, Heating, and Refrigeration News: The HVACR Contractor's Weekly Newsmagazine. Business News Publishing Co., 755 W. Big Beaver Rd., Suite 1000 Troy, MI 48084. Phone: 800-837-7370 or (248)362-3700 Fax: (248)362-0317 • URL: http://www.bnp.com • Weekly. $87.00 per year. Includes *Supplement*.

Air Conditioning Testing-Adjusting-Balancing: A Field Practice Manual. John Gladstone. Engineers Press, P.O. Box 141651 Coral Gables, FL 33114-1651. Phone: (305)856-0031 1991. $44.95. Second edition.

Air Force Aid Society., 241 18th St. S, Ste. 202, Langley Air Force Base Arlington, VA 22202. Phone: 800-769-8951 or (703)607-3034 Fax: (703)607-3022 E-mail: dvosburg@afas.org • URL: http://www.afas.org • Collects and holds funds to relieve the distress of active, retired, and selected Reserve Air Force personnel and their dependents, including those of deceased personnel. Operates through local units on all major U.S. Air Force installations worldwide. Education Loan programs are offered to members, to assist in financing post-secondary education; education grants are also offered to dependent children of active duty, retired, and deceased Air Force members.

Air Force Association., 1501 Lee Hwy. Arlington, VA 22209-1198. Phone: 800-727-3337 or (703)247-5800 Fax: (703)247-5853 E-mail: polcom@afa.org • URL: http://www.afa.org • Promotes public understanding of aerospace power and the pivotal role it plays in the security of the nation.

Air Force Historical Foundation., 1535 Command Dr., Ste. A-122, 1535 Command Dr., Suite A-122 Andrews AFB, MD 20762-7002. Phone: (301)736-1959 Fax: (301)981-3574 E-mail: afhf@earthlink.net • URL: http://www.afhistoricalfoundation.com • Preserves the history of American air power and the annals of the U.S. Air Force, its components, subsidiaries, and affiliates. Collects and disseminates historical information on air subjects.

Air Force Journal of Logistics. Available from U. S. Government Printing Office, Washington, DC 20402. Phone: (202)512-1800 Fax: (202)512-2250 E-mail: gpoaccess@gpo.gov • URL: http://www.access.gpo.gov • Quarterly. $15.00 per year. Issued by the Air Force Logistics Management Center, Air Force Department, Defense Department. Presents research and information of interest to professional Air Force logisticians.

Air Force Magazine: The Force Behind the Force. Air Force Association, 1501 Lee Highway Arlington, VA 22209-1198. Phone: (703)247-5800 Fax: (703)247-5855 E-mail: afmag@afa.mag • URL: http://www.afa.org • Monthly. $30.00 per year.

Air Force Sergeants Association., 5211 Auth Rd. Suitland, MD 20746. Phone: 800-638-0594 or (301)899-3500 Fax: (301)899-8136 E-mail: staff@hqafsa.org • URL: http://www.hqafsa.org • Any enlisted man or woman, active or retired, in the Air Force, Air National Guard, Air Force Reserve, Army Air Corps, or Army Air Forces; women auxiliaries. Works to: promote, preserve, and uphold fair and equitable legislation as it pertains to the welfare of the airmen who served and are serving in the U.S.A.F.; maintain the highest professional standards and integrity among members; promote the interests of members, the U.S., and the rest of the "free world"; promote religious, educational, and recreational activities among members, in order to develop a better understanding and mutual respect. Sponsors educational seminars, Air Force training, JOBCAP - a job placement service, and programs for retired members. Provides congressional representation, insurance, and other services.

Air Force Times. Army Times Publishing Co., 6883 Commercial Dr. Springfield, VA 22159. Phone: 800-368-5718 or (703)750-8646 Fax: (703)750-8622 E-mail: cust-svc@atpco.com • URL: http://www.armytimes.com • Weekly. $52.00 per year. In two editions: Domestic and International. *Supplement* available.

Air Freight Directory. Air Cargo Inc., 1819 Bay Ridge Ave. Annapolis, MD 21403. Phone: (410)280-8911 Fax: (410)268-3154 E-mail: aiim@aiim.org Publication includes: Directory of more than 500 motor carriers contracting with Air Cargo, Inc. for delivery and pick up of freight. Air Cargo is a ground service specialist organization jointly owned by 18 major air carriers. Entries include: Airport city and code, firm name, address, phone, and services offered. Principal content of publication is chart of service points and rates.

Air Line Pilot; The Magazine of Professional Flight Deck Crews. Air Line Pilots Association, AFL-CIO, 535 Herndon Pky. Herndon, VA 20170. Phone: (703)689-2270 Fax: (703)689-4370 E-mail: alpaemail@alpa.org • URL: http://www.alpa.org • 10 times a year. $30.00 per year.

Air Line Pilots Association, International., 1625 Massachusetts Ave. NW Washington, DC 20036. Phone: (703)689-2270 Fax: (703)689-4370 E-mail: communications@alpa.org • URL: http://www.alpa.org • Conducts collective bargaining activities of airline pilots. Promotes all aspects of aviation safety and security.

Air Market News. General Publications Co., P.O. Box 480 Hatch, NM 87937-0408. Phone: (505)267-1030 Fax: (505)267-1920 Bimonthly. Free to qualified personnel. Subject matter is news of aircraft products and services.

Air Pollution Control. BNA, Inc., 1231 25th St., N.W. Washington, DC 20037. Phone: 800-372-1033 E-mail: customercare@bna.com • URL: http://www.bna.com • Biweekly. $798.00 per year. Newsletter.

Air Pollution Research Center. University of California, Riverside

Air Pollution Research Laboratory. University of Rhode Island

Air Quality Data. U.S. Environmental Protection Agency, Washington, DC 20460. Phone: 888-372-8255 or (202)564-9828 Annual.

Air Traffic Control Association., 1101 King St., Ste. 300 Alexandria, VA 22314. Phone: (703)299-2430 Fax: (703)299-2437 E-mail: info@atca.org • URL: http://www.atca.org • Air traffic controllers; private, commercial, and military pilots; private and business aircraft owners and operators; aircraft and electronics engineers; airlines, aircraft manufacturers, and electronic and human engineering firms. Promotes the establishment and maintenance of a safe and efficient air traffic control system. Conducts special surveys and studies on air traffic control problems. Participates in aviation community conferences.

Air Transport. Air Transport Association of America, 1301 Pennsylvania Ave., NW, Ste. 1100 Washington, DC 20004-1707. Phone: (202)626-4000 Fax: (202)626-4166 E-mail: ata@air-lines.org • URL: http://www.airlines.org • Annual. $20.00.

Air Transport Association of America.

Air Transport World. Penton Media Inc., 1300 E 9th St. Cleveland, OH 44114. Phone: (216)696-7000 Fax: (216)696-1752 E-mail: information@penton.com • URL: http://www.penton.com • Monthly. Free to qualified personnel, others, $55.00 per year. Includes supplement *World Airline Reports*.

Air Transportation: A Management Perspective. Alexander Wells. Brooks/Cole Publishing Co., 511 Forest Lodge Rd. Pacific Grove, CA 93950. Phone: 800-354-9706 or (831)373-0728 Fax: (831)375-6414 E-mail: info@brookcole.com • URL: http://www.brookscole.com • 1998. $81.95. Fourth edition.

Air University Library Index to Military Periodicals. U.S. Air Force, Air University Library Maxwell Air Force Base, AL 36112-6424. Phone: (334)953-2504 Fax: (334)953-1192 E-mail: mstewart@max1.au.af.mil • URL: http://www.au.af.mil/au/aul/aul.htm • Quarterly. Free to qualified personnel. Annual cumulation.

Aircraft Electronics Association., 4217 S Hocker Independence, MO 64055-0963. Phone: (816)373-6565 Fax: (816)478-3100 E-mail: info@aea.net • URL: http://www.aea.net • Companies engaged in the sales, engineering, installation, and service of electronic aviation equipment and systems. Seeks to: advance the science of aircraft electronics; promote uniform and stable regulations and uniform standards of performance; establish and maintain a code of ethics; gather and disseminate technical data; advance the education of members and the public in the science of aircraft electronics. Offers supplement type certificates, test equipment licensing, temporary FCC licensing for new installations, spare parts availability and pricing, audiovisual technician training, equipment and spare parts loan, profitable installation, and service facility operation. Provides employment information, equipment exchange information and service assistance on member installations anywhere in the world.

Aircraft, Engines, Parts, and Equipment Industry. Available from MarketResearch.com, 641 Ave. of the Americas, Fourth Floor New York, NY 10011. Phone: 800-298-5699 or (212)807-2629 Fax: (212)807-2642 E-mail: order@ marketresearch.com • URL: http://www.marketresearch.com • 2002. $4,450.00. Published by Global Industry Analysts. Provides worldwide market research data, including profiles of major aircraft and equipment companies.

Aircraft Owners and Pilots Association.

Airline Business Report. Access Intelligence L.L.C., 4 Choke Cherry Rd., 2nd Fl. Rockville, MD 20850. Phone: 800-777-5006 or (301)354-2000 Fax: (301)309-3847 E-mail: info@ accessintel.com • URL: http://www.pbimedia.com • Description: Reports on financial aspects of the world airline industry. **Remarks:** Also available online and via e-mail.

Airline Business: The Voice of Airline Managements. Available from Reed Aerospace, 333 North Fairfax St., Suite 301 Alexandria, VA 22314. Phone: (703)836-7444 Fax: (703)836-7446 • URL: http://www.airlinebusiness.com • Monthly. $130.00 per year. Published in England by Reed Business Information. Covers management and financial topics for international airline executives.

Airline Handbook. Aerotravel Research, PO Box 3694 Cranston, RI 02910. Phone: (401)941-6140 E-mail: aiim@aiim.org Covers: 2,000 commercial airlines (scheduled and chartered) serving over 200 nations and territories worldwide. Entries include: Airline name, address of main office, phone, telex, financial keys, number of employees, routes and destinations, aircraft fleets, passenger traffic totals, company history.

Airlines. Alexander T. Wells and Franklin D. Richey. Krieger Publishing Co., P.O. Box 9542 Melbourne, FL 32902-9542. Phone: 800-724-0025 or (321)724-9542 Fax: (321)951-3671 E-mail: info@krieger-publishing.com • URL: http://www. krieger-publishing.com • 1996. $275.00. Provides an overview of the commuter airline industry, including operating and management functions.

Airman: Official Magazine of the U.S. Air Force. Available from U.S. Government Printing Office, Washington, DC 20204. Phone: (202)512-1800 Fax: (202)512-2250 E-mail: gpoaccess@gpo.gov • URL: http://www.access.gpo.gov • Monthly. $41.00 per year.

Airport Activity Statistics of Certificated Route Air Carriers. U. S. Department of Transportation. Available from U. S. Government Printing Office, Washington, DC 20402. Phone: (202)512-1800 Fax: (202)512-2250 E-mail: gpoaccess@gpo. gov • URL: http://www.access.gpo.gov • Annual. $58.00.

Airport Business. Cygnus Business Media, 1233 Janesville Ave. Fort Atkinson, WI 53538. Phone: 800-308-6397 or (920)563-6388 Fax: (920)563-1707 E-mail: rich.reiff@cygnuspub.com • URL: http://www.cygnusbzb.com • 10 times a year. $55.00 per year.

Airport/Facility Directory. U.S. National Ocean Service, SSMC4, Rm. 13632, 1305 EW Hwy. Silver Spring, MD 20910. Phone: 800-638-8972 or (301)713-3060 E-mail: nos.info@noaa.gov • URL: http://www.nos.noaa.gov • Covers: Non-military airports in the continental United States; separate volumes cover the southeast, northeast, northwest, east central, north central, southwest, and south central states (including Puerto Rico and the Virgin Islands). Entries include: Airport name, location, weather service phone number, control center frequencies, and information concerning navigational and other aids and systems.

Airports Council International - North America., 1775 K St. NW, Ste. 500 Washington, DC 20006. Phone: 888-424-7767 or (202)293-8500 Fax: (202)331-1362 E-mail: memberservices@aci-na.org • URL: http://www.aci-na.org • Represents local, regional, and state governing organizations that own and operate commercial airports in the U.S., Canada, and Bermuda. Represents a variety of industries that provide products and services to the air transportation industry.

Airports: The Weekly for Airport Users, Managers, and Suppliers. Aviation Week Business Intelligence Services, 1200 G St., N.W., Suite 200 Washington, DC 20005. Phone: 800-752-4959 or (202)383-2350 Fax: (202)383-2438 • URL: http://www.aviationnow.com/bis • Weekly. $649.00 per year. Newsletter. Covers news of worldwide airport development, financing, operations, marketing, bidding, improvements, and personnel.

AISE Steel Technology. Association of Iron and Steel Engineers, Three Gateway Center, Suite 2350 Pittsburgh, PA 15222. Phone: (412)281-6323 Fax: (412)281-4657 E-mail: subscriptions@aise.org • URL: http://www.aise.org • Monthly. $58.00 per year. Formerly *Iron and Steel Engineer.*

AJM: Authority on Jewelry Manufacturing. Manufacturing Jewelers and Silversmiths of America, Inc. Skies America Publishing Co., 9655 SW, Sunshine Beaverton, OH 97005. Phone: (503)520-1955 E-mail: ajm@ajm-magazine.com • URL: http://www.ajm-magazine.com • Monthly. $42.00 per year.

Al-Anon Family Group Headquarters, World Service Office., 1600 Corporate Landing Pkwy. Virginia Beach, VA 23454-5617. Phone: 888-4AL-ANON or (757)563-1600 or (757)563-1600 Fax: (757)563-1655 E-mail: wso@al-anon. org • URL: http://www.al-anon.alateen.org • Offers a twelve-step program for the relatives and friends of individuals with an alcohol problem. Operates Alateen for members 12-18 years of age whose lives have been adversely affected by someone else's drinking problem, usually by parents.

ALA Handbook of Organization. American Library Association, 50 E. Huron St. Chicago, IL 60611-2795. Phone: 800-545-

2433 or (312)944-6780 Fax: (312)440-9374 E-mail: ala@ala. org • URL: http://www.ala.org • Annual. Free to members; non-members, $30.00. Includes information on ALA officers, committees, divisions, sections, round tables, and state chapters. (Issued as a supplement to *American Libraries.*)

ALA Survey of Librarian Salaries. American Library Association, 50 E. Huron St. Chicago, IL 60611-2795. Phone: 800-545-2433 or (312)944-6780 Fax: (312)440-9374 E-mail: ala@ala.org • URL: http://www.ala.org • Annual. $55.00. Provides data on salaries paid to librarians in academic and public libraries. Position categories range from beginning librarian to director.

Alabama Law Institute. University of Alabama

Alabama State Data Center. University of Alabama

Alberta Research Council, Inc.

Alcohol and Drug Problems at Work: The Shift to Prevention. International Labour Organization, 1828 L St., N.W., Suite 600 Washington, DC 20036-5121. Phone: (202)653-7652 Fax: (202)653-7687 E-mail: klee@ilo.org • URL: http://www.ilo.org/publns • 2003. $9.95. Discusses workplace substance abuse initiatives for both large and small businesses.

Alcohol Research and Health. Available from U. S. Government Printing Office, Washington, DC 20402. Phone: (202)512-1800 Fax: (202)512-2250 E-mail: gpoaccess@gpo.gov • URL: http://www.access.gpo.gov • Quarterly. $25.00 per year. Issued by the National Institute on Alcohol Abuse and Alcoholism. Presents alcohol-related research findings and descriptions of alcoholism prevention and treatment programs.

Alcoholic Beverage Control: State Capitals. Wakeman-Walworth Inc., PO Box 7376 Alexandria, VA 22307-7376. Phone: (703)768-9600 Fax: (703)768-9690 E-mail: newsletters@statecapitals.com • URL: http://www.statecapitals.com • 50 times a year. $245.00 per year; print and online editions, $350.00 per year. Formerly *From the State Capitals: Alcoholic Beverage Control.*

Alcoholics Anonymous World Services., PO Box 459, Grand Central Sta., 475 Riverside Dr., 11th Fl. New York, NY 10163. Phone: (212)870-3400 Fax: (212)870-3003 E-mail: wso@al-anon.org • URL: http://www.aa.org • Individuals recovering from alcoholism. Maintains that members can solve their common problem and help others achieve sobriety through a twelve step program that includes sharing their experience, strength, and hope with each other. Self-supported through members' contributions, not an allied with any sect, denomination, political organization, or institution and does not endorse nor oppose any cause.

Alcoholism: Clinical and Experimental Research. Research Society on Alcoholism. Lippincott Williams and Wilkins, 530 Walnut St. Philadelphia, PA 19106-3621. Phone: 800-527-5597 or (410)528-4000 Fax: (215)521-8902 E-mail: custserv@lww.com • URL: http://www.lww.com • Monthly. Individuals, $331.00 per year; institutions, $639.00 per year.

Alcoholism Digest Annual. Information Planning Associates, Inc., 5205 Leesburg Pke., Ste. 505 Falls Church, VA 22041-3404. Phone: (202)820-6100 Annual. Price on application.

Alcoholism: The Health and Social Consequences of Alcohol Use: An Annnotated Bibliography with Analytical Introduction. Cecilia M. Schmitz and Richard A. Gray. Pierian Press, PO Box 1808 Ann Arbor, MI 48106-1808. Phone: 800-678-2435 or (734)434-5530 Fax: (734)434-6409 E-mail: pubinfo@pierianpress.com • URL: http://www. pierianpress.com • 1998. $40.00. Provides detailed summaries of more than 100 significant books and major articles on the subject of alcoholism. (Science and Social Responsibility Series, No. 3.)

Alcoholism Treatment Quarterly: The Practitioner's Quarterly for Individual, Group, and Family Therapy. Haworth Press, Inc., 10 Alice St. Binghamton, NY 13904-1580. Phone: 800-429-6784 or (607)722-5857 Fax: 800-895-0582 or (607)722-1424 E-mail: getinfo@haworthpressinc.com • URL: http:// www.haworthpressinc.com • Quarterly. $535.00 per year. Edited for professionals working with alcoholics and their families. Formerly *Alcoholism Counseling and Treatment.*

All About Index Funds: A Guidebook to Investment Success. Richard A. Ferri. McGraw-Hill, 1221 Ave. of the Americas New York, NY 10020. Phone: 800-722-4726 or (212)512-2000 Fax: (212)512-4502 E-mail: customer.service@ mcgraw-hill.com • URL: http://www.mcgraw-hill.com • 2002. $16.95. States that index mutual funds "routinely outperform 80 percent of managed funds." (All About Series).

All About Medicare. The National Underwriter Co., 5081 Olympic Blvd. Erlanger, KY 41018. Phone: 800-543-0874 • URL: http://www.nationalunderwriter.com • Annual. $16.95.

All About Stock Market Strategies. David Brown and Kassandra Bentley. McGraw-Hill, 1221 Ave. of the Americas New York, NY 10020. Phone: 800-722-4726 or (212)512-2000 Fax: (212)512-4502 E-mail: customer.service@mcgraw-hill.com • URL: http://www.mcgraw-hill.com • 2002. $16.95. Describes various, conservative ways of trying to obtain better than average stock investment results. (All About Series).

All About Technical Analysis. Constance Brown. McGraw-Hill, 1221 Ave. of the Americas New York, NY 10020. Phone: 800-722-4726 or (212)512-2000 Fax: (212)512-4502 E-mail: customer.service@mcgraw-hill.com • URL: http://www. mcgraw-hill.com • 2002. $16.95. Provides basic information on the use of stock price charts for trend analysis and market forecasts.

All Hands: Magazine of the United States Navy. Available from U. S. Government Printing Office, Washington, DC 20402. Phone: (202)512-1800 Fax: (202)512-2250 E-mail: gpoaccess@gpo.gov • URL: http://www.access.gpo.gov • Monthly. $42.00 per year. Contains articles of general interest concerning the U. S. Navy (http://www.navy.mil).

All States Tax Guide. Prentice Hall PTR, 240 Frisch Ct. Paramus, NJ 07652. Phone: 800-282-0693 Fax: 800-445-6991 • URL: http://www.phptr.com • Looseleaf. Periodic supplementation. Price on application. One volume summary of taxes for all states.

All States Tax Handbook. RIA, 395 Hudson St. New York, NY 10014. Phone: 800-950-1216 or 800-431-9025 E-mail: riahome@riag.com • URL: http://www.riahome.com • Annual. $53.50. Tax structures for fifty states.

All You Need to Know About the Music Business: Revised and Updated for the 21st Century. Donald S. Passman. The Free Press, 1230 Ave. of the Americas New York, NY 10020. Phone: 800-223-2348 or (212)698-7000 Fax: 800-943-9831 or (212)698-7007 E-mail: consumer.customerservice@ simonandschuster.com • URL: http://www.simonsays.com • 2003. $30.00. Covers the practical and legal aspects of record contracts, music publishing, management agreements, touring, and other music business topics.

Alliance for Acid Rain Control and Energy Policy., 444 N. Capitol St., Ste. 602 Washington, DC 20001. Phone: (202)624-5475 Fax: (202)508-3829 E-mail: caomail@hr. house.gov Former and current U.S. governors, corporate executives, public interest leaders, and academicians who are concerned about conservation issues and national energy policy. Follows implementation of acid rain control legislation. Makes use of the findings of the Center for Clean Air Policy (see separate entry) to set specific emissions goals for states, industries, and utilities and suggest emissions-reducing tactics such as emiss ions trading among industries, use of clean coal by utilities, and more efficient use of energy by industrial and utility plants. Favors enactment of comprehensive national energy legislation, including increased energy efficiency, expanded domestic energy production, protection of the environment, and increased competition in energy markets.

Alliance for Community Media., 666 11th St., N.W., Suite 740 Washington, DC 20001. Phone: (202)393-2650 Fax: (202)393-2653 E-mail: acm@alliancecm.org • URL: http:// www.alliancecm.org • Formerly National Federation of Local Cable Programmers.

Alliance for Innovative Manufacturing., Stanford University, Bldg.02-530, Rm. 225 Stanford, CA 94305-3036. Phone: (650)723-9038 Fax: (650)723-5034 E-mail: cborn@stanford. edu • URL: http://www.stanford.edu/group/aim • Development of new products and processing. Formerly Stanford Integrated Manufacturing Association.

Alliance for Nonprofit Management., 1899 L St., NW, 6th Fl. Washington, DC 20036. Phone: (202)955-8406 Fax: (202)721-0086 E-mail: alliance@allianceonline.org • URL: http://www.allianceonline.org • Members are devoted to building the capacity of nonprofit organizations in order to increase their effectiveness.

Alliance of American Insurers.

Alliance of Motion Picture and Television Producers.

Alliance of Nonprofit Mailers.

Allied Artists of America.

Allied Pilots Association., 14600 Trinity Blvd., Ste. 500, O'Connell Bldg. Fort Worth, TX 76155-2512. Phone: 800-323-1470 or (817)302-2272 Fax: (817)302-2152 E-mail: public-comment@alliedpilots.org • URL: http://www. alliedpilots.org • Independent group originating from the Air Line Pilots Association. Collective bargaining agent for the pilots of American Airlines.

Allied Trades of the Baking Industry.

Alloys Index. CSA, 7200 Wisconsin Ave. Ste. 601 Bethesda, MD 20814. Phone: 800-843-7751 or (301)961-6700 Fax: (301)961-6720 E-mail: service@csa.com • URL: http://www. csa.com • Monthly. $775.00 per year. Includes print and on-line editions.

Almanac. Penton Media Inc., 1300 E. Ninth St. Cleveland, OH 44114. Phone: (216)696-7000 Fax: (216)696-1752 E-mail: information@penton.com • URL: http://www.penton.com • Annual. $50.00. Lists equipment, products, and services for the hotel and motel industry.

Almanac of American Politics. National Journal Group, Inc., 1501 M St., N.W., Suite 300 Washington, DC 20005. Phone: 800-424-2921 or (202)739-8400 Fax: (202)833-8069 • URL: http://www.nationaljournal.com • Biennial. $54.95. Includes biographies of U.S. senators and representatives, with group ratings, key votes, and election results.

Almanac of Business and Industrial Financial Ratios. Leo Troy. Aspen Publishers, Inc., 220 Orchard Ridge Dr., Ste. 200 Gaithersburg, MD 20878. Phone: 800-234-1600 or (301)417-7500 Fax: (301)695-7931 E-mail: customer.service@ aspenpubl.com • URL: http://www.aspenpublishers.com • 2003. $125.95. Includes CD-Rom. Contains financial ratios derived from federal tax returns. Ratios for each of about 200 industries are arranged according to company asset size. (Almanac of Business and Industrial Financial Ratios Series).

Almanac of Famous People. Gale Cengage Learning, 27500 Drake Rd. Farmington Hills, MI 48331-3535. Phone: 800-877-GALE or (248)699-GALE Fax: 800-414-5043 or (248)699-8069 E-mail: gale.galeord@cengage.com • URL:

http://gale.cengage.com • 2000. $145.00. Two volumes. Seventh edition. Contains about 30,000 short biographies, with bibliographic citations. Chronological, geographic, and occupational indexes. Formerly *Biography Almanac*.

Almanac of the Canning, Freezing, Preserving Industries, Vol. Two. Edward E. Judge and Sons, Inc., P.O. Box 866 Westminster, MD 21158. Phone: (410)876-2052 Fax: (410)848-2034 E-mail: info@eejudge.com • URL: http://www.eejudge.com • Annual. $73.00. Contains U. S. food laws and regulations and detailed production statistics.

The Almanac of the Executive Branch. Maximov Publications, 80 Park Ave. New York, NY 10016. Phone: (212)973-0488 Fax: (212)464-5970 E-mail: maximov@usa.net Annual. $149.00. Provides detailed information on more than 830 key staff memebers of the executive branch of the federal government. Includes educational background, previous employment, job responsibilities, etc.

Almanac of the Federal Judiciary. Aspen Publishers, Inc., 1185 Avenue of the Americas New York, NY 10036. Phone: 800-447-1717 or (212)597-0200 Fax: (212)597-0338 E-mail: customer.service@aspenpubl.com • URL: http://www.aspenpublisher.com • Annual. $295.00 per set. Two volumes. Volume one provides information on federal district judges; volume two relates to federal circuit judges.

Almanac of the Fifty States: Basic Data Profiles with Comparative Tables. Information Publications, 3790 El Camino Real Palo Alto, CA 94306. Phone: (650)965-4449 Fax: (650)965-3801 E-mail: infopubs@wenet.net • URL: http://www.wenet.net/users/infopubs • Annual. $65.00.

Almanac of the Unelected: Staff of the U. S. Congress. Bernan Associates, 200 E 32nd St., Ste. 13B New York, NY 10016. Phone: (212)251-0819 Fax: (212)251-1042 • URL: http://www.bernan.com • Annual. $275.00. Provides detailed information on key staff members of the legislative branch of the federal government. Includes educational background, previous employment, job responsibilities, etc.

Altered Fates: The Genetic Re-Engineering of Human Life. Jeff Lyon and Peter Gorner. W. W. Norton & Co., Inc., 500 5th Ave. New York, NY 10110. Phone: 800-223-2584 or (212)354-5500 Fax: (212)869-0856 • URL: http://www.wwnorton.com • 1995. $27.50. A discussion of recent progress in genetic engineering.

Alternative Energy Resources Organization., 432 N Last Chance Gulch Helena, MT 59601-5014. Phone: (406)443-7272 Fax: (406)442-9120 E-mail: aero@aeromt.org • URL: http://www.aeromt.org • Promotes sustainable agriculture, resource conservation and transportation choices through community education and citizen representation. Provides current programs that focus on sustainable agriculture, farm improvement clubs, beginning and retiring farmers, smart growth, and a more localized food system for greater community self-reliance.

Alternative Energy Retailer. Zackin Publications, Inc., P.O. Box 2180 Waterbury, CT 06722. Phone: 800-325-6745 • URL: http://www.zackin.com • Monthly. $32.00 per year.

Aluminum Association., 1525 Wilson Blvd., Ste. 600 Arlington, VA 22209. Phone: (703)358-2960 Fax: (703)358-2961 E-mail: slarkin@aluminum.org • URL: http://www.aluminum.org • Producers of aluminum and manufacturers of semi-fabricated aluminum products. Represents members' interests in legislative activity. Conducts seminars and workshops. Provides publications on aluminum technology and the aluminum industry. Sponsors competition; compiles statistics.

Aluminum Extruders Council., 1000 N Rand Rd., Ste. 214 Wauconda, IL 60084. Phone: (847)526-2010 Fax: (847)526-3993 E-mail: mail@aec.org • URL: http://www.aec.org • Manufacturers of extruded aluminum shapes and their suppliers. Compiles statistics; provides technical assistance and develops markets. Conducts workshops for management, sales, and plant personnel.

Aluminum Industry Abstracts: A Monthly Review of the World's Technical Literature on Aluminum. Aluminum Association., 900 19th St., NW Washington, DC 20006. Phone: (202)862-5100 Fax: (202)862-5164 E-mail: slarkin@aluminum.org • URL: http://www.aluminum.org • Monthly. $975.00 per year. Includes print and online editions. Formerly *World Aluminum Abstracts*.

Aluminum Standards and Data. Aluminum Association, 900 19th St., N.W., Suite 300 Washington, DC 20006. Phone: (202)862-5100 Fax: (202)862-5164 • URL: http://www.aluminum.org • Biennial. $25.00.

Aluminum Statistical Review. Aluminum Association, 900 19th St., N.W., Suite 300 Washington, DC 20006. Phone: (202)862-5100 Fax: (202)862-5164 • URL: http://www.aluminum.org • Annual. $50.00.

AM-Appliance Manufacturer Directory. Business News Publishing Co., 755 W Big Beaver Rd., Ste. 1000 Troy, MI 48084. Phone: 800-837-7370 or (248)362-3700 Fax: (248)362-0317 • URL: http://www.bnp.com • Annual. $25.00. Formerly *Appliance Manufacturer Directory*.

AM/FM Broadcast Financial Data/TV Broadcast Financial Data. U.S. Federal Communications Commission, Washington, DC 20554. Phone: 888-225-5322 or (202)418-0500 • URL: http://www.fcc.gov • Annual. Free.

AMA Handbook of Business Letters. Jeffrey L. Seglin and Edward Coleman. AMACOM, 1601 Broadway New York, NY 10019. Phone: 800-262-9699 or (518)586-8100 Fax: (518)903-8168 E-mail: customerservice@amanet.org • URL:

http://www.amacombooks.org • 2002. $69.95. Third edition. Includes audio compact disk. Contains 300 sample letters, with advice on business correspondence.

AMA International Member and Marketing Services Guide. American Marketing Association, 311 S. Wacker Dr., Suite 5800 Chicago, IL 60606-5819. Phone: 800-262-1150 or (312)542-9000 Fax: (312)542-9001 E-mail: info@ama.org • URL: http://www.ama.org • Annual. $150.00. Lists professional members of the American Marketing Association. Also contains information on providers of marketing support services and products, including software, communications, direct marketing, promotion, research, and consulting companies. Includes geographical and alphabetical indexes. Formerly *Marketing Yellow Pages and AMA International Membership Directory*.

AMA Management Handbook. John J. Hampton, editor. AMACOM, 1601 Broadway New York, NY 10019. Phone: 800-262-9699 or (518)586-8100 Fax: (518)903-8168 E-mail: customerservice@amanet.org • URL: http://www.amacombooks.org • 1994. $110.00. Third edition. Provides 200 chapters in 16 major subject areas. Covers a wide variety of business and industrial management topics.

The Amazing Internet Challenge: How Leading Projects Use Library Skills to Organize the Web. Amy T. Wells and others. American Library Association, 50 E. Huron St. Chicago, IL 60611-2795. Phone: 800-545-2433 or (312)944-6780 Fax: (312)440-9374 E-mail: ala@ala.org • URL: http://www.ala.org • 1999. $45.00. Presents profiles of 12 digital libraries, such as the Agriculture Network Information Center and the Social Science Information Gateway. Emphasis is on how online indexes were created.

Amber Waves. Available from U. S. Government Printing Office, Washington, DC 20402. Phone: (202)512-1800 Fax: (202)512-2250 E-mail: gpoaccess@gpo.gov • URL: http://www.access.gpo.gov • Quarterly. $38.00 per year. Replaces *Agricultural Outlook; Food Review*; and *Rural America*. Provides research and analysis from the U.S. Department of Agriculture's Economic Research Service. Includes economic data on agriculture, food, trade, and environmental factors.

AMCA Directory of Licensed Products. Air Movement and Control Association, 30 W. University Dr. Arlington Heights, IL 60004. Phone: (708)394-0150 Fax: (708)253-0088 Annual. Free. Lists member manufacturers of equipment and supplies for the air and movement control industry.

America at Work. AFL-CIO, Public Affairs Dept., 815 16th St., N.W. Washington, DC 20006. Phone: (202)637-5010 Fax: (202)637-6908 E-mail: atwork@aflcio.org • URL: http://www.aflcio.org • Monthly. Membership. Formerly *AFL-CIO News*.

America on Record: A History of Recorded Sound. Andre Millard. Cambridge University Press, 40 W. 20th St. New York, NY 10011-4211. Phone: 800-872-7423 or (212)924-3900 Fax: (212)691-3239 E-mail: orders@cup.org • URL: http://www.cup.org • 1995. $22.00.

American Academy of Actuaries

American Academy of Actuaries Yearbook. American Academy of Actuaries, 1100 17th St. NW, 7th Fl. Washington, DC 20036. Phone: (202)223-8196 Fax: (202)872-1948 E-mail: lawson@actuary.org • URL: http://www.actuary.org • Annual. $25.00

American Academy of Advertising

American Academy of Dental Group Practice.

American Academy of Dental Practice Administration., c/o Kathleen Uebel, 1063 Whippoorwill Lane Palatine, IL 60067-7064. Phone: (847)934-4404 Fax: (847)934-4410 E-mail: aadpa@aol.com • URL: http://www.aadpa.org • Professional society of dentists interested in efficient administration of dental practice. Offers educational programs.

American Academy of Family Physicians., 11400 Tomahawk Creek Parkway Leawood, MO 66211-2672. Phone: 800-274-2237 or (913)906-6000 Fax: (913)906-6077 E-mail: fp@aafp.org • URL: http://www.aafp.org • Formerly American Academy of General Practice.

American Academy of Matrimonial Lawyers., 150 N. Michigan Ave., Suite 2040 Chicago, IL 60601. Phone: (312)263-6477 Fax: (312)263-7682 E-mail: aaml@aaml.org • URL: http://www.aaml.org • Members are attorneys specializing in family law.

American Academy of Matrimonial Lawyers: List of Certified Fellows. American Academy of Matrimonial Lawyers, 150 N. Michigan Ave., Suite 2040 Chicago, IL 60601. Phone: (312)263-6477 Annual. Membership.

American Academy of Medical Administrators., 701 Lee St., Ste. 600 Des Plaines, IL 60016. Phone: (847)759-8601 Fax: (847)759-8602 E-mail: info@aameda.org • URL: http://www.aameda.org • Members are executives and middle managers in health care administration.

American Academy of Optometry., 6110 Executive Blvd., Suite 506 Bethesda, MD 20852. Phone: 800-368-6263 or (301)984-1441 Fax: (301)984-4737 E-mail: aaoptom@aol.com • URL: http://www.aaopt.org • Optometrists, educators and scientists interested in optometric education and standards of care in visual problems.

American Accounting Association., 5717 Bessie Dr. Sarasota, FL 34233-2330. Phone: (941)921-7747 Fax: (941)923-4093 E-mail: office@aaahq.org • URL: http://aaahq.org • Professors and practitioners of accounting. Promotes worldwide excellence in accounting education, research and practice.

American Advertising. American Advertising Federation, 1101 Vermont Ave., N.W., Suite 500 Washington, DC 20005. Phone: (202)898-0089 Fax: (202)898-0159 E-mail: acroot@aaf.org Quarterly. Membership.

American Advertising Federation., 1101 Vermont Ave. NW, Ste. 500 Washington, DC 20005-6306. Phone: 800-999-2231 or (202)898-0089 Fax: (202)898-0159 E-mail: aaf@aaf.org • URL: http://www.aaf.org • Works to advance the business of advertising as a vital and essential part of the American economy and culture through government and public relations; professional development and recognition; community service, social responsibility and high standards; and benefits and services to members. Operates Advertising Hall of Fame, Hall of Achievement, and National Student Advertising Competition. Maintains speakers' bureau.

American Agricultural Economics Association., 555 E Wells, Ste. 1100 Milwaukee, WI 53202. Phone: (414)918-3190 Fax: (414)276-3349 E-mail: info@aaea.org • URL: http://www.aaea.org • Professional society of agricultural economists. Serves to enhance the skills, knowledge and professional contribution of those economists who serve society by solving problems related to agriculture, food, resources and economic development. Offers placement service.

American Agricultural Editors' Association., PO Box 156, PO Box 156 New Prague, MN 56071. Phone: (952)758-6502 Fax: (952)758-5813 E-mail: ageditors@aol.com • URL: http://www.ageditors.com • Editors and editorial staff members of farm publications; affiliate members are agricultural public relations and advertising personnel, and state and national agricultural officials. Maintains the AAEA Professional Improvement Foundation. Conducts educational programs.

American Alliance for Health, Physical Education, Recreation, and Dance.

American Amusement Machine Association., 450 E Higgins Rd., Ste. 201 Elk Grove Village, IL 60007. Phone: (866)372-5190 or (847)290-9088 Fax: (847)290-9121 E-mail: information@coin-op.org • URL: http://www.coin-op.org • Manufacturers and distributors of coin machines; parts suppliers and others interested in promoting and protecting the amusement machine industry. Seeks solutions to the problem of copyright infringement by foreign manufacturers, and legislative and regulatory problems facing the industry and manufacturers. Works to improve the image of the coin-operated amusement industry. Presents views to governmental decision-makers. Operates American +Amusement Machine +Charitable Foundation.

American Apparel and Footwear Association., 1601 N. Kent St., Suite 1200 Arlington, VA 22209. Phone: 800-520-2262 or (703)524-1864 Fax: (703)522-6741 E-mail: mrhowell@apparelandfootwear.org • URL: http://www.americanapparel.org • Formerly American Apparel Manufacturers Associations.

American Apparel Machinery Trade Association., Sussman Automatic Products Corp., 43-20 34th St., 43-20 34th St. Long Island City, NY 11101. Phone: (718)937-4500 Fax: (718)786-4051 E-mail: sdale@sussmancorp.com Firms engaged in the industrial sewing machine industry, including manufacturers of sewing machines, tables, motors, accessories, parts, and related items.

American Apparel Manufacturers Association Directory of Members and Associate Members. American Apparel Manufacturers Association, 1601 N Kent St., Ste. 1200 Arlington, VA 22209-2105. Phone: 800-520-2262 or (703)524-1864 Fax: (703)522-6741 E-mail: jmorgan@americanapparel.org Annual. $100.00. Lists 900 clothing manufacturers and suppliers of goods and services to apparel manufacturers.

American Arbitration Association., 1633 Broadway, 10th Fl. New York, NY 10019. Phone: 800-778-7879 or (212)716-5800 Fax: (212)716-5905 E-mail: websitemail@adr.org • URL: http://www.adr.org • Works to achieve the resolution of disputes through the use of mediation, arbitration, democratic elections, and other voluntary methods. Provides administrative services for arbitrating, mediating, or negotiating disputes and impartial administration of elections. Maintains National Roster of Arbitrators and Mediators for referrals to parties involved in disputes. Conducts skill-building sessions to promote a more complete understanding of conflict resolution processes.

American Architectural Manufacturers Association., 1827 Walden Office Sq., Ste. 550 Schaumburg, IL 60173-4287. Phone: (847)303-5664 Fax: (847)303-5774 E-mail: rwalker@aamanet.org • URL: http://www.aamanet.org • Provides performance standards, product certification and educational programs for the fenestration industry, including product testing and market research.

American Art Directory. LexisNexis Group, PO Box 933 Dayton, OH 45401-0933. Phone: 800-227-9597 or (937)865-6800 Fax: (518)487-3584 E-mail: customer.support@lexisnexis.com • URL: http://www.lexisnexis.com • Covers: over 7,000 museums, art libraries, and art organizations, and 1,700 art schools; also includes lists of state directors and supervisors of art education in schools, traveling exhibition booking agencies, corporations having art holdings for public viewing, newspapers that carry art notes, art scholarships and fellowships; and 190 national, regional, and state open art exhibitions. Entries include: For museums—Name, address, phone, fax, electronic mail address, name of curator; days and hours of operation, collection, budget, publications. For exhibits—Name, address, phone, fax, electronic mail address, name of contact; date, deadline. For schools—Name, address, phone, name of director, names of faculty members, majors or degrees offered, tuition fees; summer school or adult hobby class information. For newspapers—Name, address, phone, name of art editor.

American Artists Professional League., 47 5th Ave. New York, NY 10003. Phone: (212)645-1345 Fax: (212)645-1345 E-mail: aaplinc@gmail.com • URL: http://www.americanartistsprofessionalleague.org • Advances the cause of fine arts in America through the promotion of high standards of beauty, integrity and craftsmanship in painting, sculpture and the graphic arts.

American Association for Adult and Continuing Education.

American Association for Adult and Continuing Education: Membership Directory. American Association for Adult and Continuing Education, 4380 Forbes Blvd. Lanham, MD 20706. Phone: (301)918-1913 Fax: (301)918-1846 E-mail: aaace10@aol.com • URL: http://www.aaace.org • Annual. Price on application.

American Association for Affirmative Action.

American Association for Artificial Intelligence.

American Association for Continuity of Care., P.O. Box 532 Dunedin, FL 34697. Phone: (727)738-1030 Fax: (727)738-8099 • URL: http://www.continuityofcare.com • Members are professionals concerned with continuity of care, health care after hospital discharge, and home health care.

American Association for Public Opinion Research., P.O. Box 14263 Lenexa, KS 66285-4263. Phone: (913)310-0118 Fax: (913)310-5340 E-mail: aapor-info@goamp.com • URL: http://www.aapor.org • Members are individuals interested in methods and applications of opinion research.

American Association of Advertising Agencies.

American Association of Airport Executives.

American Association of Bioanalysts., 917 Locust St., Suite 1100 St. Louis, MO 63101-1419. Phone: (314)241-1445 Fax: (314)241-1449 E-mail: aab@aab.org • URL: http://www.aab.org • Members are owners and managers of bioanalytical clinical laboratories. Affiliated with American Board of Bioanalysis.

American Association of Collegiate Registrars and Admissions Officers.

American Association of Community Colleges.

American Association of Community Colleges Directory. American Association of Community Colleges, One Dupont Circle, N.W. Suite 410 Washington, DC 20036-1176. Phone: (202)728-0200 Fax: (202))833-2467 E-mail: bookstore@aacc.nche.edu • URL: http://www.aacc.nche.edu • Annual. $35.00. Formerly *Community, Junior and Technical College Directory*.

American Association of Cosmetology Schools/Cosmetology Educators of America.

American Association of Exporters and Importers.

American Association of Fund-Raising Counsel.

American Association of Handwriting Analysts.

American Association of Health Plans., 1129 20th St., N.W., Suite 600 Washington, DC 20036-3421. Phone: (202)728-3200 Fax: (202)331-7487 E-mail: aahp@aahp.org • URL: http://www.aahp.org • Supports the managed health care industry.

American Association of Healthcare Consultants., Five Revere Dr., Suite 200 Northbrook, IL 60062. Phone: 888-350-2242 E-mail: info@aahc.net • URL: http://www.aahc.net • Members are professional consultants who specialize in the health care industry. Formerly American Association of Hospital Consultants.

American Association of Homes and Services for the Aging., 2519 Conneticut Ave., N.W. Washington, DC 20008-1520. Phone: (202)783-2242 Fax: (202)783-2255 E-mail: info@aahsa.org • URL: http://www.aahsa.org • Committed to advancing the vision of healthy, affordable, ethical aging services for America. Formerly American Association of Homes of the Aging.

American Association of Individual Investors.

American Association of Industrial Management.

American Association of Managing General Agents.

American Association of Meat Processors.

American Association of Motor Vehicle Administrators.

American Association of Motor Vehicle Administrators: Membership Directory. American Association of Motor Vehicle Administrators, 4301 Wilson Blvd., Suite 400 Arlington, VA 22203. Phone: (703)522-4200 Fax: (703)522-1553 Annual. $100.00.

American Association of Port Authorities.

American Association of Preferred Provider Organizations., PO Box 429 Jeffersonville, IN 47131-0429. Phone: 800-642-2515 or (812)246-4376 Fax: (812)246-4630 E-mail: kgreenrose@aappo.org • URL: http://www.aappo.org • Formerly Association of Managed Healthcare Organizations.

American Association of Retired Persons.

American Association of School Administrators.

American Association of School Librarians., 50 E. Huron St. Chicago, IL 60611. Phone: 800-545-2433 or (312)280-4386 Fax: (312)664-7459 E-mail: aasl@ala.org • URL: http://www.ala.org/aasl • A division of the American Library Association.

American Association of State Highway and Transportation Officials.

American Association of Textile Chemists and Colorists.

American Association of University Administrators.

American Association of University Professors.

American Association of University Women.

American Astronautical Society., 6352 Rolling Mill Pl., Ste. 102 Springfield, VA 22152-2354. Phone: (703)866-0020 Fax: (703)866-3526 E-mail: aas@astronautical.org • URL: http://www.astronautical.org • Network of space professionals, technical and non-technical. Researchers, scientists, executives, educators, and other professionals in the field of astronautics and related areas. Promotes and supports research related to the development of astronautical sciences. Offers scholarships. Participates in student science fairs.

American Automatic Control Council., Northwestern University, 2145 Sheridan Rd., 3640 Col Glenn Highway Evanston, IL 60208-3118. Phone: (937)775-5062 Fax: (937)775-3936 E-mail: ahaddad@eec.nwv.edu • URL: http://www.a2c2.org • Control engineering divisions of: American Institute of Aeronautics and Astronautics, American Institute of Chemical Engineers, American Society of Mechanical Engineers, Association of Iron and Steel Engineers, Institute of Electrical and Electronics Engineers, Instrument Society of America, and Society for Computer Simulation International (see separate entries). Covers the field of automatic control including control of manufacturing processes, computer control, process control, navigation, and guidance.

American Automobile Association., One River Pl. Wilmington, DE 19801. Phone: 800-763-9900 or (302)299-4700 Fax: (407)444-8030 E-mail: ahaddad@eec.nwv.edu • URL: http://www.aaa.com • Federation of automobile clubs (1,000 offices) providing domestic and foreign travel services, emergency road services, and insurance. Sponsors public services for traffic safety, better highways, more efficient and safer cars, energy conservation, and improvement of motoring and travel conditions.

American Automotive Leasing Association., 675 N Washington St., Ste. 410 Alexandria, VA 22314. Phone: (703)548-0777 Fax: (703)548-1925 E-mail: peters@aalafleet.com • URL: http://www.aalafleet.com • Represents the commercial automotive fleet leasing and management industry.

American Bakers Association., 1300 I St. NW, Ste. 700 W Washington, DC 20005. Phone: (202)789-0300 Fax: (202)898-1164 E-mail: info@americanbakers.org • URL: http://www.americanbakers.org • Manufacturers and wholesale distributors of bread, rolls, and pastry products; suppliers of goods and services to bakers. Conducts seminars and expositions.

American Banker Full Text. American Banker-Bond Buyer, Database Services, One State St. Plaza New York, NY 10004. Phone: 800-221-1809 or (212)967-7000 Fax: (212)843-9600 Provides complete text online of the daily *American Banker*. Inquire as to online cost and availability.

American Banker: The Financial Services Daily. Thomson Media, One State St. Plaza New York, NY 10004. Phone: 800-221-1809 or (212)803-8200 Fax: (212)843-9635 E-mail: custserv@thomsonmedia.com • URL: http://www.thomsonmedia.com • Daily. $895.00 per year. Provides news of banking, investment products, mortgages, credit unions, finance, bank technology, and legal developments.

American Bankers Association., 1120 Connecticut Ave. NW Washington, DC 20036. Phone: 800-BAN-KERS or (202)663-5000 Fax: (202)663-7543 E-mail: custserv@aba.com • URL: http://www.aba.com • Members are principally commercial banks and trust companies; combined assets of members represent approximately 90% of the U.S. banking industry; approximately 94% of members are community banks with less than $500 million in assets. Seeks to enhance the role of commercial bankers as preeminent providers of financial services through communications, research, legal action, lobbying of federal legislative and regulatory bodies, and education and training programs. Serves as spokesperson for the banking industry; facilitates exchange of information among members. Maintains the American Institute of +Banking, an industry-sponsored adult education program. Conducts educational and training programs for bank employees and officers through a wide range of banking schools and national conferences. Maintains liaison with federal bank regulators; lobbies Congress on issues affecting commercial banks; testifies before congressional committees; represents members in U.S. postal rate proceedings. Serves as secretariat of the International Monetary Conference and the Financial Institutions Committee for the American National Standards Institute. Files briefs and lawsuits in major court cases affecting the industry. Conducts teleconferences with state banking associations on such issues as regulatory compliance; works to build consensus and coordinate activities of leading bank and financial service trade groups. Provides services to members including: public advocacy; news media contact; insurance program providing directors and officers with liability coverage, financial institution bond, and trust errors and omissions coverage; research service operated through ABA Center for Banking Information; fingerprint set processing in conjunction with the Federal Bureau of Investigation; discounts on operational and income-producing projects through the Corporation for American Banking. Conducts conferences, forums, and workshops covering subjects such as small business, consumer credit, agricultural and community banking, trust management, bank operations, and automation. Sponsors ABA Educational Foundation and the Personal +Economics Program, which educates schoolchildren and the community on banking, economics, and personal finance.

American Bankers Association Key to Routing Numbers. American Bankers Association. Thomas Financial Publishing, 4709 W Golf Rd. Skokie, IL 60076. Phone: 800-321-3373 or (847)676-9600 Fax: (847)933-8101 E-mail: customerservice@tfp.com • URL: http://www.tfp.com • Annual. $169.00. per year. Lists over 30,000 finanical institutions in the U.S. and their routing members.

American Bankruptcy Institute., 44 Canal Center Plz., Ste. 400 Alexandria, VA 22314. Phone: (703)739-0800 Fax: (703)739-1060 E-mail: sgerdano@abiworld.org • URL: http://www.abiworld.org • Attorneys, accountants, and other providers of financial services, lending institutions, credit organizations, consumer groups, federal and state governments, and other interested individuals. Provides a multidisciplinary forum for the exchange of information on bankruptcy and insolvency issues. Fosters dialogue among lawyers, businesspersons, and legislators on current and potential bankruptcy problems. Reviews existing and proposed legislation as it affects bankruptcy and insolvency. Conducts nationally televised panel discussions and research projects; provides information to the public and legislators. Maintains speakers bureau; compiles statistics. Conducts research and educational programs.

American Bankruptcy Law Journal. National Conference of Bankruptcy Judges, 235 Secret Cove Dr. Lexington, SC 29072. Phone: (803)957-6225 • URL: http://www.ncbj.org • Quarterly. $65.00.

American Bar Association., 321 N Clark St. Chicago, IL 60610. Phone: 800-285-2221 or (312)988-5000 Fax: (312)988-5522 E-mail: askaba@abanet.org • URL: http://www.abanet.org • Attorneys in good standing of the bar of any state. Conducts research and educational projects and activities to: encourage professional improvement; provide public services; improve the administration of civil and criminal justice; increase the availability of legal services to the public. Sponsors Law Day USA. Administers numerous standing and special committees such as Committee on +Soviet and +East +European +Law, providing seminars and newsletters. Operates 25 sections, including Criminal Justice, Economics of Law Practice, and Family Law. Sponsors essay competitions. Maintains library.

American Bar Association—Directory. American Bar Association, 321 N Clark St. Chicago, IL 60610. Phone: 800-285-2221 or (312)988-5000 Fax: (312)988-5177 E-mail: service@abanet.org • URL: http://www.abanet.org • Covers: Approximately 7,500 lawyers active in the affairs of the Association, including officers, members of Boards of Governors and House of Delegates, section officers and council members, committee leaders, headquarters staff, state and local bars, affiliated and other legal organizations. Entries include: Section, council, or other unit name; names, addresses, and phone numbers of officers or chairpersons and members.

American Bearing Manufacturers Association., 2025 M St. NW, Ste. 800 Washington, DC 20036-2422. Phone: (202)367-1155 Fax: (202)367-2155 E-mail: info@americanbearings.org • URL: http://www.abma-dc.org • Represents manufacturers of anti-friction bearings, balls, and rollers and major components used in anti-friction bearings. Promotes bearing standardization.

American Bee Journal. Dadant and Sons, Inc., 51 S Second St. Hamilton, IL 62341. Phone: (217)847-3324 Fax: (217)847-3660 E-mail: abj@dadant.com • URL: http://www.dadant.com • Monthly. $22.25 per year. Magazine for hobbyist and professional beekeepers.

American Beekeeping Federation., PO Box 1337 Jesup, GA 31598-1038. Phone: (912)427-4233 Fax: (912)427-8447 E-mail: info@abfnet.org • URL: http://www.abfnet.org • Commercial and avocational beekeepers, suppliers, bottlers, packers, and others affiliated with the honey industry. Promotes the industry and serves as an representative before legislative bodies; makes recommendations and helps secure appropriations for research programs. Operates the Honey Defense Fund, which works to insure the purity of honey marketed in the U.S. Sponsors American Honey Queen Program.

American Beekeeping Federation Newsletter. American Beekeeping Federation, Inc., 115 Morning Glory Dr., PO Box 1337 Jesup, GA 31598-1337. Phone: (912)427-4233 Fax: (912)427-8447 E-mail: info@abfnet.org • URL: http://www.abfnet.org • Bimonthly. $25.00 per year. Newsletter.

American Behavioral Scientist. Sage Publications, Inc., 2455 Teller Rd. Thousand Oaks, CA 91320. Phone: 800-818-7243 or (805)499-9774 Fax: 800-583-2665 or (805)499-0871 E-mail: webmaster@sagepub.com • URL: http://www.sagepub.com • Monthly. Institutions, $1,139.00 per year.

American Bench: Judges of the Nation. Forster Long, Inc., 3280 Ramos Circle Sacramento, CA 95827. Phone: 800-328-5091 or (916)362-3276 Fax: (916)362-5643 E-mail: editorial@forster-long.com Annual. $395.00. Features biographies of 18,000 members of the U.S. Judiciary at federal, state and local levels.

American Benefits Council., 1212 New York Ave. NW, Ste. 1250 Washington, DC 20005-3987. Phone: (202)289-6700 Fax: (202)289-4582 E-mail: info@abcstaff.org • URL: http://

www.americanbenefitscouncil.org • Serves as national trade association for companies concerned about federal legislation and regulations affecting all aspects of the employee benefits system. Represents the entire spectrum of the private employee benefits community and sponsors or administers retirement and health plans covering more than one hundred million Americans.

American Beverage Association., 1101 16th St. NW Washington, DC 20036-4803. Phone: (202)463-6732 Fax: (202)659-5349 E-mail: info@ameribev.org • URL: http://www.ameribev.org • Active members are bottlers and distributors of soft drinks and franchise companies; associate members are suppliers of materials and services. Conducts government affairs activities on the national and state levels, discussion of industry problems, and general improvement of operating procedures. Conducts research on beverage laws.

American Beverage Licensees., 5101 River Rd., Ste. 108 Bethesda, MD 20816-1560. Phone: 888-656-3241 or (301)656-1494 Fax: (301)656-7539 E-mail: wiles@ablusa.org • URL: http://www.ablusa.org • Federation of associations of alcohol beverage retailers.

American Bicyclist. Willow Publishing Co., 400 Skokie Blvd. Northbrook, IL 60062-2816. Phone: (847)291-1117 Fax: (847)559-4444 Monthly. Free to qualified personnel; others, $35.00 per year. Trade journal edited for bicycle retailers and wholesalers. Includes product reviews.

American Big Businesses Directory. infoUSA Inc., 5711 S 86th Cir., PO Box 27347 Omaha, NE 68127. Phone: 800-321-0869 or (402)593-4500 Fax: (402)331-1505 E-mail: help@infousa.com • URL: http://www.abii.com • Covers: 218,000 U.S. businesses with more than 100 employees, and 500,000 key executives and directors. CD-ROM version contains 160,000 top firms and 431,000 key executives. Entries include: Name, address, phone, names and titles of key personnel, number of employees, sales volume, Standard Industrial Classification (SIC) codes, subsidiaries and parent company names, stock exchanges on which traded.

American Blue Book of Funeral Directors. Kates-Boylston Publications, Inc., 1255 Rte. 70, Ste. 31-S Lakewood, NJ 08701. Phone: 800-500-4585 E-mail: customer@ucq.com • URL: http://www.kates-boylston.com • Biennial. $75.00. About 24,000 funeral homes primarily in the United States and Canada.

American Board of Medical Specialties., 1007 Church St., Suite 404 Evanston, IL 60201-5913. Phone: (847)491-9091 Fax: (847)328-3596 E-mail: info@abms.org • URL: http://www.abms.org/abms • Functions as the parent organization for U. S. medical specialty boards. Supersedes Advisory Board for Medical Specialties.

American Board of Ophthalmology.

American Board of Professional Liability Attorneys., 5712 244th St. Douglaston, NY 11362. Phone: (718)631-1400 Fax: (717)631-1456 E-mail: abpla03@aol.com • URL: http://www.abpla.org • Members are liability litigation lawyers who meet specific requirements as to experience and who pass written and oral Board examinations.

American Boat and Yacht Council.

American Boat Builders and Repairers Association.

American Book Prices Current. Bancroft-Parkman, Inc., P.O. Box 1236 Washington, CT 06793. Phone: (860)868-7408 Fax: (860)868-0080 E-mail: abpc@snet.net • URL: http://www.bookpricescurrent.com • Annual. $119.95.

American Book Publishing Record: Arranged by Dewey Decimal Classification and Indexed by Author, Title, and Subject. R. R. Bowker, 630 Central Ave. New Providence, NJ 07974. Phone: 800-526-9537 or (908)286-1090 Fax: (908)219-0098 E-mail: info@bowker.com • URL: http://www.bowker.com • Monthly. $395.00 per year. Includes annual cumulation.

American Book Trade Directory. Information Today Inc., 143 Old Marlton Pke. Medford, NJ 08055-8750. Phone: 800-300-9868 or (609)654-6266 Fax: (609)654-4309 E-mail: custserv@infotoday.com • URL: http://www.infotoday.com • Covers: Nearly 25,500 retail and antiquarian book dealers, plus 1,200 book and magazine wholesalers, distributors, and jobbers-in all 50 states and U.S. territories. Also included are sections of auctioneers of literary property, exporters/importers, booktrade associations, foreign language book dealers, book and literary appraisers, and rental library chains. Entries include: Bookstore name, address, phone, owner or manager, types and subjects of books stocked, specialty, sidelines, year established, SAN (Standard Address Number), number of volumes stocked, square footage.

American Booksellers Association., 200 White Plains Rd., Ste. 600 Tarrytown, NY 10591. Phone: 800-637-0037 or (914)591-2665 Fax: (914)591-2720 E-mail: info@bookweb.org • URL: http://www.bookweb.org • Seeks to meet the needs of members, independently owned bookstores with storefront locations, through education, information dissemination, and advocacy. Supports free speech, literacy, and programs that encourage reading.

American Bureau of Metal Statistics., P.O. Box 805 Chatham, NJ 07928. Phone: (973)701-2299 Fax: (973)701-2152 E-mail: info@abms.com • URL: http://www.abms.com • Members are metal companies. Compiles and publishes detailed statistical data on a wide variety of nonferrous metals: aluminum, copper, gold, lead, nickel, platinum, silver, tin, titanium, uranium, zinc, and others.

American Bureau of Shipping.

American Bureau of Shipping-ABS International Directory of Offices. American Bureau of Shipping, 16855 Northchase Dr. Houston, TX 77060. Phone: (281)877-6000 Fax: (281)877-5803 E-mail: abs-worldhq@eagle.org • URL: http://www.eagle.org • Annual. $520.00 per year. Quarterly supplements.

American Bus Association., 700 13th St. NW, Ste. 575 Washington, DC 20005-5923. Phone: 800-283-2877 or (202)842-1645 Fax: (202)842-0850 E-mail: abainfo@buses.org • URL: http://www.buses.org • Privately owned bus-operating firms engaged in intercity, local, charter, and tour service; state associations; motor bus manufacturers; oil, gas and tire distributors and other suppliers; travel/tourism industry destinations, attractions and organizations. Represents almost 900 motorcoach and tour operators in the United States and Canada. Its members operate charter, tour, regular route, airport express, special operations and some contract services (commuter, school transit). Another 2,400 member organizations represent the travel and tourism industry and supplies of bus products and services that work in partnership with the North American motorcoach industry. Delineates the business concerns of both U.S. and Canadian, privately owned motorcoach and tour operators. Serves the U.S. bus industry in Washington, DC and supports the government affairs activities of its Canadian members and counterpart associations. Facilitates relationships between the North American motorcoach industry and all related segments of the travel and supplier industry. In addition, it creates awareness of the motorcoach industry among consumers in North America (USA, Canada and Mexico), and communicates publicly on important issues like motorcoach and highway safety.

American Business Climate and Economic Profiles. Priscilla C. Geahigan. Gale Cengage Learning, 27500 Drake Rd. Farmington Hills, MI 48331-3535. Phone: 800-877-GALE or (248)699-GALE Fax: 800-414-5043 E-mail: gale.galeord@cengage.com • URL: http://www.galegroup.com • 1993. $170.00. Provides business, industrial, demographic, and economic figures for all states and 300 metropolitan areas. Includes production, taxation, population, growth rates, labor force data, incomes, total sales, etc.

American Business Directory. InfoUSA, Inc., 5711 South 86th Circle Omaha, NE 68127. Phone: 800-321-0869 or (402)930-3500 Fax: (402)331-0176 E-mail: help@infousa.com Provides brief online information on more than 10 million U. S. companies, including individual plants and branches. Entries typically include address, phone number, industry classification code, and contact name. Updating is quarterly. Inquire as to online cost and availability.

American Business Leaders: From Colonial Times to the Present. Neil A. Hamilton. ABC-CLIO, Inc., 130 Cremona Dr. Santa Barbara, CA 93117. Phone: 800-368-6868 or (805)968-1911 Fax: (805)685-9685 E-mail: customerservice@abc-clio.com • URL: http://www.abc-clio.com • 1999. $175.00. Two volumes. Contains biographies of 413 notable business figures. Historical coverage is from the 17th century to the 1990s.

American Business Press., 675 Third Ave., Suite 415 New York, NY 10017. Phone: (212)661-6360 Fax: (212)370-0736 E-mail: info@abumail.com • URL: http://www.americanbusinesspress.com • Members are publishers of business and technical periodicals with audited circulation. Includes a Publishing Management Committee.

American Business Values: With International Perspectives. Gerald F. Cavanaugh. Prentice Hall PTR, 240 Frisch Ct. Paramus, NJ 07652. Phone: 800-282-0693 Fax: 800-445-6991 • URL: http://www.phptr.com • 1997. $48.00. Fourth edition.

American Business Women's Association., PO Box 8728, PO Box 8728 Kansas City, MO 64114-0728. Phone: 800-228-0007 or (816)361-6621 Fax: (816)361-4991 E-mail: abwa@abwa.org • URL: http://www.abwa.org • Women in business, including women owning or operating their own businesses, women in professions, and women employed in any level of government, education, or retailing, manufacturing, and service companies. Provides opportunities for businesswomen to help themselves and others grow personally and professionally through leadership, education, networking support, and national recognition. Offers leadership training, business skills training and business education; special membership options for retired businesswomen and the Company Connection for business owners, a resume service, credit card and programs, various travel and insurance benefits. Sponsors American Business Women's Day and National Convention and regional conferences held annually.

American Butter Institute., 2101 Wilson Blvd., Ste. 400 Arlington, VA 22201. Phone: (703)243-5630 Fax: (703)841-9328 E-mail: aminer@nmpf.org • URL: http://www.butterinstitute.org • Represents butter manufacturers, processors, packagers, and distributors based on volume. Aims to promote and protect the interests and welfare of the butter industry.

American Camp Association., 5000 State Rd., 67 N Martinsville, IN 46151-7902. Phone: 800-428-CAMP or (765)342-8456 Fax: (765)342-2065 E-mail: psmith@acacamps.org • URL: http://www.acacamps.org • Camp owners, directors, program directors, businesses, and students interested in resident and day camp programming for youth and adults. Conducts camp standards. Offers educational programs in areas of administration, staffing, child development, promotion, and programming.

American Cement Directory. Bradley Pulverizer Co., 123 S 3rd St., PO Box 1318 Allentown, PA 18105-1318. Phone: 800-355-1186 or (610)434-5191 Fax: (610)770-9400 E-mail: info@bradleypulverizer.com • URL: http://www.bradleypulv.com • Covers: Approximately 100 cement manufacturing companies in the United States, Canada, Mexico, Central and South America. Entries include: Company Name, address, phone, fax, names of principal executives, capacity, capitalization, brand names and process, plant locations.

American Ceramic Society., 600 N Cleveland Ave., Ste. 210 Westerville, OH 43082. Phone: (866)721-3322 or (240)646-7054 Fax: (301)206-9789 E-mail: customerservice@ceramics.org • URL: http://www.ceramics.org • Professional society of scientists, engineers, educators, plant operators, and others interested in the glass, cements, refractories, nuclear ceramics, whitewares, electronics, engineering, and structural clay products industries. Disseminates scientific and technical information through its publications and technical meetings. Conducts continuing education courses and training such as the Precollege Education Program. Sponsors over 10 meetings yearly; encourages high school and college students' interest in ceramics. Maintains Ross C. Purdy Museum of Ceramics; offers placement service and speakers' bureau.

American Ceramic Society Bulletin. American Ceramic Society, PO Box 6136 Westerville, OH 43086-6136. Phone: (614)890-4700 Fax: (614)899-6109 E-mail: info@ceramics.org • URL: http://www.ceramics.org • Monthly. Members, $50.00 per year; non-members, $100.00 per year.

American Ceramic Society Journal. American Ceramic Society, PO Box 6136 Westerville, OH 43086-6136. Phone: (614)890-4700 Fax: (614)899-6109 E-mail: info@ceramics.org • URL: http://www.ceramics.org • Monthly. Members, $150.00 per year; non-members, $750.00 per year. Includes subscription to *Ceramic Bulletin and Abstracts*.

American Chain of Warehouses.

American Chain of Warehouses-Membership Directory. American Chain of Warehouses, 156 Flamingo Dr. Beecher, IL 60401. Phone: (708)946-9792 Fax: (708)946-9793 E-mail: bjurus@acwi.org • URL: http://www.acwi.org • Annual. Free. Controlled circulation. About 45 member public warehouses in the United States.

American Chamber of Commerce Executives.

American Chemical Society., 1155 16th St. NW Washington, DC 20036. Phone: 800-227-5558 or (202)872-4600 Fax: (202)872-4615 E-mail: help@acs.org • URL: http://portal.chemistry.org/portal/acs/corg/memberapp • Scientific and educational society of chemists and chemical engineers. Conducts: studies and surveys; special programs for disadvantaged persons; legislation monitoring, analysis, and reporting; courses for graduate chemists and chemical engineers; radio and television programming. Offers career guidance counseling; administers the Petroleum Research Fund and other grants and fellowship programs. Operates Employment Clearing Houses. Compiles statistics. Maintains Speaker's Bureau and 33 divisions.

American Chemistry Council., 1300 Wilson Blvd. Arlington, VA 22209. Phone: (703)741-5000 Fax: (703)741-6050 E-mail: aygoyer@one.net • URL: http://www.americanchemistry.com • Represents the leading companies engaged in the business of chemistry. Members apply the science of chemistry to make innovative products and services that make people's lives "better, healthier and safer." Improves environmental, health and safety performance through "Responsible Care"(R), common sense advocacy designed to address major public policy issues, and health and environmental research and product testing.

American Cinematographer Manual., 5700 Wilshire Blvd., Ste. 600 Los Angeles, CA 90036. Phone: 800-448-0145 or (323)634-3400 Fax: (323)634-3550 • URL: http://www.theasc.com • 1993. $49.95. Seventh edition. A pocket size encyclopedia of practical information about cameras, lenses, films, exposure, depth of field, lighting, special effects, etc.

American Cinematographer: The International Journal of Motion Picture ProductionTechniques. American Society of Cinematographers., 5700 Wilshire Blvd., Ste. 600 Los Angeles, CA 90036. Phone: 800-448-0145 or (323)634-3400 Fax: (323)634-3550 E-mail: ascmag@aol.com • URL: http://www.theasc.com • Monthly. $50.00 per year.

American City and County: Administration, Engineering and Operations in Relation to Local Government. Primedia Business Magazines and Media, 6151 Powers Ferry Rd., Ste. 200 Atlanta, GA 30339. Phone: 800-795-5445 or (770)955-2500 Fax: (770)618-0204 E-mail: inquiries@primemediabusiness.com • URL: http://www.primediabusiness.com • Monthly. Free to qualified personnel. Edited for mayors, city managers, and other local officials. Emphasis is on equipment and basic services.

American City and County Municipal Index: Purchasing Guide for City, Township, County Officials and Consulting Engineers. Primedia Business Magazines and Media, 6151 Powers Ferry Rd., Ste. 200 Atlanta, GA 30339. Phone: 800-795-5445 or (770)955-2500 Fax: (770)618-0204 E-mail: inquiries@primediabusiness.com • URL: http://www.primediabusiness.com • Annual. $61.95. Includes a directory of city and county governments with populations of 10,000 or more. Names and telephone numbers of municipal purchasing officials are listed. Also includes a directory of manufacturers and suppliers of materials, equipment, and services for municipalities.

American Civil Liberties Union., 125 Broad St., 18th Fl. New York, NY 10004. Phone: 888-567-ACLU or (212)549-2500 Fax: (212)549-2646 E-mail: membership@aclu.org • URL: http://www.aclu.org • Champions the rights set forth in the Bill of Rights of the U.S. Constitution: freedom of speech, press, assembly, and religion; due process of law and fair trial; equality before the law regardless of race, color, sexual orientation, national origin, political opinion, or religious belief. Conducts activities including litigation, advocacy, and public education. Sponsors litigation projects on topics such as women's rights, gay and lesbian rights, and children's rights.

American Clean Car. Crain Communications, Inc., 360 N Michigan Ave. Chicago, IL 60601-3806. Phone: 800-678-9595 or (312)649-5200 E-mail: info@crain.com • URL: http://www.crain.com • Bimonthly. $135.00 per year. Provides articles on new products and management for the carwash industry.

American Clinical Laboratory Association., 1250 H St. NW, Ste. 880 Washington, DC 20005-5943. Phone: (202)637-9466 Fax: (202)637-2050 E-mail: info@clinical-labs.org • URL: http://www.clinical-labs.org • Corporations, partnerships, or individuals owning or controlling one or more independent clinical laboratory facilities operating for a profit and licensed under the Clinical Laboratories Improvement Act of 1967 or the Clinical Laboratories Improvement Amendment of 1988, or accredited by the Medicare program. Promotes the development of uniformly high quality laboratory testing; eliminates the present inequalities in the standards applied to different segments of the clinical laboratory market; discourages the enactment of restrictive legislative or regulatory policies that may impede the free flow of commerce or operate to the detriment of the public. Examines federal and state health care and laboratory regulatory and legislative proposals and submits comments and opinions to the appropriate agencies or legislative bodies.

American Cloak and Suit Manufacturers Association.

American Cocoa Research Institute.

American Coin-Op: The Magazine for Coin-Operated Laundry and Drycleaning Businessmen. Crain Communications, Inc., 360 N Michigan Ave. Chicago, IL 60601-3806. Phone: 800-678-9595 or (312)649-5200 E-mail: info@crain.com • URL: http://www.crain.com • Monthly. Free.

American Coke and Coal Chemicals Institute.

American College of Apothecaries., 2830 Summer Oaks Dr. Bartlett, TN 38134-3811. Phone: (901)383-8119 Fax: (901)383-8882 E-mail: acaninfo@caresourcecenter.org A professional society of pharmacists.

American College of Counselors., 1124 1/2 S 5th St. Springfield, IL 62703-2314. Phone: (217)726-6220 Fax: (217)726-6220 Formerly National Alliance for Family Life.

American College of Health Care Administrators., 300 N. Lee St., No. 301 Alexandria, VA 22314. Phone: 888-882-2422 or (703)739-7900 Fax: (703)739-7901 E-mail: mtn@achca.org • URL: http://www.achca.org • Formerly American College of Nursing Home Administrators.

American College of Healthcare Executives., One N. Franklin, St., Suite 1700 Chicago, IL 60606-3491. Phone: (312)424-2800 Fax: (312)424-0023 E-mail: ache@ache.org • URL: http://www.ache.org • Formerly American College of Hospital Administrators.

American College of Medical Practice Executives., 104 Inverness Terrace E. Englewood, CO 80112-5306. Phone: 877-275-6442 Fax: (303)643-4439 E-mail: acmpe@mgma.com • URL: http://www.mgma.com/acmpe • Formerly American College of Medical Group Administrators.

American College of Occupational and Environmental Medicine-Membership Directory., 1114 N. Arlington Heights Rd. Arlington Heights, IL 60004. Phone: (847)818-1800 Fax: (847)818-9266 E-mail: acoeminfo@acoem.org Annual. $195.00. Lists 6,500 medical directories and plant physicians specializing in occupational medicine and surgery; coverage includes Canada and other foreign countries. Geographically arranged.

American College of Radiology., 1891 Preston White Dr. Reston, VA 20191-4397. Phone: 800-227-5463 or (703)648-8900 Fax: (703)295-6773 E-mail: info@acr.org • URL: http://www.acr.org • A professional society of physicians. Affiliated with International Society of Radiology.

American College of Trial Lawyers.

American College of Trust and Estate Counsel.

American Composites Manufacturers Association., 1010 N Glebe Rd., Ste. 450 Arlington, VA 22201. Phone: (703)525-0511 Fax: (703)525-0743 E-mail: info@acmanet.org • URL: http://www.acmanet.org • Companies engaged in the hand lay up or spray up of fiberglass in open molds or engaged in filament winding or resin transfer molding. Products requiring this process include boats, swimming pools, and bathroom fixtures. Conducts educational and research programs; compiles statistics. Sponsors product specialty seminars.

American Concrete Institute., PO Box 9094 Farmington Hills, MI 48333-9094. Phone: (248)848-3700 Fax: (248)848-3701 E-mail: bill.tolley@concrete.org • URL: http://www.aci-int.org • Technical and educational society of engineers, architects, contractors, educators, and others interested in improving techniques of design construction and maintenance of concrete products and structures. Offers certification program.

American Concrete Pavement Association., 500 New Jersey Ave. NW, 7th Fl. Washington, DC 20001. Phone: (202)638-2272 Fax: (202)638-2688 E-mail: acpa@pavement.com • URL: http://www.pavement.com • Contractors, cement companies, equipment manufacturers, material service suppliers, ready mixed concrete producers, consultants, trucking companies/material haulers and others allied with the concrete pavement industry. Advocates the use of concrete pavement for highways, airports, streets, and roads.

American Conference of Governmental Industrial Hygienists., 1330 Kemper Meadow Dr., Ste. 600 Cincinnati, OH 45240. Phone: (513)742-2020 or (513)742-6163 Fax: (513)742-3355 E-mail: mail@acgih.org • URL: http://www.acgih.org • Members are government employees. Formerly National Conference of Governmental Industrial Hygients.

American Congress on Surveying and Mapping.

American Consultants League., 245 NE 4th Ave., Ste. 102 Delray Beach, FL 33483. Phone: (866)344-7200 or (410)651-4869 Fax: (561)265-3542 E-mail: support@earlytorise.com • URL: http://www.americanconsultantsleague.com • Full-time and part-time consultants in varied fields of expertise. Provides assistance to consultants in establishing and managing the business component of their consultancies; offers marketing and legal advice. Maintains the Consultants Institute, which offers a home study program and bestows Certified Professional Consultants designation upon completion of program. Conducts research programs; compiles statistics. **Convention/Meeting:** none.

American Consulting Engineers Council-Membership Directory. American Consulting Engineers Council, 35 Technology Parkway, No. 150 Norcross, GA 30092-2901. Annual. $140.00. A state-by-state listing of ACEC's 5,200 consulting engineering firms with a total of over 180,000 employees.

American Consumers Association., 2633 Flossmoor Rd. Flossmoor, IL 60422. Phone: (708)957-2900 Fax: (708)957-4155 E-mail: amerconassn@ameritech.net Provides information on consumer goods and services, including product quality, cost, safety, and effectiveness. Promotes exchange of information beneficial to the health and welfare of the American consumer. Cooperates with individual or group efforts with the same goals. Offers a group insurance program and referrals on questions related to health and welfare. Issues public service announcements; conducts radio and direct mail advertising; endorses products. Compiles statistics; plans to establish a library.

American Correctional Association., 206 N Washington St., Ste. 200 Alexandria, VA 22314. Phone: 800-222-5646 or (301)918-1800 Fax: (301)918-0557 E-mail: execoffice@aca.org • URL: http://www.aca.org • Correctional administrators, wardens, superintendents, members of prison and parole boards, probation officers, psychologists, educators, sociologists, and other individuals; institutions and associations involved in the correctional field. Promotes improved correctional standards, including selection of personnel, care, supervision, education, training, employment, treatment, and post-release adjustment of inmates. Studies causes of crime and juvenile delinquency and methods of crime control and prevention through grants and contracts. Compiles statistics. Conducts research programs and training of correctional professionals. Offers accreditation of institutions and certification for correctional executive, manager, supervisor, and officer.

American Cost of Living Survey. Gale Cengage Learning, 27500 Drake Rd. Farmington Hills, MI 48331-3535. Phone: 800-877-GALE or (248)699-GALE Fax: 800-414-5043 or (248)699-8069 E-mail: gale.galeord@cengage.com • URL: http://gale.cengage.com • 2001. $245.00. Third edition. Cost of living data is provided for 455 U.S. cities and metroploitan areas.

American Cotton Shipper's Association., PO Box 3366 Memphis, TN 38173. Phone: (901)525-2272 Fax: (901)527-8303 E-mail: jonnichols@acfsa.org • URL: http://www.acsa-cotton.org • Purposes are to protect the financial well-being of exporters of U.S. grown cotton, to foster and improve international trade, and to preserve the principal of the sanctity of contracts.

American Council for Capital Formation., 1750 K St., N.W., Suite 400 Washington, DC 20006. Phone: (202)293-5811 Fax: (202)785-8165 E-mail: info@accf.org • URL: http://www.accf.org • Supports capital formation as a general concept. Formerly American Council on Capitol Gain and Estate Taxation.

American Council of Engineering Companies., 1015 15th St., 8th Fl. NW Washington, DC 20005-2605. Phone: (202)347-7474 Fax: (202)898-0068 E-mail: acec@acec.org • URL: http://www.acec.org • Represents consulting engineering firms engaged in private practice. Conducts programs concerned with public relations, business practices, governmental affairs, international practice and professional liability. Compiles statistics on office practices, insurance, employment, insurance clients served and services provided. Holds professional development seminars. Conducts educational programs; maintains speakers' bureau.

American Council of Independent Laboratories.

American Council of Life Insurance.

American Council of State Savings Supervisors., P.O. Box 1904 Leesburg, VA 20177. Phone: (703)669-5440 Fax: (703)699-5441 E-mail: amfalz@csss.org • URL: http://www.acsss.org • Members are state savings and loan supervisors. Includes a

Joint Committee on Examinations and Education.

American Council of the International Institute of Welding.

American Council on Alcoholism.

American Council on Consumer Awareness, Inc.

American Council on Consumer Interests., 415 S Duff Ave., Ste. C Ames, IA 50010-6600. Phone: (515)956-4666 Fax: (515)233-3101 E-mail: info@consumerinterests.org • URL: http://www.consumerinterests.org • Formerly Council on Consumer Information.

American Council on Education.

American Counseling Association., 5999 Stevenson Ave. Alexandria, VA 22304. Phone: 800-347-6647 or (703)823-9800 Fax: (703)823-0252 E-mail: ryep@counseling.org • URL: http://www.counseling.org • Counseling professionals in elementary and secondary schools, higher education, community agencies and organizations, rehabilitation programs, government, industry, business, private practice, career counseling, and mental health counseling. Conducts professional development institutes and provides liability insurance. Maintains Counseling and Human Development Foundation to fund counseling projects.

The American Country Club: Its Origins and Development. James M. Mayo. Rutgers University Press, 100 Joyce Kilmer Ave. Piscataway, NJ 08854-8099. Phone: 800-446-9323 or (732)445-7762 Fax: 888-471-9014 or (732)445-7039 E-mail: bksales@rci.rutgers.edu • URL: http://www.rutgerspress.rutgers.edu • 1998. $25.00.

American Culinary Federation., 180 Center Place Way St. Augustine, FL 32095. Phone: 800-624-9458 or (904)824-4468 Fax: (904)825-4758 E-mail: hcramb@acfchefs.net • URL: http://www.acfchefs.org • Aims to promote the culinary profession and provide on-going educational training and networking for members. Provides opportunities for competition, professional recognition, and access to educational forums with other culinary experts at local, regional, national, and international events. Operates the National +Apprenticeship Program for +Cooks and pastry cooks. Offers programs that address certification of the individual chef's skills, accreditation of culinary programs, apprenticeship of cooks and pastry cooks, professional development, and the fight against childhood hunger.

American Decades. Gale Cengage Learning, 27500 Drake Rd. Farmington Hills, MI 48331-3535. Phone: 800-877-GALE or (248)699-GALE Fax: 800-414-5043 or (248)699-8069 E-mail: gale.galeord@cengage.com • URL: http://gale.cengage.com • 1994-2001. $990.00. 10 volumes. $99.00 per volume. Each volume covers a decade during the period 1900-1989. "Each volume begins with an overview and chronology covering the entire decade. Subject chapters follow, each including an overview, subject-specific timeline and alphabetically arranged entries."

American Demographics: Consumer Trends for Business Leaders. Media Central, 470 Park Ave., S, 8th Fl. New York, NY 10016. Phone: 800-529-7502 E-mail: adedit@inside.com • URL: http://www.demographics.com • Monthly. $58.00 per year.

American Dental Association., 211 E Chicago Ave. Chicago, IL 60611-2678. Phone: (312)440-2500 Fax: (312)440-2800 E-mail: publicinfo@ada.org • URL: http://www.ada.org • Professional society of dentists. Encourages the improvement of the health of the public and promotes the art and science of dentistry in matters of legislation and regulations. Inspects and accredits dental schools and schools for dental hygienists, assistants, and laboratory technicians. Conducts research programs at ADA Foundation +Research Institute. Produces dental health education material used in the U.S. Sponsors National Children's Dental Health Month and Give Kids a Smile Day. Compiles statistics on personnel, practice, and dental care needs and attitudes of patients with regard to dental health. Sponsors 13 councils.

American Dental Association Journal. American Dental Association, 211 E. Chicago Ave. Chicago, IL 60611-2678. Phone: 800-947-4746 or (312)440-2500 Fax: (312)440-3538 • URL: http://www.ada.org • Monthly. Free to members; non-members, $100.00 per year; institutions, $121.00 per year.

American Dental Trade Association.

American Design Drafting Association., 105 E Main St. Newbern, TN 38059. Phone: (731)627-0802 Fax: (731)627-9321 E-mail: cadboss@gmail.com • URL: http://www.adda.org • Designers, drafters, drafting managers, chief drafters, supervisors, administrators, instructors, and students of design and drafting. Encourages a continued program of education for self-improvement and professionalism in design and drafting and computer-aided design/drafting. Informs members of effective techniques and materials used in drawings and other graphic presentations. Evaluates curriculum of educational institutions through certification program; sponsors drafter certification program.

American Dietetic Association., 120 S Riverside Plz., Ste. 2000 Chicago, IL 60606-6995. Phone: 800-877-1600 or (312)899-0040 Fax: (312)899-1979 E-mail: rmoen@eatright.org • URL: http://www.eatright.org • Represents food and nutrition professionals. Promotes nutrition, health and well-being.

American Dietetic Association Journal. American Dietetic Association. Elsevier, 655 Ave. of the Americas New York, NY 10010-1710. Phone: 800-366-2665 or (212)989-5800 Fax: 800-535-9935 or (212)633-3680 E-mail: custserv@elsevier.com • URL: http://www.elsevier.com • Monthly. Individuals, $208.00 per year; institutions, $288.00 per year.

American Disabled for Attendant Program Today., 201 S. Cherokee St. Denver, CO 80223-1836. Phone: (303)733-9324 Fax: (303)733-6211 E-mail: adapt@adapt.org • URL: http://www.adapt.org • Members are disabled individuals promoting wheelchair accessibility in all forms of public transportation.

American Doctoral Dissertations. Association of Research Libraries. UMI, 300 N. Zeeb Rd. Ann Arbor, MI 48106. Phone: 800-521-0600 or (734)761-4700 Fax: 800-864-0019 E-mail: info@il.proquest.com • URL: http://www.umi.com • Annual. Price on application.

American Driver and Traffic Safety Education Association.

American Drug Index. Facts and Comparisons, 111 W. Port Plaza, Suite 300 St. Louis, MO 6314-3098. Phone: 800-223-0554 or (314)216-2100 Fax: (314)878-5563 Annual. $69.95. Lists over 20,000 drug entries in dictionary style.

American Drycleaner. Crain Communications, Inc., 360 N Michigan Ave. Chicago, IL 60601-3806. Phone: 800-678-9595 or (312)649-5200 E-mail: info@crain.com • URL: http://www.crain.com • Monthly. Free.

American Economic Association., 2014 Broadway, Ste. 305 Nashville, TN 37203. Phone: (615)322-2595 Fax: (615)343-7590 E-mail: aeainfo@vanderbilt.edu • URL: http://www.vanderbilt.edu/AEA • Educators, business executives, government administrators, journalists, lawyers, and others interested in economics and its application to present-day problems. Encourages historical and statistical research into actual conditions of industrial life and provides a nonpartisan forum for economic discussion.

American Economic Review. American Economic Association, 2014 Broadway, Suite 305 Nashville, TN 37203. Phone: (615)322-2595 Fax: (615)343-7590 E-mail: aeainfo@vanderbilt.edu • URL: http://www.vanderbilt.edu/aea • Five times a year. Institutions, $195.00 per year. Includes *Journal of Economic Literature* and *Journal of Economic Persepective*.

American Editor. American Society of Newspaper Editors, 11690 Sunrise Valley Dr., No. B Reston, VA 20191. Phone: (703)453-1122 Fax: (703)453-1133 E-mail: asne@asne.org • URL: http://www.asne.org/ • Nine times a year. $29.00 per year. Formerly *American Society of Newspaper Editors Bulletin*.

American Egg Board., 1460 Renaissance Dr., Ste. 301 Park Ridge, IL 60068. Phone: (847)296-7043 Fax: (847)296-7007 E-mail: aeb@aeb.org • URL: http://www.aeb.org • Board of American egg producers appointed by the Secretary of Agriculture. Offers advertising, educational, research, and promotional programs designed to increase consumption of eggs and egg products. Conducts consumer educators and food-service seminars, and food safety education programs.

American Electroplaters and Surface Finishers Society.

American Enterprise Institute. American Enterprise Institute, 1150 17th St. NW Washington, DC 20036. Phone: 800-862-5801 or (202)862-5800 Fax: (202)862-7177 E-mail: cdemuth@aei.org • URL: http://www.aei.org • Economic policy, including domestic taxing, spending, and regulatory programs, and international trade and competitiveness; foreign and defense policy, including the spread of democracy and free enterprise, and the development of stable international security arrangements; social and political studies, including U.S. politics and public opinion, the Constitution and legal policy, and social welfare, educational and cultural issues.

American Entomological Society., 9301 Annapolis Rd., Ste. 300 Lanham, MD 20706. Phone: (301)731-4535 Fax: (301)731-4538 E-mail: esa@entsoc.org • URL: http://www.entsoc.org/ • Professional and amateur entomologists. Promotes the study of insects and publishes the results of research in the systematics and morphology of insects.

American Entomologist: Entomological Articles of General Interest. Entomological Society of America, 9301 Annapolis Rd. Lanham, MD 20706. Phone: (301)731-4535 Fax: (301)731-4538 E-mail: esa@entsoc.org • URL: http://www.entsoc.org • Quarterly. Individuals, $38.00 per year; institutions, $70.00 per year. Formerly *Entomological Society of America Bulletin*.

American Export Register. Thomas Publishing Co., 5 Penn Plz. New York, NY 10001. Phone: 800-699-9822 or (212)695-0500 Fax: (212)290-7362 E-mail: contact@thomaspublishing.com • URL: http://www.thomaspublishing.com • Covers: over 45,000 companies in the United States exporting products and services, United States and foreign government services to exporters and importers, chambers of commerce abroad, embassies and consulates in the U.S., and financial and transportation services such as airlines, steamship lines, freight forwarders, customs brokers, and banks, international cargo carriers and carriers, world trade centers. Entries include: Company name, address, phone, URL address, fax, markets served, contact name, product or service, company description.

American Farm Bureau Federation., 600 Maryland Ave. SW, Ste. 1000W Washington, DC 20024. Phone: 800-572-1090 or (202)406-3600 Fax: (202)406-3602 E-mail: bstallman@fb.org • URL: http://www.fb.org • Federation of 50 state farm bureaus and Puerto Rico, with membership on a family basis. Analyzes problems of members and formulates action to achieve educational improvement, economic opportunity, and social advancement. Maintains speakers' bureau; sponsors specialized education program.

American Federation of Government Employees., 80 F St., N.W. Washington, DC 20001. Phone: (202)737-8700 or (202)639-6419 Fax: (202)639-6441 E-mail: comments@afge.org • URL: http://www.afge.org • Affiliated with AFL-CIO.

American Federation of Home Health Agencies., 1320 Fenwick Lane,, Suite 100 Silver Spring, MD 20910. Fax: (301)588-4732 E-mail: afhha@his.com • URL: http://www.aft.org • Promotes home health care.

American Federation of Mineralogical Societies.

American Federation of State, County and Municipal Employees.

American Federation of Television and Radio Artists., 260 Madison Ave. New York, NY 10016-2402. Phone: (212)532-0800 Fax: (212)532-2242 E-mail: aftra@aftra.com • URL: http://www.aftra.com • Formerly American Federation of Radio Artist.

American Feed Industry Association - Alfalfa Processors Council.

American Fiber Manufacturers Association., 1530 Wilson Blvd., Ste. 690 Arlington, VA 22209-2418. Phone: (703)875-0432 Fax: (703)875-0907 E-mail: afma@afma.org • URL: http://www.fibersource.com • Producers of manufactured fibers used in apparel, household goods, industrial materials, and other types of products. Represents the industry in educational, governmental, and foreign trade matters. Distributes a video depicting production and end uses of manufactured fibers.

American Finance Association., University of California, Haas School of Business, 350 Main St., 545 Student Services Bldg. Berkeley, CA 94720-1900. Phone: 800-835-6770 or (781)388-8532 Fax: (781)388-8232 E-mail: pyle@haas.berkeley.edu • URL: http://www.afajof.org • College and university professors of economics and finance, bankers, treasurers, analysts, financiers, and others interested in financial problems; libraries and other institutions. Seeks to improve public understanding of financial problems and to provide for exchange of analytical ideas. Areas of special interest include: corporate finance, investments, banking, and international and public finance.

American Financial Directory. Accuity, 4709 W Golf Rd., Ste. 600 Skokie, IL 60076. Phone: 800-321-3373 or (847)676-9600 Fax: (847)933-8101 E-mail: custserv@accuitysolutions.com • URL: http://www.tfp.com • Covers: Approximately 23,000 banks, bank holding companies, credit unions, savings and loans, and other financial institutions and their approximately 56,000 branch offices. Entries include: Institution name, address, phone, fax, holding company affiliation, names and titles of key personnel, correspondent banks, FEDWIRE data and ABA number, balance sheet highlights, branches.

American Financial Services Association., 919 18th St. NW, Ste. 300 Washington, DC 20006-5517. Phone: (202)296-5544 Fax: (202)223-0321 E-mail: cstinebert@afsamail.org • URL: http://www.afsaonline.org • Represents companies whose business is primarily direct credit lending to consumers and/or the purchase of sales finance paper on consumer goods. Has members that have insurance and retail subsidiaries; some are themselves subsidiaries of highly diversified parent corporations. Encourages the business of financing individuals and families for necessary and useful purposes at reasonable charges, including interest; promotes consumer understanding of basic money management principles as well as constructive uses of consumer credit. Includes educational services such as films, textbooks, and study units for the classroom and budgeting guides for individuals and families. Compiles statistical reports; offers seminars.

American Firearms Industry. National Association of Federally Licensed Firearms Dealers. AFI Communications Group, Inc., 1525 S. Andrew Ave., Ste. 214 Fort Lauderdale, FL 33316. Phone: (954)467-9994 Fax: (954)463-2501 • URL: http://www.amfire.com • Monthly. $35.00 per year.

American Fisheries Society., 5410 Grosvenor Ln., Ste. 110 Bethesda, MD 20814-2199. Phone: (301)897-8616 Fax: (301)897-8096 E-mail: main@fisheries.org • URL: http://www.fisheries.org • International scientific organization of fisheries and aquatic science professionals, including fish culturists, fish biologists, water quality scientists, fish health professionals, fish technologists, educators, limnologists, and oceanographers. Promotes the development of all branches of fishery science and practice, and the conservation, development, and wise utilization of fisheries, both recreational and commercial. Strengthens professional standards by certifying fisheries scientists, stressing professional ethics, and providing forums for the exchange of scientific and management information. Represents members through written and verbal testimony before legislative and administrative bodies concerning aquatic environmental issues. Maintains over 30 committees.

American Foreign Service Association., 2101 E St. NW Washington, DC 20037. Phone: 800-704-AFSA or (202)338-4045 Fax: (202)338-6820 E-mail: member@afsa.org • URL: http://www.afsa.org • Associate membership is open to individuals and international organizations and corporations interested in foreign affairs, international trade, and economic policy. Conducts international conferences and symposia; holds monthly speaker programs. Operates the Foreign Service Club; sponsors member insurance programs. Maintains Speakers' Bureau.

American Forensic Association., Box 256 River Falls, WI 54022. Phone: 800-228-5424 or (715)425-3198 Fax: (715)425-9533 E-mail: amforensicassoc@aol.com • URL: http://www.americanforensics.org • High school and college directors of forensics and debate coaches. Promotes debate and other speech activities. Sponsors annual collegiate National Individual Events Tournament and National Debate Tournament; sells debate ballots; makes studies of professional standards and debate budgets. Supports research grants.

American Forensic Association Newsletter - Directory. American Forensic Association, P.O. Box 256 River Falls, WI 54022-0256. Phone: 800-228-5424 or (715)425-3198 Fax: (715)429-9533 Annual. Free with subscription; non-subscription, $15.00. List of 500 member teachers of argumentation and debate.

American Forest and Paper Association.

American Foundation for AIDS Research., 120 Wall St., 13th Fl. New York, NY 10005-3902. Phone: 800-392-6327 or (212)806-1600 Fax: (212)806-1601 E-mail: donors@amfar.org; teresa.coffey@amfar.org • URL: http://www.amfar.org • Purpose is to raise funds to support AIDS research.

American Foundry Society., 1695 N Penny Ln. Schaumburg, IL 60173-4555. Phone: 800-537-4237 or (847)824-0181 Fax: (847)824-7848 E-mail: jcall@afsinc.org • URL: http://www.afsinc.org • Technical, trade and management association of foundrymen, patternmakers, technologists, and educators. Sponsors foundry training courses through the Cast +Metals Institute on all subjects pertaining to the castings industry; conducts educational and instructional exhibits of foundry industry; sponsors 10 regional foundry conferences and 400 local foundry technical meetings. Maintains Technical Information Center providing literature searching and document retrieval service; and Metalcasting Abstract Service involving abstracts of the latest metal casting literature. Provides environmental services and testing; conducts research programs; compiles statistics, provides marketing information.

American Frozen Food Institute., 2000 Corporate Ridge, Ste. 1000 McLean, VA 22102. Phone: (703)821-0770 Fax: (703)821-1350 E-mail: info@affi.com • URL: http://www.affi.com • Frozen food processors and allied industry companies who work for the advancement of the frozen food industry. Seeks to improve consumer understanding and acceptance of frozen foods and to increase sales of frozen products through promotional and communications programs. Sponsors retail trade study, consumer and industry education on care and handling of frozen foods. Promotes a cooperative relationship between frozen food processors, suppliers and marketing associates. Represents the frozen food industry before federal, state and local governments. Conducts research to improve the quality of frozen food products.

American Frozen Food Institute-Membership Directory and Buyers Guide. American Frozen Food Institute, 2000 Corporate Ridge, Suite 1000 McLean, VA 22102. Phone: (703)821-0770 Fax: (703)821-1350 E-mail: info@affi.com • URL: http://www.affi.com • Annual. $100.00. 520 member frozen food processors, suppliers, brokers, and distributors.

American Fruit Grower. Meister Media, 37733 Euclid Ave. Willoughby, OH 44094-5992. Phone: 800-572-7740 or (440)942-2000 Fax: (440)975-3447 E-mail: info@meistermedia.com • URL: http://www.meistermedia.com • Monthly. $27.47 per year.

American Fruit Grower Source Book. Meister Publishing Co., 37733 Euclid Ave Willoughby, OH 44094-5992. Phone: 800-572-7740 or (440)942-2000 Fax: (440)942-0662 E-mail: info@meistermedia.com • URL: http://www.meisterpro.com • Annual. $5.00. Manufacturers and distributors of equipment and supplies for the commercial fruit growing industry.

American Funeral Director. Kates-Bolyston Publications, Inc., 1255 Rte. 70, Ste. 31-S Lakewood, NJ 08701-2716. Phone: 800-500-4585 or (732)767-9300 Fax: (732)901-8650 E-mail: customer@ucq.com • URL: http://www.kates-boylston.com • Monthly. $32.00 per year.

American Gas. American Gas Association, 400 N Capitol St., NW Washington, DC 20001. Phone: (202)824-7000 Fax: (202)824-7115 • URL: http://www.aga.org • 11 times a year. $59.00 per year. Formerly *AGA Monthly*.

American Gas Association., 400 N Capitol St. NW, Ste. 450 Washington, DC 20001. Phone: (202)824-7000 Fax: (202)824-7115 E-mail: dparker@aga.org • URL: http://www.aga.org • Advocates for local natural gas utility companies; provides a broad range of programs and services for member natural gas pipelines, marketers, gatherers, international gas companies and industry associates.

American Gear Manufacturers Association., 500 Montgomery St., Ste. 350 Alexandria, VA 22314-1581. Phone: (703)684-0211 Fax: (703)684-0242 E-mail: webmaster@agma.org • URL: http://www.agma.org • Represents manufacturers of gears, geared speed changers, and related equipment; manufacturers of gear cutting and checking equipment; teachers of mechanical engineering and gearing. Conducts educational and research programs; compiles statistics and financial data. Develops technical standards for domestic and international industry.

American Gear Manufacturers Association—News Digest. American Gear Manufacturers Association, 500 Montgomery St., Ste. 350 Alexandria, VA 22314-1581. Phone: (703)684-0211 Fax: (703)684-0242 E-mail: agma@agma.org Description: Carries information of interest to gear manufacturers and suppliers. Recurring features include news of research, a calendar of events, reports of meetings, news of educational opportunities, and columns titled Economic Review, President's Corner, and Executive Director's View.

American Gem and Mineral Suppliers Association.

American Gem Society., 8881 W Sahara Ave. Las Vegas, NV 89117. Phone: (866)805-6500 or (702)255-6500 Fax: (702)255-7420 E-mail: info@ags.org • URL: http://www.americangemsociety.org • Represents 1,600 retail and manufacturer jewelry firms in North America dedicated to proven ethics, knowledge and consumer protection. Encourages members to pursue studies in gemology; confers titles of Registered Jeweler, Registered Supplier, Certified Gemologist, and Certified Gemologist Appraiser upon those taking recognized courses and passing extensive examinations. Sponsors national promotional programs. Conducts educational programs.

American Gem Trade Association., 3030 LBJ Fwy., Ste. 840, 3030 LBJ Freeway, Ste. 840 Dallas, TX 75234. Phone: 800-972-1162 or (214)742-4367 Fax: (214)742-7334 E-mail: info@agta.org • URL: http://www.agta.org • Represents suppliers of natural colored gemstones; retail jewelers and jewelry manufacturers. Promotes natural colored gemstones; encourages high ethical standards among members and within the industry. Seeks to establish closer communication within the industry; works to protect consumers from fraud and to create a greater awareness of natural colored gemstones. Conducts seminars; maintains speakers' bureau.

American Genetic Association., 2030 SE Marine Science Dr. Newport, OR 97365. Phone: (541)867-0334 Fax: (301)695-9292 E-mail: agajoh@oregonstate.edu • URL: http://www.theaga.org • Represents biologists, zoologists, geneticists, botanists, and others engaged in basic and applied research in genetics. Explores transmission genetics of plants and animals.

American Government: Readings and Cases. Peter Woll. Longman Publishing Group, The Longman Bldg., 10 Bank St. White Plains, NY 10606-1951. Phone: 800-922-0579 or (914)993-5000 Fax: (914)997-8115 E-mail: orders@mcp.com • URL: http://www.store.awl.com • 2003. $38.80. 15th edition.

American Hardware Export Council.

American Hardware Manufacturers Association., 801 N Plaza Dr. Schaumburg, IL 60173. Phone: (847)605-1025 Fax: (847)605-1030 E-mail: info@ahma.org • URL: http://www.ahma.org • Represents the hardware, home improvement, lawn and garden, paint and decorating, and related industries.

American Health Care Association., 1201 L St. NW Washington, DC 20005. Phone: (202)842-4444 Fax: (202)842-3860 E-mail: hr@ahca.org • URL: http://www.ahcancal.org/Pages/Default.aspx • Federation of state associations of long-term health care facilities. Promotes standards for professionals in long-term health care delivery and quality care for patients and residents in a safe environment. Focuses on issues of availability, quality, affordability, and fair payment. Operates as liaison with governmental agencies, Congress, and professional associations. Compiles statistics.

American Health Care Association: Provider. American Health Care Association, 1201 L St., N.W. Washington, DC 20005. Phone: (202)842-4444 Fax: (202)842-3860 • URL: http://www.ahca.org • Monthly. $48.00 per year. Formerly *American Health Care Association Journal*.

American Helicopter Society Journal. American Helicopter Society, Inc., 217 N Washington St. Alexandria, VA 22314. Phone: (703)684-6777 Fax: (703)739-9279 E-mail: staff@avtol.org • URL: http://www.vtol.org • Quarterly. $60.00 per year.

American Highway Users Alliance., 1101 14th St. NW, Ste. 750 Washington, DC 20005. Phone: 800-483-4544 or (202)857-1200 or (202)857-1200 Fax: (202)857-1220 E-mail: info@highways.org • URL: http://www.highways.org • Broad-based consumers group for American motorists, truckers and businesses. Employs lobbying, media, communications and grassroots advocacy, promotes public policy that devotes highway use taxes to investments in safe and uncongested national highway systems.

American Home Furnishings Alliance., 317 W High Ave., 10th Fl. High Point, NC 27260. Phone: (336)884-5000 Fax: (336)884-5303 E-mail: pbowling@ahfa.us • URL: http://www.ahfa.us • Furniture manufacturers seeking to provide a unified voice for the furniture industry and to aid in the development of industry personnel. Provides: market research data; industrial relations services; costs and operating statistics; transportation information; general management and information services. Compiles statistics; develops quarterly Econometric Forecast.

American Hospital Association., 1 N Franklin Chicago, IL 60606-3421. Phone: (312)422-3000 Fax: (312)422-4796 E-mail: info@highways.org • URL: http://www.aha.org • Represents health care provider organizations. Seeks to advance the health of individuals and communities. Leads, represents, and serves health care provider organizations that are accountable to the community and committed to health improvement.

American Hotel and Lodging Association., 1201 New York Ave., N.W., No. 600 Washington, DC 20005-3931. Phone: (202)289-3180 Fax: (202)289-3199 E-mail: info@ahla.com • URL: http://www.ahla.com • Formerly American Hotel and Motel Association.

American Housing Survey for the United States in [year]. Available from U. S. Government Printing Office, Washington, DC 20402. Phone: (202)512-1800 Fax: (202)512-2250 E-mail: gpoaccess@gpo.gov • URL: http://www.access.gpo.gov • Biennial. $51.00. Issued by the U. S. Census Bureau (http://www.census.gov). Covers both owner-occupied and renter-occupied housing. Includes data on such factors as condition of building, type of mortgage, utility costs, and housing occupied by minorities. (Current Housing Reports, H150.)

American Humor Studies Association., St. Louis University, Department of English, 3800 Lindell Blvd. St. Louis, MO 63108-3414. Phone: (314)977-3068 Fax: (314)977-1514 E-mail: mcintire@slu.edu • URL: http://www.americanhumor.org • Academics, general readers, and professional humorists. Encourages the study and appreciation of American humor from interdisciplinary perspectives.

American Immigration Lawyers Association., 918 F St. NW Washington, DC 20004-1400. Phone: (202)216-2400 Fax: (202)783-7853 E-mail: executive@aila.org • URL: http://www.aila.org • Lawyers specializing in the field of immigration and nationality law. Fosters and promotes the administration of justice with particular reference to the immigration and nationality laws of the United States.

American Indonesian Chamber of Commerce., 317 Madison Ave., Room 520 New York, NY 10017-5201. Phone: (212)687-4505 Fax: (212)687-5844 E-mail: aiccny@bigplanet.com • URL: http://www.aiccusa.org • Holds briefings on new trade policies in Indonesia and offers orientation workshops to company personnel traveling in Indonesia.

American Industrial Hygiene Association., 2700 Prosperity Ave., Ste. 250 Fairfax, VA 22031. Phone: (703)849-8888 Fax: (703)207-3561 E-mail: infonet@aiha.org • URL: http://www.aiha.org • Professional society of industrial hygienists. Promotes the study and control of environmental factors affecting the health and well-being of workers. Sponsors continuing education courses in industrial hygiene, government affairs program, and public relations. Accredits laboratories. Maintains 40 technical committees and a foundation. Operates placement service. Conducts educational and research programs.

American Industrial Real Estate Association.

American Industry. Publications for Industry, 21 Russell Woods Rd. Great Neck, NY 11021. Phone: (516)487-0990 Fax: (516)487-0809 E-mail: info@publicationsforindustry.com • URL: http://www.publicationsforindustry.com • Description: Provides new product releases and information on brochures and catalogs available to industrial plant managers in the largest firms in the U.S. Recurring features include interviews, news of research, and successful use of reports.

American Industry: Structure, Conduct, Performance. Richard E. Caves. Prentice Hall PTR, 240 Frisch Ct. Paramus, NJ 07652. Phone: 800-282-0693 Fax: 800-445-6991 • URL: http://www.phptr.com • 1992. $60.00. Seventh edition.

American Inkmaker Buyers' Guide. Cygnus Business Media, Inc., 445 Broad Hollow Rd. Melville, NY 11747. Phone: 800-308-6397 or (631)845-2700 Fax: (631)845-2798 E-mail: rich.reiff@cygnuspub.com • URL: http://wwww.cygnusbzb.com • Annual. $20.00. Guide to suppliers of raw materials, equipment, and services for manufacturers of printing ink, pigments, varnishes, graphic chemicals, and similar products.

American Institute for CPCU.

American Institute for Economic Research.

American Institute for Medical and Biological Engineering.

American Institute of Aeronautics and Astronautics.

American Institute of Architects.

American Institute of Baking.

American Institute of Biological Sciences.

American Institute of Biomedical Climatology., 1050 Eagle Rd. Newtown, PA 18940. Phone: (215)968-4483 • URL: http://www.aibc.cc • Formerly American Institute of Medical Climatology.

American Institute of Building Design.

American Institute of Certified Planners.

American Institute of Certified Public Accountants.

American Institute of Chemical Engineers.

American Institute of Constructors.

American Institute of Food Distribution.

American Institute of Graphic Arts.

American Institute of Marine Underwriters.

American Institute of Parliamentarians.

American Institute of Stress., 124 Park Ave. Yonkers, NY 10703. Phone: (914)963-1200 Fax: (914)965-6267 E-mail: stress124@earthlink.net • URL: http://www.stress.org • Explores personal and social consequences of stress. Compiles research data on occupational stress and executive stress or "burn out."

American Insurance Association., 1130 Connecticut Ave. NW, Ste. 1000 Washington, DC 20036. Phone: 800-242-2302 or (202)828-7100 or (202)828-7183 Fax: (202)293-1219 E-mail: info@aiadc.org • URL: http://www.aiadc.org/aiadotnet • Represents companies providing property and casualty insurance and suretyship. Monitors and reports on economic, political, and social trends; serves as a clearinghouse for ideas, advice, and technical information. Represents members' interests before state and federal legislative and regulatory bodies; coordinates members' litigation.

American Intellectual Property Law Association., 241 18th St. S, Ste. 700 Arlington, VA 22202. Phone: (703)415-0780 Fax: (703)415-0786 E-mail: aipla@aipla.org • URL: http://www.aipla.org • Voluntary bar association of lawyers practicing in the fields of patents, trademarks, copyrights, and trade secrets. Aids in the operation and improvement of U.S. patent, trademark, and copyright systems, including the laws by which they are governed and rules and regulations under which federal agencies administer those laws. Sponsors moot court and legal writing competitions.

American International Automobile Dealers Association., 211 N Union St., Ste. 300 Alexandria, VA 22314. Phone: 800-GO-AIADA or (703)519-7800 Fax: (703)519-7810 E-mail: goaiada@aiada.org • URL: http://www.aiada.org • Trade association for America's international nameplate automobile dealerships and their employees who sell and service automobiles manufactured in the U.S. and abroad. Works to preserve a free market for international automobiles in the U.S. and is dedicated to increasing public awareness of the benefits the industry provides.

American Iron and Steel Annual Statistical Report. American Iron and Steel Institute, 1101 17th St., N.W., Suite 1300 Washington, DC 20036-4700. Phone: (202)463-6573 Fax: (202)463-6573 Annual. $100.00 per year.

American Iron and Steel Institute.

American Jobs Abroad. Gale, 27500 Drake Rd. Farmington Hills, MI 48331-3535. Phone: 800-877-4253 or (248)699-4253 Fax: 800-414-5043 or (248)699-8065 E-mail: galeord@cengage.com • URL: http://gale.cengage.com • Covers: over 800 U.S. corporations and 100 government agencies, associations, and other organizations that employ Americans overseas, generally on an ongoing or long-term basis at wages or salaries comparable to those in the U.S. Entries include: Company or organization name, address; recruiter's name, address, phone, fax, title; name of CEO; products and services; profile, annual sales, number of employees, number of U.S. employees abroad and countries where employed, application information, salaries, job categories, general requirements, length of assignment, language requirement, training, benefits. Paper back edition published by Visible Ink Press, an imprint of Gale Research.

American Journal of Agricultural Economics. American Agricultural Economics Association Blackwell Publishing, Inc., 350 Main St. Malden, MA 02148. Phone: 800-835-6770 or (781)388-8200 Fax: (781)388-8210 E-mail: subscrip@blackwellpub.com • URL: http://www.blackwellpub.com • Five times a year. $183.00 per year. Includes online edition. Provides a forum for creative and scholarly work in agriculture economics.

American Journal of Botany: Devoted to All Branches of Plant Sciences. Botanical Society of America, PO Box 299 St. Louis, MO 63166-0299. Phone: (314)577-9566 Fax: (314)577-9515 E-mail: bsa-manager@botany.org • URL: http://www.botany.org • Monthly. $295.00 per year. Includes *Plant Science Bulletin*.

American Journal of Clinical Nutrition: A Journal Reporting the Practical Application of Our World-Wide Knowledge of Nutrition. American Society for Clinical Nutrition, Inc., 9650 Rockville Pke., Rm. L-2310 Bethesda, MD 20814-3998. Phone: (301)530-7110 Fax: (301)571-1863 E-mail: secretar@ascn.faseb.org • URL: http://www.ascn.org • Monthly, Individuals, $155.00 per year; Institutions, $245.00 per year; Students, $100.00 per year. Includes online edition.

American Journal of Comparative Law. University of California, Berkeley, 890 Boalt Hall Berkeley, CA 94720-7200. Phone: (510)643-6115 Fax: (510)643-2698 • URL: http://www.comparativelaw.org • Quarterly. $30.00 per year.

American Journal of Drug and Alcohol Abuse. Marcel Dekker, Inc., 270 Madison Ave. New York, NY 10016-0602. Phone: 800-228-1160 or (212)696-9000 Fax: (212)685-4540 E-mail: journals@dekker.com • URL: http://www.dekker.com • Quarterly. Institutions, $995.00 per year; with online edition, $1,124.00 per year.

American Journal of Enology and Viticulture. American Society for Enology and Viticulture, P.O. Box 1855 Davis, CA 95617. Phone: (916)753-3142 Fax: (916)753-3318 Quarterly. $155.00 per year.

American Journal of Health-System Pharmacy. American Society of Health-System Pharmacists, 7272 Wisconsin Ave. Bethesda, MD 20814. Phone: (301)657-3000 Fax: 800-665-2747 or (301)657-1258 E-mail: custserv@ashp.org • URL: http://www.ashp.org • Semimonthly. $195.00 per year. Formerly *American Journal of Hospital Pharmacy*.

American Journal of Industrial Medicine. John Wiley and Sons, Inc., Journals, 111 River St. Hoboken, NJ 07030. Phone: 800-225-5945 or (201)748-6000 Fax: (201)748-6088 E-mail: customer@wiley.com • URL: http://www.wiley.com • Monthly. Institutions, $3,220.00 per year; with online edition, $3,381.00 per year.

American Journal of International Law., 2223 Massachusetts Ave., N.W. Washington, DC 20008-2864. Phone: (202)939-6000 Fax: (202)797-7133 • URL: http://www.asil.org • Quarterly, $140.00 per year.

American Journal of Nursing. American Nurses Association. Lippincott Williams and Wilkins, 530 Walnut St. Philadelphia, PA 19106-3621. Phone: 800-638-3030 or (215)521-8300 Fax: (215)521-8902 E-mail: custserv@lww.com • URL: http://www.lww.com • Monthly. Individuals, $39.00 per year; institutions, $129.00 per year. For registered nurses. Emphasis on the latest technological advances affecting nursing care.

American Journal of Occupational Therapy. American Occupational Therapy Association, Inc., 4720 Montgomery Ln. Bethesda, MD 20824-3425. Phone: (301)652-2682 Fax: (301)652-7711 • URL: http://www.aota.org • Six times a year. Individuals, $50.00 per year; institutions, $120.00 per year.

American Journal of Ophthalmology. Elsevier, 360 Park Ave., S. New York, NY 10010-1710. Phone: 888-437-4636 or (212)989-5800 Fax: (212)633-3990 E-mail: usinfo-f@selsevier.com • URL: http://www.elsevier.com • Monthly. Individuals, $107.00 per year; institutions, $508.00 per year; students, $145.00 per year.

American Journal of Potato Research. Potato Association of America, University of Maine, 5715 Coburn Hall, Rm. 6 Orono, ME 04469-5715. Phone: (207)581-3042 Fax: (207)581-3015 E-mail: umpotato@mail.maine.edu • URL: http://www.umaine.edu • Bimonthly. Individuals, $75.00 per year; students, $15.00 per year.Information relating to production, marketing, processing, storage, disease control, insect control and new variety releases. Formerly *American Potato Journal*.

American Judges Association., 300 Newport Ave. Williamsburg, VA 23185-4147. Phone: 800-616-6165 or (757)259-1841 Fax: (757)259-1520 E-mail: aja@ncsc.dni.us • URL: http://aja.ncsc.dni.us • Seeks to improve the administration of justice at all levels of the courts.

American Judicature Society., Drake University, The Opperman Ctr., 2700 University Ave. Des Moines, IA 50311. Phone: 800-626-4089 or (515)271-2281 Fax: (515)279-3090 E-mail: dperrault@ajs.org • URL: http://www.ajs.org • Lawyers, judges, law teachers, government officials, and citizens interested in the effective administration of justice. Conducts research; presents educational programs; offers a consultation service; sponsors and organizes citizens' conferences on judicial improvement. Coordinates the work of states in judicial discipline and removal through its Center for +Judicial Conduct Organizations.

American Laboratory. International Scientific Communications, Inc., 30 Controls Dr. Shelton, CT 06484. Phone: (203)926-9300 Fax: (203)926-9310 E-mail: iscpubs@iscpubs.com • URL: http://www.iscpubs.com • Monthly. $235.00 per year. Includes annual *Buyers' Guide*.

American Laboratory Buyers' Guide. International Scientific Communications, Inc., 30 Controls Dr. Shelton, CT 06484. Phone: (203)926-9300 Fax: (203)926-9310 E-mail: iscpubs@iscpubs.com • URL: http://www.iscpubs.com • Annual. $25.00. Manufacturers of and dealers in scientific instruments, equipment, apparatus, and chemicals worldwide.

American Land Planning Law. John Taylor and Norma Williams. West Group, 610 Opperman Dr. Eagan, MN 55123. Phone: 800-328-4880 or (651)687-7000 Fax: 800-340-9378 E-mail: bookstore@westgroup.com • URL: http://www.westgroup.com • $780.00. Eight volumes. Annual cumulative updates. (Real Property and Zoning Series).

American Land Title Association - Sections: Abstractors and Title Insurance AgenTitle Insurance and Underwriters.

American Laundry News. Crain Communications, Inc., 360 N Michigan Ave. Chicago, IL 60601-3806. Phone: 800-678-9595 or (312)649-5200 E-mail: info@crain.com • URL: http://www.crain.com • Monthly. Free. Formerly *Laundry News*.

American Law Institute., 4025 Chestnut St. Philadelphia, PA 19104-3099. Phone: 800-253-6397 or (215)243-1600 Fax: (215)243-1636 E-mail: ali@ali.org • URL: http://www.ali.org • Judges, law teachers, and lawyers. Promotes the clarification and simplification of the law and its better adaptation to social needs by continuing work on the Restatement of the Law, model and uniform codes, and model statutes. Conducts a program of continuing legal education jointly with the American Bar Association called "ALI-ABA" (see separate entry).

American Law of Mining. Rocky Mountain Mineral Law Institute. LexisNexis Matthew Bender, 1275 Broadway Albany, NY 12204. Phone: 800-424-4200 or (518)487-3000 Fax: (518)487-3584 E-mail: bookstore.support@lexisnexis.com • URL: http://www.bender.com • $768.00. Six looseleaf volumes. Periodic supplementation.

American Law Yearbook. Gale Cengage Learning, 27500 Drake Rd. Farmington Hills, MI 48331-3535. Phone: 800-877-GALE or (248)699-GALE Fax: 800-414-5043 E-mail: gale.galeord@cengage.com • URL: http://gale.cengage.com • Annual. $165.00. Serves as a yearly supplement to *West's Encyclopedia of American Law*. Describes new legal developments in many subject areas.

The American Lawyer. American Lawyer Media Inc., 345 Park Ave., S. New York, NY 10010. Phone: 800-888-8300 or (212)779-9200 Fax: (212)481-8074 • URL: http://www.americanlawyermedia.com • 10 times a year. $149.00 per year. General information for American attorneys.

American League of Lobbyists., P.O. Box 30005 Alexandria, VA 22310. Phone: (703)960-3011 Fax: (703)960-4070 E-mail: alldc.org@erols.com • URL: http://www.alldc.org • Registered lobbyists and other professionals interested in the lobbying profession.

American Leather Chemists Association., 1314 50th St., Ste. 103, P.O. Box 45300 Lubbock, TX 79412-2940. Phone: (806)744-1798 Fax: (806)744-1785 E-mail: alca@leatherchemists.org • URL: http://www.leatherchemists.org • Chemists, leather technologists, and educators concerned with the tanning and leather industry. Works to devise and perfect methods for the analysis and testing of leathers and materials used in leather manufacture. Promotes advancement of chemistry and other sciences, especially their application to problems confronting the leather industry.

American Leather Chemists Association Journal. American Leather Chemists Association, Texas Tech University, P.O. Box 45300 Lubbock, TX 79409-5300. Phone: (806)742-7296 Fax: (806)742-7298 E-mail: alca@leatherchemists.org • URL: http://www.leatherchemists.org • Monthly. Members, $8.50 per year; non-members, $115.00 per year.

American Leather Chemists Association—Membership Directory. American Leather Chemists Association, 1314 50th St., Ste. 103, P.O. Box 45300 Lubbock, TX 79412. Phone: (806)744-1798 Fax: (806)744-1785 E-mail: alca@leatherchemists.org • URL: http://www.leatherchemists.org • Covers: about 500 chemists, leather technologists, and educators concerned with the tanning and leather industry. Entries include: Personal name, address; company name, address, phone, fax.

American Legion., PO Box 1055, PO Box 1055 Indianapolis, IN 46206. Phone: 800-433-3318 or (317)630-1200 Fax: (317)630-1223 E-mail: natlcmdr@legion.org • URL: http://www.legion.org • Consists of honorably discharged wartime veterans of the U.S. armed forces. Provides a unified voice for veterans in Washington, DC. Offers free assistance with Veterans Administration claims and benefits. Sponsors American Legion baseball competition, national high school oratorical contest, and children's services; cosponsors National Education Week. Maintains museum.

The American Legion Magazine., P.O. Box 1055 Indianapolis, IN 46206. Phone: (317)630-1200 Fax: (317)630-1280 E-mail: magazine@legion.org • URL: http://www.legion.org • Monthly. Free to members; non-members, $15.00 per year.

American Legislative Process: Congress and the States. William J. Keefe and Morris Ogul, editors. Prentice Hall PTR, 240 Frisch Ct. Paramus, NJ 07652. Phone: 800-282-0693 Fax: 800-445-6991 • URL: http://www.phptr.com • 2000. $60.00. 10th edition.

American Libraries. American Library Association, 50 E. Huron St. Chicago, IL 60611-2795. Phone: 800-545-2433 or (312)944-6780 Fax: (312)440-9374 E-mail: ala@ala.org • URL: http://www.ala.org • 11 times a year. Institutions, $60.00 per year. Current news and information concerning the library industry.

American Library Association., 50 E Huron St. Chicago, IL 60611. Phone: 800-545-2433 or (312)944-6780 Fax: (312)440-9374 E-mail: ala@ala.org • URL: http://www.ala.org • Librarians, libraries, trustees, friends of libraries, and others interested in the responsibilities of libraries in the educational, social, and cultural needs of society. Promotes and improves library service and librarianship. Establishes standards of service, support, education, and welfare for libraries and library personnel; promotes the adoption of such standards in libraries of all kinds; safeguards the professional status of librarians; encourages the recruiting of competent personnel for professional careers in librarianship; promotes popular understanding and public acceptance of the value of library service and librarianship. Works in liaison with federal agencies to initiate the enactment and administration of legislation that will extend library services. Offers placement services.

American Library Association Gay, Lesbian, Bisexual and Transgendered Roundtable., 50 E Huron St. Chicago, IL 60611. Phone: 800-545-2433 E-mail: amoore@library.umass.edu • URL: http://www.ala.org • Promotes gay, lesbian, bisexual and transgendered professionals.

American Library Association Handbook of Organization and Membership Directory. American Library Association, 50 E. Huron St. Chicago, IL 60611-2795. Phone: 800-545-2433 or (312)944-6780 Fax: (312)440-9374 E-mail: membership@ala.org • URL: http://www.ala.org • Annual. $30.00. Lists about 52,000 librarians. Formerly *American Library Association Membership Directory*.

American Library Directory. Information Today Inc., 143 Old Marlton Pke. Medford, NJ 08055-8750. Phone: 800-300-9868 or (609)654-6266 Fax: (609)654-4309 E-mail: custserv@infotoday.com • URL: http://www.infotoday.com • Covers: Over 37,000 U.S. and Canadian academic, public, county, provincial, and regional libraries; library systems; medical, law, and other special libraries; and libraries for the blind and physically handicapped. Separate section lists over 350 library networks and consortia and 220 accredited and unaccredited library school programs. Entries include: For libraries—Name, supporting or affiliated institution or firm name, address, phone, fax, electronic mail address, Standard Address Number (SANs), names of librarian and department heads, income, collection size, special collections, computer hardware, automated functions, and type of catalog. For library systems—Name, location. For library schools—Name, address, phone, fax, electronic mail address, director, type of training and degrees, admission requirements, tuition, faculty size. For networks and consortia—Name, address, phone, names of affiliates, name of director, function.

American Library Directory Online. Information Today, Inc., 143 Old Marlton Pike Medford, NJ 08055-8750. Phone: 800-300-9868 or (609)654-6266 Fax: (609)654-4309 E-mail: custserv@infotoday.com • URL: http://www.infotoday.com • Provides information on more than 30,000 public, college, and special libraries in the U.S. and Canada, with annual updates. Includes library networks, consortia, organizations, and schools. Inquire as to online cost and availability.

American Lighting Association., PO Box 420288, 2050 Stemmons Fwy., PO Box 420288 Dallas, TX 75342-0288. Phone: 800-274-4448 or (214)698-9898 or (214)274-4484 Fax: (214)698-9899 E-mail: dupton@americanlightingassoc.com • URL: http://www.americanlightingassoc.com • Manufacturers, manufacturers' representatives, distributors, and retailers of residential lighting fixtures, portable lamps, component parts, accessories, and bulbs. Trains and certifies lighting consultants; conducts showroom sales seminars; disseminates marketing and merchandising information. Compiles statistics.

American Logistics Association., 1133 15th St. NW, Ste. 640 Washington, DC 20005. Phone: (202)466-2520 Fax: (202)296-4419 E-mail: membership@ala-national.org • URL: http://www.ala-national.org • Promotes, protects and ensures the continued viability of the military resale (Commissary and Exchange Benefits) and Morale, Welfare and Recreations (MWR Benefits) industries. Acts as liaison between manufacturers and the Armed Forces' purchasing agencies. Promotes cooperation between the Congress, Defense Department and the industries which it conducts business.

American Lumber Standards Committee.

American Machine Tool Distributors' Association., 1445 Research Blvd., Ste. 450 Rockville, MD 20850. Phone: 800-878-2683 or (301)738-1200 Fax: (301)738-9499 E-mail: pborden@amtda.org • URL: http://www.amtda.org • Distributors and builders of manufacturing technology. Offers technical training, sales training and management. Compiles statistics.

American Machinist: Strategies and Innovations for Competitive Manufacturing. Penton Media Inc., 1300 E. Ninth St. Cleveland, OH 44114. Phone: (216)696-7000 Fax: (216)696-1752 E-mail: infomation@penton.com • URL: http://www.penton.com • Monthly. Free to qualified personnel; others, $75.00 per year.

American Management Association., 1601 Broadway New York, NY 10019-7420. Phone: 800-262-9699 or (212)586-8100 Fax: (212)903-8168 E-mail: membership@amanet.org • URL: http://www.amanet.org • Provides educational forums worldwide where members and their colleagues learn superior, practical business skills and explore best practices of world-class organizations through interaction with each other and expert faculty practitioners. Maintains a publishing program providing tools individuals use to extend learning beyond the classroom in a process of life-long professional growth and development through education.

American Manufacturers Directory. infoUSA Inc., 5711 S 86th Cir., PO Box 27347 Omaha, NE 68127. Phone: 800-321-0869 or (402)593-4500 Fax: (402)331-1505 E-mail: help@infousa.com • URL: http://www.abbi.com • Covers: more than 150,000 manufacturing companies with 20 or more employees. CD-ROM version lists all 531,000 U.S. manufacturers, in all employee size ranges. Entries include: Company name, address, phone, contact name, Standard Industrial Classification (SIC) codes, number of employees, sales volume code, credit rating scores.

American Maritime Association., 485 Madison Ave., 15th Fl. New York, NY 10022. Phone: (646)840-0428 Fax: (212)753-8101 E-mail: membership@amanet.org U.S. flag steamship companies, which operate vessels in foreign and domestic trades. Conducts collective bargaining with the various offshore maritime unions and promotes a strong American Merchant Marine. **Publications:** none. **Convention/Meeting:** none.

American Maritime Cases. American Maritime Cases, Inc., 3600 Clipper Mill Rd., Ste. 208 Baltimore, MD 21211. Phone: (410)752-2939 Fax: (410)625-1174 E-mail: amcrptr@mindspring.com 10 times a year. $654.50 per year.

American Marketing Association., 311 S Wacker Dr., Ste. 5800 Chicago, IL 60606. Phone: 800-262-1150 or (312)542-9000 Fax: (312)542-9001 E-mail: info@ama.org • URL: http://www.marketingpower.com • Serves as a professional society of marketing and market research executives, sales and promotion managers, advertising specialists, academics, and others interested in marketing. Fosters research; sponsors seminars, conferences, and student marketing clubs; provides educational placement service and doctoral consortium.

American Meat Institute., 1150 Connecticut Ave. NW, 12th Fl. Washington, DC 20036. Phone: (202)587-4200 Fax: (202)587-4300 E-mail: memberservices@meatami.com • URL: http://www.meatami.com • Represents the interests of packers and processors of beef, pork, lamb, veal, and turkey products and their suppliers throughout North America. Provides legislative, regulatory, and public relations services. Conducts scientific research. Offers marketing and technical assistance. Sponsors educational programs.

American Medical Association., 515 N State St. Chicago, IL 60610. Phone: 800-621-8335 or (312)464-5000 Fax: (312)464-4184 E-mail: msc@ama-assn.org • URL: http://www.ama-assn.org • Represents county medical societies and physicians. Disseminates scientific information to members and the public. Informs members on significant medical and health legislation on state and national levels and represents the profession before Congress and governmental agencies. Cooperates in setting standards for medical schools, hospitals, residency programs, and continuing medical education courses. Offers physician placement service and counseling on practice management problems. Operates library that lends material and provides specific medical information to physicians. Maintains Ad-hoc committees for such topics as health care planning and principles of medical ethics.

American Medical Group Association., 1422 Duke St. Alexandria, VA 22314-3403. Phone: (703)838-0033 Fax: (703)548-1890 E-mail: dfisher@amga.org • URL: http://www.amga.org • Represents the interests of medical groups. Advocates for the medical groups and patients through innovation and information sharing, benchmarking, developing leadership, and improving patient care. Provides political advocacy, educational and networking programs and publications, benchmarking data services, and financial and operations assistance.

American Medical News. American Medical Association, 515 N State St. Chicago, IL 60610-0946. Phone: 800-262-2350 or (312)464-5000 Fax: (312)464-4184 • URL: http://www.ama-assn.org • 48 times a year. Members, $95.00 per year; non-members, $145.00 per year; institutions, $325.00 per year. Economic and legal news for the medical profession.

American Medical Political Action Committee., 515 N State St. Chicago, IL 60610. Phone: 800-621-8335 or (202)789-4587 Fax: (202)789-7449 E-mail: ampaconline@ama-assn.org • URL: http://www.ampaconline.org • Represents physicians, their spouses, and others interested in political action and participation in public affairs. Seeks to further political knowledge of its members and to provide them with means for concerted political action.

American Medical Rehabilitation Providers Association., 206 S 6th St. Springfield, IL 62701. Phone: 888-346-4624 or (217)753-1190 Fax: (217)525-1271 E-mail: czollar@13x.com • URL: http://www.amrpa.org • Rehabilitation facilities in the U.S. and Canada; agencies operating established medical, residential and vocational rehabilitation facilities. Promotes expansion and improvement of rehabilitation services to disabled persons as provided in rehabilitation facilities. Represents the concerns of rehabilitation providers before Congress and government agencies. Is concerned with quality operation of rehabilitation centers and facilities. Conducts research and development programs in national rehabilitation policy. Sponsors seminars and provides specialized education programs.

American Medical Technologists., 710 Higgins Rd. Park Ridge, IL 60068-5765. Phone: 800-275-1268 or (847)823-5169 Fax: (847)823-0458 E-mail: dfisher@amga.org • URL: http://www.amt1.com • A program of the American Medical Technologists (see separate entry). Certified assistants to physicians in office practice, clinics, hospitals, and private health care facilities. Works to establish standards of training; provides continuing education and home study programs; promotes quality care in allied health. Works with the Accrediting Bureau of Health Education Schools (see separate entry) in regard to certification examinations and student societies. Offers group insurance programs.

American Medical Women's Association., 211 N Union St., Ste. 100 Alexandria, VA 22314. Phone: 800-995-AMWA or (703)838-0500 Fax: (703)549-3864 E-mail: info@amwa-doc.org • URL: http://www.amwa-doc.org • Women holding a MD or DO degree from approved medical colleges; women interns, residents, and medical students. Promotes women's health issues in medical education and public policy. Seeks to find solutions to problems common to women studying or practicing medicine, such as career advancement and the integration of professional and family responsibilities. Provides student members with educational loans and personal counseling. Sponsors continuing medical education programs.

American Men and Women of Science A Biographical Directory of Today's Leaders in Physical, Biological and Related Sciences. Gale, 27500 Drake Rd. Farmington Hills, MI 48331. Phone: 800-877-GALE or (248)699-GALE Fax: 800-414-5043 or (248)699-8035 E-mail: gale.galeord@cengage.com • URL: http://gale.cengage.com • 2002. $950.00. 21st edition. Eight volumes. Over 119,600 United States and Canadian scientists active in the physical, biological, mathematical, computer science and engineering fields.

American Mental Health Counselors Association., 801 N Fairfax St., Ste. 304 Alexandria, VA 22314. Phone: 800-326-2642 or (703)548-6002 Fax: (703)548-4775 E-mail: mhamilton@amhca.org • URL: http://www.amhca.org • Professional counselors employed in mental health services; students. Aims to: deliver quality mental health services to children, youth, adults, families, and organizations; improve the availability and quality of counseling services through licensure and certification, training standards, and consumer advocacy. Supports specialty and special interest networks. Fosters communication among members. A division of the American Counseling Association (see separate entry).

American Meteorological Society., 45 Beacon St. Boston, MA 02108-3693. Phone: (617)227-2425 Fax: (617)742-8718 E-mail: amsinfo@ametsoc.org • URL: http://www.ametsoc.org • Professional meteorologists, oceanographers, and hydrologists; interested students and nonprofessionals. Develops and disseminates information on the atmospheric and related oceanic and hydrospheric sciences; seeks to advance professional applications. Activities include guidance service, scholarship programs, career information, certification of consulting meteorologists, and a seal of approval program to recognize competence in radio and television weathercasting. Issues statements of policy to assist public understanding on subjects such as weather modification, forecasting, tornadoes, hurricanes, flash floods, and meteorological satellites. Provides abstracting services. Prepares educational films, filmstrips, and slides for a new curriculum in meteorology at the ninth grade level. Issues monthly announcements of job openings for meteorologists.

American Military Society., PO Box 98186 Washington, DC 20090-8186. Phone: 800-379-6128 Fax: (301)925-6920 E-mail: usmcdia@atc.cc • URL: http://www.amsmilitary.org • Active or retired members of the armed services (Army, Navy, Air Force, Marine Corps, and Coast Guard), and civilians. Develops and supports activities which promote the general well-being of the members; upholds and defends the Constitution; supports national defense; and preserves the memories and traditions of the Armed Forces.

American Mineralogist: An International Journal of Earth and Planetary Materials. Mineralogical Society of America, 1015 18th St., NW, Ste. 601 Washington, DC 20036-5212. Phone: (202)775-4344 Fax: (202)775-0018 E-mail: business@minsocam.org • URL: http://www.minsocam.org • Eight times a year. $580.00 per year.

American Motor Carrier Directory. Commonwealth Business Media Inc., 400 Windsor Corporate Pk., 50 Millstone Rd., Ste. 200 East Windsor, NJ 08520-1415. Phone: 800-221-5488 or (609)371-7700 Fax: (609)371-7885 E-mail: customerservice@cbizmedia.com • URL: http://www.cbizmedia.com • Publication includes: Lists of all licensed Less Than Truckload (LTL) general commodity carriers in the United States; includes specialized motor carriers and related services; includes refrigerated carriers, heavy haulers, bulk haulers, riggers, and specified commodity carriers; state and federal regulatory bodies governing the trucking industry; tariff publishing bureaus; freight claim councils; industry associations, etc. Entries include: For carriers and services—Company name, address of headquarters and terminals, phones, tariffs followed, names of executives, insurance, and equipment information, services or commodities handled. Principal content of publication is listing of direct point-to-point services of LTL general commodity carriers throughout the United States and to Canada and Mexico.

American Motorcyclist. American Motorcyclist Association, 13515 Yarmouth Dr. Pickerington, OK 43147-8214. Phone: (614)856-1900 Fax: (614)856-1920 E-mail: ama@ama-cycle.org • URL: http://www.ama-cycle.org • Monthly. $12.50 per year.

American Motorcyclist Association., 13515 Yarmouth Dr. Pickerington, OH 43147-8214. Phone: 800-262-5646 or (614)856-1900 Fax: (614)856-1920 E-mail: ama@ama-cycle.org • URL: http://www.ama-cycle.org • Represents motorcycle enthusiasts. Acts as a rulemaking body for motorcycle competition. Promotes highway safety. Maintains museum and hall of fame.

American Moving and Storage Association. c/o John Brewer, 1611 Duke St. Alexandria, VA 22314. Phone: (703)683-7410 Fax: (703)683-7527 E-mail: amconf@amconf.org • URL: http://www.amconf.org • Members are household goods movers, storage companies, and trucking firms.

American Mushroom Institute., Washington, D.C. Office, 1 Massachusetts Ave. NW, Ste. 800 Washington, DC 20001. Phone: (202)842-4344 Fax: (202)408-7763 E-mail: ami@mwmlaw.com • URL: http://www.americanmushroom.org • Mushroom growers, processors, suppliers, and researchers united to promote the growing and marketing of cultivated mushrooms. Aims to: increase cultivated mushroom consumption; develop better and more economical methods of growing and marketing mushrooms; collect and disseminate the latest statistics and other information; foster research programs beneficial to the industry; aid members with any problems. Supports a short course on mushroom science at Penn State University and an international congress on mushroom science.

American Music Conference., 5790 Armada Dr. Carlsbad, CA 92008-4391. Phone: 800-767-6266 or (760)431-9124 or (760)366-5260 Fax: (760)438-7327 E-mail: info@amc-music.org • URL: http://www.amc-music.org • Represents associations, companies, and individuals supported by instrument manufacturers, publishers, wholesalers and retailers, educators, music industry and educator associations and other interested individuals. Promotes the importance of music, music making and music education to the general public.

American National Biography. John A. Garraty and Mark C. Carnes, editors. Oxford University Press, 198 Madison Ave. New York, NY 10016-4314. Phone: 800-445-9714 or (212)726-6000 Fax: (212)726-6446 E-mail: custserv@oup-usa.org • URL: http://www.oup-usa.org • 1999. $795.00. 24 volumes. Contains about 17,500 entries, including business leaders who were important to the American economy. Includes an index by occupation. *Supplement* available, 2002, $150.00.

American National Metric Council., 900 Mix Ave., Ste. 1 Hamden, CT 06514-5106. Phone: (203)287-9849 E-mail: anmcmetric@pi-c.com • URL: http://lamar.colostate.edu/~hillger/anmc.htm • Companies, organizations, and individuals interested in keeping up-to-date on all the latest information on the status of metric transition in the U.S. Aims to coordinate metric transition planning activities for all affected segments in the private sector of American society.

American National Standards Institute., 1819 L St. NW, 6th Fl. Washington, DC 20036. Phone: (202)293-8020 Fax: (202)293-9287 E-mail: info@ansi.org • URL: http://www.ansi.org • Industrial firms, trade associations, technical societies, labor organizations, consumer organizations, and government agencies. Serves as clearinghouse for nationally coordinated voluntary standards for fields ranging from information technology to building construction. Gives status as American National Standards to standards developed by agreement from all groups concerned, in such areas as: definitions, terminology, symbols, and abbreviations; materials, performance characteristics, procedure, and methods of rating; methods of testing and analysis; size, weight, volume, and rating; practice, safety, health, and building construction. Provides information on foreign standards and represents United States interests in international standardization work.

American Notary. American Society of Notaries, PO Box 5707 Tallahassee, FL 32314. Phone: 800-522-3392 or (850)671-5164 Fax: (850)671-5165 E-mail: mail@notaries.org • URL: http://www.notaries.org • Description: Articles of interest to notaries, educational and informative. Presents "new legislation and court decisions affecting the office of notary public, news about the American Society of Notaries," and related matters. Recurring features include Questions and Answers, and educational workshops.

American Nuclear Insurers., 95 Glastonbury Blvd. Glastonbury, CT 06033-4438. Phone: (860)682-1301 Fax: (860)659-0002 E-mail: info@nuclearinsurance.com • URL: http://www.amnucins.com • Domestic property/casualty nuclear insurance companies. Strives to ensure safe and secure insurance capacity for customers. Audits financial performance of all member companies annually, ensures compliance with guidelines.

American Nuclear Society., 555 N Kensington Ave. La Grange Park, IL 60526. Phone: 800-323-3044 or (708)352-6611 Fax: (708)352-0499 E-mail: info@nuclearinsurance.com • URL: http://www.ans.org • Physicists, chemists, educators, mathematicians, life scientists, engineers, metallurgists, managers, and administrators with professional experience in nuclear science or nuclear engineering. Works to advance science and engineering in the nuclear industry. Disseminates information; promotes research; conducts meetings devoted to scientific and technical papers; works with government agencies, educational institutions, and other organizations dealing with nuclear issues.

American Nuclear Society Transactions. American Nuclear Society, 555 N. Kensington Ave. La Grange Park, IL 60525. Phone: (708)352-6611 Fax: (708)352-0499 • URL: http://www.ans.org • Semiannual. Institutions, $800.00 per year. *Supplement* available.

American Numismatic Association., 818 N Cascade Ave. Colorado Springs, CO 80903-3279. Phone: 800-367-9723 or (719)632-2646 Fax: (719)634-4085 E-mail: ana@money.org • URL: http://www.money.org • Collectors of coins, medals, tokens, and paper money. Promotes the study, research, and publication of articles on coins, coinage, and history of money. Sponsors correspondence courses; conducts research. Maintains museum, archive, authentication service for coins, and hall of fame. Sponsors National Coin Week; operates speakers' bureau.

American Numismatic Society., 96 Fulton St. New York, NY 10038. Phone: (212)571-4470 Fax: (212)571-4479 E-mail: wartenberg@numismatics.org • URL: http://www.numismatics.org • Collectors and others interested in coins, medals, and related materials. Advances numismatic knowledge as it relates to history, art, archaeology, and economics by collecting coins, medals, tokens, decorations, and paper money. Maintains only museum devoted entirely to numismatics. Presents annual Graduate Fellowship in Numismatics. Sponsors Graduate Seminar in Numismatics, a nine-week individual study program for ten students.

American Nursery and Landscape Association., 1000 Vermont Ave. No. 300 Washington, DC 20005-4914. Phone: (202)789-2900 Fax: (202)789-1893 • URL: http://www.anla.org • Formerly Wholesale Nursery Growers of America.

American Nursery and Landscape Association Membership Directory. American Nursery and Landscape Association, 1250 Eye St., N.W., Suite 500 Washington, DC 20005. Phone: (202)789-2900 Fax: (202)789-1893 • URL: http://www.anla.org • Annual. Free to members; non-members, $250.00 per year. Lists 2,200 member firms. Formerly *American Association of Nurserymen Membership Directory.*

American Nurseryman. American Nurseryman Publishing Co., 77 Washington St., Suite 2100 Chicago, IL 60602-2904. Phone: 800-621-5727 or (312)782-5505 Fax: (312)782-3232 E-mail: subscriptions@amerinursery.com • URL: http://www.amerinursery.com • Semimonthly. $48.00 per year.

American Nurses Association., 8515 Georgia Ave., Ste. 400 Silver Spring, MD 20910. Phone: 800-274-4262 or (301)628-5000 Fax: (301)628-5001 E-mail: memberinfo@ana.org • URL: http://www.nursingworld.org • Serves as membership association representing registered nurses. Advances the nursing profession by fostering high standards of nursing practice, promoting the rights of nurses in the workplace, projecting a positive and realistic view of nursing, and by lobbying the Congress and regulatory agencies on health care issues affecting nurses and the public.

American Occupational Therapy Association., 4720 Montgomery Ln., PO Box 31220 Bethesda, MD 20824-1220.

Phone: 800-377-8555 or (301)652-2682 or (301)652-6611 Fax: (301)652-7711 E-mail: execdept@aota.org • URL: http://www.aota.org • Occupational therapists and occupational therapy assistants. Provides services to people whose lives have been disrupted by physical injury or illness, developmental problems, the aging process, or social or psychological difficulties. Occupational therapy focuses on the active involvement of the patient in specially designed therapeutic tasks and activities to improve function, performance capacity, and the ability to cope with demands of daily living.

American Oil Chemists' Society., PO Box 17190, 2211 W Bradley Ave. Urbana, IL 61803-7190. Phone: (217)359-2344 Fax: (217)351-8091 E-mail: general@aocs.org • URL: http://www.aocs.org • Chemists, biochemists, chemical engineers, research directors, plant personnel, and others in laboratories and chemical process industries concerned with animal, marine, and vegetable oils and fats, and their extraction, refining, safety, packaging, quality control, and use in consumer and industrial products such as foods, drugs, paints, waxes, lubricants, soaps, and cosmetics. Sponsors short courses; certifies referee chemists; distributes cooperative check samples; sells official reagents. Maintains 100 committees. Operates job placement service for members only.

American Optometric Association., 243 N Lindbergh Blvd. St. Louis, MO 63141-7881. Phone: 800-365-2219 or (314)991-4100 Fax: (314)991-4101 E-mail: klalexander@aoa.org • URL: http://www.aoa.org • Professional association of optometrists, students of optometry, and paraoptometric assistants and technicians. Purposes are: to improve the quality, availability, and accessibility of eye and vision care; to represent the optometric profession; to help members conduct their practices; to promote the highest standards of patient care. Monitors and promotes legislation concerning the scope of optometric practice, alternate health care delivery systems, health care cost containment, Medicare, and other issues relevant to eye/vision care. Supports the International Library, Archives and Museum of Optometry which includes references on ophthalmic and related sciences with emphasis on the history and socioeconomic aspects of optometry. Operates Vision U.S.A. program, which provides free eye care to the working poor, and the InfantSEE program, which provides free vision assessments for infants between six and twelve months of age. Conducts specialized education programs; operates placement service; compiles statistics. Maintains museum. Conducts Seal of Acceptance Program.

American Optometric Association; Contact Lens Section., 243 N. Lindbergh Blvd. St. Louis, MO 63141. Phone: (314)991-4100 Fax: (314)991-4101 • URL: http://www.aoanet.org • Members are optometrists, students of optometry and paraoptometric assistants and technicians. Formerly American Optical Association.

American Optometric Association News. American Optometric Association, 243 N. Lindbergh Blvd. St. Louis, MO 63141. Phone: (314)991-4100 Fax: (314)991-4101 E-mail: almiller@aoa.org • URL: http://www.aoanet.org • Semimonthly. Free to members; non-members, $89.00 per year.

American Orthotic and Prosthetic Association.

American Painting Contractor. Douglas Publications, Inc., 2807 N. Parham Rd., Suite 200 Richmond, VA 23294. Phone: (804)762-9600 Fax: (804)217-8999 E-mail: info@douglaspublications.com • URL: http://www.douglaspublications.com • Nine times a year. $35.00 per year.

American Payroll Association., 660 N Main Ave., Ste. 100 San Antonio, TX 78205-1217. Phone: 800-398-8681 or (210)226-4600 Fax: (210)226-4027 E-mail: apa@americanpayroll.org • URL: http://www.americanpayroll.org • Payroll employees. Works to increase members' skills and professionalism through education and mutual support. Represents the interest of members before legislative bodies. Conducts training courses. Operates speakers' bureau; conducts educational programs. Administers the certified payroll professional program of recognition.

American Peanut Council., 1500 King St., Ste. 301 Alexandria, VA 22314. Phone: (703)838-9500 Fax: (703)838-9508 E-mail: info@peanutsusa.com • URL: http://www.peanutsusa.com • Growers, shellers, brokers, processors, and manufacturers; allied businesses providing goods and services to the peanut industry. Encourages research to improve quality of peanuts.

American Peanut Council—Membership Directory. American Peanut Council Inc., 1500 King St., Ste. 301, Suite 301 Alexandria, VA 22314-2737. Phone: (703)838-9500 Fax: (703)838-9508 E-mail: peanutsusa@aol.com • URL: http://www.peanutsusa.com • Covers: about 250 growers, shellers, processors, manufacturers, brokers, and allied businesses providing goods and services to the peanut industry. Entries include: Company name, address, phone, fax, telex, e-mail, names of principal executives, subsidiary and branch names and locations, products.

American Peanut Research and Education Society.

American Pet Products Manufacturers Association, Inc.

American Petroleum Institute., 1220 L St. NW Washington, DC 20005-4070. Phone: (202)682-8000 Fax: (202)682-8033 E-mail: mediacenter@api.org • URL: http://www.api.org • Corporations in the petroleum and allied industries, including producers, refiners, marketers, and transporters of crude oil, lubricating oil, gasoline and natural gas. Provides public policy development, advocacy, research, and technical services to enhance the ability of the petroleum industry to fulfill its mission: meeting the nation's energy needs; enhancing the environmental, health, and safety performance of the industry; conducting research to advance petroleum technology, equipment, and standards; Consensus policies and collective action on issues impacting its members; and works collaboratively with all industry oil and gas associations, and other organizations, to enhance industry unity and effectiveness in its advocacy. Also provides the opportunity for standards development, technical cooperation and other activities to improve the industry's competitiveness through sponsorship of self-supporting programs.

American Petroleum Institute. Division of Statistics. Weekly Statistical Bulletin. American Petroleum Institute, Publications Section, 1220 L St., N.W. Washington, DC 20005. Phone: (202)682-8375 Fax: (202)962-4776 • URL: http://www.api.org • Weekly. $115.00 per year. Includes *Monthly Statistical Report*.

American Pharmaceutical Association-Academy of Pharmacy Practice and Management., c/o Anne Burns, 2215 Constitution Ave., N.W. Washington, DC 20037-2895. Phone: 800-237-2742 or (202)628-4410 Fax: (202)783-2351 E-mail: apha-appm@mail.aphanet.org • URL: http://www.aphanet.org • Pharmacists concerned with rendering professional services directly to the public, without regard for status of employment or environment of practice. Formerly Academy of Pharmacy Practice and Management.

American Philatelic Society., 100 Match Factory Pl. Bellefonte, PA 16823. Phone: (814)933-3803 Fax: (814)933-6128 E-mail: dngc@stamps.org • URL: http://www.stamps.org • Collectors of postage and revenue stamps, first day covers, postal history, and related philatelic items. Helps members buy and sell stamps; operates expertise service; offers stamp insurance program; circulates slide programs. Maintains hall of fame; offers correspondence courses; accredits judges for philatelic competitions. Conducts philatelic seminars.

American Places Dictionary: A Guide to Populated Places, Natural Features , and Other United States Places. Frank R. Abate, editor. Omnigraphics, Inc., 615 Griswold St. Detroit, MI 48226. Phone: 800-234-1340 or (313)961-1340 Fax: 800-875-1340 or (313)961-1383 E-mail: info@omnigraphics.com • URL: http://www.omnigraphics.com • 1994. $350.00. Four regional volumes: Northeast, South, Midwest, and West. Provides statistical data and other information on 45,000 U. S. cities, towns, townships, boroughs, and villages. Includes detailed state profiles, county profiles, and more than 10,000 name origins. Arranged by state, then by county. (Individual regional volumes are available at $100.00.)

American Planning Association., 122 S Michigan Ave., Ste. 1600 Chicago, IL 60603-6107. Phone: (312)431-9100 Fax: (312)431-9985 E-mail: customerservice@planning.org • URL: http://www.planning.org • Public and private planning agency officials, professional planners, planning educators, elected and appointed officials, and other persons involved in urban and rural development. Works to foster the best techniques and decisions for the planned development of communities and regions. Provides extensive professional services and publications to professionals and laypeople in planning and related fields; serves as a clearinghouse for information. Through Planning Advisory Service, a research and inquiry-answering service, provides, on an annual subscription basis, advice on specific inquiries and a series of research reports on planning, zoning, and environmental regulations. Supplies information on job openings and makes definitive studies on salaries and recruitment of professional planners. Conducts research; collaborates in joint projects with local, national, and international organizations.

American Planning Association Journal. American Planning Association, 122 S. Michigan Ave., Suite 1600 Chicago, IL 60603-6107. Phone: (312)431-9100 Fax: (312)431-9985 E-mail: bookservice@planning.org • URL: http://www.planning.org • Quarterly. Members, $33.00 per year; non-members $75.00 per year.

American Pomological Society Journal. American Pomological Society, c/o Dr. Robert M. Crassweller, 103 Tyson Bldg. University Park, PA 16802. Phone: (814)863-6163 Fax: (814)863-6139 E-mail: aps@psu.edu Quarterly. $30.00 per year. Presents reports and general information on fruit varieties.

American Poultry Association., 947 Grand Ave. Fillmore, CA 93015. Phone: (805)524-4046 Fax: (508)473-8769 E-mail: danderson@keygroupinc.com • URL: http://www.amerpoultryassn.com • Poultry industry. Strives to protect and promote the standard-bred poultry industry in all of its phases.

American Printer: The Graphic Arts Manager Magazine. Primedia Business Magazines and Media, 330 N Wabash Ave., Ste. 2300 Chicago, IL 60611. Phone: 800-795-5445 or (312)595-1080 Fax: (312)595-0295 E-mail: subs@primediabusiness.com • URL: http://www.primediabusiness.com • Monthly. Free to qualified personnel; others, $73.00 per year. Serves the printing and lithographic industries and allied manufacturing and service segments.

American Professional Practice Association., Association Member Service Center, Hillsboro Executive Center N, 350 Fairway Dr., Ste. 200 Deerfield Beach, FL 33441-1834. Phone: 800-221-2168 or (954)571-1877 Fax: (954)571-8582 E-mail: membership@assnservices.com • URL: http://www.appa-assn.com • Provides physicians with economic benefits and financial services including the following: unsecured loan plans, mortgage loans, group insurance discounts, accounts receivable collections, office supplies, wealth protection and a vision and dental plan.

An American Profile: Attitudes and Behaviors of the American People, 1972-1989. Gale Cengage Learning, 27500 Drake Rd. Farmington Hills, MI 48331-3535. Phone: 800-877-GALE or (248)699-GALE Fax: 800-414-5043 E-mail: gale.galeord@cengage.com • URL: http://gale.cengage.com • 1990. $89.50. A summary of responses to about 300 questions in the General Social Survey conducted annually by the National Opinion Research Center, covering family characteristics, social behavior, religion, political opinions, etc. Includes a chronology of significant world events from 1972 to 1989 and a subject-keyword index.

American Public Gas Association., 201 Massachusetts Ave. NE, Ste. C-4 Washington, DC 20002. Phone: 800-927-4204 or (202)464-2742 Fax: (202)464-0246 E-mail: bkalisch@apga.org • URL: http://www.apga.org • Publicly owned gas systems; private corporations, persons or firms dealing with public gas systems are associate members. Promotes efficiency among public gas systems and protects the interests of the gas consumer. Provides information service on federal developments affecting natural gas; surveys municipal systems.

American Public Gas Association—Directory. American Public Gas Association, 201 Massachusetts Ave. NE, Ste. C-4 Washington, DC 20002. Phone: 800-927-4204 or (202)464-2742 Fax: (202)464-0246 E-mail: lwillsdudich@apga.org Covers: about 1,000 municipally owned gas systems throughout the United States. Entries include: Name of system, address, phone, contact name, number of meters, number of employees, name of supplier of natural gas, miles of transmission and distribution lines, and date it became a municipal utility.

American Public Gas Association Public Gas News. American Public Gas Association, 11094-D Lee Highway, Suite 102 Fairfax, VA 22030. Phone: (703)352-3890 Fax: (703)352-1271 Biweekly. $45.00 per year. Formerly, *American Public Gas Association Newsletter*.

American Public Human Services Association., 810 1st St. NE, Ste. 500 Washington, DC 20002. Phone: (202)682-0100 Fax: (202)289-6555 E-mail: jerry.friedman@aphsa.org • URL: http://www.aphsa.org • Public human service agencies, their professional staff members, and others interested in public human services. Works to develop, promote and implement human service policies that improve the health and well-being of families, children and adults.

American Public Power Association., 1875 Connecticut Ave. NW, Ste. 200 Washington, DC 20009. Phone: (202)467-2900 Fax: (202)467-2910 E-mail: mrufe@appanet.org • URL: http://www.appanet.org • Municipally owned electric utilities, public utility districts, state and county-owned electric systems, and rural cooperatives. Conducts research programs; compiles statistics; offers utility education courses; sponsors competitions.

American Public Transportation Association., 1666 K St. NW, Ste. 1100 Washington, DC 20006. Phone: (202)496-4800 Fax: (202)496-4321 E-mail: info@apta.com • URL: http://www.apta.com • Motor bus and rapid transit systems; organizations responsible for planning, designing, constructing, financing, and operating transit systems; business organizations which supply products and services to transit, academic institutions, and state associations and departments of transportation. Represents the public interest in improving transit. Encourages cooperation among its members, their employees, the general public and compliance with the letter and spirit of equal opportunity principles. Seeks to: collect information relative to public transit; assist in the training, education, and professional development of all persons involved in public transit; and engage in activities which promote public transit. Provides a medium for exchange of experiences, discussion, and a comparative study of public transit affairs; Promotes research.

American Public Works Association., 2345 Grand Blvd., Ste. 700 Kansas City, MO 64108-2625. Phone: 800-848-APWA or (816)472-6100 Fax: (816)472-1610 E-mail: pking@apwa.net • URL: http://www.apwa.net • Chief administrators, commissioners, and directors of public works, city engineers, superintendents, and department heads of transportation, water, waste water, solid waste, equipment services, and buildings and grounds; federal, provincial, and state administrators and engineers; consultants and educators; associate members are equipment manufacturers' representatives, utility company officials, and contractors; student members are engineering and public administration students interested in the theory and practice of the design, construction, maintenance, administration, and operation of public works facilities and services. Conducts historical research on public works subjects and demonstrates applicability of history to current public works problems and issues through Public Works Historical Society (see separate entry). Sponsors research and education foundations.

American Railway Car Institute., 29W 140 Butterfield Rd., Ste. 103-A Warrenville, IL 60555. Phone: 888-393-0107 or (630)393-0106 Fax: (630)393-0108 E-mail: rpi@rpi.org • URL: http://www.rsiweb.org/committees/com_arci.aspx • Independent manufacturers of railroad and freight cars.

Conducts research and standardization activities, particularly in freight car design and container standards. Provides for exchange of data on new devices used in freight cars. Compiles statistics on orders, deliveries, and backlogs of railroad cars with Association of American Railroads (see separate entry). Maintains historical files.

American Railway Engineering and Maintenance of Way Association.

American Real Estate and Urban Economics Association., PO Box 1148 Portage, MI 49081-1148. Phone: (866)273-8321 Fax: (313)731-0174 E-mail: areuea@areuea.org • URL: http://www.areuea.org • Members are real estate teachers, researchers, economists, and others concerned with urban real estate and investment.

American Recreational Golf Association., 7300 W Fullerton Ave., PO Box 35215 Chicago, IL 60707-0215. Phone: (708)453-0080 Fax: (708)453-0083 E-mail: concido@ concido.com • URL: http://rentamark.com/arga/ • Initiated by the American Recreational Sports Association. Evaluates golf equipment for the sporting goods industry and offers equipment certification program. Studies trends in the golf industry. Maintains a hall of fame; sponsors competitions; conducts charitable and educational programs.

American Reference Books Annual. Bohdan S. Wynar, editor. Libraries Unlimited, Inc., 88 Post Rd., W Westport, CT 06881. Phone: 800-225-5800 Fax: (203)222-1502 E-mail: lu-books@lu.com • URL: http://www.lu.com • Annual. $125. 00.

American Rehabilitation: AR. U. S. Dept. of Health, Education, and Welfare; Rehabilitation Services Administr. Available from U. S. Government Printing Office, Washington, DC 20402. Phone: (202)512-1800 Fax: (202)512-1800 E-mail: gpoaccess@gpo.gov • URL: http://www.access.gpo.gov • Quarterly. $15.00 per year. Official publication of the Rehabilitation Services Administration. Comments on all aspects of life affecting handicapped people.

American Rehabilitation Counseling Association., PO Box 6500, Pan American Department of Rehabilitation, College of Health Sciences and Human Services, 1201 W University Dr. Brea, CA 92822. Phone: 800-347-6647 or (714)674-5728 Fax: (956)380-6499 E-mail: patricia.nunez@cna.com • URL: http://www.arcaweb.org • A division of the American Counseling Association (see separate entry). Rehabilitation counselors and interested professionals and students. Aims to improve the rehabilitation counseling profession and its services to individuals with disabilities. Promotes high standards in rehabilitation counseling, practice, research, and education. Encourages the exchange of information between rehabilitation professionals and consumer groups. Serves as liaison among members and public and private rehabilitation counselors across the country. Sponsors educational and training programs.

American Renewal Foundation., PO Box 54 Corbin, VA 22446. Phone: (703)758-4600 E-mail: info@americanrenewal.org • URL: http://www.americanrenewal.org • Explores opportunities for renewal; seeks to provide a voice in the national conversation as well as the vision of the nation's founders, through research and promotion of Christian, ethical solutions to national and global issues. Broadcasts a daily radio news show, The World from Washington, and a weekly radio show for teens called SpeakOut. Runs the web newspaper, Page One Daily. Maintains a large student program; new members are always invited to apply. Provides internship opportunities.

American Rental Association., 1900 19th St. Moline, IL 61265. Phone: 800-334-2177 or (309)764-2475 Fax: (309)764-1533 E-mail: chris.wehrman@ararental.org • URL: http://www.ararental.org • Firms engaged in the rental of event and party equipment, tools, machinery, and other products; includes independent, franchised, and chain store operators. Associates are suppliers of equipment, merchandise, and other items. Seeks to foster better business methods; promote study of economic trends in the rental industry.

American Retirees Association., PO Box 2333 Redlands, CA 92373-0781. Phone: (909)557-0107 Fax: (909)335-2711 E-mail: contactara@aol.com • URL: http://www.americanretireesassociation.org • Active, reserve, and retired members of the uniformed military services of the United States. Seeks to address what the group feels are inequities in the Uniformed Services Former Spouses' Protection Act (USFSPA). Provides advisory services to military retirees and second families adversely affected by these laws; lobbies for amendments to the USFSPA.

American Rifleman. National Rifle Association of America. NRA Publications, 11250 Waples Mill Rd. Fairfax, VA 22030-9400. Phone: 800-672-3888 or (703)267-1316 Fax: (703)267-3800 E-mail: membership@nrahq.org • URL: http://www.nra.org • Monthly. $35.00 per year.

American Risk and Insurance Association., 716 Providence Rd. Malvern, PA 19355-0728. Phone: (610)640-1997 or (610)644-2100 Fax: (610)725-1007 E-mail: aria@cpcuiia.org • URL: http://www.aria.org • Promotes education and research in the science of risk and insurance.

American Road and Transportation Association Transportation Officials and Engineers Directory. American Road and Transportation Builders Association, The ARTBA, 1010 Massachusetts Ave., N.W. Washington, DC 20001. Phone: (202)289-4434 Fax: (202)289-4435 E-mail: artbadc@aol.com • URL: http://www.artba.org • Annual. Members, $90.

00; non-members, $120.00. Lists over 5,000 administrative engineers and officials in federal, state, and county transportation agencies.

American Road and Transportation Builders Association., The ARTBA Bldg., 1010 Massachusetts Ave., N.W. Washington, DC 20001-5402. Phone: (202)289-4434 Fax: (202)289-4435 E-mail: pruane@artba.org • URL: http://www.artba.org • Promotes on-the-job training programs.

The American Safe Deposit Association., PO Box 519, 140 E Jefferson St. Franklin, IN 46131. Phone: 800-768-8678 or (317)738-4432 Fax: (317)738-5267 E-mail: tasda1@aol.com • URL: http://www.tasda.com • Federation of state and local associations of banks, trust companies, and other firms engaged in the safe deposit business.

American Salaries and Wages Survey. Gale Cengage Learning, 27500 Drake Rd. Farmington Hills, MI 48331-3535. Phone: 800-877-GALE or (248)699-GALE Fax: 800-414-5043 E-mail: gale.galeord@cengage.com • URL: http://gale.cengage.com • 2003. $195.00. Seventh edition. Arranged alphabetically by 4,402 occupational classifications. Provides salary data for different experience levels and in specific areas of the U.S. Includes cost of living data for metropolitan areas.

American Salon. National Hairdressers and Cosmetologists Association. Advanstar Communications, 545 Boylston St. Boston, MA 02116. Phone: 888-527-7008 or (617)267-6500 Fax: (617)267-6900 E-mail: info@advanstar.com • URL: http://www.advanstar.com • Monthly. $26.50 per year. Supplement available *American Salon Distributor-Manufacturer News*.

American School and University: Facilities, Purchasing, and Business Administration. Primedia Business Magazines and Media, 9800 Metcalf Ave. Overland Park, KS 66212. Phone: 800-795-5445 or (913)341-1300 Fax: (913)967-1898 E-mail: subs@primediabusiness.com • URL: http://www.primediabusiness.com • Monthly. Free to qualified personnel; others, $50.00 per year.

American School and University-Who's Who Directory and Buyers' Guide. Primedia Business Magazines and Media, 330 N Wabash Ave., Suite 2300 Chicago, IL 60611. Phone: 800-795-5445 or (312)595-1080 Fax: (312)595-0295 E-mail: subs@primediabusiness.com • URL: http://www.primediabusiness.com • Annual. $10.00. List of companies supplying products and service for physical plants and business offices of schools, colleges and universities.

American School Board Journal. National School Boards Association, 1680 Duke St. Alexandria, VA 22314-3493. Phone: (703)838-6722 Fax: (703)549-6719 • URL: http://www.asbj.com • Monthly. $54.00 per year. How to advice for community leaders who want to improve their schools.

American School Food Service Association.

American Scientific Glassblowers Society., PO Box 778 Madison, NC 27025. Phone: (336)427-2406 Fax: (336)427-2496 E-mail: natl-office@asgs-glass.org • URL: http://www.asgs-glass.org • Glassblowers with more than 5 years' experience in making scientific glass apparatus (condensers, distillation apparatus, glass-to-metal seals, and vacuum devices); junior members are glassblowers with less than 5 years' professional experience; associates are persons connected with the manufacture or use of glass or glassblowing equipment in scientific work. Seeks to gather and disseminate information concerning scientific glassblowing, apparatus, equipment, and materials.

American Seed Research Foundation., 225 Reinekers Ln., Ste. 650 Alexandria, VA 22314-2875. Phone: (703)837-8140 Fax: (703)837-9365 E-mail: natl-office@asgs-glass.org • URL: http://www.amseed.com/asrf • Breeders, producers, and distributors of seeds. Seeks to advance seed technology by supporting research on seeds.

American Seed Trade Association., 225 Reinekers Ln., Ste. 650 Alexandria, VA 22314-2875. Phone: 888-890-SEED or (703)837-8140 or (703)837-8140 Fax: (703)837-9365 E-mail: alozanom@sakata.com.mx • URL: http://www.amseed.com • Breeders, growers, assemblers, conditioners, wholesalers, and retailers of grain, grass, vegetable, flower, and other seed for planting purposes.

American Sheep Industry Association., 9785 Maroon Cir., Ste. 360 Centennial, CO 80112. Phone: (303)771-3500 Fax: (303)771-8200 E-mail: info@sheepusa.org • URL: http://www.sheepusa.org • Producers of sheep and wool. Goal is to advance the standards and profitability of the sheep industry. Conducts lobbying activities to promote legislation beneficial to the industry.

American Shipper: Ports, Transportation and Industry. Howard Publications, Inc., 300 W Adams St., Ste. 600 Jacksonville, FL 32201. Phone: (904)355-2601 Fax: (904)791-8836 E-mail: dhoward@shippers.com • URL: http://www.americanshipper.com • Monthly. $120.00 per year.

American Shoemaking. James Sutton. Shoe Trades Publishing Co., P.O. Box 198 Cambridge, MA 02140. Phone: (781)648-8160 Fax: (781)646-9832 E-mail: info@shoetrades.com Monthly. $55.00 per year.

American Shoemaking Directory. Shoe Trades Publishing Co., 241 Senneville Rd. Senneville, QC, Canada H9X 3X5. Phone: 800-973-7463 or (514)457-8787 Fax: (514)457-5832 E-mail: books@shoetrades.com Covers: Shoe manufacturers in the United States, Puerto Rico, and Canada. Entries include: Company name, address, phone, fax, names of executives, product information brand names. Also key personnel; Plant output, trade sold, and sales offices included.

American Society for Clinical Laboratory Science., 6701 Democracy Blvd., Ste. 300 Bethesda, MD 20817. Phone: (301)657-2768 Fax: (301)657-2909 E-mail: ascls@ascls.org • URL: http://www.ascls.org • Seeks to promote high standards in clincal laboratory methods. Formerly American Society for Medical Technology.

American Society for Enology and Viticulture.

American Society for Healthcare Food Service Administrators., c/o American Hospital Association, One N. Franklin St. Chicago, IL 60606. Phone: (312)422-3840 Fax: (312)422-4581 E-mail: ashfsa@aha.org • URL: http://www.ashfsa.org • Formerly American Society for Hospital Food Service Administrators.

American Society for Industrial Security.

American Society for Information Science and Technology., 1320 Fenwick Lane, No. 510 Silver Spring, MD 20910. Phone: (301)495-0900 Fax: (301)495-0810 E-mail: asis@asis.org • URL: http://www.asis.org • Members are information managers, scientists, librarians, and others who are interested in the storage, retrieval, and use of information.

American Society for Information Science and Technology Journal. American Society for Information Science and Technology. John Wiley and Sons, Inc., Journals, 111 River St. Hoboken, NJ 07030. Phone: 800-225-5945 or (201)748-6000 Fax: (201)748-6088 E-mail: custsomer@wiley.com • URL: http://www.wiley.com • 14 times a year. $1,600.00 per year; with online edition, $1,680.00 per year.

American Society for Nutritional Sciences., 9650 Rockville Pike Bethesda, MD 20814-3990. Phone: (301)634-7050 Fax: (301)634-7892 E-mail: sec@asns.org • URL: http://www.asns.org • Affiliated with American Society for Clinical Nutrition. Formerly American Institute of Nutrition.

American Society for Public Administration.

American Society for Quality.

American Society for Training and Development.

American Society of Access Professionals., 1441 Eye St. N.W., Suite 700 Washington, DC 20005-6542. Phone: (202)712-9054 Fax: (202)216-9646 E-mail: asap@bostromdc.com • URL: http://www.accesspro.org • Members are individuals concerned with safeguarding freedom of information, privacy, open meetings, and fair credit reporting laws.

American Society of Access Professionals-Membership Directory. American Society of Access Professionals, 1444 Eye St., N.W., Suite 700 Washington, DC 20005. Phone: (202)712-9054 Fax: (202)216-9646 E-mail: asap@bostromdc.com • URL: http://www.podi.com/asap • Annual. Membership.

American Society of Agricultural Consultants.

American Society of Agricultural Engineers.

American Society of Agronomy.

American Society of Animal Science.

American Society of Appraisers.

American Society of Association Executives.

American Society of Baking.

American Society of Baking Proceedings. American Society of Bakery Engineers, 1200 Cental Ave., Suite 360 Wilmette, IL 60091. Phone: (866)920-9885 or (847)920-9885 Fax: (847)920-9886 E-mail: asbe@asbe.org • URL: http://www.asbe.org • Annual. Membership.

American Society of Bariatric Physicians - Directory. American Society of Bariatric Physicians, 5453 E Evans Pl. Denver, CO 80222-5234. Phone: (303)770-2526 Fax: (303)779-4834 E-mail: info@asbp.org Annual. $50.00. Lists 1,300 physicians concerned with obesity.

American Society of Brewing Chemists.

American Society of Brewing Chemists Journal. American Society of Brewing Chemists, 3340 Pilot Knob Rd. Saint Paul, MN 55121-2097. Phone: (612)454-7250 Fax: (612)454-0766 • URL: http://www.asbcnet.org • Quarterly. Free to members; non-members, $164.00 per year; corporate members, $195.00 per year; student members, $25.00 per year.

American Society of Business Publications Editors.

American Society of Cataract and Refractive Surgery., 4000 Legato Rd., No. 850 Fairfax, VA 22033. Phone: 800-451-1339 or (703)591-2220 Fax: (703)591-0614 E-mail: ascrs@ascrs.org • URL: http://www.ascrs.org • Affiliated with American Medical Association and American Society Ophthalmic Administrators.

American Society of Cinematographers.

American Society of Civil Engineers.

American Society of Civil Engineers-Official Register. American Society of Civil Engineers, 1801 Alexander Graham Bell Dr. Reston, VA 20191-4400. Phone: 800-548-2723 or (703)295-6300 Fax: (703)295-6222 • URL: http://www.asce.org • Annual. Free.

American Society of Civil Engineers. Proceedings. American Society of Civil Engineers, 1801 Alexander Graham Bell Dr. Reston, VA 20191-4400. Phone: 800-548-2723 or (703)295-6300 Fax: (703)295-6222 • URL: http://www.asce.org • Monthly. $2,289.00 per year. Consists of the Journals of the various Divisions of the Society.

American Society of Civil Engineers: Transactions. American Society of Civil Engineers, 1801 Alexander Graham Bell Dr. Reston, VA 20191-4400. Phone: 800-548-2723 or (703)295-6300 Fax: (703)295-6222 • URL: http://www.asce.org • Annual. $254.00.

American Society of Comparative Law.

American Society of Composers, Authors and Publishers.

American Society of Consulting Planners.

American Society of Corporate Secretaries.

American Society of Criminology., 1314 Kinnear Rd., Suite 212 Columbus, OH 43212-1156. Phone: (614)292-9207 Fax: (614)292-6767 E-mail: asc41@infinet.com • URL: http://www.asc41.com • Formerly Society for the Advancement of Criminology.

American Society of Farm Managers and Rural Appraisers.

American Society of Gas Engineers.

American Society of Golf Course Architects., 111 E Wacher Dr., 18th Fl. Chicago, IL 60601. Phone: (312)372-7090 Fax: (312)372-6160 E-mail: asgca@publicis-usa.com • URL: http://www.golfdesign.org • Members are professional designers and architects of golf courses.

American Society of Health System Pharmacists., 7272 Wisconsin Ave. Bethesda, MD 20814. Phone: (301)657-3000 Fax: (301)664-8867 E-mail: ahfs@ashp.org • URL: http://www.ashp.org • Affiliated with American Hospital Association and American Nurses Association.

American Society of Heating, Refrigerating and Air Conditioning Engineers.

American Society of Indexers., 10200 W. 44th Ave., Suite 304 Wheat Ridge, CO 80033. Phone: (303)463-2887 Fax: (303)422-8894 E-mail: info@asindexing.org • URL: http://www.asindexing.org • Affiliated with the American Library Association, the American Society for Information Science, and other organizations.

American Society of Interior Designers.

American Society of International Law.

American Society of Inventors.

American Society of Journalists and Authors.

American Society of Journalists and Authors-Directory. American Society of Journalists and Authors, 1501 Broadway, Suite 302 New York, NY 10036. Phone: (212)997-0947 Fax: (212)768-7414 E-mail: staff@asja.org • URL: http://www.asja.org • Annual. $98.00. Lists 1,050 freelance nonfiction writers. Formerly *American Society of Journalists and Authors Directory of Professional Writers.*

American Society of Landscape Architects.

American Society of Landscape Architects Members' Handbook. American Society of Landscape Architects, 636 Eye St., N.W. Washington, DC 20001-3736. Phone: (202)898-2444 Fax: (202)898-1185 E-mail: email@asla.org • URL: http://www.asla.org • Annual. Members, $25.00; non-members, $250.00.

American Society of Magazine Editors.

American Society of Mechanical Engineers.

American Society of Media Photographers.

American Society of Military Comptrollers., 415 N Alfred St. Alexandria, VA 22314. Phone: 800-462-5637 or (703)549-0360 Fax: (703)549-3181 E-mail: asmchq@asmconline.org • URL: http://www.asmconline.org • Civilians and military personnel who are now or who have been involved in the overall field of military comptrollership; other interested individuals. Conducts research programs. Compiles statistics; maintains speakers' bureau. Plans to establish library.

American Society of Military Insignia Collectors., 526 Lafayette Ave. Palmerton, PA 18071-1621. Phone: (610)826-5067 Fax: (610)826-5067 E-mail: adjutant@asmic.org • URL: http://www.asmic.org • Represents oldest military insignia collectors group in the U.S. Promotes the collection and preservation of U.S. and foreign military insignia. Disseminates information on the symbolism and historical significance of insignia. Assists veterans and individuals in search of insignia.

American Society of Naval Engineers.

American Society of Newspaper Editors.

American Society of Notaries.

American Society of Pension Actuaries., 4245 N. Fairfax Dr., Suite 750 Arlington, VA 22203. Phone: (703)516-9300 Fax: (703)516-9308 E-mail: aspa@aspa.org • URL: http://www.aspa.org • Members are involved in the pension and insurance aspects of employee benefits. Includes an Insurance and Risk Management Committee, and sponsors an annual 401(k) Workshop.

American Society of Photographers - Membership Directory. American Society of Photographers, Inc., P.O. Box 316 Williamantic, CT 06226. Phone: 800-638-9609 or (860)423-1402 Fax: (860)423-9402 E-mail: ppanerl@aol.com Annual. Membership.

American Society of Plumbing Engineers.

American Society of Professional Estimators., 11141 Georgia Ave., Suite 412 Wheaton, MD 20902. Phone: 888-378-6283 or (301)929-8848 Fax: (301)929-0231 E-mail: info@aspenational.com • URL: http://www.aspenational.com • Members are construction cost estimators and construction educators.

American Society of Safety Engineers.

American Society of Sanitary Engineering.

American Society of Transportation and Logistics.

American Society of Travel Agents.

American Society of Travel Agents-Membership Directory. American Society of Travel Agents, 1101 King St. Alexandria, VA 22314. Phone: (703)739-2782 Fax: (703)684-8319 Annual. $195.00. Listings of over 13,500 worldwide members of ASTA.

American Society of Women Accountants.

American Solar Energy Society., 2400 Central Ave., Ste. G-1 Boulder, CO 80301. Phone: (303)443-3130 Fax: (303)443-

3212 E-mail: ases@ases.org • URL: http://www.ases.org • Advises industry members on financing of construction projects and represents their interests before Congress, federal agencies, and state bodies.

American Soybean Association., 12125 Woodcrest Executive Dr., Ste. 100 St. Louis, MO 63141-5009. Phone: 800-688-7692 or (314)576-1770 Fax: (314)576-2786 E-mail: scensky@asaim.soy.org • URL: http://www.soygrowers.com • Develops and implements policies to increase the profitability of its members and the entire soybean industry.

American Spa and Health Resort Association., P.O. Box 585 Lake Forest, IL 60045. Phone: (847)234-8851 Fax: (847)295-7790 Members are owners and operators of health spas.

American Speaker: Your Guide to Successful Speaking. Briefings Publishing Group, 1101 King St., Suite 110 Alexandria, VA 22314. Phone: 800-888-2084 or (703)548-3800 Fax: (703)684-2136 E-mail: customerservice@briefing.com • URL: http://www.briefings.com • Bimonthly. $399.00. Newsletter. Provides practical advice on public speaking.

American Spice Trade Association., 2025 M St. NW, Ste. 800 Washington, DC 20036. Phone: (202)367-1127 Fax: (202)367-2127 E-mail: info@astaspice.org • URL: http://www.astaspice.org • Works to foment the export of American spices. Promotes the interests of the American spice industry.

American Sports Analysis. Available from MarketResearch.com, 641 Ave. of the Americas, 3rd Fl. New York, NY 10011. Phone: 800-298-5699 or (212)807-2629 Fax: (212)807-2716 E-mail: order@marketresearch.com • URL: http://www.marketresearch.com • 2001. $375.00. Published by American Sports Data, Inc. Consumer market data. A study of participation in sports activities (golf, tennis, swimming, running, etc.) by American consumers.

American Sportscasters Association., 225 Broadway, Ste. 2030 New York, NY 10007. Phone: (212)227-8080 Fax: (212)571-0556 E-mail: lschwa8918@aol.com • URL: http://www.americansportscastersonline.com • Radio and television sportscasters. Sponsors seminars, clinics, and symposia for aspiring announcers and sportscasters. Compiles statistics. Operates Speaker's Bureau, placement service, hall of fame, and biographical archives. Maintains American Sportscaster Hall of Fame Trust. Is currently implementing Hall of Fame Museum, Community Programs.

American Sportswear and Knitting Times. National Knitwear and Sportswear Association, PO Box 230 Summit, NJ 07902-0230. Monthly. $40.00 per year. Includes *American Sportswear and Knitting Times Buyer's Guide.* Formerly *Knitting Times.*

American Sportswear and Knitting Times Buyers' Guide. National Knitwear and Sportswear Association, PO Box 230 Summit, NJ 07902-0230. Annual. $25.00. Formerly *Knitting Times Buyers' Guide.*

American Staffing Association., 277 S Washington St., Ste. 200 Alexandria, VA 22314-3675. Phone: (703)253-2020 Fax: (703)253-2053 E-mail: asa@americanstaffing.net • URL: http://www.americanstaffing.net • Promotes and represents the staffing industry through legal and legislative advocacy, public relations, education, and the establishment of high standards of ethical conduct.

American Stamp Dealers Association., 3 School St., Ste. 205 Glen Cove, NY 11542-2548. Phone: (516)759-7000 Fax: (516)759-7014 E-mail: asda@asdaonline.com • URL: http://www.asdaonline.com • Dealers and wholesalers of stamps, albums, and other philatelic materials. Sponsors National Stamp Collecting Week in November.

American Statistical Association., 732 N Washington St. Alexandria, VA 22314-1943. Phone: 888-231-3473 or (703)684-1221 Fax: (703)684-2037 E-mail: asainfo@amstat.org • URL: http://www.amstat.org • Professional society of persons interested in the theory, methodology, and application of statistics to all fields of human endeavor.

American Statistician. American Statistical Association, 1429 Duke St. Alexandria, VA 22314-3415. Phone: (703)684-1221 or 888-231-3473 Fax: (703)684-2037 E-mail: asainfo@amstat.org • URL: http://www.amstat.org • Quarterly. Individuals, $15.00 per year; libraries, $75.00 per year; students, $15.00 per year.

American Statistics Index: A Comprehensive Guide and Index to the Statistical Publications of the United States Government. Congressional Information Service, Inc., 4520 East-West Highway, Suite 800 Bethesda, MD 20814-3389. Phone: 800-638-8380 or (301)654-1550 Fax: (301)654-4033 E-mail: cisinfo@lexis-nexis.com • URL: http://www.cispubs.com • Monthly. Price varies. Quarterly and annual cumulations.

American Stock Exchange., 86 Trinity Pl. New York, NY 10006. Phone: (866)422-2639 or (212)306-1000 Fax: (212)306-1218 E-mail: amexfeedback@amex.com • URL: http://www.amex.com • Represents domestic and international equities and derivative securities market. Provides an auction marketplace that integrates service and information programs for its listed companies.

The American Stock Exchange: A Guide to Information Resources. Carol Z. Womack and Alice C. Littlejohn. Garland Publishing, Inc., 29 W. 35th St. New York, NY 10001-2299. Phone: 800-627-6273 or (212)216-7800 Fax: (212)564-7854 E-mail: info@garland.com • URL: http://www.garlandpub.com • 1995. $15.00. (Research and Information Guides in Business, Industry, and Economic Institutions Series: Vol. 7).

American Stock Exchange Directory. CCH, Inc., 2700 Lake Cook Rd. Riverwoods, IL 60015. Phone: 800-835-5224 or (847)267-7000 E-mail: cust_serv@cch.com • URL: http://www.cch.com • 2000. $30.00.

American Stock Exchange Guide. CCH, Inc., 2700 Lake Cook Rd. Riverwoods, IL 60015. Phone: 888-224-7377 or (847)267-7000 Fax: (847)267-2514 E-mail: custserv@cch.com • URL: http://www.cch.com • Annual. $490.00 per year. Monthly updates. Contains exchange rules and regulations, constitution, and a directory.

American Stock Exchange Weekly Bulletin. Nasdaq-AMEX Market Group, 86 Trinity Place New York, NY 10006-1872. Phone: (212)306-1442 Weekly. $20.00 per year. Looseleaf service.

American Subcontractors Association., 1004 Duke St. Alexandria, VA 22314-3588. Phone: 888-374-3133 or (703)684-3450 Fax: (703)836-3482 E-mail: asaoffice@asa-hq.com • URL: http://www.asaonline.com • Construction subcontractors of trades and specialties such as foundations, concrete, masonry, steel, mechanical, drywall, electrical, painting, plastering, roofing, and acoustical. Formed to deal with issues common to subcontractors. Works with other segments of the construction industry in promoting ethical practices, beneficial legislation, and education of construction subcontractors and suppliers. Manages the Foundation of the American +Subcontractors Association (FASA).

American Sugar Alliance., 2111 Wilson Blvd., Ste. 600 Arlington, VA 22201. Phone: (703)351-5055 Fax: (703)351-6698 E-mail: info@sugaralliance.org • URL: http://www.sugaralliance.org • Domestic producers, processors, and refiners of sugar beets, and sugarcane; labor organizations; allied organizations that supply goods and services to the domestic sweetener producing industry. Works to increase public awareness of the international economic and political factors influencing sweetener production; seeks increased support from consumers and the government for a U.S. sugar policy that is favorable to domestic sugar and sweetener producers; strives to maintain among domestic producers the ability to meet the sweetener needs of the U.S.

American Sugar Cane League of the U.S.A., 206 E Bayou Rd. Thibodaux, LA 70301. Phone: (985)448-3707 Fax: (985)448-3722 E-mail: lasugar@amscl.org • URL: http://www.amscl.org • Louisiana sugar cane growers and processors.

American Supply Association., 222 Merchandise Mart Plz., Ste. 1400 Chicago, IL 60654. Phone: 800-464-0314 or (312)464-0090 Fax: (312)464-0091 E-mail: info@asa.net • URL: http://www.asa.net • Represents wholesale, distributors, and manufacturers of plumbing and heating, cooling, pipes, valves, and fittings. Compiles statistics on operating costs and makes occasional studies of compensation, fringe benefits, wages, and salaries. Conducts research studies and forecasting surveys. Offers group insurance. Maintains management institutes, home study courses under the ASA Education Foundation and Endowment program, provides technology and produces a CD-ROM and internet catalogue of manufacturers.

American Supply Association Operating Performance Report. American Supply Association, 222 Merchandise Mart Place, Suite 1400 Chicago, IL 60654-1202. Phone: (312)464-0090 Fax: (312)464-0091 E-mail: info@asa.net • URL: http://www.asa.net • Annual. Members, $45.00; non-members, $150.00.

American Tanker Rate Schedule. Association of Ship Brokers and Agents-USA, 510 Sylvan Ave., Ste. 201 Englewood Cliffs, NJ 07632. Phone: (201)569-2882 Fax: (201)569-9082 E-mail: asba@asba.org • URL: http://www.asba.org • Annual. $1,500.00. Contains tanker freight rates.

American Technical Education Association. c/o North Dakota State College of Science, 800 N 6th St. Wahpeton, ND 58076-0002. Phone: (701)671-2240 or (701)671-2240 Fax: (701)671-2260 E-mail: betty.krump@ndscs.edu • URL: http://www.ateaonline.org • Dedicated to excellence in the quality of post-secondary technical education with emphasis on professional development.

American Teleservices Association., 3815 River Crossing Pkwy., Ste. 20 Indianapolis, IN 46240. Phone: 877-779-3974 or (317)816-9336 Fax: (317)218-0323 E-mail: contact@ataconnect.org • URL: http://www.ataconnect.org • Businesses involved in teleservices, telephone marketing sales, including suppliers, distributors, users, and hardware and software manufacturers; educators and teleservice businesses. Provides for the specific needs of the total telephone services community; assists in understanding and using telephone communications for marketing purposes; sponsors educational programs.

American Textile Machinery Association., 201 Park Washington Ct. Falls Church, VA 22046. Phone: (703)538-1789 Fax: (703)241-5603 E-mail: info@atmanet.org • URL: http://www.atmanet.org • Manufacturers of capital equipment for textile manufacture and interested individuals from academia, industry, banking, transportation, insurance, engineering, textiles, and other industries.

American Textile Manufacturers Institute., 1130 Connecticut Ave. NW Washington, DC 20036-3954. Phone: (202)862-0500 Fax: (202)862-0570 E-mail: info@atmanet.org • URL: http://www.textileweb.com/storefronts/amertextile.html • Textile mill firms operating machinery for manufacturing and processing cotton, man-made, wool, and silk textile products; includes spinning, weaving, bleaching, finishing, knitting, and allied plants; does not include manufacturers of hosiery or firms that produce man-made fibers and yarn by a chemical process. Operates public relations program for the industry, government relations program, textile market program, and statistical and economic information service. Holds seminars and meetings. Sponsors safety contest among textile mills.

American Tool, Die and Stamping News. Eagle Publications, Inc., 42400 Grand River Ave., Suite 103 Novi, MI 48375-2572. Phone: 800-783-3491 or (248)347-3486 Fax: (248)347-3492 • URL: http://www.ameritooldie.com • Bimonthly. Free.

American Trade Schools Directory. Croner Publications Inc., 10951 Sorrento Valley Rd., Ste. 1-D San Diego, CA 92121-1613. Phone: 800-441-4033 or (858)546-1894 Fax: 800-809-0334 E-mail: rosa@croner.com Covers: over 12,000 private and public trade, technical, and vocational schools. Entries include: School name, address, phone, contact person, year school founded, private or public, accrediting agencies, whether approved by state or Veterans Administration, home study courses offered.

American Translators Association., 225 Reinekers Ln., Ste. 590 Alexandria, VA 22314-2875. Phone: (703)683-6100 Fax: (703)683-6122 E-mail: ata@atanet.org • URL: http://www.atanet.org • Fosters the professional development of translators and interpreters and promotes the translation and interpretation professions.

American Trucking Associations., 950 N Glebe Rd., Ste. 210 Arlington, VA 22203-4181. Phone: 888-333-1759 or (703)838-1700 Fax: (703)838-1852 E-mail: atamembership@trucking.org • URL: http://www.truckline.com • Motor carriers, suppliers, state trucking associations, and national conferences of trucking companies. Works to influence the decisions of federal, state, and local government bodies; promotes increased efficiency, productivity, and competitiveness in the trucking industries; sponsors American +Trucking Associations Foundation. Provides quarterly financial and operating statistics service. Offers comprehensive accounting service for all sizes of carriers. Promotes highway and driver safety; supports highway research projects; and studies technical and regulatory problems of the trucking industry. Sponsors competitions; compiles statistics. Maintains numerous programs and services including: Management Information Systems Directory; Compensation Survey; Electronic Data Interchange Standards.

American Trucking Trends. American Trucking Associations. Trucking Information Services, Inc., 2200 Mill Rd. Alexandria, VA 22314-4677. Phone: 800-282-5463 or (703)838-1700 Fax: (703)684-5720 E-mail: ata-infocenter@trucking.org • URL: http://www.truckline.com • Annual. $45.00

American Universities and Colleges. American Council on Education USA. Walter de Gruyter, Inc., 200 Saw Mill River Rd. Hawthorne, NY 10532. Phone: (914)747-0110 Fax: (914)747-1326 E-mail: cs@degrunterny.com • URL: http://www.degruyter.com • Quadrennial. $249.50. Two volumes. Produced in collaboration with the American Council on Education. Provides full descriptions of more than 1,900 institutions of higher learning, including details of graduate and professional programs.

American Vegetable Grower. Meister Media, 37733 Euclid Ave. Willoughby, OH 44094-5992. Phone: 800-572-7740 or (440)942-2000 Fax: (440)975-3447 E-mail: info@meistermedia.com • URL: http://www.meistermedia.com • Monthly. $27.47 per year.

American Vegetable Grower—Source Book. Meister Media Worldwide, 37733 Euclid Ave. Willoughby, OH 44094-5992. Phone: 800-572-7740 or (440)942-2000 Fax: (440)975-3447 E-mail: info@meistermedia.com • URL: http://www.meisterpro.com • Publication includes: Lists of suppliers of agricultural chemicals and manufacturers and suppliers of other agricultural products, equipment, and services including packaging equipment, transportation services, direct marketing suppliers, plants and seeds, etc. Entries include: Company name, address, phone, fax, e-mail.

American Veterinary Exhibitors Association., 712 N Broadway Menomonie, WI 54751. Phone: 877-990-1836 or (480)990-1887 Fax: (715)232-9936 E-mail: avea@wwt.net Manufacturers and dealers of products for the veterinary profession. To give firms exhibiting at veterinary conventions a voice in planning the time, place, program, and facilities of such meetings; to cooperate and consult with veterinary associations in matters of mutual interest.

American Veterinary Medical Association., 1931 N Meacham Rd., Ste. 100 Schaumburg, IL 60173. Phone: 800-248-2862 or (847)925-8070 Fax: (847)925-1329 E-mail: avmainfo@avma.org • URL: http://www.avma.org • Professional society of veterinarians. Conducts educational and research programs. Provides placement service. Sponsors American +Veterinary +Medical Association Foundation (also known as AVMF Foundation) and Educational +Commission for +Foreign +Veterinary Graduates. Compiles statistics. Accredits veterinary medical education programs and veterinary technician education programs.

American Veterinary Medical Association Journal. American Veterinary Medical Association, 1931 N. Meacham Rd., Suite 100, c/o AVMA Library Schaumburg, IL 60173-4360. Phone: 800-248-2862 or (847)925-8070 Fax: (847)925-1329 E-mail: avmaininfo@avma.org • URL: http://www.avma.org • Semimonthly. $120.00 per year.

American Vocational Educational Research Association.

American Walnut Manufacturers Association., 6516 Linchmere Ln. Dublin, OH 43017. Phone: (614)923-4421 Fax: (614)923-4421 E-mail: bshardwoods1@yahoo.com • URL: http://www.walnutassociation.org • Manufacturers of hardwood veneer and lumber, especially American black walnut. Seeks to improve the sale of products made from hardwoods through advertising, promotion, sales education, and product improvement; also promotes good forest management.

American Watch Association., PO Box 464, 1201 Pennsylvania Ave. NW Washington, DC 20044. Phone: (703)759-3377 Fax: (703)759-1639 E-mail: avmainfo@avma.org Importers of watch movements, watches, and clocks; assemblers of watches, using imported or domestic movements and cases; domestic manufacturers of watch products; suppliers of goods and services.

American Watchmakers and Clockmakers Institute., 701 Enterprise Dr. Harrison, OH 45030. Phone: (866)367-2924 or (513)367-2924 Fax: (513)367-1414 E-mail: jlubic@awi-net.org • URL: http://www.awi-net.org • Formerly American Watchmakers Institute.

American Water Resources Association., PO Box 1626, PO Box 1626 Middleburg, VA 20118-1626. Phone: (540)687-8390 Fax: (540)687-8395 E-mail: info@awra.org • URL: http://www.awra.org • Engineers; natural, physical, and social scientists; other persons engaged in any aspect of the field of water resources; business concerns and other organizations; students in water resources. Includes members from 62 nations. Seeks to advance water resources research, planning, development, and management. Endeavors to collect and disseminate ideas and information relative to water resources science and technology via scientific journal, newsletter, conferences and symposia and published proceedings.

American Water Works Association., 6666 W Quincy Ave., 6666 W. Quincy Ave. Denver, CO 80235-3098. Phone: 800-926-7337 or (303)794-7711 Fax: (303)347-0804 E-mail: custsvc@awwa.org • URL: http://www.awwa.org • Water utility managers, superintendents, engineers, chemists, bacteriologists, and other individuals interested in public water supply; municipal- and investor-owned water departments; boards of health; manufacturers of waterworks equipment; government officials and consultants interested in water supply. Develops standards and supports research programs in waterworks design, construction, operation, and management. Conducts in-service training schools and prepares manuals for waterworks personnel. Maintains hall of fame. Offers placement service via member newsletter; compiles statistics. Offers training; children's services; and information center on the water utilities industry, potable water, and water reuse.

American Water Works Association Journal. American Water Works Association, 6666 W. Quincy Ave Denver, CO 80235. Phone: 800-926-7337 or (303)794-7711 Fax: (303)374-0804 • URL: http://www.awwa.org • Monthly. Free to members; libraries and governmental agencies only, $85.00 per year.

American Water Works Association—Sourcebook. American Water Works Association, 6666 W Quincy Ave. Denver, CO 80235. Phone: 800-926-7337 or (303)794-7711 Fax: (303)347-0804 E-mail: info@meistermedia.com • URL: http://www.awwa.org • Covers: member suppliers and distributors of water supply products and services, contractors for water supply projects, and engineering consultants. Entries include: Company name, address, names of executives, trade and brand names, products and services offered.

American Welding Society., 550 NW Le Jeune Rd. Miami, FL 33126. Phone: 800-443-9353 or (305)443-9353 Fax: (305)443-5647 E-mail: info@aws.org • URL: http://www.aws.org • One of several sponsors of the Welding Research Council and the Materials Properties Council. Professional engineering society in the field of welding. Sponsors seminars. Maintains over 130 technical and handbook committees, 171 sections, educational committees, and task forces.

American Wholesale Marketers Association., 2750 Prosperity Ave., Ste. 530 Fairfax, VA 22031. Phone: 800-482-2962 or (703)208-3358 Fax: (703)573-5738 E-mail: info@awmanet.org • URL: http://www.awmanet.org • Represents the interests of distributors of convenience products. Its members include wholesalers, retailers, manufacturers, brokers and allied organizations from across the U.S. and abroad. Programs include strong legislative representation in Washington and a broad spectrum of targeted education, business and information services. Sponsors the country's largest show for candy and convenience related products in conjunction with its semi-annual convention.

American Wholesalers and Distributors Directory. Gale Cengage Learning, 27500 Drake Rd. Farmington Hills, MI 48331-3535. Phone: 800-877-GALE or (248)699-GALE Fax: 800-414-5043 E-mail: gale.galeord@cengage.com • URL: http://gale.cengage.com • 2003. $250.00. 12th edition. Lists more than 30,000 national, regional, state, and local wholesalesrs.

American Wind Energy Association., 1101 14th St. NW, 12th Fl. Washington, DC 20005. Phone: (202)383-2500 Fax: (202)383-2505 E-mail: windmail@awea.org • URL: http://www.awea.org • Wind energy equipment manufacturers; project developers and dealers; individuals from industry, government, and academia; interested others. Works to: advance the art and science of using energy from the wind for human purposes; encourage the use of wind turbines and wind power plants as alternatives to current energy systems that depend on depletable fuels; facilitate the widespread use of wind as a renewable, non-polluting energy source by fostering communication within the field of wind energy and between the technical community and the public. Provides federal and state legislators with information on wind as an energy source; offers consultation to federal, state, and local government and private industry. Promotes exportation of U.S. manufactured wind energy equipment.

American Wine Society., 113 S Perry St. Lawrenceville, GA 30045. Phone: (678)377-7070 Fax: (678)377-7005 E-mail: coskery@americanwinesociety.org • URL: http://www.americanwinesociety.org • Amateur and professional winegrowers, winemakers, wine connoisseurs, wine merchants, and other interested persons. Seeks to further the knowledge, appreciation and enjoyment of wines produced on the American continent without bias toward European or other wines. Encourages legislation requiring honest labeling of both American and imported wines; fosters production of home wine-makers; seeks to further the use of American terms for American wines. Sponsors educational programs at national and local levels. Conducts wine tastings and trips to vineyards and wineries; arranges gourmet wine dinners; provides speakers on grape growing, wine-making, and wine appreciation.

American Wire Producers Association., 801 N Fairfax St., Ste. 211 Alexandria, VA 22314-1757. Phone: (703)299-4434 Fax: (703)299-9233 E-mail: info@awpa.org • URL: http://www.awpa.org • Represents manufacturers of steel wire and wire products; suppliers of wire rods, dies, machinery, and related equipment. Assures free and fair access to a global supply of wire rod and to encourage an adequate domestic supply.

American Woman's Society of Certified Public Accountants.

American Women in Radio and Television.

American Women Managers and Administrators: A Selective Biographical Dictionary of Twentieth Century Leaders in Business, Education, and Government. Judith A. Leavitt. Greenwood Publishing Group Inc., 88 Post Rd. W Westport, CT 06881. Phone: 800-225-5800 or (203)226-3571 Fax: (203)461-2214 E-mail: customer-service@greenwood.com • URL: http://www.greenwood.com • 1985. $78.50. A directory of 20th-century women who hold or have held administrative, managerial, or leadership positions in business, education, or government.

American Wood Preservers Institute., 12100 Sunset Hills Rd., Ste. 130 Reston, VA 20190-3221. Phone: 800-356-2974 or (703)204-0500 Fax: (703)204-4610 E-mail: info@awpa.org • URL: http://www.preservedwood.com • Pressure treating plants for the preservative treatment of wood products; manufacturers and distributors of standard chemical preservatives.

American Yarn Spinners Association., 2500 Lowell Rd. Gastonia, NC 28053. Phone: (704)824-3522 Fax: (704)824-0630 E-mail: info@awpa.org • URL: http://www.textileweb.com/storefronts/aysa.html • Manufacturers of combed cotton sales yarn and carded yarns spun from cotton, wool, and/or synthetics. Provides full service to the sales yarn industry.

Americana Annual. Grolier Inc., Sherman Turnpike Danbury, CT 06816. Phone: (203)797-3500 Annual. $29.95.

Americans for Common Sense., USA,. E-mail: ampaconline@ama-assn.org Bipartisan coalition of politically progressive citizens who wish to develop an issue-oriented practical political agenda to counter the activities of New Right organizations such as the Moral Majority (see separate entry). Believes that the New Right is often politically successful because individuals do not have all of the facts necessary to make a completely informed decision on the issues; helps citizens understand the complexities of current political issues by presenting alternative points of view to those adopted by the New Right; encourages individuals to avoid adopting opinions without examining alternative positions. While not taking stands on particular issues, ACS encourages progressive alternatives to New Right positions. Staff members participate in radio and television interview shows to provide a forum for public discussion of issues. Plans to make field organizers available to assist chapters with local issues, forums and news releases; also plans to organize regional seminars, develop media and outreach programs and produce film presentations. Maintains library of news clippings, public and private reference files, and publications.

Americans for Constitutional Action., USA,. E-mail: ampaconline@ama-assn.org Political action organization supported by financial contributions of individuals. Undertakes "to help elect to the Senate and House of Representatives of the United States individuals who, by their actions, have proved their allegiance to the original spirit and principles of the Constitution." Presents biennial distinguished service award to selected members of Congress. Address unknown since 1992 edition.

Americans for the Arts., 1000 Vermont Ave., N.W., 12th Fl. Washington, DC 20005. Phone: 800-321-4510 or (202)371-2830 Fax: (202)371-0424 E-mail: info@artusa.org • URL: http://www.artsusa.org • Members are arts organizations and interested individuals. Conducts research and provides information and clearinghouse services relating to the visual arts.

Americans for the Environment., 1901 Pennsylvania Ave., NW,

Ste. 1100 Washington, DC 20006. Fax: (202)797-6563 E-mail: richard.wallace@scbar.org Educational organization that encourages the public to influence the formation of environmental policy through effective use of elections. Sponsors political and electoral skills training programs for environmental and conservation activists at the national and local levels. Maintains data bank of environmental referenda; operates political trainers' bureau. **Convention/Meeting:** none.

Americans for the National Interest., 1660 L St. NW Washington, DC 20036. Phone: (202)775-9038 E-mail: richard.wallace@scbar.org A political action committee that supports candidates for office who share the views of Governor Bruce Babbitt (D-Arizona). Endorses and provides funds for candidates running for state or national office. **Publications:** none.

Americans with Disabilities Act: A Practical and Legal Guide to Impact, Enforcement, and Compliance. BNA, Inc., 1231 25th St., NW Washington, DC 20037. Phone: 800-372-1033 E-mail: customercare@bna.com • URL: http://www.bna.com • 1990. $95.00. (Special Report Series).

Americans with Disabilities Act Handbook. Henry H. Perritt. Aspen Publishers, Inc., 1185 Avenue of the Americas New York, NY 10036. Phone: 800-234-1660 or (212)597-0200 Fax: (212)597-0338 E-mail: customer.service@aspenpubl.com • URL: http://www.aspenpublishers.com • 2003. Fourth edition. Price on application.

The Americans with Disabilities Act: Overview, Regulations, and Interpretations. Nancy L. Jones. Nova Science Publishers, Inc., 400 Oser Ave., Suite 1600 Hauppauge, NY 11788-3619. Phone: (631)231-7269 Fax: (631)231-8175 E-mail: novascience@earthlink.net • URL: http://www.novapublishers.com • 2003. $29.50. Serves as a basic guide to the legal ramifications of the Act.

America's Corporate Families. Dun & Bradstreet Corp., 103 JFK Pky. Short Hills, NJ 07078. Phone: 800-234-3867 or (973)921-5500 Fax: (973)921-6056 E-mail: custserv@dnb.com • URL: http://www.dnb.com • Covers: Approximately 12,700 U.S. corporations. Ultimate companies must meet all of the following criteria for inclusion: two or more business locations, 250 or more employees at that location or in excess of $25 million in sales volume or a tangible net worth greater than $500,000, and controlling interest in one or more subsidiary company. Entries include: D&B D-U-N-S number, company name, address, phone, state of incorporation, line of business, primary/secondary SIC codes, sales volume, net worth, number of employees, current ownership date, year started, number of sites, key executives' names/titles, directors and than officers, primary bank and accounting firm, import/export designation, stock exchange symbol and indicator for publicly owned companies, parent company and location.

America's Corporate Finance Directory. LexisNexis Group, PO Box 933 Dayton, OH 45401-0933. Phone: 800-227-9597 or (937)865-6800 Fax: (518)487-3584 E-mail: customer.support@lexisnexis.com • URL: http://www.lexisnexis.com • Covers: Financial personnel and outside financial services relationships of 5,000 leading United States corporations and their wholly-owned United States subsidiaries. Entries include: Company name, address, phone, fax, telex, e-mail addresses, stock exchange information, earnings, total assets, size of pension/profit-sharing fund portfolio, number of employees, description of business, wholly-owned U.S. Subsidiaries of parent company; name and title of key executives; outside suppliers of financial services.

America's Network: A Telecommunications Magazine. Advanstar Communications, 545 Boylston St. Boston, MA 02116. Phone: 888-527-7008 or (617)267-6500 Fax: (617)267-6900 E-mail: info@advanstar.com • URL: http://www.advanstar.com • 18 times a year. $100.00 per year. Formerly *Telephone Engineer and Management.*

America's Pharmacist. National Community Pharmacists Association, 205 Daingerfield Rd. Alexandria, VA 22314-2885. Phone: 800-544-7447 or (703)683-8200 Fax: (703)683-3619 E-mail: info@ncpanet.org • URL: http://www.ncpanet.org • Monthly. $50.00 per year. Formerly *N A R D Journal.*

The Americas Society—Council of the Americas., 680 Park Ave. New York, NY 10021. Phone: (212)628-3200 Fax: (212)249-1880 E-mail: inforequest@as-coa.org • URL: http://www.americas-society.org • Members are U. S. corporations with business interests in Latin America. Formerly Council of the Americas.

America's Textiles International-The Textile Redbook. Billian/Transworld Publishing Inc., 2100 Powers Ferry Rd. Atlanta, GA 30339. Phone: 800-533-8484 or (770)955-8484 Fax: (770)955-8485 E-mail: jmetzer@billian.com • URL: http://www.billian.com • Annual. $155.00. Lists more than 6,000 textile mills and suppliers to the textile industry in North America.

America's Top Rated Cities: A Statistical Handbook. Grey House Publishing, 185 Millerton Rd. Millerton, NY 12546. Phone: 800-562-2139 or (518)789-8700 Fax: (518)789-0556 E-mail: books@greyhouse.com • URL: http://www.greyhouse.com • Annual. $195.00. Four volumes. $59.95 per volume. Each volume covers major cities in a region of the U. S.: Eastern, Southern, Central, and Western. City statistics cover the "Business Environment" (finances, employment, taxes, utilities, etc.) and the "Living Environment" (cost of living, housing, education, health care, climate, etc.).

America's Top-Rated Smaller Cities: A Statistical Handbook. Grey House Publishing, 185 Millrton Rd. Millerton, Connecticut, 12546. Phone: 800-562-2139 or (518)789-8700 Fax: (518)789-0556 E-mail: books@greyhouse.com • URL: http://www.greyhouse.com • Biennial. $160.00. Provides detailed profiles of 60 smaller U. S. cities ranging in population from 25,000 to 100,000. Includes data on cost of living, employment, income, taxes, climate, media, and many other factors.

AMS Conference Proceedings. American Meteorological Society, 45 Beacon St. Boston, MA 02108-3693. Phone: (617)227-2425 Fax: (617)742-8718 E-mail: kheideman@ametsoc.org • URL: http://www.ametsoc.org/ams • Annual.

Amusement Business: International Live Entertainment and Amusement Industry Newsletter. VNU Business Media, 770 Broadway New York, NY 10003-9595. Phone: 800-344-7119 or (646)654-4500 Fax: (646)654-7212 • URL: http://www.vnubusinessmedia.com • Weekly. $129.00 per year.

Amusement Industry Manufacturers and Suppliers International.

AMWA Journal. American Medical Writers Association, 40 W. Gude Dr., No. 101 Rockville, MD 20850-1192. Phone: (301)493-0003 • URL: http://www.amwa.org • Quarterly. $35.00 per year.

Amy Vanderbilt's Complete Book of Etiquette. Nancy Tuckerman and Nancy Dunnan. Doubleday Publishing, 1540 Broadway New York, NY 10036-4094. Phone: 800-323-9872 or (212)354-6500 Fax: (212)492-9700 • URL: http://www.doubledaybookclub.com • 1995. $32.00. Revised edition.

Analog and Digital Communications. Hwei P. Hsu. McGraw-Hill, 1221 Ave. of the Americas New York, NY 10020. Phone: 800-722-4726 or (212)512-2000 Fax: (212)512-4502 E-mail: customer.service@mcgraw-hill.com • URL: http://www.mcgraw-hill.com • 2003. $16.95. Second edition. (Schaum's Outlines Series).

Analysis and Use of Financial Statements. Gerald I. White. John Wiley and Sons, Inc., 111 River St. Hoboken, NJ 07030. Phone: 800-225-5945 or (201)748-6000 Fax: (201)748-6088 E-mail: info@wiley.com • URL: http://www.wiley.com • 2002. $123.95. Third edition. Includes analysis of financial ratios, cash flow, inventories, assets, debt, etc. Also covered are employee benefits, corporate investments, multinational operations, financial derivatives, and hedging activities

Analysis for Financial Management. Robert C. Higgins. McGraw-Hill, 1221 Ave. of the Americas New York, NY 10020. Phone: 800-722-4726 or (212)512-2000 Fax: (212)512-4502 E-mail: customer.service@mcgraw-hill.com • URL: http://www.mcgraw-hill.com • 2003. $65.94. Seventh edition. Price on application. (Finance, Insurance and Real Estate Series).

Analysis of Financial Statements. Leopold A. Bernstein and John J. Wild. McGraw-Hill, 1221 Ave. of the Americas New York, NY 10020. Phone: 800-722-4726 or (212)512-2000 Fax: (212)512-4502 E-mail: customer.service@mcgraw-hill.com • URL: http://www.mcgraw-hill.com • 1999. $65.00. Fifth edition. Includes practical examples of analysis.

Analyst's Handbook: Composite Corporate Per Share Data by Industry. Standard and Poor's, 55 Water St. New York, NY 10041. Phone: 800-221-5277 or (212)438-1000 • URL: http://www.standardandpoors.com • Annual. $795.00. Monthly updates.

Analyzing and Managing Banking Risk: A Framework for Assessing Corporate Governacial Risk Management. Hennie van Greuning and Sonja Brajovic Bratanovic. The World Bank Group, 1818 H St., NW Washington, DC 20433. Phone: 800-645-7247 or (202)473-1153 Fax: (202)477-6391 E-mail: books@worldbank.org • URL: http://www.worldbank.org • 2003. $100.00. Provides a guide to the analysis of banking risk for bank executives, bank supervisors, and risk analysts. Includes a CD-ROM with spreadsheet-based tables to assist in the interpretation and analysis of a bank's financial risk.

Analyzing Your Competition: Simple, Low-Cost Techniques for Intelligence Gathering. Michael Strenges. MarketResearch.com, 641 Ave. of the Americas, 4th Fl. New York, NY 10011. Phone: 800-298-5699 or (212)807-2629 Fax: (212)807-2676 E-mail: customerservice@marketresearch.com • URL: http://www.marketresearch.com • 1997. $95.00. Third edition. Mainly an annotated listing of specific, business information sources, but also contains concise discussions of information-gathering techniques. Indexed by publisher and title.

Anatomy of a Business Plan: A Step-by-Step Guide to Starting Smart, Building thesiness and Securing Your Company's Future. Linda J. Pinson. Dearborn Trade Publishing, A Kaplan Professional Co., 155 N. Wacker Dr. Chicago, IL 60606-1719. Phone: 800-621-9621 or (312)836-4400 Fax: (312)836-1021 E-mail: trade@dearborn.com • URL: http://www.dearborntrade.com • 2001. $21.95. Fifth edition.

and Entrepreneurs Workshop International., 1029 Castillo St. Santa Barbara, CA 93101-3736. Phone: (805)962-5722 Fax: (805)899-5722 E-mail: info@inventorsworkshop.org • URL: http://www.inventorsworkshop.org • Formerly Inventors Workshop International.

Anderson on Uniform Commercial Code. Lary Lawrence. West Group, 610 Opperman Dr. Eagan, MN 55123. Phone: 800-338-9424 or (651)687-7000 Fax: 800-340-9378 E-mail: bookstore@westgroup.com • URL: http://www.westgroup.com • $1,050.00. Annual updates.

Anderson's Manual for Notaries Public: A Complete Guide for Notaries Public and Commissioners. Anderson Publishing Co., 2035 Reading Rd. Cincinnati, OH 45205-1416. Phone:

800-582-7295 or (513)421-4142 Fax: (513)562-8110 E-mail: mail@andersonpublishing.com • URL: http://www.andersonpublishing.com • 1999. $25.00. Eighth edition.

Andrews' Professional Liability Litigation Reporter. Andrews Publications, 175 Strafford Ave., Bldg. 4, Suite 140 Wayne, PA 19087. Phone: (610)225-0510 Fax: (610)225-0501 E-mail: customer@andrewspub.com • URL: http://www.andrewspub.com • Monthly. $550.00 per year. Provides reports on lawsuits against attorneys, accountants, and investment professionals.

Animal Breeding Abstracts: A Monthly Abstract of World Literature. Available from CABI Publishing North America, 875 Massachusetts Ave. 7th Fl. Cambridge, MA 02139. Phone: 800-528-4841 or (617)395-4056 Fax: (617)354-6875 E-mail: cabi-nao@cabi.org • URL: http://www.cabi-publishing.org • Monthly. Institutions, $1,305.00 per year. Online edition available. Published in England by CABI Publishing. Provides worldwide coverage of the literature.

Animation 101. Ernest Pintoff. Michael Wiese Productions, 11288 Ventura Blvd., Suite 621 Studio City, CA 91604. Phone: 800-833-5738 or (818)379-8799 Fax: (818)986-3408 • URL: http://www.mwp.com • 1999. $16.95. Presents the history of animation from "Disney to Bakski, traditional to computer-generated." Includes comments from Stan Lee, Bill Hanna, Nick Park, and John Lasseter.

Annals of Nuclear Energy. Elsevier, 655 Ave. of the Americas New York, NY 10010-5107. Phone: 800-366-2665 or (212)989-5800 Fax: 800-535-9935 or (212)633-3680 E-mail: custserv@elsevier.com • URL: http://www.elsevier.com • 18 times a year. Qualified personnel, $98.00 per year; institutions, $3,304.00 per year. Text and summaries in English, French and German.

Annals of Probability. Institute of Mathematical Statistics, 9650 Rockville Pke. Ste. L2310 Bethesda, MD 20814-3998. Phone: (301)634-7029 Fax: (301)634-7099 E-mail: ims@imstat.org • URL: http://www.imstat.org • Quarterly. $200.00 per year.

Annals of Statistics. Institute of Mathematical Statistics, 9650 Rockville Pke., Ste. L2310 Bethesda, MD 20814-3998. Phone: (301)634-7029 Fax: (301)634-7099 E-mail: ims@imstat.org • URL: http://www.imstat.org • Bimonthly. $220.00 per year.

Anniversaries and Holidays. Bernard Trawicky. American Library Association, 50 E. Huron St. Chicago, IL 60611-2795. Phone: 800-545-2433 or (312)944-6780 Fax: (312)440-9374 E-mail: ala@ala.org • URL: http://www.ala.org • 2000. $68.00. Fifth edition. Provides information on 3,500 holidays and anniversaries.

Annotated Bibliography of Project and Team Management. Project Management Institute, Four Campus Blvd. Newtown Square, PA 19073-3299. Phone: (610)356-4600 Fax: (610)356-4647 • URL: http://www.pmibookstore.org • Provides citations and annotations on CD-ROM for selected project management literature since 1956.

Annual Benchmark Report for Retail Trade and Food Services...A Detailed Summary of Retail Sales, Purchases, Accounts Receivable, Inventories, and Food Service Sales. Available from U. S. Government Printing Office, Washington, DC 20402. Phone: (866)512-1800 or (202)512-1800 Fax: (202)512-2250 E-mail: gpoaccess@gpo.gov • URL: http://www.access.gpo.gov • Annual. $13.00. Issued by the U.S. Census Bureau. Provides detailed annual and monthly retail statistics for the most recent 10 years. Includes data for various kinds of retail outlets, including automobiles, furniture, appliances, building supplies, grocery stores, drug stores, gasoline stations, clothing, sporting goods, department stores, and restaurants.

Annual Bulletin of Housing and Building Statistics for Europe and North America. United Nations Publications, Two United Nations Plaza, Room DC2-853 New York, NY 10017. Phone: 800-253-9646 or (212)963-8302 Fax: (212)963-3489 E-mail: publications@un.org • URL: http://www.un.org/publications • Annual. $25.00. Provides basic data on housing and construction in European countries, Canada, and the U. S., including non-residential buildings, value of construction, building materials, prices, costs, and rents. Includes base years of 1990 and 1995 and recent calendar years.

Annual Bulletin of Steel Statistics for Europe, America, and Asia. United Nations Publications, Two United Nations Plaza, Room DC2-853 New York, NY 10017. Phone: 800-253-9646 or (212)963-8302 Fax: (212)963-3489 E-mail: publications@un.org • URL: http://www.un.org/publications • Annual. $90.00. Presents detailed steel data for European countries, Canada, Japan, and the U. S. Includes statistics on production, trade, raw materials, scrap, deliveries, and energy use.

Annual Bulletin of Trade in Chemical Products. Economic Commission for Europe. United Nations Publications, United Nations Concourse Level, First Ave. and 46th St. New York, NY 10017. Phone: 800-553-3210 or (212)963-7680 Fax: (212)963-4910 E-mail: bookstore@un.org • URL: http://www.un.org/publications • Annual. $47.00.

Annual Bulletin of Transport Statistics for Europe and North America. United Nations Publications, Two United Nations Plaza, Room DC2-853 New York, NY 10017. Phone: 800-253-9646 or (212)963-8302 Fax: (212)963-3489 E-mail: publications@un.org • URL: http://www.un.org/publications • Annual. $60.00. Presents detailed transportation statistics for European countries, Canada, and the U. S. Includes data on energy consumption for transport.

Annual Energy Outlook [year], with Projections to [year]. Available from U. S. Government Printing Office, Washington, DC 20402. Phone: (202)512-1800 Fax: (202)512-2250 E-mail: gpoaccess@gpo.gov • URL: http://www.access.gpo.gov • Annual. $42.00. Issued by the Energy Information Administration, U. S. Department of Energy (http://www.eia.doe.gov). Contains detailed statistics and 20-year projections for electricity, oil, natural gas, coal, and renewable energy. Text provides extensive discussion of energy issues and "Market Trends."

Annual Energy Review. Available from U. S. Government Printing Office, Washington, DC 20402. Phone: (202)512-1800 Fax: (202)512-2250 E-mail: gpoaccess@gpo.gov • URL: http://www.access.gpo.gov • Annual. $51.00. Issued by the Energy Information Administration, Office of Energy Markets and End Use, U. S. Department of Energy. Presents long-term historical as well as recent data on production, consumption, stocks, imports, exports, and prices of the principal energy commodities in the U. S.

Annual Index to Motion Picture Credits. Academy of Motion Picture Arts and Sciences, 8949 Wilshire Blvd. Beverly Hills, CA 90211-1972. Phone: (310)274-3000 Fax: (310)859-9619 E-mail: ampas@oscars.org • URL: http://www.oscars.org • Annual. $50.00.

The Annual Register: A Record of World Events. Keesing's Worldwide, LLC, 4905 Del Ray Ave., Suite 402 Bethesda, MD 20814. Phone: 800-332-3535 or (301)718-8770 Fax: (301)718-8494 E-mail: info@keesings.com • URL: http://www.keesings.com • Annual. $185.00. Published by Keesings Worldwide. Lists major economic, social, and cultural events of the past year. International coverage.

Annual Register of Grant Support: A Directory of Funding Sources. Information Today, Inc., 143 Old Marlton Pike Medford, NJ 08055-8750. Phone: 800-300-9868 or (609)654-6266 Fax: (609)654-4309 E-mail: custserv@infotoday.com • URL: http://www.infotoday.com • Annual. $229.00. Contains information on more than 3,500 corporate, private, and public organizations that provide grants in 11 major subject areas, including 61 specific sub-categories.

Annual Report of Postmaster General. U.S. Postal Service, Washington, DC 20260. Phone: (202)268-2000 Annual.

Annual Report of the Commuter Regional Airline Industry. Regional Airline Association, 2025 M St., NW, Ste. 800 Washington, DC 20036-3309. Phone: (202)367-1170 Fax: (202)367-2170 E-mail: raa@dc.sba.com • URL: http://www.raa.org • Annual. $75.00. Lists commuter and regional airlines and gives statistical information.

Annual Report of the Director. Administrative Office of the United States Courts, U.S. Supreme Court Bldg., One First St. N.W. Washington, DC 20544. Phone: (202)479-3000 Annual.

Annual Report of the Secretary of Defense. U.S. Department of Defense, Office of the Secretary, The Pentagon Washington, DC 20301. Phone: (703)545-6700 Annual.

Annual Report of the Secretary of Veterans Affairs. U.S. Department of Veterans Affairs, Washington, DC 20420. Phone: (202)273-5700 Annual. Shows monies distributed and received by the Dept. of Veterans Affairs. Describes the activities of the Department during the fiscal year.

The Annual Report on the Economic Status of the Profession. American Association of University Professors, 1012 14th St., N.W., Suite 500 Washington, DC 20005-3465. Phone: (202)737-5900 Fax: (202)737-5526 E-mail: aaup@aaup.org • URL: http://www.aaup.org • Special annual issue of *ACADEME*.

Annual Review of Biophysics and Biomolecular Structure. Annual Reviews, 4139 El Camino Way Palo Alto, CA 94303. Phone: 800-523-8635 or (650)493-4400 Fax: (650)424-0910 E-mail: service@annualreviews.org • URL: http://www.annualreviews.org • Annual. Individuals, $80.00. Includes print and online editions. Institutions, $180.00; with online edition, $216.00

Annual Review of Entomology. Annual Reviews, 4139 El Camino Way Palo Alto, CA 94303-0139. Phone: 800-523-8635 or (650)493-4400 Fax: (650)424-0910 E-mail: service@annualreviews.org • URL: http://www.annualreviews.org • Annual. Individuals, $70.00. Includes print and online editions. Institutions, $160.00; with online editions, $192.00.

Annual Review of Enviroment and Resources. Annual Reviews, 4139 El Camino Way Palo Alto, CA 94303-0139. Phone: 800-523-8635 or (650)493-4400 Fax: (650)424-0910 E-mail: serviceannualreviews.org • URL: http://www.annualreviews.org • Annual. Individuals, $89.00. Includes print and online editions. Institutions, $194.00; with online edition, $233.00.

Annual Review of Medicine: Selected Topics in the Clinical Sciences. Annual Reviews, 4139 El Camino Way Palo Alto, CA 94303-0139. Phone: 800-523-8635 or (650)493-4400 Fax: (650)424-0910 E-mail: service@annualreviews.org • URL: http://www.annualreviews.org • Annual. Individuals, $74.00. Includes print and online editions. INstitutions, $168.00; with online edition, $202.00.

Annual Review of Nuclear and Particle Science. Annual Reviews, 4139 El Camino Way Palo Alto, CA 94303-0139. Phone: 800-523-8635 or (650)493-4400 Fax: (650)424-0910 E-mail: service@annualreviews.org • URL: http://www.annualreviews.org • Annual. Individuals, $84.00. Includes print and online edition. Institutions, $189.00; with online edition, $227.00.

Annual Review of Pharmacology and Toxicology. Annual Reviews, 4139 El Camino Way Palo Alto, CA 94303-0139. Phone: 800-523-8635 or (650)493-4400 Fax: (650)424-0910 E-mail: service@annualreviews.org • URL: http://www.annualreviews.org • Annual. Individuals, $74.00. Includes print and online editions. Institutions, $173.00; with online edition, $208.00.

Annual Review of Public Health. Annual Reviews, 4139 El Camino Way Palo Alto, CA 94303-0139. Phone: 800-523-8635 or (650)493-4400 Fax: (650)424-0910 E-mail: service@annualreviews.org • URL: http://www.annualreviews.org • Annual. Individuals, $74.00. Includes print and online editions. Institutions, $163.00; with online edidtion, $215.00.

Annual Review of the Chemical Industry. United Nations Publications, United Nations Concourse Level, First Ave. and 46th St. New York, NY 10017. Phone: 800-553-3210 or (212)963-7680 Fax: (212)963-4910 E-mail: bookstore@un.org • URL: http://www.un.org/publications • Annual. $100.00.

Annual Review of United Nations Affairs. Oceana Publications, Inc., 75 Main St. Dobbs Ferry, NY 10522-1601. Phone: 800-831-0758 or (914)693-8100 Fax: (914)693-0402 E-mail: custserv@oceanalaw.com • URL: http://www.oceanalaw.com • 1999. $270.00. Three volumes.

Annual Reviews in Control. Elsevier, 655 Ave. of the Americas New York, NY 10010-5107. Phone: 800-366-2665 or (212)989-5800 Fax: 800-366-2665 or (212)633-3680 E-mail: custserv@elsevier.com • URL: http://www.elsevier.com • Annual. $471.00 per year. Formerly*Annual Review in Automatic Programming*.

Annual Society for Information Science and Technology, Information and Business Div. Martha E. Williams, editor. Information Today, Inc., 143 Old Marlton Pike Medford, NJ 08055-8750. Phone: 800-300-9868 or (609)654-6266 Fax: (609)654-4309 E-mail: custserv@infotoday.com • URL: http://www.infotoday.com • Annual. Members, $79.95; non-members, $99.95. Published on behalf of the American Society for Information Science (ASIS). Covers trends in planning, basic techniques, applications, and the information profession in general.

Annual Statement Studies. The Risk Management Association, One Liberty Place, 1650 Market St., Suite 2300 Philadelphia, PA 19103. Phone: 800-677-7621 or (215)446-4000 Fax: (215)446-4101 E-mail: member@rmahq.org • URL: http://www.rmahq.org • Annual. Median and quartile financial ratios are given for over 400 kinds of manufacturing, wholesale, retail, construction, and consumer finance establishments. Data is sorted by both asset size and sales volume. Includes a clearly written "Definition of Ratios" and an alphabetical industry index.

Annual Statement Studies: Industry Default Probabilities and Cash Flow Measures. The Risk Management Association, One Liberty Place, 1650 Market St., Suite 2300 Philadelphia, PA 19103. Phone: 800-677-7621 or (215)446-4000 Fax: (215)446-4101 E-mail: customers@rmahq.org • URL: http://www.rmahq.org • Annual. $145.00. Serves as a companion volume to the original *Annual Statement Studies*. Gives probability of default estimates on a percentage scale for more than 450 industries. Includes changes in position year-by-year for eight financial statement line items and provides percentage measures of cash flow.

Annual Statistical Reports of Independent Telephone Companies. Federal Communications Commission, 445 12th St., SW Washington, DC 20554. Phone: 888-225-5322 or (202)418-0200 Fax: (866)418-0232 E-mail: fccinfo@fcc.gov Annual.

Annual Survey of Manufactures. Available from U. S. Government Printing Office, Washington, DC 20402. Phone: (202)512-1800 Fax: (202)512-2250 E-mail: gpoaccess@gpo.gov • URL: http://www.access.gpo.gov • Annual. Prices vary. Issued by the U. S. Census Bureau as an interim update to the *Census of Manufactures*. Includes data on number of manufacturing establishments in various industries, employment, labor costs, value of shipments, capital expenditures, inventories, energy costs, and assets. (See also Census Bureau home page, http://www.census.gov/.)

Annuity and Life Insurance Shopper. United States Annuities, Eight Talmadge Rd. Jamesburg, NJ 08831-2910. Phone: 800-872-6684 or (908)521-5110 Fax: (908)521-5113 Semiannual. $25.00 per year. Provides information on rates and performance for fixed annuities, variable annuities, and term life policies issued by more than 250 insurance companies.

Annuity Market News. Thomson Media, One State St. Plaza New York, NY 10004. Phone: 800-221-1809 or (212)803-8200 Fax: (212)843-9635 E-mail: custserv@thomsonmedia.com • URL: http://www.thomsonmedia.com • Monthly. $625.00 per year. Newsletter. Edited for investment and insurance professionals. Covers the marketing, management, and servicing of variable and fixed annuity products.

Answer. Association of Teleservices International, 12 Academy Ave. Atkinson, NH 03811. Phone: (603)362-9489 Fax: (603)362-9486 E-mail: admin@atsi.org • URL: http://www.atsi.org • Bimonthly. Members, $30.00 per year; non-members, $50.00 per year.

Anti-Friction Bearings. U.S. Bureau of the Census, Washington, DC 20233-0800. Phone: (301)457-4100 Fax: (301)457-3842 • URL: http://www.census.gov • Annual.

Antiquarian Booksellers Association of America.

Antiquarian Booksellers' Association of America-Membership List. Antiquarian Booksellers' Association of America, 20 W. 44th St., 4th Fl. New York, NY 10036-6004. Phone: (212)944-8291 Fax: (212)944-8293 E-mail: abaa@panix.com • URL: http://www.abaa.org • Annual. Free. Lists about 470 rare book dealers. Send self-addressed business-size envelope with $1.43 postage.

Antique Appraisal Association of America.

Antique Automobile. Antique Automobile Club of America, 501 W. Governor Rd. Hershey, PA 17033. Phone: (717)534-1910 Fax: (717)534-9101 Membership.

Antique Dealer and Collector's Guide: The International Magazine for Dealers and Collectors. Statuscourt Ltd., P.O. Box 805 London SE1O 8TD, United Kingdom. Phone: 44 1816 914820 Fax: 44 1816 912489 E-mail: antiquedealercollectorsguide@ukbusiness.com • URL: http://www.collectiques.net • Monthly. $44.00 per year. Incorporates *Art and Antiques*.

Antique Shop Guide—Central Edition. Mayhill Publications, 27 N Jefferson St., PO Box 90 Knightstown, IN 46148. Phone: 800-876-5133 or (765)345-5133 Fax: (765)345-3398 E-mail: webmaster@mayhill-publications.com Covers: antique shops in Illinois, Indiana, Iowa, Kentucky, Michigan, Minnesota, Missouri, Ohio, Tennessee, Wisconsin, western Pennsylvania, and West Virginia. Entries include: For antique shops—Shop name, address, map reference, specialty, whether reproductions are stocked, hours and seasons open, phone. Listings for other categories have similar detail.

Antiques and Collecting Magazine. Lightner Publishing Corp., 1006 S. Michigan Ave. Chicago, IL 60605. Phone: 800-762-7576 or (312)939-4767 Fax: (312)939-0053 E-mail: lightnerpb@aol.com • URL: http://www.antiqueweek.com • Monthly. $32.00 per year.

Antitrust and Trade Regulation Report. BNA, Inc., 1231 25th St., N.W. Washington, DC 20037. Phone: 800-372-1033 E-mail: customercare@bna.com • URL: http://www.bna.com • Weekly. $1,479.00 per year. Looseleaf service.

Antitrust Basics. American Lawyer Media, Inc., 105 Madison Ave. New York, NY 10016. Phone: 800-888-8300 or (212)779-9200 Fax: (212)481-8110 E-mail: lawcatalog@amlaw.com • URL: http://www.lawcatalog.com/ • Looseleaf. $179.00. Updated as needed. Discusses "business practices consistently upheld, as well as those consistently condemned." Covers a wide variety of antitrust legal topics. (Law Journal Press).

The Antitrust Bulletin. Federal Legal Publications, Inc., 157 Chambers St. New York, NY 10007. Phone: (212)619-4949 E-mail: flp@bestweb.com Quarterly. Institutions, $85.00 per year.

Antitrust Counseling and Litigation Techniques. LexisNexis Matthew Bender, 1275 Broadway Albany, NY 12204. Phone: 800-424-4200 or (518)487-3000 Fax: (518)487-3584 E-mail: bookstore.support@lexisnexis.com • URL: http://www.bender.com • Annual. $938.00 per year. Five looseleaf volumes.

Antitrust Division Manual. Available from U. S. Government Printing Office, Washington, DC 20402. Phone: (202)512-1800 Fax: (202)512-2250 E-mail: gpoaccess@gpo.gov • URL: http://www.access.gpo.gov • Looseleaf. $60.00. Includes basic manual, with supplementary material for an indeterminate period. Serves as a guide to the operating policies and procedures of the Antitrust Division of the U. S. Department of Justice (http://www.usdoj.gov). Covers suggested methods of conducting investigations and litigation.

Antitrust-Intellectual Property Handbook. Alan J. Weinschel. Glasser Legalworks, 150 Clove Rd. Little Falls, NJ 07424. Phone: 800-308-1700 or (973)890-0008 Fax: (973)890-0042 E-mail: orders@glasserlegalworks.com • URL: http://www.glasserlegalworks.com • Looseleaf. $175.00. Periodic supplementation. Covers patent licensing, patent antitrust issues, innovation markets, intervention by government agencies, standard-setting activities, royalty arrangements, and related intellectual property/antitrust topics. Provides explanations, legal guidance, and historical background.

Antitrust Law and Economics Review. Charles E. Mueller, editor. Antitrust Law and Economics Review, Inc., P.O. Box 3532 Vero Beach, FL 32964-3532. Fax: (561)461-6007 • URL: http://www.home.mpinet.net • Quarterly. $144.50 per year.

Antitrust Law and Practice. West Publishing Co., 610 Opperman Dr. Eagan, MN 55123. Phone: 800-328-4880 or (651)687-7000 Fax: 800-340-9378 E-mail: bookstore@westgroup.com • URL: http://www.westgroup.com • Periodic supplementation. Price on application.

Antitrust Law Handbook. William C. Holmes. West Group, 610 Opperman Dr. Eagan, MN 55123. Phone: 800-328-4880 or (651)687-7000 Fax: 800-340-9378 E-mail: bookstore@westgroup.com • URL: http://www.westgroup.com • 2004. $286.50. Overview of antitrust law from procedural to substantive issues.

Antitrust Law Journal. American Bar Association, Antitrust Law Section, 750 N Lake Shore Dr. Chicago, IL 60611. Phone: 800-285-2221 or (312)988-5000 E-mail: orders@abanet.org • URL: http://www.abanet.org • Three times a year. Free to members; non-members, $40.00 per year.

Antitrust Laws and Trade Regulation. LexisNexis Matthew Bender, 1275 Broadway Albany, NY 12204. Phone: 800-424-

4200 or (518)487-3000 Fax: (518)487-3584 E-mail: bookstore.support@lexisnexis.com • URL: http://www.bender.com • $1,990.00. 11 looseleaf volumes. Periodic supplementation. Covers provisions and applications of the Sherman, Clayton, Robinson-Patman, and Federal Trade Commission Acts. Also covers state antitrust laws.

Antitrust Laws and Trade Regulation: Desk Edition. LexisNexis Matthew Bender, 1275 Broadway Albany, NY 12204. Phone: 800-424-4200 or (518)487-3000 Fax: (518)487-3584 E-mail: bookstore.support@lexisnexis.com • URL: http://www.bender.com • $709.00. Two looseleaf volumes. Periodic supplementation. The history and organization of the antitrust laws.

Antitrust Litigation Reporter: The National Journal of Record on Antitrust Litigation. Andrews Publications, 175 Strafford Ave., Bldg. 4, Suite 140 Wayne, PA 19087. Phone: (610)225-0510 Fax: (610)225-0501 E-mail: customer@andrewspub.com • URL: http://www.andrewspub.com • Monthly. $775.00 per year. Newsletter. Provides reports on federal and state antitrust statutes.

AOAC International., 481 N Frederick Ave., Ste. 500 Gaithersburg, MD 20877-2417. Phone: 800-379-2622 or (301)924-7077 Fax: (301)924-7089 E-mail: aoac@aoac.org • URL: http://www.aoac.org • Government, academic, and industry analytical scientists who develop, test, and collaboratively study methods for analyzing fertilizers, foods, feeds, pesticides, drugs, cosmetics, and other products related to agriculture and public health. Offers short courses for analytical laboratory personnel in chemical and microbiological quality assurance, lab waste management, statistics, giving expert testimony, and technical writing.

AOAC International Journal. AOAC International, 481 N. Frederick Ave., Suite 500 Gaithersberg, MD 20877. Phone: (301)924-7077 Fax: (301)924-7089 Bimonthly. Members $176.00 per year; non-members, $242.00 per year; institutions, $262.00 per year. Formerly *Association of Official Analytical Chemist Journal*.

AOPA Aviation U.S.A. Aircraft Owners and Pilots Association, 421 Aviation Way Frederick, MD 21701. Phone: 800-872-2672 or (301)695-2000 Fax: (301)695-2375 E-mail: aopahq@aopa.org • URL: http://www.aopa.org • Semiannual. Free to members. Price on Application. Primarily for pilots.

AOPA Pilot. Aircraft Owners and Pilots Association, 421 Aviation Way Frederick, MD 21701. Phone: 800-872-2672 or (301)695-2000 Fax: (301)695-2375 E-mail: aopahq@aopa.org • URL: http://www.aopa.org • Monthly. Members, $39.00 per year; qualified organizations, $21.00 per year.

APA: The Engineered Wood Association., 7011 S 19th, PO Box 11700 Tacoma, WA 98466. Phone: 888-773-2272 or (253)565-6600 Fax: (253)565-7265 E-mail: help@apawood.org • URL: http://www.apawood.org • Manufacturers of structural panel products, oriented strand board and composites. Conducts trade promotion through advertising, publicity, merchandising, and field promotion. Maintains quality supervision in accordance with U.S. product standards, APA performance standards, and APA trademarking. Conducts research to improve products, applications, and manufacturing techniques. Sponsors Engineered Wood Research Foundation; compiles statistics.

Apartment Building Income-Expense Analysis. Institute of Real Estate Management, 430 N. Michigan Ave. Chicago, IL 60611-4090. Phone: 800-837-0706 or (312)329-6000 Fax: 800-338-4736 E-mail: custserv@irem.org • URL: http://www.irem.org • Annual.

Apartment Finance Today. Alexander & Edwards Publishing, 220 Samsone St., 11th Fl. San Francisco, CA 94104. Phone: (415)546-7255 Fax: (415)249-1595 E-mail: ahe@housingfinance.com • URL: http://www.housingfinance.com • Bimonthly. $29.00 per year. Covers mortgages and financial services for apartment developers, builders, and owners.

Apartment Management Magazine. Apartment News Publications, Inc., 15502 Graham St. Huntington Beach, CA 92649-1609. Phone: (714)893-3971 Fax: (714)893-6484 Monthly. $24.00 per year. In four Los Angeles area editions, one Orange County edition.

Apartment Management Newsletter: Wealth Building Techniques for Apartment Owners and Their Managers. Apartment Management Publishing Co., Inc., 16 W 32nd St. New York, NY 10001. Phone: (212)273-0848 Monthly. $95.00 per year.

APEC-Automated Procedures for Engineering Consultants, Inc.

APICS-The Educational Society for Resource Management., 5301 Shawnee Rd. Alexandria, VA 22312-2317. Phone: 800-444-2742 or (703)354-8851 Fax: (703)354-8106 E-mail: webmaster@apicshq.org • URL: http://www.apics.org • Members are professional resource managers.

Apicultural Abstracts. International Bee Research Association, 18 North Rd. Cardiff CF10 3DT, United Kingdom. Phone: 44 2920 372409 Fax: 44 2920 665522 E-mail: mail@ibra.org.uk • URL: http://www.ibra.org.uk • Quarterly. $295.00 per year. Up-to-date summary of world literature on bees and beekeeping.

Appalachian Hardwood Manufacturers, Inc., PO Box 427 High Point, NC 27261. Phone: (336)885-8315 Fax: (336)886-8865 E-mail: info@appalachianwood.org • URL: http://www.appalachianwood.org • Promotes Appalachian hardwoods.

Apparel. VNU Business Media, 770 Broadway New York, NY 10003-9595. Phone: 800-344-7119 or (646)654-4500 Fax: (646)654-7212 • URL: http://www.vnubusinessmedia.com • Monthly. $69.00 per year. Written for executives and top managers. Formerly*Bobbin*.

Apparel Merchandising. Lebhar-Friedman, Inc., 425 Park Ave. New York, NY 10022. Phone: 800-766-6999 or (212)756-5000 E-mail: info@lf.com • URL: http://www.lf.com • Eight times a year. $24.00 per year. Reports on fashion trends in women's, men's, and children's clothing. Supplement to (DSN Retailing Today).

Apple News. U.S. Apple Association, 8233 Old Courthouse Rd., Ste. 200 Vienna, VA 22182. Phone: 800-781-4443 or (703)442-8850 Fax: (703)790-0845 E-mail: mail@notaries.org Description: Reports national and international events in the apple industry; includes statistics and article title index in each issue.

Apple Products Research and Education Council., 5775 Peachtree-Dunwoody Rd., Bldg. G, Ste. 500 Atlanta, GA 30342. Phone: (404)252-3663 Fax: (404)252-0774 E-mail: info@appleproducts.org • URL: http://www.appleproducts.org • Represents processors of apple products and suppliers to the industry. Conducts program to improve business conditions in the apple products industry and to enable the industry to serve the interests of consumers. Conducts research programs on the health benefits of apple products.

Appliance. Dana Chase Publications, Inc., 1110 Jorie Blvd., CS9019 Oakbrook, IL 60522-9019. Phone: (630)990-3484 Fax: (630)990-0078 E-mail: diane@appliance.com • URL: http://www.appliance.com • Monthly. $75.00 per year.

Appliance - Appliance Industry Purchasing Directory. Dana Chase Publications, Inc., 1110 Jorie Blvd. Oakbrook, IL 60522. Phone: (630)990-3484 Fax: (630)990-0078 E-mail: sales@appliance.com • URL: http://www.appliancemagazine.com • Annual. $40.00. Suppliers to manufacturers of consumer, commercial, and business appliances.

Appliance Manufacturer. Business News Publishing Co., 755 W Big Beaver Rd., Ste. 1000 Troy, MI 48084. Phone: 800-837-7370 or (248)362-3700 Fax: (248)362-0317 • URL: http://www.bnp.com • Monthly. $55.00 per year.

Appliance Parts Distributors Association., 4700 W Lake Ave. Glenview, IL 60025. Phone: 800-621-0298 or (847)375-4713 Fax: (866)879-7505 E-mail: apda@apda.com • URL: http://www.apda.com • Wholesale distributors of appliance parts, supplies, and accessories. Promotes the sale of appliance parts through independent parts distributors.

Appliance Service News. Gamit Enterprises, Inc., P.O. Box 809 Saint Charles, IL 60174-0809. Phone: 877-747-1625 or (630)845-9481 Fax: (630)845-9483 E-mail: info@asnews.com • URL: http://www.asnews.com • Monthly. $59.95.

Applied Calculus with Linear Programming for Business, Economics, Life Sciences, and Social Science. Michael R. Ziegler and Raymond A. Barnett. Pearson Custom Publishing, 75 Arlington St., Ste. 300 Boston, MA 02116. Phone: 800-428-4466 or (617)848-6300 Fax: (617)848-6333 • URL: http://www.pearsoncustom.com • 1999. $80.00. Fifth edition.

Applied Economics. Taylor and Francis Group, 325 Chestnut St., 8th Fl. Philadelphia, PA 19106. Phone: 800-354-1420 or (215)626-8914 E-mail: info@taylorandfrancis.com • URL: http://www.taylorandfrancis.com • 18 times a year. Institutions, $3,352.00 per year. Emphasizes quantitative studies having results of practical use. Supplements available, *Applied Financial Economics* and *Applied Economics Letters*.

Applied Economics Letters. Taylor and Francis Group, 325 Chestnut St., 8th Fl. Philadelphia, PA 19106. Phone: 800-354-1420 or (215)625-8914 E-mail: info@taylorandfrancis.com • URL: http://www.taylorandfrancis.com • 15 times a year. Individuals, $115.00 per year; institutions, $809.00 per year. Provides short accounts of new, original research in practical economics. Supplement to *Applied Economics*.

Applied Ergonomics: Human Factors in Technology and Society. Elsevier, 655 Ave. of the Americas New York, NY 10010-5107. Phone: (212)989-5800 Fax: 800-535-9935 or (212)633-3680 E-mail: custserv@elsevier.com • URL: http://www.elsevier.com • Bimonthly. Qualified personnel, $228.00 per year; institutions, $941.00 per year

Applied Financial Economics. Taylor and Francis Group, 325 Chestnut St., 8th Fl. Philadelphia, PA 19106. Phone: 800-354-1420 or (215)625-8914 E-mail: info@taylorandfrancis.com • URL: http://www.taylorandfrancis.com • Monthly. Institutions, $1,277.00 per year. Covers practical aspects of financial economics, banking, and monetary economics. Supplement to *Applied Economics*.

Applied Genetics News. BCC Research, 70 New Canaan Ave. Norwalk, CT 06850. Phone: (866)285-7216 or (203)750-9783 Fax: (203)229-0087 E-mail: info@bccresearch.com • URL: http://www.buscom.com • Description: Concerned primarily with the application of genetic research to industry and technology. Evaluates ongoing research in the areas of aging, cancer, disease, and cell differentiation. Discusses research funding and finances. Analyzes new developments in venture capital and stock price movement.

Applied Mechanics Reviews: An Assessment of World Literature in Engineering Sciences. ASME International, 3 Park Ave. New York, NY 10016-5990. Phone: 800-843-2763 or (212)591-7722 Fax: (212)591-7674 E-mail: infocentral@asme.org • URL: http://www.asme.org • Monthly. Members, $138.00 per year; non-members, $741.00 per year. Includes print and online editions.

Applied Optics. Optical Society of America, Inc., 2010 Massachusetts Ave., N.W. Washington, DC 20036-1023. Phone: 800-762-6960 or (202)223-8130 Fax: (202)223-1096 E-mail: info@osa.org • URL: http://www.osa.org • 36 times a year. $2,437.00 per year.

Applied Radiation and Isotopes. Elsevier, 360 Park Ave., S New York, NY 10010-1710. Phone: 888-437-4636 or (212)989-5800 Fax: (212)633-3990 E-mail: usinfo-f@elsevier.com • URL: http://www.elsevier.com • Monthly. Individuals, $374.00 per year; institutions, $2,546.00 per year.

Applied Research Laboratories. University of Texas at Austin

Applied Research Laboratory. Pennsylvania State University

Applied Science and Technology Index. H. W. Wilson Co., 950 University Ave. Bronx, NY 10452. Phone: 800-367-6770 or (718)588-8400 Fax: 800-590-1617 or (718)590-1617 E-mail: custserv@hwwilson.com • URL: http://www.hwwilson.com • 11 times a year. Quarterly and annual cumulations. Price varies. Indexes a wide variety of English language technical, industrial, and engineering periodicals.

Applied Science and Technology Index Online. H. W. Wilson Co., 950 University Ave. Bronx, NY 10452. Phone: 800-367-6770 or (718)588-8400 Fax: (718)590-1617 E-mail: hwwmsg@info.hwwilson.com • URL: http://www.hwwilson.com • Provides online indexing of 500 major scientific, technical, industrial, and engineering periodicals. Time period is 1983 to date. Monthly updates. Inquire as to online cost and availability.

Applying GAAP and GAAS. LexisNexis Matthew Bender, 1275 Broadway Albany, NY 12204. Phone: 800-424-4200 or (518)487-3000 Fax: (518)487-3584 E-mail: bookstore.support@bender.com • URL: http://www.bender.com • Biennial. $358.00 per year. Two looseleaf volumes. In-depth explanations of generally accepted accounting principles (GAAP) and generally accepted auditing standards (GAAS).

Applying Telecommunications and Technology from a Global Business Perspective. Jay J. Zajas and Olive D. Church. Haworth Press, Inc., 10 Alice St. Binghamton, NY 13904-1580. Phone: 800-429-6784 or (607)722-5857 Fax: 800-895-0582 or (607)722-1424 E-mail: getinfo@haworthpressinc.com • URL: http://www.haworthpressinc.com • 1997. $29.95. Provides an international, multicultural perspective.

Appraisal Institute., Headquarters Office, 550 W Van Buren St., Ste. 1000 Chicago, IL 60607. Phone: (312)335-4110 Fax: (312)335-4101 E-mail: information@appraisalinstitute.org • URL: http://www.appraisalinstitute.org • General appraisers who hold the MAI designation, and residential members who hold the SRA designation. Enforces Code of Professional Ethics and Standards of Professional Appraisal Practice. Confers one general designation, the MAI, and one residential designation, the SRA. Provides training in valuation of residential and income properties, market analysis, and standards of professional appraisal practice. Sponsors courses in preparation for state certification and licensing; offers continuing education programs for designated members.

Appraisal Journal. Appraisal Institute, 550 W Van Buren St., Ste. 1000 Chicago, IL 60607. Phone: 888-570-4545 or (312)335-4100 Fax: (312)335-4400 E-mail: info@appraisalinstitute.org • URL: http://www.appraisalinstitute.org • Quarterly. Free to members; non-members, $48.00 per year; libraries, $100.00 per year; students, $30.00 per year. Offers a broad variety of researched, documented articles.

Appraisal of Real Estate. The Appraisal Institute, 550 W Van Buren St., Ste. 1000 Chicago, IL 60607. Phone: 888-570-4545 or (312)335-4100 or (312)335-4453 Fax: (312)335-4400 E-mail: info@appraisalinstitute.org • URL: http://www.appraisalinstitute.com • 2001. 12th edition. Price on application. Provides an in-depth discussion of the driving concept of market value; guildelines for market analysis projections and updated information throughout that addresses developments affecting the movement of investment capital.

Appraisers Association of America.

Approved Drug Products, with Therapeutic Equivalence Evaluations. Available from U. S. Government Printing Office, Washington, DC 20402. Phone: (202)512-1800 Fax: (202)512-2250 E-mail: gpoaccess@gpo.gov • URL: http://www.access.gpo.gov • $108.00 for basic manual and supplemental material for an indeterminate period. Issued by the Food and Drug Administration, U. S. Department of Health and Human Services. Lists prescription drugs that have been approved by the FDA. Includes therapeutic equivalents to aid in containment of health costs and to serve State drug selection laws.

APWA Reporter. American Public Works Association, 2345 Grand Blvd., Ste. 500 Kansas City, MO 64108. Phone: 800-595-2792 or (816)472-6100 Fax: (816)472-1610 E-mail: apwa@apwa.net • URL: http://www.apwa.net • Monthly. Membership.

Aquacultural Research and Teaching Facility.

Aquaculture Magazine. Achill River Corp., P.O. Box 2329 Asheville, NC 28802. Phone: (704)254-7334 Fax: (704)253-0677 E-mail: aquamag@ioa.com • URL: http://www.aquaculturemag.com • Bimonthly. $24.00 per year.

Aquaculture Magazine. Aquill River Corp., PO Box 2329 Asheville, NC 28802. Phone: (704)254-7334 Fax: (704)253-0677 E-mail: aquamag@ioa.com • URL: http://www.aquaculturemag.com • Bimonthly. $24.00 per year.

Aqualine. Cambridge Scientific Abstracts, 7200 Wisconsin Ave., Suite 601 Bethesda, MD 20814-4823. Phone: 800-843-7751

or (301)961-6700 Fax: (301)961-6720 E-mail: support@csa. com • URL: http://www.csa.com • Provides online citations and abstracts to a wide variety of literature relating to the aquatic environment, including 400 journals, from 1960 to date. Updating is monthly. Inquire as to online cost and availability.

Aquatic Research Interactive.

Aquatic Sciences and Fisheries Abstracts: Aquatic Pollution and Environmental Quality. Food and Agriculture Organization of the United Nations. CSA, 7200 Wisconsin Ave., Suite 601 Bethesda, MD 20814. Phone: 800-843-7751 or (301)961-6700 Fax: (301)961-6720 E-mail: service@csa.com • URL: http://www.csa.com • Bimonthly. $520.00 per year. Part three. Includes print and online editions.

Aquatics International: The Source for Facility Products, Services and Management. Hanley-Wood, LLC, One Thomas Circle, NW Washington, DC 20005. Phone: 800-837-0870 or (202)452-0800 Fax: (202)785-1974 • URL: http://www.hanley-wood.com • Monthly. $10.50 per year. Edited for managers of commercial and public swimming pools, including pools in hotels, schools, theme parks, health clubs, and community centers.

Arbitration: Essential Concepts. Steven C. Bennett. American Lawyer Media, Inc., 105 Madison Ave. New York, NY 10016. Phone: 800-888-8300 or (212)779-9200 Fax: (212)481-8110 E-mail: lawcatalog@amlaw.com • URL: http://www. lawcatalog.com/ • 2002. $32.95. Provides basic explanations of arbitration law, history, and relevant case law. Describes practical procedures for arbitration in various fields (labor, employment, securities, international). (ALM Publishing).

Arbitron Radio County Coverage. Arbitron Co., 142 W. 57th St. New York, NY 10019. Phone: (212)887-1300 Fax: (212)887-1401 Ratings of radio and TV stations plus audience measurement data, updated frequently. Inquire as to online cost and availability.

Architects Handbook of Professional Practice. David Haviland. American Institute of Architects Press, 1735 New York Ave., N.W. Washington, DC 20006. Phone: 800-835-2878 or (202)626-7575 Fax: (802)864-7626 2000. $225.00. 12th edition.

Architectural Graphic Standards. Charles G. Ramsey and others. John Wiley and Sons, Inc., 111 River St. Hoboken, NJ 07030. Phone: 800-225-5945 or (201)748-6000 Fax: (201)748-6088 E-mail: info@wiley.com • URL: http://www.wiley.com • 2000. $675.00. 10th edition.

Architectural Publications Index. British Architectural Library. RIBA Publications Ltd., Finsbury Mission, 39 Moreland St. London EC1V 8BB, United Kingdom. Phone: 44 2072 510791 Fax: 44 2076 082375 • URL: http://www.ribac.co.uk • Quarterly. Individuals, $450.00 per year. Formerly *Architectural Periodicals Index.*

Architectural Record. American Institute of Architects. McGraw-Hill, 1221 Ave. of the Americas New York, NY 10020. Phone: 800-722-4726 or (212)512-2000 Fax: (212)512-4502 E-mail: customer.service@mcgraw-hill.com • URL: http://www. mcgraw-hill.com • Monthly $59.00 per year. Includes supplements *Record Interiors.* and *Record Houses.*

Architectural Review. Fenner, Reed and Jackson, P.O.Box 754 Manhasset, NY 11030-0754. Monthly. Individuals, $64.00 per year; students, $40.50 per year. Visits innovative buildings around the world.

Architectural Woodwork Institute., 46179 Westlake Dr., Ste. 120 Potomac Falls, VA 20165. Phone: (571)323-3636 Fax: (571)323-3630 E-mail: pduvic@awinet.org • URL: http:// www.awinet.org • Manufacturers of architectural woodwork products (casework, fixtures, and paneling) and associated suppliers of equipment and materials. Works to: raise industry standards; research new and improved materials and methods; publish technical data helpful in the design and use of architectural woodwork. Conducts seminars and training course.

Architecture. VNU Business Media, 770 Broadway New York, NY 10003-9595. Phone: 800-344-7119 or (646)654-4500 Fax: (646)654-7212 Monthly. $49.00 per year. Incorporates *Building Renovation.*

Archives of Environmental Health: An International Journal. Helen Dwight Reid Educational Foundation. Heldref Publications, 1319 18th St., N.W. Washington, DC 20036-1802. Phone: 800-365-9753 Fax: (202)292-6130 E-mail: subscribe@heldref.org • URL: http://www.heldref.org • Monthly. $382.00 per year. Objective documentation of the effects of environmental agents on human health.

Area Development Sites and Facility Planning: The Executive Magazine of Sites and Facility Planning. Halcyon Business Publications, Inc., 400 Post Ave. Westbury, NY 11590. Phone: (516)338-0900 Fax: (516)338-0100 • URL: http://www.area-development.com • Monthly. Free to the business trade; others, $65.00 per year. Site selection, facility planning, and plant relocation. Formerly *Area Development Magazines.*

ARF - Advertising Research Foundation., 432 Park Ave. S New York, NY 10016. Phone: (212)751-5656 Fax: (212)319-5265 E-mail: info@thearf.org • URL: http://www.thearf.org • Advertisers, advertising agencies, research organizations, associations, and the media are regular members of the foundation; colleges and universities are associate members. Objectives are to: further scientific practices and promote greater effectiveness of advertising and marketing by means of objective and impartial research; develop new research methods and techniques; analyze and evaluate existing methods and

techniques, and define proper applications; establish research standards, criteria, and reporting methods. Compiles statistics and conducts research programs.

Argonne National Laboratory Industrial - Office of Technology Transfer., 9700 S Cass Ave. Argonne, IL 60439. Phone: 800-627-2596 or (630)252-7694 Fax: (630)252-5230 E-mail: weso@anl.gov • URL: http://www.itd.anl.gov • Formerly Industrial Technology Development Center.

Argumentation and Advocacy: Journal of the American Forensic Association. American Forensic Association, P.O. Box 256 River Falls, WI 54022-0256. Phone: 800-228-5424 or (715)425-3198 Fax: (715)425-9533 • URL: http://www. americanforensic.org • Quarterly. Members, $60.00 per year; institutions, $70.00 per year; students, $20.00 per year. Formerly *American Forensic Association Journal.*

ARL: A Bimonthly Report on Research Library Issues and Actions. Association of Research Libraries, 21 Dupont Circle Washington, DC 20036. Phone: (202)296-2296 Fax: (202)872-0884 E-mail: arlh@arl.org • URL: http://www.arl. org • Bimonthly. Members, $25.00; non-members, $50.00 per year. Formerly ARL: A Bimonthly Newsletter of Research Library Issues and Actions.

ARL Annual Salary Survey. Association of Research Libraries, 21 Dupont Circle Washington, DC 20036. Phone: (202)296-2296 Fax: (202)872-0884 E-mail: arlh@arl.org • URL: http:// www.arl.org • Annual. Members, $44.00; non-members, $100.00. Statistics on salaries by institution, region, position, sex/race and other data for the 119 research libraries in ARL.

ARL Statistics. Association of Research Libraries, 21 Dupont Circle, Suite 800 Washington, DC 20036. Phone: (202)232-2466 Fax: (202)872-0884 E-mail: arlh@arl.org • URL: http:// www.arl.org • Annual. Members, $44.00; non-members, $100.00. Presents a variety of statistics for about 120 university and other major research libraries.

ARMA International-The Association of Information Management Professionals., 13725 W 109th St., Ste. 101 Lenexa, KS 66215. Phone: 800-422-2762 or (913)341-3808 Fax: (913)341-3742 • URL: http://www.arma.org • Formerly ARMA International-The Information Management Professionals.

Armed Forces Communications and Electronics Association.

Armed Forces Comptroller. American Society of Military Comptrollers, 2034 Eisenhower Ave., Suite 145 Alexandria, VA 22314. Phone: (703)549-0360 Fax: (703)549-3181 Quarterly. $18.00 per year.

Armed Forces Hostess Association., The Pentagon, Rm. ID110, 6604 Army Pentagon Washington, DC 20310-6604. Phone: (703)614-0350 Fax: (703)697-5542 E-mail: promo@afcea. org • URL: http://www.army.mil/afha/main.html • Information office operated by volunteer wives of the armed forces. Assists in welcoming service families to the Washington, DC area; provides information on living conditions at all U.S. installations in the U.S. and overseas. Maintains information files on topics ranging from animal care and camps to universities and local vacation areas.

Armed Forces Institute of Pathology., 6825 16th St. NW Washington, DC 20306-6000. Phone: (202)782-2882 Fax: (202)782-9376 E-mail: telepath@afip.osd.mil • URL: http:// www.afip.org • Chartered by the Department of Defense to: maintain a consultation service for the diagnosis of pathologic material; conduct experimental, statistical, and morphological research in pathology; provide instruction in advanced pathology and related subjects; prepare, procure, and duplicate teaching aids; operate the AFIP Repository and Research Services; maintain the National Museum of Health and Medicine and a Visual Information Service for the collection, preparation, duplication, reference, and filing of medical illustrative material. Sponsors a series of courses.

Armed Forces Journal International. Armed Forces Journal International, Inc., 8201 Greensboro Dr., Ste. 611 McLean, VA 22102-3810. Phone: (703)848-0490 Fax: (703)848-0480 E-mail: afji@afji.com • URL: http://www.afji.com • Monthly. $45.00 per year. A defense magazine for career military officers and industry executives. Covers defense events, plans, policies, budgets, and innovations.

Armed Forces Sports., The Summit Center, 4700 King St., 4th Fl., R Summit Ctr. Alexandria, VA 22302-4418. Phone: 888-875-PLAY or (703)681-7215 Fax: (703)681-7245 E-mail: afs@ cfs.army.mil • URL: http://www.armedforcessports.com • Persons serving as head of the morale and welfare activities of the U.S. Army, Navy, Marines, and Air Force. Encourages physical fitness in the armed forces through a policy of "sports for all"; has established uniform rules to govern all service sports within its jurisdiction. Conducts interservice sports championship competitions. Develops and encourages spectator interest sports for the individual services. Selects and sends military athletes and teams to national and international competitions; has representative on the Executive Board and House of Delegates of the U.S. Olympic Committee, various U.S. sports governing bodies, and the International Military Sports Council. Compiles statistics.

Army AL&T: Acquisitions, Logistics, and Technology Bulletin. Available from U. S. Government Printing Office, Washington, DC 20402. Phone: (202)512-1800 Fax: (202)512-2250 E-mail: gpoaccess@gpo.gov • URL: http:// www.access.gpo.gov • Bimonthly. $20.00 per year. Produced by the U. S. Army Materiel Command (http://www.amc.army. mil). Reports on Army research, development, and acquisition. Formerly *Army RD&A.*

Army and Air Force Mutual Aid Association., 102 Sheridan Ave., Bldg. 468 Fort Myer, VA 22211-1110. Phone: 800-336-4538 or (703)522-3060 Fax: (703)522-1336 E-mail: info@ aafmaa.com • URL: http://www.aafmaa.com • A mutual aid organization providing aid to families of deceased career Army and Airforce officers and noncommissioned officers.

Army Aviation Association of America.

Army Emergency Relief., 200 Stovall St. Alexandria, VA 22332-0001. Phone: (866)878-6378 or (703)428-0000 Fax: (703)325-7183 E-mail: aer@aerhq.org • URL: http://www. aerhq.org • A private organization whose primary purpose is to relieve distress of members of the Army (active and retired) and their dependents, and to provide assistance to needy spouses and orphans of deceased Army members; a secondary purpose is to make available educational assistance (scholarships) to unmarried dependent children of soldiers (active, retired, or deceased) who need such assistance to pursue undergraduate studies.

Army Logistician: The Professional Bulletin of United States Army Logistics. United States Army Logistics Management College. Available from U.S. Government Printing Office, Washington, DC 20401. Phone: (202)512-1800 Fax: (202)512-2250 E-mail: gpoaccess@gpo.gov • URL: http:// www.access.gpo.gov • Bimonthly. $21.00 per year.

Army Nurse Corps Association., PO Box 39235, Serna Sta. San Antonio, TX 78218-1235. Phone: (210)650-3534 Fax: (210)650-3494 E-mail: membership@e-anca.org • URL: http://e-anca.org • Army Nurse Corps officers from active, or retiree status or those serving honorably for shorter periods, or reserve duty. Provides educational and social opportunities for members; disseminates information to the public. Seeks to preserve history of the U.S. Army Nurse Corps.

The Army Officer's Guide. Keith E. Bonn. Stackpole Books, 5067 Ritter Rd. Mechanicsburg, PA 17055. Phone: 800-732-3669 Fax: (717)796-0412 E-mail: jbender@stackpolebooks.com • URL: http://www.stackpolebooks.com • 1999. $22.95. 48th edition. (Army Officer's Guide Series).

Army Reserve Magazine. Available from U. S. Government Printing Office, Washington, DC 20402. Phone: (202)512-1800 Fax: (202)512-2250 E-mail: gpoaccess@gpo.gov • URL: http://www.access.gpo.gov • Quarterly. $14.00 per year. Issued by the Army Reserve, U. S. Department of Defense.

Army Times. Army Times Publishing Co., 6883 Commercial Dr. Springfield, VA 22159. Phone: 800-368-5718 or (703)750-8646 Fax: (703)750-8699 E-mail: cust-svc@atpco.com • URL: http://www.armytimes.com • Weekly. $52.00 per year. In two editions: Domestic and International.

Arnold Air Society., AFROTC Det. 770 Clemson University, 300 Tillman Hall, Box 341352 Clemson, SC 29634. Phone: (864)656-3254 Fax: (843)521-4533 E-mail: commander@ arnold-air.org • URL: http://www.arnold-air.org • Honorary professional fraternity within AFROTC. Organizes community service projects. Sponsors Silver Wings, a nonmilitary campus service organization.

Art and Antique Dealers League of America., 1040 Madison Ave. New York, NY 10021-0111. Phone: (212)879-7558 Fax: (212)772-7197 • URL: http://www.artantiquedealersleague. com • Members are retailers and wholesalers of antiques and art objects.

Art and Antiques. Trans World Publishing Co., 2100 Powers Ferry Rd., Suite 300 Atlanta, GA 30339. Phone: (770)955-5656 Fax: (770)952-0669 E-mail: editor@antiquesmag.com • URL: http://www.artantiquesmag.com • 11 times a year. $24.95 per year. Incorporates *Antique Monthly.*

Art and Auction. Auction Guild, 11 E. 36th St., 9th Fl. New York, NY 10016-3318. Phone: (212)447-9555 Fax: (212)532-7321 E-mail: edit@artandauction.com • URL: http://www. artandauction.com • 11 times a year. $89.00 per year.

Art and Creative Materials Institute., PO Box 479 Hanson, MA 02341-0479. Phone: (781)293-4100 Fax: (781)293-0808 E-mail: debbief@acminet.com • URL: http://www.acminet. org • Members are manufacturers of school and professional art and craft materials.

The Art and Science of Leadership. Afsaneh Nahavandi. Prentice Hall PTR, 240 Frisch Ct. Paramus, NJ 07652. Phone: 800-282-0693 Fax: 800-445-6991 • URL: http://www.phptr.com • 2002. $73.33. Third edition. Includes a discussion of participative management. Emphasis is on strategic leadership.

Art Business Encyclopedia. Leonard DuBoff. Allworth Press, 10 E 23rd St., Ste. 510 New York, NY 10010. Phone: 800-491-2808 or (212)777-8395 Fax: (212)777-8261 E-mail: pub@ allworth.com • URL: http://www.allworth.com • 1994. $18. 95. Defines words, phrases, and concepts relating to the business of art, with emphasis on legal matters. Includes relevant statutes, arranged by state. Published in cooperation with the American Council for the Arts.

Art Business News. Advanstar Communications, 545 Boylston St. Boston, MA 02116. Phone: 888-527-7008 or (617)267-6500 Fax: (617)267-6900 E-mail: info@advanstar.com • URL: http://www.advanstar.com • Monthly. $43.00 per year.

Art Business News Buyer's Guide. Advanstar Communications, 545 Boylston St. Boston, MA 02116. Phone: 800-598-6008 or (617)267-6500 Fax: (617)267-6900 E-mail: info@ advanstar.com • URL: http://www.advanstar.com • Annual. $25.00. Lists companies furnishing supplies and services to art dealers and framers. Includes art by subject and media.

Art Dealers Association of America.

Art Directors Annual. Art Directors Club Inc.., 106 W 29th St.

New York, NY 10001. Phone: (212)643-1440 Fax: (212)643-4293 E-mail: info@adcny.orgnet • URL: http://www.adcny.org • Annual. $70.00. Formerly *Annual of Advertising, Editorial and Television Art and Design with the Annual Copy Awards*.

Art Directors Club., 106 W 29th St. New York, NY 10001. Phone: (212)643-1440 Fax: (212)643-4266 E-mail: info@adcglobal.org • URL: http://www.adcglobal.org • Art directors of advertising magazines and agencies, visual information specialists, and graphic designers; associate members are artists, cinematographers, photographers, copywriters, educators, journalists, and critics. Promotes and stimulates interest in the practice of art direction. Sponsors Annual Exhibition of Advertising, Editorial and Television Art and Design; International Traveling Exhibition. Provides educational, professional, and entertainment programs; on-premise art exhibitions; portfolio review program. Conducts panels for students and faculty.

Art in America. Brant Publications, Inc., 575 Broadway, 5th Fl. New York, NY 10012. Phone: 800-925-9271 or (212)941-2800 Fax: (212)941-2885 Monthly. $39.95 per year; libraries, $34.95. Comprehensive reviews of U.S. and worldwide exhibits.

Art Index. H. W. Wilson Co., 950 University Ave. Bronx, NY 10452-4224. Phone: 800-367-6770 or (718)558-8400 Fax: 800-590-1617 or (718)590-1617 E-mail: custserv@hwwilson.com • URL: http://www.hwwilson.com • Quarterly. Annual cumulations. Price varies. Subject and author index to periodicals in art, architecture, industrial design, city planning, photography, and various related topics.

Art Index Online. H. W. Wilson Co., 950 University Ave. Bronx, NY 10452. Phone: 800-367-6770 or (718)558-8400 Fax: (718)590-1617 Indexes a wide variety of art-related periodicals, 1984 to date. Monthly updates. Inquire as to online cost and availability.

Art Information Center., 55 Mercer St., 3rd Fl. New York, NY 10013. Phone: (212)966-3443 E-mail: info@adcglobal.org Serves as a clearinghouse of information on contemporary fine arts. Assists artists in finding outlets for their work; assists art dealers in finding new talent; aids curators, and collectors. Data collected is donated to the Archives of American Art. **Convention/Meeting:** none.

Art Law: The Guide for Collectors, Investors, Dealers, and Artists. Ralph E. Lerner and Judith Bresler. Practising Law Institute, 810 Seventh Ave. New York, NY 10019-5818. Phone: 800-260-4754 or (212)824-5710 E-mail: info@pli.edu 1989. $170.00. Two volumes. Second edition. Covers artist/dealer relationships, artists' rights, appraisals, museum law, tax aspects, estate planning issues, and other legal topics relating to visual art. There are six main headings: Dealers, Artwork Transactions, Artists' Rights, Collectors, Taxes and Estate Planning, and Museums and Multimedia.

Art Marketing Handbook: Marketing Art in the 21st Century. Calvin J. Goodman. Gee Tee Bee, 11901 Sunset Blvd., No. 102 Los Angeles, CA 90049. Phone: (310)476-2622 Fax: (310)472-8785 E-mail: geteebee@aol.com 2003. $65.00. Seventh enlarged revised edition. A complete guide to all aspects of the art market.

Art Marketing Sourcebook. ArtNetwork, 10647 Red Dog Rd., PO Box 1360 Nevada City, CA 95959. Phone: 800-383-0677 or (530)470-0862 Fax: (530)470-0256 E-mail: info@artmarketing.com Covers: over 2,000 representatives, consultants, galleries, architects, interior designers, museums, and specialty markets. Entries include: Company name, address, phone, description of services, style represented, mediums, years in business, types of companies dealt with, geographical limitations, number of clients, requirements for viewing slides.

Art Now Gallery Guides. Art Now Inc., 97 Grayrock Rd., PO Box 5541 Clinton, NJ 08809-5541. Phone: (908)638-5255 Fax: (908)638-8737 E-mail: artnow@galleryguide.org • URL: http://www.galleryguideonline.com • Covers: in '[M Art Now Gallery Guide—International Edition]' current exhibitions in over 1,800 museums and galleries. Separate regional editions cover metropolitan New York, Boston and New England, the Philadelphia area, the southeast, Chicago and the midwest, the southwest, California and the northwest, Latin America, and Europe. Listings are paid. Entries include: Gallery or museum name, address, phone, days and hours of operation, artist's name or name of the exhibit, medium, and dates of showing.

The Art of Asking: How to Solicit Philanthropic Gifts. Paul H. Schneiter. Fund Raising Institute, 27500 Drake Rd. Farmington Hills, MI 48331-3535. Phone: 800-877-GALE or (248)699-GALE Fax: 800-414-5043 or (248)699-8069 E-mail: galeord@gale.com • URL: http://gale.cengage.com • 1985. $25.00.

The Art of Commercial Lending. Edgar M. Morsman. Robert Morris Associates, One Liberty Place, 1650 Market St., Suite 2300 Philadelphia, PA 19103. Phone: 800-677-7621 or (215)446-4000 Fax: (215)446-4101 • URL: http://www.rmahq.org • 1997. $64.00. Describes the diverse skills required for success as a commercial lender. Covers both personal and institutional aspects.

The Art of Editing. Brian S. Brooks and others. Allyn and Bacon, Inc., 75 Arlington St., Suite 300 Boston, MA 02116. Phone: 800-922-0579 or (781)848-6000 Fax: 800-445-6991 E-mail: ab_webmaster@abacon.com • URL: http://www.abacon.com • 2000. $82.00. 7th edition.

The Art of Fund Raising. Irving R. Warner. Fund Raising Institute, 27500 Drake Rd. Farmington Hills, MI 48331-3535. Phone: 800-877-GALE or (248)699-GALE Fax: 800-414-5043 or (248)699-8069 E-mail: galeord@gale.com • URL: http://www.galegroup.com • 1991. $19.95. Third edition. Includes case histories.

The Art of M & A: A Merger-Acquisition-Buyout Guide. Stanley F. Reed and Aleandra R. Lajoux. McGraw-Hill, 1221 Ave. of the Americas New York, NY 10020. Phone: 800-722-4726 or (212)512-2000 Fax: (212)512-4502 E-mail: customer.service@mcgraw-hill.com • URL: http://www.mcgraw-hill.com • 1998. $125.00. Third edition. A how-to-do-it guide for merger and acquisition ventures. Emphasis is on legal issues.

The Art of Recording: Understanding and Crafting the Mix. William Moylan. Elsevier, 360 Park Ave., S New York, NY 10010-1710. Phone: 888-437-4636 or (212)989-5800 Fax: (212)633-3990 E-mail: usinfo-f@elsevier.com • URL: http://www.elsevier.com • 2002. $29.99. Emphasizes the ways in which recorded sound is different from live sound. Covers the recording of audio as a creative process.

The Art of the Long View: Planning for the Future in an Uncertain World. Peter Schwartz. Doubleday, 1540 Broadway New York, NY 10036-4094. Phone: 800-323-9872 or (212)354-6500 Fax: (212)492-9700 • URL: http://www.doubledaybookclub.com • 1996. $30.95. Covers strategic planning for corporations and smaller firms. Includes "The World in 2005: Three Scenarios."

The Art of 3-D Computer Animation and Imaging. Isaac V. Kerlow. John Wiley and Sons, Inc., 111 River St. Hoboken, NJ 07030. Phone: 800-225-5945 or (201)748-6000 Fax: (201)748-6088 E-mail: info@wiley.com • URL: http://www.wiley.com • 2000. $59.95. Second edition. Covers special effects, hypermedia formats, video output, the post-production process, etc. Includes full-color illustrations and step-by-step examples. (Design and Graphic Design Series).

The Art of Weaving. Else Regensteiner. Schiffer Publishing, Ltd., 4880 Lower Valley Rd. Atglen, PA 19310. Phone: (610)593-1777 Fax: (610)593-2002 E-mail: schifferbk@aol.com • URL: http://www.schifferbooks.com • 1986. $29.95.

Art Reference Services Quarterly. Haworth Press, Inc., 10 Alice St. Binghamton, NY 13904-1580. Phone: 800-429-6784 or (607)722-5857 Fax: 800-895-0582 or (607)722-1424 E-mail: getinfo@haworthpressinc.com • URL: http://www.haworthpressinc.com • Quarterly. Institutions, $110.00 per year. A journal for art librarians.

Arthur Andersen North American Business Sourcebook: The Most Comprehensive, Authoritative Reference Guide to Expanding Trade in the North American Market. Triumph Books, 601 S. LaSalle St., Suite 500 Chicago, IL 60605. Phone: 800-335-5323 or (312)939-3330 Fax: (312)663-3557 E-mail: ordering@triumphbooks.com • URL: http://www.triumpbooks.com • 1993. $195.00. Includes statistical, regulatory, economic, and directory information relating to North American trade, including information on the North American Free Trade Agreement (NAFTA). Emphasis is on exporting to Mexico and Canada.

Arthur M. Bank Center for Entrepreneurship., Babson College Babson Park, MA 02459-0310. Phone: (781)239-4623 Fax: (781)239-4178 E-mail: spinelli@babson.edu • URL: http://www.babson.edu/entrep • Sponsors annual Babson College Entrepreneurship Research Conference.

Artificial Intelligence. Winston P. Henry. Addison-Wesley, 75 Arlington St., Ste. 300 Boston, MA 02116. Phone: 800-447-2226 or (617)848-7500 • URL: http://www.aw.com • 2001. Fourth edition. Price on application.

Artificial Intelligence: A Guide to Intelligent Systems. Michael Negnevitsky. Addison-Wesley, 75 Arlington St., Ste. 300 Boston, MA 02116. Phone: 800-447-2226 or (617)848-7500 2001. $62.00.

Artificial Intelligence and Software Engineering: Understanding the Promise of the future. Darek Partridge. Fitzroy Dearborn Publishers, Inc., 919 N. Michigan Ave., Suite 760 Chicago, IL 60611. Phone: 800-850-8102 or (312)587-0131 Fax: (312)587-1049 E-mail: fitzroy@aol.com • URL: http://www.fitzroydearborn.com • 1999. $55.00. Includes applications of artificial intelligence software to banking and financial services.

Artificial Intelligence Dictionary: A Dictionary Specifically for Artificial Intelligence Users and Specialists. Ellen Thro. Slawson Communications, Inc., P.O. Box 28459 San Diego, CA 92198-0459. 1991. $24.95. Includes common lay words that lead to correct medical terms. (Lance A. Leventhal Microtrend Series).

Artificial Intelligence in Perspective. Daniel G. Bobrow, editor. MIT Press, Five Cambridge Ctr. Cambridge, MA 02142-1493. Phone: 800-356-0343 or (617)253-5646 Fax: (617)253-6779 • URL: http://www.mitpress.mit.edu • 1994. $45.00. (Special Issues of Artificial Intelligence, an International Journal Series).

Artificial Intelligence Laboratory.

Artificial Intelligence: Reality or Fantasy? Leslie Chase and Robert Landers, editors. Software and Information Industry Association, 1090 Vermont Ave. NW, 6th Fl. Washington, DC 20005. Phone: (202)289-7442 Fax: (202)289-7097 • URL: http://www.siia.net • 1984. $59.95. General information and market considerations.

Artificial Language Laboratory., Michigan State University, 405 Computer Center East Lansing, MI 48824-1042. Phone: (517)353-0870 Fax: (517)353-4766 E-mail: artlang@msu.edu • URL: http://www.msu.edu/unit/artlang/ • Research areas include speech analysis and synthesis by computer.

Artist's and Graphic Designer's Market. F&W Publications, Inc., 4700 E Galbraith Rd. Cincinnati, OH 45236. Phone: 800-289-0963 or (513)531-2690 Fax: (513)531-0798 • URL: http://www.fwpublications.com • Annual. $24.99. Lists art galleries, advertising agencies, TV producers, publishers, and other buyers of free-lance art work. Formerly *Artist's Market*.

ARTnews. Artnews LLC, 48 W. 38th St. New York, NY 10018. Phone: (212)398-1690 Fax: (212)819-0394 E-mail: info@artnewsonline • URL: http://www.artnewsonline.com • 11 times a year. $39.95 per year.

The ARTnewsletter: The International Bi-Weekly Business Report on the Art Market. ARTnews LLC, 48 W. 38th St. New York, NY 10018. Phone: (212)398-1690 Fax: (212)819-0394 E-mail: info@artnewsonline.com • URL: http://www.artnewsonline.com • Biweekly. $249.00 per year. Newsletter on forthcoming auctions, price trends, ownership squabbles, criminal cases, etc.

Arts Management. Radius Group Inc., 110 Riverside Dr., No. 4E New York, NY 10024. Phone: (212)579-2039 Fax: (212)579-2049 Five times a year. $22.00 per year. National news service for those who finance, manage and communicate the arts.

Arts Management: A Guide to Finding Funds and Winning Audiences. Alvin H. Reiss. Fund Raising Institute, 27500 Drake Rd. Farmington Hills, MI 48331-3535. Phone: 800-877-8238 or (248)699-GALE Fax: 800-414-5043 or (248)699-8069 E-mail: galeord@gale.com • URL: http://www.galegroup.com • 1992. $45.00.

ASA Newsletter. American Society of Anesthesiologists, 520 N NW Hwy. Park Ridge, IL 60068-2573. Phone: (847)825-5586 Fax: (847)825-1692 E-mail: mail@asahq.org • URL: http://www.theasa.net • Description: Reports on the educational and scientific work of the organization, which represents anesthesiologists in the U.S. Recurring features include legislative updates, reports of meetings, news of research, historical items, editorials, letters to the editor and news of members.

ASA Today. American Subcontractors Association, 1004 Duke St. Alexandria, VA 22314-3588. Phone: (703)684-3450 Fax: (703)836-3482 E-mail: asaoffice-hq@aol.com • URL: http://www.asaonline.com • Weekly. $40.00 per year.

ASBC Newsletter. American Society of Brewing Chemists, 3340 Pilot Knob Rd. Saint Paul, MN 55121. Phone: 800-328-7560 or (651)454-7250 Fax: (651)454-0766 E-mail: asbc@scisoc.org • URL: http://www.asbcnet.org • Description: Provides news items and technical reports on brewing and related matters. Recurring features include news items, abstracts of technical papers, convention news, book reviews, and membership listings and changes.

Asbestos Information Association/North America., PMB 114, 1235 Jefferson Davis Hwy. Arlington, VA 22202-3283. Phone: (703)560-2980 Fax: (703)560-2981 E-mail: aiabjpigg@aol.com Manufacturers, processors, and miners/millers of asbestos or products containing asbestos. Purposes are: to provide industry wide information on asbestos and health and on industry efforts to eliminate existing hazards; to cooperate with government agencies in developing and implementing industry wide standards for exposure to asbestos dust and for the control of asbestos dust emissions into community air and water; to exchange information on methods and techniques of asbestos dust control; to assist in the solution of problems arising from the health effects of asbestos; to increase public knowledge of the unique benefits and importance of asbestos products. Acts as central agency for the collection and dissemination of medical and technical information on asbestos-related disease, asbestos dust control, and other asbestos-related ecological considerations.

Asbestos Institute. Asbestos Institute, 1200 McGill College, Ste. 1640 Montreal, QC, Canada H3B 4G7. Phone: (514)877-9797 Fax: (514)877-9717 E-mail: info@chrysotile.com • URL: http://www.chrysotile.com • Safe of asbestos.

Asbestos Litigation Reporter: The National Journal of Record of Asbestos Litigation. Andrews Publications, 175 Strafford Ave., Bldg 4, Suite 140 Wayne, PA 19087. Phone: 800-345-1101 or (610)225-0510 Fax: (610)225-0501 E-mail: customer@andrewspub.com • URL: http://www.andrewspub.com • Semimonthly. $995.00 per year. Provides reports on legal cases involving asbestos as a health hazard.

ASBPE Editor's Notes. American Society of Business Press Editors, 710 E Ogden Ave., Ste. 600 Naperville, IL 60563-8603. Phone: (630)579-3288 Fax: (630)369-2488 E-mail: info@asbpe.org • URL: http://www.asbpe.org • Bimonthly. Membership. Newsletter.

ASCE News. American Society of Civil Engineers, 1801 Alexander Bell Dr. Reston, VA 20191-4400. Phone: 800-548-2723 or (703)295-6300 Fax: (703)295-6222 E-mail: marketing@asce.org • URL: http://www.asce.org • Description: Reports on activities of the society and news of the civil engineering profession.

ASFA Aquaculture Abstracts [Online]. Cambridge Scientific Abstracts, 7200 Wisconsin Ave., 6th Fl. Bethesda, MD 20814. Phone: 800-843-7751 or (301)961-6700 Fax: (301)961-6720 Indexing and abstracting of the literature of marine life, 1984 to present. Inquire as to online cost and availability.

ASHRAE Journal: The Magazine of the American Society of Heating, Refrigeration, Air-Conditioning, Ventilation. American Society of Heating, Refrigerating and Air

Conditioning Engineers, Inc., 1791 Tullie Circle, N.E. Atlanta, GA 30329. Phone: 800-527-4723 or (404)636-8400 Fax: (404)321-5478 E-mail: ashrae@ashrae.org • URL: http://www.ashrae.org • Monthly. Free to members; non-members, $59.00 per year.

ASHRAE Transactions. American Society of Heating, Refrigerating, and Air Conditioning Engineers, Inc., 1791 Tullie Circle, N.E. Atlanta, GA 30329. Phone: 800-527-4723 or (404)636-8400 Fax: (404)321-5478 E-mail: ashrae@ashrae.org • URL: http://wwwe.ashrae.org • Semiannual. Members, $169.00 per year; non-members, $211.00 per year.

Asia Inc.: The Region's Business Magazine. Asia, Inc., Ltd., Eight F Kinwich Centre, 32 Hollywood Rd. Central Hong Kong, Hong Kong. Phone: 852 2581-8088 Fax: 852 2581-0302 E-mail: subscriptions@team.asia-inc.com • URL: http://www.asia-inc.com • Monthly. $79.00 per year. Contains business, financial, and other news and commentary from various countries in Asia. Main sections are "At Work," "Asia Abroad: A World of Business," and "After Hours: Travel and Leisure." Text in English.

Asia/Pacific American Librarians Association., MIT Humanities Library, 77 Massachusetts Ave., Rm. 14S-222 Cambridge, MA 02139. Phone: 800-545-2433 or (617)253-9352 Fax: (617)253-3109 E-mail: baildon@mit.edu • URL: http://www.apalaweb.org • Librarians and information specialists of Asian Pacific descent working in the U.S.; interested persons. Provides a forum for discussing problems and concerns; supports and encourages library services to Asian Pacific communities; recruits and supports Asian Pacific Americans in the library and information science professions. Offers placement service; compiles statistics. Conducts fundraising for scholarships.

Asia Pacific Economic Review: Bridging Pacific Rim Business and Society. Zencore, Inc., P.O. Box 14089 Seattle, WA 98119. Phone: (206)860-4970 Fax: (206)860-4895 • URL: http://www.asialinks.com • Monthly. $35.00 per year. Includes special issues on individual countries: Taiwan, Malayasia, China/Hong Kong, Japan, and Korea.

Asia Pacific Kompass on Disc. Available from Kompass USA, Inc., 121 Whitney Ave. New Haven, CT 06510. Phone: 877-566-7277 or (203)503-6789 Fax: (203)503-6780 E-mail: mail@kompass-usa.com • URL: http://www.kompass.com • Annual. CD-ROM provides information on more than 200,000 companies in Australia, China, Hong Kong, India, Korea, Malaysia, New Zealand, Philippines, Singapore, Thailand, and Taiwan. Classification system covers approximately 50,000 products and services.

Asia Pacific Securities Handbook. Hoover's Inc., 5800 Airport Blvd. Austin, TX 78752-4204. Phone: (866)486-8666 or (512)374-4500 Fax: (512)374-4501 E-mail: salesteam@hoovers.com • URL: http://www.hoovers.com • Covers: stock exchanges and brokers in Australia, Bangladesh, China, Hong Kong, India, Indonesia, Japan, Malaysia, Nepal, New Zealand, Pakistan, Philippines, Singapore, South Korea, Sri Lanka, Taiwan, and Thailand. Entries include: Name, address, phone, fax; exchanges also list market practices, most active and highest capitalized stocks.

Asia Times Online.

Asian American Voters Coalition., 8837 Sleepy Hollow Ln. Potomac, MD 20854. E-mail: information@emilyslist.org Coalition of organizations representing 6.5 million Asian-Americans. Seeks to enhance the political influence of Asian-Americans; promotes equal treatment of Asian-Americans in the U.S. political system. Lobbies the U.S. government on immigration legislation and other matters of interest to the Asian-American community; attempts to influence party platforms and presidential candidates on issues pertinent to Asian-Americans. Sponsors voter registration and education drives; encourages Asian-Americans to run for public office. Maintains speakers' bureau; bestows award for distinguished service.

Asian Marketing Information Sourcebook. Euromonitor International, 122 South Michigan Ave., Suite 810 Chicago, IL 60603. Phone: 800-577-3876 or (312)922-1115 Fax: (312)922-1157 E-mail: info@euromonitor.com • URL: http://www.euromonitor.com • 2003. $475.00. Lists trade associations, statistical offices, government agencies, special libraries, trade journals, websites, and other sources of business information for the countries of Asia.

Asian Pacific Markets: A Guide to Company and Industry Information Sources. Washington Researchers Ltd., 1655 N. Fort Myer Dr., Suite 800 Arlington, VA 22209. Phone: (703)312-2863 Fax: (703)527-4586 E-mail: research@researchers.com • URL: http://www.washingtonresearchers.com • Irregular. $335.00. A directory of government offices, "experts," publications, and databases related to Asian markets and companies. Includes individual chapters on "the 11 most important nations in Asia." Formerly *Asian Markets*.

The Asian Wall Street Journal. Dow Jones & Co., Inc., 200 Liberty St. New York, NY 10281. Phone: 800-544-0422 or (212)416-2700 Fax: (212)416-2829 • URL: http://www.barrons.com • Daily. $970.00 per year (air mail). Published in Hong Kong. Also available in a weekly edition at $259.00 per year: *Asian Wall Street Journal Weekly*.

Asia's 7,500 Largest Companies. ELC International, 30 Eastbourne Ter. London W2 6LG, United Kingdom. Phone: 800-526-0651 or (44)71 706 0919 Fax: (44)71 723 6854 E-mail: salesteam@hoovers.com • URL: http://www.dnb.com • Covers: top 7,500 companies of Hong Kong, Indonesia, Japan, Korea, Malaysia, the Philippines, Singapore, Taiwan, Thailand, and China. Entries include: Company name, address, line of business, International SIC numbers, financial data including assets, turnover, and capital.

ASID Professional Designer. American Society of Interior Designers, 608 Massachusetts Ave., NE Washington, DC 20002. Phone: (202)546-3480 E-mail: asid@asid.org • URL: http://www.interiors.org • Bimonthly. Membership.

Aslib Proceedings: New Information Perspectives. Available from Information Today, Inc., 143 Old Marlton Pike Medford, NJ 08055-8750. Phone: 800-300-9868 or (609)654-6266 Fax: (609)654-4309 E-mail: custserv@infotoday.com • URL: http://www.infotoday.com • Ten times a year. $349.00 per year. Published in London by Aslib Covers a wide variety of information industry and library management topics.

ASM Engineered Materials Reference Book. Michael L. Bauccio, editor. ASM International, 9639 Kinsman Rd. Materials Park, OH 44073-0002. Phone: 800-336-5152 or (440)338-5151 Fax: (440)338-4634 E-mail: cust-srv@asminternational.org • URL: http://www.asminternational.org • 1994. $155.00. Third edition. Provides information on a wide range of materials, with special sections on ceramics, industrial glass products, and plastics.

ASM International., 9639 Kinsman Rd. Novelty, OH 44073-0002. Phone: 800-336-5152 or (440)338-5151 Fax: (440)338-4634 E-mail: customerservice@asminternational.org • URL: http://asmcommunity.asminternational.org/portal/site/asm • Metallurgists, materials engineers, executives in materials producing and consuming industries; teachers and students. Disseminates technical information about the manufacture, use, and treatment of engineered materials. Offers in-plant, home study, and intensive courses through Materials +Engineering Institute. Conducts career development program. Established ASM Foundation for +Education and Research.

ASM Materials Engineering Dictionary. Joseph R. Davis, editor. ASM International, 9639 Kinsman Rd. Materials Park, OH 44073-0002. Phone: 800-336-5152 or (440)338-5151 Fax: (440)338-4634 E-mail: cust-srv@asminternational.org • URL: http://www.asminternational.org • 1992. $166.00. Contains 10,000 entries, 700 illustrations, and 150 tables relating to metals, plastics, ceramics, composites, and adhesives. Includes "Technical Briefs" on 64 key material groups.

ASM Metals Reference Book. Michael L. Bauccio, editor. ASM International, 9639 Kinsman Rd. Materials Park, OH 44073-0002. Phone: 800-336-5152 or (440)338-5151 Fax: (440)338-4634 E-mail: cust-serv@asminternational.org • URL: http://www.asminternational.org • 1993. $155.00. Third edition. Includes glossary, tables, formulas, and diagrams. Covers a wide range of ferrous and nonferrous metals.

Asphalt. Asphalt Institute, P.O. Box 14052 Lexington, KY 40512-4052. Phone: (859)288-4960 Fax: (859)288-4999 E-mail: pubs@asphaltinstitute.org • URL: http://www.asphaltinstitute.org • Three times a year. Free.

Asphalt Emulsion Manufacturers Association., 3 Church Cir., PMB 250 Annapolis, MD 21401. Phone: (410)267-0023 Fax: (410)267-7546 E-mail: krissoff@aema.org • URL: http://www.aema.org • Seeks to foster: advancement and improvement of the asphalt emulsion industry; expanded and more efficient use of emulsion as a result of an improved state of the art; provision of information to users through guide specifications and answers to specific questions.

Asphalt Institute., 2696 Research Park Dr., PO Box 14052 Lexington, KY 40511-8480. Phone: (859)288-4960 Fax: (859)288-4999 E-mail: info@asphaltinstitute.org • URL: http://www.asphaltinstitute.org • Composed of petroleum asphalt/bitumen producers, manufacturers and affiliated businesses. Promotes the use, benefits, and quality performance of petroleum asphalt through environmental marketing, research, engineering, and technical development, and through the resolution of issues affecting the industry.

Asphalt Products and Markets. Available from MarketResearch.com, 641 Ave. of the Americas, 3rd Fl. New York, NY 10011. Phone: 800-298-5699 or (212)807-2629 Fax: (212)807-2716 E-mail: order@marketresearch.com • URL: http://www.marketresearch.com • 2001. $3,200.00. Published by the Freedonia Group. Market data with forecasts to 2007. Includes information on paving, coating, and roofing asphalt products.

Asphalt Roofing Manufacturers Association., 1156 15th St. NW, Ste. 900 Washington, DC 20005. Phone: (202)207-0917 Fax: (202)223-9741 E-mail: info@asphaltinstitute.org • URL: http://asphaltroofing.org • Manufacturers of asphalt shingles, rollgoods, built-up roofing systems (BUR) and modified bitumen roofing systems. Compiles statistics.

Assecuranz Compass CD-ROM. Available from Kompass USA, Inc., 121 Whitney Ave. New Haven, CT 06510. Phone: 877-566-7277 or (203)503-6789 Fax: (203)503-6780 E-mail: mail@kompass-usa.com • URL: http://www.kompass.com • Annual. CD-ROM provides detailed financial and other information on more than 21,000 insurance companies in 209 countries worldwide. Includes listings of 47,000 insurance company executives.

Assembly Buyers Guide. Reed Business Information, 360 Park Ave,. S New York, NY 10010. Phone: 800-662-7776 or (646)746-6400 E-mail: corporatecommunications@reedbusiness.com • URL: http://www.reedbusiness.com • Annual. $68.00. Lists manufacturers and suppliers of equipment relating to assembly automation, fasteners, adhesives, robotics, and power tools.

Assembly: Design and Manufacturing Technology for Better Assembled Products. Business News Publishing Co., 755 W Big Beaver Rd., Ste. 1000 Troy, MI 48084-4903. Phone: 800-837-7370 or (248)362-3700 Fax: (248)362-6317 • URL: http://www.bnp.com • Monthly. $68.00 per year. Covers assembly, fastening, and joining systems. Includes information on automation and robotics.

Assessing Competitive Intelligence Software: A Guide to Evaluating CI Technology. France Bouthillier and Kathleen Shearer. Information Today, Inc., 143 Old Marlton Pike Medford, NJ 08055-8750. Phone: 800-300-9868 or (609)654-6266 Fax: (609)654-4309 E-mail: custserv@infotoday.com • URL: http://www.infotoday.com • 2003. $39.50. Provides a 32-step methodology for making an evaluation of competitive intelligence software. (An ASIST publication: American Society for Information Science and Technology).

Assessing Service Quality: Satisfying the Expectations of Library Customers. Peter Hernon and Ellen Altman. American Library Association, 50 E. Huron St. Chicago, IL 60611-2795. Phone: 800-545-2433 or (312)944-6780 Fax: (312)440-9374 E-mail: ala@ala.org • URL: http://www.ala.org • 1998. $40.00. Discusses surveys, focus groups, and other data collection methods for measuring the quality of library service. Includes sample forms and an annotated bibliography.

Assessment Journal. International Association of Assessing Officers, 130 E. Randolph St., Suite 850 Chicago, IL 60601-6217. Phone: (312)819-6100 Fax: (312)819-6149 E-mail: ajournal@iaao.org • URL: http://www.iaao.org • Bimonthly. Free to members; non-members, $200.00 per year. Formed by merger of *Assessment* and *Valuation Legal Reporter and IAAO Update*.

Asset Allocation and Financial Market Timing: Techniques for Investment Professionals. Carroll D. Aby and Donald E. Vaughn. Greenwood Publishing Group, Inc., 88 Post Rd., W Westport, CT 06881. Phone: 800-225-5800 or (203)226-3571 Fax: (203)431-2214 E-mail: customer-service@greenwood.com • URL: http://www.greenwood.com • 1995. $79.95.

Asset Allocation: Balancing Financial Risk. Roger C. Gibson. McGraw-Hill, Two Penn Plaza New York, NY 10121. Phone: 800-722-4726 or (212)904-2000 Fax: (212)904-6096 E-mail: customer.service@mcgraw-hill.com • URL: http://www.mcgraw-hill.com • 2000. $55.00. Third edition. Provides a scholarly discussion of the fine points of investment asset allocation and financial risk management.

Asset Protection Planning Guide: A State-of-the-Art Approach to Integrated Estate Planning. Barry S. Engel and others. CCH, Inc., 2700 Lake Cook Rd. Riverwoods, IL 60015. Phone: 800-835-5224 or (847)267-7000 E-mail: cust_serv@cch.com • URL: http://www.cch.com • 2001. $99.00. Provides advice for attorneys, trust officers, accountants, and others engaged in financial planning for protection of assets.

Assets and Liabilities of Commercial Banks in the United States. U. S. Federal Reserve System, Board of Governors, Publications Services, MS-138, 20th and Constitution Ave., NW Washington, DC 20551. Phone: (202)452-3244 Fax: (202)728-5886 • URL: http://www.federalreserve.gov • Weekly. $30.00 per year. (Federal Reserve Statistical Release, H.8.)

Assisted Living Success. Virgo Publishing, Inc., PO Box 40079 Phoenix, AZ 85067-0079. Phone: (480)990-1101 Fax: (480)990-0819 E-mail: virgopub@vpico.com • URL: http://www.vpico.com • Monthly. $55.00 per year. Edited for owners, operators, and managers of assisted living facilities.

Assisted Living Today. Assisted Living Federation of America, 11200 Waples Mill Rd., Ste. 150 Fairfax, VA 22030-7407. Phone: (703)691-8100 Fax: (703)691-8106 E-mail: altoday@strattonpub.com • URL: http://www.alfa.org • Nine times a year. $30.00 per year. Covers the management, marketing, and financing of assisted living residences.

Associated Builders and Contractors.

Associated Collegiate Press. University of Minnesota, University of Minnesota, 2221 University Ave. SE, Ste. 121 Minneapolis, MN 55414. Phone: (612)625-8335 Fax: (612)626-0720 E-mail: info@studentpress.org • URL: http://www.studentpress.org/acp • Conducts annual critique of newspapers and annual critique of magazines and yearbooks. Sponsors competitions.

Associated Cooperage Industries of America.

Associated Corset and Brassiere Manufacturers.

Associated Equipment Distributors., 615 W 22nd St. Oak Brook, IL 60523. Phone: 800-388-0650 or (630)574-0650 Fax: (630)574-0132 E-mail: info@aednet.org • URL: http://www.aednet.org • Represents distributors and manufacturers of agriculture, and construction, mining, logging, forestry, public works and road maintenance equipment in the U.S., Canada, and overseas. Includes activities such as industry information and statistics, educational programs on customer service, financial management, rental management, sales management, and service and parts management program for younger executives. Maintains Washington, DC office. Oversees AED Foundation which offers industry educational programs and career/vocational services. Offers group and business insurance to members; conducts ongoing industry relations program with construction equipment manufacturers and users. Operates Market Trends Index Program, covering monthly distributor sales and inventories.

Associated General Contractors of America.

Associated General Contractors of America: Highway Division.

Associated Glass and Pottery Manufacturers.

Associated Locksmiths of America.

Associated Press Managing Editors., 450 W 33rd St. New York, NY 10001. Phone: (212)621-1838 Fax: (212)506-6102 E-mail: apme@ap.org • URL: http://www.apme.com • Represents managing editors or executives on the news or editorial staff of The Associated Press newspapers. Aims to: advance the journalism profession; examine the news and other services of the Associated Press in order to provide member newspapers with services that best suit their needs; provide a means of cooperation between the management and the editorial representatives of the members of the Associated Press. Maintains committees dealing with newspapers and news services.

Associated Press Stylebook and Libel Manual. Addison-Wesley, 75 Arlington St., Ste. 300 Boston, MA 02116. Phone: 800-447-2226 or (617)848-7500 • URL: http://www.aw.com • 1996. $14.00. Sixth edition.

Associated Specialty Contractors., 3 Bethesda Metro Ctr., Ste. 1100 Bethesda, MD 20814. Phone: (703)548-3118 Fax: (301)215-4500 E-mail: dgw@necanet.org • URL: http://www.assoc-spec-con.org • Works to promote efficient management and productivity. Coordinates the work of specialized branches of the industry in management information, research, public information, government relations and construction relations. Serves as a liaison among specialty trade associations in the areas of public relations, government relations, and with other organizations. Seeks to avoid unnecessary duplication of effort and expense or conflicting programs among affiliates. Identifies areas of interest and problems shared by members, and develops positions and approaches on such problems.

Associated Surplus Dealers., 11835 W Olympic Blvd., Ste. 550E Los Angeles, CA 90064-5810. Phone: 800-421-4511 or (310)481-7300 Fax: (310)481-1900 E-mail: dgw@necanet.org • URL: http://www.merchandisegroup.com • Represents surplus, general merchandise, and close-out dealers, manufacturers, manufacturers' representatives, and others. Promotes trade shows; provides liaison with government agencies; offers group life insurance coverage.

Associated Writing Programs The Association of Writers and Writing Programs., George Mason University, Carty House, Mail Stop 1E3 Fairfax, VA 22030. Phone: (703)933-4301 Fax: (703)933-4302 E-mail: awp@gmu.edu • URL: http://www.awpwriter.org • Supports writers and writing programs worldwide.

Association Executive Compensation and Benefits Study. American Society of Association Executives, 1575 Eye St., N.W. Washington, DC 20005-1103. Phone: (202)626-2723 Fax: (202)408-9634 E-mail: books@asaenet.org • URL: http://www.asaenet.org • 1999. $195.00. 11th edition. A salary survey.

Association for Accounting Administration., 136 S. Keowee St. Dayton, OH 45402. Phone: (937)222-0030 Fax: (937)222-5794 E-mail: aaainfo@cpaadmin.org • URL: http://www.cpaadmin.org • Members are accounting and office systems executives.

Association for Advanced Life Underwriting.

Association for Business Communication.

Association for Business Simulation and Experiential Learning.

Association for Career and Technical Education.

Association for Computational Linguistics.

Association for Computing Machinery., 1515 Broadway, 17th Fl. New York, NY 10036-5701. Phone: 800-342-6626 or (212)626-0500 Fax: (212)944-1318 E-mail: acmhelp@acm.org • URL: http://www.acm.org • Includes many Special Interest Groups.

Association for Computing Machinery Communications. Association for Computing Machinery, 1515 Broadway New York, NY 10036-5701. Phone: (212)869-7440 Fax: (212)869-0481 E-mail: acmhelp@acm.org • URL: http://www.acm.org • Monthly. Members, $36.00 per year; non-members, $174.00 per year; students, $41.00 per year.

Association for Computing Machinery Journal. Association for Computing Machinery, 1515 Broadway New York, NY 10036. Phone: (212)869-7440 Fax: (212)869-0481 E-mail: acmhelp@acm.org • URL: http://www.acm.org • Bimonthly. Members, $45.00 per year; non-members, $220.00 per year; students, $40.00 per year.

Association for Conflict Resolution., 1527 New Hampshire Ave. NW, 3rd Fl. Washington, DC 20036. Phone: (202)667-9700 Fax: (202)265-1968 E-mail: info@acresolution.org • URL: http://www.acresolution.org • Formerly Academy of Family Mediators.

Association for Continuing Higher Education.

Association for Corporate Growth.

Association for Education in Journalism and Mass Communication.

Association for Educational Communications and Technology.

Association for Facilities Engineering.

Association for Financial Counseling and Planning Education., 2121 Arlington Ave., Ste. 5 Upper Arlington, OH 43221-4339. Phone: (614)485-9650 Fax: (614)485-9621 • URL: http://www.afcpe.org • Members are researchers, academics, financial counselors and financial planners.

Association for Financial Professionals., 7315 Wisconsin Ave., Suite 600 W Bethesda, MD 20814-3211. Phone: (301)907-2862 Fax: (301)907-2864 E-mail: afp@afponline.org • URL: http://www.afponline.org • Goal is to raise the stature and visibility of the finance profession. Formerly Treasury Management Association.

Association for Financial Technology., Blendonview Office Park, 5008-2 Pine Creek Dr. Westerville, OH 43081-4899. Phone: (614)895-1208 Fax: (614)895-3466 E-mail: aft@fitech.org • URL: http://www.fitech.org • Concerned with bank computer technology.

Association for Finishing Processes of the Society of Manufacturing Engineers.

Association for Healthcare Resource and Materials Management., c/o American Hospital Association, One N Franklin St. Chicago, IL 60606-3420. Phone: (312)422-3840 Fax: (312)422-4573 E-mail: ahrmm@aha.org • URL: http://www.ahrmm.org • Members are involved with the purchasing and distribution of supplies and equipment for hospitals and other healthcare establishments. Formerly American Society for Healthcare Materials Management.

Association for Interactive Marketing., 1430 Broadway, 8th Fl. New York, NY 10018. Phone: 888-337-0008 or (212)790-1408 Fax: (212)391-9233 • URL: http://www.interactivehq.org • Members are companies engaged in various interactive enterprises, utilizing the internet, interactive television, computer communications and multimedia. Formerly Association for Interactive Media.

Association for Investment Management and Research., 560 Ray C. Hunt Dr. Charlottesville, VA 22903. Phone: 800-247-8132 or (434)951-5499 Fax: (434)951-5262 E-mail: info@aimr.org • URL: http://www.aimr.org • Members are practicing investment analysts.

Association for Investment Management and Research-Membership Directory. Association for Investment Management and Research, 560 Ray C. Hunt Dr. Charlottesville, VA 22903-0668. Phone: 800-247-8132 or (434)951-5499 Fax: (434)951-5262 E-mail: info@aimr.org • URL: http://www.aimr.org • Annual. $150.00. Lists 38,000 professional investment managers and securities analysts.

Association for Iron and Steel Technology., 186 Thorn Hill Rd. Warrendale, PA 15086-7528. Phone: (724)776-6040 Fax: (724)776-1880 E-mail: info@aist.org • URL: http://www.aistech.org • Formerly Iron and Steel Society.

Association for Library Collections and Technical Services.

Association for Management Information in Financial Services., 3895 Fairfax Court Atlanta, GA 30339. Phone: (770)444-3557 Fax: (770)444-9084 E-mail: ami@amifs.org • URL: http://www.amifs.org • Members are financial institution employees interested in management accounting and cost analysis.

Association for Postal Commerce., 1901 N Fort Myer Dr., Ste. 401 Arlington, VA 22209-1609. Phone: (703)524-0096 Fax: (703)524-1871 E-mail: info@postcom.org • URL: http://www.postcom.org • Formerly Advertising Mail Marketing Association.

Association for Quality and Participation.

Association for the Advancement of Medical Instrumentation., 1110 N. Glebe Rd., No. 220 Arlington, VA 22201-4795. Phone: 800-332-2264 or (703)525-4890 Fax: (703)525-1424 • URL: http://www.aami.org • Members are engineers, technicians, physicians, manufacturers, and others with an interest in medical instrumentation.

Association for the Advancement of Medical Instrumentation Membership Directory. c/o AAMI Foundation, 1110 N. Glebe Rd., Ste. 220 Arlington, VA 22201-4795. Phone: 800-332-2264 or (703)525-4890 Fax: (703)276-0793 E-mail: publications@aami.org • URL: http://www.aami.org • Annual. Membership. List 6,500 physicians, clinical engineers, biomedical engineersand technicians and nurses, researchers, and medical equipment manufacturers.

Association for University Business and Economic Research Membership Directory. Association for University Business and Economic Research, 801 W. Michigan St. Indianapolis, IN 46202-5151. Phone: (317)274-2204 Fax: (317)274-3312 Annual. $10.00. Member institutions in the United States and abroad with centers, bureaus, departments, etc., concerned with business and economic research.

Association for Unmanned Vehicle Systems International., 3401 Columbia Pke., Suite 400 Arlington, VA 22204. Phone: (703)920-2720 Fax: (703)920-2889 E-mail: info@auvsi.org • URL: http://www.auvsi.org • Concerned with the development of unmanned systems and robotics technologies.

The Association for Work Process Improvement., 185 Devonshire St., Suite 770 Boston, MA 02110-9555. Phone: 800-998-2974 or (617)426-1167 Fax: (617)521-8675 E-mail: info@tawpi.org • URL: http://www.tawpi.org • Members are companies that use or supply various recognition technologies equipment.

Association for Worksite Health Promotion., 60 Revere Dr., Suite 500 Northbrook, IL 60062-1577. Phone: (847)480-9574 Fax: (847)480-9282 E-mail: awhp@awhp.com • URL: http://www.awhp.com • Members are physical fitness professionals hired by major corporations to conduct health and fitness programs. Formerly Association for Fitness in Business.

Association Management. American Society of Association Executives, 1575 Eye St., N.W. Washington, DC 20005-1103. Phone: (202)626-2723 Fax: (202)371-8825 E-mail: feedback@asae.org • URL: http://www.asaenet.org • Monthly. $50.00.

Association Meeting and Event Planners Directory. Douglas Publications, Inc., 2807 Parham Rd. Richmond, VA 23294. Phone: 800-223-1797 or (804)762-9600 Fax: (804)217-8999 E-mail: info@douglaspublications.com • URL: http://www.douglaspublications.com • Annual. $650.00. Lists planners of meetings for over 8,000 national associations. Provides past and future convention locations, dates held, number of attendees, exhibit space required, and other convention information. Formerly *Association Meeting Planners*.

Association Meeting Trends. American Society of Association Executives, 1575 Eye St., N. W. Washington, DC 20005-1103. Phone: (202)626-2723 Fax: (202)408-9634 E-mail: books@asaenet.org • URL: http://www.asaenet.org • 1999. $90.00. (Management Research Series).

Association of African-American Women Business Owners.

Association of American Chambers of Commerce in Latin America., 1615 H St., N.W. Washington, DC 20062. Phone: (202)463-5485 Fax: (202)463-3126 E-mail: inbox@aaccla.org • URL: http://www.aaccla.org • Umbrella organization for American chambers of commerce in Latin America. Affiliated with U.S. Chamber of Commerce.

Association of American Colleges and Universities.

Association of American Military Uniform Collectors., PO Box 1876 Elyria, OH 44036. Phone: (440)365-5321 E-mail: aamucfl@comcast.net • URL: http://www.naples.net/clubs/aamuc • Collectors of American military and naval uniforms (1776-present). Promotes interest in uniform preservation and heritage along with patriotic interest in the U.S. armed forces. Loans uniform displays by members to various groups, including Boy Scouts of America, Girl Scouts of the U.S.A., American Legion, and Veterans of Foreign Wars of the U.S.A. branches, public schools, libraries, and public exhibitions. Reviews the books on U.S. military uniforms. **Convention/Meeting:** none.

Association of American Pesticide Control Officials.

Association of American Plant Food Control Officials.

Association of American Plant Food Control Officials Official Publication. Association of American Plant Food Control Officials, Inc., Div. of Regulatory Services. University of Kentucky, Lexington, KY 40546. Phone: (606)257-2668 Fax: (606)257-7351 E-mail: dterry@ca.uky.edu • URL: http://www.aapfco.org • Annual. $25.00.

Association of American Publishers.

Association of American Railroads.

Association of American Seed Control Officials.

Association of American Universities.

Association of American University Presses.

Association of America's Public Television Stations.

Association of Asphalt Paving Technologists.

Association of Authors' Representatives.

Association of Career Management Consulting Firms International., 204 E St., NE Washington, DC 20002. Phone: (202)547-6344 Fax: (202)547-6348 E-mail: aocfi@aocfi.org • URL: http://www.aocfi.org • Firms providing displaced employees who are sponsored by their organization, with counsel and assistance in job searching and the techniques and practices of choosing a career.

Association of Cinema and Video Laboratories.

Association of College and Research Libraries.

Association of Consulting Chemists and Chemical Engineers.

Association of Container Reconditioners-Membership and Industrial Supply Directory. Association of Container Reconditioners, 8401 Corporate Dr., Suite 140 Landover, MD 20785. Phone: 800-533-3786 or (301)577-3786 Fax: (301)577-6476 E-mail: prankin@igc.apc.org Annual. $30.00. Lists approximately 215 container reconditioners and dealers, worldwide. Also lists suppliers of machinery and accessories.

Association of Correctional Food Service Affiliates., 210 N Glenoaks Blvd., Ste. C Burbank, CA 91502. Phone: (818)843-6608 Fax: (818)843-7423 E-mail: jonnichols@acfsa.org • URL: http://www.acfsa.org • Food service professionals from federal, state and county correctional institutions and vendors that serve them. Works to advance skills and professionalism through education, information and networking.

Association of Defense Trial Attorneys.

Association of Diesel Specialists.

Association of Directory Publishers.

Association of Edison Illuminating Companies.

Association of Energy Engineers., 4025 Pleasantdale Rd., Ste. 420 Atlanta, GA 30340-4264. Phone: (770)447-5083 Fax: (770)446-3969 E-mail: info@aeecenter.org • URL: http://www.aeecenter.org • Members are engineers and other professionals concerned with energy management and cogeneration.

Association of Executive Search Consultants.

Association of Family and Conciliation Courts., c/o Ann Milne, 6515 Grand Teton Plz., Ste. 210 Madison, WI 53719-1048. Phone: (608)664-3750 Fax: (608)664-3751 E-mail: afcc@afccnet.org • URL: http://www.afccnet.org • Members are judges, attorneys, and family counselors. Promotes conciliation counseling as a complement to legal procedures.

Association of Food Industries.

Association of Free Community Papers.

Association of Fundraising Professionals., 1101 King St., Ste. 700 Alexandria, VA 22314-2967. Phone: 800-666-3863 or

(703)684-0410 Fax: (703)684-0540 • URL: http://www.afpnet.org • Formerly National Society of Fundraising Executives.

Association of Golf Merchandisers., P.O. Box 19899 Fountain Hills, AZ 85269-9899. Phone: (480)836-8250 Fax: (480)836-8251 E-mail: info@aol.com • URL: http://www.agmgolf.org • Members are vendors of gold equipment and merchandise.

Association of Governing Boards of Universities and Colleges.

Association of Government Accountants., 2208 Mount Vernon Ave. Alexandria, VA 22301-1314. Phone: 800-242-7211 or (703)684-6931 Fax: (703)548-9367 E-mail: agamembers@agacgfm.org • URL: http://www.agacgfm.org • Members are employed by federal, state, county, and city government agencies. Includes accountants, auditors, budget officers, and other government finance administrators and officials.

Association of Graduate Schools in Association of American Universities.

Association of Graduates., 3116 Academy Dr., 3116 Academy Dr. USAF Academy, CO 80840-4475. Phone: 800-232-GRAD or (719)472-0300 Fax: (719)333-4194 E-mail: aog@usafa.org • URL: http://www.usafa.org • Graduates of the United States Military Academy (West Point); membership currently includes all graduates still living. Promotes the welfare of, and raises money for the academy; helps to improve the education and training of the cadets by providing funds beyond the minimum normal appropriations. Has approximately 120 local and state chapters known as West Point Societies. Compiles statistics; offers career advisory services.

Association of Home Appliance Manufacturers.

Association of Imaging Technology and Sound., 1899 L St., NW, Ste. 600 Washington, DC 20036-3849. E-mail: katy@itsnet.org Members are individuals interested in various aspects of prerecorded videotape production. Acts as a source of general information about videotape.

Association of Independent Information Professionals., 8550 United Plz. Blvd., Ste. 1001 Baton Rouge, IL 70809. Phone: 888-544-2447 or (225)408-4400 Fax: (225)922-4611 E-mail: info@aiip.org • URL: http://www.aiip.org • Members are information brokers, document providers, librarians, consultants, database designers, webmasters, and other information professionals. Formerly International Association of Independent Information Brokers.

Association of Industrial Metallizers, Coaters and Laminators.

Association of Information and Dissemination Centers.

Association of Information Technology Professionals.

Association of Insolvency and Restructuring Advisors.

Association of International Automobile Manufacturers.

Association of International Marketing., PO Box 70 London E13 8BQ, United Kingdom. Phone: 44 208 9867539 Fax: 44 208 9867539 A multinational organization. Promotes the advancement and exchange of information and ideas in international marketing.

Association of Internet Professionals., 2929 Main St., No. 136 Santa Monica, CA 90405. Phone: (866)247-9700 or (501)423-2248 Fax: (501)423-2248 E-mail: info@association.org • URL: http://www.iproa.org • Members are interactive media professionals concerned with intetractive arts and technologies. Formerly International Interactive Communications Society.

Association of Learned and Professional Society Publishers.

Association of Life Insurance Counsel., 1300 Clinton St. Fort Wayne, IN 46801. Phone: 800-659-5589 or (219)455-2000 Fax: (219)455-4503 E-mail: membersupport@legalstaff.com • URL: http://www.legalstaff.com • Members are attorneys for life insurance companies.

Association of Local Air Pollution Control Officials.

Association of Local Television Stations., 1320 19th St., N.W., Suite 300 Washington, DC 20036. Phone: (202)887-1970 Fax: (202)887-0950 E-mail: altv@aol.com • URL: http://www.altv.com • Members are TV stations not affiliated with a major network.

Association of Management Consulting Firms., 380 Lexington Ave., No. 1700 New York, NY 10168-0002. Phone: (212)551-7887 Fax: (212)551-7934 E-mail: info@amcf.org • URL: http://www.amcf.org • Members are management consultants. One of the two divisions of the Council of Consulting Organizations.

Association of Master of Business Administration Executives.

Association of Military Colleges and Schools of the United States., 3604 Glenbrook Rd. Fairfax, VA 22031. Phone: (703)272-8406 E-mail: amcsus@cox.net • URL: http://www.amcsus.org • Comprises of military colleges and secondary schools.

Association of Military Surgeons of the U.S., 9320 Old Georgetown Rd. Bethesda, MD 20814-1653. Phone: 800-761-9320 or (301)897-8800 Fax: (301)530-5446 E-mail: amsus@amsus.org • URL: http://www.amsus.org • Physicians, dentists, veterinarians, nurses, pharmacists, dietitians, therapists, and others of commissioned rank (or grades E5 through E9) or equivalent in the Army, Navy, Air Force, Public Health Service, and Veterans Administration; Reserve and National Guard officers are also eligible for membership. Advances all phases of federal medicine and allied sciences related to federal health services. Provides group insurance.

Association of Minicomputer Users.

Association of National Advertisers.

Association of Naval Aviation., 2550 Huntington Ave., Ste. 201 Alexandria, VA 22303-1499. Phone: (703)960-2490 Fax: (703)960-4490 E-mail: ana@anahq.org • URL: http://www.anahq.org • Active or former officers and enlisted men of the aeronautical organizations of the U.S. Navy, Marines, Coast Guard, or other service personnel and civilians; industrial associates. Objectives are to stimulate and extend appreciation of naval aviation; to help the active and reserve military establishment; to merge the various diverse elements of the military, particularly in relation to problems associated with maritime aviation; to promote greater communication among the military, academic, and business communities on issues of maritime aviation. Sponsors film and videotape programs for U.S. Navy and public service television use.

Association of NROTC Colleges and Universities., University of Rochester, 33A Wallis Hall, PO Box 270041 Rochester, NY 14627-0041. Phone: (585)275-2096 Fax: (585)275-8531 E-mail: jennifer.ashbaugh@rochester.edu • URL: http://www.conferences.rochester.edu/NROTCconstitution.html • Representatives from colleges and universities that have Naval Reserve Officers Training Corps units on their campuses. Promotes NROTC training and coordinates the efforts of institutions offering this service.

Association of Oil Pipe Lines.

Association of Operative Millers.

Association of Performing Arts Presenters.

Association of Professional Material Handling Consultants.

Association of Promotion Marketing Agencies Worldwide.

Association of Publicly Traded Companies.

Association of Research Libraries.

Association of Retail Travel Agents.

Association of School Business Officials International.

Association of Schools of Journalism and Mass Communication.

Association of Ship Brokers and Agents-U.S.A., 510 Sylvan Ave., Ste. 201 Englewood Cliffs, NJ 07632-3039. Phone: (201)569-2882 Fax: (201)569-9082 E-mail: asba@asba.org • URL: http://www.asba.org • Includes a Tanker Committee.

Association of State and Interstate Water Pollution Control Administrators.

Association of Steel Distributors.

Association of Telephone Answering Services.

Association of Teleservices International., 12 Academy Ave. Atkinson, NH 03811. Phone: (866)892-2874 or (603)362-9489 Fax: (603)362-9486 E-mail: help@atsi.org • URL: http://www.atsi.org • An organization of telephone answering and voice message services.

Association of Teleservices International-Membership Directory. Association of Teleservices International, Inc., 12 Academy Ave. Atkinson, OH 03811. Phone: (603)362-9489 Fax: (603)362-9486 E-mail: admin@atsi.orgm • URL: http://www.atsi.org • Annual. $100.00. Lists 825 telephone answering services.

Association of the United States Army.

Association of the Wall and Ceiling Industries - International.

Association of Theatrical Artists and Craftspeople (ATAC)., 604 Riverside Dr. New York, NY 10031. Phone: (212)234-9001 Members are artists and craftspeople working in theatre, film, TV, and advertising. Areas of expertise include props, costumes, millinery, puppetry, display, and special effects.

Association of Theatrical Press Agents and Managers., 1560 Broadway, Ste. 700 New York, NY 10036-2501. Phone: (212)719-3666 Fax: (212)302-1585 E-mail: info@atpam.com • URL: http://www.atpam.com • A labor union for theater managers and press agents. Affiliated with AFL-CIO.

Association of Trial Lawyers of America., 1050 31st. NW Washington, DC 20007. Phone: 800-424-2725 or (202)965-3500 or (202)944-2800 Fax: (202)625-7312 E-mail: info@atlahq.org • URL: http://www.atlanet.org • Concerned with the behavioral aspects of litigation.

Association Operating Ratio Report. American Society of Association Executives The ASAE Bldg., 1575 Eye St. NW Washington, DC 20005-1103. Phone: (202)626-2723 Fax: (202)408-9634 E-mail: books@asaenet.org • URL: http://www.asaenet.org • 1997. $165.00. 10th edition. Contains comparison data from associations.

Association Trends. Martineau Corporation, 7910 Woodmont Ave., No. 1150 Bethesda, MD 20814-3062. Phone: (301)652-8666 Fax: (301)656-8654 E-mail: ads@assntrends.com Weekly. $129.00 per year. For staff executives of national, local, regional trade and professional associations. Contains news and information on association management and related issues.

Associations Canada: The Directory of Associations in Canada. Micromedia, 20 Victoria St. Toronto, ON, Canada M5C 2N8. Phone: 800-387-2689 or (416)362-5211 Fax: (416)362-6161 E-mail: info@micromedia.on.ca • URL: http://www.circ.micromedia.on.ca • Annual. $299.00. Provides detailed information in English and French on 20,000 active Canadian associations. Includes subject, keyword, personal name, and other indexes. Formerly *Directory of Associations in Canada*.

Associations Unlimited. Gale Cengage Learning, 27500 Drake Rd. Farmington Hills, MI 48331-3535. Phone: 800-877-GALE or (248)699-GALE Fax: 800-414-5043 or (248)699-8069 E-mail: galeord@gale.com • URL: http://gale.cengage.com • Semiannual. Includes all information on CD-ROM from all of the Gale *Encyclopedia of Associations* directories, plus association materials from about 2,500 of the associations-full-text documents and membership applications.

Associations Yellow Book: Who's Who at the Leading U. S. Trade and Professional Associations. Leadership Directories, Inc., 104 Fifth Ave. New York, NY 10011. Phone: (212)627-4140 Fax: (212)645-0931 E-mail: info@leadershipdirectories.com • URL: http://www.leadershipdirectories.com • Semiannual. $265.00 per year. Gives the names and titles of over 44,000 staff members in about 1,100 major associations. Six indexes are included: association name, individual name, industry, budget, acronym, and political action committee (PAC).

ASTA Agency Management. American Society of Travel Agents. Pohly and Partners Inc., 27 Melcher St., 2nd Fl. Boston, MA 02210. Phone: (617)451-1700 Fax: (617)338-7767 • URL: http://www.pohlypartners.com • Monthly. $36.00 per year.

ASTM List of Publications. American Society for Testing and Materials (ASTM), 100 Barr Harbor Dr. Conshohocken, PA 19428-2959. Phone: (610)832-9585 Fax: (610)832-9555 E-mail: service@astm.org • URL: http://www.astm.org • Annual.

ASTM Standardization News. American Society for Testing and Materials, 100 Barr Harbor Dr., W. Conshohocken, PA 19428-2959. Phone: (610)832-9500 Fax: (610)832-9555 E-mail: service@astm.org • URL: http://www.astm.org • Monthly. $18.00 per year.

Astronomy. Kalmbach Publishing Co., 21027 Crossroads Circle Waukesha, WI 53187. Phone: 800-533-6644 or (262)796-8776 Fax: (262)796-1615 • URL: http://www.kalmbach.com • Monthly. $39.95 per year.

ASU Travel Guide. Christopher Gil, editor. Airline Services Unlimited, 448 Ignacio Blvd., Ste. 333 Novato, CA 94949. Phone: (866)459-0300 or (415)898-9500 Fax: (415)898-9501 E-mail: subs@asutravelguide.com • URL: http://www.asutravelguide.com • Covers: over 3,700 listing for airlines, lodgings, tours, car rental companies, and cruise lines, which allow travel discounts to airline employees worldwide. Entries include: Name, address, and phone of facility or service; description; regular price and type and amount of discount; credit cards accepted; validity dates; booking procedures; whether parents and retired airline employees are eligible.

AT & T National Toll-Free Directories., 295 N Maple Ave. Basking Ridge, NJ 07920-1002. Phone: 800-426-8686 or (980)221-2000 • URL: http://www.tollfree.att.net • Annual. Business edition, $24.99 per year; consumer edition, $14.99 per year.

ATA Chronicle. American Translators Association, 225 Reinekers Lane, Suite 590 Alexandria, VA 22314-2875. Phone: (703)683-6100 Fax: (703)683-6122 • URL: http://www.atanet.org • Monthly. $50.00.

ATA Directory of Translaters and Interpreters. American Translators Association, 225 Reinkers Lane, Suite 590 Alexandria, VA 22314. Phone: (703)683-6100 Fax: (703)683-6122 E-mail: ata@atanet.org • URL: http://www.ata.org • Only avalible online. Over 5,000 member translators and interpreters. Formerly *ATA Translation Services Directory*.

ATEA Journal. American Technical Education Association, North Dakota State College of Science, 800 N 6th St. Wahpeton, ND 58076-0002. Phone: 800-342-4325 or (701)671-2240 Fax: (701)671-2260 E-mail: betty.krump@ndscs.edu • URL: http://www.ateaonline.org • Description: Reports on meetings, conferences, and conventions; equipment and teaching aids; news of members in the field of technical education; and reviews of books, pamphlets, and magazine articles. Recurring features include news from industry, and book reviews.

Athletic Business. Athletic Business Publications, Inc., 4130 Lien Rd. Madison, WI 53704-3602. Phone: 800-722-8764 or (608)249-0186 Fax: (608)249-1153 E-mail: editors@athleticbusiness.com • URL: http://www.athleticbusiness.com • Monthly. $55.00 per year. Published for those whose responsibility is the business of planning, financing and operating athletic/recreation/fitness programs and facilities.

Athletic Business Professional Directory. Athletic Business Publications, Inc., 4130 Lien Rd. Madison, WI 53704-3602. Phone: 800-722-8764 or (608)249-0186 Fax: (608)249-1153 E-mail: editors@athleticbusiness.com • URL: http://www.athleticbusiness.com • Monthly. $72.00 per year. $8.00 per issue. Lists consultants in athletic facility planning, with architects, engineers, and contractors. Appears in each issue of *Athletic Business*.

Athletic Management. MomentumMedia, 2488 N. Triphammer Rd. Ithaca, NY 14850-1014. Phone: (607)257-6970 Fax: (607)257-7328 E-mail: info@momentum.com Bimonthly. $24.00 per year. Formerly *College Athletic Management*.

Atlas & Gazetteer Series. DeLorme Mapping Co., Two DeLorme Dr. Yarmouth, ME 04096. Phone: 800-511-2459 Fax: 800-575-2244 E-mail: sales@delorme.com • URL: http://www.delorme.com • Dates vary. $983.50 complete ($19.95 region). Consists of 50 volumes covering all areas of the U. S. Includes detailed maps, as well as descriptions of attractions, natural areas, and historic sites. (CD-ROM versions available.)

Atmospheric Environment. Elsevier Science, 655 Ave. of the Amercias New York, NY 10010-5107. Phone: 800-366-2665 or (212)989-5800 Fax: 800-535-9935 E-mail: custserv@elsevier.com • URL: http://www.elsevier.com • 36 times a year. Qualified personnel, $431.00 per year; institutions, $5,368.00 per year. Text in English, French and German.

Atmospheric Sciences Research Center. University of Albany, State University of New York

Atomic Energy. Russian Academy of Sciences, RU. Kluwer Academic Publishers, New York, NY 10013-1522. Phone: (866)269-9527 or (212)620-8000 Fax: (212)463-0742 • URL: http://www.wkap.nl • Monthly. Institutions, $2,901.00 per year. Includes print and online editions. Formerly *Soviet Atomic Energy*.

ATP-FAR 135, Airline Transport Pilot: A Comprehensive Text and Workbook for the en Exam. K.T. Boyd. Iowa State University Press, 2121 S. State Ave. Ames, IA 50014-8300. Phone: 800-862-6657 or (515)292-0140 Fax: (515)292-3348 E-mail: orders@iowastatepress.com • URL: http://www.isupress.edu • 1994. $29.95. Third edition.

Attorneys and Agents Registered to Practice Before United States Patent and Trademark Office. U.S. Patent and Trademark Office. Available from U.S. Government Printing Office, Washington, DC 20402. Phone: (202)512-1800 Fax: (202)512-2250 E-mail: gpoaccess@gpo.gov • URL: http://www.access.gpo.gov • Annual. $56.00.

Attorneys' Dictionary of Medicine. J. E. Schmidt. LexisNexis Matthew Bender, 1275 Broadway Albany, NY 12204. Phone: 800-424-4200 or (518)487-3000 Fax: (518)487-3584 E-mail: bookstore.support@lexisnexis.com • URL: http://www.bender.com • Irregular. $673.00. Over 57,000 definitions of medical terms. Includes common lay words that lead to correct medical terms.

Attorney's Dictionary of Patent Claims: Legal Materials and Practice Commentaries. Irwin M. Aisenberg. LexisNexis Matthew Bender, 1275 Broadway Albany, NY 12204. Phone: 800-424-4200 or (518)487-3000 Fax: (518)487-3584 E-mail: bookstore.support@lexisnexis.com • URL: http://www.bender.com • $607.00. Three looseleaf volumes. Periodic supplementation. Operational guidance for bank officers, with analysis of statutory law and agency regulations.

Attorneys' Textbook of Medicine. LexisNexis Matthew Bender, 1275 Broadway Albany, NY 12204. Phone: 800-424-4200 or (518)487-3000 Fax: (518)487-3584 E-mail: bookstore.support@lexisnexis.com • URL: http://www.bender.com • Quarterly. $3,145.00 per year. 23 looseleaf volumes. Medicolegal material.

The Auctioneer. National Auctioneers Association, 8880 Ballentine Overland Park, KS 66214-1985. Phone: (913)541-8084 Fax: (913)894-5281 E-mail: hq@auchtioneers.org • URL: http://www.auctioneers.org • Monthly. Membership. News of interest to auctioneers.

AudArena Stadium International Guide and Facility Buyers Guide. San Diego Technical Books, Inc., 4240 Kearny Mesa Rd., No. 128 San Diego, CA 92111. Phone: (858)279-4990 Fax: (858)279-5088 E-mail: dan@booksmatter.com • URL: http://www.booksmatter.com • 2002. $99.00. More than 4,500 arenas, auditoriums, stadiums, exhibit halls, and coliseums in U.S., Canada and in less depth, Europe and South America. Formerly *Audarena Stadium International Guide*.

Audio. Orion Research Corp., 14555 N. Scottsdale Rd., Suite 330 Scottsdale, AZ 85254-3457. Phone: 800-844-0759 Fax: 800-375-1315 E-mail: orion@bluebook.com • URL: http://www.netzone.com • Annual. $179.00. Quotes retail and wholesale prices of used audio equipment. Original list prices and years of manufacture are also shown.

Audio Electronics. John L. Hood. Elsevier, 655 Ave. of the Americas New York, NY 10010. Phone: 800-366-2665 or (212)989-5800 Fax: 800-535-9935 or (212)633-3680 E-mail: custserv@elsevier.com • URL: http://www.elsevier.com • 1998. $54.95. Second edition.

Audio Engineer's Reference Book. Michael Talbot-Smith, editor. Elsevier, 655 Ave. of the Americas New York, NY 10010. Phone: 800-366-2665 or (212)989-5800 Fax: 800-535-9935 or (212)633-3680 E-mail: custserv@elsevier.com • URL: http://www.elsevier.com • 2001. $84.95. Second edition.

Audio Recording and Reproduction: Practical Measures for Audio Enthusiasts. Michael Talbot-Smith. Elsevier, 655 Ave. of the Americas New York, NY 10010. Phone: 800-366-2665 or (212)989-5800 Fax: 800-535-9935 or (212)633-3680 E-mail: custserv@elsevier.com • URL: http://www.elsevier.com • 1994. $29.95.

Audio Week: The Authoritative News Service of the Audio Consumer Electronics Industry. Warren Publishing, Inc., 2115 Ward Ct., NW Washington, DC 20037. Phone: (202)872-9200 Fax: (202)293-3435 • URL: http://www.warrenpub.com • Weekly. $663.00. Newsletter. Provdies audio industry news, company news, and new product information.

Audiotex Directory and Buyer's Guide. ADBG Publishing, P.O. Box 25929 Los Angeles, CA 90025. Phone: (310)479-3533 Fax: (310)479-0654 Annual. $55.00. Lists more than 1,200 voice processing product and service companies. Includes speech synthesis and recognition products.

Audit Bureau of Circulations., 900 N. Meacham Rd. Schaumburg, IL 60173-4968. Phone: (847)605-0909 Fax: (847)605-0483 E-mail: corpcomdebt@accessabc.com • URL: http://www.accessabc.com • Verifies newspaper and periodical circulation statements. Includes a Business Publications Industry Committee and a Magazine Directors Advisory Committee.

Auditing. Jack C. Robertson and Timothy J. Louwers. McGraw-Hill, 1221 Ave. of the Americas New York, NY 10020. Phone: 800-722-4726 or (212)512-2000 Fax: (212)512-4502 E-mail: customer.service@mcgraw-hill.com • URL: http://www.mcgraw-hill.com • 2001. $41.88. 10th edition.

Auditing: Integrated Approach. Alvin A. Arens. Prentice Hall PTR, 240 Frisch Ct. Paramus, NJ 07652. Phone: 800-282-0693 Fax: 800-445-6991 • URL: http://www.phptr.com • 2000. $105.00. Eighth edition.

Auditing Research Monographs. American Institute of Certified Public Accountants, 1211 Ave. of the Americas New York, NY 10036-8775. Phone: 800-862-4272 or (212)596-6200 Fax: (212)596-6213 E-mail: lmorales@aicpa.org • URL: http://www.aicpa.org • Irregular. Price varies.

Audits of Brokers and Dealers in Securities With Conforming Changes as of May 1, 1999. American Institute of Certified Public Accountants, 1211 Ave. of the Americas New York, NY 10036-8775. Phone: 800-862-4272 or (212)596-6200 Fax: (212)596-6213 E-mail: lmorales@aicpa.org • URL: http://www.aicpa.org • 1999. $42.00. Fifth edition. (Audit and Accounting Guide Series).

Author Biographies Master Index. Gale Cengage Learning, 27500 Drake Rd. Farmington Hills, MI 48331-3535. Phone: 800-877-GALE or (248)699-GALE Fax: 800-414-5043 E-mail: gale.galeord@cengage.com • URL: http://gale.cengage.com • 1997. $299.00. Fifth edition. Two volumes. Contains over 1,140,000 references tobiographies of 550,000 different authors.

Authority Collier Bankruptcy Library. LexisNexis/Matthew Bender, 1275 Broadway Albany, NY 12204. Phone: 800-424-4200 or (518)487-3000 Fax: (518)487-3584 • URL: http://www.bender.com • Periodic revisions. Price on request. CD-ROM contains updated full text of *Collier on Bankruptcy* and 13 other Collier publications. Various aspects of bankruptcy are covered, including attorney compensation, proceedings, farm insolvencies, real estate failures, family law, taxation, and business workouts.

Authority Computer and Telecommunications Law Library. LexisNexis/Matthew Bender, 1275 Broadway Albany, NY 12204. Phone: 800-424-4200 or (518)487-3000 Fax: (518)487-3584 • URL: http://www.bender.com • Quarterly. Price on request. Full text CD-ROM provides cases, analysis, sample agreements, and other information relating to computer law, telecommunications regulation (cable, broadcasting, satellite, Internet), international computer law, and computer contracts.

Authority Health Care Law Library. LexisNexis/Matthew Bender, 1275 Broadway Albany, NY 12204. Phone: 800-424-4200 or (518)487-3000 Fax: (518)487-3584 • URL: http://www.bender.com • Periodic updates. Price on request. Full text CD-ROM provides legal information, case law, and analysis relating to health care facilities, health insurance, longterm care, Medigap, and Medicare.

Authority Immigration Law Library. LexisNexis/Matthew Bender, 1275 Broadway Albany, NY 12204. Phone: 800-424-4200 or (518)487-3000 Fax: (518)487-3584 • URL: http://www.bender.com • Periodic revisions. Price on request. CD-ROM contains updated full text of *Immigration Case Reporter, Immigration Law and Procedure Treatise, INS Regulations*, and other immigration law publications issued by Matthew Bender.

Authority Intellectual Property Library. LexisNexis/Matthew Bender, 1275 Broadway Albany, NY 12204. Phone: 800-424-4200 or (518)487-3000 Fax: (518)487-3584 • URL: http://www.bender.com • Quarterly. Price on request. CD-ROM contains updated full text of *Intellectual Property Counseling and Litigation, Computer Law, International Computer Law, Nimmer on Copyright, Milgrim on Trade Secrets, Patent Litigation, Patent Licensing Transactions, Trademark Protection and Practice*, and other Matthew Bender publications relating to the law of intellectual property.

Authority on Administrative Law. LexisNexis/Matthew Bender, 1275 Broadway Albany, NY 12204. Phone: 800-424-4200 or (518)487-3000 Fax: (518)487-3584 • URL: http://www.bender.com • Periodic updates. Price on request. Full text CD-ROM provides detailed information on Federal administrative procedural law. Contains a large number of judicial, regulatory, and statutory references.

Authority Tax and Estate Planning Library. LexisNexis/Matthew Bender, 1275 Broadway Albany, NY 12204. Phone: 800-424-4200 or (518)487-3000 Fax: (518)487-3584 • URL: http://www.bender.com • Periodic revisions. Price on request. CD-ROM contains updated full text of *Bender's Payroll Tax Guide, Depreciation Handbook, Federal Income Taxation of Corporations, Tax Planning for Corporations, Modern Estate Planning, Planning for Large Estates, Murphy's Will Clauses, Tax & Estate Planning for the Elderly*, and 12 other Matthew Bender publications. The Internal Revenue Code is also included.

Authority Worker's Compensation Library. LexisNexis/Matthew Bender, 1275 Broadway Albany, NY 12204. Phone: 800-424-4200 or (518)487-3000 Fax: (518)487-3584 • URL: http://www.bender.com • Periodic revisions. Price on request. CD-ROM contains updated full text of *Larson's Workmen's Compensation, Occupational Injuries and Illnesses*, and other Matthew Bender publications relating to the law of worker's compensation.

Authors Guild., 31 E 32nd St., 7th Fl. New York, NY 10016-7923. Phone: (212)563-5904 Fax: (212)564-5363 E-mail: staff@authorsguild.org • URL: http://www.authorsguild.org • Professional book and magazine writers. Maintains legal staff to provide book and magazine contract reviews for members. Group health insurance available. Members of the guild are also members of the Authors League of America.

Authors League of America.

Auto Laundry News: The Voice of the Car Care Industry. EW Williams Publications Co., 2125 Center Ave., Suite 305 Fort Lee, NJ 07024-5898. Phone: (201)592-7007 Fax: (201)592-7171 E-mail: webeditor@ewwpi.com • URL: http://www.williamspublications.com • Monthly. $56.00 per year. Covers management, technical information, trends, and marketing for the vehicle cleaning industry. Edited for owners, operators, managers, and investors.

Autocar. Haymarket Publishing, Ltd., 38-42 Hampton Rd. Teddington TW11 OJE, United Kingdom. Phone: 44 208 943 5000 Monthly. $172.00 per year. Formerly *Autocar and Motor*.

Automated Builder Annual Buyers' Guide., 1445 Donlon St., Suite 16 Ventura, CA 93003-5640. Phone: 800-344-2537 or (805)642-9735 Fax: (805)642-8820 E-mail: info@automatedbuilder.com • URL: http://www.automatedbuilder.com • Annual. $12.00. Over 250 manufacturers and suppliers to the manufactured and pre-fabricated housing industry.

Automated Builder: The No. 1 International Housing Technology Transfer Magazine for Manufacturing and Marketing., 1445 Donlon St., Suite 16 Ventura, CA 93003-5640. Phone: 800-344-2537 or (805)642-9735 Fax: (805)642-8820 E-mail: info@automatedbuilder.com • URL: http://www.automatedbuilder.com • Monthly. $50.00 per year. Annual *Buyers' Guide* available.

Automated Imaging Association., PO Box 3724, PO Box 3724 Ann Arbor, MI 48106. Phone: 800-994-6099 or (734)994-6088 Fax: (734)994-3338 E-mail: dwhalls@robotics.org • URL: http://www.machinevisiononline.org • Represents manufacturers of machine vision components and systems, users, system integrators, universities and non-profit research groups, and financial firms that track the machine vision industry. Promotes the use and understanding of image capture and analysis technology.

Automatic Control Systems. Benjamin C. Kuo and Farid Golnaraghi. John Wiley and Sons, Inc., 111 River St. Hoboken, NJ 07030. Phone: 800-223-2336 or (201)748-6276 Fax: (201)748-8641 E-mail: info@wiley.com • URL: http://www.wiley.com • 2002. $119.95. Eighth edition.

Automatic Fire Alarm Association., PO Box 1569 Jasper, GA 30143. Phone: (678)454-3473 Fax: (678)454-3474 E-mail: fire-alarm@afaa.org • URL: http://www.afaa.org • Represents automatic fire detection and fire alarm systems industry. Membership is made up of state and regional member associations, manufacturers, installing distributors, authorities having jurisdiction, and end users. Promotes Life Safety in America through involvement in the codes and standards making process and by providing training seminars on a national basis.

Automatic Merchandiser. Cygnus Business Media, 1233 Janesville Ave. Fort Atkinson, WI 53538. Phone: 800-547-7377 or (920)563-6388 Fax: (920)563-1707 E-mail: rich.reiff@cygnuspub.com • URL: http://www.cygnusbzb.com • 11 times a year. $66.00 per year. Includes annual *Product* issue. Formerly *American Automatic Merchandiser*.

Automatic Merchandiser Blue Book Buyer's Guide. Cygnus Business Media, 1233 Janesville Ave. Fort Atkinson, WI 53538-0803. Phone: 800-547-7377 or (920)563-6388 Fax: (920)563-1707 E-mail: rich.reiff@cygnuspub.com • URL: http://www.cygnusbzb.com • Annual. $35.00. Suppliers of products, services, and equipment to the merchandise vending, contract food services, and office coffee service industries.

Automatica. Elsevier, 655 Ave. of the Americas New York, NY 10010-5107. Phone: 800-366-2665 or (212)989-5800 Fax: 800-535-9935 or (212)633-3680 E-mail: custserv@elsevier.com • URL: http://www.elsevier.com • Monthly. Qualififed personnel, $74.00 per year; institutions, $2,332.00 per year. Text in English, French, German and Russian.

Automation. Available from U. S. Government Printing Office, Washington, DC 20402. Phone: (202)512-1800 Fax: (202)512-2250 E-mail: gpoaccess@gpo.gov • URL: http://www.access.gpo.gov • Annual. Free. Issued by the Superintendent of Documents. A list of government publications on automation, computers, and related topics. Formerly *Computers and Data Processing*. (Subject Bibliography No. 51.)

Automobile Insurance Losses, Collision Coverages, Variations by Make and Series. Highway Loss Data Institute, c/o Stephen L. Oesch, 1005 N. Glebe Rd., Suite 800 Arlington, VA 22201. Phone: (703)247-1600 Fax: (703)247-1678 E-mail: iihs@highwaysafety.org • URL: http://www.carsafety.com • Semiannual. Membership.

Automobile Liability Insurance. 3d. Irvin E. Schermer and William J. Schermer. West Group, 610 Opperman Dr. Eagan, MN 55123. Phone: 800-328-4880 or (651)687-7000 Fax: 800-340-9378 E-mail: bookstore@westgroup.com • URL: http://www.westgroup.com • Seminannual. $501.00. Four looseleaf volumes.

Automobile Quarterly: The Connoisseur's Magazine of Motoring Today, Yesterday and Tomorrow. Automobile Quarterly, Inc., 1950 Classic Car Circle New Albany, IN 47150. Phone: (866)838-2886 or (812)948-2886 Fax: (812)948-2816 • URL: http://www.autoquarterly.com • Five times a year. $89.95 per year.

Automotive Aftermarket Industry Association., 7101 Wisconsin Ave., Ste. 1300 Bethesda, MD 20814-3415. Phone: (301)654-6664 Fax: (301)654-3299 E-mail: aaia@

aftermarket.org • URL: http://www.aftermarket.org • Automotive parts and accessories retailers, distributors, manufacturers, and manufacturers' representatives. Conducts research and compiles statistics. Conducts seminars and provides specialized education program.

Automotive Air Bags. Available from MarketResearch.com, 641 Ave. of the Americas, Fourth Floor New York, NY 10011. Phone: 800-298-5699 or (212)807-2629 Fax: (212)807-2642 E-mail: order@marketresearch.com • URL: http://www.marketresearch.com • 2002. $4,450.00. Published by Global Industry Analysts. Provides worldwide market research data, including profiles of major air bag manufacturers.

Automotive Engine Rebuilders Association., 500 Coventry Ln. Crystal Lake, IL 60014-7592. Phone: 888-326-2372 or (847)541-6550 Fax: (847)541-5808 E-mail: john@aera.org • URL: http://www.aera.org • Wholesalers of automotive replacement parts and equipment with machine shop operations; associate members are suppliers of parts, equipment, tools, and services to the rebuilder members. Acts as clearinghouse for automotive jobber machine shop information.

Automotive Engineering International. Society of Automotive Engineers, 400 Commonwealth Dr. Warrendale, PA 15096-0001. Phone: 877-606-7323 or (724)776-4841 Fax: (724)776-5760 E-mail: customerservice@sae.org • URL: http://www.sae.org • Monthly. $96.00 per year. Provides 86,000 automotive product planners and engineers with state-of-the-art technology that can be applied to the development of new and improved vehicles. Supplement available *Off-Highway Engineering*. Formerly *Automotive Engineering*.

Automotive Industries. Randall Publishing Co., 3200 Rice Mine Rd. NE Tuscaloosa, AL 35406. Phone: 800-633-5953 or (205)349-2990 E-mail: webmaster@randallpub.com • URL: http://www.randallpub.com • Monthly. $74.00 per year.

Automotive Market Report. Automotive Auction Publishing, Inc., 1713 Ardmore Blvd. Pittsburgh, PA 15221-4405. Phone: (412)242-3900 Biweekly. $130.00 Per Year. Current wholesale values of used vehicles.

Automotive Market Research Council., PO Box 5887, PO Box 13966 Denver, CO 80202. Phone: (303)744-4884 Fax: (919)549-4824 E-mail: info@amrc.org • URL: http://www.amrc.org • Represents manufacturers of automotive service equipment, automotive parts, components, subassemblies, accessories as original or replacement equipment, and employees whose principal responsibility is market research analysis and business planning. Promotes more complete, prompt, and accurate gathering and dissemination of marketing data; seeks to increase the reliability of forecasts of demand in the industry; works to improve the professional abilities of market analysis. Works with government agencies to improve collection of statistics.

Automotive News: Engineering, Financial, Manufacturing, Sales, Marketing, Servicing. Crain Communications, Inc., 1155 Gratiot Ave. Detroit, MI 48207-2997. Phone: 800-678-9595 or (313)446-6000 E-mail: info@crain.com • URL: http://www.crain.com • Weekly. $129.00 per year. Business news coverage of the automobile industry at the retail, wholesale, and manufacturing levels. Includes statistics.

Automotive News Market Data Book. Crain Communications, Inc., 1155 Gratiot Ave. Detroit, MI 48207-2997. Phone: 800-678-9595 or (313)446-6000 E-mail: info@crain.com • URL: http://www.crain.com • Annual. $19.95. Directory of automotive vendors and worldwide vehicle manufacturing. Formerly *Automotive News Almanac*.

Automotive Recycling. Automotive Recyclers Association, 3975 Fair Ridge Dr., Suite 20 N Fairfax, VA 22033-2924. Phone: (703)385-1001 Fax: (703)385-1494 • URL: http://www.autorecyc.org • Bimonthly. Free to members; non-members, $40.00 per year. Formerly *Dismantlers Digest*.

Automotive Service Association., PO Box 929, PO Box 929 Bedford, TX 76095-0929. Phone: 800-272-7467 or (817)283-6205 Fax: (817)685-0225 E-mail: asainfo@asashop.org • URL: http://www.asashop.org • Automotive service businesses including body, paint, and trim shops, engine rebuilders, radiator shops, brake and wheel alignment services, transmission shops, tune-up services, and air conditioning services; associate members are manufacturers and wholesalers of automotive parts, and the trade press. Represents independent business owners and managers before private agencies and national and state legislative bodies. Promotes confidence between consumer and the automotive service industry, safety inspection of motor vehicles, and better highways.

Automotive Trade Association Executives., 8400 Westpark Dr. McLean, VA 22102. Phone: (703)821-7072 Fax: (703)556-8581 E-mail: aaia@aftermarket.org • URL: http://www.atae.info • Executives of state and local automotive dealer associations.

Automotive Warehouse Distributors Association., 7101 Wisconsin Ave., Ste. 1300 Bethesda, MD 20814. Phone: (301)654-6664 Fax: (301)654-3299 E-mail: info@awda.org • URL: http://www.awda.org • Warehouse distributors of automotive parts and supplies; manufacturers of automotive parts and suppliers; publishers. Compiles statistics.

Automotive Warehouse Distributors Association-Membership Directory. Automotive Warehouse Distributors Association, 10 Laboratory Dr. Research Triangle Park, NC 27709. Phone: (919)549-4800 Fax: (919)549-4824 E-mail: info@awda.org • URL: http://www.awda.org • Annual. $200.00. Over 175 automotive parts distributors, 150 manufacturers of automotive parts, and marketing associations, manufacturer representatives, and affiliate members.

AV Guide: The Learning Media Newsletter. Educational Screen, Inc., 380 E. Northwest Highway Des Plaines, IL 60016-2282. Phone: (847)391-1024 Fax: (847)390-0408 E-mail: nferguson@sgcmail.com Monthly. $15.00 per year. Provides information on audiovisual aids. Formerly *AV Guide Newsletter*.

AV Market Place: The Complete Business Directory of Audio, Audio Visual, Computer Systems, Film, Video, and Programming, with Industry Yellow Pages. Information Today, Inc., 143 Old Marlton Pike Medford, NJ 08055-8750. Phone: 800-300-9868 or (609)654-6266 Fax: (609)654-4309 E-mail: custserv@infotoday.com • URL: http://www.infotoday.com • Annual. $195.00. Provides information on "more than 7,500 companies that create, apply, or distribute AV equipment and services for business, education, science, and government." Multimedia, virtual reality, presentation software, and interactive video are among the categories. Formerly published by R. R. Bowker.

AV Presentation—Buyer's Guide. Cygnus Business Media Inc., 3 Huntington Quadrangle, Ste. 301 N Melville, NY 11747. Phone: 800-308-6397 or (631)845-2700 Fax: (631)845-7109 E-mail: bob.stange@cygnuspub.com • URL: http://www.cygnusbzb.com • Covers: lists of film and slide laboratory services and manufacturers of media production and presentation equipment and audiovisual supplies. Entries include: Company name, address, product or service.

Available Pay Survey Reports: An Annotated Bibliography. Abbott, Langer and Associates, 548 1st St. Crete, IL 60417-9978. Phone: (708)672-4200 Fax: (708)672-4674 • URL: http://www.abbott-langer.com • 1995. $610.00. Fourth edition. Two volumes. Vol. 1, $450.00; Vol. 2, $160.00.

Avery Architectural Periodicals Index. Avery Architectural and Fine Arts Library, Columbia University New York, NY 10027. Phone: (212)854-3501 Fax: (212)854-8904 Indexes a wide range of periodicals related to architecture and design. Subjects include building design, building materials, interior design, housing, land use, and city planning. Time span: 1977 to date. *bul* URL: http://www-rlg.stanford.edu/cit-ave.html

Avery Index to Architectural Periodicals. Columbia University, Avery Architectural Library. Available from G.K. Hall Co., P.O. Box 159 Thorndike, ME 04986. Phone: 800-223-6121 or (212)654-8452 Fax: (207)448-2863 • URL: http://www.mlr.com/thorndike • Annual. $995.00.

Aviation. Available from U. S. Government Printing Office, Washington, DC 20402. Phone: (202)512-1800 Fax: (202)512-2250 E-mail: gpoaccess@gpo.gov • URL: http://www.access.gpo.gov • Annual. Free. Lists government publications. (GPO Subject Bibliography Number 18).

Aviation Consumer Action Project., 529 14th St. NW, No. 923 Washington, DC 20045. Phone: 800-588-ACAP or (202)638-4000 Fax: (202)638-0746 E-mail: info@awda.org • URL: http://www.acap1971.org • Promotes the interests of consumers in improved ground and air safety, environmental protection, affordable air fares, and expanded passenger rights. Activities include distributing passenger information leaflets and advocating passenger interests before federal regulatory agencies and the courts. Seeks: lower fares and increased competition in domestic and international air transportation; improved airline crash survivability; enhanced standards and equipment for crash prevention; elimination of unfair consumer practices; increased government accessibility.

Aviation Daily. Aviation Week Newsletter. The McGraw-Hill Cos., 1221 Ave. of the Americas New York, NY 10020. Phone: 800-752-4959 or (212)512-2000 Fax: (202)383-2438 E-mail: awgnews@mcgraw-hill.com • URL: http://www.mcgraw-hill.com • Description: Concerned with air transportation and the aviation manufacturing field. Focuses on management developments and trends with specific detail on economic, financial, and operating aspects of domestic and foreign airlines, aircraft manufacturers, and allied associations. Reports on federal legislation affecting the field, and lists relevant statistics.

Aviation Development Council., 141-07 20th Ave., Ste. 404 Whitestone, NY 11357. Phone: (718)746-0212 Fax: (718)746-1006 E-mail: root@aviationdevelopmentcouncil.org • URL: http://www.aviationdevelopmentcouncil.org • U.S. and foreign scheduled air carriers serving the New York-New Jersey metropolitan area; Port Authority of New York and New Jersey; Allied Pilots Association; and Air Line Pilots Association, International. Aims to explore, evaluate, and recommend to the proper authorities measures in various fields that will afford possible relief to people affected by noise of aircraft. Initiates public information on significant developments in the metropolitan area. Compiles runway analysis data on New York City area airports. Administers industry funded outreach programs designed to encourage local purchasing; administers "crime and security watch" programs for JFK, LGA & EWR.

Aviation Distributors and Manufacturers Association.

Aviation Law Reports. CCH, Inc., 2700 Lake Cook Rd. Riverwoods, IL 60015. Phone: 800-835-5224 or (847)267-7000 E-mail: cust_serv@cch.com • URL: http://www.cch.com • Semimonthly. $2,155.00 per year. Four looseleaf volumes.

Aviation Maintenance. PBI Media, LLC, 1201 7 Locks Rd. Potomac, MD 20854. Phone: 800-777-5006 or (301)354-2000 Fax: (310)309-3847 E-mail: clientservices@pbimedia.com • URL: http://www.pbimedia.com • Monthly. Free to qualified personnel; others, $189.00 per year. Formerly *Aviation Equipment Maintenance*.

Aviation Safety Institute., PO Box 690, 6797 N High St. Worthington, OH 43085. Phone: (614)885-4242 Fax: (614)793-1708 E-mail: 110364.3550@compuserve.com • URL: http://www.aviationsafetyinstitute.com • Acts as an independent party not aligned with industry or government to promote and improve aviation safety. Activities include: operating an anonymous hazard reporting system; conducting safety education programs and seminars; maintaining a computerized safety information system; performing safety audits and consulting services; conducting aircraft accident investigations and research projects on topics such as pilot and crew fatigue. Conducts research.

Aviation Week and Space Technology. McGraw-Hill Aviation Week Group, 1221 Ave. of the Americas New York, NY 10020. Phone: 800-722-4726 or (215)512-2000 Fax: (212)512-4502 E-mail: customer.service@mcgraw-hill.com • URL: http://www.mcgraw-hill.com • Monthly. $92.00 per year.

Avionics Engineering Center. Ohio University

Avionics Magazine The Monthly Magazine of the Global Avionics Industry. PBI Media LLC, 1201 Seven Locks Rd., Ste. 300 Potomac, MD 20859-1130. Phone: (301)424-3338 Fax: (301)309-3847 E-mail: pbi@phillips.com • URL: http://www.phillips.com • Monthly. Free to qualified personnel.

Avionics Maintenance Conference., 2551 Riva Rd., 2551 Riva Rd. Annapolis, MD 21401. Phone: 800-633-6882 or (410)266-2008 Fax: (410)266-2047 E-mail: sbuckwal@arinc.com • URL: http://www.arinc.com/amc • Avionics maintenance professionals from commercial airlines, airframe manufacturers, avionics suppliers, and government organizations. Seeks to improve safety and reliability and reduce the costs of operating and supporting avionics equipment. Contributes to reduce the growth of avionics maintenance costs per flight hour despite growth in avionics capital costs. Conducts projects such as: the establishment of a standard language source document for writing automatic test programs; definition of an economic alternative to costly dedicated automatic test systems provided by manufacturers; development of an industry standard for automated preparation of test software; specification of documentation standards for software-based avionics; coordination of technical training needs for maintenance; and development of voluntary standards for the avionics industry.

Avis Licensee Directory. Avis Licensee Association, 300 Old Country Rd., Ste. 341 Mineola, NY 11501. Phone: (516)747-4951 Fax: (516)747-0195 E-mail: bob.stange@cygnuspub.com Covers: about 125 owners of licensed Avis Rent-a-Car franchises; coverage includes Canada. Entries include: Company name, address, phone, names and titles of key officials; branch office or subsidiary names, locations, and phone numbers; name of owner, home address, phone, name of spouse (if any).

AVMA Directory. American Veterinary Medical Association, 1931 N Meacham Rd., Suite 100 Schaumburg, IL 60173-4360. Phone: 800-248-2862 or (847)925-8070 Fax: (847)925-1329 E-mail: avmainfo@avma.org • URL: http://www.avma.org • Annual. $100.00. 62,500 veterinarians; not limited to AVMA members. Formerly *American Veterinary Medical Association Directory*.

Avoiding Tax Malpractice. CCH, Inc., 2700 Lake Cook Rd. Riverwoods, IL 60015. Phone: 800-835-5224 or (847)267-7000 E-mail: cust_serv@cch.com • URL: http://www.cch.com • 2000. $75.00. Covers malpractice considerations for professional tax practitioners.

Awards and Recognition Association.

Awards, Honors, and Prizes. Gale Cengage Learning, 27500 Drake Rd. Farmington Hills, MI 48331-3535. Phone: 800-877-GALE or (248)699-GALE Fax: 800-414-5043 E-mail: gale.galeord@cengage.com • URL: http://gale.cengage.com • 2003. $525.00. Two volumes. 21th edition. Domestic volume, $275.00. International volume, $305.00.

AWO Letter. American Waterways Operators, 801 N Quincy St., Ste. 200 Arlington, VA 22203. Phone: (703)841-9300 Fax: (703)841-0389 E-mail: awgnews@mcgraw-hill.com • URL: http://www.americanwaterways.com • Description: Discusses national and local legislative, regulatory, and economic issues affecting the inland and coastal barge and towing industry.

B to B: The Magazine for Marketing and E-Commerce Strategists. Crain Communications, Inc., 711 Third Ave. New York, NY 10017-4036. Phone: 800-678-9595 or (212)210-0100 E-mail: info@crain.com • URL: http://www.crain.com • 26 times a year. $59.00 per year. Formerly *Advertising Age's Business Marketing*.

Baby and Junior: International Trade Magazine for Children's and Youth Fashions and Supplies. Verbond der Korbwaren-, Korbmoebel-und Kinderwagen-Industrie. Meisenbach GmbH, Franz-Ludwig-Str.7A 96047 Bamberg, Germany. Phone: 49 951 861126 or 49 951 861187 10 times a year. 131.00 per year. Text in German.

Babysitter's Survival Kit: A Guide for Parents and Sitters. Time-Life, Inc., 2000 Duke St. Alexandria, VA 22314. Phone: 800-950-7887 or (703)838-7000 Fax: 800-308-1083 or (703)838-7090 • URL: http://www.timelife.com • 2001. $14.95.

Back Stage: The Performing Arts Weekly. VNU Business Media, 770 Broadway New York, NY 10003-9595. Phone: 800-344-

7119 or (646)654-4500 Fax: (646)654-7212 • URL: http://www.vnubusinessmedia.com • Weekly. $95.00 per year. A theatre trade newspaper for show business professionals.

Bacon's International Directory—Western Europe. Cision US Inc., 332 S Michigan Ave., Ste. 900 Chicago, IL 60604. Phone: (866)639-5087 or (312)922-2400 Fax: (312)922-9387 E-mail: bob.stange@cygnuspub.com • URL: http://www.bacons.org • Covers: over 16,000 consumer, business, trade, and technical publications, and about 1,000 national and regional newspapers in 12 countries of western Europe. Entries include: Publication name, address, phone, telex, translation requirements for news releases, code indicating type of publicity in which interested (new products, trade literature, etc.), frequency, circulation.

Bacon's Newspaper and Magazine Directories. Bacon's Information Inc., 332 S. Michigan Ave., Ste. 900 Chicago, IL 60604. Phone: 800-621-0561 or (312)922-2400 Fax: (312)987-9773 E-mail: directories@bacons.com • URL: http://www.bacons.com • Annual. $325.00 per year. Two volumes: Magazines and Newspapers. Covers print media in the United States and Canada. Formerly *Bacon's Publicity Checker*.

Bacon's Radio/TV/Cable Directory. Bacon's Information, Inc., 322 S. Michigan Ave., Ste. 900 Chicago, IL 60604. Phone: 800-621-0561 or (312)922-2400 Fax: (312)987-9773 E-mail: directories@bacons.com • URL: http://www.bacons.com • Annual. $325.00. Includes educational and public broadcasters. Covers all United States broadcast media.

Bailey's Industrial Oil and Fat Products. Alton E. Bailey. John Wiley and Sons, Inc., 111 River St. Hoboken, NJ 07030. Phone: 800-225-5945 or (201)748-6000 Fax: (201)748-6088 E-mail: info@wiley.com • URL: http://www.wiley.com • 1996. $1,050.00. Fifth edition. $238.00 per volume. Five volumes.

Baker's Manual. Joseph Amendola. John Wiley and Sons, Inc., 111 River St. Hoboken, NJ 07030. Phone: 800-225-5945 or (201)748-6000 Fax: (201)748-6088 E-mail: info@wiley.com • URL: http://www.wiley.com • 2002. $29.95. Fifth edition.

Bakery. Entrepreneur Media, Inc., 2445 McCabe Way Irvine, CA 92614. Phone: 800-421-2300 or (949)261-2325 Fax: (949)261-0234 E-mail: entmag@entrepreneur.com • URL: http://www.entrepreneur.com • Looseleaf. $59.50. A practical guide to starting a retail bakery. Covers profit potential, start-up costs, market size evaluation, owner's time required, site selection, lease negotiation, pricing, accounting, advertising, promotion, etc. (Start-Up Business Guide No. E1158.)

Bakery, Confectionery, Tobacco Workers and Grain Millers International Union., 10401 Connecticut Ave., Room 400 Kensington, MD 20895. Phone: (301)933-8600 Fax: (301)946-8452 • URL: http://www.bctgm.org • Formerly Bakery, Confectionery and Tobacco Workers International Union.

Bakery Products. Available from MarketResearch.com, 641 Ave. of the Americas, Fourth Floor New York, NY 10011. Phone: 800-298-5699 or (212)807-2629 Fax: (212)807-2642 E-mail: order@marketresearch.com • URL: http://www.marketresearch.com • 2002. $3,850.00. Published by Global Industry Analysts. Provides worldwide market research data, including profiles of major baked food companies.

Baking and Snack. Sosland Publishing Co., 4800 Main St., Ste. 100 Kansas City, MO 64112. Phone: (816)756-1000 Fax: (816)756-0494 E-mail: web@sosland.com • URL: http://www.sosland.com • Monthly. Free to qualified personnel; others, $30.00 per year. Covers manufacturing systems and ingredients for baked goods and snack foods.

Baking Industry Sanitation Standards Committee., PO Box 3999, 1400 W. Devon Ave., Ste. 422 Manhattan, KS 66505-3999. Phone: (866)342-4772 or (785)537-4750 Fax: (785)565-6060 E-mail: bissc@bissc.org • URL: http://www.bissc.org • Industry association representing 120 bakery equipment manufacturers. Seeks to establish standards of sanitation in bakery food processing equipment. Receives advisory assistance from national and international public health and food sanitation groups. Develops and publishes sanitation standards for the baking industry. Offers an equipment certification program for bakery equipment conforming to standards (annual).

Balance. American College of Health Care Administrators, 325 S. Patrick St. Alexandria, VA 22314. Phone: 888-882-2422 or (703)739-7900 Fax: (703)739-7901 E-mail: info@achca.org • URL: http://www.achca.org • Eight times a year. Free to members; non-members, $80.00 per year. Includes research papers and articles on the administration of long term care facilities. Formerly*Continnum*.

Balance of Payments Statistics. International Monetary Fund, 700 19th St., N.W. Washington, DC 20431-0001. Phone: (202)623-7000 Fax: (202)623-4661 • URL: http://www.imf.org • Time series compiled by IMF, mid-1960's to present. Inquire as to online cost and availability.

Balanced Budgets and American Politics. James D. Savage. Cornell University Press, Sage House, 512 E. State St. Ithaca, NY 14851. Phone: 800-666-2211 or (607)277-2211 Fax: 800-688-2877 E-mail: cupress-sales@cornell.edu • URL: http://www.cornellpress.cornell.edu • 1988. $19.95. States the case for economic growth being more important than a balanced federal budget.

Baltia Kompass Business Disc. Available from Kompass USA, Inc., 121 Whitney Ave. New Haven, CT 06510. Phone: 877-566-7277 or (203)503-6789 Fax: (203)503-6780 E-mail: mail@kompass-usa.com • URL: http://www.kompass.com • Semiannual. CD-ROM provides information on more than 29,000 companies in Estonia, Latvia, and Lithuania. Classification system covers approximately 50,000 products and services.

Banishing Bureaucratese: Using Plain English in Government Writing. Judith G. Myers. Management Concepts, Inc., 8230 Leesburg Pike Vienna, VA 22182. Phone: 800-506-4450 or (703)790-9595 Fax: (703)790-1371 • URL: http://www.managementconcepts.com • 2001. $39.00. Covers plain writing style for government memos, letters, e-mail, agency communications, budget justification statements, and other bureaucratic documents.

Bank Accounting and Finance. Aspen Publishers, Inc., 1185 Ave. of the Americas New York, NY 10036. Phone: 800-234-1660 or (212)597-0200 Fax: (212)597-0338 E-mail: customer.service@aspenpubl.com • URL: http://www.aspenpublisher.com • Quarterly. $345.00 per year. Emphasis is on the practical aspects of bank accounting and bank financial management.

Bank Administration Institute., 1 N Franklin St., Ste. 1000 Chicago, IL 60606-3421. Phone: 888-284-4078 or (312)683-2464 Fax: (312)683-2373 E-mail: info@bai.org • URL: http://www.bai.org • Works to improve the competitive position of banking companies through strategic research and educational offerings.

Bank Administration Institute; Operations and Technology Commission.

Bank and Lender Litigation Reporter: The Nationwide Litigation Report of Failed National and State Banks and Savings and Loan Associations, including FDIC and FSLIC Complaints and Related Actions Among Shareholders, Officers, Directors, Ins. Andrews Publications, 175 Strafford Ave., Bldg. 4, Suite 140 Wayne, PA 19087. Phone: 800-345-1101 or (610)225-0510 Fax: (610)225-0501 E-mail: customer@andrewspub.com • URL: http://www.andrewspub.com • Semimonthly. $875.00 per year. Newsletter. Provides summaries of significant litigation and regulatory agency complaints. Formerly *Lender Liability Litigation Reporter*.

Bank and Quotation Record. William B. Dana Co., P.O. Box 1839 Daytona Beach, FL 32115-1839. Phone: (386)252-0230 Monthly. $130.00 per year.

Bank Auditing and Accounting Report. RIA Group, 395 Hudson St. New York, NY 10014. Phone: 800-950-1215 or (212)367-6300 E-mail: riahome@riag.com • URL: http://www.riahome.com • Monthly. $199.00 per year. Newsletter covering bank regulations, accounting techniques, and audit controls.

Bank Automation News. PBI Media LCC, 1201 7 Locks Rd., Ste. 300 Potomac, MD 20854. Phone: (301)354-2000 Fax: (301)309-3847 E-mail: clientservice@pbimedia.com • URL: http://www.pbimedia.com • Biweekly. $651.65 per year. Newsletter.

Bank CEO's Operating and Management Desk Reference. Thomson Media, One State St. Plaza New York, NY 10004. Phone: 800-221-1809 or (212)803-8200 Fax: (212)843-9635 E-mail: custserv@thomsonmedia.com • URL: http://www.thomsonmedia.com • $395.00. Two looseleaf volumes. Periodic updates available. Provides up-to-date information and advice on all areas of bank management. (A Sheshunoff publication.)

Bank Credit Analyst. BCA Publications Ltd., 1002 Sherbrooke St., W., 16th Fl. Montreal, QC, Canada H3A 3L6. Phone: (514)499-9706 Fax: (514)499-9709 Monthly. $695.00 per year. "The independent monthly forecast and analysis of trends in business conditions and major investment markets based on a continuous appraisal of money and credit flows." Includes many charts and graphs relating to money, credit, and securities in the U. S.

The Bank Director's Handbook. Edwin B Cox and others. Greenwood Publishing Group, Inc., 88 Post Rd., W Westport, CT 06881. Phone: 800-225-5800 or (203)226-3571 Fax: (203)431-2214 E-mail: customer-service@greenwood.com • URL: http://www.greenwood.com • 1986. $79.95. Second edition.

Bank Investment Consultant: Sales Strategies for the Financial Adviser. Thomson Media, One State St. Plaza New York, NY 10004. Phone: 800-221-1809 or (212)803-8200 Fax: (212)843-9635 E-mail: custserv@thomsonmedia.com • URL: http://www.thomsonmedia.com • Monthly. Controlled circulation. Covers sales and marketing techniques for bank investment and asset management divisions. Formerly *Bank Investment Marketing*.

Bank Investment Product News. Institutional Investor, Inc., Journals Group, 225 Park Ave., S New York, NY 10003. Phone: 800-945-2034 or (212)224-3066 Fax: (212)224-3472 E-mail: info@iijournals.com • URL: http://www.iijournals.com • Weekly. $1,195.00 per year. Newsletter. Edited for bank executives. Covers the marketing and regulation of financial products sold through banks, such as mutual funds, stock brokerage services, and insurance.

Bank Investments and Funds Management. Gerald O. Hatler. American Bankers Association, 1120 Connecticut Ave., N. W. Washington, DC 20036-3971. Phone: (202)663-5000 Fax: (202)663-7543 E-mail: custserv@aba.com • URL: http://www.aba.com • 1991. $49.00. Second edition. Focuses on portfolio management, risk analysis, and investment strategy.

Bank Loan Report. IDD Enterprises L.P., Harborside Financial Ctr., 600 Plz. II, 4th Fl. Jersey City, NJ 07311. Phone: 800-221-1809 or (212)803-8200 Fax: (212)843-9635 E-mail: custserv@americanbanker.com • URL: http://www.thomsonmedia.com • Description: Discusses banking loans and transactions made by large corporations. Recurring features include a column titled Term Sheets.

Bank Management. Timothy W. Koch and Steven S. MacDonald. Dryden Press, 301 Commerce St., Ste. 3700 Fort Worth, TX 76012. Phone: 800-447-9479 or (817)334-7500 Fax: (817)334-7844 • URL: http://www.thomson.com • 2002. Fifth edition. Price on application.

Bank Marketing for the Nineties: New Ideas from 55 of the Best Marketers in Banking. Don Wright. John Wiley and Sons, Inc., 111 River St. Hoboken, NJ 07030. Phone: 800-225-5945 or (201)748-6000 Fax: (201)748-6088 E-mail: info@wiley.com • URL: http://www.wiley.com • 1991. $175.00.

Bank Mergers & Acquisitions: The Authoritative Newsletter Providing In-Depth Analysis of the Restructuring of American Banking. SNL Financial LLC, 321 E Main St. Charlottesville, VA 22902. Phone: (804)977-1600 Fax: (804)977-4466 E-mail: subscriptions@snlnet.com • URL: http://www.snlnet.com • Monthly. $795.00 per year. Newsletter. Includes information on transactions assisted by the Federal Deposit Insurance Corporation (FDIC) for commercial banks or by the Resolution Trust Corporation (RTC) for savings and loan institutions.

Bank Operating Statistics. Federal Deposit Insurance Corp., 550 17th St., N.W. Washington, DC 20429-9990. Phone: (202)736-0000 Annual. Price on application. Based on Reports of Condition and Reports of Income.

Bank Profitability: Financial Statements of Banks. Organization for Economic Cooperation and Development. Available from OECD Publications and Information Center, 2001 L St., N. W., Suite 650 Washington, DC 20036-4922. Phone: 800-456-6323 or (202)785-6323 Fax: (202)785-0350 E-mail: washington.contact@oecd.org • URL: http://www.oecdwash.org • Annual. $85.00. Presents data for 10 years on bank profitability in OECD member countries.

Bank Rate Monitor: The Weekly Financial Rate Reporter. Advertising News Service, Inc., 11811 Federal Highway One, Ste. 101 North Palm Beach, FL 33410. Phone: (561)627-7330 Fax: (561)627-7335 E-mail: webmaster@bankrate.com • URL: http://www.bankrate.com • Weekly. $895.00 per year. Newsletter. Includes online addition and monthly supplement. Provides detailed information on interest rates currently paid by U. S. banks and savings institutions.

Bank Systems and Technology-Directory and Buyer's Guide. CMP Media LLC, 600 Community Dr. Manhasset, NY 11030. Phone: (516)562-5000 E-mail: cmp@cmp.com • URL: http://www.cmp.com • Annual. $25.00. List of more than 1,800 manufacturers, distributors, and other suppliers of equipment and materials to the banking industry.

Bank Systems and Technology: For Senior-Level Executives in Operations and Technology Management. CMP Media LLC, 600 Community Dr. Manhasset, NY 11030. Phone: (516)562-5000 E-mail: cmp@cmp.com • URL: http://www.cmp.com • 13 times a year. $65.00 per year. Focuses on strategic planning for banking executives. Formerly *Bank Systems and Equipment*.

Bank Systems Management: The Project Management Guide to Planning and Implementing Systems. Kent S. Belasco. McGraw-Hill, 1221 Ave. of the Americas New York, NY 10020. Phone: 800-772-4726 or (212)512-2000 Fax: (212)512-4502 E-mail: customer.service@mcgraw-hill.com • URL: http://www.mcgraw-hill.com • 1993. $62.50.

Bank Tax Guide. CCH, Inc., 2700 Lake Cook Rd. Riverwoods, IL 60015. Phone: 800-835-5224 or (847)267-7000 E-mail: cust_serv@cch.com • URL: http://www.cch.com • Annual. $199.00. Summarizes and explains federal tax rules affecting financial institutions.

Bank Technology Review: A Bank Manager's Guide to New Technology Products, Systems, and Applications. Tom Groenfeldt. McGraw-Hill, 1221 Ave. of the Americas New York, NY 10020. Phone: 800-772-4726 or (212)512-2000 Fax: (212)512-4502 E-mail: customer.service@mcgraw-hill.com • URL: http://www.mcgraw-hill.com • 1995. $37.50.

Bankcard Consumer News. Bankcard Holders of America, 333 Maple Ave., E., No. 2005 Vienna, VA 22180-4717. Phone: (703)389-5445 Fax: (703)481-6037 Bimonthly. $24.00 per year. Newsletter for consumers.

The Banker., Maple House, 149 ToHenham Court Rd. London W1T 7LB, United Kingdom. Phone: 44 0207 896 Fax: 44 0207 896 2586 E-mail: thebanker.ed.@ft.com • URL: http://www.thebanker.com • Monthly. $283.00 per year. Includes supplement. Published in England.

Bankers' Almanac. Reed Business Information, East Grinstead House, Windsor Court, East Grinstead West Sussex RH19 1XA, United Kingdom. Phone: 44 1342 335819 Fax: 44 1342 335998 E-mail: rbp.subscriptions@rbi.co.uk • URL: http://www.reedbusiness.co.uk • Semiannual. $1,170.00. Six volumes. Lists more than 27,000 financial institutions; international coverage. Formerly *Bankers' Almanac and Yearbook*.

Bankers' Association for Finance and Trade., 1717 Pennsylvania Ave., N.W., Ste. 450 Washington, DC 20006. Phone: (202)452-0952 Fax: (202)452-0959 E-mail: baft@baft.org • URL: http://www.baft.org • Formerly Bankers' Association for Foreign Trade.

Bankers in the Selling Role: A Consultative Guide to Cross Selling Financial Services. Linda Richardson. John Wiley and Sons, Inc., 111 River St. Hoboken, NJ 07030. Phone: 800-

225-5945 or (201)748-6000 Fax: (201)748-6088 E-mail: info@wiley.com • URL: http://www.wiley.com • 1992. $29.95. Second edition.

The Bankers: The Next Generation: The New Worlds of Money, Credit, and Banking in an Electronic Age. Martin Mayer. Dutton/Plume, 375 Hudson St. New York, NY 10014-3657. Phone: 800-526-0275 or (212)366-2000 Fax: (212)366-2666 E-mail: online@penguinputnam.com • URL: http://www.penguinputnam.com • 1998. $16.95. A popularly written discussion of the future of banks, bankers, and banking.

Banking and Finance on the Internet. Mary J. Cronin, editor. John Wiley and Sons, Inc., 111 Rive St. Hoboken, NJ 07030. Phone: 800-842-3636 or (201)748-6000 Fax: (201)748-6088 E-mail: info@wiley.com • URL: http://www.wiley.com • 1997. $45.00. Contains articles on Internet services, written by bankers, money mangers, investment analysts, and stockbrokers. Emphasis is on operations management. (Communications Series).

Banking Crimes: Fraud, Money Laundering and Embezzlement. John K. Villa. West Group, 610 Opperman Dr. Eagan, MN 55123. Phone: 800-328-4880 or (651)687-7000 Fax: 800-340-9378 E-mail: bookstore@westgroup.com • URL: http://www.westgroup.com • Annual. $280.00. Looseleaf service. Covers fraud and embezzlement.

Banking in the U. S.: An Annotated Bibliography. Jean Deuss. Scarecrow Press, Inc., 4501 Forbes Blvd., Ste. 200 Lanham, MD 20706. Phone: 800-462-6420 or (301)459-3366 Fax: 800-338-4550 or (301)429-5748 E-mail: custserv@rowman.com • URL: http://www.scarecrowpress.com • 1990. $35.00.

Banking Information Source. PROQUEST, 300 N. Zeeb Rd. Ann Arbor, MI 48103. Phone: 800-521-0600 or (734)761-4700 Fax: 800-864-0019 • URL: http://www.umi.com • Provides indexing and abstracting of periodical and other literature from 1982 to date, with weekly updates. Covers the financial services industry: banks, savings institutions, investment houses, credit unions, insurance companies, and real estate organizations. Emphasis is on marketing and management. Inquire as to online cost and availability. (Formerly *FINIS: Financial Industry Information Service*.)

Banking Law. LexisNexis Matthew Bender, 1275 Broadway Albany, NY 12204. Phone: 800-424-4200 or (518)487-3000 Fax: (518)487-3584 E-mail: bookstore.support@lexisnexis.com • URL: http://www.bender.com • $2,325.00. 20 looseleaf volumes. Periodic supplementation. Operational guidance for bank officers, with analysis of statutory law and agency regulations. Includes *Checks*, *Drafts* and *Notes* as volumes 7, 7a, 8, 8a.

Banking Law Manual: Federal Regulation of Financial Holding Companies, Banks and Thrifts. LexisNexis Matthew Bender, 1275 Broadway Albany, NY 12204. Phone: 800-424-4200 or (518)487-3000 Fax: (518)487-3584 E-mail: bookstore.support@lexisnexis.com • URL: http://www.bender.com • $254.00. Second edition. Desk reference, procedural guide, or training and management tool for the banking professional.

Banking Research Center., Northwestern University, 401 Anderson Hall, 2001 Sheridan Rd. Evanston, IL 60208. Phone: (847)491-3562 Fax: (847)491-5719 E-mail: k-hagerty@northwestern.edu Does research in the management and public regulation of financial institutions. A unit of the J. L. Kellogg Graduate School of Management.

Banking Strategies. Bank Administration Institute, 1 N Franklin St., Ste. 1000 Chicago, IL 60606-3421. Phone: (312)683-2264 Fax: (312)683-2373 E-mail: info@bai.org • URL: http://www.bai.org • Monthly. Free to qualified personnel; others, $64.50 per year. For senior bankers and financial services executives.

BANKPAC., 1120 Connecticut Ave. NW, 1120 Connecticut Ave. NW, 1120 Connecticut Ave., N.W. Washington, DC 20036. Phone: 800-BAN-KERS or (202)663-5121 Fax: (202)828-6071 E-mail: scrochet@aba.com • URL: http://www.aba.com • Members of the banking community united to help elect to the U.S. Congress, without regard to party affiliation, those who have shown an interest, understanding, and a concern for banking business and a free economic system in which it can function properly. Acts as the political action committee of the American Bankers Association (see separate entry); makes contributions for campaign expenditures in political contests for seats in the House of Representatives and the Senate; does not make contributions in presidential contests or in contests for state and local offices.

Bankruptcy: A Primer. D. Ellsworth Blanc. Nova Science Publishers, Inc., 400 Oser Ave., Suite 1600 Hauppauge, NY 11788-3619. Phone: (631)231-7269 Fax: (631)231-8175 E-mail: novascience@earthlink.net • URL: http://www.novapublishers.com • 2002. $27.50. Serves as a basic guide to liquidation, reorganization, the U. S. Bankruptcy Code, and economic issues.

Bankruptcy and Insolvency Accounting. Grant Newton. John Wiley and Sons, Inc., 111 River St. Hoboken, NJ 07030. Phone: 800-225-5945 or (201)748-6000 Fax: (201)748-6088 E-mail: info@wiley.com • URL: http://www.wiley.com • 2000. $380.00. 6th edition. Two volumes. $190.00 per volume. *2001 Supplement*, $65.00.

Bankruptcy and Insolvency Taxation. Grant W. Newton and Gilbert D. Bloom. John Wiley and Sons, Inc., 111 River St. Hoboken, NJ 07030. Phone: 800-225-5945 or (201)748-6000 Fax: (201)748-6088 E-mail: info@wiley.com • URL: http://www.wiley.com • 1993. $235.00. Second edition. 2002

cumulative supplement, $95.00.

Bankruptcy Basics. Available from U. S. Government Printing Office, Washington, DC 20402. Phone: (202)512-1800 Fax: (202)512-2250 E-mail: gpoaccess@gpo.gov • URL: http://www.access.gpo.gov • 1998. $4.25. Second edition. Issued by the Bankruptcy Judges Division, Administrative Office of the United States Courts. Provides concise explanation of five Chapters of the U.S. Bankruptcy Code: Chapter 7 (Liquidation), Chapter 9 (Municipal), Chapter 11 (Reorganization), Chapter 12 (Family Farmer), and Chapter 13 (Debt Adjustment). Includes a seven-page glossary, "Bankruptcy Terminology." (Public Information Series).

• *Bankruptcy Concepts: A Desk Reference for Lenders*. Bonnie K. Donahue. The Risk Management Association, One Liberty Place, 1650 Market St., Suite 2300 Philadelphia, PA 19103. Phone: 800-677-7621 or (215)446-4000 Fax: (215)446-4101 • URL: http://www.rmahq.org • 1994. $55.00. Designed to help loan officers deal with the intricacies of bankruptcy law. Chapters include a brief history of bankruptcy law, basic bankruptcy principles, and "Adjustments of Debts."

Bankruptcy Law Fundamentals. West Group, 610 Opperman Dr. Eagan, MN 55123. Phone: 800-328-4880 or (651)687-7000 Fax: 800-340-9378 E-mail: bookstore@westgroup.com • URL: http://www.westgroup.com • Annual. $180.00. Looseleaf service.

Bankruptcy Law Manual. West Group, 610 Opperman Dr. Eagan, MN 55123. Phone: 800-328-4880 or (651)687-7000 Fax: 800-340-9378 E-mail: bookstore@westgroup.com • URL: http://www.westgroup.com • Annual. $298.00. Looseleaf service. Complete, practical to modern bankruptcy practice and procedure.

Bankruptcy Law Reports. CCH, Inc., 2700 Lake Cook Rd. Riverwoods, IL 60015. Phone: 800-835-5224 or (847)267-7000 E-mail: cust_serv@cch.com • URL: http://www.cch.com • Biweekly. $1,150.00 per year. Three looseleaf volumes.

Bankruptcy Practice Handbook, 2d. West Group, 610 Opperman Dr. Eagan, MN 55123. Phone: 800-328-4880 or (651)687-7000 Fax: 800-340-9378 or (651)687-5827 E-mail: bookstore@westgroup.com • URL: http://www.westgroup.com • Annual. $290.00. Two looseleaf volumes.

The Bankruptcy Strategist. Law Journal Newsletter, 105 Madison Ave. New York, NY 10016. Phone: 800-603-6571 or (212)313-9300 Fax: (212)481-8110 E-mail: lawcatalog@amlaw.com • URL: http://www.lawcatalog.com/ • Description: Reports on substantive legal developments and successful strategy decisions by bankruptcy attorneys. Recurring features include a calendar of upcoming seminars.

Bankruptcy Yearbook and Almanac. New Generation Research, Inc., 225 Friend St., Suite 801 Boston, MA 02114. Phone: 800-468-3810 or (617)573-9550 Fax: (617)573-9554 Annual. Price on application.

BanxQuote Banking, Mortgage, and Finance Center. Banx-Quote, Inc.Phone: (914)722-1600 Fax: (914)722-6630 E-mail: info@banx.com • URL: http://www.banx.com • Web site quotes interest rates paid by banks around the country on various savings products, as well as rates paid by consumers for automobile loans, mortgages, credit cards, home equity loans, and personal loans. Also provided: stock quotes, indexes, stock options, futures trading data, economic indicators, and links to many other financial sites. Daily updates. Fees: Free.

Bargaining Across Borders: How to Conduct Business Successfully Anywhere in the World. Dean A. Foster. McGraw-Hill, 1221 Ave. of the Americas New York, NY 10020. Phone: 800-722-4726 or (212)512-2000 Fax: (212)512-4502 E-mail: customer.service@mcgraw-hill.com • URL: http://www.mcgraw-hill.com • 1992. $14.95. Includes a consideration of non-negotiable cultural differences.

Barometer of Business. Harris Trust and Savings Bank, 111 W. Monroe St. Chicago, IL 60690. Phone: (312)461-2121 Bimonthly. Free.

Barron's Finance & Investment Handbook. John Downes and Jordan Goodman. Barron's Educational Series, Inc., 250 Wireless Blvd. Hauppauge, NY 11788-3917. Phone: 800-645-3476 or (516)434-3311 Fax: (516)434-3723 E-mail: info@barronseduc.com • URL: http://www.barronseduc.com • 1998. $35.00. Fifth edition. Mainly concerned with personal finance, including advice on stocks, bonds, mutual funds, annuities, life insurance, real estate, futures, and collectibles. Includes a glossary of financial and investment terms.

Barron's Guide to Graduate Business Schools. Barron's Educational Series, 250 Wireless Blvd. Hauppauge, NY 11788. Phone: 800-645-3476 or (631)434-3311 Fax: (631)434-3723 E-mail: info@barronseduc.com • URL: http://www.barronseduc.com • Biennial. Contains profiles of more than 600 business schools offering graduate business degrees in the U. S. and Canada. Includes advice on choosing a school.

Barron's: The Dow Jones Business and Financial Weekly., 200 Burnett Rd. Chicopee, MA 01020. Phone: 800-544-0422 Fax: 800-975-8618 E-mail: barrons.service@dowjones.com • URL: http://www.barrons.com • Weekly. $145.00 per year.

Barter Update. Update Publicare Co., c/o Prosperity & Profits Unlimited, PO Box 570213 Houston, TX 77257. Phone: (713)867-3438 Fax: (970)292-2136 E-mail: awgnews@mcgraw-hill.com • URL: http://www.curriculumresourceonline.com • Description: Presents examples of ways to use bartering. Updates information and ideas associated with bartering. Recurring features include

news of research and ideas on barter.

BarterNews. BarterNews Publications, PO Box 3024 Mission Viejo, CA 92690. Phone: (949)831-0607 Fax: (949)831-9378 E-mail: bmeyer@barternews.com • URL: http://www.barternews.com • Quarterly. $40.00 per year. How to barter information, contacts, and other unique trades.

Basic Accounting for the Small Business: Simple, Foolproof Techniques for Keeping Your Books Straight and Staying Out of Trouble. Bobbie Kuhlmann. Pearson Custom Publishing, 75 Arlington St., Suite 300 Boston, MA 02116. Phone: 800-428-4466 or (617)848-6300 Fax: (617)848-6333 • URL: http://www.pearsoncustom.com • 1990. $120.00.

The Basic Business Library: Core Resources. Rashells S. Karp and Bernard S. Schlessinger. Greenwood Publishing Group, Inc., 88 Post Rd., W. Westport, CT 06881. Phone: 800-255-5800 or (203)226-3571 Fax: (203)431-2214 E-mail: customer-service@greenwood.com • URL: http://www.greenwood.com • 2002. $64.95. Fourth edition. Consists of three parts: (1) "Core List of Printed Business Reference Sources," (2) "The Literature of Business Reference and Business Libraries: 1976-1994," and (3) "Business Reference Sources and Services: Essays." Part one lists 200 basic titles, with annotations and evaluations.

Basic Construction Materials. Theodore Marotta. Prentice-Hall PTR, 240 Frisch Ct. Paramus, NJ 07652. Phone: 800-282-0693 Fax: 800-445-6991 • URL: http://www.phptr.com • 2001. $88.00. Sixth edition.

Basic Documents in International Law. Ian Brownlie, editor. Oxford University Press, 198 Madison Ave. New York, NY 10016. Phone: 800-451-7556 or (212)726-6000 Fax: (212)726-6440 E-mail: custserv@oup-usa.org • URL: http://www.oup-usa.org • 2002. $35.00. Fifth edition.

Basic Electronics. Bernard Grob. McGraw-Hill, 1221 Avenue of the Americas New York, NY 10020-1095. Phone: 800-722-4726 or (212)904-2000 or (212)512-2000 • URL: http://www.mcgraw-hill.com • 1997. $46.43. Eight edition.

Basic Estimating for Construction. James A. Fatzinger. Prentice Hall PTR, 240 Frisch Ct. Paramus, NJ 07652. Phone: 800-282-0693 Fax: 800-445-6991 • URL: http://www.phptr.com • 2000. $69.95. Covers electrical, plumbing, concrete, masonry, framing, etc. Includes a glossary and typical bid forms.

Basic Facts About the United Nations. United Nations Publications, United Nations Concourse Level, First Ave., 46th St. New York, NY 10017. Phone: 800-553-3210 or (212)963-7680 Fax: (212)963-4910 E-mail: bookstore@un.org • URL: http://www.un.org/publications • 2000. $12.50.

Basic Facts About Trademarks. Available from U. S. Government Printing Office, Washington, DC 20402. Phone: (202)512-1800 Fax: (202)512-2250 E-mail: gpoaccess@gpo.gov • URL: http://www.access.gpo.gov • 2001. $4.25. Issued by the Patent and Trademark Office, U. S. Department of Commerce. Includes filing requirements and sample applications.

Basic Guide to Exporting. Available from U. S. Government Printing Office, Washington, DC 20402. Phone: (202)512-1800 Fax: (202)512-2250 E-mail: gpoaccess@gpo.gov • URL: http://www.access.gpo.gov • R999. $19.00. Issued by the International Trade Administration, U. S. Department of Commerce. Discusses the costs, risks, and strategy of exporting. Includes sources of assistance and a glossary of terms used in the export business.

Basic Internet for Busy Librarians: A Quick Course for Catching Up. Laura K. Murray. American Library Association, 50 E. Huron St. Chicago, IL 60611-2795. Phone: 800-545-2433 or (312)944-6780 Fax: (312)440-9374 E-mail: ala@ala.org • URL: http://www.ala.org • 1998. $26.00. A "practical crash-course primer" for learning how to effectively navigate the Internet and the World Wide Web.

Basic Metals Processing Research Institute.

Basic Petroleum Data Book. American Petroleum Institute, Publications Section, 1220 L St., N. W. Washington, DC 20005. Phone: (202)682-8375 Fax: (202)962-4776 • URL: http://www.api.org • Three times a year. $230.00 per year.

Basic Science and Technology Statistics. Organization for Economic Cooperation and Development, OECD Washington Center, 2001 L St., N.W., Suite 650 Washington, DC 20036-4922. Phone: 800-456-6323 or (202)785-6323 Fax: (202)785-0350 E-mail: washington.contact@oecd.org • URL: http://www.oecd.org • Biennial. $84.00. Contains eight years of data on resources devoted to research and development in OECD countries. Includes both financial and personnel information.

Basic Statistics for Business and Economics. Douglas A. Lind and others. McGraw-Hill, 1221 Ave. of the Americas New York, NY 10020. Phone: 800-722-4726 or (212)512-2000 Fax: (212)512-4502 E-mail: customer.service@mcgraw-hill.com • URL: http://www.mcgraw-hill.com • 2002. Fourth edition. Price on application. (Operations and Decision Sciences Series).

Basic Statistics of the European Union. Statistical Office of the European Communities. Available from Bernan Associates, 4611-F Assembly Dr. Lanham, MD 20706-4391. Phone: 800-274-4447 or (301)459-7666 Fax: 800-865-3450 or (301)459-0056 E-mail: query@bernan.com • URL: http://www.bernan.com • Annual. Provides European demographic, economic, and other basic data. The U. S., Canada, Japan, and the Soviet

Union are included for comparative purposes. Text in Dutch, English, French, and German. Formerly *Basic Statistics of the European Community*.

Basics of Budgeting. Robert G. Finney. AMACOM, 1601 Broadway New York, NY 10019. Phone: 800-262-9699 or (518)586-8100 Fax: (518)903-8168 E-mail: customerservice@amanet.org • URL: http://www.amacombooks.org • 1993. $19.95

Battelle Memorial Institute. Battelle Memorial Institute, 505 King Ave. Columbus, OH 43201. Phone: 800-201-2011 or (614)424-5853 Fax: (614)424-5263 E-mail: solutions@battelle.org • URL: http://www.battelle.org/ • Environment and energy; national security; transportation; health and life sciences; medical, pharmaceutical, agrochemical, and consumer product development. Conducts marine research at three coastal locations: Florida Marine Research Facility (Daytona Beach), Northwest Marine Research Laboratory (Sequim, Washington), and the Ocean Sciences Laboratory (Duxbury, Massachusetts). Specialized facilities and units include: Aviation Safety Reporting System Office; the Breakthrough Center for Strategic Product Development; the Human Engineering, Ergonomics, and Organizational Research Center; and the William R. Wiley Environmental Molecular Sciences Laboratory.

Battery and EV Technology News. Business Communications Co., Inc., 25 Van Zant St. Norwalk, CT 06855-1781. Phone: (203)853-4266 Fax: (203)853-0348 E-mail: info@bccresearch.com • URL: http://www.buscom.com • Monthly. $450.00 per year. Newsletter. Technical and economic studies of electric vehicles and battery technology.

Battery Council International., 401 N Michigan Ave., 24th Fl. Chicago, IL 60611-4267. Phone: (312)644-6610 Fax: (312)527-6640 E-mail: info@batterycouncil.org • URL: http://www.batterycouncil.org • Manufacturers, suppliers of materials, and national distributors of lead-acid storage batteries. Recommends industry standards; compiles statistics.

The Battery Man: International Journal for Starting, Lighting, Ignition and Generating Systems. Independent Battery Manufacturers Association, Inc., 100 Larchwood Dr. Largo, FL 33770. Phone: 800-237-6126 or (727)586-1408 Fax: (727)586-1400 E-mail: thebatteryman@juno.com Monthly. $20.00 per year.

The Bauer Group: Reporting On and Analyzing the Performance of U. S. Banks, Thrifts, and Credit Unions. Bauer Financial Reports, Inc.Phone: 800-388-6686 or (305)445-9500 Fax: 800-230-9569 or (305)445-6775 • URL: http://www.bauerfinancial.com • Web site provides ratings (0 to 5 stars) of individual banks and credit unions, based on capital ratios and other financial criteria. Online searching for bank or credit union names is offered. Fees: Free.

BBB Wise Giving Alliance., 4200 Wilson Blvd., Ste. 800 Arlington, VA 22203-1838. Phone: (703)276-0100 Fax: (703)525-8277 E-mail: kbrannigan@cottoninc.com • URL: http://www.give.org • Supported by companies and local Better Business Bureaus operated autonomously in the United States and Puerto Rico, which are in turn supported by 270,000 local business members. Seeks to promote and foster the highest ethical relationship between businesses and the public through voluntary self-regulation, consumer and business education, and service excellence. Provides support to local Better Business Bureaus. Administers the advertising industry's self-regulatory program that monitors and investigates the truth and accuracy of national advertising claims; monitors and pre-screens advertising directed towards children. Develops information on national charitable organizations and whether they meet voluntary ethical standards for soliciting organizations. Provides information to help consumers and businesses make informed purchasing decisions and avoid costly scams and frauds; and settles consumer complaints through arbitration and other means. Operates BBB AUTO LINE, a national mediation and arbitration service providing an independent forum to resolve consumer complaints involving 32 participating auto manufacturers; Local Better Business Bureaus respond to more than 23 million requests for service annually, fielding 20 million pre-purchase inquiries and 3 million complaints.

BBB Wise Giving Council., 4200 Wilson Blvd., Ste. 800 Arlington, VA 22203-0100. Phone: (703)276-0100 Fax: (703)525-8277 E-mail: info@bbb.org • URL: http://www.give.org • Sets accountability standards and provides information for nonprofit organizations that solicit contributions from the public. Formerly National Charities Information Bureau.

BBC World Glossary of Current Affairs. Available from the Gale Group, 27500 Drake Rd. Farmington Hills, MI 48331-3535. Phone: 800-877-GALE or (248)699-GALE Fax: 800-414-5043 or (248)699-8063 E-mail: galeord@galegroup.com • URL: http://gale.cengage.com • 1991. $85.00. Published by Longman Group Ltd. Provides definitions of 7,000 terms used in world affairs. Arranged by country, with an alphabetical index.

The BBI Newsletter: A Perceptive Analysis of the Healthcare Industry and Marketplace Focusing on New Technology, Strategic Planning, and Marketshare Projections. American Health Consultants, 3525 Piedmont Rd., N.E., Bldg. 6, Suite 400 Atlanta, GA 30305. Phone: 800-688-2421 or (404)262-7436 Fax: 800-284-3291 or (404)262-5447 E-mail: custserv@ahcpub.com • URL: http://www.ahcpub.org • Monthly. $827.00 per year.

BCA Interest Rate Forecast: A Monthly Analysis and Forecast of U.S. Bond and Money Market Trends. BCA Publications, 1002 Sherbrooke St., W., 16th Fl. Montreal, QC, Canada H3A 3L6. Phone: (514)499-9706 Fax: (514)499-9709 Monthly. $695.00 per year. Formerly *Interest Rate Forecast*.

BCI Handbook. The Conference Board, Inc., 845 3rd Ave. New York, NY 10022. Phone: (212)339-0345 Fax: (212)836-9740 • URL: http://www.conference-board.org • 2001. $20.00. Provides detailed descriptions of the economic series - Business Cycle Indicators - used by The Conference Board to determine current business conditions and predict the future direction of the U. S. economy. Data sources are indicated. (A previous version was published in 1982.)

Be a Sales Superstar: 21 Great Ways to Sell More, Faster, Easier in Today's Tough Markets. Brian Tracy. Berrett-Koehler Publishers, Inc., 235 Montgomery St., Suite 650 San Francisco, CA 94104-2916. Phone: 800-929-2929 or (415)288-0260 Fax: (802)864-7626 E-mail: bkpub@bkpub.com • URL: http://www.bkconnection.com • 2003. $19.95.

The Bear Book: Survive and Profit in Ferocious Markets. John Rothchild. John Wiley and Sons, Inc., 111 River St. Hoboken, NJ 07030. Phone: 800-225-5945 or (201)748-6000 Fax: (201)748-6088 E-mail: info@wiley.com • URL: http://www.wiley.com • 1998. $24.95. Tells how to invest when the stock market is sinking.

Bearing Specialists Association., 800 Roosevelt Rd., Bldg. C, Ste. 312, Bldg. C, Ste. 312 Glen Ellyn, IL 60137. Phone: (630)858-3838 Fax: (630)790-3095 E-mail: info@bsahome.org • URL: http://www.bsahome.org • Distributors of antifriction bearings. Promotes networking and knowledge sharing and promotes the sale of bearings through authorized distributors.

Beating the Street: The Best-Selling Author of "One Up on Wall Street" Shows You How to Pick Winning Stocks and Mutual Funds. Peter Lynch and John Rothchild. Simon & Schuster Trade, 1230 Ave. of the Americas New York, NY 10020. Phone: 800-223-2348 or (212)698-7000 Fax: 800-943-9831 or (212)698-7007 E-mail: consumer.customerservice@simonandschuster.com • URL: http://www.simonsays.com • 1993. $23.00.

Beauty and Barber Supply Institute.

Beauty Salons. Available from MarketResearch.com, 641 Ave. of the Americas, 3rd Fl. New York, NY 10011. Phone: 800-298-5699 or (212)807-2629 Fax: (212)807-2716 E-mail: order@marketresearch.com • URL: http://www.marketresearch.com • 1997. $995.00. Market research report published by Specialists in Business Information. Covers beauty salon revenues, as well as sales of supplies and equipment for beauty salons and barber shops.

Beauty Supply Store. Entrepreneur Media, Inc., 2445 McCabe Way Irvine, CA 92614. Phone: 800-421-2300 or (949)261-2325 Fax: (949)261-0234 E-mail: entman@entrepreneur.com • URL: http://www.entrepreneur.com • Looseleaf. $59.50. A practical guide to starting a store for professional beauty supplies. Covers profit potential, start-up costs, market size evaluation, owner's time required, site selection, lease negotiation, pricing, accounting, advertising, promotion, etc. (Start-Up Business Guide No. E1277.)

Becker the Counterfeiter. G. F. Hill. Sanford J. Durst, 11 Clinton Ave. Rockville Centre, NY 60505. Phone: (516)766-4440 Fax: (516)766-4520 1979. $20.00.

Becoming a Fundraiser: The Principles and Practice of Library Development. Victoria Steele and Stephen D. Elder. American Library Association, 50 E Huron St. Chicago, IL 60611-2795. Phone: 800-545-2433 or (312)944-6780 Fax: (312)440-9374 E-mail: ala@ala.org • URL: http://www.ala.org • 2000. $38.00. Second edition.

Bee Biology and Systematics Laboratory. Utah State University

Bee Craft: The Official Journal of the British BeeKeepers' Association. British Bee-Keepers Association. Bee Craft Ltd., 79 Strathcona Ave. Bookham, Leatherhead KT23 4HR, United Kingdom. Phone: 44 1372 451891 E-mail: secretary@hotmail.com • URL: http://www.bee-craft.com • Monthly. $51.00 per year.

Bee Culture: The Magazine of American Beekeeping. A. I. Root Co., P.O. Box 706 Medina, OH 44258-0706. Phone: (330)725-6677 Fax: (330)725-5624 E-mail: beeculture@airoot.com • URL: http://www.airoot.com • Monthly. $20.00 per year. Articles, reports and stories about beekeeping market. Latest industry news. Formerly *Gleanings in Bee Culture*.

Bee World. International Bee Research Association, 18 North Rd. Cardiff CF10 3DT, United Kingdom. Phone: 44 029 2037 2409 Fax: 44 029 2066 5522 E-mail: mailk@ibra.org.uk • URL: http://www.ibra.org.uk • Quarterly. $85.00 per year. Authoritative articles and reviews about recent scientific and technological developments.

BEEF. National Cattlemen's Beef AssociationPhone: (303)694-0305 Fax: (303)694-2851 E-mail: cows@beef.org • URL: http://www.beef.org • Web site provides detailed information from the "Cattle and Beef Handbook," including "Beef Economics" (production, sales, consumption, retail value, foreign competition, etc.). Text of monthly newsletter is also available: "The Beef Brief-Issues & Trends in the Cattle Industry." Keyword searching is offered. Fees: Free.

Beef. Primedia Business Magazines and Media, 7900 International Dr., Ste. 300 Minneapolis, MN 55425. Phone: 800-795-5445 or (925)851-9329 Fax: (925)851-4601 E-mail: subs@primediabusiness.com • URL: http://www.primediabusiness.com • 13 times a year. $35.00 per year.

Beef Cattle and Sheep Research Center. Pennsylvania State University

Beekeeping. Devon Beekeepers Association, c/o Brian Gant, Leaf Orchard, Grange Rd. Buckfast TQ11 0EH, United Kingdom. Phone: 44 1364 642233 Fax: 44 1364 342233 E-mail: 106213.3313@compuserve.com Ten times a year. Free to members; non-members, $11.50 per year.

Beer Institute., 122 C St. NW, Ste. 350 Washington, DC 20001. Phone: 800-379-BREW or (202)737-2337 Fax: (202)737-7004 E-mail: info@beerinstitute.org • URL: http://www.beerinstitute.org • Brewers, importers, and suppliers to the industry. Committed to the development of public policy and to the values of civic duty and personal responsibility.

Beer Marketer's Insights. Beer Marketer's Insights, Inc., P.O. Box 264 West Nyack, NY 10994. Phone: (914)624-2337 Fax: (914)624-2340 • URL: http://www.beerinsights.com • Semimonthly. $485.00 per year. Newsletter for brewers and wholesalers.

Beer Statistics News. Beer Marketer's Insights, Inc., P.O. Box 264 West Nyack, NY 10994. Phone: (914)624-2337 Fax: (914)624-2340 • URL: http://www.beerinsights.com • Semimonthly. $485.00 per year. Market share and shipments by region and brewer.

Behavioral and Social Sciences Librarian. Haworth Press, Inc., 10 Alice St. Binghamton, NY 13904-1580. Phone: 800-429-6784 or (607)722-5857 Fax: 800-895-0582 or (607)722-1424 E-mail: getinfo@haworthpressinc.com • URL: http://www.haworthpressinc.com • Semiannual. Individuals, $48.00 per year; institutions, $175.00 per year; libraries, $175.00 per year.

Behavioral Medicine: An Interdisciplinary Journal of Research and Practice. Helen Dwight Reid Educational Foundation. Heldref Publications, 1319 18th St., N.W. Washington, DC 20016-1802. Phone: 800-365-9753 Fax: (202)292-6130 E-mail: subscribe@heldref.org • URL: http://www.heldref.org • Quarterly. Individuals, $69.00 per year; institutions, $129.00 per year. An interdisciplinary journal of particular interest to physicians, psychologists, nurses, educators and all who are interested in behavorial and social influences on mental and physicial health. Formerly *Journal of Human Stress*.

Being Digital. Nicholas Negroponte. Knopf Publishing Group, 299 Park Ave., 7th Fl. New York, NY 10171. Phone: 800-726-0600 or (212)751-2600 Fax: 800-659-2436 or (212)572-2593 E-mail: customerservice@randomhouse.com • URL: http://www.randomhouse.com • 1995. $30.00. A kind of history of multimedia, with visions of future technology and public participation. Predicts how computers will affect society in years to come.

BEMA, The Bakery Industry Suppliers Association.

Bender's Labor and Employment Bulletin. LexisNexis Matthew Bender, 1275 Broadway Albany, NY 12204. Phone: 800-424-4200 or (518)487-3000 Fax: (518)487-3584 E-mail: bookstore.support@lexisnexis.com • URL: http://www.bender.com • Monthly. $296.00 per year. Newsletter.

Bender's Payroll Tax Guide. LexisNexis Matthew Bender, 1275 Broadway Albany, NY 12204. Phone: 800-424-4200 or (518)487-3000 Fax: (518)487-3584 E-mail: bookstore.support@lexisnexis.com • URL: http://www.bender.com • Annual. $149.00. Guide to payroll tax planning. Includes procedures, forms, and examples.

Bender's Tax Return Manual. Ernest D. Fiore and others. LexisNexis Matthew Bender, 1275 Broadway Albany, NY 12204. Phone: 800-424-4200 or (518)487-3000 Fax: (518)487-3584 E-mail: bookstore.support@lexisnexis.com • URL: http://www.bender.com • Annual. $91.00. One looseleaf volume. Periodic supplementation. Includes all major federal tax forms and schedules.

Bendheim Center for Finance., Princeton University, 26 Prospect Ave. Princeton, NJ 08540-5296. Phone: (609)258-0770 Fax: (609)258-0771 E-mail: yacine@princeton.edu • URL: http://www.princeton.edu/~bcf/ • Research areas include securities markets, portfolio analysis, credit markets, and corporate finance. Emphasis is on quantitative and mathematical perspectives.

Benedict on Admiralty. LexisNexis Matthew Bender, 1275 Broadway Albany, NY 12204. Phone: 800-424-4200 or (518)487-3000 Fax: (518)487-3584 E-mail: bookstore.support@lexisnexis.com • URL: http://www.bender.com • Three times a year. $3,138.00. 27 looseleaf volumes. Periodic supplementation. Covers American law of the sea and shipping.

Benefits and Wages: OECD Indicators. Organization for Economic Cooperation and Development, OECD Washington Center, 2001 L St., N. W., Suite 650 Washington, DC 20036-4922. Phone: 800-456-6323 or (202)785-6323 Fax: (202)785-0350 E-mail: washington.contact@oecd.org • URL: http://www.oecd.org • Biennial. $19.00. Provides data for 28 countries on unemployment benefits and related welfare benefits. Includes a cross-country comparison of family incomes, in work and out of work. Formerly *Benefit Systems and Work Incentives*.

Benefits News Analysis. Benefits News Analysis, Inc., P.O. Box 4033 New Haven, CT 06525. Phone: (203)393-2272 Bimonthly. $89.00. Analysis of corporate employee benefit practices. Includes review of benefit program changes at a number of large corporations.

Benefits Survey. Available from Paul & Co., 814 N. Franklin St. Chicago, IL 60610. Phone: (312)337-0747 Fax: (312)337-5985 E-mail: frontdesk@ipgbook.com • URL: http://www.ipgbook.com • Annual. $99.95. Published by the Society for Human Resource Management (http://www.shrm.org). Provides five-year data, with discussion, for 200 kinds of employee benefits.

Benelux Kompass Business Disc. Available from Kompass USA, Inc., 121 Whitney Ave. New Haven, CT 06510. Phone: 877-566-7277 or (203)503-6789 Fax: (203)503-6780 E-mail: mail@kompass-usa.com • URL: http://www.kompass.com • Semiannual. CD-ROM provides information on more than 52,000 companies in Belgium, Netherlands, and Luxembourg. Classification system covers approximately 50,000 products and services.

Benn's Media Directory. Data & Information Services Div., Riverbank House, Angel Ln. Tonbridge TN91SE, United Kingdom. Phone: (44)1732 364422 Fax: (44)1732 367301 E-mail: enquiries@cmpi.biz Covers: over 38,000 daily and weekly newspapers, free newspapers, periodicals, directories, major publishers, television and radio broadcasting stations, media associations, and suppliers of services to the publishing and broadcasting industries. The United Kingdom volume covers all UK media including e-mail and internet addresses; the European and World volumes cover key media in each country in depth and detail. Entries include: For newspapers—Title, year established, affiliated publications, geographical coverage, name and address of publisher, phone, telex, fax, names and titles of key personnel, circulation, frequency. For periodicals—Title, year established and frequency, description of editorial contents, key personnel, address, phone, fax, telex. For broadcasting stations—Firm name, address, phone, waveband, personnel.

Berkeley Journal of Employment and Labor Law. University of California, Boalt Hall School of Law, 289 Simon Hall Berkeley, CA 94720-7200. Phone: (510)642-5126 E-mail: bhsa@law.berkeley.edu • URL: http://www.boalt.org • Biennial. Individuals, $36.00 per year; institutions, $47.00 per year. Formerly *Industrial Relations Law Journal.*

Berkley Center for Entrepreneurial Studies.

Best Bet Internet: Reference and Research When You Don't Have Time to Mess Around. Shirley D. Kennedy. American Library Association, 50 E. Huron St. Chicago, IL 60611-2795. Phone: 800-545-2433 or (312)944-6780 Fax: (312)440-9374 E-mail: ala@ala.org • URL: http://www.ala.org • 1997. $35.00. Provides advice for librarians and others on the effective use of World Wide Web information sources.

Best Candidate Committee.. 1400 20th St. NW, Ste. 5 Washington, DC 20036. E-mail: scrochet@aba.com To improve the quality of Congress by encouraging the selection of the "best" candidates for election. Conducts research and evaluates the performance and potential of candidates.

The Best of OPL, II: Selected Readings from the One-Person Library: 1990-1994. Andrew Berner and Guy St. Clair. Special Libraries Association, 1700 18th St., N. W. Washington, DC 20009-2514. Phone: (202)234-4700 Fax: (202)265-9317 E-mail: sla@sla.org • URL: http://www.sla.org • 1996. $36.00. Contains reprints of useful material from *The One-Person Library: A Newsletter for Librarians and Management.*

The Best of Times: A Personal and Occupational Odyssey. Paul Wasserman. Omnigraphics, Inc., 615 Griswold St. Detroit, MI 48226. Phone: 800-234-1340 or (313)961-1340 Fax: 800-875-1340 or (313)961-1383 E-mail: info@omnigraphics.com • URL: http://www.omnigraphics.com • 2000. $35.00. Autobiography of a well known librarian, educator, and reference book editor. Foreward by Frederick G. Ruffner.

Best Practices for Financial Advisors. Mary Rowland. Bloomberg, 499 Park Ave. New York, NY 10022. Phone: 800-388-2749 or (212)318-2000 Fax: (917)369-5000 • URL: http://www.bloomberg.com • 1997. $40.00. Provides advice for professional financial advisors on practice management, ethics, marketing, and legal concerns. (Bloomberg Professional Library.)

Best's Aggregates and Averages: Property-Casualty. A.M. Best Co., Inc., Ambest Rd. Oldwick, NJ 08858. Phone: (908)439-2200 Fax: (908)439-3296 E-mail: customer_service@ambest.com • URL: http://www.ambest.com • Annual. $335.00. Statistical summary of composite property casualty business. 400 pages of historical data, underwriting expenses and underwriting experience by line.

Best's Directory of Recommended Insurance Attorneys and Adjusters. A.M. Best Co., Ambest Rd. Oldwick, NJ 08858. Phone: (908)439-2200 Fax: (908)439-2688 • URL: http://www.ambest.com • Annual. $1,175.00. More than 5,000 American, Canadian, and foreign insurance defense law firms; lists 1,200 national and international insurance adjusting firms. Formerly *Best's Recommended Insurance Adjusters.*

Best's Insurance Reports. A.M. Best Co., Ambest Rd. Oldwick, NJ 08858. Phone: (908)439-2200 Fax: (908)439-3296 E-mail: customer_service@ambest.com • URL: http://www.ambest.com • Annual. $1495.00. Life-health insurance covering about 1,750 companies, and property-casualty insurance covering over 3,200 companies. Includes one year subscription to both *Best's Review* and *Best's Insurance Management Reports.*

Best's Insurance Reports: Property-Casualty. A.M. Best Co., Ambest Rd. Oldwick, NJ 08858. Phone: (908)439-2200 Fax: (908)439-3296 E-mail: customer_service@ambest.com • URL: http://www.ambest.com • Annual. $750.00. Guide to over 3,200 major property/casualty companies.

Best's Key Rating Guide. A.M. Best Co., Ambest Rd. Oldwick, NJ 08858. Phone: (908)439-2200 Fax: (908)439-3296 E-mail: customer_service@ambest.com • URL: http://www.ambest.com • Annual. $225.00. Financial information and ratings on over 3,300 major property/casualty insurers.

Best's Review: Inurance Issues and Analysis. A.M. Best Co., Ambest Rd. Oldwick, NJ 08858. Phone: (908)439-2200 Fax: (908)439-3363 E-mail: customer_service@ambest.com • URL: http://www.ambest.com • Monthly. $25.00 per year. Editorial coverage of significant industry trends, developments, and important events. Formerly *Best's Review: Property-Casualty Insurance.*

Best's Safety and Security Directory. A.M. Best Co., Ambest Rd. Oldwick, NJ 08858. Phone: (908)439-2200 Fax: (908)439-3296 E-mail: customer_service@ambest.com • URL: http://www.ambest.com • Annual. Free to members; non-members, $295.00. A manual of current industrial safety practices with a directory of manufacturers and distributors of plant safety, security and industrial hygiene products and services listed by hazard. Formerly *Best's Safety Directory.*

BestWeek: Insurance News and Analysis. A.M. Best Co., Ambest Rd. Oldwick, NJ 08858. Phone: (908)439-2200 Fax: (908)439-3296 E-mail: editor_bw@bestweek.com • URL: http://www.ambest.com • Weekly. $495.00 per year. Newsletter. Focuses on key areas of the insurance industry.

The Betrayed Profession: Lawyering at the End of the Twentieth Century. Sol M. Linowitz and Martin Mayer. John Hopkins University Press, 2715 N. Charles St. Baltimore, MD 21218-4363. Phone: 800-537-5487 or (410)516-6900 Fax: (410)516-6968 • URL: http://www.press.jhu.edu • 1996. $18.95. Reprint edition. A critical view of present-day lawyers and law firms.

Better Buys for Business: The Independent Consumer Guide to Office Equipment. What to Buy for Business, Inc., 370 Technology Dr. Malvern, PA 19355. Phone: 800-247-2185 or (805)963-3539 Fax: (805)963-3740 E-mail: orders@betterbuys.com • URL: http://www.betterbuys.com • 10 times a year. $134.00 per year. Each issue is on a particular office product, with detailed evaluation of specific models: 1. Low-Volume Copier Guide, 2. Mid-Volume Copier Guide, 3. High-Volume Copier Guide, 4. Plain Paper Fax and Low-Volume Multifunctional Guide, 5. Mid/High-Volume Multifunctional Guide, 6. Laser Printer Guide, 7. Color Printer and Color Copier Guide, 8. Scan-to-File Guide, 9. Business Phone Systems Guide, 10. Postage Meter Guide, with a Short Guide to Shredders.

Better Crops With Plant Food. Potash and Phosphate Institute, 655 Engineering Dr., Suite 110 Norcross, GA 30092-2843. Phone: (770)447-0335 Fax: (770)448-0439 Quarterly. $8.00.

Better Government Association., 11 E Adams St., Ste. 608 Chicago, IL 60603. Phone: (312)427-8330 Fax: (312)386-9203 E-mail: info@bettergov.org • URL: http://bettergov.org • Individuals and corporations concerned with major public policy questions and dedicated to promoting efficient use of tax dollars and high standards of public service. Encourages a responsive and economical government by improving government institutions' performance and maintaining high ethical standards among public officials. Uses official documents, on-the-record interviews, undercover operations, and sophisticated techniques of investigative reporting to uncover corruption. Works closely with national and local media to expose waste, inefficiency, and corruption and to educate the public on the inner workings of the government. Sponsors intern programs for students in law and investigative research.

Better Investing. National Association of Investors Corp., PO Box 220 Royal Oak, MI 48068. Phone: (248)583-6242 Fax: (248)583-4880 E-mail: awgnews@mcgraw-hill.com • URL: http://www.better-investing.org • Description: Features investment information on various corporations as seen by 10 different columnists.

Better Radio and Television. National Association for Better Broadcasting, P.O. Box 43640 Los Angeles, CA 90043. Quarterly. $6.00 per year.

Better Roads. James Informational Media, Inc., 2720 S. River Rd., Ste. 126 Des Plaines, IL 60018. Phone: 800-957-9305 or (847)391-9070 Fax: (847)391-9058 E-mail: kirk@jiminc.com • URL: http://www.jiminc.com • Monthly. Free to qualified personnel.

Better Vision Institute., 1700 Diagonal Rd., Ste. 500 Alexandria, VA 22314. Phone: 877-642-3253 or (703)548-4560 Fax: (703)548-4580 E-mail: info@thevisioncouncil.org • URL: http://www.visionsite.org • Advisory council of the Vision Council of America. Carried out in consultation with a board of eye care professionals who inform the public of the need for more adequate vision care.

Beverage Digest. John Sicher, 2 Depot Plz. Bedford Hills, NY 10507. Phone: (914)244-0700 Fax: (914)244-0774 E-mail: awgnews@mcgraw-hill.com • URL: http://www.beverage-digest.com • Description: Focuses primarily on non-alcoholic drinks. Reports on industry news in relation to pricing, marketing, competition, mergers and acquisitions, and new products.

Beverage Industry. Stagnito Communications, Inc., 155 Pfingsten

Rd., Ste. 205 Deerfield, IL 60015. Phone: (847)205-5660 Fax: (847)205-5680 E-mail: info@stagnito.com • URL: http://www.stagnito.com • Monthly. Free to qualified personnel; others, $85.05 per year. Supplement available *Beverage Industry-Annual Manual.*

Beverage Industry - Annual Manual. Stagnito Communications, Inc., 155 Pfingsten Rd., Ste. 205 Deerfield, IL 60015. Phone: (847)205-5660 Fax: (847)205-5680 E-mail: info@stagnito.com • URL: http://www.stagnito.com • Annual. $55.00. Provides statistical information on multiple beverage markets. Includes an industry directory. Supplement to *Beverage Industry.*

Beverage Industry News. BIN Publications, 171 Mayhew Way, Suite 202 Pleasant Hill, CA 94523-4348. Phone: (925)932-4999 Fax: (925)932-4966 E-mail: binmagqa.com Monthly. $49.00 per year. Incorporates *Beverage Industry News Merchandiser.*

Beverage Marketing Directory. Beverage Marketing Corp., PO Box 126 Mingo Junction, OH 43938. Phone: 800-332-6222 or (740)598-4133 Fax: (740)598-3977 E-mail: consulting@beveragemarketing.com • URL: http://www.beveragemarketing.com • Covers: About 11,000 beer wholesalers, wine and spirits wholesalers, soft drink bottlers and franchisors, breweries, wineries, distilleries, alcoholic beverage importers, bottled water companies; and trade associations, government agencies, micro breweries, juice, coffee, tea, milk companies, and others concerned with the beverage and bottling industries; coverage includes Canada. Entries include: Beverage and bottling company listings contain company name, address, phone, names of key executives, number of employees, brand names, and other information, including number of franchisees, number of delivery trucks, sales volume. Suppliers and related companies and organizations listings include similar but less detailed information.

Beverage Media. Beverage Network. Beverage Media, Ltd., 161 Ave. of the Americas New York, NY 10013. Phone: (212)734-0322 Fax: (212)620-0473 Monthly. $78.00 per year. Wholesale prices.

Beverage World Buyers Guide. VNU Business Media, 770 Broadway New York, NY 10003. Phone: 800-266-4712 or (646)654-5000 Fax: (646)654-7212 E-mail: akaplan@beverageworld.com • URL: http://www.vnubusinessmedia.com • Annual. $7.00. Lists suppliers to the beverage industry.

Beverage World: Magazine of the Beverage Industry. VNU Business Media, 770 Broadway New York, NY 10003-9595. Phone: (646)654-4500 Fax: (646)654-7212 • URL: http://www.vnubusinessmedia.com • Monthly. $79.00 per year.

Beyond Book Indexing: How to Get Started in Web Indexing, Embedded Indexing, and Other Computer-Based Media. Information Today, Inc., 143 Old Marlton Pike Medford, NJ 08055-8750. Phone: 800-300-9868 or (609)654-6266 Fax: (609)654-4309 E-mail: custserv@infotoday.com • URL: http://www.infotoday.com • 1999. $31.25. Published for the American Society of Indexers. Contains 12 chapters written by professional indexers. Part one discusses making an index by marking items in an electronic document (embedded indexing); part two is on indexing to make Web pages more accessible; part three covers CD-ROM and multimedia indexing; part four provides career and promotional advice for professionals in the field. Includes an index by Janet Perlman and a glossary.

Beyond Junk Bonds: Expanding High Yield Markets. Glenn Yago. Oxford University Press, 198 Madison Ave. New York, NY 10016-4314. Phone: 800-451-7556 or (212)726-6000 Fax: (212)726-6440 E-mail: custserv@oup-usa.org • URL: http://www.oup-usa.org • 2003. $45.00. Describes the "broadening and deepening of the high yield market over the past decade." Indicates there are now thousands of institutional buyers of lower-rated bonds, including many mutual funds.

BGF Bulletin. Banana Growers Federation Co-Operative Ltd., P.O. Box 31 Murwillumbah NSW 2484, Australia. Phone: (066)-72-2488 Fax: (066)-72-4868 Monthly. $35.00 per year. Formerly *Banana Bulletin.*

BI Research. Thomas Bishop, editor. BI Research, Inc., PO Box 133 Redding, CT 06875. Phone: (203)270-9244 E-mail: birstocks@aol.com • URL: http://www.biresearch.com • Every six weeks. $110.00 per year. Newsletter. Five to eight in-depth investment recommendations per year.

Bibliographic Guide to Business and Economics. Available from Gale Cengage Learning, 27500 Drake Rd. Farmington Hills, MI 48331-3535. Phone: 800-877-GALE or (248)699-GALE Fax: 800-414-5043 E-mail: gale.galeord@cengage.com • URL: http://gale.cengage.com • Annual. $835.00. Three volumes. Published by G. K. Hall & Co. Lists current business and economics publications cataloged by the New York Public Library and the Library of Congress.

Bibliographic Guide to Conference Publications. Available from Gale Cengage Learning, 27500 Drake Rd. Farmington Hills, MI 48331-3535. Phone: 800-877-GALE or (248)699-GALE Fax: 800-414-5043 E-mail: gale.galeord@cengage.com • URL: http://gale.cengage.com • Annual. $600.00. Two volumes. Published by G. K. Hall & Co., Lists a wide range of conference publications cataloged by the New York Public Library and the Library of Congress.

Bibliographic Guide to Government Publications: U. S. Available from Gale Cengage Learning, 27500 Drake Rd. Farmington Hills, MI 48331-3535. Phone: 800-877-GALE or

(248)699-GALE Fax: 800-414-5043 or (248)699-8069 E-mail: galeord@galegroup.com • URL: http://www.galegroup.com • Annual. $650.00. Two volumes. Published by G. K. Hall & Co. Lists U.S. government publications.

Bibliographic Guide to Government Publications: United States. Available from Gale Cengage Learning, 27500 Drake Rd. Farmington Hills, MI 48331-3535. Phone: 800-877-GALE or (248)699-GALE Fax: 800-414-5043 or (248)699-8069 E-mail: galeord@galegroup.com • URL: http://www.galegroup.com • Annual. $680.00. Two volumes. Published by G. K. Hall & Co. Lists government publications from countries other than the U. S.

Bibliographic Guide to Law. Available from Gale Cengage Learning, 27500 Drake Rd. Farmington Hills, MI 48331-3535. Phone: 800-877-GALE or (248)699-GALE Fax: 800-414-5043 E-mail: gale.galeord@cengage.com • URL: http://gale.cengage.com • Annual. $575.00. Two volumes. Published by G. K. Hall & Co. Lists legal publications cataloged by the New York Public Library and the Library of Congress.

Bibliographic Guide to Maps and Atlases. Available from Gale Cengage Learning, 27500 Drake Rd. Farmington Hills, MI 48331-3535. Phone: 800-877-GALE or (248)699-GALE Fax: 800-414-5043 E-mail: gale.galeord@cengage.com • URL: http://gale.cengage.com • Anual. $430.00. Published by G. K. Hall & Co. Lists maps and atlases cataloged by the New York Public Library and the Library of Congress.

Bibliographic Guide to Technology. Available from Gale Cengage Learning, 27500 Drake Rd. Farmington Hills, MI 48331-3535. Phone: 800-877-GALE or (248)699-GALE Fax: 800-414-5043 E-mail: gale.galeord@cengage.com • URL: http://gale.cengage.com • Annual. $575.00. Two volumes. Published by G. K. Hall & Co. Lists technology publications cataloged by the New York Public Library and the Library of Congress.

Bibliographic Index: A Subject List of Bibliographies in English and Foreign Languages. H. W. Wilson Co., 950 University Ave. Bronx, NY 10452. Phone: 800-367-6770 or (718)588-8400 Fax: 800-590-1617 or (718)590-1617 E-mail: custserv@hwwilson.com • URL: http://www.hwwilson.com • Three times a year. Third issues cumulates all three issues. Price varies.

Bibliographical Center for Research, Inc., Rocky Mountain Region., 14394 E. Evans Ave. Aurora, CO 80014-1478. Phone: 800-397-1552 or (303)751-6277 Fax: (303)751-9787 E-mail: dbrunell@bcr.org • URL: http://www.bcr.org • Fields of research include information retrieval systems, Internet technology, CD-ROM technology, document delivery, and library automation.

Bibliographical Society of America.

Bibliographical Society of the University of Virginia.

A Bibliography of Business Ethics, 1981-1985: University of Virginia. Donald G. Jones and Patricia Bennett, editors. The Edwin Mellen Press, P.O. Box 450 Lewiston, NY 14092. Phone: (716)754-2266 Fax: (716)754-4056 E-mail: imiller@mellenpress.com • URL: http://www.mellenpress.com • 1986. $99.95. (Mellen Studies in Business Series: Vol. 2).

Bicycle Dealer Showcase Buyers Guide. Skies America Publishing Co., 9655 S.W. Sunshine, Suite 500 Beaverton, OR 97005. Phone: (503)520-1955 Fax: (503)520-1275 Annual. Free to qualified personnel.

Bicycle Product Suppliers Association., PO Box 187 Montgomeryville, PA 18936. Phone: (215)393-3144 Fax: (215)893-4872 E-mail: bpsa@bpsa.org • URL: http://www.bpsa.org • Wholesalers of bicycles, bicycle parts, and accessories; vendor members are manufacturers and suppliers. Affiliate members supply services and products to bicycle retailers. Offers educational programs; compiles statistics and safety information.

Bicycles. Available from MarketResearch.com, 641 Ave. of the Americas, 3rd Fl. New York, NY 10011. Phone: 800-298-5699 or (212)807-2629 Fax: (212)807-2716 E-mail: order@marketresearch.com • URL: http://www.marketresearch.com • 2002. $3,950.00 Published by Global Industry Analysts. ProvidesU.S. and international market data for bicycles and bicycle parts. Gives profiles of major manufacturers.

Bicycling. Rodale, 33 E. Minor St. Emmaus, PA 18098-0099. Phone: 800-666-2806 or (610)967-5171 Fax: (610)967-8963 E-mail: customer_service@rodale.com • URL: http://www.rodale.com • 11 times a year. $14.94 per year. Information on buying and repairing bicycles.

Biennial Survey of Education in the United States. U.S. Department of Education, Washington, DC 20202. Phone: 800-872-5327 Biennial.

Big Book of Library Grant Money 2002-2003: Profiles of Private and Corporate Foundations and Direct Corporate Givers Receptive to Library Grant Proposals. American Library Association, 50 E Huron St. Chicago, IL 60611-2795. Phone: 800-545-2433 or (312)944-6780 Fax: (312)440-9374 E-mail: ala@ala.org • URL: http://www.ala.org • 2002. $250.00. Provides profiles, contacts, past contributions data, application procedures, and biographical information on foundation personnel. (Prepared by the Taft Group for the American Library Association.)

Billboard: The International Newsweekly of Music, Video, and Home Entertainment. VNU Business Media, 770 Broadway New York, NY 10003-9595. Phone: 800-344-7119 or (646)654-4500 Fax: (646)654-7212 • URL: http://www.vnubusinessmedia.com • 51 times a year. $299.00 per year. Newsweekly for the music and home entertainment industries.

Billboard's International Buyer's Guide. VNU Business Media, 770 Broadway New York, NY 10003-9595. Phone: 800-278-8477 or (646)654-4500 Fax: (646)654-7272 E-mail: globalc@nielsen.com • URL: http://www.watsonguptill.com • Covers: record companies; music publishers; record and tape wholesalers; services and supplies for the music-record-tape-video industry; record and tape dealer accessories, fixtures, and merchandising products; includes United States and over 65 other countries. Entries include: Company name, address, phone, names of principal executives, trade and brand names and/or list of products and services.

Billboard's International Talent and Touring Directory: The Music Industry's Worldwide Reference Source: Talent, Talent Management, Booking Agencies, Promoters, Venue Facilities, Venue Services and Products. Billboard Books, 770 Broadway New York, NY 10003. Phone: 800-745-8922 E-mail: blbd@kable.com • URL: http://www.billboard.com • Annual. $139.00. Lists entertainers, managers, booking agents, and others in the worldwide entertainment industry.

BIN Number Directory of all Visa and Mastercard Issuing Banks. Fraud and Theft Information Bureau, P.O. Box 400 Boynton Beach, FL 33425. Phone: (561)737-8700 Fax: (561)737-5800 E-mail: sales@fraudandtheftinfo.com • URL: http://www.fraudandtheftinfo.com • Annual. $1,175.00. Base edition. Semiannual updates, $360.00 per year. Numerical arrangement of about 30,000 banks worldwide. BIN numbers (also called ISO or prefix numbers) identify a credit card holder's issuing bank.

Binding Industries Association of America., 70 E Lake St., No. 300 Chicago, IL 60601. Phone: (312)372-7606 or (312)704-5000 Fax: (312)709-5025 E-mail: info@bindingindustries.org • URL: http://www.bindingindustries.org • Formerly Binding Industries of America

Bio-Base: A Master Index on Microfiche to Biographical Sketches Found in Current and Retrospective Biographical Dictionaries. Gale Cengage Learning, 27500 Drake Rd. Farmington Hills, MI 48331-3535. Phone: 800-877-GALE or (248)699-GALE Fax: 800-414-5043 E-mail: gale.galeord@cengage.com • URL: http://gale.cengage.com • $1,095.00; update, $295.00. Indexes more than 12.7 million biographical sketches.

BioCommerce Abstracts. Available from Pharmabooks Ltd., 1775 Broadway, Ste. 511 New York, NY 10019. Phone: (212)262-8230 Fax: (212)262-8234 E-mail: subsreps@pharmabooks.com Semimonthly. $996.00 per year. Quarterly cumulation. Includes CD-Rom. Emphasis is on commercial biotechnology.

Biocycle; Journal of Composting and Recycling. JG Press, Inc., 419 State Ave. Emmaus, PA 18049. Phone: (610)967-4135 E-mail: biocycle@jgpress.com • URL: http://www.jgpress.com • Monthly. $69.00 per year. Authoritative reports on the management of municipal sludge and solid wastes via recycling and composting.

Biofuels. OECD Publications and Information Center, 2001 L St., N.W., Ste. 650 Washington, DC 20036-4922. Phone: 800-456-6323 or (202)785-6323 Fax: (202)785-0350 E-mail: washington.contact@oecd.org • URL: http://www.oecdwash.org • 1994. $28.00. Produced by the International Energy Agency (IEA). Analyzes costs and greenhouse gas emissions resulting from the production and use of ethanol fuel. In addition to ethanol from corn, wheat, and sugar beets, consideration is given to diesel fuel from rapeseed oil and methanol from wood.

Biographical Dictionary of American Journalism. Joseph P. McKerns, editor. Greenwood Publishing Group Inc., 88 Post Rd., W. Westport, CT 06881. Phone: 800-225-5800 or (203)226-3571 Fax: (203)431-2214 E-mail: customer-service@greenwood.com • URL: http://www.greenwood.com • 1989. $92.95. Covers major mass media: newspapers, radio, television, and magazines. Includes reporters, editors, columnists, cartoonists, commentators, etc.

Biographical Dictionary of American Labor. Gary M. Fink, editor. Greenwood Publishing Group Inc., 88 Post Rd., W. Westport, CT 06881. Phone: 800-225-5800 or (203)226-3571 Fax: (203)431-2214 E-mail: customer-service@greenwood.com • URL: http://www.greenwood.com • 1984. $120.00.

Biographical Directory of the American Congress, 1774-1996. Joel Treese. CQ Staff Directories, Inc., P.O. Box 19994 Washington, DC 20036-0994. Phone: 800-252-1722 E-mail: staffdir@staffdirectories.com • URL: http://www.staffdirectories.com • 1996. $295.00. Provides detailed biographies of members of the Continental Congress (1774-1789) and the U. S. Congress (1789-1996). Includes presidential Cabinet members.

Biographical Encyclopedia of Hollywood Film Actors. Barry Monush. Applause Theatre & Cinema Books, 151 W. 46th St. New York, NY 10036. Phone: 800-524-4425 or (212)575-9265 Fax: (212)721-2856 E-mail: info@applausepub.com • URL: http://www.applausepub.com • 2000. $85.00. Contains detailed information on more than 1,000 film actors "from Bud Abbott to Pia Zadora." Includes film, stage, and TV credits. The author is Associate Editor of the annual, *Screen World*, and provides critical assessments.

Biography: An Interdisciplinary Quarterly. Biographical Research Center. University of Hawaii Press, Journals Dept., 2840 Kolowalu St. Honolulu, HI 96822. Phone: 888-847-7377 or (808)956-8833 Fax: 800-650-7811 or (808)988-6052 E-mail: biography@hawaii.edu • URL: http://www.hawaii.edu • Quarterly. Individuals, $30.00 per year; institutions, $50.00 per year.

Biography and Genealogy Master Index. Gale Cengage Learning, 27500 Drake Rd. Farmington Hills, MI 48331-3535. Phone: 800-877-GALE or (248)699-GALE Fax: 800-414-5043 E-mail: gale.galeord@cengage.com • URL: http://gale.cengage.com • Annual. $1,095.00. Four volumes. $295.00 per volume. Previous editions available.

Biography Index. H. W. Wilson Co., 950 University Ave, Bronx, NY 10452. Phone: 800-367-6770 or (718)588-8400 Fax: 800-590-1617 or (718)590-1617 E-mail: custserv@hwwilson.com • URL: http://www.hwwilson.com • Quarterly. $280.00 per year. Annual and biennial cumulations.

Biography Index Online. H. W. Wilson Co., 950 University Ave. Bronx, NY 10452. Phone: 800-367-6770 or (718)588-8400 Fax: (718)590-1617 An index to biographies appearing in periodicals, newspapers, current books, and other sources. Covers 1984 to date. Inquire as to online cost and availability.

Biography Master Index [Online]. Gale Cengage Learning, 27500 Drake Rd. Farmington Hills, MI 48331-3535. Phone: 800-877-GALE or (248)699-GALE Fax: 800-414-5043 or (248)699-8069 E-mail: galeord@gale.com • URL: http://gale.cengage.com • An index to biographies appearing in biographical reference volumes, both historical and current. Inquire as to online cost and availability.

Biological and Agricultural Engineering.

Biological and Agricultural Index. H. W. Wilson Co., 950 University Ave. Bronx, NY 10452. Phone: 800-367-6770 or (718)588-8400 Fax: 800-590-1617 or (718)590-1617 E-mail: custserv@hwwilson.com • URL: http://www.hwwilson.com • 11 times a year. Annual and quarterly cumulations. Price varies.

Biomedical Engineering Society., 8401 Corporate Dr., Ste. 140 Landover, MD 20785-2224. Phone: (301)459-1999 Fax: (301)459-2444 E-mail: info@bmes.org • URL: http://www.bmes.org • Biomedical, chemical, electrical, civil, agricultural and mechanical engineers, physicians, managers, and university professors representing all fields of biomedical engineering; students and corporations. Encourages the development, dissemination, integration, and utilization of knowledge in biomedical engineering.

Biomedical Products. Reed Business Information, 360 Park Ave., S New York, NY 10010. Phone: 800-446-6551 or (646)746-6400 Fax: (646)746-7028 E-mail: corporatecommunications@reedbusiness.com • URL: http://www.reedbusiness.com • Monthly. $55.90 per year. Features new products and services. Formerly *Biomedical Products*.

Biomedical Technology Information Service. Lippincott Williams & Wilkins, 530 Walnut St. Philadelphia, PA 19106-3621. Phone: 800-638-3030 or (215)521-8300 Fax: (215)521-8902 E-mail: lww@lww.com • URL: http://www.aspenpublishers.com • Description: Monitors latest advances in medical technology, including developments in medical devices and electronics. Recurring features include new technology, computer applications, legislation and regulations, new inventions, and professional activities. Also includes book reviews, letters to the editor, and a calendar of events.

BioScan: The Worldwide Biotech Industry Reporting Service. Greenwood Publishing Group, Inc., 88 Post Rd. W Westport, CT 06881. Phone: 800-225-5800 or (203)226-3571 Fax: (203)226-2540 E-mail: customer-service@greenwood.com • URL: http://www.greenwood.com • Annual. $975.00 per year. Bimonthly updates. Provides detailed information on over 1,000 U.S. and foreign companies broadly classified as biotechnological. In addition to medical technology and advanced pharmaceutical firms, includes firms doing research in food processing, waste management, agriculture, and veterinary science.

Bioscience. American Institute of Biological Sciences, 1313 Dolly Madison Blvd., Ste. 402 McLean, VA 22101. Phone: (703)790-1745 Fax: (703)790-2672 E-mail: bioscience@aibs.org • URL: http://www.aibs.org • Monthly. $267.00 per year. Includes print and online editions.

BioTechniques: The Journal of Laboratory Technology for Bioresearch. Eaton Publishing Co., 1 Research Dr., Ste. 400A Westboro, MA 01581. Phone: (508)655-8282 Fax: (508)655-9910 12 times a year. $110.00 per year.

Biotechnology. John E. Smith. Cambridge University Press, 40 W 20th St. New York, NY 10011-4211. Phone: 800-872-7423 or (212)924-3900 Fax: (212)691-3239 E-mail: orders@cup.org • URL: http://www.cup.org • 1996. $59.95. Third edition. Provides discussions of biotechnology in relation to medicine, agriculture, food, the environment, biological fuel generation, genetics, ethics, safety, etc. Includes a glossary and bibliography. (Studies in Biology Series).

Biotechnology Abstracts on CD-ROM. Thomson Derwent, Inc., 1725 Duke St., Suite 250 Alexandria, VA 22314. Phone: 800-337-9368 or (703)706-4220 Fax: (703)519-5838 E-mail: info@derwent.com • URL: http://www.derwent.com • Quarterly. Price on application. Provides CD-ROM indexing and abstracting of the world's biotechnology journal literature since 1982, including genetic engineering topics.

Biotechnology and the Law. Iver P. Cooper. West Group, 610 Opperman Dr. Eagan, MN 55123. Phone: 800-328-4880 or (651)687-7000 Fax: 800-340-9378 E-mail: bookstore@westgroup.com • URL: http://www.westgroup.com • Annual.

$424.50. Three looseleaf volumes.

Biotechnology Directory. Nature Publishing Group, 75 Varick St., 9th Fl., Houndmills New York, NY 10013-1917. Phone: 888-331-6288 or (212)726-9200 Fax: (212)696-9006 E-mail: institutions@natureny.com Covers: more than 11,000 companies, universities, research centers, and government agencies, and suppliers of products and services to the field. Entries include: Organization name, address, phone, telex, fax, contact; description of products, services, or research.

Biotechnology from A to Z. William Bains. Oxford University Press, 198 Madison Ave. New York, NY 10016. Phone: 800-451-7556 or (212)726-6000 Fax: (212)726-6440 E-mail: custserv@oup-usa.org • URL: http://www.oup-usa.org • 2004. $47.50. Third edition. Covers the terminology of biotechnology for non-specialists.

Biotechnology Industry Organization., 1201 Maryland Ave. SW, Ste. 900 Washington, DC 20024. Phone: 800-255-3304 or (202)962-9200 Fax: (202)962-9201 E-mail: info@bio.org • URL: http://www.bio.org • Represents biotechnology companies, academic institutions, state biotechnology centers and related organizations in all 50 U.S. states and 33 other nations. Members are involved in the research and development of healthcare, agricultural, industrial and environmental biotechnology products.

Biotechnology Instrumentation. Available from MarketResearch.com, 641 Ave. of the Americas, Fourth Floor New York, NY 10011. Phone: 800-298-5699 or (212)807-2629 Fax: (212)807-2642 E-mail: order@marketresearch.com • URL: http://www.marketresearch.com • 2002. $3,950.00. Published by Global Industry Analysts. Provides worldwide market research data, including profiles of major biotech instrument companies.

Biotechnology Process Engineering Center., Massachusetts Institute of Technology, 77 Massachusetts Ave., Bldg. 16, Rm. 429 Cambridge, MA 02139-4480. Phone: (617)253-0805 Fax: (617)253-2400 E-mail: lauffen@mit.edu • URL: http://www.web.mit.edu/bpec/ • Includes an Industrial Advisory Board and a Biotechnology Industrial Consortium.

BioWorld Today: The Daily Biotechnology Newspaper. American Health Consultants, Inc., BioWorld Publishing Group, 3525 Piedmont Rd., NE, Bldg. 6, Ste. 400 Atlanta, GA 30305. Phone: 800-688-2421 or (404)262-7436 Fax: 800-284-3291 or (404)262-7837 E-mail: custserv@ahcpub.com • URL: http://www.ahcpub.com • Daily. $1,897.00 per year; with online edition, $1,927.00 per year. Covers news of the biotechnology and genetic engineering industries, with emphasis on finance, investments, and marketing.

BioWorld Week: The Weekly Biotechnology Report. American Health Consultants, Inc., BioWorld Publishing Group, 3525 Piedmont Rd., N.E., Bldg. 6, Suite 400 Atlanta, GA 30305-5278. Phone: 800-688-2421 or (404)262-7436 Fax: 800-284-3291 or (404)262-7837 E-mail: custserv@ahcpub.com • URL: http://www.achpub.com • Weekly. $789.00 per year. Newsletter. Provides a weekly summary of business and financial news relating to the biotechnology and genetic engineering industries.

Biscuit and Cracker Distributors Association., 5024 Campbell Blvd., Ste. R Baltimore, MD 21236. Phone: (312)644-6610 Members are distributors and manufacturers of cookies, crackers, and related products.

Biscuit and Cracker Manufacturers Association., 8484 Georgia Ave., Suite 700 Silver Spring, MD 20910. Phone: (301)608-1552 Fax: (301)608-1557 E-mail: frooney@thebcma.org • URL: http://www.thebcma.org • Members are bakers of crackers and cookies. Formerly Biscuit Bakers Institute.

Bitter Java. Bruce A. Tate. Manning Publications Co., 209 Bruce Park Ave. Greenwich, CT 06830. Phone: 800-247-6553 or (203)629-2211 Fax: (203)661-9018 E-mail: orders@manning.com • URL: http://www.manning.com • 2002. $44.95. A guide that describes common errors in Java programming.

The Biz: The Basic Business, Legal, and Financial Aspects of the Film Industry. Schuyler M. Moore. Silman-James Press, 3624 Shannon Rd. Los Angeles, CA 90027. Phone: (323)661-9922 Fax: (323)661-9933 E-mail: silmanjamespress@earthlink.com • URL: http://www.silmanjamespress.com • 2000. $26.95. Provides information for independent filmmakers on raising money, business structure, budgeting, loans, legalities, taxation, industry jargon, and other topics. The author is an entertainment industry lawyer.

Black and White Photography: A Basic Manual. Henry Horenstein. Little, Brown and Co., Time and Life Bldg., 1271 Ave. of the Americas New York, NY 10020. Phone: 800-343-9204 or (212)522-8700 Fax: 800-286-9741 or (212)522-2067 E-mail: cust.service@littlebrown.com • URL: http://www.littlebrown.com • 1983. $24.95. Second revised edition.

Black Caucus of the American Library Association.

Black Enterprise. Earl G. Graves Publishing Co., 130 5th Ave., 10th Fl. New York, NY 10011-4399. Phone: 800-727-7777 or (212)242-8000 Fax: (212)886-9610 E-mail: customerservice@blackenterprise.com • URL: http://www.blackenterprise.com • Monthly. $17.95 per year. Covers careers, personal finances and leisure.

Black Enterprise: Top Black Businesses. Earl G. Graves Publishing Co., 130 Fifth Ave., 10th Fl. New York, NY 10011. Phone: 800-727-7777 or (212)242-8000 Fax: (212)886-9600 E-mail: customerservice@blackenterprise.com • URL: http://www.blackenterprise.com • Annual. $3.95. Lists of 100 black-owned businesses, banks, savings and loan associations, and insurance companies.

Black Tie Optional: The Ultimate Guide to Planning and Producing Successful Special Events. Harry A. Freedman and Karen F. Smith. Fund Raising Institute, 27500 Drake Rd. Farmington Hills, MI 48331-3535. Phone: 800-877-8238 or (248)699-GALE Fax: 800-414-5043 or (248)699-8069 E-mail: galeord@gale.com • URL: http://www.galegroup.com • 1994. $35.00. Includes checklists, flow charts, and worksheets.

Black's Law Dictionary. Thomas Black, editor. Kluwer Law International, 1185 Ave. of the Americas New York, NY 10036. Phone: (212)597-0200 Fax: (212)597-0338 • URL: http://www.kluwerlaw.com • 2001. $147.00. Seventh edition. Definitions of the terms and phrases of American and English jurisprudence, ancient and modern.

Black's Law Dictionary. Bryan A. Garner, editor. West Group, 610 Opperman Dr. Eagan, MN 55123. Phone: 800-328-4880 or (651)687-7000 Fax: 800-340-9378 E-mail: bookstore@westgroup.com • URL: http://www.westgroup.com • 1999. $59.95. Seventh edition. Contains a total of 30,000 legal definitions, including 4,500 new terms, 2,200 legal maxims, and 2,000 illustrative quotations from scholarly works.

Blackwell Encyclopedic Dictionary of Accounting. Rashad Abdel-khalik. Blackwell Publishing, 350 Main St. Malden, MA 02148. Phone: 800-835-6770 or (781)388-8200 Fax: 800-864-7626 or (781)388-8210 E-mail: books@blackwellpub.com • URL: http://www.blackwellpub.com • 1997. $38.95. The editor is associated with the University of Florida. Contains definitions of key terms combined with longer articles written by various U. S. and foreign business educators. Includes bibliographies and index. (Blackwell Encyclopedia of Management Series).

Blackwell Encyclopedic Dictionary of Business Ethics. Patricia H. Werhane and R. Edward Freeman. Blackwell Publishing, 350 Main St. Malden, MA 02148. Phone: 800-216-2522 or (781)388-8200 Fax: 800-864-7626 or (781)388-8210 E-mail: books@blackwellpub.com • URL: http://www.blackwellpub.com • 1997. $38.95. The editors are associated with the University of Virginia. Contains definitions of key terms combined with longer articles written by various U. S. and foreign business educators. Includes bibliographies and index. (Blackwell Encyclopedia of Management Series).

Blackwell Encyclopedic Dictionary of Finance. Dean Paxson and Douglas Wood, editors. Blackwell Publishing, 350 Main St. Malden, MA 02148. Phone: 800-216-2522 or (781)388-8200 Fax: 800-864-7626 or (781)388-8210 E-mail: books@blackwellpub.com • URL: http://www.blackwellpub.com • 1997. $110.00. The editors are associated with the University of Manchester. Contains definitions of key terms combined with longer articles written by various U. S. and foreign business educators. Includes bibliographies and index. (Blackwell Encyclopedia of Management Series).

Blackwell Encyclopedic Dictionary of International Management. John J. O'Connell, editor. Blackwell Publishers, 350 Main St. Malden, MA 02148. Phone: 800-216-2522 or (781)388-8200 Fax: 800-864-7626 or (781)388-8210 E-mail: books@blackwellpub.com • URL: http://www.blackwellpub.com • 1999. $130.95. The editor is associated with the American Graduate School of International Management. Contains definitions of key terms combined with longer articles written by various U. S. and foreign business educators. Includes bibliographies and index. (Encyclopedia of Management Series).

Blackwell Encyclopedic Dictionary of Management of Information Systems. Gordon B. Davis, editor. Blackwell Publishers, 350 Main St. Malden, MA 02148. Phone: 800-216-2522 or (781)388-8200 Fax: 800-864-7626 or (781)388-8210 E-mail: books@blackwellpub.com • URL: http://www.blackwellpub.com • 1999. $38.95. The editor is associated with the University of Minnesota. Contains definitions of key terms combined with longer articles written by various U. S. and foreign business educators. Includes bibliographies and index. (Blackwell Encyclopedia of Management Series).

Blackwell Encyclopedic Dictionary of Managerial Economics. Robert McAuliffe, editor. Blackwell Publishers, 350 Main St. Malden, MA 02148. Phone: 800-216-2522 or (781)388-8200 Fax: 800-864-7626 or (781)388-8210 E-mail: books@blackwellpub.com • URL: http://www.blackwellpub.com • 1999. $138.95. The editor is associated with Boston College. Contains definitions of key terms combined with longer articles written by various U. S. and foreign business educators. Includes bibliographies and index. *Blackwell Encyclopedia of Management Series*.

Blackwell Encyclopedic Dictionary of Marketing. Dale Littler and Barbara R. Lewis, editors. Blackwell Publishers, 350 Main St. Malden, MA 02148. Phone: 800-216-2522 or (781)388-8200 Fax: 800-864-7626 or (781)388-8210 E-mail: books@blackwellpub.com • URL: http://www.blackwellpub.com • 1997. $38.95. The editors are associated with the Manchester School of Management. Contains definitions of key terms combined with longer articles written by various U. S. and foreign business educators. Includes bibliographies and index. (Blackwell Encyclopedia of Management Series.)

Blackwell Encyclopedic Dictionary of Operations Management. Nigel Slack, editor. Blackwell Publishing, 350 Main St. Malden, MA 02148. Phone: 800-216-2522 or (781)388-8200 Fax: 800-864-7626 or (781)388-8210 E-mail: books@blackwellpub.com • URL: http://www.blackwellpub.com • 1997. $130.95. The editor is associated with the University of Warwick, England. Contains definitions of key terms combined with longer articles written by various U. S. and foreign business educators. Includes bibliographies and index. (Blackwell Encyclopedia of Management Series.)

Blackwell Encyclopedic Dictionary of Organizational Behavior. Nigel Nicholson, editor. Blackwell Publishing, 350 Main St. Malden, MA 02148. Phone: 800-216-2522 or (781)388-8200 Fax: 800-864-7626 or (781)388-8210 E-mail: books@blackwellpub.com • URL: http://www.blackwellpub.com • 1997. $130.95. The editor is associated with the London Business School. Contains definitions of key terms combined with longer articles written by various U. S. and foreign business educators. Includes bibliographies and index. *Blackwell Encyclopedia of Management Series*.

Blackwell Encyclopedic Dictionary of Strategic Management. Derek F. Channon, editor. Blackwell Publishing, 350 Main St. Malden, MA 02148. Phone: 800-216-2522 or (781)388-8200 Fax: 800-864-7626 or (781)388-8210 E-mail: books@blackwellpub.com • URL: http://www.blackwellpub.com • 1997. $128.95. The editor is associated with Imperial College, London. Contains definitions of key terms combined with longer articles written by various U. S. and foreign business educators. Includes bibliographies and index. (Blackwell Encyclopedia of Management Series.)

Bloomberg Markets. Bloomberg, 499 Park Ave. New York, NY 10022. Phone: 800-388-2749 or (212)318-2000 Fax: (917)369-5000 • URL: http://www.bloomberg.com • Monthly. Free to qualified personnel. Edited for securities dealers and investment managers.

BLR Encyclopedia of Prewritten Job Descriptions. Stephen D. Bruce. Business and Legal Reports, Inc., 141 Mill Rock Rd., E Old Saybrook, CT 06475. Phone: 800-454-0404 • URL: http://www.blr.com • $159.95. Looseleaf service. Two volumes. Covers all levels "from president to mail clerk."

Blue Book of Building and Construction. Contractors Register, Inc., Jefferson Valley, NY 10535. Phone: 800-431-2584 or (914)245-0200 Fax: (914)245-0287 E-mail: info@thebluebook.com • URL: http://www.thebluebook.com • Annual. Controlled circulation. 15 regional editions. Lists architects, contractors, subcontractors, manufacturers and suppliers of constructions materials and equipment.

Blue Book of Commercial Collection. International Association of Commercial Collectors, 4040 W. 70th St. Minneapolis, MN 55435. Phone: (952)925-0760 Fax: (952)926-1624 E-mail: iacc@collector.com • URL: http://www.commercialcollector.com • Annual. Membership.

Blue Book of Fur Farming., PO Box 655 Hopkins, MN 55343-0655. Phone: (952)949-2159 Fax: (952)934-3668 E-mail: seedtrade@seetrade.com Annual. $20.00. Lists manufacturers and suppliers of equipment and materials used in the raising of fur-bearing animals for the fur industry.

Blue Book of Stock Reports. MPL Communications Inc., 133 Richmond St., W., Suite 700 Toronto, ON, Canada M5H 3M8. Phone: (416)869-1177 Fax: (416)869-0456 Biweekly. $260.00 per year. Canadian Business Service reports on over 250 Canadian companies.

Blue Chip Economic Indicators: What Top Economists Are Saying About the U.S. Outlook for the Year Ahead. Aspen Publishers, Inc., 1185 Ave. of the Americas New York, NY 10036. Phone: 800-234-1660 or (212)597-0200 Fax: (212)597-0338 E-mail: customer.service@aspenpubl.com • URL: http://www.aspenpub.com • Monthly. $665.00 per year. Newsletter containing U. S. economic consensus forecasts.

Blue Chip Financial Forecasts: What Top Analysts are Saying About U. S. and Foreign Interest Rates, Monetary Policy, Inflation, and Economic Growth. Aspen Publishers, Inc., 1185 Ave. of the Americas New York, NY 10036. Phone: 800-234-1660 or (212)597-0200 Fax: (212)597-0338 E-mail: customer.service@aspenpubl.com • URL: http://www.aspenpublishers.com • Monthly. $665.00 per year. Newsletter. Gives forecasts about a year in advance for interest rates, inflation, currency exchange rates, monetary policy, and economic growth rates.

Blue Cross and Blue Shield Association.

Blue List of Current Municipal and Corporate Offerings. Standard and Poor's, 55 Water St. New York, NY 10041. Phone: 800-221-5277 or (212)438-1000 Fax: (212)438-4368 E-mail: clientsupport@standardandpoors.com • URL: http://www.standardandpoors.com • Daily. $940.00 per year. Compendium of municipal and corporate bond offers.

Blue Sky Law Reports. Joseph C. Long. CCH Inc., 2700 Lake Cook Rd. Riverwoods, MN 60015. Phone: 800-449-6435 or (847)267-7000 Fax: (773)886-3895 • URL: http://www.cch.com • Loosleaf service. $1,130.00 per year. Periodic supplementation. Semimonthly updates.

Blue Sky Regulation. LexisNexis Matthew Bender, 1275 Broadway Albany, NY 12204. Phone: 800-424-4200 or (518)487-3000 Fax: (518)487-3584 E-mail: bookstore.support@lexisnexis.com • URL: http://www.bender.com • $1,089.00. Four looseleaf volumes. Periodic supplementation. Covers state securities laws and regulations.

Blueprint for Franchising a Business. Steven S. Raab and Gregory Matusky. John Wiley and Sons, Inc., 111 River St. Hoboken, NJ 07030. Phone: 800-225-5945 or (201)748-6000 Fax: (201)748-6088 E-mail: info@wiley.com • URL: http://www.wiley.com • 1987. $45.00.

BMI: Music World. Broadcast Music, Inc., 320 W. 57th St. New

York, NY 10019. Phone: (212)586-2000 Quarterly. Free to qualified personnel. Formerly *BMI: The Many Worlds of Music*.

BNA Fair Employment Practices. BNA, Inc., 1231 25th St., N.W. Washington, DC 20037. Phone: 800-372-1033 E-mail: customercare@bna.com • URL: http://www.bna.com • Biweekly. $938.00 per year. Looseleaf service.

BNA Pension and Benefits Reporter. BNA, Inc., 1231 25th St., NW Washington, DC 20037. Phone: 800-372-1033 E-mail: customercare@bna.com • URL: http://www.bna.com • Weekly. $996.00 per year. Three looseleaf volumes. Legal developments affecting pensions. Formerly *BNA Pension Reporter*.

BNA Policy and Practice Series. BNA, Inc., 1231 25th St., NW Washington, DC 20037. Phone: 800-371-1033 E-mail: customercare@bna.com • URL: http://www.bna.com • Weekly. $1,965.00 per year. Three looseleaf volumes. Includes personnel management, labor relations, fair employment practice, compensation, and wage-hour laws.

BNA Policy and Practice Series: Compensation. BNA, Inc., 1231 25th St., NW Washington, DC 20037. Phone: 800-372-1033 E-mail: customercare@bna.com • URL: http://www.bna.com • Weekly. $938.00 per year.

BNA Policy and Practice Series: Wages and Hours. BNA, Inc., 1231 25th St., N.W. Washington, DC 20037. Phone: 800-372-1033 E-mail: customercare@bna.com • URL: http://www.bna.com • Weekly. $938.00 per year. Looseleaf service.

BNA's Banking Report: Legal and Regulatory Developments in the Financial Services Industry. BNA, Inc., 1231 25th St., NW Washington, DC 20037. Phone: 800-372-1033 E-mail: customercare@bna.com • URL: http://www.bna.com • Weekly. $1,221.00 per year. Two looseleaf volumes. Emphasis on federal regulations.

BNA's Patent, Trademark and Copyright Journal. BNA, Inc., 1231 25th St., N.W. Washington, DC 20037. Phone: 800-372-1033 E-mail: customercare@bna.com • URL: http://www.bna.com • Weekly. $1,495.00 per year. Looseleaf service.

BNA's SafetyNet. Bureau of National Affairs Inc., 1801 S Bell St. Arlington, VA 22202. Phone: 800-372-1033 or (202)452-4200 Fax: (202)452-4226 E-mail: customercare@bna.com • URL: http://www.bna.com • Description: Designed to help employers deal with occupational safety and health regulations, policies, standards, and practices, and to understand the effects of compliance on employee relations. Covers the establishment, management, evaluation, maintenance, and administration of health and safety programs. Carries information on recordkeeping, inspections, enforcement, employer defenses, and training.

BNA's Workers' Compensation Report. BNA, Inc., 1231 25th St., NW Washington, DC 20037. Phone: 800-372-1033 E-mail: customercare@bna.com • URL: http://www.bna.com • Biweekly. $604.00 per year. Looseleaf business and legal service.

Board Member: The Periodical for Members of the National Center for Nonprofit Boards. BoardSource, 1828 L St., NW, Ste. 900 Washington, DC 20036-5114. Phone: 800-883-6262 or (202)452-6262 Fax: (202)452-6299 • URL: http://www.boardsource.org • 10 times a year. Membership. Newsletter for trustees of nonprofit organizations.

Board of Certified Product Safety Management., 8009 Carita Court Bethesda, MD 20817. Phone: (301)469-0648 E-mail: info@chcm-chsp.org • URL: http://www.chcm.chsp.org • Evaluates qualifications of product safety managers. Formerly International Product Safety Management Certification Board.

Board of Immigration Appeals Interim Decisions. U.S. Immigration and Naturalization Service. Available from U.S. Government Printing Office, Washington, DC 20402. Phone: (202)512-1800 Fax: (202)512-2250 E-mail: gpoaccess@gpo.gov • URL: http://www.access.gpo.gov • Irregular.

Board of Research., Babson College, 204 Babson Babson Park, MA 02457-0310. Phone: (718)239-5339 Fax: (718)239-6416 E-mail: chern@babson.edu • URL: http://www.babson.edu/bor • Research areas include management, entrepreneurial characteristics, and multi-product inventory analysis.

Board of Trade of the Wholesale Seafood Merchants.

Boardwatch: Analysis of Telecom Software, Services and Strategy. Light Reading, Inc., 23 Leonard St. New York, NY 10013. Phone: (212)925-0020 • URL: http://www.boardwatch.com • Monthly. $72.00 per year. Covers World Wide Web publishing, internet technology, educational aspects of online communication, internet legalities, and other computer communication topics.

Boat and Motor Dealer. Preston Publications, Inc., 6600 W Touby Ave. Niles, IL 60714. Phone: (847)647-2900 Fax: (847)647-1155 E-mail: circulation@boatmotordealer.com • URL: http://www.prestonpub.com • 11 times a year. $48.00. Boat retailing.

Boat Owners Association of the United States., 880 S. Pickett St. Alexandria, VA 22304. Phone: 800-990-9825 or (703)823-9550 Fax: (703)461-2847 E-mail: mail@boatus.com • URL: http://www.boatus.com • Absorbed American Yachtmen's Association.

Boating. Hachette Filipacchi Media U.S., Inc., 1633 Broadway New York, NY 10019. Phone: 800-289-0399 or (212)767-4823 Fax: (212)767-4831 • URL: http://www.hfmmag.com • Monthly. $28.00 per year.

Boating Industry Buyers Guide and Directory. Ehlert Publishing Group, 6420 Sycamore Ln., Ste. 100 Maple Grove, MN 55369. Phone: (763)383-4448 Fax: (763)383-4499 E-mail: mgruhn@affinitygroup.com • URL: http://www.boatbiz.com • Monthly. $38.00 per year.

Body Fashions/Intimate Apparel Buyer's Guide. Advanstar Communications, 641 Lexington Ave., 8th Fl., 8th Fl. New York, NY 10022. Phone: 800-225-4569 or (212)951-6600 Fax: (212)951-6793 E-mail: info@advanstar.com • URL: http://www.advanstar.com • Publication includes: List of suppliers and manufacturers within the intimate apparel and hosiery industry. Entries include: Company name, address, phone.

Bogle on Mutual Funds: New Perspectives for the Intelligent Investor. John C. Bogle. McGraw-Hill, 1221 Ave. of the Americas New York, NY 10020. Phone: 800-722-4726 or (212)512-2000 Fax: (212)512-4502 E-mail: customer.service@mcgraw-hill.com • URL: http://www.mcgraw-hill.com • 1993. $25.00.

The Bond and Money Markets: Strategy, Trading, Analysis. Moorad Choudhry. Elsevier Butterworth Heinemann, 200 Wheeler Rd., Sixth Floor Burlington, MA 01803. Phone: 800-545-2522 or (781)221-2212 Fax: 800-568-5136 or (781)313-4880 E-mail: usbkinfo@elsevier.com • URL: http://www.books.elsevier.com/finance • 2003. $115.00. Serves as a reference work on corporate bonds, government bonds, currency markets, interest-rate futures, convertible securities, various kinds of derivatives, and technical analysis of financial securities.

The Bond Buyer. Veronis, Suhler and Associates Inc., One State St. Plz. New York, NY 10004. Phone: 800-935-4990 or (212)967-7000 Fax: (212)381-8166 • URL: http://www.bondbuyer.com • Daily edition, $1,897 per year. Weekly edition, $525.00 per year. Reports on new municipal bond issues.

Bond Market Association., 360 Madison Ave. New York, NY 10017-7111. Phone: (646)637-9200 Fax: (646)637-9126 E-mail: membership@bondmarkets.com • URL: http://www.bondmarkets.com • Represents securities firms and banks that underwrite, trade and sell debt securities, both domestically and internationally.

Bond Markets: Analysis and Stratgies. Frank J. Fabozzi. Prentice Hall PTR, 240 Frisch Ct. Paramus, NJ 07652. Phone: 800-282-0693 Fax: 800-445-6991 • URL: http://www.phptr.com • 1999. $115.00. Fourth edition.

Bond's Franchise Guide. Todd Publications, PO Box 500 Millwood, NY 10546. Phone: (866)896-0916 or (914)373-4750 Fax: (914)373-4750 E-mail: toddpub@aol.com • URL: http://www.toddpublications.com • Covers: 2,000 American and 500 Canadian franchisers divided into 54 business categories. Entries include: Company name, address, phone, fax, names and titles of key personnel for 1,500 franchise operations; for all entries: Company history, size, geographic distribution, financial requirements, staff, start-up assistance and training provided, ongoing royalty fees and franchiser services, and more.

Bondtalk.com: Live Talk & Analysis on the Bond Market & the Economy. Miller Tabak & Co., LLCPhone: (212)370-0040 E-mail: acrescenzi@bondtalk.com • URL: http://www.bondtalk.com • Web site provides extensive, free data on the fixed income securities market, including individual bond prices, yields, interest rates, Federal Reserve information, charts, bond market news, and economic analysis. Also offered on a fee basis is "Bondtalkpro.com: The New and Enhanced Service for Market Professionals."

Bondweek: The Newsweekly of Fixed Income and Credit Markets. Institutional Investor, Inc., Journals Group, 225 Park Ave., S New York, NY 10003. Phone: 800-945-2034 or (212)224-3066 Fax: (212)224-3472 E-mail: info@iijournals.com • URL: http://www.iijournals.com • Weekly. $2,425.00 per year. Newsletter. Includes print and online editions. Covers taxable, fixed-income securities for professional investors, including corporate, government, foreign, mortgage, and high-yield.

Book Auction Records. RoweCom UK Ltd., Cannon House, Park Farm Rd. Folkestone CT19 5EE, United Kingdom. Phone: 44 1303 850101 Fax: 44 1303 850440 • URL: http://www.dawson.co.uk • Annual. $150.00.

Book Collecting: A Comprehensive Guide. Allen Ahearn and Patricia Ahearn. Penguin Group, 375 Hudson St. New York, NY 10014. Phone: 800-788-6262 or (212)256-0017 Fax: 800-227-9604 or (212)366-2666 E-mail: online@penguinputnam.com • URL: http://www.penguinputnam.com • 2000. $45.00. Revised edition.

Book Industry Study Group., 370 Lexington Ave., Ste. 900 New York, NY 10017. Phone: (646)336-7141 Fax: (646)336-6214 E-mail: info@bisg.org • URL: http://www.bisg.org • Represents publishers, manufacturers, suppliers, wholesalers, retailers, librarians, and other engaged in the business of print and electronic media.

Book Industry Trends. Book Industry Study Group, Inc., 19 W 21st St., Ste. 905 New York, NY 10010-7000. Phone: (646)336-7141 Fax: (646)336-6214 E-mail: info@bisg.org • URL: http://www.bisg.org • Annual. $750.00.

Book Manufacturers' Institute., Two Armand Beach Dr., Ste. 1B Palm Coast, FL 32137-2612. Phone: (386)986-4552 Fax: (386)986-4553 E-mail: info@bmibook.com • URL: http://www.bmibook.com • Represents the trade association for manufacturers of books.

Book Marketing Update. Open Horizons, 328 State Rd. 240, PO Box 2887 Taos, NM 87571. Phone: 800-796-6130 or (505)751-3398 Fax: (505)751-3100 E-mail: info@bookmarket.com • URL: http://www.bookmarket.com • Description: Surveys resources for publishers interested in marketing their books to bookstores, libraries, wholesalers, catalogs, book clubs, and other special markets.

Book of ASTM Standards. ASTM, 100 Barr Harbor Dr. West Conshohocken, PA 19428. Phone: (610)832-9585 Fax: (610)832-9555 E-mail: service@astm.org • URL: http://www.astm.org • Annual. Price on application.

The Book of Coffee and Tea: A Guide to the Appreciation of Fine Coffees, Teas and Herbal Beverages. Joel Schapira and others. Saint Martin's Press, 175 Fifth Ave. New York, NY 10010. Phone: (212)726-0200 Fax: 800-672-2054 or (212)674-5151 E-mail: enquiries@stmartins.com • URL: http://www.stmartins.com • 1996. $14.95. Second revised edition.

Book of the States. Council of State Governments, 2760 Research Park Dr. Lexington, KY 40578. Phone: 800-800-1910 or (859)244-8000 Fax: (859)244-8001 E-mail: sales@csg.org • URL: http://www.csg.com • Biennial. $99.00. Includes information on state constitutions, state-by-state voting in recent elections, data on state finances, and federal-state survey articles.

Book Publishing Report: Weekly News and Analysis of Events Shaping the Book Industry. SIMBA Information, 11 Riverbend Dr., S Stamford, CT 06907-0234. Phone: 800-307-2529 or (203)358-4100 Fax: (203)358-5824 E-mail: info@simbanet.com • URL: http://www.simbanet.com • 50 times a year. $549.00 per year. Newsletter. Covers book publishing mergers, marketing, finance, personnel, and trends in general. Formerly *BP Report on the Business of Book Publishing*.

Book Repair: A How-To-Do-It Manual for Librarians. Kenneth Lavender. Neal-Schuman Publishers, Inc., 100 William St., Ste. 2004 New York, NY 10038. Phone: (866)672-6657 or (212)925-8650 Fax: (866)209-7932 or (212)219-8916 E-mail: info@neal-schuman.com • URL: http://www.neal-schuman.com • 2001. $49.95. Second edition. Covers basic book repair and conservation techniques. (How-to-Do-It Manuals Series).

Book Review Digest: An Index to Reviews of Current Books. H. W. Wilson Co., 950 University Ave. Bronx, NY 10452. Phone: 800-367-6770 or (718)588-8400 Fax: 800-590-1617 or (718)590-1617 E-mail: custserv@hwwilson.com • URL: http://www.hwwilson.com • 10 times a year. Quarterly and annual cumulation. Price varies.

Book Review Index. Gale Cengage Learning, 27500 Drake Rd. Farmington Hills, MI 48331-3535. Phone: 800-877-GALE or (248)699-GALE Fax: 800-414-5043 E-mail: gale.galeord@cengage.com • URL: http://gale.cengage.com • Annual. $310.00. Three yearly issues. An index to reviews appearing in hundreds of periodicals. Back volumes available.

Book Review Index [Online]. Gale Cengage Learning, 27500 Drake Rd. Farmington Hills, MI 48331-3535. Phone: 800-877-GALE or (248)699-GALE Fax: 800-414-5043 E-mail: galeord@gale.com • URL: http://gale.cengage.com • Cites reviews of books and periodicals in journals, 1969 to present. Inquire as to online cost and availability.

Bookkeeping Service. Entrepreneur Media, Inc., 2445 McCabe Way Irvine, CA 92614. Phone: 800-421-2300 or (949)261-2325 Fax: (949)261-0234 E-mail: entmag@entrepreneur.com • URL: http://www.entrepreneur.com • Looseleaf. $59.50. A practical guide to starting a computer-oriented bookkeeping business. Covers profit potential, start-up costs, market size evaluation, pricing, accounting, advertising, promotion, etc. (Start-Up Business Guide No. E2335.)

Booklist. American Library Association, 50 E. Huron St. Chicago, IL 60611-2795. Phone: 800-545-2433 or (312)944-6780 Fax: (312)440-9374 E-mail: ala@ala.org • URL: http://www.ala.org • 22 times a year. $79.95. Reviews library materials for school and public libraries. Incorporates *Reference Books Bulletin*.

Bookman's Price Index. Gale Cengage Learning, 27500 Drake Rd. Farmington Hills, MI 48331-3535. Phone: 800-877-GALE or (248)699-GALE Fax: 800-414-5043 E-mail: gale.galeord@cengage.com • URL: http://gale.cengage.com • Annual. 71 volumes in print. $375.00 per volume. Price guide to out more than 17,000 out-of-print and rare books.

Books and Periodicals Online: The Guide to Business and Legal Information on Databases and CD-ROM's. Nuchine Nobari, editor. Library Technology Alliance, Ltd., 264 Lexington Ave., Rm. 4C New York, NY 10016-4182. Phone: (212)686-8816 Fax: (212)686-8778 E-mail: info@booksandperiodicals.com • URL: http://www.booksandperiodicals.com • Annual. $379.00. Two volumes. 119,000 periodicals available as part of online and CD-ROM databases; international coverage.

Books in Print. R. R. Bowker, 630 Central Ave. New Providence, NJ 07974. Phone: 888-269-5372 Fax: (908)219-0098 E-mail: info@bowker.com • URL: http://www.bowker.com • Annual. $769.00. Eight volumes.

Books in Print On Disc: The Complete Books in Print System on Compact Laser Disc. Bowker Electronic Publishing, 630 Central Ave. New Providence, NJ 07974. Phone: 888-269-5372 or (908)464-6800 Fax: (908)665-3528 Monthly. $550.00 per year. The CD-ROM version of *Books in Print*, *Forthcoming Books*, and other Bowker bibliographic publications: lists the books of over 50,000 U.S. publishers. Includes books recently declared out-of-print. Also available with full text book reviews.

Books in Print Online. Bowker Electronic Publishing, 630

Central Ave. New Providence, NJ 07974. Phone: 888-269-5372 or (908)464-6800 Fax: (908)665-3528 The online version of *Books in Print*, *Forthcoming Books*, *Paperbound Books in Print*, and other Bowker bibliographic publications: lists the books of over 50,000 U. S. publishers. Includes books recently declared out-of-print. Updated monthly. Inquire as to online cost and availability.

Books in Print with Book Reviews On Disc. Bowker Electronic Publishing, 630 Central Ave. New Providence, NJ 07974. Phone: 888-269-5372 or (908)464-6800 Fax: (908)665-3528 Monthly. $2,075 per year. The CD-ROM version of *Books in Print*, *Forthcoming Books*,and other Bowker bibliographic publications, with the addition of full text book reviews from *Publishers Weekly*, *Library Journal*, *Booklist*, *Choice*, and other periodicals.

The Bookseller: The Organ of the Book Trade. J. Whitaker and Sons, Ltd., VNU Entertainment Media, Victory House, Southampton Row London WC1B 4AD, United Kingdom. Phone: 44 20 7271 0100 E-mail: info@competition-commission.qsi.gov.uk • URL: http://www.competition-commission.org • Weekly. $160.00 per year. Provides international book trade news.

Bookselling This Week. American Booksellers Association, 200 White Plains Rd., Ste. 600 Tarrytown, NY 10591. Phone: 800-637-0037 or (914)591-2665 Fax: (914)591-2720 E-mail: info@bookweb.org • URL: http://www.bookweb.org • Description: Contains information on book selling.

BookWeb. American Booksellers AssociationPhone: 800-637-0037 or (914)591-2665 Fax: (914)591-2720 E-mail: info@bookweb.org • URL: http://www.bookweb.org/bookstores • Web site provides descriptions of more than 4,500 independent bookstores, searchable by name, specialty, or zip code. Fees: Free.

Border Belt Tobacco Research Station.

The Botanical Review: Interpreting Botanical Progress. Society for Economic Botany. The New York Botanical Garden Press, Bronx, NY 10458-5126. Phone: (718)817-8721 Fax: (718)817-8842 E-mail: nygbpress@nygb.org • URL: http://www.nybg.org • Quarterly. Individuals, $82.00 per year; institutions, $96.00 per year. Reviews articles in all fields of botany.

Botanical Society of America.

The Bottom Line: Managing Library Finances. Emerald, 44 Brattle St., 4th Fl. Cambridge, MA 02138. Phone: 888-622-0075 or (617)497-2175 Fax: (617)354-6875 E-mail: jhwalther@bryancave.com Quarterly. $1,039.00 per year. Provides articles on the financial management of libraries: budgeting, funding, cost analysis, etc.

Bottom Line/Personal. Boardroom Inc., 281 Tresser Blvd., 8th Fl. Stamford, CT 06901-3246. Phone: 800-274-5611 or (203)973-5900 Fax: (203)967-3086 E-mail: info@bookweb.org • URL: http://www.boardroom.com • Description: Publishes "expert advice on how to live longer, better, richer, and wiser." Covers topical issues with a personal slant aimed at helping those involved with careers handle their personal lives more successfully. Features articles on tax issues, money information, traveling, family, friends, and general health and happiness. Contains informational items throughout on various aspects of business/personal life.

Bottomline. Hospitality Financial and Technology Professionals, 11709 Boulder Lane, Suite 110 Austin, TX 78726-1832. Phone: (512)249-5333 Fax: (512)249-1533 E-mail: hftp@hftp.org • URL: http://www.hftp.org • Bimonthly. Free to members, educational institutions and libraries; nonmembers, $50.00 per year. Contains articles on accounting, finance, information technology, and management for hotels, resorts, casinos, clubs, and other hospitality businesses.

The Bowker Annual: Library and Book Trade Almanac. Information Today, Inc., 143 Old Marlton Pike Medford, NJ 08055-8750. Phone: 800-300-9868 or (609)654-6266 Fax: (609)654-4309 E-mail: custserv@infotoday.com • URL: http://www.infotoday.com • Annual. $199.00. Reviews key trends and events and provides basic statistical information. Includes financial averages: library expenditures, salaries, and book prices. Contains lists of "best books, literary prizes, winners, and bestsellers." Formerly published by R. R. Bowker.

Bowker/Whitaker Global Books in Print On Disc. R. R. Bowker, 630 Central Ave. New Providence, NJ 07974. Phone: 888-269-5372 or (908)464-6800 Fax: (908)665-3528 Monthly. $2,055.00 per year. Provides CD-ROM listing of English language books published throughout the world, including U. S., U. K., Canada, and Australia. Combines data from R. R. Bowker's *Books in Print Plus* and J. Whitaker & Sons Ltd.'s *Bookbank*. Includes more than two million titles.

Bowker's Complete Video Directory on Disc. Bowker Electronic Publishing, 630 Central Ave. New Providence, NJ 07974. Phone: 888-269-5372 or (908)464-6800 Fax: (908)665-3528 Quarterly. $520.00 per year. An extensive CD-ROM directory of video tapes and laserdisks. Includes film reviews from *Variety*.

Boxoffice: The Business Magazine of the Global Motion Picture Industry. RLD Communication, 6640 Sunset Blvd., Ste. 100 Hollywood, CA 90028. Phone: (213)465-1186 Monthly. $40.00 per year. Provides national and local news about theater management and operations, industry trends about film production and distribution.

BPA International., 2 Corporate Dr., Ste. 900 Shelton, CT 06484. Phone: (203)447-2800 Fax: (203)447-2900 E-mail: info@

bpai.com • URL: http://www.bpai.com • Verifies business and consumer periodical circulation statements. Includes a Circulation Managers Committee. Formerly Business Publications Audit of Circulation.

Bradford's International Directory of Marketing Research Agencies. Business Research Services, Inc., 4201 Connecticut Ave., N.W., Suite 610 Washington, DC 20008. Phone: 800-845-8420 or (202)364-6973 Fax: (202)686-3228 E-mail: brspubs@sba8a.com Annual. $95.00. Over 1,700 marketing research agencies and management consultants in market research. Formerly *Bradford's Directory of Marketing Research of the United States and the World*.

Bradley Policy Research Center., University of Rochester, William E. Simon Graduate School of Business Administration Rochester, NY 14627. Phone: (585)275-2668 Fax: (585)275-0095 E-mail: hansen@simon.rochester.edu • URL: http://www.ssb.rochester.edu • Corporate control and corporate takeovers are among the research areas covered.

Brake and Frontend: The Complete Undercar Service Magazine. Babcox, 3550 Embassy Pky. Akron, OH 44333. Phone: (330)670-1234 Fax: (330)670-0874 E-mail: tfritz@babcox.com • URL: http://www.babcox.com • Monthly. $64.00 per year.

Brandeis Law Journal. University of Louisville Louis D. Brandeis School of Law. University of Louisville, 2301 S. Third St. Louisville, KY 40292. Phone: (502)852-6396 Fax: (502)852-0862 E-mail: brandies.law.journal@louisville.edu • URL: http://www.louisville.edu/law • Quarterly. $30.00 per year.

Brands and Their Companies. Gale Cengage Learning, 27500 Drake Rd. Farmington Hills, MI 48331-3535. Phone: 800-877-GALE or (248)699-GALE Fax: 800-414-5043 E-mail: gale.galeord@cengage.com • URL: http://gale.cengage.com • 2003. $895.00. 24th edition. Three volumes. Includes mid-year *Supplement*. Provides over 365,000 entries ontrade names, trademarks, and brand names of consumer-oriented products and their 80,000 manufacturers, importers, marketers, or distributors. Formerly *Trade Names Dictionary*.

Brands and Their Companies Database. Gale Cengage Learning, 27500 Drake Rd. Farmington Hills, MI 48331-3535. Phone: 800-877-GALE or (248)699-GALE Fax: 800-414-5043 or (248)699-8069 E-mail: galeord@gale.com • URL: http://gale.cengage.com • An online directory of about 400,000 domestic and international trade names, with a primary focus on consumer goods. Semiannual updates. Inquire as to online cost and availability.

Brandweek: The Newsweekly of Marketing Communications. VNU Business Media, 770 Broadway New York, NY 10003-3595. Phone: 800-344-7119 or (646)654-4500 Fax: (646)654-7212 • URL: http://www.vnubusinessmedia.com • 46 times a year. $149.00 per year. Includes articles and case studies on mass marketing and mass media. Formerly *Adweek's Marketing Week*.

Brassey's Defence Yearbook. Brassey's Inc., 22841 Quicksilver Dr. Dulles, VA 20166. Phone: (703)661-1500 Fax: (703)661-1501 E-mail: brasseymail@presswarehouse.com • URL: http://www.brasseysinc.com • 1998. $55.00.

Brazil Company Handbook: Data on Major Listed Companies. Hoovers, Inc., 5800 Airport Blvd. Austin, TX 78752-4204. Phone: 800-486-8666 or (512)374-4500 Fax: (512)374-4501 E-mail: orders@hoovers.com • URL: http://www.hoovers.com • Annual. $59.95. Contains profiles of approximately 54 publicly traded companies in Brazil. Includes information on local stock exchanges and the nation's economic situation.

Brazilian-American Chamber of Commerce., 509 W. Madison Ave., Suite 304 New York, NY 10022. Phone: (212)751-4691 Fax: (212)751-7692 E-mail: info@brazilcham.com • URL: http://www.brazilcham.com • Promotes trade between Brazil and the U.S.

Brazilian Trade Bureau of the Consulate General of Brazil in New York., 1185 Avenue of the Americas, 21st Fl. New York, NY 10036. Phone: (917)777-7777 Fax: (212)827-0225 E-mail: trade@brazilny.org • URL: http://www.braziltradeny.com • Offers assistance to American firms wishing to purchase Brazilian products, and promotes Brazilian firms and their exports. Formerly Brazilian Government Trade Bureau.

The Bread Market. Available from MarketResearch.com, 641 Ave. of the Americas, Third Floor New York, NY 10011. Phone: 800-298-5699 or (212)807-2629 Fax: (212)807-2716 E-mail: order@marketresearch.com • URL: http://www.marketresearch.com • 2000. $1,800.00. Published by Packaged Facts. Provides market data on a wide variety of packaged, frozen, and fresh- baked bread products.

Breaking Out of the Pink-Collar Ghetto: Policy Solutions for Non-College Women. Sharon H. Mastracci. M. E. Sharpe, Inc., 80 Business Park Drive Armonk, NY 10504. Phone: 800-541-6563 or (914)273-1800 Fax: (914)273-2106 E-mail: custserv@mesharpe.com • URL: http://www.mesharpe.com • 2004. $65.95. Emphasis is on innovative education and training programs for women in low-paying service jobs.

Breaking Through the Glass Ceiling: Women in Management. Linda Wirth. International Labour Organization, 1828 L St., N.W., Suite 600 Washington, DC 20036-5121. Phone: (202)653-7652 Fax: (202)653-7687 E-mail: washington@ilo.org • URL: http://www.ilo.org • 2001. $16.95. Portrays "national and international efforts to improve equal opportunities amd promote gender equality in management." Includes statistical information and discussion of earnings

gaps, recruitment of women, education, training, and career-building strategies for women.

Breaking Up America: Advertisers and the New Media World. Joseph Turow. The University of Chicago Press, 1427 E. 60th St. Chicago, IL 60637. Phone: (773)702-7700 Fax: 800-621-8476 or (773)702-9756 E-mail: custserv@press.uchicago.edu • URL: http://www.press.uchicago.edu • 1997. $22.50. A social criticism of target marketing, market segmentation, and customized media.

Bretton Woods Committee., 1726 M St. NW, Ste. 200 Washington, DC 20036. Phone: (202)331-1616 Fax: (202)785-9423 E-mail: info@brettonwoods.org • URL: http://www.brettonwoods.org • Corporate CEOs, university administrators, former government officials, state governors, association and trade union executives, and bankers. Seeks to inform and educate the public regarding the activities of the World Bank, International Monetary Fund, and other Multinational Development Banks (MDB). Promotes U.S. participation in MDBs.

Brewers Almanac. Beer Institute, 122 C St., Suite 750 Washington, DC 20001-2109. Phone: (202)737-2337 Fax: (202)737-7004 • URL: http://www.beerinst.org • Annual. $170.00.

Brewers' Association of America.

Brewers Digest. Siebel Publishing Co., Inc., P.O. Box 677 Thiensville, WI 53092. Phone: (312)463-3401 Monthly. $25.00 per year. Covers all aspects of brewing. Annual *Buyers' Guide* and *Directory* available.

Brewers Digest Annual Buyers Guide and Brewery Directory. Siebel Publishing Company, Inc., PO Box 677 Thiensville, WI 53092. Phone: (312)463-7484 Annual. $50.00. Lists all breweries throughout the western hemisphere.

Brewery and Soft Drink Workers Conference-U.S.A. and Canada., 25. Louisiana Ave., NW Washington, DC 20001. Phone: (202)624-6921 Fax: (202)624-8137 E-mail: brewery@teamster.org • URL: http://www.teamster.org • Promotes the interests of brewery and soft drink workers in the United States and Canada.

Brewing and Distilling International. Brewery Traders Publications, Ltd., 52 Glenhouse Rd. Eltham SE19 1JQ, United Kingdom. Phone: 44 20 8859 4300 Fax: 44 20 8859 5813 E-mail: bdilondon@dial.pipex.com • URL: http://www.bdinews.com • Monthly. $82.00 per year.

Brick Industry Association., 1850 Centennial Park Dr., Ste. 301 Reston, VA 20191. Phone: (703)620-0010 Fax: (703)620-3928 E-mail: brickinfo@bia.org • URL: http://www.bia.org • Manufacturers and distributors of clay brick. Promotes clay brick with the goal of increasing its market share.

Bricker's International Directory: Long-Term University- Based Executive Programs. Peterson's, Princeton Pike Corporate Center, 2000 Lennox Dr. Lawrenceville, NJ 08648. Phone: 800-338-3282 or (609)896-1800 Fax: (609)896-4544 E-mail: info@peterson's.com • URL: http://www.petersons.com • Annual. $395.00. Presents detailed information about executive education programs offered by 85 universities and nonprofit organizations in the U. S. and around the world. Includes general management and function-specific programs.

A Brief History of Cocaine. Steven B. Karch. CRC Press LLC, 2000 NW Corporate Blvd. Boca Raton, FL 33431-7372. Phone: 800-272-7737 or (561)994-0555 Fax: 800-374-3401 or (561)989-9732 E-mail: orders@crcpress.com • URL: http://www.crcpress.com • 1997. $29.95. Emphasizes the societal effects of cocaine abuse in various regions of the world.

Brink's Modern Internal Auditing. Robert R. Moeller and others. John Wiley and Sons, Inc., 111 River St. Hoboken, NJ 07030. Phone: 800-225-5945 or (201)748-6000 Fax: (201)748-6088 E-mail: info@wiley.com • URL: http://www.wiley.com • 1999. $168.00. Fifth edition.

British Year Book of International Law. Oxford University Press, 198 Madison Ave. New York, NY 10016. Phone: 800-451-7556 or (212)726-6000 Fax: (212)726-6440 E-mail: custserv@oup-usa.org • URL: http://www.oup-usa.org • Annual. Price varies.

Broadband Solutions. North American Publishing Co., 401 N. Broad St., 5th Fl. Philadelphia, PA 19108. Phone: 800-777-8074 or (215)238-5482 Fax: 800-664-1533 or (215)238-5412 E-mail: customerservice@napco.com • URL: http://www.napco.com • Monthly. Controlled circulation. Covers the high-bandwidth telecommunications industry, including new products and emerging technologies.

Broadband Technology: Newsletter on Technical Advances, Construction of New Systms and Rebuild of Existing Systems. Paul Kagan Associates, Inc., 126 Clock Tower Place Carmel, CA 93923-8746. Phone: (831)624-1536 Fax: (831)625-3225 E-mail: info@kagan.com • URL: http://www.kagan.com • Monthly. $895.00 per year. Newsletter. Contains news of cable TV technical advances. Formerly (Cable TV Technology).

Broadband Week. Reed Business Information, 360 Park Ave., S New York, NY 10010. Phone: 800-662-7776 or (646)746-6400 E-mail: corporatecommunications@reedbusiness.com • URL: http://www.reedbusiness.com • 51 times a year. $139.00 per year. Provides news and trends for all parts of the evolving broadband industry, including operations, marketing, finance, and technology. Incorporates *Broadband*.

Broadcast Cable Financial Management Association, Inc., 929 Lee St., Ste. 204 Des Plaines, IL 60016. Phone: (847)296-

0200 Fax: (847)296-7510 E-mail: mcollins@bcfm.com • URL: http://www.bcfm.com • Members are accountants and other financial personnel in the radio and television broadcasting industries. Formerly Broadcast Financial Management Association.

Broadcast Communications Dictionary. Lincoln Diamant, editor. Greenwood Publishing Group Inc., 88 Post Rd., W. Westport, CT 06881. Phone: 800-225-5800 or (203)226-3571 Fax: (203)431-2214 E-mail: customer-service@greenwood.com • URL: http://www.greenwood.com • 1989. $57.95. Third revised edition.

Broadcast Education Association., 1771 N St. NW Washington, DC 20036-2800. Phone: 888-380-7222 or (202)429-3935 Fax: (202)775-2981 E-mail: beainfo@beaweb.org • URL: http://www.beaweb.org • Universities and colleges; faculty and students; promotes improvement of curriculum and teaching methods, broadcasting research, television and radio production, and programming teaching on the college level.

Broadcast Engineering—Equipment Reference Manual. Penton Media Inc., 9800 Metcalf Ave. Overland Park, KS 66212. Phone: (866)505-7173 or (913)341-1300 Fax: (913)967-1898 E-mail: toddpub@aol.com • URL: http://www.primediabusiness.com • Publication includes: List of more than 1,400 manufacturers and distributors of communications equipment for radio, television, and recording applications. Entries include: For manufacturers—Company name, address. For distributors and dealers—Company name, address, phone, product or service provided, geographic area covered.

Broadcast Engineering: Journal of Broadcast Technology. Primedia Business Magazines and Media, 9800 Metcalf Ave. Overland Park, KS 66212. Phone: 800-795-5445 or (913)341-1300 Fax: (913)967-1898 E-mail: subs@primediabusiness.com • URL: http://www.primediabusiness.com • 10 times a year. Free to qualified personnel; others, $65.00 per year. Technical magazine for the broadcast industry.

Broadcast Investor: Newsletter on Radio-TV Station Finance. Paul Kagan Associates, Inc., 126 Clock Tower Place Carmel, CA 93923-8746. Phone: (831)624-1536 Fax: (831)625-3225 E-mail: info@kagon.com • URL: http://www.kagan.com • Monthly. $925.00 per year. Newsletter for investors in publicly held radio and television broadcasting companies.

Broadcast Music, Inc., 320 W 57th St. New York, NY 10019-3790. Phone: (212)586-2000 Fax: (212)956-2059 E-mail: newyork@bmi.com • URL: http://bmi.com • Consists of more than 90,000 writers and 50,000 publisher affiliates. Acts as steward for the performing rights of the works of its affiliates by collecting license fees from music users and making payments to the creators of the music used (based on a published schedule of payments). Maintains reciprocal agreements with 41 sister licensing organizations worldwide.

Broadcasting and Cable. Reed Business Information, 360 Park Ave., S New York, NY 10010. Phone: 800-446-6551 or (646)746-6400 Fax: (646)746-7028 E-mail: corporatecommunications@reedbusiness.com • URL: http://www.reedbusiness.com • 51 times a year. $179.00 per year; includes print and online editions. Formerly *Broadcasting*.

Broadcasting and Cable Yearbook. Gale, 27500 Drake Rd. Farmington Hills, MI 48331. Phone: 800-877-GALE or (248)699-GALE Fax: 800-414-5043 or (218)699-8035 E-mail: gale.galeord@cengage.com • URL: http://gale.cengage.com • Annual. $179.95. Provides information on U. S. and Canadian TV stations, radio stations, cable TV companies, and radio-TV services of various kinds.

Broadsource., 1828 L St., N. W., Suite 900 Washington, DC 20036. Phone: 800-883-6262 or (202)452-6262 Fax: (202)452-6299 • URL: http://www.boardsource.org • Seeks to improve the effectiveness of nonprofit boards of trustees. Formerly National Center for Nonprofit Boards.

Broadwoven Fabrics (Gray). U.S. Bureau of the Census, Washington, DC 20233-0800. Phone: (301)457-4100 Fax: (301)457-3842 • URL: http://www.census.gov • Quarterly. Provides statistical data on production, value, shipments, and consumption. Includes woolen and worsted fabrics, tire fabrics, cotton broadwoven fabrics, etc. (Current Industrial Reports, MQ-22T.)

Broker-Dealer Regulation. David A. Lipton. West Group, 610 Opperman Dr. Eagan, MN 55123. Phone: 800-328-4880 or (651)687-7000 Fax: 800-340-9378 E-mail: bookstore@westgroup.com • URL: http://www.westgroup.com • Semiannual. $429.00 per year. Looseleaf service. Focuses on the basics of stockbroker license application procedure, registration, regulation, and responsibilities. (Securities Law Series).

Broker: The Sales and Management Resource for Mortgage Originators. Thomson Media, One State St. Plaza New York, NY 10004. Phone: 800-221-1809 or (212)803-8200 Fax: (212)843-9635 E-mail: custserv@thomsonmedia.com • URL: http://www.thomsonmedia.com • Bimonthly. $48.00 per year. Edited for mortgage brokers. Emphasis is on marketing, leads to new business, and profitability.

Broker World. Insurance Publications, Inc., 9404 Reeds Rd. Overland Park, KS 66207. Phone: 800-762-3387 or (913)383-9191 Fax: (913)383-1247 E-mail: showard@brokerworld.com • URL: http://brokerworld.com • Bimonthly. $6.00 per year. Edited for independent insurance agents and brokers. Special feature issue topics include annuities, disability insurance, estate planning, and life insurance.

Brookings Institution. Brookings Institution, 1775 Massachusetts Ave. NW Washington, DC 20036. Phone: (202)797-6000 Fax: (202)797-6004 E-mail: communications@brookings.edu • URL: http://www.brookings.edu/ • Economics, including studies on what economic policies are most conducive to sustained growth of the U.S. economy, how social programs can be made more effective in an era of constrained resources, and how international economic relations can be improved; government, including studies on political institutions, the media, regulation and economic policy, and social policy; and foreign policy, including defense analysis and international economics and trade studies, and U.S. relations with, and regional studies on, the former Soviet Union, East Asia, China, the Middle East, Latin America, and Africa.

Brown's Directory of North American and International Gas Companies. Advanstar Communications, 545 Boylston St. Boston, MA 02116. Phone: 800-598-6008 or (617)267-6500 Fax: (617)267-6900 E-mail: info@advanstar.com • URL: http://www.advanstar.com • Annual. $345.00.

BUC Used Boat Price Guide. BUC International Corp., 1314 N.E. 17th Court Fort Lauderdale, FL 33305. Phone: 800-327-6929 or (954)565-6715 Fax: (954)561-3095 Semiannual. $183.00 per year. Formerly *Older Boat Price Guide*.

Budget and Economic Outlook: Fiscal Years [10-year period]. Available from U. S. Government Printing Office, Washington, DC 20402. Phone: (202)512-1800 Fax: (202)512-2250 E-mail: gpoaccess@gpo.gov • URL: http://www.access.gpo.gov • Annual. $27.00. Issued by the Congressional Budget Office (CBO). Reports on fiscal policy and provides baseline projections of federal budget for 10 years. Also offers "impartial analysis with no recommendations."

Budget of the United States Government. U.S. Office of Management and Budget. Available from U.S. Government Printing Office, Washington, DC 20402. Phone: (202)512-1800 Fax: (202)512-2250 E-mail: gpoaccess@gpo.gov • URL: http://www.access.gpo.gov • Annual. $52.00.

Budget Options. Available from U. S. Government Printing Office, Washington, DC 20402. Phone: (202)512-1800 Fax: (202)512-2250 E-mail: gpoaccess@gpo.gov • URL: http://www.access.gpo.gov • 2003. $38.00. Issued by the Congressional Budget Office (CBO). Presents both sides of the coin: major proposals to increase spending or cut taxes because of large budget surpluses, or specific options to reduce spending or increase revenues because of large deficits.

Budgeting: A How-to-Do-it Manual for Librarians. Alice S. Warner. Neal-Schuman Publishers, Inc., 100 William St., Ste. 2004 New York, NY 10038. Phone: (866)672-2667 or (212)925-8650 Fax: (866)209-7932 or (212)219-8916 E-mail: info@neal-schuman.com • URL: http://www.neal-schuman.com • 1998. $49.95. Explains six forms of budgeting suitable for various kinds of libraries. Includes a bibliography. (How-to-Do-It Manuals Series).

Builder: Buyer's Guide. Hanley-Wood, LLC., One Thomas Circle Washington, DC 20005. Phone: 800-837-0870 or (202)452-0800 Fax: (202)785-1974 • URL: http://www.hanleywood.com • Annual. $10.00. A directory of products and services for the home building and remodeling industry.

Builder: The Voice of America's Housing Industry. National Association of Home Builders of the United States, Economics, Mortgage Finance and Housing Policy Div. Hanley-Wood, LLC, One Thomas Circle NW Washington, DC 20005. Phone: (202)452-0800 Fax: (202)785-1974 • URL: http://www.hanley-wood.com • Monthly. $29.95 per year. Covers the home building and remodeling industry in general, including design, construction, and marketing.

Builders Hardware Manufacturers Association., 355 Lexington Ave., 15th Fl. New York, NY 10017. Phone: (212)297-2122 Fax: (212)370-9047 E-mail: bhma@kellencompany.com • URL: http://www.buildershardware.com • Manufacturers of builders' hardware, both contract and stock. Provides statistical services; maintains standardization program; sponsors certification programs for locks, latches, door closers, and cabinet hardware. Maintains 12 product sections.

Building a Mail Order Business: A Complete Manual for Success. William A. Cohen. John Wiley and Sons, Inc., 111 River St. Hoboken, NJ 07030. Phone: 800-225-5945 or (201)748-6000 Fax: (201)748-6088 E-mail: info@wiley.com • URL: http://www.wiley.com • 1996. $42.95. Fourth edition.

Building and Construction Trades Department - AFL-CIO.

Building and Running a Successful Research Business: A Guide for the Independent Information Professional. Mary Ellen Bates. Information Today, Inc., 143 Old Marlton Pike Medford, NJ 08055-8750. Phone: 800-300-9868 or (609)654-6266 Fax: (609)654-4309 E-mail: custserv@infotoday.com • URL: http://www.infotoday.com • 2003. $29.95. Provides practical advice for information brokers. Includes material on such topics as organization of the business, marketing, and sales promotion. (CyberAge Books).

Building Construction Cost Data. RSMeans, 63 Smiths Ln. Kingston, MA 02364-9988. Phone: 800-334-3509 Fax: 800-632-6732 • URL: http://www.rsmeans.com • Annual. $108.95. Lists over 20,000 entries for estimating.

Building Construction Handbook. Ray Chudley. Elsevier, 655 Ave. of the Americas New York, NY 10010. Phone: 800-366-2665 or (212)989-5800 Fax: 800-535-9935 or (212)633-3680 E-mail: custserv@elsevier.com • URL: http://www.elsevier.com • 2001. $34.95. Fourth edition.

Building Design and Construction: The Magazine for the Building Team. Reed Business Information, 360 Park Ave., S New York, NY 10010. Phone: 800-446-6551 or (646)746-6400 Fax: (646)746-7028 E-mail: corporatecommunications@reedbusiness.com • URL: http://www.reedbusiness.com • Monthly. $119.00 per year. For non-residential building owners, contractors, engineers and architects.

Building Material Dealer. National Lumber and Building Material Dealers Association, 40 Ivy St., SE Washington, DC 20003. Phone: 800-634-8645 or (202)547-2230 Fax: (202)547-7640 E-mail: nlbmda@dealer.org • URL: http://www.dealer.org • Monthly. $48.00 per year. Includes special feature issues on hand and power tools, lumber, roofing, kitchens, flooring, windows and doors, and insulation. Formerly *Builder Material Retailer*.

Building Officials and Code Administrators International., 4051 W Flossmoor Rd. Country Club Hills, IL 60478-5795. Phone: 800-214-4321 or (708)799-2300 Fax: 800-214-7167 E-mail: webmaster@bocai.org • URL: http://www.bocai.org • Formerly Building Officials Conference of America.

Building Officials and Code Administrators International-Membership Directory., 4051 W. Flossmoor Rd. Country Club Hills, IL 60478. Phone: (708)799-2300 Fax: (708)799-4981 E-mail: boca@bocai.org Annual. $16.00. Approximately 14,000 construction code officials, architects, engineers, trade associations, and manufacturers.

Building Operating Management: The National Magazine for Commercial and Institutional Buildings Construction, Renovation, Facility Management. Trade Press Publishing Corp., 2100 W. Florist Ave. Milwaukee, WI 53209. Phone: 800-727-7995 or (414)228-7701 Fax: (414)228-1134 • URL: http://www.tradepress.com • Monthly. Free to qualified personnel.

Building Owners and Managers Association International., 1201 New York Ave., NW, Ste. 300 Washington, DC 20005. Phone: (202)408-2662 Fax: (202)371-0181 E-mail: info@boma.org • URL: http://www.boma.org • Formerly National Association of Building Owners and Managers.

Building Parterships: Cooperarion Between the United Nations System and the Private Sector. United Nations Publications, Two United Nations Plaza, Room DC2-853 New York, NY 10017. Phone: 800-253-9646 or (212)963-8302 Fax: (212)963-3489 E-mail: publications@un.org • URL: http://www.un.org/publications • 2002. $27.50. Describes "the main types of cooperation between the UN and business." (A joint initiative of the UN Global Compact and the UN Department of Public Information in cooperation with the Prince of Wales International Business Leaders Forum).

Building Products. Hanley-Wood, LLC, One Thomas Circle, NW Washington, DC 20005. Phone: 800-837-0870 or (202)452-0800 Fax: (202)785-1974 • URL: http://www.hanley-wood.com • Quarterly. $36.00 per year. Covers building products and materials for the construction industry, including new products.

Building Research Council. University of Illinois at Urbana-Champaign, One E. Saint Mary's Rd. Champaign, IL 61820. Phone: 800-336-0616 or (217)333-1801 Fax: (217)244-2204 Integral unit of School of Architecture.

Building Service Contractors Association International., 401 N Michigan Ave., 22nd Fl. Chicago, IL 60611-4267. Phone: 800-368-3414 or (312)321-5167 Fax: (312)673-6735 E-mail: info@bscai.org • URL: http://www.bscai.org • Firms and corporations in 40 countries engaged in contracting building maintenance services including the provision of labor, purchasing materials, and janitorial cleaning and maintenance of a building or its surroundings; associate members are manufacturers of cleaning supplies and equipment. Seeks to provide a unified voice for building service contractors and to promote increased recognition by government, property owners, and the general business and professional public. Conducts continuing study and action, through committees and special task groups on areas such as public affairs, costs and ratios, uniform accounting, industrial relations and personnel, marketing and sales, contract improvement, research and planning, materials and supplies sources, group insurance, management training, statistics collection, safety, and insurance costs. Has developed a certification program for building service executives, and a registration program for building service managers.

Building Stone Institute., 551 Tollgate Rd., Ste. C Elgin, IL 60123-9357. Phone: (866)786-6313 or (847)695-0170 Fax: (847)695-0174 E-mail: margie@buildingstoneinstitute.org • URL: http://www.buildingstoneinstitute.org • Represents Natural Stone quarriers, fabricators, installers, dealers, importers, expo and restorers. Serves as a clearinghouse of information for architects, contractors, decorstors, and masons. Promotes the use of Natural Stone.

Building Stone Magazine. Building Stone Institute, P.O.Box 507 Purdys, NY 10578-0507. Phone: (914)232-5725 Fax: (914)232-5259 Bimonthly. $65.00 per year.

Building Systems Councils of NAHB., 1201 15th St., N.W. Washington, DC 20005. Phone: 800-368-5242 or (202)822-0576 Fax: (202)861-2141 E-mail: bsc@nahb.com • URL: http://www.buildingsystems.org • Formerly Home Manufacturers Councils of NAHB.

Building the Reference Collection: A How-To-Do-It Manual for

School and Public Librarians. Neal-Schuman Publishers, Inc., 100 William St., Ste. 2004 New York, NY 10038. Phone: (866)672-2667 or (212)925-8650 Fax: (866)209-7932 or (212)219-8916 E-mail: info@neal-schuman.com • URL: http://www.neal-schuman.com • 1992. $38.50. Includes a list of 300 basic reference sources. (How-to-Do-It Manuals Series).

Building the Service-Based Library Web Site: A Step-by-Step Guide to Design and Options. Kristen L. Garlock and Sherry Piontek. American Library Association, 50 E. Huron St. Chicago, IL 60611-2795. Phone: 800-545-2433 or (312)944-6780 Fax: (312)440-9374 E-mail: ala@ala.org • URL: http://www.ala.org • 1996. $30.00. Provides practical information for libraries planning a World Wide Web home page. (ALA Editions Series).

Buildings: The Source for Facilities Decision-Makers. Stamats Communications, Inc., 615 Fifth St., S.E. Cedar Rapids, IA 52406. Phone: 800-553-8878 or (319)364-6167 Fax: (319)365-5421 E-mail: info@stamats.com • URL: http://www.stamats.com • Monthly. $70.00 per year. Serves professional building ownership/management organizations.

Bull and Bear Financial Newspaper., P. O. Box 917179 Longwood, FL 32791. Phone: 800-336-2855 or (407)682-6170 Fax: (407)682-6170 • URL: http://www.thebullandbear.com • Monthly. $36.00 per year. Each issue includes a digest of advice from investment advisory newsletters.

Bulletin of Bibliography. Greenwood Publishing Group, Inc., 88 Post Rd., W Westport, CT 06881. Phone: 800-225-5800 or (203)226-3571 Fax: (203)431-2214 E-mail: customer-service@greenwood.com • URL: http://www.greenwood.com • Quarterly. $125.00 per year.

Bulletin of Labour Statistics: Supplementing the Annual Data Presented in the Year Book of Labour Statistics. International Labour Ofice., 1828 L St., NW Washington, DC 20036-5121. Phone: (202)653-7652 Fax: (202)653-7687 E-mail: washington@ilo.org • URL: http://www.ilo.org • Quarterly. $84.00 per year. Includes five *Supplements*. A supplement to *Yearbook of Labour Statistics*. Provides current labor and price index statistics for over 130 countries. Generally includes data for the most recent four years. Text in English, French and Spanish.

Bulletin of the Atomic Scientists: The Magazine of Global Security News and Analysis. Educational Foundation for Nuclear Science, 6042 S. Kimbark Ave. Chicago, IL 60637. Phone: (773)702-2555 Fax: (773)702-0275 E-mail: lrio@thebulletin.org • URL: http://www.thebulletin.org • Bimonthly. $28.00 per year.

Bulletin on Narcotics. United Nations Publications, United Nations Concourse Level, First Ave., 46th St. New York, NY 10017. Phone: 800-553-3210 or (212)963-7680 Fax: (212)963-4910 E-mail: bookstore@un.org • URL: http://www.un.org/publications • Quarterly. $10.00 per issue. Editions in Chinese, French, Russian and Spanish.

Bullinger's Postal and Shippers Guide for the United States and Canada. Alber Leland Publishing, 500 N. Skinker Blvd. Saint Luis, MO 63130. Phone: (314)725-5700 Fax: (314)725-5444 E-mail: pharig@alberland.com Annual. $375.00. Approximately 260,000 communities in the United States and Canada.

Bullion Advisory. Moneypower, 1304 Edgewood Ave. Ann Arbor, MI 48103-5522. Phone: (612)537-8096 Monthly. $36.00 per year. Specializes in gold, silver and platinum.

Bureau of Alcohol, Tobacco, and Firearms Quarterly Bulletin. Bureau of Alcohol, Tobacco, and Firearms, U.S. Department of the Treasury. Available from U.S. Government Printing Office, Washington, DC 20402. Phone: (202)512-1800 Fax: (202)512-2250 Quarterly. $25.00 per year. Laws and regulations.

Bureau of Economic Analysis (BEA). U. S. Department of Commerce, Bureau of Economic AnalysisPhone: (202)606-9900 Fax: (202)606-5310 E-mail: webmaster@bea.doc.gov • URL: http://www.bea.doc.gov • Web site includes "News Release Information" covering national, regional, and international economic estimates from the BEA. Highlights of releases appear online the same day, complete text and tables appear the next day. "Recent News Releases" section provides titles for past nine months, with links. "BEA Data and Methodology" includes "Frequently Requested NIPA Data" (national income and product accounts, such as gross domestic product and personal income). Other statistics are available. Fees: Free.

Bureau of Economic and Business Research.

Bureau of Economic and Business Research. University of Florida

Bureau of Economic Geology. University of Texas at Austin

Bureau of Educational Research and Evaluation. Mississippi State University

Bureau of Governmental Research. University of Maryland

Bureau of Wholesale Sales Representatives., 1100 Spring St. N.W., Suite 700 Atlanta, GA 30309. Phone: 800-877-1808 or (404)870-7600 Fax: (404)870-7601 E-mail: info@bwsr.com • URL: http://www.bwsr.com • Formerly Bureau of Salesmen's National Association.

Bureaucracy: What Government Agencies Do and Why They Do It. James Q. Wilson. Basic Books, 387 Park Ave. S New York, NY 10016. Phone: 800-386-5656 or (212)340-8135 Fax: (212)340-8135 E-mail: westview.orders@perseusbooks.com • URL: http://www.perseusbooksgroup.com • 2000. $24.00. Second edition.

Burglar Alarm Sales and Installation. Entrepreneur Media, Inc., 2445 McCabe Way Irvine, CA 92614. Phone: 800-421-2300 or (949)261-2325 Fax: (949)261-0234 E-mail: entmag@entrepreneur.com • URL: http://www.entrepreneur.com • Looseleaf. $59.50. A practical guide to starting a burglar alarm service. Covers profit potential, start-up costs, market size evaluation, owner's time required, pricing, accounting, advertising, promotion, etc. (Start-Up Business Guide No. E1091.)

Burlap and Jute Association.

Burley Auction Warehouse Association.

Burrelle's Media Directory: Broadcast Media. Burrelle's Information Services, 75 E Northfield Rd. Livingston, NJ 07039. Phone: 800-631-1160 Fax: (973)992-7675 • URL: http://www.burrelles.com • Annual. $550.00. Approximately 48,000 print and electronic media in North America. Provides detailed descriptions, including programming and key personnel.

Burrelle's Media Directory: Magazines and Newsletters. Burrelle's Information Services, 75 E Northfield Rd. Livingston, NJ 07039. Phone: 800-631-1160 Fax: (973)992-7675 • URL: http://www.burrelles.com • Annual. $550.00. Provides detailed descriptions of more than 13,500 magazines and newsletters published in the U. S., Canada, and Mexico. Categories are professional, consumer, trade, and college. Semiannual *Updates*. Includes CD-ROM.

Burrelle's Media Directory: Newspapers and Related Media. Burrelle's Information Services, 75 E Northfield Rd. Livingston, NJ 07039. Phone: 800-631-1160 Fax: (973)992-7675 • URL: http://www.burrelles.com • Annual. $550.00. *Daily Newspapers* volume lists more than 2,200 daily publications in the U. S., Canada, and Mexico. *Non-Daily Newspapers* volume lists more than 10,400 items published no more than three times a week. Provides detailed descriptions, including key personnel.

Burwell World Directory of Information Brokers. Helen P. Burwell, editor. Burwell Enterprises, 5619 Plumtree Dr. Dallas, TX 75252. Phone: (972)732-0160 Fax: (972)733-1951 E-mail: helen@burwellinc.com • URL: http://www.burwellinc.com • Annual. $59.50. Lists more than 1,000 information brokers, document delivery firms, free-lance librarians, and fee-based library services. Provides U. S. and international coverage (46 countries). Formerly *Directory of Fee-Based Information Services*.

Bus Ride. Friendship Publications, Inc., 1550 E Missouri Ave., Ste. 100 Phoenix, AZ 85014. Phone: 800-541-2670 or (602)265-7600 Fax: (602)265-4300 E-mail: lisa@busride.com • URL: http://www.busride.com • 10 times a year. $35.00 per year.

Business Alliance for Commerce in Hemp., PO Box 1716 El Cerrito, CA 94530. Phone: (510)215-8326 Fax: (510)234-4460 E-mail: chris@chrisconrad.com • URL: http://www.equalrights4all.org/bach/BACHcore.html • Businesses, consumers, and other individuals and organizations with an interest in hemp and hemp products. Promotes "full and unrestricted restoration of hemp as a sustainable farm crop and industrial resource"; seeks to legalize therapeutic use of marijuana and regulate adult consumption. Conducts lobbying, community organization, and outreach activities supporting hemp producers and consumers; consulting services; disseminates information on the commercial and industrial uses of hemp and the therapeutic benefits of marijuana.

Business and Acquisition Newsletter. Newsletters International, Inc., 2600 S. Gessner Rd. Houston, TX 77063. Phone: (713)783-0100 Monthly. $300.00 per year. Information about firms that want to buy or sell companies, divisions, subsidiaries, product lines, patents, etc.

Business and Administrative Communication. Kitty O. Locker. McGraw-Hill, 1221 Ave. of the Americas New York, NY 10020. Phone: 800-722-4726 or (212)512-2000 Fax: (212)512-4502 E-mail: customer.service@mcgraw-hill.com • URL: http://www.mcgraw-hill.com • 2003. Sixth edition. Price on application.

Business and Commercial Aviation. McGraw-Hill Aviation Week Group, Four International Dr. Rye Brook, NY 10573. Phone: 800-722-4726 or (914)939-0300 Fax: (914)939-1184 E-mail: customer.service@mcgraw-hill.com • URL: http://www.mcgraw-hill.com • Monthly. $52.00 per year. Supplement available: *Annual Planning Purchasing Handbook*.

Business and Finance Division Bulletin. Special Libraries Association, Business and Finance Div., 1700 18th St., N.W. Washington, DC 20009-2514. Phone: (202)234-4700 Fax: (202)265-9317 E-mail: sla@sla.org • URL: http://www.sla.org • Quarterly. $12.00 per year.

Business and Industry. Gale Cengage Learning, 27500 Drake Rd. Farmington Hills 48331-3535, England. Phone: 800-877-GALE Fax: 800-414-5043 or (248)699-8069 E-mail: galeord@galegroup.com • URL: http://www.galegroup.com • Contains online citations, abstracts, and selected fulltext from more than 1,000 trade journals, newspapers, and other publications. Provides general coverage of both manufacturing and service industries, including marketing, production, industry trends, key events, and information on specific companies. Time span is 1994 to date. Daily updates. Inquire as to online cost and availability. (Also available in a CD-ROM version.)

Business and Institutional Furniture Manufacturers Association.

Business and Management Practices. Gale Cengage Learning, 27500 Drake Rd. Farmington Hills, MI 48331-3535. Phone: 800-877-GALE or (248)699-4253 Fax: 800-414-5043 or (248)699-8069 E-mail: galeord@galegroup.com • URL: http://www.galegroup.com • Provides fulltext of management articles appearing in more than 350 relevant publications. Emphasis is on "the processes, methods, and strategies of managing a business." Time span is 1995 to date. Inquire as to online cost and availability. (Also available in a CD-ROM version.)

Business and Professional Women International.

Business and Professional Women USA., 1900 M St., NW, Ste. 310 Washington, DC 20036. Phone: (202)293-1100 Fax: (202)861-0298 E-mail: memberservices@bpwusa.org • URL: http://www.bpwusa.org • Formerly National Federation of Business and Professional Women's Clubs.

Business and Professional Women's Foundation.

Business and Society: A Journal of Interdisciplinary Exploration. International Association for Business and Society Research Committee. Sage Publications, Inc., 2455 Teller Rd. Thousand Oaks, CA 91320. Phone: 800-818-7243 or (805)499-9774 Fax: 800-583-2665 or (805)499-0871 E-mail: webmaster@sagepub.com • URL: http://www.sagepub.com • Quarterly. $402.00 per year.

Business and Society: A Managerial Approach. Heidi Vernon. McGraw-Hill, 1221 Ave. of the Americas New York, NY 10020. Phone: 800-772-4726 or (212)512-2000 Fax: (212)512-4502 E-mail: customer.service@mcgraw-hill.com • URL: http://www.mcgraw-hill.com • 1997. $110.31. Sixth edition. Emphasizes ethics and social accountability.

Business and Society Review: Journal of the Center for Business Ethics at Bentley College. Blackwell Publishing, 350 Main St., 6th Fl. Malden, MA 02148-5018. Phone: 800-835-6770 or (781)388-8200 Fax: (781)388-8232 E-mail: subscrip@blackwellpub.com • URL: http://www.blackwellpub.com • Quarterly. Institutions, $179.00 per year. Includes online edition.

Business Automation Reference Service: Office Equipment. Altech Publishing Co., 212 Cooper Center, North Park Dr. and Browning Rd. Pennsauken, NJ 08109. Monthly. $100.00 per year. Looseleaf service.

Business Brokerage. Entrepreneur Media, Inc., 2445 McCabe Way Irvine, CA 92614. Phone: 800-421-2300 or (949)261-2325 Fax: (949)261-0234 E-mail: entmag@entrepreneur.com • URL: http://www.entrepreneur.com • Looseleaf. $59.50. A practical guide to starting a brokerage service for the sale and purchase of small businesses. Covers profit potential, start-up costs, market size evaluation, owner's time required, pricing, accounting, advertising, promotion, etc. (Start-Up Business Guide No. E1317.)

Business Brokers Directory. infoUSA Inc., 5711 S 86th Cir., PO Box 27347 Omaha, NE 68127. Phone: 800-321-0869 or (402)593-4500 Fax: (402)331-1505 E-mail: help@infousa.com • URL: http://www.abii.com • Number of listings: 3,487 Entries include: Name, address, phone (including area code), size of advertisement, year first in "Yellow Pages," name of owner or manager, number of employees. Compiled from telephone company "Yellow Pages," nationwide.

Business Capital Sources. Tyler G. Hicks. IWS Inc., PO Box 186 Merrick, NY 11566-0186. Phone: 800-323-0548 or (516)766-5850 Fax: (516)766-5919 E-mail: admin@iwsmoney.com Covers: about 1,500 banks, insurance and mortgage companies, commercial finance, leasing, and venture capital firms that lend money for business investment. Entries include: Company or institution name, address, phone.

Business Committee for the Arts.

Business Communication. Betty S. Johnson and Marsha L. Bayless. Cengage Learning Custom Publishing, 5101 Madison Rd. Cincinnati, OH 45227. Phone: 800-543-0487 Fax: (513)527-9267 • URL: http://gale.cengage.com • 2001. $72.95. Third edition.

Business Communication Quarterly. Association for Business Communication, c/o Dr. Robert Myers, Baruch College, Dept. of Speech Communication, 17 Lexington Ave. New York, NY 10010. Phone: (646)312-3726 Fax: (646)349-5297 E-mail: abcrjm@cs.com • URL: http://www.theabc.org • Quarterly. Members, $65.00 per year; institutions, $160.00 per year. Features articles about teaching and writing course outlines. Description of training programs, problems, soutions, etc. Includes *Journal of Business Communcation*.

Business Communications. Sherron Bienvenu and Paul R. Timm. Prentice Hall PTR, 240 Frisch Ct. Paramus, NJ 07652. Phone: 800-282-0693 Fax: 800-445-6991 • URL: http://www.phptr.com • 2002. $90.00. Includes CD-ROM.

Business Communications Made Simple. Butterworth-Heinemann, 225 Wildwood Ave. Woburn, MA 01801. Phone: 800-366-2665 or (781)904-2500 Fax: 800-568-5136 E-mail: custserv.bh@elsevier.com • URL: http://www.bh.com • Date not set. Price on application.

Business Communications Review. Key3Media Group, Inc., 5700 Wilshire Blvd., Ste. 325 Los Angeles, CA 90036. Phone: (323)954-3000 Fax: (323)954-3010 E-mail: fknight@bcr.com • URL: http://www.bcr.com • Monthly. $45.00 per year. Edited for communications managers in large end-user companies and institutions. Includes special feature issues on intranets and network management.

Business Consumer's Advisor. Buyers Laboratory Inc., 20 Railroad Ave. Hackensack, NJ 07601-4130. Phone: (201)488-0404 Fax: (201)488-0461 E-mail: info@buyers-lab.com • URL: http://www.buyerslab.com • Description: Focuses on office equipment and supplies, offering purchasing advice and exploring methods of increasing office productivity through appropriate management of the equipment and its operators. Offers readers a chance to share their experiences, evaluate products and equipment, and gives results of Buyers Laboratory's testing.

Business Consumer's Network. Buyers Laboratory Inc., 20 Railroad Ave. Hackensack, NJ 07601. Phone: (201)488-0404 Fax: (201)488-0461 E-mail: info@buyerslab.com • URL: http://www.buyerslab.com • Monthly. $795.00 per year. Looseleaf service. Tests office equipment and issues reports. Formerly *Buyers Laboratory Report on Office Products*.

Business Council., PO Box 20147 Washington, DC 20041. Phone: (202)298-7650 Fax: (202)785-0296 E-mail: margie@buildingstoneinstitute.org • URL: http://www.businesscouncil.com • Represents business executives. Aims to serve the national interest, with the primary objectives of developing a constructive point of view on matters of public policy affecting the business interests of the country and by providing a medium for a better understanding of government problems by business. Members are former and present chief executive officers of corporations.

Business Credit. National Association of Credit Management, 8840 Columbia 100 Parkway Columbia, MD 21045. Phone: (410)740-5560 Fax: (410)740-5574 E-mail: nacm-info@nacm.org • URL: http://www.nacm.org • 10 tims a year. $48.00 per year. Formerly *Credit and Financial Management*.

Business Crimes Bulletin. American Lawyer Media, Inc., 105 Madison Ave. New York, NY 10016. Phone: 800-888-8300 or (212)779-9200 Fax: (212)481-8110 E-mail: lawcatalog@amlaw.com • URL: http://www.lawcatalog.com/ • Monthly. $229.00 per year. Newsletter. Provides news of the "multifaceted world of financial and white collar crime." Covers such items as foreign corrupt practices, mail fraud, money laundering, tax fraud, securities law violations, environmental crime, and antitrust violations. Includes developments in sentencing guidelines for white collar perpetrators. (A Law Journal Newsletter, formerly published by Leader Publications).

Business Cycle Indicators: A Monthly Report from the Conference Board. Conference Board, 845 3rd Ave. New York, NY 10022. Phone: (212)339-0345 Fax: (212)836-9740 • URL: http://www.conference-board.org • Monthly. $130.00 per year. Contains detailed business and economic statistics in tables that were formerly published by the U. S. Department of Commerce in *Survey of Current Business*, and before that, in the discontinued *Business Conditions Digest*. Includes composite indexes of leading economic indicators, coincident indicators, and lagging indicators.

Business Cycles: A Theoretical, Historical and Statistical Analysis of the Capitalist Process. Joseph A. Schumpeter. Porcupine Press, Inc., 1500 Walnut St., Ste. 1300 Philadelphia, PA 19102. Phone: (215)735-0101 Fax: (215)546-0664 1989. $24.95. Abridged edition.

Business Cycles and Depressions: An Encyclopedia. David Glasner. Garland Publishing, Inc., 29 W. 35th St. New York, NY 10001-2299. Phone: 800-627-6273 or (212)216-7800 Fax: (212)564-7854 E-mail: info@garland.com • URL: http://www.garlandpub.com • 1997. $155.00. Contains 327 alphabetical entries by various contributors. Defines and reviews all significant depressions, recessions, and financial crises in the U. S. and Europe since 1790. Includes chronologies, bibliographies, and indexes.

Business Cycles: Theory, History, Indications, and Forecasting. Victor Zarnowitz. The University of Chicago Press, 1427 E. 60th St. Chicago, IL 64720. Phone: (773)702-7700 Fax: (773)702-9756 E-mail: custserv@press.uchicago.edu • URL: http://www.press.uchicago.edu • 1992. $77.00. (National Bureau of Economic Research Monograph Series: Vol. 27).

Business Directory of Hong Kong. Estrin & Diamond Publications, 20832 Roscoe Blvd. Canoga Park, CA 91306. Phone: (818)700-6920 Fax: (818)700-6921 Annual. $180.00. Published in Hong Kong by Current Publications Ltd. Provides information on more than 12,300 Hong Kong businesses in various fields, including manufacturing, finance, services, construction, transportation, and foreign trade.

Business Economics: Designed to Serve the Needs of People Who Use Economics in Their Work. National Association for Business Economics, 1233 20th St., N.W. Suite 505 Washington, DC 20036-2304. Phone: (202)463-6223 Fax: (202)463-6239 E-mail: nabe@nabe.com • URL: http://www.nabe.com • Quarterly. $85.00 per year. Features articles on applied economics.

Business Education Forum. National Business Education Association, 1914 Association Dr. Reston, VA 20191-1596. Phone: (703)860-8300 Fax: (703)620-4483 E-mail: nbea@nbea.org • URL: http://www.nbea.org • Four times a year. Libraries, $70.00 per year. Includes *Yearbook* and *Keying In*, a newsletter.

Business English. Mary E. Guffey. South-Western, 5191 Natrop Blvd. Mason, OH 45040. Phone: 800-543-0487 or (513)229-1000 • URL: http://www.swcollege.com • 2001. $78.95. Seventh edition. (South-Western College Busines Communications Series).

Business English: A Complete Guide to Developing an Effective Business Writing Style. Andrea B. Geffner. Barron's Educational Series, Inc., 250 Wireless Blvd. Hauppauge, NY 11788-3917. Phone: 800-645-3476 or (516)434-3311 Fax: (516)434-3723 E-mail: info@barronseduc.com • URL: http://www.barronseduc.com • 2004. $16.95. Fourth edition. Covers both traditional and electronic business communication.

Business Essentials. Robert J. Ebert and Ricky W. Griffin. Prentice Hall PTR, 240 Frisch Ct. Paramus, NJ 07652. Phone: 800-282-0693 Fax: 800-445-6991 • URL: http://www.phptr.com • 2002. $73.33. Fourth edition.

Business Ethics. J. Michael Hoffman and others. McGraw-Hill, 1221 Ave. of the Americas New York, NY 10020. Phone: 800-722-4726 or (212)512-2000 Fax: (212)512-4502 E-mail: customer.service@mcgraw-hill.com • URL: http://www.mcgraw-hill.com • 2000. $39.25. Fourth edition.

Business Ethics: Roles and Responsibilities. Joseph Badaracco. McGraw-Hill, 1221 Ave. of the Americas New York, NY 10020. Phone: 800-722-4726 or (212)512-2000 Fax: (212)512-4502 E-mail: customer.service@mcgraw-hill.com • URL: http://www.mcgraw-hill.com • 1994. $63.50.

Business Ethics Survey. Available from Paul & Co., 814 N. Franklin St. Chicago, IL 60610. Phone: (312)337-0747 Fax: (312)337-5985 E-mail: frontdesk@ipgbook.com • URL: http://www.ipgbook.com • Annual. $99.95. Published by the Society for Human Resource Management (http://www.shrm.org). Provides benchmarks, with trends in business ethics data since 1997.

Business Etiquette. Marjorie Brody and Barbara Pachter. McGraw-Hill, 1221 Ave. of the Americas New York, NY 10020. Phone: 800-722-4726 or (212)512-2000 Fax: (212)512-4502 E-mail: customer.service@mcgraw-hill.com • URL: http://www.mcgraw-hill.com • 1994. $10.95. (Business Skills Express Series).

Business Etiquette: 101 Ways to Conduct Business with Charm and Savvy. Ann M. Sabath. Career Press, Inc., Three Tice Road Franklin Lakes, NJ 07417-1322. Phone: 800-227-3371 or (201)848-0310 Fax: (201)848-1727 E-mail: contact@careerpress.com • URL: http://www.careerpress.com • 2002. $12.99. Second edition. Topics include business correspondence, e-mail, current attire, telephone etiquette, social situations, and foreign business customs.

Business Facilities: The Location Advisor. Group C Communications, Inc., 44 Apple St., Ste. 3 Tinton Falls, NJ 07724. Phone: 800-524-0337 or (732)842-7433 Fax: (732)758-6634 E-mail: jstaats@groupc.com • URL: http://www.groupc.com • Monthly. Free to qualified personnel; others, $30.00 per year. Facility planning and site selection.

Business Failure Record. Dun Bradstreet Corp., 103 JFK Pky. Short Hills, NJ 07078. Phone: 800-526-0651 E-mail: custserv@dnb.com • URL: http://www.dnb.com • Annual. Free upon request. Provides historical business failure data.

Business Finance. Penton Technology and Lifestyle Media, One Penn Plz., 36th Fl. New York, NY 10119. Phone: 800-829-9028 Fax: (212)835-1605 E-mail: czelina@penton.com • URL: http://www.penton.com • Monthly. $59.00 per year. Covers trends in finance, technology, and economics for corporate financial executives.

Business Forecasting. J. Holton Wilson and Barry Keating. McGraw-Hill, 1221 Ave. of the Americas New York, NY 10020. Phone: 800-722-4726 or (212)512-2000 Fax: (212)512-4502 E-mail: customer.service@mcgraw-hill.com • URL: http://www.mcgraw-hill.com • 2001. $67.50. Fourth edition.

Business Forecasting. John E. Hanke and others. Prentice Hall PTR, 240 Frisch Ct. Paramus, NJ 07652. Phone: 800-282-0693 Fax: 800-445-6991 • URL: http://www.phptr.com • 2001. $117.33. Seventh edition.

Business Forecasting for Management. Branko Pecar. McGraw-Hill, 1221 Ave. of the Americas New York, NY 10020-1095. Phone: 800-722-4726 or (212)512-2000 Fax: (212)512-4502 E-mail: customer.service@mcgraw-hill.com • URL: http://www.mcgraw-hill.com • 1994. $14.95.

Business Forecasting Project. University of California, Los Angeles

Business Forms and Systems Manufacturers. Info USA, 5711 S 86th Circle Omaha, NE 68127. Phone: 800-321-0869 or (402)593-4600 Fax: (402)331-5481 E-mail: inquiries@infousa.com • URL: http://www.infousa.com • Annual. Price on application. Lists more than 800 suppliers and manufacturers of business forms, labels, and related equipment.

Business Forms, Labels and Systems. North American Publishing Co., 401 N. Broad St. Philadelphia, PA 19108. Phone: 800-777-8074 or (215)238-5482 Fax: 800-664-1533 or (215)238-5412 E-mail: customerservice@napco.com • URL: http://www.napco.com • Semimonthly. $95.00 per year. Formerly *Business Forms and Systems*.

Business Forms Management Association., 319 SW Washington, Ste. 710 Portland, OR 97204-2618. Phone: (503)227-3393 Fax: (503)274-7667 E-mail: bfma@bfma.org • URL: http://www.bfma.org • Persons engaged in forms management work, forms procedures analysis, forms design, or in education in this field; customer service firms selling, manufacturing, or servicing forms and supplies. Provides leadership and education to businesses in areas where the forms profession has demonstrated its special competence; promotes a broader function as a component of effective management; encourages, establishes, and maintains high standards of professional education, competence, and performance; provides a means for the sharing of information through study, programs, and research.

Business Forms on File. Facts on File Staff. Facts on File, Inc., 132 W 31st St., 17th Fl. New York, NY 10001. Phone: 800-322-8755 Fax: 800-678-3633 E-mail: custserv@factsonfile.com • URL: http://www.factsonfile.com • Annual. $126.00. Update edition, $49.50.

Business, Government, and Society: A Managerial Perspective: Text and Cases. George A. Steiner and John F. Steiner. McGraw-Hill, 1221 Ave. of the Americas New York, NY 10020. Phone: 800-722-4726 or (212)512-2000 Fax: (212)512-4502 E-mail: customer.service@mcgraw-hill.com • URL: http://www.mcgraw-hill.com • 1999. $88.75. Ninth edition. (Management Series).

Business, Government, and Society Research Institute. University of Pittsburgh

Business Guide to Modern China. Jon P. Alston and Yongxin He. Michigan State University Press, 1405 S. Harrison Rd., Suite 25 East Lansing, MI 48823-5202. Phone: (517)355-9543 Fax: (517)432-2611 E-mail: msupress@msu.edu • URL: http://www.msu.edu/press • 1997. $29.95. (International Business Series).

Business History. Frank Cass Publishers, 5804 N.E. Hassalo St. Portland, OR 97213-3644. Phone: 800-944-6190 Fax: (503)280-8832 E-mail: cass@isbs.com • URL: http://www.frankcass.com • Quarterly. Institutions, $382.00 per year. Includes print and online editions.

Business History Conference., Hagley Museum and Library, PO Box 3630, PO Box 3630 Wilmington, DE 19807-0630. Phone: (302)658-2400 Fax: (302)655-3188 E-mail: rh@udel.edu • URL: http://www.thebhc.org • Business historians and economic historians (most are from the academic community but a number of business firms are represented through their corporate historians). Brings together persons who are active historians of American and international business, with interests ranging from writing biographies of businessmen and histories of firms to the application of economic theory to analysis of the evolution of American business.

Business History of the World: A Chronology. Richard B. Robinson. Greenwood Publishing Group, Inc., 88 Post Rd., W Westport, CT 06881. Phone: 800-225-5800 or (203)226-3571 Fax: (203)431-2214 E-mail: customer-service@greenwood.com • URL: http://www.greenwood.com • 1993. $85.00. Provides "a basic chronology of the business world outside the United States from prehistory through the 1980s."

Business History Review. Harvard Business School Publishing, 300 N Beacon St. Watertown, MA 02163. Phone: 800-988-0886 or (617)783-7500 Fax: (617)783-7555 • URL: http://www.hbs.edu • Quarterly. Individuals, $50.00 per year; institutions, $100.00 per year; students, $35.00 per year.

Business Immigration Law: Strategies for Employing Foreign Nationals. American Lawyer Media, Inc., 105 Madison Ave. New York, NY 10016. Phone: 800-888-8300 or (212)779-9200 Fax: (212)481-8110 E-mail: lawcatalog@amlaw.com • URL: http://www.lawcatalog.com/ • Looseleaf. $169.00. Updated as needed. Provides step-by-step employment procedures relating to the law and regulations of the State Department, the Immigration and Naturalization Service, specific visa programs, and the Labor Department. Includes guidelines and samples of forms. (Law Journal Press).

Business Indexes. Board of Governors of the Federal Reserve System, 20th and C Sts. N.W. Washington, DC 20551. Phone: (202)452-3000 Fax: (202)452-3819 Monthly.

Business-Industry Political Action Committee., 888 16th St. NW, Ste. 305 Washington, DC 20006. Phone: (202)833-1880 Fax: (202)833-2338 E-mail: info@bipac.org • URL: http://www.bipac.org • Works as independent, bipartisan organization that works to elect pro-business candidates to Congress; has group's Business Institute for Political Analysis that carries out extensive programs of political analysis, research, and communication on campaigns and elections, and fosters business participation in the political process.

Business Information Alert: Sources, Strategies and Signposts for Information Professionals. Alert Publications, Inc., 401 W. Fullerton Parkway, Suite 1403E Chicago, IL 60614-2805. Phone: (773)525-7594 Fax: (773)525-7015 E-mail: info@alertpub.com • URL: http://www.alertpub.com • 10 times per year. Libraries, $162.00 per year. Newsletter for business librarians and information specialists.

Business Information Desk Reference: Where to Find Answers to Your Business Questions. Melvyn N. Freed and Virgil P. Diodato. Prentice Hall PTR, 340 Frisch Ct. Paramus, NJ 07652. Phone: 800-282-0693 Fax: 800-445-6991 • URL: http://www.phptr.com • 1992. $20.00. Offers a unique, question and answer approach to business information sources. Covers print sources, online databases, trade associations, and government agencies.

Business Information Handbook. David Mort. Available from Gale Cengage Learning, 27500 Drake Rd. Farmington Hills, MI 48331-3535. Phone: 800-877-GALE Fax: 800-414-5043 or (248)699-8069 E-mail: galeord@galegroup.com • URL: http://www.galegroup.com • 2003. $140.00. Published by K. G. Saur. Serves as a general guide to the world of business information.

Business Information: How to Find It, How to Use It. Michael R. Lavin. Greenwood Publishing Group, Inc., 88 Post Rd., W. Westport, CT 06881. Phone: 800-225-5800 or (203)226-3571 Fax: (203)431-2214 E-mail: customer-service@greenwood.com • URL: http://www.greenwood.com • 2001. $61.00. Third edition. Combines discussions of business research techniques with detailed descriptions of major business publications and databases. Includes title and subject indexes.

Business Insurance: Directory of 401(k) Plan Administrators.

Crain Communications, Inc., 711 Third Ave. New York, NY 10017-4036. Phone: 800-678-9595 or (212)210-0100 E-mail: info@crain.com • URL: http://www.crain.com • Annual. $4.00. Provides information on approximately 75 companies that administer 401(k) retirement plans.

Business Insurance-Directory of HMOs, POSs and PPOs. Crain Communications, 711 3rd Ave. New York, NY 10017-4036. Phone: (212)210-0100 E-mail: info@crain.com • URL: http://www.crain.com • Annual. $40.00. Provides detailed information on more than 600 managed care providers in the U. S., chiefly health maintenance organizations (HMOs) and preferred provider organizations (PPOs).

Business Insurance: Employee Benefit Consultants. Crain Communications, Inc., 711 3rd Ave. New York, NY 10017-0100. Phone: 800-678-9595 or (212)210-0100 E-mail: info@crain.com • URL: http://www.crain.com • Annual. $4.00. List of about 130 firms that offer empolyee benefit counseling services.

Business Insurance: News Magazine for Corporate Risk, Employee Benefit and Financial Executives. Crain Communications, Inc., 711 3rd Ave. New York, NY 10017-4036. Phone: 800-678-9595 or (212)210-0100 E-mail: info@crain.com • URL: http://www.crain.com • Weekly. $95.00 per year. Covers a wide variety of business insurance topics, including risk management, employee benefits, workers compensation, marine insurance, and casualty insurance.

Business Internet and Intranets: A Manager's Guide to Key Terms and Concepts. McGraw-Hill, 1221 Ave. of the Americas New York, NY 10020. Phone: 800-722-4726 or (212)512-2000 Fax: (212)512-4502 E-mail: customer.service@mcgrawhill.com • URL: http://www.mcgraw-hill.com • 1998. $39.95. Defines more than 100 words and phrases relating to the Internet or corporate intranets.

Business Interruption Coverage. American Bar Association, 750 N Lake Shore Dr. Chicago, IL 60611. Phone: 800-285-2221 or (312)988-5561 E-mail: orders@abanet.org • URL: http://www.abanet.org • 1987. $29.95. Produced by ABA Tort and Insurance Practice Section. Covers legal aspects of business interruption insurance.

Business Journals of the United States: Historical Guides to the World's Periodicals and Newspapers. William Fisher, editor. Greenwood Publishing Group, Inc., 88 Post Rd., W Westport, CT 06881. Phone: 800-225-5800 or (203)226-3571 Fax: (203)431-2214 E-mail: customer-service@greenwood.com • URL: http://www.greenwood.com • 1991. $82.95. Contains historical and descriptive essays covering over 100 leading business publications.

Business Latin America: Weekly Report to Managers of Latin American Operations. Economist Intelligence Unit, The Economist Bldg., 111 W 57th St. New York, NY 10019. Phone: 800-938-4685 or (212)554-0600 Fax: (212)586-1182 E-mail: newyork@eiu.com • URL: http://www.eiu.com • Weekly. $1,250.00 per year. Newsletter covering Latin American business trends, politics, regulations, exchange rates, economics, and finance. Provides statistical data on foreign debt, taxes, labor costs, gross domestic product (GDP), and inflation rates.

Business Law. Kevin Wardman and others. Continnum International Publishing Group, Inc., 311 Bainbridge St. Philadelphia, PA 19147. Phone: (215)925-5083 Fax: (215)925-1912 E-mail: order@transatlanticpub.com • URL: http://www.transatlanticpub.com • 2002. $99.95. Seventh edition. (Letts Higher Education List Series).

Business Law and Regulatory Environment: Concepts and Cases. Jane Mallor Frona Powell. McGraw-Hill Higher Education, 1221 Ave. of the Americas New York, NY 10020. Phone: 800-722-4726 or (212)512-2000 Fax: (212)512-4502 E-mail: customer.service@mcgraw-hill.com • URL: http://www.mcgraw-hill.com • 1997. $38.75. 10th edition. (Legal Studies in Business Series).

Business Law: Ethical, International and E-Commerce Environment. Henry R. Cheesman. Prentice Hall PTR, 240 Frisch Court Paramus, NJ 07652. Phone: 800-282-0693 Fax: 800-445-6991 • URL: http://www.phptr.com • 2000. $140.00. Fourth edition.

Business Law Monographs. LexisNexis Matthew Bender, 1275 Broadway Albany, NY 12204. Phone: 800-424-4200 or (518)487-3000 Fax: (518)487-3584 E-mail: bookstore.support@lexisnexis.com • URL: http://www.bender.com • Quarterly. $1,599.00. 38 volumes. Intended for in-house and outside corporate counsel. Each monograph concentrates on a particular subject.

Business Law: Principles and Practices. Arnold J. Goldman and William D. Sigismond. Houghton Mifflin Co., 222 Berkeley St. Boston, MA 02116. Phone: 800-733-2828 or (617)351-5000 Fax: 800-733-2098 E-mail: inquiries@hmco.com • URL: http://www.hmco.com • 2001. $64.36. Fifth edition.

Business Lawyer. American Bar Association, Business Law Section, 750 N Lake Shore Dr. Chicago, IL 60611. Phone: 800-285-2221 or (312)988-5000 Fax: (312)988-5528 E-mail: orders@abanet.org • URL: http://www.abanet.org • Quarterly. Members $99.00 per year; non-members, $149.00 per year.

Business Letters for Busy People: Time-Saving Ready-to-Use Business Letters for Any Occasion. Jim Dugger. Career Press, Inc., P.O. Box 687 Franklin Lakes, NJ 07417-1322. Phone: 800-227-3371 or (201)848-0310 Fax: (201)848-1727 E-mail: contact@careerpress.com • URL: http://www.careerpress.com • 2002. $19.99. Fourth edition.

Business Letters Ready to Go. Ann Basye. McGraw-Hill, 1221 Avenue of the Americas New York, NY 10020-1095. Phone: (212)904-2000 Fax: (212)512-2000 • URL: http://www.mcgraw-hill.com • 1998. $12.95. Includes CD-Rom. (Contemporary Books Series).

The Business Library and How to Use It: A Guide to Sources and Research Strategies for Information on Business and Management. Elizabeth Wood and others, editors. Omnigraphics, Inc., 615 Griswold St. Detroit, MI 48226. Phone: 800-234-1340 or (313)961-1340 Fax: 800-875-1340 or (313)961-1383 E-mail: info@omnigraphics.com • URL: http://www.omnigraphics.com • 1996. $28.00. Sixth edition. Explains library research methods and describes specific sources of business information. A revision of *How to Use the Business Library*, by H. Webster Johnson and others.

Business Market Association., 4131 N. Central Expy., Ste. 720 Dallas, TX 75204. Phone: 800-664-4262 or (312)822-0005 Fax: (312)822-0054 E-mail: rh@udel.edu • URL: http://www.marketing.org • Small- and medium-sized businesses. Works to bring large corporate lobbying and benefits to companies who do not have the workforce to achieve those benefits.

Business Marketing. McGraw-Hill, 1221 Ave. of the Americas New York, NY 10020. Phone: 800-722-4726 or (212)512-2000 Fax: (212)512-4502 E-mail: customer.service@mcgraw-hill.com • URL: http://www.mcgraw-hill.com • 2001. $68.00. Second edition.

Business Marketing Association and Resource Directory. Business Marketing Association, 400 N Michigan Ave., No. 1510 Chicago, IL 60611-4104. Phone: 800-664-4262 or (312)409-4262 Fax: (312)409-4266 E-mail: bma@marketing.org • URL: http://www.marketing.org • Annual. $100.00. Lists professionals in business and industrial advertising and marketing. Available online.

Business Marketing Management. Frank G. Bingham. McGraw-Hill, 1221 Ave. of the Americas New York, NY 10020. Phone: 800-722-4726 or (212)512-2000 Fax: (212)512-4502 E-mail: customer.service@mcgraw-hill.com • URL: http://www.mcgraw-hill.com • 1997. $71.95.

Business Math: Practical Applications. Cheryl Cleaves and Margie J. Hobbs. Prentice Hall PTR, 240 Frisch Ct. Paramus, NJ 07652. Phone: 800-282-0693 Fax: 800-445-6991 • URL: http://www.phptr.com • 2001. $79.93. Sixth edition.

Business Mathematics. Charles D. Miller and others. Addison-Wesley, 75 Arlington St., Ste. 300 Boston, MA 02116. Phone: 800-447-2226 or (617)848-7500 • URL: http://www.aw.com • 2002. $97.00. Ninth edition.

Business Mathematics. William L. Kindsfather and W. Alton Parish. Prentice Hall PTR, 240 Frisch Ct. Paramus, NJ 07652. Phone: 800-282-0693 Fax: 800-445-6991 • URL: http://www.phptr.com • 2003. Price on application.

Business Mathematics for College. Jeffrey Slater and Rick Ponticelli. McGraw-Hill, 1221 Ave. of the Americas New York, NY 10020. Phone: 877-833-5524 or (212)512-2000 E-mail: customer.service@mcgraw-hill.com • URL: http://www.mcgraw-hill.com • 1996. $81.56.

Business Multimedia Explained: A Manager's Guide to Key Terms and Concepts. Peter G. W. Keen. Harvard Business School Publishing, 300 N Beacon St. Watertown, MA 02163. Phone: 800-988-0886 or (617)783-7500 Fax: (617)783-7555 • URL: http://www.hbs.edu • 1997. $39.95.

Business Negotiating Basics: International Edition. Peter Economy. McGraw-Hill, 1221 Ave. of the Americas New York, NY 10020. Phone: 800-722-4726 or (212)512-2000 Fax: (212)512-4502 E-mail: customer.service@mcgraw-hill.com • URL: http://www.mcgraw-hill.com • 1994. $13.95. (Briefcase Books Series).

The Business of Banking for Bank Directors. George K. Darling and James F. Chaston. The Risk Management Association, One Liberty Place, 1650 Market St., Suite 2300 Philadelphia, PA 19103. Phone: 800-677-7621 or (215)446-4000 Fax: (215)446-4101 E-mail: customers@rmahq.org • URL: http://www.rmahq.org • 1995. $33.00. Presents basic banking concepts and issues for new directors of financial institutions. Emphasis is on the specific duties of directors.

The Business of Law: A Handbook on How to Manage Law Firms. Aspen Publishers, Inc., 1185 Ave. of the Americas New York, NY 10036. Phone: 800-234-1660 or (212)597-0200 Fax: (212)597-0338 E-mail: customer.service@aspenpubl.com • URL: http://www.aspenpublishers.com • $95.00. Looseleaf service. Periodic supplementation.

The Business of Publishing: How to Survive and Prosper in the Publishing and Bookselling Industry. Leonard Shatzkin. McGraw-Hill, 1221 Ave. of the Americas New York, NY 10020. Phone: 800-722-4726 or (212)512-2000 Fax: (212)512-4502 E-mail: customer.service@mcgraw-hill.com • URL: http://www.mcgraw-hill.com • 1995. $24.95.

The Business of Shipping. James J. Buckley and Lane C. Kendall. Cornell Maritime Press, Inc., P.O. Box 456 Centreville, MD 21617. Phone: 800-638-7641 or (410)758-1075 Fax: (410)758-6849 E-mail: cornell@crosslink.net • URL: http://www.cornellmaritimepress.com • 2001. $50.00. Seventh edition.

The Business of Special Events: Fundraising Strategies for Changing Times. Harry A. Freedman and Karen Feldman. Pineapple Press, Inc., PO Box 3899 Sarasota, FL 34230-3899. Phone: 800-746-3275 or (941)359-0886 Fax: (941)351-9988 E-mail: info@pineapplepress.com • URL: http://www.pineapplepress.com • 1998. $21.95.

The Business of Systems Integration. Andrea Prencipe and Andrew Davies, editors. Oxford University Press, 198 Madison Ave. New York, NY 10016-4314. Phone: 800-451-7556 or (212)726-6000 Fax: (212)726-6446 E-mail: custserv@oup-usa.org • URL: http://www.oup-usa.org • 2004. $74.50.

Business Organizations, Agencies, and Publications Directory. Gale Cengage Learning, 27500 Drake Rd. Farmington Hills, MI 48331-3535. Phone: 800-877-GALE or (248)699-GALE Fax: 800-414-5043 E-mail: gale.galeord@cengage.com • URL: http://gale.cengage.com • 2003. $480.00. 15th edition. Over 40,000 entries describing 39 types of business information sources. Classified by type of organization, publication, or serviceIncludes state, national, and international agencies and organizations. Master index to names and keywords. Also includes e-mail addresses and web site URL's.

Business Organizations with Tax Planning. Zolman Cavitch, editor. LexisNexis Matthew Bender, 1275 Broadway Albany, NY 12204. Phone: (518)487-3000 Fax: 800-544-6527 E-mail: bookstore.support@lexisnexis.com • URL: http://www.bender.lexisnexis.com • Quarterly. $2,750. 16 looseleaf volumes. Periodic supplementation. In-depth analytical coverage of corporation law and all relevant aspects of federal corporation taxation.

Business Periodicals Index. H. W. Wilson Co., 950 University Ave. Bronx, NY 10452. Phone: 800-367-6770 or (718)588-8400 Fax: 800-590-1617 or (718)590-1617 E-mail: custserv@hwwilson • URL: http://www.hwwilson.com • 11 times a year. Quarterly and annual cumulations. Price varies.

Business Plan: Planning for the Small Business. Alan West. Nichols Publishing Co., P.O. Box 6036 East Brunswick, NJ 08816-6036. Phone: (732)297-2862 Fax: (732)940-0549 1988. $21.95.

Business Plans Handbook. Gale Cengage Learning, 27500 Drake Rd. Farmington Hills, MI 48331-3535. Phone: 800-877-GALE or (248)699-GALE Fax: 800-414-5043 E-mail: gale.galeord@cengage.com • URL: http://gale.cengage.com • 2003. $150.00. Contains examples of detailed plans for starting or developing various kinds of businesses. Categories within plans include statement of purpose, market description, personnel requirements, financial needs, etc.

Business Plans that Work for Your Small Business. Alice H. Magos and Steve Crow, editors. CCH, Inc., 4025 West Peterson Ave. Chicago, IL 60646-6085. Phone: 800-248-3248 or (773)866-6000 Fax: 800-224-8299 or (773)866-3095 E-mail: cust_serv@cch.com • URL: http://www.onlinestore.cch.com/ • 2003. $19.95. Second edition. Part one is "Creating a Business Plan that Works" and part two is "Five Sample Business Plans."

Business Policy Game: An International Simulation. Richard V. Cotter and David J. Fritzsche. Prentice Hall PTR, 240 Frisch Ct. Paramus, NJ 07652. Phone: 800-282-0693 Fax: 800-445-6991 • URL: http://www.phptr.com • 1995. $53.33. Fourth edition.

Business Products Industry Association Membership Directory and Buyer's Guide. Independent Office Products and Furniture Dealers Association, 301 N. Fairfax St. Alexandria, VA 22314. Phone: 800-542-6672 or (703)549-9040 Fax: (703)683-7552 • URL: http://www.iopfda.org • Annual. Free to members; non-members, $80.00. 9,000 manufacturers, wholesalers, retailers and sales and marketing representatives in the office products industry.

Business-Professional Online Markets. SIMBA Information, Inc., 11 Riverbend Dr., S. Stamford, CT 06907-0234. Phone: 800-307-2529 or (203)358-4100 Fax: (203)358-5824 E-mail: info@simbanet.com • URL: http://www.simbanet.com • Annual. $1,995.00; with online edition, $3,390.00. Provides a review of current conditions in the online information industry. Profiles of major database producers and online services are included.

Business Rankings Annual. Gale Cengage Learning, 27500 Drake Rd. Farmington Hills, MI 48331-3535. Phone: 800-877-GALE or (248)699-GALE Fax: (248)699-8069 E-mail: gale.galeord@cengage.com • URL: http://gale.cengage.com • Annual. $325.00. Two volumes. Compiled by the Business Library Staff of the Brooklyn Public Library. This is a guide to lists and rankings appearing in major business publications. The top ten names are listed in each case.

Business Ratios and Formulas: A Comprehensive Guide. Steven M. Bragg. John Wiley and Sons, Inc., 111 River St. Hoboken, NJ 07030. Phone: 800-225-5945 or (201)748-6000 Fax: (201)748-6088 E-mail: bookinfo@wiley.com • URL: http://www.wiley.com • 2002. $85.00. Describes and explains a wide variety of ratios used in finance and management.

Business Records Control. Joseph S. Fosegan and Mary L. Ginn. South-Western, 5191 Natrop Blvd. Mason, OH 45040. Phone: 800-543-0487 or (513)229-1000 • URL: http://www.swcollege.com • 1999. $49.95. Eighth edition.

Business Research for Decision Making. Duane Davis. Wadsworth Publishing Co., 10 Davis Dr. Belmont, CA 94002. Phone: (650)595-2350 • URL: http://www.wadsworth.com • 1999. $62.00. Fifth edition. (Business Statistics Series).

Business Research Handbook: Methods and Sources for Lawyers and Business Professionals. Kathy E. Shimpock. Aspen Publishers, Inc., 1185 Ave. of the Americas New York, NY 10036. Phone: 800-234-1660 or (212)597-0200 Fax: 800-901-9075 or (212)597-0338 E-mail: customer.service@aspenpubl.com • URL: http://www.aspenpublishers.com • $155.00. Looseleaf service. Periodic supplementation.

Provides detailed advice on how to find business information. Describes a wide variety of data sources, both private and government.

Business Start-Ups: Smart Ideas for Your Small Business. Entrepreneur Media, Inc., 2445 McCabe Way Irvine, CA 92614. Phone: 800-421-2300 or (949)261-2325 Fax: (949)261-0234 E-mail: entmag@entrepreneur.com • URL: http://www.entrepreneur.com • Monthly. $14.97 per year. Provides advice for starting a small business. Includes business trends, new technology, E-commerce, and case histories ("real-life stories").

Business Statistics: A Decision-Making Approach. David F. Groebner and others. Prentice Hall PTR, 240 Frisch Ct. Paramus, NJ 07652. Phone: 800-282-0693 Fax: 800-445-6991 • URL: http://www.phptr.com • 2001. $115.00 Fifth edition.

Business Statistics by Example. Simon Sincich. Pearson Custom Publishing, 75 Arlington St., Ste. 300 Boston, MA 02116. Phone: 800-428-4466 or (617)848-6300 Fax: (617)848-6333 E-mail: pcp@pearsoncustom.com • URL: http://www.pearsoncustom.com • 2001. $45.00.

Business Statistics: Contemporary Decision Making. Ken Black. South-Western, 5191 Natrop Blvd. Mason, OH 45040. Phone: 800-543-0487 or (513)229-1000 • URL: http://www.swcollege.com • 2000. $107.95. Third edition.

Business Statistics for Management and Economics. Wayne W. Daniel and James C. Terrell. Houghton Mifflin Co., 222 Berkeley St. Boston, MA 02116. Phone: 800-733-2828 or (617)351-5000 Fax: 800-733-2098 E-mail: inquiries@hmco.com • URL: http://www.hmco.com • 1995. $23.96. Seventh edition.

Business Statistics for Quality and Productivity. John M. Levine. Prentice Hall PTR, 240 Frisch Ct. Paramus, NJ 07652. Phone: 800-282-0693 Fax: 800-445-6991 • URL: http://www.phptr.com • 1994. $94.07. (Prentice Hall College Title Series).

Business Statistics of the United States. Linz Audain and Cornelia J. Strawser. Bernan Associates, 4611-F Assembly Dr. Lanham, MD 20706-4391. Phone: 800-274-4888 or (301)459-7666 Fax: 800-865-3450 or (301)459-0056 E-mail: order@bernan.com • URL: http://www.bernan.com • Annual. $147.00. Based on *Business Statistics*, formerly issue by the Bureau of Economic Analysis, U. S. Department of Commerce. Provides basic data for a wide variety of U. S. industries, services, and economic indicators. Most statistics are shown annually for 30 years and monthly for the most recent four years.

Business Statistics on the Web: Find Them Fast, at Little or No Cost. Paula Berinstein. Information Today, Inc., 143 Old Marlton Pike Medford, NJ 08055-8750. Phone: 800-300-9868 or (609)654-6266 Fax: (609)654-4309 E-mail: custserv@infotoday.com • URL: http://www.infotoday.com • 2003. $29.95. Serves as a practical guide to finding and evaluating business data through the Internet. Includes advice on the organization and presentation of business statistics. (Cyber-Age Books).

Business Statistics Practice. Bruce L. Bowerman and others. McGraw-Hill, 1221 Ave. of the Americas New York, NY 10020. Phone: 800-722-4726 or (212)512-2000 Fax: (212)512-4502 E-mail: customer.service@mcgraw-hill.com • URL: http://www.mcgraw-hill.com • 2001. $68.00. Second edition.

Business Strategies. CCH, Inc., 2700 Lake Cook Rd. Riverwoods, IL 60015. Phone: 800-835-5224 or (847)267-7000 E-mail: cust_serv@cch.com • URL: http://www.cch.com • Semimonthly. $795.00 per year. Four looseleaf volumes. Semimonthly updates. Legal, tax, and accounting aspects of business planning and decision-making. Provides information on start-ups, forms of ownership (partnerships, corporations), failing businesses, reorganizations, acquisitions, and so forth. Includes *Business Strategies Bulletin*, a monthly newsletter.

Business Strategies Bulletin. CCH Inc., 4025 W Peterson Ave. Chicago, IL 60646-6085. Phone: 888-224-7377 or (847)267-7000 Fax: (773)866-3895 E-mail: info@bookweb.org • URL: http://www.cch.com • Description: Reports tax and business planning information for all sizes of business, with emphasis on small to mid-sized business advisors.

Business Strategy and Policy. McGraw-Hill, 1221 Ave. of the Americas New York, NY 10020. Phone: 800-722-4726 Fax: (212)512-4502 E-mail: customer.service@mcgraw-hill.com • URL: http://www.mcgraw-hill.com • 1999. $45.00.

Business Taxpayer Information Publications. Available from U. S. Government Printing Office, Washington, DC 20402. Phone: (202)512-1800 Fax: (202)512-2250 E-mail: gpoaccess@gpo.gov • URL: http://www.access.gpo.gov • Annual. $63.00. Two volumes, consisting of *Circular E, Employer's Tax Guide* and *Employer's Supplemental Tax Guide*. Issued by the Internal Revenue Service (http://www.irs.ustreas.gov). Includes a wide variety of business-related tax information, including withholding tables, tax calendars, self-employment issues, partnership matters, corporation topics, depreciation, and bankruptcy.

Business Technology Association., 12411 Wornall Rd., Ste. 200 Kansas City, MO 64145-1212. Phone: 800-505-2821 or (816)941-3100 Fax: (816)941-4838 E-mail: info@bta.org • URL: http://www.bta.org • Dealers and resellers of office equipment and networking products and services. Offers 60 seminars on management, service, technology, and business systems. Conducts research, provides business-supporting services and benefits, including insurance, and legal counsel.

Business to Business Advertising: A Marketing Management Approach. Charles Patti and others. McGraw-Hill, 1221 Ave. of the Americas New York, NY 10020. Phone: 800-722-4726 or (212)512-2000 Fax: (212)512-4502 E-mail: customer.service@mcgraw-hill.com • URL: http://www.mcgraw-hill.com • 1994. $39.95. (NTC Business Books Series).

Business Travel News: News and Ideas for Business Travel Management. VNU Business Media, 770 Broadway New York, NY 10010. Phone: 800-344-7119 or (646)654-4500 Fax: (646)654-7212 • URL: http://www.vnubusinessmedia.com • 29 times a year. $119.00 per year. Includes annual directory of travel sources. Formerly *Corporate Travel*.

Business 2.0. Time Inc., One California St., 29th Floor San Francisco, CA 94111. Phone: (415)293-4800 Fax: (415)293-5900 • URL: http://www.business2.com • Monthly. $30.00 per year. General business magazine emphasizing ideas, insight, and innovation.

Business 2.0 Web Guide to the Best Business Links. Business 2.0 Media Inc.Phone: (415)293-4800 E-mail: support@business2.com • URL: http://www.business2.com/webguide • Web site presents an extensive, searchable directory of links to "the best, most informative, and authoritative web pages." Twenty main categories cover business, finance, career, company information, people, and technology topics, with thousands of subtopics, all linking to Web sites recommended by experienced business researchers. Fees: Free.

Business Week. McGraw-Hill, 1221 Ave. of the Americas New York, NY 10020. Phone: 800-722-4726 or (212)512-2000 Fax: (212)512-4502 E-mail: customer.service@mcgraw-hill.com • URL: http://www.mcgraw-hill.com • Weekly. $45.97 per year. Last volume is a double issue.

Business Week China. Ministry of Foreign Economic Relations and Trade, Institute of International Tra. McGraw-Hill, 1221 Ave. of the Americas New York, NY 10020. Phone: 800-722-4726 or (212)512-2000 Fax: (212)512-4502 E-mail: customer.service@mcgraw-hill.com • URL: http://www.mcgraw-hill.com • Bimonthly. Price on application. Edited for business and government officials in the People's Republic of China. Selected Chinese translation of *Business Week*.

Business Week International: The World's Only International Newsweekly of Business. McGraw-Hill, 1221 Ave. of the Americas New York, NY 10020. Phone: 800-722-4726 or (212)512-2000 Fax: (212)512-4502 E-mail: customer.service@mcgraw-hill.com • URL: http://www.mcgraw-hill.com • Weekly. $95.00 per year.

Business Week Online. McGraw-HillPhone: (212)512-2511 Fax: (684)842-6101 • URL: http://www.businessweek.com • Web site provides complete contents of current issue of *Business Week* plus "BW Daily" with additonal business news, financial market quotes, and corporate information from Standard & Poor's. Includes various features, such as "Banking Center" with mortgage and interest data, and "Interactive Computer Buying Guide." The "Business Week Archive" is fully searchable back to 1996.

Business Week's Guide to the Best Business Schools. John A. Byrne. McGraw-Hill, 1221 Ave. of the Americas New York, NY 10020. Phone: 800-722-4726 or (212)512-2000 Fax: (212)512-4502 E-mail: customer.service@mcgraw-hill.com • URL: http://www.mcgraw-hill.com • 2002. $16.95. Seventh edition. Includes the best regional business schools. (Business Week Guide to the Best Business Schools Series).

Business Woman Magazine. National Federation of Business and Professional Women's Clubs, Inc., 2012 Massachusetts Ave. N.W. Washington, DC 20036. Phone: (202)293-1100 Fax: (202)861-0298 E-mail: businesswoman@bpwusa.org • URL: http://www.bpwusa.org • Quarterly. $12.00 per year. Focuses on the activities and interests of working women.

Business Writing at Its Best. Minerva H. Neiditz. McGraw-Hill, 1221 Ave. of the Americas New York, NY 10020. Phone: 800-722-4726 or (212)512-2000 Fax: (212)512-4502 E-mail: customer.service@mcgraw-hill.com • URL: http://www.mcgraw-hill.com • 1993. $22.50.

Businesses' Views on Red Tape: Administrative and Regulatory Burdens on Small and Medium-Sized Enterprises. Organization for Economic Cooperation and Development, OECD Washington Center, 2001 L St., N. W., Suite 650 Washington, DC 20036-4922. Phone: 800-456-6323 or (202)785-6323 Fax: (202)785-0350 E-mail: washington.contact@oecd.org • URL: http://www.oecd.org • 2001. $22.00. Based on a survey of about 8,000 firms in 11 OECD countries. Provides opinions on the costs of complying with governmental rules, regulations, and formalities.

Butane-Propane News. Butane-Propane News, Inc., P.O. Box 660698 Arcadia, CA 91006-0698. Phone: (818)357-2168 Fax: (818)303-2854 Monthly. Qualified personnel, $30.00 per year.

Buyers' Guide for the Health Care Market: A Directory of Products and Services for Health Care Institutions. Health Forum, 180 Montgomery St., Suite 1520 San Francisco, CA 94104. Phone: 800-821-2039 or (415)248-8400 Fax: (415)248-0400 • URL: http://www.healthforum.com • Annual. $17.95. Lists 1,200 suppliers and manufacturers of health care products and services for hospitals, nursing homes, and related organizations.

Buyers Guide to Outdoor Advertising. Competitive Media Reporting, 685 Third Ave., 4th Fl. New York, NY 10017. Phone: (212)991-6000 Fax: (212)949-1963 Semiannual. $475.00 per year. Lists more than 800 outdoor advertising

companies and their market rates, etc.

Buyer's Guide to the New York Market. Earnshaw Publications, Inc., 225 W 34th St. New York, NY 10001. Phone: (212)563-2742 Annual. Included with *Earnshaw's Magazine*.

Buying and Maintaining Personal Computers: A How-To-Do-It Manual for Librarians with Companion Web Site. Norman Howden. Neal-Schuman Publishers, Inc., 100 William St., Ste. 2004 New York, NY 10013. Phone: (866)672-2667 or (212)925-8650 Fax: (866)209-7932 or (212)219-8916 E-mail: info@neal-schuman.com • URL: http://www.neal-schuman.com • 2000. $45.00. Covers various aspects of buying PCs or MACs for library use, including choice of hardware, software selection, warranties, backup systems, staffing, and dealing with vendors. (How-To-Do-It Manuals Series).

Buying and Selling a Small Business: A Complete Guide to a Successful Deal. Ernest J. Honigmann. CCH, Inc., 2700 Lake Cook Rd. Riverwoods, IL 60015. Phone: 800-835-5224 or (847)267-7000 E-mail: cust_serv@cch.com • URL: http://www.cch.com • 1999. $91.95.

Buying Books: A How-To-Do-It Manual for Librarians. Audrey Eaglen. Neal-Schuman Publishers, Inc., 100 William St., Ste. 2004 New York, NY 10038. Phone: (866)672-2667 or (212)925-8650 Fax: (866)209-7932 or (212)219-8916 E-mail: info@neal-schuman.com • URL: http://www.neal-schuman.com • 2000. $45.00. Second edition. Discusses vendor selection and book ordering in the age of electronic commerce. Covers both print and electronic bibliographic sources. (How-to-Do-It Manuals Series).

Buying Serials: A How-To-Do-It Manual for Librarians. N. Bernard Basch and Judy McQueen. Neal-Schuman Publishers, Inc., 100 William St., Ste. 2004 New York, NY 10038. Phone: (866)672-2667 or (212)925-8650 Fax: (866)209-7932 or (212)219-8916 E-mail: info@neal-schuman.com • URL: http://www.neal-schuman.com • 1990. $49.95. (How-to-Do-It Manuals Series).

Buyout Financing Sources/M & A Intermediaries. Thomson Media, One State St. Plaza New York, NY 10004. Phone: 800-221-1809 or (212)803-8200 Fax: (212)843-9635 E-mail: custserv@thomsonmedia.com • URL: http://www.thomsonmedia.com • Annual. $895.00. Provides the CD-ROM combination of *Directory of Buyout Financing Sources* and *Directory of M & A Intermediaries*. Contains information on more than 1,000 financing sources (banks, insurance companies, venture capital firms, etc.) and 850 intermediaries (corporate acquirers, valuation firms, lawyers, accountants, etc.). Also includes back issues of *Buyouts Newsletter* and *Mergers & Acquisitions Report*. Fully searchable.

Buyouts: The Newsletter for Management Buyouts, Leveraged Aquisitions, and Special Situations. Thomson Financial, 195 Broadway New York, NY 10007. Phone: 800-262-6000 or (646)822-2000 Fax: (646)822-6270 E-mail: custserv@tfn.com • URL: http://www.tfn.com • Biweekly. $1,595.00 per year. Newsletter. Covers news and trends for the buyout industry. Provides information on deal makers and current buyout activity.

By the Numbers: Electronic and Online Publishing. Gale Cengage Learning, 27500 Drake Rd. Farmington Hills, MI 48331-3535. Phone: 800-877-GALE or (248)699-GALE Fax: 800-414-5043 E-mail: gale.galeord@cengage.com • URL: http://gale.cengage.com • 1997-98. $305.00. Four volumes. $85.00 per volume. Covers "high-interest" industries: 1. *By the Numbers: Electronic and Online Publishing*; 2. *By the Numbers: Emerging Industries*; 3. *By the Numbers: Nonprofits*; 4. *By the Numbers: Publishing*. Each volume provides about 600 tabulations of industry data on revenues, market share, employment, trends, financial ratios, profits, salaries, and so forth. Citations to data sources are included. (By the Numbers Series).

C E D: The Premier Magazine of Technology. Reed Business Information, 360 Park Ave., S New York, NY 10010. Phone: 800-446-6551 or (646)746-6400 Fax: (646)746-7028 E-mail: corporatecommunications@reedbusiness.com • URL: http://www.reedbusiness.com • Monthly. $54.00 per year. Formerly *Communications Engineering and Design*.

A C M Electronic Guide to Computing Literature: Bibliographic Listing, Author Index, Keyword Index, Category Index, Proper Noun Subject Index, Reviewer Index, Source Index. Association for Computing Machinery, 1515 Broadway New York, NY 10036-5701. Phone: (212)869-7440 Fax: (212)869-0481 E-mail: acmhelp@acm.org • URL: http://www.acm.org • Quarterly. Members, $175.00; non-members, $499.00 per year. A comprehensive guide to each year's computer literature (books, proceedings, journals, etc.), with an emphasis on technical material. Indexed by author, keyword, category, proper noun, reviewer, and source. Formerly *A C M Guide to Computing Literature*.

CA Search. Chemical Abstracts Service, 2540 Olentangy River Rd. Columbus, OH 43210. Phone: 800-753-4227 or (614)447-3600 Fax: (614)447-3713 Guide to chemical literature, 1967 to present. Inquire as to online cost and availability.

CA Selects: Selenium and Tellurium Chemistry. American Chemical Society. Chemical Abstracts Service, 2540 Olentangy River Rd. Columbus, OH 43202. Phone: 800-753-4227 or (614)447-3731 Fax: (614)447-3751 E-mail: help@cas.org • URL: http://www.cas.org • Semiweekly. Members, $92.00 per year; non-members, $305.00 per year. Looseleaf service. Incorporates *Selenium and Tellurium Abstracts*.

CAB Abstracts. CAB Publishing North America, 44 Brattle St. Cambridge, MA 02138. Phone: 800-528-4841 or (617)395-4056 Fax: (617)654-6875 E-mail: cabi-nao@cabi.org • URL: http://www.cabi.org • Contains 46 specialized abstract collections covering over 10,000 journals and monographs in the areas of agriculture, horticulture, forest products, farm products, nutrition, dairy science, poultry, grains, animal health, entomology, etc. Time period is 1972 to date, with monthly updates. Inquire as to online cost and availability. *CAB Abstracts on CD-ROM* also available, with annual updating.

Cabell's Directory of Publishing Opportunities in Curriculum and Methods. Cabell Publishing Co., Tobe Hahn Station, P.O. Box 5428 Beaumont, TX 77726-5428. Phone: (409)898-0575 Fax: (409)866-9554 E-mail: publish@cabells.com • URL: http://www.cabells.com • 2002. $99.95. Over 350 journals in education which will consider manuscripts for publication. Formerly *Cabell's Directory of Publishing Opportunities in Education*.

Cabell's Directory of Publishing Opportunities in Management. Cabell Publishing Co., Tobe Hahn Station, P.O. Box 5428 Beaumont, TX 77726-5428. Phone: (409)898-0575 Fax: (409)866-9554 E-mail: publish@cabells.com • URL: http://www.cabells.com • 1997. $149.95. Seventh edition. Four volumes. Over 540 scholarly periodicals in management.

Cable and Station Coverage Atlas. Warren Publishing Inc., 2115 Ward Ct., NW Washington, DC 20037. Phone: (202)872-9200 Fax: (202)293-3435 • URL: http://www.warrenpub.com • 1997. $410.00.

Cable Television Revenues. U.S. Federal Communications Commission, Washington, DC 20554. Phone: 888-225-5322 or (202)418-0500 • URL: http://www.fcc.gov • Annual.

Cable TV Facts. Cabletelevision Advertising Bureau, 830 Third Ave., FRNT. 2 New York, NY 10022-7522. Phone: (212)508-1200 Fax: (212)832-3268 Annual. $12.00. Provides statistics on cable TV and cable TV advertising in the U. S.

Cable TV Investor: Newsletter on Investments in Cable TV Systems and Publicly Held Cable TV Stocks. Paul Kagan Associates, Inc., 126 Clock Tower Place Carmel, CA 93923-8746. Phone: (831)624-1536 Fax: (831)625-3225 E-mail: info@kagan.com • URL: http://www.kagan.com • Monthly. $995.00 per year.

Cable TV Programming: Newsletter on Programs for Pay Cable TV and Analysis of Basic Cable Networks. Paul Kagan Associates, Inc., 126 Clock Tower Place Carmel, CA 93923-8746. Phone: (831)624-1536 Fax: (831)625-3225 E-mail: info@kagan.com • URL: http://www.kagan.com • Monthly. $895.00 per year.

Cabletelevision Advertising Bureau., 830 Third Ave., 2nd Fl. New York, NY 10022. Phone: (212)508-1200 Fax: (212)832-3268 E-mail: info@bta.org • URL: http://www.onetvworld.org • Ad-supported cable networks. Provides marketing and advertising support to members and promotes the use of cable by advertisers and ad agencies locally, regionally, and nationally.

The Cabot Market Letter. Cabot Heritage Corp., 176 North St., PO Box 2049 Salem, MA 01970. Phone: 800-777-2658 or (978)745-5532 Fax: (978)745-1283 E-mail: customerservice@cabot.net Description: Analyzes and recommends stock investments. Emphasizes that "optimum profits depend upon good market timing and good stock selection." Each issue follows a model portfolio made up of 12 stocks from lesser known companies chosen for their high potential for rapid, long-term growth.

CAD/CAM,CAE: Survey, Review and Buyers' Guide. Daratech, Inc., 225 Bent St. Cambridge, MA 02141-2081. Phone: (617)354-2339 Fax: (617)354-7822 E-mail: daratech@daratech.com • URL: http://www.daratech.com • $2,998.00 per year. Looseleaf service. Three editions. Mechanical edition, $972.00 per year; AEC and Plant design editon, $1,498.00 per year. Includes computer-aided engineering (CAE).

Caine Dairy Center. Utah State University

California Agricultural Experiment Station. University of California

California Farmer: The Business Magazine for Commercial Agriculture. Farm Progress Companies, 191 S. Gary Ave. Carol Stream, IL 60188. Phone: 800-441-1410 or (630)462-2224 Fax: (630)462-2869 E-mail: circhelp@farmprogress.com • URL: http://www.farmprogress.com • 15 times a year. $23.95 per year. Three editions: Northern, Southern and Central Valley.

California Institute of Technology.

California Management Review. University of California at Berkeley, S549 Haas School of Business, Ste. 1900 Berkeley, CA 94720-1900. Phone: 800-777-4726 or (510)642-7159 Fax: (510)642-1318 E-mail: cmr@haas.berkeley.edu • URL: http://www.haas.berkeley.edu/news/cmr • Quarterly. Individuals, $50.00 per year; institutions, $65.00.

Call Center. CMP Media LLC, 12 W 21st St. New York, NY 10010. Phone: (516)562-5000 E-mail: cmp@cmp.com • URL: http://www.cmp.com • Monthly. Free to qualified personnel. Emphasis is on telemarketing, selling, and customer service. Includes articles on communication technology. Formerly *Call Center Solutions*.

Callahan's Credit Union Directory. Callahan & Associates Inc., 1001 Connecticut Ave. NW, 10th Fl. Washington, DC 20036. Phone: 800-446-7453 or (202)223-3920 Fax: (202)223-6098 E-mail: callahan@creditunions.com • URL: http://www.creditunions.com • Covers: 11,843 state, federal, and U.S. credit unions; regulators, organizations, and leagues. Entries include: For credit unions—Name, address, phone, fax, chief executive officer, charter number; financial data, including total assets, loans, capital, and investments; number of members, rate of deposit growth, and routing and transit numbers. For regulators, associations and leagues—Organization or agency name, address, phone, contact.

Callmann on Unfair Competition, Trademarks and Monopolies. Louis Altman and Rudolf Callmann. West Group, 610 Opperman Dr. Eagan, MN 55123. Phone: 800-328-4880 or (651)687-7000 Fax: 800-340-9378 E-mail: bookstore@westgroup.com • URL: http://www.westgroup.com • Semiannual. $1,270.00 per year. 10 looseleaf volumes. Covers various aspects of anti-competitive behavior.

Calories and Carbohydrates: A Dictionary Listing of over 8500 Brand Names and Basic Foods with their Calorie and Carbohydrate Count. Barbara Kraus. NAL, 375 Hudson St. New York, NY 10014-3657. Phone: 800-331-4624 or (212)366-2000 Fax: (212)366-2666 E-mail: online@penguinputnam.com • URL: http://www.penguinputnam.com • 2001. $6.99. 14th revised edition.

Camera. Orion Research Corp., 14555 N. Scottsdale Rd., Suite 330 Scottsdale, AZ 85254-3457. Phone: 800-844-0759 Fax: 800-375-1315 E-mail: orion@bluebook.com • URL: http://www.netzone.com • Annual. $144.00. Quotes retail and wholesale prices of used cameras and equipment. Original list prices and years of manufacture are also shown.

Cameras. Available from MarketResearch.com, 641 Ave. of the Americas, Fourth Floor New York, NY 10011. Phone: 800-298-5699 or (212)807-2629 Fax: (212)807-2642 E-mail: order@marketresearch.com • URL: http://www.marketresearch.com • 2002. $3,950.00. Published by Global Industry Analysts. Provides worldwide market research data, including profiles of major camera companies.

Camp Directors Purchasing Guide. Klevens Publications Inc., 411 S Main St., Ste. 209 Los Angeles, CA 90013. Phone: (213)625-9000 Fax: (213)625-5002 E-mail: editor@klevenspub.com • URL: http://www.campdirectorsguide.com • Covers: suppliers of products and services used in the operation of children's summer camps. Publication includes: sporting goods, arts and crafts materials, food, food service equipment, and building and maintenance equipment. Entries include: Company name, address, phone, fax, brief description of product or service.

Campaign California., 926 J St., No. 1400 Sacramento, CA 95814. Phone: (916)447-8950 E-mail: info@bipac.org State organization that attempts to introduce new issues into the political arena such as: rebuilding the Democratic party; controlling toxic wastes; developing affordable and better child care; stopping environmental cancer; achieving low-cost housing and tenants' rights. Works to elect progressive candidates to office in California.

Campaign for America., 50 F St. NW, Ste. 1198 Washington, DC 20001. Phone: (202)628-0610 Fax: (202)628-0598 E-mail: caomail@hr.house.gov Political fund organization.

Campaign for Space Political Action Committee., PO Box 1526 Bainbridge, GA 31717. E-mail: info@bipac.org Individuals dedicated to a renewal of U.S. space efforts through direct involvement in the political process. Solicits contributions from individuals and uses these funds to assist in the election of candidates who support a strong U.S. civil space program. Believes that the technology is currently available to tap the "limitless energy and abundant natural resources which space offers," but that there is a lack of long-range national commitment to utilize sophisticated space hardware. Goals are: to maintain the United States' position as the leader in mankind's exploration and use of space; to reap the economic benefits that result from an expanded space program; to use space technology to enrich life on earth; to provide an alternative to the "limits-to-growth, closed w orld concept" now suggested as the only possible future course for mankind. Plans to maintain continued pressure on the administration and Congress to enlarge the space effort; keeps supporters informed of the status of space-related legislation.

Campaign for Working Families., PO Box 97163 Washington, DC 20090-7163. Phone: (703)671-8800 Fax: (703)671-8899 E-mail: info@cwfpac.com • URL: http://www.cwfpac.com • Represents the interests and values of America's traditional families in the political arena. Works on electing pro-family, pro-life and pro-free enterprise candidates to federal and state offices. Conducts extensive media campaigns and distribution of literature.

Campbell's List. Campbell's List Inc., 729 N Bedford Rd., Ste. 153, PO Box 428 Bedford Hills, NY 10507. Phone: 800-249-6934 or (407)644-8298 Fax: (928)438-0220 E-mail: info@campbellslist.com • URL: http://www.campbellslist.com • Covers: about 1,000 law firms in general practice that will handle referrals; international coverage. Entries include: Firm name, address, phone, and whether collection cases are accepted. A general law list. See separate listing, 'Law Lists.' Also includes court reporters and process servers by geographical arrangement.

Campground Management: Business Publication for Profitable Outdoor Recreation. Woodall Publications Corp., 8073 Constitution Dr. Syracuse, IN 46567. Phone: 800-323-9076 or (847)362-6700 E-mail: esmith@affinity.com • URL: http://www.woodalls.com • Monthly. $24.95 per year.

Camping Magazine. American Camping Association, 5000 State Rd., 67 N. Martinsville, IN 46151-7902. Phone: 800-428-2267 or (765)342-8456 Fax: (765)342-2065 E-mail: customerservice@aca-camps.org • URL: http://www.acacamps.org • Monthly. $31.00 per year.

Camping Magazine Buyer's Guide. American Camping Association, 5000 State Rd., 67 N. Martinsville, IN 46151-7902. Phone: 800-428-2267 or (765)342-8456 Fax: (765)342-2065 E-mail: customerservice@acacamps.org • URL: http://www.acacamp.org • Annual. $4.50. Over 200 firms listing camp supplies.

Can Ethics Be Taught? Perspectives, Challenges, and Approaches at the Harvard Business School. Thomas R. Piper and others. Harvard Business School Publishing, 300 N Beacon St. Watertown, MA 02163. Phone: 800-988-0886 or (617)783-7500 Fax: (617)783-7555 • URL: http://www.hbs.edu • 1993. $24.95.

Can Manufacturers Institute., 1730 Rhode Island Ave. NW, Ste. 1000 Washington, DC 20036. Phone: (202)232-4677 Fax: (202)232-5756 E-mail: clee@cancentral.com • URL: http://www.cancentral.com • Represents can makers and can industry suppliers. Aims to foster the prosperity of the industry and bring value to its members in a cost effective way.

Can You Recommend a Good Book on Indexing? Bella H. Weinberg. Information Today, Inc., 143 Old Marlton Pike Medford, NJ 08055-8750. Phone: 800-300-9868 or (609)654-6266 Fax: (609)654-4309 E-mail: custserv@infotoday.com • URL: http://www.infotoday.com • 1998. $39.50. Contains reviews of books on indexing, classified of general works, theory, book indexing, databases, thesauri, and computer-assisted (automatic) indexing. (CyberAge Books.)

Canada NewsWire. Canada NewsWire Ltd., 20 Bay St., Suite 1500 Toronto, ON, Canada M5J 2R8. Phone: 800-258-6852 or (416)863-9350 Fax: (416)863-4825 • URL: http://www.newswire.ca • Provides the complete online text of currrent press releases from more than 5,000 Canadian companies, institutions, and government agencies, including stock exchanges and the Ontario Securities Commission. Emphasis is on mining, petroleum, technology, and pharmaceuticals. Time span is 1996 to date, with daily updates. Inquire as to online cost and availability.

Canada-United States Business Association., 600 Renaissance Ctr., Ste. 1100, Ste. 1100 Detroit, MI 48243. Phone: (313)446-7013 Fax: (313)567-2164 E-mail: cheryl.clark@international.gc.ca • URL: http://www.dfait-maeci.gc.ca/canam/detroit/home_page/cusba-en.asp • Consists of supporters of business such as labor, banking, consulting, government, and academia. Promotes stronger business and trading lineages between the U.S. and Canada by providing a forum to exchange information and ideas and to build relationships. Conducts educational programs; maintains speakers' bureau, panels, and special events.

Canada Year Book. Statistics Canada, Operations and Integration Div., Circulation Management, Statistical Reference Centre (National Capital Region), Holland Ave., Main Bldg., Rm. 1500 Ottawa, ON, Canada K1A OT6. Phone: 800-263-1136 Fax: 877-287-4369 E-mail: infostats@statcan.ca • URL: http://www.statcan.ca • 2001. $75.00. Contains "fifteen chapters on the social, economic, demographic and cultural life of Canada," with more than 260 tables, charts and graphs.

Canada Year Book on CD-ROM. Statistics Canada, Publications Division, Ottawa, ON, Canada K1A OT6. Phone: 800-267-6677 or (613)951-7277 Fax: 800-899-9734 or (613)951-1582 • URL: http://www.statcan.ca • Annual. $90.00. CD-ROM in English and French provides basic statistical and other information on Canada. Contains multimedia features and search capabilities.

Canadian Almanac and Directory. Micromedia Proquest, 20 Victoria St. Toronto, ON, Canada M5C 2N8. Phone: (416)362-5211 Fax: (416)362-6161 E-mail: info@micromedia.ca • URL: http://www.micromedia.ca • Annual. $269.00. Contains general information and statistical data relating to Canada and provides information on about 60,000 Canadian agencies, associations, institutions, museums, libraries, etc.

Canadian-American Business Council., 1900 K St. NW Washington, DC 20006. Phone: (202)496-7430 Fax: (202)496-7756 E-mail: sgreenwood@mckennalong.com • URL: http://www.canambusco.org • Individuals, corporations, institutions, and organizations with an interest in trade between the United States and Canada. Promotes free trade. Gathers and disseminates information; maintains speakers' bureau.

Canadian-American Center., University of Maine - Canada House, 154 College Ave. Orono, ME 04473. Phone: (207)581-4220 Fax: (207)581-4223 E-mail: hornsby@maine.edu • URL: http://www.umaine.edu/canam/ • Research areas include Canadian-American business, economics, and trade.

Canadian Business. Canadian Business Media, 1 Mount Pleasant Rd., 11th Fl. Toronto, ON, Canada M5Y 2Y5. Phone: 800-465-0700 Fax: (416)596-2510 E-mail: service@cbmedia.ca • URL: http://www.canadianbusiness.com • Biweekly. $64.95 per year. Edited for corporate managers and executives, this is a major periodical in Canada covering a variety of business, economic, and financial topics. Emphasis is on the top 500 Canadian corporations.

Canadian Business and Current Affairs Fulltext. Micromedia Ltd., 20 Victoria St. Toronto, ON, Canada M5C 2N8. Phone: 800-387-2689 or (416)362-5211 Fax: (416)362-6161 E-mail: info@mmltd.com • URL: http://www.mmltd.com • Provides

SOURCES CITED

full-text of eight Canadian daily newspapers and more than 330 Canadian business magazines and trade journals. Indexing is 1982 to date, with selected full text from 1993. Updates are twice a month. Inquire as to online cost and availability.

Canadian Co-Operative Wool Growers Magazine. Canadian Cooperative Wool Growers, Ltd., P.O. Box 130 Carleton Place, ON, Canada K7C 3P3. Fax: (613)257-8896 E-mail: ccwghq@wool.ca • URL: http://www.wool.ca • Annual. Free to members; non-members, $3.00.

Canadian Directory of Shopping Centres. Rogers Media Publishing, 1 Mount Pleasant Rd. Toronto, ON, Canada M4Y 2Y5. Phone: (416)764-1300 Fax: (416)764-7730 • URL: http://www.rogers.com • Annual. $400.00. Two volumes (Eastern Canada and Western Canada). Describes about 2,200 shopping centers and malls, including those under development.

The Canadian Employer. MPL Communications Inc., 133 Richmond St. W, Ste. 700, 2075 Kennedy Rd. Toronto, ON, Canada M5H 3M8. Phone: 800-804-8846 or (416)869-1177 Fax: (416)869-0616 E-mail: customers@mplcomm.com • URL: http://www.carswell.com • Description: Provides information regarding Canadian employment laws.

Canadian Energy Research Institute. Canadian Energy Research Institute, 3512 33rd St. NW, No. 150 Calgary, AB, Canada T2L 2A6. Phone: (403)282-1231 Fax: (403)284-4181 E-mail: mmasri@ceri.ca • URL: http://www.ceri.ca • Economic issues relating to all forms of energy, including oil, natural gas, coal, nuclear and hydroelectric power, and alternative energy sources. Develops software such as the World Oil Market Model.

Canadian Industrial Equipment News: Reader Service On New, Improved and Redesigned Industrial Equipment and Supplies. Business Information Group, 1450 Don Mills Rd. Don Mills, ON, Canada M3B 2X7. Phone: 800-668-2374 Fax: (416)422-2214 • URL: http://www.businessinformationgroup.ca • Monthly. $68.95 per year. Supplement available. Formerly *Electrical Equipment News*.

Canadian Manufacturers and Exporters., 1 Nicholas St., Ste. 1500 Ottawa, ON, Canada K1N 7B7. Phone: (613)238-8888 Fax: (613)563-9218 E-mail: pbeatty@cme-mec.ca • URL: http://www.the-alliance.com • Formerly Alliance of Manufacturers and Exporters of Canada.

Canadian Mines Handbook. Scott's Directories, 12 Concorde Pl., Ste. 800 Toronto, ON, Canada M3C 4J2. Phone: 800-668-2374 or (416)442-2122 Fax: (416)510-6870 E-mail: customerservice@scottsdirectories.com • URL: http://www.businessinformationgroup.ca • Covers: About 2,400 mining companies in Canada, plus smelters, refineries, trade associations, related government agencies, and similar organizations. Entries include: For mining companies—Name, address, phone, names and titles of officers and directors, stock exchange and symbol, date and province of incorporation, capitalization, locations of mines and other properties, description of exploration and development, ore reserves, production statistics, financial data.

Canadian News Facts: The Indexed Digest of Canadian Current Events. MPL Communications Inc., 133 Richmond St., W., Suite 700 Toronto, ON, Canada M5H 3M8. Phone: (416)869-1177 Fax: (416)869-0456 Bimonthly. $280.00 per year. Monthly and quarterly indexes. A summary of current events in Canada.

Canadian Periodical Index. Gale Cengage Learning, 27500 Drake Rd. Farmington Hills, MI 48331-3535. Phone: 800-877-GALE or (248)699-GALE Fax: 800-414-5043 E-mail: gale.galeord@cengage.com • URL: http://gale.cengage.com • Monthly. $595.00 per year. Annual cumulation. Indexes more than 400 English and French language periodicals.

Canadian Resources and PennyMines Analyst: The Canadian Newsletter for Penny-Mines Investors Who Insist on Geological Value. MPL Communications, Inc., 133 Richmond St., W., Suite 700 Toronto, ON, Canada M5H 3M8. Phone: (416)869-1177 Fax: (416)869-0456 Weekly. $145.00 per year. Newsletter. Mainly on Canadian gold mine stocks. Formerly *Canadian PennyMines Analyst*.

Canadian Studies Program., University of Vermont, 589 Main St. Burlington, VT 05401. Phone: (802)656-3541 Fax: (802)656-8518 E-mail: canada@zoo.uvm.edu • URL: http://www.uvm.edu/~canada • Research areas include Canadian corporate strategies, telecommunications, and natural resources.

The Canadian Taxpayer. Thomson Carswell, 2075 Kennedy Rd., 2075 Kennedy Rd. Toronto, ON, Canada M1T 3V4. Phone: 800-387-5164 or (416)609-8000 Fax: (416)298-5094 E-mail: carswell.orders@thomson.com • URL: http://www.carswell.com • Description: Provides "analyses of Canadian tax trends, political appointments, tax policies and landmark cases."

Canadian Trade Index. MacRae's Blue Book, 2085 Hurontario St., Ste. 208 Mississauga, ON, Canada L5A 4G1. Phone: 877-463-6284 or (905)290-1818 Fax: (905)290-1760 E-mail: info@macraesbluebook.com • URL: http://www.ctidirectory.com • Covers: in one volumes, over 30,000 manufacturers in Canada. Also includes distributors, service companies, and exporters. Entries include: Company name, address, names and titles of key personnel, products, trademarks, number of employees, annual sales, non-manufacturing locations, subsidiaries and associates, foreign representatives, headquarters phone, ISO information, export regions.

Canadian Who's Who. University of Toronto Press, 5201 Dufferin St. Toronto, ON, Canada M3H 5T8. Phone: 800-565-9523 or (416)667-7791 Fax: 800-221-9985 or (416)667-7832 E-mail: utpbooks@utpress.utoronto.ca • URL: http://www.utpress.utoronto.ca • Annual. $185.00. Provides concise biographical information in English and French on 15,000 prominent Canadians.

CanCorp Plus Canadian Financial Database. Micromedia Ltd., 20 Victoria St. Toronto, ON, Canada M5C 2N8. Phone: 800-387-2689 or (416)362-5211 Fax: (416)362-2689 E-mail: info@mmltd.com • URL: http://www.mmltd.com • Monthly. $3,600.00 per year. Also available quarterly at $2,975.00 per year. Provides comprehensive information on CD-ROM for more than 11,000 public and private Canadian corporations. Emphasis is on detailed financial data for up to seven years.

Candy Buyers' Directory. Manufacturing Confectioner Publishing Co., 175 Rock Rd. Glen Rock, NJ 07452. Phone: (201)652-2655 Fax: (201)652-3419 E-mail: mcinfo@gomc.com Covers: Wholesale confectionery manufacturers and candy importers. Entries include: Company name, address, phone, name of sales manager (for manufacturers and importers), and products and brand names manufactured or distributed. Broker and importer listings also show territory covered and countries from which imported.

The Candy Dish. National Candy Brokers and Salesmen's Association, 710 E Ogden Ave., Suite 600 Naperville, IL 60563-8603. Phone: (630)369-2406 Fax: (630)369-2488 E-mail: ncba@b-online.com • URL: http://www.candynet.com • Monthly. Price on application. Provides industry news and event information for candy brokers and distributors.

Candy Industry Buyer's Guide. Stagnito Communications Inc., 155 Pfingsten Rd., Ste. 205 Deerfield, IL 60015. Phone: (847)405-4000 Fax: (847)405-4100 E-mail: info@stagnito.com • URL: http://www.stagnito.com • Publication includes: List of approximately 682 suppliers of ingredients, equipment, and services to the candy industry. Entries include: Company name, address, phone.

Candy Industry: The Global Magazine of Chocolate and Confectionery. Stagnito Publishing Co., 155 Pfingsten Rd., Ste. 205 Deerfield, IL 60015. Phone: (847)205-5660 Fax: (847)205-5680 E-mail: info@stagnito.com • URL: http://www.stagnito.com • Monthly. Free to qualified personnel; othres, $70.10 per year.

The Candy Market. Available from MarketResearch.com, 641 Ave. of the Americas, Third Floor New York, NY 10011. Phone: 800-298-5699 or (212)807-2629 Fax: (212)807-2716 E-mail: order@markerresearch.com • URL: http://www.marketresearch.com • 1998. $2,500.00. Published by Packaged Facts. Provides market data on chocolate and non-chocolate candy.

Cane Sugar Handbook: A Manual for Cane Sugar Manufacturers and Their Chemists. James C. Chen and Chung-Chi Chou. John Wiley and Sons, Inc., 111 River St. Hoboken, NJ 07030. Phone: 800-225-5945 or (201)748-6000 Fax: (201)748-6088 E-mail: info@wiley.com • URL: http://www.wiley.com • 1993. $400.00. 12th edition.

CANOE: Canadian Online Explorer. Canoe Limited Partnership-Phone: (416)947-2154 Fax: (416)947-2209 • URL: http://www.canoe.ca • Web site provides a wide variety of Canadian news and information, including business and financial data. Includes "Money," "Your Investment," "Technology," and "Stock Quotes." Allows keyword searching, with links to many other sites. Daily updating. Fees: Free.

CANSIM Time Series Database. Statistics Canada, Statistical Reference Center, R. H. Coats Bldg., Holland Ave. Ottawa, ON, Canada K1A 0T6. Phone: 800-263-1136 or (613)951-8116 Fax: (613)951-0581 E-mail: infostats@statcan.ca • URL: http://www.statcan.ca • CANSIM is the Canadian Socio-Economic Information Management System. Contains more than 700,000 statistical time series relating to Canadian business, industry, trade, economics, finance, labor, health, welfare, and demographics. Time period is mainly 1946 to date, with daily updating. Inquire as to online cost and availability.

Capacity of Refrigerated Warehouses. U.S. Department of Agriculture, Washington, DC 20250. Phone: (202)720-2791 Annual.

Capital Changes Reports. CCH, Inc., 2700 Lake Cook Rd. Riverwoods, IL 60015. Phone: 800-835-5224 or (847)267-7000 E-mail: cust_serv@cch.com • URL: http://www.cch.com • Weekly. $1,395.00. Six looseleaf volumes. Arranged alphabetically by company. This service presents a chronological capital history that includes reorganizations, mergers and consolidations. Recent actions are found in Volume One - "New Matters."

Capital for Shipping. Available from Informa Publishing Group Ltd., PO Box 1017 Westborough, MA 01581-6017. Phone: 800-493-4080 Fax: (508)231-0856 E-mail: enquiries@informa.com • URL: http://www.informa.com • Annual. $128.00. Published in the UK by Lloyd's List (http://www.lloydslist.com). Consists of a "Financial Directory" and a "Legal Directory," listing international ship finance providers and international law firms specializing in shipping. (Included with subscription to *Lloyd's Shipping Economist*.)

Car and Driver. Hachette Filipacchi Media U.S., Inc., 1633 Broadway New York, NY 10019. Phone: 800-289-9464 or (212)767-6000 Fax: (212)767-5600 • URL: http://www.hfmmag.com • Monthly. $11.97 per year.

Car Dealer Insider: Profit Making Secrets for the Competitive Dealer. United Communications Group, 11300 Rockville Pike, Suite 1100 Rockville, MD 20852-3030. Phone: 800-929-4824 or (301)287-2700 Fax: (301)816-8945 E-mail: webmaster@ucg.com • URL: http://www.ucg.com • Weekly. $275.00 per year. Newsletter. Provides automotive industry news, with ideas and advice for car dealers on advertising, marketing, and management. Formerly *Car and Truck Dealer Insider Newsletter*.

Car Ownership Forecasting. E.W. Allanson, editor. Gordon and Breach Publishing Group, 29 W 35th St. New York, NY 10001. Phone: 800-634-7064 or (212)216-7800 Fax: (212)564-7854 E-mail: ncarter@taylorandfrancis.com • URL: http://www.gbhap.com • 1982. $211.00. Volume one. (Transporation Studies Series).

Car Stereo. Orion Research Corp., 14555 N. Scottsdale Rd., Suite 330 Scottsdale, AZ 85254-3457. Phone: 800-844-0759 Fax: 800-375-1315 E-mail: orion@bluebook.com • URL: http://www.netzone.com • Annual. $144.00. Quotes retail and wholesale prices of used stereo sound equipment for automobiles. Original list prices and years of manufacture are also shown.

Car Wash Owners and Suppliers Association., 1822 South St. Racine, WI 53404. Phone: (262)639-2289 Fax: (262)639-4393 Formerly Car Wash Manufacturers and Suppliers Association.

Card Industry Directory and Debit Card Directory. Thomson Media, One State St. Plaza New York, NY 10004. Phone: 800-221-1809 or (212)803-8200 Fax: (212)843-9635 E-mail: custserv@thomsonmedia.com • URL: http://www.thomsonmedia.com • Annual. Price on application.

Card News: The Executive Report on the Transaction Card Marketplace. PBI Media, LLC, 1201 7 Locks Rd. Potomac, MD 20854. Phone: 800-777-5006 or (301)354-2000 Fax: (301)309-3847 E-mail: clientservices@pbimedia.com • URL: http://www.pbimedia.com • 25 times per year. $997.00 per year. Newsletter on transaction cards, debit and credit cards, automatic teller machines, etc.

Card Technology. Thomson Media, One State St. Plaza New York, NY 10004. Phone: 800-221-1809 or (212)803-8200 Fax: (212)843-9635 E-mail: custserv@thomsonmedia.com • URL: http://www.thomsonmedia.com • Monthly. $79.00 per year. Covers advanced technology for credit, debit, and other cards. Topics include smart cards, optical recognition, and card design.

CARD The Media Information Network. Rogers Media Publishing, Box 860 Markham, ON, Canada L3P 8J8. Phone: 800-26-53561 or (416)596-5523 Fax: (416)764-1755 E-mail: service@rmpublishing.com • URL: http://www.rogers.com • Covers: Radio and television stations and networks; daily and weekend newspapers; consumer, farm, and business publications; advertising agencies and international media representatives; advertising, marketing, and media associations; and transportation and out-of-home advertising. Entries include: For publications—Title, company name, address, phone, frequency, names and titles of key personnel, advertising rates, discounts, mechanical requirements, copy regulations, circulation, closing and publication dates. For broadcasting stations—Call letters, name of owning company, address, phone, name of firm or individual representing station for advertising, special features, format, facilities, affiliations, rates, participation programs. For agencies and associations—Name, address, phone, personnel.

CardTrak., PO Box 1700 Frederick, MD 21702. Phone: (301)631-9100 Fax: (301)631-9112 E-mail: cardstaff@cardweb.com • URL: http://www.cardweb.com/cardtrak • Promotes the "wise and careful" use of credit cards. A consumer organization.

Career College Association., 1101 Connecticut Ave. NW, Ste. 900 Washington, DC 20036. Phone: (202)336-6700 Fax: (202)336-6828 E-mail: cca@career.org • URL: http://www.career.org • Represents private post-secondary schools, institutes, colleges and universities that provide career-specific educational programs.

The Career Development Quarterly. National Career Development Association. American Counseling Association, 5999 Stevenson Ave. Alexandria, VA 22304-3300. Phone: 800-347-6647 or (703)823-9800 Fax: 800-473-2329 • URL: http://www.counseling.org • Quarterly. Individuals, $45.00 per year; institutions, $80.00 per year.

Career Guide to Industries. Available from U. S. Government Printing Office, Washington, DC 20402. Phone: (202)512-1800 Fax: (202)512-2250 E-mail: gpoaccess@gpo.gov • URL: http://www.access.gpo.gov • 2002. $32.00. Issued by the Bureau of Labor Statistics, U. S. Department of Labor (http://www.bls.gov). Presents background career information (text) and statistics for the 40 industries that account for 70 percent of wage and salary jobs in the U. S. Includes nature of the industry, employment data, working conditions, training, earnings, rate of job growth, outlook, and other career factors. (BLS Bulletin 2541.)

Career Legal Secretary. National Association of Legal Secretaries. West Publishing Co., 610 Opperman Dr. Eagan, MN 55123. Phone: 800-328-4880 or (651)687-7000 Fax: 800-340-9378 E-mail: bookstore@westgroup.com • URL: http://www.westgroup.com • 1997. $35.50. Fourth edition.

Career World. Weekly Reader Corp., 200 First Stamford Place Stamford, CT 06912. Phone: 800-446-3355 or (203)705-3500 E-mail: weeklyreader@weeklyreader.com • URL: http://www.weeklyreader.com • Six times a year. $33.95. per year. Up-to-the-minute, important career and vocational news for students in grades 7 thru 12.

SOURCES CITED

Careers in Golf: An Insider's Guide to Careers in the Golf Industry. Nancy Berkley. National Golf Foundation, 1150 South U.S. Highway 1, Ste. 401 Jupiter, FL 33477. Phone: 800-733-6006 or (561)744-6006 Fax: (561)744-9085 E-mail: ngf@ngf.org • URL: http://www.ngf.org • 2001. $19.95. Information on careers in golf product manufacturing, retailing, tour management, public relations, event management, course design, and instruction. Includes CD-ROM.

CARF, The Rehabilitation Accreditation Commission., 4891 E. Grant Rd. Tucson, AZ 85712. Phone: (520)325-1044 Fax: (520)318-1129 E-mail: info@carf.org • URL: http://www.carf.org • Formerly Commission on Accreditation of Rehabilitation.

Cargo Airline Association., 1220 19th St. NW, Ste. 400 Washington, DC 20036. Phone: (202)293-1030 Fax: (202)293-4377 E-mail: info@cargoair.org • URL: http://www.cargoair.org • Represents the interests of all-cargo air carriers.

Cargo Facts: The Airfreight and Express Industry Newsletter of Record. Air Cargo Management Group, 520 Pike St., Ste. 1010 Seattle, WA 98101-4058. Phone: (206)587-6537 Fax: (206)587-6540 E-mail: acmg@cargofacts.com • URL: http://www.cargofacts.com • Monthly. $345.00 per year. Newsletter. Provides analysis of developments in the air freight and express industry.

Caribbean Business. Casiano Communications, 1700 Fernandez Juncos Ave., Stop 25 San Juan 00909-2999, Puerto Rico. Phone: (787)728-3000 Fax: (787)728-5948 E-mail: cservice@casiano.com • URL: http://www.casiano.com • Weekly. $45.00 per year. Text in English.

Caring. Manitoba Association of Licensed Practical Nurses, 200-1601 Regent Ave. W. Winnipeg, MB, Canada R2C 3B3. Phone: 877-663-1212 or (204)663-1212 Fax: (204)663-1207 E-mail: carswell.orders@thomson.com • URL: http://www.nahc.org • Description: Contains educational articles, reports, and surveys pertinent to the nursing profession. Recurring features include letters to the editor, a calendar of events, reports of meetings, news of educational opportunities, board meeting highlights, and a licensed practical nurse (LPN) page.

Caring for Frail Elderly People: New Directions in Care. OECD Publications and Information Center, 2001 L St., N.W., Suite 650 Washington, DC 20036-4922. Phone: 800-456-6323 or (202)785-6323 Fax: (202)785-0350 E-mail: washington.contact@oecd.org • URL: http://www.oecdwash.org • 1994. $27.00. Discusses the problem in OECD countries of providing good quality care to the elderly at manageable cost. Includes trends in family care, housing policies, and private financing.

Carnegie Mellon Research Institute-Computer Automation and Robotics., Carnegie Mellon University, 700 Technology Dr. Pittsburgh, PA 15219. Phone: (412)268-3363 Fax: (412)368-7759 • URL: http://www.cmu.edu/cmri • Multidisciplinary research activities include expert systems applications, minicomputer and microcomputer systems design, genetic engineering, and transportation systems analysis.

The Carpenter. United Brotherhood of Carpenters and Joiners of America, 1212 Massachusetts Ave., NW Washington, DC 20005. Phone: (202)393-0580 Fax: (202)393-0580 • URL: http://www.carpenters.org • Bimonthly. Free to members; non-members, $10.00 per year.

Carpentry and Building Construction. John Feirer and others. Glencoe/McGraw-Hill, PO Box 543 Blacklick, OH 43004-0544. Phone: 800-334-7344 Fax: (614)755-5682 E-mail: customer.service@mcgraw-hill.com • URL: http://www.glencoe.com • 1999. $53.25. Fifth edition.

Carpet and Rug Industry. Rodman Publications, 70 Hilltop Rd. Ramsey, NJ 07446. Phone: (201)825-2552 Fax: (201)825-0553 • URL: http://www.happi.com • Monthly. $42.00 per year. Edited for manufacturers and distributors of carpets and rugs.

Carpet and Rug Institute., 310 Holiday Ave. Dalton, GA 30722. Phone: 800-882-8846 or (706)278-3176 Fax: (706)278-8835 • URL: http://www.carpet-rug.com • Formerly Tufted Textile Manufacturers Association.

Carpet Cleaning Service. Entrepreneur Media, Inc., 2445 McCabe Way Irvine, CA 92614. Phone: 800-421-2300 or (949)261-2325 Fax: (949)261-0234 E-mail: entmag@entrepreneur.com • URL: http://www.entrepreneur.com • Looseleaf. $59.50. A practical guide to starting a carpet cleaning business. Covers profit potential, start-up costs, market size evaluation, owner's time required, pricing, accounting, advertising, promotion, etc. (Start-Up Business Guide No. E1053.)

Carpet Cushion Council., 23 Courtney Cir. Bryn Mawr, PA 19010. Phone: (610)527-3880 Fax: (610)527-8535 E-mail: carpetcushion@msn.com • URL: http://www.carpetcushion.org • Works to promote the sale and use of separate carpet cushions; to act as public relations counsel for the industry; to maintain contact with various government agencies; to establish quality and performance standards. Compiles statistics; maintains speakers' bureau.

Carpet Flooring Retail. CMP Information, Ltd., 245 Blackfriars Rd., Ludgate House London SE1 9UR, United Kingdom. Phone: 44 20 7940 8500 Fax: 44 20 7407 7102 E-mail: enquiries@cmpinformation.com • URL: http://www.cmpinformation.com • Biweekly. $92.00 per year. Formerly *Carpet and Floorcoverings Review*.

Carpets and Rugs. Available from MarketResearch.com, 641 Ave. of the Americas, Third Floor New York, NY 10011. Phone: 800-298-5699 or (212)807-2629 Fax: (212)807-2716 E-mail: order@marketresearch.com • URL: http://www.marketresearch.com • 2001. $4,000.00. Market research data. Published by the Freedonia Group. Provides both historical data and forecasts to 2007 for various kinds of carpeting.

Carroll's County Directory. Carroll Publishing, 4701 Sangamore Rd., Ste. S-155 Bethesda, MD 20816. Phone: 800-336-4240 or (301)263-9800 Fax: (301)263-9801 E-mail: info@carrollpub.com • URL: http://www.carrollpub.com • Covers: Over 57,000 officials in more than 3,000 counties; includes elected, appointed, and career office holders. Entries include: County seat, locator phone, address, population, officials' names, titles, addresses, and phone numbers. Available as part of a "library volume" titled "Municipal/County Directory Annual Edition" (see separate entry).

Carroll's Defense Industry Charts. Carroll Publishing, 4701 Sangamore Rd., Suite S-155 Bethesda, MD 20816. Phone: 800-336-4240 or (301)263-9800 Fax: (301)263-9801 E-mail: custsvc@carrollpub.com • URL: http://www.carrollpub.com • Quarterly. $1,500.00 per year. Provides 180 large, fold-out paper charts showing personnel relationships at more than 100 major U. S. defense contractors. Charts are also available online and on CD-ROM.

Carroll's Defense Organization Charts. Carroll Publishing, 4701 Sangamore Rd., Suite S-155 Bethesda, MD 20816. Phone: 800-336-4240 or (301)263-9800 Fax: (301)263-9801 E-mail: custsvc@carrollpub.com • URL: http://www.carrollpub.com • Every six weeks. $1,500.00 per year. Provides more than 200 large, fold-out paper charts showing personnel relationships in 2,400 U. S. military offices. Charts are also available online and on CD-ROM.

Carroll's Federal & Federal Regional Directory. Carroll Publishing, 4701 Sangamore Rd., Suite S-155 Bethesda, MD 20816. Phone: 800-336-4240 or (301)263-9800 Fax: (301)263-9801 E-mail: custsvc@carrollpub.com • URL: http://www.carrollpub.com • Semiannual. $325.00 per year; with online edition, $1,200 per year. Lists more than 23,000 U. S. government officials throughout the country, including military installations.

Carroll's Federal Directory. Carroll Publishing, 4701 Sangamore Rd., Ste. S-155 Bethesda, MD 20816. Phone: 800-336-4240 or (301)263-9800 Fax: (301)263-9801 E-mail: info@carrollpub.com • URL: http://www.carrollpub.com • Covers: About 38,000 executive managers in federal government offices in Washington, DC, including executive, congressional and judicial branches; members of Congress and Congressional committees and staff. Entries include: Agency names, titles, office address (including room numbers), e-mail addresses, and telephone and fax numbers. Also available as part of a "library edition" titled "Federal Directory Annual".

Carroll's Federal Organization Charts. Carroll Publishing, 4701 Sangamore Rd., Suite S-155 Bethesda, MD 20816. Phone: 800-336-4240 or (301)263-9800 Fax: (301)263-9801 E-mail: custsvc@carrollpub.com • URL: http://www.carrollpub.com • Every six weeks. $1,000.00 per year. Provides 200 large, fold-out paper charts showing personnel relationships in 2,100 federal departments and agencies. Charts are also available online and on CD-ROM.

Carroll's Federal Regional Directory. Carroll Publishing, 4701 Sangamore Rd., Ste. S-155 Bethesda, MD 20816. Phone: 800-336-4240 or (301)263-9800 Fax: (301)263-9801 E-mail: info@carrollpub.com • URL: http://www.carrollpub.com • Covers: Over 32,000 officials in federal congressional, judicial, and executive branch departments and agencies outside the District of Columbia. Entries include: Organization or agency name; names, addresses, and phone numbers of key personnel.

Carroll's Municipal/County Directory. Carroll Publishing, 4701 Sangamore Rd., Suite S-155 Bethesda, MD 20816. Phone: 800-336-4240 or (301)263-9800 Fax: (301)263-9801 E-mail: custsvc@carrollpub.com • URL: http://www.carrollpub.com • Annual. $250.00 per year. Provides listings of about 90,000 city, town, and county officials in the U. S.

Carroll's Municipal Directory. Carroll Publishing, 4701 Sangamore Rd., Ste. S-155 Bethesda, MD 20816. Phone: 800-336-4240 or (301)263-9800 Fax: (301)263-9801 E-mail: info@carrollpub.com • URL: http://www.carrollpub.com • Covers: about 50,000 officials in more than 7,900 cities towns and villages: includes top elected council or elected board members. Entries include: Name, county name, locator phone, address, population; officials' names, titles, addresses, and phone numbers.

Carroll's State Directory. Carroll Publishing, 4701 Sangamore Rd., Ste. S-155 Bethesda, MD 20816. Phone: 800-336-4240 or (301)263-9800 Fax: (301)263-9801 E-mail: info@carrollpub.com • URL: http://www.carrollpub.com • Covers: about 73,000 state government officials in all branches of government; officers, committees and members of state legislatures; managers of boards and authorities. Entries include: Name, address, phone, fax, title.

Carroll's State Directory: CD-ROM Edition. Carroll Publishing, 4701 Sangamore Rd., Suite S-155 Bethesda, MD 20816. Phone: 800-336-4240 or (301)263-9800 Fax: (301)263-9801 E-mail: custsvc@carrollpub.com • URL: http://www.carrollpub.com • Three times a year. $325.00 per year. Provides CD-ROM listings of about 43,000 state officials, plus the text of all state constitutions and biographies of all governors. Also available online.

Cars of Revenue Freight Loaded. Association of American Railroads, American Railroads Bldg., 50 F St., N.W. Washington, DC 20001. Phone: (202)639-2100 Fax: (202)639-2156 • URL: http://www.aar.org • Weekly.

Cartography and Geographic Information Science. American Congress on Surveying and Mapping, 6 Montgomery Village Ave., Ste. 403 Gaithersburg, MD 20879. Phone: (240)632-9716 Fax: (240)632-1321 E-mail: info@acsm.net • URL: http://www.acsm.net • Quarterly. Free to members; non-members, $110.00 per year.

Case Studies in Business Ethics. Thomas Donaldson and Al Gini, editors. Prentice Hall PTR, 240 Frisch Ct. Paramus, NJ 07652. Phone: 800-282-0693 Fax: 800-445-6991 • URL: http://www.phptr.com • 1995. $49.00. Fourth edition.

Case Studies in Business, Society, and Ethics. Thomas L. Beauchamp, editor. Prentice Hall PTR, 240 Frisch Ct. Paramus, NJ 07652. Phone: 800-282-0693 Fax: 800-445-6991 • URL: http://www.phptr.com • 1997. $42.00. Fourth edition.

Case Studies in Finance: Managing for Corporate Value Creation. Robert Bruner. McGraw-Hill, 1221 Ave. of the Americas New York, NY 10020. Phone: 800-722-4726 or (212)512-2000 Fax: (212)512-4502 E-mail: customer.service@mcgraw-hill.com • URL: http://www.mcgraw-hill.com • 2002. $109.69. Fourth edition. (Finance, Insurance and Real Estate Series).

A Casebook of Grant Proposals in the Humanities. William Coleman and others, editors. Neal-Schuman Publishers, Inc., 100 William St., Ste. 2004 New York, NY 10038. Phone: (866)672-2667 or (212)925-8650 Fax: (866)209-7932 or (212)219-8916 E-mail: info@neal-schuman.com • URL: http://www.neal-schuman.com • 1982. $45.00.

Cases and Materials on Corporations-Including Partnerships and Limited Partnerships. Robert W. Hamilton. West Publishing Co., 610 Opperman Dr. Eagan, MN 55123. Phone: 800-328-2209 or (651)687-7000 Fax: 800-340-9378 E-mail: bookstore@westgroup.com • URL: http://www.westgroup.com • 2001. $83.00. Seventh edition. American Case book Series

Cases in Agribusiness Management. George J. Seperich and others. Holcomb Hathaway, Inc., 6207 N. Cattle Track Rd., Suite 5 Scottsdale, AZ 85250. Phone: (480)991-7881 Fax: (480)991-4770 E-mail: sales@hh-pub.com • URL: http://www.hh-pub.com • 1995. $28.95. Second edition.

Cases in Corporate Acquisitions, Buyouts, Mergers, and Takeovers. Gale Cengage Learning, 27500 Drake Rd. Farmington Hills, MI 48331-3535. Phone: 800-877-GALE or (248)699-GALE Fax: 800-414-5043 E-mail: gale.galeord@cengage.com • URL: http://gale.cengage.com • 1999. $350.00. Reviews and analyzes about 300 cases of both success and failure in corporate acquisitiveness.

Cases in Corporate Innovation. Gale Cengage Learning, 27500 Drake Rd. Farmington Hills, MI 48331-3535. Phone: 800-877-GALE or (248)699-GALE Fax: 800-414-5043 E-mail: gale.galeord@cengage.com • URL: http://gale.cengage.com • 2002. $310.00. Reviews and analyzes about 300 cases to illustrate both successful and failed management of innovation.

Cases in Financial Mangement: Directed Versions. Eugene Brigham and Louis Gapenski. Dryden Press, City Center Tower Two, 301 Commerce St., Suite 3700 Fort Worth, TX 76102-4137. Phone: (817)334-7500 Fax: (817)334-7844 E-mail: wlittle@harbrace.com • URL: http://www.thomson.com • 1993. $32.00.

Cases in International Finance. Gunter Duffey. Addison-Wesley, 75 Arlington St., Ste. 300 Boston, MA 02116. Phone: 800-447-2226 or (617)848-7500 • URL: http://www.aw.com • 2001. 3rd edition. Price on application.

Cases in Marketing Management. Kenneth L. Bernhardt and Thomas C. Kinnear. McGraw-Hill, 1221 Ave. of the Americas New York, NY 10020. Phone: 800-722-4726 or (212)512-2000 Fax: (212)512-4502 E-mail: customer.service@mcgraw-hill.com • URL: http://www.mcgraw-hill.com • 1997. Ninth edition. Price on application.

Cases in Portfolio Management. John W. Peavy and Katrina F. Sherrerd. Association of Investment Management and Research, 560 Ray C. Hunt Dr. Charlottesville, VA 22903. Phone: 800-247-8132 or (434)951-5499 Fax: (434)951-5262 E-mail: info@aimr.org • URL: http://www.aimr.org • 1991. $30.00.

Cases in Strategic Management. Thomas J. Wheelen and J. David Hunger. Addison-Wesley, 75 Arlington St., Ste. 300 Boston, MA 02116. Phone: 800-447-2226 or (617)-848-7500 • URL: http://www.aw.com • 1996. Fifth edition. Price on application.

Cases in Strategic Marketing: An Integrated Approach. Strickland. McGraw-Hill, 1221 Ave. of the Americas New York, NY 10020. Phone: 800-722-4726 or (212)512-2000 Fax: (212)512-4502 E-mail: customer.service@mcgraw-hill.com • URL: http://www.mcgraw-hill.com • 2000. $41.25. 12th edition.

Cases in the Management of Information Systems and Information Technology. Richard Lorette and Howard Walton. McGraw-Hill, 1221 Ave. of the Americas New York, NY 10020. Phone: 800-722-4726 or (212)512-2000 Fax: (212)512-4502 E-mail: customer.service@mcgraw-hill.com • URL: http://www.mcgraw-hill.com • 1994. $40.95.

Cases in Total Quality Management: Manufacturing and Services. Jay H. Heizer. Course Technology, Inc., One Main St. Cambridge, MA 02142. Phone: 800-648-7450 or (617)225-2595 Fax: (617)494-8008 E-mail: tucker_

malenfant@course.com • URL: http://www.course.com • 1997. $48.95. (GC Principles in Management Series.)

Cash Box: The International Music-Record Weekly. Cash Box Publishing Co., Inc., 51 E. Eighth St., Suite 155 New York, NY 10003-6494. Phone: (212)586-2640 Weekly. $185.00 per year.

Casino and Gaming Market Research Handbook. Available from MarketResearch.com, 641 Ave. of the Americas, Third Floor New York, NY 10011. Phone: 800-298-5699 or (212)807-2629 Fax: (212)807-2642 E-mail: order@marketresearch.com • URL: http://www.marketresearch.com • 2003. $375.00. Published by Terri C. Walker Consulting, Inc. Includes analysis and statistical data on casinos, lotteries, table games, electronic gaming machines, bingo, and online gambling.

Casino Chronicle: A Weekly Newsletter Focusing on the Gaming Industry. Ben Borowsky, PO Box 740465 Boynton Beach, FL 33474-0465. Phone: (561)732-6117 E-mail: casinochronicle@aol.com 48 times a year. $175.00 per year. Newsletter focusing on the Atlantic City gambling industry.

CASSIS (Patents). U. S. Patent and Trademark Office, Office of Electronic Information Products, Crystal Park 3, Suite 441 Washington, DC 20231. Phone: 800-786-9199 or (703)306-2600 Fax: (703)306-2737 E-mail: oeip@uspto.gov • URL: http://www.uspto.gov • A series of CD-ROM products, including *Patents ASSIGN* (assignment deeds, quarterly), *Patents ASSIST* (search tools, quarterly), *Patents BIB* (abstracts and search information, bimonthly), *Patents CLASS* (classifications, 1790 to date, bimonthly), *Patents SNAP* (serial number concordance, annual).

CASSIS (Trademarks). U. S. Patent and Trademark Office, Office of Electronic Information Products, Crystal Park 3, Suite 441 Washington, DC 20231. Phone: 800-786-9199 or (703)306-2600 Fax: (703)306-2737 E-mail: oeip@uspto.gov • URL: http://www.uspto.gov • CD-ROM products include *Trademarks ASSIGN* (assignment deeds, bimonthly), *Trademarks ASSIST* (search tools, single- disc), *Trademarks PENDING* (applications on file, bimonthly), *Trademarks REGISTERED* (active trademarks, 1884 to date).

Cast Metals Laboratory.

Casting Industry Suppliers Association., 14175 W Indian School Rd., Ste. B4-504 Goodyear, AZ 85395. Phone: (623)547-0920 Fax: (623)536-1486 E-mail: info@cisa.org • URL: http://www.cisa.org • Manufacturers of foundry equipment and supplies such as molding machinery, dust control equipment and systems, blast cleaning machines, tumbling equipment, and related products. Fosters better trade practices; serves as industry representative before the government and the public. Encourages member research into new processes and methods of foundry operation and disseminates reports of progress in these fields. Compiles monthly statistics on booked and billed sales.

Casualty Actuarial Society., 4350 N Fairfax Dr., Ste. 250 Arlington, VA 22203. Phone: (703)276-3100 Fax: (703)276-3108 E-mail: office@casact.org • URL: http://www.casact.org • Professional society of property/casualty actuaries. Seeks to advance the body of knowledge of actuarial science applied to property, casualty and similar risk exposures, to maintain qualification standards, promote high standards of conduct and competence, and increase awareness of actuarial science. Examinations required for membership.

Casualty Actuarial Society Yearbook. Casualty Actuarial Society, 1100 N. Glebe Rd., Suite 600 Arlington, VA 22201-4714. Phone: (703)276-3100 Fax: (703)276-3108 E-mail: office@casact.org • URL: http://www.casact.org • Annual. $40.00. Approximately 2,500 actuaries working in insurance other than life insurance.

Casualty Insurance Claims: Coverage-Investigation-Law. Pat Magarick and Ken Brownlee. West Group, 610 Opperman Dr. Eagan, MN 55123. Phone: 800-328-4880 or (651)687-7000 Fax: 800-340-9378 E-mail: bookstore@westgroup.com • URL: http://www.westgroup.com • Semiannual. $400.00 per year. Three looseleaf volumes.

Catalog Age. PRIMEDIA Business Magazine and Media, 11 Riverbend Dr. S Stamford, CT 06907. Phone: 800-795-5445 or (203)358-9900 Fax: (203)358-5823 E-mail: inquiries@primediabusiness.com • URL: http://www.primediabusiness.com • 13 times a year. Free to qualified personnel; others, $85.00 per year. Edited for catalog marketing and management personnel.

Catalog Age—Direct Sourcebook. Primedia Business, 11 River Bend Dr. S, PO Box 4949 Stamford, CT 06907-0949. Phone: 800-776-1246 or (203)358-9900 Fax: (203)358-5811 E-mail: info@stagnito.com • URL: http://www.primediabusiness.com • Publication includes: List of approximately 300 suppliers of equipment, products, and services to the direct marketing industry; related trade associations. Entries include: Name, address, phone, key personnel, geographical area covered, description of products or services, branch offices or subsidiary names and locations.

The Catalog Marketer. Maxwell Sroge Publishing Inc., 522 Forest Ave. Evanston, IL 60202. Phone: (847)866-1890 Fax: (847)866-1899 E-mail: info@catalog-news.com Description: Provides information about producing catalogs. Topics include marketing, photography, news, and telephone marketing.

Catalog of American National Standards. American National Standards Institute, 1819 L St., NW, 6th Fl. Washington, DC 20036. Phone: (202)293-8020 Fax: (202)-293-9287 E-mail: info@ansi.org • URL: http://www.ansi.org • Annual. Free to members; non-members, $20.00.

Catalog of Asphalt Institute Publications. Asphalt Institute, Research Park Drive Lexington, KY 40512. Phone: (859)288-4960 Fax: (859)288-4699 E-mail: webmaster@asphaltinstitute.org • URL: http://www.asphaltinstitute.org • Annual. Free.

Catalog of Copyright Entries. U.S. Library of Congress, Copyright Office. Available from U.S. Government Printing Office, Washington, DC 20402. Phone: (202)512-1800 Fax: (202)512-2250 Frequency and prices vary.

Catalog of Federal Domestic Assistance. U.S. Office of Management and Budget. Available from U.S. Government Printing Office, Washington, DC 20402. Phone: (202)512-1800 Fax: (202)512-2250 Annual. $87.00. Looseleaf service. Includes up-dating service for indeterminate period. Summary of financial and nonfinanacial Federal programs, projects, services and activities that provide assistance or benefits to the American public.

Catalog of U.S. Government Publications. U. S. Government Printing Office, Washington, DC 20402. Phone: 888-293-6498 or (202)512-0132 Fax: (202)512-1355 E-mail: gpoaccess@gpo.gov • URL: http://www.access.gpo.gov • Contains over 375,000 online citations to U. S. government publications, 1976 to date, with monthly updates. Corresponds to the printed *Monthly Catalog of United States Government Publications*. Inquire as to online cost and availability.

Catalogue of Statistical Materials of Developing Countries. Institute of Developing Economies/Ajia Keizai Kenkyusho, 3-2-2 Wakaba Mihana-ku 261-8545 8, Japan. Phone: 043 299 9500 E-mail: info@ide.go.jp • URL: http://www.ide.go.jp • Semiannual. Price varies. Text in English and Japanese.

Catalyst., 120 Wall St., 5th Fl. New York, NY 10005-3904. Phone: (212)514-7600 Fax: (212)514-8470 E-mail: info@catalyst.org • URL: http://www.catalystwomen.org • Works to advance women in Business and the professions. Serves as a source of information on women in business for past four decades. Helps companies and women maximize their potential. Holds current statistics, print media, and research materials on issues related to women in business.

Catering Handbook. Edith Weiss and Hal Weiss. John Wiley and Sons, Inc., 111 River St. Hoboken, NJ 07030. Phone: 800-225-5945 or (201)748-6000 Fax: (201)748-6088 E-mail: info@wiley.com • URL: http://www.wiley.com • 1990. $60.00.

Catering Industry Employee. Hotel Employees and Restaurant Employees International Union, AFL0-CIO, 1219 28th St., N.W. Washington, DC 20007-3316. Phone: (202)393-4373 Fax: (202)965-2958 • URL: http://www.hereunion.org • Quarterly. $5.00.

Catering Magazine: The Magazine for Off-Premise Caterers. GP Publishing, Inc., 609 E. Oregon Ave., Ste. 100 Phoenix, AZ 85012. Phone: 800-528-1056 or (602)265-7778 Fax: (602)265-7771 E-mail: gabeyta@gppublishing.com • URL: http://www.gppublishing.com • Bimonthly. $35.00 per year. Covers the marketing and management aspects of the catering business.

Catering Service. Entrepreneur Media, Inc., 2445 McCabe Way Irvine, CA 92614. Phone: 800-421-2300 or (949)261-2325 Fax: (949)261-0234 E-mail: entmag@entrepreneur.com • URL: http://www.entrepreneur.com • Looseleaf. $59.50. A practical guide to starting a food and beverage catering business. Covers profit potential, start-up costs, market size evaluation, owner's time required, site selection, pricing, accounting, advertising, promotion, etc. (Start-Up Business Guide No. E1215.)

Catholic Library Association., 100 North St., Ste. 224 Pittsfield, MA 01201-5109. Phone: (413)443-2252 Fax: (413)442-2252 E-mail: cla@cathla.org • URL: http://www.cathla.org • Librarians, teachers, and booksellers concerned with Catholic libraries and their specialized problems and the writing, publishing, and distribution of Catholic literature. Members represent lay and clergy in both Catholic and non-Catholic institutions.

Catholics for Christian Political Action., 1322 Vermont Ave. NW Washington, DC 20005. E-mail: info@bipac.org Catholic laymen interested in promoting the life of the family. Objectives are to voice the views of Catholics on social and political issues affecting the family, and to educate members as to where they can apply pressure to ensure that their views will be heeded. Issues of concern include war and peace, abortion, pornography, crime, drug abuse, sex education, and tax matters. Plans to conduct seminars and is in the process of organizing state and local groups. Presently inactive.

Cattle Fever Tick Research Laboratory.

Cattleman. Texas and Southwestern Cattle Raisers Association, Inc., 1301 W. Seventh Ave. Fort Worth, TX 76102. Phone: (817)332-7155 E-mail: tmccartney@texascattleraiser.org • URL: http://www.cattlemanmagazine.com • Monthly. $25.00 per year.

Cavalcade of Acts and Attractions. Amusement Business, PO Box 24970 Nashville, TN 37202. Phone: 800-449-1402 E-mail: info@amusementbusiness.com • URL: http://www.amusementbusiness.com • Annual. $85.00. Directory of personal appearance artists, touring shows and other specialized entertainment. Lists promoters, producers, managers and booking agents.

CBA., PO Box 62000 Colorado Springs, CO 80962-2000. Phone: 800-252-1950 or (719)265-9895 Fax: (719)272-3510 E-mail: info@cbaonline.org • URL: http://www.cbaonline.org • Serves as trade association for retail stores selling Christian books, Bibles, gifts, and Sunday school and church supplies. Compiles statistics; conducts specialized education programs.

CBA Marketplace. Christian Booksellers Association. CBA Service Corp., PO Box 6200 Colorado Springs, CO 80962-2000. Phone: 800-252-1950 or (719)265-9895 Fax: (719)272-3510 E-mail: info@cbaonline.org • URL: http://www.cbaonline.org • Monthly. $49.95 per year. Edited for religious book stores. Formerly *Bookstore Journal*.

CC News: The Business Newspaper for Call Center and Customer Care Professionals. United Publications, Inc., P.O. Box 995 Yarmouth, ME 04096. Phone: 800-441-6982 or (207)846-0600 Fax: (207)846-0657 E-mail: info@ccnews.com • URL: http://www.ccnews.com • Monthly. Free to qualified personnel; others, $60.00 per year. Includes news of call center technical developments.

CCH Analysis of Top Tax Issues. CCH, Inc., 2700 Lake Cook Rd. Riverwoods, IL 60015. Phone: 800-835-5224 or (847)267-7000 E-mail: cust_serv@cch.com • URL: http://www.cch.com • Annual. $49.00. Covers yearly tax changes affecting business and personal transactions, planning, and returns.

CCH Essentials: An Internet Tax Research and Primary Source Library. CCH, Inc.Phone: 800-248-3248 or (773)866-6000 Fax: 800-224-8299 or (773)866-3608 E-mail: cust_serv@cch.com • URL: http://tax.cch.com/essentials • Fee-based Web site provides full-text coverage of federal tax law and regulations, including rulings, procedures, tax court decisions, and IRS publications, announcements, notices, and penalties. Includes explanation, analysis, tax planning guides, and a daily tax news service. Searching is offered, including citation search.

CCH Financial and Estate Planning. CCH, Inc., 2700 Lake Cook Rd. Riverwoods, IL 60015. Phone: 800-525-3335 or (847)267-7000 E-mail: cust_serv@cch.com • URL: http://www.cch.com • $895.00 per year. Four looseleaf volumes. Semimonthly updates.

CCH Financial and Estate Planning Guide. CCH, Inc., 2700 Lake Cook Rd. Riverwoods, IL 60015. Phone: 800-248-3248 or (847)267-7000 E-mail: cust_serv@cch.com • URL: http://www.cch.com • Annual. $63.00. Contains four main parts: General Principles and Techniques, Special Situations, Building the Estate, and Planning Aids.

CCH Guide to Business Valuation. CCH, Inc., 2700 Lake Cook Rd. Riverwoods, IL 60015. Phone: 800-835-5224 or (847)267-7000 E-mail: cust_serv@cch.com • URL: http://www.cch.com • Looseleaf. $295.00 per year, including quarterly newsletter. Covers latest developments and trends in the evaluation of businesses.

CCH Guide to Car, Travel, Entertainment, and Home Office Deductions. CCH, Inc., 2700 Lake Cook Rd. Riverwoods, IL 60015. Phone: 800-835-5224 or (847)267-7000 E-mail: cust_serv@cch.com • URL: http://www.cch.com • Annual. $45.00. Explains how to claim maximum tax deductions for common business expenses. Includes automobile depreciation tables, lease value tables, worksheets, and examples of filled-in tax forms.

CCH Guide to Record Retention Requirements. CCH, Inc., 2700 Lake Cook Rd. Riverwoods, IL 60015. Phone: 800-835-5224 or (847)267-7000 E-mail: cust_serv@cch.com • URL: http://www.cch.com • 1999. $49.95. Covers the record-keeping provisions of the Code of Federal Regulations. Explains which records must be kept and how long to keep them.

CCIA Newsletter. Consumer Credit Insurance Association, 542 S Dearborn, No. 400 Chicago, IL 60605-1522. Phone: (312)939-2242 Fax: (312)939-8287 E-mail: info@catalog-news.com Description: Focuses on consumer credit insurance in the areas of life insurance, accident and health insurance, and property insurance. Includes news of the Association.

CD-ROM Information Products: The Evaluative Guide. Ashgate Publishing Co., 101 Cherry St., Ste. 420 Burlington, VT 05401-4405. Phone: 800-535-9544 or (802)865-7641 Fax: (802)865-7847 E-mail: adonahue@ashgate.com • URL: http://www.ashgate.com • Quarterly. $110.00 per year. Provides detailed evaluations of new CD-ROM information products.

CD-ROM Primer: The ABC's of CD-ROM. Cheryl LaGuardia. Neal-Schuman Publishers, Inc., 100 William St., Ste. 2004 New York, NY 10038. Phone: (866)672-2667 or (212)925-8650 Fax: (866)209-7932 or (212)219-8916 E-mail: info@neal-schuman.com • URL: http://www.neal-schuman.com • 1994. $49.95. Provides advice for librarians and others on CD-ROM equipment, selection, collecting, and maintenance. Includes a glossary, bibliography, and directory of suppliers.

CD-ROMS in Print. Gale Cengage Learning, 27500 Drake Rd. Farmington Hills, MI 48331-3535. Phone: 800-877-GALE or (248)699-GALE Fax: 800-414-5043 E-mail: gale.galeord@cengage.com • URL: http://gale.cengage.com • 2003. $185.00. 17th edition. Describes more than 20,000 currently available reference and multimedia CD-ROM titles and provides contact information for about 4,000 CD-ROM publishing and distribution companies. Includes several indexes.

CDC Vessel Sanitation Program (VSP): Charting a Healthier Course. U. S. Centers for Disease Control and Prevention-Phone: (770)488-7070 Fax: 888-232-6789 E-mail: vsp@cdc.gov • URL: http://www.cdc.gov/nceh/vsp/ • Web site provides details of unannounced sanitation inspections of individual cruise ships arriving at U. S. ports. Includes detailed results of the most recent inspection of each ship and results of inspections taking place in years past. There are lists of "Ships Inspected Past 2 Months" and "Ships with Not Satisfactory Scores" (passing grade is 85). CDC standards cover drinking water, food, and general cleanliness. Online searching is possible by ship name, inspection date, and numerical scores. Fees: Free.

CEC Communications (Chemical Engineering Communications). Taylor and Francis Group, 29 W 35th St. New York, NY 10001. Phone: (212)216-7800 Fax: (212)564-7854 Bimonthly. Institutions, $87.00 per year; corporations, $135.00 per year. Formerly *Chemical Engineering Communications*.

CEE News Buyers' Guide. Primedia Business Magazines and Media, 330 N Wabash Ave., Suite 2300 Chicago, IL 60611. Phone: 800-795-5445 or (312)595-1080 Fax: (312)595-0295 E-mail: subs@primediabusiness.com • URL: http://www.primediabusiness.com • Annual. $25.00. List of approximately 1,900 manufacturers of products used in the electrical construction industry; coverage includes Canada.

Celebrity Locator: How to Reach Over 6,000 Movie, TV Stars and Other Famous Ce lebrities. Axiom Information Resources, PO Box 8015 Ann Arbor, MI 48107. Phone: (313)761-4842 Fax: (734)761-3276 E-mail: axiominfo@celebritylocator.com • URL: http://www.celebritylocator.com • Biennial. $39.95. Stars, agents, networks, studios, and other celebrities. Gives names and addresses.

Celebrity Register. Gale Cengage Learning, 27500 Drake Rd. Farmington Hills, MI 48331-3535. Phone: 800-877-GALE or (248)699-GALE Fax: 800-414-5043 E-mail: gale.galeord@cengage.com • URL: http://gale.cengage.com • 1990. $115.00. 90th edition. Compiled by Celebrity Services International (Earl Blackwell). Contains profiles of 1,300 famous individuals in the performing arts, sports, politics, business, and other fields.

Cellular Phone Service. Entrepreneur Media, Inc., 2445 McCabe Way Irvine, CA 92614. Phone: 800-421-2300 or (959)261-2325 Fax: (949)261-0234 E-mail: entmag@entrepreneur.com • URL: http://www.entrepreneur.com • Looseleaf. $59.50. A practical guide to starting a business for the servicing of cellular (mobile) telephones. Covers profit potential, start-up costs, market size evaluation, owner's time required, site selection, lease negotiation, pricing, accounting, advertising, promotion, etc. (Start-Up Business Guide No. E1268.)

Cellular Telephones and Communication Equipment. Available from MarketResearch.com, 641 Ave. of the Americas, Fourth Floor New York, NY 10011. Phone: 800-298-5699 or (212)807-2629 Fax: (212)807-2642 E-mail: order@marketresearch.com • URL: http://www.marketresearch.com • 2002. $4,450.00. Published by Global Industry Analysts. Provides worldwide market research data, including profiles of major cell phone manufacturers and service providers.

CEMA Bulletin. Conveyor Equipment Manufacturers Association, 6724 Lone Oak Blvd. Naples, FL 34109. Phone: (239)514-3441 Fax: (239)514-3470 E-mail: cema@cemanet.org • URL: http://www.cemanet.org • Description: Covers information about the conveyor equipment industry. Recurring features include reports of meetings and news of members.

Cement and Concrete Research. Elsevier, 655 Ave. of the Americas New York, NY 10010-5107. Phone: 800-366-2665 or (212)989-5800 Fax: 800-535-9935 or (212)633-3680 E-mail: custserv@elsevier.com • URL: http://www.elsevier.com • Monthly. Qualified personnel, $347.00 per year; institutions, $2,147.00 per year. Text in English, French, German and Russian.

Cement Data Book: International Process Engineering in the Cement Industry. Walter H. Duda. French and European Publications, Inc., Rockefelle Center Promenade, 610 Fifth Ave. New York, NY 10020. Phone: (212)581-8810 Fax: (212)265-1094 E-mail: frenchbookstore@aol.com • URL: http://www.frencheuropean.com • Dates vary. $950.00. Three volumes. Vol.1, $375.00; vol.2, $325.00; vol.3, $250.00. Text in English and German.

Cement Employers Association., 122 E Broad St., 2nd Fl. Bethlehem, PA 18018. Phone: (610)868-8060 Fax: (610)861-2884 E-mail: emcgehee@cementemployers.com Cement companies. Aims to improve labor and employee relations.

Cement, Lime, Gypsum, and Allied Workers Division., c/o James Hickenbotham, 3112 Peters Creek Rd., North Roanoke Plaza Roanoke, VA 24019. Phone: (540)362-7110 Fax: (540)362-7116 E-mail: union2@rbnet.com • URL: http://www.boilermakers.org • Affiliated with International Brotherhood of Boilermakers, Iron Ship Builders, Blacksmiths, Forgers and Helpers.

Census Catalog and Guide. U. S. Government Printing Office, 732 N Capitol St., NW Washington, DC 20401. Phone: 888-293-6498 or (202)512-1530 Fax: (202)512-1262 E-mail: gpoaccess@gpo.gov • URL: http://www.gpoaccess.gov • Annual. Lists publications and electronic media products currently available from the U. S. Bureau of the Census, along with some out of print items. Includes comprehensive title and subject indexes. Formerly *Bureau of the Census Catalog*.

Census of Construction Industries: Roofing Siding and Sheet Metal Work Special Trade Contractors. U.S. Bureau of the Census, Washington, DC 20233-0800. Phone: (301)457-4100 Fax: (301)457-3842 • URL: http://www.census.gov • Quinquennial.

Census of Construction: Subject Bibliography No. 157. Available from U. S. Government Printing Office, Washington, DC 20402. Phone: (202)512-1800 Fax: (202)512-2250 E-mail: gpoaccess@gpo.gov • URL: http://www.access.gpo.gov • Annual. Free. Lists government publications.

Census of Governments: Subject Bibliography No. 156. Available from U. S. Government Printing Office, Washington, DC 20402. Phone: (202)512-1800 Fax: (202)512-2250 E-mail: gpoaccess@gpo.gov • URL: http://www.access.gpo.gov • Annual. Free. Lists government publications.

Center for Acoustics and Vibration. Pennsylvania State University

Center for Adult Education. Columbia University

Center for Advanced Materials Research. Brown University

Center for Advanced Phototonic and Electronic Materials., State University of New York at Buffalo, Fronczak Hall, Room 227-229, North Campus, P.O. Box 601500 Buffalo, NY 14260. Phone: (716)645-2422 Fax: (716)645-5964 E-mail: ub-capem@acsu.buffalo.edu • URL: http://www.grad.buffalo.edu/ • Does integrated optics research, including photonic circuitry.

Center for Advanced Technology in Information Management.

Center for Advanced Technology in Telecommunications., Polytechnic University, Five Metrotech Center, Rm. LC208 Brooklyn, NY 11201. Phone: (718)260-3050 Fax: (718)260-3074 E-mail: panwar@catt.poly.edu • URL: http://www.catt.poly.edu • Research fields include active media for optical communication.

Center for Aeromechanics Research. University of Texas at Austin

Center for Applied Energy Research.

Center for Applied Thermodynamics Studies.

Center for Artificial Intelligence.

Center for Arts Administration Program. Florida State University

Center for Auto Safety.

Center for Automation and Robotics Research.

Center for Automation Research.

Center for Business and Industrial Studies., University of Missouri-St. Louis, School of Business Administration, 8001 Natural Bridge Rd. St. Louis, MO 63121. Phone: (314)516-5000 • URL: http://www.umsl.edu/ • Research fields include inventory and management control. Specific projects also include development of computer software for operations in public transit systems.

Center for Canadian-American Studies., Western Washington University, Canada House High St., Ste. 516 Bellingham, WA 98225-9110. Phone: (360)650-3728 Fax: (360)650-3995 E-mail: canam@cc.wwu.edu • URL: http://www.wwu.edu/~ • Research areas include Canadian business and economics.

Center for Cement Composite Materials. University of Illinois at Urbana-Champaign

Center for Climatic Research. University of Wisconsin - Madison

Center for Communication Research.

Center for Composite Materials.

Center for Consumer Research.

Center for Corporate Citizenship., Boston College, 55 Lee Rd. Chestnut Hill, MA 02467. Phone: (617)552-4545 Fax: (617)552-8499 E-mail: cccr@bc.edu • URL: http://www.bc.edu/cccbc • Areas of study include corporate images within local communities, corporate community relations, social vision, and philanthropy. Formerly Center for Corporate Community Relations.

Center for Decision Research. University of Chicago Graduate School of Business

Center for Defense Information.

Center for Energy and Combustion Research. University of California, San Diego

Center for Energy and Environmental Studies. Carnegie Mellon University Department of Engineering and Public Policy

Center for Entrepreneurial Studies and Development, Inc., West Virginia University, College of Engineering and Mineral Resources, 1062 Maple Dr. Morgantown, WV 26506. Phone: (304)293-5551 Fax: (304)293-6707 E-mail: jbyrd@mail.cesd.wvu.edu • URL: http://www.cesd.wvu.edu • Inventory control systems included as a research field.

Center for Environmental Design Research. University of California at Berkeley

Center for Exercise Science., University of Florida, 25 Florida Gym Gainesville, FL 32611. Phone: (352)392-9575 Fax: (352)392-0316 E-mail: spowers@hhp.ufl.edu Studies fitness as it relates to the general population and as it relates to athletic performance.

Center for Exhibition Industry Research., 2301 S. Lake Shore Dr., Suite E1002 Chicago, IL 60616. Phone: (312)808-2347 Fax: (312)949-3472 E-mail: ceir@mpea.com • URL: http://www.ceir.org • Promotes the trade show as a marketing device. Formerly Trade Show Bureau.

Center for Family Business., PO Box 24219 Cleveland, OH 44124. Phone: (440)442-0800 Fax: (440)460-5407 E-mail: grummi@aol.com Members are family-owned, independent, private, and closely-held businesses. Formerly University Services Institute.

Center for Finance and Real Estate.

Center for Financial Responsibility., College of Human Sciences, Box 41162, Texas Tech University Lubbock, TX 79409-1162. Phone: (806)742-9781 Fax: (806)742-9784 E-mail: bill.gustafson@ttu.edu • URL: http://www.hs.ttu.edu/cfr/ • Research areas include financial preparation for retirement, financial education, determinants of financial satisfaction, risk tolerance, and the career preparation of retirement industry professionals.

Center for Governmental Responsibility., University of Florida, College of Law, 230 Bruton-Geer, P.O. Box 117629 Gainesville, FL 32611. Phone: (352)392-2237 Fax: (352)392-1457 • URL: http://www.law.ufl.edu/cgr • Research fields include family law.

Center for Health Administration Studies.

Center for Health and Safety Studies.

Center for Health Economics Research., 411 Waverly Oaks Rd., Suite 330 Waltham, MA 02452. Phone: (781)788-8100 Fax: (781)788-8101 E-mail: jmitchell@cher.org • URL: http://www.her-cher.org • A social science research company.

Center for Health Policy Law and Management.

Center for Health Promotion and Prevention Research., University of Texas, Houston Health Science Center, School of Public Health, 7000 Fanin St., 25th Fl. Houston, TX 77030. Phone: (713)500-9609 Fax: (713)500-9602 E-mail: chppr@sph.uth.tmc.edu • URL: http://www.sph.uth.tmc.edu/chppr • Fields of study include worksite health promotion. Formerly Center for Health Promotion Research and Development.

Center for Health Research., Wayne State University, College of Nursing, 5557 Cass Ave. Detroit, MI 48202-3515. Phone: (313)577-4134 Fax: (313)577-5777 E-mail: nursinginfo@wayne.edu • URL: http://www.nursing.wayne.edu • Studies innovation in health care organization and financing.

Center for Human Resources.

Center for Imaging Science., Rochester Institute of Technology, 54 Lomb Memorial Dr. Rochester, NY 14623. Phone: (716)475-5994 Fax: (716)475-5988 E-mail: gatley@cis.rit.edu • URL: http://www.cis.rit.edu • Activities include research in color science and digital image processing.

Center for Industrial Research and Service. Iowa State University of Science and Technology

Center for Information Systems Research. Massachusetts Institute of Technology

Center for Institutional and Intern. c/o American Council on Education

Center for Integrated Manufacturing Studies., Rochester Institute of Technology, 111 Lomb Memorial Dr. Rochester, NY 14623-5608. Phone: (716)475-5101 Fax: (716)475-5250 E-mail: wjasp@rit.edu • URL: http://www.cims.rit.edu • Research areas include electronics, imaging, printing, and publishing.

Center for Integrated Plant Systems. Michigan State University

Center for Integrated Systems., Stanford University, 420 Via Palou Mall Stanford, CA 94305-4070. Phone: (650)725-3621 Fax: (650)725-0991 E-mail: rdasher@stanford.edu • URL: http://www.cis.stanford.edu • Research programs include manufacturing science, design science, computer architecture, semiconductor technology, and telecommunications.

Center for Intelligent Machines and Robotics.

Center for Intelligent Systems, Controls, and Signal Processing.

Center for International Education and Research in Accounting. University of Illinois at Urbana-Champaign

Center for International Policy., 1755 Massachusetts Ave., N. W., Ste. 550 Washington, DC 20036. Phone: (202)232-3317 Fax: (202)232-3440 E-mail: cip@ciponline.org • URL: http://www.ciponline.org • Research subjects include the International Monetary Fund, the World Bank, and other international financial institutions. Analyzes the impact of policies on social and economic conditions in developing countries.

Center for International Private Enterprise., 1155 15th St., N.W. Ste. 700 Washington, DC 20005. Phone: (202)721-9200 Fax: (202)721-9250 E-mail: cipe@cipe.org • URL: http://www.cipe.org • Members are people involved in small businesses.

Center for International Science and Technology Policy., George Washington University, 2013 G St., N. W., Stuart Hall, Suite 201 Washington, DC 20052. Phone: (202)994-7292 Fax: (202)994-1639 E-mail: cistp@gwu.edu • URL: http://www.gwu.edu/ • Research areas include technology transfer.

Center for Labor Education and Research. University of Alabama at Birmingham

Center for Laser Applications., UT Space Institute Research Park, University of Tennessee, 411 B.H. Goethert Pky. Tullahoma, TN 37388. Phone: (931)393-7485 Fax: (931)454-2271 E-mail: dkeefer@utsi.edu • URL: http://www.cla.utsi.edu • In addition to research, provides technical assistance relating to the industrial use of lasers.

Center for Latin American Studies., University of Chicago, 5848 S. University Ave., K308 Chicago, IL 60637. Phone: (773)702-8420 Fax: (773)702-1755 E-mail: clas@uchicago.edu • URL: http://www.clas.uchicago.edu • Includes economic inquiry on Latin America.

Center for Mass Media Research.

Center for Mathematical Studies in Economics and Management Sciences.

Center for Mature Consumer Studies., Robinson College of Business, MSC4 A1370, 33 Gilmer St., Unit 4 Atlanta, GA 30303-3083. Phone: (404)651-2740 Fax: (404)651-4198 E-mail: gmoschis@gsu.edu • URL: http://www.cba.gsu.edu/

• Serves as an information resource, assisting in strategy development for reaching the mature consumer market.

Center for Media and Public Affairs.

Center for Microelectronic and Computer Engineering., Rochester Institute of Technology, 82 Lomb Memorial Dr. Rochester, NY 14623-5604. Phone: (716)475-2035 Fax: (716)475-5041 E-mail: lffeee@rit.edu • URL: http://www.microe.rit.edu • Facilities include digital computer organization/microcomputer laboratory.

Center for Migration Studies., 209 Flagg Place Staten Island, NY 10304-1122. Phone: (718)351-8800 Fax: (718)667-4598 E-mail: cms@cmsny.org • URL: http://www.cmsny.org • A nonprofit institute "committed to encourage and facilitate the study of sociodemographic, economic, political..aspects of human migration and refugee movement."

Center for National Policy.

Center for Negotiation and Conflict Resolution.

Center for Pension and Retirement Research., Miami University, Department of Economics, 109E Laws Hall Oxford, OH 45056. Phone: (513)529-2850 Fax: (513)529-3308 E-mail: swilliamson@eh.net • URL: http://www.eh.net/cprr • Research areas include pension economics, pension plans, and retirement decisions.

Center for Population and Development Studies. Harvard University

Center for Private Enterprise., Baylor University, Hankamer School of Business, P.O. Box 98003 Waco, TX 76798-8003. Phone: (254)710-2263 Fax: (254)710-1092 E-mail: jim_truitt@baylor.edu • URL: http://129.62.162.136/enterprise/ • Includes studies of entrepreneurship and women entrepreneurs.

Center for Public Interest Polling., Rutgers University, 185 Ryders Ln. New Brunswick, NJ 08901. Phone: (732)932-9384 Fax: (732)932-1551 E-mail: zukin@rci.rutgers.edu • URL: http://www.rci.rutgers.edu/ • Provides survey research and program evaluation services.

Center for Public-Private Sector Cooperation.

Center for Public Safety. Northwestern University

Center for Quality and Productivity., University of North Texas, College of Business Administration, P.P. Box 305249 Denton, TX 76203-3677. Phone: (940)565-4767 E-mail: prybutok@unt.edu • URL: http://www.coba.unt.edu • Fields of research include the management of quality systems and statistical methodology.

Center for Quality and Productivity Improvement., University of Wisconsin-Madison, 610 N. Walnut St., 575 WARF Bldg. Madison, WI 53705. Phone: (608)263-2520 Fax: (608)263-1425 E-mail: quality@engr.wisc.edu • URL: http://www.engr.wisc.edu/centers/cqpi • Research areas include quality management and industrial engineering.

Center for Real Estate Studies.

Center for Real Estate Studies. University of Florida, College of Business Administration, P.O. Box 117168 Gainesville, FL 32611-7168. Phone: (352)392-9307 Fax: (352)392-0381 E-mail: archer@notes.cba.ufl.edu • URL: http://www.ufrealestate.com • Formerly Real Estate Research Center.

Center for Research and Education in Optics and Lasers.

Center for Research and Management Services. Indiana State University

Center for Research in Regulated Industries. Rutgers University

Center for Research in Security Prices.

Center for Retail Management., Kellogg School of Management, Northwestern University, 2001 Sheridan Rd. Evanston, IL 60208. Phone: (847)467-3600 Fax: (847)467-3620 E-mail: r-blattberg@kellogg.northwestern.edu • URL: http://www.kellogg.northwestern.edu • Conducts research related to retail marketing and management.

Center for Retailing Studies., Texas A & M University, Department of Marketing, 4112 TAMU College Station, TX 77843-4112. Phone: (979)845-0325 Fax: (979)845-5230 E-mail: d-szymanski@tamu.edu • URL: http://www.crstamu.org • Research areas include retailing issues and consumer economics.

Center for Risk Management and Insurance Research.

Center for Solid State Electronics Research. Arizona State University

Center for Space Research. Massachusetts Institute of Technology

Center for Statistical Consultation and Research. University of Michigan

Center for Strategic and Budgetary Assessments., 1667 K St. NW, Ste. 900 Washington, DC 20006. Phone: (202)331-7990 Fax: (202)331-8019 E-mail: info@csbaonline.org • URL: http://www.csbaonline.org • Serves as nonpartisan independent research organization that analyzes military spending and national security policy issues. Provides timely, independent analyses of military budget and defense issues to the media, citizens' organizations, policymakers, and advocacy groups. Conducts research and educational programs. Sponsors briefings and discussions on defense and military issues. Analyzes issues such as the impact of the defense budget on other national spending priorities, the American economy, and the federal deficit; the relationship between defense spending, national security, and the development of alternatives to present national security policies. Maintains internship program.

Center for Studies in Creativity. State University of New York College at Buffalo

Center for Study of Librarianship.

Center for Study of Responsive Law., P.O. Box 19367 Washington, DC 20036. Phone: (202)387-8030 Fax: (202)234-5176 E-mail: csrl@csrl.org • URL: http://www.csrl.org • A consumer-oriented research group.

Center for the Environment., Cornell University, 200 Rice Hall Ithaca, NY 14853-5601. Phone: (607)255-7535 Fax: (607)255-0238 E-mail: cucfe@cornell.edu • URL: http://www.cfe.cornell.edu • Includes Waste Management Institute and New York State Solid Waste Combustion Institute.

Center for the Study of Aging., University of Bridgeport, Carlson Hall, 303 University Ave., Division of Counseling and Human Resources Bridgeport, CT 06601. Phone: (203)576-4175 Fax: (203)576-4200 E-mail: kaplin@bridgeport.edu Research activities include the study of Medicare and Medicaid.

Center for the Study of Higher Education. Pennsylvania State University

Center for the Study of Law, Science, and Technology., Arizona State University, College of Law, P.O. Box 877906 Tempe, AZ 85287-7906. Phone: (480)965-2554 Fax: (480)965-2427 E-mail: gary.marchant@asu.edu • URL: http://www.law.asu.edu • Studies the legal problems created by technological advances.

Center for the Study of Services., 733 15th St., N.W., Suite 820 Washington, DC 20005. Phone: 800-475-7283 or (202)347-9612 Fax: (202)347-4000 E-mail: editors@checkbook.org • URL: http://www.checkbook.org • Evaluates local consumer services and retailers in Washington, D.C. and San Francisco metropolitan areas.

Center for the Study of Sport in Society., Northeastern University, 360 Huntington Ave., Ste. 161CP Boston, MA 02115-5000. Phone: (617)373-4025 Fax: (617)373-4566 E-mail: sportinsociety@hotmail.com • URL: http://www.sportinsociety.org • Research fields include sport sociology, sport journalism, and sport business.

Center for the Study of the Presidency., 1020 19th St., NW, Ste. 250 Washington, DC 20036. Phone: (202)872-9800 Fax: (202)872-9811 E-mail: center@thepresidency.org • URL: http://www.thepresidency.org • Counsels the White House and Executive Branch on policy issues critical to strengthening presidential leadership and improving executive-congressional relations. Formerly Library of Presidential Papers.

Center for Transportation Research.

Center for Transportation Studies. Massachusetts Institute of Technology

Center for Urban and Industrial Pest Management., Purdue University, 1158 Smith Hall West Lafayette, IN 47907. Phone: (765)494-4564 Fax: (765)494-0535 E-mail: gary_bennett@entm.purdue.edu • URL: http://www.purdue.edu/entomology/urban/home • Conducts research on the control of household and structural insect pests.

Center for Urban and Regional Studies. University of North Carolina at Chapel Hill

Center for Urban Transportation Studies.

Center for Women Policy Studies., 1211 Connecticut Ave., N.W. Suite 312 Washington, DC 20036. Phone: (202)872-1770 Fax: (202)296-8962 E-mail: cwps@centerwomenpolicy.org • URL: http://www.centerwomenpolicy.org • Conducts research on the policy issues that affect the legal, economic, educational, and social status of women, including sexual harassment in the workplace, and women and AIDS.

Center for Women's Business Research., 1411 K St. N.W., Ste. 1350 Washington, DC 20005-3407. Phone: (202)638-3060 Fax: (202)638-3064 E-mail: info@womensbusinessresearch.org • URL: http://www.nfwbo.org • Provides research reports and statistical studies relating to various aspects of women-owned business enterprises. Affiliated with the National Association of Women Business Owners.

Center for Youth and Communities., Brandeis University, 60 Turner St. Waltham, MA 02453. Phone: (781)736-3770 Fax: (781)736-3773 E-mail: curnan@brandeis.org • URL: http://www.heller.brandeis.edu/chr • Formerly Center for Human Resources.

Center of International Studies. Princeton University

Center on Education and Training for Employment. The Ohio State University College of Education, 1900 Kenny Rd. Columbus, OH 43210-1090. Phone: 800-848-4815 or (614)292-4353 Fax: (614)292-1260 E-mail: chambers.2@osu.edu • URL: http://www.cete.org/products/ • Formerly National Center for Research in Vocational Education.

Center on Japanese Economy and Business., Columbia University, Graduate School of Business, 322 Uris Hall, 3022 Broadway New York, NY 10027-6902. Phone: (212)854-3976 Fax: (212)678-6958 E-mail: htp1@colombia.edu • URL: http://www.gsb.columbia.edu/japan/ • Research areas include Pacific Basin trade policy.

Central Banking: Policy, Markets, Supervision. Available from European Business Publications, Inc., P.O. Box 891 Darien, CT 06820-9859. Phone: (203)656-2701 Fax: (203)655-8332 Quarterly. $260.00 per year, including annual *Central Banking Directory*. Published in England by Central Banking Publications. Reports and comments on the activities of central banks around the world. Also provides discussions of the International Monetary Fund (IMF), the Organization for Economic Cooperation and Development (OECD), the Bank for International Settlements (BIS), and the World Bank.

Central Station Alarm Association., 440 Maple Ave., Ste. 201 Vienna, VA 22180-4723. Phone: (703)242-4670 Fax: (703)242-4675 E-mail: communications@csaaul.org • URL: http://www.csaaul.org • Individuals, firms, associations, and burglar and fire alarm corporations engaged primarily in the operation of central station burglar and fire alarm businesses. Aims to foster and improve the relationship between sellers, users, bureaus, and other agencies for the advancement of the central station electrical protection services industry.

Centre for Building Science. University of Toronto Department of Civil Engineering

A Century of Cameras. Eaton S. Lothrop. Morgan and Morgan, Inc., P.O. Box 595 Keene Valley, NY 12943-0595. Phone: (518)576-9277 Fax: (518)576-9282 E-mail: sales@morganmorgan.com • URL: http://www.morganmorgan.com • 1982. $24.00. Revised edition.

The CEO Report. United Communications Group, 11300 Rockville Pke., Ste. 1100 Rockville, MD 20852-3030. Phone: 800-929-4824 or (301)287-2700 Fax: (301)816-8945 E-mail: webmaster@ucg.com • URL: http://www.ucg.com • Description: Contains information for managers of credit unions.

Ceramic Industries International. Turret RAI plc, Armstrong House, 38 Market Square Uxbridge UB8 1TG, United Kingdom. Phone: (44)1895 454545 Fax: (44)1895 454647 Bimonthly. $94.00. per year.

Ceramic Industry Data Book Buyers' Guide. Business News Publishing Co., 755 W. Big Beaver Rd., Ste. 1000 Troy, MI 48084-4903. Phone: 800-837-7370 or (248)362-3700 Fax: (248)-362-6317 • URL: http://www.bnp.com • Annual. $25.00. Included with subscription to *Ceramic Industry*. Formerly *Ceramic Data Book*.

Ceramic Industry: The Magazine for Refractories, Traditional and Advanced Ceramic Manufacturers. Business News Publishing Co., 755 W. Big Beaver Rd., Suite 1000 Troy, MI 48084. Phone: 800-837-7370 or (248)362-3700 Fax: (248)362-0317 • URL: http://www.bnp.com • 13 times a year. $65.00 per year. Includes *Data Buyers Guide*, *Materials Handbook*, *Economic Forecast*, and *Giants in Ceramic*.

Ceramic Tile. Available from MarketResearch.com, 641 Ave. of the Americas, Third Floor New York, NY 10011. Phone: 800-298-5699 or (212)807-2629 Fax: (212)807-2716 E-mail: order@marketresearch.com • URL: http://www.marketresearch.com • 1998. $1295.00. Market research report published by Specialists in Business Information. Presents market data relative to demographics, sales growth, shipments, exports, imports, price trends, and end-use. Includes company profiles.

Ceramic Tile Distributors Association., 800 Roosevelt Rd., Bldg. C, Ste. 312, Bldg. C, Ste. 312 Glen Ellyn, IL 60137. Phone: 800-938-CTDA or (630)545-9415 Fax: (630)790-3095 E-mail: info@ctdahome.org • URL: http://www.ctdahome.org • Wholesale distributors and manufacturers of ceramic tile and related products. Promotes the increase of sales volumes in the ceramic tile industry through educational programs and networking. Promotes independent ceramic tile distributors and represents their interests. Provides technical information; compiles statistics. Sponsors competitions. Maintains insurance program for members and speakers' bureau.

Ceramics: A Potter's Handbook. Glenn C. Nelson. Wadsworth Publishing Co., 10 Davis Dr. Belmont, CA 94002. Phone: (650)595-2350 • URL: http://www.wadsworth.com • 2001. $63.95. Sixth edition.

Ceramics Abstracts/ World Ceramics Abstracts. American Ceramic Society. Cambridge Scientific Abstracts, 7200 Wisconsin Ave., Ste. 601 Bethesda, MD 20814. Phone: 800-843-7751 or (301)961-6700 Fax: (301)961-6720 E-mail: service@csa.com • URL: http://www.csa.com • Five times a year. $225.00 per year. Online edition available.

Ceramics Monthly. American Ceramic Society, PO Box 6136 Westerville, OH 43086-6136. Phone: (614)890-4700 Fax: (614)899-6100 E-mail: info@ceramics.org • URL: http://www.ceramics.org • 10 times a year. Member, $30.00 per year; non-members, $48.00 per year.

Cereal Crops Research Unit U.S. Department of Agricultural Research Service.

Cereal Disease Laboratory-U.S. Department of Agricultural Research Service.

Certified Milk Producers Association of America.

CFMA Building Profits. Construction Financial Management Association, 29 Emmons Dr., Suite F-50 Princeton, NJ 08540-1413. Phone: (609)452-8000 Fax: (609)452-0474 E-mail: info@cfma.org • URL: http://www.cfma.org • Bimonthly. Controlled circulation. Covers the financial side of the construction industry.

CFO: The Magazine for Senior Financial Executives. CFO Publishing Corp., 253 Summer St. Boston, MA 02210. Phone: (617)345-9700 Fax: (617)951-4090 E-mail: juliahomer@cfopub.com • URL: http://www.cfo.com • Monthly. $65.00 per year.

Chain Drug Review: The Reporter for the Chain Drug Store Industry. Racher Press, Inc., 220 Fifth Ave., 18th Fl. New York, NY 10001. Phone: (212)213-6000 Fax: (212)213-6106 21 times a year. $136.00 per year. Covers news and trends of concern to the chain drug store industry. Includes special articles on OTC (over-the-counter) drugs.

Chain Store Age: The NewsMagazine for Retail Executives. Lebhar-Friedman, Inc., 425 Park Ave. New York, NY 10022. Phone: 800-766-6999 or (212)756-5000 E-mail: info@lf.com • URL: http://www.lf.com • Monthly. $105.00 per year.

Formerly *Chain Store Age Executive with Shopping Center Age*.

Challenge: The Magazine of Economic Affairs. M. E. Sharpe, Inc., 80 Business Park Dr. Armonk, NY 10504. Phone: 800-541-6563 or (914)273-1800 Fax: (914)273-2106 E-mail: info@mesharpe.com • URL: http://www.mesharpe.com • Bimonthly. Individuals, $52.00 per year; institutions, $220.00 per year. Includes print and online editions. A nontechnical journal on current economic policy and economic trends.

Chamber Executive. American Chamber of Commerce Executives, 4875 Eisenhower Ave., Ste. 250 Alexandria, VA 22304. Phone: (703)998-0072 Fax: (703)212-9512 E-mail: info@acce.org • URL: http://www.acce.org • Description: Covers Chamber management issues, including economic development, international trade, membership development and retention, government relations, small business, and tourism development.

Chamber of Commerce of the Apparel Industry., 118 River Rd., Ste. 18 Harriman, NY 10926-3022. Phone: (845)781-7337 Fax: (845)781-7340 A worker's compensation group authorized by the New York State Insurance Funds.

Chamber of Shipping of America., 1730 M. St., N.W., Suite 407 Washington, DC 20036. Phone: (202)775-4399 Fax: (202)659-3795 United States based companies that own and operate tankers, dry bulk carriers, container ships and other oceangoing vessels in United States foreign and domestic commerce. Formerly United States Chamber of Shipping.

Champion. National Association of Criminal Defense Lawyers, 1150 18th St., NW, Ste. 950 Washington, DC 20036. Phone: (202)872-8600 Fax: (202)872-8690 E-mail: assist@nacdl.org • URL: http://www.criminaljustice.org • 10 times a year. $25.00 per year.

Change: The Magazine of Higher Learning. American Association of Higher Education. Heldref Publications, 1319 18th St. N.W. Washington, DC 20036-1802. Phone: 800-365-9753 or (202)296-6267 Fax: (202)296-5149 E-mail: subscribe@heldref.org • URL: http://www.heldref.org • Bimonthly. Individuals, $55.00 per year; institutions, $112.00 per year.

The Changing Role of Unions: New Forms of Representation. Phanindra V. Wunnava, editor. M. E. Sharpe, Inc., 80 Business Park Drive Armonk, NY 10504. Phone: 800-541-6563 or (914)273-1800 Fax: (914)273-2106 E-mail: custserv@mesharpe.com • URL: http://www.mesharpe.com • 2004. $74.95. Contains articles by labor economists on the future of labor unions in the U. S.

Chaos on the Shop Floor: A Worker's View of Quality, Productivity, and Management. Tom Juravich. Temple University Press, 1601 N Broad St., University Services Bldg., Rm. 305 Philadelphia, PA 19122. Phone: 800-621-2736 or (215)204-8787 Fax: 800-621-8471 or (215)204-4719 • URL: http://www.temple.edu/tempress • 1988. $19.95. (Labor and Social Change Series).

Chapter 11 Update: Monitors All Major Developments in Today's Corporate Bankruptcies and Examines Pertinent Court Decisions Related to Chapter 11 Filings. Andrews Publications, 175 Strafford Ave., Bldg. 4, Suite 140 Wayne, PA 19087. Phone: 800-345-1101 or (610)225-0510 Fax: (610)225-0501 • URL: http://www.andrewspub.com • Semimonthly. $500.00 per year. Newsletter on corporate Chapter 11 bankruptcy filings.

Chapter 13: Practice and Procedure. West Group, 620 Opperman Dr. Eagan, MN 55123. Phone: 800-328-4880 or (651)687-7000 Fax: 800-340-9378 E-mail: bookstore@westgroup.com • URL: http://www.westgroup.com • Annual. $160.00. Looseleaf service.

Characteristics of Apartments Completed. U.S. Bureau of the Census. Available from U.S. Government Printing Office, Washington, DC 20402. Phone: (202)512-1800 Fax: (202)512-2250 E-mail: gpoaccess@gpo.gov • URL: http://www.access.gpo.gov • Annual.

Characteristics of Apartments Completed: [year]. U.S. Census Bureau, Washington, DC 20233. Phone: (301)763-4636 E-mail: webmaster@census.gov • URL: http://www.census.gov • Annual. Free. Covers privately financed, nonsubsidized apartments in buildings with five units or more.

Charitable Giving and Solicitation. RIA, 395 Hudson St. New York, NY 10014. Phone: 800-950-1216 or 800-431-9025 E-mail: riahome@riag.com • URL: http://www.riahome.com • $495.00 per year. Looseleaf service. Updates 13 times a year. Bulletin discusses federal tax rules pertaining to charitable contributions.

Charitable Organizations of the U. S.: A Descriptive and Financial Information Guide. Gale Cengage Learning, 27500 Drake Rd. Farmington Hills, MI 48331-3535. Phone: 800-877-GALE or (248)699-GALE Fax: 800-414-5043 E-mail: gale.galeord@cengage.com • URL: http://gale.cengage.com • 1991. $180.00. Second edition. Describes nearly 800 nonprofit groups active in soliciting funds from the American public. Includes nearly 800 data on sources of income, administrative expenses, and payout.

Charitable Planning Primer. Ralph G. Miller and Adam Smalley. CCH, Inc., 2700 Lake Cook Rd. Riverwoods, IL 60015. Phone: 800-835-5224 or (847)267-7000 E-mail: cust_serv@cch.com • URL: http://www.cch.com • 1999. $99.00. Covers the legal and tax aspects of charitable giving and planned gifts. Includes annuity documents, tax forms, tables, and examples.

Chartcraft Monthly NYSE and ASE Chartbook. Chartcraft, Inc., 30 Church St. New Rochelle, NY 10801. Phone: (914)632-0422 Fax: (914)632-0335 Monthly. $402.00 per year. Includes all common stocks on New York and American Stock Exchanges.

Chartcraft Over-the-Counter Chartbook. Chartcraft, Inc., 30 Church St. New Rochelle, NY 10801. Phone: (914)632-0422 Fax: (914)632-0335 Quarterly. $114.00 per year. Includes more than 1,000 unlisted stocks. Long term charts.

Chartered Property and Casualty Underwriters Society Journal. Chartered Property and Casualty Underwriters Society, 720 Providence Rd. Malvern, PA 19355. Phone: 800-932-2728 or (610)251-2728 Fax: (610)251-2780 E-mail: membercenter@cpcusociety.org • URL: http://www.cpcusociety.org • Quarterly. $30.00 per year. Published by the Chartered Property and Casualty Underwriters Society (CPCU). Edited for professional insurance underwriters and agents.

Chase's Calendar of Events: The Day-by-Day Directory. McGraw-Hill, 1221 Ave. of the Americas New York, NY 10020. Phone: 800-722-4726 or (212)512-2000 Fax: (212)512-4502 E-mail: customer.service@mcgraw-hill.com • URL: http://www.mcgraw-hill.com • Annual. $52.95. Provides information for over 12,000 special days and special events throughout the world. Chronological arrangement with an alphabetical index. Formerly *Chase's Annual Events*.

The Cheap Investor: The Investor's Guide to Microcap and Turn Around Stocks Under $5 Per Share. Mathews and Associates, Inc., 2549 W. Golf Rd., Suite 350 Hoffman Estates, IL 60194-1165. Phone: (847)697-5666 Fax: (847)697-5699 Monthly. $125.00 per year. Newsletter. Gives three to six buy recommendations, updates on precious recommendations and investment tips on quality stock under $5.00. Free issue available upon request.

Check-In-Check-Out. Principles of Effective Front Office Management. Gary K. Vallen and Jerome J. Vallen. Brown and Benchmark, 25 Kessel Court Madison, WI 53711. Phone: 800-338-5578 or (608)273-0040 Fax: 800-346-2372 E-mail: customer.service@mcgraw-hill.com • URL: http://www.mhhe.com • $44.75. Looseleaf service.

The Check is Not in the Mail: How to Get Paid More, in Full, on Time, at Less Cost, and Without Losing Valued Customers. Leonard Sklār. Baroque Publishing, 783 Mediterranean Lane Redwood City, CA 94065-1758. Phone: (415)654-9138 Fax: (415)654-9139 E-mail: lenwriter@aol.com 1990. $19.95. Explains how to establish the right collection cycle, what is harassment, choosing a collection agency, and collection procedures in general.

Checklist of Library Building Design Considerations. William W. Sannwald and others. American Library Association, 50 E Huron St. Chicago, IL 60611-2795. Phone: 800-545-2433 or (312)944-6780 Fax: (312)440-9374 E-mail: ala@ala.org • URL: http://www.ala.org • 2001. $38.00. Fourth edition.

The Cheese Handbook. Bob Farand. Sterling Publishing Co., Inc., 387 Park Ave., S New York, NY 10016. Phone: (212)532-7160 E-mail: custservice@sterlingpub.com • URL: http://www.sterlingpub.com • 2001. $24.95.

Cheese Importers Association of America.

Cheese Importers Association of America Bulletin. Cheese Importer Association of America, 460 Park Ave., 11th Fl. New York, NY 10022. Phone: (212)753-7500 Fax: (212)688-2870 Irregular. Membership.

Cheese Market News. Quarne Publishing LLC, P. O. Box 620244 Middleton, WI 53562-0244. Phone: (608)831-6002 Fax: (608)831-1004 E-mail: chmarknews@aol.com Weekly. $85.00 per year. Covers market trends, legislation, and new products.

Cheese Market News—Market Directory. Quarne Publishing L.L.C., PO Box 620244 Middleton, WI 53562-0244. Phone: (608)831-6002 Fax: (608)831-1004 E-mail: info@stagnito.com • URL: http://www.cheesemarketnews.com • Publication includes: List of suppliers of equipment, ingredients and services/supplies to the cheese industry and cheese manufacturers/marketers-including variety and style of cheese. Entries include: Company name, address, phone, fax, telex, and name and title of contact.

Cheese Reporter. Richard Groves, editor. Cheese Reporter Publishing Co., Inc., 4210 E. Washington Ave. Madison, WI 53704-3742. Phone: (608)246-8430 Fax: (608)246-8431 E-mail: info@cheesereporter.com • URL: http://www.cheesereporter.com • Weekly. $80.00 per year. Reports technology, production, sales, merchandising, promotion, research and general industry news of and pertaining to the manufacture and marketing of cheese.

Chef. Talcott Communications Corp., 20 N. Wacker Dr., Suite 1865 Chicago, IL 60606. Phone: (312)849-2220 Fax: (312)849-2174 Monthly. $24.00 per year. Edited for executive chefs, food and beverage directors, caterers, banquet and club managers, and others responsible for food buying and food service. Special coverage of regional foods is provided.

Chefs de Cuisine Association of America., 155 E 55th St., Ste. 302B New York, NY 10022. Phone: (212)832-4939 Fax: (212)599-2717 E-mail: info@chefsdecuisineofamerica.com • URL: http://www.chefsdecuisineofamerica.com • Professional executive chefs; chefs who own restaurants; pastry chefs for hotels, clubs, and restaurants. Maintains 350 volume library and placement service for members.

Chem Sources—International. Chem Sources International Inc., PO Box 1824 Clemson, SC 29633. Phone: 800-222-4531 or (864)646-7840 Fax: (864)642-6168 E-mail: csinfo@chemsources.com • URL: http://www.chemssources.com • Publication includes: List of 8,000 chemical producers and distributors in 135 countries; 275,000 chemicals; and 25,000 chemical trade names. Entries include: For producers and distributors—Company name, address, phone, locations of manufacturing plants, shipping points, sales offices, telex, TWX, cable address. For agents and representatives—Name, company name and address. Principal content of publication is alphabetical listing of 200,000 organic and inorganic chemical compounds by chemical nomenclature; includes classified list of trade names for 7,000 products.

Chem Sources—USA. Chem Sources International Inc., PO Box 1824 Clemson, SC 29633. Phone: 800-222-4531 or (864)646-7840 Fax: (864)642-6168 E-mail: csinfo@chemsources.com • URL: http://www.chemsources.com • Publication includes: List of 800 United States and Canadian chemical producers and distributors; 160,000 chemicals. Entries include: company name, address, phone, locations of manufacturing plants, shipping points, e-mail addresses, sales offices, telex, fax, cable address. Principal content of directory is alphabetical listing of 160,000 chemical products by chemical nomenclature.

Chemcyclopedia. American Chemical Society, 1155 16th St., NW Washington, DC 20036. Phone: 800-227-5558 or (202)872-4600 Fax: (202)872-6067 E-mail: service@acs.org • URL: http://www.chemcyc.com • Publication includes: List of over 900 chemical manufacturers and suppliers in the United States and Canada. Entries include: Company name, address, phone, fax, telex, trade name; chemical available grades, packaging, special shipping requirements, and potential applications. Principal content of publication is technical and commercial information on about 10,000 chemicals produced and sold arranged by product group.

Chemical Abstracts. Chemical Abstracts Service, 2540 Olentangy River Rd. Columbus, OH 43202. Phone: 800-753-4227 or (614)447-3731 Fax: (614)447-3751 E-mail: help@cas.org • URL: http://www.cas.org • Weekly. $26,000.00 per year. Includes *CA Index Guide*.

Chemical and Engineering News-Career and Employment. American Chemical Society, 1155 16th St., N.W. Washington, DC 20036. Phone: 800-227-5558 or (202)872-4600 Fax: (202)776-8258 E-mail: help@cacs.org • URL: http://www.chemistry.org • Annual. $9.00.

Chemical and Engineering News: Facts and Figures. American Chemical Society, 1155 16th St., N. W. Washington, DC 20036. Phone: 800-227-5558 or (202)872-4600 Fax: (202)776-8258 E-mail: help@acs.org • URL: http://www.chemistry.org • Annual. $20.00. List of 100 largest chemical producers by total chemical sales.

Chemical and Engineering News: The Newsmagazine of the Chemical World. American Chemical Society, 1155 16th St., N.W. Washington, DC 20036. Phone: 800-227-5558 or (202)872-4600 Fax: (202)776-8258 E-mail: help@acs.org • URL: http://www.chemistry.org • Weekly. Institutions, $210.00 per year.

Chemical Coaters Association International., PO Box 54316 Cincinnati, OH 45254. Phone: 800-926-2848 or (513)624-6767 Fax: (513)624-0601 E-mail: aygoyer@one.net • URL: http://www.ccaiweb.com • Industrial users of organic finishing systems; suppliers of chemicals, equipment, and paints. Works toward the improvement of decorative, functional, and performance standards of chemical coatings. Encourages members to continue improvements in application technology. Provides coating industry with representation to public authorities and government agencies. Sponsors research and educational programs to control environmental pollution. Maintains placement service. Provides speaker's bureau.

Chemical Engineering. Chemical Week Associates, 110 Williams St. New York, NY 10038. Phone: (212)621-4900 Fax: (212)621-4800 E-mail: acortessr@chemweek.com • URL: http://www.chemweek.com • Monthly. $39.50 per year. Includes annual *Chemical Engineering Buyers Guide*.

Chemical Engineering Buyers Guide. McGraw-Hill Inc., PO Box 182604 Columbus, OH 43272. Phone: 877-833-5524 or (212)512-2000 Fax: (614)759-3749 E-mail: customer.service@mcgraw-hill.com • URL: http://www.mcgraw-hill.com • Publication includes: List of over 4,000 firms supplying equipment, materials, and services to the chemical process industries. Entries include: Company name, address, phone, fax, toll-free phone, all sales office locations and phones.

Chemical Engineering for Chemists. Richard G. Griskey. American Chemical Society, 1155 16th St., NW Washington, DC 20036. Phone: 800-227-5558 or (202)872-4600 Fax: (202)872-4615 E-mail: help@acs.org • URL: http://www.chemistry.org • 1997. $140.00. Provides basic knowledge of chemical engineering and engineering economics.

Chemical Engineering Progress. American Institute of Chemical Engineers, Three Park Ave. New York, NY 10016-5901. Phone: 800-242-4363 or (212)591-7338 Fax: (212)591-8887 E-mail: journalsedit@aiche.org • URL: http://www.aiche.org • Monthly. Individuals, $100.00 per year. Covers current advances and trends in the chemical process and related industries. Supplement available *AICh Extra*.

Chemical Equipment. Reed Business Information, 360 Park Ave., S New York, NY 10010. Phone: 800-446-6551 or (646)746-6400 Fax: (646)746-7028 E-mail: corporatecommunications@reedbusiness.com • URL: http://www.reedbusiness.com • Monthly. Free to qualified personnel. Covers the design, building, and operation of chemical process plants. Includes end-of-year *Chemical Equipment Literature Review*

Chemical Market Reporter. Schnell Publishing Co., Inc., 2 Rector St. New York, NY 10006. Phone: (212)791-4251 Fax: (212)791-4311 • URL: http://www.chemexpo.com • Weekly. $169.00 per year. Quotes current prices for a wide range of chemicals. Formerly *Chemical Marketing Reporter*.

Chemical Processing. Putman Media, 555 W. Pierce Rd., Suite 301 Itasca, IL 60143-2649. Phone: (630)467-1300 Fax: (630)467-1109 E-mail: ckappel@putnam.net • URL: http://www.chemicalprocessing.com • Monthly. Free to qualified personnel; others, $67.00 per year.

Chemical Regulation Reporter: A Weekly Review of Activity Affecting Chemical Users and Manufacturers. BNA, Inc., 1231 25th St., NW Washington, DC 20037. Phone: 800-372-1033 E-mail: customercare@bna.com • URL: http://www.bna.com • Weekly. $2,226 per year. Looseleaf service.

Chemical Sources Association., 3301 Rte. 66, Ste. 205, Bldg. C, PO Box 790 Neptune, NJ 07753. Phone: (732)922-3008 Fax: (732)922-3590 E-mail: diane@afius.org • URL: http://www.chemicalsources.org • Representatives of flavor and fragrance manufacturers. Purpose is to find suppliers and manufacturers for rare or hard-to-obtain chemicals and essential oils used in the flavor and fragrance industry. Compiles statistics.

Chemical Specialties Manufacturers Association., 1913 Eye St., N.W. Washington, DC 20006. Phone: (202)872-8110 Fax: (202)872-8114 E-mail: csma@juno.com Formerly National Association Insecticide and Disinfectant Manufacturers.

Chemical Week. Chemical Week Associates, 110 Williams St. New York, NY 10038. Phone: (212)621-4900 Fax: (212)621-4800 E-mail: acortessr@chemweek.com • URL: http://www.chemweek.com • 49 times a year. $139.00 per year. Includes annual *Buyers' Guide*.

Chemical Week-Buyers Guide. Chemical Week Associates, 110 Williams St. New York, NY 10038. Phone: (212)621-4900 Fax: (212)621-4800 • URL: http://www.chemweek.com • Annual. $115.00. About 4,200 manufacturers and suppliers of chemical raw materials to the chemical process industries. Included in subscription to *Chemical Week*.

Chemical Week: Financial Survey of the 300 Largest Companies in the U. S. Chemical Process Industries. Chemical Week Associates, 110 Williams St. New York, NY 10038. Phone: (212)621-4900 Fax: (212)621-4800 E-mail: acortessr@chemweek.cok • URL: http://www.chemweek.com • Annual. $8.00. Supersedes *Chemical Week-Chemical Week 300*.

Chemical Wholesalers Directory. infoUSA, P.O. Box 27347 Omaha, NE 68127. Phone: 800-555-6124 or (402)593-4600 Fax: (402)331-5481 E-mail: internet@infousa.com • URL: http://www.abii.com • Annual. Price on application. Lists 8,082 United States wholesalers and 1,199 Canadian wholesalers. Compiled from telephone company yellow pages.

The Chemistry and Physics of Coatings. Alastair R. Marrion, editor. Springer-Verlag, 175 Fifth Ave. New York, NY 10010. Phone: 800-777-4643 or (212)460-1500 Fax: (201)248-4505 E-mail: service@springer-ny.com • URL: http://www.springer.ny.com • 1994. $46.95. Published by The Royal Society of Chemistry. Provides an overview of paint science and technology, including environmental considerations.

Chemistry Laboratories. Rensselaer Polytechnic Institute

The Chemistry of Fragrances. D. Pybus and C. Sell. Springer-Verlag New York, Inc., 175 5th Ave. New York, NY 10010. Phone: 800-777-4643 or (212)460-1500 Fax: (212)473-6272 E-mail: service@springer-ny.com • URL: http://www.springer-ny.com • 1999. $39.00. (RSC Paperback Series). Published by The Royal Society of Chemistry.

The Chemistry of Mind-Altering Drugs: History, Pharmacology, and Cultural Context. Daniel M. Perrine. American Chemical Society, 1155 16th St., NW Washington, DC 20036. Phone: 800-227-5558 or (202)872-4600 Fax: (202)872-4615 E-mail: help@acs.org • URL: http://www.chemistry.org • 1996. $45.00. Contains detailed descriptions of the pharmacological and psychological effects of a wide variety of drugs, "from alcohol to zopiclone."

Chemistry Today and Tomorrow: The Central, Useful, and Creative Science. Ronald Breslow. Jones and Bartlett Publishers, Inc., 40 Tall Pine Dr. Sudbury, MA 01776-2256. Phone: 800-832-0034 or (978)443-5000 Fax: (978)443-8000 E-mail: info@jbpub.com • URL: http://www.jbpub.com • 1996. $37.95. Written in nontechnical language for the general reader. Discusses the various disciplines of chemistry, such as medicinal, environmental, and industrial. (Chemistry Series).

Chester F. Carlson Center for Imaging Science.

CHF Newsbriefs. Cooperative Housing Foundation, 8601 Georgia Ave., Ste. 800 Silver Spring, MD 20910-3440. Phone: (301)587-4700 Fax: (301)587-7315 E-mail: mailbox@chfhq.org • URL: http://www.chfhq.org • Description: Seeks to "help families throughout the world by focusing on the development of communities, habitat, and finance."

Chicago Board of Trade Statistical Annual. Board of Trade of the City of Chicago, 141 W. Jackson Blvd. Chicago, IL 60604. Phone: (312)435-3500 Annual.

Chicago Board of Trade: The World's Leading Futures Exchange. Chicago Board of TradePhone: (312)535-3500 Fax: (312)341-3392 E-mail: comments@cbot.com • URL: http://www.cbot.com • Web site provides a wide variety of statistics, commentary, charts, and news relating to both

agricultural and financial futures trading. For example, Web page "MarketPlex: Information MarketPlace to the World" offers prices & volume, contract specifications & margins, government reports, etc. Searching is available, with daily updates for current data. Fees: Mostly free (some specialized services are fee-based).

Chicago Board Options Exchange., 400 S LaSalle St. Chicago, IL 60605. Phone: 877-THE-CBOE or (312)786-5600 Fax: (312)786-7409 E-mail: calvinj@cboe.com • URL: http://www.cboe.com • Individuals, institutions and firms engaged in the buying and selling of various products including stock options, cash-settled index options, options on HOLDRs, options on Exchange Traded Funds and Structured Products.

Chicago Board Options Exchange. CCH, Inc., 2700 Lake Cook Rd. Riverwoods, IL 60015. Phone: 800-835-5224 or (847)267-7000 E-mail: cust_serv@cch.com • URL: http://www.cch.com • Monthly. $561.00 per year. Looseleaf service. Periodic supplementation. Rules, regulations and legal aspects for the trading of puts and calls.

The Chicago Manual of Style: The Essential Guide for Authors, Editors, and Publishers. The University of Chicago Press, 1427 E. 60th St. Chicago, IL 60637. Phone: 800-621-2736 or (773)702-7700 Fax: 800-621-8476 or (773)702-7212 E-mail: custserv@press.uchicago.edu • URL: http://www.press.uchicago.edu • 1993. $40.00. 14th edition.

Chief Executive Magazine. Chief Executive Group, Inc., 733 3rd Ave., 24th Fl. New York, NY 10017. Phone: (212)883-4628 Fax: (212)687-8456 E-mail: cevans@chiefexecutive.net • URL: http://www.chiefexecutive.net • Monthly. $95.00 per year.

Chief Executive Officers Club., 4 W 22nd St., 10th Fl. New York, NY 10010. Phone: (212)925-7911 Fax: (212)925-7463 E-mail: main@ceoclubs.org • URL: http://ceoclubs.org • Serves as a management resource for entrepreneurial managers and their professional advisers. Selects and makes available publications on developing business plans, organizing an entrepreneurial team, attracting venture capital, and obtaining patents, trademarks, and copyrights. Develops, collects, and disseminates information on business trends, new laws and regulations, and tax guidance. Conducts intensive-study courses and seminars. Has identified stages of the entrepreneurial process and, through essays and audiocassettes, addresses problems pertinent to each stage.

Chief Executive Officers Newsletter: For the Entrepreneurial Manager and the Pr ofessionals Who Advise Him. Center for Entrepreneurial Management, Inc., Penthouse, 180 Varick St. New York, NY 10014. Phone: (212)633-0060 Fax: (212)633-0063 Monthly. $96.00 per year. Looseleaf service. Formerly *Entrepreneurial Manager's Newsletter*.

Chief Executives Organization., 7920 Norfolk Ave., Ste. 400 Bethesda, MD 20814-2507. Phone: (301)656-9220 Fax: (301)656-9221 E-mail: info@ceo.org • URL: http://www.ceo.org • Invited members of the Young Presidents' Organization who have reached the age of 49, the mandatory "retirement" age for YPO. (Young Presidents' Organization comprises presidents of corporations with gross annual revenue of at least one million dollars and a minimum of 50 employees, of nonindustrial corporations with revenue of two million dollars and 25 employees, or of banking corporations with average deposits of 15 million dollars and 25 employees. Each member must have been elected president of a corporation before reaching the age of 40.) Sponsors educational programs.

Chief Warrant and Warrant Officers Association, United States Coast Guard., 200 V St. SW Washington, DC 20024. Phone: (202)554-7753 Fax: (202)484-0641 E-mail: cwoauscg@verizon.net • URL: http://www.cwoauscg.org • Individuals who currently hold or once held the rank of Warrant Officer or Chief Warrant Officer on the active, retired, and reserve rolls of the U.S. Coast Guard. Works to aid members in advancing their professional abilities. Seeks to enhance their value, loyalty, and devotion to the service; promotes its unity and morale through social association.

Child Care Service. Entrepreneur Media, Inc., 2445 McCabe Way Irvine, CA 92614. Phone: 800-421-2300 or (949)261-2325 Fax: (949)261-0234 E-mail: entmag@entrepreneur.com • URL: http://www.entrepreneur.com • Looseleaf. $59.50. A practical guide to starting a day care center for children. Covers profit potential, start-up costs, market size evaluation, owner's time required, site selection, pricing, accounting, advertising, promotion, etc. (Start-Up Business Guide No. E1058.)

Child Labor: An American History. Hugh D. Hindman. M. E. Sharpe, Inc., 80 Business Park Drive Armonk, NY 10504. Phone: 800-541-6563 or (914)273-1800 Fax: (914)273-2106 E-mail: custserv@mesharpe.com • URL: http://www.mesharpe.com • 2002. $88.95.

Children's Book Review Index. Gale Cengage Learning, 27500 Drake Rd. Farmington Hills, MI 48331-3535. Phone: 800-877-GALE or (248)699-GALE Fax: 800-414-5043 E-mail: gale.galeord@cengage.com • URL: http://gale.cengage.com • Annual. $165.00. Back volumes available. Contains more than 25,000 review citations.

Children's Bookstore. Entrepreneur Media, Inc., 2445 McCabe Way Irvine, CA 92614. Phone: 800-421-2300 or (949)261-2325 Fax: (949)261-0234 E-mail: entmag@entrepreneur.com • URL: http://www.entrepreneur.com • Looseleaf. $59.50. A practical guide to starting a children's bookstore. Covers profit potential, start-up costs, market size evaluation,

owner's time required, site selection, lease negotiation, pricing, accounting, advertising, promotion, etc. (Start-Up Business Guide No. E1293.)

Children's Clothing Store. Entrepreneur Media, Inc., 2445 McCabe Way Irvine, CA 92614. Phone: 800-421-2300 or (949)261-2325 Fax: (949)261-0234 E-mail: entmag@entrepreneur.com • URL: http://www.entrepreneur.com • Looseleaf. $59.50. A practical guide to starting a children's clothing shop. Covers profit potential, start-up costs, market size evaluation, owner's time required, site selection, lease negotiation, pricing, accounting, advertising, promotion, etc. (Start-Up Business Guide No. E1161.)

Children's Fitness Center. Entrepreneur Media, Inc., 2445 McCabe Way Irvine, CA 92614. Phone: 800-421-2300 or (949)261-2325 Fax: (949)261-0234 E-mail: entmag@entrepreneur.com • URL: http://www.entrepreneur.com • Looseleaf. $59.50. A practical guide to starting a physical fitness center for children. Covers profit potential, start-up costs, market size evaluation, owner's time required, site selection, lease negotiation, pricing, accounting, advertising, promotion, etc. (Start-Up Business Guide No. E1351.)

Chilton's Automotive Marketing: A Monthly Publication for the Retail Jobber and Distributor of Automotive Aftermarket. Reed Business Information, 360 Park Ave., S New York, NY 10010. Phone: 800-662-7776 or (646)746-6400 Fax: (610)205-1198 E-mail: corporatecommunications@reedbusiness.com • URL: http://www.reedbusiness.com • Monthly. Free to qualified personnel; others, $48.00 per year. Includes marketing of automobile batteries. Formerly *Automotive Aftermarket News*.

Chilton's Distribution: The Transportation and Business Logistics Magazine. Reed Business Information, 360 Park Ave., S New York, NY 10010. Phone: 800-662-7776 or (646)746-6400 E-mail: corporatecommunications@reedbusiness.com • URL: http://www.reedbusiness.com • Monthly. $65.00 per year.

China: A Directory and Sourcebook. Euromonitor International, Business Referene Div., 122 S. Michigan Ave., Ste. 1200 Chicago, IL 60603. Phone: 800-577-3876 or (312)922-1115 Fax: (312)922-1157 E-mail: insight@euromonitorintl.com 1998. $590.00. Second edition. Describes about 500 companies in both China and Hong Kong. Sourcebook section provides 1,000 information sources.

China Business Review. United States-China Business Council, 1818 N St., N. W., Suite 200 Washington, DC 20036-2406. Phone: (202)429-0340 Fax: (202)833-9027 E-mail: info@uschina.org • URL: http://www.uschinabusinessreview.com/r • Bimonthly. $99.00 per year. Covers trends and issues affecting U. S. investment and trade with China and Hong Kong.

China Business: The Portable Encyclopedia for Doing Business with China. Christine Genzberger and others. World Trade Press, 1450 Grant Ave., Suite 204 Novato, CA 94945. Phone: 800-833-8586 or (415)898-1124 Fax: (415)898-1080 E-mail: sales@worldtradepress.com • URL: http://www.worldtradepress.com • 1994. $24.95. Covers economic data, import/export possibilities, basic tax and trade laws, travel information, and other useful facts for doing business with the People's Republic of China. (Country Business Guides Series).

China in the World Economy: The Domestic Challenges. Organization for Economic Cooperation and Development, OECD Washington Center, 2001 L St., N. W., Suite 650 Washington, DC 20036-4922. Phone: 800-456-6323 or (202)785-6323 Fax: (202)785-0350 E-mail: washington.contact@oecd.org • URL: http://www.oecdwash.org • 2002. $120.00. Analyzes the domestic and international effects of China's entry into the World Trade Organization. (China in the Global Economy Series).

China Marketing Data and Statistics. Available from Gale Cengage Learning, 27500 Drake Rd. Farmington Hills, MI 48331-3535. Phone: 800-877-GALE or (248)699-GALE Fax: 800-414-5043 E-mail: gale.galeord@cengage.com • URL: http://gale.cengage.com • 2000. $445.00. Second edition. Two volumes. Published by Euromonitor. In addition to national statistics, includes data for 30 cities and 400 administrative areas. Major source is the Chinese State Statistical Bureau.

Chinese American Association of Commerce., 778 Clay St., Suite C San Francisco, CA 94108. Phone: (415)362-4306 Fax: (415)362-1478 Members are individuals interested in improving trade between the U. S. and the People's Republic of China.

Chinese American Librarians Association., California State University Sacramento, 2000 State University Dr. E, 605 Agriculture Dr., Mailcode 6632 Sacramento, CA 95819. Fax: (949)857-1988 E-mail: dora4ala@yahoo.com • URL: http://www.cala-web.org • Promotes better communication among Chinese American librarians in the U.S., serves as a forum for the discussion of mutual problems, and supports the development and promotion of librarianship. Maintains placement referral service.

Chisum on Patents. LexisNexis Matthew Bender, 1275 Broadway Albany, NY 12204. Phone: 800-424-4200 or (518)487-3000 Fax: (518)487-3584 E-mail: bookstore.support@lexisnexis.com • URL: http://www.bender.com • Five times a year. 2,105.00. 16 looseleaf volumes. An analysis of patent law in the U. S. Includes bibliography and glossary.

Chocolate Fads, Folklore, and Fantasies: 1,000 Chunks of Chocolate Information. Linda K. Fuller. The Haworth Press,

Inc., 10 Alice St. Binghamton, NY 13904-1580. Phone: 800-429-6784 or (607)722-5857 Fax: 800-895-0582 or (607)722-1424 E-mail: getinfo@haworthpressinc.com • URL: http://www.haworthpressinc.com • 1994. $49.95. Includes "Choco-Marketing-Mania Survey," "Media Citations: Chocolate 1979-1992," "Choco-References," and addresses of chocolate companies. (Original Book Series).

Chocolate Manufacturers Association of the U.S.A., 8320 Old Courthouse Rd., Ste. 300 Vienna, VA 22182-3811. Phone: (703)790-5750 Fax: (703)790-5752 E-mail: info@candyusa.org • URL: http://www.candyusa.org • Formerly Association of Cocoa and Chocolate Manufacturers of the U.S.

Choice Magazine: Current Reviews for Academic Libraries. Association of College Research Libraries. American Library Association, 50 E Huron St. Chicago, IL 60611-2795. Phone: 800-545-2433 or (312)280-2523 Fax: (312)280-2520 E-mail: acrl@ala.org • URL: http://www.ala.org • 11 times a year. $237.00 per year. A publication of the Association of College and Research Libraries. Contains book reviews, primarily for college and university libraries.

Choosing and Using an HMO. Ellyn Spragins. Bloomberg, 499 Park Ave. New York, NY 10022. Phone: 800-388-2749 or (212)318-2000 Fax: (917)369-5000 • URL: http://www.bloomberg.com • 1998. $19.95. Includes advice on finding a doctor, going outside the plan, and avoiding excess costs. (Bloomberg Personal Bookshelf Series.)

Chromatographia: An International Journal for Rapid Communication in Chromatography and Associated Techniques. Elsevier, 655 Ave. of the Americas New York, NY 10010-5107. Phone: 800-366-2665 or (212)989-5800 Fax: 800-535-9935 or (212)633-3680 E-mail: custserv@elsevier.com • URL: http://www.chromatographia.com • 24 times a year. $1,299.00 per year. Text in English; summaries in English, French and German.

Chronicle Financial Aid Guide. Chronicle Guidance Publications Inc., 66 Aurora St. Moravia, NY 13118-3569. Phone: 800-622-7284 or (315)497-0330 Fax: (315)497-0339 E-mail: customerservice@chronicleguidance.com • URL: http://www.chronicleguide.com • Covers: Over 1,770 financial aid programs offered primarily by private organizations, independent and AFL-CIO affiliated labor unions, and federal and state governments for high school students, undergraduate and graduate students, and adult learners. Entries include: Name of sponsoring organization, address, amount of aid, eligibility requirements, application, selection procedure.

Chronicle Four-Year College Databook. Chronicle Guidance Publications Inc., 66 Aurora St. Moravia, NY 13118-3569. Phone: 800-622-7284 or (315)497-0330 Fax: (315)497-0339 E-mail: customerservice@chronicleguidance.com • URL: http://www.chronicleguide.com • Covers: More than 825 baccalaureate, master's, doctoral, and first professional programs offered by more than 2,450 colleges and universities in the United States. Entries include: College charts section gives college name, address, phone; accreditation, enrollment, admissions, costs, financial aid; accreditation associations' names, addresses, and phone numbers. Appendices gives details on admissions and other information special to each college.

Chronicle Occupational Briefs. Chronicle Guidance Publications, Inc., 66 Aurora St. Moravia, NY 13118-3576. Phone: 800-622-7284 or (315)497-0330 Fax: (315)497-3359 Approximately 600 pamphlets about various occupations. $2.25 per pamphlet. CD-ROM edition, $149.00.

The Chronicle of Higher Education. Chronicle of Higher Education, Inc., 1255 23rd St., N.W., Suite 700 Washington, DC 20037. Phone: (202)466-1032 Fax: (202)452-1033 E-mail: letters@chronicle.com • URL: http://www.chronicle.com • 49 times a year. $82.50 per year. Includes *Almanac*. Provides news, book reviews and job listings for college professors and administrators.

Chronicle of Latin American Economic Affairs [online]. Latin America Data Base, Latin American Institute, University of New Mexico, 801 Yale Blvd., N. E. Albuquerque, NM 87131-1016. Phone: 800-472-0888 or (505)277-6839 Fax: (505)277-5989 Contains the complete text online of the weekly newsletter, *Chronicle of Latin American Economic Affairs*. Provides news and analysis of trade and economic developments in Latin America, including Caribbean countries. Time period is 1986 to date, with weekly updates. Inquire as to online cost and availability.

Chronicle of Philanthropy:The Newspaper of the Non-Profit World. Chronicle of Higher Education, Inc., 1255 23rd St., N.W., Suite 700 Washington, DC 20037. Phone: 800-728-2819 or (202)466-1032 Fax: (202)452-1033 E-mail: letters@chronicle.com • URL: http://www.chronicle.com • Biweekly. $69.50 per year.

CIES, Food Business Forum., 8455 Colesville Rd., Ste. 705 Silver Spring, MD 20910. Phone: (301)563-3383 Fax: (301)563-3386 E-mail: us.office@ciesnet.com • URL: http://www.ciesnet.com • Membership in 44 countries includes: food industry chain store firms with combined outlets of over 100,000; associations; firms supplying articles and services to chain food stores. Fosters cooperation between chain store organizations and their suppliers. Serves as a liaison between members. Assists in the exchange of trainees among member firms. Conducts studies on methods, technical progress, and the growth rate of chain store organizations throughout the world.

Cigar Association of America.

The Cigar Market. Available from MarketResearch.com, 641 Ave. of the Americas, 3rd Fl. New York, NY 10011. Phone: 800-298-5699 or (212)807-2629 Fax: (212)807-2716 E-mail: order@marketresearch.com • URL: http://www.marketresearch.com • 1997. $1,230.00. Market research report published by Packaged Facts. Who smokes cigars? Why are they smoking? Are they likely to continue? Sales projections are provided.

Cigarettes: Anatomy of an Industry from Seed to Smoke. Tara Parker-Pope. The New Press, 38 Greene St., 4th Fl. New York, NY 10013. Phone: 800-223-4830 or (212)629-8802 Fax: (212)629-8617 • URL: http://www.thenewpress.com • 2001. $24.95. Covers the history, economic ramifications, marketing strategies, and legal problems of the cigarette industry. Popularly written.

CIO: The Magazine for Chief Information Officers. CXO Media, Inc., 492 Old Connecticut Path Framingham, MA 01701-9208. Phone: 800-788-4605 or (508)935-4796 Fax: (508)879-7784 E-mail: denisep@cio.com • URL: http://www.cio.com • 23 times a year. $150.00 per year. Edited for chief information officers. Includes a monthly "Web Business" section (incorporates the former *WebMaster* periodical) and a monthly "Enterprise" section for company executives other than CIOs.

Circulation Council of DMA., 1120 Ave. of the Americas New York, NY 10036. Phone: (212)768-7277 Fax: (212)302-6714 E-mail: councils@the-dma.org • URL: http://www.the-dma.org • A division of the Direct Marketing Association. Members include publishers and circulation directors.

Circulation Management. Media Central, 470 Park Ave., S, 8th Fl. New York, NY 10016. Phone: 800-307-2529 E-mail: adedit@inside.com • URL: http://www.demographics.com • Monthly. $39.00 per year. Edited for circulation professionals in the magazine and newsletter publishing industry. Covers marketing, planning, promotion, management, budgeting, and related topics.

Citation: Current Legal Developments Relating to Medicine and Allied Professions. American Medical Association, Health Law Div. Citation Publishing Corp., P.O. Box 3538 RFD Long Grove, IL 60047. Phone: (847)438-2020 Fax: (847)438-2299 Semimonthly. $130.00 per year. Newsletter. Contains summaries of lawsuits affecting medical personnel or hospitals.

Cities for the 21st Century. OECD Publications and Information Center, 2001 L St., N.W., Suite 650 Washington, DC 20036-4922. Phone: 800-456-6323 or (202)785-6323 Fax: (202)785-0350 E-mail: washington.contact@oecd.org • URL: http://www.oecdwash.org • 1994. $39.00. Contains discussions of the economic, social, and environmental problems of today's cities.

Cities of the United States. Gale Cengage Learning, 27500 Drake Rd. Farmington Hills, MI 48331-3535. Phone: 800-877-GALE or (248)699-4253 Fax: 800-414-5043 E-mail: gale.galeord@cengage.com • URL: http://gale.cengage.com • 2001. $445.00. Fourth edition. Four regional volumes. $125.00 per volume. Detailed information is provided on 164 U. S. cities. Includes economic data, climate, geography, government, and history, with maps and photographs.

Cities of the World. Gale Cengage Learning, 27500 Drake Rd. Farmington Hills, MI 48331-3535. Phone: 800-877-GALE or (248)699-4253 Fax: 800-414-5043 E-mail: gale.galeord@cengage.com • URL: http://gale.cengage.com • 1998. $370.00. Fifth edition. Four regional volumes. $95.00 per volume. Detailed information is provided for more than 3,407 cities in 177 countries (excluding U.S.) Includes maps and photographs. Based in U.S. State Department reports.

Citizen Action Fund., 1730 Rhode Island Ave. NW, Ste. 403 Washington, DC 20036. Phone: (202)775-1580 Fax: (202)296-4054 E-mail: info@bipac.org Citizens working for economic democracy and social justice. Goal is to make the concerns of the majority of Americans felt in economic, environmental, and political decision-making. Seeks more jobs, safe and affordable energy, fair taxes, equal voting rights, and a safe and healthy community and workplace, free of toxic hazards. Conducts research, training, and educational programs.

Citizen Soldier., 267 5th Ave., No. 901 New York, NY 10016. Phone: (212)679-2250 Fax: (212)679-2252 E-mail: citizensoldier1@aol.com • URL: http://www.citizen-soldier.org • Individuals concerned with military-civilian relationships within American society. Aims to help Vietnam War veterans who may have been harmed by highly toxic herbicides (including Agent Orange) that were used in Vietnam between 1962 and 1970. Works with veterans who were exposed to low-level radiation at Nevada and South Pacific A-bomb test sites and Persian Gulf War veterans suffering from unexplained chronic ailments. Represents GIs on active duty who are victims of military racism and/or sexism. Assists GIs who have been prosecuted or otherwise punished due to positive results on drug residue urine tests that CS believes to have been inaccurate because of defective laboratory work. Seeks to protect the rights of soldiers testing positive for the AIDS antibody. Advocates for veterans suffering from Persian Gulf Syndrome. Promotes a public service campaign to inform service members of their legal rights regarding the military's HIV testing program. Works with high school and college youths to address concerns on

military recruiting practices. Maintains speakers' bureau. Advises GIs who wish alternatives to service in current Iraqi War.

Citizens for a Competitive America., 6107 Hampton Ridge Rd. Columbia, SC 29209-1308. Phone: (803)695-0940 Fax: (803)695-9729 E-mail: richard.wallace@scbar.org A political action committee that raises funds for the election campaigns of candidates who support the committee's objective of U.S. economic competitiveness.

Citizens for a Sound Economy., 1250 H St., NW, Ste. 700 Washington, DC 20005-3908. Phone: 888-564-6273 or (202)783-3870 Fax: (202)783-4687 E-mail: cse@cse.org • URL: http://www.cse.org • Absorbed Council for a Competitive Economy and Tax Foundation.

Citizens for Bush., 1156 15th St. NW, Ste. 500 Washington, DC 20005. Phone: (202)331-0541 E-mail: info@bipac.org Independent grass roots lobby organization supporting the legislative agenda and policies of President George Bush (1924-). Collaborates with several grass roots organizations to lobby Congress. Conducts seminars and legislative ratings. Maintains speakers' bureau.

Citizen's Guide on Using the Freedom of Information Act and the Privacy Act of 1974 to Request Government Records. U. S. Government Printing Office, 732 N Capitol St., NW Washington, DC 20401. Phone: 888-293-6498 or (202)512-1530 Fax: (202)512-1262 E-mail: gpoaccess@gpo.gov • URL: http://www.gpoaccess.gov • 1997. $5.00.

Citizen's Guide to the Federal Budget. Available from U. S. Government Printing Office, Washington, DC 20402. Phone: (202)512-1800 Fax: (202)512-2250 E-mail: gpoaccess@gpo.gov • URL: http://www.access.gpo.gov • Annual. $3.25. Issued by the Office of Management and Budget, Executive Office of the President (http://www.whitehouse.gov). Provides basic data for the general public about the budget of the U. S. government.

Citizens in Politics., c/o National Committee for an Effective Congress, 10 E. 39th St. New York, NY 10016. Phone: (212)686-4905 E-mail: info@bipac.org A project of National Committee for an Effective Congress (see separate entry). Artists, musicians, film and television personalities, and sports and literary figures. Acts as a referral service for celebrities who want to work on political action campaigns. Celebrities volunteer their time to attract money, attention, and votes through participation in such activities as congressional election campaigns or comedy and musical benefits that champion progressive positions on public policy issues. **Convention/Meeting:** none.

Citizens League Research Institute. Citizens League Research Institute, 1331 Euclid Ave. Cleveland, OH 44113. Phone: (216)241-5340 Fax: (216)736-7626 E-mail: staff@citizensleague.org • URL: http://www.citizensleague.org • Local government structure, performance, and financing focusing on the Greater Cleveland (7-county) region. Cooperates with public officials and civic organizations on improvement of local governmental procedures in order to obtain greater economy and efficiency in administration of public affairs.

Citrograph: Magazine of the Citrus Industry. Western Agricultural Publishing Co., Inc., 4969 E. Clinton Way, Suite 104 Fresno, CA 93727-1549. Phone: (209)252-7000 Fax: (209)252-7387 Monthly. $19.95 per year. Gives produce growing tips.

Citrus Center. Texas A & M University at Kingsville

Citrus Industry Magazine. Associated Publications Corp., 495 E. Summerlin St. Bartow, FL 33830. Phone: (813)533-4114 Monthly. $20.00 per year. Gives food growing tips.

Citrus Research and Education Center, Lake Alfred. University of Florida

Citrus Research Center and Agricultural Experiment Station. University of California at Riverside

City & Country Club Life: The Social Magazine for South Florida. Club Publications, Inc., 665 La Villa Dr. Miami, FL 33166. Phone: (305)887-1701 Fax: (305)885-1923 Five times a year. Controlled circulation.

City Planning in America: Between Promise and Despair. Mary E. Hommann. Greenwood Publishing Group, Inc., 88 Post Rd., W Westport, CT 06881. Phone: 800-225-5800 or (203)226-3571 Fax: (203)431-2214 E-mail: customerservice@greenwood.com • URL: http://www.greenwood.com • 1993. $57.95.

City Profiles USA: A Traveler's Guide to Major U. S. and Canadian Cities. Darren L. Smith, editor. Omnigraphics, Inc., Penobscot Bldg. Detroit, MI 48226. Phone: 800-234-1340 or (313)961-1340 Fax: 800-875-1340 or (313)961-1383 E-mail: info@omnigraphics.com • URL: http://www.omnigraphics.com • 2003. $130.00. A directory of information useful to business and other travelers in major cities. Includes services, facilities, attractions, and events. Arranged by city.

Civil Affairs Association., 10130 Hyla Brook Rd. Columbia, MD 21044-1705. Phone: (410)992-7724 Fax: (410)740-5046 E-mail: civilaffairs@earthlink.net • URL: http://www.-civilaffairsassoc.org • U.S. Army active and reserve officers and enlisted personnel serving in Army or Marine Corps civil affairs units or in civil affairs staff positions in major military headquarters, and international members. Advocates and promotes a strong U.S. military civil affairs capability.

Civil Engineering Database (CEDB). American Society of Civil Engineers, 1801 Alexander Bell Drive Reston, VA 20191-

4400. Phone: 800-548-2723 or (703)295-6240 Fax: (703)295-6278 Provides abstracts of the U. S. and international literature of civil engineering, 1975 to date. Inquire as to on-line cost and availability.

Civil Engineering: Engineered Design and Construction. American Society of Civil Engineers, 1801 Alexander Graham Bell Dr. Reston, VA 20191-4400. Phone: 800-548-2723 or (703)295-6300 Fax: (703)295-6222 • URL: http://www.asce.org • Monthly. $160.00 per year.

Civil Engineering Practice: Engineering Success By Analysis of Failure. David D. Piesold. McGraw-Hill, 1221 Ave. of the Americas New York, NY 10020. Phone: 800-722-4726 or (212)512-2000 Fax: (212)512-4502 E-mail: customer.service@mcgraw-hill.com • URL: http://www.mcgraw-hill.com • 1991. $52.00.

Civil Liberties. American Civil Liberties Union, 125 Broad St., 18th Fl. New York, NY 10004-2400. Phone: (212)344-3005 Fax: (212)344-3318 E-mail: info@artsusa.org • URL: http://www.aclu.org • Description: Supplies news of the legal defense, research, and public education projects of the ACLU, conducted to enable citizens to know and assert their rights. Focuses on civil liberties issues relating to freedom of expression, due process of law, equality, and privacy. Recurring features include news of significant legislation.

Civil Liberties Under the Constitution. M. Glenn Abernathy and others. University of South Carolina Press, 718 Devine St. Columbia, SC 29208. Phone: 800-768-2500 or (803)777-5243 Fax: 800-868-0740 • URL: http://www.sc.edu/uscpress • 1993. $34.95. Sixth edition.

Civil Rights Actions. LexisNexis Matthew Bender, 1275 Broadway Albany, NY 12204. Phone: 800-424-4200 or (518)487-3000 Fax: (518)487-3584 E-mail: bookstore.support@lexisnexis.com • URL: http://www.bender.com • $1,157.00. Seven looseleaf volumes. Periodic supplementation. Contains legal analysis of civil rights activities.

Civil Rights: State Capitals. Wakeman-Walworth, Inc., P.O. Box 7376 Alexandria, VA 22307-7376. Phone: (703)768-9600 Fax: (703)768-9690 E-mail: newsletters@statecapitals.com • URL: http://www.statecapitals.com • 50 times a year. $245.00 per year; print and online editions, $350.00 per year. Newsletter. Includes coverage of state affirmative action programs. Formerly *From the State Capitals: Civil Rights*.

Civil Service Employees Association., PO Box 7125, Capitol Sta., Box 7125 Albany, NY 12224-0125. Phone: 800-342-4146 or (518)257-1000 Fax: (518)462-3639 E-mail: donohue@cseainc.org • URL: http://www.csealocal1000.org • AFL-CIO. Represents state and local government employees from all public employee classifications. Negotiates work contracts; represents members in grievances; provides legal assistance for on-the-job problems; provides advice and assistance on federal, state, and local laws affecting public employees. Conducts research, training and education programs. Compiles statistics.

Civil Service Handbook: How to Get a Civil Service Job. Peterson's, 200 Lenox Dr. Lawrenceville, NJ 08648. Phone: 800-338-3282 or (609)896-1800 Fax: (609)-896-1811 E-mail: support@petersons.com • URL: http://www.petersons.com • 1999. $12.95. 14th edition. (Arco Civil Service Series).

CLAIMS. IFI/Plenum Data Corp., 3202 Kirkwood Hwy., Ste. 203 Wilmington, DE 19808. Phone: 800-331-4955 or (302)633-7200 Fax: (302)998-0733 • URL: http://www.ifiplenum.com • Includes seven separate databases: *CLAIMS/Citation, CLAIMS/Compound Registry, CLAIMS/Comprehensive Data Base, CLAIMS/Reassignment & Reexamination, CLAIMS/Reference, CLAIMS/U. S. Patent Abstracts*, and *CLAIMS/Uniterm*. Provides extensive current and historical information on U. S. Patents. Inquire as to online cost and availability.

Claims. National Underwriter Co., 5081 Olympic Blvd. Erlanger, KY 41018. Phone: 800-543-0874 or (859)692-2100 • URL: http://www.nationalunderwriter.com • Monthly. $46.00 per year. Edited for insurance adjusters, risk managers, and claims professionals. Covers investigation, fraud, insurance law, and other claims-related topics.

Classical Architecture: An Introduction to Its Vocabulary and Essentials, with a Select Glossary of Terms. James S. Curl. W. W. Norton & Co., Inc., 500 5th Ave. New York, NY 10110. Phone: 800-223-4830 or (212)354-5500 Fax: (212)869-0856 • URL: http://www.wwnorton.com • 2003. $29.95. Second edition. Covers the architectural terminology of the Renaissance, the baroque period, rococo, neoclassicism, and the modern era.

Clay Mineralogy. M. J. Wilson. John Wiley and Sons, Inc., 111 River St. Hoboken, NJ 07030. Phone: 800-225-5945 or (201)748-6000 Fax: (201)748-6088 E-mail: info@wiley.com • URL: http://www.wiley.com • 1992. $105.00.

Clay Minerals Society., 3635 Concorde Pkwy., Ste. 500 Chantilly, VA 20151-1125. Phone: (703)652-9960 Fax: (703)652-9951 E-mail: cms@clays.org • URL: http://www.clays.org • Professionals concerned with clay mineralogy and technology in industry, university research, and government. Includes students of mineralogy, geology, soil science, astronomy, physics, geochemistry, and engineering, and representatives of such firms as oil companies, instrument makers, and clay mining companies. Seeks to stimulate research and disseminate information relating to all aspects of clay science and technology. Provides a forum for exchange of information and ideas. Maintains quantities of Source and Special Clays at the Source Clays Repository.

Clays and Clay Minerals. The Clay Minerals Society, P.O. Box 460130 Aurora, CO 80046. Phone: (303)680-9002 Fax: (303)680-9003 E-mail: cms@clays.org • URL: http://www.cms.lanl.gov • Bimonthly. $235.00 per year. Includes online edition.

Cleaning Business: Published Monthly for the Self-Employed Cleaning and Maintenance Professionals. William R. Griffin, Publisher, P.O. Box 1273 Seattle, WA 98111-1273. Phone: (206)622-4241 Fax: (206)622-6876 E-mail: wgriffin@cleaningconsultants.com • URL: http://www.cleaningconsultants.com • Monthly. $20.00 per year. Formerly *Service Business*

CLEAR News. Council of Licensure, Enforcement, and Regulation. Council of State Governments, 2760 Research Park Dr., PO Box 11910 Lexington, KY 40578-1910. Phone: 800-800-1910 or (859)244-8000 Fax: (859)244-8001 E-mail: csg@csg.org • URL: http://www.csg.org • Description: Concentrates on professional licensing. Addresses such issues as reciprocity, alternatives to individual licensure, sunset, antitrust, and administrative rule-making. Recurring features include news of members, conferences, committees, programs, and legislation, and a column titled State Lines.

Clearance and Copyright: Everything the Independent Filmmaker Needs to Know. Michael C. Donaldson. Silman-James Press, 3624 Shannon Rd. Los Angeles, CA 90027. Phone: (323)661-9922 Fax: (323)661-9933 E-mail: silmanjamespress@earthlink.com • URL: http://www.silmanjamespress.com • 1996. $26.95. Covers film rights problems in pre-production, production, post-production, and final release. Includes sample contracts and forms.

Click Here! Internet Advertising: How the Pros Attract, Design, Price, Place, and Measure Ads Online. Eugene Marlow. John Wiley and Sons, Inc., 111 River St. Hoboken, NJ 07030. Phone: 800-225-5945 or (201)748-6000 Fax: (201)748-6088 E-mail: info@wiley.com • URL: http://www.wiley.com • 1997. $29.95. Covers pricing, effectiveness, Web site selection, content, and other aspects of Internet advertising. (Business Technology Series).

Climates of the States. Gale Cengage Learning, 27500 Drake Rd. Farmington Hills, MI 48331-3535. Phone: 800-877-GALE or (248)699-4253 Fax: 800-414-5043 E-mail: gale.galeord@cengage.com • URL: http://gale.cengage.com • 2002. $275.00. Fourth edition. Two volumes. State-by-state summaries of climatebased on first order weather reporting stations.

Clin-Alert. Rowman & Littlefield Education, 4501 Forbes Blvd., Ste. 200 Lanham, MD 20706. Phone: 800-462-6420 or (301)459-3366 Fax: 800-583-2665 or (301)429-5748 E-mail: custserv@rowman.com • URL: http://www.sagepub.com • Description: Reports on adverse drug reactions, drug interactions, and related therapeutic hazards. Summarizes information from leading medical and pharmaceutical journals, reporting patient history, diagnosis, treatment, dosage, author's conclusion and warning, trade names of drugs, legal actions, if any, and dispositions.

Clinical and Laboratory Standards Institute., 940 W Valley Rd., Ste. 1400 Wayne, PA 19087-1898. Phone: 877-447-1888 or (610)688-0100 Fax: (610)688-0700 E-mail: customerservice@clsi.org • URL: http://www.clsi.org • Government agencies, professional societies, clinical laboratories, and industrial firms with interests in medical testing. Purposes are to promote the development of national and international standards for medical testing and to provide a consensus mechanism for defining and resolving problems that influence the quality and cost of healthcare work performed.

Clinical Laboratory Management Association., 989 Old Eagle School Rd., Ste. 815 Wayne, PA 19087. Phone: (610)995-9580 Fax: (610)995-9568 E-mail: website@clma.org • URL: http://www.clma.org • Individuals holding managerial or supervisory positions with clinical laboratories; persons engaged in education of such individuals; manufacturers or distributors of equipment or services to clinical laboratories. Objectives are: to enhance management skills and promote more efficient and productive department operations; to further exchange of professional knowledge, new technology, and colleague experience; to encourage cooperation among those engaged in management or supervisory functions. Activities include: workshops, seminars, and expositions; dissemination of information about legislation and other topics.

Clinical Leadership and Management Review. Clinical Laboratory Management Association. Lippincott Williams and Wilkins, 530 Walnut St. Philadelphia, PA 19106-3621. Phone: 800-638-3030 or (215)521-8300 Fax: (215)521-8902 E-mail: custserv@lww.com • URL: http://www.lww.com • Bimonthly. Individuals, $132.00 per year; institutions, $181.00 per year. Formerly *Cinical Laboratory Management Review*.

Clothing Manufacturers Association of the U.S.A.

CLR (Clinical Laboratory Reference). Medical Economics Co., Five Paragon Dr. Montvale, NJ 07645-1742. Phone: 877-922-2022 or (973)944-9777 Fax: (973)847-5390 E-mail: fulfill@superfill.com • URL: http://www.medec.com • Annual. $32.00. Describes diagnostic reagents, test systems, instruments, equipment, and services for medical laboratories. Includes "Directory of Diagnostic Marketers" and "Index of Tests, Equipment, and Services."

Club Director. National Club Association, One Lafayette Center, 1120 20th St., N.W., Suite 725 Washington, DC 20036. Phone: (202)822-9822 Fax: (202)822-9808 • URL: http://

www.natlclub.org • Bimonthly. $18.00 per year. Magazine for directors, owners and managers of private clubs.

Club Industry: Buyers Guide. Primedia Business Magazines and Media, 9800 Metcalf Ave. Overland Park, KS 66212. Phone: 800-795-5445 or (913)341-1300 Fax: (913)967-1898 E-mail: subs@primediabusines.com • URL: http://www.primediabusiness.com • Annual. $25.00. A directory of over 1,000 companies furnishing equipment, supplies, and services to health and fitness clubs.

Club Management: The Resource for Successful Club Operations. Club Managers Association of America. Finan Publishing Co., 107 W. Pacific Ave. Saint Louis, MO 63119-2323. Phone: (314)961-6644 Fax: (314)961-4809 E-mail: teri@finan.com • URL: http://www.club-mgmt.com • Bimonthly. $21.95 per year.

Club Managers Association of America.

Club Manager's Guide to Private Parties and Club Functions. Joe Perdue and others. John Wiley and Sons, Inc., 111 River St. Hoboken, NJ 07030. Phone: 800-225-5945 or (201)748-6000 Fax: (201)748-6088 E-mail: info@wiley.com • URL: http://www.wiley.com • 1998. $65.00. Covers on-premises catering at clubs, including member relations, meal functions, beverage functions, room setup, staffing, etc.

CMAA Yearbook. Club Managers Association of America, 1733 King St. Alexandria, VA 22314. Phone: (703)739-9500 Fax: (703)739-0124 E-mail: cmaa@cmaa.org • URL: http://www.cmaa.org. • Annual. Membership directory.

CNA Trade Directory (Craft and Needlework Age). Krause Publications, Inc., 700 E. State St. Iola, WI 54990. Phone: 800-258-0929 or (715)445-2214 Fax: (715)445-4087 • URL: http://www.krause.com • Annual. $35.00. Lists of about 300 manufacturers and 50 publishers of books and periodicals in the craft and needlework industry.

Co-op Advertising Programs Sourcebook. National Register Publishing Co., 890 Mountain Ave., 3rd Fl. New Providence, NJ 07974. Phone: 800-473-7020 or (908)673-1001 Fax: (908)673-1189 E-mail: nrpsales@marquiswhoswho.com • URL: http://www.nationalregisterpub.com • Covers: More than 4,000 cooperative advertising programs offered by manufacturers. Entries include: Manufacturer name, address, phone; name, phone, fax of contact; products, trade names, regional variations, international availability, mechanical requirements, participation percentage, eligible media, ad specifications, reimbursement method, claim documentation, claim address.

Coal Data. National Mining Association, 1130 17th St., NW Washington, DC 20001-2133. Phone: (202)463-2625 Fax: (202)463-6125 E-mail: thowe@nma.org • URL: http://www.nma.org • Annual. Free to members; non-members, $75.00.

Coal Industry. Charles Kernot. American Educational Systems, 46 Purdy St. Harrison, NY 10528. Phone: 800-431-1579 or (914)835-0015 Fax: (914)835-0398 $710.00. Looseleaf service. Periodic supplementation.

Coal Information. Organization for Economic Cooperation and Development, OECD Washington Center, 2001 L St., N. W., Suite 650 Washington, DC 20036-4922. Phone: 800-456-6323 or (202)785-6323 Fax: (202)785-0350 E-mail: washington.contact@oecd.org • URL: http://www.oecd.org • Annual. $200.00. Presents comprehensive data from the International Energy Agency (IEA) on the world coal market, including supply, demand, production, trade, and prices. In addition to coal itself, provides country-specific data on coal-fired power stations and coal-related environmental issues.

Coal Leader: Coal's National Newspaper. Coal, Inc., P.O. Box 858 Richlands, VA 24641-0858. Phone: (276)964-6363 Fax: (276)964-6342 E-mail: coalleader@netscope.net • URL: http://www.coalleader.com • Monthly. $18.00 per year. Formerly *National Coal Leader*.

Coal Outlook. FT Energy, 1200 G St. NW, Ste. 1100 Washington, DC 20005-3830. Phone: 800-752-8878 or (202)383-2100 Fax: (202)383-2125 E-mail: orders.energy@ft.com • URL: http://www.platts.com • Description: Reports on government action affecting the coal industry. Analyzes court cases and legislation, plus market, transportation, and regulatory trends. Also provides information on production and productivity, utility coal specifications and delivered prices, overseas coal markets, union organizing activities and contract negotiations, and company news. Recurring features include statistics, coal price and consumption data, and the column titled Marketscoop. **Remarks:** Includes supplements containing price charts for steam, metallurgical, industrial, or anthracite coal. Also available via daily e-mail service.

Coal Research Center. Southern Illinois University at Carbondale

Coal Transportation Statistics. National Mining Association, 1130 17th St., NW Washington, DC 20036-4677. Phone: (202)463-2625 Fax: (202)463-6152 E-mail: thowe@nma.org • URL: http://www.nma.org • Annual, Non-profit organizations, $25.00; others, $35.00. Formerly *Coal Traffic Annual*.

Coalition of Higher Education Assistance Organizations, 1101 Vermont Ave., N.W., Suite 400 Washington, DC 20005. Phone: (202)289-3910 Fax: (202)371-0197 • URL: http://www.coheao.com • Purpose is to support student loan programs and monitor regulations.

Coalition of Labor Union Women.

The Coast Guard Reservist. Commandant, U.S. Coast Guard, 2100 2nd St., NW Washington, DC 20593. Phone: (202)267-1991 Fax: (202)267-4553 Monthly. Free.

Coast Guardsman's Manual. George E. Krietmeyer. Naval

Institute Press, Beach Hall, 291 Wood Rd. Annapolis, MD 21402-5034. Phone: 800-223-8764 or (410)268-6110 Fax: (410)269-7940 E-mail: customer@navalinstitute.org • URL: http://www.navalinstitute.org • 2000. $21.95. Ninth edition.

Coatings. National Paint and Coatings Association, 1500 Rhode Island Ave, N.W. Washington, DC 20005. Phone: (202)462-6272 Fax: (202)462-8549 E-mail: npca@paint.org • URL: http://www.paint.org • 10 times a year. $62.00 per year.

Coatings-Protective (Manufacturers) Directory. infoUSA Inc., 5711 S 86th Cir., PO Box 27347 Omaha, NE 68127. Phone: 800-321-0869 or (402)593-4500 Fax: (402)331-1505 E-mail: help@infousa.com • URL: http://www.abii.com • Number of listings: 3,246. Entries include: Name, address, phone (including area code), size of advertisement, year first in "Yellow Pages," name of owner or manager, number of employees. Compiled from telephone company "Yellow Pages," nationwide.

The Cocoa Merchants' Association of America, Inc.

Code of Federal Regulations. Office of the Federal Register, U.S. General Services Administration. Available from U.S. Government Printing Office, Washington, DC 20402. Phone: (202)512-1800 Fax: (202)512-2250 E-mail: gpoaccess@gpo.gov • URL: http://www.access.gpo.gov • $1,094.00 per year. Complete service.

Codes of Professional Responsibility: Ethic Standards in Business, Health and Law. Rena Gorlin, editor. BNA, Inc., 1231 25th St., NW Washington, DC 20037. Phone: 800-372-1033 E-mail: customercare@bna.com • URL: http://www.bna.com • 1999. $95.00. Fourth edition. Contains full text or substantial excerpts of the official codes of ethics of major professional groups in the fields of law, business, and health care.

Coffee and Cocoa International. DMG World Media Ltd., Queensway House, 2 Queensway Red Hill RH1 1QS, United Kingdom. Phone: 44 1737 855527 Fax: 44 1737 855470 • URL: http://www.dmgworldmedia.com • Seven times a year. $124.00 per year.

Coffee and Tea Market. MarketResearch.com, 641 Ave. of the Americas, 4th Fl. New York, NY 10011. Phone: 800-298-5699 or (212)807-2629 Fax: (212)807-2676 E-mail: customerservice@marketresearch.com • URL: http://www.marketresearch.com • 1999. $2,750.00. Market data with forecasts to 2004. Covers many types of coffee and tea.

Coffee and Tea Store. Entrepreneur Media, Inc., 2445 McCabe Way Irvine, CA 92614. Phone: 800-421-2300 or (949)261-2325 Fax: (949)261-0234 E-mail: entmag@entrepreneur.com • URL: http://www.entrepreneur.com • Looseleaf. $59.50. A practical guide to starting a coffee and tea store. Covers profit potential, start-up costs, market size evaluation, owner's time required, site selection, lease negotiation, pricing, accounting, advertising, promotion, etc. (Start-Up Business Guide No. E1202.)

Coffee Intelligence. Coffee Publications, P.O. Box 1315 Stamford, CT 06904. Phone: (203)969-2107 Fax: (203)327-5343 Monthly. $95.00 per year. Provides trade information for the coffee industry.

The Coffee Reporter. National Coffee Association of U.S.A Inc., 15 Maiden Lane, Suite 1405 New York, NY 10038-4003. Phone: (212)344-5596 Fax: (212)766-5815 E-mail: info@ncausa.org • URL: http://www.ncausa.org • Weekly. Free to members; non-members, $65.00 per year. Newsletter.

Coffee, Sugar and Cocoa Exchange., 1 N End Ave. New York, NY 10282-1101. Phone: (212)748-4000 E-mail: webmaster@nybot.com • URL: http://www.csce.com • Members are commodity traders.

Cognitive Science Society, Inc.

The Coin Dealer Newsletter. CDN Publications, PO Box 7939 Torrance, CA 90504. Phone: (310)515-7369 Fax: (310)515-7534 E-mail: orders@greysheet.com Description: Provides information on U.S. coinage, 1793 to present. Gives current prices and market commentary and analysis. Issues "The Monthly Supplement and Complete Series Pricing Guide" as an adjunct to the newsletter. Recurring features include columns titled The Market in Depth and This Week's Market.

Coin Laundry Association., 1315 Butterfield Rd., Ste. 212 Downers Grove, IL 60515. Phone: 877-CLA-IDEA or (630)963-5547 Fax: (630)963-5864 E-mail: info@coinlaundry.org • URL: http://www.coinlaundry.org • Manufacturers of equipment or supplies used in self-service (coin-operated) laundry or dry cleaning establishments; distributors of equipment services and supplies; owners and operators of self-service laundry and/or dry cleaning stores. Compiles statistics.

Coin Laundry Association Supplier Directory. Coin Laundry Association, 1315 Butterfield Rd., Ste. 212 Downers Grove, IL 60515. Phone: 877-CLA-IDEA or (630)963-5547 Fax: (630)963-5864 E-mail: info@coinlaundry.org • URL: http://www.coinlaundry.org • Covers: about 500 manufacturers and suppliers of products and services to the coin laundry and dry cleaning industries. Entries include: Name of firm, address, phone, e-mail, URL, products or services; distributors show area served.

Coin Prices: Complete Guide to U.S. Coin Values. Krause Publications, Inc., 700 E. State St. Iola, WI 54990-0001. Phone: 800-258-0929 or (715)445-2214 Fax: (715)445-4087 • URL: http://www.krause.com • Bimonthly. $18.98 per year. Gives current values of U. S. coins.

Coin Yearbook. British Royal Mint, Cheyenne, WY 82008-0031. Phone: 800-221-1215 Annual. $15.95

Coinage. Miller Magazines, Inc., 4880 Market St. Ventura, CA 93003-2888. Phone: (805)644-3824 Fax: (805)644-3875 E-mail: coinage@aol.com • URL: http://www.coinagemag.com • Monthly. $24.00 per year.

Coins. Krause Publications, Inc., 700 E State St. Iola, WI 54990-0001. Phone: 800-258-0929 or (715)445-2214 Fax: (715)445-4087 E-mail: info@krause.com • URL: http://www.krause.com • Monthly. $25.98 per year.

Cold Facts. Cryogenic Society of America, c/o Laurie Huget, Executive Director, 1033 S Blvd., Ste. 13 Oak Park, IL 60302-2881. Phone: (708)383-6220 Fax: (708)383-9337 E-mail: csa@huget.com • URL: http://www.cryogenicsociety.org • Description: Technical newsletter serving individuals interested in cryogenics and cryobiology.

Cold Formed Parts and Machine Institute., 25 N. Broadway Tarrytown, NY 10591. Phone: (914)332-0040 Fax: (914)332-1541 E-mail: cfpmi@cfpmi.org • URL: http://www.cfpmi.org • Formerly Tubular Rivet and Machine Institute.

Collaboratory for Research on Electronic Work., University of Michigan, 1075 Beal Ave. Ann Arbor, MI 48109-2112. Phone: (734)647-4948 Fax: (734)647-8044 E-mail: finholt@umich.edu • URL: http://www.crew.umich.edu/ • Concerned with the design and use of computer-based tools for thinking and planning in the professional office.

Collectibles Broker. Entrepreneur Media, Inc., 2445 McCabe Way Irvine, CA 92614. Phone: 800-421-2300 or (949)261-2325 Fax: (949)261-0234 E-mail: entmag@entrepreneur.com • URL: http://www.entrepreneur.com • Looseleaf. $59.50. A practical guide to starting a brokerage service for collectibles. Covers profit potential, start-up costs, market size evaluation, owner's time required, pricing, accounting, advertising, promotion, etc. (Start-Up Business Guide No. E1360.)

Collection Agency. Entrepreneur Media, Inc., 2445 McCabe Way Irvine, CA 92614. Phone: 800-421-2300 or (949)261-2325 Fax: (949)261-0234 E-mail: entmag@entrepreneur.com • URL: http://www.entrepreneur.com • Looseleaf. $59.50. A practical guide to starting a collection agency. Covers profit potential, start-up costs, market size evaluation, owner's time required, pricing, accounting, advertising, promotion, etc. (Start-Up Business Guide No. E1207.)

Collection Management: A Quarterly Journal Devoted to the Management of Library Collections. Haworth Press, Inc., 10 Alice St. Binghamton, NY 13904-1580. Phone: 800-429-6784 or (607)722-5857 Fax: 800-895-0582 or (607)722-1424 E-mail: getinfo@haworthpressinc.com • URL: http://www.haworthpressinc.com • Quarterly. $235.00 per year.

Collections and Credit Risk: The Authority for Commercial and Consumer Credit Professionals. Thomson Media, One State St. Plaza New York, NY 10004. Phone: 800-221-1809 or (212)803-8200 Fax: (212)843-9635 E-mail: custserv@thomsonmedia.com • URL: http://www.thomsonmedia.com • Monthly. $95.00 per year. Contains articles on the technology and business management of credit and collection functions. Includes coverage of bad debts, bankruptcy, and credit risk management.

Collective Bargaining Negotiations and Contracts. BNA, Inc., 1231 25th St., NW Washington, DC 20037. Phone: 800-372-1033 E-mail: customercare@bna.com • URL: http://www.bna.com • Biweekly. $1,187.00. Two looseleaf volumes.

Collector. American Collectors Association, Inc., 4040 W. 70th St. Minneapolis, MN 55435. Phone: (612)926-6547 Fax: (612)926-1624 E-mail: aca@collector.com • URL: http://www.collector.com • Monthly. Members, $30.00 per year; non-members, $60.00 per year. Provides news and education in the field of credit and collections.

Collector. Nicolas J. Barker. Collector Ltd., P.O. Box 12426 London W11 3GW, England. Phone: 44 207 7923492 Fax: 44 207 7923492 Quarterly. $68.00 per year.

College Admissions: A Selected Annotated Bibliography. Linda Sparks, compiler. Greenwood Publishing Group, Inc., 88 Post Rd., W Westport, CT 06881. Phone: 800-225-5800 or (203)226-3571 Fax: (203)431-2214 E-mail: customer-service@greenwood.com • URL: http://www.greenwood.com • 1993. $60.00. Describes about 1,000 professional or academic items relating to undergraduate college admissions in the United States. Topics include marketing and recruitment. (Popular guides are not included.) (Bibliographies and Indexes in Education Series, No.11).

College Admissions Data Handbook. Riverside Publishing/ Wintergreen Orchard House, 425 Springlake Dr. Itasca, IL 60143-2079. Phone: 800-323-9540 or (630)467-7000 Fax: (630)467-7192 E-mail: rpcwebmaster@hmco.com Covers: about 1,700 accredited four-year undergraduate and upper division institutions offering bachelor's degrees; published in a national edition and four regional editions (Northeast, Southeast, Midwest, and West). Entries include: Institution name, phone, location, names of president and admissions officer, accreditation, number of students, admission policies, Scholastic Aptitude Test and American College Test (SAT-ACT) board score distribution, costs, financial aid availability, advance placement policy, subject majors offered, degrees offered, extracurricular activities, academic calendar, religious requirements, and policies on housing, cars, alcohol, attendance, and marriage. Index volume titled 'College Admissions Index of Majors & Sports' (see separate entry).

College and Research Libraries (CRL). Association of College and Research Libraries. American Library Association, 50 E. Huron St. Chicago, IL 60611-2795. Phone: 800-545-2433 or (312)944-6780 Fax: (312)440-9374 E-mail: acrl@ala.org • URL: http://www.ala.org • Bimonthly. $60.00 per year. Supplement available *C and R L News*.

College and Research Libraries News. Association of College and Research Libraries. American Library Association, 50 E. Huron St. Chicago, IL 60611-2795. Phone: 800-545-2433 or (312)944-6780 Fax: (312)440-9374 E-mail: acrl@ala.org • URL: http://www.ala.org • 11 times per year. Free to members; non-members, $40.00 per year. Supplement to *College and Research Libraries*.

College and Undergraduate Libraries. Haworth Press, Inc., 10 Alice St. Binghamton, NY 13904-1580. Phone: 800-429-6784 or (607)722-5857 Fax: 800-895-0582 or (607)722-1424 E-mail: getinfo@haworthpressinc.com • URL: http://www.haworthpressinc.com • Semiannual. $105.00 per year. A practical journal dealing with everyday library problems.

College and University. American Association of Collegiate Registrars and Admissions Officers, One Dupont Circle, N.W., Suite 520 Washington, DC 20036-1135. Phone: (202)293-9161 Fax: (202)872-8857 E-mail: pubs@aacrao.nche.org • URL: http://www.aacrao.com • Quarterly. Free to members; non-members, $50.00 per year. Addresses issues in higher education; looks at new procedures, policies, technology; reviews new publications.

College Blue Book. Macmillan Reference USA, 12 Lunar Dr. Woodbridge, CT 06525. Phone: 800-877-4253 or (212)654-8493 Fax: 800-414-5043 or 800-414-5043 E-mail: gale.galeord@cengage.com • URL: http://gale.cengage.com • Covers: Listings and detailed descriptions of thousands of two and four year schools, their programs, degrees, financial aid sources, and scholarships.

College Blue Book CD-ROM. Available from Gale Cengage Learning, 27500 Drake Rd. Farmington Hills, MI 48331-3535. Phone: 800-877-GALE or (248)699-GALE Fax: 800-414-5043 or (248)699-8069 E-mail: galeord@galegroup.com • URL: http://www.galegroup.com • Annual. $250.00. Produced by Macmillan Reference USA. Serves as electronic version of printed *College Blue Book*. Provides detailed information on programs, degrees, and financial aid sources in the U.S. and Canada

The College Board., 45 Columbus Ave., 45 Columbus Ave. New York, NY 10023-6992. Phone: (866)392-3017 or (212)713-8000 Fax: (212)649-8442 E-mail: publicaffairs@collegeboard.org • URL: http://www.collegeboard.com • Represents the schools, colleges, universities, and other educational organizations that seeks to connect members to success and opportunity. Serves students, parents, high schools, and colleges through major programs and services in college admission, guidance, assessment, financial aid, enrollment, and teaching and learning.

College Board Review. College Board Publications, 45 Columbus Ave. New York, NY 10023. Phone: 800-323-7155 or (212)713-8000 • URL: http://www.collegeboard.com • Quarterly. $25.00 per year.

College Facts Chart. National Beta Club, 151 Beta Club Way Spartanburg, SC 29306-3012. Phone: 800-845-8281 or (864)583-4553 Fax: (864)542-9300 E-mail: betaclub@betaclub.org • URL: http://www.betaclub.org • Annual. $7.00. Reference guide to 3,500 institutions of higher education in the United States, Puerto Rico, Guam, and the Virgin Islands. Charts locate tuition and fee costs, telephone numbers and school size.

The College Handbook. The College Board, 45 Columbus Ave. New York, NY 10023-6992. Phone: (212)713-8000 • URL: http://www.collegeboard.org • 2003. $27.95. Includes CD-Rom. Over 3,200 undergraduate schools. (College Handbook Series).

College Media Advisers, Inc. University of Memphis, c/o Dept. of Journalism, MJ-300 Memphis, TN 38152-6661. Phone: (901)678-2403 Fax: (901)678-4798 E-mail: vsplbrgr@cc.memphis.edu • URL: http://www.collegemedia.org • Formerly National Council of College Publications Advisers.

College Media Review. College Media Advisors. University of Memphis, c/o Dept. of Journalism Memphis, TN 38152. Phone: (901)678-2403 Fax: (901)678-4798 E-mail: rsplbrgr@cc.memphis.edu • URL: http://www.collegemedia.org • Quarterly. Free to members; non-members, $15.00 per year.

College of Tropical Agriculture and Human Resources., University of Hawaii at Manoa, 2515 Campus Rd., Miller Hall 110 Honolulu, HI 96822. Phone: (808)956-8105 Fax: (808)956-8105 E-mail: fcs@ctahr.hawaii.edu • URL: http://www.ctahr.hawaii.edu/ • Concerned with the production and marketing of tropical food and ornamental plant products, including pineapples, bananas, coffee, and macadamia nuts.

College Press Service.

The College Store. National Association of College Stores, 500 E. Lorain St. Oberlin, OH 44074-1298. Phone: (440)775-7777 Fax: (440)775-4769 E-mail: thecollege@nacs.org • URL: http://www.nacs.org • Six times a year. Members, $54.00 per year; non-members, $64.00 per year. Formerly *College Store Journal*

College Store Executive. Executive Business Media, Inc., 825 Old Country Rd. Westbury, NY 11590. Phone: (516)334-3030 Fax: (516)334-8958 • URL: http://www.cconline.com • 10 times a year. $40.00 per year.

College Teaching: International Quarterly Journal. Helen Dwight Reid Educational Foundation. Heldref Publications, 1319 18th St., N.W. Washington, DC 20036-1802. Phone: 800-365-9753 Fax: (202)293-6130 E-mail: subscribe@

heldref.org • URL: http://www.heldref.org • Quarterly. Individuals, $47.00 per year; institutions, $93.00 per year. Practical ideas, successful methods, and new programs for faculty development.

Collier Bankruptcy Practice Guide. LexisNexis Matthew Bender, 1275 Broadway Albany, NY 12204. Phone: 800-424-4200 or (518)487-3000 Fax: (518)487-3584 $1,393.00. Six looseleaf volumes. Periodic supplementation. Strategic and procedural guide for all cases instituted under the code.

Collier on Bankruptcy. LexisNexis Matthew Bender, 1275 Broadway Albany, NY 12204. Phone: 800-833-9844 or (518)487-3000 Fax: (518)487-3584 E-mail: bookstore.support@lexisnexis. com • URL: http://www.bender.com • $2,880.00. 23 looseleaf volumes. Periodic supplementation. Detailed discussion, by the leading bankruptcy authorities, of the Bankruptcy Code as amended.

Colombian American Association., 30 Vesey St., Ste. 506 New York, NY 10007. Phone: (212)233-7776 Fax: (212)233-7779 E-mail: andean@nyct.net • URL: http://www.colombianamerican.org • Facilitates commerce and trade between the Republic of Colombia and the U.S. Fosters and advances cultural relations and goodwill between the two nations. Encourages sound investments in Colombia by Americans and in the U.S. by Colombians. Disseminates information in the U.S. concerning Colombia.

Color: A Multidisciplinary Approach. Heinrich Zollinger. John Wiley and Sons, Inc., 111 River St. Hoboken, NJ 07030. Phone: 800-225-5945 or (201)748-6000 Fax: (201)748-6088 E-mail: bookinfo@wiley.com • URL: http://www.wiley.com • 1999. $125.00. Written for a wide audience, including "interested laymen." Among the chapter headings are "Physics of Light and Color," "Chemistry of Color," "How Do We See Colors?" and "How Do We Name Colors?"

Color Association of the United States., 315 W 39th St., Studio 507 New York, NY 10018. Phone: (212)947-7774 Fax: (212)594-6987 E-mail: caus@colorassociation.com • URL: http://www.colorassociation.com • Formerly The Textile Color Card Association of America.

Color Chemistry. Heinrich Zollinger. John Wiley and Sons, Inc., 111 River St. Hoboken, NJ 07030. Phone: 800-225-5945 or (201)748-6000 Fax: (201)748-6088 E-mail: info@wiley.com • URL: http://www.wiley.com • 2003. $150.00. Third edition. Includes technical information for industrial chemists and others on dyes and pigments.

Color in the Office: Design Trends from 1950 to 1990 and Beyond. Sara O. Marberry. John Wiley and Sons, Inc., 111 River St. Hoboken, NJ 07030. Phone: 800-225-5945 or (201)748-6000 Fax: (201)748-6088 E-mail: info@wiley.com • URL: http://www.wiley.com • 1993. $90.00. Presents past, present, and future color trends in corporate office design. Features color photographs of traditional, postmodern, and neoclassical office designs. (Architecture Series).

Color Marketing Group., 5845 Richmond Hwy., No. 410 Alexandria, VA 22303. Phone: (703)329-8500 Fax: (703)329-0155 E-mail: cmg@colormarketing.org • URL: http://www.colormarketing.org • International group of professionals who forecast colors for consumer and contract markets. Examines color as it applies to the profitable marketing of products and services. Provides a forum for the exchange of ideas for all phases of color marketing, including styling, design, trends, merchandising, sales, education, and research.

Color Pigments Manufacturers Association., 300 N Washington St., Ste. 102 Alexandria, VA 22314. Phone: (703)684-4044 Fax: (703)684-1795 E-mail: cpma@cpma.com • URL: http://www.pigments.org • Manufacturers of inorganic and organic color pigments. Disseminates technical, regulatory, and legislative information on laboratory testing, toxicity, and subjects of general interest to manufacturers of pigments.

Color Publishing. PennWell Corp., Advanced Technology Div., 98 Spit Brook Rd. Nashua, NH 03062-5737. Phone: 800-331-4463 or (603)891-0123 E-mail: atd@pennwell.com • URL: http://www.pennwell.com • Bimonthly. $29.70 per year.

Color Research and Application. John Wiley and Sons, Inc., 111 River St. Hoboken, NJ 07030. Phone: 800-225-5945 or (201)748-6000 Fax: (201)748-6088 E-mail: customer@wiley.com • URL: http://www.wiley.com • Bimonthly. Institutions, $840 per year; with online edition, $882.00 per year. International coverage.

Color Science: Concepts and Methods, Quantitative Data and Formulae. Gunter Wyszecki and W. S. Stiles. John Wiley and Sons, Inc., 111 River St. Hoboken, NJ 07030. Phone: 800-225-5945 or (201)748-6000 Fax: (201)748-6088 E-mail: info@wiley.com • URL: http://www.wiley.com • 1982. $66.50. Second edition. (Pure and Applied Optics Series).

Colorado School of Mines.

Colorado School of Mines Quarterly Review. Colorado School of Mines Press, 1500 Illinois St. Golden, CO 80401-1887. Phone: (303)273-3595 Fax: (303)273-3199 E-mail: lpang@mines.edu Quarterly. $65.00 per year.

Coltrade: Colombian Government Trade Bureau., 1901 L St. NW, Ste. 700 Washington, DC 20036. Phone: (202)887-9000 Fax: (202)223-0526 E-mail: coltrade@coltrade.org • URL: http://www.coltrade.org • Promotes Colombian exports to the U. S.

Columbia Gazetteer of North America. Saul B. Cohen, editor. Columbia University Press, 61 W. 62nd St. New York, NY 10023. Phone: 800-944-8648 or (212)459-0600 Fax: 800-944-1844 or (212)459-3678 • URL: http://www.columbia.edu/cu/cup • 2000. $250.00. Contains information on 50,000 places within the U. S., Canada, Mexico, and the Caribbean. Includes 24 pages of color maps. Provides brief descriptions of natural resources and industrial activities.

Columbia Gazetteer of the World. Saul B. Cohen, editor. Columbia University Press, 61 W. 62nd St. New York, NY 10023. Phone: 800-944-8648 or (212)459-0600 Fax: 800-944-1844 or (212)459-3678 • URL: http://www.columbiabooks.edu/cu/cup • 1998. $750.00. Three volumes. Also available online (http://www.columbiagazetteer.org) and on CD-ROM.

Columbia Guide to Digital Publishing: In Print and On the Web. William E. Kasdorf, editor. Columbia University Press, 61 W 62nd St. New York, NY 10023. Phone: 800-944-8648 or (212)459-0600 Fax: 800-944-1844 or (212)459-3678 • URL: http://www.columbia.edu/cu/cup • 2002. $65.00. Covers the practical production of both written and graphic material in digital format, including archives, new technology, "information architecture," and copyright.

Columbia Guide to Online Style. Janice R. Walker and Todd W. Taylor. Columbia University Press, 61 West 62nd St. New York, NY 10023. Phone: 800-944-8648 or (212)459-0600 Fax: 800-944-1844 or (212)459-3678 • URL: http://www.columbia.edu/cu/cup • 1998. $40.50. Includes rules for bibliographic citation of online sources, formatting guidelines for online documents, and information on the electronic preparation of texts for print publication.

Columbia Institute for Tele-Information., Columbia University, Columbia Business School, 3022 Broadway, Uris Hall, Suite 1A New York, NY 10027. Phone: (212)854-4222 Fax: (212)932-1471 E-mail: webmaster@vii.org • URL: http://www.vii.org • Areas of research include private and public networking, the economics of networks, pricing of network access, and economics of technology adoption in the public network.

Columbia Journalism Review. Columbia University, Graduate School of Journalism, 2950 Broadway, Journalism Bldg. New York, NY 10027. Phone: 888-425-7782 or (212)854-1881 Fax: (212)854-8580 E-mail: subscriptions@cjr.org • URL: http://www.cjr.org • Bimonthly. $19.95 per year. Critical review of news media.

Columbia Scholastic Press Association. Columbia University, Columbia University, Mail Code 5711 New York, NY 10027-6902. Phone: (212)854-9400 Fax: (212)854-9401 E-mail: cspa@columbia.edu • URL: http://www.columbia.edu/cu/cspa • Newspapers, magazines, and yearbooks issued by schools from junior high school level through college and university, with the majority being from secondary schools. Works to promote student writing through the medium of the school publication. Improves publications in all phases. Offers critiques for each regular member. Compiles statistics. Provides consultation and referral services to student publications.

Combined Statement of Receipts, Outlays, and Balances of the United States Government. Available from U. S. Government Printing Office, Washington, DC 20402. Phone: (202)512-1800 Fax: (202)512-2250 E-mail: gpoaccess@gpo.gov • URL: http://www.access.gpo.gov • Annual. $54.00. Issued by the Financial Mangement Service, U. S. Treasury Department (http://www.fms.treas.gov). In three parts: "Fiscal Year Summary," "Details of Receipts," and "Details of Appropriations, Outlays, and Balances."

Commanderie des Cordons Bleus de France., 244 Madison Ave., No.134 New York, NY 10016-2817. Phone: (212)246-9397 E-mail: richard.wallace@scbar.org Chefs, cooks, and other culinary professionals. Encourages appreciation of good food and the establishment of high standards among culinary professionals. Promotes accuracy in the naming of dishes.

Commerce Business Daily. Industry and Trade Administration, U.S. Department of Commerce. U.S. Department of Commerce, Washington, DC 20230. Phone: (202)783-3238 Fax: (202)512-2250 E-mail: orders@greysheet.com Description: Lists notices of proposed government procurement actions, contract awards, sales of government property, and other procurement information. Includes 500-1,000 notices in each edition; notices appear in the publication only once.

Commercial and Financial Chronicle. William B. Dana Co., P.O. Box 1839 Daytona Beach, FL 32115-1839. Phone: (386)252-0230 Weekly. $140.00. per year.

Commercial Atlas and Marketing Guide. Rand McNally, 8255 N. Central Park Ave. Skokie, IL 60076-2970. Phone: (847)329-8100 Fax: (847)673-0813 • URL: http://www.randmcnally.com • Annual. $395.00. Includes maps and marketing data: population, transportation, communication, and local area business statistics. Provides information on more than 128,000 U.S. locations. (Commercial Atlas and Marketing Guide series).

Commercial Bank Management: Producing and Selling Financial Services. Peter S. Rose. McGraw-Hill, 1221 Ave. of the Americas New York, NY 10020. Phone: 800-722-4726 or (212)512-2000 Fax: (212)512-4502 E-mail: customer.service@mcgraw-hill.com • URL: http://www.mcgraw-hill.com • 2001. $110.94. Fifth edition. (Finance Series).

Commercial Building: Tranforming Plans into Buildings. Stamats Communications, 615 Fifth St., S.E. Cedar Rapids, IA 52406. Phone: 800-553-8878 or (319)364-6167 Fax: (319)365-5421 E-mail: info@stamats.com • URL: http://www.stamats.com • Bimonthly. $48.00 per year. Edited for building contractors, engineers, and architects. Includes special features on new products, climate control, plumbing, and vertical transportation.

Commercial Carrier Journal. Randall Publishing Co., 3200 Rice Mine Rd., NE Tuscaloosa, AL 35406. Phone: (205)349-2990 Fax: (205)248-1021 • URL: http://www.randallpub.com • Monthly. $45.00 per year.

Commercial Chicken Meat and Egg Production. Donald D. Bell and others. Kluwer Academic Publishers, 101 Philip Dr., Assinippi Park Norwell, MA 02061. Phone: (781)871-6600 Fax: (781)681-9045 E-mail: kluwer@wkap.com • URL: http://www.wkap.nl • 2001.$399.95. 5th edition.

Commercial Development and Marketing Association., 1900 Arch St. Philadelphia, PA 19103. Phone: (215)564-3484 Fax: (215)963-9784 E-mail: info@cdmaonline.org • URL: http://www.cdmaonline.com • Formerly Commercial Chemical Development Association.

Commercial Diode Lasers. Available from MarketResearch.com, 641 Ave. of the Americas, Fourth Floor New York, NY 10011. Phone: 800-298-5699 or (212)807-2629 Fax: (212)807-2642 E-mail: order@marketresearch.com • URL: http://www.marketresearch.com • 2001. Price on application. Published by Global Industry Analysts. Provides market research data relating to commercial diode lasers, including market projections to 2005.

Commercial Finance Association., 370 7th Ave., Ste. 1801 New York, NY 10001-3979. Phone: (212)792-9390 Fax: (212)564-6053 E-mail: info@cfa.com • URL: http://www.cfa.com • Organizations engaged in asset-based financial services including commercial financing and factoring and lending money on a secured basis to small- and medium-sized business firms. Acts as a forum for information and consideration about ideas, opportunities, and legislation concerning asset-based financial services. Seeks to improve the industry's legal and operational procedures. Offers job placement and reference services for members. Sponsors School for Field Examiners and other educational programs. Compiles statistics; conducts seminars and surveys; maintains speakers' bureau and 21 committees.

Commercial Fisheries News. Compass Publications, Fisheries Division, PO Box 37 Stonington, ME 04681. Phone: (207)367-2396 Fax: (207)367-2490 E-mail: comfish@ctel.net • URL: http://www.fish-news.com • Monthly. $21.95 per year. Covers the commercial fishing industry in New England. Includes news of marine technology, boatbuilding, fish and lobster prices, business trends, government regulation, and other topics.

Commercial Food Equipment Service Association., 2216 W Meadowview Rd., Ste. 100 Greensboro, NC 27407. Phone: 877-414-4127 or (336)346-4700 Fax: (336)346-4745 E-mail: cstrickland@cfesa.com • URL: http://www.cfesa.com • Represents firms that repair food preparation equipment used by restaurants, hotels, and institutions. Provides training and education for members and their employees.

Commercial Law Journal. Legalease Ltd, 28-33 Cato St. London W1H 5HS, United Kingdom. Phone: 44 20 7396 9292 Fax: 44 20 7396 9300 E-mail: legalease@.co.uk • URL: http://www.clla.org • 10 times a year. $99.00 per year.

Commercial Law League of America.

Commercial Leasing Law and Strategy. American Lawyer Media, Inc., 105 Madison Ave. New York, NY 10016. Phone: 800-888-8300 or (212)779-9200 Fax: (212)481-8110 E-mail: lawcatalog@amlaw.com • URL: http://www.lawcatalog.com/ • Monthly. $215.00 per year. Newsletter. Covers commercial real estate leasing developments relating to large retailers, tenant inducements, tax consequences, unbilled rent obligations, and other matters. (A Law Journal Newsletter, formerly published by Leader Publications).

Commercial Lending. George E. Ruth. American Bankers Association, 1120 Connecticut Ave., N. W. Washington, DC 20036-3971. Phone: 800-226-5377 or (202)663-5000 Fax: (202)663-7543 E-mail: custserv@aba.com • URL: http://www.aba.com • 1990. $57.00. Second edition. Discusses the practical aspects of commercial lending.

Commercial Lending Litigation News. LRP Publications, 747 Dresher Rd., Ste. 500, PO Box 980 Horsham, PA 19044-0980. Phone: 800-341-7874 or (215)784-0860 Fax: (215)784-9639 E-mail: custserve@lrp.com • URL: http://www.lrp.com • Description: Covers liability claims and their policies and procedures, case strategies, court decisions, and jury verdicts.

Commercial Lending Review. American Bankers Association. Aspen Publishers, Inc., 1185 Ave. of the Americas New York, NY 10036. Phone: 800-234-1660 or (212)597-0200 Fax: (212)597-0338 E-mail: customer.service@aspenpubl.com • URL: http://www.aspenpublishers.com • Quarterly. $315.00 per year. Edited for senior-level lending officers. Includes specialized lending techniques, management issues, legal developments, and reviews of specific industries.

Commercial Nondiode Lasers. Available from MarketResearch.com, 641 Ave. of the Americas, Fourth Floor New York, NY 10011. Phone: 800-298-5699 or (212)807-2629 Fax: (212)807-2642 E-mail: order@marketresearch.com • URL: http://www.marketresearch.com • 2001. Price on application. Published by Global Industry Analysts. Provides market research data relating to commercial nondiode lasers.

Commercial Refrigerator Manufacturers Division., 4100 N Fairfax Dr., Ste. 200 Arlington, VA 22203. Phone: (703)524-8800 Fax: (703)524-9011 E-mail: crm@ari.org • URL: http://ariadman.tempdomainname.com/crm • Manufacturers of refrigerated display cases and cabinets, food service refrigerators, and sectional cooling rooms. Seeks to provide a voice for manufacturers and suppliers to address industry developments and problems with companies who share common interests. Maintains a continuing presence within Congress and government agencies to monitor and respond to policies and regulations affecting the industry and represent the collective interests of members. Acts as a clearinghouse on information including foreign sales opportunities, technological developments, domestic markets, and other data of importance to the refrigeration industry. Provides technical information concerning regulations to governmental agencies. Conducts research to eliminate waste and increase efficiency of the production, distribution, and marketing of merchandise, products, or equipment related to the industry. Develops health and sanitation standard for retail food store refrigerators. Compiles statistics.

Commercial Review. Oregon Feed and Grain Association. Commercial Review, Inc., 2380 N.W. Roosevelt St. Portland, OR 97210. Phone: (503)226-2758 Fax: (503)244-0947 E-mail: info@oregonfeed.org • URL: http://oregonfeed.org • Weekly. $35.00 per year.

Commission European Union Bulletin. Commision of the European Communities. Bernan Associates, 4611-F Assembly Dr. Lanham, MD 20706-4391. Phone: 800-274-4447 or (301)459-2255 Fax: 800-865-3450 or (301)459-0056 E-mail: order@bernan.com • URL: http://www.bernan.com • 11 times a year. $210.00 per year. Published by the Office of Official Publications of the European Communities. Covers all main events within the Union. Supplement available. Text in Danish, Dutch, English, French, German, Greek, Italian, Spanish, Portuguese. Formerly *Bulletin of the European Communities*.

Commissioner of Patents Annual Report. U.S. Patent Office. Available from U.S. Government Printing Office, Washington, DC 20402. Phone: (202)512-1800 Fax: (202)512-2250 Annual.

Committee for a Progressive Congress., USA,. E-mail: richard. wallace@scbar.org Raises funds for Democratic Party candidates for the U.S. House of Representatives. **Convention/Meeting:** none. **Publications:** none.

Committee for a Responsible Federal Budget., 220 1/2 E St., NE Washington, DC 20002. Phone: (202)547-4484 Fax: (202)547-4476 E-mail: crfb@aol.com • URL: http://www. crfb.org • Members are corporations and others seeking to improve the federal budget process.

Committee for Economic Development., 2000 L St., N.W., Suite 700 Washington, DC 20036. Phone: (202)296-5860 Fax: (202)223-0776 E-mail: info@ced.org • URL: http://www. ced.org • Committee conducts research and formulates policy recommendations on national and international economic issues, including education and trade policy.

Committee on Human Development. University of Chicago

Commline. Numeridex, Inc., 241 Holbrook Dr. Wheeling, IL 60090, Phone: (312)541-8840 Bimonthly. Free to qualified personnel; others, $20.00 per year. Emphasizes NC/CNC (numerically controlled and computer numerically controlled machinery).

Commodities Regulation: Fraud, Manipulation, and Other Claims. Jerry W. Markham. West Group, 610 Opperman Dr. Eagan, MN 55123. Phone: 800-328-4880 or (651)687-7000 Fax: 800-340-9378 E-mail: bookstore@westgroup.com • URL: http://www.westgroup.com • Semiannual. $567.00 per year. Two looseleaf volumes. $250.00. Covers the commodity futures trading prohibitions of the Commodity Exchange Act. (Securities Law Series).

Commodity Futures Law Reports. CCH, Inc., 2700 Lake Cook Rd. Riverwoods, IL 60015. Phone: 800-835-5224 or (847)267-7000 E-mail: cust_serv@cch.com • URL: http:// www.cch.com • Semimonthly. $948.00 per year. Looseleaf service. Periodic supplementation. Includes legal aspects of financial futures and stock options trading.

Commodity Market Review. Available from Bernan Associates, 4611-F Assembly Dr. Lanham, MD 20706-4391. Phone: 800-274-4888 or (301)459-7666 Fax: 800-865-3450 or (301)459-0056 E-mail: query@bernan.com • URL: http://www.bernan. com • Annual. $18.00 Published by the Food and Agriculture Organization of the United Nations (FAO). Reviews the global outlook for over 20 specific commodities.

Commodity Markets Council., 1300 L St. NW, Ste. 1020 Washington, DC 20005. Phone: (202)842-0400 Fax: (202)789-7223 E-mail: ccochran@cmcmarkets.org • URL: http://cmcmarkets.org • Represents and supports grain exchanges, boards of trade, grain companies, milling and processing companies, transportation companies, futures commission merchants, and banks.

Commodity Trading Guide. Commodity Research Bureau, 330 South Wells St., Suite 1112 Chicago, IL 60606. Phone: 800-621-5271 or (312)554-8456 Fax: (312)939-4135 E-mail: info@crbtrader.com • URL: http://www.crbtrader.com • Annual. $22.50. Serves as a concise "Almanac, Encyclopedia, Yearbook, and Calendar for the Futures Market." Includes many price charts, tables, government report dates, contract specifications, and price outlooks.

Commodity Trading Manual. Frank S. Rose, editor. AMACOM, 1601 Broadway New York, NY 10019-7420. Phone: (212)586-8100 Fax: (212)903-8168 E-mail: cust_serv@ amanet.org • URL: http://www.amacombooks.org • 1999. $55.00. Textbook and reference manual.

Common Cause., 1133 19th St. NW, 9th Fl. Washington, DC 20036. Phone: 800-926-1064 or (202)833-1200 Fax: (202)659-3716 E-mail: grassroots@commoncause.org • URL: http://www.commoncause.org • Nonpartisan citizens' lobby. Dedicated to fighting for open, honest, and accountable government at the national, state, and local levels. Gathers and disseminates information on the effects of money in politics; lobbies for political finance and other campaign reforms.

Common Market Reports. CCH, Inc., 2700 Lake Cook Rd. Riverwoods, IL 60015. Phone: 800-835-5224 or (847)267-7000 E-mail: cust_serv@cch.com • URL: http://www.cch.com • Biweekly. $1,070.00 per year, including weekly *Euromarket News*. Looseleaf service. Four volumes. Periodic supplementation.

Common Sense on Mutual Funds: New Imperatives for the Intelligent Investor. John C. Bogle. John Wiley and Sons, Inc., 111 River St. Hoboken, NJ 07030. Phone: 800-225-5945 or (201)748-6000 Fax: (201)748-6088 E-mail: info@wiley. com • URL: http://www.wiley.com • 1999. $29.95. Provides practical, conservative advice for the average investor. Topics include asset allocation, index funds, global investing, fund selection, and taxes.

Common Stock Newspaper Abbreviations and Trading Symbols. Howard R. Jarrell. Scarecrow Press, Inc., 4501 Forbes Blvd., Ste. 200 Lanham, MD 20706. Phone: 800-462-6420 or (301)459-3366 Fax: 800-338-4550 or (301)429-5748 E-mail: custserv@rowman.com • URL: http://www.scarecrowpress. com • 1989. $60.00. Gives the meanings of financial page company name abbreviations and stock symbols.

Common Stock Newspaper Abbreviations and Trading Symbols: Supplement One. Howard R. Jarrell. Scarecrow Press, Inc., 4501 Forbes Blvd., Ste. 200 Lanham, MD 20706. Phone: 800-462-6420 or (301)459-3366 Fax: 800-338-4550 or (301)429-5748 E-mail: custserv@rowman.com • URL: http://www.scarecrowpress.com • 1991. $40.00. Provides changes and new listings occurring since the publication of Jarrell's original volume in 1989.

A Commonsense Guide to Your 401(k). Mary Rowland. Bloomberg, 499 Park Ave. New York, NY 10022. Phone: 800-388-2749 or (212)318-2000 Fax: (917)369-5000 • URL: http://www.bloomberg.com • 1997. $19.95. Explains how to use a 401(k) plan as a foundation for financial planning. (Bloomberg Personal Bookshelf Series.)

Communicating with Legal Databases: Terms and Abbreviations for the Legal Researcher. Anne L. McDonald. Neal-Schuman Publishers, Inc., 100 William St., Ste. 2004 New York, NY 10038. Phone: (866)672-2667 or (212)925-8650 Fax: (866)209-7932 or (212)219-8916 E-mail: info@neal-schuman.com • URL: http://www.neal-schuman.com • 1987. $82.50.

Communication Abstracts: An International Information Service. Sage Publications, Inc., 2455 Teller Rd. Thousand Oaks, CA 91320. Phone: 800-818-7243 or (805)499-9774 Fax: 800-583-2665 or (805)499-0871 E-mail: webmaster@ sagepub.com • URL: http://www.sagepub.com • Bimonthly. Institutions, $1,150.00 per year. Provides broad coverage of the literature of communications, including broadcasting and advertising.

Communication Booknotes Quarterly : Recent Titles in Telecommunications, Informaation, and Media. Lawrence Erlbaum Associates, Inc., 10 Industrial Ave. Mahwah, NJ 07430-2262. Phone: 800-926-6579 or (201)258-2200 Fax: (201)236-0072 E-mail: journals@erlbaum.com • URL: http://www.erlbaum. com • Bimonthly. Institutions, $395.00 per year; with online edition, $325.00 per year. Contains descriptive reviews of new publications.

Communication Briefings: A Monthly Idea Source for Decision Makers. Briefings Publishing Group, 1101 King St., Suite 110 Alexandria, VA 22314. Phone: 800-888-2084 or (703)548-3800 Fax: (703)648-2136 E-mail: customerservice@briefings.com • URL: http://www. briefings.com • Monthly. $139.00 per year. Newsletter. Presents useful ideas for communication, public relations, customer service, human resources, and employee training.

Communication Equipment, and Other Electronic Systems and Equipment. U. S. Bureau of the Census, 4700 Silver Hill Rd. Washington, DC 20233-0800. Phone: (301)763-4636 E-mail: comments@census.gov • URL: http://www.census.gov • Annual. Provides data on shipments: value, quantity, imports, and exports. (Current Industrial Reports, MA-36P.)

Communication Research. Sage Publications, Inc., 2455 Teller Rd. Thousand Oaks, CA 91320. Phone: 800-818-7243 or (805)499-9774 Fax: 800-583-2665 or (805)499-0871 E-mail: webmaster@sagepub.com • URL: http://www.sagepub.com • Bimonthly. Institutions, $599.00 per year.

Communication Technology Update. Elsevier, 655 Ave. of the Americas New York, NY 10010-5107. Phone: (212)989-5800 Fax: 800-535-9935 or (212)633-3680 • URL: http://www. elsevier.com • 2000. $36.95. 7th edition. A yearly review of developments in electronic media, telecommunications, and the Internet.

Communication World: The Magazine for Communication Professionals. International Association of Business Communicators, One Hallidie Plaza, Suite 600 San Francisco, CA 94102-2818. Phone: (415)544-4700 Fax: (415)544-4747 E-mail: ggordon@iabc.com • URL: http://www.iabc.com • Seven times a year. Free to members; libraries, $95.00 per year. Emphasis is on public relations, media relations,

corporate communication, and writing.

Communication Yearbook. International Communication Association, 8140 Burnet Rd. Austin, TX 78766. Phone: (512)454-8299 Fax: (512)451-6270 E-mail: icahdq@icahdq. org • URL: http://www.icahdq.org • Annual, Membership.

Communications. Master Brewer's Association of America, 3340 Pilot Knob Rd. Saint Paul, MN 55121-2097. Phone: (651)454-7250 Fax: (651)454-0766 E-mail: mbaa@mbaa. com • URL: http://www.mbaa.com • Bimonthly. Membership.

Communications and Information Processing Group., Rensselaer Polytechnic Institute, 7010 JEC, 110 Eighth St. Troy, NY 12180-3590. Phone: (518)276-6823 Fax: (518)276-6261 E-mail: modestin@ipl.rpi.edu • URL: http://www.ecse.rpi. edu • Includes Optical Signal Processing Laboratory and Speech Processing Laboratory.

Communications and Signal Processing Laboratory. University of Michigan

Communications Daily: The Authoritative News Service of Electronic Communications. Warren Publishing, Inc., 2115 Ward Ct., NW Washington, DC 20037. Phone: (202)872-9200 Fax: (202)293-3435 • URL: http://www.warrenpub. com • Daily. $3,006.00 per year. Newsletter. Covers telecommunications, including the telephone industry, broadcasting, cable TV, satellites, data communications, and electronic publishing. Features corporate and industry news.

Communications Media Management Association., 20423 State Rd. 7, Ste. F6-491 Boca Raton, FL 33498. Phone: (561)477-8100 Fax: (973)543-0166 E-mail: cmma@cmma.org • URL: http://www.cmma.net • Professional association of managers of communications media departments of business, education, or government. Aims to provide networking and educational opportunities for communications media managers that build peer professional relationships, facilitate leadership development, deepen managerial skills, expand technical knowledge, and develop skills in business strategy.

Communications News. Nelson Publishing Co., 2500 Tamiami Trl. N Nokomis, FL 34275. Phone: (941)966-9521 Fax: (941)966-2590 • URL: http://www.comnews.com • Monthly. Free to qualified personnel; others, $84.00 per year.

Communications News: Solutions for Today's Networking Decision Managers. Nelson Publishing, Inc., 2500 Tamiami Trail N Nokomis, FL 34275. Phone: (941)966-9521 Fax: (941)966-2590 • URL: http://www.comnews.com • Monthly. Free to qualified personnel; others, $84.00 per year. Includes coverage of "Internetworking" and "Intrenetworking." Emphasis is on emerging telecommunications technologies.

Communities: Journal of Cooperative Living. Fellowship for Intentional Communities, RR1 Box 156-W Rutledge, MO 63563-9720. Phone: (660)883-5545 Fax: (660)883-5545 E-mail: fic@fic.org • URL: http://www.fic.ic.org • Monthly. $20.00 per year.

Community and Junior College Libraries: The Journal for Learning Resources Centers. Haworth Press, Inc., 10 Alice St. Binghamton, NY 13904-1580. Phone: 800-429-6784 or (607)722-5857 Fax: 800-895-0582 or (607)722-1424 E-mail: getinfo@haworthpressinc.com • URL: http://www. haworthpressinc.com • Quarterly. $85.00 per year.

Community Associations Institute., 225 Reinekers Ln., Ste. 300 Alexandria, VA 22314. Phone: 888-CAI-4321 or (703)548-8600 Fax: (703)684-1581 E-mail: caidirect@caionline.org • URL: http://www.caionline.org • Condominium and homeowner associations, cooperatives, and association-governed planned communities of all sizes and architectural types; community or property managers and management firms; individual homeowners; community association managers and management firms; public officials; and lawyers, accountants, engineers, reserve specialists, builder/developers and other providers of professional services and products for CAs. Seeks to educate and represent America's 250,000 residential condominium, cooperative and homeowner associations and related professionals and service providers. Aims to foster vibrant, responsive, competent community associations that promote harmony, community and responsible leadership.

The Community Bank President. Siefer Consultants, Inc., 525 Cayuga St. Storm Lake, IA 50588. Phone: (712)732-7340 Fax: (712)732-7906 E-mail: info@siefer.com Monthly. $329.00 per year.

Community Banker. America's Community Bankers, 900 19th St., N.W., Suite 400 Washington, DC 20006. Phone: (202)857-3100 Fax: (202)296-8716 • URL: http://www. acbankers.org • Monthly. Price on application. Covers community banking operations and management. Formerly *America's Community Banker*.

Community College Journal. American Association of Community Colleges, One Dupont Circle, N.W., Suite 410 Washington, DC 20036-1176. Phone: (202)728-0200 Fax: (202)223-9390 E-mail: bookstore@aacc.nche.edu • URL: http://www.aacc.nche.edu • Bimonthly. $28.00 per year. Formerly *Community, Technical and Junior College Journal*.

Community College Review. Dept. of Adult and Community College Education. North Carolina State University, P.O. Box 7801 Raleigh, NC 27695-7801. Phone: (919)515-6248 Fax: (919)515-4039 E-mail: barbara__scott@nscu.edu • URL: http://www.ncsu.edu • Quarterly. $55.00 per year.

Community College Week: The Independent Voice Serving Community, Technical and Junior Colleges. Cox, Matthews & Associates, Inc., 10520 Warwick Ave., Suite B-8 Fairfax, VA

22030. Phone: (703)385-2981 Fax: (703)385-1839 E-mail: scottc@cmabiccw.com • URL: http://www.ccweek.com • Biweekly. $40.00 per year. Covers a wide variety of current topics relating to the administration and operation of community colleges.

Community Development Digest: Semi-Monthly Report on Development, Planning, Inf structure Financing. Community Services Development, Inc. CD Publications, 8204 Fenton St. Silver Springs, MD 20910-2889. Phone: 800-666-6380 or (301)588-6380 Fax: (301)588-6385 E-mail: info@cdpublications.com • URL: http://www.cdpublications.com • Semimonthly. $483.00 per year. Newsletter.

Community Development Society., 17 S High St., Ste. 200 Columbus, OH 43215. Phone: (614)221-1900 Fax: (614)221-1989 E-mail: cds@assnoffices.com • URL: http://www.comm-dev.org • Professionals and practitioners in community development; international, national, state, and local groups interested in community development efforts. Provides a forum for exchange of ideas and experiences; disseminates information to the public; advocates excellence in community programs, scholarship, and research; promotes citizen participation as essential to effective community development. Sponsors educational programs.

Community Journal. Community Service Inc., 114 E Whiteman, PO Box 243 Yellow Springs, OH 45387. Phone: (866)767-2161 or (937)767-2161 Fax: (937)767-2826 E-mail: info@communitysolution.org Description: Aims to promote the small community as a basic social institution. Publishes articles pertaining to community life with an emphasis on small towns, neighborhoods, rural life, and intentional communities. Discusses economics, education, land trusts, and other related issues. Recurring features include announcements of conferences, resources, an other events, letters to the editor, and news of the activities of the Service.

Community Leadership Association., Fanning Institute, 1240 S Lumpkin St., University of Georgia Athens, GA 30602. Phone: (706)542-0301 Fax: (706)542-7007 E-mail: info@communityleadership.org • URL: http://www.communityleadership.org • Local, regional, and state community leadership organizations. Provides for exchange of creative ideas concerning community leadership; promotes existing community leadership programs and their alumni organizations; helps establish new programs worldwide. Offers training, publications, and volunteer experts to community leadership organizations. Sponsors educational programs; compiles statistics.

Community Pharmacist: Meeting the Professional and Educational Needs of Today's Practitioner. ELF Publications, Inc., 5285 W. Louisiana Ave., Suite 112 Lakewood, CO 80232. Phone: 800-922-8513 or (303)975-0075 Fax: (303)975-0132 E-mail: elfpub@qwest.net • URL: http://www.elfpublications.com • Bimonthly. $25.00 per year. Edited for retail pharmacists in various settings, whether independent or chain-operated. Covers both pharmaceutical and business topics.

The Community Relations Report. Joe Williams Communications, 300 SE 4th St., PO Box 924 Bartlesville, OK 74005. Phone: 800-833-5946 or (918)336-2267 Fax: (918)336-2733 E-mail: joewmscomm@aol.com Description: Reports on innovative and creative corporate community relations activities throughout the country. Covers different techniques of improving community relations such as programs, activities, cultural events, and philanthropy grants. Recurring features include profiles of community relations practitioners and announcements of useful programs and books.

Compact D/SEC. Thomson Financial, 22 Thomson Place Boston, MA 02210. Phone: 877-983-4636 or (617)856-2000 Fax: (617)330-1986 E-mail: tfninfo@tfn.com • URL: http://www.tfn.com • Monthly. Provides 200 financial data items for 12,000 U. S. publicly-held corporations filing reports with the Securities and Exchange Commission. Includes company profiles.

Compact Disc Handbook. Kenneth C. Pohlmann. A-R Editions, Inc., 8551 Research Way, Ste. 180 Middleton, WI 53562. Phone: 800-736-0070 or (608)836-9000 Fax: (608)831-8200 E-mail: info@areditions.com • URL: http://www.areditions.com • 1992. $34.95. Second edition. A guide to compact disc technology, including player design and disc manufacturing. (Computer Music and Digital Audio Series).

Companies and Their Brands. Gale Cengage Learning, 27500 Drake Rd. Farmington Hills, MI 48331-3535. Phone: 800-877-GALE or (248)699-4253 Fax: 800-414-5043 E-mail: gale.galeord@cengage.com • URL: http://gale.cengage.com • 2003. $595.00. 24th edition. Two volumes. Lists companies alphabetically, with their names. (A rearrangement of the data in *Brands and Their Companies*.)

Companies Holding Nuclear Certificates. American Society of Mechanical Engineers, 3 Park Ave., 3 Park Ave. New York, NY 10016-5902. Phone: 800-843-2763 or (212)591-7158 Fax: (212)591-7739 E-mail: infocentral@asme.org • URL: http://www.asme.org • Covers: about 170 manufacturers accredited by the society's subcommittee on Nuclear Accreditation Committee for production of one or more types of pressure vessels and other components for nuclear applications. Entries include: Company name, address, and limitations of items which it is authorized by its certificate to produce.

Company of Military Historians. PO Box 910 Rutland, MA 01543-0910. Phone: (508)845-9229 E-mail: mail@military-historians.org • URL: http://www.military-historians.org •

Represents professional society of military historians, museologists, artists, writers, journalists, military personnel, teachers, researchers, and other individuals interested in the history of American military units, organization, tactics, uniforms, arms, and equipment. Maintains museum.

Company Policy and Personnel Workbook. Ardella Ramey. PSI Research, P.O. Box 3727 Central Point, OR 97502-0032. Phone: 800-228-2275 or (541)245-6502 Fax: (541)245-6505 E-mail: inforamtion@psi-research.com • URL: http://www.psi-research.com • 1999. $29.95. Fourth edition. Contains about 50 model company personnel policies for use as examples in developing a personnel manual. Explains the basic laws governing employee-employer relationships. (Successful Business Library Series).

Company Relocation Handbook: Making the Right Move. Sharon K. Ward and William Ward. Entrepreneur Media Inc., 2445 McCabe Way Irvine, CA 92614. Phone: 800-274-6229 or (949)261-2325 Fax: (949)261-7729 E-mail: gponce@entrepreneur.com • URL: http://www.entrepreneur.com • 1998. $19.95. A comprehensive guide to moving a business. (Successful Business Library Series).

Comparative Guide to American Elementary & Secondary Schools, 2002/03. Grey House Publishing, 185 Millerton Rd. Millerton, NY 12546. Phone: 800-562-2139 or (518)789-8700 Fax: (518)789-0556 E-mail: books@greyhouse.com • URL: http://www.greyhouse.com • 2002. $125.00. Second edition. Provides a "snapshot profile" of every public school district in the U. S. serving 2,500 or more students. Includes student-teacher ratios, expenditures per student, number of librarians, and socioeconomic indicators.

Comparative Guide to American Suburbs, 2003/2004. Grey House Publishing, 185 Millerton Rd. Millerton, NY 12546. Phone: 800-562-2139 or (518)789-8700 Fax: (518)789-0556 E-mail: books@greyhouse.com • URL: http://www.greyhouse.com • 2003. $130.00. Third edition. Contains detailed profiles of 1,800 suburban communities having a population of 10,000 or more and located within the 50 largest metropolitan areas. Includes ranking tables for income, unemployment, new housing permits, home prices, and crime, as well as information on school districts. (Universal Reference Publications.)

Comparative Statistics of Industrial Office Real Estate Markets. Society of Industrial and Office Realtors, 1201 New York Ave., Ste. 350 Washington, DC 20005. Phone: 888-891-7467 or (202)449-8200 Fax: (202)449-8201 E-mail: admin@sior.com • URL: http://www.sior.com • Annual. $100.00. Includes review and forecast section. Formerly *Guide to Industrial and Office Real Estate Markets*.

Compensating Executives: Drafting and Managing Tax-Advantaged Arrangements. Arthur H. Kroll. CCH, Inc., 2700 Lake Cook Rd. Riverwoods, IL 60015. Phone: 800-835-5224 or (847)267-7000 E-mail: cust_serv@cch.com • URL: http://www.cch.com • 1998. $115.00. Covers the creation and implementation of executive compensation programs. Includes sample forms, plans, and checklists.

Compensation. Robert E. Sibson. AMACOM, 1601 Broadway New York, NY 10019. Phone: 800-262-9699 or (518)586-8100 Fax: (518)903-8168 E-mail: customerservice@amanet.org • URL: http://www.amacombooks.org • 1990. $75.00. Fifth edition. Discusses planning, implementing, and managing employee compensation.

Compensation. George T. Milkovich. McGraw-Hill, 1221 Ave. of the Americas New York, NY 10020. Phone: 800-722-4267 or (212)512-2000 Fax: (212)512-4502 E-mail: customer.service@mcgraw-hill.com • URL: http://www.mcgraw-hill.com • 2001. $114.38. Seventh edition.

Compensation and Benefits Review: The Journal of Total Compensation Strategies. Sage Publications, Inc., 2455 Teller Rd. Thousand Oaks, CA 91320. Phone: 800-818-7243 or (805)499-9774 Fax: 800-583-2665 or (805)499-0871 E-mail: webmaster@sagepub.com • URL: http://www.sagepub.com • Institutions, $358.00 per year; includes print and online editions.

Compensation and Benefits Update. RIA, 395 Hudson St. New York, NY 10014. Phone: 800-950-1216 or 800-431-9025 E-mail: riahome@riag.com • URL: http://www.riahome.com • Monthly. $149.00 per year. Provides information on the latest ideas and developments in the field of employee benefits. In-depth exploration of popular benefits programs. Formerly *Benefits and Compensation Update*.

Compensation and Working Conditions. Available from U. S. Government Printing Office, Washington, DC 20402. Phone: (202)512-1800 Fax: (202)512-2250 E-mail: gpoaccess@gpo.gov • URL: http://www.access.gpo.gov • Quarterly. Issued by the Bureau of Labor Statistics, U. S. Department of Labor. Presents wage and benefit changes that result from collective bargaining settlements and unilateral management decisions. Includes statistical summaries and special reports on wage trends. Formerly *Current Wage Developments*.

Compensation Management in a Knowledge-Based World. Richard I. Henderson. Prentice Hall PTR, 240 Frisch Ct. Paramus, NJ 07652. Phone: 800-282-0693 Fax: 800-445-6991 • URL: http://www.phptr.com • 2002. $120.00. Ninth edition.

Compensation Systems in Private Law Firms. Altman Weil Publications, Inc., Two Campus Blvd. Newtown Square, PA 19073. Phone: 888-782-7297 or (610)886-2000 Fax: (610)359-0467 • URL: http://www.altmanweil.com • Annual. $325.00. Provides legal-office compensation standards ar-

ranged by region, firm size, legal specialty, and various other factors. Covers attorneys, paralegals, and other personnel.

Competitive Intelligence. Jim Underwood. John Wiley and Sons, Inc., 111 River St. Hoboken, NJ 07030. Phone: 800-225-5945 or (201)748-6000 Fax: (201)748-6088 E-mail: bookinfo@wiley.com • URL: http://www.wiley.com • 2001. $16.50. Describes the basic elements of competitive intelligence. Chapter headings include "What is Competitive Intelligence?", "Key Concepts and Thinkers," and "Ten Steps to Making It Work."

Competitive Intelligence From Black Ops to Boardrooms: How Businesses Gather, Analyze, and Use Information to Succeed in the Global Marketplace. Larry Kahaner. Simon & Schuster Trade, 1230 Ave. of the Americas New York, NY 10020. Phone: 800-223-2348 or (212)698-7000 Fax: 800-943-9831 or (212)698-7007 E-mail: consumer.customerservice@simonandschuster.com • URL: http://www.simonsays.com • 1996. $24.00. Emphasizes corporate espionage as opposed to more traditional information gathering (the author is a former licensed private investigator). Includes a "Glossary of Competitive Intelligence."

Competitive Intelligence Guide. Fuld & Co.Phone: (617)492-5900 Fax: (617)492-7108 E-mail: info@fuld.com • URL: http://www.fuld.com • Web site includes "Intelligence Index" (links to Internet sites), "Strategic Intelligence Organizer" (game-board format), "Intelligence Pyramid" (graphics), "Thoughtleaders" (expert commentary), "Intelligence System Evaluator" (interactive questionnaire), and "Reference Resource" (book excerpts from *New Competitor Intelligence*). Fees: information provided by Web site is free, but Fuld & Co. offers fee-based research and consulting services.

Competitive Intelligence Magazine. Society of Competitive Intelligence Professionals, 1700 Diagonal Rd., Ste. 520 Alexandria, VA 22314. Phone: (703)739-0696 Fax: (703)739-2524 E-mail: postmaster@scip.org • URL: http://www.scip.org • Quarterly. $49.00 per year. Covers the "legal and ethical collection and analysis of information" relating to business competition.

Competitive Telecommunications Association., 1900 M. St., N.W. Suite 800 Washington, DC 20036. Phone: (202)296-6650 Fax: (202)296-7585 E-mail: tmonroe@comptel.org • URL: http://www.comptel.org • Formerly Association of Long Distance Telephone Companies.

Complete and Easy Guide to Social Security, Healthcare Rights and Government Benefits. Faustin Jehle. Emerson-Adams Press, Inc., 1259 S.W. 14th St. Boca Raton, FL 33486. Phone: (561)750-9229 Fax: (561)394-3809 E-mail: fmurphy@emerson-adamspress.com 2000. $18.95. 16th unabridged edition.

The Complete Book of Insurance: Protecting Your Life, Health Property, and Income. Ben G. Baldwin. McGraw-Hill, 1221 Ave. of the Americas New York, NY 10020. Phone: 800-722-4726 or (212)512-2000 Fax: (212)512-4502 E-mail: customer.service@mcgraw-hill.com • URL: http://www.mcgraw-hill.com • 1991. $24.95. Provides basic information and advice on various kinds of insurance: life, health, property (fire), disability, long-term care, automobile, liability, and annuities.

Complete Book of Model Business Letters. Jack Griffin. Prentice Hall PTR, 240 Frisch Ct. Paramus, NJ 07652. Phone: 800-282-0693 Fax: 800-445-6991 • URL: http://www.phptr.com • 1997. $34.95.

Complete Book of Personal Legal Forms. Daniel Sitarz. Nova Publishing Co., 705 W Main St. Carbondale, IL 62901. Phone: 800-748-1175 or (618)457-3521 Fax: 800-338-4550 E-mail: info@novapublishing.com • URL: http://www.novapublishing.com • 2001. $24.95. Third edition. Provides more than 100 forms, including contracts, bills of sale, promissory notes, leases, deeds, receipts, and wills. Forms are also available on IBM or MAC diskettes. (Legal Self-Help Series).

Complete Book of Small Business Legal Forms. Daniel Sitarz. Nova Publishing Co., 705 W Main St. Carbondale, IL 62901. Phone: 800-748-1175 or (618)457-3521 Fax: 800-338-4550 or (618)457-2541 E-mail: info@novapublishing.com • URL: http://www.novapublishing.com • 2002. $24.95. Third edition. Includes CD-Rom and basic forms and instructions for use by small businesses in routine legal situations. Forms are also available on IBM or MAC diskettes. (Small Business Library Series).

Complete Building Equipment Maintenance Desk Book. Sheldon J. Fuchs, editor. Prentice Hall PTR, 240 Frisch Ct. Paramus, NJ 07652. Phone: 800-282-0693 Fax: 800-445-6991 • URL: http://www.phptr.com • 1992. $69.95. Second edition. *Supplement* available, $39.95.

Complete Business Statistics. Amir D. Aczel and Jayavel Sounderpandian. McGraw-Hill, 1221 Ave. of the Americas New York, NY 10020. Phone: 800-722-4726 or (212)512-2000 Fax: (212)512-4502 E-mail: customer.service@mcgraw-hill.com • URL: http://www.mcgraw-hill.com • 2001. $104.38. Fifth edition. Includes CD-ROM.

Complete Copyright: An Everyday Guide for Librarians. Carrie Russell. American Library Association, 50 East Huron St. Chicago, IL 60611-2795. Phone: 800-545-2433 or (312)944-6780 Fax: (312)440-9374 E-mail: editionsmarketing@ala.org • URL: http://www.ala.org • 2004. $50.00. Covers the fundamentals of U. S. copyright law, including the Digital Millennium Copyright Act (DMCA, 1998) and the Technology, Education, and Copyright Harmonization Act (the TEACH Act, 2002). The author is copyright specialist for the ALA Office for Information Technology Policy.

Complete Directory for People with Disabilities. Grey House Publishing, 185 Millerton Rd. Millerton, NY 12546. Phone: 800-562-2139 or (518)789-8700 Fax: (518)789-0556 E-mail: books@greyhouse.com • URL: http://www.greyhouse.com • Annual. $195.00. Provides information on a wide variety of products, goods, services, and facilities, including job training programs, rehabilitation services, and funding sources. Indexed by organization name, disability/need, and location.

Complete E-Commerce Book: Design, Build & Maintain a Successful Web-Based Business. Janice Reynolds and Roya Mofazali. CMP Books, 6600 Silacci Way Gilroy, CA 95020. Phone: 800-500-6875 or (408)848-3854 Fax: (408)848-5784 E-mail: cmp@rushorder.com • URL: http://www.cmpbooks.com • 2000. $29.95. Provides basic information for small firms wishing to do part of their business through a Web site. Covers both hardware and software for various system configurations.

Complete Federal Tax Forms. RIA, 395 Hudson St. New York, NY 10014. Phone: 800-950-1216 or 800-431-9025 E-mail: riahome@riag.com • URL: http://www.riahome.com • $605.00. Three looseleaf volumes. Periodic supplementation. Contains more than 650 reproducible Internal Revenue Service forms, with instructions.

Complete Guide to Becoming a U. S. Citizen. Eve P. Steinberg. Peterson's, 2000 Lenox Dr. Lawrenceville, NJ 08648. Phone: 800-338-3282 or (609)-896-1800 Fax: (609)-896-1811 E-mail: support@petersons.com • URL: http://www.petersons.com • 1994. $11.95.

Complete Guide to Corporate Fund Raising. Joseph Dermer and Stephen Wertheimer, editors. Fund Raising Institute, 27500 Drake Rd. Farmington Hills, MI 48331-3535. Phone: 800-877-8238 or (248)699-GALE Fax: 800-414-5043 or (248)699-8069 E-mail: galeord@gale.com • URL: http://www.galegroup.com • 1991. $19.95. Discusses the art of obtaining grants from corporate sources. Written by nine fund raising counselors.

Complete Guide to Performance Standards for Library Personnel. Carol F. Goodson. Neal-Schuman Publishers, Inc., 100 William St., Ste. 2004 New York, NY 10038. Phone: (866)672-6657 or (212)925-8650 Fax: (866)209-7932 or (212)219-8916 E-mail: info@neal-schuman.com • URL: http://www.neal-schuman.com • 1997. $55.00. Provides specific job descriptions and performance standards for both professional and paraprofessional library personnel. Includes a bibliography of performance evaluation literature, with annotations.

Complete Guide to Prescription and Non-Prescription Drugs: Side Effects, Warnings, and Vital Data for Safe Use. H. Winter Griffith. Berkley Publishing Group, 375 Hudson St. New York, NY 10014. Phone: 800-631-8571 or (212)366-2000 Fax: (212)366-2385 E-mail: online@penguinputnam.com • URL: http://www.penguinputnam.com • Annual. $17.95. A guide for consumers.

Complete Guide to Special Event Management: Business Insights, Financial Advice and Successful Strategies from Ernst and Young, Consultants to the Olympics. John Wiley and Sons, Inc., 111 River St. Hoboken, NJ 07030. Phone: 800-225-5945 or (201)748-6000 Fax: (201)748-6088 E-mail: info@wiley.com • URL: http://www.wiley.com • 1992. $39.95. Covers the marketing, financing, and general management of special events in the fields of art, entertainment, and sports.

Complete Guide to Your Real Estate Closing: Answers to All Your Questions from Opening Escrow to Negotiating Fees to Signing Closing Papers. Sandy Gadow. McGraw-Hill, 1221 Ave. of the Americas New York, NY 10020. Phone: 800-722-4726 or (212)512-2000 Fax: (212)512-4502 E-mail: customer.service@mcgraw-hill.com • URL: http://www.mcgraw-hill.com • Date not set. $19.95. Includes sample forms and work sheets, with specific real estate closing information for all 50 states. (Teach Yourself Series).

Complete Marquis Who's Who. Marquis Who's Who, 121 Chanlon Rd. New Providence, NJ 07974. Phone: 800-323-3288 or (908)464-6800 Fax: (908)665-6688 Contains information on over 825,000 prominent individuals, present and past. Semiannual updates. Inquire as to online cost and availability.

Complete Marquis Who's Who. Marquis Who's Who, Reed Reference Publishing, 121 Chanlon Rd. New Providence, NJ 07974. Phone: 800-323-3288 or (908)665-6780 Fax: 800-836-7766 or (908)665-3528 Frequency and price on application. Contains CD-ROM biographical profiles of over 800,000 notable individuals. Includes *Who's Who in America, Who Was Who in America*, and 14 regional and professional directories.

Complete Mental Health Directory. Grey House Publishing, 185 Millerton Rd., PO Box 860 Millerton, NY 12546. Phone: 800-562-2139 or (518)789-8700 Fax: (518)789-0556 E-mail: customerservice@greyhouse.com • URL: http://www.greyhouse.com • Covers: mental health resources including government agencies, professional meetings and seminars, clinic and hospital management companies, and pharmaceutical companies and their mental health product lines.

The Complete Probate Kit. Jens C. Appel and others. John Wiley and Sons, Inc., 111 River St. Hoboken, NJ 07030. Phone: 800-225-5945 or (201)748-6000 Fax: (201)748-6088 E-mail: info@wiley.com • URL: http://www.wiley.com • 1991. $35.00. A practical guide to settling estates. Provides summaries of the applicable state laws and definitions of relevant terms.

Complete Secretary's Handbook. Mary A. De Vries. Prentice Hall PTR, 240 Frisch Ct. Paramus, NJ 07652. Phone: 800-282-0693 Fax: 800-445-6991 • URL: http://www.phptr.com • 1993. $24.95. Seventh edition.

Complete Speaker's and Toastmaster's Library. Jacob M. Braude. Prentice Hall PTR, 240 Frisch Ct. Paramus, NJ 07652. Phone: 800-282-0693 Fax: 800-445-6991 • URL: http://www.phptr.com • 1992. $69.95. Second edition.

Compliance Reporter. Institutional Investor, Inc., Journals Group, 225 Park Ave., S New York, NY 10003. Phone: 800-945-2034 or (212)224-3066 Fax: (212)224-3472 E-mail: info@iijournals.com • URL: http://www.iijournals.com • Biweekly. $2,330.00 per year. Includes print and online editions. Newsletter for investment dealers and others on complying with securities laws and regulations.

Composite Catalog of Oilfield Equipment and Services. Gulf Publishing Co., 2 Greenway Plz., Ste. 1020 Houston, TX 77046. Phone: 800-231-6275 or (713)529-4301 Fax: (713)520-4433 • URL: http://www.gulfpub.com • Biennial. $750.00. Includes CD-Rom.

Composite Materials and Structures Center., Michigan State University, College of Engineering, 2100 Engineering Bldg. East Lansing, MI 48824-1226. Phone: (517)353-5466 Fax: (517)432-1634 E-mail: drzal@msu.edu • URL: http://www.egr.msu.edu/cmsc • Studies polymer, metal, and ceramic based composites.

Composite Materials Research Group.

The Composites and Adhesives Newsletter. T-C Press, P.O. Box 36006 Los Angeles, CA 90036-0006. Phone: (323)938-6923 Fax: (323)938-6923 E-mail: gps222@aol.com Quarterly. $190.00. Presents news of the composite materials and adhesives industries, with particular coverage of new products and applications.

Composites Industry Monthly. Composite Market Reports Inc., 7670 Opportunity Rd., Ste. 250 San Diego, CA 92111. Phone: (619)560-1085 Fax: (619)560-0234 E-mail: info@communitysolution.org Description: Directed toward companies seeking to diversify their line of non-aerospace applications of advanced composites. Discusses composite materials, processes, and markets worldwide with a focus on fabricators and users. Recurring features include interviews, news of research, a calendar of events, reports of meetings, and application case histories.

Composites Manufacturing Association of the Society of Manufacturing Engineers., 1 SME Dr. Dearborn, MI 48121. Phone: 800-733-4763 or (313)271-1500 Fax: (313)271-2861 E-mail: service@sme.org • URL: http://www.sme.org/cma • Members are composites manufacturing professionals and students.

Comprehensive Catalog of United States Paper Money. Gene Hessler. BNR Press, 132 E. Second St. Port Clinton, OH 43452. Phone: (419)732-6683 Fax: 800-367-9723 E-mail: ana@money.org • URL: http://www.money.org • 1992. $42.50. Fifth edtion.

Comprehensive Composite Materials. Anthony Kelly and Carl Zweben. Elsevier, 655 Ave. of the Americas New York, NY 10010-5107. Phone: 800-366-2665 Fax: 800-535-9935 or (212)633-3680 E-mail: custserv@elsevier.com • URL: http://www.elsevier.com • 2000. $2,905.50. Six volumes. Provides detailed information on a wide variety of materials used in composites, including metals, polymers, cements, concrete, carbon, ceramics, and fibers. (Pergamon Press.)

Comprehensive Day Care Programs. Stevens Administrative Center, Stevens Adm. Center, 1301 Spring Garden at 13th St., Rm. 203 Philadelphia, PA 19123. Phone: (215)351-7200 Fax: (215)351-7165 E-mail: eredd@phila.k12.pa.us Day care centers serving 3900 children of low-income families. Aims to help each child fulfill his or her own potential in intellectual, social, emotional, and physical development. Provides opportunities in self-development to parents; seeks to emphasize the parental role and responsibility in the development of the child. Services provided comprise six components: Curriculum; Food Services; Health Services; Parent Involvement; Social Services; Volunteer Services. Is funded by the School District of Philadelphia and the Pennsylvania Department of Public Welfare, under Title XX of the Federal Social Security Act.

Comprehensive Guide to the Hazardous Properties of Chemical Substances. Pradyot Patnaik. John Wiley and Sons, Inc., 111 River St. Hoboken, NJ 07030. Phone: 800-225-5945 or (201)748-6000 Fax: (201)748-6088 E-mail: info@wiley.com • URL: http://www.wiley.com • 1999. $210.00. Second edition.

Comprehensive Handbook of Psychological Assessment. Michel Hersen, editor. John Wiley and Sons, Inc., 111 River St. Hoboken, NJ 07030. Phone: 800-225-5945 or (201)748-6000 Fax: (201)748-6088 E-mail: info@wiley.com • URL: http://www.wiley.com • 2003. $500.00. Four volumes. Covers psychological testing and evaluation. Volume one: *Intellectual and Neuropsychological Assessment*. Volume two: *Personality Assessment*. Volume three: *Behavioral Assessment*. Volume four: *Industrial/Organizational Assessment*. (Individual volumes are available at $150.00.)

Compulsory Health Insurance: The Continuing American Debate. Ronald L. Numbers, editor. Greenwood Publishing Group Inc., 88 Post Rd., W Westport, CT 06881. Phone: 800-225-5800 or (203)226-3571 Fax: (203)431-2214 E-mail: customer-service@greenwood.com • URL: http://www.greenwood.com • 1982. $57.95. (Contributions in Medical History Series: No.11).

CompuMath Citation Index. Institute for Scientific Information, 3501 Market St. Philadelphia, PA 19104. Phone: 800-336-4474 or (215)386-0100 Fax: (215)386-2911 E-mail: sales@isinet.com • URL: http://www.isinet.com/isi • Three times a year. $1,090.00 per year. Provides citations to the worldwide literature of computer science and mathematics.

Compustat. Standard and Poor's, 7400 S. Alton Court, Englewood, CO 80112. Phone: 800-525-8640 or (303)771-6510 Fax: (303)721-4652 Financial data on publicly held U.S. and some foreign corporations; data held for 20 years. Inquire as to online cost and availability.

Computational Finance: Numerical Methods for Pricing Financial Instruments. George Levy. Elsevier Butterworth Heinemann, 200 Wheeler Rd., Sixth Floor Burlington, MA 01803. Phone: 800-545-2522 or (781)221-2212 Fax: 800-568-5136 or (781)313-4880 E-mail: usbkinfo@elsevier.com • URL: http://www.books.elsevier.com/finance • 2003. $89.95. Explains advanced financial modeling techniques using Windows software.

Computational Linguistics. Association for Computational Linguistics. MIT Press, Five Cambridge Center Cambridge, MA 02142-1493. Phone: 800-356-0343 or (617)253-5646 Fax: (617)258-6779 E-mail: journals-orders@mit.edu • URL: http://www.mitpress.mit.edu • Quarterly. Institutions, $150.00 per year. Includes print and online editions. Covers developments in research and applications of natural language processing.

Computer. Institute of Electrical and Electronic Engineers, Inc., Three Park Ave., 17th Fl. New York, NY 10017. Phone: 800-678-4333 or (212)419-7900 Fax: (212)752-4929 E-mail: customer-service@ieee.org • URL: http://www.ieee.org • Monthly. $1,060.00 per year. Edited for computer technology professionals.

Computer. Orion Research Corp., 14555 N. Scottsdale Rd., Suite 330 Scottsdale, AZ 85254-3457. Phone: 800-844-0759 Fax: 800-375-1315 E-mail: orion@bluebook.com • URL: http://www.netzone.com • Quarterly. $516.00 per year. $129.00 per issue. Quotes retail and wholesale prices of used computers and equipment. Original list prices and years of manufacture are also shown.

Computer Abstracts. Emerald, 875 Massachusetts Ave., 7th Fl. Cambridge, MA 02139. Fax: (617)354-6875 E-mail: america@emeraldinsight.com • URL: http://www.emeraldinsight.com • Bimonthly. $4,739.00 per year.

Computer Aided Design. Robert Becker and Carmo J. Pereira, editors. Marcel Dekker, Inc., 270 Madison Ave. New York, NY 10016. Phone: 800-228-1160 or (212)696-9000 Fax: (212)685-4540 E-mail: bookorders@dekker.com • URL: http://www.dekker.com • 1993. $250.00. (Chemical Industries Series: Vol. 51).

Computer-Aided Engineering; Data Base Applications in Design and Manufacturing. Penton Media, Inc., 1300 E. Ninth St. Cleveland, OH 44114. Phone: (216)696-7000 Fax: (216)696-1752 E-mail: information@penton.com • URL: http://www.penton.com • Quarterly. $55.00 per year.

Computer Aided Manufacturing International., 7850 N Belt Line Rd., No. 631 Irving, TX 75063-6064. Phone: (817)860-1654 Fax: (817)275-6450 E-mail: eredd@phila.k12.pa.us Companies, organizations, corporations, and individuals who are interested or engaged in computer-aided manufacturing. Seeks to develop and execute a long-range plan for the advancement of the use of computers in manufacturing. Engages in research and development activities, educational seminars, and forums for the generation and dissemination of information. Maintains library of over 1000 public-domain holdings (publications and software, including video- and magnetic tapes) relating to computer-aided design and manufacturing, cost management, and activity based costing. Compiles statistics.

Computer and Automated Systems Techincal Group of Society of Manufacturing Engin. Technical Activities Dept., 1 SME Dr. Dearborn, MI 48121. Phone: 800-733-4763 or (313)271-1500 Fax: (313)425-3400 E-mail: service@sme.org • URL: http://www.sme.org/casa • Sponsored by the Society of Manufacturing Engineers. Formerly Computer and Automated Systems Association.

Computer and Communications Industry Association., 666 11th St., N.W., Suite 600 Washington, DC 20001. Phone: (202)783-0070 Fax: (202)783-0534 E-mail: asteinem@ccianet.org • URL: http://www.ccianet.org • Formerly Computer Industry Association.

Computer and Control Abstracts. Available from INSPEC, Inc., 379 Thornall St. Edison, NJ 08337. Phone: (732)321-5575 Fax: (732)321-5702 E-mail: inspec@inspecinc.com • URL: http://www.iee.org • Monthly. $2,400.00 per year. Section C of *Science Abstracts*.

Computer and Information Science and Engineering Research Center. Ohio State University

Computer and Information Systems Abstracts Journal: An Abstract Journal Pertaining to the Theory, Design, Fabrication and Application of Computer and Information Systems. CSA, 7200 Wisconsin Ave., Suite 601 Bethesda, MD 20814. Phone: 800-843-7751 or (301)961-6700 Fax: (301)961-6720 E-mail: service@csa.com • URL: http://www.csa.com • 11 times a year. $1,750 per year.

Computer and Online Industry Litigation Reporter: The

National Journal of Record of Computer Online Industry. Andrews Publications, Inc., 175 Strafford Ave., Bldg 4, Suite 140 Wayne, PA 19087. Phone: 800-345-1101 or (610)225-0510 Fax: (610)225-0501 E-mail: customer@andrewspub.com • URL: http://www.andrewspub.com • Semimonthly. $875.00 per year. Newsletter. Provides complete text of key decisions relating to copyright, patents, trademarks, breach of contract, etc. Formerly *Computer Industry Litigation Reporter*.

Computer Animation Proceedings. Institute of Electrical and Electronic Engineers, Three Park Ave., 17th Fl. New York, NY 10016-5997. Phone: 800-678-4333 or (212)419-7900 Fax: (212)752-4929 E-mail: customer-service@ieee.org • URL: http://www.ieee.org • Annual. $110.00.

Computer Assisted Surgery: Automation, Virtual Reality, Robotics, and Radiosurgery. Theta Reports/PJB Medical Publications, Inc., 1775 Broadway, Suite 511 New York, NY 10019. Phone: (212)262-8230 Fax: (212)262-8234 E-mail: lschacterle@thetareports.com • URL: http://www.thetareports.com • 2000. $2,295.00. Contains market research data relating to surgical systems technology. (Theta Report No. 1105.)

Computer-Based Education and Instructional Design Project. Temple University

Computer Book Review., P.O. Box 61067 Honolulu, HI 96839. E-mail: cbr@bookwire.com • URL: http://www.bookwire.com/cbr • Quarterly. $30.00 per year. Includes annual index. Reviews new computer books. Back issues available.

Computer Communications Review. Association for Computing Machinery, Special Interest Group on Data Communicatio, 1515 Broadway New York, NY 10036. Phone: 800-342-6626 or (212)869-7440 Fax: (212)869-0481 E-mail: acmhelp@acm.org • URL: http://www.acm.org • Quarterly. Membership.

Computer Database. Gale Cengage Learning, 27500 Drake Rd. Farmington Hills, MI 48331-3535. Phone: 800-877-GALE or (248)699-GALE Fax: 800-414-5043 or (248)699-8069 E-mail: galeord@gale.com • URL: http://gale.cengage.com • Provides one year of full-text on CD-ROM for 150 leading computer-related publications. Also includes 70,000 product specifications and brief profiles of 13,000 computer product vendors and manufacturers.

Computer Dealers Directory. infoUSA, P.O. Box 27347 Omaha, NE 68127. Phone: 800-555-6124 or (402)593-4600 Fax: (402)331-5481 E-mail: internet@infousa.com Annual. Price on application. Lists over 30,847 computer dealers. Brand names are indicated. Compiled from telephone company yellow pages. Regional editions and franchise editions available.

Computer Economics Networking Strategies Report: Advising IT Decision Maker ractices and Current Trends. Computer Economics, Inc., 5841 Edison Place Carlsbad, CA 92008. Phone: 800-326-8100 or (760)438-8100 Fax: (760)431-1126 E-mail: access@compecon.com • URL: http://www.computereconomics.com • Monthly. $395.00 per year. Newsletter. Edited for information technology managers. Covers news and trends relating to a variety of corporate computer network and management information systems topics. Emphasis is on costs. Formerly *Intranet and Networking Strategies Report*.

Computer Economics Report: The Financial Advisor of Data Processing Users. Computer Economics, Inc., 5841 Edison Place Carlsbad, CA 92008. Phone: 800-326-8100 or (760)438-8100 Fax: (760)431-1126 E-mail: access@compecon.com • URL: http://www.computereconomics.com • Monthly. $595.00 per year. Newsletter on lease/purchase decisions, prices, discounts, residual value forecasts, personnel allocation, cost control, and other corporate computer topics. Edited for information technology (IT) executives.

Computer Fraud and Abuse Laws: An Overview of Federal Criminal Laws. Charles Doyle. Nova Science Publishers, Inc., 400 Oser Ave., Suite 1600 Hauppauge, NY 11788-3619. Phone: (631)231-7269 Fax: (631)231-8175 E-mail: novascience@earthlink.net • URL: http://www.novapublishers.com • 2002. $27.50. The author is concerned mainly with the federal computer fraud and abuse statute, 18 U.S.C. 1030.

Computer Fraud and Security. Elsevier, 655 Ave. of the Americas New York, NY 10010-5107. Phone: 800-366-2665 Fax: 800-535-9935 or (212)633-3680 E-mail: custserv@elsevier.com • URL: http://www.elsevier.com • Monthly. $833.00 per year. Newsletter. Formerly *Computer Fraud and Security Bulletin*.

Computer Glossary: The Complete Illustrated Dictionary. Alan Freedman. AMACOM, 1601 Broadway New York, NY 10019. Phone: 800-262-9699 or (518)586-8100 Fax: (518)903-8168 E-mail: customerservice@amanet.org • URL: http://www.amacombooks.org • 2000. $29.95. Ninth edition. Includes CD-Rom.

Computer Graphics. Special Interest Group on Computer Graphics. Association for Computing Machinery, 1515 Broadway New York, NY 10036-5701. Phone: (212)869-7440 Fax: (212)869-0481 E-mail: acmhelp@acm.org • URL: http://www.acm.org • Quarterly. Members, $59.00 per year; non-members, $95.00 per year; students, $50.00 per year.

Computer Graphics. Prentice Hall PTR, 240 Frisch Ct. Paramus, NJ 07652. Phone: 800-282-0693 Fax: 800-445-6991 • URL: http://www.phptr.com • 2000. $72.00.

Computer Graphics Laboratory., New York Institute of Technology, Fine Arts Old Westbury, NY 11568. Phone: (516)686-7542 Fax: (516)686-7428 E-mail: pvoci@nyit.edu

Research areas include computer graphics, computer animation, and digital sound.

Computer Graphics World. PennWell Publishing Co., Advanced Technology Div., 98 Spit Brook Rd. Nashua, NH 03062-5737. Phone: 800-331-4463 or (603)891-0123 E-mail: atd@pennwell.com • URL: http://www.pennwell.com • Monthly. $55.00 per year.

Computer Industry Almanac. Egil Juliussen and Karen Petska, editors. Computer Industry Almanac, Inc., 1013 S. Belmont Ave. Arlington Heights, IL 60005. Phone: 800-377-6810 or (847)718-0423 Fax: (847)758-1927 E-mail: info@c-i-a.com • URL: http://www.c-i-a.com • Annual. $53.00. Analyzes recent trends in various segments of the computer industry, with forecasts, employment data and industry salary information. Includes directories of computer companies, industry organizations, and publications.

Computer Languages, Systems and Structures. Elsevier, 655 Ave. of the Americas New York, NY 10010-5107. Phone: 800-366-2665 Fax: 800-535-9935 or (212)633-3680 E-mail: custserv@elsevier.com • URL: http://www.elsevier.com • Quarterly. Individuals, $208.00 per year; institutions, $951.00 per year.

Computer Law: Cases, Comments, Questions. Peter B. Maggs and others. West Publishing Co., 610 Opperman Dr. Saint Paul, MN 55164-0526. Phone: 800-338-9424 or (612)687-8000 Fax: 800-340-9378 E-mail: bookstore@westgroup.com • URL: http://www.westgroup.com • 1991. $62.50. (Amrican Casebook Series).

Computer Law: Evidence and Procedures. David Bender. Lexis-Nexis Matthew Bender, 1275 Broadway Albany, NY 12204. Phone: 800-424-4200 or (518)487-3000 Fax: (518)487-3584 E-mail: bookstore.support@lexisnexis.com • URL: http://www.bender.com • $686.00. Three looseleaf volumes. Periodic supplementation. Covers the concepts and techniques of evidence and discovery procedures as they apply to computer-based information, and to the protection of computer software under intellectual property.

Computer Law Reporter: A Monthly Journal of Computer Law and Practice, Intellectual Property, Copyright and Trademark Law. Computer Law Reporter, Inc., 1601 Connecticut Ave., N. W., Suite 602 Washington, DC 20009. Phone: (202)462-5755 Fax: (202)328-2430 Monthly. $1,650.00 per year. Newsletter.

Computer Law Strategist. American Lawyer Media Inc., 345 Park Ave., S. New York, NY 10010. Phone: 800-888-8300 or (212)779-9200 Fax: (212)481-8074 • URL: http://www.americanlawyermedia.com • Monthly. $265.00 per year. Newsletter.

Computer Letter: Business Issues in Technology. Technologic Partners, Inc., 120 Wooster St., 6th Fl. New York, NY 10012. Phone: (212)343-1900 Fax: (212)343-1915 E-mail: klein@technoglogicp.com 40 times a year. $695.00 per year. Newsletter. Computer industry newsletter with emphasis on information for investors.

Computer Literature Index: A Subject/Author Index to Computer and Data Processing Literature. EBSCO Publishing, 10 Estes St. Ipswich, MA 01938-0682. Phone: 800-653-2726 or (978)356-6500 Fax: (978)356-6565 E-mail: ep@epnet.com • URL: http://www.epnet.com • Quarterly, with annual cumulation. $245.00 per year. Contains brief abstracts of book and periodical literature covering all phases of computing, including approximately 70 specific application areas.

Computer Music Journal. MIT Press, Five Cambridge Center Cambridge, MA 02142-1493. Phone: 800-356-0343 or (617)253-5646 Fax: (617)258-6779 E-mail: journals-orders@mit.edu • URL: http://www.mitpress.mit.edu • Quarterly. Individuals, $77.00 per year; instutitions, $215.00 per year. Includes print and online editions. Covers digital sound and the musical applications of computers.

Computer Network Center.

Computer Networks. Andrew S. Tanenbaum. Prentice Hall PTR, 240 Frisch Ct. Paramus, NJ 07652. Phone: 800-282-0693 Fax: 800-445-6991 • URL: http://www.phptr.com • 2002. $89.00. Fourth edition.

Computer Parts and Supplies Directory. infoUSA, 5711 S 86th Cir. Omaha, NE 68127. Phone: 800-555-6124 or (402)593-4600 Fax: (402)331-5481 E-mail: internet@infousa.com • URL: http://www.abii.com • Annual. Price on application. Lists 7,020 companies. Compiled from telephone company yellow pages.

Computer Price Guide: The Blue Book of Used IBM Computer Prices. Computer Economics, Inc., 5841 Edison Place Carlsbad, CA 92008-6519. Phone: 800-326-8100 or (760)438-8100 Fax: (760)431-1126 E-mail: access@compecon.com • URL: http://www.computereconomics.com • Quarterly. $140.00 per year. Provides average prices of used IBM computer equipment, including "complete lists of obsolete IBM equipment." Includes a newsletter on trends in the used computer market. Edited for dealers, leasing firms, and business computer buyers.

Computer Publishing Market Forecast. SIMBA Information, 11 Riverbend Dr., S. Stamford, CT 06907-0234. Phone: 800-307-2529 or (203)358-4100 Fax: (203)358-5824 E-mail: info@simbanet.com • URL: http://www.simbanet.com • Biennial. $1,895.00. Provides market data on computer-related books, magazines, newsletters, and other publications. Includes profiles of major publishers of computer-related material.

Computer Repair Service. Entrepreneur Media, Inc., 2445 McCabe Way Irvine, CA 92614. Phone: 800-421-2300 or (949)261-2325 Fax: (949)261-0234 E-mail: entmag@entrepreneur.com • URL: http://www.entrepreneur.com • Looseleaf. $59.50. A practical guide to starting a computer repair service. Covers profit potential, start-up costs, market size evaluation, owner's time required, site selection, lease negotiation, pricing, accounting, advertising, promotion, etc. (Start-Up Business Guide No. E1256.)

Computer Reseller News: The Newsweekly for Builders of Technology Solutions. CMP Worldwide Media Networks, 600 Community Dr. Manhasset, NY 11030. Phone: (516)562-5000 • URL: http://www.cmp.com • Weekly. $199.00 per year. Includes bimonthly supplement. Incorporates *Computer Reseller Sources and Macintosh News*. Formerly *Computer Retailer News*.

Computer Review. Computer Review, 19 Pleasant St. Gloucester, MA 01930. Phone: (978)283-2100 Fax: (978)281-3125 E-mail: info@computerreview.com • URL: http://www.computerreview.com • Covers: Technology solution providers. Entries include: Company name, address, phone, fax, e-mail, product/service. Three sections—"Solution Providers", including computer hardware and software companies, telecom infrastructure and services, and Internet applications and new media; "Trends and Profiles", including products, services, and business affiliations; and the "Market Directory".

Computer Science Handbook. Allen B. Tucker. CRC Press, 2000 N.W. Corporate Blvd. Boca Raton, FL 33431. Phone: 800-272-7737 or (561)994-0555 Fax: 800-374-3401 or (561)989-9732 E-mail: orders@crcpress.com • URL: http://www.crcpress.com • 2004. $139.95. Second edition. Provides 70 chapters on 11 computer subject areas. Includes material from 150 contributing authors.

Computer Sciences. Roger Flynn, editor. Gale Cengage Learning, 27500 Drake Rd. Farmington Hills, MI 48331-3535. Phone: 800-877-GALE Fax: 800-414-5043 or (248)699-8069 E-mail: galeord@galegroup.com • URL: http://www.galegroup.com • 2002. $395.00. Four volumes. Presents a general and historical review of the impact of computers on modern society. Includes biographical information and multidisciplinary examples. (Macmillan Reference USA imprint, Macmillan Science Library.)

Computer Security: A Bibliography with Indexes. John S. Potts, editor. Nova Science Publishers, Inc., 400 Oser Ave., Suite 1600 Hauppauge, NY 11788-3619. Phone: (631)231-7269 Fax: (631)231-8175 E-mail: novascience@earthlink.net • URL: http://www.novapublishers.com • 2002. $59.00. Covers literature on computer hackers, viruses, identity theft, electronic spying, and other security issues. Includes author, title, and subject indexes.

Computer Security Basics. Deborah F. Russell and G. T. Gangemi. O'Reilly and Associates, Inc., 90 Sherman St. Cambridge, MA 02140. Phone: 800-775-7731 or (617)354-5800 Fax: (617)661-1166 E-mail: order@oreilly.com • URL: http://www.oreilly.com • 1991. $29.95. (Computer Science Series).

Computer Security Buyers Guide. Computer Security Institute, 600 Harrison St. San Francisco, CA 94107. Phone: (866)271-8529 or (818)487-4570 Fax: (818)487-4550 E-mail: csimember@espcomp.com • URL: http://www.gocsi.com • Covers: about 650 suppliers and consultants of computer security products, including communications and network security, disaster recovery, media security, personnel security, and security training. Entries include: Firm name, address, phone, name and title of contact, product or service provided.

Computer Security Digest. Jack Bologna. Computer Protection Systems Inc., PO Box 6121 Plymouth, MI 48170. Phone: (313)459-8787 Fax: (313)459-2720 E-mail: fdcr@clarknet.com Description: Provides information on computer security; company lawsuits; software viruses, failures, and piracy; and international privacy protection.

Computer Security Institute., 600 Harrison St. San Francisco, CA 94107. Phone: 800-250-2429 or (415)947-6320 Fax: (415)947-6023 E-mail: csi@techweb.com • URL: http://www.gocsi.com • Serves the information security professional.

Computer Shopper: The Computer Magazine for Direct Buyers. Media Inc., 28 E. 28th St. New York, NY 10016-7930. Phone: 800-451-1032 or (212)503-3500 Fax: (212)503-4399 E-mail: info@ziffdavis.com • URL: http://www.ziffdavis.com • Monthly. $14.99 per year. Nationwide marketplace for computer equipment.

Computer Software: Protection, Liability, Forms. L. J. Kutten. West Group, 610 Opperman Dr. Eagan, MN 55123. Phone: 800-328-4880 or (651)687-7000 Fax: 800-340-9378 E-mail: bookstore@westgroup.com • URL: http://www.westgroup.com • Semiannual. $576.00 per year. Four looseleaf volumes. Covers copyright law, patents, trade secrets, licensing, publishing contracts, and other legal topics related to computer software.

Computer Studies: Computers in Education. John Hirschbuhl and Dwight Bishop. McGraw-Hill, 1221 Ave. of the Americas New York, NY 10020. Phone: 800-722-4726 or (212)512-2000 Fax: (212)512-4502 E-mail: customer.service@mcgraw-hill.com • URL: http://www.mcgraw-hill.com • 1999. $18.44. Ninth edition. (Annual Editions Series).

Computer Video. IMAS Publishing, Inc., 5827 Columbia Pke., Ste. 310 Falls Church, VA 22041. Phone: (703)998-7600 Fax:

(703)998-2966 E-mail: adsales@imaspub.com • URL: http://www.imaspub.com • Bimonthly. $35.00 per year.

Computer Virus Crisis. Philip E. Fites and others. DIANE Publishing Co., 330 Pusey Ave. Collingdale, PA 19023-8428. Phone: 800-782-3833 or (610)461-6200 Fax: (610)461-6130 E-mail: dianepub@erols.com • URL: http://www.dianepublishing.com • 1999. $15.00. Second edition.

Computer Vision Laboratory., University of Arizona, Department of Electrical and Computer Engineering, ECE Bldg. 104, Room 230 Tucson, AZ 85721. Phone: (520)621-6191 Fax: (520)621-8076 E-mail: strickland@ece.arizona.edu • URL: http://www.ece.arizona.edu • Research areas include computer vision and speech synthesis.

Computerized Conferencing and Communications Center., New Jersey Institute of Technology, University Heights Newark, NJ 07102-1982. Phone: (973)596-3000 • URL: http://www.njit.edu • Research areas include computer conferencing software and computer-mediated communication systems.

Computerized Investing. American Association of Individual Investors, 625 N Michigan Ave. Chicago, IL 60611. Phone: 800-428-2244 or (312)280-0170 Fax: (312)280-9883 E-mail: techsupport@aaii.com • URL: http://www.aaii.org • Description: Furnishes articles on computer-aided investment analysis and investment-related software programs and database. Contains information on hardware and software, new product announcements, and editorial commentary. Recurring features include columns titled Product Reviews, New Products, Product Comparisons, BBS Update, Bookshelf, and Member Software Services.

Computers. Larry Long and Nancy Long. Prentice Hall PTR, 240 Frisch Ct. Paramus, NJ 07652. Phone: 800-282-0693 Fax: 800-445-6991 • URL: http://www.phptr.com • 2003. $46.67. Eighth edition.

Computers and Graphics: International Journal of Systems Applications in Computer Graphics. Elsevier, 655 Ave. of the Americas New York, NY 10010-5107. Phone: 800-366-2665 Fax: 800-535-9935 or (212)633-3680 E-mail: custserv@elsevier.com • URL: http://www.elsevier.com • Bimonthly. Qualified personnel, $180.00 per year; institutions, $1,760.00 per year.

Computers and Industrial Engineering: An International Journal. Elsevier, 655 Ave. of the Americas New York, NY 10010-5107. Phone: 800-366-2665 Fax: 800-535-9935 or (212)633-3680 E-mail: custserv@elsevier.com • URL: http://www.elsevier.com • Eight times a year. Qualified personnel, $83.00 per year; institutions, $2,576.00 per year.

Computers and Office and Accounting Machines. U. S. Bureau of the Census, 4700 Silver Hill Rd. Washington, DC 20233-0001. Phone: (301)763-4636 E-mail: comments@census.gov • URL: http://www.census.gov • Annual. Provides data on shipments: value, quantity, imports, and exports. (Current Industrial Reports, MA-35R.)

Computers and Security: The International Journal Devoted to the Study of the Technical and Financial Aspects of Computer Security. International Federation for Information Processing AUT Technical Committee on Computer Security. Elsevier, 655 Ave. of the Americas New York, NY 10010-5107. Phone: 800-366-2665 or (212)989-5800 Fax: 800-535-9935 or (212)633-3680 E-mail: custserv@elsevier.com • URL: http://www.elsevier.com • Eight times a year. Institutions, $760.00 per year.

Computers in Education Today. Steven L. Mandell. West Publishing Co., 610 Opperman Dr. Eagan, MN 55123. Phone: 800-328-2209 or (651)687-7000 Fax: 800-340-9378 E-mail: bookstore@westgroup.com • URL: http://www.westgroup.com • $52.00. Date not set.

Computers in Human Behavior. Elsevier, 655 Ave. of the Americas New York, NY 10010-5107. Phone: 800-366-2665 or (212)989-5800 Fax: 800-535-9935 or (212)633-3680 E-mail: custserv@elsevier.com • URL: http://www.elsevier.com • Bimonthly. Qualified personnel, $242.00 per year; institutions, $1,100.00 per year.

Computers in Libraries. Information Today, Inc., 143 Old Marlton Pike Medford, NJ 08055-8750. Phone: 800-300-9868 or (609)654-6266 Fax: (609)654-4309 E-mail: custserv@infotoday.com • URL: http://www.infotoday.com • 10 times a year. $98.95 per year.

Computers in Libraries: Buyer's Guide and Consultant Directory. Mecklermedia Corp., 16 Thorndal Cir. Darien, CT 06820-5421. Phone: (609)654-6266 Fax: (609)654-4309 E-mail: info@mecklermedia.com • URL: http://www.infotoday.com • Annual. $30.00.

Computers in the Schools: The Interdisciplinary Journal of Practice, Theory, and Applied Research. Haworth Press, Inc., 10 Alice St. Binghamton, NY 13904-1580. Phone: 800-429-6784 or (607)722-5857 Fax: 800-895-0582 or (607)722-1424 E-mail: getinfo@haworth.com • URL: http://www.haworth.com • Quarterly. $450.00 per year. Includes print and online editions.

Computers: The User Perspective. Sarah E. Hutchinson and Stacey C. Sawyer. McGraw-Hill, 1221 Ave. of the Americas New York, NY 10020. Phone: 800-722-4726 or (212)512-2000 Fax: (212)512-4502 E-mail: customer.service@mcgraw-hill.com • URL: http://www.mcgraw-hill.com • 1991. $41.95. Third edition.

Computertalk: For Contemporary Pharmacy Management. Computertalk Associates, Inc., 492 Norristown Rd., Suite 160 Blue Bell, PA 19422-2355. Phone: (610)825-7686 Fax:

(610)825-7641 E-mail: maggie@computertalk.com • URL: http://www.computertalk.com • Bimonthly. $50.00 per year. Provides detailed advice and information on computer systems for pharmacies, including a buyers' guide issue.

Computerworld: Newsweekly for Information Technology Leaders. Computerworld, Inc., 500 Old Connecticut Path Framingham, MA 01701-9171. Phone: 800-669-1002 or (508)879-0700 Fax: (508)875-8931 • URL: http://www.computerworld.com • Weekly. $190.00 per year.

Computing and Software Career Directory. Gale Cengage Learning, 27500 Drake Rd. Farmington Hills, MI 48331-3535. Phone: 800-877-GALE or (248)699-4253 Fax: 800-414-5043 E-mail: gale.galeord@cengage.com • URL: http://gale.cengage.com • 1993. $39.00. Includes career information relating to programmers, software engineers, technical writers, systems experts, and other computer specialists. Provides advice from "insiders," resume suggestions, a directory of companies that may offer entry-level positions, and a directory of career information sources. (Career Advisor Series.)

Computing Reviews. Association for Computing Machinery, 1515 Broadway New York, NY 10036-5701. Phone: (212)869-7440 Fax: (212)869-0481 E-mail: acmhelp@acm.org • URL: http://www.acm.org • Monthly. Members, $45.00 per year; non-members, $190.00 per year; students, $40.00 per year.

Computing Technology Industry Association., 1815 S Meyers Rd., Ste. 300 Oakbrook Terrace, IL 60181-5228. Phone: (630)678-8300 Fax: (630)678-8384 E-mail: information@comptia.org • URL: http://www.comptia.org • Trade association of more than 19,000 companies and professional IT members in the rapidly converging computing and communications market. Has members in more than 89 countries and provides a unified voice for the industry in the areas of e-commerce standards, vendor-neutral certification, service metrics, public policy and workforce development. Serves as information clearinghouse and resource for the industry; sponsors educational programs.

Concepts in Wine Chemistry. Yair Margalit. Wine Appreciation Guild, 360 Swift Ave. San Francisco, CA 94080-6220. Phone: 800-231-9463 or (650)866-3020 Fax: (650)866-3513 E-mail: info@wineappreciation.com • URL: http://www.wineappreciation.com • 1997. $79.95. Explains wine chemical changes in fermentation, aging, cellaring, and shipping.

Concession Profession. National Association of Concessionaires, 35 E Wacker Dr., Ste. 1816 Chicago, IL 60601. Phone: (312)236-3858 Fax: (312)236-7809 E-mail: info@naconline.org • URL: http://www.naconline.org • Covers: about 900 member equipment manufacturers, suppliers, jobber/distributors, popcorn processors, theaters, amusement parks, stadiums, rinks, and other concession operators in the United States and Canada. Entries include: For operators—Company name, address, phone, name of contact. For manufacturers and suppliers—Company name, address, phone, names and titles of up to four executives, brief description of service or products.

Concise Chemical and Technical Dictionary. Harry Bennett. Chemical Publishing Co., Inc., 527 Third Ave., No. 427 New York, NY 10016-4168. Phone: 800-786-3659 or (212)799-0090 Fax: (212)889-1537 E-mail: chempub@aol.com • URL: http://www.chemicalpublishing.com • 1986. $170.00. Fourth edition.

Concise Dictionary of Crime and Justice. Mark S. Davis. Sage Publications, Inc., 2455 Teller Rd. Thousand Oaks, CA 91320-2218. Phone: 800-818-7243 or (805)499-0721 Fax: 800-583-2665 or (805)499-0871 E-mail: info@sagepub.com • URL: http://www.sagepub.com • 2002. $64.95. Contains more than 2,000 definitions of terms relating to the criminal justice system and criminology.

Concise International Encyclopedia of Robotics:Applications and Automation. Richard C. Dorf and Shimon V. Nof, editors. John Wiley and Sons, Inc., 111 River St. Hoboken, NJ 07030. Phone: 800-225-5945 or (201)748-6000 Fax: (201)748-6088 E-mail: info@wiley.com • URL: http://www.wiley.com • 1990. $375.00.

Concord Consortium, Inc. Concord Consortium, 25 Love Ln. Concord, MA 01742. Phone: (978)405-3200 Fax: (978)405-2076 E-mail: info@concord.org • URL: http://www.concord.org • Global technology-based Science and Math education, including educational applications of networking, computers and electronics.

Concrete Construction. Hanley-Wood, LLC, One Thomas Circle, NW Washington, DC 20005. Phone: 800-837-0870 or (202)452-0800 Fax: (202)785-1974 • URL: http://www.hanley-wood.com • Monthly. $30.00 per year. Lists manufacturers or suppliers of concrete-related products and services.

Concrete Construction Buyers' Guide. Hanley-Wood, LLC, One Thomas Circle, NW Washington, DC 20005. Phone: 800-837-0870 or (202)452-0800 Fax: (202)785-1974 • URL: http://www.hanley-wood.com • Annual. $5.00. Lists sources of products and services related to building with concrete.

Concrete International. American Concrete Institute, 38800 Country Club Rd. Farmington Hills, MI 48331. Phone: (248)848-3700 Fax: (248)848-3701 E-mail: bkstore@concrete.org • URL: http://www.aci-int.org • Monthly. $126.00 per year. Covers practical technology, industry news, and business management relating to the concrete construction industry.

The Concrete Producer. Hanley-Wood, LLC, One Thomas Circle NW Washington, DC 20005. Phone: 800-837-0870 or

(202)452-0800 Fax: (202)785-1974 • URL: http://www.worldofconcrete.com • Monthly. $27.00 per year. Covers the production and marketing of various concrete products, including precast and prestressed concrete. Formerly Aberdeen's Concrete Trader.

Concrete Products. Primedia Business Magazines and Media, 330 N Wabash Ave., Ste. 2300 Chicago, IL 60606. Phone: 800-795-5445 or (312)726-2802 Fax: (312)726-2574 E-mail: subs@primediabusiness.com • URL: http://www.primediabusiness.com • Monthly. $61.00 per year. Free to qualified personnel; others, $61.00 per year.

The Concrete Yearbook. EMAP Construction Ltd., 151 Roseberry Ave. London W4 4PH, United Kingdom. Phone: 44 20 7505 6970 Fax: 44 20 7505 6970 • URL: http://www.emapconstruct.co.uk • Annual. $100.00.

Concurrent Technologies Corporation., 100 CTC Dr. Johnstown, PA 15904. Phone: 800-282-4392 or (412)269-6888 Fax: (814)262-6500 E-mail: ctc@ctc.com • URL: http://www.ctc.com • Formerly Center for Hazardous Materials Research.

Conditions in Occupational Therapy: Effect on Occupational Performance. Ruth Hansen and Ben Atchison. Lippincott Williams and Wilkins, 530 Walnut St. Philadelphia, PA 19106-3621. Phone: 800-638-3030 or (215)521-8300 Fax: (215)521-8902 E-mail: custserv@lww.com • URL: http://www.lww.com • 1999. $45.95. Second edition. Each chapter "describes a major condition that occupational therapists frequently treat." Includes case studies.

CondoBusiness. Shelter Publications, 555 Yonge St., Suite 1000 Toronto, ON, Canada M2N 6P4. Phone: (416)512-8186 Fax: (416)512-8344 E-mail: condo@mediaedge.com Monthly. $55.00 per year. Covers condominium development and administration industries.

Condos, Co-ops, and Townhomes: A Complete Guide to Finding, Buying, Maintaining, and Enjoying Your New Home. Mark B. Weiss. Dearborn Trade Publishing, A Kaplan Professional Co., 30 S Wacker Dr., Ste. 2500 Chicago, IL 60606. Phone: 800-621-9621 or (312)836-4400 Fax: (312)836-1021 E-mail: trade@dearborn.com • URL: http://www.dearborntrade.com • 2003. $18.95. Covers financing, assessments, investment for rental, common areas, homeowners associations, and other topics relating to "association-managed communities."

Conducting a Successful Capital Campaign. Kent E. Dove. John Wiley and Sons, Inc., 111 River St. Hoboken, NJ 07030. Phone: 800-225-5945 or (201)748-6000 Fax: (201)748-6088 E-mail: info@wiley.com • URL: http://www.wiley.com • 1999. $55.00. Second expanded revised edition. (Nonprofit and Public Management Series).

Confectioner: The Magazine. Stagnito Communcations, Inc., 155 Pfingsten Rd., Ste. 205 Deerfield, IL 60015. Phone: (847)205-5660 Fax: (847)205-5680 E-mail: info@stagnito.com • URL: http://www.stagnito.com • Bimonthly. $70.17 per year. Covers a wide variety of topics relating to the distribution and retailing of candy and snacks.

Confectioneries. Available from MarketResearch.com, 641 Ave. of the Americas, Fourth Floor New York, NY 10011. Phone: 800-298-5699 or (212)807-2629 Fax: (212)807-2642 E-mail: order@marketresearch.com • URL: http://www.marketresearch.com • 2002. $3,950.00. Published by Global Industry Analysts. Provides worldwide market research data, including profiles of companies producing candy and other confectionery products.

Conference Board, Inc. The Conference Board, Inc., 845 3rd Ave. New York, NY 10022. Phone: (212)339-0345 Fax: (212)980-7014 E-mail: info@conference-board.org • URL: http://www.conference-board.org • Business management practices worldwide, especially economic, and demographic in nature. Specific concerns include: corporate citizenship, including corporate contributions, diversity, environmental policy and issues, and government relations; corporate governance, including boards of directors, role of chief executives, relations with institutional investors, and shareholder input and influence; economics, including economic and financial forecasts, consumer confidence, leading economic indicators, North American outlook and trends, and global economic environment; human resources and organizational effectiveness, including organization structure and design, compensation and benefits, training and development, and communications; and performance excellence.

Conference Board of Canada., 255 Smyth Rd. Ottawa, ON, Canada K1H 8M7. Phone: (613)526-3280 Fax: (613)526-4857 E-mail: contactcboc@conferenceboard.ca • URL: http://www.conferenceboard.ca • Research areas include economics, finance, international business, and consumer buying intentions.

Conference of Consulting Actuaries., 1110 W. Lake Cook Rd., Suite 235 Buffalo Grove, IL 60089-1968. Phone: (847)419-9090 Fax: (847)419-9091 E-mail: cca@ccactuaries.org • URL: http://www.ccactuaries.org • Formerly Conference of Actuaries of Public Practice.

Conference of State Bank Supervisors., 1155 Connecticut Ave., NW, 5th Fl. Washington, DC 20036. Phone: 800-886-2727 or (202)728-5702 Fax: (202)296-1928 E-mail: nmilner@csbs.org • URL: http://www.csbs.org • Members are state officials responsible for supervision of state-chartered banking institutions.

Conference on Consumer Finance Law., Oklahoma City University School of Law, 2501 N Blackwelder Oklahoma City, OK 73106-1493. Phone: 800-633-7242 or (405)521-

5337 Fax: (405)521-5802 • URL: http://www.okcu.edu/law • Formerly Conference on Personal Finance Law.

Conference on Safe Transportation of Hazardous Articles., 7803 Hill House Ct. Fairfax Station, VA 22039. Phone: (703)451-4031 Fax: (703)451-4207 E-mail: mail@costha.com • URL: http://www.costha.com • Members are shipper associations concerned with the legal aspects of transporting hazardous materials.

Conference Papers Index. Cambridge Scientific Abstracts, 7200 Wisconsin Ave., 6th Fl. Bethesda, MD 20814. Phone: 800-843-7751 or (301)961-6700 Fax: (301)961-6720 • URL: http://www.csa.com • Citations to scientific and technical papers presented at meetings, 1973 to present. Inquire as to online cost and availability.

Confidential Reference Book of the Jewelers Board of Trade. Jewelers Board of Trade, 95 Jefferson Blvd. East Providence, RI 02888-1046. Phone: (401)467-0005 Fax: (401)467-1199 • URL: http://www.jewelersboard.com • Supplied on loan basis only to members of the Jewelers Board of Trade. Jewelry and allied product manufacturers, wholesalers and retailers; complete address, phone number and credit rating.

Congress in Print: The Weekly Catalog of Congressional Documents. Congressional Quarterly, Inc., 1414 22nd St., N.W. Washington, DC 20037. Phone: 800-432-2250 or (202)887-8500 Fax: 800-380-3810 or (202)728-1863 E-mail: customerservice@cqpress.com • URL: http://www.cq.com • 48 times a year. $198.00 per year. Newsletter.

Congressional Agenda: Millennium., 3220 N St. NW, Ste. 178 Washington, DC 20007. Phone: (202)342-9192 E-mail: grassroots@commoncause.org Raises funds for congressional representatives working to alter current administration policy trends so that programs developed in the 1970s can be adapted to present needs. Areas of specific attention include the economy, nuclear arms, and environmental preservation. Seeks to reduce interest rates, defer some proposed tax cuts, eliminate unnecessary defense expenditures, and end cuts in domestic programs that are seen as investments in future growth, such as employment training, education, transport, housing, utilities, and water systems. Works toward restoration of funding and governmental support for environmental preservation programs.

Congressional Directory. Office of Membership Grassroots Management, 1615 H St. NW Washington, DC 20062-2000. Phone: 800-638-6582 or (202)659-6000 Fax: (202)463-3190 E-mail: info@naconline.org Covers: Members of Congress. Entries include: List of members of Congress by state includes member party and home city; alphabetical list by member name includes addresses, phone, fax, e-mail, committee/subcommittee assignments, names of key staff members, and photos.

Congressional Index. CCH, Inc., 2700 Lake Cook Rd. Riverwoods, IL 60015. Phone: 800-835-5224 or (847)267-7000 E-mail: cust_serv@cch.com • URL: http://www.cch.com • Weekly when Congress is in session. $1,283.00 per year. Index to action on Public Bills from introduction to final disposition. Subject, author, and bill number indexes.

Congressional Investigations: Law and Practice. John C. Grabow. Aspen Publishers, Inc., 1185 Ave. of the Americas New York, NY 10036. Phone: 800-234-1660 or (212)597-0200 Fax: 800-901-9075 or (212)597-0338 E-mail: customer.service@aspenpubl.com • URL: http://www.aspenpublishers.com • $95.00. Looseleaf service. Periodic supplementation.

Congressional Monitor: Daily Listing of All Scheduled Congressional Committee Hearings with Witnesses. Congressional Quarterly. Inc., 1414 22nd St., N.W. Washington, DC 20037. Phone: 800-432-2250 or (202)887-8500 Fax: 800-380-3810 or (202)728-1863 E-mail: customerservice@cqpress.com • URL: http://www.cq.com • Daily. $1,349.00 per year. Weekly *Supplements.*

Congressional Quarterly Almanac. CQ Press, 1255 22nd St., NW, Ste. 400 Washington, DC 20037. Phone: 888-427-7737 or (202)729-1800 Fax: 800-380-3810 or (202)729-1863 E-mail: customerservice@cqpress.com • URL: http://www.cqpress.com • Annual. $215.00.

Congressional Record. U.S. Congress. Available from U.S. Government Printing Office, Washington, DC 20402. Phone: (202)512-1800 Fax: (202)512-2250 Daily. Indexes give names, subjects, and history of bills. Texts of bills not included.

Congressional Record Scanner. Congressional Quarterly, 1255, 22nd St. NW Washington, DC 20037. Phone: 800-432-2250 or (202)419-8500 Fax: 800-380-3810 or 800-380-3810 E-mail: customerservice@cq.com • URL: http://www.cqpress.com • Description: Contains abstracts of the Congressional Record.

Congressional Staff Directory: With Biographical Information on Members and Key Congressional Staff. CQ Press, 1255 22nd St., NW, Ste. 400 Washington, DC 20037. Phone: (866)427-7737 or (202)729-1900 Fax: 800-380-3810 E-mail: customerservice@cqpress.com • URL: http://www.cqpress.com • Three times a year. $225.00 per year. Contains more than 3,200 detailed biographies of members of Congress and their staffs. Includes committees and subcommittees. Keyword and name indexes are provided.

Congressional Yellow Book: Who's Who in Congress, Including Committees and Key Staff. Leadership Directories, Inc., 104 Fifth Ave. New York, NY 10011. Phone: (212)627-4140 Fax: (212)645-0931 E-mail: info@leadershipdirectories.com • URL: http://www.leadershipdirectories.com • Quarterly. $360.00 per year. Looseleaf. A directory of members of congress, including their committees and their key aides.

Consensus Forecasts: A Worldwide Survey. Consensus Economics Inc., 53 Upper Brook St. London W1K 2LT, United Kingdom. Phone: 44 20 7491 3211 Fax: 44 20 7409 2331 E-mail: editors@consensuseconomics.com • URL: http://www.consensuseconomics.com • Monthly. $565.00 per year. Provides a survey of more than 200 "prominent" financial and economic forecasters, covering 20 major countries. Two-year forecasts for each country include future growth, inflation, interest rates, and exchange rates. Each issue contains analysis of business conditions in various countries.

Consensus: National Futures and Financial Weekly. Consensus, Inc., PO Box 520526 Independence, MO 64052-0526. Phone: 800-383-1441 or (816)373-3700 Fax: (816)373-3701 E-mail: editor@consensus-inc.com • URL: http://www.consensus-inc.com • Weekly. $365.00 per year. Newspaper. Contains news, statistics, and special reports relating to agricultural, industrial, and financial futures markets. Features daily basis price charts, reprints of market advice, and "The Consensus Index of Bullish Market Opinion" (charts show percent bullish of advisors for various futures).

Conservation Directory: A Listing of Organizations, Agencies and Officials Concerned with Natural Resource Use and Management. National Wildlife Federation, 11100 Wildlife Center Dr. Reston, VA 20190-5362. Phone: 800-822-9919 or (703)638-6000 Fax: (703)438-6061 E-mail: info@nwf.org • URL: http://www.nwf.org • Annual. $70.00. Lists agencies and private organizations in U.S. and Canada concerned with conservation and natural resource management.

Conservative Democratic Political Action Committee., 2000 K St. NW, Ste. 500 Washington, DC 20006. E-mail: information@emilyslist.org Members of the Conservative Democratic Forum. Makes contributions to the campaigns of moderate/conservative congressional candidates.

Conservative Leadership Political Action Committee., 3128 17th St. N Arlington, VA 22201-5202. Fax: (703)352-8118 E-mail: caomail@hr.house.gov Assists in the election of conservative candidates to congressional and statewide offices. Identifies, places, and supports youth coordinators; works to organize thousands of youth votes, volunteer hours, and special activities in targeted states and congressional districts. Offers placement service that matches trained youth coordinators who are available to work full-time in a fall election cycle with conservative campaigns desiring a full-time youth effort. **Convention/Meeting:** none. **Publications:** none.

Consortium for Graduate Study in Management.

Constitution, Jefferson's Manual and Rules of the House of Representatives. U.S. Government Printing Office, Washington, DC 20402. Phone: (202)512-1800 Fax: (202)512-2250 E-mail: gpoaccess@gpo.gov. • URL: http://www.accessgpo.gov • Biennial. $58.00.

Constructing Effective Questionnaires. Robert A. Peterson. Sage Publications, Inc., 2455 Teller Rd. Thousand Oaks, CA 91320. Phone: 800-818-7243 or (805)499-9774 Fax: 800-583-2665 or (805)499-0871 E-mail: webmaster@sagepub.com • URL: http://www.sagepub.com • 1999. $86.95. Covers the construction and wording of questionnaires for survey research.

Construction Contracting. Richard H. Clough and Glenn A. Sears. John Wiley and Sons, Inc., 111 River St. Hoboken, NJ 07030. Phone: 800-225-5945 or (201)748-6000 Fax: (201)748-6088 E-mail: info@wiley.com • URL: http://www.wiley.com • 1994. $110.00. Sixth edition.

Construction Contractors' Survival Guide. Thomas C. Schleifer. John Wiley and Sons, Inc., 111 River St. Hoboken, NJ 07030. Phone: 800-225-5945 or (201)748-6000 Fax: (201)748-6088 E-mail: info@wiley.com • URL: http://www.wiley.com • 1990. $99.00. (Practical Construction Guides Series).

Construction Equipment Buyers Guide. Reed Business Information, 360 Park Ave., S New York, NY 10010. Phone: 800-446-6551 or (646)746-6400 E-mail: corporatecommunications@reedbusiness.com • URL: http://www.reedbusiness.com • Annual. $49.95.

Construction Equipment Distribution. Associated Equipment Distributors, 615 W. 22nd St. Oak Brook, IL 60521. Phone: (630)574-0650 Fax: (630)574-0132 E-mail: info@aednet.org • URL: http://www.aednet.org • Monthly. Members, $20.00 per year; non-members, $40.00 per year.

Construction Equipment Distribution-Directory. Associated Equipment Distributors, 615 W. 22nd St. Oak Brook, IL 60523. Phone: 800-388-0650 or (630)574-0650 Fax: (630)574-0132 E-mail: info@aednet.org • URL: http://www.aednet.org • Annual. $100.00 per year. Lists about 1,300 members of the association.

Construction Equipment Operation and Maintenance. Construction Publications Inc., P.O. Box 1689 Cedar Rapids, IA 52406. Phone: (319)366-1597 Fax: (319)362-8808 Bimonthly. $12.00 per year. Information for users of construction equipment and industry news.

Construction Financial Management Association., 29 Emmons Dr., Ste. F-50 Princeton, NJ 08540. Phone: (609)452-8000 Fax: (609)452-0474 E-mail: info@cfma.org • URL: http://www.cfma.org • Contractors, subcontractors, architects, real estate developers, and engineers; associate members are equipment and material suppliers, accountants, lawyers, bankers, and others involved with the financial management of the construction industry. Provides a forum for the exchange of ideas; coordinates educational programs dedicated to improving the professional standards of financial management in the construction industry. Offers expanded national programs, technical assistance, and industry representation. Conducts research programs; maintains speakers' bureau and placement service; compiles statistics.

Construction Industry Annual Financial Survey. Construction Financial Management Association, 29 Emmons Dr., Suite F-50 Princeton, NJ 08540-1413. Phone: (609)452-8000 Fax: (609)452-0474 E-mail: info@cfma.org • URL: http://www.cfma.org • Annual. $149.00. Contains key financial ratios for various kinds and sizes of construction contractors.

Construction Industry Institute. Construction Industry Institute, 3925 W Braker Ln., No. R4500 Austin, TX 78759-5316. Phone: (512)232-3000 Fax: (512)499-8101 E-mail: wcrew@mail.utexas.edu • URL: http://construction-institute.org • Management, planning, design, and technology aspects of construction project execution, as well as methods and materials of construction and craft labor techniques. Links owners, contractors, and others directly active in the construction industry with academic resources to develop techniques and databases to improve the cost, schedule, quality and safety of the constructed project, the capital investment process, and total quality of the construction industry. Identifies immediate, long-range, and breakthrough research needs; directs appropriate research and studies; collects information from engineering and construction projects; and provides implementation guides on how to get research into actual engineering and construction projects. Also addresses education needs of the industry and conducts benchmarking studies for "best practices" comparisons.

Construction Industry Manufacturers Association., 111 E. Wisconsin Ave., Ste. 1000 Milwaukee, WI 53202. Phone: (414)272-0943 Fax: (414)272-1170 E-mail: info@cfma.org • URL: http://www.cimanet.com • Manufacturers of off-highway earthmoving and construction machinery and allied equipment and components. Compiles statistics.

Construction Labor Report. BNA, Inc., 1231 25th St., NW Washington, DC 20037. Phone: 800-372-1033 E-mail: customercare@bna.com • URL: http://www.bna.com. • Weekly. $1,189.00 per year. Two looseleaf volumes.

Construction Law. LexisNexis Matthew Bender, 1275 Broadway Albany, NY 12204-4026. Phone: 800-424-4200 or (518)487-3000 Fax: 800-828-8341 or (518)487-3584 E-mail: customer.support@lexisnexis.com • URL: http://www.lexisnexis.com/matthewbender/ • Looseleaf. $935.00. Six volumes. Periodic supplementation available. Edited for lawyers who prepare construction contracts or engage in construction dispute litigation.

Construction Law Digest. LexisNexis Matthew Bender, 1275 Broadway Albany, NY 12204-4026. Phone: 800-424-4200 or (518)487-3000 Fax: 800-828-8341 or (518)487-3584 E-mail: customer.support@lexisnexis.com • URL: http://www.lexisnexis.com/matthewbender/ • Monthly. $425.00 per year. Newsletter. Provides practical information on emerging legal trends, issues, and court decisions relevant to the construction industry.

Construction Materials and Processes. Donald A. Watson. McGraw-Hill, 1221 Ave. of the Americas New York, NY 10020. Phone: 800-722-4726 or (212)512-2000 Fax: (212)512-4502 E-mail: customer.service@mcgraw-hill.com • URL: http://www.mcgraw-hill.com • 1986. $83.34. Third edition.

Construction Materials: Types, Uses, and Applications. Caleb Hornbostel. John Wiley and Sons, Inc., 111 River St. Hoboken, NJ 07030. Phone: 800-225-5945 or (201)748-6000 Fax: (201)748-6088 E-mail: infoatswiley.com • URL: http://www.wiley.com • 1991. $250.00. Second edition. (Practical Construction Guides Series).

Construction Research Center., University of Texas at Arlington, P.O. Box 19347 Arlington, TX 76019. Phone: (817)272-3701 Fax: (817)272-7575 E-mail: matthys@uta.edu Addresses the needs of the construction industry through construction research and educational programs.

Construction Sealants and Adhesives. Julian R. Panek and John P. Cook. John Wiley and Sons, Inc., 111 River St. Hoboken, NJ 07030. Phone: 800-225-5945 or (201)748-6000 Fax: (201)748-6088 E-mail: info@wiley.com • URL: http://www.wiley.com • 1991. $150.00. Third edition. (Practical Construction Guides Series).

Construction Specifier: For Commercial and Industrial Construction. Construction Specifications Institute, 99 Canal Center Plaza, Suite 300 Alexandria, VA 22314. Phone: 800-689-2900 or (703)684-0300 Fax: (703)684-0465 E-mail: membcustsrv@csinet.org • URL: http://www.csinet.org • Monthly. Free to members; non-members, $36.00 per year; libraries, $30.00 per year. Technical aspects of the construction industry.

Construction Specifier Member Directory. Construction Specifications Institute, 99 Canal Center Plz., Ste. 300 Alexandria, VA 22314. Phone: 800-689-2900 or (703)684-0300 Fax: (703)684-0465 E-mail: membcustsrv@csinet.org • URL: http://www.csinet.org • Annual. $30.00. Roster of construction specifers by the institute, and 17,200 members.

Constructor-AGC Directory of Membership and Services. Associated General Contractors of America. AGC Information, Inc., 333 John Carley St., Suite 200 Alecandria, VA 22314. Phone: (703)837-5355 Fax: (703)837-5402 • URL: http://www.agc.org • Annual. $250.00. Membership is made up of contractors and suppliers for general construction. Formerly

Associated General Contractors of America National Directory.

Constructor: The Management Magazine of the Construction Industry. Associated General Contractors of America. AGC Information, Inc., 333 John Carlye St., Suite 200 Alexandria, VA 22314-5745. Phone: (703)548-3118 Fax: (703)837-5405 E-mail: scott@agc.org • URL: http://www.agc.org • Monthly. Members, $15.00 per year; non-members, $250.00 per year. Includes *Directory*.

Consultants and Consulting Organizations Directory. Gale Cengage Learning, 27500 Drake Rd. Farmington Hills, MI 48331-3535. Phone: 800-877-GALE or (248)699-4253 Fax: 800-414-5043 E-mail: gale.galeord@cengage.com • URL: http://gale.cengage.com • 2003. $840.00. 25th edition. Three volumes. Includes mid-year *Supplement*. Lists more than 27,000 firms and individuals covering 14 general fields of consulting activity.

Consultants News: Independent Commentary on Management Consulting Since 1970. Kennedy Information, Inc., One Phoenix Mill Ln., 5th Fl. Peterborough, NH 03458. Phone: 800-531-0007 or (603)924-1006 Fax: (603)924-4460 E-mail: bookstore@kennedyinfo.com • URL: http://www.kennedyinfo.com • Monthly. $295.00 per year. Newsletter. News and ideas for management consultants.

The Consultant's Proposal, Fee, and Contract Problem-Solver. Ronald Tepper. John Wiley and Sons, Inc., 111 River St. Hoboken, NJ 07030. Phone: 800-225-5945 or (201)748-6000 Fax: (201)748-6088 E-mail: info@wiley.com • URL: http://www.wiley.com • 1993. $29.95. Provides advice for consultants on fees, contracts, proposals, and client communications. Includes case histories in 10 specific fields, such as finance, marketing, engineering, and management.

Consultative Selling: The Hanan Formula for High-Margin Sales at High Levels. Mack Hanan. AMACOM, 1601 Broadway New York, NY 10019. Phone: 800-262-9699 or (518)586-8100 Fax: (518)903-8168 E-mail: customerservice@amanet.org • URL: http://www.amacombooks.org • 1999. $27.95. Sixth revised edition. How to treat customers as friends to be helped and not as foes to be overcome.

Consulting Business. Entrepreneur Media, Inc., 2445 McCabe Way Irvine, CA 92614. Phone: 800-421-2300 or (949)261-2325 Fax: (949)261-0234 E-mail: entmag@entrepreneur.com • URL: http://www.entrepreneur.com • Looseleaf. $59.50. A practical guide to becoming a business consultant. Covers profit potential, start-up costs, market size evaluation, pricing, accounting, advertising, promotion, etc. (Start-Up Business Guide No. E1151.)

Consulting Services. Association of Consulting Chemists and Chemical Engineers Inc., PO Box 297, PO Box 297 Sparta, NJ 07871. Phone: (973)729-6671 Fax: (973)729-7088 E-mail: info@chemconsult.org • URL: http://www.chemconsult.org • Covers: about 160 member consultants in chemistry, chemical engineering, metallurgy, etc. Entries include: Individual name, address, certificate number, qualifications, affiliation, experience, facilities, staff.

Consulting-Specifiying Engineer. Reed Business Information, 360 Park Ave., S New York, NY 10010. Phone: 800-446-6551 or (646)746-6400 Fax: (646)746-7028 E-mail: corporatecommunications@reedbusiness.com • URL: http://www.reedbusiness.com • 13 times a year. $95.90 per year. Formerly *Consulting Engineer*.

Consumer and Commercial Credit: Installment Sales. Prentice Hall PTR, 240 Frisch Ct. Paramus, NJ 07652. Phone: 800-282-0693 Fax: 800-445-6991 • URL: http://www.phptr.com • Three looseleaf volumes. Periodic supplementation. Price on application. Covers secured transactions under the Uniform Commercial Code and the Uniform Consumer Credit Code. Includes retail installment sales, home improvement loans, higher education loans, and other kinds of installment loans.

Consumer Asia. Available from Gale Cengage Learning, 27500 Drake Rd. Farmington Hills, MI 48331-3535. Phone: 800-877-GALE or (248)699-GALE Fax: 800-414-5043 E-mail: gale.galeord@cengage.com • URL: http://gale.cengage.com • Annual. $1,090.00. Published by Euromonitor. Provides statistical andanalytical surveys of factors affecting Asian consumer markets: energy, labor, population, finance, debt, tourism, consumer expenditures, household characteristics, etc. Emphasis is on Hong Kong, Singapore, Taiwan, South Korea, Indonesia, and Malaysia.

Consumer Attitudes Toward Physical Fitness. Available from MarketResearch.com, 641 Ave. of the Americas, Third Floor New York, NY 10011. Phone: 800-298-5699 or (212)807-2629 Fax: (212)807-2716 E-mail: order@marketresearch.com • URL: http://www.marketresearch.com • 2002. $375.00. Published by American Sports Data, Inc. Contains market research information.

Consumer Bankers Association., 1000 Wilson Blvd., Ste. 2500 Arlington, VA 22209-3912. Phone: (703)276-1750 Fax: (703)528-1290 E-mail: membership@cbanet.org • URL: http://www.cbanet.org • Federally insured deposit-taking institutions. Sponsors Graduate School of Retail Bank Management at the university of Virginia.

Consumer Bankruptcy Law and Practice. The National Consumer Law Center, 77 Summer St., 10th Fl. Boston, MA 02110. Phone: (617)542-9595 Fax: (617)542-8028 E-mail: consumerlaw@nclc.org • URL: http://www.consumerlaw.org • 2000. $140.00. Sixth edition. (Consumer Credit and Sales Legal Practice Series).

Consumer Batteries. Available from MarketResearch.com, 641 Ave. of the Americas, Fourth Floor New York, NY 10011. Phone: 800-298-5699 or (212)807-2629 Fax: (212)807-2642 E-mail: order@marketresearch.com • URL: http://www.marketresearch.com • 2002. $4,450.00. Published by Global Industry Analysts. Provides worldwide market research data, including profiles of major battery companies. Includes the market for cellular phone and laptop computer batteries.

Consumer Behavior. Leon Schiffman and Leslie Kanut. Harcourt College Publishers, City Center Tower Two, 301 Commerce St., Suite 3700 Fort Worth, TX 76102. Phone: 800-354-9706 or (817)334-7500 Fax: 800-487-8488 or (817)334-7844 E-mail: wlittle@harbrace.com • URL: http://www.harcourtcollege.com • 2003. $120.00. Eighth edition.

Consumer China 2001. Available from Gale Cengage Learning, 27500 Drake Rd. Farmington Hills, MI 48331-3535. Phone: 800-877-GALE or (248)699-GALE Fax: 800-414-5043 E-mail: gale.galeord@cengage.com • URL: http://gale.cengage.com • Annual. $1,090.00. Published by Euromonitor. Provides demographic and consumer market data for China.

Consumer Confidence Survey. The Conference Board Inc., 845 3rd Ave. New York, NY 10022-6679. Phone: (212)759-0900 Fax: (212)980-7014 E-mail: webmaster@conference-board.org • URL: http://www.conference-board.org • Description: Publishes results of a special ongoing consumer attitude survey. Carries information on appraisal of business conditions and employment; plans to buy major durable goods such as homes, cars, and appliances; and intended vacations and chosen means of travel.

Consumer Credit. U. S. Federal Reserve System, Board of Governors, Publications Services, MS-138, 20th and Constitutution Ave. Washington, DC 20551. Phone: (202)452-3244 Fax: (202)728-5886 • URL: http://www.federalreserve.gov • Monthly. $5.00 per year. (Federal Reserve Statistical Release, G.19.)

Consumer Credit and the Law. Mary D. Pridgen. West Group, 610 Opperman Dr. Eagan, MN 55123. Phone: 800-328-4880 or (651)687-7000 Fax: 800-340-9378 E-mail: bookstore@westgroup.com • URL: http://www.westgroup.com • Annual. $280.00. Looseleaf service.

Consumer Credit and Truth-in-Lending Compliance Report. RIA, 395 Hudson St. New York, NY 10014. Phone: 800-950-1216 or 800-431-9025 E-mail: riahome@riag.com • URL: http://www.riahome.com • Monthly. $183.75 per year. Newsletter. Focuses on the latest regulatory rulings and findings involving consumer lending and credit activity. Incorporates (Consumer Lending Report).

Consumer Credit Guide. CCH, Inc., 2700 Lake Cook Rd. Riverwoods, IL 60015. Phone: 800-835-5224 E-mail: cust_serv@cch.com • URL: http://www.cch.com • Biweekly. $1,255.00 per year. Looseleaf service.

Consumer Credit Industry Association., 2911 S Shore Blvd., Ste. 130 League City, TX 77573. Phone: (281)535-7446 Fax: (281)535-7435 E-mail: jim.pangburn@anico.com • URL: http://www.cciaonline.com • Insurance companies underwriting consumer credit insurance in areas of life insurance, accident and health insurance, and property insurance.

Consumer Credit: Law Transactions and Forms. LexisNexis Matthew Bender, 1275 Broadway Albany, NY 12204. Phone: 800-424-4200 or (518)487-3000 Fax: (518)487-3584 E-mail: bookstore.support@lexisnexis.com • URL: http://www.bender.com • $849.00. Six looseleaf volumes. Periodic supplementation. Detailed treatment of the law with practical step-by-step guidance for every stage of a consumer credit transaction.

Consumer Eastern Europe. Available from Gale Cengage Learning, 27500 Drake Rd. Farmington Hills, MI 48331-3535. Phone: 800-877-GALE or (248)699-GALE Fax: 800-414-5043 E-mail: gale.galeord@cengage.com • URL: http://gale.cengage.com • Annual. $1,250.00. Published by Euromonitor. Provides demographic and consumer market data for the countries of Eastern Europe.

Consumer Education Research Center.

The Consumer Electronics Industry and the Future of American Manufacturing: How the U. S. Lost the Lead and Why We Must Get Back in the Game. Susan W. Sanderson. Economic Policy Institute, 1660 L St., N.W., Suite 1200 Washington, DC 20036. Phone: 800-374-4844 or (202)775-8810 Fax: (202)775-0819 E-mail: publications@epinet.org • URL: http://www.epinet.org • 1990. $12.00.

Consumer Europe 2000/2001. Available from Gale Cengage Learning, 27500 Drake Rd. Farmington Hills, MI 48331-3535. Phone: 800-877-GALE or (248)699-GALE Fax: 800-414-5043 E-mail: gale.galeord@cengage.com • URL: http://gale.cengage.com • Annual. $1,290.00. Published by Euromonitor. Detailed statistical tables furnish five-year data on the production, sales, distribution, consumption, and other aspects of more than 240 consumer product categories. Sixteen countries of Western Europe are included.

Consumer Expenditure Survey. Available from U. S. Government Printing Office, Washington, DC 20402. Phone: (202)512-1800 Fax: (202)512-2250 E-mail: gpoaccess@gpo.gov • URL: http://www.access.gpo.gov • Biennial. Issued by the Bureau of Labor Statistics, U. S. Department of Labor (http://www.bls.gov). Contains data on various kinds of consumer spending, according to household income, education, etc. (Bureau of Labor Statistics Bulletin.)

Consumer Federation of America., 1424 16th St., N. W., Suite 604 Washington, DC 20036. Phone: (202)387-6121 Fax: (202)265-7989 E-mail: cfa@essential.org • URL: http://www.consumerfed.org • Members are national, regional, state, and local consumer groups. Absorbed Electric Consumers Information Committee.

Consumer Finance Law Bulletin. American Financial Services Association, Legal Department, 919 18th St. NW, Ste. 300 Washington, DC 20006. Phone: (202)296-5544 Fax: (202)223-0321 E-mail: afsa@afsamail.org • URL: http://www.americanfinsvcs.org • Description: Provides a digest of recent cases in consumer finance law, covering Truth In Lending Act, Equal Credit Opportunity Act, Fair Credit Reporting Act, Fair Debt Collection Practices Act, consumer bankruptcy, state usury and consumer protection laws, and practice notes on recent regulatory activity. **Remarks:** Subscription includes membership in AFSA's Law Forum.

Consumer Finance Newsletter. Financial Publishing Co., 3975 William Richardson Dr., PO Box 570 South Bend, IN 46624. Phone: 800-247-3214 or (574)243-6040 Fax: (574)243-6060 E-mail: ksolnoky@carletoninc.com Description: Provides information on effective and pending credit insurance and installment loan regulations on the state and federal levels. Supplies news of potential state changes in regulations.

The Consumer Health Information Source Book. Alan Rees, editor. Greenwood Publishing Group, Inc., 88 Post Rd., W. Westport, CT 06881. Phone: 800-225-5800 or (203)226-3571 Fax: (203)431-2214 E-mail: customer-service@greenwood.com • URL: http://www.greenwood.com • 2003. $65.00. Seventh edition. Bibliography of current literature and guide to organizations.

Consumer Healthcare Products Association., 900 19th St. NW, Ste. 700 Washington, DC 20006. Phone: (202)429-9260 Fax: (202)223-6835 E-mail: lsuydam@chpa-info.org • URL: http://www.chpa-info.org • Marketers of nonprescription medicines and dietary supplements, which are packaged and available over-the-counter; associate members include suppliers, consultants, research and testing laboratories, advertising agencies, and media. Obtains and disseminates business, legislative, regulatory, and scientific information; conducts voluntary labeling review service to assist members in complying with laws and regulations.

Consumer Installment Credit. Board of Governors, U.S. Federal Reserve System, Publications Services, Room MS-138 Washington, DC 20551. Phone: (202)452-3244 Fax: (202)728-5886 Monthly. $5.00 per year.

Consumer International. Available from Gale Cengage Learning, 27500 Drake Rd. Farmington Hills, MI 48331-3535. Phone: 800-877-GALE or (248)699-GALE Fax: 800-414-5043 E-mail: gale.galeord@cengage.com • URL: http://gale.cengage.com • Annual. $1,290.00. Published by Euromonitor. Contains extensive consumer market, economic, and demographic data for 25 major, non-European countries, including the U. S. and Canada. Includes consumer market size (volume and value) for 150 product types in 14 categories (food, clothing, automobiles, cosmetics, appliances, etc.).

Consumer Latin America. Available from Gale Cengage Learning, 27500 Drake Rd. Farmington Hills, MI 48331-3535. Phone: 800-877-GALE or (248)699-GALE Fax: 800-414-5043 E-mail: gale.galeord@cengage.com • URL: http://gale.cengage.com • Annual. $1,090.00. Published by Euromonitor. Contains a wide variety of consumer market data relating to the countries of Latin America. Includes market forecasts.

Consumer Online Services Report. JupiterMedia, 23 Old Kings Hwy., S Darien, CT 06820. Phone: 800-488-4345 or (203)662-2800 Fax: (203)655-4686 • URL: http://www.jmm.com • Annual. $1,895.00. Market research report. Provides analysis of trends in the online information industry, with projections of growth in future years (five-year forecasts). Contains profiles of electronic media companies.

Consumer Power: How Americans Spend. Margaret Ambry. McGraw-Hill, 1221 Ave. of the Americas New York, NY 10020. Phone: 800-772-4726 or (212)512-2000 Fax: (212)512-4502 E-mail: customer.service@mcgraw-hill.com • URL: http://www.mcgraw-hill.com • 1992. $27.50. Contains detailed statistics on consumer income and spending. Nine major categories of products and services are covered, with spending data and dollar size of market for each item.

Consumer Price Indices: An ILO Manual. Ralph Turvey and others. International Labour Office, 1828 L St., NW Washington, DC 20036-5121. Phone: (202)653-7652 Fax: (202)653-7687 E-mail: washington@ilo.org • URL: http://www.ilo.org • 1990. $24.75.

Consumer Product Litigation Reporter. Andrews Publications, 175 Strafford Ave., Bldg 4, Suite 140 Wayne, PA 19087. Phone: 800-345-1101 or (610)225-0510 Fax: (610)225-0501 E-mail: customer@andrewspub.com • URL: http://www.andrewspub.com • Monthly. $725.00 per year. Newsletter. Provides reports on legislation and litigation relating to product liability.

Consumer Product Safety Guide. CCH, Inc., 2700 Lake Cook Rd. Chicago, IL 60015. Phone: 800-835-5224 or (847)267-7000 E-mail: cust_serv@cch.com • URL: http://www.cch.com • Weekly. $1,166.00 per year. Looseleaf service. Three volumes. Periodic suplementation.

Consumer Product Safety Review. Available from U. S. Government Printing Office, Washington, DC 20402. Phone: (202)512-1800 Fax: (202)512-2250 E-mail: gpoaccess@gpo. gov • URL: http://www.access.gpo.gov • Quarterly. $18.00 per year. Issued by the U. S. Consumer Product Safety Commission.

Consumer Protection and the Law. Mary D. Pridgen. West Group, 610 Opperman Dr. Eagan, MN 55123. Phone: 800-328-4880 or (651)687-7000 Fax: 340-9378 E-mail: bookstore@westgroup.com • URL: http://www.westgroup. com • Annual. $269.00. Looseleaf service. Covers advertising, sales practices, unfair trade practices, consumer fraud, and product warranties.

Consumer Reports. Consumers Union of the United States, Inc., 101 Truman Ave. Yonkers, NY 10703-1057. Phone: 800-234-1645 or (914)378-2000 Fax: (914)378-2900 • URL: http:// www.consumerreports.org • Monthly. $26.00 per year. Includes *Annual Buying Guide*.

Consumer Reports Money Book: How to Get It, Save It, and Spend It Wisely. Janet Bamford and others. Consumers Union of the United States, Inc., 101 Truman Ave. Yonkers, NY 10703-1057. Phone: 800-234-1645 or (914)378-2000 Fax: (914)378-2904 • URL: http://www.consumerreports.org • 2000. $19.95. Third edition. Covers budgeting, retirement planning, bank accounts, insurance, and other personal finance topics.

Consumer Reports Travel Letter. Consumers Union of U.S. Inc., 101 Truman Ave. Yonkers, NY 10703-1057. Phone: 800-234-1645 or (914)378-2455 Fax: (914)378-2928 E-mail: ksolnoky@carletoninc.com • URL: http://www. consumerreports.org • Description: Provides travelers with information and advice on travel goods and services. Discusses such topics as air and rail passes, air fare, hotel rates, car rental fees, and techniques for optimizing foreign exchange rates.

Consumer Research Center., Conference Board, Inc., 845 Third Ave. New York, NY 10022. Phone: (212)339-0304 Fax: (212)836-9714 E-mail: crc@conference-board.org • URL: http://www.crc-conquest.org • Conducts research on the consumer market, including elderly and working women segments.

Consumer Sourcebook: A Directory and Guide. Gale Cengage Learning, 27500 Drake Rd. Farmington Hills, MI 48331-3535. Phone: 800-877-GALE or (248)699-4253 Fax: 800-414-5043 E-mail: gale.galeord@cengage.com • URL: http:// gale.cengage.com • 2003. $305.00. 16th edition. Consumer-oriented agencies, associations, institutes, centers, etc.

Consumer USA. Available from Gale Cengage Learning, 27500 Drake Rd. Farmington Hills, MI 48331-3535. Phone: 800-877-GALE or (248)699-GALE Fax: 800-414-5043 E-mail: gale.galeord@cengage.com • URL: http://gale.cengage.com • Annual. $1,090.00. Fifth edition. Published by Euromonitor. Provides demographic and consumer market data for the United States. Forecasts to the year 2005.

The Consumer's Dictionary of Cosmetic Ingredients. Ruth Winter. Crown Publishing Group, Inc., 299 Park Ave. New York, NY 10171. Phone: 800-733-3000 or (212)751-2600 Fax: 800-659-2436 or (212)572-2165 1999. $16.00. Fifth edition. (Consumer's Dictionaries Series).

The Consumers' Directory of Continuing Care Retirement Communities. American Association of Homes and Services for the Aging, 2519 Connecticut Ave., NW Washington, DC 20008. Phone: (202)783-2242 Fax: (202)783-2255 E-mail: info@aahsa.org • URL: http://www.aahsa.org • Irregular. $30.00. Contains information on fees, services, and accreditation of about 500 U. S. retirement facilities providing lifetime housing, meals, and health care. Introductory text discusses factors to be considered in selecting a continuing care community.

Consumers Education and Protective Association International.

Consumers' Guide to Health Plans. Center for the Study of Services, 733 15th St., N. W., Suite 820 Washington, DC 20005. Phone: 800-213-7283 or (202)347-7283 Fax: (202)347-4000 E-mail: subscriptions@checkbook.org • URL: http://www.checkbook.org • 1996. $14.95. Revised edition. Presents the results of a consumer survey on satisfaction with specific managed care health insurance plans, and related information. Includes "Top-Rated Plans," "Health Plans That Chose Not to Have Their Members Surveyed," and other lists. General advice is provided on choosing a plan, finding a good doctor, getting good care, etc.

Consumers' Guide to Product Grades and Terms: From Grade A to VSOP-Definitions of 8,000 Terms Describing Food Housewares and Other Everyday Terms. Gale Cengage Learning, 27500 Drake Rd. Farmington Hills, MI 48331-3535. Phone: 800-877-GALE or (248)699-4253 Fax: 800-414-5043 E-mail: gale.galeord@cengage.com • URL: http:// gale.cengage.com • 1992. $95.00. Includes product grades and classifications defined by government agencies, such as the Food and Drug Administration (FDA), and by voluntary standards organizations, such as the American National Standards Institute (ANSI).

Consumers Guide to Varietal Wines. Wine Appreciation Guild, 360 Swift Ave. San Francisco, CA 94080-6220. Phone: 800-231-9463 or (650)866-3020 Fax: (650)866-3513 E-mail: info@wineappreciation.com • URL: http://www. wineappreciation.com • Annual. $45.00.

Consumers Reference Disc. National Information Services Corp., Wyman Towers, Suite 6, 3100 Saint Paul St. Baltimore, MD 21218. Phone: (410)243-0797 Fax: (410)243-0982 Quarterly. Provides the CD-ROM version of *Consumer Health and Nutrition Index* from Oryx Press and *Consumers Index to Product Evaluations and Information Sources* from Pierian Press. Contains citations to consumer health articles and consumer product evaluations, tests, warnings, and recalls.

Consumers' Research.

Consumer's Research Magazine: Analyzing Consumer Issues. Consumers' Research Inc., 800 Maryland Ave., N.E. Washington, DC 20002. Phone: (202)546-1713 Fax: (202)546-1638 E-mail: crmagazine@aol.com Monthly. $24.00 per year.

Consumers Union of United States.

Consumers United for Rail Equity., 1050 Thomas Jefferson St. NW, 6th Fl. Washington, DC 20007. Phone: (202)298-1844 Fax: (202)338-2416 E-mail: rcw@vnf.com • URL: http:// www.railcure.org • Coalition of railroad shippers that are captive to a single railroad for their transportation needs.

Consumption on the Woolen System and Worsted Combing. U. S. Bureau of the Census, 4700 Silver Hill Rd. Washington, DC 20233-0001. E-mail: comments@census.gov • URL: http://www.census.gov • Quarterly and annual. Provides data on consumption of fibers in woolen and worsted spinning mills, by class of fibers and end use. (Current Industrial Reports, MQ-22D.)

Contact Lens Association of Ophthalmologists., c/o John S. Massare, 721 Papworth Ave., Ste. 206 Metairie, LA 70005. Phone: (504)835-3937 Fax: (504)833-5884 E-mail: eyes@ clao.org • URL: http://www.clao.org • Affiliated with American Academy of Ophthalmology, American Medical Association and American National Standards Institute.

Contact Lens Manufacturers Association., PO Box 29398 Lincoln, NE 68529. Phone: 800-344-9060 or (402)465-4122 Fax: (402)465-4187 E-mail: clmassociation@aol.com • URL: http://www.clma.net • Represents contact lens laboratories, material, solution and equipment manufacturers in the United States and abroad. Aims to increase awareness and utilization of custom manufactured contact lenses.

Contact Lens Manufacturers Association: Directory of Members. Contact Lens Manufacturers Association, PO Box 368 Kensington, MD 20895-0368. Phone: 800-343-5367 or (301)654-2229 Annual. Membership.

Contact Lens Society of America.

Contact Lens Spectrum. Boucher Communications, Inc., 1300 Virginia Dr., Suite 400 Fort Washington, PA 19034. Phone: (215)643-8000 Fax: (215)643-8099 20 times a year. $43.00 per year. Provides news and information on clinical issues and the contact lens industry. Incorporates *Contact Lens Forum*.

Containerization and Intermodal Institute., 195 Fairfield Ave., Suite 4D West Caldwell, NJ 07006. Phone: (973)226-0160 Fax: (973)364-1212 E-mail: cii@bsya.com Formerly Containerization Institute.

Contemporary Advertising. William F. Arens. McGraw-Hill, 1221 Ave. of the Americas New York, NY 10020. Phone: 800-722-4726 or (212)512-2000 Fax: (212)512-4502 E-mail: customer.service@mcgraw-hill.com • URL: http://www. mcgraw-hill.com • 2001. $71.00. Eighth edition. Includes CD-ROM. (Marketing Series).

Contemporary Architects. Available from Gale Cengage Learning, 27500 Drake Rd. Farmington Hills, MI 48331-3535. Phone: 800-877-GALE or (248)699-GALE Fax: 800-414-5043 E-mail: gale.galeord@cengage.com • URL: http://gale. cengage.com • 1994. $190.00. Third edition. Published by St. James Press. Living architects of the world and influential architects of earlier times.

Contemporary Artists. Available from Gale Cengage Learning, 27500 Drake Rd. Farmington Hills, MI 48331-3535. Phone: 800-877-GALE or (248)699-GALE Fax: 800-414-5043 E-mail: gale.galeord@cengage.com • URL: http://gale. cengage.com • 2002. $265.00. Fifth edition. Published by St. James Press. International coverage.

Contemporary Authors. Gale Cengage Learning, 27500 Drake Rd. Farmington Hills, MI 48331-3535. Phone: 800-877-GALE or (248)699-4253 Fax: 800-414-5043 E-mail: gale. galeord@cengage.com • URL: http://gale.cengage.com • Annual. $180.00. Provides biographical information on over 112,000 modern authors, including novelists, nonfiction writers, poets, play wrights, journalists, and scriptwriters.

Contemporary Authors on CD-ROM. Gale Cengage Learning, 27500 Drake Rd. Farmington, MI 48331-3535. Phone: 800-877-GALE or (248)699-GALE Fax: 800-414-5043 or (248)699-8069 E-mail: galeord@gale.com • URL: http:// gale.cengage.com • Semiannual. $795.00 per year. Provides CD-ROM biographical and bibliographical information on about 100,000 modern authors. Includes novelists, nonfiction writers, poets, playwrights, screenwriters, editors, and journalists.

Contemporary Business: Alternate Study Guide. Louis E. Boone. Harcourt College Publishers, City Center Tower Two, 301 Commerce St., Suite 3700 Fort Worth, TX 76102. Phone: 800-354-9706 or (817)334-7500 Fax: (817)334-7844 E-mail: wlittle@harbrace.com • URL: http://www.harcourtcollege. com • 2002. 10th edition. Price on application. (Management Series).

Contemporary Business Communication. Scot Ober. Houghton Mifflin Co., 215 Park Ave. S New York, NY 10003. Phone:

(212)420-5800 Fax: 800-445-6991 or (212)420-5855 • URL: http://www.hmco.com • 2003. $106.36. Fifth edition.

Contemporary Business Law and the Legal Environment: Principles, Cases and Regulation. James Highsmith. McGraw-Hill, 1221 Ave. of the Americas New York, NY 10020. Phone: 800-722-4726 or (212)512-2000 Fax: (212)512-4502 E-mail: customer.service@mcgraw-hill.com • URL: http://www.mcgraw-hill.com • 1994. $32.81. Fifth edition.

Contemporary Business Mathematics. Southam Dietz. McGraw-Hill, 2 Penn Plz. New York, NY 10121. Phone: 800-772-4726 or (212)904-2000 • URL: http://www.mcgrawhill.com • 2001. $91.95. 13th edition. (General Business and Business Education Series).

Contemporary Designers. Gale Cengage Learning, 27500 Drake Rd. Farmington Hills, MI 48331-3535. Phone: 800-877-GALE or (248)699-4253 Fax: 800-414-5043 E-mail: gale. galeord@cengage.com • URL: http://gale.cengage.com • 1997. $190.00. Third edition. Profiles the careers and accomplishments of 685 designers from throughout the world.

Contemporary Drug Problems. Federal Legal Publications, Inc., 157 Chambers St. New York, NY 10007. Phone: (212)619-4949 E-mail: flp@bestweb.com Quarterly. Individuals, $30.00 per year; institutions, $36.00 per year.

Contemporary Fashion. St. James Press, PO Box 9187, PO Box 9187 Farmington Hills, MI 48331-9187. Phone: 800-877-4253 or (248)699-4253 Fax: 800-414-5043 or (248)699-8035 E-mail: gale.galeord@cengage.com • URL: http://gale. cengage.com • Publication includes: Contact information for designers featured. Entries include: name, address, phone, and Web site. Principal content of publication is essays evaluating contemporary clothing and accessories designers worldwide.

Contemporary Long-Term Care—Fax Directory. VNU Business Media, 770 Broadway New York, NY 10003-9595. Phone: (646)654-4420 Fax: (646)654-4420 E-mail: bmcomm@ meetingnews.com • URL: http://www.vnubusinessmedia. com • Covers: Approximately 900 manufacturers and suppliers of products and services for long-term patient care in nursing homes and retirement communities. Entries include: Company name, address, phone, fax.

Contemporary Longterm Care. Leisure Publications, 4160 Wilshire Blvd. Los Angeles, CA 90010. Phone: 800-222-7209 or (323)964-4800 Fax: (323)964-5273 E-mail: fred@ cltcmag.com • URL: http://www.cltcmag.com • Monthly. Free to qualified personnel. Edited for the long term health care industry, including retirement centers with life care, continuing care communities, and nursing homes.

Contemporary Musicians: Profiles of the People in Music. Available from Gale Cengage Learning, 27500 Drake Rd. Farmington Hills, MI 48331-3535. Phone: 800-877-GALE or (248)699-GALE Fax: 800-414-5043 E-mail: gale.galeord@ cengage.com • URL: http://gale.cengage.com • Annual. $4,305.00. 41 volumes in print. $105.00 per volume.

Contemporary Photographers. Available from Gale Cengage Learning, 27500 Drake Rd. Farmington Hills, MI 48331-3535. Phone: 800-877-GALE or (248)699-GALE Fax: 800-414-5043 E-mail: gale.galeord@cengage.com • URL: http:// gale.cengage.com • 1995. $190.00. Third edition. Provides biographical and critical information on more than 850 international photographers.

Contemporary Sales Force Management. Tony Carter. Haworth Press, Inc., 10 Alice St. Binghamton, NY 13904-1580. Phone: 800-429-6784 or (607)722-5857 Fax: 800-895-0582 or (607)722-1424 E-mail: getinfo@haworthpressinc.com • URL: http://www.haworthpressinc.com • 1997. $49.95. Emphasis is on motivation of sales personnel. Includes case studies.

Contemporary Supervision: Managing People and Technology. Betty R. Ricks and others. McGraw-Hill, 1221 Ave. of the Americas New York, NY 10020. Phone: 800-722-4726 or (212)512-2000 Fax: (212)512-4502 E-mail: customer. service@mcgraw-hill.com • URL: http://www.mcgraw-hill. com • 1994. $68.75. Second edition. (Management Series).

Contemporary Theatre, Film, and Television. Gale Cengage Learning, 27500 Drake Rd. Farmington Hills, MI 48331-3535. Phone: 800-877-GALE or (248)699-4253 Fax: 800-414-5043 E-mail: gale.galeord@cengage.com • URL: http:// gale.cengage.com • 2003. Three volumes. $185.00 per volume. Previous volumes available. Provides detailed biographical and career information on more than 11,000 currently popular performers, directors, writers, producers, designers, managers, choreographers, technicians, composers, executives, dancers, and critics.

Contemporary Women's Issues. Gale Cengage Learning, 27500 Drake Rd. Farmington Hills, MI 48331-3535. Phone: 800-877-GALE or (248)699-4253 Fax: 800-414-5043 or (248)699-8069 E-mail: galeord@galegroup.com • URL: http://www.galegroup.com • Provides fulltext articles online from 150 periodicals and a wide variety of additional sources relating to economic, legal, social, political, education, health, and other women's issues. Time span is 1992 to date. Weekly updates. Inquire as to online cost and availability. (Also available in a CD-ROM version.)

Content Delivery and Storage Association., 182 Nassau St., Ste. 204 Princeton, NJ 08542-7005. Phone: (609)279-1700 Fax: (609)279-1999 E-mail: info@contentdeliveryandstorage.org • URL: http://www.recordingmedia.org • Serves as the advocate for the growth and development of all recording media and as a forum for the exchange of information regarding global trends and innovations. Provides members an opportunity to join forces and be a strong industry voice allowing them to grow and expand their business. Encompasses all facets of the recording media.

Contests for Students: All You Need to Know to Enter and Win 600 Contests. Gale Cengage Learning, 27500 Drake Rd. Farmington Hills, MI 48331-3535. Phone: 800-877-GALE or (248)699-4253 Fax: 800-414-5043 E-mail: gale.galeord@cengage.com • URL: http://gale.cengage.com • 1999. $65.00. Second edition. details 600 regional, national, and international contests for elementary, junior high, and high school students.

Continental Europe Market Guide. Dun and Bradstreet Corp., 103 JFK Pky. Short Hills, NJ 07078. Phone: 800-234-3867 E-mail: custserv@dnb.com • URL: http://www.dnb.com • Semiannual. $1,600.00 per two volume set. Lists about 220,000 firms in 21 European countries. Includes financial strength and credit ratings. Geographic arrangement.

Contingencies: The Magazine of the Actuarial Profession. American Academy of Actuaries, 1100 17th St. NW, 7th Fl. Washington, DC 20036. Phone: (202)223-8196 Fax: (202)872-1948 E-mail: lawson@actuary.org • URL: http://www.actuary.org • Bimonthly. $30.00 per year. Provides non-technical articles on the actuarial aspects of insurance, employee benefits, and pensions.

Contingent Workforce: Business and Legal Strategies. American Lawyer Media, Inc., 105 Madison Ave. New York, NY 10016. Phone: 800-888-8300 or (212)779-9200 Fax: (212)481-8110 E-mail: lawcatalog@amlaw.com • URL: http://www.lawcatalog.com/ • Looseleaf. $169.00. Updated as needed. Covers the legal, employee benefit, and taxation aspects of alternative work arrangements (temporary employees, independent contractors, outsourcing). (Law Journal Press).

Continnum and the Publishers Association Directory of Publishing. Continnum, 22883 Quicksilver Dr. Dulles, VA 20166. Phone: 800-561-7704 or (703)661-1501 Annual. $175.00. Published in London. Provides detailed profiles of United Kingdom and British Commonwealth publishers and agencies. Includes "publishers' turnover figures."

Continuing Care News: Supporting the Transition into Post Hospital Care. Stevenson Publishing Corp., 5151 Beltline Rd., 10th Fl. Dallas, TX 75254. Phone: (972)687-6700 Fax: (972)687-6769 • URL: http://www.stevenspublishing.com • Monthly. $99.00 per year. Topics include insurance, legal issues, health business news, ethics, and case management. Includes annual *Buyer's Guide*.

Continuing Care Retirement Communities. Sylvia Sherwood and others. Johns Hopkins University Press, 2715 N. Charles St. Baltimore, MD 21218-4363. Phone: 800-537-5487 or (410)516-6900 Fax: (410)516-6968 • URL: http://www.press.jhu.edu • 1996. $44.00. Presents research based on a study of continuing care retirement communities and 2,000 residents of the communities.

The Contract and Fee-Setting Guide for Consultants and Professionals. Howard L. Shenson. John Wiley and Sons, Inc., 111 River St. Hoboken, NJ 07030. Phone: 800-225-5945 or (201)748-6000 Fax: (201)748-6088 E-mail: info@wiley.com • URL: http://www.wiley.com • 1990. $175.00.

Contract Management. National Contract Management Association, 1912 Woodford Rd. Vienna, VA 22182-3728. Phone: 800-344-8096 or (703)448-9231 • URL: http://www.ncmahq.org • Monthly. $72.00 per year.

Contract Services Association of America., 1000 Wilson Blvd., Ste. 1800 Arlington, VA 20009. Phone: (703)243-2020 Fax: (703)243-3601 E-mail: info@csa-dc.org • URL: http://www.csa-dc.org • Formerly National Council of Technical Services Industries.

Contract: The Business Magazine of Commercial and Institutional Interior Design, and Architecture, Planning and Construction. VNU Business Media, 770 Broadway New York, NY 10003-9595. Phone: 800-344-7119 or (646)654-4500 Fax: (646)654-7212 • URL: http://www.vnubusinessmedia.com • Monthly. $94.00 per year. Firms engaged in specifying furniture and furnishings for commercial installations. Formerly *Contract Design*.

Contracting with the Federal Government. Margaret M. Worthington and Louis P. Goldsman. John Wiley and Sons, Inc., 111 River St. Hoboken, NJ 07030. Phone: 800-225-5945 or (201)748-6000 Fax: (201)748-6088 E-mail: info@wiley.com • URL: http://www.wiley.com • 1998. $165.00. Fourth edition. Tells how to acquire federal contracts and execute them profitably.

Contractors Co-Op Council., 164 N Main St. Porterville, CA 93257. Phone: (559)784-5394 Fax: (714)891-5616 E-mail: clmassociation@aol.com Custom drapery merchants. Organizes cooperative advertising, warehousing, and purchasing. Sponsors workshops on computers, bookkeeping, sales, and manufacturing. Compiles statistics.

Contractors Pump Bureau, 6737 W Washington St., Ste. 2400 Milwaukee, WI 53214-5647. Phone: (866)236-0442 or (414)272-0943 Fax: (414)272-1170 E-mail: info@aem.org • URL: http://www.aem.org/CBC/ProdSpec/CPB • A bureau of the Association of Equipment Manufacturers. Manufacturers of pumping machinery and engines for the construction industry; suppliers to the manufacturers. Works toward the standardization of sizes and capacities of contractors' pumps.

Contracts for the Film and Television Industry. Mark Litwak. Silman-James Press, 3624 Shannon Rd. Los Angeles, CA 90027. Phone: (323)661-9922 Fax: (323)661-9933 E-mail: silmanjamespress@earthlink.com • URL: http://www.silmanjamespress.com • 1999. $35.95. Second expanded edition. Contains a wide variety of sample entertainment contracts. Includes material on rights, employment, joint ventures, music, financing, production, distribution, merchandising, and the retaining of attorneys.

Control Engineering Buyers Guide. Reed Business Information, 360 Park Ave., S New York, NY 10010. Phone: 800-446-6551 or (646)746-6400 Fax: (646)746-7028 E-mail: corporatecommunications@reedbusiness.com • URL: http://www.reedbusiness.com • Annual. Price on application. Contains specifications, prices, and manufacturers' listings for computer software, as related to control engineering.

Control Engineering: Covering Control, Instrumentation and Automation Systems Worldwide. Reed Business Information, 360 Park Ave., S New York, NY 10010. Phone: 800-446-6551 or (646)746-6400 Fax: (646)746-7028 E-mail: corporatecommunications@reedbusiness.com • URL: http://www.reedbusiness.com • Monthly. $109.90 per year.

Control Handbook. William S. Levine, editor. CRC Press LLC, 2000 NW Corporate Blvd. Boca Raton, FL 33431. Phone: 800-272-7737 or (561)994-0555 Fax: 800-374-3401 or (561)989-9732 E-mail: orders@crcpress.com • URL: http://www.crcpress.com • 1996. $179.95. Contains about 140 articles by various authors on automatic control, control theory, and control engineering. (Electrical Engineering Handbook Series).

Control of Banking. Prentice Hall PTR, 240 Frisch Ct. Paramus, NJ 07652. Phone: 800-282-0693 Fax: 800-445-6991 • URL: http://www.phptr.com • Two looseleaf volumes. $465.00 per year. Periodic supplementation. Banking rules and regulations affecting day-to-day operations and financial practices of banks.

Controllership: The Work of the Managerial Accountant. James D. Willson and others. John Wiley and Sons, Inc., 111 River St. Hoboken, NJ 07030. Phone: 800-225-5945 or (201)748-6000 Fax: (201)748-6088 E-mail: info@wiley.com • URL: http://www.wiley.com • 1999. $220.00. Sixth edition. *2002 Cumulative Supplement*, $70.00.

Convenience Caterers and Food Manufacturers Association., 1205 Spartan Dr. Madison Heights, MI 48071. Phone: 800-620-6422 or (248)982-5379 Fax: (248)582-3268 E-mail: ccfma@sbcglobal.net • URL: http://www.mobilecaterers.com • Firms and corporations engaged in the mobile catering business and in any other business catering to industrial feeding by mobile equipment; associate members are suppliers and manufacturers. Deals with common intra-industry problems through exchange of ideas, advice on legal problems, and safety standards and licensing regulations.

Convenience Food Store. Entrepreneur Media, Inc., 2445 McCabe Way Irvine, CA 92614. Phone: 800-421-2300 or (949)261-2325 Fax: (949)261-0234 E-mail: entmag@entrepreneur.com • URL: http://www.entrepreneur.com • Looseleaf. $59.50. A practical guide to starting a convenience food store. Covers profit potential, start-up costs, market size evaluation, owner's time required, site selection, lease negotiation, pricing, accounting, advertising, promotion, etc. (Start-Up Business Guide No. E1173.)

Convenience Store Decisions. Donohue-Meehan Publishing Co., Two Greenwood Square, Suite 410, 3331 Street Rd. Bensalem, PA 19020-2023. Phone: (215)245-4555 Fax: (215)245-4060 Monthly. $60.00 per year. Edited for headquarters and regional management personnel of convenience store chains.

Convenience Store News Buyers Guide. Bill Communications, 770 Broadway New York, NY 10003. Phone: 800-266-4712 or (646)654-4500 Fax: (646)654-7212 E-mail: cpamplin@csnews.com • URL: http://www.vnubusinessmedia.com • Annual. $200.00. Provides information on convenience store chains, including service station stores, and suppliers of products, equipment, and services to convenience stores.

Convenience Store News: The Information Source for the Industry. VNU Business Media, 770 Broadway New York, NY 10003-9595. Phone: 800-344-7119 or (646)654-4500 Fax: (646)654-7212 URL: http://www.vnubusinessmedia.com • 15 times a year. Free to qualified personnel; others, $89.00 per year. Contains news of industry trends and merchandising techniques.

Convergence: The Journal of Research Into New Media Technologies. Reed Business Information, 360 Park Ave., S New York, NY 1001. Phone: (646)746-6400 • URL: http://www.reedbusiness.com • Monthly. Individuals, $40.00 per year; institutions, $160.00 per year. Covers the merging of communications technologies. Includes telecommunications networks, interactive TV, multimedia, wireless phone service, and electronic information services.

Converted Flexible Packaging. Available from MarketResearch.com, 641 Ave. of the Americas, Third Floor New York, NY 10011. Phone: 800-298-5699 or (212)807-2629 Fax: (212)807-2716 E-mail: order@marketresearch.com • URL: http://www.marketresearch.com • 2001. $3,700.00. Published by the Freedonia Group. Market data with forecasts to the year 2006. Covers plastic, paper, and foil packaging for food and non-food products.

Convertible Securities: The Latest Instruments, Portfolio Strategies, and Valuation Analysis. John P. Calamos. McGraw-Hill, 1221 Ave. of the Americas New York, NY 10020. Phone: 800-772-4726 or (212)512-2000 Fax: (212)512-4502 E-mail: customer.service@mcgraw-hill.com • URL: http://www. mcgraw-hill.com • 1998. $65.00. Second revised edition. (Irwin Library of Investment and Finance Series).

Conveyor Equipment Manufacturers Association., 6724 Lone Oak Blvd. Naples, FL 34109. Phone: (239)514-3441 Fax: (239)514-3470 E-mail: cema@cemanet.org • URL: http://www.cemanet.org • Manufacturers and engineers of conveyors and conveying systems, and portable and stationary machinery used in the transportation of raw materials and finished products in warehouses and on assembly line operations. Aims to standardize design, manufacture, and application of conveying machinery and component parts.

Cookie and Snack Bakers Association., P.O. Box 37320 Cleveland, TN 37320. Phone: (423)472-1561 Members are bakers of snacks and cookies.

Cooking for Fifty: The Complete Reference and Cookbook. Chet Holden. John Wiley and Sons, Inc., 111 River St. Hoboken, NJ 07030. Phone: 800-225-5945 or (201)748-6000 Fax: (201)748-6088 E-mail: info@wiley.com • URL: http://www.wiley.com • 1993. $95.00. Discusses commercial cooking techniques and includes 300 "contemporary" recipes for institutional and commercial cooks.

Cooking for Profit. CP Publishing, Inc., P.O. Box 267 Fond du Lac, WI 54936-0267. Phone: (920)923-3700 Fax: (920)923-6805 Monthly. $25.00 per year. The challenge of operations management in the food service industry.

Cookware Manufacturers Association., PO Box 531335, P.O. Box 531335 Birmingham, AL 35253-1335. Phone: (205)823-3448 Fax: (205)823-3449 E-mail: hrushing@usit.net • URL: http://www.cookware.org • Represents manufacturers of cooking utensils and cooking accessories. Compiles statistics.

Cooperative Housing Bulletin. National Association of Housing Cooperatives, 1707 H St., Ste. 201 Washington, DC 20006. Phone: (202)737-0797 Fax: (202)783-7869 E-mail: info@coophousing.org • URL: http://www.coophousing.org • Bimonthly. $75.00 per year. Includes *Cooperative Housing Journal*.

Cooperative Program in Metallurgy.

Coordinated Science Laboratory. University of Illinois at Urbana-Champaign

Copier. Orion Research Corp., 14555 N. Scottsdale Rd., Suite 330 Scottsdale, AZ 85254-3457. Phone: 800-844-0759 Fax: 800-375-1315 E-mail: orion@bluebook.com • URL: http://www.netzone.com • Annual. $39.00. Quotes retail and wholesale prices of used office equipment. Original list prices and years of manufacture are also shown. Formerly *Orion Office Equipment Blue Book*.

Coping with Difficult People. Robert N. Bramson. Bantam Dell Publishing Group, 1540 Broadway New York, NY 10036-4094. Phone: 800-223-6834 or (212)782-9000 Fax: (212)492-9698 • URL: http://www.randomhouse.com • 1981. $7.50.

Copper and Brass Fabricators Council., 1050 17th St., N.W., Suite 440 Washington, DC 20036. Phone: (202)833-8575 Fax: (202)331-8267 E-mail: copbrass@aol.com Formerly Copper and Brass Fabricators Foreign Trade Association

Copper and Brass Servicenter Association.

Copper Development Association., 260 Madison Ave. New York, NY 10016. Phone: 800-CDA-DATA or (212)251-7200 Fax: (212)251-7234 E-mail: questions@cda.copper.org • URL: http://www.copper.org • Represents U.S. and foreign copper mining, smelting and refining companies, U.S. fabricating companies such as brass and wire mills, foundries, and ingot makers. Seeks to expand the uses and applications and to broaden the markets of copper and copper products. Functions in groups or divisions corresponding to principal market areas such as transportation, building construction, electrical and electronic products, industrial machinery and equipment, and consumer and general products. Provides technical service to users of copper and copper alloy products. Has industrywide responsibility for market statistics and research. Maintains 10 field offices in the U.S.

Copy Editor: Language News for the Publishing Profession. McMurry Newsletters, 1010 E. Missouri Ave. Phoenix, AZ 85014. Phone: 888-626-8779 or (602)395-5850 • URL: http://www.copyeditor.com • Bimonthly. $69.00 per year. Newsletter for professional copy editors and proofreaders. Includes such items as "Top Ten Resources for Copy Editors."

The Copyright Book: A Practical Guide. William S. Strong. MIT Press, Five Cambridge Ctr. Cambridge, MA 02142-1493. Phone: 800-356-0343 or (617)253-2864 Fax: (617)253-6779 • URL: http://www.mitpress.mit.edu • 1999. $34.95. Fifth edition.

Copyright Bulletin: Quarterly Review. Available from Bernan Associates, 4611-F Assembly Dr. Lanham, MD 20706-4391. Phone: 800-274-4447 or (301)459-7666 Fax: 800-865-3450 or (301)459-0056 E-mail: query@bernan.com • URL: http://www.bernan.com • Quarterly. Available online only.

Copyright Clearance Center., 222 Rosewood Dr. Danvers, MA 01923. Phone: (978)750-8400 Fax: (978)646-8600 E-mail: info@copyright.com • URL: http://www.copyright.com • Facilitates compliance with U.S. copyright law. Provides licensing systems for the reproduction and distribution of copyrighted materials in print and electronic formats throughout the world. Manages rights relating to over 1.75 million works and represents more than 9600 publishers and hundreds of thousands of authors and other creators, directly or through their representatives.

Copyright: Current Issues and Laws. John V. Martin, editor. Nova Science Publishers, Inc., 400 Oser Ave., Suite 1600

Hauppauge, NY 11788-3619. Phone: (631)231-7269 Fax: (631)231-8175 E-mail: novascience@earthlink.net • URL: http://www.novapublishers.com • 2002. $59.00. Contains articles by various authors on many aspects of copyright, such as copyright term extension, public domain, fair use, infringement, Internet issues, and online music delivery.

Copyright Essentials for Librarians and Educators. Kenneth D. Crews. American Library Association, 50 E Huron St. Chicago, IL 60611-2795. Phone: 800-545-2433 or (312)944-6780 Fax: (312)440-9374 E-mail: ala@ala.org • URL: http://www.ala.org • 2000. $45.00. Explains the basics of modern copyright law. Includes checklists and summaries of legislation.

Copyright Handbook: How to Protect and Use Written Works. Stephen Fishman. Nolo Press-Occidental, 501 Mission St., Suite 2 Santa Cruz, CA 95060. Phone: 800-992-6656 or (831)466-9922 Fax: (831)466-9927 E-mail: inbox@nolotech.com • URL: http://www.nolotech.com • 2002. Sixth edition. Price on application. Includes sample forms and copyright agreements.

Copyright Law in Business and Practice. John W. Hazard. West Group, 610 Opperman Dr. Eagan, MN 55123. Phone: 800-328-4880 or (651)687-7000 E-mail: bookstore@westgroup.com • URL: http://www.westgroup.com • Semiannual. $274.00 per year. Two looseleaf volumes.

Copyright Law '99 and Beyond Handbook. Glasser LegalWorks, 150 Clove Rd. Little Falls, NJ 07424. Phone: 800-308-1700 or (973)890-0008 Fax: (973)890-0042 E-mail: legalwks@aol.com • URL: http://www.glasserlegalworks.com • 1999. $95.00. Examines current trends in copyright litigation. Based on a 1999 seminar held in cooperation with the U. S. Copyright Office.

Copyright Law of the United States of America. Available from U. S. Government Printing Office, Washington, DC 20402. Phone: (202)512-1800 Fax: (202)512-2250 E-mail: gpoaccess@gpo.gov • URL: http://www.access.gpo.gov • Annual. Issued by U. S. Copyright Office, Library of Congress. Provides the text of copyright law contained in Title 17 of the U. S. Code.

Copyright Law Reports. CCH, Inc., 2700 Lake Cook Rd. Riverwoods, IL 60015. Phone: 800-835-5224 or (847)267-7000 E-mail: cust_serv@cch.com • URL: http://www.cch.com • Monthly. $768.00 per year. Two looseleaf volumes.

Copyright, Patent, Trademark and Related State Doctrines; Cases and Materials on the Law of Intellectual Property. Paul Goldstein. Foundation Press, Inc., 395 Hudson St. New York, NY 10014. Phone: (212)367-6790 E-mail: gerry.gelke@westgroup.com • URL: http://www.fdpress.com • 2002. $80.50. Fifth edition. (University Casebook Series).

Copyright Primer for Librarians and Educators. Janis H. Bruwelheide. American Library Association, 50 E. Huron St. Chicago, IL 60611-2795. Phone: 800-545-2433 or (312)944-6780 Fax: (312)440-9374 E-mail: ala@ala.org • URL: http://www.ala.org • 1995. $25.00. Second edition.

Copyright Principles, Law, and Practice. Paul Goldstein. Aspen Publishers, Inc., 1185 Avenue of the Americas New York, NY 10036. Phone: 800-234-1660 or (212)597-0200 Fax: (212)597-0338 E-mail: customer.service@aspenpubl.com • URL: http://www.aspenpublishers.com • 1989. $375.00. Three volumes.

Copyright Society of the United States of America Journal. The Copyright Society of the United States of America, 325 7th Ave., Ste. 307 New York, NY 10001. Phone: (212)354-6401 Fax: (212)354-2847 E-mail: bpannone@csusa.org • URL: http://www.csusa.org • Quarterly. Individuals, $125.00 per year; nonprofit organizations, $50.00 per year; corporations, $500.00 per year.

The Copyright Society of the U.S.A.

Copyrights, Patents, and Trademarks: Protect Your Rights Worldwide. Hoyt L. Barber. McGraw-Hill, 1221 Ave. of the Americas New York, NY 10020. Phone: 800-722-4726 or (212)512-2000 Fax: (212)512-4502 E-mail: customer.service@mcgraw-hill.com • URL: http://www.mcgraw-hill.com • 1996. $32.95. Second edition.

Copywriter's Handbook. Robert W. Bly. Henry Holt & Co., Inc., 115 W 18th St. New York, NY 10011. Phone: (212)886-9200 Fax: (212)633-0748 E-mail: info@henryholt.com • URL: http://www.henryholt.com • 1990. $16.00.

Copywriting Secrets and Tactics: How to Put More Sell into All Your Copy. Herschell G. Lewis. Dartnell Corp., 360 Hiatt Dr. Palm Beach, FL 33418. Phone: 800-621-5463 or (561)622-6520 Fax: 800-327-8635 or (561)622-2423 E-mail: cusserv@lrp.com • URL: http://www.dartnell.corp.com • $91.50. Looseleaf service.

Corbin on Contracts. LexisNexis, 125 Park Ave. New York, NY 10017. Phone: 800-437-8674 or (212)309-8100 • URL: http://www.lexisnexis.com • $999.00. 14 volumes. Includes looseleaf volume and cumulative *Supplement*.

Cordage Institute., 994 Old Eagle School Rd., Ste. 1019 Wayne, PA 19087. Phone: (610)971-4854 Fax: (610)971-4859 E-mail: info@ropecord.com • URL: http://www.ropecord.com • Represents manufacturers of natural and synthetic fiber cordage, in constructions, industry suppliers, consultants, and machinery manufacturers. Offers standard technical information and educational programs. Operates speakers' bureau. Compiles statistics.

The Core Business Web: A Guide to Key Information Sources. Gary W. White, editor. Haworth Press, Inc., 10 Alice St. Binghamton, NY 13904-1580. Phone: 800-429-6784 or (607)722-5857 Fax: 800-895-0582 or (607)722-1424 E-mail: orders@haworthpress.com • URL: http://www.haworthpress.com • 2003. $49.95. Business librarians select Web sites in 25 areas of business, such as banking, e-commerce, investments, tourism, and small business.

CORE Magazine. Congress of Racial Equality. CORE Publications, 30 Cooper Square, No. 9 New York, NY 10003-7151. Phone: (212)598-4000 Fax: (212)982-0184 Quarterly. $10.00 per year.

CoreNet Global., 260 Peachtree St., Ste. 1500 Atlanta, GA 30303-1237. Phone: 800-726-8111 or (404)589-3200 Fax: (404)589-3201 E-mail: mark.tamburro@nokia.com • URL: http://www.corenetglobal.org • Executives, attorneys, real estate department heads, architects, engineers, analysts, researchers, and anyone responsible for the management, administration, and operation of national and regional real estate departments of national and international corporations. Encourages professionalism within corporate real estate through education and communication; protects the interests of corporate realty in dealing with adversaries, public or private; maintains contact with other real estate organizations; publicizes the availability of fully qualified members to the job market. Conducts seminars, including concentrated workshops on the corporate real estate field. Compiles statistics; sponsors competitions; maintains biographical archives and placement service.

Corn and Soybean Digest. American Soybean Association. Primedia Business Magazines and Media, 7900 International Dr., Ste. 300 Minneapolis, MN 55425. Phone: 800-795-5445 or (952)851-8329 Fax: (952)851-4601 E-mail: subs@primediabusines.com • URL: http://www.primediabusiness.com • 11 times a year. $25.00 per year. Provides high acreage farmers who grow soy beans in rotation with other crops timely production, marketing and management information.

Corn Annual. Corn Refiners Association, Inc., 1701 Pennsylvania Ave., N.W., Suite 950 Washington, DC 20006. Phone: (202)331-1634 Fax: (202)331-2054 E-mail: details@corn.org • URL: http://www.corn.org • Annual. Single copies free.

Corn: Origin, History, Technology, and Production. C. Wayne Smith and others, editors. John Wiley and Sons, Inc., 111 River St. Hoboken, NJ 07030. Phone: 800-225-5945 or (201)748-6000 Fax: (201)748-6088 E-mail: info@wiley.com • URL: http://www.wiley.com • 2002. $250.00. (Crop Science Series.)

Corn Refiners Association., 1701 Pennsylvania Ave., Ste. 950 Washington, DC 20006. Phone: (202)331-1634 Fax: (202)331-2054 E-mail: info@ropecord.com • URL: http://www.corn.org • Corn refining firms that manufacture corn starches, sugars, syrups, oils, feed and alcohol by wet process.

The Cornell Hotel and Restaurant Administration Quarterly. Cornell University School of Hotel Administration. Sage Publications, Inc., 2455 Teller Rd. Thousand Oaks, CA 91320. Phone: 800-583-2665 or (805)499-0721 Fax: (805)499-0871 E-mail: info@sagepub.com • URL: http://www.sagepub.com/journal • Bimonthly. Individuals, $113.00 per year; institutions, $319.00 per year.

Corporate Acquisitions. ARCH Group, 55 Main St. Tiburon, CA 94920. Phone: (415)435-2175 Fax: (415)435-6310 E-mail: nrca@archgroup.org Description: Summaries of trends and analysis of transactions in corporate mergers and acquisitions. Recurring features include interviews, reports of meetings, book reviews, and companies listed for sale.

Corporate Acquisitions and Mergers. LexisNexis Matthew Bender, 1275 Broadway Albany, NY 12204. Phone: 800-424-4200 or (518)487-3000 Fax: (518)487-3584 E-mail: bookstore.support@lexisnexis.com • URL: http://www.bender.com • $1,286.00. Only available on CD-ROM. Four looseleaf volumes. Periodic supplementation. A guide to the antiturst, tax, corporate, securities and financial aspects of business combinations. Includes extensive forms, charts and tables.

Corporate Acquisitions, Mergers, and Divestitures. Lewis D. Solomon. Prentice Hall PTR, 240 Frisch Ct. Paramus, NJ 07652. Phone: 800-282-0693 Fax: 800-445-6991 • URL: http://www.phptr.com • Looseleaf. Periodic supplementation. Price on application. Includes how to buy a company with its own assets or earnings.

Corporate Affiliations Plus. National Register Publishing, Reed Reference Publishing, 121 Chanlon Rd. New Providence, NJ 07974. Phone: 800-323-3288 or (908)464-6800 Fax: (908)665-6688 Quarterly. $1,995.00 per year. Provides CD-ROM discs corresponding to *Directory of Corporate Affiliations* and *Corporate Finance Bluebook*. Contains corporate financial services information and worldwide data on subsidiaries and affiliates.

Corporate Board Member: The Magazine for Directors of Public Companies. Board Member Inc., 5110 Maryland Way, Ste. 250 Brentwood, TX 37027. Phone: (615)309-3200 Fax: (615)371-0899 E-mail: boardmember@boardmember.com • URL: http://www.boardmember.com • Bimonthly. $155.00 per year. Edited for board members of publicly traded corporations. Includes such topics as liability, executive compensation, mergers, corporate administration, and management succession.

Corporate Bond Desk Reference: U. S. Buyside and Sellside Profiles. Capital Access International, The Reuter Bldg., 3 Times Square New York, NY 10036. Phone: 800-866-5987 or (646)223-4130 Fax: (646)223-4123 E-mail: emaxxinfo@lipper.reuters.com • URL: http://www.capital-access.com • Annual. $395.00. Provides "detailed buyside and sellside profiles and contacts" for the the corporate bond market. (Desk Reference Series, volume one.)

Corporate Compliance Series. Joseph E. Murphy and Paul H. Dawes. West Group, 610 Opperman Dr. Eagan, MN 55123. Phone: 800-328-4880 or (651)687-7000 Fax: 800-340-9378 E-mail: bookstore@westgroup.com • URL: http://www.westgroup.com • $1,210.00. 12 looseleaf volumes. Covers criminal and civil liability problems for corporations. Includes employee safety, product liability, pension requirements, securities violations, equal employment opportunity issues, intellectual property, employee hiring and firing, and other corporate compliance topics.

The Corporate Contributions Plan: From Strategy to Budget. The Conference Board Inc., 845 Third Ave. New York, NY 10022. Phone: (212)339-0345 Fax: (212)836-9740 • URL: http://www.conference-board.org • Annual. Members, $30.00, non-members, $120.00.

Corporate Control Alert; A Report on Current Changes for Corporate Control. American Lawyer Media Inc., 345 Park Ave., S. New York, NY 10010. Phone: 800-888-8300 or (212)779-9200 Fax: (212)481-8074 • URL: http://www.americanlawyermedia.com • Monthly. $1,595 per year. A monthly mergers and acquisitions newsletter.

Corporate Controller. RIA, 395 Hudson St. New York, NY 10014. Phone: 800-950-1216 or 800-431-9025 E-mail: riahome@riag.com • URL: http://www.riahome.com • Bimonthly. $130.00 per year.

Corporate Counselor. American Lawyer Media, Inc., 105 Madison Ave. New York, NY 10016. Phone: 800-888-8300 or (212)779-9200 Fax: (212)481-8110 E-mail: lawcatalog@amlaw.com • URL: http://www.lawcatalog.com/ • Monthly. $229.00 per year. Newsletter. Covers issues involved with managing the legal department of a corporation, including relations with outside counsel. (A Law Journal Newsletter, formerly published by Leader Publications).

Corporate Creativity: How Innovation and Improvement Actually Happen. Alan G. Robinson and Sam Stern. Berrett-Koehler Pulishers, Inc., 23 Montgomery St., Ste. 650 San Francisco, CA 94104. Phone: 800-929-2929 or (415)288-0260 Fax: (415)362-2512 E-mail: bkpub@bkpub.com • URL: http://www.bkpub.com • 1997. $29.95. Describes the six "essential elements" of business creativity.

Corporate Criminal Liability. Kathleen F. Brickley. West Group, 610 Opperman Dr. Eagan, MN 55123. Phone: 800-328-4880 or (651)687-7000 Fax: 800-340-9378 E-mail: bookstore@westgroup.com • URL: http://www.westgroup.com • Annual. $365.00 per year. Three looseleaf volumes. Discusses how the general principles of criminal law apply to the corporate world. Provides a detailed analysis of liability under major federal crime statutes.

Corporate Culture and Organizational Effectiveness. Daniel R. Denison. Aviat, Inc., 10101 Wexford Court South Lyon, MI 48178. Phone: 800-421-5323 or (313)663-2386 Fax: (313)663-3670 E-mail: aviat@chamber.branch.com 1997. Second edition. Price on application.

Corporate Cultures: The Rites and Rituals of Corporate Life. Terrance E. Deal and Allan Kennedy. Perseus Books Group, 387 Park Ave. S New York, MA 10016. Phone: 800-386-5656 or (212)340-8100 Fax: (212)340-8105 E-mail: westview.orders@perseusbooks.com • URL: http://www.perseusbooksgroups.com • 1982. $15.00.

Corporate Directors' Compensation. The Conference Board, 845 3rd Ave. New York, NY 10022. Phone: (212)339-0345 Fax: (212)836-9740 • URL: http://www.conference-board.org • Irregular.

The Corporate Directory of U.S. Public Companies. Walker's Research, LLC, 1650 Borel Pl., Ste. 130 San Mateo, CA 94402. Phone: 800-258-5737 or (650)341-1110 Fax: (650)341-2351 E-mail: walkersres@aol.com • URL: http://www.walkersresearch.com • Annual. $360.00. Two volumes. Contains information on more than 10,000 publicly-traded companies, including names of executives and major subsidiaries. Includes financial and stock data.

Corporate Dividends and Stock Repurchases. Barbara Black. West Group, 610 Opperman Dr. Eagan, MN 55123. Phone: 800-328-4880 or (651)687-7000 Fax: 800-340-9378 E-mail: bookstore@westgroup.com • URL: http://www.westgroup.com • Annual. $173.00. Looseleaf service. Covers the law relating to dividends in general, illegal dividends, stock splits, stock dividends, corporate repurchases, and other dividend topics.

Corporate EFT Report (Electronic Funds Transfer). Phillips International, Inc., 7811 Montrose Rd. Potomac, MD 20854. Phone: (301)340-2100 E-mail: information@phillips.com • URL: http://www.phillips.com • Biweekly. $695.00 per year. Newsletter on subject of electronic funds transfer.

Corporate Finance. Stephen A. Ross and others. McGraw-Hill, 1221 Ave. of the Americas New York, NY 10020. Phone: 800-722-4726 or (212)512-2000 Fax: (212)512-4502 E-mail: customer.service@mcgraw-hill.com • URL: http://www.mcgraw-hill.com • 2001. $76.25. Sixth edition. (Finance, Insurance, and Real Estate Series).

Corporate Finance and the Securities Laws. Charles J. Johnson and Joseph McLaughlin. Aspen Publishers, Inc., 200 Orchard Ridge Dr., Ste. 200 Gaithersburg, MD 20878. Phone: 800-234-1660 or (301)417-7500 E-mail: customer.service@aspenpubl.com • URL: http://www.aspenpublishers.com • 1997. $175.00. Second edition.

Corporate Financial Analysis: Decisions in a Global

Environment. Diana R. Harrington and Brent D. Wilson. McGraw-Hill, 1221 Ave. of the Americas New York, NY 10020. Phone: 800-722-4726 or (212)512-2000 Fax: (212)512-4502 E-mail: customer.service@mcgraw-hill.com • URL: http://www.mcgraw-hill.com • 1993. $50.00. Fourth edition.

Corporate Financial Distress and Bankruptcy: A Complete Guide to Predicting and Avoiding Distress and Profiting from Bankruptcy. Edward I. Altman. John Wiley and Sons, Inc., 111 River St. Hoboken, NJ 07030. Phone: 800-225-5945 or (201)748-6000 Fax: (201)748-6088 E-mail: info@wiley.com • URL: http://www.wiley.com • 1993. $110.00. Second edition. Provides practical advice on analyzing the financial position of a corporation, with case studies. Includes a discussion of the junk bond market. (Finance Series).

Corporate Financial Reporting: Text and Cases. David B. Hawkins. McGraw-Hill, 1221 Ave. of the Americas New York, NY 10020. Phone: 800-772-4726 or (212)512-2000 Fax: (212)512-4502 E-mail: customer.service@mcgraw-hill.com • URL: http://www.mcgraw-hill.com • 1997. $118.13. Fourth edition.

Corporate Financing Week: The Newsweekly of Corporate Finance, Investment Banking and M and A. Institutional Investor, Inc., Journals Group, 225 Park Ave., S New York, NY 10003. Phone: (212)224-3006 Fax: (212)224-3472 E-mail: info@iijournals.com • URL: http://www.iijournals.com • Weekly. $2,550.00 per year. Includes print and online editions. Newsletter for corporate finance officers. Emphasis is on debt and equity financing, mergers, leveraged buyouts, investment banking, and venture capital.

Corporate Foundation Profiles. Foundation Center, 79 Fifth Ave., 16th St. New York, NY 10003-3076. Phone: 800-424-9836 or (212)620-4230 Fax: (212)807-3677 E-mail: communications@foundationcenter.org • URL: http://www.fdncenter.org • Covers: 235 corporate foundations in the United States that award at least $1.25 million in grants each year. Entries include: financial data on 1,131 additional corporate foundations that each give at least $66,000 in grants every year. For detailed entries—Foundation name, address, phone, contact name, detailed information on parent company; names of major donors; purpose and activities, fields of interest, giving limitations, application guidelines; names of officers, trustees, and directors; publications; financial data. For others—Foundation name, state, financial data.

Corporate Fraud. Michael J. Comer. Ashgate Publishing Co., 101 Cherry St., Ste. 420 Burlington, VT 05401-4405. Phone: 800-535-9544 or (802)865-7641 Fax: (802)865-7847 E-mail: info@ashgate.com • URL: http://www.ashgate.com • 1997. Third edition. $139.95. Examines new risks of corporate fraud related to "electronic commerce, derivatives, computerization, empowerment, downsizing, and other recent developments." Covers fraud detection, prevention, and internal control systems. Published by Gower in England.

Corporate Giving Directory: Comprehensive Profiles of America's Major Corporate Foundations and Corporate Charitable Giving Programs. Gale Cengage Learning, 27500 Drake Rd. Farmington Hills, MI 48331-3535. Phone: 800-877-8238 or (248)699-4253 Fax: 800-414-5043 E-mail: gale.galeord@cengage.com • URL: http://gale.cengage.com • Annual. $550.00. Contains detailed descriptions of the philanthropic foundations of over 1,000 major U. S. corporations. Includes grant types, priorities for giving, recent grants, and advice on approaching corporate givers.

Corporate Growth. Princeton Research Institute, Western Management Center, P.O. Box 2702 Scottsdale, AZ 85252-2702. Phone: (609)396-0305 Monthly. $198.00 per year.

Corporate Growth Report. NVST Inc., 1100 Dexter Ave. N Seattle, WA 98109. Phone: 800-910-6878 or (206)676-3802 Fax: (206)273-7401 E-mail: info@nvst.com • URL: http://www.nvst.com • Description: Reports merger, acquisition, and divestiture activity, including in-depth analysis of major transactions. Publishes statistics on seller's and buyer's sales, profits, net worth, book value and earnings per share, and multiples of earnings, sales, and net worth compared with purchase price.

Corporate Image: A Practical Guide to the Implementation of a Corporate Identity Program. Nicholas Ind. Beekman Publishers, Inc., PO Box 888 Woodstock, NY 12498-0888. Phone: 888-233-5626 or (845)679-2300 Fax: (845)679-2301 E-mail: beekman@beekmanpublishers.com • URL: http://www.beekman.net • 1992. $44.95. Revised edition.

Corporate Image: Communicating Visions and Values. Allyson LaBorde, editor. The Conference Board, 845 3rd Ave. New York, NY 10022. Phone: (212)339-0345 Fax: (212)836-9740 • URL: http://www.conference-board.org • 1993. $100.00. (Report No. 1038).

The Corporate Intranet: Create and Manage an Internal Web for your Organization. Ryan Bernard. John Wiley and Sons, Inc., 111 River St. Hoboken, NJ 07030. Phone: 800-225-5945 or (201)748-6000 Fax: (201)748-6088 E-mail: info@wiley.com • URL: http://www.wiley.com • 1997. $29.99. Second edition.

Corporate Jobs Outlook! Plunkett Research Ltd., PO Drawer 541737 Houston, TX 77254-1737. Phone: (713)932-0000 Fax: (713)932-7080 E-mail: customersupport@plunkettresearch.com • URL: http://www.plunkettresearch.

com • Description: Provides information about corporate employment opportunities. Includes salaries, benefits, and hiring policies.

Corporate Library Excellence. James M. Matarazzo. Special Libraries Association, 1700 18th St., N. W. Washington, DC 20009-2514. Phone: (202)234-4700 Fax: (202)265-9317 E-mail: sla@sla.org • URL: http://www.sla.org • 1990. $28.00.

Corporate Liquidity: Management and Measurement. Jarl G. Kallberg and Kenneth L. Parkinson. McGraw-Hill, 1221 Ave. of the Americas New York, NY 10020. Phone: 800-722-4726 or (212)512-2000 Fax: (212)512-4502 E-mail: customer.service@mcgraw-hill.com • URL: http://www.mcgraw-hill.com • 1992. $67.95. Topics include cash management and risk.

Corporate Meeting and Event Planners. Douglas Publications L.L.C., 2807 N Parham Rd., Ste. 200 Richmond, VA 23294. Phone: 800-794-6086 or (804)762-9600 Fax: (804)217-8999 E-mail: info@douglaspublications.com • URL: http://www.douglaspublications.com • Covers: Approximately 11,200 corporations that hold regular, off-site meetings arranged by nearly 14,300 corporate meeting planners. Includes companies in the United States, Puerto Rico, the Virgin Islands, and Canada. Entries include: Company name, address, phone, fax; e-mail; URL; names and titles of key personnel; geographical area served; branch/subsidiary office name and address; products and/or services provided; type of business; number of meetings; months when meetings are held; number of attendees; type of facility used; whether company utilizes services of professional speakers or entertainers.

Corporate Officers and Directors Liability Litigation Reporter: The Twice Monthly National Journal of Record of Litigation Based on Fiduciary Responsibility. Andrews Publications, 175 Strafford Ave., Bldg 4, Suite 140 Wayne, PA 19087. Phone: 800-345-1101 or (215)225-0510 Fax: (215)225-0501 E-mail: customer@andrewspub.com • URL: http://www.andrewspub.com • Semimonthly. $890.00 per year. Newsletter. Provides reports on lawsuits in the area of corporate officers' fiduciary responsibility.

Corporate, Partnership, Estate, and Gift Taxation 1997. James W. Pratt and William Kulsrud, editors. McGraw-Hill, 1221 Ave. of the Americas New York, NY 10020. Phone: 800-772-4726 or (212)512-2000 Fax: (212)512-4502 E-mail: customer.service@mcgraw-hill.com • URL: http://www.mcgraw-hill.com • 1996. $71.25. 10th edition.

Corporate Philanthropy Report. Aspen Publishers Inc., 76 9th Ave., 7th Fl. New York, NY 10011. Phone: 800-638-8437 or (212)771-0600 Fax: (212)771-0885 E-mail: customersupport@plunkettresearch.com Description: Tracks charity donations by corporations.

Corporate Practice Series. BNA, Inc., 1231 25th St., NW Washington, DC 20037. Phone: 800-372-1033 E-mail: customercare@bna.com • URL: http://www.bna.com. • Weekly. $1,937.00 per year. Looseleaf service. Series of about 30 "portfolios" on various aspects of corporate law.

Corporate Public Issues and Their Management: The Executive Systems Approach to Public Policy Formation. Issue Action Publications, Inc., 207 Loudoun St. S.E. Leesburg, VA 22075-3115. Phone: (703)777-8450 Monthly. $235.00 per year. Newsletter.

The Corporate Secretary & Governance Professional. American Society of Corporate Secretaries Inc., 521 5th Ave. New York, NY 10175. Phone: (212)681-2000 Fax: (212)681-2005 E-mail: customersupport@plunkettresearch.com Description: News items of interest to the corporate secretary. Occasional articles covering SEC briefings, ASCS events, Chapter news, etc.

Corporate Secretary's Guide. CCH, Inc., 2700 Lake Cook Rd. Riverwoods, IL 60015. Phone: 800-835-5224 or (847)267-7000 E-mail: cust_serv@cch.com • URL: http://www.cch.com • Monthly. $645.00 per year. Looseleaf service. Includes newsletter and semimonthly updates. Published in consultation with the American Society of Corporate Secretaries. Covers the duties of corporate secretaries, especially as related to taxation and securities.

Corporate Social Challenge: Cases and Commentaries. James E. Stacey and Frederick D. Sturdivant, editors. McGraw-Hill, 1221 Ave. of the Americas New York, NY 10020. Phone: 800-772-4726 or (212)512-2000 Fax: (212)512-4502 E-mail: customer.service@mcgraw-hill.com • URL: http://www.mcgraw-hill.com • 1994. $41.95. Fifth edition.

Corporate Social Responsibility: Partners for Progress. Organization for Economic Cooperation and Development, OECD Washington Center, 2001 L St., N. W., Suite 650 Washington, DC 20036-4922. Phone: 800-456-6323 or (202)785-6323 Fax: (202)785-0350 E-mail: washington.contact@oecd.org • URL: http://www.oecd.org • 2001. $25.00. Reviews the function of corporate social responsibility at the local level and its influence on economic development.

Corporate Taxation. RIA, 395 Hudson St. New York, NY 10014. Phone: 800-950-1216 or 800-431-9025 E-mail: riahome@riag.com • URL: http://www.riahome.com • Bimonthly. $400.00 per year. Analysis and guidance for practitioners. Provides ongoing coverage of currently proposed tax reform bills. Formerly (Journal of Corporate Taxation).

Corporate Taxes: Worldwide Summaries. John Wiley and Sons, Inc., 111 River St. Hoboken, NJ 07030. Phone: 800-225-5945 or (201)748-6000 Fax: (201)748-6088 E-mail: info@wiley.

com • URL: http://www.wiley.com • 2003. $105.00. Summarizes the corporate tax regulations of more than 125 countries. Provides information useful for international tax planning and foreign investments.

Corporate Travel's Blackbook. CMP Books, 460 Park Ave., S, 9th Fl. New York, NY 10016. Phone: 800-950-1314 or (212)615-2247 E-mail: mfibooks@mfi.com • URL: http://www.books.mfi.com • Annual. $15.00. Included with subscription to *Corporate Travel*. Gives sources of corporate travel packages. Formerly *Corporate Travel-Directory*.

Corporate Valuation: Tools for Effective Appraisal and Decision Making. Stephen A. Ross and others. McGraw-Hill, 1221 Ave. of the Americas New York, NY 10020. Phone: 800-772-4726 or (212)512-2000 Fax: (212)512-4502 E-mail: customer.service@mcgraw-hill.com • URL: http://www.mcgraw-hill.com • 1994. $76.95. Discusses the four most widely-used corporate appraisal methods.

Corporate Yellow Book: Who's Who at the Leading U.S. Companies. Leadership Directions, Inc., 104 Fifth Ave. New York, NY 10011. Phone: (212)627-4140 Fax: (212)645-0931 E-mail: info@leadershipdirectories.com • URL: http://www.leadershipdirectories.com • Quarterly. $360.00 per year. Lists names and titles of over 42,000 key executives in major U. S. corporations. Includes four indexes: industry, personnel, geographic by state, and company/subsidiary. Companion volume to *Financial Yellow Book*.

Corporation and Partnership Tax Return Guide (1999 Taxes). Bill Massey and others. RIA, 395 Hudson St. New York, NY 10014. Phone: 800-950-1216 or (212)367-6300 E-mail: riahome@riag.com • URL: http://www.riahome.com • 2000. $16.50. Revised edition.

Corporation for Public Broadcasting.

Corporation Forms. Prentice Hall PTR, 240 Frisch Ct. Paramus, NJ 07652. Phone: 800-282-0693 Fax: 800-445-6991 • URL: http://www.phptr.com • Looseleaf. Periodic supplementation. Price on application.

Corporation-Partnership-Fiduciary Filled-in Tax Return Forms, 2002. CCH, Inc., 2700 Lake Cook Rd. Riverwoods, IL 60015. Phone: 800-835-5224 or (847)267-7000 E-mail: cust_serv@cch.com • URL: http://www.cch.com • 2002. $34.00.

Correctional News. Emlen Publications, Inc., 1241 Andersen Dr., Ste. N San Rafael, FL 94901. Phone: 800-965-8876 or (415)460-6185 Fax: (415)460-6288 E-mail: info@emlen.com • URL: http://www.correctionalnews.com • Bimonthly. Free to qualified personnel. Only available online.

The Corrections Market. Available from MarketResearch.com, 641 Ave. of the Americas, Fourth Floor New York, NY 10011. Phone: 800-298-5699 or (212)807-2629 Fax: (212)807-2642 E-mail: order@marketresearch.com • URL: http://www.marketresearch.com • 1996. $1,375.00. Market research report published by Packaged Facts. Covers the markets for prison food service, health care, private management, and telecommunications. Includes market growth projections.

Corrections Today. American Correctional Association, 4380 Forbes Blvd. Lanham, MD 20706. Phone: 800-222-5646 or (301)918-1800 Fax: (301)918-1900 E-mail: jackg@aca.org • URL: http://www.aca.org • Bimonthly. Free to members; non-members, $35.00 per year. Includes "Annual Architecture, Construction, and Design Issue" on prisons and other correctional facilities.

Corrosion Abstracts: Abstracts of the World's Literature on Corrosion and Corrosion Mitigation. National Association of Corrosion Engineers. CSA, 7200 Wisconsin Ave., Suite 601 Bethesda, MD 20814. Phone: 800-843-7751 or (301)961-6700 Fax: (301)961-6720 E-mail: service@csa.com • URL: http://www.csa.com • Bimonthly. Individuals, $240.00 per year; institutions, $340.00 per year. Includes print and online editions. Provides abstracts of the worldwide literature of corrosion and corrosion control. Also available on CD-ROM.

Corrosion: Journal of Science and Engineering. National Association of Corrosion Engineers. NACE International, 1440 S Creek Dr. Houston, TX 77084. Phone: (281)228-6200 Fax: (281)228-6300 E-mail: pubs@mail.nace.org • URL: http://www.nace.org • Monthly. Individuals, $160.00 per year; institutions, $290.00 per year. Covers corrosion control science, theory, engineering, and practice.

Corrosion of Stainless Steels. A. John Sedriks. John Wiley and Sons, Inc., 111 River St. Hoboken, NJ 07030. Phone: 800-225-5945 or (201)748-6000 Fax: (201)748-6088 E-mail: info@wiley.com • URL: http://www.wiley.com • 1996. $105.00. Second edition. Covers the corrosion and corrosion control of stainless steels used in a variety of applications. (Corrosion Monograph Series).

Corrosion Research Center., University of Minnesota, 221 Church St., S. E. Minneapolis, MN 55455. Phone: (612)625-4048 Fax: (612)626-7246 E-mail: dshores@maroon.tc.umn.edu • URL: http://www.cems.umn.edu/crc • Research areas include the effect of corrosion on high technology materials and devices.

Cosmetic Executive Women., 286 Madison Ave., 19th Fl. New York, NY 10017. Phone: (212)685-5955 Fax: (212)685-3334 E-mail: cew@cew.org • URL: http://cew.org • Women in the cosmetic and allied industries. Unites women executives in the cosmetic field for industry awareness and business advancement. Promotes products, people, professional development and philanthropy.

Cosmetic, Toiletry and Fragrance Association., 1101 17th St., N.W., Suite 300 Washington, DC 20036. Phone: (202)331-1770 Fax: (202)331-1969 E-mail: membership@ctfa.org •

URL: http://www.ctfa.org/ • Formerly Associated Manufacturers of Toilet Articles.

Cosmetic World News: The International News Magazine of the Perfumery, Cosmetic s and Toiletries Industry. World News Publications, 130 Wigmore St. London W1H 0AT, England. Fax: (44)171 4875436 Bimonthly. $192.00 per year.

Cosmetics and Toiletries: The International Journal of Cosmetic Technology. Allured Publishing, 362 S. Schmale Rd. Carol Stream, IL 60188-2787. Phone: (630)653-2155 Fax: (630)653-2192 E-mail: allured@allured.com • URL: http://www.allured.com • Monthly. $98.00 per year.

Cosmetics: Science and Technology. M.S. Balsam and Edward Sagarin. Krieger Publishing Co., P.O. Box 9542 Melbourne, FL 32902-9542. Phone: 800-724-0025 or (321)724-9542 Fax: (321)951-3671 E-mail: info@krieger-publishing.com • URL: http://www.krieger-publishing.com • 1992. $375.00. Second edition. Three volumes. Vol. one, $135.00; vol. two, $143.50; vol. three, $163.50.

Cosmetology. Jack Rudman. National Learning Corp., 212 Michael Dr. Syosset, NY 11791. Phone: 800-645-6337 or (516)921-8888 Fax: (516)921-8743 2002. $49.95. (Occupational Competency Examination Series: OCE-13).

Cost Accounting. William K. Carter and Milton Usry. South-Western, 5191 Natorp Blvd. Mason, OH 45040. Phone: 800-543-0487 or (513)229-1000 • URL: http://www.swcollege.com • 2002. $83.95. 13th edition. (Prentice Hall Accounting Series).

Cost Accounting: A Managerial Emphasis. Charles T. Horngren. Prentice Hall PTR, 240 Frisch Ct. Paramus, NJ 07652. Phone: 800-282-0693 Fax: 800-445-6991 • URL: http://www.phptr.com • 2002. $132.00. 11th edition. (Charles T. Horngren Accounting Series).

Cost Accounting Standards Board Regulations. CCH, Inc., 2700 Lake Cook Rd. Riverwoods, IL 60015. Phone: 800-835-5224 or (847)267-7000 E-mail: cust_serv@cch.com • URL: http://www.cch.com • 2002. $27.00. Covers Federal Acquisition Regulation (FAR) cost accounting standards for both defense and civilian government contracts. Provides the rules for estimating and reporting costs for contracts of more than $500,000.

Cost Accounting Standards Guide. CCH, Inc., 2700 Lake Cook Rd. Riverwoods, IL 60015. Phone: 800-525-3335 or (847)267-7000 E-mail: cust_serv@cch.com • URL: http://www.cch.com • $385.00 per year. Looseleaf serivce. Monthly updates.

Cost Control Handbook. R. M. Wilson. Ashgate Publishing Co., 101 Cherry St., Ste. 420 Burlington, VT 05401-4405. Phone: 800-535-9544 or (802)865-7641 Fax: (802)865-7847 E-mail: adonahue@ashgate.com • URL: http://www.ashgate.com • 1983. $102.95. Second edition. Published by Gower in England.

Cost Engineering: The Journal of Cost Estimating, Cost Control, and Project Management., AACE International, 209 Prairie Ave., Suite 100 Morgantown, WV 26505. Phone: 800-858-2678 or (304)296-8444 Fax: (304)291-5728 E-mail: info@aacei.org • URL: http://www.aacei.org • Monthly. $60.00 per year. Subjects include cost estimation and cost control.

Cost Estimating. Rodney D. Stewart. John Wiley and Sons, Inc., 111 River St. Hoboken, NJ 07030. Phone: 800-225-5945 or (201)748-6000 Fax: (201)748-6088 E-mail: info@wiley.com • URL: http://www.wiley.com • 1991. $150.00. Second edition. Discusses high technology engineering cost forecasting, including the estimation of software costs. (New Dimensions in Engineering Series).

Cost Management Handbook. Barry J. Brinker. John Wiley and Sons, Inc., 111 River St. Hoboken, NJ 07030. Phone: 800-225-5945 or (201)748-6000 Fax: (201)748-6088 E-mail: info@wiley.com • URL: http://www.wiley.com • 2000. $140.00.

Cost of Doing Business for Retail Sporting Goods Stores. National Sporting Goods Association, 1601 Feehanville Dr., Ste. 300 Mount Prospect, IL 60056-6305. Phone: 800-815-5422 or (847)296-6742 Fax: (847)391-9827 E-mail: nsga1699@aol.com • URL: http://www.nsga.org • Biennial. $125.00. Includes income statements, balance sheets, sales per employee, sales per square foot, inventory turnover, etc.

Cost of Doing Business Survey. Photo Marketing Association International, 3000 Picture Place Jackson, MI 49201. Phone: (517)788-8100 Fax: (517)788-8371 • URL: http://www.pmai.org • Biennial. $225.00. Emphasis is on photographic retailing.

Cost of Personal Borrowing in the United States. Financial Publishing Co., PO Box 570 South Bend, IN 46628-9752. Phone: 800-247-3214 Fax: (574)243-6060 E-mail: sales@financial-publishing.com • URL: http://www.financial-publishing.com • Annual. $175.00.

Cotton Council International., 1521 New Hampshire Ave. NW Washington, DC 20036. Phone: (202)745-7805 Fax: (202)483-4040 E-mail: cottonusa@cotton.org • URL: http://www.cottonusa.org • Representatives of all segments of the U.S. cotton industry. Works as an international cotton sales promotion organization cooperating with cotton interests in foreign countries.

Cotton Digest International. Cotton Digest Co., Inc., P.O. Box 820768 Houston, TX 77282-0768. Phone: (713)977-1644 Fax: (713)977-8193 E-mail: cottonabb@aol.com Monthly. $40.00 per year. Formerly *Cotton Digest*.

Cotton Farming. Vance Publishing Corp., 400 Knightsbridge Parkway Lincolnshire, IL 60069. Phone: 800-255-5113 or (847)634-2600 Fax: (847)634-4379 • URL: http://www.vancepublishing.com • Nine times a year. $35.00 per year.

Cotton Grower. Meister Media, 37733 Euclid Ave. Willoughby, OH 44094-5992. Phone: 800-572-7740 or (440)942-2000 Fax: (440)975-3447 E-mail: info@meistermedia.com • URL: http://www.meistermedia.com • 10 times a year. $32.10 per year.

Cotton Incorporated., 6399 Weston Pkwy. Cary, NC 27513. Phone: (919)678-2220 Fax: (919)678-2230 E-mail: kbrannigan@cottoninc.com • URL: http://www.cottoninc.com • Represents 45,000 cotton producers for research and promotion.

Cotton International. Meister Publishing Co., 37733 Euclid Ave. Willoughby, OH 44094-5992. Phone: 800-572-7740 or (440)942-2000 Fax: (440)942-0662 E-mail: info@meisterpro.com • URL: http://www.meisterpro.com • Annual. $30.00.

Cotton: Origin, History, Technology, and Production. Joe T. Cothren and C. Wayne Smith, editors. John Wiley and Sons, Inc., 111 River St. Hoboken, NJ 07030. Phone: 800-225-5945 or (201)748-6000 Fax: (201)748-6088 E-mail: info@wiley.com • URL: http://www.wiley.com • 1999. $299.00. (Crop Science Series: Vol. 4).

Cotton Price Statistics. U.S. Department of Agriculture, Washington, DC 20250. Phone: (202)720-2791 Monthly.

Cotton's Week. National Cotton Council of America, 1918 N Pkwy., PO Box 820285 Memphis, TN 38112-5000. Phone: (901)274-9030 Fax: (901)725-0510 E-mail: info@cotton.org • URL: http://www.cotton.org/ncc • Description: Reports legislative, administrative, and economic actions and issues affecting the cotton industry from the field to the fabric. Recurring features include news of research and reports of meetings.

Cottonwood Range and Livestock Research Station. South Dakota State University

Council for Advancement and Support of Education., 1307 New York Ave. N.W., Suite 1000 Washington, DC 20005-4701. Phone: (202)328-2273 Fax: (202)387-4973 E-mail: membersservicecenter@case.org • URL: http://www.case.org • Formerly American College Public Relations Association

Council for Aid to Education.

Council for Court Excellence.

Council for Responsible Genetics., Five Upland Rd., Suite 3 Cambridge, MA 02140. Phone: (617)868-0870 Fax: (617)491-5344 E-mail: crg@gene-watch.org • URL: http://www.gene-watch.org • Concerned with the social implications of genetic engineering. Affiliated with Biotechnology Industry Organization. Formerly Committee for Responsible Genetics.

Council of American Survey Research Organizations., 170 N Country Rd., Ste. 4 Port Jefferson, NY 11777. Phone: (631)928-6954 Fax: (631)928-6041 E-mail: casro@casro.org • URL: http://www.casro.org • Members are survey research companies. Various committees are concerned with standards, survey research quality, and technology.

Council of Communication Management., 65 Enterprise Aliso Viejo, CA 92656. Phone: (866)463-6226 Fax: (949)715-6931 E-mail: membership@ccmconnection.com • URL: http://www.ccmconnection.com/ • Formerly Industrial Communication Council.

Council of Fashion Designers of America.

Council of Graduate Schools., One Dupont Circle, N.W., Suite 430 Washington, DC 20036-1173. Phone: (202)223-3791 Fax: (202)331-7157 E-mail: cflagg@cgs.nche.edu • URL: http://www.cgsnet.org • Formerly Council of Graduate Schools in the United States.

Council of Institutional Investors., 1730 Rhode Island Ave., N. W., Suite 512 Washington, DC 20036. Phone: (202)822-0800 Fax: (202)822-0801 E-mail: info@cii.org • URL: http://www.cii.org • Members are nonprofit organization pension plans and other nonprofit institutional investors.

Council of Insurance Agents and Brokers.

Council of Logistics Management.

Council of State Administrators of Vocational Rehabilitation.

Council of State Governments., 2760 Research Park Dr. Lexington, KY 40578-1910. Phone: 800-800-1910 or (859)244-8000 Fax: (859)244-8001 E-mail: web_editor@csg.org • URL: http://www.csg.org • Supersedes American Legislator Association.

Council of Writers Organizations.

Council on Career Development for Minorities., PO Box 560987 Dallas, TX 75356-0987. Phone: (214)631-3677 Fax: (214)905-2046 E-mail: ccm35@aol.com • URL: http://www.ccdm.-inc.org • Seeks to improve career counseling and placement services for minority college students.

Council on Employee Benefits., 4910 Moorland Ln. Bethesda, MD 20814. Phone: (301)664-5940 Fax: (301)664-5944 E-mail: vschieber@ceb.org • URL: http://www.ceb.org • Formerly Council on Employee Benefits Plans.

Council on Employee Relations. University of Pennsylvania

Council on Family Health., 1155 Connecticut Ave., Suite 1200B Washington, DC 20036. Phone: (202)331-7373 Fax: (202)223-6835 E-mail: cfhinfo99@aol.com • URL: http://www.cfhinfo.org • Members are drug manufacturers. Concerned with proper use of medications.

Council on Foundations., 1828 L St. NW, Ste. 300 Washington, DC 20036. Phone: (202)466-6512 Fax: (202)785-3926 E-mail: webmaster@cof.org • URL: http://www.cof.org • Formerly National Council on Community Foundations.

Council on International Educational Exchange - USA., Seven Custom House St., 3rd Fl. Portland, OR 04101. Phone: 800-407-8839 or (207)553-7600 Fax: (207)553-7699 • URL: http://www.ciee.org • Members are educational institutions and agencies that promote and sponsor international education exchange. Formerly Council on Student Travel.

Council on Licensure, Enforcement and Regulation., 403 Marquis Ave., Ste. 100 Lexington, KY 40502. Phone: (859)269-1289 Fax: (859)231-1943 E-mail: sburke@mis.net • URL: http://www.clearhq.org/ • Members are state government occupational and professional licensing officials. Formerly National Clearinghouse on Licensure, Enforcement and Regulation.

Counseling and Values. Association for Spiritual, Ethical and Religious Values in Counseling. American Counseling Association, 5999 Stevenson Ave. Alexandria, VA 22304-3300. Phone: 800-347-6647 or (703)823-9800 Fax: 800-473-2329 or (703)823-0252 • URL: http://www.counseling.org • Three times a year. Institutions, $35.00 per year.

The Counseling Psychologist. American Psychological Association. Sage Publications, Inc., 2455 Teller Rd. Thousand Oaks, CA 91320. Phone: 800-818-7243 or (805)499-9774 Fax: 800-583-2665 or (805)499-0871 E-mail: webmaster@sagepub.com • URL: http://www.sagepub • Bimonthly. Institutions, $495.00 per year.

Counseling Services: IACS Newsletter. International Association of Counseling Services, 101 S. Whiting, Suite 211 Alexandria, VA 22304. Phone: (703)823-9840 Fax: (703)823-9843 E-mail: iacs@gmu.edu Three times a year. Membership.

Counseling Today. American Counseling Association, 5999 Stevenson Ave. Alexandria, VA 22304. Phone: 800-347-6647 or (703)823-6862 Fax: 800-473-2329 or 800-473-2329 E-mail: info@cotton.org • URL: http://www.counseling.org • Description: Covers news and issues relevant to the counseling profession.

Counselor: The Magazine for Addiction Professionals. Health Communications, Inc., 3201 S. W. 15th St. Deerfield Beach, FL 33442. Phone: 800-851-9100 or (954)360-0909 Fax: (954)360-0034 E-mail: info@counselormagazine.com • URL: http://www.hci-online.com • Bimonthly. $26.00 per year. Covers both clinical and societal aspects of substance abuse.

Counselors of Real Estate., 430 N. Michigan Ave. Chicago, IL 60611-4089. Phone: (312)329-8427 Fax: (312)329-8881 E-mail: cre@interaccess.com • URL: http://www.cre.org • Formerly American Society of Real Estate Counselors.

Countdown to a New Library: Managing the Building Project. Jeannette Woodward. American Library Association, 50 E Huron St. Chicago, IL 60611-2795. Phone: 800-545-2433 or (312)944-6780 Fax: (312)440-9374 E-mail: ala@ala.org • URL: http://www.ala.org • 2000. $48.00. Explains how to work in harmony with builders and architects.

Countertrade and Offset: Weekly Intelligence on Unconventional and Reciprocal International Trade. CTO Data Services, 1512 Valley Run Durham, NC 27707-3640. Phone: (703)383-5816 Fax: (703)383-5815 24 times a year. $688.00 per year. Newsletter. Intelligence on reciprocal international trade and unconventional trade finance. Covers developments and trends in the directory publishing industry, including publisher profiles, start-ups, corporate acquisitions, and business opportunities. Includes *Directory of Countertrade Services*. Formerly *Countertrade Outlook*.

Counties USA: A Directory of United States Counties. Omnigraphics, Inc., 615 Griswold St. Detroit, MI 48226. Phone: 800-234-1340 or (313)961-1340 Fax: 800-875-1340 or (313)961-1383 E-mail: info@omnigraphics.com • URL: http://www.omnigraphics.com • 2003. $85.00. Second edition. Contains extensive economic and demographic data from the 2000 Census for about 3,100 counties of the U. S.

Countries of the World and Their Leaders Yearbook. Gale Cengage Learning, 27500 Drake Rd. Farmington Hills, MI 48331-3535. Phone: 800-877-GALE or (248)699-4253 Fax: 800-414-5043 E-mail: gale.galeord@cengage.com • URL: http://gale.cengage.com • 2003. $260.00. Two volumes. Based on U. S. State Department data covering nearly 170 countries. Features "Background Notes on countries of the World." Also includes the CIA's list of "Chiefs of State and Cabinet Members of Foreign Governments," as well as key officers at U.S. embassies and other information.

Country Data Forecasts. Bank of America, World Information Services, Dept. 3015, 555 California St. San Francisco, CA 94104. Phone: 800-645-6667 or (415)622-1446 Fax: (415)622-0909 Looseleaf, with semiannual updates. $495.00 per year. Provides detailed statistical tables for 80 countries, showing historical data and five-year forecasts of 23 key economic series. Includes population, inflation figures, debt, per capita income, foreign trade, exchange rates, and other data.

Country Finance. Economist Intelligence Unit, 111 W. 57th St., The Economist Bldg. New York, NY 10019. Phone: 800-938-4685 or (212)554-0600 Fax: (212)586-1181 E-mail: newyork@eiu.com • URL: http://www.eiu.com • Annual $425.00 per year. Discusses banking and financial conditions in each of 47 countries. Includes foreign exchange regulations, the currency outlook, sources of capital, financing techniques, and tax considerations.

Country Forecasts. The PRS Group, PO Box 248 Syracuse, NY

13057-0248. Phone: (315)431-0511 Fax: (315)431-0200 E-mail: custserv@prsgroup.com • URL: http://www.prsgroup.com • Semiannual. $695.00 per year per country. $375.00 per volume. Five-year forecasts are provided for each of 62 countries. Analyzes economic, political, and business prospects.

Country Outlooks. Pyramid Research, 58 Charles St. Cambridge, MA 02141. Phone: (617)494-1515 Fax: (617)494-8898 E-mail: customerservice@pyr.com • URL: http://www.pyr.com • Looseleaf. $495.00 per year. Covers 81 major countries, with each country updated quarterly. Provides detailed economic data and financial forecasts, including tables of key economic indicators.

Country Profile: Annual Survey of Political and Economic Background. Economist Intelligence Unit, 111 57th St. New York, NY 10019. Phone: 800-938-4685 or (212)554-0600 Fax: (212)586-1182 E-mail: newyork@eiu.com • URL: http://www.eiu.com • Annual. $245.00 per country or country group. Contains statistical tables "showing the last 6 year run of macro-economic indicators, and an overview of a country's politics, economy and industry." Covers 180 countries in 115 annual editions.

Country Report Services. The PRS Group, Post Office Box 248 East Syracuse, NY 13057-0248. Phone: (315)431-0511 Fax: (315)431-0200 Provides full text of reports describing the business risks and opportunities currently existing in more than 150 countries of the world. Contains a wide variety of statistics and forecasts relating to economics political and social conditions. Also includes demographics, tax, and currency information. Updated monthly. Inquire as to online cost and availability.

Country Reports. Economist Intelligence Unit, 111 W. 57th St. New York, NY 10019. Phone: 800-938-4685 or (212)554-0600 Fax: (212)586-1182 E-mail: newyork@eiu.com • URL: http://www.eiu.com • Quarterly. $455.00 per year per country or country group. Comprehensive economic and political information is presented for 180 countries in 99 *Country Reports*, with 12 to 18 month forecasts. Each subscription includes an annual *Country Profile* containing statistical tables.

Country Risk Monitor. Bank of America, World Information Services, Dept. 3015, 555 California St. San Francisco, CA 94104. Phone: (415)622-3456 Fax: (415)622-0909 Looseleaf, with semiannual updates. $495.00 per year. Provides rankings of 80 countries according to current and future business risk. Utilizes key economic ratios and benchmarks for countries in a manner similar to financial ratio analysis for industries.

Country Risk Service. Economist Intelligence Unit, 111 W. 57th St. New York, NY 10019. Phone: 800-938-4685 or (212)554-0600 Fax: (212)586-1182 E-mail: newyork@eiu.com • URL: http://www.eiu.com • Quarterly. $695.00 per year per country. Two-year risk forecasts are provided for each of 82 countries. Business, political, economic, and credit risks are analyzed.

County Agents Directory: The Reference Book for Agricultural Extension Workers. Doane Agricultural Services, 11701 Borman Dr., Ste. 300 St. Louis, MO 63146-4193. Phone: 800-535-2342 or (314)569-2700 Fax: (314)564-1083 • URL: http://www.edoane.com • Semiannual. $26.95. About 17,000 county agents and university agricultural extension workers.

County and City Data Book, a Statistical Abstract Supplement. U.S. Bureau of the Census. Available from U.S. Government Printing Office, Washington, DC 20402. Phone: (202)512-1800 Fax: (202)512-2250 1994. $60.00.

County and City Data Book 2000: A Statistical Abstract Supplement. Available from U. S. Government Printing Office, Washington, DC 20402. Phone: (202)512-1800 Fax: (202)512-2250 E-mail: gpoaccess@gpo.gov • URL: http://www.access.gpo.gov • 2002. $68.00. 13th edition. Issued by the U. S. Bureau of the Census (http://www.census.gov). Contains a wide variety of data on 3,141 U.S. counties, 1,078 cities, and 11,097 places of 2,500 or more inhabitants. Includes statistical information on retailing, manufacturing, banking, service industries, income, employment, housing, education, crime, and population. Updated metropolitan areas are included.

County and City Extra: Annual Metro, City and County Data Book. Deirdre A. Gaquin and Mark S. Littman. Bernan Press, 4611-F Assembly Dr. Lanham, MD 20706-4391. Phone: 800-865-3450 or (301)459-2255 Fax: 800-865-3450 or (301)459-9235 E-mail: bpress@bernan.com • URL: http://www.bernan.com • 2001. $120.00. Updates and augments data published irregularly in print form by the U. S. Census Bureau in *County and City Data Book*. Covers "every state, county, metropolitan area, and congressional district in the United States, as well as all U. S. cities with a 1990 population of 25,000 or more." Contains a wide range tic maps.

County and City Extra: Special Decennial Census Edition. Deidre A. Gaquin and Katherine A. DeBrandt, editors. Bernan Press, 4611-F Assembly Drive Lanham, MD 20706-4391. Phone: 800-274-4447 or (301)459-2255 Fax: 800-865-3450 or (301)459-0056 E-mail: order@bernan.com • URL: http://www.bernan.com • 2002. $95.00. Presents conveniently arranged population, housing, and other data from the 2000 census, with many 1980 and 1990 comparisons. Includes maps and tables with rankings of about 20 items for various geographic locations. Complements the annual *County and City Extra*.

County Business Patterns. Available from U. S. Government Printing Office, Washington, DC 20402. Phone: (202)512-1800 Fax: (202)512-2250 E-mail: gpoaccess@gpo.gov • URL: http://www.access.gpo.gov • Irregular. 52 issues containing annual data for each state, the District of Columbia, and a U. S. Summary. Produced by U.S. Bureau of the Census (http://www.census.gov). Provides local establishment and employment statistics by industry.

County News. National Association of Counties, 440 First St., N.W. Washington, DC 20001. Phone: (202)393-6226 Fax: (202)393-2630 E-mail: tgoodman@naco.org • URL: http://www.naco.org • Biweekly. $82.50 per year.

Coupon Mailer Service. Entrepreneur Media, Inc., 2445 McCabe Way Irvine, CA 92614. Phone: 800-421-2300 or (949)261-2325 Fax: (949)261-0234 E-mail: entmag@entrepreneur.com • URL: http://www.entrepreneur.com • Looseleaf. $59.50. A practical guide to starting a service for mailing business promotion discount coupons to consumers. Covers profit potential, start-up costs, market size evaluation, owner's time required, pricing, accounting, advertising, promotion, etc. (Start-Up Business Guide No. E1232.)

Court Review. American Judges Association. National Center for State Courts, 300 Newport Ave. Williamsburg, VA 23187-8798. Phone: (757)259-8798 Fax: (757)259-1520 E-mail: srockwell@ncsc.dni.us • URL: http://www.aja.ncsc.dni.us • Quarterly. Free to members; non-members, $25.00 per year.

Court System of the United States: A Bibliography. D. Ellsworth Blanc, editor. Nova Science Publishers, Inc., 400 Oser Ave., Suite 1600 Hauppauge, NY 11788-3619. Phone: (631)231-7269 Fax: (631)231-8175 E-mail: novascience@earthlink.net • URL: http://www.novapublishers.com • 2002. $69.00. Covers literature dealing with district, circuit, and appeals courts. Includes author, title, and subject indexes.

Courts, Judges and Politics: An Introduction to the Judicial Process. Walter Murphy and others, editors. McGraw-Hill, 1221 Ave. of the Americas New York, NY 10020. Phone: 800-722-4726 or (212)512-2000 Fax: (212)512-4502 E-mail: customer.service@mcgraw-hill.com • URL: http://www.mcgraw-hill.com • 2001. $56.25. Fifth edition. (Humanities, Social Sciences and World Languages Series).

Cowles Foundation for Research in Economics. Yale University

Coyle's Information Highway Handbook: A Practical File on the New Information Order. Karen Coyle. American Library Association, 50 E. Huron St. Chicago, IL 60611-2795. Phone: 800-545-2433 or (312)944-6780 Fax: (312)440-9374 E-mail: ala@ala.org • URL: http://www.ala.org • 1997. $30.00. Provides useful "essays on copyright, access, privacy, censorship, and the information marketplace."

CPA Examination Review Business Law and Professional Responibilities. Patrick R. Delaney and Debra R. Hopkins. John Wiley and Sons, Inc., 111 River St. Hoboken, NJ 07030. Phone: 800-225-5945 or (201)748-6000 Fax: (201)748-6088 E-mail: info@wiley.com • URL: http://www.wiley.com • 2001. $41.00.

The CPA Journal (Certified Public Accountants). New York State Society of Certified Public Accountants, 530 Fifth Ave., 5th Fl. New York, NY 10036-5101. Phone: 800-877-4522 or (212)719-8300 Fax: (212)719-3364 E-mail: cpaj@nysscpa.org • URL: http://www.cpajournal.com • Monthly. Individuals, $42.00 per year; students, $18.00 per year.

The CPA Letter: A News Report to Members. Public Relations-Communications. American Institute of Certified Public Accountants, 1211 Ave. of the Americas New York, NY 10036-8775. Phone: 800-862-4272 or (212)596-6200 Fax: (212)596-6213 E-mail: lmorales@aicpa.org • URL: http://www.aicpa.org • 10 times a year. Free to members; non-members, $40.00 per year.

CPA Managing Partner Report: Management News for Accounting Executives. Strafford Publications, Inc., Specialized Information Services, 590 Dutch Valley Rd., N.E. Atlanta, GA 30324. Phone: 800-926-7926 or (404)881-1141 Fax: (404)881-0074 E-mail: custserv@straffordpub.com • URL: http://www.straffordpub.com • Monthly. $396.00 per year. Newsletter. Covers practice management and professional relationships.

CPA Marketing Report. CCH Inc., 4025 W Peterson Ave., 590 Dutch Valley Rd., N.E. Chicago, IL 60646-6085. Phone: 888-224-7377 or (847)267-7000 Fax: (773)866-3895 E-mail: info@cotton.org • URL: http://www.straffordpub.com • Description: Helps public accounting firms design, implement, and evaluate effective programs to attract new clients, enhance the firm's image, improve client relations, and build sound practices.

CPA Personnel Report. Aspen Publishers Inc., 76 9th Ave., 7th Fl., 590 Dutch Valley Rd., N.E. New York, NY 10011. Phone: 800-638-8437 or (212)771-0600 Fax: (212)771-0885 E-mail: info@cotton.org • URL: http://www.straffordpub.com • Description: Helps CPA firms excel in recruiting and retaining professional and non-professional staff, in competing with other firms to attract the best talent, in making informed hiring and firing decisions, and in staying abreat of evaluation, compensation, and benefits strategies and management and motivational techniques.

The CPA Software News (Certified Public Accountant). Cygnus Business Media, 110 N Bell St., Suite 300 Shawnee, OK 74801. Phone: 800-308-6397 E-mail: rich.reiff@cygnuspub.com • URL: http://www.cygnusbzb.com • Eight times a year. $39.95 per year. Provides articles and reviews relating to computer technology and software for accountants.

CPA Technology and Internet Tax Advisor (Certified Public Accountant). Aspen Publishers, 1185 Ave. of the Americas New York, NY 10036. Phone: 800-234-1660 or (212)597-0200 Fax: 800-901-9075 or (212)597-0213 E-mail: customer.service@aspenpubl.com • URL: http://www.aspenpublishers.com • Monthly. $261.00 per year. Newsletter. Describes hardware and software products and makes recommendations. Formerly *C P A Technology and Internet Advisor*.

CPCU Society., 720 Providence Rd., 720 Providence Rd., PO Box 3009 Malvern, PA 19355-3402. Phone: 800-932-2728 or (610)251-2727 Fax: (610)251-2780 E-mail: membercenter@cpcusociety.org • URL: http://www.cpcusociety.org • Serves as a professional society of individuals who have passed national examinations of the American Institute for Chartered Property Casualty Underwriters (see separate entry), have 3 years of work experience, have agreed to be bound by a code of ethics, and have been awarded CPCU designation. Promotes education, research, social responsibility, and professionalism in the field. Holds seminars, symposia, and workshops.

CPI Detailed Report: Consumer Price Index. Available from U.S. Government Printing Office, Washington, DC 20402. Phone: (202)512-1800 Fax: (202)512-2250 Monthly. $45.00 per year. Cost of living data.

CPI Digest: Key to World Literature Serving the Coatings, Plastics, Fibers, Adhesives, and Related Industries (Chemical Process Industries). CPI Information Services, 2117 Cherokee Parkway Louisville, KY 40204. Phone: (502)456-6288 Fax: (502)454-4808 E-mail: cpidigest@mindspring.com Monthly. $397.00 per year. Abstracts of business and technical articles for polymer-based, chemical process industries. Includes a monthly list of relevant U. S. patents. International coverage.

CPI.Q: The Canadian Periodical Index Full-Text on CD-ROM. Gale Cengage Learning, 27500 Drake Rd. Farmington Hills, MI 48331-3535. Phone: 800-877-GALE or (248)699-GALE Fax: 800-414-5043 or (248)699-8069 E-mail: galeord@gale.com • URL: http://gale.cengage.com • Bimonthly. Provides CD-ROM citations from 1988 to date for more than 400 English and French language periodicals. Contains full-text coverage from 1995 to date for 150 periodicals.

CQ Weekly. CQ Press, 1255 22nd St., NW, Ste. 400 Washington, DC 20037. Phone: (866)427-7737 or (202)729-1800 Fax: 800-380-3810 or (202)728-1863 E-mail: customerservice@cqpress.com • URL: http://www.cqpress.com • 48 times a year. $1,696.00 per year. Includes annual *Almanac*. Formerly *Congressional Quarterly Weekly Report*.

Craft Businesses. Entrepreneur Media, Inc., 2445 McCabe Way Irvine, CA 92614. Phone: 800-421-2300 or (949)261-2325 Fax: (949)261-0234 E-mail: entmag@entrepreneur.com • URL: http://www.entrepreneur.com • Looseleaf. $59.50. A practical guide to starting a handicrafts-related business. Covers profit potential, start-up costs, market size evaluation, owner's time required, site selection, lease negotiation, pricing, accounting, advertising, promotion, etc. (Start-Up Business Guide No. E1304.)

Crawford Perspectives. Arch Crawford, 6890 E Sunrise Dr., Ste. 120-70 Tucson, AZ 85750-0840. Phone: (520)577-1158 Fax: (520)577-1110 E-mail: info@crawfordperspectives.com • URL: http://www.crawfordperspectives.com • Description: Publishes information on the stock market based on a "unique cycle approach using elipses instead of pure cycles to gain higher resolution in determining turning points." Employs technical analyses to back up astronomic cycles. "Ranked 1 market timer 5 year period by independent rating service".

CRB Commodity Index Report. Commodity Research Bureau., 330 S Wells St., Ste. 1114 Chicago, IL 60606. Phone: 800-621-5271 or (312)454-1801 Fax: (312)454-0239 E-mail: info@crbtrader.com • URL: http://www.crbtrader.com • Weekly. $295.00 per year. Quotes the CRB Futures Price Index and the CRB Spot Market Index for the last five business days, plus the previous week, month, and year. Includes tables and graphs.

CRB Commodity Yearbook. Commodity Research Bureau. CRB, 330 S Wells St., Ste. 1112 Chicago, IL 60606. Phone: 800-621-5271 or (312)554-8456 Fax: (312)939-4135 E-mail: info@crtrader.com • URL: http://www.crtrader.com • Annual. $99.95.

CRB Futures Market Service. Commodity Research Bureau Inc., 330 S Wells St., Ste. 612 Chicago, IL 60606-7110. Phone: 800-621-5271 or (312)554-8456 Fax: (312)939-4135 E-mail: info@crbtrader.com • URL: http://www.crbtrader.com • Description: "Discusses developments that will affect the future status of supply, demand, and price movements for the different commodities traded on the futures markets."

CRB Futures Perspective: Agricultural Edition. Commodity Research Bureau., 330 S Wells St., Suite 1112 Chicago, IL 60606. Phone: 800-621-5271 or (312)554-8456 Fax: (312)939-4135 E-mail: info@crbtrader.com • URL: http://www.crbtrader.com • Weekly. $230.00 per year. Service provides comprehensive price charts for more than 20 agricultural commodity futures, from cocoa to wheat (includes lumber). Also provides technical analysis of price movements and market commentary. Formerly part of *CRB Futures Chart Service*.

CRB Futures Perspective: Financial Edition. Commodity Research Bureau., 330 S Wells St., Suite 1112 Chicago, IL 60606. Phone: 800-621-5271 or (312)554-8456 Fax:

(312)939-4135 E-mail: info@crbtrader.com • URL: http://www.crbtrader.com • Weekly. $275.00 per year. Service provides comprehensive price charts for more than 50 financial futures, from Australian Bills to Swiss Francs (includes precious metals and oil). Also provides technical analysis of price movements and market commentary. Formerly part of *CRB Futures Chart Service*.

CRB Markets Overview. Commodity Research BureauPhone: 800-621-5271 or (312)554-8456 Fax: (312)939-4135 E-mail: info@crbtrader.com • URL: http://www.crbtrader.com/data/ • Web site provides free, detailed, current price quotes for about 100 futures contracts, covering Currencies, Energies, Financials, Grains, Meats, Metals, "Softs" (orange juice, coffee, etc.) and stock price indexes. Includes contract specifications and detailed prices of options on futures.

CRC Desk Reference for Nutrition. Carolyn D. Berdanier. CRC Press LLC, 2000 NW Corporate Blvd. Boca Raton, FL 33431. Phone: 800-272-7737 or (561)994-0555 Fax: 800-374-3401 or (561)989-9732 E-mail: orders@crcpress.com • URL: http://www.crcpress.com • 1997. $79.95. Encyclopedic, alphabetical arrangement of topics. (Desk Reference Series).

CRE Member Directory. Association of European Universities, 10, rue du Conseil General CH-1211 Geneva, Switzerland. Phone: (22)329-2251 Fax: (22)329-2821 E-mail: info@cre.unige.ch • URL: http://www.cre.org • Covers: more 1,100 Counselors of Real Estate (CREs), including many Counselors in Canada, Great Britain, Japan, Australia, Israel, Austria, France, Switzerland, New Zealand, Italy, Mexico, Puerto Rico. Entries include: Name, title, office address and phone, home address and phone, fax, areas of counseling specialty, and e-mail, where provided.

Creating a Culture of Competence. Michael Zwell. John Wiley and Sons, Inc., 111 River St. Hoboken, NJ 07030. Phone: 800-225-5945 or (201)748-6000 Fax: (201)748-6088 E-mail: info@wiley.com • URL: http://www.wiley.com • 2000. $35.95. Emphasizes employee participation to arrive at a desired change in organizational culture.

Creating a Financial Plan: A How-To-Do-It Manual for Librarians. Betty J. Turock amd Andrea Pedolsky. Neal-Schuman Publishers, Inc., 100 William St., Ste. 2004 New York, NY 10038. Phone: (866)672-6657 or (212)925-8650 Fax: (866)209-7932 or (212)219-8916 E-mail: info@neal-schuman.com • URL: http://www.neal-schuman.com • 1992. $49.95. (How-to-Do-It Manuals Series).

Creating Digital Content: A Video Production for Web, Broadcast, and Cinema. John Rice and Brian McKernan. McGraw-Hill, 1221 Ave. of the Americas New York, NY 10020. Phone: 800-722-4726 or (212)512-2000 Fax: (212)512-4502 E-mail: customer.service@mcgraw-hill.com • URL: http://www.mcgraw-hill.com • 2001. $49.95. Discusses the technicalities of digital content with a light touch, as in "Throw Another Analog on the Digital Fire." Other chapter titles are "Digital Recording," "Datacasting," "Coming to a Theatre Near You: Digital Cinema," and "The Promise of Digital Interactive Television."

Creating Newsletters, Brochures, and Pamphlets: A How-To-Do-It Manual for Librarians. Barbara A. Radke and Barbara Stein. Neal-Schuman Publishers, Inc., 100 William St., Ste. 2004 New York, NY 10038. Phone: (866)672-6657 or (212)925-8650 Fax: (866)209-7932 or (212)219-8916 E-mail: info@neal-schuman.com • URL: http://www.neal-schuman.com • 1992. $39.95. Includes desktop publishing. (How-to-Do-It Manuals Series).

Creating Policies for Results: From Chaos to Clarity. Sandra Nelson and June Garcia. American Library Association, 50 E Huron St. Chicago, IL 60611-2795. Phone: 800-545-2433 or (312)944-6780 Fax: (312)440-9374 E-mail: ala@ala.org • URL: http://www.ala.org • 2003. $50.00. Explains how to create clear, non-ambivalent public and staff policies for libraries. Covers policies relating to library organization, management, and service to patrons (Public Library Association Results Series).

Creating the Corporate Digital Library. Primary Research Group, Inc., 850 Seventh Ave., Suite 1200 New York, NY 10019. Phone: 888-455-8380 or (212)245-2327 Fax: (509)479-5787 E-mail: primarydat@primaryresearch.com • URL: http://www.primaryresearch.com • 2003. $135.00. Provides a survey of the electronic data policies of specific corporate libraries. Covers electronic journals, e-books, user training, alert services, vendor negotiation, web site development, knowledge management, outsourcing, and other topics.

Creating Web-Accessible Databases: Case Studies for Libraries, Museums, and Other Non-Profits. Julie M. Still, editor. Information Today, Inc., 143 Old Marlton Pike Medford, NJ 08055-8750. Phone: 800-300-9868 or (609)654-6266 Fax: (609)654-4309 E-mail: custserv@infotoday.com • URL: http://www.infotoday.com • 2001. $39.50. Presents case studies of successful Web projects in libraries and other institutions.

Creating Winning Marketing Plans: What Today's Managers Must Do to Succeed. Sidney J. Levy, editor. Dartnell Corp., 360 Hiatt Dr. Palm Beach, FL 33418. Phone: 800-621-5463 or (561)622-6520 Fax: (561)622-2423 E-mail: custserv@lrp.com • URL: http://www.dartnellcorp.com • 1996. $39.95. Consists of articles by 25 "Top Experts." Covers marketing objectives, customer needs, market segmentation, database marketing, consumer scanning, and other topics.

The Creative Coalition., 1100 Ave. of the Americas, 3rd Fl. New York, NY 10036. Phone: (212)512-5876 Fax: (212)512-5023 E-mail: info@thecreativecoalition.org • URL: http://www.thecreativecoalition.org • Actors, writers, directors and other arts and entertainment professionals. Aims to educate members about social and political issues, particularly in the areas of the First Amendment, arts advocacy and public education.

Creative Management. Jane Henry. Sage Publications, Inc., 2455 Teller Rd. Thousand Oaks, CA 91320. Phone: 800-818-7243 or (805)499-9774 Fax: 800-583-2665 or (805)499-0871 E-mail: webmaster@sagepub.com • URL: http://www.sagepub.com • 2001. $101.00. Second edition.

Creative Strategy in Advertising; What the Copywriter Should Know About the Creative Side of the Business. A. Jerome Jewler and Bonnie Drewniany. Wadsworth Publishing Co., 10 Davis Dr. Belmont, CA 94002. Phone: (650)595-2350 • URL: http://www.wadsworth.com • 2000. $85.95. Seventh edition. (Mass Communication Series).

Creative Strategy in Direct Marketing. Susan K. Jones. McGraw-Hill, 1221 Ave. of the Americas New York, NY 10020. Phone: 800-722-4726 or (212)512-2000 Fax: (212)512-4502 E-mail: customer.service@mcgraw-hill.com • URL: http://www.mcgraw-hill.com • 1993. $39.95. Second edition. (NTC Business Books Series).

Creative's Illustrated Guide to P-O-P Exhibits and Promotion. Magazines Creative, Inc., 42 W. 38th St., Room 601 New York, NY 10016-6210. Phone: (212)840-0160 Fax: (212)819-0945 Annual. $25.00. Lists sources of point-of-purchase displays, signs, and exhibits and sources of other promotional materials and equipment. Available online.

Creativity. Art Direction Magazine. Art Directon Book Co., Inc, 456 Glenbrook Rd. Glenbrook, CT 06906. Phone: (203)353-1441 Fax: (203)353-1371 Annual. $62.95.

Creativity Rules! A Writer's Workbook. John Vorhaus. Silman-James Press, 3624 Shannon Rd. Los Angeles, CA 90027. Phone: (323)661-9922 Fax: (323)661-9933 E-mail: silmanjamespress@earthlink.com • URL: http://www.silmanjamespress.com • 1999. $15.95. Covers the practical process of conceiving, outlining, and developing a story, especially for TV or film scripts. Includes "tactics and exercises."

Credit and Lending Dictionary. Shelley W. Geehr and Daphne Smith, editors. The Risk Management Association, One Liberty Place, 1650 Market St., Suite 2300 Philadelphia, PA 19103. Phone: 800-677-7621 or (215)446-4000 Fax: (215)446-4101 • URL: http://www.rmahq.org • 1994. $25.00.

Credit Card Management Buyers Guide. Thomson Financial (New York, New York), 195 Broadway New York, NY 10007. Phone: 888-605-3385 or (646)822-2000 Fax: (646)822-3230 E-mail: TFOnlineRequests@thomson.com • URL: http://www.thomsonmedia.com • Database covers: Credit and debit card contacts, products and services. Entries include: Company name, address, phone.

Credit Card Management: The Magazine of Electronic Payments. Thomson Media, One State St. Plaza New York, NY 10004. Phone: 800-221-1809 or (212)803-8200 Fax: (212)843-9635 E-mail: custserv@thomsonmedia.com • URL: http://www.thomsonmedia.com • Monthly. $98.00 per year. Edited for bankers and other managers of electronic payment systems.

Credit Card Users of America., P.O. Box 7100 Beverly Hills, CA 90212. Phone: (818)343-4434 Supports the rights of credit card users.

Credit Consulting. Entrepreneur Media, Inc., 2445 McCabe Way Irvine, CA 92614. Phone: 800-421-2300 or (949)261-2325 Fax: (949)261-0234 E-mail: entmag@entrepreneur.com • URL: http://www.entrepreneur.com • Looseleaf. $59.50. A practical guide to starting a consumer credit and debt counseling and consulting service. Covers profit potential, start-up costs, market size evaluation, owner's time required, pricing, accounting, advertising, promotion, etc. (Start-Up Business Guide No. E1321.)

Credit Department Management. D. Laurence Blackstone. The Risk Management Association, One Liberty Place, Suite 2300, 1650 Market St. Philadelphia, PA 19103. Phone: 800-677-7621 or (949)446-4000 Fax: (949)446-4101 • URL: http://www.rmahq.org • 1992. $65.00. Second edition.

Credit Executive Letter. American Financial Services Association, 919 18th St., NW Washington, DC 20006. Phone: (202)296-5544 Fax: (202)223-0321 E-mail: afsa@afsamail.com • URL: http://www.americanfinsvcs.org • Monthly. Members, $12.00 per year; non-members, $22.00 per year.

Credit Management Handbook. Burt Edwards and others. Ashgate Publishing Co., 101 Cherry St., Ste. 420 Burlington, VT 05401-4405. Phone: 800-535-9544 or (802)865-7641 Fax: (802)865-7847 E-mail: adonahue@ashagate.com • URL: http://www.ashgate.com • 1997. $119.95. Fourth edition. Published by Gower in England.

Credit Research Center. Georgetown University, 3240 Prospect St. NW, Ste. 300 Washington, DC 20007. Phone: (202)625-0103 Fax: (202)625-0104 E-mail: statenm@msb.edu • URL: http://www.msb.edu/prog/crc • Economic trends and public policy issues in consumer and mortgage credit, with emphasis on regulatory policy (including rate ceilings, restrictions on creditor remedies, and consumer bankruptcies), consumer behavior, medical debt, and managerial decision systems.

Credit Research Foundation., 8840 Columbia 100 Pkwy., 100 Pky. Columbia, MD 21045. Phone: (410)740-5499 Fax: (410)740-4620 E-mail: crf_info@crfonline.org • URL: http://www.crfonline.org • Represents credit, financial, and working capital executives of manufacturing and banking concerns. Aims to create a better understanding of the impact of credit on the economy. Plans, supervises, and administers research and educational programs. Conducts surveys on economic conditions, trends, policies, practices, theory, systems, and methodology. Sponsors formal educational programs in credit and financial management. Maintains library on credit, collections, and management.

Credit Risk Management. Phillips International, Inc., 7811 Montrose Rd. Potomac, MD 20854. Phone: (301)340-2100 E-mail: information@phillips.com • URL: http://www.phillips.com • Biweekly. $695.00 per year. Newsletter on consumer credit, including delinquency aspects.

Credit Risk Management: A Guide to Sound Business Decisions. H. A. Schaeffer. John Wiley and Sons, Inc., 111 River St. Hoboken, NJ 07030. Phone: 800-225-5945 or (201)748-6000 Fax: (201)748-6088 E-mail: info@wiley.com • URL: http://www.wiley.com • 2000. $95.00. Covers corporate credit policies, credit authorization procedures, and analysis of business credit applications. Includes 12 "real-life" case studies.

Credit Union Executive Journal: For Active Leaders and Managers of Credit Unions. Credit Union National Association, Inc., Communications Div. CUNA Publications, PO Box 431 Madison, WI 53705-0431. Phone: 800-356-8010 or (608)231-4000 Fax: (608)231-1869 E-mail: dorothy@cuna.org • URL: http://www.cuna.org • Bimonthly. $110.00 per year. A management journal for credit union CEOs and senior executives.

Credit Union Executives Society., PO Box 14167 Madison, WI 53708-0167. Phone: 800-252-2664 or (608)271-2664 Fax: (608)271-2303 E-mail: cues@cues.org • URL: http://www.cues.org • Advances the professional development of credit union CEOs, senior management and directors. Serves as an international membership association dedicated to the professional development of credit union CEOs, senior management and directors.

Credit Union Guide. Credit Union National Association. Prentice Hall PTR, 240 Frisch Court Paramus, NJ 07652. Phone: 800-282-0693 Fax: 800-445-6991 • URL: http://www.phptr.com • Four looseleaf volumes. Periodic supplementation. Price on application. Laws, regulations, and developments affecting credit unions.

Credit Union Journal: The Nation's Leading Independent Credit Union Newsweekly. Thomson Media, One State St. Plaza New York, NY 10004. Phone: 800-221-1809 or (212)803-8200 Fax: (212)843-9635 E-mail: custserv@thomsonmedia.com • URL: http://www.thomsonmedia.com • Weekly. $109.00 per year. Edited for credit union executives. Covers trends and developments in lending, insurance, investments, mortgages, check processing, relevant technology, and other topics.

Credit Union Magazine: For Credit Union Elected Officials, Managers and Employees. Credit Union National Association, Inc. CUNA Publications, PO Box 431 Madison, WI 53705-0431. Phone: 800-356-8010 or (608)231-4000 Fax: (608)231-1869 E-mail: dorothy@cuna.org • URL: http://www.cuna.org • Monthly. $45.00 per year. News analysis and operational information for credit union management, staff, directors, and committee executives.

Credit Union National Association., PO Box 431, PO Box 431 Madison, WI 53701-0431. Phone: 800-356-9655 or (608)231-4000 Fax: (608)231-4263 E-mail: dorothy@cuna.org • URL: http://www.cuna.org • Serves as trade association serving more than 90% of credit unions in the U.S. through their respective state leagues with a total membership of more than 77 million persons. (A credit union is a member-owned, nonprofit institution formed to encourage saving and to offer low interest loans to members, usually people working for the same employer, belonging to the same association, or living in the same community.) Promotes credit union membership, use of services, and organization of new credit unions. Seeks to perfect credit union laws; aids in the development of new credit union services, including new payment systems techniques; assists in the training of credit union officials and employees; compiles statistics, annually, by state. Offers charitable program.

Credit Union Report. Credit Union National Association, Publications Dept., PO Box 431 Madison, WI 53701-0431. Phone: 800-356-9655 Fax: (608)231-1869 • URL: http://www.cuna.org • Annual. $15.00. Credit union leagues, associations, for each of the 50 states and the District of Columbia.

CreditDisk 2.0. Fitch, Inc., One State Street Plaza New York, NY 10004. Phone: 800-753-4824 or (212)908-0800 Fax: (212)480-4435 • URL: http://www.fitchratings.com • Price and frequency on application. CD-ROM provides credit research and ratings on individual banks throughout the world, with Internet updating. Includes graphic displays of rating histories and financial ratios.

CreditWeek. Standard & Poor's, 55 Water St. New York, NY 10041. Phone: 800-852-1641 or (212)438-1000 Fax: (212)438-2000 E-mail: questions@standardandpoors.com • URL: http://www.standardandpoors.com • Description: Standard & Poor's flagship print information and news publication that covers the global credit markets. Includes insightful feature articles on market events and trends, plus columns titled Rating News and Credit Watch.

CreditWeek (Municipal Edition). Standard and Poor's, 55 Water St. New York, NY 10041. Phone: 800-221-5277 or (212)438-

1000 Fax: (212)438-4368 E-mail: clientsupport@standardandpoors.com • URL: http://www.standardandpoors.com • Weekly. Price on application. Provides news and analysis of the municipal bond market, including information on new issues.

Crime in America's Top-Rated Cities: A Statistical Profile. Grey House Publishing, 185 Milleton Rd. Millerton, NY 12546. Phone: 800-562-2139 or (518)789-8700 Fax: (518)789-0556 E-mail: books@greyhouse.com • URL: http://www.greyhouse.com • 2000. $155.00. Third edition. Contains 20-year data for major crime categories in 76 cities, suburbs, metropolitan areas, and the U. S. Also includes statistics on correctional facilities, inmates, hate crimes, illegal drugs, and other crime-related matters.

Criminal Justice Information: How to Find It, How to Use It. Dennis C. Benamati and others. Greenwood Publishing Group, Inc., 88 Post Rd., W. Westport, CT 06881. Phone: 800-225-5800 or (203)226-3571 Fax: (203)431-2214 E-mail: customer-service@greenwood.com • URL: http://www.greenwood.com • 1997. $64.95. A guide to print, electronic, and online criminal justice information resources. Includes statistical reports, directories, periodicals, monographs, databases, and other sources.

Criminal Law Advocacy Reporter. LexisNexis Matthew Bender, 1275 Broadway Albany, NY 12204. Phone: 800-424-4200 or (518)487-3000 Fax: (518)487-3584 E-mail: bookstore.support@lexisnexis.com • URL: http://www.bender.com • Monthly. $447.00 per year. Newsletter. Analysis of the latest cases and trends in criminal law and procedure.

Criminal Law Deskbook. Patrick McCloskey and Ronald Schoenberg. LexisNexis Matthew Bender, 1275 Broadway Albany, NY 12204. Phone: 800-424-4200 or (518)487-3000 Fax: (518)487-3584 E-mail: bookstore.support@lexisnexis.com • URL: http://www.bender.com • $276.00. Looseleaf service. Periodic supplementation. Discussions of the basic principles of criminal procedure, substantive law, and criminal trial strategy and tactics.

Criminal Law Reporter. BNA, Inc., 1231 25th St., NW Washington, DC 20037. Phone: 800-372-1033 E-mail: customercare@bna.com • URL: http://www.bna.com • Weekly. $896.00 per year. Includes full text of U. S. Supreme Court criminal law decisions.

Criminal Procedure Handbook. J.J. Joubert, editor. Available from Gaunt, Inc., 3011 Gulf Dr. Holmes Beach, FL 34217-2199. Phone: 800-942-8683 or (914)778-5211 Fax: (914)778-5252 E-mail: info@gaunt.com • URL: http://www.gaunt.com • 1999. $42.50. Fourth edition.

Criminology; An Interdisciplinary Journal. American Society of Criminology, 1314 Kinnear Rd. Columbus, OH 43212-1156. Phone: (614)292-9207 Fax: (614)292-6767 E-mail: asc41@infinet.com • URL: http://www.asc41.com • Quarterly. Individuals, $120.00 per year; institutions, $140.00 per year.

Crisis Response: Inside Stories on Managing Image Under Siege. Gale Cengage Learning, 27500 Drake Rd. Farmington Hills, MI 48331-3535. Phone: 800-877-GALE or (248)699-4253 Fax: 800-414-5043 E-mail: gale.galeord@cengage.com • URL: http://gale.cengage.com • 1993. $80.00. Presents first-hand accounts by media relations professionals of major business crises and how they were handled. Topics include the following kinds of crises: environmental, governmental, corporate image, communications, and product.

Critical Path Analysis and Linear Programming. Mik Wisniewski and Jonathan Klein. Palgrave Macmillan Ltd, Houndmills, Basingstoke Hampshire RG21 6XS, United Kingdom. Phone: 44 01256-302699 Fax: 44 01256-364733 E-mail: bookenquiries@palgrave.com • URL: http://www.palgrave.com • 2001. f29.99. Contains "Book 1: Linear Programming" and "Book 2: Critical Path Analysis." Chapters include "Linear Programming in the Real World" and "Critical Path Analysis Techniques." Emphasis is on software applications, with a non-mathematical orientation.

Crittenden Directory of Real Estate Financing. Crittenden Research, Inc., PO Box 1150 Novato, CA 94948. Phone: 800-421-3483 Fax: (415)382-2476 • URL: http://www.crittendennews.com • Semiannual. $399.00 per year. Includes weekly *Newsletter*. Provides information on major U. S. real estate lenders.

Crittenden Report Real Estate Financing: The Nation's Leading Weekly Newslett er on Real Estate Finance. Crittenden Research, Inc., P.O. Box 1150 Novato, CA 94948. Phone: 800-421-3483 or (415)382-2400 Fax: (415)382-2476 Weekly. $395.00 per year. Newsletter on real estate lending and mortgages. Includes semiannual *Crittenden Directory of Real Estate Financing*.

Crop Protection Chemicals Reference. Chemical and Pharmaceutical Press, Inc., 302 Fifth Ave., 5th Fl. New York, NY 10001. Phone: 800-544-7377 or (212)399-0126 Fax: (212)399-1122 1994. $130.00. 10th edition. Contains the complete text of product labels. Indexed by manufacturer, product category, pest use, crop use, chemical name, and brand name.

Crop Science: A Journal Serving the International Community. Crop Science Society of America, 677 S. Segoe Rd. Madison, WI 53711. Phone: (608)273-8080 Fax: (608)273-2021 • URL: http://www.crops.org • Bimonthly. Free to members, non-members, $241.00 per year.

Croplife. Meister Media, 37733 Euclid Ave. Willoughby, OH 44094. Phone: 800-572-7740 or (440)942-2000 Fax: (440)975-3447 E-mail: info@meistermedia.com • URL: http://www.meistermedia.com • Monthly. $36.00 per year. Formerly *Farm Chemicals*.

CropLife America., 1156 15th St. NW Washington, DC 20005. Phone: (202)296-1585 Fax: (202)463-0474 E-mail: rrunyon@croplifeamerica.org • URL: http://www.croplifeamerica.org • Fosters the interests of the general public and member companies by promoting innovative and environmentally sound manufacture, distribution and use of crop protection and production technologies for safe, high quality, affordable, abundant food, fiber and other crops.

CRS Referral Directory. Council of Residential Specialists, 430 N Michigan Ave. Ste., 300 Chicago, IL 60611. Phone: 800-462-8841 or (312)321-4400 Fax: (312)321-4400 E-mail: crshelp@crs.com • URL: http://www.crs.com • Covers: 35,000 Certified Residential Specialists (CRS). Entries include: Member name, firm name, address, phone, fax; designations held, areas of specialization, e-mail; web page address; years of experience, voicemail; 2nd business phone.

Cruise Ship Law. LexisNexis Matthew Bender, 1275 Broadway Albany, NY 12204-4026. Phone: 800-424-4200 or (518)487-3000 Fax: 800-828-8341 or (518)487-3584 E-mail: customer.support@lexisnexis.com • URL: http://www.lexisnexis.com/matthewbender/ • 2003. $198.00. Provides analysis of federal cruise ship law, relevant international treaties, and court forms. Covers the law relating to passengers, crew members, stowaways, concessionaires, shipboard medical care, cruise line bankruptcies, and other items.

Cruise Travel: Ships, Ports, Schedules, Prices. World Publishing Co., 990 Grove St. Evanston, IL 60201. Phone: (847)491-6440 Fax: (847)491-0459 E-mail: cs@centurysports.net • URL: http://www.cruisetravelmag.com • Bimonthly. $23.94 per year.

CryoGas International: The Source of Timely and Relevant Information for the Industrial Gas and Cyrogenics Industries. J. R. Campbell & Associates, Inc., Five Militia Dr. Lexington, MA 02173. Phone: (781)862-0624 Fax: (781)863-9411 E-mail: cryogas@cyrogas.com • URL: http://www.cryogas.com • 11 times a year. $150.00 per year. Reports developments in technology market development and new products for the industrial gases and cryogenic equipment industries. Formerly *Cryogenic Information Report*.

Cryogenic Engineering Conference., PO Box 500, Fermi National Lab, Kirk & Wilson Rds., PO Box 500 Batavia, IL 60510-0500. Phone: (630)840-3238 Fax: (630)840-4989 E-mail: tnicol@fnal.gov • URL: http://tdserver1.fnal.gov/nicol/cec • Represents academic, industrial and governmental researchers, and managers involved in basic and applied work in cryogenics (the branch of physics and engineering dealing with the phenomena of extreme cold). Provides a forum for a four-day presentation of papers and seminars concerning advances in the science and technology of cryogenics in areas such as superconductivity, heat transfer, insulation, instrumentation, aerospace, liquefied gases, cryo-health services, cryobiology, LNG and power generation.

Cryogenic Society of America., c/o Laurie Huget, Huget Advertising, 1033 South Blvd. Oak Park, IL 60302-2881. Phone: (708)383-6220 Fax: (708)383-9337 E-mail: csa@huget.com • URL: http://www.cryogenicsociety.gov/ • Seeks to encourage the dissemination of information on low temperature industrial technology. Formerly Helium Society.

Cryogenics: The International Journal of Low Temperature Engineering and Research. Elsevier, 655 Ave. of the Americas New York, NY 10010-5107. Phone: 800-366-2665 or (212)989-5800 Fax: 800-535-9935 or (212)633-3680 E-mail: custserv@elsevier.com • URL: http://www.elsevier.com • Monthly. Institutions, $2,169.00 per year.

Crystal Fire: The Birth of the Information Age. Michael Riordan and Lillian Hoddeson. W. W. Norton & Co., Inc., 500 5th Ave. New York, NY 10110. Phone: 800-223-2584 or (212)354-5500 Fax: (212)869-0856 • URL: http://www.wwnorton.com • 1997. $27.50. A history of the transistor, from early electronic experiments to practical development at the former Bell Telephone Laboratories. (Sloan Technology Series).

CSA Life Sciences Collection. Cambridge Scientific Abstracts, 7200 Wisconsin Ave., Suite 601 Bethesda, MD 20814. Phone: 800-843-7751 or (301)961-6700 Fax: (301)961-6720 • URL: http://www.csa.com • Includes online versions of *Biotechnology Research Abstracts, Entomology Abstracts, Genetics Abstracts*, and about 20 other abstract collections. Time period is 1978 to date, with monthly updates. Inquire as to online cost and availability.

CSANews. American Society of Agronomy, 677 S Segoe Rd. Madison, WI 53711. Phone: (608)273-8080 Fax: (608)273-2021 E-mail: headquarters@agronomy.org • URL: http://www.agronomy.org • Description: Publishes information on agronomy, crop science, soil science, and related topics. Provides news of the societies and members; reports of annual meetings; listings of publications; announcements of awards, retirements, and deaths; job listings; and a calendar of events.

CSG State Directories I. Council of State Governments, 2760 Research Park Dr., PO Box 11910 Lexington, KY 40578-1910. Phone: 800-800-1910 or (859)244-8000 Fax: (859)244-8001 E-mail: csg@csg.org • URL: http://www.csg.org • Covers: About 8,000 state legislators, elected state executive branch officials, and state supreme court judges. Entries include: Name, title, address, district, party affiliation, fax and facts about each state-motto, flower, bird, nickname, capitol address, bill status phone, land area, population, D. C. Liaison, term limits, election and session dates.

CSG State Directories II: Legislative, Leadership, Committees and Staff by Function. Council of State Governments, 2760 Research Park Dr. Lexington, KY 40578-1910. Phone: 800-800-1910 or (859)244-8000 Fax: (859)244-8001 E-mail: sales@csg.org • URL: http://www.csg.org • Annual. $49.99. Legislative leaders, committee members and staff, personnel of principal legislative staff offices. Formerly *Book of the States, Supplement Two: State Legislative Leadership, Committees, and Staff*.

CSM. CSM Marketing, Inc., 195 Smithtown Blvd. Nesconset, NY 11767-1849. Monthly. $30.00 per year. Formerly *Catalog Showroom Merchandiser*.

CSO: The Resource for Security Executives. CXO Media, Inc., 492 Old Connecticut Path Framingham, MA 01701-9208. Phone: 800-788-4605 or (508)872-0080 Fax: (508)872-6063 • URL: http://www.csoonline.com • Monthly. $64.95 per year. Edited for corporate chief security officers (CSOs). Covers a wide variety of business security issues, including computer security, identity theft, spam, physical security, loss prevention, risk management, privacy, and investigations.

CSP: The Magazine for C-Store People. CSP Information Group, 1100 Jorie Blvd. Oak Brook, IL 60523. Phone: (630)574-5075 Fax: (630)574-5175 • URL: http://www.cspnet.com • 14 times a year. $48.00 per year. Emphasizes the influence of people (both store personnel and consumers) on the C-store industry.

CTAM-Cable and Telecommunications Association for Marketing., 201 N. Union, Suite 440 Alexandria, VA 23314. Phone: (703)549-4200 Fax: (703)684-1167 E-mail: ctam@ctam.com • URL: http://www.ctam.com • Formerly CTAM, The Marketing Society for Cable and Telecommunications Industry.

CTFA News. Cosmetic, Toiletry, and Fragrance Association, 1101 17th St., N. W., Suite 300 Washington, DC 20036. Phone: (202)331-1770 Fax: (202)331-1969 E-mail: membership@ctfa.org • URL: http://www.ctfa.org • Bimonthly. Newsletter.

CTIA - The Wireless Association., 1400 16th St. NW, Ste. 600 Washington, DC 20036. Phone: (202)785-0081 Fax: (202)785-0721 E-mail: memberservices@ctia.org • URL: http://www.ctia.org • Individuals and organizations actively engaged in cellular radiotelephone communications, including: telephone companies and corporations providing radio communications; lay firms; engineering firms; consultants and manufacturers. (A cellular radiotelephone is a mobile communications device. An area is geographically divided into low frequency cells monitored by a computer that switches callers from one frequency to another as they move from cell to cell.) Objectives are to: promote, educate, and facilitate the professional interests, needs, and concerns of members with respect to the development and commercial applications of cellular technology; provide an opportunity for exchanging experience and concerns; broaden the understanding and importance of cellular communication technology. Conducts discussions, studies, and courses.

CUIS (Credit Union Information Service). United Communications Group, 11300 Rockville Pike, Suite 1100 Rockville, MD 20852-3030. Phone: 800-929-4824 or (301)287-2700 Fax: (301)816-8945 E-mail: webmaster@ucg.com • URL: http://www.ucg.com • Biweekly. $277.00 per year. Newsletter. Supplement available *CUIS Special Reoprt*.

Cumulative Index to Nursing and Allied Health Literature. CINAHL Information Systems, 1509 Wilson Terrace Glendale, CA 91209-0871. Phone: 800-959-7167 or (818)409-8005 Fax: (818)546-5679 E-mail: cinahl@cinahl.com • URL: http://www.cinahl.com • Quarterly. $365.00 per year. Includes annual*Cumulation Index*.

Cumulative List of Organizations Described in Section 170(c) of the Internal Revenue Code of 1986. Available from U. S. Government Printing Office, Washington, DC 20402. Phone: (202)512-1800 Fax: (202)512-2250 E-mail: gpoaccess@gpo.gov • URL: http://www.access.gpo.gov • Annual. $153.00 per year, including quarterly supplements. Lists about 300,000 organizations eligible for contributions deductible for federal income tax purposes. Provides name of each organization and city, but not complete address information. Arranged alphabetically by name of institution. (Office of Employee Plans and Exempt Organizations, Internal Revenue Service.)

Currency Risk Management. Gary Shoup, editor. Fitzroy Dearborn Publishers Inc, 919 N. Michigan Ave., Suite 760 Chicago, IL 60611. Phone: 800-850-8102 or (312)587-0131 Fax: (312)587-1049 E-mail: fitzroy@aol.com • URL: http://www.fitzroydearborn.com • 1998. $55.00.

Current Biography. H. W. Wilson Co., 950 University Ave. Bronx, NY 10452. Phone: 800-367-6770 or (718)588-8400 Fax: 800-590-1617 or (718)590-1617 E-mail: custserv@hwwilson.com • URL: http://www.hwwilson.com • 11 times a year. $130.00 per year. Includes profiles of business people and economists who have been prominent in the news.

Current Biography on WILSONDISC. H. W. Wilson Co., 950 University Ave. Bronx, NY 10452. Phone: 800-367-6770 or (718)588-8400 Fax: 800-590-1617 Annual. Provides *Current Biography* on CD-ROM.

Current Biography Yearbook. H. W. Wilson Co., 950 University Ave. Bronx, NY 10452. Phone: 800-367-6770 or (718)588-8400 Fax: 800-590-1617 or (718)590-1617 E-mail:

custserv@hwwilson.com • URL: http://www.hwwilson.com • Annual. $115.00. The yearly cumulation of *Current Biography*.

Current Biotechnology Abstracts. DECHEMA, c/o Neil Forsyth, Information Systems, Theodor-Heuss-Allee 25 D-60486 Frankfurt Am Main, Germany. Phone: 49 69 7564 349 Fax: 49 69 7564 201 • URL: http://www.dechema.de • Monthly. $1,229.00 per year. Reports on the latest scientific, technical and commercial advances in the field of technology.

Current Contents Connect. Institute for Scientific Information, 3501 Market St. Philadelphia, PA 19104. Phone: 800-386-4474 or (215)386-0100 Fax: (215)386-6362 • URL: http://www.isinet.com • Provides online abstracts of articles listed in the tables of contents of about 7,500 journals. Coverage is very broad, including science, social science, life science, technology, engineering, industry, agriculture, the environment, economics, and arts and humanities. Time period is two years, with weekly updates. Inquire as to online cost and availability.

Current Contents: Engineering, Computing and Technology. Thomson/ISI, 3501 Market St. Philadelphia, PA 19104. Phone: 888-216-4101 or (215)386-0100 Fax: (215)387-1125 • URL: http://www.isinet.com • Weekly. $730.00 per year. Reproductions of contents pages of technical journals. Includes *Author Index*, *Address Directory*, *Current Book Contents* and *Title Word Index*. Formerly *Current Contents: Engineering, Technology and Applied Sciences*.

Current Contents: Social and Behavioral Sciences. Thomson/ISI, 3501 Market St. Philadelphia, PA 19104. Phone: 800-216-4101 or (215)386-0100 Fax: (215)387-1125 • URL: http://www.isinet.com • Weekly. $730.00 per year. Includes *Author Index*.

Current Index to Journals in Education (CIJE). Oryx Press, 4041 N. Central Ave. Phoenix, AZ 85012-3397. Phone: (602)265-2651 Fax: (602)265-6250 E-mail: info@oryxpress.com • URL: http://www.oryxpress.com • Monthly. $245.00 per year. Semiannual cumulations, $475.00.

Current Index to Statistics: Applications, Methods, and Theory. American Statistical Association, 1429 Duke St. Alexandria, VA 22314-3415. Phone: 888-231-3473 or (703)684-1221 Fax: (703)684-2037 E-mail: asainfo@amstat.org • URL: http://www.amstat.org • Annual. Price on application. An index to journal articles on statistical applications and methodology.

Current Law Index: Multiple Access to Legal Periodicals. Gale Cengage Learning, 27500 Drake Rd. Farmington Hills, MI 48331-3535. Phone: 800-877-GALE or (248)699-4253 Fax: 800-414-5043 E-mail: gale.galeord@cengage.com • URL: http://gale.cengage.com • Monthly. $725.00 per year. Produced in cooperation with the American Association of Law Libraries. Indexes more than 900 law journals, legal newspapers, and specialty publications from the U.S., Canada, U.K., Ireland, Australia, and New Zealand.

Current Legal Forms with Tax Analysis. LexisNexis Matthew Bender, 1275 Broadway Albany, NY 12204. Phone: 800-424-4200 or (518)487-3000 Fax: (518)487-3584 E-mail: bookstore.support@lexisnexis.com • URL: http://www.bender.com • Quarterly. $2,183.00 per year. 34 looseleaf volumes.

Current Municipal Problems. West Group, 610 Opperman Dr. Eagan, MN 55123. Phone: 800-328-4880 or (651)687-7000 Fax: 800-340-9378 or (651)687-5827 E-mail: bookstore@westgroup.com • URL: http://www.westgroup.com • Quarterly. $287.50 per year. Full text journal articles on municipal law and administration. Indexing included.

Current Population Reports: Household Economic Studies, Series P-70. Available from U. S. Government Printing Office, Washington, DC 20402. Phone: (202)512-1800 Fax: (202)512-2250 E-mail: gpoaccess@gpo.gov • URL: http://www.access.gpo.gov • Irregular. $21.00 per year. Issued by the U.S. Bureau of the Census (http://www.census.gov). Each issue covers a special topic relating to household socioeconomic characteristics.

Current Population Reports: Population Characteristics, Special Studies, and Consumer Income, Series P-20, P-23, and P-60. Available from U. S. Government Printing Office, Washington, DC 20402. Phone: (202)512-1800 Fax: (202)512-2250 E-mail: gpoaccess@gpo.gov • URL: http://www.access.gpo.gov • Irregular. $80.00 per year. Issued by the U.S. Bureau of the Census (http://www.census.gov). Each issue covers a special topic relating to population or income. Series P-20, *Population Characteristics*, provides statistical studies on such items as mobility, fertility, education, and marital status. Series P-23, *Special Studies*, consists of occasional reports on methodology. Series P-60, *Consumer Income*, publishes reports on income in relation to age, sex, education, occupation, family size, etc.

Current Publications in Legal and Related Fields. American Association of Law Libraries. Fred B. Rothman and Co., 10368 W. Centennial Rd. Littleton, CO 80127. Phone: 888-361-3255 or (303)979-5657 Fax: (303)979-0707 E-mail: s_jarrett@wshein.com • URL: http://www.wshein.com • Nine times a year. $198.00 per year. Looseleaf service. Annual cumulation.

Current Trends in Information: Research and Theory. William Katz and Robin Kinder, editors. The Haworth Press, Inc., 10 Alice St. Binghamton, NY 13940-1580. Phone: 800-429-6784 or (607)722-5857 Fax: 800-895-0582 or (607)722-1424 E-mail: getinfo@haworthpressinc.com • URL: http://www.haworthpressinc.com • 1987. $49.95. (Reference Librarian Series: No. 18).

Curricula in the Atmospheric Oceanic, Hydrologic and Related Sciences - Colleges and Universities in the United States and Canada. American Meteorological Society, 45 Beacon St. Boston, MA 02108-3693. Phone: (617)227-2425 Fax: (617)742-8718 E-mail: amsinfoamericatsoc.org • URL: http://www.ametsoc.org • Free. Available online only. Includes approximately 100 schools. Formerly *Curricula in the Atmospheric and Oceanographic Sciences-Colleges and Universities in the U.S. and Canada*.

Curtains, Blinds and Valances. Rightfield Business Publications, 871 Boeke Rd. Evansville, IN 47714. Phone: 800-977-9332 or (812)477-9332 Fax: (812)479-0499 1998. $18.99. (Sew in a Weekend Series).

Custom Draperies in Interior Design. M. Neal. Prentice Hall PTR, 240 Frisch Ct. Paramus, NJ 07652. Phone: 800-282-0693 Fax: 800-445-6991 • URL: http://www.phptr.com • 1982. $40.25.

Custom Home. Hanley-Wood, LLC, One Thomas Circle, NW Washington, DC 20005. Phone: 800-837-0870 or (202)452-0800 Fax: (202)785-1974 • URL: http://www.hanley-wood.com • Seven times a year. $36.00 per year. Edited for "top of the market" custom builders, designers, and architects.

Custom Tailor. Custom Tailors and Designers Association of America, P.O. Box 53052 Washington, DC 20009-9052. Phone: (202)387-7220 Three times a year. $50.00 per year. Controlled circulation.

Custom Tailors and Designers Association of America, P.O. Box 53052 Washington, DC 20009-9052. Phone: (202)387-7220 Fax: (202)387-7713 E-mail: info@ctda.com • URL: http://www.ctda.com • Formerly Merchant Tailors and Designers Association of America.

The Customer Communicator. The Customer Service Group, 28 W 25th St., 8th Fl. New York, NY 10010. Phone: 800-232-4317 or (212)228-0246 Fax: (212)228-0376 E-mail: info@CustomerServiceGroup.com • URL: http://www.alexcommgrp.com • Description: Serves as a guideline for customer relations skills while it "boosts morale." Covers customer representative skills and provides tips on customer contact, handling complaints, checklists, and promotional contests. **Remarks:** a monthly training module.

Customer Inter@ctions Buyer's Guide and Directory. Technology Marketing Corp., One Technology Plaza Norwalk, CT 06854. Phone: 800-243-6002 or (203)852-6800 Fax: (203)853-2845 E-mail: tmc@tmcnet.com • URL: http://www.tmcnet.com • Annual. $25.00. Over 1,100 domestic and foreign suppliers of equipment, products, and services to the telecommunications/telemarketing industry. Formerly *Call Center Solutions Buyer's Guide and Directory*.

Customer Service: A Practical Approach. Elaine K. Harris. Prentice Hall PTR, 240 Frisch Ct. Paramus, NJ 07652. Phone: 800-282-0693 Fax: 800-445-6991 • URL: http://www.phptr.com • 2002. $43.00. Third edition. Covers various topics in relation to providing good customer service: problem solving; strategy; planning; communication; coping with difficult customers; motivation; leadership. Glossary, information sources, and index are included.

Customer Service Excellence: A Concise Guide for Librarians. Darlene E. Weingand. American Library Association, 50 E. Huron St. Chicago, IL 60611-2795. Phone: 800-545-2433 or (312)944-6780 Fax: (312)440-9374 E-mail: ala@ala.com • URL: http://www.ala.org • 1997. $30.00. Includes information on quality of service benchmarks, teamwork, patron-librarian conflict management, "customer service language," and other library service topics. (ALA Editions Series).

Customer Service Newsletter. The Customer Service Group, 28 W 25th St., 8th Fl. New York, NY 10010. Phone: 800-232-4317 or (212)228-0246 Fax: (212)228-0376 E-mail: info@CustomerServiceGroup.com • URL: http://www.alexcommgrp.com • Description: Reports on practical, action-oriented techniques and tactics for improving your customer service operations.

Customs Bulletin and Decisions. Available from U. S. Government Printing Office, Washington, DC 20402. Phone: (202)512-1800 Fax: (202)512-2250 E-mail: gpoaccess@gpo.gov • URL: http://www.access.gpo.gov • Weekly. $247.00 per year. Issued by U. S. Customs Service, Department of the Treasury. Contains regulations, rulings, decisions, and notices relating to customs laws.

Customs Law and Administration: Statutes and Treaties. Oceana Publications, Inc., 75 Main St. Dobbs Ferry, NY 10522-1601. Phone: 800-831-0758 or (914)693-8100 Fax: (914)693-0402 E-mail: custsvc@oceanalaw.com • URL: http://www.oceanalaw.com • $475.00. Five volumes. Looseleaf service. Periodic supplementation.

Customs Regulations of the United States. Available from U. S. Government Printing Office, Washington, DC 20402. Phone: (202)512-1800 Fax: (202)512-2250 E-mail: gpoaccess@gpo.gov • URL: http://www.access.gpo.gov • Looseleaf. $175.00. Issued by U. S. Customs Service, Department of the Treasury. Reprint of regulations published to carry out customs laws of the U. S. Includes supplementary material for an indeterminate period.

Cutting Technology. Penton Media, Inc., 1300 E 9th St. Cleveland, OH 44114. Phone: (216)696-7000 Fax: (216)696-1752 E-mail: information@penton.com • URL: http://www.penton.com • Seven times a year. Free to qualified personnel; others, $55.00 per year. Provides abstracts of the international literature of metal cutting and machining. Formerly *Cutting Tool-Machine Digest*.

Cutting Tool Engineering. CTE Publications, Inc., 400 Skokie Blvd., Suite 395 Northbrook, IL 60062-7903. Phone: (708)441-7520 Fax: (708)441-8740 Nine times a year. $30.00 per year.

C.V. Starr Center for Applied Economics.

Cyber Crime Investigator's Field Guide. Bruce Middleton. CRC Press, 2000 N.W. Corporate Blvd. Boca Raton, FL 33431. Phone: 800-272-7737 or (561)994-0555 Fax: 800-374-3401 or (561)989-9732 E-mail: orders@crcpress.com • URL: http://www.crcpress.com • 2004. $69.95. Second edition. Provides a step-by-step routine for investigating cybecrime, including the use of key forensic software, sample questions for clients, evidence collection, and examples from case studies. (Imprint: Auerbach Publications.)

Cybercrime and Cyberterrorism: Current Issues. John V. Blane. Nova Science Publishers, Inc., 400 Oser Ave., Suite 1600 Hauppauge, NY 11788-3619. Phone: (631)231-7269 Fax: (631)231-8175 E-mail: novascience@earthlink.net • URL: http://www.novapublishers.com • 2003. $29.50. Emphasizes the legal fight against cybercrime that is taking place in various countries of the world.

CyberDictionary: Your Guide to the Wired World. Spurge ink!, 16350 Ventura Blvd., Ste. 362 Encino, CA 91436. Phone: (818)705-3740 Fax: (818)705-0692 E-mail: info@spurgeink.com • URL: http://www.spurgeink.com • 1996. $17.95. Includes many illustrations.

Cyberfinance: Raising Capital for the E-Business. Martin B. Robins. CCH, Inc., 2700 Lake Cook Rd. Riverwoods, IL 60015. Phone: 800-835-5224 or (847)267-7000 E-mail: cust_serv@cch.com • URL: http://www.cch.com • 2001. $79.00. Covers the taxation, financial, and legal aspects of raising money for new Internet-based ("dot.com") companies, including the three stages of startup, growth, and initial public offering. (Solutions for Professional Advisers Series).

Cyberhound's Guide to Companies on the Internet. Gale Cengage Learning, 27500 Drake Rd. Farmington Hills, MI 48331-3535. Phone: 800-877-GALE or (248)699-4253 Fax: 800-414-5043 E-mail: gale.galeord@cengage.com • URL: http://gale.cengage.com • 1996. $79.00. Presents critical descriptions and ratings of more than 2,000 company or corporate Internet databases. Includes a glossary of Internet terms, a bibliography, and indexes. (Cyberhound's Series).

Cyberhound's Guide to Internet Libraries. Gale Cengage Learning, 27500 Drake Rd. Farmington Hills, MI 48331-3535. Phone: 800-877-GALE or (248)699-4253 Fax: 800-414-5043 E-mail: gale.galeord@cengage.com • URL: http://gale.cengage.com • 1996. 79.00. Presents critical descriptions and ratings of more than 2,000 library Internet databases. Includes a glossary of Internet terms, a bibliography, and indexes. (Cyberhound's Series).

Cyberhound's Guide to People on the Internet. Gale Cengage Learning, 27500 Drake Rd. Farmington Hills, MI 48331-3535. Phone: 800-877-GALE or (248)699-4253 Fax: 800-414-5043 E-mail: gale.galeord@cengage.com • URL: http://gale.cengage.com • 1996. $79.00. Second edition. Provides descriptions of about 5,500 Internet databases maintained by or for prominent individuals in business, the professions, entertainment, and sports. Indexed by name, subject, and keyword (master index). (Cyberhound's Series).

Cyberhound's Guide to Publications on the Internet. Gale Cengage Learning, 27500 Drake Rd. Farmington Hills, MI 48331-3535. Phone: 800-877-GALE or (248)699-4253 Fax: 800-414-5043 E-mail: gale.galeord@cengage.com • URL: http://gale.cengage.com • 1996. $79.00. Presents critical descriptions and ratings of more than 3,400 Internet databases of journals, newspapers, newsletters, and other publications. Includes a glossary of Internet terms, a bibliography, and three indexes. (Cyberhound's Series).

Cyberlaw: Intellectual Property in the Digital Millennium. American Lawyer Media, Inc., 105 Madison Ave. New York, NY 10016. Phone: 800-888-8300 or (212)779-9200 Fax: (212)481-8110 E-mail: lawcatalog@amlaw.com • URL: http://www.lawcatalog.com/ • Looseleaf. $159.00. Updated as needed. A basic guide to copyright as applied to the Internet and other electronic sources. (Law Journal Press).

Cyberquake: How the Internet will Erase Profits, Topple Market Leaders, and Shatter Business Models. Michael Sullivan-Trainor. John Wiley and Sons, Inc., 111 River St. Hoboken, NJ 07030. Phone: 800-225-5945 or (201)748-6000 Fax: (201)748-6088 E-mail: info@wiley.com • URL: http://www.wiley.com • 1997. $26.95. Predicts that the Internet will cause "an overwhelming shift in control of the worldwide marketplace" in the early 21st century. (Business Technology Series).

The CyberSkeptic's Guide to Internet Research. Information Today, Inc., 143 Old Marlton Pke. Medford, NJ 08055-8750. Phone: 800-300-9868 or (609)654-6266 Fax: (609)654-4309 E-mail: custserv@infotoday.com • URL: http://www.infotoday.com • 10 times a year. Individuals, $159.00 per year; nonprofit organizations, $134.00 per year. Newsletter. Presents critical reviews of World Wide Web sites and databases, written by information professionals. Includes "Late Breaking News" of Web sites.

Cyberspace Lawyer. Glasser Legalworks, 150 Clove Rd. Little Falls, NJ 07424. Phone: 800-308-1700 or (973)890-0008 Fax: (973)890-0042 E-mail: orders@glasserlegalworks.com • URL: http://www.glasserlegalworks.com • 11 times a year.

$300.00 per year. Newsletter. Covers various legal topics pertaining to use of the Internet. Includes advice on legal research via the Web.

Cyberspace Lexicon: An Illustrated Dictionary of Terms from Multimedia to Virtual Reality. Bob Cotton and Richard Oliver. Phaidon Press, 3 Center Plz. Boston, MA 02108. Phone: 800-759-0190 Fax: 800·286-9471 • URL: http://www.phaidon.com • 1994. $29.95. Defines more than 800 terms, with manyillustrations. Includes a bibliography.

Cybertaxation: The Taxation of E-Commerce. Karl A. Frieden. CCH, Inc., 2700 Lake Cook Rd. Riverwoods, IL 60015. Phone: 800-835-5224 or (847)267-7000 E-mail: cust_serv@cch.com • URL: http://www.cch.com • 2000. $75.00. Includes state sales and use tax issues and corporate income tax rules, as related to doing business over the Internet.

The Cybrarian's Manual. Pat Ensor, editor. American Library Association, 50 E. Huron St. Chicago, IL 60611-2795. Phone: 800-545-2433 or (312)944-6780 Fax: (312)440-9374 E-mail: ala@ala.org • URL: http://www.ala.org • 2000. $45.00. Second edition. Provides information for librarians concerning the Internet, expert systems, computer networks, client/server architecture, Web pages, multimedia, information industry careers, and other "cyberspace" topics.

Cycle Projections. Foundation for the Study of Cycles, 214 Carnegie Center, Ste. 204 Princeton, NJ 08540-6237. E-mail: cycles@cycles.org • URL: http://www.cycles.org • Monthly. $125.00 per year. Newsletter includes trend projections for stocks, commodities, real estate, and the economy. Short, intermediate, and long-term cycles are covered.

Cycle World. Hachette Filipacchi Media U.S., Inc., 1633 Broadway New York, CA 10019. Phone: 800-456-3084 or (212)767-6000 Fax: (212)767-5615 • URL: http://www.hfmmag.com • Monthly. $12.97 per year. Incorporates *Cycle*.

Cycles. Service Directions Inc., 11 Seventh St. Pelham, NY 10803. Phone: 800-666-0505 or (914)738-3800 Fax: (914)738-3241 E-mail: info@CustomerServiceGroup.com • URL: http://www.cycles.org • Description: Describes new laundry equipment, advances in laundryroom management, and analyzes problems in residential laundryrooms. Recurring features include interviews.

D & B Business Locator. Dun & Bradstreet, Inc., 103 JFK Pkwy. Short Hills, NJ 07078. Phone: 800-234-3867 or (512)794-7768 Fax: (512)794-7670 • URL: http://www.dnb.com • Quarterly. $2,495.00 per year. CD-ROM provides concise information on more than 10 million U. S. companies or businesses. Includes data on number of employees.

D and B Employment Opportunities Directory Career Guide., Dun and Bradstreet Corp., One Diamond Hill Rd. Murray Hill, NJ 07974. Phone: 800-526-0651 or (908)665-5732 Fax: (908)665-5722 E-mail: customerservice@dnb.com • URL: http://www.dnb.com • Annual. Libraries, $495.00. Lists more than 5,000 companies that have career opportunities in various fields. A Dun & Bradstreet publication.

D and B Million Dollar Directory, Dun and Bradstreet, 3 Sylvan Way Parsippany, NJ 07054-3896. Phone: 800-526-0651 or (908)665-5732 Fax: (973)605-6911 E-mail: dnbmdd@dnb.com • URL: http://www.dnbmdd.com • Annual. Commercial institutions, $1,395.00; libraries, $1,275.00. Lease basis.

D & B Women-Owned Business Directory. Dun & Bradstreet, 103 JFK Pky. Short Hills, NJ 07078. Phone: 800-234-3867 or (973)-921-5500 E-mail: custserv@dnb.com • URL: http://www.dnb.com • 2000. Price on application.

D & O Advisor: Risk Management for Directors and Officers. American Lawyer Media, Inc., 105 Madison Ave. New York, NY 10016. Phone: 800-888-8300 or (212)779-9200 Fax: (212)481-8110 E-mail: lawcatalog@amlaw.com • URL: http://www.lawcatalog.com/ • Quarterly. $125.00 per year. Covers a wide range of legal topics of concern to corporate boards and key executives.

D T T P (Documents to the People). Government Documents Round Table. American Library Association, 50 E. Huron St. Chicago, IL 60611-2795. Phone: 800-545-2433 or (312)944-6780 Fax: (312)440-9374 E-mail: ala@ala.org • URL: http://www.ala.org • Quarterly. $30.00 per year. Formerly*Documents to the People*.

Daily Graphs. Daily Graphs, Inc, P.O. Box 66919 Los Angeles, CA 90066-0919. Phone: 800-472-7479 or (310)448-6843 New York Stock Exchange edition, $363.00 per year. NASDAQ O.T.C.-American Stock Exchange edition, $363.00 per year. Both editions include the 200 leading over-the-counter stocks.

Daily Graphs. Option Guide. Daily Graphs, Inc., P.O. Box 66919 Los Angeles, CA 90066-0919. Phone: 800-472-7479 or (310)448-6843 Weekly. $300.00 per year.

Daily Labor Report. Bureau of National Affairs Inc., 1801 S Bell St. Arlington, VA 22202. Phone: 800-372-1033 or (202)452-4200 Fax: (202)452-4226 E-mail: customercare@bna.com • URL: http://www.bna.com • Description: Covers labor developments in Congress, the courts, federal agencies, unions, management, and the National Labor Relations Board.

Daily Report for Executives. BNA, Inc., 1231 25th St., NW Washington, DC 20037. Phone: 800-372-1033 E-mail: customercare@bna.com • URL: http://www.bna.com • Daily. $7,698.00 per year. Newsletter. Covers legal, regulatory, economic, and tax developments affecting corporations.

Daily Tax Report: From Today's Daily Report for Executives. BNA, Inc., 1231 25th St., NW Washington, DC 20037. Phone: 800-372-1033 E-mail: customercare@bna.com •

URL: http://www.bna.com • Daily. $2,595.00 per year. Looseleaf service. Monitors tax legislation, hearings, rulings, and court decisions.

Daily Treasury Statement: Cash and Debt Operations of the United States Treasury. Available from U. S. Government Printing Office, Washington, DC 20402. Phone: (202)512-1800 Fax: (202)512-2250 E-mail: gpoaccess@gpo.gov • URL: http://www.access.gpo.gov • Daily, except Saturdays, Sundays, and holidays. (Financial Management Service, U. S. Treasury Department.)

Daily Variety: News of the Entertainment Industry. Reed Business Information, 360 Park Ave., S New York, NY 10010. Phone: 800-446-6551 or (646)746-6400 Fax: (646)746-7028 E-mail: corporatecommunications@reedbusiness.com • URL: http://www.reedbusiness.com • Daily. $297.00 per year. Covers entire scope of the entertainment business on the East and West coast.

Daily Weather Maps (Weekly Series). U.S. Dept. of Commerce

Dairy Field—Buyer's Guide. Stagnito Communications Inc., 155 Pfingsten Rd., Ste. 205 Deerfield IL 60015. Phone: (847)405-4000 Fax: (847)405-4100 E-mail: info@stagnito.com • URL: http://www.stagnito.com • Publication includes: List of over 500 suppliers of equipment and services and distributors for the dairy processing industry. Entries include: Company or organization name, address, phone.

Dairy Field: Helping Processors Manage the Changing Industry. Stagnito Publishing Co., 155 Pfingsten Rd., Ste. 205 Deerfield, IL 60015. Phone: (847)205-5660 Fax: (847)205-5680 E-mail: info@stagnito.com • URL: http://www.stagnito.com • Monthly. Free to qualified personnel; others, $85.03 per year. Annual *Buyers Guide* available.

Dairy Foods: Innovative Ideas and Technologies for Dairy Processors. Business News Publishing Co., 755 W Big Beaver Rd., Ste. 1000 Troy, MI 48084. Phone: (248)362-3700 Fax: (248)362-0317 • URL: http://www.bnp.com • Monthly. $99.90 per year. Provides broad coverage of new developments in the dairy industry, including cheese and ice cream products. Includes an annual *Supplement*.

Dairy Foods Market Directory. Gorman Publishing Co., 8750 W Bryn Mawr Ave. Chicago, IL 60631. Phone: (312)693-3200 Fax: (248)362-0317 E-mail: info@stagnito.com • URL: http://www.bnp.com • Covers: Manufacturers of equipment, supplies and ingredients in the dairy foods industry. Entries include: Contact information.

Dairy Industry Committee., 1451 Dolley Madison Blvd., 1451 Dolley Madison Blvd. Mc Lean, VA 22101-3850. Phone: (703)761-2600 Fax: (703)761-4334 E-mail: tnicol@fnal.gov • URL: http://www.iafis.org • Federation of associations in the dairy industry. Deals with national matters common to all segments of dairy processing and distributing industry.

Dairy Management, Inc., 10255 W Higgins Rd., Ste. 900 Rosemont, IL 60018-5616. Phone: 800-853-2479 or (847)627-3252 Fax: (847)803-2077 E-mail: marykateg@rosedmi.com • URL: http://www.dairyinfo.com • Operates under the auspices of the United Dairy Industry Association. Milk producers, milk dealers, and manufacturers of butter, cheese, ice cream, dairy equipment, and supplies. Conducts programs of nutrition research and nutrition education in the use of milk and its products.

Dairy Market Statistics. U.S. Department of Agriculture, Agricultural Marketing Service, Washington, DC 20250. Phone: (202)720-2791 Annual.

Dairy Research and Education Center. Pennsylvania State University

Dairy Science Abstracts. Available from CABI Publishing North America, 875 Massachusetts Ave., 7th Fl. Cambridge, MA 02139. Phone: 800-528-4841 or (617)395-4056 Fax: (617)654-6875 E-mail: cabi-nao@cabi.org • URL: http://www.cabi-publishing.org • Monthly. Institutions, $1,305.00 per year. Online edition available. Published in England by CABI Publishing. Provides worldwide coverage of the literature.

Dalton Carpet Journal. Daily Citizen-News, P.O. Box 1167 Dalton, GA 30722-1167. Phone: (404)278-1011 Monthly. $12.00. Covers the international tufted carpet market.

Dana's New Mineralogy: The System of Mineralogy of James Dwight Dana and Edward Salisbury Dana. Richard V. Gaines and others. John Wiley and Sons, Inc., 111 River St. Hoboken, NJ 07030. Phone: 800-225-5945 or (201)748-6000 Fax: (201)748-6088 E-mail: info@wiley.com • URL: http://www.wiley.com • 1997. $375.00. Eighth edition. Provides descriptions of more than 3,650 "recognized mineral species."

Dangerous Goods Advisory Council., 1100 H St. NW, Ste. 740 Washington, DC 20005-5484. Phone: (202)289-4550 Fax: (202)289-4074 E-mail: info@dgac.org • URL: http://www.dgac.org • Represents shippers, carriers, and container manufacturers of hazardous materials, substances, and wastes, shipper and carrier associations. Works to promote safe transportation of these materials; provides assistance in answering regulatory questions, guidance to appropriate governmental resources, and advice in establishing corporate compliance and safety programs. Conducts seminars on domestic and international hazardous materials packaging and transporting; sponsors educational programs. Provides training courses.

The Darla Moore School of Business - Division of Research.

Darling Marine Center., University of Maine, 193 Clarks Cove Rd. Walpole, ME 04573. Phone: (207)563-3146 Fax:

(207)563-3119 E-mail: kevin@maine.maine.edu • URL: http://www.server.dmc.maine.edu • Formerly *Ira C. Darling Center for Research, Teaching, and Service.*

Dartnell's Advertising Manager's Handbook. David Bushko, editor. Dartnell Corp., 360 Hiatt Dr. Palm Beach, FL 33418. Phone: 800-621-5463 or (561)622-6520 Fax: (561)622-2423 E-mail: custserv@lrp.com • URL: http://www.dartnellcorp.com • 1997. $89.95. Fourth revised edition.

Dartnell's Public Relations Handbook. Robert L. Dilenschneider, editor. Dartnell Corp., 360 Hiatt Dr. Palm Beach, FL 33418. Phone: 800-621-5463 or (561)622-6520 Fax: (561)622-2423 E-mail: custserv@lrp.com • URL: http://www.dartnellcorp.com • 1996. $69.95. Fourth revised edition. Covers press releases, media kits, media contacts, crisis management, and other topics.

Dartnell's 30th Sales Force Compensation Survey 1997-1998. Christen P .Heide. Dartnell Corp., 360 Hiatt Dr. Palm Beach Gardens, FL 33418. Phone: 800-341-7874 or (561)622-6520 Fax: (561)622-2423 E-mail: custserv@lrp.com • URL: http://www.dartnellcorp.com • 1999. $159.00. 30th edition.

Data Smog: Surviving the Information Glut. David Shenk. HarperSanFrancisco, 353 Sacramento St., Ste. 500 San Francisco, CA 94111. Phone: 800-242-7737 or (415)477-4400 Fax: (415)477-4444 • URL: http://www.harpercollins.com • 1997. $14.00. A critical view of both the electronic and print information industries. Emphasis is on information overload.

Data Sources for Business and Market Analysis. John Ganly. Scarecrow Press, Inc., 4501 Forbes Blvd., Ste. 200 Lanham, MD 20706. Phone: 800-462-6420 or (301)459-3366 Fax: 800-338-4550 or (301)459-5748 E-mail: custserv@rowman.com • URL: http://www.scarecrowpress.com • 1994. $60.00. Fourth edition. Emphasis is on sources of statistics for market research, especially government sources. Relevant directories, periodicals, and research aids are included.

Data Sources: The Comprehensive Guide to the Data Processing Industry: Hardware, Data Communications Products, Software, Company Profiles. Gale Cengage Learning, 27500 Drake Rd. Farmington Hills, MI 48331-3535. Phone: 800-877-GALE or (248)699-4253 Fax: 800-414-5043 E-mail: gale.galeord@cengage.com • URL: http://gale.cengage.com • Semiannual. $455.00 per year. Two volumes. Describes hardware and software for all computer operating sysems, including prices and technical details. Lists about 75,000 products from 14,000 suppliers. Industry-specific software applications are described.

Database Marketer. SIMBA Information, 11 Riverbend Dr., S. Stamford, CT 06907-0234. Phone: 800-307-2529 or (203)358-4100 Fax: (203)358-5824 E-mail: info@simbanet.com • URL: http://www.simbanet.com • Monthly. $329.00 per year.

Datapedia of the United States: American History in Numbers. George T. Kurian, editor. Bernan Press, 4611-F Assembly Drive Lanham, MD 20706-4391. Phone: 800-865-3457 or (301)459-2255 Fax: 800-865-3450 or (301)459-9235 E-mail: bpress@bernan.com • URL: http://www.bernanpress.com • 2004. $125.00. Third edition. Based on the Census Bureau publication, *Historical Statistics of the United States*. Provides data from Colonial times to the present on agriculture, business, consumer income, energy, finance, labor, national income, population, and many other subjects. Includes "narrative highlights," maps, charts, and statistical projections.

Datapro on CD-ROM: Communications Analyst. Gartner Group, Inc., 56 Top Gallant Rd. Stamford, CT 06904. Phone: (203)316-1111 Fax: (203)316-6300 E-mail: info@gartner.com • URL: http://www.gartner.com • Monthly. Price on application. Provides detailed information on products and services for communications systems, including local area networks and voice systems.

Datapro on CD-ROM: Computer Systems Analyst. Gartner Group, Inc., 56 Top Gallant Rd. Stamford, CT 06904. Phone: (203)316-1111 Fax: (203)316-6300 E-mail: info@gartner.com • URL: http://www.gartner.com • Monthly. Price on application. Includes detailed information on specific computer hardware and software products, such as peripherals, security systems, document imaging systems, and UNIX-related products.

Datapro on CD-ROM: Computer Systems Hardware and Software. Gartner Group, Inc., 56 Top Gallant Rd. Stamford, CT 06904. Phone: (203)316-1111 Fax: (203)316-6300 E-mail: info@gartner.com • URL: http://www.gartner.com • Monthly. Price on application. CD-ROM provides product specifications, product reports, user surveys, and market forecasts for a wide range of computer hardware and software.

Datapro Software Finder. Gartner Group, Inc., 56 Top Gallant Rd. Stamford, CT 06904. Phone: (203)316-1111 Fax: (203)316-6300 E-mail: info@gartner.com • URL: http://www.gartner.com • Quarterly. $1,770.00 per year. CD-ROM provides detailed information on more than 18,000 software products for a wide variety of computers, personal to mainframe. Covers software for 130 types of business, finance, and industry. (Editions limited to either microcomputer or mainframe software are available at $995.00 per year.)

Davidson Laboratory. Stevens Institute of Technology

Davison's Textile Blue Book. Davison Publishing Company L.L. C., 3452 Lake Lynda Dr., Ste. 363 Orlando, FL 32817. Phone: 800-328-4766 or (407)380-8900 Fax: (407)380-5222 E-mail:

info@davisonpublishing.com • URL: http://www.davisonbluebook.com • Covers: Over 8,400 companies in the textile industry in the United States, Canada, and Mexico including about 4,400 textile plants. Covers mills, manufacturers, dyers, bleachers, finishers, dealers, importers, exporters, brokers, shippers, and agents for various textiles, fibers, yarns, and cordage. Also includes supplies of equipment, materials and services. Entries include: Company name, address, phone, fax, e-mail, website addresses, names of executives, description of product/service, and trade names. Mill and other production facility listings include data on equipment and capacity.

Day Care USA: The Independent Biweekly for Day Care Professionals. United Communications Group, 11300 Rockville Pike, Suite 1100 Rockville, MD 20852-3030. Phone: 800-929-4824 or (301)287-2245 Fax: (301)816-8945 E-mail: webmaster@ucg.com • URL: http://www.ucg.com • Biweekly. $239.00 per year. Newsletter. Provides current information on child day care center funding, legislation, and regulation.

Day-Trader's Manual: Theory, Art, and Science of Profitable Short-Term Investing. William F. Eng. John Wiley and Sons, Inc., 111 River St. Hoboken, NJ 07030. Phone: 800-225-5945 or (201)748-6000 Fax: (201)748-6088 E-mail: info@wiley.com • URL: http://www.wiley.com • 1992. $79.95. Covers short-term trading in stocks, futures, and options. Various technical trading systems are considered. (Finance Series, vol. 5).

Deal Engines: The Science of Auctions, Stock markets, and e-Markets. Robert E. Hall. W. W. Norton & Co., Inc., 500 Fifth Ave. New York, NY 10110. Phone: 800-223-4830 or (212)354-5500 Fax: (212)869-0856 • URL: http://www.wwnorton.com • 2003. $14.95. A practical, economic analysis of how auction markets work, whether simple (eBay) or complex (stock exchanges). Covers both theory and application. (Originally published as *Digital Dealing*.)

Dealer and Applicator. Vance Publishing Corp., 400 Knightsbridge Parkway Lincolnshire, IL 60069. Phone: 800-255-5113 or (847)634-2600 Fax: (847)634-4379 • URL: http://www.vancepublishing.com • Nine times a year. $35.00 per year. Formerly *Custom Applicator*.

Dealer Operating Analysis. Beauty and Barber Supply Institute, 271 Route 46 West, Suite F-209 Fairfield, NJ 07004. Phone: (201)808-7444 Annual.

Dealer Progress: How Smart Agribusiness is Growing. Fertilizer Institute, 501 2nd St., NE Washington, DC 20002. Phone: (202)544-8123 Fax: (202)675-8250 E-mail: information@tfi.org • URL: http://www.tfi.org • Bimonthly. Free to qualified personnel; others, $40.00 per year. Published in association with the Fertilizer Institute. Includes information on fertilizers and agricultural chemicals, including farm pesticides. Formerly *Progress*.

Dealernews—Buyers Guide. Advanstar Communications, 641 Lexington Ave., 8th Fl. New York, NY 10022. Phone: 800-225-4569 or (212)951-6600 Fax: (212)951-6793 E-mail: info@advanstar.com • URL: http://www.advanstar.com • Publication includes: List of manufacturers, distributors, OEMs, and service organizations serving the motorcycle, all-terrain vehicle, and watercraft industries. Entries include: Company name, address, phone, fax, name and title of contact, years in business, number of employees, annual sales, brand names of products; distributor entries also include territories served and branch locations.

Dealernews: The Voice of the Powersports Vehicle Industry. Advanstar Communications, 545 Boylston St. Boston, MA 02116. Phone: 888-527-7008 or (617)267-6500 Fax: (617)267-6900 E-mail: info@advanstar.com • URL: http://www.advanstar.com • 13 times a year. $40.00 per year. News concerning the power sports motor vehicle industry.

Dealerscope: Product and Strategy for Consumer Technology Retailing. North American Publishing Co., 401 N. Broad St. Philadelphia, PA 19108-1074. Phone: 800-777-8074 or (215)238-5482 Fax: 800-664-1533 or (215)238-5412 E-mail: customerservice@napco.com • URL: http://www.napco.com • Monthly. Free to qualified personnel; others, $79.00 per year. Formerly *Dealerscope Consumer Electronics Marketplace*.

Dealing Creatively with Death: A Manual of Death Education and Simple Burial. Ernest Morgan and Jennifer Morgan. Upper Access, Inc., 87 Upper Access Rd. Hinesburg, VT 05461. Phone: 800-310-8320 or (802)482-2988 Fax: (802)482-7730 E-mail: info@upperaccess.com • URL: http://www.upperaccess.com • 2001. $14.95. 14th revised edition. A humanistic approach to dying and grieving; pursuing economy, simplicity and greater sensitivity in funeral practices.

Debits and Deposit Turnover at Commercial Banks. Board of Governors, U.S. Federal Reserve System, Publications Services, Room MS-138 Washington, DC 20551. Phone: (202)452-3244 Fax: (202)728-5886 Monthly. $5.00 per year.

Debt Free: The National Bankruptcy Kit. Daniel Sitarz. Nova Publishing Co., 705 W Main St. Carbondale, IL 62901. Phone: 800-748-1175 or (618)457-3521 Fax: 800-338-4550 E-mail: info@novapublishing.com • URL: http://novapublishing.com • 1999. $19.95. Second edition. Includes basic forms and instructions for use in uncomplicated personal bankruptcy situations. (Legal Self-Help Series).

Debtor-Creditor Law. LexisNexis Matthew Bender, 1275 Broadway Albany, NY 12204. Phone: 800-424-4200 or (518)487-3000 Fax: (518)487-3584 E-mail: bookstore.support@lexisnexis.com • URL: http://www.bender.com • $2,078.00. 13 looseleaf volumes. Periodic supplementation. Covers all aspects of the creation and enforcement of the debtor-creditor relationship.

Decision Line. Decision Sciences Institute, 35 Broad St. Atlanta, GA 30303. Phone: (404)651-4073 Fax: (404)651-2804 E-mail: dsi@gsu.edu • URL: http://www.decisionsciences.org • Description: Informs business executives and faculty of research and developments in the area of decision sciences. Promotes further education in the processes of decision-making for business students. Recurring features include reports on Institute activities and programs.

Decision-Making in Forest Management. R. W. Williams, editor. State Mutual Book and Periodical Service, Ltd., PO Box 1199 Bridgehampton, NY 11932-1199. 1988. $63.00.

Decision Sciences. Decision Sciences Institute. Decision Sciences Institute, 35 Broad St. Atlanta, GA 30303. Phone: 800-835-6770 or (404)651-4073 Fax: (404)651-2804 E-mail: dsi@gsu.edu Description: Discusses the topic of decision sciences.

Decision Sciences Institute., Georgia State University, J. Mack Robinson College of Business, University Plz. Atlanta, GA 30303. Phone: (404)413-7710 Fax: (404)413-7714 E-mail: clatta@gsu.edu • URL: http://www.decisionsciences.org • Businesspersons and members of business school faculties. Maintains placement service.

Decisions in Imaging Economics: The Journal of Imaging Technology Management. Curant Communications, Inc., 6701 Center Dr. W, No. 450 Los Angeles, CA 90045-1556. Phone: (310)306-2206 Fax: (310)306-9548 Bimonthly. Controlled circulation. Edited for health care executives and radiologists concerned with the purchase and management of imaging technology.

The Decline (and Fall?) of the Income Tax: How to Make Sense of the American Tax Mess and the Flat-Tax Cures That Are Supposed to Fix It. Michael J. Graetz. W. W. Norton & Co., Inc., 500 5th Ave. New York, NY 10110. Phone: 800-223-2584 or (212)354-5500 Fax: (212)869-0856 • URL: http://www.wwnorton.com • 1997. $27.50. The author, a former U. S. Treasury official, proposes a value-added tax (VAT) to augment federal income tax. He reviews recent tax history and provides entertaining tax anecdotes.

Decorating Registry. Paint and Decorating Retailers Association, 403 Axminister Dr. Fenton, MO 63026-2941. Phone: 800-737-0107 or (636)326-2636 Fax: (636)326-1823 E-mail: info@pdra.org • URL: http://www.pdra.org • Publication includes: List of about 1,500 manufacturers, manufacturers' representatives, distributors, and suppliers of decorating merchandise; a comprehensive trademark and brand name directory; associations, societies, and trade shows related to the home decorating industry. Entries include: For companies and manufacturer representatives—Firm name, address, phone, fax, name and title of contact, trademark, brand names. For associations—Name, address, phone, statement of purpose or description of service, key personnel, trade shows sponsored with dates and locations. Principal content of publication is decorative products (coatings, wallcoverings, window treatments, flooring, sundries).

Defence & Public Service Helicopter. Shephard Press Ltd., 111 High St. Burnham SL1 7JZ, United Kingdom. Phone: 44 1628 664334 Fax: 44 1628 664075 E-mail: publishing@shephard.co.uk • URL: http://www.shephard.co.uk • Monthly. $130.00 per year. Provides international coverage of both the public service (police, emergency, etc.) and military helicopter industries and markets. Includes technical, piloting, and safety topics. Formerly *Defence Helicopter*.

Defending Pesticides in Litigation. George W. Ware and Mark J. Carpenter. West Group, 610 Opperman Dr. Eagan, MN 55123. Phone: 800-328-4880 or (651)687-7000 Fax: 800-340-9378 E-mail: bookstore@westgroup.com • URL: http://www.westgroup.com • Annual. $364.00. Discusses liability and other legal issues related to the manufacture and use of pesticides. Includes a guide to FIFRA (Federal Insecticide, Fungicide, and Rodenticide Act). (Environmental Law Series).

Defense Advisory Committee on Women in the Services., 4000 Defense Pentagon, Rm. 2C548A, 4000 Defense Pentagon, Rm. 2C548A Washington, DC 20301-4000. Phone: (703)697-2122 Fax: (703)614-6322 E-mail: dacowits@osd.mil • URL: http://www.dtic.mil/dacowits • Civilians appointed by Secretary of Defense to provide recommendations to optimize utilization and quality of life for women in U.S. armed forces. Assists the Department of Defense by advising on specified matters relating to the recruitment and retention, treatment, employment, integration, and well-being of highly qualified professional women in the Services. Advises on family issues related to the recruitment and retention of a highly qualified professional military.

Defense and Security. Available from U. S. Government Printing Office, Washington, DC 20402. Phone: (202)512-1800 Fax: (202)512-2250 E-mail: gpoaccess@gpo.gov • URL: http://www.access.gpo.gov • Annual. Free. Issued by the Superintendent of Documents. A list of government publications on defense and related topics. Formerly *Defense Supply and Logistics*. (Subject Bibliography No. 153.)

Defense Counsel Journal. International Association of Defense Counsel, One N. Franklin St., Suite 2400 Chicago, IL 60606-3401. Phone: (312)368-1494 Fax: (312)368-1854 Quarterly. $65.00 per year. Scholarly and practical articles dealing with defense of civil cases, particularly those involving insurance.

Defense Credit Union Council., South Bldg., Ste. 600, 601 Pennsylvania Ave. NW Washington, DC 20004-2601. Phone: 800-356-9655 or (202)638-3950 Fax: (202)638-3410 E-mail: dcuc1@cuna.com • URL: http://www.dcuc.org • Credit unions serving Department of Defense military and civilian personnel. Aims to assist credit unions serving DOD personnel with problems peculiar to military installations and personnel, and to maintain close liaison with DOD.

Defense Daily: The Daily of Aerospace and Defense. PBI Media, LLC, 1201 7 Locks Rd. Potomac, MD 20854. Phone: 800-777-5006 or (301)354-2000 Fax: (301)309-3847 E-mail: clientservices@pbimedia.com • URL: http://www.pbimedia.com • Daily (five times a week). $1,897.00 per year. Newsletter.

Defense Electronics. Primedia Business Magazines and Media, 6151 Powers Ferry Rd., Ste. 200 Atlanta, GA 30339-2941. Phone: 800-400-5945 or (770)955-2500 Fax: (770)955-0400 E-mail: subs@primediabusiness.com • URL: http://www.primediabusiness.com • Monthly. $52.00 per year.

The Defense Monitor. Center for Defense Information, 1779 Massachusetts Ave. NW Washington, DC 20036-2109. Phone: (202)332-6000 Fax: (202)462-4559 E-mail: info@cdi.org • URL: http://www.cdi.org • Description: Concerned with U.S. military issues such as nuclear and conventional weapons; research, development, and procurement; armed force levels; foreign commitments; arms control; annual military budget; and economic, environmental, and political implications. Provides analysis and conclusions for a single military subject in each issue, and recommends changes and areas for further study.

Defense of Narcotics Cases. David Bernheim. LexisNexis Matthew Bender, 9275 Broadway Albany, NY 12204. Phone: 800-424-4200 or (518)487-3000 Fax: (518)487-3584 E-mail: bookstore.support@lexisnexis.com • URL: http://www.bender.com • $696.00. Three looseleaf volumes. Periodic supplementation. Up-to-date coverage of all aspects of narcotics cases and related matters.

Defense Research Institute., 150 N Michigan Ave., Ste. 300 Chicago, IL 60601. Phone: 800-667-8108 or (312)795-1101 Fax: (312)795-0747 E-mail: dri@dri.org • URL: http://www.dri.org • Lawyers, claims people, adjusters, insurance companies, trade associations, corporations, and "target" defendants in civil litigation, such as doctors, pharmacists, engineers, manufacturers, and other professional and skilled personnel. Seeks to increase the knowledge and improve the skills of defense lawyers and to improve the adversary system of justice. Maintains research facilities, including files of speeches, briefs, and names of expert witnesses in various fields. Maintains Expert Witness Index.

Defense Systems Review and Military Communications. Cosgriff-Martin Publishing Group, Inc., 2595 Solano Ave. Napa, CA 94558. Phone: (707)257-8480 Monthly. $35.00 per year.

Defense Transportation Journal: Magazine of International Defense Transportation and Logistics. National Defense Transportation Association, 50 S. Pickett St., No 220 Alexandria, VA 22304-3008. Phone: (703)751-5011 Fax: (703)823-8761 • URL: http://www.brf.volpe-dot.gov • Bimonthly. Free to members; non-members, $35.00 per year.

Defined Contribution News. Aspen Publishers, Corporate Headquarters, 76 Ninth Ave., 7th Fl. New York, NY 10011. Phone: 800-638-8437 or (212)771-0600 Fax: (212)771-0885 E-mail: customer.service@aspenpubl.com • URL: http://www.iijournals.com • Description: Covers all aspects of the defined contribution pension plan market from the plan sponsor and vendor points of view. Discusses topics such as searches for investment managers; record keepers, administrators, and trustees; legislative and regulatory developments; plan profiles; sponsor forums; new vendor products; and personnel changes and DC Database.

Defining Your Market: Winning Strategies for High-Tech, Industrial, and Service Firms. Art Weinstein. Haworth Press, Inc., 10 Alice St. Binghamton, NY 13904-1580. Phone: 800-429-6784 or (607)722-5857 Fax: 800-895-0582 or (607)722-1424 E-mail: getinfo@haworthpressinc.com • URL: http://www.haworthpressinc.com • 1998. $39.95. Includes "models, frameworks, and processes" for effective industrial marketing.

Degrees and Other Awards Conferred by Institutions of Higher Education. Available from U. S. Government Printing Office, Washington, DC 20402. Phone: (202)512-1800 Fax: (202)512-2250 E-mail: gpoaccess@gpo.gov • URL: http://www.access.gpo.gov • Annual. Issued by the National Center for Education Statistics, U. S. Department of Education. Provides data on the number of degrees awarded at the associate's, bachelor's, master's, and doctor's levels. Includes fields of study and racial-ethnic-sex data by major field or discipline.

Deli News. Delicatessen Council of Southern California, Inc. Pacific Rim Publishing Co., P.O. Box 4533 Huntington Beach, CA 92605-4533. Phone: (714)375-3904 Fax: (714)375-3906 Monthly. $25.00 per year. Includes product news and comment related to cheeses, lunch meats, packaged fresh meats, kosher foods, gourmet-specialty items, and bakery products.

Delphion Research. Thomson DelphionPhone: 800-411-4811 or (630)799-0600 Fax: (630)799-0688 E-mail: support@delphion.com • URL: http://www.delphion.com • Fee-based

Web site provides more than 40 million records of full-text patent information from the U. S. Patent and Trademark Office and from about 70 foreign countries. Corporate and individual subscriptions are available.

Delta Pi Epsilon., PO Box 4340 Little Rock, AR 72214. Phone: (501)219-1866 Fax: (501)219-1876 E-mail: dpe@ipa.net • URL: http://www.dpe.org • Professional society - men and women, business education.

Delta Sigma Pi., 330 S Campus Ave. Oxford, OH 45056-2405. Phone: (513)523-1907 Fax: (513)523-7292 E-mail: centraloffice@dspnet.org • URL: http://www.dspnet.org • Professional fraternity - commerce and business administration. Operates Delta Sigma Pi Leadership Foundation. Maintains museum; sponsors competitions; offers computerized services; compiles statistics. Provides educational and career assistance.

Democracy International., 4802 Montgomery Ln., Ste. 200 Bethesda, MD 20814. Phone: (301)961-1660 Fax: (301)961-6605 E-mail: info@democracyinternational.us • URL: http://www.democracyinternational.us • Seeks to build a movement of individuals dedicated to practical action on behalf of common commitments to human rights and pluralistic democracy including freedom of speech and press, religious liberty, free political parties, and the right to contest elections. Works to develop political and economic self-determination of citizens allowing them to control their resources, choose their social systems, and end discrimination. Aims to: revive democracy where it has been destroyed; encourage and sustain democrats trying to bring democracy to dictatorships. Calls upon democracies to: increase help for democratic leaders and politicians in the Third World; provide economic sustenance to relieve human suffering; strengthen democracy where it exists. Provides a forum for democrats to express solidarity and to help each other; encourages membership in an effort to build an international force of people working to make the cause of democracy an enduring ideal. Publicizes the efforts of democratic movements in dictatorships; attempts to increase the amount of uncensored information to closed societies. **Convention/Meeting:** none.

Demographic Yearbook. United Nations, Dept. of Economic and Social Affairs. United Nations Publications, Concourse Level, First Ave., 46th St. New York, NY 10017. Phone: 800-553-3210 or (212)963-7680 Fax: (212)963-4910 E-mail: bookstore@un.org • URL: http://www.un.org/publications • Annual. $125.00. Text in English and French.

Demographics USA: County Edition. Trade Dimensions, 45 Danbury Rd. Wilton, CT 06897. Phone: 800-291-0410 or (203)563-3100 Fax: (203)563-3131 E-mail: info@tradedimensions.com • URL: http://www.tradedimensions.com • Annual. $435.00. Contains 200 statistical series for each of 3,000 counties. Includes population, household income, employment, retail sales, and consumer expenditures. Also provides Effective Buying Income, Buying Power Index, and data summaries by Metro Market, Media Market, and State. (CD-ROM version is available.)

Demographics USA: ZIP Edition. Trade Dimensions, 45 Danbury Rd. Wilton, CT 06897. Phone: 800-291-0410 or (203)563-3100 Fax: (203)563-3131 E-mail: info@tradedimenisions.com • URL: http://www.tradedimensions.com • Annual. $435.00. Contains 50 statistical series for each of 40,000 ZIP codes. Includes population, household income, employment, retail sales, and consumer expenditures. Also provides Effective Buying Income, Business Characteristics, and data summaries by state, region, and the first three digits of ZIP codes. (CD-ROM version is available.)

Demography. Population Association of America, 8630 Fenton St., Ste. 722 Silver Spring, MD 20910-3812. Phone: (301)565-6710 Fax: (301)565-7850 E-mail: info@popassoc.org • URL: http://www.popassoc.org • Quarterly. $85.00 per year.

Dental Dealers of America.

Dental Economics. Pennwell Publishing Co., Dental Economics Div., 1421 S. Sheridan Rd. Tulsa, OK 74112. Phone: 800-331-4463 or (918)835-3161 E-mail: headquarters@pennwell.com • URL: http://www.pennwell.com • Monthly. $88.00 per year.

Dental Lab Products. MEDEC Dental Communications, Two Northfield Plaza, Suite 300 Northfield, IL 60093-1219. Phone: 800-451-7838 or (847)441-3700 Fax: (847)441-3702 Bimonthly. $35.00 per year. Edited for dental laboratory managers. Covers new products and technical developments.

Dental Manufacturers of America.

Dental Practice and Finance. MEDEC Dental Communications, Two Northfield Plaza, Suite 300 Northfield, IL 60093-1219. Phone: 800-451-7838 or (847)441-3700 Fax: (847)441-3702 Bimonthly. $55.00 per year. Covers practice management and financial topics for dentists. Includes investment advice.

Dental Products Report Europe. MEDEC Dental Communications, Two Northfield Plaza, Suite 300 Northfield, IL 60093-1219. Phone: 800-451-7838 or (847)441-3700 Fax: (847)441-3702 Seven times a year. $40.00 per year. Covers new dental products for the Europea market.

Dental Products Report: Trends in Dentistry. MEDEC Dental Communications, Two Northfield Plaza, Suite 300 Northfield, IL 60093-1219. Phone: 800-451-7838 or (847)441-3700 Fax: (847)441-3702 11 times a year. $120.00 per year. Provides information on new dental products, technology, and trends in dentistry.

Dental Supplies. Available from MarketResearch.com, 641 Ave. of the Americas, Fourth Floor New York, NY 10011. Phone: 800-298-5699 or (212)807-2629 Fax: (212)807-2642 E-mail: order@marketresearch.com • URL: http://www.marketresearch.com • 2002. $3,450.00. Published by Global Industry Analysts. Provides worldwide market research data, including profiles of major dental supply companies.

Dental Trade Newsletter. American Dental Trade Association, 4222 King St., W Alexandria, VA 22302. Phone: (703)379-7755 Fax: (703)931-9429 E-mail: adta@adta.com Bimonthly. Price on application.

Dentistry Today: Equipment Buyers' Guide. Dentistry Today, Inc., Greenbook Corporate Center, 100 Passaic Ave. Fairfield, NJ 07004. Phone: (973)882-4700 Fax: (973)882-3622 • URL: http://www.dentistrytoday.com • Annual. Price on application. Provides purchasing information for more than 500 dental products.

Department of Fisheries and Allied Aquacultures.

Department of Molecular and Human Genetics.

Department of the Navy Annual Report to the Congress. U.S. Department of the Navy, Washington, DC 20350. Phone: (703)697-7391 Annual.

Deposit Account Operations and Services. The Institute of Financial Education, 55 W. Monroe St., Suite 2800 Chicago, IL 60603-5014. Phone: 800-946-0488 or (312)364-0100 Fax: (312)364-0190 E-mail: info@bai.org • URL: http://www.theinstitute.com • 1997. $49.95.

Deposit Operations. David H. Friedman. American Bankers Association, 1120 Connecticut Ave., N. W. Washington, DC 20036-3971. Phone: 800-226-5377 or (202)663-5000 Fax: (202)663-7543 E-mail: custserv@aba.com • URL: http://www.aba.com • 1992. Price on application.

Depreciation Handbook. LexisNexis Matthew Bender, 1275 Broadway Albany, NY 12204. Phone: 800-424-4200 or (518)487-3000 Fax: (518)487-3584 E-mail: bookstore.support@lexisnexis.com • URL: http://www.bender.com • Annual. $213.00. Looseleaf service. Treatment of depreciation in one volume.

Derivative Instruments: A Guide to Theory and Practice. Brian A. Eales. Elsevier Butterworth Heinemann, 200 Wheeler Rd., Sixth Floor Burlington, MA 01803. Phone: 800-545-2522 or (781)221-2212 Fax: 800-568-5136 or (781)313-4880 E-mail: usbkinfo@elsevier.com • URL: http://www.books.elsevier.com/finance • 2003. $94.95. Includes examples and spreadsheet models.

Derivatives. Imagine Software Inc.Phone: (212)317-7600 Fax: (212)317-7601 • URL: http://www.derivatives.com • Web site mainly promotes proprietary software for the use of derivatives in risk management, but also provides free access to articles on a variety of derivatives-related topics.

Derivatives: A Comprehensive Resource for Options, Futures, Interest Rate Swaps, and Mortgage Securities. Fred D. Arditti. Harvard Business School Publishing, 300 N Beacon St. Watertown, MA 02163. Phone: 800-988-0886 or (617)783-7500 Fax: (617)783-7555 • URL: http://www.hbs.edu • 1996. $60.00. Published by Harvard Business School Press. Provides detailed explanations of various kinds of financial derivatives (options, futures, swaps, etc.) and their trading tactics, uses, and risks. (Financial Management Association Survey and Synthesis Series).

Derivatives Desk Reference: Buyside and Sellside Profiles. Capital Access International, The Reuters Bldg., 3 Times Square New York, NY 10036. Phone: 800-866-5987 or (646)223-4130 Fax: (646)223-4133 E-mail: emaxxinfo@lipper.reuters.com • URL: http://www.capital-access.com • Annual. $295.00. A directory of about 900 firms active in the use of such derivatives as options, futures, currency swaps, interest rate swaps, and structured notes. Includes names of derivatives specialists in each firm.

Derivatives Handbook: Risk Management and Control. Robert J. Schwartz and Clifford W. Smith. John Wiley and Sons, Inc., 111 River St. Hoboken, NJ 07030. Phone: 800-225-5945 or (201)748-6000 Fax: (201)748-6088 E-mail: info@wiley.com • URL: http://www.wiley.com • 1997. $90.00. Some chapter topics are legal risk, risk measurement, and risk oversight. Includes "Derivatives Debacles: Case Studies of Losses in DerivativesMarkets." A glossary of derivatives terminology is provided. (Financial Engineering Series, vol. 6).

Derivatives Quarterly. Institutional Investor, Inc., Journals Group, 225 Park Ave., S New York, NY 10003. Phone: 800-945-2034 or (212)224-3066 Fax: (212)224-3472 E-mail: info@iijournals.com • URL: http://www.iijournals.com • Quarterly. Price on application. Emphasis is on the practical use of derivatives. Includes case studies to demonstrate "real-life" risks and benefits.

Derivatives Week: The Newsweekly on Derivatives Worldwide. Institutional Investor, Inc., Journals Group, 225 Park Ave., S New York, NY 10003. Phone: 800-945-2034 or (212)224-3066 Fax: (212)224-3472 E-mail: info@iijournals.com • URL: http://www.iijournals.com • Weekly. $2,475.00 per year. Includes print and online editions. Newsletter on financial derivatives linked to equities, interest rates, commodities, and currencies. Covers new products, investment opportunities, legalities, etc.

Derwent Biotechnology Abstracts. Derwent, Inc., 1725 Duke St., Suite 250 Alexandria, VA 22314. Phone: 800-451-3551 or (703)706-4220 Fax: (703)519-5829 E-mail: info@derwent.com • URL: http://www.derwent.com • Provides indexing and abstracting of the world's biotechnology journal literature since 1982, including genetic engineering topics. Monthly updates. Inquire as to online cost and availability.

Derwent Crop Protection File. Derwent, Inc., 1725 Duke St., Suite 250 Alexandria, VA 22314. Phone: 800-451-3551 or (703)706-4220 Fax: (703)519-5829 E-mail: info@derwent.com • URL: http://www.derwent.com • Provides citations to the international journal literature of agricultural chemicals and pesticides from 1968 to date, with updating eight times per year. Formerly *PESTDOC*. Inquire as to online cost and availability..

Derwent Drug File. Derwent, Inc., 1725 Duke St., Suite 250 Alexandria, VA 22314. Phone: 800-451-3551 or (703)706-4220 Fax: (703)519-5829 E-mail: info@derwent.com • URL: http://www.derwent.com • Provides indexing and abstracting of the world's pharmaceutical journal literature since 1964, with weekly updates. Formerly *RINGDOC*. Inquire as to online cost and availability.

Derwent U. S. Patents. Derwent, Inc., 1725 Duke St., Suite 250 Alexandria, VA 22314. Phone: 800-451-3551 or (703)706-4220 Fax: (703)519-5829 E-mail: info@derwent.com • URL: http://www.derwent.com • Provides citations and abstracts for more then one million U. S. patents issued since 1971. Weekly updates. Inquire as to online cost and availability.

Derwent Veterinary Drug File. Derwent, Inc., 1725 Duke St., Suite 250 Alexandria, VA 22314. Phone: 800-451-3551 or (703)706-4220 Fax: (703)519-5829 E-mail: info@derwent.com • URL: http://www.derwent.com • Provides indexing and abstracting of the world's veterinary drug literature since 1968, with monthly updates. Formerly *VETDOC*. Inquire as to online cost and availability.

Derwent World Patents Index. Derwent, Inc., 1725 Duke St., Suite 250 Alexandria, VA 22314. Phone: 800-451-3551 or (703)706-4220 Fax: (703)519-5829 E-mail: info@derwent.com • URL: http://www.derwent.com • Contains abstracts of more than 20 million patent documents from many countries. Time span varies. Weekly updates. Inquire as to online cost and availability.

Descriptive Statistical Techniques for Librarians. Arthur W. Hafner. American Library Association, 50 E. Huron St. Chicago, IL 60611-2795. Phone: 800-545-2433 or (312)944-6780 Fax: (312)440-9374 E-mail: ala@ala.org • URL: http://www.ala.org • 1997. $55.00 Second edition.

Design and Marketing of New Products. Glen Urban and John R. Hauser. Prentice Hall PTR, 240 Frisch Ct. Paramus, NJ 07652. Phone: 800-282-0693 Fax: 800-445-6991 • URL: http://www.phptr.com • 1993. $120.00. Second edition.

Design Cost Data: The Cost Estimating Magazine for Architects, Builders and Specifiers. L. M. Rector Corp., 8602 N. 40th St. Tampa, FL 33604. Phone: (813)989-9300 Fax: (813)980-3982 Bimonthly. $64.80 per year. Provides a preliminary cost estimating system for architects, contractors, builders, and developers, utilizing historical data. Includes case studies of actual costs. Formerly *Design Cost and Data*.

Design Drafting News. American Design Drafting Association, 105 E Main St. Newbern, TN 38059. Phone: (731)627-0802 Fax: (731)627-9321 E-mail: corporate@adda.org Description: Monitors new developments, techniques, and products related to design and drafting. Carries information about metrication and standards. Recurring features include news of the Association and its members, book reviews, and a calendar of events.

Design Encyclopedia. Mel Byars. John Wiley and Sons, Inc., 111 River St. Hoboken, NJ 07030. Phone: 800-225-5945 or (201)748-6000 Fax: (201)748-6088 E-mail: info@wiley.com • URL: http://www.wiley.com • 1994. $60.00. Contains more than 3,000 entries covering various aspects of design and decoration since the 19th century.

Design Management Institute., 101 Tremont St., Ste. 300 Boston, MA 02108. Phone: (617)338-6380 Fax: (617)338-6570 E-mail: dmistaff@dmi.org • URL: http://www.dmi.org • In-house design groups and consultant design firms; individuals involved in the management of designers with in-house corporate design groups or consultant design firms. Aims to share management techniques as applied to design groups, and to facilitate better understanding by business management of the role design can play in achieving business goals. Design disciplines included are: architecture, advertising, communications, exhibit design, graphics, interior design, packaging and product design. Develops and distributes design management education materials. Sponsors seminars for design professionals. Identifies critical areas of design management study; conducts surveys and research on corporate design management. Maintains design management archive. Operates Center for Research, Center for Education, and Center for +Design and Management Resources.

Design Management Journal. Design Management Institute, 29 Temple Place, 2nd Fl. Boston, MA 02111-1350. Phone: (617)338-6380 Fax: (617)338-6570 E-mail: dmistaff@dmiorg • URL: http://www.dmi.org • Quarterly. $96.00 per year. Covers the management of product-related design.

Design News OEM Directory. Reed Business Information, 360 Park Ave. S New York, NY 10010. Phone: 800-550-0827 or (646)746-6400 Fax: (781)734-8076 E-mail: corporatecommunications@reedbusiness.com • URL: http://www.reedbusiness.com • Covers: about 5,000 manufacturers and suppliers of power transmission products, fluid power products, and electrical/electronic components to the OEM (original equipment manufacturer) market in SIC groups 34-39. Entries include: Company name, address, phone, fax, url, e-mail.

Design of Concrete Structures. Arthur H. Nilson and others. McGraw-Hill, 1221 Ave. of the Americas New York, NY 10020. Phone: 800-722-4726 or (212)512-2000 Fax: (212)512-4502 E-mail: customer.service@mcgraw-hill.com • URL: http://www.mcgraw-hill.com • 2003. $134.90. 13th edition. (Construction Engineering and Project Management Series).

Design of Machine Elements and Machines. J.A. Collins. John Wiley and Sons, Inc., 111 River St. Hoboken, NJ 07030. Phone: 800-225-5945 or (201)748-6000 Fax: (201)748-6088 E-mail: info@wiley.com • URL: http://www.wiley.com • 2002. $122.95. Seventh edition.

Design Perspectives. Industrial Designers Society of America, 45195 Business Ct., Ste. 250 Dulles, VA 20166-6717. Phone: (703)707-6000 Fax: (703)759-7679 E-mail: idsa@idsa.org • URL: http://www.idsa.org • Description: The largest newsletter examining the news and trends of industrial design. Recurring features include: new and cutting-edge products, news of people and events in industrial design, resource section, reports of chapter and national activities of IDSA, and a calendar of events. The classified ad section is the largest of its kind and, for advertisers, the newsletter is the best way to reach new product decision-making VPs of industrial design.

Design Research Unit., Massachusetts College of Art, 621 Huntington Ave. Boston, MA 02115. Phone: (617)879-7733 Fax: (617)566-4034 E-mail: rstreit@massart.edu • URL: http://www.babel.massart.edu/dru • Conducts research related to the design of printed matter, including annual reports, letterheads, posters, and brochures.

Designing Organizations to Create Value: From Strategy to Structure. Jerry Zimmerman and others. McGraw-Hill, 1221 Ave. of the Americas New York, NY 10020. Phone: 800-722-4726 or (212)512-2000 Fax: (212)512-4502 E-mail: customer.service@mcgraw-hill.com • URL: http://www.mcgraw-hill.com • 2002. $29.95. Describes a process for "identifying the critical aspects of an organization's internal structure" and making administrative enhancements.

Designing the User Interface: Strategies for Effective Human-Computer Interaction. Ben Shneiderman. Addison-Wesley, 75 Arlington St., Ste. 300 Boston, MA 02116. Phone: 800-447-2226 or (617)848-7500 • URL: http://www.aw.com • 2002. $70.00. Third edition. Provides an introduction to computer user-interface design. Covers usability testing, dialog boxes, menus, command languages, interaction devices, tutorials, printed user manuals, and related subjects.

The Desktop Designer's Illustration Handbook. Marcelle L. Toor. John Wiley and Sons, Inc., 111 River St. Hoboken, NJ 07030. Phone: 800-842-3636 or (201)748-6000 Fax: (201)748-6088 E-mail: info@wiley.com • URL: http://www.wiley.com • 1996. $29.95. Serves as a guide to locating, selecting, and using illustrations for desktop publications. (ITCP Computer Science Series).

Desktop Publishing. Entrepreneur Media, Inc., 2445 McCabe Way Irvine, CA 92614. Phone: 800-421-2300 or (949)261-2325 Fax: (949)261-0234 E-mail: entmag@entrepreneur.com • URL: http://www.entrepreneur.com • Looseleaf. $59.50. A practical guide to starting a desktop publishing service. Covers profit potential, start-up costs, market size evaluation, pricing, accounting, advertising, promotion, etc. (Start-Up Business Guide No. E1288.)

Desktop Video Communications. BCR Enterprises, Inc., 999 Oakmont Plz. Dr., Ste. 100 Westmont, IL 60559-1381. Phone: 800-227-1234 or (630)986-1432 Fax: (630)323-5324 E-mail: info@bcr.com • URL: http://www.bcr.com/ • Bimonthly. Free per year. Covers multimedia technologies, with emphasis on video conferencing and the "virtual office."

DETC News. Distance Education & Training Council, 1601 18th St. NW Washington, DC 20009. Phone: (202)234-5100 Fax: (202)332-1386 E-mail: detc@detc.org • URL: http://www.detc.org • Description: Discusses issues pertaining to distance study education and reports activities of the Council. Recurring features include news of research, book reviews, news of members, and a calendar of events.

Detwiler's Directory of Health and Medical Resources. S. M. Detwiler and Associates. Information Today, Inc., 143 Old Marlton Pke. Medford, NJ 08055-8750. Phone: (609)654-6266 Fax: (609)654-4309 E-mail: custserv@infotoday.com • URL: http://www.infotoday.com • Biennial. $203.00. Lists sources of information relating to the healthcare industry, including government agencies, medical experts, directories, newsletters, research groups, associations, and mailing list producers. Four indexes are provided: subject, publication, service, and acronym.

Detwiler's Directory of Health and Medical Resources. S.M. Detwiler and Associates, PO Box 15308 Fort Wayne, IN 46885. Phone: (219)749-6534 Fax: (219)493-6717 Biennial. $195.00. Lists a wide range of healthcare information resources, including more than 2,000 corporations, associations, government agencies, publishers, licensure organizations, market research firms, foundations, and institutes, as well as 6,000 publications. Indexed by type of information, publication, acronym, and 600 subject categories.

Developing a Compensation Plan for Your Library. Paula M. Singer. American Library Association, 50 E Huron St. Chicago, IL 60611-2795. Phone: 800-545-2433 or (312)944-6780 Fax: (312)440-9374 E-mail: ala@ala.org • URL: http://www.ala.org • 2002. $38.00. Discusses a variety of pay plans for libraries, with checklists, questionnaires, case studies, and frequently asked questions. Includes samples of forms, work plans, and spreadsheets.

Developing and Managing Electronic Journal Collections: A How-To-DoIt Manual forLibrarians. Donnelyn Curtis and others. Neal-Schuman Publishers, Inc., 100 William St., Ste. 2004 New York, NY 10038. Phone: (866)672-6657 or (212)925-8650 Fax: (866)209-7932 or (212)219-8916 E-mail: info@neal-schuman.com • URL: http://www.neal-schuman.com • 2000. $55.00. Covers the acquisition, management, and integration of journals published in electronic form. (How-To-Do-It Manuals Series).

Developing Business Strategies. David A. Aaker. John Wiley and Sons, Inc., 111 River St. Hoboken, NJ 07030. Phone: 800-225-5945 or (201)748-6000 Fax: (201)748-6088 E-mail: info@wiley.com • URL: http://www.wiley.com • 2001. $39.95. Sixth edition.

Developing Countries: Definitions, Concepts, and Comparisons. Jonathan E. Sanford. Nova Science Publishers, Inc., 400 Oser Ave., Suite 1600 Hauppauge, NY 11788-3619. Phone: (631)231-7269 Fax: (631)231-8175 E-mail: novascience@earthlink.net • URL: http://www.novapublishers.com • 2003. $29.50. Describes four basic measures of levels of national development: per capita income, economic structure, social conditions (quality of life), and political freedom.

Developing E-Business Systems and Architectures: A Manager's Guide. Paul Harmon and others. Elsevier, 655 Avenue of the Americas New York, NY 10010-5107. Phone: 800-366-2665 or (212)989-5800 Fax: 800-535-9935 or (212)663-3680 E-mail: custserv@elsevier.com • URL: http://www.elsevier.com • 2000. $34.95.

Developing Java Software. Russel Winder and Graham Roberts. John Wiley and Sons, Inc., 111 River St. Hoboken, NJ 07030. Phone: 800-225-5945 or (201)748-6000 Fax: (201)748-6088 E-mail: info@wiley.com • URL: http://www.wiley.com • 2002. $55.00. Second edition. (Worldwide Computer Science Series).

Developing Reference Collections and Services in an Electronic Age: A How-To-Do-It Manual for Librarians. Kay A. Cassell. Neal-Schuman Publishers, Inc., 100 William St., Ste. 2004 New York, NY 10038. Phone: (866)672-6657 or (212)925-8650 Fax: (866)209-7932 or (212)219-8916 E-mail: info@neal-schuman.com • URL: http://www.neal-schuman.com • 1999. $55.00. Discusses print vs. electronic media for library reference services. (How-To-Do-It Manuals Series).

Development Business. United Nations Publications, Concourse Level, First Ave., 46th St. New York, NY 10017. Phone: 800-553-3210 or (212)963-7680 Fax: (212)963-4910 E-mail: dbusiness@un.org • URL: http://www.devbusiness.com • Semimonthly. $495.00 per year. Provides leads on contract opportunities worldwide for engineering firms and multinational corporations. Text in English, French, Portuguese, and Spanish.

Development Magazine. National Association of Industrial and Office Properties, Woodland Park, 2201 Cooperative Way, 3rd Fl. Herndon, VA 20171. Phone: 800-666-6780 or (703)904-7100 Fax: (703)904-7942 E-mail: naiop@naiop.org • URL: http://www.naiop.org • Quarterly. Free to members; non-members, $65.00 per year. Focuses on issues, trends and new ideas affecting the commercial and industrial real estate development industry.

The Development of Plastics. S. Mossman and P. Morris, editors. CRC Press LLC, 2000 NW Corporate Blvd. Boca Raton, FL 33431. Phone: 800-272-7737 or (561)994-0555 Fax: 800-374-3401 or (561)989-9732 E-mail: orders@crcpress.com • URL: http://www.crcpress.com • 1994. $68.00. Published by The Royal Society of Chemistry. Covers the history of plastics from the Victorian era to the present. Includes technical, scientific, and cultural perspectives.

Devil Take the Hindmost: A History of Financial Speculation. Edward Chancellor. Dutton/Plume, 375 Hudson St. New York, NY 10014-3657. Phone: 800-331-4624 or (212)366-2000 Fax: (212)366-2666 E-mail: online@penguinputnam.com • URL: http://www.penguinputnam.com • 2000. $15.00. Covers such events as the Dutch tulip mania of 1637, the South Sea bubble of 1720, and the Japanese real estate and stock market boom of the 1980's.

DFISA Reporter. Dairy and Food Industries Supply Association, Inc., 6245 Executive Blvd. Rockville, MD 20852-3906. Phone: (301)984-1444 Fax: (301)881-7832 Monthly. Free. Provides industry and association news to manufacturers of equipment products and services to the dairy and food industry.

Di Yiddishe Heim/Jewish Home. Chabad Lubavitch, 770 Eastern Parkway Brooklyn, NY 11213. Phone: (718)774-4000 E-mail: info@lubavitch.com • URL: http://www.lubavitch.com • Quarterly. $8.00 per year. Text in English and Yiddishe.

Diamond Council of America.

Diamond Dealers Club., 580 5th Ave. at 11 W 47th St. New York, NY 10036. Phone: (212)869-9777 Fax: (212)869-5164 E-mail: mhochbaum@ddcny.com • URL: http://www.nyddc.com • Seeks to foster the interests of the diamond industry, promote equitable trade principles, eliminate abuses and unfair trade practices, disseminate accurate and reliable information concerning the industry, establish uniform business ethics, and cooperate with other persons and organizations for the advancement of the trade. Maintains active trading floor for all categories of wholesale diamonds and offers all members arbitration tribunals for dispute settlement. Operates charitable program.

Diamond Manufacturers and Importers Association of America Yearbook., c/o Ben Kinzler, P.O. Box 5297 New York, NY 10185-5297. Phone: (212)944-2066 Annual.

Diamond Ring Buying Guide: How to Evaluate, Identify, and Select Diamonds and Diamond Jewelry. Renee Newman. International Jewelry Publications, 417 N. Stoneman Ave., Suite C Alhambra, CA 91801. Phone: (626)282-3781 Fax: (626)282-4807 2003. $17.95. Sixth edition. A well known gemologist explains diamond "cut, color, clarity, and carat." Color photographs are included, as well as information on diamond settings.

Diamond Walnut Growers., 1050 S Diamond St., PO Box 1727 Stockton, CA 95205. Phone: (209)467-6000 Fax: (209)467-6714 E-mail: mhochbaum@ddcny.com • URL: http://www.diamondnuts.com • Walnut processing and marketing organization.

Diamond World Review. World Federation of Diamond Bourses. International Diamond Publications, Ltd., Diamond Towers, 3A Jabotinsky Rd. 52131 Ramat Gon, Israel. Phone: 972 3 7512165 Fax: 972 3 5752201 Bimonthly. $78.00 per year. Text in English.

Diamonds. Irene Franck and David Brownstone. Scholastic Library Publishing, 7106 Saunders Court Bethesda, MD 20817. Phone: (301)983-1990 Fax: (301)983-3980 E-mail: fward@erols.com • URL: http://www.erols.com • 2003. $38.99. Price on application.

Diamonds and Conflict: Problems and Solutions. Arthur V. Levy. Nova Science Publishers, Inc., 400 Oser Ave., Suite 1600 Hauppauge, NY 11788-3619. Phone: (631)231-7269 Fax: (631)231-8175 E-mail: novascience@earthlink.net • URL: http://www.novapublishers.com • 2003. $29.50. Describes reforms and legislative initiatives that have been undertaken in efforts to stop illicit trade in diamonds ("conflict diamonds").

Diamonds and Precious Stones. Patrick Voillot. Abrams, Harry N., Inc., 100 Fifth Ave. New York, NY 10011. Phone: (212)206-7715 Fax: (212)645-8437 E-mail: webmaster@abramsbooks.com • URL: http://www.abramsbooks.com • 1998. $12.95. (Discoveries Series).

Diaper Delivery Service. Entrepreneur Media, Inc., 2445 McCabe Way Irvine, CA 92614. Phone: 800-421-2300 or (949)261-2325 Fax: (949)261-0234 E-mail: entmag@entrepreneur.com • URL: http://www.entrepreneur.com • Looseleaf. $59.50. A practical guide to starting a service for the laundering and delivery of all-cotton diapers. Covers profit potential, start-up costs, market size evaluation, owner's time required, site selection, pricing, accounting, advertising, promotion, etc. (Start-Up Business Guide No. E1364.)

Dick Davis Digest. Dick Davis Publishing, PO Box 26774 Tamarac, FL 33320. Phone: 800-654-1514 or (954)724-9826 Fax: (954)724-2952 E-mail: editorial@dickdavis.com • URL: http://www.dickdavis.com • Description: Carries excerpts from over 400 stock market letters and stock, bond, and mutual fund recommendations from leading analysts on Wall Street. Provides overview of general market trends and news of specific industries and companies. Recurring features include columns titled Personal Note, Spotlight Stock, Where's the Market Going, and The Last Word.

Dictionary of Accounting. Adrian Joliffe and P.H. Collin. Independent Publishers Group, 814 N Franklin Chicago, IL 60610. Phone: 800-888-4741 or (312)337-0747 Fax: (312)337-5985 E-mail: ussold@ipgbook.com • URL: http://www.ipgbook.com • 2002. $15.95. Second edition.

Dictionary of Accounting Terms. Joel G. Siegel. Barron's Educational Series, Inc., 250 Wireless Blvd. Hauppauge, NY 11788-3917. Phone: 800-645-3476 or (516)434-3311 Fax: (516)434-3723 E-mail: info@barronseduc.com • URL: http://www.barronseduc.com • 2000. $13.95. Third edition. (Business Dictionaries Series).

Dictionary of Agriculture: From Abaca to Zoonosis. Kathryn L. Lipton. Lynne Rienner Publishers, Inc., 1800 30th St., Suite 314 Boulder, CO 80301. Phone: (303)444-6684 Fax: (303)444-0824 E-mail: questions@rienner.com • URL: http://www.rienner.com • 1995. $75.00. Emphasis is on agricultural economics.

Dictionary of American Medical Biography. Joseph Carvalho and others. Greenwood Publishing Group Inc., 88 Post Rd., W Westport, CT 06881. Phone: 800-225-5800 or (203)226-3571 Fax: (203)431-2214 E-mail: customer-service@greenwood.com • URL: http://www.greenwood.com • 1984. $210.00. Two volumes. Vol. one, $110.00; vol. two, $110.00.

Dictionary of Architecture. James S. Curl. Oxford University Press, 198 Madison Ave. New York, NY 10016. Phone: 800-451-7556 or (212)726-6000 E-mail: custserv@oup-usa.org • URL: http://www.oup.com • 1999. $55.00. (Reference Series).

Dictionary of Architecture and Construction. Cyril M. Harris. McGraw-Hill, 1221 Ave. of the Americas New York, NY 10020. Phone: 800-722-4726 or (212)512-2000 Fax: (212)512-4502 E-mail: customer.service@mcgraw-hill.com • URL: http://www.mcgraw-hill.com • 2000. $69.95. Third edition.

Dictionary of Architecture, Building Construction and Materials. Herbert Bucksch. French and European Publications, Inc., Rockefelle Center Promenade, 610 Fifth Ave. New York, NY 10020. Phone: (212)581-8810 Fax: (212)265-1094

E-mail: liversny@aol.com • URL: http://www.frencheuropean.com • 1983. $295.00. Second edition. Volume two. Text in English and German.

Dictionary of Banking and Finance Terms: 'AAA to Zloty'. John Clark. State Mutual Book and Periodical Services Ltd., PO Box 1199 Bridgehampton, NY 11932-1199. 1998. $60.00.

Dictionary of Banking: Over 4,000 Terms Defined and Explained. Charles J. Woelfel. McGraw-Hill, 1221 Ave. of the Americas New York, NY 10020. Phone: 800-722-4726 or (212)512-2000 Fax: (212)512-4502 E-mail: customer.service@mcgraw-hill.com • URL: http://www.mcgraw-hill.com • 1994. $24.95. Contains brief definitions of more than 4,000 banking terms.

Dictionary of Banking Terms. Jack P. Friedman and Thomas Fitch. Barron's Educational Series, Inc., 250 Wireless Blvd. Hauppauge, NY 11788. Phone: 800-645-3476 or (516)434-3311 Fax: (516)434-3723 E-mail: info@barronseduc.com • URL: http://www.barronseduc.com • 2000. $13.95. Fifth edition. (Business Dictionaries Series).

Dictionary of Bibliometrics. Virgil Diodato. Haworth Press, Inc., 10 Alice St. Binghamton, NY 13904-1580. Phone: 800-429-6784 or (607)722-5857 Fax: 800-895-0582 or (607)722-1424 E-mail: getinfo@haworthpressinc.com • URL: http://www.haworthpressinc.com • 1994. $39.95. Contains detailed explanations of 225 terms, with references. (Bibliometrics is "the application of mathematical and statistical techniques to the study of publishing and professional communication.")

Dictionary of Building. Randall McMullan. GP, 6095 Marshalee Dr., Ste. 300 Elkridge, MD 21075. Phone: 888-843-4784 or (410)379-3600 Fax: (410)540-5302 E-mail: info@genphysics.com • URL: http://www.generalphysics.com/courses • 1991. $59.50.

Dictionary of Commercial, Financial and Legal Terms in Two Languages. R. Herbst. Adler's Foreign Books, Inc., 915 Foster St. Evanston, IL 60201-3199. Phone: 800-235-3771 or (847)864-0664 Fax: 800-433-9229 or (847)864-0804 E-mail: info@afb-adlers.com • URL: http://www.adlers.com • Two volumes. Vol. A, $179.50; vol. B $179.50. Text in English and German.

Dictionary of Computing. Valerie Illingworth, editor. Oxford University Press, 198 Madison Ave. New York, NY 10016. Phone: 800-451-7556 or (212)726-6000 Fax: (212)726-6440 E-mail: custserv@oup-usa.org • URL: http://www.oup-usa.org • 1997. $18.00. Fourth edition.

Dictionary of Econometrics. Adrian C. Darnell. Edward Elgar Publishing, Inc., 136 West St., Suite 202 Northampton, MA 01060. Phone: 800-390-3149 or (413)584-5551 Fax: (413)584-9933 E-mail: elgarinfo@e-elgar.com • URL: http://www.e-elgar.co.uk • 1994. $160.00. Published by Edward Elgar Publishing Co. (UK).

Dictionary of Economic Plants. J.C. Uphof. Lubrecht and Cramer, Ltd., 18 E Main St. Port Jervis, NY 12771. Phone: 800-920-9334 or (914)856-5990 E-mail: books@lubrechtcramer.com • URL: http://www.lubrechtcramer.com • 1998. $80.00. Second enlarged revised edition.

Dictionary of Economics. Donald Rutherford. Routledge, 29 W 35th St. New York, NY 10001. Phone: 800-634-7064 or (212)216-7800 Fax: 800-248-4724 or (212)564-7854 E-mail: info@routledge-ny.com • URL: http://www.routledge-ny.com • 2002. $90.00. Second edition.

Dictionary of Electronics. S.W. Amos and Roger Amos. Elsevier, 655 Ave. of the Americas New York, NY 10010-5107. Phone: 800-366-2665 or (212)989-5800 Fax: 800-535-9935 or (212)633-3680 • URL: http://www.elsevier.com • 1996. $34.95. Third edition.

Dictionary of Finance and Investment Terms. John Downes. Barron's Educational Series, Inc., 250 Wireless Blvd. Hauppauge, NY 11788. Phone: 800-645-3476 or (516)434-3311 Fax: (516)434-3723 E-mail: info@barronseduc.com • URL: http://www.barronseduc.com • 2002. $14.95. Sixth edition. Provides clear explanations of more than 5,000 business, banking, financial, investment, and tax terms. Includes a separate list of financial abbreviations and acronyms. (Business Dictionaries Series).

Dictionary of Financial Abbreviations. John Paxton. Routledge, 29 West 35th St. New York, NY 10001. Phone: 800-634-7064 or (212)216-7800 Fax: 800-248-4724 or (212)564-7854 E-mail: info@routledge-ny.com • URL: http://www.routledge-ny.com • 2002. $50.00. Provides more than 4,000 abbreviations and acronyms relating to finance, currencies, and financial organizations.

Dictionary of Food Ingredients. Robert S. Igoe and Y.H. Hui. Aspen Publishers, Inc., 1185 Avenue of the Americas New York, NY 10036. Phone: 800-234-1660 or (212)597-0200 Fax: (212)597-0338 E-mail: customer.service@aspenpubl.com • URL: http://www.aspenpublishers.com • 2001. $44.00. Fourth edition.

Dictionary of Gambling and Gaming. Thomas L. Clark. Lexik House Publishers, P.O. Box 247 Cold Spring, NY 10516. Phone: (914)424-4115 E-mail: lexik@highlands.com • URL: http://www.highlands.com • 1988. $48.00.

Dictionary of Hydraulic Machinery. A. T. Troskolanski. Elsevier, 655 Ave. of the Americas New York, NY 10010-5107. Phone: 800-366-2665 or (212)989-5800 Fax: 800-535-9935 or (212)633-3680 E-mail: custserv@elsevier.com • URL: http://www.elsevier.com • 1986. $233.00. Text in English, French, German, Italian, and Russian.

Dictionary of Information Technology and Computer Science. Tony Gunton. Blackwell Publishing, 350 Main St. Malden, MA 02148. Phone: 800-216-2522 or (781)388-8200 Fax: 800-864-7626 or (781)388-8210 E-mail: books@blackwellpub.com • URL: http://www.blackwellpub.com • 1994. $62.95. Second edition. Covers key words, phrases, abbreviations, and acronyms used in computing and data communications.

Dictionary of Insurance Terms. Harvey W. Rubin. Barron's Educational Series, Inc., 250 Wireless Blvd. Hauppauge, NY 11788. Phone: 800-645-3476 or (516)434-3311 Fax: (516)434-3723 E-mail: info@barronseduc.com • URL: http://www.barronseduc.com • 2000. $14.95. Fourth edition. Defines terms in a wide variety of insurance fields. (Business Dictionaries Series).

Dictionary of International Biography. Taylor & Francis Group, 325 Chestnut St., Ste. 800 Philadelphia, PA 19106. Phone: 800-821-8312 or (215)625-8900 Fax: (215)625-2940 E-mail: info@taylorand francis.com • URL: http://www.taylorandfrancis.com • 2001. $245.00. 29th edition. Published in England by Melrose.

Dictionary of International Business Terms. John J. Capela. Barron's Educational Series, Inc., 250 Wireless Blvd. Hauppauge, NY 11788-3917. Phone: 800-645-3476 or (631)434-3311 Fax: (631)434-3723 E-mail: info@barronseduc.com • URL: http://www.barronseduc.com • 2000. $14.95. Second edition. (Business Dictionaries Series).

Dictionary of Marketing and Advertising. Jerry M. Rosenberg. John Wiley and Sons, Inc., 111 River St. Hoboken, NJ 07030. Phone: 800-225-5945 or (201)748-6000 Fax: (201)748-6088 E-mail: info@wiley.com • URL: http://www.wiley.com • 1995. $145.00. (Business Dictionary Series).

Dictionary of Marketing Communications. Norman A. P. Govoni. Sage Publications, Inc., 2455 Teller Rd. Thousand Oaks, CA 91320-2218. Phone: 800-818-7243 or (805)499-0721 Fax: 800-583-2665 or (805)499-0871 E-mail: info@sagepub.com • URL: http://www.sagepub.com • 2003. $69.95. Contains more than 4,000 concise definitions of terms relating to advertising, sales promotion, public relations, direct marketing, and selling.

Dictionary of Marketing Terms. Betsy-Ann Toffler. Barron's Educational Series, Inc., 250 Wireless Blvd. Hauppauge, NY 11788-3917. Phone: 800-645-3476 or (516)434-3311 Fax: (516)434-3217 E-mail: info@barronseduc.com • URL: http://www.barronseduc.com • 2000. $13.95. Third edition. (Business Dictionaries Series).

Dictionary of Multimedia: Terms and Acronyms. Brad Hansen, editor. Fitzroy Dearborn Publishers, Inc., 919 N. Michigan Ave., Suite 760 Chicago, IL 60611. Phone: 800-850-8102 or (312)587-0131 Fax: (312)587-1049 E-mail: fitzroy@aol.com • URL: http://www.fitzroydearborn.com • 2002. $55.00. Third edition.

Dictionary of Natural Products. George M. Hocking. Available from Information Today, Inc., 143 Old Marlton Pike Medford, NJ 08055-8750. Phone: 800-300-9868 or (609)654-6266 Fax: (609)654-4309 E-mail: custserv@infotoday.com • URL: http://www.infotoday.com • 1997. $139.50. Published by Plexus Publishing (http://www.plexuspublishing.com). Explains terms relating to the raw materials and products used in natural, folk, or alternative medicine.

Dictionary of 1040 Deductions. LexisNexis Matthew Bender, 1275 Broadway Albany, NY 12204. Phone: 800-424-4200 or (518)487-3000 Fax: (518)487-3584 E-mail: bookstore.support@lexisnexis.com • URL: http://www.bender.com • Annual. $75.00. Organized by schedule and supported by thousands of citations. Designed to quickly answer all questions about deductions.

Dictionary of Plastics Technology. H. D. Junge. John Wiley and Sons, Inc., 111 River St. Hoboken, NJ 07030. Phone: 800-225-5945 or (201)748-0662 Fax: (201)748-6088 E-mail: info@wiley.com • URL: http://www.wiley.com • 1987. $150.00.

Dictionary of Real Estate. Jae K. Shim and others. John Wiley and Sons, Inc., 111 River St. Hoboken, NJ 07030. Phone: 800-225-5945 or (201)748-6000 Fax: (201)748-6088 E-mail: info@wiley.com • URL: http://www.wiley.com • 1995. $145.00. Contains 3,000 definitions of commercial and residential real estate terms. Covers appraisal, escrow, investment, finance, mortgages, property management, construction, legal aspects, etc. Includes illustrations and formulas. (Business Dictionary Series).

Dictionary of Real Estate Terms. Jack P. Friedman and others. Barron's Educational Series, Inc., 250 Wireless Blvd. Hauppauge, NY 11788-3917. Phone: 800-645-3476 or (516)434-3311 Fax: (516)434-3723 E-mail: info@barronseduc.com • URL: http://www.barronseduc.com • 2004. $13.95. Sixth edition. Defines more than 2,500 terms relating to real estate business, including mortgages, financing, leasing, insurance, and home buying.

Dictionary of Shipping Terms. Peter Brodie. LLP, Inc., 41-21 28th St., Rm. D Long Island City, MD 11101. Phone: 800-493-4080 • URL: http://www.informa.com • 1997. Third edition. Price on application. Published in the UK by Lloyd's List (http://www.lloydslist.com). Defines more than 2,000 words, phrases, and abbreviations related to the shipping and maritime industries.

A Dictionary of Statistical Terms. F.H. Marriott. Addison-Wesley, 75 Arlington St., Ste. 300 Boston, MA 02116. Phone: 800-447-2226 or (617)848-7500 • URL: http://www.aw.com • 1996. $76.67. Fifth edition.

Dictionary of Strategy: Strategic Management A-Z. Louise Kelly. Sage Publications, Inc., 2455 Teller Rd. Thousand Oaks, CA 91320-2218. Phone: 800-818-7243 or (805)499-0721 Fax: 800-583-2665 or (805)499-0871 E-mail: info@sagepub.com • URL: http://www.sagepub.com • 2004. $69.95. Defines more than 550 terms relating to strategy in management.

Dictionary of Taxation. Simon James. Edward Elgar Publishing, Inc., 136 West St., Suite 202 Northampton, MA 01060. Phone: 800-390-3149 or (413)584-5551 Fax: (413)584-9933 E-mail: elgarinfo@e-elgar.com • URL: http://www.e-elgar.co.uk • 1998. $65.00. Provides detailed definitions of terms relating to "various aspects of taxes and tax systems throughout the world."

Dictionary of the European Union. Available from Taylor & Francis Group, 325 Chestnut St. Philadelphia, PA 19106. Phone: 800-821-8312 or (215)625-8900 Fax: 800-248-4724 or (215)625-2940 E-mail: info@taylorandfrancis.com • URL: http://www.taylorandfrancis.com • 2002. $145.00. Published by Europa Publications (http://www.europapublications.com). Provides about 1,000 entries defining and explaining all aspects of the European Union.

Dictionary of Trade Name Origins. Adrian Room. McGraw-Hill, 1222 Ave. of the Americas New York, NY 10020. Phone: 800-722-4726 or (212)512-2000 Fax: (212)512-4502 E-mail: customer.service@mcgraw-hill.com • URL: http://www.mcgraw-hill.com • 1990. $39.95.

Die Casting Engineer. North American Die Casting Association, 9701 W. Higgins Rd., No. 880 Rosemont, IL 60018-4721. Phone: (847)292-3600 Fax: (847)292-3620 E-mail: bralower@diecasting.org • URL: http://www.diecasting.org • Bimonthly. Free to members; non-members, $55.00 per year.

Diesel and Gas Turbine Worldwide: The International Engine Power Systems Magazine. Joseph M. Kane, editor. Diesel & Gas Turbine Publications, 20855 Watertown Rd., Ste. 220 Waukesha, WI 53186-1873. Phone: (262)832-5000 Fax: (262)832-5075 10 times a year. $65.00 per year.

Diesel Progress North American Edition: For Engine, Drive and Hydraulic System Engineering and Equipment Management. Diesel and Gas Turbine Publications, 20855 Watertown Rd., Ste. 220 Waukesha, WI 53186-1873. Phone: (262)832-5000 Fax: (262)832-5075 Monthly. $75.00 per year. List of over 1,500 factory-authorized engine distributors and independent service keepers. Formerly *Diesel Progress Engines and Drives?*.

Diet and Meal Planning. Entrepreneur Media, Inc., 2445 McCabe Way Irvine, CA 92614. Phone: 800-421-2300 or (949)261-2325 Fax: (949)261-0234 E-mail: entmag@entrepreneur.com • URL: http://www.entrepreneur.com • Looseleaf. $59.50. A practical guide to starting a diet and meal planning service. Covers profit potential, start-up costs, market size evaluation, pricing, accounting, advertising, promotion, etc. (Start-Up Business Guide No. E2333.)

Dietary Managers Association., 406 Surrey Woods Dr. St. Charles, IL 60174. Phone: 800-323-1908 or (630)587-6336 Fax: (630)587-6308 E-mail: info@dmaonline.org • URL: http://www.dmaonline.org • Dietary managers united to maintain a high level of competency and quality in dietary departments through continuing education. Provides educational programs and placement service.

Dietary Supplements: Current Issues. Donna V. Porter. Nova Science Publishers, Inc., 400 Oser Ave., Suite 1600 Hauppauge, NY 11788-3619. Phone: (631)231-7269 Fax: (631)231-8175 E-mail: novascience@earthlink.net • URL: http://www.novapublishers.com • 2003. $29.50. Covers the legislative and regulatory status of vitamin and mineral supplements.

Digest of Commercial Laws of the World. N. Stephan Kinsella and Paul E. Comeaux. Oceana Publications, Inc., 75 Main St. Dobbs Ferry, NY 10522-1601. Phone: 800-831-0758 or (914)693-8100 Fax: (914)693-0402 E-mail: custsvc@oceanalaw.com • URL: http://www.oceanalaw.com • $495.00. Five volumes. Losseleaf service. Periodic supplementation.

Digest of Education Statistics. Available from U. S. Government Printing Office, Washington, DC 20402. Phone: (202)512-1800 Fax: (202)512-2250 E-mail: gpoaccess@gpo.gov • URL: http://www.access.gpo.gov • Annual. $51.00. Covers all areas of education from kindergarten through graduate school. Includes data from both government and private sources. Compiled by National Center for Education Statistics, U. S. Department of Education.

Digital Audio and Compact Disk Technology. Baert Theunisse and Luc Theunisse. Elsevier, 655 Ave. of the Americas New York, NY 10010-5107. Phone: 800-366-2665 or (212)989-5800 Fax: 800-535-9935 or (212)633-3680 E-mail: custserv@elsevier.com • URL: http://www.elsevier.com • 1995. $57.95. Third edition.

Digital Filmmaking 101: An Essential Guide to Producing Low-Budget Movies. Dale Newton and John Gaspard. Michael Wiese Productions, 11288 Ventura Blvd., Suite 621 Studio City, CA 91604. Phone: 800-833-5738 or (818)379-8799 Fax: (818)986-3408 • URL: http://www.mwp.com • 2001. $24.95. Using a light touch, covers the essentials of making a low-budget film, including scripting, budgeting, funding, equipping, casting, and recruiting a crew.

Digital Image Analysis Laboratory., University of Arizona, Dept. of Electrical and Computer Engineering Tucson, AZ 85721. Phone: (520)621-2706 Fax: (520)621-8076 E-mail: schowengerdt@ece.arizona.edu • URL: http://www.ece.arizona.edu/ • Research fields include image processing, computer vision, and artificial intelligence.

Digital Imaging: The Magazine for the Imaging Professional. Cygnus Business Media, Inc., 445 Broad Hollow Rd. Melville, NY 11747. Phone: 800-547-7377 or (631)845-2700 Fax: (631)845-2798 E-mail: rich.reiff@cygnuspub.com • URL: http://www.cygnusbzb.com • Bimonthly. $24.95 per year. Edited for business and professional users of electronic publishing products and services. Topics covered include document imaging, CD-ROM publishing, digital video, and multimedia services. Formerly *Micro Publishing News*.

Digital Information Network. Buyers Laboratory, Inc., 20 Railroad Ave. Hackensack, NJ 07601. Phone: (201)488-0404 Fax: (201)488-0461 E-mail: info@buyerslab.com • URL: http://www.buyerslab.com • Monthly. $725.00 per year. Newsletter. Information on the copier industry, including test reports on individual machines. Formerly *Digital Information Network*.

Digital Literacy: Personal Preparation for the Internet Age. Paul Gilster. John Wiley and Sons, Inc., 111 River St. Hoboken, NJ 07030. Phone: 800-225-5945 or (201)748-6000 Fax: (201)748-6088 E-mail: info@wiley.com • URL: http://www.wiley.com • 1997. $22.95. Provides practical advice for the online consumer on how to evaluate various aspects of the Internet ("digital literacy" is required, as well as "print literacy").

Digital TV Television Broadcast. United Entertainment Media, 460 Park Ave. S., 9th Fl. New York, NY 10016. Phone: (212)378-0400 Fax: (212)378-2160 E-mail: tvbcast@psn.com • URL: http://www.uemedia.com • Monthly. $52.00 per year. Contains articles on management, production, and technology for TV stations. Formerly *Digital TV*.

Digital Video. CMP Media LLC, 600 Community Dr. Manhasset, NY 11030. Phone: (516)562-5000 E-mail: cmp@cmp.com • URL: http://www.cmp.com • Monthly. $60.00 per year. Edited for professionals in the field of digital video production. Covers such topics as operating systems, videography, digital video cameras, audio, workstations, web video, software development, and interactive television.

Digital Video Magazine. CMP Media LLC, 600 Community Dr. Manhasset, NY 11030. Phone: (516)562-5000 E-mail: cmp@cmp.com • URL: http://www.cmp.com • Monthly. $29.97 per year. Edited for producers and creators of digital media. Includes topics relating to video, audio, animation, multimedia, interactive design, and special effects. Covers both hardware and software, with product reviews. Formerly *Digital Video Magazine*.

Digital X-Ray Markets: Imaging in the 21st Century. Theta Reports/PJB Medical Publications, Inc., 1775 Broadway, Suite 511 New York, NY 10019. Phone: (212)262-8230 Fax: (212)262-8234 E-mail: lschacterle@thetareports.com • URL: http://www.thetareports.com • 2000. $1,995.00. Market research data. Covers digital filmless radiography as a replacement for traditional x-ray technology. (Theta Report No. 1027.)

Dimensional Color. Lois Swirnoff. W. W. Norton & Co., Inc., 500 5th Ave. New York, NY 10110. Phone: 800-223-4830 or (212)354-5500 Fax: (212)869-0856 • URL: http://www.wwnorton.com • 2003. $39.95. Second edition. Explores the three-dimensional interaction between light, color, and surface, with 230 color illustrations. Written chiefly for architects and designers. (Previous edition was published by Van Nostrand Reinhold.)

Dinosaur Brains: Dealing with All Those Impossible People at Work. Albert J. Bernstein and Sydney C. Rozen. John Wiley and Sons, Inc., 111 River St. Hoboken, NJ 07030. Phone: 800-225-5945 or (201)748-6000 Fax: (201)748-6088 E-mail: info@wiley.com • URL: http://www.wiley.com • 1989. $29.95. How to cope with "lizard logic" and overcome the "reptile response." That is, how to deal with irrational, impulsive, and self-destructive work behavior. Covers problem bosses, manipulators, self-promoters, the old boy network, etc.

Diplomatic and Consular Officers, Retired., 1801 F St., N.W. Washington, DC 20006. Phone: 800-344-9127 or (202)682-0500 Fax: (202)842-3295 E-mail: dacor@dacorbacon.org • URL: http://www.dacorbacon.org • Formerly Retired Foreign Service Officers Association.

Diplomatic Bookshelf and Review. Arthur H. Thrower, Ltd., 44-46 S. Ealing Rd. London W5, United Kingdom. Monthly. $4.00 per year.

Diplomatic History. Society for Historians of American Foreign Relations. Blackwell Publishing, 350 Main St. Malden, MA 02148. Phone: 800-935-6770 or (781)388-8200 Fax: (781)388-8232 E-mail: subscript@blackwellpub.com • URL: http://www.blackwellpub.com • Quarterly. Institutions, $208.00 per year. Includes print and online edition.

Diplomatic List. U.S. Department of State. Department of Foreign Affairs and Trade, GPO Box 84 Canberra, Australian Capital Territory 2601, Australia. Phone: (202)512-1800 Fax: (202)512-2250 E-mail: corporatecommunications@reedbusiness.com Covers: offices of diplomatic representatives to Australia. Entries include: Diplomat name, delegation, office address, names of personnel with diplomatic status.

Diplomatic Observer. Institute for International Sociological Research, 50858 Weiner Weg Six Cologne, Germany. Monthly. $16.50 per year.

Diplomatic World Bulletin and Delegates World Bulletin: Dedicated to Serving the United Nations and the International Community. Diplomatic World Bulletin Publications, Inc., 307 E. 44th St., Suite A New York, NY 10017. Phone: (212)747-9500 Biweekly. $45.00 per year.

DIR National Minority and Women-Owned Business Directory. Diversity Information Resources Inc., 2105 Central Ave. NE Minneapolis, MN 55418. Phone: 800-627-4347 or (612)781-6819 Fax: (612)781-0109 E-mail: info@diversityinforesources.com • URL: http://www.diversityinfosources.com • Covers: Over 9,000 minority-owned companies capable of supplying their goods and services on national or regional levels. Entries include: Company name, address, phone, fax, e-mail, Web site, number of employees, year established, products or services, certification status, minority identification, annual sales, NAICS code.

Direct: Magazine for Direct Marketing Management. Primedia Business Magazines and Media, 249 W 17th St. New York, NY 10011. Phone: 800-795-5445 or (212)462-3000 Fax: (212)206-3622 E-mail: subs@primediabusiness.com • URL: http://www.primediabusiness.com • 16 times a year. Free to qualified personnel; others, $85.00 per year.

Direct Marketing Association., 1120 Ave. of the Americas New York, NY 10036-6700. Phone: (212)768-7277 Fax: (212)302-6714 E-mail: presiden@the-dma.org • URL: http://www.the-dma.org • Manufacturers, wholesalers, public utilities, retailers, mail order firms, publishers, schools, clubs, insurance companies, financial organizations, business equipment manufacturers, paper and envelope manufacturers, list brokers, compilers, managers, owners, computer service bureaus, advertising agencies, letter shops, research organizations, printers, lithographers, creators, and producers of direct mail and direct response advertising. Studies consumer and business attitudes toward direct mail and related direct marketing statistics. Offers Mail Preference Service for consumers who wish to receive less mail advertising, Mail Order Action Line to help resolve difficulties with mail order purchases, and Telephone Preference Service for people who wish to receive fewer telephone sales calls. Maintains hall of fame; offers placement service; compiles statistics. Sponsors several three-day Basic Direct Marketing Institutes, Advanced Direct Marketing Institutes, and special interest seminars and workshops. Maintains Government Affairs office in Washington, DC. Operates Direct Marketing Educational Foundation.

Direct Marketing, Direct Selling, and the Mature Consumer: A Research Study. James R. Lumpkin and others. Greenwood Publishing Group, Inc., 88 Post Rd., W Westport, CT 06881. Phone: (203)225-5800 or (203)226-3571 Fax: (203)431-2214 E-mail: customer-service@greenwood.com • URL: http://www.greenwood.com • 1989. $64.95. A study of older consumers and their use of mail order, telephone shopping, party-plans, etc.

Direct Marketing Educational Foundation., 1120 Ave. of the Americas New York, NY 10036-6700. Phone: (212)768-7277 Fax: (212)790-1561 E-mail: dmef@the-dma.org • URL: http://www.the-dma.org/dmef • Represents individuals, firms, and organizations interested in furthering college-level education in direct marketing. Functions as the collegiate arm of the direct marketing profession. Sponsors a summer internship, programs for students and professors, and campaign competition for students. Provides educational materials and course outlines to faculty members; arranges for speakers for college classes and clubs. Co-sponsors academic research competitions. Maintains hall of fame.

Direct Marketing Market Place: The Networking Source of the Direct Marketing Industry. LexisNexis, 1275 Broadway Albany, NY 12204. Phone: 800-424-4200 or (518)487-3000 E-mail: corpcomm@lexisnexis.com • URL: http://www.lexisnexis.com • Annual. $324.99. Lists direct marketers, service companies, creative sources, professional groups, photographers, paper suppliers, etc.

Direct Marketing Success: What Works and Why. Freeman F. Gosden. John Wiley and Sons, Inc., 111 River St. Hoboken, NJ 07030. Phone: 800-526-5368 or (201)748-6000 Fax: (201)748-6088 E-mail: info@wiley.com • URL: http://www.wiley.com • 1989. $24.95.

Direct Marketing: Using Direct Response Advertising to Enhance Marketing Database. Hoke Communications, Inc., 224 Seventh St. Garden City, NY 11530. Phone: 800-229-6700 or (516)746-6700 Fax: (516)294-8141 E-mail: 71410.2423@compuserve.com Monthly. $65.00 per year. Direct marketing to consumers and business.

Direct Selling Association., 1667 K St. NW, Ste. 1100 Washington, DC 20006. Phone: (202)452-8866 Fax: (202)452-9010 E-mail: info@dsa.org • URL: http://www.dsa.org • Manufacturers and distributors selling consumer products through person-to-person sales, by appointment, and through home-party plans. Products include food, gifts, house wares, dietary supplements, cosmetics, apparel, jewelry, decorative accessories, reference books, and telecommunications products and services. Offers specialized education; conducts research programs; compiles statistics. Maintains hall of fame. Sponsors Direct Selling Education Foundation (see separate entry).

Direct Selling Association World Federation News. Direct Selling Association. World Federation of Direct Selling Associations, 1275 Pennsylvania Ave., NW, Ste. 800 Washington, DC 20004. Phone: (202)347-8866 Fax: (202)347-0055 E-mail: info@wfdsa.org • URL: http://www.wfdsa.org • Six times a year. Membership.

Direction: For the Moving and Storage Industry. American Moving and Storage Association, 1611 Duke St. Alexandria, VA 22314. Phone: (703)683-7410 Fax: (703)548-1845 E-mail: amc1@erols.com Monthly. $35.00 per year. Newsletter on developments affecting the household goods movingindustry. Formerly *American Mover*.

Direction of Trade Statistics. International Monetary Fund. International Monetary Fund Publications Services, 700 19th St., N.W. Washington, DC 20431. Phone: (202)623-7000 Fax: (202)623-6278 E-mail: publicaffairs@imf.org • URL: http://www.imf.org • Quarterly. Individuals, $128.00 per year; libraries, $89.00 per year. Includes *Yearbook*.

The Director. National Funeral Directors Association. NFDA Publications, Inc., 13625 Bishops Dr. Brookfield, WI 53005-6607. Phone: 800-228-6332 or (262)789-1880 Fax: (262)789-6977 E-mail: nfda@nfda.org • URL: http://www.nfda.org • Monthly. $30.00 per year.

Directories in Print. Gale Cengage Learning, 27500 Drake Rd. Farmington Hills, MI 48331-3535. Phone: 800-877-GALE or (248)699-4253 Fax: 800-414-5043 E-mail: gale.galeord@cengage.com • URL: http://gale.cengage.com • Annual. $565.00. Two volumes. *Midyear Supplement*, $440.00. Two volumes. An annotated guide to approximately 15,500 business, industrial, professional, and scientific directories. Formerly *Directory of Directories*.

Directors & Boards., 1845 Walnut St., 9th Fl. Philadelphia, PA 19103-4709. Phone: (215)567-3200 Fax: (215)450-6078 E-mail: jkristie@directorsandboards.com • URL: http://www.directorsandboards.com • Quarterly. $295.00 per year. Edited for corporate board members and senior executive officers.

Directors and Officers Liability: Prevention, Insurance, and Indemnification. American Lawyer Media, Inc., 105 Madison Ave. New York, NY 10016. Phone: 800-888-8300 or (212)779-9200 Fax: (212)481-8110 E-mail: lawcatalog@amlaw.com • URL: http://www.lawcatalog.com/ • Looseleaf. $179.00. Updated as needed. Covers the legal risks faced by corporate directors and officers. (Law Journal Press).

Directors Guild of America., 7920 Sunset Blvd. Hollywood, CA 90046. Phone: 800-420-4173 or (310)289-2000 Fax: (310)289-2029 E-mail: dga@dga.org • URL: http://www.dga.org • Negogiates agreements for members.

Directors Guild of America Directory of Members. Directors Guild of America Inc., 7920 Sunset Blvd. Los Angeles, CA 90046. Phone: (310)289-2000 Fax: (310)289-2029 • URL: http://www.dga.org • Annual. $22.00.

Director's Monthly. National Association of Corporate Directors, 1133 21st St., NW, Ste. 700 Washington, DC 20036. Phone: (202)775-0509 Fax: (202)775-4857 E-mail: info@nacdonline.org • URL: http://www.nacdonline.org • Description: Reports current issues and events of interest to corporate directors. Covers such topics as director independence, ethics, directors, audit, compensation, nominating committees, and changing regulatory requirements. Recurring features include roundtable discussions and interviews.

Directory of Accredited Home Study Schools. Distance Education and Training Council, 1601 18th St. N.W. Washington, DC 20009. Phone: (202)234-5100 Fax: (202)332-1386 E-mail: detc@detc.org • URL: http://www.detc.org • Annual. Free. Lists accredited home study schools and the subjects they offer.

Directory of American Firms Operating in Foreign Countries. Uniworld Business Publications, 257 Central Park W, Ste. 10A New York, NY 10024-4110. Phone: (212)496-2448 Fax: (212)769-0413 E-mail: uniworldbp@aol.com • URL: http://www.uniworldbp.com • Biennial. $355.00. Three volumes. Lists approximately 3,000 American companies with more than 34,500 subsidiaries and affiliates in 190 foreign countries.

Directory of American Research and Technology: Organizations Active in Product Development for Business. Information Today, 143 Old Marlton Pke. Medford, NJ 08055. Phone: 800-300-9868 Fax: (609)654-6266 E-mail: custserv@infotoday.com • URL: http://www.infotoday.com • Annual. $359.95. Lists over 13,000 publicly and privately owned research facilities. Formerly *Industrial Research Laboratories of the U.S.*

Directory of American Scholars. Gale Cengage Learning, 27500 Drake Rd. Farmington Hills, MI 48331-3535. Phone: 800-877-GALE or (248)699-4253 Fax: 800-414-5043 E-mail: gale.galeord@cengage.com • URL: http://gale.cengage.com • 2001. $595.00. 10th edition. Six volumes. Volumes one to volume five, $145.00; volume six, $50.00. Provides biographical information and publication history for more than 24,000 scholars in the humanities.

Directory of Apparel Specialty Stores. Chain Store Guide, 3922 Coconut Palm Dr. Tampa, FL 33619-8321. Phone: 800-778-9794 or (813)627-6800 Fax: (813)627-6882 E-mail: info@csgis.com • URL: http://www.csgis.com • Annual. $335.00. 4,700 apparel and sporting goods specialty stores in the United States and Canada, operating more than 80,000 stores. Include company name, phone and fax numbers, company e-mail and web addresses and other information.

Directory of Automotive Aftermarket Suppliers. Chain Store Guide, 3922 Coconut Palm Dr. Tampa, FL 33619-8321. Phone: 800-778-9794 or (813)627-6800 Fax: (813)627-6882 E-mail: info@csgis.com • URL: http://www.csgis.com • Annual. $327.00. Covers auto supply store chains. Includes distributors.

Directory of Better Business Bureaus. Council of Better Business

SOURCES CITED

Bureaus, Inc., 4200 Wilson Blvd. No. 800 Arlington, VA 22203-1838. Phone: (703)276-0100 Fax: (703)525-8277 • URL: http://www.bbb.org • Annual. Free. Send stamped, self-addressed envelope. Lists about 185 Better Business Bureaus in the United States and Canada.

Directory of British Associations and Associations in Ireland. CBD Research Research Ltd., 15 Wickham Rd. Beckenham BR3 5JS, United Kingdom. Phone: 0208 650 7745 Fax: 0208 650 0768 E-mail: cbd@cbdresearch.com Biennial. $350.00. Lists about 7,000 national organizations of England, Wales, Scotland, Northern Ireland and the Irish Republic. Published by CBD Research.

Directory of Building Codes and Regulations. National Conference of States on Building Codes and Standards, 505 Huntmar Park Dr., Suite 210 Herndon, VA 20170. Phone: 800-362-2633 or (703)437-0100 Fax: (703)481-3596 • URL: http://www.ncsbcs.org • Annual. Optional quarterly updates. Two volumes. Members, $115.00; non-members, $150.00. In addition to information about residential and commerical building codes,includes a directory of state and majority administrators concerned with enforcement of the codes.

The Directory of Business Information Resources: Associations, Newsletters, Magazine Trade Shows. Grey House Publishing, Inc., 185 Millerton Rd. Millerton, NY 12546. Phone: 800-562-2139 or (518)789-8700 Fax: 800-248-0115 or (518)789-0556 E-mail: books@greyhouse.com • URL: http://www.greyhouse.com • Annual. $250.00. Provides concise information on associations, newsletters, magazines, and trade shows for each of 90 major industry groups. An "Entry & Company Index" serves as a guide to titles, publishers, and organizations.

Directory of Business-to-Business Catalogs. Grey House Publishing, 185 Millerton Rd. Millerton, NY 12546. Phone: 800-562-2139 or (518)789-8700 Fax: (518)789-0556 E-mail: books@greyhouse.com • URL: http://www.greyhouse.com • Annual. $165.00. Provides over 6,000 listings of U. S. mail order companies selling business or industrial products and services.

Directory of Buyout Financing Sources. Thomson Financial, 195 Broadway New York, NY 10007. Phone: 800-262-6000 or (646)822-2000 Fax: (646)822-6270 E-mail: custserv@tfn.com • URL: http://www.tfn.com • Annual. $445.00. Describes more than 1,000 U. S. and foreign sources of financing for buyout deals. Indexed by personnel, company, industry, and location.

Directory of Canadian Trademarks. Thomson & Thomson, 500 Victory Rd. North Quincy, MA 02171-3145. Phone: 800-692-8833 or (617)479-1600 Fax: (617)786-8273 E-mail: support@t-t.com • URL: http://www.thomson-thomson.com • Annual. Price on application. Provides owner, registration, and classification information for Canadian trademarks registered with the Canadian Intellectual Property Office (CIPO).

Directory of Certified Product Safety Managers. Board of Certified Product Safety Management, 8009 Carita Court Bethesda, MD 20817. Phone: (301)770-2183 Fax: (301)770-2540 E-mail: bchcm@juno.com Biennial. $15.00. Available only online. Membership directory.

Directory of Chain Restaurant Operators. Chain Store Guide, 3922 Coconut Palm Dr. Tampa, FL 33619-8321. Phone: 800-927-9292 or (813)627-6800 Fax: (813)627-6882 • URL: http://www.csgis.com • Annual. $335.00. Includes fast food establishments, and leading chain hotel copanies operating foodservice unit.

Directory of Chemical Producers - United States. SRI Consulting, 333 Ravenswood Ave. Menlo Park, CA 94025-3477. Phone: (650)859-3900 Fax: (650)859-2182 E-mail: inquiry_line@sri.com • URL: http://www.sri-chem.com • Annual. $2,070.00. Information on over 1,200 United States basic chemical producers, manufacturing nearly 7,900 chemicals in commercial quantities at 3,500 plant locations.

Directory of College Stores. B. Klein Publications, Inc., P.O. Box 6578 Delray Beach, FL 33482. Phone: (561)496-3316 Fax: (561)496-5546 1999. $95.00. Covers about 4,400 stores selling books, stationery, personal care items, gifts, etc., which serve primarily a college student population.

Directory of Companies Required to File Annual Reports with the Securities and Exchange Commission. Securities and Exchange Commission. Available from U.S. Government Printing Office, Washington, DC 20402. Phone: (202)512-1800 Fax: (202)512-2250 Annual. $46.00.

Directory of Computer and Consumer Electronics Retailers. Chain Store Guide, 3922 Coconut Palm Dr. Tampa, FL 33619-8321. Phone: 800-778-9794 or (813)627-6800 Fax: (813)627-6882 E-mail: info@csgis.com • URL: http://www.csgis.com • Annual. $335.00. Online edition, $775.00. Lists 4,500 United States and Canada companies operating almost 59,000 stores with at least $1,000,000 in sales.

Directory of Computer VAR's and Systems Integrators. Chain Store Guide, 3922 Coconut Palm Dr. Tampa, FL 33619. Phone: 800-778-9794 or (813)627-6800 Fax: (813)627-6882 E-mail: info@csgis.com • URL: http://www.csgis.com • Annual. $327.00. Provides information on computer companies that modify, enhance, or customize hardware or software. Includes systems houses, systems integrators, turnkey systems specialists, original equipment manufacturers, and value added retailers. Formerly *Directory of Value Added Resellers*.

Directory of Consumer Brands and Their Owners: Asia Pacific. Euromonitor International, Business Reference Div., 122 S Michigan Ave., Ste. 1200 Chicago, IL 60603. Phone: 800-577-3876 or (312)922-1115 Fax: (312)922-1157 E-mail: insight@euromonitorintl.com 1998. $990.00. Provides information about brands available from major Asia Pacific companies. Descriptions of companies are also included.

Directory of Consumer Brands and Their Owners: Eastern Europe. Euromonitor International, Business Reference Div., 122 S Michigan Ave., Ste. 1200 Chicago, IL 60603. Phone: 800-577-3876 or (312)922-1115 Fax: (312)922-1157 E-mail: insight@euromonitorintl.com 1998. $990.00. Provides information about brands available from major Eastern European companies. Descriptions of companies are also included.

Directory of Consumer Brands and Their Owners: Latin America. Euromonitor International, Business Reference Div., 122 S Michigan Ave., Ste. 1200 Chicago, IL 60603. Phone: 800-577-3876 or (312)922-1115 Fax: (312)922-1157 E-mail: insight@euromonitor.intl.com 1999. $990.00. Provides information about brands available from major Latin American companies. Descriptions of companies are also included.

Directory of Convenience Stores. Trade Dimensions, 45 Danbury Rd. Wilton, CT 06897. Phone: 800-291-0410 or (203)563-3000 Fax: (203)563-3131 E-mail: info@tradedimensions.com • URL: http://www.tradedimensions.com • Annual. $260.00. Provides information on over 1,400 convenience store chains having four or more convenience stores.

Directory of Conventions Regional Editions. VNU Business Media, 770 Broadway New York, NY 10003. Phone: (646)654-4500 Fax: (646)654-7212 • URL: http://www.vnubusinessmedia.com • Annual. $155.00 per volume. Four volumes. Set, $285.00. Over 14,000 meetings of North American national, regional, and state and local organizations.

Directory of Counseling Services. International Association of Counseling Services, 101 S. Whiting, Suite 211 Alexandria, VA 22304-3416. Phone: (703)823-9840 Fax: (703)823-9843 E-mail: iacs@gmu.edu Annual. $50.00. About 200 accredited services in the United States and Canada concerned with psychological educational, and vocational counseling, including those at colleges and universities and public and private agencies.

Directory of Delicatessen Products. Pacific Rim Publishing Co., P.O. Box 4533 Huntington Beach, CA 92605-4533. Phone: (714)375-3904 Fax: (714)375-3906 Annual. Included with February issue of *Deli News*. Lists suppliers of cheeses, lunch meats, packaged fresh meats, kosher foods, gourmet-specialty items, and bakery products.

Directory of Department Stores. Chain Store Guide, 3922 Coconut Palm Dr. Tampa, FL 33619-8321. Phone: 800-778-9794 or (813)627-6800 Fax: (813)627-6882 E-mail: info@csgis.com • URL: http://www.csgis.com • Annual. $327.00. Available online. Lists 214 department stores, 1,500 shoe stores, 200 jewelry stores, 95 optical stores, and 70 leather and luggage stores in the United States and Canada, with annual sales of at least $250.00.

Directory of Directors (Canada). Financial Post Datagroup, 333 King St., E. Toronto, ON, Canada M5A 4N2. Phone: 800-661-7678 or (416)350-6500 Fax: (416)350-6501 E-mail: fpdg@fpdata.finpost.com • URL: http://www.financialpost.com • Annual. $175.00. Provides brief biographical information on 16,000 directors and key officers of Canadian companies who are also Canadian residents.

Directory of Discount and General Merchandise Stores. Chain Store Guide, 3922 Coconut Palm Dr. Tampa, FL 33619-8321. Phone: 800-778-9794 or (813)627-6800 Fax: (813)627-6882 E-mail: info@csgis.com • URL: http://www.csgis.com • Annual. $327.00. Online edition, $747.00. Includes retailers and wholesalers of housewares, giftwares, novelties, toys, hobby materials, crafts, and stationery.

Directory of Electrical Wholesale Distributors. Primedia Business Magazines and Media, 9800 Metcalf Ave. Overland Park, KS 66212. Phone: 800-795-5445 or (913)341-1300 Fax: (913)967-1898 E-mail: subs@primediabusiness.com • URL: http://www.primediabusiness.com • Biennial. $1,390.00. Lists more than 10,000 locations.

Directory of Environmental Attorneys. Aspen Publishers, Inc., 1185 Ave. of the Americas New York, NY 10036. Phone: 800-234-1660 or (212)597-0200 Fax: 800-901-9075 or (212)597-0338 E-mail: customer.service@aspenpubl.com • URL: http://www.aspenpublishers.com • 1994. $195.00.

The Directory of EU Information Sources: The Red Book. Euroconfidentiel S. A., Rue de Rixensart 18 B-1332 Genval, Belgium. Phone: (32)02 652 02 84 Fax: (32)02 653 01 80 E-mail: nigel.hunt@skynet.be • URL: http://www.euroconfidential.com • Annual. $230.00. Lists publications, associations, consultants, law firms, diplomats, jounalists, and other sources of information about Europe and the European Union.

Directory of Executive Recruiters. Kennedy Information, Inc., 1 Phoenix Mill Ln., 5th Fl. Peterborough, NH 03458. Phone: 800-531-0007 or (603)924-1006 Fax: (603)924-4460 E-mail: bookstore@kennedyinfo.com • URL: http://www.kennedyinfo.com • Annual. $49.95. Contains profiles of more than 5,500 executive search firms in the U. S., Canada, and Mexico.

Directory of Federal Libraries. William R. Evinger, editor. Greenwood Publishing Group, Inc., 88 Post Rd., W. Westport, CT 06881. Phone: 800-225-5800 or (203)226-3751 Fax: (203)431-2214 E-mail: customer-service@greenwood.com • URL: http://www.greenwood.com • 1997. $99.50. Third edition. (Directory of Federal Library Series).

Directory of Foodservice Distributors. Chain Store Guide, 3922 Coconut Store Guide Tampa, FL 33619. Phone: 800-778-9794 or (813)627-6800 Fax: (813)627-6882 E-mail: info@csgis.com • URL: http://www.csgis.com • Annual. $335.00. Available online. Covers distributors of food and equipment to restaurants and institutions.

Directory of Foreign Firms Operating in the United States. Uniworld Business Publications, Inc., 257 Central Park W., Suite 10-A New York, NY 10024-4110. Phone: (212)496-2448 Fax: (212)769-0413 E-mail: uniworldbp@aol.com • URL: http://www.uniworldbp.com • Biennial. $250.00. Lists about 2,400 foreign companies and 5,700 American affiliates. 75 countries are represented.

Directory of Franchising Organizations. Prima Publishing, 3000 Lava Ridge Ct. Roseville, CA 95661. Phone: 800-632-8676 or (916)787-7000 Fax: (916)787-7003 1998. $12.95. Lists over 700 franchises with description and cost of investment.

Directory of Funparks and Attractions: International Guide to Amusement Parks, Family Entertainment Centers, Waterparks, and Attractions. Amusement Business, PO Box 24970 Nashville, TN 37202. Phone: 800-449-1402 E-mail: info@amusementbusiness.com • URL: http://www.amusementbusiness.com • Annual. $69.00. Over 2,800, amusement parks, theme parks, family entertainment centers, water parks, zoos, kiddielands and other tourist attractions in U.S., Canada and overseas. Formerly *Amusement Business Directory of Funparks and Attractions*.

Directory of Golf. National Golf Foundation, 1150 S. U.S. Highway 1, Suite 401 Jupiter, FL 33477. Phone: 800-733-6006 or (561)744-6006 Fax: (561)744-6107 E-mail: ngf@ngf.org • URL: http://www.ngf.org • Annual $60.00. Lists golf course architects, contractors, builders, appraisers, and consulting firms. Golf equipment manufacturers are also included.

Directory of Government Document Collections and Librarians. Government Documents Roundtable. American Library Association, 1301 Pennsylvania Ave., NW, Ste. 403 Washington, DC 20002. Phone: 800-638-8380 or (202)628-8410 Fax: (202)628-8419 Triennial. $57.50. A guide to federal, state, local, foreign, and international document collections in the U.S. Includes name of libratians and other government document professionals.

Directory of Graduate Programs. National Communication Association, 1765 N St., NW Washington, DC 20036-2801. Phone: (202)464-4622 Fax: (202)464-4600 E-mail: jgaudino@natcom.org • URL: http://www.natcom.org • Irregular. Available only online. Accredited institutions that offer advanced deree in 84 graduate program areas. Degrees not included are J.D., D.D.S., M.D. and some other professional degrees.

Directory of Grants for Organizations Serving People with Disabilities: A Guide to Sources of Funding in the United States for Programs and Services for Personswith Disabilities. Richard M. Eckstein. Research Grant Guides, P.O. Box 1214 Loxahatchee, FL 33470. Phone: (561)795-6129 Fax: (561)795-7794 • URL: http://www.researchgrant.com • Biennial. $59.50. Lists over 800 foundations, associations, and government agencies that grant funds to non-profit organizations for projects related to handicapped persons. Formerly *Handicapped Funding Directory*.

Directory of High Volume Independent Restaurants. Chain Store Guide, 3922 Coconut Palm Dr. Tampa, FL 33619-8321. Phone: 800-778-9794 or (813)627-6800 Fax: (813)627-6882 E-mail: info@csgis.com • URL: http://www.csgis.com • Annual. $327.00. Online edition, $775.00. Approximately 5,900 independently owned restaurants with minimum sales of at least $1 million.

Directory of Home Center Operators and Hardware Chains. Chain Store Guide, 3922 Coconut Palm Dr. Tampa, FL 33619-8321. Phone: 800-778-9794 or (813)627-6800 Fax: (813)627-6882 E-mail: info@csgis.com • URL: http://www.csgis.com • Annual. $327.00. Online edition, $747.00. Nearly 4,700 home center operators, paint and home decorating chains, and lumber and building materials companies. Covers United States and Canada.

Directory of Home Furnishings Retailers. Chain Store Guide, 3922 Coconut Palm Dr. Tampa, FL 33619. Phone: 800-778-9794 or (813)627-6800 Fax: (813)627-6882 E-mail: info@csgis.com • URL: http://www.csgis.com • Annual. $335.00. Online edition, $775.00. Includes more than 5,500 furniture retailers and wholesalers. Covers United States and Canada.

Directory of Hospital Personnel. Medical Economics Co., 5 Paragon Dr. Montvale, NJ 07645-1742. Phone: 877-922-2022 or (973)944-9777 Fax: (972)847-5390 E-mail: fulfill@superfill.com • URL: http://www.medec.com • Annual. $325.00. Lists over 200,000 healthcare professionals in 7,000 U. S. hospitals. Geographic arrangement, with indexes by personnel, hospital name, and bed size.

Directory of Hotel and Lodging Companies. American Hotel and Lodging Association, 1201 New York Ave., N. W., Suite 600 Washington, DC 20005-3931. Phone: (202)289-3100 Fax: (202)289-3199 E-mail: info@ahla.com • URL: http://www.ahla.com • Annual. $82.00. Contains listings of suppliers of products and services for the lodging industry.

Directory of Hotel and Motel Companies. HealthForum, One N.

Franklin St. Chicago, IL 60606-3421. Phone: 800-621-6902 or (312)893-6800 Fax: (312)422-4500 Annual. $79.00 per year. Lists more than 1,025 hotel, motel and resort chain companies. International coverage.

Directory of Intellectual Property Attorneys, 1995. Aspen Publishers, Inc., 1185 Ave. of the Americas New York, NY 10036. Phone: 800-234-1660 or (212)597-0200 Fax: 800-901-9075 or (212)597-0338 E-mail: customer.service@aspenpubl.com • URL: http://www.aspenpublishers.com • 1994. $195.00.

Directory of Iron and Steel Plants (The Black Book). Association of Iron and Steel Engineers, Three Gateway Center, Suite 1900 Pittsburgh, PA 15222-1004. Phone: 800-966-6323 or (412)281-6323 Fax: (412)281-4657 E-mail: directory@aise.org Biennial. $75.00. Lists executives and officials in the United States and selected overseas steel companies and plants.

Directory of Judges with Juvenile/Family Law Jurisdiction. National Council of Juvenile and Family Court Judges, PO Box 8970 Reno, NV 89507. Phone: (702)784-6012 Fax: (702)784-1084 E-mail: admin@ncjfcj.unr.edu • URL: http://www.ncjfcj.unr.edu • Irregular. $25.00. 1,400 judges who have juvenile, family, or domestic relations jurisdiction.

Directory of Juvenile and Adult Correctional Departments, Institutions, Agencies, Parole Authorities, and Probation. American Correctional Association, 4380 Forbes Blvd. Lanham, MD 20706-4322. Phone: 800-222-5646 • URL: http://www.aca.org • Annual. $90.00. Provides information on more than 4,000 correctional agencies and institutions in the U. S. and Canada. Formerly*Directory of Juvenile and Adult Correctional Agencies of the United States and Canada*.

Directory of Legislative Leaders. National Conference of State Legislatures, 7700 E 1st Pl. Denver, CO 80202-1743. Phone: (303)364-7700 Fax: (303)364-7800 E-mail: info@ncsl.org • URL: http://www.ncsl.org • Annual. $20.00. Lists state presiding officers, majority and minority leaders, and key staff members. Preferred addresses, telephone numbers, and fax numbers are included.

Directory of Library Automation Software, Systems, and Services. Information Today, Inc., 143 Old Marlton Pike Medford, NJ 08055-8750. Phone: 800-300-9868 or (609)654-6266 Fax: (609)654-4309 E-mail: custserv@infotoday.com • URL: http://www.infotoday.com • Biennial. $89.00. Provides detailed descriptions of about 330 software programs and software services for libraries.

Directory of Litigation Attorneys, 1995-1996. Aspen Publishers, Inc., 1185 Ave. of the Americas New York, NY 10036. Phone: 800-234-1660 or (212)597-0200 Fax: 800-901-9075 or (212)597-0338 E-mail: customer.service@aspenpubl.com • URL: http://www.aspenpublishers.com • 1993. $450.00. Two volumes. Includes about 40,000 attorneys, 15,000 law firms, and 100 areas of litigation specialization.

Directory of M & A Intermediaries. Thomson Financial, 195 Broadway New York, NY 10007. Phone: 800-262-6000 or (646)822-2000 Fax: (646)822-6270 E-mail: custserv@tfn.com • URL: http://www.tfn.com • Annual. $360.00. Lists more than 850 dealmakers for mergers and acquisitions, including investment banks, business brokers, and commercial banks.

Directory of Mail Order Catalogs. Grey House Publishing, 185 Millerton Rd. Millerton, NY 12546. Phone: 800-562-2139 or (518)789-8700 Fax: (518)789-0556 E-mail: books@greyhouse.com • URL: http://www.greyhouse.com • Annual. $165.00. Contains 12,000 entries for mail order companies selling consumer products throughout the U.S.

Directory of Mailing List Companies. Todd Publications, P.O. Box 635 West Nyack, NY 10960-0635. Phone: 800-747-1056 or (914)358-6213 Fax: (914)358-1059 E-mail: toddpub@aol.com • URL: http://www.toddpublications.com • Biennial. $75.00. Lists and describes approximately 1,000 of the most active list brokers, owners, managers and compilers.

Directory of Management Consultants. Kennedy Information, Inc., One Phoenix Mill Lane, 5th Fl. Peterborough, NH 03458. Phone: 800-531-0007 or (603)924-1006 Fax: (603)924-4460 E-mail: bookstore@kennedyinfo.com • URL: http://www.kennedyinfo.com • Biennial. $295.00. Contains profiles of more than 2,100 general and specialty management consulting firms in the U. S., Canada, and Mexico.

Directory of Manufacturers Supporting the Writing and Marking Instrument Industry. Writing Instrument Manufacturers Association, 17000 Commerce Pky. Ste. C Mount Laurel, NJ 08054. Phone: (856)638-0426 Fax: (856)439-0525 E-mail: wima@ahint.com • URL: http://www.wima.org • Biennial. Available only online. About 200 manufacturers; includes non-members. Formerly *Directory of Manufacturers and Products of the Handwriting and Marking Instrument Manufacturing Industry*.

Directory of Marine Diesel Engines. Institute of Marine Engineering, Science, and Technology, 80 Coleman St. London EC2R 5JB, United Kingdom. Phone: 44 20 7382 2645 Fax: 44 20 7382 2648 E-mail: info@imarest.org • URL: http://www.imarest.org • Annual. Price on application. Issued as a supplement to *Marine Engineers Review*.

Directory of Minority-Owned Professional and Personnel Services Consultants. San Francisco Redevelopment Agency, 770 Golden Gate Ave. San Francisco, CA 94102. Phone: (415)749-2400 Fax: (415)749-2590 E-mail: cheryl_towns@ci.sf.ca.us • URL: http://www.sfgov.org • Annual. Free. About 650 minority firms in Northern California.

Directory of Multinationals. Available from Gale Cengage Learning, 27500 Drake Rd. Farmington Hills, MI 48331-3535. Phone: 800-877-GALE or (248)699-GALE Fax: 800-414-5043 E-mail: gale.galeord@cengage.com • URL: http://www.galegroup.com • 2001. $775.00. Sixth edition. Two volumes. Published by Waterlow Specialist Information Publishing. Provides detailed information on multinational firms with total annual sales in excess of one billion dollars and overseas sales in excess of $500 million. Includes narrative company descriptions and statistical data.

Directory of North American Fairs, Festivals and Expositions. Amusement Business, PO Box 24970 Nashville, TN 37202. Phone: 800-449-1402 E-mail: info@amusementbusiness.com • URL: http://www.amusementbusiness.com • Annual. $79.00. Lists over 5,000 fairs, festivals and expositions in the U.S. and Canada which run three days or more.

Directory of Nursing Homes. Solucient, 300 E. Lombard St., Suite 1600 Baltimore, MD 21202. Phone: 800-568-3282 or (410)576-9600 Fax: (410)576-9429 E-mail: pubs@solucient.com • URL: http://www.solucient.com • Biennial. $125.00. Provides information on more than 15,000 nursing homes, including admission requirements, facilities, number of beds, and name of owner.

Directory of Obsolete Securities. Financial Information, Inc., 30 Montgomery St. Jersey City, NJ 07302-0473. Phone: 800-367-3441 or (201)332-5400 Fax: 800-344-3292 Annual. $655.00.

Directory of Operating Grants. Richard M. Eckstein. Research Grant Guides, P.O. Box 1214 Loxahatchee, FL 33470. Phone: (561)795-6129 Fax: (561)795-7794 • URL: http://www.researchgrant.com • Annual. $59.50. Contains profiles for approximately 800 foundations that award grants to nonprofit organizations for such operating expenses as salaries, rent, and utilities. Geographical arrangement, with indexes.

Directory of Outplacement and Career Management Firms. Kennedy Information, Inc., 1 Phoenix Mill Ln., 5th Fl. Peterborough, NH 03458. Phone: 800-531-0007 or (603)924-1006 Fax: (603)924-4460 E-mail: bookstore@kennedyinfo.com • URL: http://www.kennedyinfo.com • Annual. $149.95. Contains profiles of more than 390 firms specialize in helping "downsized" executives find new employment. Formerly *Directory of Outplacement Firms*.

Directory of Physician Groups and Networks. Dorland Healthcare Information, 1500 Walnut St., Suite 1000 Philadelphia, PA 19102. Phone: 800-784-2332 or (215)875-1212 Fax: (215)735-3966 E-mail: info@dorlandhealth.com • URL: http://www.dorlandhealth.com • Annual. $495.00. Available only online. Approximately 8,000 independent practice associations (IPAs), physician hospital organizations (PHOs), management service organizations (MSOs), physician practice management companies (PPMCs), and group practices having 20 or more physicians.

Directory of Physicians in the United States. American Medical Association, 515 N. State St. Chicago, IL 60610. Phone: 800-262-2350 or (312)464-5000 Fax: (312)464-4184 • URL: http://www.ama-asn.org • Biennial. $695.00. Four volumes. Brief information for more than 850,000 physicians. Formerly*American Medical Directory*.

Directory of Privately-Owned Hospitals,Residential Treatment Facilities and Centers, Hospital Management Companies, and Health Systems. Federation of American Health Systems, 1405 N. Pierce St., Suite 311 Little Rock, AR 72207. Phone: 800-880-3247 or (501)661-9555 Fax: (501)663-4903 • URL: http://www.americashospitals.com • Annual. $125.00. Lists approximately 1,700 privately-owned hospitals and over 80 hospital management companies in the United States, Puerto Rico, and internationally.

Directory of Regional Councils. National Association of Regional Councils, 1666 Connecticut Ave., NW, Ste. 30 Washington, DC 20009. Phone: (202)986-1032 Fax: (202)986-1038 E-mail: rsoko@narc.org • URL: http://www.narc.org • Annual. $100.00. Lists about 526 regional councils within U.S., including contacts and counties they serve. Formerly *National Association of Regional Councils-Directory of Regional Councils*.

Directory of Registered Investment Advisors. Money Market Directories, Inc., 320 E. Main St. Charlottesville, VA 22902. Phone: 800-446-2810 or (434)997-1450 Fax: (434)979-9962 • URL: http://www.mmdaccess.com • Annual. $510.00. Lists over 12,000 investment advisors and advisory firms. Indicates services offered, personnel, and amount of assets being managed. Formerly *Directory of Registered Investment Advisors with the Securities and Exchange Commission*.

Directory of Research Grants. Greenwood Publishing Group, Inc., 88 Post Rd., W Westport, CT 06881. Phone: 800-225-5800 or (203)226-3571 Fax: (203)431-2214 E-mail: customer-service@greenwood.com • URL: http://www.greenwood.com • Annual. $135.00. More than 5,100 research grants available from government, business, foundation and private sources.

Directory of Retail Chains in Canada. Rogers Media Publishing, 1 Mount Pleasant Rd. Toronto, ON, Canada M4Y 2Y5. Phone: (416)764-1300 Fax: (416)764-7730 • URL: http://www.rogers.com • Annual. $340.00. Provides detailed information on approximately 1,600 retail chains of all sizes in Canada.

Directory of Retirement Facilities. Solucient, 300 E. Lombard St., Suite 1600 Baltimore, MD 21202. Phone: 800-568-3282 or (410)576-9600 Fax: (410)576-9429 E-mail: pubs@solucient.

com • URL: http://www.solucient.com • Biennial. $125.00. Provides information on more than 14,000 "senior citizen residential alternative facilities," including both assisted living settings and independent living communities.

Directory of Single Unit Supermarket Operators. Chain Store Guide, 33619 Coconut Palm Dr. Tampa, FL 33619-8321. Phone: 800-778-9794 or (813)627-6800 Fax: (813)627-6882 E-mail: info@csgis.com • URL: http://www.csgis.com • Annual. $327.00. Online edition, $747.00. Covers more than 7,900 one-store supermarket establishments with annual sales of at least $1,000,000. Includes names of primary wholesalers.

Directory of Special Libraries and Information Centers. Gale Cengage Learning, 27500 Drake Rd. Farmington Hills, MI 48331-3535. Phone: 800-877-GALE or (248)699-4253 Fax: 800-414-5043 E-mail: gale.galeord@cengage.com • URL: http://gale.cengage.com • 2003. $975.00. 28th edition. Three volumes. Two available separately: volume one,*Directory of Special Libraries and Information Centers*, $740.00; volume two *Geographic and Personnel Indexes*, $560.00. Contains 34,000 entries from the U.S., Canada, and 80 other countries. A detailed subject index is included in volume one.

Directory of Sporting Goods and Activewear Buyers Directory. Douglas Publications, Inc., 2807 N. Parham Rd. Richmond, VA 23294. Phone: 800-223-1797 or (804)762-9600 Fax: (804)217-8999 E-mail: info@douglaspublications.com • URL: http://www.douglaspublications.com • Annual. $329.00. About 10,700 retail stores selling athletic and recreational equipment, footwear, apparel. *Salesman's Guide Directories*.

Directory of SRCC Certified Collectors and Solar Water Heating Systems Ratings. Solar Rating and Certification Corp., c/o FSEC, 1697 Clearlake Rd. Cocoa, FL 32927-5703. Phone: (321)638-1537 Fax: (321)638-1010 E-mail: srcc@fsec.ucf.edu • URL: http://www.solar-rating.org • Irregular. Free. About 20 manufacturers of solar collectors and systems certified by the Organization. Includes technical information.

Directory of Standards Laboratories. NCSL International, 1800 30th St., Ste. 305B Boulder, CO 80301-1026. Phone: (303)440-3339 Fax: (303)440-3384 E-mail: info@ncslinternational.org • URL: http://www.ncsl.org • Biennial. Available only online. Lists about 1,500 measurement standards laboratories.

Directory of State and Local Mortgage Bankers Association. Mortgage Bankers Association of America, 1919 Pennsylvania Ave., N.W. Washington, DC 20006-3438. Phone: 800-793-6222 or (202)557-2700 E-mail: communications@mbaa.org • URL: http://www.mbaa.org • Irregular. $50.00.

Directory of State Legislatures. National Conference of State Legislatures, 7700 E 1st Pl. Denver, CO 80202-1743. Phone: (303)364-7700 Fax: (303)364-7800 E-mail: info@ncsl.org • URL: http://www.ncsl.org • Annual. $85.00. Provides names, addresses, telephone numbers, and e-mail addresses of state legislators and executive officials. Available only online. Formerly *Election Results Directory*.

Directory of Statisticians. American Statistical Association, 1429 Duke St. Alexandria, VA 22314-3415. Phone: 888-231-3473 or (703)684-1211 Fax: (703)684-2037 E-mail: asainfo@amstat.org • URL: http://www.amstat.org • Triennial. Free to members; non-members, $125.00. List more than 25,000 members.

Directory of Steel Foundries and Buyers Guide. Steel Founders' Society of America, 780 McArdle Dr., Unit G Crystal Lake, IL 60014. Phone: (815)455-8240 Fax: (815)455-8241 E-mail: monroe@sfsa.org • URL: http://www.sfsa.org • Biennial. $400.00. Available only online. Lists approximately 435 steel foundries in the United States, Canada and Mexico. Formerly *Directory of Steel Foundries in the United States, Canada, and Mexico*.

Directory of Supermarket, Grocery, and Convenience Store Chains. Chain Store Guide, 3922 Coconut Palm Dr. Tampa, FL 33619-8321. Phone: 800-778-9794 or (813)627-6800 Fax: (813)627-6882 E-mail: info@csgis.com • URL: http://www.csgis.com • Annual. $327.00. Online edition, $747.00. Provides information on about 3,300 food store chains operating 120,000 individual stores. Store locations are given.

Directory of the Refractories Industry. The Refractories Institute, 650 Smithfield St., Suite 1160 Pittsburgh, PA 15222-3907. Phone: (412)281-6787 Fax: (412)281-6881 E-mail: triassn@aol.com • URL: http://www.refractoriesinstitute.org • Quadrennial. Members, $30.00; non-members, $45.00. Lists approximately 120 manufactures and suppliers of heat-resistant materials and equipment called refractories, refractory installation companies, furnace design and engineering firms, furnance builders, refractory contractors and services.

Directory of Trade and Professional Associations in the European Union - The Blue Book. Euroconfidentiel S. A., Rue de Rixensart 18 1332 Genval, Belgium. Phone: 32 2 6520284 Fax: 32 2 6530180 E-mail: info@cpinz.com • URL: http://www.cpinz.com • Annual. $160.00. Includes more than 9,000 EU-related associations.

Directory of Trust Banking. Thomson Financial Publishing, 4709 West Golf Rd. Skokie, IL 60076-1253. Phone: 800-321-3373 or (847)676-9600 Fax: (847)933-8101 E-mail: support@bankinfo.com • URL: http://www.tfp.com • Annual. $344.00. Contains profiles of bank affiliated trust companies, independent trust companies, trust investment advisors, and trust fund managers. Provides contact information for professional personnel at more than 3,000 banking and other financial institutions.

Directory of United Nations Databases and Information Systems. United Nations Publications, Available from Bernan Associates, 4611-F Assembly Dr. Lanham, MD 20706-4391. Phone: 800-274-4447 or (301)459-2255 Fax: (301)459-0056 Annual. $35.00. Nearly 38 United Nations organizations maintaining over 615 databases and information systems.

Directory of United States Exporters. Piers Publishing Group, 400 Windsor Corporate Park, 50 Millstone Rd., Suite 200 East Windsor, NJ 08520-1415. Phone: 877-203-5277 or (609)371-7700 Fax: (609)371-7883 E-mail: customerservice@cbizmedia.com • URL: http://www.pierspub.com • Annual. $2,750. Provides information on about 22,000 exporters located in the U. S.

Directory of United States Importers. Piers Publishing Group, 400 Windsor Corporate Park, 50 Millstone Rd., Suite 200 East Windsor, NJ 08520-1415. Phone: 877-203-5277 or (609)371-7700 Fax: (609)371-7883 E-mail: customerservice@cbizmedia.com • URL: http://www.pierspub.com • Annual. $2,750.00. Provides information on about 32,000 importers located in the U. S.

Directory of United States Importers/Directory of United States Exporters. Piers Publishing Group, 33 Washington St., 13th Fl. Newark, NJ 08865. Phone: 877-203-5277 or (973)848-1341 Fax: (973)848-7133 E-mail: customersvs@joc.com • URL: http://www.joc.com • Annual. $675.00. Two volumes. $475.00 per volume. Approximately 55,000 firms with import and export interests; export and import managers, agents, and merchants in the United States; World ports; consulates and embassies. Formerly *United States Importers and Exporters Directories*.

Directory of U.S. Military Bases Worldwide. William R. Evinger, editor. Greenwood Publishing Group, Inc., 88 Post Rd., W. Westport, CT 06881. Phone: 800-225-5800 or (203)226-3571 Fax: (203)431-2214 E-mail: customer-service@geenwood.com • URL: http://www.greenwood.com • 1998. $125.00. Third edition.

Directory of Venture Capital and Private Equity Firms. Grey House Publishing, 185 Millerton Rd. Millerton, NY 12546. Phone: 800-562-2139 or (518)789-8700 Fax: (518)789-0556 E-mail: books@greyhouse.com • URL: http://www.greyhouse.com • 2003. $450.00. Eighth edition. Provides detailed information on more than 3,000 U. S. and foreign sources of venture capital.

Directory of Wholesale Grocers. Chain Store Guide, 3922 Coconut Palm Dr. Tampa, FL 33619-8321. Phone: 800-778-9794 or (813)627-6800 Fax: (813)627-6882 E-mail: info@csgis.com • URL: http://www.csgis.com • Annual. $327.00. Online edition, $747.00. Profiles over 1,100 cooperatives, voluntaries, non-sponsoring wholesalers, cash and carry warehouses, and nearly 220 service merchandisers. Covers United States and Canada.

Directory of Wire Companies of North America. CRU International, 7474 Greenway Center Dr., Suite 820 Greenbelt, MD 20770. Phone: (301)441-8997 Fax: (301)441-9091 E-mail: info@wireindustrynews.com Annual. $179.00. Profiles approximately 1,050 companies in the wire industry in North America. Also profiles fiber optic companies having to do with fiber optic cables and a supplier section profiling supplier companies.

Dirty Business: Exploring Corporate Misconduct: Analysis and Cases. Maurice Punch. Sage Publications, Inc., 2455 Teller Rd. Thousand Oaks, CA 91320. Phone: 800-818-7243 or (805)499-9774 Fax: 800-583-2665 or (805)499-0871 E-mail: webmaster@sagepub.com • URL: http://www.sagepub.com • 1996. $113.00. Covers organizational misbehavior and white-collar crime. Includes "Ten Cases of Corporate Deviance."

Disability and Rehabilitation Products Markets. Theta Reports/PJB Medical Publications, Inc., 1775 Broadway, Suite 511 New York, NY 10019. Phone: (212)262-8230 Fax: (212)262-8234 E-mail: lschacterle@thetareports.com • URL: http://www.thetareports.com • 1999. $1,295.00. Market research data. Covers the market for products designed to help differently-abled people lead more active lives. Includes such items as adaptive computers, augmentative communication devices, lifts/vans, and bath/home products. Profiles of leading suppliers are included. (Theta Report No. 800.)

Disability Rights Center., PO Box 2007 Augusta, ME 04338-2007. Phone: 800-452-1948 or (207)626-2774 Fax: (207)621-1419 E-mail: advocate@drcme.org • URL: http://www.drcme.org • Represents public interest research group committed on educating society about the disability rights movement. Aims to inform the public, political activists, consumer activists, advocates, and students on the disability movement. Seeks to involve as many disabled citizens as possible in processes that directly affect their lives, to work closely with other disability-related, consumer-based advocacy groups, and to educate the public in the legitimate demands and needs of the disabled. Compiles statistics.

Disclosure SEC Database. Thomson Financial, 22 Thomson Pike Boston, MA 02210. Phone: (617)856-2000 Fax: (617)330-1986 • URL: http://www.tfn.com • Provides online information from records filed with the Securities and Exchange Commission by more than 12,000 publicly-owned companies in the U.S. Includes about 200 financial data items and information relating to executives. Time span is 1977 to date, with weekly updates. Inquire as to online cost and availability.

Discount Store News - Top Chains. Lebhar-Friedman, Inc., 425 Park Ave. New York, NY 10022. Phone: 800-766-6999 or (212)756-5000 E-mail: info@lf.com • URL: http://www.lf.com • Annual. $79.00.

Disposable Medical Supplies. Available from MarketResearch.com, 641 Ave. of the Americas, Third Floor New York, NY 10011. Phone: 800-298-5699 or (212)807-2629 Fax: (212)807-2716 E-mail: order@marketresearch.com • URL: http://www.marketresearch.com • 2001. $3,500.00. Published by the Freedonia Group. Market data with forecasts to 2007. Includes disposable syringes, catheters, kits, trays, etc.

Disposable Paper Products. Available from MarketResearch.com, 641 Ave. of the Americas, Third Floor New York, NY 10011. Phone: 800-298-5699 or (212)807-2629 Fax: (212)807-2716 E-mail: order@marketresearch.com • URL: http://www.marketresearch.com • 2001. $5,900.00. Published by Euromonitor Publications Ltd. Provides consumer market data and forecasts to 2004 for the United States, the United Kingdom, Germany, France, and Italy.

Dispute Resolution Journal. American Arbitration Association, 355 Madison Ave. New York, NY 10017-4605. Phone: 800-778-7879 or (212)716-5800 Fax: (212)716-5905 E-mail: websitemail@adr.org • URL: http://www.adr.org • Quarterly. $125.00 per year. Formerly *Arbitration Journal*.

Dissertation Abstracts International. UMI, 300 N. Zeeb Rd. Ann Arbor, MI 48106. Phone: 800-521-0600 or (734)761-4700 Fax: 800-864-0019 E-mail: info@il.proquest.com • URL: http://www.umi.com • Monthly. Price on application. Section A: Humanities and Social Sciences. Author-written summaries of current doctoral dissertations from over 500 educational institutions.

Dissertation Abstracts Online. PROQUEST, 300 N. Zeeb Rd. Ann Arbor, MI 48106. Phone: 800-521-0600 or (734)761-4700 Fax: 800-864-0019 Citations to all dissertations accepted for doctoral degrees by accredited U.S. educational institutions, 1861 to date. Includes British theses, 1988 to date. Inquire as to online cost and availability.

Distance Education and Training Council., 1601 18th St., N.W. Washington, DC 20009. Phone: (202)234-5100 Fax: (202)332-1386 E-mail: detc@detc.org • URL: http://www.detc.org • Formerly National Home Study Council.

Distilled Spirits Council of the United States.

Distributed Computing Monitor. Patricia Seybold Group, 85 Devonshire St., 5th Fl. Boston, MA 02109-3504. Phone: 800-826-2424 or (617)742-5200 Fax: (617)742-1028 E-mail: info@nacdonline.org • URL: http://www.psgroup.com • Description: Covers trends and applications within distributed network computing.

Distribution and LTL Carriers Association., 2200 Mill Rd. Alexandria, VA 22314. Phone: (703)838-1806 Fax: (703)684-8143 E-mail: dltlca@aol.com • URL: http://www.dltlca.org • Formerly Regular Common Carrier Conference.

Distribution Center Management. Alexander Research & Communications Inc., 28 W 25th St., 8th Fl. New York, NY 10010. Phone: 800-232-4317 or (212)228-0246 Fax: (212)228-0376 E-mail: info@distributionGroup.com • URL: http://www.alexcommgrp.com • Description: The monthly newsletter for distribution centers and warehouse managers with ideas and information on how to run their facilities more productively.

Distribution Channels: The Magazine for Candy, Tobacco, Grocery and General Merchandise Distributors. American Wholesalers Marketers Association, 1128 16th St. N.W. Washington, DC 20036. Phone: (202)463-2124 Fax: (202)467-0559 10 times a year. $36.00 per year. Formerly *Candy Wholesaler*.

Diversity Information Resources., 2105 Central Ave. NE Minneapolis, MN 55418. Phone: (612)781-6819 Fax: (612)781-0109 E-mail: info@diversityinforesources.com • URL: http://www.diversityinforesources.com • Promotes businesses with minority, women, veteran, service-disabled veteran and HUBZone ownership. Compiles and publishes minority and women-owned business directories to acquaint major corporations and government purchasing agents with the products and services of minority and women-owned firms. Sponsors national supplier diversity seminars.

Dividend Policy: Theory and Practice. George W. Frankfurter and Bob G. Wood. Elsevier Butterworth Heinemann, 200 Wheeler Rd., Sixth Floor Burlington, MA 01803. Phone: 800-545-2522 or (781)221-2212 Fax: 800-568-5136 or (781)313-4880 E-mail: usbkinfo@elsevier.com • URL: http://www.books.elsevier.com/finance • 2003. $59.95. Covers the history of dividends, preferred stock dividends, dividend reinvestment plans, extensive academic research, and "New Ways of Thinking About Dividends and Dividend Policy."

Division of Business and Economic Research. University of New Orleans

Division of Educational Research and Service. Louisiana Tech University

Division of Engineering Research. Michigan State University

Division of Government Research. University of New Mexico

Division of Health Services Research and Policy., University of Minnesota, Mayo Memorial Bldg. Minneapolis, MN 55455. Phone: (612)624-6151 Fax: (612)624-2196 E-mail: foote003@tc.umn.edu • URL: http://www.hsr.umn.edu • Fields of research include health insurance, consumer choice of health plans, quality of care, and long-term care.

Division of Hypertension. Cornell University

Division Officer's Guide. James Stavridis. Naval Institute Press, Beach Hall, 291 Wood Rd. Annapolis, MD 21402-5034. Phone: 800-223-8764 or (410)268-6110 Fax: (410)269-7940 E-mail: customer@navalinstitute.org • URL: http://www.navalinstitute.org • 1995. $21.95. 10th revised edition.

Divorce and Taxes. CCH, Inc., 2700 Lake Cook Rd. Riverwoods, IL 60015. Phone: 800-835-5224 or (847)267-7000 E-mail: cust_serv@cch.com • URL: http://www.cch.com • 2000. $25.00. Second edition. In addition to tax problems, topics include alimony, division of property, and divorce decrees.

Divorce Decisions Workbook: A Planning and Action Guide. Marjorie L. Engel. McGraw-Hill, 1221 Ave. of the Americas New York, NY 10020. Phone: 800-722-4726 or (212)512-2000 Fax: (212)512-4502 E-mail: customer.service@mcgraw-hill.com • URL: http://www.mcgraw-hill.com • 1992. $27.95. Covers the business, financial, legal, and tax aspects of divorce.

Divorce, Separation, and the Distribution of Property. American Lawyer Media, Inc., 105 Madison Ave. New York, NY 10016. Phone: 800-888-8300 or (212)779-9200 Fax: (212)481-8110 E-mail: lawcatalog@amlaw.com • URL: http://www.lawcatalog.com/ • Looseleaf. $169.00. Updated as needed. Covers such thorny divorce settlement issues as earning power, stock options, pensions, repayment of student loans, tort claims, closely held businesses, premarital agreement enforcement, and alimony awards. (Law Journal Press).

Divorce Yourself: The National No-Fault Divorce Kit. Daniel Sitarz. Nova Publishing Co., 705 W Main St. Carbondale, IL 62901. Phone: 800-748-1175 or (618)457-3521 Fax: 800-338-4550 E-mail: info@novapublishing.com • URL: http://www.novapublishing.com • 2002. $34.95. Fifth edition. Provides instructions, checklists, questionnaires, worksheets, and forms for use in uncomplicated divorce proceedings. Forms are also available on IBM or MAC diskettes.

DM News: The Newspaper of Direct Marketing. Courtenay Communications Corp., 100 Ave. of the Americas, 6th Fl. New York, NY 10013-1689. Phone: (212)925-7300 Fax: (212)925-8797 E-mail: dmnews@halldata.com • URL: http://www.dmnews.com • 48 times a year. $49.00 per year. Includes special feature issues on catalog marketing, telephone marketing, database marketing, and fundraising. Includes monthly supplements, *DM News International*, *DRTV News*, and *TeleServices*.

DM Review: The Premier Publication for Business Intelligence and Analytics. Thomson Media, One State St. Plaza New York, NY 10004. Phone: 800-221-1809 or (212)803-8200 Fax: (212)843-9635 E-mail: custserv@thomsonmedia.com • URL: http://www.thomsonmedia.com • Monthly. $49.00 per year. Edited for corporate executives and information technology personnel. Covers data management, business intelligence, data warehousing, systems management, data integration, knowledge management, data mining, and related topics.

DMA Direct and Interactive Marketing Buying Practices Study. Direct Marketing Association, Inc., 1120 Ave. of the Americas New York, NY 10036-6700. Phone: (212)768-7277 Fax: (212)398-6725 E-mail: lrc@the-dma.org • URL: http://www.the-dma.org • 2000. $1,295.00. Provides marketing research data relating to consumer purchasing from catalogs. "Incidence and profile of Internet buying" is also included. (Research conducted by Elrick & Lavidge.)

DMA Nonprofit Federation., 1615 L St. NW, Ste. 1100 Washington, DC 20036. Phone: (202)628-4380 Fax: (202)628-4383 E-mail: nonprofitfederation@the-dma.org • URL: http://www.the-dma.org/nonprofitfederation • Trade and lobbying group for non-profit organizations that use direct and online marketing to raise funds and communicate with members. Sponsors professional development conferences and seminars, lobbies on state and federal legislation, regulation, and standards related to direct marketing and related issues. Provides information about and participants in litigation affecting non-profits. Promotes the overall welfare of non-profits. Represents health care charities, social service agencies, religious groups, colleges and universities and fraternal organizations.

DMA State of the Catalog Industry Report. Direct Marketing Association, Inc., 1120 Ave. of the Americas New York, NY 10036-6700. Phone: (212)768-7277 Fax: (212)398-6725 E-mail: lrc@the-dma.org • URL: http://www.the-dma.org • Annual. $495.00. Provides merchandising, operating, and financial statistics on consumer and business-to-business marketing through both print and electronic (interactive) catalogs. (Produced in association with W. A. Dean & Associates.)

DMA Statistical Fact Book. Direct Marketing Association. Library and Resource Center, 1120 Ave. of the Americas New York, NY 10036-6700. Phone: (212)768-7277 Fax: (212)398-6725 E-mail: lrc@the-dma.org • URL: http://www.the-dma.org • Annual. Members, $79.95; non-members, $104.95. Provides data in five sections covering direct response advertising, media, mailing lists, market applications, and "Practical Management Information." Includes material on interactive/online marketing. (Cover title: *Direct Marketing Association's Statistical Fact Book*.)

DMA Washington Report: Federal and State Regulatory Issues of Concern. Direct Marketing Association, 1120 Ave. of the Americas New York, NY 10036-6700. Phone: (212)768-7277 Fax: (212)768-6725 E-mail: lrc@the-dma.org • URL: http://

www.the-dma.org • Monthly. Membership.

DNR: The Men's Fashion Retail Textile Authority. Fairchild Publications, Seven W. 34th St. New York, NY 10001. Phone: 800-360-1700 or (212)630-4000 E-mail: customerservice@fairchildpub.com • URL: http://www.fairchildpub.com • Daily. $85.00 per year. Formerly *Daily News Record*.

Do-It-Yourself Advertising and Promotion: How to Produce Great Ads, Brochures, Catalogs, Direct Mail, Web Sites and more. Fred E. Hahn. John Wiley and Sons, Inc., 111 River St. Hoboken, NJ 07030. Phone: 800-225-5945 or (201)748-6000 Fax: (201)748-6088 E-mail: info@wiley.com • URL: http://www.wiley.com • 2003. $19.95. Third edition. Covers magazines, newspapers, flyers, brochures, catalogs, direct mail, telemarketing, trade shows, and radio/TV promotions. Includes checklists. (Small Business Series).

Do-It-Yourself Direct Marketing: Secrets for Small Business. Mark S. Bacon. John Wiley and Sons, Inc., 111 River St. Hoboken, NJ 07030. Phone: 800-225-5945 or (201)748-6000 Fax: (201)748-6088 E-mail: info@wiley.com • URL: http://www.wiley.com • 1997. $19.95. Second edition.

Do-it-Yourself Marketing Research. George Breen and Albert B. Blankenship. Replica Books, 1200 US Hwy., 22 E Bridgewater, NJ 08807. Phone: 800-775-1800 or (908)541-7392 Fax: (908)541-7875 E-mail: btinfo@baker-taylor.com • URL: http://www.replicabooks.com • 1998. $44.95. Third edition.

Do-it-Yourself Retailing: Serving Hardware, Home Center and Building Material Retailers. National Retail Hardware Association, 5822 W. 74th St. Indianapolis, IN 46278-1787. Phone: 800-772-4424 or (317)290-0338 Fax: (317)328-4354 E-mail: contact@nrha.org • URL: http://www.nrha.org • Monthly. $50.00 per year. Formerly *DIY Retailing*.

Doane's Agricultural Report. Doane Agricultural Services, 77 Westport Plz., Ste. 250 Saint Louis, MO 63146-4193. Phone: (866)647-0918 or (314)569-2700 Fax: (314)569-1083 E-mail: doane@doane.com • URL: http://www.edoane.com • Description: Covers the marketing of commodities (such as cattle, hogs, corn, wheat, and soybeans), as well as providing agricultural, economic, management, and production information. Discusses such topics as profit management, prices, outlook, machinery, buildings, equipment, taxes, social security, law, and government.

Dr. Dobb's Journal: Software Tools for the Professional Programmer. CMP Media LLC, 600 Community Dr. Manhasset, NY 11030. Phone: (516)562-5000 E-mail: cmp@cmp.com • URL: http://www.cmp.com • Monthly. $34.95 per year. A technical publication covering software development, languages, operating systems, and applications.

Document Imaging Report. Access Intelligence L.L.C., 4 Choke Cherry Rd., 2nd Fl. Rockville, MD 20850. Phone: 800-777-5006 or (301)354-2000 Fax: (301)309-3847 E-mail: info@accessintel.com • URL: http://www.corrypub.com • Description: Aims to keep readers current with all developments in the optical media field. Reports on new products, applications, and licensing programs. Also provides coverage of the Association for Information and Image Management (AIIM), Optical Storage, and Rothchild conferences.

Document Management Industries Association., 433 E Monroe Ave. Alexandria, VA 22301-1645. Phone: 800-336-4641 or (703)836-6232 Fax: (703)836-2241 E-mail: dmia@dmia.org • URL: http://www.dmia.org • Independent distributors, manufacturers, and suppliers to the forms, business printing and document management industries. Sponsors educational and channel marketing programs. Compiles statistics.

Document Processing Technology. RB Publishing Co., 2424 American Lane Madison, WI 53704-3102. Phone: (608)241-8777 Fax: (608)241-8666 • URL: http://www.rbpub.com • Seven times a year. Controlled circulation. Edited for "high volume document printing" professionals. Covers imaging, printing, and mailing.

Documents of Title Under the Uniform Commercial Code. American Law Institute-American Bar Association Committee on Continuing Professional Education, 4025 Chestnut St. Philadelphia, PA 19104. Phone: 800-253-6397 Fax: (215)243-1664 • URL: http://www.ali-aba.org • 1990. $90.00. Second edition.

Dodge Construction News. McGraw-Hill, 1221 Ave of the Americas New York, NY 10020. Phone: 800-722-4726 or (212)512-2000 Fax: (212)512-4502 • URL: http://www.dodge.construction.com • Daily. Los Angeles, $1,392.00 per year; Chicago, $1,245.00 per year.

Dodge Reports. F. W. Dodge Group, McGraw-Hill, 1221 Ave. of the Americas New York, NY 10020. Phone: 800-393-6343 or (212)924-2063 • URL: http://www.dodge.construction.com • Daily. Price on application. Individual reports on new construction jobs.

Dodge/SCAN. F. W. Dodge Group, McGraw-Hill, 1221 Ave. of the Americas New York, NY 10020. Phone: 800-393-6343 or (212)924-2063 Fax: (212)393-6343 • URL: http://ww.dodge.construction.com • Price on application. Provides plans and specifications of new construction jobs.

DOE This Month. Available from U. S. Government Printing Office, Washington, DC 20402. Phone: (202)512-1800 Fax: (202)512-2250 E-mail: gpoaccess@gpo.gov • URL: http://www.access.gpo.gov • Monthly. $42.00 per year. Describes the U.S. Department of Energy's research and development activities and DOE publications. Includes information on nuclear energy, renewable energy sources, and synthetic fuels.

Does Financial Deregulation Work? A Critique of Free Market Approaches. Bruce Coggins. Edward Elgar Publishing, Inc., 136 West St., Suite 202 Northampton, MA 01060. Phone: 800-390-3149 or (413)584-5551 Fax: (413)584-9933 E-mail: elgarinfo@e-elgar.com • URL: http://www.e-elgar.co.uk • 1998. $95.00. Provides a critique of bank deregulation in the United States. Includes suggestions for more effective financial regulation. (New Directions in Modern Economics Series).

Does Privatization Deliver?: Highlights from a World Bank Conference. Mary M. Shirley and Ahmed Galal. The World Bank Group, 1818 H St., N. W. Washington, DC 20433. Phone: (202)477-1234 Fax: 800-645-7247 or (202)477-6391 E-mail: books@worldbank.org • URL: http://www.worldbank.org • 1994. $22.00. Includes 12 international case studies on airlines, telecommunications, electric utilities, and other industries. Presents a favorable view of privatization. (EDI Development Studies Series).

Doing Business in China: The Last Great Market. Geoffrey Murray. Saint Martin's Press, 175 Fifth Ave. New York, NY 10010. Phone: 888-330-8477 or (212)726-0200 Fax: 800-672-2054 or (212)674-5151 E-mail: enquiries@stmartins.com • URL: http://www.stmartins.com • 1994. $80.00.

Doing Business in the United States: Legal Opportunities and Pitfalls. Lawrence B. Landman. John Wiley and Sons, Inc., 111 River St. Hoboken, NJ 07030. Phone: 800-225-5945 or (201)748-6000 Fax: (201)748-6088 E-mail: info@wiley.com • URL: http://www.wiley.com • 1997. $55.00. (Essential Facts Series).

Doing Business Internationally: The Guide to Cross Cultural Success. Danielle Walker and Thomas Walker. McGraw-Hill, 1221 Ave. of the Americas New York, NY 10020. Phone: 800-722-4726 or (212)512-2000 Fax: (212)512-4502 E-mail: customer.service@mcgraw-hill.com • URL: http://www.mcgraw-hill.com • 2002. $29.95. Second edition.

Doing Exemplary Research. Ralph E. Stablein. Sage Publications, Inc., 2455 Teller Rd. Thousand Oaks, CA 91320-2218. Phone: 800-818-7243 or (805)499-0721 Fax: (805)499-0871 E-mail: info@sagepub.com • URL: http://www.sagepub.com • 1992. $43.95. Contains discussions of research methodologies.

Dollars and Cents of Shopping Centers. Urban Land Institute, 1025 Thomas Jefferson St., N.W., Suite 500 W. Washington, DC 20007-5201. Phone: 800-321-5011 or (202)624-7000 Fax: (202)624-7140 E-mail: bookstore@uli.org • URL: http://www.uli.org • Triennial. Members, $219.95; nonmembers, $239.95. Supplemental *Special Report* available.

Domestic Mail Manual. Available from U. S. Government Printing Office, Washington, DC 20402. Phone: (202)512-1800 Fax: (202)512-2250 E-mail: gpoaccess@gpo.gov • URL: http://www.access.gpo.gov • Looseleaf. $42.00 per year. Issued by U. S. Postal Service. Contains rates, regulations, classes of mail, special services, etc., for mail within the U. S.

DIrectory of U. S. Labor Organizations. BNA, Inc. ., 1231 25th St., NW Washington, DC 20037. Phone: 800-372-1033 E-mail: customercare@bna.com • URL: http://www.bna.com • Annual. $105.00. More than 150 national unions and professional and state employees associations engaged in labor representation.

Don't Die Broke: How to Turn Your Retirement Savings into Lasting Income. Margaret A. Malaspina. Bloomberg, 499 Park Ave. New York, NY 10022. Phone: 800-388-2749 or (212)318-2000 Fax: (917)369-5000 • URL: http://www.bloomberg.com • 1999. $21.95. Provides advice on such matters as retirement portfolio asset allocation and retirement spending accounts. (Bloomberg Personal Bookshelf Series).

Donut Shop. Entrepreneur Media, Inc., 2445 McCabe Way Irvine, CA 92614. Phone: 800-421-2300 or (949)261-2325 Fax: (949)261-0234 E-mail: entmag@entrepreneur.com • URL: http://www.entrepreneur.com • Looseleaf. $59.50. A practical guide to starting a doughnut shop. Covers profit potential, start-up costs, market size evaluation, owner's time required, site selection, lease negotiation, pricing, accounting, advertising, promotion, etc. (Start-Up Business Guide No. E1126.)

Door and Access Systems Manufacturers Association International., 1300 Sumner Ave. Cleveland, OH 44115-2851. Phone: (216)241-7333 Fax: (216)241-0105 E-mail: dasma@dasma.com • URL: http://www.dasma.com • Members are manufacturers of "upward-acting" garage doors and related products, both residential and commercial.

Door and Hardware Institute.

Door and Operator Industry. International Door Association, 28 Lowry Dr. West Milton, OH 45383. Phone: 800-355-4432 Fax: (937)698-6153 • URL: http://www.doors.org • Bimonthly. Free. Edited for garage door and opener dealers.

Door and Window Retailing. Jervis and Associates, 11300 US Highway 1,Suite 400 North Palm Beach, FL 33408. Phone: (908)850-8100 Fax: (908)850-6464 Bimonthly. $15.00 per year. Edited for door and window retailers. Formerly *Door and Window Business*.

Door Hardware. Available from MarketResearch.com, 641 Ave. of the Americas, Third Floor New York, NY 10011. Phone: 800-298-5699 or (212)807-2629 Fax: (212)807-2716 E-mail: order@marketresearch.com • URL: http://www.marketresearch.com • 1997. $495.00. Market research report published by Specialists in Business Information. Covers locks, closers, doorknobs, security devices, and other door hardware. Presents market data relative to demographics, sales growth, shipments, exports, imports, price trends, and end-use. Includes company profiles.

Doors. Available from MarketResearch.com, 641 Ave. of the Americas, Third Floor New York, NY 10011. Phone: 800-298-5699 or (212)807-2629 Fax: (212)807-2716 E-mail: order@marketreseach.com • URL: http://www.marketreseach.com • 1999. $2,250.00. Market research report published by Specialists in Business Information. Covers residential doors, including garage doors. Presents market data relative to demographics, sales growth, shipments, exports, imports, price trends, and end-use. Includes company profiles.

Doors and Hardware. Door and Hardware Institute, 14150 Newbrook Dr., Suite 200 Chantilly, VA 20151. Phone: (703)222-2010 Fax: (703)222-2410 E-mail: publications@dhi.org • URL: http://www.dhi.org • Monthly. $49.00 per year.

Dorland's Directory of Health Plans. Dorland Healthcare Information, 1500 Walnut St., Suite 1000 Philadelphia, PA 19102. Phone: 800-784-2332 or (215)875-1212 Fax: (215)735-3966 E-mail: chi@healthcare-info.com • URL: http://www.healthplanresearch.com • Annual. $195.00. Published in association with the American Association of Health Plans (http://www.aahp.org). Lists more than 2,400 health plans, including Health Maintenance Organizations (HMOs), Preferred Provider Organizations (PPOs), and Point of Service plans (POS). Includes the names of about 9,000 health plan executives.

Dow 40,000 Portfolio: The Stock to Own to Out Perform Today's Leading Benchmark. David Elias. McGraw Hill, 1221 Ave. of the Americas New York, NY 10020. Phone: 800-722-4726 or (212)512-2000 Fax: (212)512-4502 E-mail: customer.service@mcgraw-hill.com • URL: http://www.mcgraw-hill.com • 2000. $24.95.

Dow 40,000: Strategies for Profiting from the Greatest Bull Market in History. David Elias. Soaring Eagle Communications, 500 Essjay Rd., Ste. 220 Williamsville, NY 14221. Phone: 800-722-4726 or (716)633-3800 Fax: (716)633-3810 E-mail: elias@eliasasset.com • URL: http://www.eliasasset.com • 1999. $15.95. Predicts continuing strong growth in the U. S. economy, low interest rates, and low inflation, resulting in a level of 40,000 for the Dow Jones Industrial Average in the year 2016.

Dow Jones Averages Chart Album. Dow Theory Letters, Inc., P.O. Box 1759 La Jolla, CA 92038-1759. Phone: (858)454-0481 E-mail: staff@dowtheoryletters.com • URL: http://www.dowtheoryletters.com • Annual. $140.00. Contains one page for each year since 1885. Includes line charts of the Dow Jones industrial, transportation, utilities, and bond averages. Important historical and economic dates are shown.

Dow Jones News Service. Dow Jones and Co., Inc., Post Office Box 300 Princeton, NJ 08543-0300. Phone: 800-832-1234 or (609)520-4000 Fax: (609)520-4660 Full text and edited news stories and articles on business affairs. Inquire as to online cost and availability.

Dow 100,000: Fact or Fiction. Charles W. Kadlec. Prentice Hall PTR, 240 Frisch Ct. Paramus, NJ 07652. Phone: 800-282-0693 Fax: 800-445-6991 • URL: http://www.phptr.com • 1999. $25.00. Predicts a level of 100,000 for the Dow Jones Industrial Average in the year 2020, based mainly on a technological revolution.

Dow Theory Forecasts: Business and Stock Market. Dow Theory Forecasts, Inc., 7412 Calumet Ave. Hammond, IN 46324-2692. Phone: (219)931-6480 Fax: (219)931-6487 Weekly. $233.00 per year. Provides information and advice on blue chip and income stocks.

Dow Theory Letters. Dow Theory Letters, Inc., P.O. Box 1759 La Jolla, CA 92038-1759. Phone: (619)454-0481 E-mail: dowtheory@hotmail.com • URL: http://www.dowtheoryletter.com • 17 times a year. $250.00 per year. Newsletter on stock market trends, investing, and economic conditions.

Down Beat: Jazz, Blues and Beyond. Maher Publications, Inc., 102 N. Haven Rd. Elmhurst, IL 60126. Phone: 800-554-7470 or (630)941-2030 Fax: (630)941-3210 E-mail: service@downbeat.com • URL: http://www.downbeat.com • Monthly. $34.95 per year. Contemporary music.

Downtown Idea Exchange: Essential Information for Downtown Research and Development Center. Downtown Research and Development Center. Alexander Communications Group, Inc., 28 W 25th St., 8th Fl. New York, NY 10010. Phone: (212)228-0246 Fax: (212)228-1343 E-mail: info@alexcommgrp.com • URL: http://www.alexcommgrp.com • Semimonthly. $187.00 per year. Newsletter for those concerned with central business districts. Provides news and other information on planning, development, parking, mass transit, traffic, funding, and other topics.

Downtown Promotion Reporter. Downtown Research and Development Center. Alexander Communications Group Inc., 28 W 25th St., 8th Fl. New York, NY 10010. Phone: 800-232-4317 or (212)228-0246 Fax: (212)228-0376 E-mail: info@alexcommgrp.com • URL: http://www.alexcommgrp.com • Description: Focuses primarily on helping downtown areas be as competitive and successful as possible on a day-to-day basis. Reports on market research, retailing, advertising approaches, public relations techniques, budgeting, and organization. Provides news of promotional strategies used in cities throughout the nation. Recurring features include case studies.

Drafting Patent License Agreements. Brian G. Brunsvold and others. BNA, Inc., Bureau of National Affairs, Inc., 1231 25th

St., NW Washington, DC 20037. Phone: 800-372-1033 E-mail: customercare@bna.com • URL: http://www.bna.com • 1998. $125.00. Fourth edition.

Draperies and Window Coverings. L. C. Clark Publishing Co., Inc., 840 U.S. Highway 1, Ste. 330 North Palm Beach, FL 33408. Phone: (561)627-3993 Fax: (561)694-6578 E-mail: info@dwcdesignet.com • URL: http://www.dwcdesignet.com • 13 times a year. $33.00 per year. Published for retailers, designers, manufacturers, and distributors of window coverings.

Draperies and Window Coverings: Directory and Buyer's Guide. L. C. Clark Publishing Co., Inc., 840 U.S. Highway, Suite 330 North Palm Beach, FL 33408. Phone: 800-833-9056 or (561)627-3993 Fax: (561)627-3447 E-mail: info@dwc.designet.com • URL: http://www.dwcdesignet.com • Annual. $15.00. Includes about 2,000 manufacturers and distributors of window coverings and related products.

Dredging Industry Size Standard Committee., Patton, Boggs, 2550 M St. NW Washington, DC 20037. Phone: (202)457-6000 Fax: (202)457-6315 E-mail: info@pattonboggs.com • URL: http://www.pattonboggs.com • Provides a legislative forum for the dredging industry. Represents the interests of the industry; lobbies for favorable federal legislation.

DRG Handbook. HCIA-Sachs, Inc., 300 E. Lombard St., 17th Fl. Baltimore, MD 21202. Phone: (410)895-7526 Fax: (410)783-0575 • URL: http://www.hcia.com • Annual. $399.00. Presents summary data for all 477 DRGs (diagnosis-related groups) and the 23 MDCs (major diagnostic categories), based on information from more than 11 million Medicare patients. Ranks DRG information for 100 hospital groups according to number of beds, payor mix, case-mix, system affiliation, and profitability. Emphasis is financial. Formerly *Medicare DRG Handbook*.

DRIP Investor: Your Guide to Buying Stocks Without a Broker. Horizon Publishing, Co., LLC, 7412 Calumet Ave., Suite 200 Hammond, IN 46324-2692. Phone: (219)852-3200 Fax: (219)931-6487 Monthly. $89.00 per year. Newsletter covering the dividend reinvestment plans (DRIPs) of various publicly-owned corporations. Includes model portfolios and *Directory of Dividend Reinvestment Plans*.

Drop Shipping as a Marketing Function: A Handbook of Methods and Policies. Nicholas T. Scheel. Greenwood Publishing Group, Inc., 88 Post Rd., W. Westport, CT 06881-5007. Phone: 800-225-5800 or (203)226-3571 Fax: (203)431-2214 E-mail: customer-service@greenwood.com • URL: http://www.greenwood.com • 1990. $64.95.

Drop Shipping News., P.O. Box 7838 New York, NY 10150. Phone: (212)688-8797 E-mail: nscheel@drop-shipping-news.com • URL: http://www.drop-shipping-news.com • Monthly. Price on application. Newsletter.

Drop Shipping Source Directory of Major Consumer Product Lines. Consolidated Marketing Services, Inc., P.O. Box 1361 New York, NY 10017. Phone: (212)688-8797 E-mail: nschneel@drop-shipping-news.com • URL: http://www.drop-shipping-news.com • Irregular. $15.00. Lists over 700 firms of a wide variety of consumer products that can be drop shipped.

Drug Abuse and the Law Sourcebook. Victor G. Haddox and Gerald G. Haddox. West Group, 610 Opperman Dr. Eagan, MN 55123. Phone: 800-328-4880 or (651)687-7000 Fax: 800-340-9378 or (651)687-5827 E-mail: bookstore@westgroup.com • URL: http://www.westgroup.com • Annual. $419.00. Two looseleaf volumes. Covers drugs of abuse, criminal responsibility, possessory offenses, trafficking offenses, and related topics. (Criminal Law Series).

Drug Abuse Handbook. Steven B. Karch, editor. CRC Press LLC, 2000 NW Corporate Blvd. Boca Raton, FL 33431. Phone: 800-272-7737 or (561)994-0555 Fax: 800-374-3401 or (561)989-9732 E-mail: orders@crcpress.com • URL: http://www.crcpress.com • 1997. $129.95. Provides comprehensive coverage of drug abuse issues and trends. Edited for healthcare professionals.

Drug Abuse in Society: A Reference Handbook. Geraldine Woods. ABC-CLIO, Inc., 130 Cremona Dr. Santa Barbara, CA 93116-1911. Phone: 800-368-6868 or (805)968-1911 Fax: (805)685-9685 E-mail: customerservice@abc-clio.com • URL: http://www.abc-clio.com • 1993. $39.50. (Contemporary World Issues Series).

Drug and Alcohol Abuse Education. Editorial Resources, Inc., P.O. Box 21129 Washington, DC 20009. Phone: (202)783-2929 Monthly. $84.00 per year. Newsletter covering education, prevention, and treatment relating to abuse of drugs and alcohol.

Drug Benefit Trends: For Pharmacy Managers and Managed HealthCare Professionals. Cliggott Publishing Co., 330 Boston Post Rd. Darien, CT 06820. Phone: (203)662-6400 E-mail: editor@scp.com Monthly. Individuals, $95.00 per year; libraries, $120.00 per year; students, $40.00 per year. Covers the business of managed care drug benefits.

Drug, Chemical and Allied Trades Association., 510 Route 130, Suite B1 East Windsor, NJ 08520. Phone: 800-640-3228 or (609)448-1000 Fax: (609)448-1944 E-mail: mtimony@dcat.org • URL: http://www.dcat.org • Formerly Drug, Chemical and Allied Trades Section of the New York Board of Trade.

Drug Development Research. John Wiley and Sons, Inc., 111 River St. Hoboken, NJ 07030. Phone: 800-225-5945 or (201)748-6000 Fax: (201)748-6088 E-mail: info@wiley.com • URL: http://www.wiley.com • Monthly. Institutions, $4,295.00 per year; with online edition, $4,510.00 per year.

Drug Facts and Comparisons. Facts and Comparisons, 111 W Port Plz., Ste. 300 St. Louis, MO 63146. Phone: 800-223-0554 Fax: (314)878-5563 • URL: http://www.factsandcomparisons.com • Annual. $359.95. Provides detailed information on more than 20,000 prescription drugs and 6000 over-the-counter products. Arrangement is according to 13 therapeutic categories. Includes charts and tables.

Drug Information Association., 800 Enterprise Rd., Ste. 200 Horsham, PA 19044-3595. Phone: (215)442-6100 Fax: (215)442-6199 E-mail: dia@diahome.org • URL: http://www.diahome.org • Provides neutral, global forum promoting exchange of information critical to professional performance and achievement in the discovery, development, regulation, surveillance, or marketing of pharmaceuticals or related products.

Drug Information Fulltext. American Society of Health-System Pharmacists, 7272 Wisconsin Ave. Bethesda, MD 20814. Phone: (301)657-3000 Fax: (301)657-1641 Provides full text monographs from the *American Hospital Formulary Service* and the *Handbook On Injectable Drugs*. Inquire as to online cost and availability.

Drug Interaction Facts. Facts and Comparisons, 111 W Port Plz., Ste. 300 St. Louis, MO 63146. Phone: 800-223-0554 Fax: (314)878-5563 • URL: http://www.factsandcomparisons.com • Annual. $179.95. Contains data on the interactions of some 20,000 prescription drugs. Interactions are rated according to magnitude and likelihood of effects, from one (most severe) to five (least severe). Includes drug/drug and drug/food interactions.

Drug Product Liability. LexisNexis Matthew Bender, 1275 Broadway Albany, NY 12204. Phone: 800-424-4200 or (518)487-3000 Fax: (518)487-3584 E-mail: bookstore.support@lexisnexis.com • URL: http://www.bender.com • $803.00. Four looseleaf volumes. Periodic supplementation. All aspects of drugs: manufacturing, marketing, distribution, quality control, multiple prescription problems, drug identification, FDA coverage, etc.

Drug Store News. Lebhar-Friedman Inc., 425 Park Ave. New York, NY 10022. Phone: 800-766-6999 or (212)756-5000 E-mail: info@lf.com • URL: http://www.lf.com • Biweekly. Free to qualified personnel; others, $99.00 per year.

Drug Store News Continuing Education Quarterly. Lebhar-Friedman, Inc., 425 Park Ave. New York, NY 10022. Phone: 800-766-6999 or (212)756-5000 E-mail: info@lf.com • URL: http://www.lf.com • Quarterly. $59.95 per year. Formerly *Drug Store News Chain Pharmacy*.

Drug Testing Legal Manual and Practice Aids. Kevin B. Zeese. West Group, 610 Opperman Dr. Eagan, MN 55123. Phone: 800-328-4880 or (651)687-7000 Fax: 800-340-9378 E-mail: bookstore@westgroup.com • URL: http://www.westgroup.com • Semiannual. $394.00 per year. Two looseleaf volumes. Covers methods of testing for illegal drugs, pre-employment drug testing, technological problems, testing of school students, and related topics. (Criminal Law Series).

Drug Topics. Thomson Medical Economics, Five Paragon Dr. Montvale, NJ 07645-1742. Phone: (201)358-7200 Fax: (201)722-2680 E-mail: customer.service@medec.com • URL: http://www.medec.com • 23 times a year. $61.00 per year. Edited for retail pharmacists, hospital pharmacists, pharmacy chain store executives, wholesalers, buyers, and others concerned with drug dispensing and drug store management. Provides information on new products, including personal care items and cosmetics.

Drugs, Alcohol, and Tobacco: Learning About Addictive Behavior. Gale Cengage Learning, 27500 Drake Rd. Farmington Hills, MI 48331-3535. Phone: 800-877-GALE Fax: 800-414-5043 or (248)699-8069 E-mail: galeord@galegroup.com • URL: http://www.galegroup.com • 2002. $295.00. Three volumes. Contains 200 articles on various aspects of addiction. Includes color illustrations, a glossary, and comprehensive indexing. (Macmillan Reference USA imprint.)

Drugs and Controlled Substances: Information for Students. Gale Cengage Learning, 27500 Drake Rd. Farmington Hills, MI 48331-3535. Phone: 800-877-GALE Fax: 800-414-5043 E-mail: gale.galeord@cengage.com • URL: http://gale.cengage.com • 2002. $115.00. Arranged alphabetically by drug name. Provides detailed information on the psychological and physiological effects of addictive drugs and substances. Includes illegal drugs, addictive prescription drugs, and over-the-counter items.

Drugs of Abuse. Available from U. S. Government Printing Office, Washington, DC 20402. Phone: (202)512-1800 Fax: (202)512-2250 E-mail: gpoaccess@gpo.gov • URL: http://www.access.gpo.gov • 2003. $9.00. Issued by the Drug Enforcement Administration, U. S. Department of Justice (http://www.usdoj.gov). Provides detailed information on various kinds of narcotics, depressants, stimulants, hallucinogens, cannabis, steroids, and inhalants. Contains many color illustrations and a detailed summary of the Controlled Substances Act.

Dry Cleaning Shop. Entrepreneur Media, Inc., 2445 McCabe Way Irvine, CA 92614. Phone: 800-421-2300 or (949)261-2325 Fax: (949)851-9088 E-mail: entmag@entrepreneurmag.com • URL: http://www.entrepreneurmag.com • Looseleaf. $59.50. A practical guide to starting a dry cleaning business. Covers profit potential, start-up costs, market size evaluation, owner's time required, site selection, lease negotiation, pricing, accounting, advertising, promotion, etc. (Start-Up Business Guide No. E1037.)

Drycleaners News. Zackin Publications, Inc., P.O. Box 2180 Waterbury, CT 06722. Phone: 800-325-6745 • URL: http://www.zackin.com • Monthly. $36.00.

DSN Retailing Today. Lebhar-Friedman Inc., 425 Park Ave. New York, NY 10022. Phone: 800-766-6999 or (212)756-5000 E-mail: info@lf.com • URL: http://www.lf.com • 23 times a year. $257.00 per year. Newsletter.

DSN Retailing Today (Discount Store News). Lebhar-Friedman, Inc., 425 Park Ave. New York, NY 10022. Phone: 800-766-6999 or (212)756-5000 E-mail: info@lf.com • URL: http://www.lf.com • 23 times a year. $119.00 per year. Includes supplement *Apparel Merchandising*. Formerly (Discount Store News).

Ductile Iron Pipe Research Association., 245 Riverchase Pkwy. E, Ste. O Birmingham, AL 35244. Phone: (205)402-8700 Fax: (205)402-8730 E-mail: dia@diahome.org • URL: http://www.dipra.org • Provides engineering information about cast iron and ductile iron pipe to utility and construction engineers.

Dumb Money: Adventures of a Day Trader. Gary Wolf and Joey Anuff. Random House, Inc., 1745 Broadway New York, NY 10036. Phone: 800-726-0600 or (212)782-9000 E-mail: customerservice@randomhouse.com • URL: http://www.randomhouse.com • 2000. $9.95. An account of the day trading ordeals of one of the authors, Joey Anuff.

Dun and Bradstreet Canadian Key Business Directory. Dun and Bradstreet Corp., 103 JFK Pky. Short Hills, NJ 07078. Phone: 800-234-3867 E-mail: custserv@dnb.com • URL: http://www.dnb.com • Annual. Corporations, $495.00; libraries, $435.00. Published by Dun & Bradstreet Canada Ltd. Provides information in English and French on 20,000 leading Canadian business firms.

Dun & Bradstreet/Gale Group Industry Handbooks. Gale Cengage Learning, 27500 Drake Rd. Farmington Hills, MI 48331-3535. Phone: 800-877-GALE or (248)699-4253 Fax: 800-414-5043 E-mail: gale.galeord@cengage.com • URL: http://gale.cengage.com • 2000. $650.00. Five volumes. $130.00 per volume. Each volume covers two or more major industries: 1. *Entertainment and Hospitality*; 2. *Construction and Agriculture*; 3. *Chemicals and Pharmaceuticals*; 4. *Computers & Software and Broadcasting & Telecommunications*; 5. *Insurance and Health & Medical Services*. The following are included for each industry: overview, statistics, financial ratios, rankings, merger information, company directory, directory of associations, and consultants directory. (Dun and Bradstreet/Gale Industry Reference Handbook Series).

Dun's Asia Pacific Key Business Enterprises. Dun & Bradstreet Corp., 103 JFK Pky., 3 Sylvan Way Short Hills, NJ 07078. Phone: 800-234-3867 or (973)921-5500 Fax: (973)921-6056 E-mail: custserv@dnb.com • URL: http://www.dnbmdd.com • Covers: 30,000 leading companies in 14 Pacific Rim countries whose annual sales are $10 million and who have 500 or more employees. Entries include: Company name, address, phone, fax, telex, number of employees, import/export designation, primary and secondary Standard Industrial Classification (SIC) codes, sales volume.

Dun's Census of American Business. Dun and Bradstreet Corp., 103 JFK Pky. Short Hills, NJ 07078. Phone: 800-234-3867 E-mail: custserv@dnb.com • URL: http://www.dnb.com • Annual. $325.00.

Dun's Industrial Guide: The Metalworking Directory. Dun and Bradstreet Corp., 103 JFK Pky. Short Hills, NJ 07078. Phone: 800-234-3867 E-mail: custserv@dnb.com • URL: http://www.dnb.com • Annual. Libraries, $485; commercial institutions, $795.00. Lease basis. Three volumes. Lists about 65,000 U. S. manufacturing plants using metal and suppliers of metalworking equipment and materials. Includes names and titles of key personnel. Products, purchases, and processes are indicated.

Dun's Key Decision-Makers in Hong Kong Business., Dun and Bradstreet, 3 Sylvan Way Parsippany, NJ 07054-3896. Phone: 800-526-0651 Fax: (973)605-6911 E-mail: dnbmdd@dnb.com • URL: http://www.dnbmdd.com • Annual. $380.00. Provides information on over 8,000 major Hong Kong companies.

DV Buyer's Guide. CMP Media LLC, 600 Community Dr. Manhasset, CA 11030. Phone: (516)562-5000 • URL: http://www.cmp.com • Annual. $10.00. A directory of professional video products, including digital cameras, monitors, editing systems, and software.

DVD Assessment, No. 3. Julie B. Schwerin and Theodore A. Pine. InfoTech, Inc., 312 Main Norwich, VT 05055. Phone: (802)649-8700 Fax: (802)649-8877 E-mail: info@infotechresearch.com • URL: http://www.infotechresearch.com • 1998. $1,295.00. Third edition. Provides detailed market research data on Digital Video Discs (also known as Digital Versatile Discs). Includes history of DVD, technical specifications, DVD publishing outlook, "Industry Overview," "Market Context," "Infrastructure Analysis," "Long-Range Forecast to 2005," and emerging technologies.

DVM: The Newsmagazine of Veterinary Medicine. Advanstar Communications, Healthcare Group, 545 Boylston St. Boston, MA 02116. Phone: 888-527-7008 or (617)267-6500 Fax: (617)267-6900 E-mail: info@advanstar.com • URL: http://www.advanstar.com • Monthly. $39.00 per year.

Includes new drugs and new products.

The Dynamic Decision Maker: Five Decision Styles for Executive and Business Success. Michael J. Driver and others. HarperInformation, 10 E. 53rd St. New York, NY 10022-5299. Phone: 800-242-7737 or (212)207-7000 Fax: 800-822-4090 or (212)207-7145 • URL: http://www.harpercollins.com • 1990. $24.95. The five styles are decisive, flexible, hierarchial, integrative, and systemic.

Dynamic E-Business Implementation Management: How to Effectively Manage E-Business Implementation. Bennet P. Lientz and Kathryn P. Rea. Elsevier, 655 Avenue of the Americas New York, NY 10010-5107. Phone: 800-366-2665 or (212)989-5800 Fax: 800-535-9935 or (212)663-3680 E-mail: custserv@elsevier.com • URL: http://www.elsevier.com • 2000. $47.95. (E-Business Solutions Series).

E-Business, Internet, and Online Transactions. Michael L. Taviss and others. Glasser Legalworks, 150 Clove Rd. Little Falls, NJ 07424. Phone: 800-308-1700 or (973)890-0008 Fax: (973)890-0042 E-mail: orders@glasserlegalworks.com • URL: http://www.glasserlegalworks.com • Looseleaf. $225.00, including CD-ROM version. Periodic Supplementation. Covers the legal aspects of online content, marketing, advertising, domain names, software licensing, and other Internet issues. Includes many sample forms. (Emerging Growth Companies Series.)

E-Commerce and Internet Law: Treatise with Forms. Ian C. Ballon. Glasser Legalworks, 150 Clove Rd. Little Falls, NJ 07424. Phone: 800-308-1700 or (973)890-0008 Fax: (973)890-0042 E-mail: orders@glasserlegalworks.com • URL: http://www.glasserlegalworks.com • Three looseleaf volumes. $595.00. Periodic supplementation. Analyzes Internet legalities, including litigious matters relating to downloading, streaming, music, video, content aggregation, domain names, chatrooms, and search engines. Includes forms, contracts, checklists, sample pleadings, and an extensive glossary.

The E-Commerce Book: Building the E-Empire. Steffano Korper and Juanita Ellis. Elsevier, 655 Avenue of the Americas New York, NY 10010-5107. Phone: 800-366-2665 or (212)989-5800 Fax: 800-535-9935 or (212)663-3680 E-mail: custserv@elsevier.com • URL: http://www.elsevier.com • 2000. $41.95. Second edition. Covers the practical aspects of Internet commerce, including sales, marketing, advertising, payment systems, and security. Written for a general audience. (Communications, Networking and Multimedia Series).

E-Commerce Law and Strategy. American Lawyer Media, Inc., 105 Madison Ave. New York, NY 10016. Phone: 800-888-8300 or (212)779-9200 Fax: (212)481-8110 E-mail: lawcatalog@amlaw.com • URL: http://www.lawcatalog.com/ • Monthly. $245.00 per year. Newsletter. Covers electronic commerce contracts, licensing, copyright, fraud, taxation, etc. (A Law Journal Newsletter, formerly published by Leader Publications).

E-Commerce Law Report: Buying and Selling on the Internet. Glasser Legalworks, 150 Clove Rd. Little Falls, NJ 07424. Phone: 800-308-1700 or (973)890-0008 Fax: (973)890-0042 E-mail: orders@glasserlegalworks.com • URL: http://www.glasserlegalworks.com • Monthly. $300.00 per year. Newsletter. Provides coverage of the legal and regulatory aspects of doing business online.

E-Commerce Tax Alert. CCH Inc., 4025 W Peterson Ave. Chicago, IL 60646-6085. Phone: 888-224-7377 or (847)267-7000 Fax: (773)866-3895 E-mail: hfcustsvc@healthforum.com • URL: http://www.cch.com • Description: Print and online newsletter covering e-commerce taxation issues, including compliance and sourcing, e-cash implications, the Internet tax debate, and other topics.

E Magazine: The Environmental. Earth Action Network, Inc., 28 Knight St. Norwalk, CT 06851. Phone: (203)854-5559 Fax: (203)866-0602 E-mail: info@emagazine.com • URL: http://www.emagazine.com • Bimonthly. $20.00 per year. A popular, consumer magazine providing news, information, and commentary on a wide range of environmental issues.

E-Retailing World. VNU Business Media, 770 Broadway New York, NY 10003. Phone: (646)654-4500 Fax: (646)654-7312 • URL: http://www.billcom.com • Bimonthly. Controlled circulation. Covers various kinds of online retailing, including store-based, catalog-based, pure play, and "click-and-mortar." Includes both technology and management issues.

E: The Environmental Magazine [online]. Earth Action Network, Inc.Phone: (203)854-5559 Fax: (203)866-0602 • URL: http://www.emagazine.com • Web site provides full-text articles from *E: The Environmental Magazine* for a period of about two years. Searching is provided. Alphabetical and subject links are shown for a wide variety of environmental Web sites. Fees: Free.

eAdvertising Report. Available from MarketResearch.com, 641 Ave. of the Americas, Third Floor New York, NY 10011. Phone: 800-298-5699 or (212)807-2629 Fax: (212)807-2716 E-mail: order@marketresearch.com • URL: http://www.marketresearch.com • 2001. $495.00. Market research data published by eMarketer. Covers the growth of the Internet online advertising market. Includes future trends and Internet users' attitudes.

Earl Warren Legal Institute. University of California at Berkeley

Early American Bookbindings from the Collection of Michael Papantonio. Michael Papantonio. Oak Knoll Press, 310 Delaware St. New Castle, DE 19720. Phone: 800-996-2556 or (302)328-7232 Fax: (302)328-7274 E-mail: oakknoll@oakknoll.com • URL: http://www.oakknoll.com • 1985. $27.50. Second edition.

Earnshaw's Infants, Girls and Boys Wear Review - Children's Wear Directory. Earnshaw Publications, Inc., 225 W 34th St., Ste. 1212 New York, NY 10001. Phone: (212)563-2742 Annual. Controlled circulation.

Earth Almanac: An Annual Geophysical Review of the State of the Planet. Natalie Goldstein. Greenwood Publishing Group, Inc., 88 Post Rd., W. Westport, CT 06881. Phone: 800-225-5800 or (203)226-3571 Fax: (203)431-2214 E-mail: customer-service@greenwood.com • URL: http://www.greenwood.com • Annual. $69.95. Provides background information, statistics, and a summary of major events relating to the atmosphere, oceans, land, and fresh water.

Earth and Mineral Sciences. College of Earth and Mineral Sciences. Pennsylvania State University, 116 Deike Bldg. University Park, PA 16802. Phone: (814)863-4667 Fax: (814)863-7708 Semiannual. Free. Current research in material science, mineral engineering, geosciences, meteorology, geography and mineral economics.

Earth Data Analysis Center. University of New Mexico

Earthcare Network., 85 2nd St., 2nd Fl. San Francisco, CA 94105-3441. Phone: (415)977-5500 Fax: (415)977-5799 E-mail: information@sierraclub.org • URL: http://www.sierraclub.org • Environmental groups united for the purpose of providing mutual assistance in the conducting of environmental campaigns. Compiles and exchanges information on these campaigns and communicates with relevant authorities. Maintains liaison with Sierra Club, which acts as secretariat for the network.

East Asian Executive Reports. International Executive Reports, 717 D St. NW, Ste. 300 Washington, DC 20004-2807. Phone: (202)628-6900 Fax: (202)628-6618 E-mail: execrep@aol.com • URL: http://www.his.com • Description: Features legal, financial, and practical aspects of doing business in East Asia. Features articles on local requirements for agents and sponsors, branch offices, joint ventures, importing, government tendering, licensing, and sourcing. Reports on technology transfer, labor, product liability, taxes, investment, repatriation of profits, marketing, and financing.

East European Kompass on Disc. Available from Kompass USA, Inc., 121 Whitney Ave. New Haven, CT 06510. Phone: 877-566-7277 or (203)503-6789 Fax: (203)503-6780 E-mail: mail@kompass-usa.com • URL: http://www.kompass.com • Semiannual. CD-ROM provides information on more than 350,000 companies in Austria, Azerbaijan, Belarus, Croatia, Czech Republic, Estonia, Hungary, Latvia, Lithuania, Moldova, Poland, Romania, Russia, Slovakia, Slovenia, Ukraine, and Yugoslavia. Classification system covers approximately 50,000 products and services.

East-West Center.

Easy Access: The Reference Handbook for Writers. Michael Keene and Katherine Adams. McGraw-Hill, 1221 Ave. of the Americas New York, NY 10020. Phone: 800-722-4726 or (212)512-2000 Fax: (212)512-4502 E-mail: customer.service@mcgraw-hill.com • URL: http://www.mcgraw-hill.com • 2001. $35.31. Third edition. Covers documentation styles and "Common Writing Problems" (punctuation, grammar, and sentence construction).

EBN Benefits Sourcebook. Thomson Media, One State St. Plaza New York, NY 10004. Phone: 800-221-1809 or (212)803-8200 Fax: (212)843-9635 E-mail: custserv@thomsonmedia.com • URL: http://www.thomsonmedia.com • Annual. $36.95. Lists vendors of products and services for the employee benefits industry. Includes industry trends and statistics.

eBrands: Building an Internet Business at Breakneck Speed. Phil Carpenter. Harvard Business School Publishing, 300 N Beacon St. Watertown, MA 02163. Phone: 800-988-0886 or (617)783-7500 Fax: (617)783-7555 • URL: http://www.hbs.edu • 2000. $25.95. Emphasis is on the marketing aspects of electronic commerce.

EBRI's Databook on Employee Benefits: What is the Promise? Ken McDonnell and others. Employee Benefit Research Institute, 2121 K St., N. W., Suite 600 Washington, DC 20037. Phone: (202)659-0670 Fax: (202)775-6312 E-mail: info@ebri.org • URL: http://www.ebri.org • 1997 $99.00. Fourth edition. Contains more than 350 tables and charts presenting data on employee benefits in the U. S., including pensions, health insurance, social security, and medicare. Includes a glossary of employee benefit terms.

EBSCO Information Services. Ebsco PublishingPhone: 800-653-2726 or (978)356-6500 Fax: (978)356-6565 E-mail: ep@epnet.com • URL: http://www.epnet.com • Fee-based Web site providing Internet access to a wide variety of databases, including business-related material. Full text is available for many periodical titles, with daily updates. Fees: Apply.

Ebusiness Forum: Global Business Intelligence for the Digital Age. Economist Intelligence Unit (EIU), Economist Group-Phone: 800-938-4685 or (212)554-0600 Fax: (212)586-0248 E-mail: newyork@eiu.com • URL: http://www.ebusinessforum.com • Web site provides information relating to multinational business, with an emphasis on activities in specific countries. Includes rankings of countries for "e-business readiness," additional data on the political, economic, and business environment in 180 nations ("Doing Business in."), and "Today's News Analysis." Fees: Free, but registration is required for access to all content. Daily updates.

EC&M's Electrical Products Yearbook (Electrical Construction and Maintenance). Primedia Business Magazines and Media, 9800 Metcalf Ave. Overland Park, KS 66212. Phone: 800-795-5445 or (913)341-1300 Fax: (913)967-1898 E-mail: subs@primediabusiness.com • URL: http://www.primediabusiness.com • Annual. $10.00.

EC.COM Magazine: The Magazine for Electronic Commerce Management. Electronic Commerce Media, Inc., 227 Fuller St. Brookline, MA 02446-5757. Phone: (617)232-6596 Fax: (617)232-6674 E-mail: editor@businessforum.com • URL: http://www.businessforum.com • Monthly. $48.00 per year. Covers both technical and business issues relating to e-commerce. information

ECN Literature News (Electronic Component News). Reed Business Information, 360 Park Ave., S New York, NY 10010. Phone: 800-446-6551 or (646)746-6400 Fax: (646)746-7028 E-mail: corporatecommunications@reedbusiness.com • URL: http://www.reedbusiness.com • Bimonthly. Price on application.

ECN's Electronic Industry Telephone Directory. Reed Business Information, 360 Park Ave. S New York, NY 10010. Phone: 800-446-6551 or (646)746-6400 Fax: (646)746-7431 E-mail: corporatecommunications@reedbusiness.com • URL: http://www.reedbusiness.com • Covers: 30,000 electronics manufacturers, distributors, and representatives. Entries include: Company name, address, phone, fax, and type of establishment.

eCoatings. National Paint & Coatings Association, 1500 Rhode Island Ave. NW Washington, DC 20005-5503. Phone: (202)462-6272 Fax: (202)462-8549 E-mail: npca@paint.org • URL: http://www.coatingsmagazine.com • Description: Covers legislative, regulatory, and judicial issues affecting the paint and coatings industry. Recurring features include news of research, a calendar of events, notices of publications available, reports of meetings, and editorials.

Ecology. Ecological Society of America, 1707 H St., NW, Ste. 400 Washington, DC 20006. Phone: (202)833-8773 Fax: (202)833-8775 E-mail: esahq@esa.org • URL: http://www.sdsc.edu • Monthly. $470.00 per year. All forms of life in relation to environment.

Ecology Law Quarterly. University of California, Berkeley. Boalt Hall School of Law, Berkeley, CA 94720-7200. Phone: (510)642-1741 • URL: http://www.law.berkeley.edu • Quarterly. Individuals, $30.00 per year; institutions, $54.00 per year; students, $22.00 per year.

The Ecology of Land Use: A Bibliographic Guide. Graham Trelstad. Sage Publications, Inc., 2455 Teller Rd. Thousand Oaks, CA 91320. Phone: 800-818-7243 or (805)499-9774 Fax: 800-58302665 or (805)499-0871 E-mail: webmaster@sagepub.com • URL: http://www.sagepub.com • 1994. $10.00.

eComp: The Most Powerful Executive Compensation Online Research Tool. AON Consulting Inc.Phone: (212)441-2047 Fax: (212)441-1944 E-mail: sales@ecomp-online.com • URL: http://www.ecomponline.com • Web site provides free access to executive compensation data by company name or industry. Gives names and titles of top executives for each company, with the following information for each corporate officer: salary, bonus, long-term incentive plan data (LTIP), options granted, options expiration date, dollar value of options, and detailed options exercisable data. More extensive, customized data is available on a fee basis.

EconLit. American Economic Association, 2014 Broadway, Suite 305 Nashville, TN 37203-2418. Phone: (615)322-2595 Fax: (615)343-7590 E-mail: info@econlit.org • URL: http://www.econlit.org • Covers the worldwide literature of economics as contained in selected monographs and about 550 journals. Subjects include microeconomics, macroeconomics, economic history, inflation, money, credit, finance, accounting theory, trade, natural resource economics, and regional economics. Time period is 1969 to present, with monthly updates. Inquire as to online cost and availability.

EconLit. Available from SilverPlatter Information, Inc., 100 River Ridge Rd. Norwood, MA 02062-5026. Phone: 800-343-0064 or (781)769-2599 Fax: (781)769-8763 Monthly. Single-user, $1,600.00 per year. Provides CD-ROM citations, with abstracts, to articles from more than 500 economics journals. Time period is 1969 to date. Produced by the American Economic Association.

Econometric Analysis. William H. Greene. Prentice Hall PTR, 240 Frisch Ct. Paramus, NJ 07652. Phone: 800-282-0693 Fax: 800-445-6991 • URL: http://www.phptr.com • 2000. Fourth edition. Price on application. Includes bibliographical references.

Econometric Methods. John Johnston and John N. DiNardo. McGraw-Hill, 1221 Ave. of the Americas New York, NY 10020. Phone: 800-722-4726 or (212)512-2000 Fax: (212)512-4502 E-mail: customer.service@mcgraw-hill.com • URL: http://www.mcgraw-hill.com • 1996. $109.06. Fourth edition. Covers various models, equations, variables, relationships, and "A Smorgasbord of Computationally Intense Methods."

Econometric Models and Economic Forecasts. Robert S. Pindyck and Daniel L. Rubinfield. McGraw-Hill, 1221 Ave. of the Americas New York, NY 10020. Phone: 800-722-4726 or (212)512-2000 Fax: (212)512-4502 E-mail: customer.

service@mcgraw-hill.com • URL: http://www.mcgraw-hill. com • 1997. $110.00. Fourth edition. Includes CD-ROM.

Econometric Society., New York University, Department of Economics, 19 W 4th St., 6th Fl. New York, NY 10012. Phone: (212)998-3820 Fax: (212)995-4487 E-mail: sashi@ econometricsociety.org • URL: http://www. econometricsociety.org • Economists, statisticians, and mathematicians. Promotes studies that are directed towards unification of the theoretical and empirical approaches to economic problems and advancement of economic theory in its relation to statistics and mathematics.

Econometric Theory. Cambridge University Press, Journals Dept., 40 W. 20th St. New York, NY 10011-4221. Phone: 800-221-4512 or (212)924-3900 Fax: (212)691-3239 E-mail: information@cup.org • URL: http://www.cup.org • Bimonthly. Individuals, $152.00 per year; institutions, $440.00 per year. Devoted to the advancement of theoretical research in econometrics.

Econometrica. Blackwell Publishing, 350 Main St. Malden, MA 02148. Phone: 800-835-6770 or (781)388-8200 Fax: (781)388-8232 E-mail: subscrip@blackwellpub.com • URL: http://www.blackwellpub.com • Bimonthly. Institutions, $301.00 per year. Includes print and online editions. Published in England by Basil Blackwell Ltd.

Econometrics of Financial Markets. John Y. Campbell and others. Princeton University Press, 41 William St. Princeton, NJ 08540-5237. Phone: 800-777-4726 or (609)258-4900 Fax: (609)258-6305 • URL: http://www.pup.princeton.edu • 1996. $70.00. Written for advanced students and industry professionals. Includes chapters on "The Predictability of Asset Returns," "Derivative Pricing Models," and "Fixed-Income Securities." Provides a discussion of the random walk theory of investing and tests of the theory.

Economic Accounts for Agriculture. Organization for Economic Cooperation and Development. Available from OECD Publications and Information Center, 2001 L St., N. W., Suite 650 Washington, DC 20036-4922. Phone: 800-456-6323 or (202)785-6323 Fax: (202)785-0350 E-mail: washington. contact@oecd.org • URL: http://www.oecdwash.org • Annual. $59.00. Provides data for 14 years on agricultural output and its components, intermediate consumption, and gross value added to net income and capital formation. Relates to various commodities produced by OECD member countries.

Economic and Budget Outlook: Fiscal Years 2004-2013. Available from U. S. Government Printing Office, Washington, DC 20402. Phone: (202)512-1800 Fax: (202)512-2250 E-mail: gpoaccess@gpo.gov • URL: http://www.access.gpo.gov • 2002. $27.00. Issued by the Congressional Budget Office (http://www.cbo.gov). Contains CBO economic projections and federal budget projections annually in billions of dollars. An appendix contains "Historical Budget Data" annually from, including revenues, outlays, deficits, surpluses, and debt held by the public.

Economic and Social Progress in Latin America. Inter-American Development Bank, 1300 New York Ave., NW Washington, DC 20577. Phone: (202)623-1709 Monthly. $24.95 per year. Covers developments in Latin America affecting business and trade. Text in Spanish.

Economic and Social Progress in Latin America Report. Inter-American Development Bank, 1300 New York Ave., N. W. Washington, DC 20577. Phone: 800-548-1784 or (202)673-1709 • URL: http://www.iadb.org • Annual. $24.95. Includes surveys of economic conditions in individual Latin American countries. Text in English.

Economic and Social Survey of Asia and the Pacific. United Nations Publications, Two United Nations Plaza, Room DC2-853 New York, NY 10017. Phone: 800-253-9646 or (212)963-8302 Fax: (212)963-3489 E-mail: publications@ un.org • URL: http://www.un.org/publications • Annual. $65. 00. Emphasis is on trends in economic policy and economic development strategies.

Economic Aspects of Taxi Accessibility. Organization for Economic Cooperation and Development, OECD Washington Center, 2001 L St., N. W., Suite 650 Washington, DC 20036-4922. Phone: 800-456-6323 or (202)785-6323 Fax: (202)785-0350 E-mail: washington.contact@oecd.org • URL: http://www.oecd.org • 2001. $19.00. Contains information on taxi use in 14 countries, including use by disabled and older people. Emphasis is on affordability.

Economic Botany: Devoted to Applied Botany and Plant Utilization. Society for Economic Botany. New York Botanical Garden Press, Bronx, NY 10458-5126. Phone: (718)817-8721 Fax: (718)817-8842 E-mail: nygbpress@nygb.org • URL: http://www.nybg.org • Quarterly. Individuals, $88.00 per year; institutions, $102.00 per year. Includes *Plants and People*. Newsletter. Original research and review articles on the uses of plants.

Economic Development. Michael P. Todaro and Stephen C. Smith. Addison-Wesley, 75 Arlington St., Ste. 300 Boston, MA 02116. Phone: 800-447-2226 or (617)848-7500 • URL: http://www.aw.com • 2002. Eight edition. Price on application. (Addison-Wesley Economic Series).

Economic Development and Cultural Change. The University of Chicago Press, Journals Div., P.O. Box 37005 Chicago, IL 60637. Phone: 877-705-1878 or (773)753-3347 Fax: 877-705-1879 or (773)753-0811 E-mail: subscriptions@press. uchicago.edu • URL: http://www.journals.uchicago.edu • Quarterly. Individuals, $50.00 per year; institutions, $218.00

per year; students, $38.00 per year. Examines the economic and social forces that affect development and the impact of development on culture.

Economic Development Monitor. Whitaker Newsletters, Inc., 313 South Ave. Fanwood, NJ 07023. Phone: (908)889-6336 Fax: (908)889-6339 Biweekly. $247.00 per year. Newsletter. Covers the news of U. S. economic and industrial development, including legislation, regulation, planning, and financing.

Economic Development Quarterly: The Journal of American Revitalization. Sage Publications, Inc., 2455 Teller Rd. Thousand Oaks, CA 91320. Phone: 800-818-7243 or (805)499-9774 Fax: 800-583-2665 or (805)499-0871 E-mail: webmaster@sagepub.com • URL: http://www.sagepub.com • Quarterly. Institutions, $486.00 per year; includes print and online editions.

Economic Development Review. American Economic Development Council, 734 15th St., NW, Ste. 900 Washington, DC 20005-1013. Phone: (202)223-7800 Fax: (202)223-4745 E-mail: kburns@iedconline.org • URL: http://www.iedc.org • Quarterly. $50.00 per year.

Economic Forecasting Center., Georgia State University, College of Business Administration, University Plaza, 35 Broad St. Atlanta, GA 30303-3083. Phone: (404)651-3298 Fax: (404)651-3299 E-mail: rdhawan@gsu.edu • URL: http:// www.robinson.gsu.edu/efc/~egcenter • Concerned with national and regional economic analysis and forecasting.

Economic Geology and the Bulletin of the Society of Economic Geologists. Society of Economic Geologist. Economic Geology Publishing Co., 7811 Shaffer Parkway Littleton, CO 80127. Phone: (720)981-7882 Fax: (720)981-7874 E-mail: seg@segweb.org • URL: http://www.segweb.org • Irregular. Individuals, $75.00 per year; institutions, $145.00 per year

Economic Growth Center. Yale University

Economic History Association., Santa Clara University, Department of Economics, 500 El Camino Real Santa Clara, CA 95053-0385. Phone: (408)554-4348 or (785)864-2847 Fax: (408)554-2331 E-mail: afield@scu.edu • URL: http://eh.net/ eha • Represents scholars, teachers and students of economic history.

Economic Indicators. Council of Economic Advisors, Executive Office of the President. Available from U.S. Government Printing Office, Washington, DC 20402. Phone: (202)512-1800 Fax: (202)512-2250 E-mail: gpoaccess@gpo.gov • URL: http://www.access.gpo.gov • Monthly. $55.00 per year.

Economic Indicators Handbook: Time Series, Conversions, Documentation. Gale Cengage Learning, 27500 Drake Rd. Farmington Hills, MI 48331-3535. Phone: 800-877-GALE Fax: 800-414-5043 E-mail: gale.galeord@cengage.com • URL: http://gale.cengage.com • 2002. $205.00. Sixth edition. Provides data for about 175 U. S. economic indicators, such as the consumer price index (CPI), gross national product (GNP), and the rate of inflation. Values for series are given since inception, in both original form and adjusted for inflation. A bibliography of sources is included.

Economic Justice Report: Global Issues of Economic Justice. Ecumenical Coalition for Economic Justice, 947 Queen St., E., Suite 208 Toronto, ON, Canada M4M 1J9. Phone: (416)462-1613 Fax: (416)463-5569 E-mail: ecej@accessv. com • URL: http://www.ecej.org • Quarterly. Individuals, $30.00 per year; institutions, $40.00 per year. Reports on economic fairness in foreign trade. Formerly *Gatt-Fly Report*.

Economic Outlook: A Newsletter on Economic Issues for Financial Institutions. America's Community Bankers, 900 19th St., N.W., Suite 400 Washington, DC 20006. Phone: (202)857-3100 Fax: (202)296-8716 • URL: http://www. acbankers.org • Monthly. Members, $106.00; non-members, $212.00 per year. Statistical profiles of the savings industry. Formerly *Economic Insight*.

Economic Parables and Policies: An Introduction to Economics. Laurence S. Seidman. M. E. Sharpe, Inc., 80 Business Park Drive Armonk, NY 10504. Phone: 800-541-6563 or (914)273-1800 Fax: (914)273-2106 E-mail: custserv@ mesharpe.com • URL: http://www.mesharpe.com • 2004. $64.95. Third edition. Emphasis is on current economic policy in such areas as taxation, trade, health care, education, social security, and the environment. Popularly written.

Economic Perspectives (Chicago). Federal Reserve Bank of Chicago, Public Information Center, P.O. Box 834 Chicago, IL 60690. Phone: 888-372-2446 or (312)322-5111 Fax: (312)322-5515 • URL: http://www.chicagofed.org • Quarterly. Free.

Economic Perspectives on the Internet. Alan E. Wiseman. Nova Science Publishers, Inc., 400 Oser Ave., Suite 1600 Hauppauge, NY 11788-3619. Phone: (631)231-7269 Fax: (631)231-8175 E-mail: novascience@earthlink.net • URL: http://www.novapublishers.com • 2003. $59.00. Discusses the pricing of Internet access, pricing of goods and services sold through the Internet, network effects, and Internet taxation.

Economic Report of the President: Together with the Annual Report of the Council of Economic Advisors. Available from U. S. Government Printing Office, Washington, DC 20402. Phone: (202)512-1800 Fax: (202)512-2250 E-mail: gpoaccess@gpo.gov • URL: http://www.access.gpo.gov • Annual. $32.00. Includes about 130 pages of "Statistical Tables Relating to Income, Employment, and Production." Tables cover national income, employment, wages, productivity, manufacturing, prices, credit, finance (public

and private), corporate profits, and foreign trade.

Economic Review of Travel in America. Travel Industry Association of America, 1100 New York Ave., N.W., Suite 240 Washington, DC 20005-3934. Phone: (202)408-8422 Fax: (202)408-1255 E-mail: rmcclur@tia.org • URL: http://www. tia.org • Annual. Members, $75.00; non-members, $125.00. Presents a statistical summary of travel in the U.S., including travel expenditures, travel industry employment, tax data, international visitors, etc.

Economic Survey of Europe. United Nations Publications, Concourse Level, First Ave., 46th St. New York, NY 10017. Phone: 800-553-3210 or (212)963-7680 Fax: (212)963-4910 E-mail: bookstore@un.org • URL: http://www.un.org/ publications • Three times a year. Price varies. Provides yearly analysis and review of the European economy, including Eastern Europe and the USSR. Text in English.

Economic Survey of Latin America and the Caribbean. United Nations Publications, Two United Nations Plaza, Room DC2-853 New York, NY 10017. Phone: 800-253-9646 or (212)963-8302 Fax: (212)963-3489 E-mail: publications@ un.org • URL: http://www.un.org/publications • Annual. $50. 00. Includes reports on economic trends in 20 Latin American countries.

Economic Trends. American Hospital Association. American Hospital Publishing, One N. Franklin St. Chicago, IL 60606-3421. Phone: 800-242-2626 or (312)422-3000 Fax: (312)422-4796 • URL: http://www.aha.org • Quarterly. Members, $85.00 per year; non-members $135.00 per year. Provides statistical data on the nation's hospitals, including revenues, expenses.

Economics. William D. Nordhaus and Paul A. Samuelson. McGraw-Hill, 1221 Ave. of the Americas New York, NY 10020. Phone: 800-722-4726 or (212)512-2000 Fax: (212)512-4502 E-mail: customer.service@mcgraw-hill.com • URL: http://www.mcgraw-hill.com • 2000. $92.50. 17th edition.

Economics and Portfolio Strategy. Peter L. Bernstein, Inc., 575 Madison Ave., Suite 1006 New York, NY 10022. Phone: (212)421-8385 Fax: (212)421-8537 E-mail: info@ peterlbernsteininc.com • URL: http://www. peterlbernsteininc.com • Semimonthly. $1,700.00 per year. Provides financial analysis and insight for "institutional investors and sophisticated individual investors."

Economics Explained: Everything You Need to Know About How the Economy Works and Where It's Going. Robert L. Heilbroner and Lester C. Thurow. Peter Smith Publishing, Inc., Five Lexington Ave. Magnolia, MA 01930. Phone: (978)525-3562 Fax: (978)525-3674 1988. $27.50. Fourth revised edition.

Economics of Corporation Law and Securities Regulation. Richard A. Posner and Kenneth E. Scott. Aspen Publishers, Inc., 1185 Ave. of the Americas New York, NY 10036. Phone: 800-234-1660 or (212)597-0200 Fax: 800-901-9075 or (212)597-0338 E-mail: customer.serivce@aspenpubl.com • URL: http://www.aspenpublishers.com • 1981. $32.95.

Economics of Development. Malcolm Gillis and others. W. W. Norton and Co., Inc., 500 5th Ave. New York, NY 10110. Phone: 800-223-2584 or (212)354-5500 Fax: (212)869-0856 • URL: http://www.wwnorton.com • 2001. $105.10. Fifth edition.

Economics of Divorce: The Effect on Parents and Children. Craig A. Everett. Haworth Press, Inc., 10 Alice St. Binghamton, NY 13904-1580. Phone: 800-429-6784 or (607)722-5857 Fax: 800-895-0582 or (607)722-1424 E-mail: getinfo@ haworthpressinc.com • URL: http://www.haworthpressinc. com • 1994. $39.95. (Journal of Divorce and Remarriage Series).

Economics of Information: A Guide to Economic and Cost-Benefit Analysis for Information Professionals. Bruce R. Kingma. Libraries Unlimited, 88 Post Rd., W Westportd, CT 06881. Phone: 800-225-5800 Fax: (203)222-1205 E-mail: lu-books@lu.com • URL: http://www.lu.com • 2001. $45.00. Second edition. A technical discussion of market forces affecting the information industry. (Library and Information Science Text Series).

The Economics of Money, Banking and Financial Markets. Frederic S. Mishkin. Addison Wesley, 75 Arlington St., Ste. 300 Boston, MA 02116. Phone: 800-447-2226 or (617)-848-7500 • URL: http://www.aw.com • 2003. $110.00. Seventh edition. (Economics Series).

Economics: Principles, Problems, and Policies. Campbell R. McConnell. McGraw-Hill, 1221 Ave. of the Americas New York, NY 10020. Phone: 800-722-4726 or (212)512-2000 Fax: (212)512-4502 E-mail: customer.service@mcgraw-hill. com • URL: http://www.mcgraw-hill.com • 2001. $111.50. 14th edition.

Economics Today. Roger L. Miller. Addison-Wesley, 75 Arlington St., Ste. 300 Boston, MA 02116. Phone: 800-447-2226 or (617)848-7500 • URL: http://www.aw.com • 2003. $118.00. 11th edition. Includes CD-ROM.

The Economist. Economist Intelligence Unit, The Economist Bldg., 111 W 57th St. New York, NY 10019. Phone: 800-938-4685 or (212)554-0600 Fax: (212)586-1182 E-mail: newyork@eiu.com • URL: http://www.eiu.com • 51 times a year. $125.00 per year.

Economists and Their Theories for Students. Gale Cengage Learning, 27500 Drake Rd. Farmington Hills, MI 48331-3535. Phone: 800-877-GALE Fax: 800-414-5043 or (248)699-8069 E-mail: galeord@galegroup.com • URL:

http://www.galegroup.com • 2003. $95.00. Provides detailed information on major economic theories and the economists who developed them. Includes a glossary and chronology.

EContent: Digital Content Strategies and Resources. Online, Inc., 213 Danbury Rd. Wilton, CT 06897-4006. Phone: 800-248-8466 or (203)761-1466 Fax: (203)761-1444 E-mail: dbmag@onlineinc.com • URL: http://www.econtentmag.com • Monthly. $110.00 per year. Emphasis is on the business management and financial aspects of the digital content industry. (Formerly published by Online, Inc.)

ECRI: Emergency Care Research Institute., 5200 Butler Pike Plymouth Meeting, PA 19462-1298. Phone: (610)825-6000 Fax: (610)834-1275 E-mail: info@ecri.org • URL: http://www.ecri.org • Major research area is health care technology.

EdgarPlus: SEC Basic Filings. Thomson Financial, 22 Thomson Pike Boston, MA 02210. Phone: (617)856-2000 Fax: (617)330-1986 • URL: http://www.tfn.com • Online service provides full text of about 60,000 documents that have been filed with the U.S. Securities and Exchange Commission, 1987 to date, with daily updates. Filings include 6-K, 8-K, 10-K, 10-C, 10-Q, 20-F, and proxy statements. Inquire as to online cost and availability.

Edison Electric Institute., 701 Pennsylvania Ave. NW Washington, DC 20004-2696. Phone: 800-334-4688 or (202)508-5000 Fax: (202)508-5360 E-mail: bfarrell@eei.org • URL: http://www.eei.org • Shareholder-owned electric utility companies operating in the U.S.; international affiliates and associates worldwide.

Editing: An Annotated Bibliography. Bruce W. Speck. Greenwood Publishing Group, Inc., 88 Post Rd., W Westport, CT 06881. Phone: 800-225-5800 or (203)226-3571 Fax: (203)431-2214 E-mail: customer-service@greenwood.com • URL: http://www.greenwood.com • 1991. $67.95. (Bibliographies and Indexes in Mass Media and Communications Series, No. 4).

Editor and Publisher International Yearbook: Encyclopedia of the Newspaper Industry. Editor and Publisher Co., Inc., 770 Broadway New York, NY 10003-9595. Phone: 800-336-4380 Fax: (646)654-5370 E-mail: editorandpublisher@espcomp.com • URL: http://www.editorandpublisher.com • Annual. $150.00. Daily and Sunday newspapers in the United States and Canada.

Editor and Publisher Journalism Awards and Fellowship Directory. Editor and Publisher Co., Inc., 770 Broadway New York, NY 10003-9595. Phone: 800-336-4380 Fax: (646)654-5370 E-mail: editorandpublisher@espcomp.com • URL: http://www.editorandpublisher.com • Annual. $8.00. Over 500 cash prizes scholarships, fellowships, and grants available to journalists and students for work on special subjects or in specific fields.

Editor and Publisher Market Guide. Editor and Publisher Co., Inc., 770 Broadway New York, NY 10003-9595. Phone: 800-336-4380 Fax: (646)654-5370 E-mail: editorandpublisher@espcomp.com • URL: http://www.editorandpublisher.com • Annual. $150.00. More than 1,700 newspaper markets in the United States and Canada.

Editor and Publisher Syndicate Directory: Annual Directory of Syndicate Services. Editor and Publisher Co., Inc., 770 Broadway New York, NY 10003-9595. Phone: 800-336-4380 Fax: (646)654-5370 E-mail: editorandpublisher@espcomp.com • URL: http://www.editorandpublisher.com • Annual. $28.00. Directory of several hundred syndicates serving newspapers in the United States and abroad with news, columns, features, comic strips, editorial cartoons, etc.

Editor and Publisher - The Newsmagazine of the Fourth Estate Since 1894. Editor and Publisher Co., Inc., 770 Broadway New York, NY 10003-9595. Phone: 800-336-4380 Fax: (646)654-5370 E-mail: editorandpublisher@espcomp.com • URL: http://www.editorandpublisher.com • Weekly. $99.00 per year. Includes print and online edition. Trade journal of the newspaper industry.

Editorial Freelancers Association., 71 W 23rd St., 4th Fl. New York, NY 10010-4181. Phone: (866)929-5400 or (212)929-5400 Fax: (212)929-5439 E-mail: office@the-efa.org • URL: http://www.the-efa.org • Represents persons who work full or part-time as freelance writers or editorial freelancers. Promotes professionalism and facilitates the exchange of information and support. Conducts professional training seminars; and offers job listings.

Edmund's New Cars. Edmund Publications Corp., 2401 Colorado Blvd., Suite 250 Santa Monica, CA 90404. Phone: (310)309-6300 Fax: (310)309-6400 • URL: http://www.edmunds.com • Four times a year. Individuals, $39.96 per year; libraries, $26.80 per year. Wholesale and retail prices for all American and import models and accessories. Includes federal crash reports, leasing facts, and accident report forms. Formerly *Edmund's New Car Prices*.

Edmund's Used Cars and Trucks, Prices and Ratings. Edmund Publications Corp., 2401 Colorado Blvd., Suite 250 Santa Monica, CA 90404. Phone: (310)309-6300 Fax: (310)309-6400 • URL: http://www.edmunds.com • Four times a year. Individuals, $39.96 per year; libraries, $26.80 per year. Lists American and foreign used car prices for the past 10 years.

EDP Weekly: The Leading Weekly Computer News Summary. Computer Age and EDP News Services, 1150 Connecticut Ave., NW, Ste. 900 Washington, DC 20036. Phone: (202)862-4375 Fax: (202)659-3493 E-mail: millin@erols.com • URL: http://www.millinpubs.com • Weekly. $495.00 per year. Newsletter. Summarizes news from all areas of the computer and microcomputer industries.

Education at a Glance: OECD Indicators. Organization for Economic Cooperation and Development, OECD Washington Center, 2001 L St., N. W., Suite 650 Washington, DC 20036-4922. Phone: 800-456-6323 or (202)785-6323 Fax: (202)785-0350 E-mail: washington.contact@oecd.org • URL: http://www.oecdwash.org • Annual. $49.00. Provides comparative education statistics and indicators for OECD countries.

Education for Older Adult Learning: A Selected, Annotated Bibliography. Reva M. Greenberg. Greenwood Publishing Group, Inc., 88 Post Rd., W. Westport, CT 06881-5007. Phone: 800-225-5800 or (203)226-3571 Fax: (203)431-2214 E-mail: customer-service@greenwood.com • URL: http://www.greenwood.com • 1993. $82.95. Describes more than 700 books, articles, and other items relating to formal and informal education for older adults. (Bibliographies and Indexes in Gerontology Series, No. 20).

Education Index. H. W. Wilson Co., 950 University Ave. Bronx, NY 10452. Phone: 800-367-6770 or (718)588-8400 Fax: 800-590-1617 or (718)590-1617 E-mail: custserv@hwwilson.com • URL: http://www.hwwilson.com • 10 times a year. Quarterly and annual cumulations. Price varies.

Education Index Online. H. W. Wilson Co., 950 University Ave. Bronx, NY 10452. Phone: 800-367-6770 or (718)558-8400 Fax: (718)590-1617 Indexes a wide variety of periodicals related to schools, colleges, and education, 1984 to date. Monthly updates. Inquire as to online cost and availability.

Education Law. LexisNexis Matthew Bender, 1275 Broadway Albany, NY 12204. Phone: 800-424-4200 or (518)487-3000 Fax: (518)487-3584 E-mail: bookstore.support@lexisnexis.com • URL: http://www.bender.com • $874.00. Seven looseleaf volumes. Periodic supplementation. A reference for attorneys who represent persons having a grievance against educational institutions, and attorney representing such institutions, as well as school board members and administrators.

Education of a Speculator. Victor Niederhoffer. John Wiley and Sons, Inc., 111 River St. Hoboken, NJ 07030. Phone: 800-225-5945 or (201)748-6000 Fax: (201)748-6088 E-mail: info@wiley.com • URL: http://www.wiley.com • 1998. $18.95. An autobiography providing basic advice on speculation, investment, and the commodity futures market.

Education Statistics of the United States. Deirdre A. Gaquin and Katherine A. Debrandt. Bernan Press, 4611-F Assembly Dr. Lanham, MD 20706-4391. Phone: (301)459-2255 Fax: 800-865-3450 or (301)459-9235 E-mail: bpress@bernan.com • URL: http://www.bernan.com • 2001. $147.00. Third edition. Provides detailed county and state data, includes enrollment, educational attainment, per pupil expenditure, teacher pay and class size.

Education Technology News: Insiders Guide to Multimedia in the K-12 Classroom. Business Publishers, Inc., 8737 Colesville Rd., Suite 1100 Silver Spring, MD 20910-3928. Phone: 800-274-6737 or (301)589-5103 Fax: (301)589-8493 E-mail: bpinews@bpinews.com • URL: http://www.bpinews.com • Biweekly. $357.00 per year. Looseleaf service. Formerly *Education Computer News*.

Education Week: American Education's Newspaper of Record. Editorial Projects in Education, Inc., 6935 Arlington Rd., Suite 100 Bethesda, MD 20814-5233. Phone: 800-346-1834 Fax: (301)280-3100 E-mail: ewletter@epe.org • URL: http://www.edweek.org • 43 times a year. $79.94 per year.

Educational Administration Abstracts. Sage Publication, Inc., 2455 Teller Rd. Thousand Oaks, CA 91320. Phone: 800-818-7243 or (805)499-9774 Fax: 800-583-2665 or (805)499-0871 E-mail: webmaster@sagepub.com • URL: http://www.sagepub.com • Quarterly. Institutions, $722.00 per year.

Educational Administration Quarterly. University Council for Educational Administratiotion. Sage Publications, Inc., 2455 Teller Rd. Thousand Oaks, CA 91320. Phone: 800-818-7243 or (805)499-9774 Fax: 800-583-2665 or (805)499-0871 E-mail: webmaster@sage.pub.com • URL: http://www.sage.pub.com • Five times a year. Institutions, $489.00 per year.

Educational and Psychological Measurement: Devoted to the Development and Application of Measures of Individual Differences. Sage Publications, Inc., 2455 Teller Rd. Thousand Oaks, CA 91320. Phone: 800-818-7243 or (805)499-9774 Fax: 800-583-2665 or (805)499-0871 E-mail: webmaster@sagepub.com • URL: http://www.sagepub • Bimonthly. Institutions, $599.00 per year.

Educational Foundation for Nuclear Science.

Educational Marketer: The Educational Publishing Industry's Voice of Authority Since 1968. SIMBA Information, 11 Riverbend Dr., S Stamford, CT 06907. Phone: 800-307-2529 or (203)358-4100 Fax: (203)358-5824 E-mail: info@simbanet.com • URL: http://www.simbanet.com • Three times a month. $599.00 per year. Newsletter. Edited for suppliers of educational materials to schools and colleges at all levels. Covers print and electronic publishing, software, audiovisual items, and multimedia. Includes corporate news and educational statistics.

Educational Media and Technology Yearbook. Libraries Unlimited, Inc., 88 Post Rd., W Westport, CT 06881. Phone: 800-225-5800 Fax: (203)222-1502 E-mail: lu-books@lu.com • URL: http://www.lu.com • Annual. $75.00.

Educational Rankings Annual: A Compilation of Approximately 3,500 Published Rankings and Lists on Every Aspect of Education. Gale Cengage Learning, 27500 Drake Rd. Farmington Hills, MI 48331-3535. Phone: 800-877-GALE or (248)699-4253 Fax: 800-414-5043 E-mail: gale.galeord@cengage.com • URL: http://gale.cengage.com • Annual. $265.00. Provides national, regional, local, and international rankings of a wide variety of educational institutions, including business and professional schools.

Educational Technology Research and Development. Association for Educational Communications and Technology, 1800 N. Stonelake Dr., Suite 2 Bloomington, IN 47404. Phone: 877-677-2328 or (812)335-7675 Fax: (812)335-7678 E-mail: aect@aect.org • URL: http://www.aect.org • Quarterly. $75.00 per year.

Educational Technology: The Magazine for Managers of Change in Education. Educational Technology Publications, Inc., 700 Palisade Ave. Englewood Cliffs, NJ 07632-0564. Phone: 800-952-2665 or (201)871-4007 Fax: (201)871-4009 E-mail: edtecpubs@aol.com • URL: http://www.bookstoreread.com • Bimonthly. $139.00 per year.

Educational Testing Service., Rosedale Rd. Princeton, NJ 08541. Phone: (609)921-9000 Fax: (609)734-5410 E-mail: etsinfo@ets.org • URL: http://www.ets.org • Educational measurement and research organization, founded by merger of the testing activities of American Council on Education, Carnegie Foundation for the Advancement of Teaching, and The College Board. Provides tests and related services for schools, colleges, governmental agencies, and the professions; offers advisory services in the sound application of measurement techniques and materials; conducts educational, psychological, and measurement research. Offers a summer program in educational testing for scholars and educators from other countries, continuing education programs, and measurement, evaluation, and other instructional activities.

Educators Guide to Free Films, Filmstrips and Slides. Educators Progress Service, Inc., 214 Center St. Randolph, WI 53956. Phone: 888-951-4469 or (920)326-3126 Fax: (920)326-3127 E-mail: epsinc@centurytel.net • URL: http://www.freeteachingaids.com • Annual. $36.95. Lists educational and recreational films in all subject areas for free use by teachers and other educators. Formerly *Educators Guide to Free Filmstrips and Slides*.

Educators Guide to Free Guidance Materials. Educators Progress Service, Inc., 214 Center St. Randolph, WI 53956. Phone: 888-951-4469 or (920)326-3126 Fax: (920)326-3127 E-mail: epsinc@centurytel.net Annual. $34.95. Lists free-loan films, filmstrips, audiotapes, videotapes and free printed materials on guidance.

Educators Guide to Free Videotapes - Secondary Education. James Berger, editor. Educators Progress Service, Inc., 214 Center St. Randolph, WI 53956. Phone: 888-951-4469 or (920)326-3126 Fax: (920)326-3127 E-mail: epsince@centurytel.net • URL: http://www.freeteachingaids.com • Annual. $34.95. Lists free-loan audiotapes, videotapes and records. Formerly *Educators Guide to Free Audio and Video Materials*.

Educators Resource Directory. Grey House Publishing, 185 Millerton Rd., PO Box 860 Millerton, NY 12546. Phone: 800-562-2139 or (518)789-8700 Fax: (518)789-0556 E-mail: customerservice@greyhouse.com • URL: http://www.greyhouse.com • Covers: Publishing opportunities, state by state information on enrollment, funding and grant resources, associations and conferences, teaching jobs abroad all geared toward elementary and secondary school professionals. Also covers online databases, textbook publishers, school suppliers, plus state and federal agencies. Entries include: Contact name, address, phone, fax, description, publications. A unique compilation of over 6,500 educational resources and over 130 tables and charts of education statistics and rankings.

Edward L. Ginzton Laboratory., Stanford University, 450 Via Palou Stanford, CA 94305-4085. Phone: (650)723-0111 Fax: (650)725-9355 E-mail: dabm@ee.stanford.edu • URL: http://www.stanford.edu/group/ginzton • Research fields include low-temperature physics and superconducting electronics.

EE Product News (Electronics-Electrical). Penton Media, Inc., 1300 E 9th St. Cleveland, OH 44114. Phone: (216)696-7000 Fax: (216)696-1752 E-mail: information@penton.com • URL: http://www.penton.com • Monthly. Free to qualified personnel; others, $60.00 per year.

EEO Law and Personnel Practices. Arthur Gutman. Sage Publications, Inc., 2455 Teller Rd. Thousand Oaks, CA 91320. Phone: 800-818-7243 or (805)499-9774 Fax: 800-583-2665 or (805)499-0871 E-mail: webmaster@sagepub.com • URL: http://www.sagepub.com • 2000. $93.95. Second edition. Discusses the practical effect of federal regulations dealing with race, color, religion, sex, national origin, age, and disability. Explains administrative procedures, litigation actions, and penalties. (Management Studies Series).

EEOC Compliance Manual (Equal Employment Opportunity Commission). BNA, Inc., 1231 25th St., NW Washington, DC 20037. Phone: 800-372-1033 E-mail: customercare@bna.com • URL: http://www.bna.com • Irregular. $316.00 per year. Looseleaf service. Guide to federal Equal Employment Opportunity Commission activities.

EF Foundation for Foreign Study., EF Center Boston, One Education St. Cambridge, MA 02141. Phone: 800-447-4273 E-mail: foundation@ef.com • URL: http://www.effoundation.org • Seeks to further international understanding through cultural and academic exchange. Sponsors academic homestay programs, such as High School Year in Europe. Formerly EF Educational Foundation for Foreign Study.

Effective Clinical Practice. American College of Physicians, 190 N. Independence Mall West Philadelphia, PA 19106-1572. Phone: 800-523-1546 or (215)351-2600 Fax: (215)351-2799 E-mail: custserve@mail.acponline.org • URL: http://www.acpoline.org • Bimonthly. Individuals, $54.00 per year; institutions, $70.00 per year. Formerly *HMO Practice*.

Effective Executive's Guide to Microsoft Word 2002: The Seven Core Skills Required to Turn Word into a Business Power Tool. Pat Coleman. Redmond Technology Press, 8581 154th Ave., N.E. Redmond, WA 98052. Phone: (425)861-9628 Fax: (425)882-0160 E-mail: editor@redtechpress.com • URL: http://www.redtechpress.com • 2001. $24.95. Written to provide basic word processing skills to nontechnical business managers and executives.

Effective Physical Security: Design, Equipment, and Operations. Lawrence J. Fennelly, editor. Elsevier, 655 Ave. of the Americas New York, NY 10010-5107. Phone: 800-366-2665 or (212)989-5800 Fax: 800-535-9935 or (212)633-3680 E-mail: custserv@elsevier.com • URL: http://www.elsevier.com • 1996. $44.99. Second edition. Contains chapters written by various U. S. security equipment specialists. Covers architectural considerations, locks, safes, alarms, intrusion detection systems, closed circuit television, identification systems, etc.

Effective Project Management: How to Plan, Manage, and Deliver a Project on Time and Within Budget. Robert K. Wysocki and others. John Wiley and Sons, Inc., 111 River St. Hoboken, NJ 07030. Phone: 800-225-5945 or (201)748-6000 Fax: (201)748-6088 E-mail: info@wiley.com • URL: http://www.wiley.com • 2000. $60.00. Second edition. Selected by the Project Management Institute (PMI) as a reference for the Project Management Professional Certification Examination. Includes CD-ROM.

Effective Supervisor's Handbook. Louis V. Imundo. AMACOM, 1601 Broadway New York, NY 10019. Phone: 800-262-9699 or (518)586-8100 Fax: (518)903-8168 E-mail: customerservice@amanet.org • URL: http://www.amacombooks.org • 1992. $16.95. Second edition.

Effective Writing for Engineers, Managers, Scientists. H. J. Tichy and Sylvia Fourdrinier. John Wiley and Sons, Inc., 111 River St. Hoboken, NJ 07030. Phone: 800-526-5368 or (201)748-6000 Fax: (201)748-6088 E-mail: info@wiley.com • URL: http://www.wiley.com • 1988. $125.00. Second edition.

Egg Industry: Covering Egg Production, Processing and Marketing. Watt Publishing Co., 122 S. Wesley Ave. Mount Morris, IL 61054. Phone: (815)734-4171 Fax: (815)734-4201 • URL: http://www.wattnet.com • Monthly. Free to qualified personnel; others, $36.00 per year. Newsletter. Formerly *Poultry Tribune*.

EI Environmental Services Directory. Environmental Information Ltd., 5775 Wayzata Blvd., Ste. 820 Saint Louis Park, MN 55416. Phone: (952)831-2473 Fax: (952)831-6550 E-mail: ei@enviro-information.com • URL: http://www.envirobiz.com • Covers: Over 8,000 environmental services businesses, including waste-handling facilities, transportation firms, spill response firms, consultants, laboratories, soil boring/well drilling firms; also includes incineration services, polychlorinated biphenyl (PCB) detoxification and mobile solvent-recovery services, asbestos services and underground tank services, summaries of states' regulatory programs. Entries include: Company name, address, phone, description of services, regulatory status, on and off site processes used, type of waste handled.

EIA Publications Index/EIA Trade Directory. Electronic Industries Alliance, 2500 Wilson Blvd. Arlington, VA 22201. Phone: (703)907-7590 Fax: (703)907-7501 E-mail: cmccordy@eia.org • URL: http://www.eia.org • Annual. Free.

EIA Residential Electric Bills in Major Cities. Energy Information Administration. U.S. Department of Energy, Washington, DC 20585. Phone: (202)586-4940 Annual.

Electrial Construction and Maintenance. Primedia Business Magazines and Media, 9800 Metcalf Ave. Overland Park, KS 66212. Phone: 800-795-5445 or (913)341-1300 Fax: (913)967-1898 E-mail: subs@primediabusiness.com • URL: http://www.primediabusiness.com • Monthly. Free to qualified personnel; individuals, $30.00 per year; libraries, $25.00 per year.

Electric Lamps. U. S. Bureau of the Census, 4700 Silver Hill Rd. Washington, DC 20233-0001. Phone: (301)763-4636 E-mail: comments@census.gov • URL: http://www.census.gov • Quarterly and annual. Provides data on shipments: value, quantity, imports, and exports. (Current Industrial Reports, MQ-36B.)

Electric Perspectives. Edison Electric Institute, PO Box 266 Waldorf, MD 20604-0266. Phone: 800-334-5453 or (301)645-4222 Fax: (301)843-0159 E-mail: catalog@eei.org • URL: http://www.eei.org • Bimonthly. $50.00 per year. Covers business, financial, and operational aspects of the investor-owned electric utility industry. Edited for utility executives and managers.

Electric Power Monthly. Available from U. S. Government Printing Office, Washington, DC 20402. Phone: (202)512-1800 Fax: (202)512-2250 E-mail: gpoaccess@gpo.gov • URL: http://www.access.gpo.gov • Monthly. $137.00 per year. Issued by the Energy Information Administration, U. S. Department of Energy. Contains statistical data relating to electric utility operation, capability, fuel use, and prices.

Electric Power Supply Association., 1401 New York Ave. NW, 11th Fl. Washington, DC 20005-2110. Phone: (202)628-8200 Fax: (202)628-8260 E-mail: etsinfo@ets.org • URL: http://www.epsa.org • Represents competitive power suppliers, including generators and power marketers. Provides reliable, competitively priced electricity from environmentally responsible facilities serving global power markets. Seeks to bring the benefits of competition to all power customers.

Electric Utility Week: The Electric Utility Industry Newsletter. Platts, 2 Penn Plz. New York, NY 10121-2298. Phone: 800-752-8868 or (212)904-2977 Fax: (212)904-4209 E-mail: support@platts.com • URL: http://www.platts.com • Weekly. $1,625.00 per year. Newsletter. Formerly *Electric Week*.

Electrical and Computer Engineering. University of Texas at Austin

Electrical and Computer Engineering Industrial Institute. Purdue University School of Electrical and Computer Engineering

Electrical and Electronic Abstracts. INSPEC, Inc., 379 Thornall St. Edison, NJ 08837-2225. Phone: (732)321-5575 Fax: (732)321-5702 E-mail: inspec@iee.org • URL: http://www.iee.com • Monthly. $3,605.00 per year, with annual cumulation. *Science Abstracts. Section B*.

Electrical Apparatus: Electromechanical Bench Reference Supplement. Barks Publications, Inc., 400 N. Michigan Ave., Suite 900 Chicago, IL 60611-4104. Phone: 800-288-7493 or (312)321-9440 Fax: (312)321-1288 E-mail: eamagazine@aol.com Monthly. $24.00. Included in subscription to *Electric Apparatus Magazine*. Lists 3,000 manufacturers and distributors of electrical and electronic products. Formerly *Electrical Apparatus Magazine. Electromechanical Bench Reference Book*.

Electrical Construction Materials Directory. Underwriters Laboratories, Inc., 33 Pfingsten Rd. Northbrook, IL 60062-2096. Phone: 877-854-3577 or (847)272-8800 E-mail: customerservice.nbk@us.ul.com • URL: http://www.ul.com • Annual. $22.00. Lists construction materials manufacturers authorized to use UL label.

Electrical Contractor. National Electrical Contractors Association, Three Bethesda Metro Center, Suite 1100 Bethesda, MD 20814. Phone: (301)657-3110 Fax: (301)215-4500 E-mail: neca@necanet.org • URL: http://www.ecmag.com • Monthly. Membership.

Electrical Equipment Representatives Association., 638 W 39th St. Kansas City, MO 64111. Phone: (816)561-5323 Fax: (816)561-1249 E-mail: info2005@eera.org • URL: http://www.eera.org • Represents sales agents for manufacturers of electrical equipment used by utilities, industrial firms, and the government.

Electrical Generating Systems Association., 1650 S Dixie Hwy., Ste. 500 Boca Raton, FL 33432-7462. Phone: (561)750-5575 Fax: (561)395-8557 E-mail: e-mail@egsa.org • URL: http://www.egsa.org • Manufacturers, distributor/dealers, and manufacturers' representatives of devices used to generate electrical power through the use of an internal combustion engine or a gas turbine coupled to a generator. Conducts training programs and publishes material on On-Site Power Generation.

Electrical Wholesaling. Primedia Business Magazines and Media, 9800 Metcalf Ave. Overland Park, KS 66212. Phone: 800-795-5445 or (913)341-1300 Fax: (913)967-1898 E-mail: subs@primediabusiness.com • URL: http://www.primediabusiness.com • Monthly. $20.00 per year.

Electrical World T and D Magazine. Platts, 2 Penn Plz., 25th Fl. New York, NY 10121-2298. Phone: 800-752-8878 Fax: (212)904-4209 E-mail: support@platts.com • URL: http://www.platts.com • Monthly. Free to qualified personnel. Formerly*Electrical World*.

Electricity Information. OECD Publications and Information Center, 2001 L St., N.W., Suite 650 Washington, DC 20036-4922. Phone: 800-456-6323 or (202)785-6323 Fax: (202)785-0350 E-mail: washington.contact@oecd.org • URL: http://www.oecdwash.org • Annual. $130.00. Compiled by the International Energy Agency (IEA). Provides detailed electric power statistics for each OECD country, including data on prices, production, and consumption.

Electricity Supply Industry: Structure, Ownership, and Regulation. OECD Publications and Information Center, 2001 L St., N.W., Suite 650 Washington, DC 20036-4922. Phone: 800-456-6323 or (202)785-6323 Fax: (202)785-0350 E-mail: washington.contact@oecd.org • URL: http://www.oecdwash.org • 1994. $113.00. Discusses the "extensive reform" of the electric utility industry that is underway worldwide. Includes profiles of the electricity supply industry.

Electrochemical Analysis and Diagnostic Laboratory.

Electromedical Equipment and Irradiation Equipment, Including X-Ray. U. S. Bureau of the Census, 4700 Silver Hill Rd. Washington, DC 20233-0001. Phone: (301)763-4636 E-mail: comments@census.gov • URL: http://www.census.gov • Annual. Contains shipment quantity, value of shipment, export, and import data. (Current Industrial Report No. MA-38R.)

Electronic Banking Law and Commerce Report. Glasser Legalworks, 150 Clove Rd. Little Falls, NJ 07424. Phone: 800-308-1700 or (973)890-0008 Fax: (973)890-0042 E-mail: orders@glasserlegalworks.com • URL: http://www.glasserlegalworks.com • 10 times a year. $300.00 per year. Newsletter. Provides coverage of the legal aspects of online banking services, bank cards, and "smart phones."

Electronic Business: The Management Magazine for the Electronics Industry. Reed Business Information, 360 Park Ave., S New York, NY 10010. Phone: 800-446-6551 or (646)746-6400 Fax: (646)746-7028 E-mail: corporatecommunications@reedbusiness.com • URL: http://www.reedbusiness.com • Monthly. $100.99 per year. For the non-technical manager and executive in the electronics industry. Offers news, trends, figures and forecasts. Formerly *Electronic Business Today*.

Electronic Commerce World. Thomson Media, One State St. Plaza New York, NY 10004. Phone: 800-221-1809 or (212)803-8200 Fax: (212)843-9635 E-mail: custserv@thomsonmedia.com • URL: http://www.thomsonmedia.com • Monthly. $45.00 per year. Provides practical information on the application of electronic commerce technology. Also covers such items as taxation of e-business, cash management, copyright, and legal issues.

Electronic Commerce World: Business Solutions Through Technology Integration. EC Media Group, 2021 Coolidge St. Hollywood, FL 33020. Phone: (954)925-5900 Fax: (954)-336-4887 • URL: http://www.ecmediagroup.com • Monthly. $45.00 per year. Edited for managers and executives of business-to-business Internet commerce firms. Covers the planning, purchasing, and use of e-commerce services or products.

Electronic Design. Penton Media, Inc., 1300 E 9th St. Cleveland, OH 44114. Phone: (216)696-7000 Fax: (216)696-1752 E-mail: information@penton.com • URL: http://www.penton.com • Biweekly. Free to qualified personnel; others, $100.00 per year. Provides technical information for U.S. design engineers and managers.

Electronic Document Management Systems: A Practical Guide for Evaluators and Users. Thomas M. Koulopoulos. McGraw-Hill, 1221 Ave. of the Americas New York, NY 10020. Phone: 800-722-4726 or (212)512-2000 Fax: (212)512-4502 E-mail: customer.service@mcgraw-hill.com • URL: http://www.mcgraw-hill.com • 1995. $45.00.

Electronic Engineering Times: The Industry Newspaper for Engineers and Technical Management. CMP Publications, Inc., 600 Community Dr. Manhasset, NY 11030. Phone: (516)562-5000 Fax: (516)562-7973 E-mail: cmp@cmp.com • URL: http://www.cmp.com • Weekly. Free to qualified personnel; others, $319.00 per year.

Electronic Frontier Foundation., 454 Shotwell St. San Francisco, CA 94110-1914. Phone: (415)436-9333 Fax: (415)436-9993 E-mail: information@eff.org • URL: http://www.eff.org • Promotes the creation of legal and structural approaches to help ease the assimilation of new technologies by society. Seeks to: help policymakers develop a better understanding of issues underlying telecommunications; increase public understanding of the opportunities and challenges posed by computing and telecommunications fields. Fosters awareness of civil liberties issues arising from the advancements in new computer-based communications media and supports litigation to preserve, protect, and extend First Amendment rights in computing and telecommunications technology. Maintains speakers' bureau; conducts educational programs. Encourages and supports the development of tools to endow non-technical users with access to computer-based telecommunications.

Electronic Funds Transfer Association., 11350 Random Hills Rd., Ste. 800 Fairfax, VA 22030. Phone: (703)934-6052 Fax: (703)934-6058 E-mail: melanierenner@efta.org • URL: http://www.efta.org • Financial institutions, credit card companies, ATM owners, networks and processors, hardware and software manufacturers and e-commerce companies dedicated to the advancement of electronic payment systems and commerce.

Electronic Industries Alliance., 2500 Wilson Blvd. Arlington, VA 22201. Phone: (703)907-7500 Fax: (703)907-7501 E-mail: mflanigan@eia.org • URL: http://www.eia.org • Seeks for the competitiveness of the American producer, represents all companies involved in the design and manufacture of electronic components, parts, systems and equipment for communications, industrial, government and consumer uses.

Electronic Information Report: Empowering Industry Decision Makers Since 1979. SIMBA Information, 11 Riverbend Dr., S Stamford, CT 06907. Phone: 800-307-2529 or (203)358-4100 Fax: (203)358-5824 E-mail: info@simbanet.com • URL: http://www.simbanet.com • 46 times a year. $649.00 per year. Newsletter. Provides business and financial news and trends for online services, electronic publishing, storage media, multimedia, and voice services. Includes information on relevant IPOs (initial public offerings) and mergers. Formerly *Electronic Information Week*.

Electronic Instrument Handbook. Clyde F. Coombs. McGraw-Hill, 1221 Ave. of the Americas New York, NY 10020. Phone: 800-722-4726 or (212)512-2000 Fax: (212)512-4502 E-mail: customer.service@mcgraw-hill.com • URL: http://www.mcgraw-hill.com • 2001. $125.00. Fifth edition. (Engineering Handbook Series).

Electronic Learning. Scholastic, Inc., 557 Broadway New York, NY 10012. Phone: 800-724-6527 or (212)343-6100 Fax: (212)343-4535 • URL: http://www.scholastic.com • Eight times a year. $19.95 per year. Includes classroom applications for computers. For teachers of grades K-12.

The Electronic Library: The International Journal for the Application of Technology in Information Environments. Sage Publications, Inc., 2455 Teller Rd. Thousand Oaks, CA 91320. Phone: 800-818-7243 or (805)499-9774 Fax: 800-583-2665 or (805)499-0871 E-mail: webmaster@sagepub.com • URL: http://www.sagepub.com • Bimonthly. $469.00 per year. Incorporated*Library Computing*.

Electronic Library: The Promise and the Process. Kenneth E. Dowlin. Neal-Schuman Publishers, Inc., 100 William St., Ste. 2004 New York, NY 10038. Phone: (866)672-6657 or (212)925-8650 Fax: (866)209-7932 or (212)219-8916 E-mail: info@neal-schuman.com • URL: http://www.neal-schuman.com • 1984. $45.00. (Applications in Information Management and Technology Series).

Electronic Market Data Book. Consumer Electronics Association, CEA Market Research Dept., 2500 Wilson Blvd. Arlington, VA 22201. Phone: (703)907-7600 Fax: (703)907-7575 E-mail: cea@ce.org • URL: http://www.ce.org • Annual. Price on application.

Electronic Market Trends. Consumer Electronics Association, CEA Market Research Dept., 2500 Wilson Blvd. Arlington, VA 22201. Phone: (703)907-7022 Fax: (703)907-7767 E-mail: cea@ce.org • URL: http://www.ce.org • Monthly. Free to members; non-members, $150.00 per year.

Electronic Media Management. William E. McCavitt and others. Elsevier, 655 Ave. of the Americas New York, NY 10010-5107. Phone: 800-366-2665 or (212)989-5800 Fax: 800-535-9935 or (212)633-3680 E-mail: custserv@elsevier.com • URL: http://www.elsevier.com • 1999. $59.95. Fourth edition.

Electronic Media Ratings. Karen Buzzard. Elsevier, 655 Ave. of the Americas New York, NY 10010-5107. Phone: 800-366-2665 or (212)989-5800 Fax: 800-535-9935 or (212)633-3680 E-mail: custserv@elsevier.com • URL: http://www.elsevier.com • 1992. $22.95. Provides basic information about TV and radio audience-rating techniques. Includes glossary and bibliography. (Electronic Media Guide Series).

Electronic Messaging News: Strategies, Applications, and Standards. PBI Media, LLC, 1201 7 Locks Rd. Potomac, MD 20854. Phone: 800-777-5006 or (301)354-2000 Fax: (301)309-3847 E-mail: clientservices@pbimedia.com • URL: http://www.pbimedia.com • Biweekly. $597.00 per year. Newsletter.

Electronic Musician. Primedia Business Magazines and Media, 6400 Hollis St., Ste. 12 Emeryville, CA 94608. Phone: 800-795-5445 or (510)653-3307 Fax: (510)653-5142 E-mail: subs@primediabusiness.com • URL: http://www.primediabusiness.com • Monthly. $23.97 per year.

Electronic News. Reed Business Information, 360 Park Ave., S New York, NY 10010. Phone: 800-446-6551 or (646)746-6400 Fax: (646)746-7028 E-mail: corporatecommunications@reedbusiness.com • URL: http://www.reedbusiness.com • 51 times a year. $119.00 per year. Serves the electronic OEM industry.

Electronic Office Machines. William R. Pasewark. South-Western, 5191 Natrop Blvd. Mason, OH 45040. Phone: 800-543-0487 or (513)229-1000 • URL: http://www.swcollege.com • 1995. $25.95. Seventh edition.

Electronic Products: The Engineer's Magazine of Product Technology. Hearst Business Communications, UTP Div., 645 Stewart Ave. Garden City, NY 11530. Phone: 800-289-8696 or (516)227-1300 Fax: (516)227-1444 E-mail: lens@electronicproducts.com • URL: http://www.hearstcorp.com • Monthly. $65.00 per year.

Electronic Publishing: Applications and Implications. Myke Gluck and Elisabeth Logan, editors. Information Today, Inc., 143 Old Marlton Pike Medford, NJ 08055-8750. Phone: 800-300-9868 or (609)654-6266 Fax: (609)654-4309 E-mail: custserv@infotoday.com • URL: http://www.infotoday.com • 1997. $34.95. Provides information on copyright, preservation, standards, and other issues relating to the substitution of electronic media for paper-based print.

Electronic Publishing: For the Business Leaders Who Buy Technology. PennWell Corp., Advanced Technology Div., 98 Spit Brook Rd. Nashua, NH 03062-5737. Phone: 800-331-4463 or (603)891-0123 E-mail: atd@pennwell.com • URL: http://www.pennwell.com • Monthly. Free to qualified personnel; others, 55.00 per year. Edited for digital publishing professionals. New products are featured.

Electronic Selling: Twenty-Three Steps to E-Selling Profits. Brian Jamison and others. McGraw-Hill, 1221 Ave. of the Americas New York, NY 10020. Phone: 800-722-4726 or (212)512-2000 Fax: (212)512-4502 E-mail: customer.service@mcgraw-hill.com • URL: http://www.mcgraw-hill.com • 1997. $24.95. Covers selling on the World Wide Web, including security and payment issues. Provides a glossary and directory information. The authors are consultants specializing in Web site production.

Electronic Servicing & Technology: The How-To Magazine of Electronics. CQ Communications, Inc., 25 Newbridge Rd. Hicksville, NY 11801-2805. Phone: 800-853-9797 or (516)681-2922 Fax: (516)681-2926 E-mail: cq@cq-amateur-radio.com • URL: http://www.electronic-servicing.com • Monthly. Free to qualified personnel; others, $26.95 per year. Provides how-to technical information to technicians who service consumer electronics equipment.

Electronic Styles: A Handbook of Citing Electronic Information.

Xia Li and Nancy Crane. Information Today, Inc., 143 Old Marlton Pike Medford, NJ 08055-8750. Phone: 800-300-9868 or (609)654-6266 Fax: (609)654-4309 E-mail: custserv@infotoday.com • URL: http://www.infotoday.com • 1996. $19.99. Second edition. Covers the citing of text-based information, electronic journals, Web sites, CD-ROM items, multimedia products, and online documents.

Electronic Visualization Laboratory, University of Illinois at Chicago, Engineering Research Facility, 842 W. Taylor St., Room 2032 Chicago, IL 60607-7053. Phone: (312)996-3002 Fax: (312)413-7585 E-mail: tom@uic.edu • URL: http://www.evl.uic.edu • Research areas include computer graphics, virtual reality, multimedia, and interactive techniques.

Electronics and Communications Abstracts Journal: Comprehensive Coverage of Essential Scientific Literature. CSA, 7200 Wisconsin Ave., Suite 601 Bethesda, MD 20814. Phone: 800-843-7751 or (301)961-6700 Fax: (301)961-6720 E-mail: service@csa.com • URL: http://www.csa.com • Monthly. $1,665.00 per year. Includes print and online editions.

Electronics Fundamentals: Circuits, Devices, and Applications. Thomas L. Floyd. Prentice Hall PTR, 240 Frisch Ct. Paramus, NJ 07652. Phone: 800-282-0693 Fax: 800-445-6991 • URL: http://www.phptr.com • 2000. $110.00. Fifth edition.

Electronics Representatives Association, 300 W Adams St., Ste. 617 Chicago, IL 60606. Phone: 800-776-7377 or (312)527-3050 Fax: (312)527-3783 E-mail: info@era.org • URL: http://www.era.org • Professional field sales organizations selling components and materials; computer, instrumentation, and data communications products; audiovisual, security, land/mobile communications and commercial sound components, and consumer products to the electronics industry. Sponsors insurance programs and educational conference for members.

Electronics Research Laboratory. University of California at Berkeley

Elementary Linear Programming with Applications. Bernard Kolman and Robert E. Beck. Elsevier, 655 Avenue of the Americas New York, NY 10010-5107. Phone: 800-598-6008 or (212)989-5800 Fax: 800-535-9935 or (212)633-3680 E-mail: custserv@elsevier.com • URL: http://www.elsevier.com • 1995. $44.95. Second edition. Covers the basics of linear programming, with examples of practical applications in commerce. (Computer Science and Scientific Computing Series).

Elements of Bibliography: A Guide to Information Sources and Practical Applications. Robert B. Harmon. Scarecrow Press, Inc., 4501 Forbes Blvd., Ste. 200 Lanham, MD 20706. Phone: 800-462-6420 or (301)459-3366 Fax: (301)429-5748 E-mail: custserv@rowman.com • URL: http://www.scarecrowpress.com • 1998. $55.00. Third edition.

Elements of Bibliography: A Simplified Approach. Robert B. Harmon. Scarecrow Press, Inc., 4501 Forbes Blvd., Ste. 200 Lanham, MD 20706. Phone: 800-462-6420 or (301)459-3366 Fax: 800-338-4550 or (301)429-5748 E-mail: custserv@rowman.com • URL: http://www.scarecrowpress.com • 1989. $37.00. Revised edition.

The Elements of Editing: A Modern Guide for Editors and Journalists. Arthur Plotnik. John Wiley and Sons, Inc., 111 River St. Hoboken, NJ 07030. Phone: 800-225-5945 or (201)748-6000 Fax: (201)748-6088 E-mail: info@wiley.com • URL: http://www.wiley.com • 1986. $5.95.

Elements of Financial Risk Management. Peter F. Christoffersen. Elsevier Butterworth Heinemann, 200 Wheeler Rd., Sixth Floor Burlington, MA 01803. Phone: 800-545-2522 or (781)221-2212 Fax: 800-568-5136 or (781)313-4880 E-mail: usbkinfo@elsevier.com • URL: http://www.books.elsevier.com/finance • 2003. $79.95. Includes material on the various kinds of financial market risk, simulation methods, hedging, options, and evaluation of risk models.

Elements of Photonics. Keigo Iizuka. John Wiley and Sons, Inc., 111 River St. Hoboken, NJ 07030. Phone: 800-225-5945 or (201)748-6000 Fax: (201)748-6088 E-mail: info@wiley.com • URL: http://www.wiley.com • 2002. $200.00. Two volumes. (Pure and Applied Optics Series, vol. 41).

Elevator World. Elevator World, Inc., P.O. Box 6507 Mobile, AL 36660. Phone: 800-730-5093 or (334)479-4514 Fax: (334)479-7403 E-mail: editorial@elevator-world.com • URL: http://www.elevator-world.com • Monthly. $67.00 per year.

Elliott Wave Theorist. Robert Prechter, editor. Elliott Wave International, P.O. Box 1618 Gainesville, GA 30503. Phone: (770)536-0309 Monthly. $233.00 per year. Newsletter Formerly *Elliott Wave Commodity Forecasts*.

Elsevier's Dictionary of Automotive Engineering. A. Schellings. Elsevier, 655 Ave. of the Americas New York, NY 10010-5107. Phone: 800-366-2665 or (212)989-5800 Fax: 800-535-9935 or (212)633-3680 E-mail: custserv@elsevier.com • URL: http://www.elsevier.com • 1998. $149.50.

EM: A&WMA's Environmental Solutions That Make Good Business Sense. Air and Waste Management Association, One Gateway Center, 3rd Fl. Pittsburgh, PA 15222. Phone: 800-270-3444 or (412)232-3444 Fax: (412)232-3450 E-mail: info@awma.org • URL: http://www.awma.org • Monthly. Institutions, $299.00 per year; nonprofit and government agencies, $199.00 per year. Newsletter. Provides news of regulations, legislation, and technology relating to the environment, recycling, and waste control. Formerly *Environmental Manager*.

Embase. Elsevier Science, Inc., 360 Park Ave. S New York, NY 10010. Phone: 888-437-4636 or (212)633-3730 Fax: (212)462-1974 Worldwide medical literature, 1974 to present. Weekly updates. Inquire as to online cost and availability.

Embroidery News. Schiffli Lace and Embroidery Manufacturers Association, 22 Industrial Ave. Fairview, NJ 07022-1614. Phone: (201)943-7757 Fax: (201)943-7793 E-mail: info@schiffli.org • URL: http://www.schiffliusa.com • Description: Features articles of interest to manufacturers of machine-made lace, embroideries, eyelets, appliques, etc. Focuses on the concerns of the industry. Recurring features include a calendar of events, reports, notices of publications available, and columns titled Dropped Stitches and Thoughts to Think About.

eMedia: The Digital Studio Magazine. Online, Inc., 213 Danbury Rd. Wilton, CT 06897-4006. Phone: 800-248-8466 or (203)761-1466 Fax: (203)761-1444 Monthly. $98.00 per year. Covers video production equipment, digital video editing, electronic publishing, digital content streaming, encoding, and other topics related to digital content creation and multimedia. (Formerly published by Online, Inc.)

Emerging Markets Analyst, 1002 Sherbrooke St., W., 16th Fl. Montreal, Canada H3A 3L6. Phone: (514)499-9706 Fax: (514)499-9709 Monthly. $895.00 per year. Provides an annual overview of the emerging financial markets in 24 countries of Latin America, Asia, and Europe. Includes data on international mutual funds and closed-end funds.

Emerging Markets Debt Report. Thomson Media, One State St. Plaza New York, NY 10004. Phone: 800-221-1809 or (212)803-8200 Fax: (212)843-9635 E-mail: custserv@thomsonmedia.com • URL: http://www.thomsonmedia.com • Weekly. $895.00 per year. Newsletter. Provides information on new and prospective sovereign and corporate bond issues from developing countries. Includes an emerging market bond index and pricing data.

Emerging Markets Finance & Trade. M. E. Sharpe, Inc., 80 Business Park Drive Armonk, NY 10504. Phone: 800-541-6563 or (914)273-1800 Fax: (914)273-2106 E-mail: custserv@mesharpe.com • URL: http://www.mesharpe.com • Bimonthly. $1,150.00 per year to institutions; $140.00 to individuals. Provides research papers on developing markets in Europe, Asia, Latin America, the Middle East, and Africa.

Emerging Markets Quarterly. Institutional Investor, Inc., Journals Group, 225 Park Ave., S New York, NY 10003. Phone: 800-945-2034 or (212)224-3066 Fax: (212)224-3472 E-mail: info@iijournals.com • URL: http://www.iijournals.com • Quarterly. Price on application. Newsletter on financial markets in developing areas, such as Africa, Latin America, Southeast Asia, and Eastern Europe. Topics include institutional investment opportunities and regulatory matters. Formerly *Emerging Markets Weekly*.

Emerging Stock Markets Factbook 1999. International Finance Corp., 2121 Pennsylvania Ave., NW Washington, DC 20433. Phone: 800-645-7247 or (202)473-1000 Fax: (202)974-4384 E-mail: book@worldbank.org • URL: http://www.ifc.org • 1998. $150.00. Provides statistical profiles for emerging stock markets in various countries of the world. Includes regional, composite, and industry indexes.

Emerging Trends in Securities Law. West Group, 610 Opperman Dr. Eagan, MN 55123. Phone: 800-328-4880 or (651)687-7000 Fax: 800-340-9378 E-mail: bookstore@westgroup.com • URL: http://www.westgroup.com • Annual. $295.00. Presents a detailed chronicle of events and analysis of evolving trends.(Securities Handbook Series).

Emerson's Directory of Leading U.S. Accounting Firms. Emerson Co., 12342 Northup Way Bellevue, WA 98005. Phone: (425)869-0655 Fax: (425)869-0746 E-mail: emerson@emersoncompany.com • URL: http://www.emersoncompany.com • Biennial. $195.00. Provides information on 500 major CPA firms.

Emerson's Directory of Leading U.S. Law Firms. Emerson Co., 22 College Park Ave. Cambridge, MA 02140-1691. Phone: 800-252-1414 or (617)864-1414 Fax: (617)864-0841 E-mail: info@jhemerson.com • URL: http://www.jhemerson.com • 2000. $195.00. Provides information on major law firms in the United States.

Emerson's Directory of Leading U.S. Technology Consulting Firms. Emerson Co., 22 College Park Ave. Cambridge, MA 02140-1691. Phone: 800-252-1414 or (617)864-1414 Fax: (617)868-0841 E-mail: info@jhemerson.com • URL: http://www.jhemerson.com • 2000. $195.00. Provides information on major consulting firms specializing in technology.

EMILY's List., 1120 Connecticut Ave. NW, Ste. 1100 Washington, DC 20036-3949. Phone: 800-68-EMILY or (202)326-1400 Fax: (202)326-1415 E-mail: information@emilyslist.org • URL: http://www.emilyslist.org • Political network for Democratic women. Seeks to raise campaign funds for the election of pro-choice Democratic women to political office. (EMILY stands for Early +Money is Like Yeast.) **Convention/Meeting:** none.

The Emperor's Virtual Clothes: The Naked Truth About Internet Culture. Dinty Moore. Algonquin Books of Chapel Hill, P.O. Box 2225 Chapel Hill, NC 27515-2225. Phone: (919)967-0108 Fax: (919)933-0272 E-mail: dialogue@algonquin.com • URL: http://www.algonquin.com • 1995. $17.95. A readable consideration of both positive and negative aspects of the Internet.

Employee and Union Member Guide to Labor Law. National

Lawyers Guild. West Group, 610 Opperman Dr. Eagan, MN 55123. Phone: 800-328-4880 or (651)687-7000 Fax: 800-340-9378 E-mail: bookstore@westgroup.com • URL: http://www.westgroup.com • Semiannual. $366.00 per year. Three looseleaf volumes. Labor law for union members.

Employee Assistance Programs: An Annotated Bibliography. Donna Kemp. Garland Publishing, Inc., 29 W. 35th St. New York, NY 10001-2299. Phone: 800-627-6273 or (212)216-7800 Fax: (212)564-7854 E-mail: info@garland.com • URL: http://www.garlandpub.com • 1989. $15.00. (Public Affairs and Administration Series).

Employee Assistance Quarterly. Haworth Press, Inc., 10 Alice St. Binghamton, NY 13904-1580. Phone: 800-429-6784 or (607)722-5857 Fax: 800-895-0582 or (607)722-1424 E-mail: getinfo@haworthpressinc.com • URL: http://www.haworthpressinc.com • Quarterly. $535.00 per year. An academic and practical journal focusing on employee alcoholism and mental health problems. Formerly *Labor-Management Alcoholism Journal*.

Employee Benefit Cases. BNA, Inc., 1231 25th St., NW Washington, DC 20037. Phone: 800-372-1033 E-mail: customercare@bna.com • URL: http://www.bna.com • 50 times a year. $1,269.00 per year. Looseleaf service.

Employee Benefit News: The News Magazine for Employee Benefit Management. Thomson Media, One State St. Plaza New York, NY 10004. Phone: 800-221-1809 or (212)803-8200 Fax: (212)843-9635 E-mail: custserv@thomsonmedia.com • URL: http://www.thomsonmedia.com • Monthly. $94.00 per year. Edited for human relations directors and other managers of employee benefits.

Employee Benefit Plan Review. Charles D. Spencer and Associates, Inc., 250 S. Wacker Dr., Suite 600 Chicago, IL 60606-5834. Phone: (312)993-7900 Fax: (312)993-7910 E-mail: editor@spencernet.com • URL: http://www.spencernet.com • Monthly. $302.00 per year. Provides a review of recent events affecting the administration of employee benefit programs.

Employee Benefit Plans: A Glossary of Terms. Judith A. Sankey, editor. International Foundation of Employee Benefit Plans, 18700 W Bluemound Rd. Brookfield, WI 53045. Phone: 888-334-3327 or (262)786-6710 Fax: 888-217-5960 or (262)786-8670 E-mail: books@ifebp.org • URL: http://www.ifebp.org • 2000. $34.00. 10th edition. Contains updated and new definitions derived from all aspects of the employee benefits field in the U.S. and Canada.

Employee Benefit Research Institute. Employee Benefit Research Institute, 1100 13 St. NW, Ste. 878 Washington, DC 20005. Phone: (202)659-0670 Fax: (202)775-6312 E-mail: salisbury@ebri.org • URL: http://www.ebri.org • Employee benefits in the public and private sectors, including studies on individual retirement accounts, retirement income, flexible benefits, financing health care for the elderly, health care costs, long-term care, employee benefits and federal tax policy, social security, changing benefits, and government regulation of employee benefit plans.

Employee Benefits Digest. International Foundation of Employee Benefit Plans, 18700 W Bluemound Rd., PO Box 69 Brookfield, WI 53045. Phone: 888-334-3327 or (262)786-6700 or (262)786-6700 Fax: 888-217-5960 or (262)786-8780 E-mail: books@ifebp.org • URL: http://www.ifebp.org • Description: Covers the field of employee benefits. Recurring features include notices of publications and educational opportunities, news and announcements for members, and a review of current literature.

Employee Benefits in Medium and Large Private Establishments. Available from U. S. Government Printing Office, Washington, DC 20402. Phone: (202)512-1800 Fax: (202)512-2250 E-mail: gpoaccess@gpo.gov • URL: http://www.access.gpo.gov • Biennial. Issued by Bureau of Labor Statistics, U. S. Department of Labor. Provides data on benefits provided by companies with 100 or more employees. Covers benefits for both full-time and part-time workers, including health insurance, pensions, a wide variety of paid time-off policies (holidays, vacations, personal leave, maternity leave, etc.), and other fringe benefits.

Employee Benefits in Small Private Establishments. Available from U. S. Government Printing Office, Washington, DC 20402. Phone: (202)512-1800 Fax: (202)512-2250 E-mail: gpoaccess@gpo.gov • URL: http://www.access.gpo.gov • Biennial. $12.00. Issued by Bureau of Labor Statistics, U. S. Department of Labor. Supplies data on a wide variety of benefits provided by companies with fewer than 100 employees. Includes statistics for both full-time and part-time workers.

Employee Benefits Infosource. International Foundation of Employee Benefit Plans, P.O. Box 69 Brookfield, WI 53008-0069. Phone: 888-217-5960 or (262)786-6710 Fax: (262)786-8670 Provides citations and abstracts to the literature of employee benefits, 1986 to present. Monthly updates. Inquire as to online cost and availability.

Employee Benefits Journal. International Foundation of Employee Benefit Plans, 18700 W. Bluemound Rd. Brookfield, WI 53045. Phone: 888-334-3327 or (262)786-6700 Fax: 888-217-5960 or (262)786-8670 E-mail: journals@ifebp.org • URL: http://www.ifebp.org • Quarterly. $80.00 per year. Selected articles on timely and important benefit subjects.

Employee Benefits Law: ERISA and Beyond. American Lawyer Media, Inc., 105 Madison Ave. New York, NY 10016. Phone: 800-888-8300 or (212)779-9200 Fax: (212)481-8110 E-mail: lawcatalog@amlaw.com • URL: http://www.lawcatalog.com/ • Looseleaf. $249.00. Two volumes. Updated as needed. Explains the rules and regulations put forth by the Employee Retirement Income Security Act. Three federal agencies are involved: the Internal Revenue Service, the Labor Department, and the Pension Benefit Guaranty Corporation. (Law Journal Press).

Employee Benefits Management. CCH, Inc., 2700 Lake Cook Rd. Riverwoods, IL 60015. Phone: 800-835-5224 or (847)267-7000 E-mail: cust_serv@cch.com • URL: http://www.cch.com • Semimonthly. $839.00 per year. Looseleaf service. Emphasis on pension plans.

Employee Involvement Association., PO Box 2307 Dayton, OH 45401-2307. Phone: (937)586-3724 Fax: (937)586-3699 E-mail: eia@meinet.com • URL: http://www.eianet.org • Represents finance, commerce, industry, and government professionals. Dedicated to the worth, contributions, and benefits of employee suggestion systems and other employee involvement processes. Supports communication between employees and employer for the purpose of exchanging ideas.

Employee Involvement Association—Membership Directory. Employee Involvement Association, PO Box 2307 Dayton, OH 45401-2307. Phone: (937)586-3724 Fax: (937)586-3699 E-mail: eia@eia.meinet.com • URL: http://www.eia.com • Covers: About 400 companies, associations, and federal, state, county, and municipal government agencies operating or contemplating employee suggestion systems or other employee involvement programs. Entries include: Company, association, or agency name; address; employee involvement administrator.

Employee Involvement Association Statistical Report. Employee Involvement Association, 7925 E Lakeview Mesa, AZ 85208. Phone: (480)358-1791 Fax: (408)358-1866 E-mail: eia@assoc-mgmt.com • URL: http://www.eianet.com • Annual. 150.00.

Employee Ownership Report. National Center for Employee Ownership, 1736 Franklin St., 8th Fl. Oakland, CA 94612. Phone: (510)208-1300 Fax: (510)272-9510 E-mail: nceo@nceo.org • URL: http://www.nceo.org • Description: Provides information and news regarding employee ownership, employee stock ownership plans, participation, and communication.

Employee Policy for the Private and Public Sector: State Capitals. Wakeman-Walworth, Inc., PO Box 7376 Alexandria, VA 22307-7376. Phone: 800-876-2545 or (703)768-9600 Fax: (703)768-9690 E-mail: newsletters@statecapitals.com • URL: http://www.statecapitals.com • Weekly. $245.00 per year; print and online editions, $350.00 per year. Newsletter. Formerly *From the State Capitals: Employee Policy for the Private and Public Sector*.

Employee Relocation Council., 1717 Pennsylvania Ave. NW Washington, DC 20006. Phone: 888-801-0005 or (202)857-0857 Fax: (202)659-8631 E-mail: sselleck@njrealestate.com • URL: http://ads4homes.com/erc • Members are major corporations seeking efficiency and minimum disruption when employee transfers take place. Formerly Employee Relocation Real Estate Advisory Council.

Employee Representation: Alternatives and Future Directions. Bruce E. Kaufman and Morris Kleiner, editors. Industrial Realtions Research Association, 504 E Armory Ave. Champaign, IL 61820. Phone: (217)333-0072 Fax: (217)265-5130 E-mail: irra@uiuc.edu • URL: http://www.irra.uiuc.edu • 1993. $35.00. (Industrial Relations Research Association Series).

Employee Services Management Association., 568 Spring Rd., Ste. D Elmhurst, IL 60126-3896. Phone: (630)559-0020 Fax: (630)559-0025 E-mail: esmahq@esmassn.org • URL: http://www.esmassn.org • Corporations and governmental agencies that sponsor recreation, fitness, and service programs for their employees; associate members are manufacturers and suppliers in the employee recreation market and distributors of consumer products and services. Serves as an information resource network for members nationwide. Implements and maintains a diverse range of employee services; believes that employee services, as practical solutions to work/life issues, are essential to sound business management. Conducts programs that improves relations between employees and management, increases overall productivity, boosts morale, and reduces absenteeism and turnover. Covers the 10 Components of a Well-Rounded Employee Services Program such as employee stores, convenience services, recognition programs, recreation programs, travel services, and special events.

Employee Services Management: The Journal of Employee Services Recreation, Heal th and Education. Employee Services Management, 2211 York Rd., Ste. 207 Oak Brook, IL 60523-2371. Phone: (630)368-1280 Fax: (630)368-1286 E-mail: esmahq@esmassh.org • URL: http://www.esmassn.org • Bimonthly. Free to members; non-members, $52.00 per year.

Employee Terminations Law Bulletin. Quinlan Publishing Co., Marine Industrial Park, 23 Drydock Ave. 6th Fl. Boston, MA 02210-2387. Phone: 800-229-2084 or (617)542-0048 Fax: (617)345-9646 E-mail: info@quinlan.com Description: Advises employers on preventable errors and lawful procedure regarding employee dismissal. Reports on court decisions involving employee terminations.

Employers Council on Flexible Compensation., 927 15th St., N.W., Suite 1000 Washington, DC 20005. Phone: (202)659-4300 Fax: (202)371-1467 E-mail: info@ecfc.org • URL: http://www.ecfc.org • Promotes flexible or "cafeteria" plans for employee compensation and benefits.

Employer's Guide to Discrimination Laws. Maureen F. Moore. LexisNexis Matthew Bender, 1275 Broadway Albany, NY 12204-4026. Phone: 800-424-4200 or (518)487-3000 Fax: 800-828-8341 or (518)487-3584 E-mail: customer.support@lexisnexis.com • URL: http://www.lexisnexis.com/matthewbender/ • 2003. $28.00, including CD-ROM. Edited for business owners and managers. Provides a concise guide to federal discrimination laws relating to race, sex, age, disability, pregnancy, religion, and national origin.

Employment Agency. Entrepreneur Media, Inc., 2445 McCabe Way Irvine, CA 92614. Phone: 800-421-2300 or (949)261-2325 Fax: (949)261-0234 E-mail: entmag@entrepreneur.com • URL: http://www.entrepreneur.com • Looseleaf. $59.50. A practical guide to starting an employment agency. Covers profit potential, start-up costs, market size evaluation, owner's time required, site selection, lease negotiation, pricing, accounting, advertising, promotion, etc. (Start-Up Business Guide No. E1051.)

Employment and Earnings. Available from U. S. Government Printing Office, Washington, DC 20402. Phone: (202)512-1800 Fax: (202)512-2250 E-mail: gpoaccess@gpo.gov • URL: http://www.access.gpo.gov • Monthly. $50.00 per year, including annual supplement. Produced by the Bureau of Labor Statistics, U. S. Department of Labor. Provides current data on employment, hours, and earnings for the U. S. as a whole, for states, and for more than 200 local areas.

Employment and Training Reporter. MII Publications, Inc., 733 15th St., N.W., Suite 900 Washington, DC 20005-2112. Phone: (202)347-4822 or 800-524-8960 Fax: (202)347-4893 E-mail: service@miipublications.com • URL: http://www.millpublications.com • Weekly. $897.00 per year. Looseleaf service. Two volumes. Online edition, $747.00 per year.

Employment and Wages: Annual Averages. Available from U. S. Government Printing Office, Washington, DC 20402. Phone: (202)512-1800 Fax: (202)512-2250 E-mail: gpoaccess@gpo.gov • URL: http://www.access.gpo.gov • Annual. $53.00. Issued by the Bureau of Labor Statistics, U. S. Department of Labor. Presents a wide variety of data arranged by state and industry.

Employment Discrimination: Law and Litigation. Lexis Law Publishing, P.O. Box 7587 Charlottesville, VA 22906-7587. Phone: 800-562-1197 or (804)972-7600 Fax: (804)972-7666 E-mail: customer.support@lexis-nexis.com • URL: http://www.lexispublishing.com • $185.00 per year. Two looseleaf volumes. Periodic supplementation. Covers employment provisions of the Civil Rights Act, the Equal Pay Act, and related topics.

Employment Equity and Affirmative Action: An International Comparison. Harish C. Jain and others. M. E. Sharpe, Inc., 80 Business Park Drive Armonk, NY 10504. Phone: 800-541-6563 or (914)273-1800 Fax: (914)273-2106 E-mail: custserv@mesharpe.com • URL: http://www.mesharpe.com • 2003. $66.95. Describes and compares the affirmative action and employment equity policies of six countries: the U. S., Canada, Great Britain, India, South Africa, and Malaysia.

Employment Forms and Policies. LexisNexis Matthew Bender, 1275 Broadway Albany, NY 12204-4026. Phone: 800-424-4200 or (518)487-3000 Fax: 800-828-8341 or (518)487-3584 E-mail: customer.support@lexisnexis.com • URL: http://www.lexisnexis.com/matthewbender/ • Looseleaf. $120.00, including CD-ROM. Periodic supplementation available. Contains more than 300 forms, policies, and checklists for use by small or medium-sized businesses. Covers such topics as employee selection, payroll issues, benefits, performance appraisal, dress codes, and employee termination.

Employment Law Guide to the Americans with Disabilities Act. Mark Daniels. Prentice Hall PTR, 240 Frisch Ct. Paramus, NJ 07652. Phone: 800-282-0693 Fax: 800-445-6991 • URL: http://www.phptr.com • 1992. $95.00.

Employment Law Strategist. Law Journal Newsletter, 105 Madison Ave. New York, NY 10016. Phone: 800-603-6571 or (212)313-9300 Fax: (212)481-8110 E-mail: lawcatalog@amlaw.com • URL: http://www.lawcatalog.com/ • Monthly. 279 individuals for print version per year. Covers employment law topics, including immigration laws, repetitive stress claims, workplace violence, liability of actions of intoxicated employees, record keeping, liability for fetal injury, independent contractor, and employee issues. Monthly. 229 individuals electronic edition. Description: Reports on legal strategy and substantive developments in the area of matrimonial law, including such topics as tax considerations, custody, visitation, division of property, and valuation. Recurring features include litigation roundup and a legislative update.

Employment Litigation Reporter: The National Journal of Record for Termination Lawsuits Alleging Tort and Contract Claims Against Employers. Andrews Publications, 175 Strafford Ave., Bldg. 4, Suite 140 Wayne, PA 19087. Phone: 800-345-1101 or (610)225-0510 Fax: (610)225-0501 E-mail: customer@andrewspub.com • URL: http://www.andrewspub.com • Semimonthly. $825.00 per year. Newsletter. Provides reports on wrongful dismissal lawsuits.

Employment Outlook, 1998-2008: A Summary of BLS Projections. Available from U. S. Government Printing Office, Washington, DC 20402. Phone: (202)512-1800 Fax: (202)512-2250 E-mail: gpoaccess@gpo.gov • URL: http://

www.access.gpo.gov • 2000. $10.00. Issued by the Bureau of Labor Statistics, U. S. Department of Labor (http://www.bls.gov). Provides 1998 employment data and 2008 projections for a wide variety of managerial, professional, technical, marketing, clerical, service, agricultural, and production occupations. Includes factors affecting the employment growth of various industries. (Bureau of Labor Statistics Bulletin 2522.)

Employment Practice Guide. CCH, Inc., 2700 Lake Cook Rd. Riverwoods, IL 60015. Phone: 800-835-5224 or (847)267-7000 E-mail: cust_serv@cch.com • URL: http://www.cch.com • Weekly. $1,129.00 per year. Four looseleaf volumes.

Employment Practices Update. West Group, 610 Opperman Dr. Eagan, MN 55123. Phone: 800-328-4880 or (651)687-7000 Fax: 800-340-9378 E-mail: compandbene@westgroup.com • URL: http://www.westgroup.com • Description: Discusses such topics as employment decisions, willful violations, reduction-in-force terminations, age discrimination, and erroneous credibility determinations.

Employment Safety and Health Guide. CCH, Inc., 2700 Lake Cook Rd. Riverwoods, IL 60015. Phone: 800-835-5224 or (847)267-7000 E-mail: cust_serv@cch.com • URL: http://www.cch.com • Weekly. $1,139.00 per year. Four looseleaf volumes.

Employment Termination: Rights and Remedies. William J. Holloway and Michael J. Leech. BNA, Inc., 1231 25th St., NW Washington, DC 20037. Phone: 800-372-1033 E-mail: customercare@bna.com • URL: http://www.bna.com • 1993. $145.00. Second edition. Discusses employment contracts and wrongful-discharge claims.

EMTA-Trade Association for the Emerging Markets., 360 Madison Ave., 18th Fl. New York, NY 10017. Phone: (646)637-9100 Fax: (646)637-9128 • URL: http://www.emta.org • Promotes orderly trading markets for emerging market instruments. Formerly Emerging Markets Traders Association.

Emulsion Polymers Institute., Lehigh University, Iacocca Hall, 111 Research Dr. Bethlehem, PA 18015. Phone: (610)758-3590 Fax: (610)758-5880 E-mail: mse0@lehigh.edu • URL: http://www.lehigh.edu/ • Includes latex paint research.

Encyclopedia of Accounting Systems. Tom M. Plank and Lois R. Plank. Prentice Hall Books, 200 Old Tappan Rd. Old Tappen, NJ 07675. Phone: 800-282-0693 Fax: 800-835-5327 or (201)236-7141 • URL: http://www.prenhall.com • 1994. $132.00. Three volumes.

Encyclopedia of Advanced Materials. David Bloor and others. Elsevier, 655 Ave. of the Americas New York, NY 10010-5107. Phone: 800-366-2665 or (212)989-5800 Fax: 800-535-9935 or (212)633-3680 E-mail: custserv@elsevier.com • URL: http://www.elsevier.com • 1994. $1,534.00. Four volumes.

Encyclopedia of Aging. David J. Ekerdt, editor. Available from Gale Cengage Learning, 27500 Drake Rd. Farmington Hills, MI 48331-3535. Phone: 800-877-GALE or (248)699-4253 Fax: 800-414-5043 E-mail: gale.galeord@cengage.com • URL: http://gale.cengage.com • 2002. $450.00. Four volumes. Published by Macmillan Reference USA. Includes articles relating to the financial aspects of aging, such as housing, long-term care insurance, pensions, social security, individual retirement accounts, savings, and retirement planning.

Encyclopedia of Agriculture Science. Charles J. Arntzen and Ellen M. Ritter, editors. Elsevier, 655 Avenue of the Americas New York, NY 10010-5107. Phone: 800-366-2665 or (212)989-5800 Fax: 800-535-9935 or (212)633-3680 E-mail: custserv@elsevier.com • URL: http://www.elsevier.com • 1994. $900.00. Four volumes.

Encyclopedia of Agrochemicals. Jack R. Plimmer. John Wiley and Sons, Inc., 111 River St. Hoboken, NJ 07030. Phone: 800-225-5945 or (201)748-6000 Fax: (201)748-6088 E-mail: bookinfo@wiley.com • URL: http://www.wiley.com • 2003. $945.00. Three volumes. Includes pesticides, animal food additives, veterinary drugs, and other compounds.

Encyclopedia of AIDS: A Social, Political, Cultural, and Scientific Record of the HIV Epidemic. Raymond A. Smith, editor. Fitzroy Dearborn Publishers, Inc., 919 Michigan Ave., Ste. 760 Chicago, IL 60611. Phone: 800-850-8102 or (312)587-0131 Fax: (312)587-1049 E-mail: fitzroy@aol.com • URL: http://www.fitzroydearborn.com • 1998. $135.00. Emphasis is historical, covering the years 1981 to 1996. Includes information on AIDS law, policy, and activism.

Encyclopedia of American Facts and Dates. Gorton Carruth. HarperInformation, 10 E. 53rd St. New York, NY 10022-5299. Phone: 800-242-7737 or (212)207-7000 Fax: 800-822-4090 or (212)207-7145 • URL: http://www.harpercollins.com • 1997. $50.00. 10th edition. (Encyclopedia of American Facts and Dates Series).

Encyclopedia of American Industries. Gale Cengage Learning, 27500 Drake Rd. Farmington Hills, MI 48331-3535. Phone: 800-877-GALE or (248)699-4253 Fax: 800-414-5043 E-mail: gale.galeord@cengage.com • URL: http://gale.cengage.com • 2000. $560.00. Third edition. Two volumes. $280.00 per volume. Volume one is *Manufacturing Industries* and volume two is *Service and Non-Manufacturing Industries*. Provides the history, development, and recent status of approximately 1,000 industries. Includes statistical graphs, with industry and general indexes.

Encyclopedia of American Prisons. Carl Sifakis. Facts on File Inc., 29 W. 35th St. New York, NY 10001-2299. Phone: 800-627-6273 or (212)216-7800 Fax: (212)564-7854 E-mail: info@garland.com • URL: http://www.garlandpub.com • 2002. $75.00. Crime Library.

Encyclopedia of American Silver Manufacturers. Dorothy T. Rainwater and others. Schiffer Publishing, Ltd., 4880 Lower Valley Rd. Atglen, PA 19310. Phone: (610)593-1777 Fax: (610)593-2002 E-mail: schifferbk@aol.com • URL: http://www.schifferbooks.com • 2003. $29.95. Fifth revised edition.

Encyclopedia of Aquaculture. Robert R. Stickney. John Wiley and Sons, Inc., 111 River St. Hoboken, NJ 07030. Phone: 800-225-5945 or (201)748-6000 Fax: (201)748-6088 E-mail: info@wiley.com • URL: http://www.wiley.com • 2000. $415.00. Includes both economic and biological aspects of aquaculture and fish farming.

Encyclopedia of Associations. Gale Cengage Learning, 27500 Drake Rd. Farmington Hills, MI 48331-3535. Phone: 800-877-GALE or (248)699-4253 Fax: 800-414-5043 E-mail: gale.galeord@cengage.com • URL: http://gale.cengage.com • Annual. $1,530.00. Three volumes. Volume 1, National Organizations, $585.00; Volume 2, Geographic and Executive Indexes, $460.00; Volume 3, supplement, $485.00.

Encyclopedia of Associations CD-ROM. Gale Cengage Learning, 27500 Drake Rd. Farmington Hills, MI 48331-3535. Phone: 800-877-GALE or (248)699-GALE Fax: 800-414-5043 or (248)699-8069 E-mail: galeord@gale.com • URL: http://gale.cengage.com • Semiannual. $1,095.00 per year, single user; $1,895.00 per year, network. Available for IBM or MAC. Provides detailed CD-ROM information on over 170,000 international, national, regional, state, and local organizations. Corresponds to the various volumes and supplements that make up the Gale *Encyclopedia of Associations* series.

Encyclopedia of Associations: International Organizations. Gale Cengage Learning, 27500 Drake Rd. Farmington Hills, MI 48331-3535. Phone: 800-877-GALE or (248)699-4253 Fax: 800-414-5043 E-mail: gale.galeord@cengage.com • URL: http://gale.cengage.com • Annual. $695.00. Two volumes. Includes detailed information on approximately 24,000 international nonprofit membership organizations.

Encyclopedia of Associations [Online]. Gale Cengage Learning, 27500 Drake Rd. Farmington Hills, MI 48331-3535. Phone: 800-877-GALE or (248)669-GALE Fax: 800-414-5043 or (248)699-8069 E-mail: galeord@gale.com • URL: http://gale.cengage.com • Provides detailed information on about 170,000 U. S. and International non-profit organizations. Semiannual updates. Inquire as to online cost and availability.

Encyclopedia of Associations: Regional, State, and Local Organizations. Gale Cengage Learning, 27500 Drake Rd. Farmington Hills, MI 48331-3535. Phone: 800-877-GALE or (248)699-4253 Fax: 800-414-5043 E-mail: gale.galeord@cengage.com • URL: http://gale.cengage.com • Annual. $660.00. Five volumes. $170.00 per volume. Each volume covers a particular region of the U. S.

Encyclopedia of Banking and Finance. Charles J. Woelfel. McGraw-Hill, 1221 Ave. of the Americas New York, NY 10020. Phone: 800-722-4726 or (212)512-2000 Fax: (212)512-4502 E-mail: customer-service@mcgraw-hill.com • URL: http://www.mcgraw-hill.com • 1996. $150.00. 10th revised edition. Includes CD-ROM.

Encyclopedia of Business. Gale Cengage Learning, 27500 Drake Rd. Farmington Hills, MI 48331-3535. Phone: 800-877-GALE or (248)699-4253 Fax: 800-414-5043 E-mail: gale.galeord@cengage.com • URL: http://gale.cengage.com • 2000. $425.00. Second edition. Two volumes. Contains more than 700 signed articles covering major business disciplines and concepts. International in scope. (Encyclopedia of Business Series).

Encyclopedia of Business and Finance. Burton Kaliski, editor. Available from Gale Cengage Learning, 27500 Drake Rd. Farmington Hills, MI 48331-3535. Phone: 800-877-GALE or (248)699-GALE Fax: 800-414-5043 E-mail: gale.galeord@cengage.com • URL: http://gale.cengage.com • 2001. $275.00. Two volumes. Published by Macmillan Reference USA. Contains articles by various contributors on accounting, business administration, banking, finance, management information systems, and marketing.

Encyclopedia of Careers and Vocational Guidance. Holli Cosgrove. Fact on File Inc., 132 W 31st St., 17th Fl. New York, NY 10001. Phone: 800-322-8755 Fax: 800-678-3633 • URL: http://www.factsonfile.com • 2002. 12th edition. Price on application.

Encyclopedia of Chart Patterns. Thomas N. Bulkowski. John Wiley and Sons, Inc., 111 River St. Hoboken, NJ 07030. Phone: 800-225-5945 or (201)748-6000 Fax: (201)748-6088 E-mail: info@wiley.com • URL: http://www.wiley.com • 2000. $79.95. Provides explanations of the predictive value of various chart patterns formed by stock and commodity price movements. (Trading Series).

Encyclopedia of Climate and Weather. Stephen H. Schneider, editor. Oxford University Press, 198 Madison Ave. New York, NY 10016-4314. Phone: 800-451-7556 or (212)726-6000 Fax: (212)726-6440 E-mail: custserv@oup-usa.org • URL: http://www.oup-usa.org • 1996. $275.00. Two volumes. Contains more than 300 multidisciplinary entries, with photographs, line drawings, and charts.

Encyclopedia of Communication and Information. Available from Gale Cengage Learning, 27500 Drake Rd. Farmington Hills, MI 48331-3535. Phone: 800-877-GALE or (248)699-GALE Fax: 800-414-5043 E-mail: gale.galeord@cengage.com • URL: http://gale.cengage.com • 2001. $395.00. Three volumes. Published by Macmillan Reference USA.

Encyclopedia of Computer Science and Technology. Marcel Dekker, Inc., 270 Madison Ave. New York, NY 10016. Phone: 800-228-1160 or (212)696-9000 Fax: (212)685-4540 E-mail: bookorders@dekker.com • URL: http://www.dekker.com • Dates vary. 45 volumes. $8,775.00. $195.00 per volume. Contains scholarly articles written by computer experts. Includes bibliographies.

Encyclopedia of Corporate Meetings, Minutes and Resolutions. William Sardell, editor. Prentice Hall PTR, 240 Frisch Ct. Paramus, NJ 07652. Phone: 800-282-0693 Fax: 800-445-6991 • URL: http://www.phptr.com • 1985. $125.00. Third edition. Two volumes.

Encyclopedia of Crime and Justice. Available from Gale Cengage Learning, 27500 Drake Rd. Farmington Hills, MI 48331-3535. Phone: 800-877-GALE or (248)699-GALE Fax: 800-414-5043 E-mail: gale.galeord@cengage.com • URL: http://gale.cengage.com • 2001. $475.00. Second edition. Four volumes. Published by Macmillan Reference USA. Contains extensive information on a wide variety of topics pertaining to crime, criminology, social issues, and the courts. (A complete revision of 1982 edition.)

Encyclopedia of Crime and Punishment. David Levinson, editor. Sage Publications, Inc., 2455 Teller Rd. Thousand Oaks, CA 91320. Phone: 800-818-7243 or (805)499-9774 Fax: 800-583-2665 or (805)499-0871 E-mail: webmaster@sagepub.com • URL: http://www.sagepub.com • 2002. $600.00. Four volumes. Contains 425 signed entries dealing with civil, criminal, media, corporate, and international issues. Includes material on fraud, police science, correctional institutions, social matters, methodology, national surveys, and crime statistics.

Encyclopedia of Distributed Learning. Anna DiStefano and others, editors. Sage Publications, Inc., 2455 Teller Rd. Thousand Oaks, CA 91320-2218. Phone: 800-818-7243 or (805)499-0721 Fax: 800-583-2665 or (805)499-0871 E-mail: info@sagepub.com • URL: http://www.sagepub.com • 2004. $125.00. Contains 275 entries on contemporary continuing education and distance learning for adults in corporate, academic, and other settings.

Encyclopedia of Drugs, Alcohol, and Addictive Behavior. Available from Gale Cengage Learning, 27500 Drake Rd. Farmington Hills, MI 48331-3535. Phone: 800-877-GALE or (248)699-GALE Fax: 414-5043 E-mail: gale.galeord@cengage.com • URL: http://www.galegroup.com • 2001. $425.00. Second edition. Four volumes. Published by Macmillan Reference USA. Covers the social, economic, political, and medical aspects of addiction.

Encyclopedia of Emerging Industries. Gale Cengage Learning, 27500 Drake Rd. Farmington Hills, MI 48331-3535. Phone: 800-877-GALE or (248)699-4253 Fax: 800-414-5043 E-mail: gale.galeord@cengage.com • URL: http://gale.cengage.com • 2001. $320.00. Fourth edition. Provides detailed information on 115 "newly flourishing" industries. Includes historical background, organizational structure, significant individuals, current conditions, major companies, work force, technology trends, research developments, and other industry facts.

Encyclopedia of Energy. Cutler J. Cleveland, editor. Elsevier, Inc., 360 Park Ave. South New York, NY 10010. Phone: 888-437-4636 or (212)989-5800 Fax: (212)633-3990 E-mail: usinfo@elsevier.com • URL: http://www.books.elsevier.com/us/ • 2004. $1,560.00. Six volumes. Covers all aspects of energy sources and energy-related environmental issues.

Encyclopedia of Environmental Science. John Mongillo and Linda Zierdt-Warshaw, editors. Greenwood Publishing Group, Inc., 88 Post Rd., W. Westport, CT 06881. Phone: 800-225-5800 or (203)226-3571 Fax: (203)431-2214 E-mail: customer-service@greenwood.com • URL: http://www.greenwood.com • 2000. $99.95. Provides information on more than 1,000 topics relating to the environment. Includes graphs, tables, maps, illustrations, and 400 Web site addresses.

Encyclopedia of Environmental Science and Engineering. James R. Pfafflin and Edward N. Ziegler, editors. Gordon and Breach Publishing Group, 29 W 35th St. New York, NY 10001. Phone: 800-634-7064 or (212)216-7800 Fax: (212)564-7854 E-mail: ncarter@taylorandfrancis.com • URL: http://www.gbhap.com • $798.00. Three volumes.

Encyclopedia of Estate Planning. Robert S. Holzman. Boardroom Books, 55 Railroad Ave. Greenwich, CT 06836-2614. Phone: (203)625-5900 Fax: (203)861-7443 1995. $59.00. Second revised edition.

Encyclopedia of Food and Culture. Gale Cengage Learning, 27500 Drake Rd. Farmington Hills, MI 48331-3535. Phone: 800-877-GALE or (248)699-4253 Fax: 800-414-5043 E-mail: gale.galeord@cengage.com • URL: http://gale.cengage.com • 2002. $395.00. Three volumes. Contains 600 articles covering various aspects of food and its place in society, from agronomy to zucchini. Includes illustrations and a detailed index.

Encyclopedia of Food Science, Food Technology, and Nutrition. Robert Macrae and others, editors. Elsevier, 655 Avenue of the Americas New York, NY 10010-5107. Phone: 800-366-2665 or (212)989-5800 Fax: 800-535-9935 or (212)633-3680 E-mail: custserv@elsevier.com • URL: http://www.elsevier.com • 1993. Eight volumes. $3,056.00. $382.00 per volume.

Encyclopedia of Global Change: Environmental Change and

SOURCES CITED

Human Society. Andrew S. Goudie, editor. Oxford University Press, 198 Madison Ave. New York, NY 10016-4314. Phone: 800-451-7556 or (212)726-6000 Fax: (212)726-6440 E-mail: custserv@oup-usa.org • URL: http://www.oup-usa.org • 2001. $275.00. Two volumes. Contains 300 signed articles on a wide variety of topics relating to changes in the environment and the atmosphere. Includes bibliographies and illustrations.

Encyclopedia of Global Environmental Change. R. E. Munn. John Wiley and Sons, Inc., 111 River St. Hoboken, NJ 07030. Phone: 800-225-5945 or (201)748-6000 Fax: (201)748-6088 E-mail: info@wiley.com • URL: http://www.wiley.com • 2001. $2,400.00. Five volumes. Volume five is entitled *Social and Economic Dimensions of Global Environmental Change*.

Encyclopedia of Global Industries. Gale Cengage Learning, 27500 Drake Rd. Farmington Hills, MI 48331-3535. Phone: 800-877-GALE or (248)699-4253 Fax: 800-414-5043 E-mail: gale.galeord@cengage.com • URL: http://gale.cengage.com • 2002. $450.00. Third edition. Provides detailed statistical information on 115 industries. Coverage is international, with country and subject indexes.

Encyclopedia of Governmental Advisory Organizations. Gale Cengage Learning, 27500 Drake Rd. Farmington Hills, MI 48331-3535. Phone: 800-877-GALE or (248)699-4253 Fax: 800-414-5043 E-mail: gale.galeord@cengage.com • URL: http://gale.cengage.com • 2003. $685.00. 18th edition. Contains more than 7,300 entries describing activities and personnel. Complete contact information.

Encyclopedia of Health Care Management. Michael Stahl, editor. Sage Publications, Inc., 2455 Teller Rd. Thousand Oaks, CA 91320-2218. Phone: 800-818-7243 or (805)499-0721 Fax: 800-583-2665 or (805)499-0871 E-mail: info@sagepub.com • URL: http://www.sagepub.com • 2004. $150.00. Contains 600 entries covering "the business of health care."

Encyclopedia of Health Information Sources. Gale Cengage Learning, 27500 Drake Rd. Farmington Hills, MI 48331-3535. Phone: 800-877-GALE or (248)699-4253 Fax: 800-414-5043 E-mail: gale.galeord@cengage.com • URL: http://gale.cengage.com • 1993. $180.00. Second edition. Both print and nonprint sources of information are listed for 450 health-related topics.

Encyclopedia of Homelessness. David Levinson, editor. Sage Publications, Inc., 2455 Teller Rd. Thousand Oaks, CA 91320-2218. Phone: 800-818-7243 or (805)499-0721 Fax: 800-583-2665 or (805)499-0871 E-mail: info@sagepub.com • URL: http://www.sagepub.com • 2004. $295.00. Two volumes. Topics relating to homelessness include Causes, Health Issues, History in the United States, Legal Issues, and Organizations. Contains about 150 entries, arranged alphabetically, by various contributors. Appendices provide additional features, such as examples of homelessness in film and literaure. Includes extensive bibliographic information.

Encyclopedia of Housing. Willem van Vliet, editor. Sage Publications, Inc., 2455 Teller Rd. Thousand Oaks, CA 91320. Phone: 800-818-7243 or (805)499-9774 Fax: 800-583-2665 or (805)499-0871 E-mail: webmaster@sagepub.com • URL: http://www.sagepub.com • 1998. $216.00. Contains 500 entries covering all aspects of housing. Includes index of names and subjects.

Encyclopedia of Human Behavior. Vangipuram S. Ramachandran, editor. Elsevier, 655 Avenue of the Americas New York, NY 10010-5107. Phone: 800-366-2665 or (212)989-5800 Fax: 800-535-9935 or (212)633-3680 E-mail: custserv@elsevier.com • URL: http://www.elsevier.com • 1994. $1,000.00. Four volumes. Contains signed articles on aptitude testing, arbitration, career development, consumer psychology, crisis management, decision making, economic behavior, group dynamics, leadership, motivation, negotiation, organizational behavior, planning, problem solving, stress, work efficiency, and other human behavior topics applicable to business situations.

Encyclopedia of Information Systems. Hossein Bidgoli, editor. Elsevier, 655 Avenue of the Americas New York, NY 10010-5107. Phone: 800-366-2665 or (212)989-5800 Fax: 800-535-9935 or (212)663-3680 E-mail: custserv@elsevier.com • URL: http://www.elsevier.com • 2002. $1,200.00. Four volumes. Contains a wide range of articles relating to computers, databases, communication, and information technology. The 200 topics include coverage of hardware, software, artificial intelligence, the Internet, networks, knowledge management, electronic commerce, search engines, and systems design.

Encyclopedia of Interior Design. Joanna Banham, editor. Fitzroy Dearborn Publishers, Inc., 919 N. Michigan Ave., Suite 760 Chicago, IL 60611. Phone: 800-850-8102 or (312)587-0131 Fax: (312)587-1049 E-mail: fitzroy@aol.com • URL: http://www.fitzroydearborn.com • 1997. $295.00. Two volumes. Contains more than 500 essays on interior design topics. Includes bibliographies.

Encyclopedia of Labor History Worldwide. Gale Cengage Learning, 27500 Drake Rd. Farmington Hills, MI 48331-3535. Phone: 800-877-GALE Fax: 800-414-5043 or (248)699-8069 E-mail: galeord@galegroup.com • URL: http://www.galegroup.com • 2003. $295.00. Two volumes. Cover 300 key events, national and international, that took place in labor history over the past 200 years. Includes illustrations, maps, a glossary, a bibliography, and indexes. (St. James Press imprint.)

Encyclopedia of Law Enforcement. Larry E. Sullivan, editor. Sage Publications, Inc., 2455 Teller Rd. Thousand Oaks, CA 91320-2218. Phone: 800-818-7243 or (805)499-0721 Fax: 800-583-2665 or (805)499-0871 E-mail: info@sagepub.com • URL: http://www.sagepub.com • 2004. $295.00. Two volumes. Contains more than 400 entries by 250 contributors. Covers a wide variety of topics relating to local, state, federal, and international law enforcement and investigation.

Encyclopedia of Leadership. George R. Goethals and Georgia Sorenson, editors. Sage Publications, Inc., 2455 Teller Rd. Thousand Oaks, CA 91320-2218. Phone: 800-818-7243 or (805)499-0721 Fax: 800-583-2665 or (805)499-0871 E-mail: info@sagepub.com • URL: http://www.sagepub.com • 2004. $595.00. Four volumes. Contains articles written by "400 leading scholars and experts from 17 countries, exploring leadership theories and leadership practice." Includes many case studies and biographical essays.

Encyclopedia of Legal Information Sources. Gale Cengage Learning, 27500 Drake Rd. Farmington Hills, MI 48331-3535. Phone: 800-877-GALE or (248)699-4253 Fax: 800-414-5043 E-mail: gale.galeord@cengage.com • URL: http://gale.cengage.com • 1992. $180.00. Second edition. Lists more than 23,000 law-related information sources, including print, nonprint, and organizational.

Encyclopedia of Library and Information Science. Allen Kent and others, editors. Marcel Dekker, Inc., 270 Madison Ave. New York, NY 10016. Phone: 800-228-1160 or (212)696-9000 Fax: (212)685-4540 E-mail: bookorders@dekker.com • URL: http://www.dekker.com • 73 volumes. Dates vary. Prices vary.

Encyclopedia of Major Marketing Campaigns. Gale Cengage Learning, 27500 Drake Rd. Farmington Hills, MI 48331-3535. Phone: 800-877-GALE or (248)699-4253 Fax: 800-414-5043 E-mail: gale.galeord@cengage.com • URL: http://gale.cengage.com • 2000. $285.00. Covers 500 major marketing and advertising campaigns "of the 20th century." Examines historical context, target market, expectations, competition, strategy, development, and outcomes. Includes illustrations.

Encyclopedia of Materials: Science and Technology. K.H.J. Buschow and others, editors. Elsevier, 360 Park Ave. S New York, NY 10010-1710. Phone: 800-437-4636 or (212)633-3730 Fax: (212)633-3680 E-mail: usinfo@elsevier.com • URL: http://www.elsevier.com • 2001. $4,985.00. Eleven volumes. Provides extensive technical information on a wide variety of materials, including metals, ceramics, plastics, optical materials, and building materials. Includes more than 2,000 articles and 5,000 illustrations.

Encyclopedia of Medical Organizations and Agencies. Gale Cengage Learning, 27500 Drake Rd. Farmington Hills, MI 48331-3535. Phone: 800-877-GALE or (248)699-4253 Fax: 800-414-5043 E-mail: gale.galeord@cengage.com • URL: http://gale.cengage.com • 2001. $295.00. 11th edition. Information on over 18,000 public and private organizations in medicine and related fields.

Encyclopedia of Mental Health. Ada P. Kahn and Jan Fawcett. Facts on File, Inc., 132 W 31st St., 17th Fl. New York, NY 10001. Phone: 800-322-8755 Fax: 800-678-3633 E-mail: custserv@factsonfile.com • URL: http://www.factsonfile.com • 2001. $71.50. Second edition. Provides basic explanations of about 1,000 terms relating to mental health and mental disorders. Library of Health and Living.

Encyclopedia of Microcomputers. Allen Kent and James G. Williams, editors. Marcel Dekker, Inc., 270 Madison Ave. New York, NY 10016. Phone: 800-228-1160 or (212)696-9000 Fax: (212)685-4540 E-mail: bookorders@dekker.com • URL: http://www.dekker.com • 27 volumes. $5,265.00. $195.00 per volume. Dates vary. Contains scholarly articles written by microcomputer experts. Includes bibliographies.

Encyclopedia of New Media: An Essential Reference to Communication and Technology. Steve Jones, editor. Sage Publications, Inc., 2455 Teller Rd. Thousand Oaks, CA 91320-2218. Phone: 800-818-7243 or (805)499-0721 Fax: 800-583-2665 or (805)499-0871 E-mail: info@sagepub.com • URL: http://www.sagepub.com • 2003. $125.00. Contains more than 250 entries dealing with such areas as multimedia, broadband access, information communication technology (ICT), content filtering, wireless networks, and cyberethics.

Encyclopedia of Occupational Health and Safety. Jeanne M. Stellman. International Labour Office, 1828 L St., N.W. Washington, DC 20036-5121. Phone: (202)653-7652 Fax: (202)653-7687 E-mail: ilo@ilo.org • URL: http://www.ilo.org • 1998. $990.00. Fourth edition. Four volumes. Includes CD-Rom.

Encyclopedia of Occupational Health and Safety. International Labour Organization, 1828 L St., N.W., Suite 600 Washington, DC 20036-5121. Phone: (202)653-7652 Fax: (202)653-7687 E-mail: washington@ilo.org • URL: http://www.ilo.org • 1998. $990.00. Fourth edition. Four volumes. Includes CD-ROM. Covers safety engineering, industrial medicine, ergonomics, hygiene, epidemiology, toxicology, industrial psychology, and related topics. Includes material related to specific chemical, textile, transport, construction, manufacturing, and other industries. Indexed by subject, chemical name, and author, with a "Directory of Experts."

Encyclopedia of Physical Science and Engineering Information. Gale Cengage Learning, 27500 Drake Rd. Farmington Hills, MI 48331-3535. Phone: 800-877-GALE or (248)699-4253 Fax: 800-414-5043 E-mail: gale.galeord@cengage.com • URL: http://gale.cengage.com • 1996. $160.00. Second edition. Includes print, electronic, and other information sources for a wide range of scientific, technical, and engineering topics.

Encyclopedia of Polymer Science and Engineering. Herman F. Mark and others. John Wiley and Sons, Inc., 111 River St. Hoboken, NJ 07030. Phone: 800-526-5368 or (201)748-6000 Fax: (201)748-6088 E-mail: info@wiley.com • URL: http://www.wiley.com • 1985. $8,536.00. 22 volumes. $388.00 per volume.

Encyclopedia of Polymer Science and Technology. Corinna Czekaj. John Wiley and Sons, Inc., 111 River St. Hoboken, NJ 07030. Phone: 800-225-5945 or (201)748-6000 Fax: (201)748-6088 E-mail: info@wiley.com • URL: http://www.wiley.com • 2004. $3,600. Third edition. 12 volumes. Covers new techniques and methods, as well as "traditional topics of continuing interest."

Encyclopedia of Popular Music. Colin Larkin, editor. Available from Groves Dictionaries, Inc., 345 Park Ave. S., 10th Fl. New York, NY 10010-1707. Phone: 800-221-2123 or (212)689-9200 Fax: (212)689-9200 E-mail: grove@grovereference.com • URL: http://www.grovereference.com • 1998. $500.00. Third edition. Eight volumes. Covers a wide variety of music forms and pop culture. Includes bibliography and index.

Encyclopedia of Population. Available from Gale Cengage Learning, 27500 Drake Rd. Farmington Hills, MI 48331-3535. Phone: 800-877-GALE or (248)699-4253 Fax: 414-5043 E-mail: gale.galeord@cengage.com • URL: http://gale.cengage.com • 2003. $265.00. Two volumes. Published by Macmillan Reference USA. Formerly *Macmillan's International Encyclopedia of Population*. Covers a broad range of topics in demography and neighboring disciplines. Emphasis is on developments in population research during the past 20 years.

Encyclopedia of Prisons and Correctional Facilities. Mary Bosworth, editor. Sage Publications, Inc., 2455 Teller Rd. Thousand Oaks, CA 91320-2218. Phone: 800-818-7243 or (805)499-0721 Fax: 800-583-2665 or (805)499-0871 E-mail: info@sagepub.com • URL: http://www.sagepub.com • 2004. $295.00. Two volumes. Contains 400 entries by various "recognized authorities." Appendix includes detailed information about every federal prison in the U.S.

Encyclopedia of Psychological Assessment. Rocio Fernandez-Ballesteros, editor. Sage Publications, Inc., 2455 Teller Rd. Thousand Oaks, CA 91320-2218. Phone: 800-818-7243 or (805)499-0721 Fax: 800-583-2665 or (805)499-0871 E-mail: info@sagepub.com • URL: http://www.sagepub.com • 2003. $525.00. Two volumes. Contains about 235 alphabetically arranged entries covering various areas of applied psychology and testing.

Encyclopedia of Public Relations. Robert L. Heath, editor. Sage Publications, Inc., 2455 Teller Rd. Thousand Oaks, CA 91320-2218. Phone: 800-818-7243 or (805)499-0721 Fax: 800-583-2665 or (805)499-0871 E-mail: info@sagepub.com • URL: http://www.sagepub.com • 2004. $295.00. Two volumes. Contains about 450 entries on such topics as crisis management, ethics, public relations research, theories, jargon, mass media, public relations education, and the history of public relations.

Encyclopedia of Small Business. Gale Cengage Learning, 27500 Drake Rd. Farmington Hills, MI 48331-3535. Phone: 800-877-GALE or (248)699-4253 Fax: 800-414-5043 E-mail: gale.galeord@cengage.com • URL: http://gale.cengage.com • 2002. $450.00. Second edition. Two volumes. Contains about 600 informative entries on a wide variety of topics affecting small business. Arrangement is alphabetical.

Encyclopedia of Smart Materials. Mel Schwartz, editor. John Wiley and Sons, Inc., 111 River St. Hoboken, NJ 07030. Phone: 800-225-5945 or (201)748-6000 Fax: (201)748-6088 E-mail: info@wiley.com • URL: http://www.wiley.com • 2002. $725.00. Three volumes. Covers materials "that combine two or more functions in a single material or element."

Encyclopedia of Smoking and Tobacco. Arlene B. Hirschfelder. Greenwood Publishing Group, Inc., 88 Post Rd., W. Westport, CT 06881. Phone: 800-225-5800 or (203)226-3571 Fax: (203)431-2214 E-mail: customer-service@greenwood.com • URL: http://www.greenwood.com • 1999. $69.95. Includes information on the economics of the tobacco industry, health issues, tobacco history, advertising, legal issues, government subsidies, etc. Provides illustrations, charts, and statistical data.

Encyclopedia of Social Welfare History in North America. John M. Herrick and Paul H. Stuart, editors. Sage Publications, Inc., 2455 Teller Rd. Thousand Oaks, CA 91320-2218. Phone: 800-818-7243 or (805)499-0721 Fax: 800-583-2665 or (805)499-0871 E-mail: info@sagepub.com • URL: http://www.sagepub.com • 2004. $150.00. Includes entries on the historical aspects of charity, economic conditions, tax policy, health policy, social welfare legislation, poverty, social security, and social problems.

Encyclopedia of Software Engineering. John J. Marciniak, editor. John Wiley and Sons, Inc., 111 River St. Hoboken, NJ 07030. Phone: 800-225-5945 or (201)748-6000 Fax: (201)748-6088 E-mail: info@wiley.com • URL: http://www.wiley.com • 2002. $695.00. Second edition. Two volumes. Contains more than 500 entries covering 35 software classifications.

Encyclopedia of Space Science and Technology. Hans Mark, editor. John Wiley and Sons, Inc., 111 River St. Hoboken, NJ 07030. Phone: 800-225-5945 or (201)748-6000 Fax: (201)748-6088 E-mail: info@wiley.com • URL: http://www.wiley.com • 2003. $475.00. Two volumes. Covers astronomical background, physical principles, launch technology, control systems, rockets, space vehicles, space stations, satellites, space environment, and related topics.

Encyclopedia of Statistical Sciences. Samuel I. Kotz and others, editors. John Wiley and Sons, Inc., 111 River St. Hoboken, NJ 07030. Phone: 800-526-5368 or (201)748-6000 Fax: (201)748-6088 E-mail: info@wiley.com • URL: http://www.wiley.com • 2003. $3,725.00. 13 volumes. Includes *Supplements* and *Updates*. Price varies for each individual volume.

Encyclopedia of Technical Market Indicators. Robert W. Colby. McGraw-Hill, 1221 Ave. of the Americas New York, NY 10020. Phone: 800-722-4726 or (212)512-2000 Fax: (212)512-4502 E-mail: customer.service@mcgraw-hill.com • URL: http://www.mcgraw-hill.com • 2002. $70.00. Second edition.

Encyclopedia of Television. Horace Newcomb, editor. Fitzroy Dearborn Publishers, Inc., 919 N. Michigan Ave., Suite 760 Chicago, IL 60611. Phone: 800-850-8102 or (312)587-0131 Fax: (312)587-1049 E-mail: fitzroy@aol.com • URL: http://www.fitzroydearborn.com • 1997. $350.00. Three volumes. Contains about 1,000 entries on TV performers, programs, organizations, social issues, technical aspects, and historical details.

Encyclopedia of the European Union. Desmond Dinan, editor. Lynne Rienner Publishers, 1800 30th St., Suite 314 Boulder, CO 80301-1026. Phone: (303)444-6684 Fax: (303)444-0824 E-mail: questions@rienner.com • URL: http://www.rienner.com • 2000. $110.00. Covers "virtually every aspect" of the EU. Includes "maps, glossaries, appendixes, and a comprehensive index."

Encyclopedia of the Great Depression. Gale Cengage Learning, 27500 Drake Rd. Farmington Hills, MI 48331-3535. Phone: 800-877-GALE Fax: 800-414-5043 or (248)699-8069 E-mail: galeord@galegroup.com • URL: http://www.galegroup.com • 2003. $265.00. Two volumes. Covers about two decades of U. S. economic history, from "the farm crisis of the mid-1920s," through the gradual recovery of the 1930s, to the beginning of World War II. (Macmillan Reference USA imprint.)

Encyclopedia of the Great Depression and the New Deal. James Ciment, editor. M. E. Sharpe, Inc., 80 Business Park Drive Armonk, NY 10504. Phone: 800-541-6563 or (914)273-1800 Fax: (914)273-2106 E-mail: custserv@mesharpe.com • URL: http://www.mesharpe.com • 2001. $199.00. Two volumes. Covers the major movements, events, and people of the 1930's depression. Includes many illustrations, a bibliography, and an index.

Encyclopedia of 20th Century American Humor: Patterns, Trends and Connections. Alleen P. Nilsen and Don L. F. Nilsen. Greenwood Publishing Group, Inc., Post Rd., W. Westport, CT 06881. Phone: 800-225-5800 or (203)226-3571 Fax: (203)431-2214 E-mail: customer-service@greenwood.com • URL: http://www.greenwood.com • 2000. $69.95. Provides an A-to-Z consideration of American humor in its various forms, from early vaudeville to the Internet. Includes a bibliography, subject index, illustrations, and numerous humorous examples.

Encyclopedia of White-Collar and Corporate Crime. Lawrence M. Salinger, editor. Sage Publications, Inc., 2455 Teller Rd. Thousand Oaks, CA 91320-2218. Phone: 800-818-7243 or (805)499-0721 Fax: 800-583-2665 or (805)499-0871 E-mail: info@sagepub.com • URL: http://www.sagepub.com • 2004. $295.00. Two volumes. Covers such items as fraud, kickbacks, price fixing, tax evasion, bribery, forgery, counterfeiting, embezzlement, extortion, graft, bid rigging, and assorted scams and swindles.

Encyclopedia of Wood. U.S. Dept. of Forestry Staff. Sterling Publishing Co., Inc., 387 Park Ave., S New York, NY 10016. Phone: (212)532-7160 E-mail: custservice@sterlingpub.com • URL: http://www.sterlingpub.com • 1989. $24.95. Revised edition.

Encyclopedia of Wood: A Tree by Tree Guide to the World's Most Valuable Resource. Bill Lincoln and others. Facts on File, Inc., 132 W 31st St., 17th Fl. New York, NY 10001-2006. Phone: 800-322-8755 Fax: 800-678-3633 E-mail: custserv@factsonfile.com • URL: http://www.factsonfile.com • 1989. $29.95.

Encyclopedia of World Biography. Gale Cengage Learning, 27500 Drake Rd. Farmington Hills, MI 48331-3535. Phone: 800-877-GALE or (248)699-4253 Fax: 800-414-5043 E-mail: gale.galeord@cengage.com • URL: http://gale.cengage.com • 1998. $1,095.00. Second edition. 17 volumes. Provides biographies of about 7,000 "internationally renowned" individuals from all eras and subject fields. Includes illustrations, bibliographies, and index. *Supplement* available, $125.00.

Encyclopedic Dictionary of Gears and Gearing. David W. South. McGraw-Hill, 1221 Ave. of the Americas New York, NY 10020. Phone: 800-722-4726 or (212)512-2000 Fax: (212)512-4502 E-mail: customer.servcie@mcgraw-hill.com • URL: http://www.mcgraw-hill.com • 1994. $54.50.

Encyclopedic Dictionary of International Finance and Banking. Jae K. Shim and Michael Constas. CRC Press, 2000 N.W. Corporate Blvd. Boca Raton, FL 33431. Phone: 800-272-7737 or (561)994-0555 Fax: 800-374-3401 or (561)989-9732 E-mail: orders@crcpress.com • URL: http://www.crcpress.com • 2001. $64.95. Contains 550 detailed entries covering multinational business, international finance, money, investments, financial planning, financial economics, and banking. Includes statistics, charts, exhibits, diagrams, rules-of-thumb and checklists.

Encyclopedic Guide to Searching and Finding Health Information on the Web. P. F. Anderson and Nancy J. Allee, editors. Neal-Schuman Publishers, 100 William St., Suite 2004 New York, NY 10038. Phone: (866)672-6657 or (212)925-8650 Fax: (866)209-7932 E-mail: orders@neal-schuman.com • URL: http://www.neal-schuman.com • 2004. $395.00. Three volumes. Comprehensive guide to searching the Web for reliable information on hundreds of specific diseases, disorders, and health issues. Volume three covers Search Strategies and provides a Cumulative Index. (Published in conjunction with the Medical Library Association.)

End Point Express: Exclusive Report for Bank Operations Professionals. United Communications Group, 11300 Rockville Pike, Suite 1100 Rockville, MD 20852-3030. Phone: 800-287-2223 or (301)287-2700 Fax: (301)816-8945 E-mail: webmaster@ucg.com • URL: http://www.ucg.com • Biweekly. $247.00 per year. Newsletter. Covers bank payment systems, including checks, electronic funds transfer (EFT), point-of-sale (POS), and automated teller machine (ATM) operations. Formerly *Bank Office Bulletin*.

The Enduring Library: Technology, Tradition, and the Quest for Balance. Michael Gorman. American Library Association, 50 E Huron St. Chicago, IL 60611-2795. Phone: 800-545-2433 or (312)944-6780 Fax: (312)440-9374 E-mail: ala@ala.org • URL: http://www.ala.org • 2003. $35.00. Considers the fundamental mission of libraries, as affected by new information technologies.

Energetic Materials Research and Testing Center., New Mexico Institute of Mining and Technology, 100 South Rd. Socorro, NM 87801. Phone: (505)835-5312 Fax: (505)835-5630 E-mail: collis@emrtc.nmt.edu • URL: http://www.emrtc.nmt • Research areas include the development of industrial applications for explosives as energy sources.

Energy and Environmental Research Center. University of North Dakota

Energy and Fuels. American Chemical Society, 1155 16th St., N. W. Washington, DC 20036. Phone: 800-227-5558 or (202)872-4600 Fax: (202)776-8258 E-mail: help@acs.org • URL: http://www.chemistry.org • Bimonthly. Institutions, $852.00 per year; others, price on application. An interdisciplinary technical journal covering non-nuclear energy sources: petroleum, gas, synthetic fuels, etc.

Energy and Nuclear Sciences International Who's Who. Addison Wesley/Benjamin Cummings, 75 Arlington St., Ste. 300 Boston, MA 02116. Phone: (617)848-7500 • URL: http://www.aw-bc.com • 1990. $310.00. Third edition.

Energy and Problems of a Technical Society. Jack J. Kraushaar and Robert A. Ristinen. John Wiley and Sons, Inc., 111 River St. Hoboken, NJ 07030. Phone: 800-225-5945 or (201)748-6000 Fax: (201)748-6088 E-mail: info@wiley.com • URL: http://www.wiley.com • 1993. $64.95. Second edition.

Energy Balances of OECD Countries. Organization for Economic Cooperation and Development. Available from OECD Publications and Information Center, 2001 L St., N. W., Suite 650 Washington, DC 20036-4922. Phone: 800-456-6323 or (202)785-6323 Fax: (202)785-0350 E-mail: washington.contact@oecd.org • URL: http://www.oecdwash.org • Annual. $115.00. Presents two-year data on the supply and consumption of solid fuels, oil, gas, and electricity, expressed in oil equivalency terms. Historical tables are also provided. Relates to OECD member countries.

Energy Compass. Energy Intelligence Group, 5 E 37th St., 5th Fl. New York, NY 10016-2807. Phone: (212)532-1112 Fax: (212)532-4479 E-mail: sdp@tfn.com • URL: http://www.energyintel.com • Description: Focuses on worldwide geopolitical developments and their impact on the oil industry. Also includes marketing and trading information, political risk assessment, and current events and trends. **Remarks:** Available via fax, e-mail, or online.

Energy Conservation News. BCC Research, 70 New Canaan Ave. Norwalk, CT 06850. Phone: (866)285-7216 or (203)750-9783 Fax: (203)229-0087 E-mail: info@bccresearch.com Description: Designed to give the industrial energy manager an inside view into current conservation innovations and events in the industrial sector. Covers such topics as effective conservation programs, solar and other energy alternatives, energy efficient building design, financing, utility industry developments, and energy legislation and controls.

Energy Conversion and Management. Elsevier, 655 Ave. of the Americas New York, NY 10010-5107. Phone: 800-366-2665 or (212)989-5800 Fax: 800-535-9935 or (212)633-3680 E-mail: custserv@elsevier.com • URL: http://www.elsevier.com • 20 times a year. Institutions, $3,457.00 per year. Presents a scholarly approach to alternative or renewable energy sources. Text in English, French and German.

The Energy Daily. King Publishing Group Inc., 1325 G St. NW, Ste. 1003 Washington, DC 20005. Phone: 800-926-5464 or (202)638-4260 Fax: (202)662-9719 E-mail: kingcomm@kingpublishing.com Description: Covers the field of energy as it relates to government, policy, and industry. Discusses all forms of energy: nuclear, geothermal, coal, solar, oil, natural gas, wind, shale oil, and wave power. Includes analysis, editorial comment, and hard reporting.

Energy Institute. Pennsylvania State University

Energy Institute of the Americas.

Energy Intelligence Top 100: Ranking the World's Top Oil Companies. Energy Intelligence Group, Inc., Five E 37th St., 5th Fl. New York, NY 10016-2807. Phone: (212)532-1112 Fax: (212)532-4479 • URL: http://www.energyintel.com • Annual. $775.00. Provides detailed profiles of the world's 100 largest oil companies, with rankings by numerous key criteria. Includes both stockholder-owned and government-owned companies.

Energy Magazine. Business Communications Co., Inc., 25 Van Zant St. Norwalk, CT 06855-1781. Phone: (203)853-4266 Fax: (203)853-0348 E-mail: info@bccresearch.com • URL: http://www.buscom.com • Quarterly. $395.00 per year.

Energy Management. Paul Ocallaghan. McGraw-Hill, 1221 Ave. of the Americas New York, NY 10020. Phone: 800-722-4726 or (212)512-2000 Fax: (212)512-4502 E-mail: customer.service@mcgraw-hill.com • URL: http://www.mcgraw-hill.com • 1993. $55.00.

Energy Management and Conservation. Clive Beggs. Elsevier, 360 Park Ave., S New York, NY 10010. Phone: (212)989-5800 Fax: (212)633-3990 2000. $39.95.

Energy Management and Federal Energy Guidelines. CCH, Inc., 2700 Lake Cook Rd. Riverwoods, IL 60015. Phone: 800-835-5224 or (847)267-7000 E-mail: cust_serv@cch.com • URL: http://www.cch.com • Biweekly. $1,827.00 per year. Seven looseleaf volumes. Periodic supplementation. Reports on petroleum allocation rules, conservation efforts, new technology, and other energy concerns.

Energy Management Handbook. Wayne C. Turner. Marcel Dekker, Inc., 270 Madison Ave. New York, NY 10016. Phone: 800-228-1160 or (212)696-9000 Fax: (212)685-4540 E-mail: bookorders@dekker.com • URL: http://www.dekker.com • 2002. $165.00. Fourth edition.

Energy Prices and Taxes. International Energy Agency. OECD Publications and Information Center, 2001 L St., N.W., Suite 650 Washington, DC 20036-4922. Phone: (202)785-6323 Fax: (202)785-0350 E-mail: washington.contact@oecd.org • URL: http://www.oecdwash.org • Quarterly. $385.00 per year. Includes print and online edition. Compiled by the International Energy Agency. Provides data on prices and taxation of petroleum products, natural gas, coal, and electricity. Diskette edition, $800.00. (Published in Paris).

Energy Prices and Taxes. Organization for Economic Cooperation and Development, OECD Washington Center, 2001 L St., N. W., Suite 650 Washington, DC 20036-4922. Phone: 800-456-6323 or (202)785-6323 Fax: (202)785-0350 E-mail: washington.contact@oecd.org • URL: http://www.oecd.org • Quarterly. $355.00 per year. Includes both industrial and consumer prices for oil products, natural gas, coal, and electricity in various countries. (Also available on CD-ROM.)

Energy Services Marketing Letter: Covering Electric and Gas Utility Marketing Programs., 555 E. City Line Ave., Suite 900 Bala Cynwyd, PA 19004-1111. Phone: (610)667-2160 Fax: (610)667-5593 • URL: http://www.zeta_cross@minc.com • Monthly. $295.00 per year. Newsletter. Formerly *DSM Letter*.

Energy Sources: Recovery, Utilization, and Environmental Effects. Taylor & Francis Group, 325 Chestnut St., Suite 800 Philadelphia, PA 19106. Phone: 800-821-8312 or (215)625-8900 Fax: 800-248-4724 or (215)625-2940 E-mail: info@taylorandfrancis.com • URL: http://www.taylorandfrancis.com • Monthly. Individuals, $498.00 per year; institutions, $1,325.00 per year.

Energy Statistics of OECD Countries. Available from OECD Publications Center, 2001 L St., N.W.,, Suite 650 Washington, DC 20036-4922. Phone: 800-456-6323 or (202)785-6323 Fax: (202)785-0350 E-mail: washington.contact@oecd.org • URL: http://www.oecdwash.org • Annual. $110.00. Detailed energy supply and consumption data for OECD member countries.

Energy Statistics Yearbook. United Nations Dept. of Economic and Social Affairs. United Nations Publications, Two United Nations Plaza, Rm. DC2-853 New York, NY 10017. Phone: 800-253-9646 or (212)963-8302 Fax: (212)963-3489 Annual. $100.00. Text in English and French.

Energy Systems Handbook. McGraw Hill, 1221 Ave. of the Americas New York, NY 10020. Phone: 800-772-4726 or (212)512-2000 Fax: (212)512-4502 E-mail: customer.service@mcgraw-hill.com • URL: http://www.mcgraw-hill.com • 1999. $39.95 (Complete Construction Series).

Energy Systems Laboratory. Texas A & M University

Energy Today. Trends Publishing Inc., 1079 National Press Bldg. Washington, DC 20045. Phone: (202)333-4801 Fax: (202)393-1732 E-mail: kingcomm@kingpublishing.com • URL: http://www.newtrendspublishing.com • Description: Examines energy programs, policy, regulation, and conservation. Discusses fossil, solar, and nuclear energy and other power sources. Includes a section titled Energy Trends, which reports in brief on upcoming conferences, papers and studies, energy education, new multimedia items, and international energy news.

Energy User News: Energy Technology Buyers Guide. Business News Publishing Co., 755 W Big Beaver Rd. Troy, MI 48084. Phone: 800-866-0206 or (248)362-3700 Fax: (248)362-0317 • URL: http://www.bnp.com • Annual. $10.00. List of about

400 manufacturers, manufacturers' representatives, dealers, and distributors of energy management equipment. *Annual Review* and *Forecast* issue.

Engine Manufacturers Association., 2 N LaSalle St., Ste. 2200 Chicago, IL 60602. Phone: (312)827-8700 Fax: (312)827-8737 E-mail: ema@enginemanufacturers.org • URL: http://www.enginemanufacturers.org • Producers of internal combustion engines for all applications except those used exclusively for automobiles and aircraft. Conducts research and development programs on noise, smoke, and other emissions from internal combustion engines.

Engine Research Center. University of Wisconsin - Madison

Engineered Materials Abstracts. Cambridge Information Group, 7200 Wisconsin Ave., Suite 601 Bethesda, MD 20814. Phone: 800-843-7751 or (301)961-6700 Fax: (301)961-6720 E-mail: service@csa.com • URL: http://www.csa.com • Monthly. $995.00 per year. Provides citations to the technical and engineering literature of plastic, ceramic, and composite materials.

Engineered Materials Abstracts [online]. Cambridge Scientific Abstracts, 7200 Wisconsin Ave. Bethesda, MD 20814. Phone: 800-843-7751 or (301)961-6700 Fax: (301)961-6720 E-mail: sales@csa.com • URL: http://www.csa.com • Provides online citations to the technical and engineering literature of plastic, ceramic, and composite materials. Time period is 1986 to date, with monthly updates. (Formerly produced by ASM International.) Inquire as to online cost and availability.

Engineered Wood Technology Association., 7011 S 19th St., PO Box 11700 Tacoma, WA 98466. Phone: (253)565-6600 Fax: (253)565-7265 E-mail: ema@enginemanufacturers.org • URL: http://www.apawood.org • Represents manufacturers of construction and industrial panels and related products; associate members. Sponsors research programs on improvement in panel production processes and techniques.

Engineering and Industrial Experiment Station., University of Florida, College of Engineering Gainesville, FL 32611. Phone: (352)392-6000 Fax: (352)392-9673 E-mail: johan@eng.ufl.edu • URL: http://www.eng.ufl.edu • Research fields include chemical, civil, electrical, industrial, mechanical, and other types of engineering.

Engineering and Mining Journal Annual Buyers' Guide. Primedia Business Magazines and Media, 29 N Wacker Dr., 10th Fl. Chicago, IL 60606. Phone: 800-795-5445 or (312)726-2802 Fax: (312)726-2574 E-mail: subs@primediabusiness.com • URL: http://www.primediabusiness.com • Annual. Free to qualified subscribers; others, $69.00. List of manufacturers and suppliers of mining equipment; international coverage. Formerly *Engineering and Mining Journal Buying Directory*.

Engineering Dean's Office., University of California at Berkeley, 308 Mclaughin Hall, MC. 1702 Berkeley, CA 94720-1706. Phone: (510)642-7594 Fax: (510)643-8653 E-mail: dma@coe.berkeley.edu Research fields include civil, electrical, industrial, mechanical, and other types of engineering.

Engineering Design Graphics Journal. American Society for Engineering Education, Engineering Design Graphics Div., Purdue University, c/o Judy A. Birchman, 1419 Knoy Hall W. Lafayette, IN 47907-1419. Phone: (317)494-8206 Fax: (317)494-9267 E-mail: jabirchman@tech.purdue.edu • URL: http://www.tech.purdue.edu • Three times a year. Free to members; Non-members, $24.00 per year. Concerned with engineering graphics, computer graphics, geometric modeling, computer-aided drafting, etc.

Engineering Experiment Station., Purdue University West Lafayette, IN 47907. Phone: (765)494-5340 Fax: (765)494-9321 E-mail: richard.j.schwartz@purdue.edu • URL: http://www.ecn.purdue.edu • Research fields include chemical, civil, electrical, industrial, mechanical, and other types of engineering.

Engineering Experiment Station. Ohio State University

Engineering Index Monthly: Abstracting and Indexing Services Covering Sources ofthe World's Engineering Literature. Engineering Information Inc., One Castle Point Terrace Hoboken, NJ 07030-5996. Phone: 800-221-1044 or (201)216-8500 Fax: (201)356-6801 E-mail: customer.support@ei.org • URL: http://www.ei.org • Monthly. Institutions, $5,279.00 per year. Provides indexing and abstracting of the world's engineering and technical literature.

Engineering Plastics and Composites. William A. Woishnis and others, editors. ASM International, 9639 Kinsman Rd. Materials Park, OH 44073-0002. Phone: 800-336-5152 or (440)338-5151 Fax: (440)338-4634 E-mail: cust-srv@asminternational.org • URL: http://www.asminternational.org • 1993. $149.00. Second edition. In four sections: (1) Trade names of plastics, reinforced plastics, and resin composites; (2) Index to materials, with suppliers and other information; (3) Suppliers alphabetically, with trade names; (4) Supplier contact information. (Materials Data Series).

Engineering Systems Research Center. University of California at Berkeley

The Enlarged European Union: A Statistical Handbook. Euromonitor International, 122 South Michigan Ave., Suite 810 Chicago, IL 60603. Phone: 800-577-3876 or (312)922-1115 Fax: (312)922-1157 E-mail: info@euromonitor.com • URL: http://www.euromonitor.com • 2003. $470.00. Presents comparative statistical data for 28 countries (15 EU member states and 13 candidate countries). Covers economics, population, labor, trade, consumer markets, and other topics.

Enlisted Association of National Guard of the United States., 3133 Mt. Vernon Ave. Alexandria, VA 22305-2640. Phone: 800-234-EANG or (703)519-3846 Fax: (703)519-3849 E-mail: eangus@eangus.org • URL: http://www.memberconnections.com/eangus • Active and retired members of the U.S. National Guard. Conducts educational, legislative and charitable programs.

Eno Transportation Foundation., 1250 I St. NW, Ste. 750 Washington, DC 20005-3910. Phone: (202)879-4700 Fax: (202)879-4719 E-mail: svanbeek@enotrans.com • URL: http://www.enotrans.com • Seeks to educate the public and disseminate information about transportation in the U.S. Fosters careers in the field. Conducts research, educational programs, and policy forums; maintains museum; compiles statistics. Financed by an endowment made by William Phelps Eno.

ENR: Connecting the Industry Worldwide (Engineering News-Record). McGraw-Hill, 1221 Ave. of the Americas New York, NY 10020. Phone: 800-458-3842 or (212)512-2000 Fax: (212)904-4039 E-mail: customer.service@mcgraw.hill.com • URL: http://www.mcgraw.hill.com • Weekly. $74.00 per year.

ENR Top 400 Construction Contractors (Engineering News-Record). McGraw-Hill, 1221 Ave. of the Americas New York, NY 10020. Phone: 800-722-4726 or (212)512-2000 Fax: (212)512-4502 E-mail: customer.service@mcgraw-hill.com • URL: http://www.mcgraw-hill.com • Annual. $10.00. Lists 400 United States contractors receiving largest dollar volume of contracts in preceding calendar year.

ENR-Top International Design Firms (Engineering News Record). McGraw-Hill, 1221 Ave of the Americas New York, NY 10020. Phone: 800-722-4726 or (212)512-2000 Fax: (212)512-4502 E-mail: customer.service@mcgraw-hill.com • URL: http://www.mcgraw-hill.com • Annual. $10.00. Lists 200 firms. Includes U. S. firms. Formerly *Engineering News Record-Top International Design Firms*.

Enterprise Integration: An Architecture for Enterprise Application and Systems Integration. Fred A. Cummins. John Wiley and Sons, Inc., 111 River St. Hoboken, NJ 07030. Phone: 800-225-5945 or (201)748-6000 Fax: (201)748-6088 E-mail: info@wiley.com • URL: http://www.wiley.com • 2002. $44.99. Covers "Establishing the Enterprise Infrastructure," "Creating a Business System Domain," "Integrating with XML" (Extensible Markup Language), and related topics. Includes information on Web-based user access, system security, and enterprise intelligence support.

Entertainment Design: The Art and Technology of Show Business. Primedia Business Magazines, 32 W. 18th St. New York, NY 10011-4612. Phone: 800-827-0315 or (212)229-2965 Fax: (212)229-2084 • URL: http://www.primediabusiness.com • Monthly. $34.97 per year. Contains material on performing arts management, staging, scenery, costuming, etc. Supersedes *TCI - Theatre Crafts International*.

Entertainment Industry Economics: A Guide for Financial Analysis. Harold Vogel. Cambridge University Press, 40 W 20th St. New York, NY 10011-4211. Phone: 800-872-7423 or (212)924-3900 Fax: (212)691-3239 E-mail: orders@cup.org • URL: http://www.cup.org • 2001. $45.00. Fifth revised edition.

Entertainment Law. Jeffrey A. Helewitz and Leah K. Edwards. Delmar Learning, 5 Maxwell Dr. Clifton Park, NY 12065-8007. Phone: 800-347-7707 Fax: 800-487-8488 • URL: http://www.delmarlearning.com • 2003. $52.95. (West Legal Studies).

Entertainment Law and Business, 1989-1993: A Guide to the Law and Business Prac Entertainment Industry. Harold Orenstein and David Sinacore-Guinn. LEXIS Publishing, 701 E. Water St. Charlottesville, VA 22902. Phone: 800-446-3410 or (804)972-7600 Fax: 800-643-1280 or (804)972-7686 E-mail: custserv@michie.com • URL: http://www.lexislawpublishing.com • $180.00. Two volumes. Looseleaf Service. Periodic supplementation, $55.00.

Entertainment Law and Finance. American Lawyer Media, Inc., 105 Madison Ave. New York, NY 10016. Phone: 800-888-8300 or (212)779-9200 Fax: (212)481-8110 E-mail: lawcatalog@amlaw.com • URL: http://www.lawcatalog.com/ • Monthly. $229.00 per year. Newsletter. Covers contracts, royalties, litigation, copyright, taxation, etc., for the music industry, motion pictures, broadcasting, publishing, video, and related media. (A Law Journal Newsletter, formerly published by Leader Publications.)

Entertainment Law: Legal Concepts and Business Practices. West Group, 610 Opperman Dr. Eagan, MN 55123. Phone: 800-328-4880 or (651)687-7000 Fax: 800-340-9378 or (651)687-5827 E-mail: bookstore@westgroup.com • URL: http://www.westgroup.com • Annual. $560.00. Five looseleaf volumes.

Entertainment Marketing Letter. EPM Communications Inc., 160 Mercer St., 3rd Fl. New York, NY 10012-3212. Phone: 888-852-9467 or (212)941-0099 Fax: 888-852-3899 or (212)941-1622 E-mail: info@epmcom.com • URL: http://www.epmcom.com • Description: Reports on techniques used in the marketing of films, music, videos, television, radio, and cable features. Covers tie-in campaigns, sponsorship, intheatre advertising, and interactive telephone promotions.

Entertainment Software Association., 575 7th St. NW, Ste. 300 Washington, DC 20004. Phone: (202)223-2400 E-mail: esa@theesa.com • URL: http://www.theesa.com • Represents the interactive entertainment software publishing industry. Established an autonomous rating board to rate interactive entertainment software. Established a program to combat piracy in the United States and around the world. Represents members on industry issues at the federal and state level. Provides market research and information. **Publications:** none.

Entertainment Sourcebook: An Insider's Guide on Where to Find Everything. Applause Theatre & Cinema Books, 151 W. 46th St. New York, NY 10036. Phone: 800-524-4425 or (212)575-9265 Fax: (212)721-2856 E-mail: info@applausepub.com • URL: http://www.applausepub.com • Annual. $45.00. Compiled by the Association of Theatrical Artists and Craftspeople (http://www.entertainmentsourcebook.com/ATAC.htm). Lists more than 5,000 sources of theatrical and entertainment supplies and services, such as props, costumes, publicity agencies, scenic shops, amusement park equipment, audio/video products, balloons, wigs, make-up, magic supplies, etc.

Entomological Society of America Annals: Devoted to the Interest of Classical Entomology. Entomological Society of America, 9301 Annapolis Rd. Lanham, MD 20706. Phone: (301)731-4535 Fax: (301)731-4538 E-mail: eas@entsoc.org • URL: http://www.entsoc.org • Bimonthly. Individuals, $84.00 per year; institutions, $162.00 per year.

Entomology Abstracts. CSA, 7200 Wisconsin Ave., Ste. 601 Bethesda, MD 20814. Phone: 800-843-7751 or (301)961-6700 Fax: (301)961-6720 E-mail: service@csa.com • URL: http://www.csa.com • 11 times a year. $1,570.00 per year. Includes print and online editions.

Entrepreneur: The Small Business Authority. Entrepreneur Media, Inc., 2445 McCabe Way Irvine, CA 92614. Phone: 800-421-2300 or (949)261-2325 Fax: (949)261-0234 E-mail: entmag@entrepreneur.com • URL: http://www.entrepreneur.com • Monthly. $19.97 per year. Contains advice for small business owners and prospective owners. Includes numerous franchise advertisements.

Entrepreneur's Annual Franchise 500 Issue. Entrepreneur Media, Inc., 2445 McCabe Way Irvine, CA 92614. Phone: 800-421-2300 or (949)261-2325 Fax: (949)261-0234 E-mail: entmag@entrepreneur.com • URL: http://www.entrepreneur.com • Annual. $4.95. Provides a ranking of 500 "top franchise opportunities," based on a combination of financial strength, growth rate, size, stability, number of years in business, litigation history, and other factors. Includes 17 major business categories, further divided into about 140 very specific groups (22 kinds of fast food, for example).

Entrepreneur's Guide to Finance and Business: Wealth Creation Techniques for Growing a Business. Steven Rogers. McGraw-Hill, 1221 Ave. of the Americas New York, NY 10121. Phone: 800-722-4726 or (212)512-2000 Fax: (212)512-4502 E-mail: customer.service@mcgraw-hill.com • URL: http://www.mcgraw-hill.com • 2003. $49.95. Coverage includes entrepreneurial financing, business plan development, and structuring a deal.

The Entrepreneur's Guide to Growing Up: Taking Your Small Company to the Next Level. Edna Sheedy. Self-Counsel Press, Inc., 1704 N. State St. Bellingham, WA 98225. Phone: 877-877-6490 or (360)676-4530 Fax: (360)676-4549 E-mail: orderdesk@self-counsel.com • URL: http://www.self-counsel.com • 1993. $8.95. Discusses company structure, delegation, management information requirements, and other topics related to company growth. (Self-Counsel Business Series).

Entrepreneurship: Theory and Practice. Baylor University, Hankamer School of Business Available from Blackwell Publishing, Inc., 350 Main St. Malden, MA 02148. Phone: (781)388-8200 Fax: (781)388-8210 E-mail: subscrip@blackwellpub.com • URL: http://www.blackwellpublishers.com • Quarterly. Institutions, $280.00 per year. Includes online edition. Formerly *American Journal of Small Business*.

Entrepreneurship.com. Tim Burns. Dearborn Trade Publishing, A Kaplan Professional Co., 155 N Wacker Dr. Chicago, IL 60606. Phone: 800-621-9621 or (312)836-4400 Fax: (312)836-1021 E-mail: trade@dearborn.com • URL: http://www.dearborntrade.com • 2000. $19.95. Provides basic advice and information on the topic of dot.com startups, including business plan creation and financing.

Environment Abstracts. Congressional Information Service, Inc., 4520 East-West Highway, Ste. 800 Bethesda, MD 20814-3389. Phone: 800-638-8380 or (301)654-1550 Fax: (301)654-4033 E-mail: cisinfo@lexis-nexis.com • URL: http://www.cispubs.com • Monthly. Price varies. Provides multidisciplinary coverage of the world's environmental literature. Incorporates *Acid Rain Abstracts*.

Environment Abstracts Annual: A Guide to the Key Environmental Literature of the Year. Congressional Information Service, Inc., 4520 East-West Hwy. Bethesda, MD 20814-3389. Phone: 800-638-8380 or (301)654-1550 Fax: (301)654-4033 E-mail: cisinfo@lexis.nexis.com • URL: http://www.cispubs.com • Annual. $495.00. A yearly cumulation of *Environment Abstracts*.

Environment Abstracts on CD-ROM. LEXIS-NEXIS, 4520 East-West Highway Bethesda, MD 20814-3389. Phone: 800-638-8380 or (301)654-1550 Fax: (301)654-4033 E-mail: support@cispubs.com • URL: http://www.cispubs.com • Quarterly. $1,295.00 per year. Contains the following CD-ROM databases: *Environment Abstracts, Energy Abstracts*, and *Acid Rain Abstracts*. Length of coverage varies.

Environment Advisor. J.J. Keller & Associates, Inc., 3003 W.

Breezewood Lane Neenah, WI 54957-0368. Phone: 800-558-5011 or (414)722-2848 Fax: (414)727-7516 • URL: http://www.jjkeller.com • Monthly. $90.00 per year. Newsletter. Formerly *Hazardous Substances Advisor*.

Environment Reporter. BNA, Inc., 1231 25th St., NW Washington, DC 20037. Phone: 800-372-1033 E-mail: customercare@bna.com • URL: http://www.bna.com • Weekly. $3,166.00 per year. 18 looseleaf volumes. Covers legal aspects of wide variety of environmental concerns.

Environment Reporter. The Bureau of National Affairs, Inc. Bureau of National Affairs Inc., 1801 S Bell St. Arlington, VA 22202. Phone: 800-372-1033 or (202)452-4200 Fax: (202)452-4226 E-mail: customercare@bna.com Description: Offers a notification and reference service covering legislative, administrative, judicial, industrial, and technological developments affecting pollution control and environmental protection. Recurring features include columns titled Current Developments, Federal Laws and Regulations, Decisions.

Environment: Where Science and Policy Meet. Scientists' Institute for Public Information. Heldref Publications, 1319 18th St., N.W. Washington, DC 20036-1802. Phone: 800-365-9753 or (202)296-6267 Fax: (202)293-6130 E-mail: subscribe@heldref.org • URL: http://www.heldref.org • 10 times a year. Individuals, $48.00 per year; institutions, $98.00 per year.

Environmental Accounting: Current Issues, Abstracts, and Bibliography. United Nations Publications, Concourse Level, First Ave., 46th St. New York, NY 10017. Phone: 800-553-3210 or (212)963-7680 Fax: (212)963-4910 E-mail: bookstore@un.org • URL: http://www.un.org/publications • 1992. Provides guidelines for environmental disclosure in corporate annual reports.

Environmental Action., 6930 Carroll Ave., 6th Fl., Ste. 600 Takoma Park, MD 20912. Phone: (301)891-1100 Fax: (301)891-2218 E-mail: information@sierraclub.org National political lobby organization. Prime focuses are: solid waste; toxic substances; recycling; global warming; utility policy; ozone and acid rain. Coordinated efforts on Clean Air Act, Clean Water Act, Occupational Safety and Health Act, Toxic Substances Control Act, Resource Conservation and Recovery Act in Congress, and Superfund. Engages in educational activities and community organizing. Convention/Meeting: none.

Environmental Business Journal: Strategic Information for a Changing Industry. Environmental Business International, Inc., 4452 Park Blvd., Suite 306 San Diego, CA 92116-4039. Phone: (619)295-7685 Fax: (619)295-5743 E-mail: ebi@ebiusa.com • URL: http://www.ebiusa.com • Monthly. $495.00 per year. Newsletter. Includes both industrial and financial information relating to individual companies and to the environmental industry in general. Covers air pollution, wat es, U. S. Department of Health and Human Services. Provides conference, workshop, and symposium proceedings, as well as extensive reviews of environmental prospects.

Environmental Business Management. Klaus North. International Labour Office, 1828 L St., N.W. Washington, DC 20036-5121. Phone: (202)653-7652 Fax: (202)653-7687 E-mail: ilo@ilo.org • URL: http://www.ilo.org • 1997. $31.50. Second edition. (Management Development Series, No. 30).

Environmental Coalition on Nuclear Power., 433 Orlando Ave. State College, PA 16803. Phone: (814)237-3900 Fax: (814)237-3900 E-mail: johnsrud@uplink.net Seeks establishment of non-nuclear energy policy.

Environmental Compliance Handbook. Jacob I. Bregman and Robert D. Edell. CRC Press LLC, 2000 NW Corporate Blvd. Boca Raton, FL 33431. Phone: 800-272-7737 or (561)994-0555 Fax: 800-374-3401 or (561)989-9732 E-mail: orders@crcpress.com • URL: http://www.crcpress.com • 2001. $99.95. Second edition. Provides practical information and advice on complying with the National Environmental Policy Act (NEPA) and other federal and state environmental laws and regulations. Includes checklists, glossaries, and references.

Environmental Encyclopedia. Gale Cengage Learning, 27500 Drake Rd. Farmington Hills, MI 48331-3535. Phone: 800-877-GALE or (248)699-4253 Fax: 800-414-5043 E-mail: gale.galeord@cengage.com • URL: http://gale.cengage.com • 2003. $275.00. Third edition. Provides over 1,300 articles on all aspects of the environment. Written in non-technical style.

Environmental Engineering. Jeffrey J. Peirce. Elsevier, 655 Ave. of the Americas New York, NY 10010. Phone: 800-366-2665 or (212)989-5800 Fax: 800-535-9935 or (212)633-3680 E-mail: custserv@elsevier.com • URL: http://www.elsevier.com • 2003. $94.95. Fourth edition.

Environmental Engineering. Joseph A. Salvato and others. John Wiley and Sons, Inc., 111 River St. Hoboken, NJ 07030. Phone: 800-225-5945 or (201)748-6000 Fax: (201)748-6088 E-mail: info@wiley.com • URL: http://www.wiley.com • 2003. $240.00. Fifth edition. Written for environmental engineers, civil engineers, environmental scientists, public health professionals, and others concerned with the technical aspects of protecting the environment. Covers a wide range of topics, including sanitation management, groundwater contamination, incineration, wastewater treatment, communicable diseases, and noise control.

Environmental Engineering Center., Michigan Technological University, 1400 Townsend Dr. Houghton, MI 49931. Phone: (906)487-2520 Fax: (906)487-3167 E-mail: biology@mtu.

edu • URL: http://www.bio.mtu.edu/research • Applies biotechnological research to waste management and resource recovery.

Environmental Engineering Laboratory. Pennsylvania State University

Environmental Epidemiology and Toxicology. Nature Publishing Group, 345 Park Ave. S. New York, NY 10010-1707. Phone: (212)726-0200 Fax: (212)689-9711 E-mail: grove@grovereference.com Quarterly. Individuals, $365.00 per year; institutions, $430.00 per year. Formerly *Environmental Epidemiology and Toxicology*.

Environmental Fluid Mechanics Laboratory. Stanford University

Environmental Geology: Facing the Challenges of Our Changing Earth. Jon Erickson. Facts on File, Inc., 132 W 31st St., 17th Fl. New York, NY 10001. Phone: 800-322-8755 Fax: 800-678-3633 E-mail: custserv@factsonfile.com • URL: http://www.factsonfile.com • 2002. Revised edition. (Living Earth Series).

Environmental Hazards Management Institute. Environmental Hazards Management Institute, 10 Newmarket Rd., PO Box 932 Durham, NH 03824. Phone: (603)868-1496 Fax: (603)868-1547 E-mail: aborner@ehmi.org • URL: http://www.ehmi.org • Natural and man-made disasters, global pandemic influenza preparedness or risk avoidance and societal continuity.

Environmental Health Perspectives. Available from U. S. Government Printing Office, Washington, DC 20402. Phone: (202)512-1800 Fax: (202)512-2250 E-mail: gpoaccess@gpo.gov • URL: http://www.access.gpo.gov • Monthly. $263.00 per year. Issued by the U.S. Department of Health and Human Services (http://www.dhhs.gov). Contains original research on various aspects of the environment and human health. Includes news of environment-related legislation, regulatory actions, and technological advances.

Environmental Health Sciences Research Laboratory. Tulane University

Environmental Knowledge Base: An Electronic Bibliography Featuring Citations and Abstracts of Scientific and Popular Articles on Environmental Issues, Including Social Policy, Economics, Regulatory, and Legal Topics. Environmental Studies Institute., International Academy at Santa Barbara, PO Box 4490 Santa Barbara, CA 93140-4490. Phone: 800-530-2682 or (805)569-1436 Fax: (805)964-0890 E-mail: info@iasb.org • URL: http://www.iasb.org • Monthly. Price varies. An index to current environmental literature. Formerly *Environmental Periodicals Bibliography*.

Environmental Law in a Nutshell. Roger W. Findley. West Group, 610 Opperman Dr. Eagan, MN 55123. Phone: 800-338-9424 or (651)687-7000 Fax: 800-340-9378 E-mail: bookstore@westgroup.com • URL: http://www.westgroup.com • 2000. $23.50. Fifth edition. (Nutshell Series).

Environmental Law Institute. Environmental Law Institute, 2000 L St. NW, Ste. 620, Suite 200 Washington, DC 20036. Phone: (202)939-3800 Fax: (202)939-3868 E-mail: carothers@eli.org • URL: http://www2.eli.org/index.cfm • Legal, administrative, economic, scientific, and technical aspects of environmental policy in such areas as enforcement, air and water pollution, toxic substances, hazardous wastes, surface mining, wetlands, and environmental management. Research projects include studies on regulatory enforcement and reform, Superfund implementation, economics, international control strategies and training for professionals, and land use.

Environmental Law Reporter. Environmental Law Institute, 1616 P St., N. W., Suite 200 Washington, DC 20036. Phone: (202)328-5150 Monthly. $1,045.00 per year. Seven looseleaf volumes.

Environmental Law Reporter [online]. Environmental Law Institute, 1616 P St., N. W., Suite 200 Washington, DC 20036. Phone: 800-433-5120 or (202)939-3800 Fax: (202)939-3868 • URL: http://www.eli.org • Provides full text online of *Environmental Law Reporter*, covering administrative materials, news, pending legislation, statutes, bibliography, etc. Time periods vary. Inquire as to online cost and availability.

Environmental Management Association., PO Box 610548 Port Huron, MI 48061. Phone: (866)999-4EMA or (810)982-7271 Fax: (313)475-9229 E-mail: bdoetsch@emaweb.org • URL: http://www.emaweb.org • Individuals administering environmental sanitation maintenance programs in industrial plants, commercial and public buildings, institutions, and governmental agencies. Conducts educational programs; operates placement service; compiles statistics.

Environmental Policy Alert. Inside Washington Publishers, 1225 S Clark St. Ste. 1400, Ben Franklin Sta. Arlington, VA 22202. Phone: 800-424-9068 or (703)416-8500 Fax: (703)415-8543 E-mail: custsvc@iwpnews.com • URL: http://www.insideepa.com • Description: Tracks environmental legislation, regulation, and litigation. Recurring features include interviews and news of research.

Environmental Policy in the 1990s: Reform or Reaction? Norman Vig and Michael Kraft. CQ Press, 1255 22nd St., NW, Ste. 400 Washington, DC 20037. Phone: (866)427-7737 or (202)729-1800 Fax: 800-380-3810 or (202)728-1863 E-mail: customerservice@cq.com • URL: http://www.cqpress.com • 1996. $43.95 Third edition.

Environmental Politics and Policy. Walter A. Rosenbaum. CQ Press, 1255 22nd St., NW Washington, DC 20037. Phone:

800-432-2250 or (202)419-8500 Fax: 800-380-3810 or (202)887-6706 E-mail: customerservice@cq.com • URL: http://www.cq.com • 2001. $31.95. Fifth edition.

Environmental Regulation: State Capitals. Wakeman-Walworth, Inc., PO Box 7376 Alexandria, VA 22307-7376. Phone: 800-876-2545 or (703)768-9600 Fax: (703)768-9690 E-mail: newsletters@statecapitals.com • URL: http://www.statecapitals.com • 50 times a year. $245.00 per year; print and online editions, $350.00 per year. Newsletter. Formerly *From the State Capitals: Environmental Regulation*.

Environmental Research Institute., University of Idaho, Food Research Center 103 Moscow, ID 83844-1052. Phone: (208)885-6580 Fax: (208)885-5741 E-mail: crawford@uidaho.edu • URL: http://www.image.fs.uidaho.edu • Formerly Environmental Biotechnology Institute.

Environmental Resources Research Institute. Pennsylvania State University

Environmental Science and Technology. Kluwer Academic Publishers, New York, NY 10013-1522. Phone: (866)269-9527 or (212)620-8000 • URL: http://www.wkap.nl • Irregular. $120.00.

Environmental Toxicology: An International Journal. John Wiley and Sons, Inc. Journals, 111 River St. Hoboken, NJ 07030. Phone: 800-225-5945 or (201)748-6000 Fax: (201)748-6088 E-mail: customer@wiley.com • URL: http://www.wiley.com • Bimonthly. $700.00 per year; with online edition, $735.00 per year. Formerly *Environmental Toxicology and Water Quality*.

Environmental Viewpoints. Gale Cengage Learning, 27500 Drake Rd. Farmington Hills, MI 48331-3535. Phone: 800-877-GALE or (248)699-4253 Fax: 800-414-5043 E-mail: gale.galeord@cengage.com • URL: http://gale.cengage.com • 1993. $195.00. Three volumes. $65.00 per volume. A compendium of excerpts of about 200 articles on a wide variety of environmental topics, selected from both popular and professional periodicals. Arranged alphabetically by topic, with a subject/keyword index.

EPRI Journal. Electric Power Research Institute, 3412 Hillview Ave. Palo Alto, CA 94303. Phone: (650)855-2300 Fax: (650)855-2900 E-mail: ddietric@epri.com • URL: http://www.epri.com • Bimonthly. Free to members; non-members, $29.00 per year.

EQ: The Project Recording and Sound Magazine. United Entertainment Media, Inc., 460 Park Ave., S, 9th Fl. New York, NY 10016. Phone: (212)378-0400 Fax: (212)378-2160 E-mail: eqmagazine@aol.com • URL: http://www.uemedia.com • Monthly. $24.95 per year. Provides advice on professional music recording equipment and technique.

The Equal Employer. Y. S. Publications, Inc., P.O. Box 2172 Silver Springs, MD 20902-2172. Phone: (301)649-1231 Biweekly. $245.00 per year. Newsletter on fair employment practices.

Equal Employment Opportunity Compliance Guide. John F. Buckley. Aspen Publishers, Inc., 200 Orchard Ridge Dr., Ste. 200 Gaithersburg, MD 20878. Phone: 800-234-1660 or (301)417-7500 E-mail: customer.service@aspenpubl.com • URL: http://aspenpublishers.com • 2002. $175.00.

Equality in the Workplace: An Equal Opportunities Handbook for Trainers. Helen Collins. Blackwell Publishing, 350 Main St. Malden, MA 02148. Phone: 800-216-2522 or (781)388-8200 Fax: 800-864-7626 or (781)388-8210 E-mail: books@blackwellpub.com • URL: http://www.blackwellpub.com • 1995. $55.95. (Human Resource Management in Action Series).

Equipment Leasing. LexisNexis Matthew Bender, 1275 Broadway Albany, NY 12204. Phone: 800-424-4200 or (518)487-3000 Fax: (518)487-3584 E-mail: bookstore.support@lexisnexis.com • URL: http://www.bender.com • $478.00. Three looseleaf volumes. Periodic supplementation. Covers vital information needed to structure a transaction involving an equipment lease.

Equipment Leasing Association of America., 4301 N. Fairfax Dr., Suite 550 Arlington, VA 22203-1627. Phone: (703)527-8655 Fax: (703)527-2649 E-mail: ela@elamail.com • URL: http://www.elaonline.com • Formerly Equipment Leasing Association.

Equipment Leasing-Leveraged Leasing. Practising Law Institute, 810 Seventh Ave. New York, NY 10019-5818. Phone: 800-260-4754 or (212)824-5710 E-mail: info@pli.edu • URL: http://www.pli.edu • $350.00. Three looseleaf volumes. Annual revisions. Contains "practical analyses of the legal, tax, accounting, and financial aspects of equipment leasing." Includes forms, agreements, and checklists.

Equipment Leasing Newsletter. American Lawyer Media, Inc., 105 Madison Ave. New York, NY 10016. Phone: 800-888-8300 or (212)779-9200 Fax: (212)481-8110 E-mail: lawcatalog@amlaw.com • URL: http://www.lawcatalog.com/ • Monthly. $269.00 per year. Newsletter. Covers a wide range of legal topics relating to the leasing of business and industrial equipment, including taxation, insurance, dealing with banks, lease securitization, and letter of credit issues. (A Law Journal Newsletter, formerly published by Leader Publications).

Equipment Leasing Today. Equipment Leasing Association, 4301 N. Fairfax Ave., Suite 550 Arlington, VA 22203-1627. Phone: (703)527-8655 Fax: (703)527-2649 • URL: http://www.elaonline.com • 10 times a year. $100.00 per year. Edited for equipment leasing companies. Covers management, funding, marketing, etc.

Equipment Today. Cygnus Business Media, 1233 Janesville Ave. Fort Atkinson, WI 53538. Phone: 800-547-7377 or (920)563-6388 Fax: (920)563-1707 E-mail: rich.reiff@cygnuspub.com • URL: http://www.cygnusbzb.com • Monthly. $65.00 per year. Includes annual *Product* issue Formerly *Equipment Guide News*.

Equities: Investment News of Promising Public Companies. Equities Magazine LLC, PO Box 130 H Scarsdale, NY 10583. Phone: (914)726-6702 Fax: (914)723-0176 E-mail: equitymag@aol.com • URL: http://www.equitiesmagazine.com • Bimonthly. $21.00 per year. Formerly *OTC Review*.

The ERC Closely-Held Corporation Guide. Prentice Hall PTR, 240 Frisch Ct. Paramus, NJ 07652. Phone: 800-282-0693 Fax: 800-445-6991 • URL: http://www.phptr.com • 1983. $59.95. Second edition.

Ergonomics: An International Journal of Research and Practice in Human Factors and Ergonomics. Taylor and Francis Group, 325 Chestnut St., 8th Fl. Philadelphia, PA 19106. Phone: 800-821-8312 or (215)625-8900 Fax: 800-248-4724 or (215)625-2940 E-mail: info@taylorandfrancis.com • URL: http://www.taylorandfrancis.com • 15 times per year. Individuals, $1,210.00 per year; institutions, $2,472.00 per year.

Ergonomics and Engineering Controls Reaearch Laboratory. University of Cincinnati, Industrial Engineering Dept. Cincinnati, OH 45221-0116. Phone: (513)556-2652 Fax: (513)556-4999 E-mail: anil.mital@uc.edu Formerly Human Factors/Ergonomics Laboratory.

The Ergonomics Edge: Improving Safety, Quality, and Productivity. Dan MacLeod. John Wiley and Sons, Inc., 111 River St. Hoboken, NJ 07030. Phone: 800-225-5945 or (201)748-6000 Fax: (201)748-6088 E-mail: info@wiley.com • URL: http://www.wiley.com • 1995. $110.00. (Industrial Health and Safety Series).

ERIC. Educational Resources Information Center, 2277 Research Blvd., 6-M Rockville, MD 20850. Phone: 800-538-3742 or (301)519-5157 Fax: (301)519-6760 E-mail: accesseric@accesseric.org • URL: http://www.eric.ed.gov/ • Funded by the U. S. Department of Education, Institute of Education Sciences (formerly Office of Educational Research and Improvement). Provides access to more than one million on-line records covering education-related journal and report literature, 1966 to date. Updating is monthly. Inquire as to on-line cost and availability.

ERIC Clearinghouse for Community Colleges. University of California, Los Angeles

ERIC Clearinghouse on Adult, Career and Vocational Education. Ohio State University

ERIC Clearinghouse on Higher Education. George Washington University

ERIC on SilverPlatter. Available from SilverPlatter Information, Inc., 100 River Ridge Rd. Norwood, MA 02062-5026. Phone: 800-343-0064 or (781)769-2599 Fax: (781)769-8763 Quarterly. $700.00 per year. Produced by the Office of Educational Research and Improvement, U. S. Dept. of Education. Provides CD-ROM indexing and abstracting of a wide variety of literature relating to education. Archival discs are available from 1966.

ERISA: The Law and the Code (Employee Retirement Income Security Act). Janet K. Song and Michael G. Kushner. BNA, Inc., 1231 25th St., NW Washington, DC 20037. Phone: 800-372-1033 E-mail: customercare@bna.com • URL: http://www.bna.com • Annual. $105.00. The Employee Retirement Income Security Act, as amended, withrelevant provisions of the Internal Revenue Code.

Ernst & Young Almanac and Guide to U. S. Business Cities: 65 Leading Places to Do Business. John Wiley and Sons, Inc., 111 River St. Hoboken, NJ 07030. Phone: 800-225-5945 or (201)748-6000 Fax: (201)748-6088 E-mail: info@wiley.com • URL: http://www.wiley.com • 1994. $16.95. Provides demographic, business, economic, and site selection data for 65 major U. S. cities.

Ernst & Young Tax Guide 2002: The Official IRS Tax Guide and Usable Forms, Plus Easy-to-Use Explanation and Tax Saving Tips from America's Leading Big Six Accountants. Ernst & Young Staff. John Wiley and Sons, Inc., 605 Third Ave. New York, NY 10158-0012. Phone: 800-225-5945 or (212)850-6000 Fax: (212)850-6088 E-mail: info@wiley.com • URL: http://www.wiley.com • Annual. $16.95. (Ernst and Young Tax Guide Series).

Ernst and Young's Oil and Gas Federal Income Taxation. John R. Braden and others. CCH, Inc., 2700 Lake Cook Rd. Riverwoods, IL 60015. Phone: 800-835-5224 or (847)267-7000 E-mail: cust_serv@cch.com • URL: http://www.cch.com • Annual. $92.95. Formerly *Miller's Oil and Gas Federal Income Taxation*.

Ernst & Young's Personal Financial Planning Guide. John Wiley and Sons, Inc., 111 River St. Hoboken, NJ 07030. Phone: 800-225-5945 or (201)748-6000 Fax: (201)748-6088 E-mail: info@wiley.com • URL: http://www.wiley.com • 2001. $19.95. Fourth edition.

Escort Carrier Sailors and Airmen Association., 13114 Blue Bonnet Dr. Sun City, AZ 85375. Phone: (623)584-4794 Fax: (952)935-5454 E-mail: pyzzaz@earthlink.net • URL: http://www.escortcarriers.com • Promotes knowledge and interest in the vital role played by escort carriers during World War II and the Korean War.

eShopper: Where Style Meets the Net. Element K Journals, 65 Brighton-Henrietta Townline Rd., Ste. 3 Rochester, NY 14623. Phone: 800-223-8720 or (585)240-7301 Fax: (585)292-4392 • URL: http://www.elementkjournals.com • Bimonthly. $9.97 per year. A consumer magazine providing advice and information for "shopping on the Web."

ESOP Association., 1726 M St. NW, Ste. 501 Washington, DC 20036. Phone: (866)366-3832 or (202)293-2971 Fax: (202)293-7568 E-mail: esop@esopassociation.org • URL: http://www.esopassociation.org • Companies with employee stock ownership plans; associate members are lawyers, accountants, appraisers, actuaries, brokers, management and benefit consultants, and bankers specializing in working with ESOP. Acts as national information clearinghouse for the press and public interested in the concept of employee ownership; provides forum for the exchange of ideas, experience, and advice among members; lobbies for favorable legislation and regulation on national and state levels; produces and distributes communications material to educate employees on stock ownership. Holds seminars and roundtables. Compiles statistics; maintains speakers' bureau.

ESOP Report (Employee Stock Ownership Plan). ESOP Association, 1726 M St., N.W., Suite 501 Washington, DC 20036. Phone: (202)293-2971 Fax: (202)293-7568 • URL: http://www.esopassociation.org • Monthly. Membership. Newsletter.

The Essential Guide to Bulletin Board Systems. Patrick R. Dewey. Information Today, Inc., 143 Old Marlton Pike Medford, NJ 08055-8750. Phone: 800-300-9868 or (609)654-6266 Fax: (609)654-4309 E-mail: custserv@infotoday.com • URL: http://www.infotoday.com • 1998. $39.50. Provides details on the setup and operation of online bulletin board systems. Covers both hardware and software.

Essential Guide to the Best (and Worst) Legal Sites on the Web. Robert J. Ambrogi. American Lawyer Media, Inc., 105 Madison Ave. New York, NY 10016. Phone: 800-888-8300 or (212)779-9200 Fax: (212)481-8110 E-mail: lawcatalog@amlaw.com • URL: http://www.lawcatalog.com/ • 2001. $34.95. Sites are classified according to 25 legal subject areas and assigned 1-to-5 star ratings.

Essentials of Accounting for Governmental and Not-for-Profit Organizations. John H. Engstrom and Paul Coley. McGraw-Hill, 1221 Ave. of the Americas New York, NY 10020. Phone: 800-722-4726 or (212)512-2000 Fax: (212)512-4502 E-mail: customer.sevice@mcgraw-hill.com • URL: http://www.mcgraw-hill.com • 2003. $66.88. Seventh edition.

Essentials of Cash Management. Peter S. Adams and William Harrison, editors. The Assoiciation for Financial Professionals, 7315 Wisconsin Ave., Suite 600 W. Bethesda, MD 20814. Phone: (301)907-2862 Fax: (301)907-2864 E-mail: communications@tma-net.org • URL: http://www.tma-net.org • 1998. $95.50. Sixth edition.

Essentials of Federal Income Taxation for Individuals and Business. CCH, Inc., 2700 Lake Cook Rd. Riverwoods, IL 60015. Phone: 800-835-5224 or (847)267-7000 E-mail: cust_serv@cch.com • URL: http://www.cch.com • Annual. $72.00. Covers basic tax planning and tax reduction strategies as affected by tax law changes and IRS interpretations. Includes sample filled-in forms.

Essentials of Knowledge Management. Bryan Bergeron. John Wiley and Sons, Inc., 111 River St. Hoboken, NJ 07030. Phone: 800-225-5945 or (201)748-6000 Fax: (201)748-6088 E-mail: info@wiley.com • URL: http://www.wiley.com • 2003. $29.95. Covers current strategies, trends, and technologies in knowledge management. Includes examples of best practices. (Essentials Series).

Essentials of Managerial Finance. South-Western, City Center Tower Two, 301 Commerce St., Suite 3700 Fort Worth, TX 76102-4137. Phone: 800-354-9706 or (817)334-7500 Fax: 800-847-8488 or (817)334-7844 E-mail: wlittle@harbrace.com • URL: http://www.harcourtcollege.com • 2003. $112.95. 13th edition.

Essentials of Media Planning: A Marketing Viewpoint. Arnold M. Barban and others. McGraw-Hill, 1221 Ave. of the Americas New York, NY 10020. Phone: 800-722-4726 or (212)512-2000 Fax: (212)512-4502 E-mail: customer.service@mcgraw-hill.com • URL: http://www.mcgraw-hill.com • 1993. $29.95. Third edition. Practical guide to media analysis. (NTC Business Book Series).

Essentials of Project Management. Dennis Lock. Ashgate Publishing Co., 101 Cherry St., Ste. 420 Burlington, VT 05401-4405. Phone: 800-535-9544 or (802)865-7641 Fax: (802)865-7847 E-mail: adonahue@ashgate.com • URL: http://www.ashgate.com • 2000. $29.95. Second edition. Published by Gower in England.

Essentials of Psychological Testing. Lee J. Cronbach. Addison-Wesley, 75 Arlington St., Ste. 300 Boston, MA 02116. Phone: 800-447-2226 or (617)848-7500 • URL: http://www.aw.com • 1997. $125.00. Fifth edition.

Essentials of Real Estate Investment. David Sirota. Dearborn Trade Publishing, A Kaplan Professional Co., 155 N Wacker St. Chicago, IL 60606. Phone: 800-621-9621 or (312)836-4400 Fax: (312)836-1021 E-mail: trade@dearborn.com • URL: http://www.dearborntrade.com • 2001. $45.95. Sixth edition. Tax law revisions.

Estate and Personal Financial Planning. West Group, 610 Opperman Dr. Eagan, MN 55123. Phone: 800-328-4880 or (651)687-7000 Fax: 800-340-9378 E-mail: bookstore@westgroup.com • URL: http://www.westgroup.com • Quarterly. $980.00 per year. Newsletter.

Estate and Retirement Planning Answer Book. William D. Mitchell. Aspen Publishers, Inc., 1185 Avenue of the Americas New York, NY 10036. Phone: 800-234-1660 or (212)597-0200 Fax: (212)597-0338 E-mail: customer.service@aspenpubl.com • URL: http://www.aspenpublishers.com • 2000. $145.00. Third edition. Basic questions and answers by a lawyer.

Estate Plan Book 2000. William S. Moore. American Institute for Economic Research, PO Box 1000 Great Barrington, MA 01230-1000. Phone: (413)528-1216 Fax: (413)528-0103 E-mail: info@aier.org • URL: http://www.aier.org • 2000. $10.00. Revision of 1997 edition. Part one: "Basic Estate Planning." Part two: "Reducing Taxes on the Disposition of Your Estate." Part three: "Putting it All Together: Examples of Estate Plans." Provides succinct information on wills, trusts, tax planning, and gifts. (Economic Education Bulletin.)

Estate Planner's Alert. RIA, 395 Hudson St. New York, NY 10014. Phone: 800-950-1216 or (212)367-6300 E-mail: riahome@riag.com • URL: http://www.riahome.com • Monthly. $140.00 per year. Newsletter. Covers the tax aspects of personal finance, including home ownership, investments, insurance, retirement planning, and charitable giving. Formerly *Estate and Financial Planners Alert*.

Estate Planning. American Lawyer Media, Inc., 105 Madison Ave. New York, NY 10016. Phone: 800-888-8300 or (212)779-9200 Fax: (212)481-8110 E-mail: lawcatalog@amlaw.com • URL: http://www.lawcatalog.com/ • Looseleaf. $239.00. Two volumes. Updated as needed. Covers all legal aspects of estate planning, including wills, trusts, taxation, gifts, charitable contributions, family business considerations, and insurance. Includes forms and checklists. (Law Journal Press).

Estate Planning After The Economic Growth and Tax Relief Reconciliation Act of 2001: A Supplement to The Estate Plan Book 2000. William S. Moore. American Institute for Economic Research, PO Box 1000 Great Barrington, MA 01230-1000. Phone: (413)528-1216 Fax: (413)528-0103 E-mail: info@aier.org • URL: http://www.aier.org • 2001. Included with *The Estate Plan Book 2000* ($10.00). Contains two sections: "Major Changes Bearing on Estate Planning Under the New Act" and "Estate Planning Under the New Act" (Economic Education Bulletin).

Estate Planning and Taxation Coordinator. RIA, 395 Hudson St. New York, NY 10014. Phone: 800-950-1216 or 800-431-9025 E-mail: riahome@riag.com • URL: http://www.riahome.com • Biweekly. $1,290.00 per year. Nine looseleaf volumes. Includes *Estate Planner's Alert* and *Lifetime Planning Alert*.

Estate Planning: Inheritance Taxes. Prentice Hall PTR, 240 Frisch Ct. Paramus, NJ 07652. Phone: 800-282-0693 Fax: 800-445-6991 • URL: http://www.phptr.com • Five looseleaf volumes. Periodic supplementation. Price on application.

Estate Planning Journal. RIA, 395 Hudson St. New York, NY 10014. Phone: 800-950-1216 or 800-431-9025 • URL: http://www.riahome.com • Monthly. $295.00 per year.

Estate Planning Primer. Ralph G. Miller. ViewPlan, Inc., 2515 Camino Del Rio, S., Suite 312 San Diego, CA 92108-3716. Phone: 800-826-2127 or (619)239-3141 Fax: (619)497-0192 1994. $99.00. Eighth edition. Written for attorneys and other estate planning professionals. Includes tables, sample tax forms, legal documents, and client letters. letters

Estate Planning Program. Prentice Hall PTR, 240 Frisch Ct. Paramus, NJ 07652. Phone: 800-282-0693 Fax: 800-445-6991 • URL: http://www.phptr.com • Two looseleaf volumes. Periodic supplementation. Price on application. Includes checklists and forms.

Estate Planning Review. CCH Inc., 4025 W Peterson Ave. Chicago, IL 60646-6085. Phone: 888-224-7377 or (847)267-7000 Fax: (773)866-3895 E-mail: custsvc@iwpnews.com • URL: http://www.cch.com • Description: Monthly newsletter covering estate and financial planning issues for individuals. Includes coverage of retirement planning, insurance planning and investments.

Estate Planning Strategies After Estate Tax Reform: Insights and Analysis. Charles D. Fox and Thomas W. Aberdroth. CCH, Inc., 2700 Lake Cook Rd. Riverwoods, IL 60015. Phone: 800-835-5224 or (847)267-7000 E-mail: cust_serv@cch.com • URL: http://www.cch.com • 2001. $45.00. Produced by the Estate Planning Department of Schiff, Hardin & Waite. Covers estate planning techniques and opportunities resulting from tax legislation of 2001.

Estate Planning Under the New Law: What You Need to Know. CCH, Inc., 2700 Lake Cook Rd. Riverwoods, IL 60015. Phone: 800-835-5224 or (847)267-7000 E-mail: cust_serv@cch.com • URL: http://www.cch.com • 2001. $7.00. Booklet summarizes significant changes in estate planning brought about by tax legislation of 2001.

Estate Planning: Wills, Trusts and Forms. RIA, 395 Hudson St. New York, NY 10014. Phone: 800-950-1216 or 800-431-9025 E-mail: riahome@riag.com • URL: http://www.riahome.com • Looseleaf service. Includes bimonthly updates.

Estimating for Home Builders. Jerry Householder. Builderbooks, 1201 15th St., N. W. Washington, DC 20005-2800. Phone: 800-368-5242 or (202)822-0395 Fax: (202)822-0391 • URL: http://www.builderbooks.com • 1998. $30.80. Third edition. Describes the process of developing complete cost estimates and the shortcut methods-to ensure success in the building business.

Estimating in Building Construction. Frank R. Dagostino and Leslie Feigenbaum. Prentice Hall PTR, 240 Frisch Ct. Paramus, NJ 07652. Phone: 800-282-0693 Fax: 800-445-6991 • URL: http://www.phptr.com • 2003. Sixth edition. Price on application.

ETF Connect. Nuveen InvestmentsPhone: 800-257-8787 • URL: http://www.etfconnect.com • Free Web site makes available extensive, searchable information on individual closed-end investment funds, preferred share funds, and exchange-traded index funds. Information on a particular fund is available by name or as part of a classification (high yield, investment grade, municipal, emerging markets, global equity, etc.). Fund charts are available for various time periods, as is data concerning premiums or discounts, dividends, annualized total return, credit quality, "Top 10 Holdings," and so forth.

The Ethical Hack: A Framework for Business Value Penetration Testing. James S. Tiller. CRC Press, 2000 N.W. Corporate Blvd. Boca Raton, FL 33431. Phone: 800-272-7737 or (561)994-0555 Fax: 800-374-3401 or (561)989-9732 E-mail: orders@crcpress.com • URL: http://www.crcpress.com • 2004. $69.95. Provides practical information relating to the deliberate, "ethical hacking" of a computer system to uncover security flaws. Includes hacker technology, interpretation of results, protection of security professionals, staff politics, and details of various testing procedures. (Imprint: Auerbach Publications.)

The Ethics of Management. LaRue T. Hosmer. McGraw-Hill, 1221 Ave. of the Americas New York, NY 10020. Phone: 800-722-4726 or (212)512-2000 Fax: (212)512-4502 E-mail: customer.service@mcgraw-hill.com • URL: http://www.mcgraw-hill.com • 2002. $50.00. Fourth edition.

Ethics Resource Center., 2345 Crystal Dr., Ste. 201 Arlington, VA 22202. Phone: 800-777-1285 or (703)647-2185 Fax: (703)647-2180 E-mail: ethics@ethics.org • URL: http://www.ethics.org • Seeks to serve as a catalyst to improve the ethical practices of individuals and organizations from the classroom to the boardroom. Fulfills its mission through three distinct areas of expertise: as a leader in the fields of organizational/business ethics consulting; as a provider and facilitator of character education programs; and as an ethics information clearinghouse.

Ethnic Enrollment Data From Institutions of Higher Education. U.S. Dept. of Health and Human Services, Office for Civil Rights, Washington, DC 20201. Phone: (202)619-0671 Annual.

The EU Institutions' Register. Routledge Reference, 11 New Fetter Ln. London EC4P 4EE, United Kingdom. Phone: (44)20 70176649 Fax: (44)20 70176720 E-mail: edit.europa@tandf.co.uk • URL: http://www.euroconfidential.com • Covers: Over 5,900 key personnel in each of the major institutions, including: European Commission, European Parliament, Economic and Social Committee, Council of the European Union, Court of Justice, European Investment Bank, Court of Auditors, Committee of Regions and EU Agencies. Entries include: Contact information.

Euroguide Yearbook of the Institutions of the European Union and of the Other European Organiz. Bernan Associates, 4611-F Assembly Dr. Lanham, MD 20706-4391. Phone: 800-274-4888 or (301)459-7666 Fax: 800-865-3450 or (301)459-0056 E-mail: info@bernan.com • URL: http://www.bernan.com • Annual. Free. Published by Editions Delta. Information on public and private institutions in the European Union contributing to European integration.

Euromoney: The Monthly Journal of International Money and Capital Markets. American Educational Systems, PO Box 236 New York, NY 10024-0246. Phone: 800-431-1579 Monthly. $490.00 per year. Includes print and online editions. Supplement available *Guide to World Equity Markets*.

Europa Directory of International Organizations. Available from Taylor & Francis Group, 325 Chestnut St. Philadelphia, PA 19106. Phone: 800-821-8312 or (215)625-8900 Fax: 800-248-4724 or (215)625-2940 E-mail: info@taylorandfrancis.com • URL: http://www.taylorandfrancis.com • 2001. $250.00. Published by Europa Publications (http://www.europapublications.com). Describes about 1,700 associations and other organizations around the world.

Europa 2000: The American Business Report on Europe. Wolfe Publishing, Inc., South Nashua Station, P.O. Box 7599 Nashua, NH 03060-9883. Phone: 800-882-3876 or (603)888-0338 Fax: (603)888-5816 Monthly. $119.00 per year. Newsletter on consumer and industrial marketing in a unified European Economic Community. Includes classified business opportunity advertisements and a listing by country of forthcoming major trade shows in Europe.

Europa World Year Book. Routledge Reference, 11 New Fetter Ln. London EC4P 4EE, United Kingdom. Phone: 800-821-8312 or (44)20 70176649 Fax: (44)20 70176720 E-mail: edit.europa@tandf.co.uk • URL: http://www.taylorandfrancis.com • Covers: Background and statistical information on recent history, government, economic affairs, geography and the current situation in every country of the world as well as providing an extensive listing of national key organizations and firms and about 1,650 international organization. Entries include: For international organizations—Name, address, principal officials, organization, function, activities, financial structure. For national organizations—Lists with names, addresses, officials, and key facts as appropriate, for the government, religious bodies, newspapers, radio and television stations, banks, trade as-

sociations, transport industry, tourism and cultural organizations, universities, research institutes.

European Access. European Commission-United Kingdom Offices. Chadwyck-Healey, Inc., 300 N. Zeeb Rd. Ann Arbor, MI 48106-1346. Phone: 800-521-0600 or (734)761-4700 E-mail: info@il.proquest.com • URL: http://www.chadwyck.com • Bimonthly. $195.00 per year. Published in England. A journal providing general coverage of developments and trends within the European Community.

European Compendium of Marketing Information. Available from Gale Cengage Learning, 27500 Drake Rd. Farmington Hills, MI 48331-3535. Phone: 800-877-GALE or (248)699-GALE Fax: 800-414-5043 E-mail: gale.galeord@cengage.com • URL: http://www.galegroup.com • 1996. $350.00. Second edition. Volume two. Published by Euromonitor. Provides marketing and production statistics relating to European consumer products and services.

European Economy, Series A: Recent Economic Trends. Bernan Associates, 4611-F Assembly Dr. Lanham, MD 20706-4391. Phone: 800-274-4447 or (301)459-2255 Fax: 800-865-3450 or (301)459-0056 E-mail: order@bernan.com • URL: http://www.bernan.com • Monthly. $65.00 per year. Published by the Commission of the European Communities, Luxembourg.

European Economy, Series B: Business and Consumer Survey Results. Commission of the European Communities. Available from Bernan Associates, 4611-F Assembly Dr. Lanham, MD 20706-4391. Phone: 800-274-4888 or (301)459-2255 Fax: 800-865-3450 or (301)459-0056 E-mail: query@bernan.com • URL: http://www.bernan.com • Monthly. $65.00 per year. Published by the Commission of the European Communities, Luxembourg. Editions in English, French, German, and Italian.

European Food Marketing Directory. Euromonitor International, 224 S Michigan Ave., Ste. 1500 Chicago, IL 60604. Phone: 800-577-EURO or (312)922-1115 Fax: 800-414-5043 or (312)922-1157 E-mail: insight@euromonitorintl.com • URL: http://gale.cengage.com • Covers: The food marketing industry in Europe, including information sources, retailers, wholesalers, leading companies, and statistics. Entries include: Name, address, phone, fax, telex.

European Kompass on Disc. Available from Kompass USA, Inc., 121 Whitney Ave. New Haven, CT 06510. Phone: 877-566-7277 or (203)503-6789 Fax: (203)503-6780 E-mail: mail@kompass-usa.com • URL: http://www.kompass.com • Semiannual. CD-ROM provides information on more than 400,000 companies in Belgium, Denmark, France, Germany, Ireland, Italy, Luxembourg, Netherlands, Norway, Spain, Sweden, and UK. Classification system covers approximately 50,000 products and services.

European Management Journal. Elsevier, 655 Ave. of the Americas New York, NY 10010-5107. Phone: 800-366-2665 or (212)989-5800 Fax: 800-535-9935 or (212)633-3680 E-mail: custserv@elsevier.com • URL: http://www.elsevier.com • Bimonthly. Individuals, $140.00 per year; institutions, $690.00 per year. Covers a wide variety of topics, including management problems of the European Single Market.

European Marketing Academy., Pl. de Brouckere Plein, 31 B-1000 Brussels, Belgium. Phone: 32 2 2266660 Fax: 32 2 5121929 E-mail: jozsef.beracs@uni-corvinus.hu • URL: http://www.emac-online.org • Persons involved or interested in teaching or research in the field of marketing. Serves as forum for exchange of information concerning marketing; fosters improved dissemination of information; promotes international exchange in the field of marketing.

European Marketing Data and Statistics. Available from Gale Cengage Learning, 27500 Drake Rd. Farmington Hills, MI 48331-3535. Phone: 800-877-GALE or (248)699-GALE Fax: 800-414-5043 E-mail: gale.galeord@cengage.com • URL: http://gale.cengage.com • Annual. $530.00. Published by Euromonitor. Presents essential marketing data, including demographics and consumer expenditure patterns, for 31 European countries.

European Marketing Forecasts. Available from Gale Cengage Learning, 27500 Drake Rd. Farmington Hills, MI 48331-3535. Phone: 800-877-GALE or (248)699-GALE Fax: 800-414-5043 E-mail: gale.galeord@cengage.com • URL: http://gale.cengage.com • Annual. $1,250.00. Published by Euromonitor. Contains demographic, economic, and market forecasts for the countries of Europe to the year 2010. Forecasts include market-size data for 15 consumer product sectors (food, clothing, automobiles, consumer electronics, etc.).

European Marketing Information Sourcebook. Euromonitor International, 122 South Michigan Ave., Suite 810 Chicago, IL 60603. Phone: 800-577-3876 or (312)922-1115 Fax: (312)922-1157 E-mail: info@euromonitor.com • URL: http://www.euromonitor.com • 2003. $475.00. Lists trade associations, statistical offices, government agencies, special libraries, trade journals, websites, and other sources of business information for the countries of Europe.

European Union Annual Review of Activities, 2001/2002. Geoffrey Edwards and George Wiessala, editors. Blackwell Publishing, 350 Main St. Malden, MA 02148. Phone: 800-216-2522 or (781)388-8200 Fax: 800-864-7626 or (781)388-8210 E-mail: books@blackwellpub.com • URL: http://www.blackwellpub.com • 2002. $39.95.

European Union - Delegation of the Commission to the United States., 2300 M St. NW Washington, DC 20037. Phone: (202)862-9500 Fax: (202)429-1766 E-mail: relex-delusw-

help@cec.eu.int • URL: http://www.eurunion.org • Diplomatic delegation of the European Commission in the United States for the European Union, comprising European Community (Common Market); European Coal and Steel Community; and European Atomic Energy Community. Distributes official documents and information brochures of the European Union. Provides speakers' bureau and reference service. Represents the EU to U.S. government, international organizations, trade associations, academia, U.S. industry and the general public. Responds to all public inquiries.

European Union Encyclopedia and Directory. Taylor & Francis Group, 325 Chestnut St., Ste. 800 Philadelphia, PA 19106. Phone: 800-821-8312 or (215)625-8900 Fax: (215)625-2940 E-mail: info@taylorandfrancis.com • URL: http://www.taylorandfrancis.com • Semiannual. $600.00. Published by Europa. Provides directory information for major European Union organizations, with detailed descriptions of various groups or concepts in an "Encyclopedia" section. A statistics section contains a wide variety of data related to business, industry, and economics. Formerly *European Communities Encyclopedia and Directory*.

Europe's Top Quoted Companies: A Comparative Directory from Seventeen European Stock Exchanges. Kogan Page, 120 Pentonville Rd. London N1 9JN, England. Phone: 44 020 7278 0433 Fax: 44 020 7837 6348 E-mail: kpinfo@kogan-page.co.uk • URL: http://www.kogan-page.co.uk • Annual. $325.00. Provides detailed, 5-year financial data on 850 major European companies that are publicly traded. Includes company addresses.

Eurostat Yearbook: A Statistical View on Europe. Available from Bernan Associates, 4611-F Assembly Dr. Lanham, MD 20706-4391. Phone: 800-274-4888 or (301)459-2255 Fax: 800-865-3450 or (301)459-0056 E-mail: query@bernan.com • URL: http://www.bernan.com • Annual. $65.00. Published by European Communities (http://www.europa.eu.int/comm/eurostat/). Statistical topics include economics, national income, population, land, agriculture, environment, government, housing, and crime. Covers "every country in Europe and the European Union."

EuroWatch. LRP Publications, 747 Dresher Rd., Ste. 500, PO Box 980 Horsham, PA 19044-0980. Phone: 800-341-7874 or (215)784-0860 Fax: (215)784-9639 E-mail: custserve@lrp.com • URL: http://www.wtexec.com • Description: Provides news and analysis from European capitals and Washington, D.C. concerning how the United States' and other business interests are affected by the European Community's program to remove national barriers and create a single market for the trade and movement of goods, services, capital, and labor.

Evaluating Library Staff: A Performance Appraisal System. Patricia Belcastro. American Library Association, 50 E. Huron St. Chicago, IL 60611-2795. Phone: 800-545-2433 or (312)944-6780 Fax: (312)440-9374 E-mail: ala@ala.org • URL: http://www.ala.org • 1998. $35.00. Provides information on an appraisal system applicable to a wide variety of jobs in all types of libraries. Includes guidelines, performance appraisal forms, sample employee profiles, and a "Code of Service."

Event Planning Service. Entrepreneur Media, Inc., 2445 McCabe Way Irvine, CA 92614. Phone: 800-421-2300 or (949)261-2325 Fax: (949)261-0234 E-mail: entmag@entrepreneur.com • URL: http://www.entrepreneur.com • Looseleaf. $59.50. A practical guide to starting a social or corporate event planning service. Covers profit potential, start-up costs, market size evaluation, pricing, accounting, advertising, promotion, etc. (Start-Up Business Guide No. E1313.)

Every Landlord's Legal Guide. Marcia Stewart and others. Nolo, 950 Parker St. Berkeley, CA 94710. Phone: 800-728-3555 or (510)549-1976 Fax: 800-645-0895 or (510)548-5902 E-mail: simone@nolo.com • URL: http://www.nolo.com • 2003. $44.99. Sixth edition.

Every Manager's Guide to Information Technology: A Glossary of Key Terms and Concepts for Today's Business Leader. Peter G. W. Keen. Harvard Business School Publishing, 300 N Beacon St. Watertown, MA 02163. Phone: 800-988-0886 or (617)783-7500 Fax: (617)783-7555 • URL: http://www.hbs.edu • 1994. $18.95. Second edition. Provides definitions of terms related to computers, data communications, and information network systems. (Harvard Business Reference Series).

Every Tenant's Legal Guide. Janet Portman and Marcia Stewart. Nolo, 950 Parker St. Berkeley, CA 94710. Phone: 800-728-3555 or (510)549-1976 Fax: 800-645-0895 or (510)548-5902 E-mail: simone@nolo.com • URL: http://www.nolo.com • 2002. $29.99. Third edition.

Everyone's Money Book: Everything You Need to Know About Investing Wisely, Buying a Home. Jordan E. Goodman. Dearborn Trade Publishing, A Kaplan Professional Co., 155 N. Wacker St. Chicago, IL 60606. Phone: 800-621-9621 or (312)836-4400 Fax: (312)836-1021 E-mail: trade@dearborn.com • URL: http://www.dearborntrade.com • 2001. $30.00. Third edition. Covers investing, taxes, mortgages, retirement planning and other personal finance topics. Jordan E. Goodman is a writer for *Money* magazine.

Everything You Need to Know to Start a House Cleaning Service. Mary P. Johnson. Cleaning Consultant Services, Inc., P.O. Box 1273 Seattle, WA 98111-1273. Phone: (206)682-9748 Fax: (206)622-6876 E-mail: ccs@cleaningconsultants.com • URL: http://www.cleaningconsultants.com • 1999. $38.00. Revised edition.

SOURCES CITED

The Evolving Virtual Library: Practical and Philosophical Perspectives. Laverna M. Saunders, editor. Information Today, Inc., 143 Old Marlton Pike Medford, NJ 08055-8750. Phone: 800-300-9868 or (609)654-6266 Fax: (609)654-4309 E-mail: custserv@infotoday.com • URL: http://www.infotoday.com • 1999. $39.50. Various authors cover trends in library and school use of the Internet, intranets, extranets, and electronic databases.

eWEEK: Building the e-Business Enterprise. Element K Journals, 2165 Brighton-Henrietta Townline Rd., Ste. 3 Rochester, NY 14623. Phone: 800-223-8720 or (585)240-7301 Fax: (585)292-4392 • URL: http://www.elementkjournal.com • Weekly. $195.00 per year. Serves as an "information source for companies undertaking e-commerce and Internet-based business initiatives." Formerly *PC Week*.

Excerpta Medica: Biophysics, Bioengineering, and Medical Instrumentation. Elsevier, 655 Ave. of the Americas New York, NY 10010-5107. Phone: 800-366-2665 or (212)989-5800 Fax: 800-535-9935 or (212)633-3680 E-mail: custserv@elsevier.com • URL: http://www.elsevier.com • 16 times a year. Institutions, $2,859 per year. Section 27 of *Excerpta Medica*.

Excerpta Medica: Drug Dependence, Alcohol Abuse, and Alcoholism. Elsevier, 655 Ave. of the Americas New York, NY 10010-5107. Phone: 800-366-2665 or (212)989-5800 Fax: 800-535-9935 or (212)633-3680 E-mail: custinfo@elsevier.com • URL: http://www.elsevier.com • Bimonthly. Institutions, $1,398.00 per year. Section 40 of *Excerpta Medica*.

Excerpta Medica: Environmental Health and Pollution Control. Elsevief, 655 Ave. of the Americas New York, NY 10010-5107. Phone: 800-366-2665 or (212)989-5800 Fax: 800-535-9935 or (212)633-3680 E-mail: custserv@elsevier.com • URL: http://www.elsevier.com • 16 times a year. Institutions, $3,246.00 per year. Section 46 of *Excerpta Medica*. Covers air, water, and land pollution and noise control.

Excerpta Medica: Health Policy, Economics and Management. Elsevier, 655 Ave. of the Americas New York, NY 10010-5107. Phone: 800-366-2665 or (212)989-5800 Fax: 800-535-9935 or (212)633-3680 E-mail: custserv@elsevier.com • URL: http://www.elsevier.com • Bimonthly. Qualified personnel, $336.00 per year; institutions, $1,719.00 per year. Section 36 of *Excerpta Medica*.

Excerpta Medica: Human Genetics. Elsevier, 655 Ave. of the Americas New York, NY 10010-5107. Phone: 800-366-2665 or (212)989-5800 Fax: 800-535-9935 or (212)633-3680 E-mail: custserv@elsevier.com • URL: http://www.elsevier.com • Semimonthly. Qualified personnel, $409.00 per year; institutions, $4,140.00 per year. Section 22 of *Excerpta Medica*.

Excerpta Medica: Occupational Health and Industrial Medicine. Elsevier, 655 Ave. of the Americas New York, NY 10010-5107. Phone: 800-366-2665 or (212)989-5800 Fax: 800-535-9935 or (212)633-3680 E-mail: custserv@elsevier.com • URL: http://www.elsevier.com • Monthly. Institutions, $2,375.00 per year. Section 35 of *Excerpta Medica*.

Exchange and Commissary News. Executive Business Media, Inc., 825 Old Country Rd. Westbury, NY 11590. Phone: (516)334-3030 Fax: (516)334-8958 Monthly. $95.00 per year.

Exchange Rate Determination and Adjustment. Jagdeep S. Bhandari. Greenwood Publishing Group, Inc., 88 Post Rd., W. Westport, CT 06881-5007. Phone: 800-225-5800 or (203)226-3571 Fax: (203)431-2214 E-mail: customer-service@greenwood.com • URL: http://www.greenwood.com • 1982. $70.00.

Excise Taxes. Prentice Hall PTR, 240 Frisch Ct. Paramus, NJ 07652. Phone: 800-282-0693 Fax: 800-445-6991 • URL: http://www.phptr.com • Looseleaf. $216.00. Monthly updates. (Information Services Series)

Executive Compensation. American Lawyer Media, Inc., 105 Madison Ave. New York, NY 10016. Phone: 800-888-8300 or (212)779-9200 Fax: (212)481-8110 E-mail: lawcatalog@amlaw.com • URL: http://www.lawcatalog.com/ • Looseleaf. $189.00. Updated as needed. Covers many topics relating to the legal aspects of executive compensation, including taxation, securities law, payments in stock, fringe benefits, employment agreements, and severance arrangements. (Law Journal Press).

Executive Compensation. Michael Melbinger. CCH, Inc., 4025 West Peterson Ave. Chicago, IL 60646-6085. Phone: 800-248-3248 or (773)866-6000 Fax: 800-224-8299 or (773)866-3095 E-mail: cust_serv@cch.com • URL: http://www.onlinestore.cch.com/ • 2004. $145.00. "...describes the numerous federal statutes that govern the terms and provisions of executive compensation." Contains various samples, including an employment agreement, offer letter, retirement plan, and stock appreciation rights agreement.

Executive Compensation. Arthur H. Kroll. Prentice Hall PTR, 240 Frisch Ct. Paramus, NJ 07652. Phone: 800-282-0693 Fax: 800-445-6991 • URL: http://www.phptr.com • Three looseleaf volumes. Periodic supplementation. Price on application. Includes monthly newsletter.

Executive Compensation: A Strategic Guide for the 1990s. John J. McFadden, editor. The American College, 270 S. Bryn Mawr Ave. Bryn Mawr, PA 19010-2196. Phone: 800-421-0654 or (610)526-1000 Fax: (610)526-1310 • URL: http://www.amercoll.edu • 2001. $54.00. Sixth edition.

Executive Compensation and Taxation Coordinator. RIA, 395 Hudson St. New York, NY 10014. Phone: 800-950-1216 or 800-431-9025 E-mail: riahome@riag.com • URL: http://www.riahome.com • Monthly. $765.00 per year. Three looseleaf volumes.

Executive Compensation for Emerging Companies. Daniel Niehans and Shawn E. Lampron. Glasser Legalworks, 150 Clove Rd. Little Falls, NJ 07424. Phone: 800-308-1700 or (973)890-0008 Fax: (973)890-0042 E-mail: orders@glasserlegalworks.com • URL: http://www.glasserlegalworks.com • Looseleaf. $225.00, including CD-ROM version. Periodic Supplementation. Covers various aspects of executive compensation, with emphasis on stock option plans and stock ownership. Includes many annotated legal forms. (Emerging Growth Companies Series.)

Executive Compensation Survey Report. MidAtlantic Employees' Association, PO Box 770 Valley Forge, PA 19482. Phone: (215)666-7330 Fax: (215)666-7866 Annual. $400.00. Looseleaf service.

Executive Education.

Executive Etiquette in the New Workplace. Majabelle Y. Stewart and Marian Faux. Saint Martin's Press, 175 Fifth Ave. New York, NY 10010. Phone: 888-330-8477 or (212)726-0200 Fax: 800-672-2054 or (212)674-5151 E-mail: enquiries@stmartins.com • URL: http://www.stmartins.com • 1995. $14.95.

Executive Excellence: The Newsletter of Personal Development, Managerial Effectiveness, and Organizational Productivity. Kenneth M. Shelton, editor. Executive Excellence Publishing, 1344 E.1120 S Provo, UT 84606. Phone: (801)375-4060 Fax: (801)377-5960 E-mail: execexcl@itsnet.com • URL: http://www.eep.com • Monthly. $129.00 per year. Newsletter.

Executive Guide to Specialists in Industrial and Office Real Estate. Society of Industrial and Office Realtors, 1201 New York Ave., Ste. 350 Washington, DC 20005. Phone: 888-891-7467 or (202)449-8200 Fax: (202)449-8201 E-mail: admin@sior.com • URL: http://www.sior.com • Annual. $70.00. Approximately 1,800 specialist in industrial real estate.

Executive Recruiter News. Kennedy Information Inc., 1 Phoenix Mill Ln., 3rd Fl. Peterborough, NH 03458. Phone: 800-531-0007 or (603)924-0900 Fax: (603)924-4460 E-mail: bookstore@kennedyinfo.com • URL: http://www.kennedyinfo.com • Description: The authoritative voice of the recruiting industry, covering news, analysis, practice advice, proprietary data and opinion.

Executive Recruiting Service. Entrepreneur Media, Inc., 2445 McCabe Way Irvine, CA 92614. Phone: 800-421-2300 or (949)261-2325 Fax: (949)261-0234 E-mail: entmag@entrepreneur.com • URL: http://www.entrepreneur.com • Looseleaf. $59.50. A practical guide to starting an executive recruitment service. Covers profit potential, start-up costs, market size evaluation, owner's time required, pricing, accounting, advertising, promotion, etc. (Start-Up Business Guide No. E1228.)

Executive Remuneration. American Banker Newsletter, Thomson Financial Media, One State St. Plaza New York, NY 10004. Phone: (212)967-7000 Fax: (212)843-9600 E-mail: custserv@americanbanker.com • URL: http://www.americanbanker.com • Annual.

Executive Search Books. Kennedy Information, Inc., 1 Phoenix Mill Ln., 5th Fl. Peterborough, NH 03458. Phone: 800-531-0007 or (603)924-1006 Fax: (603)924-4460 E-mail: bookstore@kennedyinfo.com • URL: http://www.kennedyinfo.com • Annual. Free. Contains descriptions of selected books from various publishers on executive recruitment.

Executive Stock Options and Stock Appreciation Rights. American Lawyer Media, Inc., 105 Madison Ave. New York, NY 10016. Phone: 800-888-8300 or (212)779-9200 Fax: (212)481-8110 E-mail: lawcatalog@amlaw.com • URL: http://www.lawcatalog.com/ • Looseleaf. $189.00. Updated as needed. Coverage includes non-qualified stock options and incentive stock options. Contains sample forms and documents. (Law Journal Press).

Executive Wealth Advisory. National Institute of Business Management, 1750 Old Meadow Rd., Ste. 302 Mc Lean, VA 22102. Phone: 800-543-2049 or (703)905-8000 Fax: (703)905-8042 E-mail: customer@nibm.net Description: Provides investment strategies and opportunities to build personal wealth rapidly and safely.

Executive Women International., 515 S 700 E, Ste. 2A Salt Lake City, UT 84102. Phone: 877-4EWI-NOW or (801)355-2800 Fax: (801)355-2852 E-mail: ewi@executivewomen.org • URL: http://www.executivewomen.org • Individuals holding key positions in business professions. Conducts networking educational and charitable programs.

Executive's Guide to E-Business: From Tactics to Strategy. Martin Deise and others. John Wiley and Sons, Inc., 111 River St. Hoboken, NJ 07030. Phone: 800-225-5945 or (201)748-6000 Fax: (201)748-6088 E-mail: info@wiley.com • URL: http://www.wiley.com • 2000. $39.95. Covers the basic principles of doing business successfully by way of the Internet.

Exhibit Builder. Exhibit Builder, Inc., P.O. Box 4144 Woodland Hills, CA 91365. Phone: (818)225-0100 Fax: (818)225-0138 • URL: http://www.exhibitbuilder.net • Seven timees a year. $40.00 per year. For designers and builders of trade show exhibits.

Exhibit Designers and Producers Association., 5775G Peachtree-Dunwoody Rd., N.E., Suite 500 Atlanta, GA 30342. Phone: (404)303-7310 Fax: (404)252-0774 E-mail: lhoward@kellencompany.com • URL: http://www.edpa.com • Members are firms that design and build displays for trade shows.

Exhibitor Magazine Buyer's Guide to Trade Show Exhibits. Exhibitor Magazine Group, Inc., 206 S. Broadway, Suite 745 Rochester, MN 55904-6565. Phone: 888-235-6155 or (507)289-6556 Fax: (507)289-5253 • URL: http://www.exhibitornet.com • Annual. $35.00. Covers about 200 manufacturers of trade show exhibit equipment. Formerly *Buyer's Guide to Trade Show Displays*.

Expanded Shale Clay and Slate Institute., 2225 E. Murray Holladay Rd., Suite 102 Salt Lake City, UT 84117. Phone: (801)272-7070 Fax: (801)272-3377 E-mail: info@escsi.org • URL: http://www.escsi.org • Formerly Expanded Shale Institute.

Expanding Technologies, Expanding Careers: Librarianship in Transition. Ellis Mount, editor. Special Libraries Association, 1700 18th St., N. W. Washington, DC 20009-2514. Phone: (202)234-4700 Fax: (202)265-9317 E-mail: sla@sla.org • URL: http://www.sla.org • 1997. $45.00. Contains articles on alternative, non-traditional career paths for librarians, whether as entrepreneurs or employees. All the careers are related to computer-based, information retrieval and technology.

Expansion Management: Growth Strategies for Companies on the Move. Penton Media Inc., Industry Div., 1300 E. Ninth St. Cleveland, OH 44114. Phone: (216)696-7000 Fax: (216)696-1752 E-mail: information@penton.com • URL: http://www.penton.com • Monthly. Free to qualified personnel; others, $40.00 per year. Subject matter is concerned with expansion and relocation of industrial facilities.

Expenditures for Residential Improvements and Repairs. Available from U. S. Government Printing Office, Washington, DC 20402. Phone: (202)512-1800 Fax: (202)512-2250 E-mail: gpoaccess@gpo.gov • URL: http://www.access.gpo.gov • Quarterly. $16.00 per year. Bureau of the Census Construction Report, C50. Provides estimates of spending for housing maintenance, repairs, additions, alterations, and major replacements.

Expert Systems for Business: Concepts and Applications. D. V. Pigford and Gregory R. Baur. Course Technology, 25 Thompson Pl. Boston, MA 02110. Phone: 800-648-7450 or (617)757-7900 Fax: (617)621-3078 E-mail: reply@course.com • URL: http://www.course.com • 1995. $35.00. Second edition. (Introduction to Computing Series).

Explorations in Economic History. Elsevier, 655 Avenue of the Americas New York, NY 10010-5107. Phone: 800-366-2665 or (212)989-5800 Fax: 800-535-9935 or (212)633-3680 E-mail: custserv@elsevier.com • URL: http://www.elsevier.com • Quarterly. Individuals, $214.00 per year; institutions, $439.00 per year.

Explorations in Indexing and Abstracting: Pointing, Virtue, and Power. Brian C. O'Connor. Libraries Unlimited, Inc., 88 Post Rd., W Westport, CT 06881. Phone: 800-225-5800 Fax: (203)222-1205 E-mail: lu-books@lu.com • URL: http://www.lu.com • 1996. $40.00. Presents a philosophy of indexing. (Library and Information Science Text Series).

Exploring Marketing Research. William G. Zikmund. South-Western, 5191 Natorp Blvd. Mason, OH 45040. Phone: 800-543-0487 or (513)229-1000 • URL: http://www.swcollege.com • 2002. $115.95. Eighth edition.

Exploring Windows NT for Professionals. Element K Journals, 165 Brighton-Henrietta Townline Rd., Ste. 3 Rochester, NY 14623. Phone: 800-223-8720 or (585)240-7301 Fax: (585)292-4392 • URL: http://www.elementkjournals.com • Monthly. $139.00 per year. Newsletter on the Windows operating system for networks. Formerly *Exploring Windows NT*.

Explosives. Josef Kohler and others. John Wiley and Sons, Inc., 111 River St. Hoboken, NJ 07030. Phone: 800-225-5945 or (201)748-6000 Fax: (201)748-6088 E-mail: info@wiley.com • URL: http://www.wiley.com • 2002. $200.00. Fifth edition. Provides fundamental information on explosives for chemical engineers and other professionals.

Export Administration Regulations, 2004: Basic Manual. Available from U. S. Government Printing Office, Washington, DC 20402. Phone: (866)512-1800 or (202)512-1800 Fax: (202)512-2250 E-mail: gpoaccess@gpo.gov • URL: http://www.access.gpo.gov • 2004. $160.00. Looseleaf. Price includes supplements for an indeterminate period. Issued by the Bureau of Export Administration, U. S. Department of Commerce. Includes information on export policies, regulations, boycotted countries, licensing procedures, documentation requirements, and so forth.

Export America. Available from U. S. Government Printing Office, Washington, DC 20402. Phone: (202)512-1800 Fax: (202)512-2250 E-mail: gpoaccess@gpo.gov • URL: http://www.access.gpo.gov • Monthly. $61.00 per year. Issued by the International Trade Administration, U. S. Department of Conmmerce (http://www.ita.doc.gov/). Contains articles written to help American exporters penetrate overseas markets. Provides information on opportunities for trade and methods of doing international business. Formerly *Business America*.

Export-Import Financing. Harry M. Vendikian and Gerald A. Warfield. John Wiley and Sons, Inc., 111 River St. Hoboken, NJ 07030. Phone: 800-526-5368 or (201)748-6000 Fax: (201)748-6088 E-mail: info@wiley.com • URL: http://www.

wiley.com • 1996. $79.95. Fourth edition. (Frontiers in Finance Series).

Export Sales and Marketing Manual. Export Institute, 6901 W. 84th St., Suite 359 Minneapolis, MN 55438. Phone: 800-943-3171 or (612)943-1505 Fax: (612)943-1535 E-mail: info@exportinstitute.com • URL: http://www.exportinstitute.com • Annual. $315.00. Includes CD-Rom. Provides detailed information on exporting from the U. S. Includes sections on licenses, markets, pricing, agreements, shipping, payment, and other export topics.

Export Today: The Global Business and Technology Magazine. Trade Communications, Inc., 733 15th St., N.W., Suite 1100 Washington, DC 20005. Phone: (202)737-1060 Fax: (202)783-5966 E-mail: mjohn@interserv.com • URL: http://www.exporttoday.com • Monthly. $49.00 per year. Edited for corporate executives to provide practical information on international business and exporting.

Exporters' Encyclopedia. Dun and Bradstreet Information Services, 103 JFK Pky. Short Hills, NJ 07078. Phone: 800-526-0651 • URL: http://www.dnb.com • 1995. $495.00. Lease basis.

Exporting with the Internet. Peter J. Robinson and Jonathan Powell. John Wiley and Sons, Inc., 111 River St. Hoboken, NJ 07030. Phone: 800-842-3636 or (201)748-6000 Fax: (201)748-6088 E-mail: info@wiley.com • URL: http://www.wiley.com • 1997. $39.95. Explains how the Internet can help with finding overseas buyers and expediting export shipments and payments. (Business Technology Series).

Exposition Service Contractors Association., 22 Corporate Cir., No. 400 Henderson, NV 89074-7701. Phone: 877-792-3722 or (702)319-9561 or (702)450-7662 Fax: (702)450-7732 E-mail: askus@esca.org • URL: http://www.esca.org • Members are companies providing supplies and services for trade shows and conventions.

Extending the Librarian's Domain: A Survey of Emerging Occupational Opportunities for Librarians and Information Professionals. Forest W. Horton. Special Libraries Association, 1700 18th St., N. W. Washington, DC 20009-2514. Phone: (202)234-4700 Fax: (202)265-9317 E-mail: sla@sla.org • URL: http://www.sla.org • 1994. $38.00. An examination of non-traditional career possibilities for special librarians. (Occasional Papers: No. 4).

The Extraordinary Leader: Turning Good Managers into Great Leaders. John H. Zenger and Joseph Folkman. McGraw-Hill, 1221 Ave. of the Americas New York, NY 10020. Phone: 800-722-4726 or (212)512-2000 Fax: (212)512-4502 E-mail: customer.service@mcgraw-hill.com • URL: http://www.mcgraw-hill.com • 2002. $27.95. Presents a new model of leadership featuring 16 competencies.

Extraordinary Popular Delusions and the Madness of Crowds. Charles Mackay. Prometheus Books, 59 John Glenn Dr. Amherst, NY 14228-2197. Phone: 800-421-0351 or (716)691-0133 Fax: (716)691-0137 E-mail: marketing@prometheusbooks.com • URL: http://www.prometheusbooks.com • 2001. $19.00. A classic work on speculation and crowd psychology, originally published in 1841. (Great Minds Series).

The Extreme Searcher's Guide to Web Search Engines: A Handbook for the Serious Searcher. Randolph Hock. Information Today, Inc., 143 Old Marlton Pike Medford, NJ 08055-8750. Phone: 800-300-9868 or (609)654-6266 Fax: (609)654-4309 E-mail: custserv@infotoday.com • URL: http://www.infotoday.com • 2001. $24.95. Second expanded revised edition. Provides detailed information and advice on effective use of the major Internet search engines. (CyberAge Books.)

The Extreme Searcher's Internet Handbook: A Guide for the Serious Searcher. Randolph Hock. Information Today, Inc., 143 Old Marlton Pike Medford, NJ 08055-8750. Phone: 800-300-9868 or (609)654-6266 Fax: (609)654-4309 E-mail: custserv@infotoday.com • URL: http://www.infotoday.com • 2004. $24.95. Provides information on "all major areas of Internet content." Edited for both beginning and experienced searchers. (CyberAge Books).

Eye and Contact Lens: Science and Clinical Practices. University of Texas, Dept. of Ophthalmology. Lippincott Williams and Wilkins, 530 Walnut St. Philadelphia, PA 19106-3621. Phone: 800-638-3030 or (215)521-8300 Fax: (215)521-8902 E-mail: custserv@lww.com • URL: http://www.lww.com • Quarterly. Individuals, $88.00 per year; institutions, $108.00 per year. Formerly *The CLAO Journal*.

Eyecare Business: The Magazine for Progressive Dispensing. Boucher Communications, Inc., 1300 Virginia Dr. Fort Washington, PA 19034. Phone: (215)643-8000 Fax: (215)643-8099 • URL: http://www.boucher1.com • Monthly. Individuals, $75.00 per year. Covers the business side of optometry and optical retailing. Each issue features "Frames and Fashion."

F and OS Motor Carrier Annual Report: Results of Operations Class I & II Motor Carriers of Property: Regulated by the Interstate Commerce Commission. American Trucking Associations. Trucking Information Services, Inc., 2200 Mill Rd. Alexandria, VA 22314-4677. Phone: 800-282-5463 or (703)838-1700 Fax: (703)684-5720 E-mail: ata-infocenter@trucking.org • URL: http://www.truckline.com • Annual. $400.00.

F and OS Motor Carrier Quarterly Report (Financial and Operating Statistics). American Trucking Associations. Trucking Information Services, Inc., 2200 Mill Rd. Alexandria, VA 22314-4677. Phone: 800-282-5463 or (703)838-1700 Fax: (703)684-5720 • URL: http://www.truckline.com • Quarterly. $150.00 per number. Includes *Motor Carrier Annual Report*.

F & S Index. Gale Cengage Learning, 27500 Drake Rd. Farmington Hills, MI 48331-3535. Phone: 800-877-GALE or (248)699-GALE Fax: 800-414-5043 or (248)699-8069 E-mail: galeord@gale.com • URL: http://gale.cengage.com • Contains about four million citations to worldwide business, financial, and industrial or consumer product literature appearing from 1972 to date. Weekly updates. Inquire as to online cost and availability.

F & S Index: Europe. Gale Cengage Learning, 27500 Drake Rd. Farmington Hills, MI 48331-3535. Phone: 800-877-GALE or (248)699-4253 Fax: 800-414-5043 E-mail: gale.galeord@cengage.com • URL: http://gale.cengage.com • Monthly. $1,450.00 per year, including quarterly and annual cumulations. Provides annotated citations to marketing, business, financial, and industrial literature. Coverage of European business activity includes trade journals, financial magazines, business newspapers, and special reports. Formerly *Predicasts F & S Index: Europe*.

F & S Index: International. Gale Cengage Learning, 27500 Drake Rd. Farmington Hills, MI 48331-3535. Phone: 800-877-GALE or (248)699-4253 Fax: 800-414-5043 E-mail: gale.galeord@cengage.com • URL: http://gale.cengage.com • Monthly. $1,450.00 per year, including quarterly and annual cumulations. Provides annotated citations to marketing, business, financial, and industrial literature. Coverage of international business activity includes trade journals, financial magazines, business newspapers, and special reports. Areas included are Asia, Latin America, Africa, the Middle East, Oceania, and Canada.

F & S Index: United States. Gale Cengage Learning, 27500 Drake Rd. Farmington Hills, MI 48331-3535. Phone: 800-877-GALE or (248)699-4253 Fax: 800-414-5043 E-mail: gale.galeord@cengage.com • URL: http://gale.cengage.com • Monthly. $1,450.00 per year, including quarterly and annual cumulations. Provides annotated citations to marketing, business, financial, and industrial literature. Coverage of U. S. business activity includes trade journals, financial magazines, business newspapers, and special reports.

F-D-C Reports. FDC Reports, Inc., 5550 Friendship Blvd., Suite One Chevy Chase, MD 20815. Phone: 800-332-2181 or (301)657-9830 Fax: (301)656-3094 E-mail: fdcr@clark.net • URL: http://www.fdcreports.com • An online version of "The Gray Sheet" (medical devices), "The Pink Sheet" (pharmaceuticals), "The Rose Sheet" (cosmetics), "The Blue Sheet" (biomedical), and "The Tan Sheet" (nonprescription). Contains full-text information on legal, technical, corporate, financial, and marketing developments from 1987 to date, with weekly updates. Inquire as to online cost and availability.

FAA Aviation Forecasts. Federal Aviation Administration. Available from U. S. Government Printing Office, Washington, DC 20402. Phone: (202)512-1800 Fax: (202)512-2250 Annual. $44.00.

FAA Aviation News. Federal Aviation Administration. Available from U. S. Government Printing Office, Washington, DC 20402. Phone: (202)512-1800 Fax: (202)512-2250 E-mail: gpoaccess@gpo.gov • URL: http://www.access.gpo.gov • Bimonthly. $28.00. per year. Designed to help airmen become safer pilots. Includes updates on major rule changes and proposals.

FAA Historical Chronology: Civil Aviation and the Federal Government, 1926-1996. Edmund Preston, editor. Available from U. S. Government Printing Office, Washington, DC 20402. Phone: (202)512-1800 Fax: (202)512-2250 E-mail: gpoaccess@gpo.gov • URL: http://www.access.gpo.gov • 1998. $33.50. Third edition. Issued by the Federal Aviation Administration, U. S. Department of Transportation (http://www.dot.gov). Provides a compilation of historical information about the FAA and the earlier Civil Aeronautics Board (CAB). Chronological arrangement.

Fabric Filter Newsletter. The McIlvaine Co., 191 Waukegan Rd., Ste. 208 Northfield, IL 60093. Phone: (847)784-0012 Fax: (847)784-0061 E-mail: editor@mcilvainecompany.com • URL: http://www.mcilvainecompany.com • Description: Focuses on dry filtration using fabric and granular media filters. Provides information on all applications of dry filtration, from grain handling to power plants.

Fabric Science Swatch Kit, Gray. J.J. Pizzuto and others. Fairchild Books, Seven W. 34th St. New York, NY 10001. Phone: 800-932-4724 or (212)630-3880 Fax: (212)630-3868 • URL: http://www.fairchildbooks.com • 1998. $32.00. Seventh revised edition. Looseleaf service.

The Fabricator. Fabricators and Manufacturers Association International., 833 Featherstone Rd. Rockford, IL 61107-6302. Phone: (815)399-8775 Fax: (815)399-7701 E-mail: info@fmametalfab.org • URL: http://www/.fmametalfab.org • Monthly. $75.00 per year. Covers the manufacture of sheet, coil, tube, pipe, and structural metal shapes.

Fabricators and Manufacturers Association, International., 833 Featherstone Rd. Rockford, IL 61107-6302. Phone: (815)399-8700 Fax: (815)484-7701 E-mail: info@fmanet.org • URL: http://www.fmanet.org • Members are individuals concerned with metal forming, cutting, and fabricating. Includes a Sheet Metal Division and the Tube and Pipe Fabricators Association. Formerly Fabricating Manufacturers Association.

Facilities and Workplace Design: An Illustrated Guide. Quarterman Lee and others. Engineering and Management Press, 25 Technology Park Norcross, GA 30092-2988. Phone: 800-494-0460 or (770)449-0461 Fax: (770)441-3295 E-mail: cmagee@www.iienet.org • URL: http://www.iienet.org • 1996. $25.00. Written for both new and experienced designers. Features "25 illustrated tasks that can be applied to most projects."(Engineers in Business Series).

Facility Manager. International Association of Assembly Managers, Inc., 635 Fritz Dr., Ste. 100 Coppell, TX 75019-4442. Phone: 800-935-4226 or (972)906-7441 Fax: (972)906-7418 • URL: http://www.iaam.org • Quarterly. Free to members; non-members, $55.00 per year.

Factiva. Dow Jones Reuters Business Interactive, LLCPhone: 800-369-7466 or (609)452-1511 Fax: (609)520-5770 E-mail: solutions@factiva.com • URL: http://www.factiva.com • Fee-based Web site provides "global news and business information through Web sites and content integration solutions." Includes Dow Jones and Reuters newswires, The Wall Street Journal, and more than 7,000 other sources of current news, historical articles, market research reports, and investment analysis. Content includes 96 major U. S. newspapers, 900 non-English sources, trade publications, media transcripts, country profiles, news photos, etc.

Factory Automation-Related Equipment and Accessories. Available from MarketResearch.com, 641 Ave. of the Americas, Fourth Floor New York, NY 10011. Phone: 800-298-5699 or (212)807-2629 Fax: (212)807-2642 E-mail: order@marketresearch.com • URL: http://www.marketresearch.com • 2002. $3,850.00. Published by Global Industry Analysts. Provides worldwide market research data, including profiles of major automation equipment and software companies.

The Facts About Drug Use: Coping with Drugs and Alcohol in Your Family, at Work, in Your Community. The Haworth Press, Inc., 10 Alice St. Binghamton, NY 13904-1580. Phone: 800-429-6784 or (607)722-5857 Fax: 800-895-0582 or (607)722-1424 E-mail: getinfo@haworthpressinc.com • URL: http://www.haworthpressinc.com • 1992. $14.95. A comprehensive overview of drug dependence, including alcoholism.

Facts About the Cities. Allan Carpenter and Carl Provorse. H. W. Wilson Co., 950 University Ave. Bronx, NY 10452. Phone: (718)588-8400 Fax: 800-590-1617 or (718)590-1617 E-mail: custserv@hwwilson.com • URL: http://www.hwwilson.com • 1996. $100.00. Second edition. Contains a wide variety of information on 300 American cities, including cities in Puerto Rico, Guam, and the U. S. Virgin Islands. Data is provided on the workplace, taxes, revenues, cost of living, population, climate, housing, transportation, etc.

Facts and Figures on Government Finance. Tax Foundation, 1900 M St., N.W., Suite 550 Washington, DC 20036. Phone: (202)464-6200 Fax: (202)464-6201 E-mail: tf@taxfoundation.org • URL: http://www.taxfoundation.org • Annual. $45.00.

Facts-on-File World News Digest With Index. Facts on File, 132 W. 31 St., 17th Fl. New York, NY 10001. Phone: 800-322-8755 Fax: 800-678-3633 or (212)967-9196 E-mail: custserv@factsonfile.com • URL: http://ww.factsonfile.com • Weekly. $725.00 per year. Looseleaf service.

Facts-on-File Yearbook. Facts on File, Inc., 132 W 31st St., 17th Fl. New York, NY 10001. Phone: 800-322-8755 Fax: 800-678-3633 E-mail: custserv@factsonfile.com • URL: http://www.factsonfile.com • Annual. $100.00.

Faculty White Pages. Gale Cengage Learning, 27500 Drake Rd. Farmington Hills, MI 48331-3535. Phone: 800-877-GALE or (248)699-4253 Fax: 800-414-5043 E-mail: gale.galeord@cengage.com • URL: http://gale.cengage.com • 1991. $135.00. 91st edition. "Telephone book" classified arrangement of over 537,000 U. S. college faculty members in 41 subject sections. A roster of institutions is included.

Fair Employment Compliance: A Confidential Letter to Management. Management Resources, Inc., 380 Ocean Rd., Unit 2 Portsmouth, NH 03801-6051. Semimonthly. $245.00 per year. Newsletter.

Fair Employment Report. Clarity Publishing, 1894 Brown School Rd., PO Box 665 Saint Joseph, MI 49085. Phone: (616)429-8590 Fax: (616)429-8595 E-mail: editor@mcilvainecompany.com Description: Focuses on developments on the state and national levels regarding employment practices and discrimination. Emphasizes important legal decisions and governmental activities, particularly those of the Equal Employment Opportunity Commission, the Office of Federal Contract Compliance Programs, the Supreme Court, federal courts, Congress, state legislatures, state courts, and state agencies. Covers the efforts of businesses to comply with EEO, affirmative action, and diversity standards.

Fair, Square, and Legal: Safe Hiring, Managing, and Firing Practices to Keep You and Your Company Out of Court. Donald Weiss. AMACOM, 1601 Broadway New York, NY 10019. Phone: 800-262-9699 or (518)586-8100 Fax: (518)903-8168 E-mail: customerservice@amanet.org • URL: http://www.amacombooks.org • 1999. $29.95. Third edition. Covers recruiting, interviewing, sexual discrimination, evaluation of employees, disipline, defamation charges, and wrongful discharge.

The Fair Use Privilege in Copyright Law. William F. Patry. BNA,

SOURCES CITED

Inc., 1231 25th St., NW Washington, DC 20037. Phone: 800-372-1033 E-mail: customercare@bna.com • URL: http://www.bna.com • 1995. $115.00. Second edition. A comprehensive analysis of fair use.

Fairchild's Dictionary of Fashion. Charlotte Calasibetta. Fairchild Books, Seven W. 34th St. New York, NY 10001. Phone: 800-932-4724 or (212)630-3880 Fax: (212)630-3868 • URL: http://www.fairchildbooks.com • 1998. $45.00. Second revised edition.

Fairchild's Dictionary of Textiles. Phyllis B. Tortora, editor. Fairchild Books, Seven W. 34th St. New York, NY 10001. Phone: 800-932-4724 or (212)630-3880 Fax: (212)630-3868 • URL: http://www.fairchildbooks.com • 1996. $75.00. Seventh edition.

Fairplay Ports Directory. Fairplay Publications Ltd., Lombard House, 3 Princess Way Redhill RH1 1UP, United Kingdom. Phone: (44)1737 379000 Fax: (44)1737 379001 E-mail: sales@fairplay.co.uk • URL: http://www.fairplay.co.uk • Covers: 6,500 ports and over 17,700 port authorities, port agents, towage companies, repairers, and bunkerers worldwide. Entries include: Port name, address, phone, fax, name of port authority or responsible agency, location; description of facilities for navigation and cargo handling, and port service firms, including agencies, repair firms, and towage, probable charges and fees, 3,500 port plans and color atlas.

Fairplay: The International Shipping Weekly. Fairplay Publications, Ltd., PO Box 96 Coulsdon CR5 2TE, United Kingdom. Phone: 44 20 8645 2820 Fax: 44 20 8660 2524 E-mail: magazine@fairplay.co.uk • URL: http://www.fairplay.co.uk • Weekly. $465.00 per year. Provides international shipping news, commentary, market reports, reports on shipbuilding activity, advice on operational problems, and other information.

Fairplay World Shipping Directory. Fairplay Publications Ltd., Lombard House, 3 Princess Way Redhill RH1 1UP, United Kingdom. Phone: (44)1737 379000 Fax: (44)1737 379001 E-mail: sales@fairplay.co.uk • URL: http://www.fairplay.co.uk • Covers: more than 76,000 companies worldwide engaged in some aspect of shipping, including over 10,000 shipowners with fleets totalling over 45,000 vessels, shipbuilders and repairers, marine insurance shipping finance, protection and indemnity associations, marine equipment suppliers, and towing, salvage, and dredging; also lists marine organizations, shipbrokers, and consulting engineers and surveyors. Entries include: Company name, address, phone, fax, e-mail, URL, names of directors and executives, brief description of business; listings may also include associated and subsidiary companies and financial data.

Families U. S. A. Foundation., 1334 G St., N. W. Washington, DC 20005. Phone: (202)628-3030 Fax: (202)347-2417 E-mail: info@familiesusa.org • URL: http://www.familiesusa.org • Fields of interest are health care and long-term health care, including insurance. Formerly Villers Foundation.

Family Advocate. American Bar Association, Family Law Section, 750 N Lake Shore Dr. Chicago, IL 60611. Phone: 800-285-2221 or (312)988-5000 E-mail: orders@abanet.org • URL: http://www.abanet.org • Quarterly. Members $39.50; non-members, $44.50 per year. Practical advice for attorneys practicing family law.

Family Almanac. National Association of Retail Druggists. Creative Publishing, 1608 S Dakota Ave. Sioux Falls, SD 57105. Phone: 800-423-7158 or (605)336-9434 Fax: (605)338-3501 E-mail: kal1303567@aol.com Annual. Free at participating pharmacies. Formerly *NARD Almanac and Health Guide*.

Family Court Review: An Interdisciplinary Journal. Association of Family and Conciliation Courts. Sage Publications, Inc., 2455 Teller Rd. Thousand Oaks, CA 91320. Phone: 800-818-7243 or (805)499-9774 Fax: 800-583-2665 or (805)499-0871 E-mail: webmaster@sagepub.com • URL: http://www.sagepub.com • Quarterly. Institutions, $456.00 per year.

Family Economics and Nutrition Review. Available from U. S. Government Printing Office, Washington, DC 20402. Phone: (202)512-1800 Fax: (202)512-2250 E-mail: gpoaccess@gpo.gov • URL: http://www.access.gpo.gov • Semi-annual. $13.00 per year. Issued by the Consumer and Food Economics Institute, U. S. Department of Agriculture. Provides articles on consumer expenditures and budgeting for food, clothing, housing, energy, education, etc.

Family Law in a Nutshell. Harry D. Krause. West Publishing Co., 610 Opperman Dr. Eagan, MN 55123. Phone: 800-338-9424 or (651)687-7000 Fax: 800-340-9378 E-mail: bookstore@westgroup.com • URL: http://www.westgroup.com • 1995. $25.50. Third edition. (Nutshell Series).

Family Law Quarterly. American Bar Association, Family Law Section, 750 N Lake Shore Dr. Chicago, IL 60611. Phone: 800-285-2221 or (312)988-5000 Fax: (312)988-5528 E-mail: orders@abanet.org • URL: http://www.abanet.org • Quarterly. Free to members; non-members, $49.95 per year.

Family Law Reporter. Bureau of National Affairs Inc., 1801 S Bell St. Arlington, VA 22202. Phone: 800-372-1033 or (202)452-4200 Fax: (202)452-4226 E-mail: customercare@bna.com • URL: http://www.bna.com • Description: Offers a notification and reference service tracking state and federal developments affecting family law. Covers divorce, adoption, support order enforcement, parental rights termination, taxes, property division, and other topics of interest to lawyers. Recurring features include full text of selected judicial opinions; federal regulations and standards; and columns titled Current Developments, Survey and Analysis, Courts and Legislatures Report, Monographs, Reference File, Practice Aids, State Divorce Laws, and Uniform and Model Acts.

Family Law Tax Guide. CCH, Inc., 2700 Lake Cook Rd. Riverwoods, IL 60015. Phone: 800-835-5224 or (847)267-7000 E-mail: cust_serv@cch.com • URL: http://www.cch.com • Monthly. $619.00 per year. Looseleaf service.

Family Relations: State Capitals. Wakeman-Walworth, Inc., PO Box 7376 Alexandria, VA 22307-7376. Phone: 800-876-2545 or (703)768-9600 Fax: (703)768-9690 E-mail: newsletters@statecapitals.com • URL: http://www.statecapitals.com • 50 times a year. $245.00 per year.; print and online editions, $350.00 per year. Newsletter. Formerly *From the State Capitals: Family Relations*.

Family Tax Guide. Executive Reports Corp., 240 Frisch Ct. Paramus, NJ 07652. Phone: 800-282-0693 or (201)767-5059 Fax: 800-835-5327 or (201)236-7141 • URL: http://www.prenhall.com • 1985. $44.95.

Famous First Bubbles: The Fundamentals of Early Manias. Peter M. Garber. MIT Press, Five Cambridge Center Cambridge, MA 02142-1493. Phone: 800-356-0343 or (617)253-5641 Fax: (617)253-1709 E-mail: mitpr-orders@mit.edu • URL: http://www.mitpress.mit.edu • 2000. $15.95. Provides scholarly explanations of three historic price bubbles: the Dutch Tulipmania, the Mississippi Bubble, and the South Sea Bubble.

Fancy Food and Culinary Products. Talcott Communications Corp., 20 N Wacker Dr., Suite 1865 Chicago, IL 60606. Phone: (312)849-2220 Fax: (312)849-2174 Monthly. $34.00 per year. Emphasizes new specialty food products and the business management aspects of the specialty food and confection industries. Includes special issues on wine, cheese, candy, "upscale" cookware, and gifts. Formerly (Fancy Foods).

FAO Fertilizer Yearbook. United Nations Food and Agriculture Organization. Bernan Associates, 4611-F Assembly Dr. Lanham, MD 20706-4391. Phone: 800-274-4447 or (301)459-2255 Fax: 800-865-3450 or (301)459-0056 E-mail: info@bernan.com • URL: http://www.bernan.com • Annual. $36.00. Text in English, French, and Spanish. Formerly *Annual Fertilizer Review*.

FAO Fishery Series. Food and Agriculture Organization of the United States. Available from Bernan Associates, 4611-F Assembly Dr. Lanham, MD 20706-4391. Phone: 800-274-4447 or (301)459-7666 Fax: 800-865-3450 or (301)459-0056 E-mail: query@bernan.com • URL: http://www.bernan.com • Irregular. Price varies. Text in English, French, and Spanish. Incorporates *Yearbook of Fishery Statistics*.

FAO Production Yearbook. Available from Bernan Associates, 4611-F Assembly Dr. Lanham, MD 20706-4391. Phone: 800-274-4447 or (301)459-2255 Fax: 800-865-3450 or (301)459-0056 E-mail: query@bernan.com • URL: http://www.bernan.com • Annual. $45.00. Published by the Food and Agriculture Organization (http://www.fao.org). Contains worldwide data on agriculture, land use, farm crops, livestock, and agricultural prices.

FAO Quarterly Bulletin of Statistics. Food and Agriculture Organization of the United Nations. Available from UNIPUB, 4611-F Assembly Dr. Lanham, MD 20706-4391. Phone: 800-274-4888 or (301)459-2255 Fax: 800-865-3450 or (301)459-0056 • URL: http://www.unesco.org/publications • Quarterly. $20.00 per year. Provides international data on agricultural production, trade, and prices, covering the major commodities of many countries. Text in English, French, and Spanish. Formerly *FAO Monthly Bulletin of Statistics*.

FAO Trade Yearbook. Available from Bernan Associates, 4611-F Assembly Dr. Lanham, MD 20706-4391. Phone: 800-274-4888 or (301)459-2255 Fax: 800-865-3450 or (301)459-0056 E-mail: query@bernan.com • URL: http://www.bernan.com • Annual. $45.00. Published by the Food and Agriculture Organization (http://www.fao.org). Provides extensive worldwide data on exports and imports of agricultural commodities, fertilizers, tractors, and pesticides. Includes more than 130 tables of detailed statistics.

The Far East and Australasia 2000. Taylor and Francis Group, 325 Chestnut St., Ste. 800 Philadelphia, PA 19106. Phone: 800-821-8312 or (215)625-8900 Fax: (215)625-2940 E-mail: info@taylorandfrancis.com • URL: http://www.taylorandfrancis.com • Annual. $480.00. Published by Europa. Includes country statistical surveys of demographics, finance, trade, and agriculture. (Regional Surveys of the World.)

Far Eastern Economic Review. Dow Jones International Marketing Service, 420 Lexington Ave. New York, NY 10170. Phone: 800-568-7625 or (212)808-6615 Fax: (212)808-6652 Weekly. $205.00 per year (air mail). Published in Hong Kong by Review Publishing Co., a Dow Jones subsidiary (GPO Box 160, Hong Kong). Covers Asian business, economics, politics, and international relations. Includes reports on individual countries and companies, business trends, and stock price quotations.

Farm Chemicals International. Meister Media, 37733 Euclid Ave. Willoughby, OH 44094-5992. Phone: 800-572-7740 or (440)942-2000 Fax: (440)942-0662 E-mail: info@meistermedia.com • URL: http://www.meistermedia.com • Annual. $99.00. Manufacturers and suppliers of fertilizers, pesticides, and related equipment used in agribusiness.

Farm Equipment. Cygnus Business Media, 1233 Janesville Ave. Fort Atkinson, WI 53538. Phone: 800-547-7377 or (920)563-6388 Fax: (920)563-1707 E-mail: rich.reiff@cygnuspub.com • URL: http://www.cygnusbzb.com • Seven times a year. $48.00 per year. Includes annual*Product* issue.

Farm Equipment Manufacturers Association., 1000 Executive Pkwy., Ste. 100 St. Louis, MO 63141-6369. Phone: (314)878-2304 Fax: (314)878-1742 E-mail: fema@farmequip.org • URL: http://www.farmequip.org • Manufacturers of "shortlines" (specialized farm equipment).

Farm Equipment Wholesalers Association., PO Box 1347, Box 1347 Iowa City, IA 52244. Phone: (319)354-5156 Fax: (319)354-5157 E-mail: info@fewa.org • URL: http://www.fewa.org • Independent wholesaler-distributors of shortline and specialty farm equipment, light industrial tractors, lawn and garden tractors, turf care equipment, estate and park maintenance equipment, power vehicles for outdoor recreation and sports, and related supply items.

Farm Industry News. Primedia Business Magazines and Media, 7900 International Dr., Ste. 300 Minneapolis, MN 55425. Phone: 800-795-5445 or (925)851-9329 Fax: (925)851-4601 E-mail: subs@primediabusiness.com • URL: http://www.primediabusiness.com • Monthly. $25.00 per year. Includes new products for farm use.

Farm Journal: The Magazine of American Agriculture. Farm Journal Corp., 1818 Market St., 31st Fl. Philadelphia, PA 19103-3654. Phone: 800-523-1537 or (215)557-8900 Fax: (215)568-3989 E-mail: fjletters@farmjournal.com • URL: http://www.agweb.com • 12 times a year. $19.50 per year. Includes *Supplements*.

Farm Labor. U.S. Department of Agriculture, Washington, DC 20250. Phone: (202)447-2791 Monthly.

Farm Management. Michael D. Boehlje and Vernon R. Eidman. John Wiley and Sons, Inc., 111 River St. Hoboken, NJ 07030. Phone: 800-526-5368 or (201)748-6000 Fax: (201)748-6088 E-mail: info@wiley.com • URL: http://www.wiley.com • 1984. $107.95.

Farm Management. Ronald D. Kay and others. McGraw-Hill, 1221 Ave. of the Americas New York, NY 10020. Phone: 800-722-4726 or (212)512-2000 Fax: (212)512-4502 E-mail: customer.service@mcgraw-hill.com • URL: http://www.mcgraw-hill.com • 2003. $94.37. Fifth edition. (Science, Engineering and Mathematics Series).

Farm Management: Principles, Budgets, Plans. John Herbst and Duane Erickson. Stipes Publishing L.L.C, 204 W. University Ave. Champaign, IL 61820. Phone: (217)356-8391 Fax: (217)356-5753 E-mail: stipes@soltec.com • URL: http://www.stipes.com • 1996. $25.80. 10th edition.

Farm Mortgage Debt. U.S. Department of Agriculture, Economic Research Service, Washington, DC 20250. Phone: (202)720-2791 Annual.

Farm Power and Machinery Management. Donnell Hunt. Blackwell Publishing, 350 Main St. Malden, MA 02148. Phone: (781)388-8200 Fax: (781)388-8210 E-mail: subscrip@blackwellpub.com • URL: http://www.blackwellpublishing.com • 2001. $59.95. 10th edition.

Farmer's Digest. Heartland Communictions Group, Inc., 1003 Central Ave. Fort Dodge, IA 50501. Phone: 800-673-4763 10 times a year. $17.95 per year. Current information on all phases of agriculture.

FASB Accounting Standards. Financial Accounting Standards Board, 401 Merritt 7 Norwalk, CT 06856. Phone: 800-748-0659 or (203)847-0700 Fax: (203)849-9714 • URL: http://www.fasb.org • Annual. Price on application.

FASB Accounting Standards Current Text. Financial Accounting Standards Board, 401 Merritt 7 Norwalk, CT 06856. Phone: (203)847-0700 Fax: (203)849-9714 E-mail: webmaster@fasb.org • URL: http://www.fasb.org • $395.00. Three looseleaf volumes. Periodic supplementation.

FASB Accounting Standards Current Text: General Standards. Financial Accounting Standards Board, 401 Merritt 7 Norwalk, CT 06856. Phone: (203)847-0700 Fax; (203)849-9714 E-mail: webmaster@fasb.org • URL: http://www.fasb.org • Irregular. Price on application.

FASB Accounting Standards Current Text: Industries Standards. Financial Accounting Standards Board, 401 Merritt 7 Norwalk, CT 06856. Phone: (203)847-0700 Fax: (203)849-9714 E-mail: webmaster@fasb.org • URL: http://www.fasb.org • Irregular. Price on application.

FASB Accounting Standards Current Text: Professional Standards. Financial Accounting Standards Board, 401 Merritt 7 Norwalk, CT 06856. Phone: (203)847-0700 Fax: (203)849-9714 E-mail: webmaster@fasb.org • URL: http://www.fasb.org • Irregular. Price on application.

FASB Accounting Standards Current Text: Technical Practice Aids. Financial Accounting Standards Board, 401 Merritt 7 Norwalk, CT 06856. Phone: (203)847-0700 Fax: (203)849-9714 E-mail: webmaster@fasb.org • URL: http://www.fasb.org • Irregular. Price on application.

FASB Original Pronouncements. Financial Accounting Standards Board, 401 Merritt 7 Norwalk, CT 06856. Phone: (203)847-0700 Fax: (203)849-9714 E-mail: webmaster@fasb.org • URL: http://www.fasb.org • $595.00. Seven looseleaf volumes.

FASB Original Pronouncements. John Wiley and Sons, Inc., 111 River St. Hoboken, NJ 07030. Phone: 800-225-5945 or (201)748-6000 Fax: (201)748-6088 E-mail: info@wiley.com

• URL: http://www.wiley.com • 2001. $108.95. Three volumes include all the original pronouncements put forth by the Financial Accounting Standards Board since inception in 1973 and the American Institute of Certified Public Accountants.

FASB Statements of Financial Accounting Concepts. John Wiley and Sons, Inc., 111 River St. Hoboken, NJ 07030. Phone: 800-225-5945 or (201)748-6000 Fax: (201)748-6088 E-mail: info@wiley.com • URL: http://www.wiley.com • 2001. $35. 95. Contains statements of concepts issued by the Financial Accounting Standards Board.

Fashion Accessories: The Complete Twentieth Century Sourcebook. John Peacock. Thames Hudson, 500 5th Ave. New York, NY 10110. Phone: 800-223-4830 or (212)354-3763 Fax: (212)398-1252 E-mail: bookinfo@thames.wwnorton.com • URL: http://www.thamesandhudsonusa.com • 2000. $34.95.

Fashion Advertising and Promotion. Arthur A. Winters and Stanley Goodman. Fairchild Books, 7 W 34th St. New York, NY 10001. Phone: 800-932-4724 or (212)630-3868 Fax: (212)630-3880 E-mail: info@wiley.com • URL: http://www.wiley.com • 1984. $50.00

Fashion and Merchandising Fads. Frank W. Hoffmann and William G. Bailey. Haworth Press, Inc., 10 Alice St. Binghamton, NY 13904-1580. Phone: 800-429-6784 or (607)722-5857 Fax: 800-895-0582 or (607)722-1424 E-mail: getinfo@haworthpressinc.com • URL: http://www.haworthpressinc.com • 1994. $49.95. Contains descriptions of fashion industry fads or promotions from A to Z (Popular Culture Series).

Fashion Calendar. Fashion Calendar International, 153 E. 87th St. New York, NY 10128. Phone: (212)289-0420 Fax: (212)289-5917 Bimonthly. $365.00 per year.

Fashion, Fad, and Style. Gale Cengage Learning, 27500 Drake Rd. Farmington Hills, MI 48331-3535. Phone: 800-877-GALE Fax: 800-414-5043 or (248)699-8069 E-mail: galeord@galegroup.com • URL: http://www.galegroup.com • 2003. $250.00. Five volumes. Contains 500 entries covering "human decoration and adornment throughout history." Includes information on clothing, hairstyles, jewelry, and related items. (U-X-L imprint.)

Fashion Market Magazine. Fashion Market Magazine Group, Inc., 617 W 46th St., No. 2 New York, NY 10036-1906. Phone: (212)760-5100 Fax: (212)760-5112 E-mail: fashionmag@aol.com • URL: http://www.fashionmarketmagazine.com • Monthly. $59.00 per year. Covers the women's apparel industry, including photographs of "current collections of apparel available on the wholesale market." Includes news of all categories of women's clothing.

Fashion Merchandising: An Introduction. Elaine Stone. McGraw-Hill, 1221 Ave. of the Americas New York, NY 10020. Phone: 800-722-4726 or (212)512-2000 Fax: (212)512-4502 E-mail: customer.service@mcgraw-hill.com • URL: http://www.mcgraw-hill.com • 1989. $45.72. Fifth edition. (Marketing Series).

Fast Company: How Smart Business Works. Fast Company, Inc., 375 Lexington Ave. New York, NY 10017. Phone: 800-542-6029 or (212)499-2000 Fax: (212)389-5497 E-mail: subscriptions@fastcompany.com • URL: http://www.fastcompany.com • Monthly. $12.00 per year. Covers business management, with emphasis on creativity, leadership, innovation, career advancement, teamwork, the global economy, and the "new workplace."

Fast Facts About Social Security. Available from U. S. Government Printing Office, Washington, DC 20402. Phone: (202)512-1800 Fax: (202)512-2250 E-mail: gpoaccess@gpo.gov • URL: http://www.access.gpo.gov • Annual. $5.50. Issued by the Social Security Administration (http://www.ssa.gov). Provides concise data and charts relating to social security benefits, beneficiaries, disability payments, supplemental security income, and income of the aged.

Fast Food. Available from MarketResearch.com, 641 Ave. of the Americas, Third Floor New York, NY 10011. Phone: 800-298-5699 or (212)807-2629 Fax: (212)807-2716 E-mail: order@marketresearch.com • URL: http://www.marketresearch.com • 2001. $5,000.00. Published by Euromonitor Publications Ltd. Provides consumer market data for the United States, the United Kingdom, Germany, France, and Italy.

Fast Food Nation: The Dark Side of the All-American Meal. Eric Schlosser. Gale Cengage Learning, 27500 Drake Rd. Farmington Hills, MI 48331-3535. Phone: 800-877-GALE or (248)699-GALE Fax: 800-414-5043 or (248)699-8069 E-mail: gale.galeord@cengage.com • URL: http://gale.cengage.com • 2001. $30.95. Explains how the fast food industry is contributing to obesity, disease, urban sprawl, and other bad things. Special attention is given to the meatpacking industry, *E.coli*, worker injuries, fast food franchise problems, detrimental labor practices, and the effect of fast food diets on children. Companies prominently mentioned are McDonald's, Burger King, Wendy's, Taco Bell, Pizza Hut, Jack in the Box, ConAgra, and Iowa Beef Packers. Includes many research notes, a bibliography, and a detailed index.

Fastener Technology International. Initial Publications, 3869 Darrow Rd., Suite 109 Stow, OH 44224. Phone: (330)686-9544 Fax: (330)686-9563 E-mail: info@fastenertech.com • URL: http://www.fastenertech.com • Bimonthly. $40.00 per year.

Fastener Technology International Buyers' Guide. Initial Publications, Inc., 3869 Darrow Rd., Ste. 109 Stow, OH 44224. Phone: (330)686-9544 Fax: (330)686-9563 E-mail: info@fastenertech.com • URL: http://www.fastenertech.com • Annual. $40.00. Lists about 2,000 international manufacturers and distributors of fasteners and precision-formed parts.

Faster New Product Development: Getting the Right Product to Market Quickly. Milton D. Rosenau. AMACOM, 1601 Broadway New York, NY 10019. Phone: 800-262-9699 or (518)586-8100 Fax: (518)903-8168 E-mail: customerservice@amanet.org • URL: http://www.amacombooks.org • 1990. $55.00. A guide to new product development for companies of all sizes and kinds.

Fat Pipe: The Business of Marketing Broadband Services. Dagda Mor Media, Inc., 3402 Bonaire Crossing Marietta, GA 30066. Phone: (678)560-4388 Fax: (678)560-4387 E-mail: fatpipe@dagdamor.com • URL: http://www.dagdamor.com • Monthly. Controlled circulation. Edited for those who plan, develop, and market broadband Internet and telecommunications services.

Fats and Oils: Oilseed Crushings. U. S. Bureau of the Census, 4700 Silver Hill Rd. Washington, DC 20233-0001. Phone: (301)763-4636 E-mail: comments@census.gov • URL: http://www.census.gov • Monthly and annual. Provides data on shipments of cottonseed oil and soybean oil: value, quantity, imports, and exports. (Current Industrial Reports, M20J.)

Fats and Oils: Production, Consumption, and Stocks. U. S. Bureau of the Census, 4700 Silver Hill Rd. Washington, DC 20233-0001. Phone: (301)763-4636 E-mail: comments@census.gov • URL: http://www.census.gov • Monthly and annual. Covers the supply and distribution of cottonseed, soybean, and palm oils, and selected inedible products. (Current Industrial Reports, M20K.)

Fax Handbook. Gerald V. Quinn. McGraw-Hill, 1221 Ave. of the Americas New York, NY 10020. Phone: 800-722-4726 or (212)512-2000 Fax: (212)512-4502 E-mail: customer.service@mcgraw-hill.com • URL: http://www.mcgraw-hill.com • 1989. $16.95.

FAX Magazine. Technical Data Publishing Corp., 195A State, Route 33 Hartfield, VA 23071. Phone: (201)770-2633 Quarterly. Price on application.

Fax Modem Sourcebook. Andrew Margolis. John Wiley and Sons, Inc., 111 River St. Hoboken, NJ 07030. Phone: 800-225-5945 or (201)748-6000 Fax: (201)748-6088 E-mail: info@wiley.com • URL: http://www.wiley.com • 1995. $90. 00. Explains fax modem technology for both the novice and the experienced user. Includes technical programming information and international standards.

FaxUSA: A Directory of Facsimile Numbers for Business and Organizations Nationwide. Omnigraphics, Inc., 615 Griswold St. Detroit, MI 48226. Phone: 800-234-1340 or (313)961-1340 Fax: 800-875-1340 or (313)961-1383 E-mail: info@omnigraphics.com • URL: http://www.omnigraphics.com • 2004. $165.00. 11th edition. Provides more than 118,000 listings, with fax numbers, telephone numbers, and addresses.

FBI Law Enforcement Bulletin. Available from U. S. Government Printing Office, Washington, DC 20402. Phone: (202)512-1800 Fax: (202)512-2250 E-mail: gpoaccess@gpo.gov • URL: http://www.access.gpo.gov • Monthly. $36.00 per year. Issued by Federal Bureau of Investigation, U. S. Department of Justice. Contains articles on a wide variety of law enforcement and crime topics, including computer-related crime.

FCC Record. Available from U. S. Government Printing Office, Washington, DC 20402. Phone: (202)512-1800 Fax: (202)512-2250 E-mail: gpoaccess@gpo.gov • URL: http://www.access.gpo.gov • Biweekly. $678.00 per year. Produced by the Federal Communications Commission (http://www.fcc.gov). An inclusive compilation of decisions, reports, public notices, and other documents of the FCC.

FCC Report: An Exclusive Report on Domestic and International Telecommunications Policy and Regulation. Warren Publishing, Inc., 2115 Ward Ct., NW Washington, DC 20037. Phone: (202)872-9200 Fax: (202)293-3435 • URL: http://www.warrenpub.com • 26 times a year. $670.00 per year. Newsletter concerned principally with Federal Communications Commission reglations and policy.

FCIB International Bulletin (Finance, Credit and International Business). Finance, Credit and International Business-National Assoiciation of Credit Management. FCIB - NACM Corp., 8840 Columbia 100 Parkway Columbia, MD 21045-2158. Phone: 888-256-3242 or (410)423-1840 Fax: (410)423-1845 E-mail: fcib_info@fcibglobal.com • URL: http://www.fcibglobal.com • Quarterly. Membership.

FCIB-NACM Corp., 8840 Columbia 100 Pkwy. Columbia, MD 21045-2158. Phone: 888-256-3242 or (410)423-1840 Fax: (410)423-1845 E-mail: fcib_info@fcibglobal.com • URL: http://www.fcibglobal.com • Provides services to international credit and trade finance professionals, including international receivables management education, products, services and networking. Offers roundtable discussions, international trade surveys, industry groups, conferences, credit hotline, workshops and research services.

FDA Consumer. Available from U. S. Government Printing Office, Washington, DC 20402. Phone: (202)512-1800 Fax: (202)512-2250 E-mail: gpoaccess@gpo.gov • URL: http://www.access.gpo.gov • Bimonthly. $14.00 per year. Issued by the U. S. Food and Drug Administration. Provides consumer information about FDA regulations and product safety.

FDM: For Builders of Cabinets, Fixtures, Furniture, Millwork Furniture Design a nd Manufacturing. Chartwell Communications, Inc., 380 E. Northwest Highway Des Plaines, IL 60016. Phone: (847)390-6700 Fax: (847)299-7100 • URL: http://www.fdmmag.com • Monthly. Free to qualified personnel. Edited for furniture executives, production managers, and designers. Covers the manufacturing of household, office, and institutional furniture, store fixtures, and kitchen and bathroom cabinets.

FDM—The Source—Woodworking Industry Directory. Reed Business Information, 360 Pk. Ave. S New York, NY 10014. Phone: 800-662-7776 or (646)746-6400 Fax: (646)746-6734 E-mail: corporatecommunications@reedbusiness.com • URL: http://www.reedbusiness.com • Publication includes: List of over 1,800 suppliers to secondary woodworking industry; coverage includes Canada. Entries include: Company name, address, phone, fax, product lines.

FED in Print: Economics and Banking Topics. Federal Reserve Bank of Philadelphia, 10 Independence Mall Philadelphia, PA 19106-0066. Phone: (215)574-6540 Fax: (215)574-3847 • URL: http://www.phil.frb.org • Semiannual. Free. Business and banking topics.

Federal Administrative Law Judges Conference., 2020 Pennsylvania Ave. NW, PMB 260 Washington, DC 20006. Phone: (202)675-3065 Fax: (202)720-8424 E-mail: steven.glazer@ferc.gov • URL: http://www.faljc.org • Administrative law judges employed by federal agencies and departments who perform judicial functions in the federal service, presiding at administrative hearings, ruling on admissibility of evidence, making findings of fact and conclusions of law, and issuing decisions.

Federal Agency Profiles for Students. Gale Cengage Learning, 27500 Drake Rd. Farmington Hills, MI 48331-3535. Phone: 800-877-GALE or (248)699-4253 Fax: 800-414-5043 E-mail: gale.galeord@cengage.com • URL: http://gale.cengage.com • 1999. $115.00. Provides detailed descriptions of more than 175 prominent U.S. government agencies, including major activities, organizational structure, political issues, budget, and history. Includes a glossary, chronology, and index.

Federal Assistance Monitor: Semi-Monthly Report on Federal and Private Grant Opportunities. Community Development Services. CD Publications, 8204 Fenton St. Silver Spring, MD 20910. Phone: 800-666-6380 or (301)588-6380 Fax: (301)588-6385 E-mail: info@cdpublications.com • URL: http://www.cdpublications.com • Semimonthly. $339.00 per year; with online edition, $379.00 per year. Newsletter. Provides news of federal grant and loan programs for social, economic, and community purposes. Monitors grant announcements, funding, and availability. Formerly *Federal Research Report*.

Federal Aviation Regulations. Available from U. S. Government Printing Office, Washington, DC 20402. Phone: (202)512-1800 Fax: (202)512-2250 E-mail: gpoaccess@gpo.gov • URL: http://www.access.gpo.gov • Annual. Free. Lists government publications. GPO Subject Bibliography Number 12.

Federal Banking Law Reports. CCH, Inc., 2700 Lake Cook Rd. Riverwoods, IL 60015. Phone: 800-835-5244 or (847)267-7000 E-mail: cust_serv@cch.com • URL: http://www.cch.com • Weekly. $1,533.00 per year. Looseleaf service.

Federal Benefits for Veterans and Dependents (Veterans Administration). U.S. Government Printing Office, Washington, DC 20402. Phone: (202)512-1800 Fax: (202)512-2250 E-mail: gpoaccess@gpo.gov • URL: http://www.access.gpo.gov • Annual. $5.00.

Federal Carriers Reports. CCH, Inc., 2700 Lake Cook Rd. Riverwoods, IL 60015. Phone: 800-835-5224 E-mail: cust_serv@cch.com • URL: http://www.cch.com • Biweekly. $1,484.00 per year. Four looseleaf volumes. Federal rules and regulations for motor carriers, water carriers, and freight forwarders.

Federal Civil Rights Acts. West Group, 610 Opperman Dr. Eagan, MN 55123. Phone: 800-328-4880 or (651)687-7000 Fax: 800-340-9378 E-mail: bookstore@westgroup.com • URL: http://www.westgroup.com • Semiannual. $410.00 per year. Two looseleaf volumes. Covers current legislation relating to a wide range of civil rights issues, including discrimination in employment, housing, property rights, and voting.

Federal Computer Week: The Newspaper for the Government Systems Community. FCW Government Technology Group, 3141 Fairview Park Dr., Suite 777 Falls Church, VA 22042-4507. Phone: (703)876-5100 Fax: (703)876-5126 E-mail: letter@fcw.com • URL: http://www.fcw.com • 41 times a year. $95.00 per year.

Federal Consumer Information Center., General Services Administration, 1800 F St., NW, Rm. G-142 Pueblo, CO 81009. Phone: 888-8-PUEBLO Fax: (202)501-4281 E-mail: catalog.pueblo@gsa.gov • URL: http://www.pueblo.gsa.gov • A department of the General Services Administration. Established by Presidential Order in 1970 to assist federal agencies to develop, promote, and distribute information of interest to consumers and to increase public awareness of this information.

Federal Contracts Report. BNA, Inc., 1231 25th St., NW Washington, DC 20037. Phone: 800-372-1033 E-mail: customercare@bna.com • URL: http://www.bna.com • Weekly. $1,453.00 per year. Two looseleaf volumes. Developments affecting federal contracts and grants.

Federal Criminal Investigators Association., PO Box 23400 Washington, DC 20026. Phone: 800-403-3374 or (630)969-8537 Fax: 800-528-3492 or 800-528-3492 E-mail: fcianat@aol.com • URL: http://www.fedcia.org • Serves as professional fraternal organization dedicated to the advancement of federal law enforcement officers and the citizens they serve. Aims to ensure law enforcement professionals have the tools and support network to meet the challenges of future criminal investigations while becoming more community oriented. Intends to pursue mission by promoting professionalism, enhancing the image of federal officers, fostering cooperation among all law enforcement professionals, providing a fraternal environment for the advancement of the membership and community. Helps charitable programs and organizations.

Federal Deposit Insurance Corporation; Annual Report. Federal Deposit Insurance Corp., 550 17th St., N.W. Washington, DC 20429-9990. Phone: (202)736-0000, Annual. Price on application.

The Federal Employee. National Federation of Federal Employees, 1016 16th St. NW Washington, DC 20036. Phone: (202)862-4400 Fax: (202)862-4432 E-mail: customercare@bna.com • URL: http://www.nffe.org • Description: Provides news and information on issues (legislative and regulatory) affecting federal employees.

Federal Employee News Digest. Federal Employee News Digest, Inc., 1850 Centennial Park Dr., Suite 520 Reston, VA 20191. Phone: 800-989-3363 or (703)648-9551 Fax: (703)648-0265 • URL: http://www.fedforce.com • Weekly. $59.00 per year. Provides essential information for federal employees.

Federal Employees Almanac. Federal Employees New Digest, Inc., 1850 Centennial Park Dr., Suite 520 Reston, VA 20191. Phone: 800-989-3363 or (703)648-9551 Fax: (703)648-0265 • URL: http://www.fedforce.com • Annual. $11.95. Comprehensive guide for federal employees.

Federal Estate and Gift Tax Reports. CCH, Inc., 2700 Lake Cook Rd. Riverwoods, IL 60015. Phone: 800-835-5224 E-mail: cust_serv@cch.com • URL: http://www.cch.com • Weekly. $578.00. Three looseleaf volumes.

Federal Estate and Gift Taxation. RIA, 395 Hudson St. New York, NY 10014. Phone: 800-950-1216 or 800-431-9025 E-mail: riahome@riag.com • URL: http://www.riahome.com • Three times a year. $425.0 per year. Clarification and guidance on estate tax laws.

Federal Estate and Gift Taxes: Code and Regulations, Including Related Income Tax Provisions. CCH, Inc., 2700 Lake Cook Rd. Riverwoods, IL 60015. Phone: 800-835-5224 or (847)267-7000 E-mail: cust_serv@cch.com • URL: http://www.cch.com • 2000. $47.00. Revised edition. Provides full text of estate, gift, and generation-skipping tax provisions of the Internal Revenue Code.

Federal Grants and Contracts Weekly: Funding Opportunities in Research, Training and Services. Aspen Publishers, Inc., 1185 Ave. of the Americas New York, NY 10036. Phone: 800-234-1660 or (212)597-0200 Fax: (212)597-0338 E-mail: customer.service@aspenpubl.com • URL: http://www.aspenpublishers.com • 50 times a year. $450.00 per year. Newsletter.

Federal Human Resources Week: News, Strategies and Best Practices for the HR Professional. LRP Publications, 747 Dresher Rd., Suite 500 Horsham, PA 19044. Phone: 800-341-7874 or (215)784-0860 Fax: (215)784-9639 E-mail: custserv@lrp.com • URL: http://www.lrp.com • 48 times a year. $350.00 per year. Newsletter. Covers federal personnel issues, including legislation, benefits, budgets, and downsizing.

Federal Income, Gift and Estate Taxation. LexisNexis Matthew Bender, 1275 Broadway Albany, NY 12204. Phone: 800-424-4200 or (518)487-3000 Fax: (518)487-3584 E-mail: bookstore.support@lexisnexis.com • URL: http://www.bender.com • $1,220.00. Seven looseleaf volumes. Periodic supplementation.

Federal Income Taxation of Corporations Filing Consolidated Returns. LexisNexis Matthew Bender, 1275 Broadway Albany, NY 12204. Phone: 800-424-4200 or (518)487-3000 Fax: (518)487-3584 E-mail: bookstore.support@lexisnexis.com • URL: http://www.bender.com • Semiannual. $768.00. Four looseleaf volumes.

Federal Income Taxation of Inventories. LexisNexis Matthew Bender, 1275 Broadway Albany, NY 12204. Phone: 800-424-4200 or (518)487-3000 Fax: (518)487-3584 E-mail: bookstore.support@lexisnexis.com • URL: http://www.bender.com • Semiannual. $838.00 per year. Three looseleaf volumes.

Federal Income Taxation of Life Insurance Companies. LexisNexis Matthew Bender, 1275 Broadway Albany, NY 12204. Phone: 800-424-4200 or (518)487-3000 Fax: (518)487-3584 E-mail: bookstore.support@lexisnexis.com • URL: http://www.bender.com • Annual. $743.00. Three looseleaf volumes.

Federal Income Taxes of Decedents, Estates, and Trusts. CCH, Inc., 2700 Lake Cook Rd. Riverwoods, IL 60015. Phone: 800-835-5224 or (847)267-7000 E-mail: cust_serv@cch.com • URL: http://www.cch.com • 2001. $48.00. 20th revised edition. Provides rules for preparing a decedent's final income tax return. Includes discussions of fiduciary duties, grantor trusts, and bankruptcy estates.

Federal Jobs Digest., 220 White Plains Rd. Tarrytown, NY 10591. Phone: 800-824-5000 or (914)366-0333 Fax: (914)366-0059 E-mail: peter@jobsfed.com • URL: http://www.jobsfed.com • Biweekly. Individuals, $125.00 per year; libraries, $112.50 per year. Lists 15,000 immediate job openings within the federal government in each issue.

Federal Land Use Law: Limitations, Procedures, Remedies. West Group, 610 Opperman Dr. Eagan, MN 55123. Phone: 800-328-4880 or (651)687-7000 Fax: 800-340-9378 E-mail: bookstore@westgroup.com • URL: http://www.westgroup.com • Annual. $205.00 per year. Looseleaf service.

Federal Manager. Federal Managers' Association, 1641 Prince St. Alexandria, VA 22314-2818. Phone: (703)683-8700 Fax: (703)683-8707 E-mail: fma@ix.netcom.com • URL: http://www.fpmi.com • Quarterly. $24.00 per year. Formerly *Federal Managers Quarterly*.

Federal Managers Association., 1641 Prince St. Alexandria, VA 22314-2818. Phone: (703)683-8700 Fax: (703)683-8707 E-mail: info@fedmanagers.org • URL: http://www.fedmanagers.org • Represents managers and supervisors in all federal agencies. Promotes excellence in public service through effective management. Promotes and supports legislation beneficial to members, including workforce reshaping through mission analysis; compensation reform; and health and retirement benefits. Sponsors professional development program for managers as well as training seminars.

The Federal Manager's Handbook: A Guide to Rehabilitating or Removing the Problem Employee. G. Jerry Shaw and William L. Bransford. FPMI Communications, Inc., 4901 University St., Ste. 3 Huntsville, AL 35816. Phone: (256)539-1850 Fax: (256)539-0911 E-mail: books@fpmi.com • URL: http://www.fpmi.com • 1997. $29.95. Third revised edition.

Federal Personnel Manual. U.S. Office of Personnel Management. Available from U.S. Government Printing Office, Washington, DC 20402. Phone: (202)512-1800 Fax: (202)512-2250 E-mail: gpoaccess@gpo.gov • URL: http://www.access.gpo.gov • Looseleaf service. Periodic supplementation. Available in parts.

Federal Regional Yellow Book: Who's Who in the Federal Government's Departments, Agencies, Military Installations, and Service Academies Outside of Washington, DC. Leadership Directories, Inc., 104 Fifth Ave. New York, NY 10011. Phone: (212)627-4140 Fax: (212)645-0931 E-mail: info@leadershipdirectories.com • URL: http://www.leadershipdirectories.com • Semiannual. $265.00 per year. Lists over 35,000 federal officials and support staff at 8,000 regional offices.

Federal Register. Office of the Federal Register. Available from U.S. Government Printing Office, Washington, DC 20402. Phone: (202)512-1800 Fax: (202)512-2250 E-mail: gpoaccess@gpo.gov • URL: http://www.access.gpo.gov • Daily except Saturday and Sunday. $764.00 per year. Publishes regulations and legal notices issued by federal agencies, including executive orders and presidential proclamations. Issued by the National Archives and Records Administration (http://www.nara.gov).

Federal Regulatory Directory. CQ Press, 2300 N St. NW, Ste. 800 Washington, DC 20037. Phone: (866)427-7737 or (202)729-1900 Fax: 800-380-3810 or 800-380-3810 E-mail: customerservice@cqpress.com • URL: http://www.cqpress.com • Covers: Over 100 federal regulatory agencies including about 15 major agencies, about 15 smaller independent agencies, and agencies within federal departments. Entries include: For major agencies—Agency name, address, jurisdiction, description of responsibilities, list of key contacts and phone numbers, breakdown of divisions and offices with names of key officials and their phone numbers, organization chart, information sources within the agency, regional offices, analytical essays on history, recent developments, power, and outlook for agency. For other agencies—Same general information but less detail.

Federal Reserve Bank of Atlanta: Economic Review. Federal Reserve Bank of Atlanta, 1000 Peachtree St. NE Atlanta, GA 30309-3904. Phone: (404)521-8020 • URL: http://www.frbatlanta.org • Quarterly. Free.

Federal Reserve Bank of Dallas: Southwest Ecomomy Economic Review. Federal Reserve Bank of Dallas, PO Box 655906 Dallas, TX 75265-5906. Phone: 800-333-4460 or (214)922-5254 E-mail: info@dallasfed.org • URL: http://www.dallasfed.org • Quarterly. Free.

Federal Reserve Bank of Kansas City. Federal Reserve Bank of Kansas City, 925 Grand Blvd. Kansas City, MO 64198-0001. Phone: (816)881-2934 Fax: (816)881-2569 Quarterly. Free.

Federal Reserve Bank of Minneapolis: Quarterly Review. Federal Reserve Bank of Minneapolis, Research Dept., c/o The Region, PO Box 291 Minneapolis, MN 55480-0291. Phone: (612)204-6455 Fax: (612)204-5515 E-mail: err@res.mpls.frb.fed.us • URL: http://www.woodrow.mpls.frb.fed.us • Quarterly. Free.

Federal Reserve Bank of New York: Economic Policy Review. Federal Reserve Bank of New York, Public Information Office, 33 Liberty St. New York, NY 10045-0001. Phone: (212)720-6130 • URL: http://www.newyorkfed.org • Quarterly. Free.

Federal Reserve Bank of Philadelphia: Business Review. Federal Reserve Bank of Philadelphia, Research Dept., 10 Independence Mall Philadelphia, PA 19106-1574. Phone: (215)574-6000 Fax: (215)574-3847 • URL: http://www.phil.frb.org • Quarterly. Free. Contains articles on current topics in economics, finance, and banking.

Federal Reserve Bank of Richmond: Economic Quarterly. Federal Reserve Bank of Richmond, Research Dept., 701 E. Byrd St. Richmond, VA 23219. Phone: (804)697-8000 Fax: (804)697-8287 E-mail: eg@rich.frb.org • URL: http://www.rich.frb.org • Quarterly. Free. Formerly *Federal Reserve Bank of Richmond: Economic Review*.

Federal Reserve Bank of Saint Louis: Review. Federal Reserve Bank of Saint Louis, P.O. Box 442 St. Louis, MO 63166. Phone: (314)444-8320 • URL: http://www.stls.frb.org • Bimonthly. Free.

Federal Reserve Bank of San Francisco Economic Letter. Federal Reserve Bank of San Francisco. Economic Letter, PO Box 7702 San Francisco, CA 94105. Phone: 888-339-3506 or (415)974-3230 Fax: (415)974-3341 • URL: http://www.frbsf.org • 38 times a year. Free. Formerly *Federal Reserve Bank of San Francisco: Weekly Letter*.

Federal Reserve Bank of San Francisco: Economic Review. Federal Reserve Bank of San Francisco, PO Box 7702 San Francisco, CA 94120. Phone: 888-339-3506 or (415)974-3230 Fax: (415)974-3341 • URL: http://www.frbsf.org • Annual. Free.

Federal Reserve Board Publications. U.S. Board of Governors of the Federal Reserve System, Washington, DC 20551. Phone: (202)452-3000 • URL: http://www.federalreserve.gov • Semiannual. Free.

Federal Reserve Board Publications and Education Resources. Board of Governors of the Federal Reserve SystemPhone: (202)452-3000 Fax: (202)452-3819 • URL: http://www.federalreserve.gov/publications.htm • Web site provides convenient access to statistics, surveys, and research from the Federal Reserve Board. *Federal Reserve Bulletin* articles are available as abstracts or full text (PDF) currently or from six-year archives. The link "Statistics: Releases and Historical Data" offers daily, weekly, monthly, quarterly, and annual data in great detail for interest rates, foreign exchange, consumer credit, money stock measures, industrial production indexes, bank reserves, and other items. Historical tabulations are available for various time periods. Fees: Free.

Federal Reserve Bulletin. U.S. Federal Reserve System, Board of Governors, Publications Services, 20th and Constitution Ave., N.W., Room MS-127 Washington, DC 20551. Phone: (202)452-3244 Fax: (202)728-5886 • URL: http://www.federalreserve.gov • Monthly. $25.00 per year. Provides statistics on banking and the economy, including interest rates, money supply, and the Federal Reserve Board indexes of industrial production.

Federal Reserve Regulatory Service. U.S. Federal Reserve System, Board of Governors Publications Services Section, R, 20th and Constitution Ave., N.W. Washington, DC 20551. Phone: (202)452-3244 Fax: (202)728-5886 • URL: http://www.federalreserve.gov • Monthly. $200.00 per year. Looseleaf. Includes four handbooks updated monthly: *Consumer and Community Affairs, Monetary Policy and Reserve Requirements Securities, Credit Transactions and Payment Systems*. Irregular supplements.

Federal Reserve System: Background, Analyses, and Bibliography. George B. Grey, editor. Nova Science Publishers, Inc., 400 Oser Ave., Suite 1600 Hauppauge, NY 11788-3619. Phone: (631)231-7269 Fax: (631)231-8175 E-mail: novascience@earthlink.net • URL: http://www.novapublishers.com • 2002. $69.00. Provides articles by various authors on the purposes and functions of the Federal Reserve System.

Federal Reserve System: Purposes and Functions. U.S. Board of Governors of the Federal Reserve System, Washington, DC 20551. Phone: (202)452-3000 • URL: http://www.federalreserve.gov • Irregular.

Federal Securities Act of 1933-Treatise and Primary Source Material. A. A. Sommer. LexisNexis Matthew Bender, 12758 Broadway Albany, NY 12204. Phone: 800-424-4200 or (518)487-3000 Fax: (518)487-3584 E-mail: bookstore.support@lexisnexis.com • URL: http://www.bender.com • $688.00. Two looseleaf volumes. Periodic supplementation. Covers application of the Federal Securities Act of 1933 and amendments.

Federal Securities Exchange Act of 1934. A. A. Sommer. LexisNexis Matthew Bender, 1275 Broadway Albany, NY 12204. Phone: 800-424-4200 or (518)487-3000 Fax: (518)487-3584 E-mail: bookstore.support@lexisnexis.com • URL: http://www.bender.com • $688.00. Two looseleaf volumes. Periodic supplementation. Covers application of the Federal Securities Exchange Act of 1934 and amendments.

Federal Securities Law Reports. CCH, Inc., 2700 Lake Cook Rd. Riverwoods, IL 60015. Phone: 800-835-5224 or (847)267-7000 E-mail: cust_serv@cch.com • URL: http://www.cch.com • Weekly. $1,764.00 per year. Looseleaf service. Seven volumes.

Federal Staff Directory: With Biographical Information on Executive Staff Personnel. CQ Press, 1255 22nd St., NW, Ste. 400 Washington, DC 20037. Phone: (866)427-7737 or (202)729-1900 Fax: 800-380-3810 E-mail: customerservice@cqpress.com • URL: http://www.cqpress.com • Three times a year. $259.00 per year. Single copies, $149.00. Lists 35,000 staff members of federal departments and agencies, with biographies of 3,200 key executives. Includes keyword and name indexes.

Federal Tax Coordinator Library. RIA, 395 Hudson St. New York, NY 10014. Phone: 800-950-1216 or 800-431-9025 E-mail: riahome@riag.com • URL: http://www.riahome.com

• $2,125.00 per year. Available only online.

Federal Tax Course. Aspen Publishers, Inc., 1185 Ave. of the Americas New York, NY 10036. Phone: 800-638-8437 or (212)597-0200 Fax: (212)597-0338 E-mail: customer.service@aspenpubl.com • URL: http://www.apsenpublishers.com • Annual. $210.00. Provides basic reference and training for various forms of federal taxation: individual, business, corporate, partnership, estate, gift, etc.

Federal Tax Forms. CCH, Inc., 2700 Lake Cook Rd. Riverwoods, IL 60015. Phone: 800-835-5224 or (847)267-7000 E-mail: cust_serv@cch.com • URL: http://www.cch.com • Irregular. $370.00. Looseleaf service. Three volumes. Actual size reproductions of federal income tax forms.

Federal Tax Guide. CCH, Inc., 2700 Lake Cook Rd. Riverwoods, IL 60015. Phone: 800-835-5224 or (847)267-7000 E-mail: cust_serv@cch.com • URL: http://www.cch.com • Monthly. $929.00 per year. Eight looseleaf volumes. For everyday business and personal federal income tax questions. Explanation of federal tax system, income tax regulations, check lists, withholding tables, and charts.

Federal Tax Guide: Internal Revenue Code. Prentice Hall PTR, 240 Frisch Ct. Paramus, NJ 07652. Phone: 800-282-0693 Fax: 800-445-6991 • URL: http://www.phptr.com • Looseleaf. Periodic supplementation. Price on application.

Federal Tax Handbook. RIA, 395 Hudson St. New York, NY 10014. Phone: 800-950-1216 or 800-431-9025 E-mail: riahome@riag.com • URL: http://www.riahome.com • 2004. $57.00. Revised edition.

Federal Tax Manual. CCH, Inc., 2700 Lake Cook Rd. Riverwoods, IL 60015. Phone: 800-835-5224 or (847)267-7000 E-mail: cust_serv@cch.com • URL: http://www.cch.com • Monthly. $342.00 per year. Looseleaf service. Covers "basic federal tax rules and forms affecting individuals and businesses." Includes a copy of *Annuity, Depreciation, and Withholding Tables*.

Federal Tax Products. Available from U. S. Government Printing Office, Washington, DC 20402. Phone: (202)512-1800 Fax: (202)512-2250 E-mail: gpoaccess@gpo.gov • URL: http://www.access.gpo.gov • Annual. $27.00. CD-ROM issued by the Internal Revenue Service (http://www.irs.treas.gov/forms_pubs/). Provides current tax forms, instructions, and publications. Also includes older tax forms beginning with 1991.

Federal Taxation of Income, Estates and Gifts. Warren, Gorham and Lamont/RIA, 395 Hudson St. New York, NY 10014. Phone: 800-950-1215 or (212)367-6300 Fax: (914)749-5042 E-mail: customer_services@riag.com • URL: http://www.riahome.com • $1,165.00. Five looseleaf volumes. Updates three times a year. Covers aspects of income taxation of individuals, corporations, partnerships, estates, and gifts. Clear analysis to exact answers to tax questions.

Federal Taxation of Insurance Companies. Dennis P. Van Mieghem and others. Prentice Hall PTR, 240 Frisch Ct. Paramus, NJ 07652. Phone: 800-282-0693 Fax: 800-445-6991 • URL: http://www.phptr.com • $447.00 per year. Looseleaf service. Biweekly updates.

Federal Taxation of Oil and Gas Transactions. LexisNexis Matthew Bender, 1275 Broadway Albany, NY 12204. Phone: 800-424-4200 or (518)487-3000 Fax: (518)487-3584 E-mail: bookstore.support@lexisnexis.com • URL: http://www.bender.com • Semiannual. $414.00 per year. Two looseleaf volumes.

Federal Taxation of Trusts, Grantors, and Beneficiaries. John L. Peschel and Edward D. Spurgeon. RIA, 395 Hudson St. New York, NY 10014. Phone: 800-950-1216 or 800-431-9025 E-mail: riahome@riag.com • URL: http://www.riahome.com • Semiannual. $235.00 per year. Looseleaf service.

Federal Taxation Practice and Procedure Problem Supplement. Robert E. Meldman and Richard J. Sideman. CCH, Inc., 2700 Lake Cook Rd. Riverwoods, IL 60015. Phone: 800-835-5224 or (847)267-7000 E-mail: cust_serv@cch.com • URL: http://www.cch.com • 1998. $40.00. Provides information on the administrative structure of the Internal Revenue Service. Includes discussions of penalties, ethical duties, statute of limitations, litigation, and IRS collection procedures. Contains IRS standardized letters and notices.

Federal Taxes Affecting Real Estate. LexisNexis Matthew Bender, 1275 Broadway Albany, NY 12204. Phone: 800-424-4200 or (518)487-3000 Fax: (518)487-3584 E-mail: bookstore.support@lexisnexis.com • URL: http://www.bender.com • Semiannual. $261.00 per year. Two looseleaf volumes. Explains and illustrates the most important federal tax principles applying to daily real estate transactions.

Federal Taxes and the Private Club. PKF - Pannell Kerr Forster, 420 Lexington Ave. New York, NY 10170. Phone: (212)867-8000 Fax: (212)687-4346 E-mail: info@pkfny.com • URL: http://www.pkfny.com • Annual. $25.00. Provides a summary of tax issues affecting private clubs.

Federal Taxes Citator. MacMillan Publishing Co., 200 Old Tappan Rd. Old Tappan, NJ 07675. Phone: 800-223-2336 $550.00 per year. Two looseleaf volumes. Monthly supplements.

Federal Taxes: Internal Memoranda of the IRS. Prentice Hall PTR, 240 Frisch Paramus, NJ 07652. Phone: 800-282-0693 Fax: 800-445-6991 • URL: http://www.phptr.com • Looseleaf. Periodic supplementation. Price on application.

Federal Times. Army Times Publishing Co., 6883 Commercial Dr. Springfield, VA 22159. Phone: 800-368-5718 or (703)750-8646 Fax: (703)658-8314 E-mail: cust-svc@atpc.com • URL: http://www.federaltimes.com • Weekly. $52.00 per year.

Federal Withholding Tax Tables. CCH, Inc., 4025 W. Peterson Ave. Chicago, IL 60646-6085. Phone: 800-248-3248 or (773)866-6000 Fax: 800-224-8299 or (773)866-3608 • URL: http://www.cch.com • Annual. $18.00.

Federally Employed Women., 700 N Fairfax St., Ste. 510 Alexandria, VA 22314. Phone: (202)898-0994 Fax: (202)898-0994 E-mail: few@few.org • URL: http://www.few.org • Represents men and women employed by the federal government. Seeks to end sexual discrimination in government service; to increase job opportunities for women in government service and to further the potential of all women in the government; to improve the merit system in government employment; to assist present and potential government employees who are discriminated against because of sex; to work with other organizations and individuals concerned with equal employment opportunity in the government. Provides speakers and sponsors seminars to publicize the Federal Women's Program; furnishes members with information on pending legislation designed to end discrimination against working women; informs and provides members opportunities for training to improve their job potential; issues fact sheets interpreting civil service rules and regulations and other legislative issues; provides annual training conference for over 3,000 women and men.

Federation for Progress., 225 Park Ave. S., Rm. 746 New York, NY 10003. E-mail: members@aidsaction.org National and Regional Groups: 100. Multi-issue, ongoing coalition of progressive organizations composed of single-issue groups and community and labor organizers who mobilize on the grass roots level for jobs, peace, and equality.

Federation of Defense and Corporate Counsel, Inc., c/o Martha J. Streeper, 11812-A N 56th St. Tampa, MA 33617. Phone: (813)983-0022 Fax: (813)988-5837 E-mail: mmg@gte.net • URL: http://www.thefederation.org • Members are insurance lawyers and insurance company executives. Formerly Federation of Insurance and Corporate Counsel.

Federation of European Direct Marketing., Rue de l'Aurore 4, 439 Ave. de Tervueren B-1060 Brussels, Belgium. Fax: 32 2 5379984 E-mail: irene.allanson@direxions.be • URL: http://www.fedma.org • A multinational organization. Facilitates contacts and exchange of ideas and techniques among countries and members. Sponsors "Best of Europe" contest, with awards for best direct mail campaigns. Formerly European Direct Marketing Association.

Federation of Insurance and Corporate Counsel Quarterly., Marquette Univesity Law School, 1103 W. Wisconsin Ave. Milwaukee, WI 53233. Phone: (414)288-7095 Fax: (414)288-9514 Quarterly. Individuals, $40.00 per year; libraries, $34.00 per year. A journal dealing with the legal aspects of insurance.

Federation of International Civil Servants' Associations.

Federation of Organizations for Professional Women., P.O. Box 6234 Falls Church, VA 22040. Phone: (202)328-1415 Fax: (703)532-7295 E-mail: fop@hers.com • URL: http://www.fopw.org • Women's groups concerned with economic, educational and professional equality for women.

Federation of Societies for Coatings Technology., 492 Norristown Rd. Blue Bell, PA 19422-2350. Phone: (610)940-0777 Fax: (610)940-0292 E-mail: fsct@coatingstech.org • URL: http://ww.coatingstech.org • Formerly Federation of Societies for Paint Technology.

Federation of Societies for Coatings Technology: Year Book and Membership Directory. Federation of Societies for Coatings Technology, 492 Norristown Rd. Blue Bell, PA 19422-2350. Phone: (610)940-0777 Fax: (610)940-0292 E-mail: fsct@coatingstech.org • URL: http://www.coatingstech.org • Annual. $150.00. About 7,500 chemists, technicians, and supervisory production personnel in the decorative and protective coatings industry who are members of the 27 constituent societies of the federation.

Federation of Tax Administrators.

Fedstats. Federal Interagency Council on Statistical PolicyPhone: (202)395-7254 • URL: http://www.fedstats.gov • Web site features an efficient search facility for full-text statistics produced by more than 100 federal agencies, including the Census Bureau, the Bureau of Economic Analysis, and the Bureau of Labor Statistics. Boolean searches can be made within one agency or for all agencies combined. Links are offered to international statistical bureaus, including the UN, IMF, OECD, UNESCO, Eurostat, and 20 individual countries. Fees: Free.

FedWorld: A Program of the United States Department of Commerce. National Technical Information ServicePhone: (703)605-6000 Fax: (703)605-6900 E-mail: webmaster@fedworld.gov • URL: http://www.fedworld.gov • Web site offers "a comprehensive central access point for searching, locating, ordering, and acquiring government and business information." Emphasis is on searching the Web pages, databases, and government reports of a wide variety of federal agencies. Fees: Free.

Fee Income Growth Strategies. Siefer Consultants Inc., 524 Cayuga St. Storm Lake, IA 50588. Phone: 800-747-7342 or (712)732-7340 Fax: (712)732-7906 E-mail: info@siefer.com Description: Discusses the role of fees and service charges for money orders, cashier's checks, nonsufficient funds, loans, automatic teller machine cards, and other ancillary services in the profitability of financial institutions.

Feed Additive Compendium. Miller Publishing Co., 12400 Whitewater Dr., Suite 160 Minnetonka, MN 55343-2524. Phone: (952)931-0211 Fax: (952)930-1832 Annual. $265.00. Monthly updates. Covers the use of drugs as additives to livestock and poultry feed.

Feed and Feeding Digest. National Grain and Feed Association, 1250 Eye St.,N.W., Suite 1003 Washington, DC 20005. Phone: (202)289-0873 Fax: (202)289-5388 E-mail: ngfa@ngfa.org • URL: http://www.ngfa.org • Monthly. Membership.

Feed Bulletin. Jacobsen Publishing Co., 300 W. Adams St., Suite 403 Chicago, IL 60606-5108. Phone: (312)726-6600 Fax: (312)726-6654 E-mail: info@by-products.com • URL: http://www.by-products.com • Daily. $750.00 per year.

Feed Industry Red Book: Reference Book and Buyer's Guide for the Manufacturing Industry. Moffat Publishing, Inc., 317 Main St. Hopkins, MN 55343-9212. E-mail: seedtrade@skypoint.com Annual. $40.00. List of over 200 firms involved in the large animal and pet food manufacturing and distribution business, including sources of feed ingredients and suppliers of feed materials handling equipment.

Feeds and Feeding. Tilden W. Perry. Prentice Hall PTR, 240 Frisch Ct. Paramus, NJ 07652. Phone: 800-282-0693 Fax: 800-445-6991 • URL: http://www.phptr.com • 2002. $100.00. Sixth edition.

Feedstuffs: The Weekly Newspaper for Agribusiness. Farm Progress Companies, 191 S Gary Ave. Carol Stream, IL 60188. Phone: 800-441-1410 or (630)462-2224 Fax: (630)462-2869 • URL: http://www.farmprogress.com • Weekly. $135.00 per year. Newsletter.

Feminist Economics. International Association for Feminist Economics. Taylor and Francis Group, 325 Chestnut St., 8th Fl. Philadelphia, PA 19106. Phone: 800-354-1420 or (215)625-8914 E-mail: info@taylorandfrancis.com • URL: http://www.taylorandfrancis.com • Three times a year. Individuals, $68.00 per year; institutions, $184.00 per year. Includes articles on issues relating to the employment and economic opportunities of women.

Femme-Lines. Earl Barron Publications, Inc., 225 E. 36th St. New York, NY 10016. Phone: (212)683-6593 Bimonthly. $8.00 per year.

Ferrara on Insider Trading and The Wall. Ralph C. Ferrara. American Lawyer Media, Inc., 105 Madison Ave. New York, NY 10016. Phone: 800-888-8300 or (212)779-9200 Fax: (212)481-8110 E-mail: lawcatalog@amlaw.com • URL: http://www.lawcatalog.com/ • Looseleaf. $179.00. Updated as needed. Demonstrates how firms can use "Chinese Walls" and other devices to control the dissemination of material, nonpublic information by employees. Includes "suggested guidelines for deterring insider trading by employees." (Law Journal Press).

Fertilizer Industry Round Table., 1701 S Highland Ave. Baltimore, MD 21224. Phone: (410)276-4466 Fax: (410)276-0241 E-mail: peggyl@ajsackett.com • URL: http://www.firt.org • Participants include production, technical, and research personnel in the fertilizer industry. Acts as a forum for discussion of technical and production problems.

The Fertilizer Institute., Union Center Plz., 820 1st St. NE, Ste. 430 Washington, DC 20002. Phone: (202)962-0490 Fax: (202)962-0577 E-mail: informationtfi@tfi.org • URL: http://www.tfi.org • Producers, manufacturers, retailers, trading firms, and equipment manufacturers. Represents members in various legislative, educational, and technical areas. Provides information and public relations programs.

FEWA—Membership Directory. Farm Equipment Wholesalers Association, PO Box 1347 Iowa City, IA 52244. Phone: (319)354-5156 Fax: (319)354-5157 E-mail: info@fewa.org Covers: Members of the Association, including 64 wholesalers, 28 branches, and 100 associate members. Entries include: Company name, address, phone, fax, web, email, names of executives, territory served illustrated in a map, branch offices, product code, brief company profile paragraph.

Fiber and Electro Optics Research Center.

Fiber Optic Products and Applications. Available from MarketResearch.com, 641 Ave. of the Americas, Fourth Floor New York, NY 10011. Phone: 800-298-5699 or (212)807-2629 Fax: (212)807-2642 E-mail: order@marketresearch.com • URL: http://www.marketresearch.com • 2002. $3,950.00. Published by Global Industry Analysts. Provides worldwide market research data, including profiles of major companies in the field.

Fiber Optic Reference Guide. David R. Goff. Elsevier, 360 Park Ave., S New York, NY 10010-1710. Phone: 888-437-4636 or (212)989-5800 Fax: (212)633-3990 E-mail: usinfo-f@elsevier.com • URL: http://www.elsevier.com • 2002. $44.99. Third edition. A basic guide to fiber optics as utilized in telecommunications. Coverage includes fiber optic cables, light emitters, detectors, optical amplifiers, fiber for video, fiber for data transmission, interconnections, system design, testing, and future trends.

Fiber Optic Systems Design: A Practical Guide to Designing, Installing and Maintaining. John M. Simmons. McGraw Hill, 1221 Ave. of the Americas New York, NY 10020. Phone: 800-722-4726 or (212)512-2000 Fax: (212)512-4502 E-mail: customer.service@mcgraw-hill.com • URL: http://www.mcgraw-hill.com • 1991. $59.75.

Fiber Optics and Communications. Information Gatekeepers, Inc., 214 Harvard Ave., Ste. 200 Boston, MA 02134. Phone: 800-323-1088 or (617)232-3111 Fax: (617)734-8562 E-mail: info@igigroup.com • URL: http://www.igigroup.com •

SOURCES CITED

Monthly. $695.00. Emphasis on the use of fiber optics in telecommunications.

Fiber Optics News. PBI Media, LLC, 1201 7 Locks Rd. Potomac, MD 20854. Phone: 800-777-5006 or (301)344-2000 Fax: (301)309-3847 E-mail: clientservices@pbimedia.com • URL: http://www.pbimedia.com • Weekly. $797.00 per year. Newsletter.

Fiber Optics Yellow Pages: The International Optical Networks/ Fiberoptics Yellow Pages. Information Gatekeepers, Inc., 214 Harvard Ave., Ste. 200 Boston, MA 02134. Phone: 800-323-1088 or (617)232-3111 Fax: (617)734-8562 E-mail: info@igigroup.com • URL: http://www.igigroup.com • Annual. $89.95. Includes manufacturers of fiber optics products. Provides a glossary and a discussion of current uses of fiber optics. Formerly *Fiber Optics Yellow Pages*.

Fiber Organon: Featuring Manufactured Fibers. Fiber Economics Bureau, Inc., 1530 Wilson Blvd., Ste. 690 Arlington, VA 22209. Phone: 888-427-1318 or (703)875-0676 Fax: (703)875-0675 E-mail: ddezan@afma.org • URL: http://www.fibersource.com • Monthly. $300.00 per year. Summarizes "confidential producer information on the U.S. manufactured fiber market." Provides detailed statistics on production, shipments, exports, and capacity. Special issues cover worldwide data and specific end use products. (Fiber Economics Bureau is a subsidiary of the American Fiber Manufacturers Association.)

Fiber Society., North Carolina State University, College of Textiles, 2401 Research Dr. Raleigh, NC 27695-8301. Phone: (919)513-0143 Fax: (919)515-3057 E-mail: ellisom@clemson.edu • URL: http://www.thefibersociety.org • Chemists, physicists, engineers, biologists, mathematicians, and other scientists conducting research in fibers, fiber-based products, and fibrous materials. Sponsors lecture program. Sponsors conferences.

Fiberoptic Materials Research Program. Rutgers University, College of Engineering, 607 Taylor Rd. Piscataway, NJ 08854-8065. Phone: (732)445-4729 Fax: (908)445-4545 E-mail: sigel@alumnia.rutgers.edu Research fields include the communications and biomedical applications of fiber optics.

Fiberoptic Product News. Reed Business Information, 360 Park Ave., S New York, NY 10010. Phone: 800-446-6551 or (646)746-6400 Fax: (646)746-7028 E-mail: corporatecommunications@reedbusiness.com • URL: http://www.reedbusiness.com • Monthly. $167.75 per year. Includes annual *Directory* and five *European Editions*. Provides general coverage of the fiber optics industry, for both producers and users.

Fiberoptic Technology News Buying Guide. Reed Business Information, 360 Pk. Ave. S New York, NY 10014. Phone: 800-446-6551 or (646)746-6400 E-mail: corporatecommunications@reedbusiness.com • URL: http://www.reedbusiness.com • Publication includes: Over 500 manufacturers and suppliers of fiber optic products, equipment, and services. Entries include: Company name, address, phone, fax, telex, key personnel, number of employees, years in operation, description of products and services.

FiberSystems International. Available from IOP Publishing, Inc., Public Ledger Building, Suite 1035, 150 S Independence Mall West Philadelphia, PA 19106. Phone: 800-358-4677 or (215)627-0880 Fax: (215)627-0879 E-mail: custserv@iop.org • URL: http://www.iop.org • Seven times a year. Free to qualified personnel. Published in the UK by the Institute of Physics. "Covering the optical communications marketplace within the Americas and Asia." *Fibre Systems Europe* is also available, covering the business and marketing aspects of fiber optics communications in Europe.

Fibonacci Applications and Strategies for Traders. Robert Fischer. John Wiley and Sons, Inc., 111 River St. Hoboken, NJ 07030. Phone: 800-225-5945 or (201)748-6000 Fax: (201)748-6088 E-mail: info@wiley.com • URL: http://www.wiley.com • 1993. $60.00. Provides a new look at the Elliott Wave Theory and Fibonacci numbers as applied to commodity prices, business cycles, and interest rate movements. (Traders Advantage Series).

Fibre Box Association., 25 NW Point Blvd., Ste. 510 Elk Grove Village, IL 60007. Phone: (847)364-9600 Fax: (847)364-9639 E-mail: fba@fibrebox.org • URL: http://www.fibrebox.org • Works to bring together North American manufacturers of corrugated paperboard products to provide comprehensive services for the industry. Compiles statistical reports and industry forecasts; disseminates information on labor negotiations and settlements; presents industry positions to government agencies; develops performance test methods, standards and requirements; monitors environmental issues and/or regulations.

Fibre Box Industry Annual Report. Fibre Box Association, 2850 Golf Rd. Rolling Meadows, IL 60008. Phone: (847)364-9600 Fax: (847)364-9639 • URL: http://www.fibrebox.org • Annual. Free to members; non-members, $250.00.

Fibre Market News. Group Interest Enterprises. G.I.E. Media, MC, 4020 Kinross Lakes Pky., Ste. 201 Richfield, OH 44286. Phone: 800-456-0707 or (216)961-4130 Fax: (330)659-0823 E-mail: msmith@giemedia.com • URL: http://www.fibremarketnews.com • Description: Focuses on developments affecting the recycled paper industry and current market trends. Recurring features include news of research and educational opportunities, legislative updates, a calendar of events, and meeting reports.

Fibrous Materials Research Center., Drexel University, Dept. of Materials Engineering, 31st and Market St. Philadelphia, PA 19104. Phone: (215)895-1640 Fax: (215)895-6684 E-mail: fko@coe.drexel.edu • URL: http://www.fmac.coe.drexel.edu • Research fields include computer-aided design of nonwoven fabrics and design curves for industrial fibers.

Fiduciary Tax Guide. CCH, Inc., 2700 Lake Cook Rd. Riverwoods, IL 60015. Phone: 800-835-5224 or (847)267-7000 E-mail: cust_serv@cch.com • URL: http://www.cch.com • Monthly. $478.00 per year. Looseleaf service. Covers federal income taxation of estates, trusts, and beneficiaries. Provides information on gift and generation- skipping taxation.

Fiduciary Tax Return Guide 2000. RIA, 395 Hudson St. New York, NY 10014. Phone: 800-950-1216 or 800-431-9025 E-mail: riahome@riag.com • URL: http://www.riahome.com • 2000. $17.25. Revised edition.

Field Crop Abstracts: Monthly Abstract Journal on World Annual Cereal, Legume, Root, Oilseed and Fibre Crops. Available from CABI Publishing North America, 875 Massachusetts Ave., 7th Fl. Cambridge, MA 02139. Phone: 800-528-4841 or (617)395-4056 Fax: (617)354-6875 E-mail: cabi-nao@cabi.org • URL: http://www.cabi-publishing.org • Monthly. Institutions, $1,775.00 per year. Online edition available, $1,820.00 per year. Published in England by CABI Publishing, formerly Commonwealth Agricultural Bureaux. Provides worldwide coverage of the literature.

A Field Guide to Airplanes of North America. M. R. Montgomery and Gerald L. Foster. Houghton Mifflin Co., 222 Berkeley St. Boston, MA 02116. Phone: 800-733-2828 or (617)351-5000 Fax: 800-733-2098 E-mail: inquiries@hmco.com • URL: http://www.hmco.com • 1992. $18.00. Second revised edition.

Field Guide to Marketing: A Glossary to Essential Tools and Concepts for Today's Manager. McGraw-Hill, 1221 Ave. of the Americas New York, NY 10020. Phone: 800-722-4726 or (212)512-2000 Fax: (212)512-4502 E-mail: customer.service@mcgraw-hill.com • URL: http://www.mcgraw.hill.com • 1993. $29.95. Defines fundamental terms.

Field Guide to Negotiation: A Glossary of Essential Tools and Concepts for Today's Manager. Gavin Kennedy. McGraw-Hill, 1221 Ave. of the Americas New York, NY 10020. Phone: 800-722-4726 or (212)512-2000 Fax: (212)512-4502 E-mail: customerservice@mcgraw-hill.com • URL: http://www.mcgraw-hill.com • 1993. $29.95. Defines fundamental terms.

Field Guide to Project Management. David I. Cleland. John Wiley and Sons, Inc., 111 River St. Hoboken, NJ 07030. Phone: 800-225-5945 or (201)748-6000 Fax: (201)748-6088 E-mail: info@wiley.com • URL: http://www.wiley.com • 1998. $39.95. Provides 38 articles by various authors on the major aspects of project management.

Field Guide to Rocks and Minerals. Roger T. Peterson and Frederick H. Pough. Houghton Mifflin Co., 222 Berkeley St. Boston, MA 02116. Phone: 800-733-2828 or (617)351-5000 Fax: 800-733-2098 • URL: http://www.hmco.com • 1998. $20.00. Fifth edition. Data on where to find rocks and minerals, how to collect them, physical properties and various types. (Peterson Field Guide Series).

Field Guide to Strategy: A Glossary to Essential Tools and Concepts for Today's Manager. McGraw-Hill, 1221 Ave. of the Americas New York, NY 10020. Phone: 800-722-4726 or (212)512-2000 Fax: (212)512-4502 E-mail: customer.service@mcgraw-hill.com • URL: http://www.mcgraw-hill.com • 1993. $29.95. Defines fundamental terms.

FII Annual Guide to Stocks. Financial Information, Inc., 30 Montgomery St. Jersey City, NJ 07302-0473. Phone: 800-367-3441 or (201)332-5400 Fax: 800-344-3292 Annual. $2,250.00. Two volumes. Formerly *Financial Stock Guide Service: Directory of Active Stocks*.

Film and Video Budgets. Deke Simon and Michael Wiese. Michael Wiese Productions, 11288 Ventura Blvd., Suite 621 Studio City, CA 91604. Phone: 800-833-5738 or (818)379-8799 Fax: (818)986-3408 • URL: http://www.mwp.com • 2001. $26.95. Third edition. Contains detailed, sample budgets for a wide variety of productions from shoestring documentaries to expensive feature films. Includes practical explanations and information.

Film and Video Finder. National Information Center for Educational Media. c/o Plexus Publishing, Inc., 143 Old Marlton Pike Medford, NJ 08055. Phone: (609)654-6500 Fax: (609)654-4309 E-mail: info@plexuspublishing.com • URL: http://www.plexuspublishing.com • Biennial. $295.00. Contains 92,000 listings of film and video educational, technical and vocational children's programs and literary materials.

Film Finance and Distribution: A Dictionary of Terms. John W. Cones. Silman-James Press, 3624 Shannon Rd. Los Angeles, CA 90027. Phone: (323)661-9922 Fax: (323)661-9933 E-mail: silmanjamespress@earthlink.com • URL: http://www.silmanjamespress.com • 1992. $24.95. Includes commentary on practical approaches to financing and distribution for novice filmmakers.

Film Journal International. VNU Business Media, 770 Broadway New York, NY 10003. Phone: (646)654-4500 Fax: (646)654-7212 • URL: http://www.vnubusinessmedia.com • Monthly. $65.00 per year. Formerly *Film Journal*.

Film Quarterly: Quarterly of Film, Radio and Television. University of California Press, Journals Div., 2120 Berkeley Way Berkeley, CA 94704-1012. Phone: 800-777-4726 or (510)643-7154 Fax: 800-999-1958 or (510)642-9917 E-mail: journals@ucpress.com • URL: http://www.ucpress.edu/journals • Quarterly. Institutions, $102.00 per year; includes print and online editions.

Filmmaker's Dictionary. Ralph S. Singleton and James Conrad. Lone Eagle Publishing Co., LLC, 1024 N. Orange Dr. Hollywood, CA 90028. Phone: (323)308-3400 Fax: (323)308-3493 E-mail: lrossini@lfilm.com • URL: http://www.allbookstores.com • 2000. $22.95. Second edition. Defines technical terms, legal terms, industry jargon, and film slang.

Films and Audiovisual Information. Available from U. S. Government Printing Office, Washington, DC 20402. Phone: (202)512-1800 Fax: (202)512-2250 E-mail: gpoaccess@gpo.gov • URL: http://www.access.gpo.gov • Annual. Free. Issued by the Superintendent of Documents. A list of government publications on motion picture and audiovisual topics. Formerly *Motion Pictures, Films and Audiovisual Information*. (Subject Bibliography No. 73.)

Filmstrip and Slide Set Finder, 1990: A Comprehensive Index to 35mm Educational Filmstrips and Slide Sets. c/o Plexus Publishing, Inc., 143 Old Marlton Pike Medford, NJ 08055-8750. Phone: (609)654-6500 Fax: (609)654-4309 E-mail: info@plexuspublishing.com • URL: http://www.plexuspublishing.com • 1990. $225.00. Three volumes. (NICEM Series).

Filter Manufacturers Council., PO Box 13966, 10 Laboratory Dr. Research Triangle Park, NC 27709-3966. Phone: 800-993-4583 or (919)549-4800 Fax: (919)406-1306 E-mail: jdenton@mema.org • URL: http://www.filtercouncil.org • Worldwide manufacturers of filters for automotive and industrial companies. Keeps members informed of governmental actions relating to the filter industry. Provides regulatory assistance to commercial generators of used vehicular oil filters, and a forum for discussions of issues affecting the industry.

Filters and Filtration Handbook. T. Christopher Dickenson. Elsevier, 655 Ave. of the Americas New York, NY 10010-5107. Phone: 800-366-2665 or (212)989-5800 Fax: 800-535-9935 or (212)633-3680 E-mail: custserv@elsevier.com • URL: http://www.elsevier.com • 1997. $265.00. Fourth edition.

Filtration News. Eagle Publications, Inc., 42400 Grand River Ave., Suite 103 Novi, MI 48375-2572. Phone: 800-783-3491 or (248)347-3490 Fax: (248)347-3492 Bimonthly. Controlled circulation. Emphasis is on new filtration products for industrial use.

Finance and Accounting for Nonfinancial Managers. American Management Association Extension Institute, 1601 Broadway New York, NY 10019. Phone: 800-262-9699 or (518)586-8100 Fax: (518)903-8168 • URL: http://www.amanet.org • Looseleaf. $159.00. Self-study course. Emphasis is on practical explanations, examples, and problem solving. Quizzes and a case study are included.

Finance and Development. International Monetary Fund, Publication Services, 700 19th St., N.W. Washington, DC 20431. Phone: (202)623-7000 Fax: (202)623-4661 E-mail: publicaffairs@imf.org • URL: http://www.imf.org • Quarterly. Free.

Finance Companies. U. S. Federal Reserve System, Board of Governors, Publications Services, MS-138, 20th and Constitution Ave., NW Washington, DC 20551. Phone: (202)452-3244 Fax: (202)728-5886 • URL: http://www.federalreserve.gov • Monthly. $5.00 per year. (Federal Reserve Statistical Release, G.20.)

Finance for Non-Financial Managers. A. H. Millichamp. Continuum International Publishing Group, Inc., 15 E 26th St., Ste. 1703 New York, NY 10010. Phone: 800-561-7704 or (212)953-5858 Fax: (212)953-5944 E-mail: info@continnum-books.com • URL: http://www.continnumbooks.com • 2001. $24.95. Third edition. (Letts Higher Education List Series).

Financial Accounting Series. Financial Accounting Standards Board, 401 Merritt 7 Norwalk, CT 06856. Phone: (203)847-0700 Fax: (203)849-9714 E-mail: webmaster@fasb.org • URL: http://www.fasb.org • Price on application

Financial Accounting Standards: Explanation and Analysis. CCH, Inc., 2700 Lake Cook Rd. Riverwoods, IL 60015. Phone: 800-835-5224 or (847)267-7000 E-mail: cust_serv@cch.com • URL: http://www.cch.com • 1996. $56.00. 18th edition.

Financial Analysts Journal. Association for Investment Management and Research, P.O. Box 3668 Charlottesville, VA 22903-0668. Phone: 800-247-8132 or (804)951-5442 Fax: (804)951-5370 E-mail: info@aimr.org • URL: http://www.aimr.org • Bimonthly. $220.00 per year.

Financial and Accounting Guide for Not-for-Profit Organizations, Cumulative Supplement. Malvern J. Gross and Richard F. Larkin. John Wiley and Sons, Inc., 111 River St. Hoboken, NJ 07030. Phone: 800-225-5945 or (201)748-6000 Fax: (201)748-6088 E-mail: info@wiley.com • URL: http://www.wiley.com • 2000. $170.00. Sixth edition. Covers key concepts, financial statement preparation, accounting guidelines, and financial control. Includes tax laws and forms. 2003 *Supplement* available. (Nonprofit Law, Finance and Management Series).

Financial and Estate Planning: Analysis, Strategies and Checklists. CCH, Inc., 2700 Lake Cook Rd. Riverwoods, IL 60015. Phone: 800-835-5224 or (847)267-7000 E-mail: cust_serv@cch.com • URL: http://www.cch.com • 4 looseleaf volumes. Price on application. services.

Financial and Operating Results of Department and Specialty Stores. National Retail Federation. John Wiley and Sons, Inc., 111 River St. Hoboken, NJ 07030. Phone: 800-225-5945 or (201)748-6000 Fax: (201)748-6088 E-mail: customer@wiley.com • URL: http://www.wiley.com • Annual. Members, $80.00; non-members, $100.00.

Financial Counseling and Planning. Association for Financial Counseling and Planning Education, Ohio State Univ., 1787 Neil Ave., c/o Sherman Hanna, Consumer and Textile Sciences Dept. Columbus, OH 43210-1295. Phone: (614)292-4584 Fax: (614)292-7536 E-mail: hanna.1@osu.edu • URL: http://www.hec.ohio-state.edu • Semiannual. Members, $60. per year; institutional members, $100.00 per year; libraries, $60.00 per year. Disseminates scholarly research relating to finacial planning and counseling .

Financial Executive. Financial Executives International, 200 Campus Dr., Ste. 200 Florham Park, NJ 07932-0674. Phone: (973)765-1000 Fax: (973)765-1024 • URL: http://www.fei.org • Nine times a year. $59.00 per year. Published for corporate financial officers and managers.

Financial Executives International., 200 Campus Dr., PO Box 674 Florham Park, NJ 07932-0674. Phone: (973)765-1000 Fax: (973)765-1018 E-mail: mcangemi@financialexecutives.org • URL: http://www.financialexecutives.org • Professional organization of corporate financial executives performing duties of chief financial officer, controller, treasurer, or vice-president-finance. Sponsors research activities through its affiliated Financial Executives Research Foundation. Maintains offices in Toronto, Canada, and Washington, DC.

Financial Executives Research Foundation.

Financial Flows and the Developing Countries. The World Bank Group, 1818 H St., N. W. Washington, DC 20433. Phone: (202)477-1000 Fax: 800-645-7247 or (202)477-6391 E-mail: books@worldbank.org • URL: http://www.worldbank.org • Quarterly. $150.00 per year. Concerned mainly with debt, capital markets, and foreign direct investment. Includes statistical tables.

Financial History: Chronicling the History of America's Capital Markets. Museum of American Financial History, 26 Broadway New York, NY 10004. Phone: (212)908-4519 Fax: (212)908-4601 E-mail: kaguilera@financialhistory.org • URL: http://www.financialhistory.org • Quarterly. Membership. Contains articles on early stock and bond markets and trading in the U. S., with photographs and other illustrations. Current trading in rare and unusual, obsolete stock and bond certificates is featured. Formerly *Friends or Financial History*.

Financial History of the United States. Jerry W. Markham. M. E. Sharpe, Inc., 80 Business Park Dr. Armonk, NY 10504. Phone: 800-541-6563 or (914)273-1800 Fax: (914)273-2106 E-mail: info@mesharpe.com • URL: http://www.mesharpe.com • 2002. $349.00. Three volumes. Vol. 1: *From Christopher Columbus to the Robber Barons (1492-1900)*. Vol. 2: *From J. P. Morgan to the Institutional Investor (1900-1970)*. Vol. 3: *From the Age of Derivatives to the Internet (1970-2000)*. Each volume contains name and subject indexes, with cumulative indexes in volume three.

Financial Institutions. Available from U. S. Government Printing Office, Washington, DC 20402. Phone: (202)512-1800 Fax: (202)512-2250 E-mail: gpoaccess@gpo.gov • URL: http://www.access.gpo.gov • Annual. Free. Lists government publications. Formerly *Banks and Banking*. GPO Subject Bibliography No. 128.

Financial Institutions and Markets. Meir J. Kohn. Oxford University Press, Inc., 198 Madison Ave. New York, NY 10016. Phone: 800-451-7556 or (212)726-6000 Fax: (212)726-6440 E-mail: custserv@oup-usa.org • URL: http://www.oup-usa.org • 2003. $115.00. Second edition.

Financial Investigations: A Forensic Accounting Approach to Detecting and Resolving Crimes. Available from U. S. Government Printing Office, Washington, DC 20402. Phone: (202)512-1800 Fax: (202)512-2250 E-mail: gpoaccess@gpo.gov • URL: http://www.access.gpo.gov • 2002. $54.00. Two volumes: textbook and workbook. Issued by the Internal Revenue Service (http://www.irs.ustreas.gov). Serves as a text "for courses on conducting financial investigations." (IRS Publications 1714 and 1816.)

Financial Management. Financial Management Association International, University of South Florida, College of Business Administration Tampa, FL 33620-5500. Phone: (813)974-2084 Fax: (813)974-3318 E-mail: fma@coba.usf.edu • URL: http://www.fma.org • Quarterly. Individuals, $80.00 per year; libraries, $100.00 per year. Covers theory and practice of financial planning, international finance, investment banking, and portfolio management. Includes *Financial Practice* and *Education and Contempory Finance Digest*.

Financial Management Association International., University of South Florida, College of Business Administration, 4202 E Fowler Ave., BSN 3331 Tampa, FL 33620-5500. Phone: (813)974-2084 Fax: (813)974-3318 E-mail: fma@coba.usf.edu • URL: http://www.fma.org • Professors of financial management; corporate financial officers. Facilitates exchange of ideas among persons involved in financial management or the study thereof. Conducts workshops for comparison of current research projects and development of cooperative ventures in writing and research. Sponsors honorary society for superior students at 300 colleges and universities. Offers placement services.

Financial Management Association: Membership/Professional Directory. Financial Management Association, University of South Florida, College of Business Tampa, FL 33620-5500. Phone: (813)974-2084 Fax: (813)974-3318 E-mail: fma@coba.usf.edu • URL: http://www.fma.org • Annual. Membership. Lists 4,800 corporate financial officers and professors of financial management.

Financial Management for Pharmacists: A Decision-Making Approach. Norman V. Carroll. Lippincott Williams and Wilkins, 530 Walnut St. Philadelphia, PA 19106-3621. Phone: 800-638-3030 or (215)521-8300 Fax: (215)521-8902 E-mail: custserv@lww.com • URL: http://www.lww.com • 1997. $39.00. Second edition.

Financial Management Handbook. Philip Vale. Ashgate Publishing Co., 101 Cherry St., Ste. 420 Burlington, VT 05401-4405. Phone: 800-535-9544 or (802)865-7641 Fax: (802)865-7847 • URL: http://www.ashgate.com • 1988. $93.95. Third edition. Published by Gower in England.

Financial Management in Agriculture. Peter Barry and others. Prentice Hall PTR, 240 Frisch Ct. Paramus, NJ 07652. Phone: 800-282-0693 Fax: 800-445-6991 • URL: http://www.phptr.com • 2000. $62.00. Sixth edition. Includes *Casebook*.

The Financial Management of Hospitals and Healthcare Organizations. Michael Nowicki. Health Administration Press, One N. Franklin, Suite 1700 Chicago, IL 60106-3491. Phone: (312)424-2800 Fax: (312)424-0014 • URL: http://www.ache.org • 2001. $52.00. Second edition.

Financial Management of Sport-Related Organizations. Terry Haggerty and Garth Paton. Stipes Publishing L.L.C., 204 W. University Ave. Champaign, IL 61820. Phone: (217)356-8391 Fax: (217)356-5753 E-mail: stipes@soltec.com • URL: http://www.stipes.com • 1984. $4.80. (Sport and Physical Education Management Series).

Financial Management Strategies for Arts Organization. Frederick J. Turk and Robert P. Gallo. Americans for the Arts, 1000 Vermont Ave., NW, 6th Fl. Washington, DC 20005. Phone: 800-321-4510 or (202)371-2830 Fax: (202)371-0424 E-mail: info@artsusa.org • URL: http://www.artsusa.org • 1984. $16.95.

Financial Management Techniques for Small Business. Art R. DeThomas. PSI Research, P.O. Box 3727 Central Point, OR 97502-0032. Phone: 800-228-2275 or (541)245-6502 Fax: (541)245-6505 E-mail: information@psi-research.com • URL: http://www.psi-research.com • 1991. $19.95. (Successful Business Library Series).

Financial Management: Theory and Practice. Eugene F. Brigham and Michael C. Ehrhardt. Harcourt College Publishers, City Center Tower Two, 301 Commerce St., Ste. 3700 Fort Worth, TX 76102. Phone: 800-354-9706 or (817)334-7500 Fax: 800-487-8488 or (817)334-7844 E-mail: wlittle@harbrace.com • URL: http://www.harcourtcollege.com • 2002. $119.50. 10th edition. Includes CD-ROM. (Finance Series).

Financial Managers Society., 100 W Monroe, Ste. 810 Chicago, IL 60603. Phone: 800-275-4367 or (312)578-1300 Fax: (312)578-1308 E-mail: info@fmsinc.org • URL: http://www.fmsinc.org • Works for the needs of finance and accounting professionals from banks, thrifts and credit unions. Offers career-enhancing education, specialized publications, national leadership opportunities, and worldwide connections with other industry professionals.

Financial Market Trends. Organization for Economic Cooperation and Development, OECD Washington Center, 2001 L St., N. W., Suite 650 Washington, DC 20036-4922. Phone: 800-456-6323 or (202)785-6323 Fax: (202)785-0350 E-mail: washington.contact@oecd.org • URL: http://www.oecdwash.org • Quarterly. $80.00 per year. Provides analysis of developments and trends in international and national capital markets. Includes charts and graphs on interest rates, exchange rates, stock market indexes, bank stock indexes, trading volumes, and loans outstanding. Data from OECD countries includes international direct investment, bank profitability, institutional investment, and privatization.

Financial Markets and Institutions. Frederic S. Mishkin and Stanley G. Eakins. Addison-Wesley, 75 Arlington St., Ste. 300 Boston, MA 02116. Phone: 800-447-2226 or (617)848-7500 • URL: http://www.aw.com • 2002. $118.00. Fourth edition.

Financial Markets, Institutions, and Instruments. New York University, Salomon Center. Blackwell Publishing, 350 Main St., 6th Fl. Malden, MA 02148-5018. Phone: 800-835-6770 or (781)388-8200 Fax: (781)388-8232 E-mail: subscrip@blackwellpub.com • URL: http://www.blackwellpub.com • Five times a year. Institutions, $338.00 per year. Includes online edition. Edited to "bridge the gap between the academic and professional finance communities." Special fifth issue each year provides surveys of developments in four areas: money and banking, derivative securities, corporate finance, and fixed-income securities.

The Financial Numbers Game: Detecting Creative Accounting Practices. Charles W. Mulford and Eugene E. Comiskey. John Wiley and Sons, Inc., 111 River St. Hoboken, NJ 07030. Phone: 800-225-5945 or (201)748-6000 Fax: (201)748-6088 E-mail: info@wiley.com • URL: http://www.wiley.com • 2002. $39.95. Serves as a guide to financial statement analysis for investors. Explains the "creative" schemes used by corporations to boost earnings-per-share data.

Financial Options: From Theory to Practice. Stephen Figlewski. McGraw-Hill, 1221 Ave. of the Americas New York, NY 10020. Phone: 800-722-4726 or (212)512-2000 Fax: (212)512-4502 E-mail: customer.serivce@mcgraw-hill.com • URL: http://www.mcgraw-hill.com • 1992. $29.95. Includes options on financial futures.

Financial Planning and Financial Planning Ideas. Prentice Hall PTR, 240 Frisch Ct. Paramus, NJ 07652. Phone: 800-282-0693 Fax: 800-445-6991 • URL: http://www.phptr.com • Two looseleaf volumes. Periodic supplementation. Price on application.

Financial Planning Applications. Thomas P. Langdon and William J. Ruckstuhl. The American College, 270 S Bryn Mawr Ave. Bryn Mawr, PA 19010-2196. Phone: 800-421-0654 or (610)526-1000 Fax: (610)526-1310 • URL: http://www.amercoll.edu • 2003. $70.00. 19th edition. Emphasis on annuities and life insurance.

Financial Planning Association., 4100 E Mississippi Ave., Ste. 400 Denver, CO 80246-3053. Phone: 800-322-4237 or (303)759-4910 Fax: (303)759-0749 E-mail: marv.tuttle@fpanet.org • URL: http://www.fpanet.org • Works to support the financial planning process in order to help people achieve their goals and dreams. Believes that everyone needs objective advice to make smart financial decisions and that when seeking the advice of a financial planner, the planner should be a CFP professional.

Financial Planning for Libraries. Ann E. Prentice. Scarecrow Press, Inc., 4501 Forbes Blvd., Ste. 200 Lanham, MD 20706-4310. Phone: 800-462-6420 or (301)459-3366 Fax: 800-338-4550 or (301)429-5748 E-mail: custserv@rowman.com • URL: http://www.scarecrowpress.com • 1996. $36.00. Second edition. Includes examples of budgets for libraries. (Library Administration Series, No. 12).

Financial Planning for Older Clients. James E. Pearman. CCH, Inc., 2700 Lake Cook Rd. Riverwoods, IL 60015. Phone: 800-835-5224 or (847)267-7000 E-mail: cust_serv@cch.com • URL: http://www.cch.com • 2000. $49.00. Covers income sources, social security, Medicare, Medicaid, investment planning, estate planning, and other retirement-related topics. Edited for accountants, attorneys, and other financial advisors. (Solutions for Professional Advisors Series).

Financial Planning for the Utterly Confused. Joel Lerner. McGraw-Hill, 1221 Ave. of the Americas New York, NY 10020. Phone: 800-722-4726 or (212)512-2000 Fax: (212)512-4502 E-mail: customer.service@mcgraw-hill.com • URL: http://www.mcgraw-hill.com • 1998. $12.95. Fifth edition. Covers annuities, certificates of deposit, bonds, mutual funds, insurance, home ownership, retirement, social security, wills, etc.

Financial Planning: The Magazine for Financial Service Professionals. Thomson Media, One State St. Plaza New York, NY 10004. Phone: 800-221-1809 or (212)803-8200 Fax: (212)843-9635 E-mail: custserv@thomsonmedia.com • URL: http://www.thomsonmedia.com • Monthly. $79.00 per year. Edited for independent financial planners and insurance agents. Covers retirement planning, estate planning, tax planning, and insurance, including long-term healthcare considerations. Special features include a Retirement Planning Issue, Mutual Fund Performance Survey, and Variable Life and Annuity Survey.

The Financial Post: Canadian's Business Voice. Financial Post Datagroup, 333 King St., E. Toronto, ON, Canada M5A 4N2. Phone: 800-387-9011 or (416)350-6300 Fax: (416)350-6601 E-mail: fpdg@fpdata.finpost.com • URL: http://www.financialpostcanoe.ca • Daily. $200.00 per year. Provides Canadian business, economic, financial, and investment news. Features extensive price quotes from all major Canadian markets: stocks, bonds, mutual funds, commodities, and currencies. Supplement available: *Financial Post 500*. Includes annual supplement.

Financial Post Markets Canadian Demographics: Complete Demographics for Canadian Urban Markets. Financial Post Datagroup, 333 King St., E. Toronto, ON, Canada M5A 4N2. Phone: 800-661-7678 or (416)350-6516 Fax: (416)350-6501 E-mail: fpdg@fppdata.finpost.com • URL: http://www.financialpost.com • Annual. $135.00 Provides demographic and economic profiles of Canadian urban consumer regions with populations of 10,000 or more. Includes current data and projections for population, retail sales, personal income, and other market characteristics. CD-ROM available. Formerly *Canadian Markets*.

The Financial Post (Web site). National Post OnlinePhone: 800-805-1184 or (244)383-2300 Fax: (416)383-2443 • URL: http://www.nationalpost.com/financialpost/ • Provides a broad range of Canadian business news online, with daily updates. Includes news, opinion, and special reports, as well as "Investing," "Money Rates," "Market Watch," and "Daily Mutual Funds." Allows advanced searching (Boolean operators), with links to various other sites. Fees: Free.

Financial Report of the United States Government. Available from U. S. Government Printing Office, Washington, DC 20402. Phone: (202)512-1800 Fax: (202)512-2250 E-mail: gpoaccess@gpo.gov • URL: http://www.access.gpo.gov • Annual. $21.00. Issued by the U. S. Treasury Department (http://www.treas.gov). Presents information about the financial condition and operations of the federal government. Program accounting systems of various government agencies provide data for the report.

Financial Sentinel: Your Beacon to the World of Investing. Gulf Atlantic Publishing, Inc., 1947 Lee Rd. Winter Park, FL 32789-1834. Phone: (407)628-5700 Fax: (407)628-0807

Monthly. $29.95 per year. Provides "The only complete listing of all OTC Bulletin Board stocks traded, with all issues listed on the Nasdaq SmallCap Market, the Toronto, and Vancouver Stock Exchanges." Also includes investment advice and recommendations of small capitalization stocks.

Financial Services Round Table., 1001 Pennsylvania Ave. NW, Ste. 500 S Washington, DC 20004. Phone: (202)289-4322 Fax: (202)628-2507 E-mail: info@fsround.org • URL: http://www.fsround.org • Companies registered with the Federal Reserve Board under the Bank Holding Company Act of 1956.

Financial Shenanigans: How to Detect Accounting Gimmicks and Fraud in Financial Reports. Howard M. Schilit. McGraw-Hill, 1221 Ave. of the Americas New York, NY 10020. Phone: 800-722-4726 or (212)512-2000 Fax: (212)512-4502 E-mail: customer.service@mcgraw-hill.com • URL: http://www.mcgraw-hill.com • 2002. $27.95. Second edition. Tells how to interpret the footnotes and fine print in corporate annual and other reports.

Financial Statement Analysis: A Practitioner's Guide. Martin Fridson and Fernando Alvarez. John Wiley and Sons, Inc., 111 River St. Hoboken, NJ 07030. Phone: 800-225-5945 or (201)748-6000 Fax: (201)748-6088 E-mail: info@wiley.com • URL: http://www.wiley.com • 2002. $69.95. Third edition. (Finance Series).

Financial Statement Analysis: The Investor's Self Study Guide to Interpreting and Analyzing. Charles J. Woelfel. McGraw-Hill, 1221 Ave. of the Americas New York, NY 10020. Phone: 800-722-4726 or (212)512-2000 Fax: (212)512-4502 E-mail: customer.service@mcgraw-hill.com • URL: http://www.mcgraw-hill.com • 1993. $24.95. Revised edition.

Financial Statement Analysis: Theory, Application and Interpretation. Leopold A. Bernstein and John J Wild. McGraw-Hill, 1221 Ave. of the Americas New York, NY 10020. Phone: 800-722-4726 or (212)512-2000 Fax: (212)512-4502 E-mail: customer.service@mcgraw-hill.com • URL: http://www.mcgraw-hill.com • 1997. $95.31. Sixth edition.

Financial Statistics of Major Publicly Owned Electric Utilities in the U.S. U.S. Energy Information Administration, U.S. Department of Energy. Available from U.S. Government Printing Office, Washington, DC 20402. Phone: (202)512-1800 Fax: (202)512-2250 E-mail: gpoaccess@gpo.gov • URL: http://www.access.gpo.gov • Annual.

Financial Times Business Global Mining Directory. Available from Gale Cengage Learning, 27500 Drake Rd. Farmington Hills, MI 48331-3535. Phone: 800-877-GALE or (248)699-GALE Fax: 800-414-5043 E-mail: gale.galeord@cengage.com • URL: http://www.galegroup.com • Annual. $355.00. Published by Financial Times Business. Provides detailed information on 1,000 leading mining companies worldwide. Includes financial data for three years. Formerly *Financial Times Energy Yearbook: Mining*.

Financial Times Business Global Oil & Gas Directory. Available from Gale Cengage Learning, 27500 Drake Rd. Farmington Hills, MI 48331-3535. Phone: 800-877-GALE or (248)699-GALE Fax: 800-414-5043 E-mail: gale.galeord@cengage.com • URL: http://gale.cengage.com • Annual. $355.00. Published by Financial Times Business. Provides detailed information on 800 leading oil and gas companies worldwide. Includes financial data for three years. Formerly *Financial Times Energy Yearbook: Oil & Gas*.

Financial Times Currency Forecaster: Consensus Forecasts of the Worldwide Currency and Economic Outlook. Briefings Publishing Group, 1101 King St., Suite 110 Alexandria, VA 22314. Phone: 800-722-9221 or (703)518-2343 Fax: (703)648-2136 E-mail: customerservice@briefings.com • URL: http://www.briefings.com • Monthly. $695.00 per year. Newsletter. Provides forecasts of foreign currency exchange rates and economic conditions. Supplement available: *Mid-Month Global Financial Report*.

Financial Times [London]. The Financial Times, Inc., 1330 Ave. of the Americas New York, NY 10019. Phone: 800-628-8088 or (212)641-6544 Fax: (212)641-6515 E-mail: uscirculation@ft.com • URL: http://www.ft.com • Daily, except Sunday. $572.88 per year. An international business and financial newspaper, featuring news from London, Paris, Frankfurt, New York, and Tokyo. Includes worldwide stock and bond market data, commodity market data, and monetary/currency exchange information.

Financial Times: Where Information Becomes Intelligence. FT GroupPhone: 800-628-8088 • URL: http://www.ft.com • Web site provides extensive data and information relating to international business and finance, with daily updates. Includes Markets Today, Company News, Economic Indicators, Equities, Currencies, Capital Markets, Euro Prices, etc. Fees: Free (registration required).

Financial Women International., 1027 W Roselawn Ave. Roseville, MN 55113. Phone: (866)236-2007 or (651)487-7632 Fax: (651)489-1322 E-mail: info@fwi.org • URL: http://www.fwi.org • Individuals working in or with the financial services industry. Maintains FWI Educational Foundation.

Financial Women's Association of New York., 215 Park Ave. S., Suite 1713 New York, NY 10003. Phone: (212)533-2141 Fax: (212)982-3008 E-mail: fwaoffice@fwa.org • URL: http://www.fwa.org • Members are professional women in finance. Formerly Young Women's Financial Association of New York.

Financial Yellow Book: Who's Who at the Leading U. S. Financial Institutions. Leadership Directories, Inc., 104 Fifth Ave. New York, NY 10011. Phone: (212)627-4140 Fax: (212)645-0931 E-mail: info@leadershipdirectories.com • URL: http://www.leadershipdirectories.com • Semiannual. $265.00. Gives the names and titles of over 28,000 key executives in financial institutions. Includes the areas of banking, investment, money management, and insurance. Five indexes are provided: institution, executive name, geographic by state, financial service segment, and parent company.

Financing Graduate School: How to Get Money for Your Master's or Ph.D. Patricia McWade. Peterson's, Princeton Pike Corporate Center, 2000 Lenox Dr., 3rd Fl. Lawrenceville, NJ 08648. Phone: 800-338-3282 or (609)896-1800 Fax: (609)896-4594 E-mail: info@petersons.com • URL: http://www.petersons.com • 1996. $16.95. Second revised edition. Discusses the practical aspects of various types of financial aid for graduate students. Includes bibliographic and directory information.

Financing the Corporation. Richard A. Booth. West Group, 610 Opperman Dr. Eagan, MN 55123. Phone: 800-328-4880 or (651)687-7000 Fax: 800-340-9378 E-mail: bookstore@westgroup.com • URL: http://www.westgroup.com • Annual. $160.00. Looseleaf service. Covers a wide variety of corporate finance legal topics, from initial capital structure to public sale of securities.

Financing Your Small Business. Robert Walter. Barron's Educational Series, Inc., 250 Wireless Blvd. Hauppauge, NY 11788-3917. Phone: 800-645-3476 or (516)434-3311 Fax: (516)434-3723 E-mail: info@barronseduc.com • URL: http://www.barronseduc.com • 2004. $18.95. Explains various sources of capital for small businesses, including bank loans, venture capital, and initial public offerings of stock.

Find It Online: The Complete Guide to Online Research. Alan M. Schlein. Facts on Demand Press, P.O. Box 27869 Tempe, AZ 85285-7869. Phone: 800-829-8505 or (602)829-7475 Fax: 800-929-4981 or (602)829-8505 E-mail: brb@brbpub.com • URL: http://www.brbpub.com • 2002. $19.95. Third edition. Presents the general principles of online searching for information about people, phone numbers, public records, news, business, investments, etc. Covers both free and fee-based sources. (On Line Ease Series).

FINDEX [cd-rom]. Available from SilverPlatter Information, Inc., 100 River Ridge Rd. Norwood, MA 02062-5026. Phone: 800-343-0064 or (781)769-2599 Fax: (781)769-8763 Quarterly. Produced by Cambridge Scientific Abstracts. Serves as the CD-ROM version of *Findex: The Worldwide Directory of Market Research Reports, Studies, and Surveys*.

Findex: The Worldwide Directory of Market Research Reports, Studies, and Surveys. MarketResearch.com, 641 Ave. of the Americas New York, NY 10011. Phone: 800-298-5699 or (212)807-2629 Fax: (212)807-2676 E-mail: customerservice@marketresearch.com • URL: http://www.marketresearch.com • Annual. $425.00. Provides brief annotations of market research reports and related publications from about 1,000 publishers, arranged by topic. Back of book includes Report Titles by Publisher, Publishers/Distributors Directory, Subject Index, Geography Index, and Company Index. (Formerly published by Cambridge Information Group.)

Finding It on the Internet: The Internet Navigator's Guide to Search Tools and Techniques. Paul Gilster. John Wiley and Sons, Inc., 111 River St. Hoboken, NJ 07030. Phone: 800-225-5945 or (201)748-6000 Fax: (201)748-6088 E-mail: info@wiley.com • URL: http://www.wiley.com • 1996. $24.95. Second expanded revised edition. A basic guide to efficient use of the World Wide Web, search engines, e-mail, hypertext, and the Internet in general. Includes such programs or systems as Gopher, Archie, Veronica, and Jughead, with emphasis on information searching.

Finding Market Research on the Web: Best Practices of Professional Researchers. Robert I. Berkman. MarketResearch.com, 641 Ave. of the Americas, 4th Fl. New York, NY 10011. Phone: 800-298-5699 or (212)807-2629 Fax: (212)807-2676 E-mail: customerservice@marketresearch.com • URL: http://www.marketresearch.com • 2003. $279.00. Provides tips and techniques for locating useful market research data through the Internet.

Finding Statistics Online: How to Locate the Elusive Numbers You Need. Paula Berinstein. Information Today, Inc., 143 Old Marlton Pike Medford, NJ 08055-8750. Phone: 800-300-9868 or (609)654-6266 Fax: (609)654-4309 E-mail: custserv@infotoday.com • URL: http://www.infotoday.com • 1998. $29.95. Provides advice on efficient searching when looking for statistical data on the World Wide Web or from commercial online services and database producers. (Cyber-Age Books.)

FindLaw: Internet Legal Resources. FindLaw, Inc.Phone: (650)940-4300 E-mail: info@findlaw.com • URL: http://www.findlaw.com • Web site provides a wide variety of information and links relating to laws, law schools, professional development, lawyers, the U. S. Supreme Court, consultants (experts), law reviews, legal news, etc. Online searching is provided. Fees: Free.

Finishers' Management. Publication Management, Inc., 4350 DiPaolo Center, Dearlove Rd. Glenview, IL 60025. Phone: (847)699-1700 Fax: (847)699-1703 10 times a year. $35.00 per year.

Fire and Casualty Insurance Law Reports. CCH, Inc., 2700 Lake Cook Rd. Riverwoods, IL 60015. Phone: 800-835-5224 or (847)267-7000 E-mail: cust_serv@cch.com • URL: http://www.cch.com • $870.00 per year. Looseleaf service. Semimonthly updates.

Fire and Materials: An International Journal. John Wiley and Sons, Inc., Journals, 111 River St. Hoboken, NJ 07030. Phone: 800-225-5945 or (201)748-6000 Fax: (201)748-6088 E-mail: customer@wiley.com • URL: http://www.wiley.com • Bimonthly. Individuals, $1,215.00 per year; institutions, $1,620.00 per year. Published in England by John Wiley & Sons Ltd. Provides international coverage of subject matter.

Fire, Casualty and Surety Bulletin. The National Underwriter Co., 5081 Olympic Blvd. Erlanger, KY 41018. Phone: 800-543-0874 or (859)692-2100 • URL: http://www.nationalunderwriter.com • Monthly. $420.00 per year. Five looseleaf volumes.

Fire Chief: Administration, Training, Operations. Primedia Business Magazines and Media, 330 N Wabash Ave., Ste. 2300 Chicago, IL 60611. Phone: 800-795-5445 or (312)595-1080 Fax: (312)595-0295 E-mail: subs@primediabusiness.com • URL: http://www.primediabusiness.com • Monthly. $54.00 per year.

Fire Engineering: The Journal of Fire Suppression and Protection. PennWell Corp., Industrial Div., 1421 S. Sheridan Rd. Tulsa, OK 74112. Phone: 800-331-4463 or (918)835-3161 E-mail: bid@pennwell.com • URL: http://www.pennwell.com • Monthly. $19.95 per year.

Fire International: The Journal of the World's Fire Protection Services. DMG World Media Ltd., Queensway House, 2 Queensway Red Hill RH1 1QS, United Kingdom. Phone: 44 1737 855527 Fax: 44 1737 855470 • URL: http://www.dmgworldmedia.com • 10 times a year. $158.00 per year. Text in English. Summaries in French, German and Spanish.

Fire Protection Handbook. National Fire Protection Association, One Batterymarch Park Quincy, MA 02269-9101. Phone: 800-344-3555 or (617)770-3000 Fax: (617)770-0700 E-mail: library@nfpa.org • URL: http://www.nfpa.org • Irregular. Members, $112.50; non-members, $125.00.

Fire Technology: An International Journal of Fire Protection Research and Engineering. National Fire Protection Association, One Batterymarch Park Quincy, MA 02269-9101. Phone: 800-344-3555 or (617)770-3000 Fax: (617)770-0700 E-mail: library@nfpa.org • URL: http://www.nfpa.org • Quarterly. $199.00 per year.

First Call Consensus Earnings Estimates. Thomson Financial, 195 Broadway New York, NY 10007. Phone: 800-262-6000 or (646)822-2000 Fax: (646)822-6270 E-mail: custserv@tfn.com • URL: http://www.tfn.com • Online service provides corporate earnings estimates for more than 2,500 U. S. companies, based on data from leading brokerage firms. Weekly updates. Inquire as to online cost and availability.

First DataBank Blue Book. Hearst Corp., 645 Stewart Ave. Garden City, NY 11530-4709. Phone: (212)969-7568 Fax: (212)969-7564 • URL: http://www.hearstcorp.com • Annual. $65.00. List of manufacturers of prescription and over-the-counter drugs, sold in retail drug stores. Formerly *American Druggist Blue Book*.

First Have Something to Say: Writing for the Library Profession. Walt Crawford. American Library Association, 50 E Huron St. Chicago, IL 60611-2795. Phone: 800-545-2433 or (312)944-6780 Fax: (312)440-9374 E-mail: ala@ala.org • URL: http://www.ala.org • 2003. $29.00. Provides practical advice for librarian-writers on such matters as copyright, contracts, and getting published.

The First Junk Bond: A Story of Corporate Boom and Bust. Harlan D. Platt. M. E. Sharpe, Inc., 80 Business Park Dr. Armonk, NY 10504. Phone: 800-541-6543 or (914)273-1800 Fax: (914)273-2106 E-mail: info@mesharpe.com • URL: http://www.mesharpe.com • 1994. $80.95. Relates the development and history of Michael Milken's first low-quality bond issue at high interest rates. Includes a chapter, "What Have We Learned?"

First-Level Leadership: Supervising in the New Organization. American Management Association Extension Institute, 1601 Broadway New York, NY 10019. Phone: 800-262-9699 or (518)586-8100 Fax: (518)903-8168 • URL: http://www.amanet.org • Looseleaf. $139.00. Self-study course. Emphasis is on practical explanations, examples, and problem solving. Quizzes and a case study are included.

First-Line Supervision. American Management Association Extension Institute, 1601 Broadway New York, NY 10019. Phone: 800-262-9699 or (518)586-8100 Fax: (518)903-8168 • URL: http://www.amanet.org • Looseleaf. $139.00. Self-study course. Focuses on the day-to-day concerns of the first line supervisor. A self-study course.

The First-Time Sales Manager: A Survival Guide. Theodore Tyssen. Self-Counsel Press, Inc., 1704 N. State St. Bellingham, WA 98225. Phone: 877-877-6490 or (360)676-4530 Fax: (360)676-4549 E-mail: orderdesk@self-counsel.com • URL: http://www.self-counsel.com • 1994. $8.95. Provides basic information and advice for beginning sales managers. (Self Counsel Business Series).

FirstGov: Your First Click to the U. S. Government. General Services AdministrationPhone: 800-333-4636 or (202)501-0705 E-mail: public.affairs@gsa.gov • URL: http://www.firstgov.gov • Free Web site provides extensive links to federal agencies covering a wide variety of topics, such as agriculture, business, consumer safety, education, the environment, government jobs, grants, health, social security, statistics sources, taxes, technology, travel, and world affairs. Also provides links to federal forms, including IRS tax forms. Searching is offered, both keyword and advanced.

FISA-Food Industry Suppliers Association., 1207 Sunset Dr. Greensboro, NC 27408. Phone: (336)274-6311 Fax: (336)691-1839 E-mail: stella@fisanet.org • URL: http://www.fisanet.org • Distributorfs and manufacturers of equipment and supplies fro the sanitary processing industry. Formerly Food Industries Suppliers Association.

Fisheries. American Fisheries Society, 5410 Grosvenor Lane Bethesda, MD 20814. Phone: (301)897-8616 Fax: (301)897-8096 E-mail: main@fisheries.org • URL: http://www.fisheries.org • Monthly. $76.00 per year. Covers the management of fisheries and aquatic resources, including related technology.

Fisheries of the United States. Available from U. S. Government Printing Office, Washington, DC 20402. Phone: (202)512-1800 Fax: (202)512-2250 E-mail: gpoaccess@gpo.gov • URL: http://www.access.gpo.gov • Annual. $20.00. Issued by the National Marine Fisheries Service, National Oceanic and Atmospheric Administration, U. S. Department of Commerce.

Fishermen's News. Fishermen's News, Inc., Fishermen's Terminal, West Wall Bldg., Room 110 Seattle, WA 98119. Phone: (206)282-7545 Fax: (206)283-5123 Monthly. $15.00 per year.

Fitch Insights. Fitch Investors Service, Inc., One State Street Plaza New York, NY 10004. Phone: 800-753-4824 or (212)908-0500 Fax: (212)480-4435 Biweekly. $1,040.00 per year. Includes bond rating actions and explanation of actions. Provides commentary and Fitch's view of the financial markets.

Fitch Ratings Delivery Service. Fitch Inc., One State Street Plaza New York, NY 10004. Phone: 800-753-4824 or (212)908-0500 Fax: (212)480-4435 • URL: http://www.fitchratings.com • Provides online delivery of Fitch financial ratings in three sectors: "Corporate Finance" (corporate bonds, insurance companies), "Structured Finance" (asset-backed securities), and "U.S. Public Finance" (municipal bonds). Daily updates. Inquire as to online cost and availability.

Fitness Management. Leisure Publications, Inc., 4160 Wilshire Blvd. Los Angeles, CA 90010. Phone: (323)964-4800 Fax: (323)964-4837 E-mail: sales@fitnessmgmt.com • URL: http://www.fitnessworld.com • Monthly. $24.00 per year. Published for owners and managers of physical fitness centers, both commercial and corporate.

Fitness Management Products and Services Source Guide. Leisure Publications, 4160 Wilshire Blvd. Los Angeles, CA 90010. Phone: (323)964-4800 Fax: (323)964-4837 E-mail: sales@fitnessmgmt.com • URL: http://www.fitnessworld.com • Annual. $24.00. A directory of more than 1,250 fitness equipment manufacturers and suppliers of services. Includes a glossary of terms related to the fitness industry and employee wellness programs.

Fitness Motivation Institute., 26685 Sussex Hwy., Ste. B Seaford, DE 19973. Phone: 800-538-7790 E-mail: info@fmia.com • URL: http://www.fmia.com • Seeks to motivate, educate, and evaluate individuals in the area of physical fitness. Members are health and fitness professionals.

The 500 Year Delta: What Happens After What Comes Next. Jim Taylor and others. HarperInformation, 10 E. 53rd St. New York, NY 10022-5299. Phone: 800-242-7737 or (212)207-7000 Fax: 800-822-4090 or (212)207-7145 • URL: http://www.harpercollins.com • 1998. $14.00. Provides analysis of major corporate and political trends.

The Five Minute Interview: A New and Powerful Approach to Interviewing. Richard H. Beatty. John Wiley and Sons, Inc., 111 River St. Hoboken, NJ 07030. Phone: 800-526-5368 or (201)748-6000 Fax: (201)748-6088 E-mail: info@wiley.com • URL: http://www.wiley.com • 2002. $16.95. Third edition. Advice for job applicants.

The Five Rules for Successful Stock Investing: Morningstar's Guide to Building Wealth and Winning in the Market. Pat Dorsey. John Wiley and Sons, Inc., 111 River St. Hoboken, NJ 07030. Phone: 800-225-5945 or (201)748-6000 Fax: (201)748-6088 E-mail: bookinfo@wiley.com • URL: http://www.wiley.com • 2004. $24.95. Provides conservative investment advice from Morningstar's Director of Stock Analysis.

Fixed Income Almanac: The Bond Investor's Compendium of Key Market, Product, and Performance Data. Livingston G. Douglas. McGraw-Hill, 1221 Ave. of the Americas New York, NY 10020. Phone: 800-722-4726 or (212)512-2000 Fax: (212)512-4502 E-mail: customer.service@mcgraw-hill.com • URL: http://www.mcgraw-hill.com • 1993. $75.00. Presents 20 years of data in 350 graphs and charts. Covers bond market volatility, yield spreads, high-yield (junk) corporate bonds, default rates, and other items, such as Federal Reserve policy.

Fixed Income Analytics: State-of-the-Art Analysis and Valuation Modeling. Ravi E. Dattatreya, editor. McGraw-Hill, 1221 Ave. of the Americas New York, NY 10020. Phone: 800-722-4726 or (212)512-2000 Fax: (212)512-4502 E-mail: customer.service@mcgraw-hill.com • URL: http://www.mcgraw-hill.com • 1991. $69.95. Discusses the yield curve, structure and value in corporate bonds, mortgage-backed securities, and other topics. (Institutional Investor Publications).

Fixed Income Mathematics: Analytical and Statistical Techniques. Frank J. Fabozzi. McGraw-Hill, 1221 Ave. of the Americas New York, NY 10020. Phone: 800-722-4726 or (212)512-2000 Fax: (212)512-4502 E-mail: customer.service@mcgraw-hill.com • URL: http://www.mcgraw-hill.com • 1996. $65.00. Third edition. Covers the basics of fixed income analysis, as well as more advanced techniques used for complex securities.

The Flat Tax. Robert E. Hall and Alvin Rabushka. Hoover Institution Press, Stanford University Stanford, CA 94305-6010. Phone: 800-935-2882 or (650)723-3373 Fax: (650)723-8626 E-mail: digest@hoover.stanford.edu • URL: http://www.hoover.org • 1995. $14.95. Second edition. A favorable view of a flat tax as a replacement for the graduated federal income tax. (Publication Series: No. 423).

Flavor and Extract Manufacturers Association of the United States.

Flavour and Fragrance Journal. John Wiley and Sons, Inc., Journals, 111 River St. Hoboken, NJ 07030. Phone: 800-225-5945 or (201)748-6000 Fax: (201)748-6088 E-mail: customer@wiley.com • URL: http://www.wiley.com • Bimonthly. Individuals, $890.00 per year; institutions, $1,185.00 per year.

Flawless Consulting: A Guide to Getting Your Expertise Used. Peter Block. John Wiley and Sons, Inc., 111 River St. Hoboken, NJ 07030. Phone: 800-225-5945 or (201)748-6000 Fax: (201)748-6088 E-mail: info@wiley.com • URL: http://www.wiley.com • 1999. $45.00. Second edition.

Fleet Owner. Primedia Business Magazines and Media, 11 River Bend Dr., S Stamford, CT 06907. Phone: 800-795-5445 or (203)358-9900 Fax: (203)358-5811 E-mail: subs@primediabusiness.com • URL: http://www.primediabusiness.com • Monthly. $45.00 per year.

Fleet Owner Specs and Buyers' Directory. Primedia Business Magazines and Media, 11 River Bend Dr., S Stamford, CT 06907. Phone: 800-795-5445 or (203)358-9900 Fax: (203)358-5811 E-mail: subs@primediabusiness.com • URL: http://www.primediabusiness.com • Annual. $5.00. Lists of manufacturers of equipment and materials used in the operation, management, and maintenance of truck and bus fleets.

Fleet Reserve Association., 125 N West St. Alexandria, VA 22314-2709. Phone: 800-FRA-1924 or (703)683-1400 Fax: (703)549-6610 E-mail: news-fra@fra.org • URL: http://www.fra.org • Active duty enlisted personnel in the U.S. Navy, Marine Corps, Coast Guard, Fleet Reserves of the Navy, and Fleet Marine Corps and Coast Guard; retired members of these services.

Flesh Peddlers and Warm Bodies: The Temporary Help Industry and Its Workers. Robert E. Parker. Rutgers University Press, 100 Joyce Kilmer Ave. Piscataway, NJ 08854-8099. Phone: 800-446-9323 or (732)445-7762 Fax: 888-471-9014 or (732)445-7039 E-mail: bksales@rci.rutgers.edu • URL: http://www.rutgerspress.rutgers.edu • 1994. $40.00. A critical view of temporary work. (Arnold and Caroline Rose Monograph Series of the American Sociological Association).

Fletcher Corporation Forms Annotated. West Group, 610 Opperman Dr. Eagan, MN 55123. Phone: 800-328-4880 or (651)687-7000 Fax: 800-340-9378 E-mail: bookstore@westgroup.com • URL: http://www.westgroup.com • Annual. $1,263.00. 26 volumes.

Fletcher Corporation Law Adviser. West Group, 610 Opperman Dr. Eagan, MN 55123. Phone: 800-328-4880 or (651)687-7000 Fax: 800-340-9378 E-mail: compandbene@westgroup.com • URL: http://www.westgroup.com • Description: Comments on recent developments in corporation law. Discusses age discrimination, bankruptcy, civil rights, arbitration, appraisals, bylaws, derivative suits, fraud, hazardous waste, liability, mergers liens, pensions, insurance, proxies, profits, stocks, and taxation.

Flexible Packaging Association., 971 Corporate Blvd., Ste. 403 Linthicum, MD 21090-2253. Phone: (410)694-0800 Fax: (410)694-0900 E-mail: fpa@flexpack.org • URL: http://www.flexpack.org • Converters of paper, foil, and plastic packaging materials; associate members are industry suppliers. Promotes the welfare of the flexible packaging industry by: communicating with federal and state governments and the public on subjects of concern to the industry; promoting the use of flexible packaging; conducting technical, manufacturing, and statistical programs; establishing standards and specifications. Offers six lesson plans on packaging for grades 5-9. Sponsors children's services; compiles statistics.

Flight International. Reed Business Information, Quadrant House, The Quadrant, Brighton Rd. Sutton, Surrey SM2 5AS, United Kingdom. Phone: 44 208 652 3500 Fax: 44 208 652 8932 E-mail: rbi.subscriptions@qss-uk.com • URL: http://www.reedbusiness.com • Weekly. $140.00 per year. Technical aerospace coverage.

Flight Mechanics Laboratory.

Flight Research Laboratory. Kansas University Center for Research

Flight Safety Foundation., 601 Madison St., Ste. 300 Alexandria, VA 22314-1756. Phone: (703)739-6700 Fax: (703)739-6708 E-mail: wahdan@flightsafety.org • URL: http://www.flightsafety.org • Aerospace manufacturers, domestic and foreign airlines, insurance companies, fuel and oil companies, schools, and miscellaneous organizations having an interest in the promotion of safety in flight. Sponsors safety audits. Compiles statistics.

Floor Covering News. Roel Product Inc., 550 Old Country Rd., Suite 204 Hicksville, NY 11801-4116. Phone: (516)932-7860 • URL: http://www.floorcoveringnews.com • Biweekly. $25.00 per year. For retailers, distributors, contractors, and manufacturers.

Floor Covering Weekly—Annual Product Source Guide. FCW, 50 Charles Lindbergh Blvd., Ste. 100 Uniondale, NY 11553. Phone: (516)229-3600 Fax: (516)227-1342 E-mail: corporatecommunications@reedbusiness.com • URL: http://www.floorcoveringweekly.com • Publication includes: Lists of manufacturers and importers of carpet, rugs, carpet cushion, fiber, resilient wood, and ceramic floor coverings; separate listing of distributors by state, retail groups and associations. Entries include: For manufacturers—Company name, address, phone, regional sales offices, names and titles of key personnel, local distributors, products. For distributors—Company name, address, phone, manufacturers represented.

Floor Covering Weekly: The Business Newspaper of the Floor Covering Industry. FCW, 50 Charles Lindbergh Blvd., Ste. 100 Uniondale, NY 11553-4709. Phone: (516)229-3600 Fax: (516)227-1342 E-mail: dboehle@hearst.com • URL: http://www.floorcoveringweekly.com • 32 times a year. $61.00 per year.

Floor Coverings. Available from MarketResearch.com, 641 Ave. of the Americas, Fourth Floor New York, NY 10011. Phone: 800-298-5699 or (212)807-2629 Fax: (212)807-2642 E-mail: order@marketresearch.com • URL: http://www.marketresearch.com • 2002. $3,950.00. Published by Global Industry Analysts. Provides worldwide market research data, including profiles of major floor covering companies.

Flooring Buying and Resource Guide. Douglas Publications, Inc., 2807 N. Parham Rd. Richmond, VA 23294. Phone: 800-223-1797 or (804)762-9600 Fax: (804)217-8999 E-mail: info@douglaspublications.com • URL: http://www.douglaspublications.com • Annual. $42.50. Lists of manufacturers, workroom manufacturers' representatives, and distributors of floor and other interior surfacing products and equipment; carpet inspection servicecompanies' and related trade associations in the United States and Canada. Formerly *Flooring Directory and Buying Guide.*

Florafacts. Florafax International, Inc., P.O. Box 45745 Tulsa, OK 74145. Phone: (918)622-8415 Monthly. $15.00 per year.

Florida Agricultural Experiment Station. University of Florida

Florida Citrus Mutual., PO Box 89, 302 S Massachusetts Ave. Lakeland, FL 33802. Phone: (863)682-1111 Fax: (863)682-1074 E-mail: info@flcitrusmutual.com • URL: http://www.flcitrusmutual.com/content • Supplies market and price information to members; marketing of fruit is handled by affiliated shippers and processors.

Florida Department of Citrus.

Florida Gift Fruit Shippers Association., 5500 W Concord Ave. Orlando, FL 32808. Phone: 800-741-1491 or (407)295-1491 Fax: (407)290-0918 E-mail: donnag@fgfsa.com • URL: http://www.fgfsa.com • Firms packing and shipping gift fruit packages.

Florist-Buyers Directory. Florist's Transworld Delivery Association, 33031 Schoolcraft Livonia, MI 48150. Phone: 800-383-4383 Fax: (734)466-8978 Annual. $7.00. Lists 1,200 suppliers in floral industry.

Florists' Review. Florists' Review Enterprises, 3641 S.W. Plass Ave. Topeka, KS 66611-2588. Phone: (913)266-0888 Fax: (913)266-0333 Monthly. $39.00 per year.

Flour Milling and Baking Abstracts. CCFAA Technology Ltd., Station Rd. Chipping Campden, Glos. GL55 6LD, England. Phone: 44 1386 842000 Fax: 44 1386 842100 E-mail: pubs@campden.co.uk • URL: http://www.campden.co.uk • Bimonthly. Members, $275.00 per year; non-members, $325.00 per year. Includes print and online editions.

Flour Milling Products. U. S. Bureau of the Census, 4700 Silver Hill Rd. Washington, DC 20233-0001. Phone: (301)763-4636 E-mail: comments@census.gov • URL: http://www.census.gov • Monthly and annual. Covers production, mill stocks, exports, and imports of wheat and rye flour. (Current Industrial Reports, M20A.)

Flower Shop. Entrepreneur Media, Inc., 2445 McCabe Way Irvine, CA 92614. Phone: 800-421-2300 or (949)261-2325 Fax: (949)261-0234 E-mail: entmag@entrepreneur.com • URL: http://www.entrepreneura.com • Looseleaf. $59.50. A practical guide to starting a retail flower shop. Covers profit potential, start-up costs, market size evaluation, owner's time required, site selection, lease negotiation, pricing, accounting, advertising, promotion, etc. (Start-Up Business Guide No. E1143.)

Flowers &: The Beautiful Magazine About the Business of Flowers. Teleflora, Inc., 11444 W. Olympic Blvd. Los Angeles, CA 90064. Phone: 800-321-2665 or (310)966-3543 Fax: (310)966-3610 Monthly. $38.95 per year.

Fluid Abstracts: Civil Engineering. Elsevier, 655 Ave. of the Americas New York, NY 10010-5107. Phone: 800-366-2665 or (212)989-5800 Fax: 800-535-9935 or (212)633-3680 E-mail: custserv@elsevier.com • URL: http://www.elsevier.com • Monthly. Institutions, $1,709.00 per year. Includes annual cumulation. Includes the literature of coastal structures. Published in England by Elsevier Science Publishing Ltd. Formerly *Civil Engineering Hydraulics Abstracts.*

Fluid Abstracts: Process Engineering. Elsevier, 655 Ave. of the Americas New York, NY 10010-5107. Phone: 800-366-2665 or (212)989-5800 Fax: 800-535-9935 or (212)633-3680

E-mail: custserv@elsevier.com • URL: http://www.elsevier.com • Monthly. Institutions, $1,709.00 per year. Includes annual cumulation. Formerly *Pumps and Other Fluids Machinery: Abstracts*.

Fluid Controls Institute., 1300 Sumner Ave. Cleveland, OH 44115. Phone: (216)241-7333 Fax: (216)241-0105 E-mail: fci@fluidcontrolsinstitute.org • URL: http://www.fluidcontrolsinstitute.org • Works for technical advancement, promotion and understanding of a broad range of fluid control and fluid conditioning devices. Concentrates its efforts on the manufacturing and engineering aspects of control valves, solenoid valves, regulators, steam traps, pipeline strainers, secondary pressure drainers and gauges. Maintains the flexibility to adapt to changing technology by including a general products section, out of which new sections can be formed to better serve the industry and the general public.

Fluid Power Distributors Association., PO Box 1420, 1930 East Marlton Pike Ste. A-2 Cherry Hill, NJ 08034-0054. Phone: (856)424-8998 Fax: (856)424-9248 E-mail: info@fpda.org • URL: http://www.fpda.org • Represents wholesalers and manufacturers involved in the distribution of hydraulic and pneumatic equipment. Works to advance the distribution of such equipment; conducts research and educational activities. Compiles statistics.

Fluid Power Handbook and Directory. Penton Media, Inc., 1300 E 9th St. Cleveland, OH 44114. Phone: (216)696-7000 Fax: (216)931-9799 E-mail: information@penton.com • URL: http://www.penton.com • Biennial. $95.00 per year. Over 1,500 manufacturers and 3,000 distributors of fluid power products in the United States and Canada.

Fluid Power Institute.

Fluid Power Laboratory.

FLUIDEX. Elsevier Science, Inc., 360 Park Ave. S New York, NY 10010. Phone: 888-437-4636 or (212)633-3730 Fax: (212)462-1974 Produced in the Netherlands by Elsevier Science B.V. Provides indexing and abstracting of the international literature of fluid engineering and technology, 1973 to date, with monthly updates. Also known as *Fluid Engineering Abstracts*. Inquire as to online cost and availability.

Fly-Rights: A Consumer Guide to Air Travel. Available from U. S. Government Printing Office, Washington, DC 20402. Phone: (202)512-1800 Fax: (202)512-2250 E-mail: gpoaccess@gpo.gov • URL: http://www.access.gpo.gov • 1999. $4.00. 11th edition. Issued by the U. S. Department of Transportation. Explains the rights and responsibilities of air travelers.

Flying. Hachette Filipacchi Media U.S., Inc., 1633 Broadway New York, NY 10019. Phone: 800-678-0997 or (212)767-6000 Fax: (212)767-5600 • URL: http://www.hfmmag.com • Monthly. Includes three *Special Issues*. Price on application.

Flying Safety. U.S. Air Force. Available from U.S. Government Printing Office, Washington, DC 20402. Phone: (202)512-1800 Fax: (202)512-2250 E-mail: gpoaccess@gpo.gov • URL: http://www.access.gpo.gov • Monthly. $50.00 per year. Published in the interest of safer flying. Articles cover many fields of flight, aircraft engineering, training and safety measures in the air and on the ground.

FMI Annual Financial Review. Food Marketing Institute, 655 15th St., NW, No. 700 Washington, DC 20005. Phone: (202)452-8444 Fax: (202)429-4519 E-mail: fmi@fmi.org • URL: http://www.fmi.org • Annual. Members, $30.00; nonmembers, $75.00. Provides financial data on the supermarket industry.

FMRA News. American Society of Farm Managers and Rural Appraisers, 950 S Cherry St., Ste. 508 Denver, CO 80246-2664. Phone: (303)758-3513 Fax: (303)758-0190 E-mail: communications@agri-associations.org Description: Considers such topics as environmental issues, governmental regulation, technological advances, relative legislation, and other issues pertinent to rural resource properties. Recurring features include news of Society activities, educational offerings, and membership updates.

Focal Encyclopedia of Photography. Leslie Stroebel and Richard D. Zakia, editors. Elsevier, 655 Ave. of the Americas New York, NY 10010. Phone: 800-366-2665 or (212)989-5800 Fax: 800-535-9935 or (212)633-3680 E-mail: custserv@elsevier.com • URL: http://www.elsevier.com • 1996. $69.95. Third edition.

Focus Group Kit. David L. Morgan and Richard A. Krueger. Sage Publications, Inc., 2455 Teller Rd. Thousand Oaks, CA 91320. Phone: 800-818-7243 or (805)499-9774 Fax: 800-583-2665 or (805)499-0871 E-mail: webmaster@sagepub.com • URL: http://www.sagepub.com • 1997. $150.00. Six volumes. Various authors cover the basics of focus group research, including planning, developing questions, moderating, and analyzing results. (Focus Group Kit Series).

Focus Groups: A Practical Guide for Applied Research. Richard A. Krueger and Mary Anne Casey. Sage Publications, Inc., 2455 Teller Rd. Thousand Oaks, CA 91320. Phone: 800-818-7243 or (805)499-9774 Fax: 800-583-2665 or (805)499-0871 E-mail: webmaster@sagepub.com • URL: http://www.sagepub.com • 2000. $81.95. Third edition. A step-by-step guide to obtaining useful research data from a focus group.

Focus: On the Center for Research Libraries. Center for Research Libraries, 6050 S. Kenwood Ave. Chicago, IL 60637-2804. Phone: (312)955-4545 Fax: (312)955-4339 Bimonthly. Free. Newsletter. Provides news of Center activites.

Folio: The New Dynamics of Magazine Publishing. Primedia Business Magazines and Media, Overland Park, KS 10016. Phone: 800-795-5445 or (913)341-1300 Fax: (913)967-1898 E-mail: subs@primediabusiness.com • URL: http://www.primediabusiness.com • Monthly. $96.00 per year.

The Folklore of American Holidays. Gale Cengage Learning, 27500 Drake Rd. Farmington Hills, MI 48331-3535. Phone: 800-877-GALE or (248)699-4253 Fax: 800-414-5043 E-mail: gale.galeord@cengage.com • URL: http://gale.cengage.com • 1999. $140.00. Third edition. Festivals, rituals, beliefs, superstitions, etc., arranged according to holiday.

The Folklore of World Holidays. Gale Cengage Learning, 27500 Drake Rd. Farmington Hills, MI 48331-3535. Phone: 800-877-GALE or (248)699-4253 Fax: 800-414-5043 E-mail: gale.galeord@cengage.com • URL: http://gale.cengage.com • 1999. $140.00. Third edition. Contains descriptions of the important holidays in more than 150 countries.

Fontana Corrosion Center., Ohio State University, 477 Watts Halls, 2041 College Rd. Columbus, OH 43210. Phone: (614)292-9857 Fax: (614)292-9857 E-mail: fcc@osu.edu/ • URL: http://www.mse.eng.ohio-state.edu • Research areas include metal coatings and corrosion of alloys.

Food Additives. Available from MarketResearch.com, 641 Ave. of the Americas, 3rd Fl. New York, NY 10011. Phone: 800-298-5699 or (212)807-2629 Fax: (212)807-2716 E-mail: order@marketresearch.com • URL: http://www.marketresearch.com • 2002. $3,700.00. Published by the Freedonia Group. Market data with forecasts to 2006 on coloring agents, flavors, preservatives, stabilizers, etc.

Food Additives and Contaminants: Analysis, Surveillance, Evaluation, Control. Taylor and Francis Group, 325 Chestnut St., Ste. 800 Philadelphia, PA 19106. Phone: 800-821-8312 or (215)625-8900 Fax: (215)625-2940 E-mail: info@taylorandfrancis.com • URL: http://www.taylorandfrancis.com • Monthly. Institutions $2,038.00 per year.

Food and Environmental Toxicology Laboratory. University of Florida

Food and Feed Grains Institute. Kansas State University

Food Business Mergers and Acquisitions. The Food Institute, One Broadway, 2nd Fl. Elmwood Park, NJ 07407. Phone: (201)791-5570 Fax: (201)791-5222 E-mail: food1@foodinstitute.com • URL: http://www.foodinstitute.com • Annual. $285.00. Gives names, locations, and industry categories of all companies involved in food business mergers during the previous year.

Food Chemical News. CRC Press L.L.C., 2000 Corporate Blvd. NW Boca Raton, FL 33431. Phone: 800-272-7737 or (561)994-0555 Fax: (561)989-9732 E-mail: communications@agri-associations.org Description: Provides in-depth, timely coverage of the laws affecting food regulation, including additives, colors, pesticides, and allied products. Recurring features include news of research.

Food Chemicals News Directory. Food Chemical News. CRC Press LLC, 2000 NW Corporate Blvd. Boca Raton, FL 33431. Phone: 800-272-7737 or (561)994-0555 Fax: 800-374-3401 or (561)989-9732 E-mail: orders@crcpress.com • URL: http://www.crcpress.com • Semiannual. $497.00. Over 2,000 subsidiaries belonging to nearly 250 corporate parents plus an additional 3,000 independent processors. Formerly *Herald's 1,500*.

Food Distribution Magazine. Phoenix Media Network, Inc., PO Box 810425 Boca Raton, FL 33481-1768. Phone: (561)447-0810 Monthly. $49.00 per year. Edited for marketers and buyers of domestic and imported, specialty or gourmet food products, including ethnic foods, seasonings, and bakery items.

Food Distributors International., 201 Park Washington Ct. Falls Church, VA 22046. Phone: (703)532-9400 Fax: (703)538-4673 E-mail: info@ifps.org • URL: http://www.fdi.org • Comprised of food distribution companies that supply and service independent wholesale grocers and foodservice operations. Goal is to educate and inform members on industry events, government affairs, and technology.

Food Engineering and Ingredients. Reed Business Information, 360 Park Ave. S New York, NY 10010. Phone: 800-446-6551 or (646)746-6400 Fax: (646)746-7028 E-mail: corporatecommunications@reedbusiness.com • URL: http://www.reedbusiness.com • Bimonthly. Price on application. Formerly *Food Engineering International*.

Food Engineering Database. Reed Business Information, 360 Park Ave. S New York, NY 10010. Phone: 800-446-6551 or (646)746-6400 Fax: (646)746-7431 E-mail: corporatecommunications@reedbusiness.com • URL: http://www.reedbusiness.com • Covers: more than 17,000 food and beverage plants with 20 or more employees; food and beverage research and development facilities; and company headquarters. Entries include: Company name, address, number of employees, phone, Standard Industrial Classification (SIC) code codes.

Food Industries Center.

Food Industry Newsletter: All the Food News That Matters. Newsletters, Inc., P.O. Box 342730 Bethesda, MD 20827-2730. Phone: (301)469-8507 Fax: (301)469-7271 E-mail: foodltr@aol.com 26 times a year. $245.00 per year. Newsletter. A summary of key industry news for food executives.

The Food Institute Report. American Institute of Food Distribution, Inc., 1 Broadway Elmwood Park, NJ 07407. Phone: (201)791-5570 Fax: (201)791-5222 E-mail: info@foodinstitute.com • URL: http://www.foodinstitute.com • Description: Reports on developments in the food industry, including new products, the food service industry, mergers and acquisitions, current legislation and regulations, judicial decisions, and financial and marketing information.

Food Law Reports. CCH, Inc., 2700 Lake Cook Rd. Riverwoods, IL 60015. Phone: 800-835-5224 or (847)267-7000 E-mail: cust_serv@cch.com • URL: http://www.cch.com • Weekly. $1,459.00 per year. Six looseleaf volumes. Covers regulation of adulteration, packaging, labeling, and additives. Formerly *Food Drug Cosmetic Law Reports*.

Food Management: Ideas for Colleges, Healthcare, Schools, and Business Dining. Penton Media, Inc., 1300 E. Ninth St. Cleveland, OH 44114. Phone: (216)626-7000 Fax: (216)696-1752 E-mail: information@penton.com • URL: http://www.penton.com • Monthly. Free to qualified personel; others.

Food Manufacturing. Reed Business Information, 360 Park Ave., S New York, NY 10010. Phone: 800-446-6551 or (646)746-6400 Fax: (646)746-7028 E-mail: corporatecommunications@reedbusiness.com • URL: http://www.reedbusiness.com • Monthly. $86.99 per year. Edited for food processing operations managers and food engineering managers. Includes end-of-year *Food Products and Equipment Literature Review*. Formerly *Food Products and Equipment*.

Food Marketing Industry Speaks. Food Marketing Institute, 655 15th St., NW, No. 700 Washington, DC 20005. Phone: (202)452-8444 Fax: (202)429-4519 E-mail: fmi@fmi.org • URL: http://www.fmi.org • Annual. Members, $30.00; nonmembers, $75.00. Provides data on overall food industry marketing performance, including retail distribution and store operations.

Food Marketing Institute., 2345 Crystal Dr., Ste. 800 Arlington, VA 22202-4801. Phone: (202)452-8444 Fax: (202)429-4519 E-mail: info@ifps.org • URL: http://www.fmi.org • Grocery retailers and wholesalers. Maintains liaison with government and consumers. Conducts 30 educational conferences and seminars per year. Conducts research programs; compiles statistics.

Food Master. BNP Media, 2401 W Big Beaver Rd., Ste. 700 Troy, MI 48084. Phone: 800-952-6643 or (248)362-3700 Fax: (248)362-0317 E-mail: info@bnpmedia.com • URL: http://www.reedbusiness.com • Covers: over 5,000 manufacturers and distributors of equipment, ingredients, services and supplies for food processing plants. Entries include: Company name, address, phone.

Food Processing. Putman Media, 555 W. Pierce Rd., Suite 301 Itasca, IL 60143-2649. Phone: (630)467-1300 Fax: (630)467-1179 • URL: http://www.foodprocessing.com • Monthly. Free to qualified personnel; others, $89.00 per year. Edited for executive and operating personnel in the food processing industry.

Food Processing Guide and Directory. Putman Media Inc., 555 W Pierce Rd., Ste. 301 Itasca, IL 60143-2666. Phone: (630)467-1300 • URL: http://www.foodprocessing.com • Annual. $90.00. Lists over 5,390 food ingredient and equipment manufacturers.

Food Processing Machinery Association., 200 Daingerfield Rd. Alexandria, VA 22314-2800. Phone: 800-331-8816 or (703)684-1080 Fax: (703)548-6563 E-mail: info@fpmamail.com • URL: http://www.foodprocessingmachinery.com • Represents firms manufacturing machinery and providing services and supplies for the canning, freezing, food, beverage, and pharmaceutical processing industries. Produces annual exposition of food processing equipment, supplies, and services, the International Exposition for Food Processors (IEFP); offers export and marketing services for members.

Food Processing Newsletter. Putman Publishing Co., 555 W. Pierce Rd., Suite 301 Itasca, IL 60143-2649. Phone: (630)467-1300 Fax: (630)467-1123 • URL: http://www.putnampublishing.com • Weekly. $100.00 per year. Covers food processing industry news and trends.

Food Processors Institute., 1350 I St. NW Washington, DC 20005-3305. Phone: 800-355-0983 or (202)639-5945 or (202)639-5945 Fax: (202)639-5932 E-mail: fpi@fpa-food.org • URL: http://www.fpi-food.org • The education provider for the National Food Processors Association, its members, and affiliates. Presents seminars and courses that support the food processing industry, and develops publications, videos, software, and other educational materials for the continuing education of food industry and related personnel. Provides custom design workshops for specific company training needs.

Food Production-Management: Monthly Publication of the Canning, Glass-Packing, As eptic, and Frozen Food Industry. CTI Publications, Inc., 2 Oakway Rd. Timonium, MD 21093-4247. Phone: 800-468-6770 or (410)308-2080 Fax: (410)308-2079 E-mail: sales@ctipubs.com • URL: http://www.ctipubs.com • Monthly. $35.00 per year.

Food Products Association., 1350 I St. NW, Ste. 300 Washington, DC 20005. Phone: 800-355-0983 or (202)639-5900 Fax: (202)639-5932 E-mail: membership@fpa-food.org • URL: http://www.fpa-food.org • Leading authority on food science and food safety for the food industry. Members produce processed and packaged fruits and vegetables, meat and poultry, seafood, cereals, dairy products, drinks, juices, and other specialty items or provides supplies and services to food manufacturers.

Food Protein Research and Development Center. Texas A & M

University, Cater-Mattil Hall College Station, TX 77843-2476. Phone: (979)845-2741 Fax: (979)845-2744 E-mail: mrm1@tamu.edu • URL: http://www.tamu.edu/food-protein/ • Formerly Food Research Center.

Food Research Institute.

Food Safety: Is Anyone Watching? V. L. Smyth, editor. Nova Science Publishers, Inc., 400 Oser Ave., Suite 1600 Hauppauge, NY 11788-3619. Phone: (631)231-7269 Fax: (631)231-8175 E-mail: novascience@earthlink.net • URL: http://www.novapublishers.com • 2002. $59.00. Provides material by several authors on governmental oversight of the American food industry. Includes a food safety chronology of selected events, 1992-1999.

Food Science and Technology Abstracts. International Food Information Service Publishing, Lane End House, Shinfield Rd. Reading RG2 9BB, United Kingdom. Phone: 44 118 9883895 Fax: 44 118 9885065 E-mail: ifis@ifis.org • URL: http://www.dimdi.de/ • Monthly. $1,780.00 per year. Provides worldwide coverage of the literature of food technology and food production.

Food Science and Technology Abstracts [CD-ROM]. Available from SilverPlatter Information, Inc., 100 River Ridge Rd. Norwood, MA 02062-0543. Phone: 800-343-0064 or (781)769-2599 Fax: (781)769-8763 E-mail: info@silverplatter.com • URL: http://www.silverplatter.com • Quarterly. Produced by International Food Information Service (home page is http://www.ifis.org). Provides worldwide coverage on CD-ROM of the literature of food technology and production. Various types of publications are indexed, with abstracts, including about 1,800 periodicals. Time period is 1969 to date.

Food Science and Technology Abstracts [online]. IFIS North American Desk, National Food Laboratory, 6363 Clark Ave. Dublin, CA 94568. Phone: 800-336-3782 or (925)828-1440 Fax: (925)833-8795 • URL: http://www.ifis.org • Produced by International Food Information Service. Provides about 500,000 online citations, with abstracts, to the international literature of food science, technology, commodities, engineering, and processing. Approximately 2,000 periodicals are covered. Time period is 1969 to date, with monthly updates. Inquire as to online cost and availability.

Food Technology. Institute of Food Technologists, 221 N. LaSalle St. Chicago, IL 60601. Phone: 800-438-3663 or (312)782-8424 E-mail: info@ift.org • URL: http://www.ift.org • Monthly. Free to members; non-members, $82.00 per year. Articles cover food product development, food ingredients, production, packaging, research, and regulation.

Food Trade News. Best-Met Publishing Co., Inc., 5537 Twin Knolls Rd., Suite 438 Columbia, MD 21045-3240. Phone: (410)730-5013 Fax: (410)740-4680 Monthly. $36.00 per year. Reports on the retail food industry in Pennsylvania, Delaware, southern New Jersey and northern Maryland.

FOODS ADLIBRA. General Mills, Inc., Technical Information Services, Foods Adlibra Publications, 9000 Plymouth Ave. N., Minneapolis, MN 55427. Phone: (612)540-4759 Fax: (612)540-3166 Contains online citations, with abstracts, to the technical and business literature of food processing and packaging. New products and new ingredients are featured. Covers about 250 trade journals and 500 research journals from 1974 to date, with monthly updates. Inquire as to online cost and availability.

Foods Adlibra: Key to the World's Food Literature. General Mills, Inc. Foods Adlibra Publications, 9000 Plymouth Ave., N. Minneapolis, MN 55427. Phone: (612)540-4759 Fax: (612)540-3166 Semimonthly. $240.00 per year. Provides journal citations and abstracts to the literature of food technology and packaging.

Foods and Nutrition Encyclopedia. Audrey H. Ensminger and others. CRC Press, Inc., Boca Raton, FL 33431-7372. Phone: 800-272-7737 or (561)994-0555 Fax: 800-374-3401 or (561)989-9732 E-mail: order@crcpress.com • URL: http://www.crcpress.com • 1993. $309.95. Second edition. Two volumes.

Foodservice and Packaging Institute., 150 S. Washington St., Ste. 204 Falls Church, VA 22046. Phone: (703)538-2800 Fax: (703)538-2187 E-mail: fpi@fpi.org • URL: http://www.fpi.org • Members are manufacturers of one-time-use food containers. Formerly Single Service Institute.

Foodservice Consultants Society International., 455 S 4th St., Ste. 650 Louisville, KY 40202. Phone: (502)583-3783 Fax: (502)589-3602 E-mail: fcsi@fcsi.org • URL: http://www.fcsi.org • Works to promote client usage of services provided by members. Promotes ethical industry practices; disseminates information; develops accreditation programs; conducts educational and research programs; maintains speakers' bureau.

Foodservice Consultants Society International: Membership Roster. Foodservice Consultants Society International, 304 W. Liberty St., Suite 201 Louisville, KY 40202-3011. Phone: (502)583-3783 Fax: (502)589-3602 E-mail: fcsi@fcsi.org • URL: http://www.fcsi.org • Annual. $450.00. About 950 food service consultants.

Foodservice Equipment and Supplies. Reed Business Information, 360 Park Ave., S New York, NY 10010. Phone: 800-446-6551 or (646)746-6400 Fax: (646)746-7028 E-mail: corporatecommunications@reedbusiness.com • URL: http://www.reedbusiness.com • 13 times a year. $106.90 per year.

Foodservice Equipment and Supplies Product Source Guide. Reed Business Information, 360 Park Ave., S New York, NY 10010. Phone: 800-662-7776 or (646)746-6400 E-mail: corporatecommunications@reedbusiness.com • URL: http://www.reedbusiness.com • Annual. $35.00. Nearly 1,700 manufacturers of food service equipment and supplies. Formerly *Foodservice Equipment Buyer's Guide and Product Directory*.

Foodservice Equipment Distributors Association., 2250 Point Blvd., Ste. 200 Elgin, IL 60123-7887. Phone: 800-677-9605 or (224)293-6500 Fax: (224)293-6505 E-mail: feda@feda.com • URL: http://www.feda.com • Distributors of foodservice equipment, such as ovens, ranges, dishwashing machines, china, utensils, and cutlery for hotels, restaurants, and institutions. Conducts specialized education programs.

Footware. Available from MarketResearch.com, 641 Ave. of the Americas, Fourth Floor New York, NY 10011. Phone: 800-298-5699 or (212)807-2629 Fax: (212)807-2642 E-mail: order@marketresearch.com • URL: http://www.marketresearch.com • 2002. $3,950.00. Published by Global Industry Analysts. Provides worldwide market research data, including profiles of major shoe companies.

Footwear. U. S. Bureau of the Census, 4700 Silver Hill Rd. Washington, DC 20233-0001. Phone: (301)763-4636 E-mail: comments@census.gov • URL: http://www.census.gov • Quarterly. Covers production and value of shipments of leather and rubber footwear. (Current Industrial Reports, MQ-31A.)

Footwear Distributors and Retailers of America., 1319 F St., N.W., Suite 700 Washington, DC 20004. Phone: (202)737-5660 Fax: (202)638-2615 E-mail: ptmangione@fdra.org • URL: http://www.fdra.org • Formerly Volume Footwear Retailers of America.

Footwear Market. Available from MarketResearch.com, 641 Ave. of the Americas, Third Floor New York, NY 10011. Phone: 800-298-5699 or (212)807-2629 Fax: (212)807-2716 E-mail: order@marketresearch.com • URL: http://www.marketresearch.com • 2002. $1,695.00. Published by Business Trend Analysts. Provides market data on shoes for walking, running, and specific sports.

Footwear News. Fairchild Publications, Seven W. 34th St. New York, NY 10001. Phone: 800-360-1700 or (212)630-4000 E-mail: customerservice@fairchildpub.com • URL: http://www.fairchildpub.com • Weekly. Individuals, $72.00 per year; domestic retailer, $59.00 per year.

For Your Information. Western New York Library Resources Council, P.O. Box 400 Buffalo, NY 14225-0400. Phone: (716)633-0705 Fax: (716)633-1736 Bimonthly. Free.

Forbes. Forbes, Inc., 60 Fifth Ave. New York, NY 10011. Phone: 800-888-9896 or (212)620-2200 Fax: (212)620-1873 E-mail: subscriber@forbes.com • URL: http://www.forbes.com • Biweekly. $59.95 per year. Includes supplements: *Forbes ASAP* and *Forbes FYI*.

Forbes-Andrew Seybold's Wireless Outlook: A Monthly Perspective of Issues Affecting the Mobile C Computer and Communications Industries. Andrew Seybold's Outlook, Inc., 980 A University Ave. Los Gatos, CA 95032. Phone: (408)354-7900 Fax: (408)354-7980 E-mail: andys@outlook.com • URL: http://www.andyseybold.com • Monthly. $299.00 per year. Newsletter. Provides analysis of the computer industry to corporate buyers and to end users. Reports on hardware, software trends and future products. Formerly *Andrew Seybold's Outlook*.

Ford's Freighter Travel Guide. Ford's Travel Guides, 19448 Londelius st. Northridge, CA 91324-3511. Phone: (818)701-7414 Fax: (818)701-7415 E-mail: advance@pacificnet.net Covers: steamship lines which operate cargo vessels with accommodations for passengers; travel agencies which have chosen to advertise as freighter travel specialists; foreign government tourist offices in the United States, and sports and casual cruises, some on yachts, barges, and sailboats. Entries include: For steamship lines—Company name, address, phone; ships names, facilities, itineraries, fares, etc. For travel agents—Name, address, phone. For tourist bureaus—Name, address, phone, branches.

Forecasting and Management of Technology. Alan L. Porter and others. John Wiley and Sons, Inc., 111 River St. Hoboken, NJ 07030. Phone: 800-225-5945 or (201)748-6000 Fax: (201)748-6088 E-mail: info@wiley.com • URL: http://www.wiley.com • 1991. $190.00. Includes business aspects of technology. (Engineering and Management Technology Series).

Forecasting Business Trends. American Institute for Economic Research, PO Box 1000 Great Barrington, MA 01230-1000. Phone: (413)528-1216 Fax: (413)528-0103 E-mail: info@aier.org • URL: http://www.aier.org • 2000. $6.00. Summarizes methods of economic forecasting, statistical indicators, methods of analyzing business cycles, and use of leading, coincident, and lagging indicators. Includes charts, tables, and a glossary of terms. (Economic Education Bulletin.)

Forecasting Financial Markets: Exchange Rates Interest Rates and Asset Management. Christian Dunis, editor. John Wiley and Sons, Inc., 111 River St. Hoboken, NJ 07030. Phone: 800-225-5945 or (201)748-6000 Fax: (201)748-6088 E-mail: info@wiley.com • URL: http://www.wiley.com • 1996. $150.00. Examines what are said to be the more reliable or "classic" theories of continuously recurring price patterns. Practical investment applications are discussed. (Financial Economics and Quantitative Analysis Series).

Forecasts and Strategies. PBI Media, LLC, 1201 7 Locks Rd. Potomac, MD 20854. Phone: 800-777-5006 or (301)354-2000 Fax: (301)309-3847 E-mail: clientservices@pbimedia.com • URL: http://www.pbimedia.com • Monthly. $99.00 per year. Covers inflation, taxes and government controls.

Foreign Consular Offices in the United States. U.S. Department of State. Available from U.S. Government Printing Office, Washington, DC 20402. Phone: (202)512-1800 Fax: (202)512-2250 E-mail: gpoaccess@gpo.gov • URL: http://www.access.gpo.gov • Semiannual. $17.00 per copy.

Foreign Credit Insurance Association., 125 Park Ave., 14th Fl. New York, NY 10017. Phone: (212)885-1500 Fax: (212)885-1535 E-mail: service@fcia.org • URL: http://www.fcia.com • Represents marine, property, and casualty insurance companies. Insures companies against the risks of nonpayment by buyers for commercial and/or political reasons. Facilitates the financing of term credit sales, thus providing companies with support to meet competitive terms of payment offered by others.

Foreign Exchange Exposure Management: A Portfolio Approach. Niso Abuaf and Stephan Schoess. Executive Enterprises Publications Co. Inc., One Ramada Plz. New Rochelle, NY 10801-5766. 1988. $59.95.

Foreign Exchange Handbook: Managing Risk and Opportunity in Global Currency Markets. Paul Bishop and Don Dixon. McGraw-Hill, 1221 Ave. of the Americas New York, NY 10020. Phone: 800-722-4726 or (212)512-2000 Fax: (212)512-4502 E-mail: customer.service@mcgraw-hill.com • URL: http://www.mcgraw-hill.com • 1992. $69.95. Discusses factors affecting currency value, currency price forecasting, options trading, futures, credit risk, and related subjects.

Foreign Exchange Letter. Institutional Investor, Inc., Journals Group, 225 Park Ave., S New York, NY 10003. Phone: 800-945-2034 or (212)224-3066 Fax: (212)224-3472 E-mail: info@iijournals.com • URL: http://www.iijournals.com • Biweekly. $1,625.00 per year. Newsletter. Provides information on foreign exchange rates, trends, and opportunities. Edited for banks, multinational corporations, currency traders, and others concerned with money rates.

Foreign Exchange Rates. U.S. Federal Reserve System, Publications Services, 20th and Constitution Ave., N.W., Room MS-127 Washington, DC 20551. Phone: (202)452-3244 Fax: (202)728-5886 • URL: http://www.bog.frb.fed.us • Weekly, $20.00 per year; monthly, $5.00 per year.

Foreign Labor Trends. Available from U. S. Government Printing Office, Washington, DC 20402. Phone: (202)512-1800 Fax: (202)512-2250 E-mail: gpoaccess@gpo.gov • URL: http://www.access.gpo.gov • Irregular (50 to 60 issues per year, each on an individual country). $95.00 per year. Prepared by various American Embassies. Issued by the Bureau of International Labor Affairs, U. S. Department of Labor. Covers labor developments in important foreign countries, including trends in wages, working conditions, labor supply, employment, and unemployment.

Foreign Press Association., 333 E 46th St., Ste. 1K New York, NY 10017-7425. Phone: (212)370-1054 Fax: (212)370-1058 E-mail: fpanewyork@aol.com • URL: http://www.nyforeignpress.org • Represents foreign print and broadcast correspondents stationed in the U.S.

Foreign Representatives in the U. S. Yellow Book: Who's Who in the U. S. Offices of Foreign Corporations, Foreign Nations, the Foreign Press, and Intergovernmental Organizations. Leadership Directories, Inc., 104 Fifth Ave. New York, NY 10011. Phone: (212)627-4140 Fax: (212)645-0931 E-mail: info@leadershipdirectories.com • URL: http://www.leadershipdirectories.com • Annual. $265.00 per year. Lists executives located in the U. S. for 1,200 foreign companies, 300 foreign banks and other financial institutions, 175 embassies and consulates, and 375 foreign press outlets. Includes five indexes.

Foreign Service Journal. American Foreign Service Association, 2101 E St., N.W. Washington, DC 20037. Phone: 800-627-6247 or (202)338-4045 Fax: (202)338-6820 E-mail: journal@afsa.org • URL: http://www.afsa.org • Monthly. Individuals, $40.00 per year; students, $20.00 per year. Written for United States foreign service members.

Foreign Tax and Trade Briefs. LexisNexis Matthew Bender, 1275 Broadway Albany, NY 12204. Phone: 800-424-4200 or (518)487-3000 Fax: (518)487-3584 E-mail: bookstore.support@lexisnexis.com • URL: http://www.bender.com • Quarterly. $550.00 per year. Two looseleaf volumes. The latest tax and trade information for over 100 foreign countries.

Foreign Trade by Commodities (Series C). OECD Publications and Information Center, 2001 L St., N.W., Ste. 650 Washington, DC 20036-4922. Phone: 800-456-6323 or (202)785-6323 Fax: (202)785-0350 E-mail: washington.contact@oecd.org • URL: http://www.oecdwash.org • Annual. $625.00. Five volumes. Presents detailed five-year export-import data for specific commodities in OECD member countries.

Foreign Trade of the United States: Including State and Metro Area Export Data, 2000. Courtenay M. Slater. Bernan Press, 4611-F Assembly Dr. Lanham, MD 20706-4391. Phone: 800-274-4447 or (301)459-2255 Fax: 800-865-3450 or (301)459-9235 E-mail: bpress@bernan.com • URL: http://www.bernan.com • 2000. $147.00. 2001 Provides detailed national, state, and local data relating to U. S. exports and imports.

Forensic Accounting and Financial Fraud. American Management Association Extension Institute, 1601 Broadway New

York, NY 10019. Phone: 800-262-9699 or (518)586-8100 Fax: (518)903-8168 • URL: http://www.amanet.org • Looseleaf. $159.00. Self-study course. Emphasis is on practical explanations, examples, and problem solving. Quizzes and a case study are included.

Forest Chemicals Review. Kriedt Enterprises Ltd., 129 S. Cortez St. New Orleans, LA 70119-6118. Phone: (504)482-3914 Fax: (504)482-4205 E-mail: nsreview@aol.com Bimonthly. $98.00 per year. Formerly *Naval Stores Review*.

Forest Products Abstracts. CABI Publishing North America, 44 Brattle St., 4th Fl. Cambridge, MA 02138. Phone: 800-528-4841 or (617)395-4056 Fax: (617)354-6875 E-mail: cabinao@cabi.org • URL: http://www.cabi.org • Bimonthly. $770.00 per year; with online edition, $805.00 per year. Published in England by CABI Publishing. Provides worldwide coverage of forest products literature.

Forest Products and Wood Science: An Introduction. Jim L. Bowyer and others. Blackwell Publishing, 350 Main St. Malden, MA 02148. Phone: (781)388-8200 Fax: (781)388-8210 E-mail: subscrip@blackwellpub.com • URL: http://www.blackwellpublishing.com • 2002. Fourth edition. Price on application.

Forest Products Journal. Forest Products Society, 2801 Marshall Court Madison, WI 53705. Phone: (608)231-1361 Fax: (608)231-2152 E-mail: erin@forestprod.org • URL: http://www.forestprod.org • 10 times a year. $145.00 per year.

Forest Products Society, 2801 Marshall Ct. Madison, WI 53705-2295. Phone: (608)231-1361 Fax: (608)231-2152 E-mail: info@forestprod.org • URL: http://www.forestprod.org • Individuals interested in wood industry research, development, production, utilization, and distribution, from logging operations through finished products and utilization of residue as by-products. Maintains 30 technical committees.

Forest Resources Association, Inc.

Forestry Abstracts: Compiled from World Literature. Available from CABI Publishing North America, 875 Massachusetts Ave., 7th Fl. Cambridge, MA 02139. Phone: 800-528-4841 or (617)395-4056 Fax: (617)354-6875 E-mail: cabi-nao@cabi.org • URL: http://www.cabi-publishing.org • Monthly. Institutions, $1,435.00 per year. Print and online edition, $1,460.00 per year. Published in England by CABI Publishing. Provides worldwide coverage of the literature.

Forintek Canada Corporation. FPInnovations, 2665 E Mall Vancouver, BC, Canada V6T 1W5. Phone: (604)224-3221 Fax: (604)222-5690 E-mail: info@van.forintek.ca • URL: http://www.forintek.ca • Wood products, including tree quality, wood quality, utilization of damaged trees, sawing for maximum yield, productivity improvement, panel products, adhesive development, quality control, complete resource utilization, sawmill improvement, techno-economic studies, new uses for wood, biotechnology, and treated wood products. Acts as a liaison between international bodies and industry to help develop codes of standards for the forest products industry.

Formation and Financing of Emerging Companies. Daniel E. O'Connor and others. Glasser Legalworks, 150 Clove Rd. Little Falls, NJ 07424. Phone: 800-308-1700 or (973)890-0008 Fax: (973)890-0042 E-mail: orders@glasserlegalworks.com • URL: http://www.glasserlegalworks.com • Looseleaf. $225.00, including CD-ROM version. Periodic Supplementation. Covers incorporation, bylaws, indemnification, intellectual property, financing sources, venture capital, due diligence, bridge loans, investor rights, compliance, and other legal issues associated with company formation. (Emerging Growth Companies Series.)

Forms and Agreements for Architects, Engineers and Contractors. Albert Dib. West Group, 610 Opperman Dr. Eagan, MN 55123. Phone: 800-328-4880 or (651)687-7000 Fax: 800-340-9378 E-mail: bookstore@westgroup.com • URL: http://www.westgroup.com • Three times a year. $900. 00. Five looseleaf volume. Covers evaluation of construction documents and alternative clauses. Includes pleadings for litigation and resolving of claims. (Real Property Law Series).

Forms of Business Agreements and Resolutions-Annotated, Tax Tested. Prentice Hall PTR, 240 Frisch Ct. Paramus, NJ 07652. Phone: 800-282-0693 Fax: 800-445-6991 • URL: http://www.phptr.com • Three looseleaf volumes. Periodic supplementation. Price on application.

Formulary of Cosmetic Preparations. Anthony L. Hunting, editor. Micelle Press, Inc., P.O. Box 1519 Fort Washington, NY 11050-0306. Phone: (516)767-7171 Fax: (516)944-9824 E-mail: info@scholium.com • URL: http://www.scholium.com • 1991. $135.00. Two volumes. Volume one, *Decorative Cosmetics* $60.00; volume two *Creams, Lotions and Milks* $105.00.

Forthcoming Books. R. R. Bowker, 630 Central Ave. New Providence, NJ 07974. Phone: 888-269-5723 Fax: (908)219-0098 E-mail: info@bowker.com • URL: http://www.bowker.com • Bimonthly. $299.95 per year. Supplement to *Books in Print*.

Fortune Magazine. Time Inc., Business Information Group, 1271 Ave. of the Americas New York, NY 10020. Phone: 800-621-8000 or (212)522-1212 Fax: (212)522-0970 • URL: http://www.fortune.com • Biweekly. $59.95 per year. Edited for top executives and upper-level managers.

The Fortune Sellers: The Big Business of Buying and Selling Predictions. William A. Sherden. John Wiley and Sons, Inc., 111 River St. Hoboken, NJ 07030. Phone: 800-225-5945 or (201)748-6000 Fax: (201)748-6088 E-mail: info@wiley.com

• URL: http://www.wiley.com • 1997. $29.95. The author states that predictions are notoriously unreliable in any field, including the stock market, the economy, and the weather. (Forecasters in all areas don't have to be right; they just have to be interesting.)

Forum Train Europe. c/o Swiss Federal Railways, Schanzenstrasse 5 CH-3000 Bern, Switzerland. Phone: 41 512 202715 Fax: 41 512 201242 E-mail: mailbox@forumtraineurope.org • URL: http://www.forumtraineurope.org • Serves as a forum of railway undertakings and service companies for international production planning and timetable coordination of European rail traffic.

Foundation Center. Foundation Center, 79 5th Ave./16th St. New York, NY 10003-3076. Phone: 800-424-9836 or (212)620-4230 Fax: (212)807-3677 E-mail: communications@foundationcenter.org • URL: http://foundationcenter.org • Strengthens the nonprofit sector by advancing knowledge about U.S. philanthropy, maintains a comprehensive database on U.S. grantmakers and their grants, and operates research, education and training programs designed to advance philanthropy.

Foundation for American Communications.

Foundation for Cross-Connection Control and Hydraulic Research. University of Southern California

Foundation for Economic Education.

Foundation Fundamentals: A Guide for Grantseekers. The Foundation Center, 79 Fifth Ave. New York, NY 10003-3076. Phone: 800-424-9836 or (212)620-4230 Fax: (212)807-3677 E-mail: orders@fdncenter.org • URL: http://www.fdncenter.org • 1999. $24.95. Sixth edition.

Foundation Grants Index. The Foundation Center, 79 Fifth Ave. New York, NY 10003-3076. Phone: 800-424-9836 or (212)620-4230 Fax: (212)807-3677 E-mail: orders@fdncenter.org • URL: http://www.fdncenter.org • Irregular. $165.00 per year. Over 73,000 grants of $10,000 or more. Formerly *Foundation Grants Quarterly*.

Foundation Grants to Individuals. The Foundation Center, 79 Fifth Ave. New York, NY 10003-3076. Phone: 800-424-9836 or (212)620-4230 Fax: (212)807-3677 E-mail: orders@fdncenter.org • URL: http://www.fdncenter.org • Biennial. $65.00. Over 3,200 foundations that make grants to individuals.

Foundation News and Commentary: Philanthropy and the Nonprofit Sector. Council on Foundations, Inc., 1828 L St., N.W., Suite 300 Washington, DC 20036. Phone: 800-771-8187 or (202)466-6512 Fax: (202)785-3926 Bimonthly. $48.00 per year. Formerly *Foundation News*.

The Foundation 1000. Foundation Center, 79 Fifth Ave., 16th St. New York, NY 10003-3076. Phone: 800-424-9836 or (212)620-4230 Fax: (212)807-3677 E-mail: communications@foundationcenter.org • URL: http://www.fdncenter.org • Covers: the 1,000 largest corporate, community, and private foundations. Entries include: Foundation name, address, phone, name and title of contact, historical background, names and titles of key personnel, publications, detailed statements of policies and programs, application procedures, grant analysis (by subject, type of grant, and type of recipient), and listing of sample grants for latest year available.

Foundation Reporter: Comprehensive Profiles and Giving Analyses of America's Major Private Foundations. The Taft Group, 27500 Drake Rd. Farmington Hills, MI 48331-3535. Phone: 800-877-GALE or (248)699-GALE Fax: 800-414-5043 or (248)699-8063 E-mail: galeord@galegroup.com • URL: http://www.taftgroup.com • Annual. $490.00. Provides detailed information on major U. S. foundations. Eight indexes (location, grant type, recipient type, personnel, etc.)

Foundation Trusteeship: Service in the Public Interest. John Nason. The Foundation Center. 79 Fifth Ave. New York, NY 10003-3076. Phone: 800-424-9836 or (212)620-4230 Fax: (212)807-3677 E-mail: orders@fdncenter.org • URL: http://www.fdncenter.org • 1989. $19.95. Covers the roles and responsibilities of foundation boards.

Foundations of Financial Management With +Self Study Software +Powerweb. Stanley R. Block and Geoffrey A. Hirt. McGraw-Hill, 1221 Ave. of the Americas New York, NY 10020. Phone: 800-722-4726 or (212)512-2000 Fax: (212)512-4502 E-mail: customer.service@mcgraw-hill.com • URL: http://www.mcgraw-hill.com • 2002. $110.31. 10th edition. Includes CD-ROM. (Finance, Insurance and Real Estate Series).

Foundations of Robotics: Analysis and Control. Tsuneo Yoshikawa. MIT Press, Five Cambridge Ctr. Cambridge, MA 02142-1493. Phone: 800-356-0343 or (617)253-5646 Fax: (617)253-6779 • URL: http://www.mitpress.mit.edu • 1990. $52.95.

Foundry Directory and Register of Forges. Metal Bulletin PLC, 220 5th Ave., 10th Fl. New York, NY 10001. Phone: 800-638-2525 or (212)213-6202 Fax: (212)213-6619 E-mail: subscription@metalbulletin.plc.uk • URL: http://www.metalbulletin.co.uk • Biennial. $165.00. Foundries and forges in the United Kingdom and Europe; suppliers of foundry and forging equipment, raw materials and services.

Foundry Management and Technology. Penton Media, Inc., 1300 E 9th St. Cleveland, OH 44114. Phone: (216)696-7000 Fax: (216)696-1752 E-mail: information@penton.com • URL: http://www.penton.com • Monthly. Free to qualified personnel; others, $50.00 per year. Coverage includes nonferrous casting technology and production.

Foundryman's Handbook: Facts, Figures, Formulae. Elsevier, 655 Ave. of the Americas New York, NY 10010-5107. Phone: 800-366-2665 or (212)989-5800 Fax: 800-535-9935 or (212)633-3680 E-mail: custserv@elsevier.com • URL: http://www.elsevier.com • 1986. $114.00. Ninth edition.

401(k) Handbook. Thompson Publishing Group, Inc., 1725 K St., N.W., Suite 700 Washington, DC 20006. Phone: 800-444-8741 or (202)872-4000 • URL: http://www.thompson.com • Two looseleaf volumes. $387.00 per year, including monthly updates and newsletters. Provides detailed information on 401(k) retirement plan design, administration, employee communication, rollovers, federal regulations, plan loans, investment vehicles, and related topics. Includes a glossary.

The 401(k) Plan Handbook. Julie Jason. Prentice Hall PTR, 240 Frisch Ct. Paramus, NJ 07652. Phone: 800-282-0693 Fax: 800-445-6991 • URL: http://www.phptr.com • 1997. $79.95. Provides technical, legal, administrative, and investment details of 401(k) retirement plans.

FP Survey Industrials (Canada). Globe Information Services, 444 Front St., W. Toronto, ON, Canada M5V 2S9. Phone: 800-268-9128 or (416)585-5163 Fax: (416)585-5249 • URL: http://www.globeandmail.ca • Annual. $49.95. Provides information on more than 3,000 Canadian manufacturing and service companies.

FP Survey of Industrials (Canadian Firms). Financial Post Datagroup, 333 King St., E. Toronto, ON, Canada M5A 4N2. Phone: 800-661-7678 or (416)350-6500 Fax: (416)350-6501 E-mail: fpdg@fpdata.finpost.com • URL: http://www.financialpost.com • Annual. $124.95 Contains detailed information on more than 2,700 publicly owned Canadian manufacturing, retailing, and service corporations. Includes the "Financial Post 500," a ranking of the largest Canadian companies.

FPDA News. Fluid Power Distributors Association, 1930 E Marlton Pke., Ste. A-2, PO Box 1420 Cherry Hill, NJ 08003-2142. Phone: (856)424-8998 Fax: (856)424-9248 E-mail: info@fpda.org Description: Provides sales, marketing tips, and cost-cutting ideas submitted by members. Recurring features include news of the Association and its members, news of research, statistics, a calendar of events, and obituaries.

The Fragile Middle Class: Americans in Debt. Teresa A. Sullivan and others. Yale University Press, 302 Temple St. New Haven, CT 06511. Phone: 800-987-7323 or (203)432-0960 Fax: (203)432-0948 E-mail: customer.care@triliteral.org • URL: http://www.yale.edu/yup/ • 2000. $40.00. Provides an analysis of a 1991 survey of personal bankruptcies in five states of the U. S. Serves as a sequel to the authors' *As We Forgive Our Debtors* (1989), an analysis of 1981 bankruptcies.

Fragrance Foundation., 145 E 32nd St. New York, NY 10016-6002. Phone: (212)725-2755 Fax: (212)779-9058 E-mail: info@fragrance.org • URL: http://www.fragrance.org • Fragrance manufacturers, suppliers to the trade, publications, package designers, analysts, and advertising agencies. Seeks to educate consumers on the pleasures, use and care of fragrance and allied products. Initiates public relations programs.

Fragrance Foundation Reference Guide. The Fragrance Foundation Inc., 145 E 32nd St. New York, NY 10016-6002. Phone: (212)725-2755 Fax: (212)779-9058 E-mail: info@fragrance.org • URL: http://www.fragrance.org • Covers: Manufacturers of over 1100 fragrances available in the United States. Entries include: Company name, address, phone, listing of fragrances (with date of introduction and description).

Fragrances and Perfumes. Available from MarketResearch.com, 641 Ave. of the Americas, Fourth Floor New York, NY 10011. Phone: 800-298-5699 or (212)807-2629 Fax: (212)807-2642 E-mail: order@marketresearch.com • URL: http://www.marketresearch.com • 2002. $3,950.00. Published by Global Industry Analysts. Provides worldwide market research data, including profiles of major perfume companies.

Franchise Annual. Todd Publications, PO Box 500 Millwood, NY 10546. Phone: (866)896-0916 or (914)373-4750 Fax: (914)373-4750 E-mail: toddpub@aol.com Covers: Approximately 5,000 franchises, distributors, licensors and franchise consultants with U.S. or Canadian headquarters, as well as 465 overseas listings. Entries include: Company description, initial and total investment required, and government rules on franchising.

Franchise Opportunities Guide: A Comprehensive Listing of the World's Leading Franchises. International Franchise Association, 1350 New York Ave., N.W., Suite 900 Washington, DC 20005-4709. Phone: 800-543-1038 or (202)628-8000 Fax: (202)628-0812 E-mail: ifa@franchise.org • URL: http://www.franchise.org • Semiannual. $21.00 per year. More than 600 companies which offer franchises.

Franchise Opportunities Handbook. U. S. International Trade Administration, 14th St. & Constitution Ave. NW, USDOC/TOP, Rm. 1322 Washington, DC 20230. Phone: (202)377-4203 Fax: (202)512-2250 E-mail: toddpub@aol.com • URL: http://www.access.gpo.gov • Covers: over 1,400 franchisors in some 40 lines of business (auto rentals, campgrounds, foods, security systems, etc.). Entries include: Company name, address, name of contact, description of the business operation franchised, number of franchisees, date company began, amount of capital needed, whether financial assistance is available, and what training and managerial assistance are provided. Also includes general information on securing franchises and operating franchised businesses. Users of the directory are cautioned that the Commerce Department has not verified statements in the listings for the various franchisors.

The Franchise Option: How to Expand Your Business Through Franchising. Kathryn L. Boe and others. International Franchise Association, 1350 New York Ave., N.W., Suite 900 Washington, DC 20005-4709. Phone: 800-543-1038 or (202)628-8000 Fax: (202)628-0812 E-mail: ifa@franchise.org • URL: http://www.franchise.org • 1987. $24.00. Second edition.

Franchise Times. Sparks Publishing & Reporting Corp., 2000 S Colorado Blvd. Denver, CO 80222. Phone: 800-938-1044 or (303)799-1112 Fax: (303)799-1115 E-mail: ksolnoky@carletoninc.com • URL: http://www.franchisetimes.com • Description: Provides analysis and information on franchising, including trends and legal and financial aspects. Recurring features include domestic and international franchising news, questions and answers, and an editorial column.

Franchising and Licensing: Two Ways to Build Your Business. Andrew Sherman. AMACOM, 1601 Broadway New York, NY 10019. Phone: 800-262-9699 or (518)586-8100 Fax: (518)903-8168 E-mail: customerservice@amanet.org • URL: http://www.amacombooks.org • 1999. $45.00. Second edition. Written for the business person who wishes to become a franchiser. Tells how to raise capital, create a prototype, structure franchise agreements, develop operations manuals, market the franchise, and maintain good relations with franchisees.

Franchising Business and Law Alert. American Lawyer Media, Inc., 105 Madison Ave. New York, NY 10016. Phone: 800-888-8300 or (212)779-9200 Fax: (212)481-8110 E-mail: lawcatalog@amlaw.com • URL: http://www.lawcatalog.com/ • Monthly. $199.00 per year. Newsletter. Provides news of legal developments affecting both franchisors and franchisees. (A Law Journal Newsletter, formerly published by Leader Publications).

Franchising Dreams. Peter M. Birkeland. The University of Chicago Press, 1427 E 60th St. Chicago, IL 60637. Phone: 800-621-2736 or (773)702-7700 Fax: 800-621-8476 or (773)702-7212 E-mail: custserv@press.uchicago.edu • URL: http://www.press.uchicago.edu • 2002. $22.50. Provides a serious discussion of both the risks and the benefits of franchising.

Franchising: Realities and Remedies. Harold Brown. American Lawyer Media, 345 Park Ave. S New York, NY 10010-1707. Phone: (212)973-2800 Fax: (212)973-2889 • URL: http://www.lawcatalog.com • Revised edition. Price on application.

Franchising: Realities and Remedies. American Lawyer Media, Inc., 105 Madison Ave. New York, NY 10016. Phone: 800-888-8300 or (212)779-9200 Fax: (212)481-8110 E-mail: lawcatalog@amlaw.com • URL: http://www.lawcatalog.com/ • Looseleaf. $189.00. Two volumes. Updated as needed. Provides comprehensive coverage of common legal problems "faced by both franchisors and franchisees." (Law Journal Press).

Franchising World. International Franchise Association, 1350 New York Ave., N.W., Suite 900 Washington, DC 20005-4709. Phone: 800-543-1038 or (202)628-8000 Fax: (202)628-0812 E-mail: ifa@franchise.org • URL: http://www.franchise.org • Eight times a year. $18.00 per year. Formerly *Franchising Opportunities*.

Francis I. Proctor Foundation for Research in Ophthalmology.

Frasers Canadian Trade Directory. Rogers Media Publishing, One Mount Pleasant Rd., 7th Fl. Toronto, ON, Canada M4Y 2Y5. Phone: 800-265-3561 or (416)764-2000 Fax: (416)764-1746 E-mail: info@ilovepasta.org Covers: over 42,000 manufacturers and distributors and over 14,000 foreign companies with Canadian representatives. Entries include: Company name, address. Products are included for manufacturers; name and address of Canadian representative is included for foreign firms.

Fred Goss' What's Working in Direct Marketing. United Communications Group (UCG), 11300 Rockville Pike, Suite 1100 Rockville, MD 20852-3030. Phone: 888-287-2223 or (301)287-2700 Fax: (301)816-8945 E-mail: webmaster@ucg.com • URL: http://www.ucg.com • Biweekly. $242.00 per year. Newsletter. Provides ideas for direct marketing promotions.

Free Congress Research and Education Foundation., 717 2nd St. NE Washington, DC 20002. Phone: (202)546-3000 Fax: (202)543-5605 E-mail: jborda@freecongress.org • URL: http://www.freecongress.org • Brings messages of traditional values, conservative government, and institutional reform to America through publications and TV programs on America's Voice network. Includes projects such as: Judicial Selection Monitoring Project, "Taking Back Our Constitution" seminar services and the Center for Technology Policy's privacy papers.

Freedom Forum First Amendment Center., Vanderbilt Univ., 1207 18th Ave. S. Nashville, TN 37212. Phone: (615)727-1600 Fax: (615)727-1319 E-mail: info@facorg • URL: http://www.freedomforum.org • Research fields include mass communication and technological change, including mass media and the public trust.

Freedom of Information Act. Christopher L. Henry. Nova Science Publishers, Inc., 400 Oser Ave., Suite 1600 Hauppauge, NY 11788-3619. Phone: (631)231-7269 Fax: (631)231-8175 E-mail: novascience@earthlink.net • URL: http://www.novapublishers.com • 2003. $29.50. Serves as a practical guide to making a freedom of information request to the U.S. Justice Department. Includes copies of forms.

Freedom of Information Center.

FreedomWorks., 601 Pennsylvania Ave. NW, North Bldg., Ste. 700 Washington, DC 20004. Phone: 888-564-6273 or (202)783-3870 Fax: (202)942-7649 E-mail: bsteinhauser@freedomworks.org • URL: http://www.empoweramerica.org • Devoted to ensuring that government actions foster growth, economic well being and individual responsibility. Sponsors an internship program, introducing its participants to the Washington policy world, giving them a broader base of knowledge about the organization and its inner operations.

Freelance Writer's Report. Dana K. Cassell, editor. CNW Publishing, Editing & Promotion Inc., 45 Main St., PO Box A North Stratford, NH 03590. Phone: (603)922-8338 Fax: (603)922-8339 E-mail: info@writers-editors.com • URL: http://www.writers-editors.com • Description: Offers up-to-date news and information concerning effective marketing/production techniques, writing tips, self-promotion, and other topics of interest "to freelance writers who intend to earn a good income from their work and improve the quality of their work." Recurring features include interviews, book reviews, news of writing seminars, conferences, and market news. **Remarks:** Members of the Florida Freelance Writers Association receive an extra association section (4 pages).

Freelance Writing. Entrepreneur Media, Inc., 2445 McCabe Way Irvine, CA 92614. Phone: 800-421-2300 or (949)261-2325 Fax: (949)261-0234 E-mail: entmag@entrepreneur.com • URL: http://www.entrepreneur.com 3 • Looseleaf. $59.50. A practical guide to starting a freelance writing service. Covers profit potential, start-up costs, market size evaluation, pricing, accounting, advertising, promotion, etc. (Start-Up Business Guide No. E1258.)

FreeLunch.com. Economy.com, Inc.Phone: (610)696-8700 Fax: (610)696-1678 • URL: http://www.freelunch.com • Web site provides free access to more than 1.5 million economic and financial data series, covering industry, demographics, labor markets, prices, retail sales, government spending, trade, interest rates, housing starts, the stock market, and many other topics. Data is available for various time periods in either chart or table form. Searching is offered. Fees: Free, but registration required. Economy.com, Inc. also offers fee-based economic analysis at *The Dismal Scientist* site (http://www.dismal.com).

Freight Brokerage. Entrepreneur Media, Inc., 2445 McCabe Way Irvine, CA 92614. Phone: 800-421-2300 or (949)261-2325 Fax: (949)261-0234 E-mail: entmag@entrepreneur.com • URL: http://www.entrepreneur.com • Looseleaf. $59.50. A practical guide to freight transportation brokering. Covers profit potential, start-up costs, market size evaluation, pricing, accounting, advertising, promotion, etc. (Start-Up Business Guide No. E1328.)

Frequent Flyer: For Business People Who Must Travel. OAG Worldwide, 2000 Clearwater Dr. Oak Brook, IL 60523. Phone: 800-525-1138 or (630)515-5307 Fax: (630)515-3933 E-mail: custsrv@oag.com • URL: http://www.oag.com • Monthly. $89.00 per year to individuals. Also known as *OAG Frequent Flyer*. Edited for business travelers. Contains news of frequent flyer programs, airport developments, airline services, and business travel trends. Available only with *OAG Flight Guide*.

Fresh Produce Journal. Lockwood Press, Ltd., 430-438 Market Towers, 1 Nine Elms Ln. London SW8 5NN, United Kingdom. Phone: 44 20 7622 6677 Fax: 44 20 7720 2047 E-mail: info@fpj.co.uk • URL: http://www.freshinfo.com • Weekly. $148.00 per year. Formerly *Fruit Trades Journal*.

Friends of Libraries Sourcebook. Sandy Dolnick. American Library Association, 50 E. Huron St. Chicago, IL 60611-2795. Phone: 800-545-2433 or (312)944-6780 Fax: (312)440-9374 E-mail: ala@ala.org • URL: http://www.ala.org • 1996. $35.00. Third edition. Provides information and guidance relating to Friends of Libraries support groups.

Friends of the Earth., 1025 Vermont Ave., N.W., Suite 300 Washington, DC 20005. Phone: 877-843-8687 or (202)783-7400 Fax: (202)783-0444 E-mail: foe@foe.org • URL: http://www.foe.org • Promotes protection of the environment and conservation of natural resources. Affiliated with Oceanic Society.

Fringe Benefits Tax Guide. CCH, Inc., 2700 Lake Cook Rd. Riverwoods, IL 60015. Phone: 800-835-5224 or (847)267-7000 E-mail: cust_serv@cch.com • URL: http://www.cch.com • Monthly. $539.00. Looseleaf service.

FRM Weekly (Fund Raising Management). Hoke Communications, Inc., 224 Seventh St. Garden City, NY 11530. Phone: 800-229-6700 or (516)746-6700 Fax: (516)294-8141 E-mail: 71410.2423@compuserve.com Weekly. $115.00 per year.

The Froehlich-Kent Encyclopedia of Telecommunications. Fritz E. Froehlich and Allen Kent, editors. Marcel Dekker, Inc., 270 Madison Ave. New York, NY 10016. Phone: 800-228-1160 or (212)696-9000 Fax: (212)685-4540 E-mail: bookorders@dekker.com • URL: http://www.dekker.com • 18 volumes. $3,510.00. $195.00 per volume. Dates vary. Contains scholarly articles written by telecommunications experts. Includes bibliographies.

From Executive to Entrepreneur: Making the Transition. Gilbert Z. Zoghlin. AMACOM, 1601 Broadway New York, NY 10019. Phone: 800-262-9699 or (518)586-8100 Fax: (518)903-8168 E-mail: customerservice@samanet.org • URL: http://www.amacombooks.org • 1991. $24.95. A self-help guide offering psychological and financial advice to corporate employees who wish to go into business for themselves.

From GATT to the WTO: The Multilateral Trading System in the New Millennium. WTO Secretariat, editor. Kluwer Law International, 101 Philip Dr., Assinippi Park Norwell, MA 02061-1615. Phone: 800-234-1660 E-mail: sales@kluwerlaw.com • URL: http://www.kluwerlaw.com • 2000. $79.50. Published by the World Trade Organization (http://www.wto.org). A collection of essays on the future of world trade, written on the occasion of the 50th anniversary of the multilateral trading system (GATT/WTO). The authors are described as "important academics in international trade."

From Idea to Funded Project: Grant Proposals that Work. Jane C. Belcher and Julia M. Jacobsen. Greenwood Publishing Group, Inc., 88 Post Rd., W. Westport, CT 06881. Phone: 800-225-5800 or (203)226-3571 Fax: (203)431-2214 E-mail: customer-service@greenwood.com • URL: http://www.greenwood.com • 1992. $26.50. Fourth edition. Formerly *A Process for the Development of Ideas*.

From Kitchen to Market: Selling Your Gourmet Food Specialty. Stephen F. Hall. Dearborn Trade Publishing, A Kaplan Professional Co., 155 N. Wacker Dr. Chicago, IL 60606. Phone: 800-621-9621 or (312)836-4400 Fax: (312)836-1021 E-mail: trade@dearborn.com • URL: http://www.dearborntrade.com • 2000. $28.95. Third edition. Covers packaging, labeling, marketing, and distribution of specialty and gourmet food products. Includes charts, graphs, tables, guidelines, checklists, and industry examples.

From Poor Law to Welfare State: A History of Social Welfare in America. Walter I. Trattner. Simon and Schuster Trade, 1230 Ave. of the Americas New York, NY 10020. Phone: 800-223-2348 or (212)698-7000 Fax: 800-943-9831 or (212)698-7007 E-mail: consumer.customerservice@simonandschuster.com • URL: http://www.simonsays.com • 1998. $17.95. Sixth edition.

From Red Tape to Smart Tape: Administrative Simplification in OECD Countries. Organization for Economic Cooperation and Development, OECD Washington Center, 2001 L St., N. W., Suite 650 Washington, DC 20036-4922. Phone: 800-456-6323 or (202)785-6323 Fax: (202)785-0350 E-mail: washington.contact@oecd.org • URL: http://www.oecd.org • 2003. $58.00. "This report looks at a set of tools and practices commonly used by governments to make administrative regulations simpler and less burdensome to comply with." Includes information on one-stop facilitation, license/permit simplification, decision-making time limits, small business assistance, and the use of information technology (IT) for administrative simplification.

From Selling to Managing: Guidelines for the First-Time Sales Manager. Ronald Brown. AMACOM, 1601 Broadway New York, NY 10019. Phone: 800-262-9699 or (518)586-8100 Fax: (518)903-8168 E-mail: customerservice@amanet.org • URL: http://www.amacombooks.org • 1990. $17.95. Revised edition. A practical quide to the transformation of salesperson to sales manager.

From Sundials to Atomic Clocks: Understanding Time and Frequency. James Jespersen. Dover Publications, Inc., 31 E. Second St. Mineola, NY 11501. Phone: 800-223-3130 or (516)294-7000 Fax: (516)742-5049 • URL: http://www.doverpublications.com • 1999. $12.95. Second revised edition.

Front Row Advisor: Business and First Class Air Travel and the Alluring World of Free Upgrades. Diversified Specialties, Inc., 3109 Grand Ave. Coconut Grove, FL 33133-5103. Phone: 800-342-1774 or (305)362-2552 Fax: (305)774-6070 Bimonthly. $145.00 per year. Newsletter. Contains information on opportunities provided by airlines to upgrade coach seats to business class, including frequent flyer upgrades.

Frontline Solutions. Advanstar Communications, 545 Boylston St. Boston, MA 02116. Phone: 888-527-7008 or (617)267-6500 Fax: (617)267-6900 E-mail: infoadvisoryanstar.com • URL: http://www.advanstar.com • Thirteen times per year. $41.00 per year. Provides news and information about the applications and technology of automated data capture systems. Formerly (Automatic I.D. News).

Frontline Solutions Buyer's Guide. Advanstar Communications, Advanstar House Park West, Sealand Rd., Sealand Rd. Chester CH1 4RN, United Kingdom. Phone: 800-598-6008 or (44)1244 378888 Fax: (44)1244 370011 E-mail: info@advanstar.com • URL: http://www.advanstar.com • Publication includes: List of manufacturers, suppliers, consultants, value added resellers, and dealers/distributors of automatic identification and data capture software, technology, equipment, and products for bar code, biometric identification, electronic data interchange, machine vision, magnetic stripe, optical character recognition, radio frequency data communications, radio frequency identification, smart cards, and voice data entry; also includes related organizations, and sources for industry standards. Entries include: Company name, address, phone, e-mail, web address, products or services.

Frost & Sullivan Market Research Reports. Frost & Sullivan, 2525 Charleston Rd. Mountain View, CA 94043. Phone: (650)961-9000 Fax: (650)961-5042 Contains full text of Frost & Sullivan market research reports on various industries and products. Each report includes a five-year forecast.

SOURCES CITED

Frozen Food Pack Statistics. American Frozen Food Institute, 2000 Corporate Ridge, Suite 1000 McLean, VA 22102. Phone: (703)821-0770 Fax: (703)821-1350 E-mail: affi@pop.dn.net • URL: http://www.affi.com • Annual. Members, $10.00; non-members, $100.00.

Frozen Foods. Available from MarketResearch.com, 641 Ave. of the Americas, Third Floor New York, NY 10011. Phone: 800-298-5699 or (212)807-2629 Fax: (212)807-2716 E-mail: order@marketresearch.com • URL: http://www.marketresearch.com • 2000. $5,000.00. Published by Euromonitor Publications Ltd. Provides consumer market data and forecasts for the United States, the United Kingdom, Germany, France, and Italy. Contains market analyses for many kinds of frozen foods.

Fruit Juices. Available from MarketResearch.com, 641 Ave. of the Americas, Third Floor New York, NY 10011. Phone: 800-298-5699 or (212)807-2629 Fax: (212)807-2716 E-mail: order@marketresearch.com • URL: http://www.marketresearch.com • 2001. $4,500.00. Published by Euromonitor Publications Ltd. Provides consumer market data and forecasts to 2004 for the United States, the United Kingdom, Germany, France, and Italy. Includes fresh, frozen, bottled, and canned fruit and vegetable juices.

Fruit Research and Extension Center. Pennsylvania State University

FTC Freedom of Information Log (Federal Trade Commission). Washington Regulatory Reporting Associates, P.O. Box 356 Basye, VA 22810. Phone: (202)639-0581 Fax: (202)478-0260 E-mail: ftcwatch@usa.net Weekly. $451.00 per year. Newsletter listing Freedom of Information Act requests that have been submitted to the Federal Trade Commission.

Fuel and Energy Abstracts: A Summary of World Literature on All Scientific, Technical, Commercial and Environmental Aspects of Fuel and Energy. Elsevier, 655 Ave. of the Americas New York, NY 10010-5107. Phone: 800-366-2665 or (212)989-5800 Fax: 800-535-9935 or (212)633-3680 E-mail: custserv@elsevier.com • URL: http://www.elsevier.com • Bimonthly. Institutions, $1,931.00 per year.

Fuel Oil News: Source Book., Fuel Oil News, 250 S Wacker Dr., Ste. 1150 Chicago, IL 60606. Phone: (847)381-3001 Fax: (847)381-3007 E-mail: lbaron@aip.com • URL: http://www.fueloilnews.com • Annual. $28.00. Provides fuel (heating) oil industry data.

Fuel: Science and Technology of Fuel and Energy. Elsevier, 655 Ave. of the Americas New York, NY 10010-5107. Phone: 800-366-2665 or (212)989-5800 Fax: 800-535-9935 or (212)633-3680 E-mail: custserv@elsevier.com • URL: http://www.elsevier.com • 15 times a year. Qualified personnel, $98.00 per year; institutions, $2,765.00 per year.

Fulbright Scholar Program Grants for U.S. Faculty and Professionals. Council for International Exchange of Scholars, 3007 Tilden St., NW, Ste. 5L Washington, DC 20008-3009. Phone: (202)686-4000 Fax: (202)362-3442 E-mail; scholars@cies.iie.org • URL: http://www.cies.org • Annual. Free. Lists about 800 grants.

Fulfillment Management Association (FMA)., 60 E 42nd St., Ste. 1166 New York, NY 10165. Phone: (815)734-5821 Fax: (815)734-5824 • URL: http://www.fmanational.org • Members includes publishing circulation executives. Includes a Training and Education Committee and a Career Guidance Committee. Formerly Subscription Fulfillment Managers Association.

Full Disclosure: The New Lawyer's Must-Read Career Guide. Christen C. Carey. American Lawyer Media, Inc., 105 Madison Ave. New York, NY 10016. Phone: 800-888-8300 or (212)779-9200 Fax: (212)481-8110 E-mail: lawcatalog@amlaw.com • URL: http://www.lawcatalog.com/ • 2001. $19.95. "All the Things Lawyers Wish They Had Known at the Beginning of Their Careers, Rather Than at the End." Covers such topics as job hunting, job interviews, summer associate programs, law firm economics, life as a law firm associate, and gender in law firms.

Fulltext Sources Online. Information Today Inc., 143 Old Marlton Pke. Medford, NJ 08055-8750. Phone: 800-300-9868 or (609)654-6266 Fax: (609)654-4309 E-mail: custserv@infotoday.com • URL: http://www.infotoday.com • Covers: over 21,000 periodicals, newspapers, newsletters, newswires; and tv/radio transcripts available in full text online. Entries include: Name of file, online services through which available, dates of coverage, lag time if applicable. Separate list gives online service address and phone; indicates degree of online coverage and selection policy. Internet url's listed where applicable.

Fund Action. Institutional Investor, Inc., Journals Group, 225 Park Ave., S New York, NY 10003. Phone: 800-945-2034 or (212)224-3066 Fax: (212)224-3472 E-mail: info@iijournals.com • URL: http://www.iijournals.com • Weekly. $2,475.00 per year. Newsletter. Includes print and online editions. Edited for mutual fund executives. Covers competition among funds, aggregate statistics, new products, regulations, service providers, and other subjects of interest to fund managers.

Fund for a Republican Majority., PO Box 1766 Washington, DC 20013. E-mail: richard.wallace@scbar.org Political action committee that raises funds for Republican congressional candidates, particulary for the Senate.

Fund for Constitutional Government., 122 Maryland Ave., N.E., 3rd Fl. Washington, DC 20002. Phone: (202)546-3799 Fax: (202)543-3156 E-mail: funcongov@aol.com • URL:

http://www.epic.org/fcg • Provides legal and strategic counsel for government "whistleblowers."

Fund for Modern Courts., 351 W. 54th St. New York, NY 10019. Phone: (212)541-6741 Fax: (212)541-7301 E-mail: justice@moderncourts.org • URL: http://www.moderncourts.org • Members seek public support for the improvement of the judicial system.

Fund for New Priorities in America., 171 Madison Ave. New York, NY 10016. Phone: (212)685-8848 Fax: (212)685-8970 E-mail: info@fundfornewpriorities.org • URL: http://www.fundfornewpriorities.org • Believes that the United States must reorder its national priorities. Works to inform the public, to build active networks and coalitions, and to enhance participatory democracy, in pursuit of a more just, peaceful, open, and humane society. Sponsors public forums.

Fund for Stockowners Rights., PO. 65563 Washington, DC 20035. Phone: (703)241-3700 Fax: (818)223-8080 Seeks to improve methods of electing corporate boards of directors and encourages the holding of annual meetings for stockholders.

Fund for the Future Committee., 3825 Federer Pl. St. Louis, MO 63116. Phone: (314)289-3711 E-mail: information@emilyslist.org Political action committee that supports the campaigns of Republican candidates for federal office from Missouri.

Fund Governance: Legal Duties of Investment Company Directors. American Lawyer Media, Inc., 105 Madison Ave. New York, NY 10016. Phone: 800-888-8300 or (212)779-9200 Fax: (212)481-8110 E-mail: lawcatalog@amlaw.com • URL: http://www.lawcatalog.com/ • Looseleaf. $159.00. Updated as needed. Covers the legal obligations of directors of mutual funds and closed-end funds. (Law Journal Press).

Fund Raising: The Guide to Raising Money from Private Sources. Thomas Broce. University of Oklahoma Press, 4100 28th Ave., NW Norman, OK 13019-8218. Phone: 800-627-7377 or (405)325-2000 Fax: 800-735-0476 or (405)364-5798 E-mail: customerservice@oupress.com • URL: http://www.oupress.com • 1986. $27.95. Second enlarged revised edition.

FundAlarm. Roy WeitzPhone: (818)345-7516 Fax: (818)776-1562 • URL: http://www.fundalarm.com • Web site subtitle: "Know when to hold'em, know when to fold'em, know when to walk away, know when to run." Provides lists of underperforming mutual funds ("3-ALARM Funds") and severely underperforming funds ("Most Alarming 3-ALARM Funds"). Performance is based on various benchmarks. Site also provides mutual fund news, recent manager changes, and basic data for each of about 2,100 funds. Monthly updates. Fees: Free.

Fundamental Accounting Principles. Kermit D. Larson and others. McGraw-Hill, 1221 Ave. of the Americas New York, NY 10020. Phone: 800-722-4726 or (212)512-2000 Fax: (212)512-4502 E-mail: customer.service@mcgraw-hill.com • URL: http://www.mcgraw-hill.com • 2001. $36.88. 16th edition. (Ready Notes Series).

Fundamental Principles of Occupational Health and Safety. Benjamin Alli. International Labour Organization, 1828 L St., N.W., Suite 600 Washington, DC 20036-5121. Phone: (202)653-7652 Fax: (202)653-7687 E-mail: washington@ilo.org • URL: http://www.ilo.org • 2001. $14.95. A practical guide to health and safety policies in the workplace. Covers legal issues, enforcement, health surveillance, protective measures, education, and training. Includes a glossary.

Fundamental Reference Sources. James S. Sweetland and Frances N. Cheney. American Library Association, 50 E Huron St. Chicago, IL 60611-2795. Phone: 800-545-2433 or (312)944-6780 Fax: (312)440-9374 E-mail: ala@ala.org • URL: http://www.ala.org • 2001. $75.00. Third edition. Describes "the best available materials in all media for general library collections."

Fundamentals. William A. Bowditch and Kevin E. Bowditch. Goodheart-Wilcox Publishers, 18604 W Creek Dr. Tinley Park, IL 60477-6243. Phone: 800-409-3900 or (708)687-5000 Fax: 800-323-0440 E-mail: custserv@goodheartwillcox.com • URL: http://www.goodheartwillcox.com • 1997. $44.80.

Fundamentals of Computer-High Technology Law. James V. Vergari and Virginia V. Shue. American Law Institute-American Bar Association Committee on Continuing Professional Education, 4025 Chestnut St. Philadelphia, PA 19104. Phone: 800-253-6397 Fax: (215)243-1664 • URL: http://www.ali-aba.org • 1991. $29.00.

Fundamentals of Construction Estimating. David Pratt. Delmar Learning, 5 Maxwell Dr. Clifton Park, NY 12065. Phone: 800-347-7707 Fax: 800-487-4888 E-mail: info@delmar.com • URL: http://www.delmarlearning.com • 1995. $93.95. (Trade, Technology and Industry Series).

Fundamentals of Construction Estimating and Cost Accounting. Keith Collier. Prentice Hall PTR, 240 Frisch Ct. Paramus, NJ 07652. Phone: 800-282-0693 Fax: 800-445-6991 • URL: http://www.phptr.com • 2000. Third edition. Price on application.

Fundamentals of Corporate Finance. Richard A. Brealey and others. McGraw-Hill, 1221 Ave. of the Americas New York, NY 10020. Phone: 800-722-4726 or (212)512-2000 Fax: (212)512-4502 E-mail: customer.service@mcgraw-hill.com • URL: http://www.mcgraw-hill.com • 2003. Third edition. Price on application. (Finance, Insurance, and Real Estate Series).

Fundamentals of Employee Benefit Programs. Employee Benefit

Research Institute, 2121 K St., N. W., Suite 600 Washington, DC 20037. Phone: (202)659-0670 Fax: (202)775-6312 E-mail: info@ebri.org • URL: http://www.ebri.org • 1996. $49.95. Fifth edition. Provides basic explanation of employee benefit programs in both the private and public sectors, including health insurance, pension plans, retirement planning, social security, and long-term care insurance.

Fundamentals of Engineering Drawing and Design. Cecil H. Jensen and Jay D. Helsel. Glencoe/McGraw-Hill, P.O. Box 543 Balcklick, OH 43004-0544. Fax: (614)755-5682 E-mail: customer.service@mcgraw-hill.com • URL: http://www.glencoe.com • 1995. $73.56. 5th edition.

Fundamentals of Financial and Managerial Accounting. Kermit D. Larson and others. McGraw-Hill, 1221 Ave. of the Americas New York, NY 10020. Phone: 800-722-4726 or (212)512-2000 Fax: (212)512-4502 E-mail: customer.service@mcgraw-hill.com • URL: http://www.mcgraw-hill.com • 1993. $72.00.

Fundamentals of Financial Management. James C. Van Horne and John M. Wachowicz. Prentice Hall PTR, 240 Frisch Ct. Paramus, NJ 07652. Phone: 800-282-0693 Fax: 800-445-6991 • URL: http://www.phptr.com • 2000. $90.67. 11th edition.

Fundamentals of Human Resources. American Management Association Extension Institute, 1601 Broadway New York, NY 10019. Phone: 800-262-9699 or (518)586-8100 Fax: (518)903-8168 • URL: http://www.amanet.org • Looseleaf. $139.00. Self-study course on a wide range of personnel topics. Emphasis is on practical explanations, examples, and problem solving. Quizzes and a case study are included.

Fundamentals of Hydraulic Engineering Systems. Ned H. Hwang and R.J. Houghtalen. Prentice Hall PTR, 240 Frisch Ct. Paramus, NJ 07652. Phone: 800-282-0693 Fax: 800-445-6991 • URL: http://www.phptr.com • 1995. $115.00. Third edition.

Fundamentals of Investing. Lawrence J. Gitman and Michael D. Joehnk. Addison-Wesley, 75 Arlington St., Ste. 300 Boston, MA 02116. Phone: 800-447-2226 or (617)848-7500 • URL: http://www.aw.com • 2003. $101.33. Eighth edition.

Fundamentals of Management. James H. Donnelly and others. McGraw-Hill, 1221 Ave. of the Americas New York, NY 10020. Phone: 800-722-4726 or (212)512-2000 Fax: (212)512-4502 E-mail: customer.service@mcgraw-hill.com • URL: http://www.mcgraw-hill.com • 1997. $60.50. 10th edition.

Fundamentals of Managerial Economics. Mark Hirschey. South-Western, 5191 Natorp Blvd. Mason, OH 45040. Phone: 800-543-0487 or (513)229-1000 • URL: http://www.swcollege.com • 2002. $107.95. Seventh edition.

Fundamentals of Metallurgical Processes. L. Coudurier and others. Available from Franklin Book Co., Inc., 7804 Montgomery Ave. Elkins Park, PA 19027. Phone: (215)635-5252 Fax: (215)635-6155 E-mail: service@franklinbook.com • URL: http://www.franklinbook.com • 1985. $187.00. Second edition. (International Monographs on Materials and Technology Series: Volume 27).

Fundamentals of Municipal Bonds: A Basic, Definitive Text on the Municipal Securities Market. John Wiley & Sons, Inc., 111 River St. Hoboken, NJ 07030. Phone: 800-225-5945 or (201)748-6276 Fax: (201)748-8641 E-mail: bookinfo@wiley.com • URL: http://www.wiley.com • 2001. $65.00. Fifth edition. (Finance Series).

Fundamentals of Optical Fibers. John A. Buck. John Wiley and Sons, Inc., 111 River St. Hoboken, NJ 07030. Phone: 800-225-5945 or (201)748-6000 Fax: (201)748-6088 E-mail: info@wiley.com • URL: http://www.wiley.com • 1995. $99.95. (Pure and Applied Optics Series).

Fundamentals of Optoelectronics. Clifford R. Pollock. McGraw-Hill, 1221 Ave. of the Americas New York, NY 10020. Phone: 800-722-4726 or (212)512-2000 Fax: (212)512-4502 E-mail: customer.service@mcgraw-hill.com • URL: http://www.mcgraw-hill.com • 1994. $107.19.

Fundamentals of Photonics. Bahaa E. Seleh and Malvin C. Teich. John Wiley and Sons, Inc., 111 River St. Hoboken, NJ 07030. Phone: 800-225-5945 or (201)748-6000 Fax: (201)748-6088 E-mail: info@wiley.com • URL: http://www.wiley.com • 1991. $120.00. (Pure and Applied Optics Series).

Fundamentals of Private Pensions. Dan M. McGill and others. University of Pennsylvania Press, 4200 Pine St. Philadelphia, PA 19104-4011. Phone: (215)898-6261 Fax: (215)898-0404 E-mail: custserv@pobox.upenn.edu • URL: http://www.upenn.edu/pennpress • 1996. $79.95. Seventh revised edition. (Pension Research Council Publications Series).

Fundamentals of Product Liability Law for Engineers. Linda K. Enghagen. Industrial Press, Inc., 200 Madison Ave. New York, NY 10016. Phone: 888-528-7852 or (212)889-6330 Fax: (212)545-8327 E-mail: induspress@aol.com • URL: http://www.industrialpress.com • 1992. $39.95. Covers theories of liability, strategies for protection, defenses, and proving a case. Includes case histories.

Fundamentals of Professional Food Preparation: A Laboratory Text-Workbook. Donald V. Laconi. John Wiley and Sons, Inc., 111 River St. Hoboken, NJ 07030. Phone: 800-225-5945 or (201)748-6000 Fax: (201)748-6088 E-mail: info@wiley.com • URL: http://www.wiley.com • 1995. $60.00.

Fundamentals of Project Management. James P. Lewis. AMACOM, 1601 Broadway New York, NY 10019. Phone: 800-262-9699 or (518)586-8100 Fax: (518)903-8168 E-mail: customerservice@amanet.org • URL: http://www.

amacombooks.org • 2001. Second edition. Price on application.

Fundamentals of Real Estate Appraisal. William L. Ventolo and Martha R. Williams. Dearborn Trade Publishing, A Kaplan Professional Co., 155 N Wacker St. Chicago, IL 60606. Phone: 800-621-9621 or (312)836-4400 Fax: (312)836-1021 E-mail: trade@dearborn.com • URL: http://www.dearborntrade.com • 2001. $51.40. Eighth edition. Explanation of real estate appraisal.

Fundamentals of Real Estate Investment. Austin J. Jaffe. South-Western, 5191 Natrop Blvd. Mason, OH 45040. Phone: 800-543-0487 or (513)229-1000 • URL: http://www.swcollege.com • 2001. $77.95. Third edition.

Fundamentals of Risk and Insurance. Emmett J. Vaughan and Therese J. Vaughan. John Wiley and Sons, Inc., 111 River St. Hoboken, NJ 07030. Phone: 800-526-5368 or (201)748-6000 Fax: (201)748-6088 E-mail: info@wiley.com • URL: http://www.wiley.com • 2002. $115.95. Ninth edition.

Fundamentals of Robotics. David D. Ardayfio. Marcel Dekker, Inc., 270 Madison Ave. New York, NY 10016-0602. Phone: 800-228-1160 or (212)696-9000 Fax: (212)685-4540 E-mail: bookorders@dekker.com • URL: http://www.dekker.com • 1987. $75.00. (Mechanical Engineering Series: Vol. 57).

Fundamentals of Selling: Customers for Life Through Service. Charles Futrell. McGraw-Hill, 1221 Ave. of the Americas New York, NY 10020. Phone: 800-722-4736 or (212)512-2000 Fax: (212)512-4502 E-mail: customer.service@mcgraw-hill.com • URL: http://www.mcgraw-hill.com • 2003. Eighth edition. Price on application. (Marketing Series).

Fundamentals of Strategic Planning for Healthcare Organizations. Stan Williamson and others. Haworth Press, Inc., 10 Alice St. Binghamton, NY 13904-1580. Phone: 800-429-6784 or (607)722-5857 Fax: 800-895-0582 or (607)722-1424 E-mail: getinfo@haworthpressinc.com • URL: http://www.haworthpressinc.com • 1996. $49.95.

Funding Sources for Community and Economic Development 2003-2004: A Guide to Current Sources for Local Programs and Projects. Greenwood Publishing Group, Inc., 88 Post Rd., W. Westport, CT 06881. Phone: 800-225-5800 or (203)226-3571 Fax: (203)431-2214 E-mail: customer-service@greenwood.com • URL: http://www.greenwood.com • 2003. $64.95. Sixth edition. Provides information on 2,600 funding sources. Includes "A Guide to Proposal Planning." (Funding Sources for Community and Economic Development Series).

Fundraising: Hands-On Tactics for Nonprofit Groups. L. Peter Edles. McGraw-Hill, 1221 Ave. of the Americas New York, NY 10020. Phone: 800-722-4726 or (212)512-2000 Fax: (212)512-4502 E-mail: customer.service@mcgraw-hill.com • URL: http://www.mcgraw-hill.com • 1992. $16.95. Covers fundamental premises, soliciting major gifts, small gift prospecting, canvassing, telephone appeals, creating publications, direct mail, and other fund-raising topics for nonprofit organizations.

Funeral Consumers Alliance., 33 Patchen Rd. South Burlington, VT 05403. Phone: 800-765-0107 or (802)865-8300 Fax: (802)865-2626 E-mail: fca@funerals.org • URL: http://www.funerals.org • Promotes a consumer's right to choose a dignified, meaningful, affordable funeral. Provides educational material to the public and affiliates. Monitors the funeral and cemetery industry for consumers nationwide. Responds to consumer complaints. Maintains speakers' bureau.

Funeral Service "Insider". Jean DeSapio, editor. United Communications Group, 11300 Rockville Pke., Ste. 1100 Rockville, MD 20852-3030. Phone: 800-929-4824 or (301)287-2700 Fax: (301)816-8945 E-mail: webmaster@ucg.com Description: Covers the latest trends in funeral service education, legislation, franchising, marketing, and consumer purchasing. Recurring features include editorials, news of research, letters to the editor, and a calendar of events.

Funworld. International Association of Amusement Parks and Attractions, 1448 Duke St. Alexandria, VA 22314-3403. Phone: (703)836-4800 Fax: (703)836-9678 • URL: http://www.iaapa.org • 11 times a year. Members, $22.00 per year; nonmembers, $40.00 per year. Analysis and statistics of the international amusement park industry. Text in English; sections in French, German, Japanese and Spanish.

Fur Information Council of America., 8424 A Santa Monica Blvd., No. 860 West Hollywood, CA 90069. Phone: (323)848-7940 Fax: (323)848-2931 E-mail: info@fur.org • URL: http://www.fur.org • Formerly American Fur Industry.

Fur Rancher. Becker Publishing, PO Box 655 Hopkins, MN 55343. Phone: (952)949-2159 Fax: (952)934-3668 • URL: http://www.beckerpublishing.com • Quarterly. Controlled circulation. Includes *Blue Book of Fur Farming*. Covers the farm raising of animals for fur.

Fur World: The Newsmagazine of Fur and Better Outerware. Creative Marketing Plus, Inc., 19 W 21st St., Ste. 403 New York, NY 10010. Phone: (212)727-1210 Fax: (212)727-1218 • URL: http://www.cmponline.com • Semimonthly. $50.00 per year. Edited for fur retailers, ranchers, pelt dealers, and manufacturers. Provides news and statistics relating to the retail and wholesale fur business.

Furniture-Today: The Weekly Business Newspaper of the Furniture Industry. Reed Business Information, 360 Park Ave., S New York, NY 10010. Phone: 800-446-6551 or (646)746-6400 Fax: (646)746-7028 E-mail: corporatecommunications@reedbusiness.com • URL: http://www.reedbusiness.com • Weekly. $159.97 per year.

Furniture World. Towse Publishing Co., 1333A North Ave. New Rochelle, NY 10804-2807. Phone: (914)235-3095 Fax: (914)235-3278 E-mail: magazinefw@aol.com • URL: http://www.furinfo.com • Monthly. $19.00 per year. Formerly *Furniture World and Furniture Buyer and Decorator*.

Future Business Leaders of America-Phi Beta Lambda.

The Future Demographic: Global Population Trends and Forecasts to 2010 and Beyond. Euromonitor International, 122 South Michigan Ave., Suite 810 Chicago, IL 60603. Phone: 800-577-3876 or (312)922-1115 Fax: (312)922-1157 E-mail: info@euromonitor.com • URL: http://www.euromonitor.com • 2003. $470.00. Presents detailed demographic statistics and forecasts for about 200 countries. Includes age group profiles and data on consumer spending potential.

Future-Driven Library Marketing. Darlene E. Weingand. American Library Association, 50 E. Huron St. Chicago, IL 60611-2795. Phone: 800-545-2433 or (312)944-6780 Fax: (312)440-9374 E-mail: ala@ala.org • URL: http://www.ala.org • 1998. $25.00. The author discusses progressive marketing strategies for libraries. An annotated bibliography is included.

Future Libraries: Dreams, Madness, and Reality. Walt Crawford and Michael Gorman. American Library Association, 50 E. Huron St. Chicago, IL 60611-2795. Phone: 800-545-2433 or (312)944-6780 Fax: (312)440-9374 E-mail: ala@ala.org • URL: http://www.ala.org • 1995. $28.00. Discusses the "over-hyped virtual library" and electronic-publishing "fantasies." Presents the argument for the importance of books, physical libraries, and library personnel.

The Future of Money. Organization for Economic Cooperation and Development, OECD Washington Center, 2001 L St., N. W., Suite 650 Washington, DC 20036-4922. Phone: 800-456-6323 or (202)785-6323 Fax: (202)785-0350 E-mail: washington.contact@oecd.org • URL: http://www.oecdwash.org • 2002. $19.00. Discusses the inevitable trend in money from the physical to the abstract (digital or virtual money). Will cash disappear? Will virtual money threaten control of the money supply? - and so forth.

Future Survey: A Monthly Abstract of Books, Articles, and Reports Concerning Trends, Forecasts, and Ideas About the Future. World Future Society, 7910 Woodmont Ave., Suite 450 Bethesda, MD 20814-3032. Phone: 800-989-8274 or (301)656-8274 Fax: (301)951-0394 E-mail: info@wfs.org • URL: http://www.wfs.org • Monthly. Individuals, $98.00 per year; libraries, $145.00 per year. Includes author and subject indexes.

Future Survey Annual: A Guide to the Recent Literature of Trends, Forecasts, and Policy Proposals. World Future Society, 7910 Woodmont Ave., Suite 450 Bethesda, MD 20814-3032. Phone: 800-989-8274 or (301)656-8274 Fax: (301)951-0394 E-mail: info@wfs.org • URL: http://www.wfs.org • Annual. $35.00.

Futures and Derivatives Law Report: The Journal on the Law of Investment and Risk Management Products. Glasser Legalworks, 150 Clove Rd. Little Falls, NJ 07424. Phone: 800-308-1700 or (973)890-0008 Fax: (973)890-0042 E-mail: orders@glasserlegalworks.com • URL: http://www.glasserlegalworks.com • Monthly. $305.00 per year. Newsletter. Covers developments in regulation, legislation, and litigation concerning financial derivatives, futures trading, and options trading.

Futures and OTC World (Over the Counter). Russell R. Wasendorf, P.O. Box 849 Cedar Falls, IA 50613. Phone: (319)268-0441 Fax: (319)277-0880 Weekly. $435.00 per year. Newsletter. Futures market information. Includes Daily Hotline Information to update advice. Formerly *Futures and Options Factors*.

Futures Industry Association., 2001 Pennsylvania Ave. NW, Ste. 600 Washington, DC 20006. Phone: (202)466-5460 Fax: (202)296-3184 E-mail: info@futuresindustry.org • URL: http://www.futuresindustry.org • Acts as a principal spokesman for the futures and options industry. Represents all facets of the futures industry, including many international exchanges. Works to preserve the system of free and competitive markets by representing the interests of the industry in connection with legislative and regulatory issues.

Futures; The Journal of Forecasting, Planning and Policy. Elsevier, 655 Ave. of the Americas New York, NY 10010-5107. Phone: 800-366-2665 or (212)989-5800 Fax: 800-535-9935 or (212)633-3680 E-mail: custserv@elsevier.com • URL: http://www.elsevier.com • 10 times a year. Qualified personnel, $233.00 per year; institutions, $932.00 per year.

Futures Magazine SourceBook: The Most Complete List of Exchanges, Companies, Regulators, Organizations, etc., Offering Products and Services to the Futures and Options Industry. Futures Magazine, Inc., 250 S. Wacker Dr. Suite 1150 Chicago, IL 60606. Phone: 800-972-9316 or (312)977-0999 Fax: (312)977-1042 • URL: http://www.futuresmag.com • Annual. $19.50. Provides information on commodity futures brokers, trading method services, publications, and other items of interest to futures traders and money managers.

Futures Market Service. Commodity Research Bureau, Chicago, IL 60606. Phone: 800-621-5271 or (312)554-8456 Fax: (312)939-4135 E-mail: info@crbtrader.com • URL: http://www.crbtrader.com • Weekly. $155.00 per year.

Futures Markets. A. G. Malliaris, editor. Edward Elgar Publishing, Inc., 136 West St., Suite 203 Northampton, MA 01060. Phone: 800-390-3149 or (413)584-5551 Fax: (413)584-9933 E-mail: elgarinfo@e-elgar.com • URL: http://www.e-elgar.co.uk • 1997. $550.00. Three volumes. Consists of reprints of 70 articles dating from 1959 to 1993, on futures market volatility, speculation, hedging, stock indexes, portfolio insurance, interest rates, and foreign currencies. (International Library of Critical Writings in Financial Economics Series: No. 2).

Futures: News, Analysis, and Strategies for Futures, Options, and Derivatives Traders. Futures Magazine, 250 S. Wacker Dr., Suite 1150 Chicago, IL 60606. Phone: 800-972-9316 or (312)977-0999 Fax: (312)977-1042 • URL: http://www.futuresmag.com • Monthly. $39.00 per year. Edited for institutional money managers and traders, brokers, risk managers, and individual investors or speculators. Includes special feature issues on interest rates, technical indicators, currencies, charts, precious metals, hedge funds, and derivatives. Supplements available.

Futures Online. Futures Magazine Inc.Phone: (312)846-4600 Fax: (312)846-4638 • URL: http://www.futuresmag.com • Web site presents updates of *Futures* magazine and links to other futures-related sites.

Futures Research Quarterly. World Future Society, 7910 Woodmont Ave., Suite 450 Bethesda, MD 20814. Phone: 800-989-8274 or (301)656-8274 Fax: (301)951-0394 E-mail: info@wfs.org • URL: http://www.wfs.org • Quarterly. Members, $77.00 per year; others, $99.00 per year.

Futuretech. Technical Insights/John Wiley & Sons Inc., 111 River St. Hoboken, NJ 07030-5774. Phone: 800-245-6217 or (201)748-6000 Fax: (201)748-6088 E-mail: insights@wiley.com • URL: http://www.wiley.com • Description: Contains briefings on newly emerging technologies and the markets that they will create. Each issue focuses on one technology, analyzes its market impact, and provides access to developers looking for partners, licenses, or marketing agreements.

The Futurist: A Journal of Forecasts, Trends, and Ideas About the Future. World Future Society, 7910 Woodmont Ave., Suite 450 Bethesda, MD 20814. Phone: 800-989-8274 or (301)656-8274 Fax: (301)951-0394 E-mail: info@wfs.org • URL: http://www.wfs.org/ • Bimonthly. Free to members; libraries and institutions, $55.00 per year.

GAAP for Governments: Interpretation and Application of Generally Accepted Accounting Principles for State and Local Governments. John Wiley and Sons, Inc., 605 Third Ave. New York, NY 10158-0012. Phone: 800-225-5945 or (212)850-6000 Fax: (212)850-6088 E-mail: info@jwiley.com • URL: http://www.wiley.com • Annual. $134.00. (Includes CD-ROM.)

Gaining Control of the Corporate Culture. Ralph H. Kilmann and others. John Wiley and Sons, Inc., 111 River St. Hoboken, NJ 07030. Phone: 800-225-5945 or (201)748-6000 Fax: (201)748-6088 E-mail: info@wiley.com • URL: http://www.wiley.com • 1985. $48.00. (Management Series).

Gaining Word Power. Dorothy Rubin. Longman Publishing Group, The Longman Bldg., 10 Bank St. White Plains, NY 10606-1951. Phone: 800-922-0579 or (914)993-5000 Fax: (914)997-8115 E-mail: orders@mcp.com • URL: http://www.store.awl.com • 2002. $52.00. Sixth edition. Purpose of book is to help students and others build a "college-level" vocabulary, including information-age words.

Gale Biographies. Gale Cengage Learning, 27500 Drake Rd. Farmington Hills, MI 48331-3535. Phone: 800-877-GALE or (248)699-GALE Fax: 800-414-5043 or (248)699-8069 E-mail: galeord@gale.com • URL: http://gale.cengage.com • Provides online biographical profiles (text) of more than 140,000 prominent individuals, past and present, from all fields of activity. Corresponds to various Gale print sources. Quarterly updates. Inquire as to online cost and availability.

Gale Book of Averages. Gale Cengage Learning, 27500 Drake Rd. Farmington Hills, MI 48331-3535. Phone: 800-877-GALE or (248)699-4253 Fax: 800-414-5043 E-mail: gale.galeord@cengage.com • URL: http://gale.cengage.com • 1994. $75.00. Contains 1,100-1,200 statistical averages on a variety of topics, with references to published sources. Subjects include business, labor, consumption, crime, and other areas of contemporary society.

Gale Country and World Rankings Reporter. Gale Cengage Learning, 27500 Drake Rd. Farmington Hills, MI 48331-3535. Phone: 800-877-GALE or (248)699-4253 Fax: 800-414-5043 E-mail: gale.galeord@cengage.com • URL: http://gale.cengage.com • 1997. $160.00. Second edition. Provides about 3,000 statistical ranking tables and charts covering more than 235 nations. Sources include the United Nations and various government publications.

Gale Database of Publications and Broadcast Media. Gale Cengage Learning, 27500 Drake Rd. Farmington Hills, MI 48331-3535. Phone: 800-877-GALE Fax: 800-414-5043 or (248)699-8069 E-mail: galeord@galegroup.com • URL: http://www.galegroup.com • An online directory containing detailed information on over 67,000 periodicals, newspapers, broadcast stations, cable systems, directories, and newsletters. Corresponds to the following print sources: *Gale Directory of Publications and Broadcast Media; Directories in Print; City and State Directories in Print; Newsletters in Print*. Semiannual updates. Inquire as to online cost and availability.

Gale Directory of Databases. Gale Cengage Learning, 27500 Drake Rd. Farmington Hills, MI 48331-3535. Phone: 800-877-GALE or (248)699-4253 Fax: 800-414-5043 E-mail:

gale.galeord@cengage.com • URL: http://gale.cengage.com • 2003. $490.00. Two volumes. Volume 1, $315.00; volume 2, $195.00. *Volume 1: Online Databases* and *Volume 2: CD-ROM, Diskette, Magnetic Tape, Handheld, and Batch Access Database Products*.

Gale Directory of Databases [online]. Gale Cengage Learning, 27500 Drake Rd. Farmington Hills, MI 48331-3535. Phone: 800-877-GALE or (248)699-GALE Fax: 800-414-5043 or (248)699-8069 E-mail: galeord@gale.com • URL: http://gale.cengage.com • Presents the online version of the printed *Gale Directory of Databases, Volume 1: Online Databases* and *Gale Directory of Databases, Volume 2: CD-ROM, Diskette, Magnetic Tape, Handheld, and Batch Access Database Products*. Semiannual updates. Inquire as to online cost and availability.

Gale Directory of Learning Worldwide: A Guide to Faculty and Institutions of Higher Education, Research, and Culture. Gale Cengage Learning, 27500 Drake Rd. Farmington Hills, MI 48331-3535. Phone: 800-877-GALE or (248)699-4253 Fax: 800-414-5043 E-mail: gale.galeord@cengage.com • URL: http://gale.cengage.com • 2001. $425.00. Three volumes. Describes about 26,000 colleges, universities, research institutes, libraries, museums, scholarly associations, academies, and archives around the world. Arranged by country.

Gale Directory of Publications and Broadcast Media. Gale Cengage Learning, 27500 Drake Rd. Farmington Hills, MI 48331-3535. Phone: 800-877-GALE or (248)699-4253 Fax: 800-414-5043 E-mail: gale.galeord@cengage.com • URL: http://gale.cengage.com • Annual. $770.00. Five volumes. *Interedition Supplement*, Free. A guide to publications and broadcasting stations in the U. S. and Canada, including newspapers, magazines, journals, radio stations, television stations, and cable systems. Geographic arrangement. Volume three consists of statistical tables, maps, subject indexes, and title index.

Gale E-Commerce Sourcebook. Gale, 27500 Drake Rd. Farmington Hills, MI 48331-3535. Phone: 800-877-4253 or (248)699-4253 Fax: 800-414-5043 or (248)699-8065 E-mail: galeord@cengage.com • URL: http://gale.cengage.com • Covers: Over 4,700 organizations, associations, and agencies related to e-commerce such as Web site designers, government regulatory agencies, publications, and trade shows. Also covers 250 leading e-commerce companies worldwide. Entries include: Name, address, phone, fax, e-mail address, URL, and name and title of contact person. For companies—Same as above along with year of founding, company revenue, and number of employees.

Gale Encyclopedia of E-Commerce. Gale Cengage Learning, 27500 Drake Rd. Farmington Hills, MI 48331-3535. Phone: 800-877-GALE or (248)699-4253 Fax: 800-414-5043 E-mail: gale.galeord@cengage.com • URL: http://gale.cengage.com • 2002. $295.00. Two volumes. Contains about 470 entries covering Web site development, e-commerce financing, advertising, marketing, legal issues, and other topics related to doing business through the Internet. Includes a bibliography.

Gale Encyclopedia of Everyday Law. Gale Cengage Learning, 27500 Drake Rd. Farmington Hills, MI 48331-3535. Phone: 800-877-GALE Fax: 800-414-5043 E-mail: gale.galeord@cengage.com • URL: http://gale.cengage.com • 2002. $250.00. Two volumes. Contains about 200 entries providing profiles of important U. S. laws and regulations, with historical background. Includes bibliographies.

The Gale Encyclopedia of Psychology. Gale Cengage Learning, 27500 Drake Rd. Farmington Hills, MI 48331-3535. Phone: 800-877-GALE or (248)699-4253 Fax: 800-414-5043 E-mail: gale.galeord@cengage.com • URL: http://gale.cengage.com • 2001. $155.00. Second edition. Includes bibliographies arranged by topic and a glossary. More than 650 topics are covered.

Gale Encyclopedia of U.S. Economic History. Gale Cengage Learning, 27500 Drake Rd. Farmington Hills, MI 48331-3535. Phone: 800-877-GALE or (248)699-4253 Fax: 800-414-5043 E-mail: gale.galeordatsthomson.com • URL: http://gale.cengage.com • 2000. $225.00. Two volumes. Contains about 1,000 alphabetically arranged entries. Includes industry profiles, biographies, social issue profiles, geographic profiles, and chronological tables.

Gale Environmental Almanac. Gale Cengage Learning, 27500 Drake Rd. Farmington Hills, MI 48331-3535. Phone: 800-877-GALE or (248)699-4253 Fax: 800-414-5043 E-mail: gale.galeord@cengage.com • URL: http://gale.cengage.com • 1993. $115.00. Contains 15 chapters, each on a broad topic related to the environment, such as "Waste and Recycling." Each chapter has a topical overview, charts, statistics, and illustrations. Includes a glossary of environmental terms and a bibliography.

Gale Environmental Sourcebook: A Guide to Organizations, Agencies, and Publications. Gale Cengage Learning, 27500 Drake Rd. Farmington Hills, MI 48331-3535. Phone: 800-877-GALE or (248)699-4253 Fax: 800-414-5043 E-mail: gale.galeord@cengage.com • URL: http://gale.cengage.com • 1993. $115.00. Second edition. A directory of print and nonprint information sources on a wide variety of environmental topics.

Gale Five Language Dictionary of Technology: Simultaneous Translations of English, French, Spanish, German, and Italian. Gale Cengage Learning, 27500 Drake Rd. Farmington Hills, MI 48331-3535. Phone: 800-877-GALE or (248)699-4253 Fax: 800-414-5043 E-mail: gale.galeord@cengage.com • URL: http://gale.cengage.com • 1993. $75.00. Contains translations of frequently-used technological words and phrases.

Gale Guide to Internet Databases. Gale Cengage Learning, 27500 Drake Rd. Farmington Hills, MI 48331-3535. Phone: 800-877-GALE or (248)699-4253 Fax: 800-414-5043 E-mail: gale.galeord@cengage.com • URL: http://gale.cengage.com • 1999. $125.00. Sixth edition. Presents critical descriptions and ratings of more than 5,000 useful Internet databases (especially World Wide Web sites). Includes a glossary of Internet terms, a bibliography, and five indexes.

Gale State Rankings Reporter. Gale Cengage Learning, 27500 Drake Rd. Farmington Hills, MI 48331-3535. Phone: 800-877-GALE or (248)699-4253 Fax: 800-414-5043 E-mail: gale.galeord@cengage.com • URL: http://gale.cengage.com • 1996. $130.00. Second edition Provides 3,000 ranked lists of states under 35 subject headings. Sources are newspapers, periodicals, books, research institute publications, and government publications.

Gale's Guide to Nonprofits: A Gale Ready Reference Handbook. Gale Cengage Learning, 27500 Drake Rd. Farmington Hills, MI 48331-3535. Phone: 800-877-GALE or (248)699-4253 Fax: 800-414-5043 E-mail: gale.galeord@cengage.com • URL: http://gale.cengage.com • 2000. $135.00. Serves to provide a wide variety of information sources of interest to nonprofit organizations, including publications, online databases, and associations. Contains three indexes and a glossary.

Gale's Guide to the Arts: A Gale Ready Reference Handbook. Gale Cengage Learning, 27500 Drake Rd. Farmington Hills, MI 48331-3535. Phone: 800-877-GALE or (248)699-4253 Fax: 800-414-5043 E-mail: gale.galeord@cengage.com • URL: http://gale.cengage.com • 2000. $125.00. Contains descriptions of information sources of interest to nonprofit art groups, including publications, online databases, museums, government agencies, and associations. Three indexes and a glossary are provided.

Gale's Guide to the Media: A Gale Ready Reference Handbook. Gale Cengage Learning, 27500 Drake Rd. Farmington Hills, MI 48331-3535. Phone: 800-877-GALE or (248)699-4253 Fax: 800-414-5043 E-mail: gale.galeord@cengage.com • URL: http://gale.cengage.com • 2000. $125.00. Provides profiles of a wide variety of media-related organizations, publications, broadcasters, agencies, and databases, of interest to nonprofit groups. Contains three indexes and a glossary.

Gam-Anon International Service Office., PO Box 157 Whitestone, NY 11357. Phone: (718)352-1671 Fax: (718)746-2571 E-mail: info3@gam-anon.org • URL: http://www.gam-anon.org • Represents husbands, wives, relatives, and close friends of compulsive gamblers. Seeks to help members better understand the compulsive gambler and learn to cope with the problems involved. Conducts regularly scheduled meetings throughout the world to allow members to share experiences, strength, and hope, recover from the effects of compulsive gambling, and achieve a normal way of thinking and living. Maintains speakers' bureau. Sponsors social activities. Conducts open, topic, recognition, and special focus meetings.

GAMA International., 2901 Telestar Ct., Ste. 140 Falls Church, VA 22042-1205. Phone: 800-345-2687 or (703)770-8184 Fax: (703)770-8182 E-mail: gamamail@gamaweb.com • URL: http://www.gamaweb.com • Provides world-class education and training resources for individuals, companies and organizations involved with the recruitment and development of field managers, representatives and staff in the life insurance and financial services industry; advocates of the value-added role of field management and representatives in the ethical distribution of life insurance and financial products and services industry.

GAMA International Journal. GAMA International, 2901 Telestar Court, Ste. 140 Falls Church, VA 22042-1205. Phone: 800-345-2687 or (703)770-8184 Fax: (703)770-8182 E-mail: gamamail@gama.naifa.org • URL: http://www.gamaweb.com • Bimonthly. Members, $4.00 per year; non-members, $20.00 per year. Contains practical articles on the management of life insurance agencies.

Gamblers Anonymous., PO Box 17173 Los Angeles, CA 90017. Phone: 888-424-3577 or (213)386-8789 Fax: (213)386-0030 E-mail: isomain@gamblersanonymous.org • URL: http://www.gamblersanonymous.org • Men and women who have joined together in order to stop gambling and to help other compulsive gamblers do the same; is self-supporting, declines outside contributions, and neither opposes nor endorses outside causes.

Gambling Times Magazine. Gambling Times, Inc., 3883 W Century Blvd., No. 608 Inglewood, CA 90303-1003. Phone: (818)781-9355 Fax: (818)781-3125 • URL: http://www.gamblingtimes.com • Monthly. $44.00 per year.

Game, Set, Match: Winning the Negotiations Game - A Step-by-Step Approach to Getting What You Want From Any Negotiation. Henry S. Kramer. American Lawyer Media, Inc., 105 Madison Ave. New York, NY 10016. Phone: 800-888-8300 or (212)779-9200 Fax: (212)481-8110 E-mail: lawcatalog@amlaw.com • URL: http://www.lawcatalog.com/ • 2001. $19.95. Contains examples of successful negotiation, imcluding "tips, tricks, and traps."

Games, Strategies, and Managers: How Managers Can Use Game Theory to Make Better Business Decisions. John McMillan. Oxford University Press, 198 Madison Ave. New York, NY 10016-4314. Phone: 800-451-7556 or (212)726-6000 Fax: (212)726-7440 E-mail: custserv@oup-usa.org • URL: http://www.oup-usa.org • 1992. $19.95.

Garment Manufacturers Index. Klevens Publications Inc., 411 S Main St., Ste. 209 Los Angeles, CA 90013. Phone: (213)625-9000 Fax: (213)625-5002 E-mail: editor@klevenspub.com • URL: http://www.garmentindex.com • Covers: about 8,000 manufacturers and suppliers of products and services such as fabrics, trimmings, factory equipment, and sewing contractors used in the manufacture of apparel. Publication includes: fabrics, trimmings, supplies, services, equipment, and contractors. Entries include: Company name, address, phone, fax, list of products or services, brief description of product.

Gas Appliance Manufacturers Association., 2107 Wilson Blvd., Ste. 600 Arlington, VA 22201-3042. Phone: (703)525-7060 Fax: (703)525-6790 E-mail: membership@gamanet.org • URL: http://www.ahrinet.org • Composed of manufacturers of gas, oil, and electric space heating and water heating equipment for residential, commercial, and industrial applications, and associated components and accessories. Scope includes gas and oil central furnaces and boilers; gas, oil, and electric water heaters; gas space heaters; gas-fired commercial cooking equipment; gas-fired industrial heating equipment; and equipment used in the production, transmission, and distribution of natural gas.

Gas Digest: The Magazine of Gas Operations. T-P Graphics, 5731 Arboles Dr. Houston, TX 77035. Phone: (713)723-6736 Quarterly. Free. Articles and data relating to operations and management phases of natural gas operations.

Gas Facts. American Gas Association, 400 N Capitol St., NW Washington, DC 20001. Phone: (202)824-7000 Fax: (202)824-7115 • URL: http://www.aga.org • Annual. Members, $48.00; non-members, $120.00.

Gas Facts: A Statistical Record of the Gas Utility Industry. American Gas Association, Dept. of Statistics, 400 N Capitol St., NW Washington, DC 20001-1511. Phone: (202)824-7000 Fax: (202)824-7115 • URL: http://www.aga.org • Annual. Members, $40.00; non-members, $80.00.

Gas Industry Training Directory. American Gas Association, 400 N Capitol St. NW, Ste. 450 Washington, DC 20001. Phone: (202)824-7000 Fax: (202)824-7115 E-mail: ggardner@aga.org • URL: http://www.aga.org • Covers: over 600 programs available from gas transmission and distribution companies, manufacturers of gas-fired equipment, consultants, etc., and from gas associations. Entries include: Name, address, phone of source of program, name of contact, program description.

Gas Technology Institute., 1700 S Mt. Prospect Rd. Des Plaines, IL 60018-1804. Phone: (847)768-0500 Fax: (847)768-0501 E-mail: businessdevelopmentinfo@gastechnology.org • URL: http://www.gastechnology.org • Educational and research facility sponsored by companies engaged in the production, processing, transmission, and distribution of natural gas and related fuels; engineering firms; large energy consumers. Conducts contract research for government and industry in the field of non-nuclear energy technology. Offers short courses in gas production, transmission, distribution, economics, and marketing. Sponsors symposia on current topics in non-nuclear energy.

Gas Turbine World. Pequot Publishing, Inc., PO Box 447 Southport, CT 06490. Phone: (203)259-1112 Fax: (203)255-3313 Bimonthly. $90.00 per year.

Gas Utility Industry Worldwide. Midwest Publishing Co., 2230 E 49th St., Ste. E Tulsa, OK 74105-8771. Phone: 800-829-2002 or (918)582-2000 Fax: (918)587-9349 E-mail: info@midwestpub.com • URL: http://www.midwestdirectories.com • Covers: Approximately 8,000 utility companies, contractors, engineering firms, equipment manufacturers, supply companies, underground natural gas storage facilities, regulatory agencies; international coverage. Entries include: Company name, address, phone, names and titles of key personnel, description of services.

Gas Utility Manager. James Informational Media, Inc., 2720 S. River Rd., Ste. 126 Des Plaines, IL 60018. Phone: (847)391-9070 Fax: (847)391-9058 E-mail: kirk@jiminc.com • URL: http://www.jiminc.com • Monthly. $24.00 per year. Formerly *Gas Utility and Pipeline Industries*.

Gas Welding and Distributors Association., 1900 Arch St. Philadelphia, PA 19103. Phone: (215)564-3484 Fax: (215)963-9784 E-mail: gawda@gawda.org • URL: http://www.nwsa.com • Formerly *National Welding Supply Assoication*.

The Gases and Welding Distributor. Penton Media Inc., 1300 E. Ninth St. Cleveland, OH 44114. Phone: (216)696-7000 Fax: (216)696-1752 E-mail: information@penton.com • URL: http://www.penton.com • Bimonthly. Free to qualified personnel; others, $55.00 Per year. Formerly *Welding Distributor*.

Gasoline and Automotive Service Dealers Association., 9520 Seaview Ave. Brooklyn, NY 11236. Phone: (718)241-1111 Fax: (718)763-6589 E-mail: gasdal@cs.com Members are owners and operators of automobile service stations and repair shops. Formerly Gasoline Merchants.

Gates: How Microsoft's Mogul Reinvented an Industry and Made Himself the Richest Man in America. Stephen Manes and Paul Andrews. Simon & Schuster Trade, 1230 Ave. of the Americas New York, NY 10020. Phone: 800-223-2348 or (212)698-7000 Fax: 800-983-9831 or (212)698-7007 E-mail:

consumer.customerservice@simonandschuster.com • URL: http://www.simonsays.com • 1994. $15.00.

Gateway to the European Union. European UnionE-mail: pressoffice@eurostat.cec.be • URL: http://www.europa.eu.int • Web site provides access to a wide variety of EU information, including statistics (Eurostat), news, policies, publications, key issues, and official exchange rates for the euro. Includes links to the European Central Bank, the European Investment Bank, and other institutions. Fees: Free.

GATF World. Graphic Arts Technical Foundation, 200 Deer Run Sewickley, PA 15143-2600. Phone: (412)621-6941 Fax: (412)621-3049 • URL: http://www.gaft.org • Bimonthly. $75.00 per year. Technical articles of interest to the graphic communications industry. Incorporates *Graphic Arts Abstracts*.

GDL Alert. RIA, 395 Hudson St. New York, NY 10014. Phone: 800-950-1216 or 800-431-9025 E-mail: riahome@riag.com • URL: http://www.riahome.com • Monthly. $110.98 per year. Newsletter. Covers current legal developments of interest to employers. Formerly *Disabilities in the Workplace Alert*.

Gear Dynamics and Gear Noise Research Laboratory.

Gear Technology: The Journal of Gear Manufacturing. Randall Publishing, Inc., 1425 Lunt Ave. Elk Grove Village, IL 60007. Phone: (847)437-6604 Fax: (847)437-6618 E-mail: people@geartechnology.com • URL: http://www.geartechnology.com • Bimonthly. $45.00 per year. Edited for manufacturers, engineers, and designers of gears.

Gem Identification Made Easy: A Hands-on Guide to More Confident Buying and Selling. Antoinette L. Matlins and Antonio C. Bonanno. GemStone Press, Route 4 Sunset Farm Offices Woodstock, VT 05091. Phone: 800-962-4544 or (802)457-4000 Fax: (802)457-4004 E-mail: sales@gemstonepress.com • URL: http://www.gemstonepress.com • 1997. $34.95. Second revised edition.

Gemological Institute of America.

Gems and Gemology. Gemological Institute of America, 5355 Armada Dr. Carlsbad, CA 92008. Phone: 800-421-7250 or (760)603-4000 Fax: (760)603-4595 E-mail: eduinfo@gia.edu • URL: http://www.gia.edu • Quarterly. $69.95 per year.

Gemstone Buying Guide. Renee Newman and John Raimo. International Jewelry Publications, 417 N. Stoneman Ave., Suite C Alhambra, CA 91801. Phone: (626)282-3781 Fax: (626)282-4807 2003. $19.95. Second edition. Serves as a guide for evaluating, identifying, selecting, and buying gemstones of various types and colors. Includes supplier information and 281 color photographs.

Gemstones of the World. Walter Schumann. Sterling Publishing Co., Inc., 387 Park Ave., S New York, NY 10016. Phone: (212)532-7160 E-mail: custservice@sterlingpub.com • URL: http://www.sterlingpub.com • 2000. $24.95. Expanded revised edition.

Gender on Trial: Sexual Stereotypes and Work/Life Balance in the Legal Workplace. Holly English. American Lawyer Media, Inc., 105 Madison Ave. New York, NY 10016. Phone: 800-888-8300 or (212)779-9200 Fax: (212)481-8110 E-mail: lawcatalog@amlaw.com • URL: http://www.lawcatalog.com/ • 2003. $44.95. Provides an "oral history" of legal profession employment practices, based on interviews with lawyers from around the U.S., psychologists, consultants, and recruiters. Contains recommendations for "new models to help firms and individuals achieve a workplace free of gender bias for both men and women." (ALM Publishing).

General Aviation Manufacturers Association., 1400 K St. NW, Ste. 801 Washington, DC 20005. Phone: (202)393-1500 Fax: (202)842-4063 E-mail: webmaster@gama.aero • URL: http://www.gama.aero • Manufacturers of aviation airframes, engines, avionics, and components. Seeks to create a better climate for the growth of general aviation.

General Aviation News., P.O. Box 39099 Lakewood, WA 98439. Phone: 800-426-8538 or (253)471-9888 Fax: (253)471-9911 E-mail: comments@generalaviationnews.com • URL: http://www.gneralaviationnews.com • Biweekly. $29.50 per year. Formerly *Flyer*

General Federation of Women's Clubs.

General Information Concerning Patents. Available from U. S. Government Printing Office, Washington, DC 20402. Phone: (202)512-1800 Fax: (202)512-2250 E-mail: gpoaccess@gpo.gov • URL: http://www.access.gpo.gov • 2001. $4.75. Issued by Patent and Trademark Office, U. S. Department of Commerce. Provides basic information on patent applications, fees, searches, specifications, and infringement. Includes "Answers to Questions Frequently Asked."

General Robotics, Automation, Sensing and Perception (GRASP).

General Statistics. Warren Chase and Fred Brown. John Wiley and Sons, Inc., 111 River St. Hoboken, NJ 07030. Phone: 800-225-5945 or (201)748-6000 Fax: (201)748-6088 E-mail: info@wiley.com • URL: http://www.wiley.com • 1999. $98.95 Fourth edition. Includes CD-ROM.

Generic Line. Scitec Services Inc., 5324 Sinclair Rd. Columbus, OH 43229-5002. Phone: 888-838-5578 or (614)433-0648 Fax: (703)538-7660 E-mail: insights@wiley.com • URL: http://www.fda.news • Description: Focuses on the pharmaceutical industry, emphasizing generic products. Discusses regulatory, legislative, technical, and business developments of interest to generic and small pharmaceutical manufacturers. Recurring features include reports on current research and actions of pharmaceutical companies.

Generic Pharmaceutical Association., 2300 Clarendon Blvd.,

Ste. 400 Arlington, VA 22201. Phone: (703)647-2480 Fax: (703)647-2481 E-mail: info@gphaonline.org • URL: http://www.gphaonline.org • Promotes the common interests of the members and the general welfare of the pharmaceutical industry; prepares and disseminates among members and others, accurate and reliable information concerning the industry, products, needs and requirements; participates in international, federal, state and municipal legislative, regulatory and administrative proceedings with respect to law, rules and orders affecting the pharmaceutical industry; participates in scientific research and product development with intent to increase consumer access to generic products; and raises awareness and visibility of the significant benefits and value of generic drugs to the consumers.

Genetic Engineering and Biotechnology Firms Worldwide Directory. Mega-Type Publishing, 701 Sayre Dr. Princeton, NJ 08542-4602. Phone: 800-962-7004 or (609)683-0660 Fax: (609)275-8011 E-mail: biotech@megatype.com Annual. $299.00. About 6,000 firms, including major firms with biotechnology divisions as well as small independent firms.

Genetic Engineering News: The Information Source of the Biotechnology Industry. Mary Ann Liebert, Inc., Two Madison Ave. Larchmont, NY 10538. Phone: 800-654-3237 or (914)834-3100 Fax: (914)834-3688 E-mail: info@liebertpub.com • URL: http://www.liebertpub.com • 21 times a year. Institutions, $666.00 per year. Newsletter. Business and financial coverage

Genetic Technology News. Technical Insights/John Wiley & Sons Inc., 111 River St. Hoboken, NJ 07030-5774. Phone: 800-245-6217 or (201)748-6000 Fax: (201)748-6088 E-mail: insights@wiley.com • URL: http://www.wiley.com • Description: Informs corporate development and research managers of advances in genetic engineering with applications in medical, agricultural, chemical, food, and other businesses. Covers areas such as recombinant DNA, monoclonal antibodies, and interferon. Recurring features include news of research, company reports, a calendar of events, and supplements titled Market Forecasts, Patent Update, and Strategic Partners. **Remarks:** Also available as part of Biotechnology Information Package, which includes Industrial Bioprocessing (see separate listings).

Genetics Abstracts. CSA, 7200 Wisconsin Ave., Suite 601 Bethesda, MD 20814. Phone: 800-843-7751 or (301)961-6700 Fax: (301)961-6720 E-mail: servicee@csa.com • URL: http://www.csa.com • 11 times a year. $1,595.00 per year. Includes print and online editions.

Genetics Society of America., 9650 Rockville Pike Bethesda, MD 20814-3998. Phone: (866)486-4363 or (301)634-7300 Fax: (301)634-7079 E-mail: estrass@genetics-gsa.org • URL: http://www.genetics-gsa.org • Members are individuals and organizations with an interest in genetics.

GEOARCHIVE. Geosystems, P.O. Box 40, Didcot Oxon Ox11 9BX, England. Phone: 44 1235813913 Fax: 44 11235813913 Citations to literature on geoscience and water. 1974 to present. Monthly updates. Inquire as to online cost and availability.

Geographic Profile of Employment and Unemployment. Available from U. S. Government Printing Office, Washington, DC 20402. Phone: (202)512-1800 Fax: (202)512-2250 E-mail: gpoaccess@gpo.gov • URL: http://www.access.gpo.gov • Annual. $23.00. Issued by Bureau of Labor Statistics, U. S. Department of Labor. Presents detailed, annual average employment, unemployment, and labor force data for regions, states, and metropolitan areas. Characteristics include sex, age, race, Hispanic origin, marital status, occupation, and type of industry.

Geographic Reference Report: Annual Report of Costs, Wages, Salaries, and Human Resource Statistics for the United States and Canada. ERI (Economic Research Institute), 8575 164th Ave. NE, Ste. 100 Redmond, WA 98052-3679. Phone: 800-627-3697 or (425)556-0205 Fax: 800-753-4415 E-mail: info@erieri.com • URL: http://www.erieri.com • Annual. $389.00. Provides demographic and other data for each of 298 North American metropolian areas, including local salaries, wage differentials, cost-of-living, housing costs, income taxation, employment, unemployment, population, major employers, crime rates, weather, etc.

Geographical Abstracts: Human and Physical Geography. Elsevier, 655 Ave. of the Americas New York, NY 10010-5107. Phone: 800-366-2665 or (212)989-5800 Fax: 800-535-9935 or (212)633-3680 E-mail: custserv@elsevier.com • URL: http://www.elsevier.com • Monthly. Institutions, $4,213.00 per year. *Human Geography* $1,822.00 per year. Annual cumulation. *Physical Geography* $2,391.00 per year. Annual cumulation.

The Geophysical Directory. Claudia LaCalli, editor. Geophysical Directory Inc., PO Box 130508 Houston, TX 77219. Phone: 800-929-2462 or (713)529-8789 Fax: (713)529-3646 E-mail: info@geophysicaldirectory.com Covers: about 4,000 companies that provide geophysical equipment, supplies, or services, and mining and petroleum companies that use geophysical techniques; international coverage. Entries include: Company name, address, phone, fax, names of principal executives, operations, and sales personnel; similar information for branch locations.

GEOREF. American Geological Institute, 4220 King St. Alexandria, VA 22302-1507. Phone: (703)379-2480 Fax:

(703)379-7563 Bibliography and index of geology and geosciences literature, 1785 to present. Inquire as to online cost and availability.

The George Washington International Law Review. George Washington University, National Law Center, 2008 G St., N.W. Washington, DC 20052. Phone: (202)676-3874 Fax: (202)676-3876 E-mail: gwjile@gwis2.circ.gwu.edu • URL: http://www.law.gwu.edu • Quarterly. $28.00 per year. Articles dealing with a variety of topics within the area of private international comparative law and economics. Formerly *George Washington Journal of International Law and Economics*.

Geotechnical Engineering Center., University of Texas at Austin, Dept. of Civil Engineering Austin, TX 78712. Phone: (512)471-4929 Fax: (512)471-6548 E-mail: swright@mail.utexas.edu Areas of research include offshore complexes.

Geotechnical Materials Research Laboratories. Iowa State University of Science and Technology

Geothermal Laboratory.

Geothermal Resources Council., PO Box 1350 Davis, CA 95617. Phone: (530)758-2360 Fax: (530)758-2839 E-mail: grc@geothermal.org • URL: http://www.geothermal.org • Encourages research, exploration, and development of geothermal energy; promotes establishment of criteria for the development of geothermal resources compatible with the natural environment. Provides information for the public and encourages the collection and dissemination of geothermal information and data. Cooperates and communicates with national and international governmental, institutional, and private agencies. Holds technical training workshops and annual meeting. Maintains largest geothermal technical library in existence.

Geothermics: International Journal of Geothermal Research and Its Applications. Elsevier, 655 Ave. of the Americas New York, NY 10010-5107. Phone: 800-366-2665 or (212)989-5800 Fax: 800-535-9935 or (212)633-3680 E-mail: custserv@elsevier.com • URL: http://www.elsevier.com • Bimonthly. Institutions, $1,124.00 per year. Covers theory, exploration, development, and utilization of geothermal energy. Text and summaries in English and French.

Geriatric Care. Eymann Publications, P.O. Box 3577 Reno, NV 89505-3577. Phone: (775)358-1554 Fax: (775)358-1476 E-mail: eymann@care4elders.com • URL: http://www.care4elders.com • Monthly. $87.50 per year.

German American National Public Affairs., PO Box 11124 Pensacola, FL 32524. Fax: (850)478-4993 E-mail: rcw@vnf.com Seeks to represent what the committee considers to be the interests of German-Americans. Aims to "unite all Americans of German descent, and those who have the same ethical and moral values, into one politically potent force." Works to inform the public of the contributions of German-Americans to American society; opposes the "constant defamation of all things German by the American news media."

Gerontological Society of America.

Get Rich Through Multi-Level Selling: Build Your Own Sales and Distribution Organization. Gini G. Scott. Self-Counsel Press, Inc., 1704 N. State St. Bellingham, WA 98225. Phone: 877-877-6490 or (360)676-4530 Fax: (360)676-4530 E-mail: orderdesk@self-counsel.com • URL: http://www.self-counsel.com • 1998. $19.95. Third revised edition. (Self Counsel Business Series).

Getting Down to Business: Marketing and Women Lawyers. Deborah Graham. Glasser Legalworks, 150 Clove Rd. Little Falls, NJ 07424. Phone: 800-308-1700 or (973)890-0008 Fax: (973)890-0042 E-mail: orders@glasserlegalworks.com • URL: http://www.glasserlegalworks.com • 1996. $49.00. Provides advice to women lawyers concerning law firm marketing and business development. Five parts cover "The Internal Glass Ceiling", "Gender Gaps," "Clients' Attitudes," "Institutional Strategies," and "The Rules of the Game."

Getting It Printed: How to Work with Printers and Graphic Arts Services to Assure Quality, Stay on Schedule, and Control Costs. Mark Beach and Eric Kenly. F and W. Publications, Inc., 4700 E Galbraith Rd. Cincinnati, OH 45236-6709. Phone: 800-289-0963 or (513)531-2690 • URL: http://fwpublications.com • 1999. $32.99. Third edition.

Getting Started in Bonds. Sharon S. Wright. John Wiley and Sons, Inc., 111 River St. Hoboken, NJ 07030. Phone: 800-225-5945 or (201)748-6000 Fax: (201)748-6088 E-mail: info@wiley.com • URL: http://www.wiley.com • 2003. $19.95. Second edition. Serves as a primer on bonds for the individual investor. Covers government, municipal, corporate, mortgage-backed, international, and convertible bonds. Four parts: "Types of Bonds," "Fixed Income Fundamentals," "Factors Affecting Bonds," and "Fixed Income Investment Strategies". (Getting Started in...Series).

Getting Started in Futures. Todd Lofton. John Wiley and Sons, Inc., 111 River St. Hoboken, NJ 07030. Phone: 800-225-5945 or (201)748-6000 Fax: (201)748-6088 E-mail: info@wiley.com • URL: http://www.wiley.com • 2001. $19.95. Fourth edition. A general introduction to commodity and financial futures trading. Includes case studies and a glossary. (Getting Started in. Series).

Getting Started in Investment Planning Services. James E. Grant. CCH, Inc., 2700 Lake Cook Rd. Riverwoods, IL 60015. Phone: 800-835-5224 or (847)267-7000 E-mail: cust_serv@cch.com • URL: http://www.cch.com • 1999. $85.00. Second edition. Provides advice and information for lawyers and ac-

SOURCES CITED

countants who are planning to initiate fee-based investment services.

Getting Started in Mutual Funds. Alvin D. Hall. John Wiley and Sons, Inc., 111 River St. Hoboken, NJ 07030. Phone: 800-225-5945 or (201)748-6000 Fax: (201)748-6088 E-mail: info@wiley.com • URL: http://www.wiley.com • 1999. $18.95. (Getting Started in. Series).

Getting Started in Real Estate Investing. Michael C. Thomsett and others. John Wiley and Sons, Inc., 111 River St. Hoboken, NJ 07030. Phone: 800-225-5945 or (201)748-6000 Fax: (201)748-6088 E-mail: info@wiley.com • URL: http://www.wiley.com • 1998. $19.95. Second edition. (Getting Started in. Series.)

Getting Started in Stocks, Bonds, Online Investing. Alvin D. Hall. John Wiley and Sons, Inc., 111 River St. Hoboken, NJ 07030. Phone: 800-225-5945 or (201)748-6000 Fax: (201)748-6088 E-mail: info@wiley.com • URL: http://www.wiley.com • 1999. $56.85. (Getting Started in. Series).

Getting Your Book Published. Christine S. Smedley and Mitchell Allen. Sage Publications, Inc., 2455 Teller Rd. Thousand Oaks, CA 91320. Phone: 800-818-7243 or (805)499-9774 Fax: 800-583-2665 or (805)499-0871 E-mail: webmaster@sagepub.com • URL: http://www.sagepub.com • 1993. $59.95. A practical guide for academic and professional authors. Covers the initial book prospectus, contract negotiation, production procedures, and marketing. (Survival Skills for Scholars, vol. 10).

Getting Yours; The Complete Guide to Government Money. Matthew Lesko. Putnam Publishing Group, 375 Hudson St. New York, NY 10014-3657. Phone: 800-788-6262 or (212)336-2000 Fax: 800-227-9604 or (212)366-2643 E-mail: online@penguinputnam.com • URL: http://www.penguinputnam.com • 1987. $14.95. Third edition. (Penguin Handbook Series).

GFWC Clubwoman: Magazine of the General Federation of Women's Club. General Federation of Women's Clubs, 1734 N St., N.W. Washington, DC 20036. Phone: (202)347-3168 Fax: (202)835-0246 E-mail: gfwc@gfwc.org • URL: http://www.gfwc.org • Bimonthly. $6.00 per year.

Giannini Foundation of Agricultural Economics. University of California at Berkeley

Gift Association of America., 172 White Pine Way Harleysville, PA 19426-2851. Phone: (610)584-3108 Fax: (610)584-7860 E-mail: info@giftassn.com • URL: http://www.giftassn.com • Formerly Gift and Decorative Accessories Association of America.

Gift, Housewares and Home Textiles Buyers Directory. Douglas Publications, Inc., 2807 N. Parham Rd. Richmond, VA 23294. Phone: 800-223-1719 or (804)762-9600 Fax: (804)217-8999 E-mail: info@douglaspublications.com • URL: http://www.douglaspublications.com • Annual. $259.00. Lists more than 7,300 companies with names of over 15,200 buyers.

Gift/Specialty Store. Entrepreneur Media, Inc., 2445 McCabe Way Irvine, CA 92614. Phone: 800-421-2300 or (949)261-2325 Fax: (949)261-0234 E-mail: entmag@entrepreneur.com • URL: http://www.entrepreneur.com • Looseleaf. $59.50. A practical guide to starting a gift shop. Covers profit potential, start-up costs, market size evaluation, owner's time required, site selection, lease negotiation, pricing, accounting, advertising, promotion, etc. (Start-Up Business Guide No. E1218.)

Gifts and Decorative Accessories Market. Available from MarketResearch.com, 641 Ave. of the Americas, Third Floor New York, NY 10011. Phone: 800-298-5699 or (212)807-2629 Fax: (212)807-2716 E-mail: order@marketresearch.com • URL: http://www.marketresearch.com • 2001. $2,250.00. Published by Unity Marketing. Market research report covering growth trends and projections.

Gifts and Decorative Accessories: The International Business Magazine of Gifts, Tabletop, Gourmet, Home Accessories, Greeting Card and Social Stationery. Reed Business Information, 360 Park Ave., S New York, NY 10010. Phone: 800-446-6551 or (646)746-6400 Fax: (646)746-7028 E-mail: corporatecommunications@reedbusiness.com • URL: http://www.reedbusiness.com • Monthly. $53.95 per year. Includes *Annual Directory*.

Gifts and Tablewares. Business Information Group, 1450 Don Mills Rd. Don Mills, ON, Canada M3B 2X7. Phone: 800-387-0273 or (416)510-6804 Fax: (416)442-2200 E-mail: rgreif@businessinformationgroup.com • URL: http://www.businessinformationgroup.ca • Seven times a year. $47.95 per year. Includes annual *Trade Directory*.

Giftware News: The International Magazine for Gifts, China and Glass, Stationery and Home Accessories. Talcott Communications Corp., 20 N Wacker Dr., Suite 1865 Chicago, IL 60606. Phone: (312)849-2220 Fax: (312)849-2174 E-mail: giftwarenews@talcott.com • URL: http://www.giftwarenews.net • Monthly. $36.00 per year. Includes annual *Directory*.

Gilder Technology Report. George Gilder, editor. Gilder Publishing, 291A Main St. Great Barrington, MA 01230. Phone: 888-484-2727 or (413)644-2100 Fax: (413)644-2123 E-mail: info@gildertech.com • URL: http://www.gildertech.com • Monthly. $295.00 per year. Newsletter. Makes specific recommendations for investing in technology stocks. (A joint publication of Forbes Magazine and the Gilder Technology Group.)

Gilson Trademark Protection and Practice. Jerome Gilson. LexisNexis Matthew Bender, 1275 Broadway Albany, NY 12204. Phone: 800-424-4200 or (518)487-3000 Fax: (518)487-3584 E-mail: bookstore.support@lexisnexis.com • URL: http://www.bender.com • $1,279.00. 13 looseleaf volumes. Periodic supplementation. Covers U. S. trademark practice.

Giving U.S.A: The Annual Report on Philanthropy. American Association of Fund-Raising Counsel. AAFRC Trust for Philanthropy, 10293 N Meridian St., Ste. 175 Indianapolis, IN 46290. Phone: 800-462-2372 or (317)816-1613 Fax: (317)816-1633 E-mail: info@aafrc.org • URL: http://www.aafrc.com • Annual. $65.00.

Giving USA Update. American Association of Fund-Raising Counsel. AAFRC Trust for Philanthropy, 10293 N Meridian St., Ste. 175 Indianapolis, IN 46290. Phone: 800-462-2372 or (317)816-1613 or (317)816-1633 E-mail: info@aafrc.com • URL: http://www.aafrc.com • Quarterly. $110.00 per year. Legal, economic and social essays on philanthropy.

Glass and Glass Products. Available from MarketResearch.com, 641 Ave. of the Americas, Fourth Floor New York, NY 10011. Phone: 800-298-5699 or (212)807-2629 Fax: (212)807-2642 E-mail: order@marketresearch.com • URL: http://www.marketresearch.com • 2002. $3,850.00. Published by Global Industry Analysts. Provides worldwide market research data, including profiles of major glass and glass products companies.

Glass Association of North America., 2945 S.W. Wanamaker Dr., Suite A Topeka, KS 66614. Phone: (785)271-0208 Fax: (785)271-0166 E-mail: gana@glasswebsite.com • URL: http://www.glasswebsite.com • Flat Glass Jobbers Association.

Glass Digest—Buyers' Guide. Ashlee Publishing Company Inc., 18 E 41st St., 20th Fl. New York, NY 10017-6222. Phone: (212)376-7722 Fax: (212)376-7723 E-mail: ashleepub@aol.com • URL: http://www.ashlee.com • Covers: manufacturers, importers, and other suppliers who furnish the products and services used by fabricators, distributors, retailers, and installers of flat glass, architectural metal, and related products. Entries include: Supplier name, address, phone, and, when furnished, cable address, TWX, fax, and telex.

Glass Digest: Trade Magazine Serving the Flat Glass, Architectural Metal an d Allied Products Industry. Ashlee Publishing Co., Inc., 18 E. 41st St. New York, NY 10017-6222. Phone: (212)376-7722 Fax: (212)376-7723 E-mail: publisher@ashlee.com • URL: http://www.ashlee.com • Monthly. $40.00 per year.

Glass Factory Directory of North America., P.O. Box 2267 Hempstead, NY 11550-2267. Phone: (516)481-2188 E-mail: manager@glassfactorydir.com • URL: http://www.glassfactorydir.com • Annual. $30.00. Lists over 600 glass factory locations in the U.S., Canada and Mexico.

Glass Magazine. National Glass Association, 8200 Greensboro Dr., Suite 302 McLean, VA 22102. Phone: (703)442-4890 Fax: (703)442-0630 E-mail: nga@glass.org • URL: http://www.glass.org • Monthly. $34.95 per year.

Glass Molders, Pottery, Plastics, and Allied Workers International Union.

Glass Packaging Institute., 700 N Fairfax St., Ste. 510 Alexandria, VA 22314. Phone: (703)684-6359 Fax: (703)299-1543 E-mail: info@gpi.org • URL: http://www.gpi.org • Glass container manufacturers and suppliers. Promotes the manufacture, use, and recycling of glass containers and closures. Develops and evaluates testing procedures and equipment; conducts experimental activities in glass packaging; develops designs and specifications for glass containers and finishes; conducts advertising and promotional campaigns for the generic products; develops and maintains constructive relationships with various public and government agencies at the local, regional, state, and national levels.

Glass Science. Robert H. Doremus. John Wiley and Sons, Inc., 111 River St. Hoboken, NJ 07030. Phone: 800-526-5368 or (201)748-6000 Fax: (201)748-6088 E-mail: info@wiley.com • URL: http://www.wiley.com • 1994. $120.00. Second edition.

Global Data Locator. George T. Kurian. Bernan Associates, 4611-F Assembly Dr. Lanham, MD 20706-4391. Phone: 800-274-4447 or (301)459-2255 Fax: 800-865-3450 or (301)459-0056 E-mail: info@bernan.com • URL: http://www.bernan.com • 1997. $89.00. Provides detailed descriptions of international statistical sourcebooks and electronic databases. Covers a wide variety of trade, economic, and demographic topics.

Global Development Finance. The World Bank Group, 1818 H St., N. W. Washington, DC 20433. Phone: 800-645-7247 or (202)477-1234 Fax: (202)477-6391 E-mail: books@worldbank.org • URL: http://www.worldbank.org • Annual. $400.00.

The Global Drinks Market Impact Databank. M. Shanken Communications, Inc., 387 Park Ave., S New York, NY 10016. Phone: 800-344-0763 or (212)684-4424 Fax: (212)684-5424 E-mail: retailsales@mshanken.com Annual. $2,975.00. Detailed compilations of data for various segments of the liquor, beer, and soft drink industries.

Global Economic Prospects and the Developing Countries, 1999-2000. The World Bank Group, 1818 H St., N. W. Washington, DC 20433. Phone: 800-645-7247 or (202)477-1153 Fax: (202)477-6391 E-mail: books@worldbank.org • URL: http://www.worldbank.org • 2001. $25.00. Examines the economic connections between industrial and developing countries, with a different theme in each edition.

Global Economic Prospects 2004. The World Bank Group, 1818 H St., N. W. Washington, DC 20433. Phone: 800-645-7247 or (202)477-1234 Fax: (202)477-6391 E-mail: books@worldbank.org • URL: http://www.worldbank.org • 2003. $38.00. "..offers an in-depth analysis of the economic prospects of developing countries." Emphasis is on the impact of recessions and financial crises. Regional statistical data is included.

Global Employment Trends. Claire Harasty and Dorothea Schmidt. International Labour Organization, 1828 L St., N.W., Suite 600 Washington, DC 20036-5121. Phone: (202)653-7652 Fax: (202)653-7687 E-mail: washington@ilo.org • URL: http://www.ilo.org • 2003. $22.95. Provides an analysis of "current labour market trends around the world." Emphasis is on how the "global economic downturn" has affected various regions and economic groups.

Global Encyclopedia of Wine. Peter Forrestal, editor. Wine Appreciation Guild, 360 Swift Ave. South San Francisco, CA 94080. Phone: 800-231-9463 or (650)866-3020 Fax: (650)866-3513 E-mail: info@wineappreciation.com • URL: http://www.wineappreciation.com • 2001. $75.00. Includes CD-ROM. Thirty-six "leading wine experts" discuss wines from all regions of the world. Includes a wine reference table with concise descriptions, price ranges, and food compatibility of 5,000 wines. Definitions of wine terms and a detailed index are included.

Global Equity Selection Strategies. Ross P. Bruner, editor. Fitzroy Dearborn Publishers, Inc., 919 N. Michigan Ave., Suite 760 Chicago, IL 60611. Phone: 800-850-8102 or (312)587-0131 Fax: (312)587-1049 E-mail: fitzroy@aol.com • URL: http://www.fitzroydearborn.com • 1999. $65.00. Written by various professionals in the field of international investments. Contains six major sections covering growth, value, size, price momentum, sector rotation, and country allocation. (Glenlake Business Monographs).

Global Finance. Global Finance Media, Inc., 411 Fifth Ave., 7th Fl. New York, NY 10016. Phone: (212)337-5900 Fax: (212)447-7750 E-mail: srodriguez@gfmag.com • URL: http://www.gfmag.com • Monthly. $350.00 per year. Edited for corporate financial executives and money managers responsible for "cross-border" financial transactions.

Global Market Share Planner. Euromonitor International, 122 South Michigan Ave., Suite 810 Chicago, IL 60603. Phone: 800-577-3876 or (312)922-1115 Fax: (312)922-1157 E-mail: info@euromonitor.com • URL: http://www.euromonitor.com • 2003. $5,900.00. Six volumes. Second edition. Provides detailed profiles and market share rankings of major consumer product companies in North America, Latin America, Europe, South Africa, and the Asia-Pacific region. Covers firms operating in key consumer markets: beverages, food products, household products, and personal care items. (Volumes are available individually.)

Global Money Management. Aspen Publishers, Corporate Headquarters, 76 Ninth Ave., 7th Fl. New York, NY 10011. Phone: 800-638-8437 or (212)771-0600 Fax: (212)771-0885 E-mail: customer.service@aspenpubl.com • URL: http://www.iijournals.com • Description: Reports on international fund management, including investment strategies; pension fund searches; hires for consultants, managers, and custodians; performance measurement; developing markets, and significant personnel changes.

Global Power Report: An Exclusive Biweekly Covering the Cogeneration and Small Power Market. Platts, 2 Penn Plz., 25th Fl. New York, NY 10121-2298. Phone: 800-875-2887 or (212)904-2070 Fax: (212)512-4502 E-mail: suppport@platts.com • URL: http://www.platts.com • Biweekly. $1,165.00 per year. Newsletter. Covers industry trends, new projects, new contracts, rate changes, and regulations, with emphasis on the Federal Energy Regulatory Commission (FERC). Formerly *Cogeneration Report*.

Global Seed Guide: World Reference Source for the Commercial Seed Industry. Ball Publishing, 335 N River St. Batavia, IL 60510. Phone: (630)208-9080 Fax: (630)208-9350 E-mail: info@ballpublishing.com • URL: http://www.ballpublishing.com • Annual. $40.00. Includes company listings, type of business, type of seed, research centers, industry data, events calendar, and associations.

Global Seed Markets. Theta Reports, 1775 Broadway, Suite 511 New York, NY 10019. Phone: (212)262-8230 Fax: (212)262-8234 E-mail: lschacterle@thetareports.com • URL: http://www.thetareports.com • 2000. $1,040.00. Market research data. Covers the major seed sectors, including cereal crops, legumes, oilseed crops, fibre crops, and beet crops. Provides analysis of biotechnology developments. (Theta Report No. DS208E.)

Globalbase. Gale Cengage Learning, 27500 Drake Rd. Farmington Hills, MI 48331-3535. Phone: 800-877-GALE or (248)699-GALE Fax: 800-414-5043 or (248)699-8069 E-mail: galeord@gale.com • URL: http://gale.cengage.com • Provides more than one million online summaries of business, industrial, and economic news reports from more than 1,000 publications worldwide. Covers a wide range of material appearing in international trade journals, professional magazines, and newspapers. Time period is 1984 to date, with weekly updates. Inquire as to online cost and availability.

Globalization: A Bibliography with Indexes. Marina Elbakidze. Nova Science Publishers, Inc., 400 Oser Ave., Suite 1600 Hauppauge, NY 11788-3619. Phone: (631)231-7269 Fax: (631)231-8175 E-mail: novascience@earthlink.net • URL: http://www.novapublishers.com • 2002. $59.00. Covers various aspects of globalization: effect on society, trade, economics, politics, business, technology, and the environment. Includes author, title, and subject indexes.

The Globe and Mail Online. The Globe and Mail Co., 444 Front St., W. Toronto, ON, Canada M5V 2S9. Phone: 800-268-9128 or (416)585-5250 Fax: (416)585-5249 • URL: http://www.globeandmail.ca • Contains full text of more than 1.1 million news stories and articles that have appeared daily in *The Globe and Mail: Canada's National Newspaper*, including "Report on Business." Time span is 1977 to date. Daily updates of the complete newspaper are provided. Inquire as to online cost and availability.

Globe and Mail Report on Business. Globe and Mail Publishing, 444 Front St., W. Toronto, ON, Canada M5V 2S9. Phone: 800-268-9128 or (416)585-5000 Fax: (416)585-5641 E-mail: comments@globeandmail.ca • URL: http://www.globeandmail.ca • Daily. Controlled circulation. Provides general coverage of business activity in Canada, with emphasis on the economy, foreign trade, technology, and personal finance.

Globeandmail.com: Canada's Best Source for News. Bell Globemedia Publishing, Inc.Phone: 800-268-9128 or (416)585-5000 Fax: (416)585-5249 • URL: http://www.globeandmail.ca • Web site provides access to selected sections of *The Globe and Mail: Canada's National Newspaper*. Includes current news, national issues, career information, "Report on Business," and other topics. Keyword searching is offered for "a seven-day archive of the portion of the *Globe and Mail* that we publish online" (refers to the Web site). Daily updates. Fees: free.

Glossary of Geology. Robert L. Bates and Julia A. Jackson. American Geological Institute, 4220 King St. Alexandria, VA 22302-1502. Phone: (703)379-2480 Fax: (703)379-7563 E-mail: pubs@agiweb.org • URL: http://www.agiweb.org • 2000. $110.00. Fourth edition.

Glossary of Insurance Policy Terms. Organization for Economic Cooperation and Development, OECD Washington Center, 2001 L St., N. W., Suite 650 Washington, DC 20036-4922. Phone: 800-456-6323 or (202)785-6323 Fax: (202)785-0350 E-mail: washington.contact@oecd.org • URL: http://www.oecdwash.org • 1999. $30.00. "The selected topics range from insurance policy regulation/supervision to general trade issues and include technical terms related to issues such as claims, premiums, and provisions." Edited for government, academic, business, and insurance organizations.

Glossary of Terminology in Abstracting, Classification, Indexing, and Thesaurus Construction. Hans H. Wellisch. Information Today, Inc., 143 Old Marlton Pike Medford, NJ 08055-8750. Phone: 800-300-9868 or (609)654-6266 Fax: (609)654-4309 E-mail: custserv@infotoday.com • URL: http://www.infotoday.com • 2000. $20.00. Second edition. Published in conjunction with the American Society of Indexers (ASI). In addition to terms related to indexing, includes terms for the most common types of documents and their parts.

Glucksman Institute. New York University

Going Live: Starting and Running a Virtual Reference Service. Steve Coffman. American Library Association, 50 E Huron St. Chicago, IL 60611-2795. Phone: 800-545-2433 or (312)944-6780 Fax: (312)440-9374 E-mail: ala@ala.org • URL: http://www.ala.org • 2003. $42.00. Serves as a practical manual for libraries wishing to start a Web-based, always available reference service. Includes a bibliography by Bernie Sloan.

Going Private. American Lawyer Media, Inc., 105 Madison Ave. New York, NY 10016. Phone: 800-888-8300 or (212)779-9200 Fax: (212)481-8110 E-mail: lawcatalog@amlaw.com • URL: http://www.lawcatalog.com/ • Looseleaf. $169.00. Updated as needed. Discusses the legal ramifications of a publicly-owned company "going private" by way of a sale, leveraged buyout, reverse stock split, or merger. (Law Journal Press).

Going Public and the Public Corporation. Harold S. Bloomenthal and Samuel Wolff. West Group, 610 Opperman Dr. Eagan, MN 55123. Phone: 800-328-4880 or (651)687-7000 Fax: 800-340-9378 E-mail: www.bookstore@westgroup.com • URL: http://www.westgroup.com • Semiannual. $803.50 per year. Seven looseleaf volumes. Includes legal forms and documents. (Securities Law Series).

Going Public Handbook: Going Public, the Integrated Disclosure System, and Exempt Financing. Harold S. Bloomenthal. West Group, 610 Opperman Dr. Eagan, MN 55123. Phone: 800-328-4880 or (651)687-7000 Fax: 800-340-9378 E-mail: bookstore@westgroup.com • URL: http://www.westgroup.com • 2003. $304.00. Covers public financing from initiation of underwriting to closing. (Securities Handbook Series).

Going Public in Good Times and Bad: A Legal and Business Guide. Robert G. Heim. American Lawyer Media, Inc., 105 Madison Ave. New York, NY 10016. Phone: 800-888-8300 or (212)779-9200 Fax: (212)481-8110 E-mail: lawcatalog@amlaw.com • URL: http://www.lawcatalog.com/ • 2002. $29.95. Provides practical advice for corporate officers and attorneys. Covers such items as underwriter selection, registration statements, relevant securities laws, and liability concerns. Contains examples of forms needed at various stages of taking a company public.

Gold Institute., 1112 16th St. NW, Ste. 240, 101 Constitution Ave., Ste. 500E Washington, DC 20036. Phone: (202)835-0185 Fax: (202)835-0155 E-mail: info@goldinstitute.org • URL: http://www.goldinstitute.org • Miners, refiners, bullion suppliers, manufacturers of gold products, wholesalers of gold investment products. Promotes the common business interests of the gold industry as a whole by providing members with relevant, current statistical data and other information on the gold industry. Also provides early identification of changes in the operating climate for the industry, and information and statistics on the gold industry for the media and the public. Acts as a spokesperson for the industry.

Gold Newsletter. Jefferson Financial Inc., 2400 Jefferson Hwy., Ste. 600 Jefferson, LA 70121. Phone: 800-877-8847 or (504)837-3033 Fax: (504)837-4885 E-mail: info@accessintel.com Description: Reports on the relationship between gold and the economic system. Covers news of the "world gold markets, other precious metals markets, monetary reform, international economics, inflation, deflation, future of gold prices," and related economic and political matters. **Remarks:** Also available via e-mail.

Gold: Progress in Chemistry, Biotechnology, and Technology. Hubert Schmidbaur. John Wiley and Sons, Inc., 111 River St. Hoboken, NJ 07030. Phone: 800-225-5945 or (201)748-6000 Fax: (201)748-6088 E-mail: info@wiley.com • URL: http://www.wiley.com • 1999. $330.00. Covers various uses of gold, as in jewelry, decoration, electronics, and medicine. Includes detailed information on the history, chemistry, and metallurgical aspects of gold.

Goldsmiths' Kress Library of Economic Literature: A Consolidated Guide to the Microfilm Collection, 1976-1983. Primary Source Microfilm, 12 Lunar Dr. Woodbridge, CT 06525-2398. Phone: 800-444-0799 or (203)397-2600 Fax: (203)397-3892 E-mail: sales@gale.com • URL: http://www.psmedia.com • $1,200.00. Four volumes. Individual volumes, $300.00. An estimated 60,000 titles on 1,500 reels of microfilm (or fiche).

Golf Course Builders Association of America., 727 O St. Lincoln, NE 68503-1323. Phone: (402)476-4444 Fax: (402)476-4489 E-mail: gcbaa@aol.com • URL: http://www.gcbaa.org • Members are golf course builders, designers, and suppliers. Formerly Golf Course Builders Association.

Golf Course Directory. National Golf Foundation, 1150 S., U.S. Highway 1, Suite 401 Jupiter, FL 33477. Phone: 800-733-6006 or (561)744-6006 Fax: (561)744-6107 E-mail: ngf@ngf.org • URL: http://www.ngf.org • Annual. Free to members; non-members, $199.00. Three volumes. Lists about 15,000 public and private golf facilities, with information as to size, number of holes, year opened, and practice ranges.

Golf Course Management. Golf Course Superintendents Association of America, 1421 Research Park Dr. Lawrence, KS 66049-3859. Phone: 800-472-7878 or (785)841-2240 E-mail: infobox@gcsaa.org • URL: http://www.gcsaa.org • Monthly. $48.00 per year. Contains articles on golf course maintenance, equipment, landscaping, renovation, and management.

Golf Course News: The Newspaper for the Golf Course Industry. United Publications, Inc., P.O. Box 997 Yarmouth, ME 04096-1997. Phone: 800-441-6982 or (207)846-0600 Fax: (207)846-0657 Monthly. $60.00 per year. Edited for golf course superintendents, managers, architects, and developers.

Golf Course Superintendents Association of America., 1421 Research Park Dr. Lawrence, KS 66049-3859. Phone: 800-472-7878 or (785)841-2240 or (785)832-4430 Fax: (785)832-4488 E-mail: infobox@gcsaa.org • URL: http://www.gcsaa.org • Members are golf course superintendents and others concerned with golf course maintenance and improvement. Formerly National Greenkeepimg Superintendents Association.

Golf Digest: How to Play, What to Play, Where to Play. The Golf Digest Companies, 20 Westport Rd. Wilton, CT 06897. Phone: 800-727-4653 or (203)761-5100 Fax: (203)761-5129 Monthly. $14.97 per year. A high circulation consumer magazine for golfers. Editions available in various languages. Supplement available *Golf Digest Woman*.

Golf Index. Ingledue Travel Publications, 444 Burchett St. Glendale, CA 91203. Phone: (818)247-5530 Fax: (818)247-5535 Semiannual. $40.00 per year. Provides directory listings of golf courses and resorts around the world. Contains information on golf travel packages, tour operators, and tournaments.

Golf Magazine. Time Inc., Two Park Ave. New York, NY 10016. Phone: (212)779-5000 Fax: (212)481-8085 • URL: http://www.golfmagazine.com • Monthly. $19.95 per year. Popular consumer magazine for golfers.

Golf Magazine Buyers' Guide. Times4 Media Inc., Two Park Ave. New York, NY 10016-5601. Phone: 800-227-2224 or (212)779-5000 Fax: (212)779-5522 • URL: http://www.golfmagazine.com • Annual. Price on application. Lists golf club manufacturers, with description of products and prices.

Golf Manufacturers and Distributors Association., 4925 Bonnie Rd. Kettering, OH 45440-2126. Phone: (440)460-3977 Members are exhibitors at the Professional Golfers' Association annual trade show. Seeks to improve the "business habits" of professional golfers.

Golf Participation in the U. S. Available from MarketResearch.com, 641 Ave. of the Americas, Third Floor New York, NY 10011. Phone: 800-298-5699 or (212)807-2629 Fax: (212)807-2716 E-mail: order@marketresearch.com • URL: http://www.martketresearch.com • 1998. $250.00. Published by the National Golf Foundation. Market research report on consumer attitudes and industry statistics.

Golf U.S.A.: A Guide to the Best Golf Courses and Resorts. Corey Sandler. McGraw-Hill, 1221 Ave. of the Americas New York, NY 10020. Phone: 800-722-4726 or (212)512-2000 Fax: (212)512-4502 E-mail: customer.service@mcgraw-hill.com • URL: http://www.mcgraw-hill.com • 2001. $16.95. Second edition. Describes 2,500 public and private golf courses. (Econoguides Series).

Golf World Business. The Golf Digest Companies, 20 Westport Rd. Wilton, CT 06897. Phone: 800-727-4653 or (203)761-5100 Fax: (203)761-5129 E-mail: mark.murphy@golfdigest.com • URL: http://www.golfdigest.com • Nine times a year. $72.00 per year. Edited for retailers of golf equipment. Formerly *Golf Shop Operations*.

Golf World Business—Buyers' Guide. Advance Magazine Publishers Inc., 20 Westport Rd. Wilton, CT 06897. Phone: 800-438-0491 or (203)373-7176 Fax: (203)761-5135 E-mail: ashleepub@aol.com Publication includes: List of companies supplying golfing equipment, components, and apparel, accessories, golf shoes, balls, and bags, shafts, clubs, club fitting programs. Entries include: Company name and address; descriptions of products available, including model names, component materials, and suggested retail prices.

Golfdom. Elsevier, 655 Avenue of the Americas New York, NY 10010-1710. Phone: 800-598-6008 or (212)989-5800 Fax: 800-535-9935 or (212)633-5680 E-mail: custserv@elsevier.com • URL: http://www.elsevier • Monthly. $30.00 per year. Covers marketing, financing, insurance, human resources, maintenance, environmental factors, and other aspects of golf course management. *Formerly Golf Business*.

Golfweek: America's Golf Newspaper. Turnstile Publishing Co., 1500 Park Center Dr. Orlando, FL 32835. Phone: 800-830-5182 or (407)563-7000 Fax: (407)563-7076 E-mail: email@golfweek.com • URL: http://www.golfweek.com • Weekly. $69.95 per year. Includes biweekly supplement, *Golfweek's Strictly Business*, covering business and marketing for the golfing industry.

Golob's Environmental Business Report. World Information Systems, PO Box 038535, Harvard Sq. Sta., P.O. Box 535 Cambridge, MA 02238. Phone: 800-666-4430 or (617)491-5100 Fax: (617)492-3312 E-mail: info@golob.com Description: Provides news and analysis on environmental business, hazardous materials, waste management, and pollution prevention and control. Covers regulations, legislation and court decisions, new technology, contract opportunities and awards, and conferences.

Gonzo Marketing: Winning Through Worst Practices. Christopher Locke. John Wiley and Sons, Inc., 111 River St. Hoboken, NJ 07030. Phone: 800-225-5945 or (201)748-6000 Fax: (201)748-6088 E-mail: custserv@wiley.com • URL: http://www.wiley.com • 2001. $29.95. An iconoclastic, entertaining view of e-commerce advertising and marketing (banners, pop-ups, spam, etc.). States the obvious: most Web advertising is more annoying than effective.

Good Fruit Grower. Fruit Commission, 105 S. 18th St., Suite 217 Yakima, WA 98901. Phone: (509)575-2315 Fax: (509)469-9476 E-mail: getit@goodfruit.com • URL: http://www.goodfruit.com • Semimonthly. $30.00 per year.

Good Sam Recreational Vehicle Club., PO Box 6888 Englewood, CO 80155-6888. Phone: 800-234-3450 or (805)667-4100 Fax: (805)667-4454 E-mail: info@goodsamclub.com • URL: http://www.goodsamclub.com • Recreational vehicle enthusiasts who act as "Good Samaritans" on the road by aiding members in distress. Offers free benefits to members, including credit card loss protection, trip routing service, and mail forwarding. Provides comprehensive discount programs on camping fees, RV financing and insurance, tour programs, emergency road service and magazine subscriptions for members. Conducts charitable program.

Good Samaritan Coalition., c/o Hazardous Materials Advisory Council, 1110 Vermont Ave. NW, Ste. 250 Washington, DC 20005. Phone: (202)728-1460 E-mail: info@fundfornewpriorities.org Organizations supporting passage of "Good Samaritan" legislation which would protect from liability volunteer third parties who render assistance at the scene of an emergency involving hazardous material. Entities such as chemical firms, petroleum companies, and liquid propane gas dealers are often called upon to assist police and fire departments in hazardous material emergencies such as train derailments and overturned trucks. Good Samaritan legislation would protect from lawsuit those providing assistance in the event that their actions aggravate rather than alleviate the hazardous condition, provided that assistance is not rendered in a grossly negligent manner.

Goodwill Industries International, Inc.

Gourmet News: The Business Newspaper for the Gourmet Industry. United Publications, Inc., P.O. Box 1056 Yarmouth, ME 04096-1997. Phone: 800-441-6982 or (207)846-0600 Fax: (207)846-0657 E-mail: info@gourmetnews.com • URL: http://www.gourmetnews.com • Monthly. $60.00 per year. Provides news of the gourmet food industry, including specialty food stores, upscale cookware shops, and gift shops.

Gourmet Retailer. VNU Business Media, 770 Broadway New York, NY 10003-9595. Phone: 800-344-7119 or (646)654-4500 Fax: (646)654-7212 • URL: http://www.vnubusinessmedia.com • Monthly. Free to qualified personnel; others, $75.00 per year. Covers upscale food and housewares, including confectionery items, bakery operations, and coffee.

The Gourmet/Specialty Foods Market. Available from MarketResearch.com, 641 Ave. of the Americas, Third Floor New York, NY 10011. Phone: 800-298-5699 or (212)807-

2629 Fax: (212)807-2716 E-mail: order@marketresearch.com • URL: http://www.marketresearch.com • 2001. $3,299.00. Market research data. Published by Packaged Facts. Discusses current trends, with projections to 2005.

Governing: The States and Localities., 1100 Connecticut Ave. ,N.W. Suite 1300 Washington, DC 20036. Phone: 888-955-4688 or (202)862-8802 Fax: (202)862-0032 E-mail: mailbox@governing.com • URL: http://www.governing.com • Monthly. $39.95 per year. Edited for state and local government officials. Covers finance, office management, computers, telecommunications, environmental concerns, etc.

Government Affairs Yellow Book: Who's Who in Government Affairs. Leadership Directories, Inc., 104 Fifth Ave. New York, NY 10011. Phone: (212)627-4140 Fax: (212)645-6931 E-mail: info@leadershipdirectories.com • URL: http://www.leadershipdirectories.com • Semiannual. $265.00 per year. Includes in-house lobbyists of corporations and organizations, Political Action Committees (PACs), congressional liaisons, and independent lobbying firms.

Government Assistance Almanac: The Guide to Federal, Domestic, Financial and Other Programs Covering Grants, Loans, Insurance, Personal Payments and Benefits. J. Robert Dumouchel, editor. Omnigraphics, Inc., 615 Griswold St. Detroit, MI 48226. Phone: 800-234-1340 or (313)961-1340 Fax: 800-875-1340 or (313)961-1383 E-mail: info@omnigraphics.com • URL: http://www.omnigraphics.com • Annual. $235.00. Describes more than 1,400 federal assistance programs available from about 50 agencies. Includes statistics, a directory of 3,000 field offices, and comprehensive indexing.

Government Auditing Standards. Available from U. S. Government Printing Office, Washington, DC 20402. Phone: (202)512-1800 Fax: (202)512-2250 E-mail: gpoaccess@gpo.gov • URL: http://www.access.gpo.gov • 1994. $6.50. Revised edition. Issued by the U. S. General Accounting Office (http://www.gao.gov). Contains standards for CPA firms to follow in financial and performance audits of federal government agencies and programs. Also known as the "Yellow Book."

Government by Judiciary: The Transformation of the Fourteenth Amendment. Raoul Berger. Liberty Fund, Inc., 8335 Allison Pointe Trail, No. 300 Indianapolis, IN 46250-1684. Phone: 800-955-8335 or (317)842-0880 Fax: (317)579-6060 E-mail: webmaster@libertyfund.org • URL: http://www.libertyfund.org • 1997. $22.00. Second revised edition.

Government Computer News: The Newspaper Serving Computer Users Throughout the Federal Government. Business Information, Inc., 8601 Georgia Ave., Ste. 300 Silver Spring, MD 20910. Phone: 800-417-0258 or (301)650-2129 Fax: (301)350-2111 E-mail: ttemin@gcn.com • URL: http://www.gcn.com • 32 times a year. Free to qualified personnel.

Government Contract Litigation Reporter: Covers Defense Procurement Fraud Litigation As Well as False Claims Acts (Qui Tam) Litigation. Andrews Publications, 175 Strafford Ave., Bldg. 4, Suite 140 Wayne, PA 19087. Phone: 800-345-1101 or (610)225-0510 Fax: (610)225-0501 E-mail: customer@andrewspub.com • URL: http://www.andrewspub.com • Semimonthly. $875.00 per year. Newsletter. Provides reports on defense procurement fraud lawsuits.

Government Contractor. West DC Editorial, 901 15th St., NW, Ste. 200 Washington, DC 20005. Phone: (202)842-7570 Fax: (202)842-7565 E-mail: west.customer.service@cengage.com • URL: http://www.west.thomson.com • Weekly. $1,700.00 per year.

Government Contracts and Subcontract Leads Directory. Government Data Publications, Inc., 1661 McDonald Ave. Brooklyn, NY 11230. Phone: (718)627-0819 Fax: (718)998-5960 E-mail: govdata@tiac.net 1992. $89.50. Firms which received prime contracts for production of goods or services from federal government agencies during the preceeding twelve months. Formerly *Government Contracts Directory*.

Government Contracts: Law, Administration and Procedure. LexisNexis Matthew Bender, 1275 Broadway Albany, NY 12204. Phone: 800-424-4200 or (518)487-3000 Fax: (518)487-3584 E-mail: bookstore.support@lexisnexis.com • URL: http://www.bender.com • Quarterly. $1,329.00 per year. 17 looseleaf volumes. Coverage of important aspects of government contracts.

Government Contracts Reports. CCH, Inc., 2700 Lake Cook Rd. Riverwoods, IL 60015. Phone: 800-835-5224 or (847)267-7000 E-mail: cust_serv@cch.com • URL: http://www.cch.com • Weekly. $2,600.00 per year. 10 looseleaf volumes. Laws and regulations affecting government contracts.

Government Contracts Update: How to Target, Win, and Perform Government Contracts. United Communications Group (UCG), 11300 Rockville Pike, Suite 1100 Rockville, MD 20852-3030. Phone: 888-287-2223 or (301)287-2700 Fax: (301)816-8945 E-mail: webmaster@ucg.com • URL: http://www.ucg.com • Biweekly. $277.00 per year. Newsletter.

Government Discrimination: Equal Protection Law and Litigation. James A. Kushner. West Group, 610 Opperman Dr. Eagan, MN 55123. Phone: 800-328-4880 or (651)687-7000 Fax: 800-340-9378 E-mail: bookstore@westgroup.com • URL: http://www.westgroup.com • Semiannual. $244.00 per year. Looseleaf service. Covers discrimination in employment, housing, and other areas by local, state, and federal offices or agencies. (Civil Rights Series).

Government Employee Relations Report. BNA, Inc., 1231 25th St., NW Washington, DC 20037. Phone: 800-372-1033 E-mail: customercare@bna.com • URL: http://www.bna.com • Weekly. $1,144.00 per year. Three looseleaf volumes. Concerned with labor relations in the public sector.

Government Executive: Federal Government's Business Magazine. National Journal Group, Inc., 1501 M St., NW, Ste. 300 Washington, DC 20005. Phone: 800-424-2921 or (202)739-8500 Fax: (202)739-8511 E-mail: letters@govexec.com • URL: http://www.govexec.com • Monthly. $48.00 per year. Includes management of computerized information systems in the federal government.

Government Finance Officers Association. Government Finance Officers Association, 203 N LaSalle St., Ste. 2700 Chicago, IL 60601-1210. Phone: (312)977-9700 Fax: (312)977-4806 E-mail: communications@foundationcenter.org • URL: http://www.gfoa.org • Provides consulting and research services in state and local government finance and management. Areas of expertise include: accounting, budgeting, cash management, debt management, pension/benefits, revenue and expenditure forecasting, technology procurement, reengineering/privatization, and state/local fiscal relations.

Government Finance Officers Association of the United States and Canada., 203 N. LaSalle St., Ste. 2700 Chicago, IL 60601. Phone: (312)977-9700 Fax: (312)977-4806 E-mail: membership@gfoa.org • URL: http://www.gfoa.org • Formerly Municipal Finance Officers Association of United States and Canada.

Government Finance Review. Government Finance Officers Association, 180 N. Michigan Ave., Suite 800 Chicago, IL 60601. Phone: (312)977-9700 Fax: (312)977-4806 E-mail: gfr@gfoa.org Bimonthly. $30.00. per year.

Government Information on the Internet. Greg R. Notess. Bernan Associates, 4611-F Assembly Dr. Lanham, MD 20706-4391. Phone: 800-274-4447 or (301)459-2255 Fax: 800-865-3450 or (301)459-0056 E-mail: info@bernan.com • URL: http://www.bernan.com • Annual. $38.50. directory of publicly-accessible Internet sites maintained by the U. S. Government. Also includes selected foreign government sites, state sites, and non-government sites containing government-provided data.

Government Management Information Sciences., 8315 SW 183rd Ter., P.O. Box 421 Palmetto Bay, FL 33157. Phone: 800-460-7454 or (973)632-0470 Fax: (786)242-3925 E-mail: headquarters@gmis.org • URL: http://www.gmis.org • Represents state and local government agencies involved in Information Technology; while member agencies differ in many aspects, it is a homogenous group with similar interests dedicated to sharing with each other. Provides organizational support to eighteen state chapters. State chapters enable member agencies within a geographical area to develop close relationships and to foster the spirit and intent through cooperation, assistance and mutual support. Affiliated with five international sister organizations of local governments: KommITS in Sweden, SOCITM in United Kingdom, VIAG in the Netherlands, MISA in Canada, and ALGIM in New Zealand.

Government Phone Book USA: Your Comprehensive Guide to Federal, State, County, and Local Government Offices in the United States. Omnigraphics, Inc., 615 Griswold St. Detroit, MI 48226. Phone: 800-234-1340 or (313)961-1340 Fax: 800-875-1340 or (313)961-1383 E-mail: info@omnigraphics.com • URL: http://www.omnigraphics.com • Annual. $265.00. Contains more than 270,000 listings of federal, state, county, and local government offices and personnel, including legislatures. Formerly *Government Directory of Addresses and Phone Numbers*.

Government Prime Contractors Directory. Government Data Publications Inc., 2300 M St., NW Washington, DC 20037. Phone: 800-275-4688 or (718)627-0819 Fax: (718)998-5960 E-mail: gdp@govdata.com Covers: Organizations that received government prime contracts during the previous two years. Entries include: Contractor name and address, product/service; contractors with contracts of more than $500,000 are marked.

Government Primecontracts Monthly. Government Data Publications, Inc., 1155 Connecticut Ave., NW Washington, DC 20036. Phone: 800-275-4688 Fax: (718)998-5960 E-mail: gdp@govdata.com • URL: http://www.gordata.com • Monthly. $96.00 per year.

Government Product News. Penton Media, Inc., 1300 E. Ninth St. Cleveland, OH 44114. Phone: (216)696-7000 Fax: (216)696-1752 E-mail: information@penton.com • URL: http://www.penton.com • 13 times a year. $50.00 per year.

Government Publications News. Bernan Associates, 4611-F Assembly Dr. Lanham, MD 20706-4391. Phone: 800-274-4447 or (301)459-2255 Fax: 800-865-3450 or (301)459-0056 E-mail: info@bernan.com • URL: http://www.bernan.com • Monthly. Free. Controlled circulation newsletter providing information on recent publications from the U. S. Government Printing Office and selected international agencies.

Government Research Directory. Gale, 27500 Drake Rd. Farmington Hills, MI 48331-3535. Phone: 800-877-4253 or (248)699-4253 Fax: 800-414-5043 or (248)699-8065 E-mail: galeord@cengage.com • URL: http://gale.cengage.com • Covers: About 6,000 research and development facilities operated or sponsored by the United States or Canadian governments, including research centers, bureaus, and institutes; testing and experiment stations; data collection and analysis centers; government-supported user facilities; cooperative research programs; and major research-supporting service units. Entries include: Unit name, address, phone, fax, mail address, e-mail addresses, name of director, staff, year founded, parent agencies, description of activities and fields of research, special research facilities, publications, public services, and library collections.

Government Standard. American Federation of Government Employees, AFL-CIO, 80 F St., N.W. Washington, DC 20001. Phone: (202)639-6419 Fax: (202)639-6441 E-mail: communications@afge.org • URL: http://www.afge.org • Bimonthly. Membership.

Government Technology: Solutions for State and Local Government in the Information Age. E. Republic Inc., 100 Blue Ravine Rd. Folsom, CA 95630-4703. Phone: (916)363-5000 Fax: (916)363-5197 E-mail: donpears@govtech.net • URL: http://www.govtech.net • Monthly. Free to qualified personnel.

Government Union Review and Public Policy Digest. Public Service Research Foundation, 320 Maple Ave., E., Suite 4 Vienna, VA 22180-4742. Phone: (703)242-3575 Fax: (703)242-3579 E-mail: info@psrf.org • URL: http://www.psrf.org • Quarterly. $20.00 per year. Academic quarterly covering the labor relations field. Formerly *Government Union Review*.

Governmental Accounting Standards Board., 401 Merritt 7, PO Box 5116 Norwalk, CT 06856-5116. Phone: (203)847-0700 Fax: (203)849-9714 E-mail: webmaster@gasb.org • URL: http://www.gasb.org • Has established and maintains the Financial +Accounting Standards Board and the Financial +Accounting Standards Advisory Council. In 1984, organized the Governmental Accounting Standards Board and the Governmental Accounting Standards Advisory Council (see separate entries). FASB creates and improves standards of financial accounting and reporting by defining, and issuing, such standards; conducts and commissions research, statistical compilations, and other studies and surveys; holds meetings, conferences, and hearings with respect to financial accounting and reporting. FASAC consults with FASB about major technical issues, agenda of projects, assignment of priorities, and selection and organization of FASB task forces. GASB establishes accounting standards for state and local governmental entities. GASB consults with GASAC in a fashion similar to the FASB and FASAC. **Convention/Meeting:** none.

Governmental Research Association., PO Box 292300 Birmingham, AL 35229. Phone: (205)726-2482 Fax: (205)726-2900 E-mail: rancoble@nccppr.org • URL: http://www.graonline.org • Individuals professionally engaged in governmental research. Furthers research that will improve government in the public interest. Encourages development and use of effective methods of administration in government and standards for judging the results.

Governors' Staff Directory. National Governor's Association. National Governors' Association, 444 N Capitol St., Ste. 267 Washington, DC 20001-1512. Phone: (202)624-5300 Fax: (202)624-5313 E-mail: galeord@cengage.com • URL: http://www.nga.org • Publication includes: List of more than 1,000 key staff members and their titles in each of the 55 governor's offices. Entries include: Name of governor; addresses, phone numbers and fax numbers of governor's main, district, and Washington offices; names and titles of key staff members; separate listing of addresses and phone numbers of governors' chiefs of staff and media contacts; list of contacts in each office by issue area; list of NGA staff members, their titles, phone numbers, issue areas, and description of the resources NGA provides.

Gower Handbook of Customer Service. Peter Murley, editor. Ashgate Publishing Co., 101 Cherry St., Ste. 420 Burlington, VT 05401-4405. Phone: 800-535-9544 or (802)865-7641 Fax: (802)865-7847 E-mail: adonahue@ashgate.com • URL: http://www.ashgate.com • 1996. $129.95. Consists of 40 articles (chapters) written by various authors. Among the topics covered are benchmarking, customer surveys, focus groups, control groups, employee selection, incentives, training, teamwork, and telephone techniques. Published by Gower in England.

Gower Handbook of Internal Communications. Eileen Scholes, editor. Ashgate Publishing Co., 101 Cherry St., Ste. 420 Burlington, VT 05401-4405. Phone: 800-535-9544 or (802)865-7641 Fax: (802)865-7847 E-mail: adonahue@ashgate.com • URL: http://www.ashgate.com • 1997. $124.95. Consists of 38 chapters written by various authors, with case studies. Covers more than 45 communication techniques, "from team meetings to web sites." Published by Gower in England.

Gower Handbook of Management Development. Alan Mumford, editor. Ashgate Publishing Co., 101 Cherry St., Ste 420 Burlington, VT 05401-4405. Phone: 800-535-9544 or (802)865-7641 Fax: (802)865-7847 E-mail: adonahue@ashgate.com • URL: http://www.ashgate.com • 1995. $129.95. Fourth edition. Consists of 28 chapters written by various authors. Published by Gower in England.

Gower Handbook of Project Management. J. Rodney Turner and Stephen J. Simister. Ashgate Publishing Co., 101 Cherry St., Ste. 420 Burlington, VT 05401-4405. Phone: 800-535-9544 or (802)865-7641 Fax: (802)865-7847 E-mail: adonahue@ashgate.com • URL: http://www.ashgate.com • 2000. $144.95. Third edition. Consists of chapters written by various authors, with bibliographical references and index. Published by Gower in England.

Gower Handbook of Quality Management. Dennis Lock, editor. Ashgate Publishing Co., 101 Cherry St., Ste. 420 Burlington, VT 05401-4405. Phone: 800-535-9544 or (802)865-7641 Fax: (802)865-7847 E-mail: adonahue@ashgate.com • URL: http://www.ashgate.com • 1994. Second edition. Price on application. Consists of 41 chapters written by various authors. Published by Gower in England.

Gower Handbook of Training and Development. John Prior, editor. Ashgate Publishing Co., 101 Cherry St., Ste. 420 Burlington, VT 05401-4405. Phone: 800-535-9544 or (802)865-7641 Fax: (802)865-7847 E-mail: adonahue@ashgate.com • URL: http://www.ashgate.com • 1999. $144.95. Third edition. Consists of 40 chapters written by various authors. Includes glossary and index. Published by Gower in England.

GPO Access. U. S. Government Printing Office Sales Program, Bibliographic Systems BranchPhone: 888-293-6498 or (202)512-1530 Fax: (202)512-1262 E-mail: gpoaccess@gpo.gov • URL: http://www.access.gpo.gov • Web site provides searching of the GPO's Sales Product Catalog (SPC), also known as Publications Reference File (PRF). Covers all "Government information products currently offered for sale by the Superintendent of Documents." There are also specialized search pages for individual databases, such as the *Code of Federal Regulations*, the *Federal Register*, and *Commerce Business Daily*. Updated daily. Fees: Free.

GPO Sales Product Catalog. U. S. Government Printing Office, Washington, DC 20402. Phone: 888-293-6498 or (202)512-0132 Fax: (202)512-1355 E-mail: gpoaccess@gpo.gov • URL: http://www.access.gpo.gov • An online guide to federal government publications in print (currently for sale), forthcoming, and recently out-of-print. Daily updates. Inquire as to online cost and availability.

GQ: Gentleman's Quarterly for Men. Conde Nast Publications, Inc., 4 Times Sq., 5th Fl. New York, NY 10036. Phone: (212)286-2860 Fax: (212)286-7093 E-mail: gqmag@aol.com • URL: http://www.condenast.com • Monthly. $15.00 per year.

GRA Professional Directory of Who's Who in Governmental Research. Governmental Research Association, Inc., Samford University, 402 Samford Hall Birmingham, AL 35229-7017. Phone: (205)726-2482 Fax: (205)726-2900 Annual. $50.00. Lists information on governmental research organization throughout the country.

GRA Reporter. Governmental Research Association, 402 Samford Hall Birmingham, AL 35229. Phone: (205)726-2482 Fax: (205)726-2900 E-mail: James.Williams@samford.edu • URL: http://www.graonline.org • Description: Provides a research bibliography and news of members and their organizations. Recurring features include news of research, reports of meetings, and notices of publications available.

Graduate Aeronautical Laboratories. California Institute of Technology, Div. of Engineering and Applied Science

Graduate Management Admission Council., 1600 Tysons Blvd., Ste. 1400 McLean, VA 22102. Phone: (866)505-6559 or (703)749-0131 Fax: (703)749-0169 E-mail: webmaster1@gmac.com • URL: http://www.gmac.com • Graduate schools of management and business administration. Works to establish criteria for use in admission to graduate management programs. Provides professional development for academic administrators and seminars for admissions officers. Maintains Graduate +Management Admission Search Service, a program that provides institutions with the names of qualified students with desirable characteristics. Employs Educational Testing Service to develop and administer the Graduate Management Admission Test. Conducts research on student selection issues and political and social issues related to graduate management education.

Graduate Record Examinations Board., PO Box 6000, 225 Phillips Blvd., PO Box 6000 Princeton, NJ 08541-6000. Phone: (866)473-4373 or (609)771-7670 Fax: (610)290-8975 E-mail: gre-info@rosedale.org • URL: http://www.ets.org/gre • Participants are appointees of the Association of Graduate Schools in Association of American Universities, the Council of Graduate Schools, and the GRE Board. Has responsibility for the Graduate Record Examinations Program (GRE) to assist in graduate school selection. Seeks to ensure that the program is carried out in the best interests of graduate education, the students, and the schools. Educational Testing Service provides technical advice, research expertise, professional counsel, and administers the GRE. Graduate Record Examinations, first administered in 1937, were initiated as a joint venture of the Carnegie Foundation for the Advancement of Teaching and the graduate school deans of four eastern U.S. universities. The examination and programs in which they were used became the responsibility of ETS when it began operating in 1948, until 1966, when the present structure was formed in order to give broader representation to the graduate education community.

Grain and Milling Annual. Sosland Publishing Co., 4800 Main St., Ste. 100 Kansas City, MO 64112. Phone: 800-338-6201 or (816)756-1000 Fax: (816)756-0494 E-mail: worldgrain@sosland.com • URL: http://www.sosland.com • Annual. $100.00. Features listings of the major grain facilities in the U.S. and Canada. Provides an annual overview of the U.S. grain industry and a complete reference to equipment and service suppliers. Formerly *North American Grain and Milling Annual*.

Grain Elevator and Processing Society., 301 Fourth Ave., S., Ste. 365 Minneapolis, MN 55415-0026. Phone: (612)339-4625 Fax: (612)339-4644 E-mail: info@geaps.com • URL: http://www.geaps.com • Formerly Society of Grain Elevator Superintendents.

Grains: Production, Processing, Marketing. Chicago Board of Trade, 141 W. Jackson Blvd., Suite 2210 Chicago, IL 60654-2994. Phone: 800-572-3276 or (312)435-3500 E-mail: comments@cbot.com • URL: http://www.cbot.com • 1992. $12.00. Revised edition.

Grants for Arts, Culture, and the Humanities. The Foundation Center, 79 Fifth Ave. New York, NY 10003-3076. Phone: 800-424-9836 or (212)620-4230 Fax: (212)807-3677 E-mail: orders@fdncenter.org • URL: http://www.fdncenter.org • 1997. $75.00. (Grants Guides Series).

Grants for Libraries and Information Services. The Foundation Center, 79 Fifth Ave. New York, NY 10003-3076. Phone: 800-424-9836 or (212)620-4230 Fax: (212)807-3677 E-mail: orders@fdncenter.org • URL: http://www.fdncenter.org • Annual. $75.00. Foundations and organizations which have awarded grants made the preceding year for public, academic, research, special, and school libraries; for archives and information centers; for consumer information; and for philanthropy information centers.

Grants for Libraries Hotline. Quinlan Publishing Group, Marine Industrial Pk., 23 Drydock Ave., 6th Fl. Boston, MA 02210. Phone: 800-229-2084 or (617)542-0048 Fax: (617)345-9646 E-mail: info@quinlan.com • URL: http://www.quinlan.com • Monthly. $129.00 per year. Newsletter. Provides news of grants and awards specifically for libraries (http://www.grantshotline.com). Includes "Deadline Update," a list of awarding agencies or programs, approximate dollar amounts available, deadlines, contacts (telephone numbers), and dates of newsletter profiles.

Grant's Interest Rate Observer. James Grant, editor. Grant's Financial Publishing Inc., 30 Wall St. New York, NY 10005-2201. Phone: (212)809-7994 Fax: (212)809-8426 E-mail: jdiamond@grantspub.com • URL: http://www.grantspub.com • Biweekly. $725.00 per year. Newsletter containing detailed analysis of money-related topics, including interest rate trends, global credit markets, fixed-income investments, bank loan policies, and international money markets.

Grants Policy Directives. U.S. Dept. of Health, and Human Services. Available from U.S. Government Printing Office, Washington, DC 20402. Phone: (202)512-1800 Fax: (202)512-2250 E-mail: gpoaccess@gpo.gov • URL: http://www.accessgpo.gov • $219.00. Periodic supplementation. Provides guidelines on the fiscal and administrative aspects of grant management to all granting agencies of the Dept. of Health and Human Services.

Grants Register. Palgrave Macmillan Ltd., 175 5th Ave. New York, NY 10010. Phone: 888-330-8477 or (212)982-3900 Fax: 800-672-2054 E-mail: customerservice@vhpsva.com • URL: http://www.palgrave.com • Covers: over 3,500 sources in the United Kingdom, Ireland, Australia, Canada, the United States, and other English-speaking areas which award financial aid for graduate study, research, or travel, including scholarships, fellowships, grants, awards for creative work, etc. Many are not available to United States nationals. Entries include: Name of awarding organization, name of award, address, subjects, purpose, number of awards offered and their value, place and duration of tenancy, eligibility requirements, application procedure.

GrantSelect. Oryx Press, 88 Post Rd. West Westport, CT 06881. Phone: 800-225-5800 or (203)226-3571 Fax: (203)750-9790 E-mail: customer-service@greenwood.com • URL: http://www.greenwood.com • Online service provides detailed descriptions of more than 10,000 grants offered by government and organizations in the U. S. Includes grants in a wide variety of subject fields. Contains current information with daily updates. Inquire as to online cost and availability.

Grantsmanship Center Magazine: A Compendium of Resources for Nonprofit Organizations. Grantsmanship Center, P.O. Box 17220 Los Angeles, CA 90017. Phone: 800-421-9512 or (213)482-9860 Fax: (213)482-9863 E-mail: marc@tgci.com • URL: http://www.tgci.com • Irregular. Free to qualified personnel. Contains a variety of concise articles on grant-related topics, such as program planning, proposal writing, fundraising, non-cash gifts, federal project grants, benchmarking, taxation, etc.

Granville Market Letter. Joseph Granville, editor., P.O. Box 413006 Kansas City, MO 64141. Phone: 800-876-5388 46 times a year. $250.00 per year.

Graphic Artists Guild., 32 Broadway, Ste. 1114 New York, NY 10004-1612. Phone: (212)791-3400 Fax: (212)791-0333 E-mail: admin@gag.org • URL: http://gag.org • Professional graphic artists who work in the disciplines of illustration, graphic design, surface design, computer graphics, and cartoons, and create work for national magazines, newspaper syndicates, books, television, advertising, corporate and promotional materials. Aims to: raise the business and ethical standards in the industry; provide legal and educational services to members; increase public appreciation of graphic artists as professionals. Maintains professional discipline meetings and provides professional education services for each chapter.

Graphic Artists Guild Handbook of Pricing and Ethical Guidelines: Pricing and Ethical Guidelines. Graphic Artists Guild, 90 John St., Suite 403 New York, NY 10038-3202. Phone: (212)791-3400 Fax: (212)791-0333 • URL: http://www.gag.org • 2001. $34.95. 10th edition.

Graphic Arts Blue Book. Reed Business Information, 360 Pk. Ave. S New York, NY 10010. Phone: 800-446-6551 or (646)746-6400 Fax: (646)746-6734 E-mail: customerservice@vhpsva.com • URL: http://www.reedbusiness.com • Covers: printing plants, bookbinders, imagesetters, platemakers, paper merchants, paper manufacturers, printing machinery manufacturers and dealers, and others serving the graphic arts industry (Standard Industrial Classification (SIC) code 2600, 2700). Eight editions: New York edition (7,000 establishments) covers metropolitan New York and the state of New Jersey; Southeastern edition (10,500 establishments) covers Kentucky, Tennessee, Alabama, Mississippi, Virginia (except Washington suburbs), North Carolina, South Carolina, Georgia, and Florida; Northeastern edition (6,000 establishments) covers Connecticut, Maine, Massachusetts, New Hampshire, New York (upstate only), Rhode Island, and Vermont and the eastern Canadian provinces; Delaware Valley-Ohio edition (8,500 establishments) covers Pennsylvania, Maryland, Delaware, District of Columbia and its Virginia suburbs, and Ohio; Midwestern edition (13,000 establishments) covers Illinois, Indiana, Iowa, Michigan, Minnesota, Missouri, Wisconsin, North and South Dakota; Southwestern edition (5,500 establishments) covers Arizona, southern California, Hawaii, southern Nevada; Pacific Northwestern edition (5,500 establishments), covers northern California, northern Nevada, Oregon, Washington, Montana, Idaho, Wyoming, Utah, Alaska, and the western provinces of Canada. Texas central edition (8000 establishments) covering Texas, Colorado, New Mexico, Oklahoma, Louisiana, Kansas, Missouri, and Nebraska. Entries include: Company name, address, phone, names and titles of executives, name of buyer, list of products or services, year established.

Graphic Arts Monthly Sourcebook. Cahners Publishing Co., 360 Pk. Ave. S New York, NY 10010. Phone: 800-446-6551 or (646)746-6400 E-mail: corporatecommunications@reedbusiness.com • URL: http://www.reedbusiness.com • Covers: About 1,400 manufacturers and distributors of graphic arts equipment, supplies, and services, and 700 graphic arts dealers. Entries include: Company name, address, phone, name and title of contact.

Graphic Arts Monthly: The Magazine of the Printing Industry. Reed Business Information, 360 Park Ave., S New York, NY 10010. Phone: 800-662-7776 or (646)746-6400 E-mail: corporatecommunications@reedbusiness.com • URL: http://www.reedbusiness.com • Monthly. Free to qualified personnel; others, $142.99 per year.

Graphic Arts Technical Foundation., 200 Deer Run Rd. Sewickley, PA 15143-2600. Phone: 800-910-4283 or (412)741-6860 Fax: (412)741-2311 E-mail: gain@piagatf.org • URL: http://www.gain.net • Scientific, research, technical, and educational organization serving the international graphic communications industries. Conducts research in all graphic processes and their commercial applications. Conducts seminars, workshops, and forums on graphic arts and environmental subjects. Conducts educational programs, including the publishing of graphic arts textbooks and learning modules, videotapes and CD-ROMs and broadcast video seminars. Conducts training and certification program in sheet-fed offset press operating, Web Offset press operating, Image Assembly, and desktop publishing. Produces test images and quality control devices for the industry. Performs technical services for the graphic arts industry, including problem-solving, material evaluation, and plant audits.

Graphic Communications Conference of the International Brotherhood of Teamsters., 1900 L St. NW Washington, DC 20036. Phone: (202)462-1400 Fax: (202)721-0600 E-mail: webmessenger@gciu.org • URL: http://www.gciu.org • AFL-CIO; Serves as a Canadian Labour Congress.

Graphic Design: U.S.A. Kaye Publishing Corp., 120 E 56th St., Suite 440 New York, NY 10016. Phone: (212)534-5003 Fax: (212)534-4415 Monthly. $60.00.

Graphic Designer's Production Handbook. Norman Sanders and William Bevington. Hastings House Daytrips Publishers, 2601 Wells Ave., Suite 161 Fern Park, FL 32730. Phone: 800-206-7822 or (407)339-3600 Fax: (407)339-5900 E-mail: hastings_daytrips@earthlink.net • URL: http://www.hastingshousebooks.com • 1982. $12.95. Ninth edition. (Visual Communication Books Series).

Graphically Speaking: An Illustrated Guide to the Working Language of Design and Publishing. Mark Beach. Coast to Coast Books, P.O. Box 633 Manzanita, OR 97130. Phone: (503)368-5584 Fax: (503)368-5929 E-mail: mbeach@pdx.oneworld.com • URL: http://www.gettingitprinted.com • 1992. $29.50. Provides practical definitions of 2,800 terms used in printing, graphic design, publishing, and desktop publishing. Over 300 illustrations are included, about 40 in color.

Graphics, Visualization, and Usability Center. Georgia Institute of Technology, GVU Center, 801 Atlantic Dr. Atlanta, GA 30332-0280. Phone: (404)894-4488 Fax: (404)894-0673 E-mail: afb@cc.gatech.edu • URL: http://www.cc.gatech.edu/gvu/ • Research areas include computer graphics, multimedia, image recognition, interactive graphics systems, animation, and virtual realities.

Graphis Design: International Annual of Design and Illustration. Watson-Guptill Publications, 770 Broadway New York, NY 10003. Phone: 800-278-8477 or (646)654-

5000 Fax: (646)654-5487 E-mail: info@watsonguptill.com Annual. $69.00. Text in English, French, and German. Formerly *Graphis Annual*.

Graphis: International Journal of Visual Communication. Graphis Inc., 307 Fifth Ave., 10th Fl. New York, NY 10016. Phone: (212)532-9387 Fax: (212)213-3229 E-mail: carrie@graphis.com • URL: http://www.graphis.com • Bimonthly. $90.00 per year. Text in English, French and German.

Gravy Training: Inside the Real World of Business Schools. Stuart Crainer and Des Dearlove. Jossey-Bass, 989 Market St. San Francisco, CA 94103-1741. Phone: 888-378-2537 or (415)433-1740 Fax: 800-605-2665 or (415)433-0499 E-mail: jbsubs@jbp.com • URL: http://www.josseybass.com • 1999. $25.00. Provides a critical look at major American business schools. (Business and Management Series).

The Gray Sheet. F-D-C Reports Inc., 5550 Friendship Blvd., Ste. 1 Chevy Chase, MD 20815. Phone: 800-332-2181 or (301)657-9830 Fax: (301)656-3094 E-mail: fdcr@clarknet.com • URL: http://www.fdcreports.com • Description: Monitors the complex regulatory environment for devices, instrumentation, and diagnostics. Topics include device-related Congressional activity, Medicare reimbursement policies, international regulatory intiatives, enforcement and premarket approval programs at FDA's Center for Devices and Radiological Health. Recurring features include device approvals, 510(k) clearances, FDA recalls and seizures, mergers and acquisitions, and sales and earnings.

The Gray Sheet Reports: Medical Devices, Diagnostics and Instrumentation. F-D-C Reports, Inc., 5550 Friendship Blvd., Suite 1 Chevy Chase, MD 20815-7278. Phone: 800-332-2181 or (301)657-9830 Fax: (301)656-3094 • URL: http://www.fdcreports.com • Weekly. Institutions, $1,172.00 per year. Newsletter. Provides industry and financial news, including a medical sector stock index. Monitors regulatory developments at the Center for Devices and Radiological Health of the U. S. Food and Drug Administration.

Great American Trials. Gale Cengage Learning, 27500 Drake Rd. Farmington Hills, MI 48331-3535. Phone: 800-877-GALE or (248)699-4253 Fax: 800-414-5043 E-mail: gale.galeord@cengage.com • URL: http://gale.cengage.com • 2002. $170.00. Second edition. Two volumes. Contains discussions and details of momentous American trials from 1637 to 1993.

The Great Depression and New Deal Reference Library. Gale Cengage Learning, 27500 Drake Rd. Farmington Hills, MI 48331-3535. Phone: 800-877-GALE or (248)699-4253 Fax: 800-414-5043 E-mail: gale.galeord@cengage.com • URL: http://gale.cengage.com • 2002. $145.00. Three volumes. Individual volumes are available at $55.00. Includes *Great Depression and New Deal: Almanac; Great Depression and New Deal: Biographies* and *Great Depression and New Deal: Primary Sources*. (UXL imprint).

The Great Game: The Emergence of Wall Street as a World Power, 1653-2000. John S. Gordon. Gale Cengage Learning, 27500 Drake Rd. Farmington Hills, MI 48331-3535. Phone: 800-877-GALE Fax: 800-414-5043 E-mail: gale.galeord@cengage.com • URL: http://gale.cengage.com • 1999. $25.00. Provides a history of U. S. financial markets, featuring such key figures as Alexander Hamilton, Commodore Vanderbilt, J. P. Morgan, Charles Merrill, and Michael Milken.

Great Inflations of the 20th Century: Theories, Policies, and Evidence. Pierre L. Siklos, editor. Edward Elgar Publishing, Inc., 136 West St., Suite 202 Northampton, MA 01060. Phone: 800-390-3149 or (413)584-5551 Fax: (413)584-9933 E-mail: elgarinfo@e-elgar.com • URL: http://www.e-elgar.co.uk • 1995. $100.00. Contains reprints of papers on the history and economic analysis of major inflations.

Great Scouts! CyberGuides to Subject Searching on the Web. Margot Williams and others. Information Today, Inc., 143 Old Marlton Pike Medford, NJ 08055-8750. Phone: 800-300-9868 or (609)654-6266 Fax: (609)654-4309 E-mail: custserv@infotoday.com • URL: http://www.infotoday.com • 1999. $24.95. Contains descriptions of selected Web sites, arranged by subject. Covers business, investments, computers, travel, the environment, health, social issues, etc. (CyberAge Books.)

Great Toasts: From Births to Weddings to Retirement Parties and Everything in Between. Andrew Frothingham. Career Press, Inc., Three Tice Road Franklin Lakes, NJ 07417-1322. Phone: 800-227-3371 or (201)848-0310 Fax: (201)848-1727 E-mail: contact@careerpress.com • URL: http://www.careerpress.com • 2002. $13.99. Includes samples of toasts for business events.

The Greatest Direct Mail Sales Letters of All Time: Why They Succeed, How They Are Created, How You Can Create Great Sales Letters, Too. Richard S. Hodgson. Dartnell Corp., 350 Hiatt Dr. Palm Beach Gardens, FL 33418. Phone: 800-341-7874 or (561)622-6520 Fax: (561)622-2423 E-mail: custserv@lrp.com • URL: http://www.dartnellcorp.com • 1995. $69.95. Second revised edition. About 100 direct mail sales lettes on a variety of products are reprinted and analyzed.

Green Markets. Pike and Fischer, Inc., 1010 Wayne Ave., Suite 1400 Silver Spring, MD 20910-5600. Phone: 800-255-8131 or (301)562-1530 E-mail: pike@pf.com • URL: http://www.pf.com • Weekly. $915.00 per year. Newsletter including prices for potash and other agricultural chemicals.

The Green Sheet. F-D-C Reports, Inc., 5550 Friendship Blvd., Suite 1 Chevy Chase, MD 20815-7278. Phone: 800-332-2181 or (301)657-9830 Fax: (301)656-3094 E-mail: fdc.customer.service@elsevier.com • URL: http://www.fdcreports.com • Weekly. $109.00 per year. Newsletter for retailers and wholesalers of pharmaceutical products. Includes pricing developments and new drug announcements.

GreenBook. New York AMA, 60 E 42nd St., Ste. 1765 New York, NY 10165. Phone: (212)687-3280 Fax: (212)567-9242 E-mail: info@nyama.org • URL: http://www.greenbook.org • Annual. $100.00. Contains information on companies offering focus group facilities, including recruiting, moderating, and transcription services.

GreenBook Worldwide Directory of Marketing Research Companies and Services. New York AMA-Green Book, Lakewood Business Park, 4301 32nd St., Ste. E-11 Bradenton, FL 34210. Phone: 800-972-9202 or (941)752-4498 Fax: 800-879-3751 E-mail: greenbook@nyama.org • URL: http://www.greenbook.org • Annual. $250.00. Contains information in 300 categories on more than 2,500 market research companies, consultants, field services, computer services, survey research companies, etc. Indexed by specialty, industry, company, computer program, and personnel. Available online. Formerly *Greenbook Worldwide International Directory of Marketing Research Companies and Services*.

Greenhouse Grower. Meister Media, 37733 Euclid Ave. Willoughby, OH 44094-5992. Phone: 800-572-7740 or (440)942-2000 Fax: (440)975-3447 E-mail: info@meistermedia.com • URL: http://www.meistermedia.com • 14 times a year. $37.45 per year. Concerned with all crops grown under glass or plastic.

Greeting Card Association., 1156 15th St. NW, Ste. 900 Washington, DC 20005-1717. Phone: (202)393-1778 Fax: (202)331-2714 E-mail: info@greetingcard.org • URL: http://www.greetingcard.org • Publishers of greeting cards and suppliers of materials.

Greeting Cards. Available from MarketResearch.com, 641 Ave. of the Americas, Fourth Floor New York, NY 10011. Phone: 800-298-5699 or (212)807-2629 Fax: (212)807-2642 E-mail: order@marketresearch.com • URL: http://www.marketresearch.com • 2002. $3,950.00. Published by Global Industry Analysts. Provides worldwide market research data, including profiles of major greeting card companies.

Gregg Reference Manual. William A. Sabin. McGraw-Hill, Two Penn Plaza New York, NY 10121. Phone: 800-722-4726 or (212)904-2000 Fax: (212)904-6096 E-mail: customer.service@mcgraw-hill.com • URL: http://www.mcgraw-hill.com • 2004. $46.55. 10th edition. Covers grammar, usage, and style, including changes evolving from the use of computers and the Internet. (Imprint: Irwin Professional Publishing.)

Gregory C. Chow Econometric Research Program. Princeton University

Grey House Directory of Special Issues: A Guide to Business Magazines' Buyer's Guides & Directory Issues. Grey House Publishing, 185 Millerton Rd. Millerton, NY 12546. Phone: 800-562-2139 or (518)789-8700 Fax: (518)789-0556 E-mail: books@greyhouse.com • URL: http://www.greyhouse.com • 2001. $175.00. Second edition. Provides information on more than 2,500 specialized directories issued by business and trade journals, arranged according to 90 industry groups.

The Grey House Performing Arts Directory. Grey House Publishing, 185 Millerton Rd., PO Box 860 Millerton, NY 12546. Phone: 800-562-2139 or (518)789-8700 Fax: (518)789-0556 E-mail: customerservice@greyhouse.com • URL: http://www.greyhouse.com • Covers: More than 9,000 dance companies, instrumental music programs, opera companies, choral groups, theatre companies, performing arts series, and performing arts facilities. Entries include: Mailing address, telephone and fax numbers, e-mail addresses, Web sites, mission statement, key management contacts, and facility information such as capacity, season, and attendance.

Grinding and Abrasive Magazine. Abrasive Magazine, Inc., PO Box 11 Byron Center, MI 49315. Phone: (616)530-2220 Fax: (616)530-6466 E-mail: abrasivesmagazine@attbi.com • URL: http://www.abrasivesmagazine.com • Eight times a year. $27.00 per year. Formerly *Abrasive Magazine*.

Grits and Grinds. Norton Co., One New Bond St. Worcester, MA 01606. Phone: (508)795-5000 Quarterly. Free.

Grocery Headquarters: The Newspaper for the Food Industry. Trend Publishing, One E. Erie St., Suite 401 Chicago, IL 60611. Phone: 800-278-7363 or (312)654-2300 Fax: (312)654-2323 E-mail: info@groceryheadquarters.com • URL: http://www.groceryheadquarters.com • Monthly. $80.00 per year. Covers the sale and distribution of food products and other items sold in supermarkets and grocery stores. Edited mainly for retailers and wholesalers. Incorporates (Grocery Distribution).

Grocery Manufacturers of America., 1010 Wisconsin Ave., N.W., Suite 900 Washington, DC 20007. Phone: (202)337-9400 Fax: (202)337-4508 E-mail: info@gmabrands.com • URL: http://www.gmabrands.com • Members are global manufacturers of food and nonfood products sold in the United States.

Grocery Manufacturers of America, Inc., 2401 Pennsylvania Ave., NW, 2nd Fl. Washington, DC 20037. Phone: (202)337-9400 Fax: (202)337-4508 E-mail: info@gmabrands.com • URL: http://www.gmabrands.com • Absorbed Association of Sales and Marketing Companies.

Grolier Club., 47 E 60th St. New York, NY 10022. Phone: (212)838-6690 Fax: (212)838-2445 E-mail: ejh@grolierclub.org • URL: http://www.grolierclub.org • Persons concerned with the book arts. Named after Jean Grolier (1489-1565), French bibliophile. Conducts free public exhibitions per year.

Grossman on Circulation. Gordon W. Grossman. Primedia Business Magazines and Media, 9800 Metcalf Ave. Overland Park, KS 66212. Phone: 800-795-5445 or (913)341-1300 Fax: (913)967-1898 E-mail: subs@primediabusiness.com • URL: http://www.primediabusiness.com • Annual. $99.95. Covers magazine circulation management and marketing, with emphasis on circulaton incentives, such as free-issue offers, sweepstakes, premiums, "freemiums," and professional courtesy offers. Includes examples of promotions used by consumer and trade publications.

Ground Water. National Ground Water Association. Ground Water Publishing Co., 601 Dempsey Rd. Westerville, OH 43081-8978. Phone: 800-551-7379 or (614)898-7791 Fax: (614)898-7786 E-mail: ngwa@ngwa.org • URL: http://www.ngwa.org • Bimonthly. Members, $19.00 per year; nonmembers, $260.00 per year.

Group Against Smokers' Pollution., PO Box 632 College Park, MD 20741-0632. E-mail: gaspamerica@aol.com Nonsmokers who are adversely affected by tobacco smoke united to promote the rights of nonsmokers, educate the public about the problems of second-hand smoke, and regulate smoking in places where nonsmokers are exposed. Supports the establishment and enforcement of laws and other public policy measures which reduce environmental tobacco smoke. Provides information and referral services; distributes educational literature, buttons, posters, and bumper stickers. Helps members find local GASP chapters or establish a chapter.

Group Practice Journal. American Medical Group Practice Association, 1422 Duke St. Alexandria, VA 22314-3430. Phone: (703)838-0033 Fax: (703)548-1890 E-mail: roconnor@amga.org • URL: http://www.amga.org • 10 times a year. Institutions, $75.00 per year.

Growth Fund Guide: The Investor's Guide to Dynamic Growth Funds. Growth Fund Research, Inc., P.O. Box 6600 Rapid City, SD 57709. Phone: 800-621-8322 or (605)341-1971 Fax: (605)341-7260 Monthly. $99.00 per year. Newsletter. Covers no-load growth mutual funds.

Growth Stock Outlook. Charles Allmon, editor. Growth Stock Outlook Inc., 4405 East West Hwy., Ste. 305 Bethesda, MD 20814. Phone: 800-742-5476 or (301)654-5205 Fax: (301)986-0722 E-mail: James.Williams@samford.edu Description: Provides data on stock earnings, sales, price-earnings ratios, dividends, book values, returns on shareholder equity, and institutional holdings. Recommends specific companies for long-term investment. Recurring features include a stock selection guide, and a $10,000 supervised portfolio. **Remarks:** Subscription includes the supplements Junior Growth Stocks, New Issue Digest, and (see separate listings); also includes access to a telephone hotline.

GS1 US., Princeton Pike Corporate Center, 1009 Lenox Dr., Ste. 202 Lawrenceville, NJ 08648. Phone: (609)620-0200 Fax: (609)620-1200 E-mail: info@gs1us.org • URL: http://www.uc-council.org • Develops and implements standard-based, global supply chain solutions. Operates two wholly owned subsidiaries, UCCnet and RosettaNet, and co-manages the global EAN.UCC System with EAN International. Manages the United Nations Standard Products and Services Code (UNSPSC) for the United Nations Development Programme (UNDP). Evaluates the effects of brand and size demand, competitor actions, pricing policy, and shelf location of merchandise. Administers Universal Product Code and Symbol (UPC), Uniform Communications Standard (UCS), Warehouse Information Network Standard (WINS), and Voluntary Inter-Industry Communications Standard (VICSEDI).

Guerilla Trade Show Selling: New Unconventional Weapons and Tactics to Meet More People, Get More Leads, and Close More Sales. Jay C. Levinson and others. John Wiley and Sons, Inc., 111 River St. Hoboken, NJ 07030. Phone: 800-225-5945 or (201)748-6000 Fax: (201)748-6088 E-mail: info@wiley.com • URL: http://www.wiley.com • 1997. $21.95. (More People, Get More Leads and Close More Sales Series).

Guide for Authors: Manuscript, Proof, and Illustration. Payne E. Thomas. Charles C. Thomas Publishers, Ltd., 2600 S. First St. Springfield, IL 62704-9265. Phone: 800-258-8980 or (217)789-8980 Fax: (217)789-9130 E-mail: books@ccthomas.com • URL: http://www.ccthomas.com • 1993. $21.95. Fourth edition.

Guide to ACA Accredited Camps. American Camping Association, 5000 State Rd., 67 N. Martinsville, IN 46151-7902. Phone: 800-428-2267 or (765)342-8456 Fax: (765)342-2065 E-mail: bookstore@acacamps.org • URL: http://www.acacamps.org • Annual. $14.95. Lists over 2,000 summer camps. Included with subscription to *Camping Magazine*. Formerly *Guide to Accredited Camps*.

Guide to American Directories. Todd Publications, P.O. Box 635 Nyack, NY 10960. Phone: (845)358-6213 Fax: (845)358-6213 E-mail: toddpub@aol.com • URL: http://www.toddpublications.com • Biennial. $125.00. Provides more than 11,000 listings with descriptions, prices, etc.

Guide to Architecture Schools: Comprehensive Guide to Accredited Schools of Architecture in the United States and Canada. Association of Collegiate Schools of Architecture, 1735 New York Ave., N.W. Washington, DC 20006. Phone:

800-232-2724 or (202)785-2324 Fax: (202)628-0448 E-mail: info@acsa-arch.org • URL: http://www.acsa-arch.org • 1994. $19.95. Fifth edition. Descriptions of 120 accredited degree programs and related organizations in architecture. Formerly *Guide to Architecture Schools in North America*.

Guide to Arts Administration Training and Research. Americans for the Arts, One E. 53rd St. New York, NY 10022-4201. Phone: 800-321-4510 or (212)223-2787 Fax: (212)753-1325 E-mail: books@artusa.org • URL: http://www.artsusa.org • Triennial. $12.95. Lists 33 institutions.

Guide to Banks and Thrifts: A Quarterly Compilation of Financial Institutions Ratings and Analysis. Weiss Ratings, Inc., 4176 Burns Rd. Palm Beach Gardens, FL 33410. Phone: 800-289-9222 or (561)627-3300 Fax: (561)625-6685 E-mail: wr@weissinc.com • URL: http://www.weissratings.com • Quarterly. $438.00 per year. Emphasis is on rating of financial safety and relative risk. Includes annual summary.

Guide to Computer Animation: For TV, Games, Multimedia and Web. Marcia Kuperberg and others. Elsevier, 360 Park Ave., S New York, NY 10010-1710. Phone: 888-437-4636 or (212)989-5800 Fax: (212)633-3990 E-mail: usinfo-f@elsevier.com • URL: http://www.elsevier.com • 2002. $34.00. Covers the principles and techniques of digital animation, with advice on both software and hardware. (Visual Effects and Animation Series).

Guide to Computer Law. CCH, Inc., 2700 Lake Cook Rd. Riverwoods, IL 60015. Phone: 800-835-5224 or (847)267-7000 E-mail: cust_serv@cch.com • URL: http://www.cch.com • Semimonthly. $602.00 per year. Two looseleaf volumes.

Guide to Congress; Origins, History and Procedure. CQ Press, 1255 22nd St., NW, Ste. 400 Washington, DC 20037. Phone: 888-427-7737 or (202)729-1800 Fax: 800-380-3810 or (202)729-1863 E-mail: customerservice@cq.com • URL: http://www.cqpress.com • 2000. Fifth edition. Price on application.

Guide to Economic Indicators. Norman Frumkin. M. E. Sharpe, Inc., 80 Business Park Dr. Armonk, NY 10504. Phone: 800-541-6563 or (914)273-1800 Fax: (914)273-2106 E-mail: info@mesharpe.com • URL: http://www.mesharpe.com • 2000. $24.95. Third expanded revised edition. Provides detailed descriptions and sources of 50 economic indicators.

A Guide to Employee Relocation and Relocation Policy Development. Employee Relocation Council, 1720 N St., N. W. Washington, DC 20036. Phone: (202)857-0857 Fax: (202)467-4012 1987. $25.00. Second edition.

Guide to Employment Sources in the Library and Information Professions. American Library Association, Office for Human Resource Development and Recruitment, 50 E. Huron St. Chicago, IL 60611-2795. Phone: 800-545-2433 or (312)280-4282 Fax: (312)280-3256 E-mail: editionsmarketing@ala.org • URL: http://www.ala.org • Annual. Free. Associations and agencies offering library placement services.

Guide to Energy Efficient Commercial Equipment. Margaret Suozzo and others. American Council for an Energy Efficient Economy, 1001 Connecticut Ave., N. W., Suite 801 Washington, DC 20036. Phone: (202)429-0063 Fax: (202)429-0193 E-mail: info@aceee.org • URL: http://www.aceee.org • 1997. $25.00. Provides information on specifying and purchasing energy-saving systems for buildings (heating, air conditioning, lighting, and motors).

Guide to Energy Efficient Office Equipment. Loretta A. Smith and others. American Council for an Energy Efficient Economy, 1001 Connecticut Ave., N.W., Suite 801 Washington, DC 20036. Phone: (202)429-0063 Fax: (202)429-0193 E-mail: info@aceee.org • URL: http://www.aceee.org • 1996. $12.00. Second edition. Provides information on selecting, purchasing, and using energy-saving computers, monitors, printers, copiers, and other office devices.

Guide to EU Information Sources on the Internet. Euroconfidentiel S. A., Rue de Rixensart 18 B-1332 Genval, Belgium. Phone: 32 02 652 02 84 Fax: 32 02 653 01 80 • URL: http://www.euroconfidential.com • Annual. $210.00. Contains descriptions of more than 1,700 Web sites providing information relating to the European Union and European commerce and industry. Includes a quarterly e-mail newsletter with new sites and address changes.

Guide to Everyday Economic Statistics. Gary E. Clayton and Martin G. Giesbrecht. McGraw-Hill, 1221 Ave. of the Americas New York, NY 10020. Phone: 800-722-4726 or (212)512-2000 Fax: (212)512-4502 E-mail: customer.service@mcgraw-hill.com • URL: http://www.mcgraw-hill.com • 2001. $19.90. Fifth edition. Contains clear explanations of the commonly used economic indicators.

Guide to Federal Funding for Governments and Non-Profits. Government Information Services, 1725 K St., N.W., 7th Fl. Washington, DC 20006. Phone: 800-876-0226 Fax: (202)739-9657 Quarterly. $339.00 per year. Looseleaf service. Contains detailed descriptions of federal grant programs in economic development, housing, transportation, social services, science, etc. Semimonthly *Supplement* available: *Federal Grant Deadline Calendar*.

Guide to Federal Regulation of Derivatives. James Hamilton and others. CCH, Inc., 2700 Lake Cook Rd. Riverwoods, IL 60015. Phone: 800-835-5224 or (847)267-7000 E-mail: cust_serv@cch.com • URL: http://www.cch.com • 1998. $85.00. Explains the complex derivatives regulations of the Securities and Exchange Commission. Covers swap agreements, third-party derivatives, credit derivatives, mutual fund liquidity, and other topics.

Guide to Financial Reporting and Analysis. Eugene E. Comiskey and Charles W. Mulford. John Wiley and Sons, Inc., 111 River St. Hoboken, NJ 07030. Phone: 800-225-5945 or (201)748-6000 Fax: (201)748-6088 E-mail: info@wiley.com • URL: http://www.wiley.com • 2000. $75.00. Provides financial statement examples to illustrate the application of generally accepted accounting principles.

Guide to Franchising. Martin Mendelsohn. Continuum International Publishing Group, Inc., 370 Lexington Ave. New York, NY 10017-6503. Phone: 800-561-7704 or (212)953-5858 Fax: (212)953-5944 E-mail: info@continuum-books.com • URL: http://www.continuum-books.com • 1999. $32.95. Sixth edition.

A Guide to Hazardous Materials Management: Physical Characteristics, Federal Regulations, and Response Alternatives. Aileen Schumacher. Greenwood Publishing Group Inc., 88 Post Rd., W. Westport, CT 06881. Phone: 800-225-5800 or (203)226-3571 Fax: (203)431-2214 E-mail: customer-service@greenwood.com • URL: http://www.greenwood.com • 1988. $72.95.

Guide to HMOs and Health Insurers: A Quarterly Compilation of Health Insurance Company Ratings and Analysis. Weiss Ratings, Inc., 4176 Burns Rd. Palm Beach Gardens, FL 33410. Phone: 800-289-9222 or (561)627-3300 Fax: (561)625-6685 E-mail: wr@weissinc.com • URL: http://www.weissratings.com • Quarterly. $438.00 per year. Emphasis is on rating of financial safety and relative risk. Includes annual summary.

Guide to Life, Health, and Annuity Insurers: A Quarterly Compilation of Insurance Company Ratings and Analysis. Weiss Ratings, Inc., 4176 Burns Rd. Palm Beach Gardens, FL 33410. Phone: 800-289-9222 or (561)627-3300 Fax: (561)625-6685 E-mail: wr@weissinc.com • URL: http://www.weissratings.com • Quarterly. $438.00 per year. Emphasis is on rating of financial safety and relative risk. Includes annual summary.

Guide to Microforms in Print: Author-Title. Gale Group, 27500 Drake Rd. Farmington Hills, MI 48331-3535. Phone: 800-347-GALE or (248)699-4253 Fax: 800-814-5043 E-mail: gale.galeord@cengage.com • URL: http://gale.cengage.com • Annual. $450.00. Lists 166,000 publications from 417 publishers and distributors around the world. *Subject Guide*, $450.00. *Supplement* available, $185.00.

Guide to Microforms in Print: Subject Guide. Available from Gale Cengage Learning, 27500 Drake Rd. Farmington Hills, MI 48331-3535. Phone: 800-699-4253 or (248)699-4253 Fax: 800-414-5043 E-mail: gale.galeord@cengage.com • URL: http://gale.cengage.com • Annual. $450.00. Two volumes. Provides international coverage under 135 subject headings. Published by K. G. Saur.

Guide to Preparing Financial Statements. John R. Clay and others. Practitioners Publishing Co., PO Box 966 Fort Worth, TX 76101-0966. Phone: 800-323-8724 or (817)332-3709 Fax: (817)336-2433 • URL: http://www.ppc.com • 1998. Three looseleaf volumes. Price on application.

Guide to Preparing Nonprofit Financial Statements. Practitioners Publishing Co., PO Box 966 Fort Worth, TX 76101-0966. Phone: (817)332-3709 Fax: (817)336-2433 • URL: http://www.ppcnet.com • 2002. Three looseleaf volumes. Price on application.

Guide to Property and Casualty Insurers: A Quarterly Compilation of Insurance Company Ratings and Analysis. Weiss Ratings, Inc., 4176 Burns Rd. Palm Beach Gardens, FL 33410. Phone: 800-289-9222 or (561)627-3300 Fax: (561)625-6685 E-mail: wr@weissinc.com • URL: http://www.weissratings.com • Quarterly. $438.00 per year. Emphasis is on rating of financial safety and relative risk. Includes annual summary.

Guide to Record Retention Requirements in the Code of Federal Regulations. National Archives and Records Administration Office of the Federal Register. Bernan Associates, 4611-F Assembly Dr. Lanham, MD. Phone: 800-274-4447 1992. Price on application. Explains federal recordkeeping regulations for individuals and businesses.

Guide to Reference Books. Robert Balay and others. American Library Association, 50 E. Huron St. Chicago, IL 60611-2795. Phone: 800-545-2433 or (312)944-6780 Fax: (312)440-9374 E-mail: ala@ala.org • URL: http://www.ala.org • 1996. $275.00. 11th edition.

Guide to Shipbuilding, Repair, and Maintenance. Informa Marine and Transport, 69-77 Paul St. London EC2A 4LQ, United Kingdom. Phone: 44 20 7553 1000 Fax: 44 20 7553 1105 • URL: http://www.informaritime.com • Annual. Price on application. Provides worldwide coverage of shipbuilding, repair, and maintenance facilities and marine equipment suppliers for the maritime industry. (Included with subscription to *Lloyd's Ship Manager*.)

Guide to Special Issues and Indexes of Periodicals. Miriam Uhlan and Doris B. Katz, editors. Special Libraries Association, 1700 18th St., N. W. Washington, DC 20009-2514. Phone: (202)234-4700 Fax: (202)265-9317 E-mail: sla@sla.org • URL: http://www.sla.org • 1994. $59.00. Fourth edition. A listing, with prices, of the special issues of over 1700 U. S. and Canadian periodicals in business, industry, technology, science, and the arts. Includes a comprehensive subject index.

Guide to Stock Mutual Funds: A Quarterly Compilation of Mutual Fund Ratings and Analysis Covering Equity and Balanced Funds. Weiss Ratings, Inc., 4176 Burns Rd. Palm Beach Gardens, FL 33410. Phone: 800-289-9222 or (561)627-3300 Fax: (561)625-6685 E-mail: wr@weissinc.com • URL: http://www.weissratings.com • Quarterly. $438.00 per year. Emphasis is on rating of financial safety and relative risk. Includes annual summary.

Guide to Summer Camps and Summer Schools: An Objective, Comprehensive Reference Source. Porter Sargent Publishers, Inc., 11 Beacon St., Suite 1400 Boston, MA 02108. Phone: 800-342-7470 or (617)523-1670 Fax: (617)523-1021 E-mail: info@portersargent.com • URL: http://www.portersargent.com • 2002. $35.00. Over 1,300 summer camping, recreational, pioneering, and academic programs in the United States and Canada, as well as travel programs worldwide.

Guide to Superconductivity Books. Arnold Spinks, editor. Nova Science Publishers, Inc., 400 Oser Ave., Suite 1600 Hauppauge, NY 11788-3619. Phone: (631)231-7269 Fax: (631)231-8175 E-mail: novascience@earthlink.net • URL: http://www.novapublishers.com • 2002. $79.00. Covers books on superconductivity and its applications. Includes author, title, and subject indexes.

Guide to the Federal Budget 2000. Stanley E. Collender. The Century Foundation, 41 E. 70th St. New York, NY 10021. Phone: (212)535-4441 Fax: (212)535-7534 E-mail: info@tcf.org • URL: http://www.tcf.org • 1999. $22.95. A practical explanation of the federal budget for the most recent fiscal year.

Guide to the Project Management Body of Knowledge. Project Management Institute Staff. Project Management Institute, Four Campus Blvd. Newton Square, PA 19073-3299. Phone: (610)356-4600 Fax: (610)356-4647 E-mail: pmihq@pmi.org • URL: http://www.pmi.org • 2004. Price on application. Presents the fundamental tenets of project management. Covers the management of integration, scope, time, cost, quality, human resources, communications, risk, and procurement. Includes an extensive glossary. (Trial Lawyer's Series: Vol. 2).

Guide to the Use of Libraries and Information Sources. Jean K. Gates. McGraw-Hill, 1221 Ave. of the Americas New York, NY 10020. Phone: 800-722-4726 or (212)512-2000 Fax: (212)512-4502 E-mail: customer.service@mcgraw-hill.com • URL: http://www.mcgraw-hill.com • 1994. $36.56. Seventh edition. (Humanities, Social Sciences and World Languages Series).

A Guide to the World Bank. The World Bank, P. O. Box 960 Herndon, VA 20172-0960. Phone: 800-645-7247 or (703)661-1580 Fax: (703)661-1501 E-mail: books@worldbank.org • URL: http://www.worldbank.org/publications • 2003. $15.00. Covers history of the World Bank, with its organization, mission, and purpose.

Guide to U. S. Government Publications. Gale Cengage Learning, 27500 Drake Rd. Farmington Hills, MI 48331-3535. Phone: 800-877-GALE or (248)699-4253 Fax: 800-414-5043 E-mail: gale.galeord@cengage.com • URL: http://gale.cengage.com • Annual. $230.00. Catalogs "important series, periodicals, and reference tools" published annually by the federal government. Includes references to annual reports of various agencies.

Guidebook on Trading with China. United Nations Publications, Two United Nations Plaza, Room DC2-853 New York, NY 10017. Phone: 800-253-9646 or (212)963-8302 Fax: (212)963-3489 E-mail: publications@un.org • URL: http://www.un.org/publications • 1999. $75.00. Fifth edition. Serves to provide "a better understanding of China's economic policies, rules, and regulations." Includes information on China's trade and development planning.

Guidebook to Labor Relations. CCH, Inc., 2700 Lake Cook Rd. Riverwoods, IL 60015. Phone: 800-835-5224 or (847)267-7000 E-mail: cust_serv@cch.com • URL: http://www.cch.com • Annual. $12.00.

Guidebook to Managed Care and Practice Management Terminology. Norman Winegar and L. Michelle Hayter. Haworth Press, Inc., 10 Alice St. Binghamton, NY 13904-1580. Phone: 800-429-6784 or (607)722-5857 Fax: 800-895-0582 or (607)722-1424 E-mail: getinfo@haworthpressinc.com • URL: http://www.haworthpressinc.com • 1998. $39.95. Provides definitions of managed care "terminology, jargon, and concepts."

Guidebook to Pension Planning. CCH, Inc., 2700 Lake Cook Rd. Riverwoods, IL 60015. Phone: 800-835-5224 or (847)267-7000 E-mail: cust_serv@cch.com • URL: http://www.cch.com • Annual.

Guidebook to the Freedom of Information and Privacy Acts. Robert F. Bouchard and Douglas E. Franklin. West Group, 610 Opperman Dr. Eagan, MN 55123. Phone: 800-328-4880 or (651)687-7000 Fax: 800-340-9378 E-mail: bookstore@westgroup.com • URL: http://www.westgroup.com • Semiannual. $291.50 per year. Two looseleaf volumes. Includes procedures for requesting and acquiring business and government data.

Guidelines for Consumer Protection in the Context of Electronic Commerce. Organization for Economic Cooperation and Development, OECD Washington Center, 2001 L St., N. W., Suite 650 Washington, DC 20036-4922. Phone: 800-456-6323 or (202)785-6323 Fax: (202)785-0350 E-mail: washington.contact@oecd.org • URL: http://www.oecdwash.

org • 2000. $20.00. Provides a guide to effective consumer protection in online business-to-consumer transactions. Text in English and French.

Guild of Book Workers.

Guild of Book Workers-Membership List. Guild of Book Workers, 521 Fifth Ave. New York, NY 10175. Phone: (212)292-4444 Annual. $60.00. About 900 amateur and professional workers in the handbook crafts of bookbinding, calligraphy, illuminating, and decorative papermaking.

Guitars and Musical Instruments. Orion Research Corp., 14555 N. Scottsdale Rd., Suite 330 Scottsdale, AZ 85254-3457. Phone: 800-844-0759 Fax: 800-375-1315 E-mail: orion@bluebook.com • URL: http://www.netzone.com • Annual. $179.00. List of manufacturers of guitars and musical instruments. Original list prices and years of manufacture are also shown.

Guns and Ammo. PRIMEDIA Inc., 745 Fifth Ave. New York, NY 10151. Phone: 800-800-6848 or (212)448-4600 Fax: (212)252-7677 E-mail: information@primedia.com • URL: http://www.primedia.com • Monthly. $14.97 per year.

Guns Illustrated. Krause Publications Inc., 700 E State St. Iola, WI 54945-9642. Phone: 800-258-0929 or (715)445-2214 Fax: (715)445-4087 E-mail: info@krause.com • URL: http://www.krause.com • Publication includes: Lists of national and international firearms associations; manufacturers, importers, and distributors of firearms, shooting equipment, and services. Entries include: For associations—Name, address, phone, area of interest. For manufacturers and distributors—Name, address, phone, product or service provided. Principal content of publication is articles on hunting, handloading, ammunition, ballistics, collecting, gunsmithing, and customizing, as well as other related information.

Guns Magazine: Finest in the Firearms Field. Publishers Development Corp., 591 Camino de la Reina, Suite 200 San Diego, CA 92108. Phone: 888-732-2299 or (619)297-5350 Fax: (619)297-5353 E-mail: 74673.3624@compuserve.com Monthly. $19.95 per year. Annual *Supplement* available. Formerly *Guns*.

Guthrie Center for Real Estate Research.

H & R Block 2003 Income Tax Guide: Preparing America's Taxes for Over 40 Years. Simon & Schuster Trade, 1230 Ave. of the Americas New York, NY 10020. Phone: 800-223-2348 or (212)698-7000 Fax: 800-943-9831 or (212)698-7007 E-mail: consumer.customerservice@simonandschuster.com • URL: http://www.simonsays.com • 2002. $16.00. (H&R Block Income Tax Guide Series).

Hacker's Handbook: The Strategy Behind Breaking Into and Defending Networks. Susan Young and Dave Aitel. CRC Press, 2000 N.W. Corporate Blvd. Boca Raton, FL 33431. Phone: 800-272-7737 or (561)994-0555 Fax: 800-374-3401 or (561)989-9732 E-mail: orders@crcpress.com • URL: http://www.crcpress.com • 2003. $79.95. Reveals "the technical aspects of hacking that are least understood by network administrators." Practical defenses are outlined. (Imprint: Auerbach Publications.)

Hair Care Products. Available from MarketResearch.com, 641 Ave. of the Americas, Fourth Floor New York, NY 10011. Phone: 800-298-5699 or (212)807-2629 Fax: (212)807-2642 E-mail: order@marketresearch.com • URL: http://www.marketresearch.com • 2002. $3,950.00. Published by Global Industry Analysts. Provides worldwide market research data, including profiles of major hair care product companies.

Hair International/Associated Masters Barbers and Beauticians of America.

Hairdressers' Journal International. Reed Business Information, Quadrant House, The Quadrant, Brighton Rd. Sutton SM2 5AS, United Kingdom. Phone: 44 208 652 3500 Fax: 44 208 652 8975 E-mail: rbp.subscriptions@rbi.co.uk • URL: http://www.reedbusiness.com • Weekly. $112.00 per year.

Halting the Hacker: A Practical Guide to Computer Security. Donald L. Pipkin. Prentice Hall PTR, 240 Fritsch Ct. Paramus, NJ 07652. Phone: 800-282-0693 Fax: 800-445-6991 • URL: http://www.phptr.com • 2002. $44.99. Second edition. (Hewlett-Packard Professional Book Series).

Handbook for Business Writing. L. Sue Baug and others. McGraw-Hill, 1221 Ave. of the Americas New York, NY 10020. Phone: 800-722-4726 or (212)512-2000 Fax: (212)512-4502 E-mail: customer.service@mcgraw-hill.com • URL: http://www.mcgraw-hill.com • 1993. $24.95. Second edition. Covers reports, letters, memos, and proposals. (Handbook for. Series).

Handbook for Focus Group Research. Thomas L. Greenbaum. Sage Publications, Inc., 2455 Teller Rd. Thousand Oaks, CA 91320. Phone: 800-818-7243 or (805)499-9774 Fax: 800-583-2665 or (805)499-0871 E-mail: webmaster@sagepub.com • URL: http://www.sagepub • 1998. $97.95. Second edition. Includes glossary and index.

Handbook for Memo Writing. L. Sue Baugh. McGraw-Hill, 1221 Ave. of the Americas New York, NY 10020. Phone: 800-722-4726 or (212)512-2000 Fax: (212)512-4502 E-mail: customer.service@mcgraw-hill.com • URL: http://www.mcgraw-hill.com • 1995. $32.95. (NTC Business Book Series).

Handbook for Muni Bond Issuers. Joe Mysak. Bloomberg, 499 Park Ave. New York, NY 10022. Phone: 800-388-2749 or (212)318-2000 Fax: (917)369-5000 • URL: http://www.bloomberg.com • 1998. $40.00. Written primarily for the officers and attorneys of municipalities. Provides a practical explanation of the municipal bond market. (Bloomberg Professional Library.)

Handbook for No-Load Fund Investors: Everything You Need for Successful Investing Without Brokers. Sheldon Jacobs. McGraw-Hill, 1221 Ave. of the Americas New York, NY 10020. Phone: 800-722-4726 or (212)512-2000 Fax: (212)512-4502 E-mail: customer.service@mcgraw-hill.com • URL: http://www.mcgraw-hill.com • 1999. $40.00. 16th edition. Includes data on individual funds.

Handbook for Practical Letter Writing. L. Sue Baugh. McGraw-Hill, 1221 Ave. of the Americas New York, NY 10020. Phone: 800-722-4726 or (212)512-2000 Fax: (212)512-4502 E-mail: customer.service@mcgraw-hill.com • URL: http://www.mcgraw-hill.com • 1993. $12.95.

Handbook for Proofreading. Laura K. Anderson. McGraw-Hill, 1221 Ave. of the Americas New York, NY 10020. Phone: 800-722-4726 or (212)512-2000 Fax: (212)512-4502 E-mail: customer.service@mcgraw-hill.com • URL: http://www.mcgraw-hill.com • 1993. $24.95. (NTC Business Book Series).

Handbook for Public Relations Writing. Thomas Bivins. McGraw-Hill, 1221 Ave. of the Americas New York, NY 10020. Phone: 800-722-4726 or (212)904-2000 Fax: (212)512-4502 E-mail: customer.service@mcgraw-hill.com • URL: http://www.mcgraw-hill.com • 1992. $17.95. Second edition. (NTC Business Books Series).

Handbook for Sound Engineers. Glen M. Ballou, editor. Elsevier, 655 Ave. of the Americas New York, NY 10010. Phone: 800-366-2665 or (212)989-5800 Fax: 800-535-9935 or (212)633-3680 E-mail: custserv@elsevier.com • URL: http://www.elsevier.com • 2002. $120.00. Third edition. Covers fundamentals of sound, sound-system design, loudspeaker building, sound recording, audio circuits, and computer-generated music.

Handbook for Theatrical Production Managers. Robert S. Telford. Samuel French, Inc., 45 W. 25th St. New York, NY 10010-2751. Phone: (212)206-8990 Fax: (212)206-1429 E-mail: samuelfrench@earthlink.net • URL: http://www.samuelfrench.com • 1983. $8.95.

Handbook of Accounting and Auditing. John C. Burton and others. RIA, 395 Hudson St. New York, NY 10014. Phone: 800-950-1216 or 800-431-9025 E-mail: riahome@riag.com • URL: http://www.riahome.com • Annual. $310.00. Looseleaf service.

Handbook of Acoustics. Malcolm Crocker. John Wiley and Sons, Inc., 111 River St. Hoboken, NJ 07030. Phone: 800-225-5945 or (201)748-6000 Fax: (201)748-6088 E-mail: info@wiley.com • URL: http://www.wiley.com • 1998. $225.00. Covers the fundamentals of acoustics, noise control, and vibration, for engineers, architects, and designers.

Handbook of Adhesives and Sealants. Edward M. Petrie. McGraw-Hill, 1221 Ave. of the Americas New York, NY 10020. Phone: 800-722-4726 or (212)512-2000 Fax: (212)512-4502 E-mail: customer.service@mcgraw-hill.com • URL: http://www.mcgraw-hill.com • 1999. $99.95. (Handbook Series).

Handbook of Airline Statistics. National Aeronautics and Space Administration, 300 F St., SW Washington, DC 20546-0001. Phone: (202)358-0000 Fax: (202)358-3251 E-mail: info-center@hq.nasa.gov • URL: http;//www.hg.nasa.gov • Biennial.

Handbook of Alternative Investment Strategies. Thomas Schneeweis and Joseph F. Pescatore, editors. Institutional Investor, Inc., Journals Group, 225 Park Ave., S New York, NY 10003. Phone: (212)224-3066 Fax: (212)224-3472 E-mail: info@iijournals.com • URL: http://www.ijournals.com • 1999. $95.00. Covers various forms of alternative investment, including hedge funds, managed futures, derivatives, venture capital, and natural resource financing.

Handbook of Bank Accounting: Understanding and Applying Standards and Regulations. Charles J. Woelfel. McGraw-Hill, 1221 Ave. of the Americas New York, NY 10020. Phone: 800-722-4726 or (212)512-2000 Fax: (212)512-4502 E-mail: customer.service@mcgraw-hill.com • URL: http://www.mcgraw-hill.com • 1992. $65.00. "Written to meet the practical needs of senior- and middle-level bank accountants." Covers managerial accounting, the theory and practice of bank accounting, financial statement analysis, bank examinations, audits, and related topics.

Handbook of Batteries. David Linden and Thomas Reddy. McGraw-Hill, 1221 Ave. of the Americas New York, NY 10020. Phone: 800-722-4726 or (212)512-2000 Fax: (212)512-4502 E-mail: customer.service@mcgraw-hill.com • URL: http://mcgraw-hill.com • 2001. $125.00. Third edition. (Electronics Book Series).

Handbook of Budgeting. William R. Lalli. John Wiley and Sons, Inc., 111 River St. Hoboken, NJ 07030. Phone: 800-225-5945 or (201)748-6000 Fax: (201)748-6088 E-mail: info@wiley.com • URL: http://www.wiley.com • 2003. $145.00. Fifth edition.

Handbook of Business Valuation. Thomas L. West and Jeffrey D. Jones, editors. John Wiley and Sons, Inc., 111 River St. Hoboken, NJ 07030. Phone: 800-225-5945 or (201)748-6000 Fax: (201)748-6088 E-mail: info@wiley.com • URL: http://www.wiley.com • 1999. $145.00. Second edition. A collection of articles, worksheets, and appraisal techniques.

Handbook of Chemical Engineering Calculations. Nicolas P. Chopey. McGraw-Hill Professional, 1221 Ave. of the Americas New York, NY 10020. Phone: 800-722-4726 or (212)904-2000 Fax: (212)512-4502 E-mail: customer.service@mcgraw-hill.com • URL: http://www.mcgraw-hill.com • 2003. $125.00. Third edition.

Handbook of Cost Accounting. Sidney Davidson and Roman L. Weil. Prentice Hall PTR, 240 Frisch Ct. Paramus, NJ 07652. Phone: 800-282-0693 Fax: 800-445-6991 • URL: http://www.phptr.com • 1989. $79.95.

Handbook of Cost Accounting Theory and Techniques. Ahmed Righi-Belkaoui. Greenwood Publishing Group, Inc., 88 Post Rd., W. Westport, CT 06881. Phone: 800-225-5800 or (203)226-3571 Fax: (203)431-2214 E-mail: customer-service@greenwood.com • URL: http://www.greenwood.com • 1991. $94.95.

Handbook of Counseling Psychology. Steven D. Brown and Robert W. Lent, editors. John Wiley and Sons, Inc., 111 River St. Hoboken, NJ 07030. Phone: 800-225-5945 or (201)748-6000 Fax: (201)748-6088 E-mail: info@wiley.com • URL: http://www.wiley.com • 2000. $110.00. Third edition. Includes material on counseling policy, research methods, and preventive interventions, as well as group, educational, career and family counseling.

Handbook of Derivative Instruments: Investment Research, Analysis, and Portfolio Applications. Arsuo Konishi and Ravi Dattatreya, editors. McGraw-Hill, 1221 Ave. of the Americas New York, NY 10020. Phone: 800-722-4726 or (212)512-2000 Fax: (212)512-4502 E-mail: customer.service@mcgraw-hill.com • URL: http://www.mcgraw-hill.com • 1996. $80.00. Second revised edition. Contains 41 chapters by various authors on all aspects of derivative securities, including such esoterica as "Inverse Floaters," "Positive Convexity," "Exotic Options," and "How to Use the Holes in Black-Scholes."

Handbook of Digital Publishing. Michael L. Kleper. Prentice Hall PTR, 240 Frisch Ct. Paramus, NJ 07652. Phone: 800-282-0693 Fax: 800-445-6991 • URL: http://www.phptr.com • 2001. $129.99. Two volumes. Edited for the digital publishing industry. Covers print publishing, electronic documents, and Internet (Web) publishing, including basic desktop procedures. Provides information on typography, design, layout, image creation, and page creation.

Handbook of Employee Benefits: Design, Funding, and Administration. Jerry S. Rosenbloom, editor. McGraw-Hill, 1221 Ave. of the Americas New York, NY 10020. Phone: 800-722-4726 or (212)512-2000 Fax: (212)512-4502 E-mail: customer.service@mcgraw-hill.com • URL: http://www.mcgraw-hill.com • 2001. $95.00. Fourth edition.

Handbook of Enology. Pascal Ribereau-Gayon and others. John Wiley and Sons, Inc., 111 River St. Hoboken, NJ 07030. Phone: 800-225-5945 or (201)748-6000 Fax: (201)748-6088 E-mail: info@wiley.com • URL: http://www.wiley.com • 2001. $220.00. Two volumes. Vol. one, $330.00; vol. two, $180.00. Volume one is *The Microbiology of Wine and Vinifications*. Volume two is *The Chemistry of Wine Stabilization and Treatments*. Discusses the science of winemaking and associated technical problems.

Handbook of Entrepreneurial Dynamics. William B. Gartner and others, editors. Sage Publications, Inc., 2455 Teller Rd. Thousand Oaks, CA 91320-2218. Phone: 800-818-7243 or (805)499-0721 Fax: 800-583-2665 or (805)499-0871 E-mail: info@sagepub.com • URL: http://www.sagepub.com • 2004. $115.00. Covers current academic research in entrepreneurship.

Handbook of Environmental Health and Safety: Principles and Practices. Herman Koren and Michael S. Bisesi. Lewis Publishers, 2000 Corporate Blvd., N.W. Boca Raton, FL 33431. Phone: 800-272-7737 or (561)994-0555 Fax: 800-374-3401 or (561)998-9114 E-mail: orders@crcpress.com • URL: http://www.crcpress.com • 2002. Fourth edition. Two volumes. Price on application.

Handbook of Equity Derivatives. Jack C. Francis and others, editors. John Wiley and Sons, Inc., 111 River St. Hoboken, NJ 07030. Phone: 800-225-5945 or (201)748-6000 Fax: (201)748-6088 E-mail: info@wiley.com • URL: http://www.wiley.com • 1999. $105.00. Revised edition. Contains 27 chapters by various authors. Covers options (puts and calls), stock index futures, warrants, convertibles, over-the-counter options, swaps, legal issues, taxation, etc. (Financial Engineering Series).

Handbook of Family Law. Stuart J. Faber. Lega Books, 3699 Wilshire Blvd., Suite 700 Los Angeles, CA 90010-2726. Phone: (213)382-3335 1987. $56.50. Fifth revised edition. Two volumes.

Handbook of Fiber Optics: Theory and Applications. Chai Yeh. Elsevier, 655 Avenue of the Americas New York, NY 10010-5107. Phone: 800-366-2665 or (212)989-5800 Fax: 800-535-9935 or (212)633-3680 E-mail: custserv@elsevier.com • URL: http://www.elsevier.com • 1990. $165.00.

Handbook of Fixed Income Securities. Frank J. Fabozzi. McGraw-Hill, 1221 Ave. of the Americas New York, NY 10020. Phone: 800-722-4726 or (212)512-2000 Fax: (212)512-4502 E-mail: customer.service@mcgraw-hill.com • URL: http://www.mcgraw-hill.com • 2000. $99.95. Sixth edition. Topics include risk measurement, valuation techniques, and portfolio strategy.

Handbook of Fuel Cells: Fundamentals, Technology, and Applications. Wolf Vielstich, editor. John Wiley and Sons, Inc., 111 River St. Hoboken, NJ 07030. Phone: 800-225-5945 or (201)748-6000 Fax: (201)748-6088 E-mail: info@wiley.

com • URL: http://www.wiley.com • 2003. $1,225.00. Four volumes. Volume one: *Fundamentals and Survey of Systems.* Volume two: *Fuel Cell Electrocatalysis.* Volumes three and four: *Fuel Cell Technology and Applications.*

Handbook of Gem Identification. Richard T. Liddicoat, Jr. Gemological Institute of America, 5355 Armada Dr. Carlsbad, CA 92008. Phone: 800-421-7250 or (760)603-4000 Fax: (760)603-4080 • URL: http://www.gia.edu • 1987. $47.50. 12th edition.

The Handbook of Glass Manufacture. Fay V. Tooley, editor. Ashlee Publishing Co., Inc., 18 E. 41st St. New York, NY 10017-6222. Phone: (212)376-7722 Fax: (212)376-7723 E-mail: publisher@ashlee.com • URL: http://www.ashlee.com • 1985. 195.00. Revised edition. Two volumes.

Handbook of Group Counseling and Psychotherapy. Janice L. DeLucia-Waack and others, editors. Sage Publications, Inc., 2455 Teller Rd. Thousand Oaks, CA 91320-2218. Phone: 800-818-7243 or (805)499-0721 Fax: 800-583-2665 or (805)499-0871 E-mail: info@sagepub.com • URL: http://www.sagepub.com • 2004. $99.95. Contains 48 chapters by various "experts in group work."

Handbook of Human Factors and Ergonomics. Gavriel Salvendy. John Wiley and Sons, Inc., 111 River St. Hoboken, NJ 07030. Phone: 800-225-5945 or (201)748-6000 Fax: (201)748-6088 E-mail: info@wiley.com • URL: http://www.wiley.com • 1997. $275.00. Second edition.

Handbook of Hydraulics. Ernest F. Brater. McGraw-Hill, 1221 Ave. of the Americas New York, NY 10020. Phone: 800-722-4726 or (212)512-2000 Fax: (212)512-4502 E-mail: customer.service@mcgraw-hill.com • URL: http://www.mcgraw-hill.com • 1996. $84.95. Seventh edition.

Handbook of Industrial Engineering: Technology and Operations Management. Gavriel Salvendy, editor. John Wiley and Sons, Inc., 111 River St. Hoboken, NJ 07030. Phone: 800-225-5945 or (201)748-6000 Fax: (201)748-6088 E-mail: info@wiley.com • URL: http://www.wiley.com • 2001. $275.00. Third edition.

Handbook of Industrial Toxicology. E. R. Plunkett, editor. Chemical Publishing Co., Inc., 527 Third Ave., No. 427 New York, NY 10016-4168. Phone: 800-786-3659 or (212)779-0090 Fax: (212)889-1537 E-mail: chempub@aol.com • URL: http://www.chemicalpublishing.com • 1987. $100.00.

Handbook of International Economic Statistics. Available from National Technical Information Service, U. S. Department of Commerce, 5285 Port Royal Rd. Springfield, VA 22161. Phone: 800-553-6847 or (703)487-4600 Fax: (703)321-8547 E-mail: info@ntis.fedworld.gov • URL: http://www.ntis.gov • Annual. $40.00. Prepared by U. S. Central Intelligence Agency. Provides basic statistics for comparing worldwide economic performance, with an emphasis on Europe, including Eastern Europe.

Handbook of International Management. John Wiley and Sons, Inc., 111 River St. Hoboken, NJ 07030. Phone: 800-225-5945 or (201)748-6000 Fax: (201)748-6088 E-mail: info@wiley.com • URL: http://www.wiley.com • 1988. $280.00.

Handbook of International Trade and Development Statistics. United Nations Publications, United Nations Concourse Level New York, NY 10017. Phone: 800-553-3210 or (212)963-7680 Fax: (212)963-4910 E-mail: bookstore@un.org • URL: http://www.un.org/publications • Annual. $80.00. Text in English and French.

Handbook of Internet Stocks. Mergent, 60 Madison Ave., 6th Fl. New York, NY 10010. Phone: 888-411-0893 or (212)413-7700 Fax: (212)413-7670 E-mail: customerservice@mergent.com • URL: http://www.mergent.com • Annual. $19.95. Contains detailed financial information on more than 200 Internet-related corporations, including e-commerce firms and telecommunications hardware manufacturers. Lists and rankings are provided.

Handbook of Interpersonal Communication. Mark L. Knapp and John A. Daly. Sage Publications, Inc., 2455 Teller Rd. Thousand Oaks, CA 91320-2218. Phone: 800-818-7243 or (805)499-0721 Fax: 800-583-2665 or (805)499-0871 E-mail: info@sagepub.com • URL: http://www.sagepub.com • 2003. $115.00. Third edition. Includes "Computer Mediated Communications and Relationships."

Handbook of Lasers. Marvin J. Weber. CRC Press LLC, 2000 NW Corporate Blvd. Boca Raton, FL 33431-7372. Phone: 800-272-7737 or (561)994-0555 Fax: 800-374-3401 or (561)989-9732 E-mail: order@crcpress.com • URL: http://www.crcpress.com • 2000. $169.95. (Laser and Optical Science and Technology Series).

Handbook of Machine Vision Engineering. Michael Burke. John Wiley and Sons, Inc., 111 River St. Hoboken, NJ 07030. Phone: 800-225-5945 or (201)748-6000 Fax: (201)748-6088 E-mail: info@wiley.com • URL: http://www.wiley.com • 1996. $159.95. Two volumes. Volume two, $79.95; volume three, $79.95.

Handbook of Management Games and Simulations. Chris Elgood, editor. Ashgate Publishing Co., 101 Cherry St., Ste. 420 Burlington, VT 05401-4405. Phone: 800-535-9544 or (802)865-7641 Fax: (802)865-7847 E-mail: adonahue@ashgate.com • URL: http://www.ashgate.com • 1997. $109.95. Sixth edition. Published by Gower in England.

Handbook of Marketing. Barton A. Weitz and Robin Wensley, editors. Sage Publications, Inc., 2455 Teller Rd. Thousand Oaks, CA 91320-2218. Phone: 800-818-7243 or (805)499-0721 Fax: 800-583-2665 or (805)499-0871 E-mail: info@sagepub.com • URL: http://www.sagepub.com • 2003. $99.

95. Features summaries of current research in various areas of marketing.

Handbook of Materials Selection. Myer Kutz. John Wiley and Sons, Inc., 111 River St. Hoboken, NJ 07030. Phone: 800-225-5945 or (201)748-6000 Fax: (201)748-6088 E-mail: info@wiley.com • URL: http://www.wiley.com • 2002. $225.00. First section of handbook covers materials relative to the type of engineering application. Second section deals with the specific properties of materials. Covers both traditional materials and high-tech composites.

Handbook of Mathematical Economics. Elsevier, 655 Ave. of the Americas New York, NY 10010-5107. Phone: 800-366-2665 or (212)989-5800 Fax: 800-535-9935 or (212)633-3680 E-mail: custserv@elsevier.com • URL: http://www.elsevier.com • $625.00. Dates vary. Four volumes. $125.00 per volume.

Handbook of Mental Health in the Workplace. Jay C. Thomas and Michael Hersen, editors. Sage Publications, Inc., 2455 Teller Rd. Thousand Oaks, CA 91320-2218. Phone: 800-818-7243 or (805)499-0721 Fax: 800-583-2665 or (805)499-0871 E-mail: info@sagepub.com • URL: http://www.sagepub.com • 2002. $99.95. The five parts deal with general issues, working conditions, psychopathology, disruptive behavior, and organizational practice.

Handbook of Mortgage-Backed Securities. Frank J. Fabozzi. McGraw-Hill, 1221 Ave. of the Americas New York, NY 10020. Phone: 800-722-4726 or (212)512-2000 Fax: (212)512-4502 E-mail: customer.service@mcgraw-hill.com • URL: http://www.mcgraw-hill.com • 2001. $95.00. Fifth edition.

Handbook of NASDAQ Stocks. Mergent, Inc., 60 Madison Ave., 6th Fl. New York, NY 10010. Phone: 888-411-0893 or (212)413-7700 Fax: (212)413-7670 E-mail: customerservice@mergent.com • URL: http://www.mergent.com • Quarterly. $225.00 per year. Over 600 corporations, whose stocks are among the most actively, traded in dollar volume on the Nasdaq market. Formerly *Moody's Handbook of NASDAQ Stocks.*

Handbook of Nonprescription Drugs. Rosemary R. Berardi, editor. American Pharmacists Association, 2215 Constitution Ave., N. W. Washington, DC 20037-2985. Phone: 800-878-2742 or (202)628-4410 Fax: (202)783-2351 E-mail: apha-appm@aphanet.org • URL: http://www.aphanet.org • 2002. $135.00. 13th edition. Contains comprehensive, technical information on over-the-counter drugs.

Handbook of North American Industry: NAFTA and the Economies of its Member Nations. John E. Cremeans. Bernan Press, 4611-F Assembly Dr. Lanham, MD 20706-4391. Phone: 800-274-4447 or (301)459-2255 Fax: 800-865-3450 or (301)459-9235 E-mail: bpress@bernan.com • URL: http://www.bernan.com • 1999. $115.00. Second revised edition. Provides detailed industry statistics for the U.S., Canada, and Mexico.

Handbook of Occupational Safety and Health. Louis J. DiBerardinis. John Wiley and Sons, Inc, 111 River St. Hoboken, NJ 07030. Phone: 800-225-5945 or (201)748-6000 Fax: (201)748-6088 E-mail: info@wiley.com • URL: http://www.wiley.com • 1998. $170.00. Second edition.

Handbook of Pest Management in Agriculture. David Pimentel, editor. CRC Press, Inc., 2000 NW Corporate Blvd. Boca Raton, FL 33431. Phone: 800-272-7737 or (561)994-0555 Fax: 800-374-3401 or (561)989-9732 E-mail: order@crcpress.com • URL: http://www.crcpress.com • 1990. $1,229.85. Second edition. Three volumes. $409.95 per volume.

Handbook of Petrochemicals and Processes. G. Margaret Wells. Ashgate Publishing Co., 101 Cherry St., Ste. 420 Burlington, VT 05401-4405. Phone: 800-535-9544 or (802)865-7641 Fax: (802)865-7847 E-mail: adonahue@ashgate.com • URL: http://www.ashgate.com • 1999. $170.00. Second edition. Published by Gower in England.

Handbook of Pressure Sensitive Adhesive Technology. Donatas Satas. Satas and Associates, 99 Shenandoah Rd. Warwick, RI 02886. Phone: (401)884-9572 Fax: (401)884-7620 E-mail: satas@compuserve.com • URL: http://www.devicelink.com • 1999. $150.00. Third revised edition.

Handbook of Private Schools: An Annual Descriptive Survey of Independent Education. Porter Sargent Publishers, Inc., 11 Beacon St., Suite 1400 Boston, MA 02108-3099. Phone: 800-342-7470 or (617)523-1670 Fax: (617)523-1021 E-mail: info@portersargent.com 2001. $99.00. Lists more than 1,600 elementary and secondary boarding and day schools in the United States.

Handbook of Psychological Assessment. Gary Groth-Marnat. John Wiley and Sons, Inc., 111 River St. Hoboken, NJ 07030. Phone: 800-225-5945 or (201)748-6000 Fax: (201)748-6088 E-mail: info@wiley.com • URL: http://www.wiley.com • 2003. $95.00. Fourth edition. Provides information on widely used intelligence and personality tests. Covers assessment, evaluation, writing of reports, and referral.

Handbook of Public Administration. B. Guy Peters and Jon Pierre, editors. Sage Publications, Inc., 2455 Teller Rd. Thousand Oaks, CA 91320-2218. Phone: 800-818-7243 or (805)499-0721 Fax: 800-583-2665 or (805)499-0871 E-mail: info@sagepub.com • URL: http://www.sagepub.com • 2003. $125.00. Emphasis is on academic studies and public administration theory.

Handbook of Public Relations. Robert L. Heath, editor. Sage Publications, Inc., 2455 Teller Rd. Thousand Oaks, CA 91320. Phone: 800-818-7243 or (805)499-9774 Fax: 800-

583-2665 or (805)499-0871 E-mail: webmaster@sagepub.com • URL: http://www.sagepub.com • 2000. $117.00. Covers best practices, academic research, and theory. Contains articles by various advertising specialists.

Handbook of Semiconductor Technology. Kenneth A. Jackson and Wolfgang Schroter, editors. John Wiley and Sons, Inc., 111 River St. Hoboken, NJ 07030. Phone: 800-225-5945 or (201)748-6000 Fax: (201)748-6088 E-mail: info@wiley.com • URL: http://www.wiley.com • 2000. $625.00. Two volumes. Vol. one, $365.00; vol. two, $260.00. Volume one covers the electronic properties of semiconductors; volume two is on relevant materials technology.

Handbook of Services for the Handicapped. Alfred H. Katz and Knute Martin. Greenwood Publishing Group Inc., 88 Post Rd., W Westport, CT 06881. Phone: 800-225-5800 or (203)226-3571 Fax: (203)431-2214 E-mail: customer-service@greenwood.com • URL: http://www.greenwood.com • 1982. $68.50.

Handbook of Systems Engineering and Management. Andrew P. Sage and William B. Rouse, editors. John Wiley and Sons, Inc., 111 River St. Hoboken, NJ 07030. Phone: 800-225-5945 or (201)748-6000 Fax: (201)748-6088 E-mail: info@wiley.com • URL: http://www.wiley.com • 1999. $200.00. Emphasis is on information technology and systems software.

Handbook of the Nations: A Brief Guide to the Economy, Government, Land, Demographics, Communications, and National Defense Establishments of Each of 206 Nations and Other Political Entities. Gale Cengage Learning, 27500 Drake Rd. Farmington Hills, MI 48331-3535. Phone: 800-877-GALE or (248)699-4253 Fax: 800-414-5043 E-mail: gale.galeord@cengage.com • URL: http://gale.cengage.com • 2003. $180.00. 22nd edition. Includes maps and tables.

Handbook of Toxic and Hazardous Chemicals and Carcinogens. Marshall Sittig. Noyes Data Corp, 169 Kinderkomack Rd., Suite 5 Park Ridge, NJ 07676-1338. Phone: (201)505-4965 2001. $495.00. Fourth edition. Two volumes.

Handbook of Training Evaluation and Measurement Methods. Jack J. Phillips., Butterworth-Heinemann, 225 Wildwood Ave., Unit B Woburn, MA 01801. Phone: 800-366-2665 or (781)904-2500 Fax: 800-446-6520 or (781)904-2640 E-mail: custserv@bhusa.com • URL: http://www.bh.com • 1997. $55.00. Third edition. (Improving Human Performance Series).

Handbook of U. S. Labor Statistics: Employment, Earnings, Prices, Productivity, and Other Labor Data. Eva E. Jacobs, editor. Bernan Associates, 4611-F Assembly Dr. Lanham, MD 20706-4391. Phone: 800-274-4447 or (301)459-2255 Fax: 800-865-3450 or (301)459-0056 E-mail: info@bernan.com • URL: http://www.bernan.com • 1999. $74.00. Based on *Handbook of Labor Statistics,* formerly issued by the Bureau of Labor Statistics, U. S. Department of Labor. Includes the Bureau's projections of employment in the U. S. by industry and occupation. Provides a wide variety of data on the work force, prices, fringe benefits, and consumer expenditures.

Handbook of Weather, Climate, and Water: Atmospheric Chemistry, Hydrology, and Societal Impacts. Thomas D. Potter and Bradley R. Coleman. John Wiley and Sons, Inc., 111 River St. Hoboken, NJ 07030. Phone: 800-225-5945 or (201)748-6000 Fax: (201)748-6088 E-mail: info@wiley.com • URL: http://www.wiley.com • 2003. $275.00. Two volumes. $150.00 per volume. Provides a detailed weather and climate reference for "both professionals and laypersons."

Handbook of World Stock and Commodity Exchanges. Blackwell Publishing, 350 Main St. Malden, MA 02148. Phone: 800-835-6770 or (781)388-8200 Fax: (781)388-8210 E-mail: subscrip@blackwellpub.com • URL: http://www.blackwellpub.com • Annual. $265.00. Provides detailed information on over 200 stock and commodity exchanges in more than 50 countries.

Handbook on Jute. Available from Bernan Associates, 4611-F Assembly Dr. Lanham, MD 20706-4391. Phone: 800-274-4888 or (301)459-2255 Fax: 800-865-3450 or (301)459-0056 E-mail: query@bernan.com • URL: http://www.bernan.com • 1984. $30.00. Published by the Food and Agriculture Organization (http://www.fao.org). (FAO Plant Production and Protection Paper, No. 51.)

Handheld Computing: The Number One Guide to Handheld Devices. Mobile Media Group, 1670 South Amphlett Blvd., Suite 105 San Mateo, CA 94402. Phone: 888-406-4048 or (650)378-8522 Fax: (650)378-8513 E-mail: editor@hhcmag.com • URL: http://www.hhcmag.com • Nine times a year. $18.95 per year. Covers handheld devices for consumers, including PDAs, cell phones, digital cameras, MP3 players, tablet PCs, accessories, and software. Includes product reviews.

Handle with Care: Motivating and Retaining Employees - Creative, Low-Cost Ways to Raise Morale, Increase Commitment, and Reduce Turnover. Barbara A. Glanz. McGraw-Hill, 1221 Ave. of the Americas New York, NY 10020. Phone: 800-722-4726 or (212)512-2000 Fax: (212)512-4502 E-mail: customer.service@mcgraw-hill.com • URL: http://www.mcgraw-hill.com • 2002. $16.95. (Teach Yourself Series).

Handweavers Guild of America.

Hard at Work. Professional Training Associates, Inc., 600 Round Rock West Dr., Ste. 305 Round Rock, TX 78681-5018. Phone: 800-822-7824 or (512)255-6006 Fax: (512)255-7532

Monthly. $89.00 per year. Newsletter on common personnel problems of supervisors and office managers. Formerly *Practical Supervision*.

Hard Drive: Bill Gates and the Making of the Microsoft Empire. James Wallace and Jim Erickson. HarperInformation, 10 E 53rd St. New York, NY 10022-5299. Phone: 800-242-7737 or (212)207-7000 Fax: 800-822-4090 or (212)207-7145 • URL: http://www.harpercollins.com • 1992. $16.00. A biography of William H. Gates, chief executive of the Microsoft Corporation.

Hardware Age. Reed Business Information, 360 Park Ave., S New York, NY 10010. Phone: 800-662-7776 or (646)746-6400 E-mail: corporatecommunications@reedbusiness.com • URL: http://www.reedbusiness.com • Monthly. $75.00 per year.

Hardwood Distributor's Association., 2559 S Damen Ave. Chicago, IL 60608. Phone: (773)847-7444 Fax: (773)847-7833 E-mail: gaspamerica@aol.com • URL: http://www.hardwooddistributors.net • Promotes the interests of Hardwood distributors.

Hardwood Floors. National Wood Flooring Association. Athletic Business Publications, Inc., 4130 Lien Rd. Madison, WI 53704-3602. Phone: 800-722-8764 or (608)249-0186 Fax: (608)249-1153 E-mail: editors@hardwoodfloorsmag.com • URL: http://www.athleticbusiness.com • Bimonthly. $36.00 per year. Covers the marketing and installation of hardwood flooring. Published for contractors and retailers.

Hardwood Manufacturers Association., 400 Penn Center Blvd., Ste. 530 Pittsburgh, PA 15235. Phone: 800-373-9663 or (412)829-0770 Fax: (412)829-0844 E-mail: info@hardwood.org • URL: http://www.hardwoodinfo.com • Represents manufacturers of hardwood lumber and hardwood products. Conducts promotion program; compiles statistics.

Hardwood Manufacturers Association: Membership Directory. Hardwood Manufacturers Association, 400 Penn Center Blvd., Suite 530 Pittsburgh, PA 15235. Phone: 800-373-9663 or (412)829-0770 Fax: (412)829-0844 Annual. Lists over 100 companies. Price on application.

Hardwood Plywood and Veneer Association., 1825 Michael Faraday Dr. Reston, VA 20195-0789. Phone: (703)435-2900 Fax: (703)435-2537 E-mail: hpva@hpva.org • URL: http://www.hpva.org • Formerly Hardwood Plywood Manufactures Association.

Hargrave's Communications Dictionary. Frank Hargrave. Available from John Wiley and Sons, Inc., 111 River St. Hoboken, NJ 07030. Phone: 800-225-5945 or (201)748-6000 Fax: (201)748-6088 E-mail: bookinfo@wiley.com • URL: http://www.wiley.com • 2001. $140.00. Published by IEEE. Contains more than 10,000 definitions relating to voice and data communications, plus definitions in the areas of computer science, optics, networks, and the Internet. Includes acronyms, charts, equations, and drawings.

Harley Hahn's Internet and Web Yellow Pages. Harley Hahn. Osborne/McGraw-Hill, 2600 10th St., 6th Fl. Berkeley, CA 94710. Phone: 800-227-0900 E-mail: pbg. ecommerce_custserv@mcgraw-hill.com • URL: http://www.osborne.com • Annual. $34.99. Lists World Wide Web sites in more than 100 categories.

Harmonized Tariff Schedule of the United States, Annotated, Basic Manual. Available from U.S. Government Printing Office, Washington, DC 20402. Phone: (202)512-1800 Fax: (202)512-2250 E-mail: gpoaccess@gpo.gov • URL: http://www.accessgpo.gov • $84.00, including basic volumes and supplementary service for an indefinite period.

Harper's Bazaar. Hearst Corp., 1700 Broadway New York, NY 10019. Phone: 800-888-3045 or (212)903-5000 Fax: (212)262-1701 E-mail: bazaar@hearst.com • URL: http://www.hearstcorp.com • Monthly. $18.00 per year.

Harris Manufacturers Directory 2000: National Edition. Harris InfoSource, 2057 E. Aurora Rd. Twinsburg, OH 44087. Phone: 800-888-5900 or (330)425-9000 Fax: (330)425-4328 E-mail: customerservice@harrisinfo.com • URL: http://www.harrisinfo.com • Annual. $565.00. Two volumes. Provides statistical and descriptive information for about 47,062 U.S. industrial firms having 100 or more employees.

Hart's E and P (Exploration and Production). Hart Publications, Inc., 4545 Post Oak Place, Suite 210 Houston, TX 77027. Phone: (713)993-9320 Fax: (713)840-8585 E-mail: gacosta@chemweek.com • URL: http://www.hartenergynetwork.com • Monthly. Free to qualified personnel; others $149.00 per year. Edited for "decision makers" in petroleum exploration and production. Emphasis is on technology. Formerly *Petroleum Engineer International*.

Harvard Business Review. Harvard University, Graduate School of Business Administration. Harvard Business School Publishing, 300 N Beacon St. Watertown, MA 02163. Phone: 800-988-0886 or (617)783-7500 Fax: (617)783-7555 • URL: http://www.hbs.edu • Monthly. $118.00 per year.

Harvard Law Review. Harvard Law Review Association, Gannett House, 1511 Massachusetts Ave. Cambridge, MA 02138. Phone: (617)495-7889 Fax: (617)495-5053 • URL: http://www.harvardlawreview.org • Eight times a year. $45.00 per year.

Harvard Legislative Research Bureau., Harvard University, Harvard Law School, 1541 Massachusetts Ave. Cambridge, MA 02138. Phone: (617)495-4400 Fax: (617)495-1110 E-mail: pgowder@law.harvard.edu Concerned with federal and state legislation in all fields.

Harvard Management Communication Letter. Harvard Business School Publishing, 60 Harvard Way Boston, MA 02163. Phone: 800-988-0886 or (617)783-7500 Fax: (617)783-7555 E-mail: corpcustserv@hbsp.harvard.edu • URL: http://www.hbs.edu • Description: Provides information and techniques for managers on effective communication.

Harvard Management Update. Harvard Business School Publishing, 60 Harvard Way Boston, MA 02163. Phone: 800-988-0886 or (617)783-7500 Fax: (617)783-7555 E-mail: corpcustserv@hbsp.harvard.edu • URL: http://www.hbs.edu • Description: Provides information on current management techniques and trends.

Harvard Negotiation Project. Harvard University, Harvard Law School, Pound Hall Room 500 Cambridge, MA 02138. Phone: (617)495-1684 Fax: (617)495-7818 E-mail: info@pon.law.harvard.edu Seeks to improve the theory and practice of negotiation.

Hat Life Directory. Mint Publishing, 1777 Bellflower Blvd., Ste. 100 Long Beach, CA 90815. Phone: 888-372-8702 or (562)252-4010 Fax: (775)213-2689 E-mail: support@hatlife.com • URL: http://www.annun@refac.com • Covers: About 1,000 hat manufacturers, wholesalers, renovators, and importers of men's headwear, plus trade suppliers listed (SIC 2253, 2352, 5036); includes about 120 Canadian manufacturers. Entries include: Company name, address, phone, fax, trade and brand names.

Hawaii Natural Energy Institute., University of Hawaii at Manoa, 2540 Dole St., Holmes Hall 246 Honolulu, HI 96822. Phone: (808)956-8890 Fax: (808)956-2336 E-mail: hnei@hawaii.edu • URL: http://www.soest.hawaii.edu • Research areas include geothermal, wind, solar, hydroelectric, and other energy sources.

Hawley's Condensed Chemical Dictionary. Richard J. Lewis. John Wiley and Sons, Inc., 111 River St. Hoboken, NJ 07030. Phone: 800-225-5945 or (201)748-6000 Fax: (201)748-6088 E-mail: info@wiley.com • URL: http://www.wiley.com • 2002. $155.00. 14th edition. Contains information about thousands of chemicals. Entries cover properties, occurence, shipping regulations, hazards, synonyms, applications, and other characteristics. (CD-ROM edition also available.)

Hazardous and Toxic Materials: Safe Handling and Disposal. Howard H. Fawcett, editor. John Wiley and Sons, Inc., 111 River St. Hoboken, NJ 07030. Phone: 800-526-5368 or (201)748-6000 Fax: (201)748-6088 E-mail: info@wiley.com • URL: http://www.wiley.com • 1988. $160.00. Second edition.

Hazardous Chemicals Desk Reference. Richard J. Lewis. John Wiley and Sons, Inc., 111 River St. Hoboken, NJ 07030. Phone: 800-225-5945 or (201)748-6000 Fax: (201)748-6088 E-mail: info@wiley.com • URL: http://www.wiley.com • 2002. $185.00. Fifth edition. Summarizes the hazardous properties of about 5,000 chemical substances.

Hazardous Materials Dictionary. Ronald Coleman. CRC Press LLC, 2000 NW Corporate Blvd. Boca Raton, FL 33431. Phone: 800-272-7737 or (561)994-0555 Fax: 800-374-3401 or (561)989-9732 E-mail: orders@crcpress.com • URL: http://www.crcpress.com • 1994. $99.95. Second revised edition. Looseleaf service.

Hazardous Materials Newsletter. John R. Cashman, Silver Cir. Barre, VT 05641. Phone: 888-433-5366 or (802)479-2307 E-mail: info@golob.com Description: Focuses on response to and control of hazardous materials emergencies, particularly appropriate tools, equipment, materials, methods, procedures, strategies, and lessons learned. Addresses leak, fire, and spill control for incident commanders and experienced responders, including incident causes, prevention, and remedial actions; decisionmaking; scene management; control and containment; response teams; and product identification and hazards. Recurring features include incident reports, a calendar of events, description of public safety agency/commercial/industrial response team operations, coverage of research sources and resources, networking ideas, and chemical and biological agents.

Hazardous Substance Management Research Center.

Hazardous Substances Data Bank. SilverPlatter Information, Inc., 100 River Ridge Rd. Norwood, MA 02062. Phone: 800-343-0064 or (781)769-2599 Fax: (781)769-8763 Provides CD-ROM information on hazardous substances, including 140,000 chemicals in the *Registry of Toxic Effects of Chemical Substances* and 60,000 materials covered by the *Toxic Substances Control Act Initial Inventory*.

Hazardous Substances Resource Guide. Gale, 27500 Drake Rd. Farmington Hills, MI 48331-3535. Phone: 800-877-4253 or (248)699-4253 Fax: 800-414-5043 or (248)699-8065 E-mail: galeord@cengage.com • URL: http://gale.cengage.com • Publication includes: Organizations and research centers involved with hazardous substances treatment. Principal content of publication is a guide to approximately 1,200 hazardous materials and their handling, use, disposal, and health risks.

Hazardous Waste Consultant. Elsevier, 655 Ave. of the Americas New York, NY 10010-5107. Phone: 800-366-2665 or (212)989-5800 Fax: 800-535-9935 or (212)633-3680 E-mail: custserv@elsevier.com • URL: http://www.elsevier.com • Seven times a year. $798.00 per year. Discusses the technical, regulatory and legal aspects of the hazardous waste industry.

Hazardous Waste Consultant Directory of Commercial Hazardous Waste Management Facilities. Elsevier, 655 Ave. of the Americas New York, NY 10010-5107. Phone: 800-366-2665 or (212)989-5800 Fax: 800-535-9935 or (212)633-3680

E-mail: custserv@elsevier.com • URL: http://www.elsevier.com • Annual. $115.00. List of 170 facilities that process, store, and dispose of hazardous waste materials.

Hazardous Waste Litigation Reporter: The National Journal of Record of Hazardous Waste-Related Litigation. Andrews Publications, 175 Stafford Ave., Bldg. 4, Suite 140 Wayne, PA 19087. Phone: 800-345-1101 or (610)225-0510 Fax: (610)225-0501 E-mail: customer@andrewspub.com • URL: http://www.andrewspub.com • Semimonthly. $875.00 per year. Newsletter. Reports on hazardous waste legal cases.

Hazardous Waste Management. Michael D. La Gregor and others. McGraw-Hill, 1221 Ave. of the Americas New York, NY 10020. Phone: 800-722-4726 or (212)512-2000 Fax: (212)512-4502 E-mail: customer.service@mcgraw-hill.com • URL: http://www.mcgraw-hill.com • 2000. $113.75. Second edition. (Environmental Engineering and Water Resources Series).

Hazardous Waste Management in Small Businesses: Regulating and Assisting the Smaller Generator. Robert E. Deyle. Greenwood Publishing Group, Inc., 88 Post Rd., W Westport, CT 06881. Phone: 800-225-5800 or (203)226-3571 Fax: (203)431-2214 E-mail: customer-service@greenwood.com • URL: http://www.greenwood.com • 1989. $59.95. Emphasis on legal aspects.

Hazardous Waste/Superfund Week. Business Publishers Inc., 2601 University Blvd., W Ste. 200, PO Box 17592 Silver Spring, MD 20902. Phone: 800-274-6737 or (301)929-5700 Fax: (301)949-8844 E-mail: custserv@bpinews.com • URL: http://www.bpinews.com • Description: Examines issues and developments in the hazardous waste management industry. Covers legislative and regulatory actions, technology research and development, disposal site controversies, Superfund contracting, and other news of interest. Recurring features include columns titled Slants & Trends, Business and Technology News, Grants and Contracts, calendar, Around the States, Market News, and Industrial Waste Focus.

The HCEA Directory of Healthcare Meetings and Conventions. Healthcare Convention Exhibitors Association, 5775 Peachtree-Dunwoody Rd., Ste. 500, Bldg., G Atlanta, GA 30342. Phone: (404)252-3663 Fax: (404)252-0774 E-mail: hcea@kellencompany.com • URL: http://www.hcea.org • Semiannual. Free to members; non-members, $245.00 per year. Lists more than 6,000 health care meetings, most of which have an exhibit program. Formerly *Handbook-A Directory of Health Care Meetings and Conventions*.

Headquarters USA: A Directory of Contact Information for Headquarters and Other Central Offices of Major Businesses and Organizations Nationwide. Omnigraphics, Inc., 615 Griswold St. Detroit, MI 48226. Phone: 800-234-1340 or (313)961-1340 Fax: 800-875-1340 or (313)961-1383 E-mail: info@omnigraphics.com • URL: http://www.omnigraphics.com • Annual. $185.00. Two volumes. Volume one is alphabetical by name of business or organization. Volume two is classified by subject. Includes more than 112,000 businesses, organizations, agencies, institutions, and "high-profile" individuals. Listings include addresses, telephone numbers, fax numbers, and toll-free numbers and Web addresses where available. Formerly *Business Phone Book USA*.

Headwear Information Bureau., 302 W 12th St., PHC New York, NY 10014. Phone: (212)627-8333 Fax: (212)627-0067 E-mail: milicase@aol.com • URL: http://www.hatsworldwide.com • Headwear and Millinery manufacturers, importers, and suppliers for men and women's hats. Promotes the wearing of hats by women and men of all ages. Disseminates fashion information; conducts promotional and educational campaigns; handles press relations and designer store appearances. Operates speakers' bureau and charitable program; compiles statistics.

Healing the Wounds: Overcoming the Trauma of Layoffs, and Revitalizing Downsized Organizations. David M. Noer. John Wiley and Sons, Inc., 111 River St. Hoboken, NJ 07030. Phone: 800-225-5945 or (201)748-6000 Fax: (201)748-6088 E-mail: info@wiley.com • URL: http://www.wiley.com • 1993. $34.00. (Management Series).

Health Against Wealth: HMOs and the Breakdown of Medical Trust. George Anders. Gale Cengage Learning, 27500 Drake Rd. Farmington Hills, MI 48331-3535. Phone: 800-877-GALE or (248)699-GALE Fax: 800-414-5043 or (248)699-8069 E-mail: gale.galeord@cengage.com • URL: http://gale.cengage.com • 1997. $26.95. The author, a *Wall Street Journal* reporter, presents the negative side of HMO cost cutting.

Health and Environment in America's Top-Rated Cities: A Statistical Profile. Grey House Publishing, 185 Millerton Rd. Millerton, NY 12546. Phone: 800-562-2139 or (518)789-8700 Fax: (518)789-0556 E-mail: books@greyhouse.com • URL: http://www.greyhouse.com • Biennial. $125.00. Covers 75 U. S. cities. Includes statistical and other data on a wide variety of topics, such as air quality, water quality, recycling, hospitals, physicians, health care costs, death rates, infant mortality, accidents, and suicides.

The Health and Natural Product Store Market. Available from MarketResearch.com, 641 Ave. of the Americas, 3rd Fl. New York, NY 10011. Phone: 800-298-5699 or (212)807-2629 Fax: (212)807-2716 E-mail: order@marketresearch.com • URL: http://www.marketresearch.com • 1999. $2,750.00. Published by Packaged Facts. Contains market research data.

Health and Safety Science Abstracts. Institute of Safety and

Systems Management. Cambridge Information Group, 7200 Wisconsin Ave., Suite 601 Bethesda, MD 20814. Phone: 800-843-7751 or (301)961-6700 Fax: (301)961-6720 E-mail: service@csa.com • URL: http://www.csa.com • Monthly. Online edition, $850.00 year. Formerly *Safety Science Abstracts Journal*.

Health Care Benefits Law. American Lawyer Media, Inc., 105 Madison Ave. New York, NY 10016. Phone: 800-888-8300 or (212)779-9200 Fax: (212)481-8110 E-mail: lawcatalog@amlaw.com • URL: http://www.lawcatalog.com/ • Looseleaf. $169.00. Updated as needed. Covers the legal compliance aspects of employer health care plans. Includes checklists and sample forms. (Law Journal Press).

Health Care Costs. DRI/McGraw-Hill, 24 Hartwell Ave. Lexington, MA 02173. Phone: (617)863-5100 Fax: (617)860-6332 Quarterly. Price on application. Cost indexes for hospitals, nursing homes, and home healthcare agencies.

Health Care Economics. Paul J. Feldstein. Delmar Learning, 5 Maxwell Dr. Clifton Park, NY 12065-8007. Phone: 800-347-7707 Fax: 800-487-4888 E-mail: info@delmar.com • URL: http://www.delmarlearning.com • 1998. $98.95. Fifth edition.

Health Care Financing Review. Available from U. S. Government Printing Office, Washington, DC 20402. Phone: (202)512-1800 Fax: (202)512-2250 E-mail: gpoaccess@gpo.gov • URL: http://www.access.gpo.gov • Quarterly. $48.00 per year. Issued by the Health Care Financing Administration, U. S. Department of Health and Human Services. Presents articles by professionals in the areas of health care costs and financing.

Health Care Fraud and Abuse Newsletter. American Lawyer Media, Inc., 105 Madison Ave. New York, NY 10016. Phone: 800-888-8300 or (212)779-9200 Fax: (212)481-8110 E-mail: lawcatalog@amlaw.com • URL: http://www.lawcatalog.com/ • Monthly. $195.00 per year. Newsletter. Provides legal news relating mainly to fraudulent or excessive medical billing practices. Covers both civil and criminal proceedings. (A Law Journal Newsletter, formerly published by Leader Publications).

Health Care Strategic Management: The Newsletter for Hospital Strategies. Business Word, Inc., 5350 S. Roslyn St., Suite 400 Englewood, CO 80111-2125. Phone: (303)290-8500 Fax: (303)290-9025 E-mail: sandyc@businessword.com • URL: http://www.businessword.com • Monthly. $284.00 per year. Planning, marketing and resource allocation.

Health Care, Technology, and the Competitive Environment. Henry P. Brehm and Ross M. Mullner, editors. Greenwood Publishing Group, Inc., 88 Post Rd., W Westport, CT 06881. Phone: 800-225-5800 or (203)226-3571 Fax: (203)431-2214 E-mail: customer-service@greenwood.com • URL: http://www.greenwood.com • 1989. $74.95.

Health Connection., 55 W Oak Ridge Dr. Hagerstown, MD 21740. Phone: 800-548-8700 or (301)393-3290 Fax: 888-294-8405 or 888-294-8405 E-mail: sales@healthconnection.org • URL: http://www.healthconnection.org • Promotes nationwide education for the prevention of drug addiction and alcoholism through direct mailings of materials to schools, churches, and civic organizations. Participates, through exhibits, in conferences and conventions of teachers and school personnel.

Health Data Management. Thomson Media, One State St. Plaza New York, NY 10004. Phone: 800-221-1809 or (212)803-8200 Fax: (212)843-9635 E-mail: custserv@thomsonmedia.com • URL: http://www.thomsonmedia.com • Monthly. $98.00 per year. Covers the management and automation of clinical data and health care insurance claims. Provides news and analysis of various aspects of health care information technology for administrators of hospitals, clinics, and managed care plans.

Health Devices Alerts: A Summary of Reported Problems, Hazards, Recalls, and Updates. ECRI (Emergency Care Research Institute), 5200 Butler Pike Plymouth Meeting, PA 19462. Phone: (610)825-6000 Fax: (610)834-1275 E-mail: info@ecri.org • URL: http://www.ecri.org • Weekly. $3,649.40 per year. Looseleaf service. Contains reviews of health equipment problems. Includes *Health Devices Alerts Action Items, Health Devices Alerts Abstracts, Health Devices Alerts FDA Data, Health Devices Alerts Implants, Health Devices Alerts Hazards Bulletin*.

Health Devices Alerts [CD-ROM]. ECRI, 5200 Butler Pike Plymouth Meeting, PA 19462. Phone: (610)825-6000 Fax: (610)834-1275 Weekly. $2,450.00 per year. Provides CD-ROM reports of medical equipment defects, problems, failures, misuses, and recalls.

Health Devices Alerts [online]. ECRI, 5200 Butler Pike Plymouth Meeting, PA 19462. Phone: (610)825-6000 Fax: (610)834-1275 Provides online reports of medical equipment defects, problems, failures, misuses, and recalls. Time period is 1977 to date, with weekly updates. Inquire as to online cost and availability.

Health Devices Sourcebook. ECRI, 5200 Butler Pke. Plymouth Meeting, PA 19462-1298. Phone: (610)825-6000 Fax: (610)834-1275 E-mail: info@ecri.org • URL: http://www.ecri.org • Covers: Over 6,800 suppliers of patient care equipment, medical and surgical instruments, implants, clinical laboratory equipment and supplies, medical and hospital disposable supplies, and testing instruments; also lists companies that service, recondition, lease, or buy and sell used equipment; coverage includes U.S. and Canada. Entries include: Company name, address, phone, toll-free phone, fax, toll-free fax, URL, e-mail, total sales, names of key executives and contacts, product categories handled, trade names, methods of distribution, typical pricing, annual volume. Price of directory includes custom updates upon request.

Health Facilities Management. American Hospital Association. American Hospital Publishing, Inc., One N. Franklin St. Chicago, IL 60606. Phone: 800-242-2626 or (312)422-3000 Fax: (312)422-4796 • URL: http://www.aha.org • Monthly. $40.00 per year. Covers building maintenance and engineering for hospitals and nursing homes.

Health Food/Vitamin Store. Entrepreneur Media, Inc., 2445 McCabe Way Irvine, CA 92614. Phone: 800-421-2300 or (949)261-2325 Fax: (949)261-0234 E-mail: entmag@entrepreneur.com • URL: http://www.entrepreneur.com • Looseleaf. $59.50. A practical guide to starting a health food store. Covers profit potential, start-up costs, market size evaluation, owner's time required, site selection, lease negotiation, pricing, accounting, advertising, promotion, etc. (Start-Up Business Guide No. E1296.)

Health Forum Journal: Leadership Strategies for Healthcare Executives. Health Forum, One N. Franklin St., 180 Montgomery St., Ste. 1520 San Francisco, CA 94104. Phone: (415)248-8400 Fax: (415)248-0400 • URL: http://www.hospitalconnect.com • Biweekly. $65.00 per year. Covers the general management of hospitals, nursing homes, and managed care organizations. Formerly *HospitalsHealthNetworks*.

Health Forum Journal: Leadership Strategies for Healthcare Executives. Healthcare Forum, One N. Franklin St., 29th Fl. Chicago, IL 60606. Phone: (415)436-4300 Fax: (415)356-9300 • URL: http://www.healthonline.com • Bimonthly. $65.00 per year.

Health Grants and Contracts Weekly: Selected Federal Project Opportunities. Aspen Publishers, Inc., 1185 Ave. of the Americas New York, NY 10036. Phone: 800-234-1660 or (212)597-0200 Fax: (212)597-0338 E-mail: customer.service@aspenpubl.com • URL: http://www.aspenpublishers.com • 50 times a year. $459.00 per year. Newsletter. Lists new health-related federal contracts and grants.

Health Industry Buyers Guide. Lippincott Williams & Wilkins, 530 Walnut St. Philadelphia, PA 19106-3621. Phone: 800-950-0879 or (215)521-8300 Fax: (215)521-8902 E-mail: info@ecri.org Covers: 4,000 manufacturers of hospital and physician's supplies and equipment, including medical laboratory, oxygen therapy, and X-ray supplies, home health care products, and orthopedic appliances. Entries include: Manufacturer name, address, phone, fax, full product line.

Health Industry Distributors Association., 310 Montgomery St. Alexandria, VA 22314-1516. Phone: 800-549-4432 or (703)549-4432 Fax: (703)549-6495 E-mail: rowan@hida.org • URL: http://www.hida.org • Represents distributors of medical, laboratory, surgical, and other health care equipment and supplies to hospitals, physicians, nursing homes, and industrial medical departments. Conducts sales training, management seminars, and research through the HIDA Educational Foundation.

Health Industry Representatives Association., 7315 E 5th Ave. Pkwy. Denver, CO 80230. Phone: (303)756-8115 Fax: (303)341-0282 E-mail: hirainfo@comcast.net • URL: http://www.hira.org • Represents manufacturers who operate independent marketing firms under contract to manufacturers of non-competing lines and manufacturers within the health-care industry who market through independent marketing firms. Conducts special surveys at regular intervals for members. Provides panel discussions and special discounts for member firms on advertising and reference publications.

Health Industry Today: The Market Letter for Health Care Industry Vendors. Business Word, Inc., 5350 S. Roslyn St., Suite 400 Englewood, CO 80111-2125. Phone: (303)290-8500 Fax: (303)290-9025 E-mail: curthit@buisnessword.com • URL: http://www.businessword.com • Monthly. $360.00 per year; online edition, $420.00 per year.

Health Information for International Travel. Available from U. S. Government Printing Office, Washington, DC 20402. Phone: (202)512-1800 Fax: (202)512-2250 E-mail: gpoaccess@gpo.gov • URL: http://www.access.gpo.gov • Annual. Issued by Centers for Disease Control, U. S. Department of Health and Human Services. Discusses potential health risks of international travel and specifies vaccinations required by different countries.

Health Information for International Travel. U.S. Dept. of Health and Human Services, Centers for Disease Control and Prefabricated, Epidemiology Program Office, MS C-08, 1600 Clifton Rd., NE Atlanta, GA 30333. Phone: 800-843-6356 Annual. $20.00. Produced by the Centers for Disease Control and Prevention (CDC). Primarily edited for "healthcare providers who administer pre- and post-travel counseling and care." Also serves as a reference for airlines, cruise lines, and the travel industry in general. Covers such items as injuries during travel, motion sickness, disabilities, vaccines, insect repellents, and travel with children. Sometimes known as "The Yellow Book."

Health Insurance Association of America., 1201 F St., N.W., No. 500 Washington, DC 20004. Phone: (202)824-1600 Fax: (202)824-1722 E-mail: jbalda@hiaa.org • URL: http://www.hiaa.org • Members are commercial health insurers. Includes a Disability Insurance Committee, a Medicare Administration Committee, and a Long-Term Care Committee.

Health Insurance Company Financial Data. The National Underwriter Co., 5081 Olympic Blvd. Erlander, KY 41018. Phone: 800-543-0874 or (859)692-2100 • URL: http://www.nationalunderwriter.com • Annual.

Health Insurance: Current Issues and Background. William S. Stevens, editor. Nova Science Publishers, Inc., 400 Oser Ave., Suite 1600 Hauppauge, NY 11788-3619. Phone: (631)231-7269 Fax: (631)231-8175 E-mail: novascience@earthlink.net • URL: http://www.novapublishers.com • 2003. $59.00. Provides articles by various authors on the health insurance situation in America, with emphasis on the health problems of the uninsured. Includes statistical data.

Health Insurance Terminology: A Glossary of Health Insurance Terms. Margaret Lynch, editor. Health Insurance Association of America, 601 Pennsylvania Ave., NW, South Bldg., Ste. 500 Washington, DC 20004. Phone: 800-828-0111 or (202)824-1840 Fax: (202)824-1800 • URL: http://www.hiaa.org • 1992. $10.00.

Health Insurance Underwriter. National Association of Health Underwriters, 200 N 14th St., Ste. 450 Arlington, VA 22201. Phone: (703)726-0220 Fax: (703)841-7797 E-mail: info@nahu.org • URL: http://www.nahu.org • Monthly. $25.00 per year. Includes special feature issues on long-term care insurance, disability insurance, managed health care, and insurance office management.

Health Law Handbook. Alice G. Gosfield. West Group, 610 Opperman Dr. Eagan, MN 55123. Phone: 800-328-4880 or (651)687-7000 Fax: 800-340-9378 E-mail: bookstore@westgroup.com • URL: http://www.westgroup.com • Annual. $246.00.

The Health Letter. Sidney M. Wolfe, editor. North America Syndicate, PO Box 90190 Collingswood, NJ 08108. Phone: 800-443-8199 or (609)869-3464 Fax: (202)785-3584 E-mail: custserv@bpinews.com Description: Addresses health topics, with discussion of cause and effect, practical counsel, and information on normal variations. Carries news of research, briefings from current medical literature, and highlights of conferences and other events.

Health Maintenance Organization (HMO) Directory and Market Report. Firstmark, 25 Vintinner Rd. Campton, NH 03223. Phone: 800-729-2600 or (603)726-4800 Fax: (603)726-4840 E-mail: leads@firstmark.com • URL: http://www.firstmark.com • Annual. $630.00. Three looseleaf volumes. Contains information relating to over 700 HMOs. Relevant market data is also provided.

Health Management Research Center.

Health Management Technology. Nelson Publishing, Inc., 2504 Tamiami Trail N Nokomis, FL 34275. Phone: (941)966-9521 Fax: (941)966-2590 • URL: http://www.comnews.com • Monthly. $38.00 per year. Formerly *Computers in Healthcare*.

Health Marketing Quarterly. The Haworth Press, Inc., 10 Alice St. Binghamton, NY 13904-1580. Phone: 800-429-6784 or (607)722-2493 Fax: (607)722-1424 E-mail: getinfo@haworthpressinc.com • URL: http://www.haworthpressinc.com • Quarterly. $580.00 per year.

Health News Daily. F-D-C Reports Inc., 5550 Friendship Blvd., Ste. 1 Chevy Chase, MD 20815. Phone: 800-332-2181 or (301)657-9830 Fax: (301)656-3094 E-mail: fdcr@clarknet.com • URL: http://www.fdcreports.com • Description: Tracks developments in health care policy, legislation and regulation, insurance, pharmaceuticals, delivery, manufacturing, technology and treatment, funding, and research.

Health Policy and Biomedical Research: The Blue Sheet. F-D-C Reports, Inc., 5550 Friendship Blvd., Suite 1 Chevy Chase, MD 20815-7278. Phone: 800-332-2181 or (301)657-9830 Fax: (301)656-3094 E-mail: fdc.customer.service@elsevier.com • URL: http://www.fdcreports.com • 51 times a year. $716.00 per year. Newsletter. Emphasis is on news of medical research agencies and institutions, especially the National Institutes of Health (NIH).

Health Policy Institute.

Health Products Business Purchasing Guide. Cygnus Business Media, 445 Broad Hollow Rd. Melville, NY 11747. Phone: 800-308-6397 or (631)845-2700 Fax: (631)845-2798 E-mail: rich.reiff@cygnuspub.com • URL: http://www.cygnusbzb.com • Annual. $10.00. Listing of manufacturers, importers, exclusive distributors, brokers, and wholesalers of health food products, publishers of health food related books and magazines, and associations interested in the health foods industry. Formerly*Health Foods Business Purchasing Guide*.

Health Products Business: The Business Publication of the Natural Foods In dustry. Cygnus Business Media, 445 Broad Hollow Rd. Melville, NY 11747-3601. Phone: 800-308-6397 or (631)845-2700 Fax: (631)845-2798 E-mail: rich.reiff@cygnuspub.com • URL: http://www.cygnusbzb.com • Monthly. $60.00 per year.

Health Services Research and Development Center.

Health, United States, 1999: Health and Aging Chartbook. Available from U. S. Government Printing Office, Washington, DC 20402. Phone: (202)512-1800 Fax: (202)512-2250 E-mail: gpoaccess@gpo.gov • URL: http://www.access.gpo.gov • 1999. $43.00. Issued by the National Center for Health Statistics, U. S. Department of Health and Human Services. Contains 34 bar charts in color, with related statistical tables. Provides detailed data on persons over 65 years of age, including population, living arrangements, life expectancy, nursing home residence, poverty, health status, assistive devices, health insurance, and health care expenditures.

Healthcare Convention and Exhibitors Association., 5775 Peachtree-Dunwoody Rd., Bldg. G, Ste. 500 Atlanta, GA

30342. Phone: (404)252-3663 Fax: (404)252-0774 E-mail: hcea@kellencompnay.com • URL: http://www.hcea.org • Promotes more effective display of health care products at professional conventions. Formerly Health Care Exhibitors Association.

Healthcare Distribution Management Association., 901 N Glebe Rd., Ste. 1000, 1821 Michael Faraday Dr., Ste. 400 Arlington, VA 22203. Phone: (703)787-0000 Fax: (703)935-3200 E-mail: info@hdmanet.org • URL: http://www.healthcaredistribution.org • Wholesalers and manufacturers of drug and health care products and industry service providers. Seeks to secure safe and effective distribution of health care products, create and exchange industry knowledge affecting the future of distribution management, and influence standards and business processes that produce efficient health care commerce. Compiles statistics; sponsors research and specialized education programs.

Healthcare Distributor: The Industry's Multi-Market Information Resource. ELF Publications, 5285 W. Louisiana Ave., Suite 112 Lakewood, CO 80232-5976. Phone: 800-922-8513 or (303)975-0075 Fax: (303)975-0132 E-mail: elfpub@qwest.net • URL: http://www.elfpublications.com • Bimonthly. $30.00 per year. Formerly *Wholesale Drugs Magazine*.

Healthcare Executive. American College of Healthcare Executives, One N. Franklin St., Suite 1700 Chicago, IL 60606-3491. Phone: (312)424-3800 Fax: (312)424-0023 Bimonthly. $70.00 per year. Focuses on critical management issues.

Healthcare Finance for the Non-Financial Manager: Basic Guide to Financial Analysis & Control. Louis Gapenski. McGraw-Hill, 1221 Ave. of the Americas New York, NY 10020. Phone: 800-722-4726 or (212)512-2000 Fax: (212)512-4502 E-mail: customer.service@mcgraw-hill.com • URL: http://www.mcgraw-hill.com • 1994. $47.50.

Healthcare Financial Management. Healthcare Financial Management Association, 1301 Connecticut Ave., NW, Ste. 300 Washington, DC 20036-3417. Phone: 800-252-4362 or (202)296-2920 Fax: (202)223-9771 E-mail: webmaster@hfma.org • URL: http://www.hfma.org • Monthly. $102.00 per year.

Healthcare Financial Management Association., 2 Westbrook Corporate Ctr., Ste. 700 Westchester, IL 60154. Phone: 800-252-4362 or (708)531-9600 Fax: (708)531-0032 E-mail: memberservices@hfma.org • URL: http://www.hfma.org • Financial management professionals employed by hospitals and long-term care facilities, public accounting and consulting firms, insurance companies, medical groups, managed care organizations, government agencies, and other organizations. Conducts conferences, including annual conference in late June and audio teleconferences. Publishes books on healthcare financial issues. A Fellowship in Healthcare Financial Management (FHFMA) as well as the Certified Healthcare Professional (CHFP) in Finance and Accounting, Financial Management of Physician Practices, Managed Care, and Patient Financial Services are offered.

Healthcare Informatics: The Business of Healthcare Information Technology. McGraw-Hill, 1221 Ave. of the Americas New York, NY 10020. Phone: 800-722-4726 or (212)512-2000 Fax: (212)512-4502 E-mail: customer.service@mcgraw-hill.com • URL: http://www.mcgraw-hill.com • Monthly. $39.95 per year. Covers various aspects of information and computer technology for the health care industry.

Healthcare Information and Management Systems Society., 230 E. Ohio St., Suite 500 Chicago, IL 60611-3269. Phone: (312)664-4467 Fax: (312)664-6143 E-mail: himss@himss.org • URL: http://www.himss.org • Absorbed Center for Hospital Management Engineering. Formerly Hospital Management Systems Society.

Healthcare Marketing Report. HMR Publication Group, P.O. Box 76002 Atlanta, GA 30358-1002. Phone: (404)457-6105 Fax: (404)457-0049 Monthly. Price on application.

Healthcare Products Today Magazine. Health Industry Distribution Association. Douglas Publications, Inc., 2807 N. Parham Rd., Suite 200 Richmond, VA 23294. Phone: (804)762-9600 Fax: (804)217-8999 E-mail: info@douglaspublications.com • URL: http://www.douglaspublications.com • 10 times a year. $49.95 per year. Formerly*Medical Product Sales*.

Healthcare Purchasing News: A Magazine for Hospital Materials Management Central Service, Infection Control Practitioners. Thomson/Medical Economics, Five Paragon Dr. Montvale, NJ 07645-1742. Phone: (201)358-7200 Fax: (201)722-2680 E-mail: customer.service@medec.com • URL: http://www.medec.com • Monthly. $47.95 per year. Edited for personnel responsible for the purchase of medical, surgical, and hospital equipment and supplies. Features new purchasing techniques and new products. Includes news of the activities of two major purchasing associations, Health Care Material Management Society and International Association of Healthcare Central Service Materiel Management.

Healthcare QuickDisc. American Hospital Association, One North Franklin St. Chicago, IL 60606. Phone: 800-242-2626 or (312)422-3000 Fax: (312)422-4505 • URL: http://www.aha.org • Annual. AHA members, $2,800.00. Non-members, $3,750.00. CD-ROM corresponds to the printed *AHA Guide*, with additional material and extensive search capabilities (400 data fields). Provides detailed information on 6,000 hospitals and hospital systems, including utilization data.

Healthcare Risk Management. American Health Consultants Inc., PO Box 740056 Atlanta, GA 30374. Phone: 800-688-2421 or (404)262-7436 Fax: (404)262-7837 E-mail: ahc.management@thomson.com • URL: http://www.medec.com • Description: Analyzes specific legal cases and trends relevant to healthcare liability. Discusses malpractice, liability for patients, staff and visitor injury, injury prevention, biomedical engineering, and medical staff credentials. Also covers high-risk areas of hospitals, hospital-owned home health and physician practices, accreditation, Medicare reimbursement, physician liability, medical records, and claims management. Recurring features include interviews, statistics, news of research, guest columns, legal briefs, and commentaries.

HealthLeaders, Inc., 66 Music Square W. Nashville, TN 37203. Phone: (999)203-0675 or (615)385-4131 or (615)385-4979 Fax: (615)385-4979 E-mail: magazine@healthleaders.com • URL: http://www.healthleaders.coms.com • Bimonthly. $49.95 per year. Provides broad coverage of finance, marketing, management, and technology for executives in the health care industry. Includes "Roundtable" discussions of particular health care issues. F ormerly *Healthcare Business*.

Healthplan. America Association of Health Plans, 1129 20th St., N.W., Suite 600 Washington, DC 20036. Phone: (202)778-3247 Fax: (202)331-7487 E-mail: aahp@aahp.org • URL: http://www.aahp.org • Bimonthly. $75.00 per year.

Healthplan: The Magazine of Trends, Insights, and Best Practices. American Association of Health Plans, 1129 20th St., N. W., Suite 600 Washington, DC 20036. Phone: (202)778-3200 Fax: (202)331-7487 • URL: http://www.aahp.org • Bimonthly. $75.00 per year. Edited for managed care executives.

Healthstar. Medlars Management Section, National Library of Medicine, 8600 Rockville Pike Bethesda, MD 20209. Phone: 800-638-8484 or (301)496-6531 Fax: (301)480-3537 • URL: http://www.nlm.nih.gov • Provides indexing and abstracting of non-clinical literature relating to health care delivery, 1975 to date. Monthly updates. Inquire as to online cost and availability.

Healthy Prepared Foods. MarketResearch.com, 641 Ave. of the Americas, 4th Fl. New York, NY 10011. Phone: 800-298-5699 or (212)807-2629 Fax: (212)807-2676 E-mail: customerservice@marketresearch.com • URL: http://www.marketresearch.com • 1999. $2,750.00. Consumer market data on foods that are low in calories, fat, cholesterol, sodium, and sugar or high in fiber and calcium, with forecasts to 2003.

Heating/Piping/Air Conditioning Engineering: The Magazine of Mechanical Systems Engineering. Penton Media, Inc., 1300 E. Ninth St. Cleveland, OH 44114. Phone: (216)696-7000 Fax: (216)696-1752 E-mail: information@penton.com • URL: http://www.penton.com • Monthly. $65.00 per year. Covers design, specification, installation, operation, and maintenance for systems in industrial, commercial, and institutional buildings. Formerly (Heating, Piping and Air Conditioning).

Heating Systems. Available from MarketResearch.com, 641 Ave. of the Americas, Fourth Floor New York, NY 10011. Phone: 800-298-5699 or (212)807-2629 Fax: (212)807-2642 E-mail: order@marketresearch.com • URL: http://www.marketresearch.com • 2002. $3,950.00. Published by Global Industry Analysts. Provides worldwide market research data, including profiles of major heating system companies.

Heavy Duty Trucking: The Business Magazine of Trucking. Newport Communications, 38 Executive Park, Suite 300 Irvine, CA 92714. Phone: (949)261-1636 Fax: (949)261-2904 E-mail: hdtfeedback@heavytruck.com • URL: http://www.heavydutytrucking.com • Monthly. $65.00 per year.

Hebrew Immigrant Aid Society., 333 7th Ave., 16th Fl. New York, NY 10001-5004. Phone: 800-HIAS-714 or (212)967-4100 Fax: (212)967-4483 E-mail: info@hias.org • URL: http://www.hias.org • Assists refugees and migrants from Europe, North Africa, the Middle East, and other trouble areas resettle in the United States, Canada, Latin America, and Australia. Maintains offices and committees around the world to: help locate relatives and friends; prepare documents; arrange for transportation; provide reception and resettlement services. Is involved in assistance to refugees at the request of the U.S. government. Compiles statistics.

HedgeWorld Annual Compendium: The Hedge Fund Industry's Definitive Reference Guide. HedgeWorld USA, 707 Westchester Ave., Suite L-4 White Plains, NY 10604. Phone: (914)921-7800 Fax: (914)421-7717 E-mail: inquiry@hedgeworld.com • URL: http://www.hedgeworld.com • Annual. $499.00. Contains profiles of 500 domestic and offshore hedge funds with more than $50 million in assets under management. Includes articles on "The Basics of Investing in Hedge Funds," "Beyond the Basics," and other information.

HedgeWorld Service Provider League Tables & Analyses. HedgeWorld USA, 707 Westchester Ave., Suite L-4 White Plains, NY 10604. Phone: (914)921-7800 Fax: (914)421-7717 E-mail: inquiry@hedgeworld.com • URL: http://www.hedgeworld.com • Annual. $595.00. Provides quantitative and qualitative information on firms providing services to hedge funds: accountants/auditors, administrators, custodians, legal counsel, and prime brokers. Detailed categories cover banks, clearing services, consultants, derivatives business, investment companies, wealth management services, etc.

The Helicopter Annual. Helicopter Association International, 1635 Prince St. Alexandria, VA 22314. Phone: 800-435-4976 or (703)683-4646 Fax: (703)683-4745 E-mail: questions@rotor.com • URL: http://www.rotor.com • Covers: Private and corporate members of the Helicopter Association International, as well as manufacturers in the helicopter industry; international coverage. Entries include: For members—Personal or company name, address, phone, fax, name and title of contact, description of services, fleet size. For manufacturers—Company name, address, phone, fax, technical description of products.

Helicopter Association International., 1635 Prince St. Alexandria, VA 22314-2818. Phone: 800-435-4976 or (703)683-4646 Fax: (703)683-4745 E-mail: questions@rotor.com • URL: http://www.rotor.com • Owners, operators, helicopter enthusiasts, and affiliated companies in the civil helicopter industry. Receives and disseminates information concerning the use, operation, hiring, contracting, and leasing of helicopters. Maintains a collection of current helicopter service bulletins and technical data; organizes safety seminars, continuing education courses, and helicopter operator management courses; and maintains a maintenance malfunction information database.

Helicopter News. Access Intelligence L.L.C., 4 Choke Cherry Rd., 2nd Fl. Rockville, MD 20850. Phone: 800-777-5006 or (301)354-2000 Fax: (301)309-3847 E-mail: info@accessintel.com • URL: http://www.pbimedia.com • Description: Reports to company executives, military leaders, and ancillary industries on the state of the helicopter industry. Tracks buying and selling information, news of contracts, and new programs. Also concerned with related issues, including EMS (Emergency Mission Support) and insurance. Recurring features include interviews and news of technology and new products. **Remarks:** Also available online and via e-mail.

The Helping Relationship: Process and Skills. Lawrence M. Brammer and Ginger A. MacDonald. Allyn and Bacon, Inc., 75 Arlington St., Ste. 300 Boston, MA 02116. Phone: 800-922-0579 or (781)848-6000 Fax: (515)284-2607 E-mail: ab_webmaster@abacon.com • URL: http://www.abacon.com • 2002. $53.00. Eighth edition.

Herb Farming. Entrepreneur Media, Inc., 2445 McCabe Way Irvine, CA 92614. Phone: 800-421-2300 or (949)261-2325 Fax: (949)261-0234 E-mail: entmag@entrepreneur.com • URL: http://www.entrepreneur.com • Looseleaf. $59.50. A practical guide to the business side of herb farming. Covers profit potential, start-up costs, market size evaluation, owner's time required, pricing, accounting, advertising, promotion, etc. (Start-Up Business Guide No. E1282.)

Herb Quarterly. EGW Publishing Co., 1041 Shary Circle Concord, CA 94518. Phone: (925)671-9852 Fax: (925)671-0692 E-mail: herbquart@aol.com • URL: http://www.herbquarterly.com • Quarterly. $19.97 per year. A magazine for herb enthusiasts covering all aspects of herb uses.

Herb Society of America.

Herbal Drugs and Phytopharmaceuticals. Max Wichtl and Norman G. Bisset, editors. CRC Press LLC, 2000 NW Corporate Blvd. Boca Raton, FL 33431. Phone: 800-272-7737 or (561)994-0555 Fax: 800-374-3401 or (561)989-9732 E-mail: orders@crcpress.com • URL: http://www.crcpress.com • 1994. $190.00. Provides a scientific approach to the medicinal use of herbs. (English translation of original German edition.)

The Herbalist. Michael Katz. University Press of America, P.O. Box 459 New York, NY 20004. Phone: (212)969-8419 Fax: (718)624-8419 1992. $38.50.

Herbarist. Herb Society of America, Inc., 9019 Kirtland Chardon Rd. Kirkland, OH 44094. Phone: (440)256-0514 Fax: (440)256-0541 E-mail: herb@herbsociety.org • URL: http://www.herbsociety.org • Annual. Free to members; non-members, $10.00.

Herty Foundation: Research and Development Center.

HFN (Home Furnishing Network): The Newsweekly of Home Products Retailing. Fairchild Publications, Seven W. 34th St. New York, NY 10001. Phone: (212)630-4000 Fax: (212)630-3675 E-mail: customerservice@fairchildpub.com • URL: http://www.fairchildpub.com • Weekly. Individuals, $99.00 per year; institutions, $295.00 per year. Formerly *H F D-Home Furnishing Daily*.

High Performance Review: Definitive Magazine for Audiophiles and Music Lovers. High Performance Review Publishing, 296 Amherst Dr. Murfreesboro, TN 37128-6233. Phone: (615)893-9788 Fax: (615)893-9717 Quarterly. $15.00 per year.

High-Tech Materials Alert: Advanced Materials: Their Uses and Manufacture. Technical Insights, 605 Third Ave. New York, NY 10158-0012. Phone: 800-825-7550 or (212)850-8600 Fax: (212)850-8800 E-mail: insights@wiley.com • URL: http://www.wiley.com • Monthly. Institutions, $695.00 per year. Newsletter on technical developments relating to high-performance materials, including metals and ceramics. Includes market forecasts.

High Technology Fitness Research Institute., 1510 W. Montana St. Chicago, IL 60614. Phone: (773)528-1000 Fax: (773)528-1043 E-mail: bgoldman@worldhealth.net • URL: http://www.worldhealth.net • Research activities include the analysis of health and fitness products and programs on the market.

The High Yield Debt Market: Investment Performance and Economic Impact. Edward I. Altman, editor. McGraw-Hill, 1221 Ave. of the Americas New York, NY 10020. Phone: 800-

722-4726 or (212)512-2000 Fax: (212)512-4502 E-mail: customer.service@mcgraw-hill.com • URL: http://www. mcgraw-hill.com • 1990. $55.00.

High Yield Report. American Banker/Bond Buyer Inc., 1 State St. Plz. 27 Fl. New York, NY 10004. Phone: 800-221-1809 or (212)803-8200 Fax: (212)843-9600 E-mail: custserv@ americanbanker.com • URL: http://www.thomsonmedia.com • Description: Examines markets for high-yield corporate bonds, work-outs, bankruptcies, and secondary markets for distressed securities. Contains pricing information for primary and secondary markets and analysis of the high-yield sector. Reports on developments affecting the senior and subordinated debt of companies in bankruptcy or working their way out of debt, detailing proposed financial restructurings. Tracks regulatory decisions affecting trade of distressed debt and funds purchased and sold. **Remarks:** Incorporates the former Distressed Debt Report.

Higher Education and National Affairs. American Council on Education, Office of Research, One Dupont Circle, N.W. Washington, DC 20036. Phone: (202)939-9300 Fax: (202)833-4760 E-mail: web@ace.nche.edu • URL: http:// www.acenet.edu • Biweekly. $60.00 per year. Newsletter.

Highlights and Documents. Tax Analysts, 6830 N. Fairfax Dr. Arlington, VA 22213. Phone: 800-955-2444 or (703)533-4400 Fax: (703)533-4444 E-mail: cservice@tax.org • URL: http://www.tax.org • Daily. $2,249.00 per year, including monthly indexes. Newsletter. Provides daily coverage of IRS, congressional, judicial, state, and international tax developments. Includes abstracts and citations for "all tax documents released within the previous 24 to 48 hours." Annual compilation available *Highlights and Documents on Microfiche*.

Highway and Traffic Safety and Accident Research, Management, and Issues. Norman Solomon, editor. Transportation Research Board, Keck Center of the National Academies, 500 5th St., NW Washington, DC 20001. Phone: (202)334-3213 E-mail: trbsales@nas.edu • URL: http://www.trb.org • 1993. $28.00. (Record Series).

Highway Financing and Construction: State Capitals. Wakeman-Walworth, Inc., P.O. Box 7376 Alexandria, VA 22307-7376. Phone: 800-876-2545 or (703)768-9600 Fax: (703)768-9690 E-mail: newsletters@statecapitals.com • URL: http://www.statecapitals.com • 50 times a year. $345.00 per year.; print and online editions, $490.00 per year. Newsletter. Formerly *From the State Capitals: Highway Financing and Construction*.

Highway of Dreams: A Critical View Along the Information Superhighway. A. Michael Noll. Lawrence Erlbaum Associates, Inc., 10 Industrial Ave. Mahwah, NJ 07430-2262. Phone: 800-926-6579 or (201)258-2200 Fax: (201)236-0072 E-mail: orders@erlbaum.com • URL: http://www.erlbaum. com • 1996. $49.95. States that such factors as consumer needs and finance are often of more importance to the information industry than technological utopia. Includes such chapter headings as "Historical Perspective," "History Repeats," "Business Considerations," and "The Internet Exposed." (LEA's Telecommunications Series).

Highway Safety Literature., National Highway Traffic Safety Administration, 400 Seventh St. SW Washington, DC 20024-2516. Phone: (202)366-4943 Annual. $80.00.

Highway Statistics. Federal Highway Administration, U.S. Department of Transportation. Available from U.S. Government Printing Office, Washington, DC 20402. Phone: (202)512-1800 Fax: (202)512-2250 E-mail: gpoaccess@gpo. gov • URL: http://www.access.gpo.gov • Annual. $26.00.

The Highwaymen: Warriors on the Information Superhighway. Ken Auletta. Harcourt Trade Publications, 525 B St., Suite 1900 San Diego, CA 92101-4495. Phone: 800-543-1918 or (619)231-6616 Fax: 800-235-0256 E-mail: apbcs@ harcourtbrace.com • URL: http://www.harcourtbooks.com • 1998. $13.00. Revised expanded edition. Contains critical articles about Ted Turner, Rupert Murdoch, Barry Diller, Michael Eisner, and other key figures in electronic communications, entertainment, and information. (Harvest Book Series).

Highways. Good Sam club. Affinity Group, Inc., T L Enterprises, 2575 Vista Del Mar Dr. Ventura, CA 93001-3920. Phone: 800-825-6861 or (805)667-4100 Fax: (805)667-4379 • URL: http://www.rv.net • 11 times a year. Membership. Five regional editions. Formerly *Good Sam's Hi-Way Herald*.

Hine's Directory of Insurance Adjusters, Investigators, and Appraisers. Hine's, Inc., P.O. Box 143 Geneva, IL 60134-0134. Phone: (630)377-8049 Fax: (630)587-8533 Annual. $20.00. Lists selected independent insurance adjusters in the United States and Canada.

Hine's Insurance Counsel. Hine's Inc., Box 143 Geneva, IL 60134. Phone: (630)377-8049 Fax: (630)587-8533 E-mail: hines@dls.net Covers: 2,500 law firms in the United States and Canada that handle defense in litigation involving insurance and transportation companies. Entries include: Firm name, address, phone, type of practice, names of partners and associates, clients, memberships in trial organizations. An insurance law list. See separate listing, "Law Lists.".

The Hiring and Firing Book: A Complete Legal Guide for Employers. Steven M. Sack. Legal Strategies, Inc., 1795 Harvard Ave. Merrick, NY 11566. Phone: (516)377-3940 1996. $149.95. Revised edition. Covers a wide range of legal considerations relative to employment and dismissal. Includes checklists, a glossary, and samples of applications,

agreements, contracts, and other documents.

Hiring Right: A Practical Guide. Susan J. Herman. Sage Publications, Inc., 2455 Teller Rd. Thousand Oaks, CA 91320. Phone: 800-818-7243 or (805)499-9774 Fax: 800-583-2665 or (805)499-0871 E-mail: webmaster@sagepub.com • URL: http://www.sagepub.com • 1994. $77.95. A practical manual covering job definition, recruitment, interviewing, testing, and checking of references.

Hispanic American Periodicals Index. University of California, Los Angeles. Latin American Studies Center Publications, 10347 Bunche Hall Los Angeles, CA 90095. Phone: (310)825-0810 Fax: (310)206-2634 E-mail: bvalk@ucla.edu • URL: http://www.hapi.gseis.ucla.edu • Annual. $400.00. Indexes about 250 periodicals that regularly include material on Latin America. Supplement available.

The Hispanic Market. Available from MarketResearch.com, 641 Ave. of the Americas, Third Floor New York, NY 10011. Phone: 800-298-5699 or (212)807-2629 Fax: (212)807-2716 E-mail: order@marketresearch.com • URL: http://www. marketresearch.com • 2001. $2,750.00. Published by Packaged Facts. Provides consumer market data and demographics, with projections to 2006.

Hispanic Market Handbook. Gale Cengage Learning, 27500 Drake Rd. Farmington Hills, MI 48331-3535. Phone: 800-877-GALE or (248)699-4253 Fax: 800-414-5043 E-mail: gale.galeord@cengage.com • URL: http://gale.cengage.com • 1995. $95.00. Provides advice on marketing consumer items to Hispanic Americans. Includes case studies and demographic profiles. (Professional Library).

Hispanic Media and Market Source. SRDS, 1700 Higgins Rd. Des Plaines, IL 60018-5605. Phone: 800-851-7737 or (847)375-5000 Fax: (847)375-5001 • URL: http://www.srds. com • Quarterly. $295.00 per year. Provides detailed information on the following Hispanic advertising media in the U. S.: TV, radio, newspapers, magazines, direct mail, outdoor, and special events.

Historical Statistics of the United States, Colonial Times to 1970: A Statistical Abstract Supplement. U.S. Bureau of the Census. Available from U.S. Government Printing Office, Washington, DC 20402. Phone: (202)512-1800 Fax: (202)512-2250 E-mail: gpoaccess@gpo.gov • URL: http:// www.accessgpo.gov • 1975. $109.00. Two volumes.

Historical Tables, Budget of the United States Government. Available from U. S. Government Printing Office, Washington, DC 20402. Phone: (202)512-1800 Fax: (202)512-2250 E-mail: gpoaccess@gpo.gov • URL: http:// www.access.gpo.gov • Annual. $41.00. Issued by the Office of Management and Budget, Executive Office of the President (http://www.whitehouse.gov). Provides statistical data on the federal budget for an extended period of about 60 years in the past to projections of four years in the future. Includes federal debt and federal employment.

The History of Accounting: An Encyclopedia. Michael Chatfield and Richard Vangermeersch. Garland Publishing, Inc., 29 W. 35th St. New York, NY 10001-2299. Phone: 800-627-6273 or (212)216-7800 Fax: (212)564-7854 E-mail: info@garland. com • URL: http://www.garlandpub.com • 1996. $100.00. Contains more than 400 alphabetical entries by various contributors, covering the history of accounting from 750 B.C. to the modern era. Includes a bibliography for each entry and an index. (Reference Library of the Humanities Series: Vol. 1573).

The History of Black Business in America: Capitalism, Race, Entrepreneurship. Juliet E. Walker. Available from Gale Cengage Learning, 27500 Drake Rd. Farmington Hills, MI 48331-3535. Phone: 800-877-GALE or (248)699-GALE Fax: 800-414-5043 E-mail: gale.galeord@cengage.com • URL: http://gale.cengage.com • 1998. $50.00. Published by Twayne Publishers. Includes profiles of African American business pioneers. (Evolution of Modern Business Series.)

History of Interest Rates. Sidney Homer and Richard Sylla. Rutgers University Press, 100 Joyce Kilmer Ave. Piscataway, NJ 08854-8099. Phone: 800-446-9323 or (732)445-7762 Fax: 888-471-9014 or (732)445-7039 E-mail: bksales@rci.rutgers. edu • URL: http://www.rutgers.press.rutgers.edu • 1996. $79. 00. Third revised edition.

History of Rocketry and Astronautics. American Astronautical Society. Available from Univelt, Inc., 740 Metcalf St., Nos. 13+15 Escondido, CA 92025. Phone: (760)746-4005 Fax: (760)746-3139 E-mail: 76121.1532@compuserve.com • URL: http://www.univelt.com • Various volumes and prices. Covers the history of rocketry and astronautics since 1880. Prices vary. (AAS History Series).

History of the Internet: A Chronology, 1843 to the Present. Christos J. P. Moschovitis and others. ABC-CLIO, Inc., 130 Cremona Dr. Santa Barbara, CA 93117. Phone: 800-368-6868 or (805)968-1911 Fax: (805)685-9685 E-mail: customerservice@abc-clio.com • URL: http://www.abc-clio. com • 1999. $65.00. Early entries cover the history of the computer. Includes biographical information, bibliography, and glossary.

HIV/AIDS and the World of Work: An ILO Code of Practice. International Labour Organization, 1828 L St., N.W., Suite 600 Washington, DC 20036-5121. Phone: (202)653-7652 Fax: (202)653-7687 E-mail: washington@ilo.org • URL: http://www.ilo.org • 2002. $12.95. Emphasis is on protection from discrimination. Discusses the formation of appropriate policy by governments and organizations.

HMAT (Hot Mix Asphalt Technology). National Asphalt Pave-

ment Association, NAPA Building, 5100 Forbes Blvd. Lanham, MD 20706-4407. Phone: 888-468-6499 or (301)731-4748 Fax: (301)731-4621 E-mail: napa@hotmix.org • URL: http://www.hotmix.org • Bimonthly. Free.

HME News (Home Medical Equipment). United Publications, Inc., P.O. Box 997 Yarmouth, ME 04096-1997. Phone: 800-441-6982 or (207)846-0600 Fax: (207)846-0657 Monthly. Free to qualified personnel; others, $60.00 per year. Covers the home medical equipment business for dealers and manufacturers. Provides information on a wide variety of home health care supplies and equipment.

HMO Competitive Edge. InterStudy Publications, 2610 University Ave., W, Ste. 500 St. Paul, MN 55114. Phone: 800-844-3351 or (612)858-9291 Fax: (612)584-5698 Semiannual. Price on application. Provides highly detailed statistical, directory, and market information on U. S. health maintenance organizations. Consists of three parts: *The HMO Directory*, *The HMO Industry Report*, and *The Regional Market Analysis*.

Hobby Industry Association., 319 E. 54th St. Elmwood Park, NJ 07407. Phone: (201)794-1133 Fax: (201)797-0657 E-mail: hia@hobby.org • URL: http://www.hobby.org • Formerly Hobby Industry Association of America.

Hobby Shop. Entrepreneur Media, Inc., 2445 McCabe Way Irvine, CA 92614. Phone: 800-421-2300 or (949)261-2325 Fax: (949)261-0234 E-mail: entmag@entrepreneur.com • URL: http://www.entrepreneur.com • Looseleaf. $59.50. A practical guide to starting a hobby shop. Covers profit potential, start-up costs, market size evaluation, owner's time required, site selection, lease negotiation, pricing, accounting, advertising, promotion, etc. (Start-Up Business Guide No. E1132.)

Holiday Institute of Yonkers., c/o William Bickel, P.O. Box 2 Kenvil, NJ 07847-0002. E-mail: bbickel@cris.com Seeks to research, study, celebrate and promote interest in holidays in general.

Holidays and Anniversaries of the World. Gale Cengage Learning, 27500 Drake Rd. Farmington Hills, MI 48331-3535. Phone: 800-877-GALE or (248)699-4253 Fax: 800-414-5043 E-mail: gale.galeord@cengage.com • URL: http://gale. cengage.com • 1998. $125.00. Third edition. Lists 23,000 regional, national and international holidays and anniversaries. Includes birthdays of famous people, days of the saints and other days of religious significance.

Holidays, Festivals, and Celebrations of the World Dictionary: Detailing More Than 2,500 Observances from All 50 States and More Than 100 Nations. Helen Henderson and Sue Ellen Thompson, editors. Omnigraphics, Inc., 615 Griswold St. Detroit, MI 48226. Phone: 800-234-1340 or (313)961-1340 Fax: 800-875-1340 or (313)961-1383 E-mail: info@ omnigraphics.com • URL: http://www.omnigraphics.com • 2001. $98.00. Third edition.

Hollywood Creative Directory: Below-the-Line Talent. IFILMpro, 1024 N Orange Dr. Hollywood, CA 90038. Phone: 800-815-0503 or (323)308-3490 Fax: (323)308-3493 E-mail: hcd@ifilm.com • URL: http://www.ifilmpro.com • Annual. $80.00. Lists more than 6,000 cinematographers, production designers, costume designers, film editors, set decorators, and art directors and their associated 15,000 film titles.

Hollywood Creative Directory: Film Actors., 1024 N Orange Dr. Hollywood, CA 90038. Phone: 800-815-0503 or (323)308-3490 Fax: (323)468-7689 Annual. $85.00. Lists more than 6,000 film actors and their associated 15,000 film titles.

Hollywood Creative Directory: Film Directors., 1024 N Orange Dr. Hollywood, CA 90038. Phone: 800-815-0503 or (323)308-3490 Fax: (323)468-7689 Annual. $95.00. Lists more than 5,500 film directors and their associated 43,000 film titles. Includes Canadian, British, European, and Japanese directors.

Hollywood Creative Directory: Film Writers. IFILMpro, 1024 N Orange Dr. Hollywood, CA 90038. Phone: 800-815-0503 or (323)308-3490 Fax: (323)468-7689 Annual. $85.00. Lists more than 8,000 screenwriters and their associated 35,000 film titles. Includes projects in development and unsold screenplays.

Hollywood Creative Directory: International Film Buyers., 1024 N Orange Dr. Hollywood, CA 90038. Phone: 800-815-0503 or (323)308-3490 Fax: (323)468-7689 Annual. $59.95. Lists more than 1,750 film and television buyers. Worldwide coverage.

Hollywood Creative Directory: The Phone Book to Hollywood. IFILM Publishing, 1024 N Orange Dr. Hollywood, CA 90038. Phone: 800-815-0503 or (323)308-3490 Fax: (323)308-3493 E-mail: hcd@ifilm.com • URL: http://www. ifilmpro.com • Semiannual. $149.95 per year. Three issues per year. Single issue, $59.95. Lists about 9,900 talent agents, personal managers, and casting directors.

The Hollywood Reporter., 5055 Wilshire Blvd. Los Angeles, CA 90036-4396. Phone: (323)525-2000 Fax: (323)525-2377 E-mail: mailbox@hollywoodreporter.com • URL: http:// www.hollywoodreporter.com • Daily. $219.00 per year. Covers the latest news in film, TV, cable, multimedia, music, and theatre. Includes box office grosses and entertainment industry financial data.

Hollywood Women's Political Committee., 1460 4th St Ste. 212 Santa Monica, CA 90401-3414. E-mail: richard.wallace@ scbar.org Women working in the entertainment industry and related fields. Raises funds for federal political candidates, grass roots organizations, and statewide initiatives that pledge to represent the group's beliefs on nuclear disarmament, increased environmental protection, improved public education, and expanded civil rights for women. Seeks to heighten community involvement in national politics. **Publications:** none. **Convention/Meeting:** none.

Home Banking Report. JupiterMedia, 23 Old Kings Hwy., S Darien, CT 06820. Phone: 800-488-4345 or (203)662-2800 Fax: (203)655-4686 • URL: http://www.jmm.com • Annual. $695.00. Market research report. Covers banking from home by phone or online, with projections of growth in future years.

Home Business Bible: Everything You Need to Know to Start and Run Your Home-Based Business. David R. Eyler. John Wiley and Sons, Inc., 111 River St. Hoboken, NJ 07030. Phone: 800-225-5945 or (201)748-6000 Fax: (201)748-6088 E-mail: info@wiley.com • URL: http://www.wiley.com • 1994. $60.00. Includes CD-ROM.

Home Business Magazine: The Home-Based Entrepreneur's Magazine. United Marketing and Research Co., Inc., 9582 Hamilton Ave. Huntington Beach, CA 92646. Phone: (714)968-0331 Fax: (714)962-7722 E-mail: henderso@ix. netcom.com • URL: http://www.homebusinessmag.com • Bimonthly. $15.00 per year. Provides practical advice and ideas relating to the operation of a business in the home. Sections include "Marketing & Sales," "Money Corner" (financing), "Businesses & Opportunities," and "Home Office" (equipment, etc.). Includes an annual directory of more than 250 non-franchised home business opportunities, including start-up costs and information about providers.

Home Care Products Market. MarketResearch.com, 641 Ave. of the Americas, 4th Fl. New York, NY 10011. Phone: 800-298-5699 or (212)807-2629 Fax: (212)807-2716 E-mail: customerservice@marketresearch.com • URL: http://www.marketresearch.com • 2001. $3,500.00. Market data with projections to 2005. Covers a wide variety of products: wheelchairs, crutches, beds, monitoring equipment, etc.

Home Care Services Market. MarketResearch.com, 641 Ave. of the Americas, 4th Fl. New York, NY 10011. Phone: 800-298-5699 or (212)807-2629 Fax: (212)807-2676 E-mail: customerservice@marketresearch.com • URL: http://www.marketresearch.com • 1999. $3,250.00. Market data with projections. Covers a wide variety of services: primary nursing, respiratory, dialysis, infusion, etc.

Home Entertainment Installation. Entrepreneur Media, Inc., 2445 McCabe Way Irvine, CA 92614. Phone: 800-421-2300 or (949)261-2325 Fax: (949)261-0234 E-mail: entmag@ entrepreneur.com • URL: http://www.entrepreneur.com • Looseleaf. $59.50. A practical guide to starting a home entertainment installation service. Covers profit potential, start-up costs, market size evaluation, owner's time required, pricing, accounting, advertising, promotion, etc. (Start-Up Business Guide No. E1349.)

Home Fashions: Buyer's Guide. Fairchild Publications, Seven W.34th St. New York, NY 10001. Phone: (212)630-4000 E-mail: customerservice@fairchildpub.com • URL: http:// www.fairchildpub.com • Annual. $10.00. Lists manufacturers, importers, and regional sales representatives supplying bed, bath, kitchen, and table linens; window treatments; wall coverings; and fibers and fabrics.

Home Fashions Products Association., 355 Lexington Ave., 17th Fl. New York, NY 10017-6603. Phone: (212)297-2122 Fax: (212)370-9047 Members are manufacturers of curtains and draperies.

Home Health Agencies Report and Directory. SMG Marketing Group, Inc., 875 N Michigan Ave., Ste. 3100 Chicago, IL 60611. Phone: (312)642-3026 Fax: (312)642-9729 Annual. $575.00. Lists over 13,000 home healthcare agencies and corporations. Includes a market analysis and growth projections.

Home Health Care Dealer-Provider. Curant Communications, Inc., 6701 Center Dr. W, No. 450 Los Angeles, CA 90045-1556. Phone: (310)306-2206 Fax: (310)306-9548 • URL: http://www.hhcdealer.com • Bimonthly. Free. For home care dealer and home care pharmacies. Formerly *Home Health Care Dealer - Supplier.*

Home Health Care Management. Lazelle E. Benefield. Prentice Hall PTR, 240 Frisch Ct. Paramus, NJ 07652. Phone: 800-282-0693 Fax: 800-445-6991 • URL: http://www.phptr.com • 1988. $50.00.

Home Health Care Services Quarterly: The Journal of Community Care. Haworth Press, Inc., 10 Alice St. Binghamton, NY 13904-1580. Phone: 800-429-6784 or (607)722-5857 Fax: (607)722-1424 E-mail: getinfo@haworthpressinc.com • URL: http://www.haworthpressinc.com • Quarterly. $535.00 per year. An academic and practical journal focusing on the marketing and administration of home care.

Home Health Line: The Home Care Industry's National Independent Newsletter., 11300 Rockville Pike, Suite 1100 Rockville, MD 20852-3030. Phone: (301)816-8950 Fax: (301)816-8945 48 times a year. $399.00 per year. Newsletter on legislation and regulations affecting the home health care industry, with an emphasis on federal funding and Medicare programs.

Home Health Products. Stevens Publishing Corp., 5151 Beltline Rd., Ste. 1010 Dallas, TX 75240. Phone: (972)687-6700 Fax: (972)687-6769 10 times a year. $99.00 per year. Covers new medical equipment products for the home care industry.

Home Healthcare Agency Chains Directory. Firstmark Inc., 25 Vintinner Rd., PO Box 1270 Campton, NH 03223-1270. Phone: 800-729-2600 or (603)726-4800 Fax: (603)726-4840 E-mail: info@firstmark.com • URL: http://www.firstmark.

com • Description: Includes operational statistics and other data on 240 chains which own or manage home healthcare agencies. Entries include: Headquarter name, address, phone, agencies belonging to the chain, ownership type, number of employees.

Home Healthcare Nurse: The Journal for the Home Care and Hospice Professional. The Home Healthcare Nurses Association. Lippincott Williams and Wilkins, 530 Walnut St. Philadelphia, PA 19106-3621. Phone: 800-638-3030 or (215)521-8300 Fax: (215)521-8902 E-mail: custserv@lww. com • URL: http://www.lww.com • 10 times a year. Individuals, $52.95 per year; institutions, $202.95 per year. For professional nurses in the home health care field.

The Home Improvement Market. Available from MarketResearch.com, 641 Ave. of the Americas, Third Floor New York, NY 10011. Phone: 800-298-5699 or (212)807-2629 Fax: (212)807-2716 E-mail: order@marketresearch. com • URL: http://www.marketresearch.com • 1999. $2,750.00. Market research report published by Packaged Facts. Covers the market for lumber, finishing materials, tools, hardware, etc.

Home Inspection Service. Entrepreneur Media, Inc., 2445 McCabe Way Irvine, CA 92614. Phone: 800-421-2300 or (949)261-2325 Fax: (949)261-0234 E-mail: entmag@ entrepreneur.com • URL: http://www.entrepreneur.com • Looseleaf. $59.50. A practical guide to starting a home inspection service. Covers profit potential, start-up costs, market size evaluation, owner's time required, pricing, accounting, advertising, promotion, etc. (Start-Up Business Guide No. E1334.)

Home Lighting and Accessories. Doctorow Communications, Inc., 1011 Clifton Ave., Suite B1 Clifton, NJ 07013-3518. Phone: (973)779-1600 Fax: (973)779-3242 E-mail: info@ homelighting.com • URL: http://www.homelighting.com • Monthly. $30.00 per year. Trade magazine of the residential lighting industry for retailers, distributors, designers, architects, specifiers, manufacturers and all lighting professionals.

Home Lighting and Accessories Suppliers Directory. Doctorow Communications, Inc., 1011 Clifton Ave. Clifton, NJ 07013-3518. Phone: (973)779-1600 Fax: (973)779-3242 E-mail: info@homelighting.com • URL: http://www.homelighting. com • Semiannual. $6.00 per issue. Lists almost 1,000 suppliers of residential lighting fixtures and accessories.

Home Office Association of America. PO Box 51 Sagaponack, NY 11962-0051. Phone: 800-809-4622 E-mail: hoaa@aol. com • URL: http://www.hoaa.com • A for-profit organization providing advice and information to home office workers and business owners.

Home Office Connections: A Monthly Journal of News, Ideas, Opportunities, and Savings for Those Who Work at Home. Home Office Association of America, PO Box 51 East Meadow, NY 11554. Phone: 800-809-4622 or (516)997-7394 Fax: (516)997-0839 E-mail: hoaa@aol.com • URL: http:// www.hoaa.com • Monthly. Free to members; non-members, $49.00 per year.

Home Office Design: Everything You Need to Know about Planning, Organizing, and Furnishing Your Work Space. Neal Zimmerman. John Wiley and Sons, Inc., 111 River St. Hoboken, NJ 07030. Phone: 800-225-5945 or (201)748-6000 Fax: (201)748-6088 E-mail: info@wiley.com • URL: http://www. wiley.com • 1996. $19.95. Covers furniture, seating, workstations, filing, storage, task lighting, etc.

Home Recording Rights Coalition., PO Box 14267 Washington, DC 20044-4267. Phone: 800-282-8273 or (202)628-9212 Fax: (202)628-9227 E-mail: info@hrrc.org • URL: http:// www.hrrc.org • Consumers, retailers, and manufacturers of audio and video electronics products. Advocates the consumer's right to use consumer electronics equipment for private, noncommercial purposes; current issues range from new audio and video technologies to the digital information superhighway and multimedia.

Home Sewing Association., PO Box 369 Monroeville, PA 15146. Phone: (412)372-5950 Fax: (412)372-5953 E-mail: info@ sewing.org • URL: http://www.sewing.org • Manufacturers and retailers of home sewing merchandise, including fabrics, patterns, sewing machines, sewing notions, needlework, and crafts.

HomeCare Magazine Buyers' Guide. Primedia Business, 23805 Stuart Ranch Rd., PO Box 8987 Malibu, CA 90265. Phone: 800-795-5445 or (310)317-4522 Fax: (310)317-9644 E-mail: info@firstmark.com • URL: http://www.primediabusiness. com • Publication includes: List of about 800 manufacturers and distributors of home health care and rehabilitation products, as well as service providers. Entries include: Company name, address, phone, fax, web site, e-mail, names and titles of key personnel, trade names, product or service provided; also by product category.

Homecare Magazine: The Business Magazine of the Home Health Industry. Primedia Business Magazines and Media, 6151 Powers Ferry Rd., Ste. 200 Atlanta, GA 66212. Phone: 800-795-5445 or (770)955-2500 Fax: (770)618-0204 E-mail: subs@primediabusiness.com • URL: http://www. primediabusiness.com • Monthly. $69.00 per year. Edited for dealers and suppliers of home medical equipment, including pharmacies and chain stores. Includes information on new products.

Homecare News. National Association for Home Care, 228 Seventh St. SE Washington, DC 20003. Phone: (202)547-

7424 Fax: (202)547-3540 E-mail: info@accessintel.com • URL: http://www.nahc.org • Description: Reports on National Association for Home Care news plus home care industry developments for the entire industry.

Homeland Security and Defense: Weekly Intelligence for the Global Homeland Security and Defense Community. Aviation Week Business Intelligence Services, 1200 G St., N.W., Suite 200 Washington, DC 20005. Phone: 800-752-4959 or (202)383-2350 Fax: (202)383-2438 • URL: http://www. aviationnow.com/bis • Weekly. $595.00 per year. Newsletter. Emphasis is on airline and airport programs (federal, state, and local). Also covers counterterrorism, protection of military units, Department of Homeland Security activities, industrial security, communications equipment, and other topics related to homeland security.

Homemade Money: How to Turn Your Talents, Experience, and Know-How into a Profitable Homebased Business That's Perfect for You! Barbara Brabec. Evans, M and Co., Inc., 4700 E Galbraith Rd. Cincinnati, OH 45236-6709. Phone: 800-289-0963 or (513)531-2690 • URL: http:// fwpublications.com • 2003. $19.95. Second edition. Covers sales, advertising, publicity, pricing, financing, legal issues, and other topics relating to businesses operated from home.

HomeOffice: The Homebased Office Authority. Entrepreneur Media, Inc., 2445 McCabe Way Irvine, CA 92614. Phone: 800-421-2300 or (949)261-2325 Fax: (949)752-1180 E-mail: entmag@entrepreneur.com • URL: http://www.entrepreneur. com • Bimonthly. $11.97 per year. Contains advice for operating a business in the home.

Homeowner or Tenant? How to Make a Wise Choice. Lawrence S. Pratt. American Institute for Economic Research, PO Box 1000 Great Barrington, MA 01230-1000. Phone: (413)528-1216 Fax: (413)528-0103 E-mail: info@aier.org • URL: http://www.aier.org • 2002. $8.00. Provides detailed information for making rent or buy decisions. Includes "Mortgage Arithmetic," "Hints for Buyers, Sellers, and Renters," worksheets, mortgage loan interest tables, and other data. (Economic Education Bulletin.)

The Honest Herbal: A Sensible Guide to the Use of Herbs and Related Remedies. Varro E. Tyler. The Haworth Press, Inc., 10 Alice St. Binghamton, NY 13904-1580. Phone: 800-429-6784 or (607)722-5857 Fax: 800-895-0582 or (607)722-1424 E-mail: getinfo@haworthpressinc.com • URL: http://www. haworthpressinc.com • 1993. $49.95. Third edition.

Honey Bee Research Unit.

Honey Production, Annual Summary. U.S. Department of Agriculture, Washington, DC 20250. Phone: (202)720-2791 Annual.

Hong Kong Business: The Portable Encyclopedia for Doing Business with Hong Kong. Christine Genzberger and others. World Trade Press, 1450 Grant Ave., Suite 204 Novato, CA 94945. Phone: 800-833-8586 or (415)898-1124 Fax: (415)898-1080 E-mail: sales@worldtradepress.com • URL: http://www.worldtradepress.com • 1994. $24.95. Covers economic data, import/export possibilities, basic tax and trade laws, travel information, and other useful facts for doing business with Hong Kong. (Country Business Guides Series).

Hong Kong Week. Dow Jones & Co., 200 Liberty St. New York, NY 10281. Phone: 800-544-0422 or (212)416-2000 Fax: (212)416-2658 Weekly. $260.00 per year (air mail). A guide to investing in Hong Kong and China. Provides stock prices, market analysis, and commentary. Edited and published in Hong Kong by the *Asian Wall Street Journal.*

Hoover's Company Capsules on CD-ROM. Hoover's, Inc., 5800 Airport Blvd. Austin, TX 78752. Phone: 800-486-8666 or (512)374-4500 Fax: (512)374-4501 E-mail: orders@hoovers. com • URL: http://www.hoovers.com • Quarterly. $399.95 per year (single-user). Provides the CD-ROM version of *Hoover's Handbook of American Business, Hoover's Handbook of Emerging Companies, Hoover's Handbook of World Business, Hoover's Guide to Computer Companies, Hoover's Guide to Media Companies, Hoover's Handbook of Private Companies,* and various regional guides. Includes more than 11,000 profiles of companies.

Hoover's Handbook of American Business: Profiles of Major U. S. Companies. Hoover's, Inc., 5800 Airport Blvd. Austin, TX 78752-4204. Phone: 800-486-8666 or (512)374-4500 Fax: (512)374-4501 E-mail: orders@hoovers.com • URL: http:// www.hoovers.com • Annual. $195.95. Two volumes. Provides detailed profiles of more than 750 large public and private companies, including history, executives, brand names, key competitors, and up to 10 years of financial data. Includes indexes by industry, location, executive name, company name, and brand name.

Hoover's Handbook of Emerging Companies: Profiles of America's Most Exciting Growth Enterprises. Hoover's, Inc., 5800 Airport Blvd. Austin, TX 78752. Phone: 800-486-8666 or (512)374-4500 Fax: (512)374-4501 E-mail: orders@ hoovers.com • URL: http://www.hoovers.com • Annual. $125.00. Contains detailed profiles of 600 rapidly growing corporations. Includes indexes by industry, location, executive name, company name, and brand name.

Hoover's Handbook of Private Companies: Profiles of Major U. S. Private Enterprises. Hoover's, Inc., 5800 Airport Blvd. Austin, TX 78752-4204. Phone: 800-486-8666 or (512)374-4500 Fax: (512)374-4501 E-mail: orders@hoovers.com • URL: http://www.hoovers.com • Annual. $155.00. Contains profiles of 900 private companies and organizations. Includes indexes by industry, location, executive name, and product.

Hoover's Handbook of World Business: Profiles of Major European, Asian, Latin American, and Canadian Companies. Hoover's, Inc., 5800 Airport Blvd. Austin, TX 78752-4204. Phone: 800-486-8666 or (512)374-4500 Fax: (512)374-4501 E-mail: orders@hoovers.com • URL: http://www.hoovers.com • Annual. $165.00. Contains detailed profiles for approximately 300 large foreign companies. Includes indexes by industry, location, executive name, company name, and brand name.

Hoover's Masterlist of Major U. S. Companies. Hoover's, Inc., 5800 Airport Blvd. Austin, TX 78752-4204. Phone: 800-486-8666 or (512)374-4500 Fax: (512)374-4501 E-mail: orders@hoovers.com • URL: http://www.hoovers.com • 2003. $275.00. Provides brief information, including annual sales, number of employees, and chief executive, for about 5,000 U. S. companies, both public and private.

Hoover's Online. Hoover's, Inc.Phone: 800-486-8666 or (512)374-4500 Fax: (512)374-4501 • URL: http://www.hoovers.com • Web site provides stock quotes, lists of companies, and a variety of business information at no charge. In-depth company profiles are available.

Hoover's Vision: Original Thinking for Business Success. Gary Hoover. Available from Hoover's, Inc., 5800 Airport Blvd. Austin, TX 78752. Phone: 800-486-8666 or (512)374-4500 Fax: (512)374-4505 E-mail: orders@hoovers.com • URL: http://www.hoovers.com • 2001. $26.95. Published by Texere. Contains inspirational advice for entrepreneurial achievement. The author is founder of Hoover's, Inc.

Horseman and Fair World: Devoted to the Trotting and Pacing Horse. Horseman Publishing Co., Insite Communications, P.O. Box 8480 Lexington, KY 40533-8480. Phone: (606)276-4026 Fax: (606)277-8100 • URL: http://www.harnessracing.com • Weekly. $80.00 per year.

Horticultural Abstracts: Compiled from World Literature on Temperate and Tropical Fruits, Vegetables, Ornaments, Plantation Crops. Available from CABI Publishing North America, 875 Massachusetts Ave., 7th Fl. Cambridge, MA 02139. Phone: 800-528-4841 or (617)395-4056 Fax: (617)354-6875 E-mail: cabi-nao@cabi.org • URL: http://www.cabi-publishing.org • Monthly. $2,010.00 per year. Print and online edition, $2,030.00 per year. Published in England by CABI Publishing. Provides worldwide coverage of the literature of fruits, vegetables, flowers, plants, and all aspects of gardens and gardening.

Horticulture: Gardening at its Best. Krause Publications Inc., 700 E State St. Iola, WI 54990-0001. Phone: 800-258-0929 or (715)445-2214 Fax: (715)445-4087 E-mail: info@krause.com • URL: http://www.krause.com • Bimonthly. $19.95 per year.

The Hosiery Association., 7421 Carmel Executive Park, Ste. 200 Charlotte, NC 28226. Phone: (704)365-0913 Fax: (704)362-2056 E-mail: thainfo@hosieryassociation.com • URL: http://www.hosieryassociation.com • Hosiery manufacturers and suppliers. Develops standards for hosiery measurement. Sponsors annual "Celebrate Hosiery" to educate consumers on hosiery varieties. Conducts field visitations for assistance in technical areas. Compiles statistics; conducts research programs. Operates Group Purchasing Program.

Hosiery News. Hosiery Association, 3623 Latrobe Dr., Suite 130 Charlotte, NC 28211-2117. Phone: (704)365-0913 Fax: (704)362-2056 Monthly. Membership. Hosiery-related news including new offerings for retail, industry changes, legislative updates of hosiery-impacting laws, foreign trade and statistical information.

Hosiery Statistics. Hosiery Association, 3623 Latrobe Dr., Suite 130 Charlotte, NC 28211-2117. Phone: (704)365-0913 Fax: (704)362-2056 E-mail: hosierytha@aol.com • URL: http://www.hosieryassociation.com • Annual. Free to members; non-members, $50.00.

Hospital Cost Management. Prentice Hall PTR, 240 Frisch Ct. Paramus, NJ 07652. Phone: 800-282-0693 Fax: 800-445-6991 • URL: http://www.phptr.com • Looseleaf. Periodic supplementation. Price on application.

Hospital Finance Almanac. Healthcare Financial Management Association, 1301 Connecticut Ave., NW, Ste. 300 Washington, DC 20036-3417. Phone: 800-252-4362 or (202)296-2920 Fax: (202)223-9771 E-mail: webmaster@hfma.org • URL: http://www.hfma.org • Annual. $350.00. Provides five-year data relating to the financial and operating performance of the U. S. hospital industry. A consolidation of the former *Financial Report of the Hospital Industry* and *Performance Report of the Hospital Industry*.

Hospital Home Health: The Monthly Updates for Executives and Health Care Professionals. American Health Consultants, Inc., 3525 Piedmont Rd. N.E., Bldg.6, Suite 400 Atlanta, GA 30305. Phone: 800-688-2421 or (404)262-7436 Fax: 800-284-3291 or (404)262-7837 E-mail: custserv@ahcpub.com • URL: http://www.ahcpub.com • Monthly. $399.00 per year. Newsletter for hospital-based home health agencies.

Hospital Liability. American Lawyer Media, Inc., 105 Madison Ave. New York, NY 10016. Phone: 800-888-8300 or (212)779-9200 Fax: (212)481-8110 E-mail: lawcatalog@amlaw.com • URL: http://www.lawcatalog.com/ • Looseleaf. $189.00. Updated as needed. Written for attorneys representing either hospitals or patients of hospitals. Covers a wide variety of legal topics relating to hospital/physician malpractice, including the expansion of HMO liability. (Law Journal Press).

Hospital Pharmacist Report. Thomson Medical Economics, Five Paragon Dr. Montvale, NJ 07645-1742. Phone: (201)358-7200 Fax: (201)722-2680 E-mail: customer.service@medec.com • URL: http://www.medec.com • Monthly. $39.00 per year. Covers both business and clinical topics for hospital pharmacists.

Hospitality Financial and Technology Professionals., 11709 Boulder Lane, Suite 110 Austin, TX 78726. Phone: 800-646-4387 or (512)249-5333 Fax: (512)249-1533 E-mail: frank.wolfe@hftp.org • URL: http://www.hftp.org • Members are accounting and finance officers in the hotel, motel, casino, club, and other areas of the hospitality industry. Formerly International Association of Hospitality Accountants.

Hospitality Sales and Marketing Association International.

Hospitality Technology: Guiding High-Growth Businesses to Best-Choice IT Solutions. Edgell Communications, Inc., 4 Middlebury Blvd. Randolph, NJ 07869. Phone: (973)252-0100 E-mail: gedgell@edgellmail.com • URL: http://www.edgellcommunications.com • 10 times a year. Price on application. Covers information technology, computer communications, and software for foodservice and lodging enterprises.

Hot Text: Web Writing That Works. Jonathan Price and Lisa Price. New Riders Publishing, 800 E 96th St. Indianapolis, IN 46240-3770. Phone: 800-571-5840 • URL: http://www.newriders.com • 2002. $40.00. Provides practical advice on writing text for Web sites, including such details as headlines and menu design. As the attention span of many Web surfers is limited, clarity and brevity become of great importance.

Hotel and Motel Management: The Global News Magazine of the Hospitality Industry. Advanstar Communications, 545 Boylston St. Boston, MA 02116. Phone: 888-527-7008 or (617)267-6500 Fax: (617)267-6900 E-mail: info@advanstar.com • URL: http://www.advanstar.com • 21 times a year. $49.00 per year.

Hotel and Restaurant Business. Donald E. Lundberg. John Wiley and Sons, Inc., 111 River St. Hoboken, NJ 07030. Phone: 800-225-5945 or (201)748-6000 Fax: (202)748-6088 E-mail: info@wiley.com • URL: http://www.wiley.com • 1994. $65.00. Sixth edition. (Hospitality, Travel and Tourism Series).

Hotel and Travel Index: The World Wide Hotel Directory. Northstar Travel Media, 500 Plaza Dr., 4th Fl. Secaucus, NJ 07094-3626. Phone: 800-742-7076 or (201)902-2000 Fax: (201)902-2045 E-mail: secaucushelpdesk@ntmll.com • URL: http://www.northstartravelmedia.com • Quarterly. $185.00 per year. $60.00 per issue. Contains concise information on more than 41,000 hotels in the U. S. and around the world. Includes 400 maps showing location of hotels and airports.

Hotel Business. ICD Publications, 45 Research Way, Suite 106 East Setauket, NY 11733-6401. Phone: (631)246-9300 Fax: (631)246-9496 E-mail: info@hotelbusiness.com • URL: http://www.hotelbusiness.com • Semimonthly. Free to qualified personnel; others, $150.00 per year. Covers management, technology, design, business trends, new products, finance, and other topics for the hotel-motel industry.

Hotel Development. Urban Land Institute, 1025 Thomas Jefferson St., NW, Ste. 500 W Washington, DC 20007. Phone: 800-321-5011 or (202)624-7000 Fax: (202)624-7140 • URL: http://www.uli.org • 1996. $39.95. Provides practical information on developing, acquiring, and renovating hotels in urban areas. Covers market analysis, financing, construction, and management. Includes case studies.

Hotels: The Magazine of the Worldwide Hotel Industry. International Hotel Association. Reed Business Information, 360 Park Ave., S New York, NY 10010. Phone: 800-446-6551 or (646)746-4600 E-mail: corporatecommunications@reedbusiness.com • URL: http://www.reedbusiness.com • Monthly. $99.90 per year.

Hourly Precipitation Data. U.S. National Climatic Data Center, National Oceanic and Atmospheric Administration, U.S. Dept. of Commerce, Federal Bldg., Room 120, 151 Patton Ave. Ashville, NC 28801-5001. Phone: (704)271-4476 E-mail: orders@ncdc.noaa.gov • URL: http://www.ncdc.noaa.gov • Monthly. Published separately for 41 states.

House Leadership Fund., H112 Capital Washington, DC 20515. Phone: (202)225-6900 Fax: (202)226-6300 E-mail: caomail@hr.house.gov Political action committee that raises funds for the election campaigns of Democratic congressional candidates.

House Painting. Entrepreneur Media, Inc., 2445 McCabe Way Irvine, CA 92614. Phone: 800-421-2300 or (949)261-2325 Fax: (949)261-0234 E-mail: entmag@entrepreneur.com • URL: http://www.entrepreneur.com • Looseleaf. $59.50. A practical guide to starting a house painting business. Covers profit potential, start-up costs, market size evaluation, owner's time required, pricing, accounting, advertising, promotion, etc. (Start-Up Business Guide No. E1249.)

Household and Personal Products Industry - Buyers Guide. Rodman Publications, 70 Hilltop Rd. Ramsey, NJ 07446. Phone: (201)825-2552 Fax: (201)825-0553 E-mail: rodmanpub@aol.com • URL: http://www.happi.com • Annual. $12.00. Lists of suppliers to manufacturers of cosmetics, toiletries, soaps, detergents, and related household and personal products.

Household and Personal Products Industry Contract Packaging and Private Label Directory. Rodman Publications, 70 Hilltop Rd. Ramsey, NJ 07446. Phone: (201)825-2552 Fax: (201)825-0553 E-mail: rodmanpub@aol.com • URL: http://www.happi.com • Annual. $12.00. Provides information for about 450 companies offering private label or contract packaged household and personal care products, such as detergents, cosmetics, polishes, insecticides, and various aerosol items.

Household and Personal Products Industry: The Magazine for the Detergent, Soap, Cosmetic and Toiletry, Wax, Polish and Aerosol Industries. Rodman Publications, 70 Hilltop Rd. Ramsey, NJ 07446. Phone: (201)825-2552 Fax: (201)825-0553 E-mail: rodmanpub@aol.com • URL: http://www.happi.com • Monthly. $48.00 per year. Covers marketing, packaging, production, technical innovations, private label developments, and aerosol packaging for soap, detergents, cosmetics, insecticides, and a variety of other household products.

Household Cleaning Agents. Available from MarketResearch.com, 641 Ave. of the Americas, Third Floor New York, NY 10011. Phone: 800-298-5699 or (212)807-2629 Fax: (212)807-2716 E-mail: order@marketresearch.com • URL: http://www.marketresearch.com • 2001. $5,900.00. Published by Euromonitor Publications Ltd. Provides consumer market data and forecasts to 2005 for the United States, the United Kingdom, Germany, France, and Italy. Covers dishwashing detergents, floor cleaning products, scourers, polishes, bleaching products, etc.

Household Spending: Who Spends How Much On What. New Strategist Publications, Inc., 120 W. State St., 4th Fl. Ithaca, NY 14851. Phone: 800-848-0842 or (607)273-0913 Fax: (607)277-5009 E-mail: demographics@newstrategist.com • URL: http://www.newstrategist.com • 1999. $94.95. Fifth edition. Gives facts about the buying habits of U. S. consumers according to income, age, household type, and household size. Includes spending data for about 1,000 products and services.

Housewares Retail Directory. infoUSA Inc., 5711 S 86th Cir., PO Box 27347 Omaha, NE 68127. Phone: 800-321-0869 or (402)593-4500 Fax: (402)331-1505 E-mail: help@infousa.com • URL: http://www.abii.com • Number of listings: 2,992. Entries include: Name, address, phone, size of advertisement, name of owner or manager, number of employees, year first in "Yellow Pages." Compiled from telephone company "Yellow Pages," nationwide.

Housing Affairs Letter: The Weekly Washington Report on Housing. Community Development Services, Inc. CD Publications, 8204 Fenton St. Silver Spring, MD 20910-2889. Phone: 800-666-6380 or (301)588-6380 Fax: (301)588-6385 E-mail: info@cdpublications.com • URL: http://www.cdpublications.com • Weekly. $473.00 per year. Newsletter. Covers mortgage activity news, including forecasts of mortgage rates.

Housing and Commercial Real Estate News Roundup. ULI/Urban Land Institute, 1025 Thomas Jefferson St. NW, Ste. 500 W Washington, DC 20007. Phone: 800-321-5011 or (202)624-7000 Fax: (202)624-7140 E-mail: customerservice@uli.org • URL: http://www.uli.org • Description: Summarizes current developments in land use, real estate development, and related areas.

Housing and Urban Development Trends: Annual Summary. U.S. Department of Housing and Urban Development, 451 Seventh St., S.W. Washington, DC 20410. Phone: (202)708-0980 Annual.

Housing Discrimination: Law and Litigation. Robert G. Schwemm. West Group, 610 Opperman Dr. Eagan, MN 55123. Phone: 800-328-4880 or (651)687-7000 Fax: 800-340-9378 E-mail: bookstore@westgroup.com • URL: http://www.westgroup.com • Annual. $256.00. Looseleaf service. Covers provisions of the Fair Housing Act and related topics.

Housing Market Report: Forecasting Home Sales and Construction Trends Since 1976. Community Development Services, Inc., CD Publications, 8204 Fenton St. Silver Springs, MD 20910. Phone: 800-666-6380 or (301)588-6380 Fax: (301)588-6385 E-mail: info@cdpublications.com • URL: http://www.cdpublications.com • Semimonthly. $399.00 per year. Real estate outlook for U.S. housing markets.

Housing Starts. U.S. Bureau of the Census. Available from U.S. Government Printing Office, Washington, DC 20402. Phone: (202)512-1800 Fax: (202)512-2250 E-mail: gpoaccess@gpo.gov • URL: http://www.access.gpo.gov • Monthly. Construction Reports: C-20.

Housing Statistics of the United States. Patrick A. Simmons. Bernan Press, 4611-F Assembly Dr. Lanham, MD 20706-4391. Phone: 800-274-4447 or (301)459-2255 Fax: 800-865-3450 or (301)459-9235 E-mail: bpress@bernan.com • URL: http://www.bernan.com • 2000. $89.00. Third edition. (Housing Statistics of the United States Series).

Housing the Elderly Report. Community Development Services, Inc. C D Publications, 8204 Fenton St. Silver Spring, MD 20910. Phone: (301)588-6380 Fax: (301)588-6385 E-mail: info@cdpublications.com • URL: http://www.cdpublications.com • Monthly. $249.00 per year. Newsletter. Contains practical information on designing, developing, financing, managing, and marketing residential facilities for the elderly.

Housing the Elderly Report. Community Development Services, Inc. CD Publications, 8204 Fenton St. Silver Spring, MD 20910-2889. Phone: 800-666-6380 or (301)588-6380 Fax: (301)588-6385 E-mail: info@cdpublications.com • URL: http://www.cdpublications.com • Monthly. $249.00 per year. Newsletter. Edited for retirement communities, apartment projects, and nursing homes. Covers news relative to business and property management issues.

Housing the Poor: An Overview. Morton J. Schussheim. Nova

Science Publishers, Inc., 400 Oser Ave., Suite 1600 Hauppauge, NY 11788-3619. Phone: (631)231-7269 Fax: (631)231-8175 E-mail: novascience@earthlink.net • URL: http://www.novapublishers.com • 2003. $29.50. Discusses currrent and emerging housing problems affecting the poor. Covers housing rehabilitation programs, community development block grants, and other programs for low-income households.

How Advertising Works: The Role of Research. John P. Jones, editor. Sage Publications, Inc., 2455 Teller Rd. Thousand Oaks, CA 91320. Phone: 800-818-7243 or (805)499-9774 Fax: 800-583-2665 or (805)499-0871 E-mail: webmaster@sagepub.com • URL: http://www.sagepub.com • 1998. $111.00. Includes sections entitled "Research Before the Advertising Runs" and "Research After the Advertising Has Run."

How Consumers Pick a Hotel: Strategic Segmentation and Target Marketing. Dennis J. Cahill. The Haworth Press, Inc., 10 Alice St. Binghamton, NY 13904-1580. Phone: 800-429-6784 or (607)722-5857 Fax: 800-895-0582 or (607)722-1424 E-mail: getinfo@haworthpressinc.com • URL: http://www.haworthpressinc.com • 1997. $39.95.

How Our Laws Are Made. Available from U. S. Government Printing Office, Washington, DC 20402. Phone: (202)512-1800 Fax: (202)512-2250 E-mail: gpoaccess@gpo.gov • URL: http://www.access.gpo.gov • 2000. $3.75. 22nd edition. Issued by U. S. House of Representatives.

How Products Are Made. Gale Cengage Learning, 27500 Drake Rd. Farmington Hills, MI 48331-3535. Phone: 800-877-GALE or (248)699-4253 Fax: 800-414-5043 E-mail: gale.galeord@cengage.com • URL: http://gale.cengage.com • 2002. Three volumes. $115.00. Previous volumes available. Provides easy-to-read, step-by-step descriptions of how approximately 100 different products are manufactured. Items are of all kinds, both mechanical and non-mechanical.

How to Avoid Financial Tangles. American Institute for Economic Research, PO Box 1000 Great Barrington, MA 01230-1000. Phone: (413)528-1216 Fax: (413)528-0103 E-mail: info@aier.org • URL: http://www.aier.org • 2001. $8.00. Provides basic information and advice on such topics as property ownership, taxes, wills, trusts, insurance, record retention, and professional assistance. (Economic Education Bulletin.)

How to Avoid Liability: The Information Professionals' Guide to Negligence and Warrant Risks. T. R. Halvorson. Burwell Enterprises, 5619 Plumtree Dr. Dallas, TX 75252. Phone: (972)732-0160 Fax: (972)733-1951 E-mail: helen@burwellinc.com • URL: http://www.burwellinc.com • 1998. $24.50. Second edition. Provides legal advice, cases, and decisions relating to information brokers and others in the information business.

How To Be a Manager: A Practical Guide to Tips and Techniques. Robert W. Gallant. Lewis Publishers, 2000 Corporate Blvd., N.W. Boca Raton, FL 33431. Phone: 800-272-7737 or (561)994-0555 Fax: 800-374-3401 or (561)998-9114 E-mail: orders@crcpress.com • URL: http://www.crcpress.com • 1991. $69.95. A concise handbook of principles, techniques, and methods of problem solving. Covers negotiation, discipline, management ethics, training, and other subjects.

How to Become a Successful Consultant in Your Own Field. Hubert Bermont. Prima Publishing, 3000 Lava Ridge Court Roseville, CA 95661. Phone: 800-632-8676 or (916)787-7000 Fax: (916)787-7001 E-mail: sales@primapublishing.com • URL: http://www.primapublishing.com • 2000. $14.00. Third editon.

How to Build Wealth with Tax-Sheltered Investments. Kerry Anne Lynch. American Institute for Economic Research, PO Box 1000 Great Barrington, MA 01230-1000. Phone: (413)528-1216 Fax: (413)528-0103 E-mail: info@aier.org • URL: http://www.aier.org • 2000. $6.00. Provides practical information on conservative tax shelters, including defined-contribution pension plans, individual retirement accounts, Keogh plans, U. S. savings bonds, municipal bonds, and various kinds of annuities: deferred, variable-rate, immediate, and foreign-currency. (Economic Education Bulletin.)

How to Buy a House, Condo, or Co-op. Jean C. Thomsett. Consumers Union of the United States, Inc., 101 Truman Ave. Yonkers, NY 10703-1057. Phone: 800-234-1645 or (914)378-2000 Fax: (914)378-2900 • URL: http://www.consumerreports.org • 1996. $84.75. Fifth edition.

How to Buy and Understand Refracting Telescopes. Jordan Levenson. Levenson Press, P.O. Box 19606 Los Angeles, CA 90019. 1991. $43.50. Third edition.

How to Buy Stocks. Louis Engel and Henry L. Hecht. Little Brown and Co., 1271 Ave. of the Americas New York, NY 10020. Phone: 800-343-9204 or (212)522-8700 Fax: (202)522-2067 E-mail: cust.service@littlebrown.com • URL: http://www.littlebrown.com • 1994. $15.95. Eighth edition.

How to Charter a Commercial Bank. Douglas V. Austin. CCH, Inc., 2700 Lake Cook Rd. Riverwoods, IL 60015. Phone: 800-835-5224 or (847)267-7000 E-mail: cust_serv@cch.com • URL: http://www.cch.com • 1999. $350.00. Provides detailed information on how to start a commercial bank, including both technical and practical requirements.

How to Conduct Training Seminars: A Complete Reference Guide for Training Managers. Lawrence S. Munson. McGraw-Hill, 1221 Ave. of the Americas New York, NY 10020. Phone: 800-722-4726 or (212)512-2000 Fax: (212)512-4502 E-mail: customer.service@mcgraw-hill.com • URL: http://www.mcgraw-hill.com • 1992. $34.95. Second edition.

How to Cover the Gaps in Medicare: Health Insurance and Long-Term Care Options for the Retired. Robert A. Gilmour. American Institute for Economic Research, PO Box 1000 Great Barrington, MA 01230-1000. Phone: (413)528-1216 Fax: (413)528-0103 E-mail: info@aier.org • URL: http://www.aier.org • 2003. $10.00. Four parts: "The Medicare Quandry," "How to Protect Yourself Against the Medigap," "Long-Term Care Options", and "End-of-Life Decisions" (living wills). Includes discussions of long-term care insurance, retirement communities, and HMO Medicare insurance.

How to Cut Your Company's Health Care Costs. George Halvorson. Prentice Hall PTR, 240 Frisch Ct. Paramus, NJ 07652. Phone: 800-282-0693 Fax: 800-445-6991 • URL: http://www.phptr.com • 1987. $27.50.

How to Design and Install Management Incentive Compensation Plans: A Practical Guide to Installing Performance Bonus Plans. Dale Arahood. Dale Arahood and Associates, 26 W355 Keim Dr. Wheaton, IL 60187-7922. Phone: (630)-653-5443 Fax: (630)-653-5462 E-mail: darahood@aol.com 1996. $129.00. Revised edition. "This book focuses on how pay should be determined rather than how much should be paid."

How to Develop a Personnel Policy Manual. Joseph Lawson. AMACOM, 1601 Broadway New York, NY 10019. Phone: 800-262-9699 or (518)586-8100 Fax: (518)903-8168 E-mail: customerservice@amanet.org • URL: http://www.amacombooks.org • 1998. $75.00. Sixth edition.

How to Develop an Employee Handbook. Joseph W. Lawson. AMACOM, 1601 Broadway New York, NY 10019. Phone: 800-262-9699 or (518)586-8100 Fax: (518)903-8168 E-mail: customerservice@amanet.org • URL: http://www.amacombooks.org • 1997. $75.00. Second edition. Includes sample handbooks, personnel policy statements, and forms.

How to Develop and Promote Successful Seminars and Workshops: A Definitive Guide to Creating and Marketing Seminars, Workshops, Classes, and Conferences. Howard L. Shenson. John Wiley and Sons, Inc., 111 River St. Hoboken, NJ 07030. Phone: 800-225-5945 or (201)748-6000 Fax: (201)748-6088 E-mail: info@wiley.com • URL: http://www.wiley.com • 1990. $34.95.

How to Develop Multilevel Marketing Sales. Entrepreneur Media, Inc., 2445 McCabe Way Irvine, CA 92614. Phone: 800-421-2300 or (949)261-2325 Fax: (949)261-0234 E-mail: entmag@entrepreneur.com • URL: http://www.entrepreneur.com • Looseleaf. $59.50. A practical guide to starting a multilevel marketing business. Covers profit potential, start-up costs, owner's time required, pricing, accounting, advertising, market size evaluation, promotion, etc. (Start-Up Business Guide No. E1222.)

How to Do a Performance Appraisal: A Guide for Managers and Professionals. William S. Swan. John Wiley and Sons, Inc., 111 River St. Hoboken, NJ 07030. Phone: 800-225-5945 or (202)748-6000 Fax: (202)748-6088 E-mail: info@wiley.com • URL: http://www.wiley.com • 1991. $34.95. Contains advice on face-to-face discussions and offers guidelines on legal aspects.

How to Find Chemical Information: A Guide for Practicing Chemists, Educators, and Students. Robert E. Maizell. John Wiley and Sons, Inc., 111 River St. Hoboken, NJ 07030. Phone: 800-225-5945 or (201)748-6000 Fax: (201)748-6088 E-mail: info@wiley.com • URL: http://www.wiley.com • 1998. $89.95. Third edition.

How to Find Information About AIDS. Jeffrey T. Huber, editor. Haworth Press, Inc., 10 Alice St. Binghamton, NY 13904-1580. Phone: 800-429-6784 or (607)722-5857 Fax: 800-895-0582 or (607)722-1424 E-mail: getinfo@haworthpressinc.com • URL: http://www.haworthpressinc.com • 1992. $49.95. Second edition. Includes print, electronic, and organizational sources of information. Local and national hotlines are listed.

How to Find Market Research on the Web. MarketResearch.com, 641 Ave. of the Americas, 4th Fl. New York, NY 10011. Phone: 800-298-5699 or (212)807-2629 Fax: (212)807-2676 E-mail: customerservice@marketresearch.com • URL: http://www.marketresearch.com • 2001. $239.00. Analyzes and compares the online products of 80 market research publishers. Describes popular Internet search engines and provides information on useful World Wide Web sites.

How to Find Out About Financial Aid: 2002-2004. Gail A. Schlachter. Reference Service Press, 5000 Windplay Dr., Suite 4 El Dorado Hills, CA 95762. Phone: (916)939-9620 Fax: (916)939-9626 E-mail: info@rspfunding.com • URL: http://www.rspfunding.com • 2002. $37.50. Annotated bibliography of student aid directories. Author, title, subject, and geographical indexes.

How to Form a Nonprofit Corporation. Anthony Mancuso. Nolo, 950 Parker St. Berkeley, CA 94710. Phone: 800-728-3555 or (510)549-1976 Fax: 800-645-0895 or (510)548-5902 E-mail: simone@nolo.com • URL: http://www.nolo.com • 2002. $44.99. Fifth edition.

How to Form Your Own Corporation Without a Lawyer for Under $75.00. Ted Nicholas and Sean P. Melvin. Dearborn Trade Publishing, A Kaplan Professional Co., 155 N Wacker Dr. Chicago, IL 60606. Phone: 800-621-9621 or (312)836-4400 Fax: (312)836-1021 E-mail: trade@dearborn.com • URL: http://www.dearborntrade.com • 1999. $19.95. 26th edition.

How to Get Happily Published: A Complete and Candid Guide. Judith Appelbaum. HarperInformation, 10 E. 53rd St. New York, NY 10022-5299. Phone: 800-242-7737 or (212)207-7000 Fax: 800-822-4090 or (212)207-7145 • URL: http://www.harpercollins.com • 1998. $14.00. Fifth edition. Provides advice for writers on dealing with book and magazine publishers.

How to Get Results from Interviewing: A Practical Guide for Operating Management. James M. Black. Krieger Publishing Co., P.O. Box 9542 Melbourne, FL 32902-9542. Phone: 800-724-0025 or (321)724-9542 Fax: (321)951-3671 E-mail: info@krieger-publishing.com • URL: http://www.krieger-publishing.com • 1982. $22.00. Reprint of 1970 edition.

How to Get Started in Real Estate Investing. Robert Irwin. McGraw-Hill, 1221 Ave. of the Americas New York, NY 10020. Phone: 800-722-4726 or (212)512-2000 Fax: (212)515-4502 E-mail: customer.service@mcgraw-hill.com • URL: http://www.mcgraw-hill.com • 2002. $14.95. Presents basic information on real estate investing for beginners.

How to Get the Most Out of Trade Shows. Steve Miller. McGraw-Hill, 1221 Ave. of the Americas New York, NY 10020. Phone: 800-722-4726 or (212)512-2000 Fax: (212)512-4502 E-mail: customer.service@mcgraw-hill.com • URL: http://www.mcgraw-hill.com • 1999. $29.95. Third revised edition. (NTC Business Books Series).

How to Incorporate: A Handbook for Entrepreneurs and Professionals. Michael Diamond and Julia L. Williams. John Wiley and Sons, Inc., 111 River St. Hoboken, NJ 07030. Phone: 800-225-5945 or (201)748-6000 Fax: (201)748-6088 E-mail: info@wiley.com • URL: http://www.wiley.com • 2000. $24.95. Fourth edition.

How to Invest in Real Estate Using Free Money. Laurie Blum. John Wiley and Sons, Inc., 111 River St. Hoboken, NJ 07030. Phone: 800-225-5945 or (201)748-6000 Fax: (201)748-6068 E-mail: info@wiley.com • URL: http://www.wiley.com • 1991. $160.00.

How to Invest in Your First Works of Art: A Guide for the New Collector. John Carlin. Yarrow Press, 101 Monterey Ave. Pelham, NY 10803. Phone: (914)738-3884 1990. $11.95.

How to Invest Wisely. Lawrence S. Pratt. American Institute for Economic Research, PO Box 1000 Great Barrington, MA 01230-1000. Phone: (413)528-1216 Fax: (413)528-0103 E-mail: info@aier.org • URL: http://www.aier.org • 2002. $12.00. Presents a conservative policy of investing, with emphasis on dividend-paying common stocks. Gold and other inflation hedges are compared. Includes a reprint of *Toward an Optimal Stock Selection Strategy* (1997). (Economic Education Bulletin.)

How to Lie with Statistics. Darrell Huff. W. W. Norton and Co., Inc., 500 5th Ave. New York, NY 10110. Phone: 800-223-2584 or (212)354-5500 Fax: (212)869-0856 • URL: http://www.wwnorton.com • 1993. $11.00.

How to Make It Big as a Consultant. William A. Cohen. AMACOM, 1601 Broadway New York, NY 10019. Phone: 800-262-9699 or (518)586-8100 Fax: (518)903-8168 E-mail: customerservice@amanet.org • URL: http://www.amacombooks.org • 2001. $17.95. Third edition. Step-by-step instructions for finding clients, writing proposals, pricing services, etc.

How to Make it Big in the Seminar Business. Paul Karasik. McGraw-Hill, 1221 Ave. of the Americas New York, NY 10020. Phone: 800-722-4726 or (212)512-2000 Fax: (212)512-4502 E-mail: customer.service@mcgraw-hill.com • URL: http://www.mcgraw-hill.com • 1995. $15.95. Covers the organizing and marketing of seminars or workshops, including fee determination, promotion, scheduling, and evaluation.

How to Make Money in Stocks: A Winning System in Good Times or Bad. William J. O'Neil. McGraw-Hill, 1221 Ave. of the Americas New York, NY 10020. Phone: 800-722-4726 or (212)512-2000 Fax: (212)512-4502 E-mail: customer.service@mcgraw-hill.com • URL: http://www.mcgraw-hill.com • 2002. $12.95. Third edition. The author is the founder of *Investor's Business Daily*.

How to Make Tax-Saving Gifts. William S. Moore. American Institute for Economic Research, PO Box 1000 Great Barrington, MA 01230. Phone: (413)528-1216 Fax: (413)528-0103 E-mail: info@aier.org • URL: http://www.aier.org • 1999. $3.00. Provides practical advice on the tax consequences of gifts, including gifts for college tuition expenses, gifts of real estate, charitable gifts, and the use of life insurance trusts. (Economic Education Bulletin.)

How to Manage a Successful Catering Business. Manfred Ketterer. John Wiley and Sons, Inc., 111 River St. Hoboken, NJ 07030. Phone: 800-225-5945 or (201)748-6000 Fax: (201)748-6068 E-mail: info@wiley.com • URL: http://www.wiley.com • 1990. $65.00. Second edition.

How to Manage Conflict in the Organization. American Management Association Extension Institute, 1601 Broadway New York, NY 10019. Phone: 800-262-9699 or (518)586-8100 Fax: (518)903-8168 • URL: http://www.amanet.org • Looseleaf. $139.00. Self-study course. Emphasis is on practical explanations, examples, and problem solving. Quizzes and a case study are included.

How to Manage Corporate Cash Effectively. Joseph E. Finnerty. AMACOM, 1601 Broadway New York, NY 10019. Phone: 800-262-9699 or (518)586-8100 Fax: (518)903-8168 E-mail: customerservice@amanet.org • URL: http://www.

amacombooks.org • 1991. $59.95. A practical approach to cash flow problems.

How to Manage Training: A Guide to Administration, Design and Delivery. Carolyn Nilson. AMACOM, 1601 Broadway New York, NY 10019. Phone: 800-262-9699 or (518)586-8100 Fax: (518)903-8168 E-mail: customerservice@amanet.org • URL: http://www.amacombooks.org • 1991. $69.95. Looseleaf service. Presents ideas and techniques for cost-effective training.

How to Manage Your Law Office. LexisNexis Matthew Bender, 1275 Broadway Albany, NY 12204. Phone: 800-424-4200 or (518)487-3000 Fax: (518)487-3584 E-mail: bookstore.support@lexisnexis.com • URL: http://www.bender.com • Annual. $254.00. A practical guide with cutting edge information about effective techniques in law office administration.

How to Negotiate the Sale from Start to Finish. American Management Association Extension Institute, 1601 Broadway New York, NY 10019. Phone: 800-262-9699 or (518)586-8100 Fax: (518)903-8168 Looseleaf. $155.00. Self-study course. Emphasis is on practical explanations, examples, and problem solving. Quizzes and a case study are included.

How to Obtain Government Contracts. Entrepreneur Media, Inc., 2445 McCabe Way Irvine, CA 92614. Phone: 800-421-2300 or (949)261-2325 Fax: (949)261-0234 E-mail: entmag@entrepreneur.com • URL: http://www.entrepreneur.com • Looseleaf. $59.50. A practical guide to acquiring and negotiating government contracts. (Start-Up Business Guide No. E1227.)

How to Plan and Manage Warehouse Operations. American Management Association Extension Institute, 1601 Broadway New York, NY 10019. Phone: 800-262-9699 or (518)586-8100 Fax: (518)903-8168 • URL: http://www.amanet.org • Looseleaf. $159.00. Self-study course. Emphasis is on practical explanations, examples, and problem solving. Quizzes and a case study are included.

How to Plan for a Secure Retirement. Elias Zuckerman and others. Consumer Reports Books, 101 Truman Ave. Yonkers, NY 10703. Phone: 800-500-9760 or (914)378-2000 Fax: (914)378-2925 • URL: http://www.consumerreports.org • 2000. $29.95. Covers pension plans, health insurance, estate planning, retirement communities, and related topics. (Consumer Reports Money Guide.)

How to Practice Before the New IRS. Robert S. Schriebman. CCH, Inc., 2700 Lake Cook Rd. Riverwoods, IL 60015. Phone: 800-835-5224 or (847)267-7000 E-mail: cust_serv@cch.com • URL: http://www.cch.com • 1999. $115.00. Reflects changes made by the IRS Restructuring and Reform Act of 1998. Covers audits, appeals, tax court basics, refunds, penalties, etc., for tax professionals.

How to Produce Creative Advertising: Traditional Techniques and Computer Applications. Thomas Bivins and Ann Keding. McGraw Hill, 1221 Ave. of the Americas New York, NY 10020. Phone: 800-722-4726 or (212)512-2000 Fax: (212)512-4502 E-mail: customer.service@mcgraw-hill.com • URL: http://www.mcgraw-hill.com • 1993. $37.95. Covers copywriting, advertising design, and the use of desktop publishing techniques in advertising. (NTC Business Books Series).

How to Produce Creative Publications: Traditional Techniques and Computer Applications. Thomas Bivins and Ann Keding. McGraw-Hill, 1221 Ave. of the Americas New York, NY 10020. Phone: 800-722-4726 or (212)512-2000 Fax: (212)512-4502 E-mail: customer.service@mcgraw-hill.com • URL: http://www.mcgraw-hill.com • 1993. $37.95. A practical guide to the writing, designing, and production of magazines, annual reports, brochures, and newsletters by traditional methods and by desktop publishing. (NTC Business Books Series).

How to Promote, Publicize, and Advertise Your Growing Business: Getting the Word Out Without Spending a Fortune. Kim Baker and Sunny Baker. John Wiley and Sons, Inc., 111 River St. Hoboken, NJ 07030. Phone: 800-225-5945 or (201)748-6000 Fax: (201)748-6088 E-mail: info@wiley.com • URL: http://www.wiley.com • 1992. $12.95.

How to Read a Financial Report: Wringing Vital Signs Out of the Numbers. John A. Tracy. John Wiley and Sons, Inc., 111 River St. Hoboken, NJ 07030. Phone: 800-225-5945 or (201)748-6000 Fax: (201)748-6088 E-mail: info@wiley.com • URL: http://www.wiley.com • 1999. $29.95. Fifth edition.

How to Recruit and Select Successful Salesmen. Ashgate Publishing Co., 101 Cherry St., Ste. 420 Burlington, VT 05401-4405. Phone: 800-535-9544 or (802)865-7641 Fax: (802)865-7847 E-mail: adonahue@ashgate.com • URL: http://www.ashgate.com • 1983. $99.95. Revised edition. Published by Gower in England.

How to Research, Write, and Package Administrative Manuals. Leo R. Lunine. AMACOM, 1601 Broadway New York, NY 10019. Phone: 800-262-9699 or (518)586-8100 Fax: (518)903-8168 E-mail: customerservice@amanet.org • URL: http://www.amacombooks.org • 1985. $75.00.

How to Run a Small Business. McGraw-Hill, 1221 Ave. of the Americas New York, NY 10020. Phone: 800-722-4726 or (212)512-2000 Fax: (212)512-4502 E-mail: customer.service@mcgraw-hill.com • URL: http://www.mcgraw-hill.com • 1994. $27.95. Seventh edition.

How to Run Better Business Meetings: A Reference Guide for Managers. McGraw-Hill, 1221 Ave. of the Americas New York, NY 10020. Phone: 800-722-4726 or (212)512-2000

Fax: (212)512-4502 E-mail: customer.service@mcgraw-hill.com • URL: http://www.mcgraw-hill.com • 1987. Price on application. Compiled by the 3M Meeting Management Team. Covers the planning, formatting, and executing of various kinds of business meetings. Charts, checklists, diagrams, and case studies are included.

How to Save on Prescription Drugs: The AIER Guide to Prescription Drug Assistance Programs for Seniors. Kerry A. Lynch. American Institute for Economic Research, Division St. Great Barrington, MA 01230. Phone: (413)528-1216 Fax: (413)528-0103 E-mail: info@aier.org • URL: http://www.aier.org • 2003. $5.00. Contains a state-by-state directory of 39 state assistance programs offering prescription drug coverage, usually for low-income residents age 65 or older. Provides phone numbers, websites, coverage, eligibility details, and "How it works" for each state. A separate section describes five drug company discount cards. (Economic Education Bulletin.)

How to Save Time and Taxes Preparing Fiduciary Income Tax Returns. LexisNexis Matthew Bender, 1275 Broadway Albany, NY 12204. Phone: 800-424-4200 or (518)487-3000 Fax: (518)487-3584 E-mail: bookstore.support@lexisnexis.com • URL: http://www.bender.com • Biennial. $272.00 per year. Looseleaf service. Comprehensive coverage of the federal income taxation of trusts and estates.

How to Sell Your Business for More Money. Gary Schine. The Consultants Press, Ltd., PO Box 54 Rhinebeck, NY 12572. Phone: (845)876-7712 Fax: (212)873-7065 E-mail: consulinfo@aol.com • URL: http://www.consultantpress.com • 1991. $29.95.

How to Sell Your Home for Top Dollar. Michael C. Thomsett. McGraw-Hill, 1221 Ave. of the Americas New York, NY 10020. Phone: 800-722-4726 or (212)512-2000 Fax: (212)512-4502 E-mail: customer.service@mcgraw-hill.com • URL: http://www.mcgraw-hill.com • 1989. $13.00. (One Hour Guides Series).

How to Start a Home-Based Web Design Business. Jim Smith. Globe Pequot Press, 246 Goose Lane Guilford, CT 06437. Phone: 800-243-0495 or (203)458-4500 Fax: 800-820-2329 or (203)458-4604 E-mail: info@globe-pequot.com • URL: http://www.globe-pequot.com • 2004. $17.95. Second edition. Covers planning, marketing, subcontracting, setting fees, customer presentations, and other topics related to starting a freelance, web design business at home. Includes a sample customer contract. (Home-Based Business Series).

How to Succeed as an Independent Consultant. Herman Holtz. John Wiley and Sons, Inc., 111 River St. Hoboken, NJ 07030. Phone: 800-225-5945 or (201)748-6000 Fax: (201)748-6088 E-mail: info@wiley.com • URL: http://www.wiley.com • 1993. $34.95. Third edition. Covers a wide variety of marketing, financial, professional, and ethical issues for consultants. Includes bibliographic and organizational information.

How to Take the Fog Out of Business Writing. Robert Gunning and Richard A. Kallan. Dartnell Corp., 350 Hiatt Dr. Palm Beach Gardens, FL 33418. Phone: 800-341-7874 or (561)622-6520 Fax: (561)622-2423 E-mail: custserv@lrp.com • URL: http://www.dartnellcorp.com • 1994. $12.95. Includes "The 10 Principles of Clear Statement."

How to Win Arguments; More Often Than Not. William A. Rusher. University Press of America, 4501 Forbes Blvd., Ste. 200 Lanham, MD 20706. Phone: 800-462-6420 or (301)459-3366 Fax: 800-338-4550 or (301)459-2118 E-mail: custserv@rowman.com • URL: http://www.univpress.com • 1985. $25.00.

How to Write a Business Plan. American Management Association Extension Institute, 1601 Broadway New York, NY 10019. Phone: 800-262-9699 or (518)586-8100 Fax: (518)903-8168 • URL: http://www.amanet.org • Looseleaf. $159.00. Self-study course. Emphasis is on practical explanations, examples, and problem solving. Quizzes and a case study are included.

How to Write a Successful Marketing Plan: A Disciplined and Comprehensive Approach. Roman G. Hiebing. Prentice Hall PTR, 240 Fritsch Ct. Paramus, NJ 07652. Phone: 800-282-0693 Fax: 800-445-6991 • URL: http://www.phptr.com • 1999. $79.95. Second edition. The four main sections cover marketing background, the marketing plan, plan execution, and evaluation. Includes worksheets and formats.

How to Write and Present Technical Information. Charles H. Sides. Greenwood Publishing Group, Inc., 88 Post Rd., W. Westport, CT 06881. Phone: 800-225-5800 or (203)226-3571 Fax: (203)431-2214 E-mail: customer-service@greenwood.com • URL: http://www.greenwood.com • 1998. $29.95. Third edition.

How to Write Better Resumes and Cover Letters. Pat Criscito. Barron's Educational Series, Inc., 250 Wireless Blvd. Hauppauge, NY 11788. Phone: 800-645-3476 or (516)434-3311 Fax: (516)434-3723 E-mail: info@barronseduc.com • URL: http://www.barronseduc.com • 2003. $14.95.

How to Write Proposals that Produce. Joel P. Bowman and Bernadine P. Branchaw. Greenwood Publishing Group, Inc., 88 Post Rd., W. Westport, CT 06881. Phone: 800-225-5800 or (203)226-3571 Fax: (203)431-2214 E-mail: customer-service@greenwood.com • URL: http://www.greenwood.com • 1992. $23.50. An extensive guide to effective proposal writing for both nonprofit organizations and businesses. Covers writing style, intended audience, format, use of graphs, charts, and tables, documentation, evaluation, oral presentation, and related topics.

How to Write Usable User Documentation. Edmond H. Weiss. Greenwood Publishing Group, Inc., 88 Post Rd., W. Westport, CT 06881. Phone: 800-225-5800 or (203)226-3571 Fax: (203)431-2214 E-mail: customer-service@greenwood.com • URL: http://www.greenwood.com • 1991. $24.95. Second edition. Shows how to explain a product, system, or procedure. Includes a glossary and a list of books and periodicals.

Howe Laboratory of Ophthalmology. Harvard University, Massachusetts Eye and Ear Infirmary, 243 Charles St. Boston, MA 02114. Phone: (617)573-3963 Fax: (617)573-4290 • URL: http://www.howelaboratory.harvard.edu • A research unit of Harvard Medical School.

HPAC Engineering Info-Dex (Heating, Piping, Air Conditioning). Penton Media Inc., 1300 E. Ninth St. Cleveland, OH 44114-1503. Phone: (216)696-7000 Fax: (216)696-1752 E-mail: information@penton.com • URL: http://www.penton.com • Annual. $30.00. Industry directory of products, manufacturers, and trade names and a composite of catalog data for mechanical systems engineering professionals.

HPAC Techlit Selector (Heating, Piping, Air Conditioning). Penton Media, Inc., 1300 E. Ninth St. Cleveland, OH 44114. Phone: (216)696-7000 Fax: (216)696-1752 E-mail: information@penton.com • URL: http://www.penton.com • Semiannual. Free to qualified personnel. Manufacturers' catalogs and technical literature.

HR Briefing (Human Resources). Aspen Publishers, 1185 Ave. of the Americas New York, NY 10036. Phone: 800-243-1660 or (212)597-0200 Fax: 800-901-9075 or (212)597-0338 • URL: http://www.bbpnews.com • Monthly. $249.00 per year. Newsletter. Provides HR professionals and other business people with concise, up-to-date information on employment practices and trends, with an emphasis on compliance with federal employment laws.

HR Focus: The Hands-On Tool for Human Resources Professionals. American Management Association. IOMA, 29 W 35th St., 5th Fl. New York, NY 10001-2299. Phone: 800-313-8650 or (212)244-0360 Fax: (212)903-8168 E-mail: amapubs@aol.com • URL: http://www.amanet.org • Monthly. $99.00 per year. Newsletter. Covers "all aspects of HR management," including corporate culture, the impact of technology, recruiting strategies, and training. Formerly *Personnel*.

HR Magazine (Human Resources): Strategies and Solutions for Human Resource Professionals. Society for Human Resource Management, 1800 Duke St. Alexandria, VA 22314-3499. Phone: (703)548-3440 Fax: (703)535-6490 E-mail: shrm@shrm.org • URL: http://www.shrm.org • Monthly. Free to members; non-members, $70.00 per year. Formerly *Personnel Administrator*.

HR Words You Gotta Know! Essential Human Resources, Terms, Laws, Acronyms and Abbreviations for Everyone in Business. William R. Tracey, editor. AMACOM, 1601 Broadway New York, NY 10019. Phone: 800-262-9699 or (518)586-8100 Fax: (518)903-8168 E-mail: customerservice@amanet.org • URL: http://www.amacombooks.org • 1994. $17.95. Explains important human relations management terms.

HSR: Health Supplement Retailer. Virgo Publishing, Inc., PO Box 40079 Phoenix, AZ 85012. Phone: (480)990-1101 Fax: (480)990-0819 E-mail: virgopub@vpico.com • URL: http://www.vpico.com • Monthly. $50.00 per year. Covers all aspects of the vitamin and health supplement market, including new products. Includes an annual buyer's guide, an annual compilation of industry statistics, and annual guides to vitamins and herbs.

Hubert H. Humphrey Institute of Public Affairs., University of Minnesota, 300 HHH Center, 301 19th Ave., S. Minneapolis, MN 55455. Phone: (612)625-0669 Fax: (612)626-6351 E-mail: jbrandl@hhh.umn.edu • URL: http://www.hhh.umn.edu/centers • Studies strategic management in both the private and the public sectors.

Hudson Institute., 1015 15th St. NW, 6th Fl., 1015 18th St., NW, Ste. 300 Washington, DC 20005. Phone: 800-HUDSON-0 or (202)974-2400 Fax: (202)974-2410 E-mail: info@hudson.org • URL: http://www.hudson.org • Members of this research center are elected from academic, governmental, and business/industrial sectors. Studies public policy issues in areas of national security, international and domestic economics, education and employment, energy and technology, agriculture and environment, and future studies. Studies are funded through contract or grant from government agencies, private businesses, foundations, associations, and individuals. Sometimes referred to as a "think tank", the institute focuses on "providing policymakers with a broad, workable, conceptual framework within which intelligent and successful policy decisions can be developed"; seeks to determine what issues will have the greatest long-term impact and to identify issues that may become urgent though they are not yet recognized as such. Conducts briefings on policy issues to corporate and other audiences. Distributes research reports to depository libraries.

Hudson's Subscription Newsletter Directory. Newsletter Clearinghouse, 44 W Market St., PO Box 311 Rhinebeck, NY 12572. Phone: 800-572-3451 or (914)876-2081 Fax: (914)876-2561 E-mail: help@infousa.com Covers: about 4,800 newsletters available by subscription. Entries include: Title, publisher, parent company or institution, address, phone, fax, names of editor and publisher, frequency, subscription price, year founded, circulation, field or subjects.

Huenefeld Report: For Managers and Planners in Modest-Sized Book Publishing Houses. John Huenefeld, editor. Huenefeld Co., Inc., P.O. Box 665 Bedford, MA 01730-0665. Phone: (781)275-1070 Biweekly. $88.00 per year.

Hulbert Financial Digest. Hulbert Financial Digest, 5051-B Backlick Rd. Annandale, VA 22003. Phone: 888-485-2378 E-mail: orders@marketwatch.com • URL: http://www.hulbertdigest.com • Description: Provides performance ratings on more than 400 portfolios recommended by more than 145 financial newsletters, calculated on the basis of model portfolios constructed according to each newsletter's advice. Includes a timing scoreboard, analysis of newsletter performance, list of mutual funds most frequently recommended for sale or purchase, a stock market sentiment index, and a question and answer section.

Human Behavior at Work. O. Jeff Harris and Sandra Hartman. West Publishing Co., 610 Opperman Dr. Eagan, MN 55123. Phone: 800-338-9424 or (651)687-7000 Fax: 800-340-9378 E-mail: bookstore@westgroup.com • URL: http://www.westgroup.com • 1991. $55.50.

Human Communication Research. International Communication Association. Oxford University Press, Journals, 2001 Evans Rd. Cary, NC 27513. Phone: 800-852-7323 or (919)677-0977 Fax: (919)677-1714 E-mail: jnlorders@oup-usa.org • URL: http://www.oup-osa.org • Quarterly. Institutions, $294.00 per year; with online edition, $309.00 per year. A scholarly journal of interpersonal communication.

Human Factors and Aviation Medicine. Flight Safety Foundation, Inc., 601 Madison St., Suite 300 Alexandria, VA 22314-1756. Phone: (703)739-6700 Fax: (703)739-6708 E-mail: fsf@radix.net Bimonthly. Members, $120.00 per year; nonmembers, $240.00 per year.

Human Factors and Ergonomics in Manufacturing. John Wiley and Sons, Inc., Journals, 111 River Hoboken, NJ 07030. Phone: 800-225-5945 or (201)748-6000 Fax: (201)748-6088 E-mail: customer@wiley.com • URL: http://www.wiley.com • Quarterly. $649.00 per year; with online edition, $682.00 per year. Published in England by John Wiley and Sons Ltd. Formerly *International Journal of Human Factors in Manufacturing*.

Human Factors and Ergonomics Society., P.O. Box 1369 Santa Monica, CA 90406-1369. Phone: (310)394-1811 Fax: (310)394-2410 E-mail: info@hfes.org • URL: http://www.hfes.org • Formerly Human Factors Society.

Human Factors Design Handbook. Wesley E. Woodson and others. McGraw-Hill, 1221 Ave. of the Americas New York, NY 10020. Phone: 800-722-4726 or (212)512-2000 Fax: (212)512-4502 E-mail: customer.service@mcgraw-hill.com 1992. $150.00. Second edition.

Human Power, Biochemechanics, and Robotics Laboratory., Cornell University, Dept. of Theoretical and Applied Mechanics, 306 Kimball Hall Ithaca, NY 14853-1503. Phone: (607)255-7108 Fax: (607)255-2011 E-mail: ruina@cornell.edu • URL: http://www.tam.cornell.edu/~ruina • Conducts research relating to human muscle-powered machines, such as bicycles and rowers.

Human Relations. Marie Dalton and others. South-Western, 5191 Natrop Blvd. Mason, OH 45040. Phone: 800-543-0487 or (513)229-1000 • URL: http://www.swcollege.com • 2000. $49.95. Second edition.

Human Relations: Towards the Integration of Social Sciences. Tavistock Institute of Human Relations. Sage Publications, Inc., 2455 Teller Rd. Thousand Oaks, CA 91320. Phone: 800-818-7243 or (805)499-9774 Fax: 800-583-2665 or (805)499-0871 E-mail: webmaster@sagepub.com • URL: http://www.sagepub.com • Monthly. Institutions, $1,158.00 per year.

Human Resource Executive. LRP Publications, 747 Dreshner Rd., Suite 500 Horsham, PA 19044. Phone: 800-341-7874 or (215)784-0860 Fax: (215)784-9639 E-mail: custserv@lrp.com • URL: http://www.lrp.com • 16 times a year. $89.95 per year. Edited for directors of corporate human resource departments. Special issues emphasize training, benefits, retirement planning, recruitment, outplacement, workers' compensation, legal pitfalls, and oes emphasize training, benefits, retirement planning, recruitment, outplacement, workers' compensation, legal pitfalls, and other personnel topics.

Human Resource Management. David A. DeCenzo and Stephen P. Robbins. John Wiley and Sons, Inc., 111 River St. Hoboken, NJ 07030. Phone: 800-225-5945 or (201)748-6000 Fax: (201)748-6088 E-mail: info@wiley.com • URL: http://www.wiley.com • 2001. $89.95. Seventh edition.

Human Resource Management: A Strategic and Global Perspective. J.S. Black. Addison-Wesley, 75 Arlington St., Ste 300 Boston, MA 02116. Phone: 800-447-2226 or (617)848-7500 • URL: http://www.aw.com • 1997. Price on application.

Human Resource Management for Golf Course Superintendents. Robert A. Milligan and Thomas R. Maloney. John Wiley and Sons, Inc., 111 River St. Hoboken, NJ 07030-5774. Phone: 800-225-5945 or (201)748-6000 Fax: (201)748-6088 E-mail: custserv@wiley.com • URL: http://www.wiley.com • 1996. $34.95. Covers various personnel topics as related to golf course management, including organizational structure, recruitment, employee selection, training, motivation, and discipline.

Human Resource Management in Libraries: Theory and

Practice. Richard Rubin. Neal-Schuman Publishers, Inc., 100 William St., Ste. 2004 New York, NY 10038. Phone: (866)672-6657 or (212)925-8650 Fax: (866)209-7932 or (212)219-8916 E-mail: info@neal-schuman.com • URL: http://www.neal-schuman.com • 1991. $55.00. Covers such topics as performance rating, pay equity, and collective bargaining.

Human Resource Management in the Knowledge Economy: New Challenges, New Roles, New Capabilities. Mark L. Lengnick-Hall and Cynthia A. Lengnick-Hall. Berrett-Koehler Publishers, Inc., 235 Montgomery St., Suite 650 San Francisco, CA 94104-2916. Phone: 800-929-2929 or (415)288-0260 Fax: (802)864-7626 E-mail: bkpub@bkpub.com • URL: http://www.bkconnection.com • 2002. $24.95.

Human Resource Planning. Human Resource Planning Society, 317 Madison Ave., Ste. 1509 New York, NY 10017. Phone: (212)490-6387 Fax: (212)682-6851 E-mail: info@hrps.org • URL: http://www.hrps.org • Quarterly. $90.00 per year.

Human Resource Planning Society., 401 N Michigan Ave., Ste. 2200 Chicago, IL 60611. Phone: (312)321-6805 Fax: (312)673-6944 E-mail: info@hrps.org • URL: http://www.hrps.org • Human resource planning professionals representing 160 corporations and 3000 individual members, including strategic human resources planning and development specialists, staffing analysts, business planners, line managers, and others who function as business partners in the application of strategic human resource management practices. Seeks to increase the impact of human resource planning and management on business and organizational performance. Sponsors program of professional development in human resource planning concepts, techniques, and practices. Offers networking opportunities.

Human Resource Skills for the Project Manager: The Human Aspects of Project Management, Volume Two. Vijay K. Verma. Project Management Institute, Four Campus Blvd. Newton Square, PA 19073-3299. Phone: (610)356-4600 Fax: (610)356-4647 E-mail: pmihq@pmi.org • URL: http://www.pmi.org • 1996. $32.95. (Human Aspects of Project Management Series).

Human Resources. Richard B. Renckly. Barron's Educational Series, Inc., 250 Wireless Blvd. Hauppauge, NY 11788-3917. Phone: 800-645-3476 or (516)434-3311 Fax: (516)434-3723 E-mail: info@barronseduc.com • URL: http://www.barronseduc.com • 2004. $18.95. Second edition. Emphasis is on investigating, interviewing, hiring, and evaluating employees.

Human Resources Abstracts: An International Information Service. Sage Publications, Inc., 2455 Teller Rd. Thousand Oaks, CA 91320. Phone: 800-818-7243 or (805)499-9774 Fax: 800-583-2665 or (805)499-0871 E-mail: webmaster@sagepub.com • URL: http://www.sagepub.com • Quarterly. Institutions, $968.00 per year; includes print and online editions.

Human Resources and Personnel Management. William B. Werther and Keith Davis. McGraw-Hill, 1221 Aye. of the Americas New York, NY 10020. Phone: 800-722-4726 or (212)512-2000 Fax: (212)512-4502 E-mail: customer.serivce@mcgraw-hill.com • URL: http://www.mcgraw-hill.com • 1995. $91.25. Fifth edition. (Management Series).

Human Resources Glossary: A Complete Desk Reference for HR Professionals. William R. Tracey. Saint Lucie Press, 2000 Corporate Blvd., N. W. Boca Raton, FL 33431-7372. Phone: 800-272-7737 or (561)274-9906 Fax: 800-374-3401 or (561)274-9927 E-mail: information@slpress.com • URL: http://www.slpress.com • 1997. $79.95. Second edition.

Human Resources Institute. University of Alabama

Human Resources Management Whole. CCH, Inc., 2700 Lake Cook Rd. Riverwoods, IL 60015. Phone: 800-835-5224 or (847)267-7000 E-mail: cust_serv@cch.com • URL: http://www.cch.com • Nine looseleaf volumes. $1,572 per year. Includes monthly updates. Components are *Ideas and Trends Newsletter*, *Employment Relations*, *Compensation*, *Equal Employment Opportunity*, *Personnel Practices/Communications* and *OSHA Compliance*. Components are available separately.

Human Resources Research Organization. Human Resources Research Organization, 66 Canal Center Plz., Ste. 400 Alexandria, VA 22314-1591. Phone: (703)549-3611 Fax: (703)549-9025 E-mail: webmaster@humrro.orgg • URL: http://www.humrro.org • Training, training device requirements, instructional technology, recruitment and workforce analysis, personnel selection and classification, ability testing, simulation and modeling, system and job analysis, cognitive task analysis, performance appraisal, assessment centers, and program evaluation.

Human Resources Yearbook. Craig T. Norback. Prentice Hall PTR, 240 Frisch Ct. Paramus, NJ 07652. Phone: 800-282-0693 Fax: 800-445-6991 • URL: http://www.phptr.com • 1997. $75.00.

Human Rights Organizations and Periodicals Directory. Meiklejohn Civil Liberties Institute, P.O. Box 673 Berkeley, CA 94701-0673. Phone: (510)848-0599 Fax: (510)848-6008 E-mail: info@mcli.org • URL: http://www.mcli.org • Biennial. Individuals, $75.00 per year; libraries and institutions, $125.00 per year. Over 1,200 United States organizations and periodicals dedicated to improving human rights.

Human Rights Political Action Committee., 4025 Argyle Terr. NW Washington, DC 20011-5330. E-mail: info@fundfornewpriorities.org Individuals concerned about the

place of human rights in U.S. foreign policy. Is devoted solely to raising money to support candidacies of human rights activists running for Congress. **Publications:** none. **Convention/Meeting:** none.

The Human Side of Enterprise. Douglas McGregor. McGraw-Hill, 1221 Ave. of the Americas New York, NY 10020. Phone: 800-722-4726 or (212)512-2000 Fax: (212)512-4502 E-mail: customer.service@mcgraw-hill.com • URL: http://www.mcgraw-hill.com • 1985. $53.13.

Humanities Index. H. W. Wilson Co., 950 University Ave. Bronx, NY 10452. Phone: 800-367-6770 or (718)588-8400 Fax: 800-590-1617 or (718)590-1617 E-mail: custserv@hwwilson.com • URL: http://www.hwwilson.com • Quarterly. Annual cumulation. Price varies.

Hydraulic Engineering. Hsieh Wen Shen and others, editors. American Society of Civil Engineers, 1801 Alexander Graham Bell Dr. Reston, VA 20191-4400. Phone: 800-548-2723 or (703)295-6300 Fax: (703)295-6211 • URL: http://www.asce.org • 1993. $210.00. Two volumes.

Hydraulic Institute., 9 Sylvan Way Parsippany, NJ 07054. Phone: 888-786-7744 or (973)267-9700 or (973)267-9700 Fax: (973)267-9055 E-mail: info@pumps.org • URL: http://www.pumps.org • Manufacturers of pumps and products used with pumps. Compiles industry statistics, develops technical standards and meetings for pump manufacturers, creates educational programs for members and pump users worldwide and focuses on energy-savings with pumps and pumping systems through its Pump Systems Matter market transformation initiative. Provides education and tools for the effective application, testing, installation, operation and maintenance of pumps and pumping systems.

Hydraulic Tool Manufacturers Association., PO Box 5416, 198 N Brandon Dr., 198 N. Brandon Dr. Glendale Heights, IL 60139-5416. Phone: (630)893-7755 Fax: (630)790-2626 E-mail: kpolifka@wachsco.com • URL: http://www.htma.net • Manufacturers of hydraulic tools. Seeks to promote the use of portable hydraulic tools through market education, tool classification, and standardization. Has established a system for the classification of hydraulic tools based on rate of flow. Cooperates with related industry groups and standards committees; represents members to appropriate agencies or officials of the federal government. Develops research and educational programs; conducts demonstrations.

Hydraulics and Pneumatics: The Magazine of Fluid Power and Motion Control Systems. Penton Media, Inc., 1300 E. Ninth St. Cleveland, OH 44114. Phone: (216)696-7000 Fax: (216)696-1752 E-mail: information@penton.com • URL: http://www.penton.com • Monthly. $65.00 per year.

Hydro Review: A Magazine Covering the North American Hydroelectric Industry. HCI Publications, 410 Archibald St. Kansas City, MO 64111-3046. Phone: (816)931-1311 Fax: (816)931-2015 E-mail: info@hcipub.com • URL: http://www.hydroreview.com • Eight times a year. $65.00 per year. Covers hydroelectric power generation in North America. Supplement available *Industry Directory*.

Hydro Review Worldwide Industry Directory. HCI Publications, 410 Archibald St. Kansas City, MO 64111. Phone: (816)931-1311 Fax: (816)931-2015 E-mail: info@hcipub.com Annual. $20.00. Lists more than 250 manufacturers and suppliers of products and services to the hydroelectric industry worldwide. Formerly *Hydro Review-Industry Directory*.

Hydrocarbon Processing. Gulf Publishing Co., Two Greenway Plz., Ste. 1020 Houston, TX 77046. Phone: 800-231-6275 or (713)529-4301 Fax: (713)520-4433 • URL: http://www.gulfpub.com • Monthly. $120.00 per year. International edition available.

Hypertension. American Heart Association. Available from Lippincott Williams and Wilkins, 351 W. Camden St. Baltimore, MD 21201. Phone: 800-527-5597 or (410)528-4000 Fax: (410)528-4312 E-mail: custserv@lww.com • URL: http://www.lww.com • Individuals, $256.00 per year; institutions, $401.00 per year.

Hypertension Research Center. Indiana University-Purdue University at Indianapolis

Hypertension Sourcebook. Mary P. McGowan and Jo McGowan Chopra. McGraw-Hill, 1221 Ave. of the Americas New York, NY 10020. Phone: 800-722-4726 or (212)512-2000 Fax: (212)512-4502 E-mail: customer.service@mcgraw-hill.com • URL: http://www.mcgraw-hill.com • 2001. $17.95. Emphasizes recent research relating to the control and prevention of high blood pressure.

I Love Pasta. National Pasta AssociationPhone: (202)637-5888 Fax: (202)223-9741 E-mail: npa@ilovepasta.org • URL: http://www.ilovepasta.org • Web site provides a wide variety of information about pasta and the pasta industry. Includes 300 pasta recipes, pasta FAQs, and nutritional data. Industry statistics can be displayed, including data on imports, production, and per capita use in various countries. Extensive durum wheat data is provided.

IAA National & World News. International Advertising Association, 521 5th Ave. Ste. 1807 New York, NY 10175. Phone: (212)557-1133 Fax: (212)983-0455 E-mail: iaa@iaaglobal.org Description: Supplies information on Association policies and activities. Includes reviews of publications and reports from the 62 chapters worldwide.

IAFE Directory. International Association of Fairs and Expositions, P.O. Box 985 Springfield, MO 65801. Phone: 800-516-0313 or (417)862-5771 Fax: (417)862-0156 E-mail: iafg@iafenet.org • URL: http://www.fairsandexpos.com • Annual.

Free to members; non-members, $125.00. Lists more than 1,300 member agricultural fairs in the United States and Canada. Formerly *International Association of Fairs and Expositions Directory*.

IAS: Interpretation and Application of International Accounting Standards. John Wiley and Sons, Inc., 111 River St. Hoboken, NJ 07030. Phone: 800-225-5945 or (201)748-6000 Fax: (201)748-6088 E-mail: info@wiley.com • URL: http://www.wiley.com • Annual. $71.00. (Also available on CD-ROM.)

IBC's Money Fund Report. i MoneyNet Inc., PO Box 5193 Westborough, MA 01581-5193. Phone: 800-343-5413 or (508)881-2800 Fax: (508)881-0982 • URL: http://www.ibcdata.com • Weekly. $1,095.00 per year. Looseleaf. Contains detailed information on about 1,000 U. S. money market funds, including portfolios and yields. Formerly *Money Fund Report*.

Iberia Research Station. Louisiana State University

IBM Journal of Research and Development. International Business Machines Corp., 1133 Westchester Ave. White Plains, NY 10604. Phone: 800-426-4968 or (914)945-3837 Fax: (914)945-2018 • URL: http://www.ibm.com • Bimonthly. $220.00 per year.

IC Master (Integrated circuits): The Electronics Industry's Leading Source of ICInformation. IC Master, Uniondale, NY 11553-4709. Phone: (516)227-1300 Fax: (516)227-1453 E-mail: feedback@icmaster.com • URL: http://www.icmaster.com • Annual. $195.00. Semiannual supplements. Product information on 120,000 commercially available integrated circuits.

The ICAO Journal. International Civil Aviation Organization c/o Document Sales Unit, 999 University St. Montreal, QC, Canada H3C 5H7. Phone: (514)954-8022 Fax: (514)954-6769 E-mail: icaohq@icao.int • URL: http://www.icao.int • Ten times a year. $25.00 per year. Editions in English, French and Spanish.

The Ice Cream Market. MarketResearch.com, 641 Ave. of the Americas, 4th Fl. New York, NY 10011. Phone: 800-298-5699 or (212)807-2629 Fax: (212)807-2676 E-mail: customerservice@marketresearch.com • URL: http://www.marketresearch.com • 2002. $3,000.00. Market data and forecasts to 2004 on ice cream and related products (ice milk, frozen yogurt, etc.).

Ice Cream Reporter: The Newsletter for Ice Cream Executives. MarketResearch.com, 641 Ave. of the Americas, 4th Fl. New York, NY 10011. Phone: 800-298-5699 or (212)807-2629 Fax: (212)807-2676 E-mail: customerservice@marketresearch.com • URL: http://www.marketresearch.com • Monthly. $395.00 per year. Covers new products, mergers, research, packaging, etc.

Ice Cream Store. Entrepreneur Media, Inc., 2445 McCabe Way Irvine, CA 92614. Phone: 800-421-2300 or (949)261-2325 Fax: (949)261-0234 E-mail: entmag@entrepreneur.com • URL: http://www.entrepreneur.com • Looseleaf. $59.50. A practical guide to starting an ice cream shop. Covers profit potential, start-up costs, market size evaluation, owner's time required, site selection, lease negotiation, pricing, accounting, advertising, promotion, etc. (Start-Up Business Guide No. E1187.)

ICMA Newsletter. International City/County Management Association, 777 N Capital St. NE, Ste. 500 Washington, DC 20002-4201. Phone: 800-746-8780 or (202)289-4262 Fax: (202)962-3500 E-mail: amahoney@icma.org • URL: http://www.icma.org • Description: Discusses local government, professional management, and federal regulation. Publishes news of Association activities. Recurring features include news of members; reports of publications, educational workshops, positions open in public management; and two main supplements titled Nuts & Bolts and ICMA University.

ICS Cleaning Specialist (Installationa and Cleaning Specialist). Business News Publishing Co., 755 W Big Beaver Rd., Ste. 1000 Troy, MI 48084. Phone: 800-837-7370 or (248)362-3700 Fax: (248)362-0317 • URL: http://www.bnp.com • Monthly. Free to qualified personnel. Written for floor covering installers and cleaners. Formerly *Installation and Cleaning Specialist*.

ICS Cleaning Specialists Annual Trade Directory and Buying Guide. Business News Publishing Co., II, L.L.C, 22801 Ventura Blvd., Suite 115 Woodland Hills, CA 91364-1222. Phone: 800-835-4398 or (818)224-8035 Fax: (818)224-8042 E-mail: ics@bnp.com • URL: http://www.icsmag.com • Annual. $25.00. Lists about 6,000 manufacturers and distributors of floor covering installation and cleaning equipment. Formerly *Installation and Cleaning Specialists Trade Directory and Buying Guide*.

ICTA Travel Management Text Series. Institute of Certified Travel Agents, 148 Linden St. Wellesley, MA 02182. Phone: 800-542-4282 or (781)237-0280 Fax: (781)237-3860 E-mail: icta-info@icta.com • URL: http://www.icta.com • Four volumes. Volume one, *Business Management for Travel Agents*; volume two, *Personnel Management for Travel Agents*; volume three, *Marketing for Travel Agents*; volume four, *Domestic Leisure and International Tourism*.

Idaho Agricultural Experiment Station. University of Idaho

Idea Source Guide; A Monthly Report to Executives in Advertising, Merchandising and Sales Promotion. Bramlee, Inc., c/o Fred Davis, P.O. Box 366 Devon, PA 19333. Monthly. $150.00 per year. Lists new premiums and novelty products.

IDEA, The Health and Fitness Source., 6190 Cornerstone Court E., Suite 204 San Diego, CA 92121-3733. Phone: 800-999-4332 or (619)535-8979 Fax: (619)535-8234 E-mail: member@ideafit.com • URL: http://www.ideafit.com • An educational network and forum for fitness instructors, personal trainers, exercise club owners, and others. Formerly The Health and Fitness Source.

Ideas Unlimited: For Editors. Omniprint, Inc., 9700 Philadelphia Court Lanham, MD 20706-4405. Phone: 800-345-2611 or (301)731-5202 Fax: (301)731-5203 E-mail: editor@omniprint.net Monthly. $195.00 per year. Includes CD-Rom. Contains fillers for company newsletters: articles, cartoons, jokes, seasonal items, etc.

IDH—Interior Decorators Handbook. E.W. Williams Publications Co., 2125 Center Ave., Ste. 305 Fort Lee, NJ 07024-5898. Phone: (201)592-7007 Fax: (201)592-7171 E-mail: philpl@ewwpi.com • URL: http://www.williamspublications.com • Covers: Over 3,000 manufacturers and distributors of furniture, accessories, floor coverings, fabrics, wall coverings and services related to these products. Entries include: Manufacturer or distributor name, address, phone, fax, brands carried. Similar information for importers, jobbers and agents.

IEE Solutions. Institute of Industrial Engineers, 3377 Parkway Ln., Ste. 200 Norcross, GA 30092. Phone: 800-494-0460 or (770)449-0460 Fax: (770)441-3295 E-mail: jpowers@iienet.org • URL: http://www.iienet.org • Monthly. Free to members; non-members, $66.00 per year. Features articles on material handling, computers, quality control, production and inventory control, engineering economics, worker motivation, management strategies, and factory automation. Formerly *Industrial Engineers*.

IEEE Aerospace and Electronic Systems Society.

IEEE Communications Magazine. Institute of Electrical and Electronics Engineers, Inc., Three Park Ave., 17th Fl. New York, NY 10016. Phone: 800-678-4333 or (212)419-7900 Fax: (212)752-4929 E-mail: customer-service@ieee.org • URL: http://www.ieee.org • Monthly. $270.00 per year.

IEEE Computer Graphics and Applications. Insitute of Electrical and Electronics Engineers, Inc., 44 Hoes Lane Piscataway, NJ 08854-1331. Phone: 800-701-4333 E-mail: subscription-service@ieee.org • URL: http://www.ieee.org • Bimonthly. $695.00 per year.

IEEE Computer Society., 1828 L St. NW, Ste. 1202 Washington, DC 20036. Phone: (202)371-0101 Fax: (202)728-9614 E-mail: help@computer.org • URL: http://www.computer.org • Computer professionals. Promotes the development of computer and information sciences and fosters communication within the information processing community. Sponsors conferences, symposia, workshops, tutorials, technical meetings, and seminars. Operates Computer Society Press. Presents scholarships; bestows technical achievement and service awards and certificates.

IEEE Consumer Electronics Society., 4115 Clendenning Rd., 445 Hoes Ln. Gibsonia, PA 15044. Phone: 800-678-4333 or (732)981-0025 Fax: (732)981-0225 E-mail: ckobert@zbzoom.net • URL: http://www.ewh.ieee.org/soc/ces • A society of the Institute of Electrical and Electronics Engineers. Gathers and disseminates information regarding the design and manufacture of consumer electronics components and products, particularly those with recreational or educational applications.

IEEE Control Systsems Society.

IEEE Electron Devices Society., 445 Hoes Ln., PO Box 6804 Piscataway, NJ 08854. Phone: 800-678-4333 or (732)562-3926 Fax: (732)235-1626 E-mail: w.vandervort@ieee.org • URL: http://www.ieee.org/portal/pages/society/eds • A society of the Institute of Electrical and Electronics Engineers. Concerned with the theory, design, and performance of electron devices, including electron tubes, solid-state devices, integrated electron devices, energy sources, power devices, displays, and device reliability.

IEEE Engineering in Medicine and B iology Society., c/o IEEE Corporate Office, 3 Park Ave., 17th Fl. New York, NY 10016-5997. Phone: 800-678-4333 or (212)419-7900 Fax: (212)752-4929 E-mail: ieeeusa@ieee.org • URL: http://www.ieee.org • Members are engineers,technicians, physicians, manufacturers and others with an interest in medical instrumentation.

IEEE Engineering in Medicine and Biology Magazine. Institute of Electrical and Electronics Engineers, Inc., Three Park Ave., 17th Fl. New York, NY 10016. Phone: 800-678-4333 or (212)419-7900 Fax: (212)752-4929 E-mail: customer-service@ieee.org • URL: http://www.ieee.org • Six times a year, $250.00 per year. Published for biomedical engineers.

IEEE Industry Applications Magazine. Institute of Electrical and Electronics Engineers, Three Park Ave., 17th Fl. New York, NY 10016. Phone: 800-678-4333 or (212)419-7900 Fax: (212)752-4929 E-mail: customer-service@ieee.org • URL: http://www.ieee.org • Bimonthly. $190.00 per year. Covers new industrial applications of power conversion, drives, lighting, and control. Emphasis is on the petroleum, chemical, rubber, plastics, textile, and mining industries.

IEEE Lasers and Electro-Optics Society., c/o IEEE Corporate Center, Three Park Ave., 17th Fl. New York, NY 10016-5997. Phone: (212)419-7900 or (212)752-4929 E-mail: ieeeusa@ieee.org • URL: http://www.ieee.org • Fields of interest include lasers, fiber optics, optoelectronics, and photonics.

IEEE Membership Directory. Institute of Electrical and Electronics Engineers, Three Park Ave., 17th Fl. New York, NY 10016-5997. Phone: 800-678-4333 or (212)419-7900 Fax: (212)752-4929 E-mail: customer-service@ieee.org • URL: http://www.ieee.org • Annual. $190.00.

IEEE Micro. Institute of Electrical and Electronics Engineers, Inc., Three Park Ave., 17th Fl. New York, NY 10017. Phone: 800-678-4333 or (212)419-7900 Fax: (212)752-4929 E-mail: customer-service@ieee.org Bimonthly. $650.00 per year.

IEEE Multimedia Magazine. Institute of Electrical and Electronic Engineers, Inc, Three Park Ave., 17th Fl. New York, NY 10017. Phone: 800-678-4333 or (212)419-7900 Fax: (212)752-4929 E-mail: customer-service@ieee.org • URL: http://www.ieee.org • Quarterly. $560.00 per year. Provides a wide variety of technical information relating to multimedia systems and applications. Articles cover research, advanced applications, working systems, and theory.

IEEE Nuclear and Plasma Sciences Society.

IEEE Proceedings-Circuits, Devices and Systems. Institute of Electrical and Electronics Engineers, Inc., Three Park Ave., 17th Fl. New York, NY 10016-5997. Phone: 800-678-4333 or (212)419-7900 Fax: (212)752-4929 E-mail: customer-service@ieee.org • URL: http://www.ieee.org • Monthly. $720.00 per year.

IEEE Products and Publications Bulletin. Institute of Electrical and Electronics Engineers, Inc., Three Park Ave., 17th Fl. New York, NY 10017. Phone: 800-678-4333 or (212)419-7900 Fax: (212)752-4929 E-mail: customer-service@ieee.org • URL: http://www.ieee.org • Quarterly. Free. Provides information on all IEEE journals, proceedings, and other publications. Formerly *IEEE Publications Bulletin*.

IEEE Security & Privacy: Building Confidence in a Networked World. IEEE Computer Society, 10662 Los Vaqueros Circle Los Angeles, CA 90720-1264. Phone: (714)821-8380 Fax: (714)821-4010 E-mail: ieeemedia@ieee.org • URL: http://www.ieee.org • Bimonthly. $72.00 per year to individuals; $525.00 to institutions. Emphasis is on computer and netwoek security for large systems.

IEEE Software. Institute of Electrical and Electronic Engineers, Inc., Three Park Ave., 17th Fl. New York, NY 10017. Phone: 800-678-4333 or (212)419-7900 Fax: (212)752-4929 E-mail: customer-service@ieee.org • URL: http://www.ieeeorg.org • Bimonthly. $695.00 per year. Covers software engineering, technology, and development. Affiliated with the Institute of Electrical and Electronics Engineers.

IEEE Solid State Circuits Council.

IEEE Spectrum. Institute of Electrical and Electronics Engineers, Inc., Three Park Ave., 17th Fl. New York, NY 10016. Phone: 800-678-4333 or (212)419-7900 Fax: (212)752-4929 E-mail: customer-service@ieee.org • URL: http://www.ieee.org • Monthly. $195.00 per year. Includes print and online editions. Supplement available *The Institute*.

IEEE Transactions on Communications. Institute of Electrical and Electronics Engineers, Inc., Three Park Ave., 17th Fl. New York, NY 10016. Phone: 800-678-4333 or (212)419-7900 Fax: (212)752-4929 E-mail: customer-service@ieee.org • URL: http://www.ieee.org • Monthly. $600.00 per year.

IEEE Transactions on Visualization and Computer Graphics. Institute of Electrical and Electronics Engineers, Inc., Three Park Ave., 17th Fl. New York, NY 10016. Phone: 800-678-4333 or (212)419-7900 Fax: (212)752-4929 E-mail: customer-service@ieee.org • URL: http://www.ieee.org • Quarterly. $676.00 per year. Topics include computer vision, computer graphics, image processing, signal processing, computer-aided design, animation, and virtual reality.

IEG Sponsorship Sourcebook. IEG Inc., 640 N LaSalle, Ste. 450 Chicago, IL 60610-3777. Phone: 800-834-4850 or (312)944-1727 Fax: (312)944-1897 E-mail: ieg@sponsorship.com • URL: http://www.sponsorship.com • Covers: about 5,000 corporate sponsors and 1,600 major sports, events, and organizations worldwide available for commercial sponsorship; companies serving special events and sponsors (sports marketing agencies, fireworks suppliers, public relations firms, etc.). Entries include: For events—Event title, site, dates, name, and address of contact (including year-round phone number), attendance figures, event budget, and major present and past sponsors. For service firms—Company name, address, phone, contact, speciality/services. New sponsorship events are reported in "IEG Sponsorship Report", published every two weeks, which also includes a frequent "In Depth" directory of corporations and their special events contact, budget, priorities, events sponsored, etc.; $445 per year; $370 for nonprofit organizations.

IEG's Sponsorship Report: The International Newsletter of Event Sponsorship and Lifestyle Marketing. International Events Group, Inc., 640 N. LaSalle, Suite 600 Chicago, IL 60610. Phone: 800-834-4850 or (312)944-1727 Fax: (312)944-1897 E-mail: ieg@sponsorship.com • URL: http://www.sponsorship.com • Biweekly. $445.00 per year. Includes print and online editions. Newsletter reporting on corporate sponsorship of special events: sports, music, festivals, and the arts. Edited for event producers, directors, and marketing personnel.

I.E.S. Lighting Handbook. Illuminating Engineering Society of North America, 120 Wall St., 17th Fl. New York, NY 10005. Phone: (212)248-5000 Fax: (212)248-5017 E-mail: iesna@iesna.org • URL: http://www.iesna.org • Quadrennial. $389.00.

IFAP Newsletter. International Federation of Agricultural Producers, 21 rue Chaptal 75009 45 2 Paris, France. Bimonthly. Price on application.

IIHR-Hydroscience and Engineering. University of Iowa

I.I.I. Data Base Search. Insurance Information Institute, 110 Wil-

SOURCES CITED

liam St. New York, NY 10038. Phone: (212)346-5500 Fax: (212)791-1807 • URL: http://www.iii.org • Provides online citations and abstracts of insurance-related literature in magazines, newspapers, trade journals, and books. Emphasis is on property and casualty insurance issues, including highway safety, product safety, and environmental liability. Inquire as to online cost and availability.

Illuminating Engineering Society of North America., 120 Wall St., 17th Fl. New York, NY 10005-4001. Phone: (212)248-5000 Fax: (212)248-5017 E-mail: iesna@iesna.org • URL: http://www.iesna.org • Members are lighting engineers, designers, architects, and manufacturers.

Illustrated Dictionary of Building Materials and Techniques: An Invaluable Sourcebook to the Tools, Terms, Materials, and Techniques Used by Building Professionals. Paul Bianchina. John Wiley and Sons, Inc., 111 River St. Hoboken, NJ 07030. Phone: 800-225-5945 or (201)748-6000 Fax: (201)748-6088 E-mail: info@wiley.com • URL: http://www.wiley.com • 1993. $19.95. Contains 4,000 definitions of building and building materials terms, with 500 illustrations. Includes materials grades, measurements, and specifications.

Illustrated Dictionary of Cargo Handling. Peter Brodie. LLP, Inc., 41-21 28th St., Rm. D Long Island City, NY 11101. Phone: 800-493-4080 • URL: http://www.informa.com • 1991. $90.00. Second edition. Published in the UK by Lloyd's List (http://www.lloydslist.com). Provides definitions of about 600 terms relating to "the vessels and equipment used in modern cargo handling and shipping," including containerization.

Illustrated Dictionary of Historic Architecture. Cyril M. Harris, editor. Dover Publications, Inc., 31 E. Second St. Mineola, NY 11501. Phone: 800-223-3130 or (516)294-7000 Fax: (516)742-5049 • URL: http://www.doverpublications.com • 1983. $16.95.

Illustrated Dictionary of Jewelry. Harold Newman. Thames Hudson, 500 Fifth Ave. New York, NY 10110. Phone: 800-223-4830 or (212)354-3763 Fax: (212)398-1252 E-mail: bookinfo@thames.wwnorton.com • URL: http://www.thamesandhudson.usa.com • 1994. $29.95.

Illustrated Dictionary of Microcomputers. Michael Hordeski. McGraw Hill, 1221 Ave. of the Americas New York, NY 10020. Phone: 800-722-4726 or (212)512-2000 Fax: (212)512-4502 E-mail: customer.service@mcgraw-hill.com • URL: http://www.mcgraw-hill.com • 1990. $19.95. Third edition.

Illustrated Theatre Production Guide. John Holloway. Elsevier, 360 Park Ave., S New York, NY 10010-1710. Phone: 888-437-4636 or (212)989-5800 Fax: (212)633-3990 E-mail: usinfo-f@elsevier.com • URL: http://www.elsevier.com • 2002. $34.99. Covers the details of the construction of wooden, fabric, plastic, and metal scenery for stage productions.

Image Science Research Group., Worcester Polytechnic Institute, Computer Science Dept., 100 Institute Rd. Worcester, MA 01609-2208. Phone: (508)831-5357 Fax: (508)831-5776 E-mail: matt@wpi.edu • URL: http://www.cs.wpi.edu/research/isrg • Areas of research include image processing, computer graphics, and computational vision.

IMAGE Society., PO Box 6221 Chandler, AZ 85246-6221. Phone: (602)839-8709 E-mail: image@asu.edu • URL: http://image-society.org • Individuals and organizations interested in the technological advancement and application of real-time visual simulation (medical, virtual reality, telepresence, aeronautical, and automotive) and other related virtual reality technologies.

IMAGES. IMAGE Society, P.O. Box 6221 Chandler, AZ 85246-6221. Phone: (602)839-8709 E-mail: image@acu.edu • URL: http://www.public.asu.edu • Semiannual. $25.00 per year. Newsletter Provides news of virtual reality developments and the IMAGE Society.

Imaginative Events: A Sourcebook of Innovative Simulations, Exercises, Puzzles, and Games. Ken Jones. McGraw-Hill, 1221 Ave. of the Americas New York, NY 10020. Phone: 800-722-4726 or (212)512-2000 Fax: (212)512-4502 E-mail: customer.service@mcgraw-hill.com • URL: http://www.mcgraw-hill.com • 1992. $110.00. Two volumes. Vol. 1, $65.00; vol. 2, $65.00. (Training Series).

Imaging Abstracts. Royal Photographic Society of Great Britain, Imaging Science and Technology Grou. Elsevier, 655 Ave. of the Americas New York, NY 10010-5107. Phone: 800-366-2665 or (212)989-5800 Fax: 800-535-9935 or (212)633-3680 E-mail: custserv@elsevier.com • URL: http://www.elsevier.com • Bimonthly. $860.00 per year. Formerly *Photographic Abstracts*.

Imaging and Computer Vision Center., Drexel University, 32nd and Market Sts., Room 110-7 Philadelphia, PA 19104. Phone: (215)895-2279 Fax: (215)895-4987 E-mail: icvc-support@cbis.ece.drexel.edu • URL: http://www.cbis.ece.drexel.edu/icvc • Fields of research include computer vision, robot vision, and expert systems.

Imaging Business: The Voice of the Document Imaging Channel. PBI Media, LLC, 1201 7 Locks Rd. Potomac, MD 20854. Phone: 800-777-5006 or (301)354-2000 Fax: (301)309-3847 E-mail: clientservices@pbimedia.com • URL: http://www.pbimedia.com • Monthly. Free to qualified personnel. Edited for resellers of document imaging equipment.

Imaging KM: Creating and Managing the Knowledge-Based Enterprise. Knowledge Management World, PO Box 1358 Camden, ME 04843. Phone: 800-248-0588 or (207)236-8524 Fax: (207)236-6452 E-mail: hugh_keller@kmworld.com • URL: http://www.kmworld.com • 10 times a year. Free to qualified personnel; others, $48.00 per year. Covers automated and networked document image handling.

Imaging Systems Laboratory., Carnegie Mellon University, Robotics Institute, 5000 Forbes Ave. Pittsburgh, PA 15213. Phone: (412)268-3824 Fax: (412)683-3763 E-mail: rht@cs.cmu.edu Fields of research include computer vision and document interpretation.

iMarketing News: The Newspaper of E-Business and Internet Marketing. Courtenay Communications, 100 Ave. of the Americas New York, NY 10013. Phone: (212)925-7300 Fax: (212)925-8752 • URL: http://www.imarketingnews.com • Monthly. Controlled circulation.

IMF Survey. International Monetary Fund, 700 19th St. NW Washington, DC 20431. Phone: (202)623-7000 Fax: (202)623-4661 E-mail: publications@imf.org • URL: http://www.imf.org • Description: Timely news on topics of general interest in the fields of international finance, country economics, trade, and commodities. Contains information on the IMF's activities, including press releases, major management speeches, and lending activity data rates.

IMM Abstracts and Index: A Survey of World Literature on the Economic Geology and Mining of All Minerals (Except Coal), Mineral Processing, and Nonferrous Extraction Metallurgy. Institution of Mining and Metallurgy, Danum House South Parade DN1 2DY, United Kingdom. Phone: 44 1302 320486 or 44 1302 380900 E-mail: hq@imm.org.uk • URL: http://www.imm.org.uk • Bimonthly. $500.00 per year. Provides international coverage of the literature of mining and nonferrous metallurgy. Includes mineral economics, tunnelling, and rock mechanics.

Immigration Fundamentals: A Guide to Law and Practice. Practising Law Institute, 810 7th Ave. New York, NY 10019-5818. Phone: 800-260-4754 or (212)824-5710 E-mail: info@pli.edu • URL: http://www.pli.edu • $195.00. 4th edition. Includes the legal aspects of employment-based immigration, family-sponsored immigration, nonimmigrants, refugees, deportation, naturalization, and citizenship. (Basic Practice Skills Series).

Immigration History Research Center. University of Minnesota

Immigration Law and Business. Sam Bernsen. West Group, 610 Opperman Dr. Eagan, MN 55123. Phone: 800-328-4880 or (651)687-7000 Fax: 800-340-9378 E-mail: bookstore@westgroup.com • URL: http://www.westgroup.com • Three times a year. $435.00 per year. Three looseleaf volumes. Covers labor certification, temporary workers, applications, petitions, etc.

Immigration Law and Crimes. Dan Kesselbrenner and Lory D. Rosenberg. West Group, 610 Opperman Dr. Eagan, MN 55123. Phone: 800-328-4880 or (651)687-7000 Fax: 800-340-9378 E-mail: bookstore@westgroup.com • URL: http://www.westgroup.com • Semiannual. $250.00 per year. Looseleaf service. Covers legal representation of the foreign-born criminal defendant.

Immigration Law and Defense. National Lawyers Guild. West Group, 610 Opperman Dr. Eagan, MN 55123. Phone: 800-328-4880 or (651)687-7000 Fax: 800-340-9378 E-mail: bookstore@westgroup.com • URL: http://www.westgroup.com • Semiannual. $295.00 per year. Two looseleaf volumes. Covers legal defense of immigrants and aliens.

Immigration Law and Procedure. LexisNexis Matthew Bender, 1275 Broadway Albany, NY 12204. Phone: 800-424-4200 or (518)487-3000 Fax: (518)487-3584 E-mail: bookstore.support@lexisnexis.com • URL: http://www.bender.com • $1,888.00. 20 looseleaf volumes. Periodic supplementation.

Immigration Law Report. Austin T. Fragomen and Steven C. Bell. West Group, 610 Opperman Dr. Eagan, MN 55123. Phone: 800-328-4880 or (651)687-7000 Fax: 800-340-9378 E-mail: compandbene@westgroup.com • URL: http://www.westgroup.com • Description: Reports on U.S. immigration and nationality laws. Presents arguments that can be used in preparing Immigration and Naturalization Service (INS) cases and federal court cases. Carries analysis of material not readily available, such as internal INS policy statements and unpublished cases. Recurring features include reviews of recent decisions and regulations.

Immigration Procedures Handbook; A How-To Guide for Legal and Business Professionals. West Group, 610 Opperman Dr. Eagan, MN 55123. Phone: 800-328-4880 or (651)687-7000 Fax: 800-340-9378 E-mail: bookstore@westgroup.com • URL: http://www.westgroup.com • 2004. $330.00. Two volumes. How to bring foreign nationals to the U. S. on a temporary or permanent basis.

Impac., 4710 Bethesda Ave. Bethesda, MD 20814. Phone: (301)657-4600 Fax: (501)986-5782 E-mail: caomail@hr.house.gov Raises funds for Democratic candidates for public office.

Impact of Advertising Law on Business and Public Policy. Ross D. Petty. Greenwood Publishing Group, Inc., 88 Post Rd., W., Westport, CT 06881. Phone: 800-225-5800 or (203)226-3571 Fax: (203)431-2214 E-mail: customer-service@greenwood.com • URL: http://www.greenwood.com • 1992. $64.95. Analyzes cases under the Federal Trade Commission and Lanham Acts.

The Impact of Electronic Publishing: The Future for Libraries and Publishers. David J. Brown. Available from Gale Cengage Learning, 27500 Drake Rd. Farmington Hills, MI 48331-3535. Phone: 800-877-GALE Fax: 800-414-5043 or (248)699-8069 E-mail: galeord@galegroup.com • URL: http://www.galegroup.com • 2003. $80.00. Published by K. G. Saur. Explains how libraries and publishers should prepare for a significant expansion in electronic publishing.

Impact: U.S. News and Research for the Wine, Spirits, and Beer Industries. M. Shanken Communications, Inc., 387 Park Ave., S. New York, NY 10016. Phone: 800-344-0763 or (212)684-4424 Fax: (212)684-5424 E-mail: retailsales@mshanken.com • URL: http://www.mshanken.com • Semimonthly. $375.00 per year. Newsletter covering the marketing, economic, and financial aspects of alcoholic beverages.

Implement and Tractor: The Business Magazine of the Farm and Industrial Equipment Industry. Agra USA, 2302 W. First St. Cedar Falls, IA 50613. Phone: (319)277-3599 Fax: (319)277-3783 E-mail: agrausa@cfu.net • URL: http://www.agra-usa.com • Bimonthly. $35.00 per year. Includes annuals *Product File* and *Red Book*.

Import and Export. Entrepreneur Media, Inc., 2445 McCabe Way Irvine, CA 92614. Phone: 800-421-2300 or (949)261-2325 Fax: (949)261-0234 E-mail: entmag@entrepreneur.com • URL: http://www.entrepreneur.com • Looseleaf. $59.50. A practical guide to starting an import/ export business. Covers profit potential, start-up costs, market size evaluation, owner's time required, pricing, accounting, advertising promotion, etc. (Start-Up Business Guide No. E1092.)

Importcar: The Complete Import Service Magazine. Babcox Publications, Inc., 3550 Embassy Pky. Akron, OH 44333. Phone: (330)670-1234 Fax: (330)670-0874 E-mail: tfritz@babcox.com • URL: http://www.babcox.com • Monthly. $64.00 per year. Includes *Automotive Aftermarket Training Guide*. Formerly *Importcar and Truck*.

Importers Manual U. S. A.: The Single Source Reference Encyclopedia for Importined States. Edward G. Hinkelman. World Trade Press, 1450 Grant Ave., Suite 204 Novato, CA 94945. Phone: 800-833-8586 or (415)898-1124 Fax: (415)898-1080 E-mail: sales@worldtradepress.com • URL: http://www.worldtradepress.com • 1998. $87.00. Third edition. Published by World Trade Press. Covers U. S. customs regulations, letters of credit, contracts, shipping, insurance, and other items relating to importing. Includes 60 essays on practical aspects of importing.

Importing into the United States. Available from U. S. Government Printing Office, Washington, DC 20402. Phone: (202)512-1800 Fax: (202)512-2250 E-mail: gpoaccess@gpo.gov • URL: http://www.access.gpo.gov • 1998. $10.50. Issued by the U. S. Customs Service, Department of the Treasury. Formerly *Exporting to the United States*. Explains customs organization, entry of goods, invoices, assessment of duty, marking requirements, and other subjects.

Imports and Exports of Fishery Products. National Marine Fisheries Service, U.S. Department of Commerce, Washington, DC 20235. Phone: (301)713-2239 Annual.

Improving Access to Bank Information for Tax Purposes. Organization for Economic Cooperation and Development, OECD Washington Center, 2001 L St., N. W., Suite 650 Washington, DC 20036-4922. Phone: 800-456-6323 or (202)785-6323 Fax: (202)785-0350 E-mail: washington.contact@oecd.org • URL: http://www.oecdwash.org • 2000. $66.00. Discusses ways to improve the international exchange of bank account information for tax determinations.

Improving Online Public Access Catalogs. Martha M. Yee and Sara S. Layne. American Library Association, 50 E Huron St. Chicago, IL 60611-2795. Phone: 800-545-2433 or (312)944-6780 Fax: (312)440-9374 E-mail: ala@ala.org • URL: http://www.ala.org • 1998. $48.00. A practical guide to developing user-friendly online catalogs (OPACs).

Improving Poor People: The Welfare State, the "Underclass," and Urban Schools as History. Michael B. Katz. Princeton University Press, 41 William St. Princeton, NJ 08540. Phone: 800-777-4726 or (609)258-4900 Fax: (609)258-6305 • URL: http://www.pup.princeton.edu • 1995. $42.50.

In Business: The Magazine for Environmental Entrepreneuring. JG Press, Inc., 419 State Ave. Emmaus, PA 18049. Phone: (610)967-4135 • URL: http://www.jgpress.com • Bimonthly. $33.00 per year. Magazine for environmental entrepreneuring.

In Command! A Series of Messages About Getting the Most From Your Word Processor. Economics Press, Inc., 12 Daniel Road Fairfield, NJ 07004. Phone: 800-526-2554 or (973)227-1224 Fax: (973)227-9742 E-mail: info@epinc.com • URL: http://www.epinc.com • Weekly. $146.00 per year. Quantity prices available. A newsletter for word processing operators.

In Focus. National Association for Visually Handicapped, 22 W 21st St. New York, NY 10010. Phone: (212)889-3141 Fax: (212)727-2931 E-mail: staff@navh.org • URL: http://www.natoonline.org • Description: Reaches visually handicapped children through stories, poems, and drawings contributed by young readers. Covers subjects of interest to youngsters, especially those related to their experiences and hopes for the future. Also includes puzzles, contests, and items of interest to parents and educators, such as new book and symposium announcements.

In-Plant Graphics. North American Publishing Co., 401 N. Broad St. Philadelphia, PA 19108. Phone: 800-777-8074 or (215)238-5482 Fax: 800-664-1533 or (215)238-5412 E-mail: customerservice@napco.com • URL: http://www.napco.com

• Monthly. Free. Formerly *In-Plant Reproductions*.

In-Plant Printer Buyer's Guide. Innes Publishing Co., 28100 N Ashley Cir. Libertyville, IL 60048. Phone: 800-247-3306 or (847)816-7900 Fax: (847)247-8855 • URL: http://www.innespub.com • Annual. $10.00. Manufacturers of equipment for the in-plant and grahic arts industry. Formerly *In-Plant Printer and Electronic Publisher Buyer's Guide*.

In-Plant Printer: The In-Plant Management Magazine. Innes Publishing Co., P.O. Box 7280 Libertyville, IL 60048-7280. Phone: 800-247-3306 or (847)816-7900 Fax: (847)247-8855 Bimonthly. $75.00 per year. Formerly *In-Plant Printer and Electronic Publisher*.

In the Black: A History of African Americans on Wall Street. Gregory S. Bell. John Wiley and Sons, Inc., 111 River St. Hoboken, NJ 07030. Phone: 800-225-5945 or (201)748-6000 Fax: (201)748-6088 E-mail: bookinfo@wiley.com • URL: http://www.wiley.com • 2001. $24.95. Written by the son of Travers Bell, co-founder of Daniels Bell stockbrokers, the first black-owned New York Stock Exchange member firm.

Incentive: Managing and Marketing Through Motivation. VNU Business Media, 770 Broadway New York, NY 10003-9595. Phone: 800-344-7119 or (646)654-4500 Fax: (646)654-7212 • URL: http://www.vnubusinessmedia.com • Monthly. $59.00 per year.

Incentive Manufacturers Representatives Association., 1801 N. Mill St., Suite R Naerville, IL 60563. Phone: 888-285-4672 or (630)369-7786 Fax: (630)369-3773 E-mail: info@imral.org • URL: http://www.imral.org • Formerly National Premium Manufacturers Representatives.

Incentive-State of the Industry and Annual Facts Review. VNU Business Media, 770 Broadway New York, NY 10003. Phone: 800-266-4712 or (646)654-5400 Fax: (646)654-7212 E-mail: edit@incentivemag.com • URL: http://vnubusinessmedia.com • Annual. $5.00. A special issue of *Incentive* magazine.

Incentive's Buyer's Guide. VNU Business Media, 770 Broadway New York, NY 10003-9595. Phone: 800-266-4712 or (646)654-4420 Fax: (646)654-4420 E-mail: bmcomm@meetingnews.com • URL: http://www.vnubusinessmedia.com • Publication includes: List of 1,500 merchandise suppliers, hotels, cruise lines, airlines, and other companies that provide services to companies offering incentive travel and merchandise programs. Entries include: Company name, address, phone, name of sales contact, description of facilities (for hotels).

Income and Fees of Accountants in Public Practice. National Society of Accountants, 1010 N. Fairfax St. Alexandria, VA 22314-1574. Phone: 800-966-6679 or (703)549-6400 Fax: (703)549-2984 E-mail: arichman@nsacct.org • URL: http://www.nsacct.org • Triennial. Members, $35.00; non-members, $50.00.

Income of the Population 55 and Older. Available from U. S. Government Printing Office, Washington, DC 20402. Phone: (202)512-1800 Fax: (202)512-2250 E-mail: gpoaccess@gpo.gov • URL: http://www.access.gpo.gov • Biennial. $23.00. Issued by the Social Security Administration (http://www.ssa.gov). Covers major sources and amounts of income for the 55 and older population in the U. S., "with special emphasis on some aspects of the income of the population 65 and older."

Income Opportunities.Com: The Original Small Business - Home Office Magazine. Newline, 2448 E. 81st St., 5300 City Plex Tower Tulsa, OK 74137-4207. Phone: (918)491-6100 Fax: (918)491-9424 E-mail: csnatcom-publications.com • URL: http://www.eincomeopportunities.com • Monthly. $31.95 per year.

Income Tax Regulations. CCH, Inc., 2700 Lake Cook Rd. Riverwoods, IL 60015. Phone: 800-835-5224 or (847)267-7000 E-mail: cust_serv@cch.com • URL: http://www.cch.com • Annual. $119.00. Six volumes. Contains full text of official Internal Revenue Code regulations.

Incorporate in Any State. W. Dean Brown. Corporate Publishing, Co., PO Box 23830 Knoxville, TN 37933-1830. Phone: 800-677-2462 or (865)671-4854 Fax: (865)671-4857 • URL: http://www.corporatepublishingcompany.com • Annual. $24.95. Available in separate editions for every state and the District of Columbia. Includes specific instructions for creating a simple corporation in a particular state, with legal forms and sample stock certificates.

Incorporate Your Business: The National Corporation Kit. Daniel Sitarz. Nova Publishing Co., 705 W Main St. Carbondale, IL 62901. Phone: 800-748-1175 or (618)457-3521 Fax: 800-338-4550 E-mail: info@novapublishing.com • URL: http://www.novapublishing.com • 2001. $29.95. Third edition. IncludesCD-ROM and basic forms and instructions for incorporating a small business in any state. Forms are also available on IBM or MAC diskettes. (Small Business Library Series).

Inc.-The Inc. 500., 38 Commercial Wharf Boston, MA 02110. Phone: (617)248-8000 Fax: (617)248-8090 E-mail: editors@inc.com • URL: http://www.inc.com • Annual. $3.50. Information on each of the 500 fastest-growing privately held companies in the U. S. Based on percentage increase in sales over the five year period prior to compilation of current year's list.

Inc.: The Magazine for Growing Companies. INC., 38 Commercial Warf Boston, MA 02110. Phone: (617)248-8000 Fax: (617)248-8090 E-mail: editors@inc.com • URL: http://www.inc.com • 18 times a year. $14.00 per year. Edited for small office and office-in-the-home businesses with from one to 25 employees. Covers management, office technology, and lifestyle. Incorporates *Self-Employed Professional*.

Inc. Yourself: How to Profit by Setting Up Your Own Corporation. Judith H. McQuown. Career Press, Inc., Three Tice Road Franklin Lakes, NJ 07417-1322. Phone: 800-227-3371 or (201)848-0310 Fax: (201)848-1727 E-mail: contact@careerpress.com • URL: http://www.careerpress.com • 2002. $27.99. 10th revised edition. Includes information on current tax laws and other legislation affecting small corporations and individuals. Provides a step-by-step guide to forming a corporation.

Incorporating Your Business: The Complete Guide That Tells All You Should Know About Establishing and Operating a Small Corporation. McGraw-Hill, 1221 Ave. of the Americas New York, NY 10020. Phone: 800-722-4726 or (212)512-2000 Fax: (212)512-4502 E-mail: customer.service@mcgraw-hill.com • URL: http://www.mcgraw-hill.com • 1986. $14.95.

Incorporation Kit. Entrepreneur Media, Inc., 2445 McCabe Way Irvine, CA 92614. Phone: 800-421-2300 or (949)261-2325 Fax: (949)261-0234 E-mail: entmag@entrepreneur.com • URL: http://www.entrepreneur.com • Looseleaf. $59.50. A practical guide to incorporating a small business. Includes sample forms and information on how to construct bylaws and articles of incorporation. (Start-Up Business Guide No. E7100.)

INDA, Association of the Nonwoven Fabrics Industry., P.O. Box 1288 Cary, NC 27512-1288. Phone: (919)233-1210 Fax: (919)233-1282 E-mail: twritz@inda.org • URL: http://www.inda.org • Formerly International Nonwovens and Disposables Association.

Independent Action., 1511 K St. NW, Ste. 723 Washington, DC 20005. Phone: (202)628-4321 Fax: (202)628-3090 E-mail: info@fundfornewpriorities.org Seeks to build a political counterforce to the New Right and elect progressive Democrats to federal office. Plans to seek out progressive candidates and provide them with the financial and technical support they need at the early stages of the campaign process; make direct contributions to IA-endorsed candidates; make independent expenditures to counter the efforts of right-wing political action groups.

Independent Agent. Independent Insurance Agents of North America., 127 S. Peyton St. Alexandria, VA 22314. Phone: (703)683-4422 Fax: (703)683-7556 E-mail: magazine@iiaa.org • URL: http://www.independentagent.com • Monthly. $24.00 per year.

Independent Battery Manufacturers Association., 401 N Michigan Ave., 24th Fl. Chicago, IL 60611. Phone: (312)245-1074 Fax: (312)527-6640 E-mail: info@thebatteryman.com • URL: http://www.thebatteryman.com • Domestic and foreign manufacturers of lead-acid storage batteries; associate members are suppliers of battery parts and battery manufacturing equipment. Purpose is to advance the manufacture of batteries and to promote and develop standards of quality.

Independent Community Bankers of America., One Thomas Circle, N.W., Suite 400 Washington, DC 20005. Phone: 800-422-8439 or (202)659-8111 Fax: (202)659-9216 E-mail: info@icba.org • URL: http://www.icba.org • Formerly Independent Bankers Association of America.

Independent Electrical Contractors., 4401 Ford Ave., Ste. 1100 Alexandria, VA 22302-1432. Phone: 800-456-4324 or (703)549-7351 Fax: (703)549-7448 E-mail: info@ieci.org • URL: http://www.ieci.org • Independent electrical contractors, small and large, primarily open shop. Promotes the interests of members; works to eliminate "unwise and unfair business practices" and to protect its members against "unfair or unjust taxes and legislative enactments." Sponsors electrical apprenticeship programs; conducts educational programs on cost control and personnel motivation. Represents independent electrical contractors to the National Electrical Code panel. Conducts surveys on volume of sales and purchases and on type of products used. Has formulated National Pattern Standards for Apprentice Training for Electricians.

Independent Energy: The Power Industry's Business Magazine. PennWell Corp., Industrial Div., 1421 S. Sheridan Rd. Tulsa, OK 74112. Phone: 800-331-4463 or (918)835-3161 E-mail: bid@pennwell.com • URL: http://www.pennwell.com • 10 times a year. $127.00 per year. Covers non-utility electric power plants (cogeneration) and other alternative sources of electric energy.

Independent Film and Videomaker's Guide. Michael Wiese. Michael Wiese Productions, 11288 Ventura Blvd., Suite 621 Studio City, CA 91604. Phone: 800-833-5738 or (818)379-8799 Fax: (818)986-3408 • URL: http://www.mwp.com • 1999. $29.95. Second edition. Covers many aspects of the business side of independent filmmaking, such as business plan writing, financing, production, market research, distribution, presentations, and prospectus writing.

Independent Insurance Agents and Brokers of America., 127 S. Peyton Alexandria, VA 22314. Phone: 800-221-7917 or (703)683-4422 Fax: (703)683-7556 E-mail: info@iiaba.org • URL: http://www.independentagent.com • Formerly Independent Insurance Agents and Brokers of America.

Independent Medical Distributors Association., 5204 Fairmount Ave. Downers Grove, IL 60515. Phone: (866)463-2937 or (630)655-9280 Fax: (630)463-0798 E-mail: imda@imda.org • URL: http://www.imda.org • Represents sales, marketing and distribution organizations focused on bringing innovative medical technologies to market. Employs salespeople who are technically sophisticated, and who enjoy long-standing relationships with clinicians in their territories.

Independent Office Products and Furniture Dealers Association., 301 N Fairfax St. Alexandria, VA 22314. Phone: 800-542-6672 or (703)549-9040 Fax: (703)683-7552 E-mail: info@iopfda.org • URL: http://www.iopfda.org • Formerly Office Furniture Dealers Alliance.

Independent Petroleum Association of America.

Independent Publisher: Leading the World of Book Selling in New Directions. Jenkins Group, Inc., 400 W Front St., Ste. 4A Traverse City, MI 49684. Phone: 800-706-4636 or (231)933-0445 Fax: (231)933-0448 E-mail: info@bookpublishing.com • URL: http://www.bookpublishing.com • Bimonthly. Free. Covers business, finance, production, marketing, and other management topics for small publishers, including college presses. Emphasis is on book publishing.

Independent School. National Association of Independent Schools, 1620 L St., N.W., Suite 1100 Washington, DC 20036-5605. Phone: (202)973-9700 Fax: (202)973-9790 • URL: http://www.nais.org • Three times a year. $17.50 per year. An open forum for exchange of information about elementary and secondary education in general, and independent education in particular

Independent Sector., 1200 18th St. NW, Ste. 200 Washington, DC 20036. Phone: 888-860-8118 or (202)467-6100 Fax: (202)467-6101 E-mail: info@independentsector.org • URL: http://www.independentsector.org • Represents charities and foundations. Organizes corporate giving programs committed to advancement of the common good in America and around the world. Leads, strengthens, and mobilizes charitable community.

Index and Directory of Industry Standards. IHS Energy, 15 Inverness Way E. Englewood, CO 80112. Phone: 800-854-7179 or (303)736-3000 Fax: (303)736-3150 E-mail: globalcustomerservice@ihs.com • URL: http://www.global.ihs.com • Annual. $395.00 Seven volumes. Covers approximately 20,000 international and 35,000 U.S. industrial standards as well as 362 industrial organizations.

Index Medicus. National Library of Medicine. Available from U. S. Government Printing Office, Washington, DC 20402. Phone: (202)512-1800 Fax: (202)512-2250 E-mail: gpoaccess@gpo.gov • URL: http://www.access.gpo.gov • Monthly. $620.00 per year. Bibliographic listing of references to current articles from approximately 3,000 of the world's biomedical journals.

Index of Economic Articles in Journals and Collective Volumes. American Economic Association, 2014 Broadway, Suite 305 Nashville, TN 37203. Phone: (615)322-2595 Fax: (615)343-7590 E-mail: aeainfo@vanderbilt.edu • URL: http://www.vanderbilt.edu/aea • Irregular. $160.00.

Index of Majors. College Board Publications, 45 Columbus Ave. New York, NY 10023-6992. Phone: 800-323-7155 or (212)713-8000 Fax: (212)713-8143 Annual. $22.95.

Index of Patents Issued from the United States Patent and Trademark Office, Part One: List of Patentees. Available from U. S. Government Printing Office, Washington, DC 20402. Phone: (202)512-1800 Fax: (202)512-2250 E-mail: gpoaccess@gpo.gov • URL: http://www.access.gpo.gov • Annual. $160.00. Lists patentees and reissue patentees for each year.

Index of Patents Issued from the United States Patent and Trademark Office, Part Two: Index to Subjects of Invention. Available from U. S. Government Printing Office, Washington, DC 20402. Phone: (202)512-1800 Fax: (202)512-2250 E-mail: gpoaccess@gpo.gov • URL: http://www.access.gpo.gov • Annual. $71.00. A subject index to patents issued each year, arranged by class and subclass numbers. Includes a list of patent and tradmark depository libraries.

Index of Trademarks Issued from the United States Patent and Trademark Office. Available from U. S. Government Printing Office, Washington, DC 20402. Phone: (202)512-1800 Fax: (202)512-2250 E-mail: gpoaccess@gpo.gov • URL: http://www.access.gpo.gov • Annual. $98.00. Arranged alphabetically by name of registrant. The caption title is "List of Trademark Registrants."

Index to AV Producers and Distributors (Educational Audiovisual Materials). National Information Center for Educational Media. c/o Plexus Publishing, Inc., 143 Old Marlton Pike Medford, NJ 08055-8750. Phone: (609)654-6500 Fax: (609)654-4309 E-mail: info@plexuspublishing.com • URL: http://www.plexuspublishing.com • Biennial. $89.00. A directory listing about 23,300 producers and distributors of all types of audiovisual educational materials.

Index to Current Urban Documents. Greenwood Publishing Group, Inc., 88 Post Rd., W. Westport, CT 06881. Phone: 800-225-5800 or (203)226-3571 Fax: (203)431-2214 E-mail: customer-service@greenwood.com • URL: http://www.greenwood.com • Quarterly. $500.00 per year. Includes annual *cumulation*.

Index to Federal Tax Articles. RIA, 395 Hudson St. New York, NY 10014. Phone: 800-950-1216 or 800-431-9025 E-mail: riahome@riag.com • URL: http://www.riahome.com • $695.00 per year. Looseleaf service. Quarterly supplementation. Bibliographic listing of every significant article on federal income, estate and gift taxation since 1913. Lists over 36,000 articles.

Index to Foreign Legal Periodicals. American Association of Law Libraries. University of California Press, Journals Div., 2120 Berkeley Way Berkeley, CA 94704-1012. Phone: 800-777-4726 or (510)643-7154 Fax: 800-999-1958 or (510)642-9917 E-mail: journals@ucpress.com • URL: http://www.ucpress.edu/journals • Quarterly. $725.00 per year. Annual cumulation.

Index to Legal Periodicals and Books. H. W. Wilson Co., 950 University Ave. Bronx, NY 10452. Phone: 800-367-6770 or (718)588-8400 Fax: 800-590-1617 or (718)590-1617 E-mail: custserv@hwwilson.com • URL: http://www.hwwilson.com • Monthly. $490.00 per year. Quarterly and annual cumulations.

Index to Legal Periodicals and Books (Online). H. W. Wilson Co., 950 University Ave. Bronx, NY 10452. Phone: 800-367-6770 or (718)588-8400 Fax: (718)590-1617 E-mail: hwwmsg@info.hwwilson.com • URL: http://www.hwwilson.com • Broad coverage of law journals and books 1981 to date. Monthly updates. Inquire as to online cost and availability.

Index to Marquis Who's Who Publications. Marquis Who's Who, 121 Chanlon Rd. New Providence, NJ 07974. Phone: 800-521-8110 or (908)464-6800 Fax: 800-836-7766 or (908)665-6688 E-mail: info@marquiswhoswho.com • URL: http://www.marquiswhoswho.com • Annual. $115.00. A combined index to current editions of most Marquis Who's Who publications. Contains over 320,000 entries.

Index to Periodical Articles Related to Law. Glanville Publishers, Inc., 75 Main St. Dobbs Ferry, NY 10522-1601. Phone: (914)693-8100 Fax: (914)693-0402 E-mail: glanville@oceanalaw.com • URL: http://www.oceanalaw • Quarterly. $95.00 per year. Selected from journals not included in the *Index to Legal Periodicals, Current Law Index, Index to Foreign Legal Periodicals, Legal Resolve Index or Legaltrac.*

Index to Proceedings of the Economic and Social Council. United Nations Publications, United Nations Concourse Level, First Ave., 46th St. New York, NY 10017. Phone: 800-553-3210 or (212)963-7680 Fax: (212)963-4910 E-mail: bookstore@un.org • URL: http://www.un.org/publications • Irregular.

Index Veterinarius: Comprehensive Monthly Subject and Author Index to the World's Veterinary Literature. Availabe in Print and on the Internet. Available from CABI Publishing North America, 875 Massachusetts Ave., 7th Fl. Cambridge, MA 02139. Phone: 800-528-4841 or (617)395-4056 Fax: (617)354-6875 E-mail: cabi-nao@cabi.org • URL: http://www.cabi-publishing.org • Monthly. Institutions, $1,660.00 per year. Annual cumulation. Includes single site internet access. Published in England by CABI Publishing. Provides worldwide coverage of the literature.

Indexer Locater. American Society of Indexers, Inc., 10200 W 44th Ave., Ste. 304 Wheat Ridge, CO 80033. Phone: (303)463-2887 Fax: (303)422-8894 E-mail: info@asindexing.org • URL: http://www.asindexing.org • Annual. Members, $10.00; non-members, $15.00. Lists over 200 freelance indexers in the U. S. and their subject specialties. Formerly *Register of Indexers*.

The Indexer: The International Journal of Indexing. American Society of Indexers, 10200 W 44th Ave., Ste. 304 Wheat Ridge, CO 80033. Phone: (303)463-2887 Fax: (303)422-8894 E-mail: info@asindexing.org • URL: http://www.asindexing.org • Semiannual. Free to members; non-members, $65.00 per year. Devoted specifically to all aspects of indexing.

Indexer's Guide to the Internet. Lori Lathrop. Information Today, Inc., 143 Old Marlton Pike Medford, NJ 08055-8750. Phone: 800-300-9868 or (609)654-6266 Fax: (609)654-4309 E-mail: custserv@infotoday.com • URL: http://www.infotoday.com • 1999. $31.25. Second edition. Published in conjunction with the American Society of Indexers (ASI). Includes advice on useful Web sites, service providers, Web site design, and the use of search engines.

Indexing and Abstracting in Theory and Practice. F. Wilfrid Lancaster. University of Illinois at Urbana-Champaign, Graduate School of Library and Information Science,, 501 E Daniel St. Champaign, IL 61820. Phone: (217)333-7197 Fax: (217)244-3302 E-mail: gslis@alexia.lis.uiuc.edu • URL: http://www.alexia.lis.uiuc.edu • 1998. $47.50. Second revised edition. Includes indexing and abstracting exercises.

Indexing for Maximum Investment Results. Albert S. Neuberg. Fitzroy Dearborn Publishers, Inc., 919 N. Michigan Ave., Suite 760 Chicago, IL 60611. Phone: 800-850-8102 or (312)587-0131 Fax: (312)587-1049 E-mail: fitzroy@aol.com • URL: http://www.fitzroydearborn.com • 1998. $65.00. Covers the Standard & Poor's 500 and other indexing strategies for both individual and institutional investors.

Indexing from A to Z. Hans H. Wellisch. H. W. Wilson Co., 950 University Ave. Bronx, NY 10452. Phone: 800-367-6770 or (718)588-8400 Fax: 800-590-1617 or (718)590-1617 E-mail: custserv@hwwilson.com • URL: http://www.hwwilson.com • 1996. $60.00. Second enlarged revised edition. A practical guide to the indexing of books, periodicals, and non-print materials. Covers such technical topics as exhaustivity, specificity, thesauri, and keywords, and such mundane topics as contracts and fees.

Indexing Specialties: Law. Peter Kendrick and Enid L. Zafran, editors. Information Today, Inc., 143 Old Marlton Pike Medford, NJ 08055-8750. Phone: 800-300-9868 or (609)654-6266 Fax: (609)654-4309 E-mail: custserv@infotoday.com • URL: http://www.infotoday.com • 2001. $35.00. Published in conjunction with the American Society of Indexers (ASI). Includes chapters by professional legal indexers on legal cases, statutory materials, new methodologies, careers in legal indexing, and related topics.

Indexing Specialties: Medicine. L. Pilar Wyman, editor. Information Today, Inc., 143 Old Marlton Pike Medford, NJ 08055-8750. Phone: 800-300-9868 or (609)654-6266 Fax: (609)654-4309 E-mail: custserv@infotoday.com • URL: http://www.infotoday.com • 1999. $35.00. Published in conjunction with the American Society of Indexers (ASI). Includes chapters by professional medical indexers on book indexing, database indexing, reviews of published indexes, and details of such specialties as nutrition, nursing, and general medicine.

Indexing Specialties: Psychology. Becky Hornyak, editor. Information Today, Inc., 143 Old Marlton Pike Medford, NJ 08055-8750. Phone: 800-300-9868 or (609)654-6266 Fax: (609)654-4309 E-mail: custserv@infotoday.com • URL: http://www.infotoday.com • 2002. $25.00. Published in conjunction with the American Society of Indexers (ASI). Contains articles written by specialists in the area of "indexing textbooks and books aimed at clinical practitioners in the field of psychology." Includes an annotated bibliography.

Indexing: The Manual of Good Practice. Pat Booth. Available from Gale Cengage Learning, 27500 Drake Rd. Farmington Hills, MI 48331-3535. Phone: 800-877-GALE Fax: 800-414-5043 or (248)699-8069 E-mail: galeord@galegroup.com • URL: http://www.galegroup.com • 2001. $99.00. Published by K. G. Saur. Covers indexing of books, serials, graphic images, and audio sources, in addition to providing a discussion of the principles of effective indexing.

Indicators of Industrial and Services. OECD Publications and Information Center, 2001 L St., N.W., Suite 650 Washington, DC 20036-4922. Phone: 800-456-6323 or (202)785-6323 Fax: (202)785-0350 E-mail: washington.contact@oecd.org • URL: http://www.oecdwash.org • 2001-2004. Information on production, deliveries, orders, prices and employment for 17 industrial sectors in selected OECD member countries.

Individual Income Tax Returns. U.S. Department of the Treasury, Internal Revenue Service. Available from U.S. Government Printing Office, Washington, DC 20402. Phone: (202)512-1800 Fax: (202)512-2250 E-mail: gpoaccess@gpo.gov • URL: http://www.accessgpo.gov • Annual. $22.00.

The Individual Investor's Revolution: Unlock the Secrets of Wall Street and Invest Like a Pro. Charles B. Carlson. McGraw-Hill, 1221 Ave. of the Americas New York, NY 10020. Phone: 800-722-4726 or (212)904-2000 Fax: (212)512-4502 E-mail: customer.service@mcgraw-hill.com • URL: http://www.mcgraw-hill.com • 2000. $15.95. Emphasizes the growing importance of the individual investor, especially with regard to online trading (e-trading). Includes the author's favorite websites for investors and traders.

Individual Retirement Account Answer Book. Donald R. Levy and others. Aspen Publishers, Inc., 1185 Avenue of the Americas New York, NY 10036. Phone: 800-234-1660 or (212)597-0200 Fax: (212)597-0338 E-mail: customer.service@aspenpubl.com • URL: http://www.aspenpublishers.com • 2002. $195.00. Ninth edition. Periodic supplementation available. Questions and answers include information about contributions, distributions, rollovers, Roth IRAs, SIMPLE IRAs (Savings Incentive Match Plans for Employees), Education IRAs, and SEPs (Simplified Employee Pension plans). Chapters are provided on retirement planning, estate planning, and tax planning.

Individual Retirement Plans Guide. CCH, Inc., 2700 Lake Cook Rd. Riverwoods, IL 60015. Phone: 800-835-5224 or (847)267-7000 E-mail: cust_serv@cch.com • URL: http://www.cch.com • $540.00 per year. Looseleaf service. Monthly updates. Covers IRA plans (Individual Retirement Accounts), SEP plans (Simplified Employee Pensions), and Keogh plans (self-employed retirement accounts).

Individual Tax Return Guide. RIA, 395 Hudson St. New York, NY 10014. Phone: 800-950-1216 or 800-431-9025 E-mail: riahome@riag.com • URL: http://www.riahome.com • 2003. $20.00.

Individual Taxation. James W. Pratt and William N. Kulsrud. McGraw-Hill, 1221 Ave. of the Americas New York, NY 10020. Phone: 800-722-4726 or (212)512-2000 Fax: (212)512-4502 E-mail: customer.service@mcgraw-hill.com • URL: http://www.mcgraw-hill.com • 1996. $69.95. Tenth edition. Focuses on the federal income tax.

Individual Taxes 2002-2003: Worldwide Summaries. John Wiley and Sons, Inc., 111 River St. Hoboken, NJ 07030. Phone: 800-225-5945 or (201)748-6000 Fax: (201)748-6088 E-mail: info@wiley.com • URL: http://www.wiley.com • 2002. $105.00. Two volumes. Summarizes the personal tax regulations of more than 125 countries. Provides information useful for international tax planning and foreign investments.

Individuals' Filled-In Tax Return Forms. CCH, Inc., 2700 Lake Cook Rd. Riverwoods, IL 60015. Phone: 800-835-5224 or (847)267-7000 E-mail: cust_serv@cch.com • URL: http://www.cch.com • 2002. $34.00.

Industrial and Engineering Chemistry Research. American Chemical Society, 1155 16th St., NW Washington, DC 20036. Phone: 800-227-5558 or (202)872-4600 Fax: (202)872-4615 E-mail: help@acs.org • URL: http://www.chemistry.org • Monthly. Members, $169.00 per year; institutions, $1,445.00 per year; students, $127.00 per year. Available on line . Fomerly *Industrial and Engineering Chemistry Product Research and Development.*

Industrial and Labor Relations Review. Cornell University, New York State School of Industrial and Labor Relations, 158 Ives Hall Ithaca, NY 14853-3901. Phone: (607)255-3295 Fax: (607)255-8016 • URL: http://www.ilr.cornell.edu • Quarterly. Individuals, $32.00 per year; institutions, $52.00 per year; students, $16.00 per year.

Industrial and Organizational Psychology: Research and Practice. Paul E. Spector. John Wiley and Sons, Inc., 111 River St. Hoboken, NJ 07030. Phone: 800-225-5945 or (201)748-6000 Fax: (201)748-6088 E-mail: info@wiley.com • URL: http://www.wiley.com • 2002. $96.95. Third edition.

Industrial Coatings: Properties, Applications, Quality, and Environmental Compliance: Proceedings of ASM and ESD Conference. ASM International, 9639 Kinsman Rd. Materials Park, OH 44073-0002. Phone: 800-336-5152 or (440)338-5151 Fax: (440)338-4634 E-mail: cust-srv@asminternational.org • URL: http://www.asminternational.org • 1992. $90.00.

Industrial Color Testing: Fundamentals and Techniques. Hans G. Volz. John Wiley and Sons, Inc., 111 River St. Hoboken, NJ 07030. Phone: 800-225-5945 or (201)748-0662 Fax: (201)748-6088 E-mail: info@wiley.com • URL: http://www.wiley.com • 2001. $140.00. Second edition.

Industrial Commodity Statistics Yearbook. United Nations Dept. of Economic and Social Affairs. United Nations Publications, United Nations Concourse Level, First Ave., 46th St. New York, NY 10017. Phone: 800-553-3210 or (212)963-7680 Fax: (212)963-4910 E-mail: bookstore@un.org • URL: http://www.org/publications • Annual.

Industrial Computing. Industrial Computing Society. ISA Services, Inc., 67 Alexander Dr. Research Triangle Park, NC 27709. Phone: (919)549-8411 Fax: (919)549-8288 E-mail: info@isa.org • URL: http://www.isa.org • Monthly. Members $100.00 per year; non-members, $80.00 per year. Published by the Instrument Society of America. Edited for engineering managers and systems integrators. Subject matter includes industrial software, programmable controllers, artificial intelligence systems, and industrial computer networking systems.

Industrial Controls. Available from MarketResearch.com, 641 Ave. of the Americas, 3rd Fl. New York, NY 10011. Phone: 800-298-5699 or (212)807-2629 Fax: (212)807-2716 E-mail: order@marketresearch.com • URL: http://www.marketresearch.com • 2001. $4,100.00. Published by the Freedonia Group. Market data with forecasts to 2005 and 2009. Includes computerized controls and conventional controls.

Industrial Designers Society of America., 45195 Business Court, No. 250 Dulles, VA 20166. Phone: (703)707-6000 Fax: (703)787-8501 E-mail: idsa@idsa.org • URL: http://www.idsa.org • A professional society of industrial designers.

Industrial Diamond Association., PO Box 29460 Columbus, OH 43229. Phone: (614)797-2265 Fax: (614)797-2264 E-mail: tkane-ida@insight.rr.com • URL: http://www.superabrasives.org • Represents industrial diamond, CBN, CVD diamond and polycrystalline and other superabrasive manufacturers, toolmakers, end users, contractors, machine tool builders and related suppliers.

Industrial Diamond Review. De Beers Industrial Diamond Div., Charters, Sunninghill Ascot SL5 9PX, United Kingdom. Phone: 44 1344 623456 Fax: 44 1344 638236 Quarterly. Free to qualified personnel. Incorporating *Industrial Diamond Abstracts*.

Industrial Distribution Association., 1277 Lenox Pk. Blvd., Ste. 275 Atlanta, GA 30319. Phone: 877-591-6210 or (404)266-3991 Fax: 877-664-5398 or 877-664-5398 E-mail: idainc@ida-assoc.com • URL: http://www.ida-assoc.org • Distributors of industrial equipment and supplies. Conducts seminars on sales management training, inventory management, purchasing paperwork, industrial marketing, and sales profitability analysis. Maintains speakers' bureau; compiles statistics.

Industrial Distribution: For Industrial Distributors and Their Sales Personnel. Reed Business Information, 360 Park Ave., S New York, NY 10010. Phone: 800-446-6551 or (646)746-6400 Fax: (646)746-7028 E-mail: corporatecommunications@reedbusiness.com • URL: http://www.reedbusiness.com • Monthly. $109.90 per year.

Industrial Dyes: Chemistry, Properties, Applications. Klaus Hunger, editor. John Wiley and Sons, Inc., 111 River St. Hoboken, NJ 07030. Phone: 800-225-5945 or (201)748-6000 Fax: (201)748-6088 E-mail: info@wiley.com • URL: http://www.wiley.com • 2003. $185.00. Covers textile dyeing, nontextile dyeing, functional dyes, and optical brighteners. Includes health and safety aspects and examples of commercially available dyes.

Industrial Engineering Terminology. Institute of Industrial Engineering Staff. McGraw-Hill, 1221 Ave. of the Americas New York, NY 10020. Phone: 800-722-4726 or (212)512-2000 Fax: (212)512-4502 E-mail: customer.service@mcgraw-hill.com • URL: http://www.mcgraw-hill.com • 1992. $80.95. Revised edition.

Industrial Equipment News. Thomas Publishing Co., LLC, Five Penn Plaza New York, NY 10001. Phone: 800-699-9822 or (212)695-0500 Fax: (212)290-7632 E-mail: info@thomasimg.com • URL: http://www.thomaspublishing.com •

Monthly. $65.00 per year. What's new in equipment, parts and materials.

Industrial Fabric Products Review. Industrial Fabrics Association International, 1801 W. Country Rd., B Roseville, MN 55113-4061. Phone: 800-225-4324 or (651)222-2508 Fax: (651)631-9334 E-mail: generalinfo@ifai.com • URL: http://www.ifai.com • Monthly. $47.00 per year. Includes *Buyers Guide*.

Industrial Fabric Products Review Buyer's Guide: The Encyclopedia of Industrial Fabrics. Industrial Fabrics Association International, 1801 W. Country Rd., B W. Roseville, MN 55113-4061. Phone: 800-225-4324 or (651)222-2508 Fax: (651)225-9334 E-mail: generalinfo@ifai.com • URL: http://www.ifai.com • Annual. $40.00. Includes manufacturers of fabrics, fibers, and end products. Included with subscriptions to *Industrial Fabric Products Review*.

Industrial Fabrics Association International., 1801 County Rd. B W Roseville, MN 55113-4061. Phone: 800-225-4324 or (651)222-2508 Fax: (651)631-9334 E-mail: generalinfo@ifai.com • URL: http://www.ifai.com • Fiber producers, weavers, non-woven producers, coaters, laminators, finishers, and producers and manufacturers of canvas and specialty fabric end products in more than 36 countries. Provides technical, marketing, production, governmental and public relations services.

Industrial Fabrics Association International Membership Directory. Industrial Fabrics Association International, 1801 W. Country Rd., B W. Roseville, MN 55113-4061. Phone: 800-225-4324 or (651)222-2508 Fax: (651)225-9334 E-mail: generalinfo@ifai.com • URL: http://www.ifai.com • Annual. Free to members; non-members, $40.00.

Industrial Fasteners Institute., 6363 Oak Tree Blvd., 1717 E. Ninth St., Suite 1105 Independence, OH 44131. Phone: (216)241-1482 Fax: (216)241-5901 E-mail: rharris@indfast.org • URL: http://www.industrial-fasteners.org • Manufacturers of industrial fasteners and formed parts; associate members are suppliers of primary and secondary equipment, raw materials, and services used in the manufacture of fasteners and formed parts. Seeks to advance fastener and formed parts application engineering. Establishes standards and technical practices.

Industrial Heating Equipment Association., PO Box 54172 Cincinnati, OH 45254. Phone: (513)231-5613 Fax: (513)624-0601 E-mail: ihea@ihea.org • URL: http://www.ihea.org • Manufacturers of industrial furnaces, ovens, combustion equipment, atmosphere generators, induction and dielectric heating equipment, industrial heaters, process controls, fuel saving and heating devices, and heat recovery equipment.

Industrial Hydraulics. William V. Vockroth. Delmar Learning, 5 Maxwell Dr. Clifton Park, NY 12065-8007. Phone: 800-347-7707 Fax: 800-487-4888 E-mail: info@delmar.com • URL: http://www.delmarlearning.com • 1994. $37.00.

Industrial Hygiene News. Rimbach Publishing, Inc., 8650 Babcock Blvd. Pittsburgh, PA 15237-5821. Phone: 800-245-3182 or (412)364-5366 Fax: (412)369-9720 E-mail: info@rimbach.com • URL: http://www.rimbach.com • Seven times a year. Free to qualified personnel.

Industrial Hygiene News Buyer's Guide. Rimbach Publishing, Inc., 8650 Babcock Blvd. Pittsburgh, PA 15237-5821. Phone: 800-245-3182 or (412)364-5366 Fax: (412)369-9720 E-mail: info@rimbach.com • URL: http://www.rimbach.com • Annual. $50.00. Lists about 1,000 manufacturers and suppliers of products, equipment, and services to the occupational health, industrial hygiene, and high-tech safety industry.

Industrial Laser Buyers Guide. PennWell Corp., Advanced Technology Div., 98 Spit Brook Rd. Nashua, NH 03062-5737. Phone: 800-331-4463 or (603)891-0123 E-mail: atd@penwell.com • URL: http://www.pennwell.com • Annual. $104.00. Lists industrial laser suppliers by category and geographic location. (Included with subscription to *Industrial Laser Solutions*.)

Industrial Laser Solutions for Manufacturing. PennWell Corp., Advanced Technology Div., 98 Spit Brook Rd. Nashua, NH 03062-5737. Phone: 800-331-4463 or (603)891-0123 E-mail: atd@pennwell.com • URL: http://www.pennwell.com • Monthly. $300.00 per year. Covers industrial laser technology, especially machine tool applications.

Industrial Launderer. Institute of Industrial Launderers, 1300 N. 17th St., Suite 750 Arlington, VA 22209. Phone: (703)247-2600 Fax: (703)841-4750 Monthly. $100.00 per year.

Industrial Location: Principles and Policies. J.W. Harrington and Barney Warf. Routledge, 29 W. 35th St. New York, NY 10001. Phone: 800-634-7064 or (212)216-7800 Fax: 800-248-4724 E-mail: cservice@routledge-ny.com • URL: http://www.routledge-ny.com • 1995. $100.00. Second revised edition.

Industrial Maintenance and Plant Operation. Reed Business Information, 360 Park Ave., S New York, NY 10010. Phone: 800-446-6551 or (646)746-6400 Fax: (646)746-7028 E-mail: corporatecommunications@reedbusiness.com • URL: http://www.reedbusiness.com • Monthly. $95.99 per year.

Industrial Marketing Management: The International Journal of Marketing for Industrial and High-Tech Firms. Elsevier, 360 Park Ave. S New York, NY 10010-1710. Phone: 888-437-4636 or (212)989-5800 Fax: (212)633-3990 E-mail: usinfof@elsevier.com • URL: http://www.elsevier.com • Eight times a year. Qualified personnel, $127.00 per year; institutions, $816.00 per year.

Industrial Marketing Strategy. Frederick E. Webster. John Wiley

and Sons, Inc., 111 River St. Hoboken, NJ 07030. Phone: 800-225-5945 or (201)748-6000 Fax: (201)748-6088 E-mail: info@wiley.com • URL: http://www.wiley.com • 1995. $44.95. Third edition. (Marketing Management Series).

Industrial Mathematics Society., PO Box 159 Roseville, MI 48066. E-mail: ihea@ihea.org Mathematicians, scientists, engineers, and economists. To extend the understanding and application of mathematics in industry. Supports study group on mathematics of gear design. Areas of interest include applied mathematics, engineering mechanics, computers, statistics, automatic control, operations analysis, and biomechanics.

Industrial Paint and Powder Buyer's Guide. Business News Publishing, 1050 IL Route 83, Ste. 200 Bensenville, IL 60106. Phone: (248)244-6474 Annual. Free to qualified personnel; others, $15.00. List of about 2,000 manufacturers of finishing and formulating products. Formerly *Industrial Finishing Buyer's Guide*.

Industrial Paint and Powder: Coatings Manufacturing and Application. Reed Business Information, 360 Park Ave., S New York, NY 10010. Phone: 800-446-6551 or (646)746-6400 Fax: (646)746-7028 E-mail: corporatecommunications@reedbusiness.com • URL: http://www.reedbusiness.com • Monthly. $72.90 per year. Supplement available, *Annual Buyer's Guide*. Formerly *Industrial Finishing*.

Industrial Pollution Prevention Handbook. Harry M. Freeman. McGraw-Hill, 1221 Ave. of the Americas New York, NY 10020. Phone: 800-722-4726 or (212)512-2000 Fax: (212)512-4502 E-mail: customer.service@mcgraw-hill.com • URL: http://www.mcgraw-hill.com • 1994. $115.00.

Industrial Polymers Handbook: Products, Processes, Applications. Edward S. Wilks, editor. John Wiley and Sons, Inc., 111 River St. Hoboken, NJ 07030. Phone: 800-225-5945 or (201)748-6000 Fax: (201)748-6088 E-mail: info@wiley.com • URL: http://www.wiley.com • 2001. $1,400.00. Four volumes. Covers both naturally occurring and synthetic polymers that have industrial uses.

Industrial Pumps and Pumping Equipment. Available from MarketResearch.com, 641 Ave. of the Americas, Third Floor New York, NY 10011. Phone: 800-298-5699 or (212)807-2629 Fax: (212)807-2716 E-mail: order@marketresearch.com • URL: http://www.marketresearch.com • 1997. $1,195.00. Market research report published by Specialists in Business Information: Covers centrifugal, rotary, turbine, reciprocating, and other types of pumps. Presents market data relative to sales growth, shipments, exports, imports, and end-use. Includes company profiles.

Industrial Purchasing Agent. Publications for Industry, 21 Russell Woods Rd. Great Neck, NY 11021. Phone: (516)487-0990 Fax: (516)487-0809 E-mail: info@publicationsforindustry.com • URL: http://www.publicationsforindustry.com • Description: Covers new product releases pertaining to the industrial manufacturing industry. Recurring features include by-line spreads, news of research, and new literature releases.

Industrial Relations: A Journal of Economy and Society. University of California at Berkeley. Blackwell Publishing, 350 Main St. Malden, MA 02148. Phone: 800-835-6770 or (781)388-8200 Fax: (781)388-8232 E-mail: subscrip@blackwellpub.com • URL: http://www.blackwellpub.com • Bimonthly. Institutions, $862.00 per year. Includes online edition.

Industrial Relations Research Association.

Industrial Relations Research Institute.

Industrial Relations Section., Princeton University, Firestone Library Pinceton, NJ 08544. Phone: (609)258-4040 Fax: (609)258-2907 • URL: http://www.irs.princeton.edu/ • Fields of research include labor supply, manpower training, unemployment, and equal employment opportunity.

Industrial Relations Section. Massachusetts Institute of Technology

Industrial Research Institute., 2200 Clarendon Blvd., Ste. 1102 Arlington, VA 22201. Phone: (703)647-2580 Fax: (703)647-2581 E-mail: bernstein@iriinc.org • URL: http://www.iriinc.org • Manufacturers and industrial firms maintaining industrial research laboratories. Identifies and promotes effective techniques for the organization and management of research, development, and engineering in support of technological innovation.

Industrial Research Institute for Pacific Nations., California State Polytechnic University, Pomona, School of Business Administration, 3801 W. Temple Ave., Bldg. 66, Room 217 Pomona, CA 91768. Phone: (909)869-2399 Fax: (909)869-6799 E-mail: hkj@csupomona.edu • URL: http://www.hkjinacsu.edu • Conducts research on the Pacific nations marketplace.

Industrial Revolution Reference Library. Gale Cengage Learning, 27500 Drake Rd. Farmington Hills, MI 48331-3535. Phone: 800-877-GALE Fax: 800-414-5043 E-mail: gale.galeord@cengage.com • URL: http://gale.cengage.com • 2003. $165.00. Three volumes. Individual volumes are available at $55.00. Includes *Industrial Revolution: Almanac; Industrial Revolution: Biographies* and *Industrial Revolution: Primary Sources*. (UXL imprint).

Industrial Safety and Health Management. C. Ray Asfahl. Prentice Hall PTR, 240 Frisch Ct. Paramus, NJ 07652. Phone: 800-282-0693 Fax: 800-445-6991 • URL: http://www.phptr.com • 2003. $92.33. Fifth edition. (Prentice Hall International

Industrial and Systems Series).

Industrial Safety and Hygiene News: News of Safety, Health and Hygiene, Environmental, Fire, Security and Emergency Protection Equipment. Business News Publishing Co., 755 W. Big Beaver Rd., Suite 1000 Troy, MI 48084. Phone: 800-837-7370 or (248)362-3700 Fax: (248)362-0317 • URL: http://www.bnp.com • Monthly. Free to qualified personnel; others, $120.00 per year.

Industrial Supply Manufacturers Association., 1300 Sumner Ave. Cleveland, OH 44115-2851. Phone: (216)241-7333 Fax: (216)241-0105 E-mail: isma@ismaonline.org • URL: http://www.ismaonline.org • Formerly Industrial Supply and Machinery Manufacturers Association.

Industrial Truck Association., 1750 K St. NW, Ste. 460 Washington, DC 20006. Phone: (202)296-9880 Fax: (202)296-9884 E-mail: bernstein@iriinc.org • URL: http://www.indtrk.org • Manufacturers of powered industrial lift trucks; electric storage batteries, tires, engines, attachments, and hydraulic systems for powered industrial lift trucks.

Industries in Transition; A Newsletter Written for Growth Directed Management and Business Planners. Business Communications Co., Inc., 25 Van Zant St. Norwalk, CT 06855-1781. Phone: (203)853-4266 Fax: (203)853-0348 E-mail: info@bccresearch.com • URL: http://www.buscom.com • Monthly. $375.00 per year. Newsletter. Formerly *Growth Industry News*.

Industry and Product Classification Manual (SIC Basis). Available from National Technical Information Service, U. S. Department of Commerce, Technology Administration, 5285 Port Royal Rd. Springfield, VA 22161. Phone: 800-553-6847 or (703)487-4600 Fax: (703)321-8547 E-mail: info@ntis.fedworld.gov • URL: http://www.ntis.gov • 1992. Issued by U. S. Bureau of the Census. Contains extended Standard Industrial Classification (SIC) numbers used by the Census Bureau to allow a more detailed classification of industry, services, and agriculture.

Industry Coalition on Technolgy Transfer., 1400 L St., N.W. Washington, DC 20005-3502. Phone: (202)371-5994 Fax: (202)371-5950 Members are computer industry associations concerned with federal regulations on technology transfer in the computer industry.

Industry Directory. CMP Media LLC, 600 Harrison St., 6th Fl. San Francisco, CA 94107. Phone: 800-486-6508 or (415)947-6000 Fax: (415)947-6055 E-mail: cmp@cmp.com Covers: Approximately 1,800 manufacturers and distributors of bicycle products and related organizations and events; international coverage. Entries include: Company or organization name, address, phone, fax, E-mail, URL, toll-free number, name of contact, distributors list, lines distributed, and representatives.

Industry Insider. Thomson Financial, PO Box 95512 Chicago, IL 60694. Phone: 800-607-4463 or (312)288-6400 • URL: http://www.tfn.com • Contains full-text online industry research reports from more than 200 leading trade associations, covering 50 specific industries. Reports include extensive statistics and market research data. Inquire as to on-line cost and availability.

Industry Norms and Key Business Ratios. Desk Top Edition. Dun and Bradstreet Corp., 103 JFK Pky. Short Hills, NJ 07078. Phone: 800-526-0651 or (973)921-5000 E-mail: custserv@dnb.com • URL: http://www.dnb.com • Annual. Five volumes. $475.00 per volume. $1,890.00 per set. Covers over 800 kinds of businesses, arranged by Standard Industrial Classification number. More detailed editions covering longer periods of time are also available.

Industry Profile and Healthcare Factbook. Healthcare Distribution Management Association, 1821 Michael Faraday Dr., Ste. 400 Reston, VA 20190-5348. Phone: (703)787-0000 Fax: (703)787-6930 E-mail: webmaster@hdmanet.org • URL: http://www.healthcaredistribution.org • Annual. $349.00. Provides 266 statistical tables in three sections: "Industry Profile" (financial ratios related to drug distribution), "Pharmaceutical and Healthcare Distribution Trends and Facts," and "Healthcare Factbook" (expenditures, insurance utilization, company/product rankings, drug price inflation, generics, OTC, drug store data, hospital statistics, healthcare consumer summaries, etc.). Also known as *HDMA Factbook*. The Healthcare Distribution Management Association was formerly the National Wholesale Druggists' Association.

Industry's Future: Changing Patterns of Industrial Research. Herbert I. Fusfeld. American Chemical Society, 1155 16th St., N. W. Washington, DC 20036. Phone: 800-227-5558 or (202)872-4600 Fax: (202)872-4615 E-mail: help@acs.org • URL: http://www.chemistry.org • 1994. $45.00.

Industry's Guide to ISO 9000. Adedeji B. Badiru. John Wiley and Sons, Inc., 111 River St. Hoboken, NJ 07030. Phone: 800-225-5945 or (201)748-6000 Fax: (201)748-6088 E-mail: info@wiley.com • URL: http://www.wiley.com • 1995. $120.00. (Engineering and Technology Management Series).

IndustryWeek: The Management Resource. Penton Media, Inc., 1300 E. Ninth St. Cleveland, OH 44114. Phone: (216)696-7000 Fax: (216)696-1752 E-mail: information@penton.com • URL: http://www.penton.com • 22 times a year. Free to qualified personnel; others, $65.00 per year. Edited for industrial and business managers. Covers organizational and technological developments affecting industrial management.

Infant and Juvenile Manufacturers Association.

Inflation, Exchange Rates, and the World Economy: Lectures on International Monetary Economics. Warner M. Corden. The

University of Chicago Press, 1427 E. 60th St. Chicago, IL 60637. Phone: 800-621-2736 or (773)702-7700 Fax: 800-621-8476 or (773)702-7212 E-mail: custserv@press.uchicago.edu • URL: http://www.press.uchicago.edu • 1986. $22.50. Third edition. (Studies in Business and Society Series).

Influence: Clients' Guide to the Business of Lobbying. American Lawyer Media, Inc., 105 Madison Ave. New York, NY 10016. Phone: 800-888-8300 or (212)779-9200 Fax: (212)481-8110 E-mail: lawcatalog@amlaw.com • URL: http://www.lawcatalog.com/ • Monthly. $349.00 per year. Newsletter. Provides influence-related news about "lobby shops," companies, associations, and the government. Covers grass-roots campaigns, public relations strategies, new client signings, and fresh registrations. Edited for government relations personnel, public affairs professionals, and lawyers. (Legal Times).

The Influence of Disney Entertainment Parks on Architecture and Development. Stephen J. Rebori. Sage Publications, Inc., 2455 Teller Rd. Thousand Oaks, CA 91320. Phone: 800-818-7243 or (805)499-9774 Fax: 800-583-2665 or (805)499-0871 E-mail: webmaster@sagepub.com • URL: http://www.sagepub.com • 1995. $10.00. (CPL Bibliographies Series: Vol. 321).

Info Franchise Newsletter. Info Press Inc., 728 Center St., PO Box 826 Lewiston, NY 14092. Phone: 888-806-2665 or (716)754-4669 Fax: (905)688-7728 E-mail: infopress@infonews.com • URL: http://www.infonews.com • Description: Covers business format franchising in the U.S., Canada, and overseas; reports on trends, legislation and litigation, and on developments in the franchising business scene. Recurring features include lists of new franchisors, including descriptions, contact addresses and telephone numbers for each; and address changes of franchisor headquarters. Spotlights upcoming seminars, conferences and business opportunity shows.

InfoAlert: Your Expert Guide to Online Business Information. Economics Press, Inc., 12 Daniel Rd. Fairfield, NJ 07004. Phone: 800-526-2554 or (973)227-1224 Fax: (973)227-9742 E-mail: info@epinc.com • URL: http://www.epinc.com • Monthly. $129.00 per year. Newsletter. Provides information on recommended World Wide Web sites in various business, marketing, industrial, and financial areas.

InfoComm International., 11242 Waples Mill Rd., Ste. 200 Fairfax, VA 22030-6079. Phone: 800-659-7469 or (703)273-7200 Fax: (703)278-8082 E-mail: customerservice@infocomm.org • URL: http://www.infocomm.org • Represents for-profit individuals and organizations that derive revenue from the commercialization or utilization of communications technology. Ensures the credibility and desirability of its members' products and services by representing the communications industry to the public, business, education, and governments.

The Infomation Management Journal: The Journal for the Information Management Professionals. A R M A International, 13725 W 109th St., Ste. 101 Lenexa, KS 66215. Phone: 800-442-2762 or (913)341-3808 Fax: (913)341-3742 • URL: http://www.arma.org • Quarterly. Free to members; non-members, $95.00 per year; institutions and libraries, $53.00 per year. Formerly *Records management Quarterly*.

Infopreneurs: Turning Data into Dollars. H. Skip Weitzen. John Wiley and Sons, Inc., 111 River St. Hoboken, NJ 07030. Phone: 800-225-5945 or (201)748-6000 Fax: (201)748-6088 E-mail: info@wiley.com • URL: http://www.wiley.com • 1988. $19.95. Infopreneurs are entrepreneurs who market information. A how-to-do-it manual.

InForm. Victor O. Schinnerer & Company Inc., 2 Wisconsin Cir. Chevy Chase, MD 20815. Phone: 800-477-2446 or (301)961-9800 Fax: (301)451-5444 E-mail: vos.info@schinnerer.com • URL: http://www.aiim.org • Description: Reports national and state developments affecting architects and engineers.

Inform: International News on Fats, Oils, and Related Materials. American Oil Chemists Society. AOCS Press, 2211 W Bradley Ave. Champaign, IL 61821-1827. Phone: (217)359-2344 Fax: (217)351-8091 E-mail: general@aocs.org • URL: http://www.aocs.org • Monthly. Individuals, $120.00 per year; institutions, $360.00 per year. Covers a wide range of technical and business topics relating to the processing and utilization of edible oils, essential oils, and oilseeds.

The Information Advisor: Tips and Techniques for Smart Information Users. MarketResearch.com, 641 Ave. of the Americas, 3rd Fl. New York, NY 10011. Phone: 800-298-5699 or (212)807-2629 Fax: (212)807-2716 E-mail: customerservice@marketresearch.com • URL: http://www.marketresearch.com • Monthly. $159.00 per year. Newsletter. Evaluates and discusses online, CD-ROM, and published sources of business, financial, and market research information.

Information and Image Management: The State of the Industry. AIIM-The Enterprise Content Management Association, 1100 Wayne Ave., Suite 1100 Silver Spring, MD 20910-5603. Phone: 800-477-2446 or (301)587-8202 Fax: (301)587-2711 E-mail: aiim@aiim.org • URL: http://www.aiim.org • Annual. $130.00. Market data with five-year forecasts. Covers electronic imaging, micrographics supplies and equipment, software, and records management services.

Information and Management; International Journal of Information Systems Applications. Elsevier, 360 Park Ave.,

S New York, NY 10010-1710. Phone: 888-437-4636 or (212)989-5800 Fax: (212)633-3990 E-mail: usinfo-f@elsevier.com • URL: http://www.elsevier.com • Eight times a year. Institutions, $646.00 per year.

Information Bank Abstracts. New York Times Index Dept., 1133 Ave. of the Americas New York, NY 10036. Phone: (212)556-1234 Fax: (212)221-5052 • URL: http://www.nytimes.com • Provides indexing and abstracting of current affairs, primarily from the final late edition of *The New York Times* and the Eastern edition of *The Wall Street Journal*. Time period is 1969 to present, with daily updates. Inquire as to online cost and availability.

Information Broker. Helen P. Burwell, editor. Burwell Enterprises Inc., 5619 Plumtree Dr. Dallas, TX 75252. Phone: (972)732-0160 Fax: (972)733-1951 E-mail: burwellinfo@burwellinc.com • URL: http://www.burwellinc.com • Description: Covers companies that offer fee-based information services and issues related to "the business" of information brokering.

Information Broker. Entrepreneur Media, Inc., 2445 McCabe Way Irvine, CA 92614. Phone: 800-421-2300 or (949)261-2325 Fax: (949)261-0234 E-mail: entmag@entrepreneur.com • URL: http://www.entrepreneur.com • Looseleaf. $59.50. A practical guide to starting an information retrieval business. Covers profit potential, start-up costs, market size evaluation, pricing, accounting, advertising, promotion, etc. (Start-Up Business Guide No. E1237.)

Information Brokering: How to Make Money Selling Information Services. Florence M. Mason and Chris Dobson. Neal-Schuman Publishers, Inc., 100 William St., Ste. 2004 New York, NY 10038. Phone: (866)672-6657 or (212)925-8650 Fax: (866)209-7932 or (212)219-8916 E-mail: info@neal-schuman.com • URL: http://www.neal-schuman.com • 1998. $45.00. A practical guide to business plans, location, costs, fees, billing, marketing, accounting, taxes, and legal issues. Covers information brokering as a small business enterprise. (How-To-Do-It Manuals Series).

The Information Catalog. MarketResearch.com, 625 Ave. of the Americas New York, NY 10011-2020. Phone: (212)645-2000 Fax: (212)645-7681 • URL: http://www.findsvp.com • Bimonthly. Free. Mainly a catalog of market research reports from various publishers, but also includes business and marketing reference sources. Includes keyword title index. Formerly *The Information Catalog: Marketing Intelligence Studies, Competitor Reports, Business and Marketing Sources*.

Information Executive: A Monthly Publication for DPMA and the Information Systems Profession. AITP-Association of Information Technology Professional, 315 S. Northwest Highway, Suite 200 Park Ridge, IL 60068-4278. Phone: 800-224-9371 Fax: (847)825-1693 • URL: http://www.aitp.org • Monthly. $45.00 per year. Articles reporting developmental and technical aspects of EDP services, supplies, equipment, accessories and related contemporary trends and issues. Formerly *Inside DPMA*.

Information, Finance, and Services USA. Gale Cengage Learning, 27500 Drake Rd. Farmington Hills, MI 48331-3535. Phone: 800-877-GALE or (248)699-4253 Fax: 800-414-5043 E-mail: gale.galeord@cengage.com • URL: http://gale.cengage.com • 2001. $240.00. Replaces *Service Industries USA* and *Finance, Insurance, and Real Estate USA*. Presents statistics and projections relating to economic activity in a wide variety of non-manufacturing areas.

Information for Sale: How to Start and Operate Your Own Data Research Service. John H. Everett and Elizabeth P. Crowe. McGraw-Hill, 1221 Ave. of the Americas New York, NY 10020. Phone: 800-722-4726 or (212)512-2000 Fax: (212)512-4502 E-mail: customer.service@mcgraw-hill.com • URL: http://www.mcgraw-hill.com • 1988. $15.95. Second edition. A revision of *The Information Broker's Handbook*.

The Information Freeway Report: Free Business and Government Information Via Modem. Washington Researchers, Ltd., 1655 N Fort Myer Dr., Ste. 800 Arlington, VA 22209. Phone: (703)312-2863 Fax: (703)527-4586 E-mail: research@researchers.com • URL: http://www.washingtonresearchers.com • Monthly. $160.00 per year. Newsletter. Provides news of business and government databases that are available free of charge through the Internet or directly. Emphasis is on federal government databases and electronic bulletin boards (Fedworld).

Information Graphics: A Comprehensive Illustrated Reference: Visual Tools for Analyzing, Managing, and Communicating. Robert L. Harris. Oxford University Press, 198 Madison Ave. New York, NY 10016-4314. Phone: 800-451-7556 or (212)726-6000 Fax: (212)726-6440 E-mail: custserv@oup-usa.org • URL: http://www.oup-usa.org • 2000. $50.00. Provides more than 850 alphabetical entries and about 4,000 illustrations. Covers the practical application of charts, graphs, maps, diagrams, and tables.

Information Hotline. Science Associates/International Inc., 6 Hastings Rd. Marlboro, NJ 07746-1313. Phone: 800-721-1080 or (908)536-7673 Fax: (908)536-7673 E-mail: burwellinfo@burwellinc.com Description: "The oldest, most respected, continuously published newsletter." Devoted to objective coverage of trends, policy, analysis, and opinion in the information field.

Information Imagineering: Meeting at the Interface. Milton T. Wolf and others, editors. American Library Association, 50 E. Huron St. Chicago, IL 60611-2795. Phone: 800-545-2433 or (312)944-6780 Fax: (312)440-9374 E-mail: ala@ala.org •

URL: http://www.ala.org • 1997. $36.00. A collection of articles on the effect of information technology on libraries, museums, and other institutions.

Information Industry Directory. Gale, 27500 Drake Rd. Farmington Hills, MI 48331-3535. Phone: 800-877-4253 or (248)699-4253 Fax: 800-414-5043 or (248)699-8065 E-mail: galeord@cengage.com • URL: http://gale.cengage.com • Covers: Approximately 11,000 organizations, systems, and services involved in the production and distribution of information in electronic form: database producers and their products online host services, transactional services, library and information networks, bibliographic utilities, library management systems, information retrieval software, mailing list services, fee-based information on demand services, document delivery sources, data collection and analysis centers and firms, and related consultants, service companies, professional and trade associations, publishers, and research activities. Entries include: Name of parent organization, name of system of service, address, phone, toll-free phone, fax, telex, email address, year founded name of unit head, size of staff, names of any affiliated organizations, financial information. Internet access information, general description of electronic product, system, or service, subjects covered or areas of service offered, sources of data for the system, type and quantity of stored information in all forms, publications and microform products and services, computer-based products and services, other services, clientele served, availability and restrictions, name of contact.

Information Management for the Intelligent Organization: The Art of Scanning the Environment. Chun Wei Choo. Information Today, Inc., 143 Old Marlton Pike Medford, NJ 08055-8750. Phone: 800-300-9868 or (609)654-6266 Fax: (609)654-4309 E-mail: custserv@infotoday.com • URL: http://www.infotoday.com • 2001. $39.50. Third edition. Published on behalf of the American Society for Information Science (ASIS). Covers the general principles of acquiring, creating, organizing, and using information within organizations.

Information Management Report: An International Newsletter for Information Professionals and Librarians. R. R. Bowker, 630 Central Ave. New Providence, NJ 07974. Phone: 888-269-5372 Fax: (908)219-0098 E-mail: info@bowker.com • URL: http://www.bowker.com • Monthly. $505.00 per year; includes print and online editions. Incorporates *Outlook on Research Libraries*.

Information Outlook: The Monthly Magazine of the Special Libraries Association. Special Libraries Association, 1700 18th St., N. W. Washington, DC 20009-2514. Phone: (202)234-4700 Fax: (202)265-9317 E-mail: sla@sla.org • URL: http://www.sla.org • Monthly. $65.00 per year. Topics include information technology, the Internet, copyright, research techniques, library management, and professional development. Replaces *Special Libraries* and *SpeciaList*.

Information Please Business Almanac and Desk Reference. Information Please LLC, 20 Park Plaza, Ste. 1220 Boston, MA 02116. Phone: (617)832-0300 Fax: (617)956-2696 E-mail: info@infoplease.com • URL: http://www.infoplease.com • Annual. $21.95.

Information Processing and Management: An International Journal. Elsevier Science, 360 Park Ave., S New York, NY 10010-1710. Phone: 888-437-4636 or (212)988-5800 Fax: (212)633-3990 E-mail: usinfo-f@elsevier.com • URL: http://www.elsevier.com • Bimonthly. Qualified personnel, $301.00 per year; institutions, $1,196.00 per year. Text in English, French, German and Italian.

The Information Professional's Guide to Career Development Online. Sarah L. Nesbeitt and Rachel S. Gordon. Information Today, Inc., 143 Old Marlton Pike Medford, NJ 08055-8750. Phone: 800-300-9868 or (609)654-6266 Fax: (609)654-4309 E-mail: custserv@infotoday.com • URL: http://www.infotoday.com • 2001. $29.50. Provides advice to librarians and other information professionals about using online sources for career advancement. The Career Development Online Web Page (http://www.lisjobs.com/careerdev/) contains links to relevant resources.

The Information Report. Washington Researchers, 1655 N Fort Myer Dr., Ste. 800 Arlington, VA 22209. Phone: (703)312-2863 Fax: (703)527-4586 E-mail: research@researchers.com • URL: http://www.washingtonresearchers.com • Description: Contains 40-140 items in each issue identifying little-known sources of information. Lists and describes directories, special libraries, booklets, seminars, studies, and other research sources available on markets, competition, federal regulation, and economic conditions. Covers government as well as corporate sources, trade, and professional organizations.

Information Retrieval and Library Automation. Lomond Publications, Inc., P.O. Box 88 Mount Airy, MD 21771. Phone: (301)694-0123 Fax: (301)694-5151 E-mail: lomondpubs@prodigy.net • URL: http://www.lomondpubs.com • Monthly. $75.00 per year. Summarizes research events and literature worldwide.

Information Science Abstracts. American Society for Information Science. Information Today, Inc., 143 Marlton Pike Medford, NJ 08055-8750. Phone: 800-300-9868 or (609)654-6266 Fax: (609)654-4309 E-mail: custservl@infotoday.com • URL: http://www.infotoday.com • Nine times a year. $789.00 per year.

Information Science Abstracts [online]. Information Today, Inc., 143 Old Marlton Pike Medford, NJ 08055-8750. Phone: 800-

300-9868 or (609)654-6266 Fax: (609)654-4309 E-mail: custserv@infotoday.com • URL: http://www.infotoday.com • Provides indexing and abstracting of the international literature of information science, including library science, from 1966 to date. Monthly updates. Inquire as to online cost and availability.

Information Sciences Institute., University of Southern California, 4676 Admiralty Way, Suite 1001 Marina del Rey, CA 90292-6695. Phone: (310)822-1511 Fax: (310)823-6714 E-mail: schorr@isis.edu • URL: http://www.isi.edu • Research fields include online information and computer science, with emphasis on the World Wide Web.

Information Sciences; An International Journal. Elsevier Science, 360 Park Ave. S New York, NY 10010-1710. Phone: 888-467-4636 or (212)989-5800 Fax: (212)633-3990 E-mail: usinfo-f@elsevier.com • URL: http://www.elsevier.com • 36 times a year. Individuals, $106.00 per year; institutions, $3,557.00 per year. Three sections, A: Informatics and Computer Science, B: Intelligent Systems, C: Applications.

Information Security Fundamentals. Thomas R. Peltier and others. CRC Press, 2000 N.W. Corporate Blvd. Boca Raton, FL 33431. Phone: 800-272-7737 or (561)994-0555 Fax: 800-374-3401 or (561)989-9732 E-mail: orders@crcpress.com • URL: http://www.crcpress.com • 2004. $59.95. Provides basic information on computer security, employee responsibilities, and "common threats." (Imprint: Auerbach Publications.)

Information Services and Use: An International Journal. IOS Press, Inc., 5795-G Burke Centre Parkway Burke, VA 22015-0558. Phone: (703)323-5554 Fax: (703)323-3368 E-mail: iosbooks@iospress.com • URL: http://www.iospress.nl • Quarterly. Institutions, $296.00 per year.

The Information Society: An International Journal. Taylor & Francis Group, 325 Chestnut St., Ste. 800 Philadelphia, PA 19106. Phone: 800-821-8312 or (215)625-8900 Fax: (215)625-2940 E-mail: info@taylorandfrancis.com • URL: http://www.taylorandfrancis.com • Five times a year. Individuals, $105.00 per year; institutions, $285.00 per year.

Information Sources in Chemistry. Peter Rhodes and Fy Hon Rowland. K.G. Saur Publishing, Ortlerstrasse 8 D-81373 Munchen, Germany. Phone: 49 0 89 76902 0 Fax: 49 0 89 76902 150 E-mail: info@saur.de • URL: http://www.saur.de • 2003. Price on application. Evaluates information sources on a wide range of chemical topics. (Guides to Information Sources Series).

Information Sources: The Annual Directory of the Information Industry Association. Software and Information Industry Association, 1090 Vermont Ave., NW, 6th Fl. Washington, DC 20005. Phone: (202)289-7442 Fax: (202)289-7097 • URL: http://www.siia.net • Annual. Members, $75.00; non-members, $125.00.

Information Standards Quarterly: News About Library, Information Sciences, and Publishing Standards. National Information Standards Organization (NISO), 4733 Bethesda Ave., Suite 300 Bethesda, MD 20814-5248. Phone: (301)654-2512 Fax: (301)654-1721 E-mail: nisohq@niso.org • URL: http://www.niso.org • Quarterly. $80.00 per year. Newsletter. Reports on activities of the National Information Standards Organization.

Information Strategy: The Executive's Journal. Auerbach Publications, 345 Park Ave., S New York, NY 10017-1707. Phone: (212)286-1010 Fax: (212)297-9176 E-mail: orders@crcpress.com • URL: http://www.auerbach-publications.com • Quarterly. $195.00 per year.

Information Systems Audit and Control Association and Foundation., 3701 Algonquin Rd., Suite 1010 Rolling Meadows, IL 60008. Phone: (847)253-1545 Fax: (847)253-1443 E-mail: membership@isaca.org • URL: http://www.isaca.org • Formerly EDP Auditors Association.

Information Systems Concept Management. Henry C. Lucas. McGraw-Hill, 1221 Ave. of the Americas New York, NY 10020. Phone: 800-722-4726 or (212)512-2000 Fax: (212)512-4502 E-mail: customer.service@mcgraw-hill.com • URL: http://www.mcgraw-hill.com • 1994. $25.00. Fifth edition.

Information Systems; Data Bases: Their Creation, Management and Utilization. Elsevier, 360 Park Ave., S New York, NY 10010-1710. Phone: 888-437-4636 or (212)988-5800 Fax: (212)633-3990 E-mail: usinfo-f@elsevier.com • URL: http://www.elsevier.com • Eight times a year. Institutions, $1,554.00 per year.

Information Systems Laboratory., Stanford University, Packard 267 Stanford, CA 94305-9510. Phone: (650)723-4731 Fax: (650)723-8473 E-mail: denise@ee.stanford.edu • URL: http://www.isl.stanford.edu • Research fields include speech coding and recognition.

Information Systems Management. Auerbach Publications, 345 Park Ave., S New York, NY 10010-1707. Phone: (212)286-1010 Fax: (212)297-9716 E-mail: orders@crcpress.com • URL: http://www.auerbach-publications.com • Quarterly. $175.00 per year. Formerly *Journal of Information Systems Management.*

Information Systems Security. Auerbach Publications, 345 Park Ave., S New York, NY 10017. Phone: (212)286-1010 Fax: (212)297-9176 E-mail: orders@crcpress.com • URL: http://www.auerbach-publications.com • Bimonthly. $175.00 per year. Formerly *Journal of Information Systems Security.*

Information Systems Spending: An Analysis of Trends and Strategies. Computer Economics, Inc., 5841 Edison Place Carlsbad, CA 92008. Phone: 800-326-8100 or (760)438-8100 Fax: (760)431-1126 E-mail: access@compecon.com • URL: http://www.computereconomics.com • Annual. $1,595.00. Three volumes. Based on "in-depth surveys of public and private companies amd government organizations." Provides detailed data on management information systems spending, budgeting, and benchmarks. Includes charts, graphs, and analysis.

Information Technology and Management. William Cats-Baril and Ronald L. Thompson. McGraw-Hill, 1221 Ave. of the Americas New York, NY 10020. Phone: 800-722-4726 or (212)512-2000 Fax: (212)512-4502 E-mail: customer.service@mcgraw-hill.com • URL: http://www.mcgraw-hill.com • 2002. $96.25. Second edition. Covers information systems, networks, telecommunication, and database management.

Information Technology Association of America., 1401 Wilson Blvd., Suite 1100 Arlington, VA 22209. Phone: (703)522-5055 Fax: (703)525-2279 E-mail: hmiller@itaa.org • URL: http://www.itaa.org • Members are computer software and services companies. Maintains an Information Systems Integration Services Section. Formerly Software Industry Division of ADAPSO.

Information Technology Industry Council., 1250 Eye St. NW, Ste. 200 Washington, DC 20005. Phone: (202)737-8888 Fax: (202)638-4922 E-mail: rdawson@itic.org • URL: http://www.itic.org • Represents manufacturers of information technology products. Serves as secretariat and technology for ANSI-accredited standards committee x3 information technology group. Conducts public policy programs; compiles industry statistics.

Information Technology Outlook. OECD Publications and Information Center, 2001 L St., N.W., Suite 650 Washington, DC 20036-4922. Phone: 800-456-6323 or (202)785-6323 Fax: (202)785-0350 E-mail: washington.contact@oecd.org • URL: http://www.oecdwash.org • Biennial. $57.00. A review of recent developments in international markets for computer hardware, software, and services. Also examines current legal provisions for information systems security and privacy in OECD countries.

Information Technology Resellers Association., 11921 Freedom Dr., Ste. 550 Reston, VA 20190-5608. Phone: (703)904-4337 Fax: (703)736-8062 E-mail: info@itra.net • URL: http://www.itra.net • Companies that buy, sell, and lease new and used computer equipment, including central processing units and peripheral devices; associate members are companies that are actively engaged in business related to the computer industry. Promotes enhanced status of computer lessors and dealers; assures ethical business dealings for the benefit of members and their customers.

Information Times. Software and Information Industry Association, 1090 Vermont Ave. NW, 6th Fl. Washington, DC 20005. Phone: (202)289-7442 Fax: (202)289-7097 E-mail: gjohnson@siia.net • URL: http://www.spa.org • Monthly. Membership. Formerly *Friday Memo.*

Information Today: The Newspaper for Users and Producers of Electronic Information Services. Information Today, Inc., 143 Old Marlton Pike Medford, NJ 08055-8750. Phone: 800-300-9868 or (609)654-6266 Fax: (609)654-4309 E-mail: custserv@infotoday.com • URL: http://www.infotoday.com • 11 times a year. $68.95 per year.

Information Week: Business Innovation Powered by Technology. CMP Publications, Inc., 600 Community Dr. Manhasset, NY 11030. Phone: (516)562-5000 Fax: (516)733-7973 E-mail: cmpworld@cmp.com • URL: http://www.cmp.com • Weekly. $199.00 per year. The magazine for information systems management.

InfoTech Trends. Data Analysis GroupPhone: (925)462-1202 Fax: (925)462-1225 E-mail: support@infotechtrends.com • URL: http://www.infotechtrends.com • Web site provides both free and fee-based market research data on the information technology industry, including computers, peripherals, telecommunications, the Internet, software, CD-ROM/DVD, e-commerce, and workstations. Fees: Free for current (most recent year) data; more extensive information has various fee structures. Formerly *Computer Industry Forecasts.*

InfoWorld: Defining Technology for Business. InfoWorld Publishing, 155 Bovet Rd., Suite 800 San Mateo, CA 94402. Phone: 800-227-8365 or (650)572-7341 Fax: (650)312-0584 • URL: http://www.infoworld.com • Weekly. $195.00 per year. For personal computing professionals.

Infrastructure Industries USA. Gale Cengage Learning, 27500 Drake Rd. Farmington Hills, MI 48331-3535. Phone: 800-877-GALE or (248)699-4253 Fax: 800-414-5043 E-mail: gale.galeord@cengage.com • URL: http://gale.cengage.com • 2001. $260.00. Presents statistics and projections relating to economic activity in a wide variety of natural resource and construction industries.

Inheritor's Handbook: A Definitive Guide for Beneficiaries. Dan Rottenberg. Bloomberg, 499 Park Ave. New York, NY 10022. Phone: 800-388-2749 or (212)318-2000 Fax: (917)369-5000 • URL: http://www.bloomberg.com • 1998. $23.95. Covers both financial and emotional issues faced by beneficiaries. (Bloomberg Personal Bookshelf Series.)

INIS Newsletter. International Atomic Energy Agency, Division of Publications, P.O. Box 100 W-1400 Vienna, Austria. Phone: (43)1 2600 22841 Fax: (43)1 2600 29882 E-mail: inis.centreservies.unit@iaea.org • URL: http://www.iaea.org • Irregular. Free. Newsletter of the International Nuclear Information System (INIS).

Initial Public Offerings. Glasser Legalworks, 150 Clove Rd. Little Falls, NJ 07424. Phone: 800-308-1700 or (973)890-0008 Fax: (973)890-0042 E-mail: orders@glasserlegalworks.com • URL: http://www.glasserlegalworks.com • Looseleaf. $225.00, including CD-ROM version. Periodic Supplementation. Includes explanations of legal procedures for IPOs, with annotated forms. (Emerging Growth Companies Series.)

Initial Public Offerings: All You Need to Know About Taking a Company Public. David Sutton and M. William Benedetto. McGraw-Hill, 1221 Ave. of the Americas New York, NY 10020. Phone: 800-722-4726 or (212)512-2000 Fax: (212)512-4502 E-mail: customer.service@mcgraw-hill.com • URL: http://www.mcgraw-hill.com • 1990. $24.95. (Entrepreneur's Guide Series).

Ink Maker: For Manufacturers of Printing Inks and Related Graphic Arts S pecialty Colors. Cygnus Business Media, 445 Broad Hollow Rd. Melville, NY 11747. Phone: 800-308-6397 or (631)845-2700 Fax: (631)845-2798 E-mail: rich.reiff@cygnuspub.com • URL: http://www.cygnusbzb.com • Monthly. $60.00 per year. Formerly*American Inkmaker.*

Inland Marine Underwriters Association., 14 Wall St., 8th Fl. New York, NY 10005. Phone: (212)233-0550 Fax: (212)227-5102 E-mail: rthornton@imua.org • URL: http://www.imua.org • Insurance companies transacting commercial inland marine insurance in the U.S. Purposes are to provide a forum for the discussion of insurance problems of common concern; to develop underwriting and loss prevention guidelines for the protection of property; to advise with respect to legislation affecting the business. Conducts specialized education programs nationwide.

Inland River Guide Record. Waterways Journal, Inc., 319 N. Fourth St., Suite 650 Saint Louis, MO 63102. Phone: 800-366-9630 or (314)241-7354 Fax: (314)241-4207 E-mail: info@waterwaysjournal.net • URL: http://www.waterwaysjournal.net • Annual. $35.00. Covers barge and towing companies operating on Mississippi River System, Warrior-Tom Bigbee System, and Gulf Intracoastal Waterwa: all inland and Gulf Coast shipyards; public and private terminals on waterway;: contracting and dredging firms; government agencies dealing with waterways.

Innovation and Entrepreneurship: Practice and Principles. Peter F. Drucker. HarperInformation, 10 E. 53rd St. New York, NY 10022-5299. Phone: 800-242-7737 or (212)207-7000 Fax: 800-822-4090 or (212)207-7145 • URL: http://www.harpercollins.com • 1993. $16.95.

Innovation: Leadership Strategies for the Competitive Edge. Thomas D. Kuczmarski. McGraw-Hill, 1221 Ave. of the Americas New York, NY 10020. Phone: 800-722-4726 or (212)512-2000 Fax: (212)512-4502 E-mail: customer.service@mcgraw-hill.com • URL: http://www.mcgraw-hill.com • 1995. $37.95. (NTC Business Books Series).

Innovations in Education and Training International. Association for Education and Training Technology. Routledge, 11 New Fetter Ln. London EC4P 4EE, United Kingdom. Phone: 44 20 7583 9855 Fax: 44 20 7842 2298 E-mail: info@routledge.co.uk • URL: http://www.tandf.co.uk • Quarterly. Individuals, $81.00 per year; libraries and other institutions, $290.00 per year. Provides up-to-date coverage of educational and training technologies. Formerly *Educational and Training Technology International.*

Innovative Publisher: Publishing Strategies for New Markets. Emmelle Publishing Co., Inc., 370 Seventh Ave., Suite 905 New York, NY 10001. Phone: (212)714-1881 Fax: (212)714-1488 Biweekly. $69.00 per year. Provides articles and news on electronic publishing (CD-ROM or online) and desktop publishing.

The Innovator's Dilemma: When New Technologies Cause Great Firms to Fail. Clayton M. Christensen. Harvard Business School Publishing, 300 N Beacon St. Watertown, MA 02163. Phone: 800-988-0886 or (617)783-7500 Fax: (617)783-7555 • URL: http://www.hbs.edu • 1997. $27.50. Discusses management myths relating to innovation, change, and research and development. (Mangement of Innovation and Change Series).

Inquiry: The Journal of Health Care Organization, Provision, and Financing. Blue Cross and Blue Shield Association of the Rochester Area, P.O. Box 25399 Rochester, NY 14625. Phone: (716)264-9122 Fax: (716)264-9122 • URL: http://www.inquiryjournal.org • Quarterly. Individuals, $53.00 per year; institutions, $75.00 per year.

Inside Chips Ventures: The Global Report with Executive Perspective. HTE Research, Inc., 119 N. Commercial St., Suite 480 Bellingham, WA 98225-4437. Phone: (360)676-2260 Fax: (360)676-2265 E-mail: sibs@hte.sibs.com • URL: http://www.insidechips.com • Monthly. $595.00 per year. Tracks the activities of semiconductor firms worldwide. Formerly *Semiconductor Industry and Business Survey Newsletter.*

Inside Direct Mail: The Monthly Newsletter Analysis and Record of the Direct Ma reting Archive. North American Publishing Co., 401 N. Broad St. Philadelphia, PA 19108. Phone: 800-777-8074 or (215)238-5482 Fax: 800-664-1533 or (215)238-5412 E-mail: customerservice@napco.com • URL: http://www.napco.com • Monthly. $295.00 per year. Newsletter and listing of promotional mailings. Photocopies of mailings are available to subscribers. Formerly *Who's Mailing What!*

Inside Flyer. 1930 Frequent Flyer Point Colorado Springs, CO 80915. Phone: 800-767-8896 • URL: http://www.insideflyer.com • Monthly. $36.00 per year. Newsletter. Provides information relating to frequent flyer awards and air travel.

Inside Microsoft Word: Tips and Techniques for Microsoft Windows. Element K Journals, 2165 Brighton-Henrietta Townline Rd., Ste. 3 Rochester, NY 14623. Phone: 800-223-8720 or (585)240-7301 Fax: (585)292-4392 • URL: http://www.elementkjournals.com • Monthly. $87.00 per year. Newsletter on word processing with Microsoft Word for Windows. Covers applications and problem-solving.

Inside Negotiations. EFR Corp., P.O. Box 15236 Colorado Spring, FL 80935-5236. Monthly. $98.00 per year. Newsletter. Labor negotiations.

Inside Public Accounting. Hudson Sawyer Professional Services Marketing Inc., 3340 Peachtree Rd. NE, Ste. 2600 Atlanta, GA 30326. Phone: 800-945-6462 or (404)264-9977 Fax: (404)264-9968 E-mail: info@bookweb.org Description: Contains articles on CPAs and CPA firms, provides news and analysis of management strategies, politics, marketing, computers, and personnel. Email alert delivers hot and topical news to subscribers' desktops. Recurring features include interviews, commentary, reports of meetings, book reviews, and the columns titled Mergers, New Shareholders, Newsmakers, and Lawsuits.

Inside R and D: A Weekly Report on Technical Innovation. Technical Insights, 605 Third Ave. New York, NY 10158-0012. Phone: 800-825-7550 or (212)850-8600 Fax: (212)850-8800 E-mail: insights@wiley.com • URL: http://www.wiley.com • Weekly. Institutions, $840.00 per year. Concentrates on new and significant developments. Formerly *Technolog Transfer Week*.

Inside the Financial Futures Markets. Mark Powers and Mark Castelino. John Wiley and Sons, Inc., 111 River St. Hoboken, NJ 07030. Phone: 800-225-5945 or (201)748-6000 Fax: (201)748-6088 E-mail: info@wiley.com • URL: http://www.wiley.com • 1991. $55.00. Third edition. (Finance Series).

Inside the Juror: The Psychology of Juror Decision Making. Reid Hastie, editor. Cambridge University Press, 40 W 20th St. New York, NY 10011-4211. Phone: 800-872-7423 or (212)924-3900 Fax: (212)691-3239 E-mail: orders@cup.org • URL: http://www.cup.org • 1994. $29.00. (Judgement and Decision Making Series).

Inside Wordperfect for Windows. Element K Journals, 2165 Brighton-Henrietta Townline Rd., Ste. 3 Rochester, NY 14623. Phone: 800-223-8720 or (585)240-7301 Fax: (585)292-4392 • URL: http://www.elementkjournal.com • Monthly. $59.00 per year. Newsletter on word processing with Wordperfect software. Includes tips and techniques for both beginners and experts.

Insider Trading Regulation, Enforcement and Prevention. Donald C. Langevoort. West Group, 610 Opperman Dr. Eagan, MN 55123. Phone: 800-328-4880 or (651)687-7000 Fax: 800-340-9378 E-mail: bookstore@westgroup.com • URL: http://www.westgroup.com • Annual. $216.00. Two looseleaf volumes. (Securities Law Series).

An Insider's Guide to Home Health Care. Tova Navarra and Margaret Ferrer. SLACK, Inc., 6900 Grove Rd. Thorofare, NJ 08086-9447. Phone: 800-257-8290 or (856)848-1000 Fax: (856)853-6091 E-mail: customerservice@slackinc.com • URL: http://www.slackinc.org • 1996. $28.00. Covers "unexpected situations, cultural differences, and potential conflicts" for professionals in the home health care field. Emphasizes teamwork for optimal care management.

InSite 2. Intelligence Data/Thomson FinancialPhone: 800-654-0393 or (617)856-1890 Fax: (617)737-3182 E-mail: intelligence.data@tfn.com • URL: http://www.insite2.gale.com/ • Fee-based Web site consolidates information in a "Base Pack" consisting of Business InSite, Market InSite, and Company InSite. Optional databases are Consumer InSite, Health and Wellness InSite, Newsletter InSite, and Computer InSite. Includes fulltext content from more than 2,500 trade publications, journals, newsletters, newspapers, analyst reports, and other sources. Continuous updating. Formerly produced by The Gale Group.

Insolvency Law & Practice. LexisNexis Butterworths Tolley, Tolley House, Two Addiscombe Rd., Croyden Surrey CR9 5AF, England. Phone: 44 2086 622000 Fax: 44 2086 622012 E-mail: customer.services@lexisnexis.co.uk • URL: http://www.tolley.co.uk • Bimonthly. $181.00 per year. United Kingdom emphasis.

INSPEC. Institution of Electrical Engineers (IEE), London WC2R 0BL, England. Phone: 44 20 72401871 or 44 20 72407735 E-mail: postmaster@iee.org.uk • URL: http://www.iee.org.uk • Provides online citations, with abstracts, to the world literature of electrical engineering, electronics, optoelectronics, telecommunications, industrial controls, instrumentation, computer technology, information technology, and physics. Coverage includes more than 4,000 technical and scientific journals from 1969 to date, with weekly updating. (INSPEC is Information Services in Physics, Electronics, and Computing.) Inquire as to online cost and availability.

Instant Computer Arbitration Search. LRP Publications, 747 Dresher Rd. Horsham, PA 19044. Phone: 800-341-7874 or (215)784-0860 Fax: (215)784-9639 Provides citations to U. S. labor arbitration cases and a detailed directory of about 2,500 public and private labor arbitrators. Weekly updates. Cases date from 1970. Inquire as to online cost and availability.

Instant Print/Copy Shop. Entrepreneur Media, Inc., 2445 McCabe Way Irvine, CA 92614. Phone: 800-421-2300 or (949)261-2325 Fax: (949)261-0234 E-mail: entmag@entrepreneur.com • URL: http://www.entrepreneur.com • Looseleaf. $59.50. A practical guide to starting a quick printing and copying business. Covers profit potential, start-up costs, market size evaluation, owner's time required, site selection, lease negotiation, pricing, accounting, advertising, promotion, etc. (Start-Up Business Guide No. E1298.)

Instant Sign Store. Entrepreneur Media, Inc., 2445 McCabe Way Irvine, CA 92614. Phone: 800-421-2300 or (949)261-2325 Fax: (949)261-0234 E-mail: entmag@entrepreneur.com • URL: http://www.entrepreneur.com • Looseleaf. $59.50. A practical guide to starting an instant sign store. Covers profit potential, start-up costs, market size evaluation, owner's time required, site selection, lease negotiation, pricing, accounting, advertising, promotion, etc. (Start-Up Business Guide No. E1336.)

Institute for Advanced Safety Studies.

Institute for Alternative Futures., 100 N. Pitt St., Suite 235 Alexandria, VA 22314. Phone: (703)684-5880 Fax: (703)684-0640 E-mail: futurist@altfutures.com • URL: http://www.altfutures.com • Conducts studies in the future of communications, health care, bioengineering, the legal system, etc.

Institute for Case Development and Research., Simmons College, Graduate School of Management, 409 Commonwealth Ave. Boston, MA 02215. Phone: (617)521-3840 Fax: (617)521-3880 E-mail: somadm@simmons.edu • URL: http://www.simmons.edu • Studies issues and problems confronting women in management.

Institute for Communications Research.

Institute for Defense Analyses.

Institute for Economic Analysis.

Institute for Economic Research. University of Washington

Institute for Environmental Negotiation., University of Virginia, P.O. Box 400179 Charlottesville, VA 22904-4179. Phone: (434)924-1970 Fax: (434)924-0231 E-mail: ed7k@virginia.edu • URL: http://www.virginia/edu • Research activities are related to the resolution of environmental disputes through negotiation, mediation, and consensus building.

Institute for Environmental Research. Kansas State University

Institute for Fisheries Research.

Institute for Food Laws and Regulations., Michigan State University, 165 National Food Safety and Toxicology Ctr. East Lansing, MI 48224. Phone: (517)355-8295 • URL: http://www.iflr.msu.edu/ • Conducts research on the food industry, including processing, packaging, marketing, and new products.

Institute for Health, Health Care Policy, and Aging Research., Rutgers University, 30 College Ave. New Brunswick, NJ 08901-1293. Phone: (732)932-8413 Fax: (732)932-6872 E-mail: caboyer@rci.rutgers.edu • URL: http://www.ihhcpar.rutgers.edu/ • Areas of study include HMO use by older adults.

Institute for Health Policy Research., Health Science Center, University of Florida, P.O. Box 100177 Gainesville, FL 32610-0177. Phone: (352)395-8035 Fax: (352)395-8047 E-mail: admin@hpe.ufl.edu • URL: http://www.hpe.ufl.edu • Research areas include health economics, financing, and long-term care considerations.

Institute for Health Services Research and Policy Studies.

Institute for Information Science and Technology., George Washington University, 801 22nd St., N. W., 6th Fl. Washington, DC 20052. Phone: (202)994-6208 Fax: (202)994-0227 E-mail: helgert@seas.gwu.edu Research areas include computer graphics and image processing.

Institute for Information Storage Technology.

Institute for International Economics., 1750 Massachusetts Ave., N.W. Washington, DC 20036. Phone: (202)328-9000 Fax: (202)328-5432 E-mail: alreeves@iie.com • URL: http://www.iie.com • Research fields include a wide range of international economic issues, including foreign exchange rates.

Institute for Mathematics and Its Applications., University of Minnesota, 400 Lind, 206 Church St., S. E. Minneapolis, MN 55455-0436. Phone: (612)624-6066 Fax: (612)626-7370 E-mail: staff@ima.umn.edu • URL: http://www.ima.umn.edu • Research areas include various topics connected with industrial and applied mathematics.

Institute for Metal Forming. Lehigh University

Institute for Professionsals in Taxation., 3350 Peachtree Rd., N.E., Suite 280 Atlanta, GA 30326. Phone: (404)240-2300 Fax: (404)240-2315 E-mail: ipt@ipt.org • URL: http://www.ipt.org • Promotes education in the area of property taxation. Formerly Institute of Property Taxation.

Institute for Pure and Applied Physical Sciences., University of California, San Diego, 9500 Gilman Dr., Ste. 0360 La Jolla, CA 92093-0360. Phone: (858)534-3560 Fax: (858)534-7649 E-mail: mbmaple@ucsd.edu • URL: http://www.ipaps.ucsd.edu/ • Areas of study include superconductivity.

Institute for Quantitative Research in Finance., Church Street Station, P.O. Box 6194 New York, NY 10249-6194. Phone: (212)744-6825 Fax: (212)517-2259 E-mail: daleberman@compuserve Financial research areas include quantitative methods, securities analysis, and the financial structure of industries. Also known as the "Q Group."

Institute for Retired Professionals.

Institute for Social Research.

Institute for Studies in the Arts., Arizona State University, College of Fine Arts, P.O. Box 873302 Tempe, AZ 85287-3302. Phone: (480)965-9438 Fax: (480)965-0961 E-mail: trikakis@asu.edu • URL: http://www.isa.asu.edu • Research areas include the fine arts aspects of interactive media.

Institute for Supply Management.

Institute for Survey Research., Temple University Center for Public Policy, 1601 N. Broad St. Philadelphia, PA 19122. Phone: 800-827-5477 or (215)204-8355 Fax: (215)204-3797 E-mail: lenlo@temss2.isr.temple.edu • URL: http://www.temple.edu/isr • Conducts large scale in-person surveys that represent the United States househould population.

Institute for Systems Research., University of Maryland at College Park, A. V. Williams Bldg., 2nd Fl., No. 115 College Park, MD 20742-3311. Phone: (301)405-6615 Fax: (301)314-9220 E-mail: isr@isr.umd.edu • URL: http://www.isr.umd.edu/ • A National Science Foundation Engineering Research Center. Areas of research include communication systems, manufacturing systems, chemical process systems, artificial intelligence, and systems integration.

Institute for Tax Administration.

Institute for Telecommunications Studies.

Institute for the Future., 2744 Sand Hill Rd. Menlo Park, CA 94025-7020. Phone: (650)854-6322 Fax: (650)854-7850 E-mail: info@iftf.org • URL: http://www.iftf.org • Assists organizations, businesses, industry and the government in conducting long-term futures research.

Institute for the Management of Information Systems., Five Kingfisher House, New Mill Rd. Orpington, Kent BR5 3QG, England. Phone: 44 70 00023456 Fax: 44 70 00023023 E-mail: central@imis.org.uk • URL: http://www.imis.org.uk • Formerly Institute of Data Processing Management.

Institute for the Study of Business Markets., Pennsylvania State University, 402 Business Administration Bldg. University Park, PA 16802-3004. Phone: (814)863-2782 Fax: (814)863-0413 E-mail: isbm@psu.edu • URL: http://www.smeal.psu.edu/isbm/ • Research areas include international distribution channels.

Institute of Advanced Manufacturing Sciences., 1111 Edison Dr. Cincinnati, OH 45230. Phone: (513)948-2000 Fax: 800-345-4482 Fields of research include quality improvement, computer-aided design, artificial intelligence, and employee training.

Institute of Atmospheric Physics. University of Arizona

Institute of Aviation. University of Illinois

Institute of Business and Economic Research., University of California at Berkeley, Hass School of Business Berkeley, CA 94720-1900. Phone: (510)642-5905 Fax: (510)642-1420 E-mail: shapiro@haas.berkeley.edu • URL: http://www.haas.berkeley.edu/groups/iber • Research fields are business administration, economics, finance, real estate, and international development.

Institute of Certified Travel Agents.

Institute of Cultural Affairs.

Institute of Electrical and Electronics Engineers.

Institute of Food Science., Cornell University, 114 Stocking Hall Ithaca, NY 14853-7201. Phone: (607)255-7900 E-mail: cifs@cornell.edu • URL: http://www.nysaes.cornell.edu/cifs/ • Research areas include the chemistry and processing of food commodities, food processing engineering, food packaging, and nutrition.

Institute of Food Technologists., 525 W. Van Buren St., No. 1000 Chicago, IL 60607. Phone: (312)782-8424 Fax: (312)782-8348 E-mail: info@ift.org • URL: http://www.ift.org • A professional society of food scientists active in government, academia, and industry.

Institute of Human Nutrition. Columbia University

Institute of Industrial Engineers., 3377 Parkway Ln., Ste. 200 Norcross, GA 30092. Phone: 800-494-0460 or (770)449-0460 Fax: (770)441-3295 E-mail: cs@iienet.org • URL: http://www.iienet.org • Formerly American Institute of Industrial Engineers.

Institute of Industrial Relations.

Institute of Industrial Relations. University of California, Los Angeles

Institute of Internal Auditors.

Institute of International Education., 809 United Nations Plaza New York, NY 10017-3580. Phone: (212)984-5200 Fax: (212)984-5452 E-mail: info@iie.org • URL: http://www.iie.org • Promotes international educational exchange programs. Administers scholarships, fellowships, and other grants provided by over 120 sponsors.

Institute of Judicial Administration.

Institute of Labor and Industrial Relations.

Institute of Makers of Explosives., 1120 19th St., N. W., Suite 310 Washington, DC 20036. Phone: (202)429-9280 Fax: (202)293-2420 E-mail: info@ime.org • URL: http://www.ime.org • Members are manufacturers of commercial explosives.

Institute of Management Accountants., 10 Paragon Dr. Montvale, NJ 07645-1718. Phone: 800-638-4427 or (201)573-9000 Fax: (201)474-1600 E-mail: ima@imanet.org • URL: http://www.imanet.org • Formerly National Association of Accountants.

Institute of Management Consultants., 2025 M St., NW, Ste. 800 Washington, DC 20036-3309. Phone: 800-221-2557 or (202)367-1134 Fax: (202)367-2134 E-mail: office@imcusa.org • URL: http://www.imcusa.org • Provides professional services and certification to management consultants. Affiliated with Association of Management Consulting Firms.

Institute of Management, Innovation and Organization., University of California, Berkeley, F402 Haas School of Business Berkeley, CA 94720-1930. Phone: (510)642-4041 Fax: (510)642-2826 E-mail: teece@haas.berkeley.edu • URL: http://www.haas.berkeley.edu • Research areas include a wide range of business management functions.

Institute of Marine Engineers, Science and Technology., 80 Coleman St. London EC2R 5BJ, United Kingdom. Phone: 44 207 3822600 Fax: 44 207 3822670 E-mail: keith.read@imarest.org • URL: http://www.imarest.org • An international organization of marine engineers, offshore engineers, and naval architects.

Institute of Mathematical Statistics., PO Box 22718 Beachwood, OH 44122. Phone: (216)295-2340 Fax: (216)921-6703 E-mail: ims@stat.org • URL: http://www.imstat.org • Professional society of mathematicians and others interested in mathematical statistics and probability theory.

Institute of Mathematical Statistics Bulletin. Institute of Mathematical Statistics, 9650 Rockville Pke., Ste. L2310 Bethesdad, MD 20814-3998. Phone: (301)634-7029 Fax: (301)634-7099 E-mail: ims@imstat.org • URL: http://www.imstat.org • Bimonthly. $60.00 per year.

Institute of Noise Control Engineering.

Institute of Nuclear Materials Management., 60 Revere Dr., Suite 500 Northbrook, IL 60062. Phone: (847)480-9573 Fax: (847)480-9282 E-mail: inmm@inmm.org • URL: http://www.inmm.org • Affiliated with American National Standards Institute.

Institute of Nuclear Power Operations., 700 Galleria Pky. SE, Ste. 100 Atlanta, GA 30339-5957. Phone: (770)644-8000 Fax: (770)644-8549 E-mail: grillma@inpo.org An organization of electric utilities operating nuclear power plants.

Institute of Optics.

Institute of Packaging Professionals., 1601 N Bond St., No. 101 Naperville, IL 60563. Phone: 800-432-4085 or (630)544-5050 Fax: (630)544-5055 E-mail: info@iopp.org • URL: http://www.iopp.org • Members are practicing professionals in the fields of packaging and handling.

Institute of Paper Science and Technology Graphic Arts Bulletin. Cengage Learning, 500 10th St., NW Atlanta, GA 30318. Phone: (404)894-5726 Fax: (404)894-9596 E-mail: info.support@ipst.edu • URL: http://www.ipst.com • Monthly. $400.00 per volume. Formerly *Graphic Arts Literature Abstracts.*

Institute of Personality and Social Research. University of California at Berkeley

Institute of Public Administration., 411 Lafayette St., 3rd Fl. New York, NY 1003-7032. Phone: (212)992-9899 Fax: (212)995-4876 E-mail: info@theipa.org • URL: http://www.theipa.org • Formerly National Institute of Public Administration.

Institute of Real Estate Management.

Institute of Scrap Recycling Industries.

Institute of Shortening and Edible Oils., 1750 New York Ave., NW, Ste. 120 Washington, DC 20006. Phone: (202)783-7960 Fax: (202)393-1367 E-mail: info@iseo.org • URL: http://www.iseo.org • Refiners of edible vegetable oils and animal fats. Formerly Institute of Shortening Manufacturers.

Institute of State and Regional Affairs., Pennsylvania State University at Harrisburg, 777 W. Harrisburg Pike Middletown, PA 17057-4898. Phone: (717)948-6336 Fax: (717)948-6754 E-mail: xvc@psu.edu • URL: http://www.psdc.hbg.psu.edu/isra • Conducts research in environmental, general, and socioeconomic planning. Zoning is included.

Institute of Tax Consultants.

Institute of Textile Technology.

Institute of Transportation Engineers., 1099 14th St., N.W., Suite 300 W Washington, DC 20005-3438. Phone: (202)289-0222 Fax: (202)289-7722 E-mail: ite_staff@site.org • URL: http://www.ite.org • Members are professionals in surface transportation, mass transit, and traffic engineering. Formerly Institute of Traffic Engineers.

Institute of Transportation Studies. University of California at Berkeley

Institute of Urban and Regional Development., University of California at Berkeley, 316 Wurster Hall Berkeley, CA 94720-1870. Phone: (510)642-4874 Fax: (510)643-9576 E-mail: iurd@uclink.berkeley.edu • URL: http://www.ced.berkeley.edu/iurd • Research topics include the effects of changing economic trends in urban areas.

Institute on Planning, Zoning and Eminent Domain. LexisNexis, 1275 Broadway Albany, NY 12204. Phone: 800-223-1940 or (518)487-3028 Fax: 800-544-6572 or (518)462-3788 E-mail: bookstore.support@lexisnexis.com • URL: http://www.lexisnexis.com • 1971. $199.00.

Institutional and Service Textile Distributors Association., 1609 Connecticut Ave. Washington, DC 20009. Phone: (202)986-0105 Fax: (202)986-0448 E-mail: istdatextiles@aol.com • URL: http://www.istda.org • Members are wholesalers of textile products to hospitals, hotels, airlines, etc.

Institutional Buyers of Bank and Thrift Stocks: A Targeted Directory. Investment Data Corp., 4833 Rugby Ave., Ste. 600 Bethesda, MD 20814. Phone: (301)657-4271 Fax: (301)215-7104 Annual. $645.00. Provides detailed profiles of about 600 institutional buyers of bank and savings and loan stocks. Includes names of financial analysts and portfolio managers.

Institutional Buyers of Energy Stocks. Investment Data Corp., 4833 Rugby Ave., Ste. 600 Bethesda, MD 20814. Phone: (301)657-4271 Fax: (301)215-7104 Annual. $645.00. Provides detailed profiles 555 institutional buyers of petroleum-related and other energy stocks. Includes names of financial analysts and portfolio managers.

Institutional Buyers of Foreign Stocks: A Targeted Directory. Investment Data Corp., 4833 Rugby Ave., Ste. 600 Bethesda, MD 20814. Phone: (301)657-4271 Fax: (301)215-7104 Annual. $595.00. Provides detailed profiles of institutional buyers of international stocks. Includes names of financial analysts and portfolio managers.

Institutional Buyers of REIT Securities. Investment Data Corp., 4833 Rugvy Ave., Ste. 600 Bethesda, MD 20814. Phone: (301)657-4271 Fax: (301)215-7104 Semiannual. $995.00 per year. Provides detailed profiles of about 500 institutional buyers of REIT securities. Includes names of financial analysts and portfolio managers.

Institutional Buyers of Small-Cap Stocks. Investment Data Corp., 4833 Rugby Ave., Ste. 600 Bethesda, MD 20814. Phone: (301)657-4271 Fax: (301)215-7104 Annual. $295.00. Provides detailed profiles of more than 837 institutional buyers of small capitalization stocks. Includes names of financial analysts and portfolio managers.

Institutional Investor International Edition: The Magazine for International Finance and Investment. Institutional Investor, Inc., Journals Group, 225 Park Ave., S New York, NY 10003. Phone: 800-945-2034 or (212)224-3066 Fax: (212)224-3472 E-mail: info@iijournals.com • URL: http://www.iijournals.com • Monthly. $475.00 per year. Covers the international aspects of professional investing and finance. Emphasis is on Europe, the Far East, and Latin America.

Institutional Investor: The Premier of Professional Magazine Finance. Institutional Investor, Inc., Journals Group, 225 Park Ave., S New York, NY 10003. Phone: 800-945-2034 or (212)224-3066 Fax: (212)224-3472 E-mail: info@iijournals.com • URL: http://www.iijournals.com • Monthly. $445.00 per year. Includes print and online editions. Edited for portfolio managers and other investment professionals. Special feature issues include "Country Credit Ratings," "Fixed Income Trading Ranking," "All-America Research Team," and "Global Banking Ranking."

Institutional Investors Statistical Yearbook. Organization for Economic Cooperation and Development, OECD Washington Center, 2001 L St., N. W., Suite 650 Washington, DC 20036-4922. Phone: 800-456-6323 or (202)785-6323 Fax: (202)785-0350 E-mail: washington.contact@oecd.org • URL: http://www.oecdwash.org • Annual. $67.00. Provides data relating to institutional saving and investment in OECD countries. Includes investments by insurance companies, pension funds, and investment companies.

Instructional Media Development Center. University of Wisconsin at Madison

Instructional Technology Center.

Instrumentalist: A Magazine for School and College Band and Orchestra Directors, Professional Instrumentalist, Teacher-Training Specialists in Instrumental Music Education and Instrumental Teachers. The Instrumentalist Co., 200 Northfield Rd. Northfield, IL 60093-3390. Phone: 888-446-6888 or (847)446-5000 Fax: (847)446-6263 Monthly. $22.00 per year. Professional journal for school band and orchestra directors and teachers of instruments in those ensembles.

Instrumentation and Automation News: Instruments, Controls, Manufacturing Software, Electronic and Mechanical Components. Reed Business Information, 360 Park Ave., S New York, NY 10010. Phone: 800-446-6551 or (646)746-6400 Fax: (646)746-7028 E-mail: corporatecommunications@reedbusiness.com • URL: http://www.reedbusiness.com • Monthly. $61.90 per year.

Instrumentation and Control Laboratory. Princeton University

Instrumentation Systems and Automation Society., 67 Alexander Dr. Research Triangle Park, NC 27709. Phone: (919)549-8411 Fax: (919)549-8288 E-mail: info@isa.org • URL: http://www.isa.org • Members are engineers and others concerned with industrial instrumentation, systems, computers, and automation. Formerly Instrument Society of America.

Insulation Contractors Association of America.

Insulation Outlook: Business Solutions for Expanding or Relocating Companies. National Insulation Association, 99 Canal Center Palza, Suite 222 Alevandria, VA 22314. Phone: (703)683-6422 Fax: (703)549-4838 E-mail: mjones@insulation.org • URL: http://www.insulation.org • $45.00 per year. Covers site selection and related topics.

Insurance Advocate. Emanuel Levy, editor. Shea-Haarmann Cos., P.O. Box 9001 Mount Vernon, NY 10552-9001. Phone: (914)699-2020 Fax: (914)664-1503 E-mail: insuranceadvocate@cinn.com • URL: http://www.cinn.com • Weekly. $59.00 per year. News and features on all aspects of insurance business for industry professionals.

Insurance Almanac: Who, What, When and Where in Insurance. Underwriter Printing and Publishing Co., 50 E. Palisade Ave. Englewood, NJ 07631. Phone: 800-526-4700 or (201)569-8808 Fax: (201)569-8817 Annual. $175.00. Lists insurance agencies and brokerage firms; U.S. and Canadian insurance companies, adjusters, appraisers, auditors, investigators, insurance officials and insurance organizations.

Insurance and Employee Benefits Literature. Special Libraries Association, Insurance and Employee Benefits Div., 1700 18th St., N. W., 17th Fl. Washington, DC 20009-2514. Phone: (202)234-4700 Fax: (202)234-2442 E-mail: sla@sla.org • URL: http://www.sla.org • Bimonthly. $15.00 per year. Lists a wide variety of literature in all branches of the insurance industry. Includes annotations.

Insurance and Technology. CMP Media LLC, 600 Community Dr. Manhasset, NY 11030. Phone: (516)562-5000 E-mail: cmp@cmp.com • URL: http://www.cmp.com • Monthly. $65.00 per year. Covers information technology and systems management as applied to the operation of life, health, casualty, and property insurance companies.

Insurance Bar Directory. Bar Listing Publishing Co., PO Box 40580 Cleveland, OH 44140-0580. Phone: 800-533-2500 or (440)835-2000 Fax: (440)899-3037 E-mail: info@barlist.com • URL: http://www.barlist.com • Covers: law firms that handle defense insurance litigation, and general insurance practice matters. Entries include: Firm name, address, phone, names and titles of key personnel, specialty, list of clients.

Insurance Coverage Law Bulletin. American Lawyer Media, Inc., 105 Madison Ave. New York, NY 10016. Phone: 800-888-8300 or (212)779-9200 Fax: (212)481-8110 E-mail: lawcatalog@amlaw.com • URL: http://www.lawcatalog.com/ • Monthly. $199.00 per year. Newsletter. Provides news of property insurance claims management and coverage disputes. Edited for both legal and non-legal insurance professionals. (A Law Journal Newsletter, formerly published by Leader Publications).

Insurance Day. Available from Informa Publishing Group Ltd., PO Box 1017 Westborough, MA 01581-6017. Phone: 800-493-4080 Fax: (508)231-0856 E-mail: enquiries@informa.com • URL: http://www.informa.com • Three times a week. $440.00 per year. Published in the UK by Lloyd's List (http://www.lloydslist.com), A newspaper providing international coverage of property/casualty/liability insurance, reinsurance, and risk, with an emphasis on marine insurance.

Insurance Finance and Investment. Institutional Investor, Inc., Journals Group, 225 Park Ave., S New York, NY 10003. Phone: 800-945-2034 or (212)224-3066 Fax: (212)224-3472 E-mail: info@iijournals.com • URL: http://www.iijournals.com • Biweekly. $1,960.00 per year. Newsletter. Edited for insurance company investment managers.

Insurance Forum: For the Unfettered Exchange of Ideas About Insurance. Joseph M. Belth, editor. Insurance Forum, Inc., P.O. Box 245 Ellettsville, IN 47429. Phone: (812)876-6502 Monthly. $90.00 per year. Newsletter. Provides analysis of the insurance business, including occasional special issues showing the ratings of about 1,600 life-health insurance companies, as determined by four major rating services: Duff & Phelps Credit Rating Co., Moody's Investors Service, Standard & Poor's Corp., and Weiss Research, Inc.

Insurance Handbook for the Medical Offices. Marilyn T. Fordney. Elsevier, 360 Park Ave., S New York, NY 10010-1017. Phone: 888-437-4636 or (212)989-5800 Fax: (212)633-3990 E-mail: usinfo-f@elsevier.com • URL: http://www.elsevier.com • 2001. $55.00. Seventh edition.

Insurance Information Institute., 110 William St. New York, NY 10038. Phone: 800-331-9146 or (212)346-5500 Fax: (212)791-1807 E-mail: members@iii.org • URL: http://www.iii.org • Property and casualty insurance companies. Provides information and educational services to mass media, educational institutions, trade associations, businesses, government agencies, and the public.

Insurance Institute for Highway Safety., 1005 N. Glebe Rd., Ste. 800 Arlington, VA 22201-4751. Phone: (703)247-1500 Fax: (703)247-1678 E-mail: iihs@highwaysafety.org • URL: http://www.hwysafety.org • Studies highway safety, including seat belt use, air bags, property damage, vehicle recalls, and the role of alcohol and drugs.

Insurance Institute for Highway Safety, Status Report. Insurance Institute for Highway Safety, 1005 N. Glebe Rd. Arlington, VA 22201. Phone: (703)247-1500 10 times a year. Free.

Insurance Marketing: The Ins and Outs of Recruiting and Retaining More Agents. Agent Media Corp., 1255 Cleveland St., Suite 300 Clearwater, FL 33755. Phone: 800-933-9449 or (727)446-1100 Fax: (727)446-1166 Bimonthly. Controlled circulation. Provides practical advice for insurance companies on how to hire and keep sales personnel.

Insurance Marketplace: The Agents and Brokers Guide to Non-Standard and Special ty Lines, Aviation, Marine and International Insurance. The Rough Notes Co., Inc., 11690 Technology Dr. Carmel, IN 46032-5600. Phone: 800-428-4384 or (317)582-1600 Fax: 800-321-1909 or (317)816-1000 E-mail: salesrnc@roughnotes.com • URL: http://www.roughnotes.com • Annual. Included in subscription to*Rough Notes Magazine*; others, $15.95. Lists specialty, excess, and surplus insurance lines.

Insurance Networking: Strategies and Solutions for Electronic Commerce. Thomson Media, One State St. Plaza New York, NY 10004. Phone: 800-221-1809 or (212)803-8200 Fax: (212)843-9635 E-mail: custserv@thomsonmedia.com • URL: http://www.thomsonmedia.com • 10 times a year. Price on application. Covers information technology for the insurance industry, with emphasis on computer communications and the Internet.

Insurance of Accounts Handbook: A Practical Guide to the FDIC Regulations. The Institute of Financial Education, 55 W. Monroe St., Suite 2800 Chicago, IL 60603-5014. Phone: 800-946-0488 or (312)364-0100 Fax: (312)364-0190 E-mail: info2atsbai.org • URL: http://www.theinstitute.com • 1993.

$39.95. Second edition. A guide for bankers to the regulations of the Federal Deposit Insurance Corporation.

Insurance Periodicals Index. Specials Libraries Association, Insurance and Employees Benefits Div. NILS Publishing Co., 21625 Prairie St. Chatsworth, CA 91311. Phone: 800-423-5910 • URL: http://library-dialog.com • Annual. $250.00. Compiled by the Insurance and Employee Benefits Div., Special Libraries Association. A yearly index of over 15,000 articles from about 35 insurance periodicals. Arrangement is by subject, with an index to authors.

Insurance Regulation: State Capitals. Wakeman-Walworth, Inc., PO Box 7376 Alexandria, VA 22307-7376. Phone: 800-876-2545 or (703)768-9600 Fax: (703)768-9690 E-mail: newsletters@statecapitals.com • URL: http://www.statecapitals.com • 50 times a year. $245.00 per year; print and online editions, $350.00 per year. Formerly *From the State Capitals: Insurance Regulation*.

Insurance Services Office (ISO)., 545 Washington Blvd. Jersey City, NJ 07310-1686. Phone: 800-888-4476 or (201)469-2000 Fax: (201)748-1472 E-mail: info@iso.com • URL: http://www.iso.com • Provides statistical, actuarial, underwriting, and claims information to property and casualty insurance companies.

Insurance Statistics Yearbook, 1991-1998. OECD Publications and Information Center, 2001 L St., N.W., Suite 650 Washington, DC 20036-4922. Phone: 800-456-6323 or (202)785-6323 Fax: (202)785-0350 E-mail: washington.contact@oecd.org • URL: http://www.oecdwash.org • 2000. $75.00. Presents detailed statistics on insurance premiums collected in OECD countries, by type of insurance.

Insurance Words and Their Meanings: A Glossary of Insurance Terms. The Rough Notes Co., Inc., 11690 Techonology Dr. Carmel, IN 46032-5600. Phone: 800-428-4384 or (317)582-1600 Fax: (317)816-1000 E-mail: salesrnc@roughnotes.com • URL: http://www.roughnotes.com • 2001. 17th edition. Price on application.

InsuranceWeek. I.W. Publications, Inc., 2033 6th Ave., Ste. 917 Seattle, WA 98121-2568. Phone: (206)624-6965 Fax: (206)624-5021 Weekly. $30.00 per year.

Insuring Your Business: What You Need to Know to Get the Best Insurance Coverage for Your Business. Sean Mooney. Insurance Information Institute, 110 William St. New York, NY 10038. Phone: 800-331-9146 or (212)669-9200 Fax: (212)732-1916 E-mail: info@iii.org • URL: http://www.iii.org • 1992. $22.50.

InsWeb. InsWeb Corp.Phone: (916)853-3300 E-mail: info@insweb.com • URL: http://www.insweb.com • Web site offers a wide variety of advice and information on automobile, life, health, and "other" insurance. Includes glossaries of insurance terms, Standard & Poor's ratings of individual insurance companies, and "Financial Needs Estimators." Searching is available. Fees: Free.

INTECH: The International Journal of Instrumentation and Control. ISA Services, Inc., 67 Alexander Dr. Research Triangle Park, NC 27709. Phone: (919)549-8411 Fax: (919)549-8288 E-mail: info@isa.org • URL: http://www.isa.org • Monthly. $72.00 per year.

Integrated Circuits International: An International Bulletin for Suppliers and Users of Integrated Circuits. Elsevier, 360 Park Ave., S New York, NY 10010-1710. Phone: 888-437-4636 or (212)989-5800 Fax: (212)633-3990 E-mail: usinfo-f@elsevier.com • URL: http://www.elsevier.com • Monthly. $541.00 per year. For suppliers and users of integrated circuits.

Integrated Media Systems Center., University of Southern California, 3740 McClintock Ave., Suite 131 Los Angeles, CA 90089-2561. Phone: (213)740-0877 Fax: (213)740-8931 E-mail: imsc@imsc.usc.edu • URL: http://www.imsc.usc.edu • Media areas for research include education, mass communication, and entertainment.

Integrated Plant Protection Center. Oregon State University

Intellectual Property and Antitrust Law. William C. Holmes. West Group, 610 Opperman Dr. Eagan, MN 55123. Phone: 800-328-4880 or (651)687-7000 Fax: 800-340-9378 E-mail: bookstore@westgroup.com • URL: http://www.westgroup.com • Semiannual. $389.00 per year. Two looseleaf volumes. Includes patent, trademark, and copyright practices.

Intellectual Property in the International Marketplace. Melvi Simensky and others. John Wiley and Sons, Inc., 111 River St. Hoboken, NJ 07030. Phone: 800-225-5945 or (201)748-6000 Fax: (201)748-6088 E-mail: info@wiley.com • URL: http://www.wiley.com • 1999. $350.00. Second edition. Two volumes. Volume one: *Valuation, Protection, and Electronic Commerce*. Volume two: *Exploitation and Country-by-Country Profiles*. Includes contributions from lawyers and consultants in various countries. (Intellectual Property-General, Law, Accounting and Finance, Management, Licensing, Special Topics Series).

Intellectual Property Infringement Damages: A Litigation Support Handbook 2003 Cumulative Supplement. Russell L. Parr. John Wiley and Sons, Inc., 111 River St. Hoboken, NJ 07030. Phone: 800-225-5945 or (201)748-6000 Fax: (201)748-6088 E-mail: info@wiley.com • URL: http://www.wiley.com • 2003. $78.00. Second edition. Describes how to calculate damages for patent, trademark, and copyright infringement. (Intellectual Property-General, Law, Accounting and Finance, Management, Licensing and Special Topics Series).

Intellectual Property Law: Commercial, Creative, and Industrial Property. American Lawyer Media, Inc., 105 Madison Ave. New York, NY 10016. Phone: 800-888-8300 or (212)779-9200 Fax: (212)481-8110 E-mail: lawcatalog@amlaw.com • URL: http://www.lawcatalog.com/ • Looseleaf. $229.00. Two volumes. Updated as needed. Covers the legal aspects of patents, trade secrets, copyright, technology protection, software protection, databases, etc. Also "compares the basic principles of U.S. law with those of Asian and European law." (Law Journal Press).

Intellectual Property Law Review. West Group, 610 Opperman Dr. Eagan, MN 55123. Phone: 800-328-4880 or (651)687-7000 Fax: 800-340-9378 E-mail: bookstore@westgroup.com • URL: http://www.westgroup.com • 1999. $299.00. Patent, trademark, and copyright practices.

Intellectual Property Newsletter. L L Professional Publishing, 69-77 Paul St. London EC2A 4LQ, United Kingdom. Phone: 44 207 5531000 Fax: 44 207 5531593 Monthly. $261.00 per year.

Intellectual Property Owners Association., 1255 23rd St. NW, Ste. 200 Washington, DC 20037. Phone: (202)466-2396 Fax: (202)466-2893 E-mail: info@ipo.org • URL: http://www.ipo.org • Corporations, lawyers, and individuals interested in intellectual property (patents, trademarks, copyrights, and trade secrets). Seeks to support and strengthen the patent, trademark, copyright, and trade secret laws. Monitors related legislative activities.

Intellectual Property Primary Law Soucebook. LexisNexis Matthew Bender, 1275 Broadway Albany, NY 12204-4026. Phone: 800-424-4200 or (518)487-3000 Fax: 800-828-8341 or (518)487-3584 E-mail: customer.support@lexisnexis.com • URL: http://www.lexisnexis.com/matthewbender/ • Annual. $88.00. Provides federal copyright, patent, and trademark statutes and regulations.

Intellectual Property Strategist. American Lawyer Media, Inc., 105 Madison Ave. New York, NY 10016. Phone: 800-888-8300 or (212)779-9200 Fax: (212)481-8110 E-mail: lawcatalog@amlaw.com • URL: http://www.lawcatalog.com/ • Monthly. $229.00 per year. Newsletter. Covers "business and litigation tactics" in the field of intellectual property law, including international issues. (A Law Journal Newsletter, formerly published by Leader Publications).

Intellectual Property Today., 369 W Northwest Highway Palantine, IL 60067. Phone: 800-232-8078 or (847)705-7194 Fax: (847)705-7112 E-mail: ddean@iptoday.com • URL: http://www.iptoday.com • Monthly. $96.00 per year. Covers legal developments in copyright, patents, trademarks, and licensing. Emphasizes the effect of new technology on intellectual property. Formerly *Law Works*.

Intelligence Data. Thomson FinancialPhone: 800-654-0393 Fax: (617)824-2477 • URL: http://www.intelligencedata.com • Fee-based Web site provides a wide variety of information relating to competitive intelligence, strategic planning, business development, mergers, acquisitions, sales, and marketing. "Intelliscope" feature offers searching of other Thomson units, such as Investext, MarkIntel, InSite 2, and Industry Insider. Weekly updating.

Intelligence Digest: A Review of World Affairs; International Political, Economic and Strategic Intelligence. Janes Information Group, 110 N Royal St. Alexandria, VA 22314. Phone: 800-824-0768 or (703)683-3700 Fax: 800-836-0297 or (703)836-0297 E-mail: info.us@janes.com • URL: http://www.janes.com • Weekly. $240.00 per year. Provides political, strategic and economic information. Gives warnings on political trends and current affairs. Published in England.

Intelligence Essentials for Everyone. Available from U. S. Government Printing Office, Washington, DC 20402. Phone: (202)512-1800 Fax: (202)512-2250 E-mail: gpoaccess@gpo.gov • URL: http://www.access.gpo.gov • 1999. $6.50. Issued by the Joint Military Intelligence College, Defense Intelligence Agency, U. S. Department of Defense (http://www.dia.mil/). Written for "businesses worldwide." Explains how to collect, process, analyze, and manage business intelligence information.

The Intelligent Asset Allocator: How to Build Your Portfolio to Maximize Returns and Minimize Risk. William J. Bernstein. McGraw-Hill, Two Penn Plaza New York, NY 10121. Phone: 800-722-4726 or (212)904-2000 Fax: (212)904-6096 E-mail: customer.service@mcgraw-hill.com • URL: http://www.mcgraw-hill.com • 2000. $29.95. Contains popularly written, conservative advice for the average investor. Explains such items as portfolio theory, market efficiency, stock valuation models, and index investing.

Intelligent Investor: A Book of Practical Counsel. Benjamin Graham. HarperInformation, 10 E. 53rd St. New York, NY 10022-5299. Phone: 800-242-7737 or (212)207-7000 Fax: 800-822-4090 or (212)207-7145 • URL: http://www.harpercollins.com • 1997. $30.00. Fourth revised edition.

Intelligent Systems Report (ISR). Lionheart Publishing, Inc., 506 Roswell St., SE, Ste. 220 Marietta, GA 30060. Phone: (770)431-0867 Fax: (770)432-6969 E-mail: lpi@lionhrtpub.com • URL: http://www.lionrtpub.com • Monthly. $299.00 per year. Newsletter. Formed by merger of*Neural Network News*and *AI Week*.

The Intentional Entrepreneur: Bringing Technology and Engineering to the Real New Economy. David L. Bodde. M. E. Sharpe, Inc., 80 Business Park Drive Armonk, NY 10504. Phone: 800-541-6563 or (914)273-1800 Fax: (914)273-2106 E-mail: custserv@mesharpe.com • URL: http://www.mesharpe.com • 2004. $69.95. Covers the "art of entrepreneurship" for engineering and technology professionals. Includes material on marketing, business models, venture capital, and intellectual property.

Inter-American Development Bank., 1300 New York Ave. NW Washington, DC 20577. Phone: (202)623-1000 Fax: (202)623-3096 E-mail: webmaster@iadb.org • URL: http://www.iadb.org • Western Hemisphere countries; other interested countries. Seeks to help accelerate the economic and social development of members in Latin America and the Caribbean. Works to: promote the investment of public and private capital in the region; use its own capital, as well as funds raised in financial markets and other available resources, for financing high-priority projects; supplement private investment when capital is not available on reasonable terms and conditions; encourage members to direct their policies toward better use of their natural resources while fostering growth of their foreign trade and development of complementary economies in Latin America; provide technical cooperation for the preparation, financing, and execution of development plans and projects, including the study of priorities and formulation of specific project proposals; contribute to the strengthening of the institutional base of lesser-developed member countries. Fosters equitable distribution of benefits of development. Sponsors projects which alleviate poverty, expand agricultural production, finance energy projects, promote modernization, develop industry, urban renewal, and health and education, and improve development institutions. Operates Fund for Special Operations, which is used to make long-term, low-interest loans to less-developed Latin American countries and a microenterprise division, which provides financing and technical support to low-income individuals and groups who ordinarily do not have access to public or commercial credit. Also administers the Venezuelan +Trust Fund and the Social Progress +Trust Fund. Cooperates with other development and financial institutions with similar goals. Offers technical training and seminars. Operates Speakers' Bureau.

Inter-American Tropical Tuna Commission., 8604 La Jolla Shores Dr., 8604 La Jolla Shores Dr. La Jolla, CA 92037-1508. Phone: (858)546-7100 Fax: (858)546-7133 E-mail: info@iattc.org • URL: http://www.iattc.org • Appointed commissioners representing Japan, France, Nicaragua, Guatemala, Peru, Mexico, Ecuador, El Salvador, Costa Rica, Panama, Vanuatu, Venezuela and the United States. Conducts studies on Pacific Ocean tunas and dolphins associated with tunas. Recommends conservation measures to member governments in order to maintain optimum levels of tuna stock and maximum level of dolphin stock. (Dolphins are frequently caught and inadvertently killed in tuna nets.) Monitors population and mortality levels; conducts research. Provides the secretariat for the International Dolphin Conservation Program. Responsibility are met with its two programs, the Tuna-Billfish Program and the Tuna-Dolphin program. The principal responsibilities of the Tuna-Billfish program are: to study the biology of tunas and related species of the eastern Pacific Ocean to estimate the effects that fishing and natural factors have on their abundance; to recommend appropriate conservation measures so that the stocks of fish can be maintained at levels which will afford maximum sustainable catches; to collect information on compliance with Commission resolutions. The principal responsibilities of the Tuna-Dolphin program are: to monitor the abundance of dolphins and their mortality incidental to purse-seine fishing in the eastern Pacific Ocean; to study the causes of mortality of dolphins during fishing operations and promote the use of fishing techniques and equipment that minimize these mortalities; to study the effects of different modes of fishing on the various fish and other animals of the pelagic ecosystem; and to provide a secretariat for the International Dolphin Conservation Program.

Inter-American Tropical Tuna Commission Annual Report. William H. Bayliff, editor. Inter-American Tropical Tuna Commission, 8604 La Jolla Shores Dr. La Jolla, CA 92037-1508. Phone: (858)546-7100 Fax: (858)546-7133 E-mail: wbayliff@iattc.org • URL: http://www.iattc.org • Annual. Price varies. Summary of scientific research carried on during the year. Includes financial statements. Text in English and Spanish.

Inter-American Tropical Tuna Commission Bulletin. Inter-American Tropical Tuna Commission, 8604 La Jolla Shores Dr. La Jolla, CA 92037-1508. Phone: (858)546-7100 Fax: (858)546-7133 E-mail: wbayliff@iatcc.org • URL: http://www.iattc.org • Irregular. Price varies. Description of results of scientific studies. Text in English and Spanish.

Inter-Arts Center., San Francisco State University, School of Creative Arts, 1600 Holloway Ave. San Francisco, CA 94132. Phone: (415)338-1478 Fax: (415)338-6159 E-mail: jimdavis@sfsu.edu • URL: http://www.sfsu.edu/~iac • Research areas include multimedia, computerized experimental arts processes, and digital sound.

Inter-NOT: Online & Internet Statistics Reality Check. Bruce Kushnick. New Networks Institute, 826 Broadway, Suite 900 New York, NY 10003. Phone: (212)777-5418 E-mail: comments@newnetworks.com • URL: http://www.newnetworks.com • Annual. $495.00. Compares, analyzes, and criticizes statistics issued by Nielsen Media, Forrester Research, FIND/SVP, Yankelovich Partners and many others relating to online and Internet activities. For example, estimates of the number of Internet users have ranged from about 40 million down to six million. Topics include "Adjusting for the Puffery" and "The Most Plausible Statistics."

Inter-University Consortium for Political and Social Research. University of Michigan

Inter-University Seminar on Armed Forces and Society., Political Science Department, Loyola University Chicago, 6525 N Sheridan Rd. Chicago, IL 60626. Phone: (773)508-2930 Fax: (773)508-2929 E-mail: secretariat@iusafs.org • URL: http://www.iusafs.org • Individuals from both public and private life in the academic, military, and government fields who are primarily researchers. Promotes the study of armed forces and society; provides a focal point for the exchange of information on the subject; stimulates research in the field on a cross-national basis. Compiles statistics; recommends a scholar to conduct seminars and give lectures.

Interactive Computer Systems: Videotex and Multimedia. Antone F. Alber. Perseus Publishing, 11 Cambridge Center Cambridge, MA 02142. Phone: (617)252-5200 Fax: (617)252-5285 E-mail: westview.order@perseusbooks.com • URL: http://www.perseusbooks.com • 1993. $79.50.

InterActive Consumers. MarketResearch.com, 641 Ave. of the Americas, 3rd Fl. New York, NY 10011. Phone: 800-298-5699 or (212)807-2629 Fax: (212)807-2716 E-mail: order@marketresearch.com • URL: http://www.marketresearch.com • Monthly. $395.00 per year. Newsletter. Covers the emerging markets for digital content, products, and services. Includes market information on telecommuting, online services, the Internet, online investing, and other areas of electronic commerce.

Interactive Content: Consumer Media Strategies Monthly. Jupitermedia, 23 Old Kings Highway S. Darien, CT 06820. Phone: 800-488-4345 or (203)662-2800 Fax: (203)655-4686 • URL: http://www.jmm.com • Monthly. $675.00 per year; with online edition, $775.00 per year. Newsletter. Covers the broad field of providing content (information, news, entertainment) for the Internet/World Wide Web.

Interactive Home: Consumer Technology Monthly. Jupiter Communications, 627 Broadway New York, NY 10012. Phone: (212)780-6060 Fax: (212)780-6075 Monthly. $625.00 per year; with online edition, $725.00 per year. Newsletter on devices to bring the Internet into the average American home. Covers TV set-top boxes, game devices, telephones with display screens, handheld computer communication devices, the usual PCs, etc.

Interactive Marketing and P R News: News and Practical Advice on Using Interactive Advertising and Marketing to Sell Your Products. PBI Media, LLC, 1201 7 Locks Rd. Potomac, MD 20854. Phone: 800-777-5006 or (301)344-2000 Fax: (301)309-3847 E-mail: clientservices@pbimedia.com • URL: http://www.pbimedia.com • Biweekly. $495.00 per year. Newsletter. Provides information and guidance on merchandising via CD-ROM ("multimedia catalogs"), the Internet, and interactive TV. Topics include "cybermoney", addresses for e-mail marketing, "virtual malls," and other interactive subjects. Formerly *Interactive Marketing News*.

Interactive Marketing: The Future Present. Edward Forrest and Richard Mizerski, editors. McGraw-Hill, 1221 Ave. of the Americas New York, NY 10020. Phone: 800-722-4726 or (212)512-2000 Fax: (212)512-4502 E-mail: customer.service@mcgraw-hill.com • URL: http://www.mcgraw-hill.com • 1995. $47.95. Contains articles on the collection and analysis of interactive marketing data, database management, interactive media, marketing research strategies, and related topics.(NTC Business Book Series).

Interactive Multimedia and Collaborative Communications Alliance., PO Box 756 Syosset, NY 11791-0756. Phone: (516)818-8184 Fax: (516)922-2170 E-mail: staff@imcca.org • URL: http://www.imcca.org • Members are vendors and users of teleconferencing equipment. Formerly International Teleconferencing Association.

Interactive Music Handbook: The Definitive Guide to Internet Music Strategies, Enhanced CD Production and Business Development. Jodi Summers. Allworth Press, 10 E 23rd St., Ste. 510 New York, NY 10010. Phone: 800-491-2808 or (212)777-8395 Fax: (212)777-8261 E-mail: pub@allworth.com • URL: http://www.allworth.com • 1996. $19.95. Covers interactive or enhanced music CD-ROMs and online music for producers, audio technicians, and musicians. Includes case studies and interviews.

Interactive Television Demystified. Jerry C. Whitaker. McGraw-Hill, 1221 Ave. of the Americas New York, NY 10020. Phone: 800-722-4726 or (212)512-2000 Fax: (212)512-4502 E-mail: customer.service@mcgraw-hill.com • URL: http://www.mcgraw-hill.com • 2001. $49.95. Discusses the current applications and future possibilities of interactive TV, including business models. Case histories are provided. (Demystified Series).

Interactive TV Investor. Paul Kagan Associates, Inc., 126 Clock Tower Pl. Carmel, CA 93923-8746. Phone: (831)624-1536 Fax: (831)625-3225 E-mail: info@kagan.com • URL: http://www.kagan.com • Semimonthly. $895.00. Provides current information on interactive-TV applications and technical developments. Includes forecasts. Formerly *Interactive Television*.

Interactive TV Investor Buyer's Guide and Directory. Paul Kagan Associates Inc., 126 Clock Tower Pl. Carmel, CA 93923-8746. Phone: (831)624-1536 Fax: (831)625-3225 E-mail: info@kagan.com • URL: http://www.kagan.com • Annual. Price on application. (A special issue of the periodical *Convergence*.)

Interactive Update. Alexander & Associates, 38 E 29th St., 10th Fl. New York, NY 10016. Phone: (212)684-2333 Fax: (212)684-0291 E-mail: research@researchers.com Description: Provides information on the interactive entertainment industry, focusing on software.

Interest Rate Risk Measurement and Management. Sanjay K. Nawalkha and Donald R. Chambers, editors. Institutional Investor, Inc., 225 Park Ave., S New York, NY 10003. Phone: (212)224-3664 • URL: http://www.institutionalinvestor.com • 1999. $95.00. Provides interest rate risk models for fixed-income derivatives and for investments by various kinds of financial institutions.

Interest Rate Service. World Reports Ltd., 280 Madison Ave., Ste. 280 New York, NY 10016-0802. Phone: (212)679-0095 Fax: (212)679-1094 10 times a year. $950.00 per year.

Interface Culture: How New Technology Transforms the Way We Create and Communicate. Steven Johnson. HarperSanFrancisco, 353 Sacramento St., Ste. 500 San Francisco, CA 94111. Phone: 800-242-7737 or (415)477-4400 Fax: (415)477-4444 • URL: http://www.harpercollins.com • 1997. $24.00. A discussion of how computer interfaces and online technology ("cyberspace") affect society in general.

Intergovernmental Relations. Available from U. S. Government Printing Office, Washington, DC 20402. Phone: (202)512-1800 Fax: (202)512-2250 E-mail: gpoaccess@gpo.gov • URL: http://www.access.gpo.gov • Annual. Free. Lists government publications. (Subject Bibliography 211.)

Interior Design. Reed Business Information, 360 Park Ave., S New York, NY 10010. Phone: 800-446-6551 or (646)746-6400 Fax: (646)746-7028 E-mail: corporatecommunications@reedbusiness.com • URL: http://www.reedbusiness.com • Monthly. $64.95 per year. For the professional designed, provides information on trends and new products.

Interior Design Buyers Guide. Reed Business Information, 360 Park Ave., S New York, NY 10010. Phone: 800-662-7776 or (646)746-6400 E-mail: corporatecommunications@reedbusiness.com • URL: http://www.reedbusiness.com • Annual. $16.95. Included with subscription to *Interior Design*

Interior Design for Libraries: Drawing on Function and Appeal. Carol R. Brown. American Library Association, 50 E Huron St. Chicago, IL 60611-2795. Phone: 800-545-2433 or (312)944-6780 Fax: (312)440-9374 E-mail: ala@ala.org • URL: http://www.ala.org • 2002. $45.00. Covers furniture, lighting, signs, acoustics, and other items important to interior design. Contains many illustrations of library interiors, including color plates.

Interior Design Laboratory.

Interior Designer. Entrepreneur Media, Inc., 2445 McCabe Way Irvine, CA 92614. Phone: 800-421-2300 or (949)261-2325 Fax: (949)261-0234 E-mail: entmag@entrepreneur.com • URL: http://www.entrepreneur.com • Looseleaf. $59.50. A practical guide to starting an interior design and decoration business. Covers profit potential, start-up costs, market size evaluation, owner's time required, pricing, accounting, advertising, promotion, etc. (Start-Up Business Guide No. E1314.)

Interior Graphic Standards. Maryrose T. McGowan. John Wiley and Sons, Inc., 111 River St. Hoboken, NJ 07030. Phone: 800-225-5945 or (201)748-6000 Fax: (201)748-6088 E-mail: info@wiley.com • URL: http://www.wiley.com • 2003. $175.00. Provides guidelines for the planning and detailing of commercial and residential interiors. Includes more than 3,000 architectural drawings.

Interiors and Sources. L. C. Clark Publishing Co., Inc., 840 U.S. Highway 1, Ste. 330 North Palm Beach, FL 33408. Phone: (561)627-3393 Fax: (561)694-6578 E-mail: info@isdesignet.com • URL: http://www.isdesignet.com • Bimonthly. $27.00 per year. Promotes professionalism for interior designers and design firms. Includes special features on office systems, work stations, and office furniture.

Interiors and Sources: Directory and Buyer's Guide. L. C. Clark Publishing Co., Inc., 840 U.S. Highway 1, Ste. 330 North Palm Beach, FL 33408. Phone: (561)627-3393 Fax: (561)694-6578 E-mail: info@isdesignet.com • URL: http://www.isdesignet.com • Annual. $10.00. Lists sources of surface materials, furniture, lighting, etc., for interior designers.

Internal Auditing Alert. Warren, Gorham & Lamont Inc., 117 E Stevens Ave. Valhalla, NY 10595-1254. Phone: 800-950-1216 or (914)749-5000 Fax: (914)741-2412 E-mail: research@researchers.com • URL: http://www.riahome.com • Description: Presents unique coverage that includes reviews and explanations of current Institute of Internal Auditors releases, appraisals of new audit techniques, and highlights of successful audit management practices.

Internal Auditing Manual. RIA, 395 Hudson St. New York, NY 10014. Phone: 800-950-1216 or 800-431-9025 E-mail: riahome@riag.com • URL: http://www.riahome.com • Annual. $260.00. Available online.

Internal Auditor. Institute of Internal Auditors, Inc., 249 Maitland Ave. Altamonte Springs, FL 32701-4201. Phone: (407)830-7600 Fax: (407)830-4832 E-mail: custserv@theiia.org • URL: http://www.theiia.org • Bimonthly. $60.00 per year.

Internal Auditor's Handbook. Paul E. Heeschen. Institute of Internal Auditors, Inc., 247 Maitland Ave. Altamonte Springs, FL 32701-4201. Phone: (407)830-7600 Fax: (407)831-5171 • URL: http://www.theiia.org • 1984. $43.75.

Internal Revenue Bulletin. Research Institute of America, 395 Hudson St. New York, NY 10014. Phone: 800-343-8260 or (212)367-6300 Fax: (703)683-4824 E-mail: research@researchers.com • URL: http://www.access.gpo.gov • Description: Presents new treasury and IRS releases in full official text. Contains rulings and decisions, releases on treaties, tax legislation, administrative and procedural releases, disbarment and suspensions.

Internal Revenue Code. RIA, 395 Hudson St. New York, NY 10014. Phone: 800-950-1216 or 800-431-9055 Fax: (212)367-6300 E-mail: riahome@riag.com • URL: http://www.riahome.com • Annual. $86.50. Provides full text of the Internal Revenue Code (5,000 pages), including procedural and administrative provisions.

Internal Revenue Cumulative Bulletin. Available from U. S. Government Printing Office, Washington, DC 20402. Phone: (202)512-1800 Fax: (202)512-2250 E-mail: gpoaccess@gpo.gov • URL: http://www.access.gpo.gov • Semiannual. Issued by the Internal Revenue Service. Cumulates all items of a "permanent nature" appearing in the weekly *Internal Revenue Bulletin*.

Internal Revenue Manual: Audit and Administration. CCH, Inc., 2700 Lake Cook Rd. Riverwoods, IL 60015. Phone: 800-835-5224 or (847)267-7000 E-mail: cust_serv@cch.com • URL: http://www.cch.com • Irregular. $1,254.00. Six looseleaf volumes. Reproduces IRS tax administration provisions and procedures.

Internal Revenue Service Data Book. Available from U. S. Government Printing Office, Washington, DC 20402. Phone: (202)512-1800 Fax: (202)512-2250 E-mail: gpoaccess@gpo.gov • URL: http://www.access.gpo.gov • Annual. $8.00. "Contains statistical tables and organizational information previously included in the Internal Revenue Service annual report." (Internal Revenue Service Publication, 55B.)

Internal Revenue Service IRS.gov. Internal Revenue ServicePhone: 800-829-1040 or (202)622-5000 Fax: (202)622-5844 • URL: http://www.irs.gov • Web site provides a wide variety of tax information, including IRS forms and publications. Searching is available. Fees: Free.

International ABC Aerospace Directory. Jane's Information Group Ltd., Sentinel House, 163 Brighton Rd. Coulsdon CR5 2YH, United Kingdom. Phone: 800-824-0768 or (44)20 87003700 Fax: 800-836-0297 or (44)20 87631006 E-mail: customer.servicesuk@janes.com • URL: http://www.janes.com • Covers: Approximately 28,000 companies and organizations involved in the aerospace industry, including civil and military organizations, aircraft manufacturers, Civil Aviation Authorities, air force bases, leasing companies, airport authorities, engine manufacturers, distributors of components, and maintenance contractors; international coverage. Entries include: Name, address, phone, fax, names and titles of key personnel, description of products/services.

International Abstracts in Operations Research. International Federation of Operational Research Societies. Palgrave Macmillan Ltd., Houndsmill Basingstoke RG21 6XS, United Kingdom. Phone: 44 01256 329242 Fax: 44 01256 320109 E-mail: jnlsupport@palgrave.com • URL: http://www.palgrave-journals.com • Bimonthly. Institutions, $980.00 per year. Includes print and online editions.

International Academy of Trial Lawyers Roster. International Academy of Trial Lawyers, 5841 Cedar Rd., Suite 204 Minneapolis, MN 55416. Phone: (612)546-2364 Fax: (612)545-6073 E-mail: iatl@llmsi.com • URL: http://www.iatl.net • Biennial. Free. More than 2,400 trial lawyers board certified in civil and criminal trial advocacy; members of the board.

International Acronyms, Initialisms, and Abbreviations Dictionary. Gale Cengage Learning, 27500 Drake Rd. Farmington Hills, MI 48331-3535. Phone: 800-877-GALE or (248)699-4253 Fax: 800-414-5043 E-mail: gale.galeord@cengage.com • URL: http://gale.cengage.com • 2001. $250.00. Fifth edition. Contains over 210,000 English and non-English entries used internationally and in specific countries.

International Action Center., Solidarity Center, 55 W 17th St., Ste. 5C New York, NY 10011. Phone: (212)633-6646 Fax: (212)633-2889 E-mail: iacenter@action-mail.org • URL: http://www.iacenter.org • Opposes U.S. militarism. Organizes opposition to U.S. intervention abroad and to racism and political repression at home. Sponsors educational activities and research.

International Advertising Association., 275 Madison Ave., Ste. 2102 New York, NY 10016. Phone: (212)557-1133 Fax: (212)983-0455 E-mail: membership@iaaglobal.org • URL: http://www.iaaglobal.org • Global network of advertisers, advertising agencies, the media and related services, spanning 99 countries. Demonstrates to governments and consumers the benefits of advertising as the foundation of diverse, independent media. Protects and advances freedom of commercial speech and consumer choice, encourages greater practice and acceptance of advertising self-regulation, provides a forum to debate emerging professional marketing communications issues and their consequences in the fast-changing world environment, and takes the lead in state-of-the-art professional development through education and training for the marketing communications industry of tomorrow. Conducts research on such topics as restrictions and taxes on advertising, advertising trade practices and related information, and advertising expenditures around the world. Sponsors IAA Education Program. Has compiled recommendations for international advertising standards and practices.

national Advertising Association Membership Directory. International Advertising Association, 521 Fifth Ave., Suite 807 New York, NY 10175-0003. Phone: (212)557-1133 Fax: (212)983-0455 E-mail: iaa@iaaglobal.org Annual. Membership. Available only online. Over 3,600 advertisers, advertising agencies, media, and other firms involved in advertising.

national Advertising: Realities and Myths. John P. Jones, editor. Sage Publications, Inc., 2455 Teller Rd. Thousand Oaks, CA 91320. Phone: 800-818-7243 or (805)499-9774 Fax: 800-583-2665 or (805)499-0871 E-mail: webmaster@sagepub.com • URL: http://www.sagepub.com • 1999. $95.95. Includes articles by advertising professionals in 10 different countries. (Advertising Series).

national Aerospace Abstracts. American Institute of Aeronautics and Astronautics, Inc. CSA, 1801 Alexander Graham Bell Dr., Ste. 500 Reston, VA 20191. Phone: 800-639-2422 or (703)264-7500 Fax: (703)264-7551 E-mail: custserv@aiaa.org • URL: http://www.aiaa.org • 11 times a year. $2,260.00 per year. Includes print and online editions.

national Agreement on Jute and Jute Products. United Nations Publications, United Nations Concourse Level, First Ave., 46th St. New York, NY 10017. Phone: 800-553-3210 or (212)963-7680 Fax: (212)963-4910 E-mail: bookstore@un.org • URL: http://www.un.org/publications • 1992. Second revised edition. An international trade agreement.

national Agreement on Olive Oil and Table Olives. United Nations Publications, United Nations Concourse Level, First Ave., 46th St. New York, NY 10017. Phone: 800-553-3210 or (212)963-7680 Fax: (212)963-4910 E-mail: bookstore@un.org • URL: http://www.un.org/publications • 1986. Trade agreements.

rnational Air Transport Association., 703 Waterford Way, NW 62nd Ave., Ste. 600 Miami, FL 33126. Phone: (305)264-7772 Fax: (305)264-8088 E-mail: membership@iaaglobal.org • URL: http://www1.iata.org/ • Represents the airline industries; promotes safe, reliable, secure and economical air services worldwide.

rnational Airline Passengers Association., PO Box 700188 Dallas, TX 75370-0188. Phone: 800-821-4272 or (972)404-9980 Fax: (972)233-5348 E-mail: info.dallas@iapa.com • URL: http://www.iapa.com • Persons who are frequent users of airlines. Represents frequent flyers in matters of safety, comfort, convenience, and economy. Conducts semiannual survey regarding travel preferences and opinions in order to present consumers' viewpoints to airlines and government agencies. Provides discounts on hotels and car rentals. Disseminates travel information through magazines and literature. Compiles statistics. **Convention/Meeting:** none.

International Alliance of Executive and Professional Women., 8405 Grennsboro Dr., Ste. 800 McLean, VA 22102. Phone: (703)506-3284 E-mail: info@tiaw.org • URL: http://www.tiaw.org • Facilitates communication (networking) among women executives. Formerly The International Alliance, An Association of Executive and Professional Women.

rnational Amusement Industry Buyers Guide. Amusement Business, 49 Music Sq. W Nashville, TN 37203. Phone: 800-449-1402 or (646)654-5549 Fax: (615)327-1575 E-mail: info@amusementbusiness.com • URL: http://www.amusementbusiness.com • Covers: manufacturers, importers, and suppliers of amusement rides, games, and merchandise as well as food and drink equipment and supplies. Entries include: Company name, address, phone, fax, name of principal executive, list of products or services.

ernational and Comparative Law Quarterly. Oxford University Press, Journals, 2001 Evans Rd. Cary, NC 27513. Phone: 800-852-7323 or (919)677-0977 Fax: (919)677-1714 E-mail: jnlorders@oup-usa.org • URL: http://www.oup-usa.org • Quarterly. Institutions, $236.00 per year; with online edition, $248.00 per year.

ernational Animated Film Society, ASIFA - Hollywood., 2114 W Burbank Blvd. Burbank, CA 91506. Phone: (818)842-8330 Fax: (818)842-5645 E-mail: info@asifa-hollywood.org • URL: http://www.asifa-hollywood.org • Represents professional animation artists, fans, and students of animation. Works to promote and advance the art of animation.

ernational Association for Exhibition Management., 8111 LBJ Fwy., Ste. 750 Dallas, TX 75251-1313. Phone: (972)458-8002 Fax: (972)458-8119 E-mail: iaem@iaem.org • URL: http://www.iaem.org • Formerly International Association of Exposition Management.

ernational Association for Feminist Economics., c/o Barbara Krohn, 100D Roberts Hall, Bucknell University Lewisburg, PA 17837. Phone: (570)577-3637 Fax: (570)577-3451 E-mail: iaffe@bucknell.edu • URL: http://www.iaffe.org • Members are economists having a feminist viewpoint. Promotes greater economic opportunities for women.

ernational Association for Insurance Law in the United States., PO Box 9001 Mount Vernon, NY 10552. Phone: (914)699-2020 Fax: (914)699-2025 • URL: http://www.aida.org • Members are attorneys and others concerned with the international aspects of insurance law. Affiliated with International Association for Insurance Law-United Kingdom.

ernational Association for Research in Income and Wealth., c/o New York University, Dept. of Economics, Rm. 700, 269 Mercer St. New York, NY 10003. Phone: (212)924-4386 Fax: (212)366-5067 E-mail: iariw@nyu.edu • URL: http://www.econ.nyu.edu/iariw • Specialists in the field of national income accounting.

International Association of Administrative Professionals., 10502 NW Ambassador Dr. Kansas City, MO 64195-0404. Phone: (816)891-6600 Fax: (816)891-9118 E-mail: service@iaap-hq.org • URL: http://www.iaap-hq.org • Formerly Professional Secretaries International.

International Association of Agricultural Economists., c/o Walter Armbruster, 1211 W 22nd St., Ste. 216 Oak Brook, IL 60523-2197. Phone: (603)571-9393 Fax: (603)571-9580 E-mail: iaae@farmfoundation.org • URL: http://www.iaae-agecon.org/ • Formerly International Conference of Agricultural Economists.

International Association of Amusement Parks and Attractions., 1448 Duke St. Alexandria, VA 22314. Phone: (703)836-4800 Fax: (703)836-9678 E-mail: iaapa@iaapa.org • URL: http://www.iaapa.org • Formerly International Association of Amusement Parks.

International Association of Amusement Parks and Attractions International Directory and Buyers' Guide. International Association of Amusement Parks and Attractions, 1448 Duke St. Alexandria, VA 22314-3403. Phone: (703)836-4800 Fax: (703)836-4801 E-mail: iaapa@iaapa.org • URL: http://www.iaapa.org • Annual. $83.00. Over 1,800 member amusement parks, attractions and industry suppliers.

International Association of Assembly Managers., 635 Fritz Dr., Ste. 100 Coppell, TX 75019-4442. Phone: 800-935-4226 or (972)255-8020 Fax: (972)255-9582 E-mail: dexter.king@iaam.org • URL: http://www.iaam.org • Members are auditorium, theater, exhibit hall, and other facility managers. Formerly International Association of Auditorium Managers.

International Association of Assessing Officers., 130 E Randolph St. Chicago, IL 60601. Phone: (312)819-6100 Fax: (312)819-6149 E-mail: membership@iaaa.org • URL: http://www.iaao.org • Formerly National Association of Assessing Officers.

International Association of Assessing Officers: Membership Directory. International Association of Assessing Officers, 130 E. Randolph St., Suite 850 Chicago, IL 60601-6217. Phone: (312)819-6100 Fax: (312)819-6149 E-mail: webmaster@iaao.org • URL: http://www.iaao.org • Annual. $400.00. Lists about 8,500 state and local officials concerned with valuation of property tax.

International Association of Association Management Companies., 414 Plaza Dr., Suite 209 Westmont, IL 60559. Phone: (630)655-1669 Fax: (630)655-0391 E-mail: info@iaamc.org • URL: http://www.iaamc.org • Formerly Institute of Association Management Companies.

International Association of Business Communicators.

International Association of Chiefs of Police (IACP)., 515 N. Washington St. Alexandria, VA 22314. Phone: 800-843-4227 or (703)836-6767 Fax: (703)836-4543 E-mail: information@theiacp.org • URL: http://www.theiacp.org • The IACP Law Enforcement Information Management Section is concerned with law enforcement management information systems, including data processing, telecommunications, and automated systems. Formerly Chiefs of Police of the United States and Canada.

International Association of Clothing Designers and Executives., 475 Park Ave. S, 9th Fl. New York, NY 10016. Fax: (212)545-1709 E-mail: dmschmida@aol.com Formerly International Associatin of Clothing Designers.

International Association of Clothing Designers Convention Yearbook. International Association of Clothing Designers, 475 Park Ave., S, 9th Fl. New York, NY 10016. Phone: (212)545-1769 E-mail: dmschmida@aol.com Annual. Price on application. For designers of men's and boy's clothing.

International Association of Commercial Collectors., 4040 W. 70th St. Minneapolis, MN 55435. Phone: (952)925-0760 Fax: (952)926-1624 E-mail: iacc@collector.com • URL: http://www.commercialcollector.com • Collection agencies specializing in the recovery of commercial accounts receivable. Formerly American Commercial Collectors Association.

International Association of Conference Translators.

International Association of Convention and Visitor Bureaus.

International Association of Counseling Services., 101 S Whiting St., Ste. 211 Alexandria, VA 22304. Phone: (703)823-9840 Fax: (703)823-9843 E-mail: iacsinc@earthlink.net • URL: http://www.iacsinc.org • Formerly American Board on Professional Standards in Vocational Counseling.

International Association of Defense Counsel., 1 N Franklin St., Ste. 1205 Chicago, IL 60606. Phone: (312)368-1494 Fax: (312)368-1854 E-mail: office@iadclaw.org • URL: http://www.iadclaw.org • Affiliated with Defense Research Institute. Formerly International Association of Insurance Counsel.

International Association of Drilling Contractors., 15810 Park Ten Place, No. 242 Houston, TX 77210-4287. Phone: (281)578-7171 Fax: (281)578-0589 E-mail: info@iadc.org • URL: http://www.iadc.org • Includes an Offshore Committee. Formerly American Association of Oilwell Drilling Contractors.

International Association of Electrical Inspectors.

International Association of Fairs and Expositions.

International Association of Financial Crimes Investigators., 837 Embarcadero Ave., Suite 5 El Dorado Hills, CA 95762. Phone: (919)939-5000 Fax: (919)939-0395 E-mail: admin@iafci.org • URL: http://www.iafci.org • Members are officials who investigate criminal violations of credit card laws. Formerly International Association of Financial Crimes.

International Association of Financial Crimes Investigators: Membership Directory. International Association of Financial Crimes Investigators, 385 Bel Marin Keys Blvd., Suite H Novato, CA 94949-5636. Phone: (415)897-8800 Fax: (415)898-0798 Annual. Membership. About 3,500 firms and individuals engaged in investigation of fraudulent use of credit cards. Formerly *International Association of Credit Card Investigators-Membership Directory*. Formerly International Association of Credit Card Investigators.

International Association of Fire Chiefs.

International Association of Fire Fighters.

International Association of Food Industry Suppliers., 1451 Dolley Madison Blvd. McLean, VA 22101-3850. Phone: (703)761-2600 Fax: (703)761-4334 E-mail: info@iafis.org • URL: http://www.iafis.org • Formerly Dairy and Food Industries Supply Association.

International Association of Food Industry Suppliers Reporter. International Association on Food Industry Suppliers, 1451 Dolley Madison Blvd. McLean, VA 22101-3850. Phone: (703)761-2600 Fax: (703)761-4334 E-mail: info@iafis.org Monthly. Free.

International Association of Healthcare Central Service Materiel Management., 213 W. Institute Place, Suite 307 Chicago, IL 60610. Phone: 800-962-8274 or (312)440-0078 Fax: (312)440-9474 E-mail: mailbox@iahcsmm.com • URL: http://www.iahcsmm.com • Members are professional personnel responsible for management and distribution of supplies from a central service material management (purchasing) department of a hospital. Formerly International Association of Hospital Central Service Management.

International Association of Hydraulic Engineering and Research., Paseo Bajo Virgen del Puerto 3 28005 Madrid, Spain. Phone: 34 91 3357908 Fax: 34 91 3357935 E-mail: iahr@iahr.org • URL: http://www.iahr.net • Formerly International Association for Hydraulic Research.

International Association of Industrial Accident Boards and Commissions., 5610 Medical Ctr, Ste. 24 Madison, WI 53719. Phone: (608)663-6355 Fax: (608)663-1546 E-mail: fhowe@iaiabc.org • URL: http://www.iaiabc.org • Members are government agencies, insurance companies, lawyers, unions, self-insurers, and others with an interest in industrial safety and the administration of workers' compensation laws.

International Association of Jewish Vocational Services., 1845 Walnut St., No. 640 Philadelphia, PA 19103. Phone: (215)854-0233 Fax: (215)854-0212 E-mail: coheng@iajvs.org • URL: http://www.iajvs.org • Formerly National Association of Jewish Vocational Services.

International Association of Machinists and Aerospace Workers., 9000 Machinists Place Upper Marlboro, MD 20772-2687. Phone: (301)967-4500 Fax: (301)967-4595 E-mail: websteward@goiam.org • URL: http://www.iamaw.org/ • Formerly International Association of Machinists.

International Association of Meteorology and Atmospheric Sciences.

International Association of Personnel in Employment Security., 1801 Louisville Rd. Frankfort, KY 40601. Phone: 888-898-9960 or (502)223-4459 Fax: (502)233-4127 E-mail: iapes@iapes.org • URL: http://www.iapes.org • Formerly International Association of Public Employment Services.

International Association of Plastic Distributors., 4707 College Blvd., Suite 105 Leawood, KS 66211. Phone: (913)345-1005 Fax: (913)345-1006 E-mail: iapd@iapd.org • URL: http://www.iapd.org • Formerly National Association of Plastics Distributors.

International Association of Ports and Harbors.

International Association of Printing House Craftsmen.

International Association of Professional Bureaucrats., c/o Dr. James H. Boren, 2400 Jolinda Whitesboro, TX 76273. Phone: (903)564-9290 Fax: (903)564-9430 E-mail: jimboren@cox-intenet.com • URL: http://www.jimboren.com/inataprobu • Motto of Association: "When in doubt, mumble."

International Association of Refrigerated Warehouses.

International Association of Technological University Libraries.

International Association of Theoretical and Applied Limnology.

International Auction Records: Engravings, Drawings, Watercolors, Paintings, Sculpture. Archer Fields, Inc., 155 Sixth Ave. New York, NY 10013. Phone: 800-338-2665 or (212)627-1999 Fax: (212)627-9484 1993. $179.00. Back volumes available for most years.

International Authors and Writers Who's Who. Available from Taylor & Francis, Inc., 325 Chestnut St. Philadelphia, PA 19106. Phone: 800-821-8312 or (215)785-5800 Fax: (215)785-5515 E-mail: info@taylorandfrancis.com • URL: http://www.taylorandfrancis.com • Biennial. $180.00. About 8,000 authors, writers, and poets, primarily American and British but including writers from nearly 40 countries in the English-speaking world. Published by Melrose Press Ltd.

International Band and Orchestra Products Association.

International Bank Credit Analyst. BCA Publications Ltd., 1002 Sherbrooke St., W., 16th Fl. Montreal, QC, Canada H3A 3L6. Phone: (514)499-9706 Fax: (514)499-9709 Monthly. $795.00 per year. "A monthly forecast and analysis of currency movements, interest rates, and stock market developments in the principal countries, based on a continuous appraisal of money and credit trends worldwide." Includes many charts and graphs providing international coverage of money, credit, and securities.

International Banking. Peter K. Oppenheim. American Bankers Association, 1120 Connecticut Ave., N. W. Washington, DC 20036-3971. Phone: 800-226-5377 or (202)663-5000 Fax: (202)663-7543 E-mail: custserv@aba.com • URL: http://www.aba.com • 1991. $51.00. Sixth edition. Covers letters of credit, money transfers, collections, and other aspects of global banking.

International Bar Association., 1 Stephen St., 10th Fl. London W1T 1AT, United Kingdom. Phone: 44 20 76916868 Fax: 44 20 76916544 E-mail: member@int-bar.org • URL: http://www.ibanet.org • National bar associations and individual members of the legal profession working in the field of international law in 183 countries. Works to advance the science of jurisprudence; promotes uniformity in related legal fields and administration of justice under law. Seeks to establish and maintain friendly relations among members of the legal profession worldwide. Supports the legal principles and aims of the United Nations.

International Bearing Interchange (IBI Guide). Interchange, Inc., P.O. Box 16244 Saint Louis Park, MN 55416. Phone: 800-669-6208 or (612)929-6669 Biennial. $195.00. Two volumes. Cross-references for ball bearing, straight and curved roller bearings, tappered cones and cups, pillow blocks and flange units; from the latest back to 1918.

International Bee Research Association., 18 North Rd. Cardiff CF1 3DT, United Kingdom. Phone: (999)44 2920 372409 Fax: (999)44 2920 665522 E-mail: mail@ibra.org.uk • URL: http://www.ibra.org.uk • Individuals, beekeeping societies, and research organizations in 130 countries. Promotes and coordinates bee research work and research on pollination. Provides worldwide information service through publications, correspondence, and journals. Aids beekeepers and promotes beekeeping as a sustainable activity in developing countries.

International Beverage Packaging Association., Anheuser-Busch, Inc., One Ocean Spray Dr. Fort Collins, CO 80524. Phone: 888-662-3263 or (508)946-1000 Fax: (702)566-7166 E-mail: info@ibpa.org • URL: http://www.ibpa.org • Beverage industry personnel interested in the concerns of the beverage packaging industry, including soft drink, beer, bottled water, juice manufacturers and packagers, allied suppliers.

International Bibliography of Studies on Alcohol. Sarah S. Jordy, compiler. Rutgers Center of Alcohol Studies Publications, Rutgers State University of New Jersey, 607 Alison Rd. Pisataway, NJ 08854-8001. Phone: (732)445-2190 Fax: (732)445-3500 E-mail: chrouse@rci.rutgers.edu • URL: http://www.rci.rutgers.edu • $200.00. Three volumes. Volume one, *References*, 1901-1950; volume two, *Indexes*. 1901-1980; volume three, *References* and *Indexes*, 1951-1960.

International Bibliography of the Social Sciences: Economics. British Library of Political and Economic Science. Routledge, 29 W. 35th St. New York, NY 10001. Phone: 800-634-7064 or (212)216-7800 Fax: 800-248-4724 E-mail: cs@routledge.com • URL: http://www.routledge-ny.com • 1995. $250.00. (International Bibliography of the Social Sciences Series).

International Black Writers and Artists., PO Box 43576 Los Angeles, CA 90043. Phone: (213)964-3721 E-mail: ibwa_la@yahoo.com • URL: http://members.tripod.com/~ibwa/home.htm • Seeks to discover and support new black writers. Conducts research and monthly seminars in poetry, fiction, nonfiction, music, and jazz. Provides writing services and children's services. Maintains speakers' bureau. Offers referral service. Plans to establish hall of fame, biographical archives, and museum.

International Booksellers Federation., rue de la Science 10 B-1000 Brussels, Belgium. Phone: 32 2 2234940 Fax: 32 2 2234938 E-mail: ibf.booksellers@skynet.be • URL: http://www.ibf-booksellers.org • Booksellers' associations (20) are members and booksellers (200) are associate members. Promotes international cooperation among booksellers and associations of booksellers. Encourages exchange of ideas and experiences and discussion of common problems.

International Bottled Water Association., 1700 Diagonal Rd., Ste. 650 Alexandria, VA 22314. Phone: 800-WAT-ER11 or (703)683-5213 Fax: (703)683-4074 E-mail: ibwainfo@bottledwater.org • URL: http://www.bottledwater.org • Bottled water plants; distributors; manufacturers of bottled water supplies; international bottlers, distributors and suppliers. Conducts seminars and technical research.

International Bridge, Tunnel and Turnpike Association., 1146 19th St., N.W., No. 800 Washington, DC 20036. Phone: (202)659-4620 Fax: (202)659-0500 E-mail: pjones@ibbta.org • URL: http://www.ibtta.org • Formerly American Bridge, Tunnel and Turnpike Association.

International Broadcast Engineer. DMG World Media Ltd., Queensway House, 2 Queensway Red Hill RH1 1QS, United Kingdom. Phone: 44 1737 855527 Fax: 44 1737 855470 • URL: http://www.dmgworldmedia.com • Eight times a year. $119.00 per year.

International Bureau of Fiscal Documentation.

International Bureau of Weights and Measures., 2 bis Grande Rue 1-92310 Sevres, France. Phone: 33 1 45077070 Fax: 33 1 45342021 E-mail: webmaster@bipm.org • URL: http://www.bipm.org • Works for the establishment of international weights and measures standards, including international time standards. Absorbed International Time Bureau-Time Section.

International Business. Shenkar. John Wiley and Sons, Inc., 111 River St. Hoboken, NJ 07030-5774. Phone: 800-225-5945 or (201)748-6000 Fax: (201)748-6088 E-mail: custserv@wiley.com • URL: http://www.wiley.com • 2003. $88.95.

International Business and Multinational Enterprises. Stefan H. Robock and Kenneth Simmonds. McGraw-Hill, 1221 Ave. of the Americas New York, NY 10020. Phone: 800-722-4726 or (212)512-2000 Fax: (212)512-4502 E-mail: customer.service@mcgraw-hill • URL: http://www.mcgraw-hill.com • 1988. $68.50. Fourth edition.

International Business Finance: A Bibliography of Selected Business and Academic Sources. Raj Aggarwal. Greenwood Publishing Group, Inc., 88 Post Rd., W Westport, CT 06881. Phone: 800-225-5800 or (203)226-3571 Fax: (203)431-2214 E-mail: customer-service@greenwood.com • URL: http://www.greenwood.com • 1984. $72.50.

International Business Handbook. Vishnu H. Kirpalani, editor. Haworth Press, Inc., 10 Alice St. Binghamton, NY 13904-1580. Phone: 800-429-6784 or (607)722-5857 Fax: (607)722-1424 E-mail: getinfo@haworthpressinc.com • URL: http://www.haworthpressinc.com • 1990. $89.95. (International Business Series: No. 1).

International Business Information: How to Find It, How to Use It. Ruth A. Pagell and Michael Halperin. Glenlake Publishing Co., Ltd., 1261 W Glenlake Chicago, IL 60660. Phone: (773)262-9436 Fax: (773)262-9765 E-mail: info@glenlake.com • URL: http://www.glenlake.com • 2000. $65.00.

International Business Information on the Web: Searcher Magazine's Guide to Sites and Strategies for Global Business Research. Sheri R. Lanza. Information Today, Inc., 143 Old Marlton Pike Medford, NJ 08055-8750. Phone: 800-300-9868 or (609)654-6266 Fax: (609)654-4309 E-mail: custserv@infotoday.com • URL: http://www.infotoday.com • 2001. $29.95. (CyberAge Books.)

International Business Institute.

International Business Planning: Law and Taxation (United States). William P. Streng and Jeswald W. Salacuse. LexisNexis Matthew Bender, 1275 Broadway Albany, NY 12204. Phone: 800-424-4200 or (518)487-3000 Fax: (518)487-3584 E-mail: bookstore.support@lexisnexis.com • URL: http://www.bender.com • $1,483.00. Six looseleaf volumes. Periodic supplementation.

International Capital Markets and Securities Regulation. Harold S. Bloomenthal. West Group, 610 Opperman Dr. Eagan, MN 55123. Phone: 800-328-4880 or (651)687-7000 Fax: 800-340-9378 or (651)687-5827 E-mail: bookstore@westgroup.com • URL: http://www.westgroup.com • $1,083.00. Nine looseleaf volumes. Periodic supplementation. Securities regulation in industrialized nations. (Securities Law Series).

International Cast Polymer Association., 304 Bell Park Dr. Woodstock, GA 30188-1660. Phone: 800-414-4272 or (770)928-2252 Fax: (770)874-7540 E-mail: dirk@intlmarbleindustries.com • URL: http://www.icpa-hq.org • Firms and corporations that make cast polymer products (such as cast marble vanity tops and solid surface countertops); firms and corporations that supply raw materials and production equipment to manufacturers of cast polymer products. Promotes the merits of cast polymer products to their markets; works to expand these markets for the benefit of manufacturers, suppliers, and sellers of these products; firms that fabricate/install cast polymer products. Develops and promotes industry-wide standards of product quality and acceptability for the protection of purchasers of cast polymer products. Represents the cast polymer industry before government, code bodies, and regulatory agencies of all types. Defends the industry against unwarranted regulations and seeks to guarantee its source and supply of raw materials; helps members improve their skills as businessmen; educates the public on how the industry sells its products. Works to develop reliable industry-wide market data to guide members in planning operations; strives to advance the interests of the industry and of members within the boundaries set by law. Participates in standards, product testing, technical exchange, marketing and business educational activities, production data, and informal exchanges. Conducts research programs; compiles statistics.

International Center for Law in Development.

International Centre for Settlement of Investment Disputes - Annual Report. International Centre for Settlement of Investment Disputes, 1818 H St., N.W. Washington, DC 20433. Phone: (202)458-1535 Fax: (202)522-2615 • URL: http://www.worldbank.org • Annual. Free. Editions available in French and Spanish.

International Ceramic Association., 17098 Pheasant Meadow Ln. SW Prior Lake, MN 55372. Phone: (952)447-6421 E-mail: ceramicteacher@msn.com • URL: http://www.ceramic-ica.com • Manufacturers, distributors, dealers, teachers, and finished ceramists in 7 countries. Conducts promotional activities; seeks to improve relations between the industry and raw material suppliers, transportation companies, and governments. Recommends standards for sales policy and buying, pricing, and inventory; promotes standardization of entries and judging at shows. Encourages improved teaching methods; conducts pilot programs for the handicapped; organizes teachers' meetings, business seminars, and competitions. Maintains International Ceramic Association Educational Foundation. Operates hall of fame.

International Chefs' Association., GPO Box 1889 New York NY 10116-1889. Phone: (201)825-8455 E-mail: info@chefsdecuisineofamerica.com Professional chefs and cooks for restaurants, hotels, and clubs. Aims to improve the cooking profession and to guide young culinarians. Promotes international exchange. Conducts seminars, competitions, and culinary art exhibitions. Maintains placement service; bestows scholarships and Chef of the Year Award. Maintains library of 350 cookbooks.

International Cinema Technology Association., 770 Broadway 5th Fl. New York, NY 10003-9522. Phone: (646)654-768[illegible] Fax: (646)654-7694 E-mail: edith.malijan@nielsen.com • URL: http://www.internationalcinematechnologyassociation.com • Individuals in the theatre equipment industry.

International City/County Management Association., 777 N Capitol St. NE, Ste. 500 Washington, DC 20002-4201. Phone: 800-745-8780 or (202)289-4262 or (202)962-3680 Fax: (202)962-3500 E-mail: roneill@icma.org • URL: http://icma.org • International professional and educational organization for appointed administrators and assistant administrators serving cities, counties, districts, and regions. Provides publications, training, and management assistance to help local government professionals improve their skills and increase their knowledge. Collects data on local governments.

International Civil Aviation Organization Digests of Statistics. International Civil Aviation Organization c/o Document Sales Unit, 999 University St. Montreal PQ, QC, Canada H3C 5H7. Phone: (514)954-8219 Fax: (514)954-6077 E-mail: icaohq@icao.int • URL: http://www.icao@icao.int • Irregular. $54.00. Contains financial data and traffic data for international airports. Text in English, French, Russian and Spanish.

International Co-operative Alliance-Switzerland.

International Coatings and Formulation Institute.

International Code Council, Uniform Building Code. International Conference of Building Officials, 5360 Workman Mill Rd. Whittier, CA 90601-2298. Phone: 800-284-4406 or (562)669-0541 Fax: (562)699-9721 • URL: http://www.icbo.org • Triennial. Two volumes. Members, $144.55; non-members, $180.70. (International Conference of Building Officials. Uniform Building Code).

International Coffee Organization.

International Communications Agency Network., PO Box 490, 1649 Lump Gulch Rd. Rollinsville, CO 80474-0490. Phone: (303)258-9511 Fax: (303)484-4087 E-mail: info@icomagencies.com • URL: http://www.icomagencies.com • Network of non-competing advertising agencies. Provides an interchange of management information, international facilities, and branch office service for partner agencies. Provides discounts on syndicated services and access to 1000 computer databases.

The International Competitive Power Industry Directory. PennWell Corp., 1421 S Sheridan Rd. Tulsa, OK 74112. Phone: 800-331-4463 or (918)835-3161 Fax: (918)832-9201 E-mail: headquarters@pennwell.com • URL: http://www.pennwell.com • Publication includes: List of 1,400 companies active in the global power industry, providing information on developers, financial firms, law firms, engineering and construction firms, fuel suppliers, consultants, manufacturers and other suppliers of products, equipment ot the hydro, geothermal, solar and wind industries. Entries include: Company name, address, phone, fax; contact name; business area or tyope; technology used; region covered; products.

International Confederation of Art Dealers.

International Conference of Building Officials., 5360 Workman Mill Rd. Whittier, CA 90601-2298. Phone: 800-423-6587 or (562)699-0541 or (562)699-0543 Fax: (562)695-4694 • URL: http://www.icbo.org • Formerly Pacific Coast Building Officials Conference.

International Conference of Building Officials - Membership Directory. International Conference of Building Officials, 5360 Workman Mill Rd. Whittier, CA 90601-2298. Phone: 800-329-4226 or (562)699-0541 Fax: (562)699-9721 • URL: http://www.icbo.org • Annual. Price on application.

International Congress Calendar. Union of International Associations, 40, rue Washington B-1050 Brussels, Belgium. Phone: (2 6)401808 Fax: (2 6)436199 E-mail: uia@uia.be • URL: http://www.ula.org • Covers: over 12,000 scheduled international meetings; mostly covers meetings within the next two years, but extends through the next 10 years. Entries include: Name and address of sponsoring body, theme, meeting dates, meeting place, estimated number of participants, concurrent exhibition, reference to organization listing in "Yearbook of International Organizations."

International Contact Lens Clinic. Elsevier, 360 Park Ave. S New York, NY 10010-1710. Phone: 888-437-4636 or (212)989-5800 Fax: (212)633-3990 E-mail: usinfo-f@elsevier.com • URL: http://www.elsevier.com • Bimonthly. Individuals, $139.00 per year; institutions, $272.00 per year.

International Copper Association., 260 Madison Ave., 16th Fl. New York, NY 10016-2401. Phone: (212)251-7240 Fax: (212)251-7245 E-mail: info@copperinfo.com • URL: http://www.copperinfo.com • Copper producing and fabricating companies. Conducts market development and research on uses for copper through contracts with commercial, institutional, and university organizations.

International Council for Computer Communication., P.O. Box 9745 Washington, DC 20016-9745. Phone: (703)836-7787 Fax: (703)836-7787 E-mail: office@icccgovernors.org

• URL: http://www.icccgovernors.org • Affiliated with International Federation for Information Processing.

International Council for Small Business., c/o Jefferson Smurfit Center for Entrepreneurial Studies, St. Louis University, 3674 Lindell Blvd. St. Louis, MO 63108. Phone: (314)977-3628 Fax: (314)977-3627 E-mail: icsb@slu.edu • URL: http://www.icsb.org • Formerly National Committee for Small Business Management Development.

International Council of Aircraft Owner and Pilot Associations.

International Council of Shopping Centers.

International Council of Societies of Industrial Design.

International Counterpurchase Contracts. United Nations Publications, United Nations Concourse Level, First Ave., 46th St. New York, NY 10017. Phone: 800-553-3210 or (212)963-7680 Fax: (212)963-3489 E-mail: bookstore@un.org • URL: http://www.un.org/publications • 1990. Trade agreements.

International Country Risk Guide. The PRS Group, Inc., P.O. Box 248 East Syracuse, NY 13057-0248. Phone: (315)431-0511 Fax: (315)431-0200 E-mail: custserv@prsgroup.com • URL: http://www.prsgroup.com • Monthly. $3,795.00 per year. Each issue provides detailed analysis of a group of countries, covering financial risks, political trends, and economic developments. More than 130 countries are covered during the course of a year, with specific business risk point ratings assigned.

International Crude Oil Market Handbook. Energy Intelligence Group, Inc., Five E 37th St., 5th Fl. New York, NY 10016-2807. Phone: (212)532-1112 Fax: (212)532-4479 • URL: http://www.energyintel.com • Annual. $1,195.00. An overview covers "The Inner Workings of Crude Oil Markets," including a glossary of terms. Reference sections contain detailed profiles of 44 "key producing countries," legal terms, crude oil sales contracts, prices, and other information.

International Currency Review. World Reports Ltd., 280 Madison Ave., Ste. 280 New York, NY 10016. Phone: (212)679-0095 Fax: (212)679-1094 Quarterly. $475.00 per year.

International Customer Service Association., 24 Wernik Pl. Metuchen, NJ 08840. Phone: 800-360-4272 or (732)767-0330 Fax: (732)767-1423 E-mail: info@icsatoday.org • URL: http://www.icsa.com • Customer service professionals in public and private sectors united to develop the theory and understanding of customer service and management. Goals are to: promote professional development; standardize terminology and phrases; provide career counseling and placement services; establish hiring guidelines, performance standards, and job descriptions. Provides a forum for shared problems and solutions. Compiles statistics.

International Customs Tariffs Bureau., rue des Petits Carmes, 15 B-1000 Brussels, Belgium. Phone: 32 2 5018774 or 32 2 5018779 Fax: 32 2 5013147 E-mail: dir@bitd.org • URL: http://www.bitd.org • Executive instrument of the International Union for the Publication of Customs Tariffs. Translates and publishes the customs tariffs of all countries into 5 languages: English, French, German, Italian, and Spanish.

International Data Corp. (IDC)., Five Speen St. Framingham, MA 01701. Phone: (508)872-8200 Fax: (508)935-4015 E-mail: leads@idc.com • URL: http://www.idc.com • Private research firm specializing in market research related to computers, multimedia, and telecommunications.

International Defense Electronic Systems Handbook. Primedia Business Magazines and Media, 6151 Powers Ferry Rd., Ste. 200 Atlanta, GA 30339. Phone: 800-795-5445 or (770)955-2500 Fax: (770)618-0348 E-mail: subs@primediabusiness.com • URL: http://www.primediabusiness.com • Annual. $195.00. Includes information concerning federal budget for electronic military equipment. Gives descriptions of equipment.

International Desalination Association., PO Box 387 Topsfield, MA 01983. Phone: (978)887-0410 Fax: (978)887-0411 E-mail: info@idadesal.org • URL: http://www.idadesal.org • Users and suppliers of desalination equipment; water reuse and reclamation consultants. Seeks to develop and promote worldwide application of desalination and desalination technology in maintaining water supplies, controlling water pollution, and purifying, treating, and reusing water. Disseminates information on desalination-related subjects and water reuse. Encourages the establishment of standards, specifications, procedures, and the efficient use of water for energy. Conducts seminars and workshops.

International Development Association., The World Bank, 1818 H St. NW Washington, DC 20433. Phone: (202)477-6391 or (202)473-1000 Fax: (202)477-6391 E-mail: info@idadesal.org • URL: http://www.worldbank.org • Functional member of the World Bank (see separate entry); membership is open to countries of the World Bank. Promotes the economic development of the World Bank's poorer member countries by extending credits on easier terms than are normally available. Makes loans for projects aimed at strengthening the economies of developing countries in Asia, the Middle East, Africa, and the Western Hemisphere. Provides economic advice.

International Development Statistics. Organization for Economic Cooperation and Development, OECD Washington Center, 2001 L St., N. W., Suite 650 Washington, DC 20036-4922. Phone: 800-456-6323 or (202)785-6323 Fax: (202)785-0350 E-mail: washington.contact@oecd.org • URL: http://www.oecd.org • Annual. $71.00. Issued by the OECD Development Assistance Committee. CD-ROM contains data on aid to more than 180 recipient countries, including amount, origin, type, and recipients' external debt.

International Dictionary of Accounting Acronyms. Thomas W. Morris, editor. Fitzroy Dearborn Publishers, Inc., 919 N. Michigan Ave., Suite 760 Chicago, IL 60611. Phone: 800-850-8102 or (312)587-0131 Fax: (312)587-1049 E-mail: fitzroy@aol.com • URL: http://www.fitzroydearborn.com • 1999. $45.00. Defines 2,000 acronyms used in worldwide accounting and finance.

International Dictionary of Architects and Architecture. Saint James Press, 27500 Drake Rd. Farmington Hills, MI 48331-3535. Phone: 800-877-GALE or (248)699-GALE Fax: 800-414-5043 or (248)699-8063 E-mail: gale.galeord@cengage.com • URL: http://gale.cengage.com • 1993. $295.00. Two volumes. Volume one: *Architects*. Volume two: *Architecture*.

International Dictionary of Film and Filmmakers. Saint James Press, 27500 Drake Rd. Farmington Hills, MI 48232. Phone: 800-877-GALE or (248)699-GALE Fax: 800-414-5043 or (248)699-8063 E-mail: gale.galeord@cengage.com • URL: http://gale.cengage.com • 2001. $595.00. Fourth edition. Four volumes. Vol. 1:*Films*. Vol. 2: *Directors*. Vol. 3: *Actors and Actresses*. Vol. 4: *Writers and Production Artists*.

International Digital Imaging Association., PO Box 81261, PO Box 81261 Chamblee, GA 30366. Phone: (770)452-8119 Fax: (770)234-9058 E-mail: idia@bellsouth.net Represents members' interest.

International Direct Investment Statistics Yearbook. OECD Publications and Information Center, 2001 L St., N.W., Suite 650 Washington, DC 20036-4922. Phone: (202)785-6323 Fax: (202)785-0350 E-mail: washington.contact@oecd.org • URL: http://www.oecdwash.org • Annual. $76.00. Provides direct investment inflow and outflow data for OECD countries.

International Directory of Arts. Available from Gale Cengage Learning, 27500 Drake Rd. Farmington Hills, MI 48331-3535. Phone: 800-699-4253 or (248)699-GALE Fax: 800-414-5043 E-mail: gale.galeord@cengage.com • URL: http://gale.cengage.com • Annual. $305.00. Three volumes. A guide to more than 126,000 art sources and markets in 175 countries. Includes artists, collectors, dealers, galleries, museums, art schools, auctioneers, restorers, publishers, libraries, and associations. Published by K. G. Saur.

International Directory of Book Collectors. Oak Knoll Press, 414 Delaware St. New Castle, DE 19720. Phone: 800-996-2556 or (302)328-7232 Fax: (302)328-7274 E-mail: oakknoll@oakknoll.com • URL: http://www.oakknoll.com • 1992. $50.00. Over 1,500 listings. Published in England by Trigon Press.

International Directory of Company Histories. Saint James Press, 27500 Drake Rd. Farmington Hills, MI 48331-3535. Phone: 800-877-GALE or (248)699-GALE Fax: 800-414-5043 or (248)699-8063 E-mail: gale.galeord@cengage.com • URL: http://gale.cengage.com • 53 volumes. $199.00 per volume. Provides detailed histories of about 4,550 major corporations. Cumulative indexing is provided for company names, personal names, and industries.

International Directory of Corporate Art Collections. ARTnews, 48 W. 38th St. New York, NY 10018. Phone: (212)398-1690 Fax: (212)819-0394 E-mail: info@artnewsonline.com • URL: http://www.artnewsonline.com • Biennial. $109.95. Contains information on about 1,300 corporate art collections maintained or sponsored in the U. S., Canada, Europe, and Japan.

International Directory of Corporate Philanthropy. Available from Taylor & Francis Group, 325 Chestnut St. Philadelphia, PA 19106. Phone: 800-821-8312 or (215)625-8900 Fax: 800-248-4724 or (215)625-2940 E-mail: info@taylorandfrancis.com • URL: http://www.taylorandfrancis.com • Annual. $295.00. Published by Europa Publications (http://www.europapublications.com). Contains profiles of about 1,000 corporate foundations and "co-ordinating organizations" in various countries of the world. Provides details of charitable activities and philanthropic expenditures.

International Directory of Little Magazines and Small Presses. Dustbooks, P.O. Box 100 Paradise, CA 95967. Phone: 800-477-6110 or (530)877-6110 Fax: (530)877-0222 E-mail: publisher@dustbooks.com • URL: http://www.dustbooks.com • Annual. $55.00. Over 5,000 small, independent magazines, presses, and papers.

International Directory of Refrigerated Warehouses and Distribution Cente rs. International Association of Refrigerated Warehouses, 7315 Wisconsin Ave., Suite 1200N Bethesda, MD 20814. Phone: (301)652-5674 Fax: (301)652-7269 E-mail: email@iarw.org • URL: http://www.iarw.org • Annual. Free to qualified personnel; others, $150.00 per year. Lists locations/services of 1,000 public refrigerated warehouses in 30 countries. Formerly *International Directory of Public Refrigerated Warehouses*.

International Directory of the Nonwoven Fabrics Industry. INDA, Association of the Nonwoven Fabrics Industry, 1300 Crescent Green, Suite 135 Cary, NC 27511. Phone: (919)233-1210 Fax: (919)233-1282 • URL: http://www.inda.org • Biennial. Members, $195.00 per year; non-members, $275.00 per year. Lists more than 2,200 manufacturers of nonwoven fabrics and suppliers of raw material and equipment.

International District Energy Association., 24 Lyman St., Ste. 230 Westborough, MA 01581-2841. Phone: (508)366-9339 Fax: (508)366-0019 E-mail: idea@districtenergy.org • URL: http://www.districtenergy.org • Suppliers of space heating by means of steam and hot water, and air conditioning by means of steam and chilled water, via piping systems from a central station to groups of buildings.

International Door Association., PO Box 246, 28 Lowry Dr. West Milton, OH 45383-0246. Phone: 800-355-4432 or (937)698-8042 Fax: (937)698-6153 E-mail: info@longmgt.com • URL: http://www.doors.org • Individuals and companies who manufacture, sell, or install overhead garage doors and openers. Aims to promote the industry and increase training and educational opportunities. Sets a code of business practices; compiles statistics. Conducts seminars.

International Drug Report. International Narcotic Enforcement Officers Association Inc., 112 State St., Ste. 1200 Albany, NY 12207-2079. Phone: (518)463-6232 Fax: (518)432-3378 E-mail: info@ineoa.org Description: Discusses current trends in narcotic abuse and enforcement, legal decisions concerning drug abuse, and related subjects. Carries news articles, scientific reports, statistics, and agency information. Recurring features include book reviews, notices of meetings, and news from U.S. Customs and the Drug Enforcement Administration.

International Dyer. World Textile Publications Ltd., Perkins House, One Longlands St., c/o Keith Higgenbottom Bradford BD1 2TP, United Kingdom. Phone: 44 1274 378800 Fax: 44 1274 378811 E-mail: info@worldtextile.com • URL: http://www.worldtextile.com • Monthly. $90.00 per year.

International Economic Development Council., 734 15th St. NW, Ste. 900 Washington, DC 20005. Phone: (202)223-7800 Fax: (202)223-4745 E-mail: cziegler@iedconline.org • URL: http://www.iedconline.org • Works to help economic development professionals improve the quality of life in their communities. Represents all levels of government, academia, and private industry; provides a broad range of member services including research, advisory services, conferences, professional certification, professional development, publications, legislative tracking and more.

International Economic Scoreboard. The Conference Board Inc., 845 3rd Ave. New York, NY 10022-6679. Phone: (212)759-0900 Fax: (212)980-7014 E-mail: webmaster@conference-board.org • URL: http://www.conference-board.org • Description: Provides current data on the business outlook in 11 major industrial countries: Australia, Canada, France, West Germany, Italy, Japan, Korea, New Zealand, Taiwan, the United Kingdom, and the U.S. **Remarks:** A source for additional information on this indicator system and its uses is available at the Center for International Business Cycle Research, Columbia University Business School.

International Economics. Dennis R. Appleyard and Alfred J. Field. McGraw-Hill, 1221 Ave. of the Americas New York, NY 10020. Phone: 800-722-4726 or (212)512-2000 Fax: (212)512-4502 E-mail: customer.service@mcgraw-hill.com • URL: http://www.mcgraw-hill.com • 2000. $105.00. Fourth edition.

International Economics Section. Princeton University, Dept. of Economics, Fisher Hall Princeton, NJ 08544-1021. Phone: (609)258-5715 Fax: (609)258-6419 E-mail: ies@princeton.edu • URL: http://www.princeton.edu • Formerly International Finance Section.

International Employment Hotline. Carlyle Corp., PO Box 6729 Charlottesville, VA 22906-6729. Phone: 800-291-4618 or (434)985-6444 Fax: (434)985-6828 E-mail: info@ineoa.org Description: Covers the latest developments in the international job market. Summarizes hiring cycles of major employers. Lists current overseas job openings by job title, description, employer contact, and address. Recurring features include editorials and news of research.

International Encyclopedia of Business and Management. Malcolm Warner, editor. Cengage Learning, 10650 Toebben Dr. Independence, KY 41051. Phone: 800-347-7707 or (203)969-8700 Fax: 800-487-8488 E-mail: esales@cengage.com • URL: http://gale.cengage.com • 2001. $1,899.00.Second edition. Eight volumes. Contains more than 500 articles on global management issues. Includes extensive bibliographies, cross references, and an index of key words and phrases.

International Encyclopedia of Futures and Options. Fitzroy Dearborn Publishers, Inc., 919 N. Michigan Ave., Suite 760 Chicago, IL 60611. Phone: 800-850-8102 or (312)587-0131 Fax: (312)587-1049 E-mail: fitzroy@aol.com • URL: http://www.fitzroydearborn.com • 2000. $285.00. Two volumes. Covers terminology, concepts, events, individuals, and markets.

International Encyclopedia of Public Policy and Administration. Jay M. Shafritz, editor. Westview Press, 550 Central Ave. Boulder, CO 80301. Phone: 800-386-5656 or (303)444-3541 E-mail: westview.orders@perseusbooks.com • URL: http://www.westviewpress.com • 1997. $550.00. Four volumes. Covers 20 major areas, such as public administration, government budgeting, industrial policy, nonprofit management, organizational theory, public finance, labor relations, and taxation. Includes a brief bibliography for each major entry and a comprehensive index.

International Encyclopedia of the Stock Market. Michael Sheimo and Andreas Loizou, editors. Fitzroy Dearborn Publishers, Inc., 919 N. Michigan Ave., Suite 760 Chicago, IL 60611. Phone: 800-850-8102 or (312)587-0131 Fax: (312)587-1049 • URL: http://www.fitzroydearborn.com • 1999. $290.00.

Two volumes. Covers the terminology of stock exchanges around the world. Individual country entries provide details of stock exchange conditions, practices, regulation, and brokers.

International Energy Agency., 9, rue de la Federation 75739 Paris, France. Phone: 33 1 40576500 Fax: 33 1 40576559 E-mail: info@iea.org • URL: http://www.iea.org • Industrialized oil-consuming countries that carry out an international energy program designed to build and sustain strong energy economies. Seeks to improve energy supply and demand balance. Strives to develop oil-alternative energy sources. Coordinates international oil market information. Maintains an emergency oil sharing system. Compiles statistics.

International Energy Annual. Available from U. S. Government Printing Office, Washington, DC 20402. Phone: (202)512-1800 Fax: (202)512-2250 E-mail: gpoaccess@gpo.gov • URL: http://www.access.gpo.gov • Annual. $34.00. Issued by the Energy Information Administration, U. S. Department of Energy. Provides production, consumption, import, and export data for primary energy commodities in more than 200 countries and areas. In addition to petroleum products and alcohol, renewable energy sources are covered (hydroelectric, geothermal, solar, and wind).

International Executive Service Corps., 1900 M St. NW, Ste. 500 Washington, DC 20036. Phone: 800-243-4372 or (202)589-2600 Fax: (202)326-0289 E-mail: iesc@iesc.org • URL: http://www.iesc.org • Provides technical and managerial assistance to enterprises, organizations and government bodies in emerging democracies and developing countries. Focuses on the knowledge, skill and experience of its 12,000 industry experts. Maintains a network of experts that includes high-level professionals drawn from nearly every area of private enterprise, government and non-governmental organizations; Geekcorps division includes experts in communications and information technology and is committed to closing the digital divide.

International Fabricare Institute., 14700 Sweitzer Ln. Laurel, MD 20707. Phone: 800-638-2627 or (301)622-1900 Fax: (240)295-0685 E-mail: techline@ifi.org • URL: http://www.ifi.org • Retail and industrial drycleaners, hospital laundries, linen supply and drapery services, distributors and manufacturers of supplies and machinery, dry-cleaning and laundry associations, and individual launders in 43 countries. Provides washability and dry-cleanability testing for manufacturers of fabrics and related products; offers quality testing and consulting services; conducts research for members. Organizes courses in dry-cleaning, laundering, management, and maintenance. Maintains consulting service, speakers' bureau, research facilities, and library.

International Federation for Information and Documentation.

International Federation for Information Processing.

International Federation of Beekeepers' Associations.

International Federation of Freight Forwarders Associations.

International Federation of Press Cutting Agencies.

International Fertilizer Development Center., P.O. Box 2040 Muscle Shoals, AL 35662. Phone: (205)381-6600 Fax: (205)381-7408 E-mail: general@ifdc.org • URL: http://www.ifdc.org • Conducts research relating to all aspects of fertilizer production, marketing, and use. Supported by the United Nations, the World Bank, and other international agencies.

International Fiber Journal. International Media Group, Inc., 7401 Carmel Executive Park Dr., Suite 202 Charlotte, NC 28226-8275. Phone: (704)544-1969 Fax: (704)544-6559 E-mail: ifj@ifj.com • URL: http://www.ifj.com • Bimonthly. $36.00 per year. Covers manmade fiber technology and manufacturing.

International Film Guide. Variety, 5700 Wilshire Blvd. Ste. 120 Los Angeles, CA 90036. Phone: (323)857-6600 Fax: (323)932-0393 E-mail: uia@uia.be Publication includes: Lists of new films, film production companies, distributors, organizations, and government agencies concerned with film in over 70 countries of the world. Also includes film festivals, film archives, services for the industry, and film schools. Entries include: All entries include company or organization name and address; listings for festivals and other categories in foregoing list include additional details.

International Film, Television, and Video Acronyms. Matthew Stevens, editor. Greenwood Publishing Group, Inc., 88 Post Rd., W. Westport, CT 06881-5007. Phone: 800-225-5800 or (203)226-3571 Fax: (203)431-2214 E-mail: customer-service@greenwood.com • URL: http://www.greenwood.com • 1993. $85.00. A guide to 3,400 acronyms and 1,400 technical terms.

International Financial Law Review. American Educational Systems, PO Box 246 New York, NY 10024-0246. Phone: 800-431-1579 Monthly. $750.00 per year. Includes print and online editions.

International Financial Statistics. International Monetary Fund, Publications Services, 700 19th St., N.W. Washington, DC 20431. Phone: (202)623-7000 Fax: (202)623-6278 E-mail: publicaffairs@imf.org • URL: http://www.imf.org • Monthly. Individuals, $495.00 per year; students, $247.00 per year. Includes a wide variety of current data for individual countries in Europe and elsewhere. Includes *Annual* issue.

International Fire Marshals Association., 1 Batterymarch Park, PO Box 9101 Quincy, MA 02169-7471. Phone: (617)984-7423 Fax: (617)984-7056 E-mail: ifma@nfpa.org • URL: http://www.nfpa.org • Municipal, county, state, and provincial fire marshals and fire prevention bureau officials. Works for professional improvement through information exchange, meetings, and conferences. Seeks to minimize the loss of life and property by fire through fire prevention education, enforcement of fire laws, investigation of fire causes, and fire hazard regulation.

International Fire Service Training Association., Oklahoma State University, 930 N Willis Stillwater, OK 74078-8045. Phone: 800-654-4055 or (405)744-5723 Fax: (405)744-8204 E-mail: customer.service@osufpp.org • URL: http://www.ifsta.org • Educational organization formed to develop training materials for the fire service. Committee members are individuals who represent their respective fire-related fields and are considered leaders or innovators. Association committee members meet annually to validate training material for publication, add new techniques and developments, delete outmoded methods and equipment, and upgrade fire service training in general; actual publication is done for the association by Fire Protection Publications of Oklahoma State University.

International Flavors and Fragrances.

International Fluid Power Society., PO Box 1420 Cherry Hill, NJ 08034-0054. Phone: 800-303-8520 or (856)489-8983 Fax: (856)424-9248 E-mail: info@ifps.org • URL: http://www.ifps.org • Persons interested in all phases of fluid power and related motion control and its uses. Concerned with research, development, design, installation, operation, maintenance, education, and application to industry, aviation, marine, mobile, material handling, and agricultural equipment. Maintains speakers' bureau. Operates certification programs and placement service for fluid power mechanics, technicians, specialists, and engineers.

International Food Additives Council., 5775 Peachtree-Dunwoody Rd., Ste. 500G Atlanta, GA 30342. Phone: (404)252-3663 Fax: (404)252-0774 E-mail: ifac@kellencompany.com Consists of manufacturers of food additives and businesses using food additives. Aims to: gather and disseminate information on food additives; represent members' interests; provide technical and scientific assistance. Sponsors research; compiles statistics.

International Food Service Executives Association., 8155 Briar Cliff Dr. Castle Rock, CO 80108-8215. Phone: 800-893-5499 or (720)733-8001 Fax: (720)733-8999 E-mail: hq@ifsea.com • URL: http://www.ifsea.com • Owners, managers, stewards, caterers, proprietors, purchasing agents, dietitians, and other management-level personnel of hotels, clubs, restaurants, cafeterias, schools, hospitals, institutions, and airlines. Associate members are providers of goods and services to the food service industry. Seeks to raise standards in the food service industry by educating members. Underwrites scholarships; provides assistance to universities and other educational institutions establishing programs for professional food service training. Maintains Certified Food Executive Program, through which individuals in the food service industry who have demonstrated outstanding leadership capabilities receive certification training.

International Foodservice Editorial Council., PO Box 491 Hyde Park, NY 12538-0491. Phone: (845)229-6973 Fax: (845)229-6993 E-mail: info@ifeconline.com • URL: http://www.ifec-is-us.com • Key communicators within the U.S. foodservice industry, including top editors and marketing and public relations personnel for leading food companies and foodservice educational institutions. Organized to sound the marketing directions of the industry on all levels; seeks to improve communications.

International Foodservice Manufacturers Association., 2 Prudential Plz., 180 N Stetson Ave., Ste. 4400 Chicago, IL 60601. Phone: (312)540-4400 Fax: (312)540-4401 E-mail: ifma@ifmaworld.com • URL: http://www.ifmaworld.com • National and international manufacturers and processors of food, food equipment, and related products for the away-from-home food market. Associate and allied members provide support services to the industry through marketing, publishing, distribution, consulting, promotion, research, advertising, public relations, and brokering. Activities are aimed at marketing, merchandising, sales training, and market research. Compiles statistics.

International Foodservice Manufacturers Association: Membership Directory. International Foodservice Manufacturers Association, Two Prudential Plaza, 180 N. Stetson, Suite 4400 Chicago, IL 60601. Phone: (312)540-4400 Fax: (312)540-4401 E-mail: ifma@ifmaworld.com • URL: http://www.ifmaworld.com • Annual. Membership. Manufacturers of processed foods equipment and supplies for schools, hospitals, hotels, restaurants, and institutions and related services in the foodservice industry.

International Foundation Directory. Routledge Reference, 11 New Fetter Ln. London EC4P 4EE, United Kingdom. Phone: 800-821-8312 or (44)20 70176649 Fax: (44)20 70176720 E-mail: edit.europa@tandf.co.uk • URL: http://www.taylorandfrancis.com • Covers: More than 2,300 foundations, charitable and grant-making NGOs, trusts, and similar nonprofit organizations that operate on an international basis, and selected national foundations worldwide spanning over 100 countries. Entries include: Name, address, founding date, brief history and description of activities, names of officers, publications, and other details.

International Foundation for Art Research, Inc., 500 Fifth Ave., Suite 1234 New York, NY 10110. Phone: (212)391-6234 Fax: (212)391-8794 E-mail: kferg@ifar.org • URL: http://www.ifar.org • Research fields are art theft and the authenticity of art objects. Maintains an information archive on stolen art and operates an authentication service.

International Foundation for Telemetering.

International Foundation of Employee Benefit Plans., 18700 W. Bluemound Rd. Brookfield, WI 53008. Phone: 888-334-3327 or (262)786-6700 or (262)786-6710 Fax: (262)786-8670 E-mail: pr@ifebp.org • URL: http://www.ifebp.org • Formerly National Foundation of Health, Welfare and Pension Plans.

International Franchise Association., 1501 K St. NW, Ste. 350 Washington, DC 20005. Phone: (202)628-8000 Fax: (202)628-0812 E-mail: ifa@franchise.org • URL: http://www.franchise.org • Firms in 100 countries utilizing the franchise method of distribution for goods and services in all industries.

International Freighting Weekly: Sea, Air, Rail, Road. Informa UK Limited, 37-41 Mortimer St. London, United Kingdom. Phone: 44 20 7553 1000 Fax: 44 20 7553 1109 E-mail: enquiries@informa.com • URL: http://www.informa.com • Weekly. $289.00 per year. Looseleaf service.

International Gaming and Wagering Business. Gem Communications, 250 W 57th St. New York, NY 10019. Phone: 800-223-9638 or (212)246-0273 Fax: (212)246-0527 • URL: http://www.worldgaminglive.com • Monthly. $113.00 per year.

International Gaming Resource Guide. Gem Communications, 1771 E Flamingo Rd., No. 208A Las Vegas, NV 89119. Phone: (702)794-0718 Fax: (702)794-0799 E-mail: edit.europa@tandf.co.uk Publication includes: Lists of 1,800 organizations concerned with gaming and wagering establishments, including casinos, lotteries, racing commissions, race tracks, jai alai frontons, etc.; and regulatory agencies. Entries include: Listings in the 'Corporate Profiles' section (which expand selected other listings) include name, parent company name, address, mailing address (if different), phone, names and titles of key personnel. Other listings show name, address, and phone only.

International Grains Council. World Grain Statistics. International Grains Council, One Canada Square Canary Wharf E14 5AE, United Kingdom. Phone: 44 20 7513 1122 Fax: 44 20 7513 0630 E-mail: igc-fac@igc.org.uk • URL: http://www.igc.org.uk • Annual. $160.00. Text in English, French, Russian and Spanish. Formerly *International Wheat Council. World Grain Statistics*.

International Guide to Foreign Currency Management. Gary Shoup, editor. Glenlake Publishing Co., Ltd., 1261 W Glenlake Ave. Chicago, IL 60660. Phone: 800-850-8102 or (773)262-9765 Fax: (773)262-9436 E-mail: info@glenlake.com • URL: http://www.glenlake.com • 1999. $65.00. Written for corporate financial managers. Covers the market for currencies, price forecasting, exposure of various kinds, and risk management.

International Guide to Securities Market Indices. Henry Shilling, editor. Fitzroy Dearborn Publishers, Inc., 919 N. Michigan Ave., Suite 760 Chicago, IL 60611. Phone: 800-850-8102 or (312)587-0131 Fax: (312)587-1049 E-mail: fitzroy@aol.com • URL: http://www.fitzroydearborn.com • 1996. $150.00. Describes 400 stock market, bond market, and other financial price indexes maintained in various countries of the world (300 of the indexes are described in detail, including graphs and 10-year data).

International Hand Protection Association., PO Box 146 Brookville, PA 15825. Phone: (814)328-5208 Fax: (814)328-5208 E-mail: burdge@key-net.com Formerly Work Glove Manufacturers Association.

International Handbook of Convertible Securities: A Global Guide to the Convertible Market. Thomas C. Noddings and others. Fitzroy Dearborn Publishers, Inc., 919 N Michigan Ave., Ste. 760 Chicago, IL 60611. Phone: 800-850-8102 or (312)587-0131 Fax: (312)587-1049 E-mail: fitzroy@aol.com • URL: http://www.fitzroydearborn.com • 2001. $75.00. Second edition. Includes new structures for convertible securities and advanced hedging strategies.

International Handbook on Mental Health Policy. Donna R. Kemp, editor. Greenwood Publishing Group, Inc., 88 Post Rd., W Westport, CT 06881. Phone: 800-225-5800 or (203)226-3571 Fax: (203)431-2214 E-mail: customer-service@greenwood.com • URL: http://www.greenwood.com • 1993. $134.95. Provides information on critical mental health issues in 20 countries.

International Health and Temperance Association., 12501 Old Columbia Pike Silver Spring, MD 20904. Phone: (301)680-6719 Fax: (301)680-6707 E-mail: 74617.1663@compuserve.com • URL: http://www.health20-20.org • Seeks to "enlighten the public concerning the harmful effects of alcohol, tobacco and narcotics and to mount an educational campaign to solve these problems". Formerly International Temperance Association.

International Health, Racquet and Sportsclub Association., 263 Summer St. Boston, MA 02210. Phone: 800-228-4772 or (617)951-0055 Fax: (617)951-0056 E-mail: info@ihrsa.org • URL: http://www.ihrsa.org • Members are for-profit health clubs, sports clubs, and gyms. Formerly IRSA, The Association of Quality Clubs.

International Home Furnishings Representatives Association., PO Box 670 High Point, NC 27261. Phone: 800-889-3920 or (336)889-3375 Fax: (336)883-8245 E-mail: ihfra@aol.com • URL: http://www.ihfra.org • Formerly National Home

Furnishings Representatives Association.

International Housewares Association., 6400 Shafer Ct., Ste. 650 Rosemont, IL 60018. Phone: 800-843-6462 or (847)292-4200 Fax: (847)292-4211 E-mail: pbrandl@housewares.org • URL: http://www.housewares.org • Manufacturers and distributors of housewares and small appliances. Conducts annual market research survey of the housewares industry. Manages the international housewares show.

International Ice Cream Association.

International Imaging Industry Association., 701 Westchester Ave., Ste. 317W White Plains, NY 10604-3018. Phone: (914)285-4933 Fax: (914)285-4937 E-mail: i3ainfo@i3a.org • URL: http://www.i3a.org • Develops and promotes the adoption of open industry standards, addressing environmental issues and providing a voice for the industry that will benefit all users. Promotes environment, health and safety concerns; works with various government agencies including the EPA, TSA, and WTO to ensure the best interests of the imaging industry are represented.

International Income Taxation: Code and Regulations, Selected Sections. CCH, Inc., 2700 Lake Cook Rd. Riverwoods, IL 60015. Phone: 800-835-5224 or (847)267-7000 E-mail: cust_serv@cch.com • URL: http://www.cch.com • Annual. $77.00. Covers U. S. taxation of foreign entities and U. S. taxation of domestic entities having foreign income.

International Information Management Congress., 1100 Wayne Ave., Ste. 1100 Silver Spring, MD 20910-5603. Phone: (301)587-8202 Fax: (301)587-2711 E-mail: aiim@aiim.org • URL: http://www.iimc.org • Trade association for the document imaging/management industry. Seeks to communicate document-based technologies and applications to an international audience through conferences, exhibitions, publications, and various membership interactions. Promotes understanding and cooperation among organizations engaged in furthering the progress and application of document-based information systems.

International Institute for Lath and Plaster.

International Institute of Communications.

International Institute of Municipal Clerks.

International Institute of Synthetic Rubber Producers., 2077 S. Gessner Rd., Suite 133 Houston, TX 77063-1123. Phone: (713)783-7511 Fax: (713)783-7253 E-mail: info@iisrp.com • URL: http://www.iisrp.com • Formerly IISRP.

International Instrumentation and Controls Buyers Guide. Keller International Publishing, LLC, 150 Great Neck Rd. Great Neck, NY 11021. Phone: (516)829-9210 Fax: (516)829-5414 E-mail: kellpub@world.att.net • URL: http://www.kellerpubs.com • Annual. Included in subscription to *International Instrumentation and Controls*. Lists over 310 suppliers of precision instrument products and services.

International Intellectual Property Alliance., 2101 L St. NW, Ste. 1000 Washington, DC 20037. Phone: (202)833-4198 Fax: (202)331-3101 E-mail: info@iipa.com • URL: http://www.iipa.com • Comprised of six trade associations, each representing a significant segment of the U.S. copyright community. Represents over 1,300 U.S. companies producing and distributing materials protected by copyright laws globally: computer software which includes business applications software and entertainment software (such as videogame CDs and cartridges, personal computer CD-ROMs and multimedia products); theatrical films, television programs, home videos and digital representations of audiovisual works, music, records, CDs, and audiocassettes; and textbooks, tradebooks, reference and professional publications and journals (in both electronic and print media).

International Intellectual Property Association., 1255 23rd St. NW, Ste. 200 Washington, DC 20037. Phone: (202)466-2396 Fax: (202)466-2893 E-mail: herb@ipo.org • URL: http://www.ipo.org • Lawyers who have professional qualifications and interest in the international protection of patents, designs, trademarks, copyrights, and other intellectual property rights. American group of the International Association for the Protection of Industrial Property. Monitors international developments that may affect industrial property and related rights. Studies, discusses, and reports on proposed national and foreign legislation treaties and conventions that are likely to affect national and international intellectual property interests.

International Interior Design Association., 222 Merchandise Mart Plz., Ste. 567 Chicago, IL 60654. Phone: 888-799-4432 or (312)467-1950 or (312)467-1950 Fax: (312)467-0779 E-mail: iidahq@iida.org • URL: http://www.iida.org • Represents professional interior designers, including designers of commercial, healthcare, hospitality, government, retail, residential facilities; educators; researchers; representatives of allied manufacturing sources. Conducts research, student programs, and continuing education programs for members. Has developed a code of ethics for the professional design membership.

International Intertrade Index of New Imported Products. John E. Felber., P.O. Box 636 Newark, NJ 07101. Phone: (973)686-2382 Fax: (973)622-1740 Monthly. $45.00 per year. Lists new foreign products being offered to importers. Newsletter available *Foreign Trade Fairs New Products*.

International Journal for Vitamin and Nutrition Research. Hogrefe & Huber Publishers, P.O. 2487 Kirkland, WA 98083. Phone: 800-228-3749 or (425)820-1500 Fax: (425)823-8324 E-mail: verlag@hanshuber.com • URL: http://www.hhpub.com/journals • Quarterly. $202.00 per year.

International Journal of Adhesion and Adhesives. Elsevier, 360 Park Ave., S New York, NY 10010-1710. Phone: 888-437-4636 or (212)989-5800 Fax: (212)633-3990 E-mail: usinfo-f@elsevier.com • URL: http://www.elsevier.com • Six times a year. $972.00 per year. Published in England.

International Journal of Advertising: The Quarterly Review of Marketing Communications. Advertising Association. NTC Publications Ltd., Farm Rd., Henley-on-Thames Oxon RG9 1EJ, United Kingdom. Phone: 44 1491 411000 Fax: 44 1491 571188 E-mail: ijoa@ntc.co.uk • URL: http://www.warc.com • Quarterly. Price on application.

International Journal of Bank Marketing., Emerald (North America), 875 Massachusetts Ave., 7th Fl. Cambridge, MA 02139. Phone: 888-622-0075 or (617)497-2175 Fax: (617)354-6875 E-mail: america@emeraldinsight.com • URL: http://www.emeraldinsight.com • Seven times a year. $12,519.00 per year.

International Journal of Climatology. Royal Meteorological Society. John Wiley and Sons, Inc., Journals, 111 River Hoboken, NJ 07030. Phone: 800-225-5945 or (201)748-6000 Fax: (201)748-6088 E-mail: customer@wiley.com • URL: http://www.wiley.com • 15 times a year. $1,065.00 per year; institutions, $2,135.00 per year. Published in England by John Wiley and Sons Ltd.

International Journal of Communication Systems. John Wiley and Sons, Inc., Journals, 111 River Hoboken, NJ 07030. Phone: 800-225-5945 or (201)748-6000 Fax: (201)748-6088 E-mail: customer@wiley.com • URL: http://www.wiley.com • Bimonthly. Individuals, $1,055.00 per year; institutions, $1,405.00 per year. Published in England by John Wiley and Sons Ltd. Formerly *International Journal of Digital and Analog Communication Systems*.

International Journal of Electronic Commerce. M. E. Sharpe, Inc., 80 Business Park Dr. Armonk, NY 10504. Phone: 800-541-6563 or (914)273-1800 Fax: (914)273-2106 E-mail: info@mesharpe.com • URL: http://www.mesharpe.com • Quarterly. Individuals, $78.00 per year; institutions, $499.00 per year. Inlcudes print and online editions. A scholarly journal published to advance the understanding and practice of electronic commerce.

International Journal of Energy Research. John Wiley and Sons, Inc., Journals, 111 River Hoboken, NJ 07030. Phone: 800-225-5945 or (201)748-6000 Fax: (201)748-6088 E-mail: customer@wiley.com • URL: http://www.wiley.com • 15 times a year. Individuals, $2,685.00 per year; institutions, $3,500.00 per year. Published in England by John Wiley & Sons Ltd.

International Journal of Health Planning and Management. John Wiley and Sons, Inc., Journals, 111 River Hoboken, NJ 07030. Phone: 800-526-5368 or (201)748-6000 Fax: (201)748-6088 E-mail: customer@wiley.com • URL: http://www.wiley.com • Quarterly. Individuals, $960.00 per year; institutions, $1,280.00 per year. Published in England by John Wiley and Sons Ltd.

International Journal of Hospitality and Tourism Administration: A Multinationaland Cross-Cultural Journal of Applied Research. Haworth Press, Inc., 10 Alice St. Binghamton, NY 13904-1580. Phone: 800-429-6784 or (607)722-5857 Fax: 800-895-0582 or (607)722-1424 E-mail: getinfo@haworthpressinc.com • URL: http://www.haworthpressinc.com • Quarterly. $200.00 per year. Includes print and online editions. An academic journal with articles relating to lodging, food service, travel, tourism, and the hospitality/leisure industries in general. Formerly *Journal of International Hospitality, Leisure, and Tourism Management*.

International Journal of Intelligent Systems. John Wiley and Sons, Inc., Journals, 111 River St. Hoboken, NJ 07030. Phone: 800-225-5945 or (201)748-6000 Fax: (201)748-6088 E-mail: customer@wiley.com • URL: http://www.wiley.com • Monthly. $1,925.00 per year; with online edition, $2,022.00 per year.

International Journal of Machine Tools and Manufacture: Design, Research and Application. Elsevier, 360 Park Ave. S New York, NY 10010-1710. Phone: 888-437-4636 or (212)989-5800 Fax: (212)633-3990 E-mail: usinfo-f@elsevier.com • URL: http://www.elsevier.com • 15 times a year. Institutions, $2,772.00 per year.

International Journal of Mechanical Sciences. Elsevier, 360 Park Ave. S New York, NY 10010-1710. Phone: 888-437-4636 or (212)989-5800 Fax: (212)633-3990 E-mail: usinfo-f@sevier.com • URL: http://www.elsevier.com • Monthly. Qualified personnel, $228.00 per year; institutions, $2,678.00 per year.

International Journal of Powder Metallurgy. American Powder Metallurgy Institute. APMI International, 105 College Rd., E. Princeton, NJ 08540-6692. Phone: (609)452-7700 Fax: (609)987-8523 E-mail: info@mpif.org • URL: http://www.mpif.org • Eight times a year. Individuals, $85.00 per year; institutions, $180.00 per year.

International Journal of Productivity and Performance Management. Emerald, 60-62 Toller Lane, Bradford West Yorkshire BD8 9BY, United Kingdom. Phone: 44 1274 777700 Fax: 44 1274 785200 E-mail: info@emeraldinsight.com • URL: http://www.emeraldinsight.com/journals • Eight times a year. $6,069.00 per year. Provides information on management services and industrial engineering. Formerly *Work Study*.

International Journal of Refrigeration. Elsevier, 360 Park Ave. S New York, NY 10010-1710. Phone: 888-437-4636 or

(212)989-5800 Fax: (212)633-3990 E-mail: usinfo-f@elsevier.com • URL: http://www.elsevier.com • Eight times a year. Qualified personnel, $99.00 per year; institutions, $1,131.00 per year. Text in English and French.

International Journal of Robotics Research. Sage Publications, Inc., 2455 Teller Rd. Thousand Oaks, CA 91320. Phone: 800-818-7243 or (805)499-9774 Fax: 800-583-2665 or (805)499-0871 E-mail: webmaster@sagepub.com • URL: http://www.sagepub.com • Monthly. Institutions, $1,144.00 per year; includes print and online editions.

International Journal: The News and Views Paper for the Hobbyist. Levine Publications, P.O. Box 9090 Trenton, NJ 08650. Quarterly. $52.50.

International Labour Review. International Labour Office. ILO Publications Center, Nine Jay Gould Ct. Waldorf, MD 20602. Phone: (301)638-3152 Fax: (301)843-0159 E-mail: ilo@ilo.org • URL: http://www.ilo.org • Bimonthly. $80.00. Editions in English, French and Spanish.

International Law Association., Charles Clore House, 17 Russell Sq. London WC1B 5DR, United Kingdom. Phone: 44 20 73232978 Fax: 44 20 73233580 E-mail: info@ila-hq.org • URL: http://www.ila-hq.org • Lawyers and representatives in 85 countries active in the shipping, commercial, and banking industries. Fosters interest in the study, advancement and unification of international public and private law and comparative law, and in resolving legal conflicts. Conducts seminars.

International Law Institute. International Law Institute, The Foundry Bldg., 1055 Thomas Jefferson St. NW Washington, DC 20007. Phone: (202)247-6006 Fax: (202)247-6010 E-mail: kphan@ili.org • URL: http://www.ili.org • Issues of international law and development, including American and international antitrust law; trade agreements; problems of investments in foreign countries and of foreign investments in the U.S.; comparative studies on corporation and labor law, including studies of economic development, foreign investments and loans, transfer of technology, arbitration, petroleum and mining, trade, budgeting, management, and procurement, and contracting. Performs surveys of literature on U.S. trade policy instruments and their implementation, operation, and industry performance implications; also assesses U.S. international economic policy.

International Lawyer. American Bar Association, International Law and Practice Section., 740 15th St. NW Washington, DC 20005-1022. Phone: 800-285-2221 or (202)662-1660 Fax: (202)662-1669 E-mail: price@staff.abanet.org • URL: http://www.abanet.org • Quarterly. Free to members; non-members, $60.00 per year.

International Lead Zinc Research Organization., 2525 Meridian Pkwy., Ste. 100 Durham, NC 27713. Phone: (919)361-4647 Fax: (919)361-1957 E-mail: rputnam@ilzro.org • URL: http://www.ilzro.org • Seeks to develop new applications for lead and zinc. Improves current uses of lead and zinc; compiles technical information on these metals. Directs approximately 150 research programs through its contracts with universities, governments, independent laboratories, industrial companies, and member companies. Research and development projects deal with die castings, wrought zinc, alloys, galvanized steel, plating, welding, lead and zinc chemistry, environmental studies, batteries, lead for architectural uses, and other subjects. Acts as a Research organization sponsored by major producers, smelters, and refiners of lead and/or zinc from 15 countries.

International League of Electrical Associations., 2901 Metro Dr., Ste. 203 Bloomington, MN 55425. Phone: (952)854-4405 Fax: (952)854-7076 E-mail: sue@ncel.org • URL: http://www.ileaweb.org • Formerly International Association of Electric Leagues.

International Legal Materials. American Society of International Law, 2223 Massachusetts Ave., N.W. Washington, DC 20008-2864. Phone: (202)939-6000 Fax: (202)797-7133 • URL: http://www.asil.org • Bimonthly. $190.00 per year.

International Licensing Industry Merchandisers' Association., 350 Fifth Ave., Suite 1408 New York, NY 10118. Phone: (212)244-1944 Fax: (212)563-6552 E-mail: info@licensing.org • URL: http://www.licensing.org • Promotes the legal protection of licensed properties.

International Literary Market Place: The Directory of the International Book Publishing Industry. Information Today, Inc., 143 Old Marlton Pike Medford, NJ 08055-8750. Phone: 800-300-9868 or (609)654-6266 Fax: (609)654-4309 E-mail: custserv@infotoday.com • URL: http://www.infotoday.com • Annual. $219.00. Covers more than 180 countries. Listings include publishers, literary agents, major booksellers, book clubs, literary prizes, distributors, trade associations, etc. Formerly published by R. R. Bowker.

International Magnesium Association., 1000 N Rand Rd., Ste. 214 Wauconda, IL 60084. Phone: (847)526-2010 Fax: (847)526-3993 E-mail: info@intlmag.org • URL: http://www.intlmag.org • Represents manufacturers, processors, users, suppliers, and recyclers of magnesium. Works to promote the magnesium industry; develops and increases the use of magnesium and its alloys; publicizes and promotes new uses of the metal to end-use markets. Conducts research programs, compiles statistics and offers educational programs.

International Magnesium Association—Buyer's Guide. International Magnesium Association, 1000 N Rand Rd., Ste. 214 Wauconda, IL 60084. Phone: (847)526-2010 Fax: (847)526-3993 E-mail: info@intlmag.org • URL: http://

www.intlmag.org • Covers: Companies involved in the magnesium industry, including producers, die caster, processors, researchers, and suppliers. Entries include: Company name, address, phone, fax, plant locations, products and services offered.

International Mail Manual. Available from U. S. Government Printing Office, Washington, DC 20402. Phone: (202)512-1800 Fax: (202)512-2250 E-mail: gpoaccess@gpo.gov • URL: http://www.access.gpo.gov • Semiannual. $40.00 per year. Issued by U. S. Postal Service. Contains rates, regulations, classes of mail, special services, etc., for mail sent from the U. S. to foreign countries.

International Maintenance Institute., PO Box 751896 Houston, TX 77275-1896. Phone: 888-207-1773 or (281)481-0869 Fax: (281)481-8337 E-mail: iminst@swbell.net • URL: http://www.imionline.org • Persons directly engaged in maintenance in a key position (superintendent, supervisor, foreman, or manager) for chemical refineries, manufacturing firms, government agencies, institutions, and other organizations; associate members are persons indirectly engaged in maintenance in sales, service, consulting, or publications capacities. Seeks to promote the professionalism of maintenance personnel and keep members informed of developments in the field. Assembles and disseminates maintenance information related to modern cost-saving methods, processes, and equipment. Conducts plant tours; local chapters sponsor monthly meetings, lectures, and discussions on such topics as preventive maintenance, electrical specification and maintenance, purchasing procedures, painting, heating, and grounds maintenance. Maintains hall of fame.

International Management Council of the YMCA., 7502 Maple St. Omaha, NE 68134-6602. Phone: 800-688-9622 or (402)330-6310 Fax: (402)330-7424 E-mail: imcoffice@msn.com • URL: http://www.imc-ymca.org • Formerly International Management Council.

International Market Alert. United Communications Group, 11300 Rockville Pke., Ste. 1100 Rockville, MD 20852-3030. Phone: 800-929-4824 or (301)287-2700 Fax: (301)816-8945 E-mail: webmaster@ucg.com Description: Provides a fax service covering financial markets, world economy developments, foreign exchange, and U.S. interest rates.

International Marketing. Philip R. Cateora and John Graham. McGraw-Hill, 1221 Ave. of the Americas New York, NY 10020. Phone: 800-722-4726 or (212)512-2000 Fax: (212)512-4502 E-mail: customer.service@mcgraw-hill.com • URL: http://www.mcgraw-hill.com • 2001. $94.69. 11th edition. (Marketing Series).

International Marketing Data and Statistics. Available from Gale Cengage Learning, 27500 Drake Rd. Farmington Hills, MI 48331-3535. Phone: 800-877-GALE or (248)699-GALE Fax: 800-414-5043 E-mail: gale.galeord@cengage.com • URL: http://gale.cengage.com • Annual. $530.00. Published by Euromonitor. Contains statistics on population, economic factors, energy, consumer expenditures, prices, and other items affecting marketing in 158 countries of the world.

International Marketing Forecasts. Available from Gale Cengage Learning, 27500 Drake Rd. Farmington Hills, MI 48331-3535. Phone: 800-877-GALE or (248)699-GALE Fax: 800-414-5043 E-mail: gale.galeord@cengage.com • URL: http://gale.cengage.com • Annual. $1,250.00. Published by Euromonitor. Contains demographic, economic, and market forecasts to the year 2013 for major, non-European countries, including the U. S. and Canada. Forecasts include market-size data for 15 consumer product sectors, such as food, clothing, and automobiles.

International Masonry Institute., The James Brice House, 42 East St. Annapolis, MD 21401. Phone: 800-803-0295 or (410)280-1305 Fax: (301)261-2855 E-mail: masonryquestions@imiweb.org • URL: http://www.imiweb.org • Joint labor/management trust fund of the International Union of Bricklayers and Allied Craftworkers and union masonry contractors. Aims for the advancement of quality masonry construction through national and regional training, promotion, advertising and labor management relations programs in the U.S. and Canada. Provides support and materials for local/regional masonry promotion groups in the U.S. and Canada, and cooperates with national groups and organizations promoting the industry. Sponsors craft training and research programs. Offers educational programs. Maintains museum.

International Mass Retail Association., 1700 N. Moore St., Suite 2250 Arlington, VA 22209. Phone: (703)841-2300 Fax: (703)841-1184 E-mail: klasu@imra.org • URL: http://www.imra.org • Formerly National Mass Retailing Institute.

International Materials Review. ASM International, 9639 Kinsman Rd. Materials Park, OH 44073-0002. Phone: 800-336-5152 or (440)338-5151 Fax: (440)338-8091 E-mail: custsrv@asminternational.org • URL: http://www.asminternational.org • Bimonthly. $865.00 per year. Provides technical and research coverage of metals, alloys, and advanced materials. Formerly *International Metals Review*.

International Media Guide: Business-Professional: Asia/Pacific, Middle East, Africa. SRDS, 1700 Higgins Rd. Des Plaines, IL 60018-5605. Phone: 800-851-7737 or (847)375-5000 Fax: (847)375-5001 • URL: http://www.srds.com • Annual. $300.00. Provides information on 14,000 trade journals "from Africa to the Pacific Rim," including advertising rates and circulation data.

International Media Guide Business-Professional Publications: Europe. SRDS, 1700 Higgins Rd. Des Plaines, IL 60018-5605. Phone: 800-851-7737 or (847)375-5000 Fax: (847)375-5001 • URL: http://www.srds.com • Annual. $300.00. Describes 6,000 trade journals from Eastern and Western Europe, with advertising rates and circulation data.

International Media Guide: Business/Professional Publications: The Americas. SRDS, 1700 Higgins Rd. Des Plaines, IL 60018-5605. Phone: 800-851-7737 or (847)375-5605 Fax: (847)375-5001 • URL: http://www.srds.com • Annual. $300. 00. Describes trade journals from North, South, and Central America, with advertising rates and circulation data.

International Media Guide: Newspapers Worldwide. SRDS, 1700 Higgins Rd. Des Plaines, IL 60018-5605. Phone: 800-851-7737 or (847)375-5000 Fax: (847)375-5001 • URL: http://www.srds.com • Annual. $350.00. Provides advertising rates, circulation, and other details relating to newspapers in major cities of the world (covers 200 countries, including U. S.).

International Merger and Acquisition Professionals., 525 SW Fifth St. Des Moines, IA 50309. Phone: (515)282-8192 Fax: (515)282-9117 E-mail: info@imap.com • URL: http://www.imap.com • Mainly concerned with medium-sized businesses having annual sales of less than 50 million dollars.

International Microwave Power Institute., 7076 Drinkard Way Mechanicsville, VA 23111-5007. Phone: (804)559-6667 Fax: (804)559-4087 E-mail: info@impi.org • URL: http://www.impi.org • Scientists from 31 countries interested in microwave power for non-communications purposes, particularly in its applications to industrial heating processes, biomedicine, and microwave cooking and ovens. Promotes university research; provides speakers to public affairs conferences and government organizations. Offers short courses.

International Migration of the Highly Qualified: A Bibliographic and Conceptual Itinerary. Jacques Gaillard and Anne-Marie Gaillard. Center for Migration Studies, 209 Flagg Place Staten Island, NY 10304-1122. Phone: (718)351-8800 Fax: (718)667-4598 E-mail: sales@cmsny.org • URL: http://www.cmsny.org • 1998. $29.95. Includes more than 1,800 references from 1954 to 1995 on the migration patterns of skilled or highly qualified workers. (CMS Bibliographies and Documentation Series),

International Migration Review: A Quarterly Studying Sociological, Demographic, Economic, Historical, and Legislative Aspects of Human Migration Movements and Ethnic Group Relations. Center for Migration Studies, 209 Flagg Place Staten Island, NY 10304-1122. Phone: (718)351-8800 Fax: (718)667-4598 E-mail: sales@cmsny.org • URL: http://www.cmsny.org • Quarterly. Individuals, $39.00 per year; institutions, $80.00 per year.

International Military Community Executives Association.

International Mobile Air Conditioning Association Education Foundation., 6410 Southwest Blvd., Ste. 212 Fort Worth, TX 76109-3920. Phone: (817)732-4600 Fax: (817)732-9610 E-mail: info@imaca.org • URL: http://www.imaca.org • Serves the automotive, boat, and aircraft air conditioning industries. Formerly Automotive Air Conditioning Association.

International Monetary Fund., 700 19th St. NW Washington, DC 20431. Phone: (202)623-7000 Fax: (202)623-4661 E-mail: publicaffairs@imf.org • URL: http://www.imf.org • Comprises 185 national governments. Works to: facilitate monetary cooperation through consultation and collaboration among member nations; assist in the balanced expansion of trade and thus contribute to the internal development and prosperity of member nations; maintain stability in monetary exchange arrangements, particularly to avoid exchange depreciations; participate in establishing a multilateral system of payments between member nations and in eliminating exchange restrictions that hamper trade; make available the resources of the fund to provide member nations with a means of assuaging economic difficulties. Maintains the IMF Institute, which conducts training courses and seminars and provides lecturers on subjects such as compilation of statistics and formulation and execution of balance of payment policies. Offers technical assistance on monetary matters to member nations and their dependencies and to multinational institutions. Acts as a depository of information and statistical data regarding the economic affairs of member nations. Operates library, in conjunction with the World Bank, on finance and economic development.

International Monetary Fund: A Selected Bibliography. Anne C. Salda. Transaction Publishers, 309 Campus Dr. Somerset, NJ 07830. Phone: 888-999-6778 Fax: (732)748-9801 E-mail: orders@transactionpub.com • URL: http://www.transactionpub.com • 1992. $64.95.

International Monetary Fund. Annual Report on Exhange Arrangements and Exchange Restrictions. International Monetary Fund Publications Services, 700 19th St., N.W. Washington, DC 20431. Phone: (202)623-7000 Fax: (202)623-6278 E-mail: publicaffairs@imf.org • URL: http://www.imf.org • Annual. Individuals, $95.00; libraries, $47. 50.

International Monetary Fund: Overview, Issues, and Bibliography. Elisabeth P. McLellan, editor. Nova Science Publishers, Inc., 400 Oser Ave., Suite 1600 Hauppauge, NY 11788-3619. Phone: (631)231-7269 Fax: (631)231-8175 E-mail: novascience@earthlink.net • URL: http://www.novapublishers.com • 2002. $69.00. Provides articles by various authors on the basics of the IMF. Includes an extensive bibliography with author, title, and subject indexes.

International Monetary Fund Staff Papers. International Monetary Fund, Publication Services, 700 19th St., N.W. Washington, DC 20431-0001. Phone: (202)623-7000 Fax: (202)623-6278 E-mail: publicaffairs@imf.org • URL: http://www.imf.org • Quarterly. Individuals, $56.00 per year; students, $28.00 per year. Contains studies by IMF staff members on balance of payments, foreign exchange, fiscal policy, and related topics. Formerly *International Monetary Fund Staff Papers*.

International Motion Picture Almanac: Reference Tool of the Film Industry. Quigley Publishing Co., Inc., 6639 La Jolla Blvd. La Jolla, CA 92037. Phone: 800-231-8239 or (858)459-1159 Fax: (858)459-1590 E-mail: quigleypub@aol.com • URL: http://www.quigleypub.com • Annual. $130.00. Reference covering the motion picture industry.

International Municipal Lawyers Association., 1110 Vermont Ave. NW, Ste. 200 Washington, DC 20005. Phone: (202)466-5424 Fax: (202)785-1052 E-mail: info@imla.org • URL: http://www.imla.org • Seeks to promote and advance the development of local government law and. Serves as a clearinghouse of local law materials; collects and disseminates information; assists government agencies to prepare for litigation and develop new local laws; provides legal research and writing services; offers continuing legal education opportunities; conducts research programs.

International Narcotic Enforcement Officers Association., 112 State St., Suite 1200 Albany, NY 12207-2079. Phone: (518)463-6232 Fax: (518)432-3378 E-mail: inepa@iopener.net • URL: http://www.ineoa.org • Formerly National Narcotic Enforcement Officers Association.

International New Product Newsletter. International New Product Newsletter, Box 1146 Marblehead, MA 01945. Phone: (508)741-0224 Fax: (508)741-0224 E-mail: webmaster@ucg.com Description: Provides "advance news of new products and processes, primarily from sources outside the U.S." Emphasizes new products which can cut costs and improve efficiency. Recurring features include the column Special Licensing Opportunities which lists new products and processes that are available for manufacture under license, or are for sale or import.

International Newspaper Financial Executives., 21525 Ridgetop Cir., Ste. 200 Sterling, VA 20166. Phone: (703)421-4060 Fax: (703)421-4068 E-mail: infehq@infe.org • URL: http://www.infe.org • Controllers, chief accountants, auditors, business managers, treasurers, secretaries and related newspaper executives, educators, and public accountants. Conducts research projects on accounting methods and procedures for newspapers. Offers placement service; maintains speakers' bureau. Produces conferences and seminars.

International Newspaper Marketing Association., 10300 N Central Expy., Ste. 467 Dallas, TX 75231-8654. Phone: (214)373-9111 Fax: (214)373-9112 E-mail: broke.bode@inma.org • URL: http://www.inma.org • Represents individuals engaged in marketing, circulation, research, and public relations of newspapers. Conducts conferences; holds newspaper executives marketing and strategic planning seminars.

International Numismatic Society Authentication Bureau., 3386 Rasmont Rd., Apt. F Roanoke, VA 24018-6326. Fax: (610)494-2270 E-mail: broke.bode@inma.org Numismatic organizations, coin dealers, and private coin collectors from 8 countries. Offers an authentication bureau for coins from all countries and eras; holds seminars on authentication, coin grading, coin photography, and related subjects. Conducts research into microscopic characteristics of genuine coin dies.

International Oceanographic Foundation., University of Miami, Rosentiel School of Marine and Atmospheric Science Miami, FL 33149-1098. Phone: (305)361-4888 or (305)361-4697 Fax: (305)361-4711 E-mail: oceans@nbc.com • URL: http://www.rsmas.miami.edu/iof/ • Individuals interested in the sea. Encourages the protection and exploration of oceans. Topics include: game and food fish; other creatures of sea and shore; ocean currents; geology, chemistry, and physics of the sea and sea floor; submarine detection; industrial applications of oceanography.

International Oil News. William F. Bland Co., 709 Turmeric Ln. Durham, NC 27713. Phone: (919)544-1717 Fax: (919)544-1999 E-mail: mbs@PetroChemical-News.com • URL: http://www.petrochemical-news.com • Description: Covers "timely and significant developments in the international oil business, including exploration, production, transportation, refining, and marketing."

International Organization for Standardization., 1 rue de Varembe-CP56 CH-1211 Geneva 20, Switzerland. Phone: 41 22 7490111 Fax: 41 22 7490948 E-mail: rh@iso.org • URL: http://www.iso.ch/ • Members are national standards organizations. Develops and publishes international standards, including ISO 9000 quality management standards. Affiliated with American National Standards Institute.

International Personnel Management Association.

International Petroleum Encyclopedia. PennWell Corp., Industrial Div., 1421 S. Sheridan Rd. Tulsa, OK 74112. Phone: 800-331-4463 or (918)835-3161 E-mail: petroleum@pennwell.com • URL: http://www.pennwell.com • 2002. $160.00. A worldwide petroleum directory. Features statistics and a complete atlas of the international petroleum market.

International Pharmaceutical Abstracts [CD-ROM]. American Society of Health-System Pharmacists, 7272 Wisconsin Ave. Bethesda, MD 20814. Phone: (301)657-3000 Fax: (301)657-1251 Monthly. $1,795.00 per year. Contains CD-ROM indexing and abstracting of international pharmaceutical literature from 1970 to date.

International Pharmaceutical Abstracts: Key to the World's Literature of Pharmacy. American Society of Health-System Pharmacists, 7272 Wisconsin Ave. Bethesda, MD 20814. Phone: (301)657-3000 Fax: 800-665-2747 or (301)657-1251 E-mail: custserv@ashp.org • URL: http://www.ashp.org • Semimonthly. $565.50 per year.

International Pharmaceutical Abstracts [online]. American Society of Health-System Pharmacists, 7272 Wisconsin Ave. Bethesda, MD 20814. Phone: (301)657-3000 Fax: (301)657-1641 Provides online indexing and abstracting of the world's pharmaceutical literature from 1970 to date. Monthly updates. Inquire as to online cost and availability.

International Physical Fitness Association., 415 W Court St. Flint, MI 48503. Phone: 877-520-IPFA or (810)239-2166 Fax: (810)239-9390 E-mail: contact@ipfa.us • URL: http://www.ipfa.us • Physical fitness centers. Facilitates the transfer of individual memberships from one member club to another.

International Prepress Association., 7200 France Ave., S., Suite 223 Edina, MN 55435. Phone: 800-255-8141 or (612)896-1908 Fax: (612)896-0181 E-mail: info@ipa.org • URL: http://www.ipa.org • Formerly International Association of Photoplatemakers.

International Press Journal: International Press News and Views., Drawer G Kenmore, NY 14217. Quarterly. $20.00 per year.

International Private Label Directory. E. W. Williams Publications Co., 2125 Center Ave., Suite 305 Fort Lee, NJ 07024-5859. Phone: (201)592-7007 Fax: (201)592-7171 Annual. $75.00. Provides information on over 2,000 suppliers of a wide variety of private label and generic products: food, over-the-counter health products, personal care items, and general merchandise. Formerly *Private Label Directory*.

International Pulp and Paper Directory. CMP Media LLC, 600 Community Dr. Manhasset, NY 11030. Phone: (516)562-5000 E-mail: cmp@cmp.com • URL: http://www.cmp.com • Annual. $287.00. Lists over 6,000 pulp and papermills. International coverage.

International Radio and Television Society Foundation., 420 Lexington Ave., Suite 1714 New York, NY 10170. Phone: (212)867-6650 Fax: (212)867-6653 • URL: http://www.irts.org • Affiliated with National Broadcasting Society-Alpha Epsilon Pho. Formerly International Radio and Television Society.

International Radio and Television Society Newsletter. International Radio and Television Society, 420 Lexington Ave., Ste. 1714 New York, NY 10170-0002. Phone: (212)867-6650 Fax: (212)867-6653 • URL: http://www.irts.org • Quarterly.

International Railway Journal: The First International Railway and Rapid Transit Journal. Simmons-Boardman Publishing Corp., 345 Hudson St., 12th Fl. New York, NY 10014-4502. Phone: (212)620-7200 Fax: (212)633-1165 Monthly. $72.00 per year. Formerly *International Railway Journal and Rapid Transit Review*. Text in English; summaries in French, German and Spanish.

International Reciprocal Trade Association., 140 Metro Park Rochester, NY 14623-2641. Phone: (585)424-2940 Fax: (585)424-2964 E-mail: ron@irta.com • URL: http://www.irta.com • Individuals, partnerships, corporations, and firms that engage in the commercial barter industry worldwide, including local trade exchanges which act as clearinghouses, and corporate trade companies which arrange domestic and international barter transactions. Works to foster and promote the interests of the commercial barter industry through the establishment of ethical standards and self-regulation; to represent members before government agencies in matters affecting the industry; to introduce firms engaged in bartering activities; to resolve disputes between members; influence public laws and regulations affecting the industry; disseminate information and conduct public relations programs. Serves as a clearinghouse for industry and public inquiries. Compiles statistics on the segment of commercial barter accounted for by organized trade exchanges and corporate trade companies. Conducts consumer protection, educational, and training programs. Operates Corporate Barter Council as a self-governing body for the corporate trade sector. Awards professional accreditation; operates referral and placement services; maintains speakers' bureau; supports charitable programs.

International Rehabilitation Review. Rehabilitation International, 25 E 21 St., 4th Fl. New York, NY 10010. Phone: (212)420-1500 Fax: (212)505-0871 E-mail: ri@riglobal.org Description: Contains news and articles on international, national, and local developments in the fields of disability prevention and rehabilitation. Provides regular coverage of United Nations agencies, discusses the elimination of architectural and attitudinal barriers to disabled persons, and examines new trends in service delivery. Recurring features include news of research, book reviews, and a calendar of events.

International Reprographic Association., 401 N Michigan Ave. Chicago, IL 60611-4255. Phone: 800-833-4742 or (312)245-1026 Fax: (312)527-6724 E-mail: sbova@irga.com • URL:

http://www.irga.com • Commercial blue print and photocopy firms, engineering supply stores, and materials and equipment suppliers. Conducts annual photo-tech, marketing, management, and business planning seminars.

International Research Centers Directory. Gale, 27500 Drake Rd. Farmington Hills, MI 48331-3535. Phone: 800-877-4253 or (248)699-4253 Fax: 800-414-5043 or (248)699-8065 E-mail: galeord@cengage.com • URL: http://gale.cengage.com • Covers: Over 9,500 research and development facilities maintained outside the United States by governments, universities, or independent organizations, and concerned with all areas of physical, social, and life sciences, technology, business, military science, public policy, and the humanities. Entries include: Facility name, address, phone, fax, telex, e-mail, URLs, name of parent agency or other affiliation, date established, number of staff, type of activity and fields of research, special research facilities, publications, educational activities, services, and library holdings.

International Review for Business Education. SIEC-ISBE, PO Box 20457 Carson City, NV 89721. Phone: (775)882-1445 Fax: (775)882-1449 E-mail: secretary@siec-isbe.org • URL: http://www.siec-isbe.org • Semiannual. $36.00 per year. Text in English, French, German, Italian, and Spanish.

International Review of Applied Economics. Routledge, 29 W 35th St. New York, NY 10001. E-mail: info@routledge-ny.com • URL: http://www.routledge-ny.com • Quarterly. Individuals, $310.00 per year; institutions, $1,007.00 per year.

International Review of Industrial and Organizational Psychology. John Wiley and Sons, Inc., Journals, 111 River Hoboken, NJ 07030. Phone: 800-225-5945 or (201)748-6000 Fax: (201)748-6088 E-mail: customer@wiley.com • URL: http://www.wiley.com • Annual. $150.00. Published in England by John Wiley and Sons Ltd.

International Road Federation., 500 Montgomery St., 5th Fl., Madison Pl. Alexandria, VA 22314-1565. Phone: (703)535-1001 Fax: (703)535-1007 E-mail: info@irfnews.org • URL: http://www.irfnet.org • Road associations, private sector firms, and public sector firms in 70 countries. Encourages the development and improvement of highways and highway transportation and the exchange of technologies. Provides educational grants to select countries for graduate training through the International Road Educational Foundation.

International Sanitary Supply Association., 7373 N Lincoln Ave. Lincolnwood, IL 60712-1799. Phone: 800-225-4772 or (847)982-0800 Fax: (847)982-1012 E-mail: info@issa.com • URL: http://www.issa.com • Manufacturers, distributors, wholesalers, manufacturer representatives, publishers, and associate members of cleaning and maintenance supplies, chemicals, and equipment used by janitors, custodians, and maintenance workers in all types of industrial, commercial, and institutional buildings. Represents members in 83 countries. Produces videos and other educational materials. Offers specialized education seminars.

International Satellite Directory: A Complete Guide to the Satellite Communications Industry. Satnews Publishers, 800 Siesta Way Sonoma, CA 95476-4413. Phone: (707)939-9306 Fax: (707)939-9235 E-mail: design@satnews.com • URL: http://www.satnews.com • Annual. $395.00. Lists over 25,000 satellite operators, common carriers, earth stations, manufacturers, associations, etc.

International Save the Pun Foundation.

International Security Management Association., PO Box 623 Buffalo, IA 52728. Phone: 800-368-1894 or (563)381-4008 Fax: 800-568-1894 or (563)381-4283 E-mail: isma3@aol.com • URL: http://www.ismanet.com • Senior security executives of multinational business firms and chief executive officers of full service security services companies. Aims to assist senior security executives in coordinating and exchanging information about security management and to establish high business and professional standards.

International Sign Association., 707 N St. Asaph St. Alexandria, VA 22314. Phone: (703)836-4012 Fax: (703)836-8353 E-mail: lori.anderson@signs.org • URL: http://www.signs.org • Manufacturers, users, and suppliers of on-premise signs and sign products produced by more than 400,000 employees in all 50 states and 69 countries. Exists to support, promote and improve the $30 billion-a-year sign industry, which sustains the nation's nearly $3 trillion-a-year retail industry.

International Silk Association - U.S.A., One Madison St., One Madison St. East Rutherford, NJ 07073. Phone: (973)472-4200 Fax: (973)472-0222 E-mail: lori.anderson@signs.org Firms engaged in various phases of the silk industry. Promotes the use of silk in all its forms.

International Society for Community Development Newsletter., c/o Glen Leet, 54 Riverside Dr. New York, NY 10024. Phone: (212)362-7958 Fax: (212)877-7464 Semiannual. Membership.

International Society for Performance Improvement., 1400 Spring St., Suite 260 Silver Spring, MD 20910. Phone: (310)587-8570 Fax: (310)587-8573 E-mail: info@ispi.org • URL: http://www.ispi.org • Formerly National Society for Performance and Instruction.

International Society for Technology in Education.

International Society for the Performing Arts., 17 Prudy Ave. Rye, NY 10580. Phone: (914)921-1550 Fax: (914)921-1593 E-mail: info@ispa.org • URL: http://www.ispa.org • Formerly International Society of Performing Arts Administrators.

International Society of Beverage Technologists., 8110 S. Sun-coast Blvd. Homosassa, FL 34446. Phone: (352)382-2008 Fax: (352)382-2018 E-mail: isbt@bevetch.org • URL: http://www.bevtech.org • Members are professionals engaged in the technical areas of soft drink production. Formerly Society of Soft Drink Technologies.

International Society of Certified Employee Beneift Plan Specialists., 18700 W. Bluemound Rd. Brookfield, WI 53008. Phone: (262)786-8771 Fax: (262)786-8650 E-mail: iscebs@iscebs.org • URL: http://www.iscebs.org • Affiliated with International Foundation of Employee Benefit Plans.

International Society of Explosives Engineers., 30325 Bain-bridge Rd. Cleveland, OH 44139. Phone: (440)349-4400 Fax: (440)349-3788 E-mail: isee@isee.org • URL: http://www.isee.org • Formerly Society of Explosives Engineers.

International Society of Weighing and Measurement., 10 W. Kimball St. Windsor, GA 30680. Phone: (770)868-5300 Fax: (770)868-5301 E-mail: staff@iswm.org • URL: http://www.iswm.org • Formerly National Scale Men's Association.

International Society of Weighing and Measurement Membership Directory and Product Guide. International Society of Weighing and Measurement, 10 Kimball St., W. Winder, GA 30680. Phone: (770)868-5300 Fax: (770)868-5301 E-mail: staff@iswm.org • URL: http://www.iswm.org • Annual. Free to members; non-members, $50.00.

International Special Events Society., 401 N Michigan Ave. Chicago, IL 60611-4267. Phone: 800-688-4737 or (312)321-6853 Fax: (312)673-6953 E-mail: info@ises.com • URL: http://www.ises.com • Special events planners, caterers, designers, event marketers, technical experts, transportation and destination professionals. Seeks to educate, advance, and promote special events.

International Standard Industrial Classification of All Economic Activities. United Nations Publications, United Nations Concourse Level, First Ave., 46th. St. New York, NY 10017. Phone: 800-553-3210 or (212)963-7680 Fax: (212)953-4910 E-mail: bookstore@un.org • URL: http://www.un.org/publications • 1992. Third revised edition.

International Standards Desk Reference: Your Passport to World Markets. Amy Zuckerman. AMACOM, 1601 Broadway New York, NY 10019. Phone: 800-262-9699 or (518)586-8100 Fax: (518)903-8168 E-mail: customerservice@amanet.org • URL: http://www.amacombooks.org • 1996. $35.00. Provides information on standards important in export-import trade, such as ISO 9000.

International Statistical Institute., Prinses Beatrixlaan 428, PO Box 950 NL-2270 AZ Voorburg, Netherlands. Phone: 31 70 3860025 or 31 70 3375737 Fax: 31 70 3860025 E-mail: isi@cbs.nl • URL: http://isi.cbs.nl • Persons from more than 130 countries who have contributed to the development or application of statistical methods or to the administration of statistical services. Works toward the development and improvement of statistical methods and their application worldwide. Sponsors statistics course at the ISEC in Calcutta, India. Compiles and publishes information pertaining to international statistics; has established an abstracting service of statistical publications.

International Studies and Overseas Programs-Latin American Center, University of California, Los Angeles.

International Survey of Business Expectations. Dun & Bradstreet Corp., Economic Analysis Dept., 103 JFK Pky. Short Hills, NJ 07078. Phone: 800-526-0651 E-mail: custserv@dnb.com • URL: http://www.dnb.com • Quarterly. $40.00 per year. A survey of international business executives regarding their quarterly expectations for sales, profits, prices, inventories, employment, and new orders. Results are given for each of 14 major foreign countries and the U. S.

International Tax Agreements. United Nations Publications, United Nations Concourse Level, First Ave., 46th. St. New York, NY 10017. Phone: 800-553-3210 or (212)963-7680 Fax: (212)963-4910 E-mail: bookstore@un.org • URL: http://www.un.org/publications • Irregular. Price varies. Looseleaf.

International Tax Journal. Aspen Publishers, 1185 Ave. of the Americas New York, NY 10036. Phone: 800-447-1717 or (212)597-0200 Fax: (212)597-0338 E-mail: customer.service@aspenpubl.com • URL: http://www.aspenpublishers.com • Quarterly. $297.00 per year. Articles, columns and tax notes pertaining to the international tax market.

International Tax Planning Manual-Corporations. CCH, Inc., 2700 Lake Cook Rd. Riverwoods, IL 60015. Phone: 800-835-5224 or (847)267-7000 E-mail: cust_serv@cch.com • URL: http://www.cch.com • Two looseleaf volumes. Periodic supplementation. Price on application. Tax strategies for doing business in 38 major countries.

International Tax Program., Harvard University, 1563 Massachusetts Ave., Pound Hall, Room 400 Cambridge, MA 02138. Phone: (617)495-4406 Fax: (617)495-0423 E-mail: itp@law.harvard.edu • URL: http://www.law.harvard.edu/programs/itp • Studies the worldwide problems of taxation, including tax law and tax administration.

International Tax Report: Maximizing Tax Opportunities Worldwide. Informa Group PLC, Suffolk House, Church Field Rd. Sudbury C010 2YA, United Kingdom. Phone: 44 1787 378607 Fax: 44 1787 881147 • URL: http://www.monitorpress.com • Monthly. $1,100.00 per year.

International Technology Law Association., 401 Edgewater Pl., Ste. 600 Wakefield, MA 01880. Phone: (781)876-8877 Fax: (781)224-1239 E-mail: office@itechlaw.org • URL: http://

www.itechlaw.org • Lawyers, law students, and others interested in legal problems related to computer-communications technology. Aids in: contracting for computer-communications goods and services; perfecting and protecting proprietary rights chiefly in software; and taxing computer-communications goods, services, and transactions, and liability for acquisition and use of computer-communications goods and services. Provides specialized educational programs; and offers limited placement service. Holds Annual Computer Law Update.

International Telecommunications Satellite Organization.

International Television and Video Almanac: Reference Tool of the Television and Home Video Industries. Quigley Publishing Co., Inc., P.O. Box 1950 La Jolla, CA 92038. Phone: 800-231-8239 or (858)459-1159 Fax: (858)459-1590 E-mail: quigleypub@aol.com • URL: http://www.quigleypub.com • Annual. $130.00.

International Telework Association and Council., 8403 Colesville Rd., Ste. 865 Silver Spring, MD 20910. Phone: (301)650-2322 E-mail: info@workingfromanywhere.com • URL: http://www.telecommute.org • Members are individuals and organizations promoting the benefits of telecommuting and the "virtual office." Formerly Telecommuting Advisory Council/International Telework Association.

International Textile Bulletin: Dyeing-Printing-Finishing Edition. ITS Publishing, International Textile Service, Univer-Haus, Kesslerstrasse 9 CH-8952 Schlieren, Switzerland. Phone: 41 1 7384800 Fax: 41 1 7384830 E-mail: its@its-publishing.com • URL: http://www.its-publishing.com • Quarterly. $170.00 per year. Editions in Chinese, English, French, German, Italian and Spanish.

International Textile Bulletin: Nonwovens and Industrial Textiles Edition. ITS Publishing, International Textile Service, Univers-Haus, Kesslerstrasse 9 CH-8952 Schlieren, Switzerland. Phone: 41 1 7384800 Fax: 41 1 7384830 E-mail: its@its-publishing.com • URL: http://www.its-publishing.com • Quarterly. $170.00 per year. Editions in Chinese, English, French, German, Italian and Spanish.

International Textile Bulletin: Yarn and Fabric Forming Edition. ITS Publishing, International Textile Service, Univer-Haus, Kesslerstrasse 9 CH-8952 Schlieren, Switzerland. Phone: (41)1 7384800 Fax: (41)1 7384832 E-mail: circulation-management@itis-publishing.com • URL: http://www.its-publishing.com • Quarterly. $170.00 per year. Editions in Chinese, English, French, German, Italian and Spanish.

International Textile Center. Texas Tech University

International Textile Machinery Shipment Statistics. International Textile Manufacturers Federation, Am Schanzengraben 29, Postfach 8039 Zurich, Switzerland. Phone: 41 1 2017080 Fax: 41 1 2017134 E-mail: secretariat@itmf.org • URL: http://www.itmf.org • Annual. 250 Swiss francs. Formerly *International Cotton Industry Statistics*.

International Textiles: Information and Inspiration. Textile Institute. Benjamin Dent and Co., Ltd., 23 Bloomsbury Sq. London WC1A 2PJ, United Kingdom. Phone: 44 20 7637 2211 Fax: 44 20 7637 2248 10 times a year. $220.00 per year. Text in English, French and German; supplement in Japanese.

International Theatre Studies Center.

International Ticketing Association., 330 W 38th St., No. 605 New York, NY 10018. Phone: (212)629-4036 Fax: (212)629-8532 E-mail: info@intix.org • URL: http://www.intix.org • Ticket managers and directors, treasurers, financial and marketing and systems directors, and others involved in the marketing, selling, and manufacture of tickets in the performing arts and sports fields. Promotes growth and development in the ticket management industry. Works to: advance and upgrade management techniques and systems; maintain high standards of professionalism in box office management; monitor and analyze technological advances in ticket selling and accounting. Acts as an information exchange and resource center for addressing control and service issues. Provides advisory, consulting, and reference services, and job opportunity information and referral services. Compiles statistics.

International Tin Council. Quarterly Statistical Bulletin. International Tin Council, One Oxendon St. London SW1Y 4EQ, England. Quarterly. $100.00 per year. Includes eight monthly statistical summaries.

International Titanium Association., 2655 W Midway Blvd., Ste. 300, 350 Interlocken Blvd., Ste. 390 Broomfield, CO 80020-7187. Phone: (303)404-2221 Fax: (303)404-9111 E-mail: ita@titanium.org • URL: http://www.titanium.org • Represents producers, fabricators, extruders, and users of titanium (a metallic element used especially in alloys); companies performing some value-added function to titanium. Works to expand existing market, increase awareness and understanding of titanium in engineering and academic communities, and maintain an appropriate and meaningful statistics program. Maintains speakers' bureau; answers technical questions; provides application committees; sponsors educational programs.

International Titanium Association Buyers Guide. International Titanium Association, 350 Interlocken Blvd., Suite 390 Broomfield, CO 80021-3485. Phone: (303)404-2221 Fax: (303)404-9111 E-mail: info@titanium.org • URL: http://www.titanium.org • Annual. Members, $5.00; non-members, $20.00.

International Titanium Association Guide to Products and Services of Member Comp., 350 Interlocken Blvd., Suite 390 Broomfield, CO 80021-3485. Phone: (303)404-2221 Fax: (303)404-9111 E-mail: info@titanium.org • URL: http://www.titanium.org • Annual. Free. Lists about 130 titanium metal industry companies.

International Trade Alert. American Association of Exporters and Importers, 1200 G St.,NW, Ste. 800 Washington, NY 20005. Phone: (212)983-7008 Fax: (212)983-6430 E-mail: aaei5ie@aol.com Description: Reports on trade issues as they affect importers and exporters. Contains news of actions by Customs, the Federal Drug Administration (FDA), and the Department of Commerce, CITA, CPSC, FTC, and the USDA, as well as other federal agencies and departments; and the status of regulations on imported/exported products. Also contains information on legislative activity affecting importers and exporters.

International Trade and Investment Letter: Trends in U.S Policies, Trade Finance and Trading Operations. International Business Affairs Corp., 4938 Hampden Lane Bethesda, MD 20814-2914. Phone: (301)907-8647 Monthly. $240.00 per year. Newsletter.

International Trade by Commodities Statistics. Organization for Economic Cooperation and Development, OECD Washington Center, 2001 L St., N. W., Suite 650 Washington, DC 20036-4922. Phone: 800-456-6323 or (202)785-6323 Fax: (202)785-0350 E-mail: washington.contact@oecd.org • URL: http://www.oecd.org • Five times a year. $605.00 per year. Presents extensive, detailed statistical tables of OECD countries' imports and exports. Products are grouped by Standard International Trade Classification and by country.

International Trade Council., 3114 Circle Hill Rd. Alexandria, VA 22305-1606. Phone: (703)548-1234 Fax: (703)548-6216 E-mail: ita@titanium.org Companies and organizations that import and export products, commodities, and services in 300 major industries including agricultural commodities, livestock, food, farm implements, and food machinery; agencies dealing with health and medicine, housing, energy, communications, transportation, forestry, water, and sanitation. Promotes free trade and the elimination of trade barriers and facilitates logistics, research, and marketing for members. Maintains legislative and educational services to develop world trade. Conducts management, technical, and educational programs; conducts financial studies of export banking, insurance, performance bonds, and transportation costs to enable exporters to be more competitive; offers speakers' bureau. Sponsors International Development Institute; offers Opportunity/Risk Analysis Service to help members find new or expandable overseas markets for their commodities, products, services, and investments.

International Trade Reporter Export Reference Manual. BNA, Inc., 1231 25th St., NW Washington, DC 20037. Phone: 800-372-1033 E-mail: customercare@bna.com • URL: http://www.bna.com • Biweekly. $874.00 per year. Looseleaf service.

International Trade Statistics Yearbook. United Nations Statistical Office. United Nations Publications, United Nations Concourse Level, First Ave., 46th St. New York, NY 10017. Phone: 800-553-3210 or (212)963-7680 Fax: (212)963-4910 E-mail: bookstore@un.org • URL: http://www.un.org/publications • Annual. $135.00. Two volumes.

International Trademark Association., 655 3rd Ave., 10th Fl. New York, NY 10017-5617. Phone: (212)642-1700 Fax: (212)768-7796 E-mail: info@inta.org • URL: http://www.inta.org • Trademark owners; associate members are lawyers, law firms, advertising agencies, designers, market researchers, and others in the trademark industries. Seeks to: protect the interests of the public in the use of trademarks and trade names; promote the interests of members and of trademark owners generally in the use of their trademarks and trade names; disseminate information concerning the use, registration, and protection of trademarks in the United States, its territories, and in foreign countries. Maintains job bank and speakers' bureau.

International Tradeshow Directory: The Annual Statistical Directory of U.S. and Canadian Tradeshows and Public Shows. Tradeshow Week, 5700 Wilshire Blvd., Suite 120 Los Angeles, CA 90036-5804. Phone: 800-375-4212 or (323)965-2093 Fax: (323)965-5334 E-mail: aschaffer@reedbusiness.com • URL: http://www.tradesweek.com • Semiannual. Free to qualified personnel. Provides detailed information for more than 9,000 U. S. and Canadian trade shows of 5,000 square feet or more scheduled for the next four years.

International Training in Communication., 2519 Woodland Dr. Anaheim, CA 92801-2637. Phone: (714)995-3660 Fax: (714)995-6974 E-mail: itcintl@mediamatters.co.nz • URL: http://www.itcintl.com • Members are interested in speech improvement, communication, lexicology, leadership training and skill in organizational techniques and self-development.

International Travel and Tourism. H. Sorensen. Delmar Learning, 5 Maxwell Dr. Clifton Park, NJ 12065. Phone: 800-347-7707 Fax: 800-487-8488 • URL: http://www.delmarlearning.com • 1997. $86.95. (Hospitality, Travel and Tourism Series).

International Union, UAW - Community Action Program., 8000 E Jefferson Ave., Solidarity House Detroit, MI 48214. Phone: 800-243-8829 or (313)926-5000 Fax: (313)824-5750 E-mail: uaw@uaw.org • URL: http://www.uaw.org/about/works/community.html • Serves as a program of the International Union, United Automobile, Aerospace and Agricultural Implement Workers of America (UAW) (see separate entry). Informs UAW members through political education programs on topics including lobbying, the relationship between collective bargaining and the ballot box, and voluntary fundraising for political contributions. Maintains speakers' bureau; compiles statistics.

International Vital Records Handbook: Births, Marriages, Deaths. Thomas J. Kemp. Genealogical Publishing Co., Inc., 1001 N. Calvert St. Baltimore, MD 21202-3827. Phone: 800-296-6687 or (410)837-8271 Fax: 800-599-9561 or (410)752-8492 E-mail: sales@genealogical.com • URL: http://www.genealogical.com • 2000. $34.95. Fourth edition. Provides procedures and copies of forms for obtaining birth, marriage, divorce, and death records from 67 countries and territories in North America, the British Isles and other English-speaking countries and Europe.

International Warehouse Logistics Association., 2800 S River Rd., Ste. 260 Des Plaines, IL 60018-6003. Phone: 800-525-0165 or (847)813-4699 Fax: (847)813-0115 E-mail: email@iwla.com • URL: http://www.iwla.com • Fosters and promotes the growth and success of public and contract warehousing and related logistics services. Serves as the unified voice of the global outsourced warehouse logistics industry, representing 3PLs (third party logistics providers), 4PLs (fourth party logistics providers), public and contract warehouse logistics companies and their suppliers, setting standards, legal frameworks and best practices for the warehousing logistics industry for 110 years. Members of the Association receive services including legal assistance, marketing assistance and group buying programs. Owns its own insurance company (passing cost savings to members), holds an annual convention each year, and produces educational programs.

International Warehouse Logistics Association Membership Directory and Resource Guide. International Warehouse Logistics Association, 2800 S River Rd., Ste. 260 Des Plaines, IL 60018. Phone: (847)813-4699 Fax: (847)813-0115 E-mail: email@warehouselogistics.com • URL: http://www.iwia.com • Annual. Free to members, manufacturers, and distributors. Detailed listing of 500 public merchandise warehousing firms located throughout the U.S., Canada, Mexico, Costa Rica, Dominacan Republic, Panama, Venezuela, and Russia. Formerly *American Warehouse Association and Canadian Association of Warehousing and Distribution Services Membership Directory and Resource Guide*.

International Wealth Success Newsletter: The Monthly Newsletter of Worldwide Wealth Opportunities. Tyler G. Hicks, editor. International Wealth Success, Inc., 24 Canterbury Rd. Rockville Center, NY 11570-1310. Phone: (516)766-5850 Fax: (516)766-5619 Monthly. $24.00 per year. Newsletter. Provides information on a variety of small business topics, including financing, mail order, foreign opportunities, licensing, and franchises.

International Who's Who. Available from Taylor & Francis Group, 325 Chestnut St. Philadelphia, PA 19106. Phone: 800-821-8312 or (215)625-8900 Fax: 800-248-4724 or (215)625-2940 E-mail: info@taylorandfrancis.com • URL: http://www.taylorandfrancis.com • Annual. $440.00. Includes print and online editions. Published by Europa Publications (http://www.europapublications.com). Contains brief biographical information on important people in many different countries.

International Who's Who of Women. Available from Taylor and Francis, Inc., 325 Chestnut St. Philadelphia, PA 19106. Phone: 800-821-8312 or (215)625-8900 Fax: (215)625-2940 E-mail: info@taylorandfrancis.com • URL: http://www.taylorandfrancis.com • 2002. $395.00. Published by Europa. Contains biographical profiles of more than 5,000 eminent women from all countries.

International Who's Who, 2002. Taylor & Francis, 325 Chestnut St. Philadelphia, PA 19106. Phone: 800-821-8312 or (215)625-8900 Fax: (215)625-2940 E-mail: info@taylorandfrancis.com • URL: http://www.taylorandfrancis.com • 2001. $395.00. Includes CD-ROM. Provides up-to-date biographical information on important individuals in international affairs, government, diplomacy, the liberal professions, and all branches of the arts and sports. Published by Europa.

International Women's Writing Guild., PO Box 810, Gracie Sta. New York, NY 10028-0082. Phone: (212)737-7536 Fax: (212)737-9469 E-mail: dirhahn@iwwg.org • URL: http://www.iwwg.org • Women writers in 24 countries interested in expressing themselves through the written word professionally and for personal growth regardless of portfolio. Seeks to empower women personally and professionally through writing. Facilitates manuscript submissions to literary agents and independent presses. Participates in international network. Maintains dental and vision program at group rates.

Internet Alliance., 1111 19th St. NW, Ste. 1100 Washington, DC 20035-5782. Phone: (202)861-2476 Fax: (202)955-8081 E-mail: info@internetalliance.org • URL: http://www.internetalliance.org • Companies offering Internet services. Seeks to "build the confidence and trust necessary for the Internet to become the global mass market medium of the 21st century". Represents members' commercial and regulatory interests; conducts promotional activities; facilitates communication and cooperation among members.

Internet and Electronic Commerce Strategies: Using Technology to Improve Your Bottom Line. Computer Economics,

Inc., 5841 Edison Place Carlsbad, CA 92008. Phone: 800-326-8100 or (760)438-8100 Fax: (760)431-1126 E-mail: access@compecon.com • URL: http://www.computereconomics.com • Monthly. Price on application. Newsletter on management strategies for making money from the Internet. Compares online marketing with traditional marketing.

Internet and Personal Computing Abstracts. Information Today, Inc., 143 Old Marlton Pike Medford, NJ 08055-8750. Phone: 800-300-9868 or (609)654-6266 Fax: (609)654-4309 E-mail: custserv@infotoday.com • URL: http://www.infotoday.com • Contains abstracts covering a wide variety of personal and business microcomputer literature appearing in more than 100 journals and popular magazines. Time period is 1981 to date, with monthly updates. Formerly *Microcomputer Index*. Inquire as to online cost and availability.

Internet and Personal Computing Abstracts [print edition]. EBSCO Publishing, 10 Estes St. Ispwich, MA 01938. Phone: 800-653-2726 or (978)356-6500 Fax: (978)356-6565 • URL: http://www.ebsco.com • Quarterly. $269.00 per year, including cumulative index. Provides more than 10,000 abstracts annually from both trade and academic publications. Covers computer hardware, software, product reviews, Web topics, e-commerce, networks, corporate news, security, and related topics. Formerly *Microcomputer Abstracts*.

The Internet Blue Pages: The Guide to Federal Government Web Sites. Information Today, Inc., 143 Old Marlton Pike Medford, NJ 08055-8750. Phone: 800-300-9868 or (609)654-6266 Fax: (609)654-4309 E-mail: custserv@infotoday.com • URL: http://www.infotoday.com • Annual. $34.95. Provides information on more than 1,800 Web sites used by various agencies of the federal government. Includes indexes to agencies and topics. Links to all Web sites listed are available at http://www.fedweb.com. (CyberAge Books.)

Internet Book: Everything You Need to Know About Computer Networking and How the Internet Works. Douglas Comer. Prentice Hall PTR, 240 Fitsch Ct. Paramus, NJ 07652. Phone: 800-282-0693 Fax: 800-445-6991 • URL: http://www.phptr.com • 2000. $34.80. Third edition.

The Internet Bubble: Inside the Overvalued World of High-Tech Stocks, and What You Should Know to Avoid the Coming Catastrophe. Anthony Perkins and Michael C. Perkins. HarperInformation, 10 E. 53rd St. New York, NY 10022-5299. Phone: 800-242-7737 or (212)207-7000 Fax: 800-822-4090 or (212)207-7145 • URL: http://www.harpercollins.com • 2001. $28.00. Revised edition. The authors predict a shake-out in e-commerce stocks and other Internet-related investments. (HarperBusiness.)

Internet Business Intelligence: How to Build a Big Company System on a Small Company Budget. David Vine. Information Today, Inc., 143 Old Marlton Pike Medford, NJ 08055-8750. Phone: 800-300-9868 or (609)654-6266 Fax: (609)654-4309 E-mail: custserv@infotoday.com • URL: http://www.infotoday.com • 2000. $29.95. Covers the obtaining of valuable business intelligence data through use of the Internet.

Internet Business Report: Software, Tools and Platforms. Jupitermedia, 23 Old Kings Highway S. Darien, CT 06820. Phone: 800-488-4345 or (203)662-2800 Fax: (203)655-4686 • URL: http://www.jmm.com • Semimonthly. $695.00 per year; with electronic software, $795.00 per year. Newsletter. Covers Internet advertising, fee collection, and attempts in general to make the Internet/World Wide Web profitable. Includes news of how businesses are using the Internet for sales promotion and public relations.

The Internet Compendium: Guide to Resources by Subject: Subject Guides to Health and Science Resources. Joseph Janes and others, editors. Neal-Schuman Publishers, Inc., 100 William St., Ste. 2004 New York, NY 10038. Phone: (866)672-6657 or (212)925-8650 Fax: (866)209-7932 or (212)219-8916 E-mail: info@neal-schuman.com • URL: http://www.neal-schuman.com • 1995. $82.50. Editors are with the University of Michigan Internet Clearinghouse. Provides direct location access to "thousands" of Internet addresses, in a detailed subject arrangement, with critical analysis of content. Contains information databases, text archives, library catalogs, bulletin boards, newsletters, forums, etc. Includes topics in medicine, agriculture, biology, chemistry, mathematics, physics, engineering, computers, and science in general.

The Internet Compendium: Guide to Resources by Subject: Subject Guides to Social Sciences, Business, and Law Resources. Joseph Janes and others, editors. Neal-Schuman Publishers, Inc., 100 William St., Ste. 2004 New York, NY 10038. Phone: (866)672-6657 or (212)925-8650 Fax: (866)209-7932 or (212)219-8916 E-mail: info@neal-schuman.com • URL: http://www.neal-schuman.com • 1995. $82.50. Editors are with the University of Michigan Internet Clearinghouse. Provides direct location access to "thousands" of Internet addresses, in a detailed subject arrangement, with critical analysis of content. Contains information databases, text archives, library catalogs, bulletin boards, newsletters, forums, etc. Includes topics in economics, finance, taxation, history, population, civil rights law, law careers, women's studies, and so forth.

The Internet Compendium: Guide to Resources by Subject: Subject Guides to the Humanities. Joseph Janes. Neal-Schuman Publishers, Inc., 100 William St., Ste. 2004 New York, NY 10038. Phone: (866)672-6657 or (212)925-8650

Fax: (866)209-7932 or (212)219-8916 E-mail: info@neal-schuman.com • URL: http://www.neal-schuman.com • 1995. $82.50. Editors are with the University of Michigan Internet Clearinghouse. Provides direct location access to "thousands" of Internet addresses, in a detailed subject arrangement, with critical analysis of content. Contains information databases, text archives, library catalogs, bulletin boards, newsletters, forums, etc. Includes topics in literature, art, religion, philosophy, music, education, library science, games, magic, and the humanities in general.

Internet Connection: Your Guide to Government Resources. Glasser Legalworks, 150 Clove Rd. Little Falls, NJ 07424. Phone: 800-308-1700 or (973)890-0008 Fax: (973)890-0042 E-mail: legalwks@aol.com • URL: http://www.glasserlegalworks.com • 10 times a year. $89.00 per year. Newsletter (print) devoted to finding free or low-cost U. S. Government information on the Internet. Provides detailed descriptions of government Web sites.

Internet Encyclopedia. Hossein Bidgoli, editor. John Wiley and Sons, Inc., 111 River St. Hoboken, NJ 07030. Phone: 800-225-5945 or (201)748-6000 Fax: (201)748-6088 E-mail: info@wiley.com • URL: http://www.wiley.com • 2003. $750.00. Four volumes. Covers various aspects of the Internet, including information technology, electronic business, and telecommunications.

Internet Industry Magazine. Jonas Publishing, 101 W. 23rd St., Suite 2286 New York, NY 10011. Phone: (212)977-3800 Fax: (212)977-4545 • URL: http://www.internetindustry.com • Semiannual. Price on application. Lists products and services for Internet service providers. Includes Internet-related articles and interviews.

The Internet Initiative: Libraries Providing Internet Services and How They Plan, Pay, and Manage. Edward J. Valauskas and others. American Library Association, 50 E. Huron St. Chicago, IL 60611-2795. Phone: 800-545-2433 or (312)944-6780 Fax: (312)440-9374 E-mail: ala@ala.org • URL: http://www.ala.org • 1995. $27.00. Provides 18 reports on Internet services in various kinds of libraries.

Internet Insider. Ruffin Prevost. Osborne/McGraw-Hill, 2600 10th St., 6th Fl. Berkeley, CA 94710. Phone: 800-227-0900 or (510)549-6600 Fax: (510)549-6603 E-mail: pbg.ecommerce_custserv@mcgraw-hill.com • URL: http://www.osborne.com • 1995. $14.95. A colorful presentation. (Internet Series).

Internet Law and Strategy. American Lawyer Media, Inc., 105 Madison Ave. New York, NY 10016. Phone: 800-888-8300 or (212)779-9200 Fax: (212)481-8110 E-mail: lawcatalog@amlaw.com • URL: http://www.lawcatalog.com/ • Monthly. $199.00 per year. Newsletter. Primarily concerned with doing legal research online. Contains reviews of the best Web sites for lawyers. (A Law Journal Newsletter, formerly published by Leader Publications.)

Internet Law Researcher. Glasser Legalworks, 150 Clove Rd. Little Falls, NJ 07424. Phone: 800-308-1700 or (973)890-0008 Fax: (973)890-0042 E-mail: orders@glasserlegalworks.com • URL: http://www.glasserlegalworks.com • 11 times a year. $200.00 per year. Newsletter for legal professionals on how to search the Web efficiently. Provides detailed information on individual Web sites.

Internet Literacy. Fred Hofstetter. McGraw-Hill, 1221 Ave. of the Americas New York, NY 10020. Phone: 800-722-4726 or (212)512-2000 Fax: (212)512-4502 E-mail: customer.service@mcgraw-hill.com • URL: http://www.mcgraw-hill.com • 2002. $38.75. Third edition. Provides practical information on a wide variety of topics relating to Web creation and electronic publishing.

Internet Marketing and Technology Report: Advising Marketing, Sales, and Corporate Executives on Online Opportunities. Computer Economics, Inc., 5841 Edison Place Carlsbad, CA 92008. Phone: 800-326-8100 or (760)438-8100 Fax: (760)431-1126 E-mail: access@compecon.com • URL: http://www.computereconomics.com • Monthly. $387.00 per year. Newsletter. Covers strategic marketing, sales, advertising, public relations, and corporate communications, all in relation to the Internet. Includes information on "cutting-edge technology" for the Internet.

Internet Marketing Report: News and Advice to Help Companies Harness the Power of the Internet to Achieve Business Objectives. Progressive Business Publications, 370 Technology Dr. Malvern, PA 19355-1315. Phone: 800-220-5000 or (610)695-8600 Fax: (610)647-8089 E-mail: editor@pbp.com • URL: http://www.pbp.com • Semimonthly. $299.00 per year. Newsletter. Covers Internet marketing strategy, site traffic, success stories, technology, cost control, and other Web site advertising and marketing topics.

Internet Payments Report. JupiterMedia, 23 Old Kings Hwy., S Darien, CT 06820. Phone: 800-488-4345 or (203)662-2800 Fax: (203)655-4686 • URL: http://www.jmm.com • Annual. $1,095.00. Market research report. Provides data, comment, and forecasts on the collection of electronic payments ("e-money") for goods and services offered through the Internet.

Internet Plus Directory of Express Library Services. Steve Coffman and others, editors. American Library Association, 50 E Huron St. Chicago, IL 60611-2795. Phone: 800-545-2433 or (312)944-6780 Fax: (312)440-9374 E-mail: ala@ala.org • URL: http://www.ala.org • 1998. $55.00. Covers fee-based services of various U. S., Canadian, and international libraries. Paid services include online searches, faxed documents, and specialized professional research. Price ranges are

quoted. (A joint production of FISCAL, the ALA/ACRL Discussion Group of Fee-Based Information Service Centers in Academic Libraries, and FYI, the Professional Research and Rapid Information Delivery Service of the County of Los Angeles Public Library.) Formerly *FISCAL Directory of Fee-Based Information Services in Libraries*.

Internet Prophets: Enlightened E-Business Strategies for Every Budget. Mary Diffley. Information Today, Inc., 143 Old Marlton Pike Medford, NJ 08055-8750. Phone: 800-300-9868 or (609)654-6266 Fax: (609)654-4309 E-mail: custserv@infotoday.com • URL: http://www.infotoday.com • 2002. $29.95. Emphasizes the specific dollar costs of having a successful online business. The "Internet Prophets" are four individual guides for developing business on the Web, arranged according to size of budget. (CyberAge Books.)

Internet Reference Services Quarterly: A Journal of Innovative Information Practice, Technologies, and Resources. Haworth Press, Inc., 10 Alice St. Binghamton, NY 13904-1580. Phone: 800-429-6784 or (607)722-5857 Fax: 800-895-0582 or (607)722-1424 E-mail: getinfo@haworthpressinc.com • URL: http://www.haworthpressinc.com • Quarterly. $110.00 per year. Covers both theoretical research and practical applications.

Internet Research Guide: A Concise, Friendly, and Practical Handbook for Anyone Researching in the Wide World of Cyberspace. Timothy K. Maloy. Allworth Press, 10 E 23rd St., Ste. 510 New York, NY 10010. Phone: 800-491-2808 or (212)777-8395 Fax: (212)777-8261 E-mail: pub@allworth.com • URL: http://www.allworth.com • 1997. $18.95. Second revised edition. Provides "hype-free" advice on practical use of the World Wide Web.

Internet Resources: A Subject Guide. Available from American Library Association, 50 E. Huron St. Chicago, IL 60611-2795. Phone: 800-545-2433 Fax: (312)440-9374 E-mail: library@ala.org • URL: http://www.ala.org • 1995. $18.00. Published by Association of College and Research Libraries. Provides updated versions of Internet subject directories appearing originally in *College and Research Libraries News*.

Internet Resources and Services for International Business: A Global Guide. Lewis-Guodo Liu. Greenwood Publishing Group, Inc., 88 Post Rd., W. Westport, CT 06881. Phone: 800-225-5800 or (203)225-3571 Fax: (203)431-2214 E-mail: customer-service@greenwood.com • URL: http://www.greenwood.com • 1998. $62.95. Describes more than 2,500 business-related Web sites from 176 countries. Includes five major categories: general information, economics, business and trade, business travel, and contacts. Indexed by Web site name, country, and subject.

Internet Retailer: E-Business Strategies. Thomson Financial, 11 Penn Plz., 17th Fl. New York, NY 10001-2006. Phone: (212)967-7000 Fax: (212)967-7155 10 times a year. $98.00 per year. Trade journal on the selling of retail merchandise through the Internet. Provides information on pricing, payment systems, order management, fraud, digital imaging, advertising, Web trends, and other topics.

Internet Society., 1775 Wiehle Ave., Ste. 102 Reston, VA 20190-5109. Phone: (703)439-2120 Fax: (703)326-9881 E-mail: isoc@isoc.org • URL: http://www.isoc.org • Technologists, developers, educators, researchers, government representatives, and business people. Seeks to ensure global cooperation and coordination for the Internet and related internetworking technologies and applications. Supports the development and dissemination of standards for the Internet. Promotes the growth of Internet architecture and Internet-related education and research. Encourages assistance to technologically developing countries in implementing local Internet infrastructures.

Internet Taxation. Albert Tokin, editor. Nova Science Publishers, Inc., 400 Oser Ave., Suite 1600 Hauppauge, NY 11788-3619. Phone: (631)231-7269 Fax: (631)231-8175 E-mail: novascience@earthlink.net • URL: http://www.novapublishers.com • 2003. $29.50. Several authors discuss the controversial issue of local taxation of e-commerce transactions.

Internet Tools of the Profession: A Guide for Information Professionals. Hope N. Tillman, editor. Special Libraries Association, 1700 18th St., N. W. Washington, DC 20009-2514. Phone: (202)234-4700 Fax: (202)265-9317 E-mail: sla@la.org • URL: http://www.sla.org • 1997. $49.00. Second edition. Consists of 14 sections by various authors or compilers. After two introductory articles on searching the Internet, there are 12 annotated lists of useful Web sites, covering the SLA, business and finance, chemistry, education, food and agriculture, information technology, insurance and employee benefits, law, library management, metals and materials, pharmaceuticals, and telecommunications. An index is provided.

Internet World: Magazine., 16 Thorndal Cir. Darien, CT 06820-5421. Phone: 800-632-5537 or (203)559-2919 Fax: (203)559-2910 E-mail: feedback@iw.com • URL: http://www.iw.com • Semimonthly. $160.00 per year. Edited for "Internet professionals." Includes industry news, new products, e-business news, and technical developments. (Formerly *WebWeek*.)

Internet.com: The E-Business and Internet Technology Network. JupitermediaPhone: (203)226-6967 Fax: (203)454-5840 E-mail: info@internet.com • URL: http://www.internet.com • Web site provides a wide variety of information relating to Internet commerce, search engines, news, Web design, servers, browsers, Java, service providers, advertising, marketing, etc. Online searching is offered. Fees: Free. (Formerly produced by Mecklermedia Corp.)

Internship Bible. The Princeton Review, 2315 Broadway New York, NY 10024. Phone: 800-733-3000 or (212)874-8282 Fax: (212)874-0775 E-mail: helpme@review.com Covers: Approximately 850 internship programs. Entries include: Selectivity of applicant pool, compensation, location, fields of employment, duration of internship, how to apply and deadline information, organization description, and internship perks.

Interracial Council for Business Opportunity., 350 5th Ave., Ste. 2202 New York, NY 10118. • URL: http://www.mbda.gov • Provides technical and financial assistance to minority business people.

Interservice. American Logistics Association, 1133 15th St., N.W., Suite 600 Washington, DC 20005. Phone: (202)466-2520 Fax: (202)296-4419 Quarterly. $20.00 per year. Official Journal of the American Logistics Association.

Interstate Natural Gas Association of America., 10 G St., NE, Ste. 700 Washington, DC 20002. Phone: (202)216-5900 Fax: (202)216-0877 • URL: http://www.ingaa.org • Formerly Independent Natural Gas Association of America.

Interstate Tax Insights. Interstate Tax Corp., 193 East Ave. Norwalk, CT 06855-1109. Phone: (203)854-0704 Fax: (203)853-9510 Monthly. $195.00 per year. Looseleaf service. Formerly *Interstate Tax Report*.

Intimate Apparel Council.

IntraNet Professional: IntraNet Applications and Knowledge Management for Libraries and Information Professionals. Information Today, Inc., 143 Old Marlton Pike Medford, NJ 08055-8750. Phone: 800-300-9868 or (609)654-6266 Fax: (609)654-4309 E-mail: custserv@infotoday.com • URL: http://www.infotoday.com • Bimonthly. $89.95 per year. Newsletter on the use of Internet technology for local library networks.

Introducing Computers: Concepts, Systems, and Applications. Robert H. Blissmer. John Wiley and Sons, Inc., 111 River St. Hoboken, NJ 07030. Phone: 800-225-5945 or (201)748-6000 Fax: (201)748-6088 E-mail: info@wiley.com • URL: http://www.wiley.com • 1995. $38.95.

Introduction to Advertising and Promotion: An Integrated Marketing Communications Perspective. George E. Belch and Michael A. Belch. McGraw-Hill, 1221 Ave. of the Americas New York, NY 10020. Phone: 800-722-4726 or (212)512-2000 Fax: (212)512-4502 E-mail: customer.service@mcgraw-hill.com • URL: http://www.mcgraw-hill.com • 1994. $69.95. Third edition.

Introduction to Automation for Librarians. William Saffady. American Library Association, 50 E. Huron St. Chicago, IL 60611-2795. Phone: 800-545-2433 or (312)944-6780 Fax: (312)440-9374 E-mail: ala@ala.org • URL: http://www.ala.org • 1999. $60.00. Fourth edition. Provides basic information on electronic technology (computers, telecommunications) and library applications of technology.

Introduction to Biotechnology. William Thieman and Michael A. Palladino. Benjamin Cummings Publishing Co., 1301 Sansome St. San Francisco, CA 94111. Phone: 800-447-2226 or (415)402-2500 • URL: http://www.aw.com • 2003. $70.00.

An Introduction to Clay Colloid Chemistry: For Clay Technologists, Geologists and Soil Scientists. H. Van Olphen. Krieger Publishing Co., P.O. Box 9542 Melbourne, FL 32902-9542. Phone: 800-724-0025 or (321)724-9542 Fax: (321)951-3671 E-mail: info@krieger-publishing.com • URL: http://www.krieger-publishing.com • 1991. $69.50. Second edition.

Introduction to Computer Theory. Daniel I. Cohen. John Wiley and Sons, Inc., 111 River St. Hoboken, NJ 07030. Phone: 800-225-5945 or (201)748-6000 Fax: (201)748-6088 E-mail: info@wiley.com • URL: http://www.wiley.com • 1996. $98.95. Second edition.

Introduction to Ecological Economics. Robert Costanza and others. Saint Lucie Press, 2000 Corporate Blvd., N. W. Boca Raton, FL 33431-7372. Phone: 800-272-7737 or (561)274-9906 Fax: 800-374-3401 or (561)274-9927 E-mail: information@slpress.com • URL: http://www.slpress.com • 1997. $64.95. Advocates environmental policy changes on local, regional, national, and international levels.

Introduction to Financial Management. Bodil Dickerson and others. Dryden Press, 301 Commerce St., Ste. 3700 Fort Worth, TX 76012. Phone: 800-447-9479 or (817)334-7500 Fax: (817)334-7844 • URL: http://www.thomson.com • 1994. $43.50. Fourth edition. (Finance Series).

Introduction to Forest Science. Scholargy Custom Publishing, Inc., 1555 W. University Dr. Tempe, AZ 85281. Phone: 800-300-1297 or (480)731-3231 Fax: (480)731-3239 E-mail: info@scholargy.com • URL: http://www.scholargy.com • 2002. $42.57. Looseleaf service.

Introduction to Futures and Options Markets. John C. Hull. Prentice Hall PTR, 240 Frisch Ct. Paramus, NJ 07652. Phone: 800-282-0693 Fax: 800-445-6991 • URL: http://www.phptr.com • 1997. $110.00. Third edition.

Introduction to Glass Science and Technology. Springer-Verlag, 175 Fifth Ave. New York, NY 10010. Phone: 800-777-4643 or (212)460-1500 Fax: (201)348-4505 E-mail: service@springer-ny.com • URL: http://www.springer-ny.com • 1997. $49.95. Covers the basics of glass manufacture, including the physical, optical, electrical, chemical, and mechanical properties of glass. (RCS Paperback Series).

Introduction to Hospital Accounting. L. Vann Seawell. Healthcare Financial Management Educational Foundation, Two Westbrook Corporate Center, Suite 700 Westchester, IL 60154-5700. Phone: 800-252-4362 or (708)531-9600 Fax: (708)531-0032 E-mail: memberservice@hfma.org • URL: http://www.test.hfma.org • 1992. $45.00. Third edition.

Introduction to Indexing and Abstracting. Donald B. Cleveland and Ana D. Cleveland. Libraries Unlimited, Post Rd., W Westport, CT 06881. Phone: 800-225-5800 Fax: (203)222-1502 E-mail: lu-books@lu.com • URL: http://www.lu.com • 2000. $45.00. Third edition. Covers a wide variety of topics relating to indexing, including new developments and career possibilities. Includes a bibliography and a glossary.

Introduction to Industrial-Organization Psychology. Addison-Wesley, 75 Arlington St., Ste. 300 Boston, MA 02116. Phone: 800-447-2226 or (617)848-7500 • URL: http://www.aw.com • 2000. Third edition. Price on application.

Introduction to Information Systems. James A. O'Brien. McGraw-Hill, 1221 Ave. of the Americas New York, NY 10020. Phone: 800-722-4726 or (212)512-2000 Fax: (212)512-4502 E-mail: customer.service@mcgraw-hill.com • URL: http://www.mcgraw-hill.com • 2000. $87.81. 10th edition.

Introduction to Insect Pest Management. Robert L. Metcalf and William H. Luckmann. John Wiley and Sons, Inc., 111 River St. Hoboken, NJ 07030. Phone: 800-225-5945 or (201)748-6000 Fax: (201)748-6088 E-mail: info@wiley.com • URL: http://www.wiley.com • 1994. $199.00. Third edition. (Environmental Science and Technology Series).

Introduction to Laser Technology. C. Breck Hitz and others. John Wiley and Sons, Inc., 111 River St. Hoboken, NJ 07030-5774. Phone: 800-225-5945 or (201)748-6000 Fax: (201)748-6800 E-mail: consumers@wiley.com • URL: http://www.wiley.com • 2001. $79.95. Third edition. Published by the Institute of Electrical and Electronics Engineers (IEEE) (http://www.ieee.org). Provides basic information about a wide variety of commercial lasers. Edited for "professionals, students, and non-engineer executives interested in the design, sales, or applications of the laser and electro-optics industry."

Introduction to Law and the Legal System. Frank A. Schubert. Houghton Mifflin Co., 222 Berkeley St. Boston, MA 02116. Phone: (651)351-5000 Fax: (617)351-5275 • URL: http://www.hmco.com • 2000. Seventh edition. Price on application.

Introduction to Librarianship. Jean K. Gates. Neal-Schuman Publishers, Inc., 100 William St., Ste. 2004 New York, NY 10038. Phone: (866)672-6657 or (212)925-8650 Fax: (866)209-7932 or (212)219-8916 E-mail: info@neal-schuman.com • URL: http://www.neal-schuman.com • 2004. $38.50. Fourth edition.

Introduction to Linear Programming. Leonid N. Vaserstein and others. Prentice Hall, 240 Frisch Ct. Paramus, NJ 07652-5240. Phone: 800-947-7700 or (201)909-6200 Fax: 800-445-6991 or (201)909-6361 • URL: http://www.prenhall.com • 2002. $81.00. Publisher: "...enables those with little mathematical background to learn to use linear programming in their respective fields (business, economics, operations research, etc.)."

An Introduction to Linear Programming and Theory. Paul R. Thie. John Wiley and Sons, Inc., 111 River St. Hoboken, NJ 07030. Phone: 800-225-5945 or (201)748-6000 Fax: (201)748-6088 E-mail: info@wiley.com • URL: http://www.wiley.com • 1988. $104.95. Second edition.

Introduction to Mass Communication. Phillip H. Agee. Addison-Wesley, 75 Arlington St., Ste. 300 Boston, MA 02116. Phone: 800-447-2226 or (617)848-7500 • URL: http://www.aw.com • 2000. 13th edition. Price on application.

Introduction to Object-Oriented Programming with Java with Code Warrior. C. Thomas Wu. McGraw-Hill, 1221 Ave. of the Americas New York, NY 10020. Phone: 800-722-4726 or (212)512-2000 Fax: (212)512-4502 E-mail: customer.service@mcgraw-hill.com • URL: http://www.mcgraw-hill.com • 2001. $82.81. Second edition. Includes CR-ROM. (Science, Engineering and Mathematics Series).

Introduction to Option-Adjusted Spread Analysis. Tom Windas. Bloomberg, 499 Park Ave. New York, NY 10022. Phone: 800-388-2749 or (212)318-2000 Fax: (917)369-5000 • URL: http://www.bloomberg.com • 1996. $40.00. Revised edition. Discusses the limitations of traditional, yield-based, risk and return analysis of bonds. (Bloomberg Professional Library.)

Introduction to Practical Linear Programming. David J. Pannell. John Wiley and Sons, Inc., 111 River St. Hoboken, NJ 07030. Phone: 800-225-5945 or (201)748-6000 Fax: (201)748-6088 E-mail: info@wiley.com • URL: http://www.wiley.com • 1996. $105.00. Explains how to apply linear programming to real-world situations in various areas, such as agriculture, manufacturing, finance, and advertising. Includes an IBM PC diskette containing "user-friendly" software.

Introduction to Reference Work. William A. Katz. McGraw-Hill, 1221 Ave. of the Americas New York, NY 10020. Phone: 800-722-4726 or (212)512-2000 Fax: (212)512-4502 E-mail: customer.service@mcgraw-hill.com • URL: http://www.mcgraw-hill.com • 2001. $58.60. Eighth edition. Two volumes. (Introduction to Reference Works Series).

Introduction to Security. Robert J. Fischer and Gion Green. Elsevier, 655 Ave. of the Americas New York, NY 10010. Phone: 800-366-2665 or (212)989-5800 Fax: 800-535-9935 or (212)633-3680 E-mail: custserv@elsevier.com • URL http://www.elsevier.com • 2003. Seventh edition. Price on application.

Introduction to Serial Management. Marcia Tuttle. Elsevier, 360 Park Ave., S New York, NY 10010-1710. Phone: (212)989-5800 Fax: (212)633-3990 E-mail: usinfo-f@elsevier.com • URL: http://www.elsevier.com • 1983. $78.50. (Foundations in Library and Information Science Series, Vol. 11).

Introduction to the Counseling Profession. Dave Capuzzi and Douglas Gross. Allyn and Bacon, Inc., 75 Arlington St., Ste. 300 Boston, MA 02116. Phone: 800-922-0579 or (781)848-6000 Fax: (515)284-2607 E-mail: ab_webmaster@abacon.com • URL: http://www.abacon.com • 2000. $97.00. Third edition.

An Introduction to the Law of Contract. Patrick S. Atiyah. Oxford University Press, 198 Madison Ave. New York, NY 10016. Phone: 800-451-7556 or (212)726-6000 Fax: (212)726-6440 E-mail: custserv@oup.usa.org • URL: http://www.oup-usa.org • 2005. $35.00. Sixth edition. (Claredon Law Series).

Introduction to the Magee System of Technical Analysis. W.H.C. Bassetti. CRC Press, 2000 N.W. Corporate Blvd. Boca Raton, FL 33431. Phone: 800-272-7737 or (561)994-0555 Fax: 800-374-3401 or (561)989-9732 E-mail: orders@crcpress.com • URL: http://www.crcpress.com • 2002. $59.95. Serves as a basic guide to the technical analysis of stock trends promulgated by John Magee.

An Introduction to the Mathematics of Financial Derivatives. Salih N. Neftci. Elsevier, 655 Avenue of the Americas New York, NY 10010-5107. Phone: 800-366-2665 or (212)989-5800 Fax: 800-535-9935 or (212)633-3680 E-mail: custserv@elsevier.com • URL: http://www.elsevier.com • 2000. $64.95. Second edition. Covers the mathematical models underlying the pricing of derivatives. Includes explanations of basic financial calculus for students, derivatives traders, risk managers, and others concerned with derivatives.

An Introduction to the Theory and Practice of Econometrics. George G. Judge and others. John Wiley and Sons, Inc., 111 River St. Hoboken, NJ 07030. Phone: 800-526-5368 or (201)748-6000 Fax: (201)748-6088 E-mail: info@wiley.com • URL: http://www.wiley.com • 1988. $106.95. Second edition.

Introduction to the Use of Computers in Libraries: A Textbook for the Non-Technical Student. Harold C. Ogg. Information Today, Inc., 143 Old Marlton Pike Medford, NJ 08055-8750. Phone: 800-300-9868 or (609)654-6266 Fax: (609)654-4309 E-mail: custserv@infotoday.com • URL: http://www.infotoday.com • 1997. $42.50. Provides basic information on computer programs for libraries, including spreadsheets, database applications, desktop publishing, automated circulation systems, and public access online catalogs.

Introductory CD-ROM Searching: The Key to Effective Ondisc Searching. Joseph Meloche. Haworth Press, Inc., 10 Alice St. Binghamton, NY 13904-1580. Phone: 800-429-6784 or (607)722-5857 Fax: 800-895-0582 or (607)722-1424 E-mail: getinfo@haworthpressinc.com • URL: http://www.haworthpressinc.com • 1994. $49.95. Covers basic search strategies, with specific suggestions for Dialog OnDisc, Silverplatter, Wilsondisc, UMI, and others.

Introductory Concepts in Information Science. Melanie J. Norton, editor. Information Today, Inc., 143 Old Marlton Pike Medford, NJ 08055-8750. Phone: 800-300-9868 or (609)654-6266 Fax: (609)654-4309 E-mail: custserv@infotoday.com • URL: http://www.infotoday.com • 2000. $39.50. Covers the basic concepts of information science and retrieval, both practical and theoretical. Published in conjunction with the American Society for Information Science and Technology. (ASIS Monograph Series).

Inventing and Patenting Sourcebook. Gale Cengage Learning, 27500 Drake Rd. Farmington Hills, MI 48331-3535. Phone: 800-877-GALE or (248)699-4253 Fax: 800-414-5043 E-mail: gale.galeord@cengage.com • URL: http://gale.cengage.com • 1992. $120.00. Second edition. A general guide for inventors. Contains how-to-do-it text, information sources, and sample forms.

Inventory Control and Management. C. D. Waters. John Wiley and Sons, Inc., 111 River St. Hoboken, NJ 07030. Phone: 800-225-5945 or (201)748-6000 Fax: (201)748-6088 E-mail: info@wiley.com • URL: http://www.wiley.com • 2003. $50.00. Second edition.

Inventory of Electrtic Utility Power Plants in the United States. Energy Information Administration, U.S. Department of Energy. Available from U.S. Government Printing Office, Washington, DC 20402. Phone: (202)512-1800 Fax: (202)512-2250 E-mail: gpoaccess@gpo.gov • URL: http://www.access.gpo.gov • Annual. $33.00.

InvesTech Market Analyst: Technical and Monetary Investment Analysis. InvesTech Research, 2472 Birch Glen Whitefish, MT 59937-3349. Phone: 800-955-8500 or (406)862-7777 Fax: (406)862-7707 • URL: http://www.investech.com • Every three weeks. $190.00 per year. Newsletter. Provides interpretation of monetary statistics and Federal Reserve actions, especially as related to technical analysis of stock market price trends.

InvesTech Mutual Fund Advisor: Professional Portfolio Allocation. InvesTech Research, 2472 Birch Glen Whitefish, MT 59937-3349. Phone: 800-955-8500 or (406)862-7777 Fax: (406)862-7707 • URL: http://www.investech.com •

Every three weeks. $190.00 per year. Newsletter. Contains model portfolio for mutual fund investing.

InvesText. Thomson Financial, PO Box 95512 Chicago, IL 60694. Phone: 800-607-4463 or (312)288-6400 • URL: http://www.tfn.com • Provides full text online of investment research reports from more than 600 sources, including leading brokers and investment bankers. Reports are available on approximately 60,000 U. S. and international corporations. Separate industry reports cover 54 industries. Time span is 1982 to date, with daily updates. Inquire as to online cost and availability.

InvesText [CD-ROM]. Thomson Financial, PO Box 95512 Chicago, IL 60694. Phone: 800-607-4463 or (312)288-6400 • URL: http://www.investext.com • Monthly. Contains full text on CD-ROM of investment research reports from about 630 sources, including leading brokers and investment bankers. Reports are available on both U. S. and international publicly traded corporations. Separate industry reports cover more than 50 industries. Time span is 1982 to date.

Investigating Sexual Harassment: A Practical Guide to Resolving Complaints. Angela Bradbery and Rosemarie Lally. Thompson Publishing Group, Inc., 1725 K St., N.W., Suite 700 Washington, DC 20006. Phone: 800-444-8741 or (202)872-4000 • URL: http://www.thompson.com • 1998. $79.00. Provides information for employers on sexual harassment liability, investigation of complaints, basics of interviewing, and related topics.

Investigations in the Workplace. Eugene F. Ferraro. CRC Press, 2000 N.W. Corporate Blvd. Boca Raton, FL 33431. Phone: 800-272-7737 or (561)994-0555 Fax: 800-374-3401 or (561)989-9732 E-mail: orders@crcpress.com • URL: http://www.crcpress.com • 2004. $79.95. Written for security professionals, lawyers, and human resource directors. Explains how to properly conduct internal investigations in the private sector and avoid litigation. Such investigations may relate to loss prevention, asset protection, or employee rights issues. (Imprint: Auerbach Publications.)

Investigative Reporters and Editors., School of Journalism, 138 Neff Annex Columbia, MO 65211. Phone: (573)882-2042 Fax: (573)882-5431 E-mail: info@ire.org • URL: http://www.ire.org • Provides educational services to those engaged in investigative journalism.

Investing and Selling in Latin America. Judith Evans and others. Morning Light Publishing Co., 6836 Glenwood Overland Park, KS 66204. Phone: (913)677-4116 E-mail: 102673-1532@compuserve.com 1995. $60.00. Consists of one chapter for each of 12 Latin American countries. Covers a wide variety of legal, economic, and practical information relating to doing business in the region.

Investing in Call Options; An Alternative to Common Stock and Real Estate. James A. Willson. Greenwood Publishing Group, Inc., 88 Post Rd., W Westport, CT 06881. Phone: 800-225-5800 or (203)226-3571 Fax: (203)431-2214 E-mail: customer-service@greenwood.com • URL: http://www.greenwood.com • 1982. $59.95.

Investing in Education: Analysis of the 1999 World Education Indicators. Organization for Economic Cooperation and Development, OECD Washington Center, 2001 L St., N. W., Suite 650 Washington, DC 20036-4922. Phone: 800-456-6323 or (202)785-6323 Fax: (202)785-0350 E-mail: washington.contact@oecd.org • URL: http://www.oecdwash.org • 2000. $31.00. Compares educational performance data in various countries of the world, including the U. S., other OECD countries, and selected non-OECD nations. (Education and Skills Series).

Investing in IPOs: Version 2.0. Tom Taulli. Bloomberg, 499 Park Ave. New York, NY 10022. Phone: 800-388-2749 or (212)318-2000 Fax: (917)369-5000 • URL: http://www.bloomberg.com • 2001. $24.95. Second revised edition. Explains how individual investors can invest profitably in new stock offerings. (Bloomberg Personal Bookshelf Series).

Investing in Latin America: Best Stocks, Best Funds. Michael Molinski and Constance Anderson. Bloomberg, 499 Park Ave. New York, NY 10022. Phone: 800-388-2749 or (212)318-2000 Fax: (917)369-5000 • URL: http://www.bloomberg.com • 1999. $24.95. Provides Latin American stock and mutual fund recommendations for individual investors. (Bloomberg Personal Bookshelf Series).

Investing in REITs: Real Estate Investment Trusts. Ralph L. Block. Bloomberg, 499 Park Ave. New York, NY 10022. Phone: 800-388-2749 or (212)318-2000 Fax: (917)369-5000 • URL: http://www.bloomberg.com • 2002. $26.95. Revised and updated edition. A basic guide to real estate investment trusts. (Bloomberg Personal Bookshelf Series).

Investing in Small-Cap Stocks. Christopher Graja and Elizabeth Ungar. Bloomberg, 499 Park Ave. New York, NY 10022. Phone: 800-388-2749 or (212)318-2000 Fax: (917)369-5000 • URL: http://www.bloomberg.com • 1999. $26.95. Second expanded revised edition. Provides a practical strategy for investing in small-capitalization stocks. (Bloomberg Personal Bookshelf Series).

Investing in the Over-the-Counter Markets: Stocks, Bonds, IPOs. Alvin D. Hall. John Wiley and Sons, Inc., 111 River St. Hoboken, NJ 07030. Phone: 800-225-5945 or (201)748-6000 Fax: (201)748-6088 E-mail: info@wiley.com • URL: http://www.wiley.com • 1995. $29.95. Provides advice and information on investing in "unlisted" or NASDAQ (National Association of Securities Dealers Automated Quotation System) stocks, bonds, and initial public offerings (IPOs).

Investing, Licensing, and Trading. Economist Intelligence Unit, 111 W. 57th St. New York, NY 10019. Phone: 800-938-4685 or (212)554-0600 Fax: (212)586-1182 E-mail: newyork@eiu.com • URL: http://www.eiu.com • Semiannual. $345.00 per year for each country. Key laws, rules, and licensing provisions are explained for each of 60 countries. Information is provided on political conditions, markets, price policies, foreign exchange practices, labor, and export-import.

Investment Advisor: The Advisor to Advisors. Wicks Business Information, 363 Reef Rd. Fairfield, CT 06824. Phone: (203)255-4990 Fax: (203)255-4353 E-mail: info@wicksbusinessinfo.com • URL: http://www.wicksbusinessinfo.com • Monthly. $79.00 per year. Edited for professional investment advisors, financial planners, stock brokers, bankers, and others concerned with the management of assets.

Investment Banking Handbook. J. Peter Williamson. John Wiley and Sons, Inc., 111 River St. Hoboken, NJ 07030. Phone: 800-225-5945 or (201)748-6000 Fax: (201)748-6088 E-mail: info@wiley.com • URL: http://www.wiley.com • 1988. $270.00. (Frontiers in Finance Series).

Investment Company Institute., 1401 H St. NW, 12th Fl. Washington, DC 20005. Phone: (202)326-5800 Fax: (202)326-8309 E-mail: memberservices@ici.org • URL: http://www.ici.org • Represents open-end and closed-end investment companies registered under Investment Company Act of 1940; investment advisers to, and underwriters of, such companies; unit investment trust sponsors; interested others. Represents members in matters of legislation, taxation, regulation, economic research marketing, and public information. Provides a clearinghouse for information on the mutual fund industry. Compiles statistics.

Investment Company Yearbook. Thomson Financial, 195 Broadway New York, NY 10007. Phone: 800-262-6000 or (646)822-2000 Fax: (646)822-6270 E-mail: custserv@tfn.com • URL: http://www.tfn.com • Annual. $310.00. Provides an "entire history of recent events in the mutual funds industry," with emphasis on changes during the past year. About 100 pages are devoted to general information and advice for fund investors. Includes 600 full-page profiles of popular mutual funds, with brief descriptions of 10,000 others, plus 7,000 variable annuities and 500 closed-end funds. Contains a glossary of technical terms, a Web site index, and an overall book index. Also known as *Wiesenberger Investment Companies Yearbook.*

Investment Council of American Directory of Member Firms. Investment Counsel Association of America, 1050 17th St., N.W., Suite 725 Washington, DC 20036-5503. Phone: (202)293-4222 Fax: (202)293-4223 E-mail: icaa@icaa.org • URL: http://www.icaa.org • Annual. Free.

Investment Counsel Association of America.

Investment Dealers' Digest. Thomson Media, One State St. Plaza New York, NY 10004. Phone: 800-221-1809 or (212)803-8200 Fax: (212)843-9635 E-mail: custserv@thomsonmedia.com • URL: http://www.thomsonmedia.com • Weekly. $750.00 per year. Covers financial news, trends, new products, people, private placements, new issues of securities, and other aspects of the investment business. Includes feature stories.

Investment Guide. American Investment Services Inc., POB 1000 Great Barrington, MA 01230. Phone: (413)528-1216 Fax: (413)528-0103 E-mail: aaei5ie@aol.com • URL: http://www.americaninvestment.com/ • Description: Contains analyses of stock market activity and strategies for investment. Recurring features include market statistics, Dow high-yield stock investing.

Investment Management Weekly. Thomson Media, One State St. Plaza New York, NY 10004. Phone: 800-221-1809 or (212)803-8200 Fax: (212)843-9635 E-mail: custserv@thomsonmedia.com • URL: http://www.thomsonmedia.com • Weekly. $1,370.00 per year. Newsletter. Edited for money managers and other investment professionals. Covers personnel news, investment strategies, and industry trends.

Investment News: The Weekly Newspaper for Financial Advisers. Crain Communications, Inc., 711 Third Ave. New York, NY 10017-4036. Phone: 800-678-9595 or (212)210-0100 E-mail: info@crain.com • URL: http://www.crain.com • Weekly. $29.00 per year. Edited for both personal and institutional investment advisers, planners, and managers.

The Investment Reporter. MPL Communications Inc., 133 Richmond St. W, Ste. 700 Toronto, ON, Canada M5H 3M8. Phone: 800-804-8846 or (416)869-1177 Fax: (416)869-0616 E-mail: customers@mplcomm.com Description: Profiles specific companies and market trends and developments, making recommendations to assist in formulating investment strategies. Includes short articles offering advice on investment decisions.

Investment Statistics Locator. Linda H. Bentley and Jennifer J. Kiesl, editors. Greenwood Publishing Group, Inc., 88 Post Rd., W. Westport, CT 06881. Phone: 800-225-5800 or (203)226-3571 Fax: (203)431-2214 E-mail: customer-service@greenwood.com • URL: http://www.greenwood.com • 1994. $69.95. Expanded revised edition. Provides detailed subject indexing of more than 50 of the most-used sources of financial and investment data. Includes an annotated bibliography.

Investments: An Introduction to Analysis and Management. Frederick Amling. Pearson Custom Publishing, 75 Arlington St., Ste. 300 Boston, MA 02116. Phone: 800-428-4466 or

(617)848-6300 Fax: (617)848-6333 • URL: http://www.pearsoncustom.com • 1999. $94.00. Seventh edition.

Investments: Analysis and Management. Charles P. Jones. John Wiley and Sons, Inc., 111 River St. Hoboken, NJ 07030. Phone: 800-526-5368 or (201)748-6000 Fax: (201)748-6088 E-mail: info@wiley.com • URL: http://www.wiley.com • 2001. $118.95. Eighth edition.

Investor Relations Business. Thomson Media, One State St. Plaza New York, NY 10004. Phone: 800-221-1809 or (212)803-8200 Fax: (212)843-9635 E-mail: custserv@thomsonmedia.com • URL: http://www.thomsonmedia.com • Semimonthly. $495.00 per year. Covers the issues affecting stockholder relations, corporate public relations, and institutional investor relations.

Investor Responsibility Research Center, Inc. Investor Responsibility Research Center, 1350 Connecticut Ave. NW, Ste. 700 Washington, DC 20036-1702. Phone: (202)833-0700 Fax: (202)833-3555 E-mail: marketing@irrc.com • URL: http://www.irrc.org • Social, public policy, and corporate governance issues and their impact on major corporations and institutional investors. Issues studied have included anti-takeover measures, board and compensation practices, energy and the environment, the electric utility industry, military contracting, executive compensation, business in Northern Ireland, plant closings, global shareholder rights, animal testing, and voting and other actions by institutional investors. Also offers consulting and contract research.

Investor's Business Daily. Investor's Business Daily, Inc., 12655 Beatrice St. Los Angeles, CA 90066. Phone: 800-831-2525 or (310)448-6000 Fax: (310)577-7301 E-mail: custcare@investors.com • URL: http://www.investors.com • Daily. $295.00 per year. Newspaper.

The Investor's Guide to Closed-End Funds. Thomas J. Herzfeld Advisors, Inc., P.O. Box 161465 Miami, FL 33116. Phone: (305)271-1900 Fax: (305)270-7040 E-mail: herzfeld@bellsouth.net • URL: http://www.herzfeld.com • Monthly. $475.00 per year. Looseleaf service. Provides detailed information on closed-end investment funds, including charts and recommendations.

Investor's Guide to Economic Indicators. Charles R. Nelson. John Wiley and Sons, Inc., 111 River St. Hoboken, NJ 07030. Phone: 800-526-5368 or (201)748-6000 Fax: (201)748-6088 E-mail: info@wiley.com • URL: http://www.wiley.com • 1989. $17.95.

Investors Intelligence. Michael Burke, editor. Chartcraft Inc., 30 Church St., PO Box 1747 New Rochelle, NY 10801. Phone: (914)632-0422 Fax: (914)632-0335 E-mail: customers@mplcomm.com Description: Serves as a "comprehensive and authoritative Stock Market Advisory Service dedicated to bringing the investor facts, original projections, and a cross section of the recommendations of other leading Services."

Investors' Manuals. National Association of Investors Corporation, PO Box 220 Royal Oak, MI 48068. Phone: 877-275-6242 or (248)583-6242 Fax: (248)583-4880 E-mail: service@better_investing.org • URL: http://www.better-investing.org • Provides stock study tools and procedures for do-it-yourself equity investors.

The Invisible Web: Uncovering Information Sources Search Engines Can't See. Chris Sherman and Gary Price. Information Today, Inc., 143 Old Marlton Pike Medford, NJ 08055-8750. Phone: 800-300-9868 or (609)654-6266 Fax: (609)654-4309 E-mail: custserv@infotoday.com • URL: http://www.infotoday.com • 2001. $29.95. A guide to Web sites from universities, libraries, associations, government agencies, and other sources that are inadequately covered by conventional search engines (see also http://www.invisible-web.net). (CyberAge Books.)

An Invitation to Fly: Basics for the Private Pilot. Dennis Glaeser and others. Brooks/Cole, 10 Davis Dr. Belmont, CA 94002. Phone: 800-354-9706 or (650)595-2350 Fax: (650)525-0978 • URL: http://www.wadsworth.com • 2003. $77.95. Seventh edition. Prepares beginning pilots for FAA written test. (Aviation Series).

Involvement and Participation Association., 42 Colebrooke Row London N1 8Af, England. Phone: 44 207 3548040 Fax: 44 207 3548041 E-mail: involve@ipa-involve.com • URL: http://www.ip-involve.com • Promotes employee participation in the workplace.

IOMA's Report on Defined Contribution Plan Investing. Institute of Management and Administration, Inc., 29 W. 35th St., 5th Fl. New York, NY 10001-2299. Phone: (212)244-0360 Fax: (212)564-0465 E-mail: subserve@ioma.com • URL: http://www.ioma.com • Semimonthly. $1,189.90 per year. Newsletter. Edited for 401(k) and other defined contribution retirement plan managers, sponsors, and service providers. Reports on such items as investment manager performance, guaranteed investment contract (GIC) yields, and asset allocation trends.

IOMA's Report on Managing 401(k) Plans. Institute of Management and Administration, Inc., 29 W. 35th St., 5th Fl. New York, NY 10001-2299. Phone: (212)244-0360 Fax: (212)564-0465 E-mail: subserve@ioma.com • URL: http://www.ioma.com • Monthly. $269.00 per year. Includes print and online editions. Newsletter for retirement plan managers.

IP Almanac. American Lawyer Media, Inc., 105 Madison Ave. New York, NY 10016. Phone: 800-888-8300 or (212)779-9200 Fax: (212)481-8110 E-mail: lawcatalog@amlaw.com • URL: http://www.lawcatalog.com/ • Annual. $20.00.

Provides a digest of the year's most important developments in the area of intellectual property. (Also included with subscription to *IP Law and Business*).

IP Law and Business. American Lawyer Media, Inc., 105 Madison Ave. New York, NY 10016. Phone: 800-888-8300 or (212)779-9200 Fax: (212)481-8110 E-mail: lawcatalog@amlaw.com • URL: http://www.lawcatalog.com/ • Monthly. $125.00 per year. Covers intellectual property litigation and business issues. Includes annual *IP Almanac*.

IPA Magazine. Involvement and Participation Association, 42 Colebrooke Row London N1 8AF, United Kingdom. Quarterly. $57.00 per year. Formerly *Involvement of Participation*

IPOfn. IPO Financial NetworkPhone: (973)379-5100 Fax: (973)379-1696 E-mail: info@ipofinancial.com • URL: http://www.ipofinancial.com • Web site provides free information on initial public offerings: "Pricing Recap" (price performance), "Calendar Update" (weekly listing of new offerings), "Company Roster" (Web sites), "Stock Brokers" (IPO dealers), and "Brokerage Firms" (underwriters). Fees: Basic data is free. Extensive analysis and recommendations are available through fee-based telephone, fax, and database services. Daily updates.

IRA Basics. The Institute of Financial Education, 55 W. Monroe St., Suite 2800 Chicago, IL 60603-5014. Phone: 800-946-0488 or (312)364-0100 Fax: (312)364-0190 E-mail: info@bai.org • URL: http://www.theinstitute.com • 1997. $34.95. Seventh edition. A guide for bank personnel.

The IRA Reporter (Individual Retirement Account). Universal Pensions, Inc., P.O. Box 979 Brainerd, MN 56401. Phone: 800-346-3860 Fax: (218)825-5010 • URL: http://www.universalpensions.com • Monthly. $115.00 per year. Newsletter. Edited for financial planners. Provides information on the rules and regulations of individual retirement accounts (IRAs).

IRCDA/SDA., 1900 Cross Beam Dr. Charlotte, NC 28217. Phone: (704)357-3124 Fax: (704)357-3127 E-mail: info@icrda.org • URL: http://www.icrda.org • Formerly Independent Cash Register Dealers Association.

The IRE Journal (Investigative Reporters and Editors). Investigative Reporters and Editors, Inc., 138 Neff Annex, School of Journalism, University of Missouri Columbia, MO 65211. Phone: (573)882-2042 Fax: (573)882-5431 E-mail: journal@ire.org • URL: http://www.ire.org • Bimonthly. Free to members; non-members, $60.00 per year; institutions, $70.00 per year. Contains practical information relating to investigative journalism.

Iron and Steel Industry in [year]. Organization for Economic Cooperation and Development, OECD Washington Center, 2001 L St., N. W., Suite 650 Washington, DC 20036-4922. Phone: 800-456-6323 or (202)785-6323 Fax: (202)785-0350 E-mail: washington.contact@oecd.org • URL: http://www.oecd.org • Annual. $28.00. Contains yearly statistics on steel production, consumption, industry employment, investment expenditures, trade, and prices. Covers both OECD and developing countries.

IRRA-Membership Directory. Industrial Relations Research Association, Illinois, Urbana-Champaign, 121 ILR Bldg., 504 E Armory Ave. Champaign, IL 61820. Phone: (217)333-0072 Fax: (217)265-5130 E-mail: irra@uiuc.edu Quadrennial. $25.00. About 3,200 business people, union leaders, government officials, lawyers, arbitrators, academics, consultants, and others interested in labor relations.

IRRA Newsletter. Labor and Employment Relations Association, University of Illinois at Urbana-Champaign, 121 Labor and Industrial Relations Bldg., 504 E Armory Ave., 504 E Armory Ave. Champaign, IL 61820. Phone: (217)333-0072 Fax: (217)265-5130 E-mail: leraoffice@uiuc.edu Description: Presents news of meetings, elections, and programs of this Association of business, labor, and government leaders interested in researching labor and management relationships.

Irrational Exuberance. Robert J. Shiller. Princeton University Press, 41 William St. Princeton, NJ 08540. Phone: 800-777-4726 or (609)258-4900 Fax: (609)258-6305 • URL: http://www.pup.princeton.edu • 2000. $35.00. States that below-average stock market returns occur in the years following very high price-earnings ratios and very low dividend yields. 1901, 1929, 1966, and 2000 are cited as portentous years.

Irrigation and Drainage Abstracts. Available from CABI Publishing, North America, 875 Massachusetts Ave. Cambridge, MA 02139. Phone: 800-528-4841 or (617)395-4056 Fax: (617)354-6875 E-mail: cabi-nao@cabi.org • URL: http://www.cabi-publishing.org • Quarterly. Institutions, $770.00 per year; with online edition, $785.00 per year. Published in England by CABI Publishing. Provides worldwide coverage of the literature.

Irrigation Association., 6540 Arlington Blvd. Falls Church, VA 22042-6638. Phone: (703)536-7080 Fax: (703)536-7019 E-mail: deborah@irrigation.org • URL: http://www.irrigation.org • Manufacturers, distributors, dealers, designers, engineers, technicians, students, educators, sports facility managers, park and university grounds managers, golf course/resort designers and managers, government administrators, and contractors. Offers government relations, education courses, and certification programs.

Irrigation Association Membership Directory and Industry Buyers' Guide. The Irrigation Association, 6540 Arlington Blvd. Falls Church, VA 22042. Phone: (703)536-7090 Fax: (703)536-7019 E-mail: publications@irrigation.org • URL: http://www.irrigation.org • Annual. Free to members; non-members, $25.00. Includes manufacturing, distribution, contracting, consultation, research and educational information.

IRS Corporate Financial Ratios. Available from MarketResearch.com, 641 Ave. of the Americas, Fourth Floor New York, NY 10011. Phone: 800-298-5699 or (212)807-2629 Fax: (212)807-2642 E-mail: order@marketresearch.com • URL: http://www.marketresearch.com • 2002. $225.00. Published by Schonfeld & Associates, Inc. Presents 70 key financial ratios for 260 industries. Ratios are calculated from income statement and balance sheet data available from the Internal Revenue Service. Includes four asset size classes.

IRS Publications. CCH, Inc., 2700 Lake Cook Rd. Riverwoods, IL 60015. Phone: 800-835-5224 or (847)267-7000 • URL: http://www.cch.com • Irregular. $352.00. Three looseleaf volumes. Periodic supplementation. Photographic reproductions of current Internal Revenue Service tax publications intended for public use.

IRS Tax Collection Procedures. CCH, Inc., 2700 Lake Cook Rd. Riverwoods, IL 60015. Phone: 800-835-5224 or (847)267-7000 E-mail: cust_serv@cch.com • URL: http://www.cch.com • $195.00. Looseleaf service. Periodic supplementation. Covers IRS collection personnel, payment arrangements, penalties, abatements, summons, liens, etc.

Irwin Business and Investment Almanac, 1994: Dow Jones and Company Edition. Summer N. Levine and Caroline Levine. McGraw-Hill, 1221 Ave. of The Americas New York, NY 10020. Phone: 800-722-4726 or (212)512-2000 Fax: (212)512-4502 E-mail: customer.service@mcgraw-hill.com • URL: http://www.mcgraw-hill.com • 1994. $75.00. 18th edition. A review of last year's business activity. Covers a wide variety of business and economic data: stock market statistics, industrial information, commodity futures information, art market trends, comparative living costs for U. S. metropolitan areas, foreign stock market data, etc. Formerly *Business One Irwin Business and Investment Almanac*.

Irwin Handbook of Telecommunications. James H. Green. McGraw-Hill, 1221 Ave. of the Americas New York, NY 10020. Phone: 800-722-4726 or (212)512-2000 Fax: (212)512-4502 E-mail: customer.service@mcgraw-hill.com • URL: http://www.mcgraw-hill.com • 2000. $95.00. Fourth edition. Formerly *Dow Jones-Irwin Handbook of Telecommunications*.

Is It Too Late to Run Away and Join the Circus? Finding the Life You Really Want. Marti Smye. John Wiley, 111 River St. Hoboken, NJ 07030. Phone: 800-225-5945 or (201)748-6000 Fax: (201)748-6088 E-mail: info@wiley.com • URL: http://www.wiley.com • 1998. $14.95. Provides philosophical and inspirational advice on leaving corporate life and becoming self-employed as a consultant or whatever. Central theme is dealing with major changes in life style and career objectives.

ISA Directory of Instrumentation. ISA - The Instrumentation Systems and Automation Society, 67 Alexander Dr. Research Triangle Park, NC 27709. Phone: (919)549-8411 Fax: (919)549-8288 E-mail: info@isa.org • URL: http://www.isa.org • Annual. $100.00. Over 2,400 manufacturers of control and instrumentation equipment, over 1,000 manufacturers' representatives, and several hundred service companies; coverage includes Canada.

ISA-Instrumentation, Systems, and Automation Society.

ISA-The Instrumentation, Systems, and Automation Society:.

ISA Transactions. ISA-The Instrumentation, Systems and Automation Society. American Institute of Physics, PO Box 503284 Saint Louis, MO 63150-3284. Phone: 800-344-6902 or (516)576-2270 Fax: (516)349-9704 E-mail: subs@aip.org • URL: http://www.aip.org • Quarterly. $310.00 per year.

ISO Management Systems. Available from American National Standards Institute, 11 W 43rd St., 4th Fl. New York, NY 10036. Phone: (212)642-4900 Fax: (212)398-0023 • URL: http://www.ansi.org • Bimonthly. Price on application. Newsletter on quality standards. Published by the International Organization for Standardization (ISO). Text in English. Formerly *ISO 9000 and ISO 14000 News*.

ISO 9000 and the Service Sector: A Critical Interpretation of the 1994 Revisions. James L. Lamprecht. ASQ Quality Press, 600 N Plankinton Ave. Milwaukee, WI 53201. Phone: 800-248-1946 or (414)272-8575 Fax: (414)270-8810 E-mail: cs@asq.org • URL: http://www.qualitypress.asq.org • 1994. $38.00. A review of the ISO 9000 quality standards as they relate to service organizations. Includes examples of applications.

ISO 9000 Auditor's Companion. Kent A. Keeney. ASQ Quality Press, 600 N Plankinton Ave. Milwaukee, WI 53201. Phone: 800-248-1946 or (414)272-8575 Fax: (414)270-8810 E-mail: cs@asq.org • URL: http://www.qualitypress.asq.org • 1995. $30.00. Designed to help companies prepare for ISO 9000 quality management audits.

ISO 9000 Book: A Global Competitor's Guide to Compliance and Certification. John T. Rabbitt and Peter Bergh. AMACOM, 1601 Broadway New York, NY 10019. Phone: 800-262-9699 or (518)586-8100 Fax: (518)903-8168 E-mail: customerservice@amanet.org • URL: http://www.amacombooks.org • 1994. $29.95. Second edition.

ISO 9000 Handbook. Robert W. Peach. QSU Publishing Co., 3975 University Dr., Ste. 230 Fairfay, VA 22030. Phone: (866)225-3122 or (703)359-8460 Fax: (703)359-8462 E-mail: sales@qsuonline.com • URL: http://www.qsuonline.com • 2003. $99.95. Fourth edition. Includes detailed information for the ISO 9000 registration process.

ISO 9000 Made Easy: A Cost-Saving Guide to Documentation and Registration. Amy Zuckerman. AMACOM, 1601 Broadway New York, NY 10019. Phone: 800-262-9699 or (518)586-8100 Fax: (518)903-8168 E-mail: customerservice@amanet.org • URL: http://www.amacombooks.org • 1994. $75.00.

Isotopes for Medicine and the Life Sciences. S. James Adelstein and Frederick J. Manning, editors. National Academy Press, 2101 Constitution Ave., N. W., HA 384 Washington, DC 20418. Phone: 800-624-6242 or (202)334-3180 Fax: (202)334-2793 E-mail: zjones@nas.edu • URL: http://www.nap.edu • 1995. $30.00. Includes bibliographical references and a glossary.

ISPE, The Society for Life Science Professionals., 3109 W Dr. Martin Luther King, Jr. Blvd., Ste. 250 Tampa, FL 33607. Phone: (813)960-2105 Fax: (813)264-2816 E-mail: customerservice@ispe.org • URL: http://www.ispe.org • Formerly International Society of Pharmaceutical Engineers.

Israel Diamond and Precious Stones. International Diamond Publications, Ltd., Diamond Towers, 3A Jabotinsky Rd. 52520 Ramat Gon, Israel. Phone: 972 3 751 2165 Fax: 972 3 575 2201 Bimonthly. $78.00 per year. Text in English. Formerly *Israel Diamonds*.

ISSA Today. International Sanitary Supply Association, 7373 N. Lincoln Ave. Lincolnwood, IL 60712-1799. Phone: 800-225-4772 or (847)982-0800 Fax: (847)982-1012 E-mail: info@issa.com • URL: http://www.issa.com • 10 times a year. $75.00 per year.

ISWM News. International Society of Weighing and Measurement, 15245 Shady Grove Rd., Ste. 130 Rockville, MD 20850. Phone: (301)258-1115 Fax: (301)990-9771 E-mail: staff@iswm.org • URL: http://www.iswm.org • Description: Contains calendar of events, new product information, industry updates, technical articles, and association news.

IT Cost Management Strategies: The Planning Assistant for IT Directors. Computer Economics, Inc., 5841 Edison Place Carlsbad, CA 92008-6519. Phone: 800-326-8100 or (760)438-8100 Fax: (760)431-1126 E-mail: access@compecon.com • URL: http://www.computereconomics.com • Monthly. $495.00 per year. Newsletter for information technology professionals. Covers data processing costs, budgeting, financial management, and related topics.

It Was a Very Good Year: Extraordinary Moments in Stock Market History. Martin S. Fridson. John Wiley and Sons, Inc., 111 River St. Hoboken, NJ 07030. Phone: 800-225-5945 or (201)748-6000 Fax: (201)748-6088 E-mail: info@wiley.com • URL: http://www.wiley.com • 1997. $29.95. Provides details on what happened during each of the ten best years for the stock market since 1900. (Investment Series).

Italian American Librarians Caucus., 6 Peter Cooper Rd., Apt. 11G New York, NY 10010. Phone: (212)228-8438 E-mail: deborah@irrigation.org Political and national Italian and non-Italian American organizations; business, government, public, and academic information scientists. Provides guidelines and studies, for use by libraries and information centers, on Italian and Italian American materials and populations. Conducts educational, research, and charitable programs. Maintains speakers' bureau; compiles statistics.

Italian Trade Commission., 33 E 67th St. New York, NY 10021-5949. Phone: (212)980-1500 Fax: (212)758-1050 E-mail: newyork@newyork.ice.it • URL: http://www.italtrade.com • Promotes Italian exports to the United States. Assists Italian firms wishing to enter the US market as well as US firms wishing to source product in Italy. Provides assistance to Italian firms wishing to invest in the US and US firms wishing to invest in Italy. Publishes promotional material on the benefits of Italian Products such as Wine, Cheese, & Ceramic Tile. Organizes trade missions, tradeshow pavillions, seminars and special events.

ITE Journal. Institute of Transportation Engineers, 1099 14th St., N.W., Suite 300 W Washington, DC 20005-3438. Phone: (202)289-0222 Fax: (202)289-7722 E-mail: itehq@io.com • URL: http://www.ite.org • Monthly. $60.00 per year. Formerly *Transportation Engineering*.

Item Processing Report. Access Intelligence L.L.C., 4 Choke Cherry Rd., 2nd Fl. Rockville, MD 20850. Phone: 800-777-5006 or (301)354-2000 Fax: (301)309-3847 E-mail: info@accessintel.com • URL: http://www.pbimedia.com • Description: Monitors developments in the processing of remittances and checks, including image processing, optical character recognition, check truncation, hardware, and software. **Remarks:** Absorbed The Powell Report, 1992.

Izaak Walton League of America., 707 Conservation Lane Gaithersburg, MD 20878. Phone: 800-453-5463 or (301)548-0150 Fax: (301)548-0146 E-mail: general@iwla.org • URL: http://www.iwla.org • Sponsors the Acid Rain Project, an environmental protection program. Absorbed Friends of the Land.

J. K. Lasser's Choosing the Right Long-Term Care Insurance. Benjamin Lipson. John Wiley and Sons, Inc., 111 River St. Hoboken, NJ 07030. Phone: 800-225-5945 or (201)748-6000 Fax: (201)748-6088 E-mail: info@wiley.com • URL: http://www.wiley.com • 2002. $16.95. Provides practical, consumer-oriented information, with advice to be skeptical of media hype and insurance company promotions. (Practical Guides for All Your Financial Needs Series).

J. K. Lasser's Your Income Tax, 2004: For Preparing Your 2003 Tax Return. J. K. Lasser Tax Institute Staff. John Wiley and Sons, Inc., 111 River St. Hoboken, NJ 07030. Phone: 800-

526-5368 or (201)748-6000 Fax: (201)748-6088 E-mail: info@wiley.com • URL: http://www.wiley.com • 2003. $18.95.

Jake Bernstein's New Guide to Investing in Metals. Jacob Bernstein. John Wiley and Sons, Inc., 111 River St. Hoboken, NJ 07030. Phone: 800-526-5368 or (201)748-6000 Fax: (201)748-6088 E-mail: info@wiley.com • URL: http://www.wiley.com • 1991. $34.95. Covers bullion, coins, futures, options, mining stocks, and precious metal mutual funds. Includes the history of metals as an investment.

JAMA: The Journal of the American Medical Association. American Medical Association, 515 N. State St. Chicago, IL 60610. Phone: 800-262-2350 or (312)464-5000 Fax: (312)464-4814 • URL: http://www.ama-assn.org • 48 times a year. Institutions, $365.00 per year. Includes online edition.

Jane's Air Traffic Control. Jane's Information Group, Inc., 110 N Royal St. Alexandria, VA 22314. Phone: 800-824-0768 or (703)683-3700 Fax: 800-836-0297 or (703)836-0297 E-mail: info.us@janes.con • URL: http://www.janes.com • Annual. $495.00. International coverage of equipment and supplies for both civil and military airports. Formerly *Jane's Airport and ATC Equipment*.

Jane's Airport Review: The Global Airport Business Magazine. Jane's Information Group, Inc., 110 N Royal St. Alexandria, VA 22314. Phone: 800-824-0768 or (703)683-3700 Fax: 800-836-0297 or (703)836-0297 E-mail: info.us@janes.com • URL: http://www.janes.com • 10 times a year. $190.00 per year. CD-Rom edition, $775.00 per year. Edited for airport managers. Covers all aspects of airport operations.

Jane's All the World's Aircraft. Jane's Information Group, Inc., 110 N Royal St. Alexandria, VA 22314. Phone: 800-824-0768 or (703)683-3700 Fax: 800-836-0297 or (703)836-0297 E-mail: info.us@janes.com • URL: http://www.janes.com • Annual. $630.00; CD-ROM edition, $1,455.00; online edition, $1,566.00; microfiche edition, $3,075.00. Lists civil and military aircraft, helicopters, airships, and aero engines.

Jane's Avionics. Jane's Information Group Ltd., Sentinel House, 163 Brighton Rd. Coulsdon CR5 2YH, United Kingdom. Phone: 800-824-0768 or (44)20 87003700 Fax: 800-836-0297 or (44)20 87631006 E-mail: customer.servicesuk@janes.com • URL: http://www.janes.com • Covers: Civil/military airborne equipment, including radio, radar, electro-optic, and electronic warfare data processors; worldwide coverage. Entries include: Technical information on equipment, including specifications, uses. Manufacturer information contained in separate index.

Jane's Fighting Ships. Jane's Information Group Ltd., Sentinel House, 163 Brighton Rd. Coulsdon CR5 2YH, United Kingdom. Phone: 800-824-0768 or (44)20 87003700 Fax: 800-836-0297 or (44)20 87631006 E-mail: customer.servicesuk@janes.com • URL: http://www.janes.com • Covers: 164 navies of the world and ship details, weapons fits, specifications. Foreword includes an annual review of worldwide naval developments. Entries include: Major command personnel, diplomatic representatives, naval bases, shipyards, strength of fleets, etc. ; details of personnel and units; technical information about each type of ship, weapons fitted to each class.

Jane's Police and Security Equipment: The Complete Source on Worldwide Law Enforcement Equipment. Jane's Information Group, 110 N Royal St. Alexandria, VA 22314. Phone: 800-824-0768 or (703)683-3700 Fax: 800-836-0297 or (703)836-0297 E-mail: info.us@janes.com • URL: http://www.janes.com • Annual. $557.00; CD-ROM edition, $1,370.00; online edition, $1,478.00. Provides information on sources of more than 2,000 items of law enforcement equipment. Covers traffic control, riot control, communications, personal protection, surveillance, and other equipment categories. Includes detailed product descriptions.

Jane's Road Traffic Management and ITS (Intelligent Transport Systems). Jane's Information Group, Inc., 110 N Royal St. Alexandria, VA 22314. Phone: 800-824-0768 or (703)683-3700 Fax: (703)836-0297 or (703)836-0297 E-mail: info.us@janes.com • URL: http://www.janes.com • Annual. $470.00. A directory of traffic control equipment and services. Includes detailed product descriptions.

Jane's Urban Transport Systems. Jane's Information Group Ltd., Sentinel House, 163 Brighton Rd. Coulsdon CR5 2YH, United Kingdom. Phone: 800-824-0678 or (44)20 87003700 Fax: 800-836-0297 or (44)20 87631006 E-mail: customer.servicesuk@janes.com • URL: http://www.janes.com • Covers: Operating bus, metro, light rail, tram, ferry, and trolley bus transport systems; manufacturers of equipment for urban systems; experimental systems, and manufacturers of support equipment; consultants; worldwide coverage. Entries include: For systems—Name of operating company or authority, address, phone, fax, telex, names and titles of key personnel, services, equipment, finances, developments. For manufacturers—Name, address, phone, fax, telex, names and titles of key personnel, products, current contracts, new developments in equipment. For consultants—Firm name, address, phone, fax, telex, names and titles of key personnel, description of firm capabilities, past projects.

Jane's World Airlines. Jane's Information Group Ltd., Sentinel House, 163 Brighton Rd. Coulsdon CR5 2YH, United Kingdom. Phone: 800-824-0768 or (44)20 87003700 Fax: 800-836-0297 or (44)20 87631006 E-mail: customer.servicesuk@janes.com • URL: http://www.janes.com • Covers: Approximately 500 scheduled, non-scheduled, cargo, and passenger airlines; international coverage. Entries include: Airline name, address, phone, fax, fleet structure, routes operated, traffic statistics, financial data, cargo capacity, corporate structure and major subsidiaries, names and titles of executives.

Jane's World Railways. Jane's Information Group Ltd., Sentinel House, 163 Brighton Rd. Coulsdon CR5 2YH, United Kingdom. Phone: 800-824-0768 or (44)20 87003700 Fax: 800-836-0297 or (44)20 87631006 E-mail: customer.servicesuk@janes.com • URL: http://www.janes.com • Covers: Global railway industry manufacturers, railway systems, and rapid transit systems throughout various countries; freight car leasing companies; international railway associations, agencies, and consultants. Entries include: For railway systems—Governmental or private authority responsible for operation, address, names and titles of key personnel, gauges, route length, description and history, equipment, statistics. For manufacturers—Company name, address, phone, fax, telex, clients and products; names and titles of key personnel. For leasing companies—Name, address, phone, fax, names and titles of key personnel, operations and equipment. For associations—Name, address, phone, fax, telex, key officers, objectives. For consultants—Firm name, address, phone, contact name, capabilities, projects. All sections except consultants and associations include numerous drawings and photographs. Jane's World Railways continues to be the foremost information source on the railway industry, giving you a truly global perspective on the development of more than 450 railway systems in over 140 countries worldwide.

Janitorial Service. Entrepreneur Media, Inc., 2445 McCabe Way Irvine, CA 92614. Phone: 800-421-2300 or (949)261-2325 Fax: (949)261-0234 E-mail: entmag@entrepreneur.com • URL: http://www.entrepreneur.com • Looseleaf. $59.50. A practical guide to starting a janitorial service business. Covers profit potential, start-up costs, market size evaluation, owner's time required, site selection, lease negotiation, pricing, accounting, advertising, promotion, etc. (Start-Up Business Guide No. E1034.)

Japan Business: The Portable Encyclopedia for Doing Business with Japan. Christine Genzberger and others. World Trade Press, 1450 Grant Ave., Suite 204 Novato, CA 94945. Phone: 800-833-8586 or (415)898-1124 Fax: (415)898-1080 E-mail: sales@worldtradepress.com • URL: http://www.worldtradepress.com • 1994. $24.95. (Country Business Guide Series).

Japan Camera Trade News: Monthly Information on Photographic Products, Optical Instruments and Accessories. K. Eda, editor. Genyosha Publications, Inc., 4-7 Shibuya 2-chome, Shibuya-ku Tokyo 150-0002, Japan. Phone: 81 3 3407 7521 or 81 3 3407 7902 E-mail: info@genyosha.co.jp • URL: http://www.genyosha.com • Monthly. $130.00 per year. Information on the photographic industry worldwide. Text in English.

Japan Company Handbook. Toyo Keizai Inc., 1-2-1 Nihonbashi Hongokucho, Chuo-ku Tokyo 103-8345, Japan. Phone: (81)3 32465551 Fax: (81)3 32790332 E-mail: info@toyokeizai.co.jp • URL: http://www.toyokeizai.co • Covers: in two sections: over 3,939 Japanese corporations listed on the 'First Section' of Tokyo, Osaka, and Nagoya stock exchanges, listed in one volume; about 900 firms, smaller in capital but 'considered promising' and listed on the 'Second Section,' are given in a separate volume titled 'Japan Company Handbook—Second Section'; 800 over-the counter companies; and nearly 80 local market companies. Entries include: Company name, address, phone, fax, telex, description, outlook, year established, fiscal year, overseas offices, president, references, capital, other financial data, stock exchanges on which listed, underwriters, number of employees, names of major stockholders and percentage of Japanese and foreign ownership, principal products, export ratio.

Japan Economic Almanac., PO Box 15 Leonia, NJ 07605. Phone: (201)224-9480 Fax: (201)585-2343 Annual. $59.50. Lists of Japanese government agencies, and professional and trade organizations. Text in English.

Japan Economic Newswire Plus. Kyodo News International, Inc., 50 Rockefeller Plaza, Room 803 New York, NY 10020. Phone: 800-536-3510 or (212)397-3723 Fax: (212)397-3721 Provides full text in English of news items relating to business, economics, industry, trade, and finance in Japan and the Pacific Rim countries. Time period is 1982 to date, with daily updates. Inquire as to online cost and availability.

Japan External Trade Organization., 1221 Ave. of the Americas, McGraw Hill Bldg., 42nd Fl. New York, NY 10020. Phone: (212)997-0400 Fax: (212)997-0464 E-mail: epj_la@jetro.go.jp • URL: http://www.jetro.org • Supports foreign companies in export and/or investment to Japan-related business ventures. Disseminates comprehensive information on the Japanese economy and market through surveys, reports, publications, and newsletters. Conducts trade and investment promotion seminars and symposia. Sponsors trade shows and exhibitions. Provides professional business consultation services and handles trade-related inquiries and provides opportunities for international exchange.

The Japan Times., P.O. Box 144 Tokyo 100-8691, Japan. Phone: 03 3452 2099 E-mail: overseas@japantimes.co.jp Weekly. $120.00 per year. Provides news and commentary on Japan's economy, trade policies, and Japanese life in general. Regular features include "Business Briefs," "Market Reports," "Lifestyle," and "Issue Analysis." Supplement available *The Japan Times Weekly*. Text in English.

Japan Trade Directory. Japan External Trade Organization, Ark Mori Bldg., 6F 12-32, Akasaka 1-chome, Minato-ku Tokyo 107-6006, Japan. Phone: 800-877-GALE or (81)3 35825511 Fax: 800-414-5043 or (81)335872485 E-mail: customer.servicesuk@janes.com • URL: http://www.galegroup.com • Covers: nearly 2,000 Japanese firms; trade and industrial associations. Entries include: For companies—Name, address, cable address, fax, e-mail, URL, name of chief executive officer, year established, line of business, amount of capital, annual sales, number of employees, bank references, office hours, trade names, whether catalog is available, languages spoken, countries with which business relationship is desired, products desired and those available for export, contact name and phone.

Japanese Automobile Industry: An Annotated Bibliography. Sheau-Yueh J. Chao, compiler. Greenwood Publishing Group, Inc., 88 Post Rd., W Westport, CT 06881. Phone: 800-225-5800 or (203)226-3571 Fax: (203)431-2214 E-mail: customer-service@greenwood.com • URL: http://www.greenwood.com • 1994. $82.95. Describes about 600 books, articles, papers, and documents written in English. Emphasis is on material published since 1980. (Bibliographies and Indexes in Economics and Economic History Series: No. 15).

Japanese Company Factfinder: Teikoku Databank. Teikoku Databank America, Inc., 747 Third Ave., 25th Fl. New York, NY 10017. Phone: (212)421-9805 Fax: (212)421-9806 E-mail: office@teikoku.com • URL: http://www.teikoku.com • Quarterly. $1,920.00 per year to academic and public libraries. $3,200 per year to businesses. CD-ROM provides detailed financial and descriptive information on more than 186,000 Japanese companies doing business overseas.

JASA (Journal of the American Statistical Association). American Statistical Association, 1429 Duke St. Alexandria, VA 22314-3415. Phone: 888-231-3473 or (703)684-1221 Fax: (703)684-2037 E-mail: asainfo@amstat.org • URL: http://www.amstat.org • Quarterly. Members, $39.00 per year; non-members, $310.00 per year; students, $10.00 per year.

Java Cookbook: Solutions and Examples for Java Developers. Ian Darwin. O'Reilly & Associates, Inc., 90 Sherman St. Cambridge, MA 02140. Phone: 800-775-7731 or (617)354-5800 Fax: (617)661-1116 E-mail: order@oreilly.com • URL: http://www.oreilly.com • 2001. $44.95. Presents a "comprehensive collection of problems, solutions, and practical examples" for Java developers.

Java Developer's Journal. Sys-Con Media, 135 Chestnut Ridge Rd. Montvale, NJ 07645. Phone: 888-303-5282 or (201)802-3000 Fax: (201)782-9601 E-mail: info@sys-con.com • URL: http://www.sys-con.com • Monthly. $69.99 per year. Provides technical information for Java professionals.

Java FAQs. Clifford J. Berg. Prentice Hall PTR, 240 Frisch Ct. Paramus, NJ 07652. Phone: 800-282-0693 Fax: 800-445-6991 • URL: http://www.phptr.com • 2001. $26.95.

Java for Students. Douglas Bell and Mike Parr. Prentice Hall PTR, 240 Frisch Ct. Paramus, NJ 07652. Phone: 800-282-0693 Fax: 800-445-6991 • URL: http://www.phptr.com • 2001. $77.33. Third edition. A basic introduction to Java.

Java in a Nutshell. David Flanagan. O'Reilly & Associates, Inc., 90 Sherman St. Cambridgel, MA 02140. Phone: 800-775-7731 or (617)354-5800 Fax: (617)661-1166 E-mail: order@oreilly.com • URL: http://www.oreilly.com • 2002. $39.95. Fourth edition. (In a Nutshell Series).

Java in 60 Minutes a Day. R. F. Raposa. John Wiley and Sons, Inc., 111 River St. Hoboken, NJ 07030. Phone: 800-225-5945 or (201)748-6000 Fax: (201)748-6088 E-mail: info@wiley.com • URL: http://www.wiley.com • 2003. $50.00. "Includes thirty one-hour lessons that recreate a typical week-long introductory seminar." A companion Web site is offered.

Java Pro. Fawcette Technical Publications, 2600 S El Camino Real San Mateo, CA 94403-2332. Phone: 800-848-5523 or (650)387-8100 Fax: (650)570-6307 E-mail: customerservice@fawcette.com • URL: http://www.fawcette.com • Monthly. $29.95 per year. Contains technical articles for Java developers.

Java Tutorial: A Short Course on the Basics. Mary Campione and Others. Addison-Wesley, 75 Arlington St., Ste. 300 Boston, MA 02116. Phone: 800-447-2226 or (617)848-7500 • URL: http://www.aw.com • 2000. $44.99. Third edition. Presents a self-guided tour of the Java programming language. CD-ROM included. (Java Tutorial Series).

Jax Fax Travel Marketing Magazine: The Official Leisure Travel Booking Magazine. Jet Airtransport Exchange, Inc., 48 Wellington Rd. Milford, CT. Phone: (203)301-0255 Fax: (203)301-0250 E-mail: dcjaxfax@aol.com • URL: http://www.jaxfax.com • Monthly. $15.00 per year. Trade magazine for travel agents.

JCK (Jewelers' Circular Keystone). Reed Business Information, 360 Park Ave., S New York, NY 10010. Phone: 800-446-6551 or (646)746-4600 Fax: (646)746-7028 E-mail: corporatecommunications@reedbusiness.com • URL: http://www.reedbusiness.com • Monthly. $90.00 per year.

JCT:Journal of Coatings Technology. Federation of Societies for Coatings Technology, 492 Norristown Rd. Blue Bell, PA 19422-2350. Phone: (610)940-0777 Fax: (610)940-0292

E-mail: fsct@coatingstech.org • URL: http://www.coatingstech.org • Monthly. Free to members; non-members, $150.00 per year.

Jerome Lawrence and Robert E. Lee Theatre Research Institute.

Jet and Propjet: Corporate Directory. AvCom International Inc., 312 E. Murdock St. Wichita, KS 67214. Phone: (316)262-1491 Fax: (316)262-5333 E-mail: sales@avcominc.com Annual. $21.95. Owners of business jet and turboprop aircraft. Worldwide coverage. Formerly *Propjet*.

The Jewelers Board of Trade., 95 Jefferson Blvd. Providence, RI 02940. Phone: (401)467-0055 Fax: (401)467-1199 E-mail: jbtinfo@jewelersboard.com • URL: http://www.jewelersboard.com • A credit reporting and collection organization for the jewelry business.

Jewelers' Circular/Keystone-Jewelers' Directory. Reed Business Information, 360 Park Ave., S New York, NY 10010. Phone: 800-446-6551 or (646)746-6400 Fax: (646)746-7028 E-mail: corporatecommunications@reedbusines.com • URL: http://www.reedbusiness.com • Annual. $33.95. About 8,500 manufacturers, importers and wholesale jewelers providing merchandise and supplies to the jewelry retailing industry; and related trade organizations. Included with subscription to *Jewelers' Circular Keystone*.

Jewelers of America., 52 Vanderbilt Ave., 19th Fl. New York, NY 10017. Phone: 800-223-0673 or (646)658-0246 Fax: (646)658-0256 E-mail: info@jewelers.org • URL: http://www.jewelers.org • Formerly Retail Jewelers of America.

Jewelers Security Alliance of the U.S., Six E. 45th St. New York, NY 10017. Phone: 800-537-0067 or (212)687-0328 Fax: (212)808-9168 E-mail: jsa2@jewelerssecurity.org • URL: http://www.jewelerssecurity.org • Formerly Jewelers Security Alliance of U.S.

Jewelers Vigilance Committee., 25 W 45th St., Ste. 1406 New York, NY 10036. Phone: 800-JOI-NJVC or (212)997-2002 Fax: (212)997-9148 E-mail: clg@jvclegal.org • URL: http://www.jvclegal.org • Represents manufacturers, importers, wholesalers, and retailers. Combats deceptive trade practices and misleading advertising. Aims to develop and maintain high trade standards. Provides advice on markings and assists in prosecution of violations of marking, advertising, and related jewelry industry laws.

Jewelry and Gems: The Buying Guide: How to Buy Diamonds, Pearls, Precious and Other Popular Gems with Confidence and Knowledge. Antoinette L. Matlins and Antonio C. Bonanno. GemStone Press, Route 4, Sunset Farm Offices Woodstock, VT 05091. Phone: 800-962-4544 or (802)457-4000 Fax: (802)457-4004 E-mail: sales@gemstonepress.com • URL: http://www.gemstonepress.com • 2001. $24.95. Fifth edition.

Jewelry Information Center., 52 Vanderbilt Ave., 19th Fl. New York, NY 10017. Phone: 800-459-0130 or (646)658-0240 Fax: (646)658-0245 E-mail: info@jic.org • URL: http://www.jic.org • Represents retailers, wholesalers, and manufacturers of fine jewelry products. Conducts industry-wide promotional and educational programs; sponsors marketing seminars and consumer-oriented programs on radio, television, and print media.

JOACS (Journal of the American Oil Chemists' Society). American Oil Chemists' Society. AOCS Press, 2211 W Bradley Ave. Champaign, IL 61821-1827. Phone: (217)359-2344 Fax: (217)351-8091 E-mail: general@aocs.org • URL: http://www.aocs.org • Monthly. Individuals, $120.00 per year; institutions, $278.00 per year. Includes *INFORM: International News on Fats, Oils and Related Materials*.

Job & Career Books. Kennedy Information, 1 Phoenix Mill Ln., 5th Fl. Peterborough, NH 03458. Phone: 800-531-0007 or (603)924-1006 Fax: (603)924-4034 E-mail: bookstore@kennedyinfo.com • URL: http://www.kennedyinfo.com • Annual. Free. Contains descriptions of selected books from various publishers on job searching and choice of career.

Job Hunter's Sourcebook: Where to Find Employment Leads and Other Job Search Resources. Gale Cengage Learning, 27500 Drake Rd. Farmington Hills, MI 48331-3535. Phone: 800-877-GALE or (248)699-4253 Fax: 800-414-5043 E-mail: gale.galeord@cengage.com • URL: http://gale.cengage.com • 2002. $125.00. Fifth edition. Covers 206 professions and occupations.

Job Patterns for Minorities and Women in Private Industry. Available from U. S. Government Printing Office, Washington, DC 20402. Phone: (202)512-1800 Fax: (202)512-2250 E-mail: gpoaccess@gpo.gov • URL: http://www.access.gpo.gov • Annual. $61.00. Issued by the Equal Employment Opportunity Commission (http://www.eeoc.gov). "Provides statistical information on the composition of the United States workforce in private industry by sex, race, and ethnic category."

Job Safety and Health Quarterly. Available from U. S. Government Printing Office, Washington, DC 20402. Phone: (202)512-1800 Fax: (202)512-2250 E-mail: gpoaccess@gpo.gov • URL: http://www.access.gpo.gov • Quarterly. $17.00 per year. Issued by the Occupational Safety and Health Administration (OSHA), U. S. Department of Labor. Contains articles on employee safety and health, with information on current OSHA activities.

Job Search: The Total System. Kenneth Dawson and Sheryl N. Dawson. John Wiley and Sons, Inc., 111 River St. Hoboken, NJ 07030. Phone: 800-225-5945 or (201)748-6000 Fax: (201)748-6088 E-mail: info@wiley.com • URL: http://www.

wiley.com • 1988. $24.95. Second edition.

Job Seeker's Guide to Private and Public Companies. Gale Cengage Learning, 27500 Drake Rd. Farmington Hills, MI 48331-3535. Phone: 800-877-GALE or (248)699-4253 Fax: 800-414-5043 E-mail: gale.galeord@cengage.com • URL: http://gale.cengage.com • 1993. $390.00. Second edition. $99.00 per volume. Four regional volumes: *The West, The Midwest, The Northeast*, and *The South*. Covers about 15,000 companies, providing information on personnel department contacts, corporate officials, company benefits, application procedures, etc.

Jobs-Careers-Professions: A Bibliography with Indexes. Leon V. Werner. Nova Science Publishers, Inc., 400 Oser Ave., Suite 1600 Hauppauge, NY 11788-3619. Phone: (631)231-7269 Fax: (631)231-8175 E-mail: novascience@earthlink.net • URL: http://www.novapublishers.com • 2001. $59.00. Contains more than 1,500 citations to books and periodical articles on job hunting, compensation, career choice, education, mobility, supply-demand factors, and other job topics. Includes author, title, and subject indexes.

JOC Shipping Digest: For Export and Transportation Executives. Shipper Group, 33 Washington St., 13th Fl. Newark, NJ 07102. Phone: 800-223-0243 Fax: (973)848-7045 E-mail: customerservice@joc.com • URL: http://www.shippingdigest.com • Weekly. $57.00 per year. Formerly *Shipping Digest*.

The John Liner Letter. Standard Publishing Corp., 155 Federal St.,13th Fl. Boston, MA 02110-9637. Phone: 800-682-5759 or (617)457-0600 Fax: (617)457-0608 E-mail: order@standardpublishingcorp.com • URL: http://www.standardpublishingcorp.com • Description: Provides risk management and technical insurance advice for business firms, such as broadening coverage, cutting costs, and anticipating special insurance problems.

John W. Hartman Center for Sales, Advertising, and Marketing History., Special Collections Library, Duke University, P.O. Box 90185 Durham, NC 27708-0185. Phone: (919)660-5827 Fax: (919)660-5934 E-mail: hartman-center@duke.edu • URL: http://www.scriptorium.lib.duke.edu/hartman/ • Concerned with the study of the roles of sales, advertising, and marketing in society.

Joining of Composite Matrix Materials. Mel M. Schwartz. ASM International, 9639 Kinsman Rd. Materials Park, OH 44073-0002. Phone: 800-336-5152 or (440)338-5151 Fax: (440)338-4634 E-mail: cust-srv@po.asm-intl.org • URL: http://www.asminternational.org • 1994. $59.00.

Joint Committee of the States., c/o National Alcoholic Beverage Control Association, 4216 King St., W Alexandria, VA 22302. Phone: (703)578-4200 Fax: (703)820-3551 Formerly Joint Committee of the States to study Alcoholic Beverage Laws.

Joint Electron Device Engineering Council (JEDC)., 2500 Wilson Blvd. Arlington, VA 22201-3834. Phone: (703)907-7534 Fax: (703)907-7583 E-mail: arlenec@jedec.org • URL: http://www.jedec.org • Affiliated with Electronic Industries Alliance. Formerly Joint Electron Device Engineering Council.

Joint Industry Board of the Electrical Industry., 158-11 Harry Van Arsdale, Jr. Ave. Flushing, NY 11365. Phone: (718)591-2000 Fax: (718)380-7741 Concerned with labor-management relations of electrical contractors.

Joint Institute for Advancement of Flight Sciences., NASA Langley Research Center, MS 335, 227 Hunting Ave. Hampton, VA 23681-2199. Phone: (757)864-1982 Fax: (757)864-5894 E-mail: jiafs@seas.gwu.edu • URL: http://www.seas.gwu.edu/ • Conducts research in aeronautics, astronautics, and acoustics (flight-produced noise).

Joint Ventures. Glasser Legalworks, 150 Clove Rd. Little Falls, NJ 07424. Phone: 800-308-1700 or (973)890-0008 Fax: (973)890-0042 E-mail: orders@glasserlegalworks.com • URL: http://www.glasserlegalworks.com • Looseleaf. $225.00, including CD-ROM version. Periodic Supplementation. Includes explanations of legal procedures for joint ventures, with annotated forms. (Emerging Growth Companies Series.)

JOM: The Member Journal of the Minerals, Metals and Materials Society. Minerals, Metals, and Materials Society, 184 Thornhill Rd. Warrendale, PA 15086-7514. Phone: 800-759-4867 or (724)776-9000 Fax: (724)776-3770 E-mail: tmsgeneral@tms.org • URL: http://www.tms.org • Four times a year. Membership. A scholarly journal covering all phases of metals and metallurgy.

Jones Dictionary of Cable Television Terminology, Including Related Computer andSatellite Definitions. Glenn R. Jones. Jones Twenty-First Century Ltd., 9697 E Mineral Ave. Englewood, CO 80112. Phone: (303)792-3111 1988. $14.95. Third edition.

Jounal of Finacial Services Professionals. Society of Financial Services Professional, 270 S. Bryn Mawr Ave. Bryn Mawr, PA 19010-2195. Phone: 800-392-6900 or (610)526-2500 Fax: (610)526-2538 E-mail: journal@financialpro.org • URL: http://www.financialpro.org • Bimonthly. $95.00 per year. Provides information on life insurance and financial planning, including estate planning, retirement, tax planning, trusts, business insurance, long-term care insurance, disability insurance, and employee benefits. Formerly (American Society of CLU and Ch F C Journal)

The Journal of Academic Librarianship: Articles, Features, and Book Reviews for the Academic Library Professional. Elsevier, 360 Park Ave., S New York, NY 10010-1710. Phone: (212)989-5800 Fax: (212)633-3990 E-mail: usinfo-

f@elsevier.com • URL: http://www.elsevier.com • Bimonthly. Qualified personnel, $101.00 per year; institutions, $253.00 per year.

Journal of Accountancy. American Institute of Certified Public Accountants, 1211 Ave. of the Americas New York, NY 10036-8775. Phone: 800-862-4272 or (212)596-6200 Fax: (212)596-6213 E-mail: lmorales@aicpa.org • URL: http://www.aicpa.org/pubs • Monthly. Free to members; non-members, $61.00 per year.

Journal of Accounting, Auditing and Finance. New York University Vincent C. Ross Institute of Accounting Research. Greenwood Publishing Group Inc., 88 Post Rd., W Westport, CT 06881. Phone: 800-225-5800 or (203)226-3571 Fax: (203)431-2214 E-mail: customer-service@greenwood.com • URL: http://www.greenwood.com • Quarterly. Individuals, $70.00 per year; institutions, $165.00 per year.

Journal of Accounting Research. University of Chicago, Graduate School of Business Institute of Professional Accounting. Blackwell Publishing, 350 Main St. Malden, MA 02148. Phone: 800-835-6770 or (781)388-8202 Fax: (781)388-8232 E-mail: subscrip@blackwellpub.com • URL: http://www.blackwellpublishing.com • Five times a year. Institutions, $425.00 per year. Includes online edition. Annual *Supplement* available. Accepts for review unpublished research in the fields of empirical and experimental accounting.

Journal of Adhesion. Taylor & Francis Group, 325 Chestnut St., Ste. 800 Philadelphia, PA 19152. Phone: 800-821-8312 or (215)625-8900 Fax: (212)625-2940 E-mail: info@taylorandfrancis.com • URL: http://www.taylorandfrancis.com • Monthly. Three volumes. Individuals, $1,575.00 per year; institutions, $3,056.00 per year; corporations, $6,760.00 per year.

Journal of Advanced Materials. Society for the Advancement of Material and Process Engineering, P.O. Box 2459 Covina, CA 91722. Phone: (626)331-0616 Fax: (626)332-8929 E-mail: sampeibo@aol.com • URL: http://www.sampe.org • Quarterly. Individuals, $60.00 per year; institutions, $150.00 per year. Contains technical and research articles. Formerly *SAMPE Quarterly*.

Journal of Advertising. M. E. Sharpe, Inc., 80 Business Park Drive Armonk, NY 10504. Phone: 800-541-6563 or (914)273-1800 Fax: (914)273-2106 E-mail: custserv@mesharpe.com • URL: http://www.mesharpe.com • Quarterly. $90.00 per year. An academic journal devoted to advertising theory and research.

Journal of Advertising Research. Advertising Research Foundation, 641 Lexington Ave., 11th Fl. New York, NY 10022. Phone: (212)751-5656 Fax: (212)319-5265 E-mail: journal@thearf.org • URL: http://www.arfsite.org • Quarterly. Individuals, $155.00 per year; institutions, $275.00 per year.

Journal of Aging and Social Policy: A Journal Devoted to Aging and Social Policy. Haworth Press, Inc., 10 Alice St. Binghamton, NY 13904-1580. Phone: 800-429-6784 or (607)722-5857 Fax: 800-895-0582 or (607)722-1424 E-mail: getinfo@haworthpressinc.com • URL: http://www.haworthpressinc.com • Quarterly. $415.00 per year.

Journal of Agricultural and Food Information. Haworth Press, Inc., 10 Alice St. Binghamton, NY 13904-1580. Phone: 800-429-6784 or (607)722-5857 Fax: 800-895-0582 or (607)722-1424 E-mail: getinfo@haworthpressinc.com • URL: http://www.haworthpressinc.com • Quarterly. Institutions, $95.00 per year. A journal for librarians and others concerned with the acquisition of information on food and agriculture.

Journal of Aircraft: Devoted to Aeronautical Science and Technology. American Institute of Aeronautics and Astronautics, Inc., 1801 Alexander Bell Dr., Suite 500 Reston, VA 20191. Phone: 800-639-2422 or (703)264-7500 Fax: (703)264-7551 E-mail: custserv@aiaa.org • URL: http://www.aiaa.org • Bimonthly. Members, $55.00 per year; institutions, $520.00 per year. Online edition available.

Journal of Alcohol and Drug Education. American Alcohol and Drug Information Foundation, 1120 E Oakland Ave. Lansing, MI 48901-0212. Phone: (517)484-2636 Fax: (517)484-0444 • URL: http://www.unomaha.edu • Three times a year. $45.00 per year.

Journal of Alternative Investments. Institutional Investor, Inc., Journals Group, 225 Park Ave., S., 8th Fl. New York, NY 10003. Phone: 800-945-2034 or (212)224-3066 Fax: (212)224-3472 E-mail: info@iijournals.com • URL: http://www.iijournals.com • Quarterly. $540.00 per year. Includes print and online editions. Covers such items as hedge funds, private equity financing, funds of funds, real estate investment trusts, natural resource investments, foreign exchange, and emerging markets.

Journal of Animal Science. American Society of Animal Science, 1111 N. Dunlap Ave. Savoy, IL 68174. Phone: (217)356-3182 Fax: (217)398-4119 E-mail: asas@assochq.org • URL: http://www.asas.org • Monthly. $400.00 per year.

Journal of Apicultural Research. International Bee Research Association, 18 North Rd. Cardiff CF10 3DT, United Kingdom. Phone: 44 029 2037 2409 Fax: 44 029 2066 5522 E-mail: mail@ibra.org.uk • URL: http://www.ibra.org.uk • Quarterly. $225.00 per year. Primary research

Journal of Applied Behavioral Science. Sage Publications, Inc., 2455 Teller Rd. Thousand Oaks, CA 91320. Phone: 800-818-7243 or (805)499-9774 Fax: 800-583-2665 or (805)499-0871 E-mail: webmaster@sagepub.com • URL: http://www.sagepub.com • Quarterly. Institutions, $493.00 per year. Includes print and online editions.

Journal of Applied Communication Research. National Communication Association, 1765 N St., N.W. Washington, DC 20036. Phone: (202)464-4622 Fax: (202)464-4600 E-mail: jgaudino@natcom.org • URL: http://www.natcom.org • Quarterly. $110.00 per year.

Journal of Applied Econometrics. John Wiley and Sons, Inc., Journals, 111 River St. Hoboken, NJ 07030. Phone: 800-225-5945 or (201)748-6000 Fax: (201)748-6088 E-mail: customer@wiley.com • URL: http://www.wiley.com • Bimonthly. Individuals, $85.00 per year; institutions, $1,050.00 per year.

Journal of Applied Mechanics. ASME International, 3 Park Ave. New York, NY 10016-5990. Phone: 800-843-2763 or (212)591-7722 Fax: (212)591-7674 E-mail: infocentral@asme.org • URL: http://www.asme.org • Bimonthly. Members, $60.00 per year; non-members, $300.00 per year. Subscription includes online edition.

Journal of Applied Meteorology. American Meteorological Society, 45 Beacon St. Boston, MA 02108-3693. Phone: (617)227-2425 Fax: (617)742-8718 E-mail: amsinfo@ametsoc.org • URL: http://www.ametsoc.org • Monthly. Members, $55.00 per year; individuals, $365.00 per year.

Journal of Applied Polymer Science. John Wiley and Sons, Inc., Journals, 111 River St. Hoboken, NJ 07030. Phone: 800-225-5945 or (201)748-6000 Fax: (201)748-6088 E-mail: customer@wiley.com • URL: http://www.wiley.com • 56 times a year. $14,495.00 per year; with online edition, $15,220.00, four volumes.

Journal of Aquatic Food Product Technology: An International Journal Devoted to Foods from Marine and Inland Waters of the World. Haworth Press, Inc., 10 Alice St. Binghamton, NY 13904-1580. Phone: 800-429-6784 or (607)722-5857 Fax: 800-895-0582 or (607)722-1424 E-mail: getinfo@haworthpressinc.com • URL: http://www.haworthpressinc.com • Quarterly. $375.00 per year.

Journal of Architectural Education. Association of Collegiate Schools of Architecture. MIT Press, Five Cambridge Center Cambridge, MA 02142-1493. Phone: (617)253-5646 E-mail: journals-orders@mit.edu • URL: http://www.mitpress.mit.edu • Quarterly. Free to members; non-members, $50.00. Articles on architectural education, theory and practice.

Journal of Arts Management, Law, and Society. Helen Dwight Reid Educational Foundation. Publications, 1319 18th St., N.W. Washington, DC 20036-1802. Phone: 800-365-9753 or (202)296-6267 Fax: (202)292-6130 E-mail: subscribe@heldref.org • URL: http://www.helderf.org • Quarterly. Individuals, $73.00 per year; institutions, $136.00 per year. Addresses current and ongoing issues in arts policy, management, low and governance from a range of philosophical and national perspectives encompassing diverse disciplinary viewpoints. Formerly *Journal of Arts Management and Law*.

Journal of Asia-Pacific Business. Haworth Press, Inc., 10 Alice St. Binghamton, NY 13904-1580. Phone: 800-429-6784 or (607)722-5857 Fax: 800-895-0582 or (607)722-1424 E-mail: getinfo@haworthpressinc.com • URL: http://www.haworthpressinc.com • Quarterly. $225.00 per year. Includes print and online editions. An academic and practical journal concerned with marketing, finance, and other aspects of doing business in Asia.

Journal of Asian Business. Southeast Asia Business Program. University of Michigan, 914 Hill St. Ann Arbor, MI 48109-1234. Phone: (734)998-7276 Fax: (734)936-1721 E-mail: jab@umich.edu • URL: http://www.umich.edu • Quarterly. Individuals, $25.00 per year; institutions, $40.00 per year. An international academic journal covering business in all parts of Asia.

Journal of Astronautical Sciences. American Astronautical Society, 6352 Rolling Mill Place, Suite 102 Springfield, VA 22152-2354. Phone: (703)866-0020 Fax: (703)866-3526 E-mail: aas@astronautical.org • URL: http://www.astronautical.org • Quarterly. $155.00 per year.

Journal of Bank Cost and Management Accounting. Association for Management Information in Financial Services, 7950 E LaJunta Rd. Scottsdale, AZ 85255-2798. Fax: (480)515-2101 E-mail: ami@amifs.org • URL: http://www.amifs.org • Three times a year. $100.00 per year.

Journal of Behavioral Health Services and Research. Association of Behavioral Healthcare Management. Lippincott Williams and Wilkins, 530 Walnut St. Philadephia, PA 19106-3621. Phone: 800-638-3030 or (215)521-8300 Fax: (215)521-8902 E-mail: orders@lww.com Quarterly. Individuals, $81.95 per year; institutions, $231.95 per year. Pertains to the financing and organization of behavioral health services. Formerly *Journal of Mental Health Administration*.

Journal of Biotechnology. Elsevier, 360 Park Ave. S New York, NY 10010-1710. Phone: 888-437-4636 or (212)989-5800 Fax: (212)633-3990 E-mail: usinfo-f@elsevier.com • URL: http://www.elsevier.com • Semimonthly. Institutions, $3,338.00 per year. Text and summaries in English.

Journal of Broadcasting and Electronic Media. Broadcast Education Association, 1771 N St., N.W. Washington, DC 20036. Phone: 888-380-7222 or (202)429-5354 Fax: (202)775-2981 E-mail: lindlofe@uky.edu • URL: http://www.beaweb.org • Quarterly. $86.50 per year. Scholarly articles about developments, trends and research.

The Journal of Business. The University of Chicago Press, Journals Div., P.O. Box 37005 Chicago, IL 60637. Phone: 877-705-1878 or (773)753-3347 Fax: 877-705-1879 or (312)753-0811 E-mail: subcriptions@press.uchicago.edu • URL: http://www.journals.uchicago.edu • Quarterly. Individuals, $31.00 per year; institutions, $125.00 per year; students, $25.00 per year.

Journal of Business and Economic Statistics. American Statistical Association, 1429 Duke St. Alexandria, VA 22314-3415. Phone: 888-231-3473 or (703)684-1221 Fax: (703)684-2037 E-mail: asainfo@amstat.org • URL: http://www.amstat.org • Quarterly. Libraries, $90.00 per year. Emphasis is on statistical measurement and applications for business and economics.

Journal of Business and Finance Librarianship. Haworth Press, Inc., 10 Alice St. Binghamton, NY 13904-1580. Phone: 800-429-6784 or (607)722-5857 Fax: 800-895-0582 or (607)722-1424 E-mail: getinfo@haworthpressinc.com • URL: http://www.haworthpressinc.com • Quarterly. $165.00 per year.

Journal of Business and Psychology. Business Psychology Research Institute. Kluwer Academic Publishers, 101 Philip Dr., Assinippi Park Norwell, MA 02061. Phone: (781)871-6600 Fax: (781)681-9045 • URL: http://www.wkap.nl • Quarterly. Institutions, $614.00 per year; with online edition, $736.80 per year.

Journal of Business and Technical Communication. Sage Publications, Inc., 2455 Teller Rd. Thousand Oaks, CA 91320. Phone: 800-818-7243 or (805)499-9774 Fax: 800-583-2665 or (805)499-0871 E-mail: webmaster@sagepub.com • URL: http://www.sagepub.com • Institutions, $445.00 per year; includes print and online editions.

Journal of Business Communication. Association for Business Communication, Baruch College, c/o Dr. Robert J. Myers, Dept. of Speech Communication, 17 Lexington Ave. New York, NY 10010. Phone: (212)387-1620 Fax: (212)387-1655 E-mail: abcrjm@cs.com • URL: http://www.theabc.org • Quarterly. Individuals, $65.00 per year; insititutions, $160.00 per year. Includes *Association for Business Communiation Bulletin*.

Journal of Business Ethics. Kluwer Academic Publishers, 101 Phillip Dr., Assinippi Park Norwell, MA 02061. Phone: (781)871-6600 Fax: (781)681-9045 • URL: http://www.wkap.nl • 28 times a year. Institutions, $1,743.00 per year. Includes print and online editions.

Journal of Business Forecasting Methods and Systems. Graceway Publishing Co., P.O. Box 670159 Flushing, NY 11367-0159. Phone: 800-440-0499 or (516)504-7576 Fax: (516)498-2029 E-mail: ibf@ibf.org • URL: http://www.ibf.org • Quarterly. $85.00 per year. Includes articles on forecasting methods and provides actual business and economic forecasts.

The Journal of Business Research. Elsevier, 360 Park Ave. S New York, NY 10010-1710. Phone: 888-437-4636 or (212)989-5800 Fax: (212)633-3990 E-mail: usinfo-f@elsevier.com • URL: http://www.elsevier.com • Monthly. Qualified personnel, $181.00 per year; institutions, $1,471.00 per year. Covers theoretical and empirical advances in marketing, finance, international business, risk management, and other business topics.

Journal of Business Strategy. Thomson Media, One State St. Plaza New York, NY 10004. Phone: 800-221-1809 or (212)803-8200 Fax: (212)843-9635 E-mail: custserv@thomsonmedia.com • URL: http://www.thomsonmedia.com • Bimonthly. $98.00 per year. Covers managememt planning techniques and corporate strategy for senior executives.

Journal of Business-to-Business Marketing: Innovations in Basic and Applied Research for Industrial Marketing. Haworth Press, Inc., 10 Alice St. Binghamton, NY 13904-1580. Phone: 800-429-6784 or (607)722-5857 Fax: 800-895-0582 or (607)722-1424 E-mail: getinfo@haworthpressinc.com • URL: http://www.haworthpressinc.com • Quarterly. Institutions, $285.00 per year. For buyers and sellers.

The Journal of Business Venturing. Elsevier, 360 Park Ave. S New York, NY 10010-1710. Phone: 888-437-4636 or (212)989-5800 Fax: (212)633-3990 E-mail: usinfo-f@elsevier.com • URL: http://www.elsevier.com • Bimonthly. Individuals, $148.00 per year; institutions, $768.00 per year.

Journal of Career Planning and Employment: The International Magazine of Placement and Recruitment. National Association of Colleges and Employers, 62 Highland Ave. Bethlehem, PA 18017. Phone: 800-544-5272 or (610)868-1421 Fax: (610)868-0208 • URL: http://www.naceweb.org • Quarterly. Free to members; non-members, $72.00 per year. Includes *Spotlight* newsletter. Formerly *Journal of College Placement*.

Journal of Chemical and Engineering Data. American Chemical Society, 1155 16th St., NW Washington, DC 20036. Phone: 800-227-5558 or (202)872-4600 Fax: (202)776-8258 E-mail: help@acs.org • URL: http://www.chemistry.org • Bimonthly. Members, $81.00 per year; institutions, $770.00 per year; students, $61.00 per year.

Journal of Chemical Information and Computer Sciences. American Chemical Society, 1155 16th St., N.W. Washington, DC 20036. Phone: 800-227-5558 or (202)872-4600 Fax: (202)872-4615 E-mail: help@acs.org • URL: http://www.chemistry.org • Bimonthly. Members, $75.00; institutions, $531.00 per year; students, $56.00 per year. others, price on application.

Journal of Chemical Technology and Biotechnology. John Wiley and Sons, Inc., Journals, 111 River St. Hoboken, NJ 07030. Phone: 800-225-5945 or (201)748-6000 Fax: (201)748-6088 E-mail: customer@wiley.com • URL: http://www.wiley.com • Monthly. Individuals, $1,120.00 per year; institutions, $1,495.00 per year.

Journal of Clinical Laboratory Analysis. John Wiley and Sons, Inc., Journals, 111 River St. Hoboken, NJ 07030. Phone: 800-225-5945 or (201)748-6000 Fax: (201)748-6088 E-mail: customer@wiley.com • URL: http://www.wiley.com • Bimonthly. $1,225.00 per year; with online edition, $1,287.00 per year. Original articles on newly developing assays.

Journal of Clinical Ultrasound. John Wiley and Sons, Inc., Journals, 111 River St. Hoboken, NJ 07030. Phone: 800-225-5945 or (201)748-6000 Fax: (201)748-6088 E-mail: customer@wiley.com • URL: http://www.wiley.com • Nine times a year. Institutions, $895.00 per year; with online editions, $940.00 per year. Devoted exclusively to the clinical application of ultrasound in medicine.

The Journal of Commerce. Commonwealth Business Media, 400 Windsor Corporate Center, 50 Millstone Rd., Ste. 200 East Windsor, NJ 08520-1415. Phone: 800-221-5488 E-mail: jdimarino@cbizmedia.com • URL: http://www.cbizmedia.com • Weekly. $146.00 per year. Topics include transatlantic shipping, domestic shipping, customs brokers, freight forwarders, ports, air freight, containerization, and other aspects of transportation and shipping logistics. Formerly *Journal of Commerce*.

Journal of Compensation and Benefits. West Group, 610 Opperman Dr. Eagan, MN 55123. Phone: 800-340-9378 or (651)687-7000 E-mail: bookstore@westgroup.com • URL: http://www.westgroup.com • Bimonthly. $335.00 per year. Working advisor for benefits administrators, company specialists and consultants.

Journal of Computer Security. Sushil Jajodia and Jonathan K. Millen, editors. IOS Press, Inc., 5795-G Burke Centre Pkwy. Burke, VA 22015. Phone: (703)323-5554 Fax: (703)323-3668 E-mail: iosbooks@iospress.com • URL: http://www.iospress.nl • Six times a year. Institutions, $542.00 per year.

Journal of Consumer Affairs. The American Council on Consumer Interests, 415 S Duff Ave., Ste. C Ames, IA 50010-6600. Phone: (515)956-4666 Fax: (515)233-3101 E-mail: info@consumerinterests.org • URL: http://www.consumerinterests.org • Semiannual. Membership, $100.00 per year; institutions, $240.00 per year. Includes *Consumer News and Reviews*, *Advancing the Consumer Interest* and *Consumer Interest Annual*.

Journal of Consumer Research; An Interdisciplinary Quarterly. The University of Chicago Press, Journals Div., P.O. Box 37005 Chicago, IL 60637. Phone: 877-705-1878 or (773)753-3347 Fax: 877-705-1879 or (773)753-0811 E-mail: subscriptions@press.uchicago.edu • URL: http://www.journals.uchicago.edu • Quarterly. Members, $62.00 per year; non-members, $145.00 per year; institutions, $152.00 per year; students, $25.00. Covers various aspects of consumer behavior.

Journal of Convention and Event Tourism. Haworth Press, Inc., 10 Alice St. Binghamton, NY 13904-1580. Phone: 800-429-6784 or (607)722-5857 Fax: 800-895-0582 or (607)722-1424 E-mail: getinfo@haworthpressinc.com • URL: http://www.haworthpressinc.com • Quarterly. $165.00 per year. Formerly *Journal of Convention and Exhibition Management*.

Journal of Corporate Accounting and Finance. John Wiley and Sons, Inc., Journals, 111 River St. Hoboken, NJ 07030. Phone: 800-225-5945 or (201)748-6000 Fax: (201)748-6088 E-mail: customer@wiley.com • URL: http://www.wiley.com • Bimonthly. $495.00 per year; with online edition, $520.00 per year. Topics include government regulation, corporate taxation, financial risk, business valuation, and strategic planning.

Journal of Cost Management. RIA, 395 Hudson St. New York, NY 10014. Phone: 800-950-1216 or 800-431-9025 E-mail: riahome@riag.com • URL: http://www.riahome.com • Bimonthly. $230.00 per year. Includes articles on business budgeting.

Journal of Counseling and Development. American Counseling Association, 5999 Stevenson Ave. Alexandria, VA 22304-3300. Phone: 800-347-6647 or (703)823-9800 Fax: 800-473-2329 or (703)823-0252 • URL: http://www.counseling.org • Quarterly. Free to members; non-members, $140.00 per year; institutions, $175.00 per year. Contains authoritative in-depth articles on professional and scientific issues. Formerly *Personnel and Guidance Journal*.

Journal of Counseling Psychology. American Psychological Association, 750 First St., N.E. Washington, DC 20002-4242. Phone: 800-374-2721 or (202)336-5500 Fax: (202)336-6069 • URL: http://www.apa.org • Quarterly. Members, $39.00 per year; non-members, $78.00 per year; institutions, $182.00 per year.

Journal of Court Reporting. National Court Reporters Association, 8224 Old Courthouse Rd. Vienna, VA 22182-3808. Phone: 800-272-6272 or (703)556-6272 Fax: (703)556-6291 E-mail: msic@ncrahq.org • URL: http://www.ncraonline.org • 10 times a year. $49.00 per year. News and features about court reporting, reporter technology. Computer-aided transcription, real time translation captioning for the hearing-impaired, etc. Formerly *National Shorthand Reporter*.

Journal of Creative Behavior. Creative Education Foundation, Inc., 1050 Union Rd. Buffalo, NY 14224. Phone: (716)675-3181 Fax: (716)675-3209 E-mail: cefhq@cef-cpsi.org • URL: http://www.cef-cpsi.org • Quarterly. Individuals, $75.00 per year; institutions, $95.00 per year.

Journal of Crop Improvement. Haworth Press, Inc., 10 Alice St. Binghamton, NY 13904-1580. Phone: 800-429-6784 or (607)722-5857 Fax: 800-895-0582 or (607)722-1424 E-mail:

orders@haworthpress.com • URL: http://www.haworthpress.com • Semiannual. $300.00 per year to libraries; $80.00 per year to individuals. Topics include plant biotechnology, plant genetics, crop productivity, quality, safety, pest control, and environmental concerns. Formerly *Journal of Crop Production*.

Journal of Current Laser Abstracts. PennWell Corp., Advanced Technology Div., 98 Spit Brook Rd. Nashua, NH 03062-5737. Phone: 800-331-4463 or (603)891-0123 E-mail: atd@pennwell.com • URL: http://www.pennwell.com • Monthly. $495.00 per year. Covers the world's literature of lasers: industrial, medical, and military. Subscription includes annual subject and author index.

Journal of Dairy Research. Institute of Food Research. Cambridge University Press, Journals Dept., 40 W. 20th St. New York, NY 10011-4221. Phone: 800-221-4512 or (212)924-3900 Fax: (212)691-3239 E-mail: information@cup.org • URL: http://www.cup.org • Quarterly. Institutions, $446.00 per year.

Journal of Dairy Science. American Dairy Science Association, 1111 N. Dunlap Ave. Savoy, IL 61874. Phone: (217)356-3182 Fax: (217)398-4119 E-mail: jeanr@assochq.org • URL: http://www.adsa.uiuc.edu • Monthly. $400.00 per year. Provides primary scientific research on all aspects of dairy foods and dairy cattle production and management.

Journal of Derivatives. Institutional Investor, Inc., Journals Group, 225 Park Ave., S., 8th Fl. New York, NY 10003. Phone: 800-945-2034 or (212)224-3066 Fax: (212)224-3472 E-mail: info@iijournals.com • URL: http://www.iijournals.com • Quarterly. $365.00 per year. Includes print and online editions. Covers the structure and management of financial derivatives. Includes graphs, equations, and detailed analyses.

Journal of Developing Areas. Tennessee State University, 330 10th Ave., N Nashville, TN 37203-3401. Phone: (615)963-7152 Fax: (615)963-7139 E-mail: jda@tnstate.edu • URL: http://www.tnstate.edu • Semiannual. Individuals, $30.00 per year; institutions, $36.50 per year.

The Journal of Development Economics. Elsevier, 360 Park Ave. S New York, NY 10010-1710. Phone: 888-437-4636 or (212)989-5800 Fax: (212)633-3990 E-mail: usinfo-f@elsevier.com • URL: http://www.elsevier.com • Bimonthly. Individuals, $135.00 per year; institutions, $1,491.00 per year.

The Journal of Development Studies. Frank Cass Publishers, 5804 N.E. Hassalo St. Portland, OR 97213-3644. Phone: 800-944-6190 Fax: (503)280-8832 E-mail: cass@isbs.com • URL: http://www.frankcass.com • Bimonthy. Institutions, $490.00 per year. Includes print and online editions.

Journal of Dietary Supplements. Haworth Press, Inc., 10 Alice St. Binghamton, NY 13904-1580. Phone: 800-429-6784 or (607)722-5857 Fax: 800-895-0582 or (607)722-1424 E-mail: orders@haworthpress.com • URL: http://www.haworthpress.com • Quarterly. $175.00 per year to libraries; $50.00 per year to individuals. Edited with a view to both academic research and industry concerns. Sections of the journal are dedicated to health professionals, educators, dieticians, and an "Industry Spotlight." Includes book reviews and short reviews of research appearing elsewhere. Formerly *Journal of Nutraceuticals, Functional & Medical Foods*.

Journal of Divorce and Remarriage: Research and Clinical Studies in Family Theory, Family Law, Family Meditation and Family Therapy. Haworth Press, Inc., 10 Alice St. Binghamton, NY 13904-1580. Phone: 800-429-2394 or (607)722-5857 Fax: 800-895-0582 or (607)722-1424 E-mail: getinfo@haworthpressinc.com • URL: http://www.haworthpressinc.com • Quarterly. $520.00 per year. Two volumes.

Journal of Drug Education. Baywood Publishing Co., Inc., 26 Austin Ave. Amityville, NY 11701. Phone: 800-638-7819 or (631)691-1270 Fax: (631)691-1770 E-mail: info@baywood.com • URL: http://www.baywood.com • Quarterly. Individuals, $60.00 per year; institutions, $237.00 per year.

Journal of Drug Issues. Florida State University, School of Criminology and Criminal Justice, P.O. Box 66696 Tallahassee, FL 32313-6696. Phone: (850)664-7368 Fax: (850)644-9614 E-mail: jdi@garnet.fsu.edu • URL: http://www.2.criminology.fsu.edu • Quarterly. Individuals, $95.00 per year; institutions, $120.00 per year.

Journal of E-Government. Haworth Press, Inc., 10 Alice St. Binghamton, NY 13904-1580. Phone: 800-429-6784 or (607)722-5857 Fax: 800-895-0582 or (607)722-1424 E-mail: orders@haworthpress.com • URL: http://www.haworthpress.com • Quarterly. $300.00 per year to libraries; $45.00 per year to individuals. Contains material on "government usage of information technology to enhance the delivery of public services and information."

Journal of East-West Business. Haworth Press, Inc., 10 Alice St. Binghamton, NY 13904-1580. Phone: 800-429-6784 or (607)722-5857 Fax: 800-895-0582 or (607)722-1424 E-mail: getinfo@haworthpressinc.com • URL: http://www.haworthpressinc.com • Quarterly. $300.00 per year; Includes print and online editions. An academic and practical journal focusing on business in the developing regions of Asia and Eastern Europe.

Journal of Econometrics. Elsevier, 360 Park Ave. S New York, NY 10010-1710. Phone: 888-437-4636 or (212)989-5800 Fax: (212)633-3990 E-mail: usinfo-f@elsevier.com • URL: http://www.elsevier.com • Monthly. Individuals, $160.00 per year; institutions, $2,463.00 per year.

Journal of Economic History. Economic History Association. Cambridge University Press, Journals Dept., 40 W. 20th St. New York, NY 10011-4221. Phone: 800-221-4512 or (212)924-3900 Fax: (212)691-3239 E-mail: information@cup.org • URL: http://www.cup.org • Quarterly. Institutions, $144.00 per year.

Journal of Economic Literature. American Economic Association, 2014 Broadway, Suite 305 Nashville, TN 37203. Phone: (615)322-2595 Fax: (615)343-7590 E-mail: aeainfo@vandervilt.edu • URL: http://www.vanderbilt.edu/aea • Quarterly. $135.00 per year. Includes *American Economic Review* and *Journal of Economic Perspectives*.

Journal of Economic Perspectives. American Economic Association, 2014 Broadway, Suite 305 Nashville, TN 37203-2418. Phone: (615)322-2595 Fax: (615)343-7590 E-mail: aeainfo@vanderbilt.edu • URL: http://www.vanderbilt.edu/aea • Quarterly. Membership. Emphasis is on the economic analysis of public policy issues.

Journal of Economics and Business. Temple University, School of Business Administration. Elsevier, 360 Park Ave. S New York, NY 10010-1710. Phone: 888-437-4636 or (212)989-5800 Fax: (212)633-3990 E-mail: usinfo-f@elsevier.com • URL: http://www.elsevier.com • Bimonthly. Individuals, $86.00 per year; institutions, $510.00 per year. Professional and academic research primarily in economics, finance and related business disciplines.

Journal of Economics and Management Strategy. MIT Press, Five Cambridge Center Cambridge, MA 02142-1493. Phone: (617)253-5646 Fax: (617)258-6779 E-mail: journals-orders@mit.edu • URL: http://www.mitpress.mit.edu • Quarterly. Institutions, $195.00 per year. Includes print and online editions. Covers "theoretical and empirical industrial organization, applied game theory, and management strategy."

Journal of Education for Business. Helen Dwight Reid Educational Foundation. Heldref Publications, 1319 18th St., N.W. Washington, DC 20036-1802. Phone: 800-365-9753 Fax: (202)293-6130 E-mail: subscribe@heldref.org • URL: http://www.heldref.org • Bimonthly. Individuals, $51.00 per year; institutions, $87.00 per year. Features basic and applied research-based articles on business fundamentals, career education, consumer economics, distributive education, management, and trends in communications, information systems, and knowledge systems in business.

Journal of Elastomers and Plastics. Sage Publications, 2455 Teller Rd. Thousand Oaks, CA 91320. Phone: 800-818-7342 or (805)499-9774 Fax: 800-583-2665 or (805)499-0721 E-mail: webmaster@sagepub.com • URL: http://www.sagepub.com • Quarterly. Institutions, $730.00 per year. Includes print and online editions.

Journal of Electronic Defense. Association of Old Crows. Horizon House Publications, 685 Canton St. Norwood, MA 02062. Phone: 800-966-8526 or (781)769-9750 Fax: (781)762-9230 • URL: http://www.horizonhouse.com • Monthly. Free to members; non-members, $115.00 per year.

Journal of Electronic Resources in Law Libraries. Haworth Press, Inc., 10 Alice St. Binghamton, NY 13904-1580. Phone: 800-429-6784 or (607)722-5857 Fax: 800-895-0582 or (607)722-1424 E-mail: orders@haworthpress.com • URL: http://www.haworthpress.com • Quarterly. $300.00 per year to libraries; $48.00 per year to individuals.

Journal of Electronic Resources in Medical Libraries. Haworth Press, Inc., 10 Alice St. Binghamton, NY 13904-1580. Phone: 800-429-6784 or (607)722-5857 Fax: 800-895-0582 or (607)722-1424 E-mail: orders@haworthpress.com • URL: http://www.haworthpress.com • Quarterly. $240.00 per year to libraries; $75.00 per year to individuals.

Journal of Employment Counseling. National Employment Counsel Association. American Counseling Association, 5999 Stevenson Ave. Alexandria, VA 22304-3300. Phone: 800-347-6647 or (703)823-9800 Fax: 800-473-2329 or (703)823-0252 • URL: http://www.counseling.org • Quarterly. Free to members; non-members, $40.00 per year.

Journal of Energy Engineering: The International Journal. American Society of Civil Engineers, 1801 Alexander Graham Bell Dr. Reston, VA 20191-4400. Phone: 800-548-2723 or (703)295-6300 Fax: (703)295-6222 • URL: http://www.asce.org • Three times a year. Members, $40.00 per year; with online edition, $46.00 per year; non-members, $60.00 per year; with online edition, $69.00 per year.

Journal of Environmental Sciences. Chinese Academy of Sciences, Committee of Environmental Science. IOS Press, Inc., 5795-G Burke Center Parkway Burke, VA 22015. Phone: (703)323-5554 Fax: (703)323-3668 • URL: http://www.iospress.nl • Six times a year. $470.00 per year.

A Journal of Ethnicity in Substance Abuse. Haworth Press, Inc., 10 Alice St. Binghamton, NY 13904-1580. Phone: 800-429-6784 or (607)722-5857 Fax: 800-895-0582 or (607)722-1424 E-mail: getinfo@haworthpressinc.com • URL: http://www.haworthpressinc.com • Quarterly. $380.00 per year. Includes print and online editions. Edited for researchers and practitioners. Covers various areas of susbstance abuse, including alcoholism. Formerly *Drugs and Society*.

Journal of Euromarketing. Haworth Press, Inc., 10 Alice St. Binghamton, NY 13904-1580. Phone: 800-429-6784 or (607)722-5857 Fax: 800-895-0582 or (607)722-1424 E-mail: getinfo@haworthpressinc.com • URL: http://www.haworthpressinc.com • Quarterly. $435.00 per year; Includes print and online editions.

Journal of Explosives Engineering. International Society of Explosives Engineers, 30325 Bainbridge Rd. Cleveland, OH 44139-2295. Phone: (440)349-4400 Fax: (440)349-3788 E-mail: isee@isee.org • URL: http://www.isee.org • Bimonthly. $35.00 per year.

The Journal of Finance. American Finance Association. Blackwell Publishing, 350 Main St. Malden, MA 02148-5018. Phone: 800-835-6770 or (781)388-8200 Fax: (781)338-8232 E-mail: subscrip@blackwellpub.com • URL: http://www.blackwellpub.com • Bimonthly. Institutions, $304.00 per year. Includes online edition.

Journal of Financial and Quantitative Analysis. University of Washington, School of Business Administration, 115 Lewis Hall Seattle, WA 98195. Fax: (206)616-1894 • URL: http://www.depts.washington.edu • Quarterly. Individuals, $45.00 per year; libraries, $120.00 per year; students, $25.00 per year.

Journal of Financial Economics. Elsevier, 360 Park Ave. S New York, NY 10010-1710. Phone: 888-437-4636 or (212)989-5800 Fax: (212)633-3990 E-mail: usinfo-f@elsevier.com • URL: http://www.elsevier.com • Monthly. Individuals, $95.00 per year; institutions, $1,881.00 per year; students, $70.00 per year.

Journal of Financial Planning. Financial Planning Association, 3801 E. Florida Ave., Suite 708 Denver, CO 80210-2571. Phone: (303)759-4900 Fax: (303)759-0749 E-mail: journal@fpanet.org • URL: http://www.journalfp.net • 12 times a year. Free to members; non-members, $90.00 per year. Edited for professional financial and investment planners.

Journal of Fixed Income. Institutional Investor, Inc., Journals Group, 225 Park Ave., S New York, NY 10003. Phone: 800-945-2034 or (212)224-3066 Fax: (212)224-3472 E-mail: info@iijournals.com • URL: http://www.iijournals.com • Quarterly. $360.00 per year. Includes print and online editions. Covers a wide range of fixed-income investments for institutions, including bonds, interest-rate options, high-yield securities, and mortgages.

Journal of Food Products Marketing: Innovations in Food Advertising, Food Promotion, Food Publicity, Food Sales Promotion. Haworth Press, Inc., 10 Alice St. Binghamton, NY 13904-1580. Phone: 800-429-6784 or (607)722-5857 Fax: 800-895-0582 or (607)722-1424 E-mail: getinfo@haworthpressinc.com • URL: http://www.haworthpressinc.com • Semiannual. $300.00 per year.

Journal of Food Science. Institute of Food Technologists, 221 N. LaSalle St. Chicago, IL 60601. Phone: 800-438-3663 or (312)782-8424 E-mail: info@ift.org • URL: http://www.ift.org • Bimonthly. Members, $20.00 per year; non-members, $100.00 per year. A peer-reviewed research journal.

Journal of Foodservice Business Research. Haworth Press, Inc., 10 Alice St. Binghamton, NY 13904-1580. Phone: 800-429-6784 or (607)722-5857 Fax: 800-895-0582 or (607)722-1424 E-mail: getinfo@haworthpressinc.com • URL: http://www.haworthpressinc.com • Quarterly. $225.00 per year. Includes print and online editions. Formerly *Journal of Restaurant and Foodservice Marketing*.

Journal of Forecasting. John Wiley and Sons, Inc., Journals Div., 111 River Hoboken, NJ 07030. Phone: 800-526-5368 or (201)748-6000 Fax: (201)748-6088 E-mail: custserv@johnwiley.com • URL: http://www.wiley.com • Seven times a year. Individuals, $200.00 per year; institutions, $1,025.00 per year. A centralized focus on recent development in the art and science of forecasting International coverage. Published in England by John Wiley and Sons Ltd.

The Journal of Futures Markets. John Wiley and Sons, Inc., Journals, 111 River St. Hoboken, NJ 07030. Phone: 800-225-5945 or (201)748-6000 Fax: (201)748-6088 E-mail: customer@wiley.com • URL: http://www.wiley.com • Monthly. Institutions, $1,460.00 per year; with online edition, $1,533.00 per year.

Journal of Global Marketing. Haworth Press, Inc., 10 Alice St. Binghamton, NY 13904-1580. Phone: 800-429-6784 or (607)722-5857 Fax: 800-895-0582 or (607)722-1424 E-mail: getinfo@haworthpressinc.com • URL: http://www.haworthpressinc.com • Quarterly. $460.00 per year. Includes print and online editions.

The Journal of Government Financial Management. Association of Government Accountants, 2208 Mount Vernon Ave. Arlington, VA 22301-1314. Phone: 800-242-7211 or (703)684-6931 Fax: (703)548-9367 E-mail: cculkin@agacgfm.org • URL: http://www.agacgfm.org • Quarterly. $90.00 per year. Formerly*Government Accountants Journal*.

Journal of Government Information: An International Review of Policy, Issues an d Resources. Elsevier, 360 Park Ave. S New York, NY 10010-1710. Phone: 888-437-4636 or (212)989-5800 Fax: (212)633-3990 E-mail: usinfo-f@elsevier.com • URL: http://www.elsevier.com • Bimonthly. Institutions, $653.00 per year.

Journal of Healthcare Management. Foundation of the American College of Healthcare Executives. Health Administration Press, One N. Franklin, Suite 1700 Chicago, IL 60606-3491. Phone: (312)424-2800 Fax: (312)424-0014 E-mail: ache@ache.org • URL: http://www.ache.org • Bimonthly. $85.00 per year. Information on the latest trends, developments and innovations in the industry. Formerly (Hospital and Health Services Administration).

Journal of Heat Transfer. ASME International, 3 Park Ave. New York, NY 10016-5990. Phone: 800-843-2763 or (212)591-7722 Fax: (212)591-7674 E-mail: infocentral@asme.org • URL: http://www.asme.org • Quarterly. Members, $60.00 per year; non-members, $300.00 per year. Subscription includes online edition.

Journal of Herbs, Spices and Medicinal Plants. Haworth Press, Inc., 10 Alice St. Binghamton, NY 13904-1580. Phone: 800-429-6784 or (607)722-5857 Fax: 800-895-0582 or (607)722-1424 E-mail: getinfo@haworthpressinc.com • URL: http://www.haworthpressinc.com • Quarterly. $285.00 per year. An academic and practical journal on production, marketing, and other aspects of herbs and spices.

Journal of Higher Education. Ohio State University Press, 1070 Carmack Rd. Columbus, OH 43210. Phone: (614)292-6930 Fax: (614)292-2065 E-mail: moffett.8@osu.edu • URL: http://www.ohiostatepress.org • Bimonthly. Individuals, $50.00 per year; institutions, $110.00 per year. Issues important to faculty administrators and program managers in higher education.

Journal of Hospital Marketing and Public Relations. Haworth Press, Inc., 10 Alice St. Binghamton, NY 13904-1580. Phone: 800-429-6784 or (607)722-5857 Fax: 800-895-0582 or (607)722-1424 E-mail: getinfo@haworthpressinc.com • URL: http://www.haworthpressinc.com • Semiannual. $390.00 per year. Formerly *Journal of Hospital Marketing*.

Journal of Hospitality and Leisure Marketing: The International Forum for Research, Theory and Practice. Haworth Press, Inc., 10 Alice St. Binghamton, NY 13904-1580. Phone: 800-225-5945 or (607)722-5857 Fax: 800-895-0582 or (607)722-1424 E-mail: getinfo@haworthpressinc.com • URL: http://www.haworthpressinc.com • Quarterly. $315.00 per year. An academic and practical journal covering various aspects of hotel, restaurant, and recreational marketing.

Journal of Housing and Community Development. National Association of Housing and Redevelopment Officials (NAHRO), 630 Eye St., NW Washington, DC 20001. Phone: 877-866-2476 or (202)289-3500 Fax: (202)429-8181 E-mail: nahro@nahro.org • URL: http://www.nahro.org • Bimonthly. $33.00 per year. Formerly *Journal of Housing*.

Journal of Housing Economics. Elsevier, 655 Avenue of the Americas New York, NY 10010-5107. Phone: 800-366-2665 or (212)989-5800 Fax: 800-366-2665 or (212)633-3680 E-mail: custserv@elsevier.com • URL: http://www.elsevier.com • Quarterly. Individuals, $50.00 per year; institutions, $299.00 per year.

Journal of Housing for the Elderly. Haworth Press, Inc., 10 Alice St. Binghamton, NY 13904-1580. Phone: 800-429-6784 or (607)722-5857 Fax: 800-895-0582 or (607)722-1424 E-mail: getinfo@haworthpressinc.com • URL: http://www.haworthpressinc.com • Semiannual. $400.00 per year. Covers a wide variety of topics related to retirement communities and housing conditions for the elderly.

Journal of Human Resources: Education, Manpower and Welfare Economics. University of Wisconsin at Madison, Industrial Relations Research Institute. University of Wisconsin Press, 1930 Monroe St., 3rd Fl. Madison, WI 53711-2059. Phone: (608)263-0668 Fax: 800-258-3632 or (608)263-1173 E-mail: journals@uwpress.wisc.edu • URL: http://www.wisc.edu • Quarterly. Individuals, $60.00 per year; institutions, $150.00 per year. Articles on manpower, health and welfare policies as they relate to the labor market and to economic and social development.

Journal of Hydraulic Research. International Association for Hydraulic Research, P.O. Box 177 2600 MH Delft, Netherlands. Phone: 31 15 285 8819 Fax: 31 15 285 8417 E-mail: iahr@iahr.nl • URL: http://www.iahr.nl • Bimonthly. $340.00 per year. Text in English; summaries in English and French.

The Journal of Imaging Science and Technology. Society for Imaging Science and Technolgy, 7003 Kilworth Lane Springfield, VA 22151. Phone: (703)642-9090 Fax: (703)642-9094 E-mail: info@imaging.org • URL: http://www.imaging.org • Bimonthly. Individuals, $135.00 per year; institutions, $155.00 per year. Incorporates *Journal of Imaging Technology*.

Journal of Industrial Ecology. Yale University, School of Forestry and Environmental Studies. MIT Press, Five Cambridge Center Cambridge, MA 02142-1493. Phone: 800-356-0343 or (617)253-5646 Fax: (617)258-6779 E-mail: journals-orders@mit.edu • URL: http://www.mitpress.mit.edu • Quarterly. Individuals, $55.00 per year; institutions, $140.00 per year. Contains multidisciplinary articles on the relationships between industrial activity and the environment.

Journal of Industrial Textiles. Sage Publications, 2455 Teller Rd. Thousand Oaks, CA 91320. Phone: 800-818-7243 or (805)499-9774 Fax: 800-583-2665 or (805)499-0871 E-mail: webmaster@sagepub.com • URL: http://www.sagepub.com • Quarterly. Institutions, $708.00 per year. Includes print and online editions. Formerly *Journal of Coated Fabrics*.

Journal of Information Science: Principles and Practice. Institute of Information Scientists. Sage Publications, Inc., 2455 Teller Rd. Thousand Oaks, CA 91320-2218. Phone: (805)499-0721 Fax: (212)633-3990 • URL: http://www.sagepub.com • Bimonthly. $241.00 per year. Includes print and online editions.

Journal of Insurance Regulation. National Association of Insurance Commissioners, 2301 McGee St., No. 800 Kansas City, MO 64108-2604. Phone: (816)842-3600 • URL: http://www.naic.org • Quarterly. $65.00 per year.

Journal of Interactive Marketing. Direct Marketing Educational Foundation. John Wiley and Sons, Inc., Journals, 111 River St. Hoboken, NJ 07030. Phone: 800-225-5945 or (201)748-6000 Fax: (201)748-6088 E-mail: customer@wiley.com • URL: http://www.wiley.com • Quarterly. Institutions, $699.00 per year; with online edition, $734.00 per year. Exchange of ideas in the field of direct marketing. Formerly *Journal of Direct Marketing*.

Journal of International Consumer Marketing. Haworth Press, Inc., 10 Alice St. Binghamton, NY 13904-1580. Phone: 800-429-6784 or (607)722-5857 Fax: 800-895-0582 or (607)722-1424 E-mail: getinfo@haworthpressinc.com • URL: http://www.haworthpressinc.com • Quarterly. Individuals, $80.00 per year; institutions, $150.00 per year.

Journal of International Food and Agribusiness Marketing. Haworth Press, Inc., 10 Alice St. Binghamton, NY 13904-1580. Phone: 800-429-6784 or (607)722-5857 Fax: 800-895-0582 or (607)722-1424 E-mail: getinfo@haworthpressinc.com • URL: http://www.haworthpressinc.com • Semiannual. Institutions, $320.00 per year.

Journal of International Marketing. American Marketing Association, 311 S. Wacker Dr., Suite 5800 Chicago, IL 60606-5819. Phone: 800-262-1150 or (312)542-9000 Fax: (312)542-9001 E-mail: info@ama.org • URL: http://www.ama.org • Members $45.00; non-members, $80.00 per year institutions, $150.00 per year.

Journal of International Taxation. RIA, 395 Hudson St. New York, NY 10014. Phone: 800-950-1216 or 800-431-9025 E-mail: riahome@riag.com • URL: http://www.riahome.com • Monthly. $260.00 per year.

The Journal of International Trade and Economic Development. Taylor and Francis Group, 325 Chestnut St., 8th Fl. Philadelphia, PA 19106. Phone: 800-354-1420 or (215)625-8914 E-mail: info@taylorandfrancis.com • URL: http://www.taylorandfrancis.com • Quarterly. Individuals, $81.00 per year; institutions, $529.00 per year. Emphasizes the effect of trade on the economies of developing nations.

Journal of Internet Cataloging: The International Quarterly of Digital Organization, Classification, and Access. Haworth Press, Inc., 10 Alice St. Binghamton, NY 13904-1580. Phone: 800-429-6784 or (607)722-5857 Fax: 800-895-0582 or (607)722-1424 E-mail: getinfo@haworthpressinc.com • URL: http://www.haworthpressinc.com • Quarterly. $165.00 per year.

Journal of Internet Commerce. Haworth Press, Inc., 10 Alice St. Binghamton, NY 13904-1580. Phone: 800-429-6784 or (607)722-5857 Fax: 800-895-0582 or (607)722-1424 E-mail: orders@haworthpress.com • URL: http://www.haworthpress.com • Quarterly. $285.00 per year to libraries; $48.00 per year to individuals. Presents scholarly articles on marketing and other aspects of electronic commerce.

Journal of Internet Law. Aspen Publishers, Inc., 1185 Ave. of the Americas New York, NY 10036. Phone: 800-234-1660 or (212)597-0200 Fax: (212)597-0338 E-mail: customer.service@aspenpubl.com • URL: http://www.aspenpublishers.com • Monthly. $360.00 per year. Covers such Internet and e-commerce topics as domain name disputes, copyright protection, Uniform Commercial Code issues, international law, privacy regulation, electronic records, digital signatures, liability, and security.

Journal of Investing. Institutional Investor, Inc., Journals Group, 225 Park Ave., S New York, NY 10003. Phone: 800-945-2034 or (212)224-3066 Fax: (212)224-3472 E-mail: info@iijournals.com • URL: http://www.iijournals.com • Quarterly. $350.00 per year. Includes print and online editions. Edited for professional investors. Topics include equities, fixed-income securities, derivatives, asset allocation, and other institutional investment subjects.

Journal of Library Administration. Haworth Press, Inc., 10 Alice St. Binghamton, NY 13904-1580. Phone: 800-429-6784 or (607)722-2493 Fax: 800-895-0582 or (607)722-1424 E-mail: getinfo@haworthpressinc.com • URL: http://www.haworthpressinc.com • Quarterly. $265.00 per year. Two volumes. Supplement available *Monographic*. Demonstrates the application of theory to everyday problems faced by library administrators.

Journal of Library and Information Services in Distance Learning. Haworth Press, Inc., 10 Alice St. Binghamton, NY 13904-1580. Phone: 800-429-6784 or (607)722-5857 Fax: 800-895-0582 or (607)722-1424 E-mail: orders@haworthpress.com • URL: http://www.haworthpress.com • Quarterly. $150.00 per year to libraries; $48.00 per year to individuals.

Journal of Light Construction. Hanley-Wood, LLC, One Thomas Circle, NW Washington, DC 20005. Phone: 800-837-0870 or (202)452-0800 Fax: (202)785-1974 • URL: http://www.hanley-wood.com • Monthly. $35.95 per year. Provides job-site tips, techniques, and product advice for builders and contractors.

Journal of Low Temperature Physics. Kluwer Academic Publishers, 101 Philip Dr., Assinippi Park Norwell, MA 02061. Phone: (781)871-6000 Fax: (781)681-9045 • URL: http://www.wkap.nl • Semimonthly. Institutions, $1,941.00 per year; with online edition, $2,329.20 per year. Covers the science of cryogenics.

Journal of Management Education. Organizational Behavior Teaching Society. Sage Publications, Inc., 2455 Teller Rd. Thousand Oaks, CA 91320. Phone: 800-818-7243 or (805)499-9774 Fax: 800-583-2665 or (805)499-0871 E-mail: webmaster@sagepub.com • URL: http://www.sagepub.com • Bimonthly. Institutions, $397.00 per year; includes print and

online editions. A scholarly journal dealing with the teaching and training of business students and managers.

Journal of Management Information Systems. M. E. Sharpe, Inc., 80 Business Park Dr. Armonk, NY 10504. Phone: 800-541-6543 or (914)273-1800 Fax: (914)273-2106 E-mail: info@mesharpe.com • URL: http://www.mesharpe.com • Quarterly. Individuals, $88.00 per year; institutions, $599.00 per year. Includes print and online edtions. Analysis, case studies, and current research.

Journal of Maritime Law and Commerce. Jefferson Law Book Co., 2100 Huntingdon Ave. Baltimore, MD 21211. Phone: (410)727-7300 Fax: (410)783-2448 E-mail: jefflawl@juno.com • URL: http://www.jmlc.org • Quarterly. Individuals, $195.00 per year; institutions, $245.00 per year.

Journal of Marketing. American Marketing Association, 311 S. Wacker Dr., Suite 5800 Chicago, IL 60606-5819. Phone: 800-262-1150 or (312)542-9000 Fax: (312)542-9001 E-mail: info@ama.org • URL: http://www.ama.org • Quarterly. Members, $45.00; per year; non-members, $80.00 per year; institutions, $200.00 per year. Covers both marketing theory and marketing practice.

Journal of Marketing Channels: Distribution Systems, Strategy, and Management. Haworth Press, Inc., 10 Alice St. Binghamton, NY 13904-1580. Phone: 800-429-6784 or (607)722-5857 Fax: 800-895-0582 or (607)722-1424 E-mail: getinfo@haworthpressinc.com • URL: http://www.haworthpressinc.com • Quarterly. $315.00 per year. Subject matter has to do with the management of product distribution systems.

Journal of Marketing for Higher Education. Haworth Press, Inc., 10 Alice St. Binghamton, NY 13904-1580. Phone: 800-429-6784 or (607)722-5857 Fax: 800-895-0582 or (607)722-1424 E-mail: getinfo@haworthpressinc.com • URL: http://www.haworthpressinc.com • Semiannual. $365.00 per year.

Journal of Marketing Research. American Marketing Association, 311 S. Wacker Dr., Suite 5800 Chicago, IL 60606-5819. Phone: 800-262-1150 or (312)542-9000 Fax: (312)542-9001 E-mail: info@ama.org • URL: http://www.ama.org • Quarterly. Members, $45.00 per year; non-members, $80.00 per year; institutions, $200.00 per year. Provides analysis of marketing research theory and practice.

Journal of Materials Research. Materials Research Society, 506 Keystone Rd. Warrendale, PA 15086-7573. Phone: (724)779-3003 Fax: (724)779-8313 E-mail: info@mrs.org • URL: http://www.mrs.org • Monthly. $785.00 per year. Includes print and online editions. Covers the preparation, properties, and processing of advanced materials.

Journal of Mechanical Design. ASME International, 3 Park Ave. New York, NY 10016-5990. Phone: 800-843-2763 or (212)591-7722 Fax: (212)591-7674 E-mail: infocentral@asme.org • URL: http://www.asme.org • Quarterly. Members, $50.00 per year. Formerly *Journal of Mechanisms, Transmissions and Automation in Design*.

Journal of Medical Practice Management. Greenbranch Publishing, P.O. Box 208 Phoenix, MD 21131. Phone: 800-933-3711 or (410)329-9788 Fax: (410)329-1510 E-mail: ncollins@greenbrach.com Bimonthly. Individuals, $169.00 per year; institutions, $213.00 per year.

Journal of Mental Health Counseling. American Counseling Association, 5999 Stevenson Ave. Alexandria, VA 22304-3300. Phone: 800-347-6647 or (703)823-9800 Fax: 800-473-2329 or (703)823-0252 • URL: http://www.counseling.org • Quarterly. $175.00 per year. The official journal of the American Mental Health Counselors Association.

Journal of Microwave Power and Electromagnetic Energy. International Microwave Power Institute, 10210 Leatherleaf Court Manassas, VA 22111-4245. Phone: (703)257-1415 Quarterly. $195.00 per year. Formerly *Journal of Microwave Power*.

Journal of Money, Credit and Banking. Ohio State University Press, 1070 Carmack Rd. Columbus, OH 43210. Phone: (614)292-6930 Fax: (614)292-2065 E-mail: moffett.8@osu.edu • URL: http://www.ohiostatepress.org • Quarterly. $210.00 per year, with online edition, $294.00 per year. Reports major findings in the study of financial markets, monetary and fiscal policy credit markets, money and banking, portfolio management and related subjects.

Journal of Natural Fibers. Haworth Press, Inc., 10 Alice St. Binghamton, NY 13904-1580. Phone: 800-429-6784 or (607)722-5857 Fax: 800-895-0582 or (607)722-1424 E-mail: orders@haworthpress.com • URL: http://www.haworthpress.com • Quarterly. $400.00 per year to libraries; $45.00 per year to individuals. Covers applications, technology, research, and world markets relating to fibers from silk, wool, cotton, flax, hemp, jute, etc. Previously *Natural Fibres*, published annually.

Journal of New Seeds: Innovations in Production, Biotechnology, Quality, and Marketing. Haworth Press, Inc., 10 Alice St. Binghamton, NY 13904-1580. Phone: 800-429-6784 or (607)722-5857 Fax: 800-895-0582 or (607)722-1424 E-mail: orders@haworthpress.com • URL: http://www.haworthpress.com • Quarterly. $240.00 per year to libraries; $65.00 per year to individuals. Covers research and development for a new generation of seeds having a high degree of quality and productivity. Topics relating to global seed production include marketing, economics, and intellectual property rights.

Journal of Nonprofit and Public Sector Marketing. Haworth Press, Inc., 10 Alice St. Binghamton, NY 13904-1580. Phone: 800-429-6784 or (607)722-5857 Fax: 800-895-0582 or (607)722-1424 E-mail: getinfo@haworthpressinc.com •

URL: http://www.haworthpressinc.com • Semiannual. Institutions, $365.00 per year. Subject matter has to do with the promotion or marketing of the services of nonprofit organizations and governmental agencies.

Journal of Nuclear Materials Management. Institute of Nuclear Materials Management, Inc., 60 Revere Dr., Suite 500 Northbrook, IL 60062-1563. Phone: (847)480-9573 Fax: (847)480-9282 Quarterly. $100.00 per year. Summaries in English and Japanese.

Journal of Nutrition. American Society for Nutritional Science, 9650 Rockville Pike Bethesda, MD 20814-3990. Phone: 800-433-2732 or (301)634-7050 Fax: (301)571-1892 E-mail: sec@asns.org • URL: http://www.asns.org • Bimonthly. Individuals, $175.00 per year; institutions, $550.00 per year.

Journal of Nutrition Education and Behavior. Society for Nutrition Education. B. C. Decker, Inc., PO Box 620 Hamilton, ON, Canada L8N 3K7. Phone: 800-568-7281 or (905)522-7017 Fax: (905)522-7839 E-mail: info@bcdecker.com • URL: http://www.bcdecker.com • Bimonthly. Individuals, $159.00 per year; institutions, $234.00 per year.

Journal of Nutritional Science and Vitaminology. Japanese Society of Nutrition and Food Science. Center for Academic Publications, 2-4 16 Yayoi, Bunkyo-ku Tokyo 113 0032, Japan. Phone: 81 3 3817 5821 Fax: 81 3 3817 5830 E-mail: capj@crisscross.com Bimonthly. $145.00 per year. Formal *Journal of Vitaminology*.

Journal of Occupational and Organizational Psychology. The British Psychological Society, St. Andrews House, 48 Princess Rd., E Leicester LE1 7DR, United Kingdom. Phone: 44 116 254 9568 Fax: 44 116 247 0787 E-mail: journals@bps.org.uk • URL: http://www.bps.org.uk • Quarterly. Individuals, $72.00 per year; institutions, $265.00 per year. Formerly *Journal of Occupational Psychology*.

Journal of Offshore Technology. Institute of Marine Engineering, Science, and Technology, 80 Coleman St. London EC2R 5BJ, United Kingdom. Phone: 44 20 7382 2600 Fax: 44 20 7382 2669 E-mail: info@imarest.org • URL: http://www.imarest.org • Bimonthly. Free to members; non-members, $100.00 per year. Covers the latest technological developments and trends for senior offshore engineers.

Journal of Organizational Behavior Management. Haworth Press, Inc., 10 Alice St. Binghamton, NY 13904-1580. Phone: 800-429-6784 or (607)722-5857 Fax: 800-895-0582 or (607)722-1424 E-mail: getinfo@haworthpressinc.com • URL: http://www.haworthpressinc.com • Quarterly. $485.00 per year.

Journal of Organizational Excellence. Society of Competitive Intelligence Professionals. John Wiley and Sons, Inc. Journals, 111 River St. Hoboken, NJ 07030. Phone: 800-225-5945 or (201)748-6000 Fax: (201)748-6088 E-mail: customer@wiley.com • URL: http://www.wiley.com • Quarterly. Institutions, $425.00 per year; with online edition, $447.00 per year. Formerly *Competitive Intelligence Review*.

Journal of Pension Planning and Compliance. Aspen Publishers, 1185 Ave. of the Americas New York, NY 10036. Phone: 800-234-1660 or (212)597-0200 Fax: (212)597-0338 E-mail: customer.service@aspenpubl.com • URL: http://www.aspenpublishers.com • Quarterly. $265.00 per year. Technical articles and regular columns on major issues confronting the pension community.

Journal of Personal Selling and Sales Management. M. E. Sharpe, Inc., 80 Business Park Drive Armonk, NY 10504. Phone: 800-541-6563 or (914)273-1800 Fax: (914)273-2106 E-mail: custserv@mesharpe.com • URL: http://www.mesharpe.com • Quarterly. $169.00 per year. An academic journal containing peer-reviewed articles. Includes "Selling and Sales Management Abstracts" (summaries of relevant articles appearing in various publications).

Journal of Petroleum Technology. Society of Petroleum Engineers, Inc., P.O.Box 833836 Richardson, TX 75083-3836. Phone: (972)952-9393 Fax: (972)952-9435 Monthly. Free to members; non-members, $45.00 per year. Covers oil and gas exploration, drilling and production, engineering management, resevoir engineering, geothermal energy sources and emerging technologies. Also includes society news, programs, events and activities. Supplement available *SPE Computer Applications*.

Journal of Pharmaceutical, Finance, Economics and Policy. FDC Reports, 5550 Friendship Blvd., Ste. 1 Chevy Chase, MD 20815-7278. Phone: 800-332-2181 Fax: (301)656-3094 E-mail: fdc.customer.service@elsevier.com • URL: http://www.fdcreports.com • Quarterly. Institutions, $365.00 per year. Formerly *Journal of Research in Pharmaceutical Economics*.

Journal of Pharmaceutical Marketing and Management. Haworth Press, Inc., 10 Alice St. Binghamton, NY 13904-1580. Phone: 800-429-6784 or (607)722-5857 Fax: 800-895-0582 or (607)722-1424 E-mail: getinfo@haworthpressinc.com • URL: http://www.haworthpressinc.com • Quarterly. $365.00 per year.

Journal of Planning Literature. Ohio State University, Dept. of City and Regional Planning. Sage Publications, Inc., 2455 Teller Rd. Thousand Oaks, CA 91320. Phone: 800-818-7243 or (805)499-9774 Fax: 800-583-2665 or (805)499-0871 E-mail: webmaster@sagepub.com • URL: http://www.sagepub.com • Quarterly. Institutions, $682.00 per year; includes print and online editions. Provides reviews and abstracts of city and regional planning lierature.

Journal of Portfolio Management: The Journal for Investment Professionals. Institutional Investor, Inc., Journals Group, 225 Park Ave., S New York, NY 10003. Phone: 800-945-2034 or (212)224-3066 Fax: (212)224-3472 E-mail: info@iijournals.com • URL: http://www.iijournals.com • Quarterly. $410.00 per year. Includes print and online editions. Edited for professional portfolio managers. Contains articles on investment practice, theory, and models.

Journal of Poverty: Innovations on Social, Political, and Economic Inequalities. Haworth Press, Inc., 10 Alice St. Binghamton, NY 13904-1580. Phone: 800-429-6784 or (607)722-5857 Fax: 800-895-0582 or (607)722-1424 E-mail: orders@haworthpress.com • URL: http://www.haworthpress.com • Quarterly. $180.00 per year to libraries; $50.00 per year to individuals. Covers the social, emotional, and economic consequences of public assistance. Topics include welfare policy, immigrants' rights, hiring practices, managed healthcare, child support, disabilities, food programs, and affirmative action. (See also http://www.journalofpoverty.org).

Journal of Practical Estate Planning. CCH, Inc., 2700 Lake Cook Rd. Riverwoods, IL 60015. Phone: 800-835-5224 or (847)267-7000 E-mail: cust_serv@cch.com • URL: http://www.cch.com • Bimonthly. $215.00 per year. Edited for attorneys and other estate planning professionals.

Journal of Private Equity: Strategies and Techniques for Venture Investing. Institutional Investor, Inc., Journals Group, 255 Park Ave., S New York, NY 10003. Phone: 800-945-2034 or (212)224-3066 Fax: (212)224-3472 E-mail: info@iijournals.com • URL: http://www.iijournals.com • Quarterly. $450.00 per year. Includes print and online editions. Includes venture capital case histories, financial applications, foreign opportunities, industry analysis, management methods, etc.

Journal of Product Innovation Management: An International Publication of the Product Development and Management Association. Product Development and Management Association. Elsevier, 360 Park Ave. S New York, NY 10010-1710. Phone: 888-437-4636 or (212)989-5800 Fax: (212)633-3990 E-mail: usinfo-f@elsevier.com • URL: http://www.elsevier.com • Bimonthly. Institutions, $535.00 per year. Includes print and online editions. Covers new product planning and development.

Journal of Promotion Management: Innovations in Planning and Applied Research. Haworth Press, Inc., 10 Alice St. Binghamton, NY 13904-1580. Phone: 800-429-6784 or (607)722-5857 Fax: 800-895-0582 or (607)722-1424 E-mail: getinfo@haworthpressinc.com • URL: http://www.haworthpressinc.com • Semiannual. Institutions, $200.00 per year.

Journal of Property Management: The Official Publication of the Institute of Real Estate Management. Institute of Real Estate Management, 430 N. Michigan Ave. Chicago, IL 60611-4090. Phone: 800-837-0706 or (312)329-6000 Fax: 800-338-4736 E-mail: custserv@irem.org • URL: http://www.irem.org • Bimonthly. $43.95 per year.

Journal of Public Policy and Marketing. American Marketing Association, 311 S. Wacker Dr., Suite 5800 Chicago, IL 60606-5819. Phone: 800-262-1150 or (312)542-9000 Fax: (312)542-9001 E-mail: info@ama.com • URL: http://www.ama.org • Semiannual. Members, $45.00 per year; non-members, $70.00 per year; institutions, $100.00 per year. Devoted to the social and cultural impact of marketing activities.

Journal of Quality Assurance in Hospitality and Tourism: Improvements in Marketing, Management, and Development. Haworth Press, Inc., 10 Alice St. Binghamton, NY 13904-1580. Phone: 800-429-6784 or (607)722-5857 Fax: 800-895-0582 or (607)722-1424 E-mail: orders@haworthpress.com • URL: http://www.haworthpress.com • Quarterly. $240.00 per year to libraries; $50.00 per year to individuals. Includes research papers, case studies, abstracts of dissertations, book reviews, conference reviews, and Web site reviews

Journal of Quality Technology: A Quarterly Journal of Methods, Applications, and Related Topics. American Society for Quality, 600 N Plankinton Ave. Milwaukee, WI 53201. Phone: 800-248-1946 Fax: (414)272-1734 E-mail: help@asq.org • URL: http://www.asq.org • Quarterly. Members, $26.00 per year; non-members, $37.00 per year; institutions, $100.00 per year.

Journal of Range Management: Covering the Study, Management, and Use of Rangeland Ecosystems and Range Resources. Society for Range Management, 445 Union Blvd., Suite 230 Lakewood, CO 80228-1259. Phone: (303)986-3309 Fax: (303)986-3892 E-mail: srmden@ix.netcom.com • URL: http://www.uvalde.tamu.edu/jrm • Bimonthly. Institutions, $95.00 per year. Technical articles oriented towards research in range science and management.

Journal of Relationship Marketing: Innovations and Enhancement for Customer Service. Haworth Press, Inc., 10 Alice St. Binghamton, NY 13904-1580. Phone: 800-429-6784 or (607)722-5857 Fax: 800-895-0582 or (607)722-1424 E-mail: getinfo@haworthpressinc.com • URL: http://www.haworthpressinc.com • Quarterly. $325.00 per year.

The Journal of Research Administration. Society of Research Administrators, 1901 N. Moore St., Suite 1004 Arlington, VA 22209. Phone: (703)741-0140 E-mail: info@srainternational.org • URL: http://www.srainternational.org • Quarterly. Members, $35.00 per year; non-members, $45.00 per year. Formerly *SRA Journal*.

Journal of Research of the National Institute of Standards and Technology. Available from U. S. Government Printing Office, Washington, DC 20402. Phone: (202)512-1800 Fax: (202)512-2250 E-mail: gpoaccess@gpo.gov • URL: http://www.access.gpo.gov • Bimonthly. $47.00 per year. Formerly *Journal of Research of the National Bureau of Standards*.

Journal of Retailing. New York University, Leonard N. Stern School of Business. Elsevier, 360 Park Ave., S New York, NY 10010-1710. Phone: (212)989-5800 Fax: (212)633-3990 E-mail: usinfo-f@elsevier.com • URL: http://www.elsevier.com • Quarterly. Individuals, $131.00 per year; institutions, $350.00 per year.

Journal of Retirement Planning. CCH, Inc., 2700 Lake Cook Rd. Riverwoods, IL 60015. Phone: 800-835-5224 or (847)267-7000 E-mail: cust_serv@cch.com • URL: http://www.cch.com • Bimonthly. $179.00 per year. Emphasis is on retirement and estate planning advice provided by lawyers and accountants as part of their practices.

Journal of Risk and Insurance. American Risk and Insurance Association. Blackwell Publishing, Inc., 350 Main St. Malden, MA 02148. Phone: (781)388-8200 Fax: (781)388-8210 E-mail: subscrip@blackwellpub.com • URL: http://blackwellpublishers.co.uk • Quarterly. Institutions, $243.00 per year. Includes online edition.

Journal of Risk Finance: The Convergence of Financial Products and Insurance. Institutional Investor, Inc., Journals Group, 225 Park Ave., S New York, NY 10003. Phone: 800-945-2034 or (212)224-3066 Fax: (212)224-3472 E-mail: info@iijournals.com • URL: http://www.iijournals.com • Quarterly. $500.00 per year. Includes print and online editions. Covers the field of customized risk management, including securitization, insurance, hedging, derivatives, and credit arbitrage.

Journal of Robotic Systems. John Wiley and Sons, Inc., Journals, 111 River St. Hoboken, NJ 07030. Phone: 800-225-5945 or (201)748-6000 Fax: (201)748-6088 E-mail: customer@wiley.com • URL: http://www.wiley.com • Monthly. $2,075.00 per year; with online edition, $2,179.00 per year. An international journal presenting high-level, scholarly discussions and case studies on automation, taskware design and implementation of robot systems. Text in English and Japanese; summaries in English and Japanese.

Journal of Safety Research. National Safety Council. Elsevier, 360 Park Ave. S New York, NY 10010-1710. Phone: 888-437-4636 or (212)989-5800 Fax: (212)633-3990 E-mail: usinfo-f@elsevier.com • URL: http://www.elsevier.com • Quarterly. Institutions, $800.00 per year. Published in United Kingdom.

Journal of Ship Research. Society of Naval Architects and Marine Engineers, 601 Pavonia Ave. Jersey City, NJ 07306-2907. Phone: (201)798-4800 Fax: (201)798-4975 E-mail: sevans@sname.org • URL: http://www.sname.org • Quarterly. Individuals, $25.00 per year; institutions, $98.00 per year.

Journal of Small Business Management. West Virginia University Bureau of Business Research. Blackwell Publishing, Inc., 350 Main St. Malden, MA 02148. Phone: (781)388-8200 Fax: (781)388-8210 E-mail: books@blackwellpub.com • URL: http://www.blackwellpublishing.com • Quarterly. $166.00 per year. Includes print and online editions. Articles and features on small business and entrepreneurship.

Journal of Social Welfare and Family Law. Taylor & Francis Group, U.S. Psychology Press, 325 Chestnut St., Ste. 800 Philadelphia, PA 19106. Phone: 800-821-8312 or (215)625-8900 Fax: (215)625-2940 E-mail: info@taylorandfrancis.com • URL: http://www.taylorandfrancis.com • Quarterly. Individuals, $99.00 per year; institutions, $385.00 per year.

Journal of Software Maintenance and Evolution: Research and Practice. John Wiley and Sons, Inc., Journals, 111 River Hoboken, NJ 07030. Phone: 800-526-5368 or (201)748-6000 Fax: (201)748-6088 E-mail: customer@wiley.com • URL: http://www.wiley.com • Bimonthly. Individuals, $1,125.00 per year; institutions, $1,500.00 per year. Published in England by John Wiley and Sons Ltd. Provides international coverage of subject matter.

Journal of Spacecraft and Rockets: Devoted to Astronautical Science and Technology. American Institute of Aeronautics and Astronautics, Inc., 1801 Alexander Bell Dr., Suite 500 Reston, VA 20191-4344. Phone: 800-639-2422 or (703)264-7500 Fax: (703)264-7551 E-mail: custserv@aiaa.org • URL: http://www.aiaa.org • Bimonthly. Members, $45.00 per year; non-members, $165.00 per year; institutions, $330.00 per year.

Journal of Structured and Project Finance. Institutional Investor, Inc., Journals Group, 225 Park Ave., S. New York, NY 10003. Phone: 800-945-2034 or (212)224-3066 Fax: (212)224-3472 E-mail: info@iijournals.com • URL: http://www.iijournals.com • Quarterly. $365.00 per year. Includes print and online editions. Covers the financing of large-scale construction projects, such as power plants and convention centers. Formerly *Journal of Project Finance*.

Journal of Studies on Alcohol. Rutgers Center of Alcohol Studies. Alcohol Research Documentation, Inc., c/o Charles Rouse, Business Administration, 607 Allison Rd. Piscataway, NJ 08854-8001. Phone: (732)445-2190 Fax: (732)445-3500 • URL: http://www.rci.rutgers.edu • Bimonthly. Individuals, $140.00 per year; institutions, $175.00 per year.

Journal of Supply Chain Management: A Global Review of Purchasing and Supply. Institute for Supply Management, 2055 E Centennial Cir. Tempe, AZ 85285-2160. Phone: 800-

SOURCES CITED

888-6276 or (480)752-6276 Fax: (480)752-7890 E-mail: alvin.williams@usm.edu • URL: http://www.napm.org • Quarterly. $59.00 per year. Text in English. Summaries in French, German and Spanish. Formerly *International Journal of Purchasing and Materials Management*.

Journal of Sustainable Agriculture: Innovations for the Long-Term and Lasting Maintenance and Enhancement of Agricultural Resources, Production and Environmental Quality. Haworth Press, Inc., 10 Alice St. Binghamton, NY 13904-1580. Phone: 800-429-6784 or (607)722-5857 Fax: 800-895-0582 or (607)722-1424 E-mail: getinfo@haworthpressinc.com • URL: http://www.haworthpressinc.com • Quarterly. Institutions, $285.00 per year. Two volumes. An academic and practical journal concerned with resource depletion and environmental misuse.

Journal of Sustainable Forestry. Haworth Press, Inc., 10 Alice St. Binghamton, NY 13904-1580. Phone: 800-429-6784 or (607)722-5857 Fax: 800-895-0582 or (607)722-1424 E-mail: getinfo@haworthpressinc.com Quarterly. Institutions, $337.50 per year. An academic and practical journal. Topics include forest management, forest economics, and wood science.

Journal of System Safety. System Safety Society, Inc., PO Box 70 Unionville, VA 22567-0070. Phone: (504)854-8630 Quarterly. Free to members; non-members, $55.00 per year. Formerly *Hazard Prevention*.

Journal of Tax Practice and Procedure. CCH, Inc., 2700 Lake Cook Rd. Riverwoods, IL 60015. Phone: 800-835-5224 or (847)267-7000 E-mail: cust_serv@cch.com • URL: http://www.cch.com • Bimonthly. $215.00 per year. Covers the representation of taxpayers before the IRS, "from initial contact through litigation."

The Journal of Taxation: A National Journal of Current Developments, Analysis and Commentary for Tax Professionals. RIA, 395 Hudson St. New York, NY 10014. Phone: 800-950-1216 or 800-431-9025 E-mail: riahome@riag.com • URL: http://www.riahome.com • Monthly. $305.00 per year. Analysis of current tax developments for tax specialists.

Journal of Taxation of Corporate Transactions. CCH, Inc., 4025 West Peterson Ave. Chicago, IL 60646-6085. Phone: 800-248-3248 or (773)866-6000 Fax: 800-224-8299 or (773)866-3095 E-mail: cust_serv@cch.com • URL: http://www.onlinestore.cch.com/ • Bimonthly. $225.00 per year. Covers the planning and compliance issues faced by corporate taxpayers.

Journal of Taxation of Financial Products. CCH, Inc., 2700 Lake Cook Rd. Riverwoods, IL 60015. Phone: 800-835-5224 or (847)267-7000 E-mail: cust_serv@cch.com • URL: http://www.cch.com • Bimonthly. $249.00 per year.

Journal of Taxation of Global Transactions. CCH, Inc., 4025 West Peterson Ave. Chicago, IL 60646-6085. Phone: 800-248-3248 or (773)866-6000 Fax: 800-224-8299 or (773)866-3095 E-mail: cust_serv@cch.com • URL: http://www.onlinestore.cch.com/ • Quarterly. $215.00 per year. Covers tax laws affecting international business activity.

Journal of Teaching in International Business. Haworth Press, Inc., 10 Alice St. Binghamton, NY 13904-1580. Phone: 800-429-6784 or (607)722-5857 Fax: 800-895-0582 or (607)722-1424 E-mail: getinfo@haworthpressinc.com • URL: http://www.haworthpressinc.com • Quarterly. Institutions, $315.00 per year.

Journal of Technical Writing and Communication. Baywood Publishing Co., Inc., 26 Austin Ave. Amityville, NY 11701. Phone: 800-638-7819 or (631)691-1270 Fax: (631)691-1770 E-mail: info@baywood.com • URL: http://www.baywood.com • Quarterly. Individuals, $60.00 per year; institutions, $237.00 per year.

Journal of Technology Transfer. Technology Transfer Society. Kluwer Academic Publishers, 101 Philip Dr., Assinippi Park Norwell, MA 02061. Phone: (781)871-6600 Fax: (781)681-9045 • URL: http://www.wkap.nl • Quarterly. Institutions, $371.00 per year; with online edition, $445.20 per year. Topics include technology transfer ventures, models, mechanisms, and case studies.

Journal of the American Society for Information Science and Tehnology. John Wiley and Sons, Inc., Journals, 111 River St. Hoboken, NJ 07030. Phone: 800-225-5945 or (212)748-6000 Fax: (201)748-6088 E-mail: customer@wiley.com • URL: http://www.wiley.com • 14 times a year. $1,600.00 per year; with online edition, $1,680.00 per year.

Journal of the Asia Pacific Economy. Taylor and Francis Group, 325 Chestnut St., 8th Fl. Philadelphia, PA 19106. Phone: 800-354-1420 or (215)625-8914 E-mail: info@taylorandfrancis.com • URL: http://www.taylorandfrancis.com • Three times a year. Individuals, $76.00 per year; institutions, $347.00 per year. Covers economic, political, social, cultural, and historical factors affecting Asian commerce and trade.

Journal of the Atmospheric Sciences. American Meteorological Society, 45 Beacon St. Boston, MA 02108-3693. Phone: (617)227-2425 Fax: (617)742-8718 E-mail: amsinfoamericatsoc.org • URL: http://www.ametsoc.org/ams • Semimonthly. Members, $80.00 per year; institutions, $545.00 per year.

Journal of the Coin Laundry and Drycleaning Industry. Coin Laundry Association, 1315 Butterfield Rd., Suite 212 Downers Grove, IL 60515. Phone: 877-252-4332 or (630)963-5547 Fax: (630)963-5864 E-mail: info@coinlaundry.org • URL: http://www.coinlaundry.org • Monthly. $24.00 per year. Edited for owners and operators of coinoperated laundries.

Journal of Thermal Enevelope and Building Science. Sage Publications, Inc., 2455 Teller Rd. Thousand Oaks, CA 91320. Phone: 800-818-7243 or (805)499-9774 Fax: 800-583-2665 or (805)449-0871 E-mail: webmaster@sagepub.com • URL: http://www.sagepub.com • Quarterly. Institutions, $765.00 per year; includes print and online editions. Formerly *Journal of Thermal Insulation and Building Envelopes*.

Journal of Traffic Safety Education. California Association for Safety Education, 5151 State University Dr. Los Angeles, CA 90032. Phone: (213)343-4622 Quarterly. $8.00 per year.

Journal of Transnational Management Development: The Official Publication of the International Management Development Association. International Management Development Association. Haworth Press, Inc., 10 Alice St. Binghamton, NY 13904-1580. Phone: 800-429-6784 or (607)722-5857 Fax: 800-895-0582 or (607)722-1424 E-mail: getinfo@haworthpressinc.com • URL: http://www.haworthpressinc.com • Quarterly. Institutions, $375.00 per year.

Journal of Transport Economics and Policy. University of Bath, Claverton Down Bath, Avon BA2 7AY, United Kingdom. Phone: 44 1225 826302 Fax: 44 1225 826767 E-mail: turpin@turpinltd.com • URL: http://www.jtep.org • Three times a year. Individuals, $55.00 per year; institutions, $165.00 per year; students, $20.00 per year. Text in English, French, German and Spanish.

Journal of Travel and Tourism Marketing. Haworth Press, Inc., 10 Alice St. Binghamton, NY 13904-1580. Phone: 800-429-6784 or (607)722-5857 Fax: 800-895-0582 or (607)722-1424 E-mail: getinfo@haworthpressinc.com • URL: http://www.haworthpressinc.com • Quarterly. $310.00 per year.

Journal of Travel Research. University of Colorado, Business Research Div. Sage Publications, Inc., 2455 Teller Rd. Thousand Oaks, CA 91320. Phone: 800-818-7243 or (805)499-9774 Fax: 800-583-2665 or (805)499-0871 E-mail: webmaster@sagepub.com • URL: http://www.sagepub.com • Quarterly. Institutions, $350.00 per year. Includes print and online editions.

Journal of Tree Fruit Production. Haworth Press, Inc., 10 Alice St. Binghamton, NY 13904-1580. Phone: 800-429-6784 or (607)722-5857 Fax: 800-895-0582 or (607)722-1424 E-mail: getinfo@haworthpressinc.com • URL: http://www.haworthpressinc.com • Semiannual. Institutions, $95.00 per year. A research journal for tree fruit growers.

Journal of Tribology. ASME International, 3 Park Ave. New York, NY 10016-5990. Phone: 800-843-2763 or (212)591-7722 Fax: (212)591-7674 E-mail: infocentral@asme.org • URL: http://www.asme.org • Quarterly. Members, $50.00 per year; includes print and online editions. Non-members, $275.00 per year; includes print and online editons. Details lubrication and lubricants.

Journal of Turbomachinery. ASME International, 3 Park Ave. New York, NY 10016-5990. Phone: 800-843-2763 or (212)591-7722 Fax: (212)591-7674 E-mail: infocentral@asme.org • URL: http://www.asme.org • Quarterly. Members, $50.00 per year; includes print and online editions. Non-members, $250.00 per year; includes print and online editions.

Journal of Vegetable Crop Production. Haworth Press, Inc., 10 Alice St. Binghamton, NY 13904-1580. Phone: 800-429-6784 or (607)722-5857 Fax: 800-895-0582 or (607)722-1424 E-mail: getinfo@haworthpressinc.com • URL: http://www.haworthpressinc.com • Semiannual. Institutions, $225.00 per year. Covers the production and marketing of vegetables.

The Journal of Visualization and Computer Animation. John Wiley and Sons, Inc., Journals, 111 River Hoboken, NJ 07030. Phone: 800-225-5945 or (201)748-6000 Fax: (201)748-6088 E-mail: customer@wiley.com • URL: http://www.wiley.com • Quarterly. Individuals, $743.00 per year; institutions, $955.00 per year. Research papers on the technological developments (both hardware and software) that will make animation tools more accessible to end-users. International coverage. Published in England by John Wiley and Sons Ltd.

Journal of Wealth Management. Institutional Investor, Inc., Journals Group, 255 Park Ave., S New York, NY 10003. Phone: 800-945-2034 or (212)224-3066 Fax: (212)224-3472 E-mail: info@iijournals.com • URL: http://www.iijournals.com • Quarterly. $410.00 per year. Includes print and online editions. Edited for managers of wealthy individuals' investment portfolios. Formerly *Journal of Private Portfolio Management*.

Journal of Website Promotion: Innovations in Internet Business Research, Theory, and Practice. Haworth Press, Inc., 10 Alice St. Binghamton, NY 13904-1580. Phone: 800-429-6784 or (607)722-5857 Fax: 800-895-0582 or (607)722-1424 E-mail: orders@haworthpress.com • URL: http://www.haworthpress.com • Semiannual. $250.00 per year to libraries; $45.00 per year to individuals. Presents a scholarly view of such items as spam, banner ads, pop-ups, click rates, and the use of search engines for advertising.

Journal of Workers Compensation. John Liner Organization. Standard Publishing Corp., 155 Federal St. Boston, MA 02110. Phone: 800-682-5759 or (617)457-0600 Fax: (617)457-0608 E-mail: info@standardpublishingcorp.com • URL: http://www.standardpublishingcorp.com • Quarterly. $138.00 per year. Compensation topics include legal considerations, cost control, worker coverage, appropriate medical treatment, and managed care.

Journal of World Business. Columbia University, Trustees of Columbia University. Elsevier, 360 Park Ave. S New York, NY 10010-1710. Phone: (212)989-5800 Fax: (212)633-3990 E-mail: usinfo-f@elsevier.com • URL: http://www.elsevier.com • Quarterly. Individuals, $131.00 per year; institutions, $315.00 per year.

Journal of World Trade. Kluwer Academic Publishers, 101 Philip Dr., Assinippi Park Norwell, MA 02061. Phone: (781)871-6600 Fax: (781)681-9045 • URL: http://www.wkap.nl • Bimonthly. Institutions, $599.00 per year. Includes print and online editions. Formerly *Journal of World Trade Law*.

Journal Suisse d'Horlogerie et de Bijouterie Internationale. Editions Scriptar S.A., 25 Chemin du Creux-de-Corsy CH-1093 41 La Conversion-Lausanne 1093, Switzerland. Phone: 41 21 7960096 Fax: 41 21 7914084 E-mail: info@jsh.ch • URL: http://www.jsh.ch • Six times a year. $95.00. Text in English, French and German. Formery J S H- Journal Suisse d'Horlogerie e+ de Bijouterie Internationale.

Journalism and Mass Communication Directory. Association for Education in Journalism and Mass Communication, 234 Outlet Pointe Blvd., Suite A Columbia, SC 29210-5667. Phone: (803)798-0271 Fax: (803)772-3509 E-mail: aejmchq@aol.com Annual $35.00. Schools and departments of journalism and mass communication.

Journalism and Mass Communication Quarterly: Devoted to Research and Commentary in Journalism and Mass Communication. Association for Education in Journalism and Mass Communication, 234 Outlet Pointe Blvd., Suite A Columbia, SC 29210-5667. Phone: (803)798-0271 Fax: (803)772-3509 Quarterly. Individuals, $50.00 per year; institutions, $70.00 per year. Formerly *Journalism Quarterly*.

Journalism Online. Mike Ward and Andy Dickinson. Elsevier, 360 Park Ave., S New York, NY 10010-1710. Phone: 888-437-4636 or (212)989-5800 Fax: (212)633-3990 E-mail: usinfo-f@elsevier.com • URL: http://www.elsevier.com • 2002. $39.95. Covers the basic journalism skills needed for identifying, collecting, selecting, and presenting news and information for the World Wide Web.

Journalist's Road to Success: Career and Scholarship Guide. Dow Jones Newspaper Fund, Inc., PO Box 300 Princeton, NJ 08543-0300. Phone: (609)452-2820 Fax: (609)520-5804 E-mail: newsfund@wsj.dowjones.com • URL: http://www.dowjones.com • Annual. $300.00. Lists more than 400 colleges and universities offering journalism/mass communications; general journalism career information; section of minority scholarships and special training programs; section on fellowships for continuing education. Formerly *Journalism Career and Scholarship Guide*.

Judge Advocates Association., 8109 Overlake Ct. Fairfax Station, VA 22039. Phone: (703)474-7691 Fax: (202)628-0080 E-mail: jaa@jaa.org • URL: http://www.jaa.org • Active, reserve, retired and former Judge Advocates of the Army, Navy, Air Force, Marine Corps, Coast Guard and practitioners of military and veterans law. Assists in the development of military law and an efficient military and veterans legal and judicial system.

Judges' Journal. American Bar Association, Judicial Administration Div., Section of Environment, Energy and Resources, 750 N Lake Shore Dr. Chicago, IL 60611. Phone: 800-285-2221 or (312)988-5000 Fax: (312)988-5528 E-mail: orders@abanet.org • URL: http://www.abanet.org. • Quarterly. Free to members; non-members, $25.00 per year. Focuses on the court.

Judge's Peerless Food Processors. Edward E. Judge & Sons Inc., PO Box 866 Westminster, MD 21158. Phone: 800-729-5517 or (410)876-2052 Fax: (410)848-2034 E-mail: info@eejudge.com • URL: http://www.eejudge.com • Covers: over 4,000 North American plants producing frozen, refrigerated, and shelf-stable foods, fruits, vegetables, juices, preserves, jams and jellies (SIC 2033); canned specialties (SIC 2032); frozen fruits and vegetables (SIC 2037); frozen specialties (SIC 2038); pickles, sauces and salad dressings (SIC 2035); canned and cured seafood (SIC 2091); fresh or frozen packaged fish (SIC 2092); refrigerated canned and frozen meat and poultry (SIC's 2013 and 2015); meat slaughtering (SIC 2011); butler (SIC 2021); cheese (SIC 2022); ice cream (SIC 2024); fluid milk and dry milk (SIC 2026, 2023). Entries include: Company name, address, phone, divisions, subsidiaries, factories, pack volume, names and titles of key personnel, container sizes, association affiliation, brands, products by factory and process. Plant SIC codes, number of employees for each plant.

Judicature. American Judicature Society, The Opperman Center at Drake Univ., 2700 University Ave. Des Moines, IA 50311. Phone: 888-287-2513 or (515)271-2281 Fax: (515)279-3090 • URL: http://www.ajs.org • Bimonthly. Free to members; institutions, $48.00 per year.

Judicial Staff Directory: With Biographical Information on Judges and Key Court Staff. CQ Press, 1255 22nd St., NW, Ste. 400 Washington, DC 20037. Phone: (866)427-7737 or (202)729-1900 Fax: 800-380-3810 E-mail: customerservice@cqpress.com Semiannual. $450.00. $225.00 per volume. Lists 33,500 federal court personnel, including 1,900 federal judges and their staffs, including biographies of judges and key executives. Includes maps of court jurisdictions.

Judicial Yellow Book: Who's Who in Federal and State Courts.

Leadership Directories, Inc., 104 Fifth Ave. New York, NY 10011. Phone: (212)627-4140 Fax: (212)645-0931 E-mail: info@leadershipdirectories.com • URL: http://www.leadershipdirectories.com • Semiannual. $245.00 per year. Lists more than 3,200 judges and staffs in various federal courts and 1,200 judges and staffs in state courts. Includes biographical profiles of judges.

Jumbo Rate News. BauerFinancial, Inc., Gables Intl. Plz., 2655 LeJeune Rd., Penthouse One Coral Gables, FL 33134. Phone: 800-388-6686 or (305)445-9500 Fax: 800-230-9569 E-mail: customerservice@bauerfinancial.com • URL: http://www.bauerfinancial.com • Description: Reports on high-yielding, insured Jumbo CD (Certificate of Deposit) rates nationwide. Analyzes each institution by current credit-worthiness, and lists current assets and capital ratios. Provides phone numbers, contacts, methods of computation, and information on how interest is paid. Also contains financial news, insights, and commentary of interest to Jumbo CD investors. Recurring features include editorials and news of interest.

Junk Bonds: How High Yield Securities Restructured Corporate America. Glenn Yago. Oxford University Press, 198 Madison Ave. New York, NY 10016. Phone: 800-451-7556 or (212)726-6000 Fax: (212)726-6440 E-mail: custserv@oup-usa.org • URL: http://www.oup-usa.org • 1990. $35.00.

Juran's Quality Control Handbook. Joseph M. Juran and A. Blandford Godfrey, editors. McGraw-Hill, 1221 Ave. of the Americas New York, NY 10020. Phone: 800-722-4726 or (212)512-2000 Fax: (212)512-4502 E-mail: customer.service@mcgraw-hill.com • URL: http://www.mcgraw-hill.com • 1998. $150.00. Fifth edition.

Jury Manual: A Guide for Prospective Jurors. William R. Pabst. Metro Publishing, P. O. Box 270776 Houston, TX 77277. Phone: (713)666-7841 1985. $19.95.

Jury Persuasion: Psychological Strategies & Trial Techniques. Donald E. Vinson and David S. Davis. Glasser Legalworks, 150 Clove Rd. Little Falls, NJ 07424. Phone: 800-308-1700 or (973)890-0008 Fax: (973)890-0042 E-mail: orders@glasserlegalworks.com • URL: http://www.glasserlegalworks.com • 1996. $55.00. Third revised edition. Covers voir dire (questioning prospective jurors), juror selection, opening statements, visual support of oral evidence, witness likeability, and "special tactics."

JustLife., PO Box 7165 Grand Rapids, MI 49510. Phone: (616)247-1155 E-mail: richard.wallace@scbar.org Political action committee comprising Christian individuals. Supports candidates working for the establishment of what the group considers consistent, pro-life governmental policies. Advocates multilateral disarmament through negotiation; endorses governmental programs that encourage self-sufficiency of the poor (such as education and training projects to develop employable skills) and provide assistance in the areas of health care, food, and housing; opposes abortion, except when necessary to save the mother's life; believes the government should promote and offer social assistance and adoption programs as options to abortion or motherhood with inadequate economic support. Conducts educational activities. Also conducts grass roots campaign activities; makes modest campaign contributions. Maintains educational fund.

Jute and Jute Fabrics-Bangladesh. Bangladesh Jute Research Institute, Sher-e-Banglanagar Dhaka 7, Bangladesh. Monthly. $5.00 per year. Text in English.

Jute Carpet Backing Council and Burlap and Jute Association., c/o Textile Bag and Packaging Association, 322 Davis Ave. Dayton, OH 45401. Phone: 800-543-3400 or (937)476-8272 Fax: (937)258-0029 E-mail: tbpa@aol.com Affiliated with Burlap and Jute Association. Formerly Jute Carpet Backing Council.

Kane's Beverage Week: The Newsletter of Beverage Marketing. Whitaker Newsletters, Inc., 313 South Ave. Fanwood, NJ 07023. Phone: (908)889-6336 Fax: (908)889-6339 Weekly. $469.00 per year. Newsletter. Covers news relating to the alcoholic beverage industries, including social, health, and legal issues.

Kansas Agricultural Experiment Station - Performance Test Program. Kansas State University

Kansas Farmer. Farm Progress Companies, 191 S. Gary Ave. Carol Stream, IL 60188. Phone: 800-441-1410 or (630)462-2224 Fax: (630)462-2885 E-mail: circhelp@farmprogress.com • URL: http://www.farmprogress.com • 15 times a year. $23.95 per year.

Kauai Agricultural Station. University of Hawaii at Manoa

Kearneysville Tree Fruit Research and Education Center. West Virginia University

Keeping Customers for Life. Joan K. Cannie and Donald Caplin. National Institute of Business Management, 1750 Old Meadow Rd., Suite 302 McLean, VA 22102. Phone: 800-543-2055 or (703)394-4921 E-mail: customer@nibm.net • URL: http://www.nibm.net • 1996. $14.95.

Keeping Customers Happy: Strategies for Success. Jacqueline Dunckel. Self-Counsel Press, 1707 N State St. Bellingham, WA 98225. Phone: 877-877-6490 or (360)676-4530 Fax: (360)676-4549 E-mail: orderdesk@self-counsel.com • URL: http://www.self-counsel.com • 1994. $9.95. Third edition. (Business Series).

Keeping the Books: Basic Recordkeeping and Accounting for the Successful Small Business. Linda Pinson. Dearborn Trade Publishing, A Kaplan Professional Co., 155 N Wacker Dr. Chicago, IL 60606. Phone: 800-621-9621 or (312)836-4400 Fax: (312)836-1021 E-mail: trade@dearborn.com • URL: http://www.dearborntrade.com • 2001. $22.95. Fifth edition. Covers bookkeeping systems, financial statements, and IRS tax record requirements. Includes illustrations, worksheets, and forms.

Keesing's Record of World Events. Keesing's Worldwide, LLC, 4905 Del Ray Ave., Suite 402 Bethesda, MD 20814. Phone: 800-332-3535 or (301)718-8770 Fax: (301)718-8494 E-mail: info@kessings.com • URL: http://www.kessings.com • Monthly. $365.00 per year.

Kelly's Industrial Directory. Kelly's Directories, 360 Prk. Ave., S, E Grinstead House, East Grinstead New York, NY 10010. Phone: 800-018-5882 or (646)746-6400 Fax: (342)33-5745 E-mail: corporatecommunications@reedbusiness.com • URL: http://www.kellysresearch.com • Covers: Over 105,000 UK industrial companies. Entries include: Company name, address, phone, fax, telex, product or service.

Kennedy's Pocket Guide to Working with Executive Recruiters. James H. Kennedy, editor. Kennedy Information, Inc., One Phoenix Mill Ln., 5th Fl. Peterborough, NH 03458. Phone: 800-531-0007 or (603)924-0900 Fax: (603)924-4460 E-mail: bookstore@kennedyinfo.com • URL: http://www.kennedyinfo.com • 2002. $17.95. Second revised editon. Consists of 30 chapters written by various experts. Includes a glossary: "Lexicon of Executive Recruiting."

Key Abstracts: Advanced Materials. Available from INSPEC, Inc., 379 Thornall St. Edison, NJ 08337. Phone: (732)321-5575 Fax: (732)321-5702 E-mail: inspec@inspecinc.com • URL: http://www.iee.org • Monthly. $250.00 per year. Provides international coverage of journal and proceedings literature, including publications on ceramics and composite materials. Published in England by the Institution of Electrical Engineers (IEE).

Key Abstracts: Artificial Intelligence. Available from INSPEC, Inc., 379 Thornall St. Edison, NJ 08337. Phone: (732)321-5575 Fax: (732)321-5702 E-mail: inspec@inspecinc.com • URL: http://www.iee.org • Monthly. $250.00 per year. Provides international coverage of journal and proceedings literature, including material on expert systems and knowledge engineering. Published in England by the Institution of Electrical Engineers (IEE).

Key Abstracts: Business Automation. Available from INSPEC, Inc., 379 Thornall St. Edison, NJ 08337. Phone: (732)321-5575 Fax: (732)321-5702 E-mail: inspec@inspecinc.com • URL: http://www.iee.org • Monthly. $250.00 per year. Provides international coverage of journal and proceedings literature. Published in England by the Institution of Electrical Engineers (IEE).

Key Abstracts: Computer Communications and Storage. Available from INSPEC, Inc., 379 Thornall St. Edison, NJ 08337. Phone: (732)321-5575 Fax: (732)321-5702 E-mail: inspec@inspecinc.com • URL: http://www.iee.org • Monthly. $250.00 per year. Provides international coverage of journal and proceedings literature, including material on optical disks and networks. Published in England by the Institution of Electrical Engineers (IEE).

Key Abstracts: Computing in Electronics and Power. Available from INSPEC, Inc., 379 Thornall St. Edison, NJ 08357-2225. Phone: (732)321-5575 Fax: (732)321-5702 E-mail: inspec@inspecinc.com • URL: http://www.iee.org • Monthly. $250.00 per year. Provides international coverage of journal and proceedings literature. Published in England by the Institution of Electrical Engineers (IEE).

Key Abstracts: Electronic Circuits. INSPEC, Inc., 379 Thornall St. Edison, NJ 08837. Phone: (732)321-5575 Fax: (732)321-5702 E-mail: inspec@inspecinc.com • URL: http://www.iee.org • Monthly. $250.00 per year. Provides international coverage of journal and proceedings literature. Published in England by the Institution of Electrical Engineers (IEE).

Key Abstracts: Electronic Instrumentation. Available from INSPEC, Inc., 379 Thornall St. Edison, NJ 08857-2225. Phone: (732)321-5575 Fax: (732)321-5702 E-mail: inspec@inspecinc.com • URL: http://www.iee.org • Monthly. $250.00 per year. Provides international coverage of journal and proceedings literature. Published in England by the Institution of Electrical Engineers (IEE).

Key Abstracts: Factory Automation. Available from INSPEC, Inc., 379 Thornall St. Edison, NJ 08857-2225. Phone: (732)321-5572 Fax: (732)321-5702 E-mail: inspec@inspecinc.com • URL: http://www.iee.org • Monthly. $250.00 per year. Provides international coverage of journal and proceedings literature, including publications on CAD/CAM, materials handling, robotics, and factory management. Published in England by the Institution of Electrical Engineers (IEE).

Key Abstracts: High Temperature Superconductors. Available from INSPEC, Inc., 379 Thornall St. Edison, NJ 08857-2225. Phone: (732)321-5575 Fax: (732)321-5702 E-mail: inspec@inspecinc.com • URL: http://www.iee.org • Monthly. $250.00 per year. Provides international coverage of journal and proceedings literature. Published in England by the Institution of Electrical Engineers (IEE).

Key Abstracts: Machine Vision. Available from INSPEC, Inc., 379 Thornall St. Edison, NJ 08857-2225. Phone: (732)321-5575 Fax: (732)321-5702 E-mail: inspec@inspecinc.com • URL: http://www.iee.org • Monthly. $250.00 per year. Provides international coverage of journal and proceedings literature on optical noncontact sensing. Published in England by the Institution of Electrical Engineers (IEE).

Key Abstracts: Microwave Technology. Available from INSPEC, Inc., 379 Thornall St. Edison, NJ 08857-2225. Phone: (732)321-5575 Fax: (732)321-5702 E-mail: inspec@inspecinc.com • URL: http://www.iee.org • Monthly. $250.00 per year. Provides international coverage of journal and proceedings literature. Published in England by the Institution of Electrical Engineers (IEE).

Key Abstracts: Optoelectronics. Available from INSPEC, Inc., 379 Thornall St. Edison, NJ 08857-2225. Phone: (732)321-5575 Fax: (732)321-5702 E-mail: inspec@inspecinc.com • URL: http://www.iee.org • Monthly. $250.00 per year. Provides international coverage of journal and proceedings literature relating to fiber optics, lasers, and optoelectronics in general. Published in England by the Institution of Electrical Engineers (IEE).

Key Abstracts: Power Systems and Applications. Available from INSPEC, Inc., 379 Thornall St. Edison, NJ 08857-2225. Phone: (732)321-5575 Fax: (732)321-5702 E-mail: inspec@inspecinc.com • URL: http://www.iee.org • Monthly. $250.00 per year. Provides international coverage of journal and proceedings literature, including publications on electric power apparatus and machines. Published in England by the Institution of Electrical Engineers (IEE).

Key Abstracts: Robotics and Control. Available from INSPEC, Inc., 379 Thornall St. Edison, NJ 08857-2225. Phone: (732)321-5575 Fax: (732)321-5702 E-mail: inspec@inspecinc.com • URL: http://www.iee.org • Monthly. $250.00 per year. Provides international coverage of journal and proceedings literature. Published in England by the Institution of Electrical Engineers (IEE).

Key Abstracts: Semiconductor Devices. Available from INSPEC, Inc., 379 Thornall St. Edison, NJ 08857-2225. Phone: (732)321-5575 Fax: (732)321-5702 E-mail: inspec@inspecinc.com • URL: http://www.iee.org • Monthly. $250.00 per year. Provides international coverage of journal and proceedings literature. Published in England by the Institution of Electrical Engineers (IEE).

Key Abstracts: Software Engineering. Available from INSPEC, Inc., 379 Thornall St. Edison, NJ 08857-2225. Phone: (732)321-5575 Fax: (732)321-5702 E-mail: inspec@inspecinc.com • URL: http://www.iee.org • Monthly. $250.00 per year. Provides international coverage of journal and proceedings literature. Published in England by the Institution of Electrical Engineers (IEE).

Key Abstracts: Telecommunications. Available from INSPEC, Inc., 379 Thornall St. Edison, NJ 08857-2225. Phone: (732)321-5575 Fax: (732)321-5702 E-mail: inspec@inspecinc.com • URL: http://www.iee.org • Monthly. $250.00 per year. Provides international coverage of journal and proceedings literature. Published in England by the Institution of Electrical Engineers (IEE).

Key Indicators of the Labour Market. Available from Routledge, 29 W 35th St. New York, NY 10001. Phone: 800-634-7064 or (212)216-7800 Fax: 800-248-4724 E-mail: info@routledge-ny.com • URL: http://www.routledge-ny.com • Biennial. $125.00. Published by the International Labour Office (http://www.ilo.org). Provides data on 20 key indicators in 220 countries. Includes labor force statistics, employment, unemployment, part-time workers, wages, productivity, poverty indicators, and related topics.

Key Note Market Report: Home Shopping. Jupitermedia, 23 Old Kings Highway S Darien, CT 06820. Phone: (203)662-2800 Fax: (203)655-4686 • URL: http://www.jmm.com • 2001. $400.00. Market research report. Covers "interactive retailing," mainly through the Internet and television, with predictions of future trends. Formerly *Key Note Report: Home Shopping*.

Keyboard: The World's Leading Music Technology Magazine. United Entertainment Media, Inc., 460 Park Ave., S. New York, NY 10016-7315. Phone: (212)378-0400 Fax: (212)378-2160 E-mail: keyboard@uemedia.com • URL: http://www.uemedia.com • Monthly. $25.95 per year. Emphasis is on recording systems, keyboard technique, and computer-assisted music (MIDI) systems.

Keynotes. USA Section/International College of Dentists, 51 Monroe St., Ste. 1400 Rockville, MD 20850-2409. Phone: (301)251-8861 Fax: (301)738-9143 E-mail: reg-sg@icd.org • URL: http://www.aloa.org • Description: Contains news of the activities and projects of the organization, which provides networking and educational opportunities for professionals in the dental field. Recurring features include a calendar of events, reports of meetings, news of educational opportunities, and a column titled the History Corner.

Keys to Investing in Common Stocks. Barbara Apostolou and Nicholas Apostolou. Barron's Educational Series, Inc., 250 Wireless Blvd. Hauppauge, NY 11788-3917. Phone: 800-645-3476 or (516)434-3311 Fax: (516)434-3723 E-mail: info@barronseduc.com • URL: http://www.barronseduc.com • 2004. $7.95. Fourth edition. Provides basic information for the average small investor. Covers investing in both individual stocks and mutual funds.

Keystone Center. Keystone Center, 1628 St. John Rd. Keystone, CO 80435. Phone: (970)513-5800 Fax: (970)262-0152 E-mail: marketing@irrc.com • URL: http://www.keystone.org • Promotes the development of effective policy and the resolution of environmental and natural resource disputes through active facilitation of policy dialogues and information exchange between individuals in the private sector, environmental community, academia, and government.

Activities focus on negotiations for policies in the fields of energy, environment, and science/technology, including energy futures, international pesticides use, superfund, biotechnology regulation, toxic waste, public utilities, food safety, science and technology policy, and expanded access to therapeutic drugs.

Keystone Coal Industry Manual. Primedia Business, 330 North Wabash Ave., Ste. 2300 Chicago, IL 60611-3698. Phone: 800-621-9907 or (312)595-1080 Fax: (312)595-0295 E-mail: corporatecommunications@reedbusiness.com Covers: coal companies and mines, coke plants, coal preparation plants, domestic and export coal sales companies; industry organizations, steam power plants, portland cement plants, industrial coal-burning plants, consultants, mining contractors; river docks, tidewater piers, river transportation companies, railroads; financial institutions; includes list of leading coal mining companies and mines. Entries include: Company or organization name, address, names of executives; coal mine directory includes analysis, tonnage, capacity, seam mined and facilities; consultants directory includes services offered.

Keywords. SPSS Inc., 444 N Michigan Ave. Chicago, IL 60611. Phone: (312)329-2400 Fax: (312)329-3668 E-mail: reg-sg@icd.org • URL: http://www.asindexing.org • Description: Intended for users of SPSS, Inc. computer software. Offers advice and technical information on using SPSS products and carries data on new products. Recurring features include training schedules and publications ordering information.

Kika de la Garza Subtropical Agricultural Research Center.

The Kiplinger Agriculture Letter. Kiplinger Washington Editors Inc., 1729 H St. NW Washington, DC 20006. Phone: 800-544-0155 or (202)887-6491 Fax: (202)785-3648 E-mail: reg-sg@icd.org • URL: http://www.kiplinger.com • Description: Publishes information on actions and proposals by the administration, U.S. Department of Agriculture, and Congress affecting all aspects of agriculture. Includes analysis and forecasts on a broad range of issues affecting the farm/food industry, government production and price support programs, commodity production and consumption data, food marketing and processing, consumer trends, taxes, farm credit, and financial matters.

The Kiplinger Letter. Kiplinger Washington Editors Inc., 1729 H St. NW Washington, DC 20006. Phone: 800-544-0155 or (202)887-6491 Fax: (202)785-3648 E-mail: reg-sg@icd.org • URL: http://www.kiplinger.com • Description: Provides information on current events and future outlook in business, economics, legislation, politics, finance, labor, and other topics of interest to business professionals.

The Kiplinger Tax Letter. Kiplinger Washington Editors Inc., 1729 H St. NW Washington, DC 20006. Phone: 800-544-0155 or (202)887-6491 Fax: (202)785-3648 E-mail: reg-sg@icd.org • URL: http://www.kiplinger.com • Description: Reports new tax regulations, changes, decisions, and pending legislation. Includes coverage of the House Ways and Means and Senate Committees, federal monetary and fiscal policy, securities, finance, and social security.

Kiplinger's Personal Finance Magazine. Kiplinger Washington Editors, Inc., 1729 H St., N.W. Washington, DC 20006. Phone: 800-544-0155 or (202)887-6400 • URL: http://www.kiplinger.com • Monthly. $23.95 per year.

Kiplinger's Retirement Report. Kiplinger Washington Editors Inc., 1729 H St. NW Washington, DC 20006. Phone: 800-544-0155 or (202)887-6491 Fax: (202)785-3648 E-mail: reg-sg@icd.org • URL: http://www.kiplinger.com • Description: Offers information for the retired and soon-to-be-retired. Discusses such topics as money management, estate planning, health, travel and what's going on in Washington DC.

Kirk-Othmer Concise Encyclopedia of Chemical Technology. John Wiley and Sons, Inc., 111 River St. Hoboken, NJ 07030. Phone: 800-225-5945 or (201)748-6000 Fax: (201)748-6088 E-mail: info@wiley.com • URL: http://www.wiley.com • 2001. $295.00. Fourth edition. Contains abstracts of articles from the multivolume *Kirk-Othmer Encyclopedia of Chemical Technology*.

Kirk-Othmer Encyclopedia of Chemical Technology. Raymond E. Kirk and Donald F. Othmer. John Wiley and Sons, Inc., 111 River St. Hoboken, NJ 07030. Phone: 800-225-5945 or (201)748-6000 Fax: (201)748-6088 E-mail: info@wiley.com • URL: http://www.wiley.com • 1991-97. $9,895.00, prepaid. 27 volumes. Fourth edition. Four volumes are scheduled to be published each year, with individual volumes available at $415.00. (Kirk-Othmer Encyclopedia of Chemical Technology Series).

Kitchen and Bath Business. VNU Business Media, 770 Broadway New York, NY 10003-9595. Phone: 800-344-7119 or (646)654-4500 Fax: (646)654-7212 • URL: http://www.vnubusinessmedia.com • Monthly. $79.00 per year.

Kitchen and Bath Business Buyers' Guide. CMP Books, 460 Park Ave. S, 9th Fl. New York, NY 10016. Phone: 800-950-1314 or (212)615-2247 E-mail: kitchen@billcom.com • URL: http://www.kitchen-bath.com • Annual. $7.00. Guide to kitchen and bath products, supplies and services. Formerly *Kitchen and Bath Business and Buyers' Guide/Almanac*.

Kitchen Cabinet Manufacturers Association., 1899 Preston White Dr. Reston, VA 20191-5435. Phone: (703)264-1690 Fax: (703)620-6530 E-mail: info@kcma.org • URL: http://www.kcma.org • Serves as a national trade association representing cabinet and countertop manufacturers and suppliers to the industry. Promotes the cabinet manufacturing industry, develops standards for the industry, administers a testing and certification program, conducts education programs and meetings, provides management information and industry data, and engages in activities on behalf of members on legislative and regulatory issues.

Kitchen Cabinet Manufacturers Association Income and Expense Study. Kitchen Cabinet Manufacturers Association, 1899 Preston White Dr. Reston, VA 22091-4326. Phone: (703)264-1690 Fax: (703)620-6530 E-mail: dtitus@kcma.org • URL: http://www.kcma.org • Annual. Membership.

Kitchen Cabinets and Countertops. Available from MarketResearch.com, 641 Ave. of the Americas, Third Floor New York, NY 10011. Phone: 800-298-5699 or (212)807-2629 Fax: (212)807-2716 E-mail: order@marketresearch.com • URL: http://www.marketresearch.com • 2002. $2,250.00. Market research report published by Catalina Research. Covers both custom and stock cabinets. Presents market data relative to demographics, sales growth, shipments, exports, imports, price trends, and end-use. Includes company profiles.

Kleppner's Advertising Procedure. Thomas Russell and others. Prentice Hall PTR, 240 Frisch Ct. Paramus, NJ 07652. Phone: 800-282-0693 Fax: 800-445-6991 • URL: http://www.phptr.com • 2001. $115.00. 15th edition.

KM World: Creating and Managing the Knowledge-Based Enterprise (Knowledge Management). Asset Media, 18 Bayview Landing Camden, ME 04843. Phone: 800-248-0588 or (207)236-8524 Fax: (207)236-6452 E-mail: hugh_mckellar@kmworld.com • URL: http://www.kmworld.com • 10 times a year. Free to qualified personnel; others, $63.95 per year. Provides articles on knowledge management, including business intelligence, multimedia content management, document management, e-business, and intellectual property. Emphasis is on business-to-business information technology. (Knowledge Asset Media is a an affiliate of Information Today, Inc.)

KMWorld Buyer's Guide. Knowledge Asset Media, 18 Bayview St. Camden, ME 04843. Phone: 800-248-0588 or (207)236-8524 Fax: (207)236-6452 E-mail: editor@kmworld.com • URL: http://www.kmworld.com • Semiannual. Controlled circulation as part of *KMWorld*. Contains corporate and product profiles related to various aspects of knowledge management and information systems. (Knowledge Asset Media is a an affiliate of Information Today, Inc.)

Knight Center for Specialized Journalism., University of Maryland, 1117 Cole Field House College Park, MD 20742-1024. Phone: (301)405-4817 E-mail: knight@umail.umd.edu • URL: http://www.knightcenter.umd.edu/ • Research area is media coverage of complex subjects, such as economics, law, science, and medicine.

Knit Fabric Production. U.S. Bureau of the Census, Washington, DC 20233-0800. Phone: (301)457-4100 Fax: (301)457-3842 • URL: http://www.census.gov • Annual. (Current Industrial Reports MA-22K.)

Knitwear Division - American Apparel Manufacturers Association., 1601 N. Kent St., Ste. 1200 Arlington, VA 22209-2105. Formerly National Knitwear Manufacturers Association.

Knott's Handbook for Vegetable Growers. Donald N. Maynard and George J. Hochmuth. John Wiley and Sons, Inc., 111 River St. Hoboken, NJ 07030. Phone: 800-225-5945 or (201)748-6000 Fax: (201)748-6088 E-mail: info@wiley.com • URL: http://www.wiley.com • 1997. $99.00. Fourth edition. Written for commercial vegetable growers, truck farmers, horticulturists, and other professionals. Covers such topics as spacing of plants, disease control, insect pests, seeds, weeds, water management, and irrigation.

Knowledge Exchange Business Encyclopedia: Your Complete Business Advisor. Lorraine Spurge. Knowledge Exchange LLC, 16350 Ventura Blvd. Encino, CA 91436. Phone: (818)705-1269 Fax: (818)708-8764 E-mail: info@spurgeink.com • URL: http://www.spurgeink.com • 1998. $45.00. Provides definitions of business terms and financial expressions, profiles of leading industries, tables of economic statistics, biographies of business leaders, and other business information. Includes "A Chronology of Business from 3000 B.C. Through 1995." Contains illustrations and three indexes.

Knowledge Management for the Information Professional. T. Kanti Srikantaiah and Michael Koenig. Information Today, Inc., 143 Old Marlton Pike Medford, NJ 08055-8750. Phone: 800-300-9868 or (609)654-6266 Fax: (609)654-4309 E-mail: custserv@infotoday.com • URL: http://www.infotoday.com • 2000. $44.50. Contains articles by 26 contributors on the concept of "knowledge management." (ASIS Mongraph Series).

Knowledge Management Lessons Learned: What Works and What Doesn't. Michael Koenig and T. Kanti Srikantaiah, editors. Information Today, Inc., 143 Old Marlton Pike Medford, NJ 08055-8750. Phone: 800-300-9868 or (609)654-6266 Fax: (609)654-4309 E-mail: custserv@infotoday.com • URL: http://www.infotoday.com • 2003. $44.50. Contains more than 30 articles by KM experts, covering recent applications, innovations, strategy, implementation, cost analysis, training, content management, and other topics related to knowledge management. (ASIS Management Series).

Knowledge Management: The Bibliography. Paul Burden and others. Information Today, Inc., 143 Old Marlton Pike Medford, NJ 08055-8750. Phone: 800-300-9868 or (609)654-6266 Fax: (609)654-4309 E-mail: custserv@infotoday.com • URL: http://www.infotoday.com • 2000. $22.50. Provides citations to more than 1,500 articles, 150 Web sites, and 400 books. Arranged according to specific KM topics, such as "KM and E-Commerce." Published in conjunction with the American Society for Information Science and Technology (ASIST).

Koldfax. Air-Conditioning and Refrigeration Institute, 4100 Fairfax Dr., No. 200 Arlington, VA 22203. Phone: (703)524-8800 Fax: (703)528-3816 E-mail: ari@ari.org • URL: http://www.ari.org • Monthly. Membership. Newsletter.

Kompass CD-ROM Editions. Available from Kompass USA, Inc., 121 Whitney Ave. New Haven, CT 06510. Phone: 877-566-7277 or (203)503-6789 Fax: (203)503-6780 E-mail: mail@kompass-usa.com • URL: http://www.kompass.com • Semiannual or annual. Prices vary. CD-ROM versions of Kompass international trade directories are available for each of 36 major countries and nine world regions. Searching is provided for 50,000 product/service items and for many company details.

Kompass Concord CD-ROM. Available from Kompass USA, Inc., 121 Whitney Ave. New Haven, CT 06510. Phone: 877-566-7277 or (203)503-6789 Fax: (203)503-6780 E-mail: mail@kompass-usa.com • URL: http://www.kompass.com • Semiannual. CD-ROM provides information on more than 280,000 companies in 17 rapidly developing East European countries: Armenia, Azerbaijan, Belarus, Bulgaria, Czech Republic, Estonia, Hungary, Kazakhstan, Kyrgyzstan, Latvia, Lithuania, Moldova, Poland, Romania, Russia, Ukraine, and Uzbekistan. Classification system covers approximately 50,000 products and services.

Kompass International Trade Directories. Kompass International/Kompass USA, Inc., 121 Whitney Ave. New Haven, CT 06510. Phone: 877-566-7277 or (203)503-6789 Fax: (203)503-6780 E-mail: mail@kompass-usa.com • URL: http://www.kompass.com • Annual. Prices and volumes vary. Kompass directories are published internationally for each of more than 70 countries, from Algeria to Uzbekistan. The Kompass classification system covers more than 50,000 individual product and service categories, with most directories containing a tradename index and company profiles. Total number of companies in Kompass volumes is about two million.

Kompass USA. Kompass International/Kompass USA, Inc., 121 Whitney Ave. New Haven, CT 06510. Phone: 877-566-7277 or (203)503-6789 Fax: (203)503-6780 E-mail: mail@kompass-usa.com • URL: http://www.kompass.com • Annual. Price on application. Two volumes. Includes information on about 125,000 U.S. companies. Classification system covers approximately 50,000 products and services. Product and tradename indexes are provided.

Korea Trade Promotion Center., 460 Park Ave., Ste. 402 New York, NY 10022. Phone: (212)826-0900 Fax: (212)888-4930 E-mail: kotrany@ix.netcom.com • URL: http://nyc.kotra.or.kr • Works as an agency of the Korean government. Provides information about Korean export commodities and exporters, and import commodities and importers. Sponsors visits of foreign businesspersons to the Republic of Korea; arranges introductions of potential traders to Korean manufacturers and sales and buying missions of traders with the Republic of Korea. Compiles statistics; conducts economic and marketing research for distribution to Korean industry, business, and government; participates in U.S. trade shows. Maintains 35,000 volume international trade library.

Kosher Directory :Directory of Kosher Products and Services. Union of Orthodox Jewish Congregations of America (Orthodox Union), 11 Broadway New York, NY 10004. Phone: (212)563-4000 Fax: (212)564-9058 E-mail: info@ou.org • URL: http://www.ou.org • Annual. $15.00. Over 10,000 consumer, institutional and industrial products and services produced under the rabbinical supervision of the Union.

Kovels' on Antiques and Collectibles: The Newsletter for Dealers, Collectors, and Investors. Antiques Inc., 49 Richmondville Ave. Westport, CT 06880. Phone: 800-829-9158 or (216)752-2252 • URL: http://www.kovel.com • Monthly. $46.00 per year.

Kurata Thermodynamics Laboratory., University of Kansas, Dept. of Chemical and Petroleum Engineering Lawrence, KS 66045. Phone: (785)864-3860 Fax: (785)864-7399 E-mail: cshowat@ukans.edu • URL: http://www.engr.ukans.edu/~ktl • Investigates the behavior of various materials over a wide range of temperatures.

L D + A: Lighting Equipment Accessories Directory. Illuminating Engineering Society of North America, 120 Wall St., 17th Fl. New York, NY 10005. Phone: (212)248-5000 Fax: (212)248-5017 E-mail: iesna@iesna.org • URL: http://www.iesna.org • Annual. $10.00. Lists over 800 manufacturers of lighting fixtures, controls, components, mounting devices, maintenance equipment, etc.

Label Printing Industries of America., 100 Daingerfield Rd. Alexandria, VA 22314. Phone: (703)519-8100 Fax: (703)548-3227 E-mail: gain@printing.org • URL: http://www.gain.org • Affiliated with Printing Industries of America.

Labels. Available from MarketResearch.com, 641 Ave. of the Americas, Third Floor New York, NY 10011. Phone: 800-298-5699 or (212)807-2629 Fax: (212)807-2716 E-mail: order@marketresearch.com • URL: http://www.marketresearch.com • 2002. $3,900.00. Market research report published by the Freedonia Group. Covers types of label materials, methods of application, printing technology, and end-use markets. Includes company profiles and forecasts to the year 2006.

Labor and Employment Law. Labor and Employment Law Section. American Bar Association, 750 N Lake Shore Dr. Chicago, IL 60611. Phone: 800-285-2221 or (312)988-5000 E-mail: orders@abanet.org • URL: http://www.abanet.org • Quarterly. Membership.

Labor and Employment Law: Text and Cases. David P. Twomey. South-Western, 5191 Natrop Blvd. Mason, OH 45040. Phone: 800-543-0487 or (513)229-1000 • URL: http://www.swcollege.com • 2000. $93.94. 11th edition. (Business Law Series).

Labor Arbitration: An Annotated Bibliography, 1991-1996. Charles J. Coleman and others, editors. Cornell Universtiy Press, Sage House, 512 E State St. Ithaca, NY 14851. Phone: 800-666-2211 Fax: (607)277-6292 E-mail: store@cornell.edu • URL: http://www.cornellpress.cornell.edu • 1997. $27.50. (ILR Bibliography Series, No. 18).

Labor Arbitration Awards. CCH, Inc., 2700 Lake Cook Rd. Riverwoods, IL 60015. Phone: 800-835-5224 or (847)267-7000 E-mail: cust_serv@cch.com • URL: http://www.cch.com • Weekly. $1,239.00 per year. Looseleaf service.

Labor Law Journal: To Promote Sound Thinking on Labor Law Problems. CCH, Inc., 2700 Lake Cook Rd. Riverwoods, IL 60015. Phone: 800-835-5224 or (847)267-7000 E-mail: cust_serv@cch.com • URL: http://www.cch.com • Monthly. $189.00 per year.

Labor-Management Relations. Daniel Q. Mills. McGraw-Hill, 1221 Ave. of the Americas New York, NY 10020. Phone: 800-722-4726 or (212)512-2000 Fax: (212)512-4502 E-mail: customer.service@mcgraw-hill.com • URL: http://www.mcgraw-hill.com • 1993. $112.50. Fifth edition. (Management Series).

Labor Management Relations: Strikes, Lockouts, and Boycotts. West Group, 610 Opperman Dr. Eagan, MN 55123. Phone: 800-328-4880 or (651)687-7000 Fax: 800-340-9378 E-mail: bookstore@westgroup.com • URL: http://www.westgroup.com • Annual. $165.00. Looseleaf service. Covers legal issues involved in labor-management confrontations. Includes recent decisions of the National Labor Relations Board (NLRB).

Labor Policy Association.

Labor Relations. CCH, Inc., 2700 Lake Cook Rd. Riverwoods, IL 60015. Phone: 800-835-5224 or (847)267-7000 E-mail: cust_serv@cch.com • URL: http://www.cch.com • $2,589.00 per year. Seven looseleaf volumes. Weekly updates. Covers labor relations, wages and hours, state labor laws, and employment practices. Supplement available, *Labor Law Reports*. Summary Newsletter.

Labor Relations. Arthur A. Sloan and Fred Witney. Prentice Hall PTR, 240 Frisch Ct. Paramus, NJ 07652. Phone: 800-282-0693 Fax: 800-445-6991 • URL: http://www.phptr.com • 2000. $115.00. 10th edition. Emphasizes collective bargaining and arbitration.

Labor Relations Bulletin. Aspen Publishers Inc., 125 Eugene O'Neill Dr., Ste. 103 New London, CT 06320. Phone: 800-876-9105 or (860)442-4365 Fax: (860)437-3150 E-mail: customer.service@aspenpubl.com • URL: http://www.aspenpublishers.com • Description: Provides information and insight to management and labor officials to help them avoid or resolve conflicts. Recurring features include reports on current developments in labor law and relations, discipline and grievance cases based on actual arbitration, a question and answer column on labor and employment relations, and a column titled Reflections of an Arbitrator, offering the insight and experience of prominent national arbitrators.

Labor Relations: Development, Structure, Process. John A. Fossum. McGraw-Hill, 1221 Ave. of the Americas New York, NY 10020. Phone: 800-722-4726 or (212)512-2000 Fax: (212)512-4502 E-mail: customer.service@mcgraw-hill.com • URL: http://www.mcgraw-hill.com • 2001. $112.50. Eighth edition.

Labor Relations Reporter. BNA, Inc., 1231 25th St., NW Washington, DC 20037. Phone: 800-372-1033 E-mail: customercare@bna.com • URL: http://www.bna.com • Weekly. $4,998.00 per year. Looseleaf service.

Labor Research Association. Labor Research Association, 330 W 42nd St., 13th Fl. New York, NY 10001. Phone: (212)714-1677 Fax: (212)714-1674 E-mail: info@lra-ny.com • URL: http://www.laborresearch.org/about.php • Economic, social, and political conditions, focusing on labor relations.

Laboratories Medical Directory. infoUSA Inc., 5711 S 86th Cir., PO Box 27347 Omaha, NE 68127. Phone: 800-321-0869 or (402)593-4500 Fax: (402)331-1505 E-mail: help@infousa.com • URL: http://www.abii.com • Number of listings: 9,073. Entries include: Name, address, phone (including area code), size of advertisement, year first in "Yellow Pages," name of owner or manager, number of employees. Compiled from telephone company "Yellow Pages," nationwide.

Laboratory Equipment. Reed Business Information, 360 Park Ave., S New York, NY 10010. Phone: 800-446-6551 or (646)746-6400 Fax: (646)746-7028 E-mail: corporatecommunications@reedbusiness.com • URL: http://www.reedbusiness.com • 12 times a year. $105.90 per year.

Laboratory for Computer Science., Massachusetts Institute of Technology, 200 Technology Square, Bldg. NE43 Cambridge, MA 02139. Phone: (617)253-5851 Fax: (617)258-8682 E-mail: zue@mit.edu • URL: http://www.lcs.mit.edu/ • Research is in four areas: Intelligent Systems; Parallel Systems; Systems, Languages, and Networks; and Theory. Emphasis is on the application of online computing.

Laboratory for Electromagnetic and Electronic Systems., Massachusetts Institute of Technology, 77 Massachusetts Ave., Room 10-172 Cambridge, MA 02139. Phone: (617)253-4631 Fax: (617)258-6774 E-mail: jgk@mit.edu • URL: http://www.power.mit.edu/index • Research areas include heat transfer and cryogenics.

Laboratory for Energy and the Environment. Massachusetts Institute of Technology, 77 Massachusetts Ave., Bldg. E40-455 Cambridge, MA 02139-4307. Phone: (617)258-8891 Fax: (617)253-8013 E-mail: jwilmson@mit.edu • URL: http://www.lfee.mit.edu • Formerly Energy Laboratory.

Laboratory for Information and Decision Systems., Massachusetts Institute of Technology, 127 Massachusetts Ave., Bldg. 35, Room 308 Cambridge, MA 02139-4307. Phone: (617)258-8222 Fax: (617)253-3578 E-mail: chan@mit.edu • URL: http://www.justice.mit.edu • Research areas include data communication networks and fiber optic networks.

Laboratory for Manufacturing and Productivity.

Laboratory for Nuclear Science.

Laboratory for Pest Control Application Technology., Ohio State University, Ohio Agricultural Research and Development Center, 1680 Madison Ave. Wooster, OH 44691-4096. Phone: (330)263-3931 Fax: (330)263-3686 E-mail: downer.2@osu.edu • URL: http://www.oardc.ohio-state.edu/lpcat • Conducts pest control research in cooperation with the U. S. Department of Agriculture.

Laboratory of Electronics., Rockefeller University, 1230 York Ave. New York, NY 10021. Phone: (212)327-8613 Fax: (212)327-7613 E-mail: ros@rockvax.rockefeller.edu Studies the application of computer engineering and electronics to biomedicine.

Laboratory of Electronics. Rockefeller University

Labordoc. International Labour Organization, 1828 L St., N.W., Suite 801 Washington, DC 20006. Phone: (202)653-7652 Fax: (202)653-7687 Indexing of labor literature and the publications of the International Labour Organization, 1965 to present. Monthly updates. Inquire as to online cost and availability.

Labour Force Statistics. Organization for Economic Cooperation and Development. Available from OECD Publications and Information Center, 2001 L St., N. W., Suite 650 Washington, DC 20036-4922. Phone: 800-456-6323 or (202)785-6323 Fax: (202)785-0350 E-mail: washington.contact@oecd.org • URL: http://www.oecdwash.org • Annual. $98.00. Provides 21 years of data for OECD member countries on population, employment, unemployment, civilian labor force, armed forces, and other labor factors.

Lace and Embroideries Directory. Schiffli Lace and Embroidery Manufacturers Association, 20 Indus Ave., No. 26 Fairview, NJ 07022-1614. Phone: (201)943-7757 Fax: (201)943-7793 E-mail: webmaster@schiffliusa.com • URL: http://www.schiffliusa.com • Annual. $5.00. Embroidery and lace product merchandisers, producers, and industry service providers in the United States with limited international coverage. Formerly *Embroidery Directory*.

Ladies Professional Golf Association., 100 International Golf Dr. Daytona Beach, FL 32124-1092. Phone: (386)274-6200 Fax: (386)274-1099 E-mail: feedback@lpga.com • URL: http://www.lpga.com • Represents and promotes women golfers, teachers and competitors. Compiles statistics on tournaments, money winnings, and scoring.

Laffirmations: 1001 Ways to Add Humor to Your Life and Work. Joel Goodman. Health Communications, Inc., 3201 S. W. 15th St. Deerfield Beach, FL 33442-8157. Phone: 800-851-9100 or (954)360-0909 Fax: (954)360-0034 E-mail: hci@hcibooks.com • URL: http://www.hcibooks.com • 1995. $8.95. The author is director of the Humor Project, a private company promoting humor in the corporate workplace.

Lakewood Report on Positive Employee Practices. Lakewood Publications, Inc., 50 S. Ninth St. Minneapolis, MN 55402. Phone: (612)333-0471 Fax: (612)333-6526 Monthly. $128.00 per year. Newsletter. Provides news for quality improvement managers. Includes columns entitled "Eye on Quality" and "Quality Movement News." Formerly *Total Quality*.

Laminate Flooring. Available from MarketResearch.com, 641 Ave. of the Americas, Third Floor New York, NY 10011. Phone: 800-298-5699 or (212)807-2629 Fax: (212)807-2716 E-mail: order@marketresearch.com • URL: http://www.marketresearch.com • 1997. $495.00. Market research report published by Specialists in Business Information. Presents laminate flooring market data relative to demographics, sales growth, shipments, exports, imports, price trends, and end-use. Includes company profiles.

Lamme Power Systems Laboratory. Ohio State University

LAMP (Literature Analysis of Microcomputer Publications). Soft Images, 200 Route 17 Mahwah, NJ 07430. Phone: (201)529-1440 Bimonthly. $89.95 per year. Annual cumulation.

Land Economics: A Quarterly Journal Devoted to the Study of Economic and Social Institutions. University of Wisconsin at Madison. University of Wisconsin Press, Journals Div., 1930 Monroe St., 3rd Fl. Madison, WI 53711-2059. Phone: (608)263-0668 Fax: 800-258-3632 or (608)263-1173 E-mail: journals@uwpress.wisc.edu • URL: http://www.wisc.edu • Quarterly. Individuals, $59.00 per year; institutions, $166.00 per year.

Land Use and Environment Law Review. West Group, 610 Opperman Dr. Eagan, MN 55123. Phone: 800-328-4880 or (651)687-7000 Fax: 800-340-9378 E-mail: bookstore@westgroup.com • URL: http://www.westgroup.com • Annual. $330.00.

Land Use Law and Zoning Digest. American Planning Association, 122 S. Michigan Ave., Suite 1600 Chicago, IL 60603-6107. Phone: (312)431-9100 Fax: (312)431-9985 E-mail: bookservice@planning.org • URL: http://www.planning.org • Monthly. $275.00 per year. Covers judicial decisions and state laws affecting zoning and land use. Edited for city planners and lawyers. Monthly supplement available *Zoning News*.

Land Use Law Report. Business Publishers Inc., 2601 University Blvd., W Ste. 200, PO Box 17592 Silver Spring, MD 20902. Phone: 800-274-6737 or (301)929-5700 Fax: (301)949-8844 E-mail: custserv@bpinews.com • URL: http://www.bpinews.com • Description: Provides up-to-date information on court decisions, legislation, and regulations that impact today's most pressing land-use policy, planning, and legal issues. Readers receive in-depth coverage on zoning and planning policies, regulatory takings, undesirable land uses, environmental legislation, and much more. **Remarks:** Also available via e-mail.

The Landlord's Handbook: A Complete Guide to Managing Small Residential and Commercial Properties. Daniel Goodwin and Richard Rusdorf. Dearborn Trade Publishing, A Kaplan Professional Co., 30 S Wacker Dr., Ste. 2500 Chicago, IL 60606-7481. Phone: 800-621-9621 or (312)836-4400 Fax: (312)836-1021 E-mail: trade@dearborn.com • URL: http://www.dearborntrade.com • 2003. $29.95. Third edition. Covers such topics as finding good tenants, rent collection, insurance, taxes, environmental issues, leases, security deposits, and evictions.

Landscape Architecture. American Society of Landscape Architects, 636 Eye St., N.W. Washington, DC 20001-3736. Phone: (202)898-2444 Fax: (202)898-1185 E-mail: email@asla.org • URL: http://www.asla.org • Monthly. $49.00 per year.

Landscape Architecture: An Illustrated History in Timelines, Site Plans, and Biography. William A. Mann. John Wiley and Sons, Inc., 111 River St. Hoboken, NJ 07030. Phone: 800-225-5945 or (201)748-6000 Fax: (201)748-6088 E-mail: info@wiley.com • URL: http://www.wiley.com • 1993. $75.00. Includes illustrations of notable site plans and biographies of people important to landscape architecture history.

Landscape Architecture Foundation. Landscape Architecture Foundation, 818 18th St. NW, Ste. 810 Washington, DC 20006. Phone: (202)331-7070 Fax: (202)331-7079 E-mail: rfigura@lafoundation.org • URL: http://www.lafoundation.org • Landscape planning, land use planning and design, environmental planning, landscape change, landscape intervention, place-based land use planning, public participation processes.

Landscape Architecture News Digest. American Society of Landscape Architects, 636 Eye St., N.W. Washington, DC 20001-3736. Phone: (202)898-2444 Fax: (202)898-1185 E-mail: email@asla.org • URL: http://www.asla.org • 10 times a year. Free to members; non-members, $32.00 per year. Looseleaf service.

Landscape Journal: Design, Planning, and Management of the Land. Council of Education in Landscape Architecture. University of Wisconsin Press, Journal Div., 1930 Monroe St., 3rd Fl. Madison, WI 53711-2059. Phone: (608)263-0668 Fax: 800-258-3632 or (608)263-1173 E-mail: journals@uwpress.wisc.edu • URL: http://www.wisc.edu • Semiannual. Individuals, $42.00 per year; institutions, $135.00 per year.

Landscape Maintenance News. Landscape Information Services, 6401 Yellowstone, Box 2694 Casper, WY 82602. Phone: (307)265-7801 E-mail: custserv@bpinews.com Description: Provides landscape service companies with information to help them manage their services; covers changes and events in the industry. Covers image, customer service, advertising and marketing, estimating, mowing, poweraking, fertilization, weed control, maintenance, and miscellaneous services. Discusses trade shows, products and services, associations, and franchise opportunities. Recurring features include news of research, news of educational opportunities, book reviews, and notices of publications available.

Landscape Management: Commercial Magazine for Lawn, Landscape and Grounds Managers. Advanstar Communications, 545 Boylston St. Boston, MA 02116. Phone: 888-527-7008 or (617)267-6500 Fax: (617)267-6900 E-mail: info@advanstar.com • URL: http://www.advanstar.com • Monthly. $41.00 per year.

Landscape Planning: Environmental Applications. William M. Marsh. John Wiley and Sons, Inc., 111 River St. Hoboken, NJ 07030. Phone: 800-225-5945 or (201)748-6000 Fax: (201)748-6088 E-mail: info@wiley.com • URL: http://www.wiley.com • 1997. $62.95. Third edition. A handbook on environmental problems associated with landscape design, land planning, and land use. Includes techniques for obtaining data.

The Language of Banking: Terms and Phrases Used in the Financial Industry. Michael G. Hales. McFarland & Co., Inc., Publishers, PO Box 611 Jefferson, NC 28640. Phone: 800-253-2187 or (336)246-4460 Fax: (336)246-5018 E-mail: info@mcfarlandpub.com • URL: http://www.mcfarlandpub.com • 1994. $35.00. Provides detailed explanations of about

1,200 banking and finance terms.

Language of Real Estate. John Reilly. Dearborn Trade Publishing, A Kaplan Professional Co., 155 N Wacker St. Chicago, IL 60606-1719. Phone: 800-921-9621 or (312)836-4400 Fax: (312)836-1021 E-mail: trade@dearborn.com • URL: http://www.dearborntrade.com • 2000. $ 34.65. Fifth edition. Encyclopedia of real estate terms.

Language Translation Service. Entrepreneur Media, Inc., 2445 McCabe Way Irvine, CA 92614. Phone: 800-421-2300 or (949)261-2325 Fax: (949)261-0234 E-mail: entmag@entrepreneur.com • URL: http://www.entrepreneur.com • Looseleaf. $59.50. A practical guide to starting a language translation service. Covers profit potential, start-up costs, market size evaluation, pricing, accounting, advertising, promotion, etc. (Start-Up Business Guide No. E1353.)

Lapidary Journal. Primedia Enthusiast Group, 60 Chestnut Ave., Ste. 201 Devon, PA 19333-1312. Phone: 800-676-4336 or (610)964-6300 Fax: (610)293-1717 E-mail: lapidaryjournal@primediasi.com • URL: http://www.lapidaryjournal.com • Monthly. $29.95

Laptop: Mobile Solutions for Business and Life. Bedford Communications, 1410 Broadway, 21st Floor New York, NY 10018. Phone: (212)807-8220 Fax: (212)807-1098 E-mail: questions@bedfordmags.com • URL: http://www.techworthy.com • Monthly. $18.00 per year. Consumer magazine containing articles and product reviews for notebook/laptop computers, handheld computers, tablet devices, cell phones, digital cameras, and other consumer electronic products.

Laptop: Mobile Solutions for Business and Life. Bedford Communications, Inc., 1410 Broadway, 21st Fl. New York, NY 10018. Phone: 888-270-7652 or (212)807-8220 • URL: http://www.techworthy.com • Monthly. $12.00 per year. Contains informative articles and critical reviews of laptop, notebook, subnotebook, and handheld computers. Includes portable peripheral equipment, such as printers and scanners. Directory information includes company profiles (major manufacturers), product comparison charts, street price guide, list of manufacturers, and list of dealers. Formerly *Laptop Buyer's Guide and Handbook*.

Larousse Encyclopedia of Wine. Christopher Foulkes. Larousse Kingfisher Chambers, Inc. Houghton Mifflin, 215 Park Ave. S New York, NY 10003. Phone: 800-225-3362 or (212)420-5800 Fax: 800-634-7568 or (212)420-5855 • URL: http://www.lkcpub.com • 2001. $45.00. Provides information on major wine producers of the world, with emphasis on French vineyards. Includes statistics and a glossary.

Larson's Employment Discrimination. LexisNexis Matthew Bender, 1275 Broadway Albany, NY 12204. Phone: 800-424-4200 or (518)487-3000 Fax: (518)487-3584 E-mail: bookstore.support@lexisnexis.com • URL: http://www.bender.com • $1,487.00. 10 looseleaf volumes. Treatise on both substantive and procedural law governing employment discrimination based on sex, age, race, religion, national origin, etc.

Laser Biomedical Research Center., Massachusetts Institute of Technology, 77 Massachusetts Ave. Cambridge, MA 02139. Phone: (617)253-7700 Fax: (617)253-4513 E-mail: msfeld@mit.edu Concerned with the medical use of lasers.

Laser Focus World Buyers Guide. Advanced Technology Group, 1 Technology Park Dr., PO Box 989 Westford, MA 01886. Phone: 800-331-4463 or (508)692-0700 Fax: (508)692-0525 E-mail: help@infousa.com • URL: http://www.pennwell.com • Covers: over 2,000 manufacturers, suppliers, and consultants in the laser, fiber optic, electro-optic, optic, and related industries, worldwide. Entries include: Company name, address, phone, fax, e-mail, principal executives, number of employees, list of products and services, brief description of company.

Laser Focus World: The World of Optoelectronics. PennWell Corp., Advanced Technology Div., 98 Spit Brook Rd. Nashua, NH 03062-5737. Phone: 800-331-4463 or (603)891-0123 E-mail: atd@pennwell.com • URL: http://www.pennwell.com • Monthly. $165.00 per year. Covers business and technical aspects of electro-optics, including lasers and fiberoptics. Includes *Buyer's Guide*.

Laser Institute of America., 13501 Ingenuity Dr., No. 128 Orlando, FL 32826. Phone: 800-345-2737 or (407)380-1553 Fax: (407)380-5588 E-mail: webmaster@laserinstitute.org • URL: http://www.laserinstitute.org • Formerly Laser Industry Association.

Lasers: A Guide to the Book Literature. Charles Blain. Nova Science Publishers, Inc., 400 Oser Ave., Suite 1600 Hauppauge, NY 11788-3619. Phone: (631)231-7269 Fax: (631)231-8175 E-mail: novascience@earthlink.net • URL: http://www.novapublishers.com • 2002. $49.00. Provides citations to books on various kinds of lasers: chemical, dye, far infrared, tree-electron, gas, ruby, semiconductor, solid-state, and tunable. Includes author, title, and subject indexes.

Lasers in Surgery and Medicine. John Wiley and Sons, Inc., Journals, 111 River St. Hoboken, NJ 07030. Phone: 800-225-5945 or (201)748-6000 Fax: (201)748-6088 E-mail: customer@wiley.com • URL: http://www.wiley.com • 11 times a year. $1,425.00 per year; with online edition, $1,497.00 per year. Original articles in laser surgery and medicine.

The Last Word. American Consulting Engineers Council, 1015 15th St. NW, 8th Fl. Washington, DC 20005-2605. Phone: (202)347-7474 Fax: (202)898-0068 E-mail: acec@acec.org Description: Contains summaries of Council activities and legislative actions of interest to consulting engineers.

Lateral Thinking: Creativity Step by Step. Edward de Bono. HarperTrade, 10 E. 53rd St. New York, NY 10022. Phone: 800-242-7737 or (212)207-7000 Fax: 800-822-4090 or (212)207-7633 • URL: http://www.harpercollins.com • 1990. $15.00.

Latin America and the Caribbean in the World Economy. United Nations Publications, Two United Nations Plaza, Room DC2-853 New York, NY 10017. Phone: 800-253-9646 or (212)963-8302 Fax: (212)963-3489 E-mail: publications@un.org • URL: http://www.un.org/publications • 1999. $25.00. Discusses trade policy, trade activity, regional integration, and environmental protection issues.

Latin America in Graphs 1994-95: Demographic and Economic Trends. Inter-American Development Bank, 1300 New York Ave., N. W. Washington, DC 20577. Phone: (202)623-1154 Fax: (202)623-3531 E-mail: idb-books@iadb.org • URL: http://www.iadb.org • 1995. $8.00.

Latin American and Caribbean Center-Intercultural Dance and Music Institute., Florida International University, University Park, DM 353 Miami, FL 33199. Phone: (305)348-2894 Fax: (305)348-3593 E-mail: seidel@fiu.edu • URL: http://www.lacc.fiu.edu • Research fields include economic development and trade.

Latin American Business Review. Monterrey Institute of Technology. kGraduate School of Business Administration and Leadership. Haworth Press, Inc., 10 Alice St. Binghamton, NY 13904-1580. Phone: 800-429-6784 or (607)722-5857 Fax: 800-895-0582 or (607)722-1424 E-mail: getinfo@haworthpressinc.com • URL: http://www.haworthpressinc.com • Quarterly. Institutions, $200.00 per year.

Latin American Market Data and Statistics. Euromonitor International, 122 South Michigan Ave., Suite 810 Chicago, IL 60603. Phone: 800-577-3876 or (312)922-1115 Fax: (312)922-1157 E-mail: info@euromonitor.com • URL: http://www.euromonitor.com • 2003. $430.00. Provides demographic, economic, and lifestyle statistics for 43 Latin American countries.

Latin American Market Planning Report. Available from MarketResearch.com, 641 Ave. of the Americas, Third Floor New York, NY 10011. Phone: 800-298-5699 or (212)807-2629 Fax: (212)807-2716 E-mail: order@marketresearch.com • URL: http://www.marketresearch.com • 2000. $750.00.Market research report published by Strategy Research Corporation. Provides results of U. S. Hispanic Market Study covering demographics, product usage, media usage, public opinion issues, and other items.

Latin American Marketing Information Sourcebook. Euromonitor International, 122 South Michigan Ave., Suite 810 Chicago, IL 60603. Phone: 800-577-3876 or (312)922-1115 Fax: (312)922-1157 E-mail: info@euromonitor.com • URL: http://www.euromonitor.com • 2003. $475.00. Lists trade associations, statistical offices, government agencies, special libraries, trade journals, websites, and other sources of business information for the countries of Latin America.

Latin American Studies, Volume I: Multidisciplinary. National Information Services Corp., Wyman Towers, Suite Six, 3100 Saint Paul St. Baltimore, MD 21218. Phone: (410)243-0797 Fax: (410)243-0982 Semiannual. Provides more than 700,000 CD-ROM citations to scholarly literature on a wide variety of Latin American topics, including agriculture, business, demography, economics, government, and politics. Producers are the University of Texas, the University of California, and the Library of Congress.

Latin American Studies, Volume II: Current Affairs and Law. National Information Services Corp., Wyman Towers, Suite Six, 3100 Saint Paul St. Baltimore, MD 21218. Phone: (410)243-0797 Fax: (410)243-0982 Semiannual. Contains a wide variety of information on CD-ROM, from various producers, relating to Latin American business, current events, and legislation. Includes periodical citations and abstracts in *INFO-SOUTH*; the full-text newsletters, *Chronicle of Latin American Economic Affairs, Central America Update*, and *SourceMex*; and other databases. Time periods are typically 1986, 1988, or 1990 to date.

Latin America's Economy: Diversity, Trends, and Conflicts. Eliana Cardoso and Ann Helwege. MIT Press, Five Cambridge Ctr. Cambridge, MA 02142-1493. Phone: 800-356-0343 or (617)253-5646 Fax: (617)253-6779 • URL: http://www.mitpress.mit.edu • 1995. $30.00.

Latin Fund Management. Thomson Media, One State St. Plaza New York, NY 10004. Phone: 800-221-1809 or (212)803-8200 Fax: (212)843-9635 E-mail: custserv@thomsonmedia.com • URL: http://www.thomsonmedia.com • Monthly. $495.00 per year. Newsletter (also available online at www.latinfund.net). Provides news and analysis of Latin American mutual funds, pension funds, and annuities.

Latin Trade: Your Business Source for Latin America. Freedom Publications, Inc., 200 S Biscayne Blvd., Suite 1150 Miami, FL 33131. Phone: 800-783-4903 or (305)358-8373 Fax: (305)358-9166 E-mail: lattrade@aol.com • URL: http://www.latintrade.com • Monthly. $36.00 per year. English and Spanish editions. Covers various aspects of Latin American business and trade, including economic indicators, export-import, finance, commodity news, company profiles, and political developments. Formerly *U.S.-Latin Trade*.

LatinFinance. Latin American Financial Publications, Inc., 2121 Ponce de Leon Blvd., Suite 1020 Coral Gables, FL 33134. Phone: (305)448-6593 Fax: (305)448-0718 10 times a year. $235.00 per year. Includes print and online editions. Covers finance, investment, venture capital, and banking in Latin America.

Laundromat. Entrepreneur Media, Inc., 2445 McCabe Way Irvine, CA 92614. Phone: 800-421-2300 or (949)261-2325 Fax: (949)261-0234 E-mail: entmag@entrepreneur.com • URL: http://www.entrepreneur.com • Looseleaf. $59.50. A practical guide to starting a coin-operated, self-service laundry business. Covers profit potential, start-up costs, market size evaluation, owner's time required, site selection, lease negotiation, pricing, accounting, advertising, promotion, etc. (Start-Up Business Guide No. E1162.)

Law and Banking: Applications. Craig W. Smith. American Bankers Association, 1120 Connecticut Ave., N. W. Washington, DC 20036-3971. Phone: 800-226-5377 or (202)663-5000 Fax: (202)663-7543 E-mail: custserv@aba.com • URL: http://www.aba.com • 1990. $57.00. Third edition. Covers laws pertaining to collections, secured transactions, letters of credit, check processing, collateral, fraud, and default.

Law and Banking: Principles. Kathleen L. Farrell and James C. Conboy. American Bankers Association, 1120 Connecticut Ave., N. W. Washington, DC 20036-3971. Phone: 800-226-5377 or (202)663-5000 Fax: (202)663-7543 E-mail: custserv@aba.com • URL: http://www.aba.com • 2000. Fourth edition. Price on application. Discusses legal issues facing the banking industry.

Law and Contemporary Problems. Duke University, School of Law, P.O. Box 90364 Durham, NC 27708-0364. Phone: (919)613-7101 Fax: (919)613-7231 E-mail: tom@faculty.law.duke.edu • URL: http://www.law.duke.edu/ • Quarterly. $48.00 per year.

Law and Economics Center., George Mason University, School of Law, 3401 N. Fairfax Dr. Arlington, VA 22201-4498. Phone: (703)993-8028 Fax: (703)993-8088 E-mail: fbuckley@gmu.edu • URL: http://www.lawecon.org • Research fields include product liability law.

Law and Legal Information Directory. Gale Cengage Learning, 27500 Drake Rd. Farmington Hills, MI 48331-3535. Phone: 800-877-GALE or (248)699-4253 Fax: 800-414-5043 E-mail: gale.galeord@cengage.com • URL: http://gale.cengage.com • Annual. $440.00. Contains a wide range of sources of legal information, such as associations, law schools, courts, federal agencies, referral services, libraries, publishers, and research centers. There is a separate chapter for each of 23 types of information source or service.

Law and Order Magazine Police Equipment Buyer's Guide. Hendon, Inc., 130 Waukegan Rd., 2nd Fl. Deerfield, IL 60015. Phone: 800-843-9764 or (847)444-3300 Fax: (847)444-3330 E-mail: info@hendonpub.com • URL: http://www.lawandordermag.com • Annual. $15.00. Lists manufacturers, dealers, and distributors of equipment and services for police departments.

Law and Order Magazine: The Magazine for Police Management. Hendon Publishing Co., 130 Waukegan Rd. Deerfield, IL 60015. Phone: 800-843-9764 or (847)444-3300 Fax: (847)444-3333 E-mail: info@hendonpub.com • URL: http://www.hendonpub.com • Monthly. $24.95 per year. Edited for law enforcement officials. Includes special issues on communications, technology, weapons, and uniforms and equipment.

Law Books in Print: Law Books in English Published Throughout the World. Glanville Publishers, Inc., 75 Main St. Dobbs Ferry, NY 10522. Phone: (914)693-8100 Fax: (914)693-0402 E-mail: glanville@oceanalaw • URL: http://www.oceanalaw.com • Triennial. $750.00.

Law Books Published. Glanville Publishers, Inc., 75 Main St. Dobbs Ferry, NY 10522-1601. Phone: (914)693-8100 Fax: (914)693-0402 E-mail: glanville@oceanalaw.com • URL: http://www.oceanalaw.com • Semiannual. $160.00 per year. Supplement to *Law Books in Print*.

Law Dictionary for Non-Lawyers. Daniel Oran. Delmar Learning, 5 Maxwell Dr. Clifton, NY 12065. Phone: 800-347-7707 Fax: 800-487-8488 E-mail: cbutler@delmar.com • URL: http://www.delmarlearning.com • 1999. $31.95. Fourth edition.

Law Enforcement Product News. General Communications, Inc., 100 Garfield St., 3rd. Fl. Denver, CO 80206-5550. Phone: 800-291-3911 or (303)322-6400 Fax: (303)322-0627 E-mail: mlg@great.net • URL: http://www.law-enforcement.com • Bimonthly. Free. Covers new products and equipment for police departments and other law enforcement and correctional agencies.

Law Enforcement Technology. Cygnus Business Media, 1233 Janesville Ave. Fort Atkinson, WI 53538. Phone: 800-308-6397 or (920)563-6388 Fax: (920)563-1707 E-mail: rich.reiff@cygnuspub.com • URL: http://www.cygnusbzb.com • Monthly. $60.00 per year. Covers new products and technologies for police professionals. Includes special issues on weapons, uniforms, communications equipment, computers (hardware-software), vehicles, and enforcement of drug laws.

Law Enforcement Technology Directory. Cygnus Business Media, Inc., 445 Broad Hollow Rd. Melville, NY 11747. Phone: 800-308-6397 or (631)845-2700 Fax: (631)845-2736 E-mail: rich.reiff@cygnuspub.com • URL: http://www.cygnusbzb.com • Annual. $60.00 per year. $6.00 per issue; a directory of products, equipment, services, and technology for police professionals. Includes weapons, uniforms, communications equipment, and software.

Law Firm Governance: Journal of Practice Managment, Development, and Technology. Aspen Publishers, Inc., 1185 Ave. of the Americas New York, NY 10036. Phone: 800-234-1660 or (212)597-0200 Fax: (212)597-0334 E-mail: customer.care@aspenpubl.com • URL: http://www.aspenpublishers.com • Quarterly. $196.00 per year. Covers project management, strategic planning, compensation systems, advertising, etc. Regular columns include "Best Practices," "Technology Trends," and "Professional Development." Formerly *Law Governance Review*.

Law Firm Inc. American Lawyer Media, Inc., 105 Madison Ave. New York, NY 10016. Phone: 800-888-8300 or (212)779-9200 Fax: (212)481-8110 E-mail: lawcatalog@amlaw.com • URL: http://www.lawcatalog.com/ • Quarterly. $49.95 per year. Covers human resources, insurance, financing, marketing, compensation, recruitment, etc., as related to law firm management.

Law Firm Partnership and Benefits Report. American Lawyer Media, Inc., 105 Madison Ave. New York, NY 10016. Phone: 800-888-8300 or (212)779-9200 Fax: (212)481-8110 E-mail: lawcatalog@amlaw.com • URL: http://www.lawcatalog.com/ • Monthly. $215.00 per year. Newsletter. Covers personnel issues for law firms, including compensation, partnership agreements, malpractice, employment discrimination, training, health insurance, pension plans, and other matters relating to human resources management. (A Law Journal Newsletter, formerly published by Leader Publications).

Law Firms Yellow Book: Who's Who in the Management of the Leading U. S. Law Firms. Leadership Directories, Inc., 104 Fifth Ave. New York, NY 10011. Phone: (212)627-4140 Fax: (212)645-0931 E-mail: info@leadershipdirectories.com • URL: http://www.leadershipdirectories.com • Semiannual. $265.00 per year. Provides detailed information on more than 850 major U. S. law firms. Includes domestic offices, foreign offices, subsidiaries, and affiliates. There are seven indexes: geographic, subject specialty, management, administrative, law school attended, personnel, and law firm.

Law for Business. John Ashcroft and Janet Ashcroft. South-Western, 5101 Natrop Blvd. Mason, OH 45040. Phone: 800-543-0487 or (513)229-1000 • URL: http://www.swcollege.com • 2001. $82.95. 14th edition. (Business Law Series).

The Law in (Plain English) for Small Businesses. Leonard D. DuBoff. Allworth Press, 10 E 23rd St., Ste. 510 New York, NY 10010. Phone: 800-491-2808 or (212)777-8395 Fax: (212)777-8261 E-mail: pub@allworth.com • URL: http://www.allworth.com • 1998. $19.95. Third revised edition. Discusses and explains legal issues relating to the organization, financing, and operation of a small business.

The Law of Associations: An Operating Legal Manual for Executives and Counsel. George D. Webster, editor. LexisNexis Matthew Bender, 1275 Broadway Albany, NY 12204. Phone: 800-424-4200 or (518)487-3000 Fax: (518)487-3584 E-mail: bookstore.support@lexisnexis.com • URL: http://www.bender.com • Annual. $301.00. Looseleaf service. Coverage of all legal and tax aspects of non-profit associations.

The Law of Distressed Real Estate: Foreclosure, Workouts, and Procedures. West Group, 610 Opperman Dr. Eagan, MN 55123. Phone: 800-328-4880 or (651)687-7000 Fax: 800-340-9378 E-mail: bookstore@westgroup.com • URL: http://www.westgroup.com • $956.00. Five looseleaf volumes. Periodic supplementation. (Real Property LawSeries).

Law of Federal Estate and Gift Taxation-Code Commentary. West Group, 610 Opperman Dr. Eagan, MN 55123. Phone: 800-328-4880 or (651)687-7000 Fax: 800-340-9378 E-mail: bookstore@westgroup.com • URL: http://www.westgroup.com • Annual. $177.00. Looseleaf service.

The Law of Fundraising. Bruce R. Hopkins. John Wiley and Sons, Inc., 111 River St. Hoboken, NJ 07030. Phone: 800-225-5945 or (201)748-6000 Fax: (201)748-6088 E-mail: info@wiley.com • URL: http://www.wiley.com • 2002. $170.00. Third edition. Annual supplements available. Covers all aspects of state and federal nonprofit fund-raising law. Includes summaries of the relevant laws and regulations of each state. (Nonprofit Law, Finance and Management Series).

The Law of Juries. Nancy Gertner and Judith Mizner. Glasser Legalworks, 150 Clove Rd. Little Falls, NJ 07424. Phone: 800-308-1700 or (973)890-0008 Fax: (973)890-0042 E-mail: orders@glasserlegalworks.com • URL: http://www.glasserlegalworks.com • Looseleaf. $124.00. Periodic supplementation. Topics include voir dire & juror selection, peremptory challenges, trial location (venue), jury structure, jury deliberation, and jury conduct or misconduct.

The Law of Liability Insurance. LexisNexis Matthew Bender, 1275 Broadway Albany, NY 12204. Phone: 800-424-4200 or (518)487-3000 Fax: (518)487-3584 E-mail: bookstore.support@lexisnexis.com • URL: http://www.bender.com • $1,451.00. Five looseleaf volumes. Periodic supplementation. Explains the terms and phases essential for a general understanding of liability insurance, and discusses injuries to both persons and property.

Law of Professional and Amateur Sports. West Group, 610 Opperman Dr. Eagan, MN 55123. Phone: 800-328-4880 or (651)687-7000 Fax: 800-340-9378 E-mail: bookstore@westgroup.com • URL: http://www.westgroup.com • Annual. $345.00 per year. Three looseleaf volumes. Covers agent-player agreements, collective bargaining, negotiation of player contracts, taxation, and other topics.

Law of Tax-Exempt Organizations. Bruce R. Hopkins. John Wiley and Sons, Inc., 111 River St. Hoboken, NJ 07030. Phone: 800-225-5945 or (201)748-6000 Fax: (201)748-6088 E-mail: info@wiley.com • URL: http://www.wiley.com • 2003. $210.00. Eighth edition.

Law of the Sea: A Select Bibliography. United Nations Publications, Two United Nations Plaza, Room DC2-853 New York, NY 10017. Phone: 800-253-9646 or (212)963-8302 Fax: (212)963-3489 E-mail: publications@un.org • URL: http://www.un.org/publications • Annual. $17.00. Includes 23 subject categories.

Law of the Sea Bulletin. United Nations Publications, United Nations Concourse Level, First Ave., 46th St. New York, NY 10017. Phone: 800-533-3210 or (212)963-7680 Fax: (212)963-4910 E-mail: bookstore@un.org • URL: http://www.un.org/publications • Three times per year. $15.00 per issue. $40.00 per year.

Law of the Super Searchers: The Online Secrets of Top Legal Researchers. T. R. Halvorson. Information Today, Inc., 143 Old Marlton Pike Medford, NJ 08055-8750. Phone: 800-300-9868 or (609)654-6266 Fax: (609)654-4309 E-mail: custserv@infotoday.com • URL: http://www.infotoday.com • 1999. $24.95. Eight law researchers explain how to find useful legal information online. (Super Searchers Series).

Law of the Workplace: Rights of Employers and Employees. James Hunt and Patricia Strongin. BNA, Inc., Bureau of National Affairs, Inc., 1231 25th St., NW Washington, DC 20037. Phone: 800-372-1033 E-mail: customercare@bna.com • URL: http://www.bna.com • 1994. $45.00. Third edition. Wages, hours, working conditions, benefits, and so forth.

Law Technology News: Products, Systems, and Services for Legal Professionals. American Lawyer Media, Inc., 105 Madison Ave. New York, NY 10016. Phone: 800-888-8300 or (212)779-9200 Fax: (212)481-8110 E-mail: lawcatalog@amlaw.com • URL: http://www.lawcatalog.com/ • Monthly. $69.00 per year. Features descriptions of new technology products and services of interest to the legal profession.

Law.com: First in Legal News and Information. American Lawyer Media, Inc.Phone: 800-888-8300 or (212)779-9200 Fax: (212)481-8110 • URL: http://www.law.com • Web site provides free, law-related, current news (National News Sites and Regional News Sites). Free searching of martindale.com lawyer locator is offered, including lawyer ratings. Fee-based premium services for the legal profession are also available.

Lawmaking and the Legislative Process: Committees, Connections, and Compromises. Greenwood Publishing Group, Inc., 88 Post Rd., W. Westport, CT 06881. Phone: 800-225-5800 or (203)226-3571 Fax: (203)431-2214 E-mail: customer-service@greenwood.com • URL: http://www.greenwood.com • 1996. $29.95. Explains how bills are enacted into laws through the state legislative process. Provides step-by-step examples, using fictitious bills.

Lawn and Garden Market. Available from MarketResearch.com, 641 Ave. of the Americas, Third Floor New York, NY 10011. Phone: 800-298-5699 or (212)807-2629 Fax: (212)807-2716 E-mail: order@marketresearch.com • URL: http://www.marketresearch.com • 2003. $3,000.00. Published by Packaged Facts. Provides market data on garden equipment, fertilizers and other substances, and professional lawn care services.

Lawn and Landscape Magazine. Group Interest Enterprises. G.I.E., Publishers Inc., 4012 Bridge Ave. Cleveland, OH 44113-3320. Phone: 800-456-0707 or (216)961-4130 Fax: (216)961-0364 E-mail: pmorales@gie.net • URL: http://www.lawnandlandscape.com • Monthly. $30.00 per year. Supplement available. Formerly *Lawn and Landscape Maintenance*.

Lawn Care Service. Entrepreneur Media, Inc., 2445 McCabe Way Irvine, CA 92614. Phone: 800-421-2300 or (949)261-2325 Fax: (949)261-0234 E-mail: entmag@entrepreneur.com • URL: http://www.entrepreneur.com • Looseleaf. $59.50. A practical guide to starting a lawn care business. Covers profit potential, start-up costs, market size evaluation, owner's time required, pricing, accounting, advertising, promotion, etc. (Start-Up Business Guide No. E1198.)

Lawn Institute., 2 E Main St. East Dundee, IL 60118. Phone: 800-405-8873 or (847)649-5555 Fax: (847)649-5678 E-mail: info@thelawninstitue.org • URL: http://www.lawninstitute.com • Producers of lawn seed and lawn products. "Seeks to help bridge the gap between professional research and an increasingly sophisticated consumer." Promotes better lawns through use of quality materials, research, and education.

The Laws of Innkeepers: For Hotels, Motels, Restaurants, and Clubs. John E. Sherry. Cornell University Press, Sage House, 512 E. State St. Ithaca, NY 14851. Phone: 800-666-2211 E-mail: store@cornell.edu • URL: http://www.cornellpress.cornell.edu • 1993. $49.95. Third edition.

Lawyer-Pilots Bar Association., PO Box 1510 Edgewater, MD 21037. Phone: (410)571-1750 Fax: (410)571-1780 E-mail: lpba@lan2wan.com • URL: http://www.lpba.org • Lawyers who are licensed pilots and engaged in the practice of aviation law or interested in aviation. Is concerned with law, safety, and general aviation.

The Lawyer's Almanac; An Encyclopedia of Information about Law, Lawyers, and the Profession. Aspen Law, 7201 McKinney Cir. Frederick, MD 21701. Phone: 800-234-1660 Annual. $144.00. List of the 250 largest law firms.

The Lawyers Competitive Edge: The Journal of Law Office Economics and Management. West Group, 610 Opperman Dr. Eagan, MN 55123. Phone: 800-328-4880 or (651)687-7000 Fax: 800-340-9378 E-mail: bookstore@westgroup.com • URL: http://www.westgroup.com • Monthly. $322.00 per year. Newsletter.

Lawyers' List. Commercial Publishing Company Inc., 8706 Commerce Dr., PO Box 2430 Easton, MD 21601. Phone: 800-824-9911 or (410)820-8089 Fax: (410)820-4474 E-mail: info@thelawyerslist.com • URL: http://www.thelawyerslist.com • Covers: about 2,500 lawyers in general, corporate, trial, patent, trademark, and copywrite practices internationally. Entries include: Firm name, address, phone, fax, e-mail, web-site, areas of practice, branch offices, names of representative clients, names of partners and associates. A general law list. See separate listing, 'Law Lists'.

Lawyer's Register International by Specialties and Fields of Law Including a Directory of Corporate Counsel. Lawyer's Register Publishing Co., 26310 Emery Rd. Cleveland, OH 44128. Phone: 800-477-6345 or (216)591-1492 Fax: (216)591-0265 E-mail: editor@lawyersregister.com Annual. $359.00. Three volumes. Referral source for law firms.

LC MARC: Books. U. S. Library of Congress, Cataloging Distribution Service Washington, DC 20541-4912. Phone: 800-255-3666 or (202)707-6100 Fax: (202)707-1334 Contains online bibliographic records for over five million books cataloged by the Library of Congress since 1968. Updating is weekly or monthly. Inquire as to online cost and availability. (MARC is machine readable cataloging.)

LD & A: (Lighting Design and Application). Illuminating Engineering Society of North America, 120 Wall St., 17th Fl. New York, NY 10005-4001. Phone: (212)248-5000 Fax: (212)248-5017 E-mail: iesna@iesna.org • URL: http://www.iesna.org • Monthly. $39.00 per year. Information on current events, products, projects and people in the lighting industry.

LDB Interior Textiles. EW Williams Publications Co., 2125 Center Ave., Suite 305 Fort Lee, NJ 07024-5898. Phone: (201)592-7007 Fax: (201)592-7171 E-mail: webeditor@wwwpi.com • URL: http://www.williamspublications.com • Monthly. $66.00 per year. Supplement available *Linens, Domestics and Baths-Interior Textile Annual Buyer's Guide*. Formerly *Interior Textiles*.

LDB Interior Textiles Annual Buyers' Guide. E.W. Williams Publications Co., 2125 Center Ave., Ste. 305 Fort Lee, NJ 07024-5898. Phone: (201)592-7007 Fax: (201)592-7171 E-mail: philpl@ewwpi.com • URL: http://www.williamspublications.com • Covers: Over 3,000 manufacturers, importers, and suppliers of home fashions products and services, decorative fabric converters, and alternative window coverings; fabricators; manufacturer's representatives; and others allied to the home fashions trade. Entries include: For manufacturers, importers, converters, fabricators, and suppliers—Company name, address, phone, fax, contact, product line. For manufacturer's representatives—Name, address, phone, contact, lines carried. For others—Name, address, phone, fax.

Lead and Zinc Statistics. International Lead and Zinc Study Group, Two King St. London SW1Y 6QP, United Kingdom. Phone: 44 20 7484 3300 Fax: 44 20 7930 4635 E-mail: sales@ilzsg.org • URL: http://www.ilzsg.org • Monthly. $390.00 per year. Supplement available *Advance Data Service*. Text in English and French.

The Leader of the Future: New Essays by World-Class Leaders and Thinkers. Frances Hesselbein. John Wiley and Sons, Inc, 111 River St. Hoboken, NJ 07030. Phone: 800-225-5945 or (201)748-6000 Fax: (201)748-6088 E-mail: info@wiley.com • URL: http://www.wiley.com • 2000. $16.50. Contains articles on leadership by "executives, consultants, and commentators." (Management Series).

Leader to Leader. Peter F. Drucker Foundation for Nonprofit Management. Jossey-Bass, 989 Market St. San Francisco, CA 94103-1741. Phone: 888-378-2537 or (415)433-1740 Fax: 800-605-2665 or (415)433-0499 E-mail: jbsubs@jbp.com • URL: http://www.josseybass.com • Quarterly. Institutions, $199.00 per year. Contains articles on "management, leadership, and strategy" written by "leading executives, thinkers, and consultants." Covers both business and nonprofit issues.

Leaders of American Business and Industry. Gale Cengage Learning, 27500 Drake Rd. Farmington Hills, MI 48331-3535. Phone: 800-877-GALE or (248)699-4253 Fax: 800-414-5043 E-mail: gale.galeord@cengage.com • URL: http://gale.cengage.com • 2002. $145.00. Three volumes. Provides popularly written biographies of influential American entrepreneurs and business leaders, past and present. Includes detailed profiles of major companies. (UXL imprint).

Leadership Conference on Civil Rights., 1629 K St., N.W., Suite 1010 Washington, DC 20006. Phone: (202)466-3311 Fax: (202)466-3435 E-mail: webmaster@civilrights.org • URL: http://www.civilrights.org • Formerly Civil Rights Mobilization.

Leadership Library on CD-ROM: Who's Who in the Leadership of the United States. Leadership Directories, Inc., 104 Fifth Ave. New York, NY 10011. Phone: (212)627-4140 Fax: (212)645-0931 E-mail: info@leadershipdirectories.com • URL: http://www.leadershipdirectories.com • Quarterly. Including access to Internet version (weekly updates). Contains all 14 *Yellow Book* personnel directories on CD-ROM, providing contact and brief biographical information for about 400,000 individuals. Covers business, government, financial institutions, news media, law firms, associations, foreign representatives, and nonprofit organizations. Includes photographs.

Leadership Strategies: The Tools to Help You Lead Effectively. Briefings Publishing Group, 1101 King St., Suite 110 Alexandria, VA 22314. Phone: (703)548-3800 Fax: (703)684-2136 E-mail: customerservice@briefings.com • URL: http://www.briefings.com • Monthly. Free to qualified personnel. Newsletter. Includes concise articles on change management, delegation of authority, team building, conflict resolution, and other leadership topics.

Leadership: Theory and Practice. Peter G. Northouse. Sage Publications, Inc., 2455 Teller Rd. Thousand Oaks, CA 91320. Phone: 800-818-7243 or (805)499-9774 Fax: 800-583-2665 or (805)499-0871 E-mail: webmaster@sagepub.com • URL: http://www.sagepub.com • 2003. $42.95. Third edition. Considers the strengths and criticisms of specific leadership approaches, such as trait, style, situational, transformational, psychodynamic, path-goal, and others.

Leading Economic Indicators and Related Composite Indexes. The Conference Board, 845 Third Ave. New York, NY 10022. Phone: (212)339-0345 Fax: (212)836-9740 • URL: http://www.conference-board.org • Monthly. $24.00 per year. Shows monthly changes in the composite indexes of leading, coincident, and lagging economic indicators, formerly computed by the U. S. Department of Commerce. Tables present monthly data for up to 10 years, with a one-page line chart covering 18 years. (The Conference Board News.)

Leadscan: A Review of Recent Technical Literature on the Uses of lead and its Products. Clive Larson,ed. C and C Associates, Glebe House, 12 Parkside Green Meanwood,Leeds LS6 4NY 44, England. Quarterly. $110.00 per year. Provides technical articles and abstracts of recent technical and market related literature on lead and its uses.

League of Advertising Agencies.

League of American Theatres and Producers., 226 W. 47th St. New York, NY 10036. Phone: (212)764-1122 or (212)703-0200 Fax: (212)719-4389 E-mail: league@broadway.org • URL: http://www.broadway.org • Members are legitimate theater producers and owners and operators of legitimate theaters. Formerly League of New York Theatres and Producers.

League of Revolutionaries for a New America., PO Box 477113 Chicago, IL 60647. Phone: 800-691-6888 or (773)486-0028 Fax: (773)486-1728 E-mail: info@lrna.org • URL: http://www.lrna.org • Works toward a vision of a cooperative world where the full potential of all can contribute to the good of everyone.

League of Women Voters Education Fund., 1730 M St., N. W., Suite 1000 Washington, DC 20036-4508. Phone: (202)429-1965 Fax: (202)429-0854 E-mail: lwv@lwv.org • URL: http://www.lwv.org • Research fields include federal deficit issues.

Lean Manufacturing Advisor: Techniques and Technologies Supporting Lean Manufacturing and TPM. Productivity, Inc, 100 Commerce Dr., Ste. 120 Shelton, CT 06484-6220. Phone: 800-394-6868 or (203)225-0451 Fax: 800-394-6286 or (203)225-0771 E-mail: info@productivityinc.com • URL: http://www.productivityinc.com • Monthly. $167.00 per year. Formerly Productivity.

The Leap: A Memoir of Love and Madness in the Internet Gold Rush. Tom Ashbrook. Houghton Mifflin Co., 222 Berkeley St. Boston, MA 02116. Phone: 800-733-2828 or (617)351-5000 Fax: 800-733-2098 E-mail: inquiries@hmco.com • URL: http://www.hmco.com • 2000. $25.00. The author relates his personal and family tribulations while attempting to obtain financing for an eventually successful e-business startup, HomePortfolio.com.

Learn to Earn: An Introduction to the Basics of Investing and Business. Peter Lynch and John Rothchild. Simon & Schuster Trade, 1230 Ave. of the Americas New York, NY 10020. Phone: 800-223-2348 or (212)698-7000 Fax: 800-943-9831 or (212)698-7007 E-mail: consumer.customerservie@simonandschuster.com • URL: http://www.simonsays.com • 1996. $14.00.

Learned Publishing. Association of Learned and Professional Society Publishers, South House, The Street, Clapham, Worthing West Sussex BN13 3UU, England. Phone: 44 1903 871686 Fax: 44 1903 871457 E-mail: sec-gen@alpsp.org.uk • URL: http://www.alpsp.org.uk • Quarterly. Members, $60.00 per year; non-members, $80.00 per year; institutions, $170.00 per year. Articles and news of interest to publishers of academic and learned society material. Formerly *ALPSP Bulletin*.

Learning and Motivation. Elsevier, 655 Avenue of the Americas New York, NY 10010-5107. Phone: 800-366-2665 or (212)989-5800 Fax: 800-366-2665 or (212)633-3680 E-mail: custserv@elsevier.com • URL: http://www.elsevier.com • Quarterly. Individuals, $241.00 per year; institutions, $519.00 per year; students, $121.00 per year.

Learning Java. Patrick Niemeyer and Jonathon Knudsen. O'Reilly & Associates, Inc., 90 Sherman St. Cambridge, MA 02140. Phone: 800-775-7731 or (617)354-5800 Fax: (617)661-1116 E-mail: order@oreilly.com • URL: http://www.oreilly.com • 2002. $44.95. Second edition. Includes CD-ROM. Covers the essentials for programmers beginning to use Java.

Learning Web Design: A Beginner's Guide to HTML, Graphics, and Beyond. Jennifer Niederst. O'Reilly & Associates, Inc., 90 Sherman St. Cambridge, MA 02140. Phone: 800-775-7731 or (617)354-5800 Fax: (617)661-1116 E-mail: order@oreilly.com • URL: http://www.oreilly.com • 2001. $34.95. Written for beginners who have no previous knowledge of how Web design works.

Leasing Sourcebook: The Directory of the U. S. Capital Equipment Leasing Industry. Bibliotechnology Systems and Publishing Co., P.O. Box 657 Lincoln, MA 01773. Phone: (781)259-0524 Fax: (781)259-9861 E-mail: bibliotech@leasingsourcebook.com Every 12-18 months. $135.00. Lists approximately 5,200 capital equipment leasing companies.

Least Developed Countries. United Nations Publications, United Nations Concourse Level, First Ave., 46th St. New York, NY 10017. Phone: 800-533-3210 or (212)963-7680 Fax: (212)963-4910 E-mail: bookstore@un.org • URL: http://www.un.org/publications • Annual. $45.00 Report on least developed countries compiled by the United Nations Conference on Trade and Development (UNCTAD). Contains basic data.

Leather Industries of America., 1900 L St., NW, Ste 710 Washington, DC 20036. Phone: (202)296-4806 Fax: (202)296-7882 E-mail: info@leatherusa.com • URL: http://www.leatherusa.com • Formerly Tanners' Council of America.

Leather Industries Statistics. Leather Industries of America, 1900 L St., NW, Ste., 710 Washington, DC 20036. Phone: (202)296-4806 Fax: (202)296-7892 E-mail: info@leatherusa.com • URL: http://www.leatherusa.com • Annual. Free to members; non-members, $30.00. Provides detailed analysis of domestic and foreign trade.

Leather Manufacturer. Shoe Trades Publishing Co., 61 Massachusetts Ave. Arlington, MA 02474. Phone: (514)744-5858 Fax: (514)744-6377 E-mail: info@shoetrades.com Monthly. $40.00 per year. Edited for hide processors, tanners and leather finishers in the U.S. and Canada.

Leather Manufacturer Directory. Shoe Trades Publishing Co., 241 Senneville Rd. Senneville, QC, Canada H9X 3X5. Phone: 800-973-7463 or (514)457-8787 Fax: (514)457-5832 E-mail: books@shoetrades.com Covers: Tanneries, leather finishers, and hide processors and their suppliers in the United States and Canada. Entries include: Company name, address, phone, names of executives, list of products or services and over 300 companies classified by their goods and services.

Leather Research Laboratory.

Ledger Quarterly: A Financial Review for Community Association Practitioners. Community Associations Institute, 225 Reinekers Lane, Suite 300 Alexandria, VA 22314. Phone: (703)548-8600 Fax: (703)836-6907 • URL: http://www.caionline.org • Quarterly. $67.00 per year. Newsletter. Provides current information on issues affecting the finances of condominium, cooperative, homeowner, apartment, and other community housing associations.

Legal Aspects of AIDS. West Group, 610 Opperman Dr. Eagan, MN 55123. Phone: 800-328-4880 or (651)687-7000 Fax: 800-340-9378 E-mail: bookstore@westgroup.com • URL: http://www.westgroup.com • Annual. $254.50 per year. Looseleaf service. Includes issue employment discrimination, housing discrimination, and insurance. This work also "traces the historical progression of the disease and its spread."

Legal Assistant's Handbook. Thomas W. Brunner and others. BNA, Inc., Bureau of National Affairs, Inc., 1231 25th St., NW Washington, DC 20037. Phone: 800-372-1033 E-mail: customercare@bna.com • URL: http://www.bna.com • 1988. $44.00. Second edition.

Legal Ethics in the Practice of Law. Richard A. Zitrin and Carol M. Langford. LexisNexis Matthew Bender, 1275 Broadway Albany, NY 12204-4026. Phone: 800-424-4200 or (518)487-3000 Fax: 800-828-8341 or (518)487-3584 E-mail: customer.support@lexisnexis.com • URL: http://www.lexisnexis.com/matthewbender/ • 2002. $57.00. Provides "real-life examples of ethical dilemmas" occurring in the law profession.

Legal Forms for Starting and Running a Small Business. Fred Steingold. Nolo Press, 950 Parker St. Berkeley, CA 94710. Phone: 800-992-6656 or (510)549-1976 Fax: 800-645-0895 or (510)548-5902 E-mail: simone@nolo.com • URL: http://www.nolo.com • 2004. $29.99. Third edition.

Legal Guide to Independent Contractor Status. Robert W. Wood. Aspen Publishers, Inc., 200 Orchard Ridge Dr., Ste. 200 Gaithersburg, MD 20878. Phone: 800-234-1660 or (301)417-1700 E-mail: customer.service@aspenpubl.com • URL: http://www.aspenpublishers.com • 2003. Price on application. A guide to the legal and tax-related differences between employers and independent contractors. Includes examples of both "safe" and "troublesome" independent contractor designations. Penalties and fines are discussed.

Legal Information Alert: What's New in Legal Publications, Databases, and Research Techniques. Donna T. Heroy, editor. Alert Publications, Inc., 401 W Fullerton Pky., Ste. 1403E Chicago, IL 60614-3857. Phone: (773)525-7594 Fax: (773)525-7015 E-mail: info@alertpub.com • URL: http://www.alertpub.com • 10 times per year. $179.00 per year. Newsletter for law librarians and legal information specialists.

Legal Information: How to Find It, How to Use It. Kent Olson. Greenwood Publishing Group, Inc., 88 Post Rd., W. Westport, CT 06881. Phone: 800-225-5800 or (203)226-3571 Fax: (203)431-2214 E-mail: customer-service@greenwood.com • URL: http://www.greenwood.com • 1998. $64.95. Includes CD-ROM. Recommends sources for various kinds of legal information.

Legal-Legislative Reporter News Bulletin. International Foundation of Employee Benefit Plans, Inc., 18700 W. Bluemound Rd. Brookfield, WI 53008-0069. Phone: 888-334-3327 or (262)786-6700 Fax: 888-217-5960 or (262)786-8670 E-mail: books@infocenter.org • URL: http://www.ifebp.org • Monthly. $190.00 per year. Review of legislative developments, court cases, arbitration awards and administrative decisions of importance.

Legal Liability Problems in Cyberspace: Craters in the Information Highway. T. R. Halvorson. Burwell Enterprises, 5619 Plumtree Dr. Dallas, TX 75252. Phone: (972)-732-0160 Fax: (972)733-1951 E-mail: helen@burwellinc.com • URL: http://www.burwellinc.com • 1998. $24.50. Covers the legal risks and liabilities involved in doing online research as a paid professional. Includes a table of cases.

Legal Looseleafs in Print. Arlene L. Eis, editor. Infosources Publishing, 140 Norma Rd. Teaneck, NJ 07666. Phone: (201)836-7072 Fax: (201)836-7072 E-mail: aeis@carroll.com • URL: http://www.infosourcespub.com • 2001. $106.00. Lists over 3,600 titles by more than 250 publishers.

Legal Malpractice: Liability, Prevention, Litigation, Insurance. Ronald E. Mallen and Jeffrey M. Smith. West Group, 610 Opperman Dr. Eagan, MN 55123. Phone: 800-338-9424 or (651)687-7000 Fax: 800-340-9378 E-mail: bookstore@westgroup.com • URL: http://www.westgroup.com • 2000. Fifth edition. Five volumes. Periodic supplementation.

Legal Reference Services Quarterly. Haworth Press, Inc., 10 Alice St. Binghamton, NY 13904-1580. Phone: 800-429-6784 or (607)722-5857 Fax: 800-895-0582 or (607)722-1424 E-mail: getinfo@haworthpressinc.com • URL: http://www.haworth.pressinc.com • Quarterly. Institutions, $225.00 per year.

Legal Research and Law Library Management. American Lawyer Media, Inc., 105 Madison Ave. New York, NY 10016. Phone: 800-888-8300 or (212)779-9200 Fax: (212)481-8110 E-mail: lawcatalog@amlaw.com • URL: http://www.lawcatalog.com/ • Looseleaf. $169.00. Updated as needed. Covers the planning and operation of libraries for law firms, including personnel selection and selection of books, periodicals, online services, microforms, and other materials. (Law Journal Press).

Legal Resource Index. Gale Cengage Learning, 27500 Drake Rd. Farmington Hills, MI 48331-3535. Phone: 800-877-GALE or (248)699-GALE Fax: 800-414-5043 E-mail: galeord@gale.com • URL: http://gale.cengage.com • Broad coverage of law literature appearing in legal, business, and other periodicals, 1980 to date. Daily updates. Inquire as to online cost and availability.

Legal Systems of the World: A Political, Social, and Cultural Encyclopedia. Herbert M. Kritzer, editor. ABC-CLIO, Inc., 130 Cremona Drive Santa Barbara, CA 93117. Phone: 800-368-6868 or (805)968-1911 Fax: (805)685-9685 E-mail: sales@abc-clio.com • URL: http://www.abc-clio.com • 2002. $385.00. Four volumes. Describes how the courts and legal systems operate in many different countries.

Legal Thesaurus-Dictionary. William P. Statsky. West Publishing Co., College and School Div., 610 Opperman Dr. Eagan, MN 55123. Phone: 800-328-2209 or (651)687-7000 Fax: (651)687-6857 E-mail: customerservice@westgroup.com • URL: http://www.westgroup.com • 1985. $37.75. Second edition.

Legal Times. American Lawyer Media, L.P., 1730 M St., N.W., Ste. 802 Washington, DC 20036. Phone: 800-888-8300 or (202)457-0686 Fax: (202)457-0718 E-mail: legaltimes@legaltimes.com • URL: http://www.americanlawyermedia.com • Weekly. Individuals, $249.00 per year; institutions, $635.00 per year.

Legal Times: Law and Lobbying in the Nation's Capital. American Lawyer Media, Inc., 105 Madison Ave. New York, NY 10016. Phone: 800-888-8300 or (212)779-9200 Fax: (212)481-8110 E-mail: lawcatalog@amlaw.com • URL: http://www.lawcatalog.com/ • Weekly. $318.00 per year. Published in Washington, DC. Provides news relating to lawyers and the federal government. Special features cover a variety of topics relating to law firm administration.

LegalTrac. Gale Cengage Learning, 27500 Drake Rd. Farmington Hills, MI 48331-3535. Phone: 800-877-GALE or (248)699-GALE Fax: 800-414-5043 or (248)699-8069 E-mail: galeord@gale.com • URL: http://gale.cengage.com • Monthly. $5,000.00 per year. Price includes workstation. Provides CD-ROM indexing of periodical literature relating to legal matters from 1980 to date. Corresponds to online *Legal Resource Index*.

Legislative Process. Abner J. Mikva and Eric Lane. Aspen Publishers, Inc., 200 Orchard Ridge Dr., Ste. 200 Gaithersburg, MD 20878. Phone: 800-234-1660 or (301)417-7500 E-mail: customer.service@aspenpubl.com • URL: http://www.aspenpublishers.com • 2002. $56.00. Second edition.

Legislative Reference Services and Sources. Kathleen Low. Haworth Press, Inc., 10 Alice St. Binghamton, NY 13904-1580. Phone: 800-429-6784 or (607)722-5857 Fax: 800-895-0582 or (607)722-1424 E-mail: getinfo@haworthpressinc.com • URL: http://www.haworthpressinc.com • 1994. $39.95. Describes more than 100 reference sources that are frequently consulted in providing information to legislators and their staffs. Includes a discussion of online services used for legislative reference. (Library and Information Science Series).

Leisure, Recreation, and Tourism Abstracts. Available from CABI Publishing North America, 875 Massachusetts Ave. Cambridge, MA 02139. Phone: 800-528-4841 or (617)395-4056 Fax: (617)354-6875 E-mail: cabi-nao@cabi.org • URL: http://www.cabi-publishing.org • Quarterly. Members, $280.00 per year; Institutions, $610.00 per year. Includes single site internet access. Published in England by CABI Publishing. Provides coverage of the worldwide literature of travel, recreation, sports, and the hospitality industry. Emphasis is on research.

Lender Liability Law Report. RIA, 395 Hudson St. New York, NY 10014-3669. Phone: 800-950-1216 or (212)367-6300 Fax: (212)337-4207 E-mail: acec@acec.org • URL: http://www.aspratt.com • Description: Discusses the impact of relevant cases and legislation on lenders and spotlights legal landmines which lenders may encounter. Recurring features include summaries of recent cases and avoidance techniques.

Leonard Davis Institute of Health Economics., University of Pennsylvania, 3641 Locust Walk Philadelphia, PA 19104-6218. Phone: (215)898-1655 Fax: (215)898-0229 E-mail: levyj@wharton.upenn.edu • URL: http://www.upenn.edu/ldi/ • Research fields include health care management and cost-quality trade-offs.

Leonard's Annual Price Index of Art Auctions. Auction Index, Inc., 30 Valentine Pk. Newton, MA 02465. Phone: (617)964-2867 Fax: (617)969-9912 Annual. $245.00. List major auction houses.

Les Nouvelles. Licensing Executives Society International, c/o Jack Stuart Ott, 1444 W 10th St., No. 403 Cleveland, OH 44113. Phone: (216)241-3940 Fax: (216)566-9267 E-mail: acec@acec.org • URL: http://www.usa-canada.les.org • Description: Concerned with technological licensing and related subjects. Covers technology, patents, trademarks, and licensing "know-how" world-wide.

Lesko's Info-PowerIII: Over 45,000 Free and Low Cost Sources of Information. Information U.S.A. Inc., P.O. Box E Kensington, MD 20895-0418. Phone: 800-955-7693 or (301)924-0556 Fax: (301)929-8907 1996. $39.95. Third edition.

Lesly's Handbook of Public Relations and Communications. Philip Lesly. McGraw-Hill, 1221 Ave. of the Americas New York, NY 10020. Phone: 800-722-4726 or (212)512-2000 Fax: (212)512-4502 E-mail: customer.service@mcgraw-hill.com • URL: http://www.mcgraw-hill.com • 1997. $100.00. Fifth edition.

Lessons to be Learned Just in Time. James J. Cammarano. Engineering and Management Press, 25 Technology Park Norcross, GA 30092-2988. Phone: 800-494-0460 or (770)449-0461 Fax: (770)441-3295 E-mail: cmagee@www.iienet.org • URL: http://www.iienet.org • 1997. $34.95. Discusses the background, theory, and practical application of just-in-time (JIT) inventory control in manufacturing.

The Levy Institute Forecast. Forecasting Center, Blithewood, Bard College Annandale on Hudson, NY 12504-5000. Phone: 888-244-8617 or (845)758-7700 Fax: (845)758-1149 E-mail: info@levy.org Description: Provides analyses and forecasts of U.S. business conditions. Reports on production, sales, inflation, corporate profits, and interest rates.

Lexique General; A General Lexicon of Terms-United Nations as Well as General-Used by Translators, Interpreters, etc. United Nations Publications, United Nations Concourse Level, First Ave., 46th St. New York, NY 10017. Phone: 800-533-3210 or (212)963-7680 Fax: (212)963-4910 E-mail: bookstore@un.org • URL: http://www.un.org/publications • 1991. Fourth edition.

LEXIS. LEXIS-NEXIS, Post Office Box 933 Dayton, OH 45401-0933. Phone: 800-227-9597 or (937)865-6800 Fax: (937)865-6909 • URL: http://www.lexis-nexis.com • The various LEXIS databases provide full text and indexing for a wide variety of legal cases, statutes, orders, and opinions.

Lexis.com Research System. Lexis-Nexis GroupPhone: 800-227-4908 or (937)865-6800 Fax: (937)865-6909 E-mail: webmaster@prod.lexis-nexis.com • URL: http://www.lexis.com • Fee-based Web site offers extensive searching of a wide variety of legal sources. Additional features include Daily Opinion Service, lexis.com Bookstore, Career Center, CLE Center, Law Schools, and Practice Pages ("Pages specific to areas of specialty").

The Liberator: Male Call. Men's Defense Association, 17854 Lyons St. Forest Lake, MN 55025. Phone: (612)464-7663 E-mail: rdoyle@mensdefense.org • URL: http://www.mensdefense.org • Monthly. $24.00 per year. Newsletter supporting men's rights in family law. Formerly *Legal Beagle*.

Librarian-Author: A Practical Guide on How to Get Published. Betty Carol Sellen, editor. Neal-Schuman Publishers, Inc., 100 William St., Ste. 2004 New York, NY 10038. Phone: (866)672-6657 or (212)925-8650 Fax: (866)209-7932 or (212)219-8916 E-mail: info@neal-schuman.com • URL: http://www.neal-schuman.com • 1985. $38.50.

Librarian's Companion: A Handbook of Thousands of Facts on Libraries, Librarians, Books, Newspapers, Publishers, Booksellers. Vladimir F. Wertsman. Greenwood Publishing Group, Inc., 88 Post Rd., W. Westport, CT 06881-5007. Phone: 800-225-5800 or (203)226-3571 Fax: (203)431-2214 E-mail: customer-service@greenwood.com • URL: http://www.greenwood.com • 1996. $69.95. Provides international statistics on libraries and publishing. Includes directory and biographical information.

Librarian's Guide to Intellectual Property in the Digital Age: Copyrights, Patents, and Trademarks. Timothy L. Wherry. American Library Association, 50 E Huron St. Chicago, IL 60611-2795. Phone: 800-545-2433 or (312)944-6780 Fax: (312)440-9374 E-mail: ala@ala.org • URL: http://www.ala.org • 2002. $38.00. Includes lists of patent and trademark depositories, relevant Web sites, and questions & answers.

The Librarian's Internet Survival Guide: Strategies for the High-Tech Reference Desk. Irene E. McDermott. Information Today, Inc., 143 Old Marlton Pike Medford, NJ 08055-8750. Phone: 800-300-9868 or (609)654-6266 Fax: (609)654-4309 E-mail: custserv@infotoday.com • URL: http://www.infotoday.com • 2002. $29.50. Provides practical advice relating to Web reference sources, information management strategies, Internet training issues, library Web pages, and patron relations.

The Librarian's Yellow Pages: Publications, Products, and Services for Libraries and Information Centers., 2089 Boston Post Rd. Larchmont, NY 10538. Phone: 800-235-9723 Fax: (914)833-3053 E-mail: info@librariansyellowpages.com • URL: http://www.librariansyellowpages.com • Irregular. Free to librarians in the United States; others, $15.00. A classified compilation of advertisements for library items from more than 1,000 U. S. and Canadian companies. Major sections cover audio, automation, books, CD-ROMs, periodicals, and video. Subject and company indexes are included.

Libraries and Copyright: A Guide to Copyright Law in the Nineties. Laura N. Gasaway and Sarah K. Wiant. Special Libraries Association, 1700 18th St., N. W. Washington, DC 20009-2514. Phone: (202)234-4700 Fax: (202)265-9317 E-mail: sla@sla.org • URL: http://www.sla.org • 1994. $59.00. Provides practical explanations of copyright law. Includes an extensive bibliography.

Libraries and the Future: Essays on the Library in the Twenty-First Century. F. W. Lancaster, editor. Haworth Press, Inc., 10 Alice St. Binghamton, NY 13904-1580. Phone: 800-429-6784 or (607)722-5857 Fax: 800-895-0582 or (607)722-1424 E-mail: getinfo@haworthpressinc.com • URL: http://www.haworthpressinc.com • 1994. $49.95. Emphasis is on information services in libraries of the future. (Original Book Series).

Library Administration and Management Association., 50 E Huron St. Chicago, IL 60611-2795. Phone: 800-545-2433 or (312)280-5036 Fax: (312)280-5033 E-mail: lama@ala.org • URL: http://www.ala.org/lama • Affiliated with American Library Association. Formerly Library Administration Division of ALA.

The Library Administrator's Automation Handbook. Richard Boss. Information Today, Inc., 143 Old Marlton Pike Medford, NJ 08055-8750. Phone: 800-300-9868 or (609)654-6266 Fax: (609)654-4309 E-mail: custserv@infotoday.com • URL: http://www.infotoday.com • 1997. $39.50. Covers the library administrator's role in the planning, selection, and implementation of hardware and software for automated library systems.

Library Administrator's Digest. Baltimore County Public Library Foundation Inc., 320 York Rd. Towson, MD 21204-5179. Phone: (410)887-6100 Fax: (410)887-6103 E-mail: bcpl@bcpl.info Description: Designed to keep library administrators abreast of new ideas and developments, particularly in the public library field. Recurring features include editorials and letters to the editor.

Library: An Unquiet History. Matthew Battles. W. W. Norton & Co., Inc., 500 5th Ave. New York, NY 10110. Phone: 800-223-4830 or (212)354-5500 Fax: (212)869-0856 • URL: http://www.wwnorton.com • 2003. $24.95. A colorful history of libraries from very early times to the present.

Library and Information Technology Association., 50 E. Huron St. Chicago, IL 60611. Phone: 800-545-2433 or (312)280-4270 Fax: (312)280-3257 E-mail: lita@ala.org • URL: http://www.lita.org • Affiliated with the American Library Association. Formerly Information Science and Automation Division of ALA.

Library Binding Institute., 4300 S U.S. Hwy. One, No. 203-296 Jupiter, FL 33477. Phone: (561)745-6821 Fax: (561)472-8401 E-mail: dnolan@lbibinders.org • URL: http://www.lbibinders.org • Firms and certified library binders doing library binding in accordance with LBI Standard for Library Binding, including rebinding of worn volumes, prebinding of new volumes, initial hardcover binding of periodicals, and other binding principally for libraries and schools; associate members are suppliers and manufacturers of library binding materials and equipment. Certifies qualified binding companies after examination of work and investigation of experience, insurance for protection of customers' property, and examination of bank and library references. Conducts research on materials used in library binding. Conducts statistical surveys of unit production, operating statement data, and wage data.

The Library Bookseller; Books Wanted by College and University Libraries. Danna D'Esopo Jackson, editor. P.O. Box 1818 Bloomington, IN 47402-1818. Phone: (812)332-4440 Fax: (812)332-2999 E-mail: betweenl@bluemarble.net Monthly. $50.00 per year.

Library Displays Handbook. Mark Schaeffer. H. W. Wilson Co., 950 University Ave. Bronx, NY 10452-4224. Phone: 800-367-6770 or (718)588-8400 Fax: 800-590-1617 or (718)590-1617 E-mail: custserv@hwwilson.com • URL: http://www.

hwwilson.com • 1991. $65.00. Provides detailed instructions for signs, posters, wall displays, bulletin boards, and exhibits.

Library Forms Illustrated Handbook. Elizabeth Futas. Neal-Schuman Publishers, Inc., 100 William St., Ste. 2004 New York, NY 10038. Phone: (866)672-6657 or (212)925-8650 Fax: (866)209-7932 or (212)219-8916 E-mail: info@neal-schuman.com • URL: http://www.neal-schuman.com • $125.00 per year. Looseleaf service Contains forms for acquisition, cataloging, circulation, reference, online searching, interlibrary loan, bibliographic instruction, personnel, administration, budgets, software control, hardware control, statistics, and special collections.

Library Hi Tech News. MCB University Press North America, 44 Brattle St., Ste. 4 Cambridge, MA 02138-3736. Phone: 888-622-0075 or (609)654-6266 Fax: (617)354-6875 E-mail: help@mcb-usa.com • URL: http://www.infotoday.com • Description: Offers "timely and late-breaking news about all aspects of technology related to library operations." Includes "news of new products, database developments, cooperative networks, technology vendors." Recurring features include book reviews and a calendar of events.

Library Hi Tech News: The First in the Field to Identify the "Hot Topics" of Library Technology. Emerald (North America), 875 Massachusetts Ave., 7th Fl. Cambridge, MA 02139. Phone: 888-622-0075 or (617)497-2175 Fax: (617)354-6875 E-mail: america@emeraldinsight.com • URL: http://www.emeraldinsight.com • Quarterly. $319.00 per year. Provides detailed information on current and emerging library technologies.

Library Hi Tech News: Up to Date News on the Latest Developments in Library Automation. Emerald (North America), 875 Massachusetts Ave., 7th Fl. Cambridge, MA 02139. Phone: 888-622-0075 or (617)497-2175 Fax: (617)354-6875 E-mail: america@emeraldinsight.com • URL: http://www.emeraldinsight.com • 10 times a year. $389.00 per year. Newsletter. Contains news of library products and procedures, including software, hardware, and network-related items. Covers forthcoming events internationally.

Library Hotline: Breaking News for Library and Information Decision Makers. Reed Business Information, 360 Park Ave., S New York, NY 10010. Phone: 800-446-6551 or (646)746-6400 Fax: (646)746-7028 E-mail: corporatecommunications@reedbusiness.com • URL: http://www.reedbusiness.com • 50 times a year. $109.00 per year. Newsletter. News and developments affecting libraries and librarians.

Library Journal. Reed Business Information, 360 Park Ave., S New York, NY 10010. Phone: 800-446-6551 or (646)746-6400 E-mail: corporatecommunications@reedbusiness.com • URL: http://www.reedbusiness.com • 20 times a year. $134.00 per year. Includes *Buyer's Guide*, six *Supplements* and weekly *Newswire*.

Library Journal: Reference [year]: Print, CD-ROM, Online. Reed Business Information, 360 Park Ave. South New York, NY 10010. Phone: 800-662-7776 or (646)746-6400 E-mail: corporatecommunications@reedbusiness.com • URL: http://www.reedbusiness.com • Annual. Issued in November as a supplement to *Library Journal*. Lists new and updated reference material, including general and trade print titles, directories, annuals, CD-ROM titles, and online sources. Includes material from more than 200 publishers, arranged by company name, with an index by subject. Addresses include e-mail and Web information.

Library Journal Sourcebook. Reed Business Information, 360 Pk. Ave. S New York, NY 10014. Phone: 800-446-6551 or (646)746-6400 Fax: (646)746-7431 E-mail: corporatecommunications@reedbusiness.com • URL: http://www.reedbusiness.com • Publication includes: List of over 600 suppliers of products and services used by libraries from abstracting to word processing equipment. Entries include: Company name, address, phone, list of products or services. Complete listings for more than 100 architectural firms; Disaster planning for librarians

Library Literature and Information Science Index. H. W. Wilson Co., 950 University Ave. Bronx, NY 10452. Phone: 800-367-6770 or (718)588-8400 Fax: 800-590-1617 or (718)590-1617 E-mail: custserv@hwwilson.com • URL: http://www.hwwilson.com • Quarterly. Annual cumulation. Price varies.

Library Manager's Deskbook: 102 Expert Solutions to 101 Common Dilemmas. Paula P. Carson and others. American Library Association, 50 E. Huron St. Chicago, IL 60611-2795. Phone: 800-545-2433 or (312)944-6780 Fax: (312)440-9374 E-mail: ala@ala.org • URL: http://www.ala.org • 1995. $32.00. "..focuses on issues relevant to today's administrators and supervisors in all types and sizes of libraries."

Library of Investment Banking. Robert L. Kuhn, editor. McGraw-Hill, 1221 Ave. of the Americas New York, NY 10020. Phone: 800-722-4276 or (212)512-2000 Fax: (212)512-4502 E-mail: customer.service@mcgraw-hill.com • URL: http://www.mcgraw-hill.com • 1990. $475.00. Seven volumes: 1. Investing and Risk Management; 2. Capital Raising and Financial Structure; 3. Corporate and Municipal Securities; 4. Mergers, Acquisitions, and Leveraged Buyouts; 5. Mortgage and Asset Securitization; 6. International Finance and Investing; 7. Index.

Library Personnel Administration. Lowell A. Martin. Scarecrow Press, Inc., 4501 Forbes Blvd., Ste. 200 Lanham, MD 20706. Phone: 800-462-6420 or (301)459-3366 Fax: 800-338-4550 or (301)429-5748 E-mail: custserv@rowman.com • URL:

http://www.scarecrowpress.com • 1994. $35.00. (Library Administration Series: No. 11).

Library Personnel News. Office for Library Personnel Resources. American Library Association, 50 E. Huron St. Chicago, IL 60611-2795. Phone: 800-545-2433 or (312)944-6780 Fax: (312)440-9374 E-mail: ala@ala.org • URL: http://www.ala.org • Quarterly. $20.00 per year. Newsletter covering personnel trends and issues.

The Library Quarterly: A Journal of Investigation and Discussion in the Field of Library Science. University of Chicago Graduate Library School. The University of Chicago Press, Journals Div., P.O. Box 37005 Chicago, IL 60637. Phone: 877-705-1878 or (773)753-3347 Fax: 877-705-1879 or (773)753-0811 E-mail: subscriptions@press.uchicago.edu • URL: http://www.journals.uchicago.edu • Quarterly. Individuals, $40.00 per year; includes print and online editions. Institutions, $120.00 per year; includes print and online editions.

Library Research Center. University of Illinois at Urbana-Champaign

Library Resource Guide: A Catalog of Services and Suppliers for the Library Community. Information Today, Inc., 143 Old Marlton Pike Medford, NJ 08055-8750. Phone: 800-300-9868 or (609)654-6266 Fax: (609)654-4309 E-mail: custserv@infotoday.com • URL: http://www.infotoday.com • Annual. Free to libraries. An advertising directory listing several hundred manufacturers or distributors of library supplies, services, and equipment in such areas as audiovisual, automation, bar codes, binding, furniture, microfilm, shelving, and storage. Some book dealers, document delivery services, online services, and publishers are also included (http://www.libraryresource.com). Formerly published by R. R. Bowker.

Library Space Planning: A How-To-Do-It Manual for Assessing, Allocating and Recognizing Collections, Resources, and Physical Facilities. Ruth A. Fraley and Carol Lee Anderson. Neal-Schuman Publishers, Inc., 100 William St., Ste. 2004 New York, NY 10038. Phone: (866)672-6657 or (212)925-8650 Fax: (866)209-7932 or (212)219-8916 E-mail: info@neal-schuman.com • URL: http://www.neal-schuman.com • 1990. $45.00. Second edition.

Library Technology Reports: Expert Guides to Library Systems and Services. American Library Association, 50 E. Huron St. Chicago, IL 60611-2795. Phone: 800-545-2433 or (312)944-6780 Fax: (312)440-9374 E-mail: ala@ala.org • URL: http://www.ala.org • Bimonthly. $315.00 per year. Looseleaf service.

Library Trends. University of Illinois at Urbana-Champaign, Graduate School of Library and Information Science. University of Illinois Press, 501 E. Daniel St. Champaign, IL 61820. Phone: (217)333-7197 Fax: (217)244-3302 E-mail: puboff@alexia.lis.uiuc.edu • URL: http://www.lis.uiuc.edu • Quarterly. Individuals, $70.00 per year; institutions; $100.00 per year.

The Library's Legal Answer Book. Mary Minow and Tomas A. Lipinski. American Library Association, 50 E Huron St. Chicago, IL 60611-2795. Phone: 800-545-2433 or (312)944-6780 Fax: (312)440-9374 E-mail: ala@ala.org • URL: http://www.ala.org • 2003. $48.00. Includes detailed answers to more than 600 legal questions relating to libraries. Covers Internet content filters, copyright, fair use, employment issues, library liability, and other legal matters.

License to Steal: The Secret World of Wall Street Brokers and the Systematic Pluof the American Investor. Timothy Harper. DIANE Publishing Co., 330 Pusey Ave. Collingdale, PA 19023-8428. Phone: 800-782-3833 or (610)461-6200 Fax: (610)461-6130 E-mail: dianepub@erols.com • URL: http://www.dianepublishing.com • 2001. $26.00. A former stockbroker explains how brokers use persuavive and sometimes shady techniques to keep effective control of customers' accounts, regardless of losses. (HarperBusiness.)

The Licensing Book. Adventure Publishing, 1501 Broadway, Suite 500 New York, NY 10036-5503. Phone: (212)575-4510 Fax: (212)575-4521 Monthly. $36.00 per year. Contains articles about licensed product merchandising.

Licensing Executives Society., 1800 Diagonal Rd., Ste. 280 Alexandria, VA 22314. Phone: (703)836-3106 Fax: (703)836-3107 E-mail: info@les.org • URL: http://www.usa-canada.les.org • U.S. and foreign businessmen, scientists, engineers, and lawyers having direct responsibility for the transfer of technology. Maintains placement service.

Licensing Executives Society—Membership Directory. Licensing Executives Society Intl., 1800 Diagonal Rd., Ste. 280 Alexandria, VA 22314. Phone: (703)836-0026 Fax: (703)836-3107 E-mail: info@les.org • URL: http://www.les.org • Covers: About 10,000 U.S. and foreign business executives, scientists, engineers, lawyers, and new-idea scouts having direct responsibility for the licensing of technology, patents, trade marks, and know-how. Entries include: Name, address, telephone, fax, email, website.

Licensing Law Handbook. West Group, 610 Opperman Dr. Eagan, MN 55123. Phone: 800-328-4880 or (651)687-7000 Fax: 800-340-9378 E-mail: bookstore@westgroup.com • URL: http://www.westgroup.com • $299.00. Periodic supplementation.

The Licensing Letter. EPM Communications Inc., 160 Mercer St., 3rd Fl. New York, NY 10012-3212. Phone: 888-852-9467 or (212)941-0099 or (212)941-0099 Fax: 888-852-3899 or (212)941-1622 E-mail: info@epmcom.com • URL: http://www.epmcom.com • Description: Concerned with all aspects of licensed merchandising, "the business of associating someone's name, likeness or creation with someone else's product or service, for a consideration." Recurring features include statistics, research, events, mechanics, available properties, and identification of licensors, licensing agents, and licensees.

Licensing of Intellectual Property. American Lawyer Media, Inc., 105 Madison Ave. New York, NY 10016. Phone: 800-888-8300 or (212)779-9200 Fax: (212)481-8110 E-mail: lawcatalog@amlaw.com • URL: http://www.lawcatalog.com/ • Looseleaf. $169.00. Updated as needed. Includes such licensing topics as royalties, infringement, antitrust, trade secrets, and patent agreements. Examples of licensing agreements and sample forms (on CD-ROM) are included. (Law Journal Press).

Lieber on Pensions. William M. Lieber. Aspen Publishers, Inc., 1185 Ave. of the Americas New York, NY 10036. Phone: 800-234-1660 or (212)597-0200 Fax: 900-901-9075 or (212)597-0338 E-mail: customer.service@aspenpubl.com • URL: http://www.aspenpublishers.com • $595.00. Five volumes. Looseleaf service. Periodic supplementation. Organizes, describes, and analyzes ERISA and IRS pension rules. Topical arrangement.

Life and Health Insurance Law. Muirel L. Crawford. McGraw Hill, 1221 Ave. of the Americas New York, NY 10020. Phone: 800-722-4726 or (212)512-2000 Fax: (212)512-4502 • URL: http://www.mcgraw-hill.com • 1997. $118.88. Eighth edition. Covers the legal aspects of life, health, and accident insurance.

Life Communicators Association., c/o Carol Morgan, PO Box 387 East Rutherford, NJ 07073. Phone: (201)939-4739 E-mail: cmorgan@comcast.net Formerly Life Insurance Advertisers.

Life, Health, and Accident Insurance Law Reports. CCH, Inc., 2700 Lake Cook Rd. Riverwoods, IL 60015. Phone: 800-835-5224 or (847)267-7000 E-mail: cust_serv@cch.com • URL: http://www.cch.com • $835.00 per year. Looseleaf service. Monthly updates.

Life Insurance Answer Book: For Qualified Plans and Estate Planning. Gary S. Lesser and Lawrence C. Starr, editors. Aspen Publishers, Inc., 200 Orchard Ridge Dr., Ste. 200 Gaithersburg, MD 20878. Phone: 800-234-1660 or (301)474-7500 E-mail: customer.service@aspenpubl.com • URL: http://www.aspenpublishers.com • 2002. $175.00. Third edition. Four parts by various authors cover life insurance in general, qualified plans, fiduciary responsibility, and estate planning. Includes sample documents, worksheets, and information in Q&A form.

Life Insurance Fact Book. American Council of Life Insurers, 101 Constitution Ave., NW, Ste. 700 Washington, DC 20001-2133. Phone: (202)624-2000 Fax: (202)624-2319 E-mail: acli@acli.com • URL: http://www.acli.com • Biennial. $37.50 per year; with diskette, $55.00 per year.

Life Insurance from the Buyer's Point of View. American Institute for Economic Research, PO Box 1000 Great Barrington, MA 01230-1000. Phone: (413)528-1216 Fax: (413)528-0103 E-mail: info@aier.org • URL: http://www.aier.org • Annual. $8.00.

Lifetime Encyclopedia of Letters. Harold E. Meyer. Prentice Hall PTR, 240 Frisch Ct. Paramus, NJ 07652. Phone: 800-282-0693 Fax: 800-445-6991 • URL: http://www.phptr.com • 2001. $50.00. Third edition. Includes CD-ROM. Contains about 800 model letters and 400 alternative opening and closing sentences. Model letters are for sales, collection, complaints, apology, congratulations, fund raising, resignation, termination, etc.

Lifting and Transportation International. Specialized Carriers and Rigging Association. Douglas Publications, Inc., 2807 N. Parham Rd., Suite 200 Richmond, VA 23294. Phone: (804)762-9600 Fax: (804)217-8999 E-mail: info@douglaspublications.com • URL: http://www.douglaspublications.com • Nine times a year.$65.00 per year. Covers specialized trucking, including oversized loads, cranes, hauling steel, heavy rigging, etc. Serves as the official publication of the Specialized Carriers and Rigging Association.

Light Metal Age. Fellom Publishing Co., 170 S. Spruce Ave., Suite 120 South San Francisco, CA 94080. Phone: (650)588-8832 Fax: (650)588-0901 Bimonthly. $40.00 per year. Edited for production and engineering executives of the aluminum industry and other nonferrous light metal industries.

Lighting Design: An Introductory Guide for Professionals. Carl Gardner and Barry Hannaford. Ashgate Publishing Co., 101 Cherry St., Ste. 420 Burlington, VT 05401-4405. Phone: 800-535-9544 or (802)865-7641 Fax: (802)865-7847 E-mail: adonahue@ashgate.com • URL: http://www.ashgate.com • 1993. $109.95. Includes project case studies and product/effect examples. Emphasis is on commercial interior and exterior lighting. Published by Design Council Books in England.

Lighting Equipment and Fixtures. Available from MarketResearch.com, 641 Ave. of the Americas, Fourth Floor New York, NY 10011. Phone: 800-298-5699 or (212)807-2629 Fax: (212)807-2642 E-mail: order@marketresearch.com • URL: http://www.marketresearch.com • 2002. $4,450.00. Published by Global Industry Analysts. Provides worldwide market research data, including profiles of major lighting equipment companies.

Lightwave Buyers Guide. PennWell Corp., Advanced Technology Div., 98 Spit Brook Rd. Nashua, NH 03062-5737. Phone: 800-331-4463 or (603)891-0123 E-mail: atd@pennwell.com • URL: http://www.pennwell.com • Annual. $79.00. Lists manufacturers and distributors of fiberoptic systems and components.

Lightwave: Fiber Optics Technology and Applications Worldwide. PennWell Corp., Advaned Technology Div., 98 Spit Brook Rd. Nashua, NH 03062-5737. Phone: 800-331-4463 or (603)891-0123 E-mail: atd@pennwell.com • URL: http://www.pennwell.com • Monthly. $105.00 per year. Includes *Buyers Guide*.

Lilly Digest. Eli Lilly and Co., Lilly Corporate Center Indianapolis, IN 46285. Phone: (317)276-2000 • URL: http://www.lilly.com • Annual. $30.00. Includes drug store financial data.

Lilly Hospital Pharmacy Survey. Eli Lilly and Co., Lilly Corporate Center Indianapolis, IN 46285. Phone: (317)276-2000 • URL: http://www.lilly.com • Annual. $30.00. Includes financial data for drug stores located in hospitals.

Limited Partnership Investment Review. Limited Partnership Investment Review, Inc., 55 Morris Ave. Springfield, NJ 07081. Phone: (201)467-8700 Fax: (201)467-0368 Monthly. $197.00 per year. Newsletter. Formerly *Tax Shelter Investment Review*

The Limits of Liberty: Between Anarchy and Leviathan. James M. Buchanan. Liberty Fund, Inc., 8335 Allison Pointe Trail, No. 300 Indianapolis, IN 46250-1684. Phone: 800-866-3520 or (317)842-0880 Fax: (317)579-6060 E-mail: webmaster@libertyfund.org • URL: http://www.libertyfund.org • 2000. $20.00. (Collected Works of James M. Buchanan: Vol. 7).

Limousine Service. Entrepreneur Media, Inc., 2445 McCabe Way Irvine, CA 92614. Phone: 800-421-2300 or (949)261-2325 Fax: (949)261-0234 E-mail: entmag@entrepreneur.com • URL: http://www.entrepreneur.com • Looseleaf. $59.50. A practical guide to starting a limousine service. Covers profit potential, start-up costs, market size evaluation, owner's time required, site selection, lease negotiation, pricing, accounting, advertising, promotion, etc. (Start-Up Business Guide No. E1224.)

LIMRA International., 300 Day Hill Rd. Windsor, CT 06095. Phone: 800-235-4672 or (860)688-3358 Fax: (860)298-9555 E-mail: webmaster@limra.com • URL: http://www.limra.com • Life insurance and financial services companies. Conducts market, consumer, economic, financial, and human resources research; monitors industry distribution systems and product and service developments. Provides executive and field management development schools and seminars. Offers human resource development consulting services, including needs analysis and program design, evaluation, and implementation.

Lincoln Laboratory., Massachusetts Institute of Technology, 244 Wood St. Lexington, MA 02420-9108. Phone: (781)981-5500 Fax: (781)981-7086 • URL: http://www.ll.mit.edu • Multidisciplinary off-campus research unit. Research fields include solid state devices.

Lindcove Research and Extension Center. University of California

Lindey on Entertainment, Publishing and the Arts: Agreements and the Law. Alexander Lindey, editor. West Group, 610 Opperman Dr. Eagan, MN 55123. Phone: 800-328-4880 or (651)687-7000 Fax: 800-340-9378 E-mail: bookstore@westgroup.com • URL: http://www.westgroup.com • $935.00 per year. Six looseleaf volumes. Periodic supplementation. Provides basic forms, applicable law, and guidance.

Lingerie Shop. Entrepreneur Media, Inc., 2445 McCabe Way Irvine, CA 92614. Phone: 800-421-2300 or (949)261-2325 Fax: (949)261-0234 E-mail: entmag@entrepreneur.com • URL: http://www.entrepreneur.com • Looseleaf. $59.50. A practical guide to starting a lingerie store. Covers profit potential, start-up costs, market size evaluation, owner's time required, site selection, lease negotiation, pricing, accounting, advertising, promotion, etc. (Start-Up Business Guide No. E1152.)

Linn's Stamp News. Amos Press, Inc., Sidney, OH 45365. Phone: 800-448-7293 or (937)498-0801 Fax: 888-304-8388 or (937)498-0886 E-mail: linns@linns.com • URL: http://www.linns.com • Weekly. $39.90 per year.

Liquid Filtration Newsletter. The McIlvaine Co., 191 Waukegan Rd., Ste. 208 Northfield, IL 60093. Phone: (847)784-0012 Fax: (847)784-0061 E-mail: editor@mcilvainecompany.com • URL: http://www.mcilvainecompany.com • Description: Focuses on the liquid filtration industry, providing information on technical developments and reports on individual companies in the field. Recurring features include a calendar of events and a column titled New & Different.

Liquor Control Law Reporter: Federal and All States. CCH, Inc., 2700 Lake Cook Rd. Riverwoods, IL 60015. Phone: 800-835-5224 or (847)267-7000 E-mail: cust_serv@cch.com • URL: http://www.cch.com • Biweekly. $3,649.00 per year. Nine looseleaf volumes. Federal and state regulation and taxation of alcoholic beverages.

Liquor Store. Entrepreneur Media, Inc., 2445 McCabe Way Irvine, CA 92614. Phone: 800-421-2300 or (949)261-2325 Fax: (949)261-0234 E-mail: entmag@entrepreneur.com • URL: http://www.entrepreneur.com • Looseleaf. $59.50. A practical guide to starting a liquor store. Covers profit potential, start-up costs, market size evaluation, owner's time required, site selection, lease negotiation, pricing, accounting, advertising, promotion, etc. (Start-Up Business Guide No. E1024.)

LISA: Library and Information Science Abstracts. Available from Cambridge Scientific Abstracts (CSA), 7200 Wisconsin Ave., Suite 601 Bethesda, MD 20814. Phone: 800-843-7751 or (301)961-6700 Fax: (301)961-6720 E-mail: sales@csa.com • URL: http://www.csa.com/csa/factsheets/lisa.shtml • Provides abstracting and indexing of the world's library and information science literature, 1969 to date. Covers more than 440 periodicals from 68 countries. Updating is biweekly. Inquire as to online cost and availability.

LISA: Library and Information Science Abstracts. R. R. Bowker, 121 Chanlon Rd. New Providence, NJ 07974. Phone: 888-269-5372 Fax: (908)219-0098 E-mail: info@bowker.com • URL: http://www.bowker.com • 13 times a year. $1,055.00 per year; includes print and online editions.

LISA Plus. Available from Cambridge Scientific Abstracts (CSA), 7200 Wisconsin Ave., Suite 601 Bethesda, MD 20814. Phone: 800-843-7751 or (301)961-6700 Fax: (301)961-6720 E-mail: sales@csa.com • URL: http://www.csa.com • Quarterly. $2,000.00 per year. CD-ROM version of Library Information and Science Abstracts, providing abstracting and indexing of the world's library and information science literature, 1969 to date. Contains more than 180,000 citations.

List of Certificated Pilot Schools. Federal Aviation Administration. Available from U. S. Government Printing Office, Washington, DC 20402. Phone: (202)512-1800 Fax: (202)512-2250 E-mail: gpoaccess@gpo.gov • URL: http://www.access.gpo.gov • Annual $4.50.

List of Shipowners, Managers, and Managing Agents. Lloyd's Register of Shipping, Metrostar Plz., 190 Middlesex Turnpike Iselin, NJ 08830. Phone: (305)262-4070 Fax: (305)262-2006 E-mail: sales@fairplay.co.uk • URL: http://www.fairplay.co.uk • Annual. $350.00, including 10 updates per year. Published in the UK by Lloyd's Register-Fairplay Ltd. Lists 40,000 shipowners, managers, and agents worldwide. Cross-referenced with *Lloyd's Register of Ships*.

List of Worthwhile Life and Health Insurance Books. American Council of Life Insurance, 1001 Pennsylvania Ave., N. W. Washington, DC 20004-2599. Phone: (202)624-2000 Annual. Free. Books in print on life and health insurance and closely related subjects.

Literary Market Place: The Directory of the American Book Publishing Industry. Information Today, Inc., 143 Old Marlton Pike Medford, NJ 08055-8750. Phone: 800-300-9868 or (609)654-6266 Fax: (609)654-4309 E-mail: custserv@infotoday.com • URL: http://www.infotoday.com • Annual. $299.00. Two volumes. Listings include publishers, agents, ad agencies, associations, distributors, events, key executives, services, and suppliers (50 directory sections in all). Formerly published by R. R. Bowker.

Literature of the Nonprofit Sector: A Bibliography with Abstracts. The Foundation Center, 79 Fifth Ave. New York, NY 10003-3076. Phone: 800-424-9836 or (212)620-4230 Fax: (212)807-3677 E-mail: orders@fdncenter.org • URL: http://www.fdncenter.org • Dates vary. Six volumes. $45.00 per volume. Covers the literature of philanthropy, foundations, nonprofit organizations, fund-raising, and federal aid.

Literature Review. Water Environment Federation, 601 Wythe St. Alexandria, VA 22314-1994. Phone: 800-666-0206 or (703)684-2452 Fax: (703)684-2492 • URL: http://www.wef.org • Annual. Price on application.

Little Black Book of Budgets and Forecasts. Michael C. Thomsett. AMACOM, 1601 Broadway New York, NY 10019. Phone: 800-262-9699 or (518)586-8100 Fax: (518)903-8168 E-mail: customerservice@amanet.org • URL: http://www.amacombooks.org • 1988. $14.95. A concise guide to business budgeting and forecasting. (Little Black Book Series).

Little Black Book of Business Etiquette. Michael C. Thomsett. AMACOM, 1601 Broadway New York, NY 10019. Phone: 800-262-9699 or (518)586-8100 Fax: (518)903-8168 E-mail: customerservice@amanet.org • URL: http://www.amacombooks.org • 1991. $14.95. Covers company politics, chain of command, business lunches, dress codes, etc. (Little Black Book Series).

Little Black Book of Business Letters. Michael C. Thomsett. AMACOM, 1601 Broadway New York, NY 10019. Phone: 800-262-9699 or (518)586-8100 Fax: (518)903-8168 E-mail: customerservice@amanet.org • URL: http://www.amacombooks.org • 1988. $14.95. Includes examples of various kinds of business correspondence. (Little Black Book Series).

Little Black Book of Business Meetings. Michael C. Thomsett. AMACOM, 1601 Broadway New York, NY 10019. Phone: 800-262-9699 or (518)586-8100 Fax: (518)903-8168 E-mail: customerservice@amanet.org • URL: http://www.amacombooks.org • 1989. $14.95. How to run a business meeting. (Little Black Book Series).

Little Black Book of Business Reports. Michael C. Thomsett. AMACOM, 1601 Broadway New York, NY 10019. Phone: 800-262-9699 or (518)586-8100 Fax: (518)903-8168 E-mail: customerservice@amanet.org • URL: http://www.amacombooks.org • 1988. $14.95. How to write effective business reports. (Little Black Book Series).

Little Black Book of Business Statistics. Michael C. Thomsett. AMACOM, 1601 Broadway New York, NY 10019. Phone: 800-262-9699 or (518)586-8100 Fax: (518)903-8168 E-mail: customerservice@amanet.org • URL: http://www.amacombooks.org • 1990. $14.95. A practical guide to the effective use and interpretation of statistics by business managers. (Little Black Book Series).

Little Black Book of Project Management. Michael C. Thomsett. AMACOM, 1601 Broadway New York, NY 10019. Phone: 800-262-9699 or (518)586-8100 Fax: (518)903-8168 E-mail: customerservice@amanet.org • URL: http://www.amacombooks.org • 2002 $15.00. Second Edition. Gives practical advice on the day-to-day management of new projects, including budgeting and scheduling. (Little Black Book Series).

The Little Data Book. The World Bank, P. O. Box 960 Herndon, VA 20172-0960. Phone: 800-645-7247 or (703)661-1580 Fax: (703)661-1501 E-mail: books@worldbank.org • URL: http://www.worldbank.org/publications • 2003. $15.00. Contains "key development data for 208 countries," including country profiles and 54 statistical indicators relating to such factors as population, economics, trade, technology, finance, and environment.

The Little Green Data Book. The World Bank, P. O. Box 960 Herndon, VA 20172-0960. Phone: 800-645-7247 or (703)661-1580 Fax: (703)661-1501 E-mail: books@worldbank.org • URL: http://www.worldbank.org/publications • 2003. $15.00. Presents "key environmental data for over 200 countries" in such areas as water quality, air emissions, sanitation, and agriculture.

Livestock and Grain Market News Branch Weekly Summary. U.S. Dept of Agriculture. Livestock and Grain Market News Branch, 1427 S. Pioneer Way Moses Lake, WA 98837. Phone: (509)675-3611 • URL: http://www.ams.usda.gov • Weekly. $85.00 per year. Formerly *Grain and Feed Weekly Summary and Statistics*.

Livestock Market Digest. Livestock Market Digest, Inc., P.O. Box 7458 Albuquerque, NM 87194. Weekly. $20.00 per year.

Livestock Marketing Association., 10510 NW Ambassador Dr. Kansas City, MO 64153. Phone: 800-821-2048 or (816)891-0502 Fax: (816)891-7926 E-mail: lmainfo@lmaweb.com • URL: http://www.lmaweb.com • Livestock marketing businesses and livestock dealers. Sponsors annual World Livestock Auctioneer Championships. Offers management and promotional services.

Livestock, Meat, Wool, Market News. U.S. Department of Agriculture, Washington, DC 20250. Phone: (202)720-2791 Weekly.

Livestock Production Science. Elsevier, 360 Park Ave. S New York, NY 10010-1710. Phone: 888-437-4636 or (212)989-5800 Fax: (212)633-3990 E-mail: usinfo-f@elsevier.com • URL: http://www.elsevier.com • 21 times a year. Qualified personnel, $111.00 per year; institutions, $1,571.00 per year.

Livestock Weekly. Southwest Publishing, Inc., P.O. Box 3306 San Angelo, TX 76902. Phone: (915)949-4611 Fax: (915)949-4614 Weekly. $25.00 per year.

Living Logos: How U. S. Corporations Revitalize Their Trademarks. David E. Carter, editor. Art Direction Book Co., Inc., 456 Glenbrook Rd. Stamford, CT 06906-1800. Phone: (203)353-1441 Fax: (203)353-1371 1993. $22.95. Traces the history and evolution of 70 famous U. S. company logos.

The Living Trust: The Failproof Way to Pass Along Your Estate to Your Heirs Without Lawyers, Courts, or the Probate System. Henry W. Abts. McGraw-Hill, 1221 Ave. of the Americas New York, NY 10020. Phone: 800-722-4726 or (212)512-2000 Fax: (212)512-4502 E-mail: customer.service@mcgraw-hill.com • URL: http://www.mcgraw-hill.com • 2002. $24.95. Third edition.

Lloyd's Cruise International. Available from Informa Publishing Group Ltd., PO Box 1017 Westborough, MA 01581-6017. Phone: 800-493-4080 Fax: (508)237-0856 E-mail: enquiries@informa.com • URL: http://www.informa.com • Bimonthly. $217.00 per year. Published in the UK by Lloyd's List (http://www.lloydslist.com). Edited for management professionals in the cruise ship industry. Covers industry trends, technical/equipment developments, regulatory issues, new cruise ships, ship management, cruise marketing, and related topics.

Lloyd's List. Available from Informa UK Ltd., 69-77 Paul St. London EC2A 4LQ, United Kingdom. Phone: 800-493-4080 or 44 20 7553 1778 Fax: 44 20 7553 1101 • URL: http://www.informa.com • Daily. $1,698.00 per year. Published in the UK by Lloyd's List (http://www.lloydslist.com). Marine industry newspaper. Covers a wide variety of maritime topics, including global news, business/insurance, regulation, shipping markets, financial markets, shipping movements, freight logistics, and marine technology. (Also available weekly at $385.00 per year.)

Lloyd's List Ports of the World. Informa Group PLC, 37-41 Mortimer St. London W1T 3JH, United Kingdom. Phone: 44 020 7553 1000 • URL: http://www.informa.com • 2002 $442.00. Provides detailed information on more than 2,700 ports worldwide.

Lloyd's Marine Equipment Buyers' Guide. Available from Informa UK Ltd., 69-77 Paul St. London E22A 4LQ, United Kingdom. Phone: 800-493-4080 or 44 171 5531000 Fax: 44 171 5531110 • URL: http://www.informa.com • Annual. $270.00. Published in the UK by Lloyd's List (http://www.lloydslist.com). Lists more than 6,000 companies worldwide supplying over 2,000 types of marine products and services, including offshore equipment.

Lloyd's Maritime and Commercial Law Quarterly. Available from LLP Inc., Customer Service, P.O. Box 1017 Westborough, MA 01581-6017. Phone: 800-493-4080 Fax: (508)231-0856 E-mail: enquiries@informa.com • URL: http://www.informa.com • Quarterly. $255.00 per year. Published in the UK by Lloyd's List (http://www.lloydslist.com). Provides international coverage of relevant cases, decisions, and developments.

Lloyd's Maritime Atlas. Available from Informa UK Limited, Sheepen Pl. Colchester C03 3LP, United Kingdom. Phone: 440 1206 772222 E-mail: enquiries@informa.com • URL: http://www.informa.com • Biennial. $119.00. Contains more than 70 pages of world, ocean, regional, and port maps in color. Provides additional information for the planning of world shipping routes, including data on distances, port facilities, recurring weather hazards at sea, international load line zones, and sailing times.

Lloyd's Maritime Directory. Informa PLC, 27 Mortimer St., 4th Fl. London W1T 3JH, United Kingdom. Phone: (44)20 70175000 Fax: (44)20 75531100 E-mail: sales@fairplay.co.uk • URL: http://www.informa.com • Covers: Over 40,000 shipowners, managers, and operators with 75,000 vessels. Also includes Marine consultants; towing, salvage, solicitors, P&I clubs; ship building and repair firms; general maritime organizations, banking and finance and more. Entries include: Firm name, address, phone, fax, e-mail, internet; branch offices; names of principal executives; agents; parent and associated companies; and, for shipowners and lines, detailed information on ships owned, type, or capacity, etc. The former second volume of 'International Shipping and Shipbuilding Directory' is now published separately with the title 'Lloyd's List Marine Equipment Buyers' Guide' (see separate entry).

Lloyd's Maritime Law News Letter North American Edition. Informa UK Ltd., 69-77 Paul St. London EC2A 4LQ, United Kingdom. Phone: 800-493-4080 or 44 171 553 1000 Fax: 44 171 553 1110 • URL: http://www.informa.com • Biweekly. $630.00 per year. Newsletter. Published in the UK by Lloyd's List (http://www.lloydslist.com). Provides "in-depth analysis of developments in U. S. maritimne law and maritime trends."

Lloyd's Port Management. Available from Informa Publishing Group Ltd., PO Box 1017 Westborough, MA 01581-6017. Phone: 800-493-4080 Fax: (508)231-0856 E-mail: enquiries@informa.com • URL: http://www.informa.com • Quarterly. $135.00 per year. Published in the UK by Lloyd's List (http://www.lloydslist.com). Covers port management issues for port operators and users.

Lloyd's Ship Manager. LLP Inc., PO Box 1017 Westborough, MA 01581-6017. Phone: 800-493-4080 Fax: (508)231-0856 E-mail: enquiries@usa.informa.com • URL: http://www.informa.com • 10 times a year. $478.00 per year, including annual supplementary guides and directories. Published in the UK by Lloyd's List (http://www.lloydslist.com). Covers all management, technical, and operational aspects of ocean-going shipping.

Lloyd's Shipping Economist. LLP Inc., PO Box 1017 Westborough, MA 01581-6017. Phone: (508)231-0856 E-mail: enquiries@usa.informa.com Monthly. $1,446.00 per year. Published in the UK by Lloyd's List (http://www.lloydslist.com). Provides current analysis of world shipping markets, including coverage of the economics and costs of various kinds of ship operations. Statistical data and financial/legal directory listings are included.

Loan Market Week: The Newsweekly of the Loan Syndication, Trading and Investment Markets. Institutional Investor, Inc., Journals Group, 225 Park Ave., S New York, NY 10003. Phone: 800-945-2034 or (212)224-3066 Fax: (212)224-3472 E-mail: info@iijournals.com • URL: http://www.iijournals.com • Weekly. $2,370.00 per year. Newsletter. Includes print and online editions. Covers retail banking, commercial lending, foreign loans, bank technology, government regulations, and other topics related to banking. Formerly *Bank Letter*.

Local Area Networks. Gerd Keiser. McGraw Hill, Two Penn Plz. New York, NY 10121. Phone: 800-722-4726 or (212)904-2000 • URL: http://www.prenhall.com • 2001. $76.00. Second edition.

Local Area Networks in Information Management. Harry M. Kibrige. Greenwood Publishing Group, Inc., 88 Post Rd., W Westport, CT 06881. Phone: 800-225-5800 or (203)226-3571 Fax: (203)431-2214 E-mail: customer-service@greenwood.com • URL: http://www.greenwood.com • 1989. $60.00. (New Directions in Information Management Series).

Local Climatological Data. U.S. National Climatic Data Center, National Oceanic and Atmospheric Administration, U. S. Dept. of Commerce, Federal Bldg., Room 120, 151 Patton Ave. Asheville, NC 28801-5001. Phone: (704)271-4476 Fax: (704)271-4246 E-mail: orders@ncdc.noaa.gov • URL: http://www.ncdc.noaa.gov • Monthly.

Local Government Law. Chester J. Antieau. LexisNexis Matthew Bender, 1275 Broadway Albany, NY 12204. Phone: 800-424-4200 or (518)487-3000 Fax: (518)487-3584 E-mail: bookstore.support@lexisnexis.com • URL: http://www.bender.com • $1,113.00. Six looseleaf volumes. Periodic supplementation. States the principle of law for all types of local governments, and backs those principles with case citations from all jurisdictions. Examines the laws and their impact in three primary cases.

Locksmith Ledger International. Locksmith Publishing Corp., 850 Busse Highway Park Ridge, IL 60068. Phone: (708)692-5940 Fax: (708)692-4604 E-mail: lledger@aol.com • URL: http://www.simon-net.com • Monthly. $38.00 per year. Includes *Directory* issue. Formerly *Locksmith Ledger*.

Locksmith Ledger's Security Register. Locksmith Publishing Corp., Div. of ILCO UNICAN, PO Box 888 Notre Dame, IN 46556-0888. Phone: (219)243-8346 Fax: (847)692-4604 E-mail: mferrill@locksmithtraining.com • URL: http://www.simon-net.com • Publication includes: Lists of about 1,300 manufacturers, wholesalers, and distributors of security products; and nearly 80 trade associations. Entries include: For manufacturers and distributors—Company name, address, phone, name of contact, names of key personnel, products manufactured or lines handled. For trade associations—Name, address.

Lockwood-Post's Directory of the Pulp, Paper and Allied Trades. Paperloop, Four Alfred Circle Bedford, MA 01730. Phone: (866)271-8525 Fax: (818)487-4550 E-mail: info@paperloop.com Annual. $395.00. Formerly *Lockwood's Directory of the Paper and Allied Trades.*

Lodging. American Hotel and Lodging Association, 1201 New York Ave., N. W., Suite 600 Washington, DC 20005. Phone: (202)289-3100 Fax: (202)289-3129 E-mail: info@ahla.com • URL: http://www.ahla.com • Monthly. Membership. Editorial sections include news, finance, technology, foodservice, new products, human resources, marketing, design, and renovation.

The Lodging and Food Service Industry. Gerald W. Lattin and others. Educational Institute of the American Hotel & Motel Association, P.O. Box 1240 East Lansing, MI 48826-1240. Phone: 800-344-4381 or (517)372-8800 Fax: (517)372-5141 E-mail: info@ei-ahla.org • URL: http://www.eiahma.org • 1998. $60.95. Fourth revised edition. General survey of the hospitality industry.

Lodging Hospitality: Management Magazine for Hotels, Motels and Resorts. Penton Media, Inc., 1300 E. Ninth St. Cleveland, OH 44114. Phone: (216)696-7000 Fax: (216)696-1752 E-mail: information@penton.com • URL: http://www.penton.com • 16 times a year. $70.00 per year. Covers a wide variety of topics relating to hotels, motels, and resorts, including management, marketing, finance, operations, and technology.

Lodging, Restaurant and Tourism Index. Distance Learning Service. Purdue University, Consumer and Family Sciences Library, 1002 Stone Hall West Lafayette, IN 47907-1002. Phone: (765)494-2914 Fax: (765)496-2484 • URL: http://www.lib.purdue.edu • Quarterly. $265.00 per year. Provides subject indexing to 52 periodicals related to the hospitality industry. Annual bound cumulations are available. Formerly *Lodging and Restaurant Index.*

The Logic of Organizations. Bengt Abrahamsson. Sage Publications, Inc., 2455 Teller Rd. Thousand Oaks, CA 91320. Phone: 800-818-7243 or (805)499-9774 Fax: 800-583-2665 or (805)499-0871 E-mail: webmaster@sagepub.com • URL: http://www.sagepub.com • 1992. $39.95. Consists of two major sections: "The Emergence of Bureaucracy." and "Administration Theory."

Logistics Management. Reed Business Information, 360 Park Ave., S New York, NY 10010. Phone: 800-446-6551 or (646)746-6400 Fax: (646)746-7028 E-mail: corporatecommunications@reedbusiness.com • URL: http://www.reedbusiness.com • Monthly. $99.000 per year. Includes *International Shipping* and *Warehousing and Distribution*. Formerly *Logistics Management and Distribution Report.*

Logistics Management - The Association for Transportation Law, Logistics, and Policy.

Logo Power: Creating World-Class Logos and Effective Business Identities. David E. Carter. DIANE Publishing Co., 330 Pusey Ave. Collingdale, PA 19023-8428. Phone: 800-782-3833 or (610)461-6200 Fax: (610)461-6130 E-mail: dianepub@erols.com • URL: http://www.dianepublishing.com • 2001. $40.00. Explains how to plan, develop, evaluate, and implement a company logo system.

LOMA., 2300 Windy Ridge Pkwy., Ste. 600 Atlanta, GA 30339-8443. Phone: 800-275-5662 or (770)951-1770 Fax: (770)984-0441 E-mail: askloma@loma.org • URL: http://www.loma.org • Life and health insurance companies and financial services in the U.S. and Canada; and overseas in 45 countries; affiliate members are firms that provide professional support to member companies. Provides research, information, training, and educational activities in areas of operations and systems, human resources, financial planning and employee development. Administers FLMI Insurance Education Program, which awards FLMI (Fellow, Life Management Institute) designation to those who complete the ten-examination program.

London Currency Report. World Reports Ltd., 280 Madison Ave., Ste. 280 New York, NY 10016-0802. Phone: (212)679-0095 Fax: (212)679-1094 10 times a year. $950.00 per year. Formerly *Gold and Silver Survey.*

Long Range Planning. Strategic Planning Society. Elsevier, 360 Park Ave. S New York, NY 10010-1710. Phone: 888-437-4636 or (212)989-5800 Fax: (212)633-3990 E-mail: usinfo-f@elsevier.com • URL: http://www.elsevier.com • Bimonthly. Qualified personnel, $197.00 per year; institutions, $1,346.00 per year.

Long Term Care Administration; The Management of Institutional and Non-Institutional Components of the Continuum of Care. Ben Abramovice. The Haworth Press, Inc., 10 Alice St. Binghamton, NY 13904-1580. Phone: 800-429-6784 or (607)722-5857 Fax: 800-895-0582 or (607)722-1424 E-mail: getinfo@haworthpressinc.com • URL: http://www.haworthpressinc.com • 1987. $39.95. Explores the multidisciplinary nature of long-term care. (Marketing and Health Services Administration: No. 1)

Long-Term Care: An Annotated Bibliography. Theodore H. Koff. Greenwood Publishing Group, Inc., 88 Post Rd., W. Westport, CT 06881. Phone: 800-225-5800 or (203)226-3571 Fax: (203)431-2214 E-mail: customer-service@greenwood.com • URL: http://www.greenwood.com • 1995. $59.95. (Bibliographies and Indexes in Gerontology Series: No. 25).

Long-Term Care and Its Alternatives. Charles B. Inlander and others. People's Medical Society, 462 Walnut St. Allentown, PA 18102. Phone: (610)770-1670 Fax: (610)770-0607 1996. $16.95. Provides practical advice on the financing of long-term health care. The author is a consumer advocate and president of the People's Medical Society.

Long Term Care Campaign., PO Box 27394 Washington, DC 20038. Phone: (202)434-3744 or (202)434-3829 Fax: (202)434-6403 E-mail: lmainfo@lmaweb.com • URL: http://www.ltccampaign.org • Consumer, provider, business, labor, older adult, and disability groups. Works to make long term health care accessible and affordable for all families.

The Long-Term Care Market. MarketResearch.com, 641 Ave. of the Americas, 4th Fl. New York, NY 10011. Phone: 800-298-5699 or (212)807-2629 Fax: (212)807-2676 E-mail: customerservice@marketresearch.com • URL: http://www.marketresearch.com • 1999. $3,250.00. Market data with forecasts to the year 2005. Emphasis is on the over-85 age group. Covers health insurance, the nursing home industry, pharmaceuticals, healthcare supplies, etc.

Looking Fit. Virgo Publishing, Inc., PO Box 40079 Phoenix, AZ 85067-0079. Phone: (480)990-1101 Fax: (480)990-0819 E-mail: virgopub@vpico.com • URL: http://www.vpico.com • 14 times a year. $52.00 per year. Covers the business and marketing side of health clubs, aerobic studios, and tanning salons.

Looking Fit Buyers Guide. Virgo Publishing, Inc., PO Box 40079 Phoenix, AZ 85067-0079. Phone: (480)990-1101 Fax: (480)990-0819 E-mail: virgopub@vpico.com • URL: http://www.vpico.com • Annual. $4.00. Lists suppliers of products and equipment for health clubs, aerobic studios, and tanning salons.

Looking for Gold: The Modern Prospector's Handbook. Bradford Angier. Stackpole Books, Inc., 5067 Ritter Rd. Mechanicsburg, PA 17055. Phone: 800-732-3669 Fax: (717)796-0412 E-mail: jbender@stackpolebooks.com • URL: http://www.stackpolebooks.com • 1995. $16.95.

Looking Good in Print: A Guide to Basic Design for Desktop Publishing. Roger C. Parker. Paraglyph, Inc., 4015 N 78th St., No. 115 Scottsdale, AZ 85251. Phone: (602)994-3021 Fax: (602)994-3021 • URL: http://www.paraglyphpress.com • 2003. $29.99. Fifth edition. Includes CD-ROM. Covers newsletters, advertisements, brochures, manuals, and correspondence.

The Lookout. National Boating Federation, PO Box 4111 Annapolis, MD 21403. Phone: (540)659-3275 E-mail: davidg8790@aol.com • URL: http://www.n-b-f.org • Bimonthly. Newsletter. Membership.

Los Alamos National Laboratory.

Louis Rukeyser's Mutual Funds. Louis Rukeyser's Wall Street Club, PO Box 9605 McLean, VA 22102. Phone: 800-892-9702 or (703)905-8000 E-mail: customer-service@rukeyser.com • URL: http://www.rukeyser.com • Monthly. $79.00 per year. Newsletter. Provides conservative advice on mutual fund investing.

Louis Rukeyser's Wall Street. Louis Rukeyser's Wall Street Club, PO Box 9605 Mclean, VA 22102. Phone: 800-892-9702 or (703)905-8000 E-mail: customer-service@rukeyser.com • URL: http://www.rukeyser.com • Monthly. $39.50 per year. Newsletter. Gives recommendations for personal investing.

Lovejoy's College Guide. IDG Books Worldwide Inc., 10475 Crosspoint Blvd. Indianapolis, IN 46256-3386. Phone: 800-434-3422 or (317)572-3299 E-mail: lmoss@idgbooks.com Covers: 2,500 American colleges, universities, and technical institutes, and selected foreign colleges accredited by United States regional accrediting associations. Entries include: School name, location, date founded, name changes, enrollment figures, SAT/ACT figures, library size, faculty-student ratio, religious affiliation, admission information, tuition, room and board costs, scholarships and loans, athletic programs, curricula and degrees offered, special programs, summer sessions.

The Low Priced Stock Survey. Horizon Publishing Company L.L.C., 7412 Calumet Ave. Hammond, IN 46324. Phone: 800-233-5922 or (219)852-3200 Fax: (219)931-6487 E-mail: editor@mcilvainecompany.com Description: Reviews and analyzes stocks offered at a price of $20 or less. Analysis is divided into sections: Emerging Growth Opportunities, The Fundamentalist, Bargain Spotlight, Stock of the Month, and Master List Highlights. Includes weekly closes of the Dow Jones Industrials and NASDAQ, and statistics.

Low Rate and No Fee Credit Card List. Bankcard Holders of America, 560 Herndon Pky., Ste. 120 Herndon, VA 22070. E-mail: current@credit-report-bureaus-credit-reporting-agency-agencies.com Quarterly. $4.00 per copy. Lists about 50 banks offering relatively low interest rates and/or no annual fee for credit card accounts. Formerly *Low Interest Rate.*

Lowe Institute of Political Economy., Claremont McKenna College, 850 Columbia Ave. Claremont, CA 91711. Phone: (909)621-8012 Fax: (909)607-8008 E-mail: lowe@claremontmckenna.edu • URL: http://www.lowe.research.mckenna.edu/lowe • Research topics include NAFTA.

Lower Coastal Plain Research Station/Cunningham Research Station.

LP-GAS. Elsevier, 655 Avenue of the Americas New York, NY 10010-1710. Phone: 800-366-2665 or (212)989-5800 Fax: 800-535-9935 or (212)633-3680 E-mail: custserv@elsevier.com • URL: http://www.elsevier.com • Monthly. $33.00 per year. Covers the production, storage, utilization, and marketing of liquefied petroleum gas (propane). Gas appliances are included. Includes *Annual Supplement.*

Lubrication Engineering. Society of Tribiologists and Lubrication Engineers, 840 Busse Highway Park Ridge, IL 60068-2376. Phone: (847)825-5536 Fax: (847)825-1456 E-mail: stle@interaccess.com • URL: http://www.stle.org • Monthly. $70.00 per year.

Ludwig Von Mises Institute for Austrian Economics.

Luggage and Leather Goods Manufacturers of America.

Lumber Co-Operator. Northeastern Retail Lumber Association, 585 N. Greenbush Rd. Rensselaer, NY 12144-9453. Phone: 800-292-6752 or (518)286-1010 Fax: (518)286-1755 E-mail: amy@nrla.org • URL: http://www.nrla.org • Bimonthly. Members, $35.00 per year; non-members, $40.00 per year.

Lumber Production and Mill Stocks. U.S. Bureau of the Census, Washington, DC 20233-0800. Phone: (301)457-4100 Fax: (301)457-3842 • URL: http://www.census.gov • Annual. (Current Industrial Reports MA-24T).

Lumbermens Red Book: Reference Book of the Lumbermens Credit Association. Lumbermens Credit Association, 20 Wacker St., Suite 1800 Chicago, IL 60606-2905. Phone: (312)553-0943 Fax: (312)553-2149 E-mail: lumbermenscredit@compuserve.com • URL: http://www.lumbermenscredit.com • Semiannual $2,140.00 per year. Weekly supplements. Lists approximately 39,000 United States firms in the lumber and woodworking industries, with credit ratings. Available online.

Lundberg Letter. Lundberg Survey, Incorporated, PO Box 6002 Camarillo, CA 93011. Phone: (805)383-2400 Fax: (805)383-2424 E-mail: lsi@lundbergsurvey.com Description: Provides statistics and analysis of U.S. oil marketing primary data. Includes an in-depth single-subject profile of a development in the petroleum market in each issue. Discusses such topics as retail/wholesale pricing, market shares, and station characteristics nationwide and regionally.

The Lynch Municipal Bond Advisory. James F. Lynch., editor. The Lynch Municipal Bond Advisory, PO Box 25114 Sante Fe, NM 87504. Phone: (505)984-9199 Fax: (505)984-0269 E-mail: lsi@lundbergsurvey.com Description: Addresses the municipal bond market.

Machine Design: Magazine of Applied Technology for Design Engineering. Penton Media, Inc., 1300 E. Ninth St. Cleveland, OH 44114. Phone: (216)696-7000 Fax: (216)696-1752 E-mail: information@penton.com • URL: http://www.penton.com • 21 times a year. $110.00 per year. Includes *Machine Design Reference Issues* and *Penton Executive Network.*

Machine Shop Fundamentals. Stephen F. Krar. Delmar Learning, 5 Maxwell Dr. Clifton Park, NY 12065. Phone: 800-998-7498 or (518)348-2300 Fax: 800-487-4888 E-mail: info@delmar.com • URL: http://www.delmarlearning.com • 1997. $37.95. (Machine Tool Series).

Machine Tool Practices. Richard R. Kibbe. Prentice Hall PTR, 240 Frisch Ct. Paramus, NJ 07652. Phone: 800-282-0693 Fax: 800-445-6991 • URL: http://www.phptr.com • 2001. $95.00. Seventh edition.

Machine Vision and Robotics Industry Directory. Society of Manufacturing Engineers, One SME Dr. Dearborn, MI 48121. Phone: 800-733-4763 or (313)271-1500 Fax: (313)271-2861 E-mail: service@sme.org • URL: http://www.sme.org • Biennial. $25.00. Provides information on suppliers of machine vision systems, services, and equipment. Formerly *Machine Vision Industry Directory.*

Machine Vision Association of the Society of Manufacturing Engineers., 1 SME Dr. Dearborn, MI 48121. Phone: 800-733-4763 or (313)271-1500 Fax: (313)425-3400 E-mail: service@sme.org • URL: http://www.sme.org/mva • Members are professional engineers, managers, and students. Promotes the effective use of machine vision (optical sensing of actual scenes for use in machine control).

Machinery Buyers' Guide: The Annual Directory of Engineering and Products Services (United Kingdom). Findlay Publications Ltd., Franks Hall, Horton Kirby Horton Kirby DA4 9LL, United Kingdom. Phone: 44 1322 860000 Fax: 44 1322 289577 E-mail: enquiries@findlay.co.uk Annual. $200.00. About 6,000 firms offering machine tool, engineering products, machinery, industrial equipment and services worldwide.

Machinery Dealers National Association., 315 S Patrick St. Alexandria, VA 22314. Phone: 800-872-7807 or (703)836-9300 Fax: (703)836-9303 E-mail: office@mdna.org • URL: http://www.mdna.org • Dealers in used, rebuilt, and reconditioned industrial machinery.

Machinery's Handbook. Macauley and others. Industrial Press, Inc., 200 Madison Ave. New York, NY 10016. Phone: 888-528-7852 or (212)889-6330 Fax: (212)545-8327 E-mail: induspress@aol.com • URL: http://www.industrialpress.com • 2001. $149.95. 26th edition. Reference book for the mechanical engineer, draftsman, toolmaker, and machinist. Includes CD-ROM.

Mack Center on Managing Technological Innovation., University of Pennsylvania, 3620 Locust Walk, Suite 1400 Philadelphia, PA 19104. Phone: (215)898-2104 Fax: (215)573-2129 E-mail: dayg@wharton.upenn.edu • URL: http://www.emertech.wharton.upenn.edu • Conducts research related to international business. Formerly Huntsman Center for Global Competition and Innovation.

Macmillan Encyclopedia of Energy. Available from Gale Cengage Learning, 27500 Drake Rd. Farmington Hills, MI 48331-3535. Phone: 800-877-GALE or (248)699-GALE Fax: 800-414-5043 E-mail: gale.galeord@cengage.com • URL: http://gale.cengage.com • 2001. $395.00. Three volumes. Published by Macmillan Reference USA. Covers the business, technology, and history of a wide variety of energy sources.

Macmillan Encyclopedia of the Environment. Stephen R. Kellert, editor. Gale Cengage Learning, 27500 Drake Rd. Farmington Hills, MI 48331-3535. Phone: 800-877-GALE or (248)699-4253 Fax: 800-414-5043 E-mail: gale.galeord@cengage.com • URL: http://www.galeg.com • 1997. $400.00. Six volumes.

Macmillan Encyclopedia of Transportation. Available from Gale Cengage Learning, 27500 Drake Rd. Farmington Hills, MI 48331-3535. Phone: 800-877-GALE or (248)699-GALE Fax: 800-414-5043 E-mail: gale.galeord@cengage.com • URL: http://gale.cengage.com • 1999. $450.00. Six volumes. Published by Macmillan Reference USA. Covers the business, technology, and history of transportation on land, on water, in the air, and in space. Includes definitions, cross-references, and 200 color illustrations.

Macmillan Encyclopedia of Weather. Available from Gale Cengage Learning, 27500 Drake Rd. Farmington Hills, MI 48331-3535. Phone: 800-877-GALE or (248)699-GALE Fax: 800-414-5043 E-mail: gale.galeord@cengage.com • URL: http://gale.cengage.com • 2001. $140.00. Published by Macmillan Reference USA. Contains 150 entries covering the basics of weather and weather forecasting. Includes illustrations in color.

Macroeconomics and Company Planning. Continuing Professional Education Div. American Institute of Certified Public Accountants, 1211 Ave. of the Americas New York, NY 10036-8775. Phone: 800-862-4272 or (212)596-6200 Fax: (212)596-6213 E-mail: lmorales@aicpa.org • URL: http://www.aicpa.org • Looseleaf. Self-study course.

Macworld: The Macintosh Magazine for the Network Professional. Mac Publishing, L.L.C., 301 Howard St., 15th Fl. San Francisco, CA 94105. Phone: 800-217-7874 or (415)243-0505 Fax: (415)442-0766 E-mail: letters@macworld.com • URL: http://www.macworld.com • Monthly. $19.97 per year. For Macintosh personal computer users.

Made to Measure. Halper Publishing Co., 830 Mosley Rd. Highland Park, IL 60035. Phone: (847)780-2900 Fax: (847)780-2902 • URL: http://www.halper.com • Semiannual. Controlled circulation.

Magazine and Bookseller: The Retailer's Guide to Magazines and Paperbacks. North American Publishing Co., 401 N. Broad St. Philadelphia, PA 19108. Phone: 800-777-8074 or (215)238-5482 Fax: 800-664-1533 or (215)238-5412 E-mail: customerservice@napco.com • URL: http://www.napco.com • Bimonthly. Free to qualified personnel; others, $59.00 per year.

The Magazine Antiques. Brant Publications, Inc., 575 Broadway, 5th Fl. New York, NY 10012. Phone: 800-925-9271 or (212)941-2800 Fax: (212)941-2885 Monthly. Individuals, $39.95 per year; libraries, $34.95 per year. Emphasizes antique furniture, but also covers paintings, architecture, glass and textiles. Formerly *Antiques*.

The Magazine for Electronic Publishing Professionals. Publish Media, 462 Boston St. Topsfield, MA 01983-1232. Phone: (978)887-7900 Fax: (978)887-6117 E-mail: edit@publish.com • URL: http://www.publish.com • Monthly. $39.90 per year. Edited for professional publishers, graphic designers, and industry service providers. Covers new products and emerging technologies for the electronic publishing industry.

Magazine Index. Gale Cengage Learning, 27500 Drake Rd. Farmington Hills, MI 48331-3535. Phone: 800-877-GALE or (248)699-GALE Fax: 800-414-5043 or (248)699-8069 E-mail: galeord@gale.com • URL: http://gale.cengage.com • General magazine indexing (popular literature), 1973 to present. Daily updates. Inquire as to online cost and availability.

Magazine Index Plus. Gale Cengage Learning, 27500 Drake Rd. Farmington Hills, MI 48331-3535. Phone: 800-877-GALE or (248)699-GALE Fax: 800-414-5043 or (248)699-8069 E-mail: galeord@gale.com • URL: http://gale.cengage.com • Monthly. $4,000.00 per year (includes InfoTrac workstation). Provides full text on CD-ROM for about 100 popular, general interest magazines and indexing for 300 others. Includes special indexing of reviews and product evaluations. Time period is 1980 to date.

Magazine Publishers of America., 919 Third Ave., 22nd Fl. New York, NY 10022. Phone: (212)872-3700 Fax: (212)888-4217 E-mail: infocenter@magazine.org • URL: http://www.magazine.org • Members are publishers of consumer and other periodicals. Affiliated with American Society of Magazine Editors; Media Credit Association; Publishers Information Bureau. Formerly Magazine Publishers Association.

Magazines Career Directory: A Practical One-Stop Guide to Getting a Job in Publ c Relations. Visible Ink Press, 27500 Drake Rd. Farmington Hills, MI 48331. Phone: 800-877-GALE or (248)699-GALE Fax: 800-414-5043 or (248)699-8035 E-mail: gale.galeord@cengage.com • URL: http://gale.cengage.com • 1993. $39.00. Fifth edition. Includes information on magazine publishing careers in art, editing, sales, and business management. Provides advice from "insiders," resume suggestions, a directory of companies that may offer entry-level positions, and a directory of career information sources. (Career Advisor Series).

Magazines for Libraries: Reviewing the Best Publications for All Serials Collections Since 1969. R. R. Bowker, 630 Central Ave. New Providence, NJ 07974. Phone: 888-269-5372 Fax: (908)219-0098 E-mail: info@bowker.com • URL: http://www.bowker.com • 2002. 12th edition. $225.00.

Magill's Cinema Annual. Gale Cengage Learning, 27500 Drake Rd. Farmington Hills, MI 48331-3535. Phone: 800-877-GALE or (248)699-4253 Fax: 800-414-5043 E-mail: gale.galeord@cengage.com • URL: http://gale.cengage.com • Annual. $125.00. Provides reviews and facts for new films released each year in the United States. Typically covers about 300 movies, with nine indexes to title, director, screenwriter, actor, music, etc. Includes awards, obituaries, and "up-and- coming" performers of the year.

Mail Order Association of America.

Mail Order Business. Entrepreneur Media, Inc., 2445 McCabe Way Irvine, CA 92614. Phone: 800-421-2300 or (949)261-2325 Fax: (949)261-0234 E-mail: entmag@entrepreneur.com • URL: http://www.entrepreneur.com • Looseleaf. $59.50. A practical guide to starting a mail order business. Covers profit potential, start-up costs, pricing, market size evaluation, accounting, advertising, promotion, etc. (Start-Up Business Guide No. E1015.)

Mail Order Business Directory. B. Klein Publications, PO Box 6578 Delray Beach, FL 33482. Phone: (561)496-3316 Fax: (561)496-5546 E-mail: lmoss@idgbooks.com Covers: 5,000 firms in the United States and doing business by mail order and catalogs. Entries include: Name, address, phone, name of owner or contact, and products or services.

Mail Service Pharmacy Market. MarketResearch.com, 641 Ave. of the Americas, 4th Fl. New York, NY 10011. Phone: 800-298-5699 or (212)807-2629 Fax: (212)807-2676 E-mail: customerservice@marketresearch.com • URL: http://www.marketresearch.com • 1999. $3,250.00. Provides detailed market data, with forecasts to the year 2003.

Mailing and Fulfillment Service Association., 1421 Prince St. Alexandria, VA 22314-2806. Phone: 800-333-6272 or (703)836-9200 Fax: (703)548-8204 E-mail: masa-mail@mfsanet.org • URL: http://www.mfsanet.org • Formerly Mail Advertising Service Association International.

Mailing Services. Entrepreneur Media, Inc., 2445 McCabe Way Irvine, CA 92614. Phone: 800-421-2300 or (949)261-2325 Fax: (949)261-0234 E-mail: entmag@entrepreneur.com • URL: http://www.entrepreneur.com • Looseleaf. $59.50. A practical guide to starting a mailing services business. Covers profit potential, start-up costs, market size evaluation, owner's time required, site selection, pricing, accounting, advertising, promotion, etc. (Start-Up Business Guide No. E1354.)

Main Economic Indicators. OECD Publication and Information Center, 2001 L St., N.W., Suite 650 Washington, DC 20036-4910. Phone: 800-456-6323 or (202)785-6323 Fax: (202)785-0350 E-mail: washington.contact@oecd.org • URL: http://www.oecdwash.org • Monthly. $450.00 per year. "The essential source of timely statistics for OECD member countries." Includes a wide variety of business, economic, and industrial data for the 29 OECD nations.

Main Economic Indicators: Historical Statistics. OECD Publications and Information Center, 2001 L St. NW, Ste. 650 Washington, DC 20036-4922. Phone: (202)785-6323 Fax: (202)785-0350 E-mail: washington.contact@oecd.org • URL: http://www.oecdwash.org • Annual. $475.00. Includes online edition.

Main Science and Technology Indicators. OECD Publications and Information Center, 2001 L St., N.W., Suite 650 Washington, DC 20036-4922. Phone: (202)785-6323 Fax: (202)785-0350 E-mail: washington.contact@oecd.org • URL: http://www.oecdwash.org • Semiannual. $80.00 per year. Includes online edition. Provides latest available data on research and development expenditures in OECD countries. Abilingual publication.

Maine Lobstermen's Association., 21 Western Ave., Ste. 1 Kennebunk, ME 04043. Phone: (207)967-4555 or (207)363-6783 Fax: (866)407-3770 E-mail: info@mainelobstermen.org • URL: http://www.mainelobstermen.org • Licensed lobstermen and supporting business. Gives Maine's lobstermen a voice and influence at the highest levels of government.

Mainly Marketing: The Schoonmaker Report to Technical Managements. Warren K. Schoonmaker, editor. Schoonmaker Associates, 2405 Antigua Circle, Apt. E4 Coconut Creek, FL 33066-1013. Phone: (516)473-8741 Monthly. $200.00 per year. Report to technical managements focusing on methods of marketing high technology.

Maintenance Engineering Handbook. Lindley R. Higgins and R. Keith Mobley. McGraw-Hill, 1221 Ave. of the Americas New York, NY 10020. Phone: 800-722-4726 or (212)512-2000 Fax: (212)512-4502 E-mail: customer.service@mcgraw-hill.com • URL: http://www.mcgraw-hill.com • 2001. $150.00. Sixth edition. Contains about 60 chapters by various authors in 12 major sections covering all elements of industrial and plant maintenance.

Maintenance Supplies. Cygnus Business Media, 445 Broad Hollow Rd. Melville, NY 11747-3601. Phone: 800-308-6397 or (631)845-2700 Fax: (631)845-2798 E-mail: rich.reiff@cygnuspub.com • URL: http://www.cygnusbzb.com • Monthly. $60.00 per year. Geared to distributors of sanitary supplies, maintenance equipment, etc.

Maintenance Supplies Buyers' Guide. Cygnus Business Media, Inc., 445 Broad Hollow Rd. Melville, NY 11747. Phone: 800-308-6397 or (631)845-2700 Fax: (631)845-2798 E-mail: rich.reiff@cygnuspub.com • URL: http://www.cygnusbzb.com • Annual. $15.00. Approximately 1,000 manufacturers and associations for commercial, industrial, and institutional janitorial supplies; international coverage. Formerly *Maintenance Supplies Annual*.

Maize Abstracts. Available from CABI Publishing, North America, 875 Massachusetts Ave. Cambridge, MA 02139. Phone: 800-528-4841 or (617)395-4056 Fax: (617)354-6875 E-mail: cabi-nao@cabi.org • URL: http://www.cabi-publishing.org • Bimonthly. $840.00 per year. Published in England by CABI Publishing. Provides worldwide coverage of the literature.

Major Chemical and Petrochemical Companies of Europe. Available from Gale Cengage Learning, 27500 Drake Rd. Farmington Hills, MI 48331-3535. Phone: 800-877-GALE or (248)699-GALE Fax: 800-414-5043 E-mail: gale.galeord@cengage.com • URL: http://www.galegroup.com • 2003. $880.00. Fifth edition. Two volumes. Published by Graham & Whiteside Ltd., London. Includes financial, personnel, and product information for chemical companies in Western Europe.

Major Chemical and Petrochemical Companies of the World. Available from Gale Cengage Learning, 27500 Drake Rd. Farmington Hills, MI 48331-3535. Phone: 800-877-GALE or (248)699-GALE Fax: 800-414-5043 E-mail: gale.galeord@cengage.com • URL: http://www.galegroup.com • 2002. $880.00. Sixth edition. Published by Graham & Whiteside. Contains profiles of more than 7,000 important chemical and petrochemical companies in various countries. Subject areas include general chemicals, specialty chemicals, agricultural chemicals, petrochemicals, industrial gases, and fertilizers.

Major Companies of Europe. Available from Gale Cengage Learning, 27500 Drake Rd. Farmington Hills, MI 48331-3535. Phone: 800-877-GALE or (248)699-GALE Fax: 800-414-5043 E-mail: gale.galeord@cengage.com • URL: http://www.galegroup.com • 2003. $1,895.00. Four volumes. Published by Graham & Whiteside. Approximately 24,000 major companies and key executives in European countries in all lines of business.

Major Companies of Latin America and the Caribbean 2001. Available from Gale Cengage Learning, 27500 Drake Rd. Farmington Hills, MI 48331-3535. Phone: 800-877-GALE or (248)699-GALE Fax: 800-414-5043 E-mail: gale.galeord@cengage.com • URL: http://www.galegroup.com • Annual. $850.00. Published by Graham & Whiteside, London. Contains detailed information on 9,000 major companies in Central and South America and the Caribbean. Includes manufacturers, exporters, importers, service companies, and financial institutions.

Major Companies of South West Asia. Available from Gale Cengage Learning, 27500 Drake Rd. Farmington Hills, MI 48331-3535. Phone: 800-877-GALE or (248)699-GALE Fax: 800-414-5043 E-mail: gale.galeord@cengage.com • URL: http://www.galegroup.com • 2001. $570.00. Fifth edition. Published by Graham and Whiteside. Provides information on 6,000 leading businesses in India, Turkey, Pakistan, Iran and other countries of the region.

Major Companies of the Arab World. Available from Gale Cengage Learning, 27500 Drake Rd. Farmington Hills, MI 48331-3535. Phone: 800-877-GALE or (248)699-GALE Fax: 800-414-5043 E-mail: gale.galeord@cengage.com • URL: http://www.galegroup.com • Annual. $955.00. Contains basic information on companies. Published by Graham & Whiteside, London.

Major Companies of the Far East and Australasia. Gale Cengage Learning, 27500 Drake Rd. Farmington Hills, MI 48331-3535. Phone: 800-877-GALE or (248)699-4253 Fax: 800-414-5043 E-mail: gale.galeord@cengage.com • URL: http://gale.cengage.com • Annual. $1,595.00. Three volumes. Published by Graham & Whiteside. Volume one: *South East Asia*, volume two: *East Asia*, volume three: *Australia, New Zealand, and Papua New Guinea*. Includes a total of 13,000 leading companies, with the names of 81,000 senior executives. (Volumes are available individually.)

Major Employers of Europe. Available from Gale Cengage Learning, 27500 Drake Rd. Farmington Hills, MI 48331-3535. Phone: 800-877-GALE or (248)699-GALE Fax: 800-414-5043 E-mail: gale.galeord@cengage.com • URL: http://www.galegroup.com • Annual. $295.00. Published by Graham & Whiteside. Provides concise information on the top 10,000 companies in Europe, according to number of employees. Firms are indexed by country and by business activity.

Major Energy Companies of the World. Available from Gale Cengage Learning, 27500 Drake Rd. Farmington Hills, MI 48331-3535. Phone: 800-877-GALE or (248)699-GALE Fax: 800-414-5043 E-mail: gale.galeord@cengage.com • URL: http://gale.cengage.com • Annual. $880.00. Published by

SOURCES CITED

Graham & Whiteside. Contains detailed information on more than 3,300 important energy companies in various countries. Industries include electricity generation, coal, natural gas, nuclear energy, petroleum, fuel distribution, and equipment for energy production.

Major Financial Institutions of Europe. Available from Gale Cengage Learning, 27500 Drake Rd. Farmington Hills, MI 48331-3535. Phone: (248)699-GALE Fax: 800-414-5043 E-mail: gale.galeord@cengage.com • URL: http://www.galegroup.com • Annual. $510.00. Contains profiles of over 2,000 financial institutions in Europe such as banks, investment companies, and insurance companies. Formerly *Major Financial Institutions of Continental Europe*.

Major Financial Institutions of the World 2001. Available from Gale Cengage Learning, 27500 Drake Rd. Farmington Hills, MI 48331-3535. Phone: 800-877-GALE or (248)699-GALE Fax: 800-414-5043 E-mail: gale.gale@cengage.com • URL: http://www.galegroup.com • 2003. $880.00. Sixth edition. Two volumes. Published by Graham & Whiteside. Contains detailed information on more than 7,500 important financial institutions in various countries. Includes banks, investment companies, and insurance companies.

Major Food and Drink Companies of the World. Available from Gale Cengage Learning, 27500 Drake Rd. Farmington Hills, MI 48331-3535. Phone: 800-877-GALE or (248)699-GALE Fax: 800-414-5043 • URL: http://www.galegroup.com • Annual. $880.00. Two volumes. Published by Graham & Whiteside. Contains profiles and trade names for more than 9,800 important food and beverage companies in various countries. In addition to foods, includes both alcoholic and nonalcoholic drink products.

Major Household Appliances. U.S. Bureau of the Census, Washington, DC 20233-0800. Phone: (301)457-4100 Fax: (301)457-3842 • URL: http://www.census.gov • Annual. (Current Industrial Reports MA-36F.)

Major Information Technology Companies of the World 2001. Available from Gale Cengage Learning, 27500 Drake Rd. Farmington Hills, MI 48331-3535. Phone: 800-877-GALE or (248)699-GALE Fax: 800-414-5043 E-mail: gale.galeord@cengage.com • URL: http://www.galegroup.com • Annual. $880.00. Published by Graham & Whiteside. Contains profiles of more than 3,100 leading information technology companies in various countries.

Major Market Share Companies: Asia Pacific. Available from Gale Cengage Learning, 27500 Drake Rd. Farmington Hills, MI 48331-3535. Phone: 800-877-GALE or (248)699-GALE Fax: 800-414-5043 E-mail: gale.galeord@cengage.com • URL: http://www.galegroup.com • 2003. $990.00. Second edition. Published by Euromonitor. Provides consumer market share data and rankings for multinational and regional companies. Covers leading firms in Japan, China, Australia, South Korea, Indonesia, Malaysia, Philippines, and Thailand.

Major Market Share Companies: Europe. Available from Gale Cengage Learning, 27500 Drake Rd. Farmington Hills, MI 48331-3535. Phone: 800-877-GALE or (248)699-GALE Fax: 800-414-5043 or (248)699-8069 E-mail: galeord@galegroup.com • URL: http://www.galegroup.com • 2001. $990.00. Published by Euromonitor. Provides consumer market share data and rankings for multinational and regional companies. Covers leading firms in 14 European countries.

Major Market Share Companies: The Americas. Available from Gale Cengage Learning, 27500 Drake Rd. Farmington Hills, MI 48331-3535. Phone: 800-877-GALE or (248)699-GALE Fax: 800-414-5043 E-mail: gale.galeord@cengage.com • URL: http://www.galegroup.com • 2003. $990.00. Second edition. Published by Euromonitor. Provides consumer market share data and rankings for multinational and regional companies. Covers leading firms in the U.S., Canada, Mexico, Brazil, Argentina, Venezuela, and Chile.

Major Marketing Campaigns Annual. Gale Cengage Learning, 27500 Drake Rd. Farmington Hills, MI 48331-3535. Phone: 800-877-GALE or (248)699-4253 Fax: 800-414-5043 or (248)699-8069 E-mail: gale.galeord@cengage.com • URL: http://gale.cengage.com • 1999. $160.00. Describes in detail "100 major marketing initiatives of the previous calendar year." Includes illustrations.

Major Performance Rankings. Available from Gale Cengage Learning, 27500 Drake Rd. Farmington Hills, MI 48331-3535. Phone: 800-877-GALE or (248)699-GALE Fax: 800-414-5043 E-mail: gale.galeord@cengage.com • URL: http://www.galegroup.com • 2003. $1,190.00. Second edition. Published by Euromonitor. Ranks 2,500 leading consumer product companies worldwide by various kinds of business and financial data, such as sales, profit, and market share. Includes international, regional, and country rankings.

Major Pharmaceutical Companies of the World. Available from Gale Cengage Learning, 27500 Drake Rd. Farmington Hills, MI 48331-3535. Phone: 800-877-GALE or (248)699-GALE Fax: 800-414-5043 E-mail: gale.galeord@cengage.com • URL: http://www.galegroup.com • 2003. $880.00. Fifth edition. Published by Graham & Whiteside. Contains detailed information and trade names for more than 2,500 important pharmaceutical companies in various countries.

Major Telecommunications Companies of the World. Available from Gale Cengage Learning, 27500 Drake Rd. Farmington Hills, MI 48331-3535. Phone: 800-877-GALE or (248)699-GALE Fax: 800-414-5043 E-mail: gale.galeord@cengage.com • URL: http://www.galegroup.com • 2003. $885.00. Sixth edition. Published by Graham & Whiteside. Contains detailed information and trade names for more than 3,500 important telecommunications companies in various countries.

Major 20th-Century Writers: A Selection of Sketches from Contemporary Authors. Gale Cengage Learning, 27500 Drake Rd. Farmington Hills, MI 48331-3535. Phone: 800-877-GALE or (248)699-4253 Fax: 800-414-5043 or (248)699-8069 E-mail: gale.galeord@cengage.com • URL: http://gale.cengage.com • 1998. $355.00. Second edition. Five volumes. Includes important nonfiction writers and journalists.

Majority Congress Committee., c/o Rep. Jim Wright, 1236 Longworth HOB Washington, DC 20515. E-mail: information@emilyslist.org Democratic congressional political action committee.

Making Money with Vending Machines. Billy Mason. Kelso Manufacturing Co., 3676 Highway 1, S. Greenville, MS 38701. Phone: (662)332-7926 E-mail: kelso@tecinfo.com 1995. $7.00.

Making Telecommuting Happen: A Guide for Telemangers and Telecommuters. Jack M. Nilles. John Wiley and Sons, Inc., 111 River St. Hoboken, NJ 07030. Phone: 800-225-5945 or (201)748-6000 Fax: (201)748-6088 E-mail: info@wiley.com • URL: http://www.wiley.com • 1994. $25.95. Includes tips for working productively in a home environment while maintaining good relationships with workers in the corporate office.

Malcolm Wiener Center for Social Policy., Harvard University, John F. Kennedy School of Government, 79 John F. Kennedy St. Cambridge, MA 02138. Phone: (617)495-1461 Fax: (617)496-9053 E-mail: julie_wilson@harvard.edu • URL: http://www.ksg.harvard.edu/socpol • Does multidisciplinary research on health care access and financing.

Mallinckrodt Institute of Radiology - Hyperthermia Service., Washington University in Saint Louis, Radiation Oncology Center, Euclid and Forest Park Aves. St. Louis, MO 63110. Phone: (314)362-8503 Fax: (314)362-8521 • URL: http://www.mir.wustl.edu/ • Maintains laboratories for research pertaining to various kinds of radiological equipment.

Malt Advocate: Beer and Whiskey Magazine. Malt Advocate, Inc., PO Box 58 Emmaus, PA 18049-0158. Phone: (610)967-1083 Fax: (610)965-2995 E-mail: maltman999@aol.com • URL: http://www.whiskeypages.com • Quarterly. $16.00 per year. Provides information for consumers of upscale whiskey and beer.

Managed Account Reports: The Clearing House for Commodity Money Management. Managed Account Reports, Inc., 220 Fifth Ave., 19th Fl. New York, NY 10001. Phone: (212)213-6202 Fax: (212)213-1870 Monthly. $425.00 per year. Newsletter. Reviews the performance and other characteristics of commodity trading advisors and their commodity futures funds or managed accounts. Includes tables and graphs.

Managed Care: A Guide for Physicians. MediMedia USA, Inc., 275 Phillips Blvd. Trenton, NJ 08618-1426. Phone: (609)882-5700 Fax: (609)882-3213 E-mail: editors@managedcaremag.com • URL: http://www.managedcaremag.com • Monthly. $93.00 per year. Edited for physicians and managed care administrators. Includes advice on careers and the business aspects of managed care.

The Managed Care Contracting Handbook: Planning and Negotiating the Managed Care Relationship. Maria K. Todd. Available from McGraw Hill Higher Education, 1333 Burr Ridge Parkway Burr Ridge, IL 60521. • URL: http://www.mhhe.com • 1996. $65.00. Copublished by McGraw-Hill Healthcare Education Group and the Healthcare Financial Management Association. Covers managed care planning, proposals, strategy, negotiation, and contract law. Written for healthcare providers.

Managed Care Handbook: How to Prepare Your Medical Practice for the Managed Care Revolution. James R. Lyle and Hoyt Torras. Practice Management Information Corp., 4727 Wilshire Blvd., Ste. 300 Los Angeles, CA 90010. Phone: 800-633-4215 or (323)954-0224 Fax: (323)954-0253 E-mail: customer.service@pmicmail.com • URL: http://www.medicalbookstore.com • 1994. $49.95. Second edition. A management guide for physicians in private practice.

Managed Care Interface: Today's Experts Tomorrow's Health Care. Medicom International, Inc., 66 Palmer Ave., Suite 49 Bronxville, NY 10708. Phone: (914)337-7878 Fax: (914)337-5023 • URL: http://www.medicomint.com • Monthly. Individuals, $80.00 per year; institutions, $100.00 per year. Provides news and information on all aspects of the managed health care industry.

Managed Care Marketing. Engel Publishing Partners, 820 Bear Tavern Rd. West Trenton, NJ 08628. Phone: (609)530-0044 Fax: (609)530-0207 Quarterly. $24.00 per year. Edited for executives of managed health care companies and organizations.

Managed Care Outlook: The Insider's Business Briefing on Managed Health Care. Aspen Publishers, Inc., 1185 Avenue of the Americas New York, NY 10036. Phone: 800-234-1660 or (212)597-0200 Fax: (212)597-0338 E-mail: customer.service@aspenpubl.com • URL: http://www.aspenpublishers.com • 50 times a year. $632.00 per year. Newsletter relating to health maintenance organizations (HMOs), preferred provider organizations (PPOs), and other managed care systems.

Managed Healthcare Executive: The News Magazine for Managers of Healthcare Costs and Quality. Advanstar Communications, 545 Boylston St. Boston, MA 02116. Phone: 888-527-7008 or (617)267-6500 Fax: (617)267-6900 E-mail: info@advanstar.com • URL: http://www.advanstar.com • Individuals, $75.00 per year; students, $35.00 per year. Edited for managers of HMOs and other managed care organizations. Covers outcomes, quality assurance, technology, long term care, and trends in the health care industry. Formerly*Managed Healthcare*.

The Managed Medicare and Medicaid Market. MarketResearch.com, 641 Ave. of the Americas, 4th Fl. New York, NY 10011. Phone: 800-298-5699 or (212)807-2629 Fax: (212)807-2676 E-mail: customerservice@marketresearch.com • URL: http://www.marketresearch.com • 2003. $2,195.00. Market research report on medicare HMOs. Includes analysis of legal issues and the impact of managed care on older consumers. Providers such as Kaiser Permanente, Humana, and U. S. Healthcare are profiled.

Management. Luis R. Gomez-Mejia and David B. Balkin. McGraw-Hill, 1221 Ave. of the Americas New York, NY 10020. Phone: 800-722-4726 or (212)512-2000 Fax: (212)512-4502 E-mail: customer.service@mcgraw-hill.com • URL: http://www.mcgraw-hill.com • 2002. Price on application.

Management Accounting. W. Steve Albrecht. South-Western, 5191 Natrop Blvd. Mason, OH 45040. Phone: 800-543-0487 or (513)229-1000 • URL: http://www.swcollege.com • 2001. $96.95. Eighth edition.

Management Accounting for Healthcare Organizations. Bruce R. Neumann and Keith E. Boles. Teach'em, 160 E Illinois St. Chicago, IL 60611. Phone: 800-225-3775 or (312)467-0580 Fax: (312)467-9271 E-mail: bb@bonus-books.com • URL: http://www.bonus-books.com • 1998. $65.00. Fifth revised edition.

Management Advisory Services Guideline Series. American Institute of Certified Public Accountants, 1211 Ave. of the Americas New York, NY 10036-8775. Phone: 800-862-4272 or (212)596-6200 Fax: (212)596-6213 E-mail: lmorales@aicpa.org • URL: http://www.aicpa.org • Irregular. Price varies.

Management Communication Quarterly: An International Journal. Sage Publications, Inc., 2455 Teller Rd. Thousand Oaks, CA 91320. Phone: 800-818-7243 or (805)499-9774 Fax: 800-583-2665 or (805)499-0871 E-mail: webmaster@sagepub.com • URL: http://www.sagepub.com • Quarterly. Institutions, $515.00 per year; includes print and online editions. A scholarly journal on managerial and organizational communication effectiveness.

Management: Concepts, Practice, and Skills. R. Wayne Mondy and Shane R. Premeaux. Cengage Learning, 290 Harbor Dr. Stamford, CT 06902. Phone: (203)969-8700 Fax: (203)969-8700 E-mail: communcations@cengage.com • URL: http://www.thomson.com/learning • 2000. $61.95.

Management Consultant Books. Kennedy Information, 1 Phoenix Mill Ln., 5th Fl. Peterborough, NH 03458. Phone: 800-531-0007 or (603)924-1006 Fax: (603)924-4034 E-mail: bookstore@kennedyinfo.com • URL: http://www.kennedyinfo.com • Annual. Free. Contains descriptions of selected books from various publishers on management consulting.

Management Consulting: A Guide to the Profession. Milan Kubr. International Labour Organization, 1828 L St., N.W., Suite 600 Washington, DC 20036-5121. Phone: (202)653-7652 Fax: (202)653-7687 E-mail: washington@ilo.org • URL: http://www.ilo.org • 2002. $85.00. Fourth edition. Serves as a complete guide to managememt consulting, including such practical matters as contracts, client relationships, report-writing, fees, and the management of a management consulting firm.

Management Contents. Gale Cengage Learning, 27500 Drake Rd. Farmington Hills, MI 48331-3535. Phone: 800-877-GALE or (248)699-GALE Fax: 800-414-5043 or (248)699-8069 E-mail: galeord@gale.com • URL: http://gale.cengage.com • Covers a wide range of management, financial, marketing, personnel, and administrative topics. About 150 leading business journals are indexed and abstracted from 1974 to date, with monthly updating. Inquire as to online cost and availability.

Management Control in Nonprofit Organizations. Robert N. Anthony and David W. Young. McGraw-Hill, 1221 Ave. of the Americas New York, NY 10020. Phone: 800-722-4726 or (212)512-2000 Fax: (212)512-4502 E-mail: customer.service@mcgraw-hill.com • URL: http://www.mcgraw-hill.com • 2002. $115.31. Seventh edition.

Management for Strategic Business Ideas. Society of Management Accountants of Canada, 120 King St. W., Suite 850 Hamilton, ON, Canada L8P 4V2. Phone: (905)525-4100 Fax: (905)525-4533 E-mail: dfidler@managementmag.com • URL: http://www.managementmag.com • 10 times a year. $60.00 per year. Text in English and French.

A Management Guide to Leveraged Buyouts. Edward K. Crawford. John Wiley and Sons, Inc., 111 River St. Hoboken, NJ 07030. Phone: 800-225-5945 or (201)748-6000 Fax: (201)748-6088 E-mail: info@wiley.com • URL: http://www.wiley.com • 1987. $175.00. (Frontiers in Finance Series).

Management Information Systems. Raymond McLeod and George Schell. Prentice Hall PTR, 240 Frisch Ct. Paramus, NJ 07652. Phone: 800-282-0693 Fax: 800-445-6991 • URL: http://www.phptr.com • 2000. $116.67. Eighth edition.

Management Information Systems: Managing Information. Fritz J. Erickson and James A. O'Brien. McGraw-Hill, 1221 Ave. of the Americas New York, NY 10020. Phone: 800-722-4726 or (212)512-4502 Fax: (212)512-4502 E-mail: customer.service@mcgraw-hill.com • URL: http://www.mcgraw-hill.com • 1996. $72.25. Third edition.

Management Information Systems Research Center. University of Minnesota

Management Information Systems: Solving Business Problems with Information Technology. Gerald V. Post and David Anderson. McGraw-Hill, 1221 Ave. of the Americas New York, NY 10020. Phone: 800-722-4726 or (212)512-2000 Fax: (212)512-4502 E-mail: customer.service@mcgraw-hill.com • URL: http://www.mcgraw-hill.com • 2002. $75.25. Third edition. Emphasizes the use of databases in practical business applications.

Management Information Systems: With Application Cases and Internet Primer. Stephen Haag and others. McGraw-Hill, 1221 Ave. of the Americas New York, NY 10020. Phone: 800-722-4726 or (212)512-2000 Fax: (212)512-4502 E-mail: customer.service@mcgraw-hill.com • URL: http://www.mcgraw-hill.com • 2001. $107.19. Third edition. Includes CD-ROM.

Management of a Sales Force. William J. Stanton and Rosann Spiro. McGraw-Hill Higher Education, 1221 Ave. of the Americas New York, NY 10020. Phone: 800-722-4726 or (212)512-2000 Fax: (212)512-4502 E-mail: customer.service@mcgraw-hill.com • URL: http://www.mcgraw-hill.com • 1998. $113.75. 10th edition.

Management of Hazardous Materials and Wastes: Treatment, Minimization, and Environmental Impacts. Shyamal K. Majumdar and others, editors. Pennsylvania Academy of Science, Department of Biology, Lafayette College Easton, PA 18042. Phone: (610)330-5464 Fax: (610)330-5705 E-mail: leibelw@lafayette.edu 1989. $45.00.

The Management of Nonprofit Organizations. Sharon M. Oster, editor. Ashgate Publishing Co., 101 Cherry St., Ste. 420 Burlington, VT 05401-4405. Phone: 800-535-9544 or (802)865-7641 Fax: (802)865-7847 E-mail: adonahue@ashgate.com • URL: http://www.ashgate.com • 1994. $275.00. Published by Dartmouth Publisher in England.

Management of People in Hotels and Restaurants. Donald E. Lundberg and James P. Armatas. Brown and Benchmark, 25 Kessel Court Madison, WI 53711. Phone: 800-338-5578 or (608)273-0040 Fax: 800-346-2377 E-mail: customer.service@mcgraw-hill.com • URL: http://www.mhhe.com • 1992. $36.50. Fifth edition.

Management of Retail Buying. R. Patrick Cash and others. John Wiley and Sons, Inc., 111 River St. Hoboken, NJ 07030. Phone: 800-225-5945 or (201)748-6000 Fax: (201)748-6088 E-mail: info@wiley.com • URL: http://www.wiley.com • 1995. $180.00. Third edition. (National Retail Federation Series, vol. 25).

Management OHS and E. Stevens Publishing Corp., 5151 Beltline Rd., Suite 1010 Dallas, TX 75240. Phone: (972)687-6700 Fax: (972)687-6769 Monthly. Free to qualified personnel; others, $150.00 per year. Includes news, interviews, feature articles, legal developments, and reviews of literature. Includes *Buyer's Guide*.

Management Review. American Management Association, 1601 Broadway New York, NY 10019-7420. Phone: 800-262-9699 or (212)586-8100 Fax: (212)903-8168 • URL: http://www.amanet.org • Membership.

Management Science. INFORMS, 901 Elkridge Landing Rd., Suite 400 Linthicum, MD 21090-2909. Phone: 800-446-3676 or (410)850-0300 Fax: (410)684-2963 E-mail: informs@informs.org • URL: http://www.informs.org • Monthly. Individuals, $185.00 per year; institutions, $488.00 per year. Includes print and online editions. Provides an interchange of information between management and management scientists in industry, academia, the military and go vernment.

Management: Skills and Application. Lloyd L. Byars. McGraw-Hill, 1221 Ave. of the Americas New York, NY 10020. Phone: 800-722-4726 or (212)512-2000 Fax: (212)512-4502 E-mail: customer.service@mcgraw-hill.com • URL: http://www.mcgraw-hill.com • 2002. 10th edition. Price on application. An introductory text covering the principles of successful management. Arranged according to the following "Skills:" Planning, Organizing, Staffing, Directing, and Controlling. Includes a glossary of key terms and three indexes. (Irwin Professional Publishing.)

Management: Skills and Application With Powerweb. Leslie W. Rue and Lloyd L. Byars. McGraw-Hill, 1221 Ave. of the Americas New York, NY 10020. Phone: 800-722-4726 or (212)512-2000 Fax: (212)512-4502 E-mail: customer.service@mcgraw-hill.com • URL: http://www.mcgraw-hill.com • 2002. 10th edition. Price on application.

Management Strategies for Libraries: A Basic Reader. Beverly Lynch, editor. Neal-Schuman Publishers, Inc., 100 William St., Ste. 2004 New York, NY 10038. Phone: (866)672-6657 or (212)925-8650 Fax: (866)209-7932 or (212)219-8916 E-mail: info@neal-schuman.com • URL: http://www.neal-schuman.com • 1985. $55.00.

Managerial Accounting. Paul E. Dascher and others. South-Western, 5191 Natrop Blvd. Mason, OH 45040. Phone: 800-543-0487 or (513)229-1000 • URL: http://www.swcollege.com • 2001. $84.95. Second edition.

Managerial Accounting for Libraries and Other Not-for-Profit Organizations. G. Stevenson Smith. American Library Association, 50 E Huron St. Chicago, IL 60611-2795. Phone: 800-545-2433 or (312)944-6780 Fax: (312)440-9374 E-mail: ala@ala.org • URL: http://www.ala.org • 2002. $55.00. Coverage includes responsibility accounting, life cycle costing, and activity-based accounting, as opposed to traditional cost accounting for profit-based organizations.

Managerial and Decision Economics: The International Journal of Research and Progress in Management Economics. John Wiley and Sons, Inc., Journals, 111 River St. Hoboken, NJ 07030. Phone: 800-526-5368 or (201)748-6000 Fax: (201)748-6088 E-mail: customer@wiley.com • URL: http://www.wiley.com • Eight times a year. Individuals, $340.00 per year; institutions, $1,180.00 per year. Deals with economic problems in the field of managerial and decision economics. International coverage. Published in England by John Wiley and Sons Ltd.

Managerial Economics. William Sanuelson and Stephen G. Marks. John Wiley and Sons, Inc., 111 River St. Hoboken, NJ 07030. Phone: 800-225-5945 or (201)748-6000 Fax: (201)748-6088 E-mail: info@wiley.com • URL: http://www.wiley.com • 2002. $104.95. Fourth edition.

Managerial Economics. Mark Hirschey. South-Western, 5191 Natrop Blvd. Mason, OH 45040. Phone: 800-543-0487 or (513)229-1000 • URL: http://www.swcollege.com • 2002. Ninth edition. Price on application.

Managerial Economics: Analysis, Problems, Cases. Lila Truett and Dale B. Turett. John Wiley and Sons, Inc., 111 River St. Hoboken, NJ 07030. Phone: 800-225-5945 or (201)748-6000 Fax: (201)748-6088 E-mail: info@wiley.com • URL: http://www.wiley.com • 2000. $101.95. Seventh edition.

Managerial Economics and Business Strategy. Michael R. Baye. McGraw-Hill, 1221 Ave. of the Americas New York, NY 10020. Phone: 800-722-4726 or (212)512-2000 Fax: (212)512-4502 E-mail: customer.service@mcgraw-hill.com • URL: http://www.mcgraw-hill.com • 2002. $109.38. Seventh edition.

The Manager's Book of Quotations. Lewis D. and Jonathan P. Siegel Eigen. AMACOM, 1601 Broadway New York, NY 10019. Phone: 800-262-9699 or (518)586-8100 Fax: (518)903-8168 E-mail: customerservice@amanet.org • URL: http://www.amacombooks.org • 1991. $24.95. Reprint edition. Provides 5,000 modern and traditional quotations arranged by topics useful to business people for speeches and writing.

A Manager's Guide to Creative Cost Cutting: 101 Ways to Build the Bottom Line. David W. Young. McGraw-Hill, 1221 Ave. of the Americas New York, NY 10020. Phone: 800-722-4726 or (212)512-2000 Fax: (212)512-4502 E-mail: customer.service@mcgraw-hill.com • URL: http://www.mcgraw-hill.com • 2002. $16.95. Mainly concerned with reducing expenses without reducing staff. (Teach Yourself Series).

Manager's Guide to Financial Statement Analysis. Stephen F. Jablonsky and Noah P. Barsky. John Wiley and Sons, Inc., 111 River St. Hoboken, NJ 07030. Phone: 800-225-5945 or (201)748-6000 Fax: (201)748-6088 E-mail: info@wiley.com • URL: http://www.wiley.com • 2001. $49.95. Second edition. The two main sections are "Financial Statements and Business Strategy" and "Market Valuation and Business Strategy."

The Manager's Intelligence Report: An Insider's Fast Track to Better Management. Lawrence Ragan Communications, Inc., 316 N. Michigan Ave., Suite 300 Chicago, IL 60601. Phone: 800-878-5331 or (312)960-4100 Fax: (312)960-4106 E-mail: cservice@ragan.com • URL: http://www.ragan.com • Monthly. $129.00 per year. Newsletter on various aspects of management, including strategy, employee morale, and time management.

Manager's Negotiating Answer Book. George Fuller. DIANE Publishing Co., 330 Pusey Ave. Collingdale, PA 19023-8428. Phone: 800-782-3833 or (610)461-6200 Fax: (610)461-6130 E-mail: dianepubs@erol.com • URL: http://www.dianepublishing.com • 1999. $40.00.

Manager's Tool Kit: Practical Tips for Tackling 100 On-the-Job Problems. Cy Charney. AMACOM, 1601 Broadway New York, NY 10019. Phone: 800-262-9699 or (518)586-8100 Fax: (518)903-8168 E-mail: customerservice@amanet.org • URL: http://www.amacombooks.org • 1995. $17.95.

Managing a Public Relations Firm for Growth and Profit. A. C. Croft, editor. The Haworth Press, Inc., 10 Alice St. Binghamton, NY 13904-1580. Phone: 800-429-6784 or (607)722-5857 Fax: 800-895-0582 or (607)722-1424 E-mail: getinfo@haworthpressinc.com • URL: http://www.haworthpressinc.com • 1995. $39.95.

Managing and Operating a Closely-Held Corporation. Michael Diamond. John Wiley and Sons, Inc., 111 River St. Hoboken, NJ 07030. Phone: 800-526-5368 or (201)748-6000 Fax: (201)748-6088 E-mail: info@wiley.com • URL: http://www.wiley.com • 1991. $225.00.

Managing Automation. Thomas Publishing Co., LLC, Five Penn Plaza New York, NY 10001. Phone: 800-733-1127 or (212)695-0500 Fax: (212)290-7362 E-mail: info@thomasimg.com • URL: http://www.thomaspublishing.com • Monthly. Free to qualified personnel; others, $60.00 per year. Coverage includes software for manufacturing, systems planning, integration in process industry automation, computer integrated manufacturing (CIM), computer networks for manufacturing, management problems, industry news, and new products.

Managing Business Ethics: Straight Talk About How to Do It

Right. Linda K. Trevino and others. John Wiley and Sons, Inc., 111 River St. Hoboken, NJ 07030. Phone: 800-225-5945 or (201)748-6000 Fax: (201)748-6088 E-mail: info@wiley.com • URL: http://www.wiley.com • 2002. Third edition. Price on application. Includes "Ethics and the Individual," "Ethics and the Manager," and "Ethics and the Organization."

Managing Casinos: A Guide for Entrepreneurs, Management Personnel, and Aspiring Managers. Ruben Martinez. Barricade Books, Inc., 185 Bridge Plz., N, Ste. 308A Fort Lee, NJ 07024. Phone: 800-592-6657 or (201)944-7600 Fax: (201)944-6363 E-mail: customerservice@barricadebooks.com • URL: http://www.barricadebooks.com • 1995. $75.00. Covers such topics as the installation of profitable games, providing credit to players, casino business math, and understanding odds.

Managing Contingent Workers: How to Reap the Benefits and Reduce the Risk. Helen Axel and Stanley Nollen. AMACOM, 1601 Broadway New York, NY 10019. Phone: 800-262-9699 or (518)586-8100 Fax: (518)903-8168 E-mail: customerservice@amanet.org • URL: http://www.amacombooks.org • 1995. $55.00.

Managing Disability in the Workplace: An ILO Code of Practice. International Labour Organization, 1828 L St., N.W., Suite 600 Washington, DC 20036-5121. Phone: (202)653-7652 Fax: (202)653-7687 E-mail: washington@ilo.org • URL: http://www.ilo.org • 2002. $6.95. Provides concise "guidelines for employers in the management of disability-related issues in the workplace." Outlines responsibilities for improving the employment prospects of people with disabilities.

Managing Expert Systems. Efraim Tuban and Jay Liebowitz. Idea Group Publishing, 1331 E. Chocolate Ave. Hershey, PA 17033-1117. Phone: 800-345-8845 or (717)533-8845 Fax: (717)533-8661 E-mail: jtravers@idea-group.com • URL: http://www.idea-group.com • 1992. $53.50.

Managing Factory Maintenance. Joel Levitt. Industrial Press, Inc., 200 Madison Ave. New York, NY 10016. Phone: 888-528-7852 or (212)889-6330 Fax: (212)545-8327 E-mail: induspress@aol.com • URL: http://www.industrialpress.com • 1996. $39.95.

Managing Finance: A Socially Responsible Approach. David Crowther. Elsevier Butterworth Heinemann, 200 Wheeler Rd., Sixth Floor Burlington, MA 01803. Phone: 800-545-2522 or (781)221-2212 Fax: 800-568-5136 or (781)313-4880 E-mail: usbkinfo@elsevier.com • URL: http://www.books.elsevier.com/finance • 2004. $37.50. Explains how to manage an ethical approach to such items as accounting, company reports, profit analysis, costing, budgeting, performance data, and investment appraisal.

Managing Financial Risk with Forwards, Futures, Options, and Swaps. American Management Association Extension Institute, 1601 Broadway New York, NY 10019. Phone: 800-262-9699 or (518)586-8100 Fax: (518)903-8168 • URL: http://www.amanet.org • Looseleaf. $159.00. Self-study course. Emphasis is on practical explanations, examples, and problem solving. Quizzes and a case study are included.

Managing Front Office Operations. Michael L. Kasavana and Richard M. Brooks. Educational Institute of the American Hotel & Motel Association, P.O. Box 1240 East Lansing, MI 48826-1240. Phone: 800-344-4381 or (517)372-8800 Fax: (517)372-5141 E-mail: info@ei-ahla.org • URL: http://www.ei.ahma.org • 2001. $66.95. Sixth edition. Covers all aspects of the front office. Includes computer appliations throughout all phases of the guest cycle.

Managing Globally: A Complete Guide to Competing Worldwide. Carl A. Nelson. McGraw-Hill, 1221 Ave. of the Americas New York, NY 10020. Phone: 800-722-4726 or (212)512-2000 Fax: (212)512-4502 E-mail: customer.service@mcgraw-hill.com • URL: http://www.mcgraw-hill.com • 1993. $65.00. Emphasis is on global strategic management and tactics.

Managing High-Technology Programs and Projects. Russell D. Archibald. John Wiley and Sons, Inc., 111 River St. Hoboken, NJ 07030. Phone: 800-225-5945 or (201)748-6000 Fax: (201)748-6088 E-mail: info@wiley.com • URL: http://www.wiley.com • 2003. $100.00. Third edition. Written for senior executives, professional project managers, engineers, and information systems managers.

Managing Housing Letter. Community Development Services, Inc. CD Publications, 8204 Fenton St. Silver Spring, MD 20910. Phone: 800-666-6380 or (301)588-6380 Fax: (301)588-6385 E-mail: info@cdpublications.com • URL: http://www.cdpublications.com • Description: Provides news and advice for owners and managers of rental housing—public, private, and subsidized—including news from Washington and practical management tips. Recurring features include news of research.

Managing Human Resources. Arthur W. Sherman and George Bohlander. Cengage Learning, 290 Harbor Dr. Stamford, CT 06902. Phone: 800-347-7707 or (203)969-8700 Fax: 800-487-8488 or (203)969-8700 E-mail: communications@cengage.com • URL: http://www.thomson.com/learning • 2000. $50.50. 12th edition. (SWC-Management Series).

Managing More Effectively: A Professional Approach to Get the Best Out of People. Madhurendra K. Varma. Sage Publications, Inc., 2455 Teller Rd. Thousand Oaks, CA 91320. Phone: 800-818-7243 or (805)499-9774 Fax: 800-583-2665 or (805)499-0871 E-mail: webmaster@sagepub.com • URL: http://www.sagepub.com • 2001. $37.95. Second edition.

Focuses on the daily and practical application of management principles.

Managing Nonprofit Organizations in the 21th Century. James P. Gelatt. Greenwood Publishing Group, Inc., 88 Post Rd., W. Westport, CT 06881. Phone: 800-225-5800 or (203)226-3571 Fax: (203)431-2214 E-mail: customer-service@greenwood.com • URL: http://www.greenwood.com • 1992. $32.95. The author "emphasizes successful ideas and working solutions." Includes charts and tables.

Managing People in Today's Law Firm: The Human Resources Approach to Surviving Change. Ellen Weisbord and others. Greenwood Publishing Group, Inc., 88 Post Rd., W. Westport, CT 06881. Phone: 800-225-5800 or (203)226-3571 Fax: (203)431-2214 E-mail: customer-service@greenwood.com • URL: http://www.greenwood.com • 1995. $64.95.

Managing Pharmacy Practice: Principles, Strategies, and Systems. Andrew M. Peterson. CRC Press, 2000 N.W. Corporate Blvd. Boca Raton, FL 33431. Phone: 800-272-7737 or (561)994-0555 Fax: 800-374-3401 or (561)989-9732 E-mail: orders@crcpress.com • URL: http://www.crcpress.com • 2004. $69.95. Covers basic management theory and systems as applied to pharmacies. Includes discussion of current trends in managed care systems, reimbursement, formularies, and drug benefit systems.

Managing Public-Access Computers: A How-To-Do-It Manual for Librarians. Donald A. Barclay. Neal-Schuman Publishers, Inc., 100 William St., Ste. 2004 New York, NY 10038. Phone: (866)672-6657 or (212)925-8650 Fax: (866)209-7932 or (212)219-8916 E-mail: info@neal-schuman.com • URL: http://www.neal-schuman.com • 2000. $59.95. Part one covers hardware, software, and other components. Part two discusses computers users. Part three is about systems management, library policy, and legal issues. (How-to-Do-It Manuals Series).

Managing Purchasing: Making the Supply Team Work. John W. Kamuff and Kenneth H. Killen. McGraw-Hill, 1221 Ave. of the Americas New York, NY 10020. Phone: 800-722-4726 or (212)512-2000 Fax: (212)512-4502 E-mail: customer.service@mcgraw-hill.com • URL: http://www.mcgraw-hill.com • 1995. $45.00. (NAPM Professional Development Series: Vol. 2).

Managing Quality in America's Most Admired Companies. Jay W. Spechler. Engineering and Management Press, 25 Technology Park Norcross, GA 30092-2988. Phone: 800-494-0460 or (770)449-0461 Fax: (770)441-3295 E-mail: cmagee@www.iienet.org • URL: http://www.iienet.org • 1993. $49.95. Part one provides "Guidelines for Implementing Quality Management," including detailed information on the Malcolm Baldridge National Quality Award. Part two contains 30 "Case Studies of Quality Management in Leading Companies."

Managing Sales Professionals: The Reality of Profitability. Joseph P. Vaccaro. The Haworth Press, Inc., 10 Alice St. Binghamton, NY 13904-1580. Phone: 800-429-6784 or (607)722-5857 Fax: 800-895-0582 or (607)722-1424 E-mail: getinfo@haworthpressinc.com • URL: http://www.haworthpressinc.com • 1995. $49.95.

Managing Software Development Projects: Formula for Success. Neal Whitten. John Wiley and Sons, Inc., 111 River St. Hoboken, NJ 07030. Phone: 800-225-5945 or (201)748-6000 Fax: (201)748-6088 E-mail: info@wiley.com • URL: http://www.wiley.com • 1995. $70.00. Second edition.

Managing Stress: Subjectivity and Power in the Workplace. Tim Newton. Sage Publications, Inc., 2455 Teller Rd. Thousand Oaks, CA 91320-2218. Phone: 800-818-7243 or (805)499-0721 Fax: (805)499-0871 E-mail: info@sagepub.com • URL: http://www.sagepub.com • 1995. $74.50.

Managing the Non-Profit Organization: Practices and Principles. Peter F. Drucker. HarperInformation, 10 E. 53rd St. New York, NY 10022-5299. Phone: 800-242-7737 or (212)207-7000 Fax: 800-822-4090 or (212)207-7145 • URL: http://www.harpercollins.com • 1992. $16.00. General advice on strategy, leadership, marketing, and human relations for the non-profit manager.

Managing the Office Building. Mark Ingerbretsen, editor. Institute of Real Estate Management, 430 N. Michigan Ave. Chicago, IL 60611-4090. Phone: 800-837-0706 or (312)329-6000 E-mail: custserv@irem.org • URL: http://www.irem.org • 1985. $62.95. Revised edition.

Managing the Project Team: The Human Aspects of Project Management, Volume Three. Vijay K. Verma. Project Management Institute, Four Campus Blvd. Newton Square, PA 19073-3299. Phone: (610)356-4600 Fax: (610)356-4647 E-mail: pmihq@pmi.org • URL: http://www.pmi.org • 1997. $32.95. (Human Aspects of Project Management Series: Vol. 3).

Managing the Publishing Process: An Annotated Bibliography. Bruce W. Speck. Greenwood Publishing Group, Inc., 88 Post Rd., W Westport, CT 06881. Phone: 800-225-5800 or (203)226-3571 Fax: (203)431-2214 E-mail: customer-service@greenwood.com • URL: http://www.greenwood.com • 1995. $82.95. (Bibliographies and Indexes in Mass Media and Communications Series: No. 9).

Managing the Small to Mid-Sized Company: Concepts and Cases. James C. Collins and William C. Lazier. McGraw-Hill, 1221 Ave. of the Americas New York, NY 10020. Phone: 800-722-4726 or (212)512-2000 Fax: (212)512-4502 E-mail: customer.service@mcgraw-hill.com • URL: http://www.mcgraw-hill.com • 1994. $92.50.

Managing Worker's Compensation: A Guide to Injury Reduction and Effective Claim Management. Keith Wertz and others. Lewis Publishers, 2000 Corporate Blvd., N. W. Boca Raton, FL 33431. Phone: 800-272-7737 or (561)994-0555 Fax: 800-374-3401 or (561)998-9114 E-mail: orders@crcpress.com • URL: http://www.crcpress.com • 2000. $69.95. (Occupation Safety and Health Guide Series).

Managing Workplace Stress. Cary L. Cooper and Susan Cartwright. Sage Publications, Inc., 2455 Teller Rd. Thousand Oaks, CA 91320. Phone: 800-818-7243 or (805)499-9774 Fax: 800-583-2665 or (805)499-0871 E-mail: webmaster@sagepub.com • URL: http://www.sagepub.com • 1996. $70.95. Includes references and indexes. *Advanced Topics in Organizational Behavior Series, vol. 1.*

Managing World Economic Change: International Political Economy. Prentice Hall PTR, 240 Frisch Ct. Paramus, NJ 07652. Phone: 800-282-0693 Fax: 800-445-6991 • URL: http://www.phptr.com • 2000. Third edition. Price on application.

Mandel Center for Nonprofit Organizations. Case Western Reserve University, 10900 Euclid Ave. Cleveland, OH 44106-7167. Phone: (216)368-2275 Fax: (216)368-8592 • URL: http://www.cwru.edu/mandelcenter • Engages in research relating to the management of nonprofit organizations.

Manias, Panics, and Crashes: A History of Financial Crises. Charles P. Kindleberger. John Wiley and Sons, Inc., 111 River St. Hoboken, NJ 07030. Phone: 800-225-5945 or (201)748-6000 Fax: (201)748-6088 E-mail: bookinfo@wiley.com • URL: http://www.wiley.com • 2000. $19.95. Fourth edition. Provides a history of financial troubles from 1618 to modern times, with greed as a central theme. (Investment Classic Series).

Manpower Education Institute., 715 Ladd Rd. Bronx, NY 10471-1203. Phone: (718)548-4200 Fax: (718)548-4202 E-mail: info@meipublishing.com • URL: http://www.manpower-education.org • Individuals from the fields of business, labor, and education who develop educational film series for the U.S. labor force. Series includes: Ready or Not (pre-retirement planning), Your Future Is Now (high school equivalency programs), Read Your Way Up (reading skills improvement), Out of Work (for the unemployed), If You Don't Come In Sunday, Don't Come In Monday (history of the American labor movement), Plug Us In (to assist workers reentering the labor market), and Where Do I Fit In (new worker orientation).

Mansfield Stock Chart Service. R.W. Mansfield Co., Inc., 2973 Kennedy Blvd. Jersey City, NJ 07306. Phone: 877-626-7353 or (201)795-0630 Fax: (201)795-5476 Weekly. Price varies. Newsletter. Covers New York Stock Exchange, American Stock Exchange, OTC exchange, international stocks and industry groups. Partial subscriptions available.

Manual for Managing the Law Office. Prentice Hall PTR, 240 Frisch Ct. Paramus, NJ 07652. Phone: 800-282-0693 Fax: 800-445-6991 • URL: http://www.phptr.com • Looseleaf service. Price on application. (Information Services Series).

Manual for Writers of Term Papers, Theses, and Dissertations. Kate L. Turabian. The University of Chicago Press, 1427 E. 60th St. Chicago, IL 60637. Phone: 800-621-2736 or (773)702-7700 Fax: 800-621-8476 or (773)702-7212 E-mail: custserv@press.uchicago.edu • URL: http://www.press.uchicago.edu • 1996. $27.50. Sixth revised edition.

Manual of Classification. U.S. Patent Office. Available from U.S. Government Printing Office, Washington, DC 20402. Phone: (202)512-1800 Fax: (202)512-2250 E-mail: accessgpo@gpo.gov • URL: http://www.accessgpo.gov • Two volumes. Index and revised looseleaf pages for an indefinite period. Lists patent classes and subclasses.

Manual of Credit and Commercial Laws. National Association of Credit Management., 8840 Columbia, 100 Pkwy Columbia, MD 21045. Phone: 800-225-5945 or (410)740-5560 Fax: (410)740-5574 Annual. Free to members; non-members, $100.00. Formerly *Credit Manual of Commercial Laws.*

Manual of Credit and Commercial Laws. National Association of Credit Management, 8840 Columbia 100 Parkway Columbia, MD 21045. Phone: (410)740-5560 Fax: (410)740-5574 E-mail: nacm_info@nacm.org • URL: http://www.nacm.org • Annual. Free to members; non-members, $125.00. Formerly *Credit Manual of Commercial Laws.*

Manual of Mineralogy:With Minerals and Rock Exercises in Crystallography Mineralogy and Hand Speciman Petrology. Cornelius Klein and Cornelius Hurlburt. John Wiley and Sons, Inc., 111 River St. Hoboken, NJ 07030. Phone: 800-225-5945 or (201)748-6000 Fax: (201)748-6088 E-mail: info@wiley.com • URL: http://www.wiley.com • 1994. $69.95. 21st revised edition.

Manual of Oil and Gas Terms. LexisNexis Matthew Bender, 1275 Broadway Albany, NY 12204. Phone: 800-424-4200 or (518)487-3000 Fax: (518)487-3584 E-mail: bookstore.support@lexisnexis.com • URL: http://www.bender.com • $109.00. 12th edition. Defines technical, legal, and tax terms relating to the oil and gas industry

Manual of Patent Examining Procedure. U.S. Patent Office. Available from U.S. Government Printing Office, Washington, DC 20402. Phone: (202)512-1800 Fax: (202)512-2250 E-mail: accessgpo@gpo.gov • URL: http://www.accessgpo.gov • Looseleaf. $248.00. Periodic supplementation included. Information on the practices and procedures relative to the prosecution of patent applications before the Patent and Trademark Office.

Manual of Remote Working. Kevin Curran and Geoff Williams. Ashgate Publishing Co., 101 Cherry St., Ste. 420 Burlington, VT 05401-4405. Phone: 800-535-9544 or (802)865-7641 Fax: (802)865-7847 E-mail: adonahue@ashgate.com • URL: http://www.ashgate.com • 1997. Price on application. A British approach to telecommuting or "remote working." Among the chapters are "Planning a Remote Working Operation," "Human Resources," "Communication Systems," and "Project Management." Includes bibliographical references, glossary, and index. Published by Gower in England.

Manual on Employment Discrimination Law and Civil Rights Action in the Federal Courts. West Group, 610 Opperman Dr. Eagan, MN 55123. Phone: 800-328-4880 or (651)687-7000 Fax: 800-340-9378 E-mail: bookstore@westgroup.com • URL: http://www.westgroup.com • Biennial. $236.00. Two looseleaf volumes.

Manufactured Fiber Fact Book. Fiber Economics Bureau, Inc., 1530 Wilson Blvd., Ste. 690 Arlington, VA 22209. Phone: (703)875-0676 Fax: (703)875-0675 E-mail: ddezan@afma.org • URL: http://www.fibersource.com • Biennial. $5.00. Provides a general review of the history and development of the synthetic fiber industry. (Fiber Economics Bureau is a subsidiary of the American Fiber Manufacturers Association.)

Manufactured Fiber Handbook. Fiber Economics Bureau, Inc., 1530 Wilson Blvd., Ste. 690 Arlington, VA 22209. Phone: (703)875-0676 Fax: (703)875-0675 E-mail: ddezan@afma.org • URL: http://www.fibersource.com • $6,000.00 per year. Looseleaf service. Provides comprehensive data, both current and historical, on all aspects of the U.S. manufactured fiber industry. (Fiber Economics Bureau is a subsidiary of the American Fiber Manufacturers Association.)

Manufactured Fiber Review. Fiber Economics Bureau, Inc., 1530 Wilson Blvd., Ste. 690 Arlington, VA 22209. Phone: (703)875-0676 Fax: (703)875-0675 E-mail: ddezan@afma.org • URL: http://www.fibersource.com • Monthly. $350.00 per year. Provides a "quick-release four-page monthly review of the latest U.S. data on manufactured fiber." Coverage includes production, shipments, exports, and utilization rates. (Fiber Economics Bureau is a subsidiary of the American Fiber Manufacturers Association.)

Manufactured Home Merchandiser Manufactured Home Producers Guide. RLD Group, Inc., 203 N. Wabash St., Suite 800 Chicago, IL 60601-2476. Phone: (312)236-3528 Fax: (312)236-4024 Annual. $20.00. Lists about 163 manufacturers of mobil homes, modular homes and other types of manufactured housing. Includes trade associations. Formerly *Mobile/Manufactured Home Merchandiser Manufactured Home Producers Guide.*

Manufactured Homes; Making Sense of a Housing Opportunity. Thomas E. Nutt-Powell. Greenwood Publishing Group, Inc., 88 Post Rd., W. Westport, CT 06881. Phone: 800-225-5800 or (203)226-3571 Fax: (203)431-2214 E-mail: customer-service@greenwood.com • URL: http://www.greenwood.com • 1982. $69.95.

Manufactured Housing Institute., 2101 Wilson Blvd., Ste. 610 Arlington, VA 22201-3062. Phone: 800-505-5500 or (703)558-0400 Fax: (703)558-0401 E-mail: info@mfghome.org • URL: http://www.manufacturedhousing.org • Manufacturers of manufactured homes; suppliers of equipment, components, furnishings and services, financial services companies, state association organizations, retailers and community owners. Promotes sales of manufactured homes through programs and services in six key areas: government relations, technical activities, financing, public relations, site development, and community operations. Conducts research and educational programs; provides statistics.

Manufacturers' Agents for Food Service Industry., 814 Spring Rd., Ste. 211 Atlanta, GA 30339. Phone: (770)433-9844 Fax: (770)433-2450 E-mail: info@mafsi.org • URL: http://www.mafsi.org • Members are independent manufacturers' representatives who sell food service equipment and supplies. Formerly Marketing Agents for Food Service Industry.

Manufacturers' Agents National Association., 1 Spectrum Pointe, Ste. 150 Lake Forest, CA 92630-2283. Phone: 877-626-2776 or (949)859-4040 Fax: (949)855-2973 E-mail: mana@manaonline.org • URL: http://www.manaonline.org • Manufacturers' agents in all fields representing two or more manufacturers on a commission basis; associate members are manufacturers and others interested in improving the agent-principal relationship. Maintains code of ethics and rules of business and professional conduct; issues model standard form of agreement.

Manufacturers' Agents National Association - Directory of Manufacturers' Sales Agencies. Manufacturers' Agents National Association, 1 Spectrum Pointe, Ste. 150 Lake Forest, CA 92654. Phone: 877-626-2776 or (949)859-4040 Fax: (949)855-2973 E-mail: mana@manaonline.org • URL: http://www.manaonline.org • Annual. $249.00. Lists over 4,000 independent agents and firms. Price includes one year subscription to *Agency Sales Magazines*. Formerly *Manufacturers' Agents National Association-Directory of Members.*

Manufacturers Alliance/MAPI., 1600 Wilson Blvd., Ste. 1100 Arlington, VA 22209-2594. Phone: (703)841-9000 Fax: (703)841-9514 E-mail: info@mapi.net • URL: http://www.mapi.net • Manufacturing and related business service companies. Membership concentrated in the following sectors: aerospace; automotive; scientific instruments; electronics; computers and telecommunication equipment; high technology; chemicals/pharmaceuticals; oil and oil-related equipment; electrical equipment farm, construction, food, material handling, and other machinery; primary and fabricated metals. Provides member services through councils and research programs. Produces a variety of research, including economic, policy, and benchmark work to assist members in their planning, compliance, and process improvement efforts.

Manufacturers' Shipments, Inventories, and Orders. Available from U. S. Government Printing Office, Washington, DC 20402. Phone: (202)512-1800 Fax: (202)512-2250 E-mail: gpoaccess@gpo.gov • URL: http://www.access.gpo.gov • Monthly. $79.00 per year. Issued by Bureau of the Census, U. S. Department of Commerce. Includes monthly *Advance Report on Durable Goods*. Provides data on production, value, shipments, and consumption for a wide variety of manufactured products. (Current Industrial Reports, M3-1.)

Manufacturers Standardization Society of the Valve and Fittings Industry., 127 Park St., N. E. Vienna, VA 22180-4602. Phone: (703)281-6613 Fax: (703)281-6671 E-mail: info@mss-hq.com • URL: http://www.mss-hq.com • Members are valve and fitting companies. Publishes standards and specifications.

Manufacturers' Tax Alert. CCH, Inc., 2700 Lake Cook Rd. Riverwoods, IL 60015. Phone: 800-835-5224 or (847)267-7000 E-mail: cust_serv@cch.com • URL: http://www.cch.com • Monthly $297.00 per year. Newsletter. Covers the major tax issues affecting manufacturing companies. Includes current developments in various kind of federal, state, and international taxes: sales, use, franchise, property, and corporate income.

Manufacturing and Distribution USA. Gale Cengage Learning, 27500 Drake Rd. Farmington Hills, MI 48331-3535. Phone: 800-877-GALE or (248)699-4253 Fax: 800-414-5043 E-mail: gale.galeord@cengage.com • URL: http://gale.cengage.com • 2002. $395.00. Second edition. Three volumes. Presents statistics and projections relating to economic activity in more than 500 business classifications.

Manufacturing Computer Solutions., Franks Hall, Horton Kirby Dartford DA4 9LL, England. Phone: 01322 860000 Fax: 01322 289577 E-mail: bpalmer@chilton.net • URL: http://www.mcsolutions.co.uk • Monthly. $88.00 per year. Edited for managers of factory automation, emphasizing the integration of systems in manufacturing. Subjects include materials handling, CAD/CAM, specialized software for manufacturing, programmable controllers, machine vision, and automatic identification systems. Formerly *Manufacturing Systems*.

Manufacturing Computer Solutions: The Management Magazine of Integrated Manufacturing. Findlay Publications Ltd., Hadlow House, Nine High St. Orpington BR6 6BG, United Kingdom. Phone: 44 1689 854754 Fax: 44 1689 860041 Monthly. $88.00 per year.

Manufacturing Confectioner. Manufacturing Confectioner Publishing Co., 175 Rock Rd. Glen Rock, NJ 07452. Phone: (201)652-2655 Fax: (201)652-3419 Monthly. $35.00 per year. Buying guide available *Purchasing Executives' Number*.

Manufacturing Engineering. Society of Manufacturing Engineers, One SME Dr. Dearborn, MI 48121. Phone: 800-733-4763 or (313)425-3400 Fax: (313)271-2861 E-mail: service@sme.org • URL: http://www.sme.org • Monthly. $100.00 per year.

Manufacturing Jewelers and Suppliers of America., 45 Royal Little Dr. Providence, RI 02904-5305. Phone: 800-444-6572 or (401)274-3840 Fax: (401)274-0265 E-mail: mjsa@mjsainc.com • URL: http://www.mjsanic.com • Formerly Manufacturing Jewelers and Silversmiths of America.

Manufacturing Jewelers Buyers' Guide. Manufacturing Jewelers and Suppliers of America, 45 Royal Little Dr. Providence, RI 02904. Phone: 800-444-6572 or (401)274-3840 Fax: (401)274-0265 E-mail: mjsa@mjsainc.com • URL: http://www.mjsainc.com • Biennial. Free to members; nonmembers, $125.00. Lists manufacturers and suppliers and has cross-reference by products listed.

Manufacturing Processes Reference Guide. R. H. Todd and others. Industrial Press, Inc., 200 Madison Ave. New York, NY 10016. Phone: 888-528-7852 or (212)889-6330 Fax: (212)545-8327 E-mail: induspress@aol.com • URL: http://www.industrialpress.com • 1994. $46.95. Describes 130 manufacturing processes used in industry.

Manufacturing Profiles. U. S. Bureau of the CensusPhone: (301)763-4636 E-mail: webmaster@census.gov • URL: http://www.census.gov/prod/www/abs/mfg-prof.html • The Census Bureau makes available free on PDF (Portable Document Format) an annual consolidation of the entire Current Industrial Report series, presenting "all the data compiled." Contains statistics on production, shipments, inventories, consumption, exports, imports, and orders for a wide variety of manufactured products.

Manufacturing Systems: Buyers Guide. Reed Business Information, 360 Park Ave. S New York, NY 10010. Phone: 800-662-7776 or (646)746-6400 Fax: (646)746-7028 E-mail: corporatecommunications@reedbusiness.com • URL: http://www.reedbusiness.com • Annual. Price on application. Contains information on companies manufacturing or supplying materials handling systems, CAD/CAM systems, specialized software for manufacturing, programmable controllers, machine vision systems, and automatic identification systems.

Manufacturing Worldwide: Industry Analysis Statistics. Gale Cengage Learning, 27500 Drake Rd. Farmington Hills, MI 48331-3535. Phone: 800-877-GALE or (248)699-4253 Fax: 800-414-5043 E-mail: gale.galeord@cengage.com • URL: http://gale.cengage.com • 1999. $240.00. Third edition. A guide to worldwide economic activity in 500 product lines within 119 countries. Includes 37 detailed industry profiles. Name, address, phone, fax, employment, and ranking are shown for major companies worldwide in each industry sector.

Map Librarianship: An Introduction. Mary L. Larsgaard. Libraries Unlimited, Inc., 88 Post Rd., W Westport, CT 06881. Phone: 800-225-5800 Fax: (203)222-1205 E-mail: lu-books@lu.com • URL: http://www.lu.com • 1998. $68.50. Third edition.

The Map Library in the New Millennium. R. B. Parry and others, editors. American Library Association, 50 E Huron St. Chicago, IL 60611-2795. Phone: 800-545-2433 or (312)944-6780 Fax: (312)440-9374 E-mail: ala@ala.org • URL: http://www.ala.org • 2001. $75.00. Coverage includes new technologies, standards, geographical information systems, conservation, and intellectual property rights.

Maps on File. Facts on File, 132 W 31st St., 17th Fl. New York, NY 10001. Phone: 800-322-8755 Fax: 800-678-3633 E-mail: custserv@factsonfile.com • URL: http://www.factsonfile.com • Annual. $195.00. Update, $45.00. 300 country and other maps in looseleaf binder.

Marble Institute of America.

Marina Dock Age. Preston Publications, Inc., 6600 W Touhy Ave. Niles, IL 60714. Phone: (847)967-2900 Fax: (847)647-1155 E-mail: circulation@boatmotordealer.com Eight times a year. $35.00 per year. Published for owners and managers of marinas and boatyards.

Marine Corps Association., 715 Broadway St. Quantico, VA 22134. Phone: 800-336-0291 or (703)640-6161 Fax: (703)640-0823 E-mail: mca@mca-marine.org • URL: http://www.mca-marines.org • Represents active duty, reserve, retired, Fleet Reserve, honorably discharged Marines, and members of other services who have served with Marine Corps units. Disseminates information about the military arts and sciences to members; assists members' professional advancement; fosters the spirit and works to preserve the traditions of the United States Marine Corps. Maintains discount book service and group insurance plan for members. Association founded by members of the Second Provisional Marine Brigade at Guantanamo Bay, Cuba.

Marine Corps Aviation Association., PO Box 296, 715 Broadway St. Quantico, VA 22134. Phone: 800-280-3001 or (703)630-1903 Fax: (703)630-2713 E-mail: mcaa@flymcaa.org • URL: http://www.flymcaa.org • Members and former members of U.S. Marine aviation units and others with an interest in Marine Corps aviation; aerospace corporations. Aims to: perpetuate camaraderie in marine aviation; foster and encourage professional excellence and recognize important achievements in marine aviation. Conducts charitable programs.

Marine Corps League., PO Box 3070 Merrifield, VA 22116-3070. Phone: 800-625-1775 or (703)207-9588 Fax: (703)207-0047 E-mail: mclsarge@aol.com • URL: http://www.mcleague.com/mdp • Represents men and women who are serving or who have served honorably in the United States Marine Corps, and U.S. Navy Corpsmen. Preserves the traditions and promotes the interests of the United States Marine Corps. Promotes the ideals of American freedom and democracy. Preserves the history and memory of the men who have given their lives to the nation. Maintains true allegiance to American institutions. Creates a bond of comradeship between those in the service and those who have returned to civilian life. Renders assistance to all Marines and former Marines as well as to their widows and orphans.

Marine Corps Reserve Association., 8626 Lee Hwy. Fairfax, VA 22031-2135. Phone: 800-287-8780 or (703)289-1204 Fax: (703)289-1206 E-mail: mcrahq@usmcra.org • URL: http://www.usmcra.org • Marines who have served on active duty in peace or war. Seeks to: advance the professional skills of marines; represent and assist individual members; promote the interests of the U.S. Marine Corps in order to advance the welfare and preserve the security of the United States. Maintains speakers' bureau and placement service.

Marine Digest. Newman-Burrows Publishing, 1710 S. Norman St. Seattle, WA 98144-2819. Phone: (206)709-1840 Fax: (206)324-8939 Monthly. $28.00 per year. Formerly *Marine Digest*.

Marine Engineers Review (MER). Institute of Marine Engineering, Science, and Technology (IMarEST), 80 Coleman St. London EC2R 5BJ, United Kingdom. Phone: 44 20 7382 2600 Fax: 44 20 7382 2670 E-mail: info@imarest.org • URL: http://www.imarest.org • Monthly. Free to members; nonmembers, $150.00 per year. Covers marine engineering, offshore industries, and ocean shipping.

Marine Log. Simmons-Boardman Publishing Corp., 345 Hudson St., 12th Fl. New York, NY 10014-4502. Phone: (212)620-7200 Fax: (212)633-1165 • URL: http://www.marinelog.com • Monthly. $35.00 per year. Formerly *Marine Engineering-Log*.

Marine Management Holdings: Transactions. Available from Information Today, Inc., 143 Old Marlton Pike Medford, NJ 08055-8750. Phone: 800-300-9868 or (609)654-6266 Fax: (609)654-4309 E-mail: custserv@infotoday.com • URL: http://www.infotoday.com • Bimonthly. $220.00 per year. Published in London by Marine Management Holdings Ltd. Contains technical and regulatory material on a wide variety of marine and offshore topics. Formerly *Institute of Marine Engineers: Transactions*.

Marine Policy; The International Journal of Ocean Affairs. Elsevier, 360 Park Ave. S New York, NY 10010-1710. Phone: 888-437-4636 or (212)989-5800 Fax: (212)633-3990 E-mail: usinfo-f@elsevier.com • URL: http://www.elsevier.com • Bimonthly. Institutions, $882.00 per year.

Marine Pollution Bulletin: The International Journal for Marine Environmentalists, Scientists, Engineers, Administrators, Politicians, and Lawyers. Elsevier, 360 Park Ave. S New York, NY 10010-1710. Phone: 888-437-4636 or (212)989-5800 Fax: (212)633-3990 E-mail: usinfo-f@elsevier.com • URL: http://www.elsevier.com • Semimonthly. Qualified personnel, $227.00 per year; institutions, $1,149.00 per year.

Marine Technology and SNAME News. Society of Naval Architects and Marine Engineers, 601 Pavonia Ave. Jersey City, NJ 07306-2907. Phone: (201)798-4800 Fax: (201)798-4975 E-mail: sevans@sname.org • URL: http://www.sname.org • Quarterly. Individuals, $25.00 per year; institutions, $98.00 per year. Formerly *Marine Technology*.

Marine Technology Society., 5565 Sterrett Pl., Ste. 108 Columbia, MD 21044. Phone: (410)884-5330 Fax: (410)884-9060 E-mail: membership@mtsociety.org • URL: http://www.mtsociety.org • Scientists, engineers, educators, and others with professional interest in the marine sciences or related fields; includes institutional and corporate members. Disseminates marine scientific and technical information, including institutional, environmental, physical, and biological aspects; fosters a deeper understanding of the world's seas and attendant technologies. Maintains 13 sections and 29 professional committees. Conducts tutorials.

Maritime Guide. Lloyd's Register—Fairplay Ltd., Lombard House, 3 Princess Way Redhill RH1 1UP, United Kingdom. Phone: (44)1737 379000 Fax: (44)1737 379001 E-mail: info@lrfairplay.com • URL: http://www.fairplay.co.uk • Covers: international shipbuilders, marine engine builders, boilermakers, and shipbreakers; port and docking facilities; marine associations. Entries include: For shipbuilders, marine engine builders, and boilermakers—Company name, address, phone, telex. For shipbreakers—Company name, address. For port and docking facilities—Name, location, name and title of contact, services.

Maritime IT & Electronics. Institute of Marine Engineering, Science, and Technology, 80 Coleman St. London EC2R 5BJ, United Kingdom. Phone: 44 20 7382 2600 Fax: 44 20 7382 2670 E-mail: info@imarest.org • URL: http://www.imarest.org • Bimonthly. $65.00 per year. Covers modern electronic technology as applied to all areas of the maritime industry. Includes navigation systems, communications, control systems, monitoring, diagnostics, and software.

Maritime Law Association of the U.S.

Maritime Reporter and Engineering News. Maritime Activity Reports, Inc., 118 E. 25th St. New York, NY 10010. Phone: (212)477-6700 Monthly. $44.00 per year.

Market Absorption of Apartments. U.S. Bureau of the Census. Available from U.S. Government Printing Office, Washington, DC 20402. Phone: (202)512-1800 Fax: (202)512-2250 E-mail: gpoaccess@gpo.gov • URL: http://www.access.gpo.gov • Quarterly and annual. $16.00 per year. Current Housing Report H-130.

Market: Asia Pacific. Edimax, 5923 Brambletree San Antonio, TX 78247. Phone: (315)431-0511 Fax: (315)431-0200 E-mail: sdp@tfn.com • URL: http://www.prsgroup.com • Description: Concerned with demographics, lifestyles, and business opportunities in the Asia Pacific region. Profiles a particular city or country in each issue, providing consumer market trends, surveys results, and articles on direct marketing and marketing management.

Market Efficiency: Stock Market Behavior in Theory and Practice. Andrew W. Lo, editor. Edward Elgar Publishing, Inc., 136 West St., Suite 202 Northampton, MA 01060. Phone: 800-390-3149 or (413)584-5551 Fax: (413)584-9933 E-mail: elgarinfo@e-elgar.com • URL: http://www.e-elgar.co.uk • 1997. $465.00. Two volumes. Consists of reprints of 49 articles dating from 1937 to 1993, in five sections: "Theoretical Foundations," "The Random Walk Hypothesis," "Variance Bounds Tests," "Overreaction and Underreaction," and "Anomalies." (International Library of Critical Writings in Financial Economics Series: No. 3).

Market: Europe. Edimax, 5923 Brambletree San Antonio, TX 78247. Phone: (315)431-0511 Fax: (315)431-0200 E-mail: sdp@tfn.com • URL: http://www.prsgroup.com • Description: Profiles European consumers and provides ideas for marketing strategies. Reports on European conferences and summarizes articles from international periodicals. Recurring features include analyses of specific countries and cities.

The Market for Consumer Products in Southeast Asia. MarketResearch.com, 641 Ave. of the Americas, 4th Fl. New York, NY 10011. Phone: 800-298-5699 or (212)807-2629 Fax: (212)807-2676 E-mail: customerservice@marketresearch.com • URL: http://www.marketresaerch.com • 1997. $3,250.00. Market research report. Covers Asian consumer markets for food, cosmetics, pharmaceuticals, medical devices, and building materials. Market projections are provided to the year 2001.

The Market for Craft and Specialty Beer. MarketResearch.com, 641 Ave. of the Americas, 4th Fl. New York, NY 10011. Phone: 800-298-5699 or (212)807-2629 Fax: (212)807-2676 E-mail: customerservice@marketresearch.com • URL: http://www.marketresearch.com • 1997. $1,625.00. Market research report with projections. Includes brewing company profiles.

The Market for Generic Drugs. MarketResearch.com, 641 Ave. of the Americas, 4th Fl. New York, NY 10011. Phone: 800-298-5699 or (212)807-2629 Fax: (212)807-2676 E-mail: customerservice@marketresearch.com • URL: http://www.marketresearch.com • 2000. $3,250.00. Market research data. Includes a discussion of current trends in the use of generic prescription drugs to reduce healthcare costs, with forcasts to 2004.

Market for Healthy Snacks. MarketResearch.com, 641 Ave. of the Americas, 4th Fl. New York, NY 10011. Phone: 800-298-5699 or (212)807-2629 Fax: (212)807-2676 E-mail: customerservice@marketresearch.com • URL: http://www.marketresearch.com • 1996. $3,250.00. Provides market data on granola bars, dried fruit, trail mix, rice cakes, etc.

The Market for Ice Cream and Other Frozen Desserts. MarketResearch.com, 641 Ave. of the Americas, 4th Fl. New York, NY 10011. Phone: 800-298-5699 or (212)807-2629 Fax: (212)807-2676 E-mail: customerservice@marketresearch.com • URL: http://www.marketresearch.com • 2000. $2,750.00. Provides market data and discusses the impact on the ice cream industry of new technology and the Nutrition Labeling and Education Act. Includes sales projections to 2004.

The Market for Interactive Television. MarketResearch.com, 641 Ave. of the Americas, 4th Fl. New York, NY 10011. Phone: 800-298-5699 or (212)807-2629 Fax: (212)807-2676 E-mail: customerservice@marketresearch.com • URL: http://www.marketresearch.com • 2000. $995.00. Market research data.

The Market for Ophthalmic Pharmaceuticals. MarketResearch.com, 641 Ave. of the Americas, 4th Fl. New York, NY 10011. Phone: 800-298-5699 or (212)807-2629 Fax: (212)807-2676 E-mail: customerservice@marketresearch.com • URL: http://www.marketresearch.com • 1997. $2,500.00. Market research report. Covers topical and internal drugs for eye disorders, with market estimates. Includes pharmaceutical company profiles.

The Market for Pasta. MarketResearch.com, 641 Ave. of the Americas, 4th Fl. New York, NY 10011. Phone: 800-298-5699 or (212)807-2629 Fax: (212)807-2676 E-mail: customerservice@marketresearch.com • URL: http://www.marketresearch.com • 2000. $3,250.00. Provides market data on various kinds of pasta, with sales forecasts to 2004.

The Market for Physical Fitness and Exercise Equipment. MarketResearch.com, 641 Ave. of the Americas, 4th Fl. New York, NY 10011. Phone: 800-298-5699 or (212)807-2629 Fax: (212)807-2676 E-mail: customerservice@marketresearch.com • URL: http://www.marketresearch.com • 1999. $3,250.00. Provides consumer and institutional market data, with forecasts to the year 2003.

The Market for Rx-to-OTC Switched Drugs. MarketResearch.com, 641 Ave. of the Americas, 4th Fl. New York, NY 10011. Phone: 800-298-5699 or (212)807-2629 Fax: (212)807-2676 E-mail: customerservice@marketresearch.com • URL: http://www.marketresearch.com • 2000. $3,250.00. Market research report. Covers the market for over-the-counter drugs that were formerly available only by prescription. Includes profiles of relevant pharmaceutical companies.

The Market for Salted Snacks. MarketResearch.com, 641 Ave. of the Americas, 4th Fl. New York, NY 10011. Phone: 800-298-5699 or (212)807-2629 Fax: (212)807-2676 E-mail: customerservice@marketresearch.com • URL: http://www.marketresearch.com • 2002. $3,000.00. Market research report. Covers potato chips, corn chips, popcorn, nuts, pretzels, and other salted snacks. Market projections are provided to the year 2004.

The Market for Stress Management Products and Services. Available from MarketResearch.com, 641 Ave. of the Americas, Third Floor New York, NY 10011. Phone: 800-298-5699 or (212)807-2629 Fax: (212)807-2716 E-mail: order@marketresearch.com • URL: http://www.marketresearch.com • 1996. $1,195.00. Market research report published by Marketdata Enterprises. Covers anti-anxiety drugs, stress management clinics, biofeedback centers, devices, seminars, workshops, spas, institutes, etc. Includes market size projections.

The Market for Sweet Baked Goods. MarketResearch.com, 641 Ave. of the Americas, 4th Fl. New York, NY 10011. Phone: 800-298-5699 or (212)807-2629 Fax: (212)807-2676 E-mail: customerservice@marketresearch.com • URL: http://www.marketresearch.com • 2000. $2,750.00. Market research data. Covers both fresh and frozen, bakery products.

The Market for Value-Added Fresh Produce. MarketResearch.com, 641 Ave. of the Americas, 4th Fl. New York, NY 10011. Phone: 800-298-5699 or (212)807-2629 Fax: (212)807-2676 E-mail: customerservice@marketresearch.com • URL: http://www.marketresearch.com • 1999. $2,750.00. Market research report. Covers packaged salad mixes, bulk salad mixes, pre-cut fruits, and pre-cut vegetables. Market projections are provided to the year 2003.

Market: Latin America. The PRS Group, Inc., 6320 Fly Rd., Ste. 102 East Syracuse, NY 13057. Phone: (315)431-0511 Fax: (315)431-0200 E-mail: custserv@prsgroup.com • URL: http://www.prsgroup.com • Monthly. $397.00 per year ($198.00 to academic institutions). Newsletter. Provides market trend information and demographic data for Latin American countries. Includes sales trend projections for various products and services, with consumer household buying patterns and industrial expenditures. Formerly published by Market Newsletters.

Market Research Europe. Available from MarketResearch.com, 641 Ave. of the Americas, 3rd Fl. New York, NY 10011. Phone: 800-298-5699 or (212)807-2629 Fax: (212)807-2716 E-mail: order@marketresearch.com • URL: http://www.marketresearch.com • Monthly. $1,220.00 per year. Published by Euromonitor Publications. Newsletter on consumer spending in Europe.

Market Research Handbook. Statistics Reference Centre (National Capital Region), Holland Ave., Main Bldg., Rm. 1500 Ottawa, ON, Canada K1A OT6. Phone: 800-236-1136 E-mail: infostats@statcan.ca • URL: http://www.statcan.ca • Annual. $125.00. Contains a wide variety of demographic and other data relevant to Canadian markets.

Market Research Monitor. Euromonitor International, 122 South Michigan Ave., Suite 800 Chicago, IL 60603. Phone: 800-577-3876 or (312)922-1115 Fax: (312)922-1157 E-mail: info@euromonitor.com • URL: http://www.euromonitor.com • Contains full-text reports online from *Market Research Europe, Market Research Great Britain, Market Research International*, and *Retail Monitor International*. Time period is 1995 to date, with monthly updates. Inquire as to online cost and availability.

Market Research Reports. MarketResearch.com, 641 Ave. of the Americas New York, NY 10011. Phone: 800-298-5699 or (212)807-2629 Fax: (212)807-2676 E-mail: order@marketresearch.com • URL: http://www.marketresearch.com • Provides online full text of market research reports produced by FIND/SVP, Packaged Facts, Specialists in Business Information and others. Contains market data for a wide variety of industries, products, and services, including market size, forecasts, trends, structure, and opportunities. Inquire as to online cost and availability.

Market Research Toolbox: A Concise Guide for Beginners. Edward F. McQuarrie. Sage Publications, Inc., 2455 Teller Rd. Thousand Oaks, CA 91320. Phone: 800-818-7243 or (805)499-9774 Fax: 800-583-2665 or (805)499-0871 E-mail: webmaster@sagepub.com • URL: http://www.sagepub.com • 1996. $35.95.

Market Share Reporter. Available from Gale Cengage Learning, 27500 Drake Rd. Farmington Hills, MI 48331-3535. Phone: 800-877-GALE or (248)699-GALE Fax: 800-414-5043 E-mail: gale.galeord@cengage.com • URL: http://www.galegroup.com • 2002. $285.00. Sixth edition. Published by Euromonitor. Provides consumer market share data for leading companies in 30 major countries.

Market Share Reporter: An Annual Compilation of Reported Market Share Data on Companies, Products, and Services. Gale Cengage Learning, 27500 Drake Rd. Farmington Hills, MI 48331-3535. Phone: 800-877-GALE or (248)699-4253 Fax: 800-414-5043 E-mail: gale.galeord@cengage.com • URL: http://gale.cengage.com • Annual. $285.00. Contains summaries of market share reports. Actual data is given, with many charts and graphs. List more than 2,000 entries.

Market Share Reporter (MSR) [online]. Gale Cengage Learning, 27500 Drake Rd. Farmington Hills, MI 48331-3535. Phone: 800-877-GALE or (248)699-GALE Fax: 800-414-5043 or (248)699-8069 E-mail: galeord@gale.com • URL: http://gale.cengage.com • Provides online market share data for individual companies, products, and services, covering all industries. Sources include various publications, trade journals, associations, government agencies, corporate reports, investment research reports, etc. Time period is 1991 to date, with annual updates. Inquire as to online cost and availability.

Market Share Tracker. Euromonitor International, 122 South Michigan Ave., Suite 810 Chicago, IL 60603. Phone: 800-577-3876 or (312)922-1115 Fax: (312)922-1157 E-mail: info@euromonitor.com • URL: http://www.euromonitor.com • 2003. $1,190.00. Second edition. Contains market share rankings of more than 1,800 consumer product companies in 30 countries. Covers 16 kinds of products within "Drinks," "Household and Personal Care," and "Foods." Includes brand shares for leading brands. (*Global Market Share Planner*, vol. 1.)

Market Structure of Sports. Gerald W. Scully. The University of Chicago Press, 1427 E. 60th St. Chicago, IL 60637. Phone: 800-621-2736 or (773)702-7700 Fax: 800-621-8476 or (773)702-7212 E-mail: custserv@press.uchicago.edu • URL: http://www.press.uchicago.edu • 1995. $39.95.

The Marketer: Official Voice of Petroleum Marketers in Oklahoma. Oklahoma Petroleum Marketers Association, 5115 N. Western Ave. Oklahoma City, OK 73118. Phone: (405)842-6625 Fax: (405)842-9564 Quarterly. $12.00 per year.

Marketer's Guide to E-Commerce: Everything You Need to Know to Successfully Sell, Promote, and Market Your Business, Product, or Service Online. Arthur Bell and Vincent Leger. McGraw-Hill, 1221 Ave. of the Americas New York, NY 10020. Phone: 800-722-4726 or (212)512-2000 Fax: (212)512-4502 E-mail: customer.service@mcgraw-hill.com • URL: http://www.mcgraw-hill.com • 2001. $39.95. Covers website marketing strategies, including guidelines and examples. (NTC Business Books Series).

Marketing. Damico Zikmund. Cengage Learning, 290 Harbor Dr. Stamford, KY 06902. Phone: 800-347-7707 or (203)969-8700 Fax: 800-487-8488 or (203)969-8700 E-mail: communications@cengage.com • URL: http://www.thomson.com/learning • 2000. $65.00 Seventh edition. (SWC-General Business Series).

Marketing. Bruce J. Walker. McGraw-Hill, 1221 Ave. of the Americas New York, NY 10020. Phone: 800-722-4726 or (212)512-2000 Fax: (212)512-4502 E-mail: customer.service@mcgraw-hill.com • URL: http://www.mcgraw-hill.com • 2003. 13th edition. Price on application.

Marketing: A How-To-Do-It Manual for Librarians. Suzanne Walters. Neal-Schuman Publishers, Inc., 100 William St., Ste. 2004 New York, NY 10038. Phone: (866)672-6657 or (212)925-8650 Fax: (866)209-7932 or (212)219-8916 E-mail: info@neal-schuman.com • URL: http://www.neal-schuman.com • 2003. Second edition. Price on application. Includes a sample library marketing plan with worksheets. Covers market research, strategies, tactics, and evaluation. (How-to-Do-It Manuals Series).

Marketing and Advertising Reference Service (MARS). Gale Cengage Learning, 27500 Drake Rd. Farmington Hills, MI 48331-3535. Phone: 800-877-GALE or (248)699-GALE Fax: 800-414-5043 or (248)699-8069 E-mail: galeord@gale.com • URL: http://gale.cengage.com • Provides abstracts of literature relating to consumer marketing and advertising, including all forms of advertising media. Time period is 1984 to date. Daily updates. Inquire as to online cost and availability.

Marketing: Contemporary Concepts and Practices. William F. Schoell. Allyn and Bacon, Inc., 75 Arlington St., Ste. 300 Boston, MA 02116. Phone: 800-922-0579 or (781)848-6000 Fax: (515)284-2607 E-mail: ab_webmaster@abacon.com • URL: http://www.abacon.com • 1995. $110.00. Sixth edition.

Marketing for CPAs, Accountants, and Tax Professionals. William J. Winston. Haworth Press, Inc., 10 Alice St. Binghamton, NY 13904-1580. Phone: 800-429-6784 or (607)722-5857 Fax: 800-895-0582 or (607)722-1424 E-mail: getinfo@haworthpressinc.com • URL: http://www.haworthpressinc.com • 1995. $49.95. (Marketing Resources Series).

Marketing for Lawyers. American Lawyer Media, 345 Park Ave. S. New York, NY 10010. Phone: 800-888-8300 or (212)545-6170 Fax: (212)481-8161 • URL: http://www.americanlawyer.com • Monthly. $195.00 per year. Newsletter. Provides advice for law firms on attracting new clients and providing good service to present clients.

Marketing for Non-Profit Organizations. David L. Rados. Greenwood Publishing Group, Inc., 88 Post Rd., W Westport, CT 06881. Phone: 800-225-5800 or (203)226-3571 Fax: (203)431-2214 E-mail: customer-service@greenwood.com • URL: http://www.greenwood.com • 1996. $64.95. Second edition.

Marketing Health Care into the Twenty-First Century: The Changing Dynamic. Alan K. Vitberg. Haworth Press, Inc., 10 Alice St. Binghamton, NY 13904-1580. Phone: 800-429-6784 or (607)722-5857 Fax: 800-895-0582 or (607)722-1424 E-mail: getinfo@haworthpressinc.com • URL: http://www.haworthpressinc.com • 1996. $39.95. (Marketing Resources Series).

Marketing Health Services. American Marketing Association, 311 S. Wacker Dr., Suite 5800 Chicago, IL 60606-5819. Phone: 800-262-1150 or (312)542-9000 Fax: (312)542-9001 E-mail: info@ama.org • URL: http://www.ama.org • Quarterly. Members, $45.00 per year; non-members, $70.00 per year; institutions, $90.00 per year. Formerly*Journal of Health Care Marketing*.

Marketing in the Third World. Denise M. Johnson and Erdener Kaynak, editors. Haworth Press, Inc., 10 Alice St. Binghamton, NY 13904-1580. Phone: 800-429-6784 or (607)722-5857 Fax: 800-895-0582 or (607)722-1424 E-mail: getinfo@haworthpressinc.com • URL: http://www.haworthpressinc.com • 1996. $29.95. Various authors discuss marketing, advertising, government regulations, and other topics relating to business promotion in developing countries. (Also published in the *Journal of Global Marketing*, vol. 9, no. 4).

Marketing in Travel and Tourism. Victor Middleton. Elsevier, 655 Ave. of the Americas New York, NY 10010. Phone: 800-366-2665 or (212)989-5800 Fax: 800-535-9935 or (212)633-3680 E-mail: custserv@elsevier.com • URL: http://www.elsevier.com • 2001. $37.95. Third edition. Explains, with examples, the application of marketing concepts and principles to the travel industry.

Marketing Information Revolution. Robert C. Blattberg, editor. McGraw-Hill, 1221 Ave. of the Americas New York, NY 10020. Phone: 800-722-4726 or (212)512-2000 Fax: (212)512-4502 E-mail: customer.service@mcgraw-hill.com • URL: http://www.mcgraw-hill.com • 1993. $39.95. Third edition. Includes a wide variety of sources for specific kinds of marketing.

Marketing Know-How: Your Guide to the Best Marketing Tools and Sources. Primedia Business Magazines and Media, 9800 Metcalf Ave. Overland Park, KS 66212. Phone: 800-795-5445 or (913)341-1300 Fax: (913)967-1898 E-mail: subs@primediabusiness.com • URL: http://www.primediabusiness.com • 1996. $49.95. Describes more than 700 public and private sources of consumer marketing data. Also discusses market trends and provides information on such marketing techniques as cluster analysis, focus groups, and geodemographic analysis.

Marketing Magazine: Canada's Weekly Newspaper for Marketing, Advertising and Sales Executives. Rogers Media Publishing, 1 Mount Pleasant Rd. Toronto, ON, Canada M4Y 2Y5. Phone: (416)764-1593 Fax: (416)764-1419 • URL: http://www.rogers.com • Weekly. $95.00 per year. "Canada's national weekly publication dedicated to the businesses of marketing, advertising, and media." Includes annual Marketing Awards, quarterly Digital Marketing (emerging technology), Promo Marketing, and PR Quarterly (special issues on public relations).

Marketing Management for the Hospitality Industry: A Strategic Approach. Allen Z. Reich. John Wiley and Sons, Inc., 111 River St. Hoboken, NJ 07030. Phone: 800-225-5945 or (201)748-6000 Fax: (201)748-6088 E-mail: info@wiley.com • URL: http://www.wiley.com • 1997. $65.00.

Marketing Management: Knowledge and Skills. J. Paul Peter and James H. Donnelly. McGraw-Hill, 1221 Ave. of the Americas New York, NY 10020. Phone: 800-722-4726 or (212)512-2000 Fax: (212)512-4502 E-mail: customer.service@mcgraw-hill.com • URL: http://www.mcgraw-hill.com • 2003. $120.70 Seventh edition. (Marketing Series).

Marketing Management: Shaping the Profession of Marketing. American Marketing Association, 311 S. Wacker Dr., Suite 5800 Chicago, IL 60606-5819. Phone: 800-262-1150 or (312)542-9000 Fax: (312)542-9001 E-mail: info@ama.org • URL: http://www.ama.org • Quarterly. Members, $45.00 per year; non-members, $70.00 per year; institutions, $90.00 per year. Covers trends in the management of marketing, sales, and distribution.

Marketing Management: Text and Cases. Robert Dolan. McGraw Hill, 1221 Ave. of the Americas New York, NY 10020. Phone: 800-722-4726 or (212)904-2000 Fax: (212)904-2072 E-mail: customer.service@mcgraw-hill.com • URL: http://www.mcgraw-hill.com • 2001. $108.75. (Marketing Series).

Marketing Manager's Handbook. Sidney J. Levy and others. Prentice Hall PTR, 240 Frisch Ct. Paramus, NJ 07652. Phone: 800-282-0693 Fax: 800-445-6991 • URL: http://www.phptr.com • 2000. Price on application. Contains 71 chapters by various authors on a wide variety of marketing topics, including market segmentation, market research, international marketing, industrial marketing, survey methods, customer service, advertising, pricing, planning, strategy, and ethics.

Marketing News: Reporting on Marketing and Its Association. American Marketing Association, 311 S. Wacker Dr., Suite 5800 Chicago, IL 60606-5819. Phone: 800-262-1150 or (312)542-9000 Fax: (312)542-9001 E-mail: info@ama.org • URL: http://www.ama.org • Biweekly. Free to members; non-members, $100.00 per year; institutions, $130.00 per year.

Marketing on the Internet: Multimedia Strategies for the World Wide Web. Jill Ellsworth and Matthew Ellsworth. John Wiley and Sons, Inc., 111 River St. Hoboken, NJ 07030. Phone: 800-225-5945 or (201)748-6000 Fax: (201)748-6088 E-mail: info@wiley.com • URL: http://www.wiley.com • 1996. $29.99. Second expanded revised edition.

Marketing Planning: A Step-by-Step Guide. James W. Taylor. Prentice Hall PTR, 240 Frisch Ct. Paramus, NJ 07652-5240. Phone: 800-282-0693 • URL: http://www.prenhall.com • 1996. $49.95.

Marketing Planning Guide. Robert E. Stevens and others. Haworth Press, Inc., 10 Alice St. Binghamton, NY 13904-1580. Phone: 800-429-6784 or (607)722-5857 Fax: 800-895-0582 or (607)722-1424 E-mail: getinfo@haworthpressinc.com • URL: http://www.haworthpressinc.com • 1997. $49.95. Second edition. Covers market segmentation, product positioning, and other marketing planning topics.

Marketing Plans: How to Prepare Them, How to Use Them. Malcolm H. McDonald. Elsevier, 655 Ave. of the Americas New York, NY 10010. Phone: 800-366-2665 or (212)989-5800 Fax: 800-535-9935 or (212)633-3680 E-mail: custserv@elsevier.com • URL: http://www.elsevier.com • 2002. $49.99. Fifth edition.

Marketing Power: Your Guide to Successful Research. American Demographics, Inc., PO Box 2042 Marion, OH 43306-8142. Phone: 800-529-7502 • URL: http://www.demographics.com • Quarterly. Issued as a supplement to *American Demographics* and *Marketing Tools*. Describes a wide variety of current market research material issued by various publishers and available from American Demographics, Inc.

Marketing: Principles and Perspectives. William Bearden and others. McGraw-Hill, 1221 Ave. of the Americas New York, NY 10020. Phone: 800-722-4726 or (212)512-2000 Fax: (212)512-4502 E-mail: customer.service@mcgraw-hill.com • URL: http://www.mcgraw-hill.com • 2004. Fourth edition. Price on application. (Marketing Series).

The Marketing Pulse: The Exclusive Insight Provider to the Entertainment, Marketing, Advertising and Media Industries. Unlimited Positive Communications, Inc., Seven Innis Ave. New Paltz, NY 12561. Phone: (914)255-2222 Fax: (914)255-2231 E-mail: gdneml@ix.netcom Bimonthly. $300.00 per year. Newsletter concerned with advertising media forecasts and analyses. Emphasis is on TV and radio.

The Marketing Report: The Best Time-Saving Information Source for Marketing Execcutives. Progressive Business Publications, 370 Technology Dr. Malvern, PA 19355-1315. Phone: 800-220-5000 or (610)695-8600 Fax: (610)647-8089 E-mail: editor@pbp.com • URL: http://www.pbp.com • Semimonthly. $264.00 per year. Newsletter. Covers marketing ideas, problem solving, and new product development. Includes case histories.

Marketing Research. Alvin Burns and Ronald Bush. John Wiley and Sons, Inc., 111 River St. Hoboken, NJ 07030. Phone: 800-225-5945 or (201)748-6000 Fax: (201)748-6088 E-mail: info@wiley.com • URL: http://www.wiley.com • 1998. $115.00. Second edition.

Marketing Research: A Magazine of Management and Applications. American Marketing Association, 311 S. Wacker Dr., Suite 5800 Chicago, IL 60606-5819. Phone: 800-262-1150 or (312)542-9000 Fax: (312)542-9001 E-mail: info@ama.org • URL: http://www.ama.org • Quarterly. Members, $45.00 per year; non-members, $70.00 per year; institutions,$120.00 per year.

Marketing Research: An Applied Approach. Naresh K. Malhotra and David F. Birks. Prentice Hall, 240 Frisch Ct. Paramus, NJ 07652. Phone: 800-223-2336 or (201)909-6200 Fax: (201)909-6360 E-mail: pearsoned@eds.com • URL: http://www.prenhall.com • 2003. $75.00. Second edition.

Marketing Research Association., 110 National Dr., 2nd Fl., PO Box 230 Glastonbury, CT 06033-1212. Phone: (860)682-1000 Fax: (860)682-1010 E-mail: larry.brownell@mra-net.org • URL: http://www.mra-net.org • Companies and individuals involved in any area of opinion and marketing research, such as data collection, research, or as an end-user.

Marketing Research Guide. Robert E. Stevens and others. Haworth Press, Inc., 10 Alice St. Binghamton, NY 13904-1580. Phone: 800-429-6784 or (607)722-5857 Fax: 800-895-0582 or (607)722-1424 E-mail: getinfo@haworthpressinc.com • URL: http://www.haworthpressinc.com • 1997. $79.95. A practical guide to the preparation of a market research report, including worksheets, sample proposals, questionnaires, and an example of a final report. (Marketing Resources Series).

Marketing Research in a Marketing Environment. William R. Dillion and others. McGraw-Hill, 1221 Ave. of the Americas New York, NY 10020. Phone: 800-722-4726 or (212)512-2000 Fax: (212)512-4502 E-mail: customer.service@mcgraw-hill.com • URL: http://www.mcgraw-hill.com • 1993. $67.50. Third edition.

Marketing Research Process. Len T. Wright and Margaret Crimp. Prentice Hall PTR, 240 Frisch Ct. Paramus, NJ 07652. Phone: 800-282-0693 Fax: 800-445-6991 • URL: http://www.phptr.com • 2000. Fifth edition. Price on application.

Marketing Research Project Manual. Glen R. Jarboe. South-Western, 5191 Natrop Blvd. Mason, OH 45040. Phone: 800-543-0487 or (513)229-1000 • URL: http://www.swcollege.com • 1998. $32.95. Fourth edition. Covers the methodology of market research surveys. (Marketing Series).

Marketing Research That Pays Off: Case Histories of Marketing Research Leading to Success in the Marketplace. Larry Percy, editor. Haworth Press, Inc., 10 Alice St. Binghamton, NY 13904-1580. Phone: 800-429-6784 or (607)722-5857 Fax: 800-895-0582 or (607)722-1424 E-mail: getinfo@haworthpressinc.com • URL: http://www.haworthpressinc.com • 1997. $49.95.

Marketing Science Institute. Marketing Science Institute, 1000 Massachusetts Ave. Cambridge, MA 02138-5396. Phone: (617)491-2060 Fax: (617)491-2065 E-mail: mclippinger@msi.org • URL: http://www.msi.org • Marketing, including studies on marketing management and strategy, international/global marketing, impact of information technology on marketing, marketing models and methods, advertising, sales promotion, sales force, channels of distribution, consumer services marketing, business-to-business marketing, and marketing of consumer durables and packaged goods.

Marketing Strategies for the Mature Market. George P. Moschis. Greenwood Publishing Group, Inc., 88 Post Rd., W Westport, CT 06881. Phone: 800-225-5800 or (203)226-3571 Fax: (203)431-2214 E-mail: customer-service@greenwood.com • URL: http://www.greenwood.com • 1994. $64.95.

Marketing Strategy. Orville C. Walker and others. McGraw Hill, 1221 Ave. of the Americas New York, NY 10020. Phone: 800-722-4726 or (212)512-2000 Fax: (212)512-4502 E-mail: customer.service@mcgraw-hill.com • URL: http://www.mcgraw-hill.com • 1998. $73.13. Third edition.

Marketing the Law Firm. American Lawyer Media, Inc., 105 Madison Ave. New York, NY 10016. Phone: 800-888-8300 or (212)779-9200 Fax: (212)481-8110 E-mail: lawcatalog@amlaw.com • URL: http://www.lawcatalog.com/ • Monthly. $199.00 per year. Newsletter. Focuses on actions that lawyers can take to find more clients and do more business. (A Law Journal Newsletter, formerly published by Leader Publications under the title *Marketing for Lawyers*).

Marketing the Law Firm: Business Development Techniques. American Lawyer Media, Inc., 105 Madison Ave. New York, NY 10016. Phone: 800-888-8300 or (212)779-9200 Fax: (212)481-8110 E-mail: lawcatalog@amlaw.com • URL: http://www.lawcatalog.com • Looseleaf. $189.00. Updated as needed. Covers client surveys, brochures, direct mail, Web sites, seminars, newsletters, proposals, trade shows, and other marketing avenues for both large and small law firms. (Law Journal Press).

Marketing Times. Sales and Marketing Executives International, PO Box 1390 Sumas, WA 98295-1390. Phone: 800-999-1414 or (301)893-0751 Quarterly. Membership. Newsletter.

Marketing to Older Consumers: A Handbook of Information for Strategy Development. George P. Moschis. Greenwood Publishing Group, Inc., 88 Post Rd., W Westport, CT 06881. Phone: 800-225-5800 or (203)226-3571 Fax: (203)431-2214 E-mail: customer-service@greenwood.com • URL: http://www.greenwood.com • 1992. $74.95.

Marketing to the Affluent. Thomas J. Stanley. McGraw-Hill, 1221 Ave. of the Americas New York, NY 10020. Phone: 800-722-4726 or (212)512-2000 Fax: (212)521-4502 E-mail: customer.service@mcgraw-hill.com • URL: http://www.mcgraw-hill.com • 1988. $19.95. Discusses demographics, psychographics, and buying habits.

Marketing to the Emerging Minorities. EPM Communications, Inc., 160 Mercer St., 3rd. Fl. New York, NY 10012-3212. Phone: 888-852-9467 or (212)941-0099 Fax: 888-852-3899 or (212)941-1622 E-mail: info@epmcom.com • URL: http://www.epmcom.com • Monthly. $295.00 per year. Newsletter on market research relating to African American, Asian American, and U. S. Hispanic populations.

Marketing Without Advertising. Michael Phillips and Salli Rasberry. Nolo, 950 Parker St. Berkeley, CA 94710. Phone: 800-728-3555 or (510)549-1976 Fax: 800-645-0895 or (510)548-5902 E-mail: simone@nolo.com • URL: http://www.nolo.com • 2001. $24.00. Fourth edition. How to market a small business economically.

Marketing Your Indexing Services. Anne Leach, editor. Information Today, Inc., 143 Old Marlton Pike Medford, NJ 08055-8750. Phone: 800-300-9868 or (609)654-6266 Fax: (609)654-4309 E-mail: custserv@infotoday.com • URL: http://www.infotoday.com • 1998. $20.00. Second edition. Published in conjunction with the American Society of Indexers (ASI). Provides a collection of useful articles from *Key Words*, the newsletter of the American Society of Indexers.

Marketscore. CB Richard Ellis, 865 S Figueroa St., 34th Fl. Los Angeles, CA 90017. Phone: (213)438-4880 Fax: (213)438-4820 • URL: http://www.cbre.com • Quarterly. Price on application. Newsletter. Provides proprietary forecasts of commercial real estate performance in metropolitan areas.

Marking Industry Magazine. Marking Devices Publishing Co., 136 W. Vallette St., Suite 6 Elmhurst, IL 60126-4377. Phone: 888-627-5464 or (630)832-5200 Fax: (630)832-5206 • URL: http://www.markingdevices.com • Monthly. $44.00 per year. Includes annual buyer's guide *Marking Products and Equipment*.

Marking Products and Equipment Buyer's Guide. Marking Devices Publishing Co., 136 W Vallete St., Ste. 6 Elmhurst, IL 60126. Phone: 888-627-5464 or (630)852-5200 Fax: (630)832-5206 • URL: http://www.markingdevices.com • Annual. $30.00. Included in subscription to *Marking Industry Magazine*.

MarkIntel. Thomson Financial, PO Box 95512 Chicago, IL 60694. Phone: 800-607-4463 or (312)288-6400 • URL: http://www.tfsd.com • Provides the current full text online of more than 50,000 market research reports covering 54 industries, from 85 leading research firms worldwide. Reports include extensive forecasts and market analysis. Inquire as to online cost and availability.

Martin E. Segal Theatre Center.

Martin Weiss' Safe Money Report. Weiss Ratings, Inc., 4176 Burns Rd. Palm Beach Gardens, FL 33410-4606. Phone: 800-289-9222 or (561)627-3300 Fax: (561)625-6685 E-mail: wr@weissinc.com • URL: http://www.martinweiss.com • Monthly. $189.00 per year. Newsletter. Provides financial advice and current safety ratings of various banks, savings and loan companies, insurance companies, and securities dealers. Formerly (The Safe Money Report).

Martindale-Hubbell Bar Register of Preeminent Lawyers. Martindale-Hubbell, 121 Chanlon Rd. New Providence, NJ 07974. Phone: 800-526-4902 Fax: (908)771-8704 • URL: http://www.martindale.com • Annual. $195.00. Lists over 9,700 "outstanding members of the bar" in general practice and in 28 specific fields. Covers the U. S. and Canada.

Martindale-Hubbell International Dispute Resolution Directory. Martindale-Hubbell, 121 Chanlon Rd. New Providence, NJ 07974. Phone: 800-526-4902 Fax: (908)771-8704 • URL: http://www.martindale.com • Irregular. $195.00. Produced in cooperation with the American Arbitration Association. Over 45,000 judges, attorneys, law firms, and other neutral experts that specialize in dispute resolution and arbitration.

Martindale-Hubbell Law Directory. Martindale-Hubbell Inc., 121 Chanlon Rd. New Providence, NJ 07974. Phone: 800-526-4902 or (908)464-6800 Fax: (908)771-8704 E-mail: info@martindale.com • URL: http://www.martindale.com • Covers: lawyers and law firms in the United States, its possessions, and Canada, plus leading law firms worldwide; includes a biographical section by firm, and a separate list of patent lawyers, attorneys in government service, in-house counsel, and services, suppliers, and consultants to the legal profession. Entries include: For non-subscribing lawyers—Name, year of birth and of first admission to bar, code indicating college and law school attended and first degree, firm name (or other affiliation, if any) and relationship to firm, whether practicing other than as individual or in partnership. For subscribing lawyers—Above information plus complete address, phone, fax, e-mail and URL, type of practice, clients, plus additional personal details (education, certifications, etc.). A general law list. See separate listing, 'Law Lists'.

Martindale-Hubbell Law Directory on CD-ROM. Martindale-Hubbell, Reed Reference Publishing, 121 Chanlon Rd. New Providence, NJ 07974. Phone: 800-526-4902 or (908)464-

6800 Fax: (908)771-8704 Quarterly. $995.00 per year. Provides CD-ROM information on over 900,000 lawyers. International coverage.

Mason Contractors Association of America.

Masonry. Mason Contractors Association of America, 1910 S. Highland Ave., Suite 101 Lombard, IL 60148. Phone: (630)705-4200 Fax: (630)705-4209 Bimonthly. $20.00 per year.

Masonry Construction. Hanley-Wood, LLC, One Thomas Circle, NW Washington, DC 20005. Phone: 800-837-0870 or (202)452-0800 Fax: (202)785-1974 • URL: http://www.hanley-wood.com • 10 times a year. $30.00 per year. Covers masonry design, materials, equipment, and techniques.

Masonry Construction Buyers' Guide. Mason Contractors Association of America, 33 S Roselle Rd. Schaumburg, IL 60193. Phone: 800-536-2225 or (847)301-0001 Fax: (847)301-1110 E-mail: bennett@lionhrtpub.com • URL: http://www.masonrymagazine.com • Annual. $3.00. Lists manufacturers or suppliers of products and services related to masonry construction.

Masonry Design West. Pleasanton Publishing Co., 6284 Wade Court Pleasanton, CA 95688. Phone: (415)846-5623 Fax: (415)846-1753 Bimonthly. Price on application.

Mason's Manual of Legislative Procedure. American Society of Legislative Clerks and Secretaries. National Conference of State Legislatures, 7700 E 1st Fl. Denver, CO 80202-1743. Phone: (303)364-7700 Fax: (303)364-7800 E-mail: info@ncsl.org • URL: http://www.ncsl.org • 2000. $60.00. Contains parliamentary law and rules, rules of debate, rules governing motions, how to conduct business, etc.

Mass Communications Research Center.

Mass Immigration and the National Interest: Policy Directions for the New Century. Vernon M. Briggs. M. E. Sharpe, Inc., 80 Business Park Drive Armonk, NY 10504. Phone: 800-541-6563 or (914)273-1800 Fax: (914)273-2106 E-mail: custserv@mesharpe.com • URL: http://www.mesharpe.com • 2003. $69.95. Third edition. Discusses needed reforms in U. S. immigration policy, with historical background.

The Mass Media and the School Newspaper. De Witt C. Reddick. West Group, 610 Opperman Eagan, MN 55123. Phone: 800-338-9424 or (651)687-7000 Fax: 800-340-9378 E-mail: bookstore@westgroup.com • URL: http://www.westgroup.com • 1986. $24.75. Second edition. (Mass Communication Series).

Mass Media Law. Donald R. Pember. McGraw Hill, 1221 Ave. of the Americas New York, NY 10020. Phone: 800-722-4726 or (212)512-2000 Fax: (212)512-4502 E-mail: customer.service@mcgraw-hill.com • URL: http://www.mcgraw-hill.com • 2000. $62.50 12th edition. Includes CD-ROM. (Humanities, Social Sciences and World Languages Series).

Mass Merchandisers and Off-Price Apparel Buyers Directory. Douglas Publications, Inc., 2807 N. Parham Rd. Richmond, VA 23294. Phone: 800-223-1797 or (804)762-9600 Fax: (804)217-8999 E-mail: info@douglaspublications.com • URL: http://www.douglaspublications.com • Annual. $229.00. Lists buyers of clothing for major retailers. (Does not include the metropolitan New York City area.) *Salesman's Guide Directories*.

Mass Storage News: Opportunities and Trends in Data Storage and Retrieval. Corry Publishing, Inc., 5539 Peach St. Erie, PA 16506. Phone: (814)868-9935 Fax: (814)864-2037 • URL: http://www.corrypub.com • Biweekly. $597.00 per year. Newsletter. Provides descriptions of products and systems using optical storage. Formerly *Optical Memory News*.

Mass Transit: Better Transit Through Better Management. Cygnus Publishing, 1233 Janesville Ave. Fort Atkinson, WI 11747. Phone: 800-547-7377 or (920)563-6388 Fax: (920)563-1707 E-mail: rich.reiff@cygnuspub.com • URL: http://www.cygnusbzb.com • Bimonthly. 48.00 per year.

Mass Transit: Consultants. Cygnus Business Media, Inc., 1233 Janesville Ave. Fort Atkinson, WI 53538. Phone: 800-308-6397 or (920)563-6388 Fax: (920)563-1702 E-mail: rich.reiff@cygnuspub.com • URL: http://www.cygnusbzb.com • Annual. $64.00. Listings for over 300 urban transportation architects, designers, engineers, planners, consultants and other specialists serving the urban transportation industry.

Mass Transit: Supplier's Guide. Mass Transit, 1233 Janesville Ave. Fort Atkinson, WI 53538. Phone: (920)563-6388 Fax: (920)563-1702 E-mail: pbowers@airportbiz.com Eight times a year. $48.00 per year. Directory of over 800 manufacturers and distributors serving the urban transportation industry.

Master Brewers Association of the Americas., 3340 Pilot Knot Rd. Saint Paul, MN 55121-2097. Phone: (651)454-7250 Fax: (651)454-0766 E-mail: mbaa@mbaa.com • URL: http://www.mbaa.com • Formerly Master Brewers Association of America.

Master Franchising: Selecting, Negotiating, and Operating a Master Franchise. Carl E. Zwisler. CCH, Inc., 2700 Lake Cook Rd. Riverwoods, IL 60015. Phone: 800-835-5224 or (847)267-7000 E-mail: cust_serv@cch.com • URL: http://www.cch.com • 1999. $80.00. Written for franchisees, franchisers, and professional advisors. Emphasis is on international franchise transactions.

Master Handbook of Acoustics. F. Alton Everest. McGraw-Hill, 1221 Ave. of the Americas New York, NY 10020. Phone: 800-722-4726 or (212)512-2000 Fax: (212)512-4502 E-mail: customer.service@mcgraw-hill.com • URL: http://www.mcgraw-hill.com • 2001. $39.95. Fourth edition. Covers the theory of acoustics and practical applications of acoustics, as in the design of audio control rooms, recording studios, and listening rooms for the home. (Tab Electronics Series).

Master Handbook of Video Production. Jerry Whitaker. McGraw-Hill, 1221 Ave. of the Americas New York, NY 10020. Phone: 800-722-4726 or (212)512-2000 Fax: (212)512-4502 E-mail: customer.service@mcgraw-hill.com • URL: http://www.mcgraw-hill.com • 2002. $39.95. Covers such technical topics as facility design, sound isolation, production standards, video signal processing, lighting, and equipment.

MasterCard International., 2000 Purchase St. Purchase, NY 10577. Phone: 800-622-7747 or (914)249-2000 Fax: (914)249-5510 E-mail: customerservicecenter@mastercard.com • URL: http://www.mastercard.com • Represents banks and financial institutions. Serves as a licensor of the MasterCard credit card, the MasterCard business card, the Gold MasterCard credit card, and the MasterCard Travelers Cheque.

Mastering Competitive Debate. Dana Hensley and Diana Carlin. Clark Publishing, Inc., P.O. Box 19240 Topeka, KS 66619-0240. Phone: 800-845-1916 or (785)862-0218 Fax: (785)862-8224 E-mail: custservice@clarkpub.com • URL: http://www.clarkpub.com • 1999. $38.00. Fifth edition.

Mastering Management Education: Innovations in Teaching Effectiveness. Charles M. Vance, editor. Sage Publications, Inc., 2455 Teller Rd. Thousand Oaks, CA 91320. Phone: 800-818-7243 or (805)499-9774 Fax: 800-583-2665 or (805)499-0871 E-mail: webmaster@sagepub.com • URL: http://www.sagepub.com • 1993. $80.95. A collection of articles from the *Journal of Management Education*. Chapters cover lecture and discussion methods, case-study teaching, group-learning skills, and other business education topics.

Mastering Online Investing: How to Use the Internet to Become a More Successful Investor. Michael C. Thomsett. Dearborn Trading Publishing, A Kaplan Professional Co., 155 N Wacker Dr. Chicago, IL 60606. Phone: 800-621-9621 or (312)836-4400 Fax: (312)836-1021 E-mail: trade@dearborn.com • URL: http://www.dearborntrade.com • 2001. $19.95. Emphasis is on the Internet as an information source for intelligent investing, avoiding "speculation and fads."

Mastering Real Estate Mathematics. William L. Ventolo and others. Dearborn Trade Publishing, Kaplan Professional Co., 155 N Wacker Dr. Chicago, IL 60606. Phone: 800-621-9621 or (312)836-4400 Fax: (312)836-1021 E-mail: trade@dearborn.com • URL: http://www.dearborntrade.com • 2001. $31.35. Seventh edition. Step-by-step workbook written to help sharpen real estate math skills.

Mastering the Art of Marketing Professional Services: A Step-by-Step Best Practices Guide. Allan S. Boress and Michael G. Cummings. American Institute of Certified Public Accountants, 1211 Ave. of the Americas New York, NY 10036-8775. Phone: 800-862-4272 or (212)596-6200 Fax: (212)596-6213 E-mail: lmorales@aicpa.org • URL: http://www.aicpa.org • 2002. $74.00. Discusses recommended marketing practices for accounting firms, including networking, advertising, press release writing, public speaking, seminar planning, and use of trade shows.

Material Handling Equipment Distributors Association., 201 U.S. Hwy. 45 Vernon Hills, IL 60061-2398. Phone: (847)680-3500 Fax: (847)362-6989 E-mail: connect@mheda.org • URL: http://www.mheda.org • Distributors and manufacturers of material handling equipment. Aims to improve the proficiency of independent material handling distributors.

Material Handling Industry of America., 8720 Red Oak Blvd., Suite 201 Charlotte, NC 28217. Phone: 800-345-1815 or (704)676-1190 Fax: (704)676-1199 E-mail: jnofsinger@mhia.org • URL: http://www.mhia.org • Formerly Material Handling Industry.

Material Handling Management: Educating Industry on Product Handling, Flow Strategies, and Automation Technology. Penton Media, Inc., 1300 E. Ninth St. Cleveland, OH 44114. Phone: (216)696-7000 Fax: (216)696-1752 E-mail: information@penton.com • URL: http://www.penton.com • 13 times a year. Free to qualified personnel; others, $50.00 per year. Formerly *Material Handling Engineering*.

Materials Business File. Cambridge Scientific Abstracts, 7200 Wisconsin Ave. Bethesda, MD 20814. Phone: 800-843-7751 or (301)961-6700 Fax: (301)961-6720 E-mail: sales@csa.com • URL: http://www.csa.com • Provides online abstracts and citations to worldwide materials literature, covering the business and industrial aspects of metals, plastics, ceramics, and composites. Corresponds to *Steels Alert, Nonferrous Metals Alert,* and *Polymers/Ceramics/Composites Alert*. Time period is 1985 to date, with monthly updates. (Formerly produced by ASM International.) Inquire as to online cost and availability.

Materials Evaluation. American Society for Nondestructive Testing, 1711 Arlingate Ln. Columbus, OH 43228. Phone: (614)274-6003 Fax: (614)274-6899 • URL: http://www.asnt.org • Monthly. $105.00 per year. Provides up-to-date information about NDT applications and technical articles addressing nondestructive testing applications.

Materials for Occupational Education: An Annotated Source Guide. Patricia Glass Schuman, editor'. Neal-Schuman Publishers, Inc., 100 William St., Ste. 2004 New York, NY 10038. Phone: (866)672-6657 or (212)925-8650 Fax: (866)209-7932 or (212)219-8916 E-mail: info@neal-schuman.com • URL: http://www.neal-schuman.com • 1983. $39.95. Second edition. (Neal-Schuman Sourcebook Series).

Materials Handbook. John A. Vaccari and others. McGraw-Hill, 1221 Ave. of the Americas New York, NY 10020. Phone: 800-722-4726 or (212)512-2000 Fax: (212)512-4502 E-mail: customer.service@mcgraw-hill.com • URL: http://www.mcgraw-hill.com • 2002. $99.95. 15th edition. (Handbook Series).

Materials Handling and Management Society., 8720 Red Oak Blvd., Suite 201 Charlotte, NC 28217. Phone: 800-345-1815 or (704)676-1183 Fax: (704)676-1199 E-mail: bcurtis@mhia.org • URL: http://www.mhia.org/mhms • Formerly International Material Management Society.

Materials of Construction. James Lai. Kendall/Hunt Publishing Co., 4050 Westmark Dr. Dubuque, IA 52002. Phone: 800-228-0810 or (563)589-1000 Fax: 800-772-9165 or (563)589-1046 E-mail: orders@kendalhunt.com • URL: http://www.kendallhunt.com • 1999. $65.95. Second edition.

Materials Performance: Articles on Corrosion Science and Engineering Solutions for Corrosion Problems. National Association of Corrosion Engineers. NACE International, 1440 S Creek Dr. Houston, TX 77084. Phone: (281)228-6200 Fax: (281)228-6300 E-mail: pubs@mail.nace.org • URL: http://www.nace.org • Monthly. Individuals, $115.00 per year; institutions, $205.00 per year. Covers the protection and performance of materials in corrosive environments. Includes information on new materials and industrial coatings.

Materials Processing Center., Massachusetts Institute of Technology, 77 Massachusetts Ave., Room 12-007 Cambridge, MA 02139-4307. Phone: (617)253-5179 Fax: (617)258-6900 E-mail: fmpage@.mit.edu • URL: http://www.web.mit.edu/mpc • Conducts processing, engineering, and economic research in ferrous and nonferrous metals, ceramics, polymers, photonic materials, superconductors, welding, composite materials, and other materials.

Materials Properties Handbook: Titanium Alloys. R. Boyer and others, editors. ASM International, 9639 Kinsman Rd. Materials Park, OH 44073-0002. Phone: 800-336-5152 or (440)338-5151 Fax: (440)338-4634 E-mail: cust-srv@asminternational.org • URL: http://www.asminternational.org • 1994. $299.00. Covers titanium alloy applications, fabrication, properties, specifications, effects of processing, corrosion, etc.

Materials Research Center. Lehigh University

Materials Research Centres: A World Directory of Organizations and Programmes in Materials Science. Specialist Journals, 345 Park Ave., S New York, NY 10010-1707. Phone: (212)726-9333 Fax: (212)696-0052 E-mail: sjsupport@nature.com • URL: http://www.nature.com • Biennial. $445.00. Profiles of research centers in 75 countries. Materials include plastics, metals, fibers, etc.

Materials Research Society., 506 Keystone Dr. Warrendale, PA 15086-7573. Phone: (724)779-3003 Fax: (724)779-8313 E-mail: info@mrs.org • URL: http://www.mrs.org • Represents the interests of materials researchers from academia, industry, and government that promotes communication for the advancement of interdisciplinary materials research to improve the quality of life. Fosters interaction among researchers working on different classes of inorganic and organic materials and to promote interdisciplinary basic research on materials. Provides forum for industry, government, and university cooperation; conducts technical conferences, tutorial lectures. Maintains speakers' bureau.

Materials Science and Technology: A Comprehensive Treatment. R. W. Cahn and others, editors. John Wiley and Sons, Inc., 111 River St. Hoboken, NJ 07030. Phone: 800-225-5945 or (201)748-6000 Fax: (201)748-6088 E-mail: info@wiley.com • URL: http://www.wiley.com • 1997. $4,250.00. 18 volumes. Each volume covers a particular area of high-performance materials technology.

Materials Science Center. University of Wisconsin - Madison

Materials Science Citation Index. Institute for Scientific Information, 3501 Market St. Philadelphia, PA 19104. Phone: 800-336-4474 or (215)386-0100 Fax: (215)386-2911 Bimonthly. Contains current, CD-ROM citations and abstracts, providing international coverage of materials science journals.

Mathematical Finance: An International Journal of Mathematics, Statistics, and Financial Economics. Blackwell Publishing, 350 Main St. Malden, MA 02148-5018. Phone: 800-835-6770 or (781)388-8200 Fax: (781)388-8232 E-mail: subscrip@blackwellpub.com • URL: http://www.blackwellpub.com • Quarterly. Institutions, $683.00 per year. Includes online edition. Covers the use of sophisticated mathematical tools in financial research and practice.

Mathematics and Computer Education. George M. Miller, editor. MATYC Journal, Inc., P.O. Box 158 Old Bethpage, NY 11084-0158. Phone: (516)822-5475 • URL: http://www.macejournal.org • Quarterly. Individuals, $18.00 per year; institutions, $30.00 per year. Articles for high school and college teachers.

Mathematics with Applications in Management and Economics. Gordon D. Prichett and John C. Saber. McGraw-Hill, 1221 Ave. of the Americas New York, NY 10020. Phone: 800-722-4726 or (212)512-2000 Fax: (212)512-4502 E-mail: customer.service@mcgraw-hill.com • URL: http://www.mcgraw-hill.com • 1993. $72.75. Seventh revised edition.

MathSci. American Mathematical Society, 201 Charles St. Providence, RI 02904-2294. Phone: 800-321-4267 or (401)455-4000 Fax: (401)331-3842 Provides online citations, with abstracts, to the literature of mathematics, statistics, and computer science. Time period is 1940 to date, with monthly updates. Inquire as to online cost and availability.

MathSci Disc. American Mathematical Society, P.O. Box 6248 Providence, RI 02940-6248. Phone: 800-321-4267 or (401)455-4000 Fax: (401)331-3842 Semiannual. Price on application. Provides CD-ROM citations, with abstracts, to the literature of mathematics, statistics, and computer science, 1940 to date.

Matrimonial Strategist. American Lawyer Media Inc., 345 Park Ave., S. New York, NY 10010. Phone: 800-888-8300 or (212)779-2000 Fax: (212)481-8074 • URL: http://www.americanlawyermedia.com • Monthly. $175.00 per year. Newsletter on legal strategy and matrimonial law.

Maximizing Law Firm Profitability: Hiring, Training, and Developing Productive Lawyers. American Lawyer Media, Inc., 105 Madison Ave. New York, NY 10016. Phone: 800-888-8300 or (212)779-9200 Fax: (212)481-8110 E-mail: lawcatalog@amlaw.com • URL: http://www.lawcatalog.com/ • Looseleaf. $169.00. Updated as needed. (Law Journal Press).

Maximum PC (Personal Computer). Imagine Media, Inc., 150 N. Hill Dr. Brisbane, CA 94005. Phone: (415)468-4684 Fax: (415)468-4686 E-mail: webmaster@imaginemedia.com • URL: http://www.imaginemedia.com • Quarterly. $29.95 per year. Provides articles and reviews relating to multimedia hardware and software. Each issue includes a CD-ROM sampler (emphasis is on games). Formed by the merger of *Home PC* and *Boot.*

Maynard's Industrial Engineering Handbook. Kjell B. Zandin. McGraw-Hill, 1221 Ave. of the Americas New York, NY 10020. Phone: 800-722-4726 or (212)512-2000 Fax: (212)512-4502 E-mail: customer.service@mcgraw-hill.com • URL: http://www.mcgraw-hill.com • 2001. $150.00. Fifth edition. (Standard Handbooks Series).

Mayo Biomedical Imaging Resource., Mayo Clinic, 200 First St., S. W. Rochester, MN 55902. Phone: (507)284-4937 Fax: (507)284-1632 E-mail: rar@mayo.edu • URL: http://www.mayo.edu/bir • Develops three-dimensional medical imaging systems and software.

Mayo Clinic Diet Manual: A Handbook of Nutrition Practices. Jennifer K. Nelson and others. Mosby Inc., 11830 Westline Industrial Dr. Saint Louis, MO 63146. Phone: 800-325-4177 or (314)872-8370 Fax: 800-235-0256 or (314)432-1380 • URL: http://www.mosby.com • 1994. $79.00. Seventh edition.

Mayo Clinic on High Blood Pressure. Sheldon G. Sheps, editor. Mason Crest Publishers, 370 Reed Rd., Ste. 302 Broomall, PA 19008. Phone: (610)543-6200 Fax: (610)543-3878 E-mail: gbaffa@masoncrest.com • URL: http://www.masoncrest.com • 2002. $29.95. Covers diet, medications, exercise, monitoring, and alternative therapies. (Mayo Clinic on Health Series).

Mayors of America's Principal Cities. United States Conference of Mayors, 1620 Eye St., N.W. Washington, DC 20006. Phone: (202)293-7330 Fax: (202)293-2352 Semiannual. About 1,000 mayors of cities with populations of 30,000 or more.

MBA National Delinquency Survey. Mortgage Bankers Association of America, 1919 Pennsylvania Ave., N.W. Washington, DC 20006-3438. Phone: 800-793-6222 or (202)557-2700 E-mail: communications@mbaa.org • URL: http://www.mbaa.org • Quarterly. $30.00 per year. Newsletter. Provides delinquency and foreclosure data for single-family mortgage loans.

MBAA Technical Quarterly. Master Brewers Association of the Americas, 3340 Pilot Knob Rd. Saint Paul, MN 55121-2097. Phone: (651)454-7250 Fax: (651)454-0766 E-mail: mbaa@mbaa.com • URL: http://www.mbaa.com • Quarterly. $100.00 per year. Includes membership.

MBDA: Minority Business Development Agency. U. S. Department of CommercePhone: 888-324-1551 E-mail: help@mbda.gov • URL: http://www.mbda.gov • Web site provides links to a wide variety of advice and information for minority businesses. Main headings are Access to Markets, Access to Capital, Management & Technical Assistance, and Education & Training. An MBDA Resource Locator helps to locate sources of assistance in specific cities. Fees: Free. (Additional "business contracting and assistance tools" are offered to those who register with the site.)

MBEMAG. Minority Business Entrepreneur MagazinePhone: (310)540-9398 Fax: (310)792-8263 E-mail: webmaster@mbemag.com • URL: http://www.mbemag.com • Web site's main feature is the "MBE Business Resources Directory." This provides complete mailing addresses, phone, fax, and Web site addresses (URL) for more than 40 organizations and government agencies having information or assistance for ethnic minority and women business owners. Some other links are "Current Events," "Calendar of Events," and "Business Opportunities." Updating is bimonthly. Fees: Free.

MBI: The National Report on Minority, Women-Owned and Disadvantaged Business. Community Development Services, Inc. CD Publications, 8204 Fenton St. Silver Spring, MD 20910. Phone: 800-666-6380 or (301)588-6380 Fax: (301)588-6385 E-mail: info@cdpublications.com • URL: http://www.cdpublications.com • Semimonthly. $379.00 per year. Newsletter. Provides news of affirmative action, government contracts, minority business employment, and education/training for minorities in business. Formerly *Minorities in Business.*

McCarthy's Desk Encyclopedia of Intellectual Property. J. Thomas McCarthy. BNA, Inc., 1231 25th St., NW Washington, DC 20037. Phone: 800-372-1033 E-mail: customercare@bna.com • URL: http://www.bna.com • 1995. $75.00.Second edition. Defines legal terms relating to patents, trademarks, copyrights, trade secrets, entertainment, and the computer industry.

McCutcheon's Functional Materials Volumes 2. MC Publishing Co., 175 Rock Rd. Glen Rock, NJ 07452. Phone: (201)652-2655 Fax: (201)652-3419 E-mail: themc@gomc.com • URL: http://www.gomc.com • Annual. $170.00. Edited for product development, quality control and research and development chemists.

McCutcheon's Volume 1: Emulsifiers and Detergents. MC Publishing Co., 175 Rock Rd. Glen Rock, NJ 07452. Phone: (201)652-2655 Fax: (201)652-3419 E-mail: themc@gomc.com • URL: http://www.gomc.com • Annual. $190.00. Two volumes. International coverage.

McGill Centre for Intelligent Machines.

McGill's Life Insurance. Edward E. Graves, editor. The American College, 270 S. Bryn Mawr Ave. Bryn Mawr, PA 19010-2196. Phone: 800-421-0654 or (610)526-1000 Fax: (610)526-1310 • URL: http://www.amercoll.edu • 2002. $80.00. Fourth edition. Contains chapters by various authors on diverse kinds of life insurance, as well as annuities, disability insurance, long-term care insurance, risk management, reinsurance, and other insurance topics. (Huebner School Series).

McGladrey Institute of Accounting Education and Research.

McGraw-Hill Encyclopedia of Science & Technology. McGraw-Hill, 1221 Ave. of the Americas New York, NY 10020. Phone: 800-722-4726 or (212)512-2000 Fax: (212)512-4502 E-mail: customer.service@mcgraw-hill.com • URL: http://www.mcgraw-hill.com • 2002. $2,495.00. Ninth edition. 20 volumes.

McGraw-Hill Handbook of Business Letters. Roy W. Poe. McGraw-Hill, 1221 Ave. of the Americas New York, NY 10020. Phone: 800-722-4726 or (212)512-2000 Fax: (212)512-4502 E-mail: customer.service@mcgraw-hill.com • URL: http://www.mcgraw-hill.com • 1993. $59.50. Third edition. Contains about 200 model business letters in 13 categories. Writing style, organization, objective, and underlying psychology are discussed for each example.

McGraw-Hill Machining and Metalworking Handbook. Ronald A. Walsh. McGraw-Hill, 1221 Ave. of the Americas New York, NY 10020. Phone: 800-722-4726 or (212)512-2000 Fax: (212)512-4502 E-mail: customer.service@mcgraw-hill.com • URL: http://www.mcgraw-hill.com • 1998. $99.95. Second edition. Coverage includes machinery, machining techniques, machine tools, machine design, parts, fastening, and plating.

McGraw-Hill Pocket Guide to Business Finance: 201 Decision Making Tools for Managers. Joel G. Siegel. McGraw-Hill, 1221 Ave. of the Americas New York, NY 10020. Phone: 800-722-4726 or (212)512-2000 Fax: (212)512-4502 E-mail: customer.service@mcgraw-hill.com • URL: http://www.mcgraw-hill.com • 1992. $14.95. Includes ratios, formulas, models, guidelines, instructions, strategies, and rules of thumb.

McGraw-Hill Yearbook of Science and Technology. McGraw-Hill, 1221 Ave. of the Americas New York, NY 10020. Phone: 800-722-4726 or (212)512-2000 Fax: (212)512-4502 E-mail: customer.service@mcgraw-hill.com • URL: http://www.mcgraw-hill.com • Annual. $145.00.

McGraw-Hill's Big Red Book of Resumes. McGraw-Hill, 1221 Ave. of the Americas New York, NY 10020. Phone: 800-722-4726 or (212)512-2000 Fax: (212)512-4502 E-mail: customer.service@mcgraw-hill.com • URL: http://www.mcgraw-hill.com • 2002. $16.95. Contains 350 sample resumes using various approaches and styles. Includes examples of cover letters.

McGraw-Hill's Biotechnology Newswatch. McGraw-Hill, 1221 Ave. of the Americas New York, NY 10020. Phone: 800-722-4726 or (212)512-2000 Fax: (212)512-4502 E-mail: customer.service@mcgraw-hill.com • URL: http://www.mcgraw-hill.com • Semimonthly. Price on application. Newsletter.

McKnight's Long Term Care News. Thomson Medical Economics, Five Paragon Dr. Montvale, NJ 07645-1742. Phone: (201)358-7200 Fax: (201)722-2680 E-mail: customer.service@medec.com • URL: http://www.medec.com • 16 times a year. $47.95 per year. Edited for retirement housing directors and nursing home administrators.

McKnight's Long-Term Care News—Industry Directory. McKnight's Long-Term Care News, 1 Northfield Plz., Ste. 521 Northfield, IL 60093-1216. Phone: 800-558-1703 or (847)784-8706 Fax: (847)784-9346 E-mail: ltcnews@mltcn.com • URL: http://www.mcknightsonline.com • Publication includes: List of suppliers of products and services for nursing homes, as well as general information about the long-term care industry. Entries include: Company, name, address, phone, fax, name and title of contact, e-mail, web site if available.

Means Construction Cost Indexes. RSMeans, 63 Smith Ln. Kingston, MA 02364-9988. Phone: 800-334-3509 Fax: 800-632-6732 • URL: http://www.rsmeans.com • Quarterly. $237.95 per year.

Means Facilities Construction Cost Data. RSMeans, 63 Smiths Ln. Kingston, MA 02364. Phone: 800-334-3509 Fax: 800-632-6732 • URL: http://www.rsmeans.com • Annual. $236.95. Provides costs for use in building estimating.

Means Interior Cost Data. RSMeans, 63 Smiths Ln. Kingston, MA 02364. Phone: 800-334-3509 Fax: 800-632-6732 • URL: http://www.rsmeans.com • Annual. $108.95.

Means Labor Rates for the Construction Industry. RSMeans, 63 Smiths Ln. Kingston, MA 02364. Phone: 800-334-3509 Fax: (617)585-7466 • URL: http://www.rsmeans.com • Annual. $239.95. Formerly *Labor Rates for the Construction Industry.*

Means Repair and Remodeling Cost Data. RSMeans, 100 Construction Plaza Kingston, MA 02364. Phone: 800-334-3509 Fax: 800-632-6732 • URL: http://www.rsmeans.com • Annual. $95.95.

Means Residential Cost Data. RSMeans, 63 Smiths Ln. Kingston, MA 02364. Phone: 800-334-3509 Fax: 800-632-6732 • URL: http://www.rsmeans.com • Annual. $95.95.

Measurement and Evaluation in Counseling and Development. Association for Measurement and Evaluation in Counseling. American Counseling Association, 5999 Stevenson Ave. Alexandria, VA 22304-3300. Phone: 800-347-6647 Fax: 800-473-2329 • URL: http://www.counseling.org • Quarterly. Free to members; non-members, $60.00 per year.

Measurements and Control. Measurements and Data Corp., 2165 Main St. Sarasota, FL 34237. Phone: (941)366-1153 Fax: (941)366-5743 Bimonthly. $24.00 per year. Supplement available: *M & C: Measurement and Control News.*

Measuring Globalisation: The Role of Multinationals in OECD Economies. Organization for Economic Cooperation and Development, OECD Washington Center, 2001 L St., N. W., Suite 650 Washington, DC 20036-4922. Phone: 800-456-6323 or (202)785-6323 Fax: (202)785-0350 E-mail: washington.contact@oecd.org • URL: http://www.oecdwash.org • Biennial. $85.00. Two volumes. Volume one provides extensive statistics for the multinational corporate manufacturing sector. Volume two covers the services sector.

Meat and Poultry Inspection Directory. U.S. Department of Agriculture. Available from U.S. Government Printing Office, Washington, DC 20402. Phone: (202)512-1800 Fax: (202)512-2250 E-mail: gpoaccess@gpo.gov • URL: http://www.access.gpo.gov • Semiannual. $49.00 per year.

Meat and Poultry Inspection Regulations. U.S. Department of Agriculture. Available from U.S. Government Printing Office, Washington, DC 20402. Phone: (202)512-1800 Fax: (202)512-2250 E-mail: gpoaccess@gpo.gov • URL: http://www.access.gpo.gov • Looseleaf. Regulations for slaughter and processing of livestock and poultry as well as for certain voluntary services and humane slaughter.

Meat and Poultry: The Business Journal of the Meat and Poultry Industry. Sosland Publishing Co., 4800 Main St., Ste. 100 Kansas City, MO 64112. Phone: (816)756-1000 Fax: (816)756-0494 E-mail: web@sosland.com • URL: http://www.sosland.com • Monthly. $42.00 per year.

Meat Balances in OECD Countries. Organization for Economic Cooperation and Development. Available from OECD Publications and Information Center, 2001 L St., N. W., Suite 650 Washington, DC 20036-4922. Phone: 800-456-6323 or (202)785-6323 Fax: (202)785-0350 E-mail: washington.contact@oecd.org • URL: http://www.oecdwash.org • Irregular. Price varies. Presents data for seven years on meat production, trade, and consumption. Covers various categories of meat in OECD member countries. Text in French.

Meat Industry Suppliers Association., 201 Park Washington Ct. Falls Church, VA 22046-4527. Phone: (703)533-0251 Fax: (703)241-5603 E-mail: mbittle@asmii.com • URL: http://www.asmii.com • Firms supplying products and services to the meat, poultry, and seafood processing industries. Members include manufacturers and distributors of machinery, casings, seasonings, material handling and packaging equipment and materials, and other items used in slaughterhouses, packaging plants, processing plants, and supermarkets.

Meat Processing-Buyer's Guide-North American Edition. Watt Publishing Co., 122 S. Wesley Ave. Mount Morris, IL 61054. Phone: (815)734-4171 Fax: (815)734-4201 • URL: http://www.wattnet.com • Annual. $12.00. In-depth statistical review of the meat, poultry, and seafood industries with graphs and tables; governmental phonebook; listing of meat associations, list of suppliers to the industry; list of equipment, services, and supplies, list of meat processors and their respective products.

Meat Processing: North American Edition. Watt Publishing Co., 122 S. Wesley Ave. Mount Morris, IL 60154-1497. Phone: (815)734-4171 Fax: (815)734-4201 • URL: http://www.wattnet.com • Monthly. $54.00 per year.

Mechanical and Nuclear Engineering Research Laboratories. Kansas State University

Mechanical Engineering. ASME International, 3 Park Ave. New York, NY 10016-5990. Phone: 800-843-2763 or (212)591-7722 Fax: (212)591-7674 E-mail: infocentral@asme.org • URL: http://www.asme.org • Monthly. Members, $25.00 per year; non-members, $123.00 per year.

Mechanical Engineering Abstracts. CSA, 7200 Wisconsin Ave., Suite 601 Bethesda, MD 20814. Phone: 800-843-7751 or (301)961-6700 Fax: (301)961-6720 E-mail: service@csa.com • URL: http://www.csa.com • Bimonthly. $1,620.00 per year. Includes print and online editions. Formerly *ISMEC - Mechanical Engineering Abstracts*.

Mechanical Engineering Department. Stevens Institute of Technology

Mechanical Engineering Design. Joseph Shigley and others. McGraw-Hill, 1221 Ave. of the Americas New York, NY 10020. Phone: 800-722-4726 or (212)512-2000 Fax: (212)512-4502 E-mail: customer.service@mcgraw-hill.com • URL: http://www.mcgraw-hill.com • 2003. Seventh edition. Price on application.

Mechanical Engineers' Handbook. Myer P. Kutz. John Wiley and Sons, Inc., 111 River St. Hoboken, NJ 07030. Phone: 800-526-5368 or (201)748-6000 Fax: (201)748-6088 E-mail: info@wiley.com • URL: http://www.wiley.com • 1998. $250.00. Second edition.

Mechanical Engineer's Reference Book. E. H. Smith, editor. Society of Automotive Engineers, 400 Commonwealth Dr. Warrendale, PA 15096-0001. Phone: 877-606-7323 or (724)776-4841 Fax: (724)776-5760 • URL: http://www.sae.org • 1994. $135.00. 12th edition. Covers mechanical engineering principles, computer integrated engineering systems, design standards, materials, power transmission, and many other engineering topics. (Authored Series).

Mechanical Power Transmission Association., 6724 Lone Oak Blvd. Naples, FL 34109. Phone: (239)514-3441 Fax: (239)514-3470 E-mail: bob@mpta.org • URL: http://www.mpta.org • Manufacturers of multiple V-belt drive sheaves and elastomeric couplings for mechanical power transmission machinery.

Mechanism and Machine Theory. Elsevier, 360 Park Ave. S New York, NY 10010-1710. Phone: 888-437-4636 or (212)989-5800 Fax: (212)633-3990 E-mail: usinfo-f@elsevier.com • URL: http://www.elsevier.com • Monthly. Qualified personnel, $99.00 per year; institutions, $2,568.00 per year.

Med Ad News. Engel Publishing Partners, 828 A Newton-Yardley Rd. Newton, PA 18940. Phone: (215)867-0044 Fax: (215)867-0053 • URL: http://www.engelpub.com • Monthly. $225.00 per year. Covers the field of pharmaceutical advertising and marketing.

Media and Methods: Educational Products, Technologies and Programs for Schools and Universities. American Society of Educators, 1429 Walnut St. Philadelphia, PA 19102. Phone: 800-555-5657 or (215)563-6005 Fax: (215)587-9706 E-mail: michelesok@aol.com • URL: http://www.media-methods.com • Five times a year. $33.50 per year.

Media and the Law. SIMBA Information, 11 Riverbend Dr., S. Stamford, CT 06907-0234. Phone: 800-307-2529 or (203)358-4100 Fax: (203)358-5824 E-mail: info@simbanet.com • URL: http://www.simbanet.com • Semimonthly. $327.00 per year. Newsletter.

Media Communications Association International., 2810 Crossroads Dr., Ste. 3800 Madison, WI 53718. Phone: (608)443-2464 Fax: (608)443-2474 E-mail: info@mca-i.org • URL: http://www.mca-i.org • Individuals engaged in multimedia communications needs analysis, scriptwriting, producing, directing, consulting, and operations management in the video, multimedia, and film fields. Seeks to advance the benefits and image of media communications professionals.

Media Communications Association International Membership Directory. Media Communications Association International, 9202 N. Meridian St., Suite 200 Indianapolis, IN 46260-1834. Phone: (317)816-6269 Fax: (317)571-5603 E-mail: info@mca-i.org • URL: http://www.mca-i.org • Annual. Membership.

Media Device Report. Jon Peddie Associates, 100 Shoreline Hwy., Bldg. A, 2nd Fl. Mill Valley, CA 94941. Phone: 800-777-5006 or (301)354-2000 Fax: (301)309-3847 E-mail: clientservices@moodys.com • URL: http://www.pbimedia.com • Description: Covers media and electronic devices and companies, as well as business information for those devices and companies. Recurring features include a company profile, editorial articles, technology briefs, IPO's, stocks, and stock indices.

Media for Business. Robert H. Amend and Michael A. Schrader. Elsevier, 655 Ave. of the Americas New York, NY 10010. Phone: 800-366-2665 or (212)989-5800 Fax: 800-535-9935 or (212)633-3680 E-mail: custserv@elsevier.com • URL: http://www.elsevier.com • 1991. $44.95.

Media Industry Newsletter. Access Intelligence L.L.C., 4 Choke Cherry Rd., 2nd Fl. Rockville, MD 20850. Phone: 800-777-5006 or (301)354-2000 Fax: (301)309-3847 E-mail: info@accessintel.com • URL: http://www.pbimedia.com • Description: Covers the media industry, including advertising, marketing, publishing, radio, and television. Recurring features include weekly box scores of advertising pages in major magazines, salaries of top executives, earnings reports, and news of people in the industry.

Media Laboratory., Massachusetts Institute of Technology, 20 Ames St., Room E-15 Cambridge, MA 02139-4307. Phone: (617)253-0300 Fax: (617)258-6264 E-mail: casr@media.mit.edu • URL: http://www.media.mit.edu • Research areas include electronic publishing, spatial imaging, human-machine interface, computer vision, and advanced television.

Media Market Guide. Media Market Resources, 81 Main St., Ste. 2 Littleton, NH 03561. Phone: 800-242-9618 or (603)444-5720 Fax: (603)444-2872 • URL: http://www.mediamarket.com • Quarterly. $675.00 per year. Presents circulation and cost data for television, radio, magazines, newspapers and outdoor markets.

Media Math: Basic Techniques for Media Evaluation. Robert W. Hall. McGraw-Hill, 1221 Ave. of the Americas New York, NY 10020. Phone: 800-722-4726 or (212)512-2000 Fax: (212)512-4502 E-mail: customer.service@mcgraw-hill.com • URL: http://www.mcgraw-hill.com • 1988. $14.95. Second edition. (NTC Business Books Series).

The Media Monopoly. Ben H. Bagdikian. Beacon Press, 25 Beacon St. Boston, MA 02108-2892. Phone: (617)742-2110 Fax: (617)723-3097 • URL: http://www.beacon.org • 2000. $18.50. Sixth edition.

Media Rating Council., 370 Lexington Ave., Ste. 902 New York, NY 10017. Phone: (212)972-0300 Fax: (212)972-2786 E-mail: staff@mediaratingcouncil.org • URL: http://www.mediaratingcouncil.org • Broadcast and cable trade associations, media owners, advertising agencies, cable networks, and national networks including National Association of Broadcasters, Television Bureau of Advertising, Radio Advertising Bureau, Cable Advertising Bureau (see separate entries). Establishes minimum standards for electronic media ratings surveys. Commissions audits by CPA firms of the collection and processing of data gathered by audience measurement services, including A.C. Nielsen, Arbitron, Statistical Research Inc., and Mediafax. **Convention/Meeting:** none.

Media Sports Business. Kagan World Media, One Lower Ragsdale Dr. Building One, Ste. 130 Monterey, CA 93940. Phone: (831)624-1536 Fax: (831)625-3225 E-mail: info@kagan.com • URL: http://www.kagan.com • Description: Discusses the economics of national and regional cable and pay TV sports. Includes semiannual census of cable and pay sports channels, coverage of values of sports media rights, and news of other developments in the field. **Remarks:** Also available via e-mail and fax.

Media Systems Society: Understanding Industries, Strategies and Power. Joseph Turow. Addison-Wesley, 75 Arlington St., Ste. 300 Boston, MA 02116. Phone: 800-447-2226 or (617)848-7500 • URL: http://www.aw.com • 1996. $74.00. Second edition. Provides commentary on the role of U.S. mass media in a global economy.

MediaFinder CD-ROM: Oxbridge Directories of Print Media and Catalogs. Oxbridge Communications, Inc., 186 Fifth Ave., 6th Fl. New York, NY 10010. Phone: 800-955-0231 or (212)741-0231 Fax: (212)633-2938 E-mail: info@oxbridge.com • URL: http://www.mediafinder.com • Quarterly. $1,995.00 per year. CD-ROM includes about 100,000 listings from *Standard Periodical Directory*, *National Directory of Catalogs*, *National Directory of British Mail Order Catalogs*, *National Directory of German Mail Order Catalogs*, *Oxbridge Directory of Newsletters*, *National Directory of Mailing Lists*, *College Media Directory*, and *National Directory of Magazines*.

Mediaweek: The News Magazine of the Media. VNU Business Media, 770 Broadway New York, NY 10003-9595. Phone: 800-344-7119 or (646)654-4500 Fax: (646)654-7212 • URL: http://www.vnubusinessmedia.com • 47 times a year. Weekly. $149.00 per year. Published for advertising media buyers and managers.

Medical and Health Care Books and Serials in Print: An Index to Literature in Health Sciences. R. R. Bowker, 630 Central Ave. New Providence, NJ 07974. Phone: 888-269-5372 Fax: (908)219-0098 E-mail: info@bowker.com • URL: http://www.bowker.com • Annual. $359.00. Two volumes.

Medical and Health Information Directory. Gale Cengage Learning, 27500 Drake Rd. Farmington Hills, MI 48331-3535. Phone: 800-877-GALE or (248)699-GALE Fax: 800-414-5043 E-mail: gale.galeord@eengage.com • URL: http://gale.cengage.com • 2002. $675.00. Three volumes. 14th edition. Three volumes. $285.00 per volume. Vol. one covers medical organizations, agencies, and institutions; vol. two includes bibliographic, library, and database information; vol. three is a guide to services available for various medical and health problems.

Medical and Healthcare Marketplace Guide. IDD, Inc., 229 S 18th St. Philadelphia, PA 19103. Phone: 800-784-2332 or (215)790-7000 Fax: (215)735-3966 E-mail: info@dorlandhealth.com • URL: http://www.dorlandhealth.com • Annual. $595.00. Two volumes. Provides market survey summaries for about 500 specific product and service categories (volume one: "Research Reports"). Contains profiles of nearly 5,500 pharmaceutical, medical product, and healthcare service companies (volume two: "Company Profiles").

Medical Benefits. Aspen Publishers Inc., 76 9th Ave., 7th Fl. New York, NY 10011. Phone: 800-638-8437 or (212)771-0600 Fax: (212)771-0885 E-mail: info@kagan.com • URL: http://www.aspenpublishers.com • Description: Focuses on key developments, statistics, and studies relating to the health care system. Covers eight major topic areas: cost containment, employee benefits, employee health/wellness, quality of care, delivery systems, government in health care, legal issues, and health care expenditure data.

Medical Care, Medical Costs: The Search for a Health Insurance Policy. Rashi Fein. Replica Books, 1200 US Hwy., 22 E Bridgewater, NJ 08807. Phone: 800-775-1800 or (908)541-7392 Fax: (908)541-7875 E-mail: btinfo@baker-taylor.com • URL: http://www.replicabooks.com • 1999. $29.00.

Medical Claims Processing. Entrepreneur Media, Inc., 2445 McCabe Way Irvine, CA 92614. Phone: 800-421-2300 or (949)261-2325 Fax: (949)261-0234 E-mail: entmag@entrepreneur.com • URL: http://www.entrepreneur.com • Looseleaf. $59.50. A practical guide to starting a medical claims processing service. Covers profit potential, start-up costs, market size evaluation, owner's time required, site selection, pricing, accounting, advertising, promotion, etc. (Start-Up Business Guide No. E1345.)

Medical Design Technology: New Productsd, Materials and Components for Medical Device Designers. Reed Business Information, 360 Park Ave. S New York, NY 10010. Phone: 800-446-6551 or (646)746-6400 Fax: (646)749-7028 E-mail: corporatecommunications@reedbusiness.com • URL: http://www.reedbusiness.com • 10 times a year. $92.99 per year. Edited for medical technology personnel. Includes new product introductions and applications.

Medical Device and Diagnostic Industry. Canon Communications LLC, 11444 W. Olympic Blvd., Suite 900 Los Angeles, CA 90064-1549. Phone: (310)445-4200 Fax: (310)445-4299 E-mail: feedback@devicelink.com • URL: http://www.devicelink.com • Monthly. Free to qualified personnel; others, $150.00 per year.

Medical Device Register. Canon Communications L.L.C., 11444 W Olympic Blvd., Ste. 900 Los Angeles, CA 90064. Phone: 877-922-2022 or (310)445-4200 Fax: (310)445-4299 E-mail: info@cancom.com • URL: http://www.medec.com • Covers: More than 65,000 U.S. Manufacturers of medical devices and clinical laboratory products; includes OEM manufacturers. Entries include: For manufacturers—Company name, address, phone, fax, telex, names and titles of key personnel, ownership, medical product sales volume, number of employees, method of distribution, medical product subsidiaries; public company listings include annual revenues and net income.

Medical Device Technology. Elsevier, 655 Avenue of the Americas New York, NY 10010-1710. Phone: 800-366-2665 or (212)989-5800 Fax: 800-535-9935 or (212)633-3680 E-mail: custserv@elsevier.com • URL: http://www.elsevier • Ten times a year. Free to qualified personnel; others, $100.00 per year.

Medical Economics. Advanstar Medical, 5 Paragon Dr. Montvale, NJ 07645-1742. Phone: 877-922-2022 or (973)944-7777 Fax: (973)847-5390 E-mail: customer_service@medec.com • URL: http://www.medec.com • Semimonthly. $109.00 per year. Covers the financial, economic, insurance, administrative, and other non-clinical aspects of private medical practice. Provides investment and estate planning advice.

Medical Economics General Surgery-Orthopedic Surgery. Thomson Medical Economics, Five Paragon Dr. Montvale, NJ 07645-1742. Phone: (201)358-7200 Fax: (201)722-2680 E-mail: customer.service@medec.com • URL: http://www.medec.com • Monthly. $65.00 per year. Provides information and advice on practice management (non-clinical) for surgeons. Formerly *Medical Economics for Surgeons*.

Medical Electronics Laboratory., University of Wisconsin-Madison, 1300 University Ave. Madison, WI 53706. Phone: (608)262-1326 Fax: (608)262-2327 E-mail: yee@physiology.wisc.edu Develops electronic instrumentation for medical and biological research.

Medical Gloves. Available from MarketResearch.com, 641 Ave. of the Americas, Fourth Floor New York, NY 10011. Phone: 800-298-5699 or (212)807-2629 Fax: (212)807-2642 E-mail: order@marketresearch.com • URL: http://www.marketresearch.com • 2002. $3,850.00. Published by Global Industry Analysts. Provides worldwide market research data, including profiles of major medical glove companies.

Medical Group Management Association., 104 Inverness Terr. E Englewood, CO 80112-5306. Phone: 877-275-6462 or (303)799-1111 or (303)799-1111 Fax: (303)643-4439 E-mail: service@mgma.com • URL: http://www.mgma.com • Represents professionals involved in the management of medical group practices and administration of other ambulatory healthcare facilities. Provides products and services that includes education, benchmarking, surveys, national advocacy and networking opportunities for members.

Medical Group Management Association—Directory. Medical Group Management Association, 104 Inverness Ter. E Englewood, CO 80112-5306. Phone: 877-275-6462 or (303)799-1111 or (303)799-1111 Fax: (303)643-4439 E-mail: info@cancom.com • URL: http://www.mgma.com • Database covers: more than 20,000 representing over 185,000 physicians. Entries include: Group or clinic name, address, phone, size, services provided, types of specialties, statistical data; name, title, and biographical data of administrator(s).

Medical Industry Information Report. Nicholas Communications, Inc., P.O. Box 3659 Mission Viejo, CA 92690-3659. Phone: (949)859-5761 Fax: (949)859-4781 E-mail: customerservice@nickcomm.com • URL: http://www.miimagazine.com • Quarterly. $48.00 per year. Edited for executives in medical products industries, including medical devices and equipment, hospital supplies, and pharmaceuticals. Covers major trends and developments, with an emphasis on information technology.

Medical Instrumentation Laboratory., University of Wisconsin-Madison, 1415 Engineering Dr. Madison, WI 53706. Phone: (608)263-1574 Fax: (608)265-9239 E-mail: webster@engr.wisc.edu • URL: http://www.engr.wisc.edu • Research subjects include medical electrodes, medical amplifiers, bioimpedance techniques, and miniature tactile pressure sensors.

Medical Laser Report. PennWell Corp., 98 Spit Brook Rd. Nashua, NH 03062-5737. Phone: 800-331-4463 or (603)891-0123 Fax: (603)891-0574 E-mail: atd@pennwell.com • URL: http://www.pennwell.com • Description: Presents news on the medical laser industry, technology, research, and markets. Recurring features include news of research, business news and product introductions.

The Medical Letter on Drugs and Therapeutics. The Medical Letter, Inc., 1000 Main St. New Rochelle, NY 10801-7537. Phone: 800-211-2769 or (914)235-0500 Fax: (914)632-1733 E-mail: custserv@medicalletter.org • URL: http://www.medicalletter.org • Biweekly. $55.00 per year. Newsletter. Provides critical evaluation of new drugs, including effectiveness, toxicity, cost, and possible alternatives.

Medical Malpractice. David W. Louisell and Harold Williams. LexisNexis Matthew Bender, 1275 Broadway Albany, NY 12204. Phone: 800-424-4200 or (212)448-2000 E-mail: bookstore.support@lexisnexis.com • URL: http://www.bender.com • $1,063.00. Five looseleaf volumes. Periodic supplementation.

Medical Malpractice Law and Strategy. American Lawyer Media, Inc., 105 Madison Ave. New York, NY 10016. Phone: 800-888-8300 or (212)779-9200 Fax: (212)481-8110 E-mail: lawcatalog@amlaw.com • URL: http://www.lawcatalog.com/ • Monthly. $189.00 per year. Newsletter. Covers malpractice legal issues for lawyers representing physicians and for lawyers representing patients. Includes news of judicial, legislative, and medical developments affecting malpractice strategies. (A Law Journal Newsletter, formerly published by Leader Publications).

Medical Marketing and Media. Haymarket Media, Inc., 7200 W. Camino Real, Suite 215 Boca Raton, FL 33433. Phone: 800-346-2015 or (407)368-9301 Fax: (407)368-7870 • URL: http://www.pmdcentral.com • Monthly. Individuals, $96.00 per year; institutions, $108.00 per person. Contains articles on marketing, direct marketing, advertising media, and sales personnel for the healthcare and pharmaceutical industries.

Medical Product Manufacturing News. Canon Communications LLC, 11444 W. Olympic Blvd., Suite 900 Los Angeles, CA 90064-1549. Phone: (310)445-4200 Fax: (310)445-4299 E-mail: feedback@devicelink.com • URL: http://www.devicelink.com • 10 times a year. Free to qualified personnel; others, $150.00 per year. Directed at manufacturers of medical devices and medical electronic equipment. Covers industry news, service news, and new products.

Medical Product Manufacturing News Buyers Guide. Canon Communications LLC, 11444 W. Olympic Blvd., Suite 900 Los Angeles, CA 90064. Phone: (310)445-4200 Fax: (310)445-3799 E-mail: mpmn@cancom.com • URL: http://www.cancom.com • Annual. Price on application. A directory of over 3,000 medical device and medical electronic equipment. Formerly *Medical Product Manufacturing News-Buyer's Guide and Designer's Sourcebook*.

Medical Reference Services Quarterly. Haworth Press, Inc., 10 Alice St. Binghamton, NY 13904-1580. Phone: 800-429-6784 or (607)722-5857 Fax: 800-895-0582 or (607)722-1424 E-mail: getinfo@haworthpressinc.com • URL: http://www.haworthpressinc.com • Quarterly. Institutions, $275.00 per year. An academic and practical journal for medical reference librarians.

Medical Research Centres: A World Directory of Organizations and Programmes. FT Healthcare, Pabernacle Ct., 1628 Pabernacle London EC2A 4DD, United Kingdom. Phone: 44 207 3828000 Fax: 44 207 8962449 Biennial. $470.00. Two volumes. Contains profiles of more than 7,000 medical research facilities around the world. Includes medical, dental, nursing, pharmaceutical, psychiatric, and surgical research centers.

Medical Technology Stock Letter. Medical Technology Stock Letter, PO Box 40460 Berkeley, CA 94704. Phone: (510)843-1857 Fax: (510)843-0901 E-mail: mtsl@bioinvest.com • URL: http://www.bioinvest.com • Description: Specializes in investments in biotechnology companies. Offers news of the industry and recommendations for buying, selling, and holding stocks. Recurring features include news of research, a model portfolio reflecting the editors' investment strategy, and columns titled Pulse of the Market and Industry Scan. **Remarks:** Also available through e-mail.

Medicare and Coordinated Care Plans. Available from Consumer Information Center, Department 59 Pueblo, CO 81009. Free. Published by the U. S. Department of Health and Human Services. Contains detailed information on services to Medicare beneficiaries from health maintenance organizations (HMOs). (Publication No. 509-X.)

Medicare and Medicaid Claims and Procedures. Harvey L. McCormick. West Publishing Co., 610 Opperman Dr. Eagan, MN 55123. Phone: 800-338-9424 or (651)687-7000 Fax: 800-340-9378 E-mail: bookstore@westgroup.com • URL: http://www.westgroup.com • 2001. Two volumes. Third edition. Price on application.

Medicare Compliance Alert. United Communications Group, 11300 Rockville Pke., Ste. 1100 Rockville, MD 20852-3030. Phone: 800-929-4824 or (301)287-2700 Fax: (301)816-8945 E-mail: webmaster@ucg.com • URL: http://www.ucg.com • Description: Procvides news and guidance to help keep health care practices on the right side of fraud and abuse laws and regulations.

Medicare: Employer Health Plans. Available from Consumer Information Center, Department 59 Pueblo, CO 81009. Free. Published by the U. S. Department of Health and Human Services. Explains the special rules that apply to Medicare beneficiaries who have employer group health plan coverage. (Publication No. 520-Y.)

Medicare Explained. CCH, Inc., 2700 Lake Cook Rd. Riverwoods, IL 60015. Phone: 800-835-5224 or (847)267-7000 E-mail: cust_serv@cch.com • URL: http://www.cch.com • Annual. $37.50.

Medicare Handbook. Available from U. S. Government Printing Office, Washington, DC 20402. Phone: (202)512-1800 Fax: (202)512-2250 E-mail: gpoaccess@gpo.gov • URL: http://www.access.gpo.gov • Annual. $3.00. Issued by the Health Care Financing Administration, U. S. Department of Health and Human Services. Provides information on Medicare hospital insurance and medical insurance, including benefits, options, and rights. Discusses the functions of Medigap insurance, managed care plans, peer review organizations, and Medicare insurance carriers. Formerly *Medicare Handbook*.

Medicare Made Easy: Everything You Need to Know to Make Medicare Work for You. Charles B. Inlander and Michael A. Danio. Fine Communications, 322 Eighth Ave., 15th Fl. New York, NY 10001. Phone: (212)595-3500 Fax: (212)595-3779 E-mail: scott@mjfbooks.com 1999. $19.98. Revised edition. Provides basic information on Medicare claims processing and the manner in which Medicare relates to other health insurance. The author is a consumer advocate and president of the People's Medical Society.

Medicare: The Official U. S. Government Site for Medicare Information. Centers for Medicare and Medicaid Services-Phone: (202)690-6726 • URL: http://www.medicare.gov • Web site provides extensive information on Medicare health plans, publications, fraud, nursing homes, top 20 questions and answers, etc. Includes access to the National Nursing Home Database, providing summary compliance information on "every Medicare and Medicaid certified nursing home in the country." Online searching is offered. Fees: Free.

Mediphotonics Laboratory.

Medline. Medlars Management Section, National Library of Medicine, 8600 Rockville Pike Bethesda, MD 20894. Phone: 800-638-8480 or (301)496-1131 Fax: (301)480-3537 • URL: http://www.nlm.nih.gov • Provides indexing and abstracting of worldwide medical literature, 1966 to date. Weekly updates. Inquire as to online cost and availability.

MEEN Imaging Technology News. Reilly Publishing Co., 16 E. Schaumberg Rd. Schaumberg, IL 60194-3536. Phone: (847)882-6336 Fax: (847)519-0166 E-mail: rcgroup@flash.net • URL: http://www.rcgonline.com • Bimonthly. Free to qualified personnel. Provides medical electronics industry news and new product information. Formerly*Medical Electronics and Equipment News*.

Meeting and Conference Executives Alert. MCEA, 554 Strawberry Hill Rd. Centerville, MA 02632-3037. Phone: (508)771-5200 Fax: (508)775-5658 E-mail: mcea@mediaone.net Monthly. $99.00 per year. Newsletter. Formerly *Meeting Planners Alert*.

Meeting Procedures: Parliamentary Law and Rules of Order for the 21st Century. James Lochrie. Scarecrow Press, Inc., 4501 Forbes Blvd., Ste. 200 Lanham, MD 20706. Phone: 800-462-6420 or (301)459-3366 Fax: 800-338-4550 or (301)429-5748 E-mail: custserv@rowman.com • URL: http://www.scarecrowpress.com • 2003. $29.95. A simplified guide to modern meeting procedures.

The Meeting Professional. Meeting Professionals International, 4455 LBJ Freeway, Suite 1200 Dallas, TX 75244-5903. Phone: (972)702-3000 Fax: (214)712-7770 Monthly. $50.00 per year. Published for professionals in the meeting and convention industry. Contains news, features, and how-to's for domestic and international meetings management. Formerly *Meeting Manager*.

Meeting Professionals International., 3030 Lyndon B. Johnson Fwy., Ste. 1700 Dallas, TX 75234-2759. Phone: (972)702-3000 Fax: (972)702-3070 E-mail: feedback@mpiweb.org • URL: http://www.mpiweb.org • Meeting planners, full meeting consultants, and suppliers of goods and services. Works to: improve meeting method education; create an "open platform" for research and experimentation. Provides survey results, statistics, supply sources, and technical information; offers members assistance with specific problems; encourages information and idea exchange. Maintains professional code; standardizes terminology; monitors legislation affecting the industry. Maintains resource center. Conducts educational, charitable, and research programs.

Megatrends Two Thousand: Ten New Directions for the 1990's. John Naisbitt and Patricia Aburdene. Morrow Avon, 1350 Ave. of the Americas New York, NY 10019. Phone: 800-242-7737 or (212)261-6788 • URL: http://www.harpercollins.com/hc • 1991. $6.99. Social forecasting to the year 2000 and into the 21st century.

Membership and Peer Network Directory. ESM Association, 2211 York Rd., Suite 207 Oak Brook, IL 60523-2371. Phone: (630)368-1280 Fax: (630)368-1286 E-mail: esmahg@esmassn.org • URL: http://www.emassn.org • Annual. Membership. Lists more than 4,500 personnel managers, recreation directors and certified administrators in employee recreation, fitness and services. Formerly *National Employee Services and Recreation Association-Membership and Peer Network Directory*.

Membership Roster. ACA International, 4040 W 70th St. Minneapolis, MN 55439. Phone: (612)926-6547 Fax: (612)926-1624 E-mail: aca@collector.com • URL: http://www.collector.com • Annual. Membership.

Men's and Boys' Wear Buyers Directory. Douglas Publications, Inc., 2807 N. Parham Ave. Richmond, VA 23294. Phone: 800-223-1797 or (804)762-9600 Fax: (804)217-8999 E-mail: info@douglaspublications.com • URL: http://www.douglaspublications.com • Annual. $329.00. About 6,800 retail stores selling men's and boys' clothing, sportswear, furnishings, and accessories; coverage does not include New York metropolitan area. *Salesman's Guide Directories*.

Mental Health Abstracts. IFI/Plenum Data Corp., 3202 Kirkwood Hwy., Ste. 203 Wilmington, DE 19808. Phone: 800-331-4955 or (302)998-0478 Fax: (302)998-0733 • URL: http://www.ifiplenum.com • Provides indexing and abstracting of mental health and mental illness literature appearing in more than 1,200 journals and other sources from 1969 to date. Monthly updates. Inquire as to online cost and availability.

Mental Health America., 2000 N Beauregard St., 6th Fl. Alexandria, VA 22311. Phone: 800-969-6642 or (703)684-7722 Fax: (703)684-5968 E-mail: infoctr@nmha.org • URL: http://www.mentalhealthamerica.net • Addresses all aspects of mental health and mental illness and is dedicated to improving mental health, preventing mental disorders, and achieving victory over mental illnesses. Accomplishes its mission through advocacy, public education, research, and service in partnership with more than 340 affiliates across the country.

Mental Health Law Reporter. Business Publishers Inc., 2601 University Blvd., W Ste. 200, PO Box 17592 Silver Spring, MD 20902. Phone: 800-274-6737 or (301)929-5700 Fax: (301)949-8844 E-mail: custserv@bpinews.com • URL: http://www.bpinews.com • Description: Provides news and coverage of court cases pertaining to legal issues affecting mental health professionals.

Mental Measurements Yearbook. University of Nebraska-Lincoln Buros Institute of Mental Measurements, 21 Teachers College Hall Lincoln, NE 68588-0348. Phone: 800-755-1105 or (402)472-6203 Fax: (402)472-6207 E-mail: rspies@unl.edu • URL: http://www.unl.edu/buros • Biennial. $195.00 per year.

Mental Sciences Institute. University of Texas Houston Health Science Center

Merchandise and Operating Results of Department and Specialty Stores. National Retail Federation, Financial Executive Div. John Wiley and Sons, Inc., 111 River St. Hoboken, NJ 07030. Phone: 800-225-5945 or (201)748-6000 Fax: (201)748-6088 E-mail: customer@wiley.com • URL: http://www.wiley.com • Annual. Members, $80.00; non-members, $100.00.

Merck Veterinary Manual: A Handbook of Diagnosis and Therapy for the Veterinarian. Merck and Company, Inc., P.O. Box 2000 Rahway, NJ 07065. Phone: (732)726-2990 Fax: (732)750-2735 • URL: http://www.merck.com • 1998. $32.00. 8th revised edition.

Mergent Bond Record and Annual Bond Record. Mergent, Inc., 60 Madison Ave., 6th Fl. New York, NY 10010. Phone: 888-411-0893 or (212)413-7700 Fax: (212)413-7670 E-mail: customerservice@mergent.com • URL: http://www.mergent.com • Monthly. Price on application. Formerly *Moody's Bond Record and Annual Bond Record*.

Mergent Handbook of Common Stocks. Mergent, Inc., 60 Madison Ave. New York, NY 10010. Phone: 888-411-0893 or (212)413-7700 Fax: (212)413-7670 E-mail: customerservice@mergent.com • URL: http://www.mergent.com • Annual. Price on application. Facts, performance trends and financial summaries on nearly 1,000 New York Stock Exchange companies. Formerly *Moody's Handbook of Common Stocks*.

Mergent International Manual and News Reports. Mergent, Inc., 60 Madison Ave., 6th Fl. New York, NY 10010. Phone: 888-411-0893 or (212)413-7700 Fax: (212)413-7670 E-mail: customerservice@mergent.com • URL: http://www.mergent.com • Annual. Price on application. Financial and other information about 3,000 publicly-owned corporations in 100 countries. Formerly *Moody's International Manual and News Reports*.

Mergent Municipal and Government Manual. Mergent, Inc., 60 Madison Ave. New York, NY 10010. Phone: 888-411-0893 or (212)413-7700 Fax: (212)413-7670 E-mail: customerservice@mergent.com • URL: http://www.mergent.com • Annual. $3,250.00 per year. Updated weekly online.

Mergent Online. Mergent, Inc.Phone: 800-342-5647 or (704)559-7601 Fax: (704)559-6945 E-mail: customerservice@mergent.com • URL: http://www.mergentonline.com • Fee-based Web site provides detailed information on 20,000 publicly-owned companies in 100 foreign countries, as well as more than 10,000 corporations listed on the New York Stock Exchange, American Stock Exchange, NASDAQ, and U. S. regional exchanges. Searching is offered on many financial variables and text fields. Weekly updating. Formerly *FIS Online*.

Mergent OTC Unlisted Manual (Over the Counter). Mergent, 5250 77 Center Dr., Ste. 150 Charlotte, NC 28217. Phone: 800-937-1398 or (704)527-2700 Fax: (704)559-6960 E-mail: customerservice@mergent.com • URL: http://www.mergent.com • Annual, $1,995.00 per year. Includes supplement *Moody's OTC Unlisted News Report*.

Mergent's Annual Dividend Record. Mergent, Inc., 60 Madison Ave., 6th Fl. New York, NY 10010. Phone: 888-411-0893 or (212)413-7700 Fax: (212)413-7670 E-mail: customerservice@mergent.com • URL: http://www.mergent.com • Annual. $49.00. Provides detailed dividend data, including tax information, for 12,000 stocks and 18,000 mutual funds. Covers the most recent year. Formerly

Moody's Annual Dividend Record.

Mergent's Handbook of Common Stocks. Mergent, Inc., 60 Madison Ave., 6th Fl. New York, NY 10010. Phone: 888-411-0893 or (212)413-7700 Fax: (212)413-7670 E-mail: customerservice@mergent.com • URL: http://www.mergent.com • Quarterly. $350.00 per year ($100.00 per copy). Contains one-page profiles of about 1,000 major corporations listed on the New York Stock Exchange. Includes analysis, comment, stock price performance data, and 10-year financial statistics. Formerly *Moody's Handbook of Common Stocks*.

Mergent's Handbook of Dividend Achievers. Mergent, Inc., 60 Madison Ave., 6th Fl. New York, NY 10010. Phone: 888-411-0893 or (212)413-7700 Fax: (212)413-7670 E-mail: customerservice@mergent.com • URL: http://www.mergent.com • Quarterly. $160.00 per year ($45.00 per copy). Provides information on about 300 companies that have increased cash dividends for the past 10 or more consecutive years. Formerly *Moody's Handbook of Dividend Achievers*.

Mergent's Handbook of NASDAQ Stocks. Mergent, Inc., 60 Madison Ave., 6th Fl. New York, NY 10010. Phone: 888-411-0893 or (212)413-7700 Fax: (212)413-7670 E-mail: customerservice@mergent.com • URL: http://www.mergent.com • Quarterly. $350.00 per year ($100.00 per copy). Contains one-page profiles of more than 600 major companies traded on the NASDAQ National Exchange or the American Stock Exchange. Includes price performance scores, analysis, comment, and seven-year financial statistics. Formerly *Moody's Handbook of NASDAQ Stocks*.

Merger Yearbook. Thomson Media, One State St. Plaza New York, NY 10004. Phone: 800-221-1809 or (212)803-8200 Fax: (212)843-9635 E-mail: custserv@thomsonmedia.com • URL: http://www.thomsonmedia.com • Annual. $595.00. Provides detailed information on mergers and acquisitions announced or completed during the year. Includes many charts.

Mergers, Acquisitions, and Corporate Restructurings. Patrick A. Gaughan. John Wiley and Sons, Inc., 111 River St. Hoboken, NJ 07030. Phone: 800-225-5945 or (201)748-6000 Fax: (201)748-6088 E-mail: info@wiley.com • URL: http://www.wiley.com • 2001. $75.00. Third edition. Covers mergers, acquisitions, divestitures, internal reorganizations, joint ventures, leveraged buyouts, bankruptcy workouts, and recapitalizations.

Mergers, Acquisitions, and Other Restructuring Activities: An Integrated Approach to Process, Tools, Cases, and Solutions. Donald DePamphilis. Elsevier Butterworth Heinemann, 200 Wheeler Rd., Sixth Floor Burlington, MA 01803. Phone: 800-545-2522 or (781)221-2212 Fax: 800-568-5136 or (781)313-4880 E-mail: usbkinfo@elsevier.com • URL: http://www.books.elsevier.com/finance • 2003. $99.95. Second edition. Includes 18 case studies.

Mergers & Acquisitions. Glasser Legalworks, 150 Clove Rd. Little Falls, NJ 07424. Phone: 800-308-1700 or (973)890-0008 Fax: (973)890-0042 E-mail: orders@glasserlegalworks.com • URL: http://www.glasserlegalworks.com • Looseleaf. $225.00, including CD-ROM version. Periodic Supplementation. Includes explanations of M & A legal procedures, with annotated forms. (Emerging Growth Companies Series.)

Mergers and Acquisitions Advisor: Issues, Trends, and Strategies for Successful Mergers and Acquisitions. Mergers and Acquisitions Advisor, Inc., Grand Central Station, PO Box 3806 New York, NY 10164-7800. Phone: 877-996-3743 or (718)397-9157 Fax: (718)396-1351 E-mail: info@maadvisor.com • URL: http://www.maadvisor.com • Monthly. $595.00 per year. Newsletter. Discusses anticipated transactions, major trends, and the economic climate for merger activity.

Mergers and Acquisitions Handbook. Milton L. Rock and others. McGraw-Hill, 1221 Ave. of the Americas New York, NY 10020. Phone: 800-722-4726 or (212)512-2000 Fax: (212)512-4502 E-mail: customer.service@mcgraw-hill.com • URL: http://www.mcgraw-hill.com • 1994. $84.95. Second edition. The first and last word on successful mergers and acquisitions, from putting together an m&a team and targeting acquistion candidates to merging managements and benefits plans-and every step in between.

Mergers & Acquisitions Report. Thomson Media, One State St. Plaza New York, NY 10004. Phone: 800-221-1809 or (212)803-8200 Fax: (212)843-9635 E-mail: custserv@thomsonmedia.com • URL: http://www.thomsonmedia.com • Weekly. $1,295.00 per year. Newsletter. Covers pending and ongoing mergers, acquisitions, restructurings, and bankruptcies.

Mergers & Acquisitions: The Dealmaker's Journal. Thomson Media, One State St. Plaza New York, NY 10004. Phone: 800-221-1809 or (212)803-8200 Fax: (212)843-9635 E-mail: custserv@thomsonmedia.com • URL: http://www.thomsonmedia.com • Bimonthly. $475.00 per year. Provides articles on various aspects of M & A, including valuation, pricing, taxes, and strategy. Current M & A deals are listed and described.

Mergerstat Quarterly Reports. Houlihan Lokey Howard & Zukin, 1930 Century Park West Los Angeles, CA 90099-5098. Phone: 800-455-8871 or (310)553-8871 Fax: 800-554-4515 or (310)553-2173 • URL: http://www.mergerstat.com • Quarterly. $100.00 per year. Newsletter. Provides details and analysis of recent corporate merger activity. Includes "Top deals year-to-date" and rankings of financial and legal advisors.

Mergerstat Review. FactSet Mergerstat LLC, 2150 Colorado Ave., Ste. 150 Santa Monica, CA 90404. Phone: 800-455-8871 or (310)315-3100 Fax: (310)829-4855 E-mail: info@mergerstat1.com Annual. $299.00. Provides analysis of merger and acquisition activity and trends during the year. Contains statistical, industry, and geographical data, including a 25-year historical review.

Mergerstat Transaction Roster. FactSet Mergerstat LLC, 2150 Colorado Ave., Ste. 150 Santa Monica, CA 90404. Phone: 800-455-8871 or (310)315-3100 Fax: (310)829-4855 E-mail: info@mergerstate1.com • URL: http://www.mergerstat.com • Annual. $299.00. A directory of all U. S. companies that were involved in merger and acquisition activity during the year covered. Includes details of each transaction.

METADEX. Cambridge Scientific Abstracts, 7200 Wisconsin Ave. Bethesda, MD 20814. Phone: 800-843-7751 or (301)961-6700 Fax: (301)961-6720 E-mail: sales@csa.com • URL: http://www.csa.com • Covers the worldwide literature of metals, metallurgy, and materials science, 1966 to date. Includes detailed alloys indexing from 1974. Biweekly updating. Inquire as to online cost and availability. (Formerly produced by ASM International.)

METADEX Materials Collection: Metals-Polymers-Ceramics. Cambridge Scientific Abstracts, 7200 Wisconsin Ave. Bethesda, MD 20814. Phone: 800-843-7751 or (301)961-6700 Fax: (301)961-6720 E-mail: sales@csa.com • URL: http://www.csa.com • Quarterly. Provides CD-ROM citations to the worldwide literature of materials science and metallurgy. Corresponds to *Metals Abstracts, Alloys Index, Steels Alert, Nonferrous Alert, Polymers/Ceramics/Composites Alert,* and *Engineered Materials Abstracts*. (Formerly produced by ASM International.)

Metal Bulletin. Metal Bulletin, Inc., 220 Fifth Ave., 10th Fl. New York, NY 10001. Phone: 800-638-2525 or (212)213-6273 Fax: (212)213-6202 E-mail: subscriptions@metalbulletin.plc.uk • URL: http://www.metalbulletin.co.uk • Semiweekly. $1,378 per year. Provides news of international trends, prices, and market conditions for both steel and non-ferrous metal industries. (Published in England.)

Metal Bulletin Monthly. Metal Bulletin, Inc., 220 Fifth Ave., 10th Fl. New York, NY 10001. Phone: (212)213-6202 Fax: (212)213-6619 E-mail: fsubscriptions@metalbulletin.com • URL: http://www.metalbulletin.co.uk • Monthly. Price on application. Edited for international metal industry business executives and senior technical personnel. Covers business, economic, and technical developments. (Published in England.)

Metal Casting Laboratory.

Metal Center News. Sackett Business Media Inc., 1100 Jorie Blvd., Ste. 207 Oak Brook, IL 60522. Phone: (630)571-1067 Fax: (630)572-0689 E-mail: feedback@mentakenternews.com • URL: http://www.metalcenternews.com • Quadriennial 13 times a year. $99.00 per year.

Metal Finishing: Devoted Exclusively to Metallic Surface Treatments. Elsevier, 360 Park Ave. S New York, NY 10010-1710. Phone: 888-437-4636 or (212)989-5800 Fax: (212)633-3990 E-mail: usinfo-f@elsevier.com • URL: http://www.elsevier.com • Monthly. Institutions, $190.00 per year. Includes annual *Metal Finishing Guidebook and Directory*.

Metal Finishing Guidebook and Directory. Elsevier, 360 Park Ave., S New York, NY 10010-1710. Phone: 888-437-4636 or (212)989-5800 Fax: (212)633-3990 E-mail: usinfo-f@elsevier.com • URL: http://www.elsevier.com • Annual. Free to qualified personnel; others, $60.00. Included with subscription to *Metal Finishing*. Lists manufacturers and suppliers to the industry.

Metal Powder Industries Federation., 105 College Rd. E Princeton, NJ 08540-6692. Phone: (609)452-7700 Fax: (609)987-8523 E-mail: info@mpif.org • URL: http://www.mpif.org • Manufacturers of metal powders, powder metallurgy processing equipment and tools, powder metallurgy products, and refractory and reactive metals. Member associations are: Metal Injection Molding Association; Metal Powder Producers Association; Advanced Particulate Materials Association; Powder Metallurgy Equipment Association; Powder Metallurgy Parts Association; Refractory Metals Association. Promotes the science and industry of powder metallurgy and metal powder application through: sponsorship of technical meetings, seminars, and exhibits; establishment of standards; compilation of statistics; public relations; publications. Maintains speakers' bureau and placement service; conducts research.

Metal Powder Report. Elsevier, 360 Park Ave., S. New York, NY 10010-1710. Phone: 888-437-4636 or (212)989-5800 Fax: (212)633-3990 E-mail: usinfo-f@elsevier.com • URL: http://www.elsevier.com • 11 times a year. Institutions, $438.00 per year. Technical articles, company reports, up-to-date news and book reviews cover powder metallurgy worldwide.

Metal Statistics. Reed Business Information, 360 Park Ave. S New York, NY 10010. Phone: 800-662-7776 or (646)746-6400 E-mail: corporatecommunications@reedbusiness.com • URL: http://www.reedbusiness.com • Annual. $250.00. Provides statistical data on a wide variety of metals, metal products, ores, alloys, and scrap metal. Includes data on prices, production, consumption, shipments, imports, and exports.

Metalforming Digest. CSA, 7200 Wisconsin Ave., Suite 601 Bethesda, MD 20814. Phone: 800-843-7751 or (301)961-6700 Fax: (301)961-6720 E-mail: service@csa.com • URL: http://www.csa.com • Monthly. Price on application. Provides abstracts of the international literature of metal forming, including powder metallurgy, stamping, extrusion, forging, etc.

Metallurgia, The Journal of Metals Technology, Metal Forming and Thermal Processing. British Forging Industry Association. DMG World Media Ltd., Queensway House, 2 Queensway Red Hill RH1 1QS, United Kingdom. Phone: 44 1737 855527 Fax: 44 1737 855470 • URL: http://www.dmgworldmedia.com • Monthly. $157.00 per year.

Metallurgical and Materials Transactions A: Physical Metallurgy and Materials Sc. ASM International, 9639 Kinsman Rd. Materials Park, OH 44073-0002. Phone: 800-336-5152 or (440)338-5151 Fax: (440)338-4634 E-mail: cust-srv@asminternational.org • URL: http://www.asminternational.org • 13 times a year. $1,617.00 per year. Formerly *Metallurgical Transactions A- Physical Metallurgy and Materials Science*.

Metallurgical and Materials Transactions B: Process Metallurgy and Materials Processing Science. ASM International, 9639 Kinsman Rd. Materials Park, OH 44073-0002. Phone: 800-336-5152 or (440)338-5151 Fax: (440)338-4634 E-mail: cust-srv@asminternational.org • URL: http://www.asminternational.org • Bimonthly. $1,277.00 per year. Formerly *Metallurgical Transactions B: Process Metallurgy*.

Metals Abstracts. CSA, 7200 Wisconsin Ave., Suite 601 Bethesda, MD 20814. Phone: 800-843-7751 or (301)961-6700 Fax: (301)961-6720 E-mail: service@csa.com • URL: http://www.csa.com • Monthly. $3,575.00 per year. Includes print and online editions.

Metals Service Center Institute., 4201 Euclid Ave. Rolling Meadows, IL 60008-2025. Phone: (847)485-3000 Fax: (847)485-3001 E-mail: info@msci.org • URL: http://www.msci.org • Wholesalers of industrial steel products; associate members include companies manufacturing these products. Seeks to improve distribution and management performance standards of member companies through research, statistical, promotional, and public relations activities.

Meteorological and Geoastrophysical Abstracts. American Meteorological Society., 45 Beacon St. Boston, MA 02108. Phone: (617)227-2425 Fax: (617)742-8718 E-mail: mcpherson@ametsoc.org • URL: http://www.ametsoc.org • Bimonthly. $1,685.00 per year.

Metric Today. U.S. Metric Association Inc., 10245 Andasol Ave. Northridge, CA 91325-1504. Phone: (818)363-5606 Fax: (818)363-5606 E-mail: valerie.antoine@verizon.net Description: Provides news on metric system conversion in the U.S., Canada, and abroad. Covers metrication updates in industry, government, education, and consumer areas. Recurring features include news of members, metric book reviews, editorials, data on metric standards, and letters to the editor.

Metro. Bobit Publishing Co., 21061 S. Western Ave. Torrance, CA 90501. Phone: (310)533-2400 Fax: (310)533-2500 E-mail: info@metro-magazine.com • URL: http://www.bobit.com • Nine times a year. $40.00 per year. Subject matter is the management of public transportationsystems. Includes *Factbook*.

Metropolitan Home: Style for Our Generation. Hachette Filipacchi Media U.S., Inc., 1633 Broadway New York, NY 10019. Phone: 800-374-4638 or (212)767-6000 Fax: (212)767-5600 • URL: http://www.hfmmag.com • Bimonthly. $17.94 per year.

Metropolitan Life Insurance Co. Statistical Bulletin SB. Metropolitan Life Insurance Co., One Madison Ave., Area 2-D New York, NY 10010. Phone: (212)578-5014 Fax: (212)685-7987 • URL: http://www.statbull.com • Quarterly. Individuals, $50.00 per year. Covers a wide range of social, economic and demographic health concerns.

Mexico Business: The Portable Encyclopedia for Doing Business with Mexico. World Trade Press, 1450 Grant Ave., Suite 204 Novato, CA 94945-3142. Phone: 800-833-8586 or (415)898-1124 Fax: (415)898-1080 E-mail: sales@worldtradepress.com • URL: http://www.worldtradepress.com • 1994. $24.95. Covers economic data, import/export possibilities, basic tax and trade laws, travel information, and other useful facts for doing business with Mexico. Includes a special section on NAFTA. (Country Business Guides Series).

MGMA Center for Research., 104 Inverness Terrace E. Englewood, CO 80112-5306. Phone: (303)397-7879 Fax: (303)397-1827 E-mail: npiland@mgma.com • URL: http://www.mgma.com/research • Fields of research include medical group practice management. Formerly Center for Research in Ambulatory Health Care Administration.

MGMA Connexion. Medical Group Management Association, 104 Inverness Terrace E. Englewood, CO 80112-5306. Phone: 877-275-6462 or (303)759-1111 Fax: (303)643-4439 E-mail: infocenter@mgma.com • URL: http://www.mgma.com • 10 times a year. Individuals, $95.00 per year; institutions, $175.00 per year. Formerly *Medical Group Management Journal*.

MH/RV Builders News: The Magazine for Builders of Manufactured-Mobile-Modular-Marine Homes and Recreational Vehicles. Patrick Finn, editor. Dan Kamrow and Associates, Inc., P.O. Box 72367 Roselle, IL 60172. Phone: (747)891-8872 Bimonthly. Controlled circulation.

Michie on Banks on Banking, 1999. Mary J. Divine and Paul Ernest. LEXIS Publishing, 701 E. Water St. Charlottesville, VA 22902. Phone: 800-446-3410 or (804)972-7600 Fax: 800-643-1280 or (804)972-7686 E-mail: custserv@michie.com •

URL: http://www.lexislawpublishing.com • 1999. $440.00. Revised edition.

Michigan Agricultural Experiment Station. Michigan State University

Michigan Health and Social Security Research Institute., 8000 E. Jefferson Ave. Detroit, MI 48214-2699. Phone: (313)926-5321 Fax: (313)824-7220 Studies the health and social security problems of trade union members.

Michigan Institute for Environmental and Health Sciences.

Michigan Memorial-Phoenix Project., University of Michigan, Phoenix Memorial Laboratory, 2301 Bonisteel Blvd. Ann Arbor, MI 48109-2100. Phone: (734)764-1817 Fax: (734)936-1571 E-mail: pmlmail@engin.umich.edu • URL: http://www.umich.edu/~mmpp • Conducts research in peaceful uses of nuclear energy.

Microbanker Software Buyer's Guide. Microbanker Inc., PO Box 298 East Greenbush, NY 12061. Phone: (518)745-7071 Fax: (518)477-8040 E-mail: webmaster@microbanker.com • URL: http://www.microbanker.com • Covers: 600 suppliers of approximately 1,550 financial application programs for microcomputers. Entries include: Name, address, and phone of supplier; description of program, including application, hardware requirements, price, and type of documentation or software support provided.

Microcomputer Engineering. Gene H. Miller. Prentice Hall PTR, 240 Frisch Ct. Paramus, NJ 07652. Phone: 800-282-0693 Fax: 800-445-6991 • URL: http://www.phptr.com • 1998. $113.00. Second edition.

Microelectronics Laboratory.

Microform and Imaging Review. R. R. Bowker, 630 Central Ave. New Providence, NJ 07974. Phone: 888-269-5372 Fax: (908)219-0098 E-mail: info@bowker.com • URL: http://www.bowker.com • Quarterly. $198.00 per year. Evaluates scholarly micropublications for libraries. Includes articles on microform management. Text in German.

Micrographics and Hybrid Imaging Systems Newsletter: Monthly Report for Busines Excutives Who Use of Market Microfilm Services and Hybrid Imaging Services and Equipment. Microfilm Publishing. Inc., P.O. Box 950 Larchmont, NY 10538. Phone: (914)834-3044 Fax: (914)834-3993 E-mail: mngreensht@aol.com • URL: http://www.micrographicsnews.com • Monthly. $198.00 per year. A report for business executives who use or market microfilm services and equipment. Formerly *Micrographics Newsletter*.

Microkelvin Laboratory., University of Florida, Dept. of Physics, 2348 New Physics Bldg. Gainsville, FL 32611-5803. Phone: (352)392-5803 E-mail: adams@phys.ufl.edu • URL: http://www.phys.ufl.edu/~mkelvin • Focuses on electronic behavior changes in metals, insulators, and semiconductors at ultra-low temperatures.

MicroLeads Vendor Directory on Disk (Personal Computer Industry). Chromatic Communications Enterprises, Inc., PO Box 1728 Benicia, CA 94510-4728. Phone: 800-782-3475 Fax: (707)746-0542 Annual. $495.00. Includes computer hardware manufacturers, software producers, book-periodical publishers, and franchised or company-owned chains of personal computer equipment retailers, support services and accessory manufacturers, Formerly *MicroLeads U.S. Vender Directory*.

Microprocessor Report: The Insiders' Guide to Microprocessor Hardware. Reed Business Information, 360 Park Ave., S New York, NY 10010. Phone: 800-662-7776 or (646)746-6400 • URL: http://www.reedbusiness.com • 12 times a year. $695.00 per year. Newsletter. Covers the technical aspects of microprocessors from Intel, IBM, Cyrix, Motorola, and others.

Micropublishers' Trade List Annual. Chadwyck-Healey, Inc., 300 N. Zeeb Rd. Ann Arbor, MI 48106-1346. Phone: 800-521-0600 or (734)761-4700 E-mail: info@il.proquest.com • URL: http://www.chadwyck.com • Annual. $375.00. Over 250 publishers of microfilm and microfiche and their catalogs. Worldwide coverage.

Microsoft Secrets: How the World's Most Powerful Software Company Creates Technology, Shapes Markets, and Manages People. Michael A. Cusumano and Richard W. Selby. The Free Press, 1230 Ave. of the Americas New York, NY 10020. Phone: 800-223-2348 or (212)698-7000 E-mail: consumer.customerservice@simonandschuster.com • URL: http://www.simonsays.com • 1995. $30.00. Describes the internal workings of the Microsoft Corporation, including marketing, technical innovation, and human relations. Includes CD-ROM.

Microsoft Windows XP Inside Out. Ed Bott. Microsoft Press, One Microsoft Way Redmond, WA 98052-6399. Phone: 800-677-7737 or (425)882-8080 Fax: (425)936-7329 E-mail: msporder@msn.com • URL: http://www.microsoft.com • 2001. $44.99. Provides detailed coverage of both Professional and Home versions of Windows XP.

Microsoft Word Version 2002 Plain and Simple. Jerry Joyce and Marianne Moon. Microsoft Press, One Microsoft Way Redmond, WA 98052-6399. Phone: 800-677-7737 or (425)882-8080 Fax: (425)936-7329 E-mail: msporder@msn.com • URL: http://www.microsoft.com/mspress/ • 2001. $19.99. A standard manual providing detailed, step-by-step instructions for the many functions of Word 2002.

Microwave and Optical Technology Letters. John Wiley and Sons, Inc., Journals, 111 River St. Hoboken, NJ 07030. Phone: 800-225-5945 or (201)748-6000 Fax: (201)748-6088 E-mail: customer@wiley.com • URL: http://www.wiley.com

• 24 times a year. $1,690.00 per year; with online edition, $1,775.00 per year. Four volumes.

Microwave Device and Physical Electronics Laboratory. University of Utah

Microwave Journal. Horizon House Publications, Inc., 685 Canton St. Norwood, MA 02062. Phone: 800-966-8526 or (781)769-9750 Fax: (781)769-5037 • URL: http://www.horizonhouse.com • Monthly. Free to qualified personnel. International coverage.

Microwaves and RF Product Data Directory (Radio Frequency). Penton Technology and Lifestyle Media, One Penn Plz., 36th Fl. New York, NY 10119. Phone: 800-829-9028 or (212)835-1605 E-mail: czelina@penton.com • URL: http://www.penton.com • Annual. $106.00. About 2,000 manufacturers of high frequency equipment components. International coverage.

Mid-Am Antique Appraisers Association., PO Box 123 Springfield, MO 65801-0123. Phone: (417)865-7269 Fax: (417)865-7269 E-mail: info@mpif.org Antique, art, and collectible dealers. To maintain a high standard of ethics for appraising by exhibiting honesty, integrity, and professional conduct while evaluating merchandise at the current fair market value.

Middle-East/Africa Kompass on Disc. Available from Kompass USA, Inc., 121 Whitney Ave. New Haven, CT 06510. Phone: 877-566-7277 or (203)503-6789 Fax: (203)503-6780 E-mail: mail@kompass-usa.com • URL: http://www.kompass.com • Annual. CD-ROM provides information on more than 140,000 companies in Algeria, Bahrain, Cyprus, Egypt, Lebanon, Mauritania, Morocco, Oman, Saudi Arabia, South Africa, Tunisia, and United Arab Emirates. Classification system covers approximately 50,000 products and services.

Middle East Librarians Association., University of Pennsylvania Library, 3420 Walnut St., University of Washington Libraries Philadelphia, PA 19104-6206. Phone: (215)898-2196 Fax: (215)898-0559 E-mail: secretary@mela.us • URL: http://www.mela.us • Librarians and others interested in aspects of librarianship that support the study or dissemination of information about the Middle East since the rise of Islam. Facilitates communication among members through meetings and publications. Improves the quality of area librarianship through the development of standards for the profession and education of Middle East library specialists. Compiles and disseminates information concerning Middle East libraries and collections and represents the judgment of the members in matters affecting them. Encourages cooperation among members and Middle East libraries, especially in the acquisition of materials and the development of bibliographic controls.

Midwest Research Institute. Midwest Research Institute, 425 Volker Blvd. Kansas City, MO 64110-2241. Phone: (816)753-7600 Fax: (816)753-8420 E-mail: info@mriresearch.org • URL: http://www.mriresearch.org • Conducts research, development, and engineering activities in the major areas of health, chemistry, the environment, national security and defense, agriculture and food safety, and technology. Specific interests in the health area are pharmaceutical development and regulatory support, vaccine development, preclinical toxicology, metabolism studies, integrated clinical and pre-clinical drug development support, phytochemicals and designer foods, pesticide product registration support, chemistry support for toxicology, biotechnology, immunoassay development, DNA assay development, proteomics, high through-put automated assay systems, nanotechnology, food safety, seed technology, antibody production, biosensor development, electromagnetic field effects, neurobehavioral toxicology, reversal theory, and health risk behavior. In the field of chemistry, MRI focuses on analytical chemistry methods, including method development, improvement, validation, and application for programs involving immunoanalytical chemistry, exposure assessment, biological monitoring, industrial hygiene, environmental monitoring, chemical surety, site remediation, demilitarization, atmospheric chemistry, and product analysis of foods, consumer and commercial products, drinking water, and other materials. Environmental programs address environmental measurements, emission inventory development, emission factor development, modeling, water quality, waste minimization, pollution prevention, environmental control strategy development, process analysis and industry profiling, nonpoint source pollution, ambient air toxics, indoor air quality, industrial hygiene, multimedia environmental sampling and analysis, environmental impact assessment, facility assessment, environmental audits, waste processing and characterization, waste combustion, solar soil detoxification, risk analysis, regulatory support, policy analysis, cooling tower performance testing, permitting assistance, and tank and pipeline management. Technology areas include thermo electrics, microclimate conditioning systems, industrial systems evaluation, safety engineering, engineering design, prototype development, bench-scale testing, technology testing, dental biomaterial formulation, dental polymer development, pipeline coating technology, deicing chemical evaluation, traffic engineering, economic impact assessment, financial and business analysis, economic development, strategic planning, international programs, instructional material development, training program design and presentation, technology transfer, etc.

Migration World: A Bimonthly Magazine Focusing on the Newest Immigrant and Refugee Groups; Policy and Legislation; Resources. Center for Migration Studies, 209 Flagg Place Staten Island, NY 10304-1199. Phone: (718)351-8800 Fax: (718)667-4598 E-mail: sales@cmsny.org • URL: http://www.cmsny.org • Five times a year. Individuals, $31.00 per year; institutions, $50.00 per year.

Milan Experiment Station. University of Tennessee, Knoxville

The Milbank Quarterly: A Journal of Public Health and Health Care Policy. Milbank Memorial Fund. Blackwell Publishing, 350 Main St. Malden, MA 02148. Phone: 800-835-6770 or (781)388-8200 Fax: (781)388-8232 E-mail: subscrip@blackwell.com • URL: http://www.blackwellpub.com • Quarterly. Institutions, $142.00 per year. Includes print and online editions. Formerly *Health and Society*.

Military Grocer. Downey Communications, Inc., 4800 Montgomery Lane, Suite 710 Bethesda, MD 20814-5341. Phone: (301)718-7600 Fax: (301)718-7604 E-mail: grocery@downey-date.com Five times a year. $30.00 per year. Edited for managers and employees of supermarkets on military bases. (These are supermarkets administered by the Defense Commissary Agency.)

Military Helicopter Handbook. The Shephard Press Ltd., 111 High St. Burnham SL1 7JZ, United Kingdom. Phone: 44 1628 604311 Fax: 44 1628 664334 E-mail: directory@shephard.co.uk • URL: http://www.shephard.co.uk • Annual. $110.00. Data includes specifications of fighter helicopters, inventory of world helicopter forces, government contacts, directory of services & products, and listing of exhibits & conferences. Coverage is international.

Military Impacted Schools Association., 1600 Hwy. 370 Bellevue, NE 68005. Phone: 800-291-MISA or (402)293-4000 E-mail: rlindner@ngat.org • URL: http://www.militaryimpactedschoolsassociation.org • Provides the educational needs of military families, including quality of life initiatives, community and school district support, and aid funding.

Military Law Task Force., 730 N First St. San Jose, CA 95122. Phone: (619)463-2369 E-mail: info@mltf.info • URL: http://www.nlgmltf.org • Counselors, attorneys, and law students concerned with military, selective service, and veterans' law. Purposes are to: assist active-duty personnel, veterans, and those affected by selective service; provide educational and political work focused on these areas of law; offer research assistance in military and veterans law; support networking among attorneys and counselors. Operates speakers' bureau; offers informal referral services and educational materials.

Military Officer. The Military Officers Association, 201 N Washington St. Alexandria, VA 22314-2539. Phone: 800-234-6622 or (703)838-8115 Fax: (703)838-8179 E-mail: editor@moaa.org • URL: http://www.moaa.org • Monthly. $20.00 per year. Formerly *The Retired Officer*.

Military Officers Association of America., 201 N Washington St. Alexandria, VA 22314-2539. Phone: 800-245-6622 or (703)549-2311 Fax: (703)838-8173 E-mail: msc@moaa.org • URL: http://www.moaa.org • Formerly The Retired Oficers Association.

Military Prime Contract Awards and Subcontract Payments. U.S. Department of Defense, Office of the Secretary, The Pentagon Washington, DC 20301. Phone: (703)545-6700 Annual.

Military Retailing Directory. Military Retailing Publisher, 270 Ross Ave. Melbourbe Beach, FL 32951. Phone: (407)952-9171 Semiannual. $95.00 per year. Edited for use by military commissaries in making purchasing decisions. Lists sources of goods and sevices, with official military department and retail order numbers.

Military Toxics Project., PO Box 558 Lewiston, ME 04243. Phone: 877-783-5091 or (207)783-5091 Fax: (207)783-5096 E-mail: mtp@miltoxproj.org • URL: http://www.miltoxproj.org • Promotes clean up of military pollution, safeguards transportation of hazardous materials, advances development of preventative solutions to toxic, radioactive pollution from military activities.

Military Vehicle Preservation Association., PO Box 520378 Independence, MO 64052. Phone: 800-365-5798 or (816)833-6872 Fax: (816)833-5115 E-mail: hq@mvpa.org • URL: http://www.mvpa.org • Represents individuals and groups interested in the preservation, restoration, maintenance, and enjoyment of historic military vehicles. Informs the public of the historical value of collectible military vehicles; serves as a clearinghouse for technical and historical information.

Milk Industry Foundation., 1250 H St. NW, Ste. 900 Washington, DC 20005-3952. Phone: (202)737-4332 Fax: (202)331-7820 E-mail: membership@idfa.org • URL: http://www.idfa.org • Represents processors of fluid milk and milk products. Advocates before government and regulatory bodies on behalf of members.

Millennium Intelligence: Understanding and Conducting Competitive Intelligence in the Digital Age. Jerry Miller, editor. Information Today, Inc., 143 Old Marlton Pike Medford, NJ 08055-8750. Phone: 800-300-9868 or (609)654-6266 Fax: (609)654-4309 E-mail: custserv@infotoday.com • URL: http://www.infotoday.com • 1999. $29.95. Contains essays by various authors on competitive intelligence information sources, legal aspects, intelligence skills, corporate security, and other topics. (CyberAge Books.)

Miller European Accounting Guide. Aspen Publishers, 7201

McKinney Circle Frederick, MD 21704. Phone: 800-638-8437 or (301)417-7500 Fax: 800-901-9075 or (301)695-7931 E-mail: customer.service@aspenpubl.com • URL: http://www.aspenpublishers.com • Annual. $159.00. Presents analysis of accounting standards in 25 European and Eastern European countries.

Miller GAAP Financial Statement Disclosures Manual. Aspen Publishers, 7201 McKinney Circle Frederick, MD 21704. Phone: 800-638-8437 or (301)417-7500 Fax: 800-901-9075 or (301)695-7931 E-mail: customer.service@aspenpubl.com • URL: http://www.aspenpublishers.com • Annual. $105.00. Provides a detailed summary of financial report disclosure requirements, with examples. Includes a CD-ROM.

Miller GAAP Guide: A Comprehensive Restatement of All Current Promulgated Generally Accepted Accounting Principles. Aspen Publishers, Inc., 200 Orchard Ridge Dr., Ste. 200 Gaithersburg, MD 20878. Phone: 800-234-1660 or (301)417-7500 Fax: (301)695-7931 E-mail: customer.service@aspenpubl.com • URL: http://www.aspenpublishers.com • Annual. $149.00. Includes monthly *Update service*. Includes all current Financial Accounting Standards Board (FASB) statements, interpretations, and technical bulletins.

Miller GAAS Guide: A Comprehensive Restatement of Generally Accepted Auditing Standards for Auditing, Attestation, Compilation and Review and the Code of Professional Conduct. Larry P. Bailey. Aspen Publishers, 200 Orchard Ridge Dr., Ste. 200 Gaithersburg, MD 20878. Phone: 800-234-1660 or (301)417-7500 Fax: (301)695-7931 • URL: http://www.aspenpublishers.com • Annual. $139.00. Includes monthly update. Includes industry audit guides and a model audit program.

Miller International Accounting Standards Guide. Aspen Publishers, 7201 McKinney Circle Frederick, MD 21704. Phone: 800-638-8437 or (301)417-7500 Fax: 800-901-9075 or (301)695-7931 E-mail: customer.service@aspenpubl.com • URL: http://www.aspenpublishers.com • Annual. $139.00. Covers all current International Financial Reporting Standards (IFRS), International Accounting Standards (IAS), and related interpretations issued by the International Accounting Standards Board (IASB).

Miller's Antiques Shops, Fairs and Auctions. Antique Collectors' Club, 91 Market St., Suite 52, Industrial Park Wappingers Falls, NY 12590. Phone: 800-225-5231 or (914)297-0003 Fax: (914)297-0068 E-mail: info@antiquecc.com • URL: http://www.antiquecc.com • Annual. $35.00.

Milling and Baking News. Sosland Publishing Co., 4800 Main St., Ste. 100 Kansas City, MO 64112-2513. Phone: (816)756-1000 Fax: (816)756-0494 E-mail: web@sosland.com • URL: http://www.sosland.com • Weekly. $128.00 per year. News magazine for the breadstuffs industry.

Million Dollar Consulting: The Professional's Guide to Growing a Practice. Alan Weiss. McGraw-Hill, 1221 Ave. of the Americas New York, NY 10020. Phone: 800-722-4726 or (212)512-2000 Fax: (212)512-4502 E-mail: customer.service@mcgraw-hill.com • URL: http://www.mcgraw-hill.com • 2002. $15.95. Third edition. Provides step-by-step advice on raising capital, finding new clients, and setting fees.

Mind-Machine Interaction Research Center.

Mineral Commodity Summaries. Available from U. S. Government Printing Office, Washington, DC 20402. Phone: (202)512-1800 Fax: (202)512-2250 E-mail: gpoaccess@gpo.gov • URL: http://www.access.gpo.gov • Annual. $26.00. Published by the U. S. Geological Survey, Department of the Interior (http://www.usgs.gov). Contains detailed, five-year data for about 90 nonfuel minerals. Covers a wide range of statistics, including production, imports, exports, consumption, reserves, prices, tariff information, and industry employment. (Two pages are devoted to each mineral.)

Mineral Industry Research Laboratory. University of Alaska Fairbanks

Mineralogical Abstracts: A Quarterly Journal of Abstracts in English, Covering the World Literature of Mineralogy and Related Subjects. Mineralogical Society, 41 Queens Gate London SW7 5HR, United Kingdom. Phone: 44 20 7584 7516 Fax: 44 20 7823 8021 E-mail: alexia@minersoc.org • URL: http://www.minersoc.org • Quarterly. $393.00 per year.

Mineralogical Society of America.

Minerals, Metals and Materials Society., 184 Thorn Hill Dr. Warrendale, PA 15086-7514. Phone: (724)776-9000 Fax: (724)776-3770 E-mail: tmsgeneral@tms.org • URL: http://www.tms.org • Members are metallurgists, metallurgical engineers, and materials scientists. Divisions include Light Metals and Electronic, Magnetic, and Photonic Materials. Formerly The Metallurigical Society.

Minerals Yearbook. Available from U.S. Government Printing Office, Washington, DC 20402. Phone: (202)512-1800 Fax: (202)512-2250 E-mail: gpoaccess@gpo.gov • URL: http://www.access.gpo.gov • Annual. Three volumes.

Mines Magazine. Colorado School of Mines Alumni Association and the Colorado School of Mines, 1600 Arapahoe St. Golden, CO 80402-1410. Phone: 800-446-9488 or (303)273-3295 Fax: (303)273-3583 E-mail: csmaa@mines.edu • URL: http://www.alumnifriends.mines.edu • Quarterly. $30.00 per year.

MiniAtlas of Global Development. The World Bank, P. O. Box 960 Herndon, VA 20172-0960. Phone: 800-645-7247 or (703)661-1580 Fax: (703)661-1501 E-mail: books@worldbank.org • URL: http://www.worldbank.org/publications • 2003. $7.00. Presents concise data for 208 countries, based on the *World Bank Atlas* and other World Bank publications. Includes maps, tables, and graphs summarizing social, economic, and environmental statistics.

Mining and Metallurgical Society of America.

Mining Engineering. Society for Mining, Metallurgy and Exploration, P.O. Box 625002 Littleton, CO 80162-5002. Phone: (303)973-9550 Fax: (303)973-3845 Monthly. $125.00 per year. Includes *Who's Who in Mining Engineering*.

Mining for Gold on the Internet: How to Find Investment and Financial Information on the Internet. Mary Ellen Bates. McGraw-Hill, 1221 Ave. of the Americas New York, NY 10020. Phone: 800-722-4726 or (212)512-2000 Fax: (212)512-4502 E-mail: customer.service@mcgraw-hill.com • URL: http://www.mcgraw-hill.com • 2000. $24.95. Tells how to effectively search the Internet for financial advice and information. Specific websites are discussed.

Mining Machinery and Equipment. U.S. Bureau of the Census, Washington, DC 20233-0800. Phone: (301)457-4100 Fax: (301)457-3842 • URL: http://www.census.gov • Annual. (Current Industrial Reports MA35F.)

The Mining Record. The Mining Record, PO Box 370510 Denver, CO 80237. Phone: (303)770-6791 Fax: (303)770-6796 E-mail: valerie.antoine@verizon.net Description: Discusses a myriad of issues within the mining industry, particularly exploration, development, production, and milling.

Mining Week. National Mining Association, 1130 17th St., NW Washington, DC 20036-4677. Phone: (202)463-2625 Fax: (202)463-6125 E-mail: thowe@nma.org • URL: http://www.nma.org • Weekly. Free to members; non-members, $100.00 per year. Newsletter. Covers legislative, business, research, and other developments of interest to the mining industry.

Minorities in Media., P.O. Box 9198 Petersburg, VA 23806. Phone: (804)524-5935 Fax: (804)524-5757 E-mail: vthota@vsu.edu Members are minority media professionals.

Minority Broadcast Ownership. Gregory L. Rohde. Nova Science Publishers, Inc., 400 Oser Ave., Suite 1600 Hauppauge, NY 11788-3619. Phone: (631)231-7269 Fax: (631)231-8175 E-mail: novascience@earthlink.net • URL: http://www.novapublishers.com • 2002. $29.50. Provides discussion and statistical data relating to minority ownership of radio and television stations in the U.S.

Minority Business Entrepreneur., 3528 Torrance Blvd., Suite 101 Torrance, CA 90503-4803. Phone: (310)540-9398 Fax: (310)792-8263 E-mail: mbewbe@mbemag.com • URL: http://www.mbemag.com • Bimonthly. $16.00 per year. Reports on issues "critical to the growth and development of minority and women-owned firms." Provides information on relevant legislation and profiles successful women and minority entrepreneurs.

Minority Business News USA: America's Monthly News Magazine About Minority Business Enterprise and Diversity. Minority Business News, 11333 North Central Expressway, Suite 201 Dallas, TX 75243. Phone: (214)369-3200 Fax: (214)365-9393 E-mail: news@minoritybusinessnews.com • URL: http://www.minoritybusinessnews.com • Monthly. $18.00 per year. "Topics discussed include minority business certification, corporate purchasing trends, and management tips for business owners and professionals."

MIR: Management International Review: Journal of International Business. Bertelsmann Springer, Abraham-Lincoln-Str. 46 65189 Wiesbaden, Germany. Phone: 49 611 78780 Fax: 49 611 7878450 • URL: http://www.uni-hohenheim.de • Quarterly. $150.00 per year.

MIS Quarterly (Management Information Systems). University of Minnesota, School of Management. MIS Research Center, Carlson School of Management, 321 19th Ave., S. Minneapolis, MN 55455. Phone: (612)624-2035 Fax: (612)624-2029 E-mail: misq@csom.umn.edu • URL: http://www.misq.org • Quarterly. $75.00 per year.

MIT Sloan Management Review. Sloan Management Review Association. Massachusetts Institute of Technology, 50 Memorial Dr. Cambridge, MA 02142. Phone: (617)253-1000 Fax: (617)258-9344 E-mail: smr@mit.edu • URL: http://www.mitsloan.mit.edu • Quarterly. Individuals, $89.00 per year; institutions, $148.00 per year. Formerly *Sloan Management Review*.

Mix Magazine: Professional Recording, Sound, and Music Production. Primedia Business Magazine and Media, 6400 Hollis St., Ste. 12 Emeryville, CA 94608. Phone: 800-795-5445 or (510)653-3307 Fax: (510)653-5142 E-mail: subs@primediabusiness.com • URL: http://www.primediabusiness.com • Monthly. $34.97 per year.

MLA Handbook for Writers of Research Papers. Joseph Gibaldi. Modern Language Association of America, 26 Broadway, 3rd Fl. New York, NY 10004-1789. Phone: (646)576-5000 Fax: (646)458-0030 E-mail: info@mla.org • URL: http://www.mla.org • 2003. $25.00. Fifth edition. Includes style guidelines for both print and online citations. (MLA Handbook for Writers of Research Papers).

MLA Style Manual and Guide to Scholarly Publishing. Joseph Gibaldi. Modern Language Association of America, 26 Broadway, 3rd Fl. New York, NY 10004-1789. Phone: (646)576-5000 Fax: (646)458-0030 E-mail: info@mla.org • URL: http://www.mla.org • 1998. $25.00. Second edition. Covers preparation of manuscripts for publication, legal issues, basic writing principles, documentation, and use of abbreviations.

MLO (Medical Laboratory Observer). Thomson Medical Economics, Five Paragon Dr. Montvale, NJ 07645-1742. Phone: (201)358-7200 Fax: (201)722-2680 E-mail: customer.service@medec.com • URL: http://www.medec.com • Monthly. $70.00 per year. Covers management, regulatory, and technical topics for clinical laboratory administrators.

MLS: Marketing Library Services. Information Today Inc., 143 Old Marlton Pke. Medford, NJ 08055-8750. Phone: 800-300-9868 or (609)654-6266 Fax: (609)654-4309 E-mail: custserv@infotoday.com • URL: http://www.infotoday.com • Description: Tells librarians and information professionals how to actively market their services to gain clients and to justify their existence. Discusses marketing, communication skills, fundraising, promotional events, publicity, and advocacy. Recurring features include how-to articles, case studies, news, a Customer-Based Marketing column, and book reviews.

Mobile Business Advisor: Technology Strategies for Business Innovators. Advisor Media, Inc., 5675 Ruffin Rd., Suite 200 San Diego, CA 92123. Phone: 800-336-6060 or (858)278-5600 Fax: (858)278-0300 E-mail: subscribe@advisor.com • URL: http://www.advisor.com • Monthly. $39.00 per year. Covers electronic commerce management and technology, including payment technology, Web development, knowledge management, and e-business market research. Formerly *E-Buisness Advisor*.

Mobile PC. Future Network USA, 150 North Hill Drive Brisbane, CA 94005. Phone: 800-266-3312 or (415)468-4684 Fax: (415)468-4686 E-mail: editors@mobilepcmag.com • URL: http://www.mobilepcmag.com • Monthly. $20.00 per year. Provides information and detailed product reviews for consumers. Covers notebook/laptop computers, personal digital assistants (PDAs), wireless network equipment, cell phones, digital cameras, and other electronic products.

Mobility. Employee Relocation Council, 1717 Pennsylvania Ave., NW, Ste. 800 Washington, DC 20006-4665. Phone: (202)857-0857 Fax: (202)467-4012 12 times a year. $48.00 per year. Covers various aspects of the moving of corporate employees.

Mobility: Handheld and Wireless Solutions for Today's Business. Mobile Media Group, 1670 South Amphlett Blvd., Suite 105 San Mateo, CA 94402. Phone: 888-406-4048 or (650)378-8522 Fax: (650)378-8513 • URL: http://www.pdabuzz.com • Quarterly. $14.95 per year. Edited for business users of wireless handheld devices and notebook computers.

Model Business Corporation Act Annotated. American Bar Association, 750 N Lake Shore Dr. Chicago, NJ 60611. Phone: (312)988-5561 Fax: (312)988-6030 E-mail: service@abanet.org • URL: http://www.abanet.org • 1998. $600.00. Four volumes. $150.00 per volume.

The Modem Reference: The Complete Guide to PC Communications. Michael A. Banks. Information Today, Inc., 143 Old Marlton Pike Medford, NJ 08055-8750. Phone: 800-300-9868 or (609)654-6266 Fax: (609)654-4309 E-mail: custserv@infotoday.com • URL: http://www.infotoday.com • 2000. $29.95. Fourth edition. Covers personal computer data communications technology, including fax transmissions, computer networks, modems, and the Internet. Popularly written.

Moderating Focus Groups: A Practical Guide for Group Facilitation. Thomas L. Greenbaum. Sage Publications, Inc., 2455 Teller Rd. Thousand Oaks, CA 91320. Phone: 800-818-7243 or (805)499-9774 Fax: 800-583-2665 or (805)499-0871 E-mail: webmaster@sagepub.com • URL: http://www.sagepub.com • 1999. $92.95. Covers participant recruitment, characteristics of successful moderators, moderating fundamentals, and related topics.

Modern Accident Investigation and Analysis: An Executive Guide to Accident Investigation. Theodore S. Ferry. John Wiley and Sons, Inc., 111 River St. Hoboken, NJ 07030. Phone: 800-526-5368 or (201)748-6000 Fax: (201)748-6088 E-mail: info@wiley.com • URL: http://www.wiley.com • 1988. $160.00. Second edition.

Modern Auditing. William C. Boynton. John Wiley and Sons, Inc., 111 River St. Hoboken, NJ 07030. Phone: 800-526-5368 or (201)748-6000 Fax: (201)748-6088 E-mail: info@wiley.com • URL: http://www.wiley.com • 2001. $111.95. Seventh edition.

Modern Brewery Age. Business Journals, Inc., 50 Day St. Norwalk, CT 06856. Phone: 800-521-0227 or (203)853-6015 Fax: (203)852-8175 E-mail: pete@busjour.com • URL: http://www.busjour.com • Bimonthly. $85.00 per year. Annual supplement available *Blue Book*.

Modern Brewery Age Blue Book. Business Journals Inc., 50 Day St. Norwalk, CT 06854. Phone: 800-521-0227 or (203)853-6015 Fax: (203)852-8175 E-mail: stunifoo@busjour.com • URL: http://www.busjour.com • Covers: Over 3,000 breweries, beer wholesalers, importers, trade associations, regulatory agencies, and suppliers to the malt beverage industry; international coverage. Entries include: For breweries, distribution plants, wholesalers, importers and suppliers—Company name, address, names of key personnel, phone, products. For government officials—Name, address. For trade associations—Association name, address, phone.

Modern Bulk Transporter. Primedia Business Magazines and Media, 4200 S Shepherd Dr., Ste. 200 Houston, TX 77098. Phone: 800-795-5445 or (713)523-8124 Fax: (713)523-8384 E-mail: subs@primediabusiness.com • URL: http://www.primediabusiness.com • Monthly. $50.00 per year.

Modern Bulk Transporter Buyers Guide. Primedia Business Magazines and Media, 9800 Metcalf Ave. Overland Park, KS 66212. Phone: 800-441-0294 or (913)341-1300 Fax: (913)967-1898 E-mail: subs@primediabusiness.com • URL: http://www.primediabusiness.com • Annual. Controlled circulation. Suppliers of products or services for companies operating tank trucks.

Modern Business Law: The Regulatory Environment. Thomas W. Dunfee and others. McGraw-Hill, 1221 Ave. of the Americas New York, NY 10020. Phone: 800-722-4726 or (212)512-2000 Fax: (212)512-4502 E-mail: customer.service@mcgraw-hill.com • URL: http://www.mcgraw-hill.com • 1995. $132.50. Third edition.

Modern Carpentry: Building Construction Details in Easy-To-Understand Form. Willis H. Wagner and Howard S. Smith. Goodheart-Willcox Publishers, 18604 W. Creek Dr. Tinley Park, IL 60477-6243. Phone: 800-323-0440 or (708)687-5000 Fax: (708)687-5068 E-mail: custerv@goodheartwillcox.com • URL: http://www.goodheartwillcox.com • 2003. Price on application.

Modern Casting. American Foundry Society, Inc., 505 State St. Des Plaines, IL 60016-8399. Phone: 800-537-4237 or (847)824-0181 Fax: (847)824-7848 E-mail: lsmolecki@afsinc.org • URL: http://www.afsinc.org • Monthly. Free to qualified personnel; others, $50.00 per year.

Modern Casting-Buyer's Reference. American Foundry Society, Inc., 505 State St. Des Plaines, IL 60016-8399. Phone: 800-537-4237 or (847)824-0181 Fax: (847)824-7848 E-mail: lsmolecki@afsinc.org • URL: http://www.afsinc.org • Annual. $25.00. About 1,700 manufacturers, suppliers, and distributors of foundry and metal casting equipment and products. Formerly *Modern Castings - Buyer's Guide*.

Modern Dictionary of Electronics. Rudolf F. Graf. Elsevier, 655 Ave. of the Americas New York, NY 10010. Phone: 800-366-2665 or (212)989-5800 Fax: 800-535-9935 or (212)633-3680 E-mail: custserv@elsevier.com • URL: http://www.elsevier.com • 1999. $69.95. Seventh edition.

Modern Economics. Jan S. Hogendorn. Prentice Hall PTR, 240 Frisch Ct. Paramus, NJ 07652. Phone: 800-282-0693 Fax: 800-445-6991 • URL: http://www.phptr.com • 1994. $75.00.

Modern Estate Planning. Ernest D. Fiore and M. Friedlich. LexisNexis Matthew Bender, 1275 Broadway Albany, NY 12204. Phone: 800-424-4200 or (518)487-3000 Fax: (518)487-3584 E-mail: bookstore.support@lexisnexis.com • URL: http://www.bender.com • $1,008.00. Five looseleaf volumes. Periodic supplementation.

Modern Grocer. GC Publishing Co., One University Plaza, Suite 200 Hackensack, NJ 07601. Phone: (201)488-1800 Fax: (201)488-7357 • URL: http://www.moderngrocer.com • Monthly. $45.00 per year. Formerly *Modern Grocer*.

Modern Guns: Identification and Values. Russell C. Quertermous and Steven C. Quertermous. Collector Books, 5801 Kentucky Dam Rd. Paducah, KY 42003. Phone: 800-626-5420 or (270)898-6211 Fax: (270)898-8890 E-mail: info@collectorbooks.com • URL: http://www.collectorbooks.com • 2000. $14.95. 13th edition. (Modern Guns Series)

Modern Healthcare: The Newsmagazine for Adminstrators and Managers in Hospitals and Other Healthcare Institutions. Crain Communications, Inc., 360 N Michigan Ave. Chicago, IL 60601-3806. Phone: 800-678-9595 or (312)337-7700 E-mail: info@crain.com • URL: http://www.crain.com • Weekly. $145.00 per year; students, $63.00 per year.

Modern Intellectual Property. Michael A. Epstein. Aspen Publishers, Inc., 1185 Ave. of the Americas New York, NY 10036. Phone: 800-234-1660 or (212)597-0200 Fax: 800-901-9075 or (212)597-0338 E-mail: customer.service@aspenpubl.com • URL: http://www.aspenpublishers.com • 1995. Third edition. Price on application.

Modern International Economics. Wilfred Ethier. W. W. Norton & Co., Inc., 500 5th Ave. New York, NY 10110. Phone: 800-223-2584 or (212)354-5500 Fax: (212)869-0856 • URL: http://www.wwnorton.com • 1995. $106.50. Third edition.

Modern Jeweler. Cygnus Business Media, 445 Broad Hollow Rd. Melville, NY 11747-3601. Phone: 800-308-6397 or (631)845-2700 Fax: (631)845-2798 E-mail: rich.reiff@cygnuspub.com • URL: http://www.cygnusbzb.com • Monthly. $60.00 per year. Edited for retail jewelers. Covers the merchandising of jewelry, gems, and watches. Supersedes in part *Modern Jeweler*.

Modern Machine Shop. Gardner Publications, Inc., 6915 Valley Ave. Cincinnati, OH 45244-3029. Phone: 800-950-8020 or (513)527-8800 Fax: (513)527-8801 • URL: http://www.gardnerweb.com • Monthly. $50.00 per year.

Modern Machine Shop Material Working Technology Guide. Gardner Publications, Inc., 6915 Valley Ave. Cincinnati, OH 45244-3029. Phone: 800-950-8020 or (513)527-8800 Fax: (513)527-8801 E-mail: mmsmkt@gardnerweb.com • URL: http://www.gardnerweb.com • Annual. $15.00. Lists products and services for the metalworking industry. Formerly *Modern Machine Shop CNC and Software Guide*.

Modern Materials Handling. Reed Business Information, 360 Park Ave. S New York, NY 10010. Phone: 800-446-6551 or (646)746-6400 Fax: (646)746-7028 E-mail: corporatecommunications@reedbusiness.com • URL: http://www.reedbusiness.com • 14 times a year. $99.90 per year. For managers and engineers who buy or specify equipment used to move, store, control and protect products throughout the manufacturing and warehousing cycles. Includes *Casebook Directory* and *Planning Guide*. Also includes *ADC News and Solutions*.

Modern Materials Handling Casebook Directory. Reed Business Information, 360 Park Ave. S New York, NY 10010. Phone: 800-662-7776 or (646)746-6400 E-mail: corporatecommunications@reedbusiness.com • URL: http://www.reedbusiness.com • Annual. $25.00. Lists about 2,300 manufacturers of equipment and supplies in the materials handling industry. Supplement to *Modern Materials Handling*.

Modern Metals. Trend Publishing, Inc., One E. Erie St., Suite 401 Chicago, IL 60611. Phone: 800-278-7363 or (312)654-2300 Fax: (312)654-2323 • URL: http://www.modernmetals.com • Monthly. $85.00 per year. Covers management and production for plants that fabricate and finish metals of various kinds.

Modern Methods for Quality Control and Improvement. Harrison M. Wadsworth and others. John Wiley and Sons, Inc., 111 River St. Hoboken, NJ 07030. Phone: 800-526-5368 or (201)748-6000 Fax: (201)748-6088 E-mail: info@wiley.com • URL: http://www.wiley.com • 2001. $104.95. Second edition.

Modern Organizations: Theory and Practice. Ali Farazmand, editor. Greenwood Publishing Group, Inc., 88 Post Rd., W Westport, CT 06881. Phone: 800-225-5800 or (203)226-3571 Fax: (203)431-2214 E-mail: customer-service@greenwood.com • URL: http://www.greenwood.com • 2002. $67.95. Second edition.

Modern Paint and Coatings. Chemical Week Associates, 110 Williams St. New York, NY 10038. Phone: (212)621-4900 Fax: (212)621-4800 E-mail: acortessr@chemweek.com • URL: http://www.modernpaintingandcoatings.com • Monthly. $52.00 per year.

Modern Parliamentary Procedure. Ray E. Keesey. American Psychological Association, 750 1st St. NE Washington, DC 20002-4242. Phone: 800-374-2721 or (202)336-5500 Fax: (202)336-6069 • URL: http://www.apa.org • 1994. $24.95. Revised edition. A modernization and simplification of traditional, complex rules of procedure. Written for associations, clubs, community groups, and other deliberative bodies.

Modern Petroleum Technology. Richard A. Dawe, editor. John Wiley and Sons, Inc., 111 River St. Hoboken, NJ 07030. Phone: 800-225-5945 or (201)748-6000 Fax: (201)748-6088 E-mail: info@wiley.com • URL: http://www.wiley.com • 2000. $600.00. Sixth edition. Two volumes. Volume one, entitled *Upstream*, covers oil rigs and other means of obtaining raw petroleum. Volume two, *Downstream*, covers petroleum refining and end products. Edited for industry technicians, managers, and engineers.

Modern Physician: Essential Business News for the Executive Physician. Crain Communications, Inc., 360 N Michigan Ave. Chicago, IL 60601-3806. Phone: 800-678-9595 or (312)337-7700 E-mail: info@crain.com • URL: http://www.crain.com • Monthly. $45.00. Edited for physicians responsible for business decisions at hospitals, clinics, HMOs, and other health groups. Includes special issues on managed care, practice management, legal issues, and finance.

Modern Plastics Encyclopedia. McGraw-Hill, 1221 Ave. of the Americas New York, NY 10020. Phone: 800-722-4726 or (212)512-2000 E-mail: customer.service@mcgraw-hill.com • URL: http://www.mcgrawhill.com • Annual. $85.00. List of about 5,000 suppliers of over 350 types of products and services to the plastic industry in the U.S. and Canada. Included with subscription to *Modern Plastics*.

Modern Portfolio Theory and Investment Analysis and Investment Portfolio Software. Edwin J. Elton. John Wiley and Sons, Inc., 111 River St. Hoboken, NJ 07030. Phone: 800-225-5945 or (201)748-6000 Fax: (201)748-6088 E-mail: info@wiley.com • URL: http://www.wiley.com • 1998. $88.00. Fifth edition. Includes CD-Rom. The authors' central concern is that of mixing assets to achieve maximum overall return consonant with an acceptable level of risk. (Portfolio Management Series).

Modern Real Estate. Charles H. Wurtzebach and Mike E. Miles. John Wiley and Sons, Inc., 111 River St. Hoboken, NJ 07030. Phone: 800-225-5945 or (201)748-6000 Fax: (201)748-6088 E-mail: info@wiley.com • URL: http://www.wiley.com • 1994. $97.95. Fifth edition.

Modern Real Estate Practice. Fillmore W. Galaty. Dearborn Trade Publishing, Kaplan Professional Co., 155 N Wacker Dr. Chicago, IL 60606. Phone: 800-921-9621 or (312)836-4400 Fax: (312)836-1021 E-mail: trade@dearborn.com • URL: http://www.dearborntrade.com • 2002. $45.60. 16th edition. Provides essential up-to-date information to students preparing for a state licensing exam.

Modern Recording Techniques. David M. Huber and Robert Runstein. Elsevier, 655 Ave. of the Americas New York, NY 10010. Phone: 800-366-2665 or (212)989-5800 Fax: 800-535-9935 or (212)633-3680 E-mail: custserv@elsevier.com • URL: http://www.elsevier.com • 2001. $36.99. Fifth edition.

Modern Refrigeration and Air Conditioning. Andrew D. Althouse and others. Goodheart-Willcox Publishers, 18604 W. Creek Dr. Tinley Park, IL 60477-6243. Phone: 800-323-0440 or (708)687-5000 Fax: (708)687-5068 E-mail: custerv@goodheartwillcox.com • URL: http://www.goodheartwillcox.com • 2003. Price on application.

Modern Retailing: Theory and Practice. Joseph B. Mason and others. McGraw-Hill, 1221 Ave. of the Americas New York, NY 10020. Phone: 800-722-4726 or (212)512-2000 Fax: (212)512-4502 E-mail: customer.service@mcgraw-hill.com • URL: http://www.mcgraw-hill.com • 1992. $69.95. Sixth edition.

Modern Salon Magazine. Vance Publishing Corp., 400 Knightsbridge Parkway Lincolnshire, IL 60069. Phone: 800-255-5113 or (847)634-2600 Fax: (847)634-4379 • URL: http://www.vancepublishing.com • Monthly. $20.00 per year.

Modern Tire Dealer: Covering Tire Sales and Car Service., 341 Pond Dr. Akron, OH 44320. Phone: (330)867-4401 Fax: (330)867-0019 E-mail: info@mtdealer.com • URL: http://www.mtdealer.com • Monthly. $65.00 per year. Serves independent tire dealers. Cover automotive service and dealership management topics.

Modern Tire Dealer: Facts/Directory. VNU Business Media, 770 Broadway New York, NY 10003-9595. Phone: (646)654-4500 Fax: (646)654-7212 E-mail: mtd@billcom.com • URL: http://www.vnubusinessmedia.com • Annual. $30.00. Directories of tire and car service suppliers, tire shop jobbers, and national state associations.

Modern Workers Compensation. West Group, 610 Opperman Dr. Eagan, MN 55123. Phone: 800-328-4880 or (651)687-7000 Fax: 800-340-9378 E-mail: bookstore@westgroup.com • URL: http://www.westgroup.com • Quarterly. $511.00 per year. Three looseleaf volumes. Provides detailed coverage of workers' compensation law and procedure, including medical benefits, rehabilitation benefits, compensation costs, noncompensable injuries, etc.

Molasses Market News. Livestock and Seed Div., 801 Sangamon Ave. Springfield, IL 62794-9281. Phone: (217)782-4925 Fax: (217)785-5708 E-mail: custserv@infotoday.com Description: Provides the market news on molasses and its import and export.

Molecular and Environmental Toxicology Center., University of Wisconsin-Madison, Enzyme Institute, Room 290, 1710 University Ave. Madison, WI 53705. Phone: (608)263-5557 Fax: (608)262-5245 E-mail: jefcoate@facstaff.wisc.edu • URL: http://www.wisc.edu/etc/ • Formerly Environmental Toxicology Center.

Molecular Biology Institute.

Molluscan Shellfish Institute., 7918 Jones Branch Dr., Ste. 700 McLean, VA 22102. Phone: (703)752-8880 Fax: (703)752-7583 E-mail: ccfma@sbcglobal.net • URL: http://www.aboutseafood.com • A division of the National Fisheries Institute (see separate entry). Shellfish producers, processors, distributors, growers, and suppliers to the industry. Works to promote, protect, and advance the interests of the shellfish industry. Cooperates with federal, state, and municipal authorities in matters of legislation, sanitation standards, controls, and conservation.

Monell Chemical Senses Center. Monell Chemical Senses Center, 3500 Market St. Philadelphia, PA 19104-3308. Phone: (267)519-4700 Fax: (267)898-2084 E-mail: beauchamp@monell.org • URL: http://www.monell.org • Mechanisms and functions of the chemical senses (taste, smell, and chemical irritation), including studies in the areas of biochemistry, biophysics, endocrinology, physiology, ethology, neurology, behavior, genetics, psychophysics, nutrition, organic chemistry, chemical ecology, and zoology. Basic research relates to solutions of problems in health and nutrition, aging and neurodegenerative disease, environmental odors, reproduction, disease diagnosis, expansion of world food supply, and alternative means of vertebrate pest control. Projects focus on biochemistry of receptor mechanisms, sensory qualities of food, role of early diet in shaping food preferences, relationship between chemosensory function and nutritional and disease states, role of body volatiles in disease diagnosis, methods of altering salt preference, role of taste and smell in food utilization, effect of aging on taste and smell, information processing in taste and smell, role of genes in determining sensory perception and hedonic responses, and diagnosis and treatment of taste and smell disorders.

The Monell Connection: From the Monell Chemical Senses Center, a Nonprofit Scientific Institute Devoted to Research on Taste and Smell. Monell Chemical Senses Center, 3500 Market St. Philadelphia, PA 19104. Phone: (215)898-6666 Three times a year. Free. Newsletter. Includes brief summaries of selected papers describing ongoing work of Monell scientists.

Monetary Policy and Reserve Requirements Handbook. U.S. Federal Reserve System. Board of Governors Publications Services, Room MS-1, 20th and Constitution Ave., N.W. Washington, DC 20551. Phone: (202)752-3244 Fax: (202)728-5886 • URL: http://http://www.federalreserve.gov • Annual.

Money., 1271 Ave. of the Americas New York, NY 10020-1393. Phone: 800-633-9970 or (212)522-1212 Fax: (212)522-1796 E-mail: cnnmoney@money.com • URL: http://www.money.cnn.com • 13 times a year. $19.95 per year. Covers all aspects of family finance; investments, careers, shopping, taxes, insurance, consumerism, etc.

Money, Banking, and Financial Markets. Roger L. Miller and David D. VanHoose. South-Western, 5191 Natorp Blvd. Mason, OH 45040. Phone: 800-354-9706 or (513)229-1000 • URL: http://www.swcollege.com • 2003. $102.95. Second edition.

Money, Banking, and the Economy. Thomas Mayer and others.

W. W. Norton & Co., Inc., 500 5th Ave. New York, NY 10110. Phone: 800-223-2584 or (212)354-5500 Fax: (212)869-0856 • URL: http://www.wwnorton.com • 1996. $92.45. Sixth edition.

Money Income in the United States. Available from U. S. Government Printing Office, Washington, DC 20402. Phone: (202)512-1800 Fax: (202)512-2250 E-mail: gpoaccess@gpo.gov • URL: http://www.access.gpo.gov • Annual. $5.50. Issued by the U. S. Bureau of the Census. Presents data on consumer income in current and constant dollars, both totals and averages (means, medians, distributions). Includes figures for a wide variety of demographic and occupational characteristics. (Current Population Reports.)

Money: Its Origins, Development, Debasement, and Prospects. John H. Wood. American Institute for Economic Research, PO Box 1000 Great Barrington, MA 01230-1000. Phone: (413)528-1216 Fax: (413)528-0103 E-mail: info@aier.org • URL: http://www.aier.org • 1999. $10.00. A politically conservative view of monetary history, the gold standard, banking systems, and inflation. Includes a list of references. (Economic Education Bulletin.)

Money Madness: Strange Manias and Extraordinary Schemes On and Off Wall Street. John M. Waggoner. McGraw-Hill, 1221 Ave. of the Americas New York, NY 10020. Phone: 800-722-4726 or (212)512-2000 Fax: (212)512-4502 E-mail: customer.service@mcgraw-hill.com • URL: http://www.mcgraw-hill.com • 1990. $26.00.

Money Management Letter: Bi-Weekly Newsletter Covering the Pensions and Money Maagement Industry. Institutional Investor, Inc., Journals Group, 225 Park Ave., S New York, NY 10003. Phone: 800-945-2034 or (212)224-3066 Fax: (212)224-3472 E-mail: info@iijournals.com • URL: http://www.iijournals.com • Biweekly. $2,440.00 per year. Newsletter. Includes print and online editions. Edited for pension fund investment managers.

Money Management Strategies for Futures Traders. Nauzer J. Balsara. John Wiley and Sons, Inc., 111 River St. Hoboken, NJ 07030. Phone: 800-225-5945 or (201)748-6000 Fax: (201)748-6088 E-mail: info@wiley.com • URL: http://www.wiley.com • 1992. $75.00. How to limit risk and avoid catastrophic losses. (Finance Series).

Money Manager's Compliance Guide. Thompson Publishing Group, Inc., 1725 K St., N.W., Suite 700 Washington, DC 20006. Phone: (202)444-8741 • URL: http://www.thompson.com • $649.00 per year. Two looseleaf volumes. Monthly updates and newletters. Edited for investment advisers and investment companies to help them be in compliance with governmental regulations, including SEC rules, restrictions based on the Employee Retirement Income Security Act (ERISA), and regulations issued by the Commodity Futures Trading Commission (CFTC).

Money Market Directory of Pension Funds and Their Investment Managers. Money Market Directories, Inc., 320 E. Main St. Charlottesville, VA 22902. Phone: 800-446-2810 or (434)977-1450 Fax: (434)979-9962 • URL: http://www.mmdaccess.com • Annual. $1,150.00. Institutional funds and managers.

Money Reporter: The Insider's Letter for Investors Whose Interest is More Interest. MPL Communications, Inc., 133 Richmond St., W., Suite 700 Toronto, ON, Canada M5H 3M8. Phone: (416)869-1177 Fax: (416)869-0456 Biweekly. $185.00 per year. Newsletter. Supplement available, *Monthly Key Investment*.Canadian interest-bearing deposits and investments.

Money Stock Liquid Assets, and Debt Measures, in Billions of Dollars. U.S. Federal Reserve System. U.S. Board of Governors, Publications Service,, Room MS-127 Washington, DC 20551. Phone: (202)452-3244 Fax: (202)728-5886 • URL: http://www.federalreserve.gov • Weekly. $35.00 per year.

Money: Who Has How Much and Why. Andrew Hacker. Simon & Schuster Trade, 1230 Ave. of the Americas New York, NY 10020. Phone: 800-223-2348 or (212)698-7000 Fax: 800-943-9831 or (212)698-7007 E-mail: consumer.customerservice@simonandschuster.com • URL: http://www.simonsays.com • 1997. $24.50. A discourse on the distribution of wealth in America, with emphasis on the gap between rich and poor.

Moneyletter. Agora Inc., 1217 St. Paul St. Baltimore, MD 21202. Phone: 800-433-1528 or (410)223-2510 Fax: (410)223-2559 E-mail: 75127.1411@compuserve.com • URL: http://www.ibcdata.com • Description: "Provides assertive, do-it-yourself, individual investors with a unique market timing system, specific buy and sell recommendations, and portfolio allocation advice on no-load mutual funds. Features updates on economic and financial market, fund profiles, and articles on non-mutual fund financial planning issues."

The Moneypaper. Temper of the Times Communications, Inc. Temper of the Times Communications Inc., 555 Theodore Fremd Ave., Ste B-103 Rye, NY 10585. Phone: 800-388-9993 or (914)381-5400 Fax: (914)381-7206 E-mail: moneypaper@aol.com Description: Contains strategies to minimize stock sales costs and articles on investing and market trends. Includes a summary of monthly financial news drawn from over 70 financial publications and advisory services. Recurring features include columns titled Summing Up, Market Outlook, and Stocktrack.

Moneytalk. Jean Kwiatowski, 334 Highlark Dr. Larksville, PA 18704. Phone: (717)287-6498 E-mail: moneypaper@aol.com Description: Provides suggestions for saving money through the use of coupons and refund offers. Recurring features include letters to the editor and news of research.

Monopolies in America: Empire Builders and Their Enemies from Jay Gould to Bill Gates. Charles R. Geisst. DIANE Publishing Co., 330 Pusey Ave. Collingdale, PA 19023. Phone: 800-782-3833 or (610)461-6200 Fax: (610)461-6130 E-mail: dianepub@erols.com • URL: http://www.dianepublishing.com • 2000. $30.00. Provides a panoramic, historical view of U. S. trusts, monopolies, and antitrust activities.

The Montana Farmer-Stockman. Farm Progress Companies, 191 S. Gary Ave. Carol Stream, IL 60188. Phone: 800-441-1410 or (630)462-2224 Fax: (630)462-2885 E-mail: circhelp@farmprogress.com • URL: http://www.farmprogress.com • 14 times a year. $23.95 per year. Formerly *Montana Farmer*.

Montana State University-Bozeman. Montana Agricultural Experiment Station

Montana Wool Laboratory. Montana State University-Bozeman

Montford Point Marine Association., PO Box 1070 Sharon Hill, PA 19079. Phone: (202)387-8722 E-mail: info@montfordpointmarines.com • URL: http://www.montfordpointmarines.com • Represents veterans and active members of all branches of the U.S. Armed Forces. Aims to support educational assistance programs, veterans programs and promotion of community services. Works to improve the social conditions of veterans, local families, youth and the growing population of senior citizens; named after Montford Point, New River, Camp Lejeune, NC, the only base in America used for the recruit or "Boot Camp" training of black Marines, 1942-49.

Montgomery's Auditing. Vincent M. O'Reilly and others. John Wiley and Sons, Inc., 111 River St. Hoboken, NJ 073030. Phone: 800-225-5945 or (201)748-6000 Fax: (201)748-6088 E-mail: info@wiley.com • URL: http://www.wiley.com • 1999. $225.00. 12th edition. 2001 *Supplement*, $72.00. Provides comprehensive coverage of auditing strategies and methods, including detailed guidelines.

Monthly Bibliography. United Nations Publications, United Nations Concourse Level, First Ave., 46th St. New York, NY 10017. Phone: 800-533-3210 or (212)963-7680 Fax: (212)963-4910 E-mail: bookstore@un.org • URL: http://www.un.org/publications • Monthly. $125.00 per year. Text in English and French.

Monthly Bulletin of Statistics. United Nations Publications, United Nations Concourse Level, First Ave., 46th St. New York, NY 10017. Phone: 800-553-3210 or (212)963-7680 Fax: (212)963-4910 E-mail: bookstore@un.org • URL: http://www.un.org/publications • Monthly. $295.00 per year. Provides current data for about 200 countries on a wide variety of economic, industrial, and demographic subjects. Compiled by United Nations Statistical Office.

Monthly Business Failures. Dun & Bradstreet Corp., 103 JFK Pky. Short Hills, NJ 07078. Phone: 800-234-3867 E-mail: custserv@dnb.com • URL: http://www.dnb.com • Monthly. $30.00 per year. Provides number of failures and liabilities in over 100 lines of business.

Monthly Catalog of United States Government Publications. U. S. Government Printing Office, 732 N Capitol St., NW Washington, DC 20401. Phone: 888-293-6498 or (202)512-1530 Fax: (202)512-1262 E-mail: gpoaccess@gpo.gov • URL: http://www.gpoaccess.gov • Monthly. $52.00 per year. Modified in 1996. Print edition now consists of very brief entries, indexed only by key words in titles.

Monthly Climatic Data for the World. U.S. National Climatic Data Center, National Oceanic and Atmospheric Administration, U.S. Dept. of Commerce, Federal Bldg., Room 120, 151 Patton Ave. Asheville, NC 28801-5001. Phone: (704)271-4476 Fax: (704)271-4246 E-mail: orders@ncdc.noaa.gov • URL: http://www.ncdc.noaa.gov • Monthly.

Monthly Commodity Price Bulletin. United Nations Publications, United Nations Concourse Level, First Ave., 46th St. New York, NY 10017. Phone: 800-553-3210 or (212)963-7680 Fax: (212)963-4910 E-mail: bookstore@un.org • URL: http://www.un.org/publications • Monthly. $125.00 per year. Provides monthly average prices for the previous 12 months for a wide variety of commodities traded internationally.

Monthly Digest of Tax Articles. Newkirk Products Inc., 15 Corporate Circle Albany, NY 12203. Phone: (518)862-3200 Monthly. $60.00 per year.

Monthly Energy Review. Available from U. S. Government Printing Office, Washington, DC 20402. Phone: (202)512-1800 Fax: (202)512-2250 E-mail: gpoaccess@gpo.gov • URL: http://www.access.gpo.gov • Monthly. $126.00 per year. Issued by the Energy Information Administration, Office of Energy Markets and End Use, U. S. Department of Energy. Contains current and historical statistics on U. S. production, storage, imports, and consumption of petroleum, natural gas, and coal.

Monthly Labor Review. Available from U. S. Government Printing Office, Washington, DC 20402. Phone: (202)512-1800 Fax: (202)512-2250 E-mail: gpoaccess@gpo.gov • URL: http://www.access.gpo.gov • Monthly. $49.00 per year. Issued by the Bureau of Labor Statistics, U. S. Department of Labor. Contains data on the labor force, wages, work stoppages, price indexes, productivity, economic growth, and occupational injuries and illnesses.

Monthly Payment Direct Reduction Loan Schedules. Financial Publishing Co., PO Box 570 South Bend, IN 46628-9752. Phone: 800-433-0090 or (219)247-3214 Fax: (219)243-6060 E-mail: sales@financial-publishing.com • URL: http://www.finacial-publishing.com • $75.00. 13th edition. Supplement available, $30.00.

Monthly Price Review. Urner Barry Publications Inc., PO Box 389 Toms River, NJ 08754. Phone: 800-932-0617 or (732)240-5330 Fax: (732)341-0891 E-mail: mail@urnerbarry.com • URL: http://www.urnerbarry.com • Description: Provides daily price information and monthly averages on dairy, egg, and poultry products. **Remarks:** Subscription includes a supplement titled Annual Price Review.

Monthly Product Announcement. U. S. Bureau of the Census, 4700 Silver Hill Rd. Washington, DC 20233-0001. Phone: (301)763-4636 E-mail: comments@census.gov • URL: http://www.census.gov • Monthly. Lists Census Bureau publications and products that became available during the previous month.

Monthly Statement of the Public Debt of the United States. U. S, Dept. of the Treasury, Public Debt Bureau. Available from U. S. Government Printing Office, Washington, DC 20402. Phone: (202)512-1800 Fax: (202)512-2250 E-mail: gpoaccess@gpo.gov • URL: http://www.access.gpo.gov • Monthly. $42.00 per year.

Monthly Statistical Bulletin. Cigar Association of America, 1100 17th St., N.W., Suite 504 Washington, DC 20036. Phone: (202)223-8204 Fax: (202)833-0379 Monthly. Membership.

Monthly Statistical Release: Beer. U. S. Bureau of Alcohol, Tobacco, and Firearms, Washington Field Div., 607 14th St., NW, Ste. 620 Washington, DC 20005. Phone: (202)927-8810 Fax: (202)927-4024 • URL: http://www.atf.treas.gov • Monthly.

Monthly Statistical Release: Distilled Spirits. U. S. Bureau of Alcohol, Tobacco, and Firearms, Washington Field Div., 607 14th St., NW, Ste. 620 Washington, DC 20005. Phone: (202)927-8810 • URL: http://www.atf.treas.gov • 1995.

Monthly Statistical Release: Tobacco Products. U.S. Bureau of Alcohol, Tobacco, and Firearms, Washington, DC 20226. Phone: (202)927-8500 • URL: http://www.atf.treas.gov • Monthly.

Monthly Statistical Release: Wines. U.S. Bureau of Alcohol, Tobacco, and Firearms, Washington, DC 20226. Phone: (202)927-8500 • URL: http://www.atf.treas.gov • Monthly.

Monthly Statistics of International Trade. Organization for Economic Cooperation and Development, OECD Washington Center, 2001 L St., N. W., Suite 650 Washington, DC 20036-4922. Phone: 800-456-6323 or (202)785-6323 Fax: (202)785-0350 E-mail: washington.contact@oecd.org • URL: http://www.oecd.org • Monthly. $270.00 per year. Provides foreign trade data for OECD countries. Includes statistics by country and by product classification according to Standard International Trade Classification. (Also available on CD-ROM.)

Monthly Treasury Statement of Receipts and Outlays of the United States Government. Available from U. S. Government Printing Office, Washington, DC 20402. Phone: (202)512-1800 Fax: (202)512-2250 E-mail: gpoaccess@gpo.gov • URL: http://www.access.gpo.gov • Monthly. $58.00 per year. Issued by the Financial Management Service, U. S. Treasury Department.

Monthly Truck Tonnage Report. American Trucking Associations. Trucking Information Services, Inc., 2200 Mill Rd. Alexandria, VA 22314-4677. Phone: 800-282-5463 or (703)838-1700 Fax: (703)684-5720 E-mail: ata-infocenter@trucking.com • URL: http://www.truckline.com • Monthly. $50.00 per year.

Monthly Vital Statistics Report. U. S. Department of Health and Human Services, National Center for Health Statistics Hyattsville, MD 20782. Phone: (301)458-4000 E-mail: nchsquery@nchioa.em.cdc.gov • URL: http://www.cdc.gov/nchswww • Monthly. Provides data on births, deaths, cause of death, marriage, and divorce.

Monthly Weather Review. American Meteorological Society, 45 Beacon St. Boston, MA 02108-3693. Phone: (617)227-2425 Fax: (617)742-8718 E-mail: amsinfoamericatsoc.org • URL: http://www.ametsoc.org • Monthly. Members, $65.00 per year; institutions, $500.00 per year.

Moody's Bank and Finance Manual. Mergent, 5250 77 Center Dr. Charlotte, NC 28217. Phone: 800-342-5647 or (704)539-6945 • URL: http://www.mergent.com • Annual. $1,750.00 per year. Four volumes. Includes biweekly supplements in *Moody's Bank and Finance News Report*.

Moody's Bond Survey. Moody's Investors Service Inc., 99 Church St. New York, NY 10007-2787. Phone: 800-342-5647 or (212)553-1658 Fax: (212)553-0882 E-mail: clientservices@moodys.com • URL: http://www.mergent.com • Description: Presents statistical information and analysis of corporate, municipal, government, federal agency, and international bonds, preferred stock, and commercial paper. Includes ratings changes and withdrawals, calendars of recent and prospective bond offerings, and Moody's bond and preferred stock yield averages.

Moody's Corporate News: International. Moody's Investors Service, Inc., 99 Church St. New York, NY 10007-0300. Phone: 800-342-5647 or (212)553-0300 Fax: (212)553-4063 Provides financial and other business news relating to over 5,000 corporations in 100 countries, excluding the U. S. Time period is 1983 to date, with weekly updates. Inquire as to online cost and availability.

Moody's Dividend Record and Annual Dividend Record., 60 Madison Ave., 6th Fl. New York, NY 10010. Phone: 800-342-5647 or (212)413-7601 Fax: (212)413-7777 E-mail: customerservice@mergent.com • URL: http://www.mergent.com • Semiweekly. $775.00 per year. Includes annual and cumulative supplement. Formerly *Moody's Dividend Record.*

Moody's Manuals. Bank and Finance Manual, Industrial Manual, Municipal and Government Manual, OTC Industrial Manual, Public Utility Manual, Transportation Manual. Mergent Inc., 60 Madison Ave., 6th Fl. New York, NY 10010. Phone: 888-411-0893 or (212)413-7700 Fax: (212)413-7670 E-mail: customerservice@mergent.com • URL: http://www.mergent.com • Annual. Looseleaf supplements. Prices on application.

Moody's OTC Industrial Manual. Mergent, Inc., 60 Madison Ave., 6th Fl. New York, NY 10010. Phone: 888-411-0893 or (212)413-7700 Fax: (212)413-7670 E-mail: customerservice@mergent.com • URL: http://www.mergent.com • Annual, $1,995.00 per year. Includes biweekly *Moody's OTC Industrial News Report.*

Moody's Public Utility Manual. Mergent, Inc., 60 Madison Ave., 6th Fl. New York, NY 10010. Phone: 888-411-0893 or (212)413-7700 Fax: (212)413-7670 E-mail: customerservice@mergent.com • URL: http://www.mergent.com • Annual. $1,995.00. Updated weekly online. Contains financial and other information concerning publicly-held utility companies (electric, gas, telephone, water).

Morbidity and Mortality Weekly Report. Available from U. S. Government Printing Office, Washington, DC 20402. Phone: (202)512-1800 Fax: (202)512-2250 E-mail: gpoaccess@gpo.gov • URL: http://www.access.gpo.gov • Weekly. $450.00 per year (priority mail). Issued by the Centers for Disease Control (Atlanta), U. S. Department of Health and Human Services. Provides analysis and statistics on the occurrence of disease and death from all causes in the U. S.

Morgan Stanley Central Bank Directory. Central Banking Publications Ltd., 6 Langley St. London WC2H 9JA, United Kingdom. Phone: 44 207 836 3607 Fax: 44 207 836 3608 E-mail: info@centralbanking.co.uk • URL: http://www.centralbanking.co.uk • 2003. $160.00. Provides detailed information on over 160 central banks around the world. A full page is devoted to each country included. Included in subscription to *Central Banking.*

Morin Center for Banking and Financial Law., Boston University, School of Law, 765 Commonwealth Ave. Boston, MA 02215. Phone: (617)353-3023 Fax: (617)353-2444 E-mail: banklaw@bu.edu • URL: http://www.web.bu.edu/law • Research fields include banking law, regulation of depository institutions, and deposit insurance.

Morningstar American Depositary Receipts. Morningstar, Inc., 225 W. Wacker Dr. Chicago, IL 60606. Phone: 800-735-0700 or (312)696-6000 Fax: (312)696-6001 E-mail: productsupport@morningstar.com • URL: http://www.morningstar.com • Biweekly. $195.00 per year. Looseleaf. Provides detailed profiles of 700 foreign companies having shares traded in the U. S. through American Depositary Receipts (ADRs).

Morningstar Closed-End Fund 250. McGraw-Hill, 1221 Ave. of the Americas New York, NY 10020. Phone: 800-722-4726 or (212)504-2000 Fax: (212)512-4502 E-mail: customer.service@mcgraw-hill.com • URL: http://www.mcgraw-hill.com • 1996. $35.00. Second edition. Provides detailed information on 50 actively traded closed-end investment companies. Past data is included for up to 12 years, depending on life of the fund.

Morningstar FundInvestor. Morningstar, Inc., 225 W. Wacker Dr. Chicago, IL 60606. Phone: 800-735-0700 or (312)696-6000 Fax: (312)696-6001 E-mail: productsupport@morningstar.com • URL: http://www.morningstar.com • Monthly. $89.00 per year. Newsletter. Provides tables of statistical data and star ratings for leading mutual funds ("The Morningstar 500"). News of funds and financial planning advice for investors is also included.

Morningstar Guide to Mutual Funds: 5-Star Strategies for Success. Christine Benz and others. Morningstar, Inc., 225 West Wacker Drive Chicago, IL 60606. Phone: 800-735-0700 or (312)696-6000 Fax: (312)696-6001 E-mail: productsupport@morningstar.com • URL: http://www.morningstar.com • 2003. $24.95. Contains general advice on mutual funds for the small investor, including "How to Pick Mutual Funds," "How to Build a Portfolio," and "How to Monitor Your Portfolio." (Also available from John Wiley & Sons.)

Morningstar Mutual Funds. Morningstar, Inc., 225 W. Wacker Dr. Chicago, IL 60606. Phone: 800-735-0700 or (312)696-6000 Fax: (312)696-6001 E-mail: productsupport@morningstar.com • URL: http://www.morningstar.com • Biweekly. $395.00 per year. Looseleaf service. Contains detailed information and risk-adjusted ratings on over 1,240 load and no-load, equity and fixed-income mutual funds. Annual returns are provided for up to 12 years for each fund.

Morningstar StockInvestor. Morningstar, Inc., 225 West Wacker Drive Chicago, IL 60606. Phone: 800-735-0700 or (312)696-6000 Fax: (312)696-6001 E-mail: productsupport@morningstar.com • URL: http://www.morningstar.com • Monthly. $89.00 per year. Newsletter. Features about a dozen stocks in an aggressive "Hare Portfolio" and a dozen in a conservative "Tortoise Portfolio." Includes general advice on investing in stocks.

Morningstar.com: Your First Second Opinion. Morningstar, Inc. Phone: 800-735-0700 or (312)696-6000 Fax: (312)696-6001 E-mail: productsupport@morningstar.com • URL: http://www.morningstar.com • Web site provides a broad selection of information and advice on both mutual funds and individual stocks, including financial news and articles on investment fundamentals. Basic service is free, with "Premium Membership" available at $109.00 per year. Annual fee provides personal portfolio analysis, screening tools, and more extensive profiles of funds and stocks.

Mortgage & Asset-Based Desk Reference: U. S. Buyside and Sellside Profiles. Capital Access International, The Reuters BAve., 3 Times Square New York, NY 10036. Phone: 800-866-5987 or (646)223-4130 Fax: (646)223-4133 E-mail: emaxxinfo@lipper.reuters.com • URL: http://www.capital-access.com • Annual. $395.00. Provides "detailed buyside and sellside profiles and contacts" for the mortgage and asset-based securities market.

Mortgage and Real Estate Executives Report. West Group, 610 Opperman Dr. Eagan, MN 55123. Phone: 800-328-4880 or (651)687-7000 Fax: 800-340-9378 E-mail: bookstore@westgroup.com • URL: http://www.westgroup.com • Biweekly. $368.00 per year. Newsletter. Source of ideas and new updates. Covers the latest opportunities and developments.

Mortgage-Backed Securities: Developments and Trends in the Secondary Mortgage Market. Cameron L. Cowan and Kenneth G. Lore. West Group, 610 Opperman Dr. Eagan, MN 55123. Phone: 800-328-4880 or (651)687-7000 Fax: 800-340-9378 E-mail: bookstore@westgroup.com • URL: http://www.westgroup.com • 2003. $275.00. (Securities Handbook Series).

Mortgage-Backed Securities Letter. Securities Data Publishing, 395 Hudson, 3rd Fl., 40 W 57th St. New York, NY 10014. Phone: 888-605-3385 or (212)765-5311 Fax: (646)822-3230 E-mail: sdp@tfn.com • URL: http://www.thomsonmedia.com • Description: Covers developments in the structured finance markets. Analyzes transactions and their collateral; follows litigation, refinancing opportunities, and market conditions.

Mortgage Bankers Association of America.

Mortgage Banking: The Magazine of Real Estate Finance Managers and Employees. Mortgage Bankers Association of America, 1919 Pennsylvania Ave., N.W. Washington, DC 20006-3438. Phone: 800-793-6222 or (202)557-2700 E-mail: communications@mbaa.org • URL: http://www.mbaa.org • Monthly. $45.00 per year.

Mortgage Insurance Companies of America.

Mortgage Loan Disclosure Handbook: A Step-by-Step Guide with Forms. West Group, 610 Opperman Dr. Eagan, MN 55123. Phone: 800-328-4880 or (651)687-7000 Fax: 800-340-9378 E-mail: bookstore@westgroup.com • URL: http://www.westgroup.com • Annual. $363.00. Covers disclosure requirements that lenders must meet under federal laws and regulations. Discusses the Truth-in-Lending Act, RESPA (Real Estate Settlement Procedures Act), the Equal Credit Opportunity Act, and the Fair Credit Reporting Act. (Real Property Law Series).

Mortgage Servicing News: For Residential amd Commercial Servicers. Thomson Media, One State St. Plaza New York, NY 10004. Phone: 800-221-1809 or (212)803-8200 Fax: (212)843-9635 E-mail: custserv@thomsonmedia.com • URL: http://www.thomsonmedia.com • Monthly. $98.00 per year. Edited for personnel involved with processing and handling of mortgage loan payments and disbursements for such items as insurance and taxes.

Mortgage Technology. Thomson Media, One State St. Plaza New York, NY 10004. Phone: 800-221-1809 or (212)803-8200 Fax: (212)843-9635 E-mail: custserv@thomsonmedia.com • URL: http://www.thomsonmedia.com • Eight times a year. $78.00 per year. Covers the use of computers, software, automation, and technology in the mortgage industry. Includes reviews of new hardware and software products.

Morton Collectanea. University of Miami Dept. of Biology

Mosby's GenRx: The Complete Reference for Generic and Brand Drugs. Mosby, Inc., 11830 Westline Industrial Dr. Saint Louis, MO 63146. Phone: 800-325-4177 or (314)872-8370 Fax: (314)432-1380 • URL: http://www.mosby.com • 2000. $72.95. 11th edition. Provides detailed information on a wide variety of generic and brand name prescription drugs. Includes color identification pictures, prescribing data, and price comparisons. (Mosby's Physicians GenRx Series).

Mosby's GenRx [year]. CME, Inc., 2801 McGaw Ave. Irvine, CA 92614-5835. Phone: 800-933-2632 or (949)250-1008 Fax: (949)250-0445 E-mail: infostore@cmeinc.com • URL: http://www.cmeinc.com • Quarterly. $250.00. CD-ROM contains detailed monographs for more than 45,000 generic and brand name prescription drugs. Includes color pill images and customizable patient education handouts.

Mote Marine Laboratory. Mote Marine Laboratory, 1600 Ken Thompson Pky. Sarasota, FL 34236-1096. Phone: 800-691-6683 or (941)388-4441 Fax: (941)388-4312 E-mail: president@mote.org • URL: http://www.mote.org • Wetland and estuarine ecology, habitat restoration, toxic organic chemistry, physical chemistry, biochemistry, analytical chemistry, marine chemistry, fisheries, aquaculture, fish stock enhancement, benthic fauna, phytoplankton, meroplankton, ichthyoplankton, landscape ecology, marine mammals and turtles, sediments, red tide, aerosols, neurobiology, cancer resistance in sharks, elasmobranch immunology and cell culture, bioassays, toxicology, bioactive substances, corals, development of skate as a standardized laboratory animal, and reproductive patterns of sharks, skates and rays.

The Mother of All Windows 98 Books. Woody Leonhard and Barry Simon. Addison-Wesley, 75 Arlington St., Ste. 300 Boston, MA 02116. Phone: 800-447-2226 or (617)848-7500 • URL: http://www.aw.com • 1993. Price on application.

Motion Picture Association of America., 15503 Ventura Blvd. Encino, CA 91436. Phone: (818)995-6600 • URL: http://www.mpaa.org • Affiliated with Alliance of Motion Picture and Television Producers and the Motion Picture Association. Formerly Motion Picture Producers and Distributors of America.

The Motion Picture Guide Annual. CineBooks, 620 Ave. of the Americas New York, NY 10011. Phone: 800-521-8110 or (212)462-5000 Fax: (212)462-6000 Annual. $99.95. Provides detailed information on every domestic and foreign film released theatrically in the U. S. during the year covered. Includes annual Academy Award listings and film industry obituaries. Yearly volumes are available for older movies, beginning with the 1987 edition for films of 1986.

Motion Picture TV and Theatre Directory: For Services and Products. Motion Picture Enterprises Publications, Inc., P.O. Box 276 Tarrytown, NY 10591. Phone: (212)245-0969 Fax: (212)245-0974 E-mail: info@mpe.net • URL: http://www.mpe.net • Semiannual. $16.20. Companies providing products and services to the motion picture and television industries.

Motion Systems Handbook. Penton Media Inc., 1300 E. Ninth St. Cleveland, OH 44114-1503. Phone: (216)696-7000 Fax: (216)696-0836 E-mail: information@penton.com • URL: http://www.penton.com • Annual. $30.00.

Motivation and Emotion. Kluwer Academic Publishers, 101 Philip Dr., Assinippi Park Norwell, MA 02061. Phone: (781)871-6600 Fax: (781)681-9045 • URL: http://www.wkap.nl • Quarterly. Institutions, $569.00 per year; with online edition, $682.80 per year.

Motivational Manager: Strategies to Increase Morale and Productivity in the Workplace. Lawrence Ragan Communications, Inc., 316 N. Michigan Ave., Suite 300 Chicago, IL 60601. Phone: 800-878-5331 or (312)960-4100 Fax: (312)960-4106 E-mail: cservice@ragan.com • URL: http://www.ragan.com • Monthly. $119.00 per year. Newsletter. Emphasis is on participative management.

Motor Age: For the Professional Automotive Import and Domestic Service Industry. Reed Business Information, 360 Park Ave. S New York, NY 10010. Phone: 800-446-6551 or (646)746-6400 Fax: (646)746-7028 E-mail: corporatecommunications@reedbusiness.com • URL: http://www.reedbusiness.com • Monthly. $49.00 per year. Published for independent automotive repair shops and gasoline service stations.

Motor and Equipment Manufacturers Association.

Motor Carrier Permit and Tax Bulletin. J.J. Keller and Associates, Inc., 3003 W. Breezewood Lane Neenah, WI 54957. Phone: 800-327-6868 or (920)722-2848 Fax: (920)727-7526 • URL: http://www.jjkeller.com • Monthly. $125.00 per year. Looseleaf service. Formerly *Trucking Permit and Tax Bulletin.*

MOTOR: Covering the World of Automotive Service. Hearst Business Publishing, 645 Stewart Ave. Garden City, NY 11530-4709. Phone: 800-289-8696 or (516)227-1300 Fax: (516)227-1405 • URL: http://www.hearst.com • Monthly. $48.00 per year. Edited for professional automobile and light-truck mechanics. Includes industry news and market trends.

Motor Ship Directory of Shipowners and Shipbuilders. Reed Business Information, 360 Park Ave. S New York, NY 10010. Phone: 800-662-7776 or (646)746-6400 E-mail: corporatecommunications@reedbusiness.com • URL: http://www.reedbusiness.com • Annual. $120.00. Formerly *Directory of Shipowners and Shipbuilders.*

Motor Trend. PRIMEDIA Inc., 745 Fifth Ave. New York, NY 10151. Phone: 800-800-6848 or (212)745-0100 Fax: (212)745-0121 E-mail: information@primedia.com • URL: http://www.primedia.com • Monthly. $10.00. per year.

Motor Vehicle Regulation: State Capitals. Wakeman-Walworth, Inc., P.O. Box 7376 Alexandria, VA 22307-7376. Phone: 800-876-2545 or (703)768-9600 Fax: (703)768-9690 E-mail: newsletters@statecapitals.com • URL: http://www.statecapitals.com • 50 times a year. $245.00 per year; print and online editions, $350.00 per year. Formerly *From the State Capitals: Motor Vehicle Regulation.*

Motorcycle Industry Council., 2 Jenner St., Ste. 150 Irvine, CA 92618-3806. Phone: (949)727-4211 Fax: (949)727-3313 E-mail: ciannello@mic.org • URL: http://www.mic.org • Manufacturers and distributors of motorcycles and allied industries. Maintains liaison with state and federal governments. Operates collection of research documents, federal and state government documents, and trade publications. Compiles statistics.

Motorcycle Product News. Athletic Business Publications, Inc., 4130 Lien Rd. Madison, WI 53404-3602. Phone: 800-722-8764 or (608)249-0186 Fax: (608)249-1153 E-mail: editors@mpnmag.com • URL: http://www.mpnmag.com • Monthly. $55.00 per year. Edited for wholesalers and retailers of motorcycles and supplies.

Motorcycle Product News Special Buyers Guide. A.B. Publications, Inc., 4130 Lien Rd. Madison, WI 53704. Phone: 800-

722-8764 or (608)249-0186 Fax: (608)249-1153 E-mail: editors@mpnmag.com Annual. $45.00. Provides information on companies related to the motorcycle business. Formerly-*Motorcycle Product News Trade Directory*.

Motorcycle Shopper: The Source for Motorcycles, Parts, Accessories, Sidecars, Tools, Clubs, Events, and More. Payne Corp., 1353 Herndon Ave. Deltona, FL 32725-9046. Phone: 800-982-4599 or (407)860-1989 Fax: (407)574-1014 E-mail: mshopper@iag.net • URL: http://www.shopper.eurografix.com • Monthly. $19.95 per year. Contains consumer advertisements for buying, selling, and trading motorcycles and parts.

Motorcyclist. PRIMEDIA Inc., 745 Fifth Ave. New York, NY 10151. Phone: 800-800-6848 or (212)745-0100 Fax: (212)745-0121 E-mail: information@primedia.com • URL: http://www.primedia.com • Monthly. $10.00 per year.

Mount Vernon Research and Extension Unit. Washington State University

Movie Money: Understanding Hollywood's (Creative) Accounting Practices. Bill Daniels. Silman-James Press, 3624 Shannon Rd. Los Angeles, CA 90027. Phone: (323)661-9922 Fax: (323)661-9933 E-mail: silmanjamespress@earthlink.com • URL: http://www.silmanjamespress.com • 1998. $29.95. Explains the numerous amd mysterious accounting methods used by the film industry to arrive at gross and net profit figures. The authors also discuss profit participation, audits, claims, and negotiating.

Movimiento Popular Peru., 30-08 Broadway, Ste. 159 Long Island City, NY 11106. E-mail: lquispe@nyxfer.blythe.org Provides research, informational, and educational programs.

Moving and Relocation Sourcebook and Directory: Reference Guide to the 120 Largest Metropolitan Areas in the United States. Omnigraphics, Inc., 615 Griswold St. Detroit, MI 48226. Phone: 800-234-1340 or (313)961-1340 Fax: 800-875-1340 or (313)961-1383 E-mail: info@omnigraphics.com • URL: http://www.omnigraphics.com • Annual. $225.00 Provides extensive statistical and other descriptive data for the 120 largest metropolitan areas in the U. S. Includes maps and a discussion of factors to be considered when relocating.

Moving and Reorganizing a Library. Marianna Wells and Rosemary Young. Ashgate Publishing Co., 101 Cherry St., Ste. 420 Burlington, VT 05401-4405. Phone: 800-535-9544 or (802)865-7641 Fax: (802)865-7847 E-mail: adonahue@ashgate.com • URL: http://www.ashgate.com • 1997. $79.95. "This book provides detailed guidance on how to plan, design, prepare, and implement the move of a small or medium sized library from the time of the project's inception to its completion." Includes a case study and checklists. Published by Gower in England.

Moving Beyond Gridlock: Traffic and Development. Robert T. Dunphy. Urban Land Institute, 1025 Thomas Jefferson St., NW, Ste. 500 W Washington, DC 20007. Phone: 800-321-5011 or (202)624-7000 Fax: (202)624-7140 • URL: http://www.uli.org • 1996. $49.95. Describes how various regions have dealt with traffic growth. Includes case studies from seven cities.

Moving Power and Money: The Politics of Census Taking. Barbara E. Bryant and William Dunn. New Strategist Publications, Inc., 120 W. State St., 4th Fl. Ithaca, NY 14851. Phone: 800-848-0842 or (607)273-0913 Fax: (607)277-5009 E-mail: demographics@newstrategist.com • URL: http://www.newstrategist.com • 1995. $24.95. Barbara Everitt Bryant was Director of the U. S. Census Bureau from 1989 to 1993. She provides a plan for reducing the costs of census taking, improving accuracy, and overcoming public resistance to the census.

MPC Corporation. MPC Corporation, 5000 Forbes Ave. Pittsburgh, PA 15213. Phone: (412)268-2091 Fax: (412)268-5841 E-mail: rkloss@andrew.cmu.edu Engineering and technology, including cooperative studies with local industry on mass rapid transit for metropolitan areas, systems planning, and systems evaluation. Serve as administrative and coordinating agency for joint research activities of staff members of affiliated institutions.

MPT Review; Specializing in Modern Portfolio Theory. Navellier and Associates, Inc., 1 E Liberty St. Reno, NV 89501-2110. Phone: 800-861-5968 or (301)340-2100 Fax: (775)785-2323 E-mail: info@navellier.com • URL: http://www.mptreview.com • Monthly. $275.00 per year. Newsletter. Provides specific stock selection and model portfolio advice (conservative, moderately aggressive, and aggressive) based on quantitative analysis and modern portfolio theory.

MRA Blue Book Research Services Directory. Marketing Research Association, 110 National Dr., 2nd Fl. Glastonbury, CT 06033-1212. Phone: (860)682-1000 Fax: (860)682-1010 E-mail: email@mra-net.org • URL: http://www.bluebook.org • Covers: over 1,200 marketing research companies and field interviewing services. Entries include: Company name, address, phone, names of executives, services, facilities, special interviewing capabilities.

MS. Liberty Media for Women, L.L.C., 1600 Wilson Blvd., Suite 801 Arlington, VA 22209. Phone: (703)522-2214 Fax: (703)522-2219 E-mail: info@ms.magazine.com • URL: http://www.msmagazine.com • Bimonthly. $45.00 per year.

MSDN Magazine (Microsoft Systems for Developers). CMP Media LLC, 600 Community Dr. Manhasset, NY 11030. Phone: (516)562-5000 E-mail: cmp@cmp.com • URL: http://www.cmp.com • Monthly. $84.95 per year. Produced for professional software developers using Windows, MS-DOS, Visual Basic, and other Microsoft Corporation products. Incorporates *Microsoft Internet Developer*.

The MTM Association for Standards and Research.

Multi-Housing Laundry Association., 1500 Sunday Dr., Ste. 102 Raleigh, NC 27607. Phone: 800-380-3652 or (919)861-5579 Fax: (919)787-4916 E-mail: nshore@mla-online.com • URL: http://www.mla-online.com • Operating and supplier companies. Strives to provide tenants with professionally operated laundry facilities. Sponsors annual convention and trade show.

Multi-Housing News (MHN). VNU Business Media, 770 Broadway New York, NY 10003-9595. Phone: 800-344-7119 or (646)654-4500 Fax: (646)654-7212 • URL: http://www.vnubusinessmedia.com • Monthly. $80.00 per year. Individuals and firms primarily engaged in the development, construction, planning and management of multi-housing.

Multi-State Sales Tax Guide. CCH, Inc., 2700 Lake Cook Rd. Riverwoods, IL 60015. Phone: 800-835-5224 or (847)267-7000 E-mail: cust_serv@cch.com • URL: http://www.cch.com • $1,349.00 per year. Looseleaf service. Nine volumes. Periodic supplementation. Formerly *All State Sales Tax Reports*.

Multichannel News. Reed Business Information, 360 Park Ave. S New York, NY 10010. Phone: 800-446-6551 or (646)746-6400 Fax: (646)746-7028 E-mail: corporatecommunications@reedbusiness.com • URL: http://www.reedbusiness.com • 51 times a year. $139.00 per year. Covers the business, programming, market and technology concerns of cable television operators and their suppliers.

Multimedia and the Web from A to Z. David C. Leonard and Patrick M. Dillon. Greenwood Publishing Group, Inc., 88 Post Rd., W. Westport, CT 06881. Phone: 800-225-5800 or (203)226-3571 Fax: (203)431-2214 E-mail: customer-service@greenwood.com • URL: http://www.greenwood.com • 1998. $42.95. Second enlarged revised edition. Defines more than 1,500 terms relating to software and hardware in the areas of computing, online technology, telecommunications, audio, video, motion pictures, CD-ROM, and the Internet. Includes acronyms and an annotated bibliography. Formerly *Multimedia Technology from A to Z* (1994).

Multimedia Communications Laboratory., Boston University, Eight Saint Mary's St., PHO 445 Boston, MA 02215. Phone: (617)353-8042 Fax: (617)353-6440 E-mail: mcl@spiderman.bu.edu • URL: http://www.hulk.bu.edu • Research areas include interactive multimedia applications.

Multimedia: Concepts and Practice. Stephen McGloughlin. Prentice Hall Books, 200 Old Tappan Rd. Old Tappan, NJ 07675. Phone: 800-282-0693 Fax: 800-835-5327 or (201)236-7141 • URL: http://www.prenhall.com • 2000. $73.33. Includes audio compact disk. Provides basic information and instruction on multimedia graphic design, animation, video editing, sound editing, authoring, product creation, and other multimedia topics.

Multimedia Schools: A Practical Journal of Technology for Education including Multimedia, CD-ROM, Online and Internet and Hardware in K-12. Information Today, Inc., 143 Old Marlton Pike Medford, NJ 08055-8750. Phone: 800-300-9868 or (609)654-6266 Fax: (609)654-4309 E-mail: custserv@infotoday.com • URL: http://www.infotoday.com • Six times a year. $39.95 per year. Edited for school librarians, media center directors, computer coordinators, and others concerned with educational multimedia. Coverage includes the use of CD-ROM sources, the Internet, online services, and library technology.

Multinational Financial Management. Alan C. Shapiro. John Wiley and Sons, Inc., 111 River St. Hoboken, NJ 07030. Phone: 800-225-5945 or (201)748-6276 Fax: (201)748-8641 E-mail: bookinfo@wiley.com • URL: http://www.wiley.com • 2002. $106.95. Seventh edition.

Multinational Monitor. Essential Information, P. O. Box 19405 Washington, DC 20036. Phone: (202)387-8030 Fax: (202)234-5176 E-mail: monitor@essential.org • URL: http://www.multinationalmonitor.org • Monthly. Individuals, $25.00 per year; non-profit organizations, $30.00 per year; corporations, $40.00 per year. Track the activities of multinational corporations and their effects on the Third World, labor and the environment.

Municipal Bonds: The Comprehensive Review of Municipal Securities and Public Finance. Robert Lamb and Stephen Rappaport. McGraw-Hill, 1221 Ave. of the Americas New York, NY 10020. Phone: 800-722-4726 or (212)512-2000 Fax: (212)512-4502 E-mail: customer.service@mcgraw-hill.com • URL: http://www.mcgraw-hill.com • 1987. $34.95. Second edition.

Municipal Finance Journal. Civic Research Institute, 4490 U.S. Route 27 Kingston, NJ 08528. Phone: (609)683-4450 Fax: (609)683-7291 E-mail: order@civicresearchinstitute.com • URL: http://www.civicresearchinstitute.com • Quarterly. $302.00 per year. Recent tax and legal trends affecting both large and small state municipalities.

Municipal Management Series. International City-County Management Association, 777 Capitol St., N.E., Suite 500 Washington, DC 20002-4201. Phone: 800-745-8780 or (202)289-4262 Fax: (202)962-3500 • URL: http://www.icma.org • 14 volumes. Various dates, 1968 to 1988. Finance, planning, training, public relations, and other subjects.

Municipal Technical Advisory Service Library., University of Tennessee, Knoxville, Conference Center Bldg., 600 Henley St., Ste. 120 Knoxville, TN 37996-4105. Phone: (865)974-0411 Fax: (865)974-0423 E-mail: schwartzr@tennessee.edu • URL: http://www.mtas.utk.edu/library • Research areas include municipal finance, police administration, and public works.

Municipal Year Book. International City-County Management Association, 777 Capitol St., N.E., Suite 500 Washington, DC 20002-4201. Phone: 800-745-8780 or (202)289-4262 Fax: (202)962-3500 E-mail: subscriptions@icma.org • URL: http://www.icma.org • Annual. $84.95. An authoritative resume of activities and statistical data of American cities.

Municipal Yellow Book: Who's Who in the Leading City and County Governments and Local Authorities. Leadership Directories, Inc., 104 Fifth Ave. New York, NY 10011. Phone: (212)627-4140 Fax: (212)645-0931 E-mail: info@leadershipdirectories.com • URL: http://www.leadershipdirectories.com • Annual. $265.00 per year. Lists approximately 30,000 key personnel in city and county departments, agencies, subdivisions, and branches.

Murphy's Will Clauses: Annotations and Forms with Tax Effects. LexisNexis Matthew Bender, 1275 Broadway Albany, NY 12204. Phone: 800-424-4200 or (518)487-3000 Fax: (518)487-3584 E-mail: bookstore.support@lexisnexis.com • URL: http://www.bender.com • Biennial. $1,157.00 per year. Four looseleaf volumes. Over 1,400 framed will and trust clauses.

Mushroom Journal. Mushroom Growers' Association, Two Saint Paul's St. Stamford PE9 2BE, United Kingdom. Phone: 44 1780 766888 Monthly. Membership.

Mushroom News. American Mushroom Institute, One Massachusetts Ave., N.W., Suite 800 Washington, DC 20001-1401. Phone: (202)842-4344 Fax: (202)408-7763 Monthly. $275.00. Includes *News Flash*.

Music and Sound Retailer: The Newsmagazine for Musical Instrument and Sound Product Merchandisers. Testa Communications, Inc., 25 Willowdale Ave. Port Washington, NY 11050. Phone: (516)767-2500 Fax: (516)767-9335 • URL: http://www.testa.com • Monthly. Free to qualified personnel; others, $18.00 per year. Provides news and advice on the retailing of a wide range of music and sound products, including musical instruments, electronic keyboards, sound amplification systems, music software, and recording equipment.

Music Distributors Association., 1026 Northwood Dr., 262 W 38th St., Rm. 1506 Effingham, IL 62401. Phone: (217)347-6699 Fax: (217)347-6699 E-mail: geobev@consolidated.net • URL: http://www.musicdistributors.org • International distributors and suppliers of musical instruments, sheet music, and allied merchandise; manufacturers of musical merchandise.

Music Inc. Maher Publications, Inc., 102 N. Haven Rd. Elmhurst, IL 60126. Phone: 800-554-7470 or (630)941-2030 Fax: (630)941-3210 11 times a year. $16.00. per year. Music and sound retailing. Formerly *Up Beat Monthly*.

Music Index: A Subject-Author Guide to Music Periodical Literature. Harmonie Park Press, 23630 Pinewood Warren, MI 48091-4759. Phone: 800-422-4880 or (586)755-3080 Fax: (586)755-4213 E-mail: info@harmonieparkpress.com • URL: http://www.harmonieparkpress.com • Quarterly. $2,195.00 per year. Annual cummulation. Supplement available: *Music Index Subject Heading List*. Guide to current periodicals. Entries are in language of country issuing the index.

Music Industry Conference., 1806 Robert Fulton Dr., 1806 Robert Fulton Dr. Reston, VA 20191. Phone: 800-336-3768 or (703)860-4000 Fax: (703)860-1531 E-mail: geobev@consolidated.net • URL: http://www.menc.org/industry • Instrument manufacturers, music publishers, music retailers, music textbook publishers, and other music-related suppliers. Facilitates communication between MENC: The National Association for Music Education (see separate entry) and the industry; provides displays of musical instruments, publications, and other music-related products for MENC conventions.

Music Journal. Incorporated Society of Musicians, 10 Stratford Place London W8 6QD, United Kingdom. Phone: 44 20 7629 4413 Fax: 44 20 7408 1583 E-mail: membership@ism.org Monthly. $60.00 per year.

Music Library Association Notes: Quarterly Journal of the Music Library Association. Music Library Association, 8551 Research Way, Suite 180 Middleton, WI 53562. Phone: (608)836-5825 E-mail: mla@areditions.com • URL: http://www.musiclibraryassoc.org • Quarterly. Individuals, $70.00 per year; institutions, $80.00 per year. Indexes record reviews (classical).

Music Reference Services Quarterly. Haworth Press, Inc., 10 Alice St. Binghamton, NY 13904-1580. Phone: 800-429-6784 or (607)722-5857 Fax: 800-895-0582 or (607)722-1424 E-mail: getinfo@haworthpressinc.com • URL: http://www.haworthpressinc.com • Quarterly. Institutions, $95.00 per year. An academic journal for music librarians.

Music Technology Buyer's Guide. United Entertainment Media, 460 Park Ave., S, 9th Fl. New York, NY 10016. Phone: (212)378-0400 Fax: (212)378-2160 E-mail: jhurley@uemedia.com • URL: http://www.uemedia.com • $6.95. Annual. Lists more than 4,000 hardware and software music production products from 350 manufacturers. Includes synthesizers, MIDI hardware and software, mixers, microphones, music notation software, etc. Produced by the editorial staffs of *Keyboard* and *EQ* magazines.

Music Trades. Music Trades Corp., c/o Paul Majeski, 80 West St. Englewood, NJ 07631. Phone: (201)871-1965 Monthly. $14.00 per year. Includes *Purchaser's Guide to the Music Industries*.

Musical America International Directory of the Performing Arts. Commonwealth Business Media, Inc., 400 Windsor Corporate Center, 50 Millstone Rd., Suite 200 East Windsor, NJ 08520-1415. Phone: 800-221-5488 or (609)371-7700 Fax: (609)371-7883 E-mail: customerservice@cbizmedia.com • URL: http://www.cbizmedia.com • Annual. $115.00. Covers United States and Canada.

Musical Merchandise Review: Directory of Musical Instrument Dealers. Larkin Publications LLC, 50 Brook Rd. Needham, MA 02494. Phone: 800-964-5150 or (781)453-9310 Fax: (781)453-9389 E-mail: mprescott@larkinpublications.com • URL: http://www.mmrmagazine.com • Annual. $125.00. Lists retailers of musical instruments and supplies.

Musical Merchandise Review: Music Industry Directory. Larkin Publications, 50 Brook Rd. Needham, MA 02494. Phone: 800-964-5150 or (781)453-9310 Fax: (781)453-9389 E-mail: mprescott@larkinpublications.com • URL: http://www.mmrmagazine.com • Annual. $25.00. Lists about 1,500 manufacturers and distributors of musical instruments and supplies. Includes indexes to products and trade names.

Musical Merchandise Review: Pianos, Musical Instruments, Organs, Accessories. Larkin Publications, Inc., 50 Brook Rd. Needham, MA 02494. Phone: 800-964-5150 or (781)453-9310 Fax: (781)453-9389 E-mail: mprescott@larkinpublications.com • URL: http://www.mmrmagazine.com • Monthly. $32.00 per year. Edited for musical instrument dealers selling pianos, organs, band/orchestra instruments, electronic keyboards, guitars, music amplifiers, microphones, sheet music, and other musical merchandise.

Mutual Atomic Energy Liability Underwriters., 330 N. Wabash, Ste. 2611 Chicago, IL 60611. Phone: (312)467-0003 Fax: (312)467-0774 E-mail: geobev@consolidated.net Underwriting syndicate of 4 mutual casualty insurance companies writing nuclear energy liability policies.

Mutual Fund Advisor: The Top Performing Mutual Funds. Mutual Fund Advisor, Inc., One Sarasota Tower, Suite 602, 2N Tamiami Trail Sarasota, FL 34236. Phone: (813)954-5500 Fax: (813)364-8447 Monthly. Price on application. Newsletter.

Mutual Fund Buyer's Guide: Performance Ratings, Five Year Projections, Safety Ratings, Sales. Norman G. Fosback. McGraw-Hill, 1221 Ave. of the Americas New York, NY 10020. Phone: 800-722-4726 or (212)512-2000 Fax: (212)512-4502 E-mail: customer.service@mcgraw-hill.com • URL: http://www.mcgraw-hill.com • 1994. $17.95.

Mutual Fund Education Alliance (The Association of No-Load Funds)., 100 N.W. Englewood Rd., No. 130 Kansas City, MO 64118. Phone: (816)454-9422 Fax: (816)454-9322 E-mail: mfeamail@mfea.com • URL: http://www.mea.com • Formerly No-Load Mutual Fund Association.

Mutual Fund Fact Book: Industry Trends and Statistics. Investment Company Institute, 1401 H St. N.W., Suite 1200 Washington, DC 20005-2148. Phone: (202)326-5800 Fax: (202)326-5985 E-mail: ici@ici.com • URL: http://www.ici.com • 1997. $25.00. 37th edition. Industry trends and statistics.

Mutual Fund Letter. Investment Information Services, Inc., 10 S Riverside Plaza, Suite 1520 Chicago, IL 60606-3802. Phone: 800-362-6941 or (312)649-6940 Fax: (312)649-5537 Monthly. $125.00 per year. Newsletter. Provides mutual fund recommendations.

Mutual Fund Market News. Dalbar Publishing Inc., Federal Reserve Plz., 30th Fl. Boston, MA 02210. Phone: 800-221-1809 or (617)723-6400 Fax: (212)843-9635 E-mail: ve.cs@tfn.com • URL: http://www.thomsonmedia.com • Description: Provides persons in the mutual fund industry with critical information, breaking news, industry developments, new product analyses, and changes in market share. Covers all major changes of distribution for mutual funds and related products, with emphasis on banks, broker/dealers, captive sales forces, corporate and nonprofit pensions, and direct markets. Recurring features include portfolio management strategies, letters to the editor, a calendar of events and conferences, reports of industry meetings, and columns titled Hot Off the Wire, On the Move, and Newly Registered Funds.

Mutual Fund Profiles. Standard & Poor's, 55 Water St. New York, NY 10041. Phone: 800-221-5277 or (212)438-1000 • URL: http://www.standardandpoors.com • Quarterly. $158.00 per year. Produced jointly with Lipper Analytical Services. Provides detailed information on approximately 800 of the largest stock funds and taxable bond funds. In addition, contains concise data on about 2,400 smaller funds and municipal bond funds.

Mutual Fund Strategies. Progressive Investing, Inc., P.O. Box 446 Burlington, VT 05402. Phone: (802)658-3515 Monthly. $127.00 per year. Newsletter.

Mutual Fund Trends. Growth Fund Research Inc., 409 Kansas City St., PO Box 6600 Rapid City, SD 57701. Phone: 800-621-8322 or (605)341-1971 Fax: (605)341-7260 E-mail: clientservices@moodys.com Description: Provides high quality semi-log charts with multiple moving averages and relative strength line on approximately 180 top performing funds. Statistics include lows to current time and high to low. Market indicators with good records. Includes weekly telephone hot line.

Mutual Funds Interactive. Brill Editorial Services, Inc.Phone: 877-442-7455 • URL: http://www.brill.com • Web site provides specific information on individual funds in addition to general advice on mutual fund investing and 401(k) plans. Searching is provided, including links to moderated newsgroups and a chat page. Fees: Free.

Mutual Funds Update. Thomson Financial, 195 Broadway New York, NY 10007. Phone: 800-262-6000 or (646)822-2000 Fax: (646)822-6270 E-mail: custserv@tfn.com • URL: http://www.tfn.com • Monthly. $325.00 per year. Provides recent performance information and statistics for approximately 10,000 mutual funds and closed-end funds as compiled from the CDA/Wiesenberger database. Includes commentary and analysis relating to the mutual fund industry. Information is provided on new funds, name changes, mergers, and liquidations.

My Little Salesman Heavy Equipment Catalog; New and Used Equipment Guide. My Little Salesman, 2898 Chad Dr. Eugene, OR 97401. Phone: 800-493-2295 Fax: (541)342-3307 • URL: http://www.mylittlesalesman.com • Monthly. $24.95 per year.

My Little Salesman Truck and Trailer Catalog. My Little Salesman, 2895 Chad Dr. Eugene, OR 97401. Phone: 800-493-2295 or (541)341-4650 Fax: (541)342-3307 • URL: http://www.mylittlesalesman.com • Monthly. $24.95 per year. Products serving the trucking industry. Central and Western editions.

N A S D Manual. National Association of Securities Dealers, Inc. CCH, Inc., 2700 Lake Cook Rd. Riverwoods, IL 60015. Phone: 800-525-3335 or (847)267-7000 Fax: (773)886-3095 E-mail: cust_serv@cch.com • URL: http://www.cch.com • Quarterly. $452.00 per year. CD-Rom, $459.00.

NABE News. National Association for Business Economics, 1233 20th St. NW, Ste. 505 Washington, DC 20036. Phone: (202)463-6223 Fax: (202)463-6239 E-mail: nabe@nabe.com • URL: http://www.nabe.com • Description: Concerned with business economics. Serves this professional Association of persons employed by private, institutional, or government concerns in the area of business-related economic analysis. Recurring features include results of the NABE quarterly outlook survey, featured articles of timely interest, reviews of seminars and annual meetings, news from local chapters and roundtables, and personal notes.

NACAC Bulletin. National Association for College Admission Counseling, 1631 Prince St. Alexandria, VA 22314-2818. Phone: 800-822-6285 or (703)836-2222 Fax: (703)836-8015 E-mail: nabe@nabe.com • URL: http://www.nacac.com • Description: Discusses college admissions counseling, financial aid, and legislation affecting these areas. Recurring features include statistics, book reviews, news of research, a calendar of events, news of members, and columns titled Perspective, NACACTION, Capitol Outlook, News Briefs, F.Y.I., and On the Move.

NACE Directory: Who's Who in Career Services and HR/Staffing t. National Association of Colleges and Employers, 62 Highland Ave. Bethlehem, PA 18017. Phone: 800-544-5272 or (610)868-1421 Fax: (610)868-0208 Annual. Free to members; non-members, $47.95. Lists over 2,200 college placement offices and about 2,000 companies interested in recruiting college graduates. Gives names of placement and recruitment personnel. Formerly *CPC National Directory*.

NACE International: The Corrosion Society., 1440 S Creek Dr. Houston, TX 77084-4906. Phone: 800-797-6223 or (281)228-6200 Fax: (281)228-6300 E-mail: firstservice@nace.org • URL: http://www.nace.org • Serves as professional technical society dedicated to reducing the economic impact of corrosion, promoting public safety, and protecting the environment by advancing the knowledge of corrosion engineering and science. Conducts programs for technical training, sponsors technical conferences, and produces standards, publications, and software. Maintains certification program for engineers, technicians, and coating inspectors.

NACE Salary Survey: A Study of Beginning Salary Offers. National Association of Colleges and Employers, 62 Highland Ave. Bethlehem, PA 18017. Phone: 800-544-5272 or (610)868-1421 Fax: (610)868-0208 • URL: http://www.naceweb.org • Quarterly. Free to members; non-members, $220.00 per year. Formerly *PC Salary Survey*. Formerly College Placement Council, Inc.

NACHA: The Electronic Payments Association., 13450 Sunrise Valley Dr., Ste. 100 Herndon, VA 20171. Phone: 800-487-9180 or (703)561-1100 Fax: (703)787-0996 E-mail: info@nacha.org • URL: http://www.nacha.org • Automated Clearing House (ACH) association. Provides an interregional exchange for electronic debits and credits among ACHs and to establish and administer nationwide standards and operating rules for ACHs. Conducts national seminars and conferences on ACH operations and products; sponsors annual Payments and Electronic Commerce Institute; sponsors Accredited ACH Professional (AAP) program. Sponsors national marketing campaign; compiles statistics.

NADA Appraisal Guides. National Automobile Dealers Association, 8400 Westpark Dr. McLean, VA 22102. Phone: (703)821-7000 Fax: (703)821-7075 E-mail: nadainfo@nada.org • URL: http://www.nada.org • Prices and frequencies vary. Guides to prices of used cars, old used cars, motorcycles, mobile homes, recreational vehicles, and mopeds.

NADA Marine Appraisal Guide. National Automobile Dealers Association. N.A.D.A. Appraisal Guides, P.O. Box 7800 Costa Mesa, CA 92628-7800. Phone: 800-966-6232 or (714)556-8511 Fax: (714)556-8715 Three times a year. $100.00 per year. Formerly *NADA Small Boat Appraisal Guide*.

NADA'S Automotive Executive. National Automobile Dealers Association, 8400 Westpark Dr. McLean, VA 22102. Phone: (703)821-7000 Fax: (703)821-7075 E-mail: nadainfo@nada.org • URL: http://www.nada.org • Monthly. $24.00 per year.

NAEDA Equipment Dealer. North American Equipment Dealers Association, 1195 Smizer Mill Rd. Fenton, MO 63026-3480. Phone: (636)349-5000 Fax: (636)349-5443 E-mail: naeda@naeda.com • URL: http://www.naeda.com • Monthly. $40.00 per year. Covers power equipment for farm, outdoor, and industrial use. Formerly *Farm and Power Equipment Dealer*.

NAEDA Equipment Dealer Buyer's Guide. North American Equipment Dealers Association, 1195 Smizer Mill Rd. Fenton, MO 63026-3480. Phone: (636)349-5000 Fax: (636)349-5443 E-mail: naeda@naeda.com • URL: http://www.naeda.com • Annual. $28.00. List of manufacturers and suppliers of agricultural, lawn and garden, and light industrial machinery.

NAFA Annual Reference Book. National Association of Fleet Administrators, 100 Wood Ave. Suite 310 Iselin, NJ 08830-2716. Phone: (732)494-8100 Fax: (732)494-6789 E-mail: jsyp@nafa.org Annual. $45.00. Automobile manufacturers' sales and leasing representatives throughout the country.

NAFSA: Association of International Educators., 1307 New York Ave., NW, 8th Fl. Washington, DC 20005-4701. Phone: (202)737-3699 Fax: (202)737-3657 E-mail: inbox@nafsa.org • URL: http://www.nafsa.org • Members are individuals, organizations, and institutions involved with international educational interchange, including foreign student advisors, overseas educational advisers, foreign student admission officers, and U. S. students abroad. Formerly National Association for Foreign Student Affairs.

NAFSA Newsletter. NAFSA: Association of International Educators, 1307 New York Ave. NW, 8th Fl. Washington, DC 20005-4701. Phone: 800-836-4994 or (202)737-3699 Fax: (202)737-3657 E-mail: inbox@nafsa.org • URL: http://www.nafsa.org • Description: Concerned with international educational interchange. Reports on English as a second language, foreign admissions, study abroad, foreign student advising, community programming, and other subjects. Recurring features include government news, book reviews, news of members, Association news, and columns titled News and Briefs and From the Front Lines of Advocacy.

NAFTA Revisited. C. V. Anderson, editor. Nova Science Publishers, Inc., 400 Oser Ave., Suite 1600 Hauppauge, NY 11788-3619. Phone: (631)231-7269 Fax: (631)231-8175 E-mail: novascience@earthlink.net • URL: http://www.novapublishers.com • 2002. $69.00. Provides articles by various authors on the status and economic effects of the North American Free Trade Agreement. Covers worker dislocation, environmental considerations, motor truck safety, Mexican trade policy, and other issues.

NAFTA Works for America: Administration Update on the North American Free Trade Agreement, 1993-1998. Available from U. S. Government Printing Office, Washington, DC 20402. Phone: (202)512-1800 Fax: (202)512-2250 E-mail: gpoaccess@gpo.gov • URL: http://www.access.gpo.gov • 1999. $7.00. Cover title: *Bridging into the 21st Century*. Issued by the Office of the U. S. Trade Representative, Executive Office of the President (http://www.ustr.gov). Summarizes the accomplishment of NAFTA over its first five years.

NAHRO Directory of Local Agencies and Resource Guide. NAHRO, 630 Eye St., N.W. Washington, DC 20001-3736. Phone: 877-866-2476 or (202)289-3500 Fax: (202)289-4961 E-mail: nahro@nahro.org • URL: http://www.nahro.org • 1995. Members, $85.00; non-members, $100.00. Formerly *Directory of Local Agencies: Housing, Community Development, Redevelopment*.

NAIC News. National Association of Insurance Commissioners, 2301 McGee St., No. 800 Kansas City, MO 64108-2604. Phone: (816)842-3600 • URL: http://www.naic.org • Monthly. $200.00 per year. Newsletter covering insurance legislation and regulation.

Naked in Cyberspace: How to Find Personal Information Online. Carole A. Lane. Information Today, Inc., 143 Old Marlton Pike Medford, NJ 08055-8750. Phone: 800-300-9868 or (609)654-6266 Fax: (609)654-4309 E-mail: custserv@infotoday.com • URL: http://www.infotoday.com • 2002. $29.95. Second edition. Covers the availability of personal records on the Internet, including competitive intelligence data, customer characteristics, employee information, backgrounds of experts, public records, criminal records, and genealogical data. From an opposite viewpoint, advice is offered relative to the maintenance of privacy. Includes a Web directory with about 1,000 sources of information. (CyberAge Books.)

NAMIC Magazine. National Association of Mutual Insurance Cos., 3601 Vincennes Rd. Indianapolis, IN 46268. Phone: 800-336-2642 or (317)875-5250 Fax: (317)879-8408 E-mail: webmaster@namic.org • URL: http://www.namic.org • Bimonthly. $18.00 per year. Formerly *Mutual Insurance Bulletin*.

NAMM, The International Music Products Association.

Nanofabrication Facility. Pennsylvania State University, 187 Materials Research Institute University Park, PA 16802-

7003. Phone: (814)863-0627 Fax: (814)865-7173 E-mail: nanofab.psu.edu • URL: http://www.nonafab.psu.edu • Formerly Electronic Materials and Processing Research Laboratory.

Narcotic Drugs: Estimated World Requirements. International Narcotics Control Board. United Nations Publications, United Nations Concourse Level, First Ave., 46th St. New York, NY 10017. Phone: 800-553-3210 or (212)963-7680 Fax: (212)963-4910 E-mail: bookstore@un.org • URL: http://www.un.org/publications • Annual. $38.00. Includes production and utilization data relating to legal narcotics. Text in French, English and Spanish.

Narcotics and Drug Abuse A to Z. Croner Publications, 10951 Sorrento Valley Rd., Suite 1-D San Diego, CA 92121-1613. Phone: 800-441-4033 or (619)546-1894 Fax: (619)546-1855 1990. Three volumes. Price on application. Lists treatment centers.

NARDA Independent Retailer. North American Retail Dealers Association, 10 E. 22nd St., Suite 310 Lombard, IL 60148-6191. Phone: (630)953-8950 Fax: (630)953-8957 E-mail: nardanews@aol.com Monthly. $78.00. Formerly *NARDA News*.

NARDA's Cost of Doing Business Survey. North American Retail Dealers Association, 10 E. 22nd St., Suite 310 Lombard, IL 60148-6191. Rhone: (630)953-8950 Fax: (630)953-8957 E-mail: nardahq@aol.com • URL: http://www.narda.com • Annual. $295.00.

NASDAQ-AMEX Market Group Fact Book. NASD Media-Source, P.O. Box 9403 Gaithersburg, MD 20890-9403. Phone: (301)590-6142 Fax: (240)386-4838 Annual. $20.00. Published by the American Stock Exchange, Inc. Contains statistical data relating to the American Stock Exchange. Also provides the address and phone number for each company listed on the Exchange. Formerly *American Stock Exchange Fact Book*.

Nasdaq Fact Book and Company Directory. National Association of Security Dealers, Inc. Corporate Communications, 1735 K St., N.W. Washington, DC 20006-1500. Phone: (202)728-6900 Fax: (202)728-8882 Annual. $20.00. Contains statistical data relating to the Nasdaq Stock Market. Also provides corporate address, phone, symbol, stock price, and trading volume information for more than 5,000 securities traded through the National Association of Securities Dealers Automated Quotation System (Nasdaq), including Small-Cap Issues. Includes indexing by Standard Industrial Classification (SIC) number.

National Academy of Arbitrators.

National Academy of Opticianry.

National Academy of Recording Arts and Sciences.

National Academy of Television Arts and Sciences.

National Accounts of OECD Countries. OECD Publications and Information Center, 2001 L St., N.W., Suite 650 Washington, DC 20036-4910. Phone: (202)785-6323 Fax: (202)785-0350 E-mail: washington.contact@oecd.org • URL: http://www.oecdwash.org • Annual. Two volumes. Price varies.

National Accounts Statistics: Main Aggregates and Detailed Tables. United Nations Publications, United Nations Concourse Level, First Ave., 46th St. New York, NY 10017. Phone: 800-553-3210 or (212)963-7680 Fax: (212)963-4910 E-mail: bookstore@un.org • URL: http://www.un.org/publications • Annual. $160.00.

National Advertising Review Board., 70 W 36th St., 13th Fl. New York, NY 10018. Phone: (866)334-6272 or (212)705-0114 E-mail: bhopewell@narc.bbb.org • URL: http://www.narbreview.org • Individuals from industry and the public. Sponsored by the National +Advertising +Review Council for the purpose of sustaining high standards of truth and accuracy in national advertising. Aims to maintain a self-regulatory mechanism that responds constructively to public complaints about national advertising and which significantly improves advertising performance and credibility.

National Aeronautic Association of the U.S.A.

National Agri-Marketing Association., 11020 King St., Ste. 205 Overland Park, KS 66210. Phone: (913)491-6500 Fax: (913)491-6502 E-mail: agrimktg@nama.org • URL: http://www.nama.org • Persons engaged in agricultural marketing for manufacturers, advertising agencies, and the media. Promotes the highest standards of agricultural marketing; provides for the exchange of ideas; encourages the study and better understanding of agricultural advertising, selling, and marketing; works to broaden understanding of the economic importance of agriculture; encourages careers in agricultural marketing. Provides agri-marketing short courses.

National Air Carrier Association., 1000 Wilson Blvd., Ste. 1700 Arlington, VA 22209. Phone: (703)358-8060 Fax: (703)358-8070 E-mail: tzoeller@naca.cc • URL: http://www.naca.cc • Represents U.S. certificated airlines specializing in low-cost scheduled and air charter operations. Assists members in the promotion of air transportation and serves as a liaison between members and U.S. government bodies that regulate air transportation.

National Air Transportation Association., 4226 King St. Alexandria, VA 22302. Phone: 800-808-6282 or (703)845-9000 Fax: (703)845-8176 E-mail: enews@nata.aero • URL: http://www.nata.aero • Represents the interests of aviation businesses nationwide. Provides vital aviation services to the airlines, the military, and business/corporate/individual aircraft owners and operators; services includes fueling, maintenance, and flight instruction.

National Air Transportation Association Official Membership Directory. National Air Transportation Association, 4226 King St. Alexandria, VA 22302. Phone: 800-808-6282 or (703)845-9000 Fax: (703)845-8176 Annual. $95.00. List more than 1,000 regular, associate, and affliate members; regular members include airport service organizations, air taxi operators, and commuter airlines.

National Alcohol Beverage Control Association., 4401 Ford Ave., Ste. 700 Alexandria, VA 22302-1473. Phone: (703)578-4200 Fax: (703)820-3551 E-mail: info@nabca.org • URL: http://www.nabca.org • State agencies controlling the purchase, distribution, and sale of alcoholic beverages under the control system; distillery firms and trade associations are associate members.

National Antique and Art Dealers Association of America.

National Antique and Art Dealers Association of America Membership Directory. National Antique and Art Dealers Association of America, 202 E. 57th St. New York, NY 10022. Phone: (212)826-9707 Fax: (212)832-9493 Annual. Price on application. Provides a list of 46 members and their areas of specialization in the decorative arts.

National Apartment Association., 4300 Wilson Blvd., Ste. 400 Arlington, VA 22203-4168. Phone: (703)518-6141 Fax: (703)248-9440 E-mail: webmaster@naahq.com • URL: http://www.naahq.org • Federation of 155 state and local associations of industry professionals engaged in all aspects of the multifamily housing industry, including owners, builders, investors, developers, managers, and allied service representatives. Provides education and certification for property management executives, on-site property managers, maintenance personnel, property supervisors, and leasing agents. Offers a nationwide legislative network concerned with governmental decisions at the federal, state, and local levels.

National Appliance Parts Suppliers Association., 4015 W Marshall Ave., PO Box 87907 Longview, TX 75604-4916. Phone: 888-309-9676 or (903)759-3983 Fax: (360)834-3507 E-mail: info@napsaweb.org • URL: http://www.napsaweb.org • Wholesale distributors of replacement parts for major home appliance. Promotes and supports good relations among groups in the supply and distribution of appliance service parts. Sponsors Young +Executives Society of NAPSA to prepare younger generations for leadership in the appliance parts wholesale and distribution industry, and to handle problems characteristic of family businesses.

National Appliance Service Association., PO Box 2514 Kokomo, IN 46904. Phone: (765)453-1820 Fax: (765)453-1895 E-mail: nasahq@sbcglobal.net • URL: http://www.nasa1.org • Owners of factory-authorized portable appliance repair centers servicing small electrical appliances and commercial food equipment. Promotes the interests and welfare of the commercial-domestic appliance service industry.

National Architectural Accrediting Board., 1735 New York Ave. NW Washington, DC 20006. Phone: (202)783-2007 Fax: (202)783-2822 E-mail: info@naab.org • URL: http://www.naab.org • Formed by the American Institute of Architects, Association of Collegiate Schools of Architecture, and National Council of Architectural Registration Boards (see separate entries) to stimulate the improvement of architectural education. Conducts continuing program of accreditation of programs of architecture. Compiles statistics; maintains library of 100 volumes of descriptions and self-evaluations of architecture schools.

National Asphalt Pavement Association., 5100 Forbes Blvd., 5100 Forbes Blvd. Lanham, MD 20706. Phone: 888-468-6499 or (301)731-4748 or (301)731-4748 Fax: (301)731-4621 E-mail: mcervarich@hotmix.org • URL: http://www.hotmix.org • Manufacturers and producers of scientifically proportioned Hot Mix Asphalt for use in all paving, including highways, airfields, and environmental usages. Membership includes hot mix producers, paving contractors, equipment manufacturers, engineering consultants, and others. Supports research and publishes information on: producing, stockpiling, and feeding of the aggregate to the manufacturing facility; drying; methods of screening, storing, and proportioning in the manufacturing facility; production of the hot mix asphalt; transporting mix to paver; lay down procedure and rolling; general workmanship; and related construction practices and materials. Commits to product quality, environmental control, safety and health, and energy conservation. Conducts training programs on a variety of technical and managerial topics for industry personnel. Maintains speakers' bureau and Hot Mix Asphalt Hall of Fame.

National Association for Business Economics., 1233 20th St., N.W., Suite 505 Washington, DC 20036. Phone: (202)463-6223 Fax: (202)463-6239 E-mail: nabe@nabe.com • URL: http://www.nabe.com • Formerly National Association of Business Economists.

National Association for Business Economics Membership Directory. National Association for Business Economics, 1233 20th St., N.W., Suite 505 Washington, DC 20036-2304. Phone: (202)463-6223 Fax: (202)463-6239 E-mail: nabe@nabe.com • URL: http://www.nabe.com • Annual. Membership.

National Association for College Admission Counseling., 1631 Prince St. Alexandria, VA 22314-2818. Phone: 800-822-6285 or (703)836-2222 Fax: (703)836-8015 E-mail: info@nacac.com • URL: http://www.nacac.com • Formerly National Association of College Admissions Counselors.

National Association for Court Management.

National Association for Equal Opportunity in Higher Education.

National Association for Female Executives.

National Association for Home Care., 228 Seventh St., S.E. Washington, DC 20003. Phone: (202)547-7424 Fax: (202)547-3540 E-mail: exec@nahc.org • URL: http://www.nahc.org • Promotes high standards of patient care in home care services. Members are durable medical providers, medical equipment and oxygen suppliers, mainly for home health care.

National Association for Industry-Education Cooperation.

National Association for Printing Leadership., 75 W. Century Rd. Paramus, NJ 07652-1408. Phone: 800-642-6275 or (201)634-9600 Fax: (201)634-0325 E-mail: info@napl.org • URL: http://www.napl.org • Text: Formerly National Association of Printers and Lithographers.

National Association for Public Health Statistics and Information Systems., 801 Roeder Rd., Ste. 650 Silver Spring, MD 20910. Phone: (301)563-6001 Fax: (301)563-6012 E-mail: hq@napshsis.org • URL: http://www.naphsis.org • Members are officials of state and local health agencies.

National Association for Surface Finishing., 1155 15th St. NW, Ste. 500 Washington, DC 20005. Phone: (202)457-8404 Fax: (202)530-0659 E-mail: jflatley@nasf.org • URL: http://www.nasf.org • Companies manufacturing metal finishing equipment, materials, and processes, including basic metals, chemicals, and compounds; suppliers of services for metal finishing of all types; distributors. Sponsors metal finishing clinics for industrial groups; promotes the use of established standards to acquaint buyers of plated and finished products with the means of specifying a high-quality finish.

National Association for the Advancement of Colored People.

National Association for the Self-Employed., DFW Airport, P.O. Box 612067 Dallas, TX 75261-2067. Phone: 800-232-6273 Fax: 800-551-4446 • URL: http://www.nase.org • Members are very small businesses and the self-employed. Acts as an advocacy group at the state and federal levels.

National Association for the Specialty Food Trade., 120 Wall St., 27th Fl. New York, NY 10005-4001. Phone: (212)482-6440 Fax: (212)482-6459 E-mail: catalog@fancyfoodshows.com • URL: http://www.fancyfoodshows.com • Members are manufacturers, processors, importers, retailers, and brokers of specialty and gourmet food items.

National Association for Uniformed Services., 5535 Hempstead Way Springfield, VA 22151-4094. Phone: 800-842-3451 or (703)750-1342 Fax: (703)354-4380 E-mail: info@naus.org • URL: http://www.naus.org • Members of the uniformed military services, active, retired or reserve, veteran, enlisted and officers, and their spouses or widows. Develops and supports legislation that upholds the security of the U.S., sustains the morale of the uniformed services, and provides fair and equitable consideration for all service people. Protects and improves compensation, entitlements, and benefits. Provides discount rates on travel, insurance, auto rentals, charge cards, prescription medicine, and legal services.

National Association of Aluminum Distributors.

National Association of Attorneys General.

National Association of Black Owned Broadcasters.

National Association of Boards of Pharmacy.

National Association of Broadcasters., 1771 N St., NW Washington, DC 20036. Phone: (202)429-5300 Fax: (202)429-4199 E-mail: sdelanghe@nab.org • URL: http://www.nab.org • Formerly National Association of Radio and Television Broadcasters.

National Association of Business Political Action Committees., 101 Constitution Ave. NW, Ste. 800-West Washington, DC 20001. Phone: (202)341-3780 Fax: (202)478-0342 E-mail: nabpac@nabpac.org • URL: http://www.nabpac.org • Political action professionals and government affairs representatives interested in campaign finance reform issues and innovations in political action committee management.

National Association of Business Travel Agents., 3699 Wilshire Blvd., Ste. 700 Los Angeles, CA 90010. Phone: (213)382-3335 Fax: (213)480-7712 E-mail: sjfaber@earthlink.net Members specialize in corporate and business travel services.

National Association of Chain Drug Stores.

National Association of Chain Drug Stores - Communications Directory. National Association of Chain Drug Stores, 413 N Lee St. Alexandria, VA 22313-1480. Phone: (703)549-3001 Fax: (703)836-4869 • URL: http://www.nacds.org • Annual. Membership. About 150 chain drug retailers and their 31,000 individual pharmacies; 900 supplier companies; state boards of pharmacy, pharmaceutical and retail associations, colleges of pharmacy; drug trade associations.

National Association of Chemical Distributors.

National Association of College Auxiliary Services., Seven Boar's Head Lane Charlottesville, VA 22903-4610. Phone: (434)245-8425 Fax: (434)245-8453 E-mail: info@nacas.org • URL: http://www.nacas.org • Formerly Association of College Auxiliary Services.

National Association of College Stores., 500 E Lorain St. Oberlin, OH 44074. Phone: 800-622-7498 or (440)775-7777 Fax: (440)775-4769 E-mail: info@nacs.org • URL: http://www.nacs.org • Formerly College Bookstore Association.

National Association of Concessionaires., 35 E. Wacker Dr., Suite 1816 Chicago, IL 60601. Phone: (312)236-3858 Fax:

(312)236-7809 E-mail: info@naconline.org • URL: http://www.naconline.org • Formerly Popcorn and Concessions Association.

National Association of Consumer Credit Administrators., PO Box 20871 Columbus, OH 43220-0871. Phone: (614)326-1165 Fax: (614)326-1162 • URL: http://www.naccaonline.org • State government officials who administer consumer finance laws in the United States, Guam, Puerto Rico and Canada.

National Association of Container Distributors.

National Association of Convenience Stores., 1605 King St. Alexandria, VA 22314-2792. Phone: 800-966-6227 or (703)684-3600 Fax: (703)836-4564 E-mail: bremoyer@nacsonline.com • URL: http://www.nacsonline.com • Members are small retail stores that sell a variety of food and nonfood items and that usually have extended hours of opening.

National Association of Corporate Directors.

National Association of Corporate Treasurers., 11250 Roger Bacon Dr., Ste. 8 Reston, VA 20190-5202. Phone: (703)318-4227 Fax: (703)435-4390 E-mail: nact@nact.org • URL: http://www.nact.org • Members are corporate financial executives.

National Association of Counties., 440 First St., N.W., Ste. 800 Washington, DC 20001. Phone: (202)393-6226 or (202)942-4287 Fax: (202)393-2630 E-mail: tgoodman@naco.org • URL: http://www.naco.org • Formerly National Association of County Human Services Administrators.

National Association of County Park and Recreation Officials.

National Association of County Planners., c/o National Association of Counties, 440 First St., N.W., 8th Fl. Washington, DC 20001. Phone: (202)661-8807 or (202)942-4276 Fax: (202)737-0480 E-mail: jdavenpo@naco.org • URL: http://www.naco.org • Formerly National Association of County Planning Directors.

National Association of County Treasurers and Finance Officers.

National Association of Credit Management., 8815 Columbia, 100 Pky. Columbia, MD 21045-2158. Phone: 800-955-8815 or (410)740-5560 Fax: (410)740-5574 E-mail: nacm_info@nacm.org • URL: http://www.nacm.org • Formerly National Institute of Credit.

National Association of Criminal Defense Lawyers., 1150 18th St., N.W., Suite 950 Washington, DC 20036. Phone: (202)872-8600 Fax: (202)872-8690 E-mail: assist@nacdl.com • URL: http://www.criminaljustice.org • Formerly National Association of Defense Lawyers in Criminal Cases.

National Association of Decorative Fabric Distributors., 3008 Millwood Ave. Columbia, SC 29205. Phone: 800-445-8629 Fax: (803)765-0860 E-mail: info@nadfd.com • URL: http://www.nadfd.com • Formerly National Association of Upholstery Fabric Distributors.

National Association of Display Industries.

National Association of Elevator Contractors.

National Association of Environmental Professionals.

National Association of Export Companies.

National Association of Federal Credit Unions.

National Association of Flavors and Food Ingredient Systems., 3301 Rte. 66, Ste. 205, Bldg. C Neptune, NJ 07753. Phone: (732)922-3218 Fax: (732)922-3590 E-mail: info@naffs.org • URL: http://www.naffs.org • Manufacturers of fruit and syrup toppings, flavors and stabilizers for the food industry. Formerly National Association of Fruits, Flavors and Syrups.

National Association of Flight Instructors. EAA Aviation Center

National Association of Flour Distributors., c/o David Scruggs, P.O. Box 165067 Little Rock, AR 72216. Phone: (501)372-0636 Fax: (501)372-2468 Affiliated with National Association of Wholesaler-Distributors.

National Association of Government Employees., 159 Burgin Parkway Quincy, MA 02169-4213. Phone: (617)376-0220 Fax: (617)376-0285 • URL: http://www.nage.org • Supersedes Federal Employees Veterans Association.

National Association of Health Underwriters., 200 N. 14th St., Suite. 450 Arlington, VA 22201. Phone: (703)276-0220 Fax: (703)841-7797 E-mail: info@nahu.org • URL: http://www.nahu.org • Members are engaged in the sale of health and disability insurance. Formerly International Association of Health Underwriters.

National Association of Home Based Businesses., 10451 Mill Run Cir., Ste. 400 Owing Mills, MD 21117. Phone: (410)363-3698 E-mail: nahbb@msn.com • URL: http://www.usahomebusiness.com • Affiliated with International Association for Business Organizations and the Small Business Network.

National Association of Home Builders., 1201 15th St., N.W. Washington, DC 20005. Phone: 800-368-5242 or (202)266-8200 • URL: http://www.nahb.com • Members are single and multifamily home builders, commercial builders and others associated with the building industry.

National Association of Home Builders Research Center.

National Association of Housing and Redevelopment Officials., 630 Eye St., N.W. Washington, DC 20001. Phone: 877-866-2476 or (202)289-3500 Fax: (202)289-8181 E-mail: nahro@nahro.org • URL: http://www.nahro.org • Formerly National Association of Housing Officials.

National Association of Independent Insurers.

National Association of Independent Schools.

National Association of Industrial and Office Properties., 2201 Cooperative Way, 3rd Fl. Herndon, VA 20171. Phone: 800-666-6780 or (703)904-7100 Fax: (703)904-7942 E-mail: naiop@naiop.org • URL: http://www.naiop.org • Members are owners and developers of business, industrial, office, and retail properties. Formerly NAIOP - The Association of Commercial Real Estate.

National Association of Institutional Linen Management., 2130 Lexington Rd., Suite H Richmond, KY 40475. Phone: 800-669-0863 or (859)624-0177 Fax: (859)624-3580 E-mail: linda@nlmnet.org • URL: http://www.nlmnet.org • Formerly National Assoiciation of Institutional Laundry Managers.

National Association of Institutional Linen Management Membership Directory. National Association of Institutional Linen Management, 2130 Lexington Rd., Suite H Richmond, KY 40475. Phone: 800-669-0863 or (859)624-0177 Fax: (859)624-3580 • URL: http://www.nlmnet.org • Annual. $100.00. Lists managers of in-house laundries for institutions, hotels, schools, etc.

National Association of Insurance and Financial Advisors., 2901 Telestar Court Falls Church, VA 22042-1205. Phone: 877-866-2432 or (703)770-8100 Fax: (703)770-8142 E-mail: membersupport@naifa.org • URL: http://www.naifa.org • Affiliated with Association for Advanced Life Underwriting. Formerly National Association of Life Underwriters.

National Association of Insurance Commissioners., 2301 McGee St., Ste. 800 Kansas City, MO 64108-2604. Phone: (816)842-3600 Fax: (816)783-8175 E-mail: pubdist@naic.org • URL: http://www.naic.org • Members are state officials involved in the regulation of insurance companies. Formerly National Convention of Insurance Commissioners.

National Association of Insurance Women International., 1847 E 15th St. Tulsa, OK 74104. Phone: 800-766-6249 Fax: (918)743-1968 E-mail: joinnaiw@naiw.org • URL: http://www.naiw.org • Formerly Nationl Assoiciation of Insurance Women.

National Association of Investment Companies., 1300 Pennsylvania Ave., N.W., Suite 700 Washington, DC 20004. Phone: (202)289-4336 Fax: (202)289-4329 Formerly American Association of Minority Enterprise Small Business Investment Companies.

National Association of Investors Corporation., P.O. Box 220 Royal Oak, MI 48068. Phone: 877-275-6242 or (248)583-6242 Fax: (248)583-4880 E-mail: service@better-investing.org • URL: http://www.better-investing.org • Affiliated with Investment Education Institute. Formerly National Association of Investment Clubs.

National Association of Manufacturers.

National Association of Margarine Manufacturers.

National Association of Marine Services., 5458 Wagon Master Dr. Colorado Springs, CO 80917. Phone: (719)573-5946 Fax: (719)573-5952 E-mail: nams@namsshipchandler.com • URL: http://www.namsshipchandler.com • Affiliated with International Ship Suppliers Association. Formerly National Associated Marine Suppliers.

National Association of Metal Finishers., 21165 Whitfield Pl., Ste. 105 Potomac Falls, VA 20165. Phone: (703)433-2522 Fax: (703)433-0369 E-mail: namf@erols.com • URL: http://www.namf.org • Members are management personnel of metal and plastic finishing companies. Finishing includes plating, coating, polishing, rustproofing, and other processes.

National Association of Mutual Insurance Companies., 3601 Vincennes Rd. Indianapolis, IN 46268. Phone: 800-336-2642 or (317)875-5250 Fax: (317)879-8408 E-mail: services@naminc.org • URL: http://www.namic.org • Affiliated with Crop Insurance Research Bureau and the Insurance Loss Control Association.

National Association of Off-Track Betting.

National Association of Optometrists and Opticians., P.O. Box 479 Marblehead, OH 43440. Phone: (419)798-4071 or (419)798-2031 Fax: (419)798-8548 E-mail: fdrozak@cros.net Formerly National Optical Association.

National Association of Parliamentarians.

National Association of Personal Financial Advisors., 3250 N Arlington Heights Rd., Ste. 109 Arlington Heights, IL 60004. Phone: 800-366-2732 or (847)483-5400 or 888-333-6659 Fax: (847)483-5415 E-mail: info@napfa.org • URL: http://www.napfa.org • Members are full-time financial planners who are compensated on a fee-only basis.

National Association of Personnel Services., 10905 Fort Washington Rd., Ste. 400 Fort Washington, MD 20744. Phone: (301)203-6700 Fax: (301)203-4346 E-mail: conrad.taylor@recrutinglife.com • URL: http://www.napsweb.org • Members are private employment agencies. Formerly National Association of Personnel Consultants.

National Association of Photo Equipment Technicians., 3000 Picture Place Jackson, MI 49201. Phone: (517)788-8100 Fax: (517)788-8371 • URL: http://www.pmai.org • Affiliated with Photo Marketing Association International.

National Association of Pizzaria Operators., PO Box 2132 New Albany, NY 47151. Phone: 800-489-8324 or (216)766-5710 E-mail: webmaster@napa.com • URL: http://www.napo.com • Members are pizza establishment operators, food suppliers, and equipment manufacturers. Affiliated with American Society of Association Executives, Meeting Professionals International and National Restaurant Association.

National Association of Power Engineers.

National Association of Printing Ink Manufacturers., 581 Main St. Woodbridge, NJ 07095-1104. Phone: (732)855-1525 Fax: (732)855-1838 E-mail: napim@napim.org • URL: http://www.napim.org • Formerly National Association of Printing Ink Makers.

National Association of Produce Market Managers.

National Association of Professional Insurance Agents., 400 N. Washington St. Alexandria, VA 22314. Phone: (703)836-9340 Fax: (703)836-1279 E-mail: piaweb@pianet.org • URL: http://www.pianet.com • Members are independent agents in various fields of insurance. Formerly National Association of Mutual Insurance Agents.

National Association of Professional Organizers., 4700 W Lake Ave. Glenview, IL 60025. Phone: (847)375-4746 Fax: (847)734-9236 E-mail: hq@napo.net • URL: http://www.napo.net • Members are concerned with time management, productivity, and the efficient organization of documents and activities. Formerly Association of Professional Organizers.

National Association of Psychiatric Health System., 325 Seventh St., N.W., Ste. 625 Washington, DC 20004-2802. Phone: (202)393-6700 Fax: (202)783-6041 E-mail: naphs@naphs.org • URL: http://www.naphs.org • Formerly National Association of Private Psychiatric Hospitals.

National Association of Quick Printers., 2250 E Devon Ave., Ste. 302 Des Plaines, IL 60018. Phone: 800-234-0040 or (847)298-8680 Fax: (847)298-8705 E-mail: info@naqp.com • URL: http://www.naqp.com • Independent printers and printing franchise businesses; industry suppliers. Seeks to bring recognition, improved quality, and increased profits to the entire quick printing field. Provides services to members; works to advance the collective interests of the printing industries at the national and international levels.

National Association of Railroad Passengers.

National Association of Railway Business Women., 757 Aldro Rd. Hudson, WI 54016-7826. E-mail: narbwinfo@narbw.org • URL: http://www.narbw.org • Formerly Railway Business Women's Association.

National Association of Real Estate Appraisers.

National Association of Real Estate Brokers.

National Association of Real Estate Investment Trusts., 1875 Eye St., N.W. Washington, DC 20006. Phone: 800-362-7348 or (202)739-9400 Fax: (202)739-9401 E-mail: info@nareit.org • URL: http://www.nareit.com • Formerly National Association of Real Estste Investment Funds.

National Association of Realtors.

National Association of Recording Merchandisers.

National Association of Regulatory Utility Commissioners., 1101 Vermont Ave., N.W., Ste. 200 Washington, DC 20005. Phone: (202)898-2200 Fax: (202)898-2213 E-mail: cgray@naruc.com • URL: http://www.naruc.com • Formerly National Association of Railway and Utility Commissioners.

National Association of Retired Federal Employees., 606 N. Washington St. Alexandria, VA 22314-1914. Phone: 800-627-3394 or (703)838-7760 Fax: (703)838-7785 E-mail: hq@narfe.org • URL: http://www.narfe.org • Formerly National Association of Retired Civil Employees.

National Association of Rocketry., P.O. Box 177 Altoona, WI 54720. Phone: 800-262-4872 or (715)832-1946 Fax: (715)832-6432 E-mail: nar-hq@nar.org • URL: http://www.nar.org • Model rockets. Formerly Model Missile Association.

National Association of RV Parks and Campgrounds., 113 Park Ave. Falls Church, VA 22046. Phone: (703)241-8801 Fax: (703)241-1004 E-mail: lprofaizer@arvc.org • URL: http://www.arvc.org • Formerly National Campground Owners Association.

National Association of Securities Dealers (NASD)., 1735 K St., N.W. Washington, DC 20006-1506. Phone: (202)728-8000 Fax: (202)293-6260 E-mail: waltere@nasd.com • URL: http://www.nasd.com • Formerly National Association of Securities Dealers.

National Association of Service Managers., 12603 224th Ave., P.M.B., No. 17 Bristol, WI 53104. Phone: (262)857-7227 Fax: (262)857-1127 E-mail: vince@nasm.com • URL: http://www.nasm.com • Absorbed Service Managers of America.

National Association of Small Business Investment Companies., 666 11th St., N.W., No. 750 Washington, DC 20001. Phone: (202)628-5055 Fax: (202)628-5080 E-mail: nasbic@nasbic.org • URL: http://www.nasbic.org • Affiliated with Small Business Legislative Council.

National Association of Sporting Goods Wholesalers.

National Association of State Aviation Officials.

National Association of State Boards of Accountancy., 150 Fourth Ave., N., Suite. 00 Nashville, TN 37219. Phone: (615)880-4200 Fax: (615)880-4290 E-mail: communications@nasba.org • URL: http://www.nasba.org • Formerly Association of Certified Public Accountants.

National Association of State Budget Officers.

National Association of State Charity Officials., c/o Daniel Moore, Office of Attorney General, P.O. Drawer 1508 Santa Fe, NM 87504. Phone: (505)827-6693 • URL: http://www.nasconet.org • Members are state officials responsible for the administration of charitable solicitation laws.

National Association of State Departments of Agriculture.

National Association of State Development Agencies., 12884 Harbor Dr. Woodbridge, VA 22192. Phone: (703)490-6777 Fax: (703)492-4404 E-mail: spope@nasda.com • URL: http://www.nasda.com • Formerly Association of State Planning and Development Agencies.

National Association of State Directors of Veterans Affairs.

National Association of State Mental Health Program Directors.

National Association of State Procurement Officials., c/o Association Management Resources, 167 W. Main St., Suite 600 Lexington, KY 40507. Phone: (859)231-1877 or (606)231-1963 Fax: (859)514-9188 E-mail: msisler@amrinc.net • URL: http://www.naspo.org • Purchasing officials of the states and territories. Formerly National Association of State Purchasing Officials.

National Association of State Supervisors of Trade and Industrial Education.

National Association of Student Financial Aid Administrators., 1129 20th St., N.W., Suite 400 Washington, DC 20036-5020. Phone: (202)785-0453 Fax: (202)785-1487 E-mail: ask@nasfaa.org • URL: http://www.nsfaa.org • Serves as a national forum for matters related to student aid.

National Association of Superintendents of U.S. Naval Shore Establishments., 89 Pine Legde Dr. Wells, ME 04090. Phone: (207)646-7316 E-mail: admin@nasnse.org • URL: http://nasnse.org • Superintendents of production, maintenance, and public works branches of naval shore establishments. Promotes the general welfare of members professionally, intellectually, and socially; cultivates high standards of professional ethics.

National Association of Swine Records.

National Association of Tax Professionals., 720 Association Dr. Appleton, WI 54914. Phone: 800-558-3402 or (920)749-1040 Fax: 800-747-0001 E-mail: natp@natptax.com • URL: http://www.natptax.com • Promotes high professional standards for tax practitioners. Formerly National Association for Tax Practitioners.

National Association of Television Program Executives., 2425 Olympic Blvd., Suite 600E Santa Monica, CA 90404. Phone: 800-628-7346 or (310)453-4440 Fax: (310)453-5258 E-mail: info@natpe.org • URL: http://www.natpe.org • Formerly National Association of Television Program Executives.

National Association of the Physically Handicapped.

National Association of the Remodeling Industry.

National Association of Theatre Owners.

National Association of Towns and Townships., 444 N Capitol St. NW, Ste. 397 Washington, DC 20001-1202. Phone: (202)624-3550 Fax: (202)625-3554 E-mail: natat@sos.org • URL: http://www.natat.org • Provides technical and other assistance to officials of small communities. Absorbed National Association of Smaller Communities.

National Association of Uniform Manufacturers and Distributors., 1156 Ave. of the Americas, Room 700 New York, NY 10036. Phone: (212)869-0670 Fax: (212)575-2847 E-mail: nyoffice@naumd.com • URL: http://www.naumd.com • Formerly Uniform Manufacturers Exchange.

National Association of Video Distributors., 700 Frederica St., Suite 205 Owensboro, KY 42301. Phone: (270)926-6002 Fax: (270)685-6080 Members are wholesalers of home video software, both tapes and discs.

National Association of Waterfront Employers., 2011 Pennsylvania Ave., N.W., Suite 301 Washington, DC 20006. Phone: (202)296-2810 Fax: (202)331-7479 Formerly National Association of Stevedoves.

National Association of Wheat Growers.

National Association of Wholesaler-Distributors., 1725 K St., N.W., Ste. 00 Washington, DC 20006. Phone: (202)872-0885 Fax: (202)785-0586 E-mail: naw@nawd.org • URL: http://www.naw.org • Formerly National Association of Wholesalers.

National Association of Women Artists, Inc., NAWA Fifth Avenue Gallery, 80 5th Ave., Ste. 1405 New York, NY 10011. Phone: (212)675-1616 Fax: (212)675-8257 E-mail: nawomena@msn.com • URL: http://www.nawanet.org • Formerly Women's Art Club of the City of New York.

National Association of Women Business Owners., 8405 Greensboro Dr., Ste. 800 McLean, VA 22102. Phone: 800-556-2926 or (703)506-3268 Fax: (703)506-3266 E-mail: national@nawbo.org • URL: http://www.nawbo.org • Formerly Association of Women Business Owners.

National Association of Women In Construction.

National Association of Women Lawyers.

National Association of Women Lawyers. President's Newsletter. National Association of Women Lawyers, American Bar Center, MS 124, 750 N. Lake Shore Dr. Chicago, IL 60611. Phone: (312)988-6186 Fax: (312)988-6281 E-mail: nawl@staff.abanet.org • URL: http://www.abanet.org/nawl • Quarterly. Newsletter. Price on application.

National Auctioneers Association., 8880 Ballentine Overland Park, KS 66214. Phone: (913)541-8084 Fax: (913)894-5281 E-mail: info@auctioneers.org • URL: http://www.auctioneers.org • Professional auctioneers. Provides continuing education classes for auctioneers, promotes use of the auction method of marketing in both the private and public sectors. Encourages the highest ethical standards for the profession.

National Auto Auction Association., 5320 Spectrum Dr., Ste. D Frederick, MD 21703. Phone: (301)696-0400 Fax: (301)631-1359 E-mail: naaa@naaa.com • URL: http://www.naaa.com • Owners/operators of wholesale automobile and truck auctions; associate members are car and truck manufacturers, insurers of checks and titles, car and truck rental companies, publishers of auto price guide books, and others connected with the industry. Maintains hall of fame.

National Automatic Merchandising Association., 20 N Wacker Dr., Ste. 3500 Chicago, IL 60606-3102. Phone: 888-337-VEND or (312)346-0370 Fax: (312)704-4140 E-mail: rgeerdes@vending.org • URL: http://www.vending.org • Manufacturing and operating companies in the automatic vending machine industry; food service management firms; office coffee machine operators; suppliers of products and services. Compiles industry statistics.

National Automatic Merchandising Association-Directory of Members. National Automatic Merchandising Association, 20 N. Wacker Dr., Suite 3500 Chicago, IL 60606. Phone: 888-337-8363 or (312)346-0370 Fax: (312)704-4140 E-mail: sdegrave@vending.org • URL: http://www.vending.org • Annual. $150.00. Lists 2,300 vending and food service management firms, along with vending machine manufacturers and distributors and producers of other equipment and food items.

National Automobile Dealers Association., 8400 Westpark Dr. McLean, VA 22102. Phone: 800-252-6232 or (703)821-7000 Fax: (703)821-7075 E-mail: nadainfo@nada.org • URL: http://www.nada.org • Franchised new car and truck dealers. Provides representation for franchised new car and truck dealers in the areas of government, industry, and public affairs. Offers management services and retirement and insurance programs to member dealers. Maintains National +Automobile +Dealers Charitable Foundation.

National Bankers Association., 1513 P St. NW Washington, DC 20005. Phone: (202)588-5432 Fax: (202)588-5443 E-mail: nahart@nationalbankers.org • URL: http://www.nationalbankers.org • Minority banking institutions owned by minority individuals and institutions. Serves as an advocate for the minority banking industry. Organizes banking services, government relations, marketing, scholarship, and technical assistance programs. Offers placement services; compiles statistics.

National Beauty Culturists' League., 25 Logan Cir. NW Washington, DC 20005-3725. Phone: (202)332-2695 Fax: (202)332-0940 E-mail: nbcl@bellsouth.net • URL: http://www.nbcl.org • Beauticians, cosmetologists, and beauty products manufacturers. Encourages standardized, scientific, and approved methods of hair, scalp, and skin treatments. Offers scholarships and plans to establish a research center. Sponsors: National Institute of +Cosmetology, a training course in operating and designing and business techniques. Maintains hall of fame; conducts research program.

National Beer Wholesalers Association., 1101 King St., Ste. 600 Alexandria, VA 22314-2944. Phone: 800-300-6417 or (703)683-4300 Fax: (703)683-8965 E-mail: info@nbwa.org • URL: http://www.nbwa.org • Independent wholesalers of malt beverages and affiliates of the malt beverage industry. Conducts specialized education programs.

National Bicycle Dealers Association., 777 W 19th St., Ste. O Costa Mesa, CA 92627. Phone: (949)722-6909 Fax: (949)722-1747 E-mail: info@nbda.com • URL: http://www.nbda.com • Represents independent retail dealers who sell and service bicycles. Sponsors workshops and provides programs.

National Bond Summary. Pink Sheets LLC, 304 Hudson St., 2nd Fl. New York, NY 10013. Phone: 800-732-7868 or (212)896-4400 Fax: (212)868-3848 E-mail: info@pinksheets.com • URL: http://www.pinksheets.com • Monthly, with semiannual cumulations. $504.00 per year. Includes price quotes for both active and inactive issues, with transfer agents, market makers (brokers), capital changes, name changes, and other corporate information. Formerly published by the National Quotation Bureau.

National Building Cost Manual. Craftsman Book Co., 6058 Corte del Cedro Carlsbad, CA 92009. Phone: 800-829-8123 or (760)438-7828 Fax: (760)438-0398 • URL: http://www.craftsman-books.com • Annual. $23.00.

National Building Granite Quarries Association., 1220 L St. NW, Ste. 100-167 Washington, DC 20005. Phone: 800-557-2848 Fax: (603)225-4801 E-mail: ncc@chickenusa.org • URL: http://www.nbgqa.com • Represents quarriers and manufacturers of building granites. Provides specifications for designers.

National Bulk Vendors Association., 191 N Wacker Dr., Ste. 1800 Chicago, IL 60606-1615. Phone: (312)521-2400 Fax: (312)521-2300 E-mail: nbva@muchshelist.com • URL: http://www.nbva.org • Manufacturers, distributors, and operators of bulk vending merchandise and equipment.

National Bureau of Economic Research, Inc.

National Burglar and Fire Alarm Association.

National Burglar and Fire Alarm Association Members Services Directory. National Burglar and Fire Alarm Association, 8300 Colesville Rd., Suite 750 Silver Spring, MD 20910-6225. Phone: (301)585-1855 Fax: (301)585-1866 E-mail: staff@alarm.org • URL: http://www.alarm.org • Annual. Membership. Names and addresses of about 4,000 alarm security companies. Formerly *National Burglar and Fire Alarm Association-Directory of Members.*

National Business Aviation Association., 1200 18th St. NW, Ste. 400 Washington, DC 20036-2527. Phone: (202)783-9000 Fax: (202)331-8364 E-mail: info@nbaa.org • URL: http://www.nbaa.org • Companies owning and operating aircraft for business use, suppliers, and maintenance and air fleet service companies. Compiles statistics; provides literature for researchers and students.

National Business Education Association., 1914 Association Dr. Reston, VA 20191-1596. Phone: (703)860-8300 Fax: (703)620-4483 E-mail: nbea@nbea.org • URL: http://www.nbea.org • Teachers of business subjects in secondary and postsecondary schools and colleges; administrators and research workers in business education; businesspersons interested in business education; teachers in educational institutions training business teachers; high school and college students preparing for careers in business.

National Business Education Yearbook. National Business Education Association, 1914 Association Dr. Reston, VA 20191-1596. Phone: (703)860-8300 Fax: (703)620-4483 E-mail: nbea@nbea.org • URL: http://www.nbea.org • Annual. $40.00.

National Business Incubation Association., 20 E Circle Dr., No. 37198 Athens, OH 45701-3571. Phone: (740)593-4331 Fax: (740)593-1996 E-mail: info@nbia.org • URL: http://www.NBIA.org • Incubator developers and managers; corporate joint venture partners, venture capital investors; economic development professionals. (Incubators are business assistance programs providing business consulting services and financing assistance to start-up and fledgling companies.) Helps newly formed businesses to succeed. Educates businesses and investors on incubator benefits; offers specialized training in incubator formation and management. Conducts research and referral services; compiles statistics; maintains speakers' bureau; publishes information relevant to business incubation and growing companies.

National Cable and Telecommunications Association., 1724 Massachusetts Ave., N.W. Washington, DC 20036. Phone: (202)775-3550 Fax: (202)775-3675 E-mail: webmaster@ncta.com • URL: http://www.ncta.com • Affiliated with Motion Picture Association of America. Formerly National Cable Television Association.

National Cable Television Institute., 9697 E Mineral Ave. Centennial, CO 80112. Phone: (866)575-7206 or (303)797-9393 Fax: (303)797-9394 E-mail: info@jonesncti.com • URL: http://www.ncti.com • Provides comprehensive broadband training for the cable television industry. Offers career training resources and courses in areas ranging from customer service procedures to optical fiber system design, installation, and maintenance.

National Career Development Association., 305 N Beech Cir., 10820 E 45th St., Ste. 210 Broken Arrow, OK 74012. Phone: (866)367-6232 or (918)663-7060 Fax: (918)663-7058 E-mail: dpennington@ncda.org • URL: http://www.ncda.org • Represents professionals and others interested in career development or counseling in various work environments. Supports counselors, education and training personnel, and allied professionals working in schools, colleges, business/industry, community and government agencies, and in private practice. Provides publications, support for state and local activities, human equity programs, and continuing education and training for these professionals. Provides networking opportunities for career professionals in business, education, and government.

National Catalog Managers Association., 7101 Wisconsin Ave., Ste. 1300 Bethesda, MD 20814-3415. Phone: (301)654-6664 Fax: (301)654-3299 E-mail: ncma@aftermarket.org • URL: http://www.ncmacat.org • Individuals actively engaged in the management, preparation, production, and distribution of automotive product catalogs. Purposes are to: exchange practical and useful ideas in the creation, compilation, production, and distribution of catalogs; raise standards of catalogs in automotive and related industries; create a better understanding of the current developments in the field of graphics; establish a professional and fraternal relationship with colleagues; improve professional recognition of the catalog specialist; promote high standards of ethics in the cataloging industry. Operates placement service.

National Cattlemen's Beef Association., 9110 E Nichols Ave., Ste. 300 Centennial, CO 80112. Phone: (866)233-3872 or (303)694-0305 Fax: (303)694-2851 E-mail: membership@beef.org • URL: http://www.beefusa.org • Represents 149 organizations of livestock marketers, growers, meat packers, food retailers, and food service firms. Conducts extensive program of promotion, education and information about beef, veal, and associated meat products. Conducts projects such as recipe testing and development, food demonstrations, food photography, educational service to colleges, experimental meat cutting methods, merchandising programs, and preparation of materials for newspapers, magazines, radio, and television.

National Center for Computer Crime Data., 1714 Brommer St. Santa Cruz, CA 95062. Phone: (831)475-4457 Fax: (831)475-5336 E-mail: anudnic@aol.com Conducts research, compiles statistics, provides case studies and other information.

National Center for Disablity Services., 201 I.U. Willets Rd. Albertson, NY 11507. Phone: (516)465-1400 Fax: (516)747-5400 • URL: http://www.ncds.org • Seeks to improve employment opportunities for persons with disabilities.

National Center for Employee Ownership., 1736 Franklin St., 8th Fl. Oakland, CA 94612. Phone: (510)208-1300 Fax: (510)272-9510 E-mail: nceo@nceo.org • URL: http://www.nceo.org • Association promotes an increased awareness and understanding of employee ownership of companies.

National Center for Health Statistics: Monitoring the Nation's Health. National Center for Health Statistics, Centers for Disease Control and PreventioPhone: (301)458-4000 E-mail: nchsquery@cdc.gov • URL: http://www.cdc.gov/nchswww •

Web site provides detailed data on diseases, vital statistics, and health care in the U. S. Includes a search facility and links to many other health-related Web sites. "Fastats A to Z" offers quick data on hundreds of topics from Accidents to Work-Loss Days, with links to Comprehensive Data and related sources. Frequent updates. Fees: Free.

National Center for Housing Management.

National Center for Manufacturing Sciences., 3025 Boardwalk St. Ann Arbor, MI 48108. Phone: (734)995-0300 Fax: (734)995-4004 E-mail: johnd@ncms.org • URL: http://www.ncms.org • Research areas include process technology and control, machine mechanics, sensors, testing methods, and quality assurance.

National Center for Policy Analysis., 12655 N. Central Expressway, Suite 720 Dallas, TX 75243-1739. Phone: (214)386-6272 Fax: (214)386-0924 E-mail: jcgoodman@ncpa.org • URL: http://www.ncpa.org • Includes studies on medicare.

National Center for State Courts.

National Certified Pipe Welding Bureau., 1385 Piccard Dr., 1385 Piccard Dr. Rockville, MD 20850. Phone: 800-556-3653 or (301)869-5800 Fax: (301)990-9690 E-mail: nnikpourfard@mcaa.org • URL: http://www.mcaa.org/ncpwb • Contractors in the piping field. Conducts research on development in the field of certified welding for the piping industry; establishes uniform welding procedures for pipe welding; provides for interchange of records of qualified welders.

National Cheese Institute., 1250 H St. NW, Ste. 900 Washington, DC 20005-3952. Phone: (202)737-4332 Fax: (202)331-7820 E-mail: membership@idfa.org • URL: http://www.idfa.org • Represents manufacturers, processors, marketers, assemblers, and distributors of cheese and cheese products; advocates before government and regulatory bodies on behalf of members.

National Chicken Council., 1015 15th St. NW, Ste. 930 Washington, DC 20005-2622. Phone: (202)296-2622 Fax: (202)293-4005 E-mail: ncc@chickenusa.org • URL: http://www.nationalchickencouncil.com • Membership includes producers/processors of broiler chickens; distributors and allied industry. Sponsors National Chicken Cooking Contest and National Chicken Month. Compiles statistics; conducts generic promotion program for chicken; provides government relations services for member companies and the broiler industry.

National Child Labor Committee., 1501 Broadway, Ste. 1908 New York, NY 10036. Phone: (212)840-1801 Fax: (212)768-0963 E-mail: info@nationalchildlabor.org • URL: http://www.nationalchildlabor.org • Parent organization of National Committee on Employment of Youth and National Committee on the Education of Migrant Children. Provides direct and technical assistance to programs on youth-related issues, particularly education, job training, and employment.

National Child Safety Council., PO Box 1368, PO Box 1368 Jackson, MI 49204. Phone: (517)764-6070 Fax: (517)764-3068 E-mail: info@nationalchildlabor.org Furnishes complete child safety education programs through local law enforcement agencies and schools.

National Civic League., 1640 Logan St., 1445 Market, Ste. 300 Denver, CO 80203. Phone: 800-864-8622 or (303)571-4343 Fax: (303)571-4404 E-mail: ncl@ncl.org • URL: http://www.ncl.org • Community leaders, civic leaders, educators, public officials, civic organizations, libraries, nonprofits and businesses interested in community building, transforming democratic institutions and developing techniques of citizen action and participation. Serves as a clearinghouse for information on healthy communities, community renewal, local campaign, finance reform, All-American cities, city and county charters, election systems and techniques of citizen participation.

National Civic Review. National Civic League, Inc. Jossey-Bass, 989 Market St. San Francisco, CA 94103-1741. Phone: 888-378-2537 or (415)433-1740 Fax: 800-605-2665 or (415)433-0499 E-mail: jbsubs@jbp.com • URL: http://www.josseybass.com • Quarterly. Institutions, $115.00 per year; with online edition, $120.75 per year. Presents civic strategies for improving local government operations and community life.

National Clay Pipe Institute., PO Box 759 Lake Geneva, WI 53147. Phone: (262)248-9094 Fax: (262)248-1564 E-mail: info@ncpi.org • URL: http://www.ncpi.org • Manufacturers of vitrified clay sewer pipe and fittings. Promotes use of clay pipe for sanitary sewer systems. Provides engineering advisory services; conducts scientific research; acts as government liaison.

National Cleaners Association., 252 W 29th St. New York, NY 10001. Phone: (212)967-3002 Fax: (212)967-2240 E-mail: info@nca-i.com • URL: http://www.nca-i.com • Members are dry cleaning establishments.

National Club Association., 1201 15th St., Ste. 450, 1120 20th St., N.W., Suite 725 Washington, DC 20005. Phone: 800-625-6221 or (202)822-9822 Fax: (202)822-9808 E-mail: info@nationalclub.org • URL: http://www.natlclub.org • Represents the business and legal interests of private clubs. Analyzes proposed laws and regulations affecting clubs; compiles statistics and economic data; drafts model legislation; and acts as a general center of information about club matters.

National Coalition for Science and Technology., 2000 P St. NW, Ste. 305 Washington, DC 20036. Phone: (202)833-2326 E-mail: nabpac@nabpac.org Scientists, engineers, and educators. Lobbies for responsible legislation that will enable the U.S. to make greater advances in science and technology. Encourages scientists and educators to become more active in the political process. Presents Congressional Friend of Science Award to ten members of Congress every two years. Maintains membership database. Sponsors public forums on public policy issues affecting science and technology.

National Coffee Association of U.S.A., 15 Maiden Lane, Ste. 1405 New York, NY 10038-4003. Phone: (212)766-4007 Fax: (212)766-5815 E-mail: info@ncausa.org • URL: http://www.ncausa.org • Formerly Associated Coffee Industries of America.

National Committee for an Effective Congress., 122 C St., NW, Ste. 650 Washington, DC 20001. Phone: 800-547-5911 or (202)639-8300 • URL: http://www.ncec.org • Raises funds from private citizens and distributes them to its endorsed candidates for the United States Senate and House of Representatives.

National Committee for Employer Support of the Guard and Reserve., 1555 Wilson Blvd., Ste. 200 Arlington, VA 22209-2405. Phone: 800-336-4590 or (703)696-1386 Fax: (703)696-1411 E-mail: ncesgr-ombud@osd.mil • URL: http://www.esgr.org • Provides free education, consultation, and if necessary, mediation for employers of guard and reserve members. Aims to ensure the national security. Promotes cooperation and understanding between reserve component members and their civilian employers and assists in the resolution of conflicts arising from an employee's military commitment. Operates with a network of almost 4,000 volunteers throughout 56 Committees located in each state, commonwealth, territory, and the District of Columbia. Operates an ombudsman program to assist in the informal resolution of employer-employee conflicts resulting from employee participation in the National Guard and Reserve.

National Committee for Responsive Philanthropy., 2001 S St., N.W., Suite 620 Washington, DC 20009. Phone: (202)387-9177 Fax: (202)332-5084 E-mail: info@ncrp.org • URL: http://www.ncrp.org • Promotes charitable giving to new organizations working for social change or controversial issues. Formerly Committee for Responsive Philanthropy.

National Committee on Uniform Traffic Laws and Ordinances., 107 S. West St., No. 110 Alexandria, VA 22314. Phone: 800-807-5290 or (540)465-4701 Fax: (540)465-5383 E-mail: ncutloceo@rica.net • URL: http://www.ncutlo.org • Formerly National Conference on Street and Highway Safety.

National Committee to Preserve Social Security and Medicare., 10 G St., N.E., Ste. 600 Washington, DC 20002-4215. Phone: 800-966-1935 or (202)216-0420 Fax: (202)216-0451 E-mail: mailto@ncpssm.org • URL: http://www.ncpssm.org • Members are individuals concerned with Medicare and social security programs. Formerly National Committe to Preserve Social Security.

National Community Development Association., 522 21st St. NW, No. 120 Washington, DC 20006-5059. Phone: (202)293-7587 Fax: (202)887-5546 E-mail: ncda@ncdaonline.org • URL: http://www.ncdaonline.org • Represents community development program directors. Supports the interests of Community Development Block Grant Programs as well as other community and economic development issues; disseminates information; operates workshops on various aspects of housing, economic, and community development.

National Compensation Survey. Available from U. S. Government Printing Office, Washington, DC 20402. Phone: (202)512-1800 Fax: (202)512-2250 E-mail: gpoaccess@gpo.gov • URL: http://www.access.gpo.gov • Irregular. $300.00 per year. Consists of bulletins reporting on earnings for jobs in clerical, professional, technical, and other fields in 70 major metropolitan areas. Formerly *Occupational Compensation Survey*.

National Concrete Masonry Association., 13750 Sunrise Valley Dr. Herndon, VA 20171-4662. Phone: (703)713-1900 Fax: (703)713-1910 E-mail: ncma@ncma.org • URL: http://www.ncma.org • Manufacturers of concrete masonry units (concrete blocks), segmental retaining wall units and paving block; associate members are machinery, cement, and aggregate manufacturers. Conducts testing and research on masonry units and masonry assemblies. Compiles statistics.

National Confectioners Association of the U.S., 8320 Old Courthouse Rd., Ste. 300 McLean, VA 22182-3811. Phone: 800-433-1200 or (703)790-5750 Fax: (703)790-5752 E-mail: info@candyusa.org • URL: http://www.candyusa.org • Affiliated with American Cocoa Research Institute and the Chocolate Manufacturers Associations of the U.S.A.

National Confectionery Sales Association., 10225 Berea Rd., Ste. B Cleveland, OH 44102. Phone: (216)631-8200 Fax: (216)631-8210 E-mail: ttarantino@propressinc.com • URL: http://www.candyhalloffame.org • Salespersons, brokers, sales managers, wholesalers, and manufacturers in the candy industry. Maintains Candy Hall of Fame.

National Conference of Bankruptcy Judges.

National Conference of Commissioners on Uniform State Laws.

National Conference of Local Environmental Health Administrators., c/o University of Washington, Dept. of Environmental Health, Campus Box 357234 Seattle, WA 98195-7234. Phone: (206)616-2097 Fax: (206)543-8123 E-mail: ctreser@u.washington.edu • URL: http://www.depts.washington.edu/clehaweb • Affiliated with National Environmental Health Association. Formerly Conference of Local Environmental Health Administrators.

National Conference of State Legislatures., 1560 Broadway, Ste. 700, 7700 E First Pl. Denver, CO 80230. Phone: (303)364-7700 Fax: (303)364-7800 E-mail: info@ncsl.org • URL: http://www.ncsl.org • Affiliated with Council of State Governments.

National Conference of State Liquor Administrators.

National Conference of State Social Security Administrators. Social Security Div., Two Northside 75, Suite 300 Atlanta, GA 30318. Phone: (404)352-6414 Fax: (404)352-6431 E-mail: bijenkin@ers.state.ga.us • URL: http://www.ncssa.org • Formerly Conference of State Social Security Administrators.

National Conference on Citizenship.

National Conference on Weights and Measures.

National Conservative Congressional Committee., USA,. E-mail: rcw@vnf.com Political action committee whose purpose is to produce a conservative majority in the Congress in 1988. Makes contributions and places advertisements supporting conservative incumbents and opponents of liberal candidates and incumbents targeted by the group for defeat. Address unknown since 21st edition.

National Construction Estimator. Martin Kiley and William Moselle. Craftsman Book Co., 6058 Corte del Cedro Carlsbad, CA 92009. Phone: 800-829-8123 Fax: (760)438-0398 • URL: http://www.craftsman-book.com • Annual. $47.50.

National Constructors Association., 1730 M St. NW, Ste. 503 Washington, DC 20036. Phone: (703)560-2391 Fax: (703)560-2392 E-mail: nfpa@nfpa.com • URL: http://www.nccc.org • Engineering and construction contractors specializing in design and installation of chemical plants, steel mills, power plants, oil refineries, and atomic energy facilities. Serves as a clearinghouse for collecting, analyzing, and exchanging information about field labor and working conditions on industrial construction projects, wages, and safety. Negotiates union labor agreements with members of Building Constitution Trades Department. Sponsors Work +Environment +Safety Training Program.

National Consumer Law Center., 77 Summer St., 10th Fl. Boston, MA 02110. Phone: (617)542-8010 or (617)542-9500 Fax: (617)542-8028 E-mail: consumerlaw@nclc.org • URL: http://www.consumerlaw.org • Serves as a specialized resource in consumer and energy law funded by federal, state, and foundation grants and donations. Lawyers provide research, technical consulting, and in-depth assistance to legal services, private lawyers, and state agencies throughout the nation. Defines recurring patterns in the problems of low-income consumers and develops a series of alternative solutions utilizing litigation, legislation, lawyer training, and development of new service delivery systems. Seeks consultants for an interdisciplinary approach to problems. Conducts analyses of weatherization and energy assistance programs for low-income homeowners, renters, and state and federal agencies.

National Consumer Survey. Simmons Market Research Bureau, 290 Park Ave. S New York, NY 10003. Phone: (212)598-5400 Fax: (212)598-5401 • URL: http://www.smrb.com • Market and media survey data relating to the American consumer. Inquire as to online cost and availability.

National Consumers League., 1701 K St. NW, Ste. 1200 Washington, DC 20006. Phone: (202)835-3323 Fax: (202)835-0747 E-mail: info@nclnet.org • URL: http://www.nclnet.org • Identifies, protects, represents, and advances the economic and social interests of consumers and workers. Addresses issues including healthcare, food and drug safety, and consumer fraud. Promotes fairness and safety at the marketplace and in the workplace. Coordinates the Alliance Against Fraud in Telemarketing and the Child +Labor Coalition. Administers the National Fraud Information Center and Internet Fraud Watch.

National Contract Management Association., 21740 Beaumeade Cir., Ste. 125 Ashburn, VA 20147. Phone: 800-344-8096 or (571)382-0082 Fax: (703)448-0939 E-mail: couture@ncmahq.org • URL: http://www.ncmahq.org • Professional individuals concerned with administration, procurement, acquisition, negotiation and management of contracts and subcontracts. Works for the education, improvement and professional development of members and nonmembers through national and chapter programs, symposia and educational materials. Offers certification in Contract Management (CPCM, CFCM, and CCCM) designations as well as a credential program. Operates speakers' bureau.

National Cooperative Business Association., 1401 New York Ave. NW, Ste. 1100 Washington, DC 20005. Phone: (202)638-6222 Fax: (202)638-1374 E-mail: ncba@ncba.coop • URL: http://www.ncba.coop • Local, state, regional, and national cooperative business organizations including farm supply, agricultural marketing, insurance, banking, housing, health care, consumer goods and services, student, worker, fishery, and other cooperatives. Represents, strengthens, and expands cooperative businesses. Programs include: supporting the development of cooperative businesses in the U.S.; developing and providing technical assistance to cooperatives in developing nations; representing American cooperatives in Washington, DC and abroad; promoting and developing commercial relations among the world's cooperatives. Operates Cooperative Action for +Congressional Trust. Supports the Cooperative +Hall of Fame, and the Cooperative Development Foundation. Maintains hall of fame.

National Corn Growers Association., 632 Cepi Dr. Chesterfield, MO 63005-1221. Phone: (636)733-9004 Fax: (636)733-9005 E-mail: corninfo@ncga.com • URL: http://www.ncga.com • Growers of corn. Furthers the use, proper marketing, legislative position, and efficient production of corn. Conducts research and educational programs. Sponsors National Yield Contest; compiles statistics.

National Correctional Industries Association., 1202 N Charles St. Baltimore, MD 21201. Phone: 888-553-4210 or (410)230-3972 Fax: (410)230-3981 E-mail: info@nationalcia.org • URL: http://www.nationalcia.org • Professional correctional industry managers, supervisors, superintendents, and others employed in the industry. Seeks to improve the effectiveness of industrial programs as they relate to the correctional process by providing a forum for the development and exchange of ideas and by providing professional reaction and guidance concerning projected ideas and programs related to correctional industry trends. Compiles statistics.

National Corrugated Steel Pipe Association., 14070 Proton Rd., Ste. 100, LB 9, 13140 Coit Rd., Ste. 320 Dallas, TX 75244. Phone: (972)850-1907 Fax: (972)490-4219 E-mail: info@ncspa.org • URL: http://www.ncspa.org • Represents firms fabricating corrugated steel drainage pipe and structures; steel mills; allied industries. Provides engineering service in design and installation of drainage products and systems. Conducts research programs.

National Cosmetology Association., 401 N Michigan Ave., 22nd Fl. Chicago, IL 60611. Phone: (866)871-0656 or (312)527-6765 Fax: (312)464-6118 E-mail: nca1@ncacares.org • URL: http://www.ncacares.org • Owners of cosmetology salons; cosmetologists. Sponsors: National Cosmetology Month; National Beauty Show. Provides special sections for estheticians, school owners, salon owners, and nail technicians. Maintains hall of fame. Conducts educational and charitable programs.

National Cotton Council of America., 1918 N Parkway Memphis, TN 38112-0285. Phone: (901)274-9030 Fax: (901)725-0510 E-mail: info@cotton.org • URL: http://www.cotton.org/ncc • Delegates are from 19 cotton producing states.

National Cottonseed Products Association., 104 Timber Creek Dr., Ste. 200, PO Box 172267 Cordova, TN 38018-4234. Phone: (901)682-0800 Fax: (901)682-2856 E-mail: info@cottonseed.com • URL: http://www.cottonseed.com • Oil mills, refiners, dealers, brokers, chemists, and others interested in margarine, cooking fats, soaps, lubricants, cattle feed, and fertilizer. Maintains uniform trading rules covering the buying, selling, weighing, sampling, and analysis of cottonseed and its products; supports extensive research program to increase processing efficiency and to improve the quality and usefulness of cottonseed products. Conducts research programs and market development activities.

National Council for Prescription Drug Programs., 9240 E Raintree Dr. Scottsdale, AZ 85260-7519: Phone: (480)477-1000 Fax: (480)767-1042 E-mail: ncpdp@ncpdp.org • URL: http://www.ncpdp.org • Concerned with standardization of third party prescription drug programs.

National Council for Public-Private Partnerships., 1660 L. St., N.W. Washington, DC 20036. Phone: (202)467-6800 Fax: (202)467-6312 E-mail: ncppp@ncppp.org • URL: http://www.ncppp.org • Promotes private ownership of public services. Formerly Privitization Council, Inc.

National Council for Research on Women.

National Council of Agricultural Employers.

National Council of Chain Restaurants., 325 Seventh St. N.W., Suite 1000 Washington, DC 20004. Phone: (202)626-8183 Fax: (202)626-8185 E-mail: purviss@nrf.com • URL: http://www.nccr.net • Major multiunit, multistate foodservice, restaurant and lodging companies in the United States.

National Council of Commercial Plant Breeders.

National Council of Higher Education Loan Programs., 1100 Connecticut Ave. N.W., 12th Fl. Washington, DC 20036. Phone: (202)822-2106 Fax: (202)822-2142 E-mail: info@nchelp.org • URL: http://www.nchelp.org • Attempts to coordinate federal, state, and private functions in the student loan program.

National Council of Industrial Naval Air Stations., 23364 NE, 6th Ave. Lawtey, FL 32058. Phone: (904)782-1347 E-mail: adamsbk@yahoo.com Federation of local groups of government civilian employees at Industrial Naval Air Stations.

National Council of Juvenile and Family Court Judges.

National Council of Women of the United States., 777 United Nations Plaza New York, NY 10017. Phone: (212)697-1278 Fax: (212)972-0164 Works for the education, participation and advancement of women in all areas of society. Affiliated with International Council of Women.

The National Council on Aging., 300 D St., NW, Ste. 801 Washington, DC 20024. Phone: (202)479-1200 or (202)479-6674 Fax: (202)479-0735 E-mail; info@ncoa.org • URL: http://www.ncoa.org • Dedicated to improving the health and independence of older people.

National Council on Alcoholism and Drug Dependence., 20 Exchange Place, Suite 2902 New York, NY 10005-3201. Phone: 800-622-2255 or (212)269-7797 Fax: (212)269-7510 E-mail: national@ncadd.org • URL: http://www.ncadd.org • Works for the prevention and treatment of alcoholism and other drug dependence through programs of public education, information and public policy advocacy.

National Council on Compensation Insurance., 901 Peninsula Corporate Circle Boca Raton, FL 33487. Phone: 800-622-4123 or (561)893-1000 Fax: (561)893-1191 • URL: http://www.ncci.com • Members are insurance companies. Formerly National Council on Workmen's Compensation Insurance.

National Council on Crime and Delinquency.

National Council on Economic Education., 1140 Ave. of the Americas, 2nd Fl. New York, NY 10036. Phone: 800-338-1192 or (212)730-7007 Fax: (212)730-1793 E-mail: econed@ncee.net • URL: http://www.nationalcouncil.org • Formerly Joint Council in Economic Education.

National Council on Problem Gambling., 208 G St. NE Washington, DC 20002. Phone: 800-522-4700 or (202)547-9204 Fax: (202)547-9206 E-mail: ncpg@ncpgambling.org • URL: http://www.ncpgambling.org • Advocates for programs and services to assist problem gamblers and their families. Formerly National Council on Compulsive Gambling.

National Council on Public Polls., c/o Edward J. Efchak, 150 River St. Hackensack, NJ 07601. Phone: (201)646-4379 E-mail: info@ncpp.org • URL: http://www.ncpp.org • Members are public opinion polling organizations.

National Court Reporters Association., 8224 Old Courthouse Rd. Vienna, VA 22182-3808. Phone: 800-272-6272 or (703)556-6272 Fax: (703)556-6291 E-mail: msic@ncrahq.org • URL: http://www.ncraonline.org • Represents Independent state, regional, and local associations. Verbatim court reporters who work as official reporters for courts and government agencies, as freelance reporters for independent contractors, and as captioners for television programming; retired reporters, teachers of court reporting, and school officials; student court reporters. Conducts research; compiles statistics; offers several certification programs; and publishes journal.

National Credit Union Administration Rules and Regulations. Available from U. S. Government Printing Office, Washington, DC 20402. Phone: (202)512-1800 Fax: (202)512-2250 E-mail: gpoaccess@gpo.gov • URL: http://www.access.gpo.gov • Looseleaf. $130.00 for basic manual, including updates for an indeterminate period. Incorporates all amendments and revisions.

National Customs Brokers and Forwarders Association of America., 1200 18th St., N.W., Suite 901 Washington, DC 20036. Phone: (202)466-0222 Fax: (202)466-0226 E-mail: staff@ncbfaa.org • URL: http://www.ncbfaa.org • Formerly Customs Brokers and Forwarders Association of America.

National Customs Brokers and Forwarders Association of America Membership Direc tory. National Customs Brokers and Forwarders Association of America, 1200 18th St., N.W., Suite 901 Washington, DC 20036. Phone: (202)466-0222 Fax: (202)466-0226 E-mail: staff@ncbfaa.org • URL: http://www.ncbfaa.org • Annual. $25.00. Lists about 600 customs brokers, international air cargo agents, and freight forwarders in the U.S.

National Defense Industrial Association., 2111 Wilson Blvd., Ste. 400 Arlington, VA 22201-3061. Phone: (703)522-1820 or (703)247-2589 Fax: (703)522-1885 E-mail: info@ndia.org • URL: http://www.adpa.org • Concerned citizens, military and government personnel, and defense-related industry workers interested in industrial preparedness for the national defense of the United States. Operates Technology Services that provides a forum for discussion of defense industry programs and issues. Conducts 55 technical meetings per year.

National Defense: NDIA's Business and Technology Journal. National Defense Industrial Association, 2111 Wilson Blvd., Suite 400 Arlington, VA 22201-3001. Phone: (703)522-1820 Fax: (703)522-1885 • URL: http://www.ndia.org • 10 times a year. $35.00 per year.

National Defense Transportation Association., 50 S Pickett St., Ste. 220 Alexandria, VA 22304-7296. Phone: (703)751-5011 Fax: (703)823-8761 E-mail: info@ndtahq.com • URL: http://www.ndtahq.com • Men and women in the field of transportation, travel logistics and related areas in the Armed Forces, federal government, private industry and the academic sector. Dedicated to fostering a strong and efficient transportation system in support of national defense. Serves as link between government and industry on transportation matters. Operates a job placement service for members.

National Democratic Institute for International Affairs.

National Development Council., 708 Third Ave., Ste. 710 New York, NY 10017. Phone: (212)682-1106 Fax: (212)573-6118 E-mail: training@nationaldevelopmentcouncil.org • URL: http://www.nationaldevelopmentcouncil.org • Brings innovative economic development financing programs to urban and rural communities interested in local business and industrial growth, commercial revitalization, and permanent job creation. Finances professionals' work with cities, counties, and states to: build permanent systems for developing financing; train local staff; structure and negotiate financing for development projects, local business development, and industrial expansion. Conducts intensive training program for economic development professionals with courses in business credit analysis, real estate financing, loan packaging, federal financing, and program management and implementation; has provided advice to congress and federal agencies that has helped create lending programs for job creation and small business investment; has initiated and managed presidential programs for Presidents Nixon, Ford, Carter, and Reagan.

The National Dipper: The Magazine for Ice Cream Retailers., 1841 Hicks Rd., Suite C Rolling Meadows, IL 60008-1215. Phone: (847)202-4770 Fax: (847)202-4791 Bimonthly. $55.00 per year. Edited for ice cream store owners and managers. Includes industry news, new product information, statistics, and feature articles.

National Dipper Yellow Pages., 1841 Hicks Rd., Suite C Rolling Meadows, IL 60008-1215. Phone: (847)202-4770 Fax: (847)202-4791 Annual. $10.00. Special directory issue of *The National Dipper*. Lists products and services for the ice cream retail industry.

The National Directory of Catalogs. Oxbridge Communications, 186 5th Ave., 6th Fl. New York, NY 10010. Phone: 800-955-0231 or (212)741-0231 Fax: (212)633-2938 E-mail: info@oxbridge.com • URL: http://www.mediafinder.com • Annual. $645.00. Describes over 9,000 United States and Canadian catalogs within 78 subject areas.

National Directory of Community Newspapers. American Newspaper Representatives, Inc., 2075 W Big Beaver Rd., Ste. 310 Troy, MI 48084. Phone: 800-550-7557 Fax: (248)643-0606 • URL: http://www.anrinc.net • Annual. $105.00. Supersedes *National Directory of Weekly Newspapers*.

National Directory of Corporate Giving: A Guide to Corporate Giving Programs and Corporate Foundations. The Foundation Center, 79 Fifth Ave. New York, NY 10003-3076. Phone: 800-424-9836 or (212)620-4230 Fax: (212)807-3677 E-mail: orders@fdncenter.org • URL: http://www.fdncenter.org • Biennial. $195.00. Provides information on 2,895 corporations that maintain philanthropic programs (direct giving programs or company-sponsored foundations).

National Directory of Corporate Public Affairs. Columbia Books, Inc., 1825 Connecticut Ave., Suite 625 Washington, DC 20009. Phone: 888-265-0600 or (202)464-1662 E-mail: info@columbiabooks.com • URL: http://www.columbiabooks.com • Annual. $109.00. Lists about 1,900 corporations that have foundations or other public affairs activities.

National Directory of Drug and Alcohol Abuse Treatment Programs. Substance Abuse and Mental Health Services Administration, Office of Applied Studies, 5600 Fishers Lane, Room 16-105 Rockville, MD 20857. Phone: 800-729-6686 or (301)443-6239 Fax: (301)443-9847 E-mail: directory@smdi.com • URL: http://www.findtreatment.samhsa.gov • Annual. Free. Lists 11,000 federal, state, local, and privately funded agencies administering or providing drug abuse and alcoholism treatment services. Formerly *National Directory of Drug Abuse and Alcoholism Treatment and Prevention Programs*.

National Directory of HMOs. American Association of Health Plans, 1129 20th St., N. W., Suite 600 Washington, DC 20036. Phone: (202)778-3247 Fax: (202)331-7487 E-mail: aahp@aahp.org • URL: http://www.aahp.org • Annual. $125.00. Includes names of key personnel and benefit options.

National Directory of Law Enforcement Administrators, Correctional Institutio ns and Related Agencies. National Public Safety Information Bureau, 3273 Church St., Suite 201 Stevens Point, WI 54481. Phone: 800-647-7579 or (715)345-2772 Fax: (715)345-7288 E-mail: info@safetysource.com • URL: http://www.safetysource.com • Annual. $129.00. Lists a wide variety of law enforcement administrators and institutions, including city police departments, sheriffs, prosecutors, state agencies, federal agencies, correctional institutions, college campus police departments, airport police, and harbor police. Formerly*National Directory of Law Enforcement Administrators and Correctional Institutions*.

National Directory of Minority Attorneys. American Lawyer Media, Inc., 105 Madison Ave. New York, NY 10016. Phone: 800-888-8300 or (212)779-9200 Fax: (212)481-8110 E-mail: lawcatalog@amlaw.com • URL: http://www.lawcatalog.com/ • Annual. $35.00. Contains 500 listings in four sections, covering minority-owned law firms, minority lawyers at other law firms, minority corporate (in-house) lawyers, and minority lawyers in government agencies. (Minority Law Journal).

National Directory of Minority-Owned Business Firms. Available from Gale Cengage Learning, 27500 Drake Rd. Farmington Hills, MI 48331-3535. Phone: 800-877-GALE or (248)699-GALE Fax: 800-414-5043 E-mail: gale.galeord@cengage.com • URL: http://www.galegroup.com • 2003. $295.00. 12th edition. Published by Business Research Services. Includes more than 30,000 minority-owned businesses.

National Directory of Nonprofit Organizations. Available from Gale Cengage Learning, 27500 Drake Rd. Farmington Hills, MI 48331-3535. Phone: 800-877-GALE or (248)699-GALE Fax: 800-414-5043 E-mail: gale.galeord@cengage.com • URL: http://www.galegroup.com • 2003. $590.00. 16th edition. Three volumes. Published by the TAFT Group. Contains over 250,000 listings of nonprofit organizations, indexed by 260 areas of activity. Indicates income range and IRS tax filing status for each organization.

National Directory of Personnel Service Firms. National Association of Personnel Services, 10905 Fort Washington Rd., Ste. 400 Fort Washington, MD 20744-5807. Phone: (703)684-0180 Fax: (703)684-0071 E-mail: skennaugh@recruitinglife.com • URL: http://www.napsweb.org • Annual.

$15.95. Lists over 1,100 member private (for-profit) employment firms. Formerly *ACCESS*.

National Directory of Women-Owned Business Firms. Gale Cengage Learning, 27500 Drake Rd. Farmington Hills, MI 48331-3535. Phone: 800-877-GALE or (248)699-4253 Fax: 800-414-5043 E-mail: gale.galeord@cengage.com • URL: http://gale.cengage.com • 2003. $295.00. 12th edition. Published by Business Research Services. Includes more than 28,000 businesses owned by women.

National E-Mail and Fax Directory. Gale Cengage Learning, 27500 Drake Rd. Farmington Hills, MI 48331-3535. Phone: 800-877-GALE or (248)699-4253 Fax: 800-414-5043 or (248)699-8069 E-mail: gale.galeord@cengage.com • URL: http://gale.cengage.com • Annual. $160.00. Provides fax numbers, telephone numbers, and addresses for U. S. companies, organizations, government agencies, and libraries. Includes alphabetic listings and subject listings.

National Economic Development and Law Center.

National Education Association., 1201 16th St. NW Washington, DC 20036-3290. Phone: (202)833-4000 Fax: (202)822-7974 E-mail: bobchase@nea.org • URL: http://www.nea.org • Professional organization and union of elementary and secondary school teachers, college and university professors, administrators, principals, counselors, and others concerned with education.

National Electrical Contractors Association., 3 Bethesda Metro Ctr., Ste. 1100 Bethesda, MD 20814. Phone: (301)657-3110 or (301)215-4500 Fax: (301)215-4500 E-mail: webmaster@necanet.org • URL: http://www.necanet.org • Contractors erecting, installing, repairing, servicing, and maintaining electric wiring, equipment, and appliances. Provides management services and labor relations programs for electrical contractors; conducts seminars for contractor sales and training. Conducts research and educational programs; compiles statistics. Sponsors honorary society, the Academy of +Electrical +Contracting.

National Electrical Manufacturers Association., 1300 N 17th St., Ste. 1752 Rosslyn, VA 22209. Phone: (703)841-3200 Fax: (703)841-5900 E-mail: communications@nema.org • URL: http://www.nema.org • Aims to maintain and improve quality and reliability of products; insure safety standards in manufacture and use of products; organize and act upon members' interests in productivity, competition from overseas suppliers, energy conservation and efficiency, marketing opportunities, economic matters, and product liability. Develops product standards covering such matters as nomenclature, ratings, performance, testing, and dimensions; actively participates in regional and international standards process for electrical products; participates in developing National Electrical Code and National Electrical Safety Codes, and advocates their acceptance by state and local authorities; conducts regulatory and legislative analyses on issues of concern to electrical manufacturers; compiles and issues market data of all kinds, and statistical data on such factors as sales, new orders, unfilled orders, cancellations, production, and inventories. Sponsors geographical projects, advisory services, and statistical and management services.

National Electronic Distributors Association., 1111 Alderman Dr., Ste. 400 Alpharetta, GA 30005. Phone: 800-347-NEDA or (678)393-9990 Fax: (678)393-9998 E-mail: admin@nedassoc.org • URL: http://www.nedassoc.org • Represents authorized distributors and manufacturers of electronic components. Conducts research. Compiles statistical reports and surveys.

National Electronics Service Dealers Association., 3608 Pershing Ave. Fort Worth, TX 76107-4527. Phone: 800-797-9197 or (817)921-9061 Fax: (817)921-3741 E-mail: info@nesda.com • URL: http://www.nesda.com • Local and state electronic service associations and companies. Supplies technical service information on business management training to electronic service dealers. Offers certification and training programs through International Society of Certified Electronics Technicians. Conducts technical service and business management seminars.

National Elevator Industry, Inc., 1677 County Rte. 64, PO Box 838 Salem, NY 12865-0838. Phone: (518)854-3100 Fax: (518)854-3257 E-mail: info@neii.org • URL: http://www.neii.org • Serves as a trade association of the building transportation industry. Promotes safe building transportation for new and existing products and technologies, and adoption of the current codes by local government agencies.

National Employee Benefits Institute., 1350 Connecticut Ave. NW, No. 600 Washington, DC 20036. Phone: 888-822-1344 or (202)822-6432 or (202)833-7366 Fax: (202)466-5109 E-mail: memark@federlaw.com • URL: http://www.nebif.org • Fortune 1000 corporations with an interest in employee benefits legislation and regulation. Works to improve government regulation of employee benefits. Supports and introduces what the institute considers realistic legislation. Invites government spokespersons, legislators, and regulators to speak at special meetings. Conducts educational programs.

The National Estimator. Society of Cost Estimating and Analysis, 101 S. Whiting St., Suite 201 Alexandria, VA 22304. Phone: (703)751-8069 Fax: (703)461-7328 E-mail: scea@sceaonline.net • URL: http://www.sceaonline.net • Quarterly. $30.00 per year. Covers government contract estimating.

National Faculty Directory. Gale, 27500 Drake Rd. Farmington Hills, MI 48331-3535. Phone: 800-877-4253 or (248)699-4253 Fax: 800-414-5043 or (248)699-8065 E-mail: galeord@cengage.com • URL: http://gale.cengage.com • Covers: More than 740,000 (90,000 more in supplement) teaching faculty members at over 3,600 junior colleges, colleges, and universities in the United States and those in Canada that give instruction in English. Entries include: Name, department name, institution, address, and phone and fax numbers. Directory combines main edition and supplement.

National Family Business Council., 1640 W Kennedy Rd. Lake Forest, IL 60045. Phone: (847)295-1040 Fax: (847)295-1898 E-mail: jmnfbc@msn.com Serves as a consulting group and resource center on family-owned businesses. Offers consultation, speakers' bureau, and other communications with other family businesses; sponsors regional seminars on problems unique to family businesses. Conducts surveys.

National Farmers Organization., PO Box 2508 Ames, IA 50010-2000. Phone: 800-247-2110 or (515)292-2000 Fax: (515)292-7106 E-mail: nfo@nfo.org • URL: http://www.nfo.org • Nonpartisan organization of farmers who bargain collectively to obtain contracts with buyers, processors, and exporters for the sale of farm commodities. Works to continuously improve such contracts. Conducts educational programs; maintains speakers' bureau.

National Farmers Union., 5619 DTC Pkwy., Ste. 300 Greenwood Village, CO 80111-3136. Phone: 800-347-1961 or (303)337-5500 Fax: (303)771-1770 E-mail: tbuis@nfudc.org • URL: http://www.nfu.org • Farm families interested in agricultural welfare. Carries on educational, cooperative and legislative activities. Represents members' interests especially in acquiring a more equitable share of the food dollar. Assists farm families in developing self-help institutions such as cooperatives.

National Farmers Union News. National Farmers Union, 11900 E Cornell Ave. Aurora, CO 80014-3194. Phone: 800-347-1961 or (303)337-5500 Fax: (303)368-1390 E-mail: info@nfu.org • URL: http://www.nfu.org • Description: Provides news, legislation, and tax information in relation to the farming industry.

National Fastener Distributors Association., 401 N Michigan Ave. Chicago, IL 60611. Phone: 877-487-6332 or (312)527-6671 Fax: (312)673-6740 E-mail: nfda@nfda-fastener.org • URL: http://www.nfda-fastener.org • Marketers, distributors, manufacturers, and importers of the fastener industry (producers or distributors of screws, bolts, and nuts). Develops new uses for fasteners; collects and disseminates statistics and information for members; conducts membership performance surveys. Assists in the maintenance of sound and equitable relationships among members of the industry, the public, and government. Offers training and educational programs.

National Federation of Abstracting and Information Services., 1518 Walnut St., Suite 307 Philadelphia, PA 19102-3403. Phone: (215)893-1561 Fax: (215)893-1564 E-mail: nfais@nfais.org • URL: http://www.nfais.org • Formerly National Federation of Abstracting and Indexing Services.

National Federation of Federal Employees.

National Federation of Independent Business., 53 Century Blvd., Ste. 250 Nashville, TN 37214. Phone: 800-634-2669 or (615)872-5800 Fax: (615)872-5353 • URL: http://www.nfib.com • Members are independent business and professional people.

National Federation of Press Women.

National Fenestration Rating Council., 6305 Ivy Ln., Ste. 140 Greenbelt, MD 20770. Phone: (301)589-1776 Fax: (301)589-3884 E-mail: info@nfrc.org • URL: http://www.nfrc.org • Individuals, organizations, and corporations interested in production, regulation, promotion, and development of technology related to fenestration products. Develops national voluntary energy performance rating system for fenestration products; coordinates certification and labeling activities to ensure uniform rating application. Promotes consumer awareness of fenestration ratings in an effort to encourage informed purchase of windows, doors, and skylights. Conducts efficiency testing. Maintains speakers' bureau; conducts educational and research programs.

National Fire Codes. National Fire Protection Association, One Batterymarch Park Quincy, MA 02269-9101. Phone: 800-344-3555 or (617)770-3000 Fax: 800-593-6372 or (617)770-0700 E-mail: library@nfpa.org • URL: http://www.nfpa.org • Annual. Members, $710.00; non-members, $790.00. Lists over 270 codes.

National Fire Protection Association (NFPA).

National Fisherman. Diversified Business Communications, P.O. Box 7238 Rockland, ME 04112-7438. Phone: (207)842-5608 Fax: (207)842-5609 • URL: http://www.nationalfisherman.com • Monthly. $17.95 per year. American fishing industry and boat building trade.

National Five Digit Zip Code and Post Office Directory. U.S. Postal Service, National Customer Support Center, United States Postal Service, 6060 Primacy Parkway, Suite 101 Memphis, TN 38188-0001. Phone: 800-238-3150 Fax: (901)767-8853 Annual. Two volumes. Formerly *National Zip Code and Post Office Directory-*.

National Fluid Power Association., 3333 N Mayfair Rd., Ste. 211 Milwaukee, WI 53222-3219. Phone: (414)778-3344 Fax: (414)778-3361 E-mail: nfpa@nfpa.com • URL: http://www.nfpa.com • Manufacturers of components such as fittings used in transmitting power by hydraulic and pneumatic pumps, valves, cylinders, filters, seals; the components are used in industrial and mobile machinery in the material-handling, automotive, railway, aircraft, marine, aerospace, construction, agricultural, and other industries. Works to develop: American National Standards Institute and International Organization for Standardization (see separate entries); fluid power technical standards; fluid power index (industry sales); management and marketing studies. Compiles statistics. Administers and serves as secretariat to several international project groups and other fluid power organizations.

National Fluid Power Association—Reporter. National Fluid Power Association, 3333 N Mayfair Rd., Ste. 211 Milwaukee, WI 53222-3219. Phone: (414)778-3344 Fax: (414)778-3361 E-mail: nfpa@nfpa.com • URL: http://www.nfpa.com • Description: Includes articles on the fluid power market, manufacturing, people and meetings. Also includes statistics.

National Food Processors Association Research Foundation., 1350 Eye St., N.W., Suite 300 Washington, DC 20005. Phone: (202)639-5900 Fax: (202)639-5932 E-mail: nfpa@nfpa.org • URL: http://www.nfpa-food.org • Conducts research on food processing engineering, chemistry, microbiology, sanitation, preservation aspects, and public health factors.

National Foreign Trade Council., 1625 K St. NW, Ste. 200 Washington, DC 20006. Phone: (202)887-0278 Fax: (202)452-8160 E-mail: nftcinformation@nftc.org • URL: http://www.nftc.org • Manufacturers, exporters, importers, foreign investors, banks, transportation lines, and insurance, communication, law, accounting, service, and publishing firms. Works to promote and protect American foreign trade and investment. Areas of concern include the removal of arbitrary barriers to expansion of international trade and investment; a greater awareness by the government that this expansion is essential to the economic growth of the U.S.; the formation of a cohesive, consistent international economic policy.

National Forensic League., PO Box 38, PO Box 38 Ripon, WI 54971. Phone: (920)748-6206 Fax: (920)748-9478 E-mail: nfl@nflonline.org • URL: http://nflonline.org • High school honor society. Promotes the art of debate, oratory, interpretation, and extemporaneous speaking. Conducts educational and outreach programs; maintains speakers' bureau; maintains hall of fame; compiles statistics.

National Foundation for Credit Counseling., 801 Roeder Rd., Ste. 900 Silver Spring, MD 20910. Phone: 800-388-2227 or (301)589-5600 Fax: (301)495-5623 • URL: http://www.nfcc.org • Supersedes Retail Credit Institute of America.

National Foundation for Unemployment Compensation and Workers Compensation.

National Foundation of Manufactured Home Owners., 62 Hawthorne Cir., 62 Hawthorne Circle Willow Street, PA 17584. Phone: (717)284-4520 Fax: (717)284-4520 E-mail: pamhoa@aol.com • URL: http://www.manhousingfoundation.org • Represents 20,000,000 owners of mobile/manufactured homes. Serves as a unified national voice for mobile/manufactured homeowners and to improve communications among members, and research problems homeowners can experience. Maintains resources, include extensive collection of material, clearinghouse of information, especially on the purchase, set-up and maintenance of homes.

National Frozen and Refrigerated Foods Association., 4755 Linglestown Rd., Ste. 300 Harrisburg, PA 17112. Phone: (717)657-8601 Fax: (717)657-9862 E-mail: info@nfraweb.org • URL: http://www.nfraweb.org/ • Absorbed Foodservice Organizations of Distributors. Formerly National Frozen Food Association.

National Frozen and Refrigerated Foods Association Membership Directory. National Frozen and Refrigerated Foods Association, Inc., 4755 Linglestown Rd., Suite 300 Harrisburg, PA 17112. Phone: (717)657-8601 Fax: (717)657-9862 E-mail: info@nfraweb.org • URL: http://www.nfraweb.org • Annual. $195.00. Lists products, services and personnel.

National Frozen Food Dessert and Fast Food Association., P.O. Box 1116 Millbrook, NY 12545. Phone: 800-535-7748 or (845)677-9301 Fax: (845)677-3387 E-mail: director@nfdffa.org • URL: http://www.nfdffa.org • Formerly National Soft Serve and Fast Food Association.

National Funeral Directors and Morticians Association.

National Funeral Directors Association., 13625 Bishop's Dr., 13625 Bishops Dr. Brookfield, WI 53005-6607. Phone: 800-228-6332 or (262)789-1880 Fax: (262)789-6977 E-mail: nfda@nfda.org • URL: http://www.nfda.org • Federation of state funeral directors' associations with individual membership of funeral directors. Seeks to enhance the funeral service profession and promote quality services to the consumers. Conducts professional education seminars and home study courses. Compiles statistics.

National Futures Association., 300 S Riverside Plaza, No. 1800 Chicago, IL 60606-6615. Phone: 800-621-3570 or (312)781-1300 Fax: (312)781-1467 E-mail: information@nfa.futures.org • URL: http://www.nfa.futures.org • Futures commission merchants; commodity trading advisors; commodity pool operators; brokers and their associated persons. Works to: strengthen and expand industry self-regulation to include all segments of the futures industry; provide uniform standards to eliminate duplication of effort and conflict; remove unnecessary regulatory constraints to aid effective regulation. Conducts member qualification screening, financial surveillance, and registration. Monitors and enforces customer protection rules and uniform business standards. Maintains

SOURCES CITED

information center. Arbitrates customer disputes; audits non-exchange member FCM's.

National Futures Association Manual. National Futures Association, 200 W. Madison St., Suite 1600 Chicago, IL 60606. Phone: (312)781-1300 Fax: (312)781-1467 E-mail: publicaffairs@nfa.futures.org • URL: http://www.nfa.futures.org • Quarterly. Price on application. Looseleaf service. Rules and regulations concerning commodity futures trading.

National Glass Association., 8200 Greensboro Dr., Ste. 302 McLean, VA 22102-3881. Phone: (866)DIAL-NGA or (703)442-4890 Fax: (703)442-0630 E-mail: pjames@glass.org • URL: http://www.glass.org • Manufacturers, installers, retailers, distributors, and fabricators of flat, architectural, automotive, and specialty glass and metal products, mirrors, shower and patio doors, windows, and tabletops. Provides informational, educational and technical services.

National Golf Course Owners Association., 291 Seven Farms Dr. Charleston, SC 29492. Phone: 800-933-4262 or (843)881-9956 Fax: (843)881-9958 E-mail: info@ngcoa.org • URL: http://www.ngcoa.org • Owners and operators of privately owned golf courses. Assist members to develop more productive, efficient, and profitable golf operations. Provides information on taxation, destination golf, community relations, environmental regulations, and marketing. Offers group purchasing opportunities. Conducts educational seminars. Compiles statistics.

National Golf Foundation. National Golf Foundation, 1150 S U.S. Hwy. 1, Ste. 401 Jupiter, FL 33477. Phone: (561)744-6006 Fax: 800-733-6006 or (561)744-6107 E-mail: general@ngf.org • URL: http://www.ngf.org • Golf consumers, golf courses, range operations and maintenance, industry sales, and golf facility development.

National Governors Association., Hall of States, 444 N Capitol St., Ste. 267 Washington, DC 20001-1512. Phone: (202)624-5300 Fax: (202)624-5313 E-mail: webmaster@nga.org • URL: http://www.nga.org • Governors of the 50 states, Guam, American Samoa, the Virgin Islands, the Northern Mariana Islands, and Puerto Rico. Serves as vehicle through which governors influence the development and implementation of national policy and apply creative leadership to state problems. Keeps the federal establishment informed of the needs and perceptions of states. Through its Center for Best Practices, it provides a vehicle for sharing information on innovative programs among the states and providing technical assistance to governors on a wide range of issues.

National Grain and Feed Association., 1250 Eye St., N.W., Ste. 1003 Washington, DC 20005-3922. Phone: (202)289-0873 Fax: (202)289-5388 E-mail: ngfa@ngfa.org • URL: http://www.ngfa.org • Formerly Grain and Feed Dealers National Association.

National Grange., 1616 H St. NW Washington, DC 20006. Phone: 888-4-GRANGE or (202)628-3507 Fax: (202)347-1091 E-mail: info@nationalgrange.org • URL: http://www.nationalgrange.org • Rural family service organization with a special interest in agriculture. Promotes mission and goals through legislative, social, educational, community service, youth and member services programs. Sponsors needlework and stuffed toy contests.

National Grants Management Association., 11654 Plaza America Dr., No. 609 Reston, VA 20190-4700. Phone: (703)648-9023 Fax: (703)648-9024 E-mail: info@ngma.org • URL: http://www.ngma.org • Strengthens the relationship between grant-making agencies and grant recipients by empowering both sides with knowledge through training, seminars, workshops, and conferences. Focuses on federal, state, and local governments and private foundations that provide grants, grants-in-aid, cooperative agreements, and subsidies.

National Grocers Association., 1005 N Glebe Rd., Ste. 250 Arlington, VA 22201-5758. Phone: (703)516-0700 Fax: (703)516-0115 E-mail: info@nationalgrocers.org • URL: http://www.nationalgrocers.org • Independent food retailers; wholesale food distributors servicing 29,000 food stores. Promotes industry interests and works to advance understanding, trade, and cooperation among all sectors of the food industry. Represents members' interests before the government. Aids in the development of programs designed to improve the productivity and efficiency of the food distribution industry. Offers services in areas such as store planning and engineering, personnel selection and training, operations, and advertising. Sponsors seminars and in-house training. Maintains liaison with Women Grocers of America (see separate entry), which serves as an advisory arm.

National Ground Water Association., 601 Dempsey Rd. Westerville, OH 43081-8978. Phone: 800-551-7379 or (614)898-7791 Fax: (614)898-7786 E-mail: ngwa@ngwa.org • URL: http://www.ngwa.org • Ground water drilling contractors; manufacturers and suppliers of drilling equipment; ground water scientists such as geologists, engineers, public health officials, and others interested in the problems of locating, developing, preserving, and using ground water supplies. Conducts seminars, and continuing education programs. Encourages scientific education, research, and the development of standards; offers placement services; compiles market statistics. Offers charitable program. Maintains speakers' bureau.

National Ground Water Association—Membership Directory. National Ground Water Association, 601 Dempsey Rd. Westerville, OH 43081-8978. Phone: 800-551-7379 or (614)898-7791 Fax: (614)898-7786 E-mail: ngwa@ngwa.org • URL: http://www.ngwa.org • Covers: About 16,500 water well drilling contractors, manufacturers and suppliers of equipment, and related technical professionals such as geologists and engineers in the United States, Canada, Mexico, and foreign countries. Entries include: Name, office address, phone, fax.

National Guard Association of the United States., 1 Massachusetts Ave. NW Washington, DC 20001. Phone: (202)789-0031 Fax: (202)682-9358 E-mail: ngaus@ngaus.org • URL: http://www.ngaus.org • Active and Retired Officers and Warrant Officers of the Army National Guard and Air National Guard of the States, Commonwealth of Puerto Rico, the District of Columbia, Guam, and the Virgin Islands. Goals include: adequate national security and a strong Army National Guard and Air National Guard of the United States as components of the armed forces. Sponsors public affairs competition for National Guard personnel. Maintains the Museum of the National Guard, containing rare art and artifacts relating to the militia and National Guard.

National Guard Executive Directors Association., 3706 Crawford Ave. Austin, TX 78731. Phone: (512)454-7300 Fax: (512)467-6803 E-mail: rlindner@ngat.org • URL: http://www.ngeda.org • Provides a forum for the exchange of information of common interest to members and the organizations they represent; encourages states to organize and maintain a National Guard association; participates in improving the operational readiness, training and image of the National Guard on both state and national levels.

National Guide to Funding for Libraries and Information Services. The Foundation Center, 79 Fifth Ave. New York, NY 10003-3076. Phone: 800-424-9836 or (212)620-4230 Fax: (212)807-3677 E-mail: orders@fdncenter.org • URL: http://www.fdncenter.org • 2001. $115.00. Sixth edition. Contains detailed information on about 600 foundations and corporate direct giving programs providing funding to libraries. Includes indexing by type of support, subject field, location, and key personnel.

National Hardwood Lumber Association., PO Box 34518, 6830 Raleigh-LaGrange Rd. Memphis, TN 38184-0518. Phone: (901)377-1818 Fax: (901)382-6419 E-mail: info@nhla.com • URL: http://www.nhla.com • United States, Canadian and International hardwood lumber and veneer manufacturers, distributors, and consumers. Inspects hardwood lumber. Maintains inspection training school. Conducts management and marketing seminars for the hardwood industry. Promotes research in hardwood timber management and utilization. Promotes public awareness of the industry.

National Hardwood Lumber Association Membership Directory. National Hardwood Lumber Association, 6830 Raleigh-LaGrange Rd. Memphis, TN 38184-0518. Phone: 800-933-0318 or (901)377-1818 Fax: (901)382-6419 E-mail: info@natlhardwood.org • URL: http://www.natlhardwood.org • Annual. $500.00. Members are hardwood lumber and veneer manufacturers, distributors, and users.

National Hardwood Magazine. Miller Publishing Co., PO Box 34908 Memphis, TN 38184. Phone: (901)372-8280 Fax: (901)338-9058 E-mail: mktgsubs@millerpublishing.com • URL: http://www.hardwaremag.com • Monthly. $45.00 per year.

National Hay Association., 102 Treasure Island Causeway St. Petersburg, FL 33706. Phone: 800-707-0014 or (727)367-9702 Fax: (727)367-9608 E-mail: haynha@aol.com • URL: http://nationalhay.org • Hay shippers, dealers, brokers, producers, and others interested in the hay industry.

National Health Club Association., 640 Plaza Dr., Ste. 300 Highlands Ranch, CO 80129. Phone: 800-765-6422 or (303)753-6422 Fax: (303)980-8006 E-mail: haynha@aol.com • URL: http://www.nhcainsurance.com • Fitness centers and health clubs. Provides insurance and financial services to the fitness center/health club industry nationwide. Awards strength and aerobic certification.

National Health Directory. Aspen Publishers Inc., 76 9th Ave., 7th Fl. New York, NY 10011. Phone: 800-638-8437 or (212)771-0600 Fax: (212)771-0885 E-mail: ngwa@ngwa.org • URL: http://www.aspenpublishers.com • Covers: about 10,000 public health-care officials at policy-making levels. Covers federal and state agencies, and members of congress and key health committees and county and city health officials. Entries include: Agency name, address; names, titles, addresses, and phone numbers of key personnel.

National Hog Farmer. Primedia Business Magazines and Media, 7900 International Dr., Ste. 300 Minneapolis, MN 55425. Phone: 800-795-5445 or (952)851-9329 Fax: (952)851-4601 E-mail: subs@primediabusiness.com • URL: http://www.primediabusiness.com • Monthly. $115.00 per year.

National Home Center News: News and Analysis for the Home Improvement, Building Material Industry. Lebhar-Friedman, Inc., 425 Park Ave. New York, NY 10022. Phone: 800-766-6999 or (212)756-5000 E-mail: info@lf.com • URL: http://www.lf.com • 22 times a year. $99.00 per year. Includes special feature issues on hardware and tools, building materials, millwork, electrical supplies, lighting, and kitchens.

National Home Furnishings Association., 3910 Tinsley Dr., Ste. 101 High Point, NC 27265-3610. Phone: 800-888-9590 or (336)886-6100 Fax: (336)801-6102 E-mail: info@nhfa.org • URL: http://www.nhfa.org • Provides business services to help retailers of home furnishings grow their businesses. Provides educational programs for retail sales managers and trainers, for middle management, for owners and executives, and for family businesses.

National Homeowners Association., PO Box 221225 Chantilly, VA 20153. Phone: (703)581-1515 Fax: (703)581-1234 E-mail: info@nhfa.org Advocacy organization for individual homeowners. Promotes a political and economic climate favorable to American homeowners; provides legislative/regulatory liaison. Conducts political, educational, and consumer programs. Topics researched include: taxes, insurance, energy savings, home maintenance and repairs, mortgage and financing options, crime and safety precautions, and real estate practices. **Convention/Meeting:** none.

National Honey Packers and Dealers Association.

National Housing Conference., 1801 K St. NW, Ste. M-100 Washington, DC 20006-1301. Phone: (202)466-2121 Fax: (202)466-2122 E-mail: cegan@nhc.org • URL: http://www.nhc.org • Housing authority officials, community development specialists, builders, bankers, lawyers, accountants, owners, residents, insurers, architects and planners, religious organizations, labor groups, and national housing and housing related organizations. Mobilizes support for effective programs in housing and community development as well as affordable and accessible housing for all Americans. Holds educational programs.

National Human Resources Association., PO Box 7326 Nashua, NH 03060-7326. Phone: (866)523-4417 Fax: (603)891-5760 E-mail: info@humanresources.org • URL: http://www.humanresources.org • Represents human resource executives in business, industry, education, and government. Established to expand and improve the professionalism of those in human resource management.

National Hydropower Association., One Massachusetts Ave. NW, Ste. 850 Washington, DC 20001. Phone: (202)682-1700 Fax: (202)682-9478 E-mail: help@hydro.org • URL: http://www.hydro.org • Represents hydrodevelopers, dam site owners, manufacturers, utilities and municipalities, individuals from the financial community (such as bankers, brokers, and investors), civil contracting firms, architects, engineering firms, and others actively involved in the promotion and development of hydropower. Promotes the development of hydroelectric energy. Participates in the regulatory process on issues such as simplified licensing procedures, purchase power rates, removal of regulatory barriers, and timely implementation of previously adopted legislation. Informs the government about the potential of hydropower and also monitors and drafts new legislation to government regulatory and legislative bodies.

National Ice Cream Retailers Association., 1028 W Devon Ave. Elk Grove Village, IL 60007. Phone: (847)301-7500 Fax: (847)301-8402 E-mail: info@nicyra.org • URL: http://www.nicyra.org • Represents frozen dessert retailers that operate ice cream and frozen yogurt dipping stores or parlors. Provides free and frank exchange of information among members so that all may improve their operations, increase profits and prosper.

National Immigration Forum., 50 F St. NW, Ste. 300 Washington, DC 20001. Phone: (202)347-0040 Fax: (202)347-0058 E-mail: info@nicyra.org • URL: http://www.immigrationforum.org • Dedicated to extending and defending America's tradition as a nation of immigrants. Supports the reunification of families, the rescue and resettlement of refugees fleeing persecution, and the equitable treatment of immigrants under the law. Encourages immigrants to become U.S. citizens and promote cooperation and understanding between immigrants and other Americans.

National Independent Automobile Dealers Association., 2521 Brown Blvd. Arlington, TX 76006. Phone: 800-682-3837 or (817)640-3838 Fax: (817)649-5866 E-mail: mike@niada.com • URL: http://www.niada.com • Individuals, companies, or corporations licensed by their states as dealers to buy and sell used motor vehicles; associate members are businesses related to or associated with the buying or selling of motor vehicles. Gathers and disseminates information relative to the used car industry; represents used car dealers before regulatory and legislative bodies; provides educational and other programs to help used car dealers understand their responsibilities; works for the betterment of the automobile industry. Works closely with local and state independent automobile dealers' associations and others concerning dealers and the public. Maintains code of fair dealing for members. Conducts seminars, meetings, and professional training programs. Maintains speakers' bureau, services for children, and charitable programs. Sponsors competitions; compiles statistics.

National Independent Bank Equipment and Systems Association., 5300 Sequoia NW, Ste. 205 Albuquerque, NM 87120. Phone: 800-843-6082 or (505)839-7958 Fax: (505)839-0017 E-mail: nibesa@nibesa.com • URL: http://www.nibesa.com • Formerly National Independent Bank Equipment Suppliers Association.

National Industrial Security Program Operating Manual. U.S. Department of Defense. Available from U.S. Government Printing Office, Washington, DC 20402. Phone: (202)512-1800 Fax: (202)512-2250 E-mail: gpoaccess@gpo.gov • URL: http://www.accessgpo.gov • 1995.

National Industrial Transportation League., 1700 N Moore St., Ste. 1900 Arlington, VA 22209. Phone: (703)524-5011 Fax: (703)524-5017 E-mail: info@nitl.org • URL: http://www.nitl.

org • Seeks to promote adequate national and international transportation; encourages the exchange of ideas and information concerning traffic and transportation; and cooperates with regulatory agencies and other transportation companies in developing an understanding of legislation.

National Information Standards Organization., 1 N Charles St., Ste. 1905 Baltimore, MD 21201. Phone: (866)957-1593 or (301)654-2512 Fax: (301)654-1721 E-mail: nisohq@niso.org • URL: http://www.niso.org • Identifies, develops, maintains, and publishes technical standards to manage information in the changing environment used by libraries, publishers, and information services. Supports open access to NISO standards. Standards available at website.

National Institute for Automotive Service Excellence., 101 Blue Seal Dr. SE Leesburg, VA 20175. Phone: 877-273-8324 or (703)669-6600 Fax: (703)713-0727 E-mail: webmaster@asecert.org • URL: http://www.asecert.org • A public interest organization which promotes high standards in automotive service and repair. Encourages effective training programs for automobile mechanics/technicians. Affiliated with National Automotive Technicians Education Foundation.

National Institute for Fitness and Sport.

National Institute for Work and Learning., Academy for Educational Development, 1875 Connecticut Ave., N.W. Washington, DC 20009-5721. Phone: (202)884-8186 Fax: (202)884-8422 E-mail: niwl@aed.org • URL: http://www.niwl.org • Research areas include adult education, training, unemployment insurance, and career development.

National Institute of Ceramic Engineers., c/o Diane C. Folz, Virginia Polytechnic Institute and State University, Dept. of Materials Science and Engineering, 213 Holden Hall Blacksburg, VA 24061. Phone: (540)231-3897 Fax: (540)231-8919 E-mail: dfolz@vt.edu • URL: http://www.acers.org • Affiliated with Ceramic Education Council and Keramos.

National Institute of Government Purchasing.

National Institute of Hypertension Studies-Institute of Hypertension School of Research., P.O. Box 02006 Detroit, MI 48202. Phone: (313)872-0505 Fax: (313)872-0505 Formerly Institute of Hypertension Studies-Institute of Hypertension School of Research.

National Institute of Management Counsellors.

National Institute of Oilseed Products.

National Institute of Senior Housing., c/o National Council on the Aging, 409 3rd St., S.W. Washington, DC 20024. Phone: 800-424-9046 or (202)479-1200 Fax: (202)479-0735 E-mail: info@ncoa.org • URL: http://www.ncoa.org • Members are organizations and individuals concerned with the housing needs of older persons. Provides information on the development and management of housing suitable for the elderly. Affiliated with National Council on Aging.

National Institute on Community-Based Long-Term Care., c/o National Council on the Aging, 409 Third St., S.W. Washington, DC 20024. Phone: 800-424-9046 or (202)479-1200 Fax: (202)479-0735 E-mail: info@ncoa.org • URL: http://www.ncoa.org • A division of the National Council on the Aging. Seeks to promote and develop a comprehensive long-term health care system.

National Insulation Association., 99 Canal Center Plz., Ste. 222 Alexandria, VA 22314. Phone: (703)683-6422 Fax: (703)549-4838 E-mail: mjones@insulation.org • URL: http://www.insulation.org • Insulation contractors, distributors, and manufacturers.

National Insurance Association., 411 Chapel Hill St. Durham, NC 27701. E-mail: nia1921@aol.com Conducts annual Institute in +Agency +Management and Institute in +Home Office Operations. Sponsors National Insurance Week.

National Insurance Law Review. NILS Publishing Co., 21625 Prairie St. Chatsworth, CA 91311. Phone: 800-423-5910 Quarterly. $95.00 per year. Contains insurance-related articles from major law reviews.

National Interfaith Coalition on Aging., c/o National Council on the Aging, 300 D St. SW, Ste. 801 Washington, DC 20024. Phone: 800-424-9046 or (202)479-1200 Fax: (202)479-0735 E-mail: info@ncoa.org • URL: http://www.ncoa.org • Affiliated with National Council on Aging.

National Interstate Council of State Boards of Cosmetology.

National Investor Relations Institute., 8020 Towers Crescent Dr., Ste. 250 Vienna, VA 22182. Phone: (703)506-3570 Fax: (703)506-3571 E-mail: info@niri.org • URL: http://www.niri.org • Executives engaged in investor relations. Identifies the role of the investor relations practitioner; protects a free and open market with equity and access to investors of all kinds; improves communication between corporate management and shareholders, present and future. Holds professional development seminars and conducts research programs. Maintains placement service and speakers' bureau; compiles statistics.

National Jeweler. VNU Business Media, 770 Broadway New York, NY 10003-9595. Phone: 800-344-7119 or (646)654-4500 Fax: (646)654-7212 • URL: http://www.vnubusinessmedia.com • Bimonthly. $65.00 per year. For jewelry retailers.

National Journal: The Weekly on Politics and Government. National Journal Group, Inc., 1501 M St. NW, Ste. 300 Washington, DC 20005. Phone: 800-424-2921 or (202)739-8400 Fax: (202)833-8069 • URL: http://www.nationaljournal.com • Weekly $1,499.00 per year. Includes semiannual supplement *Capital Source*. A non-partisan weekly magazine on politics and government.

National Kitchen and Bath Association., 687 Willow Grove St. Hackettstown, NJ 07840. Phone: (908)852-0033 Fax: (908)852-1695 E-mail: feeback@nkba.org • URL: http://www.nkba.org • Formerly American Institute of Kitchen Dealers.

National Knitwear and Sportswear Association., 386 Park Ave. S New York, NY 10016. Phone: (212)683-7520 Fax: (212)532-0766 E-mail: nksa@pop.interport.net • URL: http://www.rtwear.com • Formerly National Knitted Outerwear Association.

National Law Journal: The Weekly Newspaper for the Profession. American Lawyer Media Inc., 345 Park Ave., S. New York, NY 10010. Phone: 800-888-8300 or (212)779-9200 • URL: http://www.americanlawyermedia.com • Weekly. $158.00 per year. News and analysis of the latest developments in the law and the law profession.

National Lawyers Guild., 132 Nassau St., Rm. 922 New York, NY 10038. Phone: (212)679-5100 Fax: (212)679-2811 E-mail: nlgno@nlg.org • URL: http://www.nlg.org • Lawyers, law students, legal workers, and jailhouse lawyers dedicated to seek economic justice, social equality, and the right to political dissent. Serves as national center for progressive legal work providing training programs to both members and nonmembers. Sponsors skills seminars in different areas of law. Maintains speakers' bureau and offers legal referrals.

National League of Cities., 1301 Pennsylvania Ave. NW Washington, DC 20004-1763. Phone: (202)626-3000 Fax: (202)626-3043 E-mail: inet@nlc.org • URL: http://www.nlc.org • Formerly American Municipal Association.

National Legal Aid and Defender Association.

National Library of Medicine (NLM). National Institutes of Health (NIH)Phone: 888-346-3656 or (301)496-1131 Fax: (301)480-3537 E-mail: access@nlm.nih.gov • URL: http://www.nlm.nih.gov • NLM Web site offers free access through MEDLINE ("PubMed") to about nine million references to articles appearing in some 4,000 biomedical journals, with abstracts. Search interfaces range from "simple keywords to advanced Boolean expressions." The NLM site offers many links to other sources of biomedical and technical information (the National Center for Biotechnology Information, for example). Fees: Free.

National Locksmith. National Publishing Co., 1533 Burgundy Parkway Streamwood, IL 60107. Phone: (708)837-2044 Monthly. $41.00.

National Lubricating Grease Institute., 4635 Wyandotte St. Kansas City, MO 64112-1509. Phone: (816)931-9480 Fax: (816)753-5026 E-mail: nlgi@nlgi.org • URL: http://www.nlgi.org • Companies manufacturing or selling all types of lubricating greases; suppliers to such companies; technical and educational organizations. Promotes research and testing for the development of better lubricating greases and improved grease lubrication engineering service to industry. Collects and disseminates technical data; conducts forums and educational program. Operates the National Lubricating +Grease Institute Research Fund.

National Luggage Dealers Association., 1817 Elmdale Ave. Glenview, IL 60025-1355. Phone: (847)998-6869 Fax: (847)998-6884 E-mail: inquiry@nlda.com • URL: http://www.nlda.com • Represents retailers of luggage, leather goods, gifts, and handbags. Buying group producing promotional materials.

National Lumber and Building Materials Dealers Association., 40 Ivy St., S.E. Washington, DC 20003. Phone: 800-634-8645 or (202)547-2230 Fax: (202)547-7640 E-mail: nikki@dealer.org • URL: http://www.dealer.org • Formerly National Retail Lumber Dealers Association.

National Management Association., 2210 Arbor Blvd. Dayton, OH 45439. Phone: (937)294-0421 Fax: (937)294-2374 E-mail: nma@nma1.org • URL: http://www.nma1.org • Business and industrial management personnel; membership comes from supervisory level, with the remainder from middle management and above. Seeks to develop and recognize management as a profession and to promote the free enterprise system. Prepares chapter programs on basic management, management policy and practice, communications, human behavior, industrial relations, economics, political education, and liberal education. Maintains speakers' bureau and hall of fame. Maintains educational, charitable, and research programs. Sponsors charitable programs.

National Marine Manufacturers Association., 1819 L St. NW, Ste. 700 Washington, DC 20036-3830. Phone: (202)861-1180 Fax: (202)861-1181 E-mail: webmaster@nmma.org • URL: http://www.nmma.org • Manufacturers of marine propulsion engines. Staff services and publications provided by National Marine Manufacturers Association (see separate entry).

National Marine Representatives Association., PO Box 360 Gurnee, IL 60031. Phone: (847)662-3167 Fax: (847)336-7126 E-mail: info@nmraonline.org • URL: http://www.nmraonline.org • Works to serve the marine industry independent sales representatives and the manufacturers selling through representatives. Serves as industry voice, networking tool and information source promoting benefits of utilizing independent marine representatives for sales. Aims to assist manufacturers find the right marine sales reps for product lines.

National Marine Representatives Association—Directory. National Marine Representatives Association, 1333 Delany Rd., Ste. 500, PO Box 360 Gurnee, IL 60031. Phone: (847)662-3167 Fax: (847)336-7126 E-mail: info@nmraonline.org • URL: http://www.mmraonline.org • Covers: Approximately 400 independent representatives selling pleasure craft and other small boats, motors, and marine accessories. Entries include: Name, address, phone, fax, e-mail, manufacturers represented, territories covered, customer classifications.

National Materials Advisory Board., 500 5th St. NW, 500 5th St. NW, MS 932 Washington, DC 20001-2736. Phone: (202)334-3505 Fax: (202)334-3718 E-mail: nmab@nas.edu • URL: http://www7.nationalacademies.org/nmab • Represents members of the board and its committees and panels appointed by the chairman of the National Research Council (see separate entry); industry, universities, research institutes, and government. Promotes the advancement of materials science and engineering in the national interest. Conducts studies on materials problem, potential approaches, and policy issues.

National Meat Association., 1970 Broadway, Ste. 825, 1970 Broadway, No. 825 Oakland, CA 94612. Phone: (510)763-1533 Fax: (510)763-6186 E-mail: staff@nmaonline.org • URL: http://www.nmaonline.org • Meat packers, processors, slaughterers, and jobbers. Promotes interests of independent meat packers in all states. Conducts group purchasing activities and administers group insurance program. Provides legal, freight rate, and contract advisory services. Offers research programs; compiles statistics.

National Mining Association., 101 Constitution Ave. NW, Ste. 500 E Washington, DC 20001-2133. Phone: (202)463-2600 Fax: (202)463-2666 E-mail: craulston@nma.org • URL: http://www.nma.org • Producers and sellers of coal and hardrock minerals, equipment manufacturers, distributors, equipment suppliers, other energy suppliers, consultants, utility companies, and coal transporters. Serves as liaison between the industry and federal government agencies. Keeps members informed of legislative and regulatory actions. Works with industry, consumers, and government agencies on mining industry issues. Seeks improved conditions for export of steam and metallurgical coal. Collects, analyzes, and distributes industry statistics; makes special studies of competitive fuels, coal and metal markets, production and consumption forecasts, and industry planning.

National Minority Supplier Development Council., 1040 Ave. of the Americas, 2nd Fl. New York, NY 10018. Phone: (212)944-2430 Fax: (212)719-9611 E-mail: nmsdc1@aol.com • URL: http://www.nmsdc.org • Provides a direct link between its 3,500 corporate members and minority-owned businesses (Black, Hispanic, Asian and Native American) and increases procurement and business opportunities for minority businesses of all sizes.

National Mortgage Directory: Lenders, Brokers & Servicers. Thomson Media, One State St. Plaza New York, NY 10004. Phone: 800-221-1809 or (212)803-8200 Fax: (212)843-9635 E-mail: custserv@thomsonmedia.com • URL: http://www.thomsonmedia.com • Annual. $479.00. Covers both residential and commercial sectors. Includes the top 400 lenders, 300 servicers, 150 mortgage brokers, commercial lenders, subprime lenders and other listings, with rankings and statistical tables.

National Motor Freight Traffic Association., 1001 N Fairfax St., Ste. 600 Alexandria, VA 22314. Phone: (866)411-6632 or (703)838-1810 or (703)838-1811 Fax: (703)683-6296 E-mail: membership@nmfta.org • URL: http://www.nmfta.org • Motor common carriers of general commodities. Represents interests of membership before the Surface Transportation Board, the Congress, the courts and state regulatory agencies.

National Naval Officers Association., PO Box 10871 Alexandria, VA 22310-0871. Phone: (703)997-1068 Fax: (703)997-1068 E-mail: webmaster@nnoa.org • URL: http://www.nnoa.org • Active, reserve, and retired Navy, Marine, and Coast Guard officers and students in college and military sea service programs. Promotes and assists recruitment, retention, and career development of minority officers in the naval service. Conducts specialized education; maintains counseling, referral, and mentorship. Makes available non-ROTC grants-in-aid. Sponsors competitions; operates charitable program.

National Newspaper Association., PO Box 7540, PO Box 7540 Columbia, MO 65205-7540. Phone: 800-829-4662 or (573)882-5800 Fax: (573)884-5490 E-mail: briansteffens@nna.org • URL: http://www.nna.org • Aims to protect, promote, and enhance community newspapers. Represents community newspapers across America; represents the industry before legislators, agencies and departments in Washington, D.C. that enact laws, rules and regulations, or conduct business, and that affect community newspapers. Promotes quality journalism and business practices at its annual convention, through its various contests and awards, and various other educational programs.

National Newspaper Index. Gale Cengage Learning, 27500 Drake Rd. Farmington Hills, MI 48331-3535. Phone: 800-877-GALE or (248)699-GALE Fax: 800-414-5043 or (248)699-8069 E-mail: galeord@gale.com • URL: http://gale.cengage.com • Citations to news items in five major newspapers, 1970 to present. Weekly updates. Inquire as to online cost and availability.

National Newspaper Publishers Association., 3200 13th St. NW Washington, DC 20010. Phone: (202)588-8764 Fax: (202)588-5302 E-mail: chairman@nnpa.org • URL: http://

SOURCES CITED

www.nnpa.org • Represents publishers of daily and weekly newspapers. Maintains Hall of Fame.

The National Notary. National Notary Association, 9350 Soto Ave. Chatsworth, CA 91313-2402. Phone: 800-876-6827 or (818)739-4000 Fax: (818)700-0920 E-mail: nna@nationalnotary.org • URL: http://www.nationalnotary.org • Bimonthly. $36.00 per year.

National Notary Association., PO Box 2402, 9350 DeSoto Ave. Chatsworth, CA 91313-2402. Phone: 800-876-6827 or (818)739-4000 Fax: 800-833-1211 E-mail: services@nationalnotary.org • URL: http://www.nationalnotary.org • Notaries public (officers empowered to witness the signing of documents, identify the signers, take acknowledgments, and administer oaths). Works to teach notaries public in the U.S. their duties, powers, limitations, liabilities, and obligations. Keeps members informed of changes in notary law; offers various services, supplies, and insurance plans to members. Maintains speakers' bureau.

National Now Times. National Organization for Women, 735 15th St., NW, 2nd Fl. Washington, DC 20005. Phone: (202)628-8669 E-mail: now@now.org • URL: http://www.now.org • Bimonthly. Free to members; non-members, $35.00 per year.

National Ocean Industries Association., 1120 G St. NW, Ste. 900 Washington, DC 20005. Phone: (202)347-6900 Fax: (202)347-8650 E-mail: mkearns@noia.org • URL: http://www.noia.org • Corporations organized to promote the common business interests of the offshore and ocean-oriented industries by: increasing public understanding of the ocean's use and its relation to the economy; encouraging interest in industrial, scientific, recreational, research, and educational activities in the field of ocean enterprise; encouraging the development and use of the resources of the ocean consistent with environmental practices and safeguards; encouraging compatible use of ocean resources; improving communication between industry and the federal government. Supports legislation and other governmental action favorable to the offshore and ocean industry and counsels against such action when it is not favorable. Seeks to expand the role of the free enterprise system in the development of ocean resources.

National Oilseed Processors Association., 1300 L St. NW, Ste. 1020 Washington, DC 20005-4168. Phone: (202)842-0463 Fax: (202)842-9126 E-mail: nopa@nopa.org • URL: http://www.nopa.org • Represents processors of oilseeds.

National Onion Association., 822 7th St., Ste. 510 Greeley, CO 80631-3941. Phone: (970)353-5895 Fax: (970)353-5897 E-mail: nopa@nopa.org • URL: http://www.onions-usa.org • Growers, brokers, grower-shippers, shippers, suppliers, and support professionals engaged in the onion industry. Promotes the onion industry. Compiles monthly statistical report of stocks-on-hand, acreage, yield, and production of onions in the U.S. Lobbies issues of importance to national onion industry.

National Onion Association—Newsletter. National Onion Association, 822 7th St., No. 510 Greeley, CO 80631. Phone: (970)353-5895 Fax: (970)353-5897 E-mail: wmininger@onions-usa.org • URL: http://www.onions-usa.org • Description: Provides information on the onion industry.

National Opinion Research Center. National Opinion Research Center, 1155 E 60th St. Chicago, IL 60637. Phone: (773)256-6000 Fax: (773)753-7886 E-mail: norcinfo@norcmail.uchicago.edu • URL: http://www.norc.uchicago.edu • Sociology, social psychology, education, demography, child studies, and policy studies, including studies of political behavior, religious attitudes, economic behavior, career development, family behavior, and survey research methodology. Research group consists of the Center on Aging, Sloan Center on Families and Work, the Data and Research and Development Center, and the Population Research Center. Conducts the General Social Survey (GSS). Maintains a national sample frame that allows national representative samples for complex, multi-year surveys.

National Optometric Association., PO Box F, PO Box F East Chicago, IN 46312. Phone: 877-394-2020 or (219)398-4483 Fax: (219)398-1077 E-mail: ddodpc@verizon.net • URL: http://www.natoptassoc.org • Represents optometrists dedicated to increasing awareness of the status of eye/vision health in the minority community and the national community at-large. Strives to make known the impact of the eye/vision dysfunction on the effectiveness and productivity of citizens and the academic proficiency of students. Conducts national minority recruiting programs, job placement, assistance programs for graduates, practitioners, and optometric organizations, and the promotion of delivery of care. Maintains speakers' bureau. Offers specialized education program.

The National Organization for Men., 11 Park Pl., Ste. 1100 New York, NY 10007. Phone: (212)686-6253 or (212)766-4030 Fax: (212)791-3056 E-mail: info@tnom.com • URL: http://www.tnom.com • Encourages rational and objective state and national divorce laws. Absorbed National Committee for Fair Divorce and Alimony Laws.

National Organization for Women., 733 15th St., N.W., 2nd Fl. Washington, DC 20005. Phone: (202)628-8669 Fax: (202)785-8576 E-mail: now@now.org • URL: http://www.now.org • Includes men and women seeking equality for women.

National Packing News. National Packing News, PO Box 829 Granby, MO 64844. Phone: (209)728-1455 Fax: (209)728-3277 E-mail: npnews@jscomm.net Description: Discusses topics that affect the food processing industry in the nation, including production, marketing, new developments and products, new plants and plant expansions, and professional appointments. Recurring features include news of research, statistics, book reviews, and obituaries. **Remarks:** Incorporates the former Eastern Packing News and Western Packing News.

National Paint and Coatings Association., 1500 Rhode Island Ave., N.W. Washington, DC 20005-5597. Phone: (202)462-6272 Fax: (202)462-8549 E-mail: npca@paint.org • URL: http://www.paint.org • Formerly National Paint, Varnish and Lacquer Association.

National Paper Trade Association., 500 Bi-County Blvd., Ste. 200E Farmingdale, NY 11735. Phone: 800-355-6782 or (631)777-2223 Fax: (631)777-2224 E-mail: bill@gonpta.com • URL: http://www.gonpta.com • Wholesale distributors and suppliers of paper, plastics and allied products.

National Paperbox Association Membership Directory. National Paperbox Association, 113 S West St., 3rd Fl. Alexandria, VA 22314-2858. Phone: (703)684-2212 Fax: (703)683-6920 E-mail: npahq@paperbox.org • URL: http://www.paperbox.org • Annual. $150.00.

National Park Hospitality Association., 1225 New York Ave. NW, Ste. 450 Washington, DC 20005. Phone: (202)682-9530 Fax: (202)682-9529 E-mail: info@nphassn.org • URL: http://parkpartners.org • Represents private concessionaires operating in the U.S. national parks. Acts as liaison between members and the National Park Service and Congress.

National Parking Association., 1112 16th St. NW, Ste. 300 Washington, DC 20036. Phone: 800-647-PARK or (202)296-4336 Fax: (202)296-3102 E-mail: info@npapark.org • URL: http://www.npapark.org • Owners and operators of off-street parking facilities; architects, traffic engineers, equipment suppliers and manufacturers, colleges, universities, municipalities, airport authorities; others with an interest in downtown parking. Provides specialized education programs; offers scholarship program through the Parking Industry Institute.

National Parliamentarian. National Association of Parliamentarians, 213 S. Main St. Independence, MO 64050-3808. Phone: 888-627-2929 or (816)833-3892 Fax: (816)833-3893 E-mail: hq@nap2.org • URL: http://www.parlimentarians.org • Quarterly. $20.00 per year. Articles and questions with answers on parliamentary procedure.

National Partnership for Women and Families., 1875 Connecticut Ave., N. W., Suite 710 Washington, DC 20009. Phone: (202)986-2600 Fax: (202)986-2539 E-mail: info@nationalpartnership.org • URL: http://www.nationalpartnership.org • Formerly Women's Legal Defense Fund.

National Pasta Association., 1156 15th St. NW, Ste. 900 Washington, DC 20005. Phone: (202)637-5888 Fax: (202)223-9741 E-mail: info@ilovepasta.org • URL: http://www.ilovepasta.org • Manufacturers of pasta in the U.S. and suppliers to the industry. Seeks to improve manufacturer and supplier efficiency. Conducts agricultural and technical research programs. Sponsors U.S. pasta product public relations program and pasta/durum wheat technical course.

National Pasta Association FYI Newsletter. National Pasta Association, 1156 15th St., NW, Ste. 900 Washington, DC 20005. Phone: (202)637-5888 Fax: (202)223-9741 • URL: http://www.ilovepasta.org • Weekly. Membership.

National Peach Council., 12 Nicklaus Ln., Ste. 101 Columbia, SC 29229. Phone: (803)788-7101 Fax: (803)865-8090 E-mail: peachcouncil@att.net • URL: http://www.nationalpeach.org • Represents peach growers, allied industries, and research and extension personnel. Lobbies the U.S. Congress on behalf of fresh market peach growers, compiles and publishes statistics on the peach industry and prepares annual preseason crop estimates.

National Pecan Shellers Association., 1100 Johnson Ferry Rd., Ste. 300 Atlanta, GA 30342. Phone: (404)252-3663 Fax: (404)252-0774 E-mail: info@ilovepecans.org • URL: http://www.ilovepecans.org • Shellers and processors of pecans. Promotes the welfare and interests of the pecan shelling and processing industry.

National Pest Management Association International., 10460 N St. Fairfax, VA 22030. Phone: 800-678-6722 or (703)352-6762 Fax: (703)352-3031 E-mail: info@pestworld.org • URL: http://www.pestworld.org • Represents firms engaged in control of insects, rodents, birds, and other pests, in or around structures, through use of insecticides, rodenticides, miticides, fumigants, and non-chemical methods. Provides advisory services on control procedures, new products, and safety and business administration practices. Promotes June as National Pest Control Month. Sponsors research, periodic technical and management seminars.

National Pest Management International.

National Petrochemical and Refiners Association.

National Petroleum Council., 1625 K St. NW, Ste. 600 Washington, DC 20006. Phone: (202)393-6100 Fax: (202)331-8539 E-mail: info@npc.org • URL: http://www.npc.org • Advisory council to the Secretary of Energy on matters relating to oil and gas.

National Pharmaceutical Association., 107 Kilmayne Dr., Ste. C Cary, NC 27511. Phone: 800-944-NPHA or (919)831-5368 Fax: (919)469-5870 E-mail: npha@npha.net • URL: http://www.npha.net • State and local associations of professional minority pharmacists. Provides a means whereby members may "contribute to their common improvement, share their experiences, and contribute to the public good".

National Pharmaceutical Council., 1894 Preston White Dr. Reston, VA 20191-5433. Phone: (703)620-6390 Fax: (703)476-0904 E-mail: info@npcnow.com • URL: http://www.npcnow.org • Pharmaceutical manufacturers producing high quality prescription medication and other pharmaceutical products. Generates research; conducts specialized educational programs, and forums.

National Plumbing Codes Handbook. R. Dodge Woodson. McGraw-Hill, 1221 Ave. of the Americas New York, NY 10020. Phone: 800-722-4726 or (212)512-2000 Fax: (212)512-4502 E-mail: customer.service@mcgraw-hill.com • URL: http://www.mcgraw-hill.com • 1997. $44.95. Second revised edition.

National Policy Association., 3424 Porter St. NW Washington, DC 20016-3126. Phone: (202)265-7685 Fax: (202)797-5516 E-mail: npa@npa1.org • URL: http://www.npa1.org • Research institution that helps private and public sector leaders from agriculture, business, labor, and academia to better understand national economic and social issues. Conducts research and analysis on national and international economic and social issues.

National Pork Producers Council., 10664 Justin Dr. Urbandale, IA 50322. Phone: (515)278-8012 Fax: (515)278-8011 E-mail: flynnk@nppc.org • URL: http://www.nppc.org • Federation of state pork producer associations. Promotes the pork industry through research programs, consumer education, and lobbying activities. Compiles statistics; maintains speakers' bureau and hall of fame.

National Ports and Waterways Institute.

National Potato Council., 1300 L St. NW, No. 910 Washington, DC 20005-4107. Phone: (202)682-9456 Fax: (202)682-0333 E-mail: spudinfo@nationalpotatocouncil.org • URL: http://www.nationalpotatocouncil.org • Commercial potato growers. Takes action on national potato legislative, regulatory, and environmental issues.

National Prepared Food Association., 485 Kinderkamack Rd., 2nd Fl. Mahwah, NJ 07430. Phone: (201)634-1870 Fax: (201)634-1871 E-mail: star1870@aol.com Manufacturers, brokers, and distributors involved in food service to restaurants, hotels and insitutions.

National Press Club., National Press Bldg., 529 14th St. NW, 14th Fl. Washington, DC 20045. Phone: (202)662-7500 Fax: (202)662-7512 E-mail: info@press.org • URL: http://www.press.org • Reporters, writers, and news people employed by newspapers, wire services, magazines, radio and television stations, and other forms of news media; former news people and associates of news people are nonvoting members. Sponsors sports, travel, and cultural events, rap sessions with news figures and authors, and newsmaker breakfasts and luncheons. Offers monthly training.

National Press Photographers Association., 3200 Croasdaile Dr., Ste. 306 Durham, NC 27705-2588. Phone: (919)383-7246 Fax: (919)383-7261 E-mail: info@nppa.org • URL: http://www.nppa.org • Professional news photographers and others whose occupation has a direct professional relationship with photojournalism, the art of news communication by photographic image through publication, television film, or theater screen. Sponsors annual television-news film workshop and annual cross-country (five locations) short course. Conducts annual competition for news photos and for television-news film, and monthly contest for still clipping and television-news film.

National Private Truck Council., 950 N Gelebe Rd., Ste. 530 Arlington, VA 22203-4183. Phone: (703)683-1300 Fax: (703)683-1217 E-mail: info@nptc.org • URL: http://www.nptc.org • Represents private motor carrier truck fleets and their suppliers.

National Propane Gas Association., 1150 17th St. NW, Ste. 310 Washington, DC 20036-4623. Phone: (202)466-7200 Fax: (202)466-7205 E-mail: info@npga.org • URL: http://www.npga.org • Represents the propane industry, including small businesses and large corporations engaged in the retail marketing of propane gas and appliances, producers and wholesalers of propane gas and equipment, manufacturers and fabricators of propane gas cylinders and tanks, propane transporters, and manufacturer's representatives. Works to promote the safe and increased use of propane; advocates in Congress and federal regulatory agencies for favorable environment for production, distributing, and marketing of propane gas. Develops safety standards and training materials for the safe use and distribution of propane gas.

National Property Management Association., 28100 U.S. Hwy. 19 N, Ste. 400 Clearwater, FL 33761. Phone: (727)736-3788 Fax: (727)736-6707 E-mail: hq@npma.org • URL: http://www.npma.org • Aims to build leadership by educating, training and promoting standards of competency and ethical behavior in the asset management of personal property. Serves property professionals throughout the United States; members represent companies and organizations in both the public and private sectors, including scientific laboratories, universities, hospitals, public school systems, and local, state and federal government agencies.

The National Provisioner: Serving Meat, Poultry, and Seafood Processors. Stagnito Communications, Inc., 155 Pfingsten Rd., Ste. 200 Deerfield, IL 60015. Phone: (847)205-5660 Fax: (847)205-5680 E-mail: info@stagnito.com • URL: http://www.stagnito.com • Monthly. Free to qualified personnel; others, $85.04 per year. Annual *Buyer's Guide* available.

Meat, poultry and seafood newsletter.

National Public Accountant. National Society of Accountants, 1010 N. Fairfax St. Alexandria, VA 22314-1574. Phone: 800-966-6679 or (703)549-6400 Fax: (703)549-2984 E-mail: arichman@nsacct.orgg • URL: http://www.nsacct.org • 10 times a year. Free to members; non-members, $20.00 per year. For accounting and tax practitioners.

National Ready Mixed Concrete Association., 900 Spring St. Silver Spring, MD 20910. Phone: 888-846-7622 or (301)587-1400 or (301)587-1400 Fax: (301)585-4219 E-mail: info@nrmca.org • URL: http://www.nrmca.org • Concrete plant manufacturers. Develops engineering standards with a view toward simplification and standardization of sizes, capacities, and other criteria associated with the manufacture of concrete plants. Performs services leading to higher quality concrete plant equipment.

National Real Estate Index. CB Richard Ellis, 865 S Figueroa St., 34th Fl. Los Angeles, CA 90017. Phone: 800-992-7257 or (213)438-4880 Fax: (213)438-4820 • URL: http://www.cbre.com • Price and frequency on application. Provides reports on commercial real estate prices, rents, capitalization rates, and trends in more than 65 metropolitan areas. Time span is 12 years. Includes urban office buildings, suburban offices, warehouses, retail properties, and apartments.

National Real Estate Investor. Primedia Business Magazines and Media, 9800 Metcalf Ave. Overland Park, KS 66212. Phone: 800-795-5445 or (913)341-1300 Fax: (913)967-1898 E-mail: subs@primediabusiness.com • URL: http://www.primediabusiness.com • Monthly. $85.00 per year. Includes annual *Directory*. Market surveys by city.

National Recreation and Park Association., 22377 Belmont Ridge Rd. Ashburn, VA 20148-4501. Phone: (703)858-0784 Fax: (703)858-0794 E-mail: info@nrpa.org • URL: http://www.nrpa.org • Formerly National Conference on State Parks.

National Referral Roster: The Nation's Directory of Residential Real Estate Firms. Stamats Communications, Inc., 615 Fifth St., S.E. Cedar Rapids, IA 54206. Phone: 800-553-8878 or (319)364-6167 Fax: (319)365-5421 E-mail: info@stamats.com • URL: http://www.stamats.com • Annual. Realtors, $95.00; non-realtors, $175.00. Formerly *National Roster of Realtors*.

National Registration Center for Study Abroad., P.O. Box 1393 Milwaukee, WI 53201. Phone: (414)278-7410 Fax: (414)271-8884 E-mail: inquire@nrcsa.com • URL: http://www.nrcsa.com • Members are foreign universities, foreign language institutions, and other institutions or organizations offering foreign study programs designed for North Americans.

National Regulatory Research Institute.

National Rehabilitation Information Center., 8201 Corporate Dr., Ste. 600 Landover, MD 20785. Phone: 800-346-2742 or (301)459-5900 Fax: (301)459-4263 E-mail: naricinfo@heitechservices.com • URL: http://www.naric.com • Aims to improve delivery of information to the rehabilitation community. Disseminates the findings of programs funded by the National Institute on Disability and Rehabilitation Research; prepares custom bibliographies; helps locate answers to reference questions; searches for relevant materials in other commercially available databases.

National Renderers Association., 801 N Fairfax St., Ste. 205 Alexandria, VA 22314-1776. Phone: (703)683-0155 Fax: (703)683-2626 E-mail: renderers@nationalrenderers.com • URL: http://nationalrenderers.org • Producers of tallow and grease products (for use in soap and lubricants), and meat meal (for use in animal feeds), obtained as by-products of the meat-packing industry. Conducts research and educational programs; provides international and domestic market development services and legislative representation.

National Research Council., 500 5th St. NW Washington, DC 20001. Phone: 800-424-5156 or (202)334-2000 Fax: (202)334-2290 E-mail: news@nas.edu • URL: http://www.nationalacademies.org/nrc • Scientists, engineers, and other professionals serving pro bono on approximately 900 study committees. Serves as an independent adviser to the federal government on scientific and technical questions of national importance; is jointly administered by the National Academy of Sciences, National Academy of Engineering, and Institute of Medicine. Carries out objectives through conferences, technical committees, surveys, collection and analysis of scientific and technical data, and administration of public and private funds for research projects and fellowships.

National Restaurant Association., 1200 17th St. NW Washington, DC 20036. Phone: 800-424-5156 or (202)331-5900 Fax: (202)331-2429 E-mail: info@dineout.org • URL: http://www.restaurant.org • Represents restaurants, cafeterias, clubs, contract foodservice management, drive-ins, caterers, institutional food services, and other members of the foodservice industry; also represents establishments belonging to non-affiliated state and local restaurant associations in governmental affairs. Supports foodservice education and research in several educational institutions. Is affiliated with the Educational Foundation of the National Restaurant Association to provide training and education for operators, food and equipment manufacturers, distributors, and educators. Has 300,000 member locations.

National Restaurant Association Educational Foundation., 175 W Jackson Blvd., Ste. 1500 Chicago, IL 60604-2702. Phone: 800-765-2122 or (312)715-1010 E-mail: info@restaurant.org • URL: http://www.nraef.org • Serves as an educational

foundation supported by the National Restaurant Association and all segments of the foodservice industry including restaurateurs, foodservice companies, food and equipment manufacturers, distributors, and trade associations. Advances the professional standards of the industry through education and research. Offers video training programs, management courses, and careers information. Conducts research and maintains hall of fame.

National Retail Federation., 325 7th St. NW, Ste. 1100 Washington, DC 20004. Phone: 800-673-4692 or (202)783-7971 Fax: (202)737-2849 E-mail: mullint@nrf.com • URL: http://www.nrf.com • Represents state retail associations, several dozen national retail associations, as well as large and small corporate members representing the breadth and diversity of the retail industry's establishment and employees. Conducts informational and educational conferences related to all phases of retailing including financial planning and cash management, taxation, economic forecasting, expense planning, shortage control, credit, electronic data processing, telecommunications, merchandise management, buying, traffic, security, supply, materials handling, store planning and construction, personnel administration, recruitment and training, and advertising and display.

National Retail Hardware Association Management Report: Cost of Doing Business Study. National Retail Hardware Association, 5822 W. 74th St. Indianapolis, IN 46278. Phone: 800-772-4424 or (317)290-0338 Fax: (317)328-4354 E-mail: contact@nrha.org • URL: http://www.nrha.org • Annual. Members, $49.00; non-members, $98.00.

National Rifle Association of America.

National Roofing Contractors Association., 10255 W Higgins Rd., Ste. 600 Rosemont, IL 60018-5607. Phone: 800-323-9545 or (847)299-9070 Fax: (847)299-1183 E-mail: nrca@nrca.net • URL: http://www.nrca.net • Roofing, roof deck, and waterproofing contractors and industry-related associate members. Assists members to successfully satisfy their customers through technical support, testing and research, education, marketing, government relations, and consultation.

National Rural Electric Cooperative Association., 4301 Wilson Blvd. Arlington, VA 22203. Phone: (703)907-5500 Fax: (703)907-5511 E-mail: nreca@nreca.coop • URL: http://www.nreca.org • Rural electric cooperative systems, public power districts, and public utility districts in 46 states. Conducts activities such as: legislative representation; energy and regulatory; management institutes; professional conferences; training and consulting services; insurance and safety programs; international program; wage and salary surveys.

National Rural Housing Coalition., 1250 Eye St. NW, Ste. 902 Washington, DC 20005. Phone: (202)393-5229 Fax: (202)393-3034 E-mail: nrhc@nrhcweb.org • URL: http://www.nrhcweb.org • Advocates for improved government and private housing programs for people in small towns and rural areas. Develops informational and educational material; gives and coordinates testimony before congressional committees; seeks improved administrative procedures within the executive branch of the federal government. Lobbies for low-income rural housing and community facilities.

National Safe Workplace Institute/Safeplaces.com.

National Safety Council., 1121 Spring Lake Dr. Itasca, IL 60143-3201. Phone: 800-621-7619 or (630)285-1121 Fax: (630)285-1613 E-mail: nrhc@nrhcweb.org • URL: http://www.nsc.org • Individuals whose professional activities are related to the safety of employees and college or university students.

National Sash and Door Jobbers Association., 10047 Robert Trent Jones Parkway New Port Richey, FL 34655-4649. Phone: 800-786-7274 or (727)372-3665 Fax: (727)372-2879 E-mail: mail@nsdja.com • URL: http://www.nsdja.com • Members are wholesale distributors of door and window products.

National Scholastic Press Association. University of Minnesota, University of Minnesota, 2221 University Ave. SE, Ste. 121 Minneapolis, MN 55414-3074. Phone: (612)625-8335 Fax: (612)626-0720 E-mail: info@studentpress.org • URL: http://www.studentpress.org/nspa • Represents publishers of high school newspapers, yearbooks, and magazines. Offers critical services for newspapers, yearbooks, and magazines.

National School Boards Association., 1680 Duke St. Alexandria, VA 22314-3493. Phone: (703)838-6722 Fax: (703)683-7590 E-mail: info@nsba.org • URL: http://www.nsba.org • Federation of state school boards associations, the Board of Education of the District of Columbia and the Virgin Islands Board of Education. Advocates equity and quality education for primary and secondary public school children through legal counsel, research studies, legislative advocacy programs, and services for members, conferences, and magazines. Provides information on topics affecting K-12 public education and school policy. Maintains library and specialized clearinghouses.

National School Supply and Equipment Association., 8300 Colesville Rd., Suite 250 Silver Spring, MD 20910. Phone: 800-395-5550 or (301)495-0240 Fax: (301)495-3330 E-mail: nssea@nssea.org • URL: http://www.nssea.org • Absorbed Education Industries Association. Formerly National School Service Institute.

National Security Political Action Committee., Washington Communications Center Boston, VA 22713. Phone: (703)484-1677 E-mail: rcw@vnf.com No further information was available for this edition Presently inactive.

National Shellfisheries Association., 14 Carter Ln., P.O. Box 350

East Quogue, NY 11942. Phone: (631)653-6327 Fax: (631)653-6327 E-mail: jdavis@bainbridge.net • URL: http://www.shellfish.org • Biologists, hydrographers, public health workers, shellfish producers, and fishery administrators. Encourages research on mollusks and crustaceans, with emphasis on those forms of economic importance known as shellfish.

National Shoe Retailers Association., 7150 Columbia Gateway Dr., Ste. G Columbia, MD 21046-1151. Phone: 800-673-8446 or (410)381-8282 Fax: (410)381-1167 E-mail: info@nsra.org • URL: http://www.nsra.org • Proprietors of independent shoe stores, and stores with major shoe departments. Provides business services and professional development programs including bankcard processing, shipping, freight discounts, free website listing, employee training; conducts research; monitors legislation.

National Shooting Sports Foundation., Flintlock Ridge Office Ctr., 11 Mile Hill Rd. Newtown, CT 06470-2359. Phone: (203)426-1320 Fax: (203)426-1087 E-mail: info@nssf.org • URL: http://www.nssf.org • Represents manufacturers of firearms and ammunition, accessories, components, gun sights, hunting clothes, and other reputable firms that make a profit from hunting and shooting; includes outdoor and gun magazine publishers. Fosters a better understanding of and more active participation in the shooting sports. Promotes firearms safety; works with state and federal agencies in providing additional hunting opportunities. Cooperates with private enterprise to create outdoor recreational facilities. Distributes literature concerning firearms safety, conservation, and recreational shooting. Finances educational programs.

National Small Business United.

National Society for Experiential Education., 9001 Braddock Rd., Ste. 380 Springfield, VA 22151. Phone: 800-803-4170 or (703)426-4268 Fax: (703)426-8400 E-mail: info@nsee.org • URL: http://www.nsee.org • Members include representatives of internship programs. Formerly National Society for Internships and Experiential Education.

National Society for the Study of Education Yearbook. National Society for the Study of Education. The University of Chicago Press, 1427 E 60th St. Chicago, IL 60637. Phone: 800-621-2736 or (773)753-3347 Fax: 800-621-8476 or (773)702-7212 E-mail: custserv@press.uchicago.edu • URL: http://www.press.uchicago.edu • Annual. Membership. Two volumes per year.

National Society of Accountants., 1010 N Fairfax St. Alexandria, VA 22314-1574. Phone: 800-966-6679 or (703)549-6400 Fax: (703)549-2984 E-mail: members@nsacct.org • URL: http://www.nsacct.org • Formerly National Society of Public Accountants.

National Society of Pershing Rifles., PO Box 25057, R PO Box 880456 Baton Rouge, LA 70894. Phone: (402)472-2472 Fax: (402)472-2478 E-mail: nhq@pershingriflessociety.org • URL: http://www.pershingriflessociety.org • Members range from military to civilian, male to female. Seeks to foster a spirit of friendship and cooperation among men and women in the military department and to maintain a highly efficient drill company.

National Society of Public Accountants - Yearbook. National Society of Accountants, 1010 N Fairfax St. Alexandria, VA 22314. Phone: 800-966-6679 or (703)549-6400 Fax: (703)549-2984 E-mail: arichman@nsacct.org • URL: http://www.nsacct.org • Annual. Free to members, government agencies and libraries; not available to others.

National Society of Scabbard and Blade., 1018 S Lewis St. Stillwater, OK 74074-4622. Phone: (405)377-4279 Fax: (405)377-2237 E-mail: ddollar@scabbardandblade.org • URL: http://www.scabbardandblade.org • Honorary and recognition fraternity - men and women, military; advanced ROTC; junior ROTC, and all-Service. Maintains speakers' bureau.

National Soil Dynamics Laboratory-U.S. Dept. of Agriculture Agricultural Research Service.

National Solid Waste Management Association Directory of Professional Services. National Solid Wastes Management Association, c/o Environmental Industry Associations, 4301 Connecticut Ave., NW. Ste. 300 Washington, DC 20008. Phone: 800-424-2869 or (202)244-4700 Fax: (202)966-4868 E-mail: jleca@envasns.org • URL: http://www.nswma.org • Annual. Lists waste management consulting firms.

National Solid Wastes Management Association., 4301 Connecticut Ave. NW. Ste. 300, 4301 Connecticut Ave., N.W., Suite 300 Washington, DC 20008-2304. Phone: 800-424-2869 or (202)244-4700 Fax: (202)966-4824 E-mail: membership@envasns.org • URL: http://www.nswma.org • Commercial firms that collect and dispose solid wastes. Acts as a forum for the discussion of specific aspects of hazardous waste transport. Promotes professionalism in the industry to minimize the risks to public health and safety. Aids in the development of industry laws and regulations. Fosters public understanding of waste transport and disposal through educational programs. Urges members to: comply with federal liability insurance requirements; employ drivers who have completed a comprehensive training program and obtained their Department of Transportation commercial vehicle operator's license and medical evaluation certificate; set limits on drivers' hours of service; and maintain transport vehicles in accordance with federal motor carrier safety regulations.

National Spa and Pool Institute., 2111 Eisenhower Ave. Alexandria, VA 22314. Phone: (703)838-0083 Fax: (703)549-0493 E-mail: memberservices@nspi.org • URL: http://www.nspi.org • Members include a wide variety of business firms and individuals involved in some way with health spas, swimming pools, or hot tubs. Formerly National Swimming Pool Institute.

National Speakers Association., 1500 S Priest Dr. Tempe, AZ 85281. Phone: (480)968-2552 Fax: (480)968-0911 E-mail: information@nsaspeaker.org • URL: http://www.nsaspeaker.org • Professional speakers. Works to increase public awareness of the speaking profession, advance the integrity and visibility of professional speakers, and provide a learning and communication vehicle to professional speakers. Sponsors workshops, conventions, and labs.

National Sporting Goods Association., 1601 Feehanville Dr., Ste. 300 Mount Prospect, IL 60056. Phone: 800-815-5422 or (847)296-6742 Fax: (847)391-9827 E-mail: info@nsga.org • URL: http://www.nsga.org • Provides services, education and information to assist member to profit in a competitive marketplace.

National Sports and Fitness Association., 1945 Palo Verde Ave., Suite 202 Long Beach, CA 90815. Phone: (562)799-8333 Fax: (562)799-3355 E-mail: info@nsfa-online.com • URL: http://www.nsfa-online.com • Members are health and fitness professionals. Formerly American Fitness Association.

National Sports Law Institute., Marquette University Law School, 1103 W. Wisconsin Ave. Milwaukee, WI 53201-1881. Phone: (414)288-7494 Fax: (414)288-5818 E-mail: matt.mitten@mu.edu • URL: http://www.marquette.edu/law/sports • Promotes ethical practices in amateur and professional sports activities.

National Sportscasters and Sportswriters Association., 322 E Innes St. Salisbury, NC 28144. Phone: (704)633-4275 Fax: (704)633-2027 Members are sportswriters and radio/TV sportscasters.

National Stock Summary. Pink Sheets LLC, 304 Hudson St., 2nd Fl. New York, NY 10013. Phone: 800-732-7868 or (212)896-4400 Fax: (212)868-3848 E-mail: info@pinksheets.com • URL: http://www.pinksheets.com • Monthly, with semiannual cumulations. $576.00 per year. Includes price quotes for both active and inactive issues, with transfer agents, market makers (brokers), capital changes, name changes, and other corporate information. Pink Sheets LLC also provides daily and weekly stock price services. Formerly published by the National Quotation Bureau.

National Stone, Sand and Gravel Association., 2101 Wilson Blvd., Ste. 100 Arlington, VA 22201. Phone: 800-342-1415 or (703)525-8788 Fax: (703)525-7782 E-mail: info@nssga.org • URL: http://www.aggregates.org • Formerly National Stone Association.

National Student Employment Association., PO Box 23606, Career Services/JLD/CWE, Collin Community College, 2200 W University Eugene, OR 97402. Phone: (541)484-6935 Fax: (541)484-6935 E-mail: claire.adams@comcast.net • URL: http://www.nsea.info • Directors, coordinators, and senior staff personnel of postsecondary educational institutions, including proprietary schools and corporate human resource directors, who are involved in student employment, internships, cooperative and experiential education, federal work-study, job location and development, and student placement. Answers problems associated with the management of student employment programs. Provides financial support for students in higher education. Creates and conducts training and professional development programs for higher education student employment professionals. Sponsors State Work Study Clearinghouse on state sponsored student employment programs. Compiles statistics. Conducts research programs. Provides legislative updates on current issues.

National Survey of State Laws. Gale Cengage Learning, 27500 Drake Rd. Farmington Hills, MI 48331-3535. Phone: 800-877-GALE or (248)699-4253 Fax: 800-414-5043 E-mail: gale.galeord@cengage.com • URL: http://gale.cengage.com • 2002. $105.00. Fourth edition. Provides concise state-by-state comparisons of current state laws on a wide variety of topics. Includes references to specific codes or statutes.

National Tank Truck Carrier Directory. National Tank Truck Carriers, Inc., 950 N Glebe Rd. Ste. 520 Arlington, VA 22203. Phone: 800-441-1414 or (703)838-1960 Fax: (703)838-8860 E-mail: info@nmraonline.org • URL: http://www.tanktruck.org • Covers: For-hire tank truck carriers serving petroleum, chemical, and other industries in the United States, Canada, Australia, England, Europe, Japan, Mexico, and South Africa. Also lists major shippers who use tank trucks, intermodal bulk facilities, industry suppliers, and state related associations affiliated with the American Trucking Associations. Entries include: Company name, address, phone, names of executives, list of products or services.

National Tank Truck Carriers., 950 N Glebe Rd., Ste. 520 Arlington, VA 22203. Phone: (703)838-1960 Fax: (703)838-8860 E-mail: jconley@tanktruck.org • URL: http://www.tanktruck.org • Common or contract "for-hire" tank truck carriers transporting liquid and dry bulk commodities, chemicals, food processing commodities, petroleum, and related products; allied industry suppliers. Promotes federal standards of construction, design, operation, and use of tank trucks and equipment. Coordinates truck transportation system for shippers of bulk commodities. Secures improvements in tank specifications. Sponsors annual schools; conducts research.

National Tax Association Proceedings of the Annual Conference on Taxation. National Tax Association-Tax Institute of America, 725 15th St., NW, Ste. 600 Washington, DC 20005-2109. Phone: (202)737-3325 Fax: (202)737-7308 E-mail: natltax@aol.com • URL: http://www.ntanet.org • Annual. Members, $85.00; individuals, $70.00; libraries, $90.00; corporations, $130.00.

National Tax Association-Tax Institute of America.

National Tax Journal. National Tax Association - Tax Institute of America, 725 15th St., NW, Ste. 600 Washington, DC 20005-2109. Phone: (202)737-3325 Fax: (202)737-7308 E-mail: natltax@aol.com • URL: http://www.ntanet.org • Quarterly. Membership. Topics of current interest in the field of taxation and public finance in the U.S. and foreign countries.

National Taxpayers Union., 108 N Alfred St. Alexandria, VA 22314. Phone: 800-829-4258 or (703)683-5700 Fax: (703)683-5722 E-mail: ntu@ntu.org • URL: http://www.ntu.org • Seeks to: reduce government spending; cut taxes; protect the rights of taxpayers. Claims to have helped generate federal budget cuts of over 120 billion dollars. Activities include research programs and an intense lobbying campaign in Washington, DC; has been a leader in the fights against government ventures such as: social security tax; guaranteed income; congressional and bureaucratic pay raises; federal subsidies; foreign aid; national health insurance. Works for a balanced federal budget/tax limitation constitutional amendment; federal pension reform; reduction of capital gains and personal income tax; social security reform. Has worked for airline deregulation; indexing of federal income tax, California's Proposition 13, Massachusetts Proposition 2 1/2, and other state tax cutting initiatives. Conducts annual voting study of congressmen and senators, rating their votes on spending and tax issues and presenting awards for best and worst records.

National Technical Services Association., 2121 Eisenhower Ave., Ste. 604 Alexandria, VA 22314-3501. Phone: (703)684-4722 Fax: (703)684-7627 E-mail: vjohnson@ntsa.com • URL: http://www.ntsa.com • Contract technical services firms that provide a variety of technical services including engineering, designing, and drafting to both industry and government. Goals are to increase understanding of the technical services industry and the role it plays in supplying engineers, draftsmen, and other contract personnel to American industry. Encourages programs in such areas as public relations, ethics, informing potential users of services provided by members, personnel classification and recruitment, technical personnel training and development, and effective utilization of technical manpower. Maintains speakers' bureau and hall of fame; conducts research programs; compiles statistics.

National Telephone Cooperative Association., 4121 Wilson Blvd., 10th Fl. Arlington, VA 22203. Phone: (703)351-2000 Fax: (703)351-2000 E-mail: frs@ntca.com • URL: http://www.ntca.org • Members are telephone cooperatives and statewide associations.

National Tooling and Machining Association.

National Tour Association., 546 E Main St. Lexington, KY 40508-2300. Phone: 800-682-8886 or (859)226-4444 Fax: (606)226-4414 E-mail: questions@ntastaff.com • URL: http://www.ntaonline.com • Formerly National Tour Brokers Association.

National Toxics Campaign., 1168 Commonwealth Ave. Boston, MA 02134. Phone: (617)232-0327 Fax: (617)232-3945 E-mail: information@sierraclub.org National labor, environmental, and citizens' groups. Purposes are to: obtain support for stronger laws against chemical contamination through canvassing and petition drives in 280 congressional districts; monitor government enforcement practices; provide legislative advocacy. Goal is to win legislation and enforcement that guarantees all Americans the right to be safe from harmful exposure to toxic substances. Maintains speakers' bureau; compiles statistics.

National Trade and Professional Associations of the United States. Columbia Books, Inc., 1825 Connecticut Ave., Ste. 625 Washington, DC 20009. Phone: 888-265-0600 or (202)464-1662 Fax: (202)464-1775 E-mail: info@columbiabooks.com • URL: http://www.columbiabooks.com • Annual. $149.00. Provides key facts on approximately 7,500 trade associations, labor and professional organizations.

National Trade Estimate Report on Foreign Trade Barriers [year]. Available from U. S. Government Printing Office, Washington, DC 20402. Phone: (202)512-1800 Fax: (202)512-2250 E-mail: gpoaccess@gpo.gov • URL: http://www.access.gpo.gov • Annual. $47.00. Issued by the Office of the United States Trade Representative. "Provides quantitative estimates of the impact of foreign practices on the value of United States exports."

National Treasury Employees Union., 1750 H St. NW, Ste. 600 Washington, DC 20006. Phone: (202)572-5500 Fax: (202)572-5641 E-mail: nteu-pr@nteu.org • URL: http://www.nteu.org • Employees of the federal government. Conducts research and educational training programs. Sponsors Federal Employees Education and Assistance Fund.

National Truck Equipment Association., 37400 Hills Tech Dr. Farmington Hills, MI 48331-3414. Phone: 800-441-NTEA or (248)489-7090 Fax: (248)489-8590 E-mail: info@ntea.com • URL: http://www.ntea.com • Serves as a trade group for commercial truck, truck body, truck equipment, trailer and accessory manufacturers and distributors. Advises members of current federal regulations affecting the manufacturing and installation of truck bodies and equipment; works to enhance the professionalism of management and improve profitability in the truck equipment business.

National Truck Equipment Association Membership Roster and Product Directory. National Truck Equipment Association, 37400 Hills Tech Dr. Farmington Hills, MI 48331-3414. Phone: 800-441-6832 or (248)489-7090 Fax: 800-700-2099 or (248)489-8950 E-mail: info@tea.com • URL: http://www.ntea.com • Annual. $50.00. Provides company information and products for over 850 of the nation's commercial truck body and equipment manufacturers and distributors.

National Turkey Federation., 1225 New York Ave., Ste., 400 Washington, DC 20005. Phone: (202)898-0100 Fax: (202)898-0203 E-mail: info@turkeyfed.org • URL: http://www.eatturkey.com • Serves as the national advocate for all segments of the turkey industry. Provides services and conducts activities that increase demand for its members' products by protecting and enhancing their ability to profitably provide wholesome, high-quality, and nutritious products.

National Underwriter. The National Underwriter Co., 5081 Olympic Blvd. Erlanger, KY 41017. Phone: 800-543-0874 or (859)692-2100 • URL: http://www.nationalunderwriter.com • Weekly. Two editions: *Life* or *Health*. $86.00 per year, each edition.

National Underwriter, Property and Casualty Edition. The National Underwriter Co., 5081 Olympic Blvd. Erlanger, KY 41017. Phone: 800-543-0874 or (859)692-2100 • URL: http://www.nationalunderwriter.com • Weekly. $92.00 per year.

National Urban League., 120 Wall St., 8th Fl. New York, NY 10005. Phone: (212)558-5300 Fax: (212)344-5332 E-mail: info@nul.org • URL: http://www.nul.org • Voluntary nonpartisan community service agency of civic, professional, business, labor, and religious leaders with a staff of trained social workers and other professionals. Aims to eliminate racial segregation and discrimination in the United States and to achieve parity for blacks and other minorities in every phase of American life. Works to eliminate institutional racism and to provide direct service to minorities in the areas of employment, housing, education, social welfare, health, family planning, mental retardation, law and consumer affairs, youth and student affairs, labor affairs, veterans' affairs, and community and minority business development. Maintains research department in Washington, DC.

National Venture Capital Association., 1655 N Ft. Myer Dr., Ste. 850 Arlington, VA 22209. Phone: (703)524-2549 Fax: (703)524-3940 E-mail: mheesen@nvca.org • URL: http://www.nvca.org • Venture capital organizations, corporate financiers, and individual venture capitalists who are responsible for investing private capital in young companies on a professional basis. Fosters a broader understanding of the importance of venture capital to the vitality of the U.S. economy and to stimulate the free flow of capital to young companies. Seeks to improve communications among venture capitalists throughout the country and to improve the general level of knowledge of the venturing process in government, universities, and the business community.

National Venture Capital Association Yearbook. Thomson Financial, 195 Broadway New York, NY 10007. Phone: 800-262-6000 or (646)822-2000 Fax: (646)822-6270 E-mail: custserv@tfn.com • URL: http://www.tfn.com • Annual. $195.00. Provides a yearly review of the U.S. venture capital industry, including statistical data.

National Water Conditions. Water Resources Div., 12201 Sunrise Valley Dr. Reston, VA 20192. Phone: (703)648-6816 Fax: (703)648-5295 E-mail: nrca@archgroup.org • URL: http://www.usgs.gov/major-sites.html • Description: Describes the month's water conditions in the U.S. and Canada, compiling data on streamflow, ground water conditions, surface water, reservoirs, the flow of large rivers, water temperatures, and dissolved solids.

National Water Resources Association., 3800 N Fairfax Dr., Ste. 4 Arlington, VA 22203. Phone: (703)524-1544 Fax: (703)524-1548 E-mail: nwra@nwra.org • URL: http://www.nwra.org • Officers of irrigation districts, canal companies, businesses, and others interested in the development, control, conservation, and utilization of water resources in the reclamation states (17 western states). Conducts legislative tracking and provides updates.

National Waterways Conference., 4650 Washington Blvd., No. 608 Arlington, VA 22201. Phone: (703)243-4090 Fax: (866)371-1390 E-mail: amy@waterways.org • URL: http://www.waterways.org • Petroleum, coal, chemical, electric power, building materials, iron and steel, and grain companies; industrial development agencies, port authorities, and other governmental bodies; water carriers; companies which build, repair, service, or insure vessels; water resource development associations, banks, chambers of commerce, and individuals. Seeks to promote a better understanding of the public value of the American waterways system. Conducts research on the economics of water transportation; sponsors an educational program to point up the diverse benefits of efficient water transport; keeps members and other waterway proponents posted on developments affecting national waterways policy.

National Wellness Institute.

National Wildlife Federation., 11100 Wildlife Center Dr. Reston, VA 20190-5362. Phone: 800-822-9919 or (703)438-6000 E-mail: info@hdmanet.org • URL: http://www.nwf.org • Serves as a member-supported conservation group, with over four million members and supporters. Federation of state and territorial affiliates, associate members and individual conservationist-contributors. Seeks to educate, inspire and assist individuals and organizations of diverse cultures to conserve wildlife and other natural resources and to protect the earth's environment in order to achieve a peaceful, equitable and sustainable future. Encourages the intelligent management of the life-sustaining resources of the earth and promotes greater appreciation of wild places, wildlife and the natural resources shared by all. Publishes educational materials and conservation periodicals.

National Women's Coalition., The Heitman Group, 1350 New York Ave. NW, Ste. 915 Washington, DC 20005. Phone: (202)347-3440 E-mail: nabpac@nabpac.org Professional and activist women drawn from business, the arts, academia, sports, and politics. Seeks to promote the rights, success, and independence of women. Believes "opportunity for all Americans can best be achieved through the policies of President Reagan, the current administration, and the Republican Party." Has initiated discussion on government policies that have benefited women.

National Women's Law Center., 11 Dupont Cir. NW, Ste. 800 Washington, DC 20036. Phone: (202)588-5180 Fax: (202)588-5185 E-mail: info@nwlc.org • URL: http://www.nwlc.org • Has "expanded the possibilities for women and girls in our country". Uses the law in all its forms: getting new laws on the books; litigating ground-breaking lawsuits all the way to the Supreme Court; and educating the public about how to make the law and public policies work for women and their families. "Takes on the issues that cut to the core of women's and girls' lives" in health, education, employment, and family economic security, with special priority given to the needs of low-income women and their families.

National Writers Association., 10940 S Parker Rd., No. 508 Parker, CO 80134. Phone: (303)841-0246 Fax: (303)841-2607 E-mail: natlwritersassn@hotmail.com • URL: http://www.nationalwriters.com • Professional full- or part-time freelance writers who specialize in business writing. Aims to serve as a marketplace whereby business editors can easily locate competent writing talent. Establishes communication among editors and writers.

National Youth Employment Coalition., 1836 Jefferson Pl. NW Washington, DC 20036. Phone: (202)659-1064 Fax: (202)659-0399 E-mail: nyec@nyec.org • URL: http://www.nyec.org • A network of over 180 community-based organizations, research organizations, public interest groups, policy analysis organizations, and others dedicated to promoting improved policies and practices related to youth employment/development, to help youth succeed in becoming lifelong learners, productive workers and self-sufficient citizens.

Nation's Cities Weekly. National League of Cities, 1301 Pennsylvania Ave. NW, Ste. 550 Washington, DC 20004. Phone: (202)626-3000 Fax: (202)626-3043 E-mail: info@nlc.org • URL: http://www.nlc.org • Description: Presents news on the latest developments in Congress, the White House, federal agencies, and other public interest groups which may affect the nation's cities.

Nations of the World: A Political, Economic, and Business Handbook. Grey House Publishing, 185 Millerton Rd. Millerton, NY 12546. Phone: 800-562-2139 or (518)789-8700 Fax: (518)789-0556 E-mail: books@greyhouse.com • URL: http://www.greyhouse.com • 2002. $135.00. Third edition. Includes descriptive data on economic characteristics, population, gross domestic product (GDP), banking, inflation, agriculture, tourism, and other factors. Covers "all the nations of the world."

Nation's Restaurant News: The Newspaper of the Food Service Industry. Lebhar-Friedman, Inc., 425 Park Ave. New York, NY 10022. Phone: 800-766-6999 or (212)756-5000 E-mail: info@lf.com • URL: http://www.lf.com • 50 times a year. $39.95 per year.

NATPE International—Media Content Directory. National Association of Television Program Executives Inc., 5757 Wilshire Bvld., Penthouse 10 Los Angeles, CA 90036-3681. Phone: 800-628-7346 or (310)453-4440 Fax: (310)453-5258 E-mail: info@natpe.org • URL: http://www.natpe.org • Covers: distributors of television programs. Entries include: Company name, address, phone, telex, fax, names and titles of key personnel, description of company, list of programs available.

NATPE: Pocket Guides Reps Groups Distributors. National Association of Television Program Executives, 2425 Olympic Blvd., Suite 600E Santa Monica, CA 90404. Phone: 800-628-7346 or (310)453-4440 Fax: (310)453-5258 E-mail: info@natpe.org • URL: http://www.natpe.org • Semiannual. Free to members; non-members, $75.00 per year. Includes station representatives, group owners (with stations owned), and program distributors.

Natural Business: The Journal of Business and Financial News for the Natural Products Industry. Natural Business Communications, 360 Interlocken Blvd., Suite 111 Broomfield, CO 80021. Phone: (303)442-8983 Fax: (303)440-7741 E-mail: info@naturalbusiness.com • URL: http://www.naturalbusiness.com • Monthly. $279.00 per year. Covers the business aspects of natural and organic products and dietary supplements, including information about private and public companies in the industry.

Natural Energy Services Association.

Natural Gas and Electricity: The Monthly Journal for Producers, Marketers, Pipels and End Users. John Wiley and Sons, Inc., 111 River St. Hoboken, NJ 07030. Phone: 800-225-5945 or (201)748-6000 Fax: (201)748-6088 E-mail: customer@wiley.com • URL: http://www.wiley.com • Monthly. Institution, $949.00 per year. Newsletter. Covers business, economic, regulatory, and high-technology news relating to the natural gas industry.

Natural Gas Information. Organization for Economic Cooperation and Development, OECD Washington Center, 2001 L St., N. W., Suite 650 Washington, DC 20036-4922. Phone: 800-456-6323 or (202)785-6323 Fax: (202)785-0350 E-mail: washington.contact@oecd.org • URL: http://www.oecd.org • Annual. $150.00. Includes international statistics relating to natural gas reserves, storage capacity, prices, consumption, trade, and pipelines. Contains detailed data for individual countries. (Also available on CD-ROM.)

Natural Gas Monthly. Energy Information Administration. Available from U.S. Government Printing Office, Washington, DC 20402. Phone: (202)512-1800 Fax: (202)512-2250 E-mail: gpoaccess@gpo.gov • URL: http://www.access.gpo.gov • Monthly. State and national data on production, storage, imports, exports and consumption of natural gas.

Natural Gas Week. Energy Intelligence Group Inc., 5 East 37th St., 5th fl. Washington, DC 20005-2150. Phone: 800-621-0050 or (202)662-0700 Fax: (202)662-0751 E-mail: oildaily@worldnet.att.com • URL: http://www.energyintel.com • Description: Covers natural gas economics, news, and analysis of gas/electric convergence.

Natural Products Association., 2112 E 4th St., Ste. 200 Santa Ana, CA 92705. Phone: 800-966-6632 or (714)460-7732 Fax: (714)460-7444 E-mail: natural@naturalproductsassoc.org • URL: http://www.naturalproductsassoc.org • Represents retailers, wholesalers, brokers, distributors and manufacturers of natural, nutritional, dietetic foods, supplements, and natural body care products.

Natural Resources Defense Council. Natural Resources Defense Council, 40 W 20th St. New York, NY 10011. Phone: (212)727-2700 Fax: (212)727-1773 E-mail: nrdcinfo@nrdc.org • URL: http://www.nrdc.org • Use of the judicial system to enforce environmental protection laws. Environmental policy studies, including studies related to public health and the environment, public lands and the coast, nuclear energy and weapons, energy conservation, and the global environment. Specific concerns include air quality, acid rain, airborne toxic pollutants, metropolitan air pollution, stratospheric ozone loss, solid waste disposal, water pollution, sewage treatment, industrial pollution, hazardous waste disposal, drinking water, pesticide policy, national forest management, agricultural resource conservation, public lands protection, irrigation policy, endangered species conservation, offshore oil leasing, shoreline protection, sea level rise, Nuclear Test Ban verification, nuclear weapons, environmental effects of nuclear production, nuclear winter, energy conservation, energy efficiency of appliances, energy efficient buildings, habitat protection, desertification, deforestation, wetlands conservation, international wildlife trade, international environmental treaties, Russian environmental law exchange, urban issues, environmental justice, Brownfield's redevelopment, and transportation.

The Natural Resources Journal. University of New Mexico, School of Law, Albuquerque, NM 87131. Phone: (505)277-0111 Fax: (505)277-4165 E-mail: inside@unm.edu • URL: http://www.unm.edu • Quarterly. $40.00 per year.

NAUMD News. National Association of Uniform Manufacturers and Distributors, 336 W 37th St., Ste. 370 New York, NY 10018. Phone: (212)736-3010 Fax: (212)736-3013 E-mail: staff@navh.org • URL: http://www.naumd.com • Description: Reports news that affects the uniform manufacturing and distributing industry. Also discusses Association programs and seminars, committee activities, and governmental trends and regulations.

Naval Affairs: In the Interest of the Enlisted Active Duty Reserve, and Retired Personnel of the U.S. Navy, Marine Corps and Coast Guard. Fleet Reserve Association, 125 N. West St. Alexandria, VA 22314-2754. Phone: (703)683-1400 Fax: (703)549-6610 E-mail: news-fra@fra.org • URL: http://www.fra.org • Free to members; non-members, $7.00 per year.

Naval Aviation News. Chief of Naval Operations Bureau of Aeronautics. Available from U.S. Government Printing Office, Washington, DC 20402. Phone: (202)512-1800 Fax: (202)512-2250 E-mail: gpoaccess@gpo.gov • URL: http://www.access.gpo.gov • Bimonthly. $23.00 per year. Articles on all phases on Navy and Marine activity.

Naval Civilian Managers Association., PO Box 215 Portsmouth, VA 23705. Phone: (757)396-2265 Fax: (757)396-7743 E-mail: clifford.elder@navy.mil Upper echelon civilian personnel in a naval organizational entity. Encourages improvement of administration and management of U.S. Navy. Compiles statistics. Maintains speakers' bureau, museum, and hall of fame.

Naval Engineers Journal. American Society of Naval Engineers, Inc., 1452 Duke St. Alexandria, VA 22314. Phone: (703)836-6727 Fax: (703)836-7491 E-mail: asnehq@navalengineers.org • URL: http://www.navalengineers.org • Bimonthly. $100 per year.

Naval Enlisted Reserve Association., 6703 Farragut Ave. Falls Church, VA 22042-2189. Phone: 800-776-9020 or (703)534-1329 Fax: (703)534-3617 E-mail: members@nera.org • URL: http://www.nera.org • Enlisted personnel of the U.S. Naval Reserve, Marine Corps Reserve, and Coast Guard Reserve on active duty, inactive duty, or retired. Works to promote career enlisted service in the "sea-going" branches of the armed services; concerned with the readiness, training, morale, and well-being of all Reservists; obtains fair and proper recognition of the contributions made by Reservists to the national defense and to obtain protection and extension of benefits and entitlements for those Reservists who are currently serving and for those who have already served satisfactorily and have retired. Works with Congress and military leaders for legislation and proposals designed to improve and enhance the effectiveness of Reserve programs; also works to provide a communications link with the public.

Naval Historical Foundation., 1306 Dahlgren Ave. SE, Washington Navy Yard Washington, DC 20374-5055. Phone: 888-880-0102 or (202)678-4333 or (202)678-4431 Fax: (202)889-3565 E-mail: nhfwny@navyhistory.org • URL: http://www.navyhistory.org • Dedicated to preserving and promoting the Navy's proud heritage, including the principal donation point for personal papers relating to naval history, a dynamic nationwide oral history program, a means for supporting the Navy's historical collections and programs, especially the Navy Museum. Provides historic research, and document and photo reproduction services.

Naval Intelligence Professionals., PO Box 11579 Burke, VA 22009-1579. Phone: (703)250-6765 E-mail: navintpro@aol.com • URL: http://www.navintpro.org • Active duty and former naval intelligence officers; enlisted personnel; civilian professionals; corporations. Objectives are to: improve naval intelligence operations; act as a clearinghouse for information on scientific and technical advances in naval intelligence; provide a forum for the exchange of ideas. Encourages readiness for those who would be involved in a national crisis mobilization.

Naval Research Logistics: An International Journal. John Wiley and Sons, Inc., 111 River St. Hoboken, NJ 07030. Phone: 800-225-5945 or (201)746-6000 Fax: (201)746-6088 E-mail: customer@wiley.com • URL: http://www.wiley.com • Eight times a year. $1,235.00 per year; with online edition, $1,297.00 per year.

Naval Reserve Association., 1619 King St. Alexandria, VA 22314-2793. Phone: (866)672-4968 or (703)548-5800 Fax: (703)683-3647 E-mail: membership@navy-reserve.org • URL: http://www.navy-reserve.org • Naval officers on active or inactive duty or retired. Maintains involvement with legislation affecting U.S. Navy and Naval Reserve. Provides Naval Officer Promotion Record Reviews. Sponsors Naval Reserve Junior Officer of the Year Programs. Offers professional education; sponsors competitions; maintains speakers' bureau.

Naval Review: Annual Review of World Seapower. U.S. Naval Institute, 291 Wood Rd. Annapolis, MD 21402. Phone: 800-223-8764 or (410)268-6110 Fax: (410)269-7940 E-mail: customer@usni.org • URL: http://www.usni.org • Annual. Price on application. Covers the previous year's events. May issue of *U.S. Naval Institute Proceedings*.

Naval Sea Cadet Corps., 2300 Wilson Blvd. Arlington, VA 22201-3308. Phone: (703)243-6910 Fax: (703)243-3985 E-mail: usmcdia@atc.cc • URL: http://www.seacadets.org • Youths aged 11-17 years interested in the Navy, Marine Corps, Coast Guard, and Merchant Marines. Works to instill good citizenship and patriotism in youth. Encourages qualities such as personal neatness, loyalty, obedience, dependability, and responsibility to others. Offers courses in physical fitness and military drill, first aid, water safety, basic seamanship, and naval history and traditions.

Navy Club of the United States of America., 6134 S 375 W Lafayette, IN 47909. Phone: 800-628-7265 or (920)336-3953 Fax: (260)432-3188 E-mail: natloffice@navyclubusa.org • URL: http://www.navyclubusa.org • Persons who are, or have been, in the active service of the U.S. Navy, Naval Reserve, Marine Corps, Marine Corps Reserve, and Coast Guard. Promotes and encourages further public interest in the U.S. Navy and its history and to uphold the spirit and ideals of the U.S. Navy. Acts as public forum for members' views on national defense. Assists Navy Recruiting Command. Conducts charitable activities.

Navy Club of the United States of America Auxiliary., 124 E Front St. Delphi, IN 46923-1508. Phone: (765)564-6147 E-mail: ncauxshipswriter@hotmail.com • URL: http://www.navyclubusa.org • Women relatives of men who have served in the United States Navy, Marine Corps, Coast Guard, and component reserve services; women who are eligible in their own right for membership in the Navy Club of the United States of America. Provides assistance to the Navy Club; promotes fraternal love and sociability; encourages interest in the U.S. Navy and its history. Activities include veterans' service, rehabilitation programs, child welfare assistance, handicapped services, and overseas relief, memorials, and community service. Supports U.S. Navy special services. Maintains museum.

SOURCES CITED

Navy League of the United States., 2300 Wilson Blvd., Ste. 200 Arlington, VA 22201-3308. Phone: 800-356-5760 or (703)528-1775 Fax: (703)528-2333 E-mail: execdirector@navyleague.org • URL: http://www.navyleague.org • Civilian organization that supports U.S. capability to keep the sea lanes open through a strong, viable Navy, Marine Corps, Coast Guard, and Merchant Marine. Seeks to awaken interest and cooperation of U.S. citizens in matters serving to aid, improve, and develop the efficiency of U.S. naval and maritime forces and equipment; acquires and disseminates information concerning the conditions of U.S. naval and maritime forces and equipment.

Navy Supply Corps Newsletter. Available from U. S. Government Printing Office, Washington, DC 20402. Phone: (202)512-1800 Fax: (202)512-2250 E-mail: gpoaccess@gpo.gov • URL: http://www.access.gpo.gov • Bimonthly. $30.00 per year. Newsletter issued by U. S. Navy Supply Systems Command. Provides news of Navy supplies and stores activities.

Navy Times: Marine Corps, Navy, Coast Guard. Army Times Publishing Co., 6883 Commercial Dr. Springfield, VA 22159-0240. Phone: 800-368-5718 or (703)750-8646 Fax: (703)750-8607 E-mail: cust-svc@atpco.com • URL: http://www.armytimes.com • Weekly. $52.00 per year. In two editions: Domestic and International. *Supplement* available.

NCBA Membership Roster. National Candy Brokers Association, 710 East Ogden Ave., Suite 600 Naperville, IL 60563-8603. Phone: (630)369-2406 Fax: (630)369-2488 E-mail: ncba@b-online.com • URL: http://www.candynet.com • Annual. $25.00. Lists broker, manufacturer, and distributor members of the National Candy Brokers Association.

NCJRS: National Criminal Justice Reference Service. U.S. Department of Justice, P.O. Box 6000 Rockville, MD 20849-6000. Phone: 800-851-3420 or (301)251-5500 Fax: (301)251-5212 References print and non-print information on law enforcement and criminal justice, 1972 to present. Monthly updates. Inquire as to online cost and availability.

NCO Guide. Robert L. Rush. Stackpole Books, Inc., 5067 Ritter Rd. Mechanicsburg, PA 17055. Phone: 800-732-3669 Fax: (717)796-0412 E-mail: jbender@stackpolebooks.com • URL: http://www.stackpolebooks.com • 2003. $18.95. 7th edition.

NCSL International., 2995 Wilderness Pl., Ste. 107 Boulder, CO 80301-5404. Phone: (303)440-3339 Fax: (303)440-3384 E-mail: info@ncsli.org • URL: http://www.ncsli.org • Representatives of measurements standards and calibration laboratories; organizations with related interests. Seeks cost reduction or solution of problems, both technical and administrative, that besiege all measurement activities in the physical sciences, engineering, and technology. Conducts conferences and meetings for presentation of papers and discussions pertaining to technical and managerial problems, operating practices, and policies for measurement standards laboratories. Works with educational organizations to develop programs for training technical personnel and professional metrologists.

NDA Pipeline(New Drug Approval). F-D-C Reports, Inc., 5550 Friendship Blvd., Suite 1 Chevy Chase, MD 20815-7278. Phone: 800-332-2181 or (301)657-9830 Fax: (301)656-3094 E-mail: fdc.customer.service@elsevier.com • URL: http://www.fdcreports.com • Annual. Available online only. Provides information on U. S. drugs in the development stage and products receiving new drug approval (NDA) from the Food and Drug Administration. Listings are company-by-company and by generic name, with orphan drug designations. Includes an industry directory.

NDT and E International; The Independent Journal of Non-Destructive Testing. Elsevier, 360 Park Ave. S New York, NY 10010-1710. Phone: 888-437-4636 or (212)989-5800 Fax: (212)633-3990 E-mail: usinfo-f@elsevier.comp • URL: http://www.elsevier.com • Eight times a year. Institutions, $727.00 per year. Formerly *NDT International*.

Nebraska Farmer. Farm Progress Companies, 191 S. Gary Ave. Carol Stream, IL 60188. Phone: 800-441-1410 or (630)462-2224 Fax: (630)462-2869 E-mail: circhelp@farmprogress.com • URL: http://www.farmprogress.com • 15 times a year. $23.95 per year.

Negotiating and Influencing Skills: The Art of Creating and Claiming Value. Brad McRae. Sage Publications, Inc., 2455 Teller Rd. Thousand Oaks, CA 91320. Phone: 800-818-7243 or (805)499-9774 Fax: 800-583-2665 or (805)499-0871 E-mail: webmaster@sagepub.com • URL: http://www.sagepub.com • 1997. $79.95. Presents a practical approach to various circumstances, based on the Harvard Project on Negotiation. Chapters include "Dealing with Difficult People and Difficult Situations." Contains a bibliography and glossary of terms.

Negotiating for Business Results. Judith E. Fisher. McGraw-Hill, 1221 Ave. of the Americas New York, NY 10020. Phone: 800-722-4726 or (212)512-2000 Fax: (212)512-4502 E-mail: customer.service@mcgraw-hill.com • URL: http://www.mcgraw-hill.com • 1993. $10.95. (Business Skills Express Series).

Negotiating to Settlement in Divorce. Sanford N. Katz, editor. Aspen Publishers, Inc., 1185 Ave. of the Americas New York, NY 10036. Phone: 800-234-1660 or (212)597-0200 Fax: 800-901-9075 or (212)597-0338 E-mail: customer.service@aspenpubl.com • URL: http://www.aspenpublishers.com • $75.00. Looseleaf service. Periodic supplementation.

Negotiation. Edward F. Sherman and others. Foundation Press, 395 Hudson St. New York, NY 10014. Phone: (212)367-6790 E-mail: gerry.gelke@westgroup.com 2001. $39.95. Second edition. (University Casebook Series).

Negotiation Basics: Concepts, Skills, and Exercises. Ralph A. Johnson. Sage Publications, Inc., 2455 Teller Rd. Thousand Oaks, CA 91320. Phone: 800-818-7243 or (805)499-9774 Fax: 800-583-2665 or (805)499-0871 E-mail: webmaster@sagepub.com • URL: http://www.sagepub.com • 1992. $77.95. Topics include goal building, the role of information, cost-benefit decision making, strategy, and creating a positive negotiating climate.

Negotiation Journal: On the Process of Dispute Settlement. Program on Negotiation. Blackwell Publishing, 350 Main St. Malden, MA 02148. Phone: 800-835-6770 or (781)388-8200 Fax: (781)388-8210 E-mail: subscrip@blackwell.com • URL: http://www.blackwellpublishing.com • Quarterly. $495.00 per year. Includes print and online editions.

Nelson Information's Directory of Institutional Real Estate. Nelson Information, 195 Broadway New York, NY 10007. Phone: 888-280-4864 or (646)822-2000 E-mail: nwlaon.pubs@tfn.com • URL: http://www.nelsoninformation.com • Annual. $400.00. Includes real estate investment managers, service firms, consultants, real estate investment trusts (REITs), and various institutional investors in real estate. Formerly *Nelson's Directory of Real Estate Investments*.

Nelson Information's Directory of Investment Managers. Nelson Information, 195 Broadway New York, NY 10007. Phone: 888-280-4864 or (646)822-2000 Fax: (914)937-0727 E-mail: nelson.pubs@tfn.com • URL: http://www.nelsoninformation.com • Annual. $595.00. Three volumes. Provides information on 2,200 investment management firms, both U.S. and foreign.

Nelson Information's Directory of Investment Research. Nelson Information, 195 Broadway New York, NY 10007. Phone: 888-280-4864 or (646)822-2000 E-mail: nelson.pubs@tfn.com • URL: http://www.nelsoninformation.com • Annual. $665.00. Three volumes. Provides information on 7,000 investment research analysts at more than 800 firms. Indexes include company name, industry, and name of person.

Nelson Information's Directory of Pension Fund Consultants. Nelson Information, 195 Broadway New York, NY 10007-3100. Phone: 888-280-4864 or (646)822-2000 E-mail: nelson.pubs@tfn.com • URL: http://www.nelsoninformation.com • Annual. $610.00. Covers the pension plan sponsor industry. More than 325 worldwide consulting firms are described. Formerly *Nelson's Guide to Pension Fund Consultants*.

Nelson Information's Directory of Plan Sponsors. Nelson Information, 195 Broadway New York, NY 10007-3100. Phone: 888-280-4864 or (646)822-2000 E-mail: nelson.pubs@tfn.com • URL: http://www.nelsoninformation.com • Annual. $610.00. Three volumes. Formerly *Nelson's Directory of Plan Sponsors and Tax-Exempt Funds*.

NERAC, Inc.

Net Crimes and Misdemeanors: Outmaneuvering the Spammers, Swindlers, and Stalkers Who Are Targeting You Online. Jayne Hitchcock. Information Today, Inc., 143 Old Marlton Pike Medford, NJ 08055-8750. Phone: 800-300-9868 or (609)654-6266 Fax: (609)654-4309 E-mail: custserv@infotoday.com • URL: http://www.infotoday.com • 2002. $24.95. Provides specific strategies and techniques for dealing with a wide range of online abusive practices. (CyberAge Books.)

Net Curriculum: An Educator's Guide to Using the Internet. Linda Joseph. Information Today, Inc., 143 Old Marlton Pike Medford, NJ 08055-8750. Phone: 800-300-9868 or (609)654-6266 Fax: (609)654-4309 E-mail: custserv@infotoday.com • URL: http://www.infotoday.com • 1999. $29.95. Covers various educational aspects of the Internet. Written for K-12 teachers, librarians, and media specialists by a columnist for *Multimedia Schools*. (CyberAge Books.)

Net Effects: How Librarians Can Manage the Unintended Consequences of the Internet. Marylaine Block, editor. Information Today, Inc., 143 Old Marlton Pike Medford, NJ 08055-8750. Phone: 800-300-9868 or (609)654-6266 Fax: (609)654-4309 E-mail: custserv@infotoday.com • URL: http://www.infotoday.com • 2003. $39.50. Contains about 50 articles by librarians on the "side effects" of Internet use in libraries, such as technology stress, threats to print sources, retraining problems, new budget demands, and legal controversies.

Net Income: Cut Costs, Boost Profits, and Enhance Operations Online. Wally Bock and Jeff Senne. John Wiley and Sons, Inc., 111 River St. Hoboken, NJ 07030. Phone: 800-225-5945 or (201)748-6000 Fax: (201)748-6088 E-mail: info@wiley.com • URL: http://www.wiley.com • 1997. $29.95. "Net Income" in this case is hoped-for Internet income. Promotes the use of the Internet, intranet, and extranet to improve business operations or start new businesses. The authors take a nontechnical, business strategy approach.

NetMag: Strategies and Solutions for the Network Professional. CMP Media LLC, 600 Community Dr. Manhasset, NY 11030. Phone: (512)562-5000 E-mail: cmp@cmp.com • URL: http://www.cmp.com • 13 times a year. Free to qualified personnel. Incorporates *Data Communications*.

Net.people: The Personalities and Passions Behind the Web Sites. Thomas E. Bleier and Eric C. Steinert. Information Today, Inc., 143 Old Marlton Pike Medford, NJ 08055-8750. Phone: 800-300-9868 or (609)654-6266 Fax: (609)654-4309 E-mail: custserv@infotoday.com • URL: http://www.infotoday.com • 2000. $19.95. Presents the personal stories of 36 Web "entrepreneurs and visionaries." (CyberAge Books.)

NetSavvy: Building Information Literacy in the Classroom. Ian Jukes and others. Corwin Press, Inc., 2455 Teller Rd. Thousand Oaks, CA 91320-2218. Phone: 800-818-7243 or (805)499-9734 Fax: (805)449-0871 E-mail: info@sagepub.com • URL: http://www.corwinpress.com • 2000. $69.95. Second edition. Provides practical advice on the teaching of computer, Internet, and technological literacy. Includes sample lesson plans and grade-level objectives. (One-Off Series).

Network and Systems Professionals Association., 7044 S. 13th St. Milwaukee, WI 53154. Phone: (414)768-8000 Fax: (414)768-8001 E-mail: sherer@naspa.com • URL: http://www.naspa.com • Members are systems programmers, communications analysts, database administrators, and other technical management personnel.

Network Buyers Guide. CMP Media LLC, 600 Community Dr. Manhasset, NY 11030. Phone: (516)562-5000 • URL: http://www.cmp.com • Annual. $5.00. Lists suppliers of products for local and wide area computer networks. Formerly *LAN Buyers Guide Issue*.

Network Computing: Computing in a Network Environment. CMP Publications, Inc., 600 Community Dr. Manhasset, NY 11030. Phone: (516)562-5000 Fax: (516)733-7973 E-mail: cmpworld@cmp.com • URL: http://www.cmp.com • Semimonthly. Free to qualified personnel.

Network: Strategies and Solutions for the Network Professional. CMP Media LLC, 600 Community Dr. Manhasset, NY 11030. Phone: (516)562-5000 E-mail: cmp@cmp.com • URL: http://www.cmp.com • 13 times a year. Free to qualified personnel. Covers network products and peripherals for computer professionals. Includes annual network managers salary survey and annual directory issue. Formerly *LAN: The Network Solutions Magazine*.

Network World: The Newsweekly of Enterprise Network Computing. Network World Inc., 118 Turnpike Rd. Southborough, MA 01772. Phone: 800-622-1108 or (508)460-3333 Fax: (508)460-6438 • URL: http://www.networkworld.com • Weekly. $129.00 per year. Includes special feature issues on enterprise Internets, network operating systems, network management, high-speed modems, LAN management systems, and Internet access providers.

Networking with the Affluent. Thomas J. Stanley. McGraw-Hill, 1221 Ave. of the Americas New York, NY 10020. Phone: 800-722-4726 or (212)512-2000 Fax: (212)512-4502 E-mail: customer.service@mcgraw-hill.com • URL: http://www.mcgraw-hill.com • 1993. $17.95. Discusses specific methods of prospecting for wealthy clients, with examples.

Never Call Your Broker on Monday: And 300 Other Financial Lessons You Can't Afford Not to Know. Nancy Dunnan. HarperInformation, 10 E. 53rd St. New York, NY 10022-5299. Phone: 800-242-7737 or (212)207-7000 Fax: 800-822-4090 or (212)207-7145 • URL: http://www.harpercollins.com • 1997. $8.50. Presents a wide range of personal finance advice, covering investments, insurance, wills, credit, real estate, etc.

New and Breaking Technologies in the Pharmaceutical and Medical Device Industries. Theta Reports, 1775 Broadway, Suite 511 New York, NY 10019. Phone: (212)262-8230 Fax: (212)262-8234 E-mail: lschacterle@thetareports.com • URL: http://www.thetareports.com • 1999. $1,695.00. Contains market research predictions of medical technology trends over the next 5 to 10 years (2004-2009), including developments in biotechnology, genetic engineering, medical device technology, therapeutic vaccines, non-invasive diagnostics, and minimally-invasive surgery. (Theta Report No. 931.)

A New Archetype for Competitive Intelligence. John J. McGonagle and Carolyn M. Vella. Greenwood Publishing Group, Inc., 88 Post Rd., W Westport, CT 06881. Phone: 800-225-5800 or (203)226-3571 Fax: (203)431-2214 E-mail: customer-service@greenwood.com • URL: http://www.greenwood.com • 1996. $64.95. Covers competitive intelligence, strategic intelligence, market intelligence, defensive intelligence, and cyber-intelligence. Includes an overview of sources and techniques for data gathering. A bibliography, glossary, and index are provided.

New Architecture: Solutions for Internet and World Wide Web Developers. CMP Media LLC, 600 Community Dr. Manhasset, NY 11030. Phone: (516)562-5000 E-mail: cmp@cmp.com • URL: http://www.cmp.com • Monthly. $34.95 per year. A technical magazine edited for Internet and World Wide Web professionals. Formerly *Web Techniques*.

New Business Incorporations. Dun & Bradstreet Corp., 103 JFK Pky. Short Hills, NJ 07078. Phone: 800-526-0651 E-mail: custserv@dnb.com • URL: http://www.dnb.com • Monthly. $25.00 per year. Gives the number of new business incorporations in each of the 50 states. Includes commentary.

New Century Family Money Book: Your Comprehensive Guide to a Lifetime of Financial Security. Jonathan D. Pond. Bantam Dell Publishing Group, 1540 Broadway New York, NY 10036-4094. Phone: 800-223-6834 or (212)782-9000 Fax: (212)492-9698 • URL: http://www.randomhouse.com • 1995. $11.00.

The New Commonsense Guide to Mutual Funds. Mary Rowland. Bloomberg, 499 Park Ave. New York, NY 10022. Phone: 800-388-2749 or (212)318-2000 Fax: (917)369-5000 • URL:

http://www.bloomberg.com • 1998. $15.95. Revised edition. Includes "Do's and Don'ts" for mutual fund investors. (Bloomberg Personal Bookshelf Series).

New Competitor Intelligence: The Complete Resource for Finding, Analyzing, and Using Information About Your Competitors. Leonard M. Fuld. John Wiley and Sons, Inc., 111 River St. Hoboken, NJ 07030. Phone: 800-225-5945 or (201)748-6000 Fax: (201)748-6088 E-mail: info@wiley.com • URL: http://www.wiley.com • 1994. $145.00. Second edition. Topics include data sources, strategy, analysis of competition, and how to establish a competitive intelligence system.

The New Direct Marketing: How to Implement a Profit-Driven Database Marketing Strategy. McGraw-Hill, 1221 Ave. of the Americas New York, NY 10020. Phone: 800-722-4726 or (212)512-2000 Fax: (212)512-4502 E-mail: customer.service@mcgraw-hill.com • URL: http://www.mcgraw-hill.com • 1999. $79.95. Third edition. Discusses the construction, analysis, practical use, and evaluation of direct marketing databases containing primary and/or secondary data.

New Directions for Higher Education. Jossey-Bass, 989 Market St. San Francisco, CA 94103-1741. Phone: 888-378-2537 or (415)433-1740 Fax: 800-605-2665 or (415)433-0499 E-mail: jbsubs@jbp.com • URL: http://www.josseybass.com • Quarterly. Institutions, $145.00 per year; with online edition, $153.00 per year. Sample issue free to librarians.

The New Economy of Nature: The Quest to Make Conservation Profitable. Gretchen E. Daily and Katherine Ellison. Island Press, PO Box 7 Covelo, CA 95428. Phone: 800-828-1302 or (707)983-6432 Fax: (707)983-6414 E-mail: service@islandpress.org • URL: http://www.islandpress.org • 2002. $25.00. Presents the stories of various individuals who successfully combined the profit motive with conservation of the environment.

New England Journal of Medicine. Massachusetts Medical Society, Publishing Div., 860 Winter St. Waltham, MA 02451. Phone: 800-843-6356 or (781)893-3800 Fax: (781)893-0413 • URL: http://www.nejm.org • Weekly. Individuals, $139.00 per year; institutions, $489.00 per year. The offical journal of the Massachusetts Medical Society.

New Equipment Digest. Penton Media, Inc., 1300 E 9th St. Cleveland, OH 44114. Phone: (216)696-7000 Fax: (216)696-1752 E-mail: information@penton.com • URL: http://www.penton.com • Monthly. Free to qualified personnel; others, $60.00 per year. Formerly *Material Handling Engineering*

New Equipment Reporter: New Products Industrial News. De Roche Publications, 12 Del Italia Irvine, CA 92714-5355. Monthly. Controlled circulation.

The New Finance: The Case Against Efficient Markets. Prentice Hall PTR, 240 Frisch Ct. Paramus, NJ 07652. Phone: 800-282-0693 Fax: 800-445-6991 • URL: http://www.phptr.com • 1998. $36.00. Second edition.

The New Financial Order: Risk in the 21st Century. Robert J. Shiller. Princeton University Press, 41 William St. Princeton, NJ 08540. Phone: 800-777-4726 or (609)258-4900 Fax: (609)258-6305 • URL: http://www.pup.princeton.edu • 2003. $29.95. By the author of *Irrational Exuberance* (2000). Recommends that risk management schemes be developed for application to the risks of everyday life, as in such chapters as "Insurance for Livelihoods and Home Values," "Inequality Insurance: Protecting the Distribution of Income," and "Intergenerational Social Security: Sharing Risks Between Young and Old."

New-Format Digital Television. Available from MarketResearch.com, 641 Ave. of the Americas, 3rd Fl. New York, NY 10011. Phone: 800-298-5699 or (212)807-2629 Fax: (212)807-2716 E-mail: order@marketresearch.com • URL: http://www.marketresearch.com • 1999. $3,995.00. Market research data. Published by Fuji- Keizai USA. Covers the developing U. S. market for digital TV.

New Hacker's Dictionary. Eric S. Raymond. MIT Press, Five Cambridge Ctr. Cambridge, MA 02142. Phone: 800-356-0343 or (617)253-5646 Fax: (617)253-6779 • URL: http://www.mitpress.mit.edu • 1996. $65.00. Third edition. Includes three classifications of hacker communication: slang, jargon, and "techspeak."

New Horizons. Horticultural Research Institute, 1000 Vermont Ave. NW, Ste. 300 Washington, DC 20005. Phone: (202)789-5980 Fax: (202)789-1893 E-mail: staff@navh.org • URL: http://www.eianet.org • Description: Explores research of the science and art of nursery, retail garden center, and landscape plant production, marketing, and care.

A New Housing Policy for America: Recapturing the American Dream. Richard C. Ferlauto and others. Temple University Press, 1601 N. Broad St., University Services Bldg., Room 305 Philadelphia, PA 19122-6099. Phone: 800-447-1656 or (215)204-8787 Fax: (215)204-4719 • URL: http://www.temple.edu/tempress • 1988. $24.95.

New Ideas About Old Age Security: Toward Sustainable Pension Systems in the 21st Century. Holzmann, editor. The World Bank Group, 1818 H St., N.W. Washington, DC 20433. Phone: (202)477-1000 Fax: (202)477-6391 E-mail: books@worldbank.org • URL: http://www.worldbank.org • 2001. $35.00. Discusses worldwide problems in dealing with the pension needs of aging populations.

The New Information Report: The International Industry Dossier. Washington Researchers, Ltd., 1655 N. Fort Myer Dr., Suite 800 Arlington, VA 22209. Phone: (703)312-2863 Fax: (703)527-4586 E-mail: research@researchers.com • URL: http://www.washingtonresearchers.com • Looseleaf service. $160.00 per year. Monthly updates. Formerly *The International Information Report*.

New Introduction to Bibliography. Philip Gaskell. Oak Knoll Press, 310 Delaware St. Newcastle, DE 19720. Phone: 800-996-2556 or (302)328-7232 Fax: (302)328-7274 E-mail: oakknoll@oakknoll.com • URL: http://www.oakknoll.com • 2000. $39.95.

The New Library Scene. Library Binding Institute, 70 E Lake St., Suite 300 Chicago, IL 60601. Phone: (312)704-5020 Fax: (312)704-5025 E-mail: info@lbibinders.org • URL: http://www.lbibinders.org • Quarterly. $24.00 per year.

New Mexico Engineering Research Institute. University of New Mexico

New One-Family Houses Sold. Available from U. S. Government Printing Office, Washington, DC 20402. Phone: (202)512-1800 Fax: (202)512-2250 E-mail: gpoaccess@gpo.gov • URL: http://www.access.gpo.gov • Monthly. $45.00 per year. Bureau of the Census Construction Report, C25. Provides data on new, privately-owned, one-family homes sold during the month and for sale at the end of the month.

New Ophthalmology: Treatments and Technologies. Theta Reports, 1775 Broadway, Suite 511 New York, NY 10019. Phone: (212)262-8230 Fax: (212)262-8234 E-mail: lschacterle@thetareports.com • URL: http://www.thetareports.com • 2000. $1,695. Provides market research data relating to eye surgery, including LASIK, cataract surgery, and associated technology. (Theta Report No. 911.)

The New Palgrave Dictionary of Money and Finance. Peter Newman and others, editors. Palgrave Macmillan, 175 Fifth Ave. New York, NY 10010. Phone: 800-221-7945 or (212)982-9300 Fax: (212)777-6359 • URL: http://www.palgrave.com • 1992. $595.00. Two volumes. Consists of signed essays on over 1,000 financial topics, each with a bibliography. Covers a wide variety of financial, monetary, and investment areas. A detailed subject index is provided.

New Plant Report. Conway Data Inc., 6625 The Corners Pkwy., Ste. 200 Norcross, GA 30092-2901. Phone: (770)446-6996 Fax: (770)263-8825 E-mail: info@sitenet.com • URL: http://www.conway.com • Description: Covers new plants and plant expansions. Provides project location, company name, product to be manufactured or service performed, NAICS code, type of facility, stage of development, and (as available) number of employees, square footage, investment amount, and contact name. **Remarks:** Also available on disk and via e-mail.

New Product Announcements Plus. Gale Cengage Learning, 27500 Drake Rd. Farmington Hills, MI 48331-3535. Phone: 800-877-GALE or 800-699-GALE Fax: 800-414-5043 or (248)699-8069 E-mail: galeord@gale.com • URL: http://gale.cengage.com • Contains the full text of new product and corporate activity press releases, with special emphasis on high technology and emerging industries. Covers 1985 to date. Weekly updates. Inquire as to online cost and availability.

New Product Development and Marketing: A Practical Guide. Italo S. Servi. Greenwood Publishing Group, Inc., 88 Post Rd., W Westport, CT 06881. Phone: 800-225-5800 or (203)226-3571 Fax: (203)431-2214 E-mail: customer-service@greenwood.com • URL: http://www.greenwood.com • 1990. $55.00. A practical guide to the creation, testing, and marketing of a new product.

New Product Development Checklists: From Mission to Market. George Gruenwald. McGraw-Hill, 1221 Ave. of the Americas New York, NY 10020. Phone: 800-722-4726 or (212)512-2000 Fax: (212)512-4502 E-mail: customer.service@mcgraw-hill.com • URL: http://www.mcgraw-hill.com • 1994. $22.95. (NTC Business Books Series).

New Products Management. C. Merle Crawford and C. Anthony Di Benedetto. McGraw-Hill, 1221 Ave. of the Americas New York, NY 10020. Phone: 800-722-4726 or (212)512-2000 Fax: (212)512-4502 E-mail: customer.service@mcgraw-hill.com • URL: http://www.mcgraw-hill.com • 1999. $97.81. Sixth edition.

The New Publicity Kit. Jeanette Smith. John Wiley and Sons, Inc., 111 River St. Hoboken, NJ 07030. Phone: 800-225-5945 or (201)748-6000 Fax: (201)748-6088 E-mail: info@wiley.com • URL: http://www.wiley.com • 1995. $19.95. Multi-media campaigns, and other forms of publicity.

New Research Centers. Gale Cengage Learning, 27500 Drake Rd. Farmington Hills, MI 48331-3535. Phone: 800-877-GALE or (248)699-4253 Fax: 800-414-5043 E-mail: gale.galeord@cengage.com • URL: http://gale.cengage.com • 2002. $420.00. 29th edition. A supplement to *Research Centers Directory*

New Riders' Official World Wide Web Yellow Pages. New Riders Publishing, 800 E 96th St. Indianapolis, IN 46240-3770. Phone: 800-571-5840 • URL: http://www.newriders.com • 1998. $34.99. Sixth edition. A broadly classified listing of Web sites, with brief descriptions of sites and a subject index to narrower topics. Includes a guide to using the Internet and a separate, alphabetical listing of more than 1,500 college and university Web sites, both U. S. and foreign. Includes CD-ROM.

The New Science of Technical Analysis. Thomas R. DeMark. John Wiley and Sons, Inc., 111 River St. Hoboken, NJ 07030. Phone: 800-225-5945 or (201)748-6000 Fax: (201)748-6088 E-mail: info@wiley.com • URL: http://www.wiley.com • 1994. $65.00. (Finance Series).

New Technical Books: A Selective List With Descriptive Annotations. New York Public Library, Science and Technology Research Center, Fifth Ave. and 42nd St., Room 120 New York, NY 10018. Phone: (212)930-0920 Fax: (212)869-7824 Bimonthly. $30.00 per year.

New Technologies and the Employment of Disabled Persons. H. Allan Hunt and Monroe Berkowitz, editors. International Labour Office, 1828 L St., N.W. Washington, DC 20036. Phone: (202)653-7652 Fax: (202)653-7687 E-mail: ilo@ilo.org • URL: http://www.ilo.org • 1992. $18.00. Discusses the development and use of new technologies to create job opportunities for the disabled in various countries.

New Uses for Obsolete Buildings. Urban Land Institute, 1025 Thomas Jefferson St., NW, Ste. 500 W Washington, DC 20007-5201. Phone: 800-321-5011 or (202)624-7000 Fax: (202)624-7140 • URL: http://www.uli.org • 1996. $65.95. Covers various aspects of redevelopment: zoning, building codes, environment, economics, financing, and marketing. Includes eight case studies and 75 descriptions of completed "adaptive use projects."

New Venture Creation: Entrepreneurship for the 21st Century. Jeffrey A. Timmons and Stephen Spinelli. McGraw-Hill, 1221 Ave. of the Americas New York, NY 10020. Phone: 800-722-4726 or (212)512-2000 Fax: (212)512-4502 E-mail: customer.service@mcgraw-hill.com • URL: http://www.mcgraw-hill.com • 2003. Sixth edition. Price on application.

New Woman. Endeavour House, 189 Shaftsbury Ave. London WC2H 8JG, United Kingdom. Phone: 020 7859 8689 E-mail: emap@subscription.co.uk • URL: http://www.newwoman.co.uk • Monthly. $57.00 per year.

The New Working Woman's Guide to Retirement Planning: Saving and Investing Now for a Secure Future. Martha P. Patterson. University of Pennsylvania Press, 4200 Pine St. Philadelphia, PA 19104-4011. Phone: (215)898-6261 Fax: (215)898-0404 E-mail: custserv@pobox.upenn.edu • URL: http://www.upenn.edu • 1999. $19.95. Second edition. Provides retirement advice for employed women, including information on various kinds of IRAs, cash balance and other pension plans, 401(k) plans, and social security. Four case studies are provided to illustrate retirement planning at specific life and career stages.

New York Cotton Exchange., 1 N End Ave., 23-10 43rd Ave. New York, NY 10282-1101. Phone: 800-HED-GEIT or (212)748-4094 E-mail: webmaster@nybot.com • URL: http://www.nybot.com • Commodity exchange - cotton and frozen concentrated orange juice. Develops new products; provides market information; compiles statistics. Collaborates with the Citrus Associates of the +New York +Cotton Exchange; operates Financial Instruments Exchange, in conjunction with the New York Stock Exchange.

New York Genealogical and Biographical Society.

New York Mercantile Exchange., World Financial Ctr., 1 N End Ave. New York, NY 10282-1101. Phone: 800-438-8616 or (212)299-2000 or (212)748-5265 Fax: (212)301-4700 E-mail: exchangeinfo@nymex.com • URL: http://www.nymex.com • Brokerage houses, businesses with commercial interests in commodities, and professional traders. Provides a mechanism for trading futures and options. Compiles trading statistics for public distribution. Operates library of government and trade publications related to commodity futures contracts currently traded. Maintains numerous committees.

New York No-Fault Arbitration Reports. American Arbitration Association, 1633 Broadway, Fl. 10 New York, NY 10019. Phone: 800-778-7879 or (212)716-5800 Fax: (212)716-5905 E-mail: websitemail@adr.org • URL: http://www.adr.org • Description: Addresses developing laws under the no-fault law in the state of New York. Summarizes awards rendered under state-sponsored arbitration.

The New York Public Library Writer's Guide to Style and Usage. Andrea Sutcliffe, editor. HarperInformation, 10 E. 53rd St. New York, NY 10022-5299. Phone: 800-242-7737 or (212)207-7000 Fax: 800-822-4090 or (212)207-7145 • URL: http://www.harpercollins.com • 1994. $40.00

New York Society of Security Analysts., 1601 Broadway, 11th Floor New York, NY 10019-7406. Phone: 800-248-0108 or (212)541-4530 Fax: (212)541-4677 E-mail: staff@nyssa.org • URL: http://www.nyssa.org • Members are portfolio managers, financial analysts, investment counselors, and other financial professionals.

New York State Agricultural Experiment Station. Cornell University

New York Stock Exchange., 11 Wall St. New York, NY 10005. Phone: (212)656-3000 Fax: (212)656-3939 E-mail: boardofdirectors@nyse.com • URL: http://www.nyse.com • Aims to "add value to the capital-raising and asset-management process by providing the highest-quality and most cost-effective self-regulated marketplace for the trading of financial instruments, promote confidence in and understanding of that process, and serve as a forum for discussion of relevant national and international policy issues".

New York Stock Exchange Fact Book. Available from Hoover's, Inc., 5800 Airport Blvd. Austin, TX 78752. Phone: 800-486-8666 or (512)374-4500 Fax: (512)374-4501 E-mail: custsupport@hoovers.com • URL: http://www.hoovers.com • Annual. $9.95. Published by the New York Stock Exchange, Inc. Contains statistical data relating to the New York Stock Exchange. Includes information on new listings and name changes.

New York Stock Exchange Guide. CCH, Inc., 2700 Lake Cook Rd. Riverwoods, IL 60015. Phone: 800-835-5224 or (847)267-7000 E-mail: cust_serv@cch.com • URL: http://www.cch.com • Monthly. $692.00 per year.

The New York Times. New York Times Co., 229 W. 43rd St. New York, NY 10036. Phone: 800-631-2580 or (212)556-1234 Fax: (212)556-4603 E-mail: hank@nytimes.com • URL: http://www.nytimes.com • Daily. $374.40 per year. Supplements available: *New York Times Book Review*, *New York Times Magazine*, *Sophisticated Traveler* and *Fashions of the Times*.

The New York Times Biographical File. New York Times Online Services, 520 Speedwell Ave Morris Plains, NY 07950. Phone: (973)829-0036 Fax: (973)829-0999 Makes available online the full text of more than 15,000 biographies that have appeared in *The New York Times* from 1980 to the present. Updating is weekly. Inquire as to online cost and availability.

The New York Times Biographical Service. UMI, 300 N. Zeeb Rd. Ann Arbor, MI 48106. Phone: 800-521-0600 or (734)761-4700 Fax: 800-864-0019 E-mail: info@il.proquest.com • URL: http://www.il.proquest.com • Monthly. Price on application. Looseleaf service.

New York Times Book Review. New York Times Co., 229 W. 43rd St. New York, NY 10036. Phone: 800-631-2580 or (212)556-1234 Fax: (212)556-4603 • URL: http://www.nytimes.com • Weekly. $54.60 per year. Supplement to *New York Times*.

The New York Times Manual of Style and Usage: The Official Style Guide Used by the Writers and Editors of the World's Most Authoriatative Newspaper. Allan M. Siegal and William G. Connolly, editors. Harmony Books, 299 Park Ave. New York, NY 10171. Phone: 800-726-0600 or (212)751-2600 Fax: (212)572-8797 • URL: http://www.randomhouse.com • 2002. $15.00. Revised edition.

New York University Annual Institute on Federal Taxation. Melvin Cornfield. LexisNexis Matthew Bender, 1275 Broadway Albany, NY 12204. Phone: 800-424-4200 or (518)487-3000 Fax: (518)487-3584 E-mail: bookstore.support@lexisnexis.com • URL: http://www.bender.com • Annual. $366.00. Two looseleaf volumes.

The New Yorker Book of Business Cartoons. Robert Mankoff, editor. Bloomberg, 499 Park Ave. New York, NY 10022. Phone: 800-388-2749 or (212)318-2000 Fax: (917)369-5000 • URL: http://www.bloomberg.com • 1998. $21.95. Contains reprints of 110 cartoons relating to business and finance. Artists are Charles Addams, George Booth, Roz Chast, William Hamilton, Edward Sorel, and other *New Yorker* cartoonists.

The Newcomen Society of the United States., 211 Welsh Pool Rd., Ste. 240 Exton, PA 19341. Phone: 800-466-7604 or (610)363-6600 Fax: (610)363-0612 E-mail: info@newcomen.org • URL: http://www.newcomen.org • Formerly Newcomen Society in North America.

News from OECD. Available from OECD Publications and Information Center, 2001 L St., N.W.,, Suite 650 Washington, DC 20036-4922. Phone: 800-456-6323 or (202)785-6323 Fax: (202)785-0350 E-mail: washington.contact@oecd.org • URL: http://www.oecdwash.org • Monthly. Free. Lists OECD's calender of activities.

News Media Yellow Book: Who's Who Among Reporters, Writers, Editors, and Producers in the Leading National News Media. Leadership Directories, Inc., 104 Fifth Ave. New York, NY 10011. Phone: (212)627-4140 Fax: (212)645-6931 E-mail: info@leadershipdirectories.com • URL: http://www.leadershipdirectories.com • Quarterly. $360.00 per year. Lists the staffs of major newspapers and news magazines, TV and radio networks, news services and bureaus, and feature syndicates. Includes syndicated columnists and programs. Seven specialized indexes are provided.

News Photographer: Dedicated to the Service and Advancement of News Photography. National Press Photographers Association, Inc., 3200 Croasdaile Dr., Suite 306 Durham, NC 27705. Phone: (919)383-7246 Fax: (919)383-7261 E-mail: info@nppa.org • URL: http://www.nppa.org • Monthly. $38.00 per year.

Newsbank. Newsbank, Inc., 58 Pine St. New Canaan, CT 06840-5426. Phone: (203)966-1100 Fax: (203)966-6254 Monthly. Price varies. Quarterly and annual cumulations. Index to articles of current interest from over 500 U.S. newspapers. Full text available on microfiche

Newsbreak. Leather Industries of America, 1000 Thomas Jefferson St., N.W., Suite 1515 Washington, DC 20007. Phone: (202)342-8086 Fax: (202)342-9063 E-mail: info@leatherusa.com • URL: http://www.leatherusa.com • Free to members and other qualified personnel. Reports on issues and events in the luggage industry.

NewsInc.: The Business of the Newspaper Business. The Cole Group, P.O. Box 719 Pacifica, CA 94044-0719. Phone: (650)994-2100 Fax: (650)994-2108 E-mail: info@colegroup.com • URL: http://www.colegroup.com • Biweekly. $425.00 per year. Newsletter. Reports on trends in mass media, especially with regard to newspaper publishing. Articles on cable TV and other competitive media are included.

Newsletter and Electronic Publishers Association., 1501 Wilson Blvd., Suite 509 Arlington, VA 22209-2403. Phone: 800-356-9302 or (703)527-2333 Fax: (703)841-0629 E-mail: nepa@newsletter.org • URL: http://www.newsletter.org • Formerly Newsletter Publishers Association.

Newsletter Database. Gale Cengage Learning, 27500 Drake Rd. Farmington Hills, MI 48331-3535. Phone: 800-877-GALE or (248)699-GALE Fax: 800-414-5043 or (248)699-8069 E-mail: galeord@gale.com • URL: http://gale.cengage.com • Contains the full text of about 600 U. S. and international newsletters covering a wide range of business and industrial topics. Time period is 1988 to date, with daily updates. Inquire as to online cost and availability.

Newsletter on Newsletters: News, Views, Trends and Techniques for the Newsletter and Specilized Information Professional., PO Box 348 Rhinebeck, NY 12572-0348. Phone: (845)876-5222 Fax: (845)876-4943 E-mail: newsonnews@aol.com Bimonthly. $196.00 per year. Newsletter.

Newsletter Publishing. Entrepreneur Media, Inc., 2392 Morse Ave. Irvine, CA 92714. Phone: 800-421-2300 or (949)261-2325 Fax: (949)851-9088 E-mail: entmag@entrepreneurmag.com • URL: http://www.entrepreneurmag.com • Looseleaf. $59.50. A practical guide to starting a newsletter. Covers profit potential, start-up costs, market size evaluation, pricing, accounting, advertising, promotion, etc. (Start-Up Business Guide No. E1067.)

Newsletters in Print. Gale Cengage Learning, 27500 Drake Rd. Farmington Hills, MI 48331-3535. Phone: 800-877-GALE or (248)699-4253 Fax: 800-414-5043 E-mail: gale.galeord@cengage.com • URL: http://gale.cengage.com • 2003. $315.00. 17th edition. Details 12,000 sources of information on a wide range of topics.

Newsline: Research News from the U. S. Travel Data Center. U.S. National Research Council, Transportation Research Board, Committee on Public Transport, ation Planning and Development, 2101 Constitution Ave., N.W. Washington, DC 20418. Phone: (202)334-2966 Monthly. $55.00 per year. Newsletter. Covers trends in the U. S. travel industry.

Newsmakers. Gale Cengage Learning, 27500 Drake Rd. Farmington Hills, MI 48331-3535. Phone: 800-877-GALE or (248)699-4253 Fax: 800-414-5043 E-mail: gale.galeord@cengage.com • URL: http://gale.cengage.com • Annual. $155.00. Three softbound issues and one hardbound annual. Biographical information on individuals currently in the news. Includes photographs. Formerly *Contemporary Newsmakers*.

Newspaper Abstracts Daily. ProQuest Inc., 300 North Zeeb Rd. Ann Arbor, MI 48103. Phone: 800-521-0600 or (734)761-4700 Fax: 800-864-0019 • URL: http://www.umi.com • Provides online coverage (citations and abstracts) of 25 major newspapers. Covers business, economics, current affairs, health, fitness, sports, education, technology, government, consumer affairs, psychology, the arts, and the social sciences. Time period is 1986 to date, with daily updates. Inquire as to online cost and availability.

Newspaper Abstracts Ondisc. PROQUEST, 300 North Zeeb Rd. Ann Arbor, MI 48103. Phone: 800-521-0600 or (734)761-4700 Fax: 800-864-0019 • URL: http://www.umi.com • Monthly. $2,950.00 per year (covers 1989 to date; archival discs are available for 1985-88). Provides cover-to-cover CD-ROM indexing and abstracting of 19 major newspapers, including the *New York Times, Wall Street Journal, Washington Post, Chicago Tribune,* and *Los Angeles Times*.

Newspaper Designer's Handbook. Timothy Harrower. McGraw-Hill, 1221 Ave. of the Americas New York, NY 10020. Phone: 800-722-4726 or (212)512-2000 Fax: (212)512-4502 E-mail: customer.service@mcgraw-hill.com • URL: http://www.mcgraw-hill.com • 2001. $50.00. Fifth edition. Includes CD-ROM. (Humanities, Social Sciences and World Language Series).

Newspaper Financial Executives Journal. International Newspaper Financial Executives, 21525 Ridgetop Circle, Ste. 200 Sterling, VA 20166-6510. Phone: (703)421-4060 Fax: (703)421-4068 • URL: http://www.infe.org • Quarterly. $100.00. Provides financially related information to newspaper executives.

The Newspaper Guild., 501 3rd St. NW, 6th Fl. Washington, DC 20001-2760. Phone: 800-585-5TNG or (202)434-7177 Fax: (202)434-1472 E-mail: guild@cwa-union.org • URL: http://www.newsguild.org • AFL-CIO; Canadian Labour Congress, and International Federation of Journalists. Sponsors Newspaper Guild International Pension Fund that provides retirement benefits to persons employed in the news industry.

Nexis.com. Lexis-Nexis GroupPhone: 800-227-4908 or (937)865-6800 Fax: (937)865-6909 E-mail: webmaster@prod.lexis-nexis.com • URL: http://www.nexis.com • Fee-based Web site offers searching of about 2.8 billion documents in some 30,000 news, business, and legal information sources. Features include a subject directory covering 1,200 topics in 34 categories and a Company Dossier containing information on more than 500,000 public and private companies. Boolean searching is offered.

NFDA Directory of Members and Resource Guide. NFDA Publications, Inc., 13625 Bishops Dr. Brookfield, WI 53005-6607. Phone: 800-228-6332 or (262)789-1880 Fax: (262)789-6977 E-mail: nfda@nfda.org • URL: http://www.nfda.org • Annual. $75.00. 14,000 members of state funeral director associations affiliated with the National Funeral Directors Association. Formerly *National Funeral Directors Association-Membership Listing and Resources*.

NFGA Directory-Yearbook., 1250 Eye St. NW, Ste. 1003 Washington, DC 20005-3922. Phone: (202)289-0873 Fax: (202)289-5388 E-mail: abawek@ngfa.org • URL: http://www.ngfa.org • Annual. Price on application.

NFPA Journal. National Fire Protection Association, One Batterymarch Park Quincy, MA 02269-9101. Phone: 800-344-3555 or (617)770-3000 Fax: (617)770-0700 E-mail: library@nfpa.org • URL: http://www.nfpa.org • Bimonthly. Membership. Incorporates *Fire Journal* and *Fire Command*.

NFPA Journal Buyers'. National Fire Protection Association, One Batterymarch Park Quincy, MA 02269. Phone: 800-344-3555 or (617)770-3000 Fax: 800-593-6372 or (617)770-0700 E-mail: library@nfpa.org • URL: http://www.nfpa.org • Annual. $30.00. Listing of fire protection equipment manufacturers.

The NGF's Executive and Par-3 Golf Course Directory. National Golf Foundation, 1150 S US Hwy. 1, Ste. 401 Jupiter, FL 33477. Phone: 888-275-4643 or (561)744-6006 Fax: (561)744-6107 E-mail: general@ngf.org • URL: http://www.ngf.org • Covers: More than 1,800 executive and par-3 golf courses in the United States. Entries include: Mailing address, telephone number, contact names, type of course, fee information, and number of holes.

NHLA Newsletter. National Hardwood Lumber Association, 6830 Raleigh-LaGrange Rd. Memphis, TN 38184-0518. Phone: 800-933-0318 or (901)377-1818 Fax: (901)382-6419 E-mail: info@lhardwood.org • URL: http://www.natlhardwood.org • Monthly. Membership. Newsletter on hardwood products, industry trends, and legislation.

Nichols Cyclopedia of Legal Forms: Annotated. West Group, 610 Opperman Dr. Eagan, MN 55123. Phone: 800-328-4880 or (651)687-7000 Fax: 800-340-9378 E-mail: bookstore@westgroup.com • URL: http://www.westgroup.com • $1,968.00. 47 volumes. Annual updates. Provides personal and business forms and alternative provisions for more than 250 subjects.

Nickel and Dimed: On Not Getting By in America. Barbara Ehrenreich. Gale Cengage Learning, 27500 Drake Rd. Farmington Hills, MI 48331-3535. Phone: (248)699-GALE Fax: 800-414-5043 or (248)699-8069 E-mail: gale.galeord@cengage.com • URL: http://gale.cengage.com • 2001. $29.95. The author temporarily became a low-wage worker to experience American life at the bottom. Dramatizes the inadequacy of the minimum wage. (Metropolitan Books.)

Nielsen Report on Television. Nielsen Media Research, 299 Park Ave. New York, NY 10171. Phone: (212)708-7500 Annual. $25.00. General statistics on television programming, plus ranking of the year's most popular shows. Pamphlet.

Nielsen Station Index. Nielsen Media Research, 770 Broadway New York, NY 10003. Phone: 800-553-3727 or (646)654-8300 Fax: (646)654-5002 E-mail: info@nielsenmedia.com • URL: http://www.nielsenmedia.com • Measures local television station audiences in about 220 U. S. geographic areas. Includes current and some historical data. Inquire as to online cost and availability.

Nielsen Television Index. Nielsen Media Research, 770 Broadway New York, NY 10003. Phone: 800-553-3727 or (646)654-8300 Fax: (646)654-5002 E-mail: info@nielsenmedia.com • URL: http://www.nielsenmedia.com • Measures national television program audiences by sampling approximately 4,000 U. S. households. Time period is 1970 to date, with weekly updates.

Nightclub & Bar Magazine: The Magazine for Nightclub and Bar Management. Oxford Publishing, 307 W. Jackson Ave. Oxford, MS 38655-2154. Phone: 800-247-3881 or (662)236-5510 Fax: (662)236-5541 E-mail: ncb@nightclub.com • URL: http://www.nightclub.com • Monthly. Free for qualified personnel; others, $30.00 per year. Provides news and business advice for owners and managers of bars, nightclubs, and themed restaurants. Includes special issues on seasonal drinks, bar technology, beer trends, appetizers, food service, etc.

The Nikkei Weekly: Japan's Leading Business Newspaper. Nikkei America, Inc., 1325 Ave. of the Americas, Suite 2500 New York, NY 10019. Phone: (212)261-6200 Fax: (212)261-6208 • URL: http://www.nikkei.co • Weekly. $129.00 per year. A newspaper in English "dedicated to all aspects of Japanese business and its influence on people, markets and political trends around the world." Includes English versions of articles appearing in leading Japanese business newspapers, such as *Nihon Keizai Shimbun, Nikkei Marketing Journal*, and *Nikkei Financial Daily*.

The Nilson Report. HSN Consultants Inc., 1110 Eugenia Pl., Ste. 100 Carpinteria, CA 93013-2080. Phone: (805)983-0448 Fax: (805)983-0792 E-mail: info@nilsonreport.com • URL: http://www.nilsonreport.com • Description: Provides information about the credit card industry.

NIMBYS and LULUs (Not-in-My-Back-Yard and Locally-Unwanted-Land-Uses). Jan Horah and Heather Scott. Sage Publications, Inc., 2455 Teller Rd. Thousand Oaks, CA 91320. Phone: 800-818-7243 or (805)499-9774 Fax: 800-583-2665 or (805)499-0871 E-mail: webmaster@sagepub.com • URL: http://www.sagepub.com • 1993. $10.00.

Nimmer on Copyright. David Nimmer. LexisNexis Matthew Bender, 1275 Broadway Albany, NY 12204. Phone: 800-424-4200 or (518)487-3000 Fax: (518)487-3584 E-mail: bookstore.support@lexisnexis.com • URL: http://www.bender.com • $1,369.00. 10 looseleaf volumes. Periodic supplementation. Analytical and practical guide on the law of literary, musical, and artistic proprerty.

9-1-1 Magazine: Public Safety Communications and Response. Official Publications, Inc., 18201 Weton Place Tustin, CA 92780. Phone: 800-231-8911 or (714)544-7776 Fax: (714)838-9233 E-mail: info@9-1-1magazine.com • URL: http://www.9-1-1magazine.com • Bimonthly. $29.95 per year. Covers technical information and applications for public safety communications personnel.

The 9 to 5 Guide to Combating Sexual Harassment: Candid Advice from 9 to 5, the National Association of Working Women. Ellen Bravo and Ellen Cassedy. John Wiley and Sons, Inc., 111 River St. Hoboken, NJ 07030. Phone: 800-225-5945 or (201)748-6000 Fax: (201)748-6088 E-mail: info@wiley.com • URL: http://www.wiley.com • 1992. $14.95.

Nine to Five: National Association of Working Women., 1430 W Peachtree St., Ste. 610 Atlanta, GA 30309. Phone: 800-522-0925 or (414)274-0925 Fax: (414)272-2870 E-mail: hotline9to5@igc.org • URL: http://www.9to5.org • Members are women office workers. Strives for the improvement of office working conditions for women and the elimination of sex and race discrimination.

Nine to Five Newsletter. 9 to 5 National Association of Working Women, 152 W Wisconsin Ave., Ste. 408 Milwaukee, WI 53203. Phone: 800-522-0925 or (414)274-0925 Fax: (414)272-2870 • URL: http://www.9to5.org • Five times a year. Free to members; individuals, $25.00 per year. A newsletter dealing with the rights and concerns of women office workers.

Ninety-Nines, International Organization of Women Pilots., Will Rogers World Airport, 7100 Terminal Dr. Oklahoma City, OK 73159. Phone: 800-994-1929 or (405)685-7969 Fax: (405)685-7985 E-mail: ihq99@cs.com • URL: http://www.ninety-nines.org • Licensed women pilots. Formerly Ninety-Nines International Women Pilots.

NIOSHTIC: National Institute for Occupational Safety and Health Technical Information Center Database. National Institute for Occupational Safety and Health, Technical Information Bra, 4676 Columbia Parkway Cincinnati, OH 45226. Phone: 800-356-4674 or (513)533-8328 Fax: (513)533-8573 Provides citations and abstracts of technical literature in the areas of industrial safety, industrial hygiene, and toxicology. Covers 1890 to date, but mostly 1973 to date. Monthly updates. (Database is also known as *Occupational Safety and Health*.) Inquire as to online cost and availability.

NLADA Directory of Legal Aid and Defender Offices in the United States and Territories. National Legal Aid and Defender Association, 1625 K St., N.W., Suite 800 Washington, DC 20006. Phone: (202)452-0620 Fax: (202)872-1031 E-mail: info@nlada.org • URL: http://www.nlada.org • Biennial. $70.00. Geographical list of approximately 3,600 legal aid and defender offices and their branches. Formerly *Directory Legal Aid and Defender Offices in the United States*.

NLGI Spokesman. National Lubricating Grease Institute, 4635 Wyandotte St. Kansas City, MO 64112. Phone: (816)931-9480 Fax: (816)753-5026 E-mail: nlgi@sound.net • URL: http://www.nlgi.net • Monthly. $24.00 per year. Information about the lubricating grease industry.

NMA. National Mining AssociationPhone: (202)463-2600 Fax: (202)463-2666 • URL: http://www.nma.org • Web site provides information on the U. S. coal and mineral industries. Includes "Salient Statistics of the Mining Industry," showing a wide variety of annual data (six years) for coal and non-fuel minerals. Publications of the National Mining Association are described and links are provided to other sites. (National Mining Association formerly known as National Coal Association.) Fees: Free.

The No-Load Fund Investor. No-Load Fund Investor Inc., 410 Sawmill River Rd., Ste. 2060, PO Box 3029 Brentwood, TN 37024. Phone: 800-706-6364 or (914)693-7420 Fax: (914)693-8067 E-mail: noload@mleesmith.com Description: Predicts which no-load and low-load funds will perform best overall in the coming year. Provides performance data for 995 no- and low-loads and recommends funds and analyzes promising new funds. Recurring features include a listing of the top 20 no-loads plus 18 model portfolios. **Remarks:** Published in conjuction with the Handbook for No-Load Investors.

No-Regrets Remodeling: Creating a Comfortable, Healthy Home That Saves Energy. Home Energy, 2124 Kittredge St., No. 95 Berkeley, CA 94704. Phone: (510)524-5405 1997. $19.95. Edited by *Home Energy* magazine. Serves as a home remodeling guide to efficient heating, cooling, ventilation, water heating, insulation, lighting, and windows.

Noise Control Engineering Journal. Institute of Noise Control Engineering, PO Box 220 Saddle River, NJ 07458. Phone: (201)760-1101 Fax: (201)236-1210 E-mail: ibo@inceusa. • URL: http://www.inceusa. • Bimonthly. $70.00 per year.

Noise Regulation Report: The Nation's Only Noise Control Publication. Great Circle Communications LLC, 204 N Main St. Galena, MD 21635. Phone: 888-828-5437 E-mail: info@noisereport.com • URL: http://www.noisereport.com • Monthly. $487.00 per year. Newsletter. Covers federal and state rules and regulations for the control of excessive noise.

Non Commissioned Officers Association of the United States of America., 10635 IH 35 N San Antonio, TX 78233. Phone: 800-662-2620 or (210)653-6161 Fax: (210)637-3337 E-mail: natdir@ncoausa.org • URL: http://www.ncoausa.org • Noncommissioned and petty officers of the United States military serving in grades E1 through E9 from all five branches of the U.S. Armed Forces; includes active duty and retired personnel, members of the Reserve and National Guard components, and personnel who held the rank of NCO/PO at the time of separation from active duty under honorable conditions. Formed for patriotic, fraternal, social, and benevolent purposes. Offers veterans job assistance, legislative representation, and grants. Conducts charitable programs.

Non-Ferrous Founders' Society., 1480 Renaissance Dr., Ste. 310 Park Ridge, IL 60068. Phone: (847)299-0950 Fax: (847)299-3598 E-mail: nffstaff@nffs.org • URL: http://www.nffs.org • Manufacturers of brass, bronze, aluminum, and other nonferrous castings.

Non-Ferrous Metal Data Yearbook. American Bureau of Metal Statistics, P.o. Box 805 Chatham, NJ 07928. Phone: (973)701-2299 Fax: (973)701-2152 E-mail: info@abms.com • URL: http://www.abms.com • Annual. $405.00. Provides worldwide data on approximately about 200 statistical tables covering many nonferrous metals. Includes production, consumption, inventories, exports, imports, and other data.

Non-Ferrous Metals Producers Committee., 2030 M St. NW, Ste. 800, 2030 M St. NW, Ste. 800, 2030 M. St., N.W., Suite 800 Washington, DC 20036. Phone: (202)466-7720 Fax: (202)466-2710 E-mail: nffstaff@nffs.org • URL: http://www.arcat.com/arcatcos/cos37/arc37679.cfm • Represents domestic copper, lead, and zinc producers. Promotes the interests of copper, lead, and zinc mining and metal industries in the U.S. with emphasis on tariffs, laws, regulations, and government policies affecting international trade and foreign imports.

Non-Foods Management: The Annual Supermarket State of the Industry Report. Millennium Media Corp., 267 Kentland Blvd., Suite 710 North Potomac, MD 20878. Phone: (301)865-8695 Fax: (301)865-8696 Annual. $45.00. Written for top management and non-foods decision makers and executives at supermarkets.

The Non-Profit Handbook: Everything You Need to Know to Start and Run Your Nonprofit Organization. Gary M. Grobman. Chronicle of Higher Education, Inc., 1255 23rd St., N.W., Suite 700 Washington, DC 20037. Phone: 800-728-2819 or (202)466-1032 Fax: (202)659-2236 E-mail: letters@chronicle.com • URL: http://www.chronicle.com • 2002. $29.95. Third edition.

Non-Profit Legal and Tax Letter. Organization Management Inc., 4289 Ellzey Dr. Ashburn, VA 20148-5026. Phone: (703)729-7052 Fax: (703)729-7053 18 times a year. $235.00 per year. Newsletter. Covers fund raising, taxation, management, postal regulations, and other topics for nonprofit organizations.

Non Store Marketing Report. Maxwell Sroge Publishing Inc., 522 Forest Ave. Evanston, IL 60202. Phone: (847)866-1890 Fax: (847)866-1899 E-mail: info@catalog-news.com Description: Source of analyses of key trends and key happeningsin the mail order, Internet, and interactive shopping business. order companies. Recurring features include an semiannual insert titled Trendwatch, which assesses the performance of publicly owned direct selling businesses, and company profiles on direct marketing businesses in the news.

Nonferrous Castings. U. S. Bureau of the Census, 4700 Silver Hill Rd. Washington, DC 20233-0001. Phone: (301)763-4636 E-mail: comments@census.gov • URL: http://www.census.gov • Annual. (Current Industrial Reports MA-33E.)

Nonprofit Almanac: A Publication Independent Sector. Virginia A. Hodgkinson and others. John Wiley and Sons, Inc., 111 River St. Hoboken, NJ 07030. Phone: 800-225-5945 or (201)748-6000 Fax: (201)748-6088 E-mail: info@wiley.com • URL: http://www.wiley.com • 1996. $35.00. Provides trends and statistics for nonprofit wages, finances, employment, and giving patterns. Includes a glossary. (Jossey-Bass Nonprofit Sector Series).

Nonprofit Counsel. John Wiley and Sons, Inc., Journals Div., 111 River St. Hoboken, NJ 07030. Phone: 800-225-5945 or (201)748-6000 Fax: (201)748-6088 E-mail: customer@wiley.com • URL: http://www.wiley.com • Monthly. Institutions, $399.00 per year; with print edition, $419.00 per year. Newsletter.

The Nonprofit Entrepreneur: Creating Ventures to Earn Income. Edward Skloot, editor. The Foundation Center, 79 Fifth Ave. New York, NY 10003-3076. Phone: 800-424-9836 or (212)620-4230 Fax: (212)807-3677 E-mail: orders@fdncenter.org • URL: http://www.fdncenter.org • 1988. $19.95. Advice on earning income through fees and service charges.

Nonprofit Issues. Donald W. Kramer, PO Box 482 Dresher, PA 19025. Phone: 888-NP-ISSUE or (215)542-7547 Fax: (215)542-7548 E-mail: cservice@ragan.com • URL: http://www.nonprofitissues.com • Description: Presents legal information for nonprofit executives and their professional advisors.

Nonprofit Management and Leadership. Jossey-Bass, 989 Market St. San Francisco, CA 94103-1741. Phone: 888-378-2537 or (415)433-1740 Fax: 800-605-2665 or (415)433-0499 E-mail: jbsubs@jbp.com • URL: http://www.josseybass.com • Quarterly. Institutions, $160.00 per year.

Nonprofit Sector Yellow Book: Who's Who in the Management of the Leading Foundations, Universities, Museums, and Other Nonprofit Organizations. Leadership Directories, Inc., 104 Fifth Ave. New York, NY 10011. Phone: (212)627-4140 Fax: (212)645-0931 E-mail: info@leadershipdirectories.com • URL: http://www.leadershipdirectories.com • Semiannual. $265.00 per year. Covers management personnel and board members of about 1,300 prominent, nonprofit organizations: foundations, colleges, museums, performing arts groups, medical institutions, libraries, private preparatory schools, and charitable service organizations.

The Nonprofit Times: The Leading Publication for Nonprofit News and Management. Davis Information Group, 240 Cedar Knolls Rd. Cedar Knolls, NJ 07927-1621. Phone: (201)734-1700 Fax: (201)734-1777 E-mail: nptimes@haven.los.com • URL: http://www.nptimes.com • Monthly. $59.00 per year. Edited for executives of nonprofit organizations. Covers fund raising, personnel, management, and technology topics. Includes an annual nonprofit salary survey.

Nonprofit World: The National Bi-Monthly Nonprofit Leadership and Management Journal. Society for Nonprofit Organizations, 5820 Canton Rd., Ste. 165 Canton, MI 48187. Phone: (734)451-3582 Fax: (734)451-5935 E-mail: info@snpo.org • URL: http://www.snpo.org • Bimonthly. Membership.

Nonwoven Disposables. Theta Reports, 1775 Broadway, Suite 511 New York, NY 10019. Phone: (212)262-8230 Fax: (212)262-8234 E-mail: lschacterle@thetareports.com • URL: http://www.thetareports.com • 1999. $1,495.00. Provides market research data, including sales projections. Covers hospital disposable items, such as surgical drapes, masks, head covers, patient gowns, and incontinence products. (Theta Report No. 922.)

Nonwoven Fabrics: Raw Materials, Manufacture, Applications, Characteristics. Wilhelm Albrecht and others. John Wiley and Sons, Inc., 111 River St. Hoboken, NJ 07030. Phone: 800-225-5945 or (201)748-6000 Fax: (201)748-6088 E-mail: info@wiley.com • URL: http://www.wiley.com • 2003. $215.00. Covers nonwoven fabric design, production planning, manufacturing, testing, and related topics.

Nonwovens Industry: The International Magazine for the Nonwoven Fabrics and Disposable Soft Goods Industry. Rodman Publications, 70 Hilltop Rd. Ramsey, NJ 07446. Phone: (201)825-2552 Fax: (201)825-0553 E-mail: rodmanpub@aol.com • URL: http://www.happi.com • Monthly. $48.00 per year.

North American Agricultural Marketing Officials., Califorinia Department of Food and Agriculture, 1220 N St., Rm. A270 Sacramento, CA 95814. E-mail: joegaines@state.tn.us • URL: http://www.naamo.org • Affiliated with National Association of Produce Market Managers and the National Association of State Departments of Agricutural. Formerly National Agricultural Marketing Officals.

North American Association of Food Equipment Manufacturers., 161 N. Clark St., Ste. 2020 Chicago, IL 60601. Phone: (312)821-0201 Fax: (312)821-0202 E-mail: info@nafem.org • URL: http://www.nafem.org • Formerly Food Equipment Manufacturers Association.

North American Building Material Distribution Association., 401 N. Michigan Ave. Chicago, IL 60611. Phone: 888-747-7862 Fax: (312)644-0310 E-mail: nbmda@sba.com • URL: http://www.nbmda.org • Formerly National Building Material Distributors Association.

North American Building Material Distribution Association-Membership. North American Building Material Distribution Association, 401 N. Michigan Ave. Chicago, IL 60611-4274. Phone: 888-747-7862 or (312)321-6845 Fax: (312)644-0310 E-mail: nbmda@sba.com • URL: http://www.nbmda.org • Annual. Free to members; non-members, $795.00. About 200 wholesale distributors of building products who are members, and 150 manufacturers in that field who are associate members and over 600 of their locations. Formerly *National Building Material Distributors Association Membership and Product Directory*.

North American Die Casting Association., 241 Holbrook Dr. Wheeling, IL 60090-5809. Phone: (847)279-0001 Fax: (847)279-0002 E-mail: nadca@diecasting.org • URL: http://www.diecasting.org • Represents producers of die castings and suppliers to the industry, product and die designers, metallurgists, and students. Develops product standards; compiles trade statistics on metal consumption trends; conducts promotional activities; provides information on chemistry, mechanics, engineering, and other arts and sciences related to die casting. Provides training materials and short, intensive courses in die casting. Maintains speakers' bureau.

North American Equipment Dealers Association., 1195 Smizer Mill Rd. Fenton, MO 63026-3480. Phone: (636)349-5000 Fax: (636)349-5443 E-mail: kindingerp@naeda.com • URL: http://www.naeda.com • Retailers of farm equipment, implements, light industrial equipment, outdoor power equipment, and related supplies. Conducts programs on management training, and governmental and trade relations.

North American Export Grain Association., 1250 I St. NW, Ste. 1003 Washington, DC 20005-3939. Phone: (202)682-4030 Fax: (202)682-4033 E-mail: info@naega.org • URL: http://www.naega.org • U.S. and Canadian exporters of grain and oilseeds from the United States.

North American Fax Directory. Dial-A-Fax Directories Corp., 930 Fox Pavilion Jenkintown, PA 19046. Phone: (215)887-5700 Fax: (215)887-7076 E-mail: berylwolk@aol.com Covers: Approximately 209,000 companies that possess facsimile machines. Entries include: Company name, address, phone, subsidiary and branch names and locations, standard industrial classification (sic) code, fax number. Subscription includes access to a database of over 500,000 firms worldwide with fax numbers.

North American Industry Classification System (NAICS). Available from Bernan Press, 4611-F Assembly Dr. Lanham, MD 20706-4391. Phone: 800-274-4888 or (301)459-2255 Fax: 800-865-3450 or (301)459-0056 E-mail: query@bernan.com • URL: http://www.bernan.com • 2002. $45.00. Issued by the Executive Office of the President, Office of Management and Budget (OMB).

North American Insulation Manufacturers Association., 44 Canal Center Plz., Ste. 310 Alexandria, VA 22314. Phone: (703)684-0084 Fax: (703)684-0427 E-mail: insulation@naima.org • URL: http://www.naima.org • Manufacturers of fiberglass, rock wool, and slag wool insulation products. Promotes energy efficiency and environmental preservation through the use of fiberglass, rock wool, and slag wool insulation products. Encourages safe production and use of insulation materials.

North American Interactive Television Markets. Available from MarketResearch.com, 641 Ave. of the Americas, 3rd Fl. New York, NY 10011. Phone: 800-298-5699 or (212)807-2629 Fax: (212)807-2716 E-mail: order@marketresearch.com • URL: http://www.marketresearch.com • 1999. $3,450.00. Published by Frost & Sullivan. Contains market research data on growth, end-user trends, and market strategies. Company profiles are included.

North American Journal of Aquaculture. American Fisheries Society, 5410 Grosvenor Lane Bethesda, MD 20814. Phone: (301)897-8616 Fax: (301)897-8096 E-mail: main@fisheries.org • URL: http://www.fisheries.org • Quarterly. $195.00 per year. Covers research and new developments relating to aquaculture.

North American Journal of Fisheries Management. American Fisheries Society, 5410 Grosvenor Lane Bethesda, MD 20814. Phone: (301)897-8616 Fax: (301)897-8096 E-mail: main@fisheries.org • URL: http://www.fisheries.org • Quarterly. $499.00 per year. Covers fisheries management trends and research.

North American Meat Processors Association., 1910 Association Dr. Reston, VA 20191. Phone: 800-368-3043 or (703)758-1900 Fax: (703)758-8001 E-mail: pkimball@namp.com • URL: http://www.namp.com • Represents wholesalers of meats and meat products to hotels, restaurants, schools, hospitals, and institutions. Conducts technical seminars.

North American Millers' Association., 600 Maryland Ave. SW, Ste. 825 W Washington, DC 20024. Phone: (202)484-2200 Fax: (202)488-7416 E-mail: generalinfo@namamillers.org • URL: http://www.namamillers.org • Millers of wheat, corn, oats, durum, and rye flour; members mill 95 percent of total U.S. capacity.

North American Packaging Association., 113 S West St., 3rd Fl. Alexandria, VA 22314. Phone: (703)684-2212 Fax: (703)683-6920 E-mail: info@paperbox.org • URL: http://www.paperbox.org • Independent package converters, including manufacturers of rigid (set-up) and folding paper boxes; suppliers to the industry. Aims to further the development, use, and sale of members' products; to deal with common industry problems; to foster greater operating economies and efficiencies. Represents the industry before legislative and regulatory bodies. Conducts technical workshops and seminars on sales, marketing, costing, computers, and management methods. Compiles statistics.

North American Retail Dealers Association., 4700 W Lake Ave. Glenview, IL 60025. Phone: 800-621-0298 or (847)375-4713 Fax: (866)879-7505 E-mail: nardasvc@narda.com • URL: http://www.narda.com • Firms engaged in the retailing of electronic and electrical devices and components. Promotes and represents members' interests. Makes available services to members including: legal and technical consulting; employee screening; bank card processing; long-distance phone discounts; financial statements analysis; in-store promotion kits; customer check authorization. Advocates for members' interests before federal regulatory bodies; disseminates information on new regulations affecting members. Conducts educational programs.

North American Retail Hardware Association., 5822 W 74th St. Indianapolis, IN 46278-1787. Phone: 800-772-4424 or (317)290-0338 Fax: (317)328-4354 E-mail: contact@nrha.org • URL: http://www.nrha.org • Represents independent family-owned hardware/home improvement retailers. Sponsors correspondence courses in hardware and building materials retailing; conducts annual cost-of-doing-business study.

North American Saving Association., 1300 Sumner Ave. Cleveland, OH 44115-2851. Phone: (216)241-7333 Fax: (216)241-0105 E-mail: nasa@sewingassociation.com • URL: http://www.sawingassociation.com • Formerly Hack and Band Saw Manufacturers Association of America.

North American Scrap Metals Directory. Recycling Today Media Group, 4020 Kinross Lakes Pky. Ste. 201 Richfield, OH 44286. Phone: 800-456-0707 or (330)523-5400 Fax: (216)961-0364 E-mail: info@carrollpub.com • URL: http://www.recyclingtoday.com • Covers: Suppliers of scrap metal materials in North America. Entries include: Contact information.

North American Securities Administrators Association., 750 1st St. NE, Ste. 1140 Washington, DC 20002-8034. Phone: 800-84-NASAA or (202)737-0900 Fax: (202)783-3571 E-mail: info@nasaa.org • URL: http://www.nasaa.org • Represents the interests of the state, provincial and territorial securities administrators in the U.S., Canada, Mexico and Puerto Rico. Provides support to its members in government relations and with federal regulators, industry SROs and other groups.

North American Simulation and Gaming Association., P.O. Box 78636 Indianapolis, IN 46278. Phone: 888-432-4263 or (317)387-1424 Fax: (317)387-1921 E-mail: info@nasaga.org • URL: http://www.nasaga.org • Members are professionals interested in the use of games and simulations for problem solving and decision-making in all types of organizations. Formerly National Gaming Council.

North American Wholesale Lumber Association - Distribution Directory. North American Wholesale Lumber Association, 3601 W. Algonquin Rd., No. 400 Rolling Meadows, IL 60008-3108. Phone: 800-527-8258 or (847)870-7470 Fax: (847)870-0201 E-mail: nawla@lumber.org • URL: http://www.lumber.org • Annual. $50.00. Over 600 wholesalers and manufacturers of lumber and related forest products.

Northeast Research and Extension Center. University of Arkansas

The Northern Miner: Devoted to the Mineral Resources Industry of Canada. Business Information Group, 1450 Don Mills Rd. Don Mills, ON, Canada M3B 2X7. Phone: 800-668-2374 Fax: (416)422-2214 • URL: http://www.businessinformationgroup.ca • Monthly. $91.50 per year.

Northern Nut Growers Association, Inc.

Northwest Farm Managers Association., PO Box 5599 Fargo, ND 58105-5599. Phone: (701)231-8914 Fax: (701)231-5632 E-mail: daakre@ndsuext.nodak.edu • URL: http://www.lib.ndsu.nodak.edu/ndirs/index.html • Represents manager-operators of commercial farms and agriculturists interested in research in farm management, marketing, and agribusiness.

Northwestern University-Media Management Center., 1007 Church St., No. 500 Evanston, IL 60201-5981. Phone: (847)491-4900 Fax: (847)491-5619 E-mail: mediamanagement@mmc.northwestern.edu • URL: http://www.mediamanagement.northwestern.edu • Research areas are related to various business aspects of the newspaper industry: management, marketing, personnel, planning, accounting, and finance. A joint activity of the J. L. Kellogg Graduate School of Management and the Medill School of Journalism.

Norton Bankruptcy Law Adviser. William L. Norton, Jr. West Group, 620 Opperman Dr. Eagan, MN 55123. Phone: 800-328-4880 or (651)687-7000 Fax: 800-340-9378 or (651)847-7302 E-mail: bookstore@westgroup.com • URL: http://www.westgroup.com • Monthly. $598.00 per year. Newsletter.

Not-for-Profit GAAP 2001: Interpretation and Application of Generally Accepted Ating Principles for Not-for-Profit Organizations. Richard F. Larkin and Marie DiTommaso. John Wiley and Sons, Inc., 111 River St. Hoboken, NJ 07030. Phone: 800-225-5945 or (201)748-6000 Fax: (201)748-6088 E-mail: info@wiley.com • URL: http://www.wiley.com • 2001. $65.00.

Notable Corporate Chronologies. Gale, 27500 Drake Rd. Farmington Hills, MI 48331-3535. Phone: 800-877-4253 or (248)699-4253 Fax: 800-414-5043 or (248)699-8065 E-mail: galeord@cengage.com • URL: http://gale.cengage.com • Covers: Company name, address, phone, fax, URL, e-mail address, and cable and telex number.

Notary Bulletin. National Notary Association, 9350 Soto Ave. Chatsworth, CA 91313-2402. Phone: 800-876-6827 or (818)739-4000 Fax: (818)700-0920 E-mail: nna@nationalnotary.org • URL: http://www.nationalnotary.org • Bimonthly. Membership. Formerly *State Notary Bulletin*.

Notary Public Practices and Glossary. Raymond C. Rothman. National Notary Association, 9350 Soto Ave. Chatsworth, CA 91313-2402. Phone: 800-876-6827 or (818)739-4000 Fax: (818)700-0920 E-mail: nna@nationalnotary.org • URL: http://www.nationalnotary.org • 1998. $22.00. Second edition.

NotiCen: Central American & Caribbean Affairs. Latin America Data Base, Latin American Institute, University of New Mexico, 801 Yale Blvd., N. E. Albuquerque, NM 87131-1016. Phone: 800-472-0888 or (505)277-6839 Fax: (505)277-6837 • URL: http://www.ladb.umn.edu/noticen • An online newsletter covering economic, trade, political, and social issues in Central America. Time period is 1986 to date, with weekly updates. Inquire as to online cost and availability. Formerly EcoCentral.

Novel and Short Story Writer's Market. F&W Publications, Inc., 4700 E Galbraith Rd. Cincinnati, OH 45236. Phone: 800-289-0963 or (513)531-2690 Fax: (513)531-0798 • URL: http://www.fwpublications.com • Annual. $24.99. List of 2,000 literary magazines, general periodicals, small presses, book publishers, and authors' agents; contests awards; and writers' organizations.

NOW Legal Defense and Education Fund., 395 Hudson St., 5th Fl. New York, NY 10014-3684. Phone: (212)925-6635 Fax: (212)226-1066 E-mail: peo@nowldef.org • URL: http://www.nowldef.org • Supersedes NOW Legal Committee.

NPES-The Association for Suppliers of Printing and Publishing and Converting Technologies., 1899 Preston White Dr. Reston, VA 22091-4367. Phone: (703)264-7200 Fax: (703)620-0994 E-mail: npes@npes.org • URL: http://www.npes.org • Formerly Association for Suppliers of Printing and Publishing and Converting Technologies.

NSF International., 789 N Dixboro Rd., PO Box 130140 Ann Arbor, MI 48113-0140. Phone: 800-NSF-MARK or (734)769-8010 Fax: (734)769-0109 E-mail: info@nsf.org • URL: http://www.nsf.org • Specializes in the areas of public health and environmental quality focusing on water quality, food safety, indoor air health and the environment. Develops standards, operates product certification and listings programs for products that meet or exceed public health safety standards. Maintains a worldwide network of auditors who conduct unannounced inspections of manufacturer facilities to ensure compliance and to protect the integrity of the NSF Certification Mark. Provides special research and testing services to industry, government, and foundations.

NSFRE-News. National Society of Fund Raising Executives, 1101 King St., Ste. 700 Alexandria, VA 22314. Phone: 800-666-FUND or (703)684-0410 Fax: (703)684-0540 E-mail: nsfre@nsfre.org Description: Covers tax-related issues affecting nonprofit organizations, conference and seminar information, educational opportunities, and chapter news.

NSGA Retail Focus. National Sporting Goods Association, 1601 Freehanville Dr., Ste. 300 Mt. Prospect, IL 60056-5780. Phone: 800-815-5422 or (847)296-6742 Fax: (847)391-9827 E-mail: nsga1699@aol.com • URL: http://www.nsga.org • Bimonthy. Membership. Covers news and marketing trends for sporting goods retailers. Formerly *NSGA Sports Retailer*.

NSPA Washington Reporter. National Society of Accountants, 1010 N. Fairfax St. Alexandria, VA 22314-1574. Phone: 800-966-6679 or (703)549-6400 Fax: (703)549-2984 E-mail: arichman@nsacct.org • URL: http://www.nsacct.org • Monthly. Membership.

NTC's Business Writer's Handbook. Arthur H. Bell. McGraw-Hill, 1221 Ave. of the Americas New York, NY 10020. Phone: 800-722-4726 or (212)512-2000 Fax: (212)512-4502 E-mail: customer.service@mcgraw-hill.com • URL: http://www.mcgraw-hill.com • 1995. $35.00. (NTC Business Books Series).

NTIS Alerts: Agriculture & Food. National Technical Information Service, U. S. Department of Commerce, Technology Administration, 5285 Port Royal Rd. Springfield, VA 22161. Phone: 800-553-6847 or (703)605-6000 Fax: (703)605-6900 E-mail: helpdesk@fedworld.gov • URL: http://www.ntis.gov • Semimonthly. $195.00 per year. Provides descriptions of government-sponsored research reports and software, with ordering information. Covers agricultural economics, horticulture, fisheries, veterinary medicine, food technology, and related subjects. Formerly *Abstract Newsletter*.

NTIS Alerts: Biomedical Technology & Human Factors Engineering. National Technical Information Service, U. S. Department of Commerce, Technology Administration, 5285 Port Royal Rd. Springfield, VA 22161. Phone: 800-553-6847 or (703)605-6000 Fax: (703)605-6900 E-mail: helpdesk@fedworld.gov • URL: http://www.ntis.gov • Semimonthly. $210.00 per year. Provides descriptions of government-sponsored research reports and software, with ordering information. Covers biotechnology, ergonomics, bionics, artificial intelligence, prosthetics, and related subjects. Formerly *Abstract Newsletter*.

NTIS Alerts: Building Industry Technology. National Technical Information Service, U. S. Department of Commerce, Technology Administration, 5285 Port Royal Rd. Springfield, VA 22161. Phone: 800-553-6847 or (703)605-6000 Fax: (703)605-6900 E-mail: helpdesk@fedworld.gov • URL: http://www.ntis.gov • Semimonthly. $210.00 per year. Provides descriptions of government-sponsored research reports and software, with ordering information. Covers architecture, construction management, building materials, maintenance, furnishings, and related subjects. Formerly *Abstract Newsletter*.

NTIS Alerts: Business & Economics. National Technical Information Service, U. S. Department of Commerce, Technology Administration, 5285 Port Royal Rd. Springfield, VA 22161. Phone: 800-553-6847 or (703)605-6000 Fax: (703)605-6900 E-mail: helpdesk@fedworld.gov • URL: http://www.ntis.gov • Text: Semimonthly. $210.00 per year.

NTIS Alerts: Communication. National Technical Information Service, U. S. Department of Commerce, Technology Administration, 5285 Port Royal Rd. Springfield, VA 22161. Phone: 800-553-6847 or (703)605-6000 Fax: (703)605-6900 E-mail: helpdesk@fedworld.gov • URL: http://www.ntis.gov • Semimonthly. $210.00 per year. . Provides descriptions of government-sponsored research reports and software, with ordering information. Covers common carriers, satellites, radio/TV equipment, telecommunication regulations, and related subjects.

NTIS Alerts: Computers, Control & Information Theory. National Technical Information Service, U. S. Department of Commerce, Technology Administration, 5285 Port Royal Rd. Springfield, VA 22161. Phone: 800-553-6847 or (703)605-6000 Fax: (703)605-6900 E-mail: helpdesk@fedworld.gov • URL: http://www.ntis.gov • Semimonthly. $235.00 per year. Provides descriptions of government-sponsored research reports and software, with ordering information. Covers computer hardware, software, control systems, pattern recognition, image processing, and related subjects. Formerly *Abstract Newsletter*.

NTIS Alerts: Electrotechnology. National Technical Information Service, U. S. Department of Commerce, Technology Administration, 5285 Port Royal Rd. Springfield, VA 22161. Phone: 800-553-6847 or (703)605-6000 Fax: (703)605-6900 E-mail: helpdesk@fedworld.gov • URL: http://www.ntis.gov • Semimonthly. $210.00 per year. Provides descriptions of government-sponsored research reports and software, with ordering information. Covers electronic components, semiconductors, antennas, circuits, optoelectronic devices, and related subjects. Formerly *Abstract Newsletter*.

NTIS Alerts: Energy. National Technical Information Service, U. S. Department of Commerce, Technology Administration, 5285 Port Royal Rd. Springfield, VA 22161. Phone: 800-553-6847 or (703)605-6000 Fax: (703)605-6900 E-mail: helpdesk@fedworld.gov • URL: http://www.ntis.gov • Semimonthly. $245.00 per year. Provides descriptions of government-sponsored research reports and software, with ordering information. Covers electric power, batteries, fuels, geothermal energy, heating/cooling systems, nuclear technology, solar energy, energy policy, and related subjects. Formerly *Abstract Newsletter*.

NTIS Alerts: Environmental Pollution & Control. National Technical Information Service, U. S. Department of Commerce, Technology Administration, 5285 Port Royal Rd. Springfield, VA 22161. Phone: 800-553-6847 or (703)605-6000 Fax: (703)605-6900 E-mail: helpdesk@fedworld.gov • URL: http://www.ntis.gov • Semimonthly. $245.00 per year. Provides descriptions of government-sponsored research reports and software, with ordering information. Covers the following categories of environmental pollution: air, water, solid wastes, radiation, pesticides, and noise. Formerly *Abstract Newsletter*.

NTIS Alerts: Government Inventions for Licensing. National Technical Information Service, U. S. Department of Commerce, Technology Administration, 5285 Port Royal Rd. Springfield, VA 22161. Phone: 800-553-6847 or (703)605-6000 Fax: (703)605-6900 E-mail: helpdesk@fedworld.gov • URL: http://www.ntis.gov • Semimonthly. $270.00 per year. Identifies new inventions available from various government agencies. Covers a wide variety of industrial and technical areas. Formerly *Abstract Newsletter*.

NTIS Alerts: Health Care. National Technical Information Service, U. S. Department of Commerce, Technology Administration, 5285 Port Royal Rd. Springfield, VA 22161. Phone: 800-553-6847 or (703)605-6000 Fax: (703)605-6900 E-mail: helpdesk@fedworld.gov • URL: http://www.ntis.gov • Semimonthly. $210.00 per year. Provides descriptions of government-sponsored research reports and software, with ordering information. Covers a wide variety of health care topics, including quality assurance, delivery organization, economics (costs), technology, and legislation. Formerly *Abstract Newsletter*.

NTIS Alerts: Manufacturing Technology. National Technical Information Service, U. S. Department of Commerce, Technology Administration, 5285 Port Royal Rd. Springfield, VA 22161. Phone: 800-553-6847 or (703)605-6000 Fax: (703)605-6900 E-mail: helpdesk@fedworld.gov • URL: http://www.ntis.gov • Semimonthly. $265.00 per year. Provides descriptions of government-sponsored research reports and software, with ordering information. Covers computer-aided design and manufacturing (CAD/CAM), engineering materials, quality control, machine tools, robots, lasers, productivity, and related subjects. Formerly *Abstract Newsletter*.

NTIS Alerts: Materials Sciences. National Technical Information Service, U. S. Department of Commerce, Technology Administration, 5285 Port Royal Rd. Springfield, VA 22161. Phone: 800-553-6847 or (703)605-6000 Fax: (703)605-6900 E-mail: helpdesk@fedworld.gov • URL: http://www.ntis.gov • Semimonthly. $220.00 per year. Provides descriptions of government-sponsored research reports and software, with ordering information. Covers ceramics, glass, coatings, composite materials, alloys, plastics, wood, paper, adhesives, fibers, lubricants, and related subjects. Formerly *Abstract Newsletter*.

NTIS Alerts: Ocean Sciences and Technology. National Technical Information Service, U. S. Department of Commerce, Technology Administration, 5285 Port Royal Rd. Springfield, VA 22161. Phone: 800-553-6847 or (703)605-6000 Fax: (703)605-6900 E-mail: helpdesk@fedworld.gov • URL: http://www.ntis.gov • Semimonthly. $210.00 per year. Provides descriptions of government-sponsored research reports and software, with ordering information. Formerly *Abstract Newsletter*.

NTIS Alerts: Transportation. National Technical Information Service, U. S. Department of Commerce, Technology Administration, 5285 Port Royal Rd. Springfield, VA 22161. Phone: 800-553-6847 or (703)605-6000 Fax: (703)605-6900 E-mail: helpdesk@fedworld.gov • URL: http://www.ntis.gov • Semimonthly. $210.00 per year. Provides descriptions of government-sponsored research reports and software, with ordering information. Covers air, marine, highway, inland waterway, pipeline, and railroad transportation. Formerly *Abstract Newsletter*.

NTIS Database. National Technical Information Service, 5285 Port Royal Rd. Springfield, VA 22161. Phone: 800-553-6847 or (703)605-6000 Fax: (703)605-6900 Contains citations and abstracts to unrestricted reports of government-sponsored research, 1964 to date. Covers a wide range of technical, engineering, business, and social science topics. Monthly updates. Inquire as to online cost and availability.

NTIS on SilverPlatter. Available from SilverPlatter Information, Inc., 100 River Ridge Rd. Norwood, MA 02062-5026. Phone: 800-343-0064 or (781)769-2599 Fax: (781)769-8763 Quarterly. $2,850.00 per year. Produced by the National Technical Information Service. Provides a CD-ROM guide to over 500,000 government reports on a wide variety of technical, industrial, and business topics.

Nuclear Energy Institute., 1776 I St. NW, Ste. 400 Washington, DC 20006-3708. Phone: (202)739-8000 Fax: (202)785-4019 E-mail: webmasterp@nei.org • URL: http://www.nei.org • Represents Electric utilities, manufacturers, industrial firms, research and service organizations, educational institutions, labor groups, and governmental agencies engaged in development and utilization of nuclear energy, especially nuclear-produced electricity, and other energy matters. Maintains speakers' bureau; compiles statistics and public attitude data.

Nuclear Engineering International. Wilmington Publishers Ltd., Wilmington House, Maidstone Rd., Wilmington Sidcup DA14 5HZ, United Kingdom. E-mail: energy@wilmington.co.uk Monthly. $341.00 per year. Text in English; summaries in French and German.

Nuclear Fuel. Platts, 2 Penn Plaza, 25th Fl. New York, NY 10121-2298. Phone: 800-752-8878 or (212)904-3070 Fax: (212)904-4209 E-mail: info@platts.com • URL: http://www.platts.com • Biweekly. $1,870.00 per year. Newsletter.

Nuclear Information and Records Management Association., 10 Almas Rd. Windham, NH 03087. Phone: (603)432-6476 Fax: (603)432-3024 E-mail: jnirma@nirma.mv.com • URL: http://www.nirma.org • Concerned with the maintenance of nuclear industry corporate records. Formerly Nuclear Records Management Association.

Nuclear Information and Resource Service., 1424 16th St., N.W., No. 404 Washington, DC 20036. Phone: (202)328-0002 Fax: (202)462-2183 E-mail: nirsnet@nirs.org • URL: http://www.nirs.org • Promotes alternatives to nuclear power. Affiliated with World Information Service on Energy.

Nuclear News. American Nuclear Society, 555 N. Kensington Ave. La Grange Park, IL 60525. Phone: (708)352-6611 Fax: (708)352-0499 • URL: http://www.ans.org • Monthly. $325.00 per year. Includes *Nuclear News Buyers Guide and 3 Special Issues*.

Nuclear News Buyers Guide. American Nuclear Society, 555 N. Kensington Ave. La Grange Park, IL 60525. Phone: 800-682-6397 or (708)352-6611 Fax: (708)352-0499 • URL: http://www.ans.org • Annual. $91.00. Lists approximately 1,500 manufacturers and suppliers of nuclear components. Included with subscription to *Nuclear News*.

Nuclear News-World List of Nuclear Power Plants. American Nuclear Society, 555 N. Kensington Ave. La Grange Park, IL 60525. Phone: 800-682-6397 or (708)352-6611 Fax: (708)352-0499 • URL: http://www.ans.org • Annual. $19.00 per copy. List of over 100 U. S. and foreign nuclear power plants that are in operation, under construction, or on order.

Nuclear Plant Journal. International Nuclear Power Industry. EQES, Inc., 799 Roosevelt Rd., Bldg. 6, Suite 208 Glen Ellyn, IL 60137-5925. Phone: (630)858-6161 Fax: (630)858-8787 Bimonthly. $120.00 per year.

Nuclear Power. Available from U. S. Government Printing Office, Washington, DC 20402. Phone: (202)512-1800 Fax: (202)512-2250 E-mail: gpoaccess@gpo.gov • URL: http://www.access.gpo.gov • Annual. Free. Lists government publications. GPO Subject Bibliography Number 200.

Nuclear Science and Engineering: Research and Development Related to Peaceful Utilization of Nuclear Energy. American Nuclear Society, 555 N. Kensington Ave. La Grange Park, IL 60525. Phone: (708)352-6611 Fax: (708)352-0499 • URL: http://www.ans.org • Nine times per year. Institutions, $900.00 per year. Includes online edition.

Nuclear Standards News. American Nuclear Society, 555 N Kensington Ave. La Grange Park, IL 60526. Phone: 800-323-3044 or (708)352-6611 Fax: (708)352-0499 E-mail: nuclear@ans.org • URL: http://www.ans.org • Description: Provides current information on nuclear standards, U.S. Nuclear Regulatory Commission (NRC) regulations and licensing issues, and developments in the domestic and international nuclear standards field. Recurring features include a calendar of standards meetings and notices of pertinent publications.

Nuclear Suppliers Association., PO Box 2038 Springfield, VA 22152. Phone: (703)451-1912 Fax: (703)451-2334 E-mail: nsanews@aol.com • URL: http://www.nuclearsuppliers.org • Companies involved in the manufacture or distribution of products and services for the nuclear industry. Promotes nuclear power and the interests of the nuclear industry.

Nuclear Technology: Applications for Nuclear Science, Nuclear Engineering and Related Arts. American Nuclear Society, 555 N. Kensington Ave. La Grange Park, IL 60525. Phone: (708)352-6611 Fax: (708)352-0499 • URL: http://www.ans.org • Institutions, $1,030.00 per year. Includes online edition.

Nuclear Waste News: Generation-Packaging-Transportation-Processing-Disposal. Business Publishers, Inc., 8737 Colesville Rd., Suite 1100 Silver Spring, MD 20910-3928. Phone: 800-274-6737 or (301)587-6300 Fax: (301)589-8493 E-mail: bpinews@bpinews.com • URL: http://www.bpinews.com • Weekly. $867.00. per year. Newsletter.

Nucleonics Week. Energy and Business Newsletters, McGraw-Hill Companies, 2 Penn Plaza, 25th Fl. New York, NY 10121-2298. Phone: 800-752-8878 or (212)904-3070 Fax: (212)904-4209 E-mail: support@platts.com • URL: http://www.platts.com • Description: Provides an overview of all international developments relating to commercial nuclear power. Offers coverage of plant construction, low-level waste issues, government policies, plant performance, services, and decommissioning, as well as "comprehensive statistical coverage of plant production and the economics of nuclear power." Recurring features include a monthly listing of nuclear power electric generation worldwide. **Remarks:** Also available in electronic format.

The Numbers You Need. Gale Cengage Learning, 27500 Drake Rd. Farmington Hills, MI 48331-3535. Phone: 800-877-GALE or (248)699-4253 Fax: 800-414-5043 E-mail: gale.galeord@cengage.com • URL: http://gale.cengage.com • 1993. $75.00. Contains mathematical equations, formulas, charts, and graphs, including many that are related to business or finance. Explanations, step-by-step directions, and examples of use are provided.

Numismatic News: The Complete Information Source for Coin Collectors. Krause Publications, Inc., 700 E. State St. Iola, WI 54990-0001. Phone: 800-258-0929 or (715)445-2214 Fax: (715)445-4087 • URL: http://www.krause.com • Weekly. $32.00 per year.

Numismatics International., PO Box 570842 Dallas, TX 75357-0842. Phone: (940)440-2213 Fax: (940)365-2072 E-mail: johnvan@grandecom.net • URL: http://www.numis.org • Numismatists, coin dealers, students, and numismatic authors in 35 countries. Works to: encourage and promote the science of numismatics; cultivate fraternal relations among collectors and numismatic students; encourage new collectors and foster the interest of youth in numismatics; stimulate and advance affiliations among collectors and kindred organizations; acquire, share, and disseminate numismatic knowledge including cultural and historical information on coins. Sponsors periodic lectures. Maintains coin collection. **Convention/Meeting:** none.

Nursery Business Retailer. Brantwood Publications, Inc., 2410 Northside Dr. Clearwater, FL 33761. Bimonthly. Price on application.

Nursery Stock and Supply Locator. American Nursery and Landscape Association, 1000 Vermont Ave., No. 300 Washington, DC 20005-4914. Phone: (202)789-2900 Fax: (202)789-1893 • URL: http://www.anla.org • Annual. $3.00.

Nursing Economics: The Journal for Health Care Leaders. Jannetti Publications, Inc., East Holly Ave. Pitman, NJ 08071. Phone: (856)256-2300 Fax: (856)589-7463 E-mail: nejrnl@ajj.com • URL: http://www.ajj.com • Bimonthly. Individuals, $54.00 per year; institutions, $70.00 per year.

Nursing Home Regulations Manual. Thompson Publishing Group, Inc., 1725 K St., N.W., Suite 700 Washington, DC 20006. Phone: 800-964-5815 or (202)872-4000 Fax: 800-999-5661 E-mail: service@thompson.com • URL: http://www.thompson.com • $295.00 per year. Looseleaf service. Includes monthly updates, newsletters and internet access. Serves as a comprehensive guide to the Nursing Home Reform Act, federal regulations, resident assessment, deficiency findings, Medicare, Medicaid, Health Care Financing Administration (HCFA) policies, and related topics for nursing home and assisted living facility owners and managers.

Nursing Homes: Long Term Care Management. Medquest Communications, LLC, 3800 Lakeside Dr., No. 201 Cleveland, OH 44114. Phone: (216)391-9100 Fax: (216)391-9200 Monthly. $95.00 per year. Covers business, finance, and management topics for nursing home directors and administrators.

Nursing Management. Springhouse Corp. Lippincott Williams and Wilkins, 530 Walnut St. Philadelphia, PA 19106-3621. Phone: 800-950-0879 or (215)521-8300 Fax: (215)521-8902 E-mail: custserv@lww.com • URL: http://www.lww.com • Monthly. Individuals, $39.95 per year; institutions, $139.00 per year. Non-clinical subject matter.

Nutrition Abstracts and Reviews, Series A: Human and Experimental. Available from CABI Publishing, North America, 875 Massachusetts Ave. Cambridge, MA 02139. Phone: 800-528-4841 or (617)395-4056 Fax: (617)354-6875 E-mail: cabi-nao@cabi.org • URL: http://www.cabi-publishing.org • Monthly. Institutions, $1,835.00 per year. Includes single site internet access. Published in England by CABI Publishing. Provides worldwide coverage of the literature.

Nutrition Abstracts and Reviews, Series B: Livestock Feeds and Feeding. Available from CABI Publishing, North America, 875 Massachusetts Ave., 7th Fl. Cambridge, MA 02139. Phone: 800-528-4841 or (617)395-4056 Fax: (617)354-6875 E-mail: cabi-nao@cabi.org • URL: http://www.cabi-publishing.org • Monthly. Institutions, $1,180.00 per year. Online edition available, $1,215.00 per year. Published in England by CABI Publishing. Provides worldwide coverage of the literature.

Nutrition Industry Executive. Vitamin Retailer Magazine, Inc., 431 Cranbury Rd. East Brunswick, NJ 08816. Phone: (732)432-9600 Fax: (732)432-9288 • URL: http://www.vitaminretailer.com • 10 times a year. $50.00 per year. Edited for manufacturers of vitamins and other dietary supplements. Covers marketing, new products, industry trends, regulations, manufacturing procedures, and related topics. Includes a directory of suppliers to the industry.

Nutrition Reviews. International Life Science Institute, One Thomas Circle, 9th Fl. Washington, DC 20005. Phone: 800-538-9601 or (202)659-0074 Fax: (202)659-8654 E-mail: ilsi@ilsi.org • URL: http://www.ilsi.org • Monthly. Individuals, $122.50 per year; institutions, $195.00 per year.

Nutrition Today. Lippincott Williams and Wilkins, 530 Walnut St. Philadelphia, PA 19106-3261. Phone: 800-527-5597 or

(215)521-8300 Fax: (215)521-8902 E-mail: custserv@lww.com • URL: http://www.lww.com • Bimonthly. Individuals, $69.00 per year; institutions, $169.00 per year.

The Nutshell. Northern Nut Growers Association, 648 Oak Hill School Rd., PO Box 427 Townsend, DE 19734-0427. Phone: (717)938-6090 Fax: (717)938-6090 E-mail: support@platts.com Description: Brings information to amateur and expert nut growers on cultural practices, new developments in propagation, and knowledge of new and better cultivars and where to get them. Contains supplements of reports on the latest practices, experiments in progress, and storage of nuts. Recurring features include letters to the editor, interviews, news of research, a calendar of events, reports of meetings, book reviews, and notices of publications available.

OAG Air Cargo Guide. OAG Worldwide, 2000 Clearwater Dr. Oakbrook, IL 60523. Phone: 800-525-1138 or (630)515-5307 Fax: (630)515-3933 E-mail: custserv@oag.com • URL: http://www.oag.com • Monthly. $239.00 per year. Shows current domestic and international air freight schedules. Diskette edition, $449.00 per year.

OAG Business Travel Planner: North America. OAG, 2000 Clearwater Dr. Oak Brook, IL 60523. Phone: 800-525-1138 or (630)515-5307 Fax: (630)515-3933 E-mail: custsvc@oag.com • URL: http://www.oag.com • Quarterly. $142.00 per year. $55.00 per issue. Arranged according to more than 14,500 destinations in the U. S., Canada, Mexico, and the Caribbean. Lists more than 31,500 hotels, with AAA ratings where available. Provides information on airports, ground transportation, coming events, and climate. Includes maps.

OAG Desktop Flight Guide, North American Edition. OAG Worldwide, 2000 Clearwater Dr. Oak Brook, IL 60521. Phone: 800-323-4000 or (630)574-6000 Fax: (630)574-6091 • URL: http://www.oag.com • Biweekly. $285.00 per year. Provides detailed airline travel schedules for the U. S., Canada, Mexico, and the Caribbean. Includes aircraft seat charts and airport diagrams. Formerly *Official Airline Guide, North American Edition*.

OAG Flight Guide: Worldwide. OAG Worldwide, 2000 Clearwater Dr. Oak Brook, IL 60521. Phone: 800-323-4000 or (630)574-6000 Fax: (630)574-6091 • URL: http://www.oag.com • Monthly. $469.00 per year. Provides detailed airline schedules for international travel. Travel within North America not included.

OAG Pocket Flight Guide. OAG Worldwide, 2000 Clearwater Dr. Oak Brook, IL 60521. Phone: 800-323-4000 or (630)574-6000 Fax: (630)574-6091 • URL: http://www.oag.com • Monthly. Price varies. Regional editions available for international areas.

OAG Travel Planner: Europe Worldwide. OAG, 2000 Clearwater Dr. Oak Brook, IL 60523. Phone: 800-525-1138 or (630)515-5307 Fax: (630)515-3933 E-mail: custsrv@oag.com • URL: http://www.oag.com • Quarterly. $149.00 per year. Arranged according to more than 13,850 destinations in Europe. Lists more than 14,700 hotels, with information on airports, ground transportation, coming events, and climate.

OAG Travel Planner Hotel and Motel Redbook: Asia Pacific. OAG, 2000 Clearwater Dr. Oak Brook, IL 60523. Phone: 800-525-1138 or (630)515-5307 Fax: (630)515-3933 E-mail: custsrv@oag.com • URL: http://www.oag.com • Quarterly. $130.00 per year. Arranged according to more than 5,000 destinations throughout Asia and the Pacific. Lists about 3,000 hotels, with information on airports, ground transportation, coming events, and climate.

OAI., 22800 Cedar Point Rd. Cleveland, OH 44142. Phone: (440)962-3000 Fax: (440)962-3120 E-mail: michaelsalkind@oai.org • URL: http://www.oai.org • Aerospace-related research, education, and technology transfers. Formerly Ohio Aerospace Institute.

Oak Ridge Associated Universities., PO Box 117, PO Box 117 Oak Ridge, TN 37831-0117. Phone: (865)576-3146 Fax: (865)241-2923 E-mail: carla.phillips@orau.org • URL: http://www.orau.org • Represents private, not-for-profit corporations and a consortium of 91 doctoral-granting colleges and universities. Serves the government, academia, and the private sector in important areas of science and technology. Manages and operates the Oak Ridge Institute for Science and Education (ORISE) for the U.S. Department of Energy. ORISE undertakes national and international programs in education, training, health, and the environment.

Oak Ridge National Laboratory.

Occupational Earnings and Wage Trends in Metropolitan Areas. U.S. Bureau of Labor Statistics, Washington, DC 20212. Phone: (202)606-5900 Three times a year.

Occupational Hazards: Magazine of Health and Environment. Penton Media, Inc., 1300 E. Ninth St. Cleveland, OH 44114. Phone: (216)696-7000 Fax: (216)696-1752 E-mail: information@penton.com • URL: http://www.penton.com • Monthly. $55.00 per year. Industrial safety and security management.

Occupational Health and Safety Letter...Towards Productivity and Peace of Mind. Business Publishers, Inc., 8737 Colesville Rd., Suite 1100 Silver Spring, MD 20910-3928. Phone: 800-274-6737 or (301)587-6300 Fax: (301)589-8493 E-mail: bpinews@bpinews.com • URL: http://www.bpinews.com • Biweekly. $317.00 per year.

Occupational Injuries and Illnesses by Industry. Bureau of Labor Statistics, U.S. Department of Labor. Available from U.S. Government Printing Office, Washington, DC 20402. Phone: (202)512-1800 Fax: (202)512-2250 E-mail: gpoaccess@gpo.gov • URL: http://www.access.gpo.gov • Annual.

Occupational Outlook Handbook. Bureau of Labor Statistics, U.S. Department of Labor. Available from U.S. Government Printing Office, Washington, DC 20402. Phone: (202)512-1800 Fax: (202)512-2250 E-mail: gpoaccess@gpo.gov • URL: http://www.access.gpo.gov • Biennial. $53.00. Issued as one of the Bureau's *Bulletin* series and kept up to date by *Occupational Outlook Quarterly*.

Occupational Outlook Quarterly. U.S. Department of Labor. Available from U.S. Government Printing Office, Washington, DC 20402. Phone: (202)512-1800 Fax: (202)512-2250 E-mail: gpoaccess@gpo.gov • URL: http://www.accessgpo.gov • Quarterly. $15.00 per year.

Occupational Projections and Training Data. Available from U. S. Government Printing Office, Washington, DC 20402. Phone: (202)512-1800 Fax: (202)512-2250 E-mail: gpoaccess@gpo.gov • URL: http://www.access.gpo.gov • Biennial. $21.00. Issued by Bureau of Labor Statistics, U. S. Department of Labor. Contains projections of employment change and job openings over the next 15 years for about 500 specific occupations. Also includes the number of associate, bachelor's, master's, doctoral, and professional degrees awarded in a recent year for about 900 specific fields of study.

Occupational Safety and Health Handbook: An Employer's Guide to OSHA Laws. LexisNexis Matthew Bender, 1275 Broadway Albany, NY 12204-4026. Phone: 800-424-4200 or (518)487-3000 Fax: 800-828-8341 or (518)487-3584 E-mail: customer.support@lexisnexis.com • URL: http://www.lexisnexis.com/matthewbender/ • Looseleaf. $115.00. Periodic supplementation available. Covers inspections, violations, the citation process, ergonomics, hazards, equipment, and other topics relating to the law enforced by the federal Occupational Safety and Health Administration (OSHA).

Occupational Safety and Health Law. Randy S. Rabinowitz. BNA Books, 1231 25th St., NW Washington, DC 20037. Phone: 800-960-1220 or (202)452-4343 Fax: (202)452-4997 E-mail: books@bna.com • URL: http://www.bnabooks.com • 2002. $265.00. Third edition.

Occupational Safety and Health Standards for General Industry. CCH, Inc., 2700 Lake Cook Rd. Riverwoods, IL 60015. Phone: 800-835-5224 or (847)267-7000 E-mail: cust_serv@cch.com • URL: http://www.cch.com • 1999. $42.95.

Occupational Therapy in Health Care: A Journal of Contemporary Practice. Haworth Press, Inc., 10 Alice St. Binghamton, NY 13904-1580. Phone: 800-429-6784 or (607)722-5857 Fax: 800-895-0582 or (607)722-1424 E-mail: getinfo@haworthpressinc.com • URL: http://www.haworthpressinc.com • Quarterly. $275.00 per year.

Occupational Therapy in Mental Health: A Journal of Psychosocial Practice and Research. Haworth Press, Inc., 10 Alice St. Binghamton, NY 13904-1580. Phone: 800-429-6784 or (607)722-5857 Fax: 800-895-0582 or (607)722-1424 E-mail: getinfo@haworthpressinc.com • URL: http://www.haworthpressinc.com • Quarterly. Institutions, $385.00 per year.

Ocean Development and International Law; The Journal of Marine Affairs. Taylor & Francis Group, 325 Chestnut St., Ste. 800 Philadelphia, PA 19106. Phone: 800-821-8312 or (215)625-8900 Fax: (215)625-2940 E-mail: info@taylorandfrancis.com • URL: http://www.taylorandfrancis.com • Quarterly. Individuals, $225.00 per year; institutions, $454.00 per year.

Ocean Engineering: An International Journal of Research and Development. Elsevier Science, 360 Park Ave. S New York, NY 10010-1710. Phone: 888-437-4636 or (212)989-5800 Fax: (212)633-3990 E-mail: usinfo-f@elsevier.com • URL: http://www.elsevier.com • 18 times a year. Qualified personnel, $261.00 per year; institutions, $2,367.00 per year.

Ocean Navigator: Marine Navigation and Ocean Voyaging. Navigator Publishing LLC, 58 Fore St. Portland, ME 04101-4842. Phone: (207)772-2466 Fax: (207)772-2879 E-mail: editors@oceannavigator.com • URL: http://www.oceannavigator.com • Bimonthly. $26.00 per year.

Ocean Oil Weekly Report: News, Analysis, and Market Trends of the Worldwide Offshore Oil and Gas Industry. PennWell Corp., Petroleum Div., 1700 W. Loop S., Suite 1000 Houston, TX 77027. Phone: 800-331-4463 or (713)621-9720 E-mail: petroleum@pennwell.com • URL: http://www.pennwell.com • Weekly. $495.00 per year. Newsletter with emphasis on the Gulf of Mexico offshore oil industry. Includes statistics.

Oceanic Abstracts. CSA, 7200 Wisconsin Ave., Suite 601 Bethesda, MD 20814. Phone: 800-843-7751 or (301)961-6700 Fax: (301)961-6720 E-mail: service@csa.com • URL: http://www.csa.com • 11 times a year. $1,645.00 per year. Includes print and online editions. Covers oceanography, marine biology, ocean shipping, and a wide range of other marine-related subject areas.

Oceanic Abstracts (Online). Cambridge Scientific Abstracts, 7200 Wisconsin Ave., 6th Fl. Bethesda, MD 20814. Phone: 800-843-7751 or (301)961-6700 Fax: (301)961-6720 Oceanographic and other marine-related technical literature, 1981 to present.Monthly updates. Inquire as to online cost and availability.

Ocular Surgery News. SLACK, Inc., 6900 Grove Rd. Thorofare, NJ 08086-9447. Phone: 800-257-8290 or (609)848-1000 Fax: (609)853-6091 E-mail: custoerservice@slackinc.com • URL: http://www.slackinc.com • Biweekly. Individuals, $399.00 per year; institutions, $384.00 per year. Formerly *IOL & Ocular Surgery News*.

O'Dwyer's Directory of Corporate Communications. J. R. O'Dwyer Co., Inc., 271 Madison Ave. New York, NY 10016. Phone: (212)679-2471 Fax: (212)683-2750 E-mail: sales@odwyer.com Annual. $130.00. Public relations departments of major corporations.

O'Dwyer's Directory of Public Relations Firms. J. R. O'Dwyer Co., Inc., 271 Madison Ave. New York, NY 10016. Phone: (212)679-2471 Fax: (212)683-2750 E-mail: sales@odwyerpr.com Triennial. $120.00. Over 9,300 corporation and public relations firms.

OECD Agricultural Outlook. Organization for Economic Cooperation and Development, OECD Washington Center, 2001 L St., N. W., Suite 650 Washington, DC 20036-4922. Phone: 800-456-6323 or (202)785-6323 Fax: (202)785-0350 E-mail: washington.contact@oecd.org • URL: http://www.oecd.org • Annual. $34.00. Provides a five-year outlook for agricultural markets in various countries of the world, including the U. S., other OECD countries, and selected non-OECD nations.

OECD Catalogue of Publications. Organization for Economic Cooperation and Development. Available from OECD Publications and Information Center, 2001 L St., N.W.,, Suite 650 Washington, DC 20036-4922. Phone: 800-456-6323 or (202)785-6323 Fax: (202)785-0350 E-mail: washington.contact@oecd.org • URL: http://www.oecdwash.org • Online only. No print edition.

OECD Communications Outlook. OECD Publications and Information Center, 2001 L St., N.W., Suite 650 Washington, DC 20036-4922. Phone: 800-456-6323 or (202)785-6323 Fax: (202)785-0350 E-mail: washington.contact@oecd.org • URL: http://www.oecdwash.org • Annual. $104.00. Provides international coverage of yearly telecommunications activity. Includes charts, graphs, and maps.

OECD Economic Outlook. OECD Publications and Information Center, 2001 L St., N.W., Suite 650 Washington, DC 20036-4922. Phone: (202)785-6323 Fax: (202)785-0350 E-mail: washington.contact@oecd.org • URL: http://www.oecdwash.org • Semiannual. Price on application. $95.00 per year. Contains a wide range of economic and monetary data relating to the member countries of the Organization for Economic Cooperation and Development. Includes about 100 statistical tables and graphs, with 24-month forecasts for each of the OECD countries. Provides extensive review and analysis of recent economic trends.

OECD Economic Survey of the United States. OECD Publications and Information Center, 2001 L St., N.W., Suite 650 Washington, DC 20036-4922. Phone: (202)785-6323 Fax: (202)785-0350 E-mail: washington.contact@oecd.org • URL: http://www.oecdwash.org • Annual. $26.00.

OECD Economic Surveys. OECD Publications and Information Center, 2001 L St., N.W., Suite 650 Washington, DC 20036-4922. Phone: (202)785-6323 Fax: (202)785-0350 E-mail: washington.contact@oecd.org • URL: http://www.oecdwash.org • Annual. $26.00 each. These are separate, yearly reviews for each of the economies of the industrialized nations that comprise the OECD. Each edition includes forecasts, analyses, and detailed statistical tables for the country being surveyed. (The combined series, one annual volume for each nation, is available at $485.00.)

OECD Employment Outlook. OECD Publications and Information Center, 2001 L St., N.W., Suite 650 Washington, DC 20036-4922. Phone: 800-456-6323 or (202)785-6323 Fax: (202)785-0350 E-mail: washington.contact@oecd.org • URL: http://www.oecdwash.org • 2000. $48.00. Outlines the employment prospects for the coming year in OECD countries. Also discusses labor force growth, job creation, labor standards, and collective bargaining.

OECD Environmental Indicators. Organization for Economic Cooperation and Development, OECD Washington Center, 2001 L St., N. W., Suite 650 Washington, DC 20036-4922. Phone: 800-456-6323 or (202)785-6323 Fax: (202)785-0350 E-mail: washington.contact@oecd.org • URL: http://www.oecd.org • Annual. $27.00. Provides statistical information relating to climate change, air pollution, biodiversity, waste management, water resources, and other environmental topics.

OECD Environmental Outlook. Organization for Economic Cooperation and Development, OECD Washington Center, 2001 L St., N. W., Suite 650 Washington, DC 20036-4922. Phone: 800-456-6323 or (202)785-6323 Fax: (202)785-0350 E-mail: washington.contact@oecd.org • URL: http://www.oecd.org • Biennial. $65.00. Contains 20-year projections of economic, social, and technological data affecting the environment.

OECD in Figures. Organization for Economic Cooperation and Development, OECD Washington Center, 2001 L St., N. W., Suite 650 Washington, DC 20036-4922. Phone: 800-456-6323 or (202)785-6323 Fax: (202)785-0350 E-mail: washington.contact@oecd.org • URL: http://www.oecd.org • Annual. $13.00. A "pocket data book" providing a summary of key statistics for OECD countries, including economic growth, employment, education, the environment, and transportation.

OECD Information Technology Outlook 2000: ICTs, E-Commerce and the Information Economy. Organization for Economic Cooperation and Development, OECD

Washington Center, 2001 L St., N. W., Suite 650 Washington, DC 20036-4922. Phone: 800-456-6323 or (202)785-6323 Fax: (202)785-0350 E-mail: washington.contact@oecd.org • URL: http://www.oecdwash.org • 2000. $72.00. Provides data on information and communications technology (ICT) and electronic commerce in 11 OECD nations (includes U. S.). Coverage includes network infrastructure, electronic payment systems, financial transaction technologies, intelligent agents, global navigation systems, and portable flat panel display technologies.

OECD Iron and Steel Industry. Organization for Economic Cooperation and Development. Available from OECD Publications and Information Center, 2001 L St., N.W.,, Suite 650 Washington, DC 20036-4922. Phone: 800-456-6323 or (202)785-6323 Fax: (202)785-0350 E-mail: washington.contact@oecd.org • URL: http://www.oecdwash.org • Annual. $34.00. Data for orders, production, manpower, imports, exports, consumption, prices and investment in the iron and steel industry in OECD member countries. Text in English and French.

OECD Main Economic Indicators. Organization for Economic Cooperation and Development, 2 rue Andre-Pascal, Cedex 16 75775 Paris, France. Phone: 331 45 248200 Fax: 331 45 241391 • URL: http://www.oecd.org • International statistics provided by OECD, 1960 to date. Monthly updates. Inquire as to online cost and availability.

OECD Nuclear Energy Data. Organization for Economic Cooperation and Development. Available from OECD Publications and Information Center, 2001 L St., N. W., Suite 650 Washington, DC 20036-4922. Phone: 800-456-6323 or (202)785-6323 Fax: (202)785-0350 E-mail: washington.contact@oecd.org • URL: http://www.oecdwash.org • Annual. $32.00. Produced by the OECD Nuclear Energy Agency. Provides a yearly compilation of basic statistics on electricity generation and nuclear power in OECD member countries. Text in English and French.

OECD Observer. Available from OECD Publications and Information Center, 2001 L St., N.W.,, Suite 650 Washington, DC 20036-4922. Phone: 800-456-6323 or (202)785-6323 Fax: (202)785-0350 E-mail: washington.contact@oecd.org • URL: http://www.oecdwash.org • Bimonthly. $50.00 per year.

OECD Oil and Gas Information. Available from OECD Publications and Information Center, 2001 L St., N.W.,, Suite 650 Washington, DC 20036-4922. Phone: 800-456-6323 or (202)785-6323 Fax: (202)785-0350 E-mail: washington.contact@oecd.org • URL: http://www.oecdwash.org • Annual. Price varies. Data on oil and gas balances, supplies, consumption by end use sector and trade of OECD countries. Text in English and French.

OECD Public Debt Markets: Trends and Recent Structural Changes. Organization for Economic Cooperation and Development, OECD Washington Center, 2001 L St., N. W., Suite 650 Washington, DC 20036-4922. Phone: 800-456-6323 or (202)785-6323 Fax: (202)785-0350 E-mail: washington.contact@oecd.org • URL: http://www.oecd.org • 2002. $49.00. Provides information on North American, Asian-Pacific, and European government bond markets. Contains chapters on individual countries, with discussion of debt management policies and techniques.

OECD Science, Technology, and Industry: Scoreboard 2003. Organization for Economic Cooperation and Development, OECD Washington Center, 2001 L St., N. W., Suite 650 Washington, DC 20036-4922. Phone: 800-456-6323 or (202)785-6323 Fax: (202)785-0350 E-mail: washington.contact@oecd.org • URL: http://www.oecd.org • 2003. $56.00. Presents data on technology trends in OECD countries. Includes more than 200 graphs relating to the performance of various countries in areas of science and technology. Issued biennially.

OECD Statistical Compendium. Organization for Economic Cooperation and Development, OECD Washington Center, 2001 L St., N. W., Suite 650 Washington, DC 20036-4922. Phone: 800-456-6323 or (202)785-6323 Fax: (202)785-0350 E-mail: washington.contact@oecd.org • URL: http://www.oecd.org • Semiannual. $1,905.00 per year for 1 to 10 users. CD-ROM contains more than 730,000 monthly, quarterly, and annual time series for OECD countries, 1960 to date. Includes fully searchable data on agriculture, food, economic indicators, national accounts, employment, energy, finance, industry, technology, and foreign trade. Results can be displayed in various forms.

OECD Steel Market and Outlook. Organization for Economic Cooperation and Development. OECD Publications and Information Center, 2001 L St., N.W.,, Suite 650 Washington, DC 20036-4910. Phone: 800-456-6323 or (202)785-6323 Fax: (202)785-0350 E-mail: washinton.contact@oecd.org • URL: http://www.oecdwash.org • Annual. Price varies.

Of Counsel: The Monthly Legal Practice Report. Aspen Law and Business, 1185 Avenue of the Americas, 37th Fl. New York, NY 10036. Phone: 800-638-8437 or (212)597-0200 Fax: (212)597-0338 E-mail: customer.service@aspenpubl.com • URL: http://www.aspenpublishers.com • 12 times a year. $445.00 per year. Newsletter on the management, marketing, personnel, and compensation of law firms.

Office Building Safety and Health. Charles D. Reese. CRC Press, 2000 N.W. Corporate Blvd. Boca Raton, FL 33431. Phone: 800-272-7737 or (561)994-0555 Fax: 800-374-3401 or (561)989-9732 E-mail: orders@crcpress.com • URL: http://www.crcpress.com • 2004. $89.95. Covers a wide variety of topics relating to office building safety, including management of emergencies, common hazards, accident prevention, environmental health issues, and security.

Office Dealer: Updating the Office Products Industry. Quality Publishing, Inc., 252 N Main St., Suite 200 Mount Airy, NC 27030. Phone: (336)783-0000 Fax: (336)783-0045 E-mail: osod@os-od.com • URL: http://www.os-od.com • Six times a year. $36.00 per year. Edited primarily for retailers of office products and office furniture. Formerly *Office Systems Dealer*.

Office Equipment Adviser: The Essential What-to-Buy and How-to-Buy Resource for Offices with One to 100 People. John Derrick. What to Buy for Business, Inc., 924 Anacapa Santa Barbara, CA 93101. Phone: (805)963-3539 Fax: (805)963-3740 E-mail: orders@betterbuys.com • URL: http://www.betterbuys.com • 1995. $24.95. Third revised edition.

Office for Sponsored Research.

Office Interior Design Guide: An Introduction for Facility and Design. Julie K. Rayfield. John Wiley and Sons, Inc., 111 River St. Hoboken, NJ 07030. Phone: 800-225-5945 or (201)748-6000 Fax: (201)748-6088 E-mail: info@wiley.com • URL: http://www.wiley.com • 1997. $70.00. (Professional Series).

Office of Academic Affairs, School of Public Health., University of Michigan, 109 S. Observatory St., 3537 SPH 1 Ann Arbor, MI 48109-2029. Phone: (734)764-5425 Fax: (734)763-5455 E-mail: sph.inquiries@umich.edu • URL: http://www.sph.umich.edu/ • Research fields include health care economics, health insurance, and long-term care.

Office of Climatology. Arizona State University

Office of Government Programs. Louisiana State University

Office of Manpower Studies. Purdue University

Office of Real Estate Research.

Office of Research Services.

Office of Sponsored Programs.

Office of Sponsored Research.

Office of Tax Policy Research.

Office of the Texas State Chemist. Texas A & M University

Office Planning and Design Desk Reference: A Guide for Architects and Design Professionals. James Rappoport and others, editors. John Wiley and Sons, Inc., 111 River St. Hoboken, NJ 07030. Phone: 800-526-5368 or (201)748-6000 Fax: (201)748-6088 E-mail: info@wiley.com • URL: http://www.wiley.com • 1991. $130.00. Covers the planning and designing of new or retrofitted office space.

Office Procedures and Technology for Colleges. Patsy J. Fulton. South-Western, 5191 Natrop Blvd. Mason, OH 45040. Phone: 800-543-0487 or (513)229-1000 • URL: http://www.swcollege.com • 1998. $39.95. 11th edition. (KF-Office Education Series).

Office Products Analyst: A Monthly Report Devoted to the Analysis of Office Products. Industry Analysts, Inc., 50 Chestnut St. Rochester, NY 14604. Phone: (716)232-5320 Fax: (716)458-3950 E-mail: theopa001@aol.com • URL: http://www.industryanalysts.com • Monthly. $195.00 per year. Newsletter. Includes user ratings of office automation equipment.

Office Professional's Quick Reference Handbook. Sheryl Lindsell-Roberts. Peterson's, 2000 Lenox Dr. Lawrenceville, NJ 08648. Phone: 800-338-3282 or (609)896-1800 Fax: (609)-896-1811 E-mail: support@petersons.com • URL: http://www.petersons.com • 1995. $9.00. Fifth revised edition.

Office Relocation Magazine. ORM Group, 354 W. Lancaster Ave., c/o J. Barthelmess Haverford, PA 19041. Phone: (610)649-6565 Fax: (610)642-8020 Bimonthly. $39.00 per year. Provides articles on the relocation of office facilities.

Office Solutions: The Magazine for Office Professionals. Quality Publishing, Inc., 252 N Main St., Suite 200 Mount Airy, NC 27030. Phone: (336)783-0000 Fax: (336)783-0045 E-mail: osod@os-od.com • URL: http://www.os-od.com • Monthly. $36.00 per year. Edited for office managers. Covers office technology, services, and new products. Formerly *Office Systems*, incorporating *Managing Office Technology*.

Office World News. BUS Publications, 366 Ramtown Greenville Rd. Howell, NJ 07731-2789. Phone: (732)785-8300 Fax: (732)785-1347 E-mail: ownews@worldnet.att.net • URL: http://www.officeworldnews.com • Monthly. Free to qualified personnel; others, $50.00 per year. Formerly *Office Products News*.

OfficePro. Stratton Publishing and Marketing Inc., 5501 Backlick Rd., Suite 240 Springfield, VA 22206. Phone: (703)914-9200 Fax: (703)914-6777 Nine times a year. $25.00 per year. Provides statistics and other information about secretaries and office trends. Formerly *Secretary*.

The Official America Online Tour Guide. Jennifer Watson and Dave Marx. John Wiley and Sons, Inc., 111 River St. Hoboken, NJ 07030-5774. Phone: 800-225-5945 or (201)748-6000 Fax: (201)748-6088 E-mail: custserv@wiley.com • URL: http://www.wiley.com • 2000. $24.99.Fifth edition. Provides a detailed explanation of the various features of versio of America Online, including electronic mail procedures and "Using the Internet."

Official Board Markets: "The Yellow Sheet". Mark Arzoumanian. Advanstar Communications, 545 Boylston St. Boston, MA 02116. Phone: 888-527-7008 or (617)267-6500 Fax: (617)267-6900 E-mail: info@advanstar.com • URL: http://www.advanstar.com • Weekly. $160.00 per year. Covers the corrugated container, folding carton, rigid box and waste paper industries.

Official Bus Guide. Russells Guides Inc., 817 2nd Ave., SE Cedar Rapids, IA 52403-2401. Phone: (319)364-6138 Fax: (319)365-8728 E-mail: russells@russellsprinting.com Publication includes: List of about 475 intercity bus companies in the U.S., Canada, and Mexico. Entries include: Company name, address, phone, executives' names and titles, list of terminals and stations with terminal managers' names. Principal content of publication is intercity operating timetables.

Official Directory of Industrial and Commercial Logistics Executives. Commonwealth Business Media, Inc., 400 Windsor Corp. Ctr., 50 Millstone Rd., Ste. 200 East Windsor, NJ 08520-1415. Phone: 800-221-5488 or (609)371-7700 Fax: (609)371-7883 E-mail: customerservice@cbizmedia.com • URL: http://www.cbizmedia.com • Annual. $205.00. CD-ROM only. About 16,000 U.S. and Canadian commercial firms with full-time or part-time traffic/transportation departments, and 28,000 traffic executives.

Official Gazette of the United States Patent and Trademark Office. Superintendent of Documents, Stop SSOM, Pulblication Customer Service Washington, DC 20402. Phone: (202)512-1806 Fax: (202)512-2168 Weekly. $110.00. Lists all trademarks currently registered and renewed trademarks in the U.S. Patent and Trademark Office.

Official Gazette of the United States Patent and Trademark Office: Patents. Available from U. S. Government Printing Office, Washington, DC 20402. Phone: (202)512-1800 Fax: (202)512-2250 E-mail: gpoaccess@gpo.gov • URL: http://www.access.gpo.gov • Weekly. Contains the Patents, Patent Office Notices, and Designs issued each week (http://www.uspto.gov). Annual indexes are sold separately.

Official Gazette of the United States Patent and Trademark Office: Trademarks. Available from U. S. Government Printing Office, Washington, DC 20402. Phone: (202)512-1800 Fax: (202)512-2250 E-mail: gpoaccess@gpo.gov • URL: http://www.access.gpo.gov • Weekly. $1,229.00 per year by first class mail. Contains Trademarks, Trademark Notices, Marks Published for Opposition, Trademark Registrations Issued, and Index of Registrants (http://www.uspto.gov).

Official Guide for GMAT Review (Graduate Management Admission Test). Graduate Management Admissions Council. Educational Testing Service, PO Box 6108 Princeton, NJ 08541-6108. Phone: (609)771-7243 Fax: (609)771-7385 E-mail: lsavadge@ets.org • URL: http://www.ets.org • 2003. 10th edition. Price on application. Provides sample tests, answers, and explanations for the Graduate Management Admission Test (GMAT).

Official Hotel Guide. Northstar Travel Media L.L.C., 100 Lighting Way, 2nd Fl. Secaucus, NJ 07094. Phone: 800-446-6551 or (201)902-2000 Fax: (201)902-2045 E-mail: secaucushelpdesk@ntmllc.com • URL: http://www.northstartravelmedia.com • Covers: in four volumes, 29,000 hotels, motels, and resorts worldwide. Volume 1 covers most of the U.S. ; Volume 2 covers the rest of the U.S. and the Western Hemisphere; Volume 3 covers Europe, the Middle East, Asia, and Africa. Volume 4 specialty travel guide includes listings of golf resorts and tennis resorts; health spas, dude ranches, bed and breakfasts, and casino & hotels in the United States; also includes lists of hotels in the Caribbean with golf, tennis, casinos, and all-inclusive. Entries include: Hotel/motel/resort name, address, phone, fax, CRS's, number of rooms or units, rates, brief description of facilities, ratings, codes indicating credit cards accepted, email and website addresses, and travel agent's commission, if any.

Official International Toy Center Directory., PO Box 173, 177 Sound Beach Ave. Old Greenwich, CT 06870-0173. Fax: (203)637-8549 E-mail: tcdnyc@aol.com Toy manufacturers and toy sales representatives who maintain permanent sales offices and showrooms at 200 5th Ave. and 1107 Broadway in New York City. "To promote the Greater Toy Center as the toy center of the world, thereby making toy buying and selling more convenient and economical."

Official Motor Shippers Guide. Official Motor Freight Guide, Inc., 1700 W. Cortland St. Chicago, IL 60622-1150. Phone: (773)278-2454 Fax: (773)489-0482 Annual. $60.50. 17 regional editions. Includes one update. Formerly *Offical Motor Freight-Shippers Guide*.

Official Railway Guide—Freight Service Edition. Commonwealth Business Media Inc., 400 Windsor Corporate Pk., 50 Millstone Rd., Ste. 200 East Windsor, NJ 08520-1415. Phone: 800-221-5488 or (609)371-7700 Fax: (609)371-7885 E-mail: customerservice@cbizmedia.com • URL: http://www.cbizmedia.com • Covers: Railways in North America offering freight service. Includes lists of railroad associations, state railroad commissions, federal regulatory agencies. Entries include: Railroad name, general office, address, phone, names of executives, list of services, schedules, maps, local sales offices and their phone numbers and executives.

Offshore: Incorporating The Oilman. PennWell Corp., Industrial Div., 1421 S. Sheridan Rd Tulsa, OK 74112. Phone: 800-331-4463 or (918)835-3161 E-mail: bid@pennwell.com • URL: http://www.pennwell.com • Monthly. $75.00 per year.

Offshore Marine Service Association., 990 N Corporate Dr., Ste. 210 Harahan, LA 70123. Phone: (504)734-7622 Fax: (504)734-7134 E-mail: kenwells@offshoremarine.org • URL: http://www.offshoremarine.org • Owners, operators, suppliers and crews of vessels servicing offshore oil and mineral installations. Seeks to advance the industry worldwide; monitors legislation and governmental regulations affecting the construction of offshore oil marine equipment and the operation of these specialized vessels, used primarily to supply and service offshore oil and gas operations worldwide. Conducts educational and personnel development and training programs; disseminates information on insurance and legal issues affecting offshore vessel operations. Maintains numerous committees representing all types of vessels engaged in the support of offshore installations.

Ohio Agricultural Research and Development Center. Ohio State University

Oil and Gas Investor. Hart Publications, Inc., 4545 Post Oak Place, Suite 210 Houston, TX 77027-3105. Phone: (713)993-9320 Fax: (713)840-8585 E-mail: hartinfo@phillips.com • URL: http://www.hartpub.com • Monthly. $259.00 per year.

Oil and Gas Journal. PennWell Corp., Industrial Div., 1421 S. Sheridan Rd. Tulsa, OK 74112. Phone: 800-331-4463 or (918)835-3161 E-mail: bid@pennwell.com • URL: http://www.pennwell.com • Weekly. $84.00 per year.

The Oil and Natural Gas Producing Industry in Your State. Independent Petroleum Association of America. Petroleum Independent Publishers, Inc., 1201 15th St., NW, No. 300 Washington, DC 20005. Phone: (202)857-4722 Fax: (202)857-4799 E-mail: rcarter@ipaa.org • URL: http://www.ipaa.org • Annual. Free to members; non-members, $50.00. Statistical issue of *Petroleum Independent*.

Oil Daily: Daily Newspaper of the Petroleum Industry. Energy Intelligence Group, Inc., Five E. 37th St., 5th Fl. New York, NY 10016-2807. Phone: (212)941-5500 Fax: (212)941-5509 • URL: http://www.energytel.com • Daily. Email, $1,595.00 per year; fax, $2,395.00 per year, online, $1,495.00 per year. Newspaper for the petroleum industry.

Oil/Energy Statistics Bulletin: And Canadian Oil Reports. Oil Statistics Co., Inc., P.O. Box 189 Whitman, MA 02382. Phone: (781)447-6407 Fax: (781)447-3977 E-mail: oilstats@compuserve.com Biweekly. $185.00 per year.

Oil Express: Inside Report on Trends in Petroleum Marketing Without the Influ nce of Advertising. United Communications Group, 11300 Rockville Pike, Suite 1100 Rockville, MD 20852-3030. Phone: 800-929-4824 or (301)287-2700 Fax: (301)816-8945 E-mail: webmaster@ucg.com • URL: http://www.ucg.com • 50 times a year. $337.00 per year. Newsletter. Provides news of trends in petroleum marketing and convenience store operations. Includes *U. S. Oil Week's Price Monitor* (petroleum product prices) and *C-Store Digest* (news concerning convenience stores operated by the major oil companies) and *Fuel Oil Update*. Formerly *U.S. Oil Week*.

Oil, Gas and Energy Quarterly. LexisNexis Matthew Bender, 1275 Broadway Albany, NY 12204. Phone: 800-424-4200 or (518)487-3000 Fax: (518)487-3584 E-mail: bookstore.support@lexisnexis.com • URL: http://www.bender.com • Quarterly. $234.00 per year. Covers latest tax ideas, techniques, and practice pointers in oil and gas taxation and accounting features.

Oil, Gas and Petrochem Equipment. PennWell Corp., Industrial Div., 1421 S. Sheridan Rd. Tulsa, OK 74112. Phone: 800-331-4463 or (918)835-3161 E-mail: bid@pennwell.com • URL: http://www.pennwell.com • Monthly. $35.00 per year.

Oil, Gas, Coal, and Electricity: Quarterly Statistics. Organization for Economic Cooperation and Development, OECD Washington Center, 2001 L St., N. W., Suite 650 Washington, DC 20036-4922. Phone: 800-456-6323 or (202)785-6323 Fax: (202)785-0350 E-mail: washington.contact@oecd.org • URL: http://www.oecd.org • Quarterly. $355.00 per year. Provides detailed data for OECD countries. Covers crude oil, nine oil product groups, hard coal, brown coal (lignite), natural gas, and electric power.

Oil Information. Organization for Economic Cooperation and Development, OECD Washington Center, 2001 L St., N. W., Suite 650 Washington, DC 20036-4922. Phone: 800-456-6323 or (202)785-6323 Fax: (202)785-0350 E-mail: washington.contact@oecd.org • URL: http://www.oecd.org • Annual. $150.00. Contains international data for major petroleum product groups. Includes statistics on supply, demand, trade, production, prices, and consumption for individual OECD countries and regions. Various time series cover about 30 years. (Also available on CD-ROM.)

Oil Market Intelligence. PIW Publications Inc., 5 E 37th St., No. 5 New York, NY 10016-2807. Phone: (212)532-1112 Fax: (212)941-5509 E-mail: sdp@tfn.com • URL: http://www.energyintel.com • Description: Provides analysis and statistics on worldwide oil markets and leading regional markets, including both the Atlantic Basin (Europe and the Americas) and Pacific Basins (East of Suez and the Far East). Covers futures and options markets and furnishes a monthly scorecard of prices for key products and crudes.

The Oil Marketing Bulletin. United Communications Group, 1300 Rockville Pke., Ste. 1100 Rockville, MD 20852-3030. Phone: (301)287-2700 Fax: (301)816-8945 E-mail: webmaster@ucg.com • URL: http://www.ucg.com • Weekly. $695.00 per year. Newsletter. Marketing information service.

Oil Price Information Service. United Comunications Group, 11300 Rockville Pike, Suite 1100 Rockville, MD 20852-3030. Phone: (301)816-8950 Fax: (301)816-8945 • URL: http://www.ucg.com • Weekly. $545.00 per year. Regional editions available at $150.00 per year. Quotes wholesale terminal prices for various petroleum products.

Oilheating: Journal of Indoor Comfort Marketing. Industry Publications, Inc., 3621 Hill Rd. Parsippany, NJ 07054. Phone: (973)331-9545 Fax: (973)331-9537 E-mail: info@oilheating.com • URL: http://www.oilheating.com • Monthly. $30.00 per year. Formerly *Fueloil and Oil Heat with Air Conditioning*

The Oilman Weekly Newsletter. PennWell Corp., Petroleum Div., 1700 W. Loop St., Ste. 1000 Houston, TX 77027. Phone: 800-736-6935 or (713)621-9720 E-mail: petroleum@pennwell.com • URL: http://www.pennwell.com • Weekly. $1,990.00 per year. Newsletter. Provides news of developments concerning the North Sea and European oil and gas businesses. Each issue contains four pages of statistical data.

Older Americans Information Directory. Grey House Publishing, 185 Millerton Rd., PO Box 860 Millerton, NY 12546. Phone: 800-562-2139 or (518)789-8700 Fax: (518)789-0556 E-mail: customerservice@greyhouse.com • URL: http://www.greyhouse.com • Covers: Information on national and state organizations, government agencies, health, research centers, libraries and information Centers, print and electronic media, disability aids and assistive devices, assisted living centers and independent living facilities, legal resources, continuing education programs, and travel information; for and about older Americans.

Older Americans Information Directory. Grey House Publshing, Inc., 185 Millerton Rd. Millerton, NY 12546. Phone: 800-562-2139 or (518)789-8700 Fax: (518)789-0556 E-mail: books@greyhouse.com • URL: http://www.greyhouse.com • 2002. $165.00. Fourth edition. Presents articles (text) and sources of information on a wide variety of aging and retirement topics. Includes an index to personal names, organizations, and subjects.

Older Americans Report. Business Publishers Inc., 2601 University Blvd., W Ste. 200, PO Box 17592 Silver Spring, MD 20902. Phone: 800-274-6737 or (301)929-5700 Fax: (301)949-8844 E-mail: custserv@bpinews.com • URL: http://www.bpinews.com • Description: Features brief articles on legislative, judicial, and federal agency activities concerning older Americans. Covers news of developments in such areas as Social Security, social services, Medicare, programs for retirement and pension funds, research projects, and the Older Americans Act. Recurring features include book reviews and a calendar of events.

Olsson Center for Applied Ethics. University of Virginia

OMB Watcher (Office of Management and Budget). O M B Watch, 1742 Connecticut Ave., N.W. Washington, DC 20009. Phone: (202)234-8494 Fax: (202)234-8584 Bimonthly. Individuals, $35.00 per year. Monitors operations of the federal Office of Management and Budget.

Omni Gazetteer of the United States of America: A Guide to 1,500,000 Place Names in the United States and Territories. Frank R. Abate, editor. Omnigraphics, Inc., 615 Griswold St. Detroit, MI 48226. Phone: 800-234-1340 or (313)961-1340 Fax: 800-875-1340 or (313)961-1383 E-mail: info@omnigraphics.com • URL: http://www.omnigraphics.com • 1991. $700.00. 11 volumes. Comprehensive listing of cities, towns, suburbs, villages, boroughs, structures, facilities, locales, historic places, and named geographic features. Population is shown where applicable. Individual regional volumes are available at $150.00.

On Becoming a Counselor: A Basic Guide for Nonprofessional Counselors and the Helping Professionals. Eugene Kennedy and Sara Charles. Crossroad Publishing Co., 481 Eighth Ave., Suite 1550 New York, NY 10001. Phone: 800-395-0690 or (212)868-1801 Fax: (212)868-2171 E-mail: ask@crossroadpublishing.com • URL: http://www.crossroadpublishing.com • 2001. $24.95. Third expanded revised edition.

On-the-Job Research: How Usable are Corporate Research Intranets? Alison J. Head and Shannon Staley. Special Libraries Association, 1700 18th St. NW, 17th Fl. Washington, DC 20009-2514. Phone: (202)234-4700 Fax: (202)234-2442 E-mail: sla@sla.org • URL: http://www.sla.org • 2002. Members, $100.00; non-members, $135.00. Presents the results of a survey of how employees at seven major corporations make use of company intranets for news and information research. Searching by individual employees generally had a success rate of less than 50 percent.

On the Mhove. Material Handling Industry of America, 8720 Red Oak Blvd., Ste. 201 Charlotte, NC 28217-3992. Phone: 800-345-1815 or (704)676-1190 Fax: (704)676-1199 • URL: http://www.mhia.org • Quarterly. Free. Formerly *MHI News*.

On Wall Street. Thomson Media, One State St. Plaza New York, NY 10004. Phone: 800-221-1809 or (212)803-8200 Fax: (212)843-9635 E-mail: custserv@thomsonmedia.com • URL: http://www.thomsonmedia.com • Monthly. $96.00 per year. Edited for securities dealers. Includes articles on financial planning, retirement planning, variable annuities, and money management, with special coverage of 401(k) plans and IRAs.

One-Hour Photo Processing Lab. Entrepreneur Media, Inc., 2445 McCabe Way Irvine, CA 92614. Phone: 800-421-2300 or (949)261-2325 Fax: (949)261-0234 E-mail: entmag@entrepreneur.com • URL: http://www.entrepreneur.com • Looseleaf. $59.50. A practical guide to starting a film developing and printing business. Covers profit potential, start-up costs, market size evaluation, owner's time required, site selection, lease negotiation, pricing, accounting, advertising, promotion, etc. (Start-Up Business Guide No. E1209.)

One Hundred Highest Yields. Advertising News Service, Inc., 11811 Federal Highway One, Ste. 101 North Palm Beach, FL 33410. Phone: (561)627-7330 Fax: (561)627-7335 E-mail: webmaster@bankrate.com • URL: http://www.bankrate.com • Weekly. $124.00 per year. Newsletter. List CD's and money markets offered by federally insured banks. National coverage.

101 Best Resumes for Grads. Jay A. Block. McGraw-Hill, 1221 Ave. of the Americas New York, NY 10020. Phone: 800-722-4726 or (212)512-2000 Fax: (212)512-4502 E-mail: customer.service@mcgraw-hill.com • URL: http://www.mcgraw-hill.com • 2002. $11.95. Contains sample resumes for recent graduates lacking significant work history or job experience. Covers 70 job categories and includes sample cover letters. (Teach Yourself Series).

101 Rules of Trading Discipline. Pejman Hamidi. McGraw-Hill, 1221 Ave. of the Americas New York, NY 10020. Phone: 800-722-4726 or (212)512-2000 Fax: (212)512-4502 E-mail: customer.service@mcgraw-hill.com • URL: http://www.mcgraw-hill.com • 2002. $39.95. Trading rules for investors or speculators are presented in three categories: "Trading Disciplines," "Market Disciplines," and "Personal Disciplines." (Teach Yourself Series).

101 Tips for Telecommuters: Successfully Manage Your Work, Team, Technology, and Family. Debra A. Dinnocenzo. Berrett-Koehler Publishers, Inc., 235 Montgomery St., Suite 650 San Francisco, CA 94104-2916. Phone: 800-929-2929 or (415)288-0260 Fax: (802)864-7626 E-mail: bkpub@bkpub.com • URL: http://www.bkconnection.com • 1999. $15.95.

175 High-Impact Cover Letters. Richard H. Beatty. John Wiley and Sons, Inc., 111 River St. Hoboken, NJ 07030. Phone: 800-225-5945 or (201)748-6000 Fax: (201)748-6088 E-mail: info@wiley.com • URL: http://www.wiley.com • 2002. $14.95. Third edition. Provides samples of cover letters for resumes.

100 Years of Wall Street. Charles R. Geisst. McGraw-Hill, 1221 Ave. of the Americas New York, NY 10020. Phone: 800-722-4726 or (212)512-2000 Fax: (212)512-4502 E-mail: customer.service@mcgraw-hill.com • URL: http://www.mcgraw-hill.com • 1999. $29.95. A popularly written, illustrated history of the American stock market. About 200 photographs, charts, cartoons, and reproductions of stock certificates are included.

The One-Person Library: A Newsletter for Librarians and Management. Information Bridges International, Inc., 447 Harris Rd. Cleveland, OH 44143-2537. Phone: (216)486-7443 Fax: (216)486-8810 E-mail: jsiess@ibi-opl.com • URL: http://www.ibi-opl.com • Monthly. $85.00 per year. Newsletter for librarians working alone or with minimal assistance. Contains reports on library literature, management advice, case studies, book reviews, and general information.

Coin World: World's #1 Publication for Coin Collectors. Amos Press, Inc., 911 Vandemark Rd. Sidney, OH 45365. Phone: 800-673-8311 E-mail: cweditor@amospress.com • URL: http://www.coinworld.com • Weekly. $36.95 per year.

1040 Preparation. Sidney Kess and others. CCH, Inc., 2700 Lake Cook Rd. Riverwoods, IL 60015. Phone: 800-835-5224 or (847)267-7000 E-mail: cust_serv@cch.com • URL: http://www.cch.com • 2001. How to prepare individual federal income tax returns.

1997 NAICS and 1987 SIC Correspondence Tables. U. S. Census BureauPhone: (301)457-4100 Fax: (301)457-1296 E-mail: naics@census.gov • URL: http://www.census.gov/epcd/www/naicstab.htm • Web site provides detailed tables for converting four-digit Standard Industrial Classification (SIC) numbers to the six-digit North American Industrial Classification System (NAICS) or vice versa: "1987 SIC Matched to 1997 NAICS" or "1997 NAICS Matched to 1987 SIC." Fees: Free.

1001 Computer Words You Need to Know. Jerry Pournelle. Oxford University Press, 198 Madison Ave. New York, NY 10016-4314. Phone: 800-451-7556 or (212)726-6000 Fax: (212)726-6446 E-mail: custserv@oup-usa.org • URL: http://www.oup-usa.org • 2004. $17.95.

One Up on Wall Street: How to Use What You Already Know to Make Money in the Market. Peter Lynch and John Rothchild. Simon and Schuster, 1230 Ave. of the Americas New York, NY 10020. Phone: 800-223-2348 or (212)698-7000 Fax: 800-943-9831 or (212)698-7007 E-mail: consumer.customerservice@simonandschuster.com • URL: http://www.simonsays.com • 2000. $14.00.

Online Banking. MarketResearch.com, 641 Ave. of the Americas, 4th Fl. New York, NY 10011. Phone: 800-298-5699 or (212)807-2629 Fax: (212)807-2676 E-mail: customerservice@marketresearch.com • URL: http://www.marketresearch.com • 2000. $3,000.00. Market research report. Includes demographics relating to the users and nonusers of online banking services. Provides market forecasts.

Online Competitive Intelligence: Move Your Business to the Top Using Cyber-Intelligence. Helen P. Burwell. Facts on Demand Press, PO Box 27869 Tempe, AZ 85285-7869. Phone: 800-929-3811 or (602)829-7475 Fax: 800-929-4981 or (602)829-8505 E-mail: brb@brbpub.com • URL: http://www.brbpub.com • 1999. $25.95. Covers the selection and use of online sources for competitive intelligence. Includes descriptions of many Internet Web sites, classified by subject. (Online Ease Series).

Online Deskbook: Online Magazine's Essential Desk Reference for Online and Internet Searchers. Mary E. Bates. Information Today, Inc., 143 Old Marlton Pike Melton, NJ 08055-8750. Phone: 800-300-9868 or (609)654-6266 Fax: (609)654-4309 E-mail: custserv@infotoday.com • URL: http://www.infotoday.com • 1995. $29.95. Covers the World Wide Web, as well as America Online, CompuServe, Dialog, Lexis-Nexis, and all other major online services. (Pemberton Press Books.)

Online Investor: Personal Investing for the Digital Age. Stock Trends, Inc., PO Box 344 Mt. Morris, IL 61054-0344. E-mail: postings@onlineinvestor.com • URL: http://www.onlineinvestor.com • Monthly. $14.95 per year. Provides advice and Web site reviews for online traders.

Online Libraries and Microcomputers. Information Intelligence, Inc., PO Box 31098 Phoenix, AZ 85046-1098. Phone: (602)996-2283 E-mail: order@infointelligence.com • URL: http://www.infointelligence.com • Ten times a year. Individuals $43.75 per year; libraries. $62.50 per year. Newsletter. Covers library automation and electronic information (online, CD-ROM). Reviews or describes new computer hardware and software for library use.

Online Marketing Handbook: How to Promote, Advertise and Sell, Your Products and Services on the Internet. Daniel S. Janal. John Wiley and Sons, Inc., 111 River St. Hoboken, NJ 07030. Phone: 800-225-5945 or (201)748-6000 Fax: (201)748-6088 E-mail: info@wiley.com • URL: http://www.wiley.com • 1999. $29.95. Revised edition. Provides step-by-step instructions for utilizing online publicity, advertising, and sales promotion. Contains chapters on interactive marketing, online crisis communication, and Web home page promotion, with numerous examples and checklists. (Business Technology Series).

Online Marketplace. Jupiter Communications, 21 Astor Pl. New York, NY 10003. Phone: 800-488-4345 or (917)534-6900 Fax: (917)534-6800 E-mail: help@mcb-usa.com • URL: http://www.jmm.com • Description: Keeps abreast of the fast-emerging developments in the digital marketplace and emerging interactive technologies. Reports on players and devices to provide the "inside scoop" on this marketplace. Topics include screen phones, interactive television, and smart cards, to name a few. Recurring features include interviews, and columns titled Tool Watch, Site Watch, and News Digest.

Online Newsletter. Information Intelligence Inc., PO Box 31098 Phoenix, AZ 85046. Phone: (602)996-2283 E-mail: rhuleatt@infointelligence.com • URL: http://www.infointelligence.com • Description: Tracks developments in the fields of CD-ROM and online services. Contains news of online/CD-ROM developments and events, mergers and acquisitions, personnel movements, telecommunications and networks, new equipment and developments, microcomputer hardware and software, new and forthcoming databases, forthcoming meetings, and publications and user aids.

The Online 100: Online Magazine's Field Guide to the 100 Most Important Online Databases. Mick O'Leary. Information Today, Inc., 143 Old Marlton Pike Medford, NJ 08055-8750. Phone: 800-300-9868 or (609)654-6266 Fax: (609)654-4309 E-mail: custserv@infotoday.com • URL: http://www.infotoday.com • 1996. $22.95. Provides detailed descriptions of 100 "important and useful" online databases in various subject areas.

Online Retrieval: A Dialogue of Theory and Practice. Geraldene Walker and Joseph Janes. Libraries Unlimited, Inc., Post Rd., W Westport, CT 06881. Phone: 800-225-5800 Fax: (203)222-1502 E-mail: lu-books@lu.com • URL: http://www.lu.com • 1999. $55.00. Second edition. Edited by Carol Tenopir. Covers a wide variety of online information topics, with emphasis on bibliographic databases. (Database Searching Series.)

Online: The Leading Magazine for Information Professionals. Information Today, Inc., 143 Old Marlton Pike Medford, NJ 08055-8750. Phone: 800-300-9868 or (609)654-6266 Fax: (609)654-4309 E-mail: custserv@infotoday.com • URL: http://www.infotoday.com • Bimonthly. $110.00 per year. Edited for librarians, Webmasters, site designers, content managers, and others concerned with knowledge/information management. Includes critical reviews of Web sites, software, search engines, and information services. (Formerly published by Online, Inc.)

The Only Investment Guide You'll Ever Need. Andrew Tobias. Harcourt Trade Publishers, 525 B St., Suite 1900 San Diego, CA 92101-4495. Phone: 800-543-1918 or (619)699-6707 Fax: 800-876-0186 • URL: http://www.harcourtbooks.com • 1999. $14.00. Expanded revised edition. An entertaining, optimistic look at investing, written for the "average" investor. Provides generally conservative advice, favoring no-load, low-expense index funds.

The Only Job-Hunting Guide You'll Ever Need: The Most Comprehensive Guide for Job Hunters and Career Switchers. Kathryn Petras and Ross Petras. Simon & Schuster Trade, 1230 Ave. of the Americas New York, NY 10020. Phone: 800-223-2348 or (212)698-7000 Fax: 800-445-6991 or (212)698-7007 E-mail: consumer.customerservice@simonandschuster.com • URL: http://www.simonsays.com • 1995. $15.00. Revised edition.

The Only Sales Promotion Techniques You'll Ever Need: Proven Tactics and Expert Insights. Tamara Block, editor. Dartnell Corp., 350 Hiatt Dr. Palm Beach Gardens, FL 33418. Phone: 800-341-7874 or (561)622-6520 Fax: (561)622-2423 E-mail: custserv@lrp.com • URL: http://www.dartnellcorp.com • 1996. $39.95. Covers sampling, sweepstakes, co-op advertising, event marketing, database management, and other topics.

OPD Chemical Buyers Directory. Schnell Publishing Company Inc., 360 Park Ave. S, 12th Fl. New York, NY 10010. Phone: (212)791-4200 Fax: (212)791-4321 E-mail: customerservice@greyhouse.com • URL: http://www.chemexpo.com • Covers: about 1,500 suppliers of chemical process materials and more than 300 companies that transport and store chemicals in the United States. Entries include: Company name, address, phone, list of products or services, telex, fax, e-mail address, internet address, branch offices.

Opening New Doors: Alternative Careers for Librarians. Ellis Mount, editor. Special Libraries Association, 1700 18th St., N. W. Washington, DC 20009-2514. Phone: (202)234-4700 Fax: (202)265-9317 E-mail: sla@sla.org • URL: http://www.sla.org • 1992. $39.00. Information professionals in careers outside the library field discuss the nature of their work, qualifications, rewards, finding a job, etc.

Operating an E-Business. Andrew McAfee. McGraw-Hill, 1221 Ave. of the Americas New York, NY 10020. Phone: 800-722-4726 or (212)512-2000 Fax: (212)512-4502 E-mail: customer.service@mcgraw-hill.com • URL: http://www.mcgraw-hill.com • 2002. $61.25. Provides case studies covering B-to-B (business-to-business) Internet endeavors, B-to-C (business-to-consumer), and the electronic business activities of traditional "bricks-and-mortar" companies. Illustrates what went right and what went wrong. The author is a professor at Harvard Business School.

Operating During Strikes: Company Experience, NLRB Policies, and Governmental Regulations. Charles R. Perry and others. Univ. of Pennsylvania, Center for Human Resources, The Wharton School, 205 Avon Rd. Haverford, PA 19041. Fax: (610)642-1576 1982. $20.00. (Labor Relations and Public Policy Series: No. 23).

Operating Results of Independent Supermarkets. Food Marketing Institute, 655 15th St., NW, No. 700 Washington, DC 20005. Phone: (202)452-8444 Fax: (202)429-4519 E-mail: fmi@fmi.org • URL: http://www.fmi.org • Annual. Members, $30.00; non-members, $75.00. Includes data on gross margins, inventory turnover, expenses, etc.

Operational Cash Flow Management and Control. Morris A. Nunes. Prentice Hall PTR, 240 Frisch Ct. Paramus, NJ 07652. Phone: 800-282-0693 Fax: 800-445-6991 • URL: http://www.phptr.com • 1982. $34.95.

Operational Research Society Journal. JSTOR, 149 Fifth Ave., 8th Fl. New York, NY 10010. Phone: 888-388-3574 or (212)358-6400 Fax: (212)358-6499 E-mail: mspinella@jstor.org • URL: http://www.jstor.org • Monthly. $1,096.00 per year. Includes print and online editions. Covers various applications of operations research, including forecasting, inventory, logistics, project management, and scheduling. Includes technical approaches (simulation, mathematical programming, expert systems, etc.).

Operations Alert. America's Community Bankers, 900 19th St. NW, Ste. 400 Washington, DC 20006. Phone: 888-872-0568 or (202)857-3100 Fax: (202)296-8716 E-mail: info@acbankers.org • URL: http://www.acbankers.org • Description: Reviews recent regulatory and product developments that affect community bank operations.

Operations and Management, Guide/Safety Manual. Helicopter Association International, 1635 Prince St. Alexandria, VA 22314-2818. Phone: (703)683-4646 Fax: (703)683-4745 E-mail: rotor@rotor.com • URL: http://www.rotor.com • Annual.

Operations Management. Institutional Investor, Inc., Journals Group, 225 Park Ave., S New York, NY 10003. Phone: 800-945-2034 or (212)224-3066 Fax: (212)224-3472 E-mail: info@iijournals.com • URL: http://www.iijournals.com • Weekly. $2,105.00 per year. Includes print and online editions. Newsletter. Edited for managers of securities clearance and settlement at financial institutions. Covers new products, technology, legalities, management practices, and other topics related to securities processing.

Operations Research. INFORMS, 901 Elkridge Landing Rd., Suite 400 Linthicum, MD 21090-2909. Phone: 800-446-3676 or (410)850-0300 Fax: (410)684-2963 E-mail: informs@informs.org • URL: http://www.informs.org • Bimonthly. Individuals, $164.00 per year; institutions, $339.00 per year.

Operations Research: A Practical Introduction. Michael W. Carter and Camille C. Price. CRC Press, 2000 N.W. Corporate Blvd. Boca Raton, FL 33431. Phone: 800-272-7737 or (561)994-0555 Fax: 800-374-3401 or (561)989-9732 E-mail: orders@crcpress.com • URL: http://www.crcpress.com • 2000. $99.95. Provides a basic guide to the use of operations research problem-solving techniques in business, industry, and engineering.

Operations Research Calculations Handbook. Dennis Blumenfeld. CRC Press, 2000 N.W. Corporate Blvd. Boca Raton, FL 33431. Phone: 800-272-7737 or (561)994-0555 Fax: 800-374-3401 or (561)989-9732 E-mail: orders@crcpress.com • URL: http://www.crcpress.com • 2001. $69.95. Contains more than 300 mathematical results and formulas used in operations research applications. Formulas are utilized in manufacturing, inventory control, and managememt science in general.

Operations Research Letters. Elsevier, 360 Park Ave., S. New York, NY 10010-1710. Phone: 888-437-4636 or (212)989-5800 Fax: (212)633-3990 E-mail: usinfo-f@elsevier.com • URL: http://www.elsevier.com • 10 times a year. Institutions, $622.00 per year.

Operations Review. Food Marketing Institute, 655 15th St., N.W. Washington, DC 20005. Phone: (202)452-8444 Fax: (202)429-4519 E-mail: fmi@fmi.org • URL: http://www.fmi.org • Quarterly. $50.00 per year. Includes operating ratios for food retailing companies.

Operative Plasterers and Cement Masons International Association of U.S. and Canada.

Ophthalmic Research Institute.

Ophthalmology. American Academy of Opthalmology. Elsevier, 360 Park Ave., S. New York, NY 10010-1710. Phone: 888-437-4636 or (212)989-5800 Fax: (212)633-3990 E-mail: usinfo-f@elsevier.com • URL: http://www.elsevier.com • Monthly. Individuals, $239.00 per year; institutions, $415.00 per year.

Ophthalmology Times: All the Clinical News in Sight. Advanstar Communications, 545 Boylston St. Boston, MA 02116. Phone: 888-527-7008 or (617)267-6500 Fax: (617)267-6900 E-mail: info@advanstar.com • URL: http://www.advanstar.com • Bimonthly. $190.00 per year.

The OPL Sourcebook: A Guide for Solo and Small Libraries. Judith A. Siess. Information Today, Inc., 143 Old Marlton Pike Medford, NJ 08055-8750. Phone: 800-300-9868 or (609)654-6266 Fax: (609)654-4309 E-mail: custserv@infotoday.com • URL: http://www.infotoday.com • 2001. $39.50. The editor of *The One-Person Library* newsletter covers a wide variety of practical topics for improving the management and efficiency of OPLs.

Opportunities for Study in Hand Bookbinding and Calligraphy. Guild of Book Workers, Inc., 521 Fifth Ave. New York, NY 10175-0038. Phone: (212)292-4444 E-mail: bcallery@flounder.com • URL: http://www.palimpsest.stanford.edu • Free. About 150 teachers, schools, and centers offering hand bookbinding and calligraphic services; international coverage.

Opportunities in Government Careers. Neale J. Baxter. McGraw-Hill, 1221 Ave. of the Americas New York, NY 10020. Phone: 800-722-4726 or (212)512-2000 Fax: (212)512-4502 E-mail: customer.service@mcgraw-hill.com • URL: http://www.mcgraw-hill.com • 2001. $15.95. Edited for students and job seekers. Includes education requirements and salary data. (VGM Career Books.)

Opportunities in Interactive TV Applications & Services: An Analysis of Market Interest & Price Sensitivity. Available from MarketResearch.com, 641 Ave. of the Americas, Third Floor New York, NY 10011. Phone: 800-298-5699 or (212)807-2629 Fax: (212)807-2642 E-mail: order@marketresearch.com • URL: http://www.marketresearch.com • 2001. $1,395. Published by TechTrends, Inc. Market research data. Includes an analysis of how much consumers are willing to pay per month for each application.

Opportunities in Journalism Careers. Jim Patten and Donald L. Ferguson. McGraw-Hill, 1221 Ave. of the Americas New York, NY 10020. Phone: 800-722-4726 or (212)512-2000 Fax: (212)512-4502 E-mail: customer.service@mcgraw-hill.com • URL: http://www.mcgraw-hill.com • 2001. $15.95. Edited for students and job seekers. Includes education requirements and salary data. (Opportunities in....Series).

Opportunities in Visual Arts Careers. Mark Salmon. McGraw-Hill, 1221 Ave. of the Americas New York, NY 10020. Phone: 800-722-4726 or (212)512-2000 Fax: (212)512-4502 E-mail: customer.service@mcgraw-hill.com • URL: http://www.mcgraw-hill.com • 2001. $15.95. Edited for students and job seekers. Includes education requirements and salary data. (Opportunities in...Series).

Opportunities Industrialization Centers of America., 1415 N Broad St. Philadelphia, PA 19122-3323. Phone: 800-621-4642 or (215)236-4500 Fax: (215)236-7480 E-mail: gsyounger@oicworld.org • URL: http://www.oicafamerica.org • Network of employment and training programs. Serves disadvantaged and unskilled workers.

Optical Engineering. SPIE-International Society for Optical Engineering, PO Box 10 Bellingham, WA 98227-0010. Phone: (360)676-3290 Fax: (360)647-1445 E-mail: spie@spie.org • URL: http://www.spie.org • Monthly. Members $55.00 per year; institutions, $550.00 per year. Technical papers and letters.

Optical Fiber Technology: Materials, Devices, and Systems. Elsevier, 655 Avenue of the Americas New York, NY 10010-5107. Phone: 800-366-2665 or (212)989-5800 Fax: 800-366-2665 or (212)633-3680 E-mail: custserv@elsevier.com • URL: http://www.elsevier.com • Quarterly. Individuals, $210.00 per year; institutions, $391.00 per year.

Optical Fibre Sensor Technology. Ken Grattan and Beverley Meggitt. Kluwer Academic Publishers, 10 Philip Dr., Assinippi Park Norwell, MA 02061. Phone: (781)871-6600 Fax: (781)681-9045 E-mail: kluwer@wkap.com • URL: http://www.wkap.nl • 2000. $145.00.

Optical Laboratories Association., 11096 Lee Hwy., Ste. A-101 Fairfax, VA 22030-5039. Phone: 800-477-5652 or (703)359-2830 Fax: (703)359-2834 E-mail: ola@ola-labs.org • URL: http://www.ola-labs.org • Represents independent, wholesale ophthalmic laboratories and suppliers serving the ophthalmic field.

Optical Publishing Industry Assessment. Julie B. Schwerin and Theodore A. Pine. InfoTech, Inc., 312 Main Norwich, VT 05055. Phone: (802)649-8700 Fax: (802)649-8877 E-mail: info@infotechresearch.com • URL: http://www.

infotechresearch.com • 1997. $1,295.00. Ninth edition. Provides market research data and forecasts to 2005 for DVD-ROM, "Hybrid ROM/Online Media," and other segments of the interactive entertainment, digital information, and consumer electronics industries. Covers both software (content) and hardware. Includes Video-CD, DVD- Video, CD-Audio, DVD-Audio, DVD-ROM, PC-Desktop, TV Set-Top, CD-R, CD-RW, DVD-R and DVD-RAM.

Optical Sciences Center.

Optical Society of America.

Optical Society of America Journal. Optical Society of America, Inc., 2010 Massachusetts Ave., N.W. Washington, DC 20036-1023. Phone: 800-762-6960 or (202)223-8130 Fax: (202)223-1096 E-mail: info@osa.org • URL: http://www.osa.org • Monthly. Part A, $1,371.00 per year; Part B, $1,371.00 per year.

Opticians Association of America., 12100 Sunset Hills Rd., Ste. 130 Reston, VA 20190. Phone: 800-443-8997 or (703)234-4072 Fax: (703)435-4390 E-mail: oaa@oaa.org • URL: http://www.oaa.org • Formerly Guild of Prescription Opticians of America.

Opticians of Association America-Reference Directory. Opticians Association of America., PO Box 6600 Springfield, VA 22150-6600. Phone: 800-443-8997 or (703)916-8856 Fax: (703)916-7966 E-mail: oaa@opticians.org • URL: http://www.opticians.org • Annual. $60.00. Lists 250 member firms with a total of 350 retail locations.

Optics. Eugene Hecht. Addison-Wesley, 75 Arlington St., Ste. 300 Boston, MA 02116. Phone: 800-447-2226 or (617)848-7500 E-mail: pearsons@eds.com • URL: http://www.awl.com • 2001. $106.95. Fourth edition. (Manchester Physics Series).

Optics and Laser Technology. Elsevier, 360 Park Ave., S. New York, NY 10010-1710. Phone: 888-437-4636 or (212)989-5800 Fax: (212)633-3990 E-mail: usinfo-f@elsevier.com • URL: http://www.elsevier.com • Eight times a year. Institutions, $1,196.00 per year. Published in United Kingdom.

Optics and Photonics News. Optical Society of America, Inc., 2010 Massachusetts Ave., N.W. Washington, DC 20036-1023. Phone: 800-762-6960 or (202)223-8130 Fax: (202)223-1096 E-mail: info@osa.org • URL: http://www.osa.org • Monthly. $99.00 per year. Includes print and online editions.

Option Advisor. Investment Research Institute Inc., 1259 Kemper Meadow Dr., Suite 100 Cincinnati, OH 45240. Phone: 800-448-2080 or (513)589-3800 Fax: (513)589-3810 E-mail: service@sir-inc.com • URL: http://www.schaeffersresearch.com • Monthly. $200.00 per year. Newsletter. Provides specific advice and recommendations for trading in stock option contracts (puts and calls).

Options., 225 S 15th St., Ste. 1635 Philadelphia, PA 19102-3916. Phone: (215)735-2202 Fax: (215)735-8097 E-mail: ola@ola-labs.org • URL: http://www.optionscareers.org • Career advising and human resource consulting service. Provides consulting and training programs on the changing workforce and workplace. Offers counseling on career issues such as job searches, career changes, and career management. Provides consultation in the areas of managing change, career management, mentoring, sexual harassment prevention gender sensitivity counseling, outplacement, managing diversity, and spouse employment assistance. Offers training to professionals. Conducts studies on employment-related issues; maintains speakers' bureau.

Options: Essential Concepts and Trading Strategies. McGraw-Hill, 1221 Ave. of the Americas New York, NY 10020. Phone: 800-722-4726 or (212)512-2000 Fax: (212)512-4502 E-mail: customer.service@mcgraw-hill.com • URL: http://www.mcgraw-hill.com • 1999. $55.00. Third edition.

Options, Futures, and Other Derivatives. John C. Hull. Prentice Hall PTR, 240 Frisch Ct. Paramus, NJ 07652. Phone: 800-282-0693 Fax: 800-445-6991 • URL: http://www.phptr.com • 2002. $135.00. Fifth edition.

Options: The International Guide to Valuation and Trading Strategies. Gordon Gemmill. McGraw-Hill, 1221 Ave. of the Americas New York, NY 10020. Phone: 800-722-4726 or (212)512-2000 Fax: (212)512-4502 E-mail: customer.service@mcgraw-hill.com • URL: http://www.mcgraw-hill.com • 1992. $37.95. Covers valuation techniques for American, European, and Asian options. Trading strategies are discussed for options on currencies, stock indexes, interest rates, and commodities.

The Options Workbook: Proven Strategies from a Market Wizard. Anthony J. Saliba. Dearborn Trade Publishing, A Kaplan Professional Co., 155 N Wacker Dr., No. 2500 Chicago, IL 60606-7481. Phone: 800-621-9621 or (312)836-4400 Fax: (312)836-1021 E-mail: trade@dearborn.com • URL: http://www.dearborntrade.com • 2001. $40.00. Emphasis is on computerized trading on the Chicago Board Options Exchange. Includes information on specific trading strategies.

Optoelectronic Computing Systems Center., University of Colorado at Boulder, Campus Box 525 Boulder, CO 80309-0525. Phone: (303)492-7135 Fax: (303)492-3674 E-mail: jneff@colorado.edu • URL: http://www.ocs.colorado.edu • Explores the advantages of optics over electronics for information processing.

Optoelectronic Devices. Safa Kasap. Addison-Wesley, 75 Arlington St., Ste. 300 Boston, MA 02116. Phone: 800-447-2226 or (617)848-7500 • URL: http://www.aw.com • 2001. $105.00.

Optoelectronics: An Introduction. John Wilson. Prentice Hall PTR, 240 Frisch Ct. Paramus, NJ 07652. Phone: 800-282-0693 Fax: 800-445-6991 • URL: http://www.phptr.com • 1998. $94.00. Third edition.

Optometric Management: The Business and Marketing Magazine for Optometry. Boucher Communications, Inc., 1300 Virginia Dr. Fort Washington, PA 19034. Phone: (215)643-8000 Fax: (215)643-8099 Monthly. $37.00 per year. Provides information and advice for optometrists on practice management and marketing.

Optometry and Vision Science-Geographical Directory, American Academy of Optometry. American Academy of Optometry, 6110 Executive Blvd., Suite 506 North Bethesda, MD 20852. Phone: (301)984-1441 Fax: (301)984-4737 E-mail: aaoptom@aol.com • URL: http://www.aaopt.org • Biennial. $25.00. List of 3,400 members; international coverage.

Optometry: Journal of the American Optometric Society. American Optometric Association, 243 N. Lindbergh Blvd. St. Louis, MO 63141. Phone: (314)991-4100 Fax: (314)991-4101 E-mail: almiller@aoa.org • URL: http://www.aoanet.org • Monthly. Free to members; non-members, $106.00 per year. Formerly *American Optometric Association Journal*.

Orders and Medals Society of America., PO Box 198 San Ramon, CA 94583. E-mail: dpeck9696@aol.com • URL: http://www.omsa.org • Persons, including 300 members outside the U.S., interested in collecting and studying insignias of the orders of knighthood and merit, the decorations of valor and honor, the medals of distinction and service, and allied material and historical data.

Oregon Wheat. Oregon Wheat Growers League, 115 SE Eighth St. Pendleton, OR 97801. Phone: (541)276-7330 Fax: (541)276-1723 E-mail: dsutor@owgl.org • URL: http://www.owgl.org • Monthly. Free to members; non-members, $15.00 per year. Deals with planting, weeds, and disease warnings, storage and marketing of wheat and barley. Specifically for Oregon growers.

Organisation for Economic Co-Operation and Development.

Organization Charts: Structures of More Than 200 Businesses and Non-Profit Organizations. Gale Cengage Learning, 27500 Drake Rd. Farmington Hills, MI 48331-3535. Phone: 800-877-GALE or (248)699-4253 Fax: 800-414-5043 E-mail: gale.galeord@cengage.com • URL: http://gale.cengage.com • 1999. $180.00. Third edition. Includes an introductory discussion of the history and use of such charts.

Organization for the Promotion and Advancement of Small Telecommunications Companies., 21 Dupont Circle, N.W., Suite 700 Washington, DC 20036. Phone: (202)659-5990 Fax: (202)659-4619 E-mail: tnb@opastco.org • URL: http://www.opastco.org • Members are small telephone companies serving rural areas. Formerly Organization for the Protection and Advancement of Small Telephone Companies.

The Organization of Industry. William F. Shughart. Cengage Learning Custom Publishing, 5101 Madison Rd. Cincinnati, OH 45227. Phone: 800-543-0487 Fax: (513)527-9267 1997. $77.95. Second edition.

Organizational Dynamics: A Quarterly Review of Organizational Behavior for Management Executives. American Management Association, 1601 Broadway New York, NY 10019-7420. Phone: 800-262-9699 or (212)586-8100 Fax: (212)903-8168 • URL: http://www.amanet.org • Quarterly. Individuals, $77.00 per year; institutions, $171.00 per year. Covers the application of behavioral sciences to business management.

Organizational Structure of Libraries. Lowell A. Martin. Scarecrow Press, Inc., 4501 Forbes Blvd., Ste. 200 Lanham, MD 20706. Phone: 800-462-6420 or (301)459-3366 Fax: 800-338-4550 or (301)429-5748 E-mail: custserv@rowman.com • URL: http://www.scarecrowpress.com • 1996. $42.00. Second edition. (Library Administration: No. 12).

Organizational Systems Research Association., Morehead State University, Dept. of Information Systems, P.O. Box 2478 Morehead, KY 40351-1689. Phone: (606)783-2718 Fax: (606)783-5025 E-mail: d.everett@morehead-st.edu • URL: http://www.osra.org • Research areas include the analysis, design, and administration of office systems. Formerly Office Systems Research Association.

Organizing Projects for Success: The Human Aspects of Project Management, Volume One. Vijay K. Verma. Project Management Institute, Four Campus Blvd. Newton Square, PA 19073-3299. Phone: (610)356-4600 Fax: (610)356-4647 E-mail: pmihq@pmi.org • URL: http://www.pmi.org • 1995. $32.95. (Human Aspects of Project Management Series: Vol. 1).

Oriental Rug Importers Association., 100 Park Plaza Dr. Secaucus, NJ 07094. Phone: (201)866-5054 Fax: (201)866-6169 E-mail: oria@oria.org • URL: http://www.oria.org • Represents wholesalers and importers of Oriental rugs. Fosters ethical business practices and promotes the best interests of the Oriental Rug Trade in the United States and in countries that produce Oriental rugs.

Oriental Rug Review. Oriental Rug Auction Review, Inc., P.O. Box 709 Meredith, NH 03253. Phone: (603)744-9191 Fax: (603)744-6933 Bimonthly. $48.00 per year.

Origination News: For Mortgage Brokers, Correspondents, Lenders, and Wholesalers. Thomson Media, One State St. Plaza New York, NY 10004. Phone: 800-221-1809 or (212)803-8200 Fax: (212)843-9635 E-mail: custserv@thomsonmedia.com • URL: http://www.thomsonmedia.com • Monthly. $78.00 per year. Edited for executives responsible for the origination and subsequent sale of mortgage loans.

OSA/SPIE/OSJ Membership Directory (Optical Societites of America and Japan). Optical Society of America, Inc., 2010 Massachusetts Ave., N.W. Washington, DC 20036-1023. Phone: 800-762-4052 or (202)223-8130 Fax: (202)223-1096 E-mail: custserv@osa.org • URL: http://www.osa.org • Annual. Only available online. List of over 20,000 persons interested in any branch of optics. Includes coverage of the Optical Society of America, the Optical Society of Japan, and the International Society for Optical Engineering. Formerly *Optical Society of American Membership Directory*.

OSH-ROM: Occupational Safety and Health Information on CD-ROM. Available from SilverPlatter Information, Inc., 100 River Ridge Rd. Norwood, MA 02062-5026. Phone: 800-343-0064 or (781)769-2599 Fax: (781)769-8763 E-mail: info@silverplatter.com • URL: http://www.silverplatter.com • Price and frequency on application. Produced in Geneva by the International Occupational Safety and Health Information Centre, International Labour Organization (http://www.ilo.org). Provides about two million citations and abstracts to the worldwide literature of industrial safety, industrial hygiene, hazardous materials, and accident prevention. Material is included from journals, technical reports, books, government publications, and other sources. Time span varies.

OSHA Required Safety Training for Supervisors. Occupational Safety and Health Administration. Business and Legal Reports, Inc., 141 Mill Rock Rd. E Old Saybrook, CT 06475. Phone: 800-454-0404 • URL: http://www.blr.com • Monthly. $99.00 per year. Newsletter. Formerly *Safetyworks for Supervisors*.

Our National Parks and the Search for Sustainability. Bob R. O'Brien. University of Texas Press, PO Box 7819 Austin, TX 78713-7819. Phone: 800-252-3206 or (512)471-7233 Fax: 800-687-6046 or (512)232-7178 E-mail: utpress@uts.cc.utexas.edu • URL: http://www.utexas.edu/utpress • 1999. $40.00. Sustainability is defined as "a balance that allows as many people as possible to visit a park that is kept in as natural a state as possible."

Outdoor Advertising Association of America., 1850 M St., NW, Ste. 1040 Washington, DC 20036. Phone: (202)833-5566 Fax: (202)833-1522 E-mail: info@oaaa.org • URL: http://www.oaaa.org • Firms owning, erecting and maintaining standardized poster panels and painted display advertising facilities. Absorbed Shelter Advertising Association.

Outdoor Amusement Business Association., 1035 S Semoran Blvd., Ste. 1045A Winter Park, FL 32792. Phone: 800-517-OABA or (407)681-9444 Fax: (407)681-9445 E-mail: oaba@aol.com • URL: http://www.oaba.org • Represents executives and employees of carnivals and fairs; ride owners; independent food and games concessionaires; manufacturers and suppliers of equipment. Promotes and lobbies on behalf of the interests of the outdoor amusement industry; provides a center for dissemination of information.

Outdoor Appliances and Power Tools. Available from MarketResearch.com, 641 Ave. of the Americas, Fourth Floor New York, NY 10011. Phone: 800-298-5699 or (212)807-2629 Fax: (212)807-2642 E-mail: order@marketresearch.com • URL: http://www.marketresearch.com • 2002. $3,950.00. Published by Global Industry Analysts. Provides worldwide market research data, including profiles of major companies in the field.

Outdoor Power Equipment Institute., 341 S Patrick St., Old Town Alexandria, VA 22314. Phone: (703)549-7600 Fax: (703)549-7604 E-mail: kreamy@opei.org • URL: http://www.opei.org • Manufacturers of lawn mowers, garden tractors, snow throwers, utility vehicles, chainsaws, motor tillers, shredder/grinders, edger/trimmers, leaf vacuums, log splitters, stump cutters, chippers and sprayers, and major components. Compiles statistics and forecasting information; sponsors industry trade shows; produces comprehensive consumer education materials on safety and other industry issues; hosts' annual member meeting; represents members' interests on important legislative and regulatory issues.

Outlook for Travel and Tourism. Travel Industry Association of America, 1100 New York Ave., N.W., Suite 240 Washington, DC 20005-3934. Phone: (202)408-8422 Fax: (202)408-1255 E-mail: rmcclur@tia.org • URL: http://www.tia.org • Annual. Members, $100.00; non-members, $175.00. Contains forecasts of the performance of the U. S. travel industry, including air travel, business travel, recreation (attractions), and accomodations.

Outlook for United States Agricultural Trade. Available from U. S. Government Printing Office, Washington, DC 20402. Phone: (202)512-1800 Fax: (202)512-2250 E-mail: gpoaccess@gpo.gov • URL: http://www.access.gpo.gov • Quarterly. $15.00 per year. Issued by the Economic Research Service, U. S. Department of Agriculture. (Situation and Outlook Reports.)

Outspokin'. National Bicycle Dealers Association, 777 W.19th St., Ste. 0 Costa Mesa, CA 92627. Phone: (949)722-6909 Fax: (949)722-1747 E-mail: info@nbda.com • URL: http://www.nbda.com • Description: Offers bicycle retailing and management tips, and provides consumer survey results. Recurring features include Association and industry news.

Outstanding Investor Digest: Perspectives and Activities of the Nation's Most Successful Money Managers. Outstanding Investor Digest, Inc., 14 E. Fourth St., Ste. 501 New York, NY 10012. Phone: (212)777-3330 $395.00 for 10 issues. Newsletter. Each issue features interviews with leading money managers.

Overeducated Worker? The Economics of Skill Utilization. Lex Borghans and Andries De Grip. Edward Elgar Publishing, Inc., 136 West St., Ste. 202 Nothampton, MA 01060-3711. Phone: 800-225-5800 or (413)584-5551 Fax: (413)584-9933 E-mail: sales@e-elgar.co.uk • URL: http://www.e-elgar.com • 2000. $95.00.

Overseas Automotive Council Membership Roster. Overseas Automotive Council, 10 Laboratory Dr. Research Triangle Park, NC 27709. Phone: (919)406-8810 Fax: (919)549-4824 E-mail: oac@mema.org • URL: http://www.oac-intl.org • Annual. $50.00 per year. Lists over 700 U.S. and overseas members. Newsletter.

Oxbridge Directory of Newsletters. Oxbridge Communications, Inc., 186 5th Ave. New York, NY 10010. Phone: 800-955-0231 or (212)741-0231 Fax: (212)633-2938 E-mail: info@oxbridge.com • URL: http://www.mediafinder.com • Annual. $845.00. Lists approximately 20,000 newsletters in the United States and Canada.

OXFAM America., 226 Causeway St., 5th Fl. Boston, MA 02114. Phone: 800-77-OXFAM or (617)482-1211 Fax: (617)728-2594 E-mail: info@oxfamamerica.org • URL: http://www.oxfamamerica.org • Autonomous development and disaster assistance organization cooperating in a worldwide network known as Oxfam, a name derived from the Oxford Committee for Famine Relief, which began in England in 1942. Provides funds for self-help projects in the poorer countries of Asia, Africa, and the Americas. Emphasizes on promoting economic and food self-reliance. Responds to emergency needs of political and natural disaster refugees by funding food, water resources, and medical aid programs. Supports development programs that address underlying causes of such disasters. Educates U.S. public about root causes of hunger; advocates for policy changes.

Oxford Companion to the Wines of North America. Bruce Cass. Oxford University Press, 198 Madison Ave. New York, NY 10016. Phone: 800-451-7556 or (212)726-6000 Fax: (212)726-6440 E-mail: custserv@oup-usa.org • URL: http://www.oup-usa.org • 2000. $49.95. Second edition. Contains approximately 3,000 entries explaining the making of wine, varieties of wine, and characteristics of vineyards.

Oxford Encyclopedia of Economic History. Joel Mokyr, editor. Oxford University Press, 198 Madison Ave. New York, NY 10016-4314. Phone: 800-451-7556 or (212)726-6000 Fax: (212)726-6446 E-mail: custserv@oup-usa.org • URL: http://www.oup-usa.org • 2003. $695.00. Five volumes. Provides extensive coverage of a wide variety of topics relating to business, industrial, and economic history.

Oxford Encyclopedia of Food and Drink in America. Andrew F. Smith, editor. Oxford University Press, 198 Madison Ave. New York, NY 10016-4314. Phone: 800-451-7556 or (212)726-6000 Fax: (212)726-6446 E-mail: custserv@oup-usa.org • URL: http://www.oup-usa.org • 2004. $250.00. Two volumes. Emphasis is on historical and cultural aspects of food and beverages in the U. S.

Oxford English Dictionary. John Simpson. Oxford University Press, 198 Madison Ave. New York, NY 10016-4314. Phone: 800-451-7556 or (212)726-6000 Fax: (212)746-6440 E-mail: custserv@oup-usa.org • URL: http://www.oup-usa.org • 2002. $1,195.00. Second edition. 20 volumes. Includes CD-Rom.

Oxford Guide to Library Research. Thomas Mann. Oxford University Press, 198 Madison Ave. New York, NY 10016. Phone: 800-451-7556 or (212)726-6000 Fax: (212)726-6440 E-mail: custserv@oup-usa.org • URL: http://www.oup-usa.org • 1998. $35.00. Covers print sources, electronic sources, and "nine research methods."

Oxford Tobacco Research Station. North Carolina Department of Agriculture and Consumer Services

Oxymorons: The Myth of the U.S. Health Care System. J. D. Kleinke. John Wiley and Sons, Inc., 111 River St. Hoboken, NJ 07030. Phone: 800-225-5945 or (201)748-6000 Fax: (201)748-6088 E-mail: info@wiley.com • URL: http://www.wiley.com • 2001. $35.00. The author is a healthcare economist who states that managed care has "left in the rubble bewildered consumers, disappointed employers, enraged patients, embittered physicians, and a raft of lawsuits." (Jossey-Bass Health Series).

P-O-P Design (Point-of-Purchase): Products and News for High-Volume Pro ducers and Designers of Displays, Signs and Fixtures. Hoyt Publishing Co., 7400 Skokie Blvd. Skokie, IL 60077-3339. Phone: (847)675-7400 Fax: (847)675-7494 E-mail: getinfo@hoytpub.com Nine times a year. $59.00 per year.

Pacific Boating Almanac. ProStar Publications, Inc., 8643 Hayden Place Culver City, CA 90232-2901. Phone: 800-481-6277 or (310)280-1010 Fax: (310)280-1025 E-mail: editor@prostarpublications.com Annual. $24.95 per volume. Three volumes. Volume one, *Pacific Northwest*; volume two, *Northern California and the Delta*; volume three *Southern California and Mexico*. Lists over 3,000 marine facilities serving recreational boating.

Pacific Coast Paper Box Manufacturers' Association., 1350 Main St., Ste. 1508 Springfield, MA 01103-1628. Phone: (413)686-9191 Fax: (413)747-7777 E-mail: paperboardpackaging@ppcnet.org • URL: http://www.ppcnet.org • Represents folding carton and rigid carton manufacturers. Furthers the success and development of paperboard packaging in the territory west of the Rocky Mountains. Offers statistical, and labor data summary

programs for members. Conducts technical and production seminars and employee training in plant and equipment operations. Sponsors student design-school competition.

Pacific Coast Shellfish Growers Association., 120 State Ave. NE, PMB No. 142 Olympia, WA 98501. Phone: (360)754-2744 Fax: (360)754-2743 E-mail: pcsga@pcsga.org • URL: http://www.pcsga.org • Oyster, clam, mussel, scallop, geoduck growers, openers, packers and shippers in Alaska, California, Oregon, Washington, Hawaii, and Mexico.

Pacific International Center for High Technology Research., 1020 Auahi St., Bldg. 5, Bay 14 Honolulu, HI 96814. Phone: (808)591-6490 Fax: (808)591-6491 E-mail: harold.masumoto@pichtr.org • URL: http://www.pichtr.org • Desalination is included as a field of research.

Pacific Salmon Commission., 1155 Robson St., Ste. 600 Vancouver, BC, Canada V6E 1B5. Phone: (604)684-8081 Fax: (604)666-8707 E-mail: paperboardpackaging@ppcnet.org • URL: http://www.psc.org • Formed by treaty between Canada and the United States for the Conservation, management and optimum production of pacific salmon.

PackagePrinting: For Printers and Converters of Labels, Flexible Packaging and Folding Cartons. North American Publishing Co., 401 N. Broad St. Philadelphia, PA 19108. Phone: 800-777-8074 or (215)238-5482 Fax: 800-664-1533 or (215)238-5412 E-mail: customerservice@napco.com • URL: http://www.napco.com • Monthly. Free to qualified personnel; others, $59.00 per year. Formerly *Package Printing and Converting*.

Packaging Digest. Reed Business Information, 360 Park Ave., S New York, NY 10010. Phone: 800-446-6551 or (646)746-6400 Fax: (646)746-7028 E-mail: corporatecommunications@reedbusiness.com • URL: http://www.reedbusiness.com • 13 times a year. $119.90 per year.

Packaging Digest Machinery/Materials Guide. Reed Business Information, 360 Park Ave. S New York, NY 10010. Phone: 800-446-6551 or (646)746-6400 Fax: (646)746-7028 E-mail: corporatecommunications@reedbusiness.com • URL: http://www.reedbusiness.com • Annual. $46.00. List of more than 3,100 manufacturers of machinery and materials for the packaging industry, and about 260 contract packagers.

Packaging Machinery Manufacturers Institute., 4350 N Fairfax Dr., Ste. 600 Arlington, VA 22203-1632. Phone: 888-275-7664 or (703)243-8555 Fax: (703)243-8556 E-mail: pmmiwebhelp@pmmi.org • URL: http://www.pmmi.org • Represents manufacturers of machinery used for all packaging operations including filling, capping, labeling, wrapping, cartoning, case loading, blister packaging, aerosol, check weighing, coding, counting, form-fill-seal, and bagging.

Packaging Technology and Science. John Wiley and Sons, Inc., Journals, 111 River St. Hoboken, NJ 07030. Phone: 800-526-5368 or (201)748-6000 Fax: (201)748-6088 E-mail: customer@wiley.com • URL: http://www.wiley.com • Bimonthly. Individuals, $650.00 per year; institutions, $1,295.00 per year. Provides international coverage of subject matter. Published in England by John Wiley & Sons Ltd.

The Packer: Devoted to the Interest of Commericial Growers, Packers, Shippers, Receivers and Retailers of Fruits, Vegetables and Other Products. Vance Publishing Corp., Produce Div., 10901 W. 84th Terrace Lenexa, KS 66214-0695. Phone: 800-255-5113 or (913)438-8700 Fax: (913)438-0691 • URL: http://www.vancepublishing.com • Weekly. $65.00 per year. *Supplments* available: *Brand Directory* and *Fresh Trends*, *Packer's Produce Availiability and Merchandising Guide* and *Produce Services Sourcebooks*.

Packer Produce Availability and Merchandising Guide. Vance Publishing Corp., Produce Div., 10901 W. 84th Terrace Lenexa, KS 66214. Phone: 800-255-5113 or (913)438-8700 Fax: (913)438-0695 • URL: http://www.vancepublishing.com • Annual. $35.00. A buyer's directory giving sources of fresh fruits and vegetables. Shippers are listed by location for each commodity.

The Page. The Cobb Group, 500 Canal View Blvd. Rochester, NY 14623-2800. Phone: 800-223-8720 or (585)240-7301 Fax: (585)292-4392 E-mail: info@nbda.com • URL: http://www.elementkjournals.com • Description: Acts as a visual guide to McIntosh computer desktop publishing.

Paint and Coatings Industry. Business News Publishing Co., 755 W. Big Beaver Rd., Suite 1000 Troy, MI 48084. Phone: 800-837-7370 or (248)362-3700 Fax: (248)362-0317 • URL: http://www.bnp.com • Monthly. Free to members, nonmembers, $55.00 per year. Includes annual *Raw Material* and *Equipment Directory and Buyers Guide*.

Paint and Decorating Retailer. Paint and Decorating Retailers Association, 403 Axminster Dr. Fenton, MO 63026-2941. Phone: 800-737-0107 or (314)326-2636 Fax: (314)326-1823 E-mail: info@pdra.org • URL: http://www.pdra.org • Monthly. $45.00 per year. Formerly *Decorating Retailer*.

Paint and Decorating Retailer's Directory of the Wallcoverings Industry: The Gold Book. Paint and Decorating Retailers Association, 403 Axminster Dr. Fenton, MO 63026-2941. Phone: 800-737-0107 or (314)326-2636 Fax: (314)326-1823 E-mail: info@pdra.org • URL: http://www.pdra.org • Annual. Membership.

Paint, Varnish, and Lacquer. U. S. Bureau of the Census, 4700 Silver Hill Rd. Washington, DC 20233-0001. Phone: (301)763-4636 E-mail: comments@census.gov • URL: http://www.census.gov • Quarterly and annual. Provides data on shipments: value, quantity, imports, and exports. Includes paint, varnish, lacquer, product finishes, and special purpose

coatings. (Current Industrial Reports, MQ-28F.)

Painting and Decorating Contractors of America., 11960 Westline Industrial Dr., Ste. 201 Saint Louis, MO 63146-2309. Phone: 800-332-7322 or (314)-514-7322 Fax: (314)-514-9417 E-mail: lwerle@pdca.org • URL: http://www.pdca.org • Painting and wallcovering contractors.

PAIS International. Public Affairs Information Service, Inc., 521 W. 43rd St. New York, NY 10036. Phone: 800-288-7247 or (212)736-6629 Fax: (212)643-2848 E-mail: inquiries@pais.org • URL: http://www.pais.org • Corresponds to the former printed publications, *PAIS Bulletin* (1976-90) and *PAIS Foreign Language Index* (1972-90), and to the current *PAIS International in Print* (1991 to date). Covers economic, political, and sociological material appearing in periodicals, books, government documents, and other publications. Updating is monthly. Inquire as to online cost and availability.

PAIS International in Print. Public Affairs Information Service, Inc., 521 W. 43rd St., 5th Fl. New York, NY 10036-4396. Phone: 800-288-7247 or (212)736-4161 Fax: (212)643-2848 E-mail: inquiries@pais.org; paisinquiries@oclc.org • URL: http://www.pais.org • Monthly. $850.00 per year; cumulations three times a year. Provides topical citations to the worldwide literature of public affairs, economics, demographics, sociology, and trade. Text in English; indexed materials in English, French, German, Italian, Portuguese and Spanish.

PAIS on CD-ROM. Public Affairs Information Service, Inc., 521 West 43rd St. New York, NY 10036. Phone: 800-288-7247 or (212)736-6629 Fax: (212)643-2848 E-mail: inquiries@pais.org • URL: http://www.pais.org • Quarterly. $1,995.00 per year. Provides a CD-ROM version of the online service, *PAIS International*. Contains over 500,000 citations to the literature of contemporary social, political, and economic issues.

Palm Beach Illustrated: The Best of Boca Raton to Vero Beach. Palm Beach Media Group, PO Box 3344 Palm Beach, FL 33480. Phone: (561)659-0210 Fax: (561)659-1736 E-mail: info@palmbeachmedia.com • URL: http://www.palmbeachillustrated.com • 10 times a year. $24.95 per year. Includes *Palm Beach Social Observer*. Formerly *Illustrated*.

Panel World. Hatton-Brown Publishers, Inc., 225 Hanrick St. Montgomery, AL 36104. Phone: 800-669-5613 or (334)834-1170 Fax: (334)834-4525 E-mail: mail@hattonbrown.com • URL: http://www.hattonbrown.com • Bimonthly. $28.00. Formerly *Plywood and Panel World*.

Panel World Directory and Buyers' Guide. Hatton-Brown Publisher, Inc., 225 Hanrick St. Montgomery, AL 36102. Phone: 800-669-5613 or (334)834-1170 Fax: (334)834-4525 E-mail: mail@hattonbrown.com • URL: http://www.hattonbrown.com • Annual. $20.00. Included with subscription to *Paper, Film and Foil Converter*. Supersedes *Plywood and Panel World Directory and Buyer's Guide*.

Panorama of European Business. Available from Bernan Associates, 4611-F Assembly Dr. Lanham, MD 20706-4391. Phone: 800-274-4888 or (301)459-2255 Fax: 800-865-3450 or (301)459-0056 E-mail: query@bernan.com • URL: http://www.bernan.com • Annual. $65.00. Presents statistical data for manufacturing and service industries in major European countries. Text in English, French and Spanish.

Paper Age. Global Publications, 77 Waldron Ave. Glen Rock, NJ 07452-2830. Phone: (201)666-2262 Fax: (201)666-9046 10 times a year. $20.00 per year.

Paper Basics: Forestry, Manufacture, Selection, Purchasing, Mathematics and Metrics, Recycling. David Saltman. Krieger Publishing Co., P.O. Box 9542 Melbourne, FL 32902-9542. Phone: 800-724-0025 or (321)724-9542 Fax: (321)951-3671 E-mail: info@krieger-publishing.com • URL: http://www.krieger-publishing.com • 1978. $29.50.

Paper, Film and Foil Converter. Primedia Business Magazines and Media, 330 N Wabash Ave., Ste. 2300 Chicago, IL 60611. Phone: 800-795-5445 or (312)595-1080 Fax: (312)595-0295 E-mail: subs@primediabusiness.com • URL: http://www.primediabusiness.com • Monthly. $88.00 per year.

Paper Industry Management Association., 15 Technology Pkwy. S Norcross, GA 30092. Phone: 877-527-5973 or (770)209-7230 Fax: (770)209-7359 E-mail: mcornell@pimaweb.org • URL: http://www.pimaweb.org • Professional organization of pulp, paper mill, and paper converting production executives.

Paper Money. Society of Paper Money Collectors, Inc., PO Box 117060 Carrollton, TX 75011. • URL: http://www.spmc.org • Bimonthly. Membership.

Paper Money of the United States: A Complete Guide with Valuations. Arthur L. Friedberg. Coin and Currency Institute, Inc., P.O. Box 1057 Clifton, NJ 07014. Phone: 800-421-1866 or (973)471-4441 Fax: (973)471-1062 E-mail: mail@coin-currency.com • URL: http://www.coin-currency.com • 2000. $38.75. 16th edition.

Paper Shipping Sack Manufacturers' Association., 520 E Oxford St. Coopersburg, PA 18036. Phone: (610)282-6845 Fax: (610)282-6921 E-mail: admin@pssma.org • URL: http://www.pssma.com • Manufacturers of multi-wall (3-4-5-6 walls) paper shipping sacks designed for packaging and shipping products in domestic and export commerce.

Paperboard Packaging Council., 700 Princess St., Ste. 202 Alexandria, VA 22314-2265. Phone: (703)836-3300 Fax: (703)836-3290 E-mail: paperboardpackaging@ppcnet.org • URL: http://www.ppcnet.org • Represents manufacturers of paperboard packaging. Sponsors public relations activities, safety programs, and biannual human resource seminars. Conducts overall industry statistical studies, marketing surveys, product reviews, and labor relations and bargaining agreement studies. Provides active technical and production service.

Paperboard Packaging Resource Directory. Advanstar Communications, 641 Lexington Ave., 8th Fl., 8th Fl. New York, NY 10022. Phone: 800-225-4569 or (212)951-6600 Fax: (212)951-6793 E-mail: info@advanstar.com • URL: http://www.advanstar.com • Covers: about 3,000 manufacturers of corrugated and solid fiber containers, folding cartons, rigid boxes, fiber cans and tubes, and fiber drums. Entries include: For manufacturers—Company name, address, phone, equipment, names of executives, plants, and type of containers manufactured.

Paperboard Packaging Worldwide. Advanstar Communications, 545 Boylston St. Boston, MA 02116. Phone: 800-527-7008 or (617)267-6500 Fax: (617)267-6900 E-mail: info@advanstar.com • URL: http://www.advanstar.com • Monthly. $39.00 per year.

PaperChem Database. Information Services Div., Institute of Paper Science and Technology, 500 Tenth St., N.W. Atlanta, GA 30318. Phone: 800-558-6611 or (404)894-5700 Fax: (404)894-4778 Worldwide coverage of the scientific and technical paper industry chemical literature, including patents, 1967 to present. Weekly updates. Inquire as to online cost and availability.

Parcel Shippers Association., 1420 King St., Ste. 620 Alexandria, VA 22314. Phone: (571)257-7617 Fax: (571)257-7613 E-mail: psa@parcelshippers.org • URL: http://www.parcelshippers.org • Wholesalers, retailers, mail order houses, and other firms using parcel post service for distribution of products. Promotes the efficient and economical distribution of small package shipments.

Parker-Coltrane Political Action Committee., 669 Federal Bldg., 231 W. Lafayette Detroit, MI 48226. Phone: (313)961-5670 E-mail: nabpac@nabpac.org Political action organization supported by financial contributions of individuals. Organized by Congressman John Conyers and others to encourage and help blacks and progressive candidates to win election to public office in the southern U.S. through direct campaign contributions and technical assistance. Conducts training sessions on methods and techniques of running for office. Initial efforts have been concentrated in Georgia, although the committee now operates throughout the South. Plans to extend operations on a national level. Presently inactive.

Parking Publications for Planners. Dennis Jenks. Sage Publications, Inc., 2455 Teller Rd. Thousand Oaks, CA 91320. Phone: 800-818-7243 or (805)499-9774 Fax: 800-583-2665 or (805)499-0871 E-mail: webmaster@sagepub.com • URL: http://www.sagepub.com • 1993. $10.00.

Parking: The Magazine of the Parking Industry. National Parking Association, 1112 16th St., N.W., Suite 300 Washington, DC 20036. Phone: (202)296-4336 Fax: (202)331-8523 E-mail: info@npapark.org • URL: http://wwwnpapark.org • 10 times a year. $95.00 per year. Includes *Product and Services Directory*.

Parks and Recreation Buyers' Guide. National Recreation and Park Association, 22377 Belmont Ridge Rd. Ashburn, VA 20148-4501. Phone: 800-626-6772 or (703)858-0784 Fax: (703)858-0794 E-mail: info@nrpa.org • URL: http://www.nrpa.org • Annual. Price upon application. List of 800 companies supplying products and services to private and governmental park and recreation agencies.

Parks Directory of the United States: A Guide to 4,700 National and State Parks, Recreation Areas, Historic Sites, Battlefields, Monuments, Forests, Preserves, Memorials, Seashores...and Other Designated Recreation Areas in the United State. Darren L. Smith, editor. Omnigraphics, Inc., 615 Griswold St. Detroit, MI 48226. Phone: 800-234-1340 or (313)961-1340 Fax: 800-875-1340 or (313)961-1383 E-mail: info@omnigraphics.com • URL: http://www.omnigraphics.com • 2001. $180.00. Third edition. Consists of three sections: National Parks, State Parks, and Park-Related Organizations and Agencies. Includes an alphabetical index and a park classification index.

Parliamentary Journal. American Institute of Parliamentarians, P.O. Box 2173 Wilmington, DE 19899-2173. Phone: (302)762-1811 Fax: (302)762-2170 E-mail: aip@parlimentaryprocedure.org • URL: http://www.parlimentaryprocedure.org • Quarterly. $20.00 per year.

Parliamentary Law and Practice for Nonprofit Organizations. Howard L. Oleck and Cami Green. American Law Institute-American Bar Association Committee on Continuing Professional Education, 4025 Chestnut St. Philadelphia, PA 19104. Phone: 800-253-6397 Fax: (215)243-1664 • URL: http://www.ali-aba.org • 1991. $20.00. Second edition. Covers meeting procedures, motions, debate, voting, nominations, elections, committees, duties of officers, rights of members, and other topics.

Participative Management: An Analysis of Its Affect on Productivity. Michael H. Swearingen. Garland Publishing, Inc., 29 W. 35th St. New York, NY 10001-2299. Phone: 800-627-6273 or (212)216-7800 Fax: (212)564-7854 E-mail: info@garland.com • URL: http://www.garlandpub.com • 1997. $35.00. (Garland Studies on Industrial Productivity).

Partnership Book: How to Write a Partnership Agreement. Ralph Warner and Dennis Clifford. Nolo, 950 Parker St. Berkeley, CA 94710. Phone: 800-728-3555 or (510)549-1976 Fax: 800-645-0895 or (510)548-5902 E-mail: simone@nolo.com • URL: http://www.nolo.com • 2001. $39.95. Sixth edition. Includes CD-Rom. (Partnership Book Series).

Partnerships and LLCs: Tax Practice and Analysis. Thomas G. Manolakas. CCH, Inc., 2700 Lake Cook Rd. Riverwoods, IL 60015. Phone: 800-835-5224 or (847)267-7000 E-mail: cust_serv@cch.com • URL: http://www.cch.com • 2000. $95.00. Covers the taxation of partnerships and limited liability companies.

Passenger Transport. American Public Transportation Association, 1666 L St., NW, 11th Fl. Washington, DC 20006. Phone: (202)496-4800 Fax: (202)496-4321 E-mail: info@apta.com • URL: http://www.apta.com • Weekly. $65.00 per year. Covers current events and trends in mass transportation.

Passport Newsletter. Remy Publishing Co., 401 N. Franklin St., 3rd Fl. Chicago, IL 60610. Phone: (312)464-0300 Fax: (312)464-0166 Monthly. $89.00 per year. Formerly *Passport*.

Pasta Industry Directory. National Pasta Association, 1156 15th St. NW, Ste. 900 Washington, DC 20005. Phone: (202)637-5888 Fax: (202)223-9741 E-mail: info@ilovepasta.org • URL: http://www.ilovepasta.org • Covers: Pasta manufacturers and industry suppliers. Entries include: contact names.

Pasta Journal. National Pasta Association, 1156 15th St., NW, Ste. 900 Washington, DC 20005-1717. Phone: (202)637-5888 Fax: (202)223-9741 • URL: http://www.ilovepasta.org • Bimonthly. $35.00 per year.

Patent and Trademark Office Society Journal. Patent and Trademark Office Society, P.O. Box 2089 Arlington, VA 22202. E-mail: contact@jptos.org • URL: http://www.jptos.org • Individuals, $20.00 per year.

Patent, Copyright, and Trademark: An Intellectual Property Desk Reference. Stephen Elias. Nolo, 950 Parker St. Berkeley, CA 94710. Phone: 800-728-3555 or (510)549-1976 Fax: 800-645-0895 or (510)548-5902 E-mail: simone@nolo.com • URL: http://www.nolo.com • 2003. $39.99. Sixth revised edition. Contains practical explanations of the legalities of patents, copyrights, trademarks, and trade secrets. Includes examples of relevant legal forms. A 1985 version was called *Nolo's Intellectual Property Law Dictionary*. (Nolo Press Self-Help Law Series).

Patent It Yourself. David R. Pressman. Nolo, 950 Parker St. Berkeley, CA 94710. Phone: 800-728-3555 or (510)549-1976 Fax: 800-645-0895 or (510)548-5902 E-mail: simone@nolo.com • URL: http://www.nolo.com • 2003. $49.99. Ninth edition. (Patent It Yourself Series).

Patent Law Basics. West Group, 610 Opperman Dr. Eagan, MN 55123. Phone: 800-328-4880 or (651)687-7000 Fax: 800-340-7378 or (651)687-5827 E-mail: bookstore@westgroup.com • URL: http://www.westgroup.com • $225.00. Looseleaf service. Annual updates. Covers Patent and Trademark Office applications, patent ownership, rights, protection, infringement, litigation, and other fundamentals of patent law.

Patent Law Handbook. West Group, 610 Opperman Dr. Eagan, MN 55123. Phone: 800-328-4880 or (651)687-7000 Fax: 800-340-9378 E-mail: bookstore@westgroup.com • URL: http://www.westgroup.com • Annual. $321.00.

Patent Strategy and Management. American Lawyer Media, Inc., 105 Madison Ave. New York, NY 10016. Phone: 800-888-8300 or (212)779-9200 Fax: (212)481-8110 E-mail: lawcatalog@amlaw.com • URL: http://www.lawcatalog.com/ • Monthly. $225.00 per year. Newsletter. Provides news of recent legal and business trends in the area of patent issuance and litigation. (A Law Journal Newsletter, formerly published by Leader Publications).

Patent, Trademark, and Copyright Laws, 2003. Jeffrey Samuels, editor. BNA, Inc., 1231 25th St., NW Washington, DC 20037. Phone: 800-372-1033 E-mail: customercare@bna.com • URL: http://www.bna.com • 2003. $115.00. Contains text of "all pertinent intellectual property legislation to date."

Patterson's American Education. Educational Directories Inc., PO Box 68097, PO Box 68097 Schaumburg, IL 60168. Phone: 800-357-6183 or (847)891-1250 Fax: (847)891-0945 E-mail: info@ediusa.com • URL: http://www.ediusa.com • Covers: Over 11,400 school districts in the United States; more than 34,000 public, private, and Catholic high schools, middle schools, and junior high schools; Approximately 300 parochial superintendents; 400 state department of education personnel. Entries include: For school districts and schools—District and superintendent Name, address, phone, fax, grade ranges, enrollment , school names, addresses, phone numbers, grade ranges, enrollment, names of principals. For postsecondary schools—School name, address, phone number, URL, e-mail, names of administrator or director of admissions. For private and Catholic high schools—name, address, phone, fax, enrollment, grades offered, name of principal. Postsecondary institutions are covered in 'Patterson's Schools Classified' (see separate entry).

Patterson's Schools Classified. Educational Directories Inc., PO Box 68097, PO Box 68097 Schaumburg, IL 60168. Phone: 800-357-6183 or (847)891-1250 Fax: (847)891-0945 E-mail: info@ediusa.com • URL: http://www.ediusa.com • Covers: Over 7,000 accredited colleges, universities, community colleges, junior colleges, career schools and teaching hospitals. Entries include: School name, address, phone, URL, e-mail, name of administrator or admissions officer, description, professional accreditation (where applicable). Updated from previous year's edition of 'Patterson's American Education' (see separate entry).

Patty's Industrial Hygiene and Toxicology. Robert L. Harris. John Wiley and Sons, Inc., 111 River St. Hoboken, NJ 07030. Phone: 800-225-5945 or (201)748-6000 Fax: (201)748-6088 E-mail: info@wiley.com • URL: http://www.wiley.com • 2001: $3,290.00. Fifth edition. Provides broad coverage of environmental factors and stresses affecting the health of workers. Contains detailed information on the effects of specific substances.

Paul Revere Society., 150 Shoreline Hwy., Bldg. E Mill Valley, CA 94941. Fax: (415)339-9383 E-mail: paulreveresociety@yahoo.com • URL: http://prosites-prs.homestead.com • Seeks to have a strong voice to the political arena; strives for the re-assertion of America's borders, language and culture. Opposes the viewpoint that English is only one of many languages in the new "Multicultural America" and that Americans share no common history or values; believes in the Sovereignty of America, that English is the national "glue", that all Americans do share in the pillars of the Bible, the U.S. Constitution, and the Bill of Rights, and that these documents stand for American's common cultural heritage.

Pay for Schools by Regulating Cannabis., PO Box 86741 Portland, OR 97286. Phone: (503)229-0428 Fax: (503)295-0883 E-mail: treefreeeco@igc.apc.org • URL: http://www.erowid.org/psychoactives/law/bills/psychoactive_bills2.shtml • Concerned citizens who believe in hemp's environmental benefits. Seeks to regulate cannabis sales in state liquor stores to fund education and drug treatment programs. Promotes hemp manufacture for paper, fabrics, oil and pharmaceutical prescriptions. Conducts educational programs; compiles statistics; maintains speakers' bureau.

Payroll Management Guide. CCH, Inc., 4025 W. Peterson Ave. Chicago, IL 60646-6085. Phone: 800-248-3248 or (773)866-6000 Fax: 800-224-8299 or (773)866-3608 • URL: http://www.cch.com • Weekly. $599.00. Eight looseleaf volumes. Covers the basics of payroll management, including employer obligations, recordkeeping, taxation, unemployment insurance, processing of new employees, and government penalties.

Paytech. American Payroll Association, 600 N Main Ave., Ste. 100 San Antonio, TX 78205-1217. Phone: (210)226-4600 Fax: (210)226-4027 E-mail: info@americanpayroll.org • URL: http://www.americanpayroll.org • Monthly. Membership. Covers the details and technology of payroll administration.

PC Graphics Handbook. Julio Sanchez and Maria P. Canton. CRC Press, 2000 N.W. Corporate Blvd. Boca Raton, FL 33431. Phone: 800-272-7737 or (561)994-0555 Fax: 800-374-3401 or (561)989-9732 E-mail: orders@crcpress.com • URL: http://www.crcpress.com • 2003. $129.95. Covers both the hardware and software specifics of PC graphics programming. Includes such practical and theoretical topics as graphics algorithms, relevant mathematics, artificial life, virtual reality, device drivers, antimation techniques, and video games.

PC Magazine: The Independent Guide to Personal Computing and the Internet. Media Inc., 28 E. 28th St. New York, NY 10016-7930. Phone: 800-451-1032 or (212)503-3500 Fax: (212)503-4399 E-mail: info@ziffdavis.com • URL: http://www.ziffdavis.com • Biweekly. $49.97 per year.

PC Management: A How-To-Do-It Manual for Librarians. Michael Schuyler and Jake Hoffman. Neal-Schuman Publishers, Inc., 100 William St., Ste. 2004 New York, NY 10038. Phone: (866)672-6657 or (212)925-8650 Fax: (866)209-7932 or (212)219-8916 E-mail: info@neal-schuman.com • URL: http://www.neal-schuman.com • 1990. $45.00. Covers the use of personal computers for library routines. Includes evaluations of software. (How-to-Do-It Manuals Series).

PC World: The No. 1 Source for Definitive How-to-Buy, How-to-Use Advice on Personal Computing Systems and Software. IDG Communications, Inc., 501 Second St., Suite 600 San Francisco, CA 94107-4133. Phone: (415)243-0500 Fax: (415)442-1891 E-mail: letters@pcworld.com • URL: http://www.pcworld.com • Monthly. $29.90 per year.

PDR Drug Guide for Mental Health Professionals. Thomson Medical Economics, Five Paragon Drive Montvale, NJ 07645-1742. Phone: 800-232-7379 or (201)358-7200 Fax: (201)722-2680 E-mail: customer.service@medec.com • URL: http://www.medec.com • Annual. $39.95. Contains detailed profiles of more than 70 "common psychotropic drugs organized by brand name." Also contains information on the psychological side effects of about 1,000 other prescription drugs.

PDR for Nutritional Supplements. Medical Economics Co., Inc., 5 Paragon Dr. Montvale, NJ 07645-1742. Phone: 877-922-2022 or (973)944-9777 Fax: (973)-847-5390 E-mail: fulfill@superfill.com • URL: http://www.medec.com • Annual. $59.95. Includes trade names, usage, adverse reactions, dosage, and other information about vitamins and minerals.

PDR Guide to Drug Interactions, Side Effects, Indications. American Medical Association. Medical Economics Co., Inc., Five Paragon Dr. Montvale, NJ 07645-1742. Phone: 877-922-2022 or (973)944-9777 Fax: (973)944-5390 E-mail: fulfill@superfill.com • URL: http://www.medec.com • Annual. $48.95. Includes a list of prescription drugs by "precise clinical situation."

PE Update. Project Equality, 7132 Main St. Kansas City, MO 64114-1406. Phone: (816)361-9222 Fax: (816)361-8997

E-mail: kirkp@projectequality.org • URL: http://www.projectequality.org • Quarterly. Membership. Formerly *Project Equality Update*.

Peace Corps Times. U. S. Peace Corps, 1111 20th St., NW, 4th Fl. Washington, DC 20526. Phone: 800-424-8580 or (202)692-1620 • URL: http://www.peacecorps.gov • Quarterly. Free to qualified personnel. Presents news of the programs and activities of the Peace Corps.

Peaceworkers Nonviolent Peaceforce., 425 Oak Grove St. Minneapolis, MN 55403. Phone: (612)871-0005 Fax: (612)871-0006 E-mail: information@nonviolentpeaceforce.org • URL: http://www.nonviolentpeaceforce.org • Promotes the widespread implementation of effective nonviolent peacemaking in conflict areas around the world. Currently working to create the Nonviolent Peaceforce, an international organization to send hundreds and eventually thousands of trained peacemakers to work in areas of conflict at the invitation of local peacemakers or human rights workers. The Peace Force will be sent to conflict areas to prevent death and destruction, and protect human rights, thus creating the space for local groups to struggle nonviolently, enter into dialogue, and seek peaceful resolution.

Peach-Times. National Peach Council, 12 Nicklaus Lane, Suite 101 Columbia, SC 29229. Phone: (803)778-7101 Fax: (803)865-8090 E-mail: charleswalker@worldnet.att.net Quarterly. Membership.

Peanut and Tree Nut Processors Association., PO Box 59811 Potomac, MD 20859-9811. Phone: (301)365-2521 Fax: (301)365-7705 E-mail: ptnpa@mindspring.com • URL: http://www.ptnpa.org • Formerly Peanut Butter Manufacturers and NutSalters Association.

The Peanut Farmer: For Commercial Growers of Peanuts and Related Agribusiness. SpecComm International, Inc., 5808 Faringdon Pl., No. 200 Raleigh, NC 27609-3930. Phone: (919)872-5040 Fax: (919)876-6531 E-mail: spec_circ@juno.com • URL: http://www.speccomm.com • Seven times a year. $15.00 per year.

Peanut Journal and Nut World. Virginia-Carolina Peanut Association. Peanut Journal Publishing Co., 2921 N. Radcliffe Lane Chesapeake, VA 23321-4551. Monthly. $8.00 per year.

Peanut Science. American Peanut Research and Education Association Society, 376 Ag Hall, Oklahoma State University Stillwater, OK 74078. Phone: (405)-372-3052 Fax: (405)624-6718 • URL: http://www.agr.okstate.edu • Semiannual. $40.00 per issue.

Pecan South. Texas Pecan Growers Association, 4348 Carter Creek Pkwy., Ste. 101 Bryan, TX 77802. Phone: (979)846-3285 Fax: (979)846-1752 E-mail: pecans@tpga.org • URL: http://www.tpga.org • Monthly. $18.00 per year.

Penguin Dictionary of Architecture and Landscape Architecture. Nikolas Pevsner and others. Penguin Group, 375 Hudson St. New York, NY 10014-3657. Phone: 800-331-4624 or (212)336-2000 Fax: (212)366-2952 • URL: http://www.penguingroup.com • 2000. $16.95. Fifth edition. (Penguin Reference Series).

Peninsular Agricultural Research Station. University of Wisconsin - Madison

The Penny Fortune Newsletter. James M. Fortune, editor. Phoenix Communications Group Ltd., 3465 Hickory Hill Dr. Colorado Springs, CO 80906. Phone: (719)576-9200 Fax: (719)576-3036 E-mail: info@nbda.com Description: Instructs small investors on how to invest modest sums of money every two weeks to build a portfolio of stocks and mutual funds.

Pension and Employee Benefits: Code-ERISA and Regulations. CCH, Inc., 2700 Lake Cook Rd. Riverwoods, IL 60015. Phone: 800-835-5224 or (847)267-7000 E-mail: cust_serv@cch.com • URL: http://www.cch.com • $123.00. Two volumes.

Pension and Profit Sharing Plans for Small or Medium Size Businesses. Aspen Publishers, Inc., 200 Orchard Ridge Dr., Ste. 200 Gaithersburg, MD 20878. Phone: 800-234-1660 or (301)417-7500 E-mail: customer.service@aspenpubl.com • URL: http://www.aspenpublishers.com • Monthly. $191.50 per year. Newsletter. Topics of interest and concern to professionals who serve small and medium size pension and profit sharing plans.

Pension Facts. American Council of Life Insurance, 1001 Pennsylvania Ave., N. W. Washington, DC 20004. Phone: (202)624-2000 Biennial. Free.

Pension Fund Investment Management: A Handbook for Sponsors and Their Advisors. Fran K. Fabozzi, editor. John Wiley and Sons, Inc., 111 River St. Hoboken, NJ 07030. Phone: 800-225-5945 or (201)748-6000 Fax: (201)748-6088 E-mail: info@wiley.com • URL: http://www.wiley.com • 1997. $95.00. Second revised edition. (Frank K. Fabozzi Series: Vol. 25).

Pension Fund Litigation Reporter. Andrews Publications, 175 Strafford Ave., Bldg 4, Suite 140 Wayne, PA 19087. Phone: 800-345-1101 or (610)225-0510 Fax: (610)225-0501 E-mail: customer@andrewspub.com • URL: http://www.andrewspub.com • Semimonthly. $750.00 per year. Newsletter. Contains reports on legal cases involving pension fund fiduciaries (trustees).

Pension Investment Report. Employee Benefit Research Institute, 2121 K St., N. W., Suite 600 Washington, DC 20037. Phone: (202)659-0670 Fax: (202)775-6312 E-mail: info@ebri.org • URL: http://www.ebri.org • Irregualr. Membership.

Pension Plan Fix-It Handbook. Thompson Publishing Group, Inc., 1725 K St., N.W., Suite 700 Washington, DC 20006. Phone: 800-444-8741 or (202)872-4000 Fax: 800-999-5661 E-mail: service@thompson.com • URL: http://www.thompson.com • Two looseleaf volumes. $499.00 per year. Two looseleaf volumes. Monthly updates and newsletters. Serves as a comprehensive guide to pension plan administration, taxation, and federal regulation. Includes both defined benefit and defined contribution plans.

Pension Plan Guide. CCH, Inc., 2700 Lake Cook Rd. Riverwoods, IL 60015. Phone: 800-835-5224 or (847)267-7000 E-mail: cust_serv@cch.com • URL: http://www.cch.com • Weekly. $1,279.00 per year. Newsletter. Formerly *Pension Plan Guide Summary*.

Pension Planning: Pensions, Profit Sharing, and Other Deferred Compensation Plans. Joseph T. Melone and others. McGraw-Hill, 1221 Ave. of the Americas New York, NY 10020. Phone: 800-722-4726 or (212)512-2000 Fax: (212)512-4502 E-mail: customer.service@mcgraw-hill.com • URL: http://www.mcgraw-hill.com • 2002. $104.38. Ninth edition.

Pension Research Council., University of Pennsylvania, 304 CPC, 3641 Locust Walk Philadelphia, PA 19104-6218. Phone: (215)898-7620 Fax: (215)898-0310 E-mail: prc@wharton.upenn.edu • URL: http://www.prc.wharton.upenn.edu/prc • Research areas include various types of private sector and public employee pension plans.

Pensions and Investments 1000 Largest Retirement Funds. Crain Communications, Inc., 711 Third Ave. New York, NY 10017-4036. Phone: 800-678-9595 or (212)210-0100 E-mail: info@crain.com • URL: http://www.crain.com • Annual. $50.00. List of the largest retirement plans in terms of total assets. Formerly *Pensions and Investments Top 100 Retirement Funds*.

Pensions and Investments: The Newspaper of Corporate and Institutional Investing. Crain Communications, Inc., 711 Third Ave. New York, NY 10017-4036. Phone: 800-678-9595 or (212)210-0100 E-mail: info@crain.com • URL: http://www.crain.com • Biweekly. $225.00 per year. Formerly *Pensions and Investment Age*.

People to People. American Public Power Association, 1875 Connecticut Ave. NW, Ste.1200 Washington, DC 20009. Phone: 800-372-1033 or (202)467-2900 Fax: (202)467-2910 E-mail: info@appanet.org • URL: http://www.bna.com • Description: Reports on public sector labor and personnel issues, especially those concerning the electric utility industry. Summarizes case studies in public labor relations.

People's Anti-War Mobilization., 39 W. 14th St., Ste. 206 New York, NY 10011. Phone: (212)633-6646 Fax: (212)633-2889 E-mail: iacenter@iacenter.org • URL: http://www.iacenter.org • Local community and welfare rights organizations, workers, and students who seek to: mobilize a mass movement to prevent U.S. military intervention abroad; pressure the federal government to reorient national priorities so that money appropriated for military use is shifted to social welfare programs. Sponsors demonstrations.

People's Medical Society., PO Box 868 Allentown, PA 18105-0868. Phone: 800-624-8773 or (610)770-1670 Fax: (610)770-0607 E-mail: cbi@peoplesmed.org • URL: http://www.peoplesmed.org • Promotes citizen involvement in the cost, quality, and management of the American health care system. Seeks to: train and encourage individuals to study local health care systems, practitioners, and institutions and promote preventive health care and medical cost control by these groups; address major policy issues and control health costs; encourage more preventive practice and research; promote self-care and alternative health care procedures; launch an information campaign to assist individuals in maintaining personal health and to prepare them for appointments with medical professionals. **Convention/Meeting:** none.

People's Republic of China Year Book. Current Publications Ltd, 1503 Enterprise Bldg., 228-238 Queens's Rd. Central Hong Kong, People's Republic of China. Phone: 22 5434702 Fax: 22 8158396 Annual. $98.00. Serves as the official yearbook of the People's Republic of China. Covers developments in various aspects of life in China, including the economy, industry, transportation, telecommunications, agriculture, technology, demographics, the legal system, health, and foreign relations. Includes many statistical tables and photographs. Text in Chinese.

Perelman's Pocket Cyclopedia of Cigars. Perelman, Pioneer and Co., 3580 Wilshire Blvd., Ste. 1290 Los Angeles, CA 90010. Phone: 888-766-5308 or (213)365-7965 Fax: (213)365-7895 E-mail: perelmanco@aol.com Annual. $12.95. Contains profiles of more than 1,000 brands of cigars marketed in the U. S.

The Perfect Interview: How to Get the Job You Really Want. John D. Drake. AMACOM, 1601 Broadway New York, NY 10019. Phone: 800-262-9699 or (518)586-8100 Fax: (518)903-8168 E-mail: customerservice@amanet.org • URL: http://www.amacombooks.org • 1996. $17.95. Second edition. Contains advice for jobseekers on how to control an interview and deal with difficult questions. Includes examples of both successful and unsuccessful interviews.

The Perfect Sales Piece: A Complete Do-It-Yourself Guide to Creating Brochures, Catalogs, Fliers, and Pamphlets. Robert W. Bly. John Wiley and Sons, Inc., 111 River St. Hoboken, NJ 07030. Phone: 800-225-5945 or (201)748-6000 Fax: (201)748-6088 E-mail: info@wiley.com • URL: http://www.wiley.com • 1994. $50.00. A guide to the use of various forms of printed literature for direct selling, sales promotion, and marketing. (Small Business Series).

Performance Analysis and Appraisal: A How-To-Do-It Manual for Librarians. Robert D. Stueart and Maureen Sullivan. Neal-Schuman Publishers, Inc., 100 William St., Ste. 2004 New York, NY 10038. Phone: (866)672-6657 or (212)925-8650 Fax: (866)209-7932 or (212)219-8916 E-mail: info@neal-schuman.com • URL: http://www.neal-schuman.com • 1991. $49.95. (How-to-Do-It Manuals Series).

Performance Budgeting for State and Local Government. Janet M. Kelly and William C. Rivenbark. M. E. Sharpe, Inc., 80 Business Park Drive Armonk, NY 10504. Phone: 800-541-6563 or (914)273-1800 Fax: (914)273-2106 E-mail: custserv@mesharpe.com • URL: http://www.mesharpe.com • 2003. $69.95. Covers performance-based management as applied to local government budgeting.

Performance Management in Government: Contemporary Illustrations. David Shand. OECD Publications and Information Center, 2001 L St., N. W., Suite 650 Washington, DC 20036-4922. Phone: 800-456-6323 or (202)785-6323 Fax: (202)785-0350 E-mail: washington.contact@oecd.org • URL: http://www.oecdwash.org • 1996. (Public Management Occasional Papers: No. 9).

Performing Arts: A Guide to the Reference Literature. Linda K. Simons. Libraries Unlimited, Inc., 88 Post Rd., W Westport, CT 06881. Phone: 800-225-5800 Fax: (203)222-1205 E-mail: lu-books@lu.com • URL: http://www.lu.com • 1994. $42.00. (Reference Sources in the Humanities Series).

Performing Arts Forum. International Society for the Performing Arts Foundation, 17 Purdy Ave., PO Box 909 Rye, NY 10580. Phone: (914)921-1550 Fax: (914)921-1593 E-mail: info@ispa.org • URL: http://www.ispa.org • Description: Directed toward producers, managers, promoters, and representatives of artists and performing arts events in the U.S. and other countries. Discusses techniques and problems involved with the development and administration of the performing arts. Recurring features include items from readers, news of research, Society reports, and notes on members.

Perfumer and Flavorist. Allured Publishing, 362 S. Schmale Rd. Carol Stream, IL 60188-2787. Phone: (630)653-2155 Fax: (630)653-2192 E-mail: allured@allured.com • URL: http://www.allured.com • Bimonthly. $135.00 per year. Provides information on the art and technology of flavors and fragrances, including essential oils, aroma chemicals, and spices.

Periodical Publications Association., PO Box 10669, PO Box 10669 Rockville, MD 20849-0669. Phone: (301)260-0929 Fax: (301)260-1647 E-mail: periodicalpubs@yahoo.com Business publications, magazines, and newspapers qualifying for periodical postage rates. Protects periodical mail rates by appropriate activity in Washington, DC. Endeavors to find solutions to postal problems of concern to members. Follows postal issues in Congress and regulation changes at United States Postal Service headquarters.

Periodical Title Abbreviations. Gale Cengage Learning, 27500 Drake Rd. Farmington Hills, MI 48331-3535. Phone: 800-877-GALE or (248)699-4253 Fax: 800-414-5043 E-mail: gale.galeord@cengage.com • URL: http://gale.cengage.com • 2002. $520.00. 14th edition. Two volumes. $260.00 per volume Vol. 1 *By Abbreviation*; vol. 2 *By Title*. Lists more than 145,000 different abbreviations.

Personal and Business Bartering. James Stout. McGraw-Hill, 1221 Ave. of the Americas New York, NY 10020. Phone: 800-722-4726 or (212)512-2000 Fax: (212)512-4502 E-mail: customer.service@mcgraw-hill.com • URL: http://www.mcgraw-hill.com • 1985. $14.95.

Personal Communications Industry Association., 500 Montgomery St., Suite 700 Alexandria, VA 22314-1561. Phone: 800-759-0300 or (703)739-0300 Fax: (703)836-1608 E-mail: ebrahiml@pcia.com • URL: http://www.pcia.com • Promotes development of industry standards for mobile telephone systems. Also concerned with the advertising and marketing of mobile telephones. Formerly National Mobile Radio System.

Personal Finance. Robert Rosefsky. John Wiley and Sons, Inc., 111 River St. Hoboken, NJ 07030. Phone: 800-526-5368 or (201)748-6000 Fax: (201)748-6088 E-mail: info@wiley.com • URL: http://www.wiley.com • 2001. $96.95. Eighth edition.

Personal Finance. KCI Communications Inc., 1750 Old Meadow Rd., Ste. 301 McLean, VA 22102. Phone: (703)394-1931 Fax: (703)905-8100 E-mail: service@kci-com.com Description: Contains articles on subjects of interest to those investigating personal finance strategies. Provides news, information, and suggestions on investment decisions. Covers stock and growth stook activity, individual retirement accounts, market trends and developments, and real estate. Recurring features include columns titled Capsule Advisory and Answers to Your Money Questions.

Personal Financial Planning. G. Victor Hallman and Jerry S. Rosenbloom. McGraw-Hill, 1221 Ave. of the Americas New York, NY 10020. Phone: 800-722-4726 or (212)512-2000 Fax: (212)512-4502 E-mail: customer.service@mcgraw-hill.com • URL: http://www.mcgraw-hill.com • 2003. $49.95. Seventh edition.

Personal Financial Planning Handbook: With Forms and Checklists. Warren, Gorham & Lamont/RIA, 395 Hudson St. New York, NY 10014. Phone: 800-950-1216 or (212)367-6300 Fax: (914)749-5042 E-mail: customer_services@riag.com • URL: http://www.riahome.com • $215.00. Looseleaf service. Biennial supplementation. Designed for professional financial planners, accountants, attorneys, insurance marketers, brokers, and bankers.

Personal Financial Planning: The Advisor's Guide. Rolf Austen. CCH, Inc., 2700 Lake Cook Rd. Riverwoods, IL 60015. Phone: 800-835-5224 or (847)267-7000 E-mail: cust_serv@cch.com • URL: http://www.cch.com • 1998. $55.95. Third edition. Covers personal taxes, investments, credit, mortgages, insurance, pensions, social security, estate planning, etc.

Personal Health Reporter. Gale Cengage Learning, 27500 Drake Rd. Farmington Hills, MI 48331-3535. Phone: 800-877-GALE or (248)699-4253 Fax: 800-414-5043 E-mail: gale.galeord@cengage.com • URL: http://gale.cengage.com • 1992. $150.00. Two volumes. Volume one, $115.00; volume two, $115.00. Presents a collection of professional and popular articles on 150 topics relating to physical and mental health conditions and treatments.

Personal Selling: Function, Theory and Practice. R. Wayne Mondy and others. Cengage Learning Custom Publishing, 5101 Madison Rd. Cincinnati, OH 45227. Phone: 800-543-0487 Fax: (513)527-9267 1999. $78.95. Fourth edition. Covers buying behavior, prospecting, presentation, objections, closing, selling as a career, and related topics. Includes a glossary.

Personal Strategies for Managing Stress. American Management Association Extension Institute, 1601 Broadway New York, NY 10019. Phone: 800-262-9699 or (518)586-8100 Fax: (518)903-8168 • URL: http://www.amanet.org • Looseleaf. $139.00. Self-study course. Emphasis is on practical explanations, examples, and problem solving. Quizzes and a case study are included.

Personnel Administration in Libraries. Sheila Creth and Frederick Duda. Neal-Schuman Publishers, Inc., 100 William St., Ste. 2004 New York, NY 10038. Phone: (866)672-6657 or (212)925-8650 Fax: (866)209-7932 or (212)219-8916 E-mail: info@neal-schuman.com • URL: http://www.neal-schuman.com • 1989. $55.00. Second edition.

Personnel Management Abstracts., 704 Island Lake Rd. Chelsea, MI 48118. Phone: (313)475-1979 Quarterly. $190.00 per year. Includes annual cumulation.

Personnel Management: Communications. Prentice Hall PTR, 240 Fritsch Paramus, NJ 07652. Phone: 800-282-0693 Fax: 800-445-6991 • URL: http://www.phptr.com • Looseleaf. Periodic supplementation. Price on application. Includes how to write effectively and how to prepare employee publications.

Personnel Management: Compensation. Prentice Hall PTR, 240 Fritsch Paramus, NJ 07652. Phone: 800-282-0693 Fax: 800-445-6991 • URL: http://www.phptr.com • Looseleaf. Periodic supplementation. Price on application.

Personnel Management: Labor Relations Guide. Prentice Hall PTR, 240 Frisch Ct. Paramus, NJ 07652. Phone: 800-282-0693 Fax: 800-445-6991 • URL: http://www.phptr.com • Three looseleaf volumes. Periodic supplementation. Price on application.

Personnel Management: Policies and Practices. Prentice Hall PTR, 240 Frisch Ct. Paramus, NJ 07652. Phone: 800-282-0693 Fax: 800-445-6991 • URL: http://www.phptr.com • Looseleaf. Periodic supplementation. Price on application.

Personnel Psychology. Personnel Psychology, Inc., 520 Ordway Ave. Bowling Green, OH 43402-2756. Phone: (419)352-1562 Fax: (419)352-2645 E-mail: ppsych@personnelpsychology.com • URL: http://www.personnelpsychology.com • Quarterly. $70.00 per year. Publishes research articles and book reviews.

Perspective. Magna Publications Inc., 2718 Dryden Dr. Madison, WI 53704-3086. Phone: 800-433-0499 or (608)246-3590 Fax: (608)246-3597 E-mail: custserv@magnapubs.com • URL: http://www.catalystwomen.org • Description: Provides administrators with guidelines for keeping their schools out of court. Examines current trends in law related to higher education, as well as past and future legal issues affecting students, faculty, administrators and the public. Recurring features include columns titled Key Case Review, Follow-Up, Resources, Legislative Note, Outside the Courts, Cross-Examination, and Cases Noted.

Perspectives on Radio and Television: Telecommunication in the United States. F. Leslie Smith and others. Lawrence Erlbaum Associates, Inc., 10 Industrial Ave., Rm. 700 Mahwah, NJ 07430-2226. Phone: 800-926-6579 or (201)258-2200 Fax: (201)236-0072 E-mail: orders@erlbaum.com • URL: http://www.erlbaum.com • 1998. Fourth edition. Price on application. (Communication Series).

Persuasive Business Speaking. Elayne Snyder. AMACOM, 1601 Broadway New York, NY 10019. Phone: 800-262-9699 or (518)586-8100 Fax: (518)903-8168 E-mail: customerservice@amanet.org • URL: http://www.amacombooks.org • 1990. $17.95. Includes ready-to-use openers, sample speeches, anecdotes, and quotes.

Pest Control. Advanstar Communications, 545 Boylston St. Boston, MA 02116. Phone: 888-527-7008 or (617)267-6500 Fax: (617)267-6900 E-mail: info@advanstar.com • URL: http://www.advanstar.com • Monthly. $44.00 per year.

Pest Control Technology. Group Interest Enterprises. GIE, Inc., Publishers, 4012 Bridge Ave. Cleveland, OH 44113. Phone: (216)961-4130 Fax: (216)961-0364 • URL: http://www.pctonline.com • Monthly. $32.00 per year. Provides technical and business management information for pest control personnel.

Pesticide Biochemistry and Physiology: An International Journal. Elsevier, 655 Avenue of the Americas New York, NY 10010-1710. Phone: 800-366-2665 or (212)989-5800 Fax: 800-535-9935 or (212)633-3680 E-mail: custserv@elsevier.com • URL: http://www.elsevier.com • Nine times a year. Individuals, $487.00 per year; institutions, $1,000.00 per year; students, $89.00 per year.

PestWeb: The Pest Control Industry Website. Univar USAPhone: 800-888-4897 or (425)889-3400 E-mail: webmaster@pestweb.com • URL: http://www.pestweb.com • Web site provides a wide variety of information on pest control products, manufacturers, associations, news, and education. Includes "Insects and Other Organisms," featuring details on 27 different kinds of pests, from ants to wasps. Online searching is offered. Fees: Free.

Pet Age: The Magazine for the Professional Retailer. Karen Long MacLeod, editor. H.H. Backer Associates, Inc., 200 S. Michigan Ave., Suite 840 Chicago, IL 60604. Phone: (312)663-4040 Fax: (312)663-5676 E-mail: petage@gol.com • URL: http://www.petage.com • Monthly. Free to qualified personnel; others, $25.00 per year.

Pet Dealer Purchasing Guide. Cygnus Business Media, Inc., 445 Broad Hollow Rd. Melville, NY 11747. Phone: 800-308-6397 or (631)845-2700 Fax: (631)845-2798 E-mail: rich.reiff@cygnuspub.com • URL: http://www.cygnusbzb.com • Annual. $75.00. Lists of manufacturers and importers of pet supplies; distributors and wholesalers of pet supples; wholesalers, breeders, and importers of pets (livestock); trade associations; publishers of pet books, records, and educational and training materials; pet care schools. Formerly *Pet Supplies Marketing Directory*.

Pet Food Institute., 2025 M St. NW, Ste. 800 Washington, DC 20036-2422. Phone: (202)367-1120 Fax: (202)367-2120 E-mail: info@petfoodinstitute.org • URL: http://www.petfoodinstitute.org • Represents the manufacturers of 97% of the commercial pet food produced in the United States. Serves as the voice of the industry before legislative and regulatory bodies at both the federal and state levels.

Pet Industry Distributors Association., 2105 Laurel Bush Rd., Ste. 200 Bel Air, MD 21015-5200. Phone: (443)640-1060 Fax: (443)640-1031 E-mail: pida@ksgroup.org • URL: http://www.pida.org • Strives to enhance the well-being of the pet product wholesaler-distributor. Promotes partnerships between suppliers and customers. Fosters the human-companion animal bond.

Pet Industry Joint Advisory Council., 1220 19th St. NW, Ste. 400 Washington, DC 20036-2438. Phone: 800-553-7387 or (202)452-1525 Fax: (202)293-4377 E-mail: info@pijac.org • URL: http://www.pijac.org • Pet retailers, manufacturers, and distributors; companion animal suppliers; pet industry trade associations. Works to monitor federal and state regulations and legislation affecting the industry. Sponsors research projects and industry-related educational programs.

Pet Product News. Fancy Publications, Three Burroughs Irvine, CA 92618. Phone: 800-365-4221 or (949)855-8822 Fax: (949)855-3045 • URL: http://www.animalnet.com • Monthly. Free to qualified personnel; others, $420.00 per year.

Pet Product News. Fancy Publications, Inc., P.O. Box 6050 Mission Viejo, CA 92690. Phone: 800-365-4421 or (949)855-8822 Fax: (949)855-3045 E-mail: ppneditor@fancypubs.com • URL: http://www.petproductnews.com • Free to qualified personnel; others, $118.00 per year. Supplement available *Pet Product News Buyer's Guide*.

Pet Shop. Entrepreneur Media, Inc., 2445 McCabe Way Irvine, CA 92614. Phone: 800-421-2300 or (949)261-2325 Fax: (949)851-9088 E-mail: entmag@entrepreneurmag.com • URL: http://www.entrepreneurmag.com • Looseleaf. $59.50. A practical guide to starting a pet store. Covers profit potential, start-up costs, market size evaluation, owner's time required, site selection, lease negotiation, pricing, accounting, advertising, promotion, etc. (Start-Up Business Guide No. E1007.)

Pet Supplies Market. Available from MarketResearch.com, 641 Ave. of the Americas, Third Floor New York, NY 10011. Phone: 800-298-5699 or (212)807-2629 Fax: (212)807-2716 E-mail: order@marketresearch.com • URL: http://www.marketresearch.com • 2001. $2,750.00. Published by Packaged Facts. Provides market data with projections to 2003 on products for dogs, cats, fish, birds, and other pets.

Peterson's College Money Handbook: The Only Complete Guide to Scholarships, College Costs, and Financial Aid at U. S. Colleges. Peterson's, Princeton Pike Corporate Center, 2000 Lenox Dr., 3rd Fl. Lawrenceville, NJ 08648. Phone: 800-338-3282 or (609)896-1800 Fax: (609)896-4544 E-mail: info@petersons.com • URL: http://www.petersons.com • 2002. $29.95. Provides information on more than 1,600 scholarships, loans, and financial aid programs.

Peterson's Computer Science and Electrical Engineering Programs. Peterson's, Princeton Pike Corporate Center, 2000 Lenox Dr. Lawrenceville, NJ 08548. Phone: 800-338-3282 or (609)896-1800 Fax: (609)895-4544 E-mail: info@petersons.com • URL: http://www.petersons.com • 1996. $24.95. A guide to 900 accredited graduate degree programs related to computers or electrical engineering at colleges and universities in the U. S. and Canada.

Peterson's Graduate and Professional Programs: Business, Education, Health, Information Studies, Law, and Social Work. Peterson's, 2000 Lenox Dr., Princeton Pike Corporate Center Lawrenceville, NJ 08648. Phone: 800-338-3282 or (609)896-1800 Fax: (609)896-4544 E-mail: info@petersons.com • URL: http://www.petersons.com • 2002. $49.95. Provides details of graduate and professional programs in business, law, information, and other fields at colleges and universities. (Peterson's Graduate and Professional Program Series). Formerly *Peterson's Guide to Graduate Programs in Business, Education, Health, Information Studies, Law and Social Work*.

Peterson's Graduate and Professional Programs in Engineering and Applied Sciences. Peterson's, 2000 Lenox Dr., Princeton Pike Corporate Center Lawrenceville, NJ 08548. Phone: 800-338-3282 or (609)896-1800 Fax: (609)896-4544 E-mail: info@petersons.com • URL: http://www.petersons.com • Annual. $49.95. Provides details of more than 3,400 graduate and professional programs in engineering and related fields at colleges and universities. (Peterson's Graduate in Professional Programs Series). Formerly *Peterson's Guide to Graduate Programs in Engineering and Professional Sciences*.

Peterson's Guide to Distance Learning Programs. Peterson's, 2000 Lenox Dr., 3rd Fl., Princeton Pike Corporate Center Lawrenceville, NJ 08548. Phone: 800-338-3282 or (609)896-1800 Fax: (609)896-1811 E-mail: info@petersons.com • URL: http://www.petersons.com • 2002. $26.95. Second revised edition. Provides detailed information on accredited college and university programs available through television, radio, computer, videocassette, and audiocassette resources. Covers U. S. and Canadian institutions.

Peterson's Guide to Four-Year Colleges. Peterson's, 2000 Lenox Dr., Princeton Pike Corporate Center Lawrenceville, NJ 08648. Phone: 800-338-3282 or (609)896-1800 Fax: (609)896-4544 E-mail: info@petersons.com • URL: http://www.petersons.com • Annual. $29.95. Provides information on more than 2,000 accredited degree-granting colleges and universities in the U. S. and Canada.

Peterson's Guide to Graduate and Professional Programs: An Overview. Peterson's, 2000 Lenox Dr., Princeton Pike Corporate Center Lawrenceville, NJ 08648. Phone: 800-338-3282 or (609)896-1800 Fax: (609)896-4544 E-mail: info@petersons.com • URL: http://www.petersons.com • Annual. $49.95. Provide details for more than 31,000 graduate programs at 1,700 colleges and universities. (Peterson's Graduate and Professional Program Series).

Peterson's Guide to MBA Programs: The Most Comprehensive Guide to U. S., Canadian, and International Business Schools. Peterson's, Princeton Pike Corporate Center, 2000 Lenox Dr. Lawrenceville, NJ 08648. Phone: 800-338-3282 or (609)896-1800 Fax: (609)896-4544 E-mail: info@petersons.com • URL: http://www.petersons.com • 2002. $29.95. Provides detailed information on about 850 graduate programs in business at 700 colleges and universities in the U. S., Canada, and other countries.

Peterson's Guide to Two-Year Colleges. Peterson's, 2000 Lenox Dr., Princeton Pike Corporate Center Princeton, NJ 08648. Phone: 800-338-3282 or (609)896-1800 Fax: (609)896-4544 E-mail: info@petersons.com • URL: http://www.petersons.com • Annual. $26.95. Provides information on more than 1,700 U. S. academic institutions granting associate degrees.

Peterson's Internships. Peterson's, Princeton Pike Corporate Ctr., 2000 Lenox Dr., PO Box 67005 Lawrenceville, NJ 08648. Phone: 800-338-3282 or (609)896-1800 Fax: (609)896-4531 E-mail: custsvc@petersons.com • URL: http://www.petersons.com • Covers: 50,000 career-oriented internship positions with over 2,000 organizations in the U.S. ranging from business to theater, communications to science. Entries include: Company name, address, phone, name and title of contact, types of internships available, number of internships offered, salary where applicable, qualifications, how to apply.

Peterson's Job Opportunities for Business Majors. Peterson's, Princeton Pike Corporate Ctr., 2000 Lenox Dr. Lawrenceville, NJ 08648. Phone: 800-338-3282 or (609)896-1800 Fax: (609)896-4544 E-mail: info@petersons.com • URL: http://www.petersons.com • 1999. $18.95. Provides career information for the 2,000 largest U. S. employers in various industries.

Peterson's Private Secondary Schools. Peterson's, 2000 Lenox Dr., Princeton Pike Corporate Ctr. Lawrenceville, NJ 08648. Phone: 800-338-3282 or (609)896-1800 Fax: (609)896-4544 E-mail: info@petersons.com • URL: http://www.petersons.com • Annual. $29.95. Provides information on more than 1,400 accredited private secondary schools in the U. S. (Peterson's Private Secondary School Series). Formerly *Peterson's Guide to Private Secondary Schools*.

Peterson's Professional Degree Programs in the Visual and Performing Arts. Peterson's, 2000 Lenox Dr., Princeton Pike Corporate Ctr. Princeton, NJ 08648. Phone: 800-338-3282 or (609)896-1800 Fax: (609)896-4544 E-mail: info@petersons.com • URL: http://www.petersons.com • Annual. $21.95. A directory of more than 900 degree programs in art, music, theater, and dance at 600 colleges and professional schools.

Peterson's Register of Higher Education. Peterson's, 2000 Lenox Dr., Princeton Pike Corporate Ctr. Lawrenceville, NJ 08648. Phone: 800-338-3282 or (609)896-1800 Fax: (609)896-4544 E-mail: info@petersons.com • URL: http://www.petersons.com • Annual. $49.95. Provides concise information on 3,700 colleges and other postsecondary educational institutions in the U. S.

Peterson's Scholarships, Grants, and Prizes: Your Complete Guide to College Aid from Private Sources. Peterson's, 2000 Lenox Dr., Princeton Pike Corporate Ctr. Lawrenceville, NJ 08648. Phone: 800-338-3282 or (609)896-1800 Fax: (609)896-4544 E-mail: info@petersons.com • URL: http://www.petersons.com • 1998. $26.95. Third edition.

Peterson's Study Abroad. Peterson's, Princeton Pike Corporate Ctr., 2000 Lenox Dr., PO Box 67005 Lawrenceville, NJ 08648. Phone: 800-338-3282 or (609)896-1800 Fax: (609)896-4531 E-mail: custsvc@petersons.com • URL: http://www.petersons.com • Covers: More than 1,800 academic year and semester Study Abroad programs. Entries include: Sponsor name, address, description of programs, course offerings, host institutions, admission requirements, costs, availability of college credit.

Peterson's Vocational and Technical Schools and Programs: East and West. Peterson's, 2000 Lenox Dr., Princeton Pike Corporate Ctr. Lawrenceville, NJ 08648. Phone: 800-338-3282 or (609)896-1800 Fax: (609)896-4544 E-mail: info@petersons.com • URL: http://www.petersons.com • Annual. $69.90. Two volumes. $34.95 per volume. Provides information on vocational schools in the eastern part of the U. S. Covers more than 370 career fields.

Petfood Industry. Watt Publishing Co., 122 S. Wesley Ave. Mount Morris, IL 61054-1497. Phone: (815)734-4171 Fax: (815)734-4201 • URL: http://www.wattnet.com • Bimonthly. $36.00 per year.

Petro Process Directory. Atlantic Communications L.L.C., 1635 W Alabama St. Houston, TX 77006. Phone: 800-654-1480 or (713)831-1768 Fax: (713)523-7804 E-mail: robg@oilonline.com • URL: http://www.oilonline.com • Covers: 9,000 companies in the United States engaged in petrochemical and refining industries; incorporating health, safety and environment; suppliers of products and services to the industry. Entries include: Company name, address, phone, fax, telex, E-mail, URL, WATS number, names and titles of key personnel, branch offices.

PetroChemical News: A Weekly News Service in English Devoted to the Worldwide Petrochemical Industry. William F. Bland Co., 709 Turmeric Ln. Durham, NC 27713. Phone: (919)544-1717 Fax: (919)544-1999 E-mail: mbs@petrochmical-news.com • URL: http://www.petrochemical-news.com • Weekly. $807.00 per year. Report of current and significant news about the petrochemical business worldwide.

Petrochemicals: The Rise of an Industry. Peter H. Spitz. John Wiley and Sons, Inc., 111 River St. Hoboken, NJ 07030. Phone: 800-526-5368 or (201)748-6000 Fax: (201)748-6088 E-mail: info@wiley.com • URL: http://www.wiley.com • 1988. $150.00.

Petroleum Abstracts. University of Tulsa, Information Services Div., 600 S. College Ave. Tulsa, OK 74104-3189. Phone: 800-247-8678 or (918)594-8000 E-mail: info@osu-tulsa.okstate.edu • URL: http://www.osu-tulsa.okstate.edu • 50 times a year. Service basis. Worldwide literature related to petroleum exploration and production.

Petroleum-Energy Business News Index Elsevier Engineering Information, Inc. Elsevier, 655 Avenue of the Americas New York, NY 10010-5107. Phone: 800-366-2665 or (212)989-5800 Fax: 800-535-9935 or (212)663-3680 E-mail: custserv@elsevier.com • URL: http://www.elsevier.com • Monthly. Members, $475.00 per year; non-members, $950.00 per year.

Petroleum Equipment Directory. Petroleum Equipment Institute, PO Box 2380 Tulsa, OK 74101-2380. Phone: (918)494-9696 Fax: (918)491-9895 E-mail: info@pei.org • URL: http://www.pei.org • Covers: over 1,600 member manufacturers, distributors, and installers of petroleum marketing equipment worldwide. Entries include: Company name, address, phone, names of executives, list of products or services.

Petroleum Equipment Institute., PO Box 2380 Tulsa, OK 74101-2380. Phone: (918)494-9696 Fax: (918)491-9895 E-mail: info@pei.org • URL: http://www.pei.org • Distributors and manufacturers of equipment used in service stations, bulk plants, and other petroleum marketing operations.

Petroleum Equipment Suppliers Association., 9225 Katy Fwy., Ste. 310 Houston, TX 77024-1510. Phone: (713)932-0168 Fax: (713)932-0497 E-mail: webmaster@pesa.org • URL: http://www.pesa.org • Promotes improvement of the petroleum equipment, service, and supply industries. Represents members' interests; cooperates with the federal government in matters of national concern; gathers and disseminates information. Conducts educational programs.

Petroleum Intelligence Weekly. PIW Publications Inc., 5 E 37th St., No. 5 New York, NY 10016-2807. Phone: (212)532-1112 Fax: (212)941-5509 E-mail: sdp@tfn.com • URL: http://www.energyintel.com • Description: Provides a "concise weekly summary and analysis of key developments in world oil and natural gas markets." Supplies highlights in petroleum news on an international scale. Concerned with OPEC (Organization of Petroleum Exporting Countries) and non-OPEC production levels, coverage of OPEC meetings and policy decisions, and quarterly demand and oil trade figures. Recurring features include analyses of emerging trends in oil and gas markets, notices of publications available, and columns titled Marketview (a weekly wrap-up of crude oil trading) and What's New Around the World (news briefs relating to the petroleum industry and market).

Petroleum Marketers Association of America., 1901 N Fort Meyer Dr., Ste. 1200 Arlington, VA 22209. Phone: (703)351-8000 Fax: (703)351-9160 E-mail: info@pmaa.org • URL: http://www.pmaa.org • Absorbed National Oil Fuel Institute and Oil Heat Institute of America. Formerly National Jobbers Council.

Petroleum Marketing Monthly. Available from U. S. Government Printing Office, Washington, DC 20402. Phone: (202)512-1800 Fax: (202)512-2250 E-mail: gpoaccess@gpo.gov • URL: http://www.access.gpo.gov • Monthly. Current information and statistics relating to a wide variety of petroleum products. (Office of Oil and Gas, Energy Information Administration, U. S. Department of Energy.)

Petroleum Statement, Annual Energy Report. Energy Information Administration. U.S. Department of Energy, Washington, DC 20585. Phone: (202)586-4940 Annual.

Petroleum Supply Annual. Available from U. S. Government Printing Office, Washington, DC 20402. Phone: (202)512-1800 Fax: (202)512-2250 E-mail: gpoaccess@gpo.gov • URL: http://www.access.gpo.gov • Annual. $78.00. Two volumes. Produced by the Energy Information Administration, U. S. Department of Energy. Contains worldwide data on the petroleum industry and petroleum products.

Petroleum Supply Monthly. Available from U. S. Government Printing Office, Washington, DC 20402. Phone: (202)512-1800 Fax: (202)512-2250 E-mail: gpoaccess@gpo.gov • URL: http://www.access.gpo.gov • Monthly. Produced by the Energy Information Administration, U. S. Department of Energy. Provides worldwide statistics on a wide variety of petroleum products. Covers production, supplies, exports and imports, transportation, refinery operations, and other aspects of the petroleum industry.

Pew Research Center for the People and the Press. Pew Charitable TrustsPhone: (202)293-3126 Fax: (202)293-2569 E-mail: mailprc@people-press.org • URL: http://www.people-press.org • Free Web site includes public opinion poll "Reports by Topic." Five broad subject areas cover business, social issues, foreign policy, news media, and politics. Searching is offered within each of these broad areas, and there are links to other major sources of public opinion poll results ("FYI Other Polls").

PGA TOUR Tournaments Association., 13000 Sawgrass Village Cir., Ste. 36 Ponte Vedra Beach, FL 32082. Phone: (904)285-4222 Fax: (904)273-5726 E-mail: suzanne@pgatta.org • URL: http://pgatta.org • Sponsors major professional golf tournaments held on the regular PGA Tour in the United States and Canada each year. Provides forum for exchange of information and ideas.

Pharma Business: The International Magazine of Pharmaceutical Business and Marketing. Engel Publishing Partners., 828 A Newton-Yardley Rd. Newton, PA 18940. Phone: 800-431-1579 or (215)867-0044 Fax: (215)867-0053 • URL: http://www.englepub.com • Six times a year. $235.00 per year. Circulated mainly in European countries. Coverage includes worldwide industry news, new drug products, regulations, and research developments.

Pharma Marketletter. Marketletter Publications Ltd., 54-55 Wilton Rd. London SW1V 1DE, United Kingdom. Phone: 44 20 78287272 Fax: 44 20 78280415 E-mail: editorial@marketletter.com • URL: http://www.marketletter.com • Fifty times a year. $525.00 per year. Newsletter. Formerly *Marketletter*.

Pharmaceutical and Medical Device Law Bulletin. American Lawyer Media, Inc., 105 Madison Ave. New York, NY 10016. Phone: 800-888-8300 or (212)779-9200 Fax: (212)481-8110 E-mail: lawcatalog@amlaw.com • URL: http://www.lawcatalog.com/ • Monthly. $199.00 per year. Newsletter. Edited for lawyers concerned with drug product or medical device litigation. Contains industry news items of special interest, reports on new products, legal case summaries, Food and Drug Administration actions, patent issues, and related news reports. (A Law Journal Newsletter, formerly published by Leader Publications).

Pharmaceutical Engineering. International Society for Pharmaceutical Engineering, Inc., 3816 W. Linebaugh Ave., Suite 412 Tampa, FL 33624-4702. Phone: (813)960-2105 Fax: (813)264-2816 E-mail: ispehq@ispe.org • URL: http://www.ispe.org • Bimonthly. $60.00 per year. Feature articles provide practical application and specification information on the design, construction, supervision and maintenance of process equipment, plant systems, instrumentation and pharmaceutical facilities.

Pharmaceutical Executive: For Global Business and Marketing Leaders. Advanstar Communications, 545 Boylston St. Boston, MA 02116. Phone: 888-527-7008 or (617)267-6500 Fax: (617)267-6900 E-mail: info@advanstar.com • URL: http://www.advanstar.com • Monthly. $64.00 per year.

Pharmaceutical Litigation Reporter: The National Journal of Record of Pharmaceutical Litigation. Andrews Publications, 175 Strafford Ave., Bldg. 4, Suite 140 Wayne, PA 19087. Phone: 800-345-1101 or (610)225-0510 Fax: (610)225-0501 E-mail: customer@andrewspub.com • URL: http://www.andrewspub.com • Monthly. $775.00 per year. Newsletter. Reports on a wide variety of legal cases involving the pharmaceutical and medical device industries. Includes product liability lawsuits.

Pharmaceutical Marketers Directory. CPS Communications Inc., 7200 W Camino Real, Ste. 215 Boca Raton, FL 33433. Phone: 800-346-2015 or (561)368-9301 Fax: (561)368-7870 E-mail: pmd@cpsnet.com • URL: http://www.pmdcentral.com • Covers: about 15,000 personnel of pharmaceutical, medical device and equipment manufacturers, and biotechnology companies; advertising agencies with clients in the healthcare field; health care publications; alternative media and healthcare industry suppliers. Entries include: Company name, address, list of personnel by job classification (with titles, phone, internet and e-mail addresses, direct dial and fax numbers).

Pharmaceutical Marketing and Management Research Program.

Pharmaceutical Marketing in the 21st Century. Mickey C. Smith, editor. Haworth Press, Inc., 10 Alice St. Binghamton, NY 13904-1580. Phone: 800-429-6784 or (607)722-5857 Fax: 800-895-0582 or (607)722-1424 E-mail: getinfo@haworthpressinc.com • URL: http://www.haworthpressinc.com • 1996. $49.95. Various authors discuss the marketing, pricing, distribution, and retailing of prescription drugs. (Pharmaceutical Marketing and Management Series, Vol. 10, Nos. 2,3&4).

Pharmaceutical News Index. ProQuest Inc., 300 N. Zeeb Rd. Ann Arbor, MI 48103. Phone: 800-521-0600 or (734)761-4700 Fax: 800-864-0019 or (734)461-6450 • URL: http://www.umi.com • Indexes major pharmaceutical industry newsletters, 1974 to present. Weekly updates. Inquire as to online cost and availability.

Pharmaceutical Processing. Reed Business Information, 360 Park Ave. S New York, NY 10010. Phone: 800-446-6551 or (646)746-6400 Fax: (646)746-7028 E-mail: corporatecommunications@reedbusiness.com • URL: http://www.reedbusiness.com • Monthly. $62.90 per year. Includes *Buyers' Guide*. Formerly *Pharmaceutical and Cosmetic Equipment*.

Pharmaceutical Processing Annual Buyers Guide. Reed Business Information, 360 Park Ave., S New York, NY 10010. Phone: 800-446-6551 or (646)746-6400 Fax: (646)746-7028 E-mail: corporatecommunications@reedbusiness.com • URL: http://www.reedbusiness.com • Annual. $69.95. Includes *Buyer's Guide*. Lists makers and distributors of supplies and equipment for the pharmaceutical manufacturing industry.

Pharmaceutical Representative. McKnight Medical Communications, 2 Northfield Plz., Ste. 300 Northfield, IL 60093. Phone: 800-451-7838 or (847)441-3700 Fax: (847)441-3701 E-mail: pr@medec.com • URL: http://www.pharmrep.com • Monthly. $37.95 per year. Edited for drug company salespeople and sales managers.

Pharmaceutical Research and Manufacturers Association., 1100 15th St., N.W., Suite 900 Washington, DC 20005. Phone: (202)835-3400 Fax: (202)835-3429 • URL: http://www.phrma.org • Formerly Pharmaceutical Manufacturers Association.

Pharmaceutical Research Manufacturers Association Annual Fact Book. Pharmaceutical Research and Manufacturers Association, 1100 15th St., N.W., Suite 900 Washington, DC 20005. Phone: (202)835-3400 Fax: (202)835-3429 • URL: http://www.phrma.org • Annual.

Pharmaceutical Technology. Advanstar Communications, 545 Boylston St. Boston, MA 02116. Phone: 888-527-7008 or (617)267-6500 Fax: (617)267-6900 E-mail: info@advanstar.com • URL: http://www.advanstar.com • Monthly. $64.00 per year. Practical hands on information about the manufacture of pharmaceutical products, focusing on applied technology.

Pharmacological and Chemical Synonyms: A Collection of Names of Drugs, Pesticides, and Other Compounds Drawn from the Medical Literature of the World. E. E. Marler. Elsevier, 360 Park Ave., S New York, NY 10010-1710. Phone: 888-437-4636 or (212)989-5800 Fax: (212)633-3990 E-mail: usinfo-f@elsevier.com • URL: http://www.elsevier.com • 1994. $272.00. Tenth edition.

Pharmacology Research Laboratory.

Pharmacopeia of Herbs. CME, Inc., 2801 McGaw Ave. Irvine, CA 92614-5835. Phone: 800-933-2632 or (949)250-1008 Fax: (949)250-0445 E-mail: infostore@cmeinc.com • URL: http://www.cmeinc.com • $149.00. Frequently updated CD-ROM provides searchable data on a wide variety of herbal medicines, vitamins, and amino acids. Includes information on clinical studies, contraindications, side-effects, phytoactivity, and 534 therapeutic use categories. Contains a 1,000 word glossary.

Pharmacopeial Forum. United States Pharmacopeial Convention, Inc., 12601 Twinbrook Parkway Rockville, MD 20852. Phone: 800-227-8772 or (301)881-0666 Fax: (301)816-8299 E-mail: jac@usp.org • URL: http://www.usp.org • Bimonthly. $469.00 per year.

Pharmacy Times: Practical Information for Today's Pharmacists. Medical World Communications, 241 Forsgate Dr. Jamesburg, NJ 08831. Phone: (732)656-1140 Fax: (732)656-1142 E-mail: cms@skaininfo.com • URL: http://www.pharmacytimes.com • Monthly. Individuals, $57.00 per year; institutions, $103.00 per year. Edited for pharmacists. Covers store management, new products, regulations, home health care products, managed care issues, etc.

Pharmacy: What It Is and How It Works. William N. Kelly. CRC Press, 2000 N.W. Corporate Blvd. Boca Raton, FL 33431. Phone: 800-272-7737 or (561)994-0555 Fax: 800-374-3401 or (561)989-9732 E-mail: orders@crcpress.com • URL: http://www.crcpress.com • 2002. $39.95. Serves as an introduction to the field of pharmacy, including a history of the profession and information on career opportunities.

Chapters are included on drug development, uses of drugs, pricing, information technology for pharmacies, and career planning.

Phelon's Discount/Jobbing Trade. Phelon, Sheldon & Marsar Inc., 15 Industrial Ave., PO Box 517 Fairview, NJ 07022-0517. Phone: 800-234-8804 or (201)941-8804 Fax: (201)941-5515 E-mail: psmpublishing@aol.com Covers: Approximately 2,050 mass merchandisers, including discount stores and discount chains, TV shopping clubs, wholesalers clubs, drug store chains, auto chains, toy store chains, audio and TV chains, leased department operators, catalog showrooms; also includes 5,000 jobbers, wholesalers, and distributors of all types of merchandise. Entries include: Company name, address, phone, names and titles of key executives, sales volume, number of stores, resident buying offices, merchandise lines with buyers' names, trade and brand names.

Philanthropy and Voluntarism: An Annotated Bibliography. Daphne N. Layton. The Foundation Center, 79 Fifth Ave. New York, NY 10003-3076. Phone: 800-424-9836 or (212)620-4230 Fax: (212)807-3577 E-mail: orders@fdncenter.org • URL: http://www.fdncenter.org • 1987. $18.50.

Philatelic Foundation., 70 W 40th St., 15th Fl. New York, NY 10018. Phone: (212)221-6555 Fax: (212)221-6208 E-mail: philatelicfoundation@verizon.net • URL: http://www.philatelicfoundation.org • Educational institution chartered by New York State Department of Education for philatelic study and research. Offers philatelic slide programs as an educational aid for schools, organized youth groups, and stamp clubs. Renders opinions on stamps and other philatelic material. Prepares exhibitions for stamp shows.

Phillips Satellite Industry Directory. PBI Media LLC, 1201 Seven Locks Rd., Suite 300 Potomac, MD 20854. Phone: 888-707-5812 or (301)340-2000 Fax: (301)762-4196 E-mail: clientservices@pbimedia.com • URL: http://www.phillips.com • Annual. $267.00. Provides information for more than 5,800 contacts and 2,000 providers of equipment and services for the satellite communications industry.

Phillips Wireless Industry Directory. Access Intelligence L.L.C., 4 Choke Cherry Rd., 2nd Fl. Rockville, MD 20850. Phone: 800-777-5006 or (301)354-2000 Fax: (301)309-3847 E-mail: info@accessintel.com • URL: http://www.wirelesstoday.com • Covers: Approximately 6,000 national and international cellular telephone companies, PCS companies, paging services, specialized mobile radio operators, and other manufacturers and distributors of products and services to the wireless communications industry. Also includes a listing of all of the PCS, MSA, and MSA license holders. Provides over 13,000 industry contacts. Entries include: For carriers—Carrier name, address, phone, names and titles of key personnel, products or services provided, geographic area covered, branch office names and locations; paging and mobile channels (in a separate list). For suppliers—Company name, address, phone, fax, names and titles of key personnel, products and services. For cellular operators—Company name, address, phone, fax, name and title of contact, plant equipment, CGSA, number of cells, description, cellular frequency, MSA/RSA name, ownership and service area.

Phillips World Satellite Almanac. Access Intelligence L.L.C., 4 Choke Cherry Rd., 2nd Fl. Rockville, MD 20850. Phone: 800-777-5006 or (301)354-2000 Fax: (301)309-3847 E-mail: info@accessintel.com • URL: http://www.pbimedia.com • Covers: all commercial satellite systems and operators (operational and planned), booking contacts, PTT decision makers, and transponder brokers. Entries include: Owner/operator/system name, corporate contact, booking contact, public relations contact, tariff information or lease price, remarks, TT&C stations, satellites, transponder details.

PHL Bulletin (Packaging, Handling, Logistics). National Institute of Packaging, Handling, and Logistics Engineers, 6902 Lyle St. Lanham, MD 20706-3454. Phone: (301)459-9105 Fax: (301)459-4925 E-mail: niphle@erols.com • URL: http://www.niphle.com • Monthly. $50.00 per year.

Phonefacts. United States Telephone Association, 1401 H St., N. W., Suite 600 Washington, DC 20005. Phone: (202)326-7300 Fax: (202)326-7333 Annual. Members, $5.00; non-members, $10.00. Presents basic statistics on the independent telephone industry in the U. S.

Phonolog. Muze, Inc., 304 Hudson St., 8th Floor New York, NY 10013. Phone: 800-456-7838 or (212)824-0300 Fax: (212)741-1246 E-mail: custsrv@muze.com • URL: http://www.muze.com • Annual. $550.00. 10 volumes. Provides detailed information on more than 370,000 titles of commercially available and out-of-print music recordings. Includes popular, jazz, and classical titles.

Photo Marketing. Photo Marketing Association International, 3000 Picture Place Jackson, MI 49201. Phone: (517)788-8100 Fax: (517)788-8371 • URL: http://www.pmai.org • Monthly. Membership.

Photographer's Market: 2000 Places to Sell Your Photographs. F&W Publications, Inc., 4700 E Galbraith Rd. Cincinnati, OH 45236. Phone: 800-289-0963 or (513)531-2690 Fax: (513)531-0798 • URL: http://www.fwpublications.com • Annual. $24.99. Lists 2,000 companies and publications that purchase original photographs.

Photographic Society of America., 3000 United Founders Blvd., Suite 103 Oklahoma City, OK 73112. Phone: (405)843-1437 Fax: (405)843-1438 E-mail: hq@psa-photo.org • URL: http://www.psa-photo.org • Formerly Associated Camera Clubs of America.

Photography in Focus. Mark Jacobs and Ken Kokrda. McGraw-Hill, 1221 Ave. of the Americas New York, NY 10020. Phone: 800-722-4726 or (212)512-2000 Fax: (212)512-4502 E-mail: customer.service@mcgraw-hill.com • URL: http://www.mcgrawhill.com • 2001. $48.64. Fifth edition.

Photoimaging Manufacturers and Distributors Association., 109 White Oak Lane, Suite 72F Old Bridge, NJ 08857. Phone: (732)679-3460 Fax: (732)679-2294 E-mail: bclarkpmda@aol.com Formerly Photographic Manufacturers and Distributors Association.

Photonics. Ralf Menzel. Springer-Verlag, 175 Fifth Ave. New York, NY 10010. Phone: 800-777-4643 or (212)460-1500 Fax: (201)948-4505 E-mail: service@springer-ny.com • URL: http://www.springer-ny.com • 2001. $89.95. "...covers the fundamental properties and the description of single photons and light beams, experimentally and theoretically." Provides basic information about modern lasers. Edited for graduate students and scientists.

The Photonics Directory. Laurin Publishing Company Inc., Berkshire Common, PO Box 4949 Pittsfield, MA 01202-4949. Phone: 800-553-0051 or (413)499-0514 Fax: (413)442-3180 E-mail: info@photonics.com • URL: http://www.photonics.com • Description: A four-book set concerning the international photonics industry, including a 'Corporate Guide' listing manufacturers and suppliers; a 'Buyers' Guide'; a technical 'Handbook' for design and applications engineers; and a 'Dictionary' of terms and abbreviations. Entries include: Company name, address, phone, fax, e-mail, description of products and services.

Photonics Research Laboratory.

Photonics Spectra. Laurin Publishing Co., Inc., Berkshire Common, PO Box 4949 Pittsfield, MA 01202-4949. Phone: 800-553-0051 or (413)499-0514 Fax: (413)442-3180 E-mail: photonics@laurin.com • URL: http://www.photonics.com • Monthly. $112.00 per year.

Physical Fitness Center. Entrepreneur Media, Inc., 2445 McCabe Way Irvine, CA 92614. Phone: 800-421-2300 or (949)261-2325 Fax: (949)851-9088 E-mail: entmag@entrepreneur.com • URL: http://www.entrepreneur.com • Looseleaf. $59.50. A practical guide to starting a physical fitness center. Covers profit potential, start-up costs, market size evaluation, owner's time required, site selection, lease negotiation, pricing, accounting, advertising, promotion, etc. (Start-Up Business Guide No. E1172.)

Physical Science Laboratory. New Mexico State University

Physician Insurers Association of America., 2275 Research Blvd., Ste. 250 Rockville, MD 20850. Phone: (301)947-9000 Fax: (301)947-9090 E-mail: ahorwich@thepiaa.org • URL: http://www.thepiaa.org • Members are cooperative physicians' professional liability insurers affiliated with state medical societies.

Physician Insurers Association of America: Membership Directory. Physician Insurers Association of America, 2275 Research Blvd., Suite 250 Rockville, MD 20850. Phone: (301)947-9000 Fax: (301)947-9090 Annual. $25.00. Lists 60 cooperative physicians' professional liability insurers affiliated with state medical societies.

Physicians & Computers. Moorhead Publications Inc., 810 S. Waukegan Rd., No. 120 Lake Forest, IL 60045-2696. Phone: (847)615-8333 Fax: (847)615-8345 Monthly. $40.00 per year. Includes material on computer diagnostics, online research, medical and non-medical software, computer equipment, and practice management.

Physicians' Desk Reference. Medical Economics Co., Five Paragon Dr. Montvale, NJ 07645-1742. Phone: 877-922-2022 or (973)944-9777 Fax: (973)-944-5390 E-mail: fulfill@superfill.com • URL: http://www.medec.com • Annual. $82.95. Generally known as "PDR". Provides detailed descriptions, effects, and adverse reactions for about 4,000 prescription drugs. Includes data on more than 250 drug manufacturers, with brand name and generic name indexes and drug identification photographs. Discontinued drugs are also listed.

Physicians' Desk Reference for Nonprescription Drugs. Medical Economics Co., Five Paragon Dr. Montvale, NJ 07645-1742. Phone: 877-922-2022 or (973)944-9777 Fax: (973)847-5390 • URL: http://www.medec.com • Annual. $49.95. Contains detailed descriptions of "commonly used" over-the-counter drug products. Includes drug identification photographs. Indexing is by product category, product name, manufacturer, and active ingredient. Formerly *Physicians' Desk Reference for Nonprescription Drugs*.

Physicians' Desk Reference for Ophthalmology. Medical Economics Co., Five Paragon Dr. Montvale, NJ 07645-1742. Phone: 888-922-2022 or (973)944-9777 Fax: (973)944-5390 E-mail: fulfill@superfill.com • URL: http://www.medec.com • Annual. $49.95. Provides detailed descriptions of ophthalmological instrumentation, equipment, supplies, lenses, and prescription drugs. Indexed by manufacturer, product name, product category, active drug ingredient, and instrumentation. Editorial discussion is included.

Physicians' Desk Reference Library on CD-ROM. Medical Economics, Five Paragon Drive Montvale, NJ 07645. Phone: 800-232-7379 or (201)358-7500 Fax: (201)722-2680 Three times a year. Contains the CD-ROM equivalent of *Physicians' Desk Reference (PDR), Physicians' Desk Reference for Nonprescription Drugs, Physicians' Desk Reference for Opthalmology*, and other PDR publications.

Physicians Financial News., 261 5th Ave., 8th Fl. New York, NY 10016. Phone: (646)472-8950 Fax: (646)472-0193 • URL: http://www.pfnpublishing.com • Monthly. $105.00 per year.

Physician's Marketing and Management. American Health Consultants, Inc., 3525 Piedmont Rd., N.E., Bldg.6, Suite 400 Atlanta, GA 30305. Phone: 800-688-2421 or (404)262-7436 Fax: 800-284-3291 or (404)262-7837 E-mail: custserv@ahcpub.com • URL: http://www.ahcpub.com • Monthly. Individuals, $299.00 per year; institutions, $323.00 per year. Newsletter. Formerly*Physician's Marketing*.

The Physics and Chemistry of Color: The Fifteen Causes of Color. Kurt Nassau. John Wiley and Sons, Inc., 111 River St. Hoboken, NJ 07030. Phone: 800-225-5945 or (201)748-6000 Fax: (201)748-6088 E-mail: info@wiley.com • URL: http://www.wiley.com • 2001. $115.00. Second edition. (Pure and Applied Optics Series).

Physics Research Center and Vitreous State Laboratory. Catholic University of America

PIA Financial Ratio Studies. Printing Industries of America, Inc., 100 Daingerfield Rd. Alexandria, VA 23314-2888. Phone: 888-868-8662 or (703)519-8100 Fax: (703)548-3227 E-mail: info@profectus.com • URL: http://www.profectus.com • Annual. $3,582.00. 18 volumes. $199.00 per volume.

PICA Bulletin: News and Analysis for the Personal Communication Industry. Personal Communications Industry Association, 500 Montgomery St., Suite 700 Alexandria, VA 22314-1561. Phone: (703)739-0300 Fax: 800-759-0300 or (703)836-1608 E-mail: ebrahim1@pica.com • URL: http://www.pica.com • Weekly. $550.00 per year.

Pictorial Price Guide to American Antiques: 2002-2003. Dorothy Hammond. Antique Collectors Club, 405 Murray Hill Pkwy East Rutherford, NJ 07073-2136. Phone: 800-526-0275 or (201)387-2136 Fax: (201)385-6521 2002 $19.95 (Pictorial Price Guide to American Antiques Series).

Picture Framing Magazine. Hobby Publications, Inc., 207 Commercial Ct. Morganville, NJ 07751. Phone: (732)536-5160 Fax: (732)536-5761 Monthly. $20.00 per year. Published for retailers, wholesalers, and manufacturers of picture frames.

PIMA Directory. Paper Industry Management Association, 15 Technology Pky. S Norcross, GA 30092. Phone: (770)209-7230 Fax: (770)209-7359 E-mail: mcornell@pimaweb.org • URL: http://www.pima-online.org • Covers: 5,000 pulp, paper mill, and paper converting production executives; affiliated supplier firms and their representatives. Entries include: Executive name, title, office address and phone, home address, and name of spouse.

Pimsleur's Checklists of Basic American Legal Publications. American Association of Law Libraries. Fred B. Rothman and Co., 10368 W Centennial Rd. Littleton, CO 80127. Phone: 888-361-3255 or (303)979-5657 Fax: (303)979-0707 E-mail: s_jarrett@wshein.com • URL: http://www.wshein.com • Irregular. $265.00. Looseleaf service.

Pine Chemicals Association., 3350 Riverwood Pkwy. SE, Ste. 1900 Atlanta, GA 30339. Phone: (770)984-5340 Fax: (770)984-5341 E-mail: wjones@pinechemicals.org • URL: http://www.pinechemicals.org • Represents manufacturers of chemical products (other than pulp, paper, and paper products) produced by, or from, wood pulp industry products. Sponsors educational and management meetings. Collects statistical data.

Pineapple Growers Association of Hawaii., 1116 Whitmore Ave. Wahiawa, HI 96786. Phone: (808)621-1220 Fax: (808)621-1213 Promotes the sale of fresh and canned pineapple products. Supersedes Pineapple Producers Cooperative Association.

The Pink Sheet: Prescription Pharmaceuticals and Biotechnology. F-D-C Reports, Inc., 5550 Friendship Blvd., Suite 1 Chevy Chase, MD 20815-7278. Phone: 800-332-2181 or (301)657-9830 Fax: (301)664-7238 E-mail: fdc.customer.service@elsevier.com • URL: http://www.fdcreports.com • 51 times a year. Institutions, $1,431.00 per year. Newsletter covering business and regulatory developments affecting the pharmaceutical and biotechnology industries. Provides information on generic drug approvals and includes a drug sector stock index.

Pipe Line and Gas Industry: Crude Oil and Products Pipelines, Gas Transmission and Gas Distribution. Gulf Publishing Co., Two Greenway Plz., Ste. 1020 Houston, TX 77046. Phone: 800-231-6275 or (713)529-4301 Fax: (713)520-4433 • URL: http://www.gulfpub.com • Monthly. Free to qualified personnel; others, $29.00 per year. International edition available.

Pipe Line Contractors Association., 1700 Pacific Ave., Ste. 4100 Dallas, TX 75201-4675. Phone: (214)969-2700 Fax: (214)969-2705 E-mail: plca@plca.org • URL: http://www.plca.org • Contractors of mainline cross-country pipeline. Associate members are equipment manufacturers, suppliers, and dealers. Represents the industry in labor negotiations.

Pipeline and Gas Journal Buyer's Guide. Oildom Publishing Co. of Texas Inc., PO Box 941669 Houston, TX 77079. Phone: (281)558-6930 Fax: (281)558-7029 E-mail: oklinger@oildompublishing.com • URL: http://www.oildompublishing.com • Annual. $75.00. Supplies and services. Lists over 700 companies supplying products and services used in construction and operation of cross-country pipeline and gas distribution systems.

Pipeline and Gas Journal: Energy Construction, Transportation and Distribution. Oildom Publishing of Texas, Inc., PO Box

941669 Houston, TX 77094-8669. Phone: (281)558-6930 Fax: (281)558-7029 E-mail: ginfo@undergroundinfo.com • URL: http://www.oildompublishing.com • Monthly. $33.00 per year. Covers engineering and operating methods on cross-country pipelines that transport crude oil products and natural gas. Includes *Energy Management Report*. Incorporates *Pipeline*.

Piping Guide: A Compact Reference for the Design and Drafting of Piping Systems. David R. Sherwood and Dennis J. Whistance. SYNTEC, Inc., 2702 Church Creek Lane Edgewater, MD 21037-1214. 1991. $89.00. Second edition.

PIRA. PIRA International Information Centre, Randalls Rd. Leatherhead, Surrey KT22 7RU, England. Phone: 44 1372 802056 Fax: 44 1372 802239 • URL: http://www.pira.co.uk • Citations and abstracts pertaining to bookbinding and other pulp, paper, and packaging industries, 1975 to present. Weekly updates. Inquire as to online cost and availability.

Pit and Quarry. Advanstar Communications, 545 Boylston St. Boston, MA 02116. Phone: 888-527-7008 or (617)267-6500 Fax: (617)267-6900 E-mail: info@advanstar.com • URL: http://www.advanstar.com • Monthly. $45.00 per year. Covers crushed stone, sand and gravel, etc.

Pit and Quarry Reference Manual and Buyers' Guide. Advanstar Communications, 545 Boylston St. Boston, MA 02116. Phone: 800-598-6008 or (617)267-6500 Fax: (617)267-6900 E-mail: info@advanstar.com • URL: http://www.advanstar.com • Annual. $25.00. Lists approximately 1,000 manufacturers and other suppliers of equipment products and services to the nonmetallic mining and quarrying industry. Absorbed: *Ready-Mix-Reference Manual*.

Pizza Today. National Association of Pizza Operators. Pete Lachapelle, 908 S 8th St., Ste. 200 Louisville, KY 40203. Phone: 800-489-8324 or (502)736-9500 Fax: (502)736-9502 E-mail: plachapelle@pizzatoday.com • URL: http://www.pizzatoday.com • Monthly. $29.95 per year. Covers both practical business topics and food topics for pizza establishments.

Pizzeria. Entrepreneur Media, Inc., 2445 McCabe Way Irvine, CA 92614. Phone: 800-421-2300 or (949)261-2325 Fax: (949)261-0234 E-mail: entmag@entrepreneur.com • URL: http://www.entrepreneur.com • Looseleaf. $59.50. A practical guide to starting a pizza shop. Covers profit potential, start-up costs, market size evaluation, owner's time required, site selection, lease negotiation, pricing, accounting, advertising, promotion, etc. (Start-Up Business Guide No. E1006.)

Placemaking: The Art and Practice of Building Communities. Lynda H. Schneekloth and Robert G. Shibley. John Wiley and Sons, Inc., 111 River St. Hoboken, NJ 07030. Phone: 800-225-5945 or (201)748-6000 Fax: (201)748-6088 E-mail: info@wiley.com • URL: http://www.wiley.com • 1995. $70.00.

Places, Towns, and Townships, 1998. Deirdre A. Gaquin and Richard W. Dodge, editors. Bernan Press, 4611-F Assembly Dr. Lanham, MD 20706-4391. Phone: 800-274-4447 or (301)459-2255 Fax: 800-865-3450 or (301)459-9235 E-mail: bpress@bernan.com • URL: http://www.bernan.com • 1997. $89.00. Second edition. Presents demographic and economic statistics from the U. S. Census Bureau and other government sources for places, cities, towns, villages, census designated places, and minor civil divisions. Contains more than 60 data categories. (Places, Towns and Townships Series).

Plan Sponsor. Asset International, Inc., 125 Greenwich Ave. Greenwich, CT 06830. Phone: (203)629-5014 Fax: (203)629-5024 Monthly. $150.00 per year. Edited for professional pension plan managers and executives. Defined contribution plans are emphasized.

Plane and Pilot. Werner Publishing Corp., 12121 Wilshire Blvd., No. 1200 Los Angeles, CA 90025-1176. Phone: 800-283-4330 or (310)820-1500 Fax: (310)826-5008 E-mail: editors@planeandpilotmag.com • URL: http://www.planeandpilotmag.com • Monthly. $9.97 per year.

Planning. American Planning Association, 122 S. Michigan Ave., Suite 1600 Chicago, IL 60603-6107. Phone: (312)431-9100 Fax: (312)431-9985 E-mail: bookservice@planning.org • URL: http://www.planning.org • Monthly. Free to members; non-members, $65.00 per year.

Planning and Zoning News. Planning and Zoning Center, Inc., 715 N. Cedar St. Lansing, MI 48906-5206. Phone: (517)886-0555 Fax: (517)886-0564 E-mail: freebury@pzcenter.com • URL: http://www.pzcenter.com • Monthly. $175.00 per year. Newsletter on planning and zoning issues in the United States.

Planning Cash Flow. American Management Association Extension Institute, 1601 Broadway New York, NY 10019. Phone: 800-262-9699 or (518)586-8100 Fax: (518)903-8168 • URL: http://www.amanet.org • Looseleaf. $139.00. Self-study course. Emphasis is on practical explanations, examples, and problem solving. Quizzes and a case study are included.

Planning for Long Term Care. McGraw-Hill, 1221 Ave. of the Americas New York, NY 10020. Phone: 800-722-4726 or (212)512-2000 Fax: (212)512-4502 E-mail: customer.service@mcgraw-hill.com • URL: http://www.mcgraw-hill.com • 2002. $14.95. Provides detailed information for consumers on long-term care insurance.

Planning for Water Source Protection. Philip M. Kappen. Sage Publications, Inc., 2455 Teller Rd. Thousand Oaks, CA 91320. Phone: 800-818-7243 or (805)499-9774 Fax: 800-583-2665 or (805)499-0871 E-mail: webmaster@sagepub.com • URL: http://www.sagepub.com • 1993. $10.00.

Planning for Your Retirement: IRA and Keogh Plans. CCH, Inc., 2700 Lake Cook Rd. Riverwoods, IL 60015. Phone: 800-835-5224 or (847)267-7000 E-mail: cust_serv@cch.com • URL: http://www.cch.com • Annual.

Plant Biotechnology Institute. National Research Council of Canada

Plant Engineering. Reed Business Information, 360 Park Ave. S New York, NY 10010. Phone: 800-446-6551 or (646)746-6400 Fax: (646)746-7028 E-mail: corporatecommunications@reedbusiness.com • URL: http://www.reedbusiness.com • 13 times a year. $131.99. per year. Includes *Plant Engineering Product Supplier Guide*.

Plant Layout and Materials Handling. James M. Apple. Krieger Publishing Co., P.O. Box 9542 Melbourne, FL 32902-9542. Phone: 800-724-0025 or (321)724-9542 Fax: (321)951-3671 E-mail: info@krieger-publishing.com • URL: http://www.krieger-publishing.com • 1991. $59.50. Reprint edition.

Plant Science Bulletin. Department of Biology, Macelwane Hall, 3507 Laclede Ave. Saint Louis, MO 63103. Phone: 800-SLU-FORU or (314)977-3900 Fax: (314)977-3658 E-mail: custserv@magnapubs.com • URL: http://www.botany.org • Description: Carries news of this Association of plant scientists, with some issues including brief articles of more general interest in the field. Recurring features include notices of awards, meetings, courses, and study and professional opportunities; annotated lists of botanical books; and book reviews.

Plant Services. Putman Media Inc., 555 W Pierce Rd., Suite 301 Itasca, IL 60143-2666. Phone: (630)467-1300 • URL: http://www.foodprocessing.com • Monthly. Free to qualified personnel.

Plants, Sites, and Parks. Reed Business Information, 360 Park Ave. S New York, NY 10010. Phone: 800-446-6551 or (646)746-6400 Fax: (646)746-7028 E-mail: corporatecommunications@reedbusiness.com • URL: http://www.reedbusiness.com • Seven times a year. Free to qualified personnel; others, $43.90 per year. Covers economic development, site location, industrial parks, and industrial development programs.

Plastics Digest on CD-ROM. Global Engineering Documents, Post Office Box 6510 Englewood, CO 80112. Phone: 800-854-7179 or (303)397-7956 Fax: (303)397-2740 Semiannual. CD-ROM index version (technical data only), $695.00 per year or $495.00 per disc. CD-ROM image version (technical data and specification sheet images), $1,295.00 per year or $995.00 per disc. Provides detailed information on the properties of 20,000 types of plastic, both current and obsolete. Time period is 1977 to date. Includes trade names and supplier names and addresses.

Plastics Engineering. Society of Plastics Engineers, Inc., 14 Fairfield Dr. Brookfield, CT 06804. Phone: (203)775-0471 Fax: (203)775-8490 E-mail: info@4spe.org • URL: http://www.4spe.org • Monthly. Free to members; non-members, $142.00 per year; corporations and libraries, $180.00 per year.

Plastics Institute of America.

Plastics News. Crain Communications, Inc., 1725 Merriman Rd., Suite 300 Akron, OH 44313-5283. Phone: 800-678-9595 or (330)836-9180 E-mail: info@crain.com • URL: http://www.crain.com • Weekly. $69.00 per year.

Plastics Pipe Institute., 105 Decker Ct., Ste. 825 Irving, TX 75062. Phone: 888-314-6774 or (469)499-1044 Fax: (469)499-1063 E-mail: info@plasticpipe.org • URL: http://www.plasticpipe.org • Manufacturers of plastic pipe and fittings and suppliers of plastic pipe raw materials. Develops technical reports and promotes trade and user acceptance. Compiles statistics; offers research programs. Conducts periodic training seminar on plastic piping.

Plastics Processing Technology. Edward A. Muccio. ASM International, 9639 Kinsman Rd. Materials Park, OH 44073-0002. Phone: 800-336-5152 or (440)338-5151 Fax: (440)338-4634 E-mail: cust-srv@asminternational.org • URL: http://www.asminternational.org • 1994. $99.00. Contains basic terminology and information on plastics for engineers, managers, technicians, purchasing agents, and students. Written to serve as a primer on plastics technology and processing.

Plastics Recognized Component Directory. Underwriters Laboratories Inc., 333 Pfingsten Rd. Northbrook, IL 60062-2096. Phone: 877-854-3577 or (847)272-8800 Fax: 877-854-3577 or (847)272-8129 E-mail: cec@us.ul.com • URL: http://www.ul.com • Covers: Companies that have qualified to use the UL recognized component marking on or in connection with materials that have been found to be in compliance with UL's requirements. Coverage includes foreign companies that manufacture for distribution in the U.S. Entries include: Company name, city, ZIP code, UL file number, type of product.

Plastics Technology Processing Handbook and Buyers' Guide. Gardner Publications Inc., 6915 Valley Ave. Cincinnati, OH 45244-3029. Phone: 800-950-8020 or (513)527-8800 Fax: (513)527-8801 • URL: http://www.gardnerweb.com • Annual. $89.00. Over 4,000 manufacturers of plastics processing equipment and materials. Included in subscription to *Plastics Technology*. Formerly *Plastcs Technology Manufacturing Handbook and Buyer's Guide*.

Plastics Technology: The Only Magazine for Plastics Processors. VNU Business Media, 770 Broadway New York, NY 10003-9595. Phone: 800-344-7119 or (646)654-4500 Fax: (646)654-7212 • URL: http://www.vnubusinessmedia.com • 13 times a year. Free to qualified personnel; others, $89.00 per year.

Plastics Week: The Global Newsletter. McGraw-Hill, 1221 Ave. of the Americas New York, NY 10020. Phone: 800-722-4726 or (212)512-2000 Fax: (212)512-4502 E-mail: customer.service@mcgraw-hill.com • URL: http://www.mcgraw-hill.com • Weekly. $530.00 per year. Newsletter. Covers international trends in plastics production, technology, research, and legislation.

Plating and Surface Finishing: Electroplating, Finishing of Metals, Organic Finishing. American Electroplaters and Surface Finishers Society, Inc., 12644 Research Parkway Orlando, FL 32826-3298. Phone: 800-334-2052 or (407)281-6441 Fax: (407)281-6446 E-mail: editors@aesf.org • URL: http://www.aesf.org • Monthly. Members, $16.00 per year; non-members, $60.00 per year.

Platinum Metals Review. Johnson Matthey PLC, 40-42 Hatton Garden London EC1N 8EE, United Kingdom. Phone: 44 20 7269 8000 Fax: 44 20 7269 8389 E-mail: jmpmr@matthey.com • URL: http://www.matthey.com • Quarterly. Free. Text in English and Japanese.

Platt's Directory of Electric Power Producers and Distributors. Platts, 2 Penn Plz. New York, NY 10125-2298. Phone: 800-752-8878 or (212)904-3070 Fax: (212)904-4209 E-mail: support@platt.com • URL: http://www.platts.com • Annual. $410.00. Over 3,500 investor-owned, municipal, rural cooperative and government electric utility systems in the U.S. and Canada. Formerly *Directory of Electric Power Producers and Distributors*.

Platt's Metals Week. Platt's, 2 Penn Plz. New York, NY 10121-2298. Phone: 800-752-8878 or (212)904-3070 Fax: (212)904-4209 E-mail: support@platts.com • URL: http://www.platts.com • Weekly. $770.00 per year.

Platt's Oilgram News. McGraw-Hill Inc., PO Box 182604 Columbus, OH 43272. Phone: 877-833-5524 or (212)512-2000 Fax: (614)759-3749 E-mail: customer.service@mcgraw-hill.com • URL: http://www.platts.com • Description: Monitors the latest developments in the politics and economics of petroleum. Covers exploration, production, supply and transportation, refining, and marketing. Recurring features include interviews, news of research, and reports of meetings. Coverage is global in scope.

Platt's Oilgram Price Report: an International Daily Oil-Gas Price and Marketing Letter. Platts, 2 Penn Plz. New York, NY 10121-2298. Phone: 800-752-8878 or (212)904-3070 Fax: (212)904-4209 E-mail: support@platts.com • URL: http://www.platts.com • Daily. Newsletter. Price on application. Prices and marketing intelligence for petroleum products. Includes weekly statistical summaries. Worldwide coverage.

Playthings—Buyers Guide. Reed Elsevier, 125 Park Ave., 23rd Fl. New York, NY 10017. Phone: 800-830-5939 or (212)309-5498 Fax: 800-526-4902 or (212)309-5480 E-mail: info@parkerdir.com Publication includes: Lists of toy manufacturers and their suppliers, designers and inventors, manufacturers' representatives, licensor, importers. Entries include: Company name, address, phone, description of products manufactured or lines carried.

Playthings: For Today's Merchandiser of Toys, Hobbies and Crafts. Reed Business Information, 360 Park Ave. S New York, NY 10010. Phone: 800-446-6551 or (646)746-6400 Fax: (646)746-7028 E-mail: corporatecommunications@reedbusiness.com • URL: http://www.reedbusiness.com • Monthly. $39.95 per year. Includes annual *Directory*. Covers the major toy and hobby categories, industry news and news products.

Pleasure Boats. Available from MarketResearch.com, 641 Ave. of the Americas, Third Floor New York, NY 10011. Phone: 800-298-5699 or (212)807-2629 Fax: (212)807-2716 E-mail: order@marketresearch.com • URL: http://www.marketresearch.com • 1997. $1,495.00. Market research report published by Specialists in Business Information. Covers inboard, outboard, sterndrive, sail, inflatable, personal watercraft, and canoes.

PlugIn Datamation: Profit and Value from Information Technology. EarthWeb, 23 Old Kings Highway Darien, CT 06820. Phone: (617)303-7906 Fax: (617)345-5486 E-mail: info@earthweb.com • URL: http://www.earthweb.com • Monthly. Price on application. Technical, semi-technical and general news covering EDP topics.

Plumbers Handbook. Howard C. Massey. Craftsman Book Co., 6058 Corte del Cedro Carlsbad, CA 92009. Phone: 800-829-8123 Fax: (760)438-0398 E-mail: jacobs@costbook.com • URL: http://www.craftsman-book.com • 1998. $32.00. Third revised edition.

Plumbing and Drainage Institute., c/o W.C. Whitehead, 45 Bristol Dr. South Easton, MA 02375. Phone: 800-589-8956 Fax: (508)230-3529 E-mail: info@pdionline.org • URL: http://www.pdionline.org • Formerly Plumbing and Drainage Manufacturers Association.

Plumbing Engineer. American Society of Plumbing Engineers., 8614 W. Catalpa Ave., No. 1007 Chicago, IL 60656-1116. Phone: (773)693-2773 Fax: (773)695-9007 E-mail: aspehq@aol.com • URL: http://www.aspe.org • Monthly. $50.00 per year.

Plumbing Fittings and Brass Goods. Available from MarketResearch.com, 641 Ave. of the Americas, Fourth Floor New York, NY 10011. Phone: 800-298-5699 or (212)807-2629 Fax: (212)807-2642 E-mail: order@marketresearch.

com • URL: http://www.marketresearch.com • 2002. $3,950. 00. Published by Global Industry Analysts. Provides worldwide market research data, including profiles of major plumbing equipment companies.

Plumbing Fixtures. U. S. Bureau of the Census, 4700 Silver Hill Rd. Washington, DC 20233-0001. Phone: (301)763-4636 E-mail: comments@census.gov • URL: http://www.census.gov • Quarterly and annual. Provides data on shipments: value, quantity, imports, and exports. Includes both metal and plastic fixtures. (Current Industrial Reports, MQ-34E.)

Plumbing-Heating-Cooling Contractors Association., PO Box 6808, PO Box 6808 Falls Church, VA 22046. Phone: 800-533-7694 or (703)237-8100 Fax: (703)237-7442 E-mail: naphcc@naphcc.org • URL: http://www.phccweb.org • Federation of state and local associations of plumbing, heating, and cooling contractors. Seeks to advance sanitation, encourage sanitary laws, and generally improve the plumbing, heating, ventilating, and air conditioning industries. Conducts apprenticeship training programs, workshops, seminars, political action committee, educational and research programs.

Plunkett's Advertising and Branding Industry Almanac. Plunkett Research, Ltd., P. O. Drawer 541737 Houston, TX 77254-1737. Phone: (713)932-0000 Fax: (713)932-7080 E-mail: info@plunkettresearch.com • URL: http://www.plunkettresearch.com • 2004. $249.99. Provides profiles of 300 leading firms in the areas of advertising, brand promotion, and corporate image, including marketing media, online advertising, and direct mail. Also covers industry trends and statistical data.

Plunkett's Airline, Hotel, and Travel Industry Almanac. Plunkett Research, Ltd., P. O. Drawer 541737 Houston, TX 77254-1737. Phone: (713)932-0000 Fax: (713)932-7080 E-mail: info@plunkettresearch.com • URL: http://www.plunkettresearch.com • Annual. $249.95. Contains profiles of 300 leading companies, including airlines, hotels, travel agencies, theme parks, cruise lines, casinos, and car rental companies.

Plunkett's Apparel and Textiles Industry Almanac. Plunkett Research, Ltd., P. O. Drawer 541737 Houston, TX 77254-1737. Phone: (713)932-0000 Fax: (713)932-7080 E-mail: info@plunkettresearch.com • URL: http://www.plunkettresearch.com • 2004. $249.99. Includes detailed profiles of 300 leading companies in such industries as clothing, footware, textile design, textile manufacturing, and apparel retailing. Also covers industry trends and statistical data.

Plunkett's Automobile Industry Almanac. Plunkett Research Ltd., PO Drawer 541737 Houston, TX 77254-1737. Phone: (713)932-0000 Fax: (713)932-7080 E-mail: customersupport@plunkettresearch.com • URL: http://www.plunkettresearch.com • Covers: 300 leading companies in the automotive industry. Entries include: Name, address, phone, fax, and key executives. Also includes analysis and information on trends, technology, and statistics in the field.

Plunkett's Biotech and Genetics Industry Almanac. Plunkett Research, Ltd., P. O. Drawer 541737 Houston, TX 77254-1737. Phone: (713)932-0000 Fax: (713)932-7080 E-mail: info@plunkettresearch.com • URL: http://www.plunkettresearch.com • Annual. $249.99. Provides detailed profiles of 400 leading biotech corporations. Includes information on current trends and research in the field of biotechnology/genetics.

Plunkett's E-Commerce and Internet Business Almanac. Plunkett Research, Ltd., P. O. Drawer 541737 Houston, TX 77254-1737. Phone: (713)932-0000 Fax: (713)932-7080 E-mail: info@plunkettresearch.com • URL: http://www.plunkettresearch.com • Annual. $249.99. Contains detailed profiles of 250 large companies engaged in various areas of Internet commerce, including e-business Web sites, communications equipment manufacturers, and Internet service providers. Includes CD-ROM.

Plunkett's Employers' Internet Sites with Careers Information. Plunkett Research, Ltd., P. O. Drawer 541737 Houston, TX 77254-1737. Phone: (713)932-0000 Fax: (713)932-7080 E-mail: info@plunkettresearch.com • URL: http://www.plunkettresearch.com • Annual. $199.99. Includes diskette.

Plunkett's Energy Industry Almanac: Complete Profiles on the Energy Industry 500 Companies. Plunkett Research Ltd., P. O. Drawer 541737 Houston, TX 77254-1737. Phone: (713)932-0000 Fax: (713)932-7080 E-mail: info@plunkettresearch.com • URL: http://www.plunkettresearch.com • Annual. $199.99. Includes major oil companies, utilities, pipelines, alternative energy companies, etc. Provides information on industry trends.

Plunkett's Engineering and Research Industry Almanac. Plunkett Research, Ltd., PO Drawer 541737 Houston, TX 77254-1737. Phone: (713)932-0000 Fax: (713)932-7080 E-mail: info@plunkettresearch.com • URL: http://www.plunkettresearch.com • Annual. $179.99. Contains detailed profiles of major engineering and technology corporations. Includes CD-ROM.

Plunkett's Financial Services Industry Almanac: The Only Comprehensive Overview of the Banking, Insurance, Credit and Investment Sectors. Plunkett Research, Ltd., P.O. Drawer 541737 Houston, TX 77254-1737. Phone: (713)932-0000 Fax: (713)932-7080 E-mail: info@plunkettresearch.com • URL: http://www.plunkettresearch.com • Annual. $229.99. Includes CD-ROM. Discusses important trends in various sectors of the financial industry. Five hundred major banking, credit card, investment, and financial services companies are profiled. (Business, Careers and Internet Reference Tools Series).

Plunkett's Food Industry Almanac. Plunkett Research Ltd., PO Drawer 541737 Houston, TX 77254-1737. Phone: (713)932-0000 Fax: (713)932-7080 E-mail: customersupport@plunkettresearch.com • URL: http://www.plunkettresearch.com • Covers: 340 leading companies in the global food industry. Entries include: Name, address, phone, fax, and key executives. Also includes analysis and information on trends, technology, and statistics in the field.

Plunkett's Health Care Industry Almanac: The Only Complete Guide to the Health Care Industry in America. Plunkett Research, Ltd., P.O. Drawer 541737 Houston, TX 77254-1737. Phone: (713)932-0000 Fax: (713)932-7080 E-mail: info@plunkettresearch.com • URL: http://www.plunkettresearch.com • Biennial. $229.99. Includes CD-ROM. Includes detailed profiles of 500 large companies providing health care products or services, with indexes by products, services, and location. Provides statistical and trend information for the health insurance industry, HMOs, hospital utilization, Medicare, medical technology, and national health expenditures.

Plunkett's InfoTech Industry Almanac: Complete Profiles on the InfoTech 500-the Leading Firms in the Movement and Management of Voice, Data, and Video. Plunkett Research, Ltd., P.O. Drawer 541737 Houston, TX 77254-1734. Phone: (713)932-0000 Fax: (713)932-7080 E-mail: info@plunkettresearch.com • URL: http://www.plunkettresearch.com • Biennial. $229.99. Includes CD-ROM. Five hundred major information companies are profiled, with corporate culture aspects. Discusses major trends in various sectors of the computer and information industry, including data on careers and job growth. Includes several indexes.

Plunkett's On-Line Trading, Finance, and Investment Web Sites Almanac. Plunkett Research, Ltd., PO Drawer 541737 Houston, TX 77254-1737. Phone: (713)932-0000 Fax: (713)932-7080 E-mail: info@plunkettresearch.com • URL: http://www.plunkettresearch.com • Annual. $149.99. Provides profiles and usefulness rankings of financial Web sites. Sites are rated from 1 to 5 for specific uses. Includes CD-ROM.

Plunkett's Real Estate and Construction Industry Almanac. Plunkett Research, Ltd., P. O. Drawer 541737 Houston, TX 77254-1737. Phone: (713)932-0000 Fax: (713)932-7080 E-mail: info@plunkettresearch.com • URL: http://www.plunkettresearch.com • 2004. $249.99. Contains profiles of 300 leading firms concerned with real estate or construction. Specialties include architecture, development, mortgages, building engineering, real estate sales, etc. Also covers industry trends and statistical data.

Plunkett's Retail Industry Almanac: Complete Profiles on the Retail 500-The Leading Firms in Retail Stores, Services, Catalogs, and On-Line Sales. Plunkett Research, Ltd., P.O. Drawer 541737 Houston, TX 77254-1737. Phone: (713)932-0000 Fax: (713)932-7080 E-mail: info@plunkettresearch.com • URL: http://www.plunkettresearch.com • 2001. $229.99. Includes CD-ROM. Provides detailed profiles of 500 major U. S. retailers. Industry trends are discussed.

Plunkett's Telecommunications Industry Almanac. Plunkett Research Ltd., PO Drawer 541737 Houston, TX 77254-1737. Phone: (713)932-0000 Fax: (713)932-7080 E-mail: customersupport@plunkettresearch.com • URL: http://www.plunkettresearch.com • Covers: 500 of the largest companies involved in telecommunications. Entries include: Name, address, phone, fax, names and titles of key personnel, subsidiary and branch names and locations, financial data, salaries and benefits, description of products/services, overview of company culture/activities.

Plunkett's Transportation and Logistics Industry Almanac. Plunkett Research, Ltd., P. O. Drawer 541737 Houston, TX 77254-1737. Phone: (713)932-0000 Fax: (713)932-7080 E-mail: info@plunkettresearch.com • URL: http://www.plunkettresearch.com • 2004. $249.99. Contains profiles of 300 leading companies in the fields of transportation, logistics, supply chain management, warehousing, distribution, and intermodal shipment systems. Includes industry trends and statistics.

PMA - The Worldwide Community of Imaging Associations., 3000 Picture Pl. Jackson, MI 49201-8853. Phone: 800-762-9287 or (517)788-8100 Fax: (517)788-8371 E-mail: pma_membership@pmai.org • URL: http://www.pmai.org • Retailers of photo and video equipment, film, and supplies; firms developing and printing film. Maintains hall of fame. Compiles statistics; conducts research and educational programs.

PMI Book of Project Management Forms. Project Management Institute, Four Campus Blvd. Newton Square, PA 19073-3299. Phone: (610)356-4600 Fax: (610)356-4647 E-mail: pmihq@pmi.org • URL: http://www.pmi.org • 1997. $49.95. Contains more than 100 sample forms for use in project management. Includes checklists, reports, charts, agreements, schedules, requisitions, order forms, and other documents.

PMMI Packaging Machinery Directory. PMMI, 4350 N Fairfax Dr., Ste. 600 Arlington, VA 22203. Phone: 888-275-7664 or (703)243-8555 Fax: (703)243-8556 E-mail: pmmiwebhelp@pmmi.org • URL: http://www.pmmi.org • Covers: 500 member companies that design, manufacture, sell, and service packaging and packaging-related converting machinery. Entries include: Company name, address, phone, names and titles of key personnel, products and services.

Pocket List of Railroad Officials. Commonwealth Business Media, 400 Windsor Corporate Ctr., 50 Millstone Rd., Ste. 200 East Windsor, NJ 08520-1415. Phone: 800-221-5488 or (609)371-7700 Fax: (609)371-7879 • URL: http://www.cbizmedia.com • Quarterly. $207.00 per year. Guide to over 30,000 officials in the freight railroad, rail transit and rail supply industries. Includes *Buyers' Guide*.

Pocket Station Listing Guide. Publications Dept., 5757 Wilshire Blvd., Penthouse 10 Los Angeles, CA 90036-3681. Phone: 800-628-7346 or (310)453-4440 Fax: (310)453-5258 E-mail: info@natpe.org • URL: http://www.natpe.org • Covers: 1,500 network-affiliated, independent, and public television stations in the U.S., Canada, and Latin America. Entries include: Station name, address, phone, fax, names and titles of key personnel, geographical area served, call letters, channel station numbers, owner, sales representative.

Podiatry Management. Kane Communications, Inc., 7000 Terminal Square, Suite 210 Upper Darby, PA 19082. Phone: (610)734-2420 Fax: (610)734-2423 Nine times a year. $30.00 per year. Non-clinical subject matter.

Point, Click & Wow! A Quick Guide to Brilliant Laptop Presentations. Claudyne Wilder and David Fine. John Wiley and Sons, Inc., 111 River St. Hoboken, NJ 07030. Phone: 800-225-5945 or (201)748-6000 Fax: (201)748-6088 E-mail: info@wiley.com • URL: http://www.wiley.com • 2002. $19.95. Second edition. Emphasis is on thorough preparation for effective presentations via a laptop computer. Provides general advice on color, graphics, animation, content, and relating to a specific audience or customer. Includes checklists and CD-ROM.

Point-of-Purchase Advertising International., 1600 Duke St., Ste. 400 Alexandria, VA 22314. Phone: (703)373-8800 Fax: (703)373-8801 E-mail: info@popai.com • URL: http://www.popai.com • Producers and suppliers of point-of-purchase advertising signs and displays and national and regional advertisers and retailers interested in use and effectiveness of signs, displays, and other point-of-purchase media. Conducts student education programs; maintains speakers' bureau.

Police: Buyer's Guide. Bobit Publications, 21061 S. Western Ave. Torrance, CA 90501. Phone: (310)533-2400 Fax: (310)533-2500 E-mail: info@policemag.com • URL: http://www.bobit.com • Annual. $3.00. Lists suppliers of products and services for police departments.

Police Chief: Buyer's Guide. Bobit Publishing, 21061 S. Western Ave. Torrance, CA 90501. Phone: (310)533-2400 Fax: (310)533-2504 E-mail: info@policemag.com • URL: http://www.policemag.com • Annual. $3.00. Contains a list of suppliers of equipment and services for police departments.

Police Chief: Professional Voice of Law Enforcement. International Association of Chiefs of Police, 515 N. Washington St., Suite 200 Alexandria, VA 22314-2340. Phone: 800-843-4227 or (703)243-6500 Fax: (703)836-4543 Monthly. $25.00 per year. Subject matter includes information on law enforcement technology and new products.

Police Executive Research Forum. Police Executive Research Forum, 1120 Connecticut Ave. NW, Ste. 930 Washington, DC 20036. Phone: 877-576-5423 or (202)466-7820 Fax: (202)466-7826 E-mail: cwexler@policeforum.org • URL: http://www.policeforum.org • Policing, including studies on community policing, operational and administrative procedures, police management, police response strategies, criminal investigations, drug abuse and enforcement, problem-oriented policing.

Police Markets of North America and the European Union. Charles LeMesurier and Marc Arnold. Jane's Information Group, Inc., 110 N Royal St. Alexandria, VA 22314. Phone: 800-824-0768 or (703)683-3700 Fax: 800-836-0297 or (703)836-0297 E-mail: info.us@janes.com • URL: http://www.janes.com • 1997. $695.00. Provides detailed market research data relative to the police and security industry. Covers a wide range of equipment and vehicle markets geographically for U. S. states, Canadian provinces, and countries. (Law Enforcement Series).

Police Misconduct and Civil Rights Law Report. National Lawyers Guild. West Group, 610 Opperman Dr. Eagan, MN 55123. Phone: 800-328-4880 or (651)687-7000 Fax: 800-340-9378 E-mail: bookstore@westgroup.com • URL: http://www.westgroup.com • $297.00. Newsletter. Periodic supplementation.

Police Science and Technology Review. Jane's Information Group, 110 N Royal St. Alexandria, VA 22314. Phone: 800-824-0768 or (703)683-3700 Fax: 800-836-0297 or (703)836-0297 E-mail: info.us@janes.com • URL: http://www.janes.com • Quarterly. $57.00 per year. Includes detailed information on technology relating to surveillance, forensics, and fingerprints.

Police: The Law Officer's Magazine. Bobit Publications, 21061 S. Western Ave. Torrance, CA 90501. Phone: (310)533-2400 Fax: (310)533-2500 E-mail: info@policemag.com • URL: http://www.bobit.com • Monthly. $25.00 per year. Edited for law enforcement professionals. Includes information on new technology and equipment.

Policy and Practice of Public Human Services. American Public Human Services Association, 810 First St., NE, Ste. 500 Washington, DC 20002. Phone: (202)682-0100 Fax:

(202)289-6555 E-mail: sbarnes@aphsa.org • URL: http://www.aphsa.org • Quarterly. $75.00 per year. Formerly *Public Welfare*.

Policy Research Institute. University of Kansas, 607 Blake Hall, 1541 Lilac Ln. Lawrence, KS 66044-3177. Phone: (785)864-9105 Fax: (785)864-3683 E-mail: thelyar@ukans.edu • URL: http://www.ukans.edu/pri • Formerly Institute for Public Policy and Business Research.

Policy Statistics Service. The National Underwriter Co.

Political Department of the AFL-CIO., 815 16th St. NW, 7th Fl. Washington, DC 20006. Phone: (202)637-5000 Fax: (202)637-5058 E-mail: feedback@aflcio.org • URL: http://www.aflcio.org • AFL-CIO members and others interested in helping to elect progressive and pro-labor candidates to public office.

Political Risk Letter. The PRS Group, 6320 Fly Rd., Ste. 102, PO Box 248 East Syracuse, NY 13057. Phone: 800-298-5699 or (315)431-0511 Fax: (315)431-0200 E-mail: custserv@prsgroup.com • URL: http://www.marketresearch.com • Description: Offers concise political and economic forecasts for both 18 month and 5 year time spans. Provides country risk forecasts and analysis on 100 countries around the world and provides indepth coverage on 20 countries.

Political Risk Yearbook. The PRS Group, Inc., P.O. Box 248 East Syracuse, NY 13057-0248. Phone: (315)431-0511 Fax: (315)431-0200 E-mail: custserv@prsgroup.com • URL: http://www.prsgroup.com • Annual. $2,415.00. Seven regional volumes; $345.00 per volume. Each volume covers a separate region of the world and assesses economic and political conditions as they relate to the risk of doing business.

Politics of Taxation: Revenue Without Representation. Susan B. Hansen. Greenwood Publishing Group, Inc, 88 Post Rd., W. Westport, CT 06881. Phone: 800-225-5800 or (203)226-3571 Fax: (203)431-2214 E-mail: customer-service@greenwood.com • URL: http://www.greenwood.com • 1983. $70.00.

Polling Report: An Independent Survey of Trends Affecting Elections, Government, and Business. Polling Report, Inc., P.O. Box 42580 Washington, DC 20015-0580. Phone: (202)237-2000 Fax: (202)237-2001 E-mail: editor@pollingreport.com • URL: http://www.pollingreport.com • Biweekly. Individuals, $195.00 per year; students, $78.00 per year. Newsletter. Reports on the results of a wide variety of public opinion polls.

Pollution A to Z. Gale Cengage Learning, 27500 Drake Rd. Farmington Hills, MI 48331-3535. Phone: 800-877-GALE Fax: 800-414-5043 or (248)699-8069 E-mail: galeord@galegroup.com • URL: http://www.galegroup.com • 2003. $195.00. Two volumes. Provides encyclopedic coverage of many aspects of environmental pollution, including air, water, noise, and soil. (Macmillan Reference USA imprint.)

Pollution Abstracts. Cambridge Information Group, 7200 Wisconsin Ave., Suite 601 Bethesda, MD 20814. Phone: 800-843-7751 or (301)961-6700 Fax: (301)961-6720 E-mail: service@csa.com • URL: http://www.csa.com • Monthly. $1,390.00 per year. Includes print and online editions; with index, $1,515.00 per year.

Pollution Abstracts [online]. Cambridge Scientific Abstracts, 7200 Wisconsin Ave., 6th Fl. Bethesda, MD 20814. Phone: 800-843-7751 or (301)961-6700 Fax: (301)961-6720 Provides indexing and abstracting of international, environmentally related literature, 1970 to date. Monthly updates. Inquire as to online cost and availability.

Pollution: Causes, Effects, and Control. R. M. Harrison. Springer-Verlag, 175 Fifth Ave. New York, NY 10010. Phone: 800-777-4643 or (212)460-1500 Fax: (201)348-4505 E-mail: service@springer-ny.com • URL: http://www.springer-ny.com • 2001. $62.00. Fourth edition. Published by The Royal Society of Chemistry. A basic introduction to pollution of air, water, and land. Includes discussions of pollution control technologies.

Pollution Engineering Buyer's Guide. BNP Media, 2401 W Big Beaver Rd., Ste. 700 Troy, MI 48084. Phone: 800-952-6643 or (248)362-3700 Fax: (248)362-0317 E-mail: info@bnpmedia.com • URL: http://www.bnp.com • Publication includes: Lists of about 32,000 suppliers of equipment and services for the environmental control field, and about 2,500 companies providing independent services as consultants, contractors, or managers for the pollution control industry and other industries concerned with the environment. Entries include: Company name, address, phone.

Pollution Engineering: Magazine of Environmental Control. Business News Publishing Co., 755 W Big Beaver Rd., Ste. 1000 Troy, MI 48084. Phone: 800-662-7776 or (248)362-3700 Fax: (248)362-0317 • URL: http://www.bnp.com • 13 times a year. $85.90 per year.

Pollution Equipment News Buyer's Guide. Rimbach Publishing, Inc., 8650 Babcock Blvd. Pittsburgh, PA 15237. Phone: 800-245-3182 or (412)364-5366 Fax: (412)369-9720 E-mail: info@rimbach.com • URL: http://www.rimbach.com • Annual. $100.00. Over 3,000 manufacturers of pollution control equipment and products.

Polymer Engineering and Science. Society of Plastics Engineers, Inc., 14 Fairfield Dr. Brookfield, CT 06804-0403. Phone: (203)775-0471 Fax: (203)775-8490 E-mail: info@4spe.org • URL: http://www.4spe.org • Monthly. Members, $330.00 per year; non-members, $470.00 per year; institutions, $915.00 per year. Includes six special issues.

Polymer Handbook. Johannes Brandup and others, editors. John Wiley and Sons, Inc., 111 River St. Hoboken, NJ 07030. Phone: 800-225-5945 or (201)748-6000 Fax: (201)748-6088 E-mail: info@wiley.com • URL: http://www.wiley.com • 2003. $197.50. Fifth edition. Emphasis is on advances in polymer science since 1989 and descriptions of polymeric materials. (Polymer Handbook Series).

Polymer Processing: Principles and Design. Donald G. Baird and Dimitria I. Collias. John Wiley and Sons, Inc., 111 River St. Hoboken, NJ 07030. Phone: 800-225-5945 or (201)748-6000 Fax: (201)748-6088 E-mail: info@wiley.com • URL: http://www.wiley.com • 1998. $105.95. A practical guide to thermoplastics.

Polymer Research Center. University of Cincinnati

Polymer Research Laboratory. University of Michigan

Pool and Spa News Source Book Directory. Leisure Publications, 4160 Wilshire Blvd. Los Angeles, CA 90010. Phone: 800-613-8223 or (323)964-4800 Fax: (323)964-4986 E-mail: poolspanews@hanley-wood.com • URL: http://www.poolspanews.com • Annual. $49.50. List of 1,500 manufacturers and distributors of pool, spa, and hot water equipment and supplies.

Pool and Spa News: The National Trade Magazine for the Swimming Poool & Spa Industry. Hanley-Wood, LLc, One Thomas Circle, NW Washington, DC 20005. Phone: 800-837-0870 or (202)452-0800 Fax: (202)785-1974 • URL: http://www.hanley-wood.com • Semimonthly. $19.97 per year.

Popcorn Institute., 401 N Michigan Ave., Ste. 2200 Chicago, IL 60611-4267. Phone: 877-POP-ALOT or (312)644-6610 Fax: 877-767-2568 or (312)527-6783 E-mail: gbertalmio@smithbucklin.com • URL: http://www.popcorn.org • Represents companies engaged in popcorn processing and trade management activities as well as government relations. Provides a platform for discussion on the popcorn industry. Maintains hall of fame for retired members who have made contributions to the industry.

Poptronics. Gernsback Publications, Inc., 275-G Marcus Blvd. Hauppage, NY 11788. Phone: (631)592-6720 Fax: (631)592-6723 E-mail: info@poptronics.com • URL: http://www.gernsback.com • Monthly. $19.99 per year. Incorporates *Electronics Now*.

Population Abstract of the U. S. Gale Cengage Learning, 27500 Drake Rd. Farmington Hills, MI 48331-3535. Phone: 800-877-GALE or (248)699-4253 Fax: 800-414-5043 E-mail: gale.galeord@cengage.com • URL: http://gale.cengage.com • 1999. $190.00. Historical emphasis. Includes a "breakdown of urban and rural population from the earliest census to the present."

Population Action International., 1300 19th St. NW, Ste. 200 Washington, DC 20036. Phone: (202)557-3400 Fax: (202)728-4177 E-mail: pai@popact.org • URL: http://www.populationaction.org • Seeks to advance policies and programs that slow population growth in order to enhance the quality of life for all ages. Advocates expansion of voluntary family planning, other reproductive health services, and educational and economic opportunities for girls and women.

Population and Development Review. Blackwell Publishing, 350 Main St., 6th Fl. Malden, MA 02148-5018. Phone: (781)388-8200 Fax: (781)388-8210 E-mail: subscript@blackwellpub.com • URL: http://www.blackwellpub.com • Quarterly. Institutions, $105.00 per year. Includes print and online editions.*Supplement* available. Text in English; summaries in English, French and Spanish.

Population and Vital Statistics Report. United Nations Publications, United Nations Concourse Level, First Ave., 46th St. New York, NY 10017. Phone: 800-553-3210 or (212)963-7680 Fax: (212)963-4910 E-mail: bookstore@un.org • URL: http://www.un.org/publications • Quarterly. $40.00 per year. Contains worldwide demographic statistics.

Population Association of America., 8630 Fenton St., Ste. 722 Silver Spring, MD 20910. Phone: (301)565-6710 Fax: (301)565-7850 E-mail: info@popassoc.org • URL: http://www.popassoc.org • Individuals interested in demography and its scientific aspects.

Population Bulletin. Population Reference Bureau, Inc., 1875 Connecticut Ave., N.W., Suite 520 Washington, DC 20009. Phone: 800-877-9881 or (202)939-5407 Fax: (202)328-3937 E-mail: popref@prb.org • URL: http://www.prb.org • Quarterly. $49.00 per year.

Population Connection., 2120 L St. NW, Ste. 500 Washington, DC 20037. Phone: 800-POP-1956 or (202)332-2200 Fax: (202)332-2302 E-mail: info@populationconnection.org • URL: http://www.populationconnection.org • Works to educate and motivate Americans to help meet global population challenge, and to mobilize support for the adoption of policies and programs necessary to stop global population growth. Participates in coalitions, influences governmental policies on the international, national, state, and local levels; works with the media; engages in teacher training and public education programs. Conducts research, interprets and applies the research of others. Maintains speakers' bureau; compiles statistics.

Population Council., 1 Dag Hammarskjold Plz. New York, NY 10017. Phone: (212)339-0500 Fax: (212)755-6052 E-mail: pubinfo@popcouncil.org • URL: http://www.popcouncil.org • Seeks to improve the well-being and reproductive health of current and future generations around the world. Helps achieve a humane, equitable, and sustainable balance between people and resources.

Population of States and Counties of the United States: 1790-1990. Available from National Technical Information Service, 5285 Port Royal Rd. Springfield, VA 22161. Phone: 800-553-6847 or (703)487-4600 Fax: (703)321-8547 E-mail: info@ntis.fedworld.gov • URL: http://www.ntis.gov • 1996. $35.00. Issued by the U. S. Census Bureau (http://www.census.gov). Provides data on the number of inhabitants of the U. S., states, territories, and counties according to 21 decennial censuses from 1790 to 1990. Includes descriptions of county origins and lists prior county names, where applicable.

Population Reference Bureau., 1875 Connecticut Ave. NW, Ste. 520 Washington, DC 20009-5728. Phone: 800-877-9881 or (202)483-1100 Fax: (202)328-3937 E-mail: popref@prb.org • URL: http://www.prb.org • Gathers, interprets, and disseminates information on the facts and implications of national and world population trends.

Population Research Center. University of Chicago

Population Studies Center. University of Michigan

Portable Power Equipment Manufacturers Association., 4330 East-West Hwy., Ste. 310 Bethesda, MD 20814. Phone: (301)652-0774 Fax: (301)654-6138 E-mail: popref@prb.org • URL: http://www.ppema.org • Manufacturers of gasoline and electric powered chain saws, monofilament trimmers, brush cutters, hand-held blowers, backpack blowers, hedge trimmers, cut-off saws, and portable gasoline-powered generators. Encourages research and development of standards.

Portable Power Tools. Time-Life, Inc., 2000 Duke St. Alexandria, VA 22314. Phone: 800-950-7887 or (703)838-7000 Fax: 800-308-1083 or (703)838-7090 • URL: http://www.timelife.com • 1992. $14.95. Contains popular descriptions of power tools for woodworking. (Art of Woodworking Series).

Portfolio Management Formulas: Mathematical Trading Methods for the Futures, Options, and Stock Markets. Ralph Vince. John Wiley and Sons, Inc., 111 River St. Hoboken, NJ 07030. Phone: 800-225-5945 or (201)748-6000 Fax: (201)748-6088 E-mail: info@wiley.com • URL: http://www.wiley.com • 1990. $90.00. Discusses optimization of trading systems by exploiting the rules of probability and making use of the principles of modern portfolio management theory. Computer programs are included. (Finance Series).

Portfolio Management in Practice. Christine Brentani. Elsevier Butterworth Heinemann, 200 Wheeler Rd., Sixth Floor Burlington, MA 01803. Phone: 800-545-2522 or (781)221-2212 Fax: 800-568-5136 or (781)313-4880 E-mail: usbkinfo@elsevier.com • URL: http://www.books.elsevier.com/finance • 2003. $40.00. Serves as a basic text on portfolio management. Among the topics covered are portfolio theory, portfolio construction, valuation methodologies, measuring returns, financial statement analysis, and financial ratios. Includes a glossary.

Portfolio Selection: Efficient Diversification of Investments. Harry M. Markowitz. Blackwell Publishing, 350 Main St. Malden, MA 02148. Phone: 800-835-6770 or (781)388-8200 Fax: (781)388-8210 E-mail: books@blackwellpub.com • URL: http://www.blackwellpub.com • 1991. $66.95. Second edition. A standard work on diversification of investments for institutions. Provides a mathematical approach.

Portland Cement Association., 5420 Old Orchard Rd. Skokie, IL 60077-1053. Phone: (847)966-6200 Fax: (847)966-8389 E-mail: info@cement.org • URL: http://www.cement.org • Companies in the U.S. and Canada. Seeks to improve and extend the uses of Portland cement and concrete through market promotion, research and development, educational programs, and representation with governmental entities. Conducts research on concrete technology and durability; concrete pavement design; load-bearing capacities, field performance, and fire resistance of concrete; transportation, building, and structural uses of concrete. Operates Construction +Technology +Laboratories, which conducts research and technical services in construction materials, products, and applications. Sponsors a public affairs program in Washington, DC.

Position Descriptions in Special Libraries. Del Sweeney and Karin Zilla, editors. Special Libraries Association, 1700 18th St., N. W. Washington, DC 20009-2514. Phone: (202)234-4700 Fax: (202)265-9317 E-mail: sla@sla.org • URL: http://www.sla.org • 1996. $41.00. Third revised edition. Provides 87 descriptions of library and information management positions.

Positive Leadership: Improving Performance Through Value-Centered Management. Lawrence Ragan Communications, Inc., 316 N. Michigan Ave. Chicago, IL 60601. Phone: 800-878-5331 or (312)960-4100 Fax: (312)960-4106 E-mail: cservice@ragan.com • URL: http://www.ragan.com • Monthly. $99.00 per year. Newsletter. Emphasis is on employee motivation, family issues, ethics, and community relations.

Postal Bulletin. Available from U. S. Government Printing Office, Washington, DC 20402. Phone: (202)512-1800 Fax: (202)512-2250 E-mail: gpoaccess@gpo.gov • URL: http://www.access.gpo.gov • Biweekly. $163.00 per year. Issued by the United States Postal Service. Contains orders, instructions, and information relating to U. S. mail service.

Postal Service. Available from U. S. Government Printing Office, Washington, DC 20402. Phone: (202)512-1800 Fax: (202)512-2250 E-mail: gpoaccess@gpo.gov • URL: http://www.access.gpo.gov • Annual. Free. Issued by the Superintendent of Documents. A list of government publica-

SOURCES CITED

tions on mail services and the post office. (Subject Bibliography No. 169.)

Postal World. United Communications Group, 11300 Rockville Pke., Ste. 1100 Rockville, MD 20852-3030. Phone: 800-929-4824 or (301)287-2700 Fax: (301)816-8945 E-mail: webmaster@ucg.com • URL: http://www.ucg.com • Description: Disseminates information to help readers run a more efficient mail operation. "Discusses how to trim postage costs, speed delivery, improve mailroom productivity, and plan for rate increases." Recurring features include an annual salary survey and periodic special reports.

Potash and Phosphate Institute., 655 Engineering Dr., No. 110 Norcross, GA 30092-2837. Phone: (770)447-0335 Fax: (770)448-0439 E-mail: ppi@ppi-ppic.org • URL: http://www.ppi-ppic.org • Formerly Potash Institute.

Potato Abstracts. Available from CABI Publishing, North America, 875 Massachusetts Ave., 7th Fl. Cambridge, MA 02139. Phone: 800-528-4841 or (617)395-4056 Fax: (617)354-6875 E-mail: cabi-nao@cabi.org • URL: http://www.cabi-publishing.org • Bimonthly. Institutions, $610.00 per year. Online edition available, $640.00 per year. Includes single site internet access. Published in England by CABI Publishing. Provides worldwide coverage of the literature.

Potato Association of America.

Potato Grower of Idaho. Harris Publishing, Inc., 360 B St. Idaho Falls, ID 83402. Phone: (208)524-7000 Fax: (208)522-5241 E-mail: info@harrispublishing.com • URL: http://www.harrispublishing.com • Monthly. $15.95 per year.

Potentials: Ideas and Products that Motivate. VNU Business Media, 770 Broadway New York, NY 10003-9595. Phone: 800-344-7119 or (646)654-4500 Fax: (646)654-7212 • URL: http://www.vnubusinessmedia.com • Monthly. $59.00 per year. Covers incentives, premiums, awards, and gifts as related to promotional activities. Formerly *Potentials in Marketing*.

Potter's Dictionary of Materials and Techniques. Frank Hamer and Janet Hamer. Gordon and Breach Publishing Group, 29 W 35th St. New York, NY 10001. Phone: 800-634-7064 or (212)216-7800 Fax: (212)564-7854 • URL: http://www.gbhap.com • 1997. $85.00. Fourth edition.

Poultry Abstracts. Available from CABI Publishing, North America, 875 Massachusetts Ave., 7th Fl. Cambridge, MA 02139. Phone: 800-528-4841 or (617)395-4056 Fax: (617)354-6875 E-mail: cabi-nao@cabi.org • URL: http://www.cabi-publishing.org • Monthly. Institutions, $760.00 per year. Online edition available. Single site internet access, $735.00 per year. Published in England by CABI Publishing. Provides worldwide coverage of the literature.

Poultry and Egg Marketing: The Bi-Monthly News Magazine of the Poultry Marketing Industry. Poultry and Egg News, 345 Green St., N.W. Gainesville, GA 30503. Phone: (770)536-2476 Fax: (770)532-4894 • URL: http://www.poultryandeggnews.com • Bimonthly. Free to qualified personnel; others, $6.00 per year. Processing and marketing of eggs and poultry products.

Poultry Science. Poultry Science Association, Inc., 1111 N. Dunlap Ave. Savoy, IL 61874. Phone: (217)356-3182 Fax: (217)398-4119 E-mail: psa@assochq.org • URL: http://www.poultryscience.org • Monthly. Members, $95.00 per year; institutions, $400.00 per year. Includes print and online editions.

Poultry Science. Colin G. Scanes and others. Prentice Hall PTR, 240 Frisch Ct. Paramus, NJ 07652. Phone: 800-282-0693 Fax: 800-445-6991 • URL: http://www.phptr.com • 2003. $100.00. Fourth edition.

Poultry Science Association., 1111 N Dunlap Ave. Savoy, IL 61874. Phone: (217)356-5285 Fax: (217)398-4119 E-mail: jcarey@poultry.tamu.edu • URL: http://www.poultryscience.org • Members are from academia, industry, and government, with many involved in the research, teaching, or extension of poultry science and related fields.

Poultry Times. Poultry and Egg News, 345 Green St., NW Gainesville, GA 30503. Phone: (770)536-2476 Fax: (770)532-4894 • URL: http://www.poultryandeggnews.com • Biweekly. $9.00 per year. Directed to grow-out operations for the egg and poultry business.

Poultry USA. Watt Publishing Co., 122 S Wesley Ave. Mount Morris, IL 61054. Phone: (815)734-4171 Fax: (815)734-4201 • URL: http://www.wattnet.com • Bionthly. $28.00 per year. Incorporate *Broiler Industry*.

Powder Coating Institute., 2121 Eisenhower Ave., Ste. 401 Alexandria, VA 22314. Phone: 800-988-COAT or (703)684-1770 Fax: (703)684-1771 E-mail: pci-info@powdercoating.org • URL: http://www.powdercoating.org • Individuals and businesses that manufacture, sell, or develop powder coating materials and equipment. Promotes the application and use of powder coating technology among industrial finishers; disseminates information to both consumers and the industry on the value and performance of powder coating; supports educational programs in the industrial coating/finishing field; updates members, governmental departments, and regulatory agencies on the activities and developments concerning the manufacture, application, and proper handling of powder coatings. Presents technical papers at conferences of related organizations and prepares articles for the media on the powder coating industry.

Powder Metallurgy. Institute of Materials, Minerals and Mining., One Carlton House Terrace London SW1Y 5DB, United Kingdom. E-mail: materials.world@iom3.org • URL: http://www.iom3.org • Quarterly. Institutions, $557.00 per Year.

Powell Monetary Analyst. Larson M. Powell, editor. Reserve Research Ltd., PO Box 4135 Portland, ME 04101. Phone: (207)774-4971 E-mail: webmaster@ucg.com Description: Offers investment advice concentrating on precious metals, gold coins, currencies, and mining stocks.

Power. McGraw-Hill Inc., PO Box 182604 Columbus, OH 43272. Phone: 877-833-5524 or (212)512-2000 Fax: (614)759-3749 E-mail: customer.service@mcgraw-hill.com • URL: http://www.mcgraw-hill.com • Description: Covers design, operation, construction, and maintenance of power plants for utilities, process industries, and manufacturers.

Power and Communication Contractors Association., 103 Oronoco St., Ste. 200 Alexandria, VA 22314. Phone: 800-542-7222 or (703)212-7734 Fax: (703)548-3733 E-mail: info@pccaweb.org • URL: http://www.pccaweb.org • Contractors engaged in electrical power and communication line construction.

Power Engineering International. PennWell Corp., Industrial Div., 1421 S. Sheridan Rd Tulsa, OK 74112. Phone: 800-331-4463 or (918)835-8161 E-mail: bid@pennwell.com • URL: http://www.pennwell.com • Monthly. $170.00 per year.

Power Equipment Trade. Hatton-Brown Publishers, Inc., 225 Hanrick St. Montgomery, AL 36104. Phone: 800-699-5613 or (334)834-1170 Fax: (334)834-4525 E-mail: mail@hattonbrown.com • URL: http://www.hattonbrown.com • 10 times a year. $40.00 per year. Formerly *Chain Saw Age and Power Equipment Trade*.

Power Generation Technology and Markets. Pasha Publishing Inc., 1600 Wilson Blvd., Suite 600 Arlington, VA 22209. Phone: (703)816-8642 Fax: (703)528-7821 Weekly. $790.00 per year. Newsletter. Formerly *Coal and Synfuels Technology*.

Power Media Yearbook. Broadcast Interview Source, 2233 Wisconsin Ave. NW Washington, DC 20007-4132. Phone: 800-932-7266 or (202)333-5000 Fax: (202)333-4904 E-mail: editor@yearbook.com Covers: Approximately 3,000 media contacts throughout the United States, including newswire services, syndicates, syndicated columnists, national newspapers, magazines, radio and television talk shows, etc. Entries include: Outlet name, address, phone, fax, names and titles of key personnel, geographical area served, and branch offices.

Power-Motion Technology Representatives Association., 1 Spectrum Pointe, Ste. 150 Lake Forest, CA 92630. Phone: 888-817-7872 or (949)859-2885 Fax: (949)855-2973 E-mail: info@ptra.org • URL: http://www.ptra.org • Manufacturers and independent manufacturers representatives in the power transmission industry. Seeks to provide a channel of communication between manufacturers' independent representatives and their principals, and other manufacturers within the industry by allowing interchange of sound business management ideas and by offering consultation on solving operational problems. Provides information and referral; compiles surveys. Offers training programs that include panels, table talk discussions, and seminars on special topics.

The Power of Gold: The History of an Obsession. Peter L. Bernstein. John Wiley and Sons, Inc., 111 River St. Hoboken, NJ 10158-0012. Phone: 800-225-5945 or (201)748-6000 Fax: (201)748-6088 E-mail: info@wiley.com • URL: http://www.wiley.com • 2000. $27.95. Covers the economic and financial history of gold from ancient times to the present.

Power Pricing: How Managing Price Transforms the Bottom Line. Robert J. Dolan and Hermann Simon. The Free Press, 1230 Ave. of the Americas New York, NY 10020. Phone: 800-223-2348 or (212)698-7000 E-mail: consumer.customerservice@simonandschuster.com • URL: http://www.simonsays.com • 1997. $40.00. Among topics included are pricing strategy, price customization, international pricing, nonlinear pricing, product-line pricing, and price bundling.

Power Resumes. Ronald Tepper. John Wiley and Sons, Inc., 111 River St. Hoboken, NJ 07030. Phone: 800-225-5945 or (201)748-6000 Fax: (201)748-6088 E-mail: info@wiley.com • URL: http://www.wiley.com • 1998. $14.95. Third edition. Offers 71 techniques for more effective resumes.

Power System Operation. Robert H. Miller. McGraw-Hill, 1221 Ave. of the Americas New York, NY 10020. Phone: 800-722-4726 or (212)512-2000 Fax: (212)512-4502 E-mail: customer.service@mcgraw-hill.com • URL: http://www.mcgraw-hill.com • 1994. $65.00. Third edition.

Power Tool Institute., 1300 Sumner Ave., 1300 Sumner Ave. Cleveland, OH 44115-2851. Phone: (216)241-7333 Fax: (216)241-0105 E-mail: pti@powertoolinstitute.com • URL: http://www.powertoolinstitute.com • Represents manufacturers of portable and stationary tools, both electric and battery operated. Distributes publications and videos on power tool safety. Offers educational programs.

Power Transmission Distributors Association., 230 W Monroe, Ste. 1410 Chicago, IL 60606-4703. Phone: (312)516-2100 Fax: (312)516-2101 E-mail: ptda@ptda.org • URL: http://www.ptda.org • Distributors and manufacturers of power transmission/motion and position control equipment. Maintains business management and continuing education resources; conducts educational programs; compiles statistics; sponsors industry summit; conducts research; cosponsors industry tradeshows.

Powerful Public Relations: A How-To Guide for Libraries. Rashelle S. Karp, editor. American Library Association, 50 E Huron St. Chicago, IL 60611-2795. Phone: 800-545-2433 or (312)944-6780 Fax: (312)440-9374 E-mail: ala@ala.org • URL: http://www.ala.org • 2002. $32.00. Provides concise coverage of library press releases, public service announcements, brochures, special events, exhibits, and use of multimedia.

PPI Detailed Report. Bureau of Labor Statistics, U.S. Department of Labor. Available from U.S. Government Printing Office, Washington, DC 20402. Phone: (202)512-1800 Fax: (202)512-2250 E-mail: gpoaccess@gpo.gov • URL: http://www.access.gpo.gov • Monthly. $55.00 per year. Formerly *Producer Price Indexes*.

PR News Casebook. Gale Cengage Learning, 27500 Drake Rd. Farmington Hills, MI 48331-3535. Phone: 800-877-GALE or (248)699-4253 Fax: 800-414-5043 E-mail: gale.galeord@cengage.com • URL: http://gale.cengage.com • 1993. $110.00. A collection of about 1,000 case studies covering major public relations campaigns and events, taken from the pages of *PR News*. Covers such issues as boycotts, new products, anniversaries, plant closings, downsizing, and stockholder relations.

PR Reporter: The Newsletter of Behavioral Public Relations, Public Affairs, and Communication Strategies. Lawrence Ragan Communications, Inc., 316 N. Michigan Ave. Chicago, IL 60601. Phone: 800-493-4867 or (312)960-4100 Fax: (312)960-4105 E-mail: publicrelations@ragan.com • URL: http://www.prexec.com • Weekly. $250.00 per year. Newsletter. Presents a "digest of theories, research, public opinion, case studies, and successful public relations techniques."

The Practical Accountant: Providing the Competitive Edge. Thomson Media, 1 State St. Plz., 27th Fl. New York, NY 10004. Phone: 800-221-1809 or (212)803-8333 Fax: (212)292-5216 E-mail: cust.serv@thomsonmedia.com • URL: http://www.thomsonmedia.com • Monthly. $65.00 per year. Covers tax planning, financial planning, practice management, client relationships, and related topics.

Practical Baking. William J. Sultan. John Wiley and Sons, Inc., 111 River St. Hoboken, NJ 07030. Phone: 800-225-5945 or (201)748-6000 Fax: (201)748-6088 E-mail: info@wiley.com • URL: http://www.wiley.com • 1990. $55.95. Fifth edition.

Practical Business Statistics: StatPad Manual. Andrew F. Siegel. McGraw-Hill, 1221 Ave. of the Americas New York, NY 10020. Phone: 800-722-4726 or (212)512-2000 Fax: (212)512-4502 E-mail: customer.service@mcgraw-hill.com • URL: http://www.mcgraw-hill.com • 1996. Third edition. $20.63.

Practical Guide to Credit and Collection. George O. Bancroft. AMACOM, 1601 Broadway New York, NY 10019. Phone: 800-262-9699 or (518)586-8100 Fax: (518)903-8168 E-mail: customerservice@amanet.org • URL: http://www.amacombooks.org • 1989. $29.95.

Practical Guide to Equal Employment Opportunity. American Lawyer Media, Inc., 105 Madison Ave. New York, NY 10016. Phone: 800-888-8300 or (212)779-9200 Fax: (212)481-8110 E-mail: lawcatalog@amlaw.com • URL: http://www.lawcatalog.com/ • Looseleaf. $199.00. Two volumes. Updated as needed. Serves as a legal manual for EEO compliance. "Volume one analyzes discrimination on the basis of race, religion, sex, age, and physical handicaps including AIDS." Provides information relating to an employer's liability in cases of sexual harassment of employees, including same-sex harassment. Covers affirmative action and reverse discrimination issues. Volume two contains model affirmative action plans, a sample EEO compliance manual, checklists, and other documents. (Law Journal Press).

Practical Guide to Foreign Direct Investment in the European Union: The Green Book. Euroconfidentiel S. A., Rue de Rixensart 18 B-1332 Genval, Belgium. Phone: (32)02 652 02 84 Fax: (32)02 653 01 80 E-mail: nigel.hunt@skynet.be • URL: http://www.euroconfidential.com • Annual. $240.00. Provides coverage of national and EU business incentives. In addition to 70 charts and tables, includes EU country profiles of taxation, labor costs, and employment regulations.

Practical Guide to Handling IRS Income Tax Audits. Ralph L. Guyette. Prentice Hall PTR, 240 Frisch Ct. Paramus, NJ 07652. Phone: 800-282-0693 Fax: 800-445-6991 • URL: http://www.phptr.com • 1986. $39.95.

Practical Guide to Tax Issues in Employment. Julia K. Brazelton. CCH, Inc., 2700 Lake Cook Rd. Riverwoods, IL 60015. Phone: 800-835-5224 or (847)267-7000 E-mail: cust_serv@cch.com • URL: http://www.cch.com • 1999. $95.00. Covers income taxation as related to labor law and tax law, including settlements and awards. Written for tax professionals.

Practical Guide to the Occupational Safety and Health Act. American Lawyer Media, Inc., 105 Madison Ave. New York, NY 10016. Phone: 800-888-8300 or (212)779-9200 Fax: (212)481-8110 E-mail: lawcatalog@amlaw.com • URL: http://www.lawcatalog.com/ • Looseleaf. $149.00. Updated as needed. Covers the practical aspects of doing business while complying with OSHA regulations. Covers inspections, enforcement, rights of employees, the possibility of criminal prosecution, and related issues. (Law Journal Press).

Practical Guide to U. S. Taxation of International Transactions. Robert E. Meldman and Michael S. Schadewald. CCH, Inc., 2700 Lake Cook Rd. Riverwoods, IL 60015. Phone: 800-835-5224 or (847)267-7000 E-mail: cust_serv@cch.com • URL: http://www.cch.com • 2000. $99.00. Third edition. Contains three parts: Basic Principles, U. S. Taxation of Foreign Income, and U. S. Taxation of Foreign Persons.

The Practical Lawyer. Committee on Continuing Professional Education. American Law Institute-American Bar Association Committee on Continuing Professional Education, 4025 Chestnut St. Philadelphia, PA 19104-3099. Phone: 800-253-6397 Fax: (215)243-1664 • URL: http://www.ali-aba.org • Eight times a year. $49.00 per year.

The Practical Real Estate Lawyer. Committee on Continuing Professional Education. American Law Institute-American Bar Association Committee on Continuing Professional Education, 4025 Chestnut St. Philadelphia, PA 19104. Phone: 800-253-6397 Fax: (215)243-1664 • URL: http://www.ali-aba.org • Bimonthly. $49.00 per year. Frequently includes legal forms for use in real estate practice.

Practical Sign Shop Operation. Bob Fitzgerald. ST Publications, Inc., 407 Gilbert Ave. Cincinnati, OH 45202-6110. Phone: 800-925-1110 or (513)421-2050 Fax: (513)421-5144 E-mail: books@stpubs.com • URL: http://www.stpubs.com • 1992. $19.95. Seventh revised edition.

Practical Strategies for Library Managers. Joan Giesecke. American Library Association, 50 E Huron St. Chicago, IL 60611-2795. Phone: 800-545-2433 or (312)944-6780 Fax: (312)440-9374 E-mail: ala@ala.org • URL: http://www.ala.org • 2001. $32.00. Covers such basic items as decision making, team-building, and effective communication with staff members.

The Practical Tax Lawyer. Committee on Continuing Professional Education. American Law Institute-American Bar Association Committee on Continuing Professional Education, 4025 Chestnut St. Philadelphia, PA 19104. Phone: 800-253-6397 Fax: (215)243-1664 • URL: http://www.ali-aba.org • Quarterly. Members, $38.50 per year; non-members, $49.00 per year.

Practical Tax Strategies. RIA, 395 Hudson St. New York, NY 10014. Phone: 800-950-1216 or 800-431-9025 E-mail: riahome@riag.com • URL: http://www.riahome.com • Monthly. $275.00. per year. Emphasis is on current tax developments as they affect accountants and their clients. Includes advice on tax software and computers. Formerly *Taxation for Accountants*.

Practical Upholstering: And the Cutting of Slip Covers. Frederick Palmer. Madison Books, Inc., USA, 200 Park Ave. S, Ste. 1109 New York, NY 10003-1503. Phone: 800-338-4550 or (212)529-3888 Fax: 800-338-4550 or (212)529-4223 • URL: http://www.univpress.com • 1982. $11.95.

The Practice of Local Government Planning. Charles Hoch and others. International City/County Management Association, 777 N. Capitol St., N.E., Suite 500 Washington, DC 20002-4201. Phone: 800-745-8780 or (202)289-4262 Fax: (202)962-3500 E-mail: subscriptions@icma.org • URL: http://www.icma.org • 2000. $42.95. Third edition. (Municipal Management Series).

Practicing Financial Planning: A Complete Guide for Professionals. Sitansu S. Mittra. R. H. Publishing, 445 Livernois Rd., Ste. 216 Rochester Hills, MI 48307. Phone: (248)650-3839 Fax: (248)650-3657 1993. $29.95. Approved for continuing education of financial planners by the International Board of Standards and Practices for Certified Financial Planners. Covers planning strategies, funds allocation, insurance considerations, risk management, ethics, and other topics.

Practising Law Institute., 810 7th Ave. New York, NY 10019-5818. Phone: 800-260-4754 or (212)824-5710 Fax: (212)581-4670 E-mail: info@pli.edu • URL: http://www.pli.edu • Provides through publications, videotapes, forums, and live and online seminars, training for lawyers throughout the country in new developments in the law and new legal techniques. Presents over 250 seminars annually.

Practitioner's Guide to GAAS. John Wiley and Sons, Inc., 111 River St. Hoboken, NJ 07030. Phone: 800-225-5945 or (201)748-6000 Fax: (201)748-6088 E-mail: info@wiley.com • URL: http://www.wiley.com • Annual. $184.95. Covers GAAS: Generally Accepted Auditing Standards, promulgated by the American Institute of Certified Public Accountants. (Includes CD-ROM.)

Pratt's Guide to Venture Capital Sources. Thomson Financial, 195 Broadway New York, NY 10007. Phone: 800-262-6000 or (646)822-2000 Fax: (646)822-6270 E-mail: custserv@tfn.com • URL: http://www.tfn.com • Annual. $625.00. Describes about 1,400 venture capital firms, including key personnel, capital under management, and recent investments. Company, personnel, and industry indexes are provided.

Precision Metalforming Association., 6363 Oak Tree Blvd. Independence, OH 44131-2556. Phone: (216)901-8800 Fax: (216)901-9190 E-mail: pma@pma.org • URL: http://www.metalforming.com • Represents the metalforming industry of North America; the industry that creates precision metal products using stamping, fabricating and other value-added processes. Its member companies include metal stampers, fabricators, spinners, slide formers and roll formers, as well as suppliers of equipment, materials and services to the industry. Members are located in 30 countries, with the majority found in North America; in 41 states of the United States as well as Canada and Mexico. Conducts technical and educational programs, compiles statistics, offers training systems, and provides legislative and regulatory assistance to members.

The Predator's Ball: The Inside Story of Drexel Burnham and the Rise of the Junk Bond Raiders. Connie Bruck. Penguin Group, 375 Hudson St. New York, NY 10014-3657. Phone: 800-331-4624 or (212)366-2000 Fax: (212)366-2952 • URL: http://www.penguingroup.com • 1989. $15.00.

Predicting Successful Hospital Mergers and Acquisitions: A Financial and Analytical Marketing Tool. David P. Angrisani and Robert L. Goldman. Haworth Press, Inc., 10 Alice St. Binghamton, NY 13904-1580. Phone: 800-429-6784 or (607)722-5857 Fax: 800-895-0582 or (607)722-1424 E-mail: getinfo@haworthpressinc.com • URL: http://www.haworthpressinc.com • 1997. $49.95.

Predicting the Future: An Introduction to the Theory of Forecasting. Nicholas Rescher. State University of New York Press, 90 State St., Ste. 700 Albany, NY 12207. Phone: (518)472-5000 Fax: (518)472-5038 E-mail: info@sunypress.edu • URL: http://www.sunypress.edu • 1997. $24.50. Provides a general theory of prediction, including the principles and methodology of forecasting. Includes "The Evaluation of Predictions and Predictors."

Predictions: Specific Investment Forecasts and Recommendations from the World's Top Financial Experts. Lee Euler, editor. Agora, Inc., P.O. Box 1936 Baltimore, MD 21203. Phone: (410)783-8499 E-mail: agorahelpdesk@agora-inc.com • URL: http://www.agora-inc.com • Monthly. $78.00 per year. Newsletter.

A Preface to Marketing Management. J. Paul Peter and James H. Donnelly. McGraw-Hill, 1221 Ave. of the Americas New York, NY 10020. Phone: 800-722-4726 or (212)512-2000 Fax: (212)512-4502 E-mail: customer.service@mcgraw-hill.com • URL: http://www.mcgraw-hill.com • 2002. $57.81. Ninth edition. (Marketing Series).

Premium, Incentive, and Travel Buyers Directory. Douglas Publications, Inc., 2807 N Parham Rd. Richmond, VA 23294. Phone: 800-223-1797 or (804)762-9600 Fax: (804)217-8999 E-mail: info@douglaspublications.com • URL: http://www.douglaspublications.com • Annual. $275.00. Lists more than 12,000 firms who purchase premiums and incentives. Provides information on about 20,000 buyers of premiums, incentive programs, and travel programs for motivation of sales personnel.

Prepared Foods. Business News Publishing Co., 755 W Big Beaver Rd., Ste. 1000 Troy, MI 48084. Phone: (248)362-3700 Fax: 800-662-7776 or (248)362-0317 • URL: http://www.bnp.com • Monthly. $99.90 per year. Edited for food manufacturing management, marketing, and operations personnel.

Prepared Foods Sourcebook. Reed Business Information, 360 Park Ave. S New York, NY 10010. Phone: 800-662-7776 or (646)746-6400 E-mail: corporatecommunications@reedbusiness.com • URL: http://www.reedbusiness.com • Annual. $75.00. Lists approximately 600 food and veverage companies.

Preparing a Successful Business Plan: How to Plan to Succeed and Secure Financial Banking. Rodger D. Touchie. Self-Counsel Press Inc., 1704 State St. Bellingham, WA 98225. Phone: 877-877-6490 or (360)676-4530 Fax: (360)676-4549 E-mail: orderdesk@self-counsel.com • URL: http://www.self-counsel.com • 2001. $16.95. Fourth edition.

Preparing for the Twenty-First Century. Paul Kennedy. Random House, Inc., 1540 Broadway New York, NY 10036. Phone: 800-726-0600 or (212)782-9000 Fax: (212)302-7985 E-mail: customerservice@randomhouse.com • URL: http://www.randomhouse.com • 1993. $16.00. A somber view of the future.

Prepress Bulletin. Bessie Halfacre, editor. International Prepress Association, 552 W. 167th St. South Holland, IL 60473. Phone: (708)596-5110 Fax: (708)596-5112 E-mail: bessieipa@earthlink.net • URL: http://www.ipa.org • Bimonthly. $20.00 per year. Provides management and technical information on the graphic arts prepress industry.

Presentations: Technology and Techniques for Effective Communication. VNU Business Media, 770 Broadway New York, NY 10003-9595. Phone: 800-344-7119 or (646)654-4500 Fax: (646)654-7212 • URL: http://www.vnubusinessmedia.com • Monthly. Free to qualified personnel; others, $69.00 per year. Covers the use of presentation hardware and software, including audiovisual equipment and computerized display systems. Includes an annual *"Buyers Guide to Presentation Products."*

Presenting Performances: A Basic Handbook for the Twenty-First Century. Thomas Wolf. Association of Performing Arts Presenters, Inc., 1112 16th St., NW, No. 400 Washington, DC 20036. Phone: (202)833-2787 Fax: (202)833-1543 2001. $21.95. Revised edition.

The Presidency: The Magazine for Higher Education Leaders. American Council on Education, Office of Research, One Dupont Cir. Washington, DC 20036-1193. Phone: (202)939-9380 Fax: (202)833-4760 E-mail: web@ace.nche.edu • URL: http://www.acenet.edu • Three times a year. Members, $27.00 per year; non-members, $30.00 per year. Formerly *Educational Record*.

Presidential Studies Quarterly. Center for the Study of the Presidency. Sage Publications, Inc., 2455 Teller Rd. Thousand Oaks, CA 91320. Phone: 800-818-7243 or (805)499-9774 Fax: 800-583-2665 or (805)499-0871 E-mail: webmaster@sagepub.com • URL: http://www.sagepub.com • Quarterly. Institutions, $255.00 per year. Includes print and online editions.

Preventing Bank Crises: Lessons from Recent Global Bank Failures. Gerand Caprio. The World Bank Group, 1818 H St., NW Washington, DC 20433. Phone: 800-645-7247 or (202)473-1153 Fax: (202)477-6391 E-mail: books@worldbank.org • URL: http://www.worldbank.org • 1998. $40.00. Examines worldwide problems with bank regulation, bank infrastructure, public accountability, and political influence.(EDI Development Studies)

Prevention: The Magazine for Better Health. Rodale, 33 E. Minor St. Emmaus, PA 18098-0099. Phone: (610)967-5171 Fax: (610)967-8963 E-mail: customer_service@rodale.com • URL: http://www.rodale.com • Monthly $15.94. per year.

Prices and Earnings Around the Globe. Union Bank of Switzerland, 299 Park Ave. New York, NY 10171-0034. Phone: (212)821-3000 Fax: (212)821-3285 • URL: http://www.ubs.com • Triennial. Free. Published in Zurich. Compares prices and purchasing power in 48 major cities of the world. Wages and hours are also compared.

Prices of Agricultural Products and Selected Inputs in Europe and North America. Economic Commission for Europe. United Nations Publications, Two United Nations Plaza, Rm. DC2-853 New York, NY 10017. Phone: 800-253-9646 or (212)963-8302 Fax: (212)963-3489 Annual.

Pricing and Capacity Determination in International Air Transport. Peter P. C. Haanappel. Kluwer Law International, 675 Massachusetts Ave. Cambridge, MA 02139. Phone: (617)354-0140 Fax: (617)354-8595 E-mail: sales@kluwerlaw.com • URL: http://www.kluwerlaw.com • 1984. $66.00.

Primer of Labor Relations. Linda G. Kahn. BNA, Inc., 1231 25th St., NW Washington, DC 20037. Phone: 800-372-1033 E-mail: customercare@bna.com • URL: http://www.bna.com • 1994. $45.00. 25th edition.

A Primer on Organizational Behavior. James L. Bowditch and Anthony F. Buono. John Wiley and Sons, Inc., 111 River St. Hoboken, NJ 07030. Phone: 800-225-5945 or (201)748-6000 Fax: (201)748-6088 E-mail: info@wiley.com • URL: http://www.wiley.com • 2000. $50.95. Fifth edition. Includes a discussion of participative management. Emphasis is on research and the theory of organizations. (Management Series).

Princeton Forrestal Center., Princeton University, 105 College Rd., E. Princeton, NJ 08540. Phone: (609)452-7720 Fax: (609)452-7485 E-mail: picus@picusassociates.com Designed to create an interdependent mix of academia and business enterprise.

Principal International Businesses: The World Marketing Directory., Dun and Bradstreet, One Diamond Hill Rd. Murray Hill, NJ 07974. Phone: 800-526-0521 or (908)665-5732 Fax: (908)665-5722 E-mail: dnbmdd@mail.dnb.com • URL: http://www.dnb.com • Annual. $5,000. Provides information about 50,000 major businesses located in over 145 countries. Geographic arrangement with company name and product indexes.

Principles and Practices of TQM. Thomas J. Cartin. ASQ Quality Press, 600 N Plankinton Ave. Milwaukee, WI 53201-3005. Phone: 800-248-1946 or (414)272-8575 Fax: (414)270-8810 E-mail: cs@asq.org • URL: http://www.qualitypress.asq.org • 1993. $28.00.

Principles of Association Management. Henry Ernstthal and Bob Jones. American Society of Association Executives, 1575 Eye St., N. W. Washington, DC 20005-1168. Phone: (202)626-2723 Fax: (202)408-9634 E-mail: books@asaenet.org • URL: http://www.asaenet.org • 2001. Fourth edition. Price on application

Principles of Auditing. O. Ray Whittington and Kurt Pany. McGraw-Hill, 1221 Ave. of the Americas New York, NY 10020. Phone: 800-722-4726 or (212)512-2000 Fax: (212)512-4502 E-mail: customer.service@mcgraw-hill.com • URL: http://www.mcgraw-hill.com • 2000. $90.31. 13th edition.

Principles of Banking. Eric N. Compton. American Bankers Association, 1120 Connecticut Ave., N. W. Washington, DC 20036-3971. Phone: 800-226-5377 or (202)663-5521 Fax: (202)663-7543 E-mail: custserv@aba.com • URL: http://www.aba.com • 2001. $65.00. Seventh edition.

Principles of Communications Satellites. Gary D. Gordon and Walter L. Morgan. John Wiley and Sons, Inc., 111 River St. Hoboken, NJ 07030. Phone: 800-225-5945 or (201)748-6000 Fax: (201)748-6088 E-mail: info@wiley.com • URL: http://www.wiley.com • 1993. $130.00.

Principles of Corporate Finance. Richard A. Brealey and Stewart C. Myers. McGraw-Hill, 1221 Ave. of the Americas New York, NY 10020. Phone: 800-722-4726 or (212)512-2000 Fax: (212)512-4502 E-mail: customer.service@mcgraw-hill.com • URL: http://www.mcgraw-hill.com • 2002. $79.50. Seventh edition. (Finance, Insurance and Real Estate Series).

Principles of Corporate Governance: Analysis and Recommendations. Mike Greenwald, editor. American Law Institute-American Bar Association Committee on Continuing Professional Education, 4025 Chestnut St. Philadelphia, PA 19104. Phone: 800-253-6397 Fax: (215)243-1664 • URL: http://www.ali-aba.org • 1994. $135.00. Two volumes. An examination of the duties and responsibilities of directors and officers of business corporations. Seven parts cover (1) definitions, (2) objectives and conduct, (3) corporate structure and oversight committees, (4) business judgment, (5) fair dealing, (6) tender offers, and (7) legal remedies.

Principles of Digital Audio. Ken C. Pohlmann. McGraw-Hill,

1221 Ave. of the Americas New York, NY 10020. Phone: 800-722-4726 or (212)512-2000 Fax: (212)512-4502 E-mail: customer.service@mcgraw-hill.com • URL: http://www.mcgraw-hill.com • 2000. $54.95. Fourth edition. Includes the details of digital audio recording, reproduction, error correction, compact disc technology, DVD, minidiscs, Internet audio, and related topics. (Video/Audio Engineering Series).

Principles of Economics. Fred M. Gottheil. South-Western, 5191 Natorp Blvd. Mason, OH 45040. Phone: 800-543-0487 or (513)229-1000 • URL: http://www.swcollege.com • 2001. $88.95. Third edition. (Economics Series).

Principles of Health and Hygiene in the Workplace. Timothy J. Key and Michael A. Mueller. Lewis Publishers, 2000 Corporate Blvd., N. W. Boca Raton, FL 33431. Phone: 800-272-7737 or (561)994-0555 Fax: 800-374-3401 or (561)998-9114 E-mail: orders@crcpress.com • URL: http://www.crcpress.com • Date not set. $69.95.

Principles of Highway Engineering and Traffic Analysis. Fred L. Mannering and Walter P. Kilareski. John Wiley and Sons, Inc., 111 River St. Hoboken, NJ 07030. Phone: 800-225-5945 or (201)748-6000 Fax: (201)748-6088 E-mail: info@wiley.com • URL: http://www.wiley.com • 1997. $68.95. Second edition.

Principles of Inventory and Materials Management. Richard J. Tersine. Prentice Hall PTR, 240 Frisch Ct. Paramus, NJ 07652. Phone: 800-282-0693 Fax: 800-445-6991 • URL: http://www.phptr.com • 1993. $45.50. Fourth edition. Includes material on just-in-time inventory systems.

Principles of Macroeconomics. Joseph E. Stiglitz and John Walsh. Norton, W.W. and Co., Inc., 500 Fifth Ave. New York, NY 10110-0017. Phone: 800-223-2584 or (212)354-5500 Fax: 800-548-6515 or (212)869-0856 • URL: http://www.norton.com • 2002. $62.00. Third edition.

Principles of Money, Banking and Financial Markets. Addison-Wesley, 75 Arlington St., Ste. 300 Boston, MA 02116. Phone: 800-447-2226 or (617)848-7500 • URL: http://www.aw.com • 2000. $67.00. 10th edition.

Principles of Operation Management. Raturi. Cengage Learning, 290 Harbor Dr. Stamford, CT 06902. Phone: 800-347-7707 or (203)969-8700 Fax: 800-487-8488 or (203)969-8700 E-mail: communications@cengage.com • URL: http://www.thomson.com/learning • 2000. $35.00. Sixth edition. (SWC-Management Series).

Principles of Project Management: Collected Handbooks from the Project Management Institute. John R. Adams and others. Project Management Institute, Four Campus Blvd. Newton Square, PA 19073-3299. Phone: (610)356-4600 Fax: (610)356-4647 E-mail: pmihq@pmi.org • URL: http://www.pmi.org • 1997. $59.95. Consists of reprints of eight "handbooks" by various authors, previously published by the Project Management Institute. Includes such topics as contract administration, conflict management, team building, and coping with stress.

Principles of Total Quality. Vincent K. Omachonu. CRC Press, 2000 N.W. Corporate Blvd. Boca Raton, FL 33431. Phone: 800-272-7737 or (561)994-0555 Fax: 800-374-3401 or (561)989-9732 E-mail: orders@crcpress.com • URL: http://www.crcpress.com • 2004. $54.95. Third edition. Covers the general management of quality control, including leadership, human resources, information analysis, strategic planning, and customer satisfaction.

Print: America's Graphic Design Magazine. Krause Publications, Inc., 700 E State St. Iola, WI 54990-4087. Phone: (715)445-2214 Fax: (715)445-4087 E-mail: info@krause.com • URL: http://www.krause.com • Bimonthly. $57.00 per year. Emphasizes creative trends.

Print Solutions Magazine. Document Management Industries Association, 433 E. Monroe Ave. Alexandria, VA 22301. Phone: (703)836-6232 Fax: (703)836-2241 E-mail: editors@formmag.com • URL: http://www.formmag.com • Monthly. Members, $29.00 per year; non-members, $49.00 per year. Formerly *Form*.

Printing Impressions. North American Publishing Co., 401 N. Broad St. Philadelphia, PA 19108. Phone: 800-777-8074 or (215)238-5482 Fax: 800-664-1533 or (215)238-5412 E-mail: customerservice@napco.com • URL: http://www.napco.com • Monthly. Free to qualified personnel; others, $90.00 per year. Annual buyer's guide *Master Specifier*.

Printing Industries of America., 100 Daingerfield Rd. Alexandria, VA 22314-2888. Phone: 800-742-2666 or (703)519-8100 Fax: (703)548-3227 E-mail: gain@printing.org • URL: http://www.printing.org • Commercial printing firms (lithography, letter-press, gravure, platemakers, typographic houses) and allied firms in the graphic arts. Formerly Printing Industry of America.

Prisoners in State and Federal Institutions. Bureau of Justice Statistics, U.S. Department of Justice. Available from U.S. Government Printing Office, Washington, DC 20402. Phone: (202)512-1800 Fax: (202)512-2250 E-mail: gpoaccess@gpo.gov • URL: http://www.accessgpo.gov • Annual.

Privacy and Information Law Report. Glasser Legalworks, 150 Clove Rd. Little Falls, NJ 07424. Phone: 800-308-1700 or (973)890-0008 Fax: (973)890-0042 E-mail: orders@glasserlegalworks.com • URL: http://www.glasserlegalworks.com • 10 times a year. $375.00 per year. Newsletter. Coverage includes the legal aspects of health record privacy, employee records, anti-spam, and privacy-enhancing technology. Provides reports on relevant court cases and consumer advocacy.

Private Asset Management. Institutional Investor, Inc., Journals Group, 225 Park Ave., S New York, NY 10003. Phone: 800-945-2034 or (212)224-3300 Fax: (212)224-3353 E-mail: info@iijournals.com • URL: http://www.iijournals.com • Biweekly. $2,335.00 per year. Newsletter. Includes print and online editions. Edited for managers investing the private assets of wealthy ("high-net-worth") individuals. Includes marketing, taxation, regulation, and fee topics.

Private Equity Week. Thomson Financial, 195 Broadway New York, NY 10007. Phone: 800-262-6000 or (646)822-2000 Fax: (646)822-6270 E-mail: custserv@tfn.com • URL: http://www.tfn.com • Weekly. $1,495.00 per year. Provides detailed information on both prospective and completed private equity transactions. Includes news, data, commentary, trends, developments, and analysis.

Private Independent Schools. Bunting and Lyon Inc., 238 N Main St. Wallingford, CT 06492. Phone: (203)269-3333 Fax: (203)269-5697 E-mail: buntingandlyon@aol.com • URL: http://www.buntingandlyon.com • Covers: 1,200 English-speaking elementary and secondary private schools and summer programs in North America and abroad. Entries include: School name, address, phone, fax, e-mail, website, enrollment, tuition and other fees, financial aid information, administrator's name and educational background, director of admission, regional accreditation, description of programs, curriculum, activities, learning differences grid.

Private Investigator. Entrepreneur Media, Inc., 2445 McCabe Way Irvine, CA 92614. Phone: 800-421-2300 or (949)261-2325 Fax: (949)261-0234 E-mail: entmag@entrepreneur.com • URL: http://www.entrepreneur.com • Looseleaf. $59.50. A practical guide to starting a private investigation agency. Covers profit potential, start-up costs, market size evaluation, pricing, accounting, advertising, promotion, etc. (Start-Up Business Guide No. E1320.)

Private Label Buyer. Stagnito Communcitions, Inc., 155 Pfingsten Rd., Ste. 205 Deerfield, IL 60015. Phone: (847)205-5660 Fax: (847)205-5680 E-mail: info@stagnito.com • URL: http://www.plnews.com • Eight times a year. $85.08 per year. Covers new private label product developments for chain stores. Formerly *Private Label News*.

Private Label International: The Magazine for Store Labels (Own Brands) and Generics. E. W. Williams Publications Co., 2125 Center Ave., Suite 305 Fort Lee, NJ 07024-5859. Phone: (201)592-7007 Fax: (201)592-7171 Semiannual. $20.00 per year. Edited for large chain store buyers and for manufacturers of private label products. Text in English; summaries in French and German.

Private Label Manufacturers Association., 630 3rd Ave., 4th Fl. New York, NY 10017. Phone: (212)972-3131 Fax: (212)983-1382 E-mail: info@plma.com • URL: http://www.plma.com • Membership consists of manufacturers, brokers, suppliers, and consultants. Educates consumers on the quality and value of private label or store brand products; promotes private label industry. Compiles statistics; conducts research programs for members.

Private Label: The Magazine for House Brands and Generics. E. W. Williams Publications Co., 2125 Center Ave., Suite 305 Fort Lee, NJ 07024-5859. Phone: (201)592-7007 Fax: (201)592-7171 Bimonthly. $36.00 per year. Edited for buyers of private label, controlled packer, and generic-labeled products. Concentrates on food, health and beauty aids, and general merchandise.

Private Pensions in OECD Countries: The United States. OECD Publications and Information Center, 2001 L St., N.W., Suite 650 Washington, DC 20036-4922. Phone: 800-456-6323 or (202)785-6323 Fax: (202)785-0350 E-mail: washington.contact@oecd.org • URL: http://www.oecdwash.org • 1993. $22.00. Provides data relating to the characteristics of private pension arrangements in the U. S.

Private Placement Letter: The Weekly for Privately Placed Fixed-Income Securities. Thomson Media, One State St. Plaza New York, NY 10004. Phone: 800-221-1809 or (212)803-8200 Fax: (212)843-9635 E-mail: custserv@thomsonmedia.com • URL: http://www.thomsonmedia.com • Weekly. $895.00 per year. Newsletter. Provides information on private financing of debt and convertible securities.

Private Power Executive. Pequot Publishing, Inc., PO Box 447 Southport, CT 06490-1112. Phone: (203)259-1812 Fax: (203)255-3313 Bimonthly. $90.00 per year. Covers private power (non-utility) enterprises, including cogeneration projects and industrial self-generation.

Private Practice. Congress of County Medical Societies (CCMS) Publishing Co., P.O. Box 1485 Shawnee, OK 74802-1485. Monthly. $18.00 per year.

Private Sector Council., 1100 New York Ave. NW, Ste. 1090 E Washington, DC 20005. Phone: (202)775-9111 Fax: (202)775-8885 E-mail: bramati@ourpublicservice.org • URL: http://www.ourpublicservice.org/psc • Serves as a nonpartisan, public service organization dedicated to improving the productivity, efficiency, and management of the federal government through a cooperative sharing of knowledge between the public and private sectors.

Privatising State-Owned Enterprises: An Overview of Policies and Practices in OECD Countries. Organization for Economic Cooperation and Development, OECD Washington Center, 2001 L St., N. W., Suite 650 Washington, DC 20036-4922. Phone: 800-456-6323 or (202)785-6323 Fax: (202)785-0350 E-mail: washington.contact@oecd.org • URL: http://www.oecd.org • 2003. $35.00. Provides information on the methods, techniques, and implementation of privatization in OECD countries. Includes case examples.

PRO. Cygnus Business Media, 1233 Janesville Ave. Fort Atkinson, WI 53538. Phone: 800-547-7377 or (920)563-6388 Fax: (920)563-1707 E-mail: rich.reiff@cygnuspub.com • URL: http://www.cygnusbzb.com • Seven times a year. $48.00 per year. For owners and operators of lawn maintenance service firms. Includes annual *Product* issue.

Pro Audio Review Gear Guide. IMAS Publishing, Inc., 5827 Columbia Pke., Ste. 310 Falls Church, VA 22041. Phone: (703)998-7600 Fax: (703)998-2966 E-mail: adsales@imaspub.com • URL: http://www.imaspub.com • Annual. Issued as February issue of *Pro Audio Review*. Contains detailed product listings of professional audio equipment and recording gear. Includes prices, specifications, and addresses of manufacturers.

Pro Audio Review: The Industry's Equipment Authority. IMAS Publishing, Inc., 5827 Columbia Pke., Ste. 310 Falls Church, VA 22041. Phone: (703)998-7600 Fax: (703)998-2966 E-mail: adsales@imaspub.com • URL: http://www.imaspub.com • Monthly. $35.00 per year. Provides critical product reviews of professional audio equipment and recording gear, including bench tests and user reports.

Pro AV: Real-World Solutions for AV Professionals., 1600 College Blvd. Overland Park, KS 66210. Phone: (913)469-1185 Fax: (913)-469-0806 • URL: http://www.proavmagazine.com • Monthly. Free. Formerly *Presenting Communications*.

Probable Tomorrows: How Science and Technology Will Transform Our Lives in the Next Twenty Years. Marvin J. Cetron and Owen L. Davies. Saint Martin's Press, 175 Fifth Ave. New York, NY 10010. Phone: 888-330-8477 or (212)674-5151 Fax: 800-672-2054 E-mail: enquiries@stmartins.com • URL: http://www.stmartins.com • 1997. $24.95. Predicts the developments in technological products, services, and "everyday conveniences" by the year 2017. Covers such items as personal computers, artificial intelligence, telecommunications, highspeed railroads, and healthcare.

Problem Loan Strategies; A Decision Process for Commercial Bankers. John E. McKinley and others. The Risk Management Association, One Liberty Place, 1650 Market St., Suite 2300 Philadelphia, PA 19103-7398. Phone: 800-677-7621 or (215)446-4000 Fax: (215)446-4101 • URL: http://www.rmahq.org • 1998. $53.00. Revised edition.

Procedures for the Automated Office. Sharon Burton and others. Prentice Hall PTR, 240 Frisch Ct. Paramus, NJ 07652. Phone: 800-282-0693 Fax: 800-445-6991 • URL: http://www.phptr.com • 2000. $60.00. Fifth edition.

Process Equipment Manufacturers Association., 201 Park Washington Ct. Falls Church, VA 22046-4527. Phone: (703)538-1796 Fax: (703)241-5603 E-mail: info@pemanet.org • URL: http://www.pemanet.org • Represents North American process equipment companies. Maintains an organization of capital equipment manufacturers. Provides a social/business base where members can meet to share and exchange views on common interests.

Process Quality Control. Ellis R. Ott and others. McGraw-Hill, 1221 Ave. of the Americas New York, NY 10020. Phone: 800-722-4726 or (212)512-2000 Fax: (212)512-4502 E-mail: customer.service@mcgraw-hill.com • URL: http://www.mcgraw-hill.com • 2000. $74.95. Third edition. (Professional Engineering Series).

Processing. Putman Media, 555 W. Pierce Rd., Suite 301 Itasca, IL 60143-2649. Phone: (630)467-1300 Fax: (630)467-1179 14 times a year. $54.00 per year. Emphasis is on descriptions of new products for all areas of industrial processing, including valves, controls, filters, pumps, compressors, fluidics, and instrumentation.

Produce Marketing Association., 1500 Casho Mill Rd., PO Box 6036 Newark, DE 19714-6036. Phone: (302)738-7100 Fax: (302)731-2409 E-mail: bsilbermann@pma.com • URL: http://www.pma.com • Represents marketers of fresh fruits, vegetables, and related products worldwide. Members are involved in the production, distribution, retail, and foodservice sectors of the industry. Works to create a favorable, responsible environment that advances the marketing of produce and floral products and services for North American buyers and sellers and their international partners.

Produce Merchandising: The Packer's Retailing and Merchandising Magazine. Vance Publishing Corp., 400 Knightsbridge Parkway Lincolnshire, IL 60069. Phone: 800-255-5113 or (847)634-2600 Fax: (847)634-4379 • URL: http://www.vancepublishing.com • Monthly. $35.00 per year. Provides information and advice on the retail marketing and promotion of fresh fruits and vegetalbe.

Produce News. Zim-Mer Trade Publications, Inc., 2185 Lemoine Ave. Fort Lee, NJ 07024. Phone: (201)592-9100 Fax: (201)592-0809 Weekly. $35.00 per year.

Producers Directory. IFILM Publishing, 1024 N Orange Dr. Hollywood, CA 90038. Phone: 800-815-0503 or (323)308-3400 Fax: (323)308-3493 E-mail: advertising@ifilm.com Covers: over 1,700 film and TV production companies, studios, networks, and TV shows, and over 7,700 creative executives within those companies. Majority of listings are located in Los Angeles and New York. Entries include: Company name, staff names and titles, address, phone, fax, e-mail address, web site address, company type, studio deals, and select credits.

Producers Guild of America.

Producer's Masterguide: The International Film Production Guide and Directory for Motion Picture, Television, Industries in the United States, the United Kingdom, Europe, the Caribbean Islands, Mexico, Israel, Morocco and Australia. 60 E. Eighth St., 34th Fl. New York, NY 10003-6514. Phone: (212)777-4002 Fax: (212)777-4101 E-mail: producers@masterguide.com • URL: http://www. producers.masterguide.com • Annual. $140.00. A standard reference guide of the professional film, television, commercial and video tape industry throughout the U.S. and Canada, Europe, the Caribbean Islands, Mexico, Israel, Morocco, Australia, etc.

Product Design and Development. Reed Business Information, 360 Park Ave. S New York, NY 10010. Phone: 800-446-6551 or (646)746-4600 Fax: (646)746-7028 E-mail: corporatecommunications@reedbusiness.com • URL: http:// www.reedbusiness.com • Monthly. Free to qualified personnel; others, $114.90 per year.

Product Distribution Law Guide. CCH, Inc., 2700 Lake Cook Rd. Riverwoods, IL 60015. Phone: 800-835-5224 or (847)267-7000 E-mail: cust_serv@cch.com • URL: http://www.cch. com • $199.00. Looseleaf service. Annual updates available. Covers the legal aspects of various methods of product distribution, including franchising.

Product Liability. American Lawyer Media, Inc., 105 Madison Ave. New York, NY 10016. Phone: 800-888-8300 or (212)779-9200 Fax: (212)481-8110 E-mail: lawcatalog@ amlaw.com • URL: http://www.lawcatalog.com/ • Looseleaf. $169.00. Updated as needed. Covers product liability litigation as viewed by both the plaintiff and the defendant. Provides detailed discussion of pre-trial and trial procedures. (Law Journal Press).

The *Product Liability Alliance*. 1325 G St. NW, Ste. 1000, 1725 K St., NW, Ste. 300 Washington, DC 20005. Phone: (202)872-0885 Fax: (202)785-0586 E-mail: naw@naw.org • URL: http://www.naw.org • Coalition of trade associations, manufacturers, and nonmanufacturing product sellers. Seeks enactment of federal product liability tort reform legislation. Supports and coordinates members' efforts in gaining passage of a product liability law. Works with the business community to develop suggestions and guidelines for such a law.

Product Liability Law and Strategy. American Lawyer Media, Inc., 105 Madison Ave. New York, NY 10016. Phone: 800-888-8300 or (212)779-9200 Fax: (212)481-8110 E-mail: lawcatalog@amlaw.com • URL: http://www.lawcatalog.com/ • Monthly. $189.00 per year. Newsletter. Contains product liability verdict and settlement reports, legislative proposal analysis, and strategies for both the plaintiff's counsel and the defendant's counsel. (A Law Journal Newsletter, formerly published by Leader Publications).

Product Safety Letter. Washington Business Information Inc., 1117 N 19th St., Ste. 200 Arlington, VA 22209-1798. Phone: (703)247-3434 Fax: (703)247-3421 E-mail: customer. service@mcgraw-hill.com Description: Follows the actions of the Consumer Product Safety Commission and other regulatory agencies and monitors developments and trends in the manufacturing industry. Offers "inside information about major regulatory trends, actions, opinions, and ideas." Spotlights stringent new rules which affect the production and sale of many common items. Recurring features include news of research and reports of meetings.

Production. Gardner Publications, Inc., 6915 Valley Ave. Cincinnati, OH 45244-4090. Phone: 800-950-8020 or (513)527-8800 Fax: (513)527-8801 Monthly. $48.00 per year. Covers the latest manufacturing management issues. Discusses the strategic and financial implications of various tecnologies as they impact factory management, quality and competitiveness.

Production and Inventory Control Handbook. James H. Greene. McGraw-Hill, 1221 Ave. of the Americas New York, NY 10020. Phone: 800-722-4726 or (212)512-2000 Fax: (212)512-4502 E-mail: customer.service@mcgraw-hill.com • URL: http://www.mcgraw-hill.com • 1997. $95.00. Third edition.

Production and Inventory Management Journal. A P I C S: The Educational Society for Resource Management, 5301 Shawnee Rd. Alexandria, VA 22312-2317. Phone: 800-444-2742 or (703)354-8851 Fax: (703)354-8106 • URL: http://www. apics.org • Quarterly. Members, $64.00 per year; nonmembers, $80.00 per year.

Production and Operations Management. Richard B. Chase. McGraw-Hill, 1221 Avenue of the Americas New York, NY 10020. Phone: 800-722-4726 or (212)512-2000 Fax: (212)512-4502 E-mail: customer.service@mcgraw-hill.com • URL: http://www.mcgraw-hill.com • 2002. $39.69. Ninth edition. Covers capacity planning, facility location, process design, inventory planning, personnel scheduling, etc.

Production and Operations Management. Production and Operations Management Society, Florida International University, EAS 2460, College of Engineering, 10555 W Flagler St. Miami, FL 33174. Phone: (305)348-1413 Fax: (305)348-6890 E-mail: poms@fiu.edu • URL: http://www.poms.org • Quarterly. Individuals, $70.00 per year; libraries, $200.00 per year.

Production and Operations Management Society. Florida International University, College of Engineering, 10555 W. Flagle St., EAS 2460 Miami, FL 33174. Phone: (305)348-1413 Fax: (305)348-6890 E-mail: poms@eng.fiu.edu • URL: http://www.poms.org • Members are professionals and

educators in fields related to operations management and production.

Production and Operations Management: Total Quality and Responsiveness. Hamid Noori and Russell Radford. McGraw-Hill, 1221 Ave. of the Americas New York, NY 10020. Phone: 800-722-4726 or (212)512-2000 Fax: (212)512-4502 E-mail: customer.service@mcgraw-hill.com • URL: http://www.mcgraw-hill.com • 1994. $70.25.

Production Technology News. Reed Business Information, 360 Park Ave. S New York, NY 10010. Phone: 800-446-6551 or (646)746-6400 Fax: (646)746-7028 E-mail: corporatecommunications@reedbusiness.com • URL: http:// www.reedbusiness.com • Monthly. $57.99. Includes *MBuyer's Guide*. Formerly *Metalworking Digest*.

Products Finishing. Gardner Publications, Inc., 6915 Valley Ave Cincinnati, OH 45244-3029. Phone: 800-950-8020 or (513)527-8800 Fax: (513)527-8801 • URL: http://www. gardnerweb.com • Monthly. $40.00 per year.

Products Finishing Directory. Gardner Publications Inc., 6915 Valley Ave. Cincinnati, OH 45244. Phone: 800-950-8020 or (513)527-8800 Fax: (513)527-8801 E-mail: buntingandlyon@aol.com • URL: http://www.gardnerweb. com • Publication includes: List of suppliers of products used in electroplating, painting, polishing, buffing, powder coating, cleaning, degreasing, and other metal finishing processes. Entries include: Company name, address, phone, e-mail, URL.

Professional and Occupational Licensing Directory. Gale Cengage Learning, 27500 Drake Rd. Farmington Hills, MI 48331-3535. Phone: 800-877-GALE or (248)699-4253 Fax: 800-414-5043 E-mail: gale.galeord@cengage.com • URL: http://gale.cengage.com • 1996. $125.00. Second edition. Provides detailed national and state information on the requirements for obtaining a license in each of about 500 occupations. Information needed to contact the appropriate licensing agency or organization is included in each case.

Professional Arts Management Institute. 110 Riverside Dr., No. 4E New York, NY 10024. Phone: (212)579-2039 or (212)787-1194 Fax: (212)579-2049 E-mail: skipreiss@aol. com • URL: http://www.artsmanagementnews.com • Intensive training program designed to supplement the knowledge and skills of both professionals and students interested in or involved in managing cultural institutions and performing arts programs. Conducts one three-day seminar per year; compiles statistics.

Professional Audiovideo Retailers Association. 2500 Wilson Blvd. Arlington, VA 22201-3834. Phone: (630)268-1500 Fax: (630)953-8957 E-mail: para@ce.org • URL: http://www. paralink.org • Retailers of specialty high end audio/video equipment. To educate the public on the value, desirability, and quality of audio equipment; to unite manufacturers for the exchange of information on the latest equipment and technological advancements in the industry. Provides computer seminar, service managers seminar, sales training course, and retail financial management course. Offers correspondence course leading to certification as professional audio specialist.

Professional Builder: Small Builders and Contractors Business Magazine. Reed Business Information, 360 Park Ave. S New York, NY 10010. Phone: 800-446-6551 or (646)746-6400 E-mail: corporatecommunications@reedbusiness.com • URL: http://www.reedbusiness.com • 11 times a year. $39.00 per year. Provides price and market forecasts on industrial products, components and materials. Office products, business systems and transportation. Includes supplement *Luxury Homes*. Formerly *Professional Builder and Remodeler*.

Professional Careers Sourcebook. Gale Cengage Learning, 27500 Drake Rd. Farmington Hills, MI 48331-3535. Phone: 800-877-GALE or (248)699-4253 Fax: 800-414-5043 E-mail: gale.galeord@cengage.com • URL: http://gale. cengage.com • 2002. $155.00. Seventh edition. Includes information sources for 129 professional and technical occupations.

Professional Carwashing and Detailing. National Trade Publications, Inc., 13 Century Hill Dr. Latham, NY 12110-2113. Phone: (518)783-1281 Fax: (518)783-1386 • URL: http:// www.carwash.com • Monthly. Free to qualified personnel. Edited for owners, operators, and managers of automatic carwashes, custom hand carwash facilities, detail shops, and coin-operated, self-service carwashes.

Professional Construction Estimators Association of America. P.O. Box 680336 Charlotte, NC 28216. Phone: 877-521-7232 or (704)987-9978 Fax: (704)987-9979 E-mail: pcea@pcea. org • URL: http://www.pcea.org • Members are building and construction cost estimators.

Professional Convention Management Association. 2301 S Lake Shore Dr., Ste. 1001 Chicago, IL 60616-1419. Phone: 877-827-7262 or (312)423-7262 Fax: (312)423-7222 E-mail: president@pcma.org • URL: http://www.pcma.org • Represents the interests of meeting management executives from associations, non-profit organizations, corporations, independent meeting planning companies, and multi-management firms who recognize the importance of meetings to their organization. Provides education, research and advocacy to advance the meetings and hospitality industry. Empowers members with the tools they need to succeed as meeting professionals and to promote the value of the industry to their organizations and the general public.

Professional Corporations and Associations. Berrien C. Eaton.

LexisNexis Matthew Bender, 1275 Broadway Albany, NY 12204. Phone: 800-424-4200 or (518)487-3000 Fax: (518)487-3584 E-mail: bookstore.support@lexisnexis.com • URL: http://www.bender.com • Semiannual. $1,432.00 per year. Six looseleaf volumes. Detailed information on forming, operating and changing a professional corporation or association.

The *Professional Cosmetologist*. John Dalton. West Group, 610 Opperman Dr. Eagan, MN 55123. Phone: 800-338-9424 or (651)687-7000 Fax: 800-340-9378 E-mail: bookstore@ westgroup.com • URL: http://www.westgroup.com • 1992. $42.50. Fourth edition.

Professional Freelance Writers Directory. The National Writers Association, 10940 S Parker Rd., No. 508 Parker, CO 80134. Phone: (303)841-0246 Fax: (303)841-2607 E-mail: natlwritersassn@hotmail.com • URL: http://www. nationalwriters.com • Database covers: about 200 professional members selected from the club's membership on the basis of significant articles or books, or production of plays or movies. Entries include: Name, address, phone (home and business numbers), special fields of writing competence, titles of books published by royalty firms, mention of contributions to specific magazines, journals, newspapers or anthologies, recent awards received, relevant activities and skills (photography, etc.).

Professional Golfers' Association of America.

Professional Lawn Care Association of America. 1000 Johnson Ferry Rd., Suite C-135 Marietta, GA 30068-6071. Phone: 800-458-3466 or (770)977-5222 Fax: (770)578-6071 E-mail: plcaa@plcaa.org • URL: http://www.plcaa.org • Members are active in the business of treating lawns with chemicals.

Professional Liability: An Economic Analysis. Roger Bowles and Philip Jones. Macmillan Publishing Co., Inc., 175 Fifth Ave. New York, NY 10010. Phone: (212)982-3900 or (212)777-6359 • URL: http://www.macmillan.com • 1989. $14.00. (David Hume Papers: No. 11).

Professional Management of Housekeeping Operations. Robert J. Martin and Tom Jones. John Wiley and Sons, Inc., 111 River St. Hoboken, NJ 07030. Phone: 800-225-5945 or (201)748-6000 Fax: (201)748-6088 E-mail: info@wiley.com • URL: http://www.wiley.com • 1998. $75.00. Third edition. For hotels and motels.

The *Professional Manager*. Institute of Industrial Engineers, 3377 Parkway Ln., Ste. 200 Norcross, GA 30092. Phone: 800-494-0460 or (770)449-0460 Fax: (770)441-3295 Bimonthly. Free to members; non-members, $24.00 per year. Features articles on the latest problem-solving techniques and trends available to industrial managers. Formerly *Industrial Management*.

Professional Negligence Law Reporter. American Association for Justice, 777 6th St. NW Washington, DC 20001. Phone: 800-424-2725 or (202)965-3500 Fax: (202)965-0030 E-mail: customer.service@mcgraw-hill.com • URL: http://www.atla. org • Description: Covers professional negligence cases, including verdicts, settlements, and court opinions. Coverage focuses on health care providers, accountants, lawyers, engineers, insurance brokers and nursing homes, among other areas. Recurring features include bylined articles, bibliographies, and indexes.

Professional Numismatists Guild. 3950 Concordia Ln., 3950 Concordia Lane Fallbrook, CA 92028. Phone: (760)728-1300 Fax: (760)728-8507 E-mail: info@pngdealers.com • URL: http://www.pngdealers.com • Represents coin dealers who have been involved full-time in the profession for at least five years. Establishes, promotes, and defends ethics in the hobby of numismatics.

Professional Photographer. Professional Photographers of America, 229 Peachtree St., NE, Ste. 2200 Atlanta, GA 30303. Phone: 800-786-6277 or (404)522-8600 Fax: (404)614-6405 E-mail: csc@ppa.com • URL: http://www. ppa.com • Monthly. $27.00 per year.

Professional Photographers of America. 229 Peachtree St., N.E., Suite 2200 Atlanta, GA 30303. Phone: 800-786-6277 or (404)522-8600 Fax: (404)614-6404 E-mail: csc@ppa.com • URL: http://www.ppa.com • Formerly Photographer's Association of America.

Professional Pilot-FBO Directory. Queensmith Communications Corp., 3014 Colvin St. Alexandria, VA 22314. Phone: 800-222-3212 or (703)370-0606 Fax: (703)370-7082 E-mail: editorial@propilotmag.com • URL: http://www.propilotmag. com • Annual. $8.00. Includes information for about 1,600 airports and fixed-base operators.

Professional Pilot Magazine. Queensmith Communications Corp., 3014 Colvin St. Alexandria, VA 22314. Phone: 800-222-3212 or (703)370-0606 Fax: (703)370-7082 E-mail: editorial@propilotmag.com • URL: http://www.propilotmag. com • Monthly. $36.00 per year. Edited for career pilots in all areas of aviation: airline, corporate, charter, and military. Includes flying technique, avionics, navigation, accident analysis, career planning, corporate profiles, and business aviation news.

Professional Practice for Interior Design. Christine M. Piotrowski. John Wiley and Sons, Inc., 111 River St. Hoboken, NJ 07030. Phone: 800-225-5945 or (201)748-6000 Fax: (201)748-6088 E-mail: info@wiley.com • URL: http://www. wiley.com • 2001. $75.00. Third edition. (Interior Design Series).

Professional Reactor Operator Society. PO Box 484 Byron, IL 61010-0484. Phone: (815)234-8140 Fax: (815)234-8140 E-mail: info@pngdealers.com • URL: http://nucpros.com •

Plenary members are licensed and certified nuclear reactor operators; associate members include equipment manufacturers and utility companies. Aims to develop a communication network between nuclear reactor operators and government agencies, Congress, and industry in order to promote safety and efficiency in nuclear facilities. Believes that the education, experience, and training of nuclear facility operators have not been fairly considered in the formation of regulations, guidelines, and decisions that affect their careers. Areas of concern include educational requirements and job stress. Plans to survey the views and concerns of members and other involved parties; also plans personal presentations of members' views, supported by scientific data, to persons in the decision-making process. Offers direct mailing service to members from advertisers and placement agencies. Compiles statistics.

Professional Resumes for Accounting, Tax, Finance and Law: A Special Gallery of Best Resumes by Professional Resume Writers. David H. Noble. JIST Publishing, 8902 Otis Ave. Indianapolis, IN 46216-1033. Phone: 800-648-5478 or (317)613-4200 Fax: 800-547-8329 or (317)613-4307 E-mail: info@jist.com • URL: http://www.jist.com • 1999. $19.95. Written for accounting, tax, law, and finance professionals. In addition to advice, provides 335 sample resumes and 22 cover letters.

Professional Safety. American Society of Safety Engineers, 1800 E Oakton St. Des Plaines, IL 60018-2187. Phone: (847)699-2929 Fax: (847)768-3434 E-mail: customerservice@asse.org • URL: http://www.asse.org • Monthly. Free to members; non-members, $60.00 per year. Emphasis is on research and technology in the field of accident prevention.

Professional Secretary's Encyclopedic Dictionary. Mary A. DeVries. Prentice Hall PTR, 240 Frisch Ct. Paramus, NJ 07652. Phone: 800-282-0693 Fax: 800-445-6991 • URL: http://www.phptr.com • 2001. $33.00. Fifth revised edition.

Professional Services Management Association., 44 Canal Center Plz., Ste. 44 Alexandria, VA 22314. Phone: (866)739-0277 or (703)739-0277 Fax: (703)549-2498 E-mail: info@psmanet.org • URL: http://www.psmanet.org • Individuals responsible for any or all aspects of business management in a professional design firm. Aims to improve the effectiveness of professional design firms through the growth and development of business management skills. Seeks to: provide a forum for the exchange of ideas and information and discussion and resolution of common problems and issues; establish guidelines for approaches to common management concerns; initiate and maintain professional relationships among members; improve recognition and practice of management as a science in professional design firms; advance and improve reputable service to clients; offer a variety of comprehensive educational programs and opportunities. Maintains speakers' bureau and placement service. Holds seminars. Conducts surveys and research programs. Compiles statistics.

Professional's Guide to Successful Management: The Eight Essentials for Running Your Firm, Practice, or Partnership. Carol A. O'Connor. McGraw-Hill, 1221 Ave. of the Americas New York, NY 10020. Phone: 800-722-4726 or (212)512-2000 Fax: (212)512-4502 E-mail: customer.service@mcgraw-hill.com • URL: http://www.mcgraw-hill.com • 1994. Price on application.

Profiles in Business and Management: An International Directory of Scholars and Their Research [CD-ROM]. Harvard Business School Publishing, 60 Harvard Way Boston, MA 02163. Phone: 800-988-0886 or (617)783-7500 Fax: (617)496-1029 • URL: http://www.hbsp.harvard.edu • Annual. $595.00. Fully searchable CD-ROM version of two-volume printed directory. Contains bibliographic and biographical information for over 5600 business and management experts active in 21 subject areas. Formerly *International Directory of Business and Management Scholars*.

Profiles of American Labor Unions. Gale Cengage Learning, 27500 Drake Rd. Farmington Hills, MI 48331-3535. Phone: 800-877-GALE or (248)699-4253 Fax: 800-414-5043 E-mail: gale.galeord@cengage.com • URL: http://gale.cengage.com • 1998. $315.00. Second edition. Provides detailed information on more than 280 national labor unions. Includes descriptions of about 800 bargaining agreements and biographies of more than 170 union officials. Local unions are also listed. Four indexes. Formerly *American Directory of Organized Labor* (1992).

Profiles of Success. International Health, Racquet, and Sportsclub Association, 263 Summer St. Boston, MA 02210. Phone: 800-228-4772 or (617)951-0055 Fax: (617)951-0056 E-mail: info@ihrsa.org • URL: http://www.ihrsa.org • Annual. Members, $125.00; non-members, $500.00. Provides detailed financial statistics for commercial health clubs, sports clubs, and gyms.

Profiles of U. S. Hospitals. Dorland Healthcare Information, 1500 Walnut St., Suite 1000 Philadelphia, PA 19102. Phone: 800-784-2332 or (215)875-1212 Fax: (215)735-3966 E-mail: info@dorlandhealth.com • URL: http://www.dorlandhealth.com • Annual. $299.00. Contains profiles of more than 6,000 community, teaching, children's, specialty, psychiatric, and rehabilitation hospitals. Emphasis is on 50 key financial and performance measures. Annual CD-ROM version with key word searching is available at $395.00.

Profit Investor Portfolio: The International Magazine of Money

and Style. Profit Publications, Inc., 69-730 Highway 111, Suite 102 Rancho Mirage, CA 92270-9822. Phone: (619)202-1545 Fax: (619)202-1544 • URL: http://www.profitinc.com • Bimonthly. $29.95 per year. A glossy consumer magazine featuring specific investment recommendations and articles on upscale travel and shopping.

Profit Sharing. Profit Sharing-401(K) Council of America, 10 S. Riverside Plaza, Suite 1610 Chicago, IL 60606-3802. Phone: (312)441-8550 Fax: (312)441-8559 Bimonthly. Membership.

Profit Sharing: Does It Make a Difference? The Productivity and Stability Effects of Profit Sharing Plans. Douglas L. Kruse. W. E. Upjohn Institute for Employment Research, 300 S. Westnedge Ave. Kalamazoo, MI 49007-4686. Phone: (269)343-5541 Fax: (269)343-3308 E-mail: webmaster@upjohninstitute.org • URL: http://www.upjohninst.org • 1993. $37.00.

Profit Sharing/401(K) Council of America., 10 S. Riverside Plaza, No. 1610 Chicago, IL 60606-3802. Phone: (312)441-8550 Fax: (312)441-8559 E-mail: psca@psca.org • URL: http://www.psca.org • Members are business firms with profit sharing and/or 401(K) plans. Affiliated with the Profit Sharing/401(K) Education Foundation. Formerly Profit Sharing Council of America.

Profit Sharing/401(K) Education Foundation., 10 S. Riverside Plaza Chicago, IL 60606-3802. Phone: (312)441-8550 Fax: (312)441-8559 E-mail: psca@psca.org • URL: http://www.psca.org • Affiliated with Profit Sharing/401(k) Council of America. Formerly Profit Sharing Research Foundation.

Profitable Investing. Richard E. Band, editor. Profitable Investing, 7811 Montrose Rd. Potomac, MD 20854. Phone: 800-211-8565 or (301)340-7788 Fax: (301)309-3847 E-mail: service@rband.com • URL: http://www.pbimedia.com • Description: Advises individuals seeking low-risk growth by providing "a wealth of information." Discusses various stocks, mutual funds, interest income, and tax issues. Contains lists of best investments.

Profitable Restaurant Management. Drysdale. Prentice Hall PTR, 240 Frisch Ct. Paramus, NJ 07652. Phone: 800-282-0693 Fax: 800-445-6991 • URL: http://www.phptr.com • 2000. Price on application.

Profiting from Real Estate Rehab. Sandra M. Brassfield. John Wiley and Sons, Inc., 111 River St. Hoboken, NJ 07030. Phone: 800-225-5945 or (201)748-6000 Fax: (201)748-6088 E-mail: info@wiley.com • URL: http://www.wiley.com • 1992. $42.95. How to fix up old houses and sell them at a profit.

Program: Electronic Library and Information Systems. Available from Information Today, Inc., 143 Old Marlton Pike Medford, NJ 08055-8750. Phone: 800-300-9868 or (609)654-6266 Fax: (609)654-4309 E-mail: custserv@infotoday.com • URL: http://www.infotoday.com • Quarterly. $339.00 per year. Published in London by Aslib: The Association for Information Management. Discusses computer applications for libraries.

Program in International Studies in Planning., Cornell University, Dept. of City Regional Planning, 106 W. Sibley Hall Ithaca, NY 14853-3901. Phone: (607)255-4331 Fax: (607)255-1971 E-mail: bdl5@cornell.edu • URL: http://www.inet.crp.cornell.edu/organizations/isp • Research activities are related to international urban and regional planning, with emphasis on developing areas.

Progress in Aerospace Sciences: An International Journal. Elsevier, 360 Park Ave., S New York, NY 10010-1710. Phone: 888-437-4636 or (212)989-5800 Fax: (212)633-3990 E-mail: usinfo-f@elsevier.com • URL: http://www.elsevier.com • Eight times a year. Institutions, $1,533.00 per year. Text in English, French and German.

Progress in Low Temperature Physics. W. P. Halperin, editor. Elsevier, 360 Park Ave., S New York, NY 10010-1710. Phone: 888-437-4636 or (212)989-5800 Fax: (212)633-3990 E-mail: usinfo-f@elsevier.com • URL: http://www.elsevier.com • 1996. $228.00. Volume 14.

Progress in Materials Science: An International Review Journal. Elsevier, 360 Park Ave., S. New York, NY 10010-1710. Phone: 888-437-4636 or (212)989-5800 Fax: (212)633-3990 E-mail: usinfo-f@elsevier.com • URL: http://www.elsevier.com • Bimonthly. $1,120.00 per year.

Progress in Oceanography. Elsevier, 360 Park Ave., S. New York, NY 10010-1710. Phone: 888-437-4636 or (212)989-5800 Fax: (212)633-3990 E-mail: usinfo-f@elsevier.com • URL: http://www.elsevier.com • 16 times a year. Qualified personnel, $175.00 per year; individuals, $168.00 per year; institutions, $2,392.00 per year.

Progress in Planning. Elsevier, 360 Park Ave, S New York, NY 10010-1710. Phone: 888-437-4636 or (212)989-5800 Fax: (212)633-3990 E-mail: usinfo-f@elsevier.com • URL: http://www.elsevier.com • Eight times a year. $755.00 per year.

Progressive Farmer. Progressive Farmer, Inc., 2100 Lakeshore Dr. Birmingham, AL 35209. Phone: (205)877-6419 Fax: (205)877-6750 E-mail: jodie@progressivefarmer.com • URL: http://www.pathfinder.com/pf • 18 times a year. $18.00 per year. 17 regional editions. Includes supplement *Rural Sportsman*.

Progressive Grocer. VNU Business Media, 770 Broadway New York, NY 10003-9595. Phone: 800-344-7119 or (646)654-4500 Fax: (646)654-7212 • URL: http://www.vnubusinessmedia.com • 18 times a year. $129.00 per year. Formerly *Supermarket Business*.

Progressive Grocer Guidebook. Trade Dimensions, 45 Danbury

Rd. Wilton, CT 06897. Phone: 800-291-0410 or (203)563-3000 Fax: (203)563-3131 E-mail: info@tradedimensions.com • URL: http://www.tradedimensions.com • Annual. $375.00. Over 800 major chain and independent food retailers and wholesalers in the United States and Canada; also includes food brokers, rack jobbers, candy and tobacco distributors, and magazine distributors.

Progressive Grocer: The Magazine of Supermarketing. VNU Business Media, 770 Broadway New York, NY 10003-9595. Phone: 800-344-7119 or (646)654-4500 Fax: (646)654-7212 • URL: http://www.vnubusinessmedia.com • 18 times a year. $129.00 per year.

Progressive Political Action Committee., 1899 L St. NW, Ste. 800 Washington, DC 20036. Phone: (202)833-3290 E-mail: iacenter@iacenter.org Contributors: 10,000. To support, by independent expenditure, the election of progressive candidates and the reelection of progressive incumbents. Actively works to defeat conservative politicians.

Progressive Railroading. Trade Press Publishing Corp., 2100 W. Florist Ave. Milwaukee, WI 53209-3799. Phone: 800-727-7995 or (414)228-7701 Fax: (414)228-1134 • URL: http://www.tradepress.com • Monthly. Free to qualified personnel. Provides feature articles, news, new product information, etc. Relative to the railroad and rail transit industry.

Project '88: Americans for the Reagan Agenda., 1667 K St. NW, Ste. 700 Washington, DC 20006. Phone: (202)785-0500 E-mail: richard.wallace@scbar.org U.S. citizens who support the economic and foreign policies of President Ronald Reagan (1911-) and his administration. Seeks a continuation of these policies beyond President Reagan's term in office by organizing grass roots support for his positions on various issues, most notably contra aid, the Strategic Defense Initiative (Star Wars), and the national budget. Plans to publish a newsletter and various briefs pertaining to current issues in foreign and domestic policy.

Project Finance Monthly. Infocast Inc., 6800 Owensmouth Ave, Ste. 300 Canoga Park, CA 91303. Phone: (818)888-4444 Fax: (818)888-4440 E-mail: service@rband.com • URL: http://www.informationforecast.com • Description: Provides information about the power industry. Includes industry news, financing, regulation, and contracts.

Project Finance: The Magazine for Global Development. American Educational Systems, PO Box 246 New York, NY 10024-0246. Phone: 800-431-1579 E-mail: aesbooks@aol.com 11 times a year. $740.00 per year. Includes print and on-line editions. Provides articles on the financing of the infrastructure (transportation, utilities, communications, the environment, etc). Coverage is international. Supplements available *World Export Credit Guide* and *Project Finance Book of Lists*. Formed by the merger of *Infrastructure Finance* and *Project and Trade Finance*.

Project Leadership. James P. Lewis. McGraw-Hill, 1221 Ave. of the Americas New York, NY 10020. Phone: 800-722-4726 or (212)512-2000 Fax: (212)512-4502 E-mail: customer.service@mcgraw-hill.com • URL: http://www.mcgraw-hill.com • 2002. $29.95. Provides detailed advice for project managers in a leadership role. (Teach Yourself Series).

Project Management. Dennis Lock. John Wiley and Sons, Inc., 111 River St. Hoboken, NJ 07030. Phone: 800-225-5945 or (201)748-6000 Fax: (201)748-6088 E-mail: info@wiley.com • URL: http://www.wiley.com • 2000. $87.95. Seventh edition.

Project Management: A Managerial Approach. Jack R. Meredith and Samuel J. Mantel. John Wiley and Sons, Inc., 111 River St. Hoboken, NJ 07030. Phone: 800-225-5945 or (201)748-6000 Fax: (201)748-6088 E-mail: info@wiley.com • URL: http://www.wiley.com • 2002. $109.95. Fifth edition. (Productions-Operations Management Series).

Project Management: A Systems Approach to Planning, Scheduling, and Controlling. Harold Kerzner. John Wiley & Sons, Inc., 111 River St. Hoboken, NJ 07030. Phone: 800-225-5945 or (201)748-6000 Fax: (201)748-6088 E-mail: info@wiley.com • URL: http://www.wiley.com • 2003. $80.00. Eighth edition. Includes chapters on time management, risk management, quality management, and program evaluation and review techniques (PERT). (Industrial Engineering Series).

Project Management Casebook. David I. Cleland and others, editors. Project Management Institute, Four Campus Newton Square, PA 19073-3299. Phone: (610)356-4600 Fax: (610)356-4647 E-mail: pmihq@pmi.org • URL: http://www.pmi.org • 1998. $69.95. Provides 50 case studies in various areas of project management.

Project Management Essential Library. Management Concepts, Inc., 8230 Leesburg Pike Vienna, VA 22182. Phone: 800-506-4450 or (703)790-9595 Fax: (703)790-1371 • URL: http://www.managementconcepts.com • 2002. $190.00. Consists of 11 separate books by various authors, covering many project management topics, including leadership, value determination, risk management, estimating, scheduling, results measurement, and quality control. (Books are available individually at $24.95.)

Project Management: How to Plan and Manage Successful Projects. Joan Knutson and Others. AMACOM, 1601 Broadway New York, NY 10019. Phone: 800-262-9699 or (518)586-8100 Fax: (518)903-8168 E-mail: customerservice@amanet.org • URL: http://www.amacombooks.org • 1991. $55.00. Covers both technical and organizational skills.

Project Management Institute., 14 Campus Blvd. Newtown Square, PA 19073-3299. Phone: (610)356-4600 Fax: (610)356-4647 E-mail: customercare@pmi.org • URL: http://www.pmi.org • Corporations and individuals engaged in the practice of project management; project management students and educators. Seeks to advance the study, teaching, and practice of project management. Establishes project management standards; conducts educational and professional certification courses; bestows Project Management Professional credential upon qualified individuals. Offers educational seminars and global congresses.

Project Management Journal. Project Management Institute, Four Campus Blvd. Newton Square, PA 19073. Phone: (610)356-4600 Fax: (610)356-4647 E-mail: pmihq@pmi.org • URL: http://www.pmi.org • Four times a year. Membership. Contains technical articles dealing with the interests of the field of project management.

Project Management Salary Survey. Project Management Institute, Four Campus Blvd. Newton Square, PA 19073-3299. Phone: (610)356-4600 Fax: (610)356-4647 E-mail: pmihq@pmi.org • URL: http://www.pmi.org • Annual. $129.00. Gives compensation data for key project management positions in North America, according to job title, level of responsibility, number of employees supervised, and various other factors. Includes data on retirement plans and benefits.

Project Management: Strategic Design and Implementation. David I. Cleland and Lewis R. Ireland. McGraw-Hill, 1221 Ave. of the Americas New York, NY 10020. Phone: 800-722-4762 or (212)512-2000 Fax: (212)512-4502 E-mail: customer.service@mcgraw-hill.com • URL: http://www.mcgraw-hill.com • 2002. $64.95. Fourth edition.

Project Management with CPM, Pert and Precedence Diagramming. Joseph J. Moder and others. Blitz Publishing Co., 1600 N. High Point Rd. Middleton, WI 53562-3635. Phone: 800-434-5595 or (608)836-7550 Fax: (608)831-5598 E-mail: wcdries@hotmail.com • URL: http://www.badgerbooks.com • 1995. $40.00. Third edition.

Project Manager's Desk Reference: A Comprehensive Guide to Project Planning, Evaluation and Control. James P. Lewis. McGraw-Hill, 1221 Ave. of the Americas New York, NY 10020. Phone: 800-722-4726 or (212)512-2000 Fax: (212)512-4502 E-mail: customer.service@mcgraw-hill.com • URL: http://www.mcgraw-hill.com • 1999. $70.00. Second edition. Includes scheduling with PERT (Program Evaluation and Review Technique), CPM (Critical Path Method), and Gantt schedules. Covers the steps for "planning, monitoring, and controlling any project."

Project on Government Oversight., 666 11th St. NW, Ste. 900 Washington, DC 20001-4542. Phone: (202)347-1122 Fax: (202)347-1116 E-mail: info@pogo.org • URL: http://www.pogo.org • Promotes accountability in government; monitors governmental agencies; exposes abuses of power, and waste and fraud committed by the government and its contractors. **Convention/Meeting:** none.

Projections of Education Statistics. Available from U. S. Government Printing Office, Washington, DC 20402. Phone: (202)512-1800 Fax: (202)512-2250 E-mail: gpoaccess@gpo.gov • URL: http://www.access.gpo.gov • Annual. $26.00. Issued by the U. S. Department of Education, National Center for Education Statistics (http://www.ed.gov). Provides 10-year projections of data relating to elementary schools, secondary schools, and institutions of higher learning. Includes projections of enrollment, graduates, classroom teachers, and expenditures.

PROMAX., 9000 W Sunset Blvd., Ste. 900 Los Angeles, CA 90069. Phone: (310)788-7600 Fax: (310)788-7616 E-mail: michael.d.benson@abc.com • URL: http://www.promax.tv • Advertising, public relations, and promotion managers of cable, radio, and television stations, systems and networks; syndicators. Seeks to: advance the role and increase the effectiveness of promotion and marketing within the industry, related industries, and educational communities. Conducts workshops and weekly fax service for members. Operates employment service. Maintains speakers' bureau, hall of fame, and resource center with print, audio, and visual materials.

PROMO Annual SourceBook: The Only Guide to the $70 Billion Promotion Industry. Primedia Business Magazines and Media, 11 River Bend Dr., S Stamford, CT 06907. Phone: 800-795-5445 or (203)358-9900 Fax: (203)358-5811 E-mail: subs@primediabusiness.com • URL: http://www.primediabusiness.com • Annual. $49.95. Lists service and supply companies for the promotion industry. Includes annual salary survey and award winning campaigns.

The PROMO 100 Promotion Agency Ranking. PROMO Magazine, 11 River Bend Dr. S Stamford, CT 06907-0949. Phone: (866)505-7173 or (203)358-4159 Fax: (203)358-5812 E-mail: kjoyce@primediabusiness.com • URL: http://www.primediabusines.com • Covers: Ranking of the top 100 U.S. Promotion agencies. Entries include: Name, address, phone, financial data, client lists, rate of growth, name of CEO, and description of product/service.

PROMO: Promotion Marketing Worldwide. Primedia Business Magazines and Media, 11 Riverbend Dr., S Stamford, CT 06907. Phone: 800-307-2529 or (203)358-9900 Fax: (203)358-5811 E-mail: subs@primediabusiness.com • URL: http://www.primediabusiness,com • Monthly. $65.00 per year. Edited for companies and agencies that utilize couponing, point-of-purchase advertising, special events, games, contests, premiums, product samples, and other unique promotional items.

Promotional Marketing. Entrepreneur Media, Inc., 2445 McCabe Way Irvine, CA 92714. Phone: 800-421-2300 or (949)261-2325 Fax: (949)261-0234 E-mail: entmag@entrepreneurmag.com • URL: http://wwww.entrepreneur.com • Looseleaf. $59.50. A practical guide to sales promotion and marketing for small businesses. (Start-Up Business Guide No. E1111.)

Promotional Products Association International., 3125 Skyway Cir. N Irving, TX 75038-3526. Phone: 888-IAM-PPAI or (972)252-0404 Fax: (972)258-3007 E-mail: membership@ppa.org • URL: http://www.ppa.org • Suppliers and distributors of promotional products including incentives, imprinted ad specialties, premiums, and executive gifts. Promotes industry contacts in 60 countries. Holds executive development and sales training seminars. Conducts research and compiles statistics. Administers industry advertising and public relations program. Maintains speakers' bureau. Conducts trade shows, regional training, publishes educational resources.

Prompt. Pasadena IBM User Group, 2303 Glen Canyon Rd. Altadena, CA 91001-3539. Phone: (818)791-1600 Fax: (818)791-1600 E-mail: 71333.130@compuserve.com Monthly. Membership. Helps users of IBM compatibles understand their system.

PROMT: Predicasts Overview of Markets and Technology. Gale Cengage Learning, 27500 Drake Rd. Farmington Hills, MI 48331-3535. Phone: 800-877-GALE or (248)699-GALE Fax: 800-414-5043 or (248)699-8069 E-mail: galeord@gale.com • URL: http://gale.cengage.com • Companies, products, applied technologies and markets. U.S. and international literature coverage, 1972 to date. Inquire as to online cost and availability. Provides abstracts from more than 1,600 publications. Weekly updates.

Proofs: Buyers' Guide and United States Manufacturers' Directory. PennWell Publishing, Dental Economics Div., PO Box 3408 Tulsa, OK 74101. Phone: 800-331-4463 or (918)835-3161 E-mail: headquarters@pennwell.com • URL: http://www.pennwell.com • Annual. $30.00. List of over 600 manufacturers of dental products and equipment; coverage includes foreign listings.

Proofs: The Magazine of Dental Sales. PennWell Corp., Industrial Div., 1421 S. Sheridan Rd. Tulsa, OK 74112. Phone: 800-331-4463 or (918)835-3161 E-mail: bid@pennwell.com • URL: http://www.pennwell.com • Five times a year. $35.00 per year.

Properties. Properties Magazine, Inc., P.O. Box 112127 Cleveland, OH 44111-8127. Phone: (216)251-0035 Fax: (216)251-0064 Monthly. $17.95 per year. News and features of interest to income property owners managers and related industries in Northeastern Ohio.

Property and Liability Insurance. Solomon S. Huebner and Kenneth Black. Prentice Hall PTR, 240 Frisch Ct. Paramus, NJ 07652. Phone: 800-282-0693 Fax: 800-445-6991 • URL: http://www.phptr.com • 2000. $72.00. Fourth edition.

Property-Casualty Insurance Facts. Insurance Information Institute, 110 William St., 24th Fl. New York, NY 10038. Phone: 800-331-9146 or (212)669-9200 Fax: (212)732-1916 E-mail: info@iii.org • URL: http://www.iii.org • Annual. $22.50. Formerly *Insurance Facts*.

Property Management Association., 7900 Wisconsin Ave., Ste. 305 Bethesda, MD 20814. Phone: (301)657-9200 Fax: (301)907-9326 E-mail: info@pma-dc.org • URL: http://www.pma-dc.org • Property management professionals who own and operate multifamily residential, commercial, retail, industrial and other income-producing properties and firms that provide goods and services used in real property management. Works to enhance the interests and welfare of property owners, managers, supervisory employees, and contractors involved in the management of multifamily residential and commercial property. Provides education and a forum for exchange of ideas on efficient methods of operation and progressive policies of management.

Property Tax Alert. State Taxation Institute, 4025 W Peterson Ave. Chicago, IL 60646-6085. Phone: 800-TELL-CCH or (847)267-7000 Fax: (773)866-3895 E-mail: cservice@ragan.com • URL: http://www.cch.com • Description: Features updates on property tax issues. Recurring features include a calendar of events and notices of publications available.

Property Tax Manual. Vertex, Inc., 1041 Old Cassatt Rd. Berwyn, PA 19312. Phone: 800-355-3500 or (610)640-4200 Fax: (610)640-5892 • URL: http://www.vertexinc.com • Price on application. Lists tax rates, assessment ratios, assessors, filing requirements, depreciation schedules, etc.

Proposal Development: How to Respond and Win the Bid. Bud Porter-Roth. PSI Research, P.O. Box 3727 Central Point, OR 97502-0032. Phone: 800-228-2275 or (541)245-6502 Fax: (541)245-6505 E-mail: information@psi-research.com • URL: http://www.psi-research.com • 1998. $21.95. Third revised edition. A step-by-step guide to the practical details of preparing, printing, and submitting business proposals of various kinds. (Successful Business Library Series).

Proposal Planning and Writing. Lynn E. Miner and Jeremy T. Miner. Greenwood Publishing Group, Inc., 88 Post Rd., W. Westport, CT 06881. Phone: 800-225-5800 or (203)226-3571 Fax: (203)431-2214 E-mail: customer-service@greenwood.com • URL: http://www.greenwood.com • 2003. $39.95. Third edition. Discusses the steps necessary to locate and obtain funding from the federal government, foundations, and corporations.

Proposal Preparation. Rodney D. Stewart and Ann L. Stewart. John Wiley and Sons, Inc., 111 River St. Hoboken, NJ 07030. Phone: 800-225-5945 or (201)748-6000 Fax: (201)748-6088 E-mail: info@wiley.com • URL: http://www.wiley.com • 1992. $150.00. Second edition. Covers proposals of various kinds. (New Dimensions in Engineering Series, vol. 6).

ProQuest Direct. ProQuest Inc.Phone: 800-889-3358 or (734)761-4700 Fax: (734)662-4554 • URL: http://proquest.com • Fee-based Web site providing Internet access to more than 3,000 periodicals, newspapers, and other publications. Many items are available full-text, with daily updates. Includes extensive corporate and financial information. Fees: Apply.

ProSales Buyer's Guide. Hanley-Wood, LLC, One Thomas Circle, NW Washington, DC 20005. Phone: 800-837-0870 or (202)452-0800 Fax: (202)785-1974 • URL: http://www.hanley-wood.com • Annual. Price on application. A directory of equipment for professional builders.

ProSales: For Dealers and Distributors Serving the Professional Contractor. Hanley-Wood LLC, One Thomas Circle NW Washington, DC 20005. Phone: 800-837-0870 or (202)452-0800 Fax: (202)785-1974 • URL: http://www.hanley-wood.com • Monthly. $36.00 per year. Includes special feature issues on selling, credit, financing, and the marketing of power tools.

ProSound News: The International Newsmagazine for the Professional Recording an d Sound Production Industry. United Entertainment Media, 460 Park Ave. S, 9th Fl. New York, NY 10016. Phone: (212)378-0400 Fax: (212)378-2158 • URL: http://www.uemedia.com • Monthly. $30.00 per year. Provides industry news for recording studios, audio contractors, sound engineers, and sound reinforcement specialists.

Prospector's Choice: The Electronic Product Profiling 10,000 Corporate and Foundation Grantmakers. Gale Cengage Learning, 27500 Drake Rd. Farmington Hills, MI 48331-3535. Phone: 800-877-GALE or (248)699-GALE Fax: 800-414-5043 or (248)699-8069 E-mail: galeord@gal.com • URL: http://gale.cengage.com • Annual. Provides detailed CD-ROM information on foundations and corporate philanthropies. Also known as *Corporate and Foundation Givers on Disk*.

Protecting Stream Corridors. Lee Nellis. Sage Publications, Inc., 2455 Teller Rd. Thousand Oaks, CA 91320. Phone: 800-818-7243 or (805)499-0774 Fax: 800-583-2665 or (805)499-0871 E-mail: webmaster@sagepub.com • URL: http://www.sagepub.com • 1993. $10.00.

Protecting Trade Secrets, Patents, Copyrights, and Trademarks. Robert C. Dorr and Christopher H. Munch. Aspen Publishers, Inc., 200 Orchard Ridge Dr., Ste. 200 Gaithersburg, MD 20878. Phone: 800-234-1660 or (301)417-7500 E-mail: customer.service@aspenpubl.com • URL: http://www.aspenpublishers.com • $165.00. Looseleaf service.

Protecting Your Practice. Katherine Vessenes. Bloomberg, 499 Park Ave. New York, NY 10022. Phone: 800-388-2749 or (212)318-2000 Fax: (917)369-5000 • URL: http://www.bloomberg.com • 1997. $60.00. Discusses legal compliance issues for financial planners. (Bloomberg Professional Library.)

Protocol (Corporate Meetings, Entertainment, and Special Events). Protocol Directory, Inc., 101 W. 12th St., Suite PHH New York, NY 10011. Phone: (212)633-6934 Fax: (212)633-6934 E-mail: protoefg@aol.com Annual. $48.00. Provides information for about 4,000 suppliers of products and services for special events, shows (entertainment), and business meetings. Geographic arrangement.

Provider: For Long Term Care Professionals. American Health Care Association, 1201 L St., N. W. Washington, DC 20005. Phone: (202)842-4444 Fax: (202)842-3860 E-mail: webmaster@ahca.org • URL: http://www.ahca.org • Monthly. $48.00 per year. Free to qualified personnel; others, $48.00 per year. Edited for medical directors, administrators, owners, and others concerned with extended care facilities and nursing homes. Covers business management, legal issues, financing, reimbursement, care planning, ethics, human resources, etc. Includes *Buyers' Guide*.

Provider: LTC Buyers' Guide. American Health Care Association, 1201 L St., NW Washington, DC 20005. Phone: 800-321-4444 or (202)842-4444 Fax: (202)842-3860 E-mail: webmaster@ahca.org • URL: http://www.ahca.org • Annual. $10.00. Lists several hundred manufacturers and suppliers of products and services for long term care (LTC) facilities.

Provincial Outlook. Conference Board of Canada, 255 Smyth Rd. Ottawa, ON, Canada K1H 8M7. Phone: (866)-711-2262 or (613)526-3280 Fax: (613)526-4857 • URL: http://www.conferenceboard.ca • Quarterly. Free to members; non-members, $2,500.00 per year. Contains detailed forecasts of economic conditions in each of the Canadian provinces.

The Prudent Speculator. Al Frank Asset Management, Inc., 32392 Coast Hwy., Ste. 260 Laguna Beach, CA 92651. Phone: 888-994-6827 or (949)497-7657 Fax: (949)499-3218 E-mail: info@alfrank.com Description: Presents a fundamental approach to stock selection and buying strategies for long-term capital gains appreciation. Provides technical analysis to aid market timing for both speculators and conservative investors. Reviews editor's personal common stock portfolio in comparison with the Dow Jones Industrials and New York Stock Exchange Composite Index. Recurring features include a column titled Currently Recommended Stocks with follow-up reviews.

The Prudent Speculator: Al Frank on Investing. Al Frank. McGraw-Hill, 1221 Ave. of the Americas New York, NY 10020. Phone: 800-722-4726 or (212)512-2000 Fax: (212)512-4502 E-mail: customer.service@mcgraw-hill.com • URL: http://www.mcgraw-hill.com • 1989. $30.00. How to be a sensible investor or speculator. Includes advice on the use of margin accounts and stock market timing.

Psychiatric Services. American Psychiatric Association. American Psychiatric Publishing, Inc., 1000 Wilson Blvd., Ste. 1825 Arlington, VA 22209-3901. Phone: 888-357-7924 Fax: (703)907-7322 E-mail: apa@psych.org • URL: http://www. psych.org • Monthly. Members, $60.00 per year; students, Non-members, $73.00 per year; institutions, $161.00 per year; Students, $40.00 per year. Includes online edition. Formerly *Hospital and Community Psychiatry*.

Psychological Abstracts. American Psychological Association. 750 First St., N. E. Washington, DC 20002-4242. Phone: 800-374-2721 or (202)336-5500 Fax: (202)336-6069 • URL: http://www.apa.org • Monthly. Members, $815.00 per year; individuals and institutions, $1,207.00 per year. Covers the international literature of psychology and the behavioral sciences. Includes journals, technical reports, dissertations, and other sources.

Psychological Symptoms. Frank J. Bruno. John Wiley and Sons, Inc., 111 River St. Hoboken, NJ 07030. Phone: 800-225-5945 or (201)748-6000 Fax: (201)748-6088 E-mail: info@wiley. com • URL: http://www.wiley.com • 1994. $29.95. Explains the meaning of common mental symptoms, what may cause them, and how to deal with them.

Psychological Testing: A Practical Introduction. Thomas P. Hogan. John Wiley and Sons, Inc., 111 River St. Hoboken, NJ 07030. Phone: 800-225-5945 or (201)748-6276 Fax: (201)748-8641 E-mail: bookinfo@wiley.com • URL: http:// www.wiley.com • 2002. $111.95.

Psychology and Marketing. John Wiley and Sons, Inc., Journals, 111 River St. Hoboken, NJ 07030. Phone: 800-225-5945 or (201)748-6000 Fax: (201)748-6088 E-mail: customer@ wiley.com • URL: http://www.wiley.com • Eight times a year. $999.00 per year; with online edition, $1,049.00 per year. Spots the latest social, economic, and cultural trends that affect marketing decisions.

Psychology for Leaders: Using Motivation, Conflict, and Power to Manage More Effectively. Dean Tjosvold and Mary Tjosvold. John Wiley and Sons, Inc., 111 River St. Hoboken, NJ 07030. Phone: 800-225-5945 or (201)748-6000 Fax: (201)748-6088 E-mail: info@wiley.com • URL: http://www. wiley.com • 1995. $32.95. (Portable MBA Series).

Psychology in Industrial Organizations. Norman R. Maier and Trudy G. Verser. Houghton Mifflin Co., 222 Berkeley St. Boston, MA 02116. Phone: 800-733-2828 or (617)351-5000 Fax: 800-733-2098 E-mail: inquiries@hmco.com • URL: http://www.hmco.com • 1982. $101.56. Five volumes. Fifth edition.

The Psychology of Decision Making: People in Organizations. Lee R. Beach. Sage Publications, Inc., 2455 Teller Rd. Thousand Oaks, CA 91320. Phone: 800-818-7243 or (805)499-9774 Fax: 800-583-2665 or (805)499-0871 E-mail: webmaster@sagepub.com • URL: http://www.sagepub.com • 1997. $97.95. Includes references and index. (Foundations for Organizational Science Series: Vol. 6).

Psychology Today. Sussex Publishers Inc., 49 E. 21st St., 11th Fl. New York, NY 10010. Phone: 800-234-8361 or (212)260-7210 Fax: (212)260-7445 Bimonthly. $18.00 per year.

Psychotropic Substances. United Nations Publications, Two United Nations Plaza, Rm. DC2-853 New York, NY 10017. Phone: 800-253-9646 or (212)963-8302 Fax: (212)963-3489 Annual. $42.00.

PsycINFO. American Psychological Association, 750 First St., N. E. Washington, DC 20002-4242. Phone: 800-374-2722 or (202)336-5650 Fax: (202)336-5568 • URL: http://www.apa. org/psycinfo • Provides indexing and abstracting of the worldwide literature of psychology and the behavioral sciences. Time period is 1967 to date, with monthly updates. Inquire as to online cost and availability.

PTC Research Foundation.

Public Accounting Report: Competitive Intelligence for Accounting Firms. Strafford Publications, Inc., Specialized Information Services, 590 Dutch Valley Rd., N.E. Atlanta, GA 30324. Phone: 800-926-7926 or (404)881-1141 Fax: (404)881-0074 E-mail: custserv@straffordpub.com • URL: http://www.straffordpub.com • 23 times a year. $360.00 per year. Newsletter. Presents news and trends affecting the accounting profession.

Public Administration and Development: An International Journal of Training, Research and Practice. John Wiley and Sons, Inc., Journals, 111 River St. Hoboken, NJ 07030. Phone: 800-225-5945 or (201)748-6000 Fax: (201)748-6088 E-mail: customer@wiley.com • URL: http://www.wiley.com • Five times a year. Individuals, $485.00 per year; institutions, $970.00 per year. Focuses on administrative practice at the local, regional and national levels. International coverage. Published in England by John Wiley and Sons Ltd.

Public Administration and Public Affairs. Nicholas L. Henry. Prentice Hall PTR, 240 Frisch Ct. Paramus, NJ 07652. Phone: 800-282-0693 Fax: 800-445-6991 • URL: http://www.phptr. com • 2003. $59.00. Ninth edition.

Public Administration: Design and Problem Solving. Jong S.

Jun. Chatelaine Press, 6454 Honey Tree Court Burke, VA 22015. Phone: 800-249-9527 or (703)569-2062 Fax: (703)569-9610 E-mail: arlene@chatpress.com • URL: http:// www.chatpress.com • 1986. $41.95.

Public Administration Review. American Society for Public Administration, 1120 G St., N.W., Suite 700 Washington, DC 20005-3885. Phone: (202)393-7878 Fax: (202)638-4952 E-mail: mhamilton@aspanet.org • URL: http://www.aspanet. org • Bimonthly. Institutions, $209.00 per year. Includes on-line edition.

Public Administration Service., 7927 Jones Branch Dr. S, No. 100 McLean, VA 22102. Phone: (703)734-8970 Fax: (703)734-4965 E-mail: info@pma-dc.org • URL: http:// www.pashq.org • Promotes improvement of public administration through research and provision of consultation services covering a full range of governmental operations in local, state, and federal units. Provides consultancy services on an international level to governments and international agencies in support of national development projects and programs. **Convention/Meeting:** none.

Public Affairs Report. Institute of Governmental Studies, 109 Moses Hall No. 2370, 109 Moses Hall Berkeley, CA 94720-2370. Phone: (510)642-6723 Fax: (510)642-5537 E-mail: igspress@uclink4.berkeley.edu • URL: http://www.igs. berkeley.edu • Description: Publishes essays on emerging governmental and public policy issues of significance to public officials and citizens in both California and the nation. Covers such subjects as pollution, politics, finance, transportation, health and housing policy, and California-Mexico trade relations. Recurring features include bibliographies.

Public Assistance and Welfare Trends: State Capitals. Wakeman-Walworth, Inc., P.O. Box 7376 Alexandria, VA 22307-7376. Phone: 800-876-2545 or (703)768-9600 Fax: (703)768-9690 E-mail: newsletters@statecapitals.com • URL: http://www. statecapitals.com • 50 times a year. $245.00 per year; print and online editions, $350.00 per year. Newsletter. Formerly *From the State Capitals: Public Assistance and Welfare Trends*.

Public Citizen., 1600 20th St. NW Washington, DC 20009. Phone: (202)588-1000 Fax: (202)588-7798 E-mail: member@citizen.org • URL: http://www.citizen.org • Formed by Ralph Nader to support the work of citizen advocates. Areas of focus include: consumer rights in the marketplace, safe products, a healthful environment and workplace, clean and safe energy sources, corporate and government accountability, and citizen empowerment. Methods for change include lobbying, litigation, monitoring government agencies, research, and public education including special reports, periodicals, expert testimony, and news media coverage. Acquires funding primarily through direct mail and also through payment for publications and court awards.

Public Citizen/Freedom of Information Clearinghouse., 1600 20th St. NW Washington, DC 20036. Phone: (202)588-1000 Fax: (202)588-7795 E-mail: member@citizen.org • URL: http://www.citizen.org/litigation/ • Promotes citizen access to government-held information.

Public Citizen's Critical Mass Energy Project., 1600 20th St. NW Washington, DC 20009. Phone: (202)588-1000 Fax: (202)547-7392 E-mail: cmep@citizen.org • URL: http:// www.citizen.org/cmep • Maintains national network of anti-nuclear groups. Affiliated with Public Citizen. Formerly Public Citizen's Critical Mass Energy and Environment Project.

Public Employment. Bureau of the Census, U.S. Department of Commerce. Available from U.S. Government Printing Office, Washington, DC 20402. Phone: (202)512-1800 Fax: (202)512-2250 Annual.

Public Finance Review. Sage Publications, Inc., 2455 Teller Rd. Thousand Oaks, CA 91320. Phone: 800-818-7243 or (805)499-9774 Fax: 800-583-2665 or (805)499-0871 E-mail: webmaster@sagepub.com • URL: http://www.sagepub.com • Bimonthly. Institutions, $599.00 per year; includes print and online editions. Formerly *Public Finance Quarterly*.

Public Human Services Directory. American Public Human Services Association, 810 1st St. NE, Ste. 500, 810 1st St. NE, Ste. 500 Washington, DC 20002. Phone: (202)682-0100 Fax: (202)289-6555 E-mail: pubs@aphsa.org • URL: http://www. aphsa.org • Covers: Federal, state, territorial, county, and major municipal public human service agencies. Entries include: Agency name, address, phone, fax, e-mail address, web site address, names of key personnel, program area.

Public Interest Profiles, 2001-2002. CQ Press, 1255 22nd St., Ste. 400 Washington, DC 20037. Phone: 800-432-2250 or (202)419-8500 Fax: 800-380-3810 E-mail: customerservice@cqpress.com • URL: http://www.cq.com • 2002. $215.00. Provides detailed information on more than 250 influential public interest and public policy organizations (lobbyists) in the U.S. Includes e-mail addresses and Web sites where available. (Public Interest Profile Series).

Public Law Education Institute. Public Law Education Institute, 454 New Jersey Ave. SE Washington, DC 20002. Phone: (202)544-8646 Investigation and legal analysis of issues relating to military justice, veterans rights and benefits, selective service, federal tort claims, federal judiciary, and freedom of information.

Public Library Association; Technology Committee., c/o American Library Association, 50 E. Huron St. Chicago, IL

60611. Phone: 800-545-2433 or (312)280-5028 Fax: (312)280-5029 E-mail: pla@pla.org • URL: http://www.pla. org • Affiliated with the American Library Association. Formerly Public Libraries Division.

Public Library Catalog: Guide to Reference Books and Adult Nonfiction. Juliette Yaakov, editor. H. W. Wilson Co., 950 University Ave. Bronx, NY 10452. Phone: 800-367-6770 or (718)558-8400 Fax: 800-590-1617 or (718)590-1617 E-mail: custserv@hwwilson.com • URL: http://www.hwwilson.com • 1999. $350.00. 11th revised edition. Contains annotations for 8,000 of the "best" reference and other nonfiction books in English. Covers a wide range of topics, including many that are related to business, economics, finance, or industry. (Standard Catalog Series).

Public Library Quarterly. The Haworth Press, Inc., 10 Alice St. Binghamton, NY 13904-1580. Phone: 800-429-6784 or (607)722-5857 Fax: 800-895-0582 or (607)722-1424 E-mail: getinfo@haworthpressinc.com • URL: http://www. haworthpressinc.com • Quarterly. Institutions, $250.00 per year.

Public Management: Devoted to the Conduct of Local Government. International City-County Management Association, 777 N. Capital, N.E., Suite 500 Washington, DC 20002-4201. Phone: 800-745-8780 or (202)289-4262 Fax: (202)962-3500 E-mail: subscriptions@icma.org • URL: http://www.icma.org • Monthly. $34.00 per year.

The Public Manager: The Journal for Practitioners. Bureaucrat, Inc., 12007 Titian Way Potomac, MD 20854. Phone: (301)279-9445 Fax: (301)251-5872 E-mail: tnovo@aol.com • URL: http://www.thepublicmanager.org • Quarterly. Individuals, $35.00 per year; institutions, $65.00 per year. Formerly *Bureaucrat*.

Public Opinion: A Bibliography with Indexes. William A. Blade, editor. Nova Science Publishers, Inc., 400 Oser Ave. Hauppauge, NY 11788. Phone: (631)231-7269 Fax: (631)231-8175 E-mail: novascience@earthlink.net • URL: http://www. novapublishers.com • 2002. $59.00. Covers public opinion "in its many forms," including polls. Author, title, and subject indexes are provided.

Public Opinion: Politics, Communication and Social Process. Carroll J. Glyn and others. Westview Press, 550 Central Ave. Boulder, CO 80301. Phone: 800-386-5656 or (303)444-3541 E-mail: westview.orders@perseusbooks.com • URL: http:// www.westviewpress.com • 1998. $75.00.

Public Opinion Polls and Survey Research: A Selected Annotated Bibliography of U.S. Guides and Studies from the 1980s. Graham R. Waldon. Garland Publishing, Inc., 29 W. 35th St. New York, NY 10001-2299. Phone: 800-627-6273 or (212)216-7800 Fax: (212)564-7854 E-mail: info@garland. com • URL: http://www.garlandpub.com • 1990. $15.00. (Public Affairs and Administration Series: vol. 24).

Public Opinion Quarterly. American Association for Public Opinion Research. The University of Chicago Press, Journals Div., P.O. Box 37005 Chicago, IL 60637. Phone: 877-705-1878 or (773)753-3347 Fax: 877-705-1879 or (773)753-0811 E-mail: subscriptions@press.uchicago.edu • URL: http:// www.journals.uchicago.edu • Quarterly. Institutions, $120.00 per year.

Public Personnel Administration: Problems and Prospects. Steven W. Hays and Richard C. Kearney, editors. Prentice Hall PTR, 240 Frisch Ct. Paramus, NJ 07652. Phone: 800-282-0693 Fax: 800-445-6991 • URL: http://www.phptr.com • 2002. $44.00.

Public Personnel Management. International Personnel Management Association, 1617 Duke St. Alexandria, VA 22314. Phone: (703)549-7100 Fax: (703)684-0948 E-mail: publications@ipma-hr.org • URL: http://www.ipma-hr.org • Quarterly. $50.00 per year.

Public Policies for Environmental Protection. Paul R. Portney, editor. Resources for the Future, 1616 P St. NW, Rm. 414 Washington, DC 20036-1400. Phone: (202)328-5000 Fax: (202)328-5024 E-mail: rffpress@rff.org • URL: http://www. rff.org • 2000. $29.95. Second edition. A discussion of issues, progress, and problems in the regulation of air pollution, water pollution, hazardous wastes, and toxic substances. Economic factors are emphasized.

Public Power. American Public Power Association, 2301 M St., N.W. Washington, DC 20037-1484. Phone: (202)467-2900 Fax: (202)467-2910 • URL: http://www.appanet.org • Bimonthly. $50.00 per year.

Public Power Annual Directory and Statistical Reprot. American Public Power Association, 2301 M St., N.W. Washington, DC 20037-1484. Phone: (202)467-2900 Fax: (202)467-2910 • URL: http://www.appanet.org • Annual. $125.00. Lists approximately 2,000 local publicly owned electric utilities in United States and possessions. Formerly *Public Power Directory of Local Publicly Owned Electric Utilities*.

Public Power Weekly. American Public Power Association, 1875 Connecticut Ave. NW, Ste.1200 Washington, DC 20009. Phone: (202)467-2900 Fax: (202)467-2910 E-mail: info@ appanet.org • URL: http://www.appanet.org • Description: Reports on legislative, regulatory, judicial, and technical developments affecting local and state-owned electric utilities. Recurring features include employment notices and news briefs.

Public Pulse: Roper's Authoritative Report on What Americans are Thinking, D oing, and Buying. Roper Starch Worldwide, 205 E. 42nd St. New York, NY 10017. Phone: (212)599-0700 Fax: (212)867-7008 Monthly. $297.00. Newsletter. Contains news of surveys of American attitudes, values, and behavior. Each issue includes a research supplement giving "complete facts and figures behind each survey question."

Public Relations. PBI Media, LLC, 1201 7 Locks Rd. Potomac, MD 20854. Phone: 800-777-5006 or (301)354-2000 Fax: (301)309-3847 E-mail: clientservices@pbimedia.com • URL: http://www.pbimedia.com • Biweekly. $397.00 per year. Newsletter on public relations and client communications for the healthcare industry. Incorporates (Healthcare PR and Marketing News).

Public Relations News. PBI Media, LLC, 1201 7 Locks Rd. Potomac, MD 20854. Phone: 800-777-5006 or (301)354-2000 Fax: (301)309-3847 E-mail: clientservices@pbimedia.com • URL: http://www.pbimedia.com • Weekly. $597.00 per year. Newsletter on public relations for business, government, and nonprofit organizations.

Public Relations Practices: Managerial Case Studies and Problems. Allen H. Center. Prentice Hall PTR, 240 Frisch Ct. Paramus, NJ 07652. Phone: 800-282-0693 Fax: 800-445-6991 • URL: http://www.phptr.com • 2002. $84.00. Sixth edition.

Public Relations Quarterly. Hudson Associates, 44 W Market St. Rhinebeck, NY 12572. Phone: (845)876-2081 Fax: (845)876-2561 E-mail: hphudson@aol.com • URL: http://www.newsletter-clearinghse.com • Quarterly. $65.00 per year. Opinion articles and case studies on the theory and practice of public relations for and by leading practitioners and academicians.

Public Relations Review: Journal of Research and Comment. Elsevier, 360 Park Ave., S New York, NY 10010-1710. Phone: 888-437-4636 or (212)989-5800 Fax: (212)633-3990 E-mail: usinfo-f@elsevier.com • URL: http://www.elsevier.com • Five times a year. Individuals, $137.00 per year; institutions, $366.00 per year. Includes annual *Bibliography*.

Public Relations Society of America., 33 Irving Pl., 3rd Fl. New York, NY 10003-2376. Phone: (212)995-2230 Fax: (212)995-0757 E-mail: hq@prsa.org • URL: http://www.prsa.org • Absorbed American Public Relations Association and National Communication Council for Human Services.

Public Relations Strategist: Issues and Trends That Affect Management. Public Relations Society of America, 33 Irving Place New York, NY 10003-2376. Phone: (212)995-2230 Fax: (212)995-0757 • URL: http://www.prsa.org • Quarterly. $48.00 per year. Provides public relations advice for corporate and government executives.

Public Relations Tactics Member Services Directory: The Blue Book. Public Relations Society of America, 33 Irving Place New York, NY 10003. Phone: (212)460-1474 Fax: (212)995-0757 E-mail: prssa@prsa.org • URL: http://www.prsa.org • Annual. Free to members; non-members, $250.00; universities, educational institutions, libraries, $375.00. About 17,000 public relations practioners in business, government, education, etc. who are members. Formerly *Public Relations Journal-Register*.

Public Relations Writer's Handbook. Merry Aronson and Donald E. Spetner. John Wiley and Sons, Inc., 111 River St. Hoboken, NJ 07030. Phone: 800-225-5945 or (201)748-6000 Fax: (201)748-6088 E-mail: info@wiley.com • URL: http://www.wiley.com • 1998. $24.95.

Public Risk. Public Risk Management Association, 1815 N. Fort Meyer Dr., Suite 1020 Arlington, VA 22209-1805. Phone: (703)528-7701 Fax: (703)528-7966 E-mail: info@primacentral.org • URL: http://www.primacentral.org • 10 times a year. $125.00 per year. Covers risk management for state and local governments, including various kinds of liabilities.

Public Risk Management Association., 500 Montgomery St., Ste. 750 Alexandria, VA 22314. Phone: (703)528-7701 Fax: (703)739-0200 E-mail: info@primacentral.org • URL: http://www.primacentral.org • Public agency risk, insurance, human resources, attorneys, and/or safety managers from cities, counties, villages, towns, school boards, and other related areas. Provides an information clearinghouse and communications network for public risk managers to share resources, ideas, and experiences. Offers information on risk, insurance, and safety management. Monitors state and federal legislative actions and court decisions that deal with immunity, tort liability, and intergovernmental risk pools. Maintains library containing current reports from governmental units on their insurance procedures, self-insurance plans, and loss control and safety programs; and copies of policy statements, job descriptions, contractual arrangements, and indemnification clauses.

Public Roads: A Journal of Highway Research and Development. Available from U.S. Government Printing Office, Washington, DC 20402. Phone: (202)512-1800 Fax: (202)512-2250 E-mail: gpoaccess@gpo.gov • URL: http://www.accessgpo.gov • Bimonthly. $26.00 per year.

Public Speaking. Michael Osborn and Suzanne Osborn. Houghton Mifflin Co., 222 Berkeley St. Boston, MA 02116. Phone: 800-733-2828 or (617)351-5000 Fax: 800-733-2098 E-mail: inquiries@hmco.com • URL: http://www.hmco.com • 2000. $34.17. Fifth edition.

Public Utilities Fortnightly. Public Utilities Reports, Inc., 8229 Boone Blvd., Suite 401 Vienna, VA 22182. Phone: 800-368-5001 or (703)847-7720 Fax: (703)847-0683 E-mail: pur_info@pur.com • URL: http://www.pur.com • 22 times a year. $139.00 per year. Management magazine for utility executives in electric, gas, telecommunications and water industries.

Public Utility Research Center. University of Florida

Public Works: City, County and State. Public Works Journal Corp., 200 S. Broad St. Ridgewood, NJ 07451. Phone: 800-524-2364 or (201)445-5800 Fax: (201)445-5170 E-mail: jkircher@pwmag.com • URL: http://www.pwmag.com • 13 times a year. Free to qualified personnel. Includes *Public Works Manual*.

Public Works Manual. Public Works Journal Corp., PO Box 688, 200 S Broad St. Ridgewood, NJ 07451. Phone: 800-524-2364 or (201)445-5800 Fax: (201)445-5170 E-mail: pw@pwmag.com • URL: http://www.pwmag.com • Publication includes: List of about 3,500 manufacturers and distributors of equipment, materials, services, computers, and software used in the design, construction, maintenance, and operation of streets and highways, water systems, wastewater and solid wastes processing, and recreation areas. Entries include: Company name, address, products. Principal content is technical articles on public works topics.

Publications of the National Institute of Standards and Technology. U.S. Government Printing Office, Washington, DC 20402. Phone: (202)512-1800 Fax: (202)512-2250 E-mail: gpoaccess@gpo.gov • URL: http://www.accessgpo.gov • Annual. Keyword and author indexes.

The Publicity Handbook: How to Maximize Publicity for Products, Services, and Organizations. David Yale. McGraw-Hill, 1221 Ave. of the Americas New York, NY 10020. Phone: 800-722-4726 or (212)512-2000 Fax: (212)512-4502 E-mail: customer.service@mcgraw-hill.com • URL: http://www.mcgraw-hill.com • 1994. $19.95. (NTC Business Books Series).

Publishers' Auxiliary. National Newspaper Association, 127-129 Neff Annex Columbia, MO 65211-1200. Phone: 800-829-4662 or (573)882-5800 Fax: (573)884-5490 • URL: http://www.nna.org • Biweekly. $85.00 per year.

Publishers' Catalogues Home Page. EBSCO PublishingPhone: (306)931-0020 Fax: (306)931-7667 E-mail: info@lights.com • URL: http://www.lights.com/publisher • Provides links to the Web home pages of about 1,700 U. S. publishers (including about 80 University presses) and publishers in 48 foreign countries. "International/Multinational Publishers" are included, such as the International Monetary Fund, the World Bank, and the World Trade Organization. Publishers are arranged in convenient alphabetical lists. Searching is offered. Fees: Free.

Publishers Directory: A Guide to New and Established Private and Special-Interest, Avant-Garde and Alternative, Organizational Association, Government and Institution Presses. Gale Cengage Learning, 27500 Drake Rd. Farmington Hills, MI 48331-3535. Phone: 800-877-GALE or (248)699-4253 Fax: 800-414-5043 E-mail: gale.galeord@cengage.com • URL: http://gale.cengage.com • 2003. $450.00. 26th edition. Contains detailed information on more than 20,000 U.S. and Canadian publishers as well as small, independent presses.

Publishers, Distributors, and Wholesalers of the United States: A Directory of Publishers, Distributors, Associations, Wholesalers, Software Producers and Manufactureres Listing Editorial and Ordering Addresses, and and ISBN Publisher Prefi. Gale, 27500 Drake Rd. Farmington Hills, MI 48331. Phone: 800-877-GALE or (248)699-GALE Fax: 800-877-GALE or (248)699-8035 E-mail: gale.galeord@cengage.com • URL: http://gale.cengage.com • Annual. $349.00. Two volumes. Lists more than 101,000 publishers, book distributors, and wholesalers. Includes museum and association imprints, inactive publishers, and publishers' fields of activity.

Publishers Information Bureau., 810 7th Ave., 24th Fl. New York, NY 10019. Phone: 888-567-3227 or (212)872-3722 Fax: (212)753-2768 E-mail: pib@magazine.org • URL: http://www.magazine.org • Measures the amount and type of advertising in magazines and reports this information monthly through printed and electronic formats; service prepared by TNSMI/Competitive Media Reporting (contracting agent).

Publishers' International ISBN Directory. International ISBN Agency, c/o EDItEUR, 39-41 North Rd. London N7 9DP, United Kingdom. Phone: 800-877-GALE or (44)20 76070021 Fax: (44)20 76070415 E-mail: brian@isbn-international.org • URL: http://www.galegroup.com • Covers: About 620,000 publishers in the United States and 218 other countries, of which about 555,000 have been assigned International Standard Book Numbers (ISBNs) by one of 140 ISBN Group Agencies. Entries include: For publishers—Name, address, phone, fax, telex, e-mail, ISBN, group, and prefix numbers. For agencies—Name, address, phone, fax, e-mail, group number, names and titles of key personnel in charge of ISBN matters. Publication is a merger of "International ISBN Publishers' Directory" and "Publishers' International Directory."

Publishers Weekly: The International News Magazine of Book Publishing. Reed Business Information, 360 Park Ave. S New York, NY 10010. Phone: 800-446-6551 or (646)746-6400 Fax: (646)746-7028 E-mail: corporatecommunications@reedbusiness.com • URL: http://www.reedbusiness.com • 51 times a year. $214.00 per year. The international news magazine of book publishing.

PubList.com: The Internet Directory of Publications. Bowes & Associates, Inc.Phone: (781)792-0999 Fax: (781)792-0988 E-mail: info@publist.com • URL: http://www.publist.com • "The premier online global resource for information about print and electronic publications." Provides online searching for information on more than 150,000 magazines, journals, newsletters, e-journals, and monographs. Database entries generally include title, publisher, format, address, editor, circulation, subject, and International Standard Serial Number (ISSN). Fees: Free.

Pulp and Paper. Paperloop, Four Alfred Circle Beford, MA 01730. Phone: (866)271-8525 Fax: (816)487-4550 E-mail: info@paperloop.com • URL: http://www.paperloop.com • 11 times a year. $135.00 per year.

Pulp and Paper Buyer's Guide. Paperloop, Four Alfred Circle Bedford, MA 01730. Phone: (866)271-8525 Fax: (818)487-4550 E-mail: info@paperloop.com • URL: http://www.paperloop.com • Annual. $75.00. Supplies and equipment.

Pulp and Paper Canada. Pulp and Paper Technical Association of Canada. Business Information Group, 1450 Don Mills Rd. Don Mills, ON, Canada M3B 2X7. Phone: 800-668-2374 Fax: (416)422-2214 • URL: http://www.businessinformationgroup.ca • Monthly. $80.00 per year.

The Pulp and Paper Industry in OECD Member Countries. Organization for Economic Cooperation and Development. Available from OECD Publications and Information Center, 2001 L St., N. W., Suite. 650 Washington, DC 20036-4922. Phone: 800-456-6323 or (202)785-6323 Fax: (202)785-0350 E-mail: washington.contact@oecd.org • URL: http://www.oecdwash.org • Annual. $31.00. Presents annual data on production, consumption, capacity, utilization, and foreign trade. Covers 33 pulp and paper products in OECD countries. Text in English and French.

Pulp and Paper International. Paperloop, Four Alfred Circle Bedford, MA 01730. Phone: (866)271-8525 Fax: (818)487-4550 E-mail: info@paperloop.com • URL: http://www.paperloop.com • Monthly. Free to qualified personnel; others, $130.00 per year.

Pulp and Paper Week. Paperloop, Four Alfred Circle Bedford, MA 01730. Phone: (866)271-8525 Fax: (818)487-4550 E-mail: info@paperloop.com • URL: http://www.paperloop.com • 48 times a year. $867.00 per year; with online edition, $1,099.00 per year. Newsletter.

Pump Application Desk Book. Paul N. Garay. Fairmont Press Inc., 700 Indian Trl. Liburn, GA 30047. Phone: 800-947-7700 or (770)925-9388 Fax: (770)381-9865 E-mail: fpinfo@fairmountprinting.com • URL: http://www.fairmountprinting.com • 1996. $88.00. Third edition.

Pumps and Compressors. U. S. Bureau of the Census, 4700 Silver Hill Rd. Washington, DC 20233-0001. Phone: (301)763-4636 E-mail: comments@census.gov • URL: http://www.census.gov • Annual. Provides data on value of manufacturers' shipments, quantity, exports, imports, etc. (Current Industrial Reports, MA-35P.)

Puns Corps. c/o Robert L. Birch., 3108 Dashiell Rd., Box 2364 Falls Church, VA 22042. Phone: (304)947-5991 E-mail: wjones@pinechemicals.org Promotes the humorous treatment of "precocious senility in bureaucratic and other contexts." Believes that the creative ambiguity inherent in puns can be used in triggering the creative imagination. Encourages training in mnemonics and other memory improvement techniques, particularly for nursing home patients. Sponsors Compliment-Your-Mirror Day and Memory Day. **Convention/Meeting:** none.

Purchasers Guide to the Music Industries. Music Trades Corp., c/o Paul Majeski, 80 West St. Englewood, NJ 07631. Phone: (201)871-1965 Annual. Available with subscription to *Music Trades*.

Purchasing and Materials Management. Michael R. Leenders and Harold E. Fearon. McGraw-Hill, 1221 Ave. of the Americas New York, NY 10020. Phone: 800-722-4726 or (212)512-2000 Fax: (212)512-4502 E-mail: customer.service@mcgraw-hill.com • URL: http://www.mcgraw-hill.com • 1996. $93.75. 11th edition.

Purchasing and Supply Management. Michael R. Leenders. McGraw-Hill, 1221 Ave. of the Americas New York, NY 10020. Phone: 800-722-4726 or (212)512-2000 Fax: (212)512-4502 E-mail: customer.service@mcgraw-hill.com • URL: http://www.mcgraw-hill.com • 2001. $112.50. 12th edition.

Purchasing/CPI Chemicals Yellow Pages. Reed Business Information, 360 Park Ave. S New York, NY 10010. Phone: 800-662-7776 or (646)746-6400 Fax: (646)746-7583 E-mail: corporatecommunications@reedbusiness.com • URL: http://www.reedbusiness.com • Annual. $85.00. Manufacturers and distributors of 10,000 chemicals and raw materials, containers and packaging, transportation services and storage facilities; includes environmental servicer companies. Formerly *CPI Purchasing-Chemicals Directory*.

Purchasing: The Magazine of Total Supply Chain Management. Reed Business Information, 360 Park Ave. S New York, NY 10010. Phone: 800-446-6551 or (646)746-6400 Fax: (646)746-7028 E-mail: corporatecommunications@reedbusiness.com • URL: http://www.reedbusiness.com • 24 times a year. $109.90 per year. Includes *Guide and Directory*.

Purchasing Today: For the Purchasing and Supply Professional. Institute for Supply Management, P.O. Box 22160 Tempe, AZ 85285-2160. Phone: 800-888-6276 or (480)752-6276 Fax: (480)752-7890 • URL: http://www.

napm.org • Monthly. Membership. Includes special issues on logistics, transportation, cost management, and supply chain management.

Putting Total Quality Management to Work: What TQM Means, How to Use It, and How to Sustain It Over the Long Run. Marshall Sashkin and Kenneth J. Kiser. Berrett-Koehler Publishers, Inc., 235 Montgomery St., Ste. 650 San Francisco, CA 94104. Phone: 800-929-2929 or (415)288-0260 Fax: (415)362-2512 E-mail: bkpub@bkpubl.com • URL: http://www.bkpub.com • 1993. $19.95. Includes control charts, flow charts, scatter diagrams, and criteria for the Baldridge Quality Award.

PVC Furniture Manufacturing. Entrepreneur Media, Inc., 2445 McCabe Way Irvine, CA 92614. Phone: 800-421-2300 or (949)261-2325 Fax: (949)261-0234 E-mail: entmag@entrepreneur.com • URL: http://www.entrepreneur.com • Looseleaf. $59.50. A practical guide to starting a business for the manufacture of plastic furniture. Covers profit potential, start-up costs, market size evaluation, owner's time required, site selection, lease negotiation, pricing, accounting, advertising, promotion, etc. (Start-Up Business Guide No. E1262.)

QSR: The Magazine of Quick Service Restaurant Success. Journalistic, Inc., 4905 Pine Cone Dr., Ste. 2 Durham, NC 27707. Phone: 800-638-0776 or (919)489-1916 Fax: (919)489-4767 • URL: http://www.qsrmagazine.com • Ten times a year. $30.00 per year. Provides news and management advice for quick-service restaurants, including franchisors and franchisees.

Quality and Reliability Engineering International. Available from John Wiley and Sons, Inc., Journals Div., 111 River St. Hoboken, NJ 07030. Phone: 800-526-5368 or (201)748-6000 Fax: (201)748-6088 E-mail: consumers@wiley.com • URL: http://www.wiley.com • Bimonthly. $1,500.00 per year. Designed to bridge the gap between existing theoretical methods and scientific research on the one hand, and current industrial practices on the other. Published in England by John Wiley and Sons Ltd.

Quality Bakers of America Cooperative Laboratory.

Quality-Buyers Guide for QA/QC Equipment, Software, and Services. Reed Business Information, 360 Park Ave. S New York, NY 10010. Phone: 800-662-7776 or (646)746-6400 Fax: (646)746-7028 E-mail: corporatecommunications@reedbusiness.com • URL: http://www.reedbusiness.com • Annual. $15.00. List of manufacturers and distributors of quality control equipment for measurement, inspection, data analysis evaluation and destructive and nondestructive testing; also lists testing laboratories, consultants, software and training organizations. Formerly *Quality Buyers Guide for Test, Inspection, Measurement and Evaluation*.

Quality Control. Dale H. Besterfield. Prentice Hall PTR, 240 Frisch Ct. Paramus, NJ 07652. Phone: 800-282-0693 Fax: 800-445-6991 • URL: http://www.phptr.com • 2000. $99.00. Sixth edition. Includes CD-ROM. Covers basic quality control concepts and procedures, including statistical process control (SPC). Includes disk.

Quality Management Journal. American Society for Quality, 600 N Plankinton Ave. Milwaukee, WI 53201. Phone: 800-248-1946 Fax: (414)272-1734 E-mail: help@asq.org • URL: http://www.asq.org • Quarterly. Members, $50.00 per year; non-members, $60.00 per year. Emphasizes research in quality control and management.

Quality Manager's Complete Guide to ISO 9000. Richard B. Clements. Prentice Hall PTR, 240 Frisch Ct. Paramus, NJ 07652. Phone: 800-282-0693 Fax: 800-445-6991 • URL: http://www.phptr.com • 2000. $79.95. (Quality Manager's Complete Guide to ISO 9000).

Quality Manager's Complete Guide to ISO 9000: 2000 Edition. Richard B. Clements. Prentice Hall PTR, 240 Frisch Ct. Paramus, NJ 07652. Phone: 800-282-0693 Fax: 800-445-6991 • URL: http://www.phptr.com • 2000. $39.95. Supplement to *Quality Manager's Complete Guide to ISO 9000*.

Quality of Cotton Report. Agricultural Marketing Service. U.S. Department of Agriculture, Washington, DC 20250. Phone: (202)720-2791 Weekly.

Quality Planning and Analysis: From Product Development Through Use. Frank M. Gryna. McGraw-Hill, 1221 Ave. of the Americas New York, NY 10020. Phone: 800-722-4726 or (212)512-2000 Fax: (212)512-4502 E-mail: customer.service@mcgraw-hill.com • URL: http://www.mcgraw-hill.com • 2000. $122.50. Fourth edition. (Industrial Engineering and Management Science Series).

Quality Progress. American Society for Quality, 600 N Plankinton Ave. Milwaukee, WI 53201. Phone: 800-248-1946 Fax: (414)272-1734 E-mail: help@asq.org • URL: http://www.asq.org • Monthly. Individuals, $60.00 per year; institutions, $120.00 per year. Covers developments in quality improvement throughout the world.

Quality Progress: QA/QC Services Directory. American Society for Quality, 600 N Plankinton Ave. Milwaukee, WI 53203. Phone: 800-248-1946 Fax: (414)272-1734 E-mail: help@asq.org • URL: http://www.asq.org • Annual. $12.00. Provides information on companies offering services related to quality management, such as consulting, inspection, auditing, calibrating, and training.

Quality Progress: Quality Assurance and Quality Control Software Directory. American Society for Quality, 600 N Plankinton Ave. Milwaukee, WI 53203. Phone: 800-248-1946 Fax: (414)272-1734 E-mail: help@asq.org • URL: http://www.asq.org • Annual. Available only online. Price on application. Covers computer software application packages related to quality management. Includes information about software companies and descriptions of programs offered. Formerly *Quality Progress Directory of Software for Quality Assurance and Quality Contol*.

Quantitative Finance. Available from American Institute of Physics, PO Box 503284 St. Louis, MO 63150-3284. Phone: 800-344-6901 Fax: (516)349-9704 E-mail: subs@aip.org • URL: http://www.aip.org • Bimonthly. $340.00 per year. Print and online edition, $765.00 per year. Published in the UK by the Institute of Physics. A technical journal on the use of quantitative tools and applications in financial analysis and financial engineering. Covers such topics as portfolio theory, derivatives, asset allocation, return on assets, risk management, price volatility, financial econometrics, market anomalies, and trading systems.

Quantum PC Report for CPAs. QNet, 5350 S. Roslyn St., Ste. 4000 Englewood, CO 80111. Phone: 800-325-8858 E-mail: info@quantum.org • URL: http://www.quantum.org • Monthly. $235.00 per year. Newsletter on personal computer software and hardware for the accounting profession.

Quarry Management: The Monthly Journal for the Quarrying, Asphalt, Concrete and Recycling Industries. QMJ Publishing Ltd., Seven Regent St. Nottingham NG1 5BS, United Kingdom. Phone: 44 115 9411315 Fax: 44 115 9484035 E-mail: mail@qmj.co.uk • URL: http://www.qmj.co.uk • Monthly. $100.00 per year.

Quarterly Analysis of Failures. Dun & Bradstreet Corp., 103 JFK Pky. Short Hills, NJ 07078. Phone: 800-526-0651 E-mail: custserv@dnb.com • URL: http://www.dnb.com • Quarterly. $20.00.

Quarterly Coal Report. Energy Information Administration, U.S. Department of Energy. Available from U.S. Government Printing Office, Washington, DC 20402. Phone: (202)512-1800 Fax: (202)512-2250 E-mail: gpoaccess@gpo.gov • URL: http://www.accessgpo.gov • Quarterly. $30.00 per year. Annual summary.

Quarterly Financial Report for Manufacturing, Mining, and Trade Corporations. U.S. Federal Trade Commission and U.S. Securities and Exchange Commission. Available from U.S. Government Printing Office, Washington, DC 20402. Phone: (202)512-1800 Fax: (202)512-2250 E-mail: gpoaccess@gpo.gov • URL: http://www.accessgpo.gov • Quarterly. $49.00 per year.

Quarterly Journal of Business and Economics. University of Nebraska at Lincoln, College of Business Administration, 138 CBA Bldg. Lincoln, NE 68588-0407. Phone: 800-742-8800 or (402)472-2310 Fax: (402)472-9777 E-mail: gjbe@unlnotes.unl.edu • URL: http://www.cba.unl.edu • Quarterly. Individuals, $24.00 per year; institutions, $45.00 per year.

Quarterly Journal of Economics. Harvard University, Dept. of Economics. MIT Press, Five Cambridge Center Cambridge, MA 02142-1493. Phone: 800-356-0343 or (617)253-5646 Fax: (617)258-6779 E-mail: journals-orders@mit.edu • URL: http://www.mitpress.mit.edu • Quarterly. Individuals, $44.00 per year; instututions, $190.00 per year; students, $28.00 per year. Includes print and online editions.

Quarterly Labour Force Statistics. Organization for Economic Cooperation and Development. Available from OECD Publications and Information Center, 2001 L St., N. W., Suite 650 Washington, DC 20036-4922. Phone: 800-456-6323 or (202)785-6323 Fax: (202)785-0350 E-mail: washington.contact@oecd.org • URL: http://www.oecdwash.org • Quarterly. $90.00 per year. Provides current data for OECD member countries on population, employment, unemployment, civilian labor force, armed forces, and other labor factors.

Quarterly Market Report. Property and Portfolio Research, 40 Court St., 3rd Fl. Boston, MA 02108. Phone: 800-992-7257 or (617)426-4446 E-mail: jack@nrei.info • URL: http://www.realestateindex.com • Quarterly. $1,000.00 per year for one property type; 2,000 per year for six property types. Newsletter. Reviews current prices, rents, capitalization rates, and occupancy trends for commercial real estate.

Quarterly Mining Review. National Mining Association, 1130 17th St., NW Washington, DC 20036-4677. Phone: (202)463-2625 Fax: (202)463-6152 E-mail: thowe@nma.org • URL: http://www.nma.org • Quarterly. $300.00 per year. Contains detailed data on production, shipments, consumption, stockpiles, and trade for coal and various minerals. (Publisher formerly National Coal Association.)

Quarterly National Accounts. OECD Publications and Information Center, 2001 L St., N.W., Suite 650 Washington, DC 20036-4910. Phone: 800-456-6323 or (202)785-6323 Fax: (202)785-0350 E-mail: washington.contact@oecd.org • URL: http://www.oecdwash.org • Quarterly. $125.00 per year. National accounts data of OECD countries.

Quarterly Operating Data of 68 Telephone Carriers. Federal Communications Commission, 445 12th St., SW Washington, DC 20554. Phone: 888-225-5322 or (202)418-0200 Fax: (202)418-0232 E-mail: fccinfo@fcc.gov Quarterly.

Quarterly Report on Money Fund Performance. IBC-Donoghue, Inc., PO Box 5193 Westborough, MA 01581-5193. Phone: 800-343-5413 or (508)881-2800 Fax: (508)881-0982 • URL: http://www.ibcdata.com • Quarterly. $525.00 per year. Provides expense ratio and yield data for about 1,000 money market funds in the U. S.

The Quarterly Review of Economics and Finance. University of Illinois at Urbana-Champaign, Bureau of Economics and Business Research. Available from JAI Press, Inc., P.O. Box 811 Stamford, CT 06904-0811. Phone: (203)323-9606 Fax: (203)357-8446 E-mail: order@jaipress.com • URL: http://www.jaipress.com • Five times a year. Individuals, $95.00 per year; institutions, $426.00 per year. Includes annual *Supplement*. Formerly *Quarterly Review of Economics and Business*.

Quebec Dairy Herd Analyses Service.

The Questers., 210 S Quince St. Philadelphia, PA 19107-5534. Phone: (215)923-5183 Fax: (212)251-0890 E-mail: wjones@pinechemicals.org • URL: http://www.questers1944.org • Promotes the study and appreciation of antiques and objects of art and their historical backgrounds; aids in the restoration and preservation of historical places. Has donated several antique pieces to the White House and has contributed financially to historic houses, villages, and foundations. Sponsors annual scholarship at Columbia University for graduate studies in the field of architectural restoration. Maintains library of 1000 volumes on history, people, and artifacts.

Questions and Answers on Real Estate. Robert W. Semenow. Prentice Hall PTR, 240 Frisch Ct. Paramus, NJ 07652. Phone: 800-282-0693 Fax: 800-445-6991 • URL: http://www.phptr.com • 1993. $24.95. Tenth edition.

Quick Caller Area Air Cargo Directory. Fourth Seacoast Publishing Co., Inc., 25300 Little Mack Ave. St. Clair Shores, MI 48081. Phone: (586)779-5570 Fax: (586)779-5547 E-mail: info@quickcalleronline.com • URL: http://www.quickcalleronline.com • Annual. $19.95 for each regional edition. Six regionals. Reference source for the air cargo industry.

Quick Frozen Foods Annual Directory of Frozen Food Processors and Buyers' Guide. Saul Beck Publications, 271 Madison Ave. New York, NY 10016. Phone: (212)557-8600 Fax: (212)986-9868 Annual. $140.00. Lists 10,500 frozen food processors; suppliers of freezing and food processing machinery, equipment, and supplies; broker locaters, refrigerated warehouses, truck and rail freight lines, and packaging systems handling frozen food.

Quick Frozen Foods International. EW Williams Publications Co., 2125 Center Ave., Suite 305 Fort Lee, NJ 07024-5898. Phone: (201)592-7007 Fax: (201)592-7171 E-mail: webeditor@ewwpi.com • URL: http://www.williamspublications.com • Quarterly. $42.00 per year. Text in English, summaries in French and German.

Quick Printing: The Information Source for Commercial Copyshops and Printshops. Cygnus Business Media, 445 Broad Hollow Rd. Melville, NY 11747-3601. Phone: 800-308-6397 or (631)845-2700 Fax: (631)845-2798 E-mail: rich.reiff@cygnuspub.com • URL: http://www.cygnusbzb.com • Monthly. $66.00 per year.

Quill and Scroll. International Honorary Society for High School Journalists. Quill and Scroll Society, School of Journalism and Mass Communication, University of Iowa Iowa City, IA 52242. Phone: (319)335-5795 Fax: (319)335-5210 • URL: http://www.uiowa.edu • Quarterly. $13.00 per year. Devoted exclusively to the field of high school publications.

Quill and Scroll Society. School of Journalism. University of Iowa

Quill: The Magazine for Journalists. Society of Professional Journalists, Eugene S. Pullman Nationalo Journalism Center, 3909 N Meridian St. Indianapolis, IN 46208. Phone: (317)927-8000 Fax: (317)920-4789 E-mail: questions@spj.org • URL: http://www.spj.org • Monthly. $35.00 per year.

The Quintessential Searcher: The Wit and Wisdom of Barbara Quint. Marylaine Block, editor. Information Today, Inc., 143 Old Marlton Pike Medford, NJ 08055-8750. Phone: 800-300-9868 or (609)654-6266 Fax: (609)654-4309 E-mail: custserv@infotoday.com • URL: http://www.infotoday.com • 2001. $19.95. Presents the sayings of Barbara Quint, editor of *Searcher* magazine, who is often critical of the online information industry. (CyberAge Books.)

R and D Contracts Monthly (Research and Development): A Continuously Up-dated Sales and R and D Tool For All Research Organizations and Manufacturers. Government Data Publications, Inc., 22001 L St., N.W. Washington, DC 20036. Phone: 800-275-4688 Fax: (718)998-5960 E-mail: gdp@govdata.com • URL: http://www.govdata.com • Monthly. $96.00 per year. Lists recently awarded government contracts. Annual *Directory* available.

R and I Blue Book (Recognition and Identification). The Engravers Journal, Inc., P.O. Box 318 Brighton, MI 48116. Phone: (810)229-5725 Fax: (810)229-8320 Annual. Price on application. Over 200 manufacturers and suppliers of trophies, plaques, engraving and marking equipment and supplies to the recognition and identification (R&I) industry. Formerly *Awards Specialist Directory*.

R E Magazine (Rural Electrification). National Rural Electric Cooperative Association, 4301 Wilson Blvd. Arlington, VA 22203-1860. Phone: (703)907-5500 Fax: (703)907-5511 E-mail: nreca@nreca.org • URL: http://www.nreca.org • Monthly. Free to members; non-members, $50.00 per year. News and information about the rural electric utility industry. Formerly *Rural Electrification*.

Radio Advertising Bureau., 1320 Greenway Dr., Ste. 500, 261 Madison Ave., 23rd Fl. Irving, TX 75038-2587. Phone: 800-232-3131 or (212)681-7214 Fax: (212)681-7217 E-mail: jhaley@rab.com • URL: http://www.rab.com • Includes radio stations, radio networks, station sales representatives, and allied industry services, such as producers, research firms, schools, and consultants. Calls on advertisers and agencies to promote the sale of radio time as an advertising medium. Sponsors program to increase professionalism of radio salespeople, awarding Certified Radio Marketing Consultant designation to those who pass examination. Sponsors regional marketing conferences. Conducts extensive research program into all phases of radio sales. Issues reports on use of radio by national, regional, and local advertisers. Speaks before conventions and groups to explain benefits of radio advertising. Sponsors Radio Creative Fund. Compiles statistics.

Radio Advertising: The Authoritative Handbook. Pete Schulberg and Bob Schulberg. McGraw Hill, 1221 Ave. of the Americas New York, NY 10020. Phone: 800-722-4726 or (212)512-2000 Fax: (212)512-4502 E-mail: customer.service@mcgraw-hill.com • URL: http://www.mcgrawhill.com • 1994. $27.95. Second edition. (NTC Business Books Series).

Radio & Records. Radio & Records, Inc., 10100 Santa Monica Blvd., 3rd Fl. Los Angeles, CA 90067-4004. Phone: (310)553-4330 Fax: (310)203-8450 E-mail: mailroom@radioandrecords.com • URL: http://www.rronline.com • Weekly. $325.00 per year. Provides news and information relating to the record industry and to regional and national radio broadcasting. Special features cover specific types of programming, such as "classic rock," "adult alternative," "oldies," "country," and "news/talk." Radio station business and management topics are included.

Radio and Television Commercial. Albert C. Book and others. McGraw Hill, 1221 Ave. of the Americas New York, NY 10020. Phone: 800-722-4726 or (212)512-2000 Fax: (212)512-4502 E-mail: customer.service@mcgraw-hill.com • URL: http://www.mcgrawhill.com • 1995. $19.95. Third revised edition. How to guide showing how to create effective radio and television advertisements. (NTC Business Books Series).

Radio Business Report: The Voice of the Radio Broadcasting Industry. Radio Business Report, Inc., P.O. Box 782 Springfield, VA 22150. Phone: (703)719-9500 Fax: (703)719-7910 E-mail: radionews@rbr.com Weekly. $89.00 per year. Covers radio advertising, FCC regulations, audience ratings, market research, station management, business conditions, and related topics.

Radio Co-op Directory. Radio Advertising Bureau, 1320 Greenway Dr., Ste. 500 Irving, TX 75038. Phone: 800-232-3131 or (972)753-6786 Fax: (972)753-6727 E-mail: info@rvda.org • URL: http://www.rab.com • Database covers: Over 5,000 manufacturers that provide cooperative allowances for radio advertising. Database includes: Company name, address, name of contact, phone, fax, allowance, accrual rate, whether plan is administered by distributor, expiration dates.

Radio Facts: The Voice of Urban Culture. RadioMan Publishing Inc., 595 Piedmont Ave., NE, Ste. 320 Studio City, CA 91604. Phone: (818)755-1611 Fax: (818)985-7386 E-mail: kevin.ross@radiofacts.com • URL: http://www.radiofacts.com • Annual. $50.00.

Radio World. IMAS Publishing Group, 5827 Columbia Pke. Ste. 310 Falls Church, VA 22041. Phone: 800-336-3045 or (703)998-7600 Fax: (703)998-2966 E-mail: adsales@imaspub.com • URL: http://www.imaspub.com • Biweekly. Free. Emphasis is on radio broadcast engineeri and equipment. Text in English, Portuguese and Spanish.

Radioisotope Laboratory. Louisiana State University

Radiological Society of North America., 820 Jorie Blvd. Oak Brook, IL 60523-2251. Phone: (630)571-2670 Fax: (630)571-7837 E-mail: informat@rsna.org • URL: http://www.rsna.org • Members are radiologists and scientists. Includes a Technical Exhibits Committee and a Scientific Exhibits Committee. Formerly Western Roentgen Society.

Radiology Business Management Association., 10300 Eaton Pl., Ste. 460 Fairfax, VA 22030. Phone: 888-224-7262 or (703)621-3355 Fax: (703)621-3356 E-mail: info@rbma.org • URL: http://www.rbma.org • Provides education, resources and solutions to manage the business of radiology. Offers an online course in radiology coding.

Ragan's Annual Report Review. Lawrence Ragan Communications Inc., 316 N Michigan Ave., Ste. 300 Chicago, IL 60601. Phone: 800-878-5331 or (312)960-4100 Fax: (312)960-4105 E-mail: cservice@ragan.com • URL: http://www.ragan.com • Description: Provides business trends, tips, and tactics.

Ragan's Journal of Business Intelligence. Lawrence Ragan Communications, Inc., 316 N. Michigan Ave., Suite 300 Chicago, IL 60601. Phone: 800-878-5331 or (312)960-4100 Fax: (312)960-4106 E-mail: cservice@ragan.com • URL: http://www.ragan.com • Bimonthly. $199.00 per year. Includes articles on competitive intelligence, knowledge management, legalities, ethics, and counterintelligence.

Railroad Facts. Association of American Railroads, American Railroads Bldg., 50 F St., N.W. Washington, DC 20001. Phone: (202)639-2100 Fax: (202)639-2156 E-mail: information@aar.org • URL: http://www.aar.org • Annual.

Railway Age. Simmons-Boardman Publishing Corp., 345 Hudson St., 12th Fl. New York, NY 10014-4502. Phone: (212)620-7200 Fax: (212)633-1165 • URL: http://www.railwayage.com • Monthly. $56.00 per year.

Railway Directory: A Railway Gazette Yearbook. Reed Business Information, Quadrant House, The Quadrant, Brighton Rd. Sutton, Surrey SM2 5AS, United Kingdom. Phone: 44 2086 528608 Fax: 44 2086 523738 E-mail: rbp.subscriptions@rbi.co.uk • URL: http://www.reedinfo.co.uk • Annual. $230.00. Lists approximately 14,000 senior personnel from railroads worldwide and over 1,800 manufacturers, suppliers and consultants in the railroad industry.

Railway Engineering-Maintenance Suppliers Association., 417 W Broad St., Ste. 203 Falls Church, VA 22046. Phone: 888-33-REMSA or (703)241-8514 Fax: (703)241-8589 E-mail: contact@remsa.org • URL: http://www.remsa.org • Provides global business development opportunities to members. Works to transfer knowledge about markets, products and the industry to members and their customers. Supports government initiatives that advance the North American railroad industry.

Railway Progress Institute., 700 N Fairfax St., No. 601 Alexandria, VA 22314. Phone: (703)836-2332 Fax: (703)548-0058 E-mail: rpi@rpi.org • URL: http://www.rpi.org • Formerly Railway Progress Institute.

Railway Supply Association., 29 W. 140 Butterfield Rd., Ste. 103A Warrenville, IL 60555. Phone: (630)393-0106 Fax: (630)393-0108 E-mail: contact@remsa.org Companies that produce railroad rolling stock equipment and components or supply rolling stock maintenance services. Seeks to improve the efficiency, safety, maintenance, and operation of railroads. Provides means for cooperation among railroads and members by enabling members to exchange information as a unified body. Encourages interest by railroads in the railway supply industry. Cooperates with Air Brake Association, Car Department Officers Association, Locomotive Maintenance Officers' Association, and International Association of Railway Operating Officers.

Railway Systems Suppliers, Inc., 9304 New LaGrange Rd., Ste. 200 Louisville, KY 40242-3671. Phone: (502)327-7774 Fax: (502)327-0541 E-mail: rssi@rssi.org • URL: http://www.rssi.org • Corporations, partnerships, and individuals engaged in the manufacture, sale, and service of products, appliances, apparatus, and devices used in railway signals, controls, and communications; engineers and contractors engaged in construction or maintenance of any such product. Collects and disseminates information of interest to members.

Railway Track and Structures. Simmons-Boardman Publishing Corp., 345 Hudson St., 12th Fl. New York, NY 10014-4502. Phone: (212)620-7200 Fax: (212)633-1165 E-mail: tjudge@rtands.com Monthly. $30.00 per year.

Raise More Money for Your Nonprofit Organization: A Guide to Evaluating and Improving Your Fundraising. Anne L. New. The Foundation Center, 79 Fifth Ave. New York, NY 10003-3076. Phone: 800-424-9836 or (212)620-4230 Fax: (212)807-3677 E-mail: orders@fdncenter.org • URL: http://www.fdncenter.org • 1991. $14.95.

Raising Money for Academic and Research Libraries: A How-To- Do-It Manual for Librarians. Barbara I. Dewey, editor. Neal-Schuman Publishers, Inc., 100 William St., Ste. 2004 New York, NY 10038. Phone: (866)672-6657 or (212)925-8650 Fax: (866)209-7932 or (212)219-8916 E-mail: info@neal-schuman.com • URL: http://www.neal-schuman.com • 1991. $45.00. (How-to-Do-It Manuals Series).

RAND. RAND, 1776 Main St., PO Box 2138 Santa Monica, CA 90407-2138. Phone: (310)393-0411 Fax: (310)393-4818 E-mail: correspondence@rand.org • URL: http://www.rand.org/ • Analysis and effective solutions that address the challenges facing the nation and the world, including critical issues surrounding education, homeland security, social security, health care and international development, as well as a range of national security issues.

Random Lengths: The Weekly Report on North American Forest Products Markets. Random Lengths Publications, Inc., P.O. Box 867 Eugene, OR 97440-0867. Phone: (541)686-9925 Fax: 800-874-7979 or (541)686-9629 E-mail: rlmail@randomlengths.com • URL: http://www.randomlengths.com • Weekly. $265.00 per year. Newsletter. Information covering the wood products industry. Supplement available *Random Lengths Midweek Market Report*.

A Random Walk Down Wall Street: The Best Investment Advice for the New Century. Burton G. Malkiel. W. W. Norton & Co., Inc., 500 Fifth Ave. New York, NY 10110. Phone: 800-223-2584 or (212)354-5500 Fax: (212)869-0856 • URL: http://www.wwnorton.com • 1999. $29.95. Seventh revised edition.

Ranking the Banks. American Banker, One State St. Plaza New York, NY 10004. Phone: 800-362-3806 or (212)967-7000 Fax: (212)843-9600 E-mail: custserv@americanbanker.com • URL: http://www.americanbanker.com • Annual. Price on application. Ranks domestic and foreign banks by 75 financial parameters.

RAPRA Abstracts. Rubber and Plastics Research Association of Great Britian. RAPRA Technology Ltd., Shawbury Shrewsbury, Shrops SY4 4NR, United Kingdom. Phone: 44 1939 250383 or 44 1939 251118 E-mail: info@rapra.net • URL: http://www.rapra.net • Monthly. $2,700.00 per year. Up-to-date survey of current international information relevant to the rubber, plastics and associated industries.

Rare Earth Bulletin. Multi-Science Publishing Co. Ltd., Five Wates Way Brentwood CM15 9TB, United Kingdom. Phone: 44 1277 224632 Fax: 44 1277 223453 E-mail: mscience@globalnet.co.uk • URL: http://www.multi-science.co.uk • Bimonthly. $318.00 per year.

Rare Earth Information Center., Iowa State University of Science and Technology, Institute for Physical Research and Technology Ames, IA 50011-3020. Phone: (515)294-2272 Fax: (515)294-3709 E-mail: ric@ameslab.gov • URL: http://www.external.ameslab.gov/ric • Collects, stores, evaluates, and makes available information on the rare earth elements, alloys, and compounds.

Rare Earth Research Conference. c/o Professor Larry Thomson, University of California/Davis, 1 Shields Ave. Davis, CA 95616. Phone: (630)252-4364 Fax: (630)252-9289 E-mail: rssi@rssi.org Researchers in chemistry, physics, metallurgy, biology, and other disciplines whose interests include the rare earth and actinide elements and/or their compounds. (The rare earth elements are those whose atomic numbers range from 58 through 71; actinide elements range from 89-103.) Purposes are to develop and disseminate information related to the science, technology, and production of the rare earth elements, alloys, and compounds; bring together persons in science, business, and government throughout the world; to study and discuss policies related to worldwide use of elements; to assist in long-range industrial and government planning involving the use of these materials.

Ratings Guide to Life, Health and Annuity Insurers. Weiss Ratings, Inc., 4176 Burns Rd. Palm Beach, FL 33410-4606. Phone: 800-289-9222 or (561)627-3300 Fax: (561)625-6685 E-mail: wr@weissinc.com • URL: http://www.weissratings.com • Quarterly. $438.00 per year. Rates life insurance companies for overall safety and financial stability.

Rauch Guide to the U. S. Ink Industry. Impact Marketing Consultants, P.O. Box 1226 Manchester Center, VT 05255. Phone: (802)362-2325 Fax: (802)362-3693 E-mail: sales@impactmarket.com • URL: http://www.impactmarket.com • 2002. $495.00. 237 leading ink manufacturers with over $1 million in annual sales; and lists of activities, organizations, and sources of information in the ink industry. Formerly *Kline Guide to the U.S. Ink Industry*.

Ray W. Herrick Laboratories.

RCR Wireless News: The Newspaper for the Wireless Communications Industry. Crain Communications, 777 E Speer Blvd. Denver, CO 80203-4214. Phone: 800-678-9595 or (303)733-2500 E-mail: info@crain.com • URL: http://www.crain.com • Weekly. $64.00 per year. Covers news of the wireless communications industry, including business and financial developments. Formerly*RCR*.

Readers' Guide Abstracts Online. H. W. Wilson Co., 950 University Ave. Bronx, NY 10452. Phone: 800-367-6770 or (718)588-8400 Fax: (718)590-1617 • URL: http://www.hwwilson.com • Indexes and abstracts general interest periodicals, 1983 to date. Weekly updates. Inquire as to online cost and availability.

Readers' Guide to Periodical Literature. H. W. Wilson Co., 950 University Ave. Bronx, NY 10452. Phone: 800-367-6770 or (718)588-8400 Fax: 800-590-1617 or (718)590-1617 E-mail: custserv@hwwilson.com • URL: http://www.hwwilson.com • Monthly. $345.00 per year. Includes annual *Cumulation*. Indexes about 250 periodicals of general interest.

Real Estate. Charles J. Jacobus. South-Western, 5191 Natorp Blvd. Mason, OH 45040. Phone: 800-543-0487 or (513)229-1000 • URL: http://www.swcollege.com • 2002. $41.95. Ninth edition.

Real Estate Appraisal. Walter R. Huber and William H. Pivar. Educational Textbook Co. Inc., P.O. Box 3597 Covina, CA 91722. Phone: (626)339-7733 Fax: (818)332-4744 • URL: http://www.etcbooks.com • 2001. Price on application.

Real Estate Brokerage: A Management Guide. John E. Cyr and others. Dearborn Trade Publishing, A Kaplan Professional Co., 155 N. Wacker St. Chicago, IL 60606-1719. Phone: 800-621-9621 or (312)836-4400 Fax: (312)836-1021 E-mail: trade@dearborn.com • URL: http://www.dearborntrade.com • 1999. $46.50. Fifth edition. Covers the industry standard on opening and operation a real brokerage office.

Real Estate Dictionary. Barbara Cox and others. South-Western, 5191 Natorp Blvd. Mason, OH 45040. Phone: 800-543-0487 or (513)229-1000 • URL: http://www.swcollege.com • 2002. $33.95.

Real Estate Economics: Journal of the American Real Estate and Urban Economics Association. MIT Press, Five Cambridge Center Cambridge, MA 02142-1493. Phone: 800-356-0343 or (617)253-5646 Fax: (617)258-6779 E-mail: journals-orders@mit.edu • URL: http://www.mitpress.mit.edu • Quarterly. Institutions, $295.00 per year. Includes print and online editions.

Real Estate Finance. Institutional Investor, Inc., Journals Group, 225 Park Ave., S New York, NY 10003. Phone: 800-945-2034 or (212)224-3066 Fax: (212)224-3472 E-mail: info@iijournals.com • URL: http://www.iijournals.com • Bimonthly. $350.00 per year. Covers real estate for professional investors. Provides information on complex financing, legalities, and industry trends.

Real Estate Finance and Investment. Institutional Investor, Inc., Journals Group, 225 Park Ave., S New York, NY 10003. Phone: 800-945-2034 or (212)224-3066 Fax: (212)224-3472 E-mail: info@iijournals.com • URL: http://www.iijournals.com • Weekly. $2,275.00 per year. Includes print and online editions. Newsletter for professional investors in commercial real estate. Includes information on financing, restructuring, strategy, and regulation.

Real Estate Finance and Investment Manual: A Guide to Money Making Strategies. Jack Cummings. Prentice Hall PTR, 240 Frisch Ct. Paramus, NJ 07652. Phone: 800-282-0693 Fax: 800-445-6991 • URL: http://www.phptr.com • 1997. $34.95. Second edition.

Real Estate Finance and Investments. William B. Brueggeman and Jeffrey Fisher. McGraw-Hill, 1221 Ave. of the Americas New York, NY 10020. Phone: 800-722-4726 or (212)512-2000 Fax: (212)512-4502 E-mail: customer.service@mcgraw-hill.com • URL: http://www.mcgraw-hill.com • 2001. 11th edition. Price on application. Covers mortgage loans, financing, risk analysis, income properties, land development, real estate investment trusts, and related topics. (Finance, Insurance and Real Estate Series).

Real Estate Financing, with Forms on Disk. American Lawyer Media, Inc., 105 Madison Ave. New York, NY 10016. Phone: 800-888-8300 or (212)779-9200 Fax: (212)481-8110 E-mail: lawcatalog@amlaw.com • URL: http://www.lawcatalog.com/ • Looseleaf. $179.00. Updated as needed. Includes forms on two diskettes. Covers loan modifications, wraparound mortgage loans, loans for condos, co-ops, and time shares, sale-leasebacks, installment sales, sales of mortgage loans, and various related topics. (Law Journal Press).

Real Estate Forum: America's Premier Real Estate Business Magazine. Real Estate Media, Inc., 520 Eighth Ave., 17th Fl. New York, NY 10018. Phone: (212)929-6900 Fax: (212)929-7124 E-mail: hoffman@remediainc.com • URL: http://www.reforum.com • Monthly. $59.95 per year. Emphasis on corporate and industrial real estate.

Real Estate Handbook. Jack C. Harris and Jack P. Friedman. Barron's Educational Series, Inc., 250 Wireless Blvd. Hauppauge, NY 11788-3917. Phone: 800-645-3476 or (631)434-3311 Fax: (631)434-3723 E-mail: info@barronseduc.com • URL: http://www.barronseduc.com • 2001. $35.00. Fifth edition.

Real Estate Index. National Association of Realtors, 430 N. Michigan Ave. Chicago, IL 60611. Phone: 800-874-6500 or (312)329-8292 Fax: (312)329-5960 E-mail: infocentral@realtors.org • URL: http://www.realtor.org • 1987. $169.00 Two volumes. Vol. one, Author-Title, $99.00; vol. two, Subject, $99.00; vol. 3, 1998 *Supplement*, $49.50.

Real Estate Investment Trusts Handbook: 1997. Peter M. Fass and others. West Group, 610 Opperman Dr. Eagan, MN 55123. Phone: 800-328-4880 or (651)687-7000 Fax: 800-340-9378 E-mail: bookstore@westgroup.com • URL: http://www.westgroup.com • 2004. $295.00. Covers the legal and tax aspects of REITs. (Securities Law Series).

Real Estate Investment Trusts: Structure, Performance, and Investment Opportunities. Su Han Chan. Oxford University Press, 198 Madison Ave. New York, NY 10016-4314. Phone: 800-451-7556 or (212)726-6000 Fax: (212)726-6440 E-mail: custserv@oup-usa.org • URL: http://www.oup-usa.org • 2002. $45.00. Covers the history of REITs, organizational structure, institutional investing, dividends, debt, and "existing scholarly research." An appendix provides "Monthly Stock Returns and Performance Index of All Publicly Traded REITs (1962-2000 and 2001-2002)." (Financial Management Association Survey and Synthesis Series).

Real Estate Investor's Answer Book. Jack Cummings. McGraw-Hill, 1221 Ave. of the Americas New York, NY 10020. Phone: 800-722-4726 or (212)512-2000 Fax: (212)512-4502 E-mail: customer.service@mcgraw-hill.com • URL: http://www.mcgraw-hill.com • 1994. $19.95. Answers key questions relating to both residential and commercial real estate investments.

Real Estate Issues. The Counselors of Real Estate, 430 N. Michigan Ave. Chicago, IL 60611. Phone: (312)329-8427 Fax: (312)329-8881 E-mail: info@cre.org • URL: http://www.cre.org • Quarterly. $48.00 per year.

Real Estate Marketing and Sales. Paddy Amyett. Prentice Hall PTR, 240 Frisch Ct. Paramus, NJ 07652. Phone: 800-282-0693 Fax: 800-445-6991 • URL: http://www.phptr.com • 2001. $33.33.

Real Estate New York., 111 Eighth Ave. New York, NY 10011-5201. Phone: (212)929-6900 Fax: (212)929-7124 E-mail: jonathan.schein@scheinpublications.com • URL: http://www.reforum.com • Ten times a year. $35.00 per year. Formerly *Better Bulidings*.

Real Estate Review. West Group, 610 Opperman Dr. Eagan, MN 55123. Phone: 800-328-4880 or (651)687-7000 Fax: 800-340-9378 E-mail: bookstore@westgroup.com • URL: http://www.westgroup.com • Quarterly. $200.00 per year. Gives inside information on the latest ideas in real estate. Provides advice from the leaders of the real estate field.

Real Estate Tax Digest. Matthew Bender & Co., LexisNexis Group, PO Box 933 Dayton, OH 45401-0933. Phone: 800-227-9597 or (937)865-6800 Fax: (518)487-3584 E-mail: customerservice.customer.support@lexisnexis.com • URL: http://www.bender.com • Description: Features articles on and analyses of legislation, Treasury regulations, federal court and Tax Court decisions, Revenue Rulings, Revenue Procedures, and selected Letter Rulings of the Internal Revenue Service pertaining to federal taxation affecting real estate activities. Includes columns titled Special Topic, New Developments, Practitioner's Corner, and Inside Washington.

Real Estate Taxation. RIA, 395 Hudson St. New York, NY 10014. Phone: 800-950-1216 or 800-431-9025 E-mail: riahome@riag.com • URL: http://www.riahome.com • Quarterly. $225.00 per year. Looseleaf service. Continuing coverage of the latest tax developments. Formerly *Journal of Real Estate Taxation*.

Real Estate Taxation: A Practitioner's Guide. David F. Windish. CCH, Inc., 2700 Lake Cook Rd. Riverwoods, IL 60015. Phone: 800-835-5224 or (847)267-7000 E-mail: cust_serv@cch.com • URL: http://www.cch.com • Date not set. $125.00. Second edition. Serves as a guide to the federal tax consequences of real estate ownership and operation. Covers mortgages, rental agreements, interest, landlord income, forms of ownership, and other tax-oriented topics.

Real Estate Transactions: Condominium Law and Practice Forms. Patrick J. Rohan and Melvin A. Reskin. LexisNexis Matthew Bender, 1275 Broadway Albany, NY 12204. Phone: 800-424-4200 or (518)487-3000 Fax: (518)487-3584 E-mail: bookstore.support@lexisnexis.com • URL: http://www.bender.com • Three times a year. $1,649.00. Eight looseleaf volumes. Guide for handling condominium transactions.

Real Estate Transactions: Cooperative Housing Law and Practice-Forms. Patrick J. Rohan and Melvin A. Reskin. LexisNexis Matthew Bender, 1275 Broadway Albany, NY 12204. Phone: 800-424-4200 or (518)487-3000 Fax: (518)487-3584 E-mail: bookstore.support@lexisnexis.com • URL: http://www.bender.com • Semiannual. $999.00 per year. Six looseleaf volumes. Covers every aspect of the creation, financing, operation, sale and tax consequences of cooperatives. (Real Estate Transaction Series).

Real Estate Transactions, Tax Planning and Consequences. Mark L. Levine. West Group, 610 Opperman Dr. Eagan, MN 55123. Phone: 800-338-9424 or (651)687-7000 Fax: 800-340-9378 E-mail: bookstore@westgroup.com • URL: http://www.westgroup.com • 1997. Periodic supplementation.

Realtor Magazine. National Association of Realtors, 430 N. Michigan Ave. Chicago, IL 60611-4087. Phone: 800-874-6500 or (312)329-8458 Fax: (312)329-5978 E-mail: infocentral@realtors.org • URL: http://www.realtormag.com • Monthly. Free to members; non-members, $54.00 per year. Provides industry news and trends for realtors. Special features include Annual Compensation Survey, Annual Technology Survey, Annual All Stars, and The Year in Real Estate.

Realty and Building. Realty and Building, Inc., 111 N. Wabash Ave. Chicago, IL 60602-2012. Phone: (312)467-1888 Fax: (312)467-0225 Biweekly. $54.00 per year.

Realty Stock Review: Market Analysis of Securities of REITS and Real Estate Companies., 92 Kennedy Rd. Tranquility, NJ 07879-0007. Phone: (908)850-1155 Semimonthly. $325.00 per year. Looseleaf service.

ReCareering Newsletter: An Idea and Resource Guide to Second Career and Relocation Planning. Publications Plus, Inc., 434 Ridge Rd. Wilimette, IL 60091-2471. Phone: (708)735-1981 Fax: (708)735-0046 Monthly. $59.00 per year. Edited for "downsized managers, early retirees, and others in career transition after leaving traditional employment." Offers advice on second careers, franchises, starting a business, finances, education, training, skills assessment, and other matters of interest to the newly unemployed.

Recent Advances and Issues in Computers. Martin K. Gay. Greenwood Publishing Group, Inc., 88 Post Rd., W. Westport, CT 06881. Phone: 800-225-5800 or (203)226-3571 Fax: (203)431-2214 E-mail: customer-service@greenwood.com • URL: http://www.greenwood.com • 2000. $49.95. Includes recent developments in computer science, computer engineering, and commercial software applications. (Oryx Frontiers of Science Series.)

Recent Advances and Issues in Environmental Science. Joan R. Callahan, editor. Greenwood Publishing Group, Inc., 88 Post Rd., W. Westport, CT 06881. Phone: 800-225-5800 or (203)226-3571 Fax: (203)431-2214 E-mail: customer-service@greenwood.com • URL: http://www.greenwood.com • 1999. $49.95. Includes environmental economic problems, such as saving jobs vs. protecting the environment. (Oryx Frontiers of Science Series.)

Recent Advances in Cryogenic Engineering. J. P. Kelley and J. Goodman, editors. American Society of Mechanical Engineers International, 3 Park Ave. New York, NY 10016-5990. Phone: 800-843-2763 or (212)591-7722 Fax: (212)591-7674 E-mail: infocentral@asme.org • URL: http://www.asme.org • 1993. $30.00.

Recent Developments in Operational Research. Manju Lata Agrawal and Kanar Sen. CRC Press, 2000 N.W. Corporate Blvd. Boca Raton, FL 33431. Phone: 800-272-7737 or (561)994-0555 Fax: 800-374-3401 or (561)989-9732 E-mail: orders@crcpress.com • URL: http://www.crcpress.com • 2002. $89.95. Major topics include mathematical programming, queuing theory, production control, statistical methods, and information technology. Covers both theoretical and practical aspects of operations research.

Reciprocity, U. S. Trade Policy, and the GATT Regime. Carolyn Rhodes. Cornell University Press, 512 E. State St. Ithaca, NY 14851. Phone: 800-666-2211 E-mail: store@cornell.edu • URL: http://www.cornellpress.cornell.edu • 1993. $42.50.

Recommendations on the Transport of Dangerous Goods. United Nations Publications, United Nations Concourse Level, First Ave., 46th St. New York, NY 10017. Phone: 800-553-3210 or (212)963-7680 Fax: (212)963-4910 E-mail: bookstore@un.org • URL: http://www.un.org/publications • 1999. $120.00. 11th edition. Covers regulations imposed by various governments and international organizations.

Recommended Bank and Thrift Report. BauerFinancial, Inc., Gables International Plaza, 2655 LeJeune Rd. Coral Gables, FL 33134. Phone: 800-388-6686 Fax: 800-230-2569 E-mail: customerservice@bauerfinancial.com • URL: http://www.bauerfinancial.com • Quarterly. $585.00 per year. Newsletter provides information on "safe, financially sound" commercial banks, savings banks, and savings and loan institutions. Various factors are considered, including tangible capital ratios and total risk-based capital ratios. (Six regional editions are also available at $150.00 per edition per year.)

Record Retailing Directory. VNU Business Media, 770 Broadway New York, NY 10003-9595. Phone: 800-278-8477 or (646)654-4500 Fax: (646)654-7272 E-mail: globalc@nielsen.com • URL: http://www.watsonguptill.com • Covers: over 7,000 independent and chain store record retailers (including audiobooks and online) in the U.S., American Samoa, Guam, and Puerto Rico. Entries include: For independents—Name, address, phone, store owner. For chain stores—Name, address, phone, fax, corporate management staff, number of outlets, year founded, corporate headquarters address and phone.

Recording Industry Association of America., 1330 Connecticut Ave., Suite 300 Washington, DC 20036. Phone: (202)775-0101 Fax: (202)775-7253 E-mail: websmaster@riaa.com • URL: http://www.riaa.com • Formerly Record Industry Association of America.

Recording Industry Sourcebook. Thomson Course Technology PTR, 25 Thomson Pl. Boston, MA 02210. Phone: 888-270-9300 or (707)554-1935 Fax: (707)554-9751 E-mail: cec@us.ul.com • URL: http://www.artistpro.com • Covers: 14,000 contacts in the music industry in over 65 categories, including record producers, publishers, promoters, attorneys, major and independent record labels, and music production facilities. Entries include: Name, address, phone, fax, name and title of contact, subsidiary and branch names and locations, background information, email, web address.

Records and Research Office. University of the Pacific, 3601 Pacific Ave. Stockton, CA 95211. Phone: (209)946-2569 Fax: (209)946-2596 E-mail: rbrodnick@upo.edu • URL: http://www.1.uop.edu/iro • Formerly Institutional Research Office.

Records Management: A Practical Guide. Judy Read Smith and others. South-Western, 5191 Natorp Blvd. Mason, OH 45040. Phone: 800-543-0487 or (513)229-1000 • URL: http://www.swcollege.com • 2001. $54.95. Seventh edition. Includes audio compact disk.

Recreation Trends and Markets: Info the 21st Century. John R. Kelly and Rodney Warnick. Sagamore Publishing, Inc., 1271 Ave. of the Americas New York, NY 10020. Phone: 800-343-9204 or (212)522-7200 Fax: 800-286-9741 • URL: http://www.warnerbooks.com • 1999. $25.00. Second edition.

Recreation Vehicle Dealers Association of North America.

Recreation Vehicle Industry Association., 1896 Preston White Dr., PO Box 2999 Reston, VA 20191. Phone: (703)620-6003 Fax: (703)620-5071 E-mail: rparsons@rvia.org • URL: http://www.rvia.org • Recreation vehicle manufacturers, manufacturers' representatives, and suppliers of accessories and equipment used by manufacturers. Seeks to provide a unified recreation vehicle organization for manufacturers and component parts suppliers of motor homes, travel trailers, truck campers, folding camping trailers, and conversion vehicles. Promotes and represents the growth and concerns of the industry to federal and state government departments, the media, and the public. Collects shipment statistics, technical data, and consumer and media information. Monitors industry compliance with safety standards and the activities of federal and state governments that affect the RV industry. Provides legal and public relations services. Sponsors market research.

Recruiter's Research Blue Book: A How-To Guide for Researchers, Consultants, Corporate Recruiters, Small Business Owners, Venture Capitalists, and Line Executives. Andrea A. Jupina. Kennedy Information, Inc., One Phoenix Mill Ln., 5th Fl. Peterborough, NH 03458. Phone: 800-531-0007 or (603)924-0900 Fax: (603)924-4460 E-mail: bookstore@kennedyinfo.com • URL: http://www.kennedyinfo.com • 2000. $179.00. Second edition. Provides detailed coverage of the role that research plays in executive recruiting. Includes such practical items as "Telephone Interview Guide," "Legal Issues in Executive Search," and "How to Create an Execuive Search Library." Covers both person-to-person research and research using printed and online business information sources. Includes an extensive directory of recommended sources. Formerly *Handbook of Executive Search Research*.

Recruiting, Interviewing, Selecting, and Orienting New Employees. Diane Arthur. AMACOM, 1601 Broadway New York, NY 10019. Phone: 800-262-9699 or (518)586-8100 Fax: (518)903-8168 E-mail: customerservice@amanet.org • URL: http://www.amacombooks.org • 1998. $59.95. Third edition. A practical guide to the basics of hiring, including legal considerations and sample forms.

Recruiting Library Staff: A How-To-Do-It Manual for Librarians. Kathleen Low. Neal-Schuman Publishers, Inc., 100 William St., Ste. 2004 New York, NY 10038. Phone: (866)672-6657 or (212)925-8650 Fax: (866)209-7932 or (212)219-8916 E-mail: info@neal-schuman.com • URL: http://www.neal-schuman.com • 1999. $45.00. Includes position description forms, sample announcements, and checklists. Discusses job fairs and other career events. (How-To-Do-It Manual for Librarians Series).

Recruiting Trends: The Monthly Newsletter for the Recruiting Executive. Kennedy Information, Inc., One Phoenix Mill Lane, 5th Fl. Peterborough, NH 03458. Phone: 800-531-0007 or (603)924-1006 Fax: (603)924-4460 E-mail: bookstore@kennedyinfo.com • URL: http://www.kennedyinfo.com • Monthly. $179.00 per year.

Recycling Sourcebook. Gale, 27500 Drake Rd. Farmington Hills, MI 48331-3535. Phone: 800-877-4253 or (248)699-4253 Fax: 800-414-5043 or (248)699-8065 E-mail: galeord@cengage.com • URL: http://gale.cengage.com • Covers: Organizations concerned with policies, programs, and implications of recycling in the U.S.; companies performing recycling services. An appendix lists products made with recycled or recyclable materials and their manufacturers. Entries include: Organization name, address, phone, description of activities and purpose.

Recycling Today. Group Interest Enterprises. G.I.E. Publishers Inc., 4012 Bridge Ave. Cleveland, OH 44113-3320. Phone: 800-456-0707 or (216)961-4130 Fax: (216)961-0364 E-mail: pmoralew@gie.net • URL: http://www.recyclingtoday.com/ • Monthly. $30.00 per year. Serves the recycling industry in all areas.

Red and White: Wine Made Simple. Max Allen. Wine Appreciation Guild, 360 Swift Ave. South San Francisco, CA 94080. Phone: 800-231-9463 or (650)866-3020 Fax: (650)866-3513 E-mail: info@wineappreciation.com • URL: http://www.wineappreciation.com • 2001. $24.95. Revised edition. A sophisticated wine primer for consumers. Includes information and advice on wine selection, grape varieties, and the matching of food and wine.

Red Book. American Monument Association, 30 Eden Alley, Ste. 301 Columbus, OH 43215. Phone: 877-922-2022 or (614)461-5852 Fax: (614)461-1497 E-mail: galeord@cengage.com • URL: http://www.medec.com • Covers: 7,000 retail monument dealers, suppliers of granite and marble, wholesalers, quarriers, funeral homes and cemeteries. Entries include: company; name, address, phone, fax; trade classification, names of owner or corporate officers and their titles. Available only to members of The American Monument Association.

Reducing Inflation: Motivation and Strategy. Christina Romer and David Romer. The University of Chicago Press, 1427 E. 60th St. Chicago, IL 60637. Phone: 800-621-2736 or (773)702-7700 Fax: 800-621-8476 or (773)702-7212 E-mail: custserv@press.uchicago.edu • URL: http://www.press.uchicago.edu • 1997. $58.00. Consists of 10 essays and comments by various economists on strategies for controlling inflation. (NBER Studies in Business Cycles Series: Vol. 30).

Reengineering Management: The Mandate for New Leadership. James Champy. DIANE Publishing Co., 330 Pusey Ave. Collingdale, PA 19023-8428. Phone: 800-782-3833 or (610)461-6200 Fax: (610)461-6130 E-mail: dianepub@erols.com • URL: http://www.dianepublishing.com • 1998. $25.00.

Reengineering Revolution: A Handbook. Michael Hammer and Steven Stanton. HarperInformation, 10 E. 53rd St. New York, NY 10022-5299. Phone: 800-242-7737 or (212)207-7000 Fax: 800-242-7737 or (212)207-7145 • URL: http://www/harpercollins.com • 1995. $17.95.

Reengineering the Bank: A Blueprint for Survival and Success. Paul H. Allen. McGraw-Hill, 1221 Ave. of the Americas New York, NY 10020. Phone: 800-722-4726 or (212)512-2000 Fax: (212)512-4502 E-mail: customer.service@mcgraw-hill.com • URL: http://www.mcgraw-hill.com • 1994. $40.00.

Reengineering the Corporation: A Manifesto for Business Revolution. Michael Hammer and James Champy. HarperInformation, 10 E. 53rd St. New York, NY 10022-5299. Phone: 800-242-7737 or (212)207-7000 Fax: 800-242-7737 or (212)207-7145 • URL: http://www.harpercollins.com • 2001. $16.00. Revised edition.

Reference and User Services Association of American Library Association: Machine Assisted Reference Section., c/o American Library Association, 50 E Huron St. Chicago, IL 60611. Phone: 800-545-2433 or (312)280-4398 Fax: (312)944-8085 E-mail: rusa@ala.org • URL: http://www.ala.org/rusa • Affiliated with American Library Association. Formerly Reference and Adult Services Division of American Library Association.

Reference and User Services Quarterly. American Library Association, Reference and Adult Services Div., 50 E. Huron St. Chicago, IL 60611-2795. Phone: 800-545-2433 or (312)944-6780 Fax: (312)440-9374 E-mail: rusa@ala.org • URL: http://www.ala.org • Quarterly. $50.00 per year. In addition to articles, includes reviews of databases, reference books, and library professional material. Formerly *RQ*.

Reference Book for World Traders, 1987. Croner Publications, Inc., 10951 Sorrento Valley Rd., Suite 1-D San Diego, CA 92121-1613. Phone: 800-441-4033 or (619)546-1894 Fax: (619)546-1955 1990. Price on application. A looseleaf handbook covering information required for planning and executing exports and imports to and from all foreign countries; kept up to date by an amendment service.

Reference Book of Corporate Managements., Dun and Bradstreet, 3 Sylvan Way Parsippany, NJ 07054-3896. Phone: 800-526-0651 Fax: (973)605-6911 E-mail: dnbmdd@dnb.com • URL: http://www.dnb.com • Annual. Libraries, $650.00 per year; others, $795.00 per year. Lease basis. Management executives at over 12,000 leading United States companies.

Reference Books Bulletin: A Compilation of Evaluations. Mary Ellen Quinn, editor. American Library Association, 50 E. Huron St. Chicago, IL 60611. Phone: 800-545-2433 or (312)944-6780 Fax: (312)440-9374 E-mail: ala@ala.org • URL: http://www.ala.org • Annual. $79.95. Contains reference book reviews that appeared during the year in *Booklist*.

The Reference Librarian. Haworth Press, Inc., 10 Alice St. Binghamton, NY 13904-1580. Phone: 800-429-6784 or (607)722-5857 Fax: 800-895-0582 or (607)722-1424 E-mail: getinfo@haworthpressinc.com • URL: http://www.haworthpressinc.com • Semiannual. Institutions, $325.00 per year. Two volumes.

Reference Manual for Telecommunications Engineering. Roger L. Freeman. John Wiley and Sons, Inc., 111 River St. Hoboken, NJ 07030. Phone: 800-225-5945 or (201)748-6000 Fax: (201)748-6088 E-mail: info@wiley.com • URL: http://www.wiley.com • 2001. $695.00. Third edition. Two volumes. Presents detailed information and specific data on the most commonly used telecommunications standards.

Reference Reviews. Available from Information Today, Inc., 143 Old Marlton Pike Medford, NJ 08055-8750. Phone: 800-300-9868 or (609)654-6266 Fax: (609)654-4309 E-mail: custserv@infotoday.com • URL: http://www.infotoday.com • Eight times a year. Price on application. Published in London by Aslib: The Association for Information Management. Incorporates*Aslib Book Guide*.

Reference Services Review: Information on All Aspects of the Reference Function. Emerald (North America), 875 Massachusetts Ave., 7th Fl. Cambridge, MA 02139. Phone: 888-622-0075 or (617)497-2175 Fax: (617)354-6875 E-mail: america@emeraldinsight.com • URL: http://www.emeraldinsight.com • Quarterly. $319.00 per year. Covers automation of library reference services, user needs, reference source evaluation, service delivery models, and related topics.

Reference Source. Sosland Publishing Co., 4800 Main St., Suite 100 Kansas City, MO 64112-2513. Phone: (816)756-1000 Fax: (816)756-0494 E-mail: web@sosland.com • URL: http://www.sosland.com • Annual. $45.00 per year. A statistical reference manual and specification guide for wholesale baking.

Reference Sources for Small and Medium-sized Libraries. Scott E. Kennedy, editor. American Library Association, 50 E. Huron St. Chicago, IL 60611-2795. Phone: 800-545-2433 or (312)944-6780 Fax: (312)440-9374 E-mail: ala@ala.org • URL: http://www.ala.org • 1999. $60.00. Sixth edition. Includes alternative (electronic) formats for reference works.

Refining and Gas Processing Industry Worldwide. Midwest Publishing Co., Tulsa, OK 74159-0468. Phone: 800-829-2002 or (918)583-2033 Fax: (918)587-9349 E-mail: info@midwestdirectories.com • URL: http://www.midwestdirectories.com • Annual. $145.00. Over 5,200 refineries, gas processing plants, engineering contractors, equipment manufacturers, supply companies and liquid terminals. Formerly *Refining and Gas Processing*.

Reforming the Bank Regulatory Structure. Andrew S. Carron. Brookings Institution Press, 1775 Massachusetts Ave., N.W. Washington, DC 20036-2188. Phone: 800-275-1447 or (202)797-6258 Fax: (202)797-6004 E-mail: bibooks@brook.edu • URL: http://www.brookings.edu • 1985. $8.95. (Studies in the Regulation of Economic Activity).

Refractories. U. S. Bureau of the Census, 4700 Silver Hill Rd. Washington, DC 20233-0001. Phone: (301)763-4636 E-mail: comments@census.gov • URL: http://www.census.gov • Annual. Provides data on value of manufacturers' shipments, quantity, exports, imports, etc. (Current Industrial Reports, MA-32C.)

Refractories Institute (TRI)., 650 Smithfield St., Ste. 1160 Pittsburgh, PA 15222-3907. Phone: (412)281-6787 Fax: (412)281-6881 E-mail: triassn@aol.com • URL: http://www.refractoriesinstitute.org • Members are producers of fire brick and other refactory materials.

Refrigerating Engineers and Technicians Association., 4700 W. Lake Ave. Glenview, IL 60625-1485. Phone: (847)375-4738 Fax: 877-218-8369 or (847)375-6338 E-mail: info@reta.com • URL: http://www.reta.com/ • Formerly National Association Practical Refrigerating Engineers.

Refrigeration. John W. Yopp Publications, Inc., P.O. Box 1147 Beaufort, SC 29901. Phone: 800-849-9677 E-mail: jcronley@jwyopp.com • URL: http://www.jwyopp.com • Monthly. $30.00 per year.

Refrigeration, Air Conditioning, and Warm Air Heating Equipment. U. S. Bureau of the Census, 4700 Silver Hill Rd. Washington, DC 20233-0001. Phone: (301)763-4636 E-mail: comments@census.gov • URL: http://www.census.gov • Annual. Provides data on quantity and value of shipments by manufacturers. Formerly *Air Conditioning and Refrigeration Equipment*. (Current Industrial Reports, MA-35M.)

Refrigeration and Air Conditioning. A.R. Trott and T. Welch. Elsevier, 655 Ave. of the Americas New York, NY 10010. Phone: 800-366-2665 or (212)989-5800 Fax: 800-535-9935 or (212)633-3680 E-mail: custserv@elsevier.com • URL: http://www.elsevier.com • 2000. $64.99. Third edition.

Refundable Bundle., Centuck Station, P.O. Box 140 Yonkers, NY 10710. Phone: (914)472-2227 E-mail: coupons50@aol.com • URL: http://www.refundlebundle.com • Bimonthly. $10.00 per year. Newsletter for grocery shoppers. Each issue provides details of new coupon and refund offers.

Refuse and Resist., 305 Madison Ave., Ste. 1166 New York, NY 10165. Phone: (212)713-5657 E-mail: info@refuseandresist.org • URL: http://www.refuseandresist.org • Participants seek to build mass resistance to the "entire agenda of repression in the U.S." Works to unite grassroots activists, prominent entertainers, teachers, plumbers, artists, student, etc. in opposition to the fundamentalist right-wing agenda. Opposes racism, restrictions on abortion rights, the escalation of the "war on women", censorship, homophobia, xenophobia, and the execution of Mumia Abu-Jamal. Has demonstrated to prevent the closing of abortion clinics and the incarceration of immigrants. Participates in debates; maintains speakers' bureau.

Regency International Directory of Private Investigators, Private Detectives, Security Guards, and Security Equipment Suppliers. Regency International Directory, 351 Cheriton Rd. Folkestone CT19 4BP, United Kingdom. Phone: 303 275222 Fax: 303 275222 E-mail: regency@hythe-printers.freeserve.co.uk Annual. $60.00. Over 5,000 detective agencies, firms specializing in security. bailiffs, and trade protection societies; worldwide coverage.

Regional Airline Association., 2025 M St. NW, Ste. 800 Washington, DC 20036-3309. Phone: (202)367-1170 Fax: (202)367-2170 E-mail: raa@raa.org • URL: http://www.raa.org • Regional air carriers engaged in the transportation of passengers, cargo, or mail on a scheduled basis; persons, companies, and organizations engaged in pursuits related to commercial aviation; colleges and universities, state and local governments, and state aviation associations. Responds to community, consumer, and public needs for air transportation and aviation facilities and to help establish a healthy business, regulatory, and legislative climate that enables members to profit through service to the nation and the flying public. Supports programs for improving safety and reliability of air transportation and air commerce; provides a forum for exchange of ideas and information.

Regional Airline World. Shephard Press Ltd., 111 High St. Burnham SL1 7JZ, United Kingdom. Phone: 800-873-2147 or 44 1628 664334 Fax: 44 1628 664075 E-mail: publishing@shephard.co.uk • URL: http://www.shephard.co.uk • 10 times a year. $130.00 per year. Covers the business, financial, and technical aspects of regional, short-haul, and commuter airline operations.

Regional Aviation Handbook. Shephard Press Ltd., 111 High St. Burnham SL1 7JZ, United Kingdom. Phone: 800-873-2147 or 44 1628 604311 Fax: 44 1628 664334 E-mail: subs@shephard.co.uk • URL: http://www.shephard.co.uk • Annual. $90.00. Edited for regional, short-haul, and commuter airlines. Includes airline operators worldwide, manufacturers of equipment and supplies, aircraft companies, leasing companies, trade associations, and other listings.

Regional Developement Services. East Carolina University

Regional Economic Development Center. University of Memphis

Regional Economic Development: Theories amd Strategies for Developing Countries. Marguerite N. Abd El-Shahid. Sage Publications, Inc., 2455 Teller Rd. Thousand Oaks, CA 91320. Phone: 800-818-7243 or (805)499-9774 Fax: 800-583-2665 or (805)499-0871 E-mail: webmaster@sagepub.com • URL: http://www.sagepub.com • 1994. $10.00.

Regional Economics and Markets: A Quarterly Analysis from the Conference Board. The Conference Board, 845 Third Ave. New York, NY 10022. Phone: (212)339-0345 Fax: (212)836-9740 • URL: http://www.conference-board.org • Quarterly. Members, $145.00 per year; non-members, $295.00 per year. Summarizes economic trends and prospects for nine geographic regions of the U. S. Provides data on key predictive indexes, including employment, housing permits, retail sales, consumer confidence, and help-wanted advertising. Charts and graphs are included.

Regional Official Guides: Tractors and Farm Equipment. Iron Solutions, LLC, 1195 Smizer Mill Rd. Fenton, MO 63026-3480. Phone: 877-266-4766 or (636)343-8000 Fax: 800-821-7270 E-mail: admin@ironsolutions.com • URL: http://www.ironsolutions.com • Quarterly. Membership.

Regional Science Association International., 2149 Grey Ave., Bevier Hall, Rm. 83, 905 S Goodwin Ave. Evanston, IL 60201. Phone: (217)333-8904 Fax: (217)333-3065 E-mail: rsai@uiuc.edu • URL: http://www.regionalscience.org • Represents academic and professional individuals concerned with the practice and advancement of urban and regional analysis and related studies.

Regions Statistical Yearbook. Bernan Associates, 4611-F Assembly Dr. Lanham, MD 20706-4391. Phone: 800-274-4447 or (301)459-2255 Fax: 800-865-3450 or (301)459-0056 E-mail: info@bernan.com • URL: http://www.bernan.com • Annual. $45.00. Published by the Commission of European Communities. Provides data on the social and economic situation in specific European areas. Includes population, employment, migration, industry, living standards, etc.

Register of International Shipowning Groups. Available from Fairplay Publications, Inc., 5201 Blue Lagoon Dr., Ste. 530 Miami, FL 33126. Phone: (305)262-4070 Fax: (305)262-2006 E-mail: sales-us@lrfairplay.com • URL: http://www.lrfairplay.com • Three times a year. $744.00 per year. Published in the UK by Lloyd's Register-Fairplay Ltd. "Provides intelligence on shipowners and managers, their subsidiary and associate companies, and owners' representatives." Includes detailed information on individual ships.

Register of Officers [United States Coast Guard]. U.S. Coast Guard, Washington, DC 20593. Phone: (202)267-2229 Annual.

Registered Representative. Primedia Business Magazines and Media, 249 W 17th St. New York, NY 10011. Phone: 800-795-5445 or (212)462-3600 Fax: (212)462-3600 E-mail: subs@primediabusiness.com • URL: http://www.

primediabusiness.com • Monthly. $48.00 per year.

Regulatory Policy and Practices: Regulating Better and Regulating Less. Fred Thompson. Greenwood Publishing Group, Inc., 88 Post Rd., W Westport, CT 06881. Phone: 800-225-5800 or (203)226-3571 Fax: (203)431-2214 E-mail: customer-service@greenwood.com • URL: http://www.greenwood.com • 1982. $68.00.

Rehabilitation International; Vocational Commission., 25 E. 21st St. New York, NY 10010. Phone: (212)420-1500 Fax: (212)505-0871 E-mail: rehabintl@rehab-international.org • URL: http://www.rehab-international.org • Formerly International Society for Rehabilitation of the Disabled.

Rehabilitation Program. University of Arizona

Reinforced Concrete Fundamentals. Phil M. Ferguson and others. John Wiley and Sons, Inc., 111 River St. Hoboken, NJ 07030. Phone: 800-225-5945 or (201)748-6000 Fax: (201)748-6088 E-mail: info@wiley.com • URL: http://www.wiley.com • 1988. $116.95. Fifth edition.

Reinventing the Bazaar: A Natural History of Markets. John McMillan. W. W. Norton & Co., Inc., 500 5th Ave. New York, NY 10110. Phone: 800-223-4830 or (212)354-5500 Fax: (212)869-0856 • URL: http://www.wwnorton.com • 2002. $25.05. Covers marketing from early times to modern times. Takes the viewpoint that markets are desirable, occur naturally, and require intelligent regulation.

Release 1.0 Esther Dysons Monthly Report. EDventure Holdings Inc., 104 5th Ave., 20th Fl. New York, NY 10011. Phone: (212)924-8800 Fax: (212)924-0240 E-mail: us@release1-0.com • URL: http://www.edventure.com • Description: Reports on technology, communications, and the Internet. Reviews and analyzes the technology business. Recurring features include a calendar of events.

Releasing an Independent Record: How to Successfully Start and Run Your Own Record Label in the 1990s. Gary Hustwit. Rockpress Publishing, 107 Norfolk St. New York, NY 10002. Phone: (212)473-9530 Fax: (212)473-9735 1998. $24.95. Sixth edition.

Reliable Financial Reporting and Internal Control: A Global Implementation Guide. Dmitris N. Chorafas. John Wiley and Sons, Inc., 111 River St. Hoboken, NJ 07030. Phone: 800-225-5945 or (201)748-6000 Fax: (201)748-6088 E-mail: info@wiley.com • URL: http://www.wiley.com • 2000. $75.00. Discusses financial reporting and control as related to doing business internationally.

Religious Conference Management Association., 7702 Woodland Dr., Ste. 120 Indianapolis, IN 46278. Phone: (317)632-1888 Fax: (317)632-7909 E-mail: rcma@rcmaweb.org • URL: http://www.rcmaweb.org • Represents persons responsible for planning and/or managing religious conventions, meetings, and assemblies; associate members are individuals who directly support the logistics of religious meetings. Promotes professional excellence through exchange of ideas, techniques, and methods of management.

Relocation Journal and Real Estate News. Mobility Services International, 124 High St. Newburyport, MA 01950. Phone: (978)463-0348 E-mail: diane@msimobility.com • URL: http://www.relojournal.com • Monthly. Free. Newsletter for real estate, building, financing and investing. Formed by the merger of *Real Estate News* and *Relocation Journal*.

Remodeling: Excellence in Professional Remodeling. Hanley-Wood, LLC, One Thomas Circle NW Washington, DC 20005. Phone: 800-837-0870 or (202)452-0800 Fax: (202)785-1974 • URL: http://www.hanley-wood.com • Monthly. $44.95 per year. Covers new products, construction, management, and marketing for remodelers.

Remodeling—Product Guide. Hanley-Wood L.L.C., 1 Thomas Cir. NW, Ste. 600 Washington, DC 20005. Phone: 800-837-0870 or (202)452-0800 or (202)452-0800 Fax: (202)785-1974 E-mail: galeord@cengage.com • URL: http://www.hanleywood.com • Publication includes: List of more than 2,000 manufacturers and suppliers serving the remodeling contracting industry; list of industry-related associations. Entries include: For manufacturers and suppliers—Company name, address, phone, name and title of contact, product line, geographical area served. For associations—Association name, address, phone, director.

Renewable Energy: An International Journal. Elsevier, 360 Park Ave., S New York, NY 10010-1710. Phone: 888-437-4636 or (212)989-5800 Fax: (212)633-3990 E-mail: usinfo-f@elsevier.com • URL: http://www.elsevier.com • 15 times a year. $1,835.00 per year. Incorporates *Solar and Wind Technology*.

Renewable Natural Resources Foundation., 5430 Grosvenor Ln. Bethesda, MD 20814-2142. Phone: (301)493-9101 Fax: (301)493-6148 E-mail: info@rnrf.org • URL: http://www.rnrf.org • Members are American Fisheries Society, American Geophysical Union, American Meteorological Society, American Society of Agronomy, American Society of Civil Engineers, Society of Landscape Architects, American Society for Photogrammetry and Remote Sensing, American Water Resources Association, Association of American Geographers, Humane Society of the United States, Society for Range Management, Society of Wood Science and Technology, Society of Environmental Toxicology and Chemistry, Soil and Water Conservation Society, Universities Council on Water Resources, and Wildlife Society. Concerned with renewable natural resources subjects and public policy alternatives. Develops 35-acre, forested Renewable Natural Resources Center, an office-park complex for natural resources and other nonprofit organizations.

Renewables for Power Generation: Status and Prospect. Organization for Economic Cooperation and Development, OECD Washington Center, 2001 L St., N. W., Suite 650 Washington, DC 20036-4922. Phone: 800-456-6323 or (202)785-6323 Fax: (202)785-0350 E-mail: washington.contact@oecd.org • URL: http://www.oecd.org • 2003. $75.00. Presents the global outlook for electrical power generation from renewable sources, including water power, wind power, solar power, and geothermal power.

Rensselaer Polytechnic Institute., Rensselaer Technology Park, 100 Jordan Rd. Troy, NY 12180. Phone: (518)283-7102 Fax: (518)283-0695 E-mail: wachom@rpi.edu • URL: http://www.rpi.edu/dept/rtp • Serves as a conduit for research interactions between Rensselaer Polytechnic Institute and private companies.

Rental Equipment Register. Primedia Business Magazines and Media', 9800 Metcalf Ave. Overland Park, KS 66212. Phone: 800-795-5445 or (913)341-1300 Fax: (913)967-1898 E-mail: subs@primediabusiness.com • URL: http://www.primediabusiness.com • Monthly. $75.00 per year.

Rental Equipment Register Buyer's Guide. Primedia Business Magazines and Media, 9800 Metcalf Ave. Overland Park, KS 66212. Phone: 800-795-5445 or (913)341-1300 Fax: (913)967-1898 E-mail: subs@primediabusiness.com • URL: http://www.primediabusiness.com • Annual. $43.95. Formerly *Rental Equipment Register Product Directory and Buyer's Guide*.

Rental Management. American Rental Association, 1900 19th St. Moline, IL 61265. Phone: 800-334-2177 or (309)764-2475 Fax: (309)764-1533 • URL: http://www.ararental.org • Monthly. Free to qualified personnel; others, $24.00 per year.

Rental Product News. Cygnus Business Media, 1233 Janesville Ave. Fort Atkinson, WI 53538. Phone: 800-547-7377 or (920)563-6388 Fax: (920)563-1707 E-mail: rich.reiff@cygnuspub.com • URL: http://www.cygnusbzb.com • Bimonthly. $48.00 per year. Includes annual *Product* issue.

Rep-Letter. Manufacturers' Agents National Association, 1 Spectrum Pointe, Ste. 150 Lake Forest, CA 92630. Phone: 877-626-2776 or (949)859-4040 Fax: (949)855-2973 E-mail: mana@manaonline.org • URL: http://www.manaonline.org • Monthly. $37.50. A bound-in monthly feature of *Agency Sales Magazine*.

Report. Robinson and Associates, 1723 Jackson St. Santa Clara, CA 95050. Phone: (408)723-7311 Monthly. $295.00 per year. Newsletter. Articles cover the artificial intelligence field. Formerly *Artificial Intelligence Report*.

Report of the International Narcotics Control Board on Its Work. United Nations Publications, United Nations Concourse Level, First Ave., 46th St. New York, NY 10017. Phone: 800-553-3210 or (212)963-7680 Fax: (212)963-4910 E-mail: bookstore@un.org • URL: http://www.un.org/publications • Annual. $20.00.

Report on Corporate Library Spending. Primary Research, 850 Seventh Ave., Ste. 1200 New York, NY 10019. Phone: (212)764-1579 Fax: (212)397-5056 E-mail: primarydat@aol.com 1995. $75.00. Provides market research data on corporate library expenditures for books, periodicals, and online/CD-ROM sources.

Report on Electronic Commerce: Online Business, Financial and Consumer Strategies and Trends. Aspen Publishers, 1185 Ave. of the Americas New York, NY 10036. Phone: 800-638-8437 or (212)597-0200 Fax: 800-561-4845 E-mail: customer.service@aspenpubl.com • URL: http://www.aspenpublishers.com • Biweekly. $1,789.00 per year. Newsletter. Includes *Daily Multimedia News Service*. Incorporates *Interactive Services Report*.

Report on Healthcare Information Management. Capital Publications, Inc., 1101 King St., Suite 444 Alexandria, VA 22314. Phone: (703)683-4100 Fax: (703)739-6501 Monthly. $358.00 per year. Newsletter. Covers management information sytems for hospitals and physicians' groups.

Report on the American Workforce. Available from U. S. Government Printing Office, Washington, DC 20402. Phone: (202)512-1800 Fax: (202)512-2250 E-mail: gpoaccess@gpo.gov • URL: http://www.access.gpo.gov • Annual. Issued by the U. S. Department of Labor (http://www.dol.gov). Appendix contains tabular statistics, including employment, unemployment, price indexes, consumer expenditures, employee benefits (retirement, insurance, vacation, etc.), wages, productivity, hours of work, and occupational injuries. Annual figures are shown for up to 50 years.

Report Writing for Business. Raymond V. Lesikar and John Pettit. McGraw-Hill, 1221 Ave. of the Americas New York, NY 10020. Phone: 800-722-4726 or (212)512-2000 Fax: (212)512-4502 E-mail: customer.service@mcgraw-hill.com • URL: http://www.mcgraw-hill.com • 1997. $83.75. 10th edition.

Reporters Committee for Freedom of the Press., 1815 N. Fort Meyer Dr., Suite 900 Arlington, VA 22209. Phone: 800-336-4243 or (703)807-2100 Fax: (703)807-2109 E-mail: rcfp@rcfp.org • URL: http://www.rcfp.org/rcfp • Concerned with protecting freedom of information rights for the working press.

Reproducible Copies of Federal Tax Forms and Instructions. Available from U. S. Government Printing Office, Washington, DC 20402. Phone: (202)512-1800 Fax: (202)512-2250 E-mail: gpoaccess@gpo.gov • URL: http://www.access.gpo.gov • Annual. $54.00. Two looseleaf volumes issued by the Internal Revenue Service (http://www.irs.gov). "Contains the most frequently requested tax forms and instructions," prepared especially for libraries.

Research Alert: A Bi-Weekly Report of Consumer Marketing Studies. EPM Communications, Inc., 160 Mercer St., 3rd Fl. New York, NY 10012-3212. Phone: 888-852-9467 or (212)941-0099 Fax: 888-852-3899 or (212)941-1622 E-mail: info@epmcom.com • URL: http://www.epmcom.com • Biweekly. $369.00 per year. Newsletter. Provides descriptions (abstracts) of new, consumer market research reports from private, government, and academic sources. Includes sample charts and tables.

Research Alert Yearbook: Vital Facts on Consumer Behavior and Attitudes. EPM Communications, Inc., 160 Mercer St., 3rd Fl. New York, NY 10012-3212. Phone: 888-852-9467 or (212)941-0099 Fax: (212)941-1622 E-mail: info@epmcom.com • URL: http://www.epmcom.com • Annual. $295.00. Provides summaries of consumer market research from the newsletters *Research Alert, Youth Markets Alert, and Minority Markets Alert*. Includes tables, charts, graphs, and textual summaries for 41 subject categories. Sources include reports, studies, polls, and focus groups.

Research and Development Associates for Military Food and Packaging Systems., 16607 Blanco Rd., No. 1506 San Antonio, TX 78232. Phone: (210)493-8024 or (210)493-8025 Fax: (210)493-8036 E-mail: rda50@flash.net • URL: http://www.militaryfood.org • Industrial firms, educational institutions and related groups engged in food, food service, distribution and container research and development.

Research and Development Expenditure in Industry. Organization for Economic Cooperation and Development, OECD Washington Center, 2001 L St., N. W., Suite 650 Washington, DC 20036-4922. Phone: 800-456-6323 or (202)785-6323 Fax: (202)785-0350 E-mail: washington.contact@oecd.org • URL: http://www.oecd.org • Annual. $51.00. Provides data for more than 10 years. Covers R&D expenditures in each of more than 50 industrial sectors in various OECD countries. Regional total for the European Union is also provided.

Research and Development Expenditures in Industry. Organization for Economic Cooperation and Development, OECD Washington Center, 2001 L St., N. W., Suite 650 Washington, DC 20036-4922. Phone: 800-456-6323 or (202)785-6323 Fax: (202)785-0350 E-mail: washington.contact@oecd.org • URL: http://www.oecd.org • Annual. $51.00. Presents research and development expenditures for OECD countries and the European Union zone. Includes about 60 industrial sectors.

Research and Development: The Voice of the Research and Development Community. Reed Business Information, 360 Park Ave., S New York, NY 10010. Phone: 800-662-7776 or (646)746-6400 E-mail: corporatecommunications@reedbusiness.com • URL: http://www.reedbusiness.com • 13 times a year. $81.90 per year.

Research and Engineering Council of NAPL.

Research and Investigation in Adult Education: Annual Register. American Association for Adult and Continuing Education, 1200 19th St., N.W., Suite 300 Washington, DC 20036. Phone: (202)429-5131 Fax: (202)223-4579 • URL: http://www.albany.edu/aaace • Annual.

Research Centers and Services Directories. Gale Cengage Learning, 27500 Drake Rd. Farmington Hills, MI 48331-3535. Phone: 800-877-GALE or (248)699-GALE Fax: 800-414-5043 or (248)699-8069 E-mail: galeord@gale.com • URL: http://gale.cengage.com • Contains profiles of about 30,000 research centers, organizations, laboratories, and agencies in 147 countries. Corresponds to the printed *Research Centers Directory, International Research Centers Directory, Government Research Directory*, and *Research Services Directory*. Updating is semiannual. Inquire as to online cost and availability.

Research Centers Directory. Gale, 27500 Drake Rd. Farmington Hills, MI 48331-3535. Phone: 800-877-4253 or (248)699-4253 Fax: 800-414-5043 or (248)699-8065 E-mail: galeord@cengage.com • URL: http://gale.cengage.com • Covers: About 13,600 university, government, and other nonprofit research organizations established on a permanent basis to carry on continuing research programs in all areas of study; includes research institutes, laboratories, experiment stations, research parks, technology transfer centers, and other facilities and activities; coverage includes Canada. Entries include: Unit name, name of parent institution, address, phone, fax, name of director, e-mail addresses, URLs, year founded, governance, staff, educational activities, public services, sources of support, annual volume of research, principal fields of research, publications, special library facilities, special research facilities.

Research Corporation Technologies. Research Corporation Technologies, 5210 E Williams Cir., Ste. 240 Tucson, AZ 85711-4410. Phone: (520)748-4400 Fax: (520)748-0025 E-mail: csouvignier@rctech.com • URL: http://www.rctech.com • Appraises, protects, develops, and commercializes inventions from colleges, universities, medical research organizations, and other research laboratories. Among the variety of inventions that have been developed and marketed are agricultural and other chemicals, chemical processes, biotechnologies, bioprocessing, diagnostics, foods and additives, pharmaceuticals, plants, vaccines, veterinary products, agricultural equipment, analytical instruments, chemicals, electronics, materials, industrial processes, machines, medical/surgical diagnostics, and optics/optical instruments. Provides incentives for invention disclosure, funds selected applied research, new business formation.

Research Foundation of Association for Investment Management and Research., 560 Ray C. Hunt Dr. Charlottesville, VA 22903-0668. Phone: 800-247-8132 or (434)951-5499 Fax: (434)951-5262 E-mail: info@aimr.com • URL: http://www.aimr.org • Affiliated with Financial Analysts Federation.

Research in Accounting Regulation. Elsevier, 360 Park Ave., S New York, NY 10010-1710. Phone: (212)989-5800 Fax: (212)633-3990 E-mail: usinfo-f@elsevier.com • URL: http://www.elsevier.com • Dates vary. Price varies. 16 volumes.

Research in Corporate Social Performance and Policy: An Annual Compilation of Research. Elsevier, 360 Park Ave., S New York, NY 10010-1710. Phone: (212)989-5800 Fax: (212)633-3990 E-mail: usinfo-f@elsevier.com • URL: http://www.elsevier.com • Dates vary. $78.50. 15 volumes.

Research in Domestic and International Agribusiness Management. Elsevier, 360 Park Ave., S New York, NY 10010-1710. Phone: (212)989-5800 Fax: (212)633-3990 E-mail: usinfo-f@elsevier.com • URL: http://www.elsevier.com • Dates vary. $73.25. 12 volumes.

Research in Experimental Economics. Elsevier, 360 Park Ave., S New York, NY 10010-1710. Phone: (212)989-5800 Fax: (212)633-3990 E-mail: usinfo-f@elsevier.com • URL: http://www.elsevier.com • Dates vary. $84.00. Nine volumes. Supplement available *An Experiment in Non-Cooperative Oligopoly*.

Research in Governmental and Nonprofit Accounting. Elsevier, 360 Park Ave., S New York, NY 10010-1710. Phone: (212)989-5800 Fax: (212)633-3990 E-mail: usinfo-f@elsevier.com • URL: http://www.elsevier.com • Dates vary. Price varies. 10 volumes.

Research in International Business and Finance. Elsevier, 360 Park Ave., S New York, NY 10010-1710. Phone: (212)989-5800 Fax: (212)633-3990 E-mail: usinfo-f@elevier.com • URL: http://www.elsevier.com • Three times a year. Individuals, $50.00 per year; institutions, $195.00 per year.

Research in Law and Economics: A Research Annual. Richard O. Zerbe. Elsevier, 360 Park Ave., S New York, NY 10010-1710. Phone: (212)989-5800 Fax: (212)633-3990 E-mail: usinfo-f@elsevier.com • URL: http://www.elsevier.com • Dates vary. $78.50. 20 volumes. Supplement available:*Economics of Nonproprietary Organizations*.

Research in Marketing: An Annual Compilation of Research. Jagdish N. Sheth, editor. Elsevier, 360 Park Ave., S New York, NY 10010-1710. Phone: (212)989-5800 Fax: (212)633-3990 E-mail: usinfo-f@elevier.com • URL: http://www.elsevier.com • Annual. Price on application.

Research in Personnel and Human Resources Management. Gerald R. Ferris, editor. Elsevier, 360 Park Ave., S New York, NY 10010-1710. Phone: (212)989-5800 Fax: (212)633-3990 E-mail: usinfo-f@elsevier.com • URL: http://www.elsevier.com • Dates vary. $78.50. 21 volumes.

Research in Philosophy and Technology. Elsevier, 360 Park Ave., S New York, NY 10010-1710. Phone: (212)989-5800 Fax: (212)633-3990 E-mail: usinfo-f@elsevier.com • URL: http://www.elsevier.com • Dates vary. Price varies. 21 volumes.

Research in Population Economics. Elsevier, 360 Park Ave., S New York, NY 10010-1710. Phone: (212)989-5800 Fax: (212)633-3990 E-mail: usinfo-f@elsevier.com • URL: http://www.elsevier.com • Irregular. $90.25. Volumes 4-9.

Research in Transportation Economics. Elsevier, 360 Park Ave., S New York, NY 10010-1710. Phone: (212)989-5800 Fax: (212)633-3990 E-mail: usinfo-f@elsevier.com • URL: http://www.elsevier.com • Dates vary. Price varies. Six volumes.

Research Institute on Addictions.

Research Laboratory of Electronics. Massachusetts Institute of Technology

Research Libraries Group., 2029 Stierlin Ct., Ste. 100 Mountain View, CA 94043-4684. Phone: 800-537-7546 or (650)691-2333 or (650)691-2333 Fax: (650)964-0943 E-mail: ric@rlg.org • URL: http://www.rlg.org • Universities, archives, historical societies, museums, and related institutions devoted to improving access to information that supports research and learning. Maintains the Research Libraries Information Network (RLIN), an online bibliographic database of more than 22 million items, including books, serials, archival materials, maps, music scores, sound recordings, films, photographs, and computer-readable files. RLIN contains the Library of Congress Name Authority and Subject Authority Files, the Art and Architecture thesaurus, and special databases for 18th-century printed material, art auction catalogs, and library collection management. CitaDel, a citation and document-delivery service, is available through RLIN.

Research on Technological Innovation, Management and Policy. Richard S. Rosenbloom and Robert A. Burgelman, editors. Elsevier, 360 Park Ave., sS New York, NY 10010-1710. Phone: (212)989-5800 Fax: (212)633-3990 E-mail: usinfo-f@elsevier.com • URL: http://www.elsevier.com • Dates vary. Prices vary. Seven volumes.

Research on Transport Economics. OECD Publications and Information Center, 2001 L St., N.W.,, Ste. 650 Washington, DC 20036-4910. Phone: (202)785-6323 Fax: (202)785-0350 E-mail: sales@oecd.org • URL: http://www.oecd.org • Annual. Quarterly $138.00. Text in French.

Research Program in Takeovers and Corporate Restructuring. University of California, Los Angeles

Research Reports. American Institute for Economic Research, PO Box 1000 Great Barrington, MA 01230-1000. Phone: (413)528-1216 Fax: (413)528-0103 E-mail: info@aier.org • URL: http://www.aier.org • Semimonthly. $59.00 per year. Newsletter. Alternate issues include charts of "Primary Leading Indicators," "Primary Roughly Coincident Indicators," and "Primary Lagging Indicators," as issued by The Conference Board (formerly provided by the U. S. Department of Commerce).

Research Services Directory: Commercial & Corporate Research Centers. Grey House Publishing, 185 Millerton Rd. Millerton, NY 12546. Phone: 800-562-2139 or (518)789-8700 Fax: (518)789-0556 E-mail: books@greyhouse.com • URL: http://www.greyhouse.com • 2003. $495.00. Ninth edition. Lists more than 8,000 independent commercial research centers and laboratories offering contract or fee-based services. Includes corporate research departments, market research companies, and information brokers.

Research Strategies: A Journal of Library Concepts and Instruction. Elsevier, 360 Park Ave., S New York, NY 10010-1710. Phone: (212)989-5800 Fax: (212)633-3990 E-mail: usinfo-f@elsevier.com • URL: http://www.elsevier.com • Quarterly. Individuals, $76.00 per year; institutions, $152.00 per year. Edited for librarians involved in bibliographic or library instruction.

Research-Technology Management: International Journal of Research Management. Industrial Research Institute, 1550 M St., N. W., Suite 1100 Washington, DC 20005-1712. Phone: (202)296-8811 Fax: (202)776-0756 • URL: http://www.iriinc.org • Bimonthly. Individuals, $65.00 per year; institutions, $150.00 per year. Covers both theoretical and practical aspects of the management of industrial research and development.

Researching Company Financial Information. Washington Researchers, Ltd., 1655 N. Fort Myer Dr., Suite 800 Arlington, VA 22209. Phone: (703)312-2863 Fax: (703)527-4586 E-mail: research@researchers.com • URL: http://www.washingtonresearchers.com • 2002. $59.00.

Researching Private Companies. Washington Researchers Ltd., 1655 N. Fort Myer Dr., Suite 800 Arlington, VA 22209. Phone: (703)312-2863 Fax: (703)527-4586 E-mail: researchers@researchers.com • URL: http://www.washingtonresearchers.com • 2002. $59.00.

Reserve Officers Association of the United States., 1 Constitution Ave. NE Washington, DC 20002-5618. Phone: 800-809-9448 or (202)479-2200 Fax: (202)547-1641 E-mail: dmccarthy@roa.org • URL: http://www.roa.org • Represents reserve members of the seven United States Uniformed Services-Army, Navy, Air Force, Marines, Coast Guard, Public Health Service, and National Oceanic and Atmospheric Administration Corps. Aims to "support and promote the development and execution of a military policy for the United States that will provide adequate National Security".

Reserves of Crude Oil, Natural Gas Liquids and Natural Gas in the United States and Canada and United States Productive Capacity. American Gas Association, 400 N Capitol St., NW Washington, DC 20001. Phone: (202)824-7000 Fax: (202)824-7115 • URL: http://www.aga.org • Annual. Price on application.

Resident and Staff Physician. Romaine Pierson Publishers, Inc., 1065 Old Country Rd., Suite 213 Westbury, NY 11090-5628. Phone: (516)883-6350 Fax: (516)883-6609 Monthly. Individuals, $83.00 per year institutions, $149.00 per year; students, $50.00 per year.

Residential Architect: Exclusively Housing. Hanley-Wood, LLC, One Thomas Circle, NW Washington, DC 20005. Phone: 800-837-0870 or (202)452-0800 Fax: (202)785-1974 • URL: http://www.hanley-wood.com • Monthly. $39.95 per year. Edited for architects specializing in home design.

Residential Mortgage Lending: From Application to Servicing. The Institute of Financial Education, 55 W. Monroe St., Suite 2800 Chicago, IL 60603-5014. Phone: 800-946-0488 or (312)364-0100 Fax: (312)364-0190 E-mail: info@bai.org • URL: http://www.theinstitute.com • 1998. $64.95. Fifth edition. A guide for bankers.

Resilient Floor Covering Institute., 115 Broad St., Ste. 201 LaGrange, GA 30240. Phone: (706)882-3833 Fax: (706)882-3880 E-mail: info@rfci.com • URL: http://www.rfci.com • Supports the manufacturers of vinyl composition tile, solid vinyl tile, or sheet vinyl and rubber tile and people who use its products. Provides technical information and data regarding the resilient flooring industry.

Resist., 259 Elm St., Ste. 201 Somerville, MA 02144. Phone: (617)623-5110 E-mail: info@resistinc.org • URL: http://www.resistinc.org • Provides grants to small progressive groups in all parts of the country; has aided groups that have organized for reproductive rights for women, gay rights, nuclear disarmament, the rights of Third World people, and work for social and economic justice.

Resistance Welding Manufacturing Alliance., 550 NW Lejeune Rd. Miami, FL 33126. Phone: (305)443-9353 Fax: (305)442-7451 E-mail: rwma@aws.org • URL: http://www.aws.org/rwma • Manufacturers, suppliers, and users of resistance welding equipment and supplies. Conducts Resistance Welding School, an annual educational program. Compiles statistics. Offers VHS tape program on basics of resistance welding.

Resort Development Handbook. Urban Land Institute, 1025 Thomas Jefferson St., NW, Ste. 500 W Washington, DC 20007-5201. Phone: 800-321-5011 or (202)624-7000 Fax: (202)624-7140 • URL: http://www.uli.org • 1997. $89.95. Covers a wide range of resort settings and amenities, with details of development, market analysis, financing, design, and operations. Includes color photographs and case studies. (ULI Development Handbook Series).

Resort Management and Operations: The Resort Resource. Finan Publishing Co., Inc., 107 W. Pacific Ave. St. Louis, MO 63119-2323. Phone: (314)961-6644 Fax: (314)961-4809 E-mail: teri@finan.com • URL: http://www.finan.com • Bimonthly. Price on application. Edited for hospitality professionals at both large and small resort facilities.

Resorts and Parks Purchasing Guide. Klevens Publications, Inc., 411 S Main St., Ste. 209 Los Angeles, CA 90013. Phone: (213)625-9000 Fax: (213)625-5002 E-mail: mailroom@stsklevenspub.com • URL: http://www.resortsparksguide.com • Annual. $85.00. Lists suppliers of products and services for resorts and parks, including national parks, amusement parks, dude ranches, golf resorts, ski areas, and national monument areas.

Resource and Energy Economics: A Journal Devoted to the Interdisciplinary Studies in the Allocation of Natural Resources. Elsevier, 360 Park Ave., S. New York, NY 10010-1710. Phone: 888-437-4636 or (212)989-5800 Fax: (212)633-3990 E-mail: usinfo-f@elsevier.com • URL: http://www.elsevier.com • Quarterly. Individuals, $75.00 per year; institutions, $583.00 per year. Text in English.

Resource Center Product Catalog. Society for Nonprofit Organizations, 5820 Canton Center Rd., Ste. 165 Canton, MI 48187. Phone: (734)451-3582 Fax: (734)451-5935 E-mail: info@snpo.org • URL: http://www.snpo.org • Included in subscription to *Non-profit World*.

Resource: LOMA's Magazine for Insurance and Financial Services Management. LOMA, 2300 Windy Ridge Parkway, Ste. 600 Atlanta, GA 30339. Phone: 800-275-5662 or (770)984-3766 Fax: (770)984-6417 E-mail: resource@loma.org • URL: http://www.loma.org • Monthly. Free to qualified personnel. Covers management topics for life insurance home and field office personnel.

Resources. Resources for the Future, 1616 P St. NW Washington, DC 20036-1400. Phone: (202)328-5000 Fax: (202)939-3460 E-mail: rffpress@rff.org • URL: http://www.rff.org • Description: Features articles on renewable resources, energy, climate, quality of the environment, and risk assessment and management. Recurring features include organizational news and book notices.

Resources, Conservation and Recycling. Elsevier, 360 Park Ave., S. New York, NY 10010-1710. Phone: 888-437-4636 or (212)989-5800 Fax: (212)633-3990 E-mail: usinfo-f@elsevier.com • URL: http://www.elsevier.com • Monthly. $1,547.00 per year.

Resources for the Future: An International Annotated Bibliography. Alan J. Mayne. Greenwood Publishing Group, Inc., 88 Post Rd., W Westport, CT 06881. Phone: 800-225-5800 or (203)226-3571 Fax: (203)431-2214 E-mail: customer-service@greenwood.com • URL: http://www.greenwood.com • 1993. $83.50. (Bibliographies and Indexes in Economics and Economic History Series, No 13).

Resources in Education. Educational Resources Information Center. Available from U.S. Government Printing Office, Washington, DC 20402. Phone: (202)512-1800 Fax: (202)512-2250 E-mail: gpoaccess@gpo.gov • URL: http://www.access.gpo.gov • Monthly. Reports on educational research.

Resources Policy; The International Journal on the Economics, Planning and Use of Non-Renewable Resources. Elsevier, 360 Park Ave., S. New York, NY 10010-1710. Phone: 888-437-4636 or (212)989-5800 Fax: (212)633-3990 E-mail: usinfo-f@elsevier.com • URL: http://www.elsevier.com • Quarterly. Institutions, $789.00 per year.

Responsibilities of Corporate Officers and Directors Under Federal Securities Law. CCH, Inc., 2700 Lake Cook Rd. Riverwoods, IL 60015. Phone: 800-835-5224 or (847)267-7000 Fax: 800-224-8299 or (773)866-3608 E-mail: cust_serv@cch.com • URL: http://www.cch.com • Annual. $79.00. Includes discussions of indemnification, "D & O" insurance, corporate governance, and insider liability.

Responsibilities of Insurance Agents and Brokers. LexisNexis Matthew Bender, 1275 Broadway Albany, NY 12204. Phone: 800-424-4200 or (518)487-3000 Fax: (518)487-3584 E-mail: bookstore.support@lexisnexis.com • URL: http://www.bender.com • Semiannual. $886.00. Four looseleaf volumes. Covers legal responsibilities of agents and federal tax consequences of insurance arrangements.

Restatement of the Law. American Law Institute-American Bar Association Committee on Continuing Professional Education, 4025 Chestnut St. Philadelphia, PA 19104. Phone: 800-253-6397 Fax: (215)243-1664 • URL: http://www.ali-aba.org • Multivolume set. Periodic supplementation. Price varies. Statements of the common law-an overview, clarification, and simplification of American law.

Restaurant Business. VNU Business Media, 770 Broadway New York, NY 10010. Phone: 800-344-7119 or (646)654-4500 Fax: (646)654-7212 • URL: http://www.vnubusinessmedia.com • Biweekly. $119.00 per year. Formerly *Fast Food*.

Restaurant Hospitality. Penton Media, Inc., 1300 E. Ninth St. Cleveland, OH 44114. Phone: (216)696-7000 Fax: (216)696-

1752 E-mail: information@penton.com • URL: http://www.penton.com • Monthly. $70.00 per year.

Restaurant Industry Operations Report. National Restaurant Association, 1200 17th St., N.W. Washington, DC 20036-3097. Phone: (202)331-5900 Fax: (202)331-2429 E-mail: info@dineout.org • URL: http://www.restaurant.org • Annual. Members, $44.95 per year; non-members, $89.95 per year.

Restaurant Start-Up. Entrepreneur Media, Inc., 2445 McCabe Way Irvine, CA 92694. Phone: 800-421-2300 or (949)261-2325 Fax: (949)261-0234 E-mail: entmag@entrepreneur.com • URL: http://www.entrepreneur.com • Looseleaf. $59.50. A practical guide to starting a restaurant. Covers profit potential, start-up costs, market size evaluation, owner's time required, site selection, lease negotiation, pricing, accounting, advertising, promotion, etc. (Start-Up Business Guide No. E1279.)

Restaurant Start-Up Guide: A 12-Month Plan for Successfully Starting a Restaurant. Peter Rainsford and David H. Bangs. Dearborn Trade Publishing, A Kaplan Professional Co., 155 N Wacker Dr. Chicago, IL 60606. Phone: 800-621-9621 or (312)836-4400 Fax: (312)836-1021 E-mail: trade@dearborn.com • URL: http://www.dearborntrade.com • 2000. $22.95. Second edition. Emphasizes the importance of advance planning for restaurant startups.

Restaurants and Institutions. Reed Business Information, 360 Park Ave. S New York, NY 10010. Phone: 800-446-6551 or (646)746-6400 Fax: (646)746-7028 E-mail: corporatecommunications@reedbusiness.com • URL: http://www.reedbusiness.com • Semimonthly. $149.00 per year. Features news, new products, recipes, menu concepts and merchandising ideas from the most successful foodservice operations around the U.S.

The Resume Kit. Richard H. Beatty. John Wiley and Sons, Inc., 111 River St. Hoboken, NJ 07030. Phone: 800-225-5945 or (201)748-6000 Fax: (201)748-6088 E-mail: info@wiley.com • URL: http://www.wiley.com • 2003. $14.95. Fifth edition. Includes information on the linear resume, a form said to be favored by outplacement firms.

Resume Writing: A Comprehensive How-To-Do-It Guide. Burdette Bostwick. John Wiley and Sons, Inc., 111 River St. Hoboken, NJ 07030. Phone: 800-225-5945 or (201)748-6000 Fax: (201)748-6088 E-mail: info@wiley.com • URL: http://www.wiley.com • 1990. $14.95. Fourth edition.

Resume Writing and Career Counseling. Entrepreneur Media, Inc., 2445 McCabe Way Irvine, CA 92614. Phone: 800-421-2300 or (949)261-2325 Fax: (949)261-0234 E-mail: entmag@entrepreneur.com • URL: http://www.entrepreneur.com • Looseleaf. $59.50. A practical guide to starting a resume writing and career counseling service. Covers profit potential, start-up costs, market size evaluation, owner's time required, site selection, pricing, accounting, advertising, promotion, etc. (Start-Up Business Guide No. E1260.)

Resumes for Banking and Financial Careers. McGraw-Hill, 1221 Ave. of the Americas New York, NY 10020. Phone: 800-722-4726 or (212)512-2000 Fax: (212)512-4502 E-mail: customer.service@mcgraw-hill.com • URL: http://www.mcgraw-hill.com • 2001. $10.95. Second edition. Contains 100 sample resumes and 20 cover letters. (VGM Professional Resumes Series.)

Resumes That Work: How to Sell Yourself on Paper. Lorretta D. Foxman. John Wiley, 111 River St. Hoboken, NJ 07030. Phone: 800-225-5945 or (201)748-6000 Fax: (201)748-6088 E-mail: info@wiley.com • URL: http://www.wiley.com • 1992. $14.95. Ninth edition.

Retail Ad World. Visual Reference Publications, Inc., 302 Fifth Ave. New York, NY 10001. Phone: 800-251-4545 or (212)279-7000 Fax: (212)279-7014 E-mail: retailreporting@retailreporting.com • URL: http://www.retailreporting.com • Monthly. $299.00 per year. Weekly report on outstanding advertising by department stores, specialty stores and shopping centers with reprints of current advertising. Formerly *Retail Rd Week*.

Retail Bakers of America., 8201 Greensboro Dr., Ste. 300, 14239 Park Ctr. Dr. McLean, VA 22102. Phone: 800-638-0924 or (703)610-9035 Fax: (703)610-9005 E-mail: info@rbanet.com • URL: http://www.rbanet.com • Independent and in-store bakeries, food service, specialty bakeries, suppliers of ingredients, tools and equipment; other. Provides information, management, production, merchandising, and small business services.

Retail Broker-Dealer Directory. Securities Data Publishing, 395 Hudson, 3rd Fl., 40 W 57th St. New York, NY 10014. Phone: 888-605-3385 or (212)765-5311 Fax: (646)822-3230 E-mail: sdp@tfn.com • URL: http://www.thomsonmedia.com • Covers: 1,300 retail brokerages serving the marketplace through the warehouse, regional, independent, bank, discount, and insurance distribution channels. Entries include: Company snapshot, key contacts, number of employees, products, specialization, financial data, assets, and other details.

Retail Confectioners International., 1807 Glenview Rd. Glenview, IL 60025. Phone: 800-545-5381 or (847)724-6120 Fax: (847)724-2719 E-mail: van@retailconfectioners.org • URL: http://www.retailconfectioners.org • Manufacturing retail confectioners who make and sell their own candies through directly owned retail candy shops; associates are suppliers to the industry. Provides education, promotion, and legislative and information service. Monitors legislative activities that affect the industry at state and national levels. Holds comprehensive two-week course and one-week specialized course on retail candy making biennially.

Retail Florist Business. Peter B. Pfahl and P. Blair Pfahl. Interstate Publishers, Inc., 510 Vermillion Danville, IL 61834-0050. Phone: 800-843-4774 or (217)446-0500 Fax: (217)446-9706 E-mail: info-ipp@ippinc.com • URL: http://www.ippinc.com • 1994. $48.75. Fifth edition.

Retail Merchandiser., 770 Broadway New York, NY 10003. Phone: (646)654-5700 Fax: (646)654-7212 • URL: http://www.billcom.com • Monthly. $55.00 per year. Mass merchandising retail industry. Formerly *Discount Merchandiser*.

Retail Pharmacy Management. McMahon Group, 545 W. 45th St., 8th Fl. New York, NY 10036. Phone: (212)957-5300 Fax: (212)957-7230 E-mail: dbron@mcmahonmed.com • URL: http://www.mcmahonmed.com • Monthly. $60.00 per year. Featues include product news for pharmacists and financial news for chain store executives. Formerly *Retail Pharmacy Management News*.

Retail Tobacco Dealers of America.

Retail Trade International. Gale Cengage Learning, 27500 Drake Rd. Farmington Hills, MI 48331-3535. Phone: 800-877-GALE or (248)699-4253 Fax: 800-414-5043 E-mail: gale.galeord@cengage.com • URL: http://gale.cengage.com • 2002. $1,990.00. 11th edition. Eight volumes. Published by Euromonitor. Presents comprehensive data on retail trends in 52 countries. Includes textual analysis and profiles of major retailers. Covers Europe, Asia, the Middle East, Africa and the Americas.

Retail Traffic. Primedia Business Magazines and Media, 249 W 17th St. New York, NY 10011. Phone: 800-795-5445 or (212)462-3600 Fax: (212)206-3622 E-mail: subs@primediabusiness.com • URL: http://www.primediabusiness.com • Monthly. $74.00 per year. Provides coverage of all phases of the shopping center industry. Formerly *Shopping Center World*.

Retail, Wholesale and Department Store Union.

Retailing Managment. Michael Levy and Barton A. Weitz. McGraw-Hill Higher Education, 1221 Ave. of the Americas New York, NY 10020. Phone: 800-722-4726 or (212)512-2000 Fax: (212)512-4502 E-mail: customer.service@mcgraw-hill.com • URL: http://www.mcgraw-hill.com • 2003. $110.63. Fifth edition.

Retailing Today. Robert Kahn and Associates, 3684 Happy Valley Rd. Lafayette, CA 94549-3040. Phone: (925)254-4434 Fax: (925)284-5612 E-mail: rffpress@rff.org Description: Focuses on general merchandise, apparel, furniture, hardware, automotive, and food retailing. Offers "original research, comments on current trends and conditions, recommendations for company policy, and emphasis on ethical conduct in business."

Rethinking Organization: New Directions in Organization Theory and Analysis. Michael Reed and Michael Hughes. Sage Publications, Inc., 2455 Teller Rd. Thousand Oaks, CA 91320. Phone: 800-818-7243 or (805)499-9774 Fax: 800-583-2665 or (805)499-0871 E-mail: webmaster@sagepub.com • URL: http://www.sagepub.com • 1992. $37.95.

Rethinking Rental Housing. John I. Gilderbloom and Richard P. Applebaum. Temple University Press, 1601 N. Broad St., University Services Bldg., Room 305 Philadelphia, PA 19122-6099. Phone: 800-447-1656 or (215)204-8787 Fax: (215)204-4719 • URL: http://www.temple.edu/tempress • 1987. $44.95. Emphasis on social and political factors.

Retired Activities Branch., Navy Personnel Command, 5720 Integrity Dr. Millington, TN 38055-6220. Phone: (866)827-5672 or (901)874-4308 Fax: (901)874-6654 E-mail: mill_retiredactivities@navy.mil • URL: http://www.npc.navy.mil/CommandSupport/RetiredActivities • A program of the U.S. Department of the Navy. Assists Navy retirees and survivors with benefits and entitlement information. Maintains speakers' bureau.

Retirement Benefits Tax Guide. CCH, Inc., 2700 Lake Cook Rd. Riverwoods, IL 60015. Phone: 800-835-5224 or (847)267-7000 E-mail: cust_serv@cch.com • URL: http://www.cch.com • $199.00. Looseleaf service.

Retirement Community Business. Great River Publishing, Inc., 91 Windy Oaks Dr. Germantown, TN 38139-5207. Phone: 800-567-6912 or (901)624-5911 Fax: (901)624-5910 Quarterly. $15.00 per year. Contains articles on management, marketing, legal concerns, development, construction, and other business-related topics.

Retirement Letter: The Money Newsletter for Mature People. Peter A. Dickinson, editor. PBI Media, LLC, 1201 7 Locks Rd. Potomac, MD 20854. Phone: 800-777-5006 or (301)354-2000 Fax: (301)309-3847 E-mail: clientservices@pbimedia.com • URL: http://www.pbimedia.com • Monthly. $49.00 per year.

Retirement Life. National Association of Retired Federal Employees, 606 N. Washington St. Alexandria, VA 24314-1914. Phone: 800-627-3394 or (703)838-7760 Fax: (703)838-7785 E-mail: hq@narfe.org • URL: http://www.narfe.org • Monthly. Free to members; non-members, $25.00 per year.

Retirement Planning Guide. Sidney Kess and Barbara Weltman. CCH, Inc., 2700 Lake Cook Rd. Riverwoods, IL 60015. Phone: 800-835-5224 or (847)267-7000 E-mail: cust_serv@cch.com • URL: http://www.cch.com • 2000. $49.00. Second edition. Presents an overview for attorneys, accountants, and other professionals of the various concepts involved in retirement planning. Includes checklists, tables, forms, and study questions.

Retirement Plans Bulletin: Practical Explanations for the IRA and Retirement Plan Professional. Universal Pensions, Inc., P.O. Box 979 Brainerd, MN 56401. Phone: 800-346-3860 Fax: (218)829-2106 Monthly. $99.00 per year. Newsletter. Provides information on the rules and regulations governing qualified (tax-deferred) retirement plans.

Retirement Research Foundation.

Reuse/Recycle. Rowman & Littlefield Education, 4501 Forbes Blvd., Ste. 200 Lanham, MD 20706. Phone: 800-462-6420 or (301)459-3366 Fax: 800-583-2665 or (301)429-5748 E-mail: custserv@rowman.com • URL: http://www.sagepub.com • Description: Contains information on "new processes, machinery, and uses for both industrial and municipal recycling." Publishes news of waste-to-energy and waste-to-materials processes, markets for recycled materials, recycling processing, plants, equipment and case history of successful projects and programs in the U.S. and Europe. Focuses on large-scale post-consumer, post-commercial and post-industrial waste recycling. Recurring features include a calendar of events.

Revenue Statistics. OECD Publications and Information Center, 2001 L St., N.W., Suite 650 Washington, DC 20036-4922. Phone: (202)785-6323 Fax: (202)785-0350 E-mail: washington.contact@oecd.org • URL: http://www.oecdwash.org • Annual. $65.00. Presents data on government revenues in OECD countries, classified by type of tax and level of government. Text in English and French.

Reverse Acronyms, Initialisms, and Abbreviations Dictionary. Gale Cengage Learning, 27500 Drake Rd. Farmington Hills, MI 48331-3535. Phone: 800-877-GALE or (248)699-4253 Fax: 800-414-5043 E-mail: gale.galeord@cengage.com • URL: http://gale.cengage.com • 2001. $235.00.

Review of Agricultural Entomology: Consisting of Abstracts of Reviews of Current Literature on Applied Entomology Throughout the World. Available from CABI Publishing, North America, 875 Massachusetts Ave., 7th Fl. Cambridge, MA 02139. Phone: 800-528-4841 or (617)395-4056 Fax: (617)354-6875 E-mail: cabi-nao@cabi.org • URL: http://www.cabi-publishing.org • Monthly. Institutions, $1,505.00 per year. Print and online edition, $1,505.00 per year. Published in England by CABI Publishing. Provides worldwide coverage of the literature. (Formerly *Review of Applied Entomology, Series A: Agricultural*.)

The Review of Economics and Statistics. Harvard University, Economics Dept. MIT Press, Five Cambridge Center Cambridge, MA 02142-1493. Phone: (617)253-5646 Fax: (617)258-6779 E-mail: journals-orders@mit.edu • URL: http://www.mitpress.mit.edu • Quarterly. Individuals, $53.00 per year; institutions, $275.00 per year; students and retired persons, $28.00 per year.

Review of Financial Economics. Elsevier, 360 Park Ave., S New York, NY 10010-1710. Phone: (212)989-5800 Fax: (212)633-3990 E-mail: usinfo-f@elsevier.com • URL: http://www.elsevier.com • Three times a year. Individuals, $95.00 per year; institutions, $350.00 per year. Formerly *Review of Business and Economic Research*.

Review of Income and Wealth. International Association for Research in Income and Wealth, c/o New York University, Dept. of Economics, 269 Mercer St., Room 700 New York, NY 10003. Phone: (212)924-4386 Fax: (212)366-5067 E-mail: iariw@nyu.edu • URL: http://www.econ.nyu.edu • Quarterly. Institutions, $200.00 per year. Includes print and online editions.

Review of International Political Economy. Taylor and Francis Group, 325 Chestnut St., 8th Fl. Philadelphia, PA 19106. Phone: 800-634-7064 or (215)625-8914 E-mail: info@taylorandfrancis.com • URL: http://www.taylorandfrancis.com • Quarterly. Individuals, $86.00 per year; institutions, $346.00 per year. Includes articles on international trade, finance, production, and consumption.

Review of Maritime Transport. United Nations Conference on Trade and Development. United Nations Publications, United Nations Concourse Level, First Ave., 46th St. New York, NY 10017. Phone: 800-553-3210 or (212)963-7680 Fax: (212)963-4910 E-mail: bookstore@un.org • URL: http://www.un.org/publications • Annual. $55.00.

Review of Medical and Veterinary Entomology. Available from CABI Publishing, North America, 875 Massachusetts Ave., 7th Fl. Cambridge, MA 02139. Phone: 800-528-4841 or (617)395-4056 Fax: (617)354-6875 E-mail: cabi-nao@cabi.org • URL: http://www.cabi-publishing.org • Monthly. Institutions, $855.00 per year. Print and online edition, $885.00 per year. Provides worldwide coverage of the literature. Formerly *Review of Applied Entomology, Series B: Medical and Veterinary*.

Review of Scientific Instruments. American Institute of Physics, Two Huntington Quadrangle, Ste. 1NO1 Melville, NY 11747-4502. Phone: 800-344-6902 or (516)576-2270 Fax: (516)349-9704 E-mail: rsi@anl.gov • URL: http://www.aip.org • Monthly. Institutions, $1,690.00 per year. Includes print and online editions.

The Review of Securities and Commodities Regulations: An Analysis of Current Laws, Regulations Affecting the Securities and Futures Industries. Standard and Poor's, 55 Water St. New York, NY 10041. Phone: 800-221-5277 or (212)438-2000 Fax: (212)438-4368 E-mail: clientsupport@standardandpoors.com • URL: http://www.standardandpoors.com • 22 times a year. $350.00 per year.

Review of Social Economy. Association for Social Economics. Taylor and Francis Group, 325 Chestnut St., 8th Fl.

Philadelphia, PA 19106. Phone: 800-354-1420 or (215)625-8914 E-mail: info@taylorandfrancis.com • URL: http://www.taylorandfrancis.com • Quarterly. Individuals, $78.00 per year; institutions, $211.00 per year. Subject matter is concerned with the relationships between social values and economics. Includes articles on income distribution, poverty, labor, and class.

Rhythms of Academic Life: Personal Accounts of Careers in Academia. M. Susan Taylor. Sage Publications, Inc., 2455 Teller Rd. Thousand Oaks, CA 91320. Phone: 800-818-7243 or (805)499-9774 Fax: 800-583-2665 or (805)499-0871 E-mail: webmaster@sagepub.com • URL: http://www.sagepub.com • 1996. $97.95. Contains articles by various authors on college teaching, research, publishing, tenure, and related topics. Contributions are described as "sometimes poignant and often humorous." (Foundations for Organizational Science Series).

RIA Federal Tax Handbook. RIA, 395 Hudson St. New York, NY 10014. Phone: 800-950-1216 or 800-431-9025 E-mail: riahome@riag.com • URL: http://www.riahome.com • Annual. $57.00.

RIC News (Rare-Earth Information Center). Rare-Earth Information Center, Institute for Physical Research and Technology, Iowa State University, 112 Wilhelm Hall Ames, IA 50011-3020. Phone: (515)294-2272 Fax: (515)294-3709 E-mail: ric@ameslab.gov • URL: http://www.ameslab.gov • Quarterly. Free. Newsletter. Containing items of current interest concerning the science and technology of the rare earth.

Rice Abstracts. Available from CABI Publishing, North America, 875 Massachusetts, 7th Fl. Cambridge, MA 02139. Phone: 800-528-4841 or (617)395-4056 Fax: (617)354-6875 E-mail: cabi-nao@cabi.org • URL: http://www.cabi-publishing.org • Quarterly. Published in England by CABI Publishing. Provides worldwide coverage of the literature.

Rice Farming. Vance Publishing Corp., 400 Knightsbridge Parkway Lincolnshire, IL 60069. Phone: 800-255-5113 or (847)634-2600 Fax: (847)634-4379 • URL: http://www.vancepublishing.com • Six times a year. $30.00 per year.

Rice Journal: For Commerical Growers of Rice and Related Agribusiness. SpecComm International, Inc., 5808 Faringdon Pl., Ste. 200 Raleigh, NC 27625-1029. Phone: (919)872-5040 Fax: (919)876-6531 E-mail: editor@ricejournal.com • URL: http://www.speccomm.com • Seven times a year. $15.00 per year.

Rice Millers' Association., 4301 N Fairfax Dr., Ste. 425, 4301 N Fairfax Dr., Ste. 425 Arlington, VA 22203. Phone: (703)236-2300 Fax: (703)236-2301 E-mail: riceinfo@usarice.com • URL: http://www.usarice.com • Represents Independent and farmer-cooperative rice milling operators. Provides economic and statistical information on production, milling, and distribution of rice. Promotes research aimed at new uses for rice products and improvements in processing, packaging, storing, and distributing rice. Maintains liaison with U.S. and foreign government agencies, congress, and foreign buyers of U.S. rice.

Rice: Origin, History, Technology, and Production. C. Wayne Smith and Robert Dilday, editors. John Wiley and Sons, Inc., 111 River St. Hoboken, NJ 07030. Phone: 800-225-5945 or (201)748-6000 Fax: (201)748-6088 E-mail: info@wiley.com • URL: http://www.wiley.com • 2002. $275.00. (Crop Science Series).

Richard C. Young's Intelligence Report. Access Intelligence L.L.C., 4 Choke Cherry Rd., 2nd Fl. Rockville, MD 20850. Phone: 800-777-5006 or (301)354-2000 Fax: (301)309-3847 E-mail: info@accessintel.com • URL: http://www.pbimedia.com • Description: Provides information for "serious, conservative investors (buy and hold as opposed to active traders)." Features investing advice and recommendations for best funds, stocks, and bonds for current or retirement income.

Rise and Fall of the Cigarette: A Social and Cultural History of Smoking in the U. S. Allan Brandt. Basic Books, 387 Park Ave. S New York, NY 10016. Phone: 800-386-5656 or (212)340-8100 Fax: (212)340-8135 E-mail: westview.order@perseusbooks.com • URL: http://www.perseusbooksgroup.com • 2000. $25.00. Second edition.

Risk and Insurance. LRP Publications, 747 Dresher Rd., Suite 500 Horsham, PA 19044-0860. Phone: 800-341-7874 or (215)784-0860 Fax: (215)784-9639 E-mail: custserve@lrp.com • URL: http://www.lrp.com • 15 times a year. Price on application. Topics include risk management, workers' compensation, reinsurance, employee benefits, and managed care.

Risk and Insurance Management Society., 655 Third Ave., 2nd Fl. New York, NY 10017. Phone: (212)286-9292 Fax: (212)986-9716 E-mail: jwaldman@rims.org • URL: http://www.rims.org • Formerly American Society of Insurance Management.

Risk Management. Risk and Insurance Management Society. Risk Management Society Publishing, Inc., 655 Third Ave., 2nd Fl. New York, NY 10017-5637. Phone: (212)286-9364 Fax: (212)922-0716 E-mail: lsullivan@rims.org • URL: http://www.rmmag.com • Monthly. $59.00 per year.

Risk Management Association., 1801 Market St., Ste. 300, 1650 Market St., Ste. 2300 Philadelphia, PA 19103-1628. Phone: 800-677-7621 or (215)446-4000 Fax: (215)446-4101 E-mail: member@rmahq.org • URL: http://www.rmahq.org/RMA • Commercial and savings banks, and savings and loan, and other financial services companies. Conducts research and professional development activities in areas of loan administration, asset management, and commercial lending and credit to increase professionalism.

Risk Management, Speculation, and Derivative Securities. Geoffrey Poitras. Elsevier Butterworth Heinemann, 200 Wheeler Rd., Sixth Floor Burlington, MA 01803. Phone: 800-545-2522 or (781)221-2212 Fax: 800-568-5136 or (781)313-4880 E-mail: usbkinfo@elsevier.com • URL: http://www.books.elsevier.com/finance • 2002. $99.95. In addition to "Risk Management Concepts" and "Speculative Concepts," topics include financial futures, forward contracts, arbitrage, spread trading, hedging, and diversification. Three appendices are devoted to mathematical concepts and calculations.

The RMA Journal. The Risk Management Association, One Liberty Place, 1650 Market St., Suite 2300 Philadelphia, PA 19103-7398. Phone: 800-677-7621 or (215)446-4000 Fax: (215)446-4101 E-mail: customers@rmahq.org • URL: http://www.rmahq.org • 10 times a year. Members, $40.00 per year; non-members, $95.00 per year. *The Journal of Lending and Credit Risk Management*.

Road and Track. Hachette Filipacchi Media U.S., Inc., 1633 Broadway New York, NY 10019. Phone: 800-876-8316 or (212)767-6000 Fax: (212)767-5600 • URL: http://www.hfmmag.com • Monthly. $11.97 per year.

Road Construction and Safety. Available from U. S. Government Printing Office, Washington, DC 20402. Phone: (202)512-1800 Fax: (202)512-2250 E-mail: gpoaccess@gpo.gov • URL: http://www.access.gpo.gov • Annual. Free. Issued by the Superintendent of Documents. A list of government publications on highway construction and traffic safety. Formerly *Highway Construction, Safety and Traffic*. (Subject Bibliography No. 3.)

The Road Information Program., 1726 M St. NW, Ste. 401 Washington, DC 20036-4521. Phone: (202)466-6706 Fax: (202)785-4722 E-mail: trip@tripnet.org • URL: http://www.tripnet.org • Conducts public education programs for the highway industry. Promotes transportation policies that relieve traffic congestion, improve air quality, make highway travel safer and enhance economic productivity.

Roads and Bridges. Scranton Gillette Communications, Inc., 380 E. Northwest Highway, Suite 200 Des Plaines, IL 60016-2282. Phone: (847)391-1000 Fax: (847)390-0408 E-mail: bwilson@sgcmail.com • URL: http://www.sgcpubs.com • Monthly. $35.00 per year. Provides information on the planning/design, administration/management, engineering and contract execution for the road and bridge industry.

Robb Report Home Entertaining & Design. CurtCo Robb Media, 29160 Heathercliff Rd., Suite 200 Malibu, CA 90265. Phone: 800-340-6541 or (310)589-7700 Fax: (310)589-7723 • URL: http://www.hedmag.com • Nine times a year. $21.95 per year. Covers "high end" home theaters, audio, video, wireless home networks, and custom installations.

Robb Report Motorcycling. CurtCo Robb Media, 29160 Heathercliff Rd., Suite 200 Malibu, CA 90265. Phone: (310)589-7700 Fax: (310)589-7723 • URL: http://www.motorcyclingmag.com • Semiannual. Price on application. Contains reviews of the "newest high-quality motorcycles."

Robb Report: The Magazine for the Luxury Lifestyle. CurtCo Robb Media, 29160 Heathercliff Rd. Malibu, CA 90265. Phone: 800-229-7622 or (310)589-7700 • URL: http://www.robbreport.com • Monthly. $65.00 per year. Consumer magazine featuring advertisements for expensive items-antique automobiles, boats, airplanes, large houses, etc.

Robb Report Worth: Wealth in Perspective. CurtCo Robb Media, 29160 Heathercliff Rd., Suite 200 Malibu, CA 90265. Phone: 800-777-1851 or (310)589-7700 Fax: (310)589-7723 • URL: http://www.worth.com • Monthly. $54.95 per year. Glossy magazine featuring articles for the affluent on personal financial management, investments, estate planning, trusts, private bankers, taxes, travel, yachts, and lifestyle. Formerly *Worth: Financial Intelligence*.

Roberts' Dictionary of Industrial Relations. BNA, Inc., 1231 25th St., NW Washington, DC 20037. Phone: 800-372-1033 E-mail: customercare@bna.com • URL: http://www.bna.com • 1993. $85.00. Fourth edition.

Robert's Rules of Order. Henry M. Roberts, editors. Perseus Books Group, 387 Park Ave. S New York, NY 10016. Phone: 800-386-5656 or (212)340-8100 Fax: (212)340-8105 E-mail: westview.orders@perseusbooks.org • URL: http://www.perseusbooksgroup.com • 2000. $35.00. 10th revised edition.

Robertson Pulp and Paper Laboratory. North Carolina State University

Robot Technology and Applications. Ulrich Rembold, editor. Marcel Dekker, Inc., 270 Madison Ave. New York, NY 10016. Phone: 800-228-1160 or (212)696-9000 Fax: (212)685-4540 E-mail: bookorders@dekker.com • URL: http://www.dekker.com • 1990. $230.00. (Manufacturing Engineering Material Processing Series: Vol. 34).

Robot Vision Laboratory.

Robotic Industries Association., PO Box 3724, PO Box 3724 Ann Arbor, MI 48106. Phone: (734)994-6088 Fax: (734)994-3338 E-mail: ria@robotics.org • URL: http://www.roboticsonline.com • Only trade group in North America organized specifically to serve the robotics industry. Member companies include robot manufacturers, users, system integrators, component suppliers, research groups, and consulting firms. Sponsors the biennial International Robots and Vision Show, develops the ANSI/RIA national robot safety standard, collects and reports robotics industry statistics.

Robotics: A Bibliography with Indexes. Peter J. Benne, editor. Nova Science Publishers, Inc., 400 Oser Ave., Suite 1600 Hauppauge, NY 11788-3619. Phone: (631)231-7269 Fax: (631)231-8175 E-mail: novascience@earthlink.net • URL: http://www.novapublishers.com • 2002. $59.00. Provides citations to books on robots in manufacturing, medical research, and other fields. Includes author, title, and subject indexes.

Robotics and Automation Laboratory.

Robotics and Computer-Integrated Manufacturing: An International Journal. Elsevier, 360 Park Ave., S. New York, NY 10010-1710. Phone: 888-437-4636 or (212)989-5800 Fax: (212)633-3990 E-mail: usinfo-f@elsevier.com • URL: http://www.elsevier.com • Bimonthly. Institutions, $1,098.00 per year.

Robotics Institute.

Robotics International of the Society of Manufacturing Engineers., 1 SME Dr. Dearborn, MI 48121. Phone: 800-733-4763 or (313)271-1500 Fax: (313)271-2861 E-mail: service@sme.org • URL: http://www.sme.org/ri • Engineers, managers, educators and government officials in 50 countries working or interested in the field of robotics. Affiliated with the Society of Manufacturing Engineers.

Rock Mechanics and Explosives Research Center.

Rock Products: The Aggregate Industry's Journal of Applied Technology. Primedia Business Magazines and Media, 330 N Wabash Ave., Ste. 2300 Chicago, IL 60611. Phone: 800-795-5445 or (312)595-1080 Fax: (312)595-0295 E-mail: subss@primediabusiness.com • URL: http://www.primediabusiness.com • Monthly. $56.00 per year.

Rocket Propulsion Elements: An Introduction to the Engineering of Rockets. George P. Sutton and Oscar Biblarz. John Wiley and Sons, Inc., 111 River St. Hoboken, NJ 07030. Phone: 800-225-5945 or (201)748-6000 Fax: (201)748-6088 E-mail: info@wiley.com • URL: http://www.wiley.com • 2000. $110.00. Seventh edition.

Rocks and Minerals: Mineralogy, Geology, Lapidary. Helen Dwight Reid Educational Foundation. Heldref Publications, 1319 18th St., N.W. Washington, DC 20036-1802. Phone: 800-365-9753 or (202)296-6267 Fax: (202)296-5149 E-mail: subscribe@heldref.org • URL: http://www.heldref.org • Bimonthly. $37.00. per year.

Rocky Mountain Coal Mining Institute., 8057 S Yukon Way Littleton, CO 80128-5510. Phone: (303)948-3300 Fax: (303)948-1132 E-mail: mail@rmcmi.org • URL: http://www.rmcmi.org • Coal industry persons, including producers, users, equipment manufacturers, suppliers, coal transporters, lawyers, bankers, and others. Promotes the use of western coal through education.

Rodney L. White Center for Financial Research., University of Pennsylvania, 3254 Steinberg Hall-Dietrich Hall Philadelphia, PA 19104. Phone: (215)898-7616 Fax: (215)573-8084 E-mail: rlwtcr@finance.wharton.upenn.edu • URL: http://www.finance.wharton.upenn.edu • Research areas include financial management, money markets, real estate finance, and international finance.

Roget's International Thesaurus. Barbara A. Kipfer, editor., 10 E. 53rd St. New York, NY 10022-5299. Phone: (212)207-7000 • URL: http://www.harpercollins.com • 2001. $20.95. Sixth edition.

The Rome, Maastricht, and Amsterdam Treaties: Comparative Texts. Available from Paul and Co. Publishers Consortium, Inc., PO Box 442 Concord, MA. Phone: 800-888-4741 or (978)369-3049 Fax: (978)369-2385 E-mail: frontdesk@ipgbook.com • URL: http://www.ipgbook.com • 1997. Price on application. Includes a comprehensive keyword index. Published in Belgium by Euroconfidential.

Roof Framing. Marshall Gross. Craftsman Book Co., 6058 Corte del Cedro Carlsbad, CA 92009. Phone: 800-829-8123 Fax: (760)438-0398 • URL: http://www.craftsman-book.com • 1989. $22.00. Revised edition. (Home Craftsman Books).

Roof Tile Institute., 230 E Ohio St., Ste. 400 Chicago, IL 60611-3265. Phone: 888-321-9236 or (312)670-4177 Fax: (312)644-8557 E-mail: info@rooftile.com • URL: http://www.ntrma.org • Members are producers of clay and concrete tile roofing. Formerly National Tile Roofing Manufacturers Association.

The Rose Sheet: Toiletries, Fragrances and Skin Care. F-D-C Reports, Inc., 5550 Friendship Blvd., Suite 1 Chevy Chase, MD 20815-7278. Phone: 800-332-2181 or (301)657-9830 Fax: (301)656-3094 E-mail: fdc.customer.service@elsevier.com • URL: http://www.fdcreports.com • 51 times a year. $916.00 per year. Newsletter. Provides industry news, regulatory news, market data, and a "Weekly Trademark Review" for the cosmetics industry.

Ross Reports Television and Film: Casting, Production, Scripts. VNU Business Media, 770 Broadway New York, NY 10003-9595. Phone: 800-344-7119 or (646)654-4500 Fax: (646)654-7212 • URL: http://www.vnubusinessmedia.com • 10 times a year. $59.00. per year. Directory, production and casting guide, designed for actors and writers. Formerly *Ross Reports Television*.

Roster of Clubs. International Training in Communication, 2519 Woodland Dr. Anaheim, CA 92801. Phone: (714)995-3600 Fax: (714)995-6974 E-mail: itcintl@itcintl.com • URL: http://www.brunnet.net • Annual. Price on application.

Rotor and Wing: Serving the Worldwide Helicopter Industry.

PBI Media, LLC, 1201 7 Locks Rd. Potomac, MD 20854. Phone: 800-777-5006 or (301)354-2000 Fax: (301)309-3847 E-mail: clientservices@pbimedia.com • URL: http://www.pbimedia.com • Monthly. Free to qualified personnel; others, $49.00 per year. Includes supplement *World Helicopter Resources*. Formerly *Rotor and Wing International*.

Rough Notes: Property, Casualty, Surety. The Rough Notes Co., Inc., 11690 Technology Dr. Carmel, IN 46032-5600. Phone: 800-428-4384 or (317)582-1600 Fax: 800-321-1909 or (317)816-1000 E-mail: salesrnc@roughnotes.com • URL: http://www.roughnotes.com • Monthly. $27.50 per year.

RSI (Roofing, Siding, Insulation). Advanstar Communications, 545 Boylston St. Boston, MA 02116. Phone: 888-527-7008 or (617)267-6500 Fax: (617)267-6900 E-mail: info@advanstar.com • URL: http://www.advanstar.com • Monthly. $44.00 per year.

RTCA., 1828 L St. NW, Ste. 805 Washington, DC 20036. Phone: (202)833-9339 Fax: (202)833-9434 E-mail: info@rtca.org • URL: http://www.rtca.org • Addresses requirements, operational concepts, and industry standards for aviation. Advances the art and science of aviation and aviation electronic systems for the benefit of the public. Products are developed by volunteers from the entire aviation community and include consensus-based recommendations addressing the implementation of new operational capabilities, performance standards, transition and implementation strategies, as well as technical guidance documents and special topic reports. Recommendations are often used as the foundation for government policy and industry business decisions. Most activities function as Federal Advisory Committees.

RTI International. RTI International, 3040 Cornwallis Rd., PO Box 12194 Research Triangle Park, NC 27709-2194. Phone: (919)485-2666 Fax: (919)541-5985 E-mail: listen@rti.org • URL: http://www.rti.org • Public health, medicine, environmental protection, electronic technology, and public policy.

Rubber and Plastics News: The Rubber Industry's International Newspaper. Crain Communications, Inc., 1725 Merriman Rd., Suite 300 Akron, OH 44313-5283. Phone: 800-678-9595 or (330)836-9180 E-mail: info@crain.com • URL: http://www.crain.com • Biweekly. $99.00 per year. Written for rubber product manufacturers.

Rubber Chemistry and Technology. American Chemical Society, Rubber Div., University of Akron Akron, OH 44309-3801. Phone: 800-227-5558 or (330)972-7814 Fax: (330)972-5269 E-mail: office@rubber.org • URL: http://www.rubber.org • Five times a year. $300.00 per year.

Rubber Manufacturers Association., 1400 K St. NW, Ste. 900 Washington, DC 20005. Phone: (202)682-4800 Fax: (202)682-4854 E-mail: info@rma.org • URL: http://www.rma.org • Manufacturers of tires, tubes, mechanical and industrial products, roofing, sporting goods, and other rubber products.

Rubber Red Book: Directory of the Rubber Industry. Lippincott, 1867 W Market St. Akron, OH 44334. Phone: (330)864-2122 Fax: (330)864-5298 E-mail: jhl@rubberworld.com • URL: http://www.rubberworld.com • Annual. $106.00. Lists manufacturers and suppliers of rubber goods in U.S., Puerto Rico and Canada.

Rubber Statistical Bulletin. International Rubber Study Group, 115 Heron House, 1st Fl., 109/115 Wembley Hill Rd. Wembley HA9 8DA, United Kingdom. Phone: 44 20 8900 5400 Fax: 44 20 8903 2848 E-mail: irsg@rubberstudy.com • URL: http://www.rubberstudy.com • 10 times a year. $1,800.00 per year. $250.00 per issue.

Rubber Technology. C. Hepburn, editor. Elsevier, 655 Ave. of the Americas New York, NY 10010. Phone: 800-366-2665 or (212)989-5800 Fax: 800-535-9935 or (212)633-3680 E-mail: custserv@elsevier.com • URL: http://www.elsevier.com • 2002. $160.00. Third edition.

Rubber World. Lippincott, 1867 W. Market St. Akron, OH 44313. Phone: (330)864-2122 Fax: (330)864-5298 E-mail: jhl@rubberworld.com • URL: http://www.rubberworld.com • 16 times a year. $34.00 per year.

Rubber World Blue Book: Materials, Compounding Ingredients and Machinery for Rubber. Don R. Smith, editor. Lippincott, 1867 W Market St. Akron, OH 44313. Phone: (330)864-2122 Fax: (330)864-5298 E-mail: jhl@rubberworld.com • URL: http://www.rubberworld.com • Annual. $111.00. Lists 700 suppliers for more than 8,000 rubber chemicals, materials and compounding ingredients.

Ruff Political Action Committee., 666 Pennsylvania Ave. SE, Ste. 402 Washington, DC 20003. Phone: (202)546-0023 Fax: (202)546-0029 E-mail: richard.wallace@scbar.org Provides campaign advice and funding for selected conservative political candidates; conducts research; lobbies conservative issues. Committee is named after chairman Howard Ruff (1931-), financial adviser and editor. **Convention/Meeting:** none.

Rundt's World Business Intelligence. S. J. Rundt and Associates, Inc., 130 E 63rd St. New York, NY 10021. Phone: (973)783-5206 Fax: (973)744-3073 E-mail: info@rundtsintelligence.com • URL: http://www.rundtsintelligence.com • Weekly. $695.00 per year. Formerly *Rundt's Weekly Intelligence*.

Running a Meeting That Works. Robert F. Miller and Marilyn Pincus. Barron's Educational Series, Inc., 250 Wireless Blvd. Hauppauge, NY 11788-3917. Phone: 800-645-3476 or (516)434-3311 Fax: (516)434-3723 E-mail: info@barronseduc.com • URL: http://www.barronseduc.com • 2004. $8.95. Third edition. A concise guide to the organization and management of effective business meetings.

Running an Indexing Business. Janet Perlman, editor. Information Today, Inc., 143 Old Marlton Pike Medford, NJ 08055-8750. Phone: 800-300-9868 or (609)654-6266 Fax: (609)654-4309 E-mail: custserv@infotoday.com • URL: http://www.infotoday.com • 2001. $31.25. Published in conjunction with the American Society of Indexers (ASI). Experienced indexers provide advice on fees, proposals, subcontractors, taxes, and other business matters.

Runzheimer Reports on Relocation. Runzheimer International, Runzheimer Park Rochester, WI 53167-0009. Phone: 800-558-1702 or (262)971-2200 Fax: (262)971-2254 E-mail: webmaster@runzheimer.com • URL: http://www.runzheimer.com • Monthly. $354.00 per year. Newsletter.

Runzheimer Reports on Travel Management. Runzheimer International, Runzheimer Park Rochester, WI 53167-0009. Phone: 800-558-1702 or (262)971-2200 Fax: (262)971-2254 E-mail: webmaster@runzheimer.com • URL: http://www.runzheimer.com • Monthly. $295.00 per year. Newsletter on the control of business travel costs.

Rupp's Insurance and Risk Management Glossary. Richard V. Rupp. NILS Publishing Co., 21625 Prairie St. Chatsworth, CA 91311. Phone: 800-423-5910 2001. $35.00. Second edition. Provides definitions of 6,400 insurance words and phrases. Includes a guide to acronyms and abbreviations.

Rural Cooperatives. Available from U. S. Government Printing Office, Washington, DC 20402. Phone: (202)512-1800 Fax: (202)512-2250 E-mail: gpoaccess@gpo.gov • URL: http://www.access.gpo.gov • Bimonthly. $21.00 per year. Issued by the U. S. Department of Agriculture. Contains articles on cooperatives in rural America. Formerly *Farmer Cooperatives*.

Rutgers Accounting Web (RAW). Rutgers University Accounting Research CenterPhone: (973)353-5172 Fax: (973)353-1283 • URL: http://www.rutgers.edu/accounting • RAW Web site provides extensive links to sources of national and international accounting information, such as the Big Six accounting firms, the Financial Accounting Standards Board (FASB), SEC filings (EDGAR), journals, publishers, software, the International Accounting Network, and "Internet's largest list of accounting firms in USA." Searching is offered. Fees: Free.

Rutgers Agricultural Research and Extension Center. Rutgers University

RV Business (Recreational Vehicle). T L Enterprises Inc., 2575 Vista Del Mar Dr. Ventura, CA 93001-3920. Phone: 800-234-3450 or (805)667-4434 Fax: (805)667-4484 E-mail: tlecs@magsserv.com • URL: http://www.rvbusiness.com • Monthly. $48.00 per year. Includes annual *Directory*. News about the entire recreational vehicle industry in the U.S.

RV Buyer's Guide (Recreational Vehicle). Affinity Group, Inc.,T L Enterprises, 2575 Vista Del Mar Dr. Ventura, CA 93001-3920. Phone: (805)667-4100 Fax: (805)667-4454 • URL: http://www.rv.net • Annual. $7.95.

The RVDA Membership Directory and Resource Guide. Recreation Vehicle Dealers Association of North America, 3930 University Dr. Fairfax, VA 22030-2515. Phone: (703)591-7130 Fax: (703)359-0152 E-mail: info@rvda.org Covers: Over 900 retail sales firms handling travel trailers, camping trailers, truck campers, and motor homes in the United States and Canada that are open for business twelve months of the year. Entries include: Company name, address, phone, and owner's or manager's name.

RxList: The Internet Drug Index. Neil SandowPhone: (707)746-8754 E-mail: info@rxlist.com • URL: http://www.rxlist.com • Web site features detailed information (cost, usage, dosage, side effects, etc.) from Mosby, Inc. for about 300 major pharmaceutical products, representing two thirds of prescriptions filled in the U. S. (3,700 other products are listed). The "Top 200" drugs are ranked by number of prescriptions filled. Keyword searching is provided. Fees: Free.

S & P MidCap 400 Directory. Standard and Poors Corp., 55 Water St. New York, NY 10041. Phone: 800-221-5277 or (212)438-1000 E-mail: clientsupport@sstandardandpoors.com • URL: http://www.standardandpoors.com • Annual. $66.00. Contains detailed profiles of the companies included in Standard & Poor's MidCap 400 Index of stock prices. Includes income and balance sheet data for up to 10 years, with growth and stability rankings for 400 midsized corporations.

S & P's Insurance Book. Standard & Poor's Ratings Group, Insurance Rating Services, 55 Water St. New York, NY 10041. Phone: 800-221-5277 or (212)438-1000 E-mail: clientsupport@standardandpoors.com • URL: http://www.standardandpoors.com • Quarterly. Price on application. Contains detailed financial analyses and ratings of various kinds of insurance companies.

S & P's Insurance Digest: Life Insurance Edition. Standard & Poor's Ratings Group, Insurance Rating Services, 55 Water St. New York, NY 10041. Phone: 800-221-5277 or (212)438-1000 E-mail: clientsupport@standardandpoors.com • URL: http://www.standardandpoors.com • Quarterly. Contains concise financial analyses and ratings of life insurance companies.

S & P's Insurance Digest: Property-Casualty and Reinsurance Edition. Standard & Poor's Ratings Group, Insurance Rating Services, 55 Water St. New York, NY 10041. Phone: 800-221-5277 or (212)438-1000 E-mail: clientsupport@standardandpoors.com • URL: http://www.standardandpoors.com • Quarterly. Contains concise financial analyses and ratings of property-casualty insurance companies.

S & P's Municipal Bond Book, with Notes, Commercial Paper, & IRBs. Standard & Poor's, 55 Water St. New York, NY 10041. Phone: 800-221-5277 or (212)438-1000 Fax: (212)438-4368 E-mail: clientsupport@standardandpoors.com • URL: http://www.standardandpoors.com • Bimonthly. $965.00 per year. Includes ratings and statistical information for about 20,000 municipal bonds, notes, commercial paper issues, and industrial revenue bonds (IRBs). The creditworthiness ("Rationales") of 200 selected municipalities and other issuers is discussed. Securities "under surveillance" by S & P are listed.

A S I S Handbook and Directory. American Society for Information Science, 1320 Fenwick Ln., Ste. 510 Silver Spring, MD 20910. Phone: (301)495-0900 Fax: (301)495-0810 E-mail: asis@asis.org • URL: http://www.asis.org • Annual. Members, $25.00; non-members, $100.00.

S. S. Huebner Foundation., University of Pennsylvania, 3733 Spruce St., Vance Hall, Suite 430 Philadelphia, PA 19104-6301. Phone: (215)898-9631 Fax: (215)573-2218 E-mail: cummins@wharton.upenn.edu • URL: http://www.rider.wharton.upenn.edu/ • Awards grants for research in various areas of insurance.

SAE Handbook. Society of Automotive Engineers, 400 Commonwealth Dr. Warrendale, PA 15096-0001. Phone: 800-832-6732 or (724)776-4841 Fax: (724)776-5760 E-mail: customerservice@sae.org • URL: http://www.sae.org • Annual. $425.00. Three volumes. Contains standards, recommended practices and information reports on ground vehicle design, manufacturing, testing and performance.

SAE International., 400 Commonwealth Dr. Warrendale, PA 15096-0001. Phone: 877-606-7323 or (724)776-4841 Fax: (724)776-5760 E-mail: custsvc@sae.org • URL: http://www.sae.org • Affiliated with Service Technicians Society. Formerly Society of Automobile Engineers.

SAEGIS Internet Search. Thomson & ThomsonPhone: 800-692-8833 or (617)479-1600 Fax: (617)786-8273 E-mail: support@thomson-thomson.com • URL: http://www.thomson-thomson.com • Fee-based Web site provides extensive, common law screening of the World Wide Web for trademarks. Searches are performed offline, with final report delivered to user's "SAEGIS Inbox." Context of trademark within each relevant Web site is indicated, and links are provided.

The Safe Deposit Bulletin. New York State Safe Deposit Association, Box 5074, Rockefeller Ctr. Sta., PO Box 5074 New York, NY 10185. Phone: (212)621-9200 Fax: (516)883-8429 E-mail: info@accessintel.com Description: Discusses topics on safe and sound business practice for safe deposit organizations. Recurring features include news of research, notices of publications available, a calendar of events, news of educational opportunities, Association news, current legal and regulatory changes, current practices and procedures and Q&A section.

Safe Trip Abroad. Available from U. S. Government Printing Office, Washington, DC 20402. Phone: (202)512-1800 Fax: (202)512-2250 E-mail: gpoaccess@gpo.gov • URL: http://www.access.gpo.gov • 2002. $2.50. Issued by the Bureau of Consular Affairs, U. S. State Department (http://www.state.gov). Provides practical advice for international travel.

Safety. Alton, L. ThyGerson. Jones and Bartlett Publishers, 40 Tall Pine Dr. Sudbury, MA 01776. Phone: 800-832-0034 or (978)443-5000 Fax: (978)443-8000 E-mail: info@jbpub.com • URL: http://www.jbpub.com • 1992. $37.75. Second edition.

Safety and Health at Work. International Labour Office, 1828 L St., N.W. Washington, DC 20036. Phone: (202)653-7652 Fax: (202)653-7687 E-mail: washington@ilo.org • URL: http://www.ilo.org • Bimonthly. $240.00 per year. Formerly *Occupational Safety and Health Abstracts*.

Safety and Health-Safety Equipment Buyers' Guide. National Safety Council, 1121 Spring Lake Dr. Itasca, IL 60143-3201. Phone: 800-621-7619 or (630)285-1121 Fax: (630)285-1315 E-mail: customerservice@nsc.org • URL: http://www.nsc.org • Annual. $5.00. Directory of manufacturers and distributors of occupational health, safety and environment products and services.

Safety and Health: The International Safety, Health and Environment Magazine. National Safety Council,, Periodicals Dept., 1121 Spring Lake Dr. Itasca, IL 60143-3201. Phone: 800-621-7619 or (630)285-1121 Fax: (630)285-1315 E-mail: info@nsc.org • URL: http://www.nsc.org • Monthly. Members, $45.00 per year; non-members, $58.50 per year. Formerly *National Safety and Health News*.

Safety Equipment Dealers Association.

Safety in Tunnels: Transport of Dangerous Goods Through Road Tunnels. Organization for Economic Cooperation and Development, OECD Washington Center, 2001 L St., N. W., Suite 650 Washington, DC 20036-4922. Phone: 800-456-6323 or (202)785-6323 Fax: (202)785-0350 E-mail: washington.contact@oecd.org • URL: http://www.oecd.org • 2001. $19.00. Discusses risks in road tunnels and the consequences of incidents.

Safety on Roads: What's the Vision? Organization for Economic Cooperation and Development, OECD Washington Center, 2001 L St., N. W., Suite 650 Washington, DC 20036-4922. Phone: 800-456-6323 or (202)785-6323 Fax: (202)785-0350

E-mail: washington.contact@oecd.org • URL: http://www.oecd.org • 2002. $22.00. Contains information on road safety programs in OECD countries. Describes the criteria that influence success or failure.

The Sage Encyclopedia of Social Science Research Methods. Michael S. Lewis-Beck and others, editors. Sage Publications, Inc., 2455 Teller Rd. Thousand Oaks, CA 91320-2218. Phone: 800-818-7243 or (805)499-0721 Fax: 800-583-2665 or (805)499-0871 E-mail: info@sagepub.com • URL: http://www.sagepub.com • 2004. $550.00. Three volumes. Includes more than 800 signed entries on such topics as basic statistics, econometrics, evaluation, linear models, data analysis, sampling, and survey design.

Sage Family Studies Abstracts. Sage Publications, Inc., 2455 Teller Rd. Thousand Oaks, CA 91320. Phone: 800-818-7243 or (805)499-9774 Fax: 800-583-2665 or (805)499-0871 E-mail: webmaster@sagepub.com • URL: http://www.sagepub.com • Quarterly. Institutions, $847.00 per year.

Sage Public Administration Abstracts. Sage Publications, Inc., 2455 Teller Rd. Thousand Oaks, CA 91320. Phone: 800-818-7243 or (805)499-9774 Fax: 800-583-2665 or (805)499-0871 E-mail: webmaster@sagepub.com • URL: http://www.sagepub.com • Quarterly. Institutions, $785.00 per year.

Sage Urban Studies Abstracts. Sage Publications, Inc., 2455 Teller Rd. Thousand Oaks, CA 91320. Phone: 800-818-7243 or (805)499-9774 Fax: 800-583-2665 or (805)499-0871 E-mail: webmaster@sagepub.com • URL: http://www.sagepub.com • Quarterly. Institutions, $797.00 per year.

Sailboat Buyers Guide. Primedia Inc. (New York, New York), 745 5th Ave. New York, NY 10151. Phone: 800-828-8130 or (212)745-0100 Fax: (212)745-0100 E-mail: information@primedia.com • URL: http://www.sailbuyersguide.com • Covers: over 2,000 sailboat and equipment manufacturers. Entries include: Firm name, address, phone; many entries have description or photo.

Salaries of Scientists, Engineers, and Technicians: A Summary of Salary Surveys. Commission on Professionals in Science and Technology. CPST Publications, 1200 New York Ave. Washington, DC 20005. Phone: (202)326-7080 Fax: (202)842-1603 Biennial. $100.00. A summary of salary surveys.

Sales and Marketing Executives International., PO Box 1390 Sumas, WA 98295-1390. Phone: 800-999-1414 or (312)893-0751 Fax: (604)855-0165 E-mail: smei@smei.org • URL: http://www.smei.org • Formerly Sales and Marketing Executives.

Sales and Marketing Management. VNU Business Media, 770 Broadway New York, NY 10003-9595. Phone: 800-344-7119 or (646)654-4500 Fax: (646)654-7212 • URL: http://www.vnubusinessmedia.com • Monthly. $48.00 per year.

Sales and Marketing Management Survey of Buying Power. VNU Business Media, 770 Broadway New York, NY 10003. Phone: 800-266-4712 or (646)654-4500 Fax: (646)654-7212 E-mail: salesandmarketing@espcomp.com • URL: http://www.vnubusinessmedia.com • Annual. $150.00.

Sales & Marketing Report: Practical Ideas for Successful Selling. Lawrence Ragan Communications, Inc., 316 N. Michigan Ave. Chicago, IL 60601. Phone: 800-878-5331 or (312)960-4100 Fax: (312)960-4106 E-mail: cservice@ragan.com • URL: http://www.ragan.com • Monthly. $119.00 per year. Newsletter. Emphasis is on sales training, staff morale, and marketing productivity.

Sales and Sales Management. Elsevier, 655 Ave. of the Americas New York, NY 10010-5107. Phone: 800-366-2665 or (212)989-5800 Fax: 800-535-9935 or (212)633-3680 E-mail: custserv@elsevier.com • URL: http://www.elsevier.com • 1998. $34.95.

Sales and Use Tax Alert. CCH, Inc., 2700 Lake Cook Rd. Riverwoods, IL 60015. Phone: 800-835-5224 or (847)267-7000 E-mail: cust_serv@cch.com • URL: http://www.cch.com • Monthly. $197.00 per year. Newsletter. Provides nationwide coverage of new developments in sales tax laws and regulations.

Sales and Use Taxation of E-Commerce: State Tax Administrators' Current Thinking, with CCH Commentary. CCH, Inc., 2700 Lake Cook Rd. Riverwoods, IL 60015. Phone: 800-835-5224 or (847)267-7000 E-mail: cust_serv@cch.com • URL: http://www.cch.com • 2000. $129.00. Provides advice and information on the impact of state sales taxes on e-commerce activity.

Sales Association of the Chemical Industry., 66 Morris Ave., Ste. 2A Springfield, NJ 07081. Phone: (973)379-1100 Fax: (973)379-6507 E-mail: veronicagaamc@earthlink.net Members are chemical sales personnel, including sales managers and executives. Formerly Salesmen's Association of the American Chemical Industry.

Sales Compensation Handbook. Stockton Colt, editor. AMACOM, 1601 Broadway New York, NY 10019. Phone: 800-262-9699 or (518)586-8100 Fax: (518)903-8168 E-mail: customerservice@amanet.org • URL: http://www.amacombooks.org • 1998. $75.00. Second edition. Topics include salespeople compensation plans based on salary, commission, bonuses, and contests.

Sales Management. William C. Moncrief and Shannon Shipp. Addison-Wesley, 75 Arlington St., Ste. 300 Boston, MA 02116. Phone: 800-447-2226 or (617)848-7500 • URL: http://www.aw.com • 1997. $130.00. Includes chapters on personal selling, organization, training, motivation, compensation, evaluation, sales forecasting, and strategy. A glossary and case histories are provided.

Sales Management: Concepts and Cases. Douglas J. Dalyrmple. John Wiley and Sons, Inc., 111 River St. Hoboken, NJ 07030. Phone: 800-225-5945 or (201)748-6000 Fax: (201)748-6088 E-mail: info@wiley.com • URL: http://www.wiley.com • 2000. $101.95 Seventh edition.

Sales Manager's Desk Book. Gene Garofalo. Prentice Hall PTR, 240 Frisch Ct. Paramus, NJ 07652. Phone: 800-282-0693 Fax: 800-445-6991 • URL: http://www.phptr.com • 1996. $69.95. Second edition. A handbook covering many aspects of selling and sales management. Includes information on telemarketing, communications technology, voice mail, and teleconferencing.

Sales Manager's Handbook. John P. Steinbrink. Dartnell Corp., 350 Hiatt Dr. Palm Beach Gardens, FL 33418. Phone: 800-341-7874 or (561)622-6520 Fax: (561)622-2423 E-mail: custserv@lrp.com • URL: http://www.dartnellcorp.com • 1989. $93.50. 14th edition.

Sales Negotiation Skills That Sell. Robert E. Kellar. AMACOM, 1601 Broadway New York, NY 10019. Phone: 800-262-9699 or (518)586-8100 Fax: (518)903-8168 E-mail: customerservice@amanet.org • URL: http://www.amacombooks.org • 1996. $17.95. Covers negotiating objectives, risk assessment, planning, strategy, tactics, and face-to-face skills.

Sales Promotion. David Horchover. John Wiley and Sons, Inc., 111 River St. Hoboken, NJ 07030. Phone: 800-597-3299 or (201)748-6000 Fax: (201)748-6088 E-mail: info@wiley.com • URL: http://www.wiley.com • 2002. $14.00. (Express Executive Series).

Sales Promotion Handbook. Tamara Brezen-Blocks and William Robinson, editors. Dartnell Corp., 350 Hiatt Dr. Palm Beach Gardens, FL 33418. Phone: 800-341-7874 or (561)622-6520 Fax: (561)622-2423 E-mail: custserv@lrp.com • URL: http://www.dartnellcorp.com • 1994. $69.95. Eighth edition. Covers licensing, tie-ins, legal aspects, event marketing, database marketing, and other topics.

Sales Prospector. Sales Prospector, PO Box 185 Lake Bluff, IL 60044-0185. Phone: 800-752-4050 or (847)899-1271 E-mail: info@accessintel.com Description: Reports on planned construction of new plants, plant additions, shopping centers, commercial and institutional buildings, relocations, mergers, acquisitions, and government contracts to provide sales leads for salesmen and other businessmen. Provides name of company, location of construction, purpose, approximate dates of start and completion, name of contractor, architect, or developer, and estimate of amount of investment. Published in 28 separate editions each month for different areas of the country, plus two editions for Canada.

Sales Representative Law Guide. CCH, Inc., 2700 Lake Cook Rd. Riverwoods, IL 60015. Phone: 800-835-5224 or (847)267-7000 E-mail: cust_serv@cch.com • URL: http://www.cch.com • $195.00 per year. Looseleaf service. Semiannual updates. Covers state laws on independent sales representation. Includes checklists and forms.

Sales Tax Rate Directory. Vertex, Inc., 1041 Old Cassatt Rd. Berwyn, PA 19312. Phone: 800-355-3500 or (610)640-4200 Fax: (610)640-5892 • URL: http://www.vertexinc.com • Annual. Price on application. U.S. and Canadian sales/use tax rates in standardized format.

Salk Institute for Biological Studies.

Salomon Center. New York University

Salt Institute., Fairfax Plz., Ste. 600, 700 N Fairfax St. Alexandria, VA 22314-2040. Phone: (703)549-4648 Fax: (703)548-2194 E-mail: dick@saltinstitute.org • URL: http://www.saltinstitute.org • Works to increase public awareness of the benefits of salt and salt products. Promotes participation in public policy as it relates to salt production, salt distribution and salt products. Fosters research in ice and snow control, agricultural feeding practices, water treatment, and salt in nutrition. Conducts public information program. Maintains Tech Data Center on salt-related materials. Sponsors industry safety contest. Compiles sales statistics.

SAM Advanced Management Journal. Society for Advancement of Management. Texas A & M University - Corpus Christi, College of Business, 6300 Ocean Dr., FC 111 Corpus Christi, TX 78412. Phone: 888-827-6077 or (361)825-6045 Fax: (361)825-2725 E-mail: moustafa@cob.tamucc.edu • URL: http://www.cob.tamucc.edu • Quarterly. $49.00. Provides information on leading business topics for practicing managers.

SAMA Group of Associations., 225 Reinekers Lane, Ste. 625 Alexandria, VA 23314. Phone: (703)836-1360 Fax: (703)836-6644 Formerly Apparatus Makers Association of America.

Samir Husni's Guide to New Consumer Magazines. Samir Husni. R. R. Bowker, 630 Central Ave. New Providence, NJ 07974. Phone: 888-269-5372 Fax: (908)219-0098 E-mail: info@bowker.com • URL: http://www.bowker.com • Annual. $95.00. A directory of more than 540 consumer magazines that began publication during the previous year. Includes names of key personnel.

SAMPE Journal. Society for the Advancement of Material and Process Engineering, P.O. Box 2459 Covina, CA 91722. Phone: (626)331-0616 Fax: (626)332-8929 E-mail: sampeibo@aol.com • URL: http://www.sampe.org • Bimonthly. Members, $78.00 per year; non-members, $80.00 per year. Provides technical information.

Samuel Zell and Robert Lurie Real Estate Center at Wharton.

SAN/LAN: Newsletter Covering Worldwide Technology Trends, Applications and Markets (Storage Area Network/Local Area Network). Information Gatekeepers, Inc., 214 Harvard Ave., Ste. 200 Boston, MA 02134. Phone: 800-323-1088 or (617)232-3111 Fax: (617)734-8562 E-mail: info@igigroup.com • URL: http://www.igigroup.com • Monthly. $695.00 per year. Cover new developments, new products, and marketing. Formerly *Local Area Networks*.

Sandhills Research Station. North Carolina Dept. of Agriculture and Consumer Services

Sandwich Shop/Deli. Entrepreneur Media, Inc., 2445 McCabe Way Irvine, CA 92614. Phone: 800-421-2300 or (949)261-2325 Fax: (949)261-0234 E-mail: entmag@entrepreneur.com • URL: http://www.entrepreneur.com • Looseleaf. $59.50. A practical guide to starting a sandwich shop and delicatessen. Covers profit potential, start-up costs, market size evaluation, owner's time required, site selection, lease negotiation, pricing, accounting, advertising, promotion, etc. (Start-Up Business Guide No. E1156.)

Sanitary Maintenance Buyers' Guide. Trade Press Publishing Corp., 2100 W. Florist Ave. Milwaukee, WI 53209. Phone: 800-727-7995 or (414)228-7701 Fax: (414)228-1134 E-mail: prograil@tradepress.com • URL: http://www.tradepress.com • Annual. $20.00. For distributors and wholesalers of sanitary supplies.

Sanitary Maintenance: The Journal of the Sanitary Supply Industry. Trade Press Publishing Corp., 2100 W. Florist Ave. Milwaukee, WI 53209-3799. Phone: 800-727-7995 or (414)228-7701 Fax: (414)228-1134 • URL: http://www.tradepress.com • Monthly. Free to qualified personnel.

Satellite Broadcasting: The Politics and Implications of the New Media. Ralph M. Negrine, editor. Taylor & Francis, 29 W. 35th St. New York, NY 10001. Phone: 800-634-7064 or (212)216-7800 Fax: (212)564-7854 E-mail: cservice@routledge.com • URL: http://www.routledge-ny.com • 1988. $65.00. Second edition.

Satellite Communications: The First Quarter Century of Service. David W. Rees. John Wiley and Sons, Inc., 111 River St. Hoboken, NJ 07030. Phone: 800-225-5945 or (201)748-6000 Fax: (201)748-6088 E-mail: info@wiley.com • URL: http://www.wiley.com • 1990. $130.00. A survey of the history of communications satellites, emphasizing business applications. (Telecommunications and Signal Processing Series).

Satellite News. Access Intelligence L.L.C., 4 Choke Cherry Rd., 2nd Fl. Rockville, MD 20850. Phone: 800-777-5006 or (301)354-2000 Fax: (301)309-3847 E-mail: info@accessintel.com • URL: http://www.phillips.com • Description: Provides business insights and analysis into the commercial satellite industry including new satellite applications, developing technologies, and unfolding partnerships. Recurring features include columns titled Satellite Spotlight, DBS News, Satellite News, Newsmaker Interiews, Satellite Circuit, and Satellite News Financial Ticker.

Satellite News: The Monthly Newsletter Covering Management, Marketing Technology and Regulation. PBI Media, Inc., 1201 7 Locks Rd. Potomac, MD 20854. Phone: 800-777-5006 or (301)344-2000 Fax: (301)309-3847 E-mail: clientservices@pbimedia.com • URL: http://www.pbimedia.com • 50 times a year. $1,097.00 per year. Newsletter. Covers business applications in space, including remote sensing and satellites. Incorporates (Space Business News).

Satellite Week: The Authoritative News Service for Satellite Communications and Allied Fields. Warren Publishing, Inc., 2115 Ward Ct., NW Washington, DC 20037. Phone: (202)872-9200 Fax: (202)293-3435 • URL: http://www.warrenpub.com • Weekly. $495.00 per year. Newsletter. Covers satellite broadcasting, telecommunications, and the industrialization of space.

SAVE International., 136 S Keowee St. Dayton, OH 45402. Phone: (937)224-7283 Fax: (937)222-5794 E-mail: info@value-eng.org • URL: http://www.value-eng.org • Value engineers and analysts. Works to promote advancement of value engineering and value analysis and its application to the research, design, development, test, evaluation, engineering, production, purchasing and distribution phases in government, private industry, and commerce. Sponsors competitions.

The Savings and Loan Crisis: An Annotated Bibliography. Pat L. Talley, compiler. Greenwood Publishing Group, Inc., 88 Post Rd., W Westport, CT 06881. Phone: 800-225-5800 or (203)226-3571 Fax: (203)431-2214 E-mail: customer-service@greenwood.com • URL: http://www.greenwood.com • 1993. $65.00. Includes 360 scholarly and popular titles (books and research papers). (Bibliographies and Indexes in Economic History, No. 14).

Savings Institutions: Mergers, Acquisitions, and Conversions. American Lawyer Media, Inc., 105 Madison Ave. New York, NY 10016. Phone: 800-888-8300 or (212)779-9200 Fax: (212)481-8110 E-mail: lawcatalog@amlaw.com • URL: http://www.lawcatalog.com/ • Looseleaf. $169.00. Updated as needed. Provides detailed information on the legal complexities of mergers and acquisitions involving savings institutions. (Law Journal Press).

Sawyer's Success Tactics for Information Businesses. Deborah C. Sawyer. Burwell Enterprises, 5619 Plumtree Dr. Dallas, TX 75252. Phone: (972)-732-0160 Fax: (972)733-1951 E-mail: helen@burwellinc.com • URL: http://www.burwellinc.com • 1998. $24.50. Covers such items as pricing, costs, and service for information brokers and others in the fee-based information business.

Sawyer's Survival Guide for Information Brokers. Deborah C. Sawyer. Burwell Enterprises, 5619 Plumtree Dr. Dallas, TX 75252. Phone: (972)732-0160 Fax: (972)733-1951 E-mail: helen@burwellinc.com • URL: http://www.burwellinc.com • 1995. $39.50. Provides practical advice for information entrepreneurs.

Sax's Dangerous Properties of Industrial Materials. Richard J. Lewis. John Wiley and Sons, Inc., 111 River St. Hoboken, NJ 07030. Phone: 800-225-5945 or (201)748-6000 Fax: (201)748-6088 E-mail: info@jwiley.com • URL: http://www.wiley.com • 1999. $545.00. 10th edition. Three volumes. Provides detailed information on the chemical, physical, and toxicity characteristics of more than 22,000 industrial materials. Hazard ratings and safety profiles are specified. Includes CD-ROM.

SBA Loan Guide. Entrepreneur Meida, Inc., 2445 McCabe Way Irvine, CA 92614. Phone: 800-421-2300 or (949)261-2325 Fax: (949)261-0234 E-mail: entmag@entrepreneur.com • URL: http://www.entrepreneur.com • Looseleaf. $59.50. A practical guide to obtaining loans through the Small Business Administration. (Start-Up Business Guide No. E1315.)

SBIC Directory and Handbook of Small Business Finance. International Wealth Success, Inc., P.O. Box 186 Merrick, NY 11570-1310. Phone: (516)766-5850 Fax: (516)766-5919 E-mail: admin@iwsmoney.com • URL: http://www.iwsmoney.com • Annual. $15.00 per year. Includes small business investment companies.

Scale Manufacturers Association., 6724 Lone Oak Blvd. Naples, FL 34109. Phone: (239)514-3441 Fax: (239)514-3470 E-mail: phil@scalemanufacturers.org • URL: http://www.scalemanufacturers.org • Manufacturers of commercial weighing equipment.

Scandinavian Kompass on Disc. Available from Kompass USA, Inc., 121 Whitney Ave. New Haven, CT 06510. Phone: 877-566-7277 or (203)503-6789 Fax: (203)503-6780 E-mail: mail@kompass-usa.com • URL: http://www.kompass.com • Semiannual. CD-ROM provides information on more than 120,000 companies in Denmark, Finland, Norway, and Sweden. Classification system covers approximately 50,000 products and services.

Schaum's Outline of Unix. Harley Hahn. McGraw-Hill, 1221 Ave. of the Americas New York, NY 10020. Phone: 800-722-4726 or (212)512-2000 Fax: (212)512-4502 E-mail: customer.service@mcgraw-hill.com • URL: http://www.mcgraw-hill.com • 1995. $7.38. (Schaum's Outline Series).

Schiffli Embroidery Manufacturers Promotion Fund., 22 Industrial Ave. Fairview, NJ 07022. Phone: (201)943-7757 Fax: (201)943-7793 E-mail: info@schiffli.org • URL: http://www.schiffli.org • Represents embroidery firms contributing to promotional activities to increase demand for laces, embroideries, emblems, and motifs manufactured on Schiffli embroidery machines. Serves as promotional arm of the Schiffli lace and embroidery industry.

The Scholarship Book: The Complete Guide to Private Scholarships, Grants, and Loans for Undergraduates. Daniel J. Cassidy. Prentice Hall PTR, 240 Frisch Ct. Paramus, NJ 07652. Phone: 800-282-0693 Fax: 800-445-6991 • URL: http://www.phptr.com • 2000. $48.00. Ninth edition. Includes CD-ROM. (Scholarship Books Series).

Scholarships, Fellowships, and Loans. Gale Cengage Learning, 27500 Drake Rd. Farmington Hills, MI 48331-3535. Phone: 800-877-GALE or (248)699-4253 Fax: 800-414-5043 E-mail: gale.galeord@cengage.com • URL: http://gale.cengage.com • 2002. $215.00. 19th edition. Describes more than 4,200 scholarships, fellowships, loans, and other educational funding sources available to U. S. and Canadian undergraduate and graduate students.

Scholastic Journalism. Tom Rolnicki and others. Blackwell Publishing, 350 Main St. Malden, MA 02148. Phone: (781)388-8200 Fax: (781)388-8210 E-mail: subscrip@blackwellpub.com • URL: http://www.blackwellpublishing.com • 2001 $44.95. 10th edition.

School Administrator's Complete Letter Book. Gerald Tomlinson. John Wiley and Sons Inc., 111 River St. Hoboken, NJ 07030. Phone: 800-225-5945 or (201)748-6276 Fax: (201)748-8641 E-mail: bookinfo@wiley.com • URL: http://www.wiley.com • 2003. $44.95. Includes CD-Rom.

School Bus Fleet. Bobit Publishing Corp., 21061 S. Western Ave. Torrance, CA 90501. Phone: (310)533-2400 Fax: (310)533-2500 E-mail: sbf@bobit.com • URL: http://www.bobit.com • Monthly. $25.00 per year. Includes *Factbook*.

School Business Affairs. Association of School Business Officials. ASBO International, 11401 N. Shore Dr. Reston, VA 20190-4200. Phone: (703)478-0405 Fax: (703)478-0205 • URL: http://www.asbointl.org • Monthly. Membership.

School Enrollment, Social and Economic Characteristics of Students. Available from U. S. Government Printing Office, Washington, DC 20402. Phone: (202)512-1800 Fax: (202)512-2250 E-mail: gpoaccess@gpo.gov • URL: http://www.access.gpo.gov • Annual. $2.25. Issued by the U. S. Bureau of the Census. Presents detailed tabulations of data on school enrollment of the civilian noninstitutional population three years old and over. Covers nursery school, kindergarten, elementary school, high school, college, and graduate school. Information is provided on age, race, sex, family income, marital status, employment, and other characteristics.

School Foodservice Who's Who. Information Central Inc., 744 Redondo Rd. Prescott, AZ 86303. Phone: (928)778-1513 Fax:

(928)778-1513 E-mail: information@primedia.com Covers: about 5,800 food service programs in public and Catholic school systems with enrollments in excess of 1,500 students. Separate listings of the biggest buyers (school districts reporting over $1.5 million/year in foodservice purchases), state school foodservice officials, and co-op buying groups and food management companies involved in food service. Entries include: School district name, address, phone, fax; food service budget, key food service executive, number of meals served daily, types of food and services, food management company, fast food brands.

School Law News: The Independent Bi-Weekly News Service on Legal Developments inEducation. Aspen Publishers, Inc., 1135 Ave. of the Americas New York, NY 10036. Phone: 800-234-1660 or (212)597-0200 Fax: (212)597-0338 E-mail: customer.service@aspenpubl.com • URL: http://www.aspenpublishers.com • Biweekly. $383.00 per year.

School Library Journal: The Magazine of Children Young Adults and School Librarians. Reed Business Information, 360 Park Ave. S New York, NY 10010. Phone: 800-446-6551 or (646)746-6400 Fax: (646)746-7028 E-mail: corporatecommunications@reedbusiness.com • URL: http://www.reedbusiness.com • Monthly. $124.00 per year. Provides news, information and reviews for librarians and media specialists who serve children and young adults in school and public libraries.

School Planning and Management. Peter Li, Inc., 2621 Dryden Rd. Dayton, OH 45439-1661. Phone: 800-523-4825 or (937)293-1415 Fax: (937)293-1310 Monthly. $23.95 per year. Formerly *School and College*.

Science and Practice of Welding: The Practice of Welding. A. C. Davies. Cambridge University Press, 40 W 20th St. New York, NY 10022-4211. Phone: 800-872-7423 or (212)924-3900 Fax: (212)691-3239 E-mail: orders@cup.org • URL: http://www.cup.org • 1993. $110.00. 10th edition.

Science and Technology Almanac. Greenwood Publishing Group, Inc., 88 Post Rd., W. Westport, CT 06881. Phone: 800-225-5800 or (203)226-3571 Fax: (203)431-2214 E-mail: customer-service@greenwood.com • URL: http://www.greenwood.com • Annual. $79.95. Covers technological news, research, and statistics.

Science and Technology Desk Reference: Answers to Frequently Asked and Difficult to Answer Reference Questions in Science and Technology. Carnegie Library of Pittsburgh, Science and Technology Department Staff, editors. Gale Cengage Learning, 27500 Drake Rd. Farmington Hills, MI 48331-3535. Phone: 800-877-GALE or (248)699-4253 Fax: 800-414-5043 E-mail: gale.galeord@cengage.com • URL: http://gale.cengage.com • 1997. $90.00. Second edition. *The Handy Science Answer Book*. Covers a wide variety of subject areas, including biology, astronomy, chemistry, geology, the environment, and health.

Science and Technology Libraries. Haworth Press, Inc., 10 Alice St. Binghamton, NY 13904-1580. Phone: 800-429-6784 or (607)722-5857 Fax: 800-895-0582 or (607)722-1424 E-mail: getinfo@haworthpressinc.com • URL: http://www.haworthpressinc.com • Quarterly. Institutions, $275.00 per year.

Science Citation Index. Thomson/ISI, 3501 Market St. Philadelphia, PA 19104. Phone: 888-216-4101 or (215)386-0100 Fax: (215)387-1125 • URL: http://www.isinet.com • Bimonthly. $15,020.00 per year. Annual cumulation. Includes *Source Index, Citation Index, Permuterm Subject Index*, and *Corporate Index*.

Science Citation Index: Compact Disc Edition. Institute for Scientific Information, 3501 Market St. Philadelphia, PA 19104. Phone: 800-336-4474 or (215)386-0100 Fax: (215)386-6362 Monthly. Provides CD-ROM indexing of the world's scientific and technical literature. Corresponds to online *Scisearch* and printed *Science Citation Index*.

Scientific and Technical Acronyms, Symbols, and Abbreviations. Uwe Erb and Harald Keller. John Wiley and Sons, Inc., 111 River St. Hoboken, NJ 07030. Phone: 800-225-5945 or (201)748-6000 Fax: (201)748-6088 E-mail: info@wiley.com • URL: http://www.wiley.com • 2001. $250.00. Contains more than 200,000 entries covering a wide variety of scientific and technical fields.

Scientific Meetings. Scientific Meetings Publications, 5214 Soledad Mountain Rd. San Diego, CA 92138. Phone: (858)270-2910 Fax: (858)270-2910 E-mail: scimeeting@access1.net Quarterly. $85.00 per year. Provides information on forthcoming scientific, technical, medical, health, engineering and management meetings held throughout the world.

The Scientist.. 3535 Market St., Ste. 200 Philadelphia, PA 19104-2645. Phone: (215)386-9601 Fax: (215)387-7542 E-mail: info@the-scientist.com • URL: http://www.the-scientist.com • Biweekly. Individuals, $29.00 per year; institutions, $58.00 per year. Contains news for scientific, research, and technical personnel.

Scisearch. Institute for Scientific Information, 3501 Market St. Philadelphia, PA 19104. Phone: 800-336-4474 or (215)386-0100 Fax: (215)386-2911 • URL: http://www.isinet.com • Broad, multidisciplinary index to the literature of science and technology, 1974 to present. Inquire as to online cost and availability. Coverage of literature is worldwide, with weekly updates.

Score Association-Service Corps of Retired Executives., c/o Service Corps of Retired Executives Association, 409 Third

St., S.W. 6th Fl. Washington, DC 20024. Phone: 800-634-0245 or (202)205-6762 Fax: (202)205-7636 • URL: http://www.score.org • Formerly Service Corps of Retired Executives.

Scott Stamp Monthly. Scott Publishing Co., 911 Vandemark Rd. Sidney, OH 45365. Phone: 800-572-6885 or (937)498-0802 Fax: (937)498-0807 E-mail: ssm@scottonline.com • URL: http://www.scottonline.com • Monthly. $17.95 per year.

Scrap. Institute of Scrap Recycling Industries, Inc., 1325 G St., N.W., Suite 1000 Washington, DC 20005-3104. Phone: (202)737-1770 Fax: (202)626-0900 • URL: http://www.isri.org • Bimonthly. Free to members; non-members, $32.95 per year. Formerly *Scrap Processing and Recycling*.

Screenwriting 101: The Essential Craft of Feature Film Writing. Neill D. Hicks. Michael Wiese Productions, 11288 Ventura Blvd., Suite 621 Studio City, CA 91604. Phone: 800-833-5738 or (818)379-8799 Fax: (818)986-3408 E-mail: mwpsales@mwp.com • URL: http://www.mwp.com • 1999. $16.95. Covers both the mechanics of screenwriting and the "practicalities of the business."

Scripps Institution of Oceanography-Integrative Oceanography Div.

Scripta Materialia. Acta Metallurgica, Inc. Elsevier, 360 Park Ave., S. New York, NY 10010-1710. Phone: 888-437-4636 or (212)989-5800 Fax: (212)633-3990 E-mail: usinfo-f@elsevier.com • URL: http://www.elsevier.com • Semimonthly. $1,358.00 per year.

Sea Power. Navy League of the United States, 2300 Wilson Blvd. Arlington, VA 22201-3308. Phone: (703)528-1775 Fax: (703)243-8251 E-mail: mail@navyleague.org • URL: http://www.navyleague.org • Monthly. Free to members; non-members $25.00 per year. Includes annual *Almanac of Seapower*.

Sea Technology Buyers Guide/Directory. Compass Publications Inc., 1501 Wilson Blvd., Ste. 1001 Arlington, VA 22209-2403. Phone: (703)524-3136 Fax: (703)841-0852 E-mail: seatechads@sea-technology.com • URL: http://www.sea-technology.com • Covers: manufacturing, service, research and development, engineering, construction, drilling, equipment lease and rental firms, and testing organizations providing goods and services to the oceanographic, offshore, marine sciences, and undersea defense industries. Eight informational sections. Entries include: Company name, contact information, executives' names, list of products and/or services.

Sea Technology: For Design Engineering and Application of Equipment and Services for the Marine Environment. Compass Publications, Inc., 1501 Wilson Blvd., Ste. 1001 Arlington, VA 22209. Phone: (703)524-3136 Fax: (703)841-0852 E-mail: seatechorder@sea-technology.com • URL: http://www.sea-technology.com • Monthly. $40.00 per year.

Seafood Business. Diversified Business Communications, 121 Free St. Portland, ME 04101. Phone: (207)842-5600 Fax: (207)842-5603 • URL: http://www.seafoodbusiness.com • Monthly. $69.00 per year. Edited for a wide range of seafood buyers, including distributors, restaurants, supermarkets, and institutions. Special issues feature information on specific products, such as salmon or lobster.

Seafood: Frozen, Canned, and Fresh. Available from MarketResearch.com, 641 Ave. of the Americas, Fourth Floor New York, NY 10011. Phone: 800-298-5699 or (212)807-2629 Fax: (212)807-2642 E-mail: order@marketresearch.com • URL: http://www.marketresearch.com • 2002. $3,850.00. Published by Global Industry Analysts. Provides worldwide market research data, including profiles of major seafood companies.

The Seafood Market. MarketResearch.com, 641 Ave. of the Americas, 4th Fl. New York, NY 10011. Phone: 800-298-5699 or (212)807-2629 Fax: (212)807-2676 E-mail: customerservice@marketresearch.com • URL: http://www.marketresearch.com • 1997. $1,625.00. Market research report. Covers fresh, frozen, and canned seafood. Market projections are provided.

Seafood Price-Current. Urner Barry Publications, Inc., P.O. Box 389 Toms River, NJ 08754. Phone: 800-932-0617 or (732)240-5330 Fax: (732)341-0891 E-mail: mail@urnerbarry.com • URL: http://www.seafoodnet.com • Semiweekly. $295.00 per year.

Sealed Insulating Glass Manufacturers Association., 401 N. Michigan Ave. Chicago, IL 60611-4267. Phone: (312)644-6610 Fax: (312)527-6783 E-mail: sigma@sba.com • URL: http://www.sigmaonline.org • Manufacturers of insulating glass; suppliers to the industry.

Search Engine Watch. Internet.com Corp.Phone: (203)662-2800 Fax: (203)655-4686 • URL: http://www.searchenginewatch.com • Web site offers information on various aspects of search engines, including new developments, indexing systems, technology, ratings and reviews of major operators, specialty services, tutorials, news, history, "Search Engine EKGs," "Facts and Fun," etc. Online searching is provided. Formerly *A Webmaster's Guide to Search Engines*.

Searcher: The Magazine for Database Professionals. Information Today, Inc., 143 Old Marlton Pike Medford, NJ 08055-8750. Phone: 800-300-9868 or (609)654-6266 Fax: (609)654-4309 E-mail: custserv@infotoday.com • URL: http://www.infotoday.com • 10 times per year. $79.95 per year. Covers a wide range of topics relating to online and CD-ROM database searching.

SEC Accounting Rules. CCH, Inc., 2700 Lake Cook Rd. Riverwoods, IL 60015. Phone: 800-525-3335 or (847)267-7000 E-mail: cust_serv@cch.com • URL: http://www.cch.com • $448.00. Looseleaf service.

SEC Financial Reporting: Annual Reports to Shareholders, Form 10-K, and Quarterly Financial Reporting. LexisNexis Matthew Bender, 1275 Broadway Albany, NY 12204. Phone: 800-424-4200 or (518)487-3000 Fax: (518)487-3584 E-mail: bookstore.support@lexisnexis.com • URL: http://www.bender.com • Annual. $254.00. Looseleaf service. Coverage of aspects of financial reporting with GAAP disclosure and Regulation S-X preparation Step-by-step procedures for preparing information for Form 10-K and annual shareholders reports.

SEC Handbook: Rules and Forms for Financial Statements and Related Disclosures. CCH, Inc., 2700 Lake Cook Rd. Riverwoods, IL 60015. Phone: 800-835-5224 or (847)267-7000 E-mail: cust_serv@cch.com • URL: http://www.cch.com • Annual. $59.00. Contains full text of rules and requirements set by the Securities and Exchange Commisssion for preparation of corporate financial statements.

SEC News Digest. U.S. Securities and Exchange Commission, Public Reference Room, 450 Fifth St., N.W., MISC-11 Washington, DC 20549. Phone: (202)272-7460 Fax: (202)272-7050 • URL: http://www.sec.gov/ • Daily.

SEC Today (Securities Exchange Commission). Washington Service Bureau, Inc., 655 15th St., N.W. Washington, DC 20005. Phone: (202)508-0600 Fax: (202)659-3655 • URL: http://www.wsb.com • Daily. $760.00 per year. Newsletter. Includes the official *SEC News Digest* from the Securities and Exchange Commission and reports on public company filing activity.

Secondary Mortgage Market: Strategies for Surviving and Thriving in Today's Challenging Markets. Jess Lederman. McGraw-Hill, 1221 Ave. of the Americas New York, NY 10020. Phone: 800-722-4726 or (212)512-2000 Fax: (212)512-4502 E-mail: customer.service@mcgraw-hill.com • URL: http://www.mcgraw-hill.com • 1992. $70.00. Revised edition.

Secretarial/Word Processing Service. Entrepreneur Media, Inc., 2445 McCabe Way Irvine, CA 92614. Phone: 800-421-2300 or (949)261-2325 Fax: (949)261-0234 E-mail: entmag@entrepreneur.com • URL: http://www.entrepreneur.com • Looseleaf. $59.50. A practical guide to starting a secretarial and word processing business. Covers profit potential, start-up costs, market size evaluation, owner's time required, site selection, pricing, accounting, advertising, promotion, etc. (Start-Up Business Guide No. E1136.)

Secrets of Closing Sales. Charles B. Roth and Roy Alexander. Prentice Hall PTR, 240 Frisch Ct. Paramus, NJ 07652. Phone: 800-282-0693 Fax: 800-445-6991 • URL: http://www.phptr.com • 1997. $16.95. Sixth edition. (Business Classics Series).

Secrets of Six-Figure Women: Seven Surprising Strategies of Successful High Earners. Barbara Stanny. HarperCollins Publishers, Inc., 10 East 53rd St. New York, NY 10022-5299. Phone: 800-242-7737 or (212)207-7000 Fax: 800-822-4090 or (212)207-7145 • URL: http://www.harpercollins.com • 2002. $23.95. Provides results of interviews with 150 women in high-paying jobs ($100,000 and over).

Secrets of the Super Net Searchers: The Reflections, Revelations and Hard-Won Wisdom of 35 of the World's Top Internet Researchers. Reva Basch. Information Today, Inc., 143 Old Marlton Pike Medford, NJ 08055-8750. Phone: 800-300-9868 or (609)654-6266 Fax: (609)654-4309 E-mail: custserv@infotoday.com • URL: http://www.infotoday.com • 1996. $29.95. Tells how to find "cyber-gems" among the "cyber-junk." (Cyber Age Books.)

Secrets of the Super Searchers: The Accumulated Wisdom of 23 of the World's Top Online Searchers. Reva Basch. Information Today, Inc., 143 Old Marlton Pike Medford, NJ 08055-8750. Phone: 800-300-9868 or (609)654-6266 Fax: (609)654-4309 E-mail: custserv@infotoday.com • URL: http://www.infotoday.com • 1993. $39.95. Contains interviews with experienced online searchers, covering such topics as pre-search interviewing, search strategy, full-text considerations, search limiting, and client relations. (Super Searchers Series).

Section for Psychiatric and Substance Abuse Services.

Section for Women in Public Administration., 1120 G St., NW, Ste. 700 Washington, DC 20005-3885. Phone: (202)393-7878 Fax: (202)638-4952 E-mail: mhamilton@aspanet.org • URL: http://www.aspanet.org • Initiates action programs appropriate to the needs and concerns of women in public administration. Formerly National Committee for Women in Public Administration.

Secured Lender. Commercial Finance Association, 225 W. 34th St. New York, NY 10122. Phone: (212)594-3490 Fax: (212)564-6053 E-mail: info@cfa.com • URL: http://www.cfa.com • Bimonthly. Members, $24.00 per year; non-members, $48.00 per year.

Securities and Federal Corporate Law Report. West Group, 610 Opperman Dr. Eagan, MN 55123. Phone: 800-328-4880 or (651)687-7000 Fax: 800-340-9378 E-mail: bookstore@westgroup.com • URL: http://www.westgroup.com • $526.00 per year. Newsletter. Periodic supplementation.

Securities Arbitration Commentator: Covering Significant Issues and Events in Securities-Commodities Arbitration. Richard P. Ryder, P.O. Box 112 Maplewood, NJ 07040. Phone: (973)761-5880 Fax: (973)761-1504 Monthly. $348.00 per year. Newsletter. Edited for attorneys and other professionals concerned with securities arbitration.

Securities, Commodities, and Federal Banking: 1999 in Review. CCH, Inc., 2700 Lake Cook Rd. Riverwoods, IL 60015. Phone: 800-835-5224 or (847)267-7000 E-mail: cust_serv@cch.com • URL: http://www.cch.com • Irregular. $57.00. Summarizes the year's significant legal and regulatory developments.

Securities Crimes. West Group, 610 Opperman Dr. Eagan, MN 55123. Phone: 800-328-4880 or (651)687-7000 Fax: 800-340-9378 E-mail: bookstore@westgroup.com • URL: http://www.westgroup.com • Annual. $225.00. Two looseleaf volumes. Analyzes the enfo of federal securities laws from the viewpoint of the defendant. Discusses Securities and Exchange Commission (SEC) investigations and federal sentencing guidelines. (Securities Law Series).

Securities Industry and Financial Markets Association., 120 Broadway, 35th Fl. New York, NY 10271-0080. Phone: (212)313-1200 Fax: (212)313-1301 E-mail: rbrockhaus@sifma.org • URL: http://www.sifma.org • Represents more than 650 member firms of all sizes, in all financial markets in the U.S. and around the world. Enhances the public's trust and confidence in the markets, delivering an efficient, enhanced member network of access and forward-looking services, as well as premiere educational resources for the professionals in the industry and the investors whom they serve. Maintains offices in New York City and Washington, DC.

Securities Industry News. Thomson Financial Corporate Communications, 22 Thomson Pl., 11F2 Boston, MA 02210. Phone: (617)856-4636 Fax: 888-280-4820 • URL: http://www.securitiesindustry.com • Weekly. $275.00 per year. Newsletter covers securities dealing and processing, including regulatory compliance, shareholder services, human resources, transaction clearing, and technology.

Securities Industry Yearbook. Securities Industry and Financial Markets Association, 120 Broadway, 35th Fl. New York, NY 10271-0080. Phone: (212)313-1200 Fax: (212)313-1301 E-mail: info@sifma.org • URL: http://www.sia.com • Covers: over 600 member securities firms, with about 480 of them covered in detail. Entries include: For firms covered in detail—Company name, name of parent company, address, phone, capital position and rank, number of offices and type, number of employees, area of specialization, names and titles of key personnel, number of registered representatives, departments with name of department head, dollar volume of underwriting and syndication by type, other financial data. For other firms—Company name, address, name of delegated liaison to the association.

Securities Law Handbook. West Group, 610 Opperman Dr. Eagan, MN 55123. Phone: 800-328-4880 or (651)687-7000 Fax: 800-340-9378 E-mail: bookstore@westgroup.com • URL: http://www.westgroup.com • Annual. $326.00. In-depth coverage of security issues. (Securities Handbook Series).

Securities Law Review. West Group, 610 Opperman Dr. Eagan, MN 55123. Phone: 800-328-4880 or (651)687-7000 Fax: 800-340-9378 E-mail: bookstore@westgroup.com • URL: http://www.westgroup.com • Annual. $326.00. Current thinking in securities law.

Securities Litigation and Regulation Reporter: The National Journal of Record ofCommodities Litigation. Andrews Publications, 175 Strafford Ave., Bldg. 4, Suite 140 Wayne, PA 19087. Phone: 800-345-1101 or (610)622-0510 Fax: (610)622-0501 E-mail: customer@andrewspub.com Semimonthly. $1,250.00 per year. Newsletter. Provides reports on litigation involving the rules and decisions of the Commodity Futures Trading Commission. Formerly *Securities and Commodities Litigation Reporter*.

Securities: Public and Private Offerings, 2d. William W. Prifti. West Group, 610 Opperman Dr. Eagan, MN 55123. Phone: 800-328-4880 or (651)687-7000 Fax: 800-340-9378 E-mail: bookstore@westgroup.com • URL: http://www.westgroup.com • Semiannual. $389.00. Three looseleaf volumes. How to issue securities. (Securities Law Series).

Securities Regulation. Joel Seligman and Louis Loss. Aspen Publishers, Inc., 1185 Ave. of the Americas New York, NY 10036. Phone: 800-234-1660 or (212)597-0200 Fax: 800-901-9075 or (212)597-0338 E-mail: customer.service@aspenpub.com • URL: http://www.aspenpublishers.com • 1995. $1,520.00. Third edition. 12 volumes. Includes 1969 supplement. Covers the fundamentals of government regulation of securities.

Securities Regulation and Law Report. BNA, Inc., 1231 25th St., N.W. Washington, DC 20037. Phone: 800-372-1033 E-mail: customercare@bna.com • URL: http://www.bna.com • Weekly. $1,479.00 per year. Looseleaf service.

Securities Week. McGraw-Hill Financial Services Co., 25 Broadway New York, NY 10004. Phone: 800-722-4726 or (212)512-2000 Fax: (212)509-8994 E-mail: info@accessintel.com • URL: http://www.mcgraw-hill.com • Description: Acts as a trade publication for Wall Street executives, publishing news stories on pertinent events and developments within the industry including those related to legislative and regulatory activity, major stock exchanges, investment banking and retail firms, institutional trading, and new products. Recurring features include reports on research departments and a column titled Financial Futures/Commodities Report.

Security Analysis. S. Cottle and Others. McGraw-Hill, 1221 Ave. of the Americas New York, NY 10020. Phone: 800-722-4726 or (212)512-2000 Fax: (212)512-4502 E-mail: customer.service@mcgraw-hill.com • URL: http://www.mcgraw-hill.com • 1988. $59.95. Fifth edition.

Security Distributing and Marketing. Business News Publishing, 755 W Big Beaver Rd., Ste. 1000 Troy, MI 48084. Phone: 800-837-7370 or (248)362-3700 Fax: (248)362-0317 • URL: http://www.bnp.com • 13 times a year. $82.00 per year. Covers applications, merchandising, new technology and management.

Security Distributing and Marketing-Security Products and Services Locater. Reed Business Information, 360 Park Ave. S New York, NY 10010. Phone: 800-662-7776 or (646)746-6400 E-mail: corporatecommunications@reedbusiness.com • URL: http://www.reedbusiness.com • Annual. $50.00. Formerly *SDM: Security Distributing and Marketing-Security Products and Services Directory*.

Security Hardwear Distributors Association., 1900 Arch St. Philadelphia, PA 19103-1498. Phone: (215)564-3484 Fax: (215)564-2175 E-mail: shda@fernley.com • URL: http://www.shda.org • Formerly National Locksmith Suppliers Association.

Security Letter. Security Letter Inc., 166 E 96th St., Apt. 3B New York, NY 10128. Phone: (212)348-1553 Fax: (212)534-2957 E-mail: info@accessintel.com Description: Contains "solution-oriented information on security and protection of assets from loss," particularly for executives concerned about the following: internal checks and controls, personnel practices, management of change, fraud and embezzlement, business crime trends, security, and urban terrorism. Recurring features include news of research, a calendar of events, semiannual FBI crime data, quarterly financial news of major companies in the security industry, book reviews, security and safety pointers, and a question-and-answer feature.

Security Management. American Society for Industrial Security, 1625 Prince St. Alexandria, VA 22314-2818. Phone: (703)519-6200 Fax: (703)519-6299 E-mail: asis@asisonline.org • URL: http://www.asisonline.com • Monthly. Members, $38.00 per year; non-members, $48.00 per year. Articles cover the protection of corporate assets, including personnel property and information security.

Security Owner's Stock Guide. Standard and Poor's, 55 Water St. New York, NY 10041. Phone: 800-221-5277 or (212)438-1000 Fax: (212)438-4368 E-mail: clientsupport@standardandpoors.com • URL: http://www.standardandpoors.com • Monthly. $125.00 per year.

Security: Product Service Suppliers Guide. Reed Business Information, 360 Park Ave., S New York, NY 10010. Phone: 800-662-7776 or (646)746-6400 E-mail: corporatecomunications@reedbusiness.com • URL: http://www.reedbusiness.com • Annual. $50.00 Includes computer and information protection products. Formerly *Security World Product Directory*.

Security Systems Administration. Cygnus Business Media, Inc., 445 Broad Hollow Rd. Melville, NY 11747. Phone: 800-547-7377 or (631)845-2700 Fax: (631)845-2798 E-mail: rich.reiff@cygnuspub.com • URL: http://www.cygnusbzb.com • Monthly. $10.00 per year.

Security: The Magazine for Buyers of Security Products, Systems and Service. Business News Publishing Co., 755 W Big Beaver Rd. Troy, MI 48084. Phone: 800-662-7776 or (248)362-3700 Fax: (248)362-0317 • URL: http://www.bnp.com • Monthly. $82.90 per year.

Security Traders Association., 420 Lexington Ave., Ste. 2334 New York, NY 10170. Phone: (212)867-7002 Fax: (212)867-7030 E-mail: traders@securitytraders.org • URL: http://www.securitytraders.org • Brokers and dealers handling listed and OTC securities, stocks, and bonds, and all securities. Conducts educational programs. Promotes the interests of members throughout the global financial markets. Provides representation of these interests in the legislative, regulatory and technological processes. Fosters goodwill and high standards of integrity in accord with the Association's founding principle.

Seed Abstracts. Available from CABI Publishing, North America, 875 Massachusetts, 7th Fl. Cambridge, MA 01239. Phone: 800-528-4841 or (617)395-4056 Fax: (617)354-6875 E-mail: cabi-nao@cabi.org • URL: http://www.cabi-publishing.org • Monthly. Institutions, $680.00 per year. Print and online edition, $700.00 per year. Published in England by CABI Publishing. Provides worldwide coverage of the literature.

The Seed Technologist Newsletter. Society of Commercial Seed Technologists, c/o Andy Evans, Ohio State University, 202 Kottman Hall, 2021 Coffey Rd. Columbus, OH 43210. Phone: (614)292-8242 • URL: http://www.zianet.com • Three times a year. $35.00 per year. Includes annual *Proceedings*.

Seed Trade News. Ball Publishing, 335 N. River St. Batavia, IL 60510. Phone: (630)208-9080 Fax: (630)208-9350 E-mail: sbruhn@seedtradenews.com • URL: http://www.seedtradenews.com • Monthly. $48.00 per year. Includes *International Seed Directory*.

Seed World. Scranton Gillette Communications, Inc., 380 E. Northwest Highway, Suite 200 Des Plaines, IL 60016-2282. Phone: (847)391-1000 Fax: (847)390-0408 E-mail: bwilson@sgcmail.com • URL: http://www.sgcpubs.com • Monthly. $30.00 per year. Provides information on the seed industry for buyers and sellers. Supplement available *Seed Trade Buyer's Guide*.

SEI Center for Advanced Studies in Management., University of Pennsylvania, 1400 Steinberg Hall-Dietrich Hall, 3620 Locust Walk Philadelphia, PA 19104-6371. Phone: (215)898-2349 Fax: (215)898-1703 E-mail: seicenter@wharton.upenn.edu • URL: http://www.seicenter.wharton.upenn.edu/seicenter • Conducts interdisciplinary management studies.

Selected Independent Funeral Homes., 500 Lake Cook Rd., Ste. 205 Deerfield, IL 60015. Phone: 800-323-4219 or (847)236-9401 Fax: (847)236-9968 E-mail: info@selectedfuneralhomes.org • URL: http://www.selectedfuneralhomes.org • Funeral directors. Aims to study, develop, and establish a standard of service for the benefit of its consumers. Provides a continuing forum for the exchange, development and dissemination of knowledge and information beneficial to members and the public.

Selected Instruments and Related Products. U.S. Bureau of the Census, Washington, DC 20233-0800. Phone: (301)457-4100 Fax: (301)457-3842 • URL: http://www.census.gov • Annual. (Current Industrial Reports, MA-38B.)

Selected Interest Rates. U.S. Federal Reserve System, Board of Governors, Publications Services, 20th and Constitution Ave., N.W. Room MS-127 Washington, DC 20551. Phone: (202)452-3244 Fax: (202)728-5886 • URL: http://www.federalreserve.gov • Weekly release, $20.00 per year.

Self. Conde Nast Publications, Inc., Four Times Sq., 5th Fl. New York, NY 10036. Phone: (212)286-2860 Fax: (212)286-8110 • URL: http://www.condenet.com • Monthly. $12.00 per year. Written for business women.

Self-Employed America. National Association for the Self-Employed, 2121 Precinct Line Rd. Hurst, TX 76054. Phone: 800-232-6273 or (817)428-4243 Fax: (817)428-4210 Bimonthly. Members, $2.00 per year; non-members, $12.00 per year. Provides articles on marketing, management, motivation, accounting, taxes, and other topics for businesses having fewer than 15 employees.

Selling by Phone: How to Reach and Sell to Customers. Linda Richardson. McGraw-Hill, 1221 Ave. of the Americas New York, NY 10020. Phone: 800-722-4726 or (212)512-2000 Fax: (212)512-4502 E-mail: customer.service@mcgraw-hill.com • URL: http://www.mcgraw-hill.com • 1995. $14.95.

Selling Through Independent Reps. Harold J. Novick. AMACOM, 1601 Broadway New York, NY 10019. Phone: 800-262-9699 or (518)586-8100 Fax: (518)903-8168 E-mail: customerservice@amanet.org • URL: http://www.amacombooks.org • 1999. $75.00. Third edition. Tells how to make good use of independent sales representatives.

Selling Through Negotiation: The Handbook of Sales Negotiation. Homer B. Smith. Marketing Education Associates, 3117 Kilkenny St. Silver Spring, MD 20904. Phone: (301)572-7478 Fax: (301)572-2960 E-mail: homsmith@erols.com 1988. $14.95.

Selling to Kids: News and Practical Advice on Successfully Marketing to Kids and Teens. EPM Communications, 160 Mercer St., 3rd Fl. New York, NY 10012. Phone: (212)941-0099 Fax: (212)941-1622 E-mail: info@epmcom.com • URL: http://www.epmcom.com • Biweekly. $495.00 per year. Newsletter. Includes market research information, news items, and case studies.

Selling to Seniors: The Monthly Report on the Mature Market. Community Development Services, Inc. CD Publications, 8204 Fenton St. Silver Spring, MD 20910-2889. Phone: 800-666-6380 or (301)588-6380 Fax: (301)588-6385 E-mail: info@cdpublications.com • URL: http://www.cdpublications.com • Monthly. $249.00 per year. Newsletter on effective ways to reach the "over 50" market.

Selling to the Affluent: The Professional's Guide to Closing the Sales That Count. Thomas Stanley. McGraw-Hill, 1221 Ave. of the Americas New York, NY 10020. Phone: 800-722-4726 or (212)512-2000 Fax: (212)512-4502 E-mail: customer.service@mcgraw-hill.com • URL: http://www.mcgraw-hill.com • 1990. $19.95.

Selling Today: Building Quality Partnerships. Gerald L. Manning and Barry L. Reece. Prentice Hall PTR, 240 Frisch Ct. Paramus, NJ 07652. Phone: 800-282-0693 Fax: 800-445-6991 • URL: http://www.phptr.com • 2000. $115.00. Eighth edition.

SEMA News. Specialty Equipment Market Association, PO Box 4910 Diamond Bar, CA 91765-0910. Phone: (909)396-0289 Fax: (909)860-0184 E-mail: sema@sema.org • URL: http://www.sema.org • Description: Covers the automotive specialty, performance equipment, and accessory sectors. Recurring features include news of government and legislative actions, new products, international markets, and member and Association activities.

Semiconductor Device Laboratory.

Semiconductor Industry Association., 181 Metro Dr., Ste. 450 San Jose, CA 95110-1344. Phone: (408)436-6600 Fax: (408)436-6646 E-mail: mailbox@sia-online.org • URL: http://www.sia-online.org/home.cfm • Companies that produce semiconductor products such as discrete components, integrated circuits, and microprocessors. Compiles industry trade statistics. Affiliate: Semiconductor Research Corporation and SEMATECH.

Semiconductor International—Semi Source. Reed Business Information, 360 Pk. Ave. S New York, NY 10014. Phone: 800-446-6551 or (646)746-6400 Fax: (646)746-6734 E-mail: corporatecommunications@reedbusiness.com • URL: http://www.reedbusiness.com • Publication includes: Lists of companies associated with the design, processing, assembly, packaging, and testing of semiconductor devices, integrated circuits, and hybrid circuits. Entries include: Company name, address, phone, fax, products.

Semiconductor International: The Industry Sourcebook for Processing, Assembly and Testing. Reed Electronics Group, 360 Park Ave., S New York, NY 10010. Phone: 800-446-6551 or (646)746-6400 Fax: (646)746-7028 E-mail: corporatecommunications@reedbusiness.com • URL: http://www.reedbusiness.com • Monthly. $131.99 per year. Devoted to processing, assembly and testing techniques.

Semiconductor Research Laboratory.

Semiconductors, Printed Circuit Boards, and Other Electronic Components. U. S. Bureau of the Census, 4700 Silver Hill Rd. Washington, DC 20233-0001. Phone: (301)763-4636 E-mail: comments@census.gov • URL: http://www.census.gov • Annual. Provides data on shipments: value, quantity, imports, and exports. (Current Industrial Reports, MA-36Q.)

Seminar Promoting. Entrepreneur Media, Inc., 2445 McCabe Way Irvine, CA 92614. Phone: 800-421-2300 or (949)261-2325 Fax: (949)261-0234 E-mail: entmag@entrepreneur.com • URL: http://www.entrepreneur.com • Looseleaf. $59.50. A practical guide to starting a seminar promotion business. Covers profit potential, start-up costs, market size evaluation, owner's time required, site selection, pricing, accounting, advertising, promotion, etc. (Start-Up Business Guide No. E1071.)

Seminars in Ultrasound, CT, and MR (Computerized Tomography and Magnetic Resonance. W.B. Saunders Co., The Curtis Center, 625 Walnut St. Philadelphia, PA 19106-3399. Phone: 800-523-1649 or (215)238-7800 Fax: (215)238-7883 • URL: http://www.elsevierhealth.com • Bimonthly. Individuals, $212.00 per year; institutions, $316.00 per year.

Senate Manual. U.S. Government Printing Office, Washington, DC 20402. Phone: (202)512-1800 Fax: (202)512-2250 E-mail: gpoaccess@gpo.gov • URL: http://www.accessgpo.gov • Biennial. $57.00.

Senior Day Care Center. Entrepreneur Media, Inc., 2445 McCabe Way Irvine, CA 92614. Phone: 800-421-2300 or (949)261-2325 Fax: (949)261-0234 E-mail: entmag@entrepreneur.com • URL: http://www.entrepreneur.com • Looseleaf. $59.50. A practical guide to starting a day care center for older adults (supervised environment for frail individuals). Covers profit potential, start-up costs, market size evaluation, owner's time required, site selection, lease negotiation, pricing, accounting, advertising, promotion, etc. (Start-Up Business Guide No. E1335.)

Senior PAC., c/o Robert Samuel, 2791 National Capital Station Washington, DC 20013-2791. Phone: (202)234-4299 E-mail: info@resistinc.org A political action committee dedicated to representing older and retired Americans. Works to strengthen and defend Social Security and Medicare programs. Supports congressional and presidential candidates who, through their statements and actions, advance the principle of "an adequate retirement income for all Americans."

Sensible Sound: Helping Audiophiles and Music Lovers to Spend Less and Get More., 403 Darwin Dr. Snyder, NY 14226-4804. Phone: 800-695-8439 or (716)833-0930 Fax: (716)833-0929 E-mail: info@sensiblesound.com • URL: http://www.sensiblesound.com • Bimonthly. $29.00 per year. High fidelity equipment review.

Sensor Technology: A Monthly Intgelligence Service. Technical Insights, 605 Third Ave. New York, NY 10158-0012. Phone: 800-825-7550 or (212)850-8600 Fax: (212)850-8800 E-mail: insights@wiley.com • URL: http://www.wiley.com • Monthly. Institutions, $685.00 per year. Newsletter on technological developments relating to industrial sensors and process control.

Sensors Buyers Guide. Advanstar Communications, Advanstar House Park West, Sealand Rd., Sealand Rd. Chester CH1 4RN, United Kingdom. Phone: 800-598-6008 or (44)1244 378888 Fax: (44)1244 370011 E-mail: info@advanstar.com • URL: http://www.advanstar.com • Covers: Lists manufacturers and vendors of sensors and transducers for use in high-technology applications engineering. Also covers related products and services. Entries include: Company name, address, phone, fax, e-mail, URL, contact person, type of sensors manufactured and/or physical, chemical, or biological characteristics utilized in sensing.

Sensors: Your Resource for Sensing, Communications, and Control. Advanstar Communications, 545 Boylston St. Boston, MA 02116. Phone: 888-527-7008 or (617)267-6500 Fax: (617)267-6900 E-mail: info@advanstar.com • URL: http://www.advanstar.com • Monthly. $70.00 per year. Edited for design, production, and manufacturing engineers involved with sensing systems. Emphasis is on emerging technology.

Serials Directory: An International Reference Book. EBSCO Publishing Inc., 10 Estes St. Ipswich, MA 01938. Phone: 800-653-2726 or (978)356-6500 Fax: (978)356-6565 E-mail: information@ebscohost.com • URL: http://www.epnet.com • Covers: Over 185,000 current and ceased periodicals and serials worldwide. Entries include: Serial title, publisher, address, phone, price, ISSN; Library of Congress, Dewey Decimal, National Library of Medicine, and Universal Decimal classification numbers; CODEN designations, description of editorial content; whether publication is peer reviewed; name of advertising manager; registration at the Copyright Clearance Center. Other format availabilities (CD-Rom), indexing and abstracting information.

Serials Directory: EBSCO CD-ROM. Ebsco Publishing, 10 Estes St. Ipswitch, MA 01938. Phone: 800-653-2726 or (978)356-6500 Fax: (978)356-6565 Quarterly. The CD-ROM version of Ebsco's *The Serials Directory: An International Reference Book*.

The Serials Librarian: The International Quarterly Journal of Theory, Research and Practice on Serial, Continuing, and Integrating Print and Electronic Resources. Haworth Press, Inc., 10 Alice St. Binghamton, NY 13904-1580. Phone: 800-429-6784 or (607)722-5857 Fax: 800-895-0582 or (607)722-1424 E-mail: getnfo@haworthpressinc.com • URL: http://www.haworthpressinc.com • Quarterly. Institutions, $275.50 per year. Two volumes.

Serials Review. JAI Press, 100 Prospect St. Stamford, CT 06904. Phone: (203)323-9606 Fax: (203)357-8446 E-mail: order@jaipress.com • URL: http://www.jaipress.com • Quarterly. Individuals, $101.00 per year; institutions, $274.00 per year.

Service Management: Strategy and Leadership in the Service Business. Richard Normann. John Wiley and Sons, Inc., 111 River St. Hoboken, NJ 07030. Phone: 800-225-5945 or (201)748-6000 Fax: (201)748-6088 E-mail: info@wiley.com • URL: http://www.wiley.com • 2001. $60.00. Third edition. Discusses the characteristics of successful service management.

Service Quality Handbook. Eberhard E. Scheuing and William F. Christopher, editors. AMACOM, 1601 Broadway New York, NY 10019. Phone: 800-262-9699 or (518)586-8100 Fax: (518)903-8168 E-mail: customerservice@amanet.org • URL: http://www.amacombooks.org • 1993. $75.00. Contains articles by various authors on the management of service to customers.

Services Marketing Quarterly. Haworth Press, Inc., 10 Alice St. Binghamton, NY 13904-1580. Phone: 800-429-6784 or (607)722-5857 Fax: 800-895-0582 or (607)722-1424 E-mail: getinfo@haworthpressinc.com • URL: http://www.haworthpressinc.com • Quarterly. Institutions, $425.00 per year. Two volumes. Supplies "how to" marketing tools for specific sectors of the expanding service sector of the economy. Formerly *Journal of Professional Services Marketing*.

Services: Statistics on International Transactions. Organization for Economic Cooperation and Development. Available from OECD Publications and Information Center, 2001 L St., N. W., Suite 650 Washington, DC 20036-4922. Phone: 800-456-6323 or (202)785-6323 Fax: (202)785-0350 E-mail: washington.contact@oecd.org • URL: http://www.oecdwash.org • Annual. $71.00. Presents a compilation and assessment of data on OECD member countries' international trade in services. Covers four major categories for 20 years: travel, transportation, government services, and other services.

Services: Statistics on Value Added and Employment. Organization for Economic Cooperation and Development, OECD Washington Center, 2001 L St., N. W., Suite 650 Washington, DC 20036-4922. Phone: 800-456-6323 or (202)785-6323 Fax: (202)785-0350 E-mail: washington.contact@oecd.org • URL: http://www.oecdwash.org • 2000. $69.00. Provides 10-year data on service industry employment and output (value added) for all OECD countries. Covers such industries as telecommunications, business services, and information technology services.

Setting National Priorities: Budget Choices for the Next Century. Robert D. Reischauer, editor. Brookings Institution Press, 1775 Massachusetts Ave., N. W. Washington, DC 20036-2188. Phone: 800-275-1447 or (202)797-6258 Fax: (202)797-6004 E-mail: bibooks@brook.edu • URL: http://www.brookings.edu • 1996. $42.95. Contains discussions of the federal budget, economic policy, and government spending policy.

Sewing Machines. Available from MarketResearch.com, 641 Ave. of the Americas, Fourth Floor New York, NY 10011. Phone: 800-298-5699 or (212)807-2629 Fax: (212)807-2642 E-mail: order@marketresearch.com • URL: http://www.marketresearch.com • 2002. $4,450.00. Published by Global Industry Analysts. Provides worldwide market research data, including profiles of major sewing machine companies.

Sex Discrimination and Sexual Harassment in the Work Place. American Lawyer Media, Inc., 105 Madison Ave. New York, NY 10016. Phone: 800-888-8300 or (212)779-9200 Fax: (212)481-8110 E-mail: lawcatalog@amlaw.com • URL: http://www.lawcatalog.com/ • Looseleaf. $169.00. Updated as needed. Considers both sides: the point of view of employers and the point of view of employees filing complaints. Coverage includes sexual harassment statutes, the Family Medical Leave Act, the Equal Pay Act, "glass ceiling" issues, pregnancy discrimination, childcare issues, reinstatement after a leave, and other legal matters. (Law Journal Press).

Sexual Harassment: A Selected, Annotated Bibliography. Lynda J. Hartell and Helena M. VonVille. Greenwood Publishing Group, Inc., 88 Post Rd., W Westport, CT 06881. Phone: 800-225-5800 or (203)226-3571 Fax: (203)431-2214 E-mail: customer-service@greenwood.com • URL: http://www.greenwood.com • 1995. $64.95. Includes articles and books on workplace sexual harassment. (Bibliographies and Indexes in Women's Studies, No. 23.)

Sexual Harassment in Employment Law. Barbara Lindemann and David D. Kadue. BNA, Inc., 1231 25th St., NW Washington, DC 20037. Phone: 800-372-1033 E-mail: customercare@bna.com • URL: http://www.bna.com • 1999. $140.00.

Sexual Harassment in the Workplace: A Guide to the Law and A Research Overview for Employers and Employees. Titus

Aaron and Judith A. Isaksen. McFarland & Co., Inc., Publishers, PO Box 611 Jefferson, NC 28640. Phone: 800-253-2187 or (336)246-4460 Fax: (336)246-5018 E-mail: info@mcfarlandpub.com • URL: http://www.mcfarlandpub.com • 1993. $32.50.

Sexual Harassment in the Workplace: How to Prevent, Investigate, and Resolve Problems in Your Organization. Ellen J. Wagner. AMACOM, 1601 Broadway New York, NY 10019. Phone: 800-262-9699 or (518)586-8100 Fax: (518)903-8168 E-mail: customerservice@amanet.org • URL: http://www.amacombooks.org • 1992. $17.95.

Sexual Harassment in the Workplace: Perspectives, Frontiers, and Response Strategies. Margaret S. Stockdale, editor. Sage Publications, Inc., 2455 Teller Rd. Thousand Oaks, CA 91320. Phone: 800-818-7243 or (805)499-9774 Fax: 800-583-2665 or (805)499-0871 E-mail: webmaster@sagepub.com • URL: http://www.sagepub.com • 1996. $103.00. Contains articles by various authors. (Women and Work Series: Vol. 5).

Sexual Harassment: Issues and Analyses. Janet V. Lewis, editor. Nova Science Publishers, Inc., 400 Oser Ave., Suite 1600 Hauppauge, NY 11788-3619. Phone: (631)231-7269 Fax: (631)231-8175 E-mail: novascience@earthlink.net • URL: http://www.novapublishers.com • 2001. $59.00. Provides articles by various authors on sexual harassment and discrimination in the workplace, in education, and in the military. Includes an index.

Sexual Harassment on the Job: What It Is and How to Stop It. William Petrocelli and Barbara K. Repa. Nolo, 950 Parker St. Berkeley, CA 94710. Phone: 800-728-3335 or (510)549-1976 Fax: (510)548-5902 E-mail: simone@nolo.com • URL: http://www.nolo.com • 1999. $24.95. Fourth edition. (Sexual Harassment on the Job: What It is and How to Stop It Series).

Sexual Orientation in the Workplace: Gays, Lesbians, Bisexuals and Heterosexuals Working Together. Amy J. Zuckerman and George F. Simons. Sage Publications, Inc., 2455 Teller Rd. Thousand Oaks, CA 91320. Phone: 800-818-7243 or (805)499-9774 Fax: 800-583-2665 or (805)499-0871 E-mail: webmaster@sagepub.com • URL: http://www.sagepub.com • 1994. $34.95. A workbook containing "a variety of simple tools and exercises" to provide skills for "working realistically and effectively with diverse colleagues."

The Seybold Report (Analyzing Publishing Technologies). Seybold Publications, 428 E. Baltimore Ave. Media, PA 19063. Phone: 800-325-3830 or (610)565-2480 Fax: (610)565-1858 Semimonthly. $595.00 per year. Newsletter. Formerly *Seybold Report on Publishing Systems*.

SFO: Stocks, Futures & Options. Wasendorf & Associates, Inc., PO Box 849 Cedar Falls, IA 50613. Phone: (319)268-0441 Fax: (319)277-1562 E-mail: info@sfomag.com • URL: http://www.sfomag.com • Monthly. $49.95 per year. Subtitle: *Official Journal for Personal Investing in Stocks, Futures, and Options*. Covers mainly speculative techniques for stocks, commodity futures, financial futures, stock index futures, foreign exchange, short selling, and various kinds of options.

Shaping the Corporate Image: An Analytical Guide for Executive Decision Makers. Marion G. Sobol and others. Greenwood Publishing Group, Inc., 88 Post Rd., W Westport, CT 06881. Phone: 800-225-5800 or (203)226-3571 Fax: (203)431-2214 E-mail: customer-service@greenwood.com • URL: http://www.greenwood.com • 1992. $59.95.

Sharing the Burden: Strategies for Public and Private Long-Term Care Insurance. Joshua M. Wiener and others. Brookings Institution Press, 1775 Massachusetts Ave., N. W. Washington, DC 20036-2188. Phone: 800-275-1447 or (202)797-6258 Fax: (202)797-6004 E-mail: bibooks@brook.edu • URL: http://www.brookings.edu • 1994. $42.95.

Sheep and Goat Science. M. E. Ensminger and Ronald B. Parker. Prentice Hall, 240 Frisch Ct. Paramus, NJ 07652. Phone: 800-282-0693 Fax: 800-445-6991 • URL: http://www.phptr.com • 2001. $69.00. Sixth edition.

Sheep Breeder and Sheepman. Mead Livestock Services, P.O. Box 796 Columbia, MO 65205. Phone: (314)442-8257 Monthly. $18.00 per year.

Sheet Metal and Air Conditioning Contractors' National Association., 4201 Lafayette Center Dr. Chantilly, VA 20151-1209. Phone: (703)803-2980 Fax: (703)803-3732 E-mail: info@smacna.org • URL: http://www.smacna.org • Formerly Sheet Metal Contractors National Association.

Sheet Metal Cutting: Collected Articles and Technical Papers. Amy Nickel, editor. Croyden Group, Ltd., 833 Featherstone Rd. Rockford, IL 61107. Phone: (815)399-8700 Fax: (815)484-7700 E-mail: info@fmametalfab.org • URL: http://www.fmametalfab.com • 1994. $33.00.

Sheet Metal Industry Promotion Plan., 6058 Royalton Rd. North Royalton, OH 44133-5104. Phone: (216)398-5600 Fax: (216)398-5576 E-mail: smacnacle@aol.com Heating, air conditioning, ventilating, roofing, and sheet metal contractors in Cuyahoga, Ashtabula, Geauga, and Lake counties of Ohio. Promotes quality sheet metal installations and pride in workmanship. Disseminates information on fabrication and erection of sheet metal construction. Has drawn up standards for mechanical sheet metal work; standards are to be adhered to by union members and participating contractors in fabrication and erection on residential, commercial, and industrial work involving sheet metal. Sponsors training classes for journeymen on sheet metal layout, heliarc welding, mechanical drawing, electric welding, balancing, and blueprint reading. **Publications:** none.

Sheldon's Major Stores and Chains. Phelon Sheldon and Marsar, Inc., 1364 Georgetowne Circle Sarasota, FL 34232-2048. Phone: 800-234-8804 or (941)342-7990 Fax: (941)342-7994 E-mail: psmpublishing@aol.com Annual. $200.00. Lists department stores and chains in, women's specialty and chains, home furnishing chains and resident buying offices in the U.S. and Canada. Formerly *Sheldon's Retail Stores*.

Shelf-Stable Food Processors Association., 1150 Connecticut Ave. NW, 12th Fl. Washington, DC 20036. Phone: (202)587-4273 Fax: (202)587-4303 E-mail: sfpa@meatami.com • URL: http://www.meatami.com/content/AboutAMI/canners. htm • Serves the shelf-stable prepared food industry. Represents the interests of shelf-stable food processors and their suppliers on issues affecting the industry. Members include companies of all sizes, from regional processors to large multi-plant operations.

Sheppard's Bookdealers in Europe: A Directory of Dealers in Secondhand and Antiquarian Books on the Continent of Europe. Richard Joseph Publishers, Ltd., PO Box 15 Torrington EX38 8ZJ, United Kingdom. Phone: 44 01805 625750 Fax: 44 01805 625376 E-mail: rjoe01@aol.com Biennial. $54.00. 1,746 dealers in antiquarian and secondhand books in 24 European countries.

Sheppard's Bookdealers in North America. Richard Joseph Publishers, Ltd., PO Box 15 Torrington EX38 82J, United Kingdom. Phone: 44 01805 625750 Fax: 44 01805 625376 E-mail: rjoe01@aol.com Biennial. $60.00. Over 3,364 dealers in antiquarian and secondhand books in the U.S. and Canada.

Ship Management. John Spruyt. LLP, Inc., 41-21 28th St., Rm D Long Island City, MA 11101. Phone: 800-493-4080 • URL: http://www.informa.com • 1994. $105.00. Second edition. Published in the UK by Lloyd's List (http://www.lloydslist. com). Covers recruitment of personnel, training, quality control, liability, safety, responsibilities of ship managers, and other topics.

Shipbuilders Council of America., 1455 F St., No. 225 Washington, DC 20005. Phone: (202)347-5462 Fax: (202)347-5464 E-mail: jmccluer@dc.bjllp.com • URL: http://www.shipbuilders.org • Absorbed Atlantic and Gulf Coasts Dry Dock Association. Formerly National Shipyard Association.

Shipcare. Available from Informa Publishing Group Ltd., PO Box 1017 Westborough, MA 01581-6017. Phone: 800-493-4080 Fax: (508)231-0856 E-mail: enquiries@informa.com • URL: http://www.informa.com • Quarterly. $206.00 per year. Published in the UK by Lloyd's List (http://www.lloydslist. com). Edited for the global ship repair, conversion, and maintenance industry. Provides news, market information, and technical analysis, including contract and pricing data.

Ships and Aircraft of the United States Fleet. U.S. Naval Institute, 291 Wood Rd. Annapolis, MD 21402-5034. Phone: 800-223-8764 or (410)268-6110 Fax: (410)269-7940 • URL: http://www.nip.org • Irregular. $85.00.

Shoe Factory Buyer's Guide: Directory of Suppliers to the Shoe Manufacturing Industry. Shoe Trades Publishing Co., P.O. Box 198 Cambridge, MA 02140. Phone: (781)648-8160 Fax: (781)646-9832 E-mail: info@shoetrades.com Annual. $59. 00. Lists over 750 suppliers and their representatives to the North American footwear industry.

Shoe Stats. Footwear Distributors and Retailers, 1319 F St. Washington, DC 20004. Phone: 800-688-7653 or (202)737-5660 Fax: (202)638-2615 E-mail: lproctor@fdra.org • URL: http://www.fdra.org • Annual. Free to members; non-members, $350.00; libraries, $225.00. Includes *Statistical Reporter*.

The SHOOT Directory for Commercial Production and Postproduction. SHOOT, 770 Broadway New York, NY 10003. Phone: (646)654-5139 Fax: (646)654-5354 • URL: http://www.shootonline.com • Annual. $79.00. Lists production companies, advertising agencies, and sources of professional television, motion picture, and audio equipment.

SHOOT: The Leading Newsweekly for Commercial Production and Postproduction. VNU Business Media, 770 Broadway New York, NY 10003-9595. Phone: 800-344-7119 or (646)654-4500 Fax: (646)654-7212 • URL: http://www. vnubusinessmedia.com • Weekly. $125.00 per year. Covers animation, music, sound design, computer graphics, visual effects, cinematography, and other aspects of television and motion picture production, with emphasis on TV commercials.

Shooting Industry. Publishers Development Corp., 591 Camino de la Reina, Suite 200 San Diego, CA 92108. Phone: 888-732-2299 or (619)297-5350 Fax: (619)297-5353 Monthly. $25.00 per year.

Shooting Industry-Buyers Guide. Publishers Development Corp., 591 Camino de la Reina, Suite 200 San Diego, CA 92108. Phone: 888-732-2299 or (619)297-5350 Fax: (619)297-5353 E-mail: 74673.3624@compuserve.com Annual. $15.00. Manufacturers, wholesalers, and importers of guns and related equipment and supplies.

Shop Talk. Mobile Air Conditioning Society, 225 S Broad St., PO Box 88 Lansdale, PA 19446. Phone: (215)631-7020 Fax: (215)631-7017 E-mail: info@macsw.org • URL: http://www. imaca.org • Description: Carries news briefs on happenings in the motor vehicle air conditioning and installed accessories industry. Publishes technical as well as management-oriented articles and listings of manuals, technical services, and training opportunities available. Recurring features include reports of meetings, company and personnel news, reports on the Association's activities and professional interest groups, and monthly supplements on specific topics.

A Shopper's Guide to Long-Term Care Insurance. Barry Leonard, editor. DIANE Publishing Co., 330 Pusey Ave. Collingdale, PA 19023-8428. Phone: 800-782-3833 or (610)461-6200 Fax: (610)461-6130 E-mail: dianepub@erols.com • URL: http://www.dianepublishing.com • 1995. $15.00. Revised edition. Provides impartial, consumer-oriented information and advice on long-term care insurance policies. Includes worksheets.

Shopping Center and Store Leases. Emanuel B. Halper. American Lawyer Media, 105 Madison Ave. New York, NY 10016. Phone: 800-537-2128 or (212)313-9343 Fax: (212)410-8110 E-mail: lawcatalog@amlaw.com • URL: http://www. lawcatalog.com • $195.00. Two looseleaf volumes. Periodic supplementation.

Shopping Center and Store Leases. American Lawyer Media, Inc., 105 Madison Ave. New York, NY 10016. Phone: 800-888-8300 or (212)779-9200 Fax: (212)481-8110 E-mail: lawcatalog@amlaw.com • URL: http://www.lawcatalog.com/ • Looseleaf. $195.00. Two volumes. Updated as needed. Provides analysis of retail leases, financing, construction issues, insurance, taxation, bankruptcy, and condemnation of property. Includes detailed information about the shopping-center business and fast-food restaurants, with many examples of lease clauses. (Law Journal Press).

Shopping Center Development Handbook. Michael D. Beyard and W. Paul O'Mara. Urban Land Institute, 1025 Thomas Jefferson St., NW, Ste. 500 W Washington, DC 20007-5201. Phone: 800-321-5011 or (202)624-7000 Fax: (202)624-7140 • URL: http://www.uli.org • 1998. $89.95. Third edition. (Development Handbook Series).

Shopping Center Directory. National Research Bureau, 33 W Wacker Dr. Chicago, IL 60606. Phone: 800-456-4555 or (312)541-0100 Fax: (312)583-5299 E-mail: information@ebscohost.com • URL: http://www.nrbonline.com • Covers: More than 40,000 shopping centers, in four regional volumes; East—Connecticut, Delaware, District of Columbia, Maine, Maryland, Massachusetts, New Hampshire, New Jersey, New York, Pennsylvania, Rhode Island, Vermont, Virginia, and West Virginia; Midwest—Illinois, Indiana, Iowa, Kansas, Kentucky, Michigan, Minnesota, Missouri, Nebraska, North Dakota, Ohio, South Dakota, and Wisconsin; South—Alabama, Arkansas, Florida, Georgia, Louisiana, Mississippi, North Carolina, Oklahoma, South Carolina, Tennessee, Texas; West—Alaska, Arizona, California, Colorado, Hawaii, Idaho, Montana, Nevada, New Mexico, Oregon, Utah, Washington, Wyoming. Entries include: Center name, address, mailing address, phone; owner, leasing agent, manager, developer, architect; year opened; physical description of center; square footage; number of stores; type of center (super-regional, regional, community, neighborhood); anchor/tenant list.

Shopping for a Better World: A Quick and Easy Guide to Socially Responsible Supermarket Shopping. Council on Economic Priorities, 30 Irving Place New York, NY 10003. Phone: 800-729-4237 Fax: (212)420-0988 Annual. $14.00. Rates 186 major corporations according to 10 social criteria: advancement of minorities, advancement of women, environmental concerns, South African investments, charity, community outreach, nuclear power, animal testing, military contracts, and social disclosure. Includes American, Japanese and British firms.

Short Course on Computer Viruses. Frederick B. Cohen. John Wiley and Sons, Inc., 111 River St. Hoboken, NJ 07030. Phone: 800-225-5945 or (201)748-6000 Fax: (201)748-6088 E-mail: info@wiley.com • URL: http://www.wiley.com • 1994. $44.95. Second edition. Includes CD-Rom. (Professional Computing Series).

A Short History of Financial Euphoria. John Kenneth Galbraith. Penguin Group, 375 Hudson St. New York, NY 10014-3657. Phone: 800-331-4624 or (212)366-2000 Fax: (212)366-2952 • URL: http://www.penguingroup.com • 1994. $13.00. An analysis of speculative euphoria and subsequent crashes, from the Holland tulip mania in 1637 to the 1987 unpleasantness in the U. S. stock market. (Whittle Series).

A Short History of the Future. W. Warren Wagar. The University of Chicago Press, 1427 E. 60th St. Chicago, IL 60637. Phone: 800-621-2736 or (773)702-7700 Fax: 800-621-8476 or (773)702-7212 E-mail: custserv@press.uchicago.edu • URL: http://www.press.uchicago.edu • 1999. $19.00. Third edition.

Short-Term Energy Outlook: Quarterly Projections. Available from U. S. Government Printing Office, Washington, DC 20402. Phone: (202)512-1800 Fax: (202)512-2250 E-mail: gpoaccess@gpo.gov • URL: http://www.access.gpo.gov • Semiannual. Issued by Energy Information Administration, U. S. Department of Energy. Contains forecasts of U. S. energy supply, demand, and prices.

Show and Sell: 133 Business Building Ways to Promote Your Trade Show Exhibit. Margit B. Weisgal. AMACOM, 1601 Broadway New York, NY 10019. Phone: 800-262-9699 or (518)586-8100 Fax: (518)903-8168 E-mail: customerservice@amanet.org • URL: http://www. amacombooks.org • 1996. $55.00. Contains information and advice on pre-show advertising and promotion, booth management, literature distribution, customer dialogue, "damage control," follow-up, evaluation, and other exhibit topics. Includes bibliography, checklists, worksheets, and index.

Show Business Law: Motion Pictures, Television, Videos. Peter Muller. Greenwood Publishing Group, Inc., 88 Post Rd., W Westport, CT 06881. Phone: 800-225-5800 or (203)226-3571 Fax: (203)431-2214 E-mail: customer-service@greenwood.com • URL: http://www.greenwood.com • 1990. $69.95.

Shutterbug. PRIMEDIA Inc., 745 Fifth Ave. New York, NY 10151. Phone: (212)745-0100 Fax: (212)745-0121 E-mail: information@primedia.com • URL: http://www.primedia.com • Monthly. $17.95 per year. Articles about new equipment, test reports on film accessories, how-to articles, etc. Annual *Buying Guide* available, $5.99.

Shuttle, Spindle, and Dyepot. Handweavers Guild of America, Inc., Two Executive Concourse, Suite 201, 3327 Duluth Hwy. Duluth, GA 30096-3301. Phone: (770)495-7702 E-mail: weavespindye@compuserve.com • URL: http://www.weavespindye.org • Quarterly. $25.00 per year.

SI: Special Issues. Trip Wyckoff, editor. Hoover's, Inc., 5800 Airport Blvd. Austin, TX 78752-3812. Phone: 800-486-8666 or (512)374-4500 Fax: (512)374-4501 E-mail: orders@hoovers.com • URL: http://www.hoovers.com • Bimonthly. $149.95 per year. Newsletter. Serves as a supplement to *Directory of Business Periodical Special Issues*. Provides current information on trade journal special issues and editorial calendars.

SIA Annual Report and Directory. Semiconductor Industry Association, 181 Metro Dr., Suite 450 San Jose, CA 95110-1344. Phone: (408)436-6600 Fax: (408)436-6646 • URL: http://www.semichips.org • Annual. Members, $105.00; nonmembers, $150.00. Provides information on key semiconductor issues. Formerly *SIA Status Report and Industry Directory*.

SIE Investment Advisory Guide. George H. Wein, editor. Select Information Exchange, 244 W 54th St., Ste. 614 New York, NY 10024. Phone: 800-743-9346 or (212)247-7123 Fax: (212)247-7326 E-mail: customerservice@stockfocus.com • URL: http://www.stockfocus.com • Annual. $2.00. Provides descriptions and prices of about 100 financial newsletters covering stocks, bonds, mutual funds, commodity futures, options, gold, and foreign investments. Offers subscription services, including short trials of any 20 investment newsletters for a total of $11.95.

Signs of the Times: The Industry Journal Since 1906. ST Media Group International, 407 Gilbert Ave. Cincinnati, OH 45202. Phone: 800-925-1110 or (513)421-2050 Fax: (513)421-5144 E-mail: customer@stmediagroup.com • URL: http://www.stmediagroup.com • 13 times a year. $36.00 per year. For designers and manufacturers of all types of signs. Features how-to-tips. Includes *Sign Erection, Maintenance Directory* and annual *Buyer's Guide*.

Silicon Snake Oil: Second Thoughts on the Information Highway. Clifford Stoll. Doubleday Publishing, 1540 Broadway New York, NY 10036-4094. Phone: 800-323-9872 or (212)354-6500 Fax: (212)492-9700 • URL: http://www.doubledaybookclub.com • 1996. $14.00. The author discusses the extravagant claims being made for online networks and multimedia.

Silver Institute., 1200 G St. NW, Ste. 800 Washington, DC 20005. Phone: (202)835-0185 Fax: (202)835-0155 E-mail: info@silverinstitute.org • URL: http://www.silverinstitute.org • Companies that mine, refine, and manufacture silver-containing products; silver bullion suppliers. Seeks to encourage the development and use of silver and silver products. Helps develop markets. Fosters research on present and prospective uses of silver. Collects and publishes statistics and other information regarding production, distribution, marketing consumption, and uses of silver and silver products.

Silver Users Association., 11240 Waples Mill Rd., No. 200 Fairfax, VA 22030. Phone: 800-245-6999 or (703)930-7790 Fax: (703)359-7562 E-mail: pmiller@mwcapitol.com • URL: http://www.silverusersassociation.org • Represents companies that make, sell and distribute products and services in which silver is an essential component. Informs members, government and the public on all the facets of the silver market in a timely manner.

Silver Wings., AFROTC Detachment 190, 229 Armory Bldg., 505 E Armory Ave. Champaign, IL 61820. Phone: (843)521-4945 Fax: (843)521-4533 E-mail: president@silver-wings.org • URL: http://www.silver-wings.org • Works as a national, co-ed, professional organization dedicated to creating proactive, knowledgeable, and effective civic leaders through community service and education about national defense. Its mission includes the following interrelated objectives: a. Personal Development b. Professional Development and c. Civic Awareness.

Silversmithing. Rupert Finegold and William Seitz. DIANE Publishing Co., 330 Pusey Ave. Collingdale, PA 19023-8428. Phone: 800-782-3833 or (610)461-6200 Fax: (610)461-6130 E-mail: dianepub@erols.com • URL: http://www.dianepublishing.com • 1997. $39.95.

Silverware, Plateware & Cutlery. Available from MarketResearch.com, 641 Ave. of the Americas, Fourth Floor New York, NY 10011. Phone: 800-298-5699 or (212)807-2629 Fax: (212)807-2642 E-mail: order@marketresearch.com • URL: http://www.marketresearch.com • 2002. $3,950.00. Published by Global Industry Analysts. Provides worldwide market research data, including profiles of major tableware companies.

The SIMBA Report on Directory Publishing. SIMBA Information, 11 Riverbend Dr., S Stamford, CT 06907. Phone: 800-307-2529 or (203)358-4100 Fax: (203)358-5824 E-mail: info@simbanet.com • URL: http://www.simbanet.com • Monthly. $359.00 per year. Newsletter.

Simulation & Gaming: An International Journal of Theory, Design and Research. Sage Publications, Inc., 2455 Teller Rd. Thousand Oaks, CA 91320. Phone: 800-818-7243 or (805)499-9774 Fax: 800-583-2665 or (805)499-0871 E-mail: webmaster@sagepub.com • URL: http://www.sagepub.com • Quarterly. Institutions, $5155.00 per year; includes print and online editions.

Singapore Business: The Portable Encyclopedia for Doing Business with Singapore. Christine Genzberger and others. World Trade Press, 1450 Grant Ave., Suite 204 Novato, CA 94945. Phone: 800-833-8586 or (415)898-1124 Fax: (415)898-1080 E-mail: sales@worldtradepress.com • URL: http://www.worldtradepress.com • 1994. $24.95. Covers economic data, import/export possibilities, basic tax and trade laws, travel information, and other useful facts for doing business with Singapore. (Country Business Guides Series).

Site Selection. Conway Data, Inc., 35 Technology Parkway, Suite 150 Norcross, GA 30092. Phone: (770)446-6996 Fax: (770)263-8825 • URL: http://www.conway.com • Bimonthly. Six volumes, $22.00 per volume. $85.00 per set. Each of the six issues per year is a separate directory: *Geo-Corporate* (facility planners), *Geo-Economic* (area development officials), *Geo-Labor* (labor force data), *Geo-Life* (quality of life information), *GeoPolitical* (government agencies), and *Geo-Sites* (industrial/office parks). Formerly *Site Selection and Industrial Development*.

6,000 Years of Housing. Norbert Schoenauer. W. W. Norton & Co., Inc., 500 Fifth Ave. New York, NY 10110. Phone: 800-223-4830 or (212)354-5500 Fax: (212)869-0856 • URL: http://www.wwnorton.com • 2000. $50.00. Revised edition. Presents the story of housing from early nomadic societies to the present.

16 Million Businesses Phone Directory. Info USA., 5711 South 86th Circle Omaha, NE 68127. Phone: 800-321-0869 or (402)593-4500 Fax: (402)331-0176 Annual. $29.95. Provides more than 16 million yellow pages telephone directory listings on CD-ROM for all ZIP Code areas of the U. S.

The Skeptical Business Searcher: The Information Advisor's Guide to Evaluating Web Data, Sites, and Sources. Robert Berkman. Information Today, Inc., 143 Old Marlton Pike Medford, NJ 08055-8750. Phone: 800-300-9868 or (609)654-6266 Fax: (609)654-4309 E-mail: custserv@infotoday.com • URL: http://www.infotoday.com • 2003. $29.95. Covers free Internet sources of company backgrounds, sales data, earnings, SEC documents, competitive intelligence information, poll data, business news, economic statistics, etc. The author is editor of *The Information Advisor* newsletter. (CyberAge Books).

Sky and Telescope: The Essential Magazine of Astronomy. Sky Publishing Co., 49 Bay State Rd. Cambridge, MA 02138. Phone: 800-253-0245 or (617)864-7360 Fax: (617)864-6117 E-mail: skytel@skypub.com • URL: http://www.skypub.com • Monthly. $39.95 per year. Reports astronomy and space science for amateurs and professionals. Many "how to" features.

SLA Annual Salary Survey. Special Libraries Association, 1700 18th St., N. W. Washington, DC 20009-2514. Phone: (202)234-4700 Fax: (202)265-9317 E-mail: sla@sla.org • URL: http://www.sla.org • Annual. Members, $45.00; nonmembers, $125.00. Provides data on salaries for special librarians in the U. S. and Canada, according to location, job title, industry, budget, and years of experience.

SLIG Buyers' Guide: Starting, Lighting, Ignition, Generating Systems. Independent Battery Manufacturers Association, 100 Larchwood Dr. Largo, FL 33770. Phone: 800-237-6126 or (727)586-1408 Fax: (727)586-1400 E-mail: thebatteryman@juno.com Biennial. $25.00 per year. Over 1,900 manufacturers and rebuilders of heavy-duty storage batteries.

Sludge Newsletter: The Newsletter on Municipal Wastewater and Biosolids. Business Publishers, Inc., 8737 Colesville Rd., Suite 1100 Silver Spring, MD 20910-3928. Phone: 800-274-6737 or (301)587-6300 Fax: (301)589-8493 E-mail: bpinews@bpinews.com • URL: http://www.bpinews.com • Biweekly. $409.00 per year. per year. Newsletter. Monitors sludge management developments in Washington and around the country.

Small Business Accounting Simplefied. Daniel Sitarz. Nova Publishing Co., 705 W Main St. Carbondale, IL 62901. Phone: 800-748-1175 or (618)457-3521 Fax: 800-338-4550 E-mail: info@novapublishing.com • URL: http://www.novapublishing.com • 2002. $22.95. Third edition. Includes basic forms and instructions for small business accounting and bookkeeping. (Small Business Library Series).

Small Business Administration. Annual Report. U.S. Government Printing Office, Washington, DC 20402. Phone: (202)512-1800 Fax: (202)512-2250 E-mail: gpoaccess@gpo.gov • URL: http://www.accessgpo.gov • Annual. Two volumes.

Small Business Development Center.

Small Business IPOs: From Concept to Closing. Robert W. Walter. CCH, Inc., 4025 West Peterson Ave. Chicago, IL 60646-6085. Phone: 800-248-3248 or (773)866-6000 Fax: 800-224-8299 or (773)866-3095 E-mail: cust_serv@cch.com • URL: http://www.onlinestore.cch.com/ • 2004. $85.00. Edited mainly for lawyers. Provides a step-by-step guide to taking a relatively small firm public. Covers use of investment bankers, valuation, letter of intent, due diligence, dealing with the SEC, and other topics. Appendices include samples of various forms, letters, and agreements.

Small Business Legal Smarts. Deborah L. Jacobs. Bloomberg, 499 Park Ave. New York, NY 10022. Phone: 800-388-2749 or (212)318-2000 Fax: (917)369-5000 • URL: http://www.bloomberg.com • 1998. $16.95. Discusses common legal problems encountered by small business owners. (Small Business Series).

Small Business Management: An Entrepreneurial Emphasis. Justin Longenecker. Cengage Learning, 10650 Toebben Dr. Independence, KY 41051. Phone: 800-347-7707 or (859)525-6620 Fax: (859)525-0978 • URL: http://gale.cengage.com • 1999. $94.95. 11th edition. (Small Business Management Series).

Small Business Management Fundamentals. John Burgess. McGraw-Hill, 1221 Ave. of the Americas New York, NY 10020. Phone: 800-722-4726 or (212)512-2000 Fax: (212)512-4502 E-mail: customer.service@mcgraw-hill.com • URL: http://www.mcgraw-hill.com • 1993. $45.93. Sixth edition.

Small Business Opportunities. Harris Publications, Inc., 1115 Broadway New York, NY 10010. Phone: (212)807-7100 Fax: (212)924-8416 • URL: http://www.sbomag.com • Bimonthly. $11.97.

Small Business Retirement Savings Advisor. U. S. Department of LaborPhone: (202)219-8921 • URL: http://www.dol.gov/elaws/pwbaplan.htm • Web site provides "answers to a variety of commonly asked questions about retirement saving options for small business employers." Includes a comparison chart and detailed descriptions of various plans: 401(k), SEP-IRA, SIMPLE-IRA, Payroll Deduction IRA, Keogh Profit-Sharing, Keogh Money Purchase, and Defined Benefit. Searching is offered. Fees: Free.

Small Business Sourcebook. Gale Cengage Learning, 27500 Drake Rd. Farmington Hills, MI 48331-3535. Phone: 800-877-GALE or (248)699-4253 Fax: 800-414-5043 E-mail: gale.galeord@cengage.com • URL: http://gale.cengage.com • 2003. $380.00. 17th edtion. Two volumes. Information sources for about 100 kinds of small businesses.

Small Business Survival Guide: How to Manage Your Cash, Profits and Taxes. Robert E. Fleury. Sourcebooks, Inc., 1935 Brookdale Rd., Ste. 139 Naperville, IL 60563. Phone: 800-432-7444 or (630)961-3900 Fax: (630)961-2168 E-mail: info@sourcebooks.com • URL: http://www.sourcebooks.com • 1995. $17.95. Third revised edition. (Small Business Series).

Small Business Tax News. Inside Mortgage Finance Publications, PO Box 42387 Washington, DC 20015. Phone: (301)951-1240 Fax: (301)656-1709 E-mail: service@imfpubs.comm • URL: http://www.imfpubs.com • Monthly. $175.00 per year. Newsletter. Formerly *Small Business Tax Control*.

The Small Business Tax Review. A/N Group Inc., 17 Scott Dr. Melville, NY 11747. Phone: (631)549-4090 Fax: (631)385-9858 E-mail: angroup@pb.net • URL: http://www.smbiz.com • Description: Reports tax news on such topics as new laws, court cases, IRS rulings, fringe benefits, and business and individual taxes, with emphasis on smaller businesses. Advises on financial planning and technical aspects of small business management.

Small Fruits Review. Haworth Press, Inc., 10 Alice St. Binghamton, NY 13904-1580. Phone: 800-429-6784 or (607)722-5857 Fax: 800-895-0582 or (607)722-1424 E-mail: getinfo@haworthpressinc.com • URL: http://www.haworthpressinc.com • Quarterly. Institutions $200.00 per year. An academic and practical journal focusing on the marketing of grapes, berries, and other small fruit. Formerly *Journal of Small Fruit and Viticulture*.

Small Law Firm Economic Survey. Altman Weil Publications, Inc., Two Campus Blvd. Newtown Square, PA 19073. Phone: 888-782-7297 or (610)886-2000 Fax: (610)359-0467 • URL: http://www.altmanweil.com • Annual. $395.00. Provides aggregate data (benchmarks) on the economics, finances, billing, and staffing of law offices in the U. S. having "less than 12 lawyers."

Small Libraries: A Handbook for Successful Management. Sally Gardner. McFarland and Co., Inc., Publishers, PO Box 611 Jefferson, NC 28640. Phone: 800-253-2187 or (336)246-4460 Fax: (336)246-5018 E-mail: info@macfarlandpub.com • URL: http://www.mcfarlandpub.com • 2002. $35.00. Second revised edition. Covers personnel (including volunteers), buildings, collections, service policies, community politics, and other topics.

Small Time Operator: How to Start Your Own Small Business, Keep Your Books, Pay Your Taxes, and Stay Out of Trouble. Bernard Kamoroff. Bell Springs Publishing, 106 State St. Willits, CA 95490. Phone: 800-515-8050 or (707)459-6372 Fax: (707)459-8614 E-mail: info@bellsprings.com • URL: http://www.bellsprings.com • 2001. $16.95. 26th edition. Concise, practical advice. Includes bookkeeping forms.

Small Towns Institute., PO Box 13530, PO Box 517 Burton, WA 98013-3530. Phone: (509)925-1830 Fax: (509)963-1753 E-mail: pmiller@mwcapitol.com Individuals and institutions interested in small town problems and potentials. Collects, assembles, and disseminates information on small town living, especially in regard to planning, revitalization, and environmental programs. Provides research data on topics such as historic preservation and arts development for small towns, innovative job resources, and improving the quality of life in community development projects.

Smart Business for the New Economy. Element K Journals, 2165 Brighton-Henrietta Townline Rd., Ste. 3 Rochester, NY 14623. Phone: 800-223-8720 or (585)240-7301 Fax: (585)292-4392 • URL: http://www.elementkjournal.com • Monthly. $12.00 per year. Provides practical advice for doing business in an economy dominated by technology and electronic commerce.

Smart Choices: A Practical Guide to Making Better Decisions. John S. Hammond and others. Harvard Business School Publishing, 300 N Beacon St. Watertown, MA 02163. Phone: 800-988-0886 or (617)783-7500 Fax: (617)783-7555 • URL: http://www.hbs.edu • 1998. $22.50. Provides a systematic approach to effective decision-making. Eight fundamentals of decision-analysis are described, involving problems, objectives, alternatives, consequences, tradeoffs, uncertainty, risks, and choices.

Smart Computing. Sandhills Publishing Co., 131 West Grand Drive Lincoln, NE 68501. Phone: 800-733-3809 or (402)479-2141 Fax: (402)479-2104 E-mail: feedback@sandhills.com • URL: http://www.smartcomputing.com • Monthly. $29.00 per year. Provides basic computer advice "in plain English." Includes reviews of hardware and software.

Smart Hiring: The Complete Guide for Recruiting Employees. Robert W. Wendover. Leadership Resources, Inc., 15200 E. Girard Ave., Suite 2300 Aurora, CO 80014-5039. 1989. $17.95.

Smart Libraries Newsletter: An Innovative Overview of Library Automation. American Library Association, 50 E. Huron St. Chicago, IL 60611-2795. Phone: 800-545-2433 or (312)944-6780 Fax: (312)440-9374 E-mail: ala@ala.org • URL: http://www.ala.org • Monthly. $144.00 per year. Articles and news briefs covering all aspects of library automation. Formerly *Library Systems Newsletter*.

Smart Money Guide to Long-Term Investing: How to Build Real Wealth for Retirement and Other Future Goals. Nellie S. Huang and Peter Finch. John Wiley and Sons, Inc., 111 River St. Hoboken, NJ 07030. Phone: 800-225-5945 or (201)748-6000 Fax: (201)748-6088 E-mail: bookinfo@wiley.com • URL: http://www.wiley.com • 2002. $24.95. The authors are associated with *Smart Money* magazine. Their book emphsizes the importance of effective asset allocation through the years and recommends specific stock and bond mutual funds for retirement, including "The Best and Worst Funds for Your 401(k)."

Smart Questions to Ask Your Financial Advisers. Lynn Brenner. Bloomberg, 499 Park Ave. New York, NY 10022. Phone: 800-388-2749 or (212)318-2000 Fax: (917)369-5000 • URL: http://www.bloomberg.com • 1997. $19.95. Provides practical advice on how to deal with financial planners, stockbrokers, insurance agents, and lawyers. Some of the areas covered are investments, estate planning, tax planning, house buying, prenuptial agreements, divorce arrangements, loss of a job, and retirement. (Bloomberg Personal Bookshelf Series).

Smart Services: Competitive Information Strategies, Solutions, and Success Stories for Service Businesses. Deborah C. Sawyer. Information Today, Inc., 143 Old Marlton Pike Medford, NJ 08055-8750. Phone: 800-300-9868 or (609)654-6266 Fax: (609)654-4309 E-mail: custserv@infotoday.com • URL: http://www.infotoday.com • 2002. $29.95. Covers the use of competitive information by service-oriented firms. (CyberAge Books.)

Smart TV and Sound: Interactive Television and DVD-MP3-Internet Audio and Video-Satellite Television. York Publishing, P.O. 4591 Chico, CA 95927. Phone: (530)891-8410 Fax: (530)891-8443 E-mail: editorial@smarttvandsound.com • URL: http://www.smarttvmag.com • Semiannual. $14.97 per year. Consumer magazine covering WebTV, PC/TV appliances, DVD players, "Smart TV," advanced VCRs, and other topics relating to interactive television, the Internet, and multimedia. Formerly *Smart TV*.

Smarter Insurance Solutions. Janet Bamford. Bloomberg, 499 Park Ave. New York, NY 10022. Phone: 800-388-2749 or (212)318-2000 Fax: (917)369-5000 • URL: http://www.bloomberg.com • 1996. $19.95. Provides practical advice to consumers, with separate chapters on the following kinds of insurance: automobile, homeowners, health, disability, and life. (Bloomberg Personal Bookshelf Series).

SmartMoney: The Wall Street Journal Magazine of Personal Business. Hearst Communications, Inc., 1755 Broadway New York, NY 10019. Phone: 800-444-4204 or (212)765-7323 Fax: (212)245-7276 E-mail: editors@smartmoney.com • URL: http://www.hearstcorp.com • Monthly. $15.00 per year. Includes *Stock Trader's Almanac*.

Smithells Metals Reference Book. William F. Gale and Terry C. Totemeier. Elsevier, 655 Ave. of the Americas New York, NY 10010-5107. Phone: 800-366-2665 or (212)989-5800 Fax: 800-535-9935 or (212)633-3680 E-mail: custserv@elsevier.com • URL: http://www.elsevier.com • 2003. $195.00. Eighth edition.

Smokeshop., 26 Broadway, Fl. 9M New York, NY 10004. Phone: (212)391-2060 Fax: (212)827-0945 E-mail: circulation@lockwoodpublications.com • URL: http://www.lockwoodpublications.com • Bimonthly. $32.00 per year.

Smoking and Politics: Policy Making and the Federal Bureaucracy. A. Lee Fritschler and James M. Hoepler. Prentice Hall PTR, 240 Frisch Ct. Paramus, NJ 07652. Phone: 800-282-0693 Fax: 800-445-6991 • URL: http://www.phptr.com • 1995. $44.00. Fifth edition.

Smoking: The Health Consequences of Tobacco Use. Richard A. Gray and Cecilia M. Schmitz. Pierian Press, PO Box 1808 Ann Arbor, MI 48106-1808. Phone: 800-678-2435 or (734)434-5530 Fax: (734)434-6409 E-mail: pubinfo@pierianpress.com • URL: http://www.pierianpress.com • 1995. $30.00. (Science and Social Responsibility Series: No. 2).

SMPTE Motion Imaging Journal. Society of Motion Picture and Television Engineers, 595 W. Hartsdale Ave. White Plains, NY 10607-1824. Phone: (914)761-1100 Fax: (914)761-3115 E-mail: smpte@smpte.org • URL: http://www.smpte.org • Monthly. Membership. Formerly *SMPTE Journal*.

Snack Food and Wholesale Baker's Buyer's Guide. Stagnito Publishing Co., 155 Pfingsten Rd., Ste. 205 Deerfield, IL 60015. Phone: (847)205-5660 Fax: (847)205-5680 E-mail: info@stagnito.com • URL: http://www.stagnito.com • Annual. $55.00. Lists approximately 900 companies that provide supplies and services to the snack food industry. Formerly *Snack Food Buyer's Guide*.

Snack Food and Wholesale Bakery: The Magazine That Defines the Snack Food Industry. Stagnito Publishing Co., 155 Pfingsten Rd., Ste. 205 Deerfield, IL 60015. Phone: (847)205-5660 Fax: (847)205-5680 E-mail: info@stagnito.com • URL: http://www.stagnito.com • Monthly. Free to qualified personnel; others, $85.06 per year. Provides news and information for producers of pretzels, potato chips, cookies, crackers, nuts, and other snack foods. Includes *Annual Buyers Guide* and *State of Industry Report*.

Snack Food Association., 1600 Wilson Blvd., Ste. 650 Arlington, VA 22209. Phone: 800-628-1334 or (703)836-4500 Fax: (703)836-8262 E-mail: sfa@sfa.org • URL: http://www.sfa.org • Manufacturers of potato chips, pretzels, corn chips, tortilla chips, popcorn, cheese snacks, pork rinds, cookies, crackers, nuts, meat snacks, fruit snacks, and grain-based snacks; associate members are suppliers and distributors of fats and oils, packaging supplies, machinery, seasonings, and potato and corn growers.

Snips. Business News Publishing Co., 755 W Big Beaver Rd., Ste. 1000 Troy, MI 48084. Phone: 800-837-7370 or (248)362-3700 Fax: (248)362-0317 • URL: http://www.bnp.com • Monthly. $18.00 per year. Provides information for heating, air conditioning, sheet metal and ventilating contractors, wholesalers, manufacturers representatives and manufacturers.

Soap and Cosmetics. Cygnus Business Media, 445 Broad Hollow Rd. Melville, NY 11747-3601. Phone: 800-308-6397 or (631)845-2700 Fax: (631)845-2798 E-mail: rich.reiff@cygnuspub.com • URL: http://www.cygnusbzb.com • Monthly. $60.00 per year. Formerly *Soap, Cosmetics, Chemical Specialities*.

The Soap and Detergent Association., 1500 K St., NW, Ste. 300 Washington, DC 20005. Phone: (202)347-2900 Fax: (202)347-4110 E-mail: info@cleaning101.com • URL: http://www.cleaning101.com • Represents over 100 North American manufacturers of household, industrial and institutional cleaning projucts, their ingredients and finished packaging. Formerly Glycerine and Oleochemicals Association.

Soap/Cosmetics/Blue Book. Cygnus Business Media, Inc., 445 Broad Hollow Rd. Melville, NY 11747. Phone: 800-547-7377 or (631)845-2700 Fax: (631)845-2798 E-mail: rich.reiff@cygnuspub.com • URL: http://www.cygnusbzb.com • Annual. $15.00. Sources of raw materials, equipment and services for the soap, cosmetic and chemical specialities. Formerly*Blue Book of the Soap, Detergent, Cosmetic, and Chemical Specialty Industries*.

Sober for Good: New Solutions for Drinking Problems - Advice from Those Who Have Succeeded. Anne M. Fletcher. Houghton Mifflin Co., 222 Berkeley St. Boston, MA 02116. Phone: 800-733-2828 or (617)351-5000 Fax: 800-733-2098 E-mail: inquiries@hmco.com • URL: http://www.hmco.com • 2001. $25.00. Describes the various methods that problem drinkers have used to attain sobriety.

Social Democrats, U.S.A., 815 15th St. NW, Ste. 921 Washington, DC 20005. Phone: (202)638-1515 Fax: (202)457-0029 E-mail: info@socialdemocrats.org • URL: http://www.socialdemocrats.org • Serves as political action and education organization of young people, students, and trade unionists. Supports Independent and Democratic liberal-labor candidates for public office. Seeks realignment of the major political parties in the U.S. Maintains speakers' bureau. Supports "greater democratic decision-making over the social forces that control our everyday economic lives." Recommends democratic economic planning to ease pains of the economic crisis and to allocate resources in the public interest. Favors public aid to education and increased public investment in such areas as national health care, mass transit, low-cost housing, and new sources of energy. Supports trade unionism. Believes in foreign policy that supports democratic movements and governments.

Social Sciences Citation Index. ISI, 3501 Market St. Philadelphia, PA 19104. Phone: 800-336-4474 or (215)386-0100 Fax: (215)386-2911 E-mail: custserv@isinet.com • URL: http://www.isinet.com • Monthly. Price on request. Provides CD-ROM indexing of articles appearing in 1700 leading social science journals worldwide, with additional selections from more than 5700 other journals. Time span is 1992 to date. Coverage includes economics, business, finance, management, communications, demographics, library and information science, political science, sociology, and many other subjects.

Social Sciences Citation Index. Thomson/ISI, 3501 Market St. Philadelphia, PA 19104. Phone: 888-216-4101 or (215)386-0100 Fax: (215)387-1125 • URL: http://www.isinet.com • Three times a year. $6,900 per year. Annual cumulation. Includes *Source Index*, *Citation Index*, *Permuterm Subject Index*, and *Corporate Index*.

Social Sciences Citation Index: Compact Disc Edition with Abstracts. Institute for Scientific Information, 3501 Market St. Philadelphia, PA 19104. Phone: 800-336-4474 or (215)386-0100 Fax: (215)386-6362 Monthly. Provides CD-ROM indexing and abstracting of "significant articles" from 1,700 social science journals worldwide, with additional selections from 3,200 other journals, 1986 to date. Includes economics, business, finance, management, communications, demographics, information and library science, political science, sociology, and many other subjects.

Social Sciences Index. H. W. Wilson Co., 950 University Ave. Bronx, NY 10452. Phone: 800-367-6770 or (718)588-8400 Fax: 800-590-1617 or (718)590-1617 E-mail: custserv@hwwilson.com • URL: http://www.hwwilson.com • Quarterly, with annual cumulation. Price varies. Indexes more than 400 periodicals covering economics, environmental policy, government, insurance, labor, health care policy, plannning, public administration, public welfare, urban studies, women's issues, criminology, and related topics.

Social Scisearch. Institute for Scientific Information, 3501 Market Street Philadelphia, PA 19104. Phone: 800-336-4474 or (215)386-0100 Fax: (215)386-2911 • URL: http://www.isinet.com • Broad, multidisciplinary index to the literature of the social sciences, 1972 to present. Weekly updates. Worldwide coverage. Inquire as to online cost and availability.

Social Security Benefits, Including Medicare. CCH, Inc., 2700 Lake Cook Rd. Riverwoods, IL 60015. Phone: 800-835-5224 or (847)267-7000 E-mail: cust_serv@cch.com • URL: http://www.cch.com • Annual. $11.00.

Social Security Bulletin. Social Security Administration. Available from U.S. Government Printing Office, Washington, DC 20402. Phone: (202)512-1800 Fax: (202)512-2250 E-mail: gpoaccess@gpo.gov • URL: http://www.access.gpo.gov • Quarterly. $27.00 per year. Annual statistical supplement.

Social Security Claims and Procedures. Harvey L. McCormick. West Group, 610 Opperman Dr. Eagan, MN 55123. Phone: 800-338-9424 or (651)687-7000 Fax: 800-340-9378 E-mail: bookstore@westgroup.com • URL: http://www.westgroup.com • 1991. Two volumes. Fourth edition. Price on application.

Social Security Explained. CCH, Inc., 2700 Lake Cook Rd. Riverwoods, IL 60015. Phone: 800-835-5224 or (847)267-7000 E-mail: cust_serv@cch.com • URL: http://www.cch.com • Annual. $37.00.

Social Security Handbook. Available from U. S. Government Printing Office, Washington, DC 20402. Phone: (202)512-1800 Fax: (202)512-2250 E-mail: gpoaccess@gpo.gov • URL: http://www.access.gpo.gov • Annual. $53.00. Issued by the Social Security Administration (http://www.ssa.gov). Provides detailed information about social security programs, including Medicare, with brief descriptions of related programs administered by agencies other than the Social Security Administration.

Social Security Manual. The National Underwriter Co., 5801 Olympic Blvd. Erlanger, KY 41017. Phone: 800-543-0874 or (859)692-2100 • URL: http://www.nationalunderwriter.com • Annual. $22.95.

Social Security, Medicare, and Government Pensions: Get the Most Out of Your Retirement and Medical Benefits. Joseph Matthews and Dorothy M. Berman. Nolo, 950 Parker St. Berkeley, CA 94710. Phone: 800-728-3555 or (510)549-1976 Fax: 800-645-0895 or (510)548-5902 E-mail: simone@nolo.com • URL: http://www.nolo.com • 2002. $29.99. Eighth edition. In addition to the basic topics, includes practical information on Supplemental Security Income (SSI), disability benefits, veterans benefits, 401(k) plans, Medicare HMOs, medigap insurance, Medicaid, and how to appeal decisions. (Social Security, Medicare and Pensions Series).

Social Security Online: The Official Web Site of the Social Security Administration. U. S. Social Security AdministrationPhone: 800-772-1213 or (410)965-7700 • URL: http://www.ssa.gov • Web site provides a wide variety of online information relating to social security and Medicare. Topics include benefits, disability, employer wage reporting, personal earnings statements, statistics, government financing, social security law, and public welfare reform legislation.

Social Security Practice Guide. LexisNexis Matthew Bender, 1275 Broadway Albany, NY 12204. Phone: 800-424-4200 or (518)487-3000 Fax: (518)487-3584 E-mail: bookstore.support@lexisnexis.com • URL: http://www.bender.com • Irregular. $1,027.00. Four looseleaf volumes. Periodic supplementation. Complete, practical guide on all substantive and procedural aspects of social security practice. Prepared under the supervision of the National Organization of Social

Security Claimants' Representatives (NOSSCR).
Social Security Programs Throughout the World. Available from U. S. Government Printing Office, Washington, DC 20402. Phone: (202)512-1800 Fax: (202)512-2250 E-mail: gpoaccess@gpo.gov • URL: http://www.access.gpo.gov • Annual. Issued by the Social Security Administration (http://www.ssa.gov). Presents basic information on more than 170 social security systems around the world.
Social Statistics of the United States. Mark S. Littman, editor. Bernan Press, 4611-F Assembly Dr. Lanham, MD 20706-4391. Phone: 800-274-4447 or (301)459-2255 Fax: 800-865-3450 or (301)459-9235 E-mail: bpress@bernan.com • URL: http://www.bernan.com • 2000. $65.00. Includes statistical data on population growth, labor force, occupations, environmental trends, leisure time use, income, poverty, taxes, and other economic or demographic topics.
Social Trends and Indicators USA. Monique D. Magee, editor. Gale Cengage Learning, 27500 Drake Rd. Farmington Hills, MI 48331-3535. Phone: 800-877-GALE or (248)699-4253 Fax: 800-414-5043 E-mail: gale.galeord@cengage.com • URL: http://gale.cengage.com • 2003. $450.00. Four volumes. Includes data on labor, economics, the health care industry, crime, leisure, population, education, social security, and many other topics. Sources include various government agencies and major publications.
Social Welfare Research Institute. Boston College
Society for Advancement of Management., Texas A&M University-Corpus Christi, College of Business, 6300 Ocean Dr. Corpus Christi, TX 78412. Phone: 888-827-6077 or (361)825-6045 or (361)825-5574 Fax: (361)825-2725 E-mail: moustafa@falcon.tamucc.edu • URL: http://www.enterprise.tamucc.edu/sam/ • Professional organization of management executives in industry, commerce, government and education. Absorbed Industrial Methods Society.
Society for Computer Simulation International., PO Box 17900 San Diego, CA 92177-1810. Phone: (858)277-3888 Fax: (858)277-3930 E-mail: info@scs.org • URL: http://www.scs.org • Formerly Society for Computer Simulation.
Society for Economic Botany., PO Box 7075 Lawrence, KS 66044. Phone: 800-627-0629 or (785)843-1235 Fax: (785)843-1274 E-mail: info@econbot.org • URL: http://www.econbot.org • Botanists, anthropologist, pharmacologists and others interested in scientific studies of useful plants. Affiliated with American Association for the Advancement of Science and the Botanical Society of America.
Society for Foodservice Management.
Society for Health Strategy and Market Development-Directory of Membership and Services. Society for Healthcare Strategy and Market Development. American Hospital Association, One N. Franklin St., 31st Fl. Chicago, IL 60606. Phone: 800-242-2626 or (312)422-3888 Fax: (312)422-4579 E-mail: stratsoc@aha.org • URL: http://www.stratsociety.org • Annual. Membership.
Society for Historians of American Foreign Relations Newsletter. Society for Historians of American Foreign Relations, c/o Tennessee Technological University, Dept. of History Cookeville, TN 38505. Phone: (931)372-3332 Fax: (931)372-6142 Quarterly. $15.00 per year.
Society for Human Resource Management., 1800 Duke St. Alexandria, VA 22314. Phone: 800-283-7476 or (703)548-3440 Fax: (703)535-6490 • URL: http://www.shrm.org • Affiliated with Human Resource Certification Institute; Media Human Resources Association and SHRM Global Forum. Formerly American Society for Personnel Administration.
Society for Imaging Science and Technology., 7003 Kilworth Lane Springfield, VA 22151. Phone: (703)642-9090 Fax: (703)642-9094 E-mail: info@imaging.org • URL: http://www.imaging.org • Individuals apply photography and imaging to science, engineering and industry. Formerly Society of Photographic Scientists and Engineering.
Society for Industrial and Applied Mathematics.
Society for Information Management., 401 N. Michigan Ave. Chicago, IL 60621-4267. Phone: 800-387-9746 or (312)527-6734 or (312)644-6610 Fax: (312)245-1081 E-mail: info@simnet.org • URL: http://www.simnet.org • Formerly Society for Management Information Systems.
Society for International Development USA.
Society for International Numismatics.
Society for Mining, Metallurgy, and Exploration., 8307 Shaeffer Pky. Littleton, CO 80127. Phone: 800-763-3132 or (303)973-9550 or (303)948-4210 Fax: (303)973-3845 E-mail: sme@smenet.org • URL: http://www.smenet.org • Affiliated with American Institute of Mining and the Mettallurgical and Petroleum Engineers. Formerly Society of Mining Engineers.
Society for Nonprofit Organizations., 5820 Canton Rd., No. 165 Canton, MI 48187. Phone: 800-424-7367 or (734)451-3582 Fax: (734)451-5935 E-mail: info@snpo.org • URL: http://www.snpo.org • The society is dedicated to bringing together those who serve in the nonprofit world in order to build a strong network of professionals throughout the country.
Society for Range Management., 445 Union Blvd., Ste. 230 Lakewood, CO 80228-1259. Phone: (303)986-3309 Fax: (303)986-3892 E-mail: srmweb@rangelands.org • URL: http://www.rangelands.org • Formerly American Society of Range Management.
Society for Technical Communication., 901 N. Stuart St., Suite 904 Arlington, VA 22203-1822. Phone: (703)522-4114 Fax: (703)522-2075 E-mail: stc@stc.org • URL: http://www.stc.org • Formerly Society of Technical Writers and Publishers.
Society for the Advancement of Material and Process Engineering., 1161 Parkview Dr. Covina, CA 91722-3748. Phone: 800-562-7360 or (626)331-0616 Fax: (626)332-8929 E-mail: sampeibo@sampe.org • URL: http://www.sampe.org • Formerly Society of Aerospace Material and Process Engineers.
Society for the Eradication of Television., PO Box 10491 Oakland, CA 94610-0491. Phone: (510)763-8712 E-mail: set.info@webwm.com • URL: http://www.webwm.com/set • Encourages the removal of television sets from homes.
Society for the History of Technology.
Society of Actuaries.
Society of Actuaries Yearbook. Society of Actuaries, 475 N. Martingale Rd., Suite 800 Schaumburg, IL 60173-2226. Phone: (847)706-3500 Fax: (847)706-3599 E-mail: bhaynes@soa.org • URL: http://www.soa.org • Annual. Price on application. Includes alphabetical list of actuaries.
Society of Air Force Physicians., PO Box 64, R Bolling Air Force Base, R 110 Luke Ave., Ste. 405 Devine, TX 78016-0064. Phone: (830)665-4048 Fax: (830)665-9658 E-mail: safp2002@aol.com • URL: http://www.acponline.org/about_acp/chapters/usaf/officers.htm • Air Force internists, family practitioners, and specialists in emergency medicine, dermatology, allergy/immunology, and neurology. Seeks to foster advancement of the art and science of medicine in the Air Force; encourage clinical and laboratory investigation; disseminate information.
Society of American Business Editors and Writers, Inc., c/o University of Missouri,, School of Journalism, 134 Neff Annex Columbia, MO 65211-1200. Phone: (573)882-7862 or (573)882-8985 Fax: (573)884-1372 E-mail: sabew@missouri.edu • URL: http://www.sabew.org • Affiliated with Association for Education in Journalism and Mass Communication. Formerly Society of American Business and Economic Writers.
Society of American Florists., 1601 Duke St. Alexandria, VA 22314-3406. Phone: 800-336-4743 or (703)836-8700 Fax: (703)836-8705 E-mail: memberinfo@safnow.org • URL: http://www.safnow.org • Members are growers, wholesalers, retailers and allied tradesmen in the floral industry. Formerly SAF-The Center for Commercial Floriculture.
Society of American Graphic Artists., 32 Union Square, Room 1214 New York, NY 10003. Phone: (212)260-5706 • URL: http://www.clt.astate.edu • Formerly Society of American Erchers, Engravers, Lithographers and Woodcutters.
Society of American Registered Architects.
Society of Broadcast Engineers., 9247 N Meridian St., Ste. 305 Indianapolis, IN 46260. Phone: (317)846-9000 Fax: (317)846-9120 E-mail: jporay@sbe.org • URL: http://www.sbe.org • Broadcast engineers, students and broadcast professionals in closely allied fields. Formerly Institute of Braodcast Engineers.
Society of Cable Telecommunications Engineers., 140 Philips Rd. Exton, PA 19341-1318. Phone: 800-542-5040 or (610)363-6888 Fax: (610)363-5898 E-mail: info@scte.org • URL: http://www.scte.org • Formerly Society of Cable Television Engineers.
Society of Certified Credit Executives.
Society of Commercial Seed Technologists., 101 E State St., No. 214, c/o Anita Hall Ithaca, NY 14850. Phone: (607)256-3313 Fax: (607)256-3313 E-mail: scst@twcny.rr.com • URL: http://www.seedtechnology.net • Affiliated with Association of Official Seed Analysts.
Society of Competitive Intelligence Professionals., 1700 Diagonal Rd., Suite 600 Alexandria, VA 22314. Phone: (703)739-0696 Fax: (703)739-2524 E-mail: info@scip.org • URL: http://www.scip.org • Members are professionals involved in competitor intelligence and analysis. Formerly Society of Competitor Intelligence Professionals.
Society of Consumer Affairs Professionals in Business., 675 Washington St., Ste. 200 Alexandria, VA 22314. Phone: (703)519-3700 Fax: (703)549-4886 E-mail: socap@socap.org • URL: http://www.socap.org • Members are managers of consumer affairs departments of business firms.
Society of Corporate Meeting Professionals., 217 Ridgemount Ave. San Antonio, TX 78209. Phone: (210)822-6522 Fax: (210)822-9838 E-mail: info@scmp.org • URL: http://www.scmp.org • Members are company and corporate meeting planners. Formerly Society of Company Meeting Planners.
Society of Cosmetic Chemists., 120 Wall St., Suite 2400 New York, NY 10005. Phone: (212)668-1500 Fax: (212)668-1504 E-mail: scc@scconline.org • URL: http://www.scconline.org • Affiliated with International Federation of Societies o Cosmetic Chemists.
Society of Cost Estimating and Analysis., 101 S Whiting St., Ste. 201 Alexandria, VA 22304. Phone: (703)751-3013 Fax: (703)461-7328 E-mail: scea@sceaonline.net • URL: http://www.sceaonline.net • Members are engaged in government contract estimating and pricing.
Society of Craft Designers.
Society of Economic Geologists.
Society of Experimental Test Pilots.
Society of Financial Service Professionals.
Society of Fire Protection Engineers.
Society of Government Meeting Professionals., 908 King St. Alexandria, VA 22314. Phone: 800-827-8916 or (703)549-8916 Fax: (703)549-0708 E-mail: membership@sgmp.org • URL: http://www.sgmp.org • Members are individuals involved in the planning of government meetings. Formerly Society of Government Meeting Professionals.
Society of Illustrators., 128 E 63rd St. New York, NY 10021-7303. Phone: (212)838-2560 Fax: (212)838-2561 E-mail: sil901@aol.com • URL: http://www.societyillustrators.org • Professional society of illustrators and art directors.
Society of Incentive and Travel Executives., 401 N Michigan Ave. Chicago, IL 60611. Phone: (312)321-5148 Fax: (312)527-6783 • URL: http://www.site-intl.org • Members include both users and suppliers of incentive travel. Formerly Society of Incentive Travel Executives.
Society of Independent Gasoline Marketers of America., 11911 Freedom Dr., Ste. 590 Reston, VA 20190. Phone: (703)709-7000 Fax: (703)709-7007 E-mail: sigma@sigma.org • URL: http://www.sigma.org • Chain gasoline marketers, wholesale and retail.
Society of Indexers.
Society of Industrial and Office Realtors.
Society of Leather Technologists and Chemists Journal. Society of Leather Technologies and Chemists, Grooms Cottage Bosherston SA71 5DN, United Kingdom. Phone: 44 1604 639306 Fax: 44 1604 635932 E-mail: office@sltc.org • URL: http://www.sltc.org • Bimonthly. $75.00 per year. Scientific, technical, historical and commercial papers on leather and allied industries.
Society of Manufacturing Engineers.
Society of Medical Consultants to the Armed Forces., 5 Southern Way Fredericksburg, VA 22406. Phone: (540)548-2019 Fax: (540)361-2589 E-mail: margo@smcaf.org • URL: http://www.smcaf.org • Professional society of physicians and surgeons who have been in active military service and who have acted as consultants to the Surgeons General of the Army, Navy, or Air Force. Preserves and encourages the association of civilian consultants and military medical personnel and assists in the development and maintenance of the highest standards of medical practice in the Armed Forces.
Society of Medical-Dental Management Consultants.
Society of Medical-Dental Management Consultants: Membership Directory. Society of Medical-Dental Management Consultants, 3646 E. Ray Rd., B16-45 Phoenix, AZ 85044. Phone: 800-826-2264 Fax: (602)759-3530 E-mail: chuck@smdmc.org • URL: http://www.smdmc.org • Annual. Free. About 100 consultants in business and financial aspects of the management of medical and dental practices.
Society of Military Orthopaedic Surgeons., 8610 N New Braunfels Ave., Ste. 705 San Antonio, TX 78217. Phone: 888-329-1239 or (210)829-1239 Fax: (210)829-5513 E-mail: j.bennett@trueresearch.org • URL: http://www.trueresearch.org/somos • Orthopedic surgeons who have served in the active or reserve military. Seeks to stimulate scholarly contribution by military medical residents; act as clearinghouse; provides opportunities for consultation with and contributions of surgeons who are retired from the military; furthers the continuing education of orthopedic surgeons and residents. Presents scientific papers at annual meeting.
Society of Military Otolaryngologists - Head and Neck Surgeons., 9231 Shadow Lawn Cir. Converse, TX 78109. Phone: (210)945-9006 Fax: (210)945-9024 E-mail: spearce@worldnet.att.net Otolaryngologists, head and neck surgeons and residents in training of the U.S. Army, Air Force, Navy, and former active duty members. Purposes are to further the social and professional contacts of military otolaryngologists and to advance the science and art of the field.
Society of Motion Picture and Television Engineers., 595 W Hartsdale Ave. White Plains, NY 10607. Phone: (914)761-1100 Fax: (914)761-3115 E-mail: smpte@smpte.org • URL: http://www.smpte.org • Professional engineers and technicians in motion poctures, television, motion imaging and allied arts and sciences.
Society of Naval Architects and Marine Engineers.
Society of Paper Money Collectors.
Society of Petroleum Engineers., 222 Palisades Creek Dr. Richardson, TX 75080. Phone: 800-456-6863 or (972)952-9393 Fax: (972)952-9435 E-mail: spedal@spe.org • URL: http://www.spe.org • Formerly Petroleum Branch of AIME.
Society of Plastics Engineers.
Society of Professional Investigators.
Society of Professional Journalists., 3909 N. Meridian St. Indianapolis, IN 46208-4011. Phone: (317)927-8000 Fax: (317)920-4789 E-mail: questions@spj.org • URL: http://www.spj.org • Affiliated with Sigma Delta Chi Foundation. Absorbed Economics News Broadcaster Association.
Society of Publication Designers., 60 E. 42nd St., Suite 721 New York, NY 10165. Phone: (212)983-8585 Fax: (212)983-6043 E-mail: spdnyc@aol.com • URL: http://www.spd.org • Supersedes Society of Publication Designers.
Society of Recreation Executives., PO Box 520 Gonzalez, FL 35260-0520. Phone: 800-281-9186 or (850)937-8354 Fax: (850)937-8356 E-mail: rltresource@spydee.net Members are corporate executives employed in the recreation, leisure and travel industries.
Society of Research Administrators International., 1901 N Moore St., Ste. 1004 Arlington, VA 22209. Phone: (703)741-0140 Fax: (703)741-0142 E-mail: info@srainternational.org • URL: http://www.srainternational.org • Dedicated to advancing the profession and improving the efficiency and effectiveness of research administration.
Society of the Fifth Division., PO Box 1422 Bridgeview, IL 60455. Phone: (708)839-0608 E-mail: wiskey_sour@

hotmail.com • URL: http://www.societyofthefifthdivision.com • Works to perpetuate and memorialize the valiant acts and patriotic deeds of the Fifth Division.

Society of the Plastics Industry.

Society of the 3rd Infantry Division., 1515 Ramblewood Dr. Hanover Park, IL 60133-2230. Phone: (302)239-1525 E-mail: roster3id@warfoto.com • URL: http://www.warfoto.com/3rdiv.htm • Past and present members of the 3rd Infantry Division of the U.S. Army and attached and supporting units; families of veterans of the division. Fosters and strengthens associations and friendships formed during service with the Third Infantry Division. Honors the Third Infantry Division War Dead and perpetuates their memory. Encourages and achieves the mutual benefit and support resulting from a close and cooperative alliance between the Society and the Third Infantry Division, U.S. Army. Supports the government of the United States. Assists in the maintenance of monuments dedicated to the Third Infantry Division. Organizes and conducts wreath laying and memorial ceremonies.

Society of Tribologists and Lubrication Engineers., 840 Busse Hwy. Park Ridge, IL 60068-2376. Phone: (847)825-5536 Fax: (847)825-1456 E-mail: information@sstle.org • URL: http://www.stle.org • Formerly American Society of Lubrication Engineers.

Society of Vacuum Coaters.

Society of Wine Educators.

Society of Women Engineers., 230 E Ohio St., Ste. 400 Chicago, IL 60611-3265. Phone: (312)596-5223 Fax: (312)596-5252 E-mail: hq@swe.org • URL: http://www.swe.org • Educational and service organization representing both students and professional women in engineering and technical fields. Affiliated with American Association of Engineering Societies.

Sociological Abstracts. Cambridge Information Group, 7200 Wisconsin Ave., Suite 601 Bethesda, MD 20814. Phone: 800-843-7751 or (301)961-6700 Fax: (301)961-6720 E-mail: service@csa.com • URL: http://www.csa.com • Bimonthly. $720.00 per year; with cumulative index, $860.00 per year. Includes print and online editions. A compendium of non-evaluative abstracts covering the field of sociology and related disciplines.

Sock Shop. Entrepreneur Media, Inc., 2445 McCabe Way Irvine, CA 92614. Phone: 800-421-2300 or (949)261-2325 Fax: (949)261-0234 E-mail: entmag@entrepreneur.com • URL: http://www.entrepreneur.com • Looseleaf. $59.50. A practical guide to starting a store that sells stockings of various kinds. Covers profit potential, start-up costs, market size evaluation, owner's time required, site selection, lease negotiation, pricing, accounting, advertising, etc. (Start-Up Business Guide No. E1340.)

Soft Drink Letter. Whitaker Newsletters Inc., 313 South Ave., Ste. 202, PO Box 192 Fanwood, NJ 07023-0192. Phone: 800-359-6049 or (908)889-6336 Fax: (908)889-6339 E-mail: angroup@pb.net Description: Covers news pertaining to the beverage industry with emphasis on soft drinks, mixers, and bottled water. Includes reports on new products and federal/state regulations, interviews with leading industry executives, marketing trends, and advertising and marketing research.

Soft Drinks (Excluding Juices). Available from MarketResearch.com, 641 Ave. of the Americas, Fourth Floor New York, NY 10011. Phone: 800-298-5699 or (212)807-2629 Fax: (212)807-2642 E-mail: order@marketresearch.com • URL: http://www.marketresearch.com • 2002. $3,950.00. Published by Global Industry Analysts. Provides worldwide market research data, including profiles of major soft drink companies.

Soft-Letter: Trends and Strategies in Software Publishing. UCG Technologies, 11300 Rockville Pike, Ste. 1100 Rockville, MD 20852-3030. Phone: (301)287-2718 Fax: (301)924-3944 E-mail: jtarter@softletter.com • URL: http://www.softletter.com • Semimonthly. $395.00 per year. Newsletter on the software industry, including new technology and financial aspects.

SoftBase: Reviews, Companies, and Products. Information Sources, Inc., Post Office Box 8120 Berkeley, CA 94707. Phone: (510)525-6220 Fax: (510)525-1568 Describes and reviews business software packages. Inquire as to online cost and availability.

Software and Information Industry Association., 1090 Vermont Ave. NW, 6th Fl. Washington, DC 20005. Phone: (202)289-7442 Fax: (202)289-7097 • URL: http://www.siia.net • A trade association for the software and digital content industry. Affiliated with Massachusetts Software and Internet Council.

Software Development. CMP Media LLC, 600 Harrison St. San Francisco, CA 94107. Phone: (415)947-6161 Fax: (415)947-6070 • URL: http://www.sdmagazine.com • Monthly. $39.00 per year. Edited for professional software developers and managers.

Software Digest: The Independent Comparative Ratings Report for PC and LAN Software. NSTL, 670 Sentry Pky, 2nd Fl. Blue Bell, PA 19422. Phone: 800-257-2402 or (610)832-8400 Fax: (610)941-9952 • URL: http://www.nstl.com • 12 times a year. $450.00 per year. Critical evaluations of personal computer software.

Software Economics Letter: Maximizing Your Return on Corporate Software. Computer Economics, Inc., 5841 Edison Place Carlsbad, CA 92008-6519. Phone: 800-326-8100 or (760)438-8100 Fax: (760)431-1126 E-mail: access@compecon.com • URL: http://www.computereconomics.com • Monthly. $395.00 per year. Newsletter for information systems managers. Contains data on business software trends, vendor licensing policies, and other corporate software management issues.

The Software Encyclopedia: A Guide for Personal, Professional, and Business Users. Gale, 27500 Drake Rd. Farmington Hills, MI 48331. Phone: 800-877-GALE or (248)699-GALE Fax: 800-414-5043 or (248)699-8035 E-mail: gale.galeord@cengage.com • URL: http://gale.cengage.com • Annual. $335.00. Two volumes. Volume one lists software programs by title and producer. Volume two provides information on programs according to application and operating system. Includes prices and requirements for hardware and memory.

Software Engineering. Ian Sommerville. Addison-Wesley, 75 Arlington St., Ste. 300 Boston, MA 02116. Phone: 800-447-2226 or (617)848-7500 • URL: http://www.aw.com • 2000. $98.00. Sixth edition. (International Computer Science Series).

Software for Indexing. Sandi Schroeder, editor. Information Today, Inc., 143 Old Marlton Pike Medford, NJ 08055-8750. Phone: 800-300-9868 or (609)654-6266 Fax: (609)654-4309 E-mail: custserv@infotoday.com • URL: http://www.infotoday.com • 2003. $35.00. Published in conjunction with the American Society of Indexers (ASI). Material by professional indexers covers dedicated indexing programs, embedded software, online indexing, Web indexing, database software, customized software, automatic indexing, and other indexing software topics.

Software Magazine. Wiesner Publishing, Inc., 7009 S. Potomac St., Suite 200 Englewood, CA 80112. Phone: 800-669-5613 or (303)397-7600 Fax: (303)397-7619 • URL: http://www.softwaremaqazine.com • Monthly. Free to qualified personnel; others, $42.00 per year.

Software Store. Entrepreneur Media, Inc., 2445 McCabe Way Irvine, CA 92614. Phone: 800-421-2300 or (949)261-2325 Fax: (949)261-0234 E-mail: entmag@entrepreneur.com • URL: http://www.entrepreneur.com • Looseleaf. $59.50. A practical guide to opening a computer software retail establishment. Covers profit potential, start-up costs, market size evaluation, owner's time required, site selection, lease negotiation, pricing, accounting, advertising, promotion, etc. (Start-Up Business Guide No. E1261.)

SOHO Journal (Small Office Home Office). National Association for the Cottage Industry, P.O. Box 14850 Chicago, IL 60614. Phone: (312)472-8116 Members, $25.00 per year; libraries, $35.00 per year. Newsletter on business in thehome. Formerly *Mind Your Own Business at Home.*

Soil and Plant Tissue Testing Laboratory. University of Massachusetts at Amherst

Soil Science: An Interdisciplinary Approach to Soils Research. Lippincott Williams and Wilkins, 530 Walnut St. Philadelphia, PA 19106-3621. Phone: 800-527-5597 or (410)528-4000 Fax: (215)521-8902 E-mail: custserv@lww.com • URL: http://www.lww.com • Monthly. Individuals, $182.00 per year; institutions, $336.00 per year.

Solar Energy. Available from U. S. Government Printing Office, Washington, DC 20402. Phone: (202)512-1800 Fax: (202)512-2250 E-mail: gpoaccess@gpo.gov • URL: http://www.access.gpo.gov • Annual. Free. Lists government publications. GPO Subject Bibliography Number 9.

Solar Energy and Energy Conversion Laboratory.

Solar Energy Center.

Solar Energy Industries Association., 805 15th St. NW, Ste. 510 Washington, DC 20005. Phone: (202)682-0556 Fax: (202)682-0559 E-mail: info@seia.org • URL: http://www.seia.org • Manufacturers, installers, distributors, contractors, and engineers of solar energy systems and components. Aims to accelerate and foster commercialization of solar energy conversion for economic purposes. Maintains Solar +Energy +Research and +Education Foundation. Compiles statistics; offers computerized services.

Solar Energy: International Journal for Scientists, Engineers and Technologists Energy and Its Application. International Solar Energy Society. Elsevier, 360 Park Ave., S. New York, NY 10010-1710. Phone: 888-437-4636 or (212)989-5800 Fax: (212)633-3990 E-mail: usinfo-f@elsevier.com • URL: http://www.elsevier.com • 18 times a year. $2,304.00 per year.

The Solar Home: How to Design and Build a House You Heat with the Sun. Mark Freeman. Stackpole Books, 5067 Ritter Rd. Mechanicsburg, PA 17055. Phone: 800-732-3669 Fax: (717)796-0412 E-mail: jbender@stackpolebooks.com • URL: http://www.stackpolebooks.com • 1994. $14.95. (How-To Guides).

Soldiers. Available from U. S. Government Printing Office, Washington, DC 20402. Phone: (202)512-1800 Fax: (202)512-2250 E-mail: gpoaccess@gpo.gov • URL: http://www.access.gpo.gov • Monthly. $38.00 per year. Provides information on the policies, plans, operations, and technical developments of the U.S. Department of the Army (http://www.army.mil).

SOLE-The International Society of Logistics., 8100 Professional Pl., Ste. 111 Hyattsville, MD 20785. Phone: (301)459-8446 Fax: (301)459-1522 E-mail: solehq@sosle.org • URL: http://www.sole.org • Concerned with designing, supplying, and maintaining resources to support objectives, plans, and operations. Formerly Society of Logistics Engineers.

Solid State and Superconductivity Abstracts. CSA, 7200 Wisconsin Ave., Suite 601 Bethesda, MD 20814. Phone: 800-843-7751 or (301)961-6700 Fax: (301)961-6720 E-mail: service@csa.com • URL: http://www.csa.com • Bimonthly. $1,695.00 per year. Includes print and online editions. Formerly *Solid State Abstracts Journal.*

Solid-State Device and Materials Research Laboratory.

Solid State Electronic Devices. Prentice Hall PTR, 240 Frisch Ct. Paramus, NJ 07652. Phone: 800-282-0693 Fax: 800-445-6991 • URL: http://www.phptr.com • 1999. $107.00. Fifth edition. (Solid State Physical Electronics Series).

Solid State Technology. PennWell Corp., Advanced Technology Div., 98 Spit Brook Rd. Nashua, NH 03062-5737. Phone: 800-331-4463 or (603)891-0123 E-mail: atd@pennwell.com • URL: http://www.pennwell.com • Monthly. $217.00 per year. Covers the technical and business aspects of semiconductor and integrated circuit production. Includes *Buyers Guide.*

Solid Waste Association of North America., 1100 Wayne Ave. Silver Spring, MD 20907. Phone: 800-467-9262 or (301)585-2898 Fax: (301)589-7068 E-mail: info@swana.org • URL: http://www.swana.org • Members are officials from both public agencies and private companies. Attempts to improve waste management services to the public and industry. Formerly Governmental Refuse Collection and Disposal Association.

Solid Waste Handbook: A Practical Guide. William D. Robinson, editor. John Wiley and Sons, Inc., 111 River St. Hoboken, NJ 07030. Phone: 800-225-5945 or (201)748-6000 Fax: (201)748-6088 E-mail: info@wiley.com • URL: http://www.wiley.com • 1986. $275.00.

Solid Waste Report: Resource Recovery-Recycling-Collection-Disposal. Business Publishers, Inc., 8737 Colesville Rd., Suite 1100 Silver Spring, MD 20910-3928. Phone: 800-274-6737 or (301)587-6300 Fax: (301)589-8493 E-mail: bpinews@bpinews.com • URL: http://www.bpinews.com • Weekly. $627.00 per year. Newsletter. Covers regulation, business news, technology, and international events relating to solid waste management.

The SOLO Librarian's Sourcebook. Judith A. Siess. Information Today, Inc., 143 Old Marlton Pike Medford, NJ 08055-8750. Phone: 800-300-9868 or (609)654-6266 Fax: (609)654-4309 E-mail: custserv@infotoday.com • URL: http://www.infotoday.com • 1997. $39.50. Covers management and other aspects of one-librarian libraries.

Solutions! The Official Publication of TAPPI and PIMA. Technical Association of the Pulp and Paper Industry, P.O. Box 105113 Atlanta, GA 30348. Phone: (770)446-1400 Fax: (770)446-6947 E-mail: dmeadows@tappi.org • URL: http://www.tappi.org • Monthly. Membership. Formerly *TAPPI Journal.*

Sound and Communications. Testa Communications, Inc., 25 Willowdale Ave. Port Washington, NY 11050. Phone: (516)767-2500 Fax: (516)767-9335 • URL: http://www.testa.com • Monthly. $15.00 per year. A business, news and technical journal for contractors, consultants, engineers and system managers who design, install and purchase sound and communications equipment.

Sound and Communications: The Blue Book. Testa Communications Inc., 25 Willowdale Ave. Port Washington, NY 11050. Phone: (516)767-2500 Fax: (516)767-9335 • URL: http://www.testa.com • Annual. $15.00. Included with subscription. Approximately 1,000 suppliers of sound and communications equipment; including audio/video products in the United States and Canada.

Sound and Recording: An Introduction. Francis Rumsey and Tim McCormick. Elsevier, 655 Ave. of the Americas New York, NY 10010-5107. Phone: 800-366-2665 or (212)989-5800 Fax: 800-535-9935 or (212)633-3680 E-mail: custserv@elsevier.com • URL: http://www.elsevier.com • 2002. $42.99. Fourth edition. Covers the theory and principles of sound recording and reproduction, with chapters on amplifiers, microphones, mixers, and other components. (Music Technology Series).

Sound and Vibration Buyer's Guide., P.O. Box 40416 Bay Village, OH 44140. Phone: (440)835-0101 Fax: (440)835-9303 E-mail: sv@mindspring.com • URL: http://www.sandvmag.com • Annual. Free to qualified personnel. Lists of manufacturers of products for noise and vibration control, dynamic measurements instrumentation, and dynamic testing equipment.

Sound and Vibration (S/V). Acoustical Publications, Inc., 27101 E Oviatt Rd. Bay Village, OH 44140. Phone: (440)835-0101 Fax: (440)835-9303 E-mail: sv@mindspring.com Monthly. Free to qualified personnel; others, $60.00 per year.

Sound & Vision: Home Theater- Audio- Video- MultimediaMovies- Music. Hachette Filipacchi Media U.S., Inc., 1633 Broadway New York, NY 10019. Phone: 800-876-9011 or (212)767-6000 Fax: (212)767-5615 E-mail: soundandvision@hfmus.com • URL: http://www.hfmmag.com • 10 times a year. $24.00 per year. Popular magazine providing explanatory articles and critical reviews of equipment and media (CD-ROM, DVD, videocassettes, etc.). Supplement available *Stero Review's Sound and Vision Buyers Guide.* Replaces *Stereo Review* and *Video Magazine.*

Sound Check: The Basics of Sound and Sound Systems. Tony Moscal. Hal Leonard Corp., PO Box 13819 Milwaukee, WI 53213. Phone: 800-524-4425 or (414)774-3630 Fax: (414)774-3259 E-mail: halinfo@halleonard.com • URL: http://www.halleonard.com • 1994. $14.95. Explains the fundamentals of sound and related electronics.

Sound Synthesis and Sampling. Martin Russ. Elsevier, Inc., 360 Park Ave. South New York, NY 10010. Phone: 888-437-4636 or (212)989-5800 Fax: (212)633-3990 E-mail: usinfo@ elsevier.com • URL: http://www.books.elsevier.com/us/ • 2004. $44.95. Second edition. Covers "the underlying principles and practical techniques applied to both commercial and research synthesizers." Includes software examples, examples of representative instruments, a glossary, and a "jargon guide." (Imprint: Focal Press.)

Source Book of Health Insurance Data, 1997-1998. Health Insurance Association of America, 601 Pennsylvania Ave., NW, South Bldg., Ste. 500 Washington, DC 20004. Phone: 800-828-0111 or (202)824-1840 Fax: (202)824-1800 • URL: http://www.hiaa.org • 1998. $35.00. Data on health insurance, medical care costs, morbidity and health manpower in the U. S.

Source Directory. Elevator World Inc., 356 Morgan Ave., PO Box 6507 Mobile, AL 36606. Phone: 800-730-5093 or (251)479-4514 Fax: (251)479-7043 E-mail: editorial@elevator-world. com • URL: http://www.elevator-world.com • Publication includes: Lists of over 700 elevator manufacturers/suppliers, contractors and consultants; and 130 elevator/escalator trade associations; international coverage. Entries include: For firms—Company name, address, phone, URL, e-mail, fax, names of marketing and engineering contacts, list of products or services, description or history, market area. For consultants—Name, address, phone, area of specialization. For contractors—Name, address, phone, URL, e-mail, name of key personnel, company statement, area of operation. For trade associations—Name, address, phone, URL, e-mail, names of key personnel, responsibilities, statement of purpose (when available).

Source OECD. Economic Outlook Statistics., 2001 L St., NW, Ste. 650 Washington, DC 20036-4922. Phone: 800-456-6323 or (202)785-6323 or (202)822-3865 Fax: (202)785-0350 E-mail: washington.contact@oecd.org 2000. $325.00. Includes country and global forecasts of over 170 economic and business variables. Actual data is shown for two years, with forecasts up to ten years.

Sourcebook America. Gale Cengage Learning, 27500 Drake Rd. Farmington Hills, MI 48331-3535. Phone: 800-877-GALE or (248)699-GALE Fax: 800-414-5043 or (248)699-8069 E-mail: galeord@gale.com • URL: http://gale.cengage.com • Annual. $995.00. Produced by CACI Marketing Systems. A combination on CD-ROM of *The Sourcebook of ZIP Code Demographics* and *The Sourcebook of County Demographics*. Provides detailed population and socio-economic data (about 75 items) for each of 3,141 U. S. counties and approximately 30,000 ZIP codes, plus states, metropolitan areas, and media market areas. Includes forecasts to the year 2004.

The Sourcebook of County Demographics. Available from Gale Cengage Learning, 27500 Drake Rd. Farmington Hills, MI 48331-3535. Phone: 800-877-GALE or (248)699-GALE Fax: 800-414-5043 E-mail: gale.galeord@cengage.com • URL: http://gale.cengage.com • Annual. $395.00. Published by ESRI Business Information Solutions. Contains demographic and socio-economic data (70 characteristics) for each U. S. county.

Sourcebook of Criminal Justice Statistics. Available from U. S. Government Printing Office, Washington, DC 20402. Phone: (202)512-1800 Fax: (202)512-2250 E-mail: gpoaccess@gpo. gov • URL: http://www.access.gpo.gov • Annual. $56.00. Issued by the Bureau of Justice Statistics, U. S. Department of Justice (http://www.usdoj.gov/bjs). Contains both crime data and corrections statistics.

The Sourcebook of ZIP Code Demographics. Available from Gale Cengage Learning, 27500 Drake Rd. Farmington Hills, MI 48331-3535. Phone: 800-877-GALE or (248)699-GALE Fax: 800-414-5043 E-mail: gale.galeord@cengage.com • URL: http://gale.cengage.com • Annual. $495.00. Published by ESRI Business Information Systems. Presents detailed statistical profiles of every ZIP code in America. Each profile contains data on more than 70 variables with 2003 updates and 2008 forecasts.

Sourcebook of Zip Code Demographics. ESRI Business Information Solutions, 8620 Westwood Center Dr. Vienna, VA 22182-2214. Phone: 800-292-2224 or (703)679-4185 Fax: (703)679-3371 E-mail: msgw@caci.com • URL: http://www. demographics.caci.com • 2002. $495.00. 16th edition. Provides data on 75 demographic and socio-economic characteristics for each ZIP code in the U. S.

Sourcebooks America CD-ROM. CACI Marketing Systems, 1100 N. Glebe Rd., Suite 200 Arlington, VA 22201-4714. Phone: 800-292-2224 or (703)841-7800 Fax: (703)243-6272 Annual. $1,250.00. Provides the CD-ROM version of *The Sourcebook of ZIP Code Demographics: Census Edition* and *The Sourcebook of County Demographics: Census Edition*.

SourceMex. Latin America Data Base, Latin American Institute, University of New Mexico, 801 Yale Blvd., N. E. Albuquerque, NM 87131-1016. Phone: 800-472-0888 or (505)277-6839 Fax: (505)277-6837 An online newsletter covering economic conditions in Mexico, including foreign trade, public finances, foreign debt, agriculture, and the oil industry. Time period is 1990 to date, with weekly updates. Inquire as to online cost and availability.

Sources of Supply/Buyers Guide. William O. Dannhausen Corp., 720 S River Rd., Ste. 126 Des Plaines, IL 60068-4152. Phone: (847)823-3145 Fax: (847)696-3445 E-mail: dan@

dannhausen.com • URL: http://www.dannhausen.com • Annual. $90.00. About 2,200 mills and converters, 2,700 merchants and 500 manufacturers' representatives in paper, films, foils, and allied lines.

Southern Christian Leadership Conference., PO Box 89128, PO Box 89128 Atlanta, GA 30312. Phone: (404)522-1420 Fax: (404)527-4333 E-mail: president@sclcnational.org • URL: http://www.sclcnational.org • Nonsectarian coordinating and service agency for local organizations seeking full citizenship rights, equality, and the integration of African-Americans in all aspects of life in the U.S. and subscribing to the Ghandian philosophy of nonviolence. Works primarily in 16 southern and border states to improve civic, religious, economic, and cultural conditions. Fosters nonviolent resistance to all forms of racial injustice, including state and local laws and practices. Conducts leadership training program embracing such subjects as registration and voting, social protest, use of the boycott, picketing, nature of prejudice, and understanding politics. Sponsors citizenship education schools to teach reading and writing, help persons pass literacy tests for voting, and provide information about income tax forms, tax-supported resources, aid to handicapped children, public health facilities, how government is run, and social security. Conducts Crusade for the Ballot, which aims to double the black vote in the South through increased voter registrations. Sponsors lectures; disseminates literature.

Southern, Lumberman. Hatton-Brown Publishers, Inc., 225 Hanrick St. Montgomery, AL 36104. Phone: (334)834-1170 Fax: (334)834-4525 Monthly. $23.00 per year. Controlled circulation. A magazine for the sawmill industry.

Southwest Research Institute. Southwest Research Institute, PO Box 28510, 6220 Culebra Rd. San Antonio, TX 78228-0510. Phone: (210)684-5111 Fax: (210)522-3547 E-mail: bd@swri. org • URL: http://www.swri.org • Automation, robotics, intelligent systems, space sciences, environmental sciences and engineering, bioengineering, micro encapsulation, chemistry, plant machinery and piping dynamics, radiolocation sciences and development, communications, electromagnetic compatibility, electronic systems, geophysical instrumentation, nondestructive evaluation research, nuclear waste regulatory analysis, fluid dynamics and hydraulics, offshore systems, structural analysis and testing, terminal ballistics and blast effects, materials development, solid mechanics, nonmetallic materials, engine systems engineering, engine emissions analysis and control, fuels and lubricants evaluation, fluids and lubrication technology, alternate energy systems, alternate fuels, mining systems engineering, vehicle and highway safety, and fire research.

Souvenir and Gift Novelty Trade Association., 7000 Terminal Sq., Ste. 210 Upper Darby, PA 19082. Phone: (610)734-2420 Fax: (610)734-2423 E-mail: souvnovmag@aol.com Formerly Souvenir and Novelty Trade Association.

Soya and Oilseed Bluebook. Soyatech, Inc., Seven Pleasant St, Bar Harbour, ME 04609. Phone: 800-424-7692 or (207)288-4969 Fax: (207)288-5264 E-mail: data@soyatech.comm • URL: http://www.soyatech.com • Annual. $70.00. Includes quarterly *Bluebook Update*. Formerly *Soya Bluebook Plus*.

Soyabean Abstracts. Available from CABI Publishing, North America, 875 Massachusetts, 7th Fl. Cambridge, MA 02139. Phone: 800-528-4841 or (617)395-4056 Fax: (617)354-6875 E-mail: cabi-nao@cabi.org • URL: http://www.cabi-publishing.org • Bimonthly. $450.00 per year. Internet access only. Published in England by CABI Publishing. Provides worldwide coverage of the literature.

Space Institute. University of Tennessee

Space Planning in the Special Library. Caryl Masyr and Roberta Freifeld. Special Libraries Association, 1700 18th St., N. W. Washington, DC 20009-2514. Phone: (202)234-4700 Fax: (202)265-9317 E-mail: sla@sla.org • URL: http://www.sla. org • 1991. $23.00. Provides practical advice for planners of new libraries, renovations, and relocations.

Space Sciences. Patricia Dasch, editor. Gale Cengage Learning, 27500 Drake Rd. Farmington Hills, MI 48331-3535. Phone: 800-877-GALE Fax: 800-414-5043 or (248)699-8069 E-mail: galeord@galegroup.com • URL: http://www. galegroup.com • 2002. $395.00. Four volumes. Includes business and economic aspects of aerospace technology. (Macmillan Reference USA imprint, Macmillan Science Library,)

Space, Telecommunications and Radioscience Laboratory. Stanford University

Space Times. American Astronautical Society, 6352 Rolling Mill Pl., Ste. 102 Springfield, VA 22152-2354. Phone: (703)866-0020 Fax: (703)866-3526 E-mail: aas@astronautical.org • URL: http://www.astronautical.org • Description: Discusses current topics in astronautics, Society events, national and international space programs, and related items of interest to those in the field. Recurring features include a calendar of events, book reviews, editorials, and feature articles on space exploration: past, present, and future.

The Special Event Magazine. Primedia Business Magazines and Media, 11 River Bend Dr., S Stamford, CT 06907. Phone: 800-795-5445 or (203)358-9900 Fax: (203)358-5811 E-mail: subs@primediabusiness.com • URL: http://www. primediabusiness.com • Monthly. $48.00 per year. Edited for professionals concerned with parties, meetings, galas, and special events of all kinds and sizes. Provides practical ideas for the planning of special events. Formerly *Special Events*.

Special Interest Autos. Watering Inc., Special Interest Publica-

tions, P.O. Box 904 Bennington, VT 05201. Phone: (802)442-3101 Fax: (802)447-1561 E-mail: hmnmail@hemmings.com • URL: http://www.hemmings.com • Bimonthly. $19.95 per year.

Special Interest Group for Computer Science Education., c/o Association for Computing Machinery, 1515 Broadway New York, NY 10036-5701. Phone: 800-342-6626 or (212)626-0500 E-mail: acmhelp@acm.org • URL: http://www.acm.org • Concerned with education relating to computer science and technology on various levels, ranging from secondary school to graduate degree programs.

Special Interest Group for Design Automation.

Special Interest Group on Applied Computing., c/o Association for Computing Machinery, 1515 Broadway New York, NY 10036. Phone: 800-342-6626 or (212)626-0500 Fax: (212)302-5826 E-mail: sigs@acm.org • URL: http://www. acm.org/sigapp • Concerned with "innovative applications, technology transfer, experimental computing, strategic research, and the management of computing." Publishes a semiannual newsletter, *Applied Computing Review*.

Special Interest Group on Artificial Intelligence.

Special Interest Group on Computers and Society.

Special Interest Group on Computers and the Physically Handicapped., c/o Association for Computing Machinery, 1515 Broadway New York, NY 10036. Phone: 800-342-6626 or (212)869-7440 Fax: (212)944-1318 E-mail: acmhelp@ acm.org • URL: http://www.acm.org/sigcaph • Members are physically disabled computer professionals.

Special Interest Group on Design Automation., c/o Association for Computing Machinery, 1515 Broadway New York, NY 10036. Phone: 800-342-6626 or (212)869-7440 Fax: (212)944-1318 E-mail: acmhelp@acm.org • URL: http:// www.acm.org/sigda • Concerned with computer-aided design systems and software. Publishes the semiannual *SIGDA Newsletter*.

Special Interest Group on Electronic Sound Technology., c/o Association for Computing Machinery, 1515 Broadway New York, NY 10036. Phone: 800-342-6626 or (212)626-0603 Fax: (212)944-1318 E-mail: barish@acm.org • URL: http:// www.acm.org/sigsound • Concerned with software, algorithms, hardware, and applications relating to digitally generated audio.

Special Interest Group on Hypertext, Hypermedia, and Web., c/o Association for Computing Machinery, 1515 Broadway New York, NY 10036. Phone: 800-342-6626 or (212)869-7440 Fax: (212)944-1318 E-mail: acmhelp@acm.org • URL: http://www.acm.org/sigweb • Concerned with the design, use, and evaluation of hypertext and hypermedia systems. Provides a multi-disciplinary forum for the promotion, dissemination, and exchange of ideas relating to research technologies and applications. Publishes the *SIGWEB Newsletter* three times a year.

Special Interest Group on Information Retrieval.

Special Interest Group on Management of Data., c/o Association for Computing Machinery, 1515 Broadway New York, NY 10036. Phone: 800-342-6626 or (212)869-7440 Fax: (212)944-1318 E-mail: acmhelp@acm.org • URL: http:// www.acm.org/sigmod • Focuses on network architecture, protocols, and distributed systems. Publishes a quarterly newsletter *Computer Communication Review*. Formerly Special Interest Group on Data Communication.

Special Interest Group on Multimedia., c/o Association for Computing Machinery, 1515 Broadway New York, NY 10036. Phone: 800-342-6626 or (212)626-0500 Fax: (212)305-5826 E-mail: sigs@acm.org • URL: http://www. acm.org/sigmm • Concerned with multimedia computing, communication, storage, and applications.

Special Interest Group on Operating Systems.

Special Interest Group on Programming Languages.

Special Interest Group on Security, Audit, and Control.

Special Interest Group on Software Engineering., c/o Association for Computing Machinery, 1515 Broadway New York, NY 10036. Phone: 800-342-6626 or (212)869-7440 Fax: (212)944-1318 E-mail: acmhelp@acm.org • URL: http:// www.acm.org/sigsoft • Concerned with all aspects of software development and maintenance. Publishes *Software Engineering Notes*, a bimonthly newsletter.

Special Interest Group Profiles for Students. Gale Cengage Learning, 27500 Drake Rd. Farmington Hills, MI 48331-3535. Phone: 800-877-GALE or (248)699-4253 Fax: 800-414-5043 E-mail: gale.galeord@cengage.com • URL: http:// gale.cengage.com • 1999. $115.00. Provides detailed descriptions for more than 175 lobbies, political action committees, civic action groups, and political parties. Includes a glossary, chronology, and index.

Special Libraries: A Guide for Management. Cathy A. Porter and Elin B. Christianson. Special Libraries Association, 1700 18th St., N. W. Washington, DC 20009-2514. Phone: (202)234-4700 Fax: (202)265-9317 E-mail: sla@sla.org • URL: http://www.sla.org • 1997. $42.00. Fourth edition. Provides basic information for the managers of business and other organizations on starting, staffing, and maintaining a special library.

Special Libraries and Information Centers: An Introductory Text. Ellis Mount and Renee Massoud. Special Libraries Association, 1700 18th St., N. W. Washington, DC 20009-2514. Phone: (202)234-4700 Fax: (202)265-9317 E-mail: sla@sla. org • URL: http://www.sla.org • 1999. $49.00. Fourth edition. Descriptions of 13 outstanding libraries and information centers. Includes audio cassette.

Special Libraries Association., 331 S Patrick St. Alexandria, VA 22314-3501. Phone: (703)647-4900 Fax: (703)647-4901 E-mail: sla@sla.org • URL: http://www.sla.org • International association of information professionals who work in special libraries serving business, research, government, universities, newspapers, museums, and institutions that use or produce specialized information. Seeks to advance the leadership role of special librarians. Offers consulting services to organizations that wish to establish or expand a library or information services. Conducts strategic learning and development courses, public relations, and government relations programs. Provides employment services. Operates knowledge exchange on topics pertaining to the development and management of special libraries. Maintains Hall of Fame.

Special Libraries Association; Information Technology Division.

Special Situations Newsletter: In-Depth Survey of Under-Valued Stocks. Charles Howard Kaplan, 26 Broadway, Suite 200 New York, NY 10004-1703. Phone: 800-756-1811 or (201)418-4411 Fax: (201)418-5085 Monthly. $75.00 per year. Newsletter. Principal content is "This Month's Recommendation," a detailed analysis of one special situation stock.

Specialty Advertising. Entrepreneur Media, Inc., 2445 McCabe Way Irvine, CA 92614. Phone: 800-421-2300 or (949)261-2325 Fax: (949)261-0234 E-mail: entmag@entrepreneur.com • URL: http://www.entrepreneur.com • Looseleaf. $59.50. A practical guide to starting a business dealing in advertising specialties. Covers profit potential, market size evaluation, start-up costs, pricing, accounting, advertising, promotion, etc. (Start-Up Business Guide No. E1292.)

Specialty Baker's Voice. Specialty Bakery Owners of America, 1568 Ralph Ave. Brooklyn, NY 11236-3129. Phone: (212)227-7754 Monthly. $25.00 per year.

Specialty Food Industry Directory. Phoenix Media Network, Inc., P.O. Box 810425 Boca Raton, FL 33481. Phone: (561)447-0810 Annual. Included in subscription to Food Distribution Magazine. Lists manufacturers and suppliers of specialty foods, and services and equipment for the specialty food industry. Featured food products include legumes, sauces, spices, upscale cheese, specialty beverages, snack foods, baked goods, ethnic foods, and specialty meats.

Specialty Occupational Outlook: Professions. Gale Cengage Learning, 27500 Drake Rd. Farmington Hills, MI 48331-3535. Phone: 800-877-GALE or (248)699-42533 Fax: 800-414-5043 E-mail: gale.galeord@cengage.com • URL: http://gale.cengage.com • 1994. $75.00. Provides information on 150 professional occupations. (Career Information Guide Series).

Specialty Occupational Outlook: Trade and Technical. Gale Cengage Learning, 27500 Drake Rd. Farmington Hills, MI 48331-3535. Phone: 800-877-GALE or (248)699-4253 Fax: 800-414-5043 E-mail: gale.galeord@cengage.com • URL: http://gale.cengage.com • 1995. $75.00. Provides information on 150 "high-interest" careers that do not require a bachelor's degree.

Specialty Tools and Fasteners Distributors Association.

Spectra. National Communication Association, 1765 N St. NW Washington, DC 20036. Phone: (202)464-4622 Fax: (202)464-4600 E-mail: iwang@natcom.org • URL: http://www.ags.org • Description: Discusses forensics, interpretation, interpersonal communication, rhetoric and public address, communication theory, mass media, theater, speech and language sciences, and job advertising. Recurring features include official business of the Association, news briefs concerning members, and notices of available materials.

Spectrum: Journal of State Government. Council of State Governments, 2760 Research Park Dr. Lexington, KY 40578. Phone: 800-800-1910 or (859)244-8000 Fax: (859)244-8001 E-mail: sales@csg.org • URL: http://www.csg.org • Quarterly. $49.99 per year. Formerly *Journal of State Government.*

Speech Index: An Index to Collections of World Famous Orations and Speeches for Various Occasions, 1966-1980. Charity Mitchell. Scarecrow Press, Inc., 4501 Forbes Blvd., Ste. 200 Lanham, MD 20706. Phone: 800-462-6420 or (301)459-3366 Fax: 800-338-4550 or (301)429-5748 E-mail: custserv@rowman.com • URL: http://www.scarecrowpress.com • 1982. $82.50. Fourth edition.

Speech Synthesis and Recognition. John Holmes and Wendy Holmes. Routledge, 29 W 35th St. New York, NY 10001. Phone: 800-634-7064 or (212)216-7800 Fax: 800-248-4727 E-mail: info@routledge-ny.com • URL: http://www.routledge.ny.com • 2001. $72.00.

Spices and Seasonings. Available from MarketResearch.com, 641 Ave. of the Americas, Third Floor New York, NY 10011. Phone: 800-298-5699 or (212)807-2629 Fax: (212)807-2716 E-mail: order@marketresearch.com • URL: http://www.marketresearch.com • 1999. $2,250.00. Market research data. Published by Specialists in Business Information. Covers salt, pepper, garlic, salt substitutes, seasoning mixes, etc.

SPIE-The International Society for Optical Engineering., P.O. Box 10 Bellingham, WA 98227-0010. Phone: (360)676-3290 Fax: (360)647-1445 E-mail: spie@spie.org • URL: http://www.spie.org • Formerly Society of Photo-Optical Instrumentation Engineers.

Spilled Milk: A Special Collection from The Journal of Commercial Bank Lending on Loans that Went Sour. The Risk Management Association, One Liberty Place, 1650 Market

St., Suite 2300 Philadelphia, PA 19103-7398. Phone: 800-677-7621 or (215)446-4000 Fax: (215)446-4101 • URL: http://www.rmahq.org • 1987. $16.75. Two volumes.

Sportbil. International Sport Summit, 6550 Rock Spring Dr., Suite 500 Bethesda, MD 20817-1126. Fax: (301)493-0536 Annual. Price on application. A yearly review of the business of sport.

Sporting Arms and Ammunition Manufacturers Institute., 11 Mile Hill Rd., c/o Flintlock Ridge Office Ctr. Newtown, CT 06470-2359. Phone: (203)426-4358 Fax: (203)426-1087 E-mail: info@nssf.org • URL: http://www.nssf.org • Producers of firearms, ammunition and propellants.

Sporting Goods Business: The National Newsmagazine of the Sporting Goods Industry. VNU Business Media, 770 Broadway New York, NY 10003-9595. Phone: 800-344-7119 or (646)654-4500 Fax: (646)654-7212 • URL: http://www.vnubusinessmedia.com • 16 times a year. Free to qualified personnel; others, $65.00 per year. The national news magazine of the sporting goods industry.

Sporting Goods Dealer: The Voice of Team Dealers Since 1899. VNU Business Media, 770 Broadway New York, NY 10003-9595. Phone: 800-344-7119 or (646)654-4500 Fax: (646)654-7212 E-mail: vnubusinessmedia.com • URL: http://www.vnu.com • Quarterly. $38.00 per year. Covers the merchandising of sports products to consumers, as well as to schools, colleges, and professional teams.

Sporting Goods Manufacturers Association., 1150 17th St. NW, Ste. 850 Washington, DC 20036. Phone: (202)775-1762 Fax: (202)296-7462 E-mail: info@sgma.com • URL: http://www.sgma.com • Manufacturers of athletic clothing, footwear, and sporting goods. Seeks to increase sports participation and create growth in the sporting goods industry. Owns and operates the largest sports products trade show in the world.

Sporting Goods Store. Entrepreneur Media, Inc., 2445 McCabe Way Irvine, CA 92614. Phone: 800-421-2300 or (949)261-2325 Fax: (949)261-0234 E-mail: entmag@entrepreneur.com • URL: http://www.entrepreneur.com • Looseleaf. $59.50. A practical guide to starting a retail sporting goods business. Covers profit potential, start-up costs, market size evaluation, owner's time required, site selection, lease negotiation, pricing, accounting, advertising, promotion, etc. (Start-Up Business Guide No. E1286.)

Sports and Entertainment Litigation Reporter. Andrews Publications, 175 Strafford Ave., Bldg. 4, Suite 140 Wayne, PA 19087. Phone: 800-345-1101 or (610)225-0510 Fax: (610)225-0501 E-mail: customer@andrewspub.com • URL: http://www.andrewspub.com • Monthly. $899.00 per year. Newsletter. Provides reports on lawsuits involving films, TV, cable broadcasting, stage productions, radio, and other areas of the entertainment business. Formerly *Sports and Entertainment Litigation Reporter.*

Sports, Convention, and Entertainment Facilities. David C. Petersen. Urban Land Institute, 1025 Thomas Jefferson St., NW, Ste. 500 W Washington, DC 20007-5201. Phone: 800-321-5011 or (202)624-7000 Fax: (202)624-7140 • URL: http://www.uli.org • 1996. $61.95. Provides advice and information on developing, financing, and operating amphitheaters, arenas, convention centers, and stadiums. Includes case studies of 70 projects.

Sports Industry News: Management and Finance, Regulation and Litigation, Media and Marketing. Game Point Publishing, P. O. Box 946 Camden, ME 04843. Weekly. $244.00 per year. Newsletter. Covers ticket promotions, TV rights, player contracts, concessions, endorsements, etc.

Sports Market Place. Sports Careers, 2990 E Northern Ave., Ste. D107 Phoenix, AZ 85028. Phone: 800-776-7877 or (602)485-5555 Fax: (602)485-5556 E-mail: support@sportscareers.com • URL: http://www.sportsmarketplace.com • Covers: manufacturers, organizations, professional sports teams, broadcasting networks, sports arenas, syndicators, publications, trade shows, marketing services, corporate sports sponsors, and other groups concerned with the business and promotional aspects of sports generally and with air sports, arm wrestling, auto sports, badminton, baseball, basketball, biathlon, bowling, boxing, curling, equestrian, exercise, fencing, field hockey, football, golf, gymnastics, ice hockey, lacrosse, martial arts, paddleball, paddle tennis, platform tennis, pentathlon, racquetball, rowing, rugby, running/jogging, skiing, soccer, softball, squash, swimming, table tennis, tennis, track and field, volleyball, water sports, weightlifting, and wrestling. Entries include: Name of company or organization, address, fax, e-mail, URL, name of key personnel with titles, and description of products or services.

Sports Trend. Shore-Verrone, Inc., 1115 Northmeadow Pkwy., No. 100 Roswell, GA 30076-3857. Phone: 800-241-9034 or (770)569-1540 • URL: http://www.svi-atl.com • Monthly. $75.00 per year. Formerly *Sports Merchandiser.*

Spotlight. World Affairs Council of Northern California, 312 Sutter St., Ste. 200 San Francisco, CA 94108. Phone: (415)293-4600 Fax: (415)982-5028 E-mail: schools@wacsf.org Description: Includes one major and 30-40 brief annotated reviews of books on international relations, world politics, and economics. Includes transcripts of council programs.

Spray Equipment Directory. infoUSA, 5711 S 86th Cir. Omaha, NE 68127. Phone: 800-555-6124 or (402)593-4600 Fax: (402)331-5481 E-mail: internet@infousa.com • URL: http://www.abii.com • Annual. Price on application.

Spray Technology and Marketing: The Magazine of Spray Pressure Packaging. Industry Publications, Inc., 3621 Hill Rd. Parsippany, NJ 07054. Phone: (973)331-9545 Fax: (973)331-

9547 E-mail: info@spraytechnology.com • URL: http://www.spraytechnology.com • Monthly. $30.00 per year. Formerly *Aerosol Age.*

Spraying—Insect Control Directory. infoUSA Inc., 5711 S 86th Cir., PO Box 27347 Omaha, NE 68127. Phone: 800-321-0869 or (402)593-4500 Fax: (402)331-1505 E-mail: help@infousa.com • URL: http://www.infousa.com • Number of listings: 1,287. Entries include: Name, address, phone, size of advertisement, name of owner or manager, number of employees, year first in "Yellow Pages." Compiled from telephone company "Yellow Pages," nationwide.

SRC Green Book of 5 Trend 35-Year Charts. Securities Research Co., 400 Talcott Ave. Watertown, MA 02472-2700. Phone: 877-388-4502 or (781)235-0900 Fax: (617)235-9684 E-mail: src@babson.com • URL: http://www.babson.com • Annual. $150.00. Chart book presents statistical information on the stocks of 400 leading companies over a 35-year period. Each full page chart is in semi-log format to avoid visual distortion. Also includes charts of 12 leading market averages or indexes and 39 major industry groups.

SRDS Business Publication Advertising Source. SRDS, 1700 Higgins Rd. Des Plaines, IL 60018-5605. Phone: 800-851-7737 or (847)375-5000 Fax: (847)375-5001 • URL: http://www.srds.com • Monthly. $714.00 per year. Issued in three parts: (1) U. S. Business Publications, (2) U. S. Healthcare Publications, and (3) International Publications. Provides detailed advertising rates, profiles of editorial content, management names, "Multiple Publications Publishers," circulation data, and other trade journal information. Formerly *Business Publication Advertising Source.*

SRDS Circulation [year]. SRDS, 1700 Higgins Rd. Des Plaines, IL 60018-5605. Phone: 800-851-7737 or (847)375-5000 Fax: (847)375-5001 • URL: http://www.srds.com • Annual. $297.00. Contains detailed statistical analysis of newspaper circulation by metropolitan area or county and data on television viewing by area. Includes maps. Formerly *Circulation Year.*

SRDS Community Publication Advertising Source. SRDS, 1700 Higgins Rd. Des Plaines, IL 60018-5605. Phone: 800-851-7737 or (847)375-5000 Fax: (847)375-5001 • URL: http://www.srds.com • Semiannual. $186.00 per year. Provides advertising rates for weekly community newspapers, shopping guides, and religious newspapers, with circulation data and other information.

SRDS Consumer Magazine Advertising Source. SRDS, 1700 Higgins Rd. Des Plaines, IL 60018-5605. Phone: 800-851-7737 or (847)375-5000 Fax: (847)375-5001 • URL: http://www.srds.com • Annual. $699.00 per year. Contains advertising rates and other data for U. S. consumer magazines and agricultural publications. Also provides consumer market data for population, households, income, and retail sales. Formerly *Consumer Magazine and Advertising Source.*

SRDS Direct Marketing List Source. SRDS, 1700 Higgins Rd. Des Plaines, IL 60018-5605. Phone: 800-851-7737 or (847)375-5000 Fax: (847)375-5001 • URL: http://www.srds.com • Bimonthly. $561.00 per year. Provides detailed information and rates for business, farm, and consumer mailing lists (U. S., Canadian, and international). Includes current postal information and directories of list brokers, compilers, and managers. Formerly *Direct Mail List Source.*

SRDS Interactive Advertising Source. SRDS, 1700 Higgins Rd. Des Plaines, IL 60018-5605. Phone: 800-851-7737 or (847)375-5000 Fax: (847)375-5001 • URL: http://www.srds.com • Quarterly. $569.00 per year. Provides descriptive profiles, rates, audience, personnel, etc., for producers of various forms of interactive or multimedia advertising: online/Internet, CD-ROM, interactive TV, interactive cable, interactive telephone, interactive kiosk, and others.

SRDS International Media Guides. SRDS, 1700 Higgins Rd. Des Plaines, IL 60018-5605. Phone: 800-851-7737 or (847)375-5000 Fax: (847)375-5001 E-mail: info@intlmag.org • URL: http://www.srds.com • Covers: In five volumes (Newspapers worldwide, Consumer magazines worldwide, Business Publications: Asia-Pacific/Middle East/Africa, Business Publications: Europe, Business Publications: (The Americas), advertising rates and data for 20,000 newspapers, consumer magazines and business publications worldwide. Entries include: contact names, addresses, phone and fax numbers, and e-mail.

SRDS Lifestyle Market Analyst. SRDS, 1700 Higgins Rd. Des Plaines, IL 60018-5605. Phone: 800-851-7737 or (847)375-5000 Fax: (847)375-5001 • URL: http://www.srds.com • Annual. $440.00. Published in conjunction with EQUIFAX. Provides extensive lifestyle data on interests, activities, and hobbies within specific geographic and demographic markets. Formerly *Lifestyle Market Analyst.*

SRDS Newspaper Advertising Source. SRDS, 1700 Higgins Rd. Des Plaines, IL 60018-5605. Phone: 800-851-7737 or (847)375-5000 Fax: (847)375-5001 • URL: http://www.srds.com • Monthly. $700.00 per year. Lists newspapers geographically, with detailed information on advertising rates, special features, personnel, circulation, etc. Includes a section on college newspapers. Also provides consumer market data for population, households, income, and retail sales. Formerly *Newspaper Advertising Source.*

SRDS Out-of-Home Advertising Source. SRDS, 1700 Higgins Rd. Des Plaines, IL 60018-5605. Phone: 800-851-7737 or (847)375-5000 Fax: (847)375-5001 • URL: http://www.srds.com • Annual. $341.00. Provides detailed information on non-traditional or "out-of-home" advertising media: outdoor, aerial, airport, mass transit, bus benches, school, hotel, in-flight, in-store, theater, stadium, taxi, truckstop, kiosk, shopping malls, and others. Formerly*Advertising Options Plus*.

SRDS Print Media Production Source. SRDS, 1700 Higgins Rd. Des Plaines, IL 60018-5605. Phone: 800-851-7737 or (847)375-5000 Fax: (847)375-5001 • URL: http://www.srds. com • Quarterly. $808.00 per year. Contains details of printing and mechanical production requirements for advertising in specific trade journals, consumer magazines, and newspapers. Formerly *Print Media Production Source*.

SRDS Radio Advertising Source. SRDS, 1700 Higgins Rd. Des Plaines, IL 60018-5605. Phone: 800-851-7737 or (847)375-5000 Fax: (847)375-5001 • URL: http://www.srds.com • Quarterly. $535.00 per year. Contains detailed information on U. S. radio stations, networks, and corporate owners, with maps of market areas. Includes key personnel. Formerly*Radio Advertising Rates and Data*.

SRDS Technology Media Source. SRDS, 1700 Higgins Rd. Des Plaines, IL 60018-5605. Phone: 800-851-7737 or (847)375-5000 Fax: (847)375-5001 • URL: http://www.srds.com • Annual. $312.00. Contains detailed information on business publications, consumer magazines, and direct mail lists that may be of interest to "technology marketers." Emphasis is on aviation and telecommunications. Formerly*Technology Media Source*.

SRDS TV and Cable Source. SRDS, 1700 Higgins Rd. Des Plaines, IL 60018-5605. Phone: 800-851-7737 or (847)375-5000 Fax: (847)375-5001 • URL: http://www.srds.com • Quarterly. $525.00 per year. Provides detailed information on U. S. television stations, cable systems, networks, and group owners, with maps and market data. Includes key personnel.

SRI International. SRI International, 333 Ravenswood Ave. Menlo Park, CA 94025-3493. Phone: (650)859-2000 Fax: (650)859-4111 E-mail: inquiry.line@sri.com • URL: http://www.sri.com • Physical and life sciences, engineering, industrial management, business, social sciences, and public policy. Areas of research include biosciences, economics, energy, engineering systems and development, environment, health, industry consulting, information and communications, public policy, national security, and physical, life, and social sciences.

Sri Lanka Journal of Tea Science. Tea Research Institute of Sri Lanka, Saint Coombs Talawakele, Sri Lanka. Phone: 052 8385 Fax: 052 8311 Semiannual. $20.00 per year. Text in English. Formerly *Tea Quarterly*.

SSA Publications on CD-ROM. Available from U. S. Government Printing Office, Washington, DC 20402. Phone: (202)512-1800 Fax: (202)512-2250 E-mail: gpoaccess@gpo.gov • URL: http://www.access.gpo.gov • Monthly. $238.00 per year. Provides updated text of three Social Security Administration publications: *Program Operations Manual; Social Security Handbook; Social Security Rulings*.

Staffing for Results: A Guide to Working Smarter. Diane Mayo and Jeanne Goodrich. American Library Association, 50 E Huron St. Chicago, IL 60611-2795. Phone: 800-545-2433 or (312)944-6780 Fax: (312)440-9374 E-mail: ala@ala.org • URL: http://www.ala.org • 2002. $42.00. Written for the Public Library Association. Emphasizes work measurement in libraries for the sake of efficiency and productivity.

Stained Glass Association of America., 10009 E 62nd St. Raytown, MO 64133. Phone: 800-888-7422 or (816)737-2090 Fax: (816)737-2801 E-mail: sgaa@stainedglass.org • URL: http://www.stainedglass.org • Formerly National Ornamental Glass Manufacturers Association.

Stainless Steels, 87: Proceedings of Conference, University of York, 14-16 September, 87. Available from Ashgate Publishing Co., 101 Cherry St., Ste. 420 Burlington, VT 05401-4405. Phone: 800-535-9544 or (802)865-7641 Fax: (802)865-7847 E-mail: info@ashgate.com • URL: http://www.ashgate.com • 1988. $94.50. Published by Institute of Materials.

Stamp Collector. Krause Publications, Inc., 700 State St. Iola, WI 54990-0001. Phone: 800-258-0929 or (715)445-2214 Fax: (715)445-4087 • URL: http://www.krause.com • Biweekly. $32.98 per year. Newspaper.

Stamp Exchangers Directory. Levine Publications, Box 9090 Trenton, NJ 08650. E-mail: support@sportscareers.com Covers: over 1000 people who are interested in exchanging stamps, coins, and other collectibles with Americans; international coverage. Entries include: Name, address, item collected.

Stamps: The Weekly Magazine of Philately. American Publishing Co. of New York, 85 Canisteo St. Hornell, NY 14843. Phone: (607)324-2212 Fax: (607)324-1753 Weekly. $23.50 per year.

Standard and Poor's Bond Guide. Standard and Poor's, 55 Water St. New York, NY 10041. Phone: 800-221-5277 or (212)438-1000 Fax: (212)438-4368 E-mail: clientsupport@standardandpoors.com • URL: http://www.standardandpoors.com • Monthly. $239.00 per year.

Standard & Poor's Corporate Descriptions. Standard & Poor's Corp., 55 Water St. New York, NY 10041. Phone: 800-221-5277 or (212)438-1000 Fax: (212)438-7290 Provides current, detailed financial and other information on approximately 12,000 publicly held U. S. and foreign corporations. Corresponds to the printed *Standard & Poor's Corporation Records*. Updating is twice a month. Inquire as to online cost and availability.

Standard and Poor's Corporate Registered Bond Interest Record. Standard and Poor's, 55 Water St. New York, NY

10041. Phone: 800-221-5277 or (212)438-1000 • URL: http://www.standardandpoors.com • Annual. $2,600.00 per year. Weekly updates.

Standard & Poor's Corporations. Available from Dialog OnDisc, 11000 Regency Parkway, Suite 10 Cary, NC 27511. Phone: 800-334-2564 or (919)462-8600 Fax: (919)468-9890 E-mail: ondisc@dialog.com • URL: http://products.dialog.com/products/ondisc/ • Monthly. Price on application. Produced by Standard & Poor's. Contains three CD-ROM files: Executives, Private Companies, and Public Companies, providing detailed information on more than 70,000 business executives, 55,000 private companies, and 12,000 publicly-traded corporations.

Standard and Poor's Daily News Online. Standard and Poor's Corp., 55 Water St. New York, NY 10041. Phone: 800-221-5277 or (212)438-1000 Fax: (212)438-7290 Full text of business news and other information, 1984 to present. Inquire as to online cost and availability.

Standard and Poor's Daily Stock Price Records. Standard and Poor's, 55 Water St. New York, NY 10041. Phone: 800-221-5277 or (212)438-1000 Fax: (212)438-4368 E-mail: clientsupport@standardandpoors.com • URL: http://www.standardandpoors.com • Quarterly. New York Stock Exchange, $420.00 per year; American Stock Exchange, $441.00 per year; NASDAQ, $530.00 per year.

Standard and Poor's Directory of Bond Agents. Standard and Poor's, 55 Water St. New York, NY 10041. Phone: 800-221-5277 or (212)438-1000 Fax: (212)438-4368 • URL: http://www.standardandpoors.com • Bimonthly. $1,250.00 per year. *Supplement available*.

Standard and Poor's Dividend Record. Standard and Poor's, 55 Water St. New York, NY 10041. Phone: 800-221-5277 or (212)438-2000 Fax: (212)438-4368 • URL: http://www.standardandpoors.com • Daily. $825.00 per year.

Standard & Poor's 500 Guide. McGraw-Hill, 1221 Ave. of the Americas New York, NY 10020. Phone: 800-722-4726 or (212)512-2000 Fax: (212)512-4502 E-mail: customer.service@mcgraw-hill.com • URL: http://www.mcgraw-hill.com • Annual. $27.95. Contains detailed profiles of the companies included in Standard & Poor's 500 Index of stock prices. Includes income and balance sheet data for up to 10 years, with growth and stability rankings for 500 major corporations.

Standard & Poor's Industry Surveys. Standard & Poor's, 55 Water St. New York, NY 10041. Phone: 800-221-5277 or (212)438-1000 Fax: (212)438-4368 E-mail: clientsupport@standardandpoors.com • URL: http://www.standardandpoors.com • Semiannual. $1,800.00. Two looseleaf volumes. Includes monthly *Supplements*. Provides detailed, individual surveys of 52 major industry groups. Each survey is revised on a semiannual basis. Also includes "Monthly Investment Review" (industry group investment analysis) and monthly "Trends & Projections" (economic analysis).

Standard and Poor's Ratings Handbook. Standard & Poor's, 55 Water St. New York, NY 10041. Phone: 800-221-5277 or (212)438-1000 Fax: (212)438-4368 E-mail: clientsupport@standardandpoors.com • URL: http://www.standardandpoors.com • Monthly. $275.00 per year. Newsletter. Provides news and analysis of international credit markets, including information on new bond issues. Formerly *Credit Week International Ratings*.

Standard & Poor's Register: Biographical. Standard & Poor's Corp., 55 Water St. New York, NY 10041. Phone: 800-221-5277 or (212)438-1000 Fax: (212)438-7290 Contains brief biographies of approximately 70,000 business executives and directors. Corresponds to the biographical volume of *Standard & Poor's Register of Corporations, Directors, and Executives*. Updated twice a year. Inquire as to online cost and availability.

Standard & Poor's Register: Corporate. Standard & Poor's Corp., 55 Water St. New York, NY 10041. Phone: 800-221-5277 or (212)438-1000 Fax: (212)438-7290 Contains brief descriptions, with names of key executives, of about 55,000 public and private U. S. companies. Corresponds to the corporate volume of *Standard & Poor's Register of Corporations, Directors, and Executives*. Updated quarterly. Inquire as to online cost and availability.

Standard and Poor's Register of Corporations, Directors and Executives. Standard and Poor's, 55 Water St. New York, NY 10041. Phone: 800-221-5277 or (212)438-1000 E-mail: clientsupport@standardandpoors.com • URL: http://www.standardandpoors.com • Annual. $675.00. Looseleaf service. Lease basis. Periodic supplementation. Over 55,000 public and privately held corporations in the U.S.

Standard and Poor's Security Dealers of North America. Standard & Poor's, 55 Water St. New York, NY 10041. Phone: 800-221-5277 or (212)438-1000 E-mail: clientsupport@standardandpoors.com • URL: http://www.standardandpoors.com • Semiannual. $480.00 per year; with *Supplements* every six weeks. Geographical listing of over 12,000 stock, bond, and commodity dealers.

Standard and Poor's Semi-Weekly Called Bond Record. Standard & Poor's, 55 Water St. New York, NY 10041. Phone: 800-221-5277 or (212)438-1000 Fax: (212)438-4368 E-mail: clientsupport@standardandpoors.com • URL: http://www.standardandpoors.com • Semiweekly. $1,175.00 per year.

Standard & Poor's SmallCap 600 Guide. McGraw-Hill, 1221 Ave. of the Americas New York, NY 10020. Phone: 800-722-4726 or (212)512-2000 Fax: (212)512-4502 E-mail:

customer.service@mcgraw-hill.com • URL: http://www.mcgraw-hill.com • Monthly. $24.95. Contains detailed profiles of the companies included in Standard & Poor's SmallCap 600 Index of stock prices. Includes income and balance sheet data for up to 10 years, with growth and stability rankings for 600 small capitalization corporations.

Standard & Poor's Statistical Service. Current Statistics. Standard & Poor's, 55 Water St. New York, NY 10041. Phone: 800-221-5277 or (212)438-1000 Fax: (212)438-4368 E-mail: clientsupport@standardandpoors.com • URL: http://www.standardandpoors.com • Monthly. $688.00 per year. Includes 10 *Basic Statistics* sections, *Current Statistics Supplements* and *Annual Security Price Index Record*.

Standard & Poor's Stock and Bond Guide. McGraw-Hill, 1221 Ave. of the Americas New York, NY 10020. Phone: 800-722-4726 or (212)512-2000 Fax: (212)512-4502 E-mail: customer.service@mcgraw-hill.com • URL: http://www.mcgraw-hill.com • Annual. $24.95. Contains concise data on 6,000 stocks, 7,000 bonds, and 700 mutual funds. Includes year-end prices, earnings estimates for stocks, and debt ratings for bonds.

Standard & Poor's Stock Reports: NASDAQ and Regional Exchanges. Standard & Poor's, 55 Water St. New York, NY 10041. Phone: 800-221-5277 or (212)438-1000 Fax: (212)438-0040 E-mail: clientsupport@standardandpoors.com • URL: http://www.standardandpoors.com • Irregular. $1,100.00 per year. Looseleaf service. Provides two pages of financial details and other information for each corporation included.

Standard & Poor's Stock Reports: New York Stock Exchange. Standard & Poor's, 55 Water St. New York, NY 10041. Phone: 800-221-5277 or (212)438-1000 Fax: (212)438-0040 E-mail: clientsupport@standardandpoors.com • URL: http://www.standardandpoors.com • Irregular. $1,295.00 per year. Looseleaf service. Provides two pages of financial details and other information for each corporation with stock listed on the N. Y. Stock Exchange.

Standard Business Forms for the Entrepreneur. Entrepreneur Media, Inc., 2445 McCabe Way Irvine, CA 92614. Phone: 800-421-2300 or (949)261-2325 Fax: (949)261-0234 E-mail: entmag@entrepreneur.com • URL: http://www.entrepreneur.com • Looseleaf. $59.50. A practical collection of forms useful to entrepreneurial small businesses. (Start-Up Business Guide No. E1319.)

Standard Directory of Advertisers: Business Classifications Edition. National Register Publishing, 121 Chanlon Rd. New Providence, NJ 07974. Phone: 800-521-8100 Annual $799.00; with supplements, $899.00. Arranged by product or service. Provides information on the advertising programs of over 14,000 companies, including advertising/marketing personnel and the names of advertising agencies used.

Standard Directory of Advertisers: Geographic Edition. National Register Publishing, 121 Chanlon Rd. New Providence, NJ 07974. Phone: 800-521-8110 Annual $659.00; with supplements, $759.00. Arranged geographically by state. Provides information on the advertising programs of over 20,000 companies, including advertising/marketing personnel and the names of advertising agencies used. Includes *Advertiser/Agency* supplement.

Standard Directory of Advertising Agencies: The Agency Red Book. National Register Publishing, 121 Chanlon Rd. New Providence, NJ 07974. Phone: 800-521-8110 Semiannual $969.00. Information on nearly 10,800 Provides advertising agencies and branch offices. Includes annual billings by media and names of clients. Includes *Advertiser/Agency* supplement.

Standard Directory of International Advertisers and Agencies: The International Red Book. National Register Publishing, 121 Chanlon Rd. New Providence, NJ 07974. Phone: 800-521-8110 Annual. $629.00. Includes more than 5,000 foreign companies and their advertising agencies. Geographic, company name, personal name, and trade name indexes are provided.

Standard Handbook for Civil Engineers. Frederick S. Merritt and others. McGraw-Hill, 1221 Ave. of the Americas New York, NY 10020. Phone: 800-722-4726 or (212)512-2000 Fax: (212)512-4502 E-mail: customer.service@mcgraw-hill.com • URL: http://www.mcgraw-hill.com • 2003. $150.00. Fifth edition. (Scientic, Technical and Medical Series).

Standard Handbook for Electrical Engineers. Douglas G. Fink. McGraw-Hill, 1221 Ave. of the Americas New York, NY 10020. Phone: 800-722-4726 or (212)512-2000 Fax: (212)512-4502 E-mail: customer.service@mcgraw-hill.com • URL: http://www.mcgraw-hill.com • 1999. $150.00. 14th edtion. (Engineering and Technology Management Series).

Standard Handbook of Audio and Radio Engineering. Jerry C. Whitaker and K. Blair Benson. McGraw-Hill, 1221 Ave. of the Americas New York, NY 10020. Phone: 800-722-4726 or (212)512-2000 Fax: (212)512-4502 E-mail: customer.service@mcgraw-hill.com • URL: http://www.mcgraw-hill.com • 2002. $125.00. Second edition. Emphasis is on audio. Covers such topics as DVD, MP3, sound reproduction, amplification, noise reduction, and Internet audio.

Standard Handbook of Hazardous Waste Treatment and Disposal. Harry M. Freeman, editor. McGraw-Hill, 1221 Ave. of the Americas New York, NY 10020. Phone: 800-722-4726 or (212)512-2000 Fax: (212)512-4502 E-mail: customer.service@mcgraw-hill.com • URL: http://www.mcgraw-hill.com • 1997. $140.00. Second expanded revised edition.

Standard Handbook of Plant Engineering. Robert C. Rosaler, editor. McGraw-Hill Professional, 1221 Ave. of the Americas New York, NY 10020. Phone: 800-722-4726 or (212)512-2000 Fax: (212)512-4502 E-mail: customer.service@mcgraw-hill.com • URL: http://www.mcgraw-hill.com • 2002. $125.00. Third edition. (Handbook Series).

Standard Handbook of Power Plant Engineering. Thomas C. Elliott and others. McGraw-Hill, 1221 Ave. of the Americas New York, NY 10020. Phone: 800-722-4726 or (212)512-2000 Fax: (212)512-4502 E-mail: customer.service@mcgraw-hill.com • URL: http://www.mcgraw-hill.com • 1997. $115.00. Second edition.

Standard Handbook of Structural Details for Building Construction. Morton Newman. McGraw-Hill, 1221 Ave. of the Americas New York, NY 10020. Phone: 800-722-4726 or (212)512-2000 Fax: (212)512-4502 E-mail: customer.service@mcgraw-hill.com • URL: http://www.mcgraw-hill.com • 1993. $99.95. Second edition.

Standard Handbook of Video and Television Engineering. Jerry C. Whitaker. McGraw-Hill, 1221 Ave. of the Americas New York, NY 10020. Phone: 800-722-4726 or (212)512-2000 Fax: (212)512-4502 E-mail: customer.service@mcgraw-hill.com • URL: http://www.mcgraw-hill.com • 2000. $150.00. Fourth edition. Covers the design, production, installation, operation, and maintenance of video recording or TV broadcasting facilities.

Standard Highway Signs, as Specified in the Manual on Uniform Traffic Control Devices. Available from U. S. Government Printing Office, Washington, DC 20402. Phone: (202)512-1800 Fax: (202)512-2250 E-mail: gpoaccess@gpo.gov • URL: http://www.access.gpo.gov • Looseleaf. $153.00. Issued by the U. S. Department of Transportation (http://www.dot.gov). Includes basic manual, with updates for an indeterminate period. Contains illustrations of typical standard signs approved for use on streets and highways, and provides information on dimensions and placement of symbols.

Standard Industrial Classification Manual. U.S. Department of Commerce, Bureau of the Census. Available from U.S. Government Printing Office, Washington, DC 20402. Phone: (202)512-1800 Fax: (202)512-2250 E-mail: gpoaccess@gpo.gov • URL: http://www.accessgpo.gov • 1987. $36.00.

Standard Occupational Classification Manual. Available from Bernan Associates, 4611-F Assembly Dr. Lanham, MD 20706-4391. Phone: 800-274-4888 or (301)459-2255 Fax: 800-865-3450 or (301)459-0056 E-mail: query@bernan.com • URL: http://www.bernan.com • 2000. $38.00. Replaces the *Dictionary of Occupational Titles*. Produced by the federal Office of Management and Budget, Executive Office of the President. "Occupations are classified based on the work performed, and on the required skills, education, training, and credentials for each one." Six-digit codes contain elements for 23 Major Groups, 96 Minor Groups, 451 Broad Occupations, and 820 Detailed Occupations. Designed to reflect the occupational structure currently existing in the U. S.

Standard Periodical Directory. Oxbridge Communications Inc., 186 5th Ave. New York, NY 10010. Phone: 800-955-0231 or (212)741-0231 Fax: 800-414-5043 or (212)633-2938 E-mail: info@oxbridge.com • URL: http://www.galegroup.com • Covers: 58,000 magazines, journals, newsletters, directories, house organs, association publications, etc. in the United States and Canada. Entries include: Publication current and former title; publisher name, address, phone; names and titles of key personnel; circulation and advertising rates; description of contents; ISSN, year founded, frequency; subscription rates, print method, page size, number of pages.

Standard Textbook of Cosmetology 2000: A Practical Course on the Scientific Fundals of Beauty Culture for Students and Practicing Cosmetologists. Constance V. Kibbe. Delmar Learning, 5 Maxwell Dr. Clifton Park, NY 12065. Phone: 800-347-7707 or (518)464-3500 Fax: (518)464-0357 • URL: http://www.delmarlearning.com • 1999. $57.95. Ninth deluxe edition. (Standard Texts of Cosmetology).

Standards Action. American National Standards Institute Inc., 1819 L St. NW, 6th Fl., Ste. 600 Washington, DC 20016. Phone: (202)293-8020 Fax: (202)293-9287 E-mail: storemanager@ansi.org • URL: http://www.ansi.org • Description: Lists new and proposed American National Standards and draft international standards of the International Organization for Standardization (ISO), International Electrotechnical Commission (IEC), European Committee for Standardization (CEN), and European Committee for Electrotechnical Standardization (CENELEC). Lists proposed foreign government regulations from countries that signed the General Agreement on Tariffs and Trade (GATT) Standards Code. Provides listing for registration of organization names in the United States. **Remarks:** Subscription includes ANSI Reporter (see separate listing).

Standards Activities of Organizations in the United States. Available from U. S. Government Printing Office, Washington, DC 20402. Phone: (202)512-1800 Fax: (202)512-2250 E-mail: gpoaccess@gpo.gov • URL: http://www.access.gpo.gov • 1996. Prepared by the Office of Standards Code and Information, National Institute of Standards and Technology, U. S. Dept. of Commerce. Describes the activities of over 750 U. S. organizations that develop and publish standards. Formerly *Directory of United States Standardization Activities*.

Standards Engineering. Standards Engineering Society, 13340 S.W. 96th Ave. Miami, FL 33176. Phone: (305)971-4798 Fax:

(305)971-4799 E-mail: director@ses-standards.org • URL: http://www.ses-standards.org • Bimonthly. $45.00 per year.

Standards Engineering Society., 13340 SW 96th Ave. Miami, FL 33176. Phone: (305)971-4798 Fax: (305)971-4799 E-mail: admin@ses-standards.org • URL: http://www.ses-standards.org • Engineers, teachers, executives, and scholars interested in practicing standardization. Seeks to further standardization as a means of enhancing general welfare and to promote knowledge and use of approved standards issued by regularly constituted standardizing bodies.

Stanford Research Park., Stanford University, 2770 Sand Hill Rd. Menlo Park, CA 94025. Phone: (650)926-0200 Links research resources of Stanford University with private enterprise.

Stanger Report: A Guide to Partnership Investing. Robert A. Stanger and Co., 1129 Broad St., 2nd Fl. Shrewsbury, NJ 07702-4314. Phone: (732)389-3600 Fax: (732)389-1751 E-mail: info@rastanger.com • URL: http://www.rastanger.com • Quarterly. $447.00 per year. Newsletter providing analysis of limited partnership investments.

Star Service: The Critical Guide to Hotels and Cruise Ships. New Concepts Canada, 7311 Schaefer Ave. Richmond, BC, Canada V6Y 2W7. Phone: 888-975-7888 or (604)272-1174 Fax: (604)272-4574 E-mail: sales@newconcepts.ca • URL: http://www.newconcepts.ca • $210.00. Looseleaf. Quarterly updates. Provides "honest and unbiased descriptions of accommodations, facilities, amenities, ambience, appearance, and service" for more than 10,000 hotels worldwide and 150 cruise ships. Ship information includes history, passenger profiles, crew profiles, and other data.

Start and Run a Successful Craft Business: A Step-by-Step Business Plan. William G. Hynes. Self-Counsel Press, Inc., 1704 N. State St. Bellingham, WA 98225. Phone: 877-877-6490 or (360)676-4530 Fax: (360)676-4549 E-mail: orderdesk@self-counsel.com • URL: http://www.self-counsel.com • 2002. $14.95. Seventh revised edition. (Start and Run a Profitable Series: Vol. 6).

Start Right in E-Business: A Step-by-Step Guide to Successful E-Business Implementation. Bennet P. Lientz and Kathryn P. Rea. Elsevier, 655 Avenue of the Americas New York, NY 10010-5107. Phone: 800-366-2665 or (212)989-5800 Fax: 800-535-9935 or (212)633-3680 E-mail: custserv@elsevier.com • URL: http://www.elsevier.com • 2000. $47.95. (E-Business Solutions Series).

Start, Run, and Profit From Your Own Home-Based Business. Gregory Kishel and Patricia Kishel. John Wiley and Sons, Inc., 111 River St. Hoboken, NJ 07030. Phone: 800-225-5945 or (201)748-6000 Fax: (201)748-6088 E-mail: info@wiley.com • URL: http://www.wiley.com • 1991. $16.95.

Start-Up and Emerging Companies: Planning, Financing, and Operating the Successful Business, with Forms on Disk. American Lawyer Media, Inc., 105 Madison Ave. New York, NY 10016. Phone: 800-888-8300 or (212)779-9200 Fax: (212)481-8110 E-mail: lawcatalog@amlaw.com • URL: http://www.lawcatalog.com/ • Looseleaf. $289.00. Two volumes. Updated as needed. Covers a wide variety of business and legal topics relating to new enterprises. Provides information on venture financing, formation of corporations, tax laws, limited liability companies, employee benefits, contracts, and accounting. Includes a CD-ROM containing more than 75 sample legal forms, clauses, agreements, organizational resolutions, and checklists. (Law Journal Press).

Start-Up Business Guides. Entrepreneur Media, Inc., 2445 McCabe Way Irvine, CA 92614. Phone: 800-421-2300 or (949)261-2325 Fax: (949)261-0234 E-mail: entmag@entrepreneur.com • URL: http://www.entrepreneur.com • Looseleaf. $59.50 each. Practical guides to starting a wide variety of small businesses.

Starting an Indexing Business. Enid L. Zafran, editor. Information Today, Inc., 143 Old Marlton Pike Medford, NJ 08055-8750. Phone: 800-300-9868 or (609)654-6266 Fax: (609)654-4309 E-mail: custserv@infotoday.com • URL: http://www.infotoday.com • 2000. $30.00. Third edition. Published in conjunction with the American Society of Indexers (ASI). Covers fees, contractual forms, indexing as a business in the home, publisher expectations, career concerns, and related topics.

Starting and Running a Nonprofit Organization. Joan Hummel. University of Minnesota Press, 111 Third Ave., S. Suite 290 Minneapolis, MN 55401-2520. Phone: 800-621-2736 or (612)627-1970 Fax: (612)627-1980 E-mail: ump@staff.tc.umn.edu • URL: http://www.upress.umn.edu • 1996. $14.95. Second revised edition.

Starting on a Shoestring: Building a Business Without a Bankroll. Arnold S. Goldstein. John Wiley and Sons, Inc., 111 River St. Hoboken, NJ 07030. Phone: 800-225-5945 or (201)748-6000 Fax: (201)748-6088 E-mail: info@wiley.com • URL: http://www.wiley.com • 2002. $19.95. Fourth edition. Includes chapters on venture capital and Small Business Administration (SBA) loans.

Startup: An Entrepreneur's Guide to Launching and Managing a New Venture. William J. Stolze. Rock Beach Press, 1255 University Press Rochester, NY 14607. Phone: (716)442-0888 1989. $24.95.

State and Local Communications Report. Aspen Publishers, 1185 Ave. of the Americas New York, NY 10036. Phone: 800-234-1660 or (212)597-0200 Fax: 800-561-4845 • URL: http://www.aspenpublishers.com • Biweekly. $645.00 per year.

Newsletter. Formerly *Telecommunications Week*.

State and Metropolitan Area Data Book. Available from U. S. Government Printing Office, Washington, DC 20402. Phone: (202)512-1800 Fax: (202)512-2250 E-mail: gpoaccess@gpo.gov • URL: http://www.access.gpo.gov • 1998. Issued by the U. S. Bureau of the Census. Presents a wide variety of statistical data for U. S. regions, states, counties, metropolitan areas, and central cities, with ranking tables. Time period is 1970 to 1990.

State and Regional Associations of the United States. Columbia Books, Inc., 1825 Connecticut Ave., Suite 625 Washington, DC 20009. Phone: 888-265-0600 or (202)464-1662 Fax: (202)464-1775 E-mail: info@columbiabooks.com • URL: http://www.comlubiabooks.com • Annual. $149.00. Provides information on over 7,400 state and regional business associations, professional societies, and labor unions

State Budget Actions, 2000. Corina Eckl and Arturo Perez. National Conference of State Legislatures, 7700 E 1st Pl. Denver, CO 80202-1743. Phone: (303)364-7700 Fax: (303)364-7800 E-mail: info@ncsl.org • URL: http://www.ncsl.org • 2000. $35.00. Presents yearly summaries of state spending priorities and fiscal climates. Includes end-of-year general fund balances and other information on state funds.

State Capitals. Wakeman-Walworth, Inc., P.O. Box 7376 Alexandria, VA 22307-7376. Phone: 800-876-2545 or (703)768-9600 Fax: (703)768-9690 E-mail: newsletters@statecapitals.com • URL: http://www.statecapitals.com • Irregular. Prices may vary. A group of 39 newsletters, with each publication having its own subtitle and topic of relevance to state government.

State Government Affairs Council., 515 King St., Ste. 325 Alexandria, VA 22314. Phone: (703)684-0967 Fax: (703)684-0968 E-mail: stategov@sgac.org • URL: http://www.sgac.org • Businesses and organizations of businesses operating in multiple states. Each member has an established officer, employee or department who represents the company or organization in state legislative, regulatory or public affairs matters. Seeks to improve the state legislative process through interaction with major state governmental conferences. Acts as liaison with National Conference of State Legislatures, Council of State Governments (see separate entries) and governors' associations. Through State +Government +Affairs Council Foundation program, conducts educational programs on issues of public policy concern in order to further understanding between private sector business and state legislatures and agencies.

State Government News: The Monthly Magazine Covering All Facets of State Government. Council of State Governments, 2760 Research Park Dr. Lexington, KY 40578. Phone: 800-800-1910 or (859)244-8000 Fax: (859)244-8001 E-mail: sales@csg.org • URL: http://www.csg.org • Monthly. $39.00 per year.

State Guard Association of the United States., PO Box 1416 Fayetteville, GA 30214-1416. Phone: (770)460-1215 Fax: (770)261-9099 E-mail: director@sgaus.org • URL: http://www.sgaus.org • Active and retired officers and enlisted personnel of State Defense Forces (SDF) including State Guard, State Military Reserve, National Reserve, Defense Force, Guard Reserve, and other militia. Promotes the SDF in states where they exist; lobbies on behalf of SDF before state and federal governments; fosters exchange among states to keep members abreast of changes in laws pertaining to the SDF. Seeks to educate the public and disseminates information on the history and mission of the militia and to advocate a viable state militia system.

State Income Tax Alert. State Taxation Institute, 4025 W Peterson Ave. Chicago, IL 60646-6085. Phone: 800-TELL-CCH or (847)267-7000 Fax: (773)866-3895 E-mail: cservice@ragan.com • URL: http://www.cch.com • Description: Features updates on state income tax issues. Recurring features include a calendar of events, book reviews, and news of educational opportunities.

State Legislative Report. National Conference of State Legislatures, 7700 E First Pl. Denver, CO 80230. Phone: (303)364-7700 Fax: (303)364-7800 E-mail: books@ncsl.org • URL: http://www.ncsl.org • Description: Contains briefings on topics of state legislative concerns covering a broad range of policy issues.

State Legislatures. National Conference of State Legislatures, 7700 E First Pl. Denver, CO 80230. Phone: (303)364-7700 Fax: (303)364-7800 E-mail: books@ncsl.org • URL: http://www.ncsl.org • Description: Provides a national perspective on government and policy in the each state. Features articles on public policy issues.

The State of Food and Agriculture. Available from Bernan Associates, 4611-F Assembly Dr. Lanham, MD 20706-4391. Phone: 800-274-4447 or (301)459-2255 Fax: 800-865-3450 or (301)459-0056 E-mail: query@bernan.com • URL: http://www.bernan.com • Annual. $55.00. Published by the Food and Agriculture Organization of the United Nations (FAO). A yearly review of world and regional agricultural and food activities. Includes tables and graphs. Text in English.

State of the World [year]. Worldwatch Institute, 1776 Massachusetts Ave., N.W. Washington, DC 20036-1904. Phone: 888-544-2303 or (202)452-1999 Fax: (202)296-7365 E-mail: wwpub@worldwatch.org • URL: http://www.worldwatch.org • Annual. $16.95. Provides yearly analysis of factors influencing the global environment.

State Profiles: The Population and Economy of Each U. S.

State. Courtenay Slater and Others. Bernan Press, 4611-F Assembly Dr. Lanham, MD 20706-4391. Phone: 800-274-4447 or (301)459-2255 Fax: 800-865-3450 or (301)459-9235 E-mail: bpress@bernan.com • URL: http://www.bernan.com • 1999. $89.00. Presents charts, tables, and text in an eight-page profile for each state. Covers population, labor force, income, poverty, employment, wages, industry, trade, housing, education, health, taxes, and government finances. (The Population and Economy of Each United States Series).

State Tax Actions. National Conference of State Legislatures, 444 N Capitol St., NW, Ste. 515 Washington, DC 20001. Phone: (202)624-5400 Fax: (202)737-1069 E-mail: info@ncsl.org • URL: http://www.ncsl.org • Annual. $35.00. Summarizes yearly tax changes by type and by state.

State Tax Notes. Tax Analysts, 6830 N. Fairfax Dr. Arlington, VA 22213. Phone: 800-955-2444 or (703)533-4400 Fax: (703)533-4444 E-mail: cservice@tax.org • URL: http://www.tax.org • Weekly. $949.00 per year, including annual CD-ROM. Newsletter. Covers tax developments in all states. Provides state tax document summaries and citations.

State Yellow Book: Who's Who in the Executive and Legislative Branches of the 50 Governments. Leadership Directories, Inc., 104 Fifth Ave. New York, NY 10011. Phone: (212)627-4140 Fax: (212)645-6931 E-mail: info@leadershipdirectories.com • URL: http://www.leadershipdirectories.com • Quarterly. $360.00 per year. Lists more than 37,000 elected and administrative officials by state, District of Columbia, and U. S. Territory. Includes state profiles, with historical and statistical data. County population and per capita income is also included.

The Statesman's Yearbook: Statistical and Historical Annual of the States of the World. Saint Martin's Press, 175 5th Ave. New York, NY 10010. Phone: 800-221-7945 or (212)674-5151 E-mail: enquiries@stmartins.com • URL: http://www.stmartins.com • Annual. $120.00.

Station Representatives Association., 16 W. 77th St. No. 9-E New York, NY 10024-5126. Phone: (212)362-8868 Fax: (212)362-4999 E-mail: srajerry@aol.com Sales representatives for television stations concerned with the sale of "spot" advertising. **Publications:** none.

Statistical Abstract of Latin America. University of California, Los Angeles, Latin American Center, 10343 Bunche Hall Los Angeles, CA 90095. Phone: (310)825-6634 Fax: (310)206-6859 E-mail: lacpubs@isop.ucla.edu • URL: http://www.isop.ucla.edu • Annual. $325.00. Two volumes.

Statistical Abstract of the United States. Available from U. S. Government Printing Office, Washington, DC 20402. Phone: (202)512-1800 Fax: (202)512-2250 E-mail: gpoaccess@gpo.gov • URL: http://www.access.gpo.gov • Annual. $51.00. Issued by the U. S. Bureau of the Census.

Statistical Abstract of the United States on CD-ROM. Hoover's, Inc., 5800 Airport Blvd. Austin, TX 78752. Phone: 800-486-8666 or (512)374-4500 Fax: (512)374-4501 E-mail: orders@hoovers.com • URL: http://www.hoovers.com • Annual. $49.95. Provides all statistics from official print version, plus expanded historical data, greater detail, and keyword searching features.

Statistical Abstract of the World. Gale Cengage Learning, 27500 Drake Rd. Farmington Hills, MI 48331-3535. Phone: 800-877-GALE or (248)699-4253 Fax: 800-414-5043 E-mail: gale.galeord@cengage.com • URL: http://gale.cengage.com • 1997. $85.00. Third edition. Provides data on a wide variety of economic, social, and political topics for about 200 countries. Arranged by country.

Statistical Annual: Grains, Options on Agricultural Futures. Chicago Board of Trade, Education and Marketing Services Dept., 141 W. Jackson Blvd. Chicago, IL 60604-2994. Phone: 800-572-3276 or (312)435-3500 E-mail: comments@cbot.com • URL: http://www.cbot.com • Annual. Includes historical data on Wheat Futures, Options on Wheat Futures, Corn Futures, Options on Corn Futures, Oats Futures, Soybean Futures, Options on Soybean Futures, Soybean Oil Futures, Soybean Meal Futures.

Statistical Annual: Interest Rates, Metals, Stock Indices, Options on Financial Futures, Options on Metals Futures. Chicago Board of Trade, Education and Marketing Services Dept., 141 W. Jackson Blvd. Chicago, IL 60604-2994. Phone: 800-572-3276 or (312)435-3542 E-mail: comments@cbot.com • URL: http://www.cbot.com • Annual. Includes historical data on GNMA CDR Futures, Cash-Settled GNMA Futures, U. S. Treasury Bond Futures, U. S. Treasury Note Futures, Options on Treasury Note Futures, NASDAQ-100 Futures, Major Market Index Futures, Major Market Index MAXI Futures, Municipal Bond Index Futures, 1,000-Ounce Silver Futures, Options on Silver Futures, and Kilo Gold Futures.

Statistical Bulletin of the International Office of Cocoa, Chocolate and Sugar Confectionary. International Office of Cocoa, Chocolate and Sugar Confectionary, Ave. de Cortenbergh 172 B-1040 Brussels, Belgium. Phone: (322)-7351072 Fax: (322)-7363623 Annual.

Statistical Forecasts of the United States. Gale Cengage Learning, 27500 Drake Rd. Farmington Hills, MI 48331-3535. Phone: 800-877-GALE or (248)699-4253 Fax: 800-414-5043 E-mail: gale.galeord@cengage.com • URL: http://gale.cengage.com • 1995. $115.00. Second edition. Provides both long-term and short-term statistical forecasts relating to basic items in the U. S.: population, employment, labor, crime, education, and health care. Data in the form of charts, graphs,

and tables has been taken from a wide variety of government and private sources. Includes a subject index and an "Index of Forecast by Year."

Statistical Handbook of Working America. Gale Cengage Learning, 27500 Drake Rd. Farmington Hills, MI 48331-3535. Phone: 800-877-GALE or (248)699-4253 Fax: 800-414-5043 E-mail: gale.galeord@cengage.com • URL: http://gale.cengage.com • 1997. $130.00. Second edition. Provides statistics, rankings, and forecasts relating to a wide variety of careers, occupations, and working conditions.

Statistical Handbook on Aging Americans. Renee Schick. Greenwood Publishing Group, Inc., 88 Post Rd., W. Westport, CT 06881. Phone: 800-225-5800 or (203)226-3571 Fax: (203)431-2214 E-mail: customer-service@greenwood.com • URL: http://www.greenwood.com • 1994. $69.95. Second edition. Provides data on demographics, social characteristics, health, employment, economic conditions, income, pensions, and social security. Includes bibliographic information and a glossary. (Statistical Handbook Series).

Statistical Handbook on Consumption and Wealth in the United States. Greenwood Publishing Group, Inc., 88 Post Rd., W. Westport, CT 06881. Phone: 800-225-5800 or (203)226-3571 Fax: (203)431-2214 E-mail: customer-service@greenwood.com • URL: http://www.greenwood.com • 1999. $69.95. Provides more than 400 graphs, tables, and charts dealing with basic income levels, income inequalities, spending patterns, taxation, subsidies, etc. (Statistical Handbook Series).

Statistical Handbook on Poverty in the Developing World. Chandrika Kaul. Greenwood Publishing Group, Inc., 88 Post Rd., W. Wesport, CT 06881. Phone: 800-225-5800 or (203)226-3571 Fax: (203)431-2214 E-mail: customer-service@greenwood.com • URL: http://www.greenwood.com • 1999. $69.95. Provides international coverage, including special sections on women and children, and on selected cities. (Statistical Handbooks Series).

Statistical Handbook on Technology. Paula Bernstein. Greenwood Publishing Group, Inc., 88 Post Rd., W. Westport, CT 06881. Phone: 800-225-5800 or (203)226-3571 Fax: (203)431-2214 E-mail: customer-service@greenwood.com • URL: http://www.greenwood.com • 1999. $69.95. Provides statistical data on such items as the Internet, online services, computer technology, recycling, patents, prescription drug sales, telecommunications, and aerospace. Includes charts, tables, and graphs. Edited for the general reader. (Statistical Handbook Series).

Statistical Handbook on the American Family. Bruce A. Chadwick and Tim B. Heaton. Greenwood Publishing Group, Inc., 88 Post Rd., W. Westport, CT 06881. Phone: 800-225-5800 or (203)226-3571 Fax: (203)431-2214 E-mail: customer-service@greenwood.com • URL: http://www.greenwood.com • 1998. $69.95. Second edition. Includes data on education, health, politics, employment, expenditures, social characteristics, the elderly, and women in the labor force. Historical statistics on marriage, birth, and divorce are shown from 1900 on. A list of sources and a subject index are provided. (Statistical Handbooks Series).

Statistical Handbook on U. S. Hispanics. Frank L. Schick and Renee Schick, editors. Greenwood Publishing Group, Inc., 88 Post Rd., W. Westport, CT 06881. Phone: 800-225-5800 or (203)226-3571 Fax: (203)431-2214 E-mail: customer-service@greenwood.com • URL: http://www.greenwood.com • 1991. $69.95. Includes data on demographics, employment, income, assets, etc. (Statistical Handbooks Series).

Statistical Handbook on Women in America. Cynthia M. Taeuber, editor. Greenwood Publishing Group, Inc., 88 Post Rd., W. Westport, CT 06881. Phone: 800-225-5800 or (203)226-3571 Fax: (203)431-2214 E-mail: customer-service@greenwood.com • URL: http://www.greenwood.com • 1996. $69.95. Second edition. Includes data on demographics, employment, earnings, economic status, educational status, marriage, divorce, household units, health, and other topics. (Statistical Handbook Series).

Statistical Indicators for Asia and the Pacific. United Nations Publications, United Nations Concourse Level New York, NY 10017. Phone: 800-553-3210 or (212)963-7680 Fax: (212)963-4910 E-mail: bookstore@un.org • URL: http://www.un.org/publications • Quarterly. $80.00 per year. Provides data on economic and demographic trends in the region. Text in English.

Statistical Information on the Financial Services Industry. American Bankers Association, 1120 Connecticut Ave., N. W. Washington, DC 20036-3971. Phone: 800-226-5377 or (202)663-5000 Fax: (202)663-7543 E-mail: custserv@aba.com • URL: http://www.aba.com • Annual. Members, $150.00; non-members, $275.00. Presents a wide variety of data relating to banking and financial services, including consumer economics, personal finance, credit, government loans, capital markets, and international banking.

Statistical Methods for the Information Professional: A Practical, Painless Approach to Understanding, Using, and Interpreting Statistics. Liwen Vaughan. Information Today, Inc., 143 Old Marlton Pike Medford, NJ 08055-8750. Phone: 800-300-9868 or (609)654-6266 Fax: (609)654-4309 E-mail: custserv@infotoday.com • URL: http://www.infotoday.com • 2001. $39.50. Published in conjunction with the American Society for Information Science and Technology (ASIST).

A Statistical Portrait of the United States: Social Conditions and Trends. Mark S. Littman, editor. Bernan Press, 4611-F Assembly Dr. Lanham, MD 20706-4391. Phone: 800-274-4447

or (301)459-2255 Fax: 800-865-3450 or (301)459-0056 E-mail: bpress@bernan.com • URL: http://www.bernan.com • 1998. $89.00. Covers "social, economic, and environmental trends in the United States over the past 25 years." Includes statistical tables, graphs, and analysis relating to such topics as population, income, poverty, wealth, labor, housing, education, healthcare, air/water quality, and government. (Statistical Portrait of the United States: Social Conditions and Trends Series).

Statistical Quality Control: Strategies and Tools for Continual Improvement. Johannes Ledolter and Claude W. Burrill. John Wiley and Sons, Inc., 111 River St. Hoboken, NJ 07030. Phone: 800-225-5945 or (201)748-6000 Fax: (201)748-6088 E-mail: info@wiley.com • URL: http://www.wiley.com • 1998. $104.95.

Statistical Record of Black Americans. Gale Cengage Learning, 27500 Drake Rd. Farmington Hills, MI 48331-3535. Phone: 800-877-GALE or (248)699-4253 Fax: 800-414-5043 E-mail: gale.galeord@cengage.com • URL: http://gale.cengage.com • 1996. $130.00. Fourth edition. Contains more than 1,000 statistical graphs, tables, and lists arranged in 16 broad subject chapters. Covers population, housing, business, income, education, etc. Includes an extensive bibliography and a detailed subject index.

Statistical Record of Older Americans. Gale Cengage Learning, 27500 Drake Rd. Farmington Hills, MI 48331-3535. Phone: 800-877-GALE Fax: 800-414-5043 E-mail: gale.galeord@cengage.com • URL: http://gale.cengage.com • 1996. $130.00. Second edition. Includes income and pension data.

Statistical Record of the Environment. Gale Cengage Learning, 27500 Drake Rd. Farmington Hills, MI 48331-3535. Phone: 800-877-GALE or (248)699-4253 Fax: 800-414-5043 E-mail: gale.galeord@cengage.com • URL: http://gale.cengage.com • 1996. $130.00. Third edition. Provides over 875 charts, tables, and graphs of major environmental statistics, arranged by subject. Covers population growth, hazardous waste, nuclear energy, acid rain, pesticides, and other subjects related to the environment. A keyword index is included. (Gale Environmental Library Series).

Statistical Record of Women Worldwide. Gale Cengage Learning, 27500 Drake Rd. Farmington Hills, MI 48331-3535. Phone: 800-877-GALE or (248)699-4253 Fax: 800-414-5043 E-mail: gale.galeord@cengage.com • URL: http://gale.cengage.com • 1995. $130.00. Second edition. Includes employment data and other economic statistics relating to women in the U. S. and internationally.

Statistical Reference Centre., Holland Ave., Room 1500 Ottawa, ON, Canada K1A OT6. Phone: 800-263-1136 or (613)951-8116 Fax: 877-287-4369 E-mail: infostats@statcan.ca • URL: http://www.statcan.ca • Issues compilations of census data and other facts relating to Canadian business, finance, industry, economics, and society in general. Statistics Canada is the country's national statistical agency, required to collect data according to the Statistics Act.

Statistical Reference Index: A Selective Guide to American Statistical Publications from Sources Other than the United States Government. Congressional Information Service, Inc., 4520 East-West Highway Bethesda, MD 20814-3389. Phone: 800-638-8380 or (301)654-1550 Fax: (301)654-4033 E-mail: cisinfo@lexis-nexis.com • URL: http://www.cispubs.com • Monthly. Price varies. Quarterly and annual cumulations. Service basis.

Statistical Report on Road Accidents. Organization for Economic Cooperation and Development, OECD Washington Center, 2001 L St., N. W., Suite 650 Washington, DC 20036-4922. Phone: 800-456-6323 or (202)785-6323 Fax: (202)785-0350 E-mail: washington.contact@oecd.org • URL: http://www.oecd.org • Annual. $20.00. Provides data from various countries on road accidents resulting in injuries or fatalities. Includes 12-year statistical trends.

Statistical Reports. National Alcoholic Beverage Control Association, 4216 King St., W. Alexandria, VA 22302. Phone: (703)578-4200 Fax: (703)820-3551 E-mail: tschultz@nabca.org • URL: http://www.nabca.org • Monthly. Price on application. Includes quarterly and annual cumulations.

Statistical Techniques in Business and Economics. Douglas A. Lind and others. McGraw-Hill, 1221 Ave. of the Americas New York, NY 10020. Phone: 800-722-4726 or (212)512-2000 Fax: (212)512-4502 E-mail: customer.service@mcgraw-hill.com • URL: http://www.mcgraw-hill.com • 2001. 11th edition. Price on application.

Statistical Theory and Method Abstracts. International Statistical Institute, Princes Beatrixlaan 2270 AZ Voorburg, Netherlands. Phone: 31 70 337 5737 Fax: 31 70 386 0025 E-mail: isi@cbs.nl • URL: http://www.cbs.nl • Quarterly. Members, $100.00 per year; non-members, $140.00 per year. Worldwide coverage of published papers on mathematical statistics and probability.

Statistical Yearbook. United Nations Publications, United Nations Concourse Level, First Ave., 46th St. New York, NY 10017. Phone: 800-553-3210 or (212)963-7680 Fax: (212)963-4910 E-mail: bookstore@un.org • URL: http://www.un.org/publications • Annual. $125.00. Contains statistics for about 200 countries on a wide variety of economic, industrial, and demographic topics. Compiled by United Nations Statistical Office.

Statistical Yearbook for Asia and the Pacific. United Nations Publications, United Nations Concourse Level, First Ave., 46th St. New York, NY 10017. Phone: 800-553-3210 or

(212)963-7680 Fax: (212)963-4910 E-mail: bookstore@un. org • URL: http://www.un.org/publications • Annual. $90.00. Includes 56 countries of the region. Contains data on national accounts, trade, industry, banking, wages, consumption, population, and other economic and demographic subjects. Text in English and French.

Statistical Yearbook for Latin America and the Caribbean. Available from United Nations Publications, United Nations Concourse Level, First Ave., 46th St. New York, NY 10017. Phone: 800-553-3210 or (212)963-7680 Fax: (212)963-4910 E-mail: bookstore@un.org • URL: http://www.un.org/ publications • Annual. $79.00. Issued by the Economic Commission for Latin America and the Caribbean. Includes a wide variety of economic, industrial, and trade data for Latin American nations. Text in English and Spanish.

Statistical YearBook of the Electric Utility Industry. Edison Electric Institute, PO Box 266 Waldorf, MD 20604-0266. Phone: 800-334-5453 or (301)645-4222 Fax: (301)843-0159 E-mail: catalog@eei.org • URL: http://www.eei.org • Annual. Members, $270.00; non-members, $550.00.

Statistical Yearbook of the Immigration and Naturalization Service. Available from U. S. Government Printing Office, Washington, DC 20402. Phone: (202)512-1800 Fax: (202)512-2250 E-mail: gpoaccess@gpo.gov • URL: http:// www.access.gpo.gov • Annual. $40.00. Provides data on legal immigrants, deportable aliens, refugees, persons naturalized, political asylum cases, foreign tourists, and foreign students.

Statistics Canada! Statistics CanadaPhone: 800-263-1136 or (613)951-8116 Fax: 877-287-4369 • URL: http://www. statcan.ca • Web site in English and French provides basic statistical information relating to economic and social conditions in Canada: "The Land," "The People," "The Economy," "The State." Includes daily news, latest indicators, products and services, and links to other sites. Keyword searching is provided. Fees: Free.

Statistics for Management. Richard I. Levin and David S. Rubin. Prentice Hall PTR, 240 Frisch Ct. Paramus, NJ 07652. Phone: 800-282-0693 Fax: 800-445-6991 • URL: http://www.phptr. com • 1997. $93.33. Seventh edition.

Statistics for People Who Think They Hate Statistics. Neil J. Salkind. Sage Publications, Inc., 2455 Teller Rd. Thousand Oaks, CA 91320-2218. Phone: 800-818-7243 or (805)499-0721 Fax: 800-583-2665 or (805)499-0871 E-mail: info@ sagepub.com • URL: http://www.sagepub.com • 2004. $84. 95. Second edition. Serves as a clearly-written introduction to a wide variety of statistical procedures. Includes a glossary.

Statistics for the Environment: Statistical Aspects of Health and the Environment. Vic Barnett and others. John Wiley and Sons, Inc., 111 River St. Hoboken, NJ 07030. Phone: 800-225-5945 or (201)748-6000 Fax: (201)748-6088 E-mail: info@wiley.com • URL: http://www.wiley.com • 1999. $180. 00. Two volumes. Vol. 3, $205.00; vol. 4, $225.00. Contains articles on the statistical analysis and interpretation of environmental monitoring and sampling data. Areas covered include meteorology, pollution of the environment, and forest resources. (Statistics for the Environment Series).

Statistics of Income Bulletin. Available from U.S. Government Printing Office, Washington, DC 20402. Phone: (202)512-1800 Fax: (202)512-2250 E-mail: gpoaccess@gpo.gov • URL: http://www.access.gpo.gov • Quarterly. $44.00 per year. Current data compiled from tax returns relating to income, assets, and expenses of individuals and businesses. (U. S. Internal Revenue Service).

Statistics of Income: Corporation Income Tax Returns. U.S. Internal Revenue Service. Available from U.S. Government Printing Office, Washington, DC 20402. Phone: (202)512-1800 Fax: (202)512-2250 E-mail: gpoaccess@gpo.gov • URL: http://www.access.gpo.gov • Annual. $26.00.

Statistics of Paper, Paperboard and Wood Pulp. American Forest and Paper Association, 1111 19th St., N.W. Washington, DC 20036. Phone: (202)463-2700 Fax: (202)463-2785 Annual. $395.00. Formerly *Statistics of Paper and Paperboard*.

Statistics of World Trade in Steel. United Nations Economic Commission for Europe. Available from United Nations Publications, United Nations Concourse Level, First Ave., 46th St. New York, NY 10017. Phone: 800-553-3210 or (212)963-7680 Fax: (212)963-4910 E-mail: bookstores@un. org • URL: http://www.un.org/publications • Annual. $90.00

Statistics on Alcohol, Drug, and Tobacco Use: A Selection of Statistical Charts, Graphs and Tables about Alcohol, Drug and Tobacco Use from a Variety of Published Sources with Explanatory Comments. Gale Cengage Learning, 27500 Drake Rd. Farmington Hills, MI 48331-3535. Phone: 800-877-GALE or (248)699-4253 Fax: 800-414-5043 E-mail: gale.galeord@cengage.com • URL: http://gale.cengage.com • 1995. $85.00. Includes graphs, charts, and tables arranged within subject chapters. Citations to data sources are provided. (Statistics on...Series: vol. 1).

Statistics on Crime, Justice, and Punishment. Gale Cengage Learning, 27500 Drake Rd. Farmington Hills, MI 48331-3535. Phone: 800-877-GALE or (248)699-4253 Fax: 800-414-5043 E-mail: gale.galeord@cengage.com • URL: http:// gale.cengage.com • 1996. $850.00. Volume three. Includes graphs, charts, and tables arranged within subject chapters. Citations to data sources are provided. (Statistics on...Series: vol. 3).

Statistics on Occupational Wages and Hours of Work and on Food Prices. International Labour Organization, 1828 L St.,

N.W., Suite 600 Washington, DC 20036-5121. Phone: (202)653-7652 Fax: (202)653-7687 E-mail: klee@ilo.org • URL: http://www.ilo.org/publns • Annual. $28.00. Provides international data on wages and hours for 159 occupations within 49 industries. Includes retail prices for 93 food items.

Statistics on Weapons and Violence: A Selection of Statistical Charts, Graphs and Tables about Weapons and Violence from a Variety of Published Sources with Explanatory Comments. Gale Cengage Learning, 27500 Drake Rd. Farmington Hills, MI 48331-3535. Phone: 800-877-GALE or (248)699-4253 Fax: 800-414-5043 E-mail: gale.galeord@cengage.com • URL: http://gale.cengage.com • 1995. $85. 00. Includes graphs, charts, and tables arranged within subject chapters. Citations to data sources are provided. (Statistics for Students Series).

Statistics Sources: A Subject Guide to Data on Industrial, Business, Social, Educational, Financial and Other Topics for the U. S. and Selected Foreign Countries. Gale Cengage Learning, 27500 Drake Rd. Farmington Hills, MI 48331-3535. Phone: 800-877-GALE or (248)699-4253 Fax: 800-414-5043 E-mail: gale.galeord@cengage.com • URL: http:// gale.cengage.com • 2003. $515.00. 27th edition. Two volumes. Lists sources of statistical information for more than 20,000 topics.

Staying Wealthy: Strategies for Protecting Your Assets. Brian H. Breuel. Bloomberg, 499 Park Ave. New York, NY 10022. Phone: 800-388-2749 or (212)318-2000 Fax: (917)369-5000 • URL: http://www.bloomberg.com • 1998. $21.95. Presents ideas for estate planning and personal wealth preservation. Includes case studies. (Bloomberg Personal Bookshelf Series).

Steam Electric Market Analysis. National Mining Association, 1130 17th St., NW Washington, DC 20036-4677. Phone: (202)463-2625 Fax: (202)463-6152 E-mail: thowe@nma.org • URL: http://www.nma.org • Monthly. Free to members; non-members, $300.00 per year. Covers 400 major electric power plants, with detailed data on coal consumption and stockpiles. Shows percent of power generated by fuel type. (Publisher formerly National Coal Association.)

Steel Door Institute., 30200 Detroit Rd. Cleveland, OH 44145-1967. Phone: (440)899-0010 Fax: (440)892-1404 E-mail: info@steeldoor.org • URL: http://www.steeldoor.org • Represents manufacturers of standard, all-metal doors and frames used in commercial applications. Aims to promote the use of steel doors and frames in the construction industry.

Steel Founders' Society of America., 205 Park Ave. Barrington, IL 60010. Phone: (847)382-8240 Fax: (847)382-8287 E-mail: monroe@sfsa.org • URL: http://www.sfsa.org • Manufacturers of steel casting. Provides technical support and research. Abosorbed Alloy Casting Institute.

Steel Mill Products. U.S. Bureau of the Census, Washington, DC 20233-0800. Phone: (301)457-4100 Fax: (301)457-3842 • URL: http://www.census.gov • Annual. (Current Industrial Reports MA-33B).

Steel Shipping Container Institute., S-1101 14th St. NW Washington, DC 20005. Phone: (202)408-1900 Fax: (202)408-1972 E-mail: ssci_office@steelcontainers.com • URL: http://www.steelcontainers.com • Manufacturers of steel drums, barrels, pails, accessories, fittings, equipment, and materials used by the industry. Underwrites U.S. Bureau of Census monthly report on steel pail and drum production. Sponsors development programs on container design, safety features, testing, quality control, and product protection systems.

Steel Times International. DMG World Media Ltd., Queensway House, 2 Queensway Red Hill RH1 1QS, United Kingdom. Phone: 44 1737 855527 Fax: 44 1737 855470 • URL: http:// www.dmgworldmedia.com • Bimonthly. $182.00 per year. Includes *Iron and Steel Directory*.

Step-By-Step Electronic Design: The How-To Newsletter for Electronic Designers. Dynamic Graphics, Inc., 6000 N. Forest Park Dr. Peoria, IL 61614-3592. Phone: 800-255-8800 or (309)688-2300 Fax: (309)688-8515 E-mail: sxsgl@aol.com Monthly. $48.00 per year.

Step Inside Design: The World of Design from Inside Out. Dynamic Graphics, Inc., 6000 N. Forest Park Dr. Peoria, IL 61614-3592. Phone: 800-255-8800 or (309)688-2300 Fax: (309)698-8515 E-mail: sxsgl@aol.com Bimonthly. $42.00 per year. Formerly*Step-by-Step Graphics*.

Steps to Small Business Start-Up: Everything You Need to Know to Turn Your Idea into a Successful Business. Linda Pinson and Jerry Jinnett. Dearborn Trade Publishing, A Kaplan Professional Co., 30 S Wacker Dr., Ste. 2500 Chicago, IL 60606. Phone: 800-621-9621 or (312)836-4400 Fax: (312)836-1021 E-mail: trade@dearborn.com • URL: http:// www.dearborntrade.com • 2003. $22.95. Fifth edition. Covers such topics as location, legal structure, cash flow, financing, appropriateness, taxes, and insurance. Includes charts, sample calculations, spreadsheets, and forms.

Stereophile: For the High Fidelity Stereo Perfectionist. PRIMEDIA Inc., 745 Fifth Ave. New York, NY 10151. Phone: 800-800-6848 or (212)745-0100 Fax: (212)745-0121 E-mail: information@primedia.com • URL: http://www.primedia. com • Monthly. $12.97 per year. Review of high-end audio products.

Stock Index Futures: Buying and Selling the Market Averages. Charles Sutcliffe. Cengage Learning, 290 Harbor Dr. Stamford, CT 06902. Phone: 800-347-7707 or (203)969-8700 Fax: 800-487-8488 or (203)969-8700 E-mail:

communications@cengage.com • URL: http://www.thomson. com/learning • 1998. $37.95. Third edition.

Stock Index Options: How to Use and Profit from Indexed Options in Volatile and Uncertain Markets. Scot G. Barenblat and Donald T. Mesler. McGraw-Hill, 1221 Ave. of the Americas New York, NY 10020. Phone: 800-722-4726 or (212)512-2000 Fax: (212)512-2072 E-mail: customer. service@mcgraw-hill.com • URL: http://www.mcgraw-hill. com • 1991. $29.95. Revised editon.

Stock Market Crashes and Speculative Manias. Eugene N. White, editor. Edward Elgar Publishing, Inc., 136 West St., Suite 202 Northampton, MA 01060. Phone: 800-390-3149 or (413)584-5551 Fax: (413)584-9933 E-mail: elgarinfo@e-elgar.com • URL: http://www.e-elgar.co.uk • 1996. $255.00. Contains reprints of 23 articles dating from 1905 to 1994. (International Library of Macroeconomic and Financial History Series: No. 13).

Stock Market Values and Yields 2000. RIA, 395 Hudson St. New York, NY 10014. Phone: 800-950-1216 or 800-431-9025 E-mail: riahome@riag.com • URL: http://www.riahome.com • 2000. $22.00. Revised edition. Gives year-end prices and dividends for tax purposes.

Stockman's Handbook. R. M. Ensminger. Prentice Hall, 240 Frisch Ct. Paramus, NJ 07652. Phone: 800-223-2336 or (201)909-6200 Fax: (201)909-6360 E-mail: pearsoned@eds. com • URL: http://www.prenhall.com • 2002. $85.00. Seventh edition.

Stocks, Bonds, Bills, and Inflation Yearbook. Ibbotson Associates, 225 N. Michigan Ave., Suite 700 Chicago, IL 60601-7676. Phone: 800-758-3557 or (312)616-1620 Fax: (312)616-0404 Annual. $92.00. Provides detailed data from 1926 to the present on inflation and the returns from various kinds of financial investments, such as small-cap stocks and long-term government bonds.

Stocks for the Long Run: The Definitive Guide to Financial Market Returns and Long-Term Investment Strategies. Jeremy J. Siegel. McGraw-Hill, 1221 Ave. of the Americas New York, NY 10020. Phone: 800-722-4726 or (212)512-2000 Fax: (212)512-4502 E-mail: customer.service@mcgraw-hill.com • URL: http://www.mcgraw-hill.com • 2002. $29.95. Third revised edition. A favorable view of a buy-and-hold strategy for stock market investors. (Teach Yourself Series).

Stores. National Retail Federation. NRF Enterprises, Inc., 325 Seventh St., NW, Ste. 1000 Washington, DC 20004-2802. Phone: 800-673-4692 or (202)626-8101 Fax: (202)626-8191 • URL: http://www.stores.org • Monthly. Individuals $49.00 per year; institutions, $120.00 per year.

Storm Data. U.S. National Climatic Data Center, National Oceanic and Atmospheric Administration, U.S. Dept of Commerce, Federal Bldg., Room 120, 151 Patton Ave. Asheville, NC 28801-5001. Phone: (704)271-4476 E-mail: orders@ ncdc.noaa.gov • URL: http://www.ncdc.noaa.gov • Monthly.

Straight Talk on Investing: What You Need to Know. Jack Brennan. John Wiley and Sons, Inc., 111 River St. Hoboken, NJ 07030. Phone: 800-225-5945 or (201)748-6000 Fax: (201)748-6088 E-mail: info@wiley.com • URL: http://www. wiley.com • 2002. $22.95. Provides basic, conservative advice for the small investor. Emphasis is on long-term goals and investment planning.

StraightTalk. The Conference Board, 845 Third Ave. New York, NY 10022. Phone: (212)339-0345 Fax: (212)836-9740 • URL: http://www.conference-board.org • 10 times a year. Members, $195.00 per year; non-members, $395.00 per year. Newsletter. Provides analysis of domestic and international economic issues. Includes coverage of interest rate trends and the currency exchange outlook.

The Strategic Bond Investor: Strategies and Tools to Unlock the Power of the Bond Market. Anthony Crescenzi. McGraw-Hill, 1221 Ave. of the Americas New York, NY 10020. Phone: 800-722-4726 or (212)512-2000 Fax: (212)512-4502 E-mail: customer.service@mcgraw-hill.com • URL: http://www. mcgraw-hill.com • 2002. $29.95. Covers management strategies for fixed-income investment portfolios. (Teach Yourself Series).

Strategic Finance. Institute of Management Accountants, Ten Paragon Dr. Montvale, NJ 07645-1718. Phone: 800-638-4427 or (201)573-9000 Fax: (201)573-0639 E-mail: info@ strategicfinancemag.com • URL: http://www. strategicfinancemag.com • Monthly. Institutions, $140.00 per year; non-profit libraries, $70,00 per year. Provides articles on corporate finance, cost control, cash flow, budgeting, corporate taxes, and other financial management topics.

Strategic Health Care Marketing. Health Care Communications, 11 Heritage Ln., PO Box 594 Rye, NY 10580. Phone: (914)967-6741 Fax: (914)967-3054 E-mail: healthcomm@ aol.com • URL: http://www.strategichealthcare.com • Description: Provides news and analysis on health care services marketing, and business development. Covers strategies and techniques used by marketing innovators. Recurring features include interviews, news of research, a calendar of events, reports of meetings, and notices of publications available.

Strategic Hotel Motel Marketing. Christopher W. L. Hart and David Troy. Educational Institute of the American Hotel & Motel Association, P.O. Box 1240 East Lansing, MI 48826-1240. Phone: 800-344-4381 or (517)372-8800 Fax: (517)372-5141 E-mail: info@ei-ahla.org • URL: http://www.ei.ahma. org • 1998. $59.95. Third edition.

Strategic Leadership Forum., 230 E Ohio St., No. 400, PO Box 5329 Chicago, IL 60611-3265. Phone: (403)240-1245 Fax: (403)240-0776 E-mail: ssci_office@steelcontainers.com • URL: http://www.strategicleadershipforum.org • Professional society primarily comprised of executives involved in international strategic management and planning. Conducts education programs. Maintains numerous committees.

Strategic Management. Fred R. David. Prentice Hall PTR, 240 Frisch Ct. Paramus, NJ 07652. Phone: 800-282-0693 Fax: 800-445-6991 • URL: http://www.phptr.com • 2002. $80.00. Ninth edition.

Strategic Management for Academic Libraries: A Handbook. Robert M. Hayes. Greenwood Publishing Group, Inc., 88 Post Rd., W Westport, CT 06881. Phone: 800-225-5800 or (203)226-3571 Fax: (203)431-2214 E-mail: customer-service@greenwood.com • URL: http://www.greenwood.com • 1993. $69.95. (Library Management Collection).

Strategic Management for Public Libraries: A Handbook. Robert M. Hayes and Virginia A. Walter. Greenwood Publishing Group, Inc., 88 Post Rd., W Westport, CT 06881. Phone: 800-225-5800 or (203)226-3571 Fax: (203)431-2214 E-mail: customer-service@greenwood.com • URL: http://www.greenwood.com • 1996. $69.95. (Greenwood Library Management Collection).

Strategic Management for Today's Libraries. Marilyn G. Mason. American Library Association, 50 E. Huron St. Chicago, IL 60611-2795. Phone: 800-545-2433 or (312)944-6780 Fax: (312)440-9374 E-mail: ala@ala.org • URL: http://www.ala.org • 1999. $35.00. (ALA Editions Series).

Strategic Management: Formulation, Implementation, and Control. John A. Pearce and Richard B. Robinson. McGraw-Hill, 1221 Ave. of the Americas New York, NY 10020. Phone: 800-722-4726 or (212)512-2000 Fax: (212)512-4502 E-mail: customer.service@mcgraw-hill.com • URL: http://www.mcgraw-hill.com • 2002. Eighth edition. Price on application.

Strategic Management in Non-Profit Organizations: An Administrator's Handbook. Robert D. Hay. Greenwood Publishing Group, Inc., 88 Post Rd., W Westport, CT 06881. Phone: 800-225-5800 or (203)226-3571 Fax: (203)431-2214 E-mail: customer-service@greenwood.com • URL: http://www.greenwood.com • 1990. $84.95.

Strategic Management Journal. John Wiley and Sons, Inc., Journals, 111 River St. Hoboken, NJ 07030. Phone: 800-526-5368 or (201)748-6000 Fax: (201)748-6088 E-mail: customer@wiley.com • URL: http://www.wiley.com • Monthly. Individuals, $315.00 per year; institutions, $1,325.00 per year. Original refereed material concerned with all aspects of strategic management. Devoted to the development and improvement of both theory and practice. Provides international coverage.

Strategic Market Management. David A. Aaker. John Wiley and Sons, Inc., 111 River St. Hoboken, NJ 07030. Phone: 800-225-5945 or (201)748-6000 Fax: (201)748-6088 E-mail: info@wiley.com • URL: http://www.wiley.com • 2001. $57.95. Sixth edition.

Strategic Marketing. David W. Cravens and Nigel Percy. McGraw-Hill, 1221 Ave. of the Americas New York, NY 10020. Phone: 800-722-4726 or (212)512-2000 Fax: (212)412-4502 E-mail: customer.service@mcgraw-hill.com • URL: http://www.mcgraw-hill.com • 2002. $110.00. Seventh edition. (Marketing Series).

Strategic Marketing Problems: Cases and Comments. Roger A. Kerin and Robert A. Peterson. Prentice Hall PTR, 240 Frisch Ct. Paramus, NJ 07652. Phone: 800-282-0693 Fax: 800-445-6991 • URL: http://www.phptr.com • 2003. $113.33. 10th edition.

Strategic Planning: A How-To-Do-It Manual for Librarians. M. E. Jacob. Neal-Schuman Publishers, Inc., 100 William St., Ste. 2004 New York, NY 10038. Phone: (866)672-6657 or (212)925-8650 Fax: (866)209-7932 or (212)219-8916 E-mail: info@neal-schuman.com • URL: http://www.neal-schuman.com • 1990. $45.00. (How-to-Do-It Manuals Series).

Strategic Planning: A Practical Guide. Peter J. Rea and Harold Kerzner. John Wiley and Sons, Inc., 111 River St. Hoboken, NJ 07030. Phone: 800-225-5945 or (201)748-6000 Fax: (201)748-6088 E-mail: info@wiley.com • URL: http://www.wiley.com • 1997. $90.00. Covers strategic planning for manufacturing firms, small businesses, and large corporations. (Industrial Engineering Series).

Strategic Planning Institute., 1030 Massachusetts Ave. Newton Center, MA 01238-5388. Phone: (617)491-9200 Fax: (617)491-1634 Conducts research in business information and strategy.

Strategic Planning Plus: An Organizational Guide. Roger Kaufman. Sage Publications, Inc., 2455 Teller Rd. Thousand Oaks, CA 91320. Phone: 800-818-7243 or (805)499-9774 Fax: 800-583-2665 or (805)499-0871 E-mail: webmaster@sagepub.com • URL: http://www.sagepub • 1992. $80.95.

Strategic Trading in the Foreign Exchange Markets. Gary Klopfenstein. Fitzroy Dearborn Publishers, Inc., 919 N. Michigan Ave., Suite 760 Chicago, IL 60611. Phone: 800-850-8102 or (312)587-0131 Fax: (312)587-1049 E-mail: fitzroy@aol.com • URL: http://www.fitzroydearborn.com • 2000. $65.00. Describes the tactics of successful foreign exchange traders.

Strategy and Business., 101 Park Ave. New York, NY 10178. Phone: (212)551-6222 Fax: (212)551-6008 E-mail: editors@strategy-business.com • URL: http://www.strategy-business.com • Quarterly. $38.00 per year.

Strategy-Specific Decision Making: A Guide for Executing Competitive Strategy. William G. Forgang. M. E. Sharpe, Inc., 80 Business Park Drive Armonk, NY 10504. Phone: 800-541-6563 or (914)273-1800 Fax: (914)273-2106 E-mail: custserv@mesharpe.com • URL: http://www.mesharpe.com • 2004. $72.95. Includes a bibliography and case studies in the area of competitive strategy.

Stratis Health.

Streetsmart Guide to Short Selling: Techniques the Pros Use to Profit in Any Market. Tom Taulli. McGraw-Hill, 1221 Ave. of the Americas New York, NY 10020. Phone: 800-722-4726 or (212)512-2000 Fax: (212)512-4502 E-mail: customer.service@mcgraw-hill.com • URL: http://www.mcgraw-hill.com • 2002. $29.95. Provides the details of short sale procedures and offers practical advice for individual investors or traders. (Teach Yourself Series).

Stress: A Bibliography with Indexes. Clarke M. Ivanich, editor. Nova Science Publishers, Inc., 400 Oser Ave., Suite 1600 Hauppauge, NY 11788-3619. Phone: (631)231-7269 Fax: (631)231-8175 E-mail: novascience@earthlink.net • URL: http://www.novapublishers.com • 2002. $59.00. Provides book and journal citations to the literature of emotional stress. Includes author, title, and subject indexes.

Stress and Burnout in Library Service. Janette S. Caputo. Greenwood Publishing Group, Inc., 88 Post Rd., W. Westport, CT 06881. Phone: 800-225-5800 or (203)226-3571 Fax: (203)431-2214 E-mail: customer-service@greenwood.com • URL: http://www.greenwood.com • 1991. $24.95. Discusses symptoms of stress in library staff members and ways of dealing with stress. Includes self-help checklists and a list of references for further information.

Stress and Health. John Wiley and Sons, Inc., Journals, 111 River St. Hoboken, NJ 07030. Phone: 800-526-5368 or (201)748-6000 Fax: (201)748-6088 E-mail: customer@wiley.com • URL: http://www.wiley.com • Five times a year. Individuals, $310.00 per year; institutions, $620.00 per year. A forum for discussion of all aspects of stress which affect the individual in both health and disease. Provides international coverage. Formerly*Stress Medicine*.

Stress and Well-Being at Work: Assessments and Interventions for Occupational Mental Health. James C. Quick and others, editors. American Psychological Association, 750 1st St. NE Washington, DC 20002-4242. Phone: 800-374-2721 or (202)336-5500 Fax: (202)336-6069 • URL: http://www.apa.org • 1992. $19.95.

Strike! Jeremy Brecher. South End Press, Seven Brookline St., No. 1 Cambridge, MA 02139-4146. Phone: 800-533-8478 or (617)547-4002 Fax: (617)547-1333 E-mail: southend@southendpress.org • URL: http://www.southendpress.org • 1997. $40.00. Fourth revised edition. (Classics Series: Vol. 1.)

Structural Statistics for Industry and Services: Core Data. Organization for Economic Cooperation and Development, OECD Washington Center, 2001 L St., N. W., Suite 650 Washington, DC 20036-4922. Phone: 800-456-6323 or (202)785-6323 Fax: (202)785-0350 E-mail: washington.contact@oecd.org • URL: http://www.oecd.org • Annual. $63.00. Provides annual data for eight years for both industrial and service sectors. Industries include mining, manufacturing, utilities, and construction. Statistics for OECD countries cover production, value added, investment, employment, wages, hours worked, and number of establishments.

Structures and Composites Laboratory. Stanford University

Student Aid News: The Independent Biweekly News Service on Student Financial Assistance Programs. Aspen Publishers, Inc., 1135 Ave. of the Americas New York, NY 10036. Phone: 800-234-1660 or (212)597-0200 Fax: (212)597-0338 E-mail: customer.service@aspenpubl.com • URL: http://www.aspenpublishers.com • Biweekly. $383.00 per year. Newsletter on federal student aid programs.

Student Coalition for the Right to Drink., USA,. E-mail: info@socialdemocrats.org A federation of state coalitions of students opposed to the establishment of a federal drinking age of 21, viewing it as contrary to the interest of college students (most of whom are under 21), and as an unnecessary form of government regulation. Works to have both the federal drinking age and voting age constitutionally mandated at age 18.

The Student Guide: Financial Aid. U.S. Dept. of Education, Federal Student Aid Information Center, P.O. Box 84 Washington, DC 20044-0084. Phone: 800-322-3213 • URL: http://www.ed.gov/prog-info/sfa/studentguide • Annual. Describes financial aid for college and vocational school students. Available online.

Studies in American Humor. American Human Studies Association, c/o Joseph Alvarez, P.O. Box 35009 Charlotte, NC 28235-5009. Phone: (704)330-4097 Fax: (704)330-5930 E-mail: joe_alvarez@cpcc.cc.nc.us Annual. Membership.

Studio Business Book: A Guide to Professional Recording Studio Business and Management. Jim Mandell. artistpro.com, LLC, 236 Georgia St., Suite 100 Vallejo, CA 94590. Phone: (707)554-1935 Fax: (707)554-9751 E-mail: patrick@artistpro.com • URL: http://www.artistpro.com • 1995. $34.95. Second expanded edition. Includes information on business plans, studio equipment, financing, expenses, rate setting, and personnel.

Studio for Creative Inquiry., Carnegie Mellon University, College of Fine Arts Pittsburgh, PA 15213-3890. Phone: (412)268-3454 Fax: (412)268-2829 E-mail: mmbm@andrew.cmu.edu/ • URL: http://www.cmu.edu/studio/ • Research areas include artificial intelligence, virtual reality, hypermedia, multimedia, and telecommunications, in relation to the arts.

Studio Photography and Design. Cygnus Business Media, Inc., 445 Broad Hollow Rd. Melville, NY 11747. Phone: 800-308-6397 or (631)845-2700 Fax: (631)845-2798 E-mail: rich.reiff@cygnuspub.com • URL: http://www.cygnusbzb.com • Monthly. Free to qualified personnel; others, $60.00 per year. Incorporates *Comercial Image*.

Study Abroad: Scholarships and Higher Education Courses Worldwide. Available from Bernan Associates, 4611-F Assembly Dr. Lanham, MD 20706. Phone: 800-274-4888 or (301)459-2255 Fax: 800-865-3450 or (301)459-0056 E-mail: query@bernan.com • URL: http://www.bernan.com • Biennial. $34.95 provides information on a wide variety of scholarships, fellowships, and educational exchange programs in over 100 countries. Text in English, French, and Spanish. Published by the United Nations Educational, Scientific, and Cultural Organization (UNESCO).

Study Abroad, 2003. Jerry S. Carlson and others. Peterson's, Princeton Pike Corporate Ctr., 2000 Lennox Dr. Lawrenceville, NJ 08648. Phone: (609)896-1800 E-mail: custsvc@petersons.com • URL: http://www.petersons.com • 2002. $29.95. 10th edition.

Study on the Operation and Effects of the North American Free Trade Agreement. Available from U. S. Government Printing Office, Washington, DC 20402. Phone: (202)512-1800 Fax: (202)512-2250 E-mail: gpoaccess@gpo.gov • URL: http://www.access.gpo.gov • 1997. $17.00. Produced by the Executive Office of the President (http://www.whitehouse.gov). Presents a generally favorable view of the effects of NAFTA on the U. S. and Mexican economies.

Studying Your Workforce: Applied Research Methods and Tools for the Training and Development Practitioner. Alan Clardy. Sage Publications, Inc., 2455 Teller Rd. Thousand Oaks, CA 91320. Phone: 800-818-7243 or (805)499-9774 Fax: 800-583-2665 or (805)499-0871 E-mail: webmaster@sagepub.com • URL: http://www.sagepub.com • 1997. $79.95. Describes how to apply specific research methods to common training problems. Emphasis is on data collection methods: testing, observation, surveys, and interviews. Topics include performance problems and assessment.

Style: Toward Clarity and Grace. Joseph M. Williams. The University of Chicago Press, 1427 E. 60th St. Chicago, IL 60637. Phone: 800-621-2736 or (773)702-7700 Fax: 800-621-8476 or (773)702-7212 E-mail: custserv@press.uchicago.edu • URL: http://www.press.uchicago.edu • 1990. $17.95.

Subject Bibliography: Art and Artists. Available from U. S. Government Printing Office, Washington, DC 20402. Phone: (202)512-1800 Fax: (202)512-2250 E-mail: gpoaccess@gpo.gov • URL: http://www.access.gpo.gov • Annual. Free. Lists books, pamphlets, periodicals, and other government publications on art-related topics. (Subject Bibliography No. SB-107.)

Subject Bibliography Index: A Guide to U. S. Government Information. Available from U. S. Government Printing Office, Washington, DC 20402. Phone: (202)512-1800 Fax: (202)512-2250 E-mail: gpoaccess@gpo.gov • URL: http://www.access.gpo.gov • Annual. Free. Issued by the Superintendent of Documents. Lists currently available subject bibliographies by title and by topic. Each *Subject Bibliography* describes government books, periodicals, posters, pamphlets, and subscription services available for sale from the Government Printing Office.

Subject Collections: A Guide to Special Book Collections and Subject Emphasis in Libraries. Lee Ash and William G. Miller, editors. R. R. Bowker, 630 Central Ave. New Providence, NJ 07974. Phone: 888-269-5372 Fax: (908)219-0098 E-mail: info@bowker.com • URL: http://www.bowker.com • Irregular. $275.00. Two volumes. A guide to special book collections and subject emphases as reported by university, college, public and special libraries in th United States and Canada.

Subject Directory of Special Libraries and Information Centers. Gale Cengage Learning, 27500 Drake Rd. Farmington Hills, MI 48331-3535. Phone: 800-877-GALE or (248)699-4253 Fax: 800-414-5043 E-mail: gale.galeord@cengage.com • URL: http://gale.cengage.com • Annual. $960.00. Three volumes, available separately: volume one, *Business, Government, and Law Libraries*, $375.00; volume two, *Computer, Engineering, and Law Libraries*, $375.00; volume three, *Health Sciences Libraries*, $375.00. Altogether, 14,000 entries from the *Directory of Special Libraries and Information Centers* are arranged in 14 subject chapters.

Subject Encyclopedias: User's Guide, Review Citations, and Keyword Index. Allan N. Mirwis. Greenwood Publishing Group, Inc., 88 Post Rd., W. Westport, CT 06881. Phone: 800-225-5800 or (203)226-3571 Fax: (203)431-2214 E-mail: customer-service@greenwood.com • URL: http://www.greenwood.com • 1999. $300.00. Two volumes. $150.00 per volume. Volume one describes 1,000 subject encyclopedias; volume two provides a keyword index to articles appearing in 100 selected encyclopedias.

Subject Guide to Books in Print. R. R. Bowker, 630 Central Ave. New Providence, NJ 07974. Phone: 888-269-5372 Fax: (908)219-0098 E-mail: info@bowker.com • URL: http://

www.bowker.com • Annual. $525.00. Six volumes.

Subject Indexing: An Introductory Guide. Trudi Bellardo. Special Libraries Association, 1700 18th St, N. W. Washington, DC 20009-2514. Phone: (202)234-4700 Fax: (202)265-9317 E-mail: sla@sla.org • URL: http://www.sla.org • 1991. $85.00. A self-study guide to creating subject indices for a variety of materials and formats.

Submersible Wastewater Pump Association., 1866 Sheridan Rd., Ste. 201 Highland Park, IL 60035-2545. Phone: (847)681-1868 Fax: (847)681-1869 E-mail: swpaexdir@sbcglobal.net • URL: http://www.swpa.org • Represents manufacturers of submersible wastewater pumps and pumping systems for municipal and industrial applications; manufacturers of component parts and accessory items for those pumps and systems, and companies who provide services to users of those products, including consulting engineers, distributors, rep organizations, service shops, systems packagers and publishers.

Substance Abuse: A Comprehensive Textbook. Joyce Lowinson and others. Lippincott Williams and Wilkins, 530 Walnut St. Philadelphia, PA 19106-3621. Phone: 800-638-3030 or (215)521-8300 Fax: (215)521-8902 E-mail: custserv@lww.com • URL: http://www.lww.com • 1997. $179.00. Third edition. Covers the medical, psychological, socioeconomic, and public health aspects of drug and alcohol abuse.

Successful Advertising Research Methods. Jack B. Haskins and Alice Gagnard-Kendrick. McGraw-Hill, 1221 Ave. of the Americas New York, NY 10020. Phone: 800-722-4726 or (212)512-2000 Fax: (212)512-4502 E-mail: customer.service@mcgraw-hill.com • URL: http://www.mcgraw-hill.com • 1994. $49.95. (NTC Business Books Series).

The Successful Benefits Communicator. Lawrence Ragan Communications Inc., 316 N Michigan Ave., Ste. 300 Chicago, IL 60601. Phone: 800-878-5331 or (312)960-4100 Fax: (312)960-4105 E-mail: cservice@ragan.com • URL: http://www.ioma.com • Description: Offers ideas, techniques, and tips for those who communicate benefits information.

Successful Business Plan: Secrets and Strategies. Rhonda M. Abrams. Rhonda, Inc., 555 Bryant St., No. 180 Palo Alto, CA 94301. Phone: (650)941-9120 E-mail: info@rhondaonline.com • URL: http://www.rhondaonline.com • 1999. $27.95. Third edition. (Successful Business Library Series).

Successful Catering. Bernard Splaver. John Wiley and Sons, Inc., 111 River St. Hoboken, NJ 07030. Phone: 800-225-5945 or (201)748-6000 Fax: (201)748-6088 E-mail: info@wiley.com • URL: http://www.wiley.com • 1991. $70.00. Third edition.

Successful Cold Call Selling. Lee Boyan. AMACOM, 1601 Broadway New York, NY 10019. Phone: 800-262-9699 or (518)586-8100 Fax: (518)903-8168 E-mail: customerservice@amanet.org • URL: http://www.amacombooks.org • 1989. $16.95. Second edition.

Successful Cost Control Strategies for CEOs, Managers, and Administrators. Siefer Consultants, Inc., 525 Cayuga St. Storm Lake, IA 50588. Phone: (712)732-7340 Fax: (712)732-7906 E-mail: info@siefer.com Monthly. $279.00 per year. Newsletter. Provides a variety of ideas on business budgeting and controlling company expenses. Formerly *Employee Cost Conrol Strategies for CEOs, Managers, and Administrators*.

Successful Dealer. Kona Communications, Inc., 707 Lake Cook Rd., Suite 300 Deerfield, IL 60015. Phone: (847)498-3180 Fax: (847)498-3197 Bimonthly. $50.00 per year. For truck and heavy duty equipment dealers.

Successful Meetings: The Authority on Meetings and Incentive Travel Management. VNU Business Media, 770 Broadway New York, NY 10003-9595. Phone: 800-344-7119 or (646)654-5400 Fax: (646)654-7212 • URL: http://www.vnubusinessmedia.com • Monthly. $79.00 per year.

Successful Mergers, Acquisitions, and Strategic Alliances: How to Bridge Corporate Cultures. Irene Rodgers and others. McGraw-Hill, 1221 Ave. of the Americas New York, NY 10020. Phone: 800-722-4726 or (212)512-2000 Fax: (212)512-4502 E-mail: customer.service@mcgraw-hill.com • URL: http://www.mcgraw-hill.com • 2002. $39.95. Provides advice on mergers involving companies in different countries.

Successful Telemarketing: Opportunities and Techniques for Increasing Sales and Profits. Bob Stone. McGraw-Hill, 1221 Ave. of the Americas New York, NY 10020. Phone: 800-722-4726 or (212)512-2000 Fax: (212)512-4502 E-mail: customer.service@mcgraw-hill.com • URL: http://www.mcgraw-hill.com • 1995. $39.95. Second edition. Includes case histories and examples of effective telemarketing. (NTC Business Books Series).

Sugar and Sweetener Situation and Outlook. Available from U. S. Government Printing Office, Washington, DC 20402. Phone: (202)512-1800 Fax: (202)512-2250 E-mail: gpoaccess@gpo.gov • URL: http://www.access.gpo.gov • Three times per year. $18.00 per year. Issued by Economic Research Service, U. S. Department of Agriculture. Provides current statistical information on supply, demand, and prices.

Sugar Association., 1300 L St. NW, Ste. 1001 Washington, DC 20005. Phone: (202)785-1122 Fax: (202)785-5019 E-mail: sugar@sugar.org • URL: http://www.sugar.org • Represents processors, refiners, and growers of beet sugar and cane sugar. Disseminates scientifically based information on the nutritional and health aspects of sucrose. Promotes research. Sponsors educational programs on sugar and its role in a balanced diet.

Sugar Bulletin. American Sugar Cane League of the U.S.A., 206 E Bayou Rd. Thibodaux, LA 70302. Phone: (504)448-3707 Fax: (504)448-3722 Monthly. Free to members; non-members, $15.00 per year.

Sugar Journal: Covering the World's Sugar Industry. Kriedt Enterprises Ltd., 129 S. Cortez St. New Orleans, LA 70119-6118. Phone: (504)482-3914 Fax: (504)482-4205 E-mail: romney@sugarjournal.com • URL: http://www.sugarjournal.com • Monthly. $45.00 per year. A monthly technical publication designed to inform sugar beet and cane farms, factories, and refineries throughout the world about the latest developments in the sugar industry.

Sugar Producer: Representing the Sugar Beet Industry in the United States. Harris Publishing, Inc., 360 B St. Idaho Falls, ID 83402. Phone: (208)524-7000 Fax: (208)522-5241 E-mail: info@harrispublishing.com • URL: http://www.harrispublishing.com • Seven times a year. $10.95 per year. Supplies sugar beet growers with information to assist them in production of quality sugar beet crops.

Sugar y Azucar. RUSPAM Communications, Inc., 452 Hudson Terrace Englewood, NJ 07632. Phone: (201)871-9200 Fax: (201)871-9639 E-mail: sugarpublications@compuserve.com Monthly. $75.00 per year. Text in English and Spanish

Sugar y Azucar Yearbook. RUSPAM Communications, Inc., 452 Hudson Terrace Englewood, NJ 07632. Phone: (201)871-9200 Fax: (201)871-9639 E-mail: sugarpublications@compuserve.com Annual. $75.00. List of over 1,700 cane sugar mills and refineries-international coverage.

Suggested State Legislation. Council of State Governments, 2760 Research Park Dr. Lexington, KY 40578. Phone: 800-800-1910 or (859)244-8000 Fax: (859)244-8001 E-mail: sales@csg.org • URL: http://www.csg.org • Annual. $59.00. A source of legislative ideas and drafting assistance for state government officials.

Sulphur: Covers All Aspects of World Sulphur and Sulphuric Acid Industry. British Sulphur Publishing, 31 Mount Pleasant London WC1X 0AD, United Kingdom. Phone: 44 20 7837 5600 Fax: 44 20 7837 0292 E-mail: smoore@cruint.tcom.co.uk • URL: http://www.cru.co.uk • Bimonthly. $520.00 per year.

The Sulphur Institute., 1140 Connecticut Ave. NW, Ste. 612 Washington, DC 20036. Phone: (202)331-9660 Fax: (202)293-2940 E-mail: sulphur@sulphurinstitute.org • URL: http://www.sulphurinstitute.org • International organization supported by the sulphur industry to promote and expand the use of sulphur in all forms worldwide.

Summary of Commentary on Current Economic Conditions by Federal Reserve District [the Beige Book]. Board of Governors of the Federal Reserve SystemPhone: (202)452-3000 Fax: (202)452-3819 • URL: http://www.federalreserve.gov/fomc/beigebook/2004/ • Free Web site provides current "anecdotal information" eight times a year on economic conditions within each of the 12 Federal Reserve Districts, plus an extensive national *Summary*. Text is based on the opinions of bank officials, business executives, economists, financial market experts, and others. Typically contains views of consumer spending, manufacturing, services, credit, employment, prices, wages, and the economy in general. Usually referred to as the Beige Book.

Summary of Health Information for International Travel. U. S. Department of Health and Human Services, Centers for Disease Control and Prevention, 1600 Clifton Rd. Atlanta, GA 30333. Phone: 800-311-3435 or (404)639-3311 • URL: http://www.cdc.gov • Biweekly. Formerly *Weekly Summary of Health Information for International Travel*.

Summary of International Travel to the United States. International Trade Administration, Tourism Industries. U.S. Dept. of Commerce, Washington, DC 20230. Phone: (202)482-3809 Fax: (202)482-2877 • URL: http://www.tinet.ita.doc.gov • Monthly. Quarterly and annual versions available. Provides statistics on air travel to the U.S. from each of 90 countries. Formerly *Summary and Analysis of International Travel to the United States*.

Summary of Labor Arbitration Awards. American Arbitration Association, Inc., 335 Madison Ave. New York, NY 10017. Phone: 800-778-7879 or (212)716-5800 Fax: (212)716-5905 E-mail: websitemail@adr.org • URL: http://www.adr.org • Monthly. $120.00 per year.

Summary of Sanitation Inspections of International Cruise Ships. Centers for Disease Control and Prevention (CDC), 1600 Clifton Rd. Atlanta, GA 30333. Phone: (404)639-3311 Fax: 800-311-3435 • URL: http://www.cdc.gov • Biweekly. Apply. "All passenger cruise ships arriving at U. S. ports are subject to unannounced inspection..to achieve levels of sanitation that will minimize the potential for gastrointestinal disease outbreaks on these ships." Individual ships are listed, with sanitation rating and date of inspection. (CDC Document No. 510051.)

Summers on Oil and Gas. West Group, 610 Opperman Dr. Eagan, MN 55123. Phone: 800-338-9424 or (651)687-7000 Fax: 800-340-9378 E-mail: bookstore@westgroup.com • URL: http://www.westgroup.com • $625.00. Annual updates. Legal aspects of the petroleum industry.

Sump and Sewage Pump Manufacturers Association., PO Box 647 Northbrook, IL 60065-0647. Phone: (847)559-9233 Fax: (847)559-9235 • URL: http://www.sspma.org • Formerly Sump Pump Manufacturers Association.

The Suncare Products Market. Available from MarketResearch.com, 641 Ave. of the Americas, 3rd Fl. New York, NY 10011. Phone: 800-298-5699 or (212)807-2629 Fax: (212)807-2716 E-mail: order@marketresearch.com • URL: http://www.marketresearch.com • 2001. $2,100.00. Published by Packaged Facts. Provides market data on sun screen lotions, after-sun products, and sunless tanning cosmetics, with sales projections.

Sunkist Growers., PO Box 7888 Van Nuys, CA 91409-7888. Phone: (818)986-4800 Fax: (818)379-7511 E-mail: info@sunkistgrowers.com • URL: http://www.sunkist.com • Serves as a citrus fruit marketing cooperative.

Super Searcher, Author, Scribe: Successful Writers Share Their Internet Research Secrets. Loraine Page. Information Today, Inc., 143 Old Marlton Pike Medford, NJ 08055-8750. Phone: 800-300-9868 or (609)654-6266 Fax: (609)654-4309 E-mail: custserv@infotoday.com • URL: http://www.infotoday.com • 2002. $24.95. Presents the results of interviews with 14 leading journalists, book authors, writing teachers, and professional literary researchers. Tips, techniques, and sources for searching the Web are featured. (Super Searchers Series).

Super Searchers Cover the World: The Online Secrets of International Business Researchers. Mary E. Bates. Information Today, Inc., 143 Old Marlton Pike Medford, NJ 08055-8750. Phone: 800-300-9868 or (609)654-6266 Fax: (609)654-4309 E-mail: custserv@infotoday.com • URL: http://www.infotoday.com • 2001. $24.95. Presents interviews with 15 experts in the area of online searching for international business information. (Super Searchers Series).

Super Searchers Do Business: The Online Secrets of Top Business Researchers. Mary E.Bates. Information Today, Inc., 143 Old Marlton Pike Medford, NJ 08055-8750. Phone: 800-300-9868 or (609)654-6266 Fax: (609)654-4309 E-mail: custserv@infotoday.com • URL: http://www.infotoday.com • 1999. $24.95. Presents the results of interviews with "11 leading researchers who use the Internet and online services to find critical business information." (Super Searchers Series.)

Super Searchers Go to the Source: The Interviewing and Hands-On Information Strategies of Top Primary Researchers - Online, On the Phone, and In Person. Risa Sacks. Information Today, Inc., 143 Old Marlton Pike Medford, NJ 08055-8750. Phone: 800-300-9868 or (609)654-6266 Fax: (609)654-4309 E-mail: custserv@infotoday.com • URL: http://www.infotoday.com • 2001. $24.95. Explains how information-search experts use various print, electronic, and live sources for competitive intelligence and other purposes. (Super Searchers Series).

Super Searchers in the News: The Online Secrets of Journalists and News Researchers. Paula J. Hane. Information Today, Inc., 143 Old Marlton Pike Medford, NJ 08055-8750. Phone: 800-300-9868 or (609)654-6266 Fax: (609)654-4309 E-mail: custserv@infotoday.com • URL: http://www.infotoday.com • 2000. $24.95. Contains online searching advice from 10 professional news researchers and fact checkers. (Super Searchers Series).

Super Searchers Make It On Their Own: Top Independent Information Professionals Share Their Secrets for Starting and Running a Research Business. Suzanne Sabroski. Information Today, Inc., 143 Old Marlton Pike Medford, NJ 08055-8750. Phone: 800-300-9868 or (609)654-6266 Fax: (609)654-4309 E-mail: custserv@infotoday.com • URL: http://www.infotoday.com • 2002. $24.95. Presents discussions by "11 of the world's top research entrepreneurs" on the practical aspects of being in business as an information broker or other information provider. (Super Searchers Series).

Super Searchers on Competitive Intelligence: The Online and Offline Secrets of Top CI Researchers. Margaret M. Carr. Information Today, Inc., 143 Old Marlton Pike Medford, NJ 08055-8750. Phone: 800-300-9868 or (609)654-6266 Fax: (609)654-4309 E-mail: custserv@infotoday.com • URL: http://www.infotoday.com • 2003. $24.95. Presents the views of business intelligence experts from 15 major corporations and organizations. Contains information on sources for "monitoring competitive forces." (Super Searchers Series).

Super Searchers on Health and Medicine: The Online Secrets of Top Health and Medical Researchers. Susan M. Detwiler. Information Today, Inc., 143 Old Marlton Pike Medford, NJ 08055-8750. Phone: 800-300-9868 or (609)654-6266 Fax: (609)654-4309 E-mail: custserv@infotoday.com • URL: http://www.infotoday.com • 2000. $24.95. Provides the results of interviews with 10 experts in online searching for medical research data and healthcare information. Discusses both traditional sources and Web sites. (Super Searchers Series).

Super Searchers on Madison Avenue: Top Advertising and Marketing Professionals Share Their Online Research Strategies. Grace A. Villamora. Information Today, Inc., 143 Old Marlton Pike Medford, NJ 08055-8750. Phone: 800-300-9868 or (609)654-6266 Fax: (609)654-4309 E-mail: custserv@infotoday.com • URL: http://www.infotoday.com • 2003. $24.95. Provides research "tips, techniques, and resources" from 13 information professionals working in advertising and marketing. (Super Searchers Series).

Super Searchers on Mergers & Acquisitions: The Online Secrets of Top Corporate Researchers and M & A Professionals. Jan Tudor. Information Today, Inc., 143 Old Marlton Pike Medford, NJ 08055-8750. Phone: 800-300-9868 or (609)654-6266 Fax: (609)654-4309 E-mail: custserv@infotoday.com • URL: http://www.infotoday.com • 2001. $24.95. Presents the results of interviews with 13 "top M & A information pros." Covers the finding, evaluating, and delivering of relevant data on companies and industries. (Super Searchers Series).

Super Searchers on Wall Street: Top Investment Professionals Share Their Online Research Secrets. Amelia Kassel. Information Today, Inc., 143 Old Marlton Pike Medford, NJ 08055-8750. Phone: 800-300-9868 or (609)654-6266 Fax: (609)654-4309 E-mail: custserv@infotoday.com • URL: http://www.infotoday.com • 2000. $24.95. Gives the results of interviews with "10 leading financial industry research experts." Explains how online information is used by stock brokers, investment bankers, and individual investors. Includes relevant Web sites and other sources. (Super Searchers Series).

Superconductivity. John B. Ketterson and Shengnian Song. Cambridge University Press, 40 W 20th St. New York, NY 10011-4211. Phone: 800-872-7423 or (212)924-3900 Fax: (212)691-3239 E-mail: orders@cup.org • URL: http://www.cup.org • 1999. $140.00.

Superconductivity: An Annotated Bibliography with Abstracts. A. Bisarsh, editor. Nova Science Publishers, Inc., 400 Oser Ave., Suite 1600 Hauppauge, NY 11743-6682. Phone: (631)231-7269 Fax: (631)231-8175 E-mail: novascience@earthlink.net • URL: http://www.nexusworld.com • 1998. $115.00.

Superconductivity: The Next Revolution? Gianfranco Vidali. Cambridge University Press, 40 W 20th St. New York, NY 10011-4211. Phone: 800-872-7423 or (212)924-3900 Fax: (212)691-3239 E-mail: orders@cup.org • URL: http://www.cup.org • 1993. $20.00.

Superconductor and Cyroelectronics. WestTech, 478 Wilshire Blvd., Ste. 205 Los Angeles, CA 90036-4225. Phone: 800-446-7778 or (323)937-1211 Fax: (323)937-1030 E-mail: info@superconductorweek.com • URL: http://www.superconductorweek.com • Quarterly. $22.00 per year.

Superconductor Week: The Newsletter of Record in the Field of Superconductivity. WestTech, 5478 Wilshire Blvd., Ste. 205 Los Angeles, CA 90036-4225. Phone: 800-446-7778 or (323)937-1211 Fax: (323)937-1030 E-mail: info@superconductorweek.com • URL: http://www.superconductorweek.com • 30 times a year. $437.00 per year. Newsletter. Covers applications of superconductivity and cryogenics, including new markets and products.

Supermarket News: The Industry's Weekly Newspaper. Fairchild Publications, Seven W. 34th St. New York, NY 10001. Phone: 800-204-4515 or (212)630-4000 E-mail: customerservice@fairchildpub.com • URL: http://www.fairchildpub.com • Weekly. Individuals, $196.00 per year; retailers, $45.00 per year; manufacturers, $89.00 per year.

Superstudy of Sports Participation. Available from MarketResearch.com, 641 Ave. of the Americas, Third Floor New York, NY 10011. Phone: 800-298-5699 or (212)807-2629 Fax: (212)807-2716 E-mail: order@marketresearch.com • URL: http://www.marketresearch.com • 2002. $700.00. Three volumes. Published by American Sports Data, Inc. Provides market research data on 102 sports and activities. Vol. 1: *Physical Fitness Activities*. Vol. 2: *Recreational Sports*. Vol. 3: *Outdoor Activities*. (Volumes are available separately at $295.00.)

Supertrader's Almanac-Reference Manual: Reference Guide and Analytical Techniques for Investors. Frank A. Taucher, c/o 5212 E 69th Pl. Tulsa, OK 74136-3402. Phone: 800-878-7442 or (918)493-2897 Fax: (918)493-3892 E-mail: taucher@supertraderalmanac.com • URL: http://www.supertraderalmanac.com • 1991. $55.00. Explains technical methods for the trading of commodity futures, and includes data on seasonality, cycles, trends, contract characteristics, highs and lows, etc.

Supervision in the Hospitality Industry. Jack E. Miller and others. John Wiley and Sons, Inc., 111 River St. Hoboken, NJ 07030. Phone: 800-225-5945 or (201)748-6000 Fax: (201)748-6088 E-mail: info@wiley.com • URL: http://www.wiley.com • 2002. $70.00. Fourth edition. Principles of communication, motivation, recruiting, training, etc.

Supply Chain Systems: The Resource for Supply Chain Automation. Helmers Publishing, Inc., 174 Concord St. Peterborough, NH 03458. Phone: (603)924-9631 Fax: (603)924-7408 E-mail: dandrews@helmers.com • URL: http://www.scs-mag.com • Monthly. Free to qualified personnel; others, $55.00 per year. Covers trends in automatic identification technology and management. Formerly *ID Systems7*.

Supply, Distribution Manufacturing and Service: Supply and Service Companies and Equipment Manufacturers. Midwest Publishing Co., P.O. Box 4468 Tulsa, OK 74159-0468. Phone: 800-829-2002 or (918)583-2000 Fax: (918)587-9349 E-mail: info@midwestdirectories.com • URL: http://www.midwestdirectories.com • Annual. $115.00. Two volumes. 8,000 oil well supply stores, service companies, and equipment manufacturers. Formerly *Directory of Oil Well Supply Companies*.

Supporting Emotional Needs of the Gifted.

Sure-Hire Resumes. Robbie M. Kaplan. Impact Publications, 9104 Manassas Dr., Suite N Manassas, VA 20111-5211. Phone: 800-361-1055 or (703)361-7300 Fax: (703)335-9486 E-mail: info@impactpublications.com • URL: http://www.impactpublications.com • 1998. $14.95. Second edition. Includes sample cover letters and 25 sample resumes.

Surface Coatings: Science and Technology. Swaraj Paul, editor. John Wiley and Sons, Inc., 111 River St. Hoboken, NJ 07030. Phone: 800-225-5945 or (201)748-6000 Fax: (201)748-6088 E-mail: info@wiley.com • URL: http://www.wiley.com •

1996. $375.00. Second edition.

Surface Finishing Technology. ASM International, 9639 Kinsman Rd. Materials Park, OH 44073-0002. Phone: 800-336-5152 or (440)338-5151 Fax: (440)338-4634 E-mail: cust-srv@asminternational.org • URL: http://www.asminternational.org • Monthly. Members, $130.00 per year; non-members, $160.00 per year. Provides abstracts of the international literature of metallic and nonmetallic industrial coating and finishing. Formerly *Cleaning-Finishing-Coating Digest*.

Surface Treatment Technology Abstracts. Finishing Publications Ltd., 105 Whitney Dr. Stevenage SG1 4BL, United Kingdom. Phone: 44 1438 745115 Fax: 44 1438 364536 E-mail: finpubs@compuserve.com • URL: http://www.finpus.demon.co.uk • Bimonthly. $880.00 per year. Includes *Printed Circuits* and *Electronics Coating Abstracts*.

Surgical Products. Reed Business Information, 360 Park Ave., S New York, NY 10010. Phone: 800-446-6551 or (646)746-6400 Fax: (646)746-7028 E-mail: corporatecommunications@reedbusiness.com • URL: http://www.reedbusiness.com • Monthly. $41.90 per year. Covers new Technology and products for surgeons and operation rooms.

Surplus Record: Machinery and Equipment Directory. Surplus Record, Inc., 20 N. Wacker Dr. Chicago, IL 60606. Phone: (312)372-9077 Fax: (312)372-6537 E-mail: surplus@surplusrecord.com • URL: http://www.surplusrecord.com • Monthly. $33.00 per year. Lists over 46,000 items of used and surplus machine tools, chemical processing and electrical equipment.

Survey and Analysis of Employee Relocation Policies and Costs. Runzheimer International, Runzheimer Park Rochester, WI 53167-0009. Phone: 800-558-1702 or (262)971-2200 Fax: (262)971-2254 E-mail: webmaster@runzheimer.com • URL: http://www.runzheimer.com • Annual. Based on surveys of relocation administrators.

The Survey Kit. Arlene Fink, editor. Sage Publications, Inc., 2455 Teller Rd. Thousand Oaks, CA 91320-2218. Phone: 800-818-7243 or (805)499-0721 Fax: 800-583-2665 or (805)499-0871 E-mail: info@sagepub.com • URL: http://www.sagepub.com • 2003. $130.00. Second edition. Ten volumes. Covers various survey research topics, such as in-person interviews, telephone interviewing, focus groups, content analysis, sampling, database management, and Internet surveys. Each volume contains a glossary.

Survey of Advanced Technology: A Strategic Analysis of Today's Leading-edge Information Technologies. I.T. Works, Innovation Center, Technology Park 3 9052 Gent, Belgium. Phone: 32 09 241 5613 Fax: 32 09 241 5656 E-mail: custserv@compecon.com • URL: http://www.itworks.be • Annual. $795.00. Surveys the corporate use (or neglect) of advanced computer technology. Topics include major technology trends and emerging technologies.

Survey of Business Travelers. Travel Industry Association of America, 1100 New York Ave., N. W., Suite 240 Washington, DC 20005-3934. Phone: (202)408-8422 Fax: (202)408-1255 E-mail: rmcclur@tia.org • URL: http://www.tia.org • Biennial. Members, $100.00 per year; non-members, $175.00 per year.

Survey of Current Business. Available from U. S. Government Printing Office, Washington, DC 20402. Phone: (202)512-1800 Fax: (202)512-2250 E-mail: gpoaccess@gpo.gov • URL: http://www.access.gpo.gov • Monthly. $63.00 per year. Issued by Bureau of Economic Analysis, U. S. Department of Commerce. Presents a wide variety of business and economic data.

Survey of Industry Activity. Equipment Leasing Association of America, 4301 N. Fairfax Ave., Suite 550 Arlington, VA 22203-1627. Phone: (703)527-8655 Fax: (703)527-2649 • URL: http://www.elaonline.com • Annual. Provides financial and statistical data on the equipment leasing industry. Price on application.

Survey of Law Firm Economics: A Management and Planning Tool. Altman Weil Publications, Inc., Two Campus Blvd. Newtown Square, PA 19073. Phone: 888-782-7297 or (610)886-2000 Fax: (610)359-0467 • URL: http://www.altmanweil.com • Annual. $995.00. Provides aggregate economic statistics and financial data (benchmarks) relating to the legal profession in the U. S. Includes income, expenses, hourly rates, billable hours, compensation, staffing, data by states, and trends. Most information is arranged by region, firm size, years of experience, and other factors.

Survey of Mortgage Lending Activity. U.S. Department of Housing and Urban Development, 451 Seventh St., S.W. Washington, DC 20410. Phone: (202)708-0980 Monthly.

Survey of Salaries. AACSB International-The Association to Advance Collegiate Schools of Business, 600 Emerson Rd., Suite 300 Saint Louis, MO 63141-6762. Phone: (314)872-8481 Fax: (314)872-8495 E-mail: webmaster@aacsb.edu • URL: http://www.aacsb.edu • Annual. $25.00, Reports aggregate salary data of business school administrators and faculty. Text in English and Spanish.

Survey Research. Survey Research Laboratory, 615 CUPPAH MC 336, 412 S Peoria Chicago, IL 60607. Phone: (312)996-5300 Fax: (312)996-3358 E-mail: info@srl.uic.edu • URL: http://www.srl.uic.edu • Description: Contains "descriptions of current survey research projects by academic and not-for-profit survey research organizations; news from survey research centers; descriptions of recent methodological publications

on survey research." Recurring features include news of research and columns titled Current Research, Personnel Notes, and New Methodological Publications.

Survey Research Center., University of California at Berkeley, 2538 Channing Way Berkeley, CA 94720-5100. Phone: (510)642-6578 Fax: (510)643-8292 E-mail: hbrady@bravo.berkeley.edu • URL: http://www.grad.berkeley.edu • Research areas include the utilization and development of survey methods.

Survey Research Handbook: Guidelines and Strategies for Conducting a Survey. Pamela L. Alreck and Robert B. Settle. McGraw-Hill, 1221 Ave. of the Americas New York, NY 10020. Phone: 800-722-4726 or (212)512-2000 Fax: (212)512-4502 E-mail: customer.service@mcgraw-hill.com • URL: http://www.mcgraw-hill.com • 1994. $50.00. Second edition. Consists of four major parts: 1: Planning and Designing the Survey, 2. Developing Survey Instruments, 3. Collecting and Processing Data, 4. Interpreting and Reporting Results. Includes a glossary and index. (Marketing Series).

Survey Research Laboratory., University of Illinois at Chicago, 412 S. Peoria St. Chicago, IL 60607. Phone: (312)996-5300 Fax: (312)996-3358 E-mail: info@srl.uic.edu • URL: http://www.srl.uic.edu • Research areas include survey methodology and sampling techniques.

Surveying and Land Information Systems: Devoted to the Advancement of the Sciences of Surveying and Mapping. American Congress on Surveying and Mapping, 6 Montgomery Village Ave., Ste. 403 Gaithersburg, MD 20879. Phone: (240)632-9716 Fax: (240)632-1321 E-mail: info@acsm.net • URL: http://www.acsm.net • Quarterly. Free to members; non-members, $110.00 per year. Formerly *Surveying and Mapping*.

Surviving Job Stress: How to Overcome Workday Pressures. John B. Arden. Career Press, Inc., Three Tice Road Franklin Lakes, NJ 07417. Phone: 800-227-3371 or (201)848-0310 Fax: (201)848-1727 E-mail: contact@careerpress.com • URL: http://www.careerpress.com • 2002. $14.99. Includes information on stress-related medical problems, nutrition issues, and the side effects of medication for stress.

Surviving Your Dissertation: A Comprehensive Guide to Content and Process. Kjell E. Rudestam and Rae R. Newton. Sage Publications, Inc., 2455 Teller Rd. Thousand Oaks, CA 91320. Phone: 800-818-7243 or (805)499-9774 Fax: 800-583-2665 or (805)499-0871 E-mail: webmaster@sagepub.com • URL: http://www.sagepub.com • 2000. $72.95. Second edition. Provides general advice on how to successfully complete a dissertation or thesis.

Sustainability Perspectives for Resources and Business. Orie L. Loucks and others. Saint Lucie Press, 2000 Corporate Blvd., N. W. Boca Raton, FL 33431-7372. Phone: 800-272-7737 or (561)274-9906 Fax: 800-374-3401 or (561)274-9927 E-mail: information@slpress.com • URL: http://www.slpress.com • 1998. $54.95. Discusses the business and economic aspects of environmental protection.

Sustainable Buildings Industry Council., 1112 16th St. NW, Ste. 240 Washington, DC 20036. Phone: (202)628-7400 Fax: (202)393-5043 E-mail: sbic@sbicouncil.org • URL: http://www.sbicouncil.org • Works to advance the design, affordability, energy performance, and environmental soundness of commercial, institutional, and residential buildings nationwide. Offers professional training, consumer education, and energy analysis tools. Provides accurate, easy-to-use guidelines, software, and general information about energy conservation measures, energy efficient equipment and appliances, daylighting, and sustainable architecture. Active in presenting workshops and seminars geared toward improving building energy performance in cities and towns throughout the nation.

Swap and Derivative Financing: The Global Reference to Products Pricing Applications and Markets. Satyajit Das. McGraw-Hill, 1221 Ave. of the Americas New York, NY 10020. Phone: 800-722-4726 or (212)512-2000 Fax: (212)512-4502 E-mail: customer.service@mcgraw-hill.com • URL: http://www.mcgraw-hill.com • 1993. $99.95. Second revised edition.

Swap Literacy. Elizabeth Ungar. Bloomberg, 499 Park Ave. New York, NY 10022. Phone: 800-388-2749 or (212)318-2000 Fax: (917)369-5000 • URL: http://www.bloomberg.com • 1996. $40.00. Written for corporate finance officers. Provides basic information on arbitrage, hedging, and speculation, involving interest rate, currency, and other types of financial swaps. (Bloomberg Professional Library.)

Swaps and Financial Engineering: A Self-Study Guide to Mastering and Applying Swaps and Financial Engineering. McGraw-Hill, 1221 Ave. of the Americas New York, NY 10020. Phone: 800-722-4726 or (212)512-2000 Fax: (212)512-4502 E-mail: customer.servicemcgraw-hill.com • URL: http://www.mcgraw-hill.com • 1994. $55.00.

SWE. Anne Perusek, editor. Society of Women Engineers, 230 E Ohio St., Ste. 400 Chicago, IL 60611-3645. Phone: (312)596-5223 Fax: (312)596-5252 • URL: http://www.swe.org • Bimonthly. Members, $10.00 per year; non-members, $20.00 per year. Covers technical articles, continuing development, career guidance and recruitment and product advertising. Formerly *U.S. Woman Engineer*.

Sweaty Palms: The Neglected Art of Being Interviewed. H. Anthony Medley. Ten Speed Press, P.O. Box 7123 Berkeley, CA 94707. Phone: 800-841-2665 or (510)559-1600 Fax: (510)559-1629 E-mail: order@tenspeed.com • URL: http://

www.tenspeed.com • 1992. $12.95. Revised edition.

Sweetener Users Association., 3231 Valley Ln. Falls Church, VA 22044. Phone: (703)532-2683 Fax: (703)532-9361 E-mail: info@acmanet.org Industrial users of sugar and other sweeteners; companies and associations in the sweetener industry. Seeks legislative or administrative actions which will result in more market-oriented sweetener prices and an adequate and reliable supply of domestic and imported sugar. **Publications:** none.

Swimming Pool/Spa Age—Product Directory. Primedia Business, 6151 Powers Ferry Rd., Ste. 200 Atlanta, GA 30339. Phone: (770)995-2500 Fax: (770)618-0204 E-mail: csg@csg.org • URL: http://www.age.poolspa.com • Covers: about 2,000 manufacturers of swimming pool and spa equipment and supplies, and suppliers of services for the industry; manufacturers of spas and hot tubs; distributors and manufacturers' representatives; and pool industry associations. Entries include: Company or association name, address, phone, name and title of contact, branch offices.

Switchboard. Switchboard, Inc.Phone: (508)898-8000 Fax: (508)898-1755 E-mail: webmaster@switchboard.com • URL: http://www.switchboard.com • Web site provides telephone numbers and street addresses for more than 100 million business locations and residences in the U. S. Broad industry categories are available. Fees: Free.

Syllabus: New Directions in Educational Technology. Syllabus Press, 9121 Oakdale Ave., Suite 101 Chatsworth, CA 91311-6526. Phone: (818)734-1520 or (408)261-7280 Fax: (818)734-1522 • URL: http://www.syllabus.com • 10 times a year. $24.00 per year. Covers the use of advanced technology in higher education systems, including video, multimedia, the Internet, distance learning systems, and electronic publishing.

SYNERJY: A Directory of Renewable Energy. Synerjy, P.O. Box 1854, Cathedral Station New York, NY 10025. Phone: (212)865-9595 E-mail: info@synerjy.com • URL: http://www.synerjy.com • Semiannual. Individuals, $30.00 per year; others, $62.00 per year. Includes organizations, publishers, and other resources. Lists articles, patents, government publications, research groups and facilities.

Synthetic Organic Chemical Manufacturers Association., 1850 M St. NW, Ste. 700 Washington, DC 20036-5810. Phone: (202)721-4100 Fax: (202)296-8120 E-mail: info@socma.com • URL: http://www.socma.com • Represents manufacturers of synthetic organic chemicals, which are products manufactured from coal, natural gas, crude petroleum, and certain natural substances such as vegetable oils, fats, proteins, carbohydrates, rosin, grains, and their derivatives.

Synthetic Organic Chemicals: United States Production and Sales. International Trade Commission. Available from U.S. Government Printing Office, Washington, DC 20402. Phone: (202)512-1800 Fax: (202)512-2250 E-mail: gpoaccess@gpo.gov • URL: http://www.accessgpo.gov • Annual.

Sys Admin: The Journal for Unix System Administrators. CMP Media LLC, 600 Community Dr. Manhasset, NY 11030. Phone: (516)562-5000 E-mail: cmp@cmp.com • URL: http://www.cmp.com • Monthly. $39.00 per year. Provides technical information for managers of Unix systems.

System Integration. Jeffrey O. Grady. CRC Press LLC, 2000 NW Corporate Blvd. Boca Raton, FL 33431-7372. Phone: 800-272-7737 or (561)994-0555 Fax: 800-374-3401 or (561)989-9732 E-mail: orders@crcpress.com • URL: http://www.crcpress.com • 1994. $139.95. (Systems Engineering Series).

System of National Accounts Glossary. Organization for Economic Cooperation and Development, OECD Washington Center, 2001 L St., N. W., Suite 650 Washington, DC 20036-4922. Phone: 800-456-6323 or (202)785-6323 Fax: (202)785-0350 E-mail: washington.contact@oecd.org • URL: http://www.oecd.org • 2000. $24.00. Contains "precise definitions of the terms commonly used in national accounting."

Systems Analysis and Design. Kenneth E. Kendall and Julie E. Kendall. Prentice Hall PTR, 240 Frisch Ct. Paramus, NJ 07652. Phone: 800-282-0693 Fax: 800-445-6991 • URL: http://www.phptr.com • 2002. $75.00. Fifth edition.

Systems Approach to Computer-Integrated Design and Manufacturing. Nanua Singh. John Wiley and Sons, Inc., 111 River St. Hoboken, NJ 07030. Phone: 800-225-5945 or (201)748-6000 Fax: (201)748-6088 E-mail: info@wiley.com • URL: http://www.wiley.com • 1995. $105.95.

Systems User. Caulfield Publishing Ltd, 308 E. Van Buren St. Janesville, WI 53545-4047. Monthly. $62.00 per year.

T and D Magazine. American Society for Training and Development, 1640 King St. Alexandria, VA 22313. Phone: 800-628-2873 or (703)683-8100 Fax: (703)683-1523 E-mail: subscriberservice@astd.org • URL: http://www.astd.org • Monthly. Free to members; non-members, $85.00 per year.

T H E Journal (Technological Horizons in Education). Ed Warnshuis Ltd., 17501 17th St., Suite 230 Tustin, CA 92680-3670. Phone: (714)730-4011 Fax: (714)730-3739 E-mail: cedwards@thejournal.com • URL: http://www.thejournal.com • 11 times a year. $29.00 per year. For educators of all levels.

T W I C E: This Week in Consumer Electronics. Reed Business Information, 360 Park Ave., S New York, NY 10010. Phone: 800-446-6551 or (646)746-6400 Fax: (646)746-7028 E-mail: corporatecommunications@reedbusiness.com • URL: http://www.reedbusiness.com • 29 times a year. $129.90 per year. Contains marketing and manufacturing news relating to a wide variety of consumer electronic products, including video, audio, telephone, and home office equipment.

Tablebase. Gale Cengage Learning, 27500 Drake Rd. Farmington Hills 48331-3535, England. Phone: 800-877-GALE Fax: 800-414-5043 or (248)699-8069 E-mail: galeord@galegroup.com • URL: http://www.galegroup.com • Provides online numerical tabular data from a wide variety of business, organization, and government sources, including about 1,000 trade journals. Includes industry and individual company statistics relating to products, market share, sales forecasts, production, exports, market trends, etc. Time span is 1997 to date. Weekly updates. Inquire as to online cost and availability. (Also available in a CD-ROM version.)

Tables of Redemption Values for United States Savings Bonds, Series EE and Series E. Available from U. S. Government Printing Office, Washington, DC 20402. Phone: (202)512-1800 Fax: (202)512-2250 E-mail: gpoaccess@gpo.gov • URL: http://www.access.gpo.gov • Semiannual. $12.00 per year. Issued by the Public Debt Bureau, U. S. Treasury Department.

The Tabletop Market. Available from MarketResearch.com, 641 Ave. of the Americas, Third Floor New York, NY 10011. Phone: 800-298-5699 or (212)807-2629 Fax: (212)807-2716 E-mail: order@marketresearch.com • URL: http://www.marketresearch.com • 2000. $2,750.00. Published by Packaged Facts. Provides market data on dinnerware, glassware, and flatware, with projections to 2002.

Taft Monthly Portfolio. Taft Group, 27500 Drake Rd. Farmington Hills, MI 48331-3535. Phone: 800-877-GALE or (248)699-GALE Fax: 800-414-5043 or (248)699-8069 E-mail: gale.galeord@cengage.com • URL: http://gale.cengage.com • Monthly. $75.00 per year. New ideas and proven techniques used by universitites, hospitals and a wide range of other nonprofit organizations to raise philanthropic gifts. Formerly *FRI Monthly Portfolio*.

Tag and Label Manufacturers Institute., 40 Shuman Blvd., Suite 295 Naperville, IL 60563. Phone: 800-533-8564 or (630)357-9222 Fax: (630)357-0192 E-mail: office@tlmi.com • URL: http://www.tlmi.com • Formerly Tag Manufacturers Institute.

TAGA Newsletter. Technical Association of the Graphic Arts, 200 Deer Run Rd. Sewickley, PA 15143-2324. Phone: (412)259-1706 Fax: (412)741-2311 E-mail: info@srl.uic.edu Description: Disseminates information in the graphic arts industry to members which is international in scope. Recurring features include interviews, news of research, reports of meetings, news of educational opportunities, and standards updates.

Tailhook Association., 9696 Businesspark Ave. San Diego, CA 92131. Phone: 800-322-4665 or (858)689-9223 Fax: (858)578-8839 E-mail: thookassn@aol.com • URL: http://www.tailhook.org • Individuals who have been designated as Naval Aviators or Naval Flight Officers and have made carrier landings; other individuals who have made carrier landings or who have the background and interest to support the objectives of the association. Seeks to foster, develop, study, and support U.S. aircraft carriers and aircrews, and their role in the nation's defense system.

Taiwan Business: The Portable Encyclopedia for Doing Business with Taiwan. Christine Genzberger and others. World Trade Press, 1450 Grant Ave., Suite 204 Novato, CA 94945. Phone: 800-833-8586 or (415)898-1124 Fax: (415)898-1080 E-mail: sales@worldtradepress.com • URL: http://www.worldtradepress.com • 1994. $24.95. Covers economic data, import/export possibilities, basic tax and trade laws, travel information, and other useful facts for doing business with Taiwan. (Country Business Guide Series).

The Take-Charge Assistant. American Management Association, 1601 Broadway New York, NY 10019. Phone: 800-262-9699 or (212)586-8100 Fax: (212)903-8168 E-mail: cust-serv@amanet.org • URL: http://www.amanet.org • Description: Features career and professional guidance, tips, and problem solving.

Tampa Bay Rare Fruit Council International., c/o Charles Novak, 2812 N Wilder Rd. Plant City, FL 33565-2669. • URL: http://www.rarefruit.org • Individuals in 34 countries interested in propagating and raising tropical fruit plants. Formerly Rare Fruit Council.

The Tan Sheet: Nonprescription Pharmaceuticals and Nutritionals. F-D-C Reports, Inc., 5550 Friendship Blvd., Suite 1 Chevy Chase, MD 20815-7278. Phone: 800-332-2181 or (301)657-9830 Fax: (301)656-3094 E-mail: fdc.customer.service@elsevier.com • URL: http://www.fdcreports.com • Weekly. $1,220.00 per year. Newsletter covering over-the-counter drugs and vitamin supplements. Emphasis is on regulatory activities of the U. S. Food and Drug Administration (FDA).

Tanker Market Quarterly. Available from Informa Publishing Group Ltd., PO Box 1017 Westborough, MA 01581-6017. Phone: 800-493-4080 Fax: (508)231-0856 E-mail: enquiries@informa.com • URL: http://www.informa.com • Quarterly. $495.00 per year. Published in the UK by Lloyd's List (http://www.lloydslist.com). Provides supply and demand information "required to make accurate market decisions." Includes detailed graphs and analytical commentary.

Tanker Operations: A Handbook for the Person-in-Charge. Mark Huber and G.S Marton. Cornell Maritime Press, Inc., P.O. Box 456 Centreville, MD 21617. Phone: 800-638-7641 or (410)758-1075 Fax: (410)758-6849 E-mail: cornell@crosslink.net • URL: http://www.cornellmaritimepress.com • 2001. $50.00. Fourth edition.

Tanker Register. Clarkson Research Studies, 12 Camomile St. London EC3A 7BP, United Kingdom. Phone: (44)207 3343134 Fax: (44)207 5220330 E-mail: crs@clarksons.co.uk Covers: More than 4,282 tankers and combined carriers throughout the world having deadweight tonnage exceeding 10,000, and their owners and managers. Entries include: Ship name, owner or manager, where registered, when and where built, tonnage, draft, capacity, engines, etc.

TAPPI - Technical Association of the Pulp and Paper Industry.

Tapping the Government Grapevine: The User-Friendly Guide to U. S. Government Information Sources. Judith S. Robinson, editor. Greenwood Publishing Group, Inc., 88 Post Rd., W. Westport, CT 06881. Phone: 800-225-5800 or (203)226-3571 Fax: (203)431-2214 E-mail: customer-service@greenwood.com • URL: http://www.greenwood.com • 1998. $47.95. Third edition. Includes source information on statistics, regulations, patents, technology, nonprint items, bibliographies, and indexes. A special chapter by Karen Smith covers "Foreign and International Documents."

Target Marketing: The Leading Magazine for Integrated Database Marketing. North American Publishing Co., 401 N. Broad St. Philadelphia, PA 19108. Phone: 800-777-8074 or (215)238-5482 Fax: 800-664-1533 or (215)238-5412 E-mail: customerservice@napco.com • URL: http://www.napco.com • Monthly. $65.00 per year. Dedicated to direct marketing excellence. Formerly *Zip Target Marketing*.

Taunton's Fine Homebuilding. Taunton Press, Inc., 63 S Main St. Newtown, CT 06470. Phone: 800-477-8727 or (203)426-8171 Fax: (203)426-7184 E-mail: fh@taunton.com • URL: http://www.taunton.com • Bimonthly $37.95. Special interest magazine written by builders for builders - professional and homeowners. Formerly *Fine Homebuilding*.

Tax Administrators News. Federation of Tax Administrators, Hall of the States, 444 N Capitol St., NW, Ste. 348 Washington, DC 20001. Phone: (202)624-5890 Fax: (202)624-7888 E-mail: cust-serv@amanet.org • URL: http://www.taxadmin.org • Description: Focuses on state tax legislation and administration. Covers research results and federal legislation that affects state taxation. Recurring features include state-by-state news of tax changes and innovations in administration, announcements of conferences and meetings, profiles of state revenue commissioners, and special sections on motor fuel taxes and technology in tax administration.

Tax-Advantaged Securities Law Report. Robert J. Haft. West Group, 610 Opperman Dr. Eagan, MN 55123. Phone: 800-328-4880 or (651)687-7000 Fax: 800-340-9378 E-mail: compandbene@westgroup.com • URL: http://www.westgroup.com • Description: Devotes each issue to one or two articles on federal or major state law concerning tax-advantaged securities. Presents explanation and analysis of new decisions, laws, rulings, and regulations. Gives practical advice and cautions for selected tax investments.

The Tax Adviser: A Magazine of Tax Planning, Trends and Techniques. American Institute of Certified Public Accountants, 1211 Ave. of the Americas New York, NY 10036-8775. Phone: 800-862-4272 or (212)596-6200 Fax: (212)596-6213 E-mail: lmorales@aicpa.org • URL: http://www.aicpa.org/pubs • Monthly. Members, $71.00 per year; non-members, $98.00 per year. Newsletter.

Tax Analysts., 400 S Maple Ave., Ste. 400 Falls Church, VA 22046. Phone: 800-955-2444 or (703)533-4400 Fax: (703)533-4444 E-mail: cservice@tax.org • URL: http://www.tax.org • Reviews all tax law developments, federal, state, international comprehensively; compiles statistics. **Convention/Meeting:** none.

Tax Analysts [Web site]. Tax AnalystsPhone: 800-955-3444 or (703)533-4400 Fax: (703)533-4444 • URL: http://www.tax.org • The three main sections of Tax Analysts home page are "Tax News" (Today's Tax News, Feature of the Week, Tax Snapshots, Tax Calendar); "Products & Services" (Product Catalog, Press Releases); and "Public Interest" (Discussion Groups, Tax Clinic, Tax History Project). Fees: Free for coverage of current tax events; fee-based for comprehensive information. Daily updating.

The Tax Directory. Tax Analysts, 400 S Maple Ave., Ste. 400 Falls Church, VA 22046. Phone: 800-955-2444 or (703)533-4400 Fax: (703)533-4444 E-mail: cservice@tax.org • URL: http://www.tax.org • Covers: Volume One—Approximately 15,000 federal and state government tax legislators, policymakers, administrators, and employees; tax regulation attorneys; over 500 international tax officials with central banks, ministries of finance, foreign embassies and consulate, and chambers of commerce; over 300 tax and business journalists and editors working for magazines, journals, newspapers, television, and radio; tax sections of over 100 trade and professional associations; state CPA, bar, and enrolled agent associations. Volume Two—Over 5,000 corporate tax managers of large U.S. and international firms. Entries include: For government and international officials—Name, title, address, phone, fax, email and website. For corporate tax managers—Name, address, phone, fax, email, website, and company name. For journalists—Name, address, phone, fax, email, website, and name of publication/network. For organizations and associations—Name, address, phone, fax, email, website, budget, membership, background information, and description of purpose.

The Tax Directory [CD-ROM]. Tax Analysts, 6830 North Fairfax Drive Arlington, VA 22213. Phone: 800-955-3444 or (703)533-4400 Fax: (703)533-4444 E-mail: taxdir@tax.org • URL: http://www.tax.org • Quarterly. Provides *The Tax Directory* listings on CD-ROM, covering federal, state, and international tax officials, tax practitioners, and corporate tax executives.

The Tax Executive. Tax Executives Institute, 1200 G St., N.W., No. 300 Washington, DC 20005-3814. Phone: (202)638-5601 Fax: (202)638-5607 • URL: http://www.tei.org • Bimonthly. $120.00 per year. Professional journal for corporate tax executives.

Tax Executives Institute., 1200 G St. NW, Ste. 300 Washington, DC 20005-3814. Phone: (202)638-5601 Fax: (202)638-5607 E-mail: administration@tei.org • URL: http://www.tei.org • Professional society of executives administering and directing tax affairs for corporations and businesses. Maintains TEI +Education Fund.

Tax Foundation. Tax Foundation, 2001 L St. NW, Ste. 1050 Washington, DC 20036. Phone: (202)464-6200 Fax: (202)464-6201 E-mail: hodge@taxfoundation.org • URL: http://www.taxfoundation.org • Fiscal and management aspects of federal, state, and local government, including studies on government expenditures, the federal budget, taxation, and international competitiveness. Serves as a national information agency for individuals and organizations concerned with problems of government expenditures, taxation, and debt.

Tax Guide for Small Business. U.S. Department of the Treasury, Internal Revenue Service. Available from U.S. Government Printing Office, Washington, DC 20402. Phone: (202)512-1800 Fax: (202)512-2250 E-mail: gpoaccess@gpo.gov • URL: http://www.accessgpo.gov • Annual. $8.00.

Tax Legislation 2001: Law, Explanation, and Analysis. CCH, Inc., 2700 Lake Cook Rd. Riverwoods, IL 60015. Phone: 800-835-5224 or (847)267-7000 E-mail: cust_serv@cch.com • URL: http://www.cch.com • 2001. $42.50. Provides explanation and interpretation of federal tax legislation enacted in 2001.

Tax Legislation 2002: Highlights. CCH, Inc., 2700 Lake Cook Rd. Riverwoods, IL 60015. Phone: 800-835-5224 or (847)267-7000 E-mail: cust_serv@cch.com • URL: http://www.cch.com • 2002. $7.00. Booklet summarizes significant changes in U. S. tax law resulting from the legislation of 2001.

Tax Management Compensation Planning Journal. BNA Tax Management, 1231 25th St., NW Washington, DC 20037. Phone: 800-223-7270 or (202)785-7191 Fax: (202)785-7195 • URL: http://www.bnatax.com • Monthly. $426.00 per year. Formerly *Compensation Planning Journal*.

Tax Management International Forum. BNA, Inc., 1231 25th St., NW Washington, DC 20037. Phone: 800-372-1033 E-mail: customercare@bna.com • URL: http://www.bna.com • Quarterly. $370.00 per year.

Tax Management International Journal: A Monthly Professional Review of Current International Tax Developments. BNA Tax Management, 1231 25th St., N.W. Washington, DC 20037. Phone: 800-223-7270 or (202)785-7191 Fax: (202)785-7195 E-mail: customercare@bna.com • URL: http://www.bnatax.com • Monthly. $426.00 per year. Semiannual *Index*.

Tax Management Weekly Report. Tax Management Inc., 1250 23rd St. NW Washington, DC 20037-1164. Phone: 800-223-7270 or (202)785-7195 Fax: (202)833-7297 E-mail: tm@bna.com • URL: http://www.bnatax.com • Description: Covers developments affecting taxation and the tax aspects of accounting. Includes summaries of federal cases including the U.S. Tax Court, synopses of IRS general counsel and technical advice memoranda, analysis of selected IRS revenue rulings, procedures and private letter rulings, and status reports of Treasury Department actions on pending regulations. Covers topics in financial planning, including memoranda on current financial and tax planning strategies.

Tax Notes International. Tax Analysts, 6830 N. Fairfax Dr. Arlington, VA 22213. Phone: 800-955-2444 or (703)533-4400 Fax: (703)533-4444 E-mail: cservice@tax.org • URL: http://www.tax.org • Weekly. $949.00 per year. Newsletter. Provides "news and in-depth reports on a variety of international tax topics." Summarizes tax statutes, regulations, rulings, court decisions, and treaties from various countries of the world.

Tax Notes: The Weekly Tax Service. Tax Analysts, 6830 N. Fairfax Dr. Arlington, VA 22213. Phone: 800-955-2444 or (703)533-4400 Fax: (703)533-4444 E-mail: cservice@tax.org • URL: http://www.tax.org • Weekly. $1,699.00 per year. Includes an *Annual* and 1985-1996 compliations on CD-ROM. Newsletter. Covers "tax news from all federal sources," including congressional committees, tax courts, and the Internal Revenue Service. Each issue contains "summaries of every document that pertains to federal tax law," with citations. Commentary is provided.

Tax Planning and Compliance for Tax-Exempt Organizations: Forms, Checklists, Procedures. Jody Blazek. John Wiley and Sons, Inc., 111 River St. Hoboken, NJ 07030. Phone: 800-225-5945 or (201)748-6000 Fax: (201)748-6088 E-mail: info@wiley.com • URL: http://www.wiley.com • 1999. $165.00. Third edition. 2002 *Supplement*, $70.00. (Nonprofit, Law, Finance, and Management Series).

Tax Planning for Corporations and Shareholders: Forms. LexisNexis Matthew Bender, 1275 Broadway Albany, NY 12204. Phone: 800-424-4200 or (518)487-3000 Fax: (518)487-3584 E-mail: bookstore.support@lexisnexis.com • URL: http://www.bender.com • Annual. $236.00. Looseleaf service.

Tax Planning for Highly Compensated Individuals. RIA Group, 395 Hudson St. New York, NY 10014. Phone: 800-950-1216 or 800-431-9025 E-mail: riahome@riag.com • URL: http://www.riahome.com • $235.00. Looseleaf service. Biennial supplementation.

Tax Planning for Individuals and Small Businesses. Sidney Kess. CCH, Inc., 2700 Lake Cook Rd. Riverwoods, IL 60015. Phone: 800-835-5224 or (847)267-7000 E-mail: cust_serv@cch.com • URL: http://www.cch.com • 2002. $52.00. Second edition. Includes illustrations, charts, and sample client letters. Edited primarily for accountants and lawyers.

Tax Policy and the Economy. MIT Press, Five Cambridge Ctr. Cambridge, MA 02142-1493. Phone: (617)253-5646 Fax: (617)253-6779 • URL: http://www.mitpress.mit.edu • Annual. $58.00. Reviews "issues in the current tax debate." Produced by the National Bureau of Economic Research. (NBER Tax Policy and the Economy Series).

Tax Practice. Tax Analysts, 6830 N. Fairfax Dr. Arlington, VA 22213. Phone: 800-955-2444 or (703)533-4400 Fax: (703)533-4444 E-mail: cservice@tax.org • URL: http://www.tax.org • Weekly. $199.00 per year. Newsletter. Covers news affecting tax practitioners and litigators, with emphasis on federal court decisions, rules and regulations, and tax petitions. Provides a guide to Internal Revenue Service audit issues.

Tax Preparation Service. Entrepreneur Media, Inc., 2445 McCabe Way Irvine, CA 92614. Phone: 800-421-2300 or (949)261-2325 Fax: (949)261-0234 E-mail: entmag@entrepreneur.com • URL: http://www.entrepreneur.com • Looseleaf. $59.50. A practical guide to starting a business for the preparation of income tax returns. Covers profit potential, start-up costs, market size evaluation, owner's time required, site selection, lease negotiation, pricing, accounting, advertising, promotion, etc. (Start-Up Business Guide No. E2332.)

The Tax Reform Act of 1986 and Its Impact on the Real Estate Industry. Marilyn Hankel. Sage Publications, Inc., 2455 Teller Rd. Thousand Oaks, CA 91320. Phone: 800-818-7243 or (805)499-9774 Fax: 800-583-2665 or (805)499-0871 E-mail: webmaster@sagepub.com • URL: http://www.sagepub.com • 1993. $10.00.

Tax Strategies for the Self-Employed. Alan D. Campbell and others. CCH, Inc., 2700 Lake Cook Rd. Riverwoods, IL 60015. Phone: 800-835-5224 or (847)267-7000 E-mail: cust_serv@cch.com • URL: http://www.cch.com • 2000. $95.00. Covers accounting methods, start-up expenses, transportation deductions, depreciation, pension deductions, tax penalties, and other topics related to tax planning for the self-employed.

Tax Year in Review. CCH, Inc., 2700 Lake Cook Rd. Riverwoods, IL 60015. Phone: 800-835-5224 or (847)267-7000 E-mail: cust_serv@cch.com • URL: http://www.cch.com • Annual. Covers the year's "major new legislative and regulatory changes."

Taxation and Revenue Policies: State Capitals. Wakeman-Walworth, Inc., P.O. Box 7376 Alexandria, VA 22307-7376. Phone: 800-876-2545 or (703)768-9600 Fax: (703)768-9690 E-mail: newsletters@statecapitals.com • URL: http://www.statecapitals.com • 50 times a year. $345.00 per year; print and online edition, $490.00 per year. Formerly *From the State Capitals: Taxation and Revenue Policies*.

Taxation of Securities Transactions. LexisNexis Matthew Bender, 1275 Broadway Albany, NY 12204. Phone: 800-424-4200 or (518)487-3000 Fax: (518)487-3584 E-mail: bookstoer.support@lexisnexis.com • URL: http://www.bender.com • Semiannual. $307.00. Looseleaf service. Covers taxation of a wide variety of securities transactions, including those involving stocks, bonds, options, short sales, new issues, mutual funds, dividend distributions, foreign securities, and annuities.

Taxes on Parade. CCH, Inc., 2700 Lake Cook Rd. Riverwoods, IL 60015. Phone: 800-835-5224 or (847)267-7000 E-mail: cust_serv@cch.com • URL: http://www.cch.com • Weekly. $129.00 per year. Newsletter.

Taxes-Property: State Capitals. Wakeman-Walworth, Inc., P.O. Box 7376 Alexandria, VA 22307-7376. Phone: 800-876-2545 or (703)768-9600 Fax: (703)768-9690 E-mail: newsletters@statecapitals.com • URL: http://www.statecapitals.com • 50 times a year. $345.00 per year; print and online edition, $490.00. Formerly *From the State Capitals: Taxes-Property*.

Taxes: The Tax Magazine. CCH, Inc., 2700 Lake Cook Rd. Riverwoods, IL 60015. Phone: 800-835-5224 or (847)267-7000 E-mail: cust_serv@cch.com • URL: http://www.cch.com • Monthly. $215.00. per year. Mainly for accountants and lawyers.

Taxi and Livery Management. International Taxicab and Livery Association, 3849 Farragut Ave. Kensington, MD 20895-2004. Phone: (301)946-5701 Fax: (301)946-4641 E-mail: itla@itla-info.org • URL: http://www.taxinetwork.com • Quarterly. $16.00 per year.

Taxicab and Transportation Service Directory. infoUSA, 5711 S 86th Cir. Omaha, NE 68127. Phone: 800-555-6124 or (402)593-4600 Fax: (402)331-5481 E-mail: internet@infousa.com • URL: http://www.abii.com • Annual. Price on application. Provides a geographical list for over 9,065 taxicab companies. Compiled from telephone company yellow pages. Formerly *Taxicab Directory*.

Taxicab, Limousine and Paratransit Association., 3849 Farragut Ave. Kensington, MD 20895. Phone: (301)946-5701 Fax: (301)946-4641 E-mail: info@tlpa.org • URL: http://www.tlpa.org • Formerly International Taxicab and Livery Association.

Taxing Wages. Organization for Economic Cooperation and Development, OECD Washington Center, 2001 L St., N. W., Suite 650 Washington, DC 20036-4922. Phone: 800-456-6323 or (202)785-6323 Fax: (202)785-0350 E-mail: washington.contact@oecd.org • URL: http://www.oecd.org • Annual. $52.00. Contains data on income tax and social security levies collected from employees and employers in OECD countries. Includes marginal and effective tax burden figures for various family income levels and statistics on cash transfers paid as family benefits.

TAXNET.PRO. CarswellPhone: 800-387-5164 or (416)609-3800 Fax: (416)298-5082 E-mail: orders@carswell.com • URL: http://www.carswell.com/taxnetpro.asp • Fee-based Web site provides complete coverage of Canadian tax law and regulation, including income tax, provincial taxes, accounting, and payrolls. Daily updates. Base price varies according to product.

TCA - The Information Technology and Telecommunications Association-Sacramento Valley.

Tea and Coffee Trade Journal. Lockwood Publications, 26 Broadway, Fl. 9M New York, NY 10004. Phone: (212)391-2060 Fax: (212)827-0945 E-mail: circulation@lockwoodpublications.com • URL: http://www.lockwoodpublications.com • Monthly. $30.00 per year. Current trends in coffee roasting and tea packing industry.

Tea Council of the United States of America., 420 Lexington Ave., Suite 825 New York, NY 10170. Phone: (212)986-6998 Fax: (212)697-8658 E-mail: simrany@teasusa.com • URL: http://www.teausa.com • Affiliated with Tea Association of the U.S.A. Companies and countries trading tea in the United States.

Teach Yourself Copywriting. J. Jonathan Gabay. McGraw-Hill, 1221 Ave. of the Americas New York, NY 10020. Phone: 800-722-4726 or (212)512-2000 Fax: (212)512-4502 E-mail: customer.service@mcgraw-hill.com • URL: http://www.mcgraw-hill.com • 2001. $14.95. Second edition. Includes material on copywriting for e-commerce websites.

Teach Yourself Desktop Publishing. Christopher Lumgair. McGraw-Hill, 1221 Ave. of the Americas New York, NY 10020. Phone: 800-722-4726 or (212)512-2000 Fax: (212)512-4502 E-mail: customer.service@mcgraw-hill.com • URL: http://www.mcgraw-hill.com • 2001. $10.95. Describes current desktop publishing software and techniques.

Teach Yourself Java. Chris Wright. McGraw-Hill, 1221 Ave. of the Americas New York, NY 10020. Phone: 800-722-4726 or (212)512-2000 Fax: (212)512-4502 E-mail: customer.service@mcgraw-hill.com • URL: http://www.mcgraw-hill.com • 2001. $12.95. Second edition. Covers the basics of designing websites and interactive pages.

Teaching Business Studies. David Needham and others. McGraw-Hill, 1221 Ave. of the Americas New York, NY 10020. Phone: 800-722-4726 or (212)512-2000 Fax: (212)512-4502 E-mail: customer.service@mcgraw-hill.com • URL: http://www.mcgraw-hill.com • 1992. $15.99.

Teaching Information Literacy: 35 Practical, Standards-based Exercises for College Students. Joanna M. Burkhardt and others. American Library Association, 50 E Huron St. Chicago, IL 60611-2795. Phone: 800-545-2433 or (312)944-6780 Fax: (312)440-9374 E-mail: ala@ala.org • URL: http://www.ala.org • 2003. $35.00. Provides a step-by-step guide for teaching students the intricacies of library and online research.

Team Leader. LRP Publications, 747 Dresher Rd., Ste. 500, PO Box 980 Horsham, PA 19044-0980. Phone: 800-341-7874 or (215)784-0860 Fax: (215)784-9639 E-mail: custserve@lrp.com • URL: http://www.dartnellcorp.com • Description: Keeps business team leaders up to date on team-leading techniques and provides solutions to team-oriented issues.

Teambuilding and Total Quality: A Guidebook to TQM Success. Gene Milas. Engineering and Management Press, 25 Technology Park Norcross, GA 30092-2988. Phone: 800-494-0460 or (770)449-0461 Fax: (770)441-3295 E-mail: cmagee@www.iienet.org • URL: http://www.iienet.org • 1997. $29.95. A practical, how-to-do-it guide to total quality management in industry. The importance of employee involvement is stressed.

Teamwork: Your Personal Guide to Working Successfully with People. Dartnell Corp., 350 Hiatt Dr. Palm Beach Gardens, FL 33418. Phone: 800-341-7874 or (561)622-6520 Fax: (561)622-2423 E-mail: custserv@lrp.com • URL: http://www.dartnellcorp.com • Biweekly. $76.70 per year. Provides advice for employees on human relations, motivation, and team spirit.

Technical Analysis Explained: The Successful Investor's Guide to Spotting Investment Trends and Turning Points. Martin J. Pring. McGraw-Hill, 1221 Ave. of the Americas New York, NY 10020. Phone: 800-722-4726 or (212)512-2000 Fax: (212)512-4502 E-mail: customer.service@mcgraw-hill.com • URL: http://www.mcgraw-hill.com • 2002. $55.00. Fourth edition.

Technical Analysis from A to Z: Covers Every Trading Tool from the Absolute Breadth Index to Zig Zag. Steven B. Achelis. McGraw-Hill, 1221 Ave. of the Americas New York, NY

10020. Phone: 800-722-4726 or (212)512-2000 Fax: (212)512-4502 E-mail: customer.service@mcgraw-hill.com • URL: http://www.mcgraw-hill.com • 2000. $39.95. Second edition. Provides definitions and explanations of more than 100 technical indicators used in attempts to predict stock and commodity price trends. Includes a general introduction to technical analysis.

Technical Analysis of Stock Trends. John Magee and others. Saint Lucie Press, 2000 Corporate Blvd., NW Boca Raton, FL 33431-7372. Phone: 800-272-9906 or (561)274-9906 Fax: (561)274-9927 E-mail: information@slpress.com • URL: http://www.slpress.com • 2001. $99.95. Eighth edition. Standard manual of technical analysis.

Technical Analysis of Stocks & Commodities: The Traders Magazine. Technical Analysis, Inc., 4757 California Ave., S.W. Seattle, WA 98116-4499. Phone: 800-832-4642 or (206)938-0570 Fax: (206)938-1307 E-mail: mail@traders.com • URL: http://www.traders.com • 13 times a year. $64.95 per year. Covers use of personal computers for stock trading, price movement analysis by means of charts, and other technical trading methods.

Technical Association of the Graphic Arts., 68 Lomb Memorial Dr. Rochester, NY 14623-5604. Phone: (585)475-7470 Fax: (585)475-2250 E-mail: tagaofc@aol.com • URL: http://www.taga.org • Formerly Technical Association of the Lithographic Industry.

Technical Communication. Society for Technical Communication, 901 N. Stuart St., Suite 904 Arlington, VA 22203-1822. Phone: (703)522-4114 • URL: http://www.stc-va.org • Quarterly. $60.00 per year. Production of technical literature.

Technical Education and Training Abstracts. Taylor and Francis Group, 325 Chestnut St., Ste. 800 Philadelphia, PA 19106. Phone: 800-354-1420 Fax: (215)625-8914 • URL: http://www.taylorandfrancis.com • Quarterly. Individuals, $283.00 per year; institutions, $920.00 per year. Published in England. Formerly *Technical Education Abstracts*.

Technical Education News. Glencoe-McGraw Hill, 8787 Orion Pl. Columbus, OH 43240-4027. Phone: 800-334-7344 Fax: (614)755-5682 E-mail: customer.service@mcgraw-hill.com • URL: http://www.glencoe.com • Semiannual. Free to qualified personnel.

Technical Report Writing Today. Steven E. Pauley and Daniel Riordan. Houghton Mifflin Co., 222 Berkeley St. Boston, MA 02116. Phone: 800-733-2828 or (617)351-5000 Fax: 800-733-2098 E-mail: inquiries@hmco.com • URL: http://www.hmco.com • 1999. Seventh edition. Price on application.

Technical Services Quarterly: New Trends in Computers, Automation, and Advanced Technologies in the Technical Operation of Libraries and Information Centers. Haworth Press, Inc., 10 Alice St. Binghamton, NY 13904-1580. Phone: 800-429-6784 or (607)722-5857 Fax: 800-895-0582 or (607)722-1424 E-mail: getinfo@haworthpressinc.com • URL: http://www.haworthpressinc.com • Quarterly. Institutions, $375.00 per year.

Technical Trends: The Indicator Accuracy Service. Technical Trends Inc., P.O. Box 792 Wilton, CT 06897. Phone: 800-736-0229 or (203)762-0229 Fax: (203)761-1504 • URL: http://www.capecod.net/techtrends • 40 times a year. $147.00 per year. Technical investment newsletter.

TECHniques. Informix Software, 16011 College Blvd., PO Box 15998 Lenexa, KS 66215-0998. Phone: 800-826-9972 or (913)599-7100 Fax: (703)683-7424 E-mail: custserve@lrp.com • URL: http://www.acteonline.org • Eight times a year. Free to members; non-members, $45.00 per year. Formerly *Vocational Educational Journal*

Techniques of Financial Analysis: A Modern Approach. Erich A. Helfert. McGraw-Hill, 1221 Ave. of the Americas New York, NY 10020. Phone: 800-722-4726 or (212)512-2000 Fax: (212)512-4502 E-mail: customer.serivce@mcgraw-hill.com • URL: http://www.mcgraw-hill.com • 1996. $32.00. Ninth edition.

Technological Forecasting and Social Change: An International Journal of the Dragon Project. Elsevier, 655 Ave. of the Americas New York, NY 10010-1710. Phone: 888-437-4636 or (212)989-5800 Fax: (212)633-3990 E-mail: usinfo-f@elsevier.com • URL: http://www.elsevier.com • Nine times a year. Individuals, $131.00 per year; institutions, $839.00 per year.

Technology and Learning: The Leading Magazine of Electronic Education. CMP Media LLC, 600 Community Dr. Manhasset, NY 11030. Phone: (516)562-5000 E-mail: cmp@cmp.com • URL: http://www.cmp.com • Eight times a year. $29.95 per year. Covers all levels of computer/electronic education-elementary to college. Formerly *Classroom Computer Learning*.

Technology and Teaching. Les Lloyd, editor. Information Today, Inc., 143 Old Marlton Pike Medford, NJ 08055-8750. Phone: 800-300-9868 or (609)654-6266 Fax: (609)654-4309 E-mail: custserv@infotoday.com • URL: http://www.infotoday.com • 1997. $42.50. Contains multimedia computer application case studies relating to college level curricula and teaching.

Technology Based Learning and Research., Arizona State University, College of Education, Community Service Center Tempe, AZ 85287-0908. Phone: (480)965-4960 Fax: (480)946-1423 E-mail: bitter@asu.edu • URL: http://tblr.ed.asu.edu/ • Research activities are related to computer literacy.

Technology Forecasts and Technology Surveys. Technology Forecasts, 205 S. Beverly Dr.,, Suite 208 Beverly Hills, CA 90212. Phone: (310)273-3486 Fax: (310)858-8272 Monthly. $192.00 per year. Newsletter. Information on major breakthroughs in advanced technologies along with forecasts of effects on future applications and markets.

Technology in Society: An International Journal. Elsevier, 360 Park Ave., S. New York, NY 10010-1710. Phone: 888-437-4636 or (212)989-5800 Fax: (212)633-3990 E-mail: usinfo-f@elsevier.com • URL: http://www.elsevier.com • Quarterly. Individuals, $233.00 per year; institutions, $981.00 per year.

Technology Investing. Michael Murphy, editor. PBI Media, Inc., 1201 7 Locks Rd. Potomac, MD 20854. Phone: 800-777-5006 or (301)354-2000 Fax: (301)309-3847 E-mail: clientservices@pbimedia.com • URL: http://www.pbimedia.com • Monthly. $195.00 per year. Newsletter. Provides specific recommendations for investing in high technology companies.

Technology Law Alert: Monthly Newsletter Covering Computer-Related Law and Tax Issues. Roditti Reports Corp., P.O. Box 2066 New York, NY 10021-5013. Phone: (212)879-3325 Fax: (212)879-4496 • URL: http://www.computerlawandtax.com • Monthly. $297.00 per year. Newsletter. Formerly*Computer Law and Tax Report*.

Technology Review: MITs National Magazine of Technology and Policy. Massachusetts Institute of Technology, One Main St., 7th Fl. Cambridge, MA 02142. Phone: (617)475-8000 Fax: (617)475-8042 E-mail: trcomments@mit.edu • URL: http://www.techreview.com • Ten times a year. $30.00 per year. Examines current technological issues facing society.

Technology Transfer Highlights. Argonne National Laboratory Industrial Technology Development Div., 9700 S Cass Ave. Argonne, IL 60439. Phone: 800-627-2596 or (630)252-2000 Fax: (630)252-5230 E-mail: partners@anl.gov • URL: http://www.anl.gov • Description: Provides information on federally-developed technology available for transfer and commercialization.

Technology Transfer Society., 2005 Arthur Ln. Austin, TX 78704. Phone: (512)447-4409 Fax: (512)447-1814 E-mail: t2s@t2s.org • URL: http://www.t2society.org • Individuals, institutions, and other professional societies involved in the process of technology transfer. Encourages development of technology assessment, transfer, utilization, and forecasting techniques; disseminates information on these new techniques. Seeks to develop an environment for and promote the enhancement of professional competence in the field. Establishes standards and ethics; defines terms. Acts as a liaison among disciplines within the technological community such as scientific, management, engineering, and other professional societies. Provides a nonprofit capability to accept charitable contributions, contracts, and grants for the performance of pilot technological transfer programs that will aid the nation.

TechTrends: For Leaders in Education and Training. Association for Educational Communications and Technology, 1800 N. Stonelake Dr., Suite 2 Bloomington, IN 47404. Phone: 877-677-2328 or (812)335-7675 Fax: (812)335-7678 E-mail: aect@aect.org • URL: http://www.aect.org • Bimonthly. $65.00 per year.

Teenage Economic Power. Available from MarketResearch.com, 641 Ave. of the Americas, 3rd Fl. New York, NY 10011. Phone: 800-298-5699 or (212)807-2629 Fax: (212)807-2716 E-mail: order@marketresearch.com • URL: http://www.marketresearch.com • 2001. $1,200.00. Published by Rand Youth Poll. Provides consumer market data on the 13-year to 19-year age group. Gives results of an extensive survey of teenage attitudes toward shopping and spending.

Telco Business Report: Executive Briefings on the Bell Operating Companies, Regional Holding Companies and Independent Telcos. Briefings Publishing Group, 1101 King St., Suite 110 Alexandria, VA 22314. Phone: 800-722-9221 or (703)518-2343 Fax: (703)739-6490 E-mail: customerservice@briefings.com • URL: http://www.briefings.com • 26 times a year. $759.00 per year. Newsletter. Covers long-distance markets, emerging technologies, strategies of Bell operating companies, and other telephone business topics.

Telecom Made Easy: Money-Saving, Profit-Building Solutions for Home Businesses, Telecommuters. June Langhoff. Aegis Publishing Group, Ltd., 796 Aquidneck Ave. Newport, RI 02842. Phone: 800-828-6961 or (401)849-4200 Fax: (401)849-4231 E-mail: aegis@aegisbooks.com • URL: http://www.aegisbooks.com • 2001. $19.95. Fouth revised edition.

Telecommunication Transmission Handbook. Roger L. Freeman. John Wiley and Sons, Inc., 111 River St. Hoboken, NJ 07030. Phone: 800-225-5945 or (201)748-6000 Fax: (201)748-6088 E-mail: info@wiley.com • URL: http://www.wiley.com • 1998. $198.00. Fourth edition. (Telecommunications and Signal Processing Series).

Telecommunications., PO Box 3255 Northbrook, IL 60065-3255. Phone: (847)291-5216 Fax: (847)291-4816 E-mail: tc@omeda.com • URL: http://www.omeda.com • Monthly. Free to qualified personnel; others, $145.00 per year. International coverage.

Telecommunications. Warren Hioki. Prentice Hall PTR, 240 Frisch Ct. Paramus, NJ 07652. Phone: 800-282-0693 Fax: 800-445-6991 • URL: http://www.phptr.com • 2000. $120.00. Fourth edition.

Telecommunications and Signal Processing Research Center. University of Texas at Austin

Telecommunications Directory. Gale, 27500 Drake Rd. Farmington Hills, MI 48331-3535. Phone: 800-877-4253 or (248)699-4253 Fax: 800-414-5043 or (248)699-8065 E-mail: galeord@cengage.com • URL: http://gale.cengage.com • Covers: Two volumes-North America and International, Cover approximately 6,000 national and international voice and data communications networks, electronic mail services, teleconferencing facilities and services, facsimile services, Internet access providers, videotex and teletext operations, transactional services, local area networks, audiotex services, microwave systems/networkers, satellite facilities, and others involved in telecommunications, including related consultants, advertisers/marketers; associations, regulatory bodies, and publishers. Entries include: Company or organization name, address, phone, fax, year established, name and title of contact, executive officers and board of directors, function or type of service; geographical area served; NAICS and SIC codes; number of employees; general description, including telecommunications-related activities; product/service; specific applications; means of access and equipment required; publications; intended market and availability; pricing; stock exchanges traded and ticker symbols; financial figures.

Telecommunications Engineer's Reference Book. Fraidoon Mazda. Elsevier, 655 Ave. of the Americas New York, NY 10010-5107. Phone: 800-366-2665 or (212)989-5800 Fax: 800-535-9935 or (212)633-3680 E-mail: custserv@elsevier.com • URL: http://www.elsevier.com • 1998. $170.00. Second edition.

Telecommunications Industry Association., 2500 Wilson Blvd., Ste. 300 Arlington, VA 22201-3834. Phone: 800-799-6682 or (703)907-7700 Fax: (703)907-7727 E-mail: gseiffert@tiaonline.org • URL: http://www.tiaonline.org • Serves the communications and IT industry, with proven strengths in standards development, domestic and international public policy, and trade shows. Facilitates business development and opportunities and a competitive market environment; provides a forum for member companies, the manufacturers and suppliers of products and services used in global communications. Represents the communications sector of the Electronic Industries Alliance.

Telecommunications: Issues in Focus. Agnes S. Corwall, editor. Nova Science Publishers, Inc., 400 Oser Ave., Suite 1600 Hauppauge, NY 11788-3619. Phone: (631)231-7269 Fax: (631)231-8175 E-mail: novascience@earthlink.net • URL: http://www.novapublishers.com • 2002. $69.00. Provides reviews of many aspects of telecommunications, including broadband, wireless, access fees, encryption, telemarketing, telephone bills, remote sensing, and regulation. Includes an index.

Telecommunications Policy. Elsevier, 360 Park Ave., S. New York, NY 10010-1710. Phone: 888-437-4636 or (212)989-5800 Fax: (212)633-3990 E-mail: usinfo-f@elsevier.com • URL: http://www.elsevier.com • 11 times a year. Individuals, $267.00 per year; institutions, $1,077.00 per year.

Telecommunications Regulation: Cable, Broadcasting, Satellite, and the Internet. LexisNexis Matthew Bender, 1275 Broadway Albany, NY 12204. Phone: 800-424-4200 or (518)487-3000 Fax: (518)487-3584 E-mail: bookstore.support@lexisnexis.com • URL: http://www.bender.com • Semiannual. $826.00. Four looseleaf volumes. Covers local, state, and federal regulation, with emphasis on the Telecommunications Act of 1996. Includes regulation of television, telephone, cable, satellite, computer communication, and on-line services. Formerly *Cable Television Law*.

Telecommunications Reports., 1333 H St. NW, Ste. 100 E Washington, DC 20005. Phone: 800-822-6338 or (202)842-6060 Fax: (202)842-3023 E-mail: customerservice@tr.com • URL: http://www.tr.com • Weekly. Institutions, $1,695.00 per year. Includes *TR Daily*. Regulatory newsletter.

TeleCommunicator. Association of Teleservices International, 12 Academy Ave. Atkinson, NH 03811. Phone: (866)896-2874 or (603)362-9489 Fax: (603)362-9486 E-mail: admin@atsi.org • URL: http://www.atsi.org • Description: Contains news concerning telephone company, legislative and governmental actions, and Association activities.

Telecommute! Go to Work Without Leaving Home. Lisa Shaw. John Wiley and Sons, Inc., 111 River St. Hoboken, NJ 07030. Phone: 800-225-5945 or (201)748-6000 Fax: (201)748-6088 E-mail: info@wiley.com • URL: http://www.wiley.com • 1996. $14.95. Includes "Are You Right for Telecommuting?" and "How to Negotiate with Your Boss."

Telecommuters, the Workforce of the Twenty-First Century: An Annotated Bibliography. Teri R. Switzer. Scarecrow Press, Inc., 4501 Forbes Blvd., Ste. 200 Lanham, MD 20706. Phone: 800-462-6420 or (301)459-3366 Fax: 800-388-4550 or (301)429-5748 E-mail: custserv@rowman.com • URL: http://www.scarecrowpress.com • 1996. $34.00. Covers material published since 1970.

Telecommuting, Teleworking, and Alternative Officing. Gil Gordon AssociatesPhone: (732)329-2266 Fax: (732)329-2703 • URL: http://www.gilgordon.com • Web site includes "About Telecommuting" (questions and answers), "Worldwide Resources" (news groups, publications, conferences), and "Technology" (virtual office, intranets, groupware). Other features include monthly updates and an extensive list of telecommuting/telework related books. Fees: Free.

Telecons. Applied Business Telecommunications, 2300 Territorial Rd. Saint Paul, MN 55114. Phone: (651)643-6595 Fax: (651)643-6596 E-mail: service@abcominc.com • URL: http://www.abcominc.com • Bimonthly. $30.00 per year.

Topics include teleconferencing, videoconferencing, distance learning, telemedicine, and telecommuting.

Telehealth Buyer's Guide. Miller Freeman, 600 Harrison St. San Francisco, CA 94107. Phone: (415)905-2200 Fax: (415)905-2232 • URL: http://www.telehealthmag.com • Annual. $10.00. Lists sources of telecommunications and information technology products and services for the health care industry.

Telemarketer. Actel Marketing, 163 Third Ave., Suite 303 New York, NY 10003. Phone: (212)674-2545 Semimonthly. $285.00 per year. Newsletter.

Telemarketing Law Guide. CCH, Inc., 4025 West Peterson Ave. Chicago, IL 60646-6085. Phone: 800-248-3248 or (773)866-6000 Fax: 800-224-8299 or (773)866-3095 E-mail: cust_serv@cch.com • URL: http://www.onlinestore.cch.com/ • Looseleaf. $700.00. Quarterly updates available. Contains detailed information on federal do-not-call legislation, various state laws, court decisions, and penalties.

Telematics and Informatics: An International Journal on Telecommunications and Internet Technology. Elsevier, 360 Park Ave., S. New York, NY 10010-1710. Phone: 888-437-4636 or (212)989-5800 Fax: (212)633-3990 E-mail: usinfo-f@elsevier.com • URL: http://www.elsevier.com • Four times a year. Institutions, $938.00 per year.

Telephone Answering Service. Entrepreneur Media, Inc., 2445 McCave Way Irvine, CA 92614. Phone: 800-421-2300 or (949)261-2325 Fax: (949)851-9088 E-mail: entmag@entrepreneurmag.com • URL: http://www.entrepreneurmag.com • Looseleaf. $59.50. A practical guide to starting a telephone answering service. Covers profit potential, start-up costs, market size evaluation, owner's time required, pricing, accounting, advertising, promotion, etc. (Start-Up Business Guide No. E1148).

The Telephone Industry Directory. Access Intelligence L.L.C., 4 Choke Cherry Rd., 2nd Fl. Rockville, MD 20850. Phone: 800-777-5006 or (301)354-2000 Fax: (301)309-3847 E-mail: info@accessintel.com • URL: http://www.pbimedia.com • Covers: 7,000 companies and 14,000 contacts in the telephone industry.

Telephone Management Strategist. Buyers Laboratory, Inc., 20 Railroad Ave. Hackensack, NJ 07601. Phone: (201)489-6439 Fax: (201)489-9365 E-mail: info@buyerslab.com • URL: http://www.buyerslab.com • Monthly. $125.00 per year. Newsletter. Information on business telecommunications.

Telephone Selling Report: Providing Proven Sales Ideas You Can Use. Art Sobczak, editor. Business By Phone, Inc., 13254 Stevens St. Omaha, NE 68137-1728. Phone: (402)895-9399 Fax: (402)896-3353 • URL: http://www.businessbyphone.com • Bimonthly. $69.00 per year. Newsletter. How-to newsletter providing proven ideas, tips, and techniques for telephone prospecting and selling.

Telephony: Intelligence for the Broadband Economy. Primedia Business Magazines and Media, 330 N Wabash Ave., Ste. 2300 Chicago, IL 60611. Phone: 800-795-5445 or (312)595-1080 Fax: (312)595-0295 E-mail: subs@primediabusiness.com • URL: http://www.primediabusiness.com • Biweekly. $114.00 per year.

Teleselling: A Self-Teaching Guide. James D. Porterfield. John Wiley and Sons, Inc., 111 River St. Hoboken, NJ 07030. Phone: 800-225-5945 or (201)748-6000 Fax: (201)748-6088 E-mail: info@wiley.com • URL: http://www.wiley.com • 1996. $24.95. Second revised edition. Provides practical information and advice on selling by telephone, including strategy, prospecting, script development, and performance evaluation. (Self-Teaching Guides Series, vol. 135).

Teleselling Techniques That Close the Sale. Flyn L. Penoyer. AMACOM, 1601 Broadway New York, NY 10019. Phone: 800-262-9699 or (518)586-8100 Fax: (518)903-8168 E-mail: customerservice@amanet.org • URL: http://www.amacombooks.org • 1997. $19.95.

TeleTrends. International Telework Association Council, 8403 Colesville Rd., Ste. 865 Silver Spring, MD 20910. Phone: (301)650-2322 E-mail: info@workfromanywhere.com • URL: http://www.telecommute.org • Quarterly. Newsletter. Price on application.

Television and Cable Factbook. Warren Publishing, Inc., 2115 Ward Ct., NW Washington, DC 20037. Phone: (202)872-9200 Fax: (202)293-3435 • URL: http://www.warrenpub.com • Annual. $595.00. Three volumes. Weekly updates. Commercial and noncommercial television stations and networks.

Television Bureau of Advertising.

Television Digest with Consumer Electronics. Warren Publishing, Inc., 2115 Ward Ct. NW Washington, DC 20037. Phone: (202)872-9200 Fax: (202)293-3435 Weekly. $944.00 per year. Newsletter featuring new consumer entertainment products utilizing electronics. Also covers the television broadcasting and cable TV industries, with corporate and industry news.

Television International Magazine. TVI Publishing, P.O. Box 8471 University City, CA 91618-8471. Phone: (213)462-1099 E-mail: tvi@smartgo.com • URL: http://www.tvinews.com • Bimonthly. $42.00 per year.

Television Production Handbook. Herbert Zettl. Wadsworth Publishing Co., 10 Davis Dr. Belmont, CA 94002. Phone: (650)595-2350 • URL: http://www.wadsworth.com • 2000. $95.95. Seventh edition. (Radio/TV/Film Series).

Television Quarterly. National Academy of Television Arts and Sciences, 111 W. 57th St., Ste. 1020 New York, NY 10019. Phone: (212)586-8424 Fax: (212)246-8129 • URL: http://www.emmys.org • Quarterly. Individuals, $30.00 per year; students, $22.00 per year.

Television Week. Crain Communications, Inc., 711 3rd Ave. New York, NY 10017-4036. Phone: 800-678-9595 or (212)210-0100 E-mail: info@crain.com • URL: http://www.crain.com • Weekly. $119.00 per year. Formerly *Electronic Media*.

Temporary Help Service. Entrepreneur Media, Inc., 2445 McCabe Way Irvine, CA 92614. Phone: 800-421-2300 or (949)261-2325 Fax: (949)261-0234 E-mail: entmag@entrepreneur.com • URL: http://www.entrepreneur.com • Looseleaf. $59.50. A practical guide to starting an employment agency for temporary workers. Covers profit potential, start-up costs, market size evaluation, owner's time required, site selection, lease negotiation, pricing, accounting, advertising, promotion, etc. (Start-Up Business Guide No. E1189.)

Tennessee Agricultural Experiment Station. University of Tennessee, Knoxville

Tennis Industry. Tennis Industry Inc., 79 Madison Ave., 8th Fl. New York, NY 10016. Phone: (212)636-2721 Fax: (212)636-2720 E-mail: tennisind@aol.com • URL: http://www.tennisindustry.com • Bimonthly. $22.00 per year. Edited for retailers serving the "serious tennis enthusiast." Provides news of apparel, rackets, equipment, and court construction.

Tenting Directory. Woodall Publications Corp., 2575 Vista Del Mar Dr. Ventura, CA 93001. Phone: 877-680-6155 or (805)667-4097 Fax: (805)667-4468 E-mail: info@woodallpub.com • URL: http://www.woodalls.com • Covers: campgrounds in the U.S. and Canada that have tent sites and tent rentals. Entries include: Name of campground, driving directions, facilities, base rate, recreational activities, season, phone.

TESS: (The Educational Software Selector). EPIE Institute, 103-3 W Montauk Highway Hampton Bays, NY 11946-4006. Phone: 888-776-7730 or (516)728-9100 Fax: (516)728-9228 E-mail: epieinst@aol.com • URL: http://www.epie.org • Semiannual. $82.50 per year. Lists over 900 suppliers of educational software for Mackintosh, Apple II, MS-DOS and Windows compatible computers and videodisc players. Formerly *The Latest and Best of TESS: The Educational Software Selector*.

Test and Measurement World Annual Buyer's Guide. Reed Business Information, 360 Park Ave.S New York, NY 10010. Phone: 800-662-7776 or (646)746-6400 E-mail: corporatecommunications@reedbusiness.com • URL: http://www.reedbusiness.com • Annual. $29.95. List of suppliers of test, measurement, inspection, and monitoring products and services.

Test and Measurement World: The Magazine for Quality in Electronics. Reed Electronics Group, 360 Park Ave., S New York, NY 10010. Phone: 800-446-6551 or (646)746-6400 Fax: (646)746-7028 E-mail: corporatecommunications@reedbusiness.com • URL: http://www.reedbusiness.com • 15 times a year. $93.99 per year.

Tests: A Comprehensive Reference for Assessments in Psychology, Education and Business. Available from Gale Cengage Learning, 27500 Drake Rd. Farmington Hills, MI 48331-3535. Phone: 800-877-GALE or (248)699-GALE Fax: 800-414-5043 E-mail: gale.galeord@cengage.com • URL: http://www.galegroup.com • 2003. $96.00. Fifth edition. List nearly 200 publishers for over 2,000 tests. Published by Pro-Ed Inc.

Tests in Print. Linda L. Murphy and others. University of Nebraska-Lincoln Buros Institute of Mental Measurements, 21 Teachers College Hall Lincoln, NE 68588-0484. Phone: 800-755-1105 or (402)472-6203 Fax: (402)472-6207 E-mail: rspies@unl.edu • URL: http://www.unl.edu/buros • Quinquennial. Price varies. Two volumes. Lists over 4,000 testing instruments.

Texas Agricultural Experiment Station at Sonora. Texas A & M University

Texas Agricultural Market Research Center. Texas A & M University

Texas Longhorn Breeders Association of America., 2315 N Main St., Ste. 402 Fort Worth, TX 76164. Phone: (817)625-6241 Fax: (817)625-1388 E-mail: tlbaa@tlbaa.org • URL: http://www.tlbaa.org • Individuals, firms and organizations interested in the Texas Longhorn breed of cattle.

Texas Transportation Institute., Texas A & M University System, CE/TTI, Room 801 B College Station, TX 77843-3135. Phone: (979)845-1713 Fax: (979)845-9356 E-mail: herbert-richardson@tamu.edu • URL: http://www.tii.tamu.edu • Concerned with all forms and modes of transportation. Research areas include transportation economics, highway construction, traffic safety, public transportation, and highway engineering.

Texas Transportation Institute, Systems Planning. Texas A & M University

Textile Bag and Packaging Association., Drawer 8 Dayton, OH 45401. Phone: 800-543-3400 or (937)476-8272 Fax: (937)258-0029 E-mail: tbpa@aol.com Formerly Textile Bag Packaging Association.

Textile Care Allied Trades Association., 271 Rte. 46 W, No. D203 Fairfield, NJ 07004. Phone: (973)244-1790 Fax: (973)244-4455 E-mail: info@tcata.org • URL: http://www.tcata.org • Represents Manufacturers and distributors of laundry and dry-cleaning machinery, and supplies.

Textile Distributors Association., 980 Ave. of the Americas New York, NY 10018-3617. Phone: (212)868-2210 Fax: (212)868-2214 E-mail: tda104@msn.com Distributors or converters of fabrics made predominantly of man-made and natural fibers and blends for all end uses. Member services include routing assistance and Trademark and +Copyright Bureau.

Textile Fibers and By-Products Association., 1531 Industrial Dr. Griffin, GA 30224-0008. Phone: (770)412-2325 or (770)227-9236 Fax: (770)227-6321 E-mail: info@tfbpa.org • URL: http://www.tfbpa.org • Firms purchasing and marketing textile fiber by-products, commonly designated as textile waste.

Textile Hi-Lights. American Textile Manufacturers Institute, Inc., 1130 Connecticut Ave., NW, Ste. 1200 Washington, DC 20036-3954. Phone: (202)862-0500 Fax: (202)862-0570 • URL: http://www.atmi.org • Quarterly. $125.00 per year. Monthly *Supplements*.

Textile Horizons: Providing Essential Reading for All Present and Future Decision Makers in Textiles and Fashion Worldwide. World Textile Publications Ltd., c/o Keith Higgenbottom, Perkins House, 1 Longlands St. Bradford BD1 2TP, United Kingdom. Bimonthly. $115.00 per year.

Textile Industries. Billian Publishing Inc., 2100 Powers Ferry Rd. Atlanta, GA 30339. Phone: 800-533-8484 or (770)955-8484 Fax: (770)955-8485 E-mail: jmetzer@billian.com • URL: http://www.billian.com • Monthly. $43.00 per year. Formerly *America's Textiles International*.

Textile Institute., St. James's Buildings, 1st Fl., 79 Oxford St. Manchester M1 6FQ, United Kingdom. Phone: 44 161 2371188 Fax: 44 161 2361991 E-mail: tiihq@textileinst.org.uk • URL: http://www.texi.org • Companies and individuals in 100 countries involved in management, science, technology, design, information transfer, and marketing of textiles including clothing and footwear. Promotes interests of the textile industry worldwide; serves professional interests of members; confers qualifications and recognizes achievements in research, application of ideas, education, business, and public affairs. Maintains Information Service to collect information relating to textile industrial and economic conditions in different countries and economic sectors.

Textile Processors, Service Trades, Health Care, Professional and Technical Employees International Union.

Textile Research Journal. TRI/Princeton (Textile Research Institute), 601 Prospect Ave. Princeton, NJ 08540. Phone: (609)924-3150 E-mail: infotriennialprinceton.org • URL: http://www.triprinceton.org • Monthly. Individuals, $325.00 per year; college and university libraries, $500.00 per year.

Textile Technology Digest. Institute of Textile Technology, 2551 Ivy Rd. Charlottesville, VA 22903-4614. Phone: (804)296-5511 Fax: (804)977-5400 • URL: http://www.itt.edu • Annual. $535.00. Provides indexing and abstracting of a wide variety of textile technology literature.

Textile Technology Digest [CD-ROM]. Textile Information Center, Institute of Textile Technology, 2551 Ivy Rd. Charlottesville, VA 22903-4614. Phone: (804)296-5511 Fax: (804)977-5400 Quarterly. Provides CD-ROM indexing and abstracting of worldwide journals and monographs in various areas of textile technology, production, and management. Covers 1978 to date.

Textile Technology Digest [online]. Institute of Textile Technology, 2551 Ivy Rd. Charlottesville, VA 22903-4614. Phone: (804)296-5511 Fax: (804)977-5400 Contains indexing and abstracting of more than 300 worldwide journals and monographs in various areas of textile technology, production, and management. Time period is 1978 to date, with monthly updating. Inquire as to online cost and availability.

Textile Terms and Definitions. J.E. McIntyre and Paul N. Daniels, editors. Available from State Mutual Book and Periodical Service Ltd., PO Box 1199 Bridgehampton, NY 11932-1199. 1996. $180.00. 10th edition. Published by the Textile Insitute (UK). Includes more than 1,000 definitions of textile processes, fiber types, and end products. Illustrated.

Textile World. Biilian Publishing Inc., 2100 Powers Ferry Rd. Atlanta, GA 30339. Phone: 800-533-8484 or (770)955-8484 Fax: (770)955-8485 E-mail: jmetzer@billian.com • URL: http://www.billian.com • Monthly. Free to qualified personnel.

Textile World Blue Book. Primedia Business Magazines and Media, 2100 Powers Ferry Rd., Suite 200 Atlanta, GA 30339. Phone: 800-533-8484 or (770)955-2500 Fax: (770)955-8485 • URL: http://www.primediabusiness.com • Annual. $160.00. Provides information on more than 5,200 textile mills in the U. S., Canada, and Mexico, including number of employees and names of about 17,000 key personnel. Also provides data on 2,500 suppliers of equipment and products for textile mills. Also known as *Official North American Textile World Blue Book*, formerly *Textile Red Book*.

Textiles and Materials., Philadelphia University, Schoolhouse Lane and Henry Ave. Philadelphia, PA 19144-5497. Phone: (215)951-2751 Fax: (215)951-2651 E-mail: brooksteind@philau.edu • URL: http://www.philaau.edu/schools • Many research areas, including industrial and nonwoven textiles.

Theatre Design and Technology. U. S. Institute for Theatre Technology, 6443 Ridings Rd. Syracuse, NY 13206-1111. Phone: 800-938-7448 or (315)463-6463 Fax: (866)398-7448 or (315)463-6525 E-mail: info@office.usitt.org • URL: http://www.usitt.org • Quarterly. $48.00 per year. Covers developments in theatre lighting, sound, scenic design, costuming, and safety.

Theatre Journal. Association for Theatre in Higher Education. Johns Hopkins University Press, Journals Publishing Div., 2715 N. Charles St. Baltimore, MD 21218-4363. Phone: 800-548-1784 or (410)516-6900 Fax: (410)516-6968 • URL:

http://www.press.jhu.edu • Quarterly. Individuals, $35.00 per year; institutions, $108.00 per year. Contains material on theatre history, theatre news, and reviews of books and plays.

Theatrical Index. Theatrical Index Ltd., 888 8th Ave., 16th Fl. New York, NY 10019. Phone: (212)586-6343 Fax: (212)307-6162 E-mail: theatricalindex@nyc.rr.com Covers: theatrical presentations in pre-production stage which are seeking investors; also covers producers, agents, and theaters. Entries include: For productions—Production name, brief details, contact. For agents and producers—Name, address, phone. For theaters—Name, address, box office and backstage phone numbers.

Theories of Macro-Organizational Behavior: A Handbook of Ideas and Explanations. Conor Vibert. M. E. Sharpe, Inc., 80 Business Park Drive Armonk, NY 10504. Phone: 800-541-6563 or (914)273-1800 Fax: (914)273-2106 E-mail: custserv@mesharpe.com • URL: http://www.mesharpe.com • 2004. $64.95. Presents summaries of 30 major theories of organizational behavior and economic organization.

The Theory and Practice of Econometrics. George G. Judge and others. John Wiley and Sons, Inc., 111 River St. Hoboken, NJ 07030. Phone: 800-225-5945 or (201)748-6000 Fax: (201)748-6088 E-mail: info@wiley.com • URL: http://www.wiley.com • 1985. $109.95. Second edition. (Probability and Statistics Series).

Theory of Corporate Finance. Michael J. Brennan, editor. Edward Elgar Publishing, Inc., 136 West St., Suite 202 Northampton, MA 01060. Phone: 800-390-3149 or (413)584-5551 Fax: (413)584-9933 E-mail: elgarinfo@e-elgar.com • URL: http://www.e-elgar.co.uk • 1996. $760.00. Two volumes. Consists of reprints of 46 articles dating from 1976 to 1994. (International Library of Critical Writings in Financial Economics Series: Vol. 1).

Thermophysical Properties Research Laboratory., 3080 Kent Ave. West Lafayette, IN 47906. Phone: (765)463-1581 Fax: (765)463-5235 E-mail: rtaylor@tprl.com • URL: http://www.tprl.com • Studies the thermophysical properties of materials from cryogenic to very high temperatures.

TheStreet.com: Your Insider's Look at Wall Street. TheStreet.com, Inc.Phone: 800-562-9571 or (212)321-5000 Fax: (212)321-5016 • URL: http://www.thestreet.com • Web site offers "Free Sections" and "Premium Sections" ($24.95 per month). Both sections offer iconoclastic advice and comment on the stock market, but premium service displays a more comprehensive selection of news and analysis. There are many by-lined articles. "Search the Site" is included.

Thinking Like Your Editor: How to Write Great Serious Nonfiction and Get It Published. Susan Rabiner and Alfred Fortunato. W. W. Norton & Co., Inc., 500 Fifth Ave. New York, NY 10110. Phone: 800-223-4830 or (212)354-5500 Fax: (212)869-0856 • URL: http://www.wwnorton.com • 2003. $14.95. Emphasizes the importance of submitting an effective proposal. The authors operate the Susan Rabiner Literary Agency in New York.

Third World Handbook. Guy Arnold. Fitzroy Dearborn Publishers, Inc., 919 Michigan Ave., Suite 760 Chicago, IL 60611. Phone: 800-850-8102 or (312)587-0131 Fax: (312)587-1049 E-mail: fitzroy@aol.com • URL: http://www.fitzroydearborn.com • 1994. $45.00. Second revised edition. Published by Cassell Publications. Discusses background, organizations, and movements within each country and region. Includes maps and photographs.

33 Metalproducing: For Primary Producers of Steel, Aluminum, and Copper-Base Alloys. Penton Media, Inc., 1300 E 9th St. Cleveland, OH 44114. Phone: (216)696-7000 Fax: (216)696-1752 E-mail: information@penton.com • URL: http://www.penton.com • Monthly. $65.00 per year. Covers metal production technology and methods and industry news. Includes a bimonthly *Nonferrous Supplement*.

Thomas A. Roe Institute for Economic Policy Studies., Heritage Foundation, 214 Massachusetts Ave., N. E. Washington, DC 20002. Phone: (202)546-4400 Fax: (202)544-8328 E-mail: staff@heritage.org • URL: http://www.heritage.org/department/roe • Concerned with the financing of Medicare.

Thomas Cook Overseas Timetable: Railway, Road and Shipping Services Outside Europe. Thomas Cook Publishing Co., Thorpe Wood, PO Box 227 Peterborough PE3 GPU, United Kingdom. Phone: 44 1733 503571 Fax: 44 1733 503596 Bimonthly. $76.20. per year. International railroad passenger schedules. Text in English; summaries in French, German, Italian and Spanish.

Thomas Food and Beverage Market Place. Grey House Publishing, 185 Millerton Rd. Millerton, NY 12546. Phone: 800-562-2139 or (518)789-8700 Fax: (518)789-0556 E-mail: books@greyhouse.com • URL: http://www.greyhouse.com • 2004. $495.00. Three volumes. Contains more than 40,000 entries covering food companies, beverages, food equipment, warehouse companies, food brokers, wholesalers, importers, and exporters. Formerly *Thomas Food Industry Register*.

Thomas Register of American Manufacturers. Thomas Publishing Co., Inc., Five Penn Plaza New York, NY 10001. Phone: 800-699-9822 or (212)695-0500 Fax: (212)290-7362 E-mail: info@thomasimg.com • URL: http://www.thomaspublishing.com • Annual. $149.00. 34 volumes. A three-part system offering information on a wide variety of industrial equipment and supplies. Lists more than 151,000 industrial product and services companies.

Thomas Register Online. Thomas Publishing Co., Inc., Five Penn Plaza New York, NY 10001. Phone: (212)290-7277 Fax: (212)629-1140 • URL: http://www.thomasregister.com • Provides concise information on approximately 194,000 U. S. companies, mainly manufacturers, with over 50,000 product classifications. Indexes over 115,000 trade names. Information is updated semiannually. Inquire as to online cost and availability.

Thomson Bank Directory. Accuity, 4709 W Golf Rd., Ste. 600 Skokie, IL 60076. Phone: 800-321-3373 or (847)676-9600 Fax: (847)933-8101 E-mail: custserv@accuitysolutions.com • URL: http://www.tfp.com • Covers: in five volumes, about 11,000 banks and 50,000 branches of United States banks, and 60,000 foreign banks and branches engaged in foreign banking; Federal Reserve system and other United States government and state government banking agencies; 500 largest North American and International commercial banks; paper and automated clearinghouses. Volumes 1 and 2 contain North American listings; volumes 3 and 4, international listings (also cited as 'Thomson International Bank Directory'); volume 5, Worldwide Correspondents Guide containing key correspondent data to facilitate funds transfer. Entries include: For domestic banks—Bank name, address, phone, telex, cable, date established, routing number, charter type, bank holding company affiliation, memberships in Federal Reserve System and other banking organizations, principal officers by function performed, principal correspondent banks, and key financial data (deposits, etc.). For international banks—Bank name, address, phone, fax, telex, cable, SWIFT address, transit or sort codes within home country, ownership, financial data, names and titles of key personnel, branch locations. For branches—Bank name, address, phone, charter type, ownership and other details comparable to domestic bank listings.

Thomson Credit Union Directory. Credit Union National Association, Inc. Accuity, 4709 W Golf Rd., Ste. 600 Skokie, IL 60076. Phone: 800-321-3373 or (847)676-9600 Fax: (847)933-8101 E-mail: custserv@accuitysolutions.com • URL: http://www.tfp.com • Covers: Approximately 12,000 credit unions and head offices and over 6,000 branches. Entries include: Institution name, address, phone, fax, routing and transit number, managing officer, financial data, charter number, year established, number of members, number of employees.

Thomson Derivatives and Risk Management Directory. Cengage Learning, 290 Harbor Dr. Stamford, CT 06902. Phone: 800-347-7707 or (203)969-8700 Fax: 800-487-8488 or (203)969-8700 E-mail: communications@cengage.com • URL: http://www.thomson.com/learning • 1998. $247.00. Lists "over 9,000 contacts at more than 4,000 institutions." (Thomson Derivatives and Risk Management Directory 1999 Series: Vol. 1).

Thomson Savings Directory. Accuity, 4709 W Golf Rd., Ste. 600 Skokie, IL 60076. Phone: 800-321-3373 or (847)676-9600 Fax: (847)933-8101 E-mail: custserv@accuitysolutions.com • URL: http://www.tfp.com • Covers: nearly 2,000 savings institutions and their 13,000 branch offices. Entries include: Institution name, address, phone, fax, type, identification of mutual or stock ownership, type of insurance, routing number, number of employees, names and titles of key personnel, branch office locations, financial and operational data.

Thomson World Bank Directory. Accuity, 4709 W Golf Rd., Ste. 600 Skokie, IL 60076. Phone: 800-321-3373 or (847)676-9600 Fax: (847)933-8101 E-mail: custserv@accuitysolutions.com • URL: http://www.tfp.com • Covers: Over 10,000 international banks and their branches in around 200 countries around the globe, including the top 1,000 U.S. Banks. Entries include: Institution name, address, phone, fax, key banking officers by functional title, directors, data established, expanded statement of condition, including a profit and loss account and historic performance ratios.

303 Software Programs to Use in Your Library: Descriptions, Evaluations, and Practical Advice. Patrick R. Dewey. American Library Association, 50 E. Huron St. Chicago, IL 60611-2795. Phone: 800-545-2433 or (312)944-6780 Fax: (312)440-9374 E-mail: ala@ala.org • URL: http://www.ala.org • 1997. $36.00. Contains profiles of a wide variety of software (21 categories) that may be useful in libraries. Includes prices, company addresses, glossary, bibliography, and an index.(101 Micro Series).

Thriving as a Broker in the 21st Century. Thomas J. Dorsey. Bloomberg, 499 Park Ave. New York, NY 10022. Phone: 800-388-2749 or (212)318-2000 Fax: (917)369-5000 • URL: http://www.bloomberg.com • 1999. $39.95. Provides advice for stockbrokers operating in today's rapidly changing financial environment. (Bloomberg Professional Library).

Thunderbird International Business Review. Thunderbird American Graduate School of International Management. John Wiley and Sons, Inc., Journals, 111 River St. Hoboken, NJ 07030. Phone: 800-225-5945 or (201)748-6000 Fax: (201)748-6088 E-mail: customer@wiley.com • URL: http://www.wiley.com • Bimonthly. $499.00 per year; with online edition, $532.00 per year. Formerly *International Executive*.

TIA Directory and Desk Reference. Telecommunications Industry Association, 2500 Wilson Blvd., Suite 300 Arlington, VA 22201-3834. Phone: (703)907-7700 Fax: (703)907-7727 • URL: http://www.tiaonline.org • Annual. Members, $50.00; non-members, $100.00. Lists manufacturers and suppliers of interconnect telephone equipment. Formerly *Multimedia Telecommunications Sourcebook*.

Tight Money Timing: The Impact of Interest Rates and the Federal Reserve on the Stock Market. Wilfred R. George. Greenwood Publishing Group, Inc., 88 Post Rd., W Westport, CT 06881. Phone: 800-225-5800 or (203)226-3571 Fax: (203)431-2214 E-mail: customer-service@greenwood.com • URL: http://www.greenwood.com • 1982. $55.00.

Tile and Decorative Surfaces: Directory and Purchasing Guide. Ashlee Publishing Co. Inc., 18 E 41st St. New York, NY 10017. Phone: (212)376-7722 Fax: (212)376-7723 E-mail: publisher@ashlee.com • URL: http://www.ashlee.com • Annual. $6.00. Lists more than 2,000 manufacturers and distributors of the products and tile setting materials.

Tile and Decorative Surfaces: The Voice of America's Tile Market. Ashlee Publishing Co., Inc., 18 E. 41st St., 20th Fl. New York, NY 10017-6222. Phone: (212)376-7722 Fax: (212)376-7723 E-mail: publisher@ashlee.com • URL: http://www.ashlee.com • Monthly. $50.00 per year.

Tile Design and Installation. Business News Publishing Co., 755 W. Big Beaver Rd., Suite 1000 Troy, MI 48084. Phone: 800-837-7370 or (248)362-3700 Fax: (248)362-0317 • URL: http://www.bnp.com • Quarterly. $55.00 per year. Formerly *Tile World*.

Timber Bulletin. Economic Commission for Europe. United Nations Publications, United Nations Concourse Level, First Ave., 46th St. New York, NY 10017. Phone: 800-553-3210 or (212)963-7680 Fax: (212)963-4910 E-mail: bookstore@un.org • URL: http://www.un.org/publications • Irregular. Price on application. Contains international statistics on forest products, including price, production, and foreign trade data.

Timber Construction Manual. American Institute of Timber Construction. John Wiley and Sons, Inc., 111 River St. Hoboken, NJ 07030. Phone: 800-225-5945 or (201)748-6000 Fax: (201)748-6088 E-mail: info@wiley.com • URL: http://www.wiley.com • 1994. $160.00. Fourth edition.

Timber Harvesting. Hatton Brown Publishers, Inc., 225 Hanrick St. Montgomery, AL 36104. Phone: 800-669-5613 or (334)834-1170 Fax: (334)834-4525 E-mail: mail@hattonbrown.com • URL: http://www.hattonbrown.com • 10 times a year. $40.00 per year.

Timber Harvesting—Logger's Resource Guide. Hatton-Brown Publishers Inc., 225 Hanrick St., PO Box 2268 Montgomery, AL 36102. Phone: 800-669-5613 or (334)834-1170 Fax: (334)834-4525 E-mail: dianne@hattonbrown.com • URL: http://www.hattonbrown.com • Publication includes: List manufacturers and distributors of equipment used in harvesting and handling timber, logging trade organizations and trade associations. Entries include: Firm name, division or subsidiary name, address, fax, phone, e-mail, website, year company established, names and titles of key personnel.

Tin International. Tin Magazines Ltd., Kingston Lane Uxbridge UB8 3PJ, United Kingdom. Monthly. $215.00 per year. News and analysis for the international tin industry.

Tin: Its Production and Marketing. William Robertson. Greenwood Publishing, P.O. Box 459 New York, NY 10004. Phone: (212)969-8419 1982. $60.00. (Contributions in Economics and Economic istory Series: No. 51).

Tin: Its Production and Marketing. William Robertson. Greenwood Publishing Group, Inc., 88 Post Rd., W Westport, CT 06881. Phone: 800-225-5800 or (203)226-3571 Fax: (203)431-2214 E-mail: customer-service@greenwood.com • URL: http://www.greenwood.com • 1982. $60.00. (Contributions in Economics and Economic History Series: No. 51).

Tips and Traps for Saving on All Your Real Estate Taxes. Robert Irwin and Norman Lane. McGraw-Hill, 1221 Ave. of the Americas New York, NY 10020. Phone: 800-722-4726 or (212)512-2000 Fax: (212)512-4052 E-mail: customer.service@mcgraw-hill.com • URL: http://www.mcgraw-hill.com • 1992. $12.95.

Tips and Traps When Buying a Franchise. Mary E. Tomzack. Source Book Publications, 1814 Franklin St., Suite 820 Oakland, CA 94612. Phone: (510)839-5471 Fax: (510)547-3245 1999. $19.95. Second edition. Provides specific cautionary advice and information for prospective franchisees.

Tips and Traps When Mortgage Hunting. Robert Irwin. McGraw-Hill, 1221 Ave. of the Americas New York, NY 10020. Phone: 800-722-4726 or (212)512-2000 Fax: (212)512-4502 E-mail: customer.service@mcgraw-hill.com • URL: http://www.mcgraw-hill.com • 1998. $14.95. Second revised edition. Contains practical advice for home buyers and small real estate investors.

Tire and Rim Association.

Tire and Rim Association Year Book. Tire and Rim Association, Inc., Crown Pointe, 175 Montrose Ave., W Copley, OH 44321. Phone: (303)666-8121 Fax: (303)666-8340 E-mail: tireandrim@aol.com Annual. $55.00.

Tire Business. Crain Communications, Inc., 1725 Merriman Rd., Suite 300 Akron, OH 44313-5283. Phone: 800-678-9595 or (330)836-9180 E-mail: info@crain.com • URL: http://www.crain.com • Semimonthly. $71.00 per year. Edited for independent tire retailers and wholesalers.

Tire Industry Association., 1532 Pointer Ridge Pl., Ste. G Bowie, MD 20716-1874. Phone: 800-876-8372 or (301)430-7280 Fax: (301)430-7283 E-mail: info@tireindustry.org • URL: http://www.tireindustry.org • Corporations engaged in all sectors of the replacement tire industry. Seeks to advance members' interests. Serves as a clearinghouse on economic and regulatory issues affecting the replacement tire industry; conducts educational programs; sponsors lobbying activities.

Tire Industry Safety Council., 1400 K St. NW, Ste. 900

Washington, DC 20005. Phone: (202)682-4800 Fax: (202)682-4854 E-mail: info@rma.org • URL: http://www.rma.org • Represents companies and organizations in the rubber industry producing rubber or rubber-related products.

Tire Review: The Authority on Tire Dealer Profitability. Babcox Publications, Inc., 3550 Embassy Pky. Akron, OH 44333. Phone: (330)670-1234 Fax: (330)670-0874 E-mail: jsmith@babcox.com • URL: http://www.babcox.com • Monthly. $64.00. Includes *LiftGuide, Custom Wheel and Tire Style Guide, Sourcebook and Directory and NTDRA Show.*

Tires. Available from MarketResearch.com, 641 Ave. of the Americas, Fourth Floor New York, NY 10011. Phone: 800-298-5699 or (212)807-2629 Fax: (212)807-2642 E-mail: order@marketresearch.com • URL: http://www.marketresearch.com • 2002. $3,950.00. Published by Global Industry Analysts. Provides worldwide market research data, including profiles of major tire companies.

Titanium: A Statistical Review. International Titanium Association, 350 Interlocken Blvd., Suite 390 Broomfield, CO 80021-3485. Phone: (303)404-2221 Fax: (303)404-9111 • URL: http://www.titanium.org • Annual. Free to members; non-members, $100.00.

Titanium: A Technical Guide. Matthew J. Donachie, editor. ASM International, 9639 Kinsman Rd. Materials Park, OH 44073-0002. Phone: 800-336-5152 or (440)338-5151 Fax: (440)338-4634 E-mail: cust-srv@asminternational.org • URL: http://www.asminternational.org • 2000. $160.00. Second edition. Provides coverage of all major, technical aspects of titanium and titanium alloys.

Titanium Newsletter. Titanium Development Association, 4141 Arapahoe Ave., Ste. 100 Boulder, CO 80303. Phone: (303)443-7515 Fax: (303)443-4406 E-mail: admin@atsi.org • URL: http://www.titanium.org • Description: Presents news on the titanium industry. Covers corporate and Association activities, personnel changes, and legislative news. Recurring features include news of research, news of members, a calendar of events, product information, and columns titled Ti News Pipeline and Ti Reference Library.

Titanium Technology: Present Status and Future Trends. F. H. Froes and others. International Titanium Association, 350 Interlocken Blvd., Suite 390 Broomfield, CO 80021-3485. Phone: (303)404-2221 Fax: (303)404-9111 E-mail: info@titanium.org • URL: http://www.titanium.org • 1985. $19.95.

Title News. American Land Title Association, 1828 L St. NW, Ste. 705 Washington, DC 20036-5104. Phone: 800-787-ALTA or (202)296-3671 Fax: 800-329-2582 or (202)223-5843 E-mail: service@alta.org • URL: http://www.alta.org • Description: Provides information for title companies and property investors.

Tlargi Rubber Technology Foundation. University of Southern California

TMA Tobacco Tax Guide: Summaries of Key Provisions of Tobacco Tax Laws, All Tobacco Products, All States. Tobacco Merchant's Association of the United States, Inc., 231 Clarksville Rd., Suite 6 Princeton, NJ 08543-8019. Phone: (609)275-4900 Fax: (609)275-8379 Looseleaf service. Members, $750.00 per year; non-members, $2,250.00 per year. Quarterly updates.

The Toastmaster: For Better Listening, Thinking, Speaking. Suzanne Frey, editor. Toastmasters International, PO Box 9052 Mission Viejo, CA 92690. Phone: (949)858-8255 Fax: (949)858-1207 • URL: http://www.toastmasters.org • Monthly. Membership. Provides information and "how-to" articles on communication and leadership.

Toastmasters International., PO Box 9052, PO Box 9052 Mission Viejo, CA 92690-9052. Phone: 800-993-7732 or (949)858-8255 Fax: (949)858-1207 E-mail: tminfo@toastmasters.org • URL: http://www.toastmasters.org • Men and women who wish to improve their communication and leadership skills. Sponsors clubs in corporate, government, and military facilities, as well as local communities in over 90 countries. Sponsors annual World Championship of Public Speaking. Special activities include: advanced communication and leadership program; youth leadership programs for junior and senior high school students; Gavel Clubs in schools, prisons, and other institutions.

Toastmasters International Club Directory. Toastmasters International, PO Box 9052 Mission Viejo, CA 92690. Phone: (949)858-8255 Fax: (949)858-1207 • URL: http://www.toastmasters.org • Annual. Price on application. Lists toastmasters clubs across the world.

Tobacco Abstracts: World Literature on Nicotiana. Tobacco Literature Service, North Carolina State University, Budler Bldg., 3210 Faucette Dr., Rms. 204-206 Raleigh, NC 27695. Phone: (919)515-2836 E-mail: cbridges@cals1.cals.ncsu.edu Bimonthly. $120.00 per year.

Tobacco and Health Research Institute. University of Kentucky

Tobacco Associates., 8452 Holly Leaf Dr. McLean, VA 22102. Phone: (703)821-1255 Fax: (703)821-1511 E-mail: taw@tobaccoassociatesinc.org • URL: http://www.tobaccoassociatesinc.org • Represents U.S. flue-cured producers in export promotion and market development.

Tobacco Association of the U.S., 3716 National Dr., Suite 114 Raleigh, NC 27612. Phone: (919)782-5151 Fax: (919)781-0915 Buyers, packers, and distributors of American leaf tobacco and manufacturers of tobacco products.

Tobacco-Cigarette News. International Press Cutting Service, P.O. Box 121 Allahabad 211 001, Uttar Pradesh, India. Phone: (91)532 622392 Weekly. $85.00 per year. Text in English. Formerly *Tobacco News.*

Tobacco Industry Litigation Reporter: The National Journal of Record of Litigation Affecting the Tobacco Industry. Andrews Publications, 175 Strafford Ave., Bldg. 4, Suite 140 Wayne, PA 19087. Phone: 800-345-1101 or (610)225-0510 Fax: (610)225-0501 E-mail: customer@andrewspub.com • URL: http://www.andrewspub.com • Monthly. $725.00 per year. Newsletter. Reports on major lawsuits brought against tobacco companies.

Tobacco International. Lockwood Publications, Inc., 26 Broadway, Fl. 9M New York, NY 10004. Phone: (212)391-2060 Fax: (212)827-0945 E-mail: circulation@lockwoodpublications.com • URL: http://www.lockwoodpublications.com • Weekly. $32.00 per year.

Tobacco International Buyers' Guide and Directory. Lockwood Publications, Inc., 26 Broadway, Fl. 9M New York, NY 10004. Phone: (212)391-2060 Fax: (212)827-0945 E-mail: circulation@lockwoodpublications.com • URL: http://www.lockwoodpublications.com • Annual. $40.00. Formerly *Tobacco Internatonal Directory and Buyers' Guide.*

Tobacco Market Review. U.S. Department of Agriculture, Agricultural Marketing Service, Washington, DC 20250. Phone: (202)720-2791 Annual.

Tobacco Merchants Association., PO Box 8019 Princeton, NJ 08543-8019. Phone: (609)275-4900 Fax: (609)275-8379 E-mail: tma@tma.org • URL: http://www.tma.org • Manufacturers of tobacco products, leaf dealers, suppliers, distributors, and others related to the tobacco industry. Maintains records of trademarks.

Tobacco Reporter: Devoted to All Segments of the International Tobacco Trade Processing, Trading, Manufacturing. Spec-Comm International, Inc., 5808 Faringdon Pl., Ste. 200 Raleigh, NC 27609-3930. Phone: (919)872-5040 Fax: (919)876-6531 • URL: http://www.speccomm.com • Monthly. $36.00 per year.

Tobacco Retailers Almanac. Retail Tobacco Dealers of America Inc., 12 Galloway Ave., Ste. 1-B Cockeysville, MD 21030. Phone: (410)328-1674 Fax: (410)628-1679 E-mail: info@rtda.org • URL: http://www.rtda.org • Annual. Price on application. Lists virtually every tobacco related product available (including cigars, cigarettes, pipes, tobacco, lighters and gift items).

Tobacconists' Association of America., 1211 Tutor Ln. Evansville, IN 47715-4001. Phone: (812)479-8070 Fax: (812)479-5939 E-mail: t_a_a@hotmail.com • URL: http://www.t-a-a.org • Retail tobacco merchants.

Tobe Report. Tobe, 501 Fifth Ave., Suite 1208 New York, NY 10017. Phone: (212)867-8677 Fax: (212)867-8662 E-mail: report@tobereport.com • URL: http://www.tobereport.com • 38 times a year. Price on application. Edited for fashion retailers. Provides detailed information and analysis relating to current trends in the women's, children's, and men's apparel and accessories markets.

Today's Chemist at Work. American Chemical Society, 1155 16th St., N. W. Washington, DC 20036. Phone: 800-227-5558 or (202)872-4600 Fax: (202)776-8258 E-mail: help@acs.org • URL: http://www.chemistry.org • Monthly. Institutions, $200.00 per year; others, price on application. Provide pracrtical information for chemists on day-to-day operations. Product coverage includes chemicals, equipment, apparatus, instruments, and supplies.

Today's Facility Manager: The Magazine of Facilities-Interior Planning Team. Group C Communications, 44 Apple St., Ste. 3 Tinton Falls, NJ 07724. Phone: 800-524-0337 or (732)842-7433 Fax: (732)758-6634 E-mail: jstaats@groupc.com • URL: http://www.groupc.com • Monthly. $30.00 per year. Covers office design, furnishings, and furniture, including open plan systems. Formerly *Business Interiors.*

Today's Insurance Professionals. National Association of Insurance Women, 1847 E. 15th St. Tulsa, OK 74159. Phone: 800-766-6249 or (918)744-5195 Fax: (918)743-1968 E-mail: joinnaiw@naiw.org • URL: http://www.naiw.org • Quarterly. Free to members; non-members, $15.00 per year. Provides advice on professional and personal development in the insurance business. Formerly *Today's Insurance Woman.*

Tollways. International Bridge, Tunnel and Turnpike Association, 1146 19th St. NW, Ste. 800 Washington, DC 20036-3725. Phone: (202)659-4620 Fax: (202)659-0500 E-mail: info@ibtta.org Description: Focuses on trends, developments, and news about the worldwide toll industry for members.

Tools and Techniques of Financial Planning. Stephan Leimberg and others. National Underwriter Co., 5081 Olympic Blvd. Erlanger, KY 41017. Phone: 800-543-0874 or (859)-692-2100 • URL: http://www.nationalunderwriter.com • 2004. $74.95.

Tools of the Trade. Hanley-Wood, LLC, One Thomas Circle, NW Washington, DC 20005. Phone: 800-837-0870 or (202)452-0800 Fax: (202)785-1974 • URL: http://www.hanley-wood.com • Five times a year. $19.80 per year. Provides advice and information on tools for the construction industry. Includes product tests and evaluations.

Tools of the Trade Annual Buyers Guide. Hanley-Wood, LLC, One Thomas Circle, NW Washington, DC 20005. Phone: 800-837-0870 or (202)452-0800 Fax: (202)737-1974 • URL: http://www.hanley-wood.com • Annual. Price on application. A directory of tools for the construction industry.

Top CEOs: Forbe's Executive Pay Survey. Forbes Magazine, 60 Fifth Ave. New York, NY 10011. Phone: 800-888-9698 or (212)620-2200 • URL: http://www.forbes.com • 2001. $4.95. List of 800 firms. May issue of *Forbes Magazine.*

Top Contacts: Major Owners, Leasing Agents, and Managers. National Research Bureau, Inc., 200 W. Jackson Blvd., No. 2700 Chicago, IL 60606-6910. Phone: 800-456-4555 or (312)583-5250 • URL: http://www.nrbonline.com • Annual. $305.00. Contains information on more than 1,300 owners, agents, and managers, each with control of three or more shopping centers.

Top Executive Compensation. The Conference Board, 845 3rd Ave. New York, NY 10022. Phone: (212)339-0345 Fax: (212)836-9740 • URL: http://www.conference-board.org • Annual. Members, $55.00; non-members, $195.00. Provides data on compensation of highest paid executives in major corporations.

The Top 500 Design Firms Sourcebook. McGraw-Hill, 1221 Ave. of the Americas New York, NY 10020. Phone: 800-722-4726 or (212)512-2000 Fax: (212)512-4502 E-mail: customer.service@mcgraw-hill.com • URL: http://www/mcgraw-hill.com • Annual. $25.00. Lists 500 leading architectural, engineering and speciality design firms selected on basis of annual billings. Formerly *ENR Directory of Design Firms.*

The Top 5,000 European Companies 2002. Available from Gale Cengage Learning, 27500 Drake Rd. Farmington Hills, MI 48331-3535. Phone: 800-877-GALE or (248)699-GALE Fax: 800-414-5043 E-mail: gale.galeord@cengage.com • URL: http://www.galegroup.com • 2002. $645.00. Third edition. Published by Graham & Whiteside. In addition to about 5,000 manufacturing and service companies, includes the 500 largest banks in Europe and the 100 largest insurance companies.

The Top 5,000 Global Companies 2002. Available from Gale Cengage Learning, 27500 Drake Rd. Farmington Hills, MI 48331-3535. Phone: 800-877-GALE or (248)699-GALE Fax: 800-414-5043 E-mail: gale.galeord@cengage.com • URL: http://www.galegroup.com • 2002. $730.00. Third edition. Published by Graham & Whiteside. Includes about 5,000 manufacturing and service companies worldwide, plus the world's 500 largest banks and 100 largest insurance companies.

Topical Reference Books: Authoritative Evaluations of Recommended Resources in Specialized Subject Areas. Marion Sader, editor. Greenwood Publishing Group, Inc., 88 Post Rd. W Westport, CT 06881. Phone: 800-225-5800 or (203)226-3571 Fax: (203)431-2214 E-mail: customer-service@greenwood.com • URL: http://www.greenwood.com • 1991. $109.00. Ranks 2,000 reference books ("Core Titles," "New and Noteworthy," "Supplementary"). (Buying Guide Series).

Topicator: Classified Guide to Articles in the Advertising/Communications/Marketing Periodical Press., P.O. Box 757 Terrebonne, OR 97760-0757. Phone: (541)923-7334 Bimonthly. $110.00 per year. An index of major articles appearing in 20 leading magazines in the advertising, communications, and marketing fields.

Total Business Budgeting: A Step-by-Step Guide with Forms. Robert Rachlin. John Wiley and Sons, Inc., 111 River St. Hoboken, NJ 07030. Phone: 800-225-5945 or (201)748-6000 Fax: (201)748-6088 E-mail: info@jwiley.com • URL: http://www.wiley.com • 1999. $90.00. Second edition.

Total Business Planning: A Step-by-Step Guide with Forms. E. James Burton. John Wiley and Sons, Inc., 111 River St. Hoboken, NJ 07030. Phone: 800-225-5945 or (201)748-6000 Fax: (201)748-6088 E-mail: info@wiley.com • URL: http://www.wiley.com • 1999. $29.95. Second edition. How to construct and activate an internal business plan, whether short-term or long-term. Includes CD-ROM.

Total Customer Service: The Ultimate Weapon. William H. Davidow and Bro Uttal. HarperTrade, 10 E. 53rd St. New York, NY 10022-5299. Phone: 800-242-7737 or (212)207-7000 Fax: 800-822-4090 or (212)207-7633 • URL: http://www.harpercollins.com • 1990. $13.00.

Total Quality Management Handbook. John L. Hradesky. McGraw-Hill, 1221 Ave. of the Americas New York, NY 10020. Phone: 800-722-4726 or (212)512-2000 Fax: (212)512-4502 E-mail: customer.service@mcgraw-hill.com • URL: http://www.mcgraw-hill.com • 1994. $74.50.

Total Telemarketing: Complete Guide to Increasing Sales and Profits. Robert J. McHatton. John Wiley and Sons, Inc., 111 River St. Hoboken, NJ 07030. Phone: 800-225-5945 or (201)748-6000 Fax: (201)748-6088 E-mail: info@wiley.com • URL: http://www.wiley.com • 1988. $16.95.

The Touche Ross Personal Financial Planning and Investment Workbook. John R. Connell and others. Prentice Hall, 1 Lake St. Upper Saddle River, NJ 07458. Phone: 800-282-0693 Fax: 800-835-5327 or (201)236-7141 • URL: http://www.prenhall.com • 1989. $39.95. Third edition.

Tough-Minded Leadership. Joe D. Batten. AMACOM, 1601 Broadway New York, NY 10019. Phone: 800-262-9699 or (518)586-8100 Fax: (518)903-8168 E-mail: customerservice@amenet.org • URL: http://www.amacombooks.org • 1989. $15.95.

Tourism Planning. David Marcouiller. Sage Publications, Inc., 2455 Teller Rd. Thousand Oaks, CA 91320. Phone: 800-818-7243 or (805)499-9774 Fax: 800-583-2665 or (805)449-0871 E-mail: webmaster@sagepub.com • URL: http://www.sagepub.com • 1995. $10.00. (Bibliographies Series No. 316).

Tourism Policy and International Tourism in OECD Member

Countries. Available from OECD Publications and Information Center, 2001 L St., N.W.,, Suite 700 Washington, DC 20036-4922. Phone: 800-456-6323 or (202)785-6323 Fax: (202)785-0350 E-mail: washington.contact@oecd.org • URL: http://www.oecdwash.org • Annual. $50.00. Reviews developments in the international tourism industry in OECD member countries. Includes statistical information.

Tourism: Principles, Practices, Philosophies. Charles R. Goeldner. John Wiley and Sons, Inc., 111 River St. Hoboken, NJ 07030. Phone: 800-225-5945 or (201)748-6000 Fax: (201)748-6088 E-mail: info@wiley.com • URL: http://www.wiley.com • 2002. $70.00. Ninth edition. General review of the travel industry.

Tourist Attractions and Parks Magazine Buyers Guide. Kane Communications, Inc., 10 E. Athens Ave., Ste. 208 Ardmore, PA 19003. Phone: (610)734-2420 Fax: (610)734-2423 E-mail: kanecominc@aol.com • URL: http://www.tapmag.com • Annual. $10.00. Lists companies making products or services for leisure facilities.

Towards a Sustainable Energy Future. Organization for Economic Cooperation and Development, OECD Washington Center, 2001 L St., N. W., Suite 650 Washington, DC 20036-4922. Phone: 800-456-6323 or (202)785-6323 Fax: (202)785-0350 E-mail: washington.contact@oecd.org • URL: http://www.oecdwash.org • 2001. $100.00. Prepared by the International Energy Agency (IEA). Describes various policies for promoting sustainable energy, especially as related to economic development. Discusses "growing concerns about climate change and energy-supply security."

Towards Electronic Journals: Realities for Scientists, Librarians, and Publishers. Carol Tenopir and Donald W. King. Special Libraries Association, 1700 18th St., N. W. Washington, DC 20009-2514. Phone: (202)234-4700 Fax: (202)265-9317 E-mail: sla@sla.org • URL: http://www.sla.org • 2000. $59.00. Discusses journals in electronic form vs. traditional (paper) scholarly journals, including the impact of subscription prices.

Town and Country. Hearst Corp., 1700 Broadway New York, NY 10019-5970. Phone: 800-289-8696 or (212)903-5000 E-mail: tnc@hearst.com • URL: http://www.hearstcorp.com • Monthly. $24.00 per year.

Township Atlas of the United States. Gale Cengage Learning, 27500 Drake Rd. Farmington Hills, MI 48331-3535. Phone: 800-877-GALE or (248)699-4253 Fax: 800-414-5043 E-mail: gale.galeord@cengage.com • URL: http://gale.cengage.com • 2000. $85.00. Fourth edition. Covers the 48 contiguous states. Includes state maps, county maps, townships, subdivisions, and indexes.

Toxic Chemicals Laboratory. Cornell University

Toxic Substances Controls Guide. Mary D. Worobec and Cheryl Hogue. BNA, Inc., 1231 25th St., NW Washington, DC 20037. Phone: 800-372-1033 E-mail: customercare@bna.com • URL: http://www.bna.com • 1992. 45.00. Second edition. Emphasis on legal aspects.

Toxline. National Library of Medicine, 8600 Rockville Pike Bethesda, MD 20894. Phone: 800-638-8484 or (301)496-6531 Fax: (301)480-3537 Abstracting service covering human and animal toxicity studies, 1965 to present (older studies available in *Toxback* file). Monthly updates. Inquire as to online cost and availability.

Toy Industry Association., 1115 Broadway, Ste. 400 New York, NY 10010. Phone: (212)675-1141 Fax: (212)633-1429 E-mail: info@toyassociation.org • URL: http://www.toy-tia.org • Provides business services to U.S. manufacturers and importers of toys. Manages American International Toy Fair; represents the industry before Federal, State and Local government on issues of importance; provides legal and legislative counsel; conducts educational programs; compiles industry statistics.

TPG Briefing on Local Exchange Statistics. Warren Communication News, 2115 Ward Court, N. W. Washington, DC 20037. Phone: 800-771-9202 or (202)872-9200 Fax: (202)293-3435 E-mail: customerservice@warren-news.com • URL: http://www.warren-news.com • Annual. $325.00. Contains statistics on local telephone companies: revenues, expenses, debt, income, advertising, access lines, network usage, etc. Provides "Current Information on Major Competitors."

Tracking America's Economy. Norman Frumkin. M. E. Sharpe, Inc., 80 Business Park Drive Armonk, NY 10504. Phone: 800-541-6563 or (914)273-1800 Fax: (914)273-2106 E-mail: custserv@mesharpe.com • URL: http://www.mesharpe.com • 2004. $72.95. Fourth edition. Provides detailed explanations of the meaning and methodology of the leading U. S. economic indicators. Covers such topics as employment data, financial indicators, productivity, housing, government spending, balance of payments, and taxation.

Trade-a-Plane., 174 4th St. Crossville, TN 38555. Phone: 800-423-9030 or (931)484-5137 Fax: (931)484-2532 E-mail: subs@trade-a-plane.com • URL: http://www.trade-a-plane.com • 36 times a year. $42.00 per year. Subject matter is aircraft for sale or trade.

Trade and Development Report and Overview. Available from United Nations Publications, United Nations Concourse Level, First Ave., 46th St. New York, NY 10017. Phone: 800-553-3210 or (212)963-7680 Fax: (212)963-4910 E-mail: bookstore@un.org • URL: http://www.un.org/publications • Annual. $45.00. Yearly overview of trends in international trade, including an analysis of the economic and trade situation in developing countries. Published by the United Nations Conference on Trade and Development (UNCTAD).

Trade and Employment in Developing Countries. Anne O. Krueger, editor. The University of Chicago Press, 1427 E. 60th St. Chicago, IL 60637. Phone: 800-621-2736 or (773)702-7700 Fax: 800-621-8476 or (773)702-7212 E-mail: custserv@press.uchicago.edu • URL: http://www.press.uchicago.edu • Two volumes. Vol. 2, 1982, $35.00; Vol. 3, 1983, $16.00. (National Bureau of Economic Research Project Report Series).

Trade & Industry Database. Gale Cengage Learning, 27500 Drake Rd. Farmington Hills, MI 48331-3535. Phone: 800-877-GALE or (248)699-GALE Fax: 800-414-5043 or (248)699-8069 E-mail: galeord@gale.com • URL: http://gale.cengage.com • Provides indexing of business periodicals, January 1981 to date. Daily updates. (Full text articles from some periodicals are available online, 1983 to date. Inquire as to online cost and availability).

Trade Associations amd Professional Bodies of Continental Europe. Available from Gale Cengage Learning, 27500 Drake Rd. Farmington Hills, MI 48331-3535. Phone: 800-877-GALE or (248)699-GALE Fax: 800-414-5043 E-mail: gale.galeord@cengage.com • URL: http://www.galegroup.com • 2003. $290.00. Second edition. Published by Graham & Whiteside. Provides detailed information on more than 3,600 business and professional organizations in Europe.

Trade Book Publishing: Analysis by Category. Kathleen Martucci and others. SIMBA Information, Inc., 11 Riverbend Dr., S. Stamford, CT 06907-0234. Phone: 800-307-2529 or (203)358-4100 Fax: (203)358-5824 E-mail: info@simbanet.com • URL: http://www.simbanet.com • 1998. $1,495.00. 6th revised edition. Reviews current conditions in the book publishing industry, including analysis of market segments, retailing aspects, and profiles of major publishers.

Trade Channel. Trade Channel Europe, Nieuw Guineastraat 30 2022 PA Haarlem, Netherlands. Phone: (31)23 5319022 Fax: (31)23 5317974 E-mail: sales_nl@tradechannel.com • URL: http://www.tradechannel.com • Monthly. $88.00 per year. Features export "offers" and import "wants." Worldwide coverage. Technical products and consumer products. Each edition $88.00 per year. Formerly *Export Channel*.

Trade Dimensions' Market Scope. Trade Dimensions, 55 Greens Farms Rd. Westport, CT 06880. Phone: 800-291-0410 or (203)222-5750 Fax: (203)222-5701 E-mail: info@tradedimensions.com • URL: http://www.tradedimensions.com • Covers: Market share for over 1,400 supermarket chains and wholesalers. Entries include: Company name, location, number of stores in the area, market share. Syndicated market areas include 52 AC Nielsen Scantrack markets, all 64 IRI InfoScan markets, all 205 DMAs (Designated Market Areas) and 100 MSAs (government-defined), plus 48 Trad Dimensions markets.

Trade Directories of the World. Croner Publications, Inc., 10951 Sorrento Valley Rd., Suite 1-D San Diego, CA 92121-1613. Phone: 800-441-4033 or (858)546-1894 Fax: (858)546-1955 Annual. 100.00. Looseleaf service. Monthly supplements. Lists over 3,300 publications.

Trade Directory of Mexico. Available from Hoovers, Inc., 5800 Airport Blvd. Austin, TX 78752. Phone: 800-486-8666 or (512)374-4500 Fax: (512)374-4501 E-mail: custsupport@hoovers.com • URL: http://www.hoovers.com • Annual. $99.95. Published by IMF Editora. Contains profiles of 6,000 Mexican companies involved in foreign trade. Includes profile of Mexico and of the individual states.

Trade Directory of Mexico. Mexican Foreign Trade Bank, Hoover's Inc., 1033 La Posada Dr., Ste. 250 Austin, TX 78752. Phone: (512)374-4500 Fax: (512)374-4501 Annual. $100.00. Provides information on more than 6,000 Mexican companies involved in foreign trade. Lists forwarding agencies, customs brokers, consulting groups, transportation companies, and other trade-related Mexican organizations.

Trade Policy Agenda. Available from U. S. Government Printing Office, Washington, DC 20402. Phone: (202)512-1800 Fax: (202)512-2250 E-mail: gpoaccess@gpo.gov • URL: http://www.access.gpo.gov • Annual. $45.00. Lists U. S. trade agreements "that afford increased foreign market access or reduce foreign barriers."

Trade Policy Review - Japan. Bernan Press, 4611-F Assembly Dr. Lanham, MD 20706-4391. Phone: 800-274-4447 or (301)459-2255 Fax: 800-865-3450 or (301)459-0056 E-mail: bpress@bernan.com • URL: http://www.bernan.com • 1999. $60.00. Available in English, French, or Spanish versions. Provides WTO analysis of Japan's overall economic environment, trade policy objectives, and "policy developments affecting trade and investment."

Trade Policy Reviews. Bernan Press, 4611-F Assembly Dr. Lanham, MD 20706-4391. Phone: 800-274-4447 or (301)459-2255 Fax: 800-865-3450 or (301)459-9235 E-mail: bpress@bernan.com • URL: http://www.bernan.com • Annual. Price varies for each country's review (31 are available). Each review describes "trade policies, practices, and macroeconomic situations." Prepared by the Trade Policy Review Board of the World Trade Organization.

Trade Secret Protection in an Information Age. Gale R. Peterson. Glasser LegalWorks, 150 Clove Rd. Little Falls, NJ 07424. Phone: 800-308-1700 or (973)890-0008 Fax: (973)890-0042 E-mail: legalwks@aol.com • URL: http://www.glasserlegalworks.com • Looseleaf. $149.00, including sample forms on disk. Periodic supplementation available. Covers trade secret law relating to computer software, online databases, and multimedia products. Explanations are based on more than 1,000 legal cases. Sample forms on disk include work-for-hire examples and covenants not to compete.

Trade Secrets. American Lawyer Media, Inc., 105 Madison Ave. New York, NY 10016. Phone: 800-888-8300 or (212)779-9200 Fax: (212)481-8110 E-mail: lawcatalog@amlaw.com • URL: http://www.lawcatalog.com/ • Looseleaf. $169.00. Updated as needed. Covers the legal protection of trade secrets, including information on the Economic Espionage Act of 1996. Includes a CD-ROM with samples of applicable legal forms. (Law Journal Press).

Trade Show Center. Global Sources/Trade Media Holdings Ltd. [Singapore]Phone: (656)574-2800 E-mail: service@globalsources.com • URL: http://www.globalsources.com/TRADESHW/TRDSHFRM.HTM • Free Web site provides current, detailed information on more than 1,000 major trade shows worldwide, including events in the U. S., but with an emphasis on "Asia and Greater China." Searching is offered by product, supplier, country, and month of year. Includes links to "Trade Information."

Trade Show Exhibitors Association., 2301 S Lake Shore Dr., Ste. 1005, 2301 S Lakeshore Dr., No. 1005 Chicago, IL 60616. Phone: (312)842-8732 Fax: (312)842-8744 E-mail: tsea@tsea.org • URL: http://www.tsea.org • Exhibitors working to improve the effectiveness of trade shows as a marketing tool. Purposes are to promote the progress and development of trade show exhibiting; to collect and disseminate trade show information; conduct studies, surveys, and stated projects designed to improve trade shows; to foster good relations and communications with organizations representing others in the industry; to undertake other activities necessary to promote the welfare of member companies. Sponsors Exhibit +Industry +Education Foundation and professional exhibiting seminars; the forum series of educational programs on key issues affecting the industry. Maintains placement services; compiles statistics.

Trade Show Exhibitors Association Membership Directory and Industry Buyer's Guide. Trade Show Exhibitors Association, 2301 S Lake Shore Dr., No. 1005 Chicago, IL 60616-1419. E-mail: tsea@tsea.org • URL: http://www.tsea.org • Annual. Free to members; non-members, $99.00. Provides listings and details for approximately 2,300 exhibit professionals.

Trade Shows Worldwide: An International Directory of Events, Facilities and Suppliers. Gale Cengage Learning, 27500 Drake Rd. Farmington Hills, MI 48331-3535. Phone: 800-877-GALE or (248)699-4253 Fax: 800-414-5043 E-mail: gale.galeord@cengage.com • URL: http://gale.cengage.com • 2003. $355.00. 19th edition. Provides detailed information from over 75 countries on more than 10,800 trade shows and exhibitions. Separate sections are provided for trade shows/exhibitions, for sponsors/organizers, and for services, facilities, and information sources. Indexing is by date, location, subject, name, and keyword.

Trade Union World. International Confederation of Free Trade Unions, Bd. Emil Jacqmain 155, Bte. One 1210 Brussels, Belgium. Phone: 32 2 2240211 Fax: 32 2 2015815 E-mail: internetpo.icftu.org • URL: http://www.ictfu.org • Monthly. $60.00 per year. Formerly *Free Labour World*.

Tradeline Exclusive Reports. Tradeline, Inc., P.O. Box 1568 Orinda, CA 94563. Phone: (925)254-1744 Fax: (925)254-1093 E-mail: fmdm@fmdata.com • URL: http://www.tradelineinc.com • Monthly. $120.00 per year. Newsletter. Covers the planning, design, construction, and renovation of of a variety of corporate facilities. Formerly *FM Data Monthly*.

Trademark Manual of Examining Procedure. Available from U. S. Government Printing Office, Washington, DC 20402. Phone: (202)512-1800 Fax: (202)512-2250 E-mail: gpoaccess@gpo.gov • URL: http://www.access.gpo.gov • $168.00 for basic manual and semiannual changes for an indeterminate period. Covers "practices and procedures" relating to the processing of applications to register trademarks in the U. S. Patent and Trademark Office.

The Trademark Reporter. International Trademark Association, 1133 6th Ave. New York, NY 10036-6710. Phone: (212)768-9887 Fax: (212)768-7796 E-mail: tmr@inta.org • URL: http://www.inta.org • Bimonthly. Free to members; libraries, $60.00 per year. Contains articles on trademark developments, trademark law, and the use of trademarks.

The Trademarker Reporter. International Trademark Association, 1133 6th Ave. New York, NY 10036-6710. Phone: (212)768-9887 Fax: (212)768-7796 E-mail: tmr@inta.org • URL: http://www.inta.org • Bimonthly. Free to members; others, $50.00 per year. Newsletter.

TRADEMARKSCAN: International Register. Thomson & Thomson, 500 Victory Rd. North Quincy, MA 02171-3145. Phone: 800-692-8833 or (617)479-1600 Fax: (617)786-8273 • URL: http://www.thomson-thomson.com • Supplies current information on more than 400,000 trademarks registered with the World Intellectual Property Organization. Updates are monthly. Inquire as to online cost and availability. (TRADEMARKSCAN also maintains extensive databases for individual countries: Canada, U. K., Germany, Italy, France, and others.)

TRADEMARKSCAN: U. S. Federal. Thomson & Thomson, 500 Victory Rd. North Quincy, MA 02171-3145. Phone: 800-692-8833 or (617)479-1600 Fax: (617)786-8273 • URL: http://www.thomson-thomson.com • Provides information on more than two million trademarks registered and pending at the U.

S. Patent and Trademark Office. Time period is 1884 to date for active trademarks, with updates twice a week. Graphic images are show. Inquire as to online cost and availability.

TRADEMARKSCAN: U. S. Federal [CD-ROM]. Thomson & Thomson, 500 Victory Rd. North Quincy, MA 02171-1545. Phone: 800-692-8833 or (617)479-1600 Fax: (617)786-8273 Monthly. $7,500.00 per year. Contains information on CD-ROM for more than two million trademarks from the U. S. Patent and Trademark Office. For active trademarks, time period is 1884 to date. Graphic images are shown for many of the records.

TRADEMARKSCAN: U. S. State. Thomson & Thomson, 500 Victory Rd. North Quincy, MA 02171-3145. Phone: 800-692-8833 or (617)479-1600 Fax: (617)786-8273 • URL: http://www.thomson-thomson.com • Contains information on more than 970,000 trademarks registered with the Office of the Secretary of State in all 50 states and in Puerto Rico. Time period is 1900 to date for active trademarks, with weekly updates. Inquire as to online cost and availability.

TRADEMARKSCAN: U. S. State [CD-ROM]. Thomson & Thomson, 500 Victory Rd. North Quincy, MA 02171-1545. Phone: 800-692-8833 or (617)479-1600 Fax: (617)786-8273 Monthly. $3,500.00 per year. Provides information on CD-ROM for more than one million trademarks registered with the Office of the Secretary of State in all 50 states and in Puerto Rico. For active trademarks, time period is 1900 to date.

Trader Vic: Methods of a Wall Street Master. Victor Sperandeo and T. Sullivan Brown. John Wiley and Sons, Inc., 111 River St. Hoboken, NJ 07030. Phone: 800-225-5945 or (201)748-6000 Fax: (201)748-6088 E-mail: info@wiley.com • URL: http://www.wiley.com • 1993. $22.95.

Traders Magazine. Thomson Media, One State St. Plaza New York, NY 10004. Phone: 800-221-1809 or (212)803-8200 Fax: (212)843-9635 E-mail: custserv@thomsonmedia.com • URL: http://www.thomsonmedia.com • Monthly. $60.00 per year. Edited for institutional buy side and sell side equity traders. Covers industry news, market trends, regulatory developments, and personnel news. Serves as the official publication of the Security Traders Association.

Tradeshow and Exhibit Manager. Goldstein and Associates, 1150 Yale St., Suite 12 Santa Monica, CA 90403-4738. Phone: (310)828-1309 Fax: (310)829-1169 Bimonthly. $80.00 per year. Edited for exhibit, tradeshow, and exposition managers. Covers design trends, site selection, shipping problems, industry news, etc. Supplement available *Tradeshow Directory*.

Tradeshow and Exhibit Manager Buyer's Guide. Goldstein and Associates, 1150 Yale St., Suite 12 Santa Monica, CA 90403. Phone: (310)828-1309 Fax: (310)829-1169 Annual. $10.00. Lists about 1,000 suppliers providing products and services for exhibits and tradeshows.

Tradeshow Week: Since 1971, the Only Weekly Source of News and Statistics on the Tradeshow Industry. Reed Business Information, 360 Park Ave. S New York, NY 10010. Phone: 800-446-6551 or (646)746-6400 Fax: (646)746-7028 E-mail: corporatecommunications@reedbusiness.com • URL: http://www.reedbusiness.com • 50 times a year. $419.00 per year; includes 18 *Supplements and 7 Websites*. Edited for corporate and association trade show and exhibit managers. Includes show calendars and labor rates.

Trading and Exchanges: Market Microstructure for Practitioners. Larry Harris. Oxford University Press, 198 Madison Ave. New York, NY 10016-4314. Phone: 800-451-7556 or (212)726-6000 Fax: (212)726-6440 E-mail: custserv@oup-usa.org • URL: http://www.oup-usa.org • 2002. $95.00. Explains the function and workings of modern stock markets. Covers such topics as liquidity, volatility, speculation, market efficiency, stock indexes, and the structure of trading. (Financial Management Association Survey and Synthesis Series).

Trading and Investing in Bond Options: Risk Management, Arbitrage, and Value Investing. M. Anthony Wong. John Wiley and Sons, Inc., 111 River St. Hoboken, NJ 07030. Phone: 800-225-5945 or (201)748-6000 Fax: (201)748-6088 E-mail: info@wiley.com • URL: http://www.wiley.com • 1991. $55.00. Covers dealing, trading, and investing in U. S. government bond futures options (puts and calls). (Finance Series).

Trading Cycles. R.E. Andrews, editor. Andrews Publications, Inc., 156 Shadow Creek Lane Paso Robles, CA 93446-1922. Phone: (408)778-2925 Monthly. $97.99 per year. Newsletter. Technical investment newsletter. Formerly *Andrews Trading Cycles*.

Trading Financial Futures: Markets, Methods, Strategies, and Tactics. John W. Labuszewski and John E. Nyhoff. John Wiley and Sons, Inc., 111 River St. Hoboken, NJ 07030. Phone: 800-225-5945 or (201)748-6000 Fax: (201)748-6088 E-mail: info@wiley.com • URL: http://www.wiley.com • 1997. $49.95. Second edition. (Finance Series).

Trading for a Living: Psychology, Trading Tactics, Money Management. Alexander Elder. John Wiley and Sons, Inc., 111 River St. Hoboken, NJ 07030. Phone: 800-225-5945 or (201)748-6000 Fax: (201)748-6088 E-mail: info@wiley.com • URL: http://www.wiley.com • 1993. $70.00. Covers technical and chart methods of trading in commodity and financial futures, options, and stocks. Includes Elliott Wave Theory, oscillators, moving averages, point-and- figure, and other technical approaches. (Finance Series).

Trading to Win: The Psychology of Mastering the Markets. Ari Kiev. John Wiley and Sons, Inc., 111 River St. Hoboken, NJ 07030. Phone: 800-225-5945 or (201)748-6000 Fax: (201)748-6088 E-mail: info@wiley.com • URL: http://www.wiley.com • 1998. $39.95. A mental health guide for stock, bond, and commodity traders. Tells how to keep speculative emotions in check, overcome self-doubt, and focus on a winning strategy. (Trading Series).

Traffic Engineering and Control: The International Journal of Traffic Management and Transportation Planning. Printerhall Ltd., 29 Newman St. London W1P 3PE, England. Phone: 44 171 6363956 Fax: 44 171 4367016 Monthly. $120.00 per year. Provides authoritative articles on planning, engineering and management of highways for safe and efficient operation.

Traffic Safety: The Magazine for Traffic Safety Professionals. National Safety Council, Periodicals Dept., 1121 Spring Lake Dr. Itasca, IL 60143-3201. Phone: 800-621-7619 or (630)285-1121 Fax: (630)285-1315 E-mail: info@nsc.org • URL: http://www.nsc.org • Bimonthly. Members, $24.00 per year; non-members, $31.20 per year.

Traffic World: The Logistics News Weekly n. Journal of Commerce, Inc., 1270 National Press Bldg. Washington, DC 20045. Phone: 888-215-6084 or (202)783-1101 E-mail: customerservice@cbizmedia.com • URL: http://www.trafficworld.com • Weekly. $174.00 per year.

Trailer Body Builders Buyers Guide. Primedia Business Magazines and Media, 4200 S. Shepherd Dr., Suite 200 Houston, TX 77098. Phone: 800-441-0294 or (713)523-8124 Fax: (713)523-8384 • URL: http://www.primediabusiness.com • Annual. Controlled circulation. List of 8,000 products used by original equipment manufacturers of truck trailers and truck bodies.

Trailer Life Campground and RV Services Directory. Trailer Life Publishing Co., Inc.., 2575 Vista Del Mar Dr. Ventura, CA 93001-3920. Phone: 800-234-3450 or (805)667-4100 Fax: (805)667-4301 Annual. $19.95. Describes and rates over 18,000 RV campgrounds, service centers and tourist attractions.

Trailer Life: RVing At Its Best. Good Sam Club. Affinity Group Inc., T L Enterprises, 2575 Vista Del Mar Dr. Ventura, CA 93001. Phone: 800-825-6861 Fax: (805)667-4484 E-mail: info@trailerlife.com • URL: http://www.rv.net • Monthly. $22.00 per year.

Training and Development Organizations Directory. Gale Cengage Learning, 27500 Drake Rd. Farmington Hills, MI 48331-3535. Phone: 800-877-GALE or (248)699-4253 Fax: 800-414-5043 E-mail: gale.galeord@cengage.com • URL: http://gale.cengage.com • 1994. $415.00. Sixth edition.

Training and Development Yearbook. Carolyn Nilson. Prentice Hall PTR, 240 Frisch Ct. Paramus, NJ 07652. Phone: 800-282-0693 Fax: 800-445-6991 • URL: http://www.phptr.com • 2002. $130.00. Includes reprints of journal articles on employee training and development. (Training and Development Yearbook Series).

Training for Non-Trainers: A Do-It-Yourself Guide for Managers. Carolyn Nilson. AMACOM, 1601 Broadway New York, NY 10019. Phone: 800-262-9699 or (518)586-8100 Fax: (518)903-8168 E-mail: customerservice@amanet.org • URL: http://www.amacombooks.org • 1990. $16.95.

Training: The Magazine of Covering the Human Side of Business. VNU Business Media, 770 Broadway New York, NY 10003-9595. Phone: (646)654-4500 Fax: (646)654-7212 • URL: http://www.vnubusinessmedia.com • Monthly. $78.00 per year.

Trains; The Magazine of Railroading. Kalmbach Publishing Co., 21027 Crossroads Circle Waukesha, WI 53187. Phone: 800-533-6644 or (262)796-8776 Fax: (262)796-1615 • URL: http://www.kalmbach.com • Monthly. $39.95 per year.

Transdex Index. UMI, 300 N Zeeb Rd. Ann Arbor, MI 48106. Phone: 800-521-0600 or (734)761-4700 Fax: 800-864-0019 E-mail: info@il.proquest.com • URL: http://www.umi.com • Monthly. Price on application.

Transform: Reinventing Business with Content and Collaboration Technologies. CMP Media LLC, 600 Community Dr. Manhasset, NY 11030. Phone: (516)562-5000 E-mail: cmp@cmp.com • URL: http://www.cmp.com • Monthly. $25.00 per year. Emphasis is on descriptions of new imaging products, including CD-ROM items. Formerly *Imaging and Document Solutions*.

Transit Fact Book. American Public Transportation Association, 1666 K St. NW, Ste. 1100 Washington, DC 20006. Phone: (202)496-4800 Fax: (202)496-4324 E-mail: info@apta.com • URL: http://www.apta.com • Annual. Free.

Transitions Abroad: The Guide to Learning, Living, and Working Overseas. Transitions Abroad Publishing, Inc., 18 Hulst Rd. Amherst, MA 01004. Phone: 800-293-0373 or (413)256-3414 Fax: (413)256-0373 E-mail: info@transitionsabroad.com • URL: http://www.transitionsabroad.com • Bimonthly. $28.00 per year, including annual directory of information sources. Provides practical information and advice on foreign education and employment. Supplement available *Overseas Travel Planner*.

Translating and the Computer. Available from Information Today, Inc., 143 Old Marlton Pike Medford, NJ 08055-8750. Phone: 800-300-9868 or (609)654-6266 Fax: (609)654-4309 E-mail: custserv@infotoday.com • URL: http://www.infotoday.com • Annual. Members, $50.00; non-members, $57.50. Published in London by Aslib: The Association for Information Management. Includes papers from the annual International Conference on Translating and the Computer.

Transnational Accounting. Dieter Ordelheide and others, editors. Groves Dictionaries, Inc., 345 Park Ave. S., 10th Fl. New York, NY 10010-1707. Phone: 800-221-2123 or (212)689-9200 Fax: (212)689-9200 E-mail: grove@grovereference.com • URL: http://www.grovereference.com • 2001. $685.00. Second edition. Three volumes. Published by Macmillan (UK). Provides detailed descriptions of financial accounting principles and practices in 14 major countries (10 European, plus the U. S., Canada, Australia, and Japan). Includes tables, exhibits, index, and a glossary of 244 accounting terms in eight languages.

Transnational Bank Behavior and the International Debt Crisis. United Nations Publications, United Nations Concourse Level, First Ave., 46th St. New York, NY 10017. Phone: 800-553-3210 or (212)963-7680 Fax: (212)963-4910 E-mail: bookstore@un.org • URL: http://www.un.org/publications • 1990.

Transnational Corporations. United Nations Conference on Trade and Development. United Nations Publications, United Nations Concourse Level, First Ave., 46th St. New York, NY 10017. Phone: 800-553-3210 or (212)963-7608 Fax: (212)963-4910 E-mail: bookstore@un.org • URL: http://www.un.org/publications • Three times a year. $45.00 per year. Reports on both governmental and non-governmental aspects of multinational corporations. Issued by the United Nations Centre on Transnational Corporations (UNCTC). Formerly *CTC Reporter*.

Transport Topics. American Trucking Associations Inc., 2200 Mill Rd. Alexandria, VA 22314-4677. Phone: 800-517-7370 or (703)838-1700 Fax: (703)683-2292 E-mail: media@trucking.org • URL: http://www.ttnews.com • Description: Covers news of the trucking transportation industry.

Transportation. Rob Bowden. Gale, 27500 Drake Rd. Farmington Hills, MI 48331. Phone: 800-877-GALE or (248)699-GALE Fax: 800-414-5043 or (248)699-8035 E-mail: gale.galeorder@cengage.com • URL: http://gale.cengage.com • 2004.

Transportation and Distribution: Integrating Logistics in Supply Chain Management. Penton Media, Inc., 1300 E. Ninth St. Cleveland, OH 44114. Phone: (216)696-7000 Fax: (216)696-1752 E-mail: information@penton.com • URL: http://www.penton.com • Monthly. Free to qualified personnel; others, $50.00 per year. Essential information on transportation and distribution practices in domestic and international trade.

Transportation Builder. American Road and Transportation Builders Association. Heartland Custom Publishers Group, 1003 Central Ave. Fort Dodge, IA 50501. Phone: 800-247-2000 or (515)955-1600 Fax: 800-247-2000 Monthly. $50.00 per year.

Transportation Center.

Transportation Clubs International., PO Box 2223 Ocean Shores, WA 98569. Phone: 877-858-8627 Fax: (360)289-3188 E-mail: info@transportationclubsinternational.com • URL: http://www.transportationclubsinternational.com • Men and women in the traffic and transportation fields, including railroads, bus lines, trucking firms, and traffic managers of industrial firms. Sponsors National Transportation Week.

Transportation, Elevator and Grain Merchants Association., 1300 L St. NW, Ste. 1020 Washington, DC 20005. Phone: (202)842-0400 Fax: (202)789-7223 E-mail: jkinnaird@ngtc.org • URL: http://www.grainnet.com • Formerly Terminal Elevator Grain Association.

Transportation Engineering and Planning. C. S. Papacostas and Panos D. Prevedouros. Prentice Hall PTR, 240 Frisch Ct. Paramus, NJ 07652. Phone: 800-282-0693 Fax: 800-449-6991 • URL: http://www.phptr.com • 2000. $115.00. Third edition.

Transportation Institute., 5201 Auth Way Camp Springs, MD 20746-4211. Phone: (301)423-3335 Fax: (301)423-0634 E-mail: info@trans-inst.org • URL: http://www.trans-inst.org • U.S. deep-sea and inland waters shipping, towing and dredging companies devoted to research and education on a broad range of transportation problems, with emphasis on problems related to the nation's citizen-owned and citizen-manned Merchant Marine. Addresses the need for halting the decline of deep-sea commerce aboard vessels flying the American flag and the need for full development of water-borne commerce on the Great Lakes. Supports utilizing America's 25,000-mile long network of inland waterways to meet the domestic transportation needs of a growing nation and the need for revitalizing the American fishing industry to halt the incursion of foreign fishing fleets on U.S. spawning grounds. Supports the need for a national oceanographic policy to ensure maximum exploitation of the wealth of the sea. Conducts ongoing research.

Transportation Journal. American Society of Transportation and Logistics, Inc., 1700 N Moore St., Ste. 1900 Arlington, VA 22209-1904. Phone: (703)524-5011 Fax: (703)524-5017 E-mail: astl@nitl.org • URL: http://www.astl.org • Quarterly. $61.95 per year.

Transportation Planning Handbook. John D. Edwards. Institute of Transportation Engineers, 1099 14th St. NW, Ste. 300 W Washington, DC 20005-3438. Phone: (202)289-0222 Fax: (202)289-7722 E-mail: itehq@io.com • URL: http://www.ite.org • 1999. $100.00. Second edition.

Transportation Quarterly: An Independent Journal for Better Transportation Policy. Eno Transportation Foundation, 1634 Eye St., N.W., Suite 500 Washington, DC 20006-4003. Phone: (202)879-4700 Fax: (202)879-4719 Quarterly. $55.00

per year. To qualify a written request must be submitted.

Transportation Research Center. University of Florida

Transportation Research Information Services (TRIS). Transportation Research Board, Highway Research Information, Keck Center of the National Academies, 500 5th St., NW Washington, DC 20001. Phone: (202)334-3213 Fax: (202)334-2003 E-mail: trbsales@nas.edu • URL: http://www.trb.org • Monthly. Price on application.

Transportation Research Institute., University of Michigan, 2901 Baxter Rd. Ann Arbor, MI 48109-2150. Phone: (734)764-6504 Fax: (734)936-1081 E-mail: umtri@umich.edu • URL: http://www.umtri.umich.edu • Research areas include highway safety, transportation systems, and shipbuilding.

Transportation Review Part E: Logistics and Transportation Review. University of British Columbia Centre for Transportation Studies. Elsevier, 360 Park Ave., S New York, NY 10010-1710. Phone: 888-437-4636 or (212)989-5800 Fax: (212)633-3990 E-mail: usinfo.f@elsevier.com • URL: http://www.elsevier.com • Bimonthly. Individuals, $213.00 per year; institutions, $897.00 per year.

Transportation Science. INFORMS, 901 Elkridge Landing Rd., Ste. 400 Linthicum, MD 21090-2909. Phone: 800-446-3676 or (410)850-0300 Fax: (410)684-2963 E-mail: informs@informs.org • URL: http://www.informs.org • Quarterly. Individuals, $155.00 per year. Includes print and online editions. Institutions, $221.00 per year. Includes print and online editions.

Transportation Statistics Annual Report. Available from U. S. Government Printing Office, Washington, DC 20402. Phone: (202)512-1800 Fax: (202)512-2250 E-mail: gpoaccess@gpo.gov • URL: http://www.access.gpo.gov • Annual. $43.00. Issued by the U. S. Bureau of Transportation Statistics, Transportation Department (http://www.bts.gov). Summarizes national data for various forms of transportation, including airlines, railroads, and motor vehicles. Information on the use of roads and highways is included.

Transportation Systems Institute., University of Central Florida, Dept. of Civil and Environmental Engineering, P.O. Box 162450 Orlando, FL 32816-2450. Phone: (407)823-2988 Fax: (407)823-3315 E-mail: haldeek@pegasus.cc.ucf.edu • URL: http://www.catss.ucf.edu/tsi • Research areas include mass transportation systems.

Transportation Telephone Tickler. Journal of Commerce, 33 Washington St., 13th Fl., 50 Millstone Rd., Ste. 300 Newark, NJ 07102-3107. Phone: 888-215-6084 or (973)848-7158 Fax: (973)837-7004 E-mail: customerservice@cbizmedia.com • URL: http://www.tickleronline.com • Covers: 24,000 companies and agents in North American port districts which provide transportation services ranging from air freight forwarding to warehousing. Published in a four-volume national edition and 7 regional editions. Entries include: Company name, headquarters and branch addresses, phone and fax numbers, names of key personnel, e-mail and web addresses.

Travel Agency. Entrepreneur Media, Inc., 2445 McCabe Way Irvine, CA 92614. Phone: 800-421-2300 or (949)261-2325 Fax: (949)261-0234 E-mail: entmag@entrepreneur.com • URL: http://www.entrepreneur.com • Looseleaf. $59.50. A practical guide to starting a travel agency. Covers profit potential, start-up costs, market size evaluation, owner's time required, site selection, lease negotiation, pricing, accounting, advertising, promotion, etc. (Start-Up Business Guide No. E1154.)

Travel Agent: The National Newsweekly Magazine of the Travel Industry. Advanstar Communications, 545 Boylston St. Boston, MA 02116. Phone: 888-527-7008 or (617)267-6500 Fax: (617)267-6900 E-mail: info@advanstar.com • URL: http://www.advanstar.com • 51 times a year. 250.00 per. year.

Travel and Leisure. American Express Publishing Corp., 1120 Ave. of the Americas New York, NY 10036. Phone: (212)382-5600 Fax: (212)768-1568 • URL: http://www.travelandleisure.com • Monthly. $39.00 per year. In three regional editions and one demographic edition.

Travel and Tourism. Available from U. S. Government Printing Office, Washington, DC 20402. Phone: (202)512-1800 Fax: (202)512-2250 E-mail: gpoaccess@gpo.gov • URL: http://www.access.gpo.gov • Annual. Free. Issued by the Superintendent of Documents. A list of government publications on the travel industry and tourism. Formerly *Mass Transit, Travel and Tourism*. (Subject Bibliography No. 302.)

Travel and Tourism Research Association., P.O. Box 2133 Boise, ID 83701. Phone: (208)429-9511 Fax: (208)429-9512 E-mail: ttra@worldnet.att.net • URL: http://www.ttra.com • Members are travel directors, airline officials, hotels, government agencies, and others interested in the travel field.

Travel Industry Association of America., 1100 New York Ave., N.W., Suite 450 Washington, DC 20005. Phone: (202)408-8422 Fax: (202)408-1255 E-mail: membership@tia.org • URL: http://www.tia.org • Corporations engaged in the hospitality and travel industry.

Travel Industry Association of America-Research Dept., 1100 New York Ave., N.W., No. 450 Washington, DC 20005-3934. Phone: (202)408-8422 Fax: (202)408-1255 E-mail: feedback@tia.org • URL: http://www.tia.org • Conducts economic, statistical, and market research relating to the U. S. travel industry. Affiliated with the Travel Industry Association of America.

Travel Law. American Lawyer Media, Inc., 105 Madison Ave. New York, NY 10016. Phone: 800-888-8300 or (212)779-9200 Fax: (212)481-8110 E-mail: lawcatalog@amlaw.com • URL: http://www.lawcatalog.com/ • Looseleaf. $149.00. Updated as needed. Emphasis is on the legal rights of travelers, including a consideration of class action suits. Includes such matters as tour operator liability, hotel responsibilities, overbooking by airlines, and frequent-flyer issues. (Law Journal Press).

Travel Management Daily. Cahners Business Information, 500 Plaza Dr. Secaucus, NJ 07094. Phone: 800-742-7076 or (201)902-7788 Fax: (201)902-1991 E-mail: tmdsecaucus@cahners.com • URL: http://www.northstartravelmedia.com • Description: E-mail and internet publication which offers news and advice for those who work in the travel industry.

Travel Manager's Executive Briefing. American Business Publishing, 1913 Atlantic Ave., Ste. F4 Manasquan, NJ 08736. Phone: 800-516-4343 or (732)292-1100 Fax: (732)292-1111 E-mail: media@trucking.org • URL: http://www.themcic.com • Description: Follows developments in the field of travel and expense cost control. Recurring features include news of discounted air fares, car rentals, and hotel bills; case histories of other companies cutting costs; travel alternatives, phone savings, planning for meetings; and trends in government legislation affecting business travel costs.

Travel Smart: Pay Less, Enjoy More. Dunan Communications, Inc., PO Box 397 Dobbs Ferry, NY 10522. Phone: 800-327-3633 or (914)693-8300 Monthly. $39.00 per year. Newsletter. Provides information and recommendations for travelers. Emphasis is on travel value and opportunities for bargains. Incorporates*Joy of Travel*.

Travel Trade News Edition: The Business Paper of the Travel Industry. Travel Trade Publications, 15 W. 44th St., 6th Fl. New York, NY 10036. Phone: (212)730-6600 Fax: (212)730-7137 E-mail: travelcat@aol.com • URL: http://www.traveltrade.com • Weekly. $10.00 per year. Formerly *Travel Trade*.

Travel Weekly. Northstar Travel Media, LLC, 500 Plaza Dr., 4th Fl. Secaucus, NJ 07096. Phone: (201)902-2000 Fax: (201)902-2045 E-mail: secausushelpdesk@ntmllc.com • URL: http://www.northstartravelmedia.com • Weekly. $266.00 per year. Includes cruise guides, a weekly "Business Travel Update," and special issues devoted to particular destinations and areas. Edited mainly for travel agents and tour operators.

Travelware. Business Journals, Inc., 50 Day St. Norwalk, CT 06856. Phone: 800-521-0227 or (203)853-6015 Fax: (203)852-8175 E-mail: chris@busjour.com • URL: http://www.busjour.com • Seven times a year. $32.00. Formerly *Luggage and Travelware*.

Travelware Resources Directory. Business Journals, Inc., 50 Day St. Norwalk, CT 06856. Phone: (203)853-6015 Fax: (203)852-8175 E-mail: lorrief@busjour.com • URL: http://www.busjour.com • Annual. $20.00. Manufacturers of trunks, luggage, brief cases, and personal leather goods are listed. Formerly *Luggage and Travelware Directory*.

Travelware Suppliers Directory. Business Journals Inc., 50 Day St. Norwalk, CT 06854. Phone: (203)853-6015 Fax: (203)852-8175 E-mail: stunifoo@busjour.com • URL: http://www.busjour.com • Covers: 500 manufacturers and importers that supply hardware, leather, fabrics, and other components to the luggage and leather goods industry (SIC 3161). Entries include: Company name, address, phone, fax, telex, name of principal executive, sales offices/showrooms/reps, email, URL.

Treasury and Risk Management. Wicks Business Information, 363 Reef Rd. Fairfield, CT 06430. Phone: (203)255-4990 Fax: (203)255-4353 E-mail: info@wickbusinessinfo.com • URL: http://www.wicksbusinessinfo.com • 10 times a year. $64.00 per year. Covers risk management tools and techniques. Incorporates *Treasury*.

Treasury Bulletin. Available from U. S. Government Printing Office, Washington, DC 20402. Phone: (202)512-1800 Fax: (202)512-2250 E-mail: gpoaccess@gpo.gov • URL: http://www.access.gpo.gov • Quarterly. $45.00 per year. Issued by the Financial Management Service, U. S. Treasury Department. Provides data on the federal budget, government securities and yields, the national debt, and the financing of the federal government in general.

Treasury Manager's Report: Strategic Information for the Financial Executive. PBI Media, LLC, 1201 7 Locks Rd. Potomac, MD 20854. Phone: 800-777-5006 or (301)354-2000 Fax: (301)309-3847 E-mail: clientservices@pbimedia.com • URL: http://www.pbimedia.com • Biweekly. $630.00. Newsletter reporting on legal developments affecting the operations of banks, savings institutions, and other financial service organizations. Formerly *Financial Services Law Report*.

Trends and Developments in Business Administration Programs. Donald L. Joyal. Greenwood Publishing Group, Inc., 88 Post Rd., W Westport, CT 06881. Phone: 800-225-5800 or (203)226-3571 Fax: (203)431-2214 E-mail: customer-service@greenwood.com • URL: http://www.greenwood.com • 1982. $52.50.

Trends in International Migration. Organization for Economic Cooperation and Development, OECD Washington Center, 2001 L St., N. W., Suite 650 Washington, DC 20036-4922. Phone: 800-456-6323 or (202)785-6323 Fax: (202)785-0350 E-mail: washington.contact@oecd.org • URL: http://www.oecdwash.org • 2001. $59.00. Contains detailed data on population migration flows, channels of immigration, and migrant nationalities. Includes demographic analysis.

Trends in Mutual Fund Activity. Investment Company Institute, 1401 H St., N. W., Suite 1200 Washington, DC 20005-2148. Phone: (202)326-5800 Fax: (202)326-5806 • URL: http://www.ici.org • Monthly. $225.00 per year. Contains statistical tables showing fund industry sales, redemptions, assets, cash, and other data.

Trends in the Hotel Industry. PKF Consulting, 425 California St., Suite 1650 San Francisco, CA 94104. Phone: (415)421-5378 Fax: (415)956-7708 • URL: http://www.pkfc.com • Quarterly. $150.00 per year.

Trends in the Hotel Industry: U.S.A. Edition. PKF Consulting, 425 California St., Suite 1650 San Francisco, CA 94104. Phone: 800-633-4931 or (415)421-5378 Fax: (415)956-7708 Annual. $225.00. Provides detailed financial analysis of hotel operations in the U. S. (PKF is Pannell Kerr Forster.)

The Trends Journal: The Authority on Trends Management. Gerald Celente, editor. Trends Research Institute, P.O. Box 660 Rhinebeck, NY 12572-0660. Phone: (845)876-6700 Fax: (845)758-5252 E-mail: gcelente@trendsresearch.com • URL: http://www.trendsresearch.com • Quarterly. $185.00 per year. Newsletter. Provides forecasts on a wide variety of economic, social, and political topics. Includes "Hot Trends to Watch."

TRI/Princeton. TRI/Princeton, 601 Prospect Ave., PO Box 625 Princeton, NJ 08542. Phone: (609)430-4820 Fax: (609)683-7149 E-mail: info@triprinceton.org • URL: http://www.triprinceton.org • Physics, chemistry, and engineering as related to raw materials, processes, and products of polymer, fiber, and textile systems with special strengths in: surface physics and chemistry; micro and nano structure characterization; fluid flow in porous materials; resins and composites; process-structure-property relationships; human hair chemistry, physics, and mechanics; on-line monitoring of spin finish; dye transport; fabric wear and soiling; modeling of sorption and transport phenomena; and instrument design and development.

Trial. Association of Trial Lawyers of America, 1050 31st St., N.W. Washington, DC 20007-4499. Phone: 800-424-2725 or (202)965-3500 Fax: (202)625-7312 E-mail: info@atlahq.org • URL: http://www.atla.org • Monthly. $79.00 per year.

Trial Lawyers Quarterly. New York State Trial Lawyers Association, 132 Nassau St.,, Suite 200 New York, NY 10038. Phone: (212)349-5890 Fax: (212)608-2310 Quarterly. $50.00 per year.

Triangle. Florida Citrus Mutual, PO Box 89 Lakeland, FL 33802. Phone: (863)682-1111 Fax: (863)682-1074 E-mail: tmdsecaucus@cahners.com • URL: http://www.fl-citrus-mutual.com • Description: Contains items of interest to citrus growers, including statistical data, market information, ongoing scientific research, and action by various government agencies. Recurring features include weather forecasts, market information, production statistics, news of research, a calendar of events, and reports of meetings.

Tribology International; The Practice and Technology of Lubrication, Wear Prevention and Friction Control. Elsevier, 360 Park Ave., S. New York, NY 10010-1710. Phone: 888-437-4636 or (212)989-5800 Fax: (212)633-3990 E-mail: usinfo-f@elsevier.com • URL: http://www.elsevier.com • Monthly. Qualified personnel, $173.00 per year; institutions, $1,528.00 per year.

TRIS: Transportation Research Information Service. National Research Council, 500 5th St. NW Washington, DC 20001. Phone: (202)334-2934 Fax: (202)334-2003 • URL: http://www.ntl.bts.gov/tris/ • Contains abstracts and citations to a wide range of transportation literature, 1968 to present, with monthly updates. Includes references to the literature of air transportation, highways, ships and shipping, railroads, trucking, and urban mass transportation. Formerly *TRIS-ON-LINE*. Inquire as to online cost and availability.

Tropical Research and Education Center.

The Trouble with Computers: Usefulness, Useability, and Productivity. Thomas K. Landauer. MIT Press, Five Cambridge Ctr. Cambridge, MA 02142-1493. Phone: 800-356-0343 or (617)253-5646 Fax: (617)253-6779 • URL: http://www.mitpress.mit.edu • 1995. $30.00. A critical view of computers and how they are being used.

Troubled and Problematic Bank and Thrift Report. BauerFinancial, Inc., Gables International Plaza, 2655 LeJeune Rd. Coral Gables, FL 33134. Phone: 800-388-6686 Fax: 800-230-2569 E-mail: customerservice@bauerfinancial.com • URL: http://www.bauerfinancial.com • Quarterly. $225.00 per year. Newsletter provides information on seriously undercapitalized ("Troubled") banks and savings institutions, as defined by a federal Prompt Corrective Action Rule. "Problematic" banks and thrifts are those meeting regulatory capital levels, but showing negative trends.

Troubleshooting and Repairing Color Television Systems. Robert Goodman. McGraw-Hill, 1221 Ave. of the Americas New York, NY 10020. Phone: 800-722-4726 or (212)512-2000 Fax: (212)512-4502 E-mail: customer.service@mcgraw-hill.com • URL: http://www.mcgraw-hill.com • 1997. $24.95

Troubleshooting and Repairing Solid-State TVs. Homer Davidson. McGraw-Hill, 1221 Ave. of the Americas New York, NY 10020. Phone: 800-722-4726 or (212)512-2000 Fax: (212)512-4502 E-mail: customer.service@mcgraw-hill.com • URL: http://www.mcgraw-hill.com • 1996. $44.95. Third editionl. (Tab Electronics Technician Library).

Truck Trailer Manufacturers Association., 1020 Princess St. Alexandria, VA 22314-2247. Phone: (703)549-3010 Fax:

(703)549-3014 E-mail: ttma@erols.com • URL: http://www.ttmanet.org • Manufacturers of commercial trailers; manufacturers of supplies for the truck trailer industry.

Truck Trailer Manufacturers Association Membership Directory. Truck Trailer Manufacturers Association, 1020 Princess St. Alexandria, VA 22314. Phone: (703)549-3010 Fax: (703)549-3014 Annual. $135.00. About 100 trucks and tank trailer manufacturers and 120 suppliers to the industry.

Truck Trailers. U. S. Bureau of the Census, 4700 Silver Hill Rd. Washington, DC 20233-0001. Phone: (301)763-4636 E-mail: comments@census.gov • URL: http://www.census.gov • Monthly and annual. Provides data on shipments of truck trailers and truck trailer vans: value, quantity, imports, and exports. (Current Industrial Reports, M37L.)

Trust Administration and Taxation. LexisNexis Matthew Bender, 1275 Broadway Albany, NY 12204. Phone: 800-424-4200 or (518)487-3000 Fax: (518)487-3584 E-mail: bookstore.support@lexisnexis.com • URL: http://www.bender.com • Semiannual. $1,007.00. Four looseleaf volumes. Text on establishment, administration, and taxation of trusts.

Trust Department Administration and Operations. LexisNexis Matthew Bender, 1275 Broadway Albany, NY 12204. Phone: 800-424-4200 or (518)487-3000 Fax: (518)487-3584 E-mail: bookstore.support@lexisnexis.com • URL: http://www.bender.com • Biennial. $360.00 per year. Two looseleaf volumes. A procedural manual, training guide and idea source.

Trust Letter. American Bankers Association, 1120 Connecticut Ave. NW, 1120 Connecticut Ave., N. W. Washington, DC 20036-3971. Phone: 800-226-5377 or (202)663-5000 Fax: (202)663-5201 E-mail: custserv@aba.com • URL: http://www.aba.com • Description: Contains updates of national legislation and regulation that impacts the trust and investment businesses. Reports on significant industry happenings, important research, and provides coverage of ABA legislative/regulatory testimony and committee activities, especially in the areas of taxation, securities, and employee benefits.

Trust Management Update. American Bankers Association, 1120 Connecticut Ave., N.W. Washington, DC 20036-3971. Phone: 800-338-0626 or (202)226-5377 Fax: (202)663-7543 E-mail: custserv@aba.com • URL: http://www.aba.com • Bimonthly. $95.00 per year.

Trustee: The Magazine for Hospital Governing Boards. American Hospital Association. American Hospital Publishing, Inc., One N Franklin St., 27th Fl. Chicago, IL 60606-3421. Phone: 800-242-2626 or (312)422-3000 Fax: (312)422-4796 • URL: http://www.aha.com • 10 times a year. $40.00 per year. Emphasis is on community health care.

Trusts and Estates. Primedia Business Magazines and Media, 6151 Powers Ferry Rd., Ste. 200 Atlanta, GA 30339. Phone: 800-795-5445 or (770)955-2500 Fax: (770)618-0204 E-mail: subs@primediabusiness.com • URL: http://www.primediabusiness.com • Monthly. $139.00 per year. Includes annual *Directory*.

Trusts and Estates - Directory of Trust Institutions. Primedia Business Magazines and Media, 249 W 17th St. New York, NY 10011. Phone: 800-795-5445 or (212)462-3600 Fax: (212)367-8345 E-mail: subs@primediabusiness.com • URL: http://www.primediabusiness.com • Annual. $79.95. Lists approximately 5,000 trust departments in U.S. and Canadian banks.

TRW Business Credit Profiles. Experian, 475 Anton Blvd. Costa Mesa, CA 92626. Phone: 888-397-3742 or (714)830-7000 Provides credit history (trade payments, payment trends, payment totals, payment history, etc.) for public and private U. S. companies. Key facts and banking information are also given. Updates are weekly. Inquire as to online cost and availability.

Tulane Maritime Law Journal. Tulane University, School of Law, John Giffen Weinmann Hall, 6329 Freret St. New Orleans, LA 70118. Phone: (504)865-5959 Fax: (504)865-8878 E-mail: lbecnel@law.tulane.edu • URL: http://www.law.tulane.edu/journals • Semiannual. $28.00 per year. Formerly *Maritime Lawyer*.

Tulsa (Petroleum Abstracts). Information Services, 600 S. College, Harwell 101 Tulsa, OK 74104. Phone: 800-247-8678 or (918)631-2297 Fax: (918)599-9361 Worldwide literature in the petroleum and natural gas areas, 1965 to present. Inquire as to online cost and availability. Includes petroleum exploration patents. Updated weekly.

Turning Your Human Resources Department into a Profit Center. Michael W. Mercer. AMACOM, 1601 Broadway New York, NY 10019. Phone: 800-262-9699 or (518)586-8100 Fax: (518)903-8168 E-mail: customerservice@amanet.org • URL: http://www.amacombooks.org • 1989. $59.95. Concerned with costs, employee efficiency, and productivity.

The TV Guide. Gemstar-TV Guide International, 1211 Avenue of the Americas New York, NY 10036. Phone: 800-866-1400 or (610)293-8500 Fax: (610)688-6216 • URL: http://www.tvguide.com • Weekly. $46.28 per year.

TV Technology. IMAS Publishing Group, 5827 Columbia Pke., Ste. 310 Falls Church, VA 22041. Phone: 800-336-3045 or (703)998-7600 Fax: (703)998-2966 E-mail: adsales@imaspub.com Biweekly. $75.00 per year. International coverage available.

Twentieth Anniversary Mobilization., USA,. E-mail: info@socialdemocrats.org Civil rights, labor, and peace organizations and others joined together in a national effort to concentrate on three key issues: jobs, peace, and freedom. Sponsored a March on Washington on Aug. 27, 1983 commemorating the 20th anniversary of Martin Luther King's "I Have a Dream" speech. Works for legislative passage designating January 15 as a national holiday honoring Martin Luther King's birthday. Promotes the work of the coalition on state and local levels.

21.C: Scanning the Future: A Magazine of Culture, Technology, and Science. International Publishers Distributors, P.O. Box 200029, Riverfront Plaza Station Newark, NJ 07102-0301. Phone: 800-545-8398 or (973)643-7500 Fax: (973)643-7676 • URL: http://www.21c.com • Quarterly. $24.00 per year. Contains multidisciplinary articles relating to the 21st century.

20/20 Vision National Project., 8403 Colesville Rd., Ste. 860 Silver Spring, MD 20910. Phone: 800-669-1782 or (301)587-1782 Fax: (301)587-1848 E-mail: vision@2020vision.org • URL: http://www.2020vision.org • Promotes citizen involvement in influencing public policies that endorse protection of the environment, an increase in national and global security, reduction of military spending, and the support of individual economic and social needs. Encourages individual political activism by providing convenient, simple, effective activities designed to take less than 20 minutes to complete. (Organization name is derived from the belief that an individual's contribution of 20 minutes a month and $20 a year can have a significant impact on public policy.) Maintains network of local lobbying groups; provides training and promotional materials to local organizers.

The 22 Immutable Laws of Branding: How to Build a Product or Service Into a World-Class Brand. Al Ries and Laura Ries. HarperInformation, 10 E 53rd St. New York, NY 10022-5299. Phone: 800-242-7737 or (212)207-7000 Fax: 800-822-4090 or (212)207-7145 1998. $25.00. Provides advice on attaining positive brand recognition.

Twin Plant News: The Magazine of the Maquiladora Industry. Nibbe, Hernandez and Associates, Inc., 4110 Rio Bravo Dr., No. 108 El Paso, TX 79902. Phone: (915)532-1567 Fax: (915)544-7556 Monthly. $85.00 per year. Focuses on Mexican labor laws, taxes, economics, industrial trends, and culture. Industries featured include electronic components, plastics, automotive supplies, metals, communications, and packaging.

Type Directors Club., 347 W 36 St., Ste. 603 New York, NY 10018. Phone: (212)633-8943 Fax: (212)633-8944 E-mail: director@tdc.org • URL: http://www.tdc.org • Serves as a professional society of typographic designers, type directors, and teachers of typography; sustaining members are individuals with interests in typographic education. Seeks to stimulate research and disseminate information. Provides speakers, classes and offers presentations on history and new developments in typography.

U. S. Almanac of International Trade. Bernan Press, 4611-F Assembly Dr. Lanham, MD 20706-4391. Phone: 800-274-4447 or (301)459-2255 Fax: 800-865-3450 or (301)459-0056 E-mail: bpress@bernan.com • URL: http://www.bernan.com • 2000. $225.00. Fifth edition. Provides directory information on individuals and organizations concerned with foreign trade. Contains four sections dealing with: U. S. government, foreign governments, international organizations, and trade-related groups. Formerly *Washington Almanac of International Trade and Business*.

The U. S. Asian American Market. Available from MarketResearch.com, 641 Ave. of the Americas, Fourth Floor New York, NY 10011. Phone: 800-298-5699 or (212)807-2629 Fax: (212)807-2642 E-mail: order@marketresearch.com • URL: http://www.marketresearch.com • 2002. $2,700.00. Published by Packaged Facts. Provides market research data pertaining to Asian American consumers: Chinese, Japanese, Korean, Vietnamese, Filipino, and Asian Indian.

U. S. Banker. Thomson Media, One State St. Plaza New York, NY 10004. Phone: 800-221-1809 or (212)803-8200 Fax: (212)843-9635 E-mail: custserv@thomsonmedia.com • URL: http://www.thomsonmedia.com • Monthly. $65.00 per year. Edited for bank executives and managers. Covers a wide variety of banking and financial topics.

U. S. Business Advisor. Small Business AdministrationPhone: (202)205-6600 Fax: (202)205-7064 • URL: http://www.business.gov • Web site provides "a one-stop electronic link to all the information and services government provides for the business community." Covers about 60 federal agencies that exist to assist or regulate business. Detailed information is provided on financial assistance, workplace issues, taxes, regulations, international trade, and other business topics. Searching is offered. Fees: Free.

U. S. Census Bureau: The Official Statistics. U. S. Bureau of the CensusPhone: (301)763-4100 Fax: (301)763-4794 • URL: http://www.census.gov • Web site is "Your Source for Social, Demographic, and Economic Information." Contains "Current U. S. Population Count," "Current Economic Indicators," and a wide variety of data under "Other Official Statistics." Keyword searching is provided. Fees: Free.

U. S. Cheese Market. Available from MarketResearch.com, 641 Ave. of the Americas, Third Floor New York, NY 10011. Phone: 800-298-5699 or (212)807-2629 Fax: (212)807-2716 E-mail: order@marketresearch.com • URL: http://www.marketresearch.com • 2002. $2,950.00. Market research data published by Packaged Facts. Includes projections to 2006.

The U. S. College Market. Available from MarketResearch.com, 641 Ave. of the Americas, Third Floor New York, NY 10011. Phone: 800-298-5699 or (212)807-2629 Fax: (212)807-2642 E-mail: order@marketresearch.com • URL: http://www.marketresearch.com • 2001. $2,799.00. Published by Packaged Facts. Market research report on college students as consumers.

U. S. Commercial and Residential Cleaning Services Industry. Available from MarketResearch.com, 641 Ave. of the Americas, Third Floor New York, NY 10011. Phone: 800-298-5699 or (212)807-2629 Fax: (212)807-2716 E-mail: order@marketresearch.com • URL: http://www.marketresearch.com • 2001. $2,025.00. Market research report published by Marketdata Enterprises. Covers commercial contract cleaning services and residential services. Provides actual industry and market statistics and forecasts to the year 2005.

U. S. Copyrights. Available from DIALOG, 11000 Regency Pkwy., Ste. 400 Cary, NC 27511. Phone: 800-334-2564 or (919)462-8600 Fax: (919)468-9890 • URL: http://www.dialog.com • Provides access to registration details for all active copyright registrations on file at the U. S. Copyright Office since 1978. Contains information on initial registration, renewal, assignments, and ownership status. Weekly updates. Inquire as to online cost and availability.

U. S. Credit Bureaus and Collection Agencies: An Industry Analysis. Available from MarketResearch.com, 641 Ave. of the Americas, 3rd Fl. New York, NY 10011. Phone: 800-298-5699 or (212)807-2629 Fax: (212)807-2716 E-mail: order@marketresearch.com • URL: http://www.marketresearch.com • 2003. $1,435.00. Market research report published by Marketdata Enterprises. Includes forecasts of industry growth to the year 2006 and provides profiles of Dun & Bradstreet, Equifax, Experion, and TransUnion.

U. S. Exports of Merchandise on CD-ROM. U. S. Bureau of the Census, Foreign Trade Div.,, Washington, DC 20233-0800. Phone: (301)763-4636 Fax: (301)457-3842 Monthly. $1,200 per year. Provides export data in the most extensive detail available, including product, quantity, value, shipping weight, country of destination, customs district of exportation, etc.

U. S. Floor Coverings Industry. Available from MarketResearch.com, 641 Ave. of the Americas, Third Floor New York, NY 10011. Phone: 800-298-5699 or (212)807-2629 Fax: (212)807-2716 E-mail: order@marketresearch.com • URL: http://www.marketresearch.com • 2000. $1,795.00. Market research report published by Specialists in Business Information. Covers carpets, hardwood flooring, and tile. Presents market data relative to demographics, sales growth, shipments, exports, imports, price trends, and end-use. Includes company profiles.

U. S. FullText. MicroPatent, 250 Dodge Ave. East Haven, CT 06512-3358. Phone: 800-648-6787 or (203)466-5055 Fax: (203)466-5054 E-mail: info@micropat.com • URL: http://www.micropat.com • Monthly. Contains complete text on CD-ROM of all patents issued by the U. S. Patent and Trademark Office. Archival discs are available from 1975.

U. S. Glass, Metal, and Glazing. Key Communications, Inc., P.O. Box 569 Garrisonville, VA 22463. Phone: (540)720-5584 Fax: (540)720-5687 E-mail: usglass@glass.com • URL: http://www.usglassmag.com • Monthly. $35.00 per year. Edited for glass fabricators, glaziers, distributors, and retailers. Special feature issues are devoted to architectural glass, mirror glass, windows, storefronts, hardware, machinery, sealants, and adhesives. Regular topics include automobile glass and fenestration (window design and placement).

U. S. Glass, Metal, and Glazing: Buyers Guide. Key Communications, Inc., P.O. Box 569 Garrisonville, VA 22463. Phone: (540)720-5584 Fax: (540)720-5687 E-mail: info@glass.com • URL: http://www.glass.com • Annual. $25.00. A directory of about 3,000 supplies and equipment for the glass fabrication and installation industry.

U. S. Government Books: Publications for Sale by the Government Printing Office. U. S. Government Printing Office, 732 N Capitol St., SW Washington, DC 20401. Phone: 888-293-6498 or (202)512-1530 Fax: (202)512-1262 E-mail: gpoaccess@gpo.gov • URL: http://www.gpoaccess.gov • Quarterly. Free. Describes best selling government documents and "new titles that reflect today's news and consumer issues."

U. S. Government Information Catalog of New and Popular Titles. U. S. Government Printing Office, 732 N. Capitol St., NW Washington, DC 20401. Phone: 888-293-6498 or (202)512-1530 Fax: (202)512-1262 E-mail: gpoaccess@gpo.gov • URL: http://www.gpoaccess.gov • Irregular. Free. Includes recently issued and popular publications, periodicals, and electronic products.

U. S. Government Information for Business. U. S. Government Printing Office, 732 N Capitol St., SW Washington, DC 20401. Phone: 888-293-6498 or (202)512-1530 Fax: (202)512-1262 E-mail: gpoaccess@gpo.gov • URL: http://www.gpoaccess.gov • Annual. Free. A selected list of currently available publications, periodicals, and electronic products on business, trade, labor, federal regulations, economics, and other topics. Also known as *Business Catalog*.

U. S. Government Periodicals Index. Congressional Information Service, Inc., 4520 East-West Highway Bethesda, MD 20814-3389. Phone: 800-638-8380 or (301)654-1550 Fax: (301)654-4033 E-mail: cisinfo@lexis-nexis.com • URL: http://www.cispubs • Quarterly. $995.00 per year; with annual cumulation, $1,295.00 per year. An index to approximately 180 periodicals issued by various agencies of the federal government.

U. S. Herbal Supplement Market. Available from MarketResearch.com, 641 Ave. of the Americas, Third Floor New York, NY 10011. Phone: 800-298-5699 or (212)807-2629 Fax: (212)807-2716 E-mail: order@marketresearch.com • URL: http://www.marketresearch.com • 2001. $2,750.00. Market research data published by Packaged Facts. Includes forecasts to 2005.

U. S. Home Theater Market. Available from MarketResearch.com, 641 Ave. of the Americas, 3rd Fl. New York, NY 10011. Phone: 800-298-5699 or (212)807-2629 Fax: (212)807-2716 E-mail: order@marketresearch.com • URL: http://www.marketresearch.com • 1997. $1,3750.00. Market research report published by Packaged Facts. Covers big-screen TV, high definition TV, audio equipment, and video sources. Market projections are provided.

U. S. Housing Markets. Hanley-Wood, LLC, One Thomas Circle, N.W. Washington, DC 20005. Phone: 800-837-0870 or (202)452-0800 Fax: (202)785-1974 • URL: http://www.hanley-wood.com • Monthly. $345.00 per year. Includes eight interim reports. Provides data on residential building permits, apartment building completions, rental vacancy rates, sales of existing homes, average home prices, housing affordability, etc. All major U. S. cities and areas are covered.

U. S. Immigration and Migration Reference Library. Gale Cengage Learning, 27500 Drake Rd. Farmington Hills, MI 48331-3535. Phone: 800-877-GALE Fax: 800-414-5043 or (248)699-8069 E-mail: galeord@galegroup.com • URL: http://www.galegroup.com • 2003. $250.00. Five volumes. Includes *Almanac* (2 vols.), *Biographies* (2 vols.), and *Primary Sources*. Provides detailed history and information relating to U. S. immigration from "earliest times" to the present. (U-X-L imprint.)

U. S. Imports of Merchandise (CD-ROM). U. S. Bureau of the Census, Foreign Trade Division, Washington, DC 20233-0800. Phone: (301)763-4636 Fax: (301)457-3842 Monthly. $1,200 per year. Provides import data in the most extensive detail available, including product, quantity, value, shipping weight, country of origin, customs district of entry, rate provision, etc.

U. S. Industry and Trade Outlook. Available from National Technical Information Service, 5285 Port Royal Rd. Springfield, VA 22161. Phone: 800-553-6847 or (703)605-6000 Fax: (703)605-6900 E-mail: helpdesk@ntis.gov • URL: http://www.ntis.gov • Annual. $69.95. Produced by the International Trade Administration, U. S. Department of Commerce, in a "public-private" partnership with DRI/McGraw-Hill and Standard & Poor's. Provides basic data, outlook for the current year, and "Long-Term Prospects" (five-year projections) for a wide variety of products and services. Includes high technology industries. Formerly *U. S. Industrial Outlook*.

U. S. Industry Profiles: The Leading 100. Gale Cengage Learning, 27500 Drake Rd. Farmington Hills, MI 48331-3535. Phone: 800-877-GALE or (248)699-4253 Fax: 800-414-5043 E-mail: gale.galeord@cengage.com • URL: http://gale.cengage.com • 1998. $130.00. Second edition. Contains detailed profiles, with statistics, of 100 industries in the areas of manufacturing, construction, transportation, wholesale trade, retail trade, and entertainment.

U. S. Insurance: Life, Accident, and Health. Sheshunoff Information Services, Inc., 505 Barton Springs Rd., Suite 1200 Austin, TX 78704. Phone: 800-456-2340 or (512)472-2244 Fax: (512)305-6576 • URL: http://www.sheshunoff.com • Monthly. Price on application. CD-ROM provides detailed, current information on the financial characteristics of more than 2,300 life, accident, and health insurance companies.

U. S. Insurance: Property and Casualty. Sheshunoff Information Services, Inc., 505 Barton Springs Rd., Suite 1200 Austin, TX 78704. Phone: 800-456-2340 or (512)472-2244 Fax: (512)305-6576 • URL: http://www.sheshunoff.com • Monthly. Price on application. CD-ROM provides detailed, current financial information on more than 3,200 property and casualty insurance companies.

The U. S. Kids Market. Available from MarketResearch.com, 641 Ave. of the Americas, Fourth Floor New York, NY 10011. Phone: 800-298-5699 or (212)807-2629 Fax: (212)807-2642 E-mail: order@marketresearch.com • URL: http://www.marketresearch.com • 2002. $3,000.00. Published by Packaged Facts. Provides market research data on American consumers aged 5 to 14.

The U. S. Market for Assisted-Living Facilities. MarketResearch.com, 641 Ave. of the Americas, 4th Fl. New York, NY 10011. Phone: 800-298-5699 or (212)807-2629 Fax: (212)807-2676 E-mail: customerservice@marketresearch.com • URL: http://www.marketresearch.com • 1997. $2,750.00. Market research report. Includes market demographics and estimates of future revenues. Facility operators such as Emeritus, Manor Care, and Marriott Senior Living are profiled.

The U. S. Market for Catalog Shopping. Available from MarketResearch.com, 641 Ave. of the Americas, Third Floor New York, NY 10011. Phone: 800-298-5699 or (212)807-2629 Fax: (212)807-2716 E-mail: order@marketresearch.com • URL: http://www.marketresearch.com • 1997. $1,375.00. Market research report published by Packaged Facts. Includes analysis of catalog shopping market by age, ethnic groups, and income.

The U. S. Market for Funeral and Cremation Services. Available from MarketResearch.com, 641 Ave. of the Americas, Third Floor New York, NY 10011. Phone: 800-298-5699 or (212)807-2629 Fax: (212)807-2716 E-mail: order@marketresearch.com • URL: http://www.marketresearch.com • 1997. $1,375.00. Market research report published by Packaged Facts. Includes information on multinational funeral service chains.

The U. S. Market for Home Medical Tests. Available from MarketResearch.com, 641 Ave. of the Americas, Third Floor New York, NY 10011. Phone: 800-298-5699 or (212)807-2629 Fax: (212)807-2716 E-mail: order@marketresearch.com • URL: http://www.marketresearch.com • 1997. $1,375.00. Market research report published by Packaged Facts. Covers the market for diagnostic products used in the home and the effect of regulation.

The U. S. Market for Plastic Payment Cards. Available from MarketResearch.com, 641 Ave. of the Americas, Third Floor New York, NY 10011. Phone: 800-298-5699 or (212)807-2629 Fax: (212)807-2716 E-mail: order@marketresearch.com • URL: http://www.marketresearch.com • 1998. $1,375.00. Market research report published by Packaged Facts. Covers credit cards, charge cards, debit cards, and smart cards. Provides profiles of Visa, Mastercard, American Express, Discover, Diners Club, and others.

The U. S. Market for Vitamins, Supplements, and Minerals. Available from MarketResearch.com, 641 Ave. of the Americas, 3rd Fl. New York, NY 10011. Phone: 800-298-5699 or (212)807-2629 Fax: (212)807-2716 E-mail: order@marketresearch.com • URL: http://www.marketresearch.com • 2002. $3,000.00. Market research report published by Packaged Facts. Includes company profiles and sales forecasts to the year 2005.

U. S. Market Trends and Forecasts. Gale Cengage Learning, 27500 Drake Rd. Farmington Hills, MI 48331-3535. Phone: 800-877-GALE or (248)699-4253 Fax: 800-414-5043 E-mail: gale.galeord@cengage.com • URL: http://gale.cengage.com • 2002. $325.00. Third edition. Provides graphic representation of market statistics by means of pie charts and tables for each of 30 major industries and 400 market segments. Includes market forecasts and historical overviews.

U. S. Master Accounting Guide. John C. Wisdom. CCH, Inc., 2700 Lake Cook Rd. Riverwoods, IL 60015. Phone: 800-835-5224 or (847)267-7000 E-mail: cust_serv@cch.com • URL: http://www.cch.com • 1999. $52.95. Summarizes key accounting, business, and financial information from various sources. Includes digests, tables, charts, formulas, ratios, examples, and explanatory text. (Master Guide Series).

U. S. Master Auditing Guide. CCH, Inc., 2700 Lake Cook Rd. Riverwoods, IL 60015. Phone: 800-835-5224 or (847)267-7000 E-mail: cust_serv@cch.com • URL: http://www.cch.com • 2002. $65.00. Covers such topics as auditing standards, audit management, compliance, consulting, governmental audits, forensic auditing, and fraud. Includes checklists, charts, graphs, and sample reports.

U. S. Master Compensation Tax Guide. Dennis R. Lassila and Bob G. Kilpatrick. CCH, Inc., 2700 Lake Cook Rd. Riverwoods, IL 60015. Phone: 800-835-5224 or (847)267-7000 E-mail: cust_serv@cch.com • URL: http://www.cch.com • 2001. $57.00. Third edition. Provides concise coverage of taxes on salaries, bonuses, fringe benefits, other current compensation, and deferred compensation (qualified and nonqualified).

U. S. Master Depreciation Guide. CCH, Inc., 4025 W. Peterson Ave. Chicago, IL 60646-6085. Phone: 800-248-3248 or (773)866-6000 Fax: 800-224-8299 or (773)866-3608 • URL: http://www.cch.com • Annual. $52.00. Contains explanations of ADR (asset depreciation range), ACRS (accelerated cost recovery system), and MACRS (modified accelerated cost recovery system). Includes the historical background of depreciation.

U. S. Master Employee Benefits Guide. CCH, Inc., 2700 Lake Cook Rd. Riverwoods, IL 60015. Phone: 800-835-5224 or (847)267-7000 E-mail: cust_serv@cch.com • URL: http://www.cch.com • $56.95. Seventh edition. Explains federal tax and labor laws relating to health care benefits, disability benefits, workers' compensation, employee assistance plans, etc.

U. S. Master Estate and Gift Tax Guide. CCH, Inc., 2700 Lake Cook Rd. Riverwoods, IL 60015. Phone: 800-835-5224 or (847)267-7000 E-mail: cust_serv@cch.com • URL: http://www.cch.com • Annual. $55.00. Covers federal estate and gift taxes, including generation-skipping transfer tax plans. Includes tax tables and sample filled-in tax return forms.

U. S. Master GAAP Guide. Bill D. Jarnagin. CCH, Inc., 2700 Lake Cook Rd. Riverwoods, IL 60015. Phone: 800-835-5224 or (847)267-7000 E-mail: cust_serv@cch.com • URL: http://www.cch.com • 2000. $62.95. Covers the generally accepted accounting principles (GAAP) contained in the professional pronouncements of the Accounting Principles Board (APB) or the Financial Accounting Standards Board (FASB). Includes general discussions, flow charts, and detailed examples. Arranged by topic.

U. S. Master Multistate Corporate Tax Guide. CCH, Inc., 2700 Lake Cook Rd. Riverwoods, IL 60015. Phone: 800-835-5224 or (847)267-7000 E-mail: cust_serv@cch.com • URL: http://www.cch.com • Annual. $72.00. Provides corporate income tax information for 47 states, New York City, and the District of Columbia.

U. S. Master Pension Guide. CCH, Inc., 2700 Lake Cook Rd. Riverwoods, IL 60015. Phone: 800-835-5224 or (847)267-7000 E-mail: cust_serv@cch.com • URL: http://www.cch.com • Annual. $56.95. Explains IRS rules and regulations applying to 401(k) plans, 403(k) plans, ESOPs (employee stock ownership plans), IRAs, SEPs (simplified employee pension plans), Keogh plans, and nonqualified plans.

U. S. Master Property Tax Guide. CCH, Inc., 2700 Lake Cook Rd. Riverwoods, IL 60015. Phone: 800-835-5224 or (847)267-7000 E-mail: cust_serv@cch.com • URL: http://www.cch.com • Annual. $72.00. Provides state-by-state coverage of "key property tax issues and concepts," including exemptions, assessments, taxpayer remedies, and property tax calendars.

U. S. Master Sales and Use Tax Guide. CCH, Inc., 4025 W. Peterson Ave. Chicago, IL 60646-6085. Phone: 800-248-3248 or (773)866-6000 Fax: 800-224-8299 or (773)866-3608 • URL: http://www.cch.com • Annual. $69.00. Contains concise information on sales and use taxes in all states and the District of Columbia.

U. S. Master Tax Guide. CCH, Inc., 2700 Lake Cook Rd. Riverwoods, IL 60015. Phone: 800-835-5224 or (847)267-7000 • URL: http://www.cch.com • $184.00. Looseleaf service. Periodic supplementation.Provides concise information on personal and business income tax, with cross-references to the Internal Revenue Code and Income Tax Regulations.

U. S. Master Tax Guide on CD-ROM. CCH, Inc., 4025 West Peterson Ave. Chicago, IL 60646-6085. Phone: 800-248-3248 or (773)866-6000 Fax: 800-224-8299 or (773)866-3608 • URL: http://www.cch.com • Annual. CD-ROM version of the printed *U. S. Master Tax Guide*. Includes search commands, link commands, and on-screen prompts.

U. S. Patents Fulltext. Available from DIALOG, 11000 Regency Parkway, Ste. 400 Cary, NC 27511. Phone: 800-334-2564 or (919)462-8600 Fax: (919)468-9890 • URL: http://www.dialog.com • Contains complete text of patents issued by the U. S. Patent and Trademark Office since 1971. Weekly updates. Inquire as to online cost and availability.

U. S. Pharmacist. Jobson Publishing LLC, 100 Ave. of the Americas New York, NY 10013-1678. Phone: 800-747-1652 or (212)274-7000 Fax: (212)431-0500 E-mail: uspharmacist@jobson.com • URL: http://www.uspharmacist.com • Monthly. $30.00 per year. Covers a wide variety of topics for independent, chain store, hospital, and other pharmacists.

U. S. Securities and Exchange Commission.Phone: 800-732-0330 or (202)942-7040 Fax: (202)942-9634 E-mail: webmaster@sec.gov • URL: http://www.sec.gov • SEC Web site offers free access through EDGAR to text of official corporate filings, such as annual reports (10-K), quarterly reports (10-Q), and proxies. (EDGAR is "Electronic Data Gathering, Analysis, and Retrieval System.") An example is given of how to obtain executive compensation data from proxies. Text of the daily *SEC News Digest* is offered, as are links to other government sites, non-government market regulators, and U. S. stock exchanges. Search facilities are extensive. Fees: Free.

U. S. Supreme Court Bulletin. CCH, Inc., 2700 Lake Cook Rd. Riverwoods, IL 60015. Phone: 800-835-5224 or (847)267-7000 E-mail: cust_serv@cch.com • URL: http://www.cch.com • Monthly and on each decision day while the Court is in session.

U. S. Survey of Business Expectations. Dun & Bradstreet Corp., 103 JFK Pky. Short Hills, NJ 07078. Phone: 800-526-0651 E-mail: custserv@dnb.com • URL: http://www.dnb.com • Quarterly. 40.00 per year. A survey of 3,000 U. S. business executives as to their expectations for next quarter's sales, profits, prices, inventories, employment, exports, and new orders.

U. S. Trade Policy: History, Theory, and the WTO. William A. Lovett and others. M. E. Sharpe, Inc., 80 Business Park Drive Armonk, NY 10504. Phone: 800-541-6563 or (914)273-1800 Fax: (914)273-2106 E-mail: custserv@mesharpe.com • URL: http://www.mesharpe.com • 2004. $66.95. Second edition. Discusses the consequences of free trade and the activities of the World Trade Organization. Covers U. S. trade history from colonial times to recent years.

The U. S. Tweens Market. Available from MarketResearch.com, 641 Ave. of the Americas, Third Floor New York, NY 10011. Phone: 800-298-5699 or (212)807-2629 Fax: (212)807-2642 E-mail: order@marketresearch.com • URL: http://www.marketresearch.com • 2001. $2,750.00. Published by Packaged Facts. Market research report on American consumers aged 8 to 14.

UCC Bulletin. West Group, 610 Opperman Dr. Eagan, MN 55123. Phone: 800-328-4880 or (651)687-7000 Fax: 800-340-9378 E-mail: bookstore@westgroup.com • URL: http://www.westgroup.com • Monthly. $560.00 per year. Newsletter. Includes case summaries of recent UCC decisions.

UCLA Film and Television Archive-Research and Study Center., University of California, Los Angeles, 405 Hilgard Ave., 46 Powell Library Los Angeles, CA 90095-1517. Phone: (310)206-5388 Fax: (310)206-5392 E-mail: arsc@ucla.edu • URL: http://www.cinema.ucla.edu/ • Research areas include animation.

Uhlig's Corrosion Handbook. R. Winston Revie and Herbert H.

Uhlig, editors. John Wiley and Sons, Inc., 111 River St. Hoboken, NJ 07030. Phone: 800-225-5945 or (201)748-6000 Fax: (201)748-6088 E-mail: info@wiley.com • URL: http://www.wiley.com • 2000. $248.00. Second edition. Covers the basics of corrosion science and the use of modern materials for corrosion control. (Electrochemical Society Series, vol. 39).

UK Coal. OECD Publications and Information Center, OECD Washington Center, 2001 L St., N.W.,Suite 650 Washington, DC 20036-4922. Phone: 800-456-6323 or (202)785-6323 Fax: (202)785-0350 E-mail: washington.contact@oecd.org • URL: http://www.oecdwash.org • Annual. $200.00. A yearly report on world coal market trends and prospects.

Uker's International Tea and Coffee Directory and Buyers' Guide. Lockwood Trade Publications, Inc., 26 Broadway, Fl. 9M New York, NY 10004. Phone: (212)391-2060 Fax: (212)827-0945 E-mail: circulation@lockwookpublications.com • URL: http://www.lockwoodpublications.com • Annual. $40.00. Lists firms which export and import tea and coffee.

ULI Market Profiles: North America. Urban Land Institute, 1025 Thomas Jefferson St., N. W., Suite 500 W. Washington, DC 20007-5201. Phone: 800-321-5011 or (202)624-7000 Fax: (202)624-7140 E-mail: bookstore@uli.org • URL: http://www.uli.org • Annual. Members, $249.95; non-members, $299.95. Provides real estate marketing data for residential, retail, office, and industrial sectors. Covers 76 U. S. metropolitan areas and 13 major foreign metropolitan areas.

Ullmann's Encyclopedia of Industrial Chemistry. Matthias Bonet and others, editors. John Wiley and Sons, Inc., 111 River St. Hoboken, NJ 07030. Phone: 800-225-5945 or (201)748-6000 Fax: (201)748-6088 E-mail: info@wiley.com • URL: http://www.wiley.com • 2003. $4,500.00. Sixth edition. 40 volumes.

Ulrich's International Periodicals Directory Online. Bowker Electronic Publishing, 630 Central Ave. New Providence, NJ 07974. Phone: 888-269-5372 or (908)464-6800 Fax: (908)665-3528 Includes over 275,000 periodicals currently published worldwide and publications discontinued. Corresponds to *Ulrich's International Periodcals Directory, Irregular Serials and Annuals, Bowker International Serials Database Update*, and *Sources of Serials*. Inquire as to online cost and availability.

Ulrich's on Disc: The Complete International Serials Database on Compact Laser Disc. Bowker Electronic Publishing, 630 Central Ave. New Providence, NJ 07974. Phone: 888-269-5372 or (908)464-6800 Fax: (908)665-3528 Quarterly. $950.00 per year. The CD-ROM version of *Ulrich's International Periodicals Directory* and *Magazines for Libraries*.

Ulrich's Periodicals Directory. R.R. Bowker L.L.C., 630 Central Ave., Cantelupe Rd. New Providence, NJ 07974. Phone: 888-269-5372 or (908)286-1090 Fax: (908)219-0098 E-mail: info@diversityinforesources.com • URL: http://www.bowker.com • Covers: nearly 186,000 current periodicals and newspapers published worldwide. Entries include: In main list—Publication title; Dewey Decimal Classification number, Library of Congress Classification Number (where applicable), CODEN designation (for sci-tech serials), British Library Document Supply Centre shelfmark number, country code, ISSN; subtitle, language(s) of text, year first published, frequency, subscription prices, sponsoring organization, publishing company name, address, phone, fax, e-mail and website addresses, editor and publisher names; regular features (reviews, advertising, abstracts, bibliographies, trade literature, etc.), indexes, circulation, format, brief description of content; availability of microforms and reprints; whether refereed; CD-ROM availability with vendor name; online availability with service name; services that index or abstract the periodical, with years covered; advertising rates and contact; right and permissions contact name and phone; availability through document deliver

Ulrichsweb.com. R. R. BowkerPhone: 888-269-5372 or (908)464-6800 Fax: (908)464-3553 E-mail: info@bowker.com • URL: http://www.ulrichsweb.com • Web site provides fee-based access to about 250,000 serials records from the *Ulrich's International Periodicals Directory* database. Includes periodical evaluations from *Library Journal* and *Magazines for Libraries*. Monthly updates.

The Ultimate Digital Library: Where the New Information Players Meet. Andrew K. Pace. American Library Association, 50 E Huron St. Chicago, IL 60611-2795. Phone: 800-545-2433 or (312)944-6780 Fax: (312)440-9374 E-mail: ala@ala.org • URL: http://www.ala.org • 2003. $35.00. Discusses how libraries can remain competitive within the new digital information world.

Ultimate Guide to Raising Money for Growing Companies. Michael C. Thomsett. McGraw-Hill, 1221 Ave. of the Americas New York, NY 10020. Phone: 800-722-4726 or (212)512-2000 Fax: (212)512-4502 E-mail: customer.service@mcgraw-hill.com • URL: http://www.mcgraw-hill.com • 1990. $45.00. Discusses the preparation of a practical business plan, how to manage cash flow, and debt vs. equity decisions.

Ultrasonic Imaging, An International Journal. Dynamedia, Inc., Two Fulham Court Silver Spring, MD 20902. Phone: 800-468-4680 or (301)649-3447 Fax: (301)649-3447 Quarterly. $325.00 per year.

Ultrasonic Industry Association., PO Box 2307 Dayton, OH 45401-2307. Phone: (937)586-3725 Fax: (937)586-3699 E-mail: uia@ultrasonics.org • URL: http://www.ultrasonics.org • Manufacturers and users of ultrasonic equipment and component parts for ultrasonic equipment. Promotes the ultrasonic industry; cooperation with government on legislation and relations affecting ultrasonic equipment; collection and dissemination of information; research into use and safety of ultrasonic products; establishment of liaison with other organizations in the field.

Ultrasonics: The World's Leading Journal Covering the Science and Technology of Ultrasound. Elsevier, 360 Park Ave., S. New York, NY 10010-1710. Phone: 888-437-4636 or (212)989-5800 Fax: (212)633-3990 E-mail: usinfo-f@elsevier.com • URL: http://www.elsevier.com • 10 times a year. Institutions, $131.00 per year; institutions, $1,461.00 per year.

Ultrasound in Medicine and Biology. Elsevier, 360 Park Ave., S. New York, NY 10010-1710. Phone: 888-437-4636 or (212)989-5800 Fax: (212)633-3990 E-mail: usinfo-f@elsevier.com • URL: http://www.elsevier.com • Monthly. Institutions, $1,305.00 per year.

UN Chronicle. United Nations Pulications, Sales and Marketing Section, Roon DC2-0853 New York, NY 10017. Phone: 800-253-9646 or (212)963-8302 Fax: (212)963-3489 E-mail: publications@un.org • URL: http://www.un.org/publications • 11 times a year. $25.00 per year. Editions in English, French and Spanish.

The Unabashed Librarian: The "How I Run My Library Good" Letter. Maurice J. Freedman, P.O. Box 325 Mount Kisco, NY 10549. Fax: (914)244-0941 E-mail: editor@unabashedlibrarian.com • URL: http://www.unabashedlibrarian.com • Quarterly. $57.50 per year. Newsletter. Provides practical library management ideas and library humor.

Unabridged Dictionary of Occupational and Environmental Safety and Health with CD-ROM. Jeffrey W. Vincoli and Kathryn L. Bazan. Lewis Publishers, 2000 Corporate Blvd., N. W. Boca Raton, FL 33431. Phone: 800-272-7737 or (561)994-0555 Fax: 800-374-3401 or (561)998-9114 1999. $89.95.

UNCTAD Commodity Yearbook. United Nations Conference on Trade and Development. United Nations Publications, United Nations Concourse Level, First Ave., 46th St. New York, NY 10017. Phone: 800-253-9646 or (212)963-7608 Fax: (212)963-3489 E-mail: bookstore@un.org • URL: http://www.un.org/publications • Annual.

UNCTAD Handbook of Statistics. United Nations Conference on Trade and Development. United Nations Publications, Two United Nations Plaza, Room DC2-853 New York, NY 10017. Phone: 800-253-9646 or (212)963-8302 Fax: (212)963-3489 E-mail: publications@un.org • URL: http://www.un.org/publications • Annual. $80.00. Contains a "comprehensive collection of statistical data relevant to the analysis of world trade, investment, and development." Includes rankorderings, growth rates, and 20-year time series.

Understanding Business. William G. Nickels. McGraw-Hill, 1221 Ave. of the Americas New York, NY 10020. Phone: 800-722-4726 or (212)512-2000 Fax: (212)512-4502 E-mail: customer.service@mcgraw-hill.com • URL: http://www.mcgraw-hill.com • 2001. $56.25. Sixth edition.

Understanding Business Statistics. John E. Hanke and Arthur G. Reitsch. McGraw-Hill, 1221 Ave. of the Americas New York, NY 10020. Phone: 800-722-4726 or (212)512-2000 Fax: (212)512-4502 E-mail: customer.service@mcgraw-hill.com • URL: http://www.mcgraw-hill.com • 1993. $71.25. Second edition.

Understanding Corporate Bonds. Harold Kerzner. McGraw-Hill, 1221 Ave. of the Americas New York, NY 10020. Phone: 800-722-4726 or (212)512-2000 Fax: (212)512-4502 E-mail: customer.service@mcgraw-hill.com • URL: http://www.mcgraw-hill.com • 1991. $24.95. A general introduction to investing in corporate bonds. Includes a discussion of high-risk (junk) bonds.

Understanding Economics Today. Gary M. Walton and Frank C. Wykoff. McGraw-Hill, 1221 Ave. of the Americas New York, NY 10020. Phone: 800-722-4726 or (212)512-2000 Fax: (212)512-4502 E-mail: customer.service@mcgraw-hill.com • URL: http://www.mcgraw-hill.com • 2000. $82.19. Seventh edition.

Understanding Financial Derivatives: How to Protect Your Investments. Donald Strassheim. McGraw-Hill, 1221 Ave. of the Americas New York, NY 10020. Phone: 800-722-4726 or (212)512-2000 Fax: (212)512-4502 E-mail: customer.service@mcgraw-hill.com • URL: http://www.mcgraw-hill.com • 1996. $40.00. Covers three basic risk management instruments: options, futures, and swaps. Includes advice on equity index options, financial futures contracts, and over-the-counter derivatives markets.

Understanding Financial Statements. Lyn M. Fraser and Aileen Orminston. Prentice Hall PTR, 240 Frisch Ct. Paramus, NJ 07652. Phone: 800-282-0693 Fax: 800-445-6991 • URL: http://www.phptr.com • 2003. $42.67. Seventh edition. Emphasis is on the evaluation and interpretation of financial statements.

Understanding Object-Oriented Programming with Java. Timothy Budd. Addison-Wesley, 75 Arlington St., Ste. 300

Boston, MA 02116. Phone: 800-447-2226 or (617)848-7500 • URL: http://www.aw.com • 1999. $85.00. Second revised edition.

Understanding the Census: A Guide for Marketers, Planners, Grant Writers, and Other Data Users. Michael R. Lavin. Epoch Books, Inc., 22 Byron Ave. Kenmore, NY 14223. Phone: (716)837-4341 1996. $49.95. Contains basic explanations of U. S. Census "concepts, methods, terminology, and data sources." Includes practical advice for locating and using Census data.

Understanding Toxicology: Chemicals, Their Benefits and Uses. Bruno H. Schiefer and others. CRC Press LLC, 2000 NW Corporate Blvd. Boca Raton, FL 33431-7372. Phone: 800-272-7737 or (561)994-0555 Fax: 800-374-3401 or (561)989-9732 E-mail: orders@crcpress.com • URL: http://www.crcpress.com • 1997. $39.95. Provides a basic introduction to chemical interactions and toxicology for the general reader.

Understanding Wine Technology: The Science of Wine Explained. David Bird. Wine Appreciation Guild, 360 Swift Ave. South San Francisco, CA 94080. Phone: 800-231-9463 or (650)866-3020 Fax: (650)866-3513 E-mail: info@wineappreciation.com • URL: http://www.wineappreciation.com • 2001. $30.00. Provides basic information on vineyards, grape processing, fermentation, stabilization, wine quality control, and bottling. Includes color illustrations, diagrams, graphs, index, and glossary.

UNDOC: Current Index (United Nations Documents). United Nations Publications, United Nations Concourse Level, Sales and Marketing Section, Room DC2-0853 New York, NY 10017. Phone: 800-553-3210 or (212)963-7680 Fax: (212)963-4810 E-mail: bookstore@un.org • URL: http://www.un.org/publications • Quarterly. $150.00. Annual cumulation on microfiche. Text in English.

Unemployment Insurance Claims Weekly Report. U.S. Department of Labor, Employment and Training Administration, Washington, DC 20210. Phone: (202)219-6050 Weekly.

UNESCO Statistical Yearbook. Bernan Press, 4611-F Assembly Dr. Lanham, MD 20706-4391. Phone: 800-274-4447 or (301)459-2255 Fax: 800-865-3450 or (301)459-9235 E-mail: bpress@bernan.com • URL: http://www.bernan.com • 1998. $95.00. Co-published by Bernan Press and the United Nations Educational, Scientific, and Cultural Organization (http://www.unesco.org). Presents statistical data from more than 200 countries on education, technology, research, broadcasting, cinema, book publishing, newspapers, libraries, museums, and population. Includes charts, maps, and graphs.

Unified Abrasives Manufacturers Association - Bonded Division., c/o Wherry Associates, 30200 Detroit Ave. Cleveland, OH 44145-1967. Phone: (440)899-0010 Fax: (440)892-1404 E-mail: contact@uama.org • URL: http://www.uama.org • Formerly Grinding Wheel Institute.

Uniform and Textile Service Association., 1300 N. 17th St., Suite 750 Arlington, VA 22209. Phone: (703)247-2600 Fax: (703)841-4750 E-mail: info@utsa.com • URL: http://www.utsa.com • Formerly Institute of Industrial Launderers.

Uniform Crime Reports for the United States. Federal Bureau of Investigation, U.S. Department of Justice. Available from U.S. Government Printing Office, Washington, DC 20402. Phone: (202)512-1800 Fax: (202)512-2250 E-mail: gpoaccess@gpo.gov • URL: http://www.accessgpo.gov • Annual. $45.00.

Uniform System of Accounts for the Lodging Industry. Timothy J. Eaton, editor. Educational Institute of the American Hotel & Motel Association, P.O. Box 1240 East Lansing, MI 48826-1240. Phone: 800-344-4381 or (517)372-8800 Fax: (517)372-5141 E-mail: info@el-ahla.org • URL: http://www.ei.ahma.org • 1996. $55.95. 9th revised edition.

Uniformed Services Academy of Family Physicians., 1503 Santa Rosa Rd. Richmond, VA 23229. Phone: (804)968-4436 Fax: (804)968-4418 E-mail: tschulte@vafp.org • URL: http://www.usafp.org • Family physicians, teachers of family medicine, medical students, and residents in the armed services, public health service, or Indian health service. Sponsors continuing education program. Sponsors educational programs.

Uniforms: Why We Are What We Wear. Paul Fussell. Houghton Mifflin Co., 222 Berkeley St. Boston, MA 02116. Phone: 800-733-2828 or (617)351-5000 Fax: 800-733-2098 E-mail: inquiries@hmco.com • URL: http://www.hmco.com • 2002. $22.00. Provides an informal discussion of the cultural, social, and historical significance of uniforms. Popularly written.

Union Labor Report. Bureau of National Affairs Inc., 1801 S Bell St. Arlington, VA 22202. Phone: 800-372-1033 or (202)452-4200 Fax: (202)452-4226 E-mail: customercare@bna.com • URL: http://www.bna.com • Description: Covers legal, legislative, and regulatory developments and trends affecting management and labor in the workplace.

Union of Orthodox Jewish Congregations of America.

Unique Homes: The Global Resource of Luxury Real Estate. Unique Homes, Inc., 2020 Santa Monica Blvd., Ste. 460 Santa Monica, CA 90404. Phone: 800-732-4092 or (310)453-0500 Fax: (310)453-0511 • URL: http://www.uniquehomes.com • Six times a year. $29.97 per year. Homes for sale.

Unique 3-in-1 Research and Development Directory. Government Data Publications, Inc., 2300 M St., NW Washington, DC 20037. Phone: 800-275-4688 or (718)627-0819 Fax: (718)998-5960 E-mail: gdp@govdata.com • URL: http://www.govdata.com • Annual. $15.00. Government contractors in the research and development fields. Included with subscription to *R and D Contracts Monthly*. Formerly *Research and Development Directory*.

Unite!-The Union of Needletrades, Industrial and Textile Employees.

UNITE!-Union of Needletrades, Industrial and Textile Employees.

United Abrasives Manufacturers Association - Coated Division., c/o Wherry Associates, 30200 Detroit Rd. Cleveland, OH 44145-1967. Phone: (440)899-0010 Fax: (440)892-1404 E-mail: contact@uama.org • URL: http://www.uama.org • Formerly Coated Abrasives Manufacturers Institute.

United Brotherhood of Carpenters and Joiners of America.

United Dairy Industry Association., O'Hare International Center, 10255 W Higgins Rd., Ste. 900 Rosemont, IL 60018. Phone: (847)803-2000 Fax: (847)803-2077 E-mail: info@gs1us.org Aims to promote the sale and consumption of U.S.-produced milk and milk products. Sponsors the advertising and sales promotion campaigns of the American Dairy Association and the nutrition research and education programs of the National Dairy Council. Maintains reference library. **Publications:** none.

United Food and Commercial Workers International Union.

United Food and Commercial Workers Union International.

United Fresh Fruit and Vegetable Association.

United Furniture Workers Insurance Fund., 1910 Air Lane Dr., PO Box 100037 Nashville, TN 37210. Phone: (615)889-8860 Fax: (615)889-8860 E-mail: info@gs1us.org • URL: http://ufwip.com • AFL-CIO. A division of International Union of Electronic, Electrical, Salaried, Machine, and Furniture Workers.

United Kingdom Committee of International Association., c/o R.G. Ainsworth, Lower Common House, The Avenue Bucklebury RG7 6NS, United Kingdom. Phone: 44 118 9712489 E-mail: r.ainsworth@btinternet.com Formerly United Kingdom National Committee of the International Association on Water Pollution Research and Control.

United Mine Workers of America., 8315 Lee Highway Fairfax, VA 22031. Phone: (703)208-7200 • URL: http://www.umwa.org • Formerly International Union United Mine Workers in America.

The United Nations and Drug Abuse Control. United Nations Publications, United Nations Concourse Level, First Ave., 46th St. New York, NY 10017. Phone: 800-253-9646 or (212)963-7608 Fax: (212)963-4910 E-mail: bookstore@un.org • URL: http://www.un.org/publications • 1992. An overview of international drug control efforts.

United Nations Association of the United States of America., 801 Second Ave., 2nd Fl. New York, NY 10017. Phone: (212)907-1300 Fax: (212)682-9185 E-mail: unahq@unausa.org • URL: http://www.unausa.org • Absorbed Conference Group of U.S. National Organizations on the United Nations.

United Nations Disarmament Yearbook. United Nations Publications, Two United Nations Plaza, Rm. DC2-853 New York, NY 10017. Phone: 800-253-9646 or (212)963-8302 Fax: (212)963-3489 E-mail: bookstore@un.org • URL: http://www.un.org/publications • Annual. $55.00.

United Press International., 1510 H St. NW Washington, DC 20005. Phone: 800-796-4874 or (202)898-8188 Fax: (202)898-8048 E-mail: hguerra@upi.com • URL: http://www.upi.com • Gathers news and photographs of current events to distribute to newspapers, periodicals, cable systems, and radio and television stations throughout the world; maintains 204 local news bureaus in 79 countries. Provides speakers.

United Producers., PO Box 29800, PO Box 29800 Columbus, OH 43229. Phone: 800-456-3276 or (614)890-6666 Fax: (614)839-8659 E-mail: erayburn@uproducers.com • URL: http://www.uproducers.com • Cooperative marketing organization for livestock producers in the Midwest. Conducts livestock marketing program. Owns Illinois Livestock Marketing Company. Works with Illinois, Iowa, and Missouri farm bureaus.

United States Agricultural Trade: Trends, Policy, and Direction. Larry V. Fedorov, editor. Nova Science Publishers, Inc., 400 Oser Ave., Suite 1600 Hauppauge, NY 11788-3619. Phone: (631)231-7269 Fax: (631)231-8175 E-mail: novascience@earthlink.net • URL: http://www.novapublishers.com • 2003. $59.00. Includes data on the impact of NAFTA on the import and export of farm products.

U.S. Armor Association., PO Box 607 Fort Knox, KY 40121-0607. Phone: (502)942-8624 Fax: (502)942-6219 E-mail: mgavula@bellsouth.net • URL: http://www.usarmor-assn.org • U.S. Army officers, noncommissioned officers, enlisted men, and veterans of all components. Disseminates professional knowledge of military art and science, especially mobile ground warfare.

United States Army Warrant Officers Association., 462 Herndon Pkwy., Ste. 207 Herndon, VA 20170-5235. Phone: 800-587-2962 or (703)742-7727 Fax: (703)742-7728 E-mail: usawoa@cavtel.net • URL: http://www.penfed.org/usawoa • Active duty, National Guard, Reserve, and retired U.S. Army warrant officers. Promotes the technical and social welfare of warrant officers. Recommends Army improvement programs. Circulates professional information among warrant officers. Stimulates patriotism, devotion to duty, and comradeship among members.

United States Association of Former Members of Congress., 233 Pennsylvania Ave., S.E., Suite 200 Washington, DC 20003-1107. Phone: (202)543-8676 Fax: (202)543-7145 E-mail: usafmcl@mindspring.com • URL: http://www.usafmc.org • Formerly Former Members of Congress.

United States Association of Independent Gymnastic Clubs., 22 River Terrace, Ste. 2D New York, NY 10282. Phone: 800-480-0201 or (212)227-9792 Fax: (212)227-9793 E-mail: usaigcpsnyz@aol.com • URL: http://www.usaigc.com • Members include gym clubs and manufacturers of gymnastic equipment.

U.S. Banker. IMG Media, 11 Penn Plz, 17th Fl. New York, NY 10001-2006. Phone: 800-535-8403 or (212)967-7000 Fax: (212)967-7155 E-mail: custserv@americanbanker.com • URL: http://www.usbanker.com • Monthly. $79.00 per year. Covers technology innovation for the banking industry, including online banking. Incorporates *Future Banker*.

The U.S. Beer Market: Impact Databank Review and Forecast. M. Shanken Communications, Inc., 387 Park Ave., S New York, NY 10016. Phone: 800-344-0763 or (212)684-4424 Fax: (212)684-5424 E-mail: retailsales@mshanken.com • URL: http://www.mshanken.com • Annual. $845.00. Includes industry commentary and statistics.

United States Beet Sugar Association., 1156 15th St. NW, Ste. 1019 Washington, DC 20005. Phone: (202)296-4820 Fax: (202)331-2065 E-mail: hguerra@upi.com • URL: http://www.beetsugar.org • Represents beet sugar processing companies.

United States Business History, 1602-1988: A Chronology. Richard B. Robinson. Greenwood Publishing Group, Inc., 88 Post Rd. W Westport, CT 06881. Phone: 800-225-5800 or (203)226-3571 Fax: (203)431-2214 E-mail: customer-service@greenwood.com • URL: http://www.greenwood.com • 1990. $99.95.

United States Census of Agriculture. U.S. Bureau of the Census, Washington, DC 20233-0800. Phone: (301)457-4100 Fax: (301)457-3842 • URL: http://www.census.gov • Quinquennial. Results presented in reports, tape, CD-ROM, and Diskette files.

United States Census of Construction Industries. U.S. Bureau of the Census, Washington, DC 20233-0800. Phone: (202)512-1800 Fax: (202)512-2250 • URL: http://www.census.gov • Quinquennial. Results presented in reports, tape, and CD-ROM files.

United States Census of Governments. Bureau of the Census, U.S. Department of Commerce. Available from U.S. Government Printing Office, Washington, DC 20402. Phone: (202)512-1800 Fax: (202)512-2250 E-mail: gpoaccess@gpo.gov • URL: http://www.accessgpo.gov • Quinquennial.

United States Census of Manufactures. U.S. Bureau of the Census, Washington, DC 20233-0800. Phone: (301)457-4100 Fax: (301)457-3842 • URL: http://www.census.gov • Quinquennial. Results presented in reports, tape, CD-ROM, and Diskette files.

United States Census of Mineral Industries. Bureau of the Census, U.S. Department of Commerce. Available from U.S. Government Printing Office, Washington, DC 20402. Phone: (202)512-1800 Fax: (202)512-2250 E-mail: gpoaccess@gpo.gov • URL: http://www.accessgpo.gov • Quinquennial.

United States Census of Population. Bureau of the Census, U.S. Department of Commerce. Available from U.S. Government Printing Office, Washington, DC 20402. Phone: (202)512-1800 Fax: (202)512-2250 E-mail: gpoaccess@gpo.gov • URL: http://www.accessgpo.gov • Quinquennial.

United States Census of Retail Trade. U.S. Bureau of the Census, Washington, DC 20233-0800. Phone: (301)457-4100 Fax: (301)457-3842 • URL: http://www.census.gov • Quinquennial.

United States Census of Service Industries. U.S. Bureau of the Census, Washington, DC 20233-0800. Phone: (301)457-4100 Fax: (301)457-3842 • URL: http://www.census.gov • Quinquennial. Various reports available.

United States Census of Transportation. Bureau of the Census, U.S. Department of Commerce. Available from U.S. Government Printing Office, Washington, DC 20402. Phone: (202)512-1800 Fax: (202)512-2250 E-mail: gpoaccess@gpo.gov • URL: http://www.accessgpo.gov • Quinquennial.

United States Census of Wholesale Trade. Bureau of the Census, U.S. Department of Commerce. Available from U.S. Government Printing Office, Washington, DC 20402. Phone: (202)512-1800 Fax: (202)512-2250 E-mail: gpoaccess@gpo.gov • URL: http://www.accessgpo.gov • Quinquennial.

United States Coast Guard Auxiliary.

United States Coast Guard Chief Petty Officer Association.

United States Coast Guard Marine Safety Council Proceedings. U.S. Coast Guard, Washington, DC 20593. Phone: (202)267-2229 Bimonthly.

United States Code. U.S. Congress. Available from U.S. Government Printing Office, Washington, DC 20402. Phone: (202)512-1800 Fax: (202)512-2250 E-mail: gpoaccess@gpo.gov • URL: http://www.accessgpo.gov • Continual supplements. Price varies. Permanent and general public law of the United States from 1789 to the codification date.

United States Code Annotated: Crimes and Criminal Procedures. West Group, 610 Opperman Dr. Eagan, MN 55123. Phone: 800-338-9424 or (612)687-7000 Fax: 800-340-9378 E-mail: bookstore@westgroup.com • URL: http://www.westpub.com • $3,125.00. 15 volumes. Annual cumulation. Arranged in parallel fashion to *United States Code*. Gives abstracts of relevant federal and state court decisions pertaining to each section of the code. Supplemented by annual pocket parts.

U.S. Committee on Irrigation and Drainage., 1616 17th St., No. 483 Denver, CO 80202. Phone: (303)628-5430 Fax: (303)628-5431 E-mail: stephens@uscid.org • URL: http://www.uscid.org • Formerly U.S. Committee on Irrigation, Drainage and Flood Control.

United States Conference of Mayors., 1620 Eye St., N. W. Washington, DC 20006. Phone: (202)293-7330 Fax: (202)293-2352 E-mail: info@usmayors.org • URL: http://www.usmayors.org • Promotes improved municipal government, with emphasis on federal cooperation.

United States Council for International Business., 1212 Ave. of the Americas, 21st Fl. New York, NY 10036. Phone: (212)354-4480 Fax: (212)575-0327 E-mail: info@uscib.org • URL: http://www.uscib.org • Formerly United States Council of the International Chamber of Commerce.

U.S. Custom House Guide. Commonwealth Business Media Inc., 400 Windsor Corporate Pk., 50 Millstone Rd., Ste. 200 East Windsor, NJ 08520-1415. Phone: 800-221-5488 or (609)371-7700 Fax: (609)371-7885 E-mail: customerservice@cbizmedia.com • URL: http://www.cbizmedia.com • Publication includes: List of ports having customs facilities, customs officials, port authorities, chambers of commerce, embassies and consulates, foreign trade zones, and other organizations; related trade services. Entries include: For each principal port—Name of organization or agency, address, phone, fax, names and titles of key personnel; description and limitations of port facilities. For service firms—Company name, address, phone, fax. Principal content is U.S. tariff schedules and customs regulations, and a "How to Import" manual.

United States Department of State Indexes of Living Costs Abroad, Quarters Allowances, and Hardship Differentials. Available from U. S. Government Printing Office, Washington, DC 20402. Phone: (202)512-1800 Fax: (202)512-2250 E-mail: gpoaccess@gpo.gov • URL: http://www.access.gpo.gov • Quarterly. $15.00 per year. Provides data on the difference in living costs between Washington, DC and each of 160 foreign cities.

The U.S. Distilled Spirits Market: Impact Databank Market Review and Forecast. M. Shanken Communications, Inc., 387 Park Ave., S New York, NY 10016. Phone: 800-684-4065 or (212)684-4424 Fax: (212)684-5424 E-mail: retailsales@mshanken.com • URL: http://www.mshanken.com • Annual. $865.00. Includes industry commentary and statistics.

United States Durum Growers Association., 2409 Jackson Ave. Bismarck, ND 58501. Phone: 800-463-8786 or (701)214-3203 Fax: (701)250-1730 E-mail: dawn@durumgrowers.com • URL: http://www.durumgrowers.com • Durum wheat growers. Cooperates with other organizations to promote favorable conditions for the production and marketing of durum wheat.

U.S. Energy Association., 1300 Pennsylvania Ave. NW, Ste. 550, Mailbox 142 Washington, DC 20004-3022. Phone: (202)312-1230 Fax: (202)682-1682 E-mail: kgrover@usea.org • URL: http://www.usea.org • One of 100 national committees representing the energy interests of industry, government, professional and technical societies, educational institutions, and legal and other professional service organizations. Supports World Energy Council objectives, which are: to provide for broad consideration of energy resources, policy, management, technology, use, and conservation as they relate to the total energy picture of the U.S. and the world; to publish data on energy resources and their utilization; to hold conferences and forums for those concerned with surveying, developing, or using energy resources. Conducts special energy seminars.

U.S. Energy Association; Research and Development Committee.

United States Equal Employment Opportunity Commission Annual Report: Job Patterns for Minorities and Women in Private Industry. U.S. Equal Employment Opportunity Commission, Washington, DC 20507. Phone: (202)663-4900 Annual.

United States Export Administration Regulations. Available from U. S. Government Printing Office, Washington, DC 20402. Phone: (202)512-1800 Fax: (202)512-2250 E-mail: gpoaccess@gpo.gov • URL: http://www.access.gpo.gov • $132.00. Looseleaf. Includes basic manual and supplementary bulletins for one year. Issued by the Bureau of Export Administration, U. S. Department of Commerce (http://www.doc.gov). Consists of export licensing rules and regulations.

United States Golf Association (USGA)., P.O. Box 708 Far Hills, NJ 07931. Phone: (908)234-2300 Fax: (908)234-9687 E-mail: usga@usga.org • URL: http://www.usga.org • Members are established golf courses and clubs. Serves as governing body for golf in the U. S. and provides rules and regulations. Affiliated with USGA Green Section.

United States Government Annual Report, Fiscal Year. Available from U. S. Government Printing Office, Washington, DC 20402. Phone: (202)512-1800 Fax: (202)512-2250 E-mail: gpoaccess@gpo.gov • URL: http://www.access.gpo.gov • Annual. $5.00. Issued by the Financial Management Service, U. S. Treasury Department (http://www.fms.treas.gov). Contains the official report on the receipts and outlays of the federal government. Presents budgetary results at the summary level.

United States Government Manual. National Archives and

Records Administration. Office of the Federal Register, c/o The National Archives and Records Administration, 8601 Adelphi Rd. College Park, MD 20740-6001. Phone: (866)272-6272 or (301)837-0482 Fax: (301)837-0483 E-mail: fedreg.info@nara.gov • URL: http://www.accessgpo.gov • Description: Provides information on the agencies of the executive, judicial, and legislative branches of the Federal government. Contains a section on terminated or transferred agencies.

United States Government Printing Office Style Manual. U. S. Government Printing Office, 732 N Capitol St., NW Washington, DC 20401. Phone: 888-293-6498 or (202)512-1530 Fax: (202)512-1262 E-mail: gpoaccess@gpo.gov • URL: http://www.gpoaccess.gov • 2000. $41.00. 29th edition. Supersedes the 1984 edition (28th). Designed to achieve uniformity in the style and form of government printing.

United States Government Purchasing and Sales Directory. U.S. Small Business Administration. Available from U.S. Government Printing Office, Washington, DC 20402. Phone: (202)512-1800 Fax: (202)512-2250 E-mail: gpoaccess@gpo.gov • URL: http://www.accessgpo.gov • 1994. $24.00.

U.S. Government Subscriptions. U. S. Government Printing Office, 732 N Capitol St., SW Washington, DC 20401. Phone: 888-293-6498 or (202)512-1530 Fax: (202)512-1262 E-mail: gpoaccess@gpo.gov • URL: http://www.gpoaccess.gov • Quarterly. Free. Includes agency and subject indexes.

U.S. Grains Council., 1400 K St. NW, Ste. 1200 Washington, DC 20005. Phone: (202)789-0789 Fax: (202)898-0522 E-mail: grains@grains.org • URL: http://www.grains.org • Federation of feed grain producer organizations, seed trade associations, and organizations of grain processors, exporters, dealers and related agribusiness manufacturers. Maintains 10 international offices for development of foreign markets in over 80 countries for barley, corn, grain sorghum and related products.

United States Hide, Skin and Leather Association., 1700 N. Moore St., Suite 1600 Arlington, VA 22209. Phone: (703)841-5485 Fax: (703)841-9656 E-mail: lcondon@ushsla.org • URL: http://www.meatami.org • Affilicated with American Meat Institute.

United States Immigration Laws, General Information. U.S. Immigration and Naturalization Service. Available from U.S. Government Printing Office, Washington, DC 20402. Phone: (202)512-1800 Fax: (202)512-2250 E-mail: gpoaccess@gpo.gov • URL: http://www.accessgpo.gov • Irregular.

United States Institute for Theatre Technology., 6443 Ridings Rd. Syracuse, NY 13206-1111. Phone: 800-938-7488 or (315)463-6463 Fax: (315)463-6525 E-mail: info@office.usitt.org • URL: http://www.usitt.org • Members include acousticians, architects, costumers, educators, engineers, lighting designers, and others.

United States International Air Travel Statistics. U. S. Department of Transportation, Center for Transportation Information, Kendall Square Cambridge, MA 02142. Phone: (617)494-2000 Fax: (617)494-2497 Provides detailed statistics on air passenger travel between the U. S. and foreign countries for both scheduled and charter flights. Time period is 1975 to date, with monthly updates. Inquire as to online cost and availability.

United States Law Week: A National Survey of Current Law. BNA, Inc., 1231 25th St., NW Washington, DC 20037. Phone: 800-372-1033 E-mail: customercare@bna.com • URL: http://www.bna.com • Weekly. $1,152.00 per year. Covers U.S. Supreme Court proceedings and gives full text of decisions. Also provides detailed reports on important legislative and regulatory actions.

United States Marine Corps Drill Instructors Association., PO Box 5401 Parris Island, SC 29905. Phone: (912)632-4557 Fax: (912)632-4557 E-mail: usmcdia@atc.cc • URL: http://www.usmcdiassn.com • Present and former U.S. Marine Corps drill instructors. Fosters a spirit of comradery through social and recreational activities. Promotes the welfare of elderly, disabled, and needy veterans; sponsors patriotic, charitable, and educational programs. Maintains living memorial monument fund; conducts blood drives and active participants' toys 4 tots.

U.S. Mayor. U.S. Conference of Mayors, 1620 Eye St. NW Washington, DC 20006. Phone: (202)293-7330 Fax: (202)293-2352 E-mail: info@usmayors.org Description: Provides a national forum for issues that affect cities in the U.S. Contains ideas in public programs and coverage of innovative projects. Recurring features include letters to the editor, interviews, a calendar of events, and reports of meetings.

U.S. Metric Association., 10245 Andasol Ave. Northridge, CA 91325-1504. Phone: (818)363-5606 Fax: (818)363-5606 E-mail: valerie.antoine@verizon.net • URL: http://lamar.colostate.edu/~hillger • Scientists, engineers, teachers, government and industry personnel, students, and laymen interested in promoting greater use of the metric system of measurement; appointed by the U.S. Department of Commerce to represent the private sector on government metric committees. Aids teachers, consumers, government, and industry in implementing the metric system. Maintains a Certified Metrication Specialist Board which is responsible for screening qualified applicants to work with metric system units. Distributes educational fliers on the metric system. Compiles statistics.

United States-Mexico Chamber of Commerce., 1300 Pennsylvania Ave., Suite 270 Washington, DC 20004-3021. Phone: 800-876-2624 or (202)371-8680 Fax: (202)371-8686 E-mail: news-hq@usmc.org • URL: http://www.usmoc.org • Works to promote trade and investment between the U. S. and Mexico.

United States National Credit Union Administration NCUA Quarterly. National Credit Union Administration

United States Naval Institute., 291 Wood Rd. Annapolis, MD 21402. Phone: 800-233-8764 or (410)268-6110 Fax: (410)571-1703 E-mail: customer@usni.org • URL: http://www.navalinstitute.org • Regular, reserve, and retired professionals in the Navy, Marine Corps, and Coast Guard; civilians interested in the advancement of the knowledge of sea power and in advancing professional, literary, and scientific knowledge in the naval and maritime services. Conducts oral history and color print program.

U.S. Pastry Alliance., 462 Broadway New York, NY 10013. Phone: 888-272-7879 E-mail: bsteinhauser@freedomworks.org Pastry chefs. Dedicated to the advancement of professional pastry making through education, networking, and communication.

United States Patent and Trademark Office. U. S. Department of CommercePhone: 800-786-9199 or (703)308-4357 Fax: (703)305-7786 • URL: http://www.uspto.gov • Web site provides extensive information about patents and trademarks, with advanced search facilities for specific documents or names. "Special Pages" are available for "How to Search," "Trademarks-Logos-Brands," "Inventor Resources," and other topics. A complete fee schedule is available for filing applications, appeals, copies, etc.

United States Personal Chef Association., 610 Quantum Rd. NE Rio Rancho, NM 87124. Phone: 800-995-2138 or (505)994-6372 E-mail: customerservice@uspca.com • URL: http://www.uspca.com • Promotes the personal chef; committed in advancing the profession of personal chef as a legitimate career choice in the culinary arts field; ensures the credibility of the personal chef with the industry-wide implementation of Educational Standards of Knowledge.

United States Pharmacopeia., 12601 Twinbrook Pkwy. Rockville, MD 20852-1790. Phone: 800-822-8772 or (301)881-0666 Fax: (301)816-8299 E-mail: webmaster@usp.org • URL: http://www.usp.org • Promotes the public health by establishing and disseminating officially recognized standards of quality and authoritative information for the use of medicines and other health care technologies by health professionals, patients and consumers. Helps to monitor quality and prevent medication errors through national reporting programs. Achieves its goals through the contributions of volunteers representing pharmacy, medicine, and other health care professions, as well as science, academia, the U.S. government, the pharmaceutical industry, and consumer organizations.

United States Pharmacopeia National Formulary. United States Pharmacopeial Convention, 12601 Twinbrook Parkway Rockville, MD 20852. Phone: 800-227-8772 or (301)881-0666 Fax: (301)816-8148 E-mail: jac@usp.org • URL: http://www.usp.org • Quinquennial.

United States Postal Service: Make Your Mark. U. S. Postal ServicePhone: (202)268-2000 E-mail: webmaster@email.usps.com • URL: http://www.usps.com • Web site contains detailed information on U. S. mail services and post offices, including ZIP codes, postage rates, stamps, addressing, Express Mail tracking, and consumer postal information in general. Links are provided to the State Department for passport procedures and to the IRS for tax forms.

U.S. Postal Service Revenue and Cost Analysis Report. U.S. Postal Service, Rates and Classification Dept., 475 L'Enfant Plaza W., SW., Rm. 5300 Washington, DC 20260-1300. Phone: (202)268-2000 Annual.

United States Professional Tennis Association., 3535 Briarpark Dr., Ste. 1, 3535 Briarpark Dr., Suite 1 Houston, TX 77042. Phone: 800-USPTA-4U or (713)978-7782 Fax: (713)978-7780 E-mail: uspta@uspta.org • URL: http://www.uspta.com • Professional tennis instructors, tennis-teaching professionals and college coaches. Seeks to improve tennis instruction in the United States; maintains placement bureau and library. Offers specialized education; sponsors competitions; administrates an adult tennis league and a nationwide program to introduce children ages 3-10 to tennis. Sponsors annual "Tennis Across America" program each spring.

U.S. Rail News. Business Publishers Inc., 2601 University Blvd., W Ste. 200, PO Box 17592 Silver Spring, MD 20902. Phone: 800-274-6737 or (301)929-5700 Fax: (301)949-8844 E-mail: custserv@bpinews.com • URL: http://www.bpinews.com • Description: Reports developments in all aspects of the rail transportation industry. Covers topics such as deregulation, mergers and acquisitions, labor relations, and financial management. Recurring features include news briefs and a calendar of related conferences and meetings.

U.S. Real Estate Register. Barry Inc., PO Box 551 Wilmington, MA 01887-0551. Phone: 800-752-1269 or (978)658-0441 Fax: (978)657-8691 E-mail: sales@barryinc.com • URL: http://www.usrealestateregister.com • Covers: real estate departments of large national companies, industrial economic/development organizations, utilities, real estate brokers, and railroads involved in commercial and industrial real estate development. Entries include: Company or organization name, address; many listings include name of contact.

United States Securities and Exchange Commission Annual Report. U.S. Government Printing Office, Washington, DC 20402. Phone: (202)512-1800 Fax: (202)512-2250 E-mail: gpoaccess@gpo.gov • URL: http://www.accessgpo.gov • Annual. The Commission maintains a Web site at http://www.sec.gov

The U.S. Skincare Market. Available from MarketResearch.com, 641 Ave. of the Americas, 3rd Fl. New York, NY 10011. Phone: 800-298-5699 or (212)807-2629 Fax: (212)807-2716 E-mail: order@marketresearch.com • URL: http://www.marketresearch.com • 2001. $2,750.00. Published by Packaged Facts. Provides market data on skincare products such as moisturizers, cleansers, and toners, with sales projections to 2005.

United States Statutes at Large. U.S. Office of the Federal Register. Available from U.S. Government Printing Office, Washington, DC 20402. Phone: (202)512-1800 Fax: (202)512-2250 E-mail: gpoaccess@gpo.gov • URL: http://www.accessgpo.gov • Annual. Price varies. Congressional acts and presidential proclamations issued during the Congressional session. For all laws in force at a specific date, refer to *United States Code*.

United States Telecom Association., 607 14th St. NW, Ste. 400 Washington, DC 20005. Phone: (202)326-7300 Fax: (202)315-3603 E-mail: membership@ustelecom.org • URL: http://www.usta.org • Local operating telephone companies or telephone holding companies. Members represent a total of 114 million access lines. Conducts educational and training programs. Maintains 21 committees.

United States Tennis Association., 70 W Red Oak Ln. White Plains, NY 10604. Phone: 800-990-8782 or (914)696-7000 Fax: (914)696-7167 E-mail: eliezer@usta.com • URL: http://www.usta.com • Federation of local tennis clubs, educational institutions, recreation departments, and other groups and individuals interested in the promotion of tennis. Works to develop tennis as a means of healthful recreation and physical fitness and maintain high standards of fair play and sportsmanship. Sanctions thousands of tennis tournaments for all age groups throughout the U.S. each year. Sponsors Junior Program for boys and girls under 18 years of age; U.S. national tennis team; national championships for various age groups; National Circuit tournament for pro and amateur players; Davis Cup, Fed Cup, Olympics international matches; and adult recreational leagues. Compiles statistics on leading professional and amateur players.

United States Timber Production, Trade, Consumption, And Price Statistics. Forest Service. U.S. Department of Agriculture, Washington, DC 20250. Phone: (202)205-2791 Annual.

United States Tuna Foundation., 7918 Jones Branch Dr., Ste. 700 McLean, VA 22102. Phone: (703)752-8880 Fax: (202)331-9686 E-mail: eliezer@usta.com • URL: http://www.tunafacts.com • Represents tuna boat owners, fishermen, processors, fishermen's unions, and cannery workers' unions. Analyzes all matters related to or affecting the industry as a whole.

United States Waterborne Exports and General Imports. U.S. Bureau of the Census, Washington, DC 20233-0800. Phone: (301)457-4100 Fax: (301)457-3842 • URL: http://www.census.gov • Quarterly and annual.

U.S. Wheat Associates., 3103 10th St. N, Ste. 300 Arlington, VA 22201. Phone: (202)463-0999 Fax: (703)524-4399 E-mail: info@uswheat.org • URL: http://www.uswheat.org • Works as the industry export market development organization.

The U.S. Wine Market: Impact Databank Review and Forecast. M. Shanken Communications, Inc., 387 Park Ave., S New York, NY 10016. Phone: 800-344-0763 or (212)684-4424 Fax: (212)684-5424 E-mail: retailsales@mshanken.com • URL: http://www.mshanken.com • Annual. $845.00. Includes industry commentary and statistics.

United Steelworkers of America. Aluminum, Brick and Glassworkers Division.

United Way Annual Report. United Way of America, 701 N. Fairfax St. Alexandria, VA 22314. Phone: (703)836-7100 Fax: (703)683-7840 • URL: http://www.unitedway.org • Annual. Price on application.

United Way of America., 701 N. Fairfax St. Alexandria, VA 22314. Phone: (703)836-7112 Fax: (703)683-7840 • URL: http://www.national.unitedway.org • Formerly United Community Funds and Councils of America.

United Weighers Association., PO Box 1027 Floral Park, NY 11002. Phone: (516)352-2673 Fax: (516)352-3569 E-mail: info@uswheat.org Weighers and supervisors of raw commodities (sugar, coffee, cocoa, rubber, tin, and wool) imported to U.S. by ship.

Universal Cooperatives., 1300 Corporate Center Curve Eagan, MN 55121. Phone: (651)239-1000 Fax: (651)239-1080 E-mail: info@ucoop.com • URL: http://www.ucoop.com • Works as a federation of regional agricultural cooperative associations. Engages in buying, manufacturing, importing and distributing activities. Focuses on tires, batteries, and accessories; twine; farm supplies; lubricants; animal health products; agricultural chemicals.

The Universal Healthcare Almanac: A Complete Guide for the Healthcare Professional - Facts, Figures, Analysis. Silver & Cherner, Ltd., 10221 N. 32nd St., Suite D Phoenix, AZ

85028-3849. Phone: (602)996-2220 Fax: (602)996-2330 E-mail: uhaeditor@aol.com $195.00 per year. Looseleaf service. Quarterly updates. Includes a wide variety of health care statistics: national expenditures, hospital data, health insurance, health professionals, vital statistics, demographics, etc. Years of coverage vary, with long range forecasts provided in some cases.

University Aviation Association., 3410 Skyway Dr. Auburn, AL 36830. Phone: (334)844-2434 Fax: (334)844-2432 E-mail: uaamail@uaa.aero • URL: http://www.uaa.aero • Professional organization of educators, industry representatives, institutions and corporations interested in promoting aviation education at the higher education level. Fosters exchange and dissemination of information among colleges and governmental and industrial organizations in the aerospace field. Supports aerospace-oriented teacher education. Sponsors research programs and compiles statistics.

University Business: Solutions for Today's Higher Education. Educational Media Inc., 488 Main Ave. Norwalk, CT 06851. Phone: (203)847-7200 Fax: (203)846-1866 E-mail: general@universitybusiness.com • URL: http://www.universitybusiness.com • 10 times a year. $60.00 per year. Edited for college administrators, including managers of business services, finance, computing, and telecommunications. Includes information on relevant technological advances.

University Continuing Education Association., 1 Dupont Cir., Ste. 615 Washington, DC 20036. Phone: (202)659-3130 Fax: (202)785-0374 E-mail: kjkohl@ucea.edu • URL: http://www.ucea.edu • Institutions of higher education, both public and private, that offer professional and continuing education programs, both degree and non-degree, to nontraditional students at the pre and post baccalaureate levels. Offers accelerated learning opportunities to practitioners through professional development seminars, modules and conferences. Collects and disseminates data on continuing education programs and trends. Compiles statistics on the field. Only those individuals who work for a member institution are eligible to become professional members.

University of California, San Diego., Scripps Institution of Oceanography, Integrative Oceanography Div., 9500 Gilman Dr. La Jolla, CA 92093-0227. Phone: (858)534-2068 Fax: (858)534-6500 E-mail: evenriek@ucsd.edu • URL: http://www.mlrg.ucsd.edu/ • Formerly *Marine Life Research Group*.

University Professors for Academic Order.

University Science and Engineering Libraries. Ellis Mount. Greenwood Publishing Group, Inc., 88 Post Rd., W Westport, CT 06881. Phone: 800-225-5800 or (203)226-3571 Fax: (203)431-2214 E-mail: customer-service@greenwood.com • URL: http://www.greenwood.com • 1985. $67.00. Second edition. (Contributions in Librarianship and Information Science Series: No. 49).

UNIX and Windows 2000 Integration Toolkit: A Complete Guide for System Administrators and Developers. Rawn Shah. John Wiley and Sons, Inc., 111 River St. Hoboken, NJ 07030. Phone: 800-225-5945 or (201)748-6000 Fax: (201)748-6088 E-mail: info@jwiley.com • URL: http://www.wiley.com • 2000. $49.99. Includes CD-ROM.

UNIX and Windows 2000: Interoperability Guide. Alan Roberts. Prentice Hall PTR, 240 Frisch Ct. Paramus, NJ 07652. Phone: 800-282-0693 Fax: 800-445-6991 • URL: http://www.phptr.com • 2001. $34.99. (Hewlett-Packard Professional Books).

Unix Secrets. James Armstrong., New York, NY 10158-0012. Phone: 800-225-5945 or (212)850-6000 Fax: (212)850-6088 E-mail: bookinfo@wiley.com • URL: http://www.wiley.com • 1999. $39.99. Second edition. (UNIX Secrets Series).

UNIX System Administration Handbook. Evi Nemeth and others. Prentice Hall PTR, 240 Frisch Ct. Paramus, NJ 07652. Phone: 800-282-0693 Fax: 800-445-6991 • URL: http://www.phptr.com • 1995. $110.00. Second edition. Includes CD-ROM.

UNIX Unbounded: A Beginning Approach. Amir Afzal. Prentice Hall PTR, 240 Frisch Ct. Paramus, NJ 07652. Phone: 800-282-0693 Fax: 800-445-6991 • URL: http://www.phptr.com • 2002. $96.00. Fourth edition.

UNIX Weekend Crash Course. Arthur Griffith. John Wiley and Sons, Inc., 111 River St. Hoboken, NJ 07030. Phone: 800-225-5945 or (201)748-6000 Fax: (201)748-6088 E-mail: info@wiley.com • URL: http://www.wiley.com • 2002. $24.99. Covers UNIX in 30 "easy lessons" (15 hours). Topics range from "The Many Flavors of UNIX" to "Archiving and Compressing Files." Includes CD-ROM with general UNIX utilities and resources, security utilities, code examples, and an assessment test to gauge progress. (Weekend Crash Course Series).

Unmasking Administrative Evil. Guy B. Adams and Danny L. Balfour. M. E. Sharpe, Inc., 80 Business Park Drive Armonk, NY 10504. Phone: 800-541-6563 or (914)273-1800 Fax: (914)273-2106 E-mail: custserv@mesharpe.com • URL: http://www.mesharpe.com • 2004. $59.95. Revised edition. Discusses bureaucratic mismanagement and the resulting evil or even tragedy.

Unofficial Business Traveler's Pocket Guide: 249 Tips Even the Best Business Travelers May Not Know. Christopher J. McGinnis. McGraw-Hill, 1221 Ave. of the Americas New York, NY 10020. Phone: 800-722-4726 or (212)512-2000 Fax: (212)512-4502 E-mail: customer.service@mcgraw-hill.com • URL: http://www.mcgraw-hill.com • 1998. $10.95. Arranged by subject categories, such as airports, frequent traveler programs, eating, and staying well.

Upgrade. Software and Information Industry Association, 1730 M St., NW, Ste. 700 Washington, DC 20036-4510. Phone: (202)452-1600 Fax: (202)223-8756 E-mail: orders@siia.net • URL: http://www.siia.net • Monthly. $79.00 per year. Covers news and trends relating to the software, information, and Internet industries. Formerly *SPA News* from Software Publisers Association.

Upholstered Furniture Action Council., Box 2436 High Point, NC 27261. Phone: (336)885-5065 Fax: (336)885-5072 E-mail: info@ufac.org • URL: http://www.ufac.org • Conducts research and disseminates information regarding the development and adoption of voluntary guidelines for production of more cigarette-resistant upholstered furniture; educates the public in the safe use of smoking materials. Maintains speakers' bureau; compiles statistics.

Upholstering Fundamentals. Clois E. Kicklighter and Joan C. Klicklighter. Goodheart-Willcox Publishers, 18604 W. Creek Dr. Tinley Park, IL 60477-6243. Phone: 800-323-0440 or (708)687-5000 Fax: (708)687-5068 E-mail: custserv@goodheartwillcox.com • URL: http://www.goodheartwillcox.com • 2000. $33.28. *Answer Key?*, $4.00.

Upjohn Center for Clinical Pharmacology. University of Michigan

Uranium: Resources, Production, and Demand. Organization for Economic Cooperation and Development, OECD Washington Center, 2001 L St., N. W., Suite 650 Washington, DC 20036-4922. Phone: 800-456-6323 or (202)785-6323 Fax: (202)785-0350 E-mail: washington.contact@oecd.org • URL: http://www.oecd.org • Annual. $77.00. Produced by the OECD Nuclear Energy Agency and the International Atomic Energy Agency. Provides detailed statistics and trend analysis for uranium based on official information from 49 countries.

Urban Affairs Review. Sage Publications, Inc., 2455 Teller Rd. Thousand Oaks, CA 91320. Phone: 800-818-7243 or (805)499-9774 Fax: 800-583-2665 or (805)499-0871 E-mail: webmaster@sagepub.com • URL: http://www.sagepub.com • Bimonthly. Institutions, $601.00 per year; includes print and online editions. Formerly *Urban Affairs Quarterly*.

Urban Economics and Land Use in America: The Transformation of Cities in the Twentieth Century. Alan Rabinowitz. M. E. Sharpe, Inc., 80 Business Park Drive Armonk, NY 10504. Phone: 800-541-6563 or (914)273-1800 Fax: (914)273-2106 E-mail: custserv@mesharpe.com • URL: http://www.mesharpe.com • 2004. $72.95. Covers suburbanization and its problems from 1900 to modern times.

Urban Environment Conference., 7620 Morningside Dr. NW Washington, DC 20012. Phone: (202)726-8111 E-mail: information@sierraclub.org National labor, minority, and environmental organizations. Lobbies in Washington, DC, and at a grass roots level for strong environmental and occupational health laws. Offers educational programs to enable minorities, workers, and others to participate more effectively in decisions affecting their health and interests.

Urban Institute. Urban Institute, 2100 M St. NW Washington, DC 20037. Phone: (202)833-7200 Fax: (202)728-0232 E-mail: paffairs@ui.urban.org • URL: http://www.urban.org • Domestic, social, and economic affairs, including multidisciplinary studies and government program evaluations in the areas of tax and budget reform, education policy, health policy, crime and justice, housing and community development, labor and human services, income security and retirement, welfare reform, international activities, nonprofit sector and philanthropy, public finance, productivity and economic development, social services, and immigration. Also conducts research programs on employment and training, children's issues and family policy, minorities and social policy, poverty, state and local governments, and community impact and demography.

Urban Land Institute. Urban Land Institute, 1025 Thomas Jefferson St. NW, Ste. 500 W Washington, DC 20007. Phone: (202)624-7000 Fax: (202)624-7140 E-mail: customerservice@uli.org • URL: http://www.uli.org • Urban land use policy, planning, and development issues, including studies on central city problems, industrial development, new community development, residential developments of all types, taxation, smart growth, shopping center development and economics, metropolitan and urbanized area growth and development, mixed use development, and environmental factors affecting development.

Urban Land: News and Trends in Land Development. Urban Land Institute, 1025 Thomas Jefferson St., NW, Ste. 500 W Washington, DC 20007-5201. Phone: 800-321-5011 or (202)624-7000 Fax: (202)624-7140 • URL: http://www.uli.org • Monthly. Membership.

Urban Parks and Open Space. Gayle L. Berens and others. Urban Land Institute, 1025 Thomas Jefferson St., NW, Ste. 500 W Washington, DC 20007-5201. Phone: 800-321-5011 or (202)624-7000 Fax: (202)624-7140 • URL: http://www.uli.org • 1997. $40.95. Covers financing, design, management, and public-private partnerships relative to the development of open space for new urban parks. Includes color illustrations and the history of urban parks.

Urban Revitalization: Policies and Prgrams. Timothy E. Joder. Sage Publications, Inc., 2455 Teller Rd. Thousand Oaks, CA 91320. Phone: 800-818-7243 or (805)499-9774 Fax: 800-583-2665 or (805)499-0871 E-mail: webmaster@sagepub.com • URL: http://www.sagepub.com • 1995. $76.95.

Urban Transport News: Management-Funding Terrorism-Ridership-Technology. Business Publishers, Inc., 8737 Colesville Rd., Suite 1100 Silver Spring, MD 20910-3928. Phone: 800-274-6737 or (301)587-6300 Fax: (301)589-8493 E-mail: bpinews@bpinews.com • URL: http://www.bpinews.com • 25 times a year. $437.00 per year. Newsletter. Provides current news from Capitol Hill, the White House, the Dept. of Transportation, as well as transit operations and industries across the country.

Urethanes Technology. Crain Communications, Inc., New Garden House, 78 Hatton Garden London EC1N 8JD, United Kingdom. Phone: 44 207 457 1440 E-mail: info@crain.com • URL: http://www.crain.com • Bimonthly. $108.00 per year. Covers the international polyurethane industry.

Urethanes Technology. Crain Communications Ltd., 34 Southwark Bridge Rd. London SE1 9EU, United Kingdom. Phone: 800-678-9595 or 44 207 4571400 Fax: 44 207 4571400 E-mail: info@crain.com • URL: http://www.crain.co.uk • Bimonthly. $108.00 per year.

US Apple Association., 8233 Old Courthouse Rd., Ste. 200 Vienna, VA 22182. Phone: 800-781-4443 or (703)442-8850 Fax: (703)790-0845 E-mail: jdaly@usapple.org • URL: http://www.usapple.org • Formerly International Apple Institute.

US Workders Flint Glass Conference.

USA Funds., 555 Fairmount Ave., Ste. 310 Towson, MD 21286. Phone: 800-824-7044 or (317)849-6510 Fax: (317)951-5072 E-mail: contact@usafunds.org • URL: http://www.usafunds.org • USA Funds is a nonprofit corporation guaranteeing low-cost loans from about 10,000 lenders. Approximately 1,000 colleges participate.

U.S.A. Oil Industry Directory. PennWell Publishing Co., 1455 W Loop S, Ste. 400 Houston, TX 77027. Phone: 800-736-6935 or (713)621-9720 Fax: (713)963-6296 E-mail: petroleum@pennwell.com • URL: http://www.pennwell.com • Covers: over 4,000 associations, brokers/dealers, drilling contractors, explorers, producers, gas processors/treaters, government agencies, marketing companies, refineries, and other companies related to the oil industry. Entries include: Name, address, phone, fax, e-mail, URL, key personnel, and brief company synopsis.

USA Today Weather Book. Jack Williams. Random House, Inc., 1745 Broadway New York, NY 10036. Phone: 800-726-0600 or (212)782-9000 Fax: 800-659-2436 E-mail: customerservice@randomhouse.com • URL: http://www.randomhouse.com • 1997. $20.00. Contains a state-by-state guide to U. S. climate, with color illustrations. Author (weather editor of *USA Today*) includes discussions of weather patterns and computerized forecasting.

USA Trade. U. S. Department of Commerce, Economics and Statistics Administration, Office of Business Analysis Washington, DC 20230. Phone: 800-782-8872 or (202)482-1986 Fax: (202)482-2164 Monthly. $650.00 per year. Provides over 150,000 trade-related data series on CD-ROM. Includes full text of many government publications. Specific data is included on national income, labor, price indexes, foreign exchange, technical standards, and international markets. Website address is http://www.stat-usa.gov/

USAN and the USP Dictionary of Drug Names. United States Pharmacopeial Convention, 12601 Twinbrook Parkway Rockville, MD 20852. Phone: 800-227-8772 or (301)881-0666 Fax: (301)816-8299 E-mail: jac@usp.org • URL: http://www.usp.org • Annual. $279.00. Adopted names, brand names, compendial and other generic names, CAS Registry Numbers, molecular weights, and other information.

USDA. United States Department of AgriculturePhone: (202)720-2791 E-mail: agsec@usda.gov • URL: http://www.usda.gov • The USDA home page has six sections: News and Information; What's New; About USDA; Agencies; Opportunities; Search and Help. Keyword searching is offered from the USDA home page and from various individual agency home pages. Agencies are the Economic Research Service, Agricultural Marketing Service, National Agricultural Statistics Service, National Agricultural Library, and about 12 others. Updating varies. Fees: Free.

Used Book Store. Entrepreneur Media, Inc., 2445 McCabe Way Irvine, CA 92614. Phone: 800-421-2300 or (949)261-2325 Fax: (949)261-0234 E-mail: entmag@entrepreneur.com • URL: http://www.entrepreneur.com • Looseleaf. $59.50. A practical guide to starting a used book store. Covers profit potential, start-up costs, market size evaluation, owner's time required, site selection, lease negotiation, pricing, accounting, advertising, promotion, etc. (Start-Up Business Guide No. E1117.)

Used Car Dealer. National Independent Automobile Dealers Association, 2521 Brown Blvd. Arlington, TX 76006-5203. Phone: 800-682-3837 or (817)640-3838 Fax: (817)649-5866 E-mail: mike@niada.com • URL: http://www.niada.com • Monthly. Free to members; non-members, $60.00 per year.

Used-Car Rental Agency. Entrepreneur Media, Inc., 2445 McCabe Way Irvine, CA 92614. Phone: 800-421-2300 or (949)261-2325 Fax: (949)261-0234 E-mail: entmag@entrepreneur.com • URL: http://www.entrepreneur.com • Looseleaf. $59.50. A practical guide to starting a used-car rental business. Covers profit potential, start-up costs, market size evaluation, owner's time required, site selection, lease negotiation pricing, accounting, advertising, promotion, etc. (Start-Up Business Guide No. E1108.)

Used Car Sales. Entrepreneur Media, Inc., 2445 McCabe Way Irvine, CA 92614. Phone: 800-421-2300 or (949)261-2325 Fax: (949)261-0234 E-mail: entmag@entrepreneur.com •

URL: http://www.entrepreneur.com • Looseleaf. $59.50. A practical guide to getting started in the business of selling used cars. Covers profit potential, start-up costs, market size evaluation, owner's time required, site selection, lease negotiation, pricing, accounting, advertising, etc. (Start-Up Business Guide No. E2330.)

Used Equipment Directory. Penton Technology and Lifestyle Media Inc., 45 Eisenhower Dr., 5th Fl., Ste. 550 Paramus, NJ 07652. Phone: 800-526-6052 or (201)843-6511 Fax: (201)845-2482 E-mail: information@penton.com • URL: http://www.penton.com • Publication includes: List of 800 dealers in used metalworking, electrical, power, process, and material handling equipment, woodworking and machine tools. Entries include: Company name, address, phone; principal executive; types of equipment handled; description of machinery offered. Principal content is approximately 30,000 paid listings of used equipment for sale, classified by type.

U.S.English., 1747 Pennsylvania Ave. NW, Ste. 1050 Washington, DC 20006. Phone: 800-873-4547 or (202)833-0100 Fax: (202)833-0108 E-mail: info@usenglish.org • URL: http://www.us-english.org • Aims to preserve the common bond by making English the official language of government in the U.S. Promotes opportunities for people living here to learn English.

USENIX Association., 2560 9th St., Ste. 215, 2560 Ninth St., Ste. 215 Berkeley, CA 94710. Phone: (510)528-8649 Fax: (510)548-5738 E-mail: office@usenix.org • URL: http://www.usenix.org • Individuals with an interest in Advanced Computing Systems in a professional or technical capacity; and (commercial computer firms) institutions, colleges and universities, and research institutes. Promotes innovation in advanced computing systems; fosters the development of research and technological information pertaining to advanced computer systems.

Using Bar Code: Why It's Taking Over. David J. Collins and Nancy N. Whipple. Data Capture Press, 225 Water St. Plymouth, MA 02360. Phone: 800-733-7592 or (508)746-5120 Fax: (508)746-7193 E-mail: inquiry@datacaptureinstitute.com • URL: http://www.datacaptureinstitute.com • 1994. $34.95. Second edition.

Using Computers: A Gateway to Information. Gary B. Shelley and others. Course Technology, 25 Thompson Place Boston, MA 02210. Phone: 800-648-7450 or (617)757-7900 E-mail: reply@course.com • URL: http://www.course.com • 1995. $44.00. Second edition.

Using Desktop Publishing to Create Newsletters, Library Guides, and Web Pages: A How-To-Do-It Manual for Librarians. John Maxymuk. Neal-Schuman Publishers, Inc., 100 William St., Ste. 2004 New York, NY 10038. Phone: (866)672-6657 or (212)925-8650 Fax: (866)209-7932 or (212)219-8916 E-mail: info@neal-schuman.com • URL: http://www.neal-schuman.com • 1997. $55.00. Includes more than 90 illustrations. (How-to-Do-It Manuals Series).

Using Econometrics: A Practical Guide. Addison-Wesley, 75 Arlington St., Ste. 300 Boston, MA 02116. Phone: 800-447-2226 or (617)848-7500 • URL: http://www.aw.com • 2000. $114.00. Fourth edition. (Economics Series).

Using Government Documents: A How-To-Do-It Manual for School Librarians. Melody S. Kelly. Neal-Schuman Publishers, Inc., 100 William St., Ste. 2004 New York, NY 10038. Phone: (866)672-6657 or (212)925-8650 Fax: (866)209-7932 or (212)219-8916 E-mail: info@neal-schuman.com • URL: http://www.neal-schuman.com • 1992. $27.50. (How-to-Do-It Manuals Series).

Using Government Information Sources, Electronic and Print. Marilyn K. Moody and Jean L. Sears. Greenwood Publishing Group, Inc., 88 Post Rd., W. Westport, CT 06881. Phone: 800-225-5800 or (203)226-3571 Fax: (203)431-2214 E-mail: customer-service@greenwood.com • URL: http://www.greenwood.com • 2001. $125.00. Third edition. Contains detailed information in four sections on subject searches, agency searches, statistical searches, and special techniques for searching. Appendixes give selected agency and publisher addresses, telephone numbers, and computer communications numbers.

Using Technical Analysis: A Step-by-Step Guide to Understanding and Applying Stock Market. Clifford Pistolese. McGraw-Hill, 1221 Ave. of the Americas New York, NY 10020. Phone: 800-722-4726 or (212)512-2000 Fax: (212)512-4502 E-mail: customer.service@mcgraw-hill.com • URL: http://www.mcgraw-hill.com • 1994. $32.95. Revised edition.

Using Technology to Increase Student Learning. Linda E. Reksten. Corwin Press, Inc., 2455 Teller Rd. Thousand Oaks, CA 91320-2218. Phone: 800-818-7243 or (805)499-9734 Fax: (805)449-0871 E-mail: info@sagepub.com • URL: http://www.corwinpress.com • 2000. $74.95. Emphasis is on the use of computer technology in schools. (Technology Series).

Using the Agricultural, Environmental, and Food Literature. Barbara S. Hutchinson and Antoinette P. Greider, editors. Marcel Dekker, Inc., 270 Madison Ave. New York, NY 10016. Phone: 800-228-1160 or (212)696-9000 Fax: (212)685-4540 E-mail: bookorders@dekker.com • URL: http://www.dekker.com • 2002. $125.00. Serves as a guide to both print and electronic sources of information.

Using the Financial and Business Literature. Thomas P. Slavens. Marcel Dekker, Inc., 270 Madison Ave. New York, NY 10016. Phone: 800-228-1160 or (212)696-9000 Fax:

(212)685-4540 E-mail: bookorders@dekker.com • URL: http://www.dekker.com • 2004. $165.00. Provides detailed descriptions of both print and electronic information sources. (Books in Library and Information Science Series/64.)

Using Windows for Library Administration. Kenneth E. Marks and Steven P. Nielson. Information Today, Inc., 143 Old Marlton Pike Medford, NJ 08055-8750. Phone: 800-300-9868 or (609)654-6266 Fax: (609)654-4309 E-mail: custserv@infotoday.com • URL: http://www.infotoday.com • 1997. $34.95. Contains details on the use of Microsoft Windows software applications for library management: spreadsheets, desktop publishing, project planning, forms, etc.

Utilities Industry Litigation Reporter: National Coverage of the Many Types of Litigation Stemming From the Transmission and Distribution of Energy By Publicly and Privately Owned Utilities. Andrews Publications, 175 Strafford Ave., Bldg. 4, Suite 140 Wayne, PA 19087. Phone: 800-345-1101 or (610)225-0510 Fax: (610)225-0501 E-mail: customer@andrewspub.com • URL: http://www.andrewspub.com • Monthly. $775.00 per year. Newsletter. Reports on legal cases involving the generation or distribution of energy.

Utility Automation. PennWell Corp., Industrial Div., 1421 S. Sheridan Rd. Tulsa, OK 74112. Phone: 800-331-4643 or (918)835-3161 E-mail: bid@pennwell.com • URL: http://www.pennwell.com • 10 times a year. $69.00 per year; schools and public libraries, $10.00 per year. Covers new information technologies for electric utilities, including automated meter reading, distribution management systems, and customer information systems.

Utility Automation Buying Guide. Pennwell Corp., Industrial Div., 1421 S. Sheridan Rd. Tulsa, OK 74112. Phone: 800-331-4643 or (918)835-3161 E-mail: bid@pennwell.com • URL: http://www.pennwell.com • Annual. Price on application. A directory of information technology products and services for electric utility companies.

Utility Communicators International., 1818 Country Creek Ct., 5525 E Grandview Dr. Magnolia, TX 77354. Phone: (936)271-5005 Fax: (936)271-5060 E-mail: eboardman@att.net • URL: http://www.uci-online.com • Advertising and public relations directors of electric, gas, water, telephone, and other utility companies and allied industries. Sponsors utility advertising/communications contest.

Vacation Study Abroad. Institute of International Education Inc., 809 United Nations Plz. New York, NY 10017-3580. Phone: 800-445-0443 or (212)883-8200 Fax: (212)984-5452 E-mail: iiebooks@iie.org • URL: http://www.iie.org • Covers: more than 2,200 college-level and adult education summer and short-term courses sponsored by United States and foreign colleges, language schools, and private and public organizations. Courses run from as briefly as two weeks to three months. Entries include: Name of institution or other sponsor, inclusive dates, subjects offered, orientation information, language of instruction, whether United States college credit is offered and how much, related travel, housing, costs, scholarships, work-study or internship opportunities, deadline, phone, fax, e-mail, website and address for application.

Vacuum Cleaner Manufacturers Association., 1300 Sumner Ave. Cleveland, OH 44115. Phone: (216)241-7333 Fax: (216)241-0105 E-mail: eboardman@att.net • URL: http://www.vacuumcleaners.org • Manufacturers of household electric floor-care products, including vacuum cleaners and soil extractors. Publications: none.

Valuating Information Intangibles: Measuring the Bottom Line Contribution of Librarians and Information Professionals. Frank H. Portugal. Special Libraries Association, 1700 18th St., N. W. Washington, DC 20009-2514. Phone: (202)234-4700 Fax: (202)265-9317 E-mail: sla@sla.org • URL: http://www.sla.org • 2000. $79.00. Focuses on the importance of the intangible aspects of appraising information resources and services.

Valuation: Measuring and Managing the Value of Companies. Tom Copeland and others. John Wiley and Sons, Inc., 111 River St. Hoboken, NJ 07030. Phone: 800-225-5945 or (201)748-6000 Fax: (201)748-6088 E-mail: info@wiley.com • URL: http://www.wiley.com • 2000. $115.00. Third editon. A practical guide to economic value analysis for bankers, accountants, financial analysts, and others concerned with company valuation. Includes CD-ROM. (Frontiers in Finance Series).

Valuation Strategies in Divorce: Cumulative Supplement. Robert D. Feder. Aspen Publishers, Inc., 200 Orchard Ridge Dr., Ste. 200 Gaithersburg, MD 20878. Phone: 800-234-1660 or (301)417-7500 Fax: (201)748-6088 E-mail: customer.service@aspenpubl.com • URL: http://www.aspenpublishers.com • 2002. Fourth edition. Explains the basic principles of asset valuation in divorce cases. Discusses financial statements, tax returns, retirement benefits, real estate, and personal property.

Value Line Convertible Data Base. Value Line Publishing, Inc., 220 East 42nd St. New York, NY 10017. Phone: 800-654-0508 or (212)907-1550 Fax: (212)907-1922 Provides online data for about 600 convertible bonds and other convertible securities: price, yield, premium, issue size, liquidity, and maturity. Information is current, with weekly updates. Inquire as to online cost and availability.

The Value Line Investment Survey. Value Line Publishing, Inc., 220 E 42nd St., 6th Fl. New York, NY 10017-5891. Phone: 800-223-0818 or (212)907-1500 Fax: (212)818-9474 • URL:

http://www.valueline.com • Weekly. $570.00 per year. Newsletter. Provides detailed information and ratings for 1,700 stocks actively-traded in the U. S.

Value Line Mutual Fund Survey. Value Line Publishing, Inc., 220 E 42nd St., 6th Fl. New York, NY 10017-5891. Phone: 800-223-0818 or (212)907-1500 Fax: (212)818-9474 • URL: http://www.valueline.com • Every three weeks. $345.00 per year. Looseleaf service. Provides ratings and detailed performance information for 2,300 equity and fixed income funds.

Value Line Options: the All-in-One Service for Listed Options. Value Line Publishing, Inc., 220 E 42nd St., 6th Fl. New York, NY 10017-5891. Phone: 800-223-0818 or (212)907-1500 Fax: (212)818-9747 E-mail: vloptions@valueline.com • URL: http://www.valueline.com • Weekly. $445.00 per year. Formerly *Value Line Option and Convertible Survey*.

The Value of a Dollar: Millenium Edition. Scott Derks, editor. Grey House Publishing, Inc., 185 Millerton Rd. Millerton, NY 12546. Phone: 800-562-2139 or (518)789-8700 Fax: (518)789-0556 E-mail: books@greyhouse.com • URL: http://www.greyhouse.com • 1999. $135.00. Second edition.

The Value of a Dollar: Millennium Edition, 1860-1999. Grey House Publishing, 185 Millerton Rd. Millerton, NY 12546. Phone: 800-562-2139 or (518)789-8700 Fax: (518)789-0556 E-mail: books@greyhouse.com • URL: http://www.greyhouse.com • 1999. $135.00. Second edition. Shows the actual prices of thousands of items available to consumers from the Civil War era to recent years. Includes selected data on consumer expenditures, investments, income, and jobs. (Universal Reference Publications.)

Value of New Construction Put in Place. U.S. Bureau of the Census. Available from U.S. Government Printing Office, Washington, DC 20402. Phone: (202)512-1800 Fax: (202)512-2250 E-mail: gpoaccess@gpo.gov • URL: http://www.access.gpo.gov • Monthly. $42.00 per year.

Value Retail News: The Journal of Outlet and Off-Price Retail and Development. Off-Price Specialists, Inc. Value Retail News, 29399 U.S. Highway 19 N., Suite 370 Clearwater, FL 33773-2138. Phone: (727)536-4047 Fax: (727)536-4389 Monthly. Members, $144.00 per year; non-members, $175.00 per year. Provides news of the off-price and outlet store industry. Emphasis is on real estate for outlet store centers.

Value Shift: Merging Social and Financial Imperatives to Achive Superior Performance. Lynn S. Paine. McGraw-Hill, 1221 Ave. of the Americas New York, NY 10020. Phone: 800-722-4726 or (212)512-2000 Fax: (212)512-4502 E-mail: customer.service@mcgraw-hill.com • URL: http://www.mcgraw-hill.com • 2002. $27.95. Emphasizes the financial merits of corporate social responsibility. (Teach Yourself Series).

Valuing a Business: Analysis and Appraisal of Closely Held Companies. Shannon P. Pratt and others. McGraw-Hill, 1221 Ave. of the Americas New York, NY 10020-1095. Phone: 800-722-4726 or (212)512-2000 Fax: (212)512-4502 E-mail: customer.service@mcgraw-hill.com • URL: http://www.mcgraw-hill.com • 2000. $95.00. Fourth edition. Includes information on how to appraise partial interests and how to write a valuation report.

Valuing Professional Practices: A Practitioner's Guide. Robert Reilly and Robert Schweihs. CCH, Inc., 2700 Lake Cook Rd. Riverwoods, IL 60015. Phone: 800-835-5224 or (847)267-7000 E-mail: cust_serv@cch.com • URL: http://www.cch.com • 1997. $99.00. Provides a basic introduction to estimating the dollar value of practices in various professional fields.

Valve Manufacturers Association of America., 1050 17th St., N.W., Suite 280 Washington, DC 20036. Phone: (202)331-8105 Fax: (202)296-0378 E-mail: vma@vma.org • URL: http://www.vma.org • Formerly Valve Manufacturers Association.

Van Dean Manual. Delmar Learning, 5 Maxwell Dr. Clifton Park, NY 12065. Phone: 800-998-7498 or (518)464-3500 Fax: (518)464-0357 • URL: http://www.delmarlearning.com • 1990. $36.95. (Cosmetology Series).

Vanguard Retirement Investing Guide: Charting Your Course to a Secure Retirement. McGraw-Hill, 1221 Ave. of the Americas New York, NY 10020. Phone: 800-722-4726 or (212)512-2000 Fax: (212)512-4502 E-mail: customer.service@mcgraw-hill.com • URL: http://www.mcgraw-hill.com • 1995. $24.95. Second edition. Covers saving and investing for future retirement. Topics include goal setting, investment fundamentals, mutual funds, asset allocation, defined contribution retirement savings plans, social security, and retirement savings strategies. Includes glossary and worksheet for retirement saving.

Vanity Fair. Conde Nast Publications, Inc., Four Times Square New York, NY 10034. Phone: 800-289-9330 or (212)286-2860 Fax: (212)880-8289 • URL: http://www.condenet.com • Monthly. $18.00 per year.

Vapor Trail's Boating News and International Yachting and Cruiser and Manufacturers Report. Gemini Productions, Ltd., 8962 Bainford Dr. Huntington Beach, CA 92646. Phone: (714)833-8003 Monthly. $24.00 per year.

Variety International Film Guide. Peter Cowie, editor. Silman-James Press, 3624 Shannon Rd. Los Angeles, CA 90027. Phone: (323)661-9922 Fax: (323)661-9933 E-mail: silmanjamespress@earthlink.net • URL: http://www.silmanjamespress.com • Annual. $24.95. Covers the "who, what, where, and when of the international film scene." Includes information from 70 countries on film festivals, top-grossing films, awards, schools, etc.

Variety: The International Entertainment Weekly. Reed Business Information, 360 Park Ave., S New York, NY 10010. Phone: 800-446-6551 or (646)746-6400 Fax: (646)746-7028 E-mail: corporatecommunications@reedbusiness.com • URL: http://www.reedbusiness.com • 50 times a year. $259.00 per year. Contains national and international news of show business, with emphasis on motion pictures and television. Includes *Market* and *Special Focus* issues.

Vatel Club., BP 271 L-9003 Ettelbruck, Luxembourg. Phone: (352)80 24 53 Fax: (352)80 98 97 E-mail: secretary@vatel.lu • URL: http://www.vatel.lu • Social club for chefs, cooks, and other members of the culinary profession.

Vegetable Growing: Traditional Methods. Arthur Billitt. Trans-Atlantic Publications, Inc., 311 Bainbridge St. Philadelphia, PA 19147. Phone: (215)925-5083 Fax: (215)925-1912 E-mail: order@transatlanticpub.com 1988. $55.00. Third edition.

Vegetables and Specialties Situation and Outlook. Available from U. S. Government Printing Office, Washington, DC 20402. Phone: (202)512-1800 Fax: (202)512-2250 E-mail: gpoaccess@gpo.gov • URL: http://www.access.gpo.gov • Three times a year. Issued by the Economic Research Service of the U. S. Department of Agriculture. Provides current statistical information on supply, demand, and prices.

Vehicle Leasing. Entrepreneur Media, Inc., 2445 McCabe Way Irvine, CA 92614. Phone: 800-421-2300 or (949)261-2325 Fax: (949)261-0234 E-mail: entmag@entrepreneur.com • URL: http://www.entrepreneur.com • Looseleaf. $59.50. A practical guide to starting an automobile leasing business. Covers profit potential, start-up costs, market size evaluation, owner's time required, site selection, lease negotiation, pricing, accounting, advertising, promotion, etc. (Start-Up Business Guide No. E2329.)

Vending Machines. U. S. Bureau of the Census, 4700 Silver Hill Rd. Washington, DC 20233-0001. Phone: (301)763-4636 E-mail: comments@census.gov • URL: http://www.census.gov • Annual. Provides data on value of manufacturers' shipments, quantity, exports, imports, etc. (Current Industrial Reports, MA-35U.)

Vending Times Buyers Guide and Directory. Vending Times Inc., 1375 Broadway, 6th Fl. New York, NY 10018. Phone: (212)302-4700 Fax: (212)221-3311 E-mail: subscriptions@vendingtimes.net • URL: http://www.vendingtimes.com • Annual. $35.00. Formerly *Vending Times International Buyers Guide and Directory*.

Vending Times Census of the Industry. Vending Times, Inc., 1375 Broadway, 6th Fl. New York, NY 10018. Phone: (212)302-4700 Fax: (212)221-3311 E-mail: subscriptions@vendingtimes.net • URL: http://www.vendingtimes.com/census • Annual. $25.00.

Vending Times: Vending-Feeding-Coffee Service-Music and Games. Vending Times, Inc., 1375 Broadway, 6th Fl. New York, NY 10018-7001. Phone: (212)302-4700 Fax: (212)221-3311 • URL: http://www.vendingtimes.com • Monthly. $35.00 per year. Incorporates *V-T Music and Games*.

Venezuela Company Handbook: Data on Major Listed Companies. Hoovers, Inc., 5800 Airport Blvd. Austin, TX 78752-3812. Phone: 800-486-8666 or (512)374-4500 Fax: (512)374-4501 E-mail: orders@hoovers.com • URL: http://www.hoovers.com • Annual. $29.95. Published by IMF Editora. Contains profiles of publicly traded companies in Venezuela. Includes information on local stock exchanges and the nation's economic situation. Text in English.

Venezuelan American Association of the United States., 30 Vesey St., Rm. 506 New York, NY 10007. Phone: (212)233-7776 Fax: (212)233-7779 E-mail: andean@nyct.net • URL: http://www.venezuelanamerican.org • Facilitates trade and investment between the U.S. and Venezuela. Formerly Venezuelan Chamber of Commerce of the United States.

Venture Capital: An Authoritative Guide for Investors, Entrepreneurs, and Managers. Douglas A. Lindgren. McGraw-Hill, 1221 Ave. of the Americas New York, NY 10020. Phone: 800-722-4726 or (212)512-2000 Fax: (212)512-4502 E-mail: customer.service@mcgraw-hill.com • URL: http://www.mcgraw-hill.com • 1998. $65.00.

Venture Capital Directory (Small Business Administation). Forum Publishing Co., 383 E. Main St. Centerport, NY 11721. Phone: (516)754-5000 Fax: (516)754-0630 E-mail: forum383@aol.com Annual. $12.95. Over 500 members of the Small Business Administration and the Small Business Investment. Companies that provide funding for small and minority businesses.

Venture Capital Journal. Venture Economics Inc., 195 Broadway New York, NY 10007. Phone: 888-605-3385 or (646)822-2000 Fax: (646)822-3230 E-mail: ve.cs@tfn.com • URL: http://www.tfn.com • Description: Hard news, analysis and data on the North American private equity market.

Vertical File Index: Guide to Pamphlets and References to Current Topics. H. W. Wilson Co., 950 University Ave. Bronx, NY 10452. Phone: 800-367-6770 or (718)588-8400 Fax: 800-590-1617 or (718)590-1617 E-mail: custserv@hwwilson.com • URL: http://www.hwwilson.com • 11 times a year. $115.00 per year. A subject and title index to selected pamphlet material.

Vertiflite. American Helicopter Society, Inc., 217 N. Washington St. Alexandria, VA 22314. Phone: (703)684-6777 Fax: (703)739-9279 E-mail: staff@vtol.org • URL: http://www.vtol.org/journal • Quarterly. $55.00 per year.

Vertiflite-American Helicopter Society Membership Directory. American Helicopter Society, Inc., 217 N. Washington St. Alexandria, VA 22314. Phone: (703)684-6777 Fax: (703)739-9279 E-mail: staff@vtol.org • URL: http://www.vtol.org • Annual. $45.00. Lists over 6,000 individuals and 150 companies concerned with vertical take off and landing craft.

Veterans Benefits Manual. LexisNexis Matthew Bender, 1275 Broadway Albany, NY 12204-4026. Phone: 800-424-4200 or (518)487-3000 Fax: 800-828-8341 or (518)487-3584 E-mail: customer.support@lexisnexis.com • URL: http://www.lexisnexis.com/matthewbender/ • 2003. $125.00. Compiled by the National Veterans Legal Service Program. Explains a wide range of benefits available from the U. S. Department of Veterans Affairs.

Veterans of Foreign Wars of the United States., 406 W. 34th St. Kansas, MO 64111. Phone: (816)756-3390 Fax: (816)968-1157 E-mail: info@vfw.org • URL: http://www.vfw.org • Affiliated with Ladies Auxiliary to the Veterans of Foreign Wars of the United States.

Veterinary Economics: Business Solutions for Practicing Veterinarians. Thomson Veterinary Healthcare Communications, 8033 Flint Lenexa, KS 66214. Phone: 800-255-6864 or (913)492-4300 Fax: (913)492-4157 E-mail: ve@vetmedpub.com • URL: http://www.vetmetpub.com • Monthly. Free to qualified personnel; others, $42.00 per year. Provides business management and financial articles for veterinarians.

VFW Magazine: Ensuring Rights, Recognition, and Remembrance. Veterans of Foreign Wars of the United States: Ensuring Rights Recognition and Remembrance, 406 W. 34th St. Kansas City, MO 64111. Phone: (816)756-3390 Fax: (816)968-1149 E-mail: info@vfw.org • URL: http://www.vfw.org • 11 times a year. Free to members; nonmembers,$10.00 per year. Events and general features.

Via Satellite. PBI Media, LLC, 1201 7 Locks Rd. Potomac, MD 20854. Phone: 800-777-5006 or (301)354-2000 Fax: (301)309-3847 E-mail: clientservices@pbimedia.com • URL: http://www.pbimedia.com • Monthly. $49.00 per year. Covers the communications satellite industry.

Vickers Directory of Institutional Investors. Vickers Stock Research Corp., 226 New York Ave. Huntington, NY 11743. Phone: 800-645-5043 or (631)-423-7710 Fax: (631)423-7715 E-mail: clientservices@vickers-stock.com • URL: http://www.vickers-stock.com • Semiannual. $195.00 per year. Detailed alphabetical listing of more than 4,000 U. S., Canadian, and foreign institutional investors. Includes insurance companies, banks, endowment funds, and investment companies. Formerly *Directory of Institutional Investors*.

Vickers On-Line. Vickers Stock Research Corp., 226 New York Ave. Huntington, NY 11743. Phone: 800-645-5043 or (516)423-7710 Fax: (516)423-7715 Provides detailed online information relating to insider trading and the securities holdings of institutional investors. Daily updates. Inquire as to online cost and availability.

Vickers Weekly Insider Report. Vickers Stock Research Corp., 98 Pratt Oval Glen Cove, NY 11542. Phone: 800-645-5043 or (516)945-0020 Fax: (516)945-0030 E-mail: sales@vickers-stock.com Description: Reports on stock insider transactions and maintains portfolios based on insider buy signals-96 up 68%.

Video and Television. Orion Research Corp., 14555 N. Scottsdale Rd., Suite 330 Scottsdale, AZ 85254-3457. Phone: 800-844-0759 Fax: 800-375-1315 E-mail: orion@bluebook.com • URL: http://www.netzone.com • Annual. $144.00. Quotes retail and wholesale prices of used video and TV equipment. Original list prices and years of manufacture are also shown.

Video Engineering. Arch Luther and Andrew Inglis. McGraw-Hill, 1221 Ave. of the Americas New York, NY 10020. Phone: 800-722-4726 or (212)512-2000 Fax: (212)512-4502 E-mail: customer.service@mcgraw-hill.com • URL: http://www.mcgraw-hill.com • 2000. $65.00. Third edition. Covers such topics as digital postproduction technology, streaming video on the Internet, digital HDTV, digital cameras, and satellite TV systems.

Video Investor. Kagan World Media, One Lower Ragsdale Dr. Building One, Ste. 130 Monterey, CA 93940. Phone: (831)624-1536 Fax: (831)625-3225 E-mail: info@kagan.com • URL: http://www.kagan.com • Description: Reports videocassette industry developments, including sales statistics and forecasts. Provides news of related conventions and events and focuses on sales and rentals of film product, performance of retail outlets, market shares of suppliers and distributors, the sale of chains and outlets, hardware revenues and sales, and laser disk technologies. **Remarks:** Also available via e-mail and fax.

Video Librarian: The Video Review Magazine. Video Librarian, 8705 Honeycomb Court, N.W. Seabeck, WA 98380. Phone: 800-692-2270 or (360)830-9345 Fax: (360)830-9346 E-mail: vidlib@videolibrarian.com • URL: http://www.videolibrarian.com • Bimonthly. $64.00 per year. $99.00 per year with online access to archives (15,000 reviews). Edited for public and school libraries. Each issue includes reviews of hundreds of video DVDs or cassettes, in various subject areas.

Video Recorder Dealers Directory. infoUSA, P.O. Box 27347 Omaha, NE 68127. Phone: 800-555-6124 or (402)593-4600 Fax: (402)331-5481 E-mail: internet@infousa.com Annual. Price on application. Lists over 1,106 dealers. Compiled from U.S. yellow pages.

Video Software Dealers Association., 16530 Ventura Blvd., Ste.

400 Encino, CA 91436-4551. Phone: 800-955-8732 or (818)385-1500 Fax: (818)385-0567 E-mail: vsdaoffice@vsda.org • URL: http://www.vsda.org • Retailers and distributors of videocassettes and videodiscs; associate members are major studios or independent companies that produce video programming and manufacturers of video games, accessories, and other goods and services for the video software industry. Represents and acts as spokesperson for the video software merchandising industry. Conducts statistical survey of video retailing; offers legal counsel representing members' interests in Washington, DC. Offers seminars on management and inventory control.

Video Source Book. Gale, 27500 Drake Rd. Farmington Hills, MI 48331-3535. Phone: 800-877-4253 or (248)699-4253 Fax: 800-414-5043 or (248)699-8065 E-mail: galeord@cengage.com • URL: http://gale.cengage.com • Covers: Approximately 160,000 videos covering more than 120,000 complete programs available from more than 2,100 distributors. Entries include: Video title, release year, description, run time, format, audience, MPAA rating, credits, producer, awards, distributor, price. Distributor's address and phone are given in a separate list.

Video Store Magazine. Advanstar Communications, 545 Boylston St. Boston, MA 02116. Phone: 888-527-7008 or (617)267-6500 Fax: (617)267-6900 E-mail: info@advanstar.com • URL: http://www.advanstar.com • Weekly. $105.99 per year.

Video Systems: Equipment Buyer's Guide. Primedia Business Magazines and Media, 9800 Metcalf Ave. Overland Park, KS 66212. Phone: 800-795-5445 or (913)341-1300 Fax: (913)967-1898 E-mail: subs@primediabusiness.com • URL: http://www.primediabusiness.com • Annual. $10.00. Lists approximately 1,000 manufacturers and suppliers of professional video equipment.

Video Systems: Guide to Production Services. Primedia Business Magazines and Media, 9800 Metcalf Ave. Overland Park, KS 66212. Phone: 800-795-5445 or (913)341-1300 Fax: (913)967-1898 E-mail: subs@primediabusiness.com • URL: http://www.primediabusiness.com • Annual. $10.00. Lists about 1,000 firms offering services to videotape production companies. Price on application.

Video Systems: The Magazine for Video Professionals. Primedia Business Magazines and Media, 9800 Metcalf ave. Overland Park, KS 66212. Phone: 800-795-5445 or (913)341-1300 Fax: (913)967-1898 E-mail: subs@primediabusiness.com • URL: http://www.primediabusiness.com • Monthly. $70.00 per year.

Video Technology News. Access Intelligence L.L.C., 4 Choke Cherry Rd., 2nd Fl. Rockville, MD 20850. Phone: 800-777-5006 or (301)354-2000 Fax: (301)309-3847 E-mail: info@accessintel.com • URL: http://www.pbimedia.com • Description: Reports on video technologies from a business point of view. Provides industry analyses and forecasts, reports on new products and emerging media trends. Covers legal and regulatory developments. **Remarks:** Incorporates the former FutureHome Technology News, merged December 1992.

Video Week: Devoted to the Business of Program Sales and Distribution for Videocassettes, Disc, Pay TV and Allied News Media. Warren Publishing Inc., 2115 Ward Ct., NW Washington, DC 20037. Phone: (202)872-9200 Fax: (202)293-3435 • URL: http://www.warrenpub.com • Weekly. $907.00 per year. Newsletter. Covers video industry news and corporate developments.

Videocassette Rental Store. Entrepreneur Media, Inc., 2445 McCabe Way Irvine, CA 92614. Phone: 800-421-2300 or (949)261-2325 Fax: (949)261-0234 E-mail: entmag@entrepreneur.com • URL: http://www.entrepreneur.com • Looseleaf. $59.50. A practical guide to starting a videocassette rental store. Covers profit potential, start-up costs, market size evaluation, owner's time required, site selection, lease negotiation, pricing, accounting, advertising, promotion, etc. (Start-Up Business Guide No. E1192.)

Videography. United Entertainment Media, 460 Park Ave. S., 9th Fl. New York, NY 10016. Phone: (212)378-0400 Fax: (212)378-2160 E-mail: mfoley@uemedia.com • URL: http://www.uemedia.com • Monthly. $72.00 per year. Edited for the professional video production industry. Covers trends in technique and technology.

Videolog. Muze, Inc., 304 Hudson St., 8th Floor New York, NY 10013. Phone: 800-456-7838 or (212)824-0300 Fax: (212)741-1246 E-mail: custsrv@muze.com • URL: http://www.muze.com • Annual. $250.00. Five volumes. Provides detailed information on more than 170,000 VHS and DVD video titles. Includes a "Directory of Stars and Directors" and 13 category sections.

Vinyl Sheet and Floor Tile. Available from MarketResearch.com, 641 Ave. of the Americas, 3rd Fl. New York, NY 10011. Phone: 800-298-5699 or (212)807-2629 Fax: (212)807-2716 E-mail: order@marketresearch.com • URL: http://www.marketresearch.com • 1997. $495.00. Market research report published by Specialists in Business Information. Presents vinyl flooring market data relative to demographics, sales growth, shipments, exports, imports, price trends, and end-use. Includes company profiles.

Violence at Work. Duncan Chappell and Vittorio Di Martino. International Labour Organization, 1828 L St., N.W., Suite 600 Washington, DC 20036-5121. Phone: (202)653-7652 Fax: (202)653-7687 E-mail: klee@ilo.org • URL: http://www.ilo.org/publns • 2000. $23.00. Second edition. Discusses guidelines, practices, and international legislation aimed at establishing violence-free workplace environments. Problems covered include aggression, assault, physical abuse, and sexual harassment.

Virtual Office Survival Handbook: What Telecommuters and Entrepreneurs Need to Succeed in Today's Nontraditional Workplace. Alice Bredin. John Wiley and Sons, Inc., 111 River St. Hoboken, NJ 07030. Phone: 800-225-5945 or (201)748-6000 Fax: (201)748-6088 E-mail: info@jwiley.com • URL: http://www.wiley.com • 1996. $16.95. Presents broad coverage of telecommuting considerations, including workplace customizing and the evaluation of electronic office equipment. Coping with distractions and psychological issues are discussed.

Virtual Realism. Michael Heim. Oxford University Press, 198 Madison Ave. New York, NY 10016. Phone: 800-451-7556 or (212)726-6000 Fax: (212)726-6440 E-mail: custserv@oup-usa.org • URL: http://www.oup-usa.org • 1998. $21.00. Discusses computer simulation and human/computer interaction.

Virtual Reality Annual International Symposium. IEEE Computer Society, 10662 Los Vacqueros Circle Los Alamitos, CA 90720-1264. Phone: 800-272-6657 or (714)821-8380 Fax: (714)821-4010 E-mail: csinfo@computer.org • URL: http://www.computer.org • Annual. $70.00.

Virtual Reality: Computers Mimic the Physical World. Sean M. Grady. Facts on File, Inc., 132 W 31st St., 17th Fl. New York, NY 10001. Phone: 800-322-8755 Fax: 800-678-3633 E-mail: custserv@factsonfile.com • URL: http://www.factsonfile.com • 1998. $25.00. (Science Sourcebooks Series.)

Virtual Reference Training: The Complete Guide to Providing Anytime, Anywhere Answers. Buff Hirko and Mary Bucher Ross. American Library Association, 50 East Huron St. Chicago, IL 60611-2795. Phone: 800-545-2433 or (312)944-6780 Fax: (312)440-9374 E-mail: editionsmarketing@ala.org • URL: http://www.ala.org • 2004. $42.00. Serves as a guide to effective, online library reference service. Emphasis is on staff training and "14 core competencies."

The Visible Librarian: Asserting Your Value with Marketing and Advocacy. Judith A. Siess. American Library Association, 50 E Huron St. Chicago, IL 60611-2795. Phone: 800-545-2433 or (312)944-6780 Fax: (312)440-9374 E-mail: ala@ala.org • URL: http://www.ala.org • 2003. $34.00. Contains practical advice on library public relations and marketing of services. The author is editor of *The One-Person Library: A Newsletter for Librarians and Management*.

Vision Research Center in Ophthalmology.

Vision: Revista Latinoamericana. Vision, Inc., 13 E. 75th St. New York, NY 10021. Phone: (915)203-6734 Fax: (915)254-8546 Semimonthly. $124.00 per year. A popular newsmagazine covering Latin American politics, economics, business, and culture. Text in Spanish.

Visons. Unified Abrasives Manufacturers Association, c/o Wherry Associates, 30200 Detroit Rd. Cleveland, OH 44145-1967. Phone: (440)889-0010 Fax: (440)892-1404 Irregular. Newsletter. Price on application.

The Visual Display of Quantitative Information. Edward R. Tufte. Graphics Press, P.O. Box 430 Cheshire, CT 06410. Phone: 800-822-2454 or (203)272-9187 Fax: (203)272-8600 2001. $40.00. Second edition. A classic work on the graphic display of numerical data, including many illustrations. The two parts are "Graphical Practice," and "Theory of Data Graphics."

Visual Sciences Center.

Vital and Health Statistics. Available from U. S. Government Printing Office, Washington, DC 20402. Phone: (202)512-1800 Fax: (202)512-2250 E-mail: gpoaccess@gpo.gov • URL: http://www.access.gpo.gov • Annual. Free. Lists government publications. (GPO Subject Bibliography Number 121).

Vital Signs [year]: The Trends That Are Shaping Our Future. Worldwatch Institute, 1776 Massachusetts Ave., N.W. Washington, DC 20036-1904. Phone: (202)452-1999 Fax: (202)296-7365 E-mail: worldwatch@worldwatch.org • URL: http://www.worldwatch.org • Annual. $14.95. Provides access to selected indicators showing social, economic, and environmental trends throughout the world. Includes data relating to food, energy, transportation, finance, population, and other topics.

Vital Speeches of the Day. City News Publishing Co., Inc., P.O. Box 1247 Mount Pleasant, SC 29465-1247. Phone: (843)881-8733 Fax: (843)881-4007 E-mail: vitalspeeches@awod.com • URL: http://www.votd.com • Bimonthly. $45.00 per year.

Vital Statistics of the United States. Public Health Service, U.S. Dept. of Health and Human Services. Available from U.S. Government Printing Office, Washington, DC 20402. Phone: (202)512-1800 Fax: (202)512-2250 E-mail: gpoaccess@gpo.gov • URL: http://www.access.gpo.gov • Annual.

Vital Statistics of the United States: Births, Life Expectancy, Deaths, and Selected Health Data. Helmut F. Wendel and Christopher S. Wendel, editors. Bernan Press, 4611-F Assembly Drive Lanham, MD 20706-4391. Phone: 800-865-3457 or (301)459-2255 Fax: 800-865-3450 or (301)459-9235 E-mail: bpress@bernan.com • URL: http://www.bernanpress.com • 2004. $95.00. Serves as "the successor to the National Center for Health Statistics' discontinued compendia, *Vital Statistics of the United States*." Contains both recent and historical data.

Vital Statistics of the United States: Life Tables. Available from U. S. Government Printing Office, Washington, DC 20402. Phone: (202)512-1800 Fax: (202)512-2250 E-mail: gpoaccess@gpo.gov • URL: http://www.access.gpo.gov • Annual. $64.00. Produced by the National Center for Health Statistics, Public Health Service, U. S. Department of Health and Human Services. Provides detailed data on expectation of life by age, race, and sex. Historical data is shown annually from the year 1900. (Vital Statistics, volume 2.)

Vitamin Book. Simon and Schuster Trade Bantam, 1230 Ave. of the Americas New York, NY 10020. Phone: 800-223-2348 or (212)698-7000 Fax: 800-943-9831 or (212)698-7007 E-mail: consumer.customerservice@simonandschuster.com • URL: http://www.simonsays.com • 1999. $6.99. Revised edition.

Vitamin Retailer: The Dietary Supplement Industry's Leading Magazine. Vitamin Retailer Magazine, Inc., 431 Cranbury Rd. East Brunswick, NJ 08816. Phone: (732)432-9600 Fax: (732)432-9288 E-mail: info@vitaminretailer.com • URL: http://www.vitaminretailer.com • Monthly. $60.00 per year. Edited for retailers of vitamins, herbal remedies, minerals, antioxidants, essential fatty acids, and other food supplements.

VM & SD (Visual Merchandising and Store Design). International Authority on Visual Merchandising and Store Design. S T Publications, Inc., 407 Gilbert Ave. Cincinnati, OH 45202. Phone: 800-925-1110 or (513)421-2050 Fax: (513)421-5144 E-mail: cwinters@stpubs.com • URL: http://www.visualstore.com • Monthly. $39.00 per year. Ideas for retailers on store design and display. Includes *Buyers' Guide*. Formerly *Visual Merchandising and Store Design*.

VNU Business Media. ADWEEK Directories, 770 Broadway New York, NY 10003-9595. Phone: (646)654-4500 Fax: (646)654-7212 • URL: http://www.vnubusinessmedia.com • Annual. $100.00. Presents cost, circulation, and audience statistics for various mass media segments, including television, radio, magazines, newspapers, telephone yellow pages, and cinema.

Vocational and Rehabilitation Research Institute., 3304 33rd St., N.W. Calgary, AB, Canada T2L 2A6. Phone: (403)284-1121 Fax: (403)284-1146 E-mail: vrri@cadvision.com • URL: http://www.vrri.org • Associated with University of Calgary.

Vocational Careers Sourcebook. Gale Cengage Learning, 27500 Drake Rd. Farmington Hills, MI 48331-3535. Phone: 800-877-GALE or (248)699-4253 Fax: 800-414-5043 E-mail: gale.galeord@cengage.com • URL: http://gale.cengage.com • 2002. $135.00. Fifth edition. A companion volume to *Professional Careers Sourcebook*. Includes information sources for 139 occupations that typically do not require a four-year college degree. Compiled in cooperation with InfoPLACE of the Cuyahoga County Public Library, Ohio.

Vocational Evaluation and Work Adjustment Association.

Vocational Training News: The Independent Weekly Report on Employment, Training, and Vocational Education. Aspen Publishers, Inc., 1135 Ave. of the Americas New York, NY 10036. Phone: 800-234-1660 or (212)597-0200 Fax: (212)597-0338 E-mail: customer.service@aspenpubl.com • URL: http://www.aspenpub.com • Biweekly. $377.00 per year. Newsletter. Emphasis is on federal job training and vocational education programs. Formerly *Manpower and Vocational Education Weekly*.

Vogue. Conde Nast Publications, Inc., Four Times Square New York, NY 10034. Phone: 800-289-9330 or (212)286-2860 Fax: (212)286-6921 • URL: http://www.condenet.com • Monthly. $18.00 per year.

Volunteers in Technical Assistance., 1600 Wilson Blvd., Suite 710 Arlington, VA 22209. Phone: (703)276-1800 Fax: (703)243-1865 E-mail: vita@vita.org • URL: http://www.vita.org • Formerly Volunteers for International Technical Assistance.

W. E. Upjohn Institute for Employment Research., 300 S. Westnedge Ave. Kalamazoo, MI 49007-4686. Phone: (616)343-5541 Fax: (616)343-3308 E-mail: eberts@we.upjohninst.org • URL: http://www.upjohninst.org • Research fields include unemployment, unemployment insurance, worker's compensation, labor productivity, profit sharing, the labor market, economic development, earnings, training, and other areas related to employment.

W. W. Hansen Experimental Physics Laboratory., Stanford University, 445 Via Palou St. Stanford, CA 94305-4085. Phone: (650)723-0280 Fax: (650)725-8311 • URL: http://www.hepl.stanford.edu • Conducts large-scale cryogenic research.

WaferNews Confidential. PennWell Corp., Advanced Technology Div., 98 Spit Brook Rd. Nashua, NH 03062-5737. Phone: 800-331-4463 or (603)891-0123 E-mail: atd@pennwell.com • URL: http://www.pennwell.com • 50 times a year. $799.00 per year. Newsletter. Covers developments and trends in the semiconductor equipment industry.

Wageweb: Salary Survey Data On-Line. HRPDI: Human Resources Programs Development and ImprovementPhone: (804)363-1792 Fax: (804)594-3721 E-mail: salaries@wageweb.com • URL: http://www.wageweb.com • Web site provides salary information for more than 170 benchmark positions, including (for example) 29 information management jobs. Data shows average minimum, median, and average maximum compensation for each position, based on salary surveys. Fees; Free for national salary data; $169.00 per year for more detailed information (geographic, organization size, specific industries).

Waland Window Trends. Cygnus Business Media, Inc., 445 Broad Hollow Rd. Melville, NY 11747. Phone: 800-547-7377 or (631)845-2700 Fax: (631)845-2798 E-mail: rich.reiff@cygnuspub.com • URL: http://www.cygnusbzb.com • Monthly $36.00 per year. Edited for retailers of interior decoration products, with an emphasis on wallcoverings. Formerly *Wallcoverings, Windows and Interior Fashion*.

Walden's ABC Guide. Walden-Mott Corp., 225 N Franklin Tpke. Ramsey, NJ 07446. Phone: (201)818-8630 or (201)818-8630 Fax: (201)818-8720 E-mail: walden@walden-mott.com • URL: http://www.walden-mott.com • Covers: about 7,662 firms which manufacture, convert, and sell paper products and their suppliers. Entries include: Company name, address, phone, names of executives, and products and services offered.

Walker's Building Estimator's Reference Book. Frank R. Walker Co., 1989 University Lane, Unit C Lisle, IL 60532. Phone: 800-458-3737 or (630)971-8989 Fax: (630)971-0586 E-mail: info@frankwalker.com • URL: http://www.frankrwalker.com • 2002. $75.00. 27th edition.

Walker's Manual of Unlisted Stocks. Walker's Manual, LLC, 1650 Borel Pl., Ste. 130 San Mateo, CA 94402. Phone: 800-258-5737 or (650)341-1110 Fax: (650)341-2351 E-mail: walkersres@aol.com • URL: http://www.walkersresearch.com • Annual. $99.00. Provides information on 500 over-the-counter stocks,including many "penny stocks" trading at less than $5.00 per share.

The Wall Fashions. Grace McNamara, Inc., 4215 White Bear Parkway, Suite 100 Saint Paul, MN 55110-7635. Phone: (651)293-1544 Fax: (651)653-4308 E-mail: barb@gracemcnamara.com • URL: http://www.gwmcnamara.com • Monthly. $39.00 per year. News, events, trends, marketing, and merchandising covering the wallcovering industry. Formerly *The Wall Paper*.

Wall Street: A History. Charles R. Geisst. Oxford University Press, 198 Madison Ave. New York, NY 10016. Phone: 800-451-7556 or (212)726-6000 Fax: (212)726-6440 E-mail: custserv@oup-usa.org • URL: http://www.oup-usa.org • 1997. $18.95. Presents the history of the U. S. stock market according to four distinct eras: 1790 to the Civil War, the Civil War to 1929, 1929 to 1954, and from 1954 to recent years.

Wall Street and Technology: For Senior-Level Executives in Technology and Information Management in Securities and Invesment Firms. CMP Media LLC, 600 Community Dr. New York, NY 10030. Phone: (512)562-5000 E-mail: cmp@cmp.com • URL: http://www.cmp.com • Monthly. $85.00 per year. Includes material on the use of computers in technical investment strategies. Formerly *Wall Computer Review*.

The Wall Street Digest. Donald H. Rowe, 2 N Tamiami Trl., 2 N Tamiami Trl. Sarasota, FL 34236. Phone: 800-785-5050 or (941)954-5500 Fax: (941)364-8447 E-mail: info@accessintel.com • URL: http://www.wallstreetdigest • Description: Covers major investment areas, including stocks and bonds; foreign currencies; gold, silver, and other precious metals; real estate; tax shelters; and estate planning. Recurring features include "a digest of the month's best" investment and financial seminars, newsletter reviews, and statistics.

The Wall Street Journal. Dow Jones & Co., Inc., 200 Liberty St. New York, NY 10281. Phone: 800-544-0422 Fax: (212)416-2000 • URL: http://www.wsj.com • Daily. $189.00 per year. Covers news and trends relating to business, industry, finance, the economy, and international commerce. Provides extensive price and other data for the securities, commodity, options, futures, foreign exchange, and money markets.

Wall Street Journal/Europe. Dow Jones & Co., Inc., 1155 Ave. of the Americas New York, NY 10036. Phone: 800-544-0422 • URL: http://www.dowsjones.com • Daily. $300.00 per year (air mail). Published in Europe. Text in English.

Wall Street Journal Guide to Business Style and Usage. Paul R. Martin, editor. The Free Press, 1230 Ave. of the Americas New York, NY 10020. Phone: 800-223-2348 or (212)698-7000 Fax: 800-943-9831 or (212)698-7007 E-mail: consumer.customerservice@simonandschuster.com • URL: http://www.simonsays.com • 2002. $30.00. Contains definitions and explanations relating to grammar, spelling, punctuation, and the use of specialized business terms. (Wall Street Journal Book Series).

Wall Street Journal Guide to Planning Your Financial Future: The Easy-to-Read Guide to Lifetime Planning for Retirement. Kenneth M. Morris and Virginia B. Morris. Simon & Schuster Trade, 1230 Ave. of the Americas New York, NY 10020. Phone: 800-223-2348 or (212)698-7000 Fax: 800-943-9831 or (212)698-7007 E-mail: ssonline_feedback@simonsays.com • URL: http://www.simonsays.com • 2002. $15.95. Third edition. (Wall Street Journal Guides Series).

Wall Street Journal Guide to the Top Business Schools. Simon & Schuster, Inc., 1230 Ave. of the Americas New York, NY 10020. Phone: 800-223-2348 or (212)698-7000 Fax: 800-943-9831 or (212)698-7007 E-mail: consumer.customerservice@simonandschuster.com • URL: http://www.simonandschuster.com • Annual. $17.00. Rankings are based on surveys of recruiters of MBA graduates. Includes detailed descriptions of the leading U.S. business schools and information for applicants.

Wall Street Journal Interactive Edition. Dow Jones & Co., Inc. Phone: 800-369-2834 or (212)416-2000 Fax: (212)416-2658 E-mail: inquiries@interactive.wsj.com • URL: http://www.wsj.com • Fee-based Web site providing online searching of worldwide information from the *The Wall Street Journal*.

Includes "Company Snapshots," "The Journal's Greatest Hits," "Index to Market Data," "Journal Links," etc. Financial price quotes are available. Fees: $49.00 per year; $29.00 per year to print subscribers.

Wall Street Letter: Newsweekly for Investment Banking and Brokerage Community. Institutional Investor, Inc., Journals Group, 225 Park Ave., S New York, NY 10003. Phone: 800-945-2034 or (212)224-3066 Fax: (212)224-3472 E-mail: info@iijournals.com • URL: http://www.iijournals.com • Weekly. $2,665.00 per year. Includes print and online editions. Newsletter for stock brokers and companies providing services for stock brokers. Emphasis is on regulatory matters.

Wall Street Transcript: A Professional Publication for the Business and Financial Community. Wall Street Transcript Corp., 100 Wall St. New York, NY 10005-4301. Phone: (212)952-7400 Fax: (212)668-9842 E-mail: transcript@twst.com • URL: http://www.twst.com • Weekly. $1,890.00. per year. Provides reprints of investment research reports.

Wallcoverings Association., 401 N Michigan Ave., Ste. 2200 Chicago, IL 60611. Phone: (312)644-6610 Fax: (312)527-6705 E-mail: rpietrzak@smithbucklin.com • URL: http://www.wallcoverings.org • Manufacturers, converters, distributors, and suppliers in the wallcoverings industry.

Wallstreetlawyer.com: Securities in the Electronic Age. Glasser Legalworks, 150 Clove Rd. Little Falls, NJ 07424. Phone: 800-308-1700 or (973)890-0008 Fax: (973)890-0042 E-mail: orders@glasserlegalworks.com • URL: http://www.glasserlegalworks.com • Monthly. $345.00 per year. Newsletter. Covers the latest regulatory developments in capital raising, disclosure, and enforcement.

Want's Federal-State Court Directory. Want Publishing Co., Graybar Bldg. - Grand Central, 420 Lexington Ave., Ste. 300 New York, NY 10170. Phone: (212)687-3774 Fax: (212)687-3779 E-mail: rwant@wantpublishing.com • URL: http://www.wantpublishing.com • Covers: All federal court judges and clerks of court, and United States attorneys and magistrates, judges; state supreme court chief justices and state court administrators; Supreme Court Chief Justices of Canada and other nations. Entries include: Judge, clerk, probation office, or magistrate's name, address, phone.

Ward's Auto World. Primedia Business Magazines and Media, 300 Town Center, Suite 2750 Southfield, MI 48075-1212. Phone: (248)357-0800 Fax: (248)357-0810 E-mail: subs@primediabusiness.com • URL: http://www.primediabusiness.com • Monthly. Free to members; non-members, $55.00 per year. In-depth news and analysis of the automotive industry.

Ward's AutoInfoBank. Ward's Communications, Inc., 3000 Town Center, Suite 2750 Southfield, MI 48075. Phone: (248)357-0800 Fax: (248)357-0810 Provides weekly, monthly, quarterly, and annual statistical data from 1980 to date for U. S. and imported cars and trucks. Covers production, shipments, sales, inventories, optional equipment, etc. Updating varies by series. Inquire as to online cost and availability.

Ward's Automotive Reports. Ward's Communications, 3000 Town Ctr., Ste. 2750 Southfield, MI 48075. Phone: (248)799-2622 Fax: (248)357-0810 E-mail: wards@primediabusiness.com • URL: http://www.primediabusiness.com • Description: Reports "vital statistical information and exclusive news of critical interest" to the automotive industry. **Remarks:** Subscription includes Ward's Automotive Yearbook. Ward's Communications, Inc. is a subsidiary of Intertec Publishing Corp..

Ward's Automotive Yearbook. Ward's Communications, 300 Town Center, Suite 2750 Southfield, MI 48075. Phone: (248)357-0800 Fax: (248)357-0810 E-mail: wards@primediabusiness.com • URL: http://www.wardsauto.com • Annual. $425.00. Comprehensive statistical information on automotive production, sales, truck data and suppliers. Included with subscription to *Ward's Automotive Reports*.

Ward's Business Directory of U. S. Private and Public Companies. Gale Cengage Learning, 27500 Drake Rd. Farmington Hills, MI 48331-3535. Phone: 800-877-GALE or (248)699-4253 Fax: 800-414-5043 E-mail: gale.galeord@cengage.com • URL: http://gale.cengage.com • 2002. $2,765. 00. 45th edition. Eight volumes. *Ward's* contains basic information on about 120,000 business firms, of which 90 percent are private companies. Includes mid-year *Supplement*. Volumes available individually. Prices vary.

Ward's Private Company Profiles: Excerpts and Articles on 150 Privately Held U. S. Companies. Gale Cengage Learning, 27500 Drake Rd. Farmington Hills, MI 48331-3535. Phone: 800-877-GALE or (248)699-4253 Fax: 800-414-5043 E-mail: gale.galeord@cengage.com • URL: http://gale.cengage.com • 1994. $139.00. Second edition. A collection of detailed information on 150 private companies.

Warehouse Management Handbook. James A. Tompkins. McGraw-Hill, 1221 Ave. of the Americas New York, NY 10020. Phone: 800-722-4726 or (212)512-2000 Fax: (212)512-4502 E-mail: customer.service@mcgraw-hill.com • URL: http://www.mcgraw-hill.com • 1997. $89.95. Second edition. Covers site selection, order fulfillment, inventory control systems, storage space determination, equipment maintenance programs, and other warehousing topics.

Warehouse Management's Guide to Public Warehousing. Reed Business Information, 360 Park Ave. S New York, NY 10010. Phone: 800-446-6551 or (646)746-6400 Fax: (646)746-7028 E-mail: corporatecommunications@reedbusiness.com • URL: http://www.reedbusiness.com • Annual. $55.00. List of

general merchandise,contract and refrigerated warehouses.

Warehousing Distribution Directory. Commonwealth Business Media Inc., 400 Windsor Corporate Pk., 50 Millstone Rd., Ste. 200 East Windsor, NJ 08520-1415. Phone: 800-221-5488 or (609)371-7700 Fax: (609)371-7885 E-mail: customerservice@cbizmedia.com • URL: http://www.cbizmedia.com • Publication includes: List of about 800 warehousing and consolidation companies and firms offering trucking, trailer on flatcar, container on flatcar, and piggyback carrier services. Entries include: Name of firm, address, phone, name and title of contact, services, insurance provided, bank references, territory covered, restrictions, number of staff, and branches or subsidiaries with their locations.

Warman's Antiques and Collectibles Price Guide. Krause Publications, Inc., 700 E. State St. Iolao, WI 54990-0001. Phone: 800-258-0929 or (715)445-2214 Fax: (715)445-4087 • URL: http://www.krause.com • Annual. $19.99. Manufacturer profiles, key events, current status, collector's clubs, museums, resources available for Americana and collectibles.

WARN Act: A Manager's Compliance Guide to Workforce Reductions. Joseph A. Brislin. BNA, Inc., 1231 25th St., NW Washington, DC 20037. Phone: 800-372-1033 E-mail: customercare@bna.com • URL: http://www.bna.com • 1990. $195.00.

Warren's Cable Regulation Monitor: The Authoritative Weekly News Service Covering Federal, State, and Local Cable Activities and Trends. Warren Publishing, Inc., 2115 Ward Ct., NW Washington, DC 20037. Phone: (202)872-9200 Fax: (202)293-3435 • URL: http://www.warrenpub.com • Weekly. $594.00 per year. Newsletter. Emphasis is on Federal Communications Commission regulations affecting cable television systems. Covers rate increases made by local systems and cable subscriber complaints filed with the FCC.

Warren's Forms of Agreements. LexisNexis Matthew Bender, 1275 Broadway Albany, NY 12204. Phone: 800-424-4200 or (518)487-3000 Fax: (518)487-3584 E-mail: bookstore.support@lexisnexis.com • URL: http://www.bender.com • Biennial. $1,110.00. Eight looseleaf volumes. A compact source of forms that business transaction lawyers are most frequently asked to document.

Washington: A Comprehensive Directory of the Key Institutions and Leaders in th e National Capitol Area. Columbia Books, Inc., 1825 Connecticut Ave., N. W., Suite 625 Washington, DC 20009-5724. Phone: 888-265-0600 or (202)464-1662 Fax: (202)464-1775 E-mail: info@columbiabooks.com • URL: http://www.columbiabooks.com • Annual. $149.00. Provides information on about 5,000 Washington, DC key businesses, government offices, non-profit organizations, and cultural institutions, with the names of about 25,000 principal executives. Includes Washington media, law offices, foundations, labor unions, international organizations, clubs, etc.

The Washington Agricultural Record. Washington Agricultural Record, Box 25001, Georgetown Sta., P.O. Box 25001 Washington, DC 20007. Phone: 800-382-9989 or (202)333-8190 Fax: (202)337-3809 E-mail: wards@primediabusiness.com Description: Focuses on Washington farm issues and developments, reporting international congressional and United States Department of Agriculture (U.S.D.A.) news and international agricultural developments.

Washington Drug Letter. Washington Business Information Inc., 1117 N 19th St., Ste. 200 Arlington, VA 22209-1798. Phone: (703)247-3434 Fax: (703)247-3421 E-mail: wards@primediabusiness.com • URL: http://www.fdanews.com • Description: Focuses on regulation and legislation affecting prescription and proprietary drugs. Monitors Food & Drug Administration (FDA) actions and new drug applications, manufacturing procedures, advertising and labeling, compliance cases, research, and testing rules.

Washington Information Directory. CQ Press, 2300 N St. NW, Ste. 800 Washington, DC 20037. Phone: (866)427-7737 or (202)729-1900 Fax: 800-380-3810 or 800-380-3810 E-mail: customerservice@cqpress.com • URL: http://www.cq.com • Covers: 5,000 governmental agencies, congressional committees, and non-governmental associations considered competent sources of specialized information. Entries include: Name of agency, committee, or association; address, phone, fax, and Internet; annotation concerning function or activities of the office; and name of contact.

Washington International Arts Letter. Allied Business Consultants Inc., 317 Fairchild St. Iowa City, IA 52245-2115. E-mail: wards@primediabusiness.com Description: Publishes information about cultural developments; personalities in the arts; and the workings and actions of the National Endowments of the Arts and Humanities, Congress, and federal offices as they affect this field. Recurring features include announcements of jobs, scholarships, grants, and other forms of assistance available in the arts and humanities; bibliographies; publications reviews; and listings of names and addresses of businesses and organizations that contribute to the arts.

Washington International Business Report: An Analytical Review and Outlook on Major Government Developments Impacting International Trade and Investment. International Business-Government Counsellors, Inc., 818 Connecticut Ave., N.W., 12th Fl. Washington, DC 20006-

2702. Phone: (202)872-8181 Fax: (202)872-8696 E-mail: arobbins@ibgc.com • URL: http://www.ibgc.com • Monthly. $288.00 per year. Newsletter.

Washington Representatives: Lobbyists, Foreign Agents, Consultants, Legal Advisors, Public Affairs, and Government Relations. Columbia Books, Inc., 1825 Connecticut Ave., Suite 625 Washington, DC 20009. Phone: 888-265-0600 or (202)464-1662 Fax: (202)464-1775 E-mail: info@columbiabooks.com • URL: http://www.columbiabooks.com • Annual. $149.00. Over 17,000 individuals and law or public relations firms registered as lobbyists, foreign agents, or otherwise acting as representatives in Washington, DC, for companies, associations, labor unions, and special interest groups; legislative affairs personnel of federal government agencies and departments and the White House.

Waste Age. Environmental Industry Association. Primedia Business Magazines and Media, 6151 Powers Ferry Rd., Ste. 200 Atlanta, GA 30339. Phone: 800-795-5445 or (770)955-2500 Fax: (770)618-0204 E-mail: subs@primediabusiness.com • URL: http://www.primediabusiness.com • Monthly. Price on application.

Waste Age Buyers' Guide. Primedia Business Magazines and Media, 6151 Powers Ferry Rd., Ste. 200 Atlanta, GA 30339. Phone: 800-795-5445 or (770)955-2500 Fax: (770)618-0348 E-mail: subs@primediabusiness.com • URL: http://www.primediabusiness.com • Annual. $64.95. Manufacturers of equipment and supplies for the waste management industry.

Waste Management: Industrial-Radioactive-Hazardous. Elsevier, 360 Park Ave., S. New York, NY 10010-1710. Phone: 888-437-4636 or (212)989-5800 Fax: (212)633-3990 E-mail: usinfo-f@elsevier.com • URL: http://www.elsevier.com • 10 times a year.Individuals, $120.00 per year; institutions, $1,646.00 per year. Formerly *Nuclear and Chemical Waste Management*.

Waste Management Research and Education Institute., University of Tennessee, Knoxville, Conference Center Bldg., Suite 311 Knoxville, TN 37996-4134. Phone: (865)974-4251 Fax: (865)974-1838 E-mail: kdavis17@utk.edu • URL: http://www.eerc.ra.utk.edu/divisions/wmrei • Research fields include chemical, nuclear, and solid waste management, especially waste policy and environmental biotechnology studies.

Waste Treatment and Disposal. Paul T. Williams. John Wiley and Sons, Inc., 111 River St. Hoboken, NJ 07030. Phone: 800-225-5945 or (201)748-6000 Fax: (201)748-6088 E-mail: info@wiley.com • URL: http://www.wiley.com • 1998. $200.00.

Waste Treatment Technology News. BCC Research, 70 New Canaan Ave. Norwalk, CT 06850. Phone: (866)285-7216 or (203)750-9783 Fax: (203)229-0087 E-mail: info@bccresearch.com • URL: http://www.buscom.com • Description: Profiles existing and developing industrial waste treatment techniques. Follows governmental action such as Superfund legislation and EPA (Environmental Protection Agency) activities. Focuses on the research and development of waste treatment technologies, listing recent patents in the field. Recurring features include news of research.

Watch and Clock Review. Golden Bell Press Inc., 2403 Champa St. Denver, CO 80205. Phone: (303)296-1600 Fax: (303)295-2159 10 times a year. $19.50 per year. Formerly *American Horologist and Jeweler*.

Watch Officer's Guide: A Handbook for All Deck Watch Offices. James Stavridis. U.S. Naval Institute, Beach Hall, 291 Wood Rd. Annapolis, MD 21402. Phone: 800-223-8764 or (410)268-6110 Fax: (410)269-7940 E-mail: customer@usni.org • URL: http://www.nip.org • 1999. $21.95. 14th edition.

The Watch Repairer's Manual. Henry B. Fried. American Watchmakers Institute, 701 Enterprise Dr. Harrison, OH 45030. Phone: (513)367-9800 Fax: (513)367-1414 $35.00. 1986. Fourth revised edition.

Water, Air and Soil Pollution: An International Journal of Environmental Pollution. Kluwer Academic Publishers, 101 Philip Dr., Assinippi Park Norwell, MA 02061. Phone: (866)269-9527 or (781)871-6600 Fax: (781)681-9045 • URL: http://www.wkap.nl • 32 times a year. Institutions, $3,985.00. Includes print and online editions.

Water and Environment Manager. Chartered Institution of Water and Environmental Management. Terence Dalton Ltd., Arbons House, Water St. Lavenham CO10 9RN, United Kingdom. Phone: 44 1787 249290 Fax: 44 1787 248267 E-mail: postmaster@lavenhambroup.co.uk 10 times a year. $90.00 per year. Formerly *Chartered Institution of Water and Environmental Management Newsletter*.

Water and Wastes Digest. Scranton Gillette Communications, Inc., 380 E. Northwest Highway, Suite 200 Des Plaines, IL 60016-2282. Phone: (847)391-1000 Fax: (847)390-0408 E-mail: bwilson@sgcmail.com • URL: http://www.sgcpubs.com • 12 times a year. Free to qualified personnel; others, $40.00 per year. Exclusively designed to serve engineers, consultants, superintendents, managers and operators who are involved in water supply, waste water treatment and control.

Water and Wastewater Equipment Manufacturers Association., P.O. Box 17402 Washington, DC 20041. Phone: (703)444-1777 Fax: (703)444-1779 E-mail: info@wwema.org • URL: http://www.wwema.org • Formerly Water and Sewage Works Manufacturers Association.

Water Desalination Report. Maria C. Smith, PO Box 10 Tracys Landing, MD 20779-0010. Phone: (301)261-5010 Fax: (301)261-5010 E-mail: info@bccresearch.com • URL: http://

www.waterdesal.com • Description: Concentrates on the activities of government and industry worldwide concerning the desalination of seawater and brackish water. Discusses such topics as problems with water supply and reuse, resource planning, and pollution control. Reports on federal budgets, regulation, new and future programs, opportunities in business, and research. Recurring features include book reviews and a schedule of activities.

Water Encyclopedia. Frits Von Der Leeden and others, editors. Lewis Publishers, 2000 Corporate Blvd., N.W. Boca Raton, FL 33431. Phone: 800-272-7737 or (561)994-0555 Fax: 800-374-3401 or (561)998-9114 E-mail: orders@crdpress.com • URL: http://www.crcpress.com • 1990. $249.95. Second edition. Covers a wide variety of topics relating to water. (Geraghty and Miller Environmental Science and Engineering Series).

Water Engineering and Management. Scranton Gillette Communications, Inc., 380 E. Northwest Highway, Suite 200 Des Plaines, IL 60016-2282. Phone: (847)391-1000 Fax: (847)390-0408 E-mail: bwilson@sgcmail.com • URL: http://www.sgcpubs.com • Monthly. $40.00 per year.

Water Environment Federation., 601 Wythe St. Alexandria, VA 22314-1994. Phone: 800-666-0206 or (703)684-2400 Fax: (703)684-2492 E-mail: wbertera@wef.org • URL: http://www.wef.org • Technical societies representing chemists, biologists, ecologists, geologists, operators, educational and research personnel, industrial wastewater engineers, consultant engineers, municipal officials, equipment manufacturers, and university professors and students dedicated to the enhancement and preservation of water quality and resources. Seeks to advance fundamental and practical knowledge concerning the nature, collection, treatment, and disposal of domestic and industrial wastewaters, and the design, construction, operation, and management of facilities for these purposes. Disseminates technical information; and promotes good public relations and regulations that improve water quality and the status of individuals working in this field. Conducts educational and research programs.

Water Environment Research. Water Environment Federation, 601 Wythe St. Alexandria, VA 22314-1994. Phone: 800-666-0206 or (703)684-2400 Fax: (703)684-2492 E-mail: kroy@wef.org • URL: http://www.wef.org • Bimonthly. Members, $158.00 per year; non-members, $404.00 per year. Formerly *Water Pollution Control Federation. Research Journal.*

Water Operation and Maintenance Bulletin., Denver Federal Center, Bldg. 67 Denver, CO 80225. Phone: (303)234-3217 Quarterly.

Water Quality Association., 4151 Naperville Rd. Lisle, IL 60532-1088. Phone: (630)505-0160 Fax: (630)505-9637 E-mail: info@wqa.org • URL: http://www.wqa.org • Individuals or firms engaged in the manufacture and/or assembly and distribution and/or retail selling of water treatment equipment, supplies, and services. Promotes the acceptance and use of industry equipment, products, and services. Provides activities, programs, and services designed to improve economy and efficiency within the industry. Conducts expositions and certification and equipment validation programs. Compiles statistics.

Water Research. International Association on Water Quality. Elsevier, 360 Park Ave., S. New York, NY 10010-1710. Phone: 888-437-4636 or (212)989-5800 Fax: (212)633-3990 E-mail: usinfo-f@elsevier.com • URL: http://www.elsevier.com • 20 times a year. Institutions, $4,537.00 per year.

Water Resources Center. University of Delaware

Water Resources: Distribution, Use and Management. John R. Mather. John Wiley and Sons, Inc., 111 River St. Hoboken, NJ 07030. Phone: 800-225-5945 or (201)748-6000 Fax: (201)748-6088 E-mail: info@wiley.com • URL: http://www.wiley.com • 1983. $199.00. (Environmental Science and Technology Series).

Water Science and Technology. International Association on Water Quality. Elsevier, 360 Park Ave., S. New York, NY 10010-1710. Phone: 888-437-4636 or (212)989-5800 Fax: (212)633-3990 E-mail: usinfo-f@elsevier.com • URL: http://www.elsevier.com • 24 times a year. $4,495.00 per year. Includes print and online editions.

Water Systems Council., 1101 30th St. NW, Ste. 500, 1101 30th St. NW, Ste. 500 Washington, DC 20007. Phone: 888-395-1033 or (202)625-4387 Fax: (202)625-4363 E-mail: wsc@watersystemcouncil.org • URL: http://www.watersystemscouncil.org • Manufacturers of pitless adapters and units for water wells. Promotes sound principles of pitless equipment construction and installation; maintains standards. Seeks to educate customers and users of pitless adapters. Conducts workshops for local health officials. Maintains speakers' bureau and library of state water well regulations.

Water Treatment Equipment and Supplies. Available from MarketResearch.com, 641 Ave. of the Americas, Fourth Floor New York, NY 10011. Phone: 800-298-5699 or (212)807-2629 Fax: (212)807-2642 E-mail: order@marketresearch.com • URL: http://www.marketresearch.com • 2002. $3,850.00. Published by Global Industry Analysts. Provides worldwide market research data, including profiles of major water treatment supply companies.

Water Well Journal. National Ground Water Association, 601 Dempsey Rd. Westerville, OH 43081-8978. Phone: 800-551-7379 or (614)898-7791 Fax: (614)898-7786 E-mail: ngwa@ngwa.org • URL: http://www.ngwa.org • Monthly. Free to qualified personnel; others, $65.00 per year.

Waterfront Revitalization. Eric J. Fournier. Sage Publications, Inc., 2455 Teller Rd. Thousand Oaks, CA 91320 8. Phone: 800-818-7423 or (805)499-9774 Fax: 800-583-2665 or (805)449-0871 E-mail: webmaster@sagepub.com • URL: http://www.sagepub.com • 1994. $10.00. (CPL Bibliographies Series, No. 310).

Waterway Guide—The Yachtman's Bible. Primedia Business, 6151 Powers Ferry Rd., Ste. 200 Atlanta, GA 30339. Phone: 800-795-5445 or (770)955-2500 Fax: (770)618-0204 E-mail: inquiries@primediabusiness.com • URL: http://www.primediabusiness.com • Covers: inland and coastal waterways in the eastern half of the United States; published in three editions. Northern edition covers coastal waterways from the Delaware Bay to the U.S.-Canadian border; plus New York canals, Champlain Waterways, and St. Lawrence River; Middle Atlantic edition covers waterways from the Chesapeake Bay to the Florida-Georgia line; Southern edition covers intracoastal waterways from the Florida-Georgia line to the Texas-Mexico border and the Bahamas. Entries include: Name of marine facility, location, navigation information and courses, points of interest, anchorages.

Waterways Journal: Devoted to the Marine Profession and Commercial Interest of All Inland Waterways. Waterways Journal, Inc., 319 N. Fourth St., Suite 650 Saint Louis, MO 63102. Phone: 800-366-9630 or (314)241-7354 Fax: (314)241-4207 • URL: http://www.waterwaysjournal.net • Weekly. $32.00 per year. Weekly business journal serving nation's inland marine industry. Supplement available *Annual Review Number*.

Wealth Ranking Annual. Mark W. Scott. The Taft Group, 27500 Drake Rd. Farmington Hills, MI 48331-3535. Phone: 800-877-GALE or (248)699-GALE Fax: 800-414-5043 or (248)699-8063 E-mail: gale.galeord@galegroup.com • URL: http://www.group.com • Contains reprints of wealth rankings and compensation lists appearing in periodicals and newspapers. Includes about 600 lists naming more than 6,000 individuals.

The Weather Almanac: A Reference Guide to Weather, Climate, and Air Quality in the United States and Its Key Cities, Comprising Statistics, Principles, and Terminology. Gale Cengage Learning, 27500 Drake Rd. Farmington Hills, MI 48331-3535. Phone: 800-877-GALE or (248)699-4253 Fax: 800-414-5043 E-mail: gale.galeord@cengage.com • URL: http://gale.cengage.com • 2001. $165.00. 10th edition. Weather reports for 108 major U.S. cities and a climatic overview of the country.

Weather America: A Thirty-Year Summary of Statistical Data and Weather Trends. David Garoogian, editor. Grey House Publishing, 185 Millerton Rd. Millerton, NY 12546. Phone: 800-562-2139 or (518)789-8700 Fax: (518)789-0556 E-mail: books@greyhouse.com • URL: http://www.greyhouse.com • 2000. $175.00. Second edition. Contains detailed climatological data for 4,000 national and cooperative weather stations in the U. S. Organized by state, with an index to cities. (Universal Reference Publications.)

Weather and Climate Report. Nautilus Press, Inc., 1201 National Press Bldg. Washington, DC 20045. Phone: (202)347-6643 Monthly. $95.00 per year. Newsletter.

Weather Modification Association., PO Box 26926 Fresno, CA 93729-6926. Phone: (559)434-3486 Fax: (559)434-3486 E-mail: wxmod@comcast.net • URL: http://www.weathermodification.org • Individuals and organizations interested in weather modification problems; universities and non-profit research institutes; public utilities, power and water companies, and districts; private meteorological firms, government agencies, and foreign organizations; and other groups and firms. Encourages scientific research; coordinates efforts of different weather modification projects and encourages standardization of weather modification recording procedures. Renders technical assistance in developing legislation pertaining to weather modification.

Weather of U.S. Cities. Gale Cengage Learning, 27500 Drake Rd. Farmington Hills, MI 48331-3535. Phone: 800-877-GALE or (248)699-4253 Fax: 800-414-5043 E-mail: gale.galeord@cengage.com • URL: http://gale.cengage.com • 1996. $235.00. Fifth edition.

Weatherwise: The Magazine About the Weather. Helen Dwight Reid Educational Foundation. Heldref Publications, 1319 18th St., N.W. Washington, DC 20036-1802. Phone: 800-365-9753 Fax: (202)292-6130 E-mail: subscribe@heldref.org • URL: http://www.heldref.org • Bimonthly. Individuals, $38.00 per year; institutions, $80.00 per year. Popular magazine devoted to weather.

Web Feet: The Internet Traveler's Desk Reference. RockHill Communications, 14 Rock Hill Rd. Bala Cynwyd, PA 19004. Phone: 888-762-5445 or (610)667-2040 Fax: (610)667-2291 E-mail: info@rockhillcommunications.com • URL: http://www.rockhillcommunications.com • Monthly. $165.00 per year. Looseleaf service. Serves as a subject guide to the "best" Web sites.

The Web Library: Building a World Class Personal Library with Free Web Resources. Nicholas G. Tomaiuolo. Information Today, Inc., 143 Old Marlton Pike Medford, NJ 08055-8750. Phone: 800-300-9868 or (609)654-6266 Fax: (609)654-4309 E-mail: custserv@infotoday.com • URL: http://www.infotoday.com • 2003. $24.95. Provides advice on obtaining free, useful information and literature by way of the Internet. (CyberAge Books).

Web Marketing Update: Quick, Actionable, Internet Intelligence for Marketing Executives. Computer Economics, Inc., 5841 Edison Place Carlsbad, CA 92008. Phone: 800-326-8100 or (760)438-8100 Fax: (760)431-1126 E-mail: access@compecon.com • URL: http://www.computereconomics.com • Monthly. $347.00 per year. Newsletter on various aspects of promoting or selling products and services through an Internet Web site: technology, advertising, strategy, customer base, cost projections, search engines, etc.

Web of Deception: Misinformation on the Internet. Anne P. Mintz, editor. Information Today, Inc., 143 Old Marlton Pike Medford, NJ 08055-8750. Phone: 800-300-9868 or (609)654-6266 Fax: (609)654-4309 E-mail: custserv@infotoday.com • URL: http://www.infotoday.com • 2002. $24.95. Barbara Quint, Susan M. Detwiler, and others discuss the spread of intentionally misleading or erroneous information by Web sites. Provides advice on the evaluation of Internet sources. (CyberAge Books.)

The Web of Inclusion: Building an Organization for Everyone. Sally Helgesen. Doubleday Publishing, 1540 Broadway New York, NY 10036-4094. Phone: 800-323-9872 or (212)354-6500 Fax: (212)492-9700 • URL: http://www.doubledaybookclub.com • 1995. $24.95.

Web Site Source Book: A Guide to Major U. S. Businesses, Organizations, Agencies, Institutions, and Other Information Resources on the World Wide Web. Omnigraphics, Inc., 615 Griswold St. Detroit, MI 48226. Phone: 800-234-1340 or (313)961-1340 Fax: 800-875-1340 or (313)961-1383 E-mail: info@omnigraphics.com • URL: http://www.omnigraphics.com • 2004. $150.00. Ninth edition. About 84,000 Web sites are arranged alphabetically by business or organization and by 1,350 subject categories. Surface mail addresses, phone numbers, fax numbers, and e-mail addresses are included.

Web Style Guide: Basic Design Principles for Creating Web Sites. Patrick J. Lynch and Sarah Horton. Yale University Press, 302 Temple St. New Haven, CT 06511. Phone: 800-987-7323 or (203)432-0948 Fax: (203)432-0948 E-mail: customer.care@triliteral.org • URL: http://www.yale.edu/yup • 2002. $35.00. Second edition. Covers design of content, interface, page layout, graphics, and multimedia aspects.

The Webb Report: A Newsletter on Sexual Harassment. Susan L. Webb, editor. Pacific Resource Development Group, Inc., 1651 NE 185th St. Seattle, WA 98155. Phone: 800-767-3062 E-mail: pacres@shadesofgray.com • URL: http://www.shadesofgray.com • Monthly. $120.00 per year. Contains news and information on sexual harassment issues and court cases. Provides guidelines for supervisors and employees as to what constitutes harassment.

WebFinance. Thomson Media, One State St. Plaza New York, NY 10004. Phone: 800-221-1809 or (212)803-8200 Fax: (212)843-9635 E-mail: custserv@thomsonmedia.com • URL: http://www.thomsonmedia.com • Semimonthly. $995.00 per year. Newsletter (also available online at www.webfinance.net). Covers the Internet-based provision of online financial services by banks, online brokers, mutual funds, and insurance companies. Provides news stories, analysis, and descriptions of useful resources.

Weekly Board of Trade, Cotton Exchange. New York Cotton Exchange, One North End Ave. New York, NY 10282-1101. Phone: (212)748-8000 E-mail: webmaster@nybot.com • URL: http://www.nyce.com • Weekly. $100.00 per year.

Weekly Business Failures. Dun & Bradstreet Corp., 103 JFK Pky. Short Hills, NJ 07078. Phone: 800-526-0651 E-mail: custserv@dnb.com • URL: http://www.dnb.com • Weekly. $445.00 per year.

Weekly Insiders Dairy and Egg Letter. Urner Barry Publications, Inc., P.O. Box 389 Toms River, NJ 08754. Phone: 800-932-0617 or (732)240-5330 Fax: (732)341-0891 E-mail: mail@urnerbarry.com • URL: http://www.unerbarry.com • Weekly. $173.00 per year.

The Weekly of Business Aviation. Aviation Week Newsletter. McGraw-Hill, 1221 Ave. of the Americas New York, NY 10020. Phone: 800-722-4726 or (212)512-2000 Fax: (212)512-4502 E-mail: customer.service@mcgraw-hill.com • URL: http://www.mcgraw-hill.com • Weekly. $595.00 per year.

Weekly Petroleum Status Report. Energy Information Administration. Available from U.S. Government Printing Office, Washington, DC 20402. Phone: (202)512-1800 Fax: (202)512-2250 E-mail: gpoaccess@gpo.gov • URL: http://www.accessgpo.gov • Weekly. Current statistics in the context of both historical information and selected prices and forecasts.

Weekly Statistical Summary. National Mining Association, 1130 17th St., N. W. Washington, DC 20036-4677. Phone: (202)463-2625 Fax: (202)463-6152 E-mail: thowe@nma.org • URL: http://www.nma.org • Weekly. Newsletter. Free to members; non-members, $100.00 per year. A detailed report on coal production and consumption.

Weekly Summary of the National Labor Relations Board Cases. Available from U. S. Government Printing Office, Washington, DC 20402. Phone: (202)512-1800 Fax: (202)512-2250 E-mail: gpoaccess@gpo.gov • URL: http://www.access.gpo.gov • Weekly. $237.00 per year. Issued by the Division of Information, National Labor Relations Board.

WEFA Industrial Monitor. John Wiley and Sons, Inc., 605 Third Ave. New York, NY 10158-0012. Phone: 800-225-5945 or (212)850-6000 Fax: (212)850-6088 E-mail: info@wiley.com • URL: http://www.wiley.com • Annual. $65.00. Prepared by industry analysts at WEFA, an economic forecasting and consulting firm (originally Wharton Econometric Forecasting Associates). Contains discussions of the outlook for major U. S. industries, with many 10-year forecasts (WEFA Web site is http://www.wefa.com).

Weidenbaum Center on the Economy, Government, and Public Policy. Washington University in Saint Louis, One Brookings Dr., CB 1027 St. Louis, MO 63130-4899. Phone: (314)935-5630 Fax: (314)935-5688 • URL: http://www.wc.wustl.edu • Research activity includes the study of corporate takeovers. Formerly Center for the Study of American Business.

Weighing and Measurement. Key Markets Publishing Co., P.O. Box 270 Roscoe, IL 61073-0270. Phone: (815)636-7739 Fax: (815)636-7741 Bimonthly. $30.00 per year. Provides information relating to industrial weighing methods.

Weight Loss and Diet Control Market. Available from MarketResearch.com, 641 Ave. of the Americas, Third Floor New York, NY 10011. Phone: 800-298-5699 or (212)807-2629 Fax: (212)807-2716 E-mail: order@marketresearch.com • URL: http://www.marketresearch.com • 2002. $795.00. Market research report published by Marketdata Enterprises. Covers commercial diet programs, medical plans, nonprescription appetite suppressants low-calorie foods, artifical sweeteners, health clubs, and diet books. Includes forecasts to the year 2006.

Welcome to the Foundation Center. The Foundation Center-Phone: (212)620-4230 or (212)807-3679 Fax: (212)807-3677 E-mail: mfn@fdncenter.org • URL: http://www.fdncenter.org • Web site provides a wide variety of information about foundations, grants, and philanthropy, with links to philanthropic organizations. "Grantmaker Information" link furnishes descriptions of available funding.

Weldasearch. The Welding Institute, Abington Hall, Abington Cambridge CB1 6AL, England. Phone: (122)3-891162 Fax: (122)3-892588 Contains abstracts of international welding literature, 1967 to date. Inquire as to online cost and availability.

Welding and Metal Fabrication. Media Scores Ltd., Oaks House, 12-22 West St. Epson KT18 7RG, United Kingdom. Phone: 44 1372 730020 10 times a year. $168.00 per year.

Welding Design and Fabrication. Penton Media, Inc., 1300 E. Ninth St. Cleveland, OH 44114. Phone: (216)696-7000 Fax: (216)696-1752 E-mail: information@penton.com • URL: http://www.penton.com • Monthly. Free to qualified personnel; others, $75.00 per year.

Welding in the World. International Institute of Welding. Elsevier, 360 Park Ave., S. New York, NY 10010-1710. Phone: 888-437-4636 or (212)989-5800 Fax: (212)633-3990 E-mail: usinfo-f@elsevier.com • URL: http://www.elsevier.com • Semimonthly. $449.00 per year. Text in English and French.

Welding Journal. American Welding Society, 550 N.W. LeJeune Rd. Miami, FL 33126. Phone: 800-443-9353 or (305)443-9353 Fax: (305)443-7559 E-mail: info@awsparc.amweld.org • URL: http://www.amweld.org • Monthly. Membership.

Welding Research Abroad. Welding Research Council, Three Park Ave., 27th Fl. New York, NY 10016-5902. Phone: (212)705-7956 10 times a year. $1,100.00. Includes *Progress Reports*, *WRC Bulletins*, *WRC News* and *Welding Journal*.

Welding Research Council., PO Box 1942 New York, NY 10156. Phone: (216)658-3847 Fax: (216)658-3854 E-mail: mprager@forengineers.org • URL: http://forengl.securesites.net/wrc • Established by the Engineering Foundation under the sponsorship of the major engineering societies to conduct needed cooperative research in welding and closely allied fields, to disseminate research information, to promote welding research in the universities, and to provide a means for cooperation with similar agencies abroad. Activities include administration of large projects by specific committees, as well as sponsorship of small grants-in-aid by the University +Research Committee to foster interest in welding research in universities. The council is guided by 24 corporation executives who establish broad policies and prepare overall budgets for its projects. In itself, or through its committees, the Council is considered the welding research arm of eight engineering societies and six trade associations. In addition, it acts in an advisory capacity to the public utility industry, aerospace industry, and the Atomic Energy Commission. Financed by subscriptions from corporations, associations, and government departments; it has more than 900 scientists affiliated with its work, which is carried out in some 45 laboratories. Acts as one of the two sponsor body representatives of the American Council of the International Institute of Welding.

Welding Research Council Yearbook. Welding Research Council, Three Park Ave., 27th Fl. New York, NY 10016-5902. Phone: (212)705-7956 Annual. Membership.

Welfare, the Working Poor, and Labor. Louise Simmons, editor. M. E. Sharpe, Inc., 80 Business Park Drive Armonk, NY 10504. Phone: 800-541-6563 or (914)273-1800 Fax: (914)273-2106 E-mail: custserv@mesharpe.com • URL: http://www.mesharpe.com • 2004. $66.95. Presents material by various authors on poverty, welfare reform, and the market for low-wage labor.

Wellness Center., 2315 Stockton Blvd., 2315 Stockton Blvd. Sacramento, CA 95817. Phone: (916)734-9797 Fax: (916)734-2011 E-mail: mprager@forengineers.org • URL: http://www.wellness.ucdavis.edu • Individuals concerned with wellness and preventive health care; firms, institutions, and organizations with wellness centers or employee assistance programs. Educates health practitioners and the public on methods of developing healthier lifestyles through the prevention and treatment of degenerative diseases and other health disorders. Provides professional training workshops in wellness counseling, an approach that integrates many scientific and medical disciplines, to assist members with problems related to weight control, stress, alcoholism, personal relationships, drug addiction, and other physical, mental, or social problems. Conducts individual and group counseling sessions and support groups. Provides speakers on topics such as wellness, lifestyle changes, longevity, diseases and alternative therapies. **Convention/Meeting:** none.

Western Fruit Grower: The Business Magazine of the Western Produce Industry. Meister Media, 37733 Euclid Ave. Willoughby, OH 44094-5992. Phone: 800-572-7740 or (440)942-2000 Fax: (440)975-3447 E-mail: info@meistermedia.com • URL: http://www.meistermedia.com • Monthly. $15.95 per year. Covers the commercial fruit industry in 13 western states.

Western Grower and Shipper: The Business Magazine of the Western Product Industry. Western Growers Association., 17620 Fitch St. Irvine, CA 92658. Phone: (949)863-1000 Fax: (949)863-9028 E-mail: ddewees@wga.com • URL: http://www.wga.com • Monthly. $18.00 per year.

Western Growers Association—Membership Directory. Western Growers Association, PO Box 2130, PO Box 2130 Newport Beach, CA 92658. Phone: 800-333-4942 or (949)863-1000 Fax: (949)863-9028 E-mail: blewis@wga.com • URL: http://www.wga.com • Covers: 2,700 growers, shippers, packers, brokers, and distributors of fruits, vegetables, nuts, and allied industries in California and Arizona. Entries include: Company name, address, phone and fax, names of executives, list of commodities.

West's Business Law: Text and Cases, Legal, Ethical, Regulatory and International Environment. Kenneth Clarkson. South-Western, 5191 Natrop Blvd. Mason, OH 45040. Phone: 800-543-0487 or (513)229-1000 • URL: http://www.swcollege.com • 2000. $125.95. Eighth edition.

West's Encyclopedia of American Law. Available from Gale Cengage Learning, 27500 Drake Rd. Farmington Hills, MI 48331-3535. Phone: 800-877-GALE or (248)699-GALE Fax: 800-414-5043 E-mail: gale.galeord@cengage.com • URL: http://www.galegroup.com • 2003. $1,195.00. Second edition. 12 volumes. Published by West Group. Covers a wide variety of legal topics for the general reader.

West's Legal Forms. West Group, 610 Opperman Dr. Eagan, MN 55123. Phone: 800-338-9424 or (651)687-7000 Fax: 800-340-9378 E-mail: bookstore@westgroup.com • URL: http://www.westgroup.com • $1,938.00. Multivolume set. Annual cumulation.

WFDSA Directory of Members (World Federation of Direct Selling Association). World Federation of Direct Selling Associations, 1275 Pennsylvania Ave., NW, Ste. 800 Washington, DC 20004. Phone: (202)347-8866 Fax: (202)347-0055 E-mail: info@dsa.org • URL: http://www.org • Annual. Price on application.

What America's Small Companies Pay Their Sales Forces and How They Make It Pay Off. Christen P. Heide. Dartnell Corp., 360 Hiatt Dr. Palm Beach Gardens, FL 33418. Phone: 800-341-7874 or (561)622-6520 Fax: (561)622-2423 E-mail: custserv@lrp.com • URL: http://www.dartnellcorp.com • 1997. $29.95. Provides advice on attracting, motivating, and retaining productive sales personnel. Includes sales position descriptions and "latest sales compensation figures for companies under $5 million in sales."

What Color is Your Parachute? 2003: A Practical Manual for Job Hunters and Career Changers. Richard N. Bolles. Ten Speed Press, P.O. Box 7123 Berkeley, CA 94707. Phone: 800-841-2665 or (510)559-1600 Fax: (510)559-1629 E-mail: order@tenspeed.com • URL: http://www.tenspeed.com • 2002. $27.95. Revised edition. Features non-traditional job searching methods. (What Color is Your Parachute? Series).

What Corporate and General Practitioners Should Know About Intellectual Property Litigation. Raphael V. Lupo and Donna M. Tanguay. American Law Institute-American Bar Association, Committee on Continuing Professional Education, 4025 Chestnut St. Philadelphia, PA 19104. Phone: 800-253-6397 Fax: (215)243-0319 • URL: http://www.ali-aba.org • 1991. $34.00. A lawyer's guide to patents, trademarks, copyrights, and trade secrets.

What the IRS Doesn't Want You to Know: A CPA Reveals the Tricks of the Trade. Martin Kaplan. John Wiley and Sons, Inc., 111 River St. Hoboken, NJ 07030-5744. Phone: 800-225-5945 or (201)-748-6000 Fax: (201)748-6088 E-mail: custserv@wiley.com • URL: http://www.wiley.com • 2003. $18.95. Ninth edition. Explains how to legally pay as little income tax as possible.

What Will Be: How the New World of Information Will Change Our Lives. Michael L. Dertouzos. DIANE Publishing Co., 330 Pusey Ave. Collingdale, PA 19023. Phone: 800-782-3833 or (610)461-6200 Fax: (610)461-6130 E-mail: dianepub@erols.com 1997. $25.00. A discussion of the "information market place" of the future, including telecommuting, virtual reality, and computer recognition of speech. The author is director of the MIT Laboratory for Computer Science.

What Will Recession Mean to You? C. Edgar Murray, editor. American Institute for Economic Research, PO Box 1000 Great Barrington, MA 01230-1000. Phone: (413)528-1216 Fax: (413)528-0103 E-mail: info@aier.org • URL: http://www.aier.org • 2001. $6.00. A revision of *What Will the Next Recession Mean to You?* (1998). Covers the history of U. S. recessions, future recessions, forecasting, and "Coping with a Recession." (Economic Education Bulletin.)

What Works on Wall Street: A Guide to the Best Performing Investment Strategies of All Time. James P. O'Shaughnessy. McGraw-Hill, 1221 Ave. of the Americas New York, NY 10020. Phone: 800-722-4726 or (212)512-2000 Fax: (212)512-4502 E-mail: customer.service@mcgraw-hill.com • URL: http://www.mcgraw-hill.com • 1998. $49.95. Second revised edition. Examines investment strategies over a 43-year period and concludes that large capitalization, high-dividend-yield stocks produce the best results. Includes digital audio.

What You Need to Know About Mutual Funds. Kenneth M. Lefkowitz. American Institute for Economic Research, PO Box 1000 Great Barrington, MA 01230-1000. Phone: (413)528-1216 Fax: (413)528-0103 E-mail: info@aier.org • URL: http://www.aier.org • 2001. $6.00. Provides conservative advice on investing in mutual funds, unit investment trusts, closed-end investment companies, and other funds. Includes a glossary and lists of recommended information sources.

What Your Car Really Costs: How to Keep a Financially Safe Driving Record. American Institute for Economic Research, PO Box 1000 Great Barrington, MA 01230-1000. Phone: (413)528-1216 Fax: (413)528-0103 E-mail: info@aier.org • URL: http://www.aier.org • 2002. $6.00. Contains "Should You Buy or Lease?," "Should You Buy New or Used?," "Dealer Trade-in or Private Sale?," "Lemon Laws," and other car buying information. Includes rankings of specific models for resale value, 1995 to 2001. (Economic Education Bulletin.)

What's in a Name? Advertising and the Concept of Brands. John P. Jones and Jan S. Slater. M. E. Sharpe, Inc., 80 Business Park Drive Armonk, NY 10504. Phone: 800-541-6563 or (914)273-1800 Fax: (914)273-2106 E-mail: custserv@mesharpe.com • URL: http://www.mesharpe.com • 2003. $79.95. Second edition. Covers brand identity and loyalty from the viewpoint of modern marketing theory.

What's New in Advertising and Marketing. Special Libraries Association, Advertising and Marketing Div., c/o John Patton, Suffolk Cooperative Library System, 627 N. Sunrise Service Rd. Bellport, NY 11713. Phone: (516)286-1600 Fax: (516)286-1647 Quarterly. Non-profit organizations, $20.00 per year; corporations, $30.00 per year. Lists and briefly describes a wide variety of free or inexpensive material relating to advertising, marketing, and media.

Wheat, Barley, and Triticale Abstracts. Available from CABI Publishing, North America, 875 Massachusetts Ave., 7th Fl. Cambridge, MA 02139. Phone: 800-528-4841 or (617)395-4056 Fax: (617)354-6875 E-mail: cabi-nao@cabi.org • URL: http://www.cabi-publishing.org • Bimonthly. Institutions, $1,235.00 per year. Print and online editions, $1,250.00 per year. Published in England by CABI Publishing. Provides worldwide coverage of the literature of wheat, barley, and rye.

Wheat Facts. National Association of Wheat Growers, 415 Second St., N.E., Suite 300 Washington, DC 20002. Phone: (202)547-7800 Fax: (202)546-2638 E-mail: wheatworld@wheatworld.org • URL: http://www.wheatworld.org • Annual. Price on application.

Wheat Life. Washington Association of Wheat Growers, 109 E. First St. Ritzville, WA 99169-2394. Phone: (509)659-0610 11 times a year. $12.00 per year. Covers research, marketing information, and legislative and regulatory news pertinent to the wheat and barley industries of the Pacific Northwest.

Wheels of Fortune: The History of Speculation from Scandal to Respectability. Charles R. Geisst. John Wiley and Sons, Inc., 111 River St. Hoboken, NJ 07030. Phone: 800-225-5945 or (201)748-6000 Fax: (201)748-6088 E-mail: bookinfo@wiley.com • URL: http://www.wiley.com • 2002. $29.95. Provides a colorful history of speculation in the U. S. commodity futures markets from 1850 to about 2000.

When Talk Works: Profiles of Mediators. Deborah M. Kolb. John Wiley and Sons, Inc., 111 River St. Hoboken, NJ 07030. Phone: 800-225-5945 or (201)748-6000 Fax: (201)748-6088 E-mail: info@wiley.com • URL: http://www.wiley.com • 1997. $38.00. Provides interview-based profiles of expert mediators in labor, business, education, family matters, community relations, foreign affairs, and other fields. (Business Management Series).

When Technology Fails. Gale Cengage Learning, 27500 Drake Rd. Farmington Hills, MI 48331-3535. Phone: 800-877-GALE or (248)699-4253 Fax: 800-414-5043 E-mail: gale.galeord@cengage.com • URL: http://gale.cengage.com • 1994. $85.00. The stories of about 100 important technological disasters, accidents, and failures in the 20th century, caused by faults in design, construction, planning, and testing. Arranged in broad subject categories, with a keyword index.

When Work Doesn't Work Anymore: Women, Work, and Identity. Elizabeth P. McKenna. Doubleday Publishing, 1540 Broadway New York, NY 10036-4094. Phone: 800-323-9872 or (212)354-6500 Fax: (212)492-9700 • URL: http://www.doubledaybookclub.com • 1998. $12.95. A popularly written discussion of the conflict between corporate culture and the traditional, family roles of women.

When You Lose Your Job: Laid Off, Fired, Early Retired, Relocated, Demoted. Cliff Hakim. Berrett-Koehler Publishers, Inc., 235 Montgomery St., Ste. 650 San Francisco, CA 94104. Phone: 800-929-2929 or (415)288-0260 Fax: (415)362-2512 E-mail: bkpub@bkpub.com • URL: http://www.bkpub.com • 1993. $14.95. A guide to overcoming job loss. Covers emotional responses, as well as practical matters such as networking, resumes, and preparing for interviews.

Where the Suckers Moon: The Life and Death of an Advertising Campaign. Randall Rothenberg. Random House, Inc., 1540 Broadway New York, NY 10036. Phone: 800-726-0600 or (212)782-9000 E-mail: customerservice@randomhouse.com • URL: http://www.randomhouse.com • 1995. $16.00. Presents the story of an advertising agency's failed automobile campaign.

Where to Buy Hardwood Plywood, Veneer, and Engineered Hardwood Flooring. Hardwood Plywood and Veneer Association, P.O. 2789 Reston, VA 20195-0789. Phone: (703)435-2900 Fax: (703)435-2537 E-mail: hpva@hpva.org • URL: http://www.hpva.org • Annual. Free. Lists about 190 member manufacturers, prefinishers, and suppliers of hardwood veneer and plywood.

Where to Go When the Bank Says No: Alternatives to Financing Your Business. David R. Evanson. Bloomberg, 499 Park Ave. New York, NY 10022. Phone: 800-388-2749 or (212)318-2000 Fax: (917)369-5000 • URL: http://www.bloomberg.com • 1998. $24.95. Emphasis is on obtaining business financing in the $250,000 to $15,000,000 range. Business plans are discussed. (Bloomberg Small Business Series).

Where to Write for Vital Records: Births, Deaths, Marriages, and Divorces. Available from U. S. Government Printing Office, Washington, DC 20402. Phone: (202)512-1800 Fax: (202)512-2250 E-mail: gpoaccess@gpo.gov • URL: http://www.access.gpo.gov • 2002. $3.00. Issued by the National Center for Health Statistics, U. S. Department of Health and Human Services. Arranged by state. Provides addresses, telephone numbers, and cost of copies for various kinds of vital records or certificates. (DHHS Publication No. PHS 93-1142.)

Whirly-Girls - International Women Helicopter Pilots., PO Box 265 Pinehurst, TX 77362. Phone: (650)462-1441 Fax: (650)323-3840 E-mail: tcoreywg@aol.com • URL: http://www.whirlygirls.org • Women helicopter pilots. Stimulates interest among women in rotary-wing aircraft.

White Collar Crime: Business and Regulatory Offenses. American Lawyer Media, Inc., 105 Madison Ave. New York, NY 10016. Phone: 800-888-8300 or (212)779-9200 Fax: (212)481-8110 E-mail: lawcatalog@amlaw.com • URL: http://www.lawcatalog.com/ • Looseleaf. $249.00. Updated as needed. Covers such legal matters as criminal tax cases, securities fraud, computer crime, mail fraud, bank embezzlement, criminal antitrust activities, extortion, perjury, the criminal liability of corporations, and RICO (Racketeer Influenced and Corrupt Organization Act). (Law Journal Press).

White-Collar Crime Reporter: Information and Analyses Concerning White-Collar Practice. Andrews Publications, 175 Strafford Ave., Bldg 4, Suite 140 Wayne, PA 19087. Phone: 800-345-1101 or (610)225-0510 Fax: (610)225-0501 E-mail: customer@andrewspub.com • URL: http://www.andrewspub.com • 10 times a year. $550.00 per year. Newsletter. Provides information on trends in white collar crime.

Whittington's Dictionary of Plastics. James F. Carley, editor. CRC Press LLC., 2000 NW Corporate Blvd. Boca Raton, FL 33431. Phone: 800-272-7737 or (561)994-0555 Fax: 800-374-3401 or (561)989-9732 E-mail: orders@crcpress.com • URL: http://www.crcpress.com • 1993. $129.95. Third expanded revised edition.

Who Audits America: A Directory of Publicly Held Corporations and the Accounting Firms Who Audit Them. Data Financial Press, P.O. Box 668 Menlo Park, CA 94026. Phone: (415)321-4553 Fax: (707)598-3560 1994. $155.00. 12,000 publicly held corporations that report to the Securities and Exchange Commission, and their accounting firms.

Who Cares for Them? Workers in the Home Care Industry. Penny H. Feldman and others. Greenwood Publishing Group, Inc., 88 Post Rd., W. Westport, CT 06881-5007. Phone: 800-225-5800 or (203)226-3571 Fax: (203)431-2214 E-mail: customer-service@greenwood.com • URL: http://www.greenwood.com • 1990. $67.95. (Contributions to the Study of Aging Series: No.16).

Who Knows Who: Networking Through Corporate Boards. Jeannette E. Glynn. Who Knows Who Publishing, 568 62nd St., Unit A Oakland, CA 94609-1245. Phone: (510)601-1556 1998. $165.00. Fifth edition. Shows the connections between the board members of major U. S. corporations and major foundations and nonprofit organizations.

Who Owns Whom. Dun & Bradstreet Corp., 103 JFK Pky., 103 JFK Pky. Short Hills, NJ 07078. Phone: 800-234-3867 or (973)921-5500 Fax: (973)921-6056 E-mail: custserv@dnb.com • URL: http://www.dnb.com • Covers: In four regional volumes, approximately 320,000 company affiliates and subsidiaries of more than 23,000 companies in Australia and the Far East, North America, the United Kingdom and Ireland, and Continental Europe. Entries include: Ultimate parent and country, parent name, address, phone, place of incorporation, Standard Industrial Classification (SIC) code, trade investments, direct subsidiaries.

Who Owns Whom: Australasia, Asia, Middle East and Africa. Dun & Bradstreet Corp., 103 JFK Pky. Short Hills, NJ 07078. Phone: 800-526-0651 E-mail: custserv@dnb.com • URL: http://www.dnb.com • Annual. $550.00. Two volumes. Published in England by Dun & Bradstreet Ltd. Provides information on 32,000 parent companies and their foreign and domestic subsidiaries. Parent companies are located in Singapore, Hong Kong, Japan, the Philippines, South Korea, Taiwan, Thailand, Papua New Guinea, Malaysia, Indonesia, New Zealand, and Australia. Formerly *Who Owns Whom: Australasia and Far East*.

Who Writes What in Life and Health Insurance. The National Underwriter Co., 5081 Olympic Blvd. Erlanger, KY 41017. Phone: 800-543-0874 or (859)692-2100 • URL: http://www.nationalunderwriter.com • Annual. $9.95.

Wholesale Commodity Report. Financial Times, 14 E. 60th St. New York, NY 10022. Phone: (212)641-6500 Weekly. $144.00 to $165.00 per year depending on postal rates.

Wholesale Florists and Florist Suppliers Association Membership Directory. Wholesale Florists and Florist Suppliers Association, 147 Old Solomons Island Rd., Suite 302 Annapolis, MD 21401. Phone: 800-289-3372 or (410)573-0400 Fax: (410)573-5001 E-mail: jwanko@wffsa.org • URL: http://www.wffsa.org • Free to members; non-members, $100.00.

Wholesale Florists and Florist Suppliers of America., 147 Old Solomons Island Rd., Suite 302 Annapolis, MD 21401-3838. Phone: (410)573-0400 Fax: (410)573-5001 E-mail: j.wanko@wffsa.org • URL: http://www.wffsa.org • Formerly Wholesale Commission Florists.

The Wholesaler. TMB Publishing, Inc., 1838 Techny Court Northbrook, IL 60062. Phone: (847)564-1127 Fax: (847)564-1264 E-mail: info@tmbpublishing.com • URL: http://www.thewholesaler.com • Monthly. $75.00 per year. Edited for wholesalers and distributors of plumbing, piping, heating, and air conditioning equipment.

The Wholesaler "The Wholesaling 100". TMB Publishing, Inc., 1838 Techny Court Northbrook, IL 60062. Phone: (847)564-1127 Fax: (847)564-1264 E-mail: info@tmbpublishing.com • URL: http://www.thewholesaler.com • Annual. $25.00. Provides information on the 100 leading wholesalers of plumbing, piping, heating, and air conditioning equipment.

Who's Who Among African Americans. Gale Cengage Learning, 27500 Drake Rd. Farmington Hills, MI 48331-3535. Phone: 800-877-GALE or (248)699-4253 Fax: 800-414-5043 E-mail: gale.galeord@cengage.com • URL: http://gale.cengage.com • 2002. $195.00. 15th edition. Includes many business leaders.

Who's Who: An Annual Biographical Dictionary. Saint Martin's Press, 175 Fifth Ave. New York, NY 10010. Phone: 800-221-7945 or (212)674-5151 E-mail: enquiries@stmartin.com • URL: http://www.stmartins.com • Annual. $275.00. Over 29,000 prominent individuals worldwide, but with emphasis on the United Kingdom.

Who's Who in America. Marquis Who's Who, 121 Chanlon Rd. New Providence, NJ 07974. Phone: 800-473-7020 or (908)673-1001 Fax: (908)673-1189 E-mail: susan.towne@marquiswhoswho.com • URL: http://www.marquiswhoswho.com • Annual. $575.00. Three volumes. Contains over 90,000 concise biographies, with a Geographic/Professional Index.

Who's Who in American Art. Available from Reed Elsevier, 121 Chanlon Rd. New Providence, NJ 07974. Phone: (908)464-6800 Fax: (908)464-3553 • URL: http://www.reed-elsevier.com • Biennial. $229.00. Lists about 11,800 people active in visual arts. Published by Marquis Who's Who.

Who's Who in American Education. Marquis Who's Who, 121 Chanlon Rd. New Providence, NJ 07974. Phone: 800-473-7020 or (908)673-1001 Fax: (908)673-1189 E-mail: susan.towne@marquiswhoswho.com • URL: http://www.marquiswhoswho.com • Biennial. $159.95. Contains over 27,000 concise biographies of teachers, administrators, and other individuals involved in all levels of American education.

Who's Who in American Law. Marquis Who's Who, 121 Chanlon Rd. New Providence, NJ 07974. Phone: 800-473-7020 or (908)673-1001 Fax: (908)673-1189 E-mail: susan.towne@marquiswhoswho.com • URL: http://www.marquiswhoswho.com • Biennial. $295.00. Contains over 23,000 concise biographies of American lawyers, judges, and others in the legal field.

Who's Who in American Politics. Marquis Who's Who, 121 Chanlon Rd. New Providence, NJ 07974. Phone: 800-473-7020 or (908)673-1000 Fax: (908)673-1189 E-mail: susan.towne@marquiswhoswho.com • URL: http://www.marquiswhoswho.com • Biennial. $275.00. Two volumes. Contains about 27,000 biographical sketches of local, state, and national elected or appointed individuals.

Who's Who in Art. Available from Gale Cengage Learning, 27500 Drake Rd. Farmington Hills, MI 48331-3535. Phone: 800-877-4253 or (248)699-4253 Fax: 800-414-5043 E-mail: gale.galeord@cengage.com • URL: http://gale.cengage.com • Biennial. $140.00 per year. Contains about 3,000 brief biographies of artists, designers, curators, critics, and other art-related individuals. International coverage, with British emphasis. Published by Art Trade Press.

Who's Who in Art Materials/NAMTA Membership. National Art Materials Trade Association, 15806 Brookway Dr., Ste. 300 Huntersville, NC 28078. Phone: (704)982-6244 Fax: (704)982-6247 E-mail: info@namta.org • URL: http://www.namta.org • Annual. Free to members; non-members, $110.00 per year. Lists retailers and manufacturers of artists' supplies.

Who's Who in Association Management. American Society of Association Executives, 1575 Eye St., N.W. Washington, DC 20005-1103. Phone: (202)626-2723 Fax: (202)408-9634 E-mail: asea@asea.org • URL: http://www.asaenet.org • Annual. $160.00. Lists paid executives who are members of the association and suppliers of products and services to the association.

Who's Who in Canadian Business. University of Toronto Press, 241 College St. Toronto, ON, Canada M4Y 2W8. Phone: (416)978-2239 Fax: (416)921-6353 E-mail: books@utpress.utoronto.ca • URL: http://www.uoftbookstorestore.com • Annual. $179.95. Contains brief biographies of 5,200 individuals prominent in Canadian business.

Who's Who in Engineering. American Association of Engineering Societies, 1828 L St. NW, Ste. 906 Washington, DC 20036. Phone: 888-400-2237 or (202)296-2237 Fax: (202)296-1151 E-mail: aaes@aaes.org • URL: http://www.aaes.org • 1995. $250.00. Lists about 15,000 engineers who have received professional recognition for outstanding achievement.

Who's Who in Finance and Industry. Marquis Who's Who, 121 Chanlon Rd. New Providence, NJ 07974. Phone: 800-473-7020 or (908)673-1001 Fax: (908)673-1189 E-mail: susan.towne@marquiswhoswho.com • URL: http://www.marquiswhoswho.com • Biennial. $259.95. Provides over 21,000 concise biographies of business leaders in all fields.

Who's Who in Insurance. Underwriter Printing and Publishing Co., 50 E. Palisade Ave. Englewood, NJ 07631. Phone: 800-526-4700 or (201)569-8808 Fax: (201)569-8817 Annual. $150.00. Contains over 5,000 biographies of insurance officials, leading agents and brokers, and high-ranking company officials.

Who's Who in International Banking. Bowker-Saur, 121 Chanlon Rd. New Providence, NJ 07974. Phone: 800-521-8110 or (908)464-6800 Fax: (908)464-3553 E-mail: info@bowker.com • URL: http://www.bowker.com • Irregular. $400.00. Contains biographical sketches of about 4,000 bankers. Worldwide coverage.

Who's Who in Metal Forming and Fabricating. Fabricators and Manufacturers Association International, 833 Featherstone Rd. Rockford, IL 61107-6302. Phone: (815)399-8700 Fax: (815)484-7700 E-mail: info@fmametalfab.org • URL: http://www.fmametalfab.org • Annual. Free to members; non-members, $200.00. Lists members of the Fabricators and Manufacturers Association (FMA), International; and members of the Tube and Pipe Association. Includes five indexes. Formerly *FMA Member Resource Directory*.

Who's Who in Packaging. Institute of Packaging Professionals, 1601 N Bond St., Ste. 101 Naperville, IL 60563. Phone: 800-432-4085 or (630)544-5050 Fax: (630)544-5055 E-mail: info@iopp.org • URL: http://www.iopp.org • Annual. Price on application. Formerly *Who's Who and What's What in Packaging*.

Who's Who in Professional Imaging. Professional Photographers of America, Inc., 229 Peachtree St., N.E., Suite 2200 Atlanta, GA 30303. Phone: 800-786-6277 or (404)522-8600 Fax: (404)614-6405 E-mail: csc@ppa.com • URL: http://www.ppa-world.org • Annual. $110.00. Lists over 18,000 members. Formerly *Buyers Guide to Qualified Photographers*.

Who's Who in Risk Management. Underwriter Printing and Publishing Co., 50 E. Palisade Ave. Englewood, NJ 07631. Phone: 800-526-4700 or (201)569-8808 Fax: (201)569-8817 Annual. $95.00. Contains specialized biographies of insurance buyers for large business and industrial firms throughout the U.S.

Who's Who in Science and Engineering. Marquis Who's Who, 121 Chanlon Rd. New Providence, NJ 07974. Phone: 800-473-7020 or (908)673-1000 Fax: (908)673-1189 E-mail: susan.towne@marquiswhoswho.com • URL: http://www.marquiswhoswho.com • Biennial. $269.00. Provides concise biographical information on 35,000 prominent engineers and scientists. International coverage, with geographical and professional indexes.

Who's Who in Special Libraries. Special Libraries Association, 1700 18th St, N. W. Washington, DC 20009-2514. Phone: (202)234-4700 Fax: (202)265-9317 E-mail: sla@sla.org • URL: http://www.sla.org • Annual. $125.00. Available only online. About 14,000 librarians of libraries and special collections having a specific subject focus.

Who's Who in Technology [Online]. Gale Cengage Learning, 27500 Drake Rd. Farmington Hills, MI 48331-3535. Phone: 800-877-GALE or (248)669-GALE Fax: 800-414-5043 or (248)699-8069 E-mail: galeord@gale.com • URL: http://gale.cengage.com • Provides online biographical profiles of over 25,000 American scientists, engineers, and others in technology-related occupations. Inquire as to online cost and availability.

Who's Who in the Egg and Poultry Industries. Watt Publishing Co., 122 S. Wesley Ave. Mount Morris, IL 61054. Phone: (815)734-4171 Fax: (815)734-4201 • URL: http://www.wattnet.com • Annual. $100.00. Producers, processors, and distributors of poultry meat and eggs in the United States; manufacturers of supplies and equipment for the poultry industry; breeders and hatcheries; refrigerated public warehouses;. food chain buyers of poultry meat and eggs; related government agencies; poultry associations.

Who's Who in the Securities Industry. Economist Publishing Co., 11 N Wabash Ave., Ste. 1120 Chicago, IL 60602-2012. Phone: 800-843-3266 or (312)467-1888 Fax: (312)467-0225 Annual. $15.00. Lists about 1,000 investment bankers.

Who's Who in the Snack Food Industry. Snack Food Association, 1711 King St., Suite 1 Alexandria, VA 22314. Phone: 800-628-1334 or (703)836-4500 Fax: (703)836-8262 E-mail: sfa@sfa.org • URL: http://www.snax.com • Annual. $150. 00. A directory of more than 800 snack food manufacturers and suppliers to the industry.

Who's Who in the Southern Furniture Industry. American Furniture Manufacturers Association, P.O. Box HP-7 High Point, NC 27261. Phone: (336)884-5000 Fax: (336)884-5303 E-mail: accounts@afma4u.org • URL: http://www.afma4u. org • Annual. $50.00. Lists about 400 manufacturers of furniture and their suppliers.

Who's Who in the Wall and Ceiling Industry. Association of the Wall and Ceiling Industries International, 803 W Broad St., Ste. 600 Falls Church, VA 22046. Phone: (703)534-8300 Fax: (703)534-8307 E-mail: info@awci.org • URL: http://www. awci.org • Annual. $45.00. Contractors, manufacturers, suppliers, unions, organizations, and periodicals affiliated with the industry.

Who's Who in the World. Marquis Who's Who, 121 Chanlon Rd. New Providence, NJ 07974. Phone: 800-473-7020 or (908)673-1000 Fax: (908)673-1189 E-mail: susan.towne@ marquiswhoswho.com • URL: http://www.marquiswhoswho. com • Annual. $329.95. Provides biographical profiles of about 35,000 prominent individuals. International coverage.

Who's Who in World Petrochemicals and Plastics. Reed Business Information, 360 Park Ave. S New York, NY 10010. Phone: 800-446-6551 or (646)746-6400 E-mail: corporatecommunications@reedbusiness.com • URL: http:// www.reedbusiness.com • Annual. $175.00. Names, addresses, telephone numbers, and company affiliations of individuals active in the petrochemical business. Formerly *Who's Who in World Petrochemicals*.

Who's Who-Masa's Buyers' Guide to Blue Ribbon Mailing Service. Mailing and Fulfillment Service Association, 1421 Prince St. Alexandria, VA 22314-2806. Phone: 800-333-6272 or (703)836-9200 Fax: (703)548-8204 E-mail: mfsa-mail@ mfsanet.org • URL: http://www.mfsanet.org • Annual. Free. Member firms that provide printing, addressing, inserting, sorting, and other mailing services, and mailing list brokers.

Who's Who of American Women. Marquis Who's Who, 121 Chanlon Rd. New Providence, NJ 07974. Phone: 800-473-7020 or (908)673-1001 Fax: (908)673-1189 E-mail: susan. towne@marquiswhoswho.com • URL: http://www. marquiswhoswho.com • Biennial. $275.00. Provides over 25,000 biographical profiles of important women, including individuals prominent in business, finance, and industry.

Who's Who: The CTFA Membership Directory (Cosmetics Industry). Cosmetic, Toiletry, and Fragrance Association, 1101 17th St., N. W., Suite 300 Washington, DC 20036-4702. Phone: (202)331-1770 Fax: (202)331-1969 E-mail: membership@ctfa.org • URL: http://www.ctfa.org • Annual. Free to members; non-members, $100.00. Lists 600 member companies, with key personnel, products, and services.

Why Entreprenuers Fail: Avoid the 20 Fatal Pitfalls of Running Your Own Business. James W. Halloran. Waterview Press, Inc., 3208 E Colonial Dr., No. 301 Orlando, FL 32803. Phone: (407)599-7200 Fax: 800-726-0585 or (407)629-0662 E-mail: waterviewpress@mindspring.com 1999. $17.00. Second revised edition.

Why Leaders Can't Lead: The Unconscious Conspiracy Continues. Warren Bennis. John Wiley and Sons, Inc., 111 River St. Hoboken, NJ 07030. Phone: 800-225-5945 or (201)748-6000 Fax: (201)748-6088 E-mail: info@wiley.com • URL: http://www.wiley.com • 1997. $22.95.

Why This Horse Won't Drink: How to Win and Keep Employee Commitment. Ken Matejka. AMACOM, 1601 Broadway New York, NY 10019. Phone: 800-262-9699 or (518)586-8100 Fax: (518)903-8168 E-mail: customerservice@amanet. org • URL: http://www.amacombooks.org • 1990. $22.95. How to set up programs to build trust and change behavior.

Wiley Dictionary of Civil Engineering and Construction. Len F. Webster, editor. John Wiley and Sons, Inc., 111 River St. Hoboken, NJ 07030. Phone: 800-225-5945 or (201)748-6000 Fax: (201)748-6088 E-mail: info@wiley.com • URL: http:// www.wiley.com • 1997. $85.00. Provides more than 30,000 definitions in the fields of civil engineering, construction, architecture, forestry, mining, and public works. (Professional Series).

Wiley Encyclopedia of Electrical and Electronics Engineering. John G. Webster, editor. John Wiley and Sons, Inc., 111 River St. Hoboken, NJ 07030. Phone: 800-225-5945 or (201)748-6000 Fax: (201)748-6088 E-mail: info@wiley.com • URL: http://www.wiley.com • 1999. $9,630.00. 25 volumes. Includes *Supplement I*and*Supplement II*. Contains about 1,400 articles, each with bibliography. Arrangement is according to 64 categories.

Wiley Encyclopedia of Energy and the Environment. Attilio Bisio and Sharon Boots. John Wiley and Sons, Inc., 111 River St. Hoboken, NJ 07030. Phone: 800-225-5945 or (201)748-6000 Fax: (201)748-6088 E-mail: info@wiley.com • URL: http://www.wiley.com • 1996. $285.00. Abriged edition. Two volumes. Covers a wide variety of energy and environmental topics, including legal and policy issues. (Encyclopedia of Energy and the Environment Series: Vol. 2).

Wiley Encyclopedia of Environmental Pollution and Cleanup. Robert A. Meyers, editor. John Wiley and Sons, Inc., 111 River St. Hoboken, NJ 07030. Phone: 800-225-5945 or (201)748-6000 Fax: (201)748-6088 E-mail: info@wiley.com • URL: http://www.wiley.com • 1999. $350.00. Two volumes. Presents generally nontechnical, basic coverage of environmental hazards and methods of detection and cleanup, with consideration of risk assessment, regulatory policy, and economic factors.

Wiley Encyclopedia of Food Science and Technology. Frederick J. Francis, editor. John Wiley and Sons, Inc., 111 River St. Hoboken, NJ 07030. Phone: 800-225-5945 or (201)748-6000 Fax: (201)748-6088 E-mail: info@wiley.com • URL: http:// www.wiley.com • 2000. $1,650.00. Second edition. Four volumes. Contains about 400 entries. Coverage includes biotechnology, genetic engineering, nutrition, regulatory matters, food safety, labeling, food substitutes (sugar, fat, dairy), and many other topics.

Wiley Encyclopedia of Packaging Technology. Aaron Brody and Kenneth Marsh, editors. John Wiley and Sons, Inc., 111 River St. Hoboken, NJ 07030. Phone: 800-225-5945 or (201)748-6000 Fax: (201)748-6088 E-mail: info@wiley.com • URL: http://www.wiley.com • 1997. $330.00. Second edition.

Wiley Encyclopedia of Telecommunications and Signal Processing. John G. Proakis, editor. John Wiley and Sons, Inc., 111 River St. Hoboken, NJ 07030. Phone: 800-225-5945 or (201)748-6000 Fax: (201)748-6088 E-mail: info@wiley. com • URL: http://www.wiley.com • 2002. $1,250.00. Five volumes. Contains about 300 articles covering both fundamentals and recent advances in telecommunications and signal processing. Emphasis is on material for electrical engineers.

Willing's Press Guide. Romeike, Romeike House, 16-22 Baltic St. W London EC1Y 0UL, United Kingdom. Phone: 800-877-GALE or (44)1494 797225 Fax: 800-414-5043 or (44)20 74905640 E-mail: info@romeike.com • URL: http://gale. cengage.com • Covers: almost 20,000 United Kingdom print media titles, publishers, and broadcasters; over 30,000 periodicals and newspapers in the United Kingdom, with listings for major publications in Europe, the Americas, Australasia, Africa, the Far East, and the Middle East; also includes services and suppliers section to publishers in the United Kingdom. Entries include: For periodicals—Publication title, name of publisher, address, frequency, subscription price, advertising rates, editorial contact names, phone, names and titles of key personnel, circulation. For services—Name, address.

Williston on Contracts. Richard A. Lord. West Group, 610 Opperman Dr. Eagan, MN 55123. Phone: 800-328-4880 or (651)687-7000 Fax: 800-340-9378 E-mail: bookstore@ westgroup.com • URL: http://www.westgroup.com • $1,963. 00. 23 volumes. Periodic supplementation. Encyclopedic coverage of contract law.

Wilson Business Abstracts Online. H. W. Wilson Co., 950 University Ave. Bronx, NY 10452. Phone: 800-367-6770 or (718)588-8400 Fax: (718)590-1617 E-mail: hwwmsg@info. hwwilson.com • URL: http://ww.hwwilson.com • Indexes and abstracts 600 major business periodicals, plus the *Wall Street Journal* and the business section of the *New York Times*. Indexing is from 1982, abstracting from 1990, with the two newspapers included from 1993. Updated weekly. Inquire as to online cost and availability. (*Business Periodicals Index* without abstracts is also available online.)

Wilson Social Sciences Abstracts Online. H. W. Wilson Co., 950 University Ave. Bronx, NY 10452. Phone: 800-367-6770 or (718)588-8400 Fax: (718)590-1617 E-mail: hwwmsg@info. hwwilson.com • URL: http://www.hwwilson.com • Provides online abstracting and indexing of more than 500 periodicals covering area studies, community health, public administration, public welfare, urban studies, and many other social science topics. Time period is 1994 to date for abstracts and 1983 to date for indexing, with updates weekly. Inquire as to online cost and availability.

WILSONDISC: Applied Science and Technology Abstracts. H. W. Wilson Co., 950 University Ave. Bronx, NY 10452. Phone: 800-367-6770 or (718)588-8400 Fax: 800-590-1617 Monthly. Includes unlimited access to the online version of *Applied Science and Technology Abstracts* through WILSONLINE. Provides CD-ROM indexing and abstracting of 500 prominent scientific, technical, engineering, and industrial periodicals. Indexing coverage is provided from 1983 to date and abstracting from 1993 to date.

WILSONDISC: Art Index. H. W. Wilson Co., 950 University Ave. Bronx, NY 10452. Phone: 800-367-6770 or (718)588-8400 Fax: 800-590-1617 Monthly. Provides CD-ROM indexing of art-related literature from 1982 to date. Price includes online service.

WILSONDISC: Biography Index. H. W. Wilson Co., 950 University Ave. Bronx, NY 10452. Phone: 800-367-6770 or (718)588-8400 Fax: 800-590-1617 Quarterly. Includes unlimited online access to *Biography Index* through WILSONLINE. Provides CD-ROM indexing of biographical information appearing in books, critical studies, fiction, periodicals, obituaries, and other printed sources. Time period is 1984 to date. Corresponds to the printed and online *Biography Index*.

WILSONDISC: Biological and Agricultural Index. H. W. Wilson Co., 950 University Ave. Bronx, NY 10452. Phone: 800-367-6770 or (718)588-8400 Fax: 800-590-1617 Monthly. Includes unlimited online access to *Biological and Agricultural Index* through WILSONLINE. Provides CD-ROM indexing of over 250 periodicals covering agriculture, agricultural chemicals, biochemistry, biotechnology, entomology, horticulture, and related topics.

WILSONDISC: Business Periodicals Index. H. W. Wilson Co., 950 University Ave. Bronx, NY 10452. Phone: 800-367-6770 or (718)588-8400 Fax: 800-590-1617 Monthly. Provides CD-ROM indexing of business periodicals from 1982 to date. Price includes online service.

WILSONDISC: Education Index. H. W. Wilson Co., 950 University Ave. Bronx, NY 10452. Phone: 800-367-6770 or (718)588-8400 Fax: 800-590-1617 Monthly. Provides CD-ROM indexing of education-related literature from 1983 to date. Price includes online service.

WILSONDISC: Index to Legal Periodicals and Books. H. W. Wilson Co., 950 University Ave. Bronx, NY 10452. Phone: 800-367-6770 or (718)588-8400 Fax: 800-590-1617 Monthly. Includes unlimited online access to *Index to Legal Periodicals* through WILSONLINE. Contains CD-ROM indexing of more than 1,400 English language legal periodicals from 1981 to date and 2,500 books.

WILSONDISC: Library Literature and Information Science Index. H. W. Wilson Co., 950 University Ave. Bronx, NY 10452. Phone: 800-367-6770 or (718)588-8400 Fax: 800-590-1617 Quarterly. Includes unlimited access to the online version of *Library Literature*. Provides CD-ROM indexing of about 300 periodicals, covering a wide range of topics having to do with libraries, library management, and the information industry.

WILSONDISC: Readers' Guide to Periodical Literature. H. W. Wilson Co., 950 University Ave. Bronx, NY 10452. Phone: 800-367-6770 or (718)588-8400 Fax: 800-590-1617 Monthly. $1,095.00 per year, including unlimited online access to *Readers' Guide to Periodical Literature* through WILSONLINE. Provides CD-ROM indexing of about 270 general interest periodicals. Covers 1983 to date. (*Readers' Guide Abstracts* also available on CD-ROM at $1,995 per year.)

WILSONDISC: Wilson Business Abstracts. H. W. Wilson Co., 950 University Ave. Bronx, NY 10452. Phone: 800-367-6770 or (718)588-8400 Fax: 800-590-1617 E-mail: hwwmsg@ info.hwwilson.com • URL: http://www.hwwilson.com • Monthly. Includes unlimited online access to *Wilson Business Abstracts* through WILSONLINE. Provides CD-ROM "cover-to-cover" abstracting and indexing of over 600 prominent business periodicals. Indexing is from 1982, abstracting from 1990. (*Business Periodicals Index* without abstracts is available on CD-ROM at $1,495 per year.)

WILSONDISC: Wilson Social Sciences Abstracts. H. W. Wilson Co., 950 University Ave. Bronx, NY 10452. Phone: 800-367-6770 or (718)588-8400 Fax: 800-590-1617 E-mail: hwwmsg@info.hwwilson.com • URL: http://www.hwwilson. com • Monthly. Includes unlimited online access to *Social Sciences Index* through WILSONLINE. Provides CD-ROM indexing from 1983 and abstracting from 1994 of more than 500 periodicals covering economics, area studies, community health, public administration, public welfare, urban studies, and many other topics related to the social sciences.

WilsonWeb Periodicals Databases. H. W. WilsonPhone: 800-367-6770 or (718)588-8400 Fax: 800-590-1617 or (718)992-8003 E-mail: custserv@hwwilson.com • URL: http://www. hwwilson.com/ • Web sites provide fee-based access to *Wilson Business Full Text, Applied Science & Technology Full Text, Biological & Agricultural Index, Library Literature & Information Science Full Text*, and *Readers' Guide Full Text, Mega Edition*. Daily updates.

WIMA Bulletin. Writing Instrument Manufacturers Association, 17000 Commerce Pky., Ste. C Mount Laurel, NJ 08054. Phone: (856)638-0426 Fax: (856)439-0525 E-mail: wima@ ahint.com • URL: http://www.wima.org • 50 times a year. Price on application.

WIMA Directory. Writing Instrument Manufacturers Association, 17000 Commerce Pky., Ste. C Mount Laurel, NJ 08054. Phone: (856)638-0426 Fax: (856)439-0525 E-mail: wima@ ahint.com • URL: http://www.wima.org • Semiannual. $50. 00. Lists manufacturers, suppliers and products of the writing industry.

Win Government Contracts for Your Small Business. John DiGiacomo and James Kleckner. CCH, Inc., 4025 West Peterson Ave. Chicago, IL 60646-6085. Phone: 800-248-3248 or (773)866-6000 Fax: 800-224-8299 or (773)866-3095 E-mail: cust_serv@cch.com • URL: http://www.onlinestore.cch.com/ • 2003. $24.95. Second edition. Provides 10 "easy-to-understand steps" to obtain government contracts. Appendices include a glossary, sample forms, and other information.

WIN News: All the News that is Fit to Print By, For and About Women. Women's International Network, 187 Grant St. Lexington, MA 02173-2140. Phone: (781)862-9431 Fax: (781)862-9431 E-mail: winnews@igc.org • URL: http:// www.feminist.com • Quarterly. Individuals $35.00 per year; institutions, $48.00 per year. World-wide communication system by, for and about women of all backgrounds, beliefs, nationalities and age-groups.

Win-Win Negotiating: Turning Conflict into Agreement. Fred E. Jandt. John Wiley and Sons, Inc., 111 River St. Hoboken, NJ 07030. Phone: 800-225-5945 or (201)748-6000 Fax: (201)748-6088 E-mail: info@wiley.com • URL: http://www.

wiley.com • 1987. $24.95. (Sound Business Cassette Books).

Window and Door Manufacturers Association., 1400 E Touhy Ave., No. 470 Des Plaines, IL 60018. Phone: 800-223-2301 or (847)299-5200 Fax: (847)299-1286 E-mail: admin@wdma.com • URL: http://www.wdma.org • Members are manufacturers of wooden door and window products. Absorbed Ponderosa Pine Woodwork Association. Formerly National Wood Window and Door Association.

Window Coverings Association of America., 3550 McKelvey Rd., No. 202 C Bridgeton, MO 63044-2535. Phone: 888-298-9222 or (314)770-0229 Fax: (314)770-0263 E-mail: info@wcaa.org • URL: http://www.wcaa.org • Members are manufacturers of venetian blinds, vertical blinds, and pleated shades.

Window Fashions. Grace McNamara Publishing, Inc., 4215 White Bear Parkway, Suite 100 St. Paul, MN 55110-7635. Phone: (651)293-1544 Fax: (651)653-4308 E-mail: bloberg@gwmcnamara.com • URL: http://www.gwmcnamara.com • Monthly. $39.00 per year. Published for designers and retailers of draperies, blinds, and shades.

Window Fashions Magazine: Design and Education Magazine. Grace McNamara Publishing, Inc., 4215 White Bear Parkway, Suite 100 St. Paul, MN 55110-7635. Phone: (651)293-1544 Fax: (651)653-4308 E-mail: barb@gracemcnamara.com • URL: http://www.gwmcnamara.com • Monthly. $39.00 per year. A directory of suppliers, manufacturers, and fabricators of vertical blinds, soft shades, curtains, draperies, and other window treatment items. Appears as a regular feature of *Window Fashions Magazine* and covers a different product category each month.

Window Treatments. Karla J. Nielson. John Wiley and Sons, Inc., 111 River St. Hoboken, NJ 07030. Phone: 800-225-5945 or (201)748-6000 Fax: (201)748-6088 E-mail: info@wiley.com • URL: http://www.wiley.com • 1989. $85.00.

Window Washing Service. Entrepreneur Media, Inc., 2445 McCabe Way Irvine, CA 92614. Phone: 800-421-2300 or (949)261-2325 Fax: (949)261-0234 E-mail: entmag@entrepreneur.com • URL: http://www.entrepreneur.com • Looseleaf. $59.50. A practical guide to starting a window cleaning business. Covers profit potential, start-up costs, market size evaluation, owner's time required, pricing, accounting, advertising, promotion, etc. (Start-Up Business Guide No. E1012.)

Windows. Available from MarketResearch.com, 641 Ave. of the Americas, Third Floor New York, NY 10011. Phone: 800-298-5699 or (212)807-2629 Fax: (212)807-2716 E-mail: order@marketresearch.com • URL: http://www.marketresearch.com • 2001. $2,250.00. Market research report published by Specialists in Business Information. Covers metal, wood, and vinyl windows. Presents market data relative to demographics, sales growth, shipments, exports, imports, price trends, and end-use. Includes company profiles.

Windows and .Net Magazine. Penton Media, Inc., 1300 E 9th St. Cleveland, OH 44114. Phone: (216)696-7000 Fax: (216)696-1752 E-mail: subs@winntmag.com • URL: http://www.win2000mag.net • 14 times a year. $49.95 per year. Edited for information systems personnel developing business applications for Windows NT software. Formerly *Windows2000Magazine.*

Windows Developer's Network: Application Development from Windows to Web. CMP Media LLC, 600 Community Dr. Manhasset, NY 11030. Phone: (516)562-5000 E-mail: cmp@cmp.com • URL: http://www.cmp.com • Monthly. $34.99 per year. Edited for advanced programming developers. Formerly *Windows Developer's Journal.*

Windows in Financial Services., 162 Fifth Ave., Suite 1015 New York, NY 10010. Phone: (212)206-9393 Fax: (212)206-9778 • URL: http://www.windowsfs.com • Quarterly. $39.00 per year. Covers information technology applications and products for Microsoft Windows users in the financial sector.

Windows ME Annoyances. David Karp. O'Reilly & Associates, Inc., 90 Sherman St. Cambridge, MA 02140. Phone: 800-775-7731 or (617)354-5800 Fax: (617)661-1116 E-mail: order@oreilly.com • URL: http://www.oreilly.com • 2001. $29.95. A critical but helpful view of Windows Millennium Edition.

Windows ME: The Missing Manual - The Book That Should Have Been in the Box. David Pogue. O'Reilly & Associates, Inc., 90 Sherman St. Cambridge, MA 02140. Phone: 800-775-7731 or (617)354-5800 Fax: (617)661-1116 E-mail: order@oreilly.com • URL: http://www.oreilly.com • 2000. $19.95. Popularly written explanation of Windows ME features. (Pogue Press.)

Windows Millennium Edition: The Complete Reference. John R. Levine and Margaret L. Young. McGraw-Hill, 1221 Ave. of the Americas New York, NY 10020. Phone: 800-722-4726 or (212)512-2000 Fax: (212)512-4502 E-mail: customer.service@mcgraw-hill.com • URL: http://www.mcgraw-hill.com • 2000. $39.99. (Complete Reference Series).

Windows 98 Bible. Alan Simpton and others. John Wiley and Sons, Inc., 111 River St. Hoboken, NJ 07030. Phone: 800-225-5945 or (201)748-6000 Fax: (201)748-6088 E-mail: bookinfo@wiley.com • URL: http://www.wiley.com • 1998. $39.99.

Windows 98 for Busy People. Ron Mansfield and Peter Weverka. Macmillian Inc., 175 5th Ave. New York, NY 10010. Phone: (212)982-3900 Fax: (212)777-6359 • URL: http://www.macmillan.com • 1999. $19.99. Second edition.

Windows 98 in a Nutshell. Tim O'Reilly. O'Reilly & Associates,

Inc., 90 Sherman St. Cambridge, MA 02140. Phone: 800-775-7731 or (617)354-5800 Fax: (617)661-1116 E-mail: order@oreilly.com • URL: http://www.oreilly.com • 1999. $24.95. (In a Nutshell Series).

Windows 95 is Driving Me Crazy! A Practical Guide to Windows 95 Headaches, Hassles, Bugs, Potholes, and Installation Problems. Kay Y. Nelson. Peachpit Press, 1249 Eighth St. Berkeley, CA 94710. Phone: 800-283-9444 or (510)524-2178 Fax: (510)524-2221 E-mail: tell@peachpit.com • URL: http://www.peachpit.com • 1996. $24.95. Includes many illustrations.

Windows NT Administration and Security. Richard O. Hudson. Prentice Hall PTR, 240 Frisch Ct. Paramus, NJ 07652. Phone: 800-282-0693 Fax: 800-455-6991 • URL: http://www.phptr.com • 2001. $95.00.

Windows NT Server Concise. Jerry Dixon and J. Scott Reeves. New Riders Publishing, 800 E 96th St. Indianapolis, IN 46240-3770. Phone: 800-571-5840 • URL: http://www.newriders.com • Date not set. $19.99.

Windows 2000: A Beginner's Guide. Martin S. Matthews. McGraw-Hill, 1221 Ave. of the Americas New York, NY 10020. Phone: 800-772-4726 or (212)512-2000 Fax: (212)512-4502 E-mail: customer.service@mcgraw-hill.com • URL: http://www.mcgraw-hill.com • 2000. $39.99. (Network Professional's Library).

Windows 2000 Commands Pocket Reference. Aeleen Frisch. O'Reilly & Associates, Inc., 90 Sherman St. Cambridge, MA 02140. Phone: 800-775-7731 or (617)354-5800 Fax: (617)661-1116 E-mail: order@oreilly.com • URL: http://www.oreilly.com • 2001. $9.95. (Pocket Reference Series).

Windows 2000 Performance Guide: Help for Windows 2000 Administrators. Mark Friedman. O'Reilly & Associates, Inc., 90 Sherman St. Cambridge, MA 02140. Phone: 800-775-7731 or (617)354-5800 Fax: (617)661-1116 E-mail: order@oreilly.com • URL: http://www.oreilly.com • 2002. $44.95.

Windows 2000 Professional Reference. Karanjit Siyan. Gale Group, 27500 Drake Rd. Farmington Hills, MI 48333-9187. Phone: 800-877-GALE or (248)699-4253 Fax: 800-414-5043 E-mail: gale.galeord@cengage.com • URL: http://gale.cengage.com • 2000. $75.00. Third edition.

Windows 2000 Quick Fixes. Jim Boyce. O'Reilly & Associates, Inc., 90 Sherman St. Cambridge, MA 02140. Phone: 800-775-7731 or (617)354-5800 Fax: (617)661-1116 E-mail: order@oreilly.com • URL: http://www.oreilly.com • 2000. $29.95. Covers troubleshooting for Windows 2000, both Professional Edition and Server Edition.

Windows 2000 System Administration Handbook. David Watts and others. Prentice Hall PTR, 240 Frisch Ct. Paramus, NJ 07652. Phone: 800-282-0693 Fax: 800-445-6691 • URL: http://www.phptr.com • 2000. $59.99. (Microsoft Technologies Series).

Windows XP Home Edition: The Missing Manual - The Book That Should Have Been in the Box. David Pogue. O'Reilly & Associates, Inc., 90 Sherman St. Cambridge, MA 02140. Phone: 800-775-7731 or (617)354-5800 Fax: (617)661-1116 E-mail: order@oreilly.com • URL: http://www.oreilly.com • 2002. $24.95. The title says it all. David Pogue is a computer and technology columnist for *The New York Times.*

Windows XP in a Nutshell. David A. Karp and others. O'Reilly & Associates, Inc., 90 Sherman St. Cambridge, MA 02140. Phone: 800-775-7731 or (617)354-5800 Fax: (617)661-1116 E-mail: order@oreilly.com • URL: http://www.oreilly.com • 2002. $29.95.

Windows XP in 10 Steps or Less. Bill Hatfield and Bradley L. Jones. John Wiley and Sons, Inc., 111 River St. Hoboken, NJ 07030. Phone: 800-225-5945 or (201)748-6000 Fax: (201)748-6088 E-mail: info@wiley.com • URL: http://www.wiley.com • 2003. $24.99. Explains more than 250 Windows XP procedures that require no more than 10 steps each. Includes tips, warnings, and cross-references.

Windows XP Professional Network Administration. Toby J. Velte. McGraw-Hill, 1221 Ave. of the Americas New York, NY 10020. Phone: 800-722-4726 or (212)512-2000 Fax: (212)512-4502 E-mail: customer.service@mcgraw-hill.com • URL: http://www.mcgrawhill.com • 2002. $49.99. Covers design, implementation, administration, configuration, networking, functionality, remote desktop assistance, and other matters. (Networking Series).

Wine and Spirits Guild of America.

Wine and Spirits Wholesalers of America., 805 15th St., N.W., Suite 430 Washington, DC 20005. Phone: (202)371-9792 Fax: (202)789-2405 E-mail: juanita.duggan@wswa.org • URL: http://www.wswa.org • Wholesale distributors of domestic and imported wine and distilled spirits. Affiliated with Wine and Spirits Shippers Association.

Wine Business Monthly: Grower and Seller News. Wine Business Communications, Inc., 110 W. Napa St. Sonoma, CA 94576. Phone: (707)939-0822 Fax: (707)939-0833 E-mail: info@winebusiness.com • URL: http://www.winebusiness.com • Monthly. $39.00 per year; students, $24.00 per year. Edited for executives in the North American wine making industry. Covers marketing, finance, export-import, management, new technology, etc.

Wine Enthusiast., Eight Saw Mill River Rd. Hawthorne, NY 10532. Phone: 800-829-5901 or (914)345-8463 Fax: (914)345-3028 E-mail: winenthmag@aol.com • URL: http://www.wineenthusiast.com • 13 times a year. $32.95 per year. Covers domestic and world wine. Formerly *Wine Times.*

Wine Institute., 425 Market St., Ste. 1000, 425 Market St., Suite

1000 San Francisco, CA 94105. Phone: (415)512-0151 Fax: (415)442-0742 E-mail: tcoreywg@aol.com • URL: http://www.wineinstitute.org • Initiates and advocates state, federal, and international public policy to enhance the environment for the responsible consumption and enjoyment of wine.

Wine: Nutritional and Therapeutic Benefits. Thomas R. Watkins, editor. American Chemical Society, 1155 16th St., N. W. Washington, DC 20036. Phone: 800-227-5558 or (202)872-4600 Fax: (202)872-4615 E-mail: help@acs.org • URL: http://www.chemistry.org • 1997. $95.00. A review of wine chemistry, agronomic practice at vineyards, and the potential health benefits of wine drinking. (ACS Symposium Series, No. 661.)

The Wine Spectator. M. Shanken Communications, Inc., 387 Park Ave., S New York, NY 10016. Phone: 800-344-0763 or (212)684-4424 Fax: (212)684-5424 E-mail: retailsales@mshanken.com • URL: http://www.mshanken.com • 18 times a year. $45.00 per year. Wine ratings.

Winemaking Basics. Cornelius S. Ough. Haworth Press, Inc., 10 Alice St. Binghamton, NY 13904-1580. Phone: 800-429-6784 or (607)722-5857 Fax: 800-895-0582 or (607)722-1424 E-mail: getinfo@haworthpressinc.com • URL: http://www.haworthpressinc.com • 1992. $59.95. Covers all practical aspects of commercial winemaking from harvesting grapes to bottling and storage.

Winery Technology and Operations: A Handbook for Small Wineries. Yair Margalit. Wine Appreciation Guild, 360 Swift Ave. San Francisco, CA 94080-6220. Phone: 800-231-9463 or (650)866-3020 Fax: (650)866-3513 E-mail: info@wineappreciation.com • URL: http://www.wineappreciation.com • 1990. $29.95. Covers a wide variety of topics from grape harvest to wine bottling, including aging and quality control.

Wines and Vines: Annual Directory/Buyer's Guide. The Hiaring Co., 1800 Lincoln Ave. San Rafael, CA 94901-1298. Phone: (415)453-9700 Fax: (415)453-2517 E-mail: geninfo@winesandvines.com • Annual. $95.00. List of wineries and wine bottlers in the United States, Canada, and Mexico; also lists industry suppliers.

Wines and Vines: The Authoritative Voice of the Grape and Wine Industry. Hiaring Co., 1800 Lincoln Ave. San Rafael, CA 94901-1298. Phone: (415)453-9700 Fax: (415)453-2517 E-mail: geninfo@winesandvines.com • URL: http://www.winesandvines.com • Monthly. $32.50 per year.

Winning is the Only Thing: Sports in America Since 1945. Randy Roberts and James Olson. Johns Hopkins University Press, 2715 N Charles St. Baltimore, MD 21218-4363. Phone: 800-537-5487 or (410)516-6900 Fax: (410)516-6968 • URL: http://www.press.jhu.edu/press • 1989. $16.95. (American Moments Series).

Winning Numbers: How to Use Business Facts and Figures to Make Your Point and Get Ahead. Michael C. Thomsett. AMACOM, 1601 Broadway New York, NY 10019. Phone: 800-262-9699 or (518)586-8100 Fax: (518)903-8168 E-mail: customerservice@amanet.org • URL: http://www.amacombooks.org • 1990. $22.95. A short course in financial communication, or finance for the nonfinancial manager.

The Winning Portfolio: Choosing Your 10 Best Mutual Funds. Paul B. Farrell. Bloomberg, 499 Park Ave. New York, NY 10022. Phone: 800-388-2749 or (212)318-2000 Fax: (917)369-5000 • URL: http://www.bloomberg.com • 1999. $15.95. Tells how to select 10 from among the 10,000 mutual funds that are available. (Bloomberg Personal Bookshelf Series).

Wire and Cable Technology International Buyers' Guide. Initial Publications, Inc., 3869 Darrow Rd., Ste. 109 Stow, OH 44224. Phone: (330)686-9544 Fax: (330)686-9563 E-mail: info@wiretech.com • Annual. $40.00. About 2,000 companies listed by product categories. Formerly *Wire Tech Buyers' Guide.*

Wire Association International., 1570 Boston Post Rd., PO Box 578 Guilford, CT 06437. Phone: (203)453-2777 Fax: (203)453-8384 E-mail: tcoreywg@aol.com • URL: http://www.wirenet,org • Finances educational and research activities that will enhance the scientific endeavors of the wire industry.

Wire Industry: International Monthly Journal. Publex International Ltd., 110 Station Rd., E Oxted, Surrey RH8 0QA, United Kingdom. Phone: 44 1883 717755 Fax: 44 1883 714554 Monthly. $151.00 per year. News, information and technical articles on manufacture of wire, wire products and cable. International coverage.

Wire Industry Suppliers Association., 201 Park Washington Ct. Falls Church, VA 22046. Phone: (703)538-1797 Fax: (703)241-5603 E-mail: atmahq@aol.com Firms engaged in the designing, building, and selling of machinery and equipment for use in plants producing wire or wire products. Includes wire and rod drawing machinery and accessories, shaping and flattening mills, stranding, cabling cutting off, pointing straightening, armoring, bending, forming, and cold heading equipment.

Wire: International Technical Journal for the Wire and Cable Industries and All Areas of Wire Processing. Meisenbach GMBH, Franz-Ludwig-Str 7A 96047 Bamberg, Germany. Phone: 49 951 861125 Fax: 49 951 861161 E-mail: wire@meisenbach.de • URL: http://www.meisenbach.de • Bimonthly. $118.00 per year. (English edition of *Draht-Welt.*)

Wire Journal International. Wire Association International. Wire Journal, Inc., 1570 Boston Rd. Guilford, CT 06437-0578.

Phone: (203)453-2777 Fax: (203)453-8384 Monthly. $75.00 per year.

Wire Journal International Reference Guide. Wire Association International. Wire Journal Inc., 1570 Boston Post Rd., PO Box 578 Guilford, CT 06437. Phone: (203)453-2777 Fax: (203)453-8384 E-mail: info@romeike.com Covers: Manufacturers and suppliers of steel and nonferrous rods, strip, wire, wire products, electrical wire and cable, fiber optics, and machinery and equipment to the industry (SIC 33). Entries include: Company name, address, phone, fax, e-mail and website addresses, year established, number of employees, names of executives, trade and brand names, product indices and geographical cross reference.

Wire Reinforcement Institute., 942 Main St., Ste. 300 Hartford, CT 06103. Phone: 800-552-4974 or 800-552-4974 Fax: (860)808-3009 E-mail: wwrinfo@wirereinforcementinstitute.org • URL: http://www.wirereinforcementinstitute.org • Manufacturers of steel welded wire reinforcement (WWR), sometimes referred to as fabric, mesh or WWF and wire products for concrete construction. Works to disseminate technical information and extend the use of welded wire reinforcement through scientific and market research, consumer education, engineering, product development, and general construction technology. Provides technical service to users and specifiers of welded wire reinforcement such as architects, consulting engineers, contractors, and governmental department engineers. Conducts research programs on properties and performance of welded wire reinforcement.

Wirebound Box Manufacturers Association., PO Box 531335 Mountain Brook, AL 35253-1335. Phone: (205)823-3448 Fax: (205)823-3449 E-mail: hrushing@usit.net Manufacturers of wirebound boxes and crates.

Wired. Wired Ventures Ltd., 660 Third St., 1st Fl. San Francisco, CA 94107. Phone: 800-769-4733 or (415)276-8400 Fax: (415)276-8500 E-mail: subscriptions@wired.com • URL: http://www.wired.com • Monthly. $10.00 per year. Edited for creators and managers in various areas of electronic information and entertainment, including multimedia, the Internet, and video. Often considered to be the primary publication of the "digital generation."

Wired for the Future: Developing Your Library Technology Plan. Diane Mayo and others. American Library Association, 50 E. Huron St. Chicago, IL 60611-2795. Phone: 800-545-2433 or (312)944-6780 Fax: (312)440-9374 E-mail: ala@ala.org • URL: http://www.ala.org • 1998. $38.00. Describes various technologies and applications available to libraries.

Wired Neighborhood. Stephen Doheny-Farina. Yale University Press, PO Box 2307 Dayton, OH 45401-2307. Phone: 800-987-7323 or (973)586-3724 Fax: (973)586-3699 E-mail: eia@eia.meinet.com • URL: http://www.yale.edu/yup/ • 1996. $40.00. The author examines both the hazards and the advantages of "making the computer the center of our public and private lives," as exemplified by the Internet and telecommuting.

Wired News. Lycos, Inc.Phone: (415)276-8400 Fax: (415)276-8500 E-mail: newsfeedback@wired.com • URL: http://www.wired.com • Provides summaries and full-text of "Top Stories" relating to the Internet, computers, multimedia, telecommunications, and the electronic information industry in general. These news stories are placed in the broad categories of Politics, Business, Culture, and Technology. Affiliated with *Wired* magazine. Fees: Free.

Wireless Business and Technology: Your Source for Unwired Technology. SYS-CON Media, Inc., 135 Chesnut Ridge Rd. Montvale, NJ 07654. Phone: (201)802-3000 Fax: (201)782-9601 E-mail: info@sys-con.com • URL: http://www.sys-con.com • Monthly. $49.99 per year. Trade journal for mobile radio and telephone dealers.

Wireless Data Networks. Gupta. Prentice Hall PTR, 240 Frisch Ct. Paramus, NJ 07652. Phone: 800-282-0693 Fax: 800-445-6991 • URL: http://www.phptr.com • 2000. Price on application. Presents market research information relating to cellular data networks, paging networks, packet radio networks, satellite systems, and other areas of wireless communication. Contains "summaries of recent developments and trends in wireless markets."

Wireless Data News. Access Intelligence L.L.C., 4 Choke Cherry Rd., 2nd Fl. Rockville, MD 20850. Phone: 800-777-5006 or (301)354-2000 Fax: (301)309-3847 E-mail: info@accessintel.com • URL: http://www.pbimedia.com • Description: Provides analysis of technology, applications, marketing, and competition in the mobile communications industry. Scope is international. Recurring features include news of research.

Wireless Dealers Association., 9746 Tappenbeck Dr. Houston, TX 77055-4102. Phone: 800-624-6918 or (713)467-0077 Fax: 800-820-2284 or 800-820-2284 E-mail: topbox@wirelessindustry.com • URL: http://www.wirelessdealers.com • Individuals involved in the cellular mobile telephone industry including agents, carriers, dealers, distributors, manufacturers, and consultants. Works to: foster members' financial and professional success in the cellular industry; make available skills improvement and educational materials necessary for professional growth; develop a more professional structure conducive to career success. Promotes benefits of cellular telephones and services to current and prospective cellular users. Conducts marketing and sales training seminars. Offers customized primary training materials.

Wireless Review: Intelligence for Competitive Providers. Primedia Business Magazines and Media, 330 N Wabash Ave., Ste. 2300 Chicago, IL 60611. Phone: 800-795-5445 or (312)595-1080 Fax: (312)595-0295 E-mail: subs@primediabusiness.com • URL: http://www.primediabusiness.com • Semimonthly. $48.00 per year. Covers business and technology developments for wireless service providers. Includes special issues on a wide variety of wireless topics. Formed by merger of *Cellular Business* and *Wireless World*.

Wireless Week. Reed Business Information, 360 Park Ave., S New York, NY 10010 2345. Phone: 800-446-6551 or (646)746-6400 Fax: (646)746-7028 E-mail: corporatecommunications@reedbusiness.com • URL: http://www.reedbusiness.com • 50 times a year. $99.00 per year. Covers news of cellular telephones, mobile radios, communications satellites, microwave transmission, and the wireless industry in general. Includes annual *Directory*.

Wisconsin Agricultural Experiment Station. University of Wisconsin - Madison

Wisconsin Center for Film and Theater Research., University of Wisconsin-Madison, 816 State St. Madison, WI 53706. Phone: (608)264-6466 Fax: (608)264-6472 • URL: http://www.shsw.wisc.edu/archives/wcftr • Studies the performing arts in America, including theater, cinema, radio, and television.

Wisconsin Cheese Makers' Association., 8030 Excelsior Dr., Ste. 305 Madison, WI 53717-1950. Phone: (608)828-4550 Fax: (608)828-4551 E-mail: office@wischeesemakersassn.org • URL: http://www.wischeesemakersassn.org • Active licensed cheese plants; active licensed cheese making employees; suppliers of goods and services to the industry. Seeks to educate members for better work in the art of making cheese, the care and management of factories, and the sale of the product. Works to curb competency in the business and enforce laws that will protect the manufacturer against deceitful imitations.

Wise Giving Guide. BBB Wise Giving Alliance, 4200 Wilson Blvd., Ste. 800 Arlington, VA 22203-1838. Phone: (703)276-0100 Fax: (703)525-8277 E-mail: info@bbb.org • URL: http://www.give.org • Quarterly. Single copy free; individuals, $25.00 per year. Evaluates 400 national charities against a set of standards concerning management, government and budget.

Women Against Military Madness., 310 E 38th St., Ste. 222 Minneapolis, MN 55409-1337. Phone: (612)827-5364 Fax: (612)827-6433 E-mail: wamm@mtn.org • URL: http://www.worldwidewamm.org • Advocates a "radical shift in our nations priorities away from militarism, military spending, arms trade, military intervention, and the militarization of schools".

Women and Careers: Issues and Challenges. Carol W. Konek and Sally L. Kitch. Sage Publications, Inc., 2455 Teller Rd. Thousand Oaks, CA 91320. Phone: 800-818-7243 or (805)499-9774 Fax: 800-583-2665 or (805)499-0871 E-mail: webmaster@sagepub.com • URL: http://www.sagepub.com • 1993. $77.95. Based on a major survey assessing women's experiences in the workplace.

Women and Philanthropy., 1015 18th St., N.W., Suite 202 Washington, DC 20036. Phone: (202)887-9660 Fax: (202)861-5483 E-mail: webmaster@womenphil.org • URL: http://www.womenphil.org • Purpose is to increase the amount of money given to programs benefiting women.

Women and Sexual Harassment: A Guide to the Legal Protections of Title VII and the Hostile Environment Claim. Anja A. Chan. Haworth Press, Inc., 10 Alice St. Binghamton, NY 13904-1580. Phone: 800-429-6784 or (607)722-5857 Fax: 800-895-0582 or (607)722-1424 E-mail: Getinfo@haworthpressinc.com • URL: http://www.haworthpressinc.com • 1994. $29.95. Emphasis is on hostile environment claims under Title VII of the Civil Rights Act of 1964. Discusses employer liability, the statute of limitations, remedies, discovery and evidence, and related claims. Includes a research guide and lists of primary and secondary sources.

Women and the Economy: A Reader. Ellen Mutari and Deborah M. Figart, editors. M. E. Sharpe, Inc., 80 Business Park Drive Armonk, NY 10504. Phone: 800-541-6563 or (914)273-1800 Fax: (914)273-2106 E-mail: custserv@mesharpe.com • URL: http://www.mesharpe.com • 2003. $69.95. A collection of essays presenting a feminist approach to economic issues.

Women and the Law. Carol H. Lefcourt, editor. West Group, 610 Opperman Dr. Eagan, MN 55123. Phone: 800-328-4880 or (651)687-7000 Fax: 800-340-9378 E-mail: bookstore@westgroup.com • URL: http://www.westgroup.com • Annual. $302.00. Looseleaf service. Covers such topics as employment discrimination, pay equity (comparable worth), sexual harassment in the workplace, property rights, and child custody issues.

Women and Work: Exploring Race, Ethnicity, and Class. Mary Romero. Sage Publications, Inc., 2455 Teller Rd. Thousand Oaks, CA 91320. Phone: 800-818-7243 or (805)499-9774 Fax: 800-583-2665 or (805)499-0871 E-mail: webmaster@sagepub.com • URL: http://www.sagepub.com • 1997. $103.00. Contains articles by various authors, including material on the historical and economic background of women in the workplace. (Women and Work: Vol. 6.)

Women as Managers: Strategies for Success. Economics Press, Inc., 12 Daniel Rd. Fairfield, NJ 07004. Phone: 800-526-2554 or (973)227-1224 Fax: (973)227-9742 E-mail: info@epinc.com • URL: http://www.epinc.com • Biweekly. $69.00 per year. Newsletter. Covers management skills and techniques leading to higher career levels. Discusses problems women face on the job.

Women Breaking Through: Overcoming the Final 10 Obstacles at Work. Deborah J. Swiss. Peterson's, 2000 Lenox Dr., Princeton Pike Corporate Ctr. Lawrenceville, NJ 08648. Phone: 800-338-3282 or (609)896-1800 Fax: (609)896-4544 E-mail: info@petersons.com • URL: http://www.petersons.com • 1996. $24.95. Discusses specific strategies for women to use to advance beyond the middle management level. Based on a survey of 300 women "on the leading edge of change."

Women Chefs and Restaurateurs., 455 S Fourth St., Ste. 650 Louisville, KY 40202. Phone: 877-927-7787 or (502)581-0300 Fax: (502)589-3602 E-mail: dsacksteder@hqtrs.com • URL: http://www.womenchefs.org • Seeks to educate and advance women in the restaurant industry.

Women Employed Institute. Women Employed Institute, 111 N Wabash, 13th Fl. Chicago, IL 60602. Phone: (312)782-3902 Fax: (312)782-5249 E-mail: info@womenemployed.org • URL: http://www.womenemployed.org • Economic status of working women, working women and the law, sexual harassment in the workplace, equal employment opportunity, women's access to vocational education and job training, comparable worth, working mothers, and career development.

Women Entrepreneurs: Moving Beyond the Glass Ceiling. Dorothy P. Moore and E. Holly Buttner. Sage Publications, Inc., 2455 Teller Rd. Thousand Oaks, CA 91320. Phone: 800-818-7243 or (805)499-9774 Fax: 800-583-2665 or (805)499-0871 E-mail: webmaster@sagepub.com • URL: http://www.sagepub.com • 1997. $79.95. Contains profiles of "129 successful female entrepreneurs who previously worked in corporate environments."

Women Executives in Public Relations., FDR Station, PO Box 7657 New York, NY 10150-7657. Phone: (212)289-7375 Fax: (212)289-7375 • URL: http://www.wepr.org • Formerly Committee on Women in Public Relations.

Women, Gender, and Work: What is Equality and How Do We Get There? Martha F. Loutfi, editor. International Labour Organization, 1828 L St., N.W., Suite 600 Washington, DC 20036-5121. Phone: (202)653-7652 Fax: (202)653-7687 E-mail: washington@ilo.org • URL: http://www.ilo.org • 2001. $26.95. A collection of articles from the *International Labour Review* covering such topics as equal opportunity for women, family concerns, legal issues, the glass ceiling, wage inequality, and sexual harassment in the workplace. Includes statistical data.

Women in Cable and Telecommunications., 230 W. Monroe St., Suite 2630 Chicago, IL 60606-4702. Phone: (312)634-2330 Fax: (312)634-2345 E-mail: information@wict.org • URL: http://www.wict.org • Formerly Women in Cable.

Women in Management: Trends, Issues, and Challenges in Managerial Diversity. Ellen A. Fagenson, editor. Sage Publications, Inc., 2455 Teller Rd. Thousand Oaks, CA 91320. Phone: 800-818-7243 or (805)499-9774 Fax: 800-583-2665 or (805)499-0871 E-mail: webmaster@sagepub.com • URL: http://www.sagepub.com • 1993. $46.95. Includes material from 22 contributors on topics related to the experiences of women managers. (Women and Work Series: Vol. 4).

Women in the World of Work: Statistical Analysis and Projections to the Year 2000. Shirley Nuss and others. International Labour Office, 1828 L St. NW Washington, DC 20036-5121. Phone: (202)653-7652 Fax: (202)653-7687 E-mail: ilo@ilo.org • URL: http://www.ilo.org • 1989. $18.00. (Women, Work, and Development Series, No. 18).

Women Lawyers Journal. National Association of Women Lawyers, American Bar Center, MS 124, 750 N. Lake Shore Dr. Chicago, IL 60611-4479. Phone: (312)988-6186 Fax: (312)988-6281 E-mail: nawl@staff.abanet.org • URL: http://www.abanet.org/nawl • Quarterly. $16.00 per year.

Women, Men, the Family and HIV/AIDS: A Sociological Perspective on the Epidemic in America. Carole A. Campbell. Cambridge University Press, 40 W 20th St. New York, NY 10011-4221. Phone: 800-221-4512 or (212)924-3900 Fax: (212)691-3239 E-mail: orders@cup.org • URL: http://www.cup.org • 1999. $21.00.

Women of the Street: Making It on Wall Street-The World's Toughest Business. Sue Herera. John Wiley and Sons, Inc., 111 River St. Hoboken, NJ 07030. Phone: 800-225-5945 or (201)748-6000 Fax: (201)748-6088 E-mail: info@wiley.com • URL: http://www.wiley.com • 1998. $16.95. The author is a CNBC business television anchorperson.

Women Studies Abstracts. Transaction Publishers, 35 Berrue Circle Piscataway, NJ 08854-8042. Phone: 888-999-6778 or (732)445-2280 Fax: (732)445-3138 E-mail: trans@transactionpub.com • URL: http://www.transactionpub.com • Quarterly. Individuals, $102.00 per year; institutions, $240.00 per year.

Women's Accessories Store. Entrepreneur Media, Inc., 2445 McCabe Way Irvine, CA 92614. Phone: 800-421-2300 or (949)261-2325 Fax: (949)261-0234 E-mail: entmag@entrepreneur.com • URL: http://www.entrepreneur.com • Looseleaf. $59.50. A practical guide to starting a women's clothing accessories shop. Covers profit potential, start-up costs, market size evaluation, owner's time required, site selection, lease negotiation, pricing, accounting, advertising, promotion, etc. (Start-Up Business Guide No. E1333.)

Women's and Children's Wear Buyers Directory. Douglas Publications, Inc., 2807 N. Parham Rd. Richmond, VA 23294. Phone: 800-223-1797 or (804)762-9600 Fax: (804)217-8999 E-mail: info@douglaspublications.com • URL: http://www.douglaspublications.com • Annual. $329.00. About 10,500 retail stores selling women's dresses, coats, sportswear, intimate apparel, and women's accessories, infants' to teens wear, and accessories; coverage does not include New York metropolitan area. *Salesman's Guide Directories*

Women's Apparel Shop. Entrepreneur Media, Inc., 2445 McCabe Way Irvine, CA 92614. Phone: 800-421-2300 or (949)261-2325 Fax: (949)261-0234 E-mail: entmag@entrepreneur.com • URL: http://www.entrepreneur.com • Looseleaf. $59.50. A practical guide to starting a women's clothing store. Covers profit potential, start-up costs, market size evaluation, owner's time required, site selection, lease negotiation, pricing, accounting, advertising, promotion, etc. (Start-Up Business Guide No. E1107.)

Women's Army Corps Veterans' Association., PO Box 5577 Fort McClellan, AL 36205-0577. Phone: (256)820-6824 E-mail: info@armywomen.org • URL: http://www.armywomen.org • Veterans of the United States Women's Army Corps and Women's Army Auxiliary Corps, women soldiers and officers of the line who are on a tour of active duty with, or have been honorably discharged from, the United States Army, and women who have served honorably or are serving in the United States Reserve or Army National Guard. Seeks "to be of service to all veterans and the communities in which we live and promote justice, tolerance, peace and goodwill". Conducts hospital and community service programs. Supports the U.S. Army Women's Museum at Ft. Lee, VA. Has assisted in the establishment of Women's Army Corps Veterans Redwood Memorial Grove in Big Basin Redwoods State Park, CA. Conducts charitable projects and educational programs.

Women's Council of Realtors., 430 N Michigan Ave. Chicago, IL 60611. Phone: 800-245-8512 or (312)329-8483 Fax: (312)329-3290 E-mail: wcr@wcr.org • URL: http://www.wcr.org • Formerly Women's Council of Realtors of the National Association of Realtors.

Women's Information Directory. Gale, 27500 Drake Rd. Farmington Hills, MI 48331-3535. Phone: 800-877-4253 or (248)699-4253 Fax: 800-414-5043 or (248)699-8065 E-mail: galeord@cengage.com • URL: http://gale.cengage.com • Covers: Nearly 10,800 sources of information for and about women in the U.S., including national, state, and local organizations; publishers and booksellers of women's materials; newspapers, magazines, newsletters, other directories, and videos; museums; awards, honors, and prizes; government agencies and assistance programs; research centers; women's studies programs at colleges and universities; consultants; scholarships and other financial aids; electronic resources; and library collections. Entries include: Organization or publication name, address, phone, name and title of contact, description of services, activities, etc.

Women's Law Project., 125 S 9th St., No. 300 Philadelphia, PA 19107. Phone: (215)928-9801 Fax: (215)928-9848 E-mail: info@womenslawproject.org • URL: http://www.womenslawproject.org/pages/contact_us.htm • Serves as feminist law firm working to challenge sex discrimination in the law and in legal and social institutions through litigation, public education, research and writing, representation of women's groups, and individual counseling. Specializes in the areas of family law, education, employment, reproductive rights, violence against women, and sex-based insurance rates.

Women's National Book Association., PO Box 237, 26 W 17th St., No. 504 New York, NY 10150. Phone: (212)208-4629 Fax: (212)208-4629 E-mail: publicity@bookbuzz.com • URL: http://www.wnba-books.org • Women and men who work with and value books. Exists to promote reading and to support the role of women in the book community.

Women's Rights Law Reporter. Rutgers University School of Law, 123 Washington St. Newark, NJ 07102. Phone: (973)353-5320 • URL: http://www.info.rutgers.edu • Three times a year. Individuals $20.00 per year; institutions, $40.00 per year; students, $15.00 per year. Provides analysis and commentary on legal issues affecting women, including gender-based discrimination.

Women's Studies International Forum: A Multidisciplinary Journal for the Rapid Publication of Research Communications and Review Articles in Women's Studies. Elsevier, 360 Park Ave., S. New York, NY 10010-1710. Phone: 888-437-4636 or (212)989-5800 Fax: (212)633-3990 E-mail: usinfo-f@elsevier.com • URL: http://www.elsevier.com • Bimonthly. Individuals, $122.00 per year; institutions $585.00 per year; students, $38.00 per year.

Women's Studies Quarterly: The First U.S. Journal Devoted to Teaching about Women. Feminist Press, CUNY Graduate Center, 365 Fifth Ave., Ste. 5406 New York, NY 10016. Phone: (212)817-7920 Fax: (212)817-1593 E-mail: jroncker@gc.cuny.edu • URL: http://www.feministpress.org • Four times a year. Individuals, $30.00 per year; institutions, $40.00 per year. Provides coverage of issues and events in women's studies and feminist education, including in-depth articles on research about women and current projects to transform traditional curricula. Includes two double thematic issues.

Women's Undergarments. Available from MarketResearch.com, 641 Ave. of the Americas, Third Floor New York, NY 10011. Phone: 800-298-5699 or (212)807-2629 Fax: (212)807-2716 E-mail: order@marketresearch.com • URL: http://www.marketresearch.com • 1997. $995.00. Published by Specialists in Business Information, Inc. Provides market data with forecasts of sales to the year 2005 for various kinds of women's underwear.

Wood and Paper Science., North Carolina State University, P.O. Box 8005 Raleigh, NC 27695. Phone: (919)515-5807 Fax: (919)515-6302 E-mail: mike_kocurek@ncsu.edu • URL: http://www.cfr.ncsu.edu/wps/ • Studies the mechanical and engineering properties of wood, wood finishing, wood anatomy, wood chemistry, etc.

Wood and Wood Products: Furniture, Cabinets, Woodworking and Allied Products Management and Operations. Vance Publishing Corp., 400 Knightsbridge Parkway Lincolnshire, IL 60069. Phone: 800-255-5113 or (847)634-2600 Fax: (847)634-4379 • URL: http://www.vancepublishing.com • 13 times a year. $55.00 per year.

Wood Component Manufacturers Association., 741 Butlers Gate, Ste. 100 Marietta, GA 30068. Phone: (770)565-6660 Fax: (770)565-6663 E-mail: wcma@woodcomponents.org • URL: http://www.woodcomponents.org • Manufacturers of wood parts for the furniture, kitchen cabinet, and building industries, including interior trim moldings, stair treads and risers, thresholds, and paneling; industrial users. Establishes grading rules and standards. Offers seminars in cost accounting, marketing, and production techniques. Conducts plant tours among members.

Wood Digest. Cygnus Business Media, 1233 Janesville Ave. Fort Atkinson, WI 53538. Phone: 800-308-6397 or (920)563-6388 Fax: (920)536-1707 E-mail: rich.reiff@cygnuspub.com • URL: http://www.cygnusbzb.com • Monthly. $60.00 per year. Formerly *Furniture Wood Digest*.

Wood Digest-Showcase. Cygnus Business Media, 1233 Janesville Ave. Fort Atkinson, WI 53538. Phone: 800-547-7377 or (920)563-6388 Fax: (920)563-1702 E-mail: galeord@cengage.com • URL: http://www.cygnusbzb.com • Publication includes: List of suppliers of materials, machinery, tools, and services for woodworking, cabinetry, casegoods, and furniture manufacturing processes (SIC 24, 25, 37, and 39). Entries include: Company name, phone number, photograph of product, services.

Wood Flooring. Available from MarketResearch.com, 641 Ave. of the Americas, Third Floor New York, NY 10011. Phone: 800-298-5699 or (212)807-2629 Fax: (212)807-2716 E-mail: order@marketresearch.com • URL: http://www.marketresearch.com • 1999. $2,250.00. Market research report published by Specialists in Business Information. Presents hardwood flooring market data relative to demographics, sales growth, shipments, exports, imports, price trends, and end-use. Includes company profiles.

Wood Machinery Manufacturers of America., 1900 Arch St. Philadelphia, PA 19103-1498. Phone: 800-289-9662 or (215)564-3484 Fax: (215)963-9785 E-mail: wmma@fernley.com • URL: http://www.wmma.org • Formerly Woodworking Machinery Manufacturers of America.

Wood Products Manufacturers Association., PO Box 761 Westminster, MA 01473-0761. Phone: (978)874-5445 Fax: (978)874-9946 E-mail: wcma@woodcomponents.org • URL: http://www.wpma.org • Manufacturers of component parts, turned and shaped wood products, moulding, millwork, manufacturer's representatives, wholesalers, suppliers of lumber, machinery, and service providers in the industry.

Wood Research Laboratory.

Wood Technology-Equipment Catalog and Buyers' Guide. CMP Media, Inc., 600 Community Dr. Manhasset, NY 11030. Phone: (516)562-5000 E-mail: cmp@cmp.com • URL: http://www.cmp.com • Annual. $55.00. Formerly *Forest Industries-Lumber Review and Buyers' Guide*.

Woodturner's Bible. Percy Blandford. McGraw-Hill, 1221 Ave. of the Americas New York, NY 10020. Phone: 800-722-4726 or (212)512-2000 Fax: (212)512-4502 E-mail: customer.service@mcgraw-hill.com • URL: http://www.mcgraw-hill.com • 1990. $26.95. Third edition.

Wool Record. World Textile Publications Ltd., Perkins House,, One Longlands St., c/o Keith Higgenbottom, Bradford Bradford BDI 2TP, United Kingdom. E-mail: info@worldtextile.com • URL: http://www.worldtextile.com • Monthly. $115.00 per year.

The Wool Sack. Mid-States Wool Growers Cooperative, 9449 Basil Western Rd. Canal Winchester, OH 43110-9728. Semiannual. Free. Newsletter. Information on lamb production and the wool industry.

Woolmark Company., 1156 Ave. of the Americas, Ste. 701 New York, NY 10036. Phone: 800-986-WOOL or (212)221-8161 Fax: (212)221-8152 E-mail: stuart.mccullough@wool.com • URL: http://www.woolmark.com • Sponsored by the wool growers of Australia to carry out global promotional and research programs. Works with American mills, apparel, upholstery fabric, carpet, and other end-product manufacturers and retailers at promotional and technical levels; conducts programs of product and market development; provides wool industry with marketing and statistical information; offers technical advice to increase manufacturing efficiency and assist in the introduction at the commercial level of new processes and products. Maintains Technical Services Center that tests and evaluates chemical and finishing processes developed to add new performance characteristics to wool products and to create new market outlets. **Convention/Meeting:** none.

Work and Health: Strategies for Maintaining a Vital Workforce. Aspen Publishers, Inc., 1185 Avenue of the Americas New York, NY 10036. Phone: 800-234-1660 or (212)597-0200 Fax: (212)597-0338 E-mail: customer.service@aspenpubl.com • URL: http://www.aspenpublishers.com • 1989. $79.00.

Work and Occupations: An International Sociological Journal. Sage Publications, Inc., 2455 Teller Rd. Thousand Oaks, CA 91320. Phone: 800-818-7243 or (805)499-9774 Fax: 800-583-2665 or (805)499-0871 E-mail: webmaster@sagepub.com • URL: http://www.sagepub.com • Quarterly. $499.00 per year. Includes print and online editions.

Work in America: An Encyclopedia of History, Policy, and Society. Carl E. Van Horn and Herbert A. Schaffner. ABC-CLIO, Inc., 130 Cremona Drive Santa Barbara, CA 93117. Phone: 800-368-6868 or (805)968-1911 Fax: (805)685-9685 E-mail: sales@abc-clio.com • URL: http://www.abc-clio.com • 2003. $185.00. Two volumes. Contains 265 A-Z entries covering work in the U. S. from the Industrial Revolution to modern times. Covers labor-related topics in economics, history, law, welfare, employment policy, and other areas.

Work Simplification: An Analyst's Handbook. Pierre Theriault. Engineering and Management Press, 25 Technology Park Norcross, GA 30092-2988. Phone: 800-494-0460 or (770)449-0461 Fax: (770)441-3295 E-mail: cmagee@www.iienet.org • URL: http://www.iienet.org • 1996. $25.00. A basic guide to work simplification as an industrial management technique.

Workboat. Diversified Business Communications, 121 Free St. Portland, ME 04101. Phone: (207)842-5600 Fax: (207)842-5603 • URL: http://www.seafoodbusiness.com • Monthly. $49.00 per year. Covers equipment, products, and services for commercial boats such as tugboats, ferries, fireboats, fishing boats, and excursion boats.

Workers' Compensation Law Bulletin. Quinlan Publishing Co., Marine Industrial Park, 23 Drydock Ave. 6th Fl. Boston, MA 02210-2387. Phone: 800-229-2084 or (617)542-0048 Fax: (617)345-9646 E-mail: info@quinlan.com Description: Summarizes in layman's terms recent court cases deriving from the worker compensation law, with specific identification of cases and brief explanations of the court decisions.

Workers' Compensation Monitor. LRP Publications, 747 Dresher Rd., Ste. 500, PO Box 980 Horsham, PA 19044-0980. Phone: 800-341-7874 or (215)784-0860 Fax: (215)784-9639 E-mail: custserve@lrp.com • URL: http://www.lrp.com • Description: Suggests ways to reduce workers' compensation costs and improve your return-to-work programs. Provides proven solutions your colleagues have implemented to resolve their challenges. Keeps readers up-to-date on the latest developments in national workers' compensation issues including benefits, insurance coverage, legislative reform and costs.

Worker's Compensation: The Survival Guide for Business. LexisNexis Matthew Bender, 1275 Broadway Albany, NY 12204-4026. Phone: 800-424-4200 or (518)487-3000 Fax: 800-828-8341 or (518)487-3584 E-mail: customer.support@lexisnexis.com • URL: http://www.lexisnexis.com/matthewbender/ • Looseleaf. $100.00. Periodic supplementation available. Edited for business managers and executives. Covers the basics of worker's compensation, including accident prevention, post-accident activities, accident investigation, medical management, insurance issues, and recent legislation. Includes a glossary, checklists, sample letters, a sample employers liability insurance policy, and statistics.

Workforce: H R Trends and Tools for Business Results. Crain Communications, Inc., 245 Fischer Ave., Ste. B2 Costa Mesa, CA 92626-4537. Phone: (714)751-1883 Fax: (714)751-4106 E-mail: tostiv@workforcemag.com • URL: http://www.workforceonline • Monthly. $59.00 per year. Edited for human resources managers. Covers employee benefits, compensation, relocation, recruitment, training, personnel legalities, and related subjects. Supplements include bimonthly "New Product News" and semiannual "Recruitment/Staffing Sourcebook." Formerly *Personnel Journal*.

Working Americans, 1880-1999, Volume One: The Working Class. Scott Derks, editor. Grey House Publishing, 185 Millerton Rd. Millerton, NY 12546. Phone: 800-562-2139 or (518)789-8700 Fax: (518)789-0556 E-mail: books@greyhouse.com • URL: http://www.greyhouse.com • 2000. $375.00. Provides detailed information on the lifestyles and economic life of working class families in the 12 decades from 1880 to 1999. Includes such items as selected consumer prices, income, family finances, budgets, life at home, jobs, and working conditions. (Universal Reference Publications.)

Working Americans, 1880-1999, Volume Two: The Middle Class. Scott Derks, editor. Grey House Publishing, 185 Millerton Rd. Millerton, NY 12546. Phone: 800-562-2139 or (518)789-8700 Fax: (518)789-0556 E-mail: books@greyhouse.com • URL: http://www.greyhouse.com • 2000. $135.00. Three volumes. Furnishes details of the social and economic lives of middle class Americans during the years 1880 to 1999. Describes such items as selected consumer prices, income, family finances, budgets, life at home, jobs, and working conditions. (Universal Reference Publications.)

Working from Home: Everything You Need to Know About Living and Working Under the Same Roof. Paul Edwards and Sarah Edwards. The Putnam Publishing Group, 375 Hudson St. New York, NY 10014. Phone: 800-788-6262 or (212)366-2000 Fax: 800-227-9604 or (212)366-2643 E-mail: online@penguinputnam.com • URL: http://www.penguinputnam.com • 1999. $18.95. Fifth revised expanded edition.

Working Mother. Working Mother Media, 260 Madison Ave. New York, NY 10016. Phone: 800-627-0690 or (212)351-6400 Fax: (212)351-6487 E-mail: subscripbers@workingmother.com • URL: http://www.workingmother.com • 10 times a year. $19.97 per year.

Working Options. Association of Part-Time Professionals, 701 W Broad St., Ste. 400 Falls Church, VA 22046-3220. Phone: (703)734-7975 Fax: (703)734-7405 E-mail: lemans@erols.com Description: Advocates alternative work schedules, particularly part-time employment for professionals. Topics include job sharing, older workers, personnel policies, employee benefits, insurance, chapter news, and legislative news. Also provides how-to information on part-time employment and profiles employees and employers who have used flexible work schedules and part-time employment to their advantage. Recurring features include news about the Association and a column titled Point of View, the Executive Director's Corner and Members' Mail Box.

Working Press of the Nation. R. R. Bowker, 630 Central Ave. New Providence, NJ 07974. Phone: 888-269-5372 Fax: (908)219-0098 E-mail: info@bowker.com • URL: http://www.bowker.com • Annual. $530.00. $295.00 per volume. Three volumes: (1) *Newspaper Directory*; (2) *Magazine and Internal Publications Directory*; (3) *Radio and Television Directory*. Includes names of editors and other personnel.

Working USA: The Journal of Labor and Society. M. E. Sharpe, Inc., 80 Business Park Drive Armonk, NY 10504. Phone: 800-541-6563 or (914)273-1800 Fax: (914)273-2106 E-mail: custserv@mesharpe.com • URL: http://www.mesharpe.com • Quarterly. $160.00 per year to institutions; $45.00 to individuals. Provides a wide range of material on employment, labor markets, societal issues, and present-day labor unions.

Working with Faculty to Design Undergraduate Information Literacy Programs: A How-To-Do-It Manual for Librarians. Rosemary M. Young and Stephana Harmony. Neal-Schuman Publishers, Inc., 100 William St., Ste. 2004 New York, NY 10038. Phone: (866)672-6657 or (212)925-8650 Fax: (866)209-7932 or (212)219-8916 E-mail: info@neal-schuman.com • URL: http://www.neal-schuman.com • 1999. $45.00. Includes sample forms, surveys, evaluations, and assignments for credit courses or single sessions. (How-to-Do-It Manuals Series).

Working with Tax-Sheltered Annuities: 403(b) Plans Explained. Steven Leventhal. CCH, Inc., 2700 Lake Cook Rd. Riverwoods, IL 60015. Phone: 800-835-5224 or (847)267-7000 E-mail: cust_serv@cch.com • URL: http://www.cch.com • 2001. $75.95. Fourth edition. Emphasis is on legal aspects of tax-deferred annuities.

Working Women: A World Survey. Available from MarketResearch.com, 641 Ave. of the Americas, Fourth Floor New York, NY 10011. Phone: 800-298-5699 or (212)807-2629 Fax: (212)807-2642 E-mail: order@marketresearch.com • URL: http://www.marketresearch.com • 2001. $3,500.00. Published by Euromonitor International. Worldwide market research data on consumer spending patterns of women in the work force, with forecasts to 2005.

Workplace Sexual Harassment. Anne Levy and Michele A. Paludi. Prentice Hall PTR, 240 Frisch Ct. Paramus, NJ 07652. Phone: 800-282-0693 Fax: 800-445-6991 • URL: http://www.phptr.com • 2001. $38.20. Second edition. A management guide to confronting and preventing sexual harassment in organizations. Includes case studies and training materials.

Workplace Substance Abuse Advisor. LRP Publications, 747 Dresher Rd., Ste. 500, PO Box 980 Horsham, PA 19044-0980. Phone: 800-341-7874 or (215)784-0860 Fax: (215)784-9639 E-mail: custserve@lrp.com • URL: http://www.lrp.com • Description: Reviews federal, state, and local laws and regulations concerning alcohol and drug use, testing, and policies. Discusses significant court decisions. Contains information on the drug enforcement budgets at all levels of government. Examines employee assistance plans and other educational programs designed to help substance abusers.

Workshops: Designing and Facilitating Experiential Learning. Jeff E. Brooks-Harris and Susan R. Stock-Ward. Sage Publications, Inc., 2455 Teller Rd. Thousand Oaks, CA 91320. Phone: 800-818-7243 or (805)499-5774 Fax: 800-583-2665 or (805)499-0871 E-mail: webmaster@sagepub.com • URL: http://www.sagepub.com • 1999. $80.95. Presents a practical approach to designing, running, and evaluating workshops in business, adult education, and other areas. Includes references.

World Agricultural Economics and Rural Sociology Abstracts: Abstracts of World Literature. Available from CABI Publishing, North America, 875 Massachusetts Ave., 7th Fl. Cambridge, MA 02139. Phone: 800-528-4841 or (617)395-4056 Fax: (617)354-6875 E-mail: cabi-nao@cabi.org • URL: http://www.cabi-publishing.org • Monthly. Institutions, $1,425.00 per year. Print and online edition, $1,460.00 per year. Published in England by CABI Publishing. Provides worldwide coverage of the literature.

World Agricultural Supply and Demand Estimates. Available from U. S. Government Printing Office, Washington, DC 20402. Phone: (202)512-1800 Fax: (202)512-2250 E-mail: gpoaccess@gpo.gov • URL: http://www.access.gpo.gov • Monthly. $52.00 per year. Issued by the Economics and Statistics Service and the Foreign Agricultural Service of the U. S. Department of Agriculture. Consists mainly of statistical data and tables.

World Agrochemical Markets. Theta Reports, 1775 Broadway, Suite 511 New York, NY 10019. Phone: (212)262-8230 Fax: (212)262-8234 E-mail: lschacterle@thetareports.com • URL: http://www.thetareports.com • 2000. $1,040.00. Market research data. Covers the demand for crop protection products in 11 countries having major markets and 20 countries having minor markets. (Theta Report No. DS196E.)

World Air Transport Statistics. International Air Transport Association, 800 Place Victoria Montreal PQ, QC, Canada H4Z 1M1. Phone: (514)874-0202 Fax: (514)874-9632 E-mail: sales@iata.org • URL: http://www.iata.org.charts • Annual. $225.00.

The World Almanac and Book of Facts. World Almanac Books, 512 7th Ave., 22nd Fl. New York, NY 10018. Phone: (646)312-6800 Fax: (646)312-6839 • URL: http://www.worldalmanac.com • Annual. $11.95.

World Animal Health Markets. Theta Reports, 1775 Broadway, Suite 511 New York, NY 10019. Phone: (212)262-8230 Fax: (212)262-8234 E-mail: lschacterle@thetareports.com • URL: http://www.thetareports.com • 2000. $830.00. Market research data. Covers the market for animal health products in 15 major countries, including the U.S. (Theta Report No. SR198E.)

World Antique Dealers Association., 818 Marion Ave., 818 Marion Ave. Mansfield, OH 44906. Phone: (419)756-4374 Fax: (419)756-4979 E-mail: drjm@richnet.net Antique dealers, educators, authors, auctioneers, show managers, and museum professionals dedicated to the promotion and preservation of the antiques profession and fair and honest representation of antiques. Seeks to build a more professional and reliable approach to the purchase and sale of antiques. Establishes standards to clearly price merchandise, refund purchase money if merchandise is found to be other than represented. Receives and transmits pertinent information, actively engages in curbing unethical practices, and promotes the dignity of the antiques profession. Conducts seminars and study groups.

World Association for Public Opinion Research., University of Texas Pan American, 1405 Driftwood 1 Mission, TX 78572. Phone: (956)618-4048 Fax: (956)618-4943 E-mail: ghanem@panam.edu • URL: http://www.unl.edu/wapor • Members are opinion survey research experts, both academic and commercial. Promotes the use of objective, scientific, public opinion methodology and research. International emphasis.

World Association of Alcohol Beverage Industries., P.O. Box 45-1057 Garland, TX 75045. Phone: 800-466-6920 or (972)675-3246 Fax: (972)675-3673 E-mail: woodgateh@aol.com • URL: http://www.waabi.org • Volunteer men and women working together for personal growth and for the benefit of the legal alcohol beverage industry. Formerly National Women's Association of Allied Beverage Industries.

World at Work Membership Directory. American Compensation Association, 14040 N. Northsight Blvd. Scottsdale, AZ 85260. Phone: 877-951-9191 or (480)951-9191 Fax: (480)483-8352 E-mail: customerrelations@worldatwork.org • URL: http://www.worldatwork.org • Annual. Free to members; non-members, $150.00. Covers 20,000 member benefits and compensation professionals in Canada and United States.

The World Bank Atlas. World Bank Group, 1818 H St., NW Washington, DC 20433. Phone: (202)477-1000 Fax: (202)477-6391 E-mail: books@worldbank.org • URL: http://www.worldbank.org • Annual. $10.00. Contains "color maps, charts, and graphs representing the main social, economic, and environmental indicators for 209 countries and territories" (publisher).

World Bank Group., 1818 H St. NW Washington, DC 20433. Phone: (202)473-1000 or (202)473-1000 Fax: (202)477-6391 E-mail: wbannualreport@worldbank.org • URL: http://www.worldbank.org • Comprises of the International Bank for Reconstruction and Development, the International Development Association, International Finance Corporation and the Multilateral Investment Guarantee Agency. Established by the United Nations to assist in raising the standards of living in developing countries by channeling financial resources from developed countries. Emphasis is placed on investments which foster active participation in the development process. Programs concentrate on rural and urban development, agriculture, and education. Activities include improving water and sewage facilities, building low-cost housing, and increasing the productivity of small industries. Assists organizations with identifying, designing, and executing development projects; offers financial aid to national development institutions. Encourages discussion on common development problems such as income distribution, rural poverty, unemployment, excessive population growth, and rapid urbanization. Conducts research programs on topics including economic planning and public utilities. Works in association with the United Nations Development Program and executes many UNDP projects.

World Banking Abstracts: The International Journal of the Financial Services Industry. Institution of European Finance. Blackwell Publishing Ltd., 9600 Garsington Rd. Oxford 0X4 2DQ, United Kingdom. Phone: 44 1865 778315 Fax: 44 1865 471775 E-mail: customerservice@oxon.blackwellpublishing.com Bimonthly. Institutions, $1,393.00 per year. Includes print and online editions. Provides worldwide coverage of articles appearing in over 400 financial publications.

World Business Directory. Gale, 27500 Drake Rd. Farmington Hills, MI 48331-3535. Phone: 800-877-4253 or (248)699-4253 Fax: 800-414-5043 or (248)699-8065 E-mail: galeord@cengage.com • URL: http://www.galegroup.com • Covers: nearly 140,000 companies in over 180 countries involved in international trade. Entries include: Company name, address, phone, fax, telex, names and titles of key personnel, financial data, number of employees, type of company, fiscal year end, year founded, product description, Standard Industrial Classification (SIC) codes, parent company.

World Business Directory 2001. Gale Cengage Learning, 27500 Drake Rd. Farmington Hills, MI 48331-3535. Phone: 800-877-GALE or (248)699-4253 Fax: 800-414-5043 E-mail: gale.galeord@cengage.com • URL: http://gale.cengage.com • 2003. $645.00. Four volumes. 11th edition. Covers about 136,000 companies in 180 countries.

World Business Rankings Annual. Gale Cengage Learning, 27500 Drake Rd. Farmington Hills, MI 48331-3535. Phone: 800-877-GALE or (248)699-4253 Fax: 800-414-5043 E-mail: gale.galeord@cengage.com • URL: http://gale.cengage.com • 1998. $189.00. Provides 2,500 ranked lists of international companies, compiled from a variety of published sources. Each list shows the "top ten" in a particular category. Keyword indexing, a country index, and citations are provided.

World Cartography. United Nations, Department of Economic and Social Affairs. United Nations Publications, United Nations Concourse Level, First Ave., 46th St. New York, NY 10017. Phone: 800-553-3210 or (212)963-7680 Fax: (212)963-3489 E-mail: bookstore@un.org • URL: http://www.un.org/publications • Various volumes. Price on application.

World Chamber of Commerce Directory., P.O. Box 1029 Loveland, CO 80539. Phone: (970)663-3231 Fax: (970)663-6187 E-mail: worldchamberdirectory@compuserve.com Annual. $50.00.

World Class Quality: Using Design of Experiments to Make It Happen. Keki R. Bhote and Adi K. Bhote. AMACOM, 1601 Broadway New York, NY 10019. Phone: 800-262-9699 or (518)586-8100 Fax: (518)903-8168 E-mail: customerservice@amanet.org • URL: http://www.amacombooks.org • 1999. $45.00. Second revised expanded edition. An explanation of seven Shainin techniques for quality control. Exercises and case studies are included.

World Class Warehousing and Material Handling. Edward Frazelle. McGraw-Hill, 1221 Ave. of the Americas New York, NY 10020. Phone: 800-722-4726 or (212)512-2000 Fax: (212)512-4502 E-mail: customer.service@mcgraw-hill.com • URL: http://www.mcgraw-hill.com • 2001. $49.95. (Logistics Management Library).

World Cogeneration: A Power Source for Partnering in the 90's. Dick Flanagan, Two Penn Plaza, Suite 1500 New York, NY 10121. Phone: (212)432-7300 Five times a year. $36.00 per year. Edited for managers and executives of independent and cogeneration electric power plants. Provides analysis of industry trends.

World Consumer Expenditure Patterns. Euromonitor International, 122 South Michigan Ave., Suite 810 Chicago, IL 60603. Phone: 800-577-3876 or (312)922-1115 Fax: (312)922-1157 E-mail: info@euromonitor.com • URL: http://www.euromonitor.com • 2003. $1,190.00. Contains detailed consumer expenditure data for 71 countries. Covers 70 specific categories within the areas of food, beverages, tobacco, clothing, housing, appliances, health, transportation, leisure, etc. Provides 10 years of data and includes consumer price indexes.

World Consumer Income and Expenditure Patterns. Available from Gale Cengage Learning, 27500 Drake Rd. Farmington Hills, MI 48331-3535. Phone: 800-877-GALE or (248)699-GALE Fax: 800-414-5043 E-mail: gale.galeord@cengage.com • URL: http://gale.cengage.com • Annual. $1,090.00. Two volumes. Published by Euromonitor. Provides data for countries worldwide on consumer income, earning power, spending patterns, and savings. Expenditures are detailed for product or service categories.

World Consumer Income Patterns. Euromonitor International, 122 South Michigan Ave., Suite 810 Chicago, IL 60603. Phone: 800-577-3876 or (312)922-1115 Fax: (312)922-1157 E-mail: info@euromonitor.com • URL: http://www.euromonitor.com • 2003. $1,190.00. Provides detailed data on household income in 71 countries (10-year statistics). Covers income by age, sex, and level of education, with further data on savings, earnings, and average taxes.

World Consumer Lifestyles Databook: Key Trends. Euromonitor International, 122 South Michigan Ave., Suite 810 Chicago, IL 60603. Phone: 800-577-3876 or (312)922-1115 Fax: (312)922-1157 E-mail: info@euromonitor.com • URL: http://www.euromonitor.com • 2003. $1,190.00. Second edition. Covers 71 countries. Presents statistical data relating to such consumer lifestyle characteristics as family size, household income, family expenditures, home ownership, shopping habits, eating habits, drinking habits, savings, transportation, travel, health characteristics, and education.

World Consumer Markets. Gale Cengage Learning, 27500 Drake Rd. Farmington Hills, MI 48331-3535. Phone: 800-877-GALE or (248)699-4253 Fax: 800-414-5043 or (248)699-8069 E-mail: galeord@gale.com • URL: http://gale.cengage.com • Annual. $2,500.00. Pblished by Euromonitor. Provides five- year historical data, current data, and forecasts, on CD-ROM for 330 consumer products in 55 countries. Market data is presented in a standardized format for each country.

World Cosmetics and Toiletries Data and Statistics. Euromonitor International, 122 South Michigan Ave., Suite 810 Chicago, IL 60603. Phone: 800-577-3876 or (312)922-1115 Fax: (312)922-1157 E-mail; info@euromonitor.com • URL: http://www.euromonitor.com • 2004. $650.00. Provides five-year data for a wide variety of cosmetics and toiletries in 52 countries. Includes market size, consumer expenditures, price indicators, and retail distribution data for such items as perfume, shampoo, sun products, soap, deodorants, toothpaste, hair care products, and skin care products.

World Cosmetics and Toiletries Marketing Directory. Available from Gale Cengage Learning, 27500 Drake Rd. Farmington Hills, MI 48331-3535. Phone: 800-877-GALE or (248)699-GALE Fax: 800-414-5043 E-mail: gale.galeord@cengage.com • URL: http://www.galegroup.com • 2002. $1,190.00. Third edition. Three volumes. Published by Euromonitor. Provides detailed descriptions of the world's cosmetics and toiletries companies. Includes consumers market research data.

World Cost of Living Survey. Gale Cengage Learning, 27500 Drake Rd. Farmington Hills, MI 48331-3535. Phone: 800-877-GALE or (248)699-4253 Fax: 800-414-5043 E-mail: gale.galeord@cengage.com • URL: http://gale.cengage.com • 1999. $275.00. Second edition. Arranged by country and then by city within each country. Provides cost of living data for many products and services. Includes indexes and an annotated bibliography.

World Council of Credit Unions, Inc., 5710 Mineral Point Rd. Madison, WI 53705. Phone: (608)231-7130 Fax: (608)238-8020 E-mail: mail@woccu.org • URL: http://www.woccu.org • A worldwide representative organization of credit unions. Supersedes World Division CUNA International.

World Currrency Yearbook. International Currency Analysis, Inc., 7595 Baymeadows Cir. W, Apt. 2714 Jacksonville, FL 32256-1864. Annual. $250.00. Directory of more than 110 central banks worldwide.

World Database of Business Information Sources on CD-ROM. Gale Cengage Learning, 27500 Drake Rd. Farmington Hills, MI 48331-3535. Phone: 800-877-GALE or (248)699-4253 Fax: 800-414-5043 or (248)699-8069 E-mail: galeord@gale.com • URL: http://gale.cengage.com • Annual. Produced by Euromonitor. Presents Euromonitor's entire information source database on CD-ROM. Contains a worldwide total of about 35,000 publications, organizations, libraries, trade fairs, and online databases.

World Database of Consumer Brands and Their Owners on CD-ROM. Gale Cengage Learning, 27500 Drake Rd. Farmington Hills, MI 48331-3535. Phone: 800-877-GALE or (248)669-GALE Fax: 800-414-5043 or (248)699-8069 E-mail: galeord@gale.com • URL: http://gale.cengage.com • Annual. $3,190.00. Produced by Euromonitor. Provides detailed information on CD-ROM for about 10,000 companies and 80,000 brands around the world. Covers 1,000 product sectors.

World Development. Elsevier, 360 Park Ave., S. New York, NY 10010-1710. Phone: 888-437-4636 or (212)989-5800 Fax: (212)633-3990 E-mail: usinfo-f@elsevier.com • URL: http://www.elsevier.com • Monthly. Qualified personnel, $286.00 per year; institutions, $1,887.00 per year; students, $84.00 per year.

World Development Indicators. The World Bank Group, 1818 H St., N. W. Washington, DC 20433. Phone: 800-645-7247 or (202)477-1234 Fax: (202)477-6391 E-mail: books@worldbank.org • URL: http://www.worldbank.org • Annual. $60.00. Provides data and information on the people, economy, environment, and markets of 148 countries. Emphasis is on statistics relating to major development issues.

World Development Report [CD-ROM]. The World Bank, Office of the Publisher, 1818 H St., N. W. Washington, DC 20433. Phone: 800-645-7247 or (202)477-1234 Fax: (202)477-6391 E-mail: books@worldbank.org • URL: http://www.worldbank.org • Annual. CD-ROM includes the current edition of *World Development Report* and 21 previous editions.

World Development Report 2004. The World Bank Group, 1818 H St., N. W. Washington, DC 20433. Phone: (202)477-1000 Fax: (202)477-6391 E-mail: books@worldbank.org • URL: http://www.worldbank.org • Annual. $26.00. Covers history, conditions, and trends relating to economic globalization and localization. Includes selected data from *World Development Indicators* for 132 countries or economies. Key indicators are provided for 78 additional countries or economies.

The World Directory of Business Information Libraries. Available from Gale Cengage Learning, 27500 Drake Rd. Farmington Hills, MI 48331-3535. Phone: 800-877-GALE or (248)699-GALE Fax: 800-414-5043 E-mail: gale.galeord@cengage.com • URL: http://www.galegroup.com • 2003.

$650.00. Fifth edition. Published by Euromonitor. Provides detailed information on 2,000 major business libraries in 180 countries. Emphasis is on collections relevant to consumer goods and services markets.

World Directory of Business Information Web Sites. Available from Gale Cengage Learning, 27500 Drake Rd. Farmington Hills, MI 48331-3535. Phone: 800-877-GALE or (248)699-GALE Fax: 800-414-5043 E-mail: gale.galeord@cengage.com • URL: http://www.galegroup.com • 2003. $690.00. Sixth edition. Published by Euromonitor. Provides detailed descriptions of a wide variety of business-related Web sites. More than 1,500 sites are included from around the world. Covers statistics sources, market research, company information, rankings, surveys, economic data, etc.

World Directory of Manufactured Fiber Producers. Fiber Economics Bureau, Inc., 1530 Wilson Blvd., Ste. 690 Arlington, DC 22209. Phone: 888-427-1318 or (703)875-0676 Fax: (703)875-0675 E-mail: ddezan@afma.org • URL: http://www.fibersource.com • Annual. Print edition, $135.00. Print edition with CD-ROM, $195.00. Provides information on 2,000 fiber producers in 75 countries. (Fiber Economics Bureau is a subsidiary of the American Fiber Manufacturers Association.)

World Directory of Marketing Information Sources. Available from Gale Cengage Learning, 27500 Drake Rd. Farmington Hills, MI 48331-3535. Phone: 800-877-GALE or (248)699-GALE Fax: 800-414-5043 E-mail: gale.galeord@cengage.com • URL: http://www.galegroup.com • 2003. $650.00. Fourth edition. Published by Euromonitor. Provides details on approximately 6,000 sources of marketing information, including publications, libraries, associations, market research companies, online databases, and governmental organizations. Coverage is worldwide.

World Directory of Non-Official Statistical Sources. Gale Group, Inc., 27500 Drake Rd. Farmington Hills, MI 48331-3535. Phone: 800-877-GALE or (248)699-4253 Fax: 800-414-5043 E-mail: gale.galeord@cengage.com • URL: http://gale.cengage.com • 2002. $650.00. Fourth edition. Provides detailed descriptions of more than 4,000 regularly published, non-governmental statistics sources. Includes surveys, studies, market research reports, trade journals, databank compilations, and other print sources. Coverage is international, with four indexes.

World Directory of Trade and Business Associations. Available from Gale Cengage Learning, 27500 Drake Rd. Farmington Hills, MI 48331-3535. Phone: 800-877-GALE or (248)699-GALE Fax: 800-414-5043 E-mail: gale.galeord@cengage.com • URL: http://www.galegroup.com • 2003. $650.00. Fourth edition. Published by Euromonitor. Provides detailed information on approximately 3,000 trade associations in various countries of the world. Includes subject and geographic indexes.

World Directory of Trade and Business Journals. Euromonitor International, 122 South Michigan Ave., Suite 810 Chicago, IL 60603. Phone: 800-577-3876 or (312)922-1115 Fax: (312)922-1157 E-mail: info@euromonitor.com • URL: http://www.euromonitor.com • 2003. $650.00. Second edition. Contains descriptions of more than 2,300 trade and business journals published in various countries of the world.

World Drinks Data and Statistics. Euromonitor International, 122 South Michigan Ave., Suite 810 Chicago, IL 60603. Phone: 800-577-3876 or (312)922-1115 Fax: (312)922-1157 E-mail: info@euromonitor.com • URL: http://www.euromonitor.com • 2004. $650.00. Provides five-year data for both alcoholic and non-alcoholic beverages in 52 countries. Includes market size, consumer expenditures, price indicators, and retail distribution data for beer, wine, spirits, tea, coffee, soft drinks, fruit juices, bottled water, and other drinks.

World Drinks Marketing Directory. Euromonitor International, 224 S Michigan Ave., Ste. 1500 Chicago, IL 60604. Phone: 800-577-EURO or (312)922-1115 Fax: 800-414-5043 or (312)922-1157 E-mail: insight@euromonitorintl.com • URL: http://www.galegroup.com • Covers: 500 retailers and wholesalers, 1,000 manufacturers, over 2,000 international and European organizations, statistical agencies, market research companies, trade journals and associations, databases, and trade fairs in the beverage industry worldwide. Entries include: Company name, address, phone, telex, number of employees, parent company and subsidiary names, financial data, products and brand names handled; retailers and wholesalers include type of outlets, names and titles of key personnel.

World Drug Report. United Nations Publications, Two United Nations Plaza, Room DC2-853 New York, NY 10017. Phone: 800-253-9646 or (212)963-8302 Fax: (212)963-3489 E-mail: publications@un.org • URL: http://www.un.org/publications • Annual. $25.00. Issued by the United Nations Office for Drug Control and Crime Prevention. Includes maps, graphs, charts, and tables.

World Economic and Social Survey: Trends and Policies in the World Economy. United Nations Publications, Two United Nations Plaza, Room DC2-853 New York, NY 10017. Phone: 800-253-9646 or (212)963-8302 Fax: (212)963-3489 E-mail: publications@un.org • URL: http://www.un.org/publications • Annual. $55.00. Includes discussion and "an extensive statistical annex of economic, trade, and financial indicators, incorporating current data and forecasts."

The World Economic Factbook. Available from Gale Cengage Learning, 27500 Drake Rd. Farmington Hills, MI 48331-

3535. Phone: 800-877-GALE or (248)699-GALE Fax: 800-414-5043 E-mail: gale.galeord@cengage.com • URL: http://gale.cengage.com • Annual. $530.00. Published by Euromonitor. Presents key economic facts and figures for each of 200 countries, including details of chief industries, export-import trade, currency, political risk, household expenditures, and the economic situation in general.

World Economic Outlook: A Survey by the Staff of the International Monetary Fund. International Monetary Fund, Publications Services, 700 19th St., N.W. Washington, DC 20431. Phone: (202)623-7000 Fax: (202)623-6278 E-mail: publicaffairs@imf.org • URL: http://www.imf.org • Semiannual. $78.00 per year. Presents international statistics combined with forecasts and analyses of the world economy.

World Economic Prospects: A Planner's Guide to International Market Conditions. Available from Gale Cengage Learning, 27500 Drake Rd. Farmington Hills, MI 48331-3535. Phone: 800-877-GALE or (248)699-GALE Fax: 800-414-5043 or (248)699-8069 E-mail: gale.galeord@cengage.com • URL: http://www.galegroup.com • 2002. $490.00. Second edition. Published by Euromonitor. Ranks countries by specific economic characteristics, such as gross domestic product (GDP) per capita and short term growth prospects. Discusses the economic situation, prospects, and market potential of each of the countries.

World Economic Situation and Prospects. United Nations Publications, Two United Nations Plaza, Room DC2-853 New York, NY 10017. Phone: 800-253-9646 or (212)963-8302 Fax: (212)963-3489 E-mail: publications@un.org • URL: http://www.un.org/publications • Annual. $15.00. Serves as a supplement and update to the UN *World Economic and Social Survey*.

The World Economy: A Millennial Perspective. Angus Maddison. Organization for Economic Cooperation and Development, OECD Washington Center, 2001 L St., N. W., Suite 650 Washington, DC 20036-4922. Phone: 800-456-6323 or (202)785-6323 Fax: (202)785-0350 E-mail: washington.contact@oecd.org • URL: http://www.oecdwash.org • 2001. $63.00. "...covers the development of the entire world economy over the past 2000 years," including data on world population and gross domestic product (GDP) since the year 1000, and exports since 1820. Focuses primarily on the disparity in economic performance among nations over the very long term. More than 200 statistical tables and figures are provided.

World Employment Report. International Labour Organization, 1828 L St., N.W., Suite 600 Washington, DC 20036-5121. Phone: (202)653-7652 Fax: (202)653-7687 E-mail: klee@ilo.org • URL: http://www.ilo.org/publns • Annual. $34.95. Contains detailed information on the world employment situation and world employment trends.

World Encyclopedia of Library and Information Services. Robert Wedgeworth, editor. American Library Association, 50 E. Huron St. Chicago, IL 60611-2795. Phone: 800-545-2433 or (312)944-6780 Fax: (312)440-9374 E-mail: ala@ala.org • URL: http://www.ala.org • 1993. $200.00. Third edition. Contains about 340 articles from various contributors.

World Energy and Nuclear Directory. Specialist Journals, 345 Park Ave., S New York, NY 10010-1707. Phone: (212)726-9333 Fax: (212)696-0052 E-mail: sjsupport@nature.com • URL: http://www.nature.com • Biennial. $385.00. Lists 5,000 public and private, international research and development organizations functioning in a wide variety of areas related to energy.

World Energy Outlook. OECD Publications and Information Center, 2001 L St., N.W., Suite 650 Washington, DC 20036-4922. Phone: 800-456-6323 or (202)785-6323 Fax: (202)785-0350 E-mail: washington.contact@oecd.org • URL: http://www.oecdwash.org • Annual. $150.00. Provides detailed, 15-year projections by the International Energy Agency (IEA) for world energy supply and demand.

World Environment Report: News and Information on International Resource Management. Business Publishers, Inc., 8737 Colesville Rd., Suite 1100 Silver Spring, MD 20910-3928. Phone: 800-274-6737 or (301)587-6300 Fax: (301)589-8493 E-mail: bpinews@bpinews.com • URL: http://www.bpinews.com • Biweekly. $494.00 per year. Newsletter on international developments having to do with the environment, energy, pollution control, waste management, and toxic substances.

World Factbook. U.S. National Technical Information Service, 5285 Port Royal Rd. Springfield, VA 22161. Phone: 800-553-6847 or (703)605-6060 Fax: (703)605-6880 E-mail: orders@ntis.fedworld.gov • URL: http://www.ntis.gov • Annual. $83.00. Prepared by the Central Intelligence Agency. For all countries of the world, provides current economic, demographic, geographic, communications, government, defense force, and illicit drug trade information (where applicable).

World Fleet Statistics. Available from Fairplay Publications, Inc., 5201 Blue Lagoon Dr., Ste. 530 Miami, FL 33126. Phone: (305)262-4070 Fax: (305)262-2006 E-mail: sales-us@lrfairplay.com • URL: http://www.lrfairplay.com • Annual. $215.00. Published in the UK by Lloyd's Register-Fairplay Ltd. Provides data on the "world fleet of propelled seagoing merchant ships of 100 gross tonnage and above." Includes five-year summaries.

World Food Data and Statistics. Euromonitor International, 122 South Michigan Ave., Suite 810 Chicago, IL 60603. Phone:

800-577-3876 or (312)922-1115 Fax: (312)922-1157 E-mail: info@euromonitor.com • URL: http://www.euromonitor.com • 2004. $650.00. Provides five-year data for a wide variety of food products in 52 countries. Includes market size, consumer expenditures, price indicators, and retail distribution data for many kinds of meat, fish, fruits, vegetables, dairy products, baked goods, condiments, canned food, and frozen food.

World Food Logistics Organization. World Food Logistics Organization, 1500 King St., Ste. 201 Alexandria, VA 22314. Phone: (703)373-4300 Fax: (703)373-4301 E-mail: bhudson@iarw.org • URL: http://www.wflo.org • Food storage.

World Food Marketing Directory. Euromonitor International, 224 S Michigan Ave., Ste. 1500 Chicago, IL 60604. Phone: 800-577-EURO or (312)922-1115 Fax: 800-414-5043 or (312)922-1157 E-mail: insight@euromonitorintl.com • URL: http://www.galegroup.com • Covers: Over 2,000 retailers and wholesalers, 1,600 manufacturers, over 2,000 international and European organizations, statistical agencies, trade journals and associations, databases, and trade fairs in the grocery and food industries worldwide. Entries include: Company name, address, phone, telex, names of parent company and subsidiaries, number of employees, financial data, products and brand names handled; retailers and wholesalers include type of outlet, names and titles of key personnel.

World Future Society., 7910 Woodmont Ave., Ste. 450 Bethesda, MD 20814. Phone: 800-989-8274 or (301)656-8274 Fax: (301)951-0394 E-mail: info@wfs.org • URL: http://www.wfs.org • Helps individuals, organizations, and communities see, understand, and respond appropriately and effectively to change. Raises awareness of change and encourages development of creative solutions through media, meetings, and dialogue among its members. Serves as a neutral forum for exploring possible, probable, and preferable futures.

World Futures Studies Federation., 2nd Floor, Main Administration Bldg., University of St. La Salle, La Salle Ave., PO Box 249 Bacolod City 6100, Philippines. Phone: 34 4353857 Fax: 34 4353857 E-mail: secretariat@worldfutures. org • URL: http://www.worldfutures.org • Institutions, scholars, policymakers, and individuals involved in futures studies. Promotes futures studies and innovative interdisciplinary analyses. Encourages the exchange of information and opinion through organized research projects.

World Futures Studies Federation Membership Directory. World Futures Studies Federation, c/o Marianne Rugard Jarvstrat, Sec. Gen., De Lavalsgatan 6, P.O. Box 249 Trollhattan, Sweden. Phone: (46)709 906923 E-mail: secretariat@wfsf. org Publication includes: List of over 700 member individuals and 60 institutions with an interest in the study of the world's future. Entries include: Name, address, phone, fax, e-mail.

World Gas Handbook. Energy Intelligence Group, Inc., Five E 37th St., 5th Fl. New York, NY 10016-2807. Phone: (212)532-1112 Fax: (212)532-4479 • URL: http://www.energyintel.com • Annual. $1,250.00. Contains the gas industry structure, policies, markets, and production data for each of about 50 countries. Also includes detailed profiles of 56 major gas producers.

World Guide to Libraries. Available from Gale Cengage Learning, 27500 Drake Rd. Farmington Hills, MI 48331-3535. Phone: 800-877-GALE or (248)699-GALE E-mail: gale.galeord@cengage.com • URL: http://www.galegroup.com • 2003. $465.00. 17th edition. Two volumes. Provides information on more than 43,000 academic, government, and public libraries in 200 countries. Published by K. G. Saur.

World Guide to Special Libraries. Available from Gale Cengage Learning, 27500 Drake Rd. Farmington Hills, MI 48331-3535. Phone: 800-877-GALE or (248)699-GALE Fax: 800-414-5043 E-mail: gale.galeord@cengage.com • URL: http://www.galegroup.com • 2001. $400.00. Fifth edition. Two volumes. Published by K. G. Saur. Classifies more than 38,000 libraries in 183 countries under 750 subject headings.

World Highways. International Road Federation, 1010 Massachusetts Ave., N.W., Suite 410 Washington, DC 20001. Phone: (202)371-5544 Fax: (202)371-5565 E-mail: info@irfnet.org • URL: http://www.irfnet.org • Eight times a year. $165.00 per year. Text in English, French, German and Spanish.

World History of Beekeeping and Honey Hunting. Eva Crane. Taylor & Francis, 29 W 35th St. New York, NY 10001. Phone: 800-634-7064 or (212)216-7800 Fax: (212)564-7854 E-mail: cservice@routledge.com • URL: http://www.routledge-ny.com • 1999. $140.00. Provides a wide variety of information on beekeeping and the honey industry.

The World in 2020: Power, Culture, and Prosperity. Hamish McRae. Harvard Business School Publishing, 300 N Beacon St. Watertown, MA 02163. Phone: 800-988-0886 or (617)783-7500 Fax: (617)783-7555 • URL: http://www.hbs.edu • 1995. $14.95. States that the best predictor of economic success will be a nation's creativity and social responsibility.

World Interactive Television and Video Transmission Overview. Primary Research, 850 Seventh Ave., Ste. 1200 New York, NY 10019. Phone: (212)764-1579 Fax: (212)397-5056 E-mail: primarydat@aol.com 1994. Contains market research data. Price on application.

World Investment Report. United Nations Publications, Two United Nations Plaza, Room DC2-853 New York, NY 10017. Phone: 800-253-9646 or (212)963-8302 Fax: (212)963-3489

E-mail: publications@un.org • URL: http://www.un.org/publications • Annual. $49.00. Concerned with foreign direct investment, economic development, regional trends, transnational corporations, and globalization.

World Labour Report. International Labour Office., 1828 L St. NW, Ste. 600 Washington, DC 20036-5121. Phone: (202)653-7652 Fax: (202)653-7687 E-mail: ilopubs@tascol.com • URL: http://www.ilo.org/pubns • Irregular. Price varies. Volume eight. International coverage. Reviews significant recent events and labor policy developments in the following areas: employment, human rights, labor relations, and working conditions.

World Leading Global Brand Owners. Euromonitor International, 122 South Michigan Ave., Suite 810 Chicago, IL 60603. Phone: 800-577-3876 or (312)922-1115 Fax: (312)922-1157 E-mail: info@euromonitor.com • URL: http://www.euromonitor.com • 2003. $1,190.00. Second edition. Contains detailed profiles of multinational consumer product companies. Includes sales, market share, brand names, and financial information. (*Global Market Share Planner*, vol. 3.)

World Leisure Journal: Official Publication of the World Leisure and Recr eation Association. World Leisure and Recreation Association, WLRA Secretariat, Site 81C Comp O Okanagan Falls, BC, Canada V0H 1R0. Phone: (250)497-6578 Fax: (250)497-6578 E-mail: secretariat@worldleisure.com • URL: http://www.worldleisure.org • Quarterly. Libraries $80.00 per year. Formerly *World Leisure and Recreation*.

World Market Share Reporter: A Compilation of Reported World Market Share Data and Rankngs on Companies, Products, and Services. Gale Cengage Learning, 27500 Drake Rd. Farmington Hills, MI 48331-3535. Phone: 800-877-GALE or (248)699-4253 Fax: 800-414-5043 E-mail: gale.galeord@cengage.com • URL: http://gale.cengage.com • 2001. $340.00. Fifth edition. Provides market share data for companies, products, and industries in countries or regions other than North America and Mexico.

World Marketing Data and Statistics on CD-ROM. Gale Cengage Learning, 27500 Drake Rd. Farmington Hills, MI 48331-3535. Phone: 800-877-GALE or (248)699-GALE Fax: 800-414-5043 or (248)699-8069 E-mail: galeord@gale.com • URL: http://gale.cengage.com • Annual. $1,750.00. Published by Euromonitor. Provides demographic, marketing, socioeconomic, and political data on CD-ROM for each of 209 countries.

World Marketing Forecasts on CD-ROM. Gale Cengage Learning, 27500 Drake Rd. Farmington Hills, MI 48331-3535. Phone: 800-877-GALE or (248)699-4253 Fax: 800-414-5043 or (248)699-8069 E-mail: galeord@gale.com • URL: http://gale.cengage.com • Annual. $2,500.00. Produced by Euromonitor. Provides detailed forecast data for the years to 2012 on CD-ROM for 54 countries in all parts of the world. Covers a wide range of social, demographic, economic, and market factors. Includes specific forecasts for many kinds of consumer products.

World Meetings: Outside United States and Canada. Gale Group, 27500 Drake Rd. Farmington Hills, MI 48331-3535. Phone: 800-877-GALE or (248)699-4253 E-mail: gale.galeord@cengage.com • URL: http://gale.cengage.com • Three times a year. $195.00 per year

World Meetings: United States and Canada. Gale Cengage Learning, 27500 Drake Rd. Farmington Hills, MI 48331-3535. Phone: 800-877-4253 or (248)699-4253 Fax: 800-414-5043 E-mail: gale.galeord@cengage.com • URL: http://gale.cengage.com • Three times a year. $195.00 per year.

World Metal Statistics. World Bureau of Metal Statistics, 27a High St. Ware SG12 9BA, United Kingdom. Phone: 44 1920 461274 Fax: 44 1920 464258 E-mail: 100010.2037@compuserve.com Monthly. $980.00 per year.

World Meteorological Organization., 7bis, ave. de la Paix CH-1211 Geneva, Switzerland. Phone: 41 22 7308111 Fax: 41 22 7308181 E-mail: wmo@wmo.int • URL: http://www.wmo.ch • States, territories, and groups of territories. Supports international cooperation in establishing networks for meteorological observations and hydrological and geophysical observations related to meteorology. Promotes the creation of centers offering meteorological services and systems to facilitate exchange of information. Encourages uniform publication of observations and statistics and the application of meteorology as it involves aviation, shipping, water problems, and agriculture. Fosters activities in operational hydrology and cooperation between meteorological and hydrological services. Organizes courses in meteorology and operational hydrology.

World Migration Report. United Nations Publications, Two United Nations Plaza, Room DC2-853 New York, NY 10017. Phone: 800-253-9646 or (212)963-8302 Fax: (212)963-3489 E-mail: publications@un.org • URL: http://www.un.org/publications • Annual. $39.00. Analyzes major trends in world migration, including individual country profiles.

World Non-Agricultural Pesticide Markets. Theta Reports, 1775 Broadway, Suite 511 New York, NY 10019. Phone: (212)262-8230 Fax: (212)262-8234 E-mail: lschacterle@thetareports.com • URL: http://www.thetareports.com • 2000. $1,670.00. Market research data. Includes home/garden pesticides, herbicides, professional pest-control products, and turf pesticides. (Theta Report No. DS191E.)

World of Computer Science. Gale Cengage Learning, 27500 Drake Rd. Farmington Hills, MI 48331-3535. Phone: 800-877-GALE or (248)699-4253 Fax: 800-414-5043 E-mail:

gale.galeord@cengage.com • URL: http://gale.cengage.com • 2002. $160.00. Alphabetical arrangement. Contains 650 entries covering discoveries, theories, concepts, issues, ethics, and people in the broad area of computer science and technology.

World of Criminal Justice. Gale Cengage Learning, 27500 Drake Rd. Farmington Hills, MI 48331-3535. Phone: 800-877-GALE or (248)699-4253 Fax: 800-414-5043 E-mail: gale.galeord@cengage.com • URL: http://gale.cengage.com • 2002. $160.00. Two volumes. Contains both topical and biographical entries relating to the criminal justice system and criminology.

World of Invention: History's Most Significant Inventions and the People Beh ind Them. Gale Cengage Learning, 27500 Drake Rd. Farmington Hills, MI 48331-3535. Phone: 800-877-GALE or (248)699-4253 Fax: 800-414-5043 E-mail: gale.galeord@cengage.com • URL: http://gale.cengage.com • 1999. $115.00. Second edition.

The World of Learning. Available from Taylor and Francis, Inc., 325 Chestnut St. Philadelphia, PA 19106. Phone: 800-821-8312 or (215)625-8900 Fax: (215)625-2940 E-mail: info@taylorandfrancis.com • URL: http://www.taylorandfrancis.com • Annual. $525.00. Covers about 30,000 colleges, libraries, museums, learned societies, academies, and research institutions throughout the world. Published by Europa Publications.

World of Winners: A Current and Historical Perspective on Awards and Their Winners. Gale Cengage Learning, 27500 Drake Rd. Farmington Hills, MI 48331-3535. Phone: 800-877-GALE or (248)699-4253 Fax: 800-414-5043 E-mail: gale.galeord@cengage.com • URL: http://gale.cengage.com • 1991. $99.00. Second edition. Lists 100,000 recipients of 2,500 awards, honors, and prizes in 12 subject categories. Indexed by organization, recipient, and award. Covers all years for each award.

World Oil. Gulf Publishing Co., Two Greenway Plz., Ste. 1020 Houston, TX 77046. Phone: 800-231-6275 or (713)529-4301 Fax: (713)520-4433 • URL: http://www.gulfpub.com • Monthly. $130.00 per year. Covers worldwide oil and gas exploration, drilling and production.

World Oil Tanker Trends. Jacobs and Partners Ltd., 18 Mansell St. London E1 IAA, United Kingdom. Phone: 44 171 4592100 Fax: 44 171 4592199 Semiannual. $520.00 per year.

World Online Markets. JupiterMedia, 23 Old Kings Hwy. S Darien, CT 06820. Phone: 800-488-4345 or (203)662-2800 Fax: (203)655-4686 • URL: http://www.jmm.com • Annual. $1,895.00. Market research report. Provides broad coverage of worldwide Internet and online information business activities, including country-by-country data. Includes company profiles and five-year forecasts or trend projections.

World Opinion Update. Survey Research Consultants International, Inc. Survey Research Consultants International Inc., 156 Bulkley St. Williamstown, MA 01267. Phone: (413)458-5338 Fax: (413)414-1527 E-mail: custserve@lrp.com • URL: http://www.worldopinionupdate.com • Description: Gives tabular results of recent public opinion polls conducted in many countries on international public affairs subjects: sociological, political, economic, military, and religious. Recurring features include statistics.

World Patent Information: International Journal for Patent Documentation, Clasification and Statistics. European Commission BEL. Elsevier, 360 Park Ave., S New York, NY 10010-1710. Phone: 888-437-4636 or (212)989-5800 Fax: (212)633-3990 E-mail: usinfo-f@elsevier.com • URL: http://www.elsevier.com • Quarterly. $656.00 per year.

World Population Chart. United Nations Publications, United Nations Concourse Level, First Ave., 46th St. New York, NY 10017. Phone: 800-553-3210 or (212)963-7680 Fax: (212)963-3489 E-mail: bookstore@un.org • URL: http://www.un.org/publications • 1998. $5.95. Shows population, birth rate, death rate, etc., for all countries of the world, with forecasts to the year 2015 and to the year 2050.

World Population Data Sheet. Population Reference Bureau, Inc., 1875 Connecticut Ave., N.W., Suite 520 Washington, DC 20009. Phone: 800-877-9881 or (202)939-5407 Fax: (202)328-3937 E-mail: popref@prb.org • URL: http://www.prb.org • Annual. $4.50

World Population Projections to 2150. United Nations Publications, Two United Nations Plaza, Room DC2-853 New York, NY 10017. Phone: 800-253-9646 or (212)963-8302 Fax: (212)963-3489 E-mail: publications@un.org • URL: http://www.un.org/publications • 1998. $15.00. Presents very long-range population projections for eight major areas of the world: Africa, Asia, China, Europe, India, Latin America, North America, and Oceania.

World Press Encyclopedia. Gale Cengage Learning, 27500 Drake Rd. Farmington Hills, MI 48331-3535. Phone: 800-877-GALE or (248)699-4253 Fax: 800-414-5043 E-mail: gale.galeord@cengage.com • URL: http://gale.cengage.com • 2003. $325.00. Second edition. Two volumes. Comprehensive essays cover the background and economic framework of newspapers and other news media in about 200 countries. Covers relevant legal issues, censorship, government relations, education in journalism, status of news agencies, cable, Internet, and other media topics.

World Press Review: News and Views from Around the World. Stanley Foundation, 700 Broadway, 3rd Fl. New York, NY 10003-9536. Phone: (212)982-8880 Fax: (212)982-6968 E-mail: tschure@worldpress.com • URL: http://www.

worldpress.com • Monthly. $26.97 per year. International news and information on a wide variety of subjects that do not appear in other American publications.

World Pumps. Elsevier, 360 Park Ave., S. New York, NY 10010-1710. Phone: 888-437-4636 or (212)989-5800 Fax: (212)633-3990 E-mail: usinfo-f@elsevier.com • URL: http://www.elsevier.com • Monthly. Institutions, $307.00 per year. Text in English, French and German.

World Radio TV Handbook. World Radio TV Handbook, PO Box 290 Oxford OX2 7FT, United Kingdom. Phone: 800-278-8479 or (646)654-5500 Fax: (646)654-5487 or (44)1865 514405 E-mail: sales@wrth.com • URL: http://www.watsonguptill.com • Covers: 25,000 radio and television stations worldwide; national regulatory bodies. Entries include: For stations—Name, frequency, address, phone, telex, name and title of contact and key personnel, description of programming. For agencies—Name, address, phone.

World Retail Directory and Sourcebook. Available from Gale Cengage Learning, 27500 Drake Rd. Farmington Hills, MI 48331-3535. Phone: 800-877-GALE or (248)699-GALE Fax: 800-414-5043 E-mail: gale.galeord@cengage.com • URL: http://www.galegroup.com • 2003. $1,250.00. Fifth edition. Published by Euromonitor. Provides information on more than 2,400 retailers around the world. Information sources, conferences, trade fairs, and special libraries are also listed.

World Robotics: Statistics, Market Analysis, Forecasts, Case Studies, and Profitability of Robot Investment. United Nations Publications, Two United Nations Plaza, Room DC2-853 New York, NY 10017. Phone: 800-253-9646 or (212)963-8302 Fax: (212)963-3489 E-mail: publications@un.org • URL: http://www.un.org/publications • Annual. $120.00. Presents international data on industrial robots and service robots. Statistical tables allow uniform comparison of numbers for 20 countries, broken down by type of application, type of robot, and other variables.

World Semiconductor Trade Statistics. Semiconductor Industry Association, 181 Metro Dr. San Jose, CA 95110. Phone: (408)436-6600 Fax: (408)436-6646 E-mail: mailbox@sia-online.org • URL: http://www.semichips.org • Monthly. $2,200.00 per year. Provides data on all world semiconductor markets including industry forecasts.

World Shipbuilding Statistics. Available from Fairplay Publications, Inc., 5201 Blue Lagoon Dr., Ste. 530 Miami, FL 33126. Phone: (305)262-4070 Fax: (305)262-2006 E-mail: sales-us@lrfairplay.com • URL: http://www.lrfairplay.com • Quarterly. $215.00 per year. Published in the UK by Lloyd's Register-Fairplay Ltd. Contains detailed, current data on shipbuilding orders placed and completions.

World Statistics Pocketbook. United Nations Publications, United Nations Concourse Level, First Ave., 46st St. New York, NY 10017. Phone: 800-553-3210 or (212)963-7680 Fax: (212)963-3489 Annual $10.00.

World Surface Coatings Abstracts. Paint Research Association, Eight Waldgreave Rd. Teddington TW11 8EP, United Kingdom. Phone: 44 20 8977 4427 Fax: 44 20 8943 4705 E-mail: coatings@pra.org.uk • URL: http://www.pra.org.uk • 13 times a year. Members, $1,230.00 per year; non-members, $1,695.00 per year.

World Surface Coatings Abstracts [Online]. Paint Research Association of Great Britain, Waldegrave Rd. Teddington, Middlesex TW11 8LD 4, England. Phone: 44 20 86144800 Fax: 44 20 89434705 Indexing and abstracting of the literature of paint and surface coatings, 1976 to present. Monthly updates. Inquire as to online cost and availability.

World Textile Abstracts. Elsevier, 360 Park Ave., S. New York, NY 10010-1710. Phone: 888-437-4636 or (212)989-5800 Fax: (212)633-3990 E-mail: usinfo-f@elsevier.com • URL: http://www.elsevier.com • Monthly. Institutions $1,696.00 per year. Digests of articles published in the world's textile literature. Includes subscription to *World Textile Digest*.

World Textiles. Elsevier Science, Inc., 360 Park Ave. S New York, NY 10010. Phone: 888-437-4636 or (212)633-3730 Fax: (212)633-3680 • URL: http://www.elsevier.com • Provides abstracting and indexing from 1970 of worldwide textile literature (periodicals, books, pamphlets, and reports). Includes U. S., European, and British patent information. Updating is monthly. Inquire as to online cost and availability.

World Tobacco. DMG World Media Ltd., Queensway House, 2 Queensway Red Hill RH1 1QS, United Kingdom. Phone: 44 1737 855527 Fax: 44 1737 855470 • URL: http://www.dmgworldmedia.com • Six times a year. $132.00 per year.

World Trade Analyzer. Statistics Canada, International Trade Division, Ottawa, ON, Canada K1A OT6. Phone: 800-263-1136 or (613)951-8116 Fax: 800-899-9734 or (613)951-0117 • URL: http://www.statcan.ca • Annual. CD-ROM provides 20 years of export-import data for 800 commodities traded by the 180 member countries of the United Nations.

World Trade Annual. United Nations Statistical Office. Walker and Co., 435 Hudson St. New York, NY 10014-3941. Phone: (212)727-8300 Fax: (212)727-0984 Annual. Prices vary.

World Trade Atlas CD-ROM. Global Trade Information Services, Inc., 2218 Devine St. Columbia, SC 29205. Phone: 800-982-4847 or (803)765-1860 Fax: (803)799-5589 E-mail: trade@gtis.com • URL: http://www.gtis.com • Monthly. $4,920.00 per year. ($3,650.00 per year with quarterly updates.) Provides government statistics on trade between the U. S. and each of more than 200 countries. Includes import-export data, trade balances, product information, market share, price data, etc. Time period is the most recent three years.

World Trade Centers Association., 420 Lexington Ave., Ste. 518 New York, NY 10170. Phone: 800-937-8886 or (212)432-2626 Fax: (212)488-0064 E-mail: wtca@wtca.org • URL: http://world.wtca.org/portal/site/wtcaonline • Regular members are organizations involved in the development or operation of a World Trade Center (WTC). Affiliate members are Chambers of Commerce, clubs, exhibit facilities or other international trade related organizations. Encourages expansion of world trade and international business relationships.

World Trade: For U.S. Executives with Global Vision. BNP Media, 2401 W. Big Beaver Rd., Ste. 700 Troy, MI 48084. Phone: 800-640-7071 or (248)362-3700 Fax: (248)244-6439 E-mail: info@worldtrademag.com • URL: http://www.worldtrademag.com • Monthly. $24.00 per year. Edited for senior management of U. S. companies engaged in international business and trade.

World Trade Issues. Lambert S. Martin, editor. Nova Science Publishers, Inc., 400 Oser Ave., Suite 1600 Hauppauge, NY 11788-3619. Phone: (631)231-7269 Fax: (631)231-8175 E-mail: novascience@earthlink.net • URL: http://www.novapublishers.com • 2002. $69.00. Provides articles by various authors on foreign trade and the influence of globalization, including discussion of the World Trade Organization. Emphasis is on Asian countries and Latin America.

World Trade Organization Dispute Settlement Decisions: Bernan's Annotated Reporter. Bernan Press, 4611-F Assembly Dr. Lanham, MD 20706-4391. Phone: 800-274-4447 or (301)459-2255 Fax: 800-865-3450 or (301)459-9235 E-mail: bpress@bernan.com • URL: http://www.bernan.com • Dates vary. $75.00 per volume. Contains all World Trade Organization Panel Reports and Appellate Decisions since the establishment of the WTO in 1995. Includes such cases as "The Importation, Sale, and Distribution of Bananas."

World Trade Organization Trade Policy Review. Bernan Press, 4611-F Assembly Dr. Lanham, MD 20706-4391. Phone: 800-274-4447 or (301)459-7666 Fax: 800-865-3450 or (301)459-0056 E-mail: info@bernan.com • URL: http://www.bernan.com • Annual. $95.00. CD-ROM provides detailed trade information for each of 40 countries. Includes search capabilities, hypertext links, charts, tables, and graphs.

World Trade Review: Economics, Law, International Institutions. Cambridge University Press, 40 W 20th St. New York, NY 10011-4211. Phone: 800-872-7423 or (212)924-3900 Fax: (212)691-3239 E-mail: information@cup.org • URL: http://www.cup.org • Three times a year. Individuals, $48.00 pr year; institutions, $200.00 per year. Published in conjunction with the World Trade Organization (http://www.wto.org). Covers "issues of relevance to the multilateral trading system."

World Trademark Law and Practice. LexisNexis Matthew Bender, 1275 Broadway Albany, NY 12204. Phone: 800-424-4200 or (518)487-3000 Fax: (518)487-3584 E-mail: bookstore.support@lexisnexis.com • URL: http://www.bender.com • $849.00. Five looseleaf volumes. Periodic supplementation. A guide to international trademark practice with detailed coverage of 35 major jurisdictions and summary coverage for over 100.

World Watch: Working for a Sustainable Future. Worldwatch Institute, 1776 Massachusetts Ave., N.W. Washington, DC 20036-1904. Phone: (202)452-1999 Fax: (202)296-7365 E-mail: worldwatch@worldwatch.org • URL: http://www.worldwatch.org • Bimonthly. $25.00 per year. Emphasis is on environmental trends, including developments in population growth, climate change, human behavior, the role of government, and other factors.

World Who is Who and Does What in Environment and Conservation. Nicholas Polunin and Lynn M. Curme. Stylus Publishing, LLC, Herndon, VA 20176. Phone: (703)661-1504 Fax: (703)-661-1547 E-mail: styluspub@aol.co • URL: http://styluspub.com • 1997. $95.00. Provides biographies of 1,300 individuals considered to be leaders in environmental and conservation areas.

World Wide Pet Industry Association., 135 W Lemon Ave. Monrovia, CA 91016-2809. Phone: 800-999-7295 or (626)447-2222 Fax: (626)447-8350 E-mail: info@wwpia.org • URL: http://www.wwpia.org • Manufacturers, retailers, and distributors of pet food and services and of avian, aquarium, and companion animal care products, equipment, and services. Seeks to advance the economic interests of members; promotes responsible pet ownership. Conducts trade shows, certificate training courses, and seminars for pet shop retailers, grooming establishments, and veterinary clinics.

WorldatWork., 14040 N Northsight Blvd. Scottsdale, AZ 85260. Phone: 877-951-9191 or (480)951-9191 Fax: (480)483-8352 E-mail: customerrelations@worldatwork.org • URL: http://www.worldatwork.org • Dedicated to knowledge leadership in compensation, benefits and total rewards, focusing on disciplines associated with attracting, retaining and motivating employees. Offers CCP, CBP, and GRP certification and education programs, conducts surveys, research and provides networking opportunities.

Worldmark Encyclopedia of National Economies. Gale Cengage Learning, 27500 Drake Rd. Farmington Hills, MI 48331-3535. Phone: 800-877-GALE or (248)699-4253 Fax: 800-414-5043 E-mail: gale.galeord@cengage.com • URL: http://gale.cengage.com • 2002. $325.00. Four volumes. Covers both the current and historical development of the economies of 200 foreign nations. Includes analysis and statistics.

Worldmark Yearbook. Gale Cengage Learning, 27500 Drake Rd. Farmington Hills, MI 48331-3535. Phone: 800-877-GALE or (248)699-4253 Fax: 800-414-5043 E-mail: gale.galeord@cengage.com • URL: http://gale.cengage.com • 2001. $295.00. Three volumes. Covers economic, social, and political events in about 230 countries. Includes statistical data, directories, and a bibliography.

World's Greatest Brands: An International Review by Interbrand. John Wiley and Sons, Inc., 111 River St. Hoboken, NJ 07030. Phone: 800-225-5945 or (201)748-6000 Fax: (201)748-6088 E-mail: info@wiley.com • URL: http://www.wiley.com • 1992. $49.95. Compiled by Interbrand. Provides details on 330 of the most successful international brand names and trademarks. Includes color illustrations.

The World's Largest Market: A Business Guide to Europe 1992. Robert Williams and others. AMACOM, 1601 Broadway New York, NY 10019. Phone: 800-262-9699 or (518)586-8100 Fax: (518)903-8168 E-mail: customerservice@amanet.org • URL: http://www.amacombooks.org • 1991. $19.95. Reprint edition. Provides information on agencies, organizations programs, and regulations relevant to the forthcoming 1992 unified European Community.

World's Major Multinationals. Euromonitor International, 224 S Michigan Ave., Ste. 1500 Chicago, IL 60604. Phone: 800-577-EURO or (312)922-1115 Fax: 800-414-5043 or (312)922-1157 E-mail: insight@euromonitorintl.com • URL: http://www.galegroup.com • Covers: List of major multinational companies. Entries include: Company name, address, phone; performance analysis; list of subsidiaries; market share; net profit and turnover; leading brands; and merger and acquisition information.

Worldscope. Thomson Financial, 22 Thomson Pike Boston, MA 02210. Phone: (617)856-2000 Fax: (617)330-1986 • URL: http://www.tfn.com • Online service provides detailed financial and other information on more than 32,000 publicly-owned companies in 50 countries. Includes business description, balance sheets, earnings statements, senior officers, major shareholders, financial ratios, and 20-year historical data. Monthly updates. Inquire as to online cost and availability.

Worldtariff Guidebook on Customs Tariff Schedules of Import Duties. Worldtariff Division, Morse Agri-Energy Associates, 220 Montgomery St., Suite 432 San Francisco, CA 94104. Phone: 800-556-9334 or (415)391-7501 Fax: (415)391-7537 Looseleaf. Over 60 volumes. Prices vary. Consists generally of volumes for individual countries and volumes for broad classes of products, such as clothing. (Country volumes are typically $500.00 each.)

Worldwatch Institute. Worldwatch Institute, 1776 Massachusetts Ave. NW Washington, DC 20036-1904. Phone: (202)452-1999 or (202)452-1999 Fax: (202)296-7365 E-mail: worldwatch@worldwatch.org • URL: http://www.worldwatch.org • Global trends in the availability and management of both human and natural resources, including research in energy, food policy, population, development, technology, the environment, economics, toxics, and recycling.

Worldwide Branch Location of Multinational Companies. Gale Cengage Learning, 27500 Drake Rd. Farmington Hills, MI 48331-3535. Phone: 800-877-GALE or (248)699-4253 Fax: 800-414-5043 E-mail: gale.galeord@cengage.com • URL: http://gale.cengage.com • 1993. $270.00. A guide to subsidiaries, sales offices, manufacturing facilities, and other corporate units operating outside the headquarters country. Includes over 500 leading multinational companies and their 20,000 branch locations.

Worldwide Government Directory. MacFarlane Management Services Inc., 1410 Highland Bluff Atlanta, GA 30339. Phone: 800-877-GALE or (770)226-8844 Fax: 800-414-5043 or (770)956-0408 E-mail: macfmgt@earthlink.net • URL: http://www.galegroup.com • Covers: 32,000 key elected and appointed government officials in 196 nations and 100 international agencies. Entries include: Head of state, key government ministers, address, phone, and areas of responsibility.

Worldwide History of Telecommunications. Anton Huurdeman. John Wiley and Sons, Inc., 111 River St. Hoboken, NJ 07030. Phone: 800-225-5945 or (201)748-6000 Fax: (201)748-6088 E-mail: info@wiley.com • URL: http://www.wiley.com • 2003. $125.00. Covers the evolution and history of telecommunications from before 1800 to 2000. Topics include telegraph, telephone, radio, satellite transmission, optical fiber transmission, electronic switching, telefax, multimedia, and many other subjects. Includes a two-century chronology, worldwide statistics, a glossary, and an index.

Worldwide Offshore Petroleum Directory. PennWell Corp., Petroleum Div., 1700 W. Loop S., Suite 1000 Houston, TX 77027. Phone: 800-736-6935 or (713)621-9720 E-mail: petroleum@pennwell.com • URL: http://www.pennwell.com • Annual. $135.00. Lists about 5,800 companies.

Worldwide Petrochemical Directory. PennWell Corp., Petroleum Div., 1700 W. Loop S., Suite 1000 Houston, TX 77027. Phone: 800-736-6935 or (713)621-9720 E-mail: petroleum@pennwell.com • URL: http://www.pennwell.com • Annual. $165.00. Do more than 3,400 petrochemical plants; separate section on new construction; worldwide coverage. Formerly *Refining and Petrochemical Technology Yearbook*.

Worldwide Refining and Gas Processing Directory. PennWell Corp., Petroeum Div., 1700 W Loop S, Ste. 1000 Houston,

TX 77027. Phone: 800-331-4463 or (713)621-9720 E-mail: petroleum@pennwell.com • URL: http://www.pennwell.com • Annual. $165.00. Lists over 1,000 crude oil refineries, 1,300 gas processing plants and over 600 engineering and construction firms which build and service these plants; worldwide coverage.

Worldwide Trade Secrets Law. Terrence F. MacLaren, editor. West Group, 610 Opperman Dr. Eagan, MN 55123. Phone: 800-328-4880 or (651)687-7000 Fax: 800-340-9378 E-mail: bookstore@westgroup.com • URL: http://www.westgroup.com • $440.00. Three looseleaf volume. Annual supplementation.

Worst Pills Best Pills News. Public Citizen, 1600 20th St., N. W. Washington, DC 20009. Phone: (202)588-1000 Fax: (202)785-3584 E-mail: slittle@citizen.org • URL: http://www.citizen.org • Monthly. $20.00 per year. Newsletter. Provides pharmaceutical news and information for consumers, with an emphasis on harmful drug interactions.

WRC Progress Reports. Welding Research Council, Three Park Ave., 27th Fl. New York, NY 10016-5902. Phone: (212)591-7956 Fax: (212)591-7183 • URL: http://www.foregineers.org/wrc • Bimonthly. $1,100 per year. Includes *Welding Research Abroad; WRC Bulletins*, *WRC News* and *Welding Journal*.

The Writer. Kalmbach Publishing Co., 21027 Crossroads Circle Waukesha, WI 53187. Phone: 800-533-6644 or (262)796-8776 Fax: (262)796-1615 • URL: http://www.kalmbach.com • Monthly. $29.00 per year. Freelance writers.

Writers' and Artists' Yearbook: A Directory for Writers, Artists, Playwrights, Writers for Film, Radio and Television, Photographers and Composers. Mid Point Trade Books, 1263 Southwest Blvd. Kansas City, KS 66103. Phone: 800-537-8894 or (913)362-7400 Fax: (913)362-7401 Annual. $25.00. A worldwide guide to markets for various kinds of writing and artwork. Published in England by A O C Black. Formerly*International Writers' and Artists' Yearbook*.

Writer's Digest. F&W Publications, Inc., 4700 E Galbraith Rd. Cincinnati, OH 45236. Phone: 800-289-0963 or (513)531-2690 Fax: (513)531-0798 • URL: http://www.fwpublications.com • Monthly. $19.96 per year.

Writers Directory. infoUSA Inc., 5711 S 86th Cir., PO Box 27347 Omaha, NE 68127. Phone: 800-321-0869 or (402)593-4500 Fax: 800-414-5043 or (402)331-1505 E-mail: help@infousa.com • URL: http://gale.cengage.com • Number of listings: 2,400. Entries include: Name, address, phone, size of advertisement, name of owner or manager, number of employees, year first in "Yellow Pages." Compiled from telephone company "Yellow Pages," nationwide.

Writer's Guide to Book Editors, Publishers, and Literary Agents, Who They Are, What They Want, and How to Win Them Over. Prima Publishing, 3000 Lava Ridge Ct. Roseville, CA 95765. Phone: 800-632-8676 or (916)787-7000 Fax: (916)787-7001 E-mail: sales@primapublishing.com • URL: http://www.primapublishing.com • Annual. $27.95; with CD-ROM, $49.95. Directory for authors includes information on publishers' response times and pay rates.

The Writer's Handbook. Kalmbach Publishing Co., PO Box 1612, 21027 Crossroads Cir. Waukesha, WI 53186-4055. Phone: 800-533-6644 or (262)796-8776 Fax: (262)796-1615 E-mail: customerservice@kalmbach.com Publication includes: compilation of 50-plus articles for publication, many by recognized authors and editors. Features list of 3,000-plus markets for the sale of manuscripts (fiction, nonfiction, poetry, drama, greeting card), plus lists of American literary agents, writers' organizations, literary contests, and writing conferences. Entries include: Markets— name of firm or publication, contact information, editorial preferences, payment rate. Agents—agency name, contact information, submission guidelines, commission rates. Organizations—name, contact information, description of purpose and activities. Contests—name, contact information, prize or award, deadline. Conferences—name, contact information, date/place, description of workshops/activities.

Writer's Market. Writer's Digest Books, 4700 E Galbraith Rd., PO Box 420235 Cincinnati, OH 45236. Phone: 800-258-0929 or (513)531-2222 Fax: (513)531-4082 E-mail: writersdig@fwpubs.com • URL: http://www.fwpublications.com • Covers: Over 8,000 buyers of books, articles, short stories, plays, gags, verse, fillers, and other original written material. Includes book and periodical publishers, greeting card publishers, play producers and publishers, audiovisual material producers, syndicates, and contests and awards. Entries include: Name and address of buyer, phone, payment rates, editorial requirements, reporting time, how to break in.

Writing and Designing Manuals: Operator Manuals, Service Manuals, Manuals for International Markets. Patricia A. Robinson and Ryn Etter. Lewis Publishers, 2000 Corporate Blvd., N. W. Boca Raton, FL 33431. Phone: 800-272-7737 or (407)994-0555 Fax: (407)998-9114 E-mail: orders@crcpress.com • URL: http://www.crcpress.com • 2000. $69.95. Third edition. Includes planning, organization, format, visuals, writing strategies, and other topics.

Writing and Marking Instruments. Available from MarketResearch.com, 641 Ave. of the Americas, Fourth Floor New York, NY 10011. Phone: 800-298-5699 or (212)807-2629 Fax: (212)807-2642 E-mail: order@marketresearch.com • URL: http://www.marketresearch.com • 2002. $3,950.00. Published by Global Industry Analysts. Provides worldwide market research data, including profiles of major companies in the field.

Writing Business Letters for Dummies. Sheryl Lindsell-Roberts. John Wiley, 111 River St. Hoboken, NJ 07030. Phone: 800-225-5945 or (201)748-6000 Fax: (201)748-6088 E-mail: info@wiley.com • URL: http://www.wiley.com • 1999. $21.99. (For Dummies Series).

Writing Effective Business Plans. Entrepreneur Media, Inc., 2445 McCabe Way Irvine, CA 92614. Phone: 800-421-2300 or (949)261-2325 Fax: (949)261-0234 E-mail: entmag@entrepreneur.com • URL: http://www.entrepreneur.com • Looseleaf. $49.50. A step-by-step guide. Includes a sample business plan.

Writing Instrument Manufacturers Association., 15000 Commerce Pkwy., Ste. C Mount Laurel, NJ 08054-2212. Phone: (856)638-0426 Fax: (856)439-0525 E-mail: wima@ahint.com • URL: http://www.wima.org • Manufacturers of handwriting and marking instruments and parts; industry suppliers. Conducts activities in government and public relations; offers product certification program. Compiles import and export statistics, annual total industry sales, and quarterly industry product sales with detailed breakdowns. Collects information on trademarks.

Writing That Works: How to Write Effective E-Mails, Letters, Resumes, Presentations, Plans, Reports and Other Business Communications. Kenneth Roman. HarperInformation, 10 E. 53rd St. New York, NY 10022-5299. Phone: 800-242-7737 or (212)207-7000 Fax: 800-822-4090 or (212)207-7145 • URL: http://www.harpercollins.com • 2000. $13.00. Third edition.

Writing That Works: The Business Communications Report. Writing That Works, 7481 Huntsman Blvd., Suite 720 Springfield, VA 22153-1648. Phone: (703)643-2200 Fax: (703)643-2329 E-mail: concepts@writingthatworks.com Monthly. $119.00 per year.

Written Communication: A Quarterly Journal of Research, Theory, and Application. Sage Publications, Inc., 2455 Teller Rd. Thousand Oaks, CA 91320. Phone: 800-818-7243 or (805)499-9774 Fax: 800-583-2665 or (805)499-0871 E-mail: webmaster@sagepub.com • URL: http://www.sagepub.com • Quarterly. Institutions, $499.00 per year; includes print and online editions.

WTO Annual Report (World Trade Organization). Available from Bernan Associates, 4611-F Assembly Drive Lanham, MD 20706-4391. Phone: 800-274-4888 or (301)459-2255 Fax: 800-865-3450 or (301)459-0056 E-mail: query@bernan.com • URL: http://www.bernan.com • Annual. $80.00. Two volumes ($40.00 per volume). Published by the World Trade Organization. Volume one: *Annual Report*. Volume two: *International Trade Statistics*.

WTO Focus. World Trade Organization, Publications Service, 154 Rue de Lausanne 1211 Geneva 10, Switzerland. Phone: 41 22 739 51 11 Fax: 41 22 739 54 58 E-mail: enquiries@wto.org • URL: http://www.wto.org • Newsletter. Free. 10 times a year. Text in English. Provides current news about activities relating to the World Trade Organization (WTO) and the General Agreement on Tariffs and Trade (GATT). Formerly *GATT Focus*.

WWD: The Retailer's Daily Newspaper (Women's Wear Daily). Fairchild Publications, Seven W. 34th St. New York, NY 10001. Phone: (866)357-4414 or (212)630-4000 E-mail: custservice@fairchildpub.com • URL: http://www.fairchildpub.com • Daily. Individuals, $195.00 per year; retailers, $99.00 per year; manufacturers, $135.00 per year.

X-Change. Virgo Publishing, Inc., PO Box 40079 Phoenix, AZ 85067-0079. Phone: (480)990-1101 Fax: (480)990-0819 E-mail: virgopub@vpico.com • URL: http://www.vpico.com • 18 times per year. $70.00 per year. Edited for local telecommunications exchange services, both wireline and wireless.

X-Ray Films and Chemicals. Available from MarketResearch.com, 641 Ave. of the Americas, Fourth Floor New York, NY 10011. Phone: 800-298-5699 or (212)807-2629 Fax: (212)807-2642 E-mail: order@marketresearch.com • URL: http://www.marketresearch.com • 2002. $3,450.00. Published by Global Industry Analysts. Provides worldwide market research data, including profiles of major x-ray supply companies.

Yale Daily News Guide to Internships 2000: The Essential Guide to Landing an Internship that Launches Your Career. John Anselmi and others. Simon & Schuster Trade, 1230 Ave. of the Americas New York, NY 10020. Phone: 800-223-2348 or (212)698-7000 Fax: (212)698-7007 E-mail: customerservice@simonandschuster.com • URL: http://www.simonsays.com • 1999. Annual. $25.00. Lists internships in various fields.

Yale Law Journal. Yale Journal Co., Inc., P.O. Box 208215 New Haven, CT 06520-8215. Phone: (203)432-1666 Fax: (203)432-7482 • URL: http://www.yale.edu • Eight times a year. $40.00 per year.

Yard and Garden. Cygnus Business Media, Inc., 1233 Janesville Ave. Fort Atkinson, WI 53538. Phone: 800-547-7377 or (920)563-6388 Fax: (920)563-1702 E-mail: rich.reiff@cygnuspub.com • URL: http://www.cygnusbzb.com • Nine times a year. $48.00. Includes retailers and distributors of lawn and garden power equipment, lawn and plant care products, patio furniture, etc. Arranged by type of product. Includes a *Product* issue.

Yearbook. Association of Government Accountants, 2200 Mount Vernon Ave. Arlington, VA 22301-1314. Phone: (703)684-6931 Fax: (703)548-9367 E-mail: jmccumber@agacgfm.org • URL: http://www.agacgfm.org • Annual.

Yearbook of Agriculture. U.S. Department of Agriculture. Available from U.S. Government Printing Office, Washington, DC 20402. Phone: (202)512-1800 Fax: (202)512-2250 E-mail: gpoaccess@gpo.gov • URL: http://www.access.gpo.gov • Annual.

Yearbook of Forest Products. Food and Agriculture Organization of the United Nations. Available from Bernan Associates, 4611-F Assembly Dr. Lanham, MD 20706-4391. Phone: 800-274-4888 or (301)459-7666 Fax: 800-865-3450 or (301)459-0056 E-mail: query@bernan.com • URL: http://www.bernan.com • Annual. $57.00. Test in English, French, and Spanish.

Yearbook of International Organizations. Available from Gale Cengage Learning, 27500 Drake Rd. Farmington Hills, MI 48331-3535. Phone: 800-877-GALE or (248)699-GALE E-mail: gale.galeord@cengage.com • URL: http://www.galegroup.com • Annual. $1,460,00. Five volumes. Vol. 1 *Organization Descriptions and Cross-References*; Vol. 2 *Geographic*; Vol. 4 *Bibliographic*; Vol. 5 *Statistics, Visualizations and Patterns*. Published by K. G. Saur.

Yearbook of International Organizations PLUS. R. R. Bowker, 630 Central Ave. New Providence, NJ 07974. Phone: 888-269-5372 or (908)464-6800 Fax: (908)665-3528 Annual. Compiled by the Union of International Organizations, Brussels. Includes the *Yearbook of International Organizations* and *Who's Who in International Organizations*.

Yearbook of Labour Statistics. Available from Bernan Associates, 4611-F Assembly Dr. Lanham, MD 20706-4391. Phone: 800-274-4888 or (301)459-2255 Fax: 800-865-3450 or (301)459-0056 E-mail: query@bernan.com • URL: http://www.bernan.com • Annual. $168.00. Published by the International Labour Organizaton (http://www.ilo.org). Provides data for more than 180 countries on employment, unemployment, wages, hours of work, cost of labor, strikes, industrial accidents, and consumer prices.

Yearbook of the International Law Commission. Available from United Nations Publications, United Nations Concourse Level, First Ave., 46th St. New York, NY 10017. Phone: 800-553-3210 or (212)963-7680 Fax: (212)963-3489 E-mail: bookstore@un.org • URL: http://www.un.org/publications • Annual. $90.00. Two volumes. Volume one, $35.00; volume two, $55.00.

Yellow Pages and Directory Report: The Newsletter for the Yellow Page and Directory Publishing Industry. SIMBA Information, 11 Riverbend Dr., S Stamford, CT 06907. Phone: 800-307-2529 or (203)358-4100 Fax: (203)358-5824 E-mail: info@simbanet.com • URL: http://www.simbanet.com • 22 times a year. $689.00 per year. Newsletter. Covers the yellow pages publishing industry, including electronic directory publishing, directory advertising, and special interest directories.

Yes, You Can Achieve Financial Independence. James E. Stowers and others. Stowers Innovations, Inc., 4500 Main St. Kansas City, MO 64111-1834. Phone: 800-234-3445 or (816)753-8887 Fax: (816)753-7787 E-mail: info@stowers-innovations.com • URL: http://www.stowerinnovations.com • 2000. $34.00. Third revised edition.

Yes, You Can Time the Market! Ben Stein and Phil DeMuth. John Wiley and Sons, Inc., 111 River St. Hoboken, NJ 07030. Phone: 800-225-5945 or (201)748-6000 Fax: (201)748-6088 E-mail: bookinfo@wiley.com • URL: http://www.wiley.com • 2003. $24.95. Despite the title, provides generally conservative advice for investors. Timing, in this case, relates to long-term trends and valuations.

Young Presidents' Organization., 600 E Las Colinas Blvd., Ste. 1000, 451 S Decker, Ste. 200 Irving, TX 75039. Phone: 800-773-7976 or (972)587-1500 Fax: (972)650-4777 E-mail: membership@ypo.org • URL: http://www.ypo.org • Presidents or chief executive officers of corporations with minimum of 50 employees; each member must have been elected president before his/her 40th birthday and must retire by June 30th the year after his/her 50th birthday. Assists members in becoming better presidents through education and idea exchange. Conducts courses for members and spouses, in business, arts and sciences, world affairs, and family and community life, during a given year at various locations, including graduate business schools.

Your Dream Home: A Comprehensive Guide to Buying a House, Condo, or Co-op. Marguerite Smith. Warner Books, Inc., Time and Life Bldg., 1271 Ave of the Americas New York, NY 10020. Phone: 800-343-9204 or (212)522-8700 Fax: (212)522-2067 E-mail: cust.serv@twbg.com • URL: http://www.warnerbooks.com • 1997. $10.99. (Money, America's Financial Advisor Series).

Your Federal Income Tax. U.S. Department of the Treasury, Internal Revenue Service. Available from U.S. Government Printing Office, Washington, DC 20402. Phone: (202)512-1800 Fax: (202)512-2250 E-mail: gpoaccess@gpo.gov • URL: http://www.accessgpo.gov • Annual. $25.00. Layman's guide to income tax preparation.

Your Telephone Personality. Economics Press, Inc., 12 Daniel Rd. Fairfield, NJ 07004. Phone: 800-526-2554 or (973)227-1224 Fax: (973)227-9742 E-mail: info@epinc.com • URL: http://www.epinc.com • Biweekly. $33.00 per year. Telephone skills for office employees.

Youth for Understanding International Exchange., 6400 Goldboro Rd. Ste. 100 Bethesda, MD 20817. Phone: (866)493-

8872 or (240)235-2100 Fax: (240)235-2104 E-mail: admissions@yfo.org • URL: http://www. youthforunderstanding.org • Provides educational opportunities for young people and adults through international student exchange. Administers study abroad scholarship programs in cooperation with other governments, the U. S. Senate, the U. S. Information Agency, and various educational organizations.

Youth Markets Alert. EPM Communications Inc., 160 Mercer St., 3rd Fl. New York, NY 10012-3212. Phone: 888-852-9467 or (212)941-0099 or (212)941-0099 Fax: 888-852-3899 or (212)941-1622 E-mail: info@epmcom.com • URL: http://www.epmcom.com • Description: Features information and research results related to young consumers from elementary school through high school.

Zacks Analyst Directory: Listed by Broker. Zacks Investment Research, 155 N. Wacker Dr. Chicago, IL 60606. Phone: 800-767-3771 or (312)630-9880 Fax: (312)630-9898 E-mail: info@zacks.com • URL: http://www.zacks.com • Quarterly. $395.00 per year. Lists stockbroker investment analysts and gives the names of major U. S. corporations covered by those analysts.

Zacks Analyst Directory: Listed by Company. Zacks Investment Research, 155 N. Wacker Dr. Chicago, IL 60606. Phone: 800-767-3771 or (312)630-9880 Fax: (312)630-9898 E-mail: info@zacks.com • URL: http://www.zacks.com • Quarterly. $395.00 per year. Lists major U. S. corporations and gives the names of stockbroker investment analysts covering those companies.

Zacks Analyst Watch. Zacks Investment Research, 155 N. Wacker Dr. Chicago, IL 60606. Phone: 800-767-3771 or (312)630-9880 Fax: (312)630-9898 E-mail: info@zacks.com • URL: http://www.zacks.com • Biweekly. $250.00 per year. Provides the results of research by stockbroker investment analysts on major U. S. corporations.

Zacks Earnings Estimates. Zacks Investment Research, 155 N. Wacker Drive Chicago, IL 60606. Phone: 800-767-3771 or (312)630-9880 Fax: (312)630-9898 E-mail: support@zacks.com • URL: http://www.zacks.com • Provides online earnings projections for about 6,000 U. S. corporations, based on

investment analysts' reports. Data is mainly from 200 major brokerage firms. Time span varies according to online provider, with daily or weekly updates. Inquire as to online cost and availability.

Zacks Earnings Forecaster. Zacks Investment Research, 155 N. Wacker Dr. Chicago, IL 60606. Phone: 800-767-3771 or (312)630-0954 Fax: (312)630-9898 E-mail: info@zacks.com • URL: http://www.zacks.com • Biweekly. $495.00 per year. (Also available monthly at $375.00 per year.) Provides estimates by stockbroker investment analysts of earnings per share of individual U. S. companies.

Zacks EPS Calendar. Zacks Investment Research, 155 N. Wacker Dr. Chicago, IL 60606. Phone: 800-767-3771 or (312)630-9880 Fax: (312)630-9898 E-mail: info@zacks.com • URL: http://www.zacks.com • Biweekly. $1,250.00 per year. (Also available monthly at $895.00 per year.) Lists anticipated reporting dates of earnings per share for major U. S. corporations.

Zacks Profit Guide. Zacks Investment Research, 155 N. Wacker Dr. Chicago, IL 60606. Phone: 800-767-3771 or (312)630-9880 Fax: (312)630-9898 E-mail: info@zacks.com • URL: http://www.zacks.com • Quarterly. $375.00 per year. Provides analysis of total return and stock price performance of major U. S. companies.

Zincscan: A Review of Recent Technical Literature On the Use of Zinc and Its Products. C & C Associates, 12 Parkside Green Meanwood Leeds LS6 4NY, England. Quarterly. $125.00. per year. Provides technical articles and abstracts of recent technical and market related literature on zinc. Formerly *Zinc Abstracts*.

Zip Code Mapbook of Metropolitan Areas. ESRI Business Information Solutions, 8620 Westwood Center Dr. Vienna, VA 22182-2214. Phone: 800-292-2224 or (703)679-4185 Fax: (703)679-3371 E-mail: msgw@caci.com • URL: http://www.demographics.caci.com • 1992. $195.00. Second edition. Contains Zip Code two-color maps of 326 metropolitan areas. Includes summary statistical profiles of each area: population characteristics, employment, housing, and income.

Zoning and Planning Deskbook, 2d. Douglas W. Kmiec. West

Group, 610 Opperman Dr. Eagan, MN 55123. Phone: 800-328-4880 or (651)687-7000 Fax: 800-340-9378 E-mail: bookstore@westgroup.com • URL: http://www.westgroup.com • $220.00. Two looseleaf volumes. Annual supplementation. Emphasis is on legal issues.

Zoning and Planning Law Handbook. West Group, 610 Opperman Dr. Eagan, MN 55123. Phone: 800-328-4880 or (651)687-7000 Fax: 800-340-9378 E-mail: bookstore@westgroup.com • URL: http://www.westgroup.com • $264.50.

Zoning and Planning Law Report. West Group, 610 Opperman Dr. Eagan, MN 55123. Phone: 800-328-4880 or (651)687-7000 Fax: 800-340-9378 E-mail: bookstore@westgroup.com • URL: http://www.westgroup.com • Monthly. $483.00 per year. Newsletter.

Zoning Bulletin. Quinlan Publishing Co., Inc., Marine Industrial Pk., 23 Drydock St., 6th Fl. Boston, MA 02210. Phone: 800-229-2084 or (617)542-0048 Fax: (617)345-9646 E-mail: info@quinlan.com • URL: http://www.quinlan.com • Semimonthly. $89.00 per year. Newsletter dealing with zoning legal issues.

Zoning News. American Planning Association, 122 S. Michigan Ave., Suite 1600 Chicago, IL 60603-6107. Phone: (312)431-9100 Fax: (312)431-9985 E-mail: bookservice@planning.org • URL: http://www.planning.org • Monthly. $60.00 per year.

Zoological Action Committee., USA,. E-mail: info@usenglish.org Zoological institutions, animal suppliers and interested individuals. Lobbies in Washington, DC and state capitals on behalf of zoos, aquariums, oceanariums, private animal breeders and zoological suppliers. Presently inactive.

The ZPG Reporter. Population Connection, 2120 L St. NW, Ste. 500 Washington, DC 20036-2290. Phone: 800-767-1956 or (202)332-2200 Fax: (202)332-2302 E-mail: info@populationconnection.org • URL: http://www.populationconnection.org • Description: Reports on population growth and related social, environmental, and economic issues. Tracks legislative developments. Recurring features include interviews, news of research, book reviews, and regular columns.